Index

Dynamic Distribution Ltd.

HOW TO USE AND CONDITION GUIDE

Isn't it great? Every year this book gets bigger and better with all the new sets coming out. But even more exciting is that every year there are more attractive choices and, subsequently, more interest in the cards we love so much. This edition has been enhanced and expanded from the previous edition. The cards you collect–who appears on them, what they look like, where they are from, and (most important to most of you) what their current values are–are enumerated within. Many of the features contained in the other Beckett Price Guides have been incorporated into this volume since condition grading, terminology, and many other aspects of collecting are common to the card hobby in general. We hope you find the book both interesting and useful in your collecting pursuits.

The *Beckett Hockey Card Price Guide* has been successful where other attempts have failed because it is complete, current, and valid. This Price Guide contains not just one, but two prices by condition for all hockey cards listed. These account for most of the hockey cards in existence. The prices were added to the card lists just prior to printing and reflect not the author's opinions or desires, but the going retail prices for each card based on the active market (sports memorabilia conventions and shows, sports card shops, mail-order catalogs, local club meetings, auction results, and other firsthand reports of actual realized prices).

What is the best price guide available on the market today? Of course card sellers will prefer the price guide with the highest prices, while card buyers will naturally prefer the one with the lowest prices. Accuracy, however, is the true test. Use the price guide used by more collectors and dealers than all the others combined because it's not the lowest and not the highest – but the most accurate guide, and is produced with integrity.

To facilitate your use of this book, read the complete introductory section on the following pages before going to the pricing pages. Every collectible field has its own terminology; we've tried to capture most of these terms and definitions in our glossary. Please read carefully the section on grading and the condition of your cards, as you will not be able to determine which price column is appropriate for a given card without first knowing its condition.

HOW TO COLLECT

Each collection is personal and reflects the individuality of its owner. There are no set rules on how to collect cards. Since card collecting is a hobby or leisure pastime, what you collect, how much you collect, and how much time and money you spend collecting are entirely up to you. The funds you have available for collecting and your own personal taste should determine how you collect.

It is impossible to collect every card ever produced. Therefore, beginners as well as intermediate and advanced collectors usually specialize in some way. One of the reasons this hobby is popular is that individual collectors can define and tailor their collecting methods to match their own tastes.

Many collectors select complete sets from particular years, acquire only certain players, some collectors are only interested in the first cards or Rookie Cards of certain players, and others collect cards by team.

Remember, this is a hobby so pick a style of collecting that appeals to you.

GLOSSARY/LEGEND

Our glossary defines terms most frequently used in the card collecting hobby. Many of these terms are common to other types of sports memorabilia collecting. Some terms may have several meanings depending on the use and context.

Cabinet Card – Popular and highly valuable photographs on thick card stock produced in the 19th and early 20th century.

Checklist – A list of the cards contained in a particular set. The list is always in numerical order if the cards are numbered. Some unnumbered sets are artificially numbered in alphabetical order or by team.

CL – Checklist card. A card that lists, in order, the cards and players in the set or series.

CO – Coach.

Common Card – The typical card of any set. It has no premium value accruing from the subject matter, numerical scarcity, popular demand, or anomaly.

Convention – A gathering of sealers and collectors at a single location of the purpose of buying, selling and trading sports memorabilia items. Conventions are open to the public and sometimes feature

DETERMINING VALUE

Why are some cards more valuable than others? Obviously, the economic laws of supply and demand are applicable to card collecting just as they are to any other field where a commodity is bought, sold or traded in a free, unregulated market.

Supply (the number of cards available on the market) is less than the total number of cards originally produced since attrition diminishes that original quantity. Each year a percentage of cards is typically thrown away, destroyed or otherwise lost to collectors. This percentage is much, much smaller today than it was in the past because more and more people have become increasingly aware of the value of their cards.

For those who collect only Mint condition cards, the supply of older cards can be quite small indeed. Until recently, collectors were not so conscious of the need to preserve the condition of their cards. For this reason, it is difficult to know exactly how many 1953 Topps are currently available, Mint or otherwise. It is generally accepted that there are fewer 1953 Topps available than 1963, 1973 or 1983 Topps cards. If demand were equal for each of these sets, the law of supply and demand would increase the price for the least available sets. Demand, however, is never equal for all sets, so price correlations can be complicated. The demand for a card is influenced by many factors. These include: (1) the age of the card; (2) the number of cards printed; (3) the player(s) portrayed on the card; (4) the attractiveness and popularity of the set; and (5) the physical condition of the card.

In general, (1) the older the card, (2) the fewer the number of the cards printed, (3) the more famous, popular and talented the player, (4) the more attractive and popular the set, and (5) the better the condition of the card, the higher the value of the card will be. There are exceptions to all but one of these factors: the condition of the card. Given two cards similar in all respects except condition, the one in the best condition will always be valued higher.

While those guidelines help to establish the value of a card, the countless exceptions and peculiarities make any simple, direct mathematical formula to determine card values impossible.

REGIONAL VARIATION

Since the market varies from region to region, card prices of local players may be higher. This is known as a regional premium. How significant the premium is and if there is any premium at all depends on the local popularity of the team and the player.

The largest regional premiums usually do not apply to superstars, who often are so well-known nationwide that the prices of their key cards are too high for local dealers to realize a premium.

Lesser stars often command the strongest premiums. Their popularity is concentrated in their home region, creating local demand that greatly exceeds overall demand.

Regional premiums can apply to popular retired players and sometimes can be found in the areas where the players grew up or starred in college.

A regional discount is the converse of a regional premium. Regional discounts occur when a player has been so popular in his region for so long that local collectors and dealers have accumulated quantities of his key cards. The abundant supply may make the cards available in that area at the lowest prices anywhere.

GLOSSARY/LEGEND

autograph guests, door prizes, contests, or seminars. They are frequently referred to as "shows."

COR – Corrected.

Dealer – A person who engages in the buying, selling and trading sports collectibles or supplies. A dealer may also be a collector, but as a dealer, his main goal it to earn a profit.

Die-Cut – A card with part of its stock partial cut, allowing one or more parts to be folded or removed. After removal or appropriate folding, the remaining part of the card can frequently be made to stand up.

DK – Diamond King.

DP – Draft pick or Double print. A double print is a card that was printed in double the quantity compared to other cards in the same series.

ERR – Error card. A card with erroneous information, spelling or depiction on either side of the card. Most errors are not corrected by the manufacturer.

High Number – The cards in the last series of a set in a year in which such high-numbered cards were printed or distributed in significantly less amounts than the lower numbered cards. Not all years have high numbers in terms of this definition.

HOF – Hall of Fame or a card that pictures of

HOW TO USE AND CONDITION GUIDE

SET PRICES

A somewhat paradoxical situation exists in the price of a complete set vs. the combined cost of the individual cards in the set. In nearly every case, the sum of the prices for the individual cards is higher than the cost for the complete set. This is prevalent especially in the cards of the last few years. The reasons for this apparent anomaly stem from the habits of collectors and from the carrying costs to dealers. Today, each card in a set normally is produced in the same quantity as all other cards in its set.

Many collectors pick up only stars, superstars and particular teams. As a result, the dealer is left with a shortage of certain player cards and an abundance of others. He therefore incurs an expense in simply "carrying" these less desirable cards in stock. On the other hand, if he sells a complete set, he gets rid of large numbers of cards at one time. For this reason, he generally is willing to receive less money for a complete set. By doing this, he recovers all of his costs and also makes a profit.

The disparity between the price of the complete set and the sum of the individual cards also has been influenced by the fact that some of the major manufacturers now are pre-collating card sets. Since "pulling" individual cards from the sets involves a specific type of labor (and cost), the singles or star card market is not affected significantly by pre-collation.

Set prices also do not include rare card varieties, unless specifically stated. Of course, the prices for sets do include one example of each type for the given set, but this is the least expensive variety.

CONDITION GUIDE

The most widely used grades are defined on page 22. Obviously, many cards will not perfectly fit one of the definitions. Therefore, categories between the major grades known as in-between grades are used, such as Good to Very Good (G-Vg), Very Good to Excellent (VgEx), and Excellent-Mint to Near Mint (ExMt-NrMt). Such grades indicate a card with all qualities of the lower category but with at least a few qualities of the higher category.

This Price Guide book lists each card and set in three grades, with the middle grade valued at about 40-45% of the top grade, and the bottom grade valued at about 10-15% of the top grade.

The value of cards that fall between the listed columns can also be calculated using a percentage of the top grade. For example, a card that falls between the top and middle grades (Ex, ExMt or NrMt in most cases) will generally be valued at anywhere from 50% to 90% of the top grade.

Similarly, a card that falls between the middle and bottom grades (G-Vg, Vg or VgEx in most cases) will generally be valued at anywhere from 20% to 40% of the top grade.

There are also cases where cards are in better condition than the top grade or worse than the bottom grade. Cards that grade worse than the lowest grade are generally valued at 5-10% of the top grade.

When a card exceeds the top grade by one – such as NrMt-Mt when the top grade is NrMt, or Mint when the top grade is NrMt-Mt – a premium of up to 50% is possible, with 10-20% the usual norm.

When a card exceeds the top grade by two – such as Mint when the top grade is NrMt, or NrMt-Mt when the top grade is ExMt – a premium of 25-50% is the usual norm. But certain condition sensitive cards or sets, particularly those

GLOSSARY/LEGEND

Hall of Famer (HOFer).

IA – In action.

Insert – A card or any other sports collectible contained and sold in the same package along with a card or cards from a major set. An insert card may or may not be numbered in the same sequence as the major set. Many times the inserts are randomly inserted in packs.

JSY – Jersey.

Major Set – A set produced by a national manufacturer of cards.

Multi-Player Card – A single card depicting two or more players.

Parallel – A card that is similar in design to its counterpart from a basic set, but offers a distinguishing quality.

RC Rookie Card.

Redemption – A program established by multiple card manufacturers that allows collectors to main in a special card (usually a random insert) in return for special cards, sets, or other prizes not available through conventional channels.

Refractor – A card that features a design element that enhances its color or appearance by deflecting light.

ROY – Rookie of the Year.

Series – The entire set of cards issued by a particular manufacturer in a particular year. Within a particular set, a series can refer to a group of consecutively

from the pre-war era, can bring premiums of up to 100% or even more.

Unopened packs, boxes and factory-collated sets are considered Mint in their unknown (and presumed perfect) state. Once opened, however, each card can be graded (and valued) in its own right by taking into account any defects that may be present in spite of the fact that the card has never been handled.

GENERAL CARD FLAWS

CENTERING

Current centering terminology uses numbers representing the percentage of border on either side of the main design. Obviously, centering is diminished in importance for borderless cards.

Slightly Off-Center (60/40)

A slightly off-center card is one that upon close inspection is found to have one border bigger than the opposite border. This degree once was offensive to only purists, but now some hobbyists try to avoid cards that are anything other than perfectly centered.

Off-Center (70/30)

An off-center card has one border that is noticeably more than twice as wide as the opposite border.

Badly Off-Center (80/20 or worse)

A badly off-center card has virtually no border on one side of the card.

Miscut

A miscut card actually shows part of the adjacent card in its larger border and consequently a corresponding amount of its card is cut off.

CORNER WEAR

Corner wear is the most scrutinized grading criteria in the hobby.

Corner with a slight touch of wear

The corner still is sharp, but there is a slight touch of wear showing. On a dark-bordered card, this shows as a dot of white.

Fuzzy corner

The corner still comes to a point, but the point has just begun to fray. A slightly "dinged" corner is considered the same as a fuzzy corner.

Slightly rounded corner

The fraying of the corner has increased to where there is only a hint of a point. Mild layering may be evident. A "dinged" corner is considered the same as a slightly rounded corner.

Rounded corner

The point is completely gone. Some layering is noticeable.

Badly rounded corner

The corner is completely round and rough. Severe layering is evident.

CREASES

A third common defect is the crease. The degree of creasing in a card is difficult to show in a drawing or picture. On giving the specific condition of an expensive card for sale, the seller should note any creases additionally. Creases can be categorized as to severity according to the following scale.

Light Crease

A light crease is a crease that is barely noticeable upon close inspection. In fact, when cards are in plastic sheets or holders, a light crease may not be seen (until the card is taken out of the holder). A light crease on the front is much more serious than a light crease on the card back only.

Medium Crease

A medium crease is noticeable when held and studied at arm's length by the naked eye, but does

GLOSSARY/LEGEND

numbered cards printed at the same time.

Set – One of each of the entire run of cards of the same type produced by a particular manufacturer during a single year.

Skip-Numbered – A set that has many unissued card numbers between the lowest and highest number in the set. A major set in which only a few numbers were not printed is not considered to be skip-numbered.

SP – Single or Short Print. A short print is a card that was printed in less quantity compared to the other cards in the same series.

TP – Triple print. A card that was printed in triple the quantity compared to the other cards in the same series.

UER – Uncorrected error.

VAR – Variation card. One of two or more cards from the same series, with the same card number, that differ from one and other in some way. This sometimes occurs when the manufacture notices an error in one or more of the cards, corrects the mistake, and then resumes the printing process. In some cases, on of the variations may be relatively scarce.

*** –** Used to denote multi-sport set or an announced print run of a particular card.

not overly detract from the appearance of the card. It is an obvious crease, but not one that breaks the picture surface of the card.

Heavy Crease: A heavy crease is one that has torn or broken through the card's picture surface, e.g., puts a tear in the photo surface.

ALTERATIONS

Deceptive Trimming

This occurs when someone alters the card in order (1) to shave off edge wear, (2) to improve the sharpness of the corners, or (3) to improve centering – obviously their objective is to falsely increase the perceived value of the card to an unsuspecting buyer. The shrinkage usually is evident only if the trimmed card is compared to an adjacent full-sized card or if the trimmed card is itself measured.

Obvious Trimming

Obvious trimming is noticeable and unfortunate. It is usually performed by non-collectors who give no thought to the present or future value of their cards.

Deceptively Retouched Borders

This occurs when the borders (especially on those cards with dark borders) are touched up on the edges and corners with magic marker or crayons of appropriate color in order to make the card appear to be Mint.

MISCELLANEOUS CARD FLAWS

The following are common minor flaws that, depending on severity, lower a card's condition by one to four grades and often render it no better than Excellent-Mint: bubbles (lumps in surface), gum and wax stains, diamond cutting (slanted borders), notching, off-centered backs, paper wrinkles, scratched-off cartoons or puzzles on back, rubber band marks, scratches, surface impressions and warping.

The following are common serious flaws that, depending on severity, lower a card's condition at least four grades and often render it no better than Good: chemical or sun fading, erasure marks, mildew, miscutting (severe off-centering), holes, bleached or retouched borders, tape marks, tears, trimming, water or coffee stains and writing.

GRADES

Mint (Mt)

A card with no flaws or wear. The card has four perfect corners, 55/45 or better centering from top to bottom and from left to right, original gloss, smooth edges and original color borders. A Mint card does not have print spots, color or focus imperfections.

Near Mint-Mint (NrMt-Mt)

A card with one minor flaw. Any one of the following would lower a Mint card to Near Mint-Mint: one corner with a slight touch of wear, barely noticeable print spots, color or focus imperfections. The card must have 60/40 or better centering in both directions, original gloss, smooth edges and original color border.

Near Mint (NrMt)

A card with one minor flaw. Any one of the following would lower a Mint card to Near Mint: one fuzzy corner or two to four corners with slight touches of wear, 70/30 to 60/40 centering, slightly rough edges, minor print spots, color or focus imperfections. The card must have original gloss and original color borders.

Excellent-Mint (ExMt)

A card with two or three fuzzy, but not rounded, corners and centering no worse than 80/20. The card may have no more than two of the following: slightly rough edges, very slightly discolored borders, minor print spots, color or focus imperfections. The card must have original gloss.

Excellent (Ex)

A card with four fuzzy but definitely not rounded corners and centering no worse than 70/30. The card may have a small amount of original gloss lost, rough edges, slightly discolored borders and minor print spots, color or focus imperfections.

Very Good (Vg)

A card that has been handled but not abused: slightly rounded corners with slight layering, slight notching on edges, a significant amount of gloss lost from the surface but no scuffing and moderate discoloration of borders. The card may have a few light creases.

Good (G), Fair (F), Poor (P)

A well-worn, mishandled or abused card: badly rounded and layered corners, scuffing, most or all original gloss missing, seriously discolored borders, moderate or heavy creases, and one or more serious flaws. The grade of Good, Fair or Poor depends on the severity of wear and flaws. Good, Fair and Poor cards generally are used only as fillers.

1989-90 Action Packed Prototypes

This three-card set was produced by Action Packed to show the NHL and NHLPA a sample in order to obtain a license for hockey cards. The cards are unnumbered and listed below in alphabetical order. Reportedly only 1000 cards of Gretzky and Lemieux were produced and only 300 of Yzerman. These cards are standard size with the rounded corners.

COMPLETE SET (4) 125.00 300.00
1 Wayne Gretzky 50.00 100.00
2 Mario Lemieux 30.00 75.00
3 Mario Lemieux 30.00 75.00
White border
4 Steve Yzerman 50.00 100.00

1993 Action Packed HOF Induction

This special limited edition standard-size set was produced by Action Packed to commemorate the 1993 Hockey Hall Of Fame induction on November 16, 1993, and honors the ten inductees. It was given to attendees at the induction and was on sale at the Hockey Hall of Fame. This set was released in a special black cardboard display featuring all ten cards (in two rows of five) and which could be placed in a black cardboard sleeve with the Hall of Fame logo and the words "1993 Hockey Hall of Fame Induction, November 16, 1993" printed in silver letters on the front. The back of the sleeve gives the set serial number out of a total of 5,000 sets produced.

COMPLETE SET (10) 8.00 20.00
1 Edgar Laprade .75 2.00
2 Guy Lapointe 2.00 5.00
3 Billy Smith 3.00 8.00
4 Steve Shutt 2.00 5.00
5 John D'Amico .40 1.00
6 Al Shaver .20 .50
7 Seymour Knox III .20 .50
8 Frank Griffiths .20 .50
9 Fred Page .20 .50
10 Al Strachan .20 .50

1993 Action Packed Prototypes

Both prototype cards measure the standard size and feature Bobby Hull. The first card has a borderless embossed color photo, while the second card has the same design but is all in gold. Both cards feature a silver Stanley Cup in the upper right corner. The horizontal backs carry biographical (in English and French) and statistical information, the Blackhawks logo on a puck, and the word "Prototype" printed vertically on the left. The cards are numbered on the back with a "BH" prefix.

COMPLETE SET (2) 3.00 8.00
1 Bobby Hull 1.50 4.00
(Color)
2 Bobby Hull 2.00 5.00
(Gold)

1994 Action Packed Badge of Honor Promos

Issued to herald the release of a new product, each of these four pins measures approximately 1 1/2" by 1". They were packaged together in a cardboard sleeve which carries a checklist on its back. On a bronze background, the fronts feature color player portraits with a gold border. The player's last name appears in gold lettering at the bottom. The Action Packed logo is above the picture, while the year 1994 inside a puck and hockey sticks icon is below. The backs carry the copyrights "Action Packed 1994" and "NHL 1994", and "NHLPA 1994." The pins are unnumbered and checklisted below in alphabetical order. By all accounts, the actual set these pins were designed to promote never was released.

COMPLETE SET (4) 10.00 25.00
1 Sergei Fedorov 4.00 10.00
2 Doug Gilmour 2.00 5.00
3 Mike Modano 3.00 8.00
4 Patrick Roy 5.00 12.00

1994-95 Action Packed Big Picture Promos

These four standard-size cards were issued to preview a proposed (but never released) Action Packed product, "Big Picture" cards. The fronts have borderless embossed color action photos. On a team color-coded background, the backs have a color close-up inside a gold foil circle, the player's name and team in gold foil lettering, and player profile. The front and back are hinged at the top, and the card opens up to reveal a 5 3/4" by 6 1/2" mini-poster, with a movie-frame design.

COMPLETE SET (4) 8.00 20.00
BP1 Jeremy Roenick 1.25 3.00
BP2 John Vanbiesbrouck 1.25 3.00
BP3 Jaromir Jagr 4.00 10.00
BP4 Steve Yzerman 4.00 10.00

1994-95 Action Packed Mammoth

The cards measure approximately 7 1/2" by 10 1/2". The fronts have borderless embossed color action photos with rounded corners. The player's last name is gold foil stamped on the bottom. The backs carry a color player cutout superimposed over the team logo. Player biography, profile and career totals are superimposed over the cutout. The player's name, team and position appear in a black bar alongside the left. The cards were issued in a plastic sleeve and are individually numbered out of 25,000 on the back.

COMPLETE SET (16) 4.80 12.00
MM1 Chris Chelios 1.00 2.50
MM2 Brett Hull 1.25 3.00
MM3 Pavel Bure 2.50 6.00
MM4 Adam Oates .75 2.00

1956 Adventure R749

This set features athletes from across the realm of sporting endeavours, but includes just the one hockey card listed below. The cards were slightly undersized, at 2 1/2 by 3 1/2.

63 Gordie Howe 50.00 100.00
Chuck Rayner

1990-91 Alberta International Team Canada

This 24-card set features the Canadian National Team and a bonus card of Vladislav Tretiak, the honorary captain of the Soviet Olympic team during the Pre-Olympic Hockey Tour. The cards are slightly smaller than standard size, measuring approximately 2 7/16" by 3 1/2".

COMPLETE SET (24) 4.80 12.00
1 Craig Billington .30 .75
2 Doug Dadswell .30 .75
3 Greg Andrusak .20 .50
4 Karl Dykhuis .20 .50
5 Gord Hynes .20 .50
6 Ken MacArthur .20 .50
7 Jim Paek .20 .50
8 Brad Schlegel .20 .50
9 Dave Archibald .20 .50
10 Stu Barnes .30 .75
11 Brad Bennett .20 .50
12 Todd Brost .20 .50
13 Jose Charbonneau .20 .50
14 Jason Lafreniere .20 .50
15 Chris Lindberg .20 .50
16 Ken Priestlay .20 .50
17 Stephane Roy .20 .50
18 Randy Smith .20 .50
19 Todd Strueby .20 .50
20 Vladislav Tretiak 1.25 3.00
21 Dave King CO .20 .50
22 Checklist Card .02 .10
NNO Title Card .02 .10

1991-92 Alberta International Team Canada

Sponsored by Alberta Lotteries, this 24-card standard-size set features the Canadian National Team. The fronts feature posed player photos on the ice that are full-bleed on the left and bottom. The cards are unnumbered and checklisted below in alphabetical order.

COMPLETE SET (24) 4.80 12.00
1 Dave Archibald .20 .50
2 Todd Brost .20 .50
3 Sean Burke .75 2.00
4 Terry Crisp ACO .20 .50
5 Kevin Dahl .20 .50
6 Karl Dykhuis .20 .50
7 Wayne Fleming AGM/ACO .02 .10
8 Curt Giles .20 .50
9 Gord Hynes .20 .50
10 Fabian Joseph .20 .50
11 Joe Juneau .40 1.00
12 Trevor Kidd .40 1.00
13 Dave King GM/CO .20 .50
14 Chris Kontos .20 .50
15 Chris Lindberg .20 .50
16 Kent Manderville .20 .50
17 Adrien Plavsic .20 .50
18 Dan Ratushny .20 .50
19 Stephane Roy .20 .50
20 Brad Schlegel .20 .50
21 Scott Scissons .20 .50
22 Randy Smith .20 .50
23 Jason Woolley .30 .75
24 Title Card .02 .10

1992-93 Alberta International Team Canada

This 22-card set features the Canadian National Team as well as bonus cards of Mike Myers, honorary captain of the team, and of Vladislav Tretiak, honorary captain of Russia's National Team. The cards are slightly smaller than standard size, measuring 2 1/2" by 3 7/16". The cards are unnumbered and checklisted below in alphabetical order.

COMPLETE SET (22) 8.00 20.00
1 Dominic Amodeo .20 .50
2 Mark Astley .20 .50
3 Adrian Aucoin .40 1.00
4 Mark Bassen .20 .50
5 Eric Bellerose .20 .50
6 Mike Brewer .20 .50
7 Danny Dube CO .02 .10
8 Mike Fountain .30 .75
9 Todd Hlushko .20 .50
10 Hank Lammens .20 .50
11 Derek Laxdal .20 .50
12 Derek Mayer .20 .50
13 Keith Morris .20 .50
14 Mike Myers SNL 4.00 10.00
15 Jackson Penney .20 .50
16 Garth Premak .20 .50
17 Tom Renney CO .20 .50
18 Allain Roy .30 .75
19 Stephane Roy .20 .50
20 Trevor Sim .20 .50
21 Vladislav Tretiak 1.25 3.00
22 Title Card .02 .10

1993-94 Alberta International Team Canada

This 23-card standard-size set features players on the 1994 Canadian National Hockey Team. The cards are unnumbered and checklisted below in alphabetical order.

COMPLETE SET (23) 12.00 30.00
1 Adrian Aucoin .30 .75
2 Todd Brost .20 .50
3 Dany Dube ACO .02 .10
4 David Harlock .20 .50
5 Corey Hirsch .30 .75
6 Todd Hlushko .20 .50
7 Fabian Joseph .20 .50
8 Paul Kariya 6.00 15.00
9 Chris Kontos .20 .50
10 Manny Legace 2.00 5.00
11 Brett Lindros .20 .50
12 Ken Lovsin .20 .50
13 Jason Marshall .20 .50
14 Derek Mayer .20 .50
15 Dwayne Norris .20 .50
16 Tom Renney CO .20 .50
17 Russ Romaniuk .20 .50
18 Brian Savage .60 1.50
19 Trevor Sim .20 .50
20 Chris Therien .30 .75
21 Todd Warriner .20 .50
22 Craig Woodcroft .20 .50
23 Title Card .02 .10

1992-93 All World Mario Lemieux Promos

This set consists of six standard-size cards. All cards feature the same color action photo of Mario Lemieux, skating with stick in both hands. On the first three cards, the top of the photo is oval-shaped and framed by yellow stripes. The space above the oval as well as the stripe at the bottom carrying player information are purple. The outer border is green. Inside green borders, the horizontal back has a color close-up photo, biography and statistics. On the second three cards listed below, the player photo is tilted slightly to the right and framed by a thin green border. Yellow stripes above and below the picture carry information, and the outer border is black-and-white speckled. The back has a similar design and displays a close-up color head shot and biographical and statistical information on a pastel green panel. All cards are numbered as number 1. The cards were issued three different ways, in Spanish, French, and English. The design and concept of these cards is very similar to the 1992 All World Troy Aikman promos.

COMPLETE SET (6) 10.00 25.00
COMMON CARD (1A-1F) 2.00 5.00

1993 American Licorice Sour Punch Caps

Printed in Canada and sponsored by the American Licorice Co., these individually wrapped cards were inserted in specially-marked packages of 4 1/2 oz. Sour Punch Candy Straws. Each package contained one card, measuring the standard size with two punch-out caps, each measuring 1 1/2" in diameter. One cap carries the Sour Punch logo and where appropriate, a flavor, while the other cap features a color player portrait with a black border. The cards are numbered on the front, and the backs are blank. There is a special promotion cap featuring Bobby Hull with no number, but the letter "P." This promo cap was used by the American Licorice sales brokerage as a sales sample.

COMPLETE SET (8) 4.80 12.00
1 Theo Fleury .50 1.25
Sour Apple Cap
2 Guy Lafleur 1.00 2.50
Blue Raspberry Cap
3 Chris Chelios .50 1.25
Strawberry Cap
4 Stan Mikita .50 1.25
Sour Apple Cap
5 Rocket Richard 1.00 2.50
Strawberry Cap
6 Steve Thomas .20 .50
Blue Raspberry Cap
7 Checklist 1 .08 .25
Sour Punch Cap Logo
8 Checklist 2 .08 .25
Sour Punch Cap Logo
P Bobby Hull 1.00 2.50
Sour Punch Cap Logo

2007 Americana Promos

DISTRIBUTED AT TRADE SHOWS
PR Patrick Roy 1.25 3.00
Sports Legends

2007 Americana Sports Legends

RANDOM INSERTS IN PACKS
STATED PRINT RUN 500 SERIAL #'d SETS
6 Tony Esposito 1.50 4.00
9 Patrick Roy 4.00 10.00

2007 Americana Sports Legends Material

RANDOM INSERTS IN PACKS
PRINT RUNS B/WN 25-500 COPIES PER
6 Tony Esposito Jsy/500 4.00 10.00

2007 Americana Sports Legends Signature

RANDOM INSERTS IN PACKS
PRINT RUNS B/WN 25-50 COPIES PER
6 Tony Esposito/25 15.00 40.00
9 Patrick Roy/25 50.00 100.00

2007 Americana Sports Legends Signature Material

*MTL: .5X TO 1.2X BASIC SIG
RANDOM INSERTS IN PACKS
PRINT RUNS B/WN 25-50 COPIES PER

1924-28 Anonymous NHL

Honestly, we're not quite sure what to make of this checklist, which was provided by vintage expert Mike Jaspersen. It is thought that there are probably cards from at least two and possibly three different sets in this checklist, but because there are no distinguishing marks, it is impossible to accurately state to which single set each card belongs. It's noteworthy that at least two different sets appear to have been issued during the 1925-26 season as several players appear on two distinct cards with different numbers that only played that season. If anyone has further info and can help sort these very important cards out, please contact us at hockeymag@beckett.com. Because so little is known about these sets, they are checklisted below without pricing.

COMPLETE SET (?)
1 Billy Boucher
1 George Hainsworth
2 Billy Coutu
2 Billy Boucher
3 Sylvio Mantha
3 Georges Vezina
4 Roland Paulhus
(white background
4 Sylvio Mantha
4 Roland Paulhus
5 Alphonse Lacroix
5 George Prodgers
6 Albert Leduc
7 Wildor Larochelle UER
(first name listed as Victor
7 Wildor Larochelle VAR
(no border
8 Aurele Joliat
9 Howie Morenz
10 Hec Lepine
10 Amby Moran
11 Alphonse Lacroix
12 Herb Rheaume
12 Art Gagne
13 Pit Lepine
14 Bill Holmes
15 Leo Dandurand
16 Frank Nighbor
16 Alex Connell
17 Cy Denneny
17 King Clancy
18 King Clancy
19 Billy Boucher
19 Hec Kilrea
20 Hec Kilrea
21 Hooley Smith
22 Alex Smith
22 Alex Smith VAR
(no border
25 Ed Gorman
28 Alex Connell
31 Carson Cooper
31 Sprague Cleghorn
32 Carson Cooper
36 Hugo Harrington
38 Herb Mitchell
39 Charles Stewart
39 Herb Mitchell
40 Red Stuart
41 Lloyd Cook
41 Sprague Cleghorn
42 Billy Coutu VAR
(no border
42 Billy Coutu
46 Odie Cleghorn VAR
(no border, Montreal
46 Odie Cleghorn
46 Odie Cleghorn VAR
(no border, Pittsburgh
47 Louis Berlinquette
47 Roy Worters
48 Hib Milks
52 Hib Milks
57 Odie Cleghorn
61 Pete Bellefeuille
76 Charlie Langlois
77 Jake Forbes
79 Billy Burch
82 Joe Simpson VAR
(Montreal
82 Joe Simpson VAR
(Americans
91 Dutch Cain VAR
(Bruins
91 Dunc Munro
91 Dutch Cain VAR
(Maroons
92 Dunc Munro
95 Clint Benedict
96 Reg Noble
97 Nels Stewart
100 Sam Rothschild UER
(name misspelled Rotchild
121 Harry Holmes
127 Clem Loughlin
129 Johnny Sheppard
136 Gord Fraser
138 Dick Irvin

1993 Anti-Gambling Postcards *

Each card measures 5" x 7" and is part of a multi-sport set which was created to allow voters to express their opinion to legislators on sports team-based lotteries in the U.S.

NNO Andy Moog .75 2.00
NNO Chris Chelios 2.00 5.00

2005-06 Artifacts

This 342-card set was released in a mix of product specific unopened and through inserts in Rookie Update. Cards numbered 1-242 were in the unopened product while cards 243-342 were inserts in Rookie Update. The unopened product came in five-card packs, with a $9.99 SRP, which came 10 packs to a box. Cards numbered 1-100 feature veterans in team alphabetical order while cards 101-150 feature retired greats in alphabetical order and All-Stars (151-200) in team alphabetical order. All cards 101-200 were issued to a stated print run of 899 serial numbered sets. Cards numbered 201-342 are all Rookie Cards and all issued to 750 serial numbered sets with cards 201-242 in the unopened product and cards 243-342 in the Rookie Update packs.

COMP.SET w/o SP'S (100) 15.00 30.00
AL/AS PRINT RUN 899 SER.#'d SETS
RC PRINT RUN 750 SER.#'d SETS
GOLD & AUTO 1/1's EXIST
1 Jean-Sebastien Giguere .12 .30
2 Sergei Fedorov .20 .50
3 Joffrey Lupul .08 .20
4 Dany Heatley .20 .50
5 Ilya Kovalchuk .20 .50
6 Kari Lehtonen .12 .30
7 Andrew Raycroft .12 .30
8 Joe Thornton .25 .60
9 Glen Murray .08 .20
10 Sergei Samsonov .12 .30
11 Patrice Bergeron .08 .20
12 Martin Biron .12 .30
13 Maxim Afinogenov .08 .20
14 Chris Drury .12 .30
15 Jarome Iginla .20 .50
16 Miikka Kiprusoff .12 .30
17 Jordan Leopold .08 .20
18 Eric Staal .08 .20
19 Justin Williams .08 .20
20 Erik Cole .08 .20
21 Tuomo Ruutu .08 .20
22 Eric Daze .12 .30
23 Tyler Arnason .08 .20
24 Joe Sakic .30 .75
25 Rob Blake .12 .30
26 David Aebischer .12 .30
27 Milan Hejduk .15 .40
28 Alex Tanguay .12 .30
29 Geoff Sanderson .08 .20
30 Rick Nash .20 .50
31 Nikolai Zherdev .12 .30
32 Mike Modano .25 .60
33 Bill Guerin .12 .30
34 Brenden Morrow .12 .30
35 Marty Turco .12 .30
36 Manny Legace .12 .30
37 Pavel Datsyuk .15 .40
38 Brendan Shanahan .15 .40
39 Steve Yzerman .60 1.50
40 Henrik Zetterberg .15 .40
41 Ty Conklin .12 .30
42 Ryan Smyth .08 .20
43 Stephen Weiss .08 .20
44 Roberto Luongo .20 .50
45 Olli Jokinen .12 .30
46 Alexander Frolov .08 .20
47 Dustin Brown .08 .20
48 Luc Robitaille .12 .30
49 Dwayne Roloson .12 .30
50 Marian Gaborik .25 .60
51 Mike Ribeiro .08 .20
52 Michael Ryder .08 .20
53 Jose Theodore .15 .40
54 Saku Koivu .15 .40
55 Steve Sullivan .08 .20
56 Jordin Tootoo .08 .20
57 Tomas Vokoun .12 .30
58 Martin Brodeur .60 1.50
59 Scott Gomez .08 .20
60 Jeff Friesen .08 .20
61 Patrik Elias .12 .30
62 Tom Poti .08 .20
63 Mark Messier .15 .40
64 Jaromir Jagr .25 .60
65 Mark Parrish .08 .20
66 Rick DiPietro .12 .30
67 Alexei Yashin .08 .20
68 Daniel Alfredsson .12 .30
69 Dominik Hasek .30 .75
70 Marian Hossa .15 .40
71 Jason Spezza .15 .40
72 Martin Havlat .12 .30
73 Robert Esche .12 .30
74 Keith Primeau .12 .30
75 Simon Gagne .12 .30
76 Michal Handzus .08 .20
77 Brett Hull .20 .50
78 Mike Comrie .12 .30
79 Shane Doan .08 .20
80 Marc-Andre Fleury .12 .30
81 Mario Lemieux .75 2.00
82 Mark Recchi .12 .30
83 Evgeni Nabokov .12 .30
84 Patrick Marleau .12 .30
85 Jonathan Cheechoo .12 .30
86 Mike Sillinger .08 .20
87 Doug Weight .12 .30
88 Keith Tkachuk .15 .40
89 Brad Richards .12 .30
90 Fredrik Modin .08 .20
91 Martin St. Louis .12 .30
92 Vincent Lecavalier .15 .40
93 Ed Belfour .15 .40
94 Owen Nolan .12 .30
95 Mats Sundin .15 .40
96 Nik Antropov .08 .20
97 Ed Jovanovski .12 .30
98 Markus Naslund .15 .40
99 Trevor Linden .08 .20
100 Olaf Kolzig .12 .30
101 Glenn Anderson AL 1.50 4.00
102 Bill Barber AL 1.50 4.00
103 Jean Beliveau AL 2.00 5.00
104 Mike Bossy AL 2.00 5.00
105 Johnny Bower AL 2.00 5.00
106 Scotty Bowman AL 1.50 4.00
107 Johnny Bucyk AL 2.00 5.00
108 Wayne Cashman AL 1.50 4.00
109 Gerry Cheevers AL 1.50 4.00
110 Don Cherry AL 1.50 4.00
111 Bobby Clarke AL 2.00 5.00
112 Gordie Howe AL 2.50 6.00
113 Wayne Gretzky AL 4.00 10.00
114 Marcel Dionne AL 1.50 4.00
115 Phil Esposito AL 1.50 4.00
116 Tony Esposito AL 2.00 5.00
117 Grant Fuhr AL 2.00 5.00
118 Bernie Geoffrion AL 2.00 5.00
119 Clark Gillies AL 1.50 4.00
120 Butch Goring AL 1.50 4.00
121 Glenn Hall AL 2.00 5.00
122 Paul Henderson AL 1.50 4.00
123 Ron Hextall AL 1.50 4.00
124 Al Iafrate AL 1.50 4.00
125 Red Kelly AL 2.00 5.00
126 Jari Kurri AL 2.00 5.00
127 Guy LaFleur AL 2.00 5.00
128 Igor Larionov AL 1.50 4.00
129 Reggie Leach AL 1.50 4.00
130 Hakan Loob AL 1.50 4.00
131 Frank Mahovlich AL 1.50 4.00
132 Rick Martin AL 1.50 4.00
133 Lanny McDonald AL 1.50 4.00
134 Stan Mikita AL 2.00 5.00
135 Dickie Moore AL 2.00 5.00
136 Ken Morrow AL 1.50 4.00
137 Larry Murphy AL 1.50 4.00
138 Cam Neely AL 2.00 5.00
139 Mats Naslund AL 1.50 4.00
140 Bob Nystrom AL 1.50 4.00
141 Terry O'Reilly AL 2.00 5.00
142 Brad Park AL 1.50 4.00
143 Gilbert Perreault AL 2.00 5.00
144 Rene Robert AL 1.50 4.00
145 Derek Sanderson AL 1.50 4.00
146 Denis Savard AL 1.50 4.00
147 Peter Stastny AL 1.50 4.00
148 Thomas Steen AL 1.50 4.00
149 Dave Taylor AL 1.50 4.00
150 Bryan Trottier AL 1.50 4.00
151 Sergei Fedorov AS 2.00 5.00
152 Ilya Kovalchuk AS 2.00 5.00
153 Dany Heatley AS 2.00 5.00
154 Joe Thornton AS 2.00 5.00
155 Glen Murray AS 1.50 4.00
156 Jarome Iginla AS 2.00 5.00
157 Eric Daze AS 1.50 4.00
158 Joe Sakic AS 2.00 5.00
159 Rob Blake AS 1.50 4.00
160 Milan Hejduk AS 1.50 4.00
161 Alex Tanguay AS 1.50 4.00
162 Rick Nash AS 2.00 5.00
163 Mike Modano AS 2.00 5.00
164 Bill Guerin AS 1.50 4.00
165 Marty Turco AS 1.50 4.00
166 Brendan Shanahan AS 1.50 4.00
167 Steve Yzerman AS 3.00 8.00
168 Pavel Datsyuk AS 1.50 4.00
169 Roberto Luongo AS 2.00 5.00
170 Luc Robitaille AS 1.50 4.00
171 Marian Gaborik AS 2.00 5.00
172 Jose Theodore AS 1.50 4.00
173 Saku Koivu AS 1.50 4.00
174 Tomas Vokoun AS 1.50 4.00
175 Martin Brodeur AS 2.00 5.00
176 Scott Gomez AS 1.50 4.00
177 Patrik Elias AS 1.50 4.00
178 Mark Messier AS 2.00 5.00
179 Jaromir Jagr AS 2.00 5.00
180 Alexei Yashin AS 1.50 4.00
181 Mark Parrish AS 1.50 4.00
182 Dominik Hasek AS 2.00 5.00
183 Marian Hossa AS 1.50 4.00
184 Daniel Alfredsson AS 1.50 4.00
185 Keith Primeau AS 1.50 4.00
186 Simon Gagne AS 1.50 4.00
187 Brett Hull AS 1.50 4.00
188 Shane Doan AS 1.50 4.00
189 Mario Lemieux AS 3.00 8.00
190 Mark Recchi AS 1.50 4.00
191 Evgeni Nabokov AS 1.50 4.00
192 Keith Tkachuk AS 1.50 4.00
193 Martin St. Louis AS 1.50 4.00
194 Vincent Lecavalier AS 1.50 4.00
195 Ed Belfour AS 1.50 4.00
196 Mats Sundin AS 1.50 4.00
197 Owen Nolan AS 1.50 4.00
198 Markus Naslund AS 1.50 4.00
199 Ed Jovanovski AS 1.50 4.00
200 Olaf Kolzig AS 1.50 4.00
201 Corey Perry RC 6.00 15.00
202 Braydon Coburn RC 3.00 8.00
203 Hannu Toivonen RC 4.00 10.00
204 Thomas Vanek RC 12.00 30.00
205 Dion Phaneuf RC 40.00 100.00
206 Cam Ward RC 8.00 20.00
207 Brent Seabrook RC 5.00 12.00
208 Wojtek Wolski RC 6.00 15.00
209 Gilbert Brule RC 4.00 10.00
210 Jussi Jokinen RC 4.00 10.00
211 Jim Howard RC 5.00 12.00
212 Brad Winchester RC 3.00 8.00
213 Rostislav Olesz RC 3.00 8.00
214 George Parros RC 3.00 8.00
215 Matt Foy RC 3.00 8.00
216 Alexander Perezhogin RC 3.00 8.00
217 Ryan Suter RC 3.00 8.00
218 Zach Parise RC 8.00 20.00
219 Henrik Lundqvist RC 12.00 30.00
220 Robert Nilsson RC 3.00 8.00
221 Andrej Meszaros RC 3.00 8.00
222 Jeff Carter RC 10.00 25.00
223 David Leneveu RC 3.00 8.00
224 Sidney Crosby RC 75.00 150.00
225 Ryane Clowe RC 3.00 8.00
226 Jeff Woywitka RC 3.00 8.00
227 Evgeny Artykuhin RC 3.00 8.00
228 Alexander Steen RC 4.00 10.00
229 Rob McVicar RC 3.00 8.00
230 Alexander Ovechkin RC 60.00 120.00
231 Peter Budaj RC 6.00 15.00
232 Rene Bourque RC 3.00 8.00
233 Yann Danis RC 3.00 8.00
234 Eric Nystrom RC 2.00 5.00
235 Mike Richards RC 8.00 20.00
236 Kevin Nastiuk RC 2.00 5.00
237 Petteri Nokelainen RC 2.00 5.00
238 Ryan Getzlaf RC 6.00 15.00
239 Johan Franzen RC 2.50 6.00
240 Brandon Bochenski RC 2.00 5.00
241 Patrick Eaves RC 3.00 8.00
242 Jim Slater RC 2.00 5.00
243 Dustin Penner RC 3.00 8.00
244 Zenon Konopka RC 2.00 5.00
245 Michael Wall RC 2.00 5.00
246 Adam Berkhoel RC 2.00 5.00
247 Andrew Alberts RC 2.00 5.00
248 Milan Jurcina RC 2.00 5.00
249 Ben Walter RC 2.00 5.00
250 Jordan Sigalet RC 3.00 8.00
251 Nathan Paetsch RC 2.00 5.00
252 Chris Thorburn RC 2.00 5.00
253 Daniel Paille RC 2.00 5.00
254 Mark Giordano RC 2.00 5.00
255 Niklas Nordgren RC 2.00 5.00
256 Andrew Ladd RC 3.00 8.00
257 Chad Larose RC 2.00 5.00
258 Danny Richmond RC 2.00 5.00
259 Duncan Keith RC 6.00 15.00
260 Cam Barker RC 2.00 5.00
261 Martin St. Pierre RC 2.00 5.00
262 Corey Crawford RC 2.00 5.00
263 James Wisniewski RC 2.00 5.00
264 Brad Richardson RC 2.00 5.00
265 Vitaly Kolesnik RC 2.00 5.00
266 Alexandre Picard RC 2.00 5.00
267 Ole-Kristian Tollefsen RC 2.00 5.00

268 Steven Goertzen RC 2.00 5.00
269 Geoff Platt RC 2.00 5.00
270 Joakim Lindstrom RC 2.00 5.00
271 Junior Lessard RC 2.00 5.00
272 Vojtech Polak RC 2.00 5.00
273 Brett Lebda RC 2.00 5.00
274 Kyle Quincey RC 2.00 5.00
275 Valtteri Filppula RC 2.00 5.00
276 Danny Syvret RC 2.00 5.00
277 Kyle Brodziak RC 2.00 5.00
278 J-F Jacques RC 2.00 5.00
279 Matt Greene RC 2.00 5.00
280 Anthony Stewart RC 2.00 5.00
281 Greg Jacina RC 2.00 5.00
282 Petr Taticek RC 2.00 5.00
283 Yanick Lehoux RC 2.00 5.00
284 Jeff Tambellini RC 2.00 5.00
285 Petr Kanko RC 2.00 5.00
286 Richard Petiot RC 2.00 5.00
287 Mikko Koivu RC 4.00 10.00
288 Derek Boogaard RC 2.00 5.00
289 Jonathan Ferland RC 2.00 5.00
290 Maxim Lapierre RC 2.00 5.00
291 Jean-Philippe Cote RC 2.00 5.00
292 Andrei Kostitsyn RC 5.00 12.00
293 Greg Zanon RC 2.00 5.00
294 Kevin Klein RC 2.00 5.00
295 Pekka Rinne RC 2.00 5.00
296 Barry Tallackson RC 2.00 5.00
297 Cam Janssen RC 2.00 5.00
298 Jason Ryznar RC 2.00 5.00
299 Jeremy Colliton RC 2.00 5.00
300 Chris Campoli RC 2.00 5.00
301 Bruno Gervais RC 2.00 5.00
302 Petr Prucha RC 4.00 10.00
303 Ryan Hollweg RC 2.00 5.00
304 Al Montoya RC 3.00 8.00
305 Brian McGrattan RC 2.00 5.00
306 Christoph Schubert RC 2.00 5.00
307 R.J. Umberger RC 3.00 8.00
308 Stefan Ruzicka RC 2.00 5.00
309 Ben Eager RC 2.00 5.00
310 Alexandre Picard RC 2.00 5.00
311 Keith Ballard RC 2.00 5.00
312 Matt Jones RC 2.00 5.00
313 Maxime Talbot RC 2.00 5.00
314 Erik Christensen RC 2.00 5.00
315 Ryan Whitney RC 2.00 5.00
316 Colby Armstrong RC 3.00 8.00
317 Josh Gorges RC 2.00 5.00
318 Dimitri Patzold RC 2.00 5.00
319 Steve Bernier RC 5.00 10.00
320 Grant Stevenson RC 2.00 5.00
321 Doug Murray RC 2.00 5.00
322 Jay McClement RC 2.00 5.00
323 Jeff Hoggan RC 2.00 5.00
324 Colin Hemingway RC 2.00 5.00
325 Dennis Wideman RC 2.00 5.00
326 Lee Stempniak RC 3.00 8.00
327 Chris Beckford-Tseu RC 2.00 5.00
328 Gerald Coleman RC 2.00 5.00
329 Nick Tarnasky RC 2.00 5.00
330 Paul Ranger RC 2.00 5.00
331 Darren Reid RC 2.00 5.00
332 Ryan Craig RC 2.00 5.00
333 Andrew Wozniewski RC 2.00 5.00
334 Staffan Kronwall RC 2.00 5.00
335 Jay Harrison RC 2.00 5.00
336 Kevin Bieksa RC 2.00 5.00
337 Rick Rypien RC 2.00 5.00
338 Rob McVicar 2.00 5.00
339 Tomas Mojzis RC 2.00 5.00
340 Tomas Fleischmann RC 2.00 5.00
341 Jakub Klepis RC 2.00 5.00
342 Mike Green RC 3.00 8.00

2005-06 Artifacts Blue

*1-100: 4X TO 10X BASE HI
*101-200: .5X TO 1.25X
PRINT RUN 75 SER.#'d SETS

2005-06 Artifacts Green

*1-100: 10X TO 25X BASE HI
*101-200: .75X TO 2X
PRINT RUN 25 SER.#'d SETS

2005-06 Artifacts Pewter

*1-100: 4X TO 10X BASE HI
*101-200: .5X TO 1.25X
PRINT RUN 100 SER.#'d SETS

2005-06 Artifacts Red

*1-100: 5X TO 12X BASE HI
*101-200: .6X TO 1.5X
PRINT RUN 50 SER.#'d SETS

2005-06 Artifacts Auto Facts

UNLISTED STARS 8.00 20.00
PRINT RUN 100 SER.#'d SETS
PEWTER PRINT RUN 10 SETS
BLUE PRINT RUN 1 SET
PEWTER/BLUE NOT PRICED
DUE TO SCARCITY
AFHE Milan Hejduk 8.00 20.00
AFES Eric Staal 10.00 25.00
AFBB Brad Boyes 4.00 10.00
AFSC Dave Schultz 6.00 15.00
AFML Manny Legace 6.00 15.00
AFDK Dave Taylor 4.00 10.00
AFSU Mats Sundin 10.00 25.00
AFHZ Henrik Zetterberg 8.00 20.00
AFJG Jean-Sebastien Giguere 6.00 15.00
AFRY Michael Ryder 8.00 20.00
AFJT Joe Thornton 15.00 40.00
AFBM Bryan McCabe 4.00 10.00
AFMO Brendan Morrison 4.00 10.00
AFMH Martin Havlat 8.00 20.00
AFDL David Legwand 4.00 10.00
AFNY Bob Nystrom 4.00 10.00
AFWC Wayne Cashman 4.00 10.00
AFCP Chris Pronger 6.00 15.00
AFMR Mike Ribeiro 4.00 10.00
AFTR Tuomo Ruutu 6.00 15.00
AFMF Marc-Andre Fleury 12.00 30.00
AFAR Andrew Raycroft 6.00 15.00
AFDC Don Cherry 12.00 30.00
AFJW Justin Williams 4.00 10.00
AFRS Ryan Smyth 6.00 15.00
AFGL Georges Laraque 4.00 10.00
AFAH Ales Hemsky 6.00 15.00
AFIK Ilya Kovalchuk 12.00 30.00
AFBC Bobby Clarke 8.00 20.00
AFSS Steve Sullivan 4.00 10.00
AFNH Nathan Horton 4.00 10.00
AFSW Stephen Weiss 4.00 10.00
AFSL Martin St. Louis 6.00 15.00
AFJR Jeremy Roenick 10.00 25.00
AFVL Vincent Lecavalier 10.00 25.00
AFNO Mika Noronen 4.00 10.00
AFTC Ty Conklin 4.00 10.00
AFMT Marty Turco 6.00 15.00
AFHO Marcel Hossa 4.00 10.00
AFDU Dustin Brown 4.00 10.00
AFTL Trevor Linden 12.00 30.00
AFAM Antti Miettinen 4.00 10.00
AFBL Brian Leetch 8.00 20.00
AFJI Jarome Iginla 15.00 40.00
AFST Matt Stajan 6.00 15.00
AFNA Nikolai Antropov 4.00 10.00
AFEC Erik Cole 4.00 10.00
AFAF Alexander Frolov 6.00 15.00
AFGF Grant Fuhr 10.00 25.00
AFBO Mike Bossy 10.00 25.00
AFGW Gump Worsley 8.00 20.00
AFRE Robert Esche 8.00 20.00
AFRN Rick Nash 10.00 25.00
AFCE Christian Ehrhoff 4.00 10.00
AFMA Maxim Afinogenov 6.00 15.00
AFBR Brad Richards 6.00 15.00
AFKH Ken Hodge 4.00 10.00
AFMM Mike Modano 10.00 25.00
AFCO Bob Cole 4.00 10.00
AFCD Chris Drury 6.00 15.00
AFRL Roberto Luongo 12.00 30.00
AFLN Ladislav Nagy 4.00 10.00
AFLR Luc Robitaille 6.00 15.00
AFRK Ryan Kesler 4.00 10.00
AFKD Kris Draper 6.00 15.00
AFZC Zdeno Chara 4.00 10.00
AFRB Rob Blake 4.00 10.00
AFJS Jason Spezza 8.00 20.00
AFPB Patrice Bergeron 8.00 20.00
AFJK Jari Kurri 8.00 20.00
AFRF Ruslan Fedotenko 4.00 10.00
AFMP Mark Popovic 4.00 10.00
AFTH Trent Hunter 4.00 10.00
AFKL Kari Lehtonen 10.00 25.00
AFRM Ryan Miller 6.00 15.00
AFMN Markus Naslund 8.00 20.00
AFCN Cam Neely 12.00 30.00
AFJL Joffrey Lupul 6.00 15.00
AFDA David Aebischer 6.00 15.00
AFTC Tony Salmelainen 4.00 10.00
AFRZ Richard Zednik 4.00 10.00
AFAT Alex Tanguay 6.00 15.00
AFSK Saku Koivu 8.00 20.00
AFDM Darren McCarty 8.00 20.00
AFNZ Nikolai Zherdev 4.00 10.00
AFJC Jonathan Cheechoo 10.00 25.00
AFDS Denis Savard 6.00 15.00
AFHS Marian Hossa 8.00 20.00
AFMG Marian Gaborik 15.00 40.00
AFJB Jay Bouwmeester 4.00 10.00
AFSG Simon Gagne 8.00 20.00
AFPW Peter Worrell 4.00 10.00
AFRH Ron Hextall 20.00 40.00
AFMC Mike Cammalleri 6.00 15.00
AFBI Martin Biron 6.00 15.00
AFPS Philippe Sauve 4.00 10.00

2005-06 Artifacts Auto Facts Copper

*COPPER: .75 TO 1.25 VALUE BASE
PRINT RUN 75 SER.#'d SETS
AFGH Gordie Howe 50.00 125.00
AFMB Martin Brodeur 40.00 100.00
AFDH Dominik Hasek 20.00 50.00
AFWG Wayne Gretzky 100.00 200.00

2005-06 Artifacts Auto Facts Silver

*SILVER: .5X TO 1.25X BASIC AUTO
PRINT RUN 50 SER.#'d SETS
AFGH Gordie Howe 60.00 150.00
AFWG Wayne Gretzky 150.00 250.00
AFMB Martin Brodeur 50.00 125.00
AFDH Dominik Hasek 25.00 60.00

2005-06 Artifacts Frozen Artifacts

COMMON CARD 2.00 5.00
UNLISTED STARS 3.00 8.00
PRINT RUN 275 SER.#'d SETS
*COPPER/SILVER: .5X TO 1.25X HI
COPPER PRINT RUN 125 SER.#'d SETS
SILVER PRINT RUN 50 SER.#'d SETS
*MAROON: .75X TO 2X
MAROON PRINT RUN 25 SER.#'d SETS
PEWTER PRINT RUN 10 SER.#'d SETS
GOLD & AUTO 1/1's EXIST
UNDER 25 NOT PRICED DUE TO SCARCITY
FABG Bernie Geoffrion 3.00 8.00
FAMG Marian Gaborik 4.00 10.00
FAMH Martin Havlat 2.00 5.00
FARE Mark Recchi 2.00 5.00
FADW Doug Weight 2.00 5.00
FAGR Gary Roberts 2.00 5.00
FARB Ray Bourque 5.00 12.00
FAAM Al MacInnis 2.00 5.00
FADS Darryl Sittler 3.00 8.00
FADR Derek Roy 2.00 5.00
FAGU Bill Guerin 2.00 5.00
FAAF Alexander Frolov 2.00 5.00
FAJB Jean Beliveau 4.00 10.00
FAON Owen Nolan 2.00 5.00
FAWG Wayne Gretzky 15.00 40.00
FAMO Alexander Mogilny 2.00 5.00
FARD Rick DiPietro 2.00 5.00
FARL Roberto Luongo 4.00 10.00
FAHZ Henrik Zetterberg 3.00 8.00
FAMT Marty Turco 2.00 5.00
FAPK Paul Kariya 3.00 8.00
FABO Jay Bouwmeester 2.00 5.00
FAEL Eric Lindros 3.00 8.00
FASL Martin St. Louis 2.00 5.00
FARH Ron Hextall 6.00 15.00
FASA Denis Savard 2.00 5.00
FABC Bobby Clarke 2.00 5.00
FABS Borje Salming 3.00 8.00
FAEB Ed Belfour 3.00 8.00
FATE Tony Esposito 3.00 8.00
FAJT Jocelyn Thibault 2.00 5.00
FADC Dan Cloutier 2.00 5.00
FADU Dustin Brown 2.00 5.00
FAJK Jari Kurri 3.00 8.00
FAML Mario Lemieux 10.00 25.00
FAKD Kris Draper 3.00 8.00
FABH Brett Hull 3.00 8.00
FARA Bill Ranford 2.00 5.00
FAJL Joffrey Lupul 2.00 5.00
FAJO Jose Theodore 4.00 10.00
FAJW Justin Williams 2.00 5.00
FABT Bryan Trottier 2.00 5.00
FADH Dominik Hasek 5.00 12.00
FABM Brendan Morrison 2.00 5.00
FANH Nathan Horton 2.00 5.00
FABR Brad Richards 2.00 5.00
FAHO Marcel Hossa 2.00 5.00
FACO Chris Osgood 2.00 5.00
FAMR Mike Ribeiro 2.00 5.00

2005-06 Artifacts Frozen Artifacts Patches

*PATCHES: 2X TO 5X FA BASE
PATCH PRINT RUN 50 SER.#'d SETS
SILVER PATCH PRINT RUN 5 SETS
DUAL PATCH PRINT RUN 15 SETS
PEWTER & AUTO 1/1's EXIST
UNDER 25 NOT PRICED DUE TO SCARCITY
FPMG Marian Gaborik 15.00 40.00
FPML Mario Lemieux 25.00 60.00
FPWG Wayne Gretzky 60.00 150.00
FPRB Ray Bourque 20.00 50.00
FPDH Dominik Hasek 15.00 40.00

2005-06 Artifacts Frozen Artifacts Dual

*DUAL: 1X TO 2.5X FA BASE
DUAL PRINT RUN 65 SER.#'d SETS
*DUAL COPPER: 1X TO 2.5X FA BASE
COPPER PRINT RUN 50 SER.#'d SETS
*DUAL SILVER: 1.25X TO 3X FA BASE
SILVER PRINT RUN 25 SER.#'d SETS
MAROON PRINT RUN 15 SER.#'d SETS
PEWTER PRINT RUN 10 SER.#'d SETS
GOLD & AUTO 1/1'S EXIST
UNDER 25 NOT PRICED DUE TO SCARCITY

2005-06 Artifacts Goalie Gear

PRINT RUN 50 SER.#'d SETS
SILVER PATCH PRINT RUN 5 SETS
DUAL PATCH PRINT RUN 15 SETS
PEWTER, AUTO & DUAL AUTO 1/1's EXIST
UNDER 25 NOT PRICED DUE TO SCARCITY
FGDH Dominik Hasek 25.00 60.00
FGRD Rick DiPietro 8.00 20.00
FGEB Ed Belfour 12.00 30.00
FGMT Marty Turco 8.00 20.00
FGRA Bill Ranford 12.00 30.00
FGJO Jose Theodore 15.00 40.00
FGRL Roberto Luongo 10.00 25.00
FGCO Chris Osgood 8.00 20.00
FGJT Jocelyn Thibault 8.00 20.00
FGTE Tony Esposito 8.00 20.00
FGGC Gerry Cheevers 8.00 20.00

2005-06 Artifacts Remarkable Artifacts

PRINT RUN 1 SET
DUAL PRINT RUN 1 SET
NOT PRICED DUE TO SCARCITY

2005-06 Artifacts Treasured Patches

*PATCHES: 2X TO 5X TS BASE
PATCH PRINT RUN 50 SER.#'d SETS
SILVER PATCH PRINT RUN 5 SETS
DUAL PATCH PRINT RUN 15 SETS
PEWTER, AUTO & DUAL AUTO 1/1's EXIST
UNDER 25 NOT PRICED DUE TO SCARCITY
TPSY Steve Yzerman 30.00 80.00
TPMB Martin Brodeur 30.00 80.00
TPML Mario Lemieux 30.00 80.00
TPMG Marian Gaborik 20.00 50.00
TPHA Dominik Hasek 25.00 60.00
TPJS Joe Sakic 15.00 40.00
TPMM Mike Modano 20.00 50.00
TPPF Peter Forsberg 20.00 50.00
TPJJ Jaromir Jagr 25.00 60.00
TPWG Wayne Gretzky 100.00 250.00

2005-06 Artifacts Treasured Swatches

PRINT RUN 275 SER.#'d SETS
*COPPER/SILVER: .5X TO 1.25X HI
COPPER PRINT RUN 125 SER.#'d SETS
SILVER PRINT RUN 50 SER.#'d SETS
*MAROON: .75X TO 2X
MAROON PRINT RUN 25 SER.#'d SETS
PEWTER PRINT RUN 10 SER.#'d SETS
BLUE & AUTO 1/1's EXIST
UNDER 25 NOT PRICED DUE TO SCARCITY
TSSY Steve Yzerman 8.00 20.00
TSPF Peter Forsberg 4.00 10.00
TSZP Zigmund Palffy 2.00 5.00
TSBS Brendan Shanahan 3.00 8.00
TSSF Sergei Fedorov 3.00 8.00
TSVL Vincent Lecavalier 3.00 8.00
TSRN Rick Nash 4.00 10.00
TSTS Teemu Selanne 3.00 8.00
TSBL Brian Leetch 3.00 8.00
TSPE Patrik Elias 2.00 5.00
TSMG Marian Gaborik 4.00 10.00
TSHA Dominik Hasek 5.00 12.00
TSSU Mats Sundin 3.00 8.00
TSJI Jarome Iginla 3.00 8.00
TSKP Keith Primeau 2.00 5.00
TSMM Mike Modano 4.00 10.00
TSEB Ed Belfour 3.00 8.00
TSTR Tuomo Ruutu 2.00 5.00
TSSK Saku Koivu 3.00 8.00
TSRS Ryan Smyth 2.00 5.00
TSMH Milan Hejduk 3.00 8.00
TSSL Martin St. Louis 2.00 5.00
TSHO Marian Hossa 3.00 8.00
TSMP Michael Peca 2.00 5.00
TSMD Marc Denis 2.00 5.00
TSMB Martin Brodeur 10.00 25.00
TSSS Scott Stevens 2.00 5.00
TSDH Dany Heatley 3.00 8.00
TSJP Jason Spezza 3.00 8.00
TSSD Shane Doan 2.00 5.00
TSCJ Curtis Joseph 3.00 8.00
TSML Mario Lemieux 10.00 25.00
TSIK Ilya Kovalchuk 4.00 10.00
TSTB Todd Bertuzzi 3.00 8.00
TSJG Jean-Sebastien Giguere 2.00 5.00
TSCP Chris Pronger 2.00 5.00
TSJR Jeremy Roenick 3.00 8.00
TSNK Nikolai Khabibulin 3.00 8.00
TSDA Daniel Alfredsson 2.00 5.00
TSJJ Jaromir Jagr 5.00 12.00
TSMN Markus Naslund 3.00 8.00
TSST Matt Stajan 2.00 5.00
TSPD Pavel Datsyuk 3.00 8.00
TSMS Mark Messier 3.00 8.00
TSJS Joe Sakic 5.00 12.00
TSJT Joe Thornton 4.00 10.00
TSJO Jose Theodore 3.00 8.00
TSAT Alex Tanguay 2.00 5.00
TSWG Wayne Gretzky 15.00 40.00

2005-06 Artifacts Treasured Swatches Dual

*DUAL: 1X TO 2.5X TS BASE
DUAL PRINT RUN 65 SER.#'d SETS
*DUAL COPPER: 1X TO 2.5X TS BASE
COPPER PRINT RUN 60 SER.#'d SETS
*DUAL SILVER: 1.25X TO 3X TS BASE
SILVER PRINT RUN 25 SER.#'d SETS
MAROON PRINT RUN 15 SER.#'d SETS
PEWTER PRINT RUN 10 SER.#'d SETS
BLUE & AUTO 1/1'S EXIST
UNDER 25 NOT PRICED DUE TO SCARCITY

2006-07 Artifacts

This 272-card set was issued in four-card packs which came 10 to a box. Cards numbered 1-100 featured NHL veterans while cards 101-150 featured retired greats and cards 151-200 featured NHL all-stars. All cards between 101 and 200 were issued to a stated print run of 999 serial numbered sets. Cards numbered 201-272 feature NHL rookies and those were broken down into cards 201-230 with a print run of 999 serial numbered sets and cards 231-272 with a stated print run of 599 serial numbered sets. Those cards 231-272 were issued as redemptions from cards in packs.

COMP.SET w/o SPs (100)
AS/LEGEND PRINT RUN 999 #'d SETS
RC PRINT RUN 999 #'d SETS
RC (231-272) PRINT RUN 599 #'d SETS
1 Alexander Ovechkin 1.25 3.00
2 Olaf Kolzig .40 1.00
3 Roberto Luongo .60 1.50
4 Markus Naslund .30 .75
5 Brendan Morrison .20 .50
6 Mats Sundin .30 .75
7 Darcy Tucker .20 .50
8 Alexander Steen .25 .60
9 Andrew Raycroft .25 .60
10 Michael Peca .20 .50
11 Brad Richards .30 .75
12 Vincent Lecavalier .30 .75
13 Martin St. Louis .30 .75
14 Keith Tkachuk .25 .60
15 Doug Weight .20 .50
16 Patrick Marleau .25 .60
17 Joe Thornton .50 1.25
18 Jonathan Cheechoo .30 .75
19 Vesa Toskala .25 .60
20 Mark Recchi .20 .50
21 Sidney Crosby 1.50 4.00
22 Marc-Andre Fleury .30 .75
23 Colby Armstrong .20 .50
24 Shane Doan .25 .60
25 Curtis Joseph .30 .75
26 Jeremy Roenick .30 .75
27 Mike Richards .30 .75
28 Peter Forsberg .50 1.25
29 Simon Gagne .30 .75
30 Jeff Carter .30 .75
31 Jason Spezza .30 .75
32 Dany Heatley .30 .75
33 Daniel Alfredsson .25 .60
34 Martin Gerber .30 .75
35 Brendan Shanahan .30 .75
36 Jaromir Jagr .50 1.25
37 Henrik Lundqvist .50 1.25
38 Petr Prucha .20 .50
39 Miroslav Satan .20 .50
40 Rick DiPietro .30 .75
41 Alexei Yashin .20 .50
42 Patrik Elias .20 .50
43 Martin Brodeur 1.00 2.50
44 Brian Gionta .20 .50
45 Paul Kariya .30 .75
46 Tomas Vokoun .25 .60
47 Saku Koivu .30 .75
48 Cristobal Huet .30 .75
49 Michael Ryder .25 .60
50 Alex Kovalev .20 .50
51 Pavol Demitra .20 .50
52 Marian Gaborik .50 1.25
53 Manny Fernandez .30 .75
54 Alexander Frolov .20 .50
55 Rob Blake .25 .60
56 Nathan Horton .20 .50
57 Olli Jokinen .20 .50
58 Todd Bertuzzi .25 .60
59 Ed Belfour .75 2.00
60 Ales Hemsky .20 .50
61 Joffrey Lupul .20 .50
62 Ryan Smyth .25 .60
63 Henrik Zetterberg .30 .75
64 Pavel Datsyuk .30 .75
65 Nicklas Lidstrom .30 .75
66 Dominik Hasek .40 1.00
67 Mike Modano .30 .75
68 Marty Turco .25 .60
69 Brenden Morrow .25 .60
70 Eric Lindros .30 .75
71 Fredrik Modin .20 .50
72 Rick Nash .30 .75
73 Sergei Fedorov .25 .60
74 Joe Sakic .60 1.50
75 Milan Hejduk .25 .60
76 Jose Theodore .30 .75
77 Marek Svatos .20 .50
78 Martin Havlat .25 .60
79 Nikolai Khabibulin .30 .75
80 Tuomo Ruutu .30 .75
81 Eric Staal .25 .60
82 Cam Ward .50 1.25
83 Rod Brind'Amour .25 .60
84 Jarome Iginla .50 1.25
85 Miikka Kiprusoff .30 .75
86 Dion Phaneuf .40 1.00
87 Alex Tanguay .25 .60
88 Ryan Miller .30 .75
89 Chris Drury .25 .60
90 Daniel Briere .25 .60
91 Brad Boyes .20 .50
92 Patrice Bergeron .25 .60
93 Zdeno Chara .20 .50
94 Marc Savard .20 .50
95 Ilya Kovalchuk .40 1.00
96 Marian Hossa .25 .60
97 Kari Lehtonen .30 .75
98 Teemu Selanne .30 .75
99 Jean-Sebastien Giguere .30 .75
100 Chris Pronger .25 .60
101 Glenn Anderson 1.50 4.00
102 Jean Beliveau 1.25 3.00
103 Bob Bourne 1.00 2.50
104 Mike Bossy 1.25 3.00
105 Richard Brodeur 1.25 3.00
106 Johnny Bucyk 1.50 4.00
107 Gerry Cheevers 3.00 8.00
108 Don Cherry 1.50 4.00
109 Wendel Clark 1.00 2.50
110 Bobby Clarke 1.50 4.00
111 Phil Esposito 1.50 4.00
112 Tony Esposito 2.50 6.00
113 Grant Fuhr 2.50 6.00
114 Doug Gilmour 1.00 2.50
115 Peter Stastny 1.00 2.50
116 Glenn Hall 2.50 6.00
117 Ron Hextall 3.00 8.00
118 Guy Lafleur 1.50 4.00
119 Guy Lapointe 1.00 2.50
120 Reggie Leach 1.00 2.50
121 Ted Lindsay 1.00 2.50
122 Lanny McDonald 1.25 3.00
123 Joe Mullen 1.00 2.50
124 Kirk Muller 1.00 2.50
125 Cam Neely 1.25 3.00
126 Bob Nystrom 1.00 2.50
127 Terry O'Reilly 1.00 2.50
128 Bernie Parent 2.50 6.00
129 Gilbert Perreault 1.00 2.50
130 Denis Potvin 1.25 3.00
131 Bill Ranford 2.50 6.00
132 Derek Sanderson 1.25 3.00
133 Denis Savard 1.25 3.00
134 Steve Shutt 1.00 2.50
135 Darryl Sittler 1.00 2.50
136 Billy Smith 2.00 5.00
137 Thomas Steen 1.00 2.50
138 Rick Vaive 1.00 2.50
139 Ron Ellis 1.00 2.50
140 Doug Wilson 1.25 3.00
141 Wayne Gretzky 6.00 15.00
142 Patrick Roy 5.00 12.00
143 Gordie Howe 6.00 15.00
144 Ray Bourque 1.50 4.00
145 Al MacInnis 1.00 2.50
146 Mike Krushelnyski 1.00 2.50
147 Mario Lemieux 5.00 12.00
148 Bob Probert 1.25 3.00
149 Dave Williams 1.25 3.00
150 Clark Gillies 1.00 2.50
151 Teemu Selanne 1.50 4.00
152 Ilya Kovalchuk 2.00 5.00
153 Marian Hossa 1.50 4.00
154 Patrice Bergeron 1.25 3.00
155 Cristobal Huet 1.50 4.00
156 Ryan Miller 1.50 4.00
157 Miikka Kiprusoff 1.50 4.00
158 Jarome Iginla 2.50 6.00
159 Eric Staal 1.25 3.00
160 Nikolai Khabibulin 1.50 4.00
161 Joe Sakic 3.00 8.00
162 Alex Tanguay 1.25 3.00
163 Rick Nash 1.50 4.00
164 Mike Modano 1.50 4.00
165 Marty Turco 1.25 3.00
166 Henrik Zetterberg 1.50 4.00
167 Pavel Datsyuk 1.50 4.00
168 Brendan Shanahan 1.50 4.00
169 Ales Hemsky 1.00 2.50
170 Chris Pronger 1.25 3.00
171 Roberto Luongo 3.00 8.00
172 Olli Jokinen 1.00 2.50
173 Alexander Frolov 1.00 2.50
174 Marian Gaborik 2.50 6.00
175 Saku Koivu 1.50 4.00
176 Michael Ryder 1.25 3.00
177 Paul Kariya 1.50 4.00
178 Tomas Vokoun 1.25 3.00
179 Martin Brodeur 5.00 12.00
180 Patrik Elias 1.00 2.50
181 Brian Gionta 1.00 2.50
182 Miroslav Satan 1.00 2.50
183 Jaromir Jagr 2.50 6.00
184 Henrik Lundqvist 2.50 6.00
185 Dany Heatley 1.50 4.00
186 Ed Belfour 4.00 10.00
187 Jason Spezza 1.50 4.00
188 Peter Forsberg 2.50 6.00
189 Simon Gagne 1.50 4.00
190 Shane Doan 1.25 3.00
191 Sidney Crosby 8.00 20.00
192 Marc-Andre Fleury 1.50 4.00
193 Joe Thornton 2.50 6.00
194 Patrick Marleau 1.25 3.00
195 Jonathan Cheechoo 1.50 4.00
196 Martin St. Louis 1.50 4.00
197 Vincent Lecavalier 1.50 4.00
198 Brad Richards 1.50 4.00
199 Mats Sundin 1.50 4.00
200 Markus Naslund 1.50 4.00
201 Dustin Byfuglien RC 4.00 10.00
202 Yan Stastny RC 2.00 5.00
203 Mark Stuart RC 2.00 5.00
204 Eric Fehr RC 2.50 6.00
205 Bill Thomas RC 2.00 5.00
206 Joel Perrault RC 2.00 5.00
207 Carsen Germyn RC 2.00 5.00
208 Ryan Potulny RC 2.50 6.00
209 David Printz RC 2.00 5.00
210 Rob Collins RC 2.00 5.00
211 Steve Regier RC 2.00 5.00
212 Matt Koalska RC 2.00 5.00
213 Masi Marjamaki RC 2.00 5.00
214 Konstantin Pushkarev RC 2.00 5.00
215 Ben Ondrus RC 2.00 5.00
216 Brendan Bell RC 2.00 5.00
217 Ian White RC 2.00 5.00
218 Jeremy Williams RC 2.00 5.00
219 Marc-Antoine Pouliot RC 2.50 6.00
220 Noah Welch RC 2.00 5.00
221 Michel Ouellet RC 3.00 8.00
222 Shea Weber RC 2.50 6.00
223 Jarkko Immonen RC 2.00 5.00
224 David Liffiton RC 2.00 5.00
225 Tomas Kopecky RC 2.50 6.00
226 Billy Thompson RC 2.00 5.00
227 Filip Novak RC 2.00 5.00
228 Matt Carle RC 2.50 6.00
229 Erik Reitz RC 2.00 5.00
230 Miroslav Kopriva RC 2.00 5.00
231 Ryan Shannon 2.50 6.00
232 Benoit Pouliot RC 3.00 8.00
233 Phil Kessel RC 8.00 20.00
234 Drew Stafford RC 3.00 8.00
235 Dustin Boyd RC 3.00 8.00
236 Josh Hennessey RC 2.50 6.00
237 Dave Bolland RC 5.00 12.00
238 Paul Stastny RC 10.00 25.00
239 Fredrik Norrena RC 2.50 6.00
240 Loui Eriksson RC 2.50 6.00
241 Derek Meech RC 2.50 6.00
242 Ladislav Smid RC 2.50 6.00
243 Janis Sprukts RC 2.50 6.00
244 Anze Kopitar RC 6.00 15.00
245 Niklas Backstrom RC 2.50 6.00
246 G. Latendresse RC 8.00 20.00
247 Alexander Radulov RC 6.00 15.00
248 Travis Zajac RC 4.00 10.00
249 Blake Comeau RC 2.50 6.00
250 Nigel Dawes RC 2.50 6.00
251 Alexei Kaigorodov RC 2.50 6.00
252 Martin Houle RC 3.00 8.00
253 Enver Lisin RC 2.50 6.00
254 Evgeni Malkin RC 30.00 60.00
255 M-E Vlasic RC 2.50 6.00
256 Marek Schwarz RC 5.00 12.00
257 Karri Ramo RC 2.50 6.00
258 Kris Newbury RC 2.50 6.00
259 Luc Bourdon RC 3.00 8.00
260 Darren Machesney RC 2.50 6.00
261 Jordan Staal RC 10.00 25.00
262 Patrick O'Sullivan RC 3.00 8.00
263 Patrik Thoresen RC 2.50 6.00
264 Mikhail Grabovski RC 2.50 6.00
265 Jesse Schultz RC 2.50 6.00
266 Michael Blunden RC 2.50 6.00
267 David Booth RC 2.50 6.00
268 Brandon Prust RC 2.50 6.00
269 Matt Lashoff RC 2.50 6.00
270 Niklas Grossman RC 2.50 6.00
271 Joe Pavelski RC 8.00 20.00
272 Clarke MacArthur RC 2.50 6.00

2006-07 Artifacts Gold

*1-100: 3X to 8X BASE HI
*101-230: .5X to 1.5X
*GOLD RCs (201-230): .6X TO 1.5X
STATED PRINT RUN 50 SER. #'d SETS
21 Sidney Crosby 12.00 30.00
191 Sidney Crosby S 20.00 50.00

2006-07 Artifacts Bronze

*1-100 5X TO 12X HI
*101-230 .75X TO 2X HI
*BRONZE RCs (201-230): 1.4X TO 4X
PRINT RUN 25 SER. #'d SETS
21 Sidney Crosby 15.00 40.00
191 Sidney Crosby S 25.00 60.00

2006-07 Artifacts Platinum

STATED PRINT RUN 10 SER.#'d SETS
NOT PRICED DUE TO SCARCITY

2006-07 Artifacts Radiance

COMPLETE SET (230)
PRINT RUN 1/1
NOT PRICED DUE TO SCARCITY

2006-07 Artifacts Silver

*RED 1-100 2X TO 5X HI
*RED 101-230 SAME AS BASE
*SILVER RCs (201-230): .5X TO 1.2X
PRINT RUN 100 SER. #'d SETS

2006-07 Artifacts Auto-Facts

The Billy Smith card mistakenly pictures Chico Resch.

STATED ODDS 1:10
GOLD 1/1s EXIST
GOLDS NOT PRICED DUE TO SCARCITY
AFAA Adrian Aucoin 3.00 8.00
AFAH Ales Hemsky 5.00 12.00
AFAK Andrei Kostitsyn 8.00 20.00
AFAO Alexander Ovechkin SP 75.00 150.00
AFAP Alexandre Picard 3.00 8.00
AFBB Bob Bourne 3.00 8.00
AFBC Bobby Clarke 8.00 20.00
AFBE Jean Beliveau SP 40.00 100.00
AFBI Martin Biron 3.00 8.00
AFBL Brett Lebda 3.00 8.00
AFBN Bob Nystrom 3.00 8.00
AFBO Jay Bouwmeester 10.00 25.00
AFBP Bob Probert 8.00 20.00
AFBR Brad Boyes 2.50 6.00
AFBS Billy Smith UER 8.00 20.00
AFBU Johnny Bucyk SP 6.00 15.00
AFBW Ben Walter 3.00 8.00
AFBY Mike Bossy 6.00 15.00
AFCA Jeff Carter 6.00 15.00
AFCD Chris Drury 5.00 12.00
AFCG Clark Gillies 5.00 12.00
AFCK Chuck Kobasew 3.00 8.00
AFCN Cam Neely 10.00 25.00
AFCP Corey Perry 5.00 12.00
AFDA David Aebischer 6.00 15.00
AFDB Doug Bodger 3.00 8.00
AFDE Derek Boogaard 5.00 12.00
AFDP Dion Phaneuf 12.00 30.00
AFDR Dwayne Roloson 6.00 15.00
AFDS Denis Savard 5.00 12.00
AFDW Doug Wilson 3.00 8.00
AFFP Fernando Pisani 3.00 8.00
AFGA Glenn Anderson SP 6.00 15.00
AFGF Grant Fuhr SP 15.00 40.00
AFGL Guy Lafleur SP 20.00 50.00
AFHO Gordie Howe 25.00 60.00
AFHR Ryan Hollweg 3.00 8.00
AFHZ Henrik Zetterberg SP 15.00 40.00
AFIK Ilya Kovalchuk SP 15.00 40.00
AFJB Jaroslav Balastik 3.00 8.00
AFJC Jonathan Cheechoo 8.00 20.00
AFJH Jeff Halpern 3.00 8.00
AFJI Jarome Iginla SP 15.00 40.00
AFJL Joffrey Lupul SP 8.00 20.00
AFJM Joe Mullen 5.00 12.00
AFJT Jose Theodore SP 12.00 30.00
AFKD Kris Draper 3.00 8.00
AFKM Kirk Muller 3.00 8.00
AFLE Reggie Leach 8.00 20.00
AFLN Ladislav Nagy 3.00 8.00
AFLS Lee Stempniak 3.00 8.00
AFMA Marian Gaborik SP 20.00 50.00
AFMB Martin Brodeur SP 75.00 175.00
AFMC Mike Cammalleri 3.00 8.00
AFMG Martin Gerber 5.00 12.00
AFMI Mike Richards 8.00 20.00
AFMK Miikka Kiprusoff SP 15.00 40.00
AFML Mario Lemieux SP 200.00 350.00

AFMR Michael Ryder 5.00 12.00
AFMS Marek Svatos 5.00 12.00
AFMT Mikael Tellqvist 5.00 12.00
AFNH Nathan Horton 5.00 12.00
AFOJ Olli Jokinen 3.00 8.00
AFPB Pierre-Marc Bouchard SP 25.00 50.00
AFPE Phil Esposito SP 50.00 125.00
AFPM Patrick Marleau 8.00 20.00
AFRA Ray Bourque SP 25.00 60.00
AFRB Rob Blake SP 25.00 50.00
AFRE Ron Ellis 5.00 12.00
AFRF Ruslan Fedotenko 3.00 8.00
AFRG Ryan Getzlaf 6.00 15.00
AFRH Ron Hextall SP 20.00 50.00
AFRI Richard Brodeur 5.00 12.00
AFRK Rostislav Klesla 3.00 8.00
AFRL Rod Langway 3.00 8.00
AFRM Ryan Malone SP 12.00 30.00
AFRO Mike Ribeiro 3.00 8.00
AFRS Ryan Smyth 12.00 30.00
AFRY Ryan Miller 15.00 30.00
AFSC Sidney Crosby 125.00 225.00
AFSG Scott Gomez 3.00 8.00
AFSH Scott Hartnell 3.00 8.00
AFSS Steve Shutt 3.00 8.00
AFSW Stephen Weiss 3.00 8.00
AFTE Tony Esposito SP 20.00 50.00
AFTH Joe Thornton SP 25.00 50.00
AFTL Ted Lindsay 6.00 15.00
AFTS Tomas Steen 3.00 8.00
AFTV Thomas Vanek 10.00 25.00
AFVO Tomas Vokoun 5.00 12.00
AFWC Wendel Clark 20.00 50.00
AFWG Wayne Gretzky SP 125.00 200.00
AFWI Dave Williams 5.00 12.00
AFWR Wade Redden SP 15.00 40.00
AFZC Zdeno Chara 5.00 12.00

2006-07 Artifacts Auto-Facts Gold

COMPLETE SET (95)
PRINT RUN 1/1
NOT PRICED DUE TO SCARCITY
AFAA Adrian Aucoin
AFAH Ales Hemsky
AFAK Andrei Kostitsyn
AFAO Alexander Ovechkin
AFAP Alexandre Picard
AFBB Bob Bourne
AFBC Bobby Clarke
AFBE Jean Beliveau
AFBI Martin Biron
AFBL Brett Lebda
AFBN Bob Nystrom
AFBO Jay Bouwmeester
AFBP Bob Probert
AFBR Brad Boyes
AFBS Billy Smith
AFBU Johnny Bucyk
AFBW Ben Walter
AFBY Mike Bossy
AFCA Jeff Carter
AFCD Chris Drury
AFCG Clark Gillies
AFCK Chuck Kobasew
AFCN Cam Neely
AFCP Corey Perry
AFDA David Aebischer
AFDB Doug Bodger
AFDE Derek Boogaard
AFDP Dion Phaneuf
AFDR Dwayne Roloson
AFDS Denis Savard
AFDW Doug Wilson
AFFP Fernando Pisani
AFGA Glenn Anderson
AFGF Grant Fuhr
AFGL Guy Lafleur
AFHO Gordie Howe
AFHR Ryan Hollweg
AFHZ Henrik Zetterberg
AFIK Ilya Kovalchuk
AFJB Jaroslav Balastik
AFJC Jonathan Cheechoo
AFJH Jeff Halpern
AFJI Jarome Iginla
AFJL Joffrey Lupul
AFJM Joe Mullen
AFJT Jose Theodore
AFKD Kris Draper
AFKM Kirk Muller
AFLE Reggie Leach
AFLN Ladislav Nagy
AFLS Lee Stempniak
AFMA Marian Gaborik
AFMB Martin Brodeur
AFMC Mike Cammalleri
AFMG Martin Gerber
AFMI Mike Richards
AFMK Miikka Kiprusoff
AFML Mario Lemieux
AFMR Michael Ryder
AFMS Marek Svatos
AFMT Mikael Tellqvist
AFNH Nathan Horton
AFOJ Olli Jokinen
AFPB Pierre-Marc Bouchard
AFPE Phil Esposito
AFPM Patrick Marleau
AFRA Ray Bourque
AFRB Rob Blake
AFRE Ron Ellis
AFRF Ruslan Fedotenko
AFRG Ryan Getzlaf
AFRH Ron Hextall
AFRI Richard Brodeur
AFRK Rostislav Klesla
AFRL Rod Langway
AFRM Ryan Malone
AFRO Mike Ribeiro
AFRS Ryan Smyth
AFRY Ryan Miller
AFSC Sidney Crosby
AFSG Scott Gomez
AFSH Scott Hartnell
AFSS Steve Shutt
AFSW Stephen Weiss
AFTE Tony Esposito
AFTH Joe Thornton
AFTL Ted Lindsay
AFTS Tomas Steen
AFTV Thomas Vanek
AFVO Tomas Vokoun
AFWC Wendel Clark
AFWG Wayne Gretzky
AFWI Dave Williams
AFWR Wade Redden
AFZC Zdeno Chara

2006-07 Artifacts Autographed Radiance Parallel

COMPLETE SET (111)
STATED PRINT RUN 1/1
NOT PRICED DUE TO SCARCITY

2006-07 Artifacts Frozen Artifacts

PRINT RUN 250 SER. #'d SETS
FAAO Adam Oates 2.00 5.00
FAAT Alex Tanguay 2.50 6.00
FABG Brian Gionta 2.50 6.00
FABM Brenden Morrow 2.50 6.00
FABP Brad Park 2.50 6.00
FABR Bill Ranford 2.50 6.00
FABS Brad Stuart 2.00 5.00
FACC Chris Chelios 2.50 6.00
FACD Chris Drury 2.50 6.00
FACK Chuck Kobasew 2.00 5.00
FACP Chris Pronger 2.50 6.00
FACW Cam Ward 3.00 8.00
FADA Daniel Alfredsson 2.50 6.00
FADS Darryl Sittler 2.50 6.00
FAES Eric Staal 3.00 8.00
FAGA Glenn Anderson 2.50 6.00
FAHZ Henrik Zetterberg 3.00 8.00
FAJB Jay Bouwmeester 2.50 6.00
FAJC Jeff Carter 2.50 6.00
FAJI Jarome Iginla 4.00 10.00
FAJL Joffrey Lupul 2.50 6.00
FAJO Jonathan Cheechoo 2.50 6.00
FAJS Joe Sakic 5.00 12.00
FALM Lanny McDonald 2.50 6.00
FAMC Bryan McCabe 2.00 5.00
FAMH Milan Hejduk 2.50 6.00
FAMK Miikka Kiprusoff 3.00 8.00
FAMM Mike Modano 3.00 8.00
FAMO Brendan Morrison 2.50 6.00
FAMR Mark Recchi 2.00 5.00
FANL Nicklas Lidstrom 2.50 6.00
FAPB Patrice Bergeron 3.00 8.00
FAPD Pavol Demitra 2.00 5.00
FAPE Patrik Elias 2.00 5.00
FAPM Patrick Marleau 2.50 6.00
FAPR Patrick Roy 10.00 25.00
FAPS Peter Stastny 2.00 5.00
FARB Rod Brind'Amour 2.50 6.00
FARL Roberto Luongo 4.00 10.00
FARM Ryan Miller 3.00 8.00
FARS Ryan Smyth 3.00 8.00
FASG Simon Gagne 3.00 8.00
FASK Saku Koivu 3.00 8.00
FASP Jason Spezza 3.00 8.00
FASS Steve Shutt 2.50 6.00
FASU Steve Sullivan 2.00 5.00
FASW Stephen Weiss 2.00 5.00
FATS Teemu Selanne 3.00 8.00
FATV Tomas Vokoun 3.00 8.00
FAWC Wendel Clark 3.00 8.00

2006-07 Artifacts Frozen Artifacts Blue

*BLUE .75X TO 1.5X HI
PRINT RUN 50 SER. #'d SETS

2006-07 Artifacts Frozen Artifacts Platinum

PRINT RUN 10 SER. #'d SETS
NOT PRICED DUE TO SCARCITY

2006-07 Artifacts Frozen Artifacts Red

*RED .5X TO 1.25X HI
PRINT RUN 100 SER. #'d SETS

2006-07 Artifacts Frozen Artifacts Patches Blue

PRINT RUN 25 SER. #'d SETS
BLUE SAME PRICE AS RED

2006-07 Artifacts Frozen Artifacts Patches Gold

PRINT RUN 10 SER. #'d SETS
NOT PRICED DUE TO SCARCITY

2006-07 Artifacts Frozen Artifacts Patches Platinum

PRINT RUN 5 SER. #'d SETS
NOT PRICED DUE TO SCARCITY

2006-07 Artifacts Frozen Artifacts Patches Red

PRINT RUN 35 SER. #'d SETS
FAAO Adam Oates 12.00 25.00
FAAT Alex Tanguay 15.00 40.00
FABG Brian Gionta 10.00 25.00
FABM Brenden Morrow 15.00 40.00
FABP Brad Park 10.00 25.00
FABR Bill Ranford 15.00 40.00
FABS Brad Stuart 10.00 25.00
FACC Chris Chelios 15.00 40.00
FACD Chris Drury 15.00 40.00
FACK Chuck Kobasew 10.00 25.00
FACP Chris Pronger 15.00 40.00
FACW Cam Ward 15.00 40.00
FADA Daniel Alfredsson 15.00 40.00
FADS Darryl Sittler 15.00 40.00
FAES Eric Staal 15.00 40.00
FAGA Glenn Anderson 15.00 40.00
FAHZ Henrik Zetterberg 15.00 40.00
FAJB Jay Bouwmeester 10.00 25.00
FAJC Jeff Carter 15.00 40.00
FAJI Jarome Iginla 20.00 50.00
FAJL Joffrey Lupul 10.00 25.00
FAJO Jonathan Cheechoo 10.00 25.00
FAJS Joe Sakic 30.00 60.00
FALM Lanny McDonald 15.00 40.00
FAMC Bryan McCabe 10.00 25.00
FAMH Milan Hejduk 15.00 40.00
FAMK Miikka Kiprusoff 20.00 50.00
FAMM Mike Modano 20.00 50.00
FAMO Brendan Morrison 10.00 25.00
FAMR Mark Recchi 10.00 25.00
FANL Nicklas Lidstrom 15.00 40.00
FAPB Patrice Bergeron 15.00 40.00
FAPD Pavol Demitra 10.00 25.00
FAPE Patrik Elias 10.00 25.00
FAPM Patrick Marleau 15.00 40.00
FAPR Patrick Roy 50.00 100.00
FAPS Peter Stastny 10.00 25.00
FARB Rod Brind'Amour 15.00 40.00
FARL Roberto Luongo 20.00 50.00
FARM Ryan Miller 15.00 40.00
FARS Ryan Smyth 15.00 40.00
FASG Simon Gagne 15.00 40.00
FASK Saku Koivu 15.00 40.00
FASP Jason Spezza 15.00 40.00
FASS Steve Shutt 15.00 40.00
FASU Steve Sullivan 10.00 25.00
FASW Stephen Weiss 10.00 25.00
FATS Teemu Selanne 15.00 40.00
FATV Tomas Vokoun 15.00 40.00
FAWC Wendel Clark 15.00 40.00

2006-07 Artifacts Frozen Artifacts Autographed Black

PRINT RUN 1/1
NOT PRICED DUE TO SCARCITY
FABR Bill Ranford
FACD Chris Drury
FACK Chuck Kobasew
FACP Chris Pronger
FADS Darryl Sittler
FAGA Glenn Anderson
FAHZ Henrik Zetterberg
FAJB Jay Bouwmeester
FAJC Jeff Carter
FAJI Jarome Iginla
FAJL Joffrey Lupul
FAJO Jonathan Cheechoo
FAMH Milan Hejduk
FAMK Miikka Kiprusoff
FAPM Patrick Marleau
FAPR Patrick Roy
FAPS Peter Stastny
FARL Roberto Luongo
FARM Ryan Miller
FARS Ryan Smyth
FASK Saku Koivu
FASS Steve Shutt
FASW Stephen Weiss
FATV Tomas Vokoun
FAWC Wendel Clark

2006-07 Artifacts Frozen Artifacts Patches Autographed Black Tag Parallel

PRINT RUN 1/1
NOT PRICED DUE TO SCARCITY
FACD Chris Drury
FACK Chuck Kobasew
FACP Chris Pronger
FADS Darryl Sittler
FAGA Glenn Anderson
FAHZ Henrik Zetterberg
FAJB Jay Bouwmeester
FAJC Jeff Carter
FAJI Jarome Iginla
FAJL Joffrey Lupul
FAJO Jonathan Cheechoo
FAMH Milan Hejduk
FAMK Miikka Kiprusoff
FAPM Patrick Marleau
FAPR Patrick Roy
FAPS Peter Stastny
FARL Roberto Luongo
FARM Ryan Miller
FARS Ryan Smyth
FASK Saku Koivu
FASS Steve Shutt
FASW Stephen Weiss
FATV Tomas Vokoun
FAWC Wendel Clark

2006-07 Artifacts Treasured Patches Black

TSAF Alexander Frolov
TSAH Ales Hemsky
TSAK Alex Kovalev
TSAM Al MacInnis
TSAO Alexander Ovechkin
TSAR Jason Arnott
TSBB Bob Bourne
TSBC Bobby Clarke
TSBG Bill Guerin
TSBL Rob Blake
TSBP Bob Probert
TSBS Borje Salming
TSCJ Curtis Joseph
TSCN Cam Neely
TSDG Doug Gilmour
TSDW Dave Williams
TSEB Ed Belfour
TSEL Eric Lindros
TSGF Grant Fuhr
TSIK Ilya Kovalchuk
TSJA Jason Allison
TSJG Jean-Sebastien Giguere
TSJJ Jaromir Jagr
TSJN Joe Nieuwendyk
TSJT Joe Thornton
TSKP Keith Primeau
TSKT Keith Tkachuk
TSMB Martin Brodeur
TSMF Manny Fernandez
TSMH Marian Hossa
TSML Mario Lemieux
TSMM Mike Modano
TSMN Markus Naslund
TSMR Mark Recchi
TSMT Marty Turco
TSNK Nikolai Khabibulin
TSOK Olaf Kolzig
TSPF Peter Forsberg
TSPK Paul Kariya
TSRB Ray Bourque
TSRN Rick Nash
TSRV Rick Vaive
TSRY Michael Ryder
TSSC Sidney Crosby
TSSF Sergei Fedorov
TSSG Scott Gomez
TSSK Saku Koivu
TSSN Scott Niedermayer
TSWE Doug Weight

2006-07 Artifacts Treasured Patches Blue

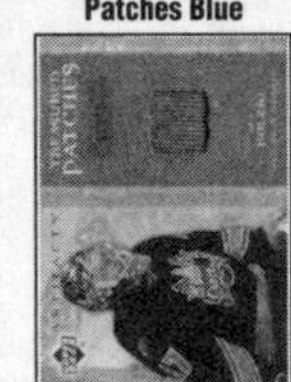

*BLUE SAME PRICE AS RED
PRINT RUN 25 SER. #'d SETS

2006-07 Artifacts Treasured Patches Platinum

COMPLETE SET (50)
PRINT RUN 5 SER. #'d SETS
NOT PRICED DUE TO SCARCITY

2006-07 Artifacts Treasured Patches Red

PRINT RUN 35 SER. #'d SETS
TSAF Alexander Frolov 10.00 25.00
TSAH Ales Hemsky 10.00 25.00
TSAK Alex Kovalev 8.00 20.00
TSAM Al MacInnis 8.00 20.00
TSAO Alexander Ovechkin 50.00 100.00
TSAR Jason Arnott 8.00 20.00
TSBB Bob Bourne 8.00 20.00
TSBC Bobby Clarke 15.00 40.00
TSBG Bill Guerin 8.00 20.00
TSBL Rob Blake 10.00 25.00
TSBN Bob Nystrom 8.00 20.00
TSBP Bob Probert 15.00 40.00
TSBS Borje Salming 15.00 40.00
TSCJ Curtis Joseph 15.00 40.00
TSCN Cam Neely 15.00 40.00
TSDG Doug Gilmour 15.00 40.00
TSDW Dave Williams 15.00 40.00
TSEB Ed Belfour 15.00 40.00
TSEL Eric Lindros 15.00 40.00
TSGF Grant Fuhr 15.00 40.00
TSIK Ilya Kovalchuk 20.00 50.00
TSJA Jason Allison 8.00 20.00
TSJG Jean-Sebastien Giguere 10.00 25.00
TSJJ Jaromir Jagr 20.00 50.00
TSJN Joe Nieuwendyk 10.00 25.00
TSJT Joe Thornton 20.00 50.00
TSKP Keith Primeau 8.00 20.00
TSKT Keith Tkachuk 10.00 25.00
TSMB Martin Brodeur 25.00 60.00
TSMF Manny Fernandez 10.00 25.00
TSMH Marian Hossa 15.00 40.00
TSML Mario Lemieux 30.00 80.00
TSMM Mike Modano 20.00 50.00
TSMN Markus Naslund 15.00 40.00
TSMR Mark Recchi 8.00 20.00
TSMT Marty Turco 15.00 40.00
TSNK Nikolai Khabibulin 15.00 40.00
TSOK Olaf Kolzig 20.00 50.00
TSPF Peter Forsberg 20.00 50.00
TSPK Paul Kariya 15.00 40.00
TSRB Ray Bourque 15.00 40.00
TSRN Rick Nash 15.00 40.00
TSRV Rick Vaive 8.00 20.00
TSRY Michael Ryder 15.00 40.00
TSSC Sidney Crosby 75.00 150.00
TSSF Sergei Fedorov 15.00 40.00
TSSG Scott Gomez 8.00 20.00
TSSK Saku Koivu 15.00 40.00
TSSN Scott Niedermayer 10.00 25.00
TSWE Doug Weight 10.00 25.00

2006-07 Artifacts Treasured Patches Autographed Black Tag Parallel

PRINT RUN 1/1
NOT PRICED DUE TO SCARCITY
TSAF Alexander Frolov
TSAH Ales Hemsky
TSAO Alexander Ovechkin
TSBB Bob Bourne
TSBL Rob Blake
TSBP Bob Probert
TSBS Borje Salming
TSCN Cam Neely
TSDW Dave Williams
TSGF Grant Fuhr
TSIK Ilya Kovalchuk
TSJT Joe Thornton
TSMB Martin Brodeur
TSMH Marian Hossa
TSML Mario Lemieux
TSMN Markus Naslund
TSMT Marty Turco
TSRB Ray Bourque
TSRN Rick Nash
TSRY Michael Ryder
TSSC Sidney Crosby
TSSG Scott Gomez
TSSK Saku Koivu
TSWE Doug Weight

2006-07 Artifacts Treasured Swatches

PRINT RUN 250 SER. #'d SETS
TSAF Alexander Frolov 2.00 5.00
TSAH Ales Hemsky 2.50 6.00
TSAK Alex Kovalev 2.00 5.00
TSAM Al MacInnis 2.00 5.00
TSAO Alexander Ovechkin 10.00 25.00
TSAR Jason Arnott 2.00 5.00
TSBB Bob Bourne 2.00 5.00
TSBC Bobby Clarke 3.00 8.00
TSBG Bill Guerin 2.00 5.00
TSBL Rob Blake 2.50 6.00
TSBN Bob Nystrom 2.00 5.00
TSBP Bob Probert 4.00 10.00
TSBS Borje Salming 2.50 6.00
TSCJ Curtis Joseph 3.00 8.00
TSCN Cam Neely 3.00 8.00
TSDG Doug Gilmour 3.00 8.00
TSDW Dave Williams 2.50 6.00
TSEB Ed Belfour 3.00 8.00
TSEL Eric Lindros 3.00 8.00
TSGF Grant Fuhr 3.00 8.00
TSIK Ilya Kovalchuk 5.00 12.00
TSJA Jason Allison 2.00 5.00
TSJG Jean-Sebastien Giguere 2.50 6.00
TSJJ Jaromir Jagr 5.00 12.00
TSJN Joe Nieuwendyk 2.00 5.00
TSJT Joe Thornton 5.00 12.00
TSKP Keith Primeau 2.00 5.00
TSKT Keith Tkachuk 3.00 8.00
TSMB Martin Brodeur 8.00 20.00
TSMF Manny Fernandez 2.50 6.00
TSMH Marian Hossa 3.00 8.00
TSML Mario Lemieux 12.00 30.00
TSMM Mike Modano 5.00 12.00
TSMN Markus Naslund 3.00 8.00
TSMR Mark Recchi 2.00 5.00
TSMT Marty Turco 3.00 8.00
TSNK Nikolai Khabibulin 3.00 8.00
TSOK Olaf Kolzig 3.00 8.00
TSPF Peter Forsberg 5.00 12.00
TSPK Paul Kariya 3.00 8.00
TSRB Ray Bourque 5.00 12.00
TSRN Rick Nash 4.00 10.00
TSRV Rick Vaive 2.00 5.00
TSRY Michael Ryder 2.50 6.00
TSSC Sidney Crosby 15.00 40.00
TSSF Sergei Fedorov 3.00 8.00
TSSG Scott Gomez 3.00 8.00
TSSK Saku Koivu 3.00 8.00
TSSN Scott Niedermayer 2.00 5.00
TSWE Doug Weight 2.00 5.00

2006-07 Artifacts Treasured Swatches Black

PRINT RUN 1/1
NOT PRICED DUE TO SCARCITY
TSAF Alexander Frolov
TSAH Ales Hemsky
TSAK Alex Kovalev
TSAM Al MacInnis
TSAO Alexander Ovechkin
TSAR Jason Arnott
TSBB Bob Bourne
TSBC Bobby Clarke
TSBG Bill Guerin
TSBL Rob Blake
TSBN Bob Nystrom
TSBP Bob Probert
TSBS Borje Salming
TSCJ Curtis Joseph
TSCN Cam Neely
TSDG Doug Gilmour
TSDW Dave Williams
TSEB Ed Belfour
TSEL Eric Lindros
TSGF Grant Fuhr
TSIK Ilya Kovalchuk
TSJA Jason Allison
TSJG Jean-Sebastien Giguere
TSJJ Jaromir Jagr
TSJN Joe Nieuwendyk
TSJT Joe Thornton
TSKP Keith Primeau
TSKT Keith Tkachuk
TSMB Martin Brodeur
TSMF Manny Fernandez
TSMH Marian Hossa
TSML Mario Lemieux
TSMM Mike Modano
TSMN Markus Naslund
TSMR Mark Recchi
TSMT Marty Turco
TSNK Nikolai Khabibulin
TSOK Olaf Kolzig
TSPF Peter Forsberg
TSPK Paul Kariya
TSRB Ray Bourque
TSRN Rick Nash
TSRV Rick Vaive
TSRY Michael Ryder
TSSC Sidney Crosby
TSSF Sergei Fedorov
TSSG Scott Gomez
TSSK Saku Koivu
TSSN Scott Niedermayer
TSWE Doug Weight

2006-07 Artifacts Treasured Swatches Blue

*BLUE: .75X TO 1.5X HI
PRINT RUN 50 SER. #'d SETS

2006-07 Artifacts Treasured Swatches Platinum

PRINT RUN 10 SER. #'d SETS
NOT PRICED DUE TO SCARCITY

2006-07 Artifacts Treasured Swatches Red

*RED: .50X TO 1.25X HI
PRINT RUN 100 SER. #'d SETS

2006-07 Artifacts Treasured Swatches Autographed Black

PRINT RUN 1/1
NOT PRICED DUE TO SCARCITY
TSAF Alexander Frolov
TSAH Ales Hemsky
TSAO Alexander Ovechkin
TSBB Bob Bourne
TSBL Rob Blake
TSBN Bob Nystrom
TSBP Bob Probert
TSBS Borje Salming
TSCN Cam Neely
TSDW Dave Williams
TSGF Grant Fuhr
TSIK Ilya Kovalchuk
TSJT Joe Thornton
TSMB Martin Brodeur
TSMH Marian Hossa
TSML Mario Lemieux
TSMN Markus Naslund
TSMT Marty Turco
TSRB Ray Bourque
TSRN Rick Nash
TSRV Rick Vaive
TSRY Michael Ryder
TSSC Sidney Crosby
TSSG Scott Gomez
TSSK Saku Koivu
TSWE Doug Weight

2006-07 Artifacts Tundra Tandems

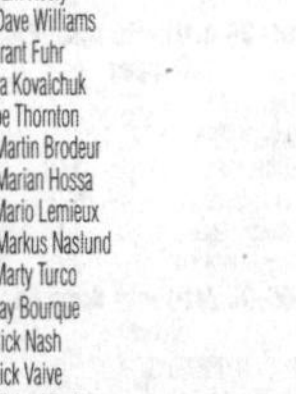

PRINT RUN 125 SER. #'d SETS
TTAB Andrew Raycroft 3.00 8.00
Bryan McCabe
TTAD Maxim Afinogenov 3.00 8.00
Chris Drury
TTAG Glenn Anderson 30.00 80.00
Wayne Gretzky/50
TTAK Glenn Anderson 3.00 8.00
Mike Krushelnyski
TTAM Matt Stajan 3.00 8.00
Alexander Steen
TTAS Sergei Samsonov 3.00 8.00
Alex Kovalev
TTBB Brad Boyes 4.00 10.00
Patrice Bergeron
TTBE Martin Brodeur 6.00 15.00
Patrik Elias
TTBJ Brendan Shanahan 6.00 15.00
Jaromir Jagr
TTBN Bob Nystrom 3.00 8.00
Bob Bourne
TTBO Johnny Bucyk 6.00 15.00
Ray Bourque
TTBR Brian Rolston 3.00 8.00
Pierre-Marc Bouchard
TTCA Cam Neely 5.00 12.00
Adam Oates
TTCE Curtis Joseph 4.00 10.00
Ed Jovanovski
TTCG Wendel Clark 8.00 20.00
Doug Gilmour
TTCL Dino Ciccarelli 3.00 8.00
Rod Langway
TTCN Mike Comrie 3.00 8.00
Ladislav Nagy
TTCR Cam Neely 8.00 20.00
Ray Bourque
TTDB Darryl Sittler 8.00 20.00
Borje Salming
TTDD Daniel Alfredsson 4.00 10.00
Dany Heatley
TTDH Tomas Holmstrom 4.00 10.00
Pavel Datsyuk
TTDO Trevor Daley 3.00 8.00
Steve Ott
TTDR Richard Brodeur 4.00 10.00
Dave Williams
TTDW Kris Draper 3.00 8.00
Jason Williams
TTEJ Ed Belfour 4.00 10.00
Jay Bouwmeester
TTFB Rob Blake 3.00 8.00
Alexander Frolov
TTFG Peter Forsberg 5.00 12.00
Simon Gagne
TTFP Manny Fernandez 3.00 8.00
Mark Parrish
TTFR Grant Fuhr 6.00 15.00
Bill Ranford
TTGC Simon Gagne 4.00 10.00
Jeff Carter
TTGD Marian Gaborik 4.00 10.00
Pavol Demitra
TTGG Scott Gomez 3.00 8.00
Brian Gionta
TTGP Guy Lafleur 6.00 15.00
Peter Stastny
TTHD Henrik Sedin 4.00 10.00
Daniel Sedin
TTHK Marian Hossa 5.00 12.00
Ilya Kovalchuk
TTHO Dominik Hasek 6.00 15.00
Chris Osgood
TTHP Marcel Hossa 3.00 8.00
Petr Prucha
TTHS Milan Hejduk 3.00 8.00
Marek Svatos
TTHU Scott Hartnell 3.00 8.00
Scottie Upshall
TTIT Jarome Iginla 5.00 12.00
Alex Tanguay
TTJA Joe Mullen 3.00 8.00
Al MacInnis
TTJH Jason Spezza 4.00 10.00
Dany Heatley
TTJJ Joffrey Lupul 3.00 8.00
Jarret Stoll
TTKA Paul Kariya 3.00 8.00
Jason Arnott
TTKH Nikolai Khabibulin 3.00 8.00
Martin Havlat
TTKK Saku Koivu 4.00 10.00
Alex Kovalev
TTKL Ilya Kovalchuk 4.00 10.00
Kari Lehtonen
TTKO Olaf Kolzig 10.00 25.00
Alexander Ovechkin
TTKP Miikka Kiprusoff 6.00 15.00
Dion Phaneuf
TTLB Guy Lafleur 15.00 40.00
Jean Beliveau
TTLC Mario Lemieux 40.00 80.00
Sidney Crosby
TTLM John LeClair 3.00 8.00
Mark Recchi
TTLN Markus Naslund 5.00 12.00
Roberto Luongo
TTLR Vincent Lecavalier 5.00 12.00
Brad Richards
TTLS Guy Lafleur 5.00 12.00
Steve Shutt
TTLZ Luc Robitaille 3.00 8.00
Zigmund Palffy
TTMB Ryan Miller 5.00 12.00
Martin Biron
TTMC Larry Murphy 3.00 8.00
Chris Chelios
TTME Lanny McDonald 4.00 10.00
Ron Ellis
TTML Mike Modano 4.00 10.00
Eric Lindros
TTMM Lanny McDonald 3.00 8.00
Al MacInnis
TTMR Miroslav Satan 3.00 8.00
Rick DiPietro
TTMS Glen Murray 3.00 8.00
Marc Savard
TTMT Bryan McCabe 4.00 10.00
Darcy Tucker
TTNF Rick Nash 4.00 10.00
Sergei Fedorov
TTNG Scott Niedermayer 3.00 8.00

Jean-Sebastien Giguere
TTNH Nicklas Lidstrom 5.00 12.00
Henrik Zetterberg
TTNO Markus Naslund 3.00 8.00
Mattias Ohlund
TTNP Chris Pronger 4.00 10.00
Scott Niedermayer
TTNR Joe Nieuwendyk 3.00 8.00
Gary Roberts
TTNY Mike York 3.00 8.00
Trent Hunter
TTOT Olli Jokinen 3.00 8.00
Todd Bertuzzi
TTPJ Patrick Roy 12.00 30.00
Joe Sakic
TTPK Patrick Roy 10.00 25.00
Kirk Muller
TTPM Patrick Marleau 3.00 8.00
Mark Bell
TTPT Pascal Leclaire 3.00 8.00
Ty Conklin
TTRB Patrick Roy 10.00 25.00
Ray Bourque
TTRD Shane Doan 3.00 8.00
Jeremy Roenick
TTRK Tuomo Ruutu 3.00 8.00
Nikolai Khabibulin
TTRM Mark Recchi 3.00 8.00
Ryan Malone
TTRR Mike Ribeiro 3.00 8.00
Michael Ryder
TTRS Ryan Smyth 3.00 8.00
Shawn Horcoff
TTSF Martin St. Louis 3.00 8.00
Ruslan Fedotenko
TTSJ Sami Kapanen 3.00 8.00
Joni Pitkanen
TTSM Marc Denis 3.00 8.00
Sean Burke
TTSP Teemu Selanne 5.00 12.00
Corey Perry
TTST Joe Sakic 8.00 20.00
Jose Theodore
TTSV Darryl Sittler 5.00 12.00
Rick Vaive
TTSW Eric Staal 5.00 12.00
Cam Ward
TTTC Joe Thornton 8.00 20.00
Jonathan Cheechoo
TTTG Keith Tkachuk 3.00 8.00
Bill Guerin
TTTM Marty Turco 3.00 8.00
Brenden Morrow
TTTO Mats Sundin 4.00 10.00
Michael Peca
TTTW Doug Weight 3.00 8.00
Keith Tkachuk
TTVE Tomas Vokoun 3.00 8.00
Martin Erat
TTWA Wade Redden 3.00 8.00
Andrej Meszaros
TTWB Justin Williams 3.00 8.00
Rod Brind'Amour
TTWG Doug Weight 3.00 8.00
Bill Guerin
TTWS Denis Savard 3.00 8.00
Doug Wilson
TTZM Zdeno Chara 3.00 8.00
Milan Jurcina

2006-07 Artifacts Tundra Tandems Black

COMPLETE SET (100)
PRINT RUN 1/1
NOT PRICED DUE TO SCARCITY

2006-07 Artifacts Tundra Tandems Blue

*BLUE: .75X TO 1.5X HI
PRINT RUN 25 SER. #'d SETS
TTAG Glenn Anderson 75.00 125.00
Wayne Gretzky
TTKO Olaf Kolzig 30.00 75.00
Alexander Ovechkin
TTLC Mario Lemieux 60.00 100.00
Sidney Crosby
TTPJ Patrick Roy 25.00 60.00
Joe Sakic
TTRB Patrick Roy 25.00 60.00
Ray Bourque

2006-07 Artifacts Tundra Tandems Gold

PRINT RUN 10 SER. #'d SETS
NOT PRICED DUE TO SCARCITY

2006-07 Artifacts Tundra Tandems Red

*RED: .50X TO 1.25X HI
PRINT RUN 50 SER. #'d SETS

2006-07 Artifacts Tundra Tandems Dual Patches Red

PRINT RUN 25 SER. #'d SETS
NOT PRICED DUE TO SCARCITY
TTLC Mario Lemieux 100.00 175.00
Sidney Crosby

2007-08 Artifacts

COMP.SET w/o SPs (100) 12.00 30.00
101-140 STARS/LEG PRINT RUN 1499
141-200 ROOKIES PRINT RUN 999
201-242 ROOKIES PRINT RUN 599
1 Ryan Miller .30 .75
2 Thomas Vanek .25 .60
3 Chris Drury .25 .60
4 Daniel Briere .30 .75
5 Zach Parise .25 .60
6 Patrik Elias .20 .50
7 Martin Brodeur .75 2.00
8 Marian Hossa .30 .75
9 Ilya Kovalchuk .40 1.00
10 Kari Lehtonen .30 .75
11 Dany Heatley .40 1.00
12 Ray Emery .25 .60
13 Jason Spezza .30 .75
14 Daniel Alfredsson .25 .60
15 Sidney Crosby 1.50 4.00
16 Evgeni Malkin .75 2.00
17 Marc-Andre Fleury .30 .75
18 Jordan Staal .40 1.00
19 Jaromir Jagr .50 1.25
20 Henrik Lundqvist .40 1.00
21 Martin Straka .20 .50
22 Vincent Lecavalier .30 .75
23 Brad Richards .25 .60
24 Martin St. Louis .25 .60
25 Alexei Yashin .20 .50
26 Rick DiPietro .25 .60
27 Miroslav Satan .20 .50
28 Mats Sundin .30 .75
29 Andrew Raycroft .25 .60
30 Darcy Tucker .25 .60
31 Alexander Steen .20 .50
32 Saku Koivu .25 .60
33 Guillaume Latendresse .25 .60
34 Cristobal Huet .25 .60
35 Michael Ryder .20 .50
36 Eric Staal .30 .75
37 Cam Ward .30 .75
38 Ray Whitney .20 .50
39 Nathan Horton .20 .50
40 Olli Jokinen .20 .50
41 Tomas Vokoun .30 .75
42 Patrice Bergeron .25 .60
43 Marc Savard .20 .50
44 Tim Thomas .40 1.00
45 Alexander Ovechkin 1.00 2.50
46 Olaf Kolzig .30 .75
47 Alexander Semin .30 .75
48 Simon Gagne .30 .75
49 Martin Biron .25 .60
50 Jeff Carter .25 .60
51 Henrik Zetterberg .30 .75
52 Pavel Datsyuk .30 .75
53 Nicklas Lidstrom .30 .75
54 Tomas Holmstrom .25 .60
55 Jean-Sebastien Giguere .30 .75
56 Chris Pronger .30 .75
57 Ryan Getzlaf .25 .60
58 Teemu Selanne .30 .75
59 Markus Naslund .30 .75
60 Roberto Luongo .50 1.25
61 Henrik Sedin .20 .50
62 Daniel Sedin .20 .50
63 Chris Mason .25 .60
64 Alexander Radulov .30 .75
65 Paul Kariya .30 .75
66 Peter Forsberg .40 1.00
67 Jonathan Cheechoo .25 .60
68 Joe Thornton .40 1.00
69 Evgeni Nabokov .25 .60
70 Mike Modano .30 .75
71 Marty Turco .30 .75
72 Mike Ribeiro .20 .50
73 Marian Gaborik .40 1.00
74 Pavol Demitra .20 .50
75 Pierre-Marc Bouchard .20 .50
76 Jarome Iginla .50 1.25
77 Dion Phaneuf .30 .75
78 Miikka Kiprusoff .40 1.00
79 Alex Tanguay .25 .60
80 Joe Sakic .60 1.50
81 Milan Hejduk .25 .60
82 Paul Stastny .30 .75
83 Brad Boyes .25 .60
84 Manny Legace .25 .60
85 Doug Weight .20 .50
86 Rick Nash .30 .75
87 Pascal Leclaire .25 .60
88 Sergei Fedorov .30 .75
89 Ales Hemsky .20 .50
90 Dwayne Roloson .25 .60
91 Shawn Horcoff .20 .50
92 Martin Havlat .25 .60
93 Nikolai Khabibulin .30 .75
94 Tuomo Ruutu .20 .50
95 Anze Kopitar .30 .75
96 Alexander Frolov .25 .60
97 Mike Cammalleri .25 .60
98 Shane Doan .20 .50
99 Mikael Tellqvist .25 .60
100 Zbynek Michalek .20 .50
101 Wayne Gretzky L 6.00 15.00
102 Mario Lemieux L 4.00 10.00
103 Gordie Howe L 3.00 8.00
104 Bobby Orr L 5.00 12.00
105 Mark Messier L 2.50 6.00
106 Patrick Roy L 4.00 10.00
107 Ray Bourque L 1.50 4.00
108 Gilbert Perreault L 1.00 2.50
109 Bobby Clarke L 1.25 3.00
110 Guy Lafleur L 1.25 3.00
111 Don Cherry L 1.50 4.00
112 Ron Hextall L 2.00 5.00
113 Grant Fuhr L 2.00 5.00
114 Larry Robinson L 1.50 4.00
115 Cam Neely L 1.25 3.00
116 Bernie Parent L 1.50 4.00
117 Frank Mahovlich L 2.00 5.00
118 Tony Esposito L 2.00 5.00
119 Phil Esposito L 2.00 5.00
120 Stan Mikita L 1.00 2.50
121 Sidney Crosby S 6.00 15.00
122 Joe Sakic S 2.50 6.00
123 Martin Brodeur S 3.00 8.00
124 Dany Heatley S 1.50 4.00
125 Joe Thornton S 1.50 4.00
126 Henrik Zetterberg S 1.25 3.00
127 Jaromir Jagr S 2.00 5.00
128 Simon Gagne S 1.25 3.00
129 Jarome Iginla S 2.00 5.00
130 Roberto Luongo S 2.50 6.00
131 Alexander Ovechkin S 4.00 10.00
132 Ilya Kovalchuk S 1.50 4.00
133 Mats Sundin S 1.25 3.00
134 Rick Nash S 1.25 3.00
135 Patrice Bergeron S 1.25 3.00
136 Saku Koivu S 1.00 2.50
137 Henrik Lundqvist S 1.50 4.00
138 Evgeni Malkin S 3.00 8.00
139 Vincent Lecavalier S 1.25 3.00
140 Ryan Miller S 1.25 3.00
141 Jeff Finger RC 2.50 6.00
142 Colin Fraser RC 2.50 6.00
143 Pierre Parenteau RC 2.50 6.00
144 David Koci RC 2.50 6.00
145 Bryan Bickell RC 2.50 6.00
146 Jonas Nordqvist RC 2.50 6.00
147 Tomas Popperle RC 3.00 8.00
148 Curtis Glencross RC 2.50 6.00
149 Marc Methot RC 2.50 6.00
150 David Krejci RC 5.00 12.00
151 Jonathan Sigalet RC 2.50 6.00
152 Petr Kalus RC 3.00 8.00
153 Jaroslav Halak RC 8.00 20.00
154 Duncan Milroy RC 2.50 6.00
155 Jannik Hansen RC 2.50 6.00
156 Jeff Schultz RC 2.50 6.00
157 Jamie Hunt RC 2.50 6.00
158 Daniel Carcillo RC 3.00 8.00
159 Andy Greene RC 2.50 6.00
160 Mark Fraser RC 2.50 6.00
161 Rod Pelley RC 2.50 6.00
162 David Clarkson RC 2.50 6.00
163 Aaron Rome RC 2.50 6.00
164 Kent Huskins RC 2.50 6.00
165 Bryan Melin RC 2.50 6.00
166 Drew Miller RC 2.50 6.00
167 David Moss RC 4.00 10.00
168 Tomi Maki RC 2.50 6.00
169 Scott Munroe RC 2.50 6.00
170 Nathan Guenin RC 2.50 6.00
171 Ryan Parent RC 3.00 8.00
172 Frans Nielsen RC 2.50 6.00
173 Lauri Tukonen RC 2.50 6.00
174 Yutaka Fukufuji RC 3.00 8.00
175 John Zeiler RC 2.50 6.00
176 Gabe Gauthier RC 2.50 6.00
177 Shay Stephenson RC 2.50 6.00
178 Joe Piskula RC 2.50 6.00
179 Jack Johnson RC 4.00 10.00
180 Tom Gilbert RC 3.00 8.00
181 Mathieu Roy RC 2.50 6.00
182 Zack Stortini RC 2.50 6.00
183 Bryan Young RC 2.50 6.00
184 Sebastien Bisaillon RC 2.50 6.00
185 Rob Schremp RC 3.00 8.00
186 Martin Lojek RC 2.50 6.00
187 Rich Peverley RC 2.50 6.00
188 Ryan Callahan RC 4.00 10.00
189 Daniel Girardi RC 2.50 6.00
190 Brandon Dubinsky RC 4.00 10.00
191 Matt Ellis RC 2.50 6.00
192 Patrick Kaleta RC 2.50 6.00
193 Mark Mancari RC 3.00 8.00
194 Danny Bois RC 2.50 6.00
195 Tomas Plihal RC 3.00 8.00
196 Tobias Stephan RC 3.00 8.00
197 Joel Lundqvist RC 2.50 6.00
198 Chris Conner RC 2.50 6.00
199 Krys Barch RC 2.50 6.00
200 Joel Ward RC 2.50 6.00
201 T. J. Hensick RC 5.00 12.00
202 Jonathan Toews RC 30.00 60.00
203 Kris Russell RC 6.00 15.00
204 Tuukka Rask RC 10.00 25.00
205 Carey Price RC 30.00 60.00
206 Mason Raymond RC 10.00 25.00
207 Nicklas Backstrom RC 15.00 40.00
208 Peter Mueller RC 12.00 30.00
209 Nicklas Bergfors RC 5.00 12.00
210 Bobby Ryan RC 15.00 40.00
211 Curtis McElhinney RC 5.00 12.00
212 Steve Downie RC 5.00 12.00
213 Casey Borer RC 4.00 10.00
214 Martin Hanzal RC 5.00 12.00
215 Jonathan Bernier RC 10.00 25.00
216 Matt Smaby RC 4.00 10.00
217 Sam Gagner RC 8.00 20.00
218 Stefan Meyer RC 4.00 10.00
219 Ville Koistinen RC 4.00 10.00
220 Marc Staal RC 10.00 25.00
221 Kyle Chipchura RC 6.00 15.00
222 Mike Weber RC 4.00 10.00
223 Nick Foligno RC 6.00 15.00
224 Devin Setoguchi RC 8.00 20.00
225 Matt Niskanen RC 4.00 10.00
226 James Sheppard RC 4.00 10.00
227 Bryan Little RC 6.00 15.00
228 Tyler Kennedy RC 6.00 15.00
229 Erik Johnson RC 8.00 20.00
230 Jiri Tlusty RC 10.00 25.00
231 Patrick Kane RC 30.00 60.00
232 Andrew Cogliano RC 10.00 25.00
233 David Jones RC 4.00 10.00
234 Anton Stralman RC 5.00 12.00
235 Brian Elliott RC 5.00 12.00
236 Tobias Enstrom RC 6.00 15.00
237 David Perron RC 6.00 15.00
238 Chris Bourque RC 5.00 12.00
239 Ondrej Pavelec RC 6.00 15.00
240 Milan Lucic RC 10.00 25.00
241 Jack Skille RC 6.00 15.00
242 Sergei Kostitsyn RC 12.00 30.00

2007-08 Artifacts Blue

*BLUE: 8X TO 20X
*BLUE STARS/LEG: 2X TO 5X
*BLUE RCs (141-200): 1X to 2.5X
*BLUE RCs (201-242): .8X TO 2X
STATED PRINT RUN 25 #'d SETS

2007-08 Artifacts Bronze

STATED PRINT RUN 10 #'d SETS
NOT PRICED DUE TO SCARCITY

2007-08 Artifacts Gold

*GOLD: 4X TO 10X
*GOLD LEG/STARS: 1.5X TO 4 X
*GOLD ROOKIES (141-200): .8X TO 2X
*GOLD ROOKIES (201-242): .6X TO 1.5X
STATED PRINT RUN 50 SERIAL #'d SETS

2007-08 Artifacts Silver

*SILVER: 3X TO 8X BASE
*SILVER LEG/STARS: 1.2X TO 3X BASE
*SILVER ROOKIES (141-200): .6X TO 1.5X BASE
*SILVER ROOKIES (201-242): .5X TO 1.2X BASE
STATED PRINT RUN 100 #'d SETS

2007-08 Artifacts Silver Rainbow

STATED PRINT RUN 1 SERIAL #'d SET
NOT PRICED DUE TO SCARCITY

2007-08 Artifacts Auto-Facts

STATED ODDS: 1:10
AFAF Alexander Frolov 4.00 10.00
AFAK Andrei Kostitsyn 4.00 10.00
AFAL Andrew Ladd 4.00 10.00
AFAM Al MacInnis 5.00 12.00
AFAN Andrew Raycroft 5.00 12.00
AFAO Alex Ovechkin SP 60.00 150.00
AFAT Alex Tanguay 5.00 12.00
AFBC Bobby Clarke 6.00 15.00
AFBG Butch Goring 4.00 10.00
AFBI Martin Biron 5.00 12.00
AFBM Brendan Morrison 4.00 10.00
AFBO Ray Bourque SP 12.00 30.00
AFBP Bernie Parent SP 12.00 30.00
AFBR Brad Richardson 2.50 6.00
AFBS Borje Salming SP 8.00 20.00
AFBY Brad Boyes 5.00 12.00
AFCH Erik Christensen 4.00 10.00
AFCM Clarke MacArthur 4.00 10.00
AFCP Chris Pronger 6.00 15.00
AFDB Daniel Briere 6.00 15.00
AFDE Denis Potvin 5.00 12.00
AFDL David Leneveu 5.00 12.00
AFDP Dion Phaneuf 6.00 15.00
AFDS Drew Stafford 5.00 12.00
AFDT Darcy Tucker SP 8.00 20.00
AFDU Dustin Brown 4.00 10.00
AFEC Erik Cole 4.00 10.00
AFEM Evgeni Malkin 25.00 60.00
AFES Eric Staal 6.00 15.00
AFGA Glenn Anderson 5.00 12.00
AFGB Gilbert Brule SP 6.00 15.00
AFGC Gerry Cheevers 10.00 25.00
AFGH Gordie Howe SP 30.00 60.00
AFGL Guillaume Latendresse 5.00 12.00
AFGP Gilbert Perreault 5.00 12.00
AFHA Dale Hawerchuk 5.00 12.00
AFHE Milan Hejduk 5.00 12.00
AFHL Henrik Lundqvist 8.00 20.00
AFHZ Henrik Zetterberg 6.00 15.00
AFIK Ilya Kovalchuk 8.00 20.00
AFJA Jason Arnott 4.00 10.00
AFJB Johnny Bucyk 4.00 10.00
AFJC Jeff Carter 4.00 10.00
AFJK Jari Kurri SP
AFJR Jeremy Roenick 4.00 10.00
AFJS Jarret Stoll 4.00 10.00
AFKL Kari Lehtonen 6.00 15.00
AFKM Kirk Muller 4.00 10.00
AFLA Guy Lafleur 15.00 40.00
AFLM Lanny McDonald SP
AFLR Luc Robitaille 5.00 12.00
AFMB Martin Brodeur SP 60.00 120.00
AFMC Mike Cammalleri 5.00 12.00
AFMG Marian Gaborik 8.00 20.00
AFMH Martin Havlat 5.00 12.00
AFMI Mike Bossy 5.00 12.00
AFMK Miikka Kiprusoff 8.00 20.00
AFML Mario Lemieux SP 60.00 150.00
AFMM Mark Messier SP 150.00 250.00
AFMR Mike Richards 8.00 20.00
AFNB Niklas Backstrom 5.00 12.00
AFNZ Nikolai Zherdev 4.00 10.00
AFOR Bobby Orr SP
AFPE Corey Perry 5.00 12.00
AFPK Phil Kessel 6.00 15.00
AFPO Patrick O'Sullivan 5.00 12.00
AFPR Patrick Roy SP 75.00 150.00
AFPS Paul Stastny 6.00 15.00
AFRA Bill Ranford 5.00 12.00
AFRB Richard Brodeur 5.00 12.00
AFRE Ron Ellis 4.00 10.00
AFRH Ron Hextall 10.00 25.00
AFRM Ryan Malone 4.00 10.00
AFRN Rick Nash 6.00 15.00
AFSC Sidney Crosby 75.00 150.00
AFSG Scott Gomez 4.00 10.00
AFST Peter Stastny 5.00 12.00
AFTL Ted Lindsay SP 8.00 20.00
AFTV Tomas Vokoun 6.00 15.00
AFTW Tiger Williams 5.00 12.00
AFWC Wayne Cashman 5.00 12.00
AFWG Wayne Gretzky SP 150.00 300.00
AFZC Zdeno Chara 4.00 10.00

2007-08 Artifacts Frozen Artifacts

STATED PRINT RUN 299 #'d SETS
FAAK Alex Kovalev 3.00 8.00
FAAO Alexander Ovechkin 15.00 40.00
FAAR Andrew Raycroft 4.00 10.00
FAAS Alexander Steen 3.00 8.00
FAAT Alex Tanguay 4.00 10.00
FAAY Alexei Yashin 3.00 8.00
FABB Brad Boyes 4.00 10.00
FABF Bernie Federko 3.00 8.00
FABG Brian Gionta 3.00 8.00
FABM Brendan Morrison 3.00 8.00
FABR Bill Ranford 4.00 10.00
FABS Billy Smith 5.00 12.00
FACC Chris Chelios 3.00 8.00
FACD Chris Drury 4.00 10.00
FACI Dino Ciccarelli 4.00 10.00
FACJ Curtis Joseph 4.00 10.00
FACN Cam Neely 5.00 12.00
FACP Chris Pronger 5.00 12.00
FACW Cam Ward 5.00 12.00
FADA Daniel Alfredsson 4.00 10.00
FADC Dan Cloutier 4.00 10.00
FADH Dale Hawerchuk 4.00 10.00
FADL David Legwand 3.00 8.00
FADP Rick DiPietro 4.00 10.00
FADS Darryl Sittler 4.00 10.00
FADW Doug Weight 3.00 8.00
FAEB Ed Belfour 5.00 12.00
FAEM Evgeni Malkin 12.00 30.00
FAES Eric Staal 5.00 12.00
FAGA Glenn Anderson 4.00 10.00
FAGL Guy Lafleur 12.00 30.00
FAHA Dominik Hasek 6.00 15.00
FAHZ Henrik Zetterberg 5.00 12.00
FAIK Ilya Kovalchuk 6.00 15.00
FAJB Jay Bouwmeester 3.00 8.00
FAJC Jonathan Cheechoo 4.00 10.00
FAJI Jarome Iginla 8.00 20.00
FAJL Jere Lehtinen 3.00 8.00
FAJO Joe Sakic 10.00 25.00
FAJS Jason Spezza 5.00 12.00
FAKL Kari Lehtonen 5.00 12.00
FAKT Keith Tkachuk 4.00 10.00
FALM Lanny McDonald 4.00 10.00
FALR Larry Robinson 6.00 15.00
FAMC Bryan McCabe 3.00 8.00
FAMH Marian Hossa 5.00 12.00
FAML Mario Lemieux 15.00 40.00
FAMO Brenden Morrow 4.00 10.00
FARI Brad Richards 4.00 10.00
FASA Borje Salming 4.00 10.00
FASH Brendan Shanahan 4.00 10.00

2007-08 Artifacts Frozen Artifacts Gold

*GOLD: .6X TO 1.5X BASE
STATED PRINT RUN 50 #'d SETS

2007-08 Artifacts Frozen Artifacts Icy Blue

*ICY BLUE: .8X TO 2X BASE
STATED PRINT RUN 25 #'d SETS

2007-08 Artifacts Frozen Artifacts Red

STATED PRINT RUN 10 SERIAL #'d SETS
NOT PRICED DUE TO SCARCITY

2007-08 Artifacts Frozen Artifacts Silver

*SILVER: .5X TO 1.2X BASE
STATED PRINT RUN 100 #'d SETS

2007-08 Artifacts Frozen Artifacts Patches Bronze

STATED PRINT RUN 50 SERIAL #'d SETS
FAAK Alex Kovalev 6.00 15.00
FAAO Alexander Ovechkin 30.00 80.00
FAAR Andrew Raycroft 8.00 20.00
FAAS Alexander Steen 6.00 15.00
FAAT Alex Tanguay 8.00 20.00
FABB Brad Boyes 8.00 20.00
FABF Bernie Federko 6.00 15.00
FABG Brian Gionta 6.00 15.00
FABM Brendan Morrison 6.00 15.00
FABR Bill Ranford 8.00 20.00
FABS Billy Smith 10.00 25.00
FACC Chris Chelios 6.00 15.00
FACD Chris Drury 8.00 20.00
FACI Dino Ciccarelli 8.00 20.00
FACJ Curtis Joseph 8.00 20.00
FACN Cam Neely 10.00 25.00
FACP Chris Pronger 10.00 25.00
FACW Cam Ward 10.00 25.00
FADA Daniel Alfredsson 8.00 20.00
FADC Dan Cloutier 8.00 20.00
FADH Dale Hawerchuk 8.00 20.00
FADL David Legwand 6.00 15.00
FADP Rick DiPietro 8.00 20.00
FADW Doug Weight 6.00 15.00
FAEB Ed Belfour 10.00 25.00
FAEM Evgeni Malkin 25.00 60.00
FAES Eric Staal 10.00 25.00
FAGA Glenn Anderson 8.00 20.00
FAHA Dominik Hasek 12.00 30.00
FAHZ Henrik Zetterberg 10.00 25.00
FAIK Ilya Kovalchuk 12.00 30.00
FAJB Jay Bouwmeester 6.00 15.00
FAJC Jonathan Cheechoo 8.00 20.00
FAJI Jarome Iginla 15.00 40.00
FAJL Jere Lehtinen 6.00 15.00
FAJO Joe Sakic 20.00 50.00
FAJS Jason Spezza 10.00 25.00
FAKL Kari Lehtonen 10.00 25.00
FAKT Keith Tkachuk 8.00 20.00
FALM Lanny McDonald 8.00 20.00
FALR Larry Robinson 12.00 30.00
FAMC Bryan McCabe 6.00 15.00
FAMH Marian Hossa 10.00 25.00
FAML Mario Lemieux 30.00 80.00
FAMO Brenden Morrow 8.00 20.00
FARI Brad Richards 8.00 20.00
FASA Borje Salming 8.00 20.00
FASH Brendan Shanahan 10.00 25.00

2007-08 Artifacts Frozen Artifacts Patches Gold

*GOLD: .5X TO 1.2X BASE
STATED PRINT RUN 25 SERIAL #'d SETS

2007-08 Artifacts Frozen Artifacts Patches Red

STATED PRINT RUN 10 SERIAL #'d SETS
NOT PRICED DUE TO SCARCITY

2007-08 Artifacts Frozen Artifacts Patches Purple Tags

STATED PRINT RUN 1 SERIAL #'d SET
NOT PRICED DUE TO SCARCITY

2007-08 Artifacts Gold Rainbow Autographs

STATED PRINT RUN 1 SERIAL #'d SET
NOT PRICED DUE TO SCARCITY

2007-08 Artifacts Treasured Patches Bronze

*PATCHES BRONZE: .8X TO 2X SWATCHES
STATED PRINT RUN 50 SERIAL #'d SETS

2007-08 Artifacts Treasured Patches Gold

*PATCHES GOLD: 1.5X TO 4X SWATCHES
STATED PRINT RUN 50 SERIAL #'d SETS

2007-08 Artifacts Treasured Patches Red

STATED PRINT RUN 10 SERIAL #'d SETS
NOT PRICED DUE TO SCARCITY

2007-08 Artifacts Treasured Patches Purple Tags

STATED PRINT RUN 1 SERIAL #'d SET
NOT PRICED DUE TO SCARCITY

2007-08 Artifacts Treasured Swatches

STATED PRINT RUN 299 SERIAL #'d SETS
TSAF Alexander Frolov 3.00 8.00
TSAH Ales Hemsky 3.00 8.00
TSAK Alex Kovalev 3.00 8.00
TSAM Al MacInnis 4.00 10.00
TSAO Alexander Ovechkin 15.00 40.00
TSBB Bob Bourne 3.00 8.00
TSBG Bill Guerin 3.00 8.00
TSBL Rob Blake 4.00 10.00
TSBN Bob Nystrom 3.00 8.00
TSBR Brad Richards 4.00 10.00
TSBS Borje Salming 4.00 10.00
TSCJ Curtis Joseph 4.00 10.00
TSCN Cam Neely 5.00 12.00
TSDB Daniel Briere 5.00 12.00
TSDG Doug Gilmour 4.00 10.00
TSDH Dany Heatley 6.00 15.00
TSDW Doug Weight 3.00 8.00
TSEB Ed Belfour 5.00 12.00
TSEL Eric Lindros 5.00 12.00
TSGO Scott Gomez 3.00 8.00
TSIK Ilya Kovalchuk 6.00 15.00
TSJG Jean-Sebastien Giguere 5.00 12.00
TSJJ Jaromir Jagr 8.00 20.00
TSJT Joe Thornton 6.00 15.00
TSKT Keith Tkachuk 4.00 10.00
TSMB Martin Brodeur 12.00 30.00
TSMF Manny Fernandez 4.00 10.00
TSMH Marian Hossa 5.00 12.00
TSMM Mike Modano 5.00 12.00
TSMN Markus Naslund 5.00 12.00
TSMR Mark Recchi 3.00 8.00
TSMT Marty Turco 5.00 12.00
TSNK Nikolai Khabibulin 5.00 12.00
TSOK Olaf Kolzig 5.00 12.00
TSPF Peter Forsberg 6.00 15.00
TSPK Paul Kariya 6.00 15.00
TSRB Ray Bourque 6.00 15.00
TSRN Rick Nash 5.00 12.00
TSRY Michael Ryder 3.00 8.00
TSSC Sidney Crosby 25.00 60.00
TSSF Sergei Fedorov 5.00 12.00
TSSG Simon Gagne 5.00 12.00
TSSK Saku Koivu 4.00 10.00
TSSN Scott Niedermayer 3.00 8.00
TSSS Steve Shutt 4.00 10.00
TSTH Tomas Holmstrom 4.00 10.00
TSTS Teemu Selanne 5.00 12.00
TSTW Tiger Williams 4.00 10.00
TSVL Vincent Lecavalier 5.00 12.00
TSWG Wayne Gretzky 25.00 60.00

2007-08 Artifacts Treasured Swatches Gold

*GOLD: .6X TO 1.5X BASE
STATED PRINT RUN 50 SERIAL #'d SETS

2007-08 Artifacts Treasured Swatches Icy Blue

*ICY BLUE: .8X TO 2X BASE
STATED PRINT RUN 25 SERIAL #'d SETS

2007-08 Artifacts Treasured Swatches Purple

STATED PRINT RUN 1 SERIAL #'d SET
NOT PRICED DUE TO SCARCITY

2007-08 Artifacts Treasured Swatches Red

STATED PRINT RUN 10 SERIAL #d SETS
NOT PRICED DUE TO SCARCITY

2007-08 Artifacts Treasured Swatches Silver

*SILVER: .5X TO 1.2X BASE
STATED PRINT RUN 100 SERIAL #'d SETS

2007-08 Artifacts Tundra Tandems

STATED PRINT RUN 125 SER.#'d SETS
TTAL Al MacInnis 5.00 12.00
Lanny McDonald
TTAM Alexander Steen 4.00 10.00
Matt Stajan
TTBB Ed Belfour 6.00 15.00
Jay Bouwmeester
TTBC Steve Bernier 4.00 10.00
Matt Carle
TTBE Martin Biron 5.00 12.00
Robert Esche
TTBK Patrice Bergeron 6.00 15.00
Phil Kessel
TTBM Ray Bourque 8.00 20.00
Al MacInnis
TTBO Kevin Bieksa 4.00 10.00
Mattias Ohlund
TTBP Borje Salming 8.00 20.00
Peter Forsberg
TTBS Martin Brodeur 15.00 40.00
Scott Stevens
TTBT Peter Budaj 6.00 15.00
Jose Theodore
TTCF Sidney Crosby 30.00 80.00
Marc-Andre Fleury
TTCG Jonathan Cheechoo 5.00 12.00
Bill Guerin
TTCM Sidney Crosby 30.00 80.00
Evgeni Malkin
TTCR Corey Perry 5.00 12.00
Ryan Getzlaf
TTDG Chris Drury 5.00 12.00
Scott Gomez
TTDH Daniel Sedin 4.00 10.00
Henrik Sedin
TTDJ Shane Doan 4.00 10.00
Ed Jovanovski
TTDL Pavel Datsyuk 6.00 15.00
Nicklas Lidstrom
TTDR Pavol Demitra 4.00 10.00
Brian Rolston
TTER Eric Staal 6.00 15.00
Rod Brind'Amour
TTFM Bernie Federko 4.00 10.00
Joe Mullen
TTFT Manny Fernandez 8.00 20.00
Tim Thomas
TTFV Peter Forsberg 8.00 20.00
Tomas Vokoun
TTGC Simon Gagne 6.00 15.00
Jeff Carter
TTGE Brian Gionta 4.00 10.00
Patrik Elias
TTGK Marian Gaborik 8.00 20.00
Mikko Koivu
TTGL Wayne Gretzky 30.00 80.00
Mario Lemieux
TTGS Jean-Sebastien Giguere 6.00 15.00
Teemu Selanne
TTHA Dany Heatley 8.00 20.00
Daniel Alfredsson
TTHB Martin Havlat 4.00 10.00
Peter Bondra
TTHC Dale Hawerchuk 5.00 12.00
Dino Ciccarelli
TTHL Gordie Howe 20.00 50.00
Mario Lemieux
TTHO Dominik Hasek 8.00 20.00
Chris Osgood
TTHR Ales Hemsky 5.00 12.00
Dwayne Roloson
TTHS Milan Hejduk 5.00 12.00
Marek Svatos
TTHW Nathan Horton 4.00 10.00
Stephen Weiss
TTIH Ilya Kovalchuk 8.00 20.00
Marian Hossa
TTIT Jarome Iginla 10.00 25.00
Alex Tanguay
TTJJ Curtis Joseph 5.00 12.00
Ed Jovanovski
TTJL Jussi Jokinen 4.00 10.00
Jere Lehtinen
TTJM Joe Sakic 12.00 30.00
Milan Hejduk
TTJP Joe Sakic 20.00 50.00
Patrick Roy
TTJS Jaromir Jagr 10.00 25.00
Martin Straka
TTKA Jari Kurri 6.00 15.00
Glenn Anderson
TTKF Anze Kopitar 6.00 15.00
Alexander Frolov

TTKK Alex Kovalev / Andrei Kostitsyn 4.00 10.00
TTKP Miikka Kiprusoff / Dion Phaneuf 8.00 20.00
TTKR Saku Koivu / Michael Ryder 5.00 12.00
TTKT Paul Kariya / Keith Tkachuk 6.00 15.00
TTLA David Legwand / Jason Arnott 4.00 10.00
TTLC Nicklas Lidstrom / Chris Chelios 6.00 15.00
TTLH Kari Lehtonen / Marian Hossa 6.00 15.00
TTLN Roberto Luongo / Markus Naslund 10.00 25.00
TTLR Vincent Lecavalier / Brad Richards 6.00 15.00
TTLS Manny Legace / Curtis Sanford 5.00 12.00
TTLV Pascal Leclaire / David Vyborny 5.00 12.00
TTMB Mats Sundin / Borje Salming 6.00 15.00
TTML Brendan Morrison / Trevor Linden 5.00 12.00
TTMM Mike Modano / Joe Mullen 6.00 15.00
TTMO Guy Lafleur / Larry Robinson 15.00 40.00
TTMP Martin Brodeur / Patrik Elias 15.00 40.00
TTMR Mike Modano / Mike Ribeiro 6.00 15.00
TTMS Glen Murray / Marc Savard 4.00 10.00
TTMW Bryan McCabe / Ian White 4.00 10.00
TTNF Rick Nash / Sergei Fedorov 6.00 15.00
TTNT Evgeni Nabokov / Vesa Toskala 5.00 12.00
TTNY Brendan Witt / Trent Hunter 4.00 10.00
TTOK Alexander Ovechkin / Olaf Kolzig 20.00 50.00
TTOM Alexander Ovechkin / Evgeni Malkin 15.00 40.00
TTPA Peter Stastny / Anton Stastny 4.00 10.00
TTPB Gilbert Perreault / Daniel Briere 6.00 15.00
TTPG Zach Parise / Brian Gionta 5.00 12.00
TTPN Chris Pronger / Scott Niedermayer 6.00 15.00
TTPP Fernando Pisani / Marc-Antoine Pouliot 4.00 10.00
TTRB Patrick Roy / Ray Bourque 20.00 50.00
TTRG Wade Redden / Martin Gerber 5.00 12.00
TTRH Michael Ryder / Chris Higgins 5.00 12.00
TTRJ Ray Bourque / Johnny Bucyk 8.00 20.00
TTSB Billy Smith / Bob Bourne 6.00 15.00
TTSD Martin St. Louis / Marc Denis 5.00 12.00
TTSE Jason Spezza / Patrick Eaves 6.00 15.00
TTSF Mats Sundin / Peter Forsberg 8.00 20.00
TTSG Miroslav Satan / Bill Guerin 4.00 10.00
TTSH Jarret Stoll / Shawn Horcoff 4.00 10.00
TTSK Brent Seabrook / Duncan Keith 6.00 15.00
TTSL Brendan Shanahan / Henrik Lundqvist 8.00 20.00
TTSR Mats Sundin / Andrew Raycroft 6.00 15.00
TTSS Darryl Sittler / Borje Salming 5.00 12.00
TTST Joe Sakic / Pierre Turgeon 12.00 30.00
TTSW Denis Savard / Doug Wilson 8.00 20.00
TTTM Joe Thornton / Patrick Marleau 8.00 20.00
TTTS Ryan Smyth / Jose Theodore 6.00 15.00
TTTZ Marty Turco / Sergei Zubov 6.00 15.00
TTWB Doug Weight / Brad Boyes 5.00 12.00
TTWP Tiger Williams / Bob Probert 5.00 12.00
TTWW Cam Ward / Justin Williams 6.00 15.00
TTYS Alexei Yashin / Miroslav Satan 4.00 10.00
TTZH Henrik Zetterberg / Tomas Holmstrom 6.00 15.00

2007-08 Artifacts Tundra Tandems Black

STATED PRINT RUN 1 SERIAL #'d SET
NOT PRICED DUE TO SCARCITY

2007-08 Artifacts Tundra Tandems Icy Blue

*ICY BLUE: .5X TO 1.2X BASE
STATED PRINT RUN 50 SERIAL #'d SETS

2007-08 Artifacts Tundra Tandems Metallic Purple

*SINGLES: .4X TO 1X BASIC CARDS
RANDOM INSERTS IN RETAIL PACKS

2007-08 Artifacts Tundra Tandems Red

*RED: .6X TO 1.5X BASE
STATED PRINT RUN 25 SERIAL #'d SETS

2007-08 Artifacts Tundra Tandems Patches Black

STATED PRINT RUN 1 SERIAL #'d SET
NOT PRICED DUE TO SCARCITY

2007-08 Artifacts Tundra Tandems Patches Icy Blue

SILVER: 1X TO 2.5X BASIC TANDEMS
STATED PRINT RUN 25 SERIAL #'d SETS

2007-08 Artifacts Tundra Tandems Patches Red

STATED PRINT RUN 10 SERIAL #'d SETS
NOT PRICED DUE TO SCARCITY

2007-08 Artifacts Tundra Tandems Patches Silver

SILVER: .8X TO 2X BASIC TANDEMS
STATED PRINT RUN 35 SERIAL #'d SETS

2007-08 Artifacts Tundra Trios Blue

STATED PRINT RUN 75 #'d SETS
T3AMV Thomas Vanek / Maxim Afinogenov / Ryan Miller 10.00 25.00
T3ASD Jason Arnott / Steve Sullivan / J.P. Dumont 6.00 15.00
T3ASH Dany Heatley / Jason Spezza / Daniel Alfredsson 12.00 30.00
T3BLK Martin Brodeur / Roberto Luongo / Miikka Kiprusoff 15.00 40.00
T3BWH Nathan Horton / Jay Bouwmeester / Stephen Weiss 6.00 15.00
T3CHD Dominik Hasek / Pavel Datsyuk / Chris Chelios 12.00 30.00
T3CMS Sidney Crosby / Jordan Staal / Evgeni Malkin 25.00 60.00
T3DGK Marian Gaborik / Mikko Koivu / Pavol Demitra 12.00 30.00
T3FCK Alexander Frolov / Anze Kopitar / Mike Cammalleri 10.00 25.00
T3GEP Brian Gionta / Patrik Elias / Zach Parise 8.00 20.00
T3GRC Simon Gagne / Jeff Carter / Mike Richards 12.00 30.00
T3GYS Bill Guerin / Miroslav Satan / Alexei Yashin 6.00 15.00
T3HRK Martin Havlat / Nikolai Khabibulin / Tuomo Ruutu 10.00 25.00
T3ITK Jarome Iginla / Miikka Kiprusoff / Alex Tanguay 15.00 40.00
T3JJD Shane Doan / Curtis Joseph / Ed Jovanovski 8.00 20.00
T3KHL Ilya Kovalchuk / Marian Hossa / Kari Lehtonen 12.00 30.00
T3KPK Alex Kovalev / Andrei Kostitsyn / Alexander Perezhogin 6.00 15.00
T3KRH Saku Koivu / Michael Ryder / Chris Higgins 8.00 20.00
T3LBS Georges Laraque / Jody Shelley / Donald Brashear 6.00 15.00
T3LGH Wayne Gretzky / Gordie Howe / Mario Lemieux 50.00 120.00
T3LHZ Henrik Zetterberg / Nicklas Lidstrom / Tomas Holmstrom 10.00 25.00
T3LMK Trevor Linden / Brendan Morrison / Ryan Kesler 8.00 20.00
T3LRC Mario Lemieux / Sidney Crosby / Mark Recchi 50.00 120.00
T3LRS Vincent Lecavalier / Martin St. Louis / Brad Richards 10.00 25.00
T3LTC Sidney Crosby / Joe Thornton / Vincent Lecavalier 50.00 120.00
T3LZB Pascal Leclaire / Gilbert Brule / Nikolai Zherdev 8.00 20.00
T3MCB Patrick Marleau / Matt Carle / Steve Bernier 8.00 20.00
T3MCT Glen Murray / Zdeno Chara / Tim Thomas 12.00 30.00
T3MGM Lanny McDonald / Doug Gilmour / Al MacInnis 8.00 20.00
T3MLR Mike Modano / Eric Lindros / Mike Ribeiro 10.00 25.00
T3MRM Mike Modano / Joe Mullen / Jeremy Roenick 10.00 25.00
T3MSW Borje Salming / Lanny McDonald / Tiger Williams 8.00 20.00
T3NBO Ray Bourque / Cam Neely / Adam Oates 12.00 30.00
T3NPG Ryan Getzlaf / Scott Niedermayer / Corey Perry 8.00 20.00
T3NSS Markus Naslund / Henrik Sedin / Daniel Sedin 10.00 25.00
T3OGF Alexander Ovechkin / Mike Green / Eric Fehr 30.00 80.00
T3PRB Pierre-Marc Bouchard / Brian Rolston / Mark Parrish 6.00 15.00
T3PSB Billy Smith / Denis Potvin / Bob Bourne 25.00 60.00
T3RBB Patrick Roy / Ed Belfour / Martin Brodeur 30.00 80.00
T3REE Ray Emery / Wade Redden / Patrick Eaves 8.00 20.00
T3RLR Patrick Roy / Guy Lafleur / Larry Robinson 30.00 80.00
T3RSS Andrew Raycroft / Alexander Steen / Matt Stajan 8.00 20.00
T3SBK Patrice Bergeron / Phil Kessel / Marc Savard 10.00 25.00
T3SDG Martin Straka / Chris Drury / Scott Gomez 8.00 20.00
T3SHB Joe Sakic / Milan Hejduk / Peter Budaj 20.00 50.00
T3SJL Brendan Shanahan / Jaromir Jagr / Henrik Lundqvist 15.00 40.00
T3SNF Mats Sundin / Peter Forsberg / Markus Naslund 12.00 30.00
T3SPG Teemu Selanne / Jean-Sebastien Giguere / Chris Pronger 10.00 25.00
T3SRH Ales Hemsky / Dwayne Roloson / Jarret Stoll 8.00 20.00
T3STM Mats Sundin / Darcy Tucker / Bryan McCabe 10.00 25.00
T3TCM Joe Thornton / Jonathan Cheechoo / Milan Michalek 12.00 30.00
T3TKL Miikka Kiprusoff / Kari Lehtonen / Vesa Toskala 12.00 30.00
T3TKS Keith Tkachuk / Paul Kariya / Lee Stempniak 10.00 25.00
T3VHB Dominik Hasek / Tomas Vokoun / Peter Budaj 12.00 30.00
T3VNF Rick Nash / Sergei Fedorov / David Vyborny 10.00 25.00
T3WLB Doug Weight / Manny Legace / Brad Boyes 8.00 20.00
T3WPP Tiger Williams / Bob Probert / Willi Plett 8.00 20.00
T3WSW Eric Staal / Cam Ward / Justin Williams 10.00 25.00
T3ZLT Marty Turco / Sergei Zubov / Jere Lehtinen 10.00 25.00

2007-08 Artifacts Tundra Trios Red

STATED PRINT RUN 10 SERIAL #'d SETS
NOT PRICED DUE TO SCARCITY

2008-09 Artifacts

This set was released on October 28, 2008. The base set consists of 302 cards. Cards 1-200 feature veterans, with cards 101-200 serial numbered of 999. Cards 201-260 are rookies serial numbered of 999, and cards 271-312 are exchange cards serial numbered of 750.

COMP.SET w/o SPs (100) 12.00 30.00
LEG/S PRINT RUN 999 SERIAL #'d SETS
RC PRINT RUN 999 SERIAL #'d SETS
STATED PRINT RUN 750 SERIAL #'d SETS
1 Alexander Ovechkin 1.00 2.50
2 Nicklas Backstrom .50 1.25
3 Markus Naslund .25 .60
4 Roberto Luongo .40 1.00
5 Daniel Sedin .25 .60
6 Henrik Sedin .25 .60
7 Mats Sundin .25 .60
8 Vesa Toskala .25 .60
9 Alexander Steen .25 .60
10 Vincent Lecavalier .25 .60
11 Martin St. Louis .25 .60
12 Paul Kariya .25 .60
13 Manny Legace .20 .50
14 Brad Boyes .20 .50
15 Joe Thornton .40 1.00
16 Patrick Marleau .20 .50
17 Evgeni Nabokov .20 .50
18 Jonathan Cheechoo .25 .60
19 Peter Stastny .25 .60
20 Mario Lemieux .60 1.50
21 Sidney Crosby 1.25 3.00
22 Marc-Andre Fleury .25 .60
23 Evgeni Malkin .60 1.50
24 Jordan Staal .40 1.00
25 Peter Mueller .30 .75
26 Shane Doan .15 .40
27 Daniel Briere .25 .60
28 Simon Gagne .20 .50
29 Mike Richards .40 1.00
30 Jason Spezza .30 .75
31 Dany Heatley .30 .75
32 Daniel Alfredsson .20 .50
33 Mark Messier .50 1.25
34 Marian Hossa .40 1.00
35 Henrik Lundqvist .50 1.25
36 Brendan Shanahan .25 .60
37 Brian Leetch .30 .75
38 Rick DiPietro .25 .60
39 Bill Guerin .15 .40
40 Mike Bossy .25 .60
41 Zach Parise .25 .60
42 Martin Brodeur .50 1.25
43 Jason Arnott .15 .40
44 J.P. Dumont .15 .40
45 Patrick Roy .75 2.00
46 Carey Price .75 2.00
47 Saku Koivu .25 .60
48 Alex Tanguay .20 .50
49 Alex Kovalev .25 .60
50 Larry Robinson .25 .60
51 Marian Gaborik .40 1.00
52 Josh Harding .20 .50
53 Anze Kopitar .25 .60
54 Jack Johnson .20 .50
55 Tomas Vokoun .25 .60
56 Nathan Horton .15 .40
57 Wayne Gretzky 1.25 3.00
58 Andrew Cogliano .40 1.00
59 Sam Gagner .40 1.00
60 Ales Hemsky .15 .40
61 Dustin Penner .15 .40
62 Jari Kurri .25 .60
63 Gordie Howe 1.00 2.50
64 Nicklas Lidstrom .25 .60
65 Henrik Zetterberg .50 1.25
66 Pavel Datsyuk .25 .60
67 Dominik Hasek .40 1.00
68 Mike Modano .25 .60
69 Brad Richards .20 .50
70 Marty Turco .20 .50
71 Rick Nash .25 .60
72 Nikolai Zherdev .15 .40
73 Paul Stastny .25 .60
74 Joe Sakic .40 1.00
75 Peter Forsberg .40 1.00
76 Ryan Smyth .20 .50
77 Patrick Kane .60 1.50
78 Jonathan Toews .75 2.00
79 Patrick Sharp .15 .40
80 Bobby Hull .50 1.25
81 Eric Staal .40 1.00
82 Cam Ward .25 .60
83 Miikka Kiprusoff .25 .60
84 Jarome Iginla .50 1.25
85 Dion Phaneuf .25 .60
86 Mike Cammalleri .25 .60
87 Thomas Vanek .25 .60
88 Ryan Miller .25 .60
89 Drew Stafford .25 .60
90 Gilbert Perreault .25 .60
91 Bobby Orr .75 2.00
92 Tim Thomas .25 .60
93 Phil Kessel .25 .60
94 Marc Savard .15 .40
95 Ilya Kovalchuk .30 .75
96 Kari Lehtonen .15 .40
97 Teemu Selanne .25 .60
98 Jean-Sebastien Giguere .25 .60
99 Scott Niedermayer .15 .40
100 Ryan Getzlaf .30 .75
101 Dale Hawerchuk LEG .75 2.00
102 Rod Langway LEG 1.00 2.50
103 Johnny Bower LEG 1.00 2.50
104 Borje Salming LEG .75 2.00
105 Frank Mahovlich LEG .75 2.00
106 Bernie Federko LEG .60 1.50
107 Al MacInnis LEG 1.00 2.50
108 Peter Stastny LEG .75 2.00
109 Mario Lemieux LEG 2.00 5.00
110 Joe Mullen LEG .75 2.00
111 Bobby Clarke LEG .75 2.00
112 Ron Hextall LEG .75 2.00
113 Andy Bathgate LEG .75 2.00
114 Brian Leetch LEG 1.00 2.50
115 Walt Tkaczuk LEG .50 1.25
116 Mike Bossy LEG .75 2.00
117 Bob Bourne LEG .50 1.25
118 Clark Gillies LEG .60 1.50
119 Jean Beliveau LEG 1.25 3.00
120 Scotty Bowman LEG .75 2.00
121 Guy Lafleur LEG 1.50 4.00
122 Steve Shutt LEG .75 2.00
123 Larry Robinson LEG .75 2.00
124 Patrick Roy LEG 2.50 6.00
125 Dino Ciccarelli LEG .50 1.25
126 Marcel Dionne LEG .75 2.00
127 Bernie Nicholls LEG .50 1.25
128 Luc Robitaille LEG .60 1.50
129 Grant Fuhr LEG .75 2.00
130 Wayne Gretzky LEG 4.00 10.00
131 Jari Kurri LEG .75 2.00
132 Alex Delvecchio LEG 1.00 2.50
133 Gordie Howe LEG 3.00 8.00
134 Red Kelly LEG 1.00 2.50
135 Ted Lindsay LEG .75 2.00
136 Doug Wilson LEG .50 1.25
137 Tony Esposito LEG .75 2.00
138 Bobby Hull LEG 1.50 4.00
139 Denis Savard LEG .75 2.00
140 Stan Mikita LEG .75 2.00
141 Lanny McDonald LEG .75 2.00
142 Gilbert Perreault LEG .75 2.00
143 Ray Bourque LEG 1.50 4.00
144 Johnny Bucyk LEG .75 2.00
145 Don Cherry LEG 2.00 5.00
146 Phil Esposito LEG 1.25 3.00
147 Cam Neely LEG 1.00 2.50
148 Willie O'Ree LEG .75 2.00
149 Bobby Orr LEG 2.50 6.00
150 Terry O'Reilly LEG .75 2.00
151 Alexander Ovechkin S 3.00 8.00
152 Roberto Luongo S 1.25 3.00
153 Henrik Sedin S .75 2.00
154 Mats Sundin S .75 2.00
155 Vincent Lecavalier S .75 2.00
156 Martin St. Louis S .75 2.00
157 Paul Kariya S .75 2.00
158 Joe Thornton S 1.25 3.00
159 Patrick Marleau S .60 1.50
160 Sidney Crosby S 4.00 10.00
161 Evgeni Malkin S 2.00 5.00
162 Marc-Andre Fleury S .75 2.00
163 Simon Gagne S .60 1.50
164 Daniel Briere S .75 2.00
165 Dany Heatley S 1.00 2.50
166 Jason Spezza S 1.00 2.50
167 Daniel Alfredsson S .60 1.50
168 Markus Naslund S .75 2.00
169 Brendan Shanahan S .75 2.00
170 Martin Brodeur S 1.50 4.00
171 Zach Parise S .75 2.00
172 Carey Price S 2.50 6.00
173 Saku Koivu S .75 2.00
174 Marian Gaborik S 1.25 3.00
175 Josh Harding S .60 1.50
176 Anze Kopitar S .75 2.00
177 Sam Gagner S 1.25 3.00
178 Andrew Cogliano S 1.25 3.00
179 Henrik Zetterberg S 1.50 4.00
180 Chris Osgood S .75 2.00
181 Pavel Datsyuk S .75 2.00
182 Mike Modano S .75 2.00
183 Marty Turco S .60 1.50
184 Rick Nash S .75 2.00
185 Joe Sakic S 1.25 3.00
186 Peter Forsberg S 1.25 3.00
187 Paul Stastny S .75 2.00
188 Patrick Kane S 2.00 5.00
189 Jonathan Toews S 2.50 6.00
190 Eric Staal S 1.25 3.00
191 Jarome Iginla S 1.50 4.00
192 Miikka Kiprusoff S .75 2.00
193 Ryan Miller S .75 2.00
194 Thomas Vanek S .75 2.00
195 Patrice Bergeron S .75 2.00
196 Ilya Kovalchuk S 1.00 2.50
197 Teemu Selanne S .75 2.00
198 Jean-Sebastien Giguere S .75 2.00
199 Ryan Getzlaf S 1.00 2.50
200 Scott Niedermayer S .50 1.25
201 Derick Brassard RC 6.00 15.00
202 Mark Fistric RC 2.50 6.00
203 Alex Goligoski RC 6.00 15.00
204 Claude Giroux RC 6.00 15.00
205 Jon Filewich RC 2.50 6.00
206 Robbie Earl RC 2.50 6.00
207 Ilya Zubov RC 3.00 8.00
208 Steve Mason RC 8.00 20.00
209 Brian Boyle RC 3.00 8.00
210 Shawn Matthias RC 3.00 8.00
211 Ryan Stone RC 3.00 8.00
212 Teddy Purcell RC 3.00 8.00
213 Mike Iggulden RC 2.50 6.00
214 Tim Ramholt RC 2.50 6.00
215 Kyle Okposo RC 6.00 15.00
216 Sami Lepisto RC 3.00 8.00
217 Colin Stuart RC 2.50 6.00
218 Brandon Nolan RC 4.00 10.00
219 Andrew Murray RC 2.50 6.00
220 Kevin Doell RC 2.00 5.00
221 Tim Conboy RC 2.50 6.00
222 Pascal Pelletier RC 2.50 6.00
223 Chris Minard RC 3.00 8.00
224 Joey Mormina RC 2.50 6.00
225 Peter Vandermeer RC 2.00 5.00
226 Darryl Boyce RC 2.50 6.00
227 Cody McLeod RC 2.50 6.00
228 Corey Locke RC 3.00 8.00
229 Jordan Hendry RC 2.50 6.00
230 Mike Brown RC 4.00 10.00
231 B.J. Crombeen RC 2.50 6.00
232 David Brine RC 2.50 6.00
233 Joe Jensen RC 2.50 6.00
234 Kyle Greentree RC 4.00 10.00
235 Zach Fitzgerald RC 3.00 8.00
236 Marc-Andre Gragnani RC 2.50 6.00
237 Andrew Ebbett RC 3.00 8.00
238 Erik Ersberg RC 3.00 8.00
239 Jonathan Ericsson RC 5.00 12.00
240 Theo Peckham RC 3.00 8.00
241 Tyler Plante RC 3.00 8.00
242 Niklas Hjalmarsson RC 5.00 12.00
243 Tom Sestito RC 2.50 6.00
244 Tom Cavanagh RC 2.50 6.00
245 Alex Foster RC 2.50 6.00
246 Kyle Turris RC 6.00 15.00
247 Brian Lee RC 3.00 8.00
248 Justin Abdelkader RC 6.00 15.00
249 Adam Pineault RC 3.00 8.00
250 Boris Valabik RC 4.00 10.00
251 Darren Helm RC 5.00 12.00
252 Matt D'Agostini RC 5.00 12.00
253 Mattias Ritola RC 4.00 10.00
254 Dan LaCosta RC 4.00 10.00
255 Danny Taylor RC 3.00 8.00
256 Clay Wilson RC 2.00 5.00
257 Jordan LaVallee RC 3.00 8.00
258 Mike Mole RC 2.50 6.00
259 Jack Hillen RC 2.50 6.00
260 Garrett Stafford RC 4.00 10.00
271 Karl Alzner RC 6.00 15.00
272 Cory Schneider RC 8.00 20.00
273 Luke Schenn RC 12.00 30.00
274 Steven Stamkos RC 30.00 80.00
275 Alex Pietrangelo RC 6.00 15.00
276 Jamie McGinn RC 4.00 10.00
277 Dustin Jeffery RC 6.00 15.00
278 Mikkel Boedker RC 6.00 15.00
279 Luca Sbisa RC 6.00 15.00
280 Zach Smith RC 3.00 8.00
281 Corey Potter RC 6.00 15.00
282 Josh Bailey RC 6.00 15.00
283 Petr Vrana RC 5.00 12.00
284 Patric Hornqvist RC 4.00 10.00
285 Max Pacioretty RC 10.00 25.00
286 Colton Gillies RC 4.00 10.00
287 Drew Doughty RC 12.00 30.00
288 Michael Frolik RC 8.00 20.00
289 Tim Sestito RC 3.00 8.00
290 Patrik Berglund RC 10.00 25.00
291 Fabian Brunnstrom RC 6.00 15.00
292 Jakub Voracek RC 8.00 20.00
293 Chris Stewart RC 5.00 12.00
294 Viktor Tikhonov RC 4.00 10.00
295 Brandon Sutter RC 5.00 12.00
296 Brett Sutter RC 4.00 10.00
297 Tim Kennedy RC 6.00 15.00
298 Blake Wheeler RC 10.00 25.00
299 Zach Bogosian RC 8.00 20.00
300 Brendan Mikkelson RC 2.50 6.00
301 Justin Pogge RC 8.00 20.00
302 Zach Boychuk RC 6.00 15.00
303 Nathan Gerbe RC 8.00 20.00
304 Nikita Filatov RC 15.00 40.00
305 James Neal RC 6.00 15.00
306 Kenndal McArdle RC 4.00 10.00
307 Ben Maxwell RC 6.00 15.00
308 T.J. Oshie RC 10.00 25.00
309 Ty Wishart RC 4.00 10.00
310 Nikolai Kulemin RC 4.00 10.00
311 Simeon Varlamov RC 20.00 50.00
312 Michal Repik RC 5.00 12.00

2008-09 Artifacts Black Rainbow

STATED PRINT RUN 1 SERIAL #'d SET
NOT PRICED DUE TO SCARCITY

2008-09 Artifacts Blue

*BLUE (1-100): 3X TO 8X BASE
*BLUE LEG/S (101-200): 1.2X TO 3X BASE
*BLUE RCs (201-260): .8X TO 2X BASE
STATED PRINT RUN 50 SERIAL #'d SETS

2008-09 Artifacts Gold Spectrum

STATED PRINT RUN 5 SERIAL #'d SETS
NOT PRICED DUE TO SCARCITY

2008-09 Artifacts Silver Spectrum

STATED PRINT RUN 10 SERIAL #'d SETS
NOT PRICED DUE TO SCARCITY

2008-09 Artifacts Auto-Facts

STATED ODDS 1:10
AFAK Anze Kopitar 6.00 15.00
AFAO Alexander Ovechkin 60.00 120.00
AFAP Alexandre Picard 4.00 10.00
AFAR Andrew Raycroft 6.00 15.00
AFBB Brian Boyle 6.00 15.00
AFBC Chris Bourque 5.00 12.00
AFBJ Johnny Bower 8.00 20.00
AFBL Michael Blunden 4.00 10.00
AFBN Bob Nystrom 5.00 12.00
AFBO Bobby Orr 125.00 200.00
AFBR Bobby Ryan 10.00 25.00
AFCA Daniel Carcillo 4.00 10.00
AFCB Casey Borer 6.00 15.00
AFCD Chris Drury 12.00 30.00
AFCG Claude Giroux 12.00 30.00
AFCH Kyle Chipchura 4.00 10.00
AFCK Chris Kunitz 6.00 15.00
AFCM Clarke MacArthur 4.00 10.00
AFCN Cam Neely 15.00 40.00
AFCP Corey Perry 6.00 15.00
AFCW Cam Ward 10.00 25.00
AFDA David Perron 5.00 12.00
AFDB Dan Boyle 5.00 12.00
AFDC Dan Cleary 6.00 15.00
AFDE Derick Brassard 12.00 30.00
AFDH Dany Heatley 8.00 20.00
AFDP Dustin Penner 4.00 10.00
AFDR Drew Stafford 6.00 15.00
AFDS Daniel Sedin 6.00 15.00
AFEJ Erik Johnson 8.00 20.00
AFEM Evgeni Malkin 15.00 40.00
AFEN Eric Nystrom 4.00 10.00
AFES Tony Esposito 10.00 25.00
AFGH Gordie Howe
AFGL Guillaume Latendresse 5.00 12.00
AFGP Gilbert Perreault 6.00 15.00
AFHA Dominik Hasek 10.00 25.00
AFHS Henrik Sedin 6.00 15.00
AFHZ Henrik Zetterberg 12.00 30.00
AFIK Ilya Kovalchuk
AFIZ Ilya Zubov 6.00 15.00
AFJA Jared Boll 5.00 12.00
AFJB Johnny Bucyk 6.00 15.00
AFJC Jeff Carter 6.00 15.00
AFJF Jon Filewich 5.00 12.00
AFJH Josh Harding 5.00 12.00
AFJI Jarome Iginla
AFJJ Jack Johnson 5.00 12.00
AFJL Joffrey Lupul 4.00 10.00
AFJO Johnny Boychuk 4.00 10.00
AFJP Jason Pominville 5.00 12.00
AFJS Jack Skille 5.00 12.00
AFJT Jonathan Toews 20.00 50.00
AFKA Patrick Kane 15.00 40.00
AFKC Kyle Calder 4.00 10.00
AFLE Mario Lemieux
AFLK Lukas Kaspar 4.00 10.00
AFMA Martin Brodeur 60.00 120.00
AFMB Mike Bossy 6.00 15.00
AFME Mark Messier 40.00 80.00
AFMH Marian Hossa 10.00 25.00
AFML Matt Lashoff 4.00 10.00
AFMM Mike Modano 10.00 25.00
AFMR Mike Ribeiro 4.00 10.00
AFMT Maxime Talbot 5.00 12.00
AFNA Evgeni Nabokov 6.00 15.00
AFNF Nick Foligno 6.00 15.00
AFNH Nathan Horton 4.00 10.00
AFNK Niklas Kronwall 5.00 12.00
AFOP Ondrej Pavelec 5.00 12.00
AFPB Peter Budaj 5.00 12.00
AFPE Patrik Elias 4.00 10.00
AFPK Phil Kessel 6.00 15.00
AFPR Carey Price 20.00 50.00
AFPS Paul Stastny 6.00 15.00
AFRB Ray Bourque 25.00 60.00
AFRE Robbie Earl 5.00 12.00
AFRG Ryan Getzlaf 8.00 20.00
AFRL Rod Langway 8.00 20.00
AFRN Rick Nash 12.00 30.00
AFRO Dwayne Roloson 5.00 12.00
AFRS Ryan Smyth 5.00 12.00
AFSC Sidney Crosby 75.00 150.00
AFSD Steve Downie 6.00 15.00
AFSE Devin Setoguchi 6.00 15.00
AFSG Sam Gagner 10.00 25.00
AFSH James Sheppard 6.00 15.00
AFSK Sergei Kostitsyn 6.00 15.00
AFSM Steve Mason 15.00 40.00
AFST Jordan Staal 10.00 25.00
AFTE Tobias Enstrom 6.00 15.00
AFTH T.J. Hensick 5.00 12.00
AFTJ Joe Thornton 15.00 40.00
AFTK Tyler Kennedy 5.00 12.00
AFTL Jiri Tlusty 6.00 15.00
AFTO Tomas Kaberle 4.00 10.00
AFTR Tuukka Rask 6.00 15.00
AFTV Tomas Vokoun 6.00 15.00
AFVL Vincent Lecavalier 6.00 15.00
AFWG Wayne Gretzky 150.00 250.00

2008-09 Artifacts Black Rainbow Autographs

STATED PRINT RUN 1 SERIAL #'d SET
NOT PRICED DUE TO SCARCITY

2008-09 Artifacts Frozen Artifacts Dual

STATED PRINT RUN 199 SERIAL #'d SETS
FADAK Anze Kopitar 4.00 10.00
FADAM Al MacInnis 5.00 12.00
FADAO Adam Oates 4.00 10.00
FADAS Alexander Semin 4.00 10.00
FADAT Alex Tanguay 3.00 8.00
FADBB Brad Boyes 3.00 8.00
FADBG Bill Guerin 2.50 6.00
FADBS Brendan Shanahan 4.00 10.00
FADCC Chris Chelios 5.00 12.00
FADCN Cam Neely 5.00 12.00
FADCW Cam Ward 4.00 10.00
FADDA Daniel Alfredsson 3.00 8.00
FADDB Daniel Briere 4.00 10.00
FADDC Dino Ciccarelli 2.50 6.00
FADDH Dominik Hasek 6.00 15.00
FADDP Dion Phaneuf 4.00 10.00
FADDS Daniel Sedin 4.00 10.00
FADDT Darcy Tucker 3.00 8.00
FADEM Evgeni Malkin 10.00 25.00
FADEN Evgeni Nabokov 4.00 10.00
FADES Eric Staal 6.00 15.00
FADHA Dale Hawerchuk 4.00 10.00
FADHE Dany Heatley 5.00 12.00
FADHL Henrik Lundqvist 8.00 20.00
FADHS Henrik Sedin 4.00 10.00

FADIK Ilya Kovalchuk 5.00 12.00
FADJC Jonathan Cheechoo 4.00 10.00
FADJG Jean-Sebastien Giguere 4.00 10.00
FADJS Joe Sakic 6.00 15.00
FADJT Joe Thornton 6.00 15.00
FADKO Alex Kovalev 4.00 10.00
FADMB Martin Brodeur 8.00 20.00
FADMF Manny Fernandez 4.00 10.00
FADMG Marian Gaborik 6.00 15.00
FADMK Miikka Kiprusoff 4.00 10.00
FADMM Mark Messier 8.00 20.00
FADMN Markus Naslund 4.00 10.00
FADMO Mike Modano 4.00 10.00
FADMS Marc Savard 2.50 6.00
FADOV Alexander Ovechkin 15.00 40.00
FADPF Peter Forsberg 6.00 15.00
FADPR Patrick Roy 12.00 30.00
FADRB Ray Bourque 8.00 20.00
FADSA Borje Salming 4.00 10.00
FADSC Sidney Crosby 20.00 50.00
FADSP Jason Spezza 5.00 12.00
FADSU Mats Sundin 4.00 10.00
FADTV Thomas Vanek 4.00 10.00

2008-09 Artifacts Frozen Artifacts Dual Black

STATED PRINT RUN 1 SERIAL #'d SET
NOT PRICED DUE TO SCARCITY

2008-09 Artifacts Frozen Artifacts Dual Blue

*BLUE: .8X TO 2X BASE
STATED PRINT RUN 50 SERIAL #'d SETS

2008-09 Artifacts Frozen Artifacts Dual Red

STATED PRINT RUN 10 SERIAL #'d SETS
NOT PRICED DUE TO SCARCITY

2008-09 Artifacts Frozen Artifacts Jersey/Patch Combo

STATED PRINT RUN 50 SERIAL #'d SETS
FADAK Anze Kopitar 6.00 15.00
FADAM Al MacInnis 8.00 20.00
FADAO Adam Oates 6.00 15.00
FADAS Alexander Semin 6.00 15.00
FADAT Alex Tanguay 5.00 12.00
FADBB Brad Boyes 5.00 12.00
FADBG Bill Guerin 4.00 10.00
FADBS Brendan Shanahan 6.00 15.00
FADCC Chris Chelios 8.00 20.00
FADCN Cam Neely 8.00 20.00
FADCW Cam Ward 6.00 15.00
FADDA Daniel Alfredsson 5.00 12.00
FADDB Daniel Briere 6.00 15.00
FADDC Dino Ciccarelli 4.00 10.00
FADDH Dominik Hasek 10.00 25.00
FADDP Dion Phaneuf 6.00 15.00
FADDS Daniel Sedin 6.00 15.00
FADDT Darcy Tucker 5.00 12.00
FADEM Evgeni Malkin 15.00 40.00
FADEN Evgeni Nabokov 6.00 15.00
FADES Eric Staal 10.00 25.00
FADHA Dale Hawerchuk 6.00 15.00
FADHE Dany Heatley 8.00 20.00
FADHL Henrik Lundqvist 12.00 30.00
FADHS Henrik Sedin 6.00 15.00
FADIK Ilya Kovalchuk 8.00 20.00
FADJC Jonathan Cheechoo 6.00 15.00
FADJG Jean-Sebastien Giguere 6.00 15.00
FADJS Joe Sakic 10.00 25.00
FADJT Joe Thornton 10.00 25.00
FADKO Alex Kovalev 6.00 15.00
FADMB Martin Brodeur 12.00 30.00
FADMF Manny Fernandez 6.00 15.00
FADMG Marian Gaborik 10.00 25.00
FADMK Miikka Kiprusoff 6.00 15.00
FADMM Mark Messier 12.00 30.00
FADMN Markus Naslund 6.00 15.00
FADMO Mike Modano 6.00 15.00
FADMS Marc Savard 4.00 10.00
FADOV Alexander Ovechkin 25.00 60.00
FADPF Peter Forsberg 10.00 25.00
FADPR Patrick Roy 20.00 50.00
FADRB Ray Bourque 12.00 30.00
FADSA Borje Salming 6.00 15.00
FADSC Sidney Crosby 30.00 80.00
FADSP Jason Spezza 8.00 20.00
FADSU Mats Sundin 6.00 15.00
FADTV Thomas Vanek 6.00 15.00

2008-09 Artifacts Frozen Artifacts Jersey/Patch Combo Black

STATED PRINT RUN 1 SERIAL #'d SET
NOT PRICED DUE TO SCARCITY

2008-09 Artifacts Frozen Artifacts Jersey/Patch Combo Blue

STATED PRINT RUN 10 SERIAL #'d SETS
NOT PRICED DUE TO SCARCITY

2008-09 Artifacts Frozen Artifacts Jersey/Patch Combo Gold

*GOLD: .8X TO 2X BASE
STATED PRINT RUN 25 SERIAL #'d SETS

2008-09 Artifacts Frozen Artifacts Jersey/Patch Combo Silver

*SILVER: .6X TO 1.5X BASE
STATED PRINT RUN 35 SERIAL #'d SETS

2008-09 Artifacts Frozen Artifacts Jersey/Tag Patch Combo Black

STATED PRINT RUN 1 SERIAL #'d SET
NOT PRICED DUE TO SCARCITY

2008-09 Artifacts Treasured Swatches Dual

STATED PRINT RUN 199 SERIAL #'d SETS
TSDAH Ales Hemsky 2.50 6.00
TSDAO Alexander Ovechkin 15.00 40.00
TSDAS Alexander Steen 4.00 10.00
TSDBB Bob Bourne 2.50 6.00
TSDBL Brian Leetch 5.00 12.00
TSDBM Brendan Morrison 2.50 6.00

TSDBR Brad Richards 3.00 8.00
TSDBS Brendan Shanahan 4.00 10.00
TSDCD Chris Drury 4.00 10.00
TSDCP Chris Pronger 3.00 8.00
TSDCW Cam Ward 4.00 10.00
TSDDH Dany Heatley 5.00 12.00
TSDDS Daniel Sedin 4.00 10.00
TSDES Eric Staal 6.00 15.00
TSDGA Glenn Anderson 3.00 8.00
TSDGP Gilbert Perreault 4.00 10.00
TSDHS Henrik Sedin 4.00 10.00
TSDJC Jonathan Cheechoo 4.00 10.00
TSDJI Jarome Iginla 8.00 20.00
TSDJM Joe Mullen 4.00 10.00
TSDJR Jeremy Roenick 4.00 10.00
TSDJS Jordan Staal 6.00 15.00
TSDJT Jonathan Toews 12.00 30.00
TSDKA Paul Kariya 4.00 10.00
TSDKL Kari Lehtonen 2.50 6.00
TSDKT Keith Tkachuk 3.00 8.00
TSDLM Lanny McDonald 4.00 10.00
TSDLR Luc Robitaille 3.00 8.00
TSDLU Roberto Luongo 6.00 15.00
TSDMB Martin Brodeur 8.00 20.00
TSDMO Brenden Morrow 3.00 8.00
TSDMS Mats Sundin 4.00 10.00
TSDMT Marty Turco 3.00 8.00
TSDNB Nicklas Backstrom 8.00 20.00
TSDPB Pierre-Marc Bouchard 2.50 6.00
TSDPD Pavol Demitra 2.50 6.00
TSDPE Patrik Elias 2.50 6.00
TSDPK Patrick Kane 10.00 25.00
TSDPL Pascal Leclaire 3.00 8.00
TSDPM Patrick Marleau 3.00 8.00
TSDPS Paul Stastny 4.00 10.00
TSDRD Rick DiPietro 4.00 10.00
TSDRG Ryan Getzlaf 5.00 12.00
TSDRN Rick Nash 4.00 10.00
TSDSA Miroslav Satan 2.50 6.00
TSDSD Shane Doan 2.50 6.00
TSDST Peter Stastny 4.00 10.00
TSDTS Teemu Selanne 4.00 10.00

2008-09 Artifacts Treasured Swatches Dual Black

STATED PRINT RUN 1 SERIAL #'d SET
NOT PRICED DUE TO SCARCITY

2008-09 Artifacts Treasured Swatches Dual Blue

*BLUE: .8X TO 2X BASE
STATED PRINT RUN 50 SERIAL #'d SETS

2008-09 Artifacts Treasured Swatches Dual Gold

*GOLD: .6X TO 1.5X BASE
STATED PRINT RUN 75 SERIAL #'d SETS

2008-09 Artifacts Treasured Swatches Dual Red

STATED PRINT RUN 1 SERIAL #'d SET
NOT PRICED DUE TO SCARCITY

2008-09 Artifacts Treasured Swatches Dual Silver

*SILVER: .5X TO 1.2X BASE
STATED PRINT RUN 100 SERIAL #'d SETS

2008-09 Artifacts Treasured Swatches Jersey/Patch Combo

STATED PRINT RUN 50 SERIAL #'d SETS
TSDAH Ales Hemsky 4.00 10.00
TSDAO Alexander Ovechkin 25.00 60.00
TSDAS Alexander Steen 6.00 15.00
TSDBB Bob Bourne 4.00 10.00
TSDBL Brian Leetch 8.00 20.00
TSDBM Brendan Morrison 4.00 10.00
TSDBR Brad Richards 5.00 12.00
TSDBS Brendan Shanahan 6.00 15.00
TSDCD Chris Drury 6.00 15.00
TSDCP Chris Pronger 5.00 12.00
TSDCW Cam Ward 6.00 15.00
TSDDH Dany Heatley 8.00 20.00
TSDDS Daniel Sedin 6.00 15.00
TSDES Eric Staal 10.00 25.00
TSDGA Glenn Anderson 5.00 12.00
TSDGP Gilbert Perreault 6.00 15.00
TSDHS Henrik Sedin 6.00 15.00
TSDJC Jonathan Cheechoo 6.00 15.00
TSDJI Jarome Iginla 12.00 30.00
TSDJM Joe Mullen 6.00 15.00
TSDJR Jeremy Roenick 6.00 15.00
TSDJS Jordan Staal 10.00 25.00
TSDJT Jonathan Toews 20.00 50.00
TSDKA Paul Kariya 6.00 15.00
TSDKL Kari Lehtonen 4.00 10.00
TSDKT Keith Tkachuk 5.00 12.00
TSDLM Lanny McDonald 6.00 15.00
TSDLR Luc Robitaille 5.00 12.00
TSDLU Roberto Luongo 10.00 25.00
TSDMB Martin Brodeur 12.00 30.00
TSDMO Brenden Morrow 5.00 12.00
TSDMS Mats Sundin 6.00 15.00
TSDMT Marty Turco 5.00 12.00
TSDNB Nicklas Backstrom 12.00 30.00
TSDPB Pierre-Marc Bouchard 4.00 10.00
TSDPD Pavol Demitra 4.00 10.00
TSDPE Patrik Elias 4.00 10.00
TSDPK Patrick Kane 15.00 40.00
TSDPL Pascal Leclaire 5.00 12.00
TSDPM Patrick Marleau 5.00 12.00
TSDPS Paul Stastny 6.00 15.00
TSDRD Rick DiPietro 6.00 15.00
TSDRG Ryan Getzlaf 8.00 20.00
TSDRN Rick Nash 6.00 15.00
TSDSA Miroslav Satan 4.00 10.00
TSDSD Shane Doan 4.00 10.00
TSDST Peter Stastny 6.00 15.00
TSDTS Teemu Selanne 6.00 15.00

2008-09 Artifacts Treasured Swatches Jersey/Patch Combo Blue

STATED PRINT RUN 10 SERIAL #'d SETS
NOT PRICED DUE TO SCARCITY

2008-09 Artifacts Treasured Swatches Jersey/Patch Combo Silver

*SILVER: .6X TO 1.5X BASE
STATED PRINT RUN 35 SERIAL #'d SETS

2008-09 Artifacts Tundra Tandems

STATED PRINT RUN 100 SERIAL #'d SETS
TTAR Shea Weber 4.00 10.00
Jason Arnott
TTAS Daniel Alfredsson 8.00 20.00
Jason Spezza
TTBD Brent Seabrook 5.00 12.00
Duncan Keith
TTBJ Jack Johnson 6.00 15.00
Rob Blake
TTBL Martin Brodeur 12.00 30.00
Roberto Luongo
TTBN Martin Biron 6.00 15.00
Antero Niittymaki
TTBR Mike Richards 10.00 25.00
Daniel Briere
TTBS Drew Stafford 6.00 15.00
Steve Bernier
TTBT Darcy Tucker 5.00 12.00
Jason Blake
TTCL Nicklas Lidstrom 8.00 20.00
Chris Chelios
TTCM Sidney Crosby 30.00 80.00
Evgeni Malkin
TTCR Jonathan Cheechoo 6.00 15.00
Michael Ryder
TTDF Pavel Datsyuk 10.00 25.00
Sergei Fedorov
TTDG Marian Gaborik 10.00 25.00
Pavol Demitra
TTDM Shane Doan 8.00 20.00
Peter Mueller
TTDS Mike Modano 6.00 15.00
Doug Weight
TTDZ Pavel Datsyuk 12.00 30.00
Henrik Zetterberg
TTEC Eric Staal 10.00 25.00
Cam Ward
TTEM Eric Staal 10.00 25.00
Marc Staal
TTEP Patrik Elias 6.00 15.00
Zach Parise
TTFB Peter Forsberg 12.00 30.00
Nicklas Backstrom
TTFM Marc-Andre Fleury 15.00 40.00
Evgeni Malkin
TTFS Peter Forsberg 10.00 25.00
Borje Salming
TTGB Simon Gagne 6.00 15.00
Daniel Briere
TTGD Scott Gomez 6.00 15.00
Chris Drury
TTGH Simon Gagne 8.00 20.00
Dany Heatley
TTGK Marian Gaborik 6.00 15.00
Mikko Koivu
TTGL Wayne Gretzky 30.00 80.00
Mario Lemieux
TTGM Wayne Gretzky 30.00 80.00
Mark Messier
TTGS Miroslav Satan 4.00 10.00
Bill Guerin
TTHG Ales Hemsky 10.00 25.00
Sam Gagner
TTHM Gordie Howe 25.00 60.00
Mark Messier
TTHO Dominik Hasek 10.00 25.00
Chris Osgood
TTHV Nathan Horton 6.00 15.00
Tomas Vokoun
TTIK Jarome Iginla 12.00 30.00
Miikka Kiprusoff
TTJJ Erik Johnson 8.00 20.00
Barret Jackman
TTJL Henrik Lundqvist 12.00 30.00
Vesa Toskala
TTJO Jordan Staal 10.00 25.00
Ryan Malone
TTJS Olli Jokinen 6.00 15.00
Saku Koivu
TTKB Paul Kariya 6.00 15.00
Brad Boyes
TTKF Sergei Fedorov 10.00 25.00
Viktor Kozlov
TTKJ Anze Kopitar 6.00 15.00
Jack Johnson
TTKK Alex Kovalev 6.00 15.00
Andrei Kostitsyn
TTKL Ilya Kovalchuk 8.00 20.00
Kari Lehtonen
TTKP Saku Koivu 20.00 50.00
Carey Price
TTKT Miikka Kiprusoff 6.00 15.00
Vesa Toskala
TTLG Rod Langway 8.00 20.00
Mike Green
TTLH Nicklas Lidstrom 6.00 15.00
Tomas Holmstrom
TTLM Mario Lemieux 15.00 40.00
Evgeni Malkin
TTLN Rick Nash 6.00 15.00
Pascal Leclaire
TTLS Steve Shutt 6.00 15.00
Larry Robinson
TTLT Joe Thornton 10.00 25.00
Vincent Lecavalier
TTMC Patrick Marleau 6.00 15.00
Jonathan Cheechoo
TTMK Ryan Kesler 4.00 10.00
Brendan Morrison
TTMP Mike Modano 6.00 15.00
Zach Parise
TTMR Mike Modano 6.00 15.00
Brad Richards
TTMS Lanny McDonald 6.00 15.00
Borje Salming
TTMT Joe Thornton 10.00 25.00
Patrick Marleau
TTMV Ryan Miller 6.00 15.00
Thomas Vanek
TTMW Marian Gaborik 10.00 25.00
Pierre-Marc Bouchard
TTNK Cam Neely 8.00 20.00
Phil Kessel
TTNL Roberto Luongo 10.00 25.00
Markus Naslund
TTNY Rick DiPietro 6.00 15.00
Bill Guerin
TTOE Alexander Edler 5.00 12.00
Mattias Ohlund
TTOM Alexander Ovechkin 25.00 60.00
Evgeni Malkin
TTOS Adam Oates 6.00 15.00
Marc Savard
TTPF Simon Gagne 5.00 12.00
Martin Biron
TTPN Scott Niedermayer 5.00 12.00
Chris Pronger
TTPP Paul Stastny 6.00 15.00
Peter Stastny
TTPR Paul Stastny 6.00 15.00
Ryan Smyth
TTPS Drew Stafford 6.00 15.00
Daniel Paille
TTRC Wade Redden 4.00 10.00
Mike Commodore
TTRD Marcel Dionne 6.00 15.00
Luc Robitaille
TTRL Michael Ryder 5.00 12.00
Guillaume Latendresse
TTRM Mike Ribeiro 5.00 12.00
Brenden Morrow
TTRP Patrick Roy 20.00 50.00
Carey Price
TTRS Luc Robitaille 6.00 15.00
Steve Shutt
TTSA Steve Sullivan 4.00 10.00
Jason Arnott
TTSB Patrice Bergeron 6.00 15.00
Marc Savard
TTSF Joe Sakic 10.00 25.00
Peter Forsberg
TTSG Teemu Selanne 6.00 15.00
Jean-Sebastien Giguere
TTSH Shawn Horcoff 5.00 12.00
Jarret Stoll
TTSJ Jonathan Cheechoo 6.00 15.00
Milan Michalek
TTSK Jari Kurri 6.00 15.00
Teemu Selanne
TTSM Saku Koivu 6.00 15.00
Mikko Koivu
TTSO Alexander Ovechkin 25.00 60.00
Alexander Semin
TTSR Joe Sakic 20.00 50.00
Patrick Roy
TTSS Henrik Sedin 6.00 15.00
Daniel Sedin
TTSW Marek Svatos 4.00 10.00
Wojtek Wolski
TTTB Peter Budaj 6.00 15.00
Jose Theodore
TTTK Patrick Kane 20.00 50.00
Jonathan Toews
TTTL Manny Legace 5.00 12.00
Keith Tkachuk
TTTM Mats Sundin 6.00 15.00
Alexander Steen
TTTT Joe Thornton 20.00 50.00
Jonathan Toews
TTVB Tomas Vokoun 6.00 15.00
Jay Bouwmeester
TTVP Vincent Lecavalier 6.00 15.00
Paul Ranger
TTWB Rod Brind'Amour 5.00 12.00
Justin Williams
TTWH Stephen Weiss 4.00 10.00
Nathan Horton
TTWL Ryan Whitney 4.00 10.00
Kristopher Letang
TTZG Sergei Gonchar 6.00 15.00
Sergei Zubov

2008-09 Artifacts Tundra Tandems Bronze

*BRONZE: .5X TO 1.2X BASE
STATED PRINT RUN 75 SERIAL #'d SETS

2008-09 Artifacts Tundra Tandems Gold

*GOLD: .8X TO 2X BASE
STATED PRINT RUN 25 SERIAL #'d SETS

2008-09 Artifacts Tundra Tandems Red

STATED PRINT RUN 10 SERIAL #'d SETS
NOT PRICED DUE TO SCARCITY

2008-09 Artifacts Tundra Tandems Silver

*SILVER: .6X TO 1.5X BASE
STATED PRINT RUN 50 SERIAL #'d SETS

2008-09 Artifacts Tundra Tandems Patches Copper

STATED PRINT RUN 35 SERIAL #'d SETS
TTAR Jason Arnott 6.00 15.00
Shea Weber
TTAS Daniel Alfredsson 12.00 30.00
Jason Spezza
TTBD Brent Seabrook 8.00 20.00
Duncan Keith
TTBJ Rob Blake 10.00 25.00
Jack Johnson
TTBL Martin Brodeur 20.00 50.00
Roberto Luongo
TTBN Martin Biron 10.00 25.00
Antero Niittymaki
TTBR Daniel Briere 15.00 40.00
Mike Richards
TTBS Steve Bernier 10.00 25.00
Drew Stafford
TTBT Jason Blake 8.00 20.00
Darcy Tucker
TTCL Chris Chelios 12.00 30.00
Nicklas Lidstrom
TTCM Sidney Crosby 50.00 120.00
Evgeni Malkin
TTCR Jonathan Cheechoo 10.00 25.00
Michael Ryder
TTDF Pavel Datsyuk 15.00 40.00
Sergei Fedorov
TTDG Pavol Demitra 15.00 40.00
Marian Gaborik
TTDM Shane Doan 12.00 30.00
Peter Mueller
TTDS Mike Modano 10.00 25.00
Doug Weight
TTDZ Pavel Datsyuk 20.00 50.00
Henrik Zetterberg
TTEC Eric Staal 15.00 40.00
Cam Ward
TTEM Eric Staal 15.00 40.00
Marc Staal
TTEP Patrik Elias 10.00 25.00
Zach Parise
TTFB Peter Forsberg 20.00 50.00
Nicklas Backstrom
TTFM Marc-Andre Fleury 25.00 60.00
Evgeni Malkin
TTFS Peter Forsberg 15.00 40.00
Borje Salming
TTGB Simon Gagne 10.00 25.00
Daniel Briere
TTGD Scott Gomez 10.00 25.00
Chris Drury
TTGH Simon Gagne 12.00 30.00
Dany Heatley
TTGK Marian Gaborik 10.00 25.00
Mikko Koivu
TTGL Mario Lemieux 50.00 120.00
Wayne Gretzky
TTGM Wayne Gretzky 50.00 120.00
Mark Messier
TTGS Bill Guerin 6.00 15.00
Miroslav Satan
TTHG Ales Hemsky 15.00 40.00
Sam Gagner
TTHO Dominik Hasek 15.00 40.00
Chris Osgood
TTHV Tomas Vokoun 10.00 25.00
Nathan Horton
TTIK Jarome Iginla 20.00 50.00
Miikka Kiprusoff
TTJJ Barret Jackman 12.00 30.00
Erik Johnson
TTJL Henrik Lundqvist 20.00 50.00
Vesa Toskala
TTJR Ryan Malone 15.00 40.00
Jordan Staal
TTJS Saku Koivu 10.00 25.00
Olli Jokinen
TTKB Paul Kariya 10.00 25.00
Brad Boyes
TTKF Viktor Kozlov 15.00 40.00
Sergei Fedorov
TTKJ Anze Kopitar 10.00 25.00
Jack Johnson
TTKK Alex Kovalev 10.00 25.00
Andrei Kostitsyn
TTKL Ilya Kovalchuk 12.00 30.00
Kari Lehtonen
TTKP Saku Koivu 30.00 80.00
Carey Price
TTKT Vesa Toskala 10.00 25.00
Miikka Kiprusoff
TTLG Rod Langway 12.00 30.00
Mike Green
TTLH Nicklas Lidstrom 10.00 25.00
Tomas Holmstrom
TTLM Mario Lemieux 25.00 60.00
Evgeni Malkin
TTLN Pascal Leclaire 10.00 25.00
Rick Nash
TTLS Larry Robinson 10.00 25.00
Steve Shutt
TTLT Vincent Lecavalier 15.00 40.00
Joe Thornton
TTMC Patrick Marleau 10.00 25.00
Jonathan Cheechoo
TTMK Brendan Morrison 6.00 15.00
Ryan Kesler
TTMP Mike Modano 10.00 25.00
Zach Parise
TTMR Mike Modano 10.00 25.00
Brad Richards
TTMS Lanny McDonald 10.00 25.00
Borje Salming
TTMT Patrick Marleau 15.00 40.00
Joe Thornton
TTMV Ryan Miller 10.00 25.00
Thomas Vanek
TTMW Marian Gaborik 15.00 40.00
Pierre-Marc Bouchard
TTNK Cam Neely 12.00 30.00
Phil Kessel
TTNL Markus Naslund 15.00 40.00
Roberto Luongo
TTNY Bill Guerin 10.00 25.00
Rick DiPietro
TTOE Mattias Ohlund 8.00 20.00
Alexander Edler
TTOS Marc Savard 10.00 25.00
Adam Oates
TTPF Simon Gagne 8.00 20.00
Martin Biron
TTPN Chris Pronger 8.00 20.00
Scott Niedermayer
TTPP Peter Stastny 10.00 25.00
Paul Stastny
TTPR Ryan Smyth 10.00 25.00
Paul Stastny
TTPS Daniel Paille 10.00 25.00
Drew Stafford
TTRC Wade Redden 6.00 15.00
Mike Commodore
TTRD Luc Robitaille 10.00 25.00
Marcel Dionne
TTRL Michael Ryder 8.00 20.00
Guillaume Latendresse
TTRM Mike Ribeiro 8.00 20.00
Brenden Morrow
TTRP Patrick Roy 30.00 80.00
Carey Price
TTRS Luc Robitaille 10.00 25.00
Steve Shutt
TTSA Jason Arnott 6.00 15.00
Steve Sullivan
TTSB Marc Savard 10.00 25.00
Patrice Bergeron
TTSF Joe Sakic 15.00 40.00
Peter Forsberg
TTSG Teemu Selanne 10.00 25.00
Jean-Sebastien Giguere
TTSH Jarret Stoll 8.00 20.00
Shawn Horcoff
TTSJ Jonathan Cheechoo 10.00 25.00
Milan Michalek
TTSK Teemu Selanne 10.00 25.00
Jari Kurri
TTSM Saku Koivu 10.00 25.00
Mikko Koivu
TTSR Patrick Roy 30.00 80.00
Joe Sakic
TTSS Henrik Sedin 10.00 25.00
Daniel Sedin
TTSW Marek Svatos 6.00 15.00
Wojtek Wolski
TTTB Jose Theodore 10.00 25.00
Peter Budaj
TTTK Jonathan Toews 30.00 80.00
Patrick Kane
TTTL Keith Tkachuk 8.00 20.00
Manny Legace
TTTM Mats Sundin 10.00 25.00
Alexander Steen
TTTT Joe Thornton 30.00 80.00
Jonathan Toews
TTVB Tomas Vokoun 10.00 25.00
Jay Bouwmeester
TTVP Vincent Lecavalier 10.00 25.00
Paul Ranger
TTWB Justin Williams 8.00 20.00
Rod Brind'Amour
TTWH Stephen Weiss 6.00 15.00
Nathan Horton
TTWL Ryan Whitney 6.00 15.00
Kristopher Letang
TTZG Sergei Zubov 10.00 25.00
Sergei Gonchar

2008-09 Artifacts Tundra Tandems Patches Gold

STATED PRINT RUN 5 SERIAL #'d SETS
NOT PRICED DUE TO SCARCITY

2008-09 Artifacts Tundra Tandems Patches Silver

STATED PRINT RUN 10 SERIAL #'d SETS
NOT PRICED DUE TO SCARCITY

2008-09 Artifacts Tundra Trios Gold

STATED PRINT RUN 75 SERIAL #'d SETS
T3ASE Jason Spezza 12.00 30.00
Daniel Alfredsson
Wade Redden
T3ASR Shea Weber 6.00 15.00
Jason Arnott
Steve Sullivan
T3BFP Patrik Elias 10.00 25.00
Zach Parise
Martin Brodeur
T3BKJ Anze Kopitar 10.00 25.00
Dustin Brown
Jack Johnson
T3BSW Eric Staal 15.00 40.00
Rod Brind'Amour
Cam Ward
T3CLO Dino Ciccarelli 12.00 30.00
Adam Oates
Rod Langway
T3FCM Sidney Crosby 50.00 120.00
Evgeni Malkin
Marc-Andre Fleury
T3FKM Mark Messier 10.00 25.00
Jari Kurri
Grant Fuhr
T3GBK Marian Gaborik 10.00 25.00
Mikko Koivu
Pierre-Marc Bouchard
T3GBR Simon Gagne 15.00 40.00
Mike Richards
Martin Biron
T3GSD Miroslav Satan 10.00 25.00
Bill Guerin
Rick DiPietro
T3HKL Ilya Kovalchuk 12.00 30.00
Bobby Holik
Kari Lehtonen
T3HLD Pavel Datsyuk 15.00 40.00
Nicklas Lidstrom
Dominik Hasek
T3ICK Jarome Iginla 10.00 25.00
Mike Cammalleri
Miikka Kiprusoff
T3JDM Shane Doan 12.00 30.00
Peter Mueller
Ed Jovanovski
T3KKP Saku Koivu 30.00 80.00
Alex Kovalev
Carey Price
T3KLB Paul Kariya 10.00 25.00
Brad Boyes
Manny Legace
T3KOM Alexander Ovechkin 40.00 100.00
Evgeni Malkin
Ilya Kovalchuk
T3KTK Patrick Kane 30.00 80.00
Jonathan Toews
Nikolai Khabibulin
T3LAM Mark Messier 12.00 30.00
Brian Leetch
Glenn Anderson
T3LBR Ray Bourque 20.00 50.00
Larry Robinson
Rod Langway
T3LGM Wayne Gretzky 50.00 120.00
Mario Lemieux
Mark Messier
T3LNB Rick Nash 10.00 25.00
Gilbert Brule
Pascal Leclaire
T3LSD Vincent Lecavalier 10.00 25.00
Martin St. Louis
Marc Denis
T3MMM Lanny McDonald 10.00 25.00
Al MacInnis
Joe Mullen
T3MRM Mike Modano 10.00 25.00
Jeremy Roenick
Joe Mullen
T3MRT Mike Modano 10.00 25.00
Brad Richards
Marty Turco
T3MVS Thomas Vanek 10.00 25.00
Drew Stafford
Ryan Miller
T3NBO Cam Neely 20.00 50.00
Adam Oates
Ray Bourque
T3NLS Markus Naslund 15.00 40.00
Henrik Sedin
Roberto Luongo
T3RBL Patrick Roy 30.00 80.00
Martin Brodeur
Roberto Luongo
T3RHG Ales Hemsky 15.00 40.00
Sam Gagner
Dwayne Roloson
T3SBS Joe Sakic 15.00 40.00
Paul Stastny
Peter Budaj
T3SBT Patrice Bergeron 10.00 25.00
Marc Savard
Tim Thomas
T3SJL Brendan Shanahan 20.00 50.00
Marc Staal
Henrik Lundqvist
T3SNG Teemu Selanne 10.00 25.00
Scott Niedermayer
Jean-Sebastien Giguere
T3STS Mats Sundin 10.00 25.00
Alexander Steen
Vesa Toskala
T3STT Joe Thornton 30.00 80.00
Joe Sakic
Jonathan Toews
T3SWV Denis Savard 10.00 25.00
Rick Vaive
Doug Wilson
T3TNC Joe Thornton 15.00 40.00
Jonathan Cheechoo
Evgeni Nabokov
T3TSB Bryan Trottier 8.00 20.00
Billy Smith
Bob Bourne
T3VWH Stephen Weiss 10.00 25.00
Nathan Horton
Tomas Vokoun

2008-09 Artifacts Tundra Trios Patches Blue

STATED PRINT RUN 10 SERIAL #'d SETS
NOT PRICED DUE TO SCARCITY

2009-10 Artifacts

COMP.SET w/o SPs (100)	12.00	30.00
(101-135) PRINT RUN 999 SER.#'d SETS		
(136-150) PRINT RUN 999 SER.#'d SETS		
(151-200) PRINT RUN 999 SER.#'d SETS		
(201-242) PRINT RUN 699 SER.#'d SETS		
1 Henrik Lundqvist	.50	1.25
2 Chris Osgood	.30	.75
3 Jason Spezza	.30	.75
4 Brian Campbell	.20	.50
5 Kris Versteeg	.30	.75
6 Wojtek Wolski	.15	.40
7 Simon Gagne	.25	.60
8 Phil Kessel	.25	.60
9 Eric Staal	.30	.75
10 Doug Weight	.15	.40
11 Pavel Datsyuk	.25	.60
12 Niklas Backstrom	.25	.60
13 Zach Parise	.25	.60
14 Steven Stamkos	.60	1.50
15 Olli Jokinen	.15	.40
16 Jonas Hiller	.30	.75
17 Cam Ward	.25	.60
18 Henrik Zetterberg	.50	1.25
19 Miikka Kiprusoff	.25	.60
20 Roberto Luongo	.60	1.50
21 Andrei Kostitsyn	.20	.50
22 Patrice Bergeron	.20	.50
23 Jeff Carter	.25	.60
24 Carey Price	.60	1.50
25 Teemu Selanne	.25	.60
26 Chris Drury	.20	.50
27 Thomas Vanek	.20	.50
28 Patrick Kane	.50	1.25
29 Peter Budaj	.25	.60
30 Daniel Alfredsson	.25	.60
31 Joe Thornton	.50	1.25
32 Patrick Marleau	.25	.60
33 Tim Thomas	.25	.60
34 Blake Wheeler	.30	.75
35 Jason Arnott	.15	.40
36 Shane Doan	.20	.50
37 Nathan Horton	.15	.40
38 Jonathan Toews	.60	1.50
39 Ryan Kesler	.20	.50
40 Patrick O'Sullivan	.20	.50
41 Tomas Kaberle	.15	.40
42 Jordan Staal	.30	.75
43 Tomas Vokoun	.25	.60
44 Dany Heatley	.50	1.25
45 Patrik Berglund	.50	1.25
46 Vincent Lecavalier	.30	.75
47 David Backes	.25	.60
48 Derick Brassard	.25	.60
49 Patrik Elias	.25	.60
50 Martin St. Louis	.25	.60
51 Ray Whitney	.15	.40
52 Evgeni Nabokov	.25	.60
53 Martin Brodeur	.60	1.50
54 Evgeni Malkin	.60	1.50
55 Pierre-Marc Bouchard	.20	.50
56 Nicklas Backstrom	.50	1.25
57 Shea Weber	.20	.50
58 Bobby Ryan	.30	.75
59 Mikhail Grabovski	.20	.50
60 Sidney Crosby	1.25	3.00
61 Nicklas Lidstrom	.30	.75
62 Brad Richards	.20	.50
63 Jason Pominville	.25	.60
64 Rick DiPietro	.25	.60
65 Ales Hemsky	.20	.50
66 Marty Turco	.20	.50
67 Mason Raymond	.15	.40
68 Ilya Kovalchuk	.30	.75
69 Mike Modano	.25	.60
70 Ryan Getzlaf	.40	1.00
71 Alexander Frolov	.20	.50
72 Steve Mason	.40	1.00
73 Zach Bogosian	.30	.75
74 Bryan Little	.25	.60
75 David Booth	.15	.40
76 Nikolai Zherdev	.15	.40
77 Alexander Ovechkin	1.00	2.50
78 Mike Richards	.50	1.25
79 Ryan Miller	.25	.60
80 J.P. Dumont	.15	.40
81 Jarome Iginla	.50	1.25
82 Sam Gagner	.30	.75
83 Anze Kopitar	.25	.60
84 Milan Hejduk	.20	.50
85 Drew Doughty	.50	1.25
86 Peter Mueller	.30	.75
87 Marc Staal	.20	.50
88 Andrei Markov	.20	.50
89 Simeon Varlamov	.50	1.25
90 Rick Nash	.25	.60
91 Marc-Andre Fleury	.25	.60
92 Dion Phaneuf	.40	1.00
93 Paul Stastny	.20	.50
94 Tomas Plekanec	.20	.50
95 Andrew Cogliano	.30	.75
96 Mikko Koivu	.25	.60
97 Jakub Voracek	.25	.60
98 Luke Schenn	.40	1.00
99 Devin Setoguchi	.20	.50
100 Paul Kariya	.25	.60
101 Denis Potvin L	.60	1.50
102 Steve Shutt L	.75	2.00
103 Dale Hawerchuk L	.75	2.00
104 Stan Mikita L	1.25	3.00
105 Mario Lemieux L	2.00	5.00
106 Denis Savard L	.75	2.00
107 Alex Delvecchio L	1.00	2.50
108 Johnny Bucyk L	1.25	3.00
109 Ted Lindsay L	.75	2.00
110 Clark Gillies L	.75	2.00
111 Red Kelly L	.75	2.00
112 Gilbert Perreault L	.75	2.00
113 Jean Beliveau L	1.25	3.00
114 Mark Messier L	1.50	4.00
115 Guy Carbonneau L	1.25	3.00
116 Steve Yzerman L	2.50	6.00
117 Frank Mahovlich L	1.00	2.50
118 Lanny McDonald L	.75	2.00
119 Peter Stastny L	.75	2.00
120 Larry Robinson L	1.00	2.50
121 Bobby Orr L	3.00	8.00
122 Cam Neely L	1.25	3.00
123 Rogie Vachon L	1.25	3.00
124 Phil Esposito L	1.50	4.00
125 Johnny Bower L	1.00	2.50
126 Luc Robitaille L	.75	2.00
127 Patrick Roy L	2.50	6.00
128 Doug Gilmour L	.75	2.00
129 Mike Bossy L	.75	2.00
130 Bobby Clarke L	1.25	3.00
131 Ray Bourque L	1.25	3.00
132 Al MacInnis L	.75	2.00
133 Bobby Hull L	2.00	5.00
134 Gordie Howe L	3.00	8.00
135 Wayne Gretzky L	4.00	10.00
136 Alexander Ovechkin S	3.00	8.00
137 Jonathan Toews S	2.00	5.00
138 Henrik Zetterberg S	1.50	4.00
139 Joe Thornton S	1.50	4.00
140 Evgeni Malkin S	2.00	5.00
141 Henrik Lundqvist S	1.50	4.00
142 Pavel Datsyuk S	.75	2.00
143 Martin Brodeur S	2.00	5.00
144 Ilya Kovalchuk S	1.00	2.50
145 Patrick Kane S	1.50	4.00
146 Carey Price S	2.00	5.00
147 Jeff Carter S	.75	2.00
148 Vincent Lecavalier S	1.00	2.50
149 Jarome Iginla S	1.50	4.00
150 Sidney Crosby S	4.00	10.00
151 Chris Durno RC	2.00	5.00
152 Peter Regin RC	3.00	8.00
153 Kevin Quick RC	1.50	4.00
154 Kurtis McLean RC	2.00	5.00
155 Mike Santorelli RC	1.50	4.00
156 Alexander Sulzer RC	1.50	4.00
157 Troy Bodie RC	2.00	5.00
158 Matt Beleskey RC	2.50	6.00
159 Kevin Westgarth RC	2.00	5.00
160 John Scott RC	2.50	6.00
161 Mikael Backlund RC	4.00	10.00
162 Byron Bitz RC	2.00	5.00
163 Bryan Rodney RC	2.00	5.00
164 Tim Wallace RC	1.50	4.00
165 Ben Lovejoy RC	4.00	10.00
166 Riley Armstrong RC	2.00	5.00
167 Jaime Sifers RC	2.00	5.00
168 Sean Collins RC	2.00	5.00
169 Riku Helenius RC	2.50	6.00
170 Ville Leino RC	3.00	8.00
171 Michal Neuvirth RC	6.00	15.00
172 Artem Anisimov RC	3.00	8.00
173 Davis Drewiske RC	2.50	6.00
174 David Schlemko RC	2.00	5.00
175 Luca Caputi RC	3.00	8.00
176 Jakub Petruzalek RC	2.50	6.00
177 Ryan Vesce RC	2.00	5.00
178 Jay Beagle RC	2.50	6.00
179 Jhonas Enroth RC	3.00	8.00
180 Brandon Segal RC	2.00	5.00
181 Tim Stapleton RC	2.50	6.00
182 Jesse Joensuu RC	3.00	8.00
183 David Van Der Gulik RC	2.00	5.00
184 Antti Niemi RC	8.00	20.00
185 Grant Lewis RC	2.00	5.00
186 Cal O'Reilly RC	2.50	6.00
187 Brian Salcido RC	2.00	5.00
188 Phil Oreskovic RC	2.50	6.00
189 Kris Chucko RC	2.00	5.00
190 Joel Rechlicz RC	2.50	6.00
191 Andrew MacDonald RC	2.00	5.00
192 Spencer Machacek RC	2.00	5.00
193 T.J. Galiardi RC	3.00	8.00
194 Michael Sauer RC	2.00	5.00
195 Yannick Weber RC	3.00	8.00
196 Christian Hanson RC	3.00	8.00
197 Ivan Vishnevskiy RC	3.00	8.00
198 Taylor Chorney RC	2.50	6.00
199 John Negrin RC	2.00	5.00
200 Matt Pelech RC	2.50	6.00
201 John Carlson RC	6.00	15.00
202 Michael Grabner RC	4.00	10.00
203 Jonas Gustavsson RC	8.00	20.00
204 Victor Hedman RC	6.00	15.00
205 Lars Eller RC	5.00	12.00
206 Logan Couture RC	6.00	15.00
207 Mark Letestu RC	3.00	8.00
208 Shawn Heshka RC	4.00	10.00
209 James van Riemsdyk RC	8.00	20.00
210 Erik Karlsson RC	10.00	25.00
211 Michael Del Zotto RC	6.00	15.00
212 John Tavares RC	20.00	50.00
213 Matthew Corrente RC	3.00	8.00
214 Colin Wilson RC	6.00	15.00
215 Mathieu Carle RC	4.00	10.00
216 Danny Irmen RC	2.50	6.00
217 Andrei Loktionov RC	4.00	10.00
218 Dmitry Kulikov RC	3.00	8.00
219 Devan Dubnyk RC	4.00	10.00
220 Jakub Kindl RC	4.00	10.00
221 Jamie Benn RC	5.00	12.00
222 Ryan Stoa RC	3.00	8.00
223 Matt Duchene RC	12.00	30.00
224 Matt Gilroy RC	4.00	10.00
225 Viktor Stalberg RC	5.00	12.00
226 Sergei Shirokov RC	5.00	12.00
227 Tyler Myers RC	12.00	30.00
228 Brad Marchand RC	4.00	10.00
229 Evander Kane RC	8.00	20.00
230 MacGregor Sharp RC	3.00	8.00
231 Ryan O'Reilly RC	6.00	15.00
232 Daniel Larsson RC	4.00	10.00
233 Ryan O'Marra RC	2.50	6.00
234 Bobby Sanguinetti RC	2.50	6.00
235 Jason Demers RC	2.50	6.00
236 Tyler Ennis RC	8.00	20.00
237 Tyler Bozak RC	8.00	20.00
238 Benn Ferriero RC	3.00	8.00
239 Mikko Lehtonen RC	3.00	8.00
240 Anton Khudobin RC	3.00	8.00
241 Tyler Eckford RC	2.50	6.00
242 James Reimer RC	3.00	8.00

2009-10 Artifacts Black

STATED PRINT RUN 5 SER.#'d SETS
NOT PRICED DUE TO SCARCITY

2009-10 Artifacts Gold

*SINGLES: 1.5X TO 4X BASIC CARDS
*LEG/STARS: 1X TO 2.5X BASIC CARDS
*ROOKIES: .6X TO 1.5X BASIC CARDS
STATED PRINT RUN 50 SER.#'d SETS

2009-10 Artifacts Gold Spectrum

STATED PRINT RUN 10 SER.#'d SETS
NOT PRICED DUE TO SCARCITY

2009-10 Artifacts Silver

*SINGLES: 1X TO 2.5X BASIC CARDS
*LEGENDS/STARS: .8X TO 2X BASIC
*ROOKIES: .5X TO 1.2X BASIC
STATED PRINT RUN 75 SER.#'d SETS

2009-10 Artifacts Silver Spectrum

*SINGLES: 2X TO 5X BASIC CARDS
*LEG/STARS: 1.2X TO 3X BASIC CARDS
*ROOKIES: .8X TO 2X BASIC CARDS
STATED PRINT RUN 25 SER.#'d SETS

2009-10 Artifacts Autofacts

AFAC Andrew Cogliano	8.00	20.00
AFAE Andrew Ebbett	5.00	12.00
AFAM Al MacInnis	6.00	15.00
AFAO Adam Oates	6.00	15.00
AFAT Alex Tanguay	5.00	12.00
AFBB Bob Bourne	5.00	12.00
AFBG Brian Gionta	6.00	15.00
AFBL Brian Lee	6.00	15.00
AFBM Brenden Morrow	5.00	12.00
AFBO Brian Boyle	5.00	12.00
AFBP Pierre-Marc Bouchard	5.00	12.00
AFCA Mike Cammalleri	6.00	15.00
AFCG Clark Gillies	6.00	15.00
AFCH Don Cherry	15.00	40.00
AFCR Sidney Crosby	75.00	150.00
AFCS Cory Stillman	5.00	12.00
AFDA Matt D'Agostini	8.00	20.00
AFDB David Booth	4.00	10.00
AFDC David Clarkson	4.00	10.00
AFDD Drew Doughty	12.00	30.00
AFDG Daniel Girardi	4.00	10.00
AFDH Dale Hawerchuk	6.00	15.00
AFDJ David Jones	4.00	10.00
AFDL Dan LaCosta	5.00	12.00
AFDP David Perron	5.00	12.00
AFDS Darryl Sittler	8.00	20.00
AFDU Dustin Boyd	4.00	10.00
AFDW Doug Weight	4.00	10.00
AFEL Patrik Elias	5.00	12.00
AFEM Evgeni Malkin	40.00	80.00
AFEN Evgeni Nabokov	6.00	15.00
AFES Phil Esposito	12.00	30.00
AFFB Fabian Brunnstrom	6.00	15.00
AFFI Mark Fistric	4.00	10.00
AFFM Frank Mahovlich		
AFGA Glenn Anderson	6.00	15.00
AFGH Gordie Howe	25.00	60.00
AFHE Dany Heatley	12.00	30.00
AFHM Milan Hejduk	6.00	15.00
AFJB Jean Beliveau		
AFJD Jeff Drouin-Deslauriers	4.00	10.00
AFJE Jonathan Ericsson	6.00	15.00
AFJG Jean-Sebastien Giguere	6.00	15.00
AFJJ Jack Johnson	5.00	12.00
AFJK Jari Kurri	6.00	15.00
AFJM Joe Mullen	5.00	12.00
AFJP Jason Pominville	6.00	15.00
AFJS Jack Skille	4.00	10.00
AFJT Joe Thornton	12.00	30.00
AFKC Kyle Chipchura	4.00	10.00
AFKD Kris Draper	4.00	10.00
AFKL Kari Lehtonen	6.00	15.00
AFKT Kyle Turris	8.00	20.00
AFLI Bryan Little	6.00	15.00
AFLR Larry Robinson	8.00	20.00
AFLS Luke Schenn	10.00	25.00
AFMB Mike Bossy	6.00	15.00
AFMC Bryan McCabe	5.00	12.00
AFMD Marcel Dionne	8.00	20.00
AFMF Marc-Andre Fleury	12.00	30.00
AFMH Martin Havlat	5.00	12.00
AFMI Mike Iggulden	4.00	10.00
AFMK Miikka Kiprusoff		
AFML Milan Lucic	6.00	15.00
AFMT Matt Lashoff	4.00	10.00
AFMM Milan Michalek	4.00	10.00
AFMO Mike Modano	6.00	15.00
AFMP Michael Peca	5.00	12.00
AFMR Mason Raymond	4.00	10.00
AFNK Nikolai Khabibulin	6.00	15.00
AFNZ Nikolai Zherdev	4.00	10.00
AFPB Peter Budaj	6.00	15.00
AFPE Dustin Penner	4.00	10.00
AFPI Alex Pietrangelo	5.00	12.00
AFPK Phil Kessel	6.00	15.00
AFPM Patrick Marleau		
AFPO Denis Potvin	5.00	12.00
AFPR Patrick Roy	50.00	100.00
AFRB Rob Blake	6.00	15.00
AFRC Ryane Clowe	4.00	10.00
AFRH Ron Hextall	12.00	30.00
AFRI Mattias Ritola	5.00	12.00
AFRK Rostislav Klesla	6.00	15.00
AFRM Mike Ribeiro	4.00	10.00
AFRV Rogie Vachon		
AFRY Ryan Miller	6.00	15.00
AFSA Derek Sanderson	4.00	10.00
AFSC Marek Schwarz	4.00	10.00
AFSE Devin Setoguchi	5.00	12.00
AFSH James Sheppard	6.00	15.00
AFSS Steven Stamkos	15.00	40.00
AFTG Tom Gilbert	4.00	10.00
AFTS Tom Sestito	4.00	10.00
AFTV Thomas Vanek	6.00	15.00
AFTW Ty Wishart	6.00	15.00
AFVF Vallteri Filppula	6.00	15.00
AFWI Doug Wilson	4.00	10.00
AFZB Zach Boychuk	8.00	20.00

2009-10 Artifacts Frozen Artifacts

STATED PRINT RUN 199 SER.#'d SETS		
FAAM Al MacInnis	5.00	12.00
FABC Bobby Clarke	8.00	20.00
FABL Brian Leetch	5.00	12.00
FABN Bernie Nicholls	3.00	8.00
FABO Mike Bossy	5.00	12.00
FABR Rob Blake	5.00	12.00
FABS Borje Salming	5.00	12.00
FABU Johnny Bucyk	8.00	20.00
FACJ Curtis Joseph	12.00	30.00
FACN Cam Neely	8.00	20.00
FADC Dino Ciccarelli	3.00	8.00
FADG Doug Gilmour	5.00	12.00
FADH Dale Hawerchuk	5.00	12.00
FADW Doug Weight	3.00	8.00
FAFM Frank Mahovlich	6.00	15.00
FAGA Glenn Anderson	5.00	12.00
FAGC Guy Carbonneau	8.00	20.00
FAGF Grant Fuhr	6.00	15.00
FAGH Gordie Howe	20.00	50.00
FAGP Gilbert Perreault	5.00	12.00
FAJK Jari Kurri	5.00	12.00
FAJS Joe Sakic	10.00	25.00
FALM Lanny McDonald	5.00	12.00
FALR Larry Robinson	6.00	15.00
FAMB Martin Brodeur	12.00	30.00
FAML Mario Lemieux	12.00	30.00
FAMM Mark Messier	10.00	25.00
FAMO Mike Modano	5.00	12.00
FAMS Mats Sundin	5.00	12.00
FANI Scott Niedermayer	3.00	8.00
FANL Nicklas Lidstrom	6.00	15.00
FAPE Phil Esposito	10.00	25.00
FAPK Paul Kariya	5.00	12.00
FAPR Patrick Roy	15.00	40.00
FAPS Peter Stastny	5.00	12.00
FARB Ray Bourque	8.00	20.00
FARH Ron Hextall	10.00	25.00
FARL Rod Langway	4.00	10.00
FARO Luc Robitaille	5.00	12.00
FASF Sergei Fedorov	10.00	25.00
FASH Brendan Shanahan	5.00	12.00
FASK Saku Koivu	5.00	12.00
FASS Steve Shutt	5.00	12.00
FATE Tony Esposito	8.00	20.00
FATS Teemu Selanne	5.00	12.00
FAWG Wayne Gretzky	25.00	60.00
FAWI Doug Wilson	3.00	8.00

2009-10 Artifacts Frozen Artifacts Black

STATED PRINT RUN 1 SER.#'d SETS
NOT PRICED DUE TO SCARCITY

2009-10 Artifacts Frozen Artifacts Blue

*SINGLES: .6X TO 1.5X BASIC INSERTS
STATED PRINT RUN 25 SER.#'d SETS

2009-10 Artifacts Frozen Artifacts Copper

*SINGLES: .5X TO 1.2X BASIC INSERTS
STATED PRINT RUN 50 SER.#'d SETS

2009-10 Artifacts Frozen Artifacts Jersey-Patch

*SINGLES: .8X TO 2X BASIC INSERTS
STATED PRINT RUN 35 SER.#'d SETS

2009-10 Artifacts Frozen Artifacts Jersey-Patch Black

STATED PRINT RUN 1 SER.#'d SETS
NOT PRICED DUE TO SCARCITY

2009-10 Artifacts Frozen Artifacts Jersey-Patch Blue

*SINGLES: 1X TO 2.5X BASIC INSERTS
STATED PRINT RUN 25 SER.#'d SETS

2009-10 Artifacts Frozen Artifacts Jersey-Patch Red

STATED PRINT RUN 5 SER.#'d SETS
NOT PRICED DUE TO SCARCITY

2009-10 Artifacts Frozen Artifacts Red

STATED PRINT RUN 5 SER.#'d SETS
NOT PRICED DUE TO SCARCITY

2009-10 Artifacts Frozen Artifacts Retail

*SINGLES: .4X TO 1X BASIC INSERTS

2009-10 Artifacts Treasured Swatches

STATED PRINT RUN 199 SER.#'d SETS		
TSAK Alex Kovalev	5.00	12.00
TSAO Alexander Ovechkin	20.00	50.00
TSBR Brad Richards	4.00	10.00
TSBW Blake Wheeler	6.00	15.00
TSCD Chris Drury	4.00	10.00
TSCP Carey Price	12.00	30.00
TSDD Drew Doughty	10.00	25.00
TSDH Dany Heatley	10.00	25.00
TSDP Dion Phaneuf	8.00	20.00
TSDS Daniel Sedin	6.00	15.00
TSEM Evgeni Malkin	12.00	30.00
TSEN Evgeni Nabokov	5.00	12.00
TSES Eric Staal	6.00	15.00
TSGA Marian Gaborik	8.00	20.00
TSHL Henrik Lundqvist	10.00	25.00
TSIK Ilya Kovalchuk	6.00	15.00
TSJB Jay Bouwmeester	5.00	12.00
TSJC Duncan Keith	4.00	10.00
TSJI Jarome Iginla	10.00	25.00
TSJP Jason Pominville	5.00	12.00
TSJS Jason Spezza	6.00	15.00
TSJT Jonathan Toews	12.00	30.00
TSKO Anze Kopitar	5.00	12.00
TSLS Luke Schenn	8.00	20.00
TSMA Patrick Marleau	5.00	12.00
TSMF Marc-Andre Fleury	5.00	12.00
TSMG Mike Green	10.00	25.00
TSMH Marian Hossa	8.00	20.00
TSMK Miikka Kiprusoff	5.00	12.00
TSMN Markus Naslund	5.00	12.00
TSMR Mike Richards	10.00	25.00
TSMS Marc Savard	3.00	8.00
TSMT Marty Turco	4.00	10.00
TSNB Nicklas Backstrom	10.00	25.00
TSOJ Olli Jokinen	3.00	8.00
TSPD Pavel Datsyuk	5.00	12.00
TSPL Pascal Leclaire	5.00	12.00
TSPM Peter Mueller	6.00	15.00
TSPS Paul Stastny	5.00	12.00
TSRD Rick DiPietro	5.00	12.00
TSRG Ryan Getzlaf	8.00	20.00
TSRL Roberto Luongo	12.00	30.00
TSRM Ryan Miller	5.00	12.00
TSRN Rick Nash	5.00	12.00
TSSC Sidney Crosby	25.00	60.00
TSSE Devin Setoguchi	4.00	10.00
TSSM Martin St. Louis	5.00	12.00
TSST Jordan Staal	6.00	15.00
TSSV Marek Svatos	3.00	8.00
TSWR Wade Redden	3.00	8.00

2009-10 Artifacts Treasured Swatches Black

STATED PRINT RUN 1 SER.#'d SETS
NOT PRICED DUE TO SCARCITY

2009-10 Artifacts Treasured Swatches Blue

*SINGLES: .6X TO 1.5X BASIC INSERTS
STATED PRINT RUN 25 SER.#'d SETS

2009-10 Artifacts Treasured Swatches Copper

*SINGLES: .5X TO 1.2X BASIC INSERTS
STATED PRINT RUN 50 SER.#'d SETS

2009-10 Artifacts Treasured Swatches Jersey-Patch

*SINGLES: .8X TO 2X BASIC INSERTS
STATED PRINT RUN 35 SER.#'d SETS

2009-10 Artifacts Treasured Swatches Jersey-Patch Black

STATED PRINT RUN 1 SER.#'d SETS
NOT PRICED DUE TO SCARCITY

2009-10 Artifacts Treasured Swatches Jersey-Patch Blue

*SINGLES: 1X TO 2.5X BASIC INSERTS
STATED PRINT RUN 25 SER.#'d SETS

2009-10 Artifacts Treasured Swatches Jersey-Patch Red

STATED PRINT RUN 5 SER.#'d SETS
NOT PRICED DUE TO SCARCITY

2009-10 Artifacts Treasured Swatches Red

STATED PRINT RUN 5 SER.#'d SETS
NOT PRICED DUE TO SCARCITY

2009-10 Artifacts Treasured Swatches Retail

*SINGLES: .4X TO 1X BASIC INSERTS

2009-10 Artifacts Tundra Tandems

STATED PRINT RUN 100 SER.#'d SETS		
TTBE Martin Brodeur	15.00	40.00
Patrik Elias		
TTBK Anze Kopitar	6.00	15.00
Dustin Brown		
TTCM Evgeni Malkin	30.00	80.00
Sidney Crosby		
TTCR Chris Chelios	8.00	20.00
Brian Rafalski		
TTDM Peter Mueller	8.00	20.00
Shane Doan		
TTDT Teemu Selanne	6.00	15.00
Dale Hawerchuk		
TTED David Perron	5.00	12.00
Erik Johnson		
TTFM Bernie Federko	5.00	12.00
Joe Mullen		
TTFS Marc-Andre Fleury	8.00	20.00
Jordan Staal		
TTFT Tim Thomas	6.00	15.00
Manny Fernandez		
TTGA Nikolai Zherdev	10.00	25.00
Marian Gaborik		
TTGF Doug Gilmour	10.00	25.00
Theoren Fleury		
TTGR Mike Richards	12.00	30.00
Simon Gagne		
TTGS Teemu Selanne	10.00	25.00
Ryan Getzlaf		
TTHB David Booth	4.00	10.00
Nathan Horton		
TTHH Ron Hextall	12.00	30.00
Mark Howe		
TTHZ Henrik Zetterberg	12.00	30.00
Tomas Holmstrom		
TTIB Jay Bouwmeester	12.00	30.00
Jarome Iginla		
TTJD Drew Doughty	12.00	30.00
Jack Johnson		
TTJK Olli Jokinen	6.00	15.00
Miikka Kiprusoff		
TTJP Pascal Leclaire	6.00	15.00
Jason Spezza		
TTKL Ilya Kovalchuk	8.00	20.00
Bryan Little		
TTKT Paul Kariya	6.00	15.00
Keith Tkachuk		
TTKW Phil Kessel	8.00	20.00
Blake Wheeler		
TTLC Sidney Crosby	30.00	80.00
Mario Lemieux		
TTLD Pavel Datsyuk	8.00	20.00
Nicklas Lidstrom		
TTLM Mark Messier	12.00	30.00
Brian Leetch		
TTLS Steven Stamkos	15.00	40.00
Vincent Lecavalier		
TTMF Grant Fuhr	12.00	30.00
Mark Messier		
TTMS Patrick Marleau	6.00	15.00
Devin Setoguchi		
TTMT Mike Modano	6.00	15.00
Marty Turco		
TTNB Ray Bourque	10.00	25.00
Cam Neely		
TTNK Jari Kurri	6.00	15.00
Bernie Nicholls		
TTNL Markus Naslund	12.00	30.00
Henrik Lundqvist		
TTNU Rick Nash	6.00	15.00
R.J. Umberger		
TTOB Nicklas Backstrom	25.00	60.00
Alexander Ovechkin		
TTOD Kris Draper	8.00	20.00
Chris Osgood		
TTOG Sam Gagner	8.00	20.00
Patrick O'Sullivan		
TTPB Brent Seabrook	5.00	12.00
Patrick Sharp		
TTPC David Clarkson	6.00	15.00
Zach Parise		
TTPS Drew Stafford	6.00	15.00
Jason Pominville		
TTPW Paul Stastny	6.00	15.00
Wojtek Wolski		
TTRG Luc Robitaille	30.00	80.00
Wayne Gretzky		
TTRS Denis Savard	20.00	50.00
Patrick Roy		
TTRV Derek Roy	6.00	15.00
Thomas Vanek		
TTSB Joe Sakic	12.00	30.00
Ray Bourque		
TTSG Doug Gilmour	6.00	15.00
Mats Sundin		
TTSH Jason Spezza	12.00	30.00
Dany Heatley		
TTSL Mats Sundin	15.00	40.00
Roberto Luongo		
TTSS Mats Sundin	6.00	15.00
Borje Salming		
TTSW Cam Ward	8.00	20.00
Eric Staal		
TTTG Jose Theodore	12.00	30.00
Mike Green		
TTTK Patrick Kane	15.00	40.00
Jonathan Toews		
TTWD Rick DiPietro	6.00	15.00
Doug Weight		
TTWS Shea Weber	5.00	12.00
Steve Sullivan		

2009-10 Artifacts Tundra Tandems Gold

STATED PRINT RUN 1 SER.#'d SETS
NOT PRICED DUE TO SCARCITY

2009-10 Artifacts Tundra Tandems Patches

*SINGLES: .8X TO 2X BASIC INSERTS
STATED PRINT RUN 35 SER.#'d SETS

2009-10 Artifacts Tundra Tandems Patches Gold

STATED PRINT RUN 1 SER.#'d SETS
NOT PRICED DUE TO SCARCITY

2009-10 Artifacts Tundra Tandems Patches Red

STATED PRINT RUN 15 SER.#'d SETS
NOT PRICED DUE TO SCARCITY

2009-10 Artifacts Tundra Tandems Patches Silver

STATED PRINT RUN 5 SER.#'d SETS
NOT PRICED DUE TO SCARCITY

2009-10 Artifacts Tundra Tandems Red

*SINGLES: .5X TO 1.2X BASIC INSERTS
STATED PRINT RUN 50 SER.#'d SETS

2009-10 Artifacts Tundra Tandems Silver

*SINGLES: .6X TO 1.5X BASIC INSERTS
STATED PRINT RUN 25 SER.#'d SETS

2009-10 Artifacts Tundra Trios

STATED PRINT RUN 75 SER.#'d SETS		
TRIASW Jason Arnott	8.00	20.00
Steve Sullivan		
Shea Weber		
TRIBEP Zach Parise	25.00	60.00
Patrik Elias		
Martin Brodeur		
TRIBHS Stephen Weiss	6.00	15.00
Nathan Horton		
David Booth		
TRIBKP Dion Phaneuf	15.00	40.00
Miikka Kiprusoff		
Jay Bouwmeester		
TRIBSW Eric Staal	12.00	30.00
Rod Brind'Amour		
Cam Ward		
TRICGM Sidney Crosby	50.00	120.00
Mark Messier		
Wayne Gretzky		
TRICMS Sidney Crosby	50.00	120.00
Jordan Staal		
Evgeni Malkin		
TRIDMB Peter Mueller	12.00	30.00
Shane Doan		
Mikkel Boedker		
TRIEJM Eric Staal	12.00	30.00
Jordan Staal		
Marc Staal		
TRIFCT Manny Fernandez	10.00	25.00
Tim Thomas		
Zdeno Chara		
TRIFKD Alexander Frolov	20.00	50.00
Drew Doughty		
Anze Kopitar		
TRIGCK Scott Gomez	10.00	25.00
Andrei Kostitsyn		
Mike Cammalleri		
TRIGFL Kristopher Letang	10.00	25.00
Marc-Andre Fleury		
Sergei Gonchar		
TRIGOB Mike Green	40.00	100.00
(Nicklas Backstrom		
Alexander Ovechkin		
TRIGRC Mike Richards	20.00	50.00
Simon Gagne		
Jeff Carter		
TRIHOD Tomas Holmstrom	12.00	30.00
Pavel Datsyuk		
Chris Osgood		
TRIJIB Jay Bouwmeester	20.00	50.00
Olli Jokinen		
Jarome Iginla		
TRIKGG Jean-Sebastien Giguere	15.00	40.00
Saku Koivu		
Ryan Getzlaf		
TRIKLL Bryan Little	10.00	25.00
Ilya Kovalchuk		
Kari Lehtonen		
TRIKTP Keith Tkachuk	10.00	25.00
Paul Kariya		
David Perron		
TRILBE Alexander Edler	25.00	60.00
Kevin Bieksa		
Roberto Luongo		
TRILGH Gordie Howe	50.00	120.00
Wayne Gretzky		
Mario Lemieux		
TRILHZ Tomas Holmstrom	20.00	50.00
Henrik Zetterberg		
Nicklas Lidstrom		
TRILSS Steven Stamkos	25.00	60.00
Vincent Lecavalier		
Martin St. Louis		
TRIMGP Carey Price	25.00	60.00
Andrei Markov		
Brian Gionta		
TRIMNC Jonathan Cheechoo	10.00	25.00
Evgeni Nabokov		
Patrick Marleau		
TRIMRT Marty Turco	10.00	25.00
Brad Richards		
Mike Modano		
TRINLZ Markus Naslund	20.00	50.00
Henrik Lundqvist		
Nikolai Zherdev		
TRINSS Mats Sundin	20.00	50.00
Joe Sakic		
Owen Nolan		
TRIOCG Patrick O'Sullivan	12.00	30.00
Andrew Cogliano		
Sam Gagner		
TRIPMV Thomas Vanek	10.00	25.00
Jason Pominville		
Ryan Miller		
TRIPRS Jason Pominville	10.00	25.00
Derek Roy		
Drew Stafford		
TRISHS Paul Stastny	20.00	50.00
Milan Hejduk		
Joe Sakic		
TRISJK Olli Jokinen	10.00	25.00
Teemu Selanne		
Jari Kurri		
TRISLH Jason Spezza	20.00	50.00
Pascal Leclaire		
Dany Heatley		
TRISTK Patrick Kane	25.00	60.00
Jonathan Toews		
Patrick Sharp		
TRITSS Vesa Toskala	15.00	40.00

Matt Stajan
Luke Schenn
TRIWDT Doug Weight 10.00 25.00
Rick DiPietro
Jeff Tambellini

2009-10 Artifacts Tundra Trios Patches

STATED PRINT RUN 10 SER.#'d SETS
NOT PRICED DUE TO SCARCITY

2001-02 Atomic

Released in late November 2001, this 125-card base set featured die-cut cards printed on styrene stock and carried an SRP of $5.99 for a 5-card hobby pack. Rookies were short printed to just 500 copies each and were inserted at a rate of 1:21. Retail packs contained 3 cards.

COMP.SET w/o SP's (100) 30.00 60.00
SP STAT.PRINT RUN 500 SER.#'d SETS
1 Paul Kariya .60 1.50
2 Steve Shields .50 1.25
3 Milan Hnilicka .30 .75
4 Patrik Stefan .30 .75
5 Jason Allison .30 .75
6 Byron Dafoe .50 1.25
7 Bill Guerin .50 1.25
8 Sergei Samsonov .50 1.25
9 Joe Thornton 1.00 2.50
10 Martin Biron .50 1.25
11 Tim Connolly .30 .75
12 J-P Dumont .50 1.25
13 Jarome Iginla .75 2.00
14 Marc Savard .30 .75
15 Roman Turek .50 1.25
16 Ron Francis .50 1.25
17 Arturs Irbe .50 1.25
18 Jeff O'Neill .30 .75
19 Tony Amonte .50 1.25
20 Steve Sullivan .30 .75
21 Jocelyn Thibault .50 1.25
22 Rob Blake .50 1.25
23 Chris Drury .50 1.25
24 Peter Forsberg 1.50 4.00
25 Milan Hejduk .60 1.50
26 Patrick Roy 3.00 8.00
27 Joe Sakic 1.25 3.00
28 Alex Tanguay .50 1.25
29 Marc Denis .50 1.25
30 Geoff Sanderson .30 .75
31 Ed Belfour .60 1.50
32 Mike Modano 1.00 2.50
33 Joe Nieuwendyk .50 1.25
34 Pierre Turgeon .50 1.25
35 Sergei Fedorov 1.00 2.50
36 Dominik Hasek 1.25 3.00
37 Brett Hull .75 2.00
38 Luc Robitaille .50 1.25
39 Brendan Shanahan .60 1.50
40 Steve Yzerman 3.00 8.00
41 Mike Comrie .50 1.25
42 Tommy Salo .50 1.25
43 Ryan Smyth .30 .75
44 Pavel Bure .60 1.50
45 Valeri Bure .30 .75
46 Roberto Luongo .75 2.00
47 Zigmund Palffy .50 1.25
48 Felix Potvin .60 1.50
49 Manny Fernandez .50 1.25
50 Marian Gaborik 1.25 3.00
51 Saku Koivu .60 1.50
52 Yanic Perreault .30 .75
53 Jose Theodore .75 2.00
54 Mike Dunham .50 1.25
55 David Legwand .50 1.25
56 Jason Arnott .30 .75
57 Martin Brodeur 1.50 4.00
58 Patrik Elias .50 1.25
59 Mariusz Czerkawski .30 .75
60 Rick DiPietro .50 1.25
61 Michael Peca .30 .75
62 Alexei Yashin .30 .75
63 Theo Fleury .30 .75
64 Brian Leetch .50 1.25
65 Eric Lindros .60 1.50
66 Mark Messier .60 1.50
67 Daniel Alfredsson .50 1.25
68 Martin Havlat .50 1.25
69 Marian Hossa .60 1.50
70 Patrick Lalime .50 1.25
71 Roman Cechmanek .50 1.25
72 John LeClair .60 1.50
73 Mark Recchi .50 1.25
74 Jeremy Roenick .75 2.00
75 Sean Burke .50 1.25
76 Daymond Langkow .30 .75
77 Johan Hedberg .50 1.25
78 Alexei Kovalev .50 1.25
79 Mario Lemieux 4.00 10.00
80 Martin Straka .30 .75
81 Brent Johnson .50 1.25
82 Chris Pronger .50 1.25
83 Keith Tkachuk .60 1.50
84 Doug Weight .50 1.25
85 Evgeni Nabokov .50 1.25
86 Owen Nolan .50 1.25
87 Teemu Selanne .60 1.50
88 Nikolai Khabibulin .60 1.50
89 Vincent Lecavalier .60 1.50
90 Brad Richards .50 1.25
91 Curtis Joseph .60 1.50
92 Alexander Mogilny .50 1.25
93 Mats Sundin .60 1.50
94 Markus Naslund .60 1.50
95 Daniel Sedin .30 .75
96 Henrik Sedin .30 .75
97 Peter Bondra .60 1.50
98 Jaromir Jagr 1.00 2.50
99 Olaf Kolzig .50 1.25
100 Adam Oates .50 1.25
101 Ilja Bryzgalov RC 5.00 12.00
102 Timo Parssinen RC 5.00 12.00
103 Dany Heatley SP 8.00 20.00
104 Ilya Kovalchuk RC 20.00 50.00
105 Kamil Piros RC 5.00 12.00
106 Erik Cole RC 8.00 20.00
107 Vaclav Nedorost RC 5.00 12.00
108 Pavel Datsyuk RC 15.00 40.00
109 Niklas Hagman RC 5.00 12.00
110 Kristian Huselius RC 8.00 20.00
111 Jaroslav Bednar RC 5.00 12.00
112 Pascal Dupuis RC 5.00 12.00
113 Martin Erat RC 5.00 12.00
114 Scott Clemmensen RC 5.00 12.00
115 Radek Martinek RC 5.00 12.00
116 Dan Blackburn RC 6.00 15.00
117 Ivan Ciernik RC 5.00 12.00
118 Chris Neil RC 5.00 12.00
119 Pavel Brendl SP 5.00 12.00
120 Jiri Dopita RC 5.00 12.00
121 Krystofer Kolanos RC 5.00 12.00
122 Mark Rycroft RC 5.00 12.00
123 Jeff Jillson RC 5.00 12.00
124 Nikita Alexeev RC 5.00 12.00
125 Brian Sutherby RC 5.00 12.00
NNO Mats Sundin
NNO Keith Tkachuk
NNO Johan Hedberg

2001-02 Atomic Blue

STATED ODDS 1:161
PRINT RUN LIMITED TO PLAYER'S JSY #
NOT PRICED DUE TO SCARCITY

2001-02 Atomic Gold

*GOLD: 3X TO 8X BASIC CARD
STATED ODDS 2:21 HOBBY PACKS
PRINT RUN 200 SER.#'d SETS

2001-02 Atomic Premiere Date

*STARS: 5X TO 12X BASIC CARD
*SP's: .5X TO 1X BASIC CARD
STATED ODDS 1:21 HOBBY PACKS
STATED PRINT RUN 90 SER.#'d SETS

2001-02 Atomic Red

*RED: 2.5X TO 6X BASIC CARD
STATED ODDS 4:25 RETAIL
STATED PRINT RUN 290 SER.#'d SETS

2001-02 Atomic Blast

STATED ODDS 1:321 HOBBY/1:481 RETAIL
STATED PRINT RUN 55 SER.#'d SETS
1 Paul Kariya 8.00 20.00
2 Peter Forsberg 12.50 30.00
3 Joe Sakic 10.00 25.00
4 Steve Yzerman 25.00 60.00
5 Mike Comrie 8.00 20.00
6 Pavel Bure 6.00 15.00
7 Alexei Yashin 8.00 20.00
8 Eric Lindros 10.00 25.00
9 Mario Lemieux 30.00 80.00
10 Jaromir Jagr 8.00 20.00

2001-02 Atomic Core Players

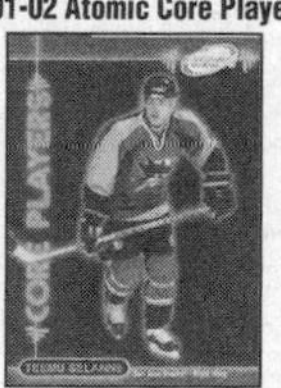

COMPLETE SET (20) 40.00 80.00
STATED ODDS 1:21 HOBBY/1:25 RETAIL
1 Paul Kariya 1.25 3.00
2 Joe Thornton 2.00 5.00
3 Patrick Roy 6.00 15.00
4 Mike Modano 2.00 5.00
5 Steve Yzerman 6.00 15.00
6 Pavel Bure 1.50 4.00
7 Zigmund Palffy 1.00 2.50
8 Marian Gaborik 2.50 6.00
9 Saku Koivu 1.25 3.00
10 Martin Brodeur 3.00 8.00
11 Alexei Yashin 1.00 2.50
12 Mark Messier 1.50 4.00
13 Marian Hossa 1.25 3.00
14 John LeClair 1.50 4.00
15 Mario Lemieux 8.00 20.00
16 Chris Pronger 1.00 2.50
17 Teemu Selanne 1.25 3.00
18 Vincent Lecavalier 1.25 3.00
19 Curtis Joseph 1.25 3.00
20 Jaromir Jagr 2.00 5.00

2001-02 Atomic Jerseys

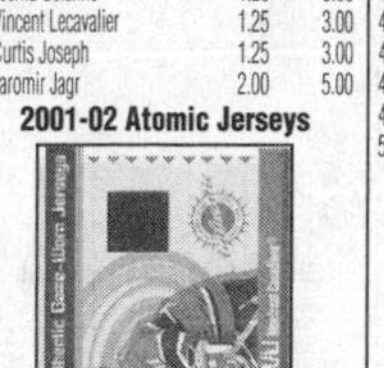

Please note that card #46 does not exist.

STATED ODDS 3:21
1 Jean-Sebastien Giguere 3.00 8.00
2 Steve Rucchin 3.00 8.00
3 Byron Dafoe 3.00 8.00
4 Erik Rasmussen 3.00 8.00
5 Phil Housley 3.00 8.00
6 Marc Savard 3.00 8.00
7 Jeff Shantz 3.00 8.00
8 Tony Amonte 3.00 8.00
9 Eric Daze 3.00 8.00
10 Jocelyn Thibault 3.00 8.00
11 Peter Forsberg 6.00 15.00
12 Dave Reid 3.00 8.00
13 Patrick Roy 12.00 30.00
14 Joe Sakic 8.00 20.00
15 Lyle Odelein 3.00 8.00
16 Ed Belfour 3.00 8.00
17 Benoit Hogue 3.00 8.00
18 Jyrki Lumme 3.00 8.00
19 Mike Modano 3.00 8.00
20 Sergei Zubov 3.00 8.00
21 Mathieu Dandenault 3.00 8.00
22 Dominik Hasek 6.00 15.00
23 Darren McCarty 3.00 8.00
24 Chris Osgood 3.00 8.00
25 Brendan Shanahan 3.00 8.00
26 Steve Yzerman 10.00 25.00
27 Valeri Bure 3.00 8.00
28 Wade Flaherty 3.00 8.00
29 Felix Potvin 3.00 8.00
30 Sergei Zholtok 3.00 8.00
31 Benoit Brunet 3.00 8.00
32 Jeff Hackett 3.00 8.00
33 Saku Koivu 3.00 8.00
34 Mike Dunham 3.00 8.00
35 Tom Fitzgerald 3.00 8.00
36 Scott Walker 3.00 8.00
37 Scott Niedermayer 3.00 8.00
38 Mariusz Czerkawski 3.00 8.00
39 Chris Terreri 3.00 8.00
40 Guy Hebert 3.00 8.00
41 Mike York 3.00 8.00
42 Mika Alatalo 3.00 8.00
43 Rene Corbet 3.00 8.00
44 Jan Hrdina 3.00 8.00
45 Mario Lemieux 12.00 30.00
47 Teemu Selanne 3.00 8.00
48 Mats Sundin 3.00 8.00
49 Dimitri Yushkevich 3.00 8.00
50 Jaromir Jagr 6.00 15.00

2001-02 Atomic Patches

STATED ODDS 1:21 HOBBY
PRINT RUNS VARY
1 Jean-Sebastien Giguere/403 6.00 15.00
2 Steve Rucchin/303 6.00 15.00
3 Byron Dafoe/128 6.00 15.00
4 Erik Rasmussen/153 6.00 15.00
5 Phil Housley/106 6.00 15.00
6 Marc Savard/403 6.00 15.00
7 Jeff Shantz/203 6.00 15.00
8 Tony Amonte/403 6.00 15.00
9 Eric Daze/328 6.00 15.00
10 Jocelyn Thibault/328 6.00 15.00
12 Dave Reid/328 6.00 15.00
13 Patrick Roy/53 40.00 100.00
14 Joe Sakic/308 12.00 30.00
15 Lyle Odelein/153 6.00 15.00
16 Ed Belfour/48 20.00 50.00
17 Benoit Hogue/123 6.00 15.00
18 Jyrki Lumme/303 6.00 15.00
19 Mike Modano/128 12.00 30.00
20 Sergei Zubov/268 6.00 15.00
21 Mathieu Dandenault/178 6.00 15.00
22 Dominik Hasek/283 10.00 25.00
23 Darren McCarty/16
24 Chris Osgood/203 6.00 15.00
26 Steve Yzerman/53 30.00 80.00
27 Valeri Bure/428 6.00 15.00
28 Wade Flaherty/302 6.00 15.00
29 Felix Potvin/103 10.00 25.00
30 Sergei Zholtok/138 6.00 15.00
33 Saku Koivu/53 15.00 40.00
34 Mike Dunham/193 6.00 15.00
35 Tom Fitzgerald/378 6.00 15.00
36 Scott Walker/428 6.00 15.00
37 Scott Niedermayer/478 6.00 15.00
38 Mariusz Czerkawski/503 6.00 15.00
39 Chris Terreri/153 6.00 15.00
40 Guy Hebert/115 6.00 15.00
41 Mike York/403 6.00 15.00
42 Mika Alatalo/228 6.00 15.00
43 Rene Corbet/53 12.00 30.00
44 Jan Hrdina/353 6.00 15.00
46 Kevin Stevens/353 6.00 15.00
47 Teemu Selanne/153 8.00 20.00
48 Mats Sundin/203 8.00 20.00
49 Dimitri Yushkevich/128 6.00 15.00
50 Jaromir Jagr/78 15.00 40.00

2001-02 Atomic Power Play

COMPLETE SET (36) 15.00 30.00
STATED ODDS 1:1
1 Paul Kariya .50 1.25
2 Patrik Stefan .25 .60
3 Sergei Samsonov .40 1.00
4 Joe Thornton .75 2.00
5 Jarome Iginla .60 1.50
6 Jeff O'Neill .25 .60
7 Tony Amonte .40 1.00
8 Peter Forsberg 1.25 3.00
9 Milan Hejduk .50 1.25
10 Joe Sakic 1.00 2.50
11 Mike Modano .75 2.00
12 Sergei Fedorov .75 2.00
13 Brendan Shanahan .50 1.25
14 Steve Yzerman 2.50 6.00
15 Mike Comrie .40 1.00
16 Pavel Bure .50 1.25
17 Zigmund Palffy .40 1.00
18 Marian Gaborik 1.00 2.50
19 Saku Koivu .50 1.25
20 Jason Arnott .25 .60
21 Alexei Yashin .25 .60
22 Theo Fleury .25 .60
23 Eric Lindros .50 1.25
24 Mark Messier .50 1.25
25 Marian Hossa .50 1.25
26 John LeClair .50 1.25
27 Mario Lemieux 3.00 8.00
28 Chris Pronger .40 1.00
29 Keith Tkachuk .50 1.25
30 Teemu Selanne .50 1.25
31 Vincent Lecavalier .50 1.25
32 Mats Sundin .50 1.25
33 Daniel Sedin .25 .60
34 Henrik Sedin .25 .60
35 Peter Bondra .50 1.25
36 Jaromir Jagr .75 2.00

2001-02 Atomic Rookie Reaction

COMPLETE SET (10) 10.00 25.00
STATED ODDS 1:41
1 Dany Heatley 2.00 5.00
2 Ilya Kovalchuk 6.00 15.00
3 Vaclav Nedorost .40 1.00
4 Rostislav Klesla .75 2.00
5 Rick DiPietro 2.00 5.00
6 Pavel Brendl .40 1.00
7 Jiri Dopita .40 1.00
8 Kris Beech .40 1.00
9 Johan Hedberg .75 2.00
10 Nikita Alexeev .40 1.00

2001-02 Atomic Statosphere

COMPLETE SET (20) 40.00 80.00
STATED ODDS 1:21 HOBBY/1:25 RETAIL
CARDS 1-10 AVAIL. HOBBY ONLY/
CARDS 11-20 AVAIL. RETAIL ONLY
1 Patrick Roy 6.00 15.00
2 Ed Belfour 1.25 3.00
3 Dominik Hasek 2.50 6.00
4 Martin Brodeur 3.00 8.00
5 Rick DiPietro 1.00 2.50
6 Mike Richter 1.25 3.00
7 Roman Cechmanek 1.00 2.50
8 Johan Hedberg 1.00 2.50
9 Evgeni Nabokov 1.00 2.50
10 Curtis Joseph 1.25 3.00
11 Peter Forsberg 3.00 8.00
12 Joe Sakic 2.50 6.00
13 Brett Hull 1.50 4.00
14 Pavel Bure 1.50 4.00
15 Zigmund Palffy 1.00 2.50
16 Alexei Yashin 1.00 2.50
17 Alexei Kovalev 1.00 2.50
18 Mario Lemieux 8.00 20.00
19 Martin Straka 1.00 2.50
20 Jaromir Jagr 2.00 5.00

2001-02 Atomic Team Nucleus

COMPLETE SET (15) 30.00 60.00
STATED ODDS 1:21 HOBBY/1:25 RETAIL
1 Bill Guerin 2.00 5.00
Sergei Samsonov
Joe Thornton
2 Jarome Iginla 2.00 5.00
Serge Savard
Roman Turek
3 Ron Francis 2.00 5.00
Arturs Irbe
Jeff O'Neill
4 Peter Forsberg 4.00 10.00
Patrick Roy
Joe Sakic
5 Ed Belfour 2.00 5.00
Mike Modano
Joe Nieuwendyk
6 Dominik Hasek 4.00 10.00
Brendan Shanahan
Steve Yzerman
7 Mike Comrie 2.00 5.00
Tommy Salo
Ryan Smyth
8 Jason Arnott 2.00 5.00
Martin Brodeur
Patrik Elias
9 Rick DiPietro 2.00 5.00
Mike Peca
Alexei Yashin
10 Theo Fleury 2.00 5.00
Eric Lindros
Mark Messier
11 Johan Hedberg 2.00 5.00
Alexei Kovalev
Mario Lemieux
12 Evgeni Nabokov 2.00 5.00
Owen Nolan
Teemu Selanne
13 Curtis Joseph 2.00 5.00
Alexander Mogilny
Mats Sundin
14 Markus Naslund 2.00 5.00
Daniel Sedin
Henrik Sedin
15 Peter Bondra 2.00 5.00
Jaromir Jagr
Adam Oates

2001-02 Atomic Toronto Fall Expo

Available only by wrapper redemption at the 2001 Toronto Fall Expo, this 25-card set paralleled the Atomic rookies, but carried a Fall Expo gold stamp. Each card was serial numbered out of 500.

COMPLETE SET (25) 30.00 80.00
STATED PRINT RUN 500 SETS
101 Ilja Bryzgalov 2.00 5.00
102 Timo Parssinen .75 2.00
103 Dany Heatley 4.00 10.00
104 Ilya Kovalchuk 8.00 20.00
105 Kamil Piros .75 2.00
106 Erik Cole 2.00 5.00
107 Vaclav Nedorost .75 2.00
108 Pavel Datsyuk 4.00 10.00
109 Niklas Hagman .75 2.00
110 Kristian Huselius 2.00 5.00
111 Jaroslav Bednar .75 2.00
112 Pascal Dupuis .75 2.00
113 Martin Erat .75 2.00
114 Scott Clemmensen 1.25 3.00
115 Radek Martinek .75 2.00
116 Dan Blackburn 1.25 3.00
117 Ivan Ciernik .75 2.00
118 Chris Neil 1.25 3.00
119 Pavel Brendl .75 2.00
120 Jiri Dopita .75 2.00
121 Krystofer Kolanos .75 2.00
122 Mark Rycroft .75 2.00
123 Jeff Jillson .75 2.00
124 Nikita Alexeev .75 2.00
125 Brian Sutherby .75 2.00

2002-03 Atomic

Released in mid-November, this 125-card set sported a die-cut design. Cards 101-125 were shortprinted to just 1300 copies each. Cards 126-131 were available in packs of Private Stock Reserve at a rate of 1:9 hobby packs and 1:49 retail.

COMP.SET w/o SP's (100) 25.00 60.00
SP PRINT RUN 1300 SER.#'d SETS
126-131 AVAIL. 1:9 PVT.STK HBBY PACKS
1 Jean-Sebastien Giguere .30 .75
2 Paul Kariya .60 1.50
3 Adam Oates .30 .75
4 Dany Heatley .75 2.00
5 Ilya Kovalchuk .75 2.00
6 Glen Murray .20 .50
7 Sergei Samsonov .30 .75
8 Joe Thornton 1.00 2.50
9 Martin Biron .30 .75
10 J-P Dumont .20 .50
11 Miroslav Satan .20 .50
12 Craig Conroy .20 .50
13 Jarome Iginla .75 2.00
14 Roman Turek .30 .75
15 Erik Cole .20 .50
16 Ron Francis .30 .75
17 Arturs Irbe .30 .75
18 Jeff O'Neill .20 .50
19 Mark Bell .20 .50
20 Eric Daze .30 .75
21 Jocelyn Thibault .30 .75
22 Rob Blake .30 .75
23 Chris Drury .30 .75
24 Peter Forsberg 1.00 2.50
25 Steven Reinprecht .20 .50
26 Patrick Roy 2.50 6.00
27 Joe Sakic 1.25 3.00
28 Marc Denis .30 .75
29 Espen Knutsen .20 .50
30 Ray Whitney .20 .50
31 Jason Arnott .20 .50
32 Bill Guerin .30 .75
33 Mike Modano 1.00 2.50
34 Marty Turco .30 .75
35 Pavel Datsyuk .60 1.50
36 Sergei Fedorov .60 1.50
37 Brett Hull .60 1.50
38 Curtis Joseph .60 1.50
39 Nicklas Lidstrom .60 1.50
40 Brendan Shanahan .60 1.50
41 Steve Yzerman 2.00 5.00
42 Mike Comrie .30 .75
43 Tommy Salo .30 .75
44 Ryan Smyth .20 .50
45 Kristian Huselius .20 .50
46 Roberto Luongo .75 2.00
47 Stephen Weiss .20 .50
48 Jason Allison .20 .50
49 Zigmund Palffy .30 .75
50 Felix Potvin .60 1.50
51 Andrew Brunette .20 .50
52 Manny Fernandez .30 .75
53 Marian Gaborik 1.25 2.50
54 Doug Gilmour .30 .75
55 Saku Koivu .60 1.50
56 Yanic Perreault .20 .50
57 Jose Theodore .60 1.50
58 Denis Arkhipov .20 .50
59 Mike Dunham .30 .75
60 Martin Brodeur 1.50 4.00
61 Patrik Elias .30 .75
62 Joe Nieuwendyk .30 .75
63 Chris Osgood .30 .75
64 Michael Peca .20 .50
65 Alexei Yashin .20 .50
66 Dan Blackburn .30 .75
67 Pavel Bure .60 1.50
68 Eric Lindros .60 1.50
69 Mike Richter .30 .75
70 Daniel Alfredsson .30 .75
71 Marian Hossa .30 .75
72 Patrick Lalime .30 .75
73 Roman Cechmanek .20 .50
74 Simon Gagne .30 .75
75 Jeremy Roenick .60 1.50
76 Tony Amonte .30 .75
77 Daniel Briere .20 .50
78 Sean Burke .30 .75
79 Johan Hedberg .30 .75
80 Mario Lemieux 2.50 6.00
81 Alexei Morozov .20 .50
82 Brent Johnson .30 .75
83 Chris Pronger .30 .75
84 Keith Tkachuk .30 .75
85 Patrick Marleau .30 .75
86 Evgeni Nabokov .30 .75
87 Owen Nolan .30 .75
88 Teemu Selanne .60 1.50
89 Nikolai Khabibulin .30 .75
90 Vincent Lecavalier .60 1.50
91 Ed Belfour .30 .75
92 Alexander Mogilny .30 .75
93 Gary Roberts .20 .50
94 Mats Sundin .60 1.50
95 Todd Bertuzzi .30 .75
96 Dan Cloutier .30 .75
97 Markus Naslund .30 .75
98 Peter Bondra .30 .75
99 Jaromir Jagr 1.00 2.50
100 Olaf Kolzig .30 .75
101 Stanislav Chistov RC 2.00 5.00
102 Martin Gerber RC 2.50 6.00
103 Alexei Smirnov RC 1.50 4.00
104 Chuck Kobasew RC 2.50 6.00
105 Rick Nash RC 6.00 15.00
106 Dmitri Bykov RC 2.00 5.00
107 Henrik Zetterberg RC 6.00 15.00
108 Kari Haakana RC 2.00 5.00
109 Ales Hemsky RC 4.00 10.00
110 Alex Henry RC 2.00 5.00
111 Jay Bouwmeester RC 3.00 8.00
112 Alexander Frolov RC 4.00 10.00
113 P-M Bouchard RC 4.00 10.00
114 Sylvain Blouin RC 2.00 5.00
115 Ron Hainsey RC 2.00 5.00
116 Adam Hall RC 2.00 5.00
117 Scottie Upshall RC 2.00 5.00
118 Mike Danton SP 2.00 5.00
119 Ray Schultz RC 2.00 5.00
120 Anton Volchenkov RC 2.00 5.00
121 Dennis Seidenberg RC 2.00 5.00
122 Patrick Sharp RC 2.00 5.00
123 Dick Tarnstrom RC 2.00 5.00
124 Alexander Svitov RC 2.00 5.00
125 Steve Eminger RC 2.00 5.00
126 Jordan Leopold RC 2.00 5.00
127 Stephane Veilleux RC 1.50 4.00
128 Jason Spezza RC 8.00 20.00
129 Radovan Somik RC 1.50 4.00
130 Jeff Taffe RC 1.50 4.00
131 Tom Koivisto RC 1.50 4.00

2002-03 Atomic Blue

*STARS: 1.25X TO 3X BASIC CARDS
*ROOKIES: .5X TO 1.25X
STATED ODDS 1:6 US
PRINT RUN 175 SER.#'d SETS

2002-03 Atomic Gold

*GOLD: X TO X BASIC CARDS
*ROOKIES: .6X TO 1.5X
STATED ODDS 1:11 HOBBY
PRINT RUN 99 SER.#'d SETS

2002-03 Atomic Red

*STARS:1.5X TO 4X BASIC CARDS
*ROOKIES: .6X TO 1.5X
STATED ODDS 1:6
PRINT RUN 125 SER.#'d SETS

2002-03 Atomic Cold Fusion

COMPLETE SET (24) 30.00 60.00
STATED ODDS 1:11
1 Paul Kariya .75 2.00
2 Dany Heatley 1.00 2.50
3 Ilya Kovalchuk 1.00 2.50
4 Joe Thornton 1.25 3.00
5 Jarome Iginla 1.00 2.50
6 Jeff O'Neill .60 1.50
7 Eric Daze .60 1.50
8 Peter Forsberg 2.00 5.00
9 Joe Sakic 1.50 4.00
10 Pavel Datsyuk .75 2.00
11 Brendan Shanahan 1.25 3.00
12 Steve Yzerman 3.00 8.00
13 Mike Comrie .60 1.50
14 Kristian Huselius .60 1.50
15 Saku Koivu .75 2.00
16 Pavel Bure 1.00 2.50
17 Eric Lindros .75 2.00
18 Daniel Alfredsson .60 1.50
19 Simon Gagne .75 2.00
20 Mario Lemieux 5.00 12.00
21 Teemu Selanne .75 2.00
22 Mats Sundin .75 2.00
23 Markus Naslund .75 2.00
24 Jaromir Jagr 1.25 3.00

2002-03 Atomic Denied

COMPLETE SET (20) 20.00 40.00
STATED ODDS 1:41
1 Jean-Sebastien Giguere .75 2.00
2 Roman Turek .75 2.00
3 Arturs Irbe .75 2.00
4 Jocelyn Thibault .75 2.00
5 Patrick Roy 5.00 12.00
6 Marty Turco .75 2.00
7 Curtis Joseph 1.00 2.50
8 Roberto Luongo 1.50 4.00
9 Felix Potvin 1.00 2.50
10 Jose Theodore 1.00 2.50
11 Martin Brodeur 2.50 6.00
12 Chris Osgood .75 2.00
13 Mike Richter .75 2.00
14 Patrick Lalime .75 2.00
15 Roman Cechmanek .75 2.00
16 Sean Burke .75 2.00
17 Brent Johnson .75 2.00
18 Evgeni Nabokov .75 2.00
19 Nikolai Khabibulin 1.00 2.50
20 Ed Belfour 1.00 2.50

2002-03 Atomic Hobby Parallel

*STARS: .75X TO 2X BASIC CARDS
*ROOKIES: .25X TO .75X
STATED ODDS 3:4
PRINT RUN 775 SER.#'d SETS

2002-03 Atomic Jerseys

STATED ODDS 4:21
1 Adam Oates 2.00 5.00

2 Roman Turek 2.00 5.00
3 Jason Arnott 2.00 5.00
4 Bill Guerin 2.00 5.00
5 Scott Young 2.00 5.00
6 Dominik Hasek 8.00 20.00
7 Brett Hull 4.00 10.00
8 Curtis Joseph 3.00 8.00
9 Luc Robitaille 3.00 8.00
10 Ryan Smyth 2.00 5.00
11 Jose Theodore 6.00 15.00
12 Jeff Friesen 2.00 5.00
13 Oleg Tverdovsky 2.00 5.00
14 Alexei Yashin 2.00 5.00
15 Pavel Bure 4.00 10.00
16 Mark Messier 4.00 10.00
17 John LeClair 2.00 5.00
18 Daymond Langkow 2.00 5.00
19 Mario Lemieux 12.00 30.00
20 Pavol Demitra 2.00 5.00
21 Ray Ferraro 2.00 5.00
22 Tom Barrasso 2.00 5.00
23 Darcy Tucker 2.00 5.00
24 Jaromir Jagr 8.00 20.00
25 Robert Lang 2.00 5.00

2002-03 Atomic Patches

*PATCHES: 1X TO 2.5X JERSEY

2002-03 Atomic National Pride

COMP.CANADA SET (10) 20.00 40.00
COMP.US SET (10) 8.00 15.00
STATED ODDS 1:21
C1-C10 AVAIL.CANADA PACKS ONLY
U1-U10 AVAIL.US PACKS ONLY
C1 Paul Kariya .75 2.00
C2 Jarome Iginla 1.00 2.50
C3 Rob Blake .60 1.50
C4 Joe Sakic 1.50 4.00
C5 Curtis Joseph .75 2.00
C6 Brendan Shanahan 1.00 2.50
C7 Steve Yzerman 4.00 10.00
C8 Martin Brodeur 2.00 5.00
C9 Mario Lemieux 5.00 12.00
C10 Chris Pronger .60 1.50
U1 Bill Guerin .60 1.50
U2 Mike Modano 1.25 3.00
U3 Chris Chelios .75 2.00
U4 Brett Hull 1.00 2.50
U5 Brian Leetch .60 1.50
U6 Mike Richter .60 1.50
U7 Jeremy Roenick 1.00 2.50
U8 Tony Amonte .60 1.50
U9 Keith Tkachuk .75 2.00
U10 Tom Barrasso .60 1.50

2002-03 Atomic Power Converters

COMPLETE SET (20) 15.00 40.00
STATED ODDS 1:21
1 Dany Heatley 1.50 4.00
2 Ilya Kovalchuk 1.50 4.00
3 Miroslav Satan 1.25 3.00
4 Jarome Iginla 1.50 4.00
5 Ron Francis 1.25 3.00
6 Sami Kapanen .75 2.00
7 Nicklas Lidstrom 1.25 3.00
8 Luc Robitaille 1.25 3.00
9 Jason Allison .75 2.00
10 Zigmund Palffy .75 2.00
11 Andrew Brunette .75 2.00
12 Alexei Yashin .75 2.00
13 Pavel Bure 1.25 3.00
14 Eric Lindros 1.25 3.00
15 Daniel Briere .75 2.00
16 Pavol Demitra .75 2.00
17 Keith Tkachuk 1.25 3.00
18 Todd Bertuzzi 1.25 3.00
19 Markus Naslund 1.25 3.00
20 Peter Bondra 1.25 3.00

2002-03 Atomic Super Colliders

COMPLETE SET (16) 12.00 30.00
STATED ODDS 1:21
1 Ilya Kovalchuk 2.00 5.00
2 Joe Thornton 2.00 5.00
3 Jarome Iginla 2.00 5.00
4 Erik Cole .75 2.00
5 Jason Arnott .75 2.00
6 Brendan Shanahan 1.25 3.00
7 Ryan Smyth .75 2.00
8 Jason Allison .75 2.00
9 Michael Peca .75 2.00
10 Eric Lindros 1.25 3.00
11 Jeremy Roenick 1.25 3.00
12 Chris Pronger .75 2.00
13 Keith Tkachuk .75 2.00
14 Owen Nolan .75 2.00
15 Gary Roberts .75 2.00
16 Todd Bertuzzi 1.25 3.00

1998-99 Aurora

The 1998-99 Pacific Aurora set was issued in one series with a total of 200 standard size cards. The six-card packs retail for $2.99 each. The fronts feature color game-action photos with a smaller head-shot of the featured player in the upper right hand corner. The super-thick card also offers a challenging trivia question on the back.

COMPLETE SET (200) 25.00 50.00
1 Travis Green .07 .20
2 Guy Hebert .20 .50
3 Paul Kariya .25 .60
4 Steve Rucchin .07 .20
5 Tomas Sandstrom .07 .20
6 Teemu Selanne .25 .60
7 Jason Allison .07 .20
8 Ray Bourque .40 1.00
9 Anson Carter .20 .50
10 Byron Dafoe .20 .50
11 Ted Donato .07 .20
12 Dave Ellett .07 .20
13 Dimitri Khristich .07 .20
14 Sergei Samsonov .20 .50
15 Matthew Barnaby .07 .20
16 Michal Grosek .07 .20
17 Dominik Hasek .50 1.25
18 Brian Holzinger .07 .20
19 Michael Peca .07 .20
20 Miroslav Satan .20 .50
21 Dixon Ward .07 .20
22 Alexei Zhitnik .07 .20
23 Andrew Cassels .07 .20
24 Theo Fleury .07 .20
25 Jarome Iginla .30 .75
26 Marty McInnis .07 .20
27 Derek Morris .07 .20
28 Michael Nylander .07 .20
29 Cory Stillman .07 .20
30 Kevin Dineen .07 .20
31 Nelson Emerson .07 .20
32 Martin Gelinas .07 .20
33 Sami Kapanen .07 .20
34 Trevor Kidd .20 .50
35 Robert Kron .07 .20
36 Jeff O'Neill .07 .20
37 Keith Primeau .07 .20
38 Tony Amonte .20 .50
39 Chris Chelios .25 .60
40 Eric Daze .20 .50
41 Jeff Hackett .20 .50
42 Jean-Yves Leroux .07 .20
43 Jeff Shantz .07 .20
44 Alexei Zhamnov .07 .20
45 Adam Deadmarsh .07 .20
46 Peter Forsberg .60 1.50
47 Valeri Kamensky .07 .20
48 Claude Lemieux .07 .20
49 Eric Messier .07 .20
50 Sandis Ozolinsh .07 .20
51 Patrick Roy 1.25 3.00
52 Joe Sakic .50 1.25
53 Ed Belfour .25 .60
54 Derian Hatcher .07 .20
55 Brett Hull .30 .75
56 Jamie Langenbrunner .07 .20
57 Jere Lehtinen .07 .20
58 Mike Modano .40 1.00
59 Joe Nieuwendyk .20 .50
60 Darryl Sydor .07 .20
61 Sergei Zubov .07 .20
62 Sergei Fedorov .40 1.00
63 Vyacheslav Kozlov .20 .50
64 Igor Larionov .20 .50
65 Nicklas Lidstrom .25 .60
66 Darren McCarty .07 .20
67 Chris Osgood .20 .50
68 Brendan Shanahan .25 .60
69 Steve Yzerman 1.25 3.00
70 Kelly Buchberger .07 .20
71 Mike Grier .07 .20
72 Bill Guerin .20 .50
73 Roman Hamrlik .07 .20
74 Boris Mironov .07 .20
75 Janne Niinimaa .07 .20
76 Ryan Smyth .20 .50
77 Doug Weight .20 .50
78 Dino Ciccarelli .20 .50
79 Dave Gagner .07 .20
80 Ed Jovanovski .07 .20
81 Viktor Kozlov .07 .20
82 Paul Laus .07 .20
83 Scott Mellanby .07 .20
84 Ray Whitney .07 .20
85 Rob Blake .20 .50
86 Stephane Fiset .20 .50
87 Yanic Perreault .07 .20
88 Luc Robitaille .20 .50
89 Jamie Storr .20 .50
90 Jozef Stumpel .20 .50
91 Vladimir Tsyplakov .07 .20
92 Shayne Corson .07 .20
93 Vincent Damphousse .07 .20
94 Saku Koivu .25 .60
95 Mark Recchi .20 .50
96 Martin Rucinsky .07 .20
97 Brian Savage .07 .20
98 Jocelyn Thibault .20 .50
99 Andrew Brunette .20 .50
100 Mike Dunham .20 .50
101 Tom Fitzgerald .07 .20
102 Sergei Krivokrasov .07 .20
103 Denny Lambert .07 .20
104 Mikhail Shtalenkov .07 .20
105 Darren Turcotte .07 .20
106 Dave Andreychuk .20 .50
107 Jason Arnott .07 .20
108 Martin Brodeur .60 1.50
109 Patrik Elias .20 .50
110 Bobby Holik .07 .20
111 Randy McKay .07 .20
112 Scott Niedermayer .07 .20
113 Scott Stevens .20 .50
114 Bryan Berard .07 .20
115 Jason Dawe .07 .20
116 Trevor Linden .20 .50
117 Zigmund Palffy .20 .50
118 Robert Reichel .07 .20
119 Tommy Salo .20 .50
120 Bryan Smolinski .07 .20
121 Adam Graves .07 .20
122 Wayne Gretzky 1.50 4.00
123 Alexei Kovalev .07 .20
124 Brian Leetch .25 .60
125 Mike Richter .25 .60
126 Ulf Samuelsson .07 .20
127 Kevin Stevens .20 .50
128 Daniel Alfredsson .20 .50
129 Andreas Dackell .07 .20
130 Igor Kravchuk .07 .20
131 Shawn McEachern .07 .20
132 Chris Phillips .07 .20
133 Damian Rhodes .20 .50
134 Alexei Yashin .07 .20
135 Rod Brind'Amour .20 .50
136 Alexandre Daigle .07 .20
137 Eric Desjardins .07 .20
138 Chris Gratton .20 .50
139 Ron Hextall .20 .50
140 John LeClair .25 .60
141 Eric Lindros .25 .60
142 John Vanbiesbrouck .20 .50
143 Dainius Zubrus .07 .20
144 Brad Isbister .07 .20
145 Nikolai Khabibulin .20 .50
146 Jeremy Roenick .30 .75
147 Cliff Ronning .07 .20
148 Keith Tkachuk .25 .60
149 Rick Tocchet .20 .50
150 Oleg Tverdovsky .07 .20
151 Stu Barnes .07 .20
152 Tom Barrasso .20 .50
153 Kevin Hatcher .07 .20
154 Jaromir Jagr .40 1.00
155 Darius Kasparaitis .07 .20
156 Alexei Morozov .07 .20
157 Martin Straka .07 .20
158 Jim Campbell .07 .20
159 Geoff Courtnall .07 .20
160 Grant Fuhr .20 .50
161 Al MacInnis .20 .50
162 Jamie McLennan .20 .50
163 Chris Pronger .20 .50
164 Pierre Turgeon .20 .50
165 Tony Twist .07 .20
166 Jeff Friesen .07 .20
167 Tony Granato .07 .20
168 Patrick Marleau .07 .20
169 Marty McSorley .07 .20
170 Owen Nolan .20 .50
171 Marco Sturm .07 .20
172 Mike Vernon .20 .50
173 Karl Dykhuis .07 .20
174 Mikael Renberg .20 .50
175 Stephane Richer .20 .50
176 Alexander Selivanov .07 .20
177 Paul Ysebaert .07 .20
178 Rob Zamuner .07 .20
179 Sergei Berezin .20 .50
180 Tie Domi .07 .20
181 Mike Johnson .20 .50
182 Curtis Joseph .25 .60
183 Igor Korolev .07 .20
184 Mathieu Schneider .07 .20
185 Mats Sundin .25 .60
186 Todd Bertuzzi .25 .60
187 Donald Brashear .07 .20
188 Pavel Bure .25 .60
189 Mark Messier .25 .60
190 Alexander Mogilny .20 .50
191 Mattias Ohlund .20 .50
192 Garth Snow .20 .50
193 Brian Bellows .07 .20
194 Peter Bondra .20 .50
195 Sergei Gonchar .07 .20
196 Calle Johansson .07 .20
197 Joe Juneau .20 .50
198 Olaf Kolzig .20 .50
199 Adam Oates .20 .50
200 Richard Zednik .07 .20
S108 Martin Brodeur SAMPLE .07 .20

1998-99 Aurora Atomic Laser Cuts

COMPLETE SET (20) 25.00 50.00
STATED ODDS 4:37 HOBBY
1 Paul Kariya .75 2.00
2 Teemu Selanne .75 2.00
3 Sergei Samsonov .60 1.50
4 Dominik Hasek 1.50 4.00
5 Peter Forsberg 2.00 5.00
6 Patrick Roy 4.00 10.00
7 Joe Sakic 1.50 4.00
8 Mike Modano 1.25 3.00
9 Sergei Fedorov 1.25 3.00
10 Brendan Shanahan .75 2.00
11 Steve Yzerman 4.00 10.00
12 Martin Brodeur 2.00 5.00
13 Wayne Gretzky 5.00 12.00
14 John LeClair .75 2.00
15 Eric Lindros .75 2.00
16 Jaromir Jagr 1.25 3.00
17 Mats Sundin .75 2.00
18 Pavel Bure .75 2.00
19 Mark Messier .75 2.00
20 Peter Bondra .60 1.50

1998-99 Aurora Championship Fever

COMPLETE SET (50) 15.00 40.00
STATED ODDS 1:1
UNPRICED COPPER PRINT RUN 20
*ICE BLUE/100: 6X TO 15X BASIC INSERTS
ICE BLUE PRINT RUN 100 SETS
*RED: .8X TO 2X BASIC INSERTS
RED STATED ODDS 1:4 TREAT
*SILVER/250: 2.5X TO 6X BASIC INSERTS
SILVER PRINT RUN 250
M.BRODEUR ICE BLUE AU 1/1 EXISTS
M.BRODEUR COPPER AU 1/1 EXISTS
M.BRODEUR RED AU 1/1 EXISTS
1 Paul Kariya .30 .75
2 Teemu Selanne .30 .75
3 Ray Bourque .50 1.25
4 Byron Dafoe .25 .60
5 Sergei Samsonov .25 .60
6 Dominik Hasek .60 1.50
7 Michael Peca .25 .60
8 Theo Fleury .25 .60
9 Keith Primeau .25 .60
10 Chris Chelios .30 .75
11 Peter Forsberg .75 2.00
12 Patrick Roy 1.50 4.00
13 Joe Sakic .60 1.50
14 Ed Belfour .30 .75
15 Mike Modano .50 1.25
16 Sergei Fedorov .50 1.25
17 Nicklas Lidstrom .30 .75
18 Chris Osgood .25 .60
19 Brendan Shanahan .30 .75
20 Steve Yzerman 1.50 4.00
21 Doug Weight .25 .60
22 Dino Ciccarelli .25 .60
23 Rob Blake .25 .60
24 Saku Koivu .30 .75
25 Mark Recchi .25 .60
26 Martin Brodeur .75 2.00
27 Patrik Elias .25 .60
28 Trevor Linden .25 .60
29 Zigmund Palffy .25 .60
30 Wayne Gretzky 2.00 5.00
31 Mike Richter .30 .75
32 Daniel Alfredsson .25 .60
33 Damian Rhodes .25 .60
34 Alexei Yashin .25 .60
35 John LeClair .30 .75
36 Eric Lindros .30 .75
37 Dainius Zubrus .25 .60
38 Keith Tkachuk .30 .75
39 Tom Barrasso .25 .60
40 Jaromir Jagr .50 1.25
41 Grant Fuhr .25 .60
42 Pierre Turgeon .25 .60
43 Patrick Marleau .25 .60
44 Mike Vernon .25 .60
45 Rob Zamuner .25 .60
46 Mats Sundin .30 .75
47 Pavel Bure .30 .75
48 Mark Messier .30 .75
49 Peter Bondra .25 .60
50 Olaf Kolzig .25 .60
NNO M.Brodeur Gold AU/97 75.00 150.00

1998-99 Aurora Cubes

COMPLETE SET (20) 40.00 100.00
ONE PER HOBBY BOX
1 Paul Kariya 1.50 4.00
2 Teemu Selanne 1.50 4.00
3 Dominik Hasek 3.00 8.00
4 Peter Forsberg 3.00 8.00
5 Patrick Roy 6.00 15.00
6 Joe Sakic 3.00 8.00
7 Mike Modano 2.50 6.00
8 Sergei Fedorov 2.50 6.00
9 Brendan Shanahan 1.50 4.00
10 Steve Yzerman 5.00 12.00
11 Martin Brodeur 4.00 10.00
12 Wayne Gretzky 8.00 20.00
13 John LeClair 1.50 4.00
14 Eric Lindros 1.50 4.00
15 Jaromir Jagr 2.50 6.00
16 Mats Sundin 1.50 4.00
17 Pavel Bure 1.50 4.00
18 Mark Messier 1.50 4.00
19 Peter Bondra 1.25 3.00
20 Olaf Kolzig 1.25 3.00

1998-99 Aurora Front Line Copper

COPPER/80 ODDS 1:97 CANADIAN
COPPER PRINT RUN 80
UNPRICED ICE BLUE PRINT RUN 15
UNPRICED RED PRINT RUN 5
1 Dominik Hasek 30.00 80.00
2 Peter Forsberg 30.00 80.00
3 Patrick Roy 50.00 125.00
4 Joe Sakic 30.00 80.00
5 Steve Yzerman 50.00 125.00
6 Daniel Alfredsson 10.00 25.00
7 Eric Lindros 20.00 50.00
8 Jaromir Jagr 25.00 60.00
9 Wayne Gretzky 75.00 200.00
10 Tie Domi 10.00 25.00

1998-99 Aurora Man Advantage

COMPLETE SET (20) 50.00 100.00
STATED ODDS 1:73
1 Paul Kariya 2.00 5.00
2 Teemu Selanne 2.00 5.00
3 Ray Bourque 3.00 8.00
4 Michael Peca .75 2.00
5 Peter Forsberg 5.00 12.00
6 Joe Sakic 4.00 10.00
7 Mike Modano 3.00 8.00
8 Joe Nieuwendyk 1.50 4.00
9 Brendan Shanahan 2.00 5.00
10 Steve Yzerman 10.00 25.00
11 Shayne Corson .75 2.00
12 Zigmund Palffy 1.50 4.00
13 Wayne Gretzky 12.50 30.00
14 John LeClair 2.00 5.00
15 Eric Lindros 2.00 5.00
16 Jaromir Jagr 3.00 8.00
17 Mats Sundin 2.00 5.00
18 Pavel Bure 2.00 5.00
19 Mark Messier 2.00 5.00
20 Peter Bondra 1.50 4.00

1998-99 Aurora NHL Command

STATED ODDS 1:361
1 Teemu Selanne 3.00 8.00
2 Dominik Hasek 6.00 15.00
3 Peter Forsberg 8.00 20.00
4 Patrick Roy 15.00 40.00
5 Mike Modano 5.00 12.00
6 Steve Yzerman 15.00 40.00
7 Martin Brodeur 8.00 20.00
8 Wayne Gretzky 20.00 50.00
9 Eric Lindros 3.00 8.00
10 Jaromir Jagr 5.00 12.00

1999-00 Aurora

Cards feature one large color action photo, and one small color action photo on each cardfront. Card backs feature current statistics with another color action photo. Cardstock is thicker than most cards and were available at both hobby and retail outlets.

COMPLETE SET (150) 20.00 40.00
*STRIPED: .4X TO 1X BASIC CARDS
1 Guy Hebert .20 .50
2 Paul Kariya .25 .60
3 Marty McInnis .07 .20
4 Steve Rucchin .07 .20
5 Teemu Selanne .25 .60
6 Andrew Brunette .20 .50
7 Kelly Buchberger .07 .20
8 Damian Rhodes .07 .20
9 Jason Allison .07 .20
10 Ray Bourque .40 1.00
11 Anson Carter .20 .50
12 Byron Dafoe .20 .50
13 Sergei Samsonov .20 .50
14 Joe Thornton .40 1.00
15 Curtis Brown .07 .20
16 Dominik Hasek .50 1.25
17 Joe Juneau .20 .50
18 Michael Peca .20 .50
19 Miroslav Satan .20 .50
20 Valeri Bure .07 .20
21 Jean-Sebastien Giguere .20 .50
22 Phil Housley .07 .20
23 Jarome Iginla .30 .75
24 Cory Stillman .07 .20
25 Ron Francis .20 .50
26 Arturs Irbe .20 .50
27 Sami Kapanen .07 .20
28 Keith Primeau .07 .20
29 Ray Sheppard .20 .50
30 Tony Amonte .20 .50
31 J-P Dumont .20 .50
32 Doug Gilmour .20 .50
33 Jocelyn Thibault .20 .50
34 Alexei Zhamnov .07 .20
35 Adam Deadmarsh .07 .20
36 Chris Drury .20 .50
37 Theo Fleury .07 .20
38 Peter Forsberg .60 1.50
39 Milan Hejduk .30 .75
40 Claude Lemieux .07 .20
41 Patrick Roy 1.25 3.00
42 Joe Sakic .50 1.25
43 Ed Belfour .25 .60
44 Brett Hull .30 .75
45 Jamie Langenbrunner .07 .20
46 Jere Lehtinen .20 .50
47 Mike Modano .40 1.00
48 Joe Nieuwendyk .20 .50
49 Chris Chelios .25 .60
50 Sergei Fedorov .40 1.00
51 Nicklas Lidstrom .25 .60
52 Darren McCarty .07 .20
53 Chris Osgood .20 .50
54 Brendan Shanahan .25 .60
55 Steve Yzerman 1.25 3.00
56 Bill Guerin .07 .20
57 Mike Grier .20 .50
58 Tommy Salo .20 .50
59 Ryan Smyth .20 .50
60 Doug Weight .20 .50
61 Pavel Bure .25 .60
62 Sean Burke .20 .50
63 Viktor Kozlov .07 .20
64 Rob Niedermayer .07 .20
65 Mark Parrish .07 .20
66 Ray Whitney .07 .20
67 Donald Audette .07 .20
68 Rob Blake .07 .20
69 Zigmund Palffy .20 .50
70 Luc Robitaille .20 .50
71 Jamie Storr .20 .50
72 Jozef Stumpel .07 .20
73 Shayne Corson .07 .20
74 Jeff Hackett .07 .20
75 Saku Koivu .25 .60
76 Martin Rucinsky .07 .20
77 Brian Savage .07 .20
78 Mike Dunham .07 .20
79 Sergei Krivokrasov .07 .20
80 David Legwand .20 .50
81 Cliff Ronning .07 .20
82 Scott Walker .07 .20
83 Jason Arnott .07 .20
84 Martin Brodeur .60 1.50
85 Patrik Elias .20 .50
86 Bobby Holik .20 .50
87 Brendan Morrison .07 .20
88 Petr Sykora .07 .20
89 Mariusz Czerkawski .07 .20
90 Kenny Jonsson .07 .20
91 Felix Potvin .25 .60
92 Mike Watt .07 .20
93 Adam Graves .07 .20
94 Brian Leetch .25 .60
95 John MacLean .07 .20
96 Petr Nedved .20 .50
97 Mike Richter .25 .60
98 Magnus Arvedson .07 .20
99 Marian Hossa .25 .60
100 Shawn McEachern .07 .20
101 Ron Tugnutt .20 .50
102 Alexei Yashin .07 .20
103 Rod Brind'Amour .20 .50
104 Eric Desjardins .07 .20
105 John LeClair .25 .60
106 Eric Lindros .25 .60
107 Mark Recchi .20 .50
108 John Vanbiesbrouck .20 .50
109 Nikolai Khabibulin .20 .50
110 Teppo Numminen .07 .20
111 Jeremy Roenick .30 .75
112 Rick Tocchet .20 .50
113 Keith Tkachuk .25 .60
114 Matthew Barnaby .07 .20
115 Tom Barrasso .07 .20
116 Jaromir Jagr .40 1.00
117 Alexei Kovalev .07 .20
118 Martin Straka .07 .20
119 Vincent Damphousse .07 .20
120 Jeff Friesen .07 .20
121 Patrick Marleau .20 .50
122 Steve Shields .20 .50
123 Mike Vernon .20 .50
124 Pavol Demitra .20 .50
125 Grant Fuhr .20 .50
126 Al MacInnis .20 .50
127 Chris Pronger .20 .50
128 Pierre Turgeon .20 .50
129 Chris Gratton .07 .20
130 Kevin Hodson .20 .50
131 Vincent Lecavalier .07 .20
132 Paul Mara .07 .20
133 Darcy Tucker .07 .20
134 Sergei Berezin .20 .50
135 Mike Johnson .20 .50
136 Curtis Joseph .25 .60
137 Yanic Perreault .07 .20
138 Mats Sundin .25 .60
139 Steve Thomas .07 .20
140 Mark Messier .25 .60
141 Bill Muckalt .20 .50
142 Alexander Mogilny .20 .50
143 Markus Naslund .25 .60
144 Mattias Ohlund .07 .20
145 Garth Snow .20 .50
146 Peter Bondra .20 .50
147 Sergei Gonchar .07 .20
148 Benoit Gratton RC .07 .20
149 Olaf Kolzig .20 .50
150 Adam Oates .20 .50

1999-00 Aurora Premiere Date

*PREMIERE DATE/60: 15X TO 40X BASIC CARDS
PREMIERE DATE PRINT RUN 60
*STRIPED/60: .4X TO 1X BASIC PD/60

1999-00 Aurora Canvas Creations

COMPLETE SET (10) 60.00 150.00
STATED ODDS 1:193
1 Paul Kariya 6.00 15.00
2 Teemu Selanne 6.00 15.00
3 Dominik Hasek 12.00 30.00
4 Peter Forsberg 10.00 25.00
5 Patrick Roy 25.00 60.00
6 Steve Yzerman 20.00 50.00
7 Pavel Bure 6.00 15.00
8 John LeClair 4.00 10.00
9 Eric Lindros 6.00 15.00
10 Jaromir Jagr 8.00 20.00

1999-00 Aurora Championship Fever

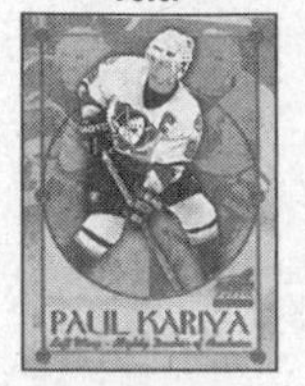

Martin Brodeur autographed 197 copies of his insert card and one each of the parallel cards; these were inserted randomly.

COMPLETE SET (20) 40.00 80.00
STATED ODDS 4:25
UNPRICED COPPER PRINT RUN 20
*ICE BLUE/100: 3X TO 8X BASIC INSERTS
ICE BLUE STATED PRINT RUN 100
*SILVER/250: 1X TO 2.5X BASIC INSERTS
SILVER STATED PRINT RUN 250
1 Paul Kariya .60 1.50
2 Teemu Selanne .60 1.50
3 Ray Bourque 1.00 2.50
4 Dominik Hasek 1.25 3.00
5 Michael Peca .50 1.25
6 Theo Fleury .50 1.25
7 Peter Forsberg 1.50 4.00
8 Patrick Roy 3.00 8.00
9 Joe Sakic 1.50 4.00
10 Ed Belfour .60 1.50
11 Mike Modano 1.00 2.50
12 Brendan Shanahan .60 1.50
13 Steve Yzerman 3.00 8.00
14 Pavel Bure .60 1.50
15 Martin Brodeur 1.50 4.00
16 John LeClair .60 1.50
17 Eric Lindros .60 1.50
18 Jaromir Jagr 1.00 2.50
19 Curtis Joseph .60 1.50
20 Mats Sundin .60 1.50
NNO M.Brodeur AU/197 30.00 80.00

1999-00 Aurora Complete Players

COMPLETE SET (10) 150.00 300.00
HOBBY/RETAIL PRINT RUN 299
*HOBBY PARALLEL 25: 2.5X TO 6X BASIC INSERTS
*RETAIL PARALLEL 25: 2.5X TO 6X BASIC INSERTS
HOB/RET PARALLEL PRINT RUN 25
1 Paul Kariya 10.00 25.00
2 Teemu Selanne 10.00 25.00
3 Dominik Hasek 12.50 30.00
4 Peter Forsberg 15.00 40.00
5 Patrick Roy 30.00 80.00
6 Mike Modano 12.50 30.00
7 Steve Yzerman 40.00 100.00
8 John LeClair 10.00 25.00
9 Eric Lindros 10.00 25.00
10 Jaromir Jagr 10.00 25.00

1999-00 Aurora Glove Unlimited

COMPLETE SET (20) 50.00 100.00
STATED ODDS 2:25
1 Guy Hebert 1.50 4.00
2 Byron Dafoe 1.50 4.00
3 Dominik Hasek 4.00 10.00
4 Arturs Irbe 1.50 4.00
5 Jocelyn Thibault 1.50 4.00
6 Patrick Roy 12.50 25.00

7 Ed Belfour 2.00 5.00
8 Chris Osgood 1.50 4.00
9 Tommy Salo 1.50 4.00
10 Jeff Hackett 1.50 4.00
11 Martin Brodeur 6.00 12.00
12 Felix Potvin 2.00 5.00
13 Mike Richter 2.00 5.00
14 Ron Tugnutt 1.50 4.00
15 John Vanbiesbrouck 1.50 4.00
16 Nikolai Khabibulin 1.50 4.00
17 Grant Fuhr 1.50 4.00
18 Steve Shields 1.50 4.00
19 Curtis Joseph 2.00 5.00
20 Olaf Kolzig 1.50 4.00

1999-00 Aurora Styrotechs

COMPLETE SET (20) 25.00 60.00
STATED ODDS 1:25
1 Paul Kariya 1.25 3.00
2 Teemu Selanne 1.25 3.00
3 Dominik Hasek 3.00 8.00
4 Theo Fleury .75 2.00
5 Peter Forsberg 3.00 8.00
6 Patrick Roy 8.00 20.00
7 Ed Belfour 1.25 3.00
8 Mike Modano 2.00 5.00
9 Brendan Shanahan 1.25 3.00
10 Steve Yzerman 6.00 15.00
11 Pavel Bure 1.25 3.00
12 Martin Brodeur 5.00 12.00
13 Alexei Yashin .40 1.00
14 John LeClair .40 1.00
15 Eric Lindros 1.25 3.00
16 Keith Tkachuk .75 2.00
17 Jaromir Jagr 3.00 8.00
18 Curtis Joseph 1.25 3.00
19 Mats Sundin 1.25 3.00
20 Mark Messier 1.50 4.00

2000-01 Aurora

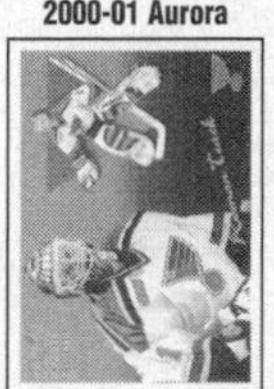

Released as a 150-card set, Aurora base cards feature a white borderd card with two player photos on the card front. A full color action photo appears set against a background that fades from green to blue, top to bottom, and a smaller brown tone player action photo set against a blue triangle. Cards are highlighted with bronze foil. Aurora was packaged in 36-pack boxes with each pack containing six cards. A parallel with a striped background was also created and inserted randomly. The striped set was complete at 50 cards and was skip numbered.

COMPLETE SET (150) 20.00 40.00
*STRIPED: .75X TO 2X BASIC CARD
1 Guy Hebert .20 .50
2 Paul Kariya .25 .60
3 Steve Rucchin .08 .20
4 Teemu Selanne .25 .60
5 Andrew Brunette .20 .50
6 Scott Fankhouser .20 .50
7 Damian Rhodes .20 .50
8 Patrik Stefan .08 .20
9 Jason Allison .08 .20
10 Anson Carter .20 .50
11 Paul Coffey .25 .60
12 Byron Dafoe .20 .50
13 John Grahame .20 .50
14 Sergei Samsonov .20 .50
15 Joe Thornton .40 1.00
16 Maxim Afinogenov .08 .20
17 Martin Biron .20 .50
18 Doug Gilmour .20 .50
19 Dominik Hasek .50 1.25
20 Michael Peca .20 .50
21 Miroslav Satan .20 .50
22 Fred Brathwaite .20 .50
23 Valeri Bure .08 .20
24 Jarome Iginla .30 .75
25 Derek Morris .08 .20
26 Marc Savard .20 .50
27 Rod Brind'Amour .20 .50
28 Ron Francis .20 .50
29 Arturs Irbe .20 .50
30 Sami Kapanen .08 .20
31 Tony Amonte .20 .50
32 Eric Daze .20 .50
33 Steve Sullivan .08 .20
34 Jocelyn Thibault .20 .50
35 Alexei Zhamnov .20 .50
36 Ray Bourque .50 1.25
37 Chris Drury .20 .50
38 Peter Forsberg .60 1.50
39 Milan Hejduk .25 .60
40 Patrick Roy 1.25 3.00
41 Joe Sakic .50 1.25
42 Alex Tanguay .20 .50
43 Ed Belfour .25 .60
44 Brett Hull .25 .75
45 Mike Modano .40 1.00
46 Brenden Morrow .20 .50
47 Joe Nieuwendyk .20 .50
48 Chris Chelios .25 .60
49 Sergei Fedorov .40 1.00
50 Nicklas Lidstrom .25 .60
51 Chris Osgood .25 .60
52 Brendan Shanahan .25 .60
53 Pat Verbeek .08 .20
54 Steve Yzerman 1.25 3.00
55 Mike Grier .08 .20
56 Bill Guerin .20 .50
57 Tommy Salo .20 .50
58 Ryan Smyth .20 .50
59 Doug Weight .20 .50
60 Pavel Bure .25 .60
61 Trevor Kidd .20 .50
62 Viktor Kozlov .20 .50
63 Roberto Luongo .30 .75
64 Ray Whitney .20 .50
65 Rob Blake .20 .50
66 Stephane Fiset .20 .50
67 Zigmund Palffy .20 .50
68 Luc Robitaille .20 .50
69 Jamie Storr .20 .50
70 Jozef Stumpel .20 .50
71 Jeff Hackett .20 .50
72 Saku Koivu .25 .60
73 Trevor Linden .20 .50
74 Martin Rucinsky .08 .20
75 Jose Theodore .30 .75
76 Mike Dunham .20 .50
77 Patric Kjellberg .08 .20
78 David Legwand .20 .50
79 Cliff Ronning .08 .20
80 Jason Arnott .08 .20
81 Martin Brodeur .60 1.50
82 Patrik Elias .20 .50
83 Scott Gomez .08 .20
84 John Madden .08 .20
85 Scott Stevens .20 .50
86 Petr Sykora .08 .20
87 Tim Connolly .08 .20
88 Mariusz Czerkawski .08 .20
89 Brad Isbister .08 .20
90 Mark Parrish .08 .20
91 John Vanbiesbrouck .20 .50
92 Theo Fleury .08 .20
93 Adam Graves .08 .20
94 Jan Hlavac .20 .50
95 Brian Leetch .20 .50
96 Mark Messier .25 .60
97 Petr Nedved .20 .50
98 Mike Richter .20 .50
99 Daniel Alfredsson .20 .50
100 Radek Bonk .08 .20
101 Marian Hossa .25 .60
102 Shawn McEachern .20 .50
103 Vaclav Prospal .08 .20
104 Brian Boucher .25 .60
105 Eric Desjardins .20 .50
106 Simon Gagne .25 .60
107 John LeClair .25 .60
108 Eric Lindros .25 .60
109 Mark Recchi .20 .50
110 Shane Doan .20 .50
111 Joe Juneau .08 .20
112 Jeremy Roenick .30 .75
113 Keith Tkachuk .25 .60
114 Jean-Sebastien Aubin .20 .50
115 Jan Hrdina .08 .20
116 Jaromir Jagr .40 1.00
117 Alexei Kovalev .08 .20
118 Martin Straka .08 .20
119 Pavol Demitra .20 .50
120 Dallas Drake .08 .20
121 Michal Handzus .20 .50
122 Al MacInnis .20 .50
123 Chris Pronger .20 .50
124 Roman Turek .20 .50
125 Pierre Turgeon .25 .60
126 Vincent Damphousse .08 .20
127 Jeff Friesen .08 .20
128 Patrick Marleau .25 .60
129 Owen Nolan .20 .50
130 Steve Shields .20 .50
131 Dan Cloutier .20 .50
132 Matt Elich RC .20 .50
133 Mike Johnson .08 .20
134 Vincent Lecavalier .25 .60
135 Kevin Weekes .20 .50
136 Nikolai Antropov .08 .20
137 Tie Domi .08 .20
138 Jeff Farkas .08 .20
139 Curtis Joseph .25 .60
140 Mats Sundin .25 .60
141 Steve Thomas .08 .20
142 Andrew Cassels .08 .20
143 Steve Kariya .08 .20
144 Markus Naslund .25 .60
145 Felix Potvin .25 .60
146 Peter Bondra .25 .60
147 Jeff Halpern .08 .20
148 Olaf Kolzig .20 .50
149 Adam Oates .20 .50
150 Chris Simon .08 .20

2000-01 Aurora Premiere Date

*PREM.DATE STARS: 20X TO 50X BASIC CARD
STATED PRINT RUN 50 SER.#'d SETS
*PINSTRIPES: .4X TO 1X BASIC INSERTS

2000-01 Aurora Autographs

23 Valeri Bure/300 6.00 15.00
37 Chris Drury/250 8.00 20.00
42 Alex Tanguay/500 8.00 20.00
46 Brenden Morrow/500 6.00 15.00
55 Mike Grier/500 6.00 15.00
75 Jose Theodore/500 12.50 30.00
78 David Legwand/500 8.00 20.00
81 Martin Brodeur/197 40.00 80.00
115 Jean-Sebastien Aubin/500 8.00 20.00
135 Nikolai Antropov/500 6.00 15.00
148 Olaf Kolzig/250 8.00 20.00

2000-01 Aurora Canvas Creations

COMPLETE SET (10) 60.00 100.00
STATED ODDS 1:361
1 Paul Kariya 2.00 5.00
2 Peter Forsberg 6.00 15.00
3 Patrick Roy 12.50 30.00
4 Mike Modano 3.00 8.00
5 Steve Yzerman 10.00 25.00
6 Pavel Bure 2.00 5.00
7 Martin Brodeur 12.50 30.00
8 John LeClair 2.00 5.00
9 Jaromir Jagr 3.00 8.00
10 Curtis Joseph 2.00 5.00

2000-01 Aurora Championship Fever

COMPLETE SET (20) 30.00 60.00
STATED ODDS 4:37
*COPPER STARS: 10X TO 25X BASIC CARDS
COPPER PRINT RUN 90 SER.#'d SETS
*PLAT.BLUE STARS: 10X TO 25X BASIC CARDS
BLUE PRINT RUN 92 SER.#'d SETS
*SILVER STARS: 6X TO 15X BASIC CARDS
SILVER PRINT RUN 221 SER.#'d SETS
1 Paul Kariya .75 2.00
2 Teemu Selanne .75 2.00
3 Dominik Hasek 1.50 4.00
4 Ray Bourque 1.50 4.00
5 Peter Forsberg 2.00 5.00
6 Patrick Roy 4.00 10.00
7 Ed Belfour .75 2.00
8 Brett Hull 1.00 2.50
9 Mike Modano 1.25 3.00
10 Sergei Fedorov 1.25 3.00
11 Brendan Shanahan .75 2.00
12 Steve Yzerman 4.00 10.00
13 Pavel Bure .75 2.00
14 Martin Brodeur 2.00 5.00
15 Scott Gomez .75 2.00
16 Mark Messier .75 2.00
17 Brian Boucher .75 2.00
18 John LeClair .75 2.00
19 Jaromir Jagr 1.25 3.00
20 Curtis Joseph .75 2.00
NNO J.LeClair AU/197 15.00 40.00

2000-01 Aurora Dual Game-Worn Jerseys

STATED PRINT RUN 200 SER.#'d SETS
1 Petr Sykora 15.00 40.00
Saku Koivu
2 John Vanbiesbrouck 15.00 40.00
Roberto Luongo
3 S.Yzerman/B.Shanahan 20.00 50.00
4 Jaromir Jagr 15.00 40.00
Peter Bondra

2000-01 Aurora Game-Worn Jerseys

1 Paul Coffey 5.00 12.00
2 Brendan Shanahan 5.00 12.00
3 Steve Yzerman 12.50 30.00
4 Roberto Luongo 10.00 25.00
5 Saku Koivu 5.00 12.00
6 John Vanbiesbrouck 5.00 12.00
7 Mark Messier 10.00 25.00
8 Petr Sykora 5.00 12.00
9 Eric Lindros 6.00 15.00
10 Peter Bondra 5.00 12.00

2000-01 Aurora Game-Worn Jersey Patches

STATED PRINT RUN 10 SER.#'d SETS
NOT PRICED DUE TO SCARCITY

2000-01 Aurora Scouting Reports

COMPLETE SET (20) 50.00 100.00
STATED ODDS 2:37 HOBBY
1 Paul Kariya 2.00 5.00
2 Teemu Selanne 2.00 5.00
3 Patrik Stefan 1.50 4.00
4 Joe Thornton 3.00 8.00
5 Peter Forsberg 5.00 12.00
6 Milan Hejduk 2.00 5.00
7 Brett Hull 2.50 6.00
8 Ed Belfour 2.00 5.00
9 Sergei Fedorov 3.00 8.00
10 Brendan Shanahan 2.00 5.00
11 Pavel Bure 2.00 5.00
12 Roberto Luongo 2.50 6.00
13 Martin Brodeur 5.00 12.00
14 Scott Gomez 1.50 4.00
15 Marian Hossa 1.50 4.00
16 Brian Boucher 2.00 5.00
17 John LeClair 2.00 5.00
18 Vincent Lecavalier 2.00 5.00
19 Curtis Joseph 2.00 5.00
20 Mats Sundin 2.00 5.00

2000-01 Aurora Styrotechs

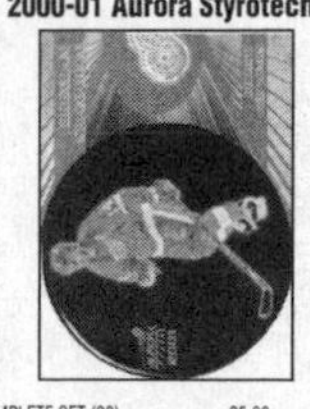

COMPLETE SET (20) 25.00 60.00
A VERSION ODDS 1:37 HOBBY
B VERSION ODDS 1:37 RETAIL
1A Paul Kariya 1.00 2.50
1B Teemu Selanne 1.00 2.50
2A Doug Gilmour 1.00 2.50
2B Dominik Hasek 2.50 6.00
3A Peter Forsberg 2.50 6.00
3B Patrick Roy 8.00 20.00
4A Joe Sakic 2.50 6.00
4B Ray Bourque 2.00 5.00
5A Brett Hull 1.00 2.50
5B Mike Modano 2.00 5.00
6A Brendan Shanahan 1.00 2.50
6B Steve Yzerman 6.00 15.00
7A Scott Gomez .40 1.00
7B Martin Brodeur 4.00 10.00
8A John LeClair .40 1.00
8B Brian Boucher .40 1.00
9A Jaromir Jagr 3.00 8.00
9B Jean-Sebastien Aubin .40 1.00
10A Curtis Joseph 1.00 2.50
10B Mats Sundin 1.00 2.50

1996 Avalanche Photo Pucks

COMPLETE SET (5) 6.00 15.00
1 Claude Lemieux 2.00 5.00
Peter Forsberg
2 Joe Sakic 1.50 4.00
Adam Deadmarsh
3 Patrick Roy 2.00 5.00
Adam Foote
4 Valeri Kamensky 1.25 3.00
Mike Ricci
5 Colorado Avalanche 1.25 3.00

1997 Avalanche Pins

This set of promotional giveaway pins was sponsored by Denver Post. One pin was given out per special event night.

1 Team Logo .40 1.00
2 Joe Sakic 1.50 4.00
3 Patrick Roy 2.50 6.00
4 Marc Crawford CO .40 1.00
5 Peter Forsberg 1.50 4.00
6 Claude Lemieux .40 1.00
7 Olympic Break .40 1.00
8 Sandiz Ozolinsh .40 1.00
9 Adam Foote .75 2.00

1999-00 Avalanche Pins

Released as a limited edition set in conjunction with the Denver Post, this 8-pin set commemorates the inagural season of the Pepsi Center. These pins were available for purchase on April 2 at the Pepsi Center vs. the Dallas Stars. Each pin was shrinkwraped with an oversized card featuring the respective player and logos of both the Pepsi Center and The Denver Post.

COMPLETE SET (8)
1 Joe Sakic 1.50 4.00
2 Adam Foote 1.25 3.00
3 Adam Deadmarsh .40 1.00
4 Patrick Roy 2.50 6.00
5 Peter Forsberg 2.00 5.00
6 Sandis Ozolinsh .40 1.00
7 Chris Drury .40 1.00
8 Milan Hejduk 1.25 3.00

1999-00 Avalanche Team Issue

This set was issued as a promotional giveaway by the Avs. Each card in this set measures 3 1/2" x 5" and card backs are blank. The cards are unnumbered, so are listed below alphabetically.

COMPLETE SET (24) 8.00 20.00
1 Greg DeVries .08 .25
2 Adam Deadmarsh .20 .50
3 Marc Denis .40 1.00
4 Chris Dingman .08 .25
5 Chris Drury .40 1.00
6 Adam Foote .20 .50
7 Peter Forsberg 1.25 3.00
8 Alexei Gusarov .08 .25
9 Milan Hejduk .60 1.50
10 Sami Helenius .08 .25
11 Dan Hinote .30 .75
12 Jon Klemm .15 .40
13 Eric Messier .08 .25
14 Aaron Miller .08 .25
15 Jeff Odgers .08 .25
16 Sandis Ozolinsh .20 .50
17 Shjon Podein .08 .25
18 Dave Reid .08 .25
19 Brian Rolston .20 .50
20 Patrick Roy 2.00 5.00
21 Joe Sakic .75 2.00
22 Martin Skoula .20 .50
23 Alex Tanguay .60 1.50
24 Stephane Yelle .15 .40

2001-02 Avalanche Team Issue

This 23-card set measured approx. 3 1/2" X 5". Each card carried the players jersey number, name and position diagonally along the bottom of the card with the team logo at the top.

COMPLETE SET (22) 15.00 30.00
1 David Aebischer .75 2.00
2 Stephane Yelle .40 1.00
3 Rob Blake .75 2.00
4 Shjon Podein .40 1.00
5 Scott Parker .40 1.00
6 Brian Willsie .40 1.00
7 Brad Larsen .40 1.00
8 Radim Vrbata .40 1.00
9 Rick Berry .40 1.00
10 Adam Foote .40 1.00
11 Chris Drury .40 1.00
12 Alex Tanguay .75 2.00
13 Dan Hinote .40 1.00
14 Eric Messier .40 1.00
15 Joe Sakic 1.25 3.00
16 Pascal Trepanier .40 1.00
17 Martin Skoula .40 1.00
18 Steven Reinprecht .40 1.00
19 Patrick Roy 2.00 5.00
20 Milan Hejduk .75 2.00
21 Todd Gill .40 1.00
22 Greg DeVries .40 1.00
23 Peter Forsberg 1.50 4.00

2002-03 Avalanche Postcards

This postcard sized set was used as a promotional item by the team and featured player action photos on team colored card fronts. Card backs were blank.

COMPLETE SET (18) 10.00 25.00
1 Mike Keane .40 1.00
2 Riku Hahl .60 1.50
3 Scott Parker .60 1.50
4 David Aebischer .60 1.50
5 Steven Reinprecht .40 1.00
6 Greg deVries .40 1.00
7 Eric Messier .40 1.00
8 Peter Forsberg 2.00 5.00
9 Joe Sakic 2.00 5.00
10 Martin Skoula .40 1.00
11 Adam Foote .40 1.00
12 Derek Morris .40 1.00
13 Brian Willsie .40 1.00
14 Jeff Shantz .40 1.00
15 Milan Hejduk .60 1.50
16 Rob Blake .60 1.50
17 Dan Hinote .40 1.00
18 Bryan Muir .40 1.00

2003-04 Avalanche Team Issue

These team issued cards were sponsored by Conoco and each handed out at one home game each. This checklist may be incomplete. Any additional information can be forwarded to hockeymag@beckett.com.

COMPLETE SET (20) 12.00 25.00
1 David Aebischer .40 1.00
2 Rob Blake .75 2.00
3 Jim Cummins .40 1.00
4 Adam Foote .40 1.00
5 Peter Forsberg 1.25 3.00
6 Chris Gratton .40 1.00
7 Riku Hahl .40 1.00
8 Milan Hejduk .75 2.00
9 Dan Hinote .40 1.00
10 Paul Kariya .75 2.00
11 Steve Konowalchuk .40 1.00
12 John-Michael Liles .40 1.00
13 Andrei Nikolishin .40 1.00
14 Joe Sakic 1.25 3.00
15 Phil Sauve .40 1.00
16 Teemu Selanne .75 2.00
17 Karlis Skrastins .40 1.00
18 Marek Svatos .75 2.00
19 Alex Tanguay .75 2.00
20 Peter Worrell .40 1.00

2006-07 Avalanche Postcards

COMPLETE SET (21) 15.00 30.00
1 Tyler Arnason .40 1.00
2 Patrice Brisebois .40 1.00
3 Andrew Brunette .40 1.00
4 Peter Budaj .75 2.00
5 Brett Clark .40 1.00
6 Milan Hejduk .75 2.00
7 Ken Klee .40 1.00
8 Ian Laperriere .40 1.00
9 Jordan Leopold .40 1.00
10 Brett McLean .40 1.00
11 Brad Richardson .40 1.00
12 Mark Rycroft .40 1.00
13 Joe Sakic 2.00 5.00
14 Kurt Sauer .40 1.00
15 Karlis Skrastins .40 1.00
16 Paul Stastny 2.00 5.00
17 Marek Svatos .75 2.00
18 Jose Theodore .75 2.00
19 Pierre Turgeon .40 1.00
20 Ossi Vaananen .40 1.00
21 Wojtek Wolski .75 2.00
22 Ken Klee
23 Paul Stastny
24 Antii Laaksonen
25 Brett Clark
26 Brad May
27 Pierre Lacroix
28 Jeff Hackett
29 Tony Granato
30 Jacques Cloutier
31 Francois Giguere
32 Joel Quenneville

2003-04 Backcheck: A Hockey Retrospective

Produced by the National Library of Canada, this sepia-toned set features a look back at some early photos from hockey's history.

COMPLETE SET (20) 8.00 20.00
1 Choosing Sides .20 .50
2 Outdoor Game .20 .50
3 Early Skating .20 .50
4 Ottawa Rebels .40 1.00
5 Renfrew hockey team .40 1.00
6 Oxford Canadian Hockey Club .40 1.00
7 Gore Bay Hockey Club .40 1.00
8 Ottawa Silver Seven .75 2.00
9 Maurice Richard 2.00 5.00
10 Clarence Campbell .40 1.00
11 Bodychecking .20 .50
12 Asahi Athletic Club .40 1.00
13 Lester B. Pearson .20 .50
14 Prisoners' hockey team .40 1.00
15 Sydney Millionaires .40 1.00
16 Jacques Plante 2.00 5.00
17 Shinny .20 .50
18 Montreal Canadiens 1942 .75 2.00
19 Eva Ault .20 .50
20 Orillia Hockey Club .40 1.00

1995-96 Bashan Super Stickers

COMPLETE SET (135) 15.00 30.00
1 Oleg Tverdovsky TC .08 .25
2 Paul Kariya .60 1.50
3 Chad Kilger .08 .25
4 Oleg Tverdovsky .08 .25
5 Adam Oates TC .08 .25
6 Ray Bourque .60 1.50
7 Cam Neely .60 1.50
8 Adam Oates .20 .50
9 Kevin Stevens .20 .50
10 Dominik Hasek TC .08 .25
11 Pat LaFontaine .20 .50
12 Dominik Hasek .75 2.00
13 Alexei Zhitnik .08 .25
14 Theo Fleury TC .08 .25
15 Theo Fleury .40 1.00
16 Phil Housley .08 .25
17 Trevor Kidd .20 .50
18 Joe Nieuwendyk .20 .50
19 Zarley Zalapski .08 .26
20 Ed Belfour TC .08 .25
21 Jeremy Roenick .60 1.50
22 Chris Chelios .40 1.00
23 Ed Belfour .60 1.50
24 Joe Murphy .08 .25
25 Patrick Poulin .08 .25
26 Peter Forsberg TC .08 .25
27 Joe Sakic .75 2.00
28 Peter Forsberg 1.00 2.50
29 Sandis Ozolinsh .08 .25
30 Mike Ricci .08 .25
31 Valeri Kamensky .08 .25
32 Mike Modano TC .08 .25
33 Mike Modano .60 1.50
34 Kevin Hatcher .08 .25
35 Andy Moog .20 .50
36 Sergei Fedorov TC .08 .25
37 Steve Yzerman 1.25 3.00
38 Sergei Fedorov .60 1.50
39 Paul Coffey .40 1.00
40 Keith Primeau .08 .25
41 Nick Lidstrom .40 1.00
42 Bill Ranford TC .08 .25
43 Doug Weight .08 .25
44 Jason Arnott .08 .25
45 Bill Ranford .20 .50
46 John Vanbiesbrouck TC .08 .25
47 John Vanbiesbrouck .40 1.00
48 Stu Barnes .08 .25
49 Scott Mellanby .08 .25
50 Rob Niedermayer .08 .25
51 Geoff Sanderson TC .08 .25
52 Brendan Shanahan .40 1.00
53 Geoff Sanderson .08 .25
54 Sean Burke .20 .50
55 Jeff O'Neill .08 .25
56 Rob Blake TC .08 .25
57 Wayne Gretzky 2.00 5.00
58 Rob Blake .20 .50
59 Rick Tocchet .20 .50
60 Dimitri Khristich .08 .25
61 Kelly Hrudey .20 .50
62 Vincent Damphousse TC .08 .25
63 Pierre Turgeon .08 .25
64 Mark Recchi .20 .50
65 Saku Koivu .40 1.00
66 Patrick Roy 1.50 4.00
67 Vincent Damphousse .08 .25
68 Scott Stevens TC .08 .25
69 Stephane Richer .08 .25
70 Martin Brodeur 1.25 3.00
71 Scott Niedermayer .08 .25
72 Scott Stevens .08 .25
73 Matt Schneider TC .08 .25
74 Kirk Muller .08 .25
75 Mathieu Schneider .08 .25
76 Derek King .08 .25
77 Wendel Clark .20 .50
78 Mark Messier TC .08 .25
79 Brian Leetch .40 1.00
80 Mark Messier .60 1.50
81 Alexei Kovalev .08 .25
82 Luc Robitaille .40 1.00
83 Mike Richter .40 1.00
84 Radek Bonk TC .08 .25
85 Dan Quinn .08 .25
86 Alexandre Daigle .08 .25
87 Steve Duchesne .08 .25
88 Radek Bonk .08 .25
90 Eric Lindros .60 1.50
91 Mikael Renberg .08 .25
92 John LeClair .20 .50
93 Eric Desjardins .08 .25
94 Rod Brind'Amour .08 .25
95 Ron Francis TC .08 .25
96 Jaromir Jagr .75 2.00
97 Mario Lemieux 1.50 4.00
98 Ron Francis .20 .50
99 Sergei Zubov .08 .25
100 Al MacInnis TC .08 .25
101 Brett Hull .60 1.50
102 Al MacInnis .20 .50
103 Dale Hawerchuk .20 .50
104 Chris Pronger .40 1.00
105 Craig Janney TC .08 .25
106 Craig Janney .08 .25
107 Pat Falloon .08 .25
108 Arturs Irbe .40 1.00
109 Ulf Dahlen .08 .25
110 Owen Nolan .20 .50
111 Brian Bradley TC .08 .25
112 Roman Hamrlik .08 .25
113 Brian Bradley .08 .25
114 Chris Gratton .08 .25
115 Brian Bellows .08 .25
116 Doug Gilmour TC .08 .25
117 Doug Gilmour .40 1.00
118 Mats Sundin .60 1.50
119 Dave Andreychuk .08 .25
120 Felix Potvin .40 1.00
121 Larry Murphy .08 .25
122 Alex Mogilny TC .08 .25
123 Pavel Bure .40 1.00
124 Alex Mogilny .20 .50
125 Trevor Linden .20 .50
126 Jeff Brown .08 .25
127 Kirk McLean .20 .50
128 Jim Carey TC .08 .25
129 Joe Juneau .08 .25
130 Peter Bondra .20 .50
131 Jim Carey .20 .50
132 Calle Johansson .08 .25
133 Teemu Selanne TC .08 .25
134 Teemu Selanne .60 1.50
135 Alexei Zhamnov .08 .25
136 Keith Tkachuk .40 1.00

1995-96 Bashan Super Stickers Die-Cut

COMPLETE SET (25) 8.00 20.00
1 Pierre Turgeon .08 .25
2 Patrick Roy 1.50 4.00
3 Pat LaFontaine .20 .50
4 Joe Sakic 1.00 2.50
5 Paul Coffey .40 1.00
6 Ray Bourque .60 1.50
7 Brian Leetch .40 1.00
8 Joe Juneau .08 .25
9 Jeremy Roenick .60 1.50
10 Chris Chelios .40 1.00
11 Brett Hull .60 1.50
12 Paul Kariya .40 1.00
13 Jason Arnott .08 .25
14 Pavel Bure .40 1.00
15 Steve Duchesne .08 .25
16 Martin Brodeur 1.25 3.00
17 Eric Lindros .60 1.50
18 Mikael Renberg .08 .25
19 Felix Potvin .40 1.00
20 Roman Hamrlik .08 .25
21 Wayne Gretzky 2.00 5.00
22 Brendan Shanahan .60 1.50
23 Jaromir Jagr .75 2.00
24 Mario Lemieux 1.50 4.00
25 Steve Yzerman 1.25 3.00

1968 Bauer Ads

These oversized cards are approximately 8" x 10" and feature full color fronts, with blank backs. They were issued as premiums with Bauer skates. Since they are unnumbered, they are checklisted below in alphabetical order.

COMPLETE SET (21) 300.00 600.00
1 Andy Bathgate 12.50 25.00
2 Gary Bergman 12.50 25.00
3 Charlie Burns 12.50 25.00
4 Ray Cullen 12.50 25.00
5 Gary Dornhoeffer 12.50 25.00
6 Kent Douglas 12.50 25.00
7 Tim Ecclestone 12.50 25.00
8 Bill Flett 12.50 25.00
9 Ed Giacomin 20.00 40.00
10 Ted Harris 12.50 25.00
11 Paul Henderson 20.00 40.00
12 Ken Hodge 12.50 25.00
13 Harry Howell 12.50 25.00
14 Earl Ingarfield 12.50 25.00
15 Gilles Marotte 12.50 25.00
16 Doug Mohns 12.50 25.00
17 Bobby Orr 75.00 150.00
18 Claude Provost 12.50 25.00
19 Gary Sabourin 12.50 25.00
20 Brian Smith 12.50 25.00
21 Bob Woytowich 12.50 25.00

1991-92 BayBank Bobby Orr

These promotional cards were sponsored by BayBank and measure approximately 2 1/2" by 3 1/2". A player card and a sponsor advertisement were packaged inside a hockey puck-shaped holder (bearing the Bruins logo) and passed out to ticket holders on BayBank

Night at the Bruins game. The fronts of the first two cards have a color action player photo framed by a blue and green inner border design. The white outer border on card 1 is slightly thicker than on card 2, and the positions of the player's name and the sponsor name are reversed when one compares the two cards. The third card has a green border. Against a pale green background, the back presents biography, statistics (career and playoffs), and career awards. The card number appears in a green box in the upper left corner.

COMPLETE SET (4)	12.00	30.00
1 Bobby Orr (Skating with Flyer in pursuit)	3.00	8.00
2 Bobby Orr (Skating alone with puck)	3.00	8.00
3 Bobby Orr (Skating behind the net)	3.00	8.00
NNO Bobby Orr (8 1/2" by 11") (Skating without puck)	4.00	10.00

1995 BayBank Bobby Orr

This set consists of a 10" by 8" sheet, featuring a color action photo of Bobby Orr, and a standard-size card carrying the same picture. The sheet has a blank back; the card back salutes the Boston Bruins on the 25th Anniversary of the 1970 Stanley Cup Championship.

COMPLETE SET (2)	6.00	15.00
1 Bobby Orr (Oversized card)	4.00	10.00
2 Bobby Orr (Regular size card)	2.00	5.00

1971-72 Bazooka

The 1971-72 Bazooka set contains 36 cards. The cards, nearly identical in design to the 1971-72 Topps and O-Pee-Chee hockey cards, were distributed in 12 three-card panels as the bottoms of Bazooka bubble gum boxes. The cards are numbered at the bottom of each obverse. The cards are blank backed and are about 2/3 the size of standard cards. The panels of three are in numerical order, e.g., cards 1-3 are a panel, cards 4-6 form a panel, etc. The prices below refer to cut-apart individual cards; values for panels are 50 percent more than the values below. This is one of the scarcest sets in the trading card hobby, and because of the lack of confirmed sales, prices below are based on dealer buy prices.

COMPLETE SET (36)	4500.00	9000.00
1 Phil Esposito	375.00	750.00
2 Frank Mahovlich	200.00	400.00
3 Ed Van Impe	25.00	50.00
4 Bobby Hull	500.00	1000.00
5 Henri Richard	150.00	300.00
6 Gilbert Perreault	375.00	750.00
7 Alex Delvecchio	125.00	250.00
8 Denis DeJordy	75.00	150.00
9 Ted Harris	30.00	60.00
10 Gilles Villemure	75.00	150.00
11 Dave Keon	150.00	300.00
12 Derek Sanderson	150.00	300.00
13 Orland Kurtenbach	30.00	60.00
14 Bob Nevin	30.00	60.00
15 Yvan Cournoyer	100.00	200.00
16 Andre Boudrias	25.00	50.00
17 Frank St.Marseille	25.00	50.00
18 Norm Ullman	100.00	200.00
19 Garry Unger	40.00	80.00
20 Pierre Bouchard	25.00	50.00
21 Roy Edwards	75.00	150.00
22 Ralph Backstrom	30.00	60.00
23 Guy Trottier	25.00	50.00
24 Serge Bernier	25.00	50.00
25 Bert Marshall	25.00	50.00
26 Wayne Hillman	25.00	50.00
27 Tim Ecclestone	25.00	50.00
28 Walt McKechnie	25.00	50.00
29 Tony Esposito	375.00	750.00
30 Rod Gilbert	100.00	200.00
31 Walt Tkaczuk	30.00	60.00
32 Roger Crozier	75.00	150.00
33 Ken Schinkel	25.00	50.00
34 Ron Ellis	25.00	50.00
35 Stan Mikita	300.00	600.00
36 Bobby Orr	1250.00	2500.00

1994 Be A Player Magazine

Cards were inserted into the NHLPA's Be A Player magazine. Cards are full color and are larger than standard size.

COMPLETE SET (4)	4.00	10.00
1 Paul Kariya	2.00	5.00
2 Felix Potvin	.60	1.50
3 Joe Sakic	1.25	3.00
4 Teemu Selanne	.75	2.00

1994-95 Be A Player

This set was issued by Upper Deck in conjunction with the NHL Players Association. The set contained 180 standard-size cards, each numbered with an "R" prefix. The card backs contained text and personal information. The set was released in hobby (blue) and retail (purple) packaging. Production total for both was announced at 1,995 cases. Each box was individually numbered on the side. Each pack included 11 cards and one autographed card. Suggested retail was $5.95 per pack. The NNO Wayne Gretzky promo card was included as a premium in an NHLPA hockey tips video. The card is slightly different from his R99 regular issue card. This set was not licensed by the National Hockey League and did not use any NHL team logos.

COMPLETE SET (180)	20.00	40.00
R1 Doug Gilmour	.07	.20
R2 Joel Otto	.02	.10
R3 Kirk Muller	.02	.10
R4 Marty McInnis	.02	.10
R5 Dave Gagner	.02	.10
R6 Geoff Courtnall	.02	.10
R7 Dale Hawerchuk	.07	.20
R8 Mike Modano	.25	.60
R9 Roman Hamrlik	.02	.10
R10 Marty McSorley	.07	.20
R11 Teemu Selanne	.15	.40
R12 Jeremy Roenick	.20	.50
R13 Glenn Healy	.07	.20
R14 Darren Turcotte	.02	.10
R15 Derian Hatcher	.02	.10
R16 Enrico Ciccone	.02	.10
R17 Tony Amonte	.07	.20
R18 Mark Recchi	.07	.20
R19 Eric Weinrich	.02	.10
R20 John Vanbiesbrouck	.07	.20
R21 Nick Kypreos	.02	.10
R22 Gilbert Dionne	.02	.10
R23 Theo Fleury	.02	.10
R24 Todd Gill	.02	.10
R25 Jari Kurri	.02	.10
R26 Brad May	.02	.10
R27 Russ Courtnall	.02	.10
R28 Bill Ranford	.07	.20
R29 Steve Yzerman	.75	2.00
R30 Alexandre Daigle	.02	.10
R31 Mike Hudson	.02	.10
R32 Ray Bourque	.25	.60
R33 Dave Andreychuk	.07	.20
R34 Jason Arnott	.02	.10
R35 Pavel Bure	.15	.40
R36 Keith Tkachuk	.15	.40
R37 Scott Niedermayer	.02	.10
R38 Johan Garpenlov	.02	.10
R39 Dino Ciccarelli	.07	.20
R40 Rob Blake	.07	.20
R41 Dave Manson	.02	.10
R42 Adam Foote	.07	.20
R43 Chris Pronger	.15	.40
R44 Scott Lachance	.02	.10
R45 Adam Oates	.07	.20
R46 Brian Leetch	.15	.40
R47 Guy Hebert	.07	.20
R48 Brett Hull	.20	.50
R49 Mike Ricci	.07	.20
R50 Dave Ellett	.02	.10
R51 Owen Nolan	.07	.20
R52 Craig Janney	.02	.10
R53 Trevor Linden	.07	.20
R54 Ray Sheppard	.02	.10
R55 Rob Niedermayer	.07	.20
R56 Kevin Haller	.02	.10
R57 Jeff Norton	.02	.10
R58 Martin Brodeur	.40	1.00
R59 Robb Stauber	.02	.10
R60 Sylvain Turgeon	.02	.10
R61 Pat Verbeek	.02	.10
R62 Steve Smith	.02	.10
R63 Jaromir Jagr	.25	.60
R64 Steve Duchesne	.02	.10
R65 Tie Domi	.07	.20
R66 Sylvain Lefebvre	.02	.10
R67 Guy Carbonneau	.02	.10
R68 Alexander Mogilny	.07	.20
R69 Mario Lemieux	1.25	3.00
R70 Neil Wilkinson	.02	.10
R71 Curtis Joseph	.15	.40
R72 Wendel Clark	.07	.20
R73 Kirk McLean	.07	.20
R74 Mikael Renberg	.02	.10
R75 Shawn McEachern	.02	.10
R76 Mats Sundin	.15	.40
R77 Craig Simpson	.02	.10
R78 Phil Housley	.07	.20
R79 Pat LaFontaine	.15	.40
R80 Pierre Turgeon	.07	.20
R81 Felix Potvin	.15	.40
R82 Kevin Stevens	.02	.10
R83 Steve Chiasson	.02	.10
R84 Robert Petrovicky	.02	.10
R85 Joe Juneau	.07	.20
R86 Brendan Shanahan	.15	.40
R87 Joe Sacco	.02	.10
R88 David Reid	.02	.10
R89 Louie DeBrusk	.02	.10
R90 Darryl Sydor	.02	.10
R91 Paul Coffey	.15	.40
R92 Alexei Yashin	.02	.10
R93 Jason Arnott	.02	.10
R94 Gary Suter	.02	.10
R95 Luc Robitaille	.07	.20
R96 Joe Sakic	.30	.75
R97 Chris Chelios	.15	.40
R98 Tony Granato	.02	.10
R99 Wayne Gretzky	1.50	4.00
R100 Joe Juneau	.07	.20
R101 Curtis Joseph	.15	.40
R102 Vincent Damphousse	.02	.10
R103 Paul Kariya	.15	.40
R104 Brendan Shanahan	.15	.40
R105 Eric Desjardins	.07	.20
R106 Eric Lindros	.15	.40
R107 Kirk McLean	.07	.20
R108 Mike Ricci	.07	.20
R109 Chris Chelios	.15	.40
R110 Chris Gratton	.02	.10
R111 Doug Gilmour	.07	.20
R112 Vincent Damphousse	.02	.10
R113 Mark Osborne	.02	.10
R114 Mike Modano	.15	.40
R115 Steve Yzerman	.75	2.00
R116 Garry Valk	.02	.10
R117 Adam Graves	.02	.10
R118 Doug Weight	.07	.20
R119 Rob Niedermayer	.07	.20
R120 Craig Simpson	.02	.10
R121 Patrick Roy	1.25	3.00
R122 Ronnie Stern	.02	.10
R123 Jiri Slegr	.02	.10
R124 Darren Turcotte	.02	.10
R125 Vladimir Malakhov	.02	.10
R126 Paul Kariya	.15	.40
R127 Mike Gartner	.07	.20
R128 Scott Niedermayer	.02	.10
R129 Dino Ciccarelli	.07	.20
R130 Martin Brodeur TN	.20	.50
R131 Kevin Hatcher	.02	.10
R132 Pat LaFontaine	.07	.20
R133 Joel Otto	.02	.10
R134 Jason Arnott	.02	.10
R135 John Vanbiesbrouck	.07	.20
R136 Derian Hatcher	.02	.10
R137 Brendan Shanahan	.15	.40
R138 Felix Potvin	.15	.40
R139 Trevor Linden	.07	.20
R140 Ken Baumgartner	.02	.10
R141 Denis Leary	.02	.10
R142 Wendel Clark	.07	.20
R143 Cam Neely	.15	.40
R144 Jeremy Roenick	.20	.50
R145 Sergei Fedorov	.25	.60
R146 Scott Stevens	.07	.20
R147 Wayne Gretzky	1.50	4.00
R148 Darius Kasparaitis	.02	.10
R149 Brian Leetch	.15	.40
R150 Marty McSorley	.07	.20
R151 Paul Kariya	.15	.40
R152 Peter Forsberg	.50	1.25
R153 Brett Lindros	.02	.10
R154 Kenny Jonsson	.02	.10
R155 Jason Allison	.02	.10
R156 Aaron Gavey	.02	.10
R157 Jamie Storr	.07	.20
R158 Viktor Kozlov	.07	.20
R159 Valeri Bure	.02	.10
R160 Oleg Tverdovsky	.07	.20
R161 Brent Gretzky	.02	.10
R162 Todd Harvey	.02	.10
R163 Todd Warriner	.02	.10
R164 Jeff Friesen	.07	.20
R165 Adam Deadmarsh	.07	.20
R166 Ken Baumgartner	.02	.10
R167 Terry Carkner	.02	.10
R168 Tie Domi	.07	.20
R169 Steve Larmer	.07	.20
R170 Larry Murphy	.07	.20
R171 Steve Thomas	.02	.10
R172 Alexei Yashin	.02	.10
R173 Felix Potvin	.15	.40
R174 Curtis Joseph	.15	.40
R175 Rob Zamuner	.02	.10
R176 Wayne Gretzky	2.00	5.00
R177 Pavel Bure	.15	.40
R178 Eric Lindros	.15	.40
R179 Patrick Roy	1.25	3.00
R180 Doug Gilmour	.07	.20
NNO Wayne Gretzky PROMO	4.00	10.00

1994-95 Be A Player 99 All-Stars

COMPLETE SET (19)	30.00	80.00
STATED ODDS 1:14		
G1 Wayne Gretzky	12.00	30.00
G2 Paul Coffey	2.00	5.00
G3 Rob Blake	2.00	5.00
G4 Pat Conacher	1.00	2.50
G5 Russ Courtnall	1.00	2.50
G6 Sergei Fedorov	2.00	5.00
G7 Grant Fuhr	2.00	5.00
G8 Todd Gill	1.00	2.50
G9 Tony Granato	1.00	2.50
G10 Brett Hull	3.00	8.00
G11 Charlie Huddy	1.00	2.50
G12 Steve Larmer	2.00	5.00
G13 Kelly Hrudey	2.00	5.00
G14 Al MacInnis	2.00	5.00
G15 Marty McSorley	2.00	5.00
G16 Jari Kurri	2.00	5.00
G17 Kirk Muller	1.00	2.50
G18 Rick Tocchet	2.00	5.00
G19 Steve Yzerman	6.00	15.00

1994-95 Be A Player Autographs

These authentic signature cards were issued one per foil pack. All autographs were guaranteed by the National Hockey League Players Association. The Jiri Slegr card (#119) was only available through a mail-in offer. The set is considered complete without it. Reportedly, most players signed approximately 2,400 of each card (including Slegr). Players who signed fewer are indicated below with parenthesis indicating approximately how many cards they signed.

ONE SIGNATURE CARD PER PACK		
STATED PRINT RUN 300-2400		
1 Doug Gilmour (1250)	6.00	15.00
2 Adam Foote	2.00	5.00
3 Martin Brodeur	20.00	50.00
4 Alexander Semak	2.00	5.00
5 Dale Hawerchuk	4.00	10.00
6 Derek King	2.00	5.00
7 Mark Recchi	4.00	10.00
8 Fredrik Olausson	2.00	5.00
9 Dave McLlwain	2.00	5.00
10 Marc Bergevin	2.00	5.00
11 Teemu Selanne (600)	75.00	200.00
12 Jeremy Roenick (600)	30.00	80.00
13 Eric Lacroix	2.00	5.00
14 Marty McInnis	2.00	5.00
15 Kris King	2.00	5.00
16 Bill Ranford	4.00	10.00
17 Gary Roberts	2.00	5.00
18 Mark Osborne	2.00	5.00
19 Dmitri Mironov	2.00	5.00
20 John Vanbiesbrouck (600)	30.00	80.00
21 Alexei Zhamnov	2.00	5.00
22 Brad May	2.00	5.00
23 Doug Lidster	2.00	5.00
24 Mikael Renberg	2.00	5.00
25 Kris Draper	4.00	10.00
26 Darryl Sydor	4.00	10.00
27 Claude Lemieux	2.00	5.00
28 Doug Brown	2.00	5.00
29 Louie DeBrusk	2.00	5.00
30 Andy Moog	6.00	15.00
31 Donald Audette	2.00	5.00
32 Ray Bourque (600)	60.00	150.00
33 Brian Rolston	2.00	5.00
34 Ted Drury	2.00	5.00
35 Darren Turcotte	2.00	5.00
36 Gary Shuchuk	2.00	5.00
37 Mike Ricci	2.00	5.00
38 Kirk Maltby	2.00	5.00
39 Doug Bodger	2.00	5.00
40 Kirk Muller	2.00	5.00
41 Sylvain Lefebvre	2.00	5.00
42 Brent Grieve	2.00	5.00
43 Bill Houlder	2.00	5.00
44 Neil Wilkinson	2.00	5.00
45 Donald Dufresne	2.00	5.00
46 Brian Leetch (600)	30.00	80.00
47 Bryan Smolinski	2.00	5.00
48 Kevin Hatcher	2.00	5.00
49 Steven Rice	2.00	5.00
50 Bill Guerin	4.00	10.00
51 Grant Jennings	2.00	5.00
52 Dave Andreychuk	4.00	10.00
53 Sean Burke	4.00	10.00
54 Nick Kypreos	2.00	5.00
55 Drake Berehowsky	2.00	5.00
56 Kevin Haller	2.00	5.00
57 Bill Berg	2.00	5.00
58 Chris Simon	2.00	5.00
59 Owen Nolan (Wrong birthdate blacked out on back)	4.00	10.00
60 Don Sweeney	2.00	5.00
61 Johan Garpenlov	2.00	5.00
62 Garry Galley	2.00	5.00
63 Pat LaFontaine	4.00	10.00
64 Craig Berube	2.00	5.00
65 Dave Ellett	2.00	5.00
66 Robert Kron	2.00	5.00
67 Alexander Godynyuk	2.00	5.00
68 Markus Naslund	6.00	15.00
69 Joel Otto	2.00	5.00
70 Igor Ulanov	2.00	5.00
71 Pat Verbeek	2.00	5.00
72 Craig MacTavish	2.00	5.00
73 Gary Leeman	2.00	5.00
74 Kevin Todd	2.00	5.00
75 Mike Sullivan	2.00	5.00
76 Rob Pearson	2.00	5.00
77 Dave Gagner	2.00	5.00
78 Dirk Graham	2.00	5.00
79 Joe Sacco	2.00	5.00
80 Jassen Cullimore	2.00	5.00
81 Glen Featherstone	2.00	5.00
82 Scott Lachance	2.00	5.00
83 Kerry Huffman	2.00	5.00
84 Troy Loney	2.00	5.00
85 Rob Gaudreau	2.00	5.00
86 Brendan Shanahan (600)	75.00	150.00
87 Joe Murphy	2.00	5.00
88 Scott Niedermayer	4.00	10.00
89 Dan Quinn	2.00	5.00
90 Jeff Norton	2.00	5.00
91 Jim Dowd	2.00	5.00
92 Ray Ferraro	2.00	5.00
93 Shawn Burr	2.00	5.00
94 Denis Savard	4.00	10.00
95 Dave Manson	2.00	5.00
96 Joe Nieuwendyk	4.00	10.00
97 Tony Amonte	4.00	10.00
98 James Patrick	2.00	5.00
99 Guy Hebert	2.00	5.00
100 Peter Zezel	2.00	5.00
101 Shawn McEachern	2.00	5.00
102 Dave Lowry	2.00	5.00
103 David Reid	2.00	5.00
104 Todd Gill	2.00	5.00
105 John Cullen	2.00	5.00
106 Guy Carbonneau	2.00	5.00
107 Jeff Beukeboom	2.00	5.00
108 Wayne Gretzky (300)	200.00	400.00
109 Curtis Joseph	6.00	15.00
110 Jason Arnott	2.00	5.00
112 Gary Suter	2.00	5.00
113 Luc Robitaille	6.00	15.00
114 Tony Granato	2.00	5.00
115 Steve Yzerman (600)	100.00	200.00
116 Chris Gratton	2.00	5.00
117 Doug Weight	4.00	10.00
118 Garry Valk	2.00	5.00
119 Jiri Slegr	8.00	20.00
120 Vincent Damphousse	2.00	5.00
121 Vladimir Malakhov	2.00	5.00
122 Craig Simpson	2.00	5.00
123 Theoren Fleury	4.00	10.00
124 Dave Poulin	2.00	5.00
125 Derian Hatcher	2.00	5.00
126 Jimmy Waite	2.00	5.00
127 Norm Maciver	2.00	5.00
128 Glenn Healy	2.00	5.00
129 Jocelyn Lemieux	2.00	5.00
130 Steve Chiasson	4.00	10.00
131 Keith Jones	2.00	5.00
132 Enrico Ciccone	2.00	5.00
133 Martin Lapointe	2.00	5.00
134 John MacLean	2.00	5.00
135 Geoff Courtnall	2.00	5.00
136 David Shaw	2.00	5.00
137 Steve Duchesne	2.00	5.00
138 Dean Evason	2.00	5.00
139 Eric Weinrich	2.00	5.00
140 Kelly Hrudey	4.00	10.00
141 Ted Donato	2.00	5.00
142 Darius Kasparaitis	2.00	5.00
143 Tie Domi	4.00	10.00
144 Terry Carkner	2.00	5.00
145 Steve Thomas	2.00	5.00
146 Steve Larmer	2.00	5.00
147 Rob Zamuner	2.00	5.00
148 Larry Murphy	2.00	5.00
149 Ken Baumgartner	2.00	5.00
150 Alexei Yashin (600)	15.00	40.00
151 Paul Kariya (600)	60.00	150.00
152 Todd Harvey	2.00	5.00
153A Viktor Kozlov (VK variation)	4.00	10.00
153B Viktor Kozlov (Full Signature)	75.00	200.00
154 Brent Gretzky	2.00	5.00
155 Petr Klima	2.00	5.00
156 Kent Manderville	2.00	5.00
157 Mike Eagles	2.00	5.00
158 Valeri Kamensky	2.00	5.00
159 Thomas Steen	2.00	5.00
160 Michal Pivonka	2.00	5.00
161 Steve Heinze	2.00	5.00
162 Nicklas Lidstrom	6.00	15.00
163 Uwe Krupp	2.00	5.00
164 Pat Elynuik	2.00	5.00
165 Mike Peca	4.00	10.00
166 Sylvain Cote	2.00	5.00
167 Trevor Kidd	2.00	5.00
168 Patrick Poulin	2.00	5.00
169 Shane Churla	2.00	5.00
170 Scott Mellanby	2.00	5.00
171 Mike Sillinger	2.00	5.00
172 Shayne Corson	2.00	5.00
173 Micah Aivazoff	2.00	5.00
174 Robert Lang	2.00	5.00
175 Rod Brind'Amour	4.00	10.00
176 Troy Murray	2.00	5.00
177 Mike Krushelnyski	2.00	5.00
178 Sergio Momesso	2.00	5.00

1994-95 Be A Player Up Close and Personal

This 10-card set was inserted two per box (1:8 packs) in Be A Player product. The cards featured an "Up Close" photo of the player and Roy Firestone, a popular ESPN show host. The text on the back was written by Firestone. The cards are numbered with an "UC" prefix.

COMPLETE SET (10)	20.00	50.00
STATED ODDS 1:14		
UC1 Wayne Gretzky	10.00	25.00
UC2 Eric Lindros	1.00	2.50
UC3 Pavel Bure	1.00	2.50
UC4 Teemu Selanne	1.00	2.50
UC5 Steve Yzerman	4.00	10.00
UC6 Jeremy Roenick	1.25	3.00
UC7 Sergei Fedorov	1.50	4.00
UC8 Patrick Roy	6.00	15.00
UC9 Paul Kariya	1.00	2.50
UC10 Doug Gilmour	.50	1.25

1995-96 Be A Player

This 225-card set was released in June 1996. It was released by Upper Deck, in conjunction with the NHLPA. The set was not licensed by the NHL, hence the absence of logos and insignia from player uniforms, and the color changes on the sweaters of players from Colorado and the Islanders. Suggested retail was $7.99 per ten-card pack, although packs tended to sell for more due to the allure of the one-per-pack autographs.

COMPLETE SET (225)	15.00	40.00
1 Brett Hull	.40	1.00
2 Jyrki Lumme	.05	.15
3 Shean Donovan	.05	.15
4 Yuri Khmylev	.05	.15
5 Stephane Matteau	.05	.15
6 Basil McRae	.05	.15
7 Dimitri Yushkevich	.05	.15
8 Ron Francis	.10	.30
9 Keith Carney	.05	.15
10 Brad Dalgarno	.05	.15
11 Bob Carpenter	.05	.15
12 Kevin Stevens	.05	.15
13 Patrick Flatley	.05	.15
14 Craig Muni	.05	.15
15 Travis Green	.10	.30
16 Derek Plante	.05	.15
17 Mike Craig	.05	.15
18 Chris Pronger	.25	.60
19 Bret Hedican	.05	.15
20 Mathieu Schneider	.05	.15
21 Chris Therien	.05	.15
22 Greg Adams	.05	.15
23 Arturs Irbe	.10	.30
24 Zigmund Palffy	.10	.30
25 Peter Douris	.05	.15
26 Bob Sweeney	.05	.15
27 Chris Terreri	.10	.30
28 Alexei Zhitnik	.05	.15
29 Jay Wells	.05	.15
30 Andrew Cassels	.05	.15
31 Radek Bonk	.05	.15
32 Brian Bellows	.10	.30
33 Frantisek Kucera	.05	.15
34 Valeri Bure	.05	.15
35 Randy Wood	.05	.15
36 Dimitri Khristich	.05	.15
37 Randy Ladouceur	.05	.15
38 Nelson Emerson	.05	.15
39 Bryan Marchment	.05	.15
40 Kevin Lowe	.10	.30
41 Trevor Linden	.10	.30
42 Neal Broten	.10	.30
43 Tom Chorske	.05	.15
44 Patrice Brisebois	.05	.15
45 Wayne Presley	.05	.15
46 Murray Craven	.05	.15
47 Craig Janney	.05	.15
48 Ken Daneyko	.05	.15
49 Dino Ciccarelli	.10	.30
50 Jason Dawe	.05	.15
51 Brad McCrimmon	.05	.15
52 Randy McKay	.05	.15
53 Rudy Poeschek	.05	.15
54 Calle Johansson	.05	.15
55 Wendel Clark	.10	.30
56 Rob Ray	.25	.60
57 Garth Snow	.10	.30
58 Joe Juneau	.05	.15
59 Craig Wolanin	.05	.15
60 Ray Sheppard	.05	.15
61 Oleg Tverdovsky	.05	.15
62 Geoff Sanderson	.05	.15
63 Mike Ridley	.05	.15
64 David Oliver	.05	.15
65 Russ Courtnall	.05	.15
66 Joe Reekie	.05	.15
67 Ken Wregget	.10	.30
68 Teppo Numminen	.05	.15
69 Mikhail Shtalenkov	.05	.15
70 Luke Richardson	.05	.15
71 Brent Gilchrist	.05	.15
72 Phil Housley	.10	.30
73 Greg Johnson	.05	.15
74 Sean Hill	.05	.15
75 Karl Dykhuis	.05	.15
76 Tim Cheveldae	.10	.30
77 Shjon Podein	.05	.15
78 Rene Corbet	.05	.15
79 Ronnie Stern	.05	.15
80 Mike Donnelly	.05	.15
81 Randy Cunneyworth	.05	.15
82 Rick Tocchet	.10	.30
83 Dallas Drake	.05	.15
84 Cam Russell	.05	.15
85 Daren Puppa	.10	.30
86 Benoit Brunet	.05	.15
87 Paul Ranheim	.05	.15
88 Bob Rouse	.05	.15
89 Todd Elik	.05	.15
90 Darcy Wakaluk	.10	.30
91 Cliff Ronning	.05	.15
92 Pat Conacher	.05	.15
93 Todd Krygier	.05	.15
94 Dave Babych	.05	.15
95 Pat Falloon	.05	.15
96 Don Beaupre	.10	.30
97 Wayne Gretzky	2.00	5.00
98 Chris Joseph	.05	.15
99 Vyacheslav Kozlov	.10	.30
100 Brent Fedyk	.05	.15
101 Tim Taylor	.05	.15
102 Mike Eastwood	.05	.15
103 Mike Keane	.05	.15
104 Grant Ledyard	.05	.15
105 Rob Dimaio	.05	.15
106 Martin Straka	.05	.15
107 Scott Young	.05	.15
108 Zarley Zalapski	.05	.15
109 Steve Leach	.05	.15
110 Jody Hull	.05	.15
111 Lyle Odelein	.05	.15
112 Bob Corkum	.05	.15
113 Rob Blake	.10	.30
114 Randy Burridge	.05	.15
115 Keith Primeau	.05	.15
116 Glen Wesley	.05	.15
117 Brian Bradley	.05	.15
118 Andrei Kovalenko	.05	.15
119 Patrik Juhlin	.05	.15
120 John Tucker	.05	.15
121 Stephane Fiset	.10	.30
122 Mike Hough	.05	.15
123 Steve Smith	.05	.15
124 Tom Barrasso	.10	.30
125 Ray Whitney	.10	.30
126 Benoit Hogue	.05	.15
127 Stu Barnes	.05	.15
128 Craig Ludwig	.10	.30
129 Curtis Leschyshyn	.05	.15
130 John LeClair	.25	.60
131 Dennis Vial	.05	.15
132 Cory Stillman	.05	.15
133 Roman Hamrlik	.10	.30
134 Al MacInnis	.10	.30
135 Igor Korolev	.05	.15
136 Rick Zombo	.05	.15
137 Zdeno Ciger	.05	.15
138 Brian Savage	.05	.15
139 Paul Ysebaert	.05	.15
140 Brent Sutter	.05	.15
141 Ed Olczyk	.05	.15
142 Adam Creighton	.05	.15
143 Jesse Belanger	.05	.15
144 Glen Murray	.05	.15
145 Alexander Selivanov	.05	.15
146 Trent Yawney	.05	.15
147 Bruce Driver	.05	.15
148 Michael Nylander	.05	.15
149 Martin Gelinas	.05	.15
150 Yanic Perreault	.05	.15
151 Craig Billington	.10	.30
152 Pierre Turgeon	.10	.30
153 Mike Modano	.50	1.25
154 Joe Mullen	.10	.30
155 Todd Ewen	.05	.15
156 Petr Nedved	.10	.30
157 Dominic Roussel	.10	.30
158 Murray Baron	.05	.15
159 Robert Dirk	.05	.15
160 Tomas Sandstrom	.05	.15
161 Brian Holzinger	.25	.60
162 Ken Klee RC	.05	.15
163 Radek Dvorak RC	.25	.60
164 Marcus Ragnarsson	.10	.30
165 Aaron Gavey	.05	.15
166 Jeff O'Neill	.05	.15
167 Chad Kilger RC	.10	.30
168 Todd Bertuzzi RC	.75	2.00
169 Robert Svehla	.05	.15
170 Eric Daze	.10	.30
171 Daniel Alfredsson RC	.75	2.00
172 Shane Doan RC	.75	2.00
173 Kyle McLaren	.10	.30
174 Saku Koivu	.25	.60
175 Jere Lehtinen	.10	.30
176 Nikolai Khabibulin	.10	.30
177 Niklas Sundstrom	.10	.30
178 Ed Jovanovski	.25	.60
179 Jason Bonsignore	.05	.15
180 Kenny Jonsson	.05	.15
181 Vitali Yachmenev	.05	.15
182 Alexei Kovalev	.05	.15
183 Sandis Ozolinsh	.05	.15
184 Rob Niedermayer	.10	.30
185 Richard Park	.05	.15
186 Adam Deadmarsh	.05	.15
187 Sergei Krivokrasov	.05	.15
188 Alexandre Daigle	.05	.15
189 Jim Carey	.10	.30
190 Todd Marchant	.05	.15
191 Mike Richter	.25	.60
192 Dominik Hasek	.50	1.25
193 Chris Osgood	.10	.30
194 Ed Belfour	.25	.60
195 Felix Potvin	.25	.60
196 Grant Fuhr	.25	.60
197 Patrick Roy	1.25	3.00
198 Ron Hextall	.10	.30
199 Jocelyn Thibault	.25	.60
200 Kirk McLean	.10	.30
201 Jari Kurri	.25	.60
202 Bobby Holik	.05	.15
203 Mats Sundin	.25	.60
204 Alexander Mogilny	.10	.30
205 Valeri Karpov	.05	.15
206 Igor Larionov	.05	.15
207 Valeri Zelepukin	.05	.15
208 Jozef Stumpel	.05	.15
209 Sergei Nemchinov	.05	.15
210 Peter Bondra	.10	.30
211 Chris Chelios	.25	.60
212 Adam Graves	.05	.15
213 Dale Hunter	.10	.30
214 Tony Twist	.10	.30
215 Keith Tkachuk	.25	.60
216 Vladimir Konstantinov	.10	.30
217 Sandy McCarthy	.05	.15
218 Jamie Macoun	.05	.15
219 Scott Stevens	.10	.30
220 Mark Tinordi	.05	.15
221 Bob Probert	.10	.30
222 Gino Odjick	.05	.15
223 Ulf Samuelsson	.05	.15
224 Stu Grimson	.10	.30
225 Marty McSorley	.05	.15

1995-96 Be A Player Autographs

These authentic signed cards were inserted at a rate of one per pack. Every seventh pack featured a special signed card which was distinguished by unique die-cut corners. The card fronts are the same as the regular cards, but the backs of the signed cards feature a certificate of authenticity. Although production numbers were not officially revealed, documents suggest approximately 3,000 regular and 400 die-cut versions of each signed card were released. The quantities of the Wayne Gretzky cards (#S97) were intially reported at 802 signed and 99 die-cut copies. Upper Deck later announced the actual numbers as being 648 regular and 234 die-cut. The Mike Richter card (#191) was not inserted in packs, but was made available through a mail-in offer. The set is considered complete without this card.

BASE AU ESTIMATED PRINT RUN 3000		
S1 Brett Hull	10.00	25.00
S2 Jyrki Lumme	2.00	5.00
S3 Shean Donovan	2.00	5.00
S4 Yuri Khmylev	2.00	5.00
S5 Stephane Matteau	2.00	5.00
S6 Basil McRae	2.00	5.00
S7 Dimitri Yushkevich	2.00	5.00
S8 Ron Francis	4.00	10.00
S9 Keith Carney	2.00	5.00
S10 Brad Dalgarno	2.00	5.00
S11 Bob Carpenter	2.00	5.00
S12 Kevin Stevens	2.00	5.00
S13 Pat Flatley	2.00	5.00
S14 Craig Muni	2.00	5.00
S15 Travis Green	2.00	5.00
S16 Derek Plante	2.00	5.00
S17 Mike Craig	2.00	5.00
S18 Chris Pronger	6.00	15.00
S19 Bret Hedican	2.00	5.00
S20 Mathieu Schneider	2.00	5.00
S21 Chris Therien	2.00	5.00
S22 Greg Adams	2.00	5.00
S23 Arturs Irbe	4.00	10.00
S24 Zigmund Palffy	4.00	10.00
S25 Peter Douris	2.00	5.00
S26 Bob Sweeney	2.00	5.00
S27 Chris Terreri	2.00	5.00
S28 Alexei Zhitnik	2.00	5.00
S29 Jay Wells	2.00	5.00
S30 Andrew Cassels	2.00	5.00

S31 Radek Bonk	2.00	5.00
S32 Brian Bellows	2.00	5.00
S33 Frantisek Kucera	2.00	5.00
S34 Valeri Bure	2.00	5.00
S35 Randy Wood	2.00	5.00
S36 Dimitri Khristich	2.00	5.00
S37 Randy Ladouceur	2.00	5.00
S38 Nelson Emerson	2.00	5.00
S39 Bryan Marchment	2.00	5.00
S40 Kevin Lowe	4.00	10.00
S41 Trevor Linden	4.00	10.00
S42 Neal Broten	4.00	10.00
S43 Tom Chorske	2.00	5.00
S44 Patrice Brisebois	2.00	5.00
S45 Wayne Presley	2.00	5.00
S46 Murray Craven	2.00	5.00
S47 Craig Janney	2.00	5.00
S48 Ken Daneyko	2.00	5.00
S49 Dino Ciccarelli	4.00	10.00
S50 Jason Dawe	2.00	5.00
S51 Brad McCrimmon	2.00	5.00
S52 Randy McKay	2.00	5.00
S53 Rudy Poeschek	2.00	5.00
S54 Calle Johansson	2.00	5.00
S55 Wendel Clark	4.00	10.00
S56 Rob Ray	4.00	10.00
S57 Garth Snow	4.00	10.00
S58 Joe Juneau	4.00	10.00
S59 Craig Wolanin	2.00	5.00
S60 Ray Sheppard	2.00	5.00
S61 Oleg Tverdovsky	2.00	5.00
S62 Geoff Sanderson	2.00	5.00
S63 Mike Ridley	2.00	5.00
S64 David Oliver	2.00	5.00
S65 Russ Courtnall	2.00	5.00
S66 Joe Reekie	2.00	5.00
S67 Ken Wregget	4.00	10.00
S68 Teppo Numminen	2.00	5.00
S69 Mikhail Shtalenkov	2.00	5.00
S70 Luke Richardson	2.00	5.00
S71 Brent Gilchrist	2.00	5.00
S72 Phil Housley	2.00	5.00
S73 Greg Johnson	2.00	5.00
S74 Sean Hill	2.00	5.00
S75 Karl Dykhuis	2.00	5.00
S76 Tim Cheveldae	2.00	5.00
S77 Shjon Podein	2.00	5.00
S78 Rene Corbet	2.00	5.00
S79 Ron Stern	2.00	5.00
S80 Mike Donnelly	2.00	5.00
S81 Randy Cunneyworth	2.00	5.00
S82 Rick Tocchet	4.00	10.00
S83 Dallas Drake	2.00	5.00
S84 Cam Russell	2.00	5.00
S85 Daren Puppa	2.00	5.00
S86 Benoit Brunet	2.00	5.00
S87 Paul Ranheim	2.00	5.00
S88 Bob Rouse	2.00	5.00
S89 Todd Elik	2.00	5.00
S90 Darcy Wakaluk	2.00	5.00
S91 Cliff Ronning	2.00	5.00
S92 Pat Conacher	2.00	5.00
S93 Todd Krygier	2.00	5.00
S94 Dave Babych	2.00	5.00
S95 Pat Falloon	2.00	5.00
S96 Don Beaupre	4.00	10.00
S97 Wayne Gretzky/648*	100.00	250.00
S98 Chris Joseph	2.00	5.00
S99 Vyacheslav Kozlov	4.00	10.00
S100 Brent Fedyk	2.00	5.00
S101 Tim Taylor	2.00	5.00
S102 Mike Eastwood	2.00	5.00
S103 Mike Keane	2.00	5.00
S104 Grant Ledyard	2.00	5.00
S105 Rob Dimaio	2.00	5.00
S106 Martin Straka	2.00	5.00
S107 Scott Young	2.00	5.00
S108 Zarley Zalapski	2.00	5.00
S109 Steve Leach	2.00	5.00
S110 Jody Hull	2.00	5.00
S111 Lyle Odelein	2.00	5.00
S112 Bob Corkum	2.00	5.00
S113 Rob Blake	4.00	10.00
S114 Randy Burridge	2.00	5.00
S115 Keith Primeau	2.00	5.00
S116 Glen Wesley	2.00	5.00
S117 Brian Bradley	2.00	5.00
S118 Andrei Kovalenko	2.00	5.00
S119 Patrik Juhlin	2.00	5.00
S120 John Tucker	2.00	5.00
S121 Stephane Fiset	4.00	10.00
S122 Mike Hough	2.00	5.00
S123 Steve Smith	2.00	5.00
S124 Tom Barrasso	4.00	10.00
S125 Ray Whitney	2.00	5.00
S126 Benoit Hogue	2.00	5.00
S127 Stu Barnes	2.00	5.00
S128 Craig Ludwig	2.00	5.00
S129 Curtis Leschyshyn	2.00	5.00
S130 John LeClair	6.00	15.00
S131 Dennis Vial	2.00	5.00
S132 Cory Stillman	2.00	5.00
S133 Roman Hamrlik	2.00	5.00
S134 Al MacInnis	4.00	10.00
S135 Igor Korolev	2.00	5.00
S136 Rick Zombo	2.00	5.00
S137 Zdeno Ciger	2.00	5.00
S138 Brian Savage	2.00	5.00
S139 Paul Ysebaert	2.00	5.00
S140 Brent Sutter	2.00	5.00
S141 Ed Olczyk	2.00	5.00
S142 Adam Creighton	2.00	5.00
S143 Jesse Belanger	2.00	5.00
S144 Glen Murray	2.00	5.00
S145 Alexander Selivanov	2.00	5.00
S146 Trent Yawney	2.00	5.00
S147 Bruce Driver	2.00	5.00
S148 Michael Nylander	2.00	5.00
S149 Martin Gelinas	2.00	5.00
S150 Yanic Perreault	2.00	5.00
S151 Craig Billington	4.00	10.00
S152 Pierre Turgeon	4.00	10.00
S153 Mike Modano	10.00	25.00
S154 Joe Mullen	4.00	10.00
S155 Todd Ewen	2.00	5.00
S156 Petr Nedved	2.00	5.00
S157 Dominic Roussel	2.00	5.00
S158 Murray Baron	2.00	5.00
S159 Robert Dirk	2.00	5.00
S160 Tomas Sandstrom	2.00	5.00
S161 Brian Holzinger	2.00	5.00
S162 Ken Klee	2.00	5.00
S163 Radek Dvorak	2.00	5.00
S164 Marcus Ragnarsson	2.00	5.00
S165 Aaron Gavey	2.00	5.00
S166 Jeff O'Neill	2.00	5.00
S167 Chad Kilger	2.00	5.00
S168 Todd Bertuzzi	6.00	15.00
S169 Robert Svehla	2.00	5.00
S170 Eric Daze	2.00	5.00
S171 Daniel Alfredsson	6.00	15.00
S172 Shane Doan	4.00	10.00
S173 Kyle McLaren	2.00	5.00
S174 Saku Koivu	6.00	15.00
S175 Jere Lehtinen	4.00	10.00
S176 Nikolai Khabibulin	4.00	10.00
S177 Niklas Sundstrom	2.00	5.00
S178 Ed Jovanovski	4.00	10.00
S179 Jason Bonsignore	2.00	5.00
S180 Kenny Jonsson	2.00	5.00
S181 Vitali Yachmenev	2.00	5.00
S182 Alexei Kovalev	4.00	10.00
S183 Sandis Ozolinsh	2.00	5.00
S184 Rob Niedermayer	4.00	10.00
S185 Richard Park	2.00	5.00
S186 Adam Deadmarsh	2.00	5.00
S187 Sergei Krivokrasov	2.00	5.00
S188 Alexandre Daigle	2.00	5.00
S189 Jim Carey	4.00	10.00
S190 Todd Marchant	4.00	10.00
S191 Mike Richter Mail In	75.00	150.00
S192 Dominik Hasek	12.50	30.00
S193 Chris Osgood	4.00	10.00
S194 Ed Belfour	6.00	15.00
S195 Felix Potvin	6.00	15.00
S196 Grant Fuhr	6.00	15.00
S197 Patrick Roy	40.00	100.00
S198 Ron Hextall	4.00	10.00
S199 Jocelyn Thibault	4.00	10.00
S200 Kirk McLean	4.00	10.00
S201 Jari Kurri	4.00	10.00
S202 Bobby Holik	4.00	10.00
S203 Mats Sundin	15.00	40.00
S204 Alexander Mogilny	4.00	10.00
S205 Valeri Karpov	2.00	5.00
S206 Igor Larionov	2.00	5.00
S207 Valeri Zelepukin	2.00	5.00
S208 Jozef Stumpel	2.00	5.00
S209 Sergei Nemchinov	2.00	5.00
S210 Peter Bondra	4.00	10.00
S211 Chris Chelios	6.00	15.00
S212 Adam Graves	2.00	5.00
S213 Dale Hunter	4.00	10.00
S214 Tony Twist	6.00	15.00
S215 Keith Tkachuk	4.00	10.00
S216 Vladimir Konstantinov	25.00	50.00
S217 Sandy McCarthy	2.00	5.00
S218 Jamie Macoun	2.00	5.00
S219 Scott Stevens	4.00	10.00
S220 Mark Tinordi	2.00	5.00
S221 Bob Probert	4.00	10.00
S222 Gino Odjick	2.00	5.00
S223 Ulf Samuelsson	2.00	5.00
S224 Stu Grimson	4.00	10.00
S225 Marty McSorley	2.00	5.00

1995-96 Be A Player Autographs Die Cut

*DIE CUT/400: .6X TO 1.5X BASE AU/3000		
ONE AUTOGRAPH PER PACK		
DIE CUT AU ESTIMATED PRINT RUN 400		
S97 Wayne Gretzky/234*	300.00	500.00

1995-96 Be A Player Gretzky's Great Memories

COMPLETE SET (10)	40.00	80.00
COMMON GRETZKY (GM1-GM10)	4.00	10.00
GRETZKY MEMORIES STATED ODDS 1:15		

1995-96 Be A Player Lethal Lines

COMPLETE SET (15)	30.00	60.00
STATED ODDS 1:7		
LL1 Keith Tkachuk	1.50	4.00
LL2 Wayne Gretzky	6.00	15.00
LL3 Brett Hull	2.00	5.00
LL4 Eric Daze	1.50	4.00
LL5 Saku Koivu	1.50	4.00
LL6 Daniel Alfredsson	1.50	4.00
LL7 Pavel Bure	1.50	4.00
LL8 Sergei Fedorov	1.50	4.00
LL9 Alexander Mogilny	1.50	4.00
LL10 Paul Kariya	1.50	4.00
LL11 Mario Lemieux	5.00	12.00
LL12 Jaromir Jagr	2.00	5.00
LL13 Brendan Shanahan	1.50	4.00
LL14 Eric Lindros	1.50	4.00
LL15 Alexei Kovalev	1.25	3.00

1996-97 Be A Player

This 220-card set was issued by Pinnacle in two series and was distributed in eight-card packs with a suggested retail price of $6.99. For the first time, the series was licensed by the NHL, as well as the NHLPA, and thus the players were allowed to be seen in their own uniforms. Promotional cards were issued to dealers in six-card and two-card packs. These cards mirror those in the regular set save for the addition of the word PROMO written on the card back. The numbering, however, is the same as the base cards. The P prefix has been added for checklist purposes only.

COMPLETE SET (220)	10.00	25.00
COMP.SERIES 1 (110)	6.00	15.00
COMP.SERIES 2 (110)	6.00	15.00
1 Todd Gill	.08	.25
2 Dave Andreychuk	.08	.25
3 Igor Kravchuk	.08	.25
4 Tom Fitzgerald	.08	.25
5 Jeremy Roenick	.40	1.00
6 Peter Popovic	.08	.25
7 Andy Moog	.20	.50
8 Steven Rice	.08	.25
9 Darren Langdon	.08	.25
10 Mark Fitzpatrick	.20	.50
11 Alexei Zhamnov	.08	.25
12 Luc Robitaille	.20	.50
13 Michal Pivonka	.08	.25
14 Kevin Hatcher	.08	.25
15 Stephane Yelle	.08	.25
16 Bill Ranford	.20	.50
17 Jamie Baker	.08	.25
18 Sean Burke	.20	.50
19 Al Iafrate	.08	.25
20 Mark Recchi	.20	.50
21 Rod Brind'Amour	.20	.50
22 Doug Gilmour	.20	.50
23 Mike Wilson	.08	.25
24 Barry Potomski RC	.08	.25
25 Mike Gartner	.20	.50
26 Jason Wiemer	.08	.25
27 Scott Lachance	.08	.25
28 Joe Murphy	.08	.25
29 Bill Guerin	.08	.25
30 Byron Dafoe	.20	.50
31 Esa Tikkanen	.08	.25
32 Ken Baumgartner	.08	.25
33 Valeri Kamensky	.20	.50
34 J.J. Daigneault	.08	.25
35 Ulf Dahlen	.08	.25
36 Jason Allison	.08	.25
37 Ted Donato	.08	.25
38 Pat Verbeek	.08	.25
39 Miroslav Satan	.08	.25
40 Eric Desjardins	.20	.50
41 Dave Karpa	.08	.25
42 Jeff Hackett	.20	.50
43 Doug Brown	.08	.25
44 Gord Murphy	.08	.25
45 Kelly Hrudey	.20	.50
46 Kelly Miller	.08	.25
47 Tie Domi	.20	.50
48 Alexei Yashin	.08	.25
49 German Titov	.08	.25
50 Stephane Richer	.20	.50
51 Corey Hirsch	.20	.50
52 Brad May	.08	.25
53 Joe Nieuwendyk	.20	.50
54 Sylvain Lefebvre	.08	.25
55 Brian Leetch	.30	.75
56 Petr Svoboda	.08	.25
57 Dave Manson	.08	.25
58 Jason Woolley	.08	.25
59 Scott Niedermayer	.08	.25
60 Kelly Chase	.08	.25
61 Guy Hebert	.20	.50
62 Shayne Corson	.08	.25
63 Jon Casey	.20	.50
64 Rob Zettler	.08	.25
65 Mikael Andersson	.08	.25
66 Tony Amonte	.20	.50
67 Johan Garpenlov	.08	.25
68 Denny Lambert	.08	.25
69 Jim McKenzie	.08	.25
70 Darren Turcotte	.08	.25
71 Eric Weinrich	.08	.25
72 Troy Mallette	.08	.25
73 Donald Audette	.08	.25
74 Philippe Boucher	.08	.25
75 Shawn Chambers	.08	.25
76 Joel Otto	.08	.25
77 Tommy Salo	.20	.50
78 Olaf Kolzig	.30	.75
79 Adrian Aucoin	.08	.25
80 Alek Stojanov	.08	.25
81 Robert Reichel	.08	.25
82 Marc Bureau	.08	.25
83 Alexander Godynyuk	.08	.25
84 Bill Berg	.08	.25
85 Marc Bergevin	.08	.25
86 Kevin Kaminski	.08	.25
87 Uwe Krupp	.08	.25
88 Boris Mironov	.08	.25
89 Bob Bassen	.08	.25
90 Darryl Shannon	.08	.25
91 Mikael Renberg	.08	.25
92 Mike Stapleton	.08	.25
93 David Roberts	.08	.25
94 Peter Zezel	.08	.25
95 Mathieu Dandenault	.08	.25
96 Bobby Dollas	.08	.25
97 Don Sweeney	.08	.25
98 Niklas Andersson	.08	.25
99 Pat Jablonski	.20	.50
100 John Slaney	.08	.25
101 Kevin Todd	.08	.25
102 Jamie Pushor	.08	.25
103 Andreas Johansson RC	.08	.25
104 Corey Schwab	.20	.50
105 Todd Simpson RC	.08	.25
106 Landon Wilson	.08	.25
107 Daniel Goneau RC	.20	.50
108 David Wilkie	.08	.25
109 Andreas Dackell RC	.08	.25
110 Marek Malik	.08	.25
111 Mark Messier	.30	.75
112 Francois Leroux	.08	.25
113 Michal Sykora	.08	.25
114 Rob Zamuner	.08	.25
115 Craig Berube	.08	.25
116 Mike Ricci	.08	.25
117 Adam Burt	.08	.25
118 Alexander Karpovtsev	.08	.25
119 Shawn McEachern	.08	.25
120 Shawn Antoski	.08	.25
121 Dave Reid	.08	.25
122 Todd Warriner	.08	.25
123 Markus Naslund	.20	.50
124 Martin Rucinsky	.08	.25
125 Bob Carpenter	.08	.25
126 Dean McAmmond	.08	.25
127 Trevor Kidd	.20	.50
128 Martin Lapointe	.08	.25
129 Enrico Ciccone	.08	.25
130 Dixon Ward	.08	.25
131 Jason Muzzatti	.20	.50
132 Bryan Smolinski	.08	.25
133 Norm Maciver	.08	.25
134 Fredrik Olausson	.08	.25
135 Daniel Lacroix	.08	.25
136 Mike Peluso	.08	.25
137 Andrei Nikolishin	.08	.25
138 Rhett Warrener	.08	.25
139 Ray Ferraro	.08	.25
140 Glenn Healy	.20	.50
141 Steve Duchesne	.08	.25
142 Tony Granato	.08	.25
143 Cory Cross	.08	.25
144 Jon Klemm	.08	.25
145 Sami Kapanen	.08	.25
146 Grant Marshall	.08	.25
147 Matthew Barnaby	.08	.25
148 Lyle Odelein	.08	.25
149 Joe Dziedzic	.08	.25
150 Sergei Gonchar	.08	.25
151 Doug Zmolek	.08	.25
152 Sean O'Donnell RC	.08	.25
153 Scott Thornton	.08	.25
154 Steve Heinze	.08	.25
155 Garry Valk	.08	.25
156 Jeff Finley	.08	.25
157 Trent Klatt	.08	.25
158 Jeff Beukeboom	.08	.25
159 Theo Fleury	.08	.25
160 Dana Murzyn	.08	.25
161 Tommy Albelin	.20	.50
162 Bryan McCabe	.08	.25
163 Shaun Van Allen	.08	.25
164 Rick Tabaracci	.20	.50
165 Kevin Miller	.08	.25
166 Mariusz Czerkawski	.08	.25
167 Gerald Diduck	.08	.25
168 Brad McCrimmon	.08	.25
169 Stephane Matteau	.08	.25
170 Scott Daniels	.08	.25
171 Scott Mellanby	.20	.50
172 Sandy Moger	.08	.25
173 Steve Konowalchuk	.08	.25
174 Doug Weight	.20	.50
175 Darren McCarty	.08	.25
176 Darryl Sydor	.08	.25
177 Dave Ellett	.08	.25
178 Bob Boughner RC	.08	.25
179 Derek Armstrong	.08	.25
180 Gary Suter	.08	.25
181 Donald Brashear	.08	.25
182 Chris Tamer	.08	.25
183 Darrin Shannon	.08	.25
184 Stanislav Neckar	.08	.25
185 Brent Severyn	.08	.25
186 Steve Rucchin	.08	.25
187 Jeff Norton	.08	.25
188 Steven Finn	.08	.25
189 Kjell Samuelsson	.08	.25
190 Jeff Friesen	.08	.25
191 Shawn Burr	.08	.25
192 Paul Laus	.08	.25
193 Jeff Odgers	.08	.25
194 Keith Jones	.08	.25
195 Richard Matvichuk	.08	.25
196 Adam Foote	.08	.25
197 Bob Errey	.08	.25
198 Ryan Smyth	.20	.50
199 Mark Janssens	.08	.25
200 Claude Lapointe	.08	.25
201 Brian Noonan	.08	.25
202 Damian Rhodes	.20	.50
203 Dale Hawerchuk	.20	.50
204 Bill Lindsay	.08	.25
205 Brian Skrudland	.08	.25
206 Curtis Joseph	.30	.75
207 Jon Rohloff	.08	.25
208 Doug Bodger	.08	.25
209 Steve Sullivan RC	.20	.50
210 Ricard Persson	.08	.25
211 Dwayne Roloson RC	1.25	3.00
212 Mike Dunham	.20	.50
213 Marcel Cousineau RC	.08	.25
214 Eric Fichaud	.20	.50
215 Matt Johnson	.08	.25
216 Fredrik Modin RC	.08	.25
217 Denis Pederson	.08	.25
218 Kevin Hodson RC	.20	.50
219 Drew Bannister	.08	.25
220 Mike Grier RC	.50	1.25
P44 Gord Murphy PROMO	.08	.25
P52 Brad May PROMO	.08	.25
P55 Brian Leetch PROMO	.08	.25
P67 Johan Garpenlov PROMO	.08	.25
P89 Bob Bassen PROMO	.08	.25
P91 Mikael Renberg PROMO	.08	.25
P119 Shawn MacEachern PROMO	.08	.25
P176 Darryl Sydor PROMO	.08	.25
P181 Donald Brashear PROMO	.08	.25
P217 Denis Pederson PROMO	.08	.25
P218 Kevin Hodson PROMO	.08	.25
P219 Drew Bannister PROMO	.08	.25

1996-97 Be A Player Autographs

These autographs were inserted one per pack. Gold foil distinguishes them from base cards. Alexei Zhamnov did not sign, and thus the set is considered complete at 219 cards. A silver parallel version of the autograph set existed as well. The cards were distinguishable by the silver foil backing on the card fronts. Although no odds were published, these cards were inserted at a rate of about 1:30 packs.

ONE AUTO CARD PER PACK		
*SILVER AUTO: .6X TO 1.5X BASIC AU		
SILVER AU STATED ODDS 1:7		
1 Todd Gill	1.50	4.00
2 Dave Andreychuk	3.00	8.00
3 Igor Kravchuk	1.50	4.00
4 Tom Fitzgerald	1.50	4.00
5 Jeremy Roenick	6.00	15.00
6 Peter Popovic	1.50	4.00
7 Andy Moog	2.50	6.00
8 Steven Rice	1.50	4.00
9 Darren Langdon	1.50	4.00
10 Mark Fitzpatrick	2.50	6.00
12 Luc Robitaille	6.00	15.00
13 Michal Pivonka	1.50	4.00
14 Kevin Hatcher	1.50	4.00
15 Stephane Yelle	1.50	4.00
16 Bill Ranford	3.00	8.00
17 Jamie Baker	1.50	4.00
18 Sean Burke	3.00	8.00
19 Al Iafrate	2.50	6.00
20 Mark Recchi	3.00	8.00
21 Rod Brind'Amour	3.00	8.00
22 Doug Gilmour	6.00	15.00
23 Mike Wilson	1.50	4.00
24 Barry Potomski	1.50	4.00
25 Mike Gartner	3.00	8.00
26 Jason Wiemer	1.50	4.00
27 Scott Lachance	1.50	4.00
28 Joe Murphy	1.50	4.00
29 Bill Guerin	3.00	8.00
30 Byron Dafoe	2.50	6.00
31 Esa Tikkanen	1.50	4.00
32 Ken Baumgartner	1.50	4.00
33 Valeri Kamensky	1.50	4.00
34 J.J. Daigneault	1.50	4.00
35 Ulf Dahlen	1.50	4.00
36 Jason Allison	1.50	4.00
37 Ted Donato	1.50	4.00
38 Pat Verbeek	1.50	4.00
39 Miroslav Satan	3.00	8.00
40 Eric Desjardins	2.50	6.00
41 Dave Karpa	1.50	4.00
42 Jeff Hackett	2.50	6.00
43 Doug Brown	1.50	4.00
44 Gord Murphy	1.50	4.00
45 Kelly Hrudey	2.50	6.00
46 Kelly Miller	1.50	4.00
47 Tie Domi	3.00	8.00
48 Alexei Yashin	1.50	4.00
49 German Titov	1.50	4.00
50 Stephane Richer	1.50	4.00
51 Corey Hirsch	2.50	6.00
52 Brad May	1.50	4.00
53 Joe Nieuwendyk	3.00	8.00
54 Sylvain Lefebvre	1.50	4.00
55 Brian Leetch	5.00	12.00
56 Petr Svoboda	1.50	4.00
57 Dave Manson	1.50	4.00
58 Jason Woolley	1.50	4.00
59 Scott Niedermayer	1.50	4.00
60 Kelly Chase	1.50	4.00
61 Guy Hebert	2.50	6.00
62 Shayne Corson	1.50	4.00
63 Jon Casey	2.50	6.00
64 Rob Zettler	1.50	4.00
65 Mikael Andersson	1.50	4.00
66 Tony Amonte	3.00	8.00
67 Johan Garpenlov	1.50	4.00
68 Denny Lambert	1.50	4.00
69 Jim McKenzie	1.50	4.00
70 Darren Turcotte	1.50	4.00
71 Eric Weinrich	1.50	4.00
72 Troy Mallette	1.50	4.00
73 Donald Audette	1.50	4.00
74 Philippe Boucher	1.50	4.00
75 Shawn Chambers	1.50	4.00
76 Joel Otto	1.50	4.00
77 Tommy Salo	2.50	6.00
78 Olaf Kolzig	3.00	8.00
79 Adrian Aucoin	1.50	4.00
80 Alek Stojanov	1.50	4.00
81 Robert Reichel	1.50	4.00
82 Marc Bureau	1.50	4.00
83 Alexander Godynyuk	1.50	4.00
84 Bill Berg	1.50	4.00
85 Marc Bergevin	1.50	4.00
86 Kevin Kaminski	1.50	4.00
87 Uwe Krupp	1.50	4.00
88 Boris Mironov	1.50	4.00
89 Bob Bassen	1.50	4.00
90 Darryl Shannon	1.50	4.00
91 Mikael Renberg	1.50	4.00
92 Mike Stapleton	1.50	4.00
93 David Roberts	1.50	4.00
94 Peter Zezel	1.50	4.00
95 Mathieu Dandenault	1.50	4.00
96 Bobby Dollas	1.50	4.00
97 Don Sweeney	1.50	4.00
98 Niklas Andersson	1.50	4.00
99 Pat Jablonski	1.50	4.00
100 John Slaney	1.50	4.00
101 Kevin Todd	1.50	4.00
102 Jamie Pushor	1.50	4.00
103 Andreas Johansson	1.50	4.00
104 Corey Schwab	1.50	4.00
105 Todd Simpson	1.50	4.00
106 Landon Wilson	1.50	4.00
107 Daniel Goneau	1.50	4.00
108 David Wilkie	1.50	4.00
109 Andreas Dackell	1.50	4.00
110 Marek Malik	1.50	4.00
111 Mark Messier	30.00	80.00
112 Francois Leroux	1.50	4.00
113 Michal Sykora	1.50	4.00
114 Rob Zamuner	1.50	4.00
115 Craig Berube	1.50	4.00
116 Mike Ricci	2.50	6.00
117 Adam Burt	1.50	4.00
118 Alexander Karpovtsev	1.50	4.00
119 Shawn McEachern	1.50	4.00
120 Shawn Antoski	1.50	4.00
121 Dave Reid	1.50	4.00
122 Todd Warriner	1.50	4.00
123 Markus Naslund	4.00	10.00
124 Martin Rucinsky	1.50	4.00
125 Bob Carpenter	1.50	4.00
126 Dean McAmmond	1.50	4.00
127 Trevor Kidd	2.50	6.00
128 Martin Lapointe	2.50	6.00
129 Enrico Ciccone	1.50	4.00
130 Dixon Ward	1.50	4.00
131 Jason Muzzatti	1.50	4.00
132 Bryan Smolinski	1.50	4.00
133 Norm Maciver	1.50	4.00
134 Fredrik Olausson	1.50	4.00
135 Daniel Lacroix	1.50	4.00
136 Mike Peluso	1.50	4.00
137 Andrei Nikolishin	1.50	4.00
138 Rhett Warrener	1.50	4.00
139 Ray Ferraro	1.50	4.00
140 Glenn Healy	1.50	4.00
141 Steve Duchesne	1.50	4.00
142 Tony Granato	1.50	4.00
143 Cory Cross	1.50	4.00
144 Jon Klemm	1.50	4.00
145 Sami Kapanen	1.50	4.00
146 Grant Marshall	1.50	4.00
147 Matthew Barnaby	2.50	6.00
148 Lyle Odelein	1.50	4.00
149 Joe Dziedzic	1.50	4.00
150 Sergei Gonchar	1.50	4.00
151 Doug Zmolek	1.50	4.00
152 Sean O'Donnell	1.50	4.00
153 Scott Thornton	1.50	4.00
154 Steve Heinze	1.50	4.00
155 Garry Valk	1.50	4.00
156 Jeff Finley	1.50	4.00
157 Trent Klatt	1.50	4.00
158 Jeff Beukeboom	1.50	4.00
159 Theo Fleury	1.50	4.00
160 Dana Murzyn	1.50	4.00
161 Tommy Albelin	1.50	4.00
162 Bryan McCabe	1.50	4.00
163 Shaun Van Allen	1.50	4.00
164 Rick Tabaracci	2.50	6.00
165 Kevin Miller	1.50	4.00
166 Mariusz Czerkawski	1.50	4.00
167 Gerald Diduck	1.50	4.00
168 Brad McCrimmon	1.50	4.00
169 Stephane Matteau	1.50	4.00
170 Scott Daniels	1.50	4.00
171 Scott Mellanby	1.50	4.00
172 Sandy Moger	1.50	4.00
173 Steve Konowalchuk	1.50	4.00
174 Doug Weight	2.50	6.00
175 Darren McCarty	3.00	8.00
176 Darryl Sydor	1.50	4.00
177 Dave Ellett	1.50	4.00
178 Bob Boughner	1.50	4.00
179 Derek Armstrong	1.50	4.00
180 Gary Suter	1.50	4.00
181 Donald Brashear	1.50	4.00
182 Chris Tamer	1.50	4.00
183 Darrin Shannon	1.50	4.00
184 Stanislav Neckar	1.50	4.00
185 Brent Severyn	1.50	4.00
186 Steve Rucchin	1.50	4.00
187 Jeff Norton	1.50	4.00
188 Steven Finn	1.50	4.00
189 Kjell Samuelsson	1.50	4.00
190 Jeff Friesen	1.50	4.00
191 Shawn Burr	1.50	4.00
192 Paul Laus	1.50	4.00
193 Jeff Odgers	1.50	4.00
194 Keith Jones	1.50	4.00
195 Richard Matvichuk	1.50	4.00
196 Adam Foote	1.50	4.00
197 Bob Errey	1.50	4.00
198 Ryan Smyth	3.00	8.00
199 Mark Janssens	1.50	4.00
200 Claude Lapointe	1.50	4.00
201 Brian Noonan	1.50	4.00
202 Damian Rhodes	2.50	6.00
203 Dale Hawerchuk	3.00	8.00
204 Bill Lindsay	1.50	4.00
205 Brian Skrudland	1.50	4.00
206 Curtis Joseph	10.00	20.00
207 Jon Rohloff	1.50	4.00
208 Doug Bodger	1.50	4.00
209 Steve Sullivan	2.50	6.00
210 Ricard Persson	1.50	4.00
211 Dwayne Roloson	3.00	8.00
212 Mike Dunham	3.00	8.00
213 Marcel Cousineau	1.50	4.00
214 Eric Fichaud	1.50	4.00
215 Matt Johnson	1.50	4.00
216 Fredrik Modin	1.50	4.00
217 Denis Pederson	1.50	4.00
218 Kevin Hodson	2.50	6.00
219 Drew Bannister	1.50	4.00
220 Mike Grier	1.50	4.00

1996-97 Be A Player Biscuit In The Basket

COMPLETE SET (25)	25.00	60.00
STATED ODDS 1:17		
1 Wayne Gretzky	6.00	15.00
2 Mario Lemieux	4.00	10.00
3 Eric Lindros	1.25	3.00
4 Theo Fleury	.75	2.00
5 Peter Forsberg	2.00	5.00
6 Keith Tkachuk	.75	2.00
7 Sergei Fedorov	1.50	4.00
8 Mike Modano	1.50	4.00
9 Jaromir Jagr	2.00	5.00
10 Brendan Shanahan	1.25	3.00
11 Teemu Selanne	1.25	3.00
12 Mats Sundin	1.25	3.00
13 Steve Yzerman	3.00	8.00
14 Brett Hull	1.50	4.00
15 Zigmund Palffy	.75	2.00
16 Joe Sakic	2.50	6.00
17 John LeClair	.40	1.00
18 Pavel Bure	1.25	3.00
19 Mark Messier	1.25	3.00
20 Paul Kariya	1.25	3.00
21 Jason Arnott	.40	1.00
22 Saku Koivu	1.25	3.00
23 Daniel Alfredsson	.75	2.00
24 Alexander Mogilny	.75	2.00
25 Owen Nolan	.75	2.00

1996-97 Be A Player Lemieux Die Cut

This two-card set commemorated the career of future Hall-of-Famer, Mario Lemieux, with a special interlocking, all-foil Dufex, die-cut insert. The first card was randomly inserted in Series 1 packs with it's matching, interlocking counterpart inserted in Series 2 packs. Only 66 of each card was produced and sequentially numbered.

STATED PRINT RUN 66 SER.#'d SETS		
1 Mario Lemieux	100.00	200.00
2 Mario Lemieux	100.00	200.00

1996-97 Be A Player Lindros Die Cut

This two-card set honored the superstar center, Eric Lindros, with a special interlocking, all-foil Dufex, die-cut insert. Each card carried an authentic autograph. The first card was randomly inserted in Series 1 packs with it's matching, interlocking counterpart inserted in Series 2 packs. Only 88 of each card was produced and sequentially numbered.

RANDOM INSERTS IN PACKS		
STATED PRINT RUN 88 SER.#'d SETS		
1 Eric Lindros AU	60.00	150.00
2 Eric Lindros AU	60.00	150.00

1996-97 Be A Player Link to History

Randomly inserted at an approximate rate of 1:2 packs, cards from this 20-card set featured ten top rookie standouts matched with their 10 mega-star veteran counterparts. The first five rookie "Links" appeared in Series I with the second five veteran "Links" and featured silver foil with blue accents. The second five rookie "Links" appeared in Series II with the first five veteran "Links" and featured silver foil with red accents.

COMPLETE SET (20)	8.00	20.00
COMP.SERIES 1 (10)	4.00	10.00
COMP.SERIES 2 (10)	4.00	10.00
STATED ODDS 1:2		
1A Jarome Iginla	.50	1.25
1B Teemu Selanne	.40	1.00
2A Harry York	.20	.50
2B Peter Forsberg	1.00	2.50
3A Sergei Berezin	.40	1.00
3B Brendan Shanahan	.40	1.00
4A Ethan Moreau	.40	1.00
4B Pavel Bure	.40	1.00
5A Rem Murray	.20	.50
5B Jason Arnott	.20	.50
6A Jamie Langenbrunner	.20	.50
6B Paul Kariya	.40	1.00
7A Jim Campbell	.40	1.00
7B Eric Lindros	.40	1.00
8A Jonas Hoglund	.20	.50
8B Pat LaFontaine	.40	1.00
9A Wade Redden	.20	.50
9B Steve Yzerman	2.00	5.00
10A Patrick Lalime	.40	1.00
10B John Vanbiesbrouck	.30	.75
2B Peter Forsberg PROMO	2.00	5.00

1996-97 Be A Player Link to History Autographs

An authentic autograph and gold foil on each card front make these parallel cards easy to identify from their more common Link to History counterparts. Exact odds per pack were not released, but they're significantly tougher to pull than the non-autographed cards. Because of a delayed return, Ethan Moreau's cards were inserted in Series II packs only; Teemu Selanne's autographed cards replaced them in Series I packs. A silver parallel version of the autograph was also created. The cards were distinguishable by the silver foil backing on the card fronts. Although no odds were published, these cards were inserted at a rate of about 1:30 packs.

*SILVER AUTO: .8X TO 2X BASIC AU

Card	Low	High
1A Jarome Iginla	15.00	40.00
1B Teemu Selanne	6.00	15.00
2A Harry York	1.50	4.00
2B Peter Forsberg	15.00	40.00
3A Sergei Berezin	4.00	10.00
3B Brendan Shanahan	6.00	15.00
4A Ethan Moreau	1.50	4.00
4B Pavel Bure	6.00	15.00
5A Rem Murray	1.50	4.00
5B Jason Arnott	1.50	4.00
6A Jamie Langenbrunner	1.50	4.00
6B Paul Kariya	15.00	40.00
7A Jim Campbell	4.00	10.00
7B Eric Lindros	6.00	15.00
8A Jonas Hoglund	1.50	4.00
8B Pat LaFontaine	1.50	4.00
9A Wade Redden	1.50	4.00
9B Steve Yzerman	20.00	50.00
10A Patrick Lalime	4.00	10.00
10B John Vanbiesbrouck	5.00	12.00

1996-97 Be A Player Messier Die Cut

This two-card set featured superstar, Mark Messier, with a special interlocking, all-foil Dufex, die-cut insert. Each card was personally autographed. The first card was randomly inserted in Series 1 packs with it's matching, interlocking counterpart inserted in Series 2 packs. Only 11 of each card was produced and sequentially numbered.

UNPRICED MESSIER PRINT RUN 11

1 Mark Messier AU

2 Mark Messier AU

1996-97 Be A Player Stacking the Pads

Card	Low	High
COMPLETE SET (15)	12.00	30.00
STATED ODDS 1:35		
1 Patrick Lalime	.75	2.00
2 Chris Osgood	.75	2.00
3 Ron Hextall	.75	2.00
4 John Vanbiesbrouck	.75	2.00
5 Martin Brodeur	2.50	6.00
6 Felix Potvin	1.25	3.00
7 Nikolai Khabibulin	.75	2.00
8 Jim Carey	.75	2.00
9 Grant Fuhr	.75	2.00
10 Mike Richter	1.25	3.00
11 Dominik Hasek	2.00	5.00
12 Andy Moog	.75	2.00
13 Patrick Roy	4.00	10.00
14 Curtis Joseph	1.25	3.00
15 Jocelyn Thibault	.75	2.00

1997-98 Be A Player

The 1997-98 Be A Player set was issued by Pinnacle in two series totalling 250 cards and was distributed in eight-card packs with a suggested retail price of $6.99. The fronts featured color action photos of players with a heavy emphasis on rookies and Calder Trophy candidates in a white and net-shadow border. The backs carried a head photo with player information and career statistics.

Card	Low	High
COMPLETE SET (250)	6.00	15.00
1 Eric Lindros	.25	.60
2 Martin Brodeur	.60	1.50
3 Saku Koivu	.25	.60
4 Felix Potvin	.25	.60
5 Adam Oates	.15	.40
6 Rob DiMaio	.08	.25
7 Jari Kurri	.15	.40
8 Andrew Cassels	.08	.25
9 Trevor Linden	.15	.40
10 Jocelyn Thibault	.15	.40
11 Chris Chelios	.25	.60
12 Paul Coffey	.25	.60
13 Nikolai Khabibulin	.15	.40
14 Robert Lang	.08	.25
15 Brett Hull	.30	.75
16 Mike Sillinger	.08	.25
17 Lyle Odelein	.08	.25
18 Bryan Berard	.08	.25
19 Craig Muni	.08	.25
20 Kris Draper	.08	.25
21 Ed Jovanovski	.15	.40
22 Keith Tkachuk	.25	.60
23 Dean Malkoc	.08	.25
24 Cory Stillman	.08	.25
25 Chris Osgood	.08	.25
26 Dainius Zubrus	.08	.25
27 Yves Racine	.08	.25
28 Eric Cairns RC	.08	.25
29 Dan Bylsma	.08	.25
30 Chris Terreri	.08	.25
31 Bill Huard	.08	.25
32 Warren Rychel	.08	.25
33 Scott Walker	.08	.25
34 Brian Holzinger	.08	.25
35 Roman Turek	.08	.25
36 Ron Tugnutt	.15	.40
37 Mike Richter	.25	.60
38 Mattias Norstrom	.08	.25
39 Joe Sacco	.08	.25
40 Derek King	.08	.25
41 Brad Werenka	.08	.25
42 Paul Kruse	.08	.25
43 Mike Knuble RC	.08	.25
44 Mike Peca	.08	.25
45 Jean-Yves Leroux RC	.08	.25
46 Ray Sheppard	.08	.25
47 Reid Simpson	.08	.25
48 Rob Brown	.08	.25
49 Dave Babych	.08	.25
50 Scott Pellerin	.08	.25
51 Bruce Gardiner RC	.08	.25
52 Adam Deadmarsh	.08	.25
53 Curtis Brown	.08	.25
54 Jason Marshall	.08	.25
55 Gerald Diduck	.08	.25
56 Mick Vukota	.08	.25
57 Kevin Dean	.08	.25
58 Adam Graves	.08	.25
59 Craig Conroy	.08	.25
60 Cale Hulse	.08	.25
61 Dimitri Khristich	.08	.25
62 Chris Wells	.08	.25
63 Travis Green	.08	.25
64 Tyler Wright	.08	.25
65 Chris Simon	.08	.25
66 Mikhail Shtalenkov	.08	.25
67 Anson Carter	.15	.40
68 Zarley Zalapski	.08	.25
69 Per Gustafsson	.08	.25
70 Jayson More	.08	.25
71 Steve Thomas	.08	.25
72 Todd Marchant	.08	.25
73 Gary Roberts	.08	.25
74 Richard Smehlik	.08	.25
75 Aaron Miller	.08	.25
76 Daren Puppa	.08	.25
77 Garth Snow	.15	.40
78 Greg DeVries	.08	.25
79 Randy Burridge	.08	.25
80 Jim Cummins	.08	.25
81 Rich Pilon	.08	.25
82 Chris McAlpine	.08	.25
83 Joe Sakic	.50	1.25
84 Ted Drury	.08	.25
85 Brent Gilchrist	.08	.25
86 Dallas Eakins RC	.08	.25
87 Bruce Driver	.08	.25
88 Jamie Huscroft	.08	.25
89 Jeff Brown	.08	.25
90 Janne Laukkanen	.08	.25
91 Ken Klee	.08	.25
92 Peter Bondra	.15	.40
93 Ian Moran	.08	.25
94 Stephane Quintal	.08	.25
95 Jason York	.08	.25
96 Todd Harvey	.08	.25
97 Slava Kozlov	.08	.25
98 Kevin Haller	.08	.25
99 Alexei Zhamnov	.08	.25
100 Craig Johnson	.08	.25
101 Mike Keane	.08	.25
102 Craig Rivet	.08	.25
103 Roman Vopat	.08	.25
104 Jim Johnson	.08	.25
105 Ray Whitney	.08	.25
106 Ron Sutter	.08	.25
107 Jamie McLennan	.15	.40
108 Kris King	.08	.25
109 Lance Pitlick RC	.08	.25
110 Mike Dunham	.15	.40
111 Jim Dowd	.08	.25
112 Geoff Sanderson	.15	.40
113 Vladimir Vujtek	.08	.25
114 Tim Taylor	.08	.25
115 Sandis Ozolinsh	.08	.25
116 Scott Daniels	.08	.25
117 Bob Corkum	.08	.25
118 Kirk McLean	.15	.40
119 Darcy Tucker	.08	.25
120 Dennis Vaske	.08	.25
121 Kirk Muller	.08	.25
122 Jay McKee	.08	.25
123 Jere Lehtinen	.08	.25
124 Ruslan Salei	.08	.25
125 Al MacInnis	.08	.25
126 Ulf Samuelsson	.08	.25
127 Rick Tocchet	.15	.40
128 Nick Kypreos	.08	.25
129 Joel Bouchard	.08	.25
130 Jeff O'Neill	.08	.25
131 Daniel McGillis RC	.08	.25
132 Sean Pronger	.08	.25
133 Vladimir Malakhov	.08	.25
134 Petr Sykora	.08	.25
135 Zigmund Palffy	.15	.40
136 Joe Reekie	.08	.25
137 Chris Gratton	.08	.25
138 Craig Billington	.15	.40
139 Steve Washburn	.08	.25
140 Robert Kron	.08	.25
141 Larry Murphy	.08	.25
142 Shean Donovan	.08	.25
143 Scott Young	.08	.25
144 Janne Niinimaa	.15	.40
145 Ken Belanger RC	.08	.25
146 Pavol Demitra	.15	.40
147 Roman Hamrlik	.08	.25
148 Lonny Bohonos	.08	.25
149 Mike Eagles	.08	.25
150 Kelly Buchberger	.08	.25
151 Mattias Timander	.08	.25
152 Benoit Hogue	.08	.25
153 Joey Kocur	.08	.25
154 Mats Lindgren	.08	.25
155 Aki Berg	.08	.25
156 Tim Sweeney	.08	.25
157 Vincent Damphousse	.08	.25
158 Dan Kordic	.08	.25
159 Darius Kasparaitis	.08	.25
160 Randy McKay	.08	.25
161 Steve Staios	.08	.25
162 Brendan Witt	.08	.25
163 Paul Ysebaert	.08	.25
164 Greg Adams	.08	.25
165 Kent Manderville	.08	.25
166 Steve Dubinsky	.08	.25
167 David Nemirovsky	.08	.25
168 Todd Bertuzzi	.25	.60
169 Frederic Chabot RC	.08	.25
170 Dmitri Mironov	.08	.25
171 Pat Peake	.08	.25
172 Ed Ward	.08	.25
173 Jeff Shantz	.08	.25
174 Dave Gagner	.08	.25
175 Randy Cunneyworth	.08	.25
176 Daymond Langkow	.15	.40
177 Alex Hicks RC	.08	.25
178 Darby Hendrickson	.08	.25
179 Mike Sullivan	.08	.25
180 Anders Eriksson	.08	.25
181 Turner Stevenson	.08	.25
182 Shane Churla	.08	.25
183 Dave Lowry	.08	.25
184 Joe Juneau	.08	.25
185 Bob Essensa	.08	.25
186 James Black	.08	.25
187 Michal Grosek	.08	.25
188 Tomas Holmstrom	.08	.25
189 Ian Laperriere	.08	.25
190 Terry Yake	.08	.25
191 Jason Smith	.08	.25
192 Sergei Zholtok	.08	.25
193 Doug Houda	.08	.25
194 Guy Carbonneau	.08	.25
195 Terry Carkner	.08	.25
196 Alexei Gusarov	.08	.25
197 Vladimir Tsyplakov	.08	.25
198 Jarrod Skalde	.08	.25
199 Marty Murray	.08	.25
200 Aaron Ward	.08	.25
201 Bobby Holik	.08	.25
202 Steve Chiasson	.08	.25
203 Brantt Myhres	.08	.25
204 Eric Messier RC	.15	.40
205 Rene Corbet	.08	.25
206 Mathieu Schneider	.08	.25
207 Tom Chorske	.08	.25
208 Doug Lidster	.08	.25
209 Igor Ulanov	.08	.25
210 Blair Atcheynum RC	.08	.25
211 Sebastien Bordeleau	.08	.25
212 Alexei Morozov	.15	.40
213 Vaclav Prospal RC	.40	1.00
214 Brad Bombardir RC	.08	.25
215 Mattias Ohlund	.15	.40
216 Chris Dingman RC	.08	.25
217 Erik Rasmussen	.08	.25
218 Mike Johnson RC	.15	.40
219 Chris Phillips	.08	.25
220 Sergei Samsonov	.15	.40
221 Patrick Marleau	.30	.75
222 Alyn McCauley	.15	.40
223 Ryan VandenBussche RC	.08	.25
224 Daniel Cleary	.08	.25
225 Magnus Arvedson RC	.08	.25
226 Brad Isbister	.08	.25
227 Pascal Rheaume RC	.08	.25
228 Patrik Elias RC	.60	1.50
229 Krzysztof Oliwa RC	.08	.25
230 Tyler Moss RC	.08	.25
231 Jamie Rivers	.08	.25
232 Joe Thornton	.40	1.00
233 Steve Shields RC	.15	.40
234 Dave Scatchard RC	.15	.40
235 Patrick Cote RC	.08	.25
236 Rich Brennan RC	.08	.25
237 Boyd Devereaux	.08	.25
238 Per Johan Axelsson RC	.08	.25
239 Craig Millar RC	.08	.25
240 Juha Ylonen	.08	.25
241 Donald MacLean RC	.08	.25
242 Jaroslav Svejkovsky	.08	.25
243 Marco Sturm RC	.40	1.00
244 Steve McKenna RC	.08	.25
245 Derek Morris RC	.30	.75
246 Dean Chynoweth	.08	.25
247 Alexander Mogilny	.15	.40
248 Ray Bourque	.40	1.00
249 Ed Belfour	.25	.60
250 John LeClair	.25	.60
P3 Saku Koivu PROMO	.75	2.00

1997-98 Be A Player Autographs

Inserted one per pack, this 250-card set was an autographed gold foil enhanced parallel version of the base set. Die-cut and limited prismatic die-cut parallel autographed versions of the base set were also produced. Die-cut auto stated odds were 1:7. The prismatic parallel had a stated print run of 100 sets.

ONE AUTO PER PACK
*DIE CUT: 1X TO 2X BASIC AUTO
*DIE CUT: .6X TO 1.25X BASIC AU SP
DIE CUT STATED ODDS 1:7
*PRISM: 1.5X TO 3X BASIC AUTO
*PRISM: .75X TO 1.5X BASIC AU SP
PRISMATIC PRINT RUN 100 SETS

Card	Low	High
1 Eric Lindros SP	10.00	25.00
2 Martin Brodeur SP	50.00	100.00
3 Saku Koivu	3.00	8.00
4 Felix Potvin	3.00	8.00
5 Adam Oates	2.00	5.00
6 Rob DiMaio	1.00	2.50
7 Jari Kurri	4.00	10.00
8 Andrew Cassels	1.00	2.50
9 Trevor Linden	1.00	2.50
10 Jocelyn Thibault	2.00	5.00
11 Chris Chelios	2.00	5.00
12 Paul Coffey	4.00	10.00
13 Nikolai Khabibulin	4.00	10.00
14 Robert Lang	1.00	2.50
15 Brett Hull SP	30.00	60.00
16 Mike Sillinger	1.00	2.50
17 Lyle Odelein	1.00	2.50
18 Bryan Berard	1.00	2.50
19 Craig Muni	1.00	2.50
20 Kris Draper	1.00	2.50
21 Ed Jovanovski	1.00	2.50
22 Keith Tkachuk	2.00	5.00
23 Dean Malkoc	1.00	2.50
24 Cory Stillman	1.00	2.50
25 Chris Osgood	2.00	5.00
26 Dainius Zubrus	1.00	2.50
27 Yves Racine	1.00	2.50
28 Eric Cairns	1.00	2.50
29 Dan Bylsma	1.00	2.50
30 Chris Terreri	1.00	2.50
31 Bill Huard	1.00	2.50
32 Warren Rychel	1.00	2.50
33 Scott Walker	1.00	2.50
34 Brian Holzinger	1.00	2.50
35 Roman Turek	1.00	2.50
36 Ron Tugnutt	2.00	5.00
37 Mike Richter	2.00	5.00
38 Mattias Norstrom	1.00	2.50
39 Joe Sacco	1.00	2.50
40 Derek King	1.00	2.50
41 Brad Werenka	1.00	2.50
42 Paul Kruse	1.00	2.50
43 Mike Knuble	1.00	2.50
44 Mike Peca	2.00	5.00
45 Jean-Yves Leroux	1.00	2.50
46 Ray Sheppard	1.00	2.50
47 Reid Simpson	1.00	2.50
48 Rob Brown	1.00	2.50
49 Dave Babych	1.00	2.50
50 Scott Pellerin	1.00	2.50
51 Bruce Gardiner	1.00	2.50
52 Adam Deadmarsh	1.00	2.50
53 Curtis Brown	1.00	2.50
54 Jason Marshall	1.00	2.50
55 Gerald Diduck	1.00	2.50
56 Mick Vukota	1.00	2.50
57 Kevin Dean	1.00	2.50
58 Adam Graves	1.00	2.50
59 Craig Conroy	1.00	2.50
60 Cale Hulse	1.00	2.50
61 Dimitri Khristich	1.00	2.50
62 Chris Wells	1.00	2.50
63 Travis Green	1.00	2.50
64 Tyler Wright	1.00	2.50
65 Chris Simon	1.00	2.50
66 Mikhail Shtalenkov	1.00	2.50
67 Anson Carter	1.00	2.50
68 Zarley Zalapski	1.00	2.50
69 Per Gustafsson	1.00	2.50
70 Jayson More	1.00	2.50
71 Steve Thomas	1.00	2.50
72 Todd Marchant	1.00	2.50
73 Gary Roberts	1.00	2.50
74 Richard Smehlik	1.00	2.50
75 Aaron Miller	1.00	2.50
76 Daren Puppa	2.00	5.00
77 Garth Snow	2.00	5.00
78 Greg DeVries	1.00	2.50
79 Randy Burridge	1.00	2.50
80 Jim Cummins	1.00	2.50
81 Rich Pilon	1.00	2.50
82 Chris McAlpine	1.00	2.50
83 Joe Sakic SP	40.00	80.00
84 Ted Drury	1.00	2.50
85 Brent Gilchrist	1.00	2.50
86 Dallas Eakins	1.00	2.50
87 Bruce Driver	1.00	2.50
88 Jamie Huscroft	1.00	2.50
89 Jeff Brown	1.00	2.50
90 Janne Laukkanen	1.00	2.50
91 Ken Klee	1.00	2.50
92 Peter Bondra	2.00	5.00
93 Ian Moran	1.00	2.50
94 Stephane Quintal	1.00	2.50
95 Jason York	1.00	2.50
96 Todd Harvey	1.00	2.50
97 Slava Kozlov	2.00	5.00
98 Kevin Haller	1.00	2.50
99 Alexei Zhamnov	1.00	2.50
100 Craig Johnson	1.00	2.50
101 Mike Keane	1.00	2.50
102 Craig Rivet	1.00	2.50
103 Roman Vopat	1.00	2.50
104 Jim Johnson	1.00	2.50
105 Ray Whitney	1.00	2.50
106 Ron Sutter	1.00	2.50
107 Jamie McLennan	2.00	5.00
108 Kris King	1.00	2.50
109 Lance Pitlick	1.00	2.50
110 Mike Dunham	2.00	5.00
111 Jim Dowd	1.00	2.50
112 Geoff Sanderson	1.00	2.50
113 Vladimir Vujtek	1.00	2.50
114 Tim Taylor	1.00	2.50
115 Sandis Ozolinsh	1.00	2.50
116 Scott Daniels	1.00	2.50
117 Bob Corkum	1.00	2.50
118 Kirk McLean	2.00	5.00
119 Darcy Tucker	1.00	2.50
120 Dennis Vaske	1.00	2.50
121 Kirk Muller	1.00	2.50
122 Jay McKee	1.00	2.50
123 Jere Lehtinen	2.00	5.00
124 Ruslan Salei	1.00	2.50
125 Al MacInnis SP	12.50	30.00
126 Ulf Samuelsson	1.00	2.50
127 Rick Tocchet	2.00	5.00
128 Nick Kypreos	1.00	2.50
129 Joel Bouchard	1.00	2.50
130 Jeff O'Neill	1.00	2.50
131 Daniel McGillis	1.00	2.50
132 Sean Pronger	1.00	2.50
133 Vladimir Malakhov	1.00	2.50
134 Petr Sykora	1.00	2.50
135 Zigmund Palffy	2.00	5.00
136 Joe Reekie	1.00	2.50
137 Chris Gratton	1.00	2.50
138 Craig Billington	2.00	5.00
139 Steve Washburn	1.00	2.50
140 Robert Kron	1.00	2.50
141 Larry Murphy	1.00	2.50
142 Shean Donovan	1.00	2.50
143 Scott Young	1.00	2.50
144 Janne Niinimaa	1.00	2.50
145 Ken Belanger	1.00	2.50
146 Pavol Demitra	2.00	5.00
147 Roman Hamrlik	1.00	2.50
148 Lonny Bohonos	1.00	2.50
149 Mike Eagles	1.00	2.50
150 Kelly Buchberger	1.00	2.50
151 Mattias Timander	1.00	2.50
152 Benoit Hogue	1.00	2.50
153 Joey Kocur	1.00	2.50
154 Mats Lindgren	1.00	2.50
155 Aki Berg	1.00	2.50
156 Tim Sweeney	1.00	2.50
157 Vincent Damphousse	1.00	2.50
158 Dan Kordic	1.00	2.50
159 Darius Kasparaitis	1.00	2.50
160 Randy McKay	1.00	2.50
161 Steve Staios	1.00	2.50
162 Brendan Witt	1.00	2.50
163 Paul Ysebaert	1.00	2.50
164 Greg Adams	1.00	2.50
165 Kent Manderville	1.00	2.50
166 Steve Dubinsky	1.00	2.50
167 David Nemirovsky	1.00	2.50
168 Todd Bertuzzi	2.00	5.00
169 Frederic Chabot	1.00	2.50
170 Dmitri Mironov	1.00	2.50
171 Pat Peake	1.00	2.50
172 Ed Ward	1.00	2.50
173 Jeff Shantz	1.00	2.50
174 Dave Gagner	1.00	2.50
175 Randy Cunneyworth	1.00	2.50
176 Daymond Langkow	1.00	2.50
177 Alex Hicks	1.00	2.50
178 Darby Hendrickson	1.00	2.50
179 Mike Sullivan	1.00	2.50
180 Anders Eriksson	1.00	2.50
181 Turner Stevenson	1.00	2.50
182 Shane Churla	1.00	2.50
183 Dave Lowry	1.00	2.50
184 Joe Juneau	1.00	2.50
185 Bob Essensa	1.00	2.50
186 James Black	1.00	2.50
187 Michal Grosek	1.00	2.50
188 Tomas Holmstrom	1.00	2.50
189 Ian Laperriere	1.00	2.50
190 Terry Yake	1.00	2.50
191 Jason Smith	1.00	2.50
192 Sergei Zholtok	1.00	2.50
193 Doug Houda	1.00	2.50
194 Guy Carbonneau	1.00	2.50
195 Terry Carkner	1.00	2.50
196 Alexei Gusarov	1.00	2.50
197 Vladimir Tsyplakov	1.00	2.50
198 Jarrod Skalde	1.00	2.50
199 Marty Murray	1.00	2.50
200 Aaron Ward	1.00	2.50
201 Bobby Holik	1.00	2.50
202 Steve Chiasson	1.00	2.50
203 Brantt Myhres	1.00	2.50
204 Eric Messier	1.00	2.50
205 Rene Corbet	1.00	2.50
206 Mathieu Schneider	1.00	2.50
207 Tom Chorske	1.00	2.50
208 Doug Lidster	1.00	2.50
209 Igor Ulanov	1.00	2.50
210 Blair Atcheynum	1.00	2.50
211 Sebastien Bordeleau	1.00	2.50
212 Alexei Morozov	1.00	2.50
213 Vaclav Prospal	1.00	2.50
214 Brad Bombardir	1.00	2.50
215 Mattias Ohlund	1.00	2.50
216 Chris Dingman	1.00	2.50
217 Erik Rasmussen	1.00	2.50
218 Mike Johnson	1.00	2.50
219 Chris Phillips	1.00	2.50
220 Sergei Samsonov	3.00	8.00
221 Patrick Marleau	4.00	10.00
222 Alyn McCauley	1.00	2.50
223 Ryan Vandenbussche	1.00	2.50
224 Daniel Cleary	1.00	2.50
225 Magnus Arvedson	1.00	2.50
226 Brad Isbister	1.00	2.50
227 Pascal Rheaume	1.00	2.50
228 Patrik Elias	3.00	8.00
229 Krzysztof Oliwa	2.00	5.00
230 Tyler Moss	1.00	2.50
231 Jamie Rivers	1.00	2.50
232 Joe Thornton	10.00	25.00
233 Steve Shields	2.00	5.00
234 Dave Scatchard	1.00	2.50
235 Patrick Cote	1.00	2.50
236 Rich Brennan	1.00	2.50
237 Boyd Devereaux	1.00	2.50
238 Per Johan Axelsson	1.00	2.50
239 Craig Millar	1.00	2.50
240 Juha Ylonen	1.00	2.50
241 Donald MacLean	1.00	2.50
242 Jaroslav Svejkovsky	1.00	2.50
243 Marco Sturm	2.00	5.00
244 Steve McKenna	1.00	2.50
245 Derek Morris	1.00	2.50
246 Dean Chynoweth	1.00	2.50
247 Alexander Mogilny SP	12.50	30.00
248 Ray Bourque SP	20.00	50.00
249 Ed Belfour SP	20.00	50.00
250 John LeClair SP	12.50	30.00

1997-98 Be A Player One Timers

Card	Low	High
COMPLETE SET (20)	12.50	30.00
STATED ODDS 1:7		
1 Wayne Gretzky	2.50	6.00
2 Keith Tkachuk	.40	1.00
3 Eric Lindros	.75	2.00
4 Brendan Shanahan	.75	2.00
5 Paul Kariya	.75	2.00
6 Brett Hull	.75	2.00

Card	Low	High
7 Jaromir Jagr	1.25	3.00
8 Teemu Selanne	.75	2.00
9 John LeClair	.40	1.00
10 Mike Modano	.75	2.00
11 Peter Forsberg	1.25	3.00
12 Pavel Bure	.75	2.00
13 Peter Bondra	.40	1.00
14 Saku Koivu	.75	2.00
15 Pat LaFontaine	.40	1.00
16 Patrik Elias	.40	1.00
17 Richard Zednik	.40	1.00
18 Mike Johnson	.40	1.00
19 Marco Sturm	.40	1.00
20 Joe Thornton	1.25	3.00

1997-98 Be A Player Stacking the Pads

Card	Low	High
COMPLETE SET (15)	15.00	40.00
STATED ODDS 1:15		
1 Guy Hebert	.75	2.00
2 Dominik Hasek	2.00	5.00
3 Felix Potvin	1.00	2.50
4 Patrick Roy	4.00	10.00
5 Ed Belfour	1.00	2.50
6 Chris Osgood	.75	2.00
7 Curtis Joseph	1.00	2.50
8 John Vanbiesbrouck	.75	2.00
9 Jocelyn Thibault	.75	2.00
10 Mike Richter	1.00	2.50
11 Martin Brodeur	3.00	8.00
12 Garth Snow	.75	2.00
13 Nikolai Khabibulin	.75	2.00
14 Tommy Salo	.75	2.00
15 Byron Dafoe	.75	2.00

1997-98 Be A Player Take A Number

Card	Low	High
COMPLETE SET (20)	30.00	60.00
STATED ODDS 1:15		
1 Ray Bourque	2.00	5.00
2 Eric Daze	.75	2.00
3 Ed Belfour	1.00	2.50
4 Patrick Roy	5.00	12.00
5 Sergei Fedorov	1.25	3.00
6 John Vanbiesbrouck	.75	2.00
7 Doug Gilmour	.75	2.00
8 Wayne Gretzky	6.00	15.00
9 Bryan Berard	.75	2.00
10 Eric Lindros	1.00	2.50
11 Paul Coffey	1.00	2.50
12 Jeremy Roenick	1.25	3.00
13 Brett Hull	1.25	3.00
14 Pierre Turgeon	.75	2.00
15 Keith Primeau	.75	2.00
16 Daren Puppa	.75	2.00
17 Mark Messier	1.00	2.50
18 Alexander Mogilny	.75	2.00
19 Joe Sakic	2.00	5.00
20 Jaromir Jagr	1.50	4.00

1998-99 Be A Player

The 1998-99 Be A Player set was issued in two series totalling 300 cards and was distributed in eight-card packs with an SRP of $6.99. The fronts featured color action photos of players with a heavy emphasis on rookies and Calder Trophy candidates printed on 30 pt. card stock with a full foil treatment. The backs carried a head photo with player information and career statistics. A gold-foiled parallel version was also created and inserted into random packs.

Card	Low	High
COMPLETE SET (300)	80.00	200.00
COMP.SERIES 1 (150)	40.00	100.00
COMP.SERIES 2 (150)	40.00	100.00
1 Jason Marshall	.25	.60
2 Paul Kariya	.60	1.50
3 Teemu Selanne	.60	1.50
4 Guy Hebert	.50	1.25
5 Ted Drury	.25	.60
6 Byron Dafoe	.50	1.25
7 Rob Dimaio	.25	.60
8 Ray Bourque	1.00	2.50
9 Joe Thornton	1.00	2.50
10 Sergei Samsonov	.50	1.25
11 Dimitri Khristich	.25	.60
12 Michael Peca	.25	.60
13 Jason Woolley	.25	.60
14 Matthew Barnaby	.25	.60
15 Brian Holzinger	.25	.60
16 Dixon Ward	.25	.60
17 Tyler Moss	.25	.60
18 Jarome Iginla	.75	2.00
19 Marty McInnis	.25	.60
20 Andrew Cassels	.25	.60
21 Jason Wiemer	.25	.60
22 Trevor Kidd	.25	.60
23 Keith Primeau	.25	.60
24 Sami Kapanen	.25	.60
25 Robert Kron	.25	.60
26 Glen Wesley	.25	.60
27 Jeff Hackett	.50	1.25
28 Tony Amonte	.50	1.25
29 Alexei Zhamnov	.25	.60
30 Eric Weinrich	.25	.60
31 Jeff Shantz	.25	.60
32 Christian Laflamme	.25	.60
33 Adam Foote	.25	.60
34 Patrick Roy	3.00	8.00
35 Peter Forsberg	1.50	4.00
36 Adam Deadmarsh	.25	.60
37 Joe Sakic	1.25	3.00
38 Eric Lacroix	.25	.60
39 Guy Carbonneau	.25	.60
40 Mike Modano	1.00	2.50
41 Roman Turek	.25	.60
42 Mike Keane	.25	.60
43 Sergei Zubov	.25	.60
44 Jere Lehtinen	.25	.60
45 Sergei Fedorov	1.00	2.50
46 Steve Yzerman	3.00	8.00
47 Chris Osgood	.50	1.25
48 Larry Murphy	.25	.60
49 Vyacheslav Kozlov	.25	.60
50 Darren McCarty	.25	.60
51 Boris Mironov	.25	.60
52 Roman Hamrlik	.25	.60
53 Bill Guerin	.50	1.25
54 Mike Grier	.25	.60
55 Todd Marchant	.25	.60
56 Ray Whitney	.25	.60
57 Dave Gagner	.25	.60
58 Scott Mellanby	.25	.60
59 Robert Svehla	.25	.60
60 Viktor Kozlov	.25	.60
61 Luc Robitaille	.50	1.25
62 Yanic Perreault	.25	.60
63 Jozef Stumpel	.50	1.25
64 Sandy Moger	.25	.60
65 Ian Laperriere	.25	.60
66 Jocelyn Thibault	.50	1.25
67 Dave Manson	.25	.60
68 Mark Recchi	.50	1.25
69 Patrick Poulin	.25	.60
70 Benoit Brunet	.25	.60
71 Turner Stevenson	.25	.60
72 Mike Dunham	.50	1.25
73 Tom Fitzgerald	.25	.60
74 Darren Turcotte	.25	.60
75 Brad Smyth	.25	.60
76 J.J. Daigneault	.25	.60
77 Dave Andreychuk	.50	1.25
78 Jason Arnott	.25	.60
79 Martin Brodeur	1.50	4.00
80 Randy McKay	.25	.60
81 Patrik Elias	.50	1.25
82 Kevin Dean	.25	.60
83 Tommy Salo	.25	.60
84 Scott Lachance	.25	.60
85 Bryan Berard	.50	1.25
86 Robert Reichel	.25	.60
87 Kenny Jonsson	.25	.60
88 Kevin Stevens	.25	.60
89 Mike Richter	.60	1.50
90 Wayne Gretzky	4.00	10.00
91 Adam Graves	.25	.60
92 Alexei Kovalev	.25	.60
93 Ulf Samuelsson	.25	.60
94 Radek Bonk	.25	.60
95 Wade Redden	.25	.60
96 Damian Rhodes	.50	1.25
97 Bruce Gardiner	.25	.60
98 Daniel Alfredsson	.50	1.25
99 Ron Hextall	.25	.60
100 Eric Lindros	.60	1.50
101 Chris Gratton	.50	1.25
102 Dainius Zubrus	.25	.60
103 Luke Richardson	.25	.60
104 Petr Svoboda	.25	.60
105 Rick Tocchet	.25	.60
106 Teppo Numminen	.25	.60
107 Jeremy Roenick	.75	2.00
108 Nikolai Khabibulin	.50	1.25
109 Brad Isbister	.25	.60
110 Peter Skudra	.25	.60
111 Alexei Morozov	.25	.60
112 Kevin Hatcher	.25	.60
113 Darius Kasparaitis	.25	.60
114 Stu Barnes	.25	.60
115 Martin Straka	.25	.60
116 Andrei Zyuzin	.25	.60
117 Marcus Ragnarsson	.25	.60
118 Murray Craven	.25	.60
119 Marco Sturm	.25	.60
120 Patrick Marleau	.25	.60
121 Shawn Burr	.25	.60
122 Grant Fuhr	.50	1.25
123 Chris Pronger	.50	1.25
124 Geoff Courtnall	.25	.60
125 Jim Campbell	.25	.60
126 Pavol Demitra	.50	1.25
127 Todd Gill	.25	.60

128 Cory Cross .25 .60
129 Daymond Langkow .50 1.25
130 Alexander Selivanov .25 .60
131 Mikael Renberg .50 1.25
132 Rob Zamuner .25 .60
133 Stephane Richer .25 .60
134 Fredrik Modin .25 .60
135 Derek King .25 .60
136 Mats Sundin .60 1.50
137 Mike Johnson .25 .60
138 Alyn McCauley .25 .60
139 Jason Smith .25 .60
140 Markus Naslund .60 1.50
141 Alexander Mogilny .50 1.25
142 Mattias Ohlund .25 .60
143 Donald Brashear .25 .60
144 Garth Snow .50 1.25
145 Brian Bellows .25 .60
146 Peter Bondra .25 .60
147 Joe Juneau .50 1.25
148 Steve Konowalchuk .25 .60
149 Ken Klee .25 .60
150 Michal Pivonka .25 .60
151 Steve Rucchin .25 .60
152 Stu Grimson .25 .60
153 Tomas Sandstrom .25 .60
154 Fredrik Olausson .25 .60
155 Travis Green .25 .60
156 Jason Allison .25 .60
157 Steve Heinze .25 .60
158 Rob Tallas .25 .60
159 Darren Van Impe .25 .60
160 Ken Baumgartner .25 .60
161 Peter Ferraro .25 .60
162 Dominik Hasek 1.25 3.00
163 Geoff Sanderson .25 .60
164 Miroslav Satan .25 .60
165 Rob Ray .25 .60
166 Alexei Zhitnik .25 .60
167 Phil Housley .25 .60
168 Theo Fleury .25 .60
169 Ken Wregget .25 .60
170 Valeri Bure .25 .60
171 Rico Fata .25 .60
172 Arturs Irbe .25 .60
173 Sean Hill .25 .60
174 Ron Francis .25 .60
175 Jeff O'Neill .25 .60
176 Paul Ranheim .25 .60
177 Paul Coffey .60 1.50
178 Doug Gilmour .50 1.25
179 Eric Daze .50 1.25
180 Chris Chelios .25 .60
181 Bob Probert .25 .60
182 Mark Fitzpatrick .25 .60
183 Alexei Gusarov .25 .60
184 Sylvain Lefebvre .25 .60
185 Craig Billington .25 .60
186 Valeri Kamensky .25 .60
187 Milan Hejduk RC 1.50 4.00
188 Sandis Ozolinsh .25 .60
189 Brett Hull .75 2.00
190 Ed Belfour .25 .60
191 Darryl Sydor .25 .60
192 Sergei Gusev RC .25 .60
193 Joe Nieuwendyk .25 .60
194 Derian Hatcher .25 .60
195 Brendan Shanahan .60 1.50
196 Tomas Holmstrom .25 .60
197 Nicklas Lidstrom .60 1.50
198 Martin Lapointe .25 .60
199 Igor Larionov .25 .60
200 Kris Draper .25 .60
201 Kelly Buchberger .25 .60
202 Andrei Kovalenko .25 .60
203 Josef Beranek .25 .60
204 Mikhail Shtalenkov .25 .60
205 Pat Falloon .25 .60
206 Mark Parrish RC .60 1.50
207 Terry Carkner .25 .60
208 Rob Niedermayer .25 .60
209 Sean Burke .25 .60
210 Oleg Kvasha RC .60 1.50
211 Pavel Bure .60 1.50
212 Rob Blake .25 .60
213 Vladimir Tsyplakov .25 .60
214 Stephane Fiset .25 .60
215 Steve Duchesne .25 .60
216 Patrice Brisebois .25 .60
217 Vincent Damphousse .25 .60
218 Saku Koivu .60 1.50
219 Jose Theodore .75 2.00
220 Brett Clark RC .25 .60
221 Martin Rucinsky .25 .60
222 Vladimir Malakhov .25 .60
223 Sergei Krivokrasov .25 .60
224 Scott Walker .25 .60
225 Greg Johnson .25 .60
226 Cliff Ronning .25 .60
227 Eric Fichaud .25 .60
228 Bob Carpenter .25 .60
229 Scott Daniels .25 .60
230 Brian Rolston .25 .60
231 Sergei Brylin .25 .60
232 Scott Niedermayer .25 .60
233 Bryan Smolinski .25 .60
234 Trevor Linden .25 .60
235 Eric Brewer .25 .60
236 Zigmund Palffy .25 .60
237 Sergei Nemchinov .25 .60
238 Brian Leetch .25 .60
239 Mathieu Schneider .25 .60
240 Niklas Sundstrom .25 .60
241 Manny Malhotra .50 1.25
242 Jeff Beukeboom .25 .60
243 Petr Nedved .25 .60
244 Ron Tugnutt .25 .60
245 Shaun Van Allen .25 .60
246 Alexei Yashin .25 .60
247 Jason York .25 .60
248 Shawn McEachern .25 .60
249 Marian Hossa .60 1.50
250 John LeClair .60 1.50
251 Rod Brind'Amour .25 .60
252 John Vanbiesbrouck .50 1.25
253 Eric Desjardins .50 1.25
254 Valeri Zelepukin .25 .60
255 Karl Dykhuis .25 .60
256 Keith Tkachuk .60 1.50
257 Dallas Drake .25 .60
258 Oleg Tverdovsky .25 .60
259 Jyrki Lumme .25 .60
260 Jimmy Waite .25 .60
261 Jaromir Jagr 1.00 2.50
262 German Titov .25 .60
263 Robert Lang .25 .60
264 Brad Werenka .25 .60
265 Rob Brown .25 .60
266 Bobby Dollas .25 .60
267 Jeff Friesen .25 .60
268 Andy Sutton RC .25 .60
269 Steve Shields .25 .60
270 Mike Ricci .25 .60
271 Joe Murphy .25 .60
272 Tony Granato .25 .60
273 Jamie McLennan .50 1.25
274 Al MacInnis .25 .60
275 Pierre Turgeon .25 .60
276 Kelly Chase .25 .60
277 Craig Conroy .25 .60
278 Scott Young .25 .60
279 Vincent Lecavalier 1.25 3.00
280 Wendel Clark .25 .60
281 Daren Puppa .25 .60
282 Sandy McCarthy .25 .60
283 Daniil Markov .25 .60
284 Curtis Joseph .60 1.50
285 Sergei Berezin .50 1.25
286 Steve Sullivan .25 .60
287 Tomas Kaberle RC .75 2.00
288 Kris King .25 .60
289 Igor Korolev .25 .60
290 Mark Messier .60 1.50
291 Bill Muckalt RC .25 .60
292 Todd Bertuzzi .60 1.50
293 Brad May .25 .60
294 Peter Zezel .25 .60
295 Dmitri Mironov .25 .60
296 Adam Oates .25 .60
297 Calle Johansson .25 .60
298 Craig Berube .25 .60
299 Sergei Gonchar .25 .60
300 Andrei Nikolishin .25 .60

1998-99 Be A Player Press Release

This 300-card set paralleled the basic series, but carried a gold foil "Press Release" stamp on the card fronts. The cards were rumored to be available only to members of the media.

*SINGLES: 20X TO 50X BASIC CARDS
ISSUED AS MEDIA PROMOS

1998-99 Be A Player Gold

*VETERANS: 2X TO 5X BASIC CARDS
*ROOKIES: 1.2X TO 3X BASIC CARDS
RANDOM INSERTS IN PACKS

1998-99 Be A Player Autographs

Inserted one per pack, this 300-card set was an autographed version of the base set. SP's had a stated print run of 450 except for the Gretzky card which was reported to be limited to 90 copies. A gold-foil parallel to the set was also created and inserted in random packs. Gold SP's had a stated print run of 50 except for the Gretzky gold parallel which was numbered out of 9.

OVERALL AUTO ODDS ONE PER PACK
SILVER SP PRINT RUN 90-450
1 Jason Marshall 1.50 4.00
2 Paul Kariya SP 15.00 40.00
3 Teemu Selanne SP 20.00 50.00
4 Guy Hebert 4.00 10.00
5 Ted Drury 1.50 4.00
6 Byron Dafoe 1.50 4.00
7 Rob Dimaio 1.50 4.00
8 Ray Bourque SP 20.00 50.00
9 Joe Thornton 8.00 20.00
10 Sergei Samsonov 4.00 10.00
11 Dimitri Khristich 1.50 4.00
12 Michael Peca 1.50 4.00
13 Jason Woolley 1.50 4.00
14 Matthew Barnaby 1.50 4.00
15 Brian Holzinger 1.50 4.00
16 Dixon Ward 1.50 4.00
17 Tyler Moss 1.50 4.00
18 Jarome Iginla 8.00 20.00
19 Marty McInnis 1.50 4.00
20 Andrew Cassels 1.50 4.00
21 Jason Wiemer 1.50 4.00
22 Trevor Kidd 4.00 10.00
23 Keith Primeau 1.50 4.00
24 Sami Kapanen 1.50 4.00
25 Robert Kron 1.50 4.00
26 Glen Wesley 1.50 4.00
27 Jeff Hackett 4.00 10.00
28 Tony Amonte SP 6.00 15.00
29 Alexei Zhamnov 1.50 4.00
30 Eric Weinrich 1.50 4.00
31 Jeff Shantz 1.50 4.00
32 Christian Laflamme 1.50 4.00
33 Adam Foote 1.50 4.00
34 Patrick Roy SP 40.00 100.00
35 Peter Forsberg SP 20.00 50.00
36 Adam Deadmarsh 1.50 4.00
37 Joe Sakic SP 30.00 80.00
38 Eric Lacroix 1.50 4.00
39 Guy Carbonneau 1.50 4.00
40 Mike Modano SP 15.00 40.00
41 Roman Turek 1.50 4.00
42 Mike Keane 1.50 4.00
43 Sergei Zubov 1.50 4.00
44 Jere Lehtinen 4.00 10.00
45 Sergei Fedorov SP 10.00 25.00
46 Steve Yzerman SP 40.00 100.00
47 Chris Osgood 4.00 10.00
48 Larry Murphy 1.50 4.00
49 Vyacheslav Kozlov 4.00 10.00
50 Darren McCarty 4.00 10.00
51 Boris Mironov 1.50 4.00
52 Roman Hamrlik 1.50 4.00
53 Bill Guerin 1.50 4.00
54 Mike Grier 1.50 4.00
55 Todd Marchant 1.50 4.00
56 Ray Whitney 1.50 4.00
57 Dave Gagner 1.50 4.00
58 Scott Mellanby 1.50 4.00
59 Robert Svehla 1.50 4.00
60 Viktor Kozlov 1.50 4.00
61 Luc Robitaille 6.00 15.00
62 Yanic Perreault 1.50 4.00
63 Jozef Stumpel 1.50 4.00
64 Sandy Moger 1.50 4.00
65 Ian Laperriere 1.50 4.00
66 Jocelyn Thibault 4.00 10.00
67 Dave Manson 1.50 4.00
68 Mark Recchi SP 6.00 15.00
69 Patrick Poulin 1.50 4.00
70 Benoit Brunet 1.50 4.00
71 Turner Stevenson 1.50 4.00
72 Mike Dunham 4.00 10.00
73 Tom Fitzgerald 1.50 4.00
74 Darren Turcotte 1.50 4.00
75 Brad Smyth 1.50 4.00
76 J.J. Daigneault 1.50 4.00
77 Dave Andreychuk 4.00 10.00
78 Jason Arnott 1.50 4.00
79 Martin Brodeur SP 30.00 80.00
80 Randy McKay 1.50 4.00
81 Patrik Elias 4.00 10.00
82 Kevin Dean 1.50 4.00
83 Tommy Salo 4.00 10.00
84 Scott Lachance 1.50 4.00
85 Bryan Berard 1.50 4.00
86 Robert Reichel 1.50 4.00
87 Kenny Jonsson 1.50 4.00
88 Kevin Stevens 1.50 4.00
89 Mike Richter SP 10.00 25.00
90 Wayne Gretzky/90 200.00 400.00
91 Adam Graves 1.50 4.00
92 Alexei Kovalev 4.00 10.00
93 Ulf Samuelsson 1.50 4.00
94 Radek Bonk 1.50 4.00
95 Wade Redden 1.50 4.00
96 Damian Rhodes 1.50 4.00
97 Bruce Gardiner 1.50 4.00
98 Daniel Alfredsson 4.00 10.00
99 Ron Hextall 4.00 10.00
100 Eric Lindros SP 8.00 20.00
101 Chris Gratton 1.50 4.00
102 Dainius Zubrus 1.50 4.00
103 Luke Richardson 1.50 4.00
104 Petr Svoboda 1.50 4.00
105 Rick Tocchet 4.00 10.00
106 Teppo Numminen 1.50 4.00
107 Jeremy Roenick SP 12.00 30.00
108 Nikolai Khabibulin 4.00 10.00
109 Brad Isbister 1.50 4.00
110 Peter Skudra 1.50 4.00
111 Alexei Morozov 1.50 4.00
112 Kevin Hatcher 1.50 4.00
113 Darius Kasparaitis 1.50 4.00
114 Stu Barnes 1.50 4.00
115 Martin Straka 1.50 4.00
116 Andrei Zyuzin 1.50 4.00
117 Marcus Ragnarsson 1.50 4.00
118 Murray Craven 1.50 4.00
119 Marco Sturm 1.50 4.00
120 Patrick Marleau 4.00 10.00
121 Shawn Burr 1.50 4.00
122 Grant Fuhr 4.00 10.00
123 Chris Pronger 4.00 10.00
124 Geoff Courtnall 1.50 4.00
125 Jim Campbell 1.50 4.00
126 Pavol Demitra 4.00 10.00
127 Todd Gill 1.50 4.00
128 Cory Cross 1.50 4.00
129 Daymond Langkow 1.50 4.00
130 Alexander Selivanov 1.50 4.00
131 Mikael Renberg 1.50 4.00
132 Rob Zamuner 1.50 4.00
133 Stephane Richer 1.50 4.00
134 Fredrik Modin 1.50 4.00
135 Derek King 1.50 4.00
136 Mats Sundin SP 15.00 40.00
137 Mike Johnson 1.50 4.00
138 Alyn McCauley 1.50 4.00
139 Jason Smith 1.50 4.00
140 Markus Naslund 6.00 15.00
141 Alexander Mogilny SP 6.00 15.00
142 Mattias Ohlund 1.50 4.00
143 Donald Brashear 1.50 4.00
144 Garth Snow 1.50 4.00
145 Brian Bellows 1.50 4.00
146 Peter Bondra SP 6.00 15.00
147 Joe Juneau 1.50 4.00
148 Steve Konowalchuk 1.50 4.00
149 Ken Klee 1.50 4.00
150 Michal Pivonka 1.50 4.00
151 Steve Rucchin 1.50 4.00
152 Stu Grimson 1.50 4.00
153 Tomas Sandstrom 1.50 4.00
154 Fredrik Olausson 1.50 4.00
155 Travis Green 1.50 4.00
156 Jason Allison 1.50 4.00
157 Steve Heinze 1.50 4.00
158 Rob Tallas 1.50 4.00
159 Darren Van Impe 1.50 4.00
160 Ken Baumgartner 1.50 4.00
161 Peter Ferraro 1.50 4.00
162 Dominik Hasek SP 25.00 60.00
163 Geoff Sanderson 1.50 4.00
164 Miroslav Satan 4.00 10.00
165 Rob Ray 4.00 10.00
166 Alexei Zhitnik 1.50 4.00
167 Phil Housley 1.50 4.00
168 Theo Fleury SP 10.00 25.00
169 Ken Wregget 1.50 4.00
170 Valeri Bure 1.50 4.00
171 Rico Fata 1.50 4.00
172 Arturs Irbe 4.00 10.00
173 Sean Hill 1.50 4.00
174 Ron Francis SP 8.00 20.00
175 Jeff O'Neill 1.50 4.00
176 Paul Ranheim 1.50 4.00
177 Paul Coffey SP 10.00 25.00
178 Doug Gilmour SP 8.00 20.00
179 Eric Daze 1.50 4.00
180 Chris Chelios SP 10.00 25.00
181 Bob Probert 4.00 10.00
182 Mark Fitzpatrick 1.50 4.00
183 Alexei Gusarov 1.50 4.00
184 Sylvain Lefebvre 1.50 4.00
185 Craig Billington 1.50 4.00
186 Valeri Kamensky 1.50 4.00
187 Milan Hejduk 6.00 15.00
188 Sandis Ozolinsh 1.50 4.00
189 Brett Hull SP 15.00 40.00
190 Ed Belfour SP 12.00 30.00
191 Darryl Sydor 1.50 4.00
192 Sergei Gusev 1.50 4.00
193 Joe Nieuwendyk SP 6.00 15.00
194 Derian Hatcher 1.50 4.00
195 Brendan Shanahan SP 8.00 20.00
196 Tomas Holmstrom 4.00 10.00
197 Nicklas Lidstrom 6.00 15.00
198 Martin Lapointe 4.00 10.00
199 Igor Larionov 1.50 4.00
200 Kris Draper 1.50 4.00
201 Kelly Buchberger 1.50 4.00
202 Andrei Kovalenko 1.50 4.00
203 Josef Beranek 1.50 4.00
204 Mikhail Shtalenkov 1.50 4.00
205 Pat Falloon 1.50 4.00
206 Mark Parrish 1.50 4.00
207 Terry Carkner 1.50 4.00
208 Rob Niedermayer 1.50 4.00
209 Sean Burke 4.00 10.00
210 Oleg Kvasha 1.50 4.00
211 Pavel Bure SP 15.00 40.00
212 Rob Blake 4.00 10.00
213 Vladimir Tsyplakov 1.50 4.00
214 Stephane Fiset 1.50 4.00
215 Steve Duchesne 1.50 4.00
216 Patrice Brisebois 1.50 4.00
217 Vincent Damphousse 1.50 4.00
218 Saku Koivu 6.00 15.00
219 Jose Theodore 8.00 20.00
220 Brett Clark 1.50 4.00
221 Martin Rucinsky 1.50 4.00
222 Vladimir Malakhov 1.50 4.00
223 Sergei Krivokrasov 1.50 4.00
224 Scott Walker 1.50 4.00
225 Greg Johnson 1.50 4.00
226 Cliff Ronning 1.50 4.00
227 Eric Fichaud 1.50 4.00
228 Bob Carpenter 1.50 4.00
229 Scott Daniels 1.50 4.00
230 Brian Rolston 1.50 4.00
231 Sergei Brylin 1.50 4.00
232 Scott Niedermayer 1.50 4.00
233 Bryan Smolinski 1.50 4.00
234 Trevor Linden 4.00 10.00
235 Eric Brewer 1.50 4.00
236 Zigmund Palffy SP 6.00 15.00
237 Sergei Nemchinov 1.50 4.00
238 Brian Leetch SP 6.00 15.00
239 Mathieu Schneider 1.50 4.00
240 Niklas Sundstrom 1.50 4.00
241 Manny Malhotra 1.50 4.00
242 Jeff Beukeboom 1.50 4.00
243 Petr Nedved 1.50 4.00
244 Ron Tugnutt 1.50 4.00
245 Shawn Van Allen 1.50 4.00
246 Alexei Yashin 1.50 4.00
247 Jason York 1.50 4.00
248 Shawn McEachern 1.50 4.00
249 Marian Hossa 6.00 15.00
250 John LeClair SP 8.00 20.00
251 Rod Brind'Amour 4.00 10.00
252 John Vanbiesbrouck 4.00 10.00
253 Eric Desjardins 1.50 4.00
254 Valeri Zelepukin 1.50 4.00
255 Karl Dykhuis 1.50 4.00
256 Keith Tkachuk 4.00 10.00
257 Dallas Drake 1.50 4.00
258 Oleg Tverdovsky 1.50 4.00
259 Jyrki Lumme 1.50 4.00
260 Jimmy Waite 1.50 4.00
261 Jaromir Jagr SP 20.00 50.00
262 German Titov 1.50 4.00
263 Robert Lang 1.50 4.00
264 Brad Werenka 1.50 4.00
265 Rob Brown 1.50 4.00
266 Bobby Dollas 1.50 4.00
267 Jeff Friesen 1.50 4.00
268 Andy Sutton 1.50 4.00
269 Steve Shields 4.00 10.00
270 Mike Ricci 1.50 4.00
271 Joe Murphy 1.50 4.00
272 Tony Granato 1.50 4.00
273 Jamie McLennan 1.50 4.00
274 Al MacInnis SP 10.00 25.00
275 Pierre Turgeon 1.50 4.00
276 Kelly Chase 1.50 4.00
277 Craig Conroy 1.50 4.00
278 Scott Young 1.50 4.00
279 Vincent Lecavalier 8.00 20.00
280 Wendel Clark 4.00 10.00
281 Daren Puppa 1.50 4.00
282 Sandy McCarthy 1.50 4.00
283 Daniil Markov 1.50 4.00
284 Curtis Joseph SP 10.00 25.00
285 Sergei Berezin 1.50 4.00
286 Steve Sullivan 1.50 4.00
287 Tomas Kaberle 1.50 4.00
288 Kris King 1.50 4.00
289 Igor Korolev 1.50 4.00
290 Mark Messier SP 50.00 100.00
291 Bill Muckalt 1.50 4.00
292 Todd Bertuzzi 6.00 15.00
293 Brad May 1.50 4.00
294 Peter Zezel 1.50 4.00
295 Dmitri Mironov 1.50 4.00
296 Adam Oates SP 6.00 15.00
297 Calle Johansson 1.50 4.00
298 Craig Berube 1.50 4.00
299 Sergei Gonchar 1.50 4.00
300 Andrei Nikolishin 1.50 4.00

1998-99 Be A Player Autographs Gold

*GOLD: .8X TO 2X SILVER AU
*GOLD: .6X TO 1.5X SILVER AU SP
GOLD SP ANNC'd PRINT RUN 50
90 Wayne Gretzky/9*

1998-99 Be A Player All-Star Game Used Sticks

ANNOUNCED PRINT RUN 100 SETS
S1 Eric Lindros 15.00 40.00
S2 Peter Forsberg 25.00 60.00
S3 Teemu Selanne 15.00 40.00
S4 Mike Modano 15.00 40.00
S5 Mats Sundin 15.00 40.00
S6 Patrick Roy 40.00 100.00
S7 Paul Kariya 15.00 40.00
S8 Martin Brodeur 30.00 80.00
S9 Steve Yzerman 40.00 100.00
S10 Mark Messier 15.00 40.00
S11 Brett Hull 15.00 40.00
S12 Joe Sakic 25.00 60.00
S13 Alexander Mogilny 15.00 40.00
S14 Sergei Fedorov 20.00 50.00
S15 Ray Bourque 25.00 60.00
S16 Jeremy Roenick 15.00 40.00
S17 Jaromir Jagr 30.00 80.00
S18 Dominik Hasek 15.00 40.00
S19 Chris Chelios 15.00 40.00
S20 John LeClair 15.00 40.00
S21 Brendan Shanahan 15.00 40.00
S22 Ed Belfour 15.00 40.00
S23 Wayne Gretzky 125.00 300.00

1998-99 Be A Player All-Star Game Used Jerseys

ANNOUNCED PRINT RUN 100 SETS
AS1 Eric Lindros 12.50 30.00
AS2 Peter Forsberg 20.00 50.00
AS3 Teemu Selanne 12.50 30.00
AS4 Mike Modano 12.50 30.00
AS5 Mats Sundin 12.50 30.00
AS6 Patrick Roy 30.00 80.00
AS7 Paul Kariya 12.50 30.00
AS8 Martin Brodeur 25.00 60.00
AS9 Steve Yzerman 30.00 80.00
AS10 Mark Messier 12.50 30.00
AS11 Paul Coffey 12.50 30.00
AS12 Brett Hull 12.50 30.00
AS13 Joe Sakic 15.00 40.00
AS14 Alexander Mogilny 8.00 20.00
AS15 Sergei Fedorov 15.00 40.00
AS16 Ray Bourque 20.00 50.00
AS17 Jeremy Roenick 12.50 30.00
AS18 Jaromir Jagr 15.00 40.00
AS19 Pavel Bure 12.50 30.00
AS20 Dominik Hasek 20.00 50.00
AS21 Chris Chelios 12.50 30.00
AS22 John LeClair 12.50 30.00
AS23 Brendan Shanahan 12.50 30.00
AS24 Ed Belfour 12.50 30.00
AS25 Wayne Gretzky 100.00 200.00

1998-99 Be A Player All-Star Legend Gordie Howe

Randomly inserted in packs, this two-card set honored Hall-of-Famer Gordie Howe. One card in the set carried a piece of Howe's Detroit Red Wings jerseys embedded in the cards. Each card was autographed by Gordie Howe and eahc card was limited to just 90 copies.

ANNOUNCED PRINT RUN 90
GH1 Gordie Howe GJ AU 125.00 250.00
GH2 Gordie Howe AU 100.00 200.00

1998-99 Be A Player All-Star Milestones

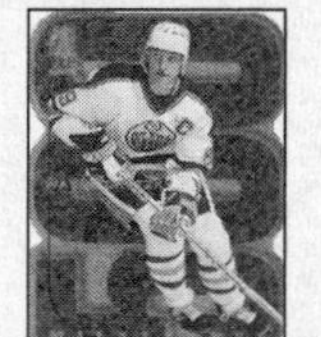

COMPLETE SET (22) 50.00 100.00
RANDOM INSERTS IN PACKS
M1 Wayne Gretzky 4.00 10.00
M2 Mark Messier 2.00 5.00
M3 Dino Ciccarelli 1.50 4.00
M4 Steve Yzerman 3.00 8.00
M5 Dave Andreychuk 1.50 4.00
M6 Brett Hull 2.50 6.00
M7 Wayne Gretzky 4.00 10.00
M8 Mark Messier 2.00 5.00
M9 Dino Ciccarelli 1.50 4.00
M10 Steve Yzerman 3.00 8.00
M11 Bernie Nicholls 1.50 4.00
M12 Ron Francis 1.50 4.00
M13 Ray Bourque 2.50 6.00
M14 Paul Coffey 2.00 5.00
M15 Adam Oates 1.50 4.00
M16 Phil Housley 1.50 4.00
M17 Dale Hunter 1.50 4.00
M18 Luc Robitaille 1.50 4.00
M19 Doug Gilmour 1.50 4.00
M20 Larry Murphy 1.50 4.00
M21 Dave Andreychuk 1.50 4.00
M22 Al MacInnis 1.50 4.00

1998-99 Be A Player Playoff Game Used Jerseys

ANNOUNCED PRINT RUN 100 SETS
UNPRICED JSY AUTO PRINT RUN 10
G1 Wayne Gretzky 100.00 200.00
G2 Mats Sundin 12.50 30.00
G3 Jeremy Roenick 12.50 30.00
G4 Eric Lindros 12.50 30.00
G5 John LeClair 12.50 30.00
G6 Joe Sakic 15.00 40.00
G7 Peter Forsberg 20.00 50.00
G8 Patrick Roy 40.00 100.00
G9 Martin Brodeur 25.00 60.00
G10 Pavel Bure 12.50 30.00
G11 Teemu Selanne 12.50 30.00
G12 Paul Kariya 12.50 30.00
G13 Ray Bourque 20.00 50.00
G14 Brendan Shanahan 12.50 30.00
G15 Steve Yzerman 30.00 80.00
G16 Sergei Fedorov 15.00 40.00
G17 Mike Modano 12.50 30.00
G18 Brett Hull 12.50 30.00
G19 Ed Belfour 12.50 30.00
G20 Mark Messier 12.50 30.00
G21 Alexander Mogilny 8.00 20.00
G22 Tony Amonte 8.00 20.00
G23 Jaromir Jagr 15.00 40.00
G24 Alexei Yashin 8.00 20.00

1998-99 Be A Player Playoff Highlights

COMPLETE SET (18) 60.00 125.00
H1 Mark Messier 2.00 5.00
H2 Peter Forsberg 5.00 12.00
H3 Wayne Gretzky 12.50 30.00
H4 Martin Brodeur 5.00 12.00
H5 Jaromir Jagr 3.00 8.00
H6 Mike Richter 2.00 5.00
H7 Steve Yzerman 10.00 25.00
H8 Patrick Roy 10.00 25.00
H9 Paul Coffey 2.00 5.00
H10 Joe Sakic 4.00 10.00
H11 John Vanbiesbrouck 2.00 5.00
H12 Pavel Bure 2.00 5.00
H13 Chris Osgood 2.00 5.00
H14 Chris Chelios 2.00 5.00
H15 Curtis Joseph 2.00 5.00
H16 Brian Leetch 2.00 5.00
H17 Sergei Fedorov 3.00 8.00
H18 Doug Gilmour 2.00 5.00

1998-99 Be A Player Playoff Legend Mario Lemieux

Randomly inserted in packs, this 4-card set was limited to a print run of just 66 sets. Each card featured one or two pieces of game-used memorabilia and an autograph from Mario Lemieux.

STATED PRINT RUN 66 CARDS
L1 All-Star Jersey/AU Card 150.00 300.00
L2 Penguins Jersey/AU Card 150.00 300.00
L3 All-Star Jsy/Stick/AU Card 200.00 400.00
L4 Peng.Jsy/Stick/AU Card 200.00 400.00

1998-99 Be A Player Playoff Practice Used Jerseys

ANNOUNCED PRINT RUN 100 SETS
P1 Brett Hull 10.00 25.00
P2 Alexander Mogilny 6.00 15.00
P3 Ray Bourque 15.00 40.00
P4 Pavel Bure 10.00 25.00
P5 Steve Yzerman 30.00 80.00
P6 Ed Belfour 10.00 25.00
P7 Jaromir Jagr 12.50 30.00
P8 Sergei Fedorov 12.50 30.00
P9 Teemu Selanne 10.00 25.00
P10 Eric Lindros 10.00 25.00
P11 Tony Amonte 8.00 20.00
P12 Jeremy Roenick 10.00 25.00
P13 John LeClair 10.00 25.00
P14 Mike Modano 10.00 25.00
P15 Joe Sakic 12.50 30.00
P16 Patrick Roy 30.00 80.00
P17 Mark Messier 10.00 25.00
P18 Paul Kariya 10.00 25.00
P19 Martin Brodeur 20.00 50.00
P20 Mats Sundin 25.00 60.00
P21 Brendan Shanahan 10.00 25.00
P22 Peter Forsberg 20.00 50.00
P23 Alexei Yashin 6.00 15.00
P24 Wayne Gretzky 100.00 150.00

1998-99 Be A Player Atlanta National

*SINGLES: 1.2X TO 3X BASIC CARDS
AVAILABLE AT ATLANTA NATIONAL '99
AVAILABLE VIA PACK REDEMPTION ONLY

1998-99 Be A Player Toronto Fall Expo

These cards were made available as a wrapper redemption at the Fall Expo '99 show in Toronto, Ontario. These cards parallel the 1998-99 Be A Player set, but were serial numbered out of 5 and carry an embossed Toronto Fall Expo logo. Due to the limited distribution of these cards, there is not a significant amount of market data to price them, though they do have secondary market interest.

UNPRICED FALL EXPO PRINT RUN 5

1998-99 Be A Player Toronto Spring Expo

Available via wrapper redemption at the Be A Player booth during the 1999 Toronto Spring Expo Show. Each wrapper was exchanged for one random card from 1998-99 Be A Player Series II that was serial-numbered out of 25 and embossed with the Spring Expo logo.

*SINGLES: 15X TO 40X BASIC CARDS

1998-99 Be A Player Tampa Bay All-Star Game

These cards were only available to children during the special kid's preview at the 1999 NHL All-Star Game in Tampa Bay. These cards parallel the 1998-99 Be A Player Series I, and each card was hand serial-numbered to 50 with an embossed silver All-Star logo.

*SINGLES: 10X TO 25X BASIC CARDS

2005-06 Be A Player

Released in August 2005, Be A Player was produced by Upper Deck for the first time. Each pack contained 5 cards including one autograph card and carried a $20 SRP, each box carried 10 packs.

COMPLETE SET (90) 15.00 40.00
1 Jean-Sebastien Giguere .60 1.50
2 Joffrey Lupul .50 1.25
3 Ilya Kovalchuk 1.00 2.50
4 Dany Heatley .75 2.00
5 Kari Lehtonen .75 2.00
6 Glen Murray .50 1.25
7 Joe Thornton 1.25 3.00
8 Andrew Raycroft .60 1.50
9 Miroslav Satan .50 1.25
10 Chris Drury .60 1.50
11 Daniel Briere .60 1.50
12 Jarome Iginla .60 1.50
13 Miikka Kiprusoff .75 2.00
14 Martin Gelinas .25 .60
15 Erik Cole .50 1.25
16 Eric Staal .60 1.50
17 Tuomo Ruutu .50 1.25
18 Eric Daze .60 1.50
19 Joe Sakic 1.50 4.00
20 Peter Forsberg 1.25 3.00
21 Milan Hejduk .75 2.00
22 Rob Blake .60 1.50
23 Alex Tanguay .60 1.50
24 Rick Nash 1.00 2.50
25 Nikolai Zherdev .60 1.50
26 Todd Marchant .25 .60
27 Marty Turco .60 1.50
28 Brenden Morrow .60 1.50
29 Mike Modano .75 2.00
30 Brendan Shanahan .75 2.00
31 Nicklas Lidstrom .75 2.00
32 Pavel Datsyuk .75 2.00
33 Steve Yzerman 2.00 5.00
34 Curtis Joseph .75 2.00
35 Ryan Smyth .60 1.50
36 Jason Smith .25 .60
37 Ty Conklin .60 1.50
38 Olli Jokinen .60 1.50
39 Roberto Luongo 1.25 3.00
40 Jay Bouwmeester .50 1.25
41 Zigmund Palffy .60 1.50
42 Luc Robitaille .60 1.50
43 Alexander Frolov .60 1.50
44 Marian Gaborik .75 2.00
45 Dwayne Roloson .60 1.50
46 Saku Koivu .75 2.00
47 Jose Theodore .60 1.50
48 Michael Ryder .60 1.50
49 Tomas Vokoun .60 1.50
50 Steve Sullivan .50 1.25
51 Jordin Tootoo .25 .60
52 Martin Brodeur 1.25 3.00
53 Patrik Elias .60 1.50
54 Scott Gomez .60 1.50
55 Rick DiPietro .60 1.50
56 Mike Peca .50 1.25

57 Trent Hunter .50 1.25
58 Jaromir Jagr 1.25 3.00
59 Bobby Holik .50 1.25
60 Dan Blackburn .40 1.00
61 Marian Hossa .60 1.50
62 Jason Spezza .75 2.00
63 Daniel Alfredsson .60 1.50
64 Keith Primeau .50 1.25
65 Simon Gagne .75 2.00
66 Robert Esche .60 1.50
67 Brett Hull .50 1.25
68 Shane Doan .50 1.25
69 Mike Comrie .40 1.00
70 Marc-Andre Fleury .60 1.50
71 Mark Recchi .60 1.50
72 Mario Lemieux 2.00 5.00
73 Patrick Marleau .60 1.50
74 Jonathan Cheechoo .75 2.00
75 Evgeni Nabokov .60 1.50
76 Chris Pronger .60 1.50
77 Doug Weight .60 1.50
78 Keith Tkachuk .75 2.00
79 Martin St. Louis .60 1.50
80 Vincent Lecavalier .75 2.00
81 Nikolai Khabibulin .75 2.00
82 Brad Richards .60 1.50
83 Dave Andreychuk .50 1.25
84 Gary Roberts .25 .60
85 Mats Sundin .75 2.00
86 Joe Nieuwendyk .60 1.50
87 Markus Naslund .75 2.00
88 Brendan Morrison .50 1.25
89 Ed Jovanovski .60 1.50
90 Olaf Kolzig .60 1.50

2005-06 Be A Player First Period

*STARS: 2X TO 5X BASIC CARDS
PRINT RUN 100 SER.#'d SETS

2005-06 Be A Player Second Period

*STARS: 5X TO 12X BASIC CARDS
PRINT RUN 50 SER.#'d SETS

2005-06 Be A Player Third Period

PRINT RUN 10 SER.#'d SETS
NOT PRICED DUE TO SCARCITY

2005-06 Be A Player Overtime

PRINT RUN 1 SER.#'d SET
NOT PRICED DUE TO SCARCITY

2005-06 Be A Player Class Action

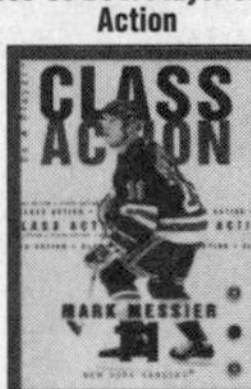

COMPLETE SET
PRINT RUN 299 SER.#'d SETS
CA1 Keith Tkachuk 2.50 6.00
CA2 Dany Heatley 2.50 6.00
CA3 Ilya Kovalchuk 3.00 8.00
CA4 Joe Thornton 4.00 10.00
CA5 Jarome Iginla 2.00 5.00
CA6 Peter Forsberg 4.00 10.00
CA7 Joe Sakic 5.00 12.00
CA8 Rick Nash 3.00 8.00
CA9 Mike Modano 2.50 6.00
CA10 Steve Yzerman 5.00 12.00
CA11 Mats Sundin 2.50 6.00
CA12 Martin St. Louis 2.00 5.00
CA13 Jose Theodore 2.50 6.00
CA14 Miikka Kiprusoff 2.50 6.00
CA15 Martin Brodeur 4.00 10.00
CA16 Mark Messier 1.50 4.00
CA17 Markus Naslund 2.50 6.00
CA18 Jeremy Roenick 2.50 6.00
CA19 Brett Hull 2.00 5.00
CA20 Mario Lemieux 10.00 25.00

2005-06 Be A Player Dual Signatures

STATED ODDS 1:10
AR D.Andreychuk/L.Robitaille 8.00 20.00
BD Daniel Briere 8.00 20.00
Chris Drury
BF Martin Brodeur 40.00 100.00
Marc-Andre Fleury
BS Brian Rafalski 5.00 12.00
Scott Niedermayer
DK Dany Heatley 10.00 25.00
Kari Lehtonen
DL Kris Draper 20.00 50.00
Nicklas Lidstrom
DR M.Denis/D.Roloson 8.00 20.00
DT E.Daze/J.Thibault 5.00 12.00
FL Marc Andre Fleury 20.00 50.00
Roberto Luongo
GB Bill Guerin 5.00 12.00
Brenden Morrow
GD Bill Guerin/C.Drury 5.00 12.00
HH Marian Hossa 12.00 30.00
Dominik Hasek
HR Marian Hossa 8.00 20.00
Wade Redden
HT Gordie Howe 125.00 250.00
Joe Thornton
IM Jarome Iginla 10.00 25.00
Patrick Marleau
JE J.Spezza/E.Staal 12.00 30.00
KC K.Tkachuk/C.Pronger 10.00 25.00
LI Martin St. Louis 12.00 30.00
Jarome Iginla
LL Martin St.Louis 12.50 30.00
Vincent Lecavalier
LP Nicklas Lidstrom 20.00 50.00
Chris Pronger
LW Roberto Luongo 8.00 20.00
Stephen Weiss
MA Michael Peca 5.00 12.00
Adrian Aucoin
MC P.Marleau/J.Cheechoo 8.00 20.00
ND R.Nash/M.Denis 12.00 30.00
NL Markus Naslund 12.00 30.00
Trevor Linden
NT R.Nash/J.Thornton 15.00 40.00
PA Paul Kariya 12.00 30.00
Alex Tanguay
PE Keith Primeau 5.00 12.00
Robert Esche
PP Michael Peca 5.00 12.00
Mark Parrish
RB Luc Robitaille 5.00 12.00
Dustin Brown
RJ Rob Blake 5.00 12.00
Jay Bouwmeester
RL Roberto Luongo 20.00 50.00
Kari Lehtonen
RR Michael Ryder 5.00 12.00
Mike Ribeiro
RT Michael Ryder 8.00 20.00
Jose Theodore
SB Joe Sakic 25.00 60.00
Rob Blake
SR J.Spezza/M.Ryder 12.00 30.00
SS R.Smyth/J.Smith 8.00 20.00
ST Mike Sillinger 5.00 12.00
Keith Tkachuk
TL Marty Turco 10.00 25.00
Roberto Luongo
TM Joe Thornton 10.00 25.00
Glen Murray
TP Joe Thornton 10.00 25.00
Keith Primeau
TR Jose Theodore 8.00 20.00
Mike Ribeiro
VR Vincent Lecavalier 10.00 25.00
Ruslan Fedotenko

2005-06 Be A Player Ice Icons

PRINT RUN 99 SER.#'d SETS
ICE1 Martin Brodeur 12.00 30.00
ICE2 Mario Lemieux 20.00 50.00
ICE3 Joe Sakic 10.00 25.00
ICE4 Peter Forsberg 8.00 20.00
ICE5 Steve Yzerman 12.00 30.00

2005-06 Be A Player Outtakes

PRINT RUN 499 SER.#'d SETS
OT1 Jean-Sebastien Giguere 1.50 4.00
OT2 Sergei Fedorov 2.00 5.00
OT3 Dany Heatley 2.00 5.00
OT4 Ilya Kovalchuk 2.50 6.00
OT5 Andrew Raycroft 1.50 4.00
OT6 Joe Thornton 3.00 8.00
OT7 Chris Drury 1.50 4.00
OT8 Jarome Iginla 2.00 5.00
OT9 Miikka Kiprusoff 2.00 5.00
OT10 Eric Staal 1.50 4.00
OT11 Tuomo Ruutu 1.25 3.00
OT12 Peter Forsberg 3.00 8.00
OT13 Rob Blake 1.50 4.00
OT14 Alex Tanguay 1.50 4.00
OT15 Joe Sakic 4.00 10.00
OT16 Nikolai Zherdev 1.50 4.00
OT17 Rick Nash 2.50 6.00
OT18 Mike Modano 2.00 5.00
OT19 Marty Turco 1.50 4.00
OT20 Pavel Datsyuk 2.00 5.00
OT21 Brendan Shanahan 2.00 5.00
OT22 Steve Yzerman 5.00 12.00
OT23 Ryan Smyth 1.50 4.00
OT24 Roberto Luongo 3.00 8.00
OT25 Luc Robitaille 1.50 4.00
OT26 Marian Gaborik 2.50 6.00
OT27 Saku Koivu 2.00 5.00
OT28 Jose Theodore 2.00 5.00
OT29 Tomas Vokoun 1.50 4.00
OT30 Steve Sullivan 1.25 3.00
OT31 Martin Brodeur 5.00 12.00
OT32 Jaromir Jagr 3.00 8.00
OT33 Mark Messier 1.25 3.00
OT34 Michael Peca 1.25 3.00
OT35 Daniel Alfredsson 1.50 4.00
OT36 Jason Spezza 2.00 5.00
OT37 Jeremy Roenick 2.00 5.00
OT38 Simon Gagne 2.00 5.00
OT39 Shane Doan 1.25 3.00
OT40 Mario Lemieux 6.00 15.00
OT41 Patrick Marleau 1.50 4.00
OT42 Keith Tkachuk 2.00 5.00
OT43 Chris Pronger 1.50 4.00
OT44 Vincent Lecavalier 2.00 5.00
OT45 Martin St. Louis 1.50 4.00
OT46 Mats Sundin 2.00 5.00
OT47 Ed Belfour 2.00 5.00
OT48 Markus Naslund 2.00 5.00
OT49 Ed Jovanovski 1.50 4.00
OT50 Olaf Kolzig 1.50 4.00

2005-06 Be A Player Quad Signatures

STATED ODDS 1:180
BLTG Martin Brodeur 250.00 500.00
Roberto Luongo
Jose Theodore
Jean Sebastien Giguere
BLUE Chris Pronger 30.00 80.00
Keith Tkachuk
Eric Weinrich
Mike Sillinger
BOST Joe Thornton 60.00 150.00
Andrew Raycroft
Glen Murray
Patrice Bergeron
COLO Alex Tanguay 75.00 150.00
Joe Sakic
David Aebischer
Vincent Damphousse
GDEF Chris Pronger 100.00 200.00
Nicklas Lidstrom
Rob Blake
Jay Bouwmeester
GOAL Martin Brodeur 150.00 300.00
Jose Theodore
Jean-Sebastien Giguere
Marc-Andre Fleury
HAWK Tuomo Ruutu 30.00 80.00
Eric Daze
Jocelyn Thibault
Bryan Berard
HSNT Heatly/Sakic/Nash/Thorntn
IMPL Jarome Iginla 50.00 100.00
Patrick Marleau
Keith Primeau
Martin St. Louis
ITLB Iginla/Tangy/St.Lou/Bergrn 50.00 125.00
MAPL Sundn/Stajn/McCbe/Robrts 125.00 200.00
MONT Theo/Ryder/Ribeiro/Souray 125.00 250.00
OTWA Marian Hossa 100.00 200.00
Wade Redden
Peter Bondra
Dominik Hasek
RBSS Ruutu/Bergrn/Staal/Stajan 60.00 125.00
SCCH Andrychk/St.Lou/Richrds/Stllmn 60.00 100.00
SDPH Ryan Smyth 30.00 80.00
Eric Daze
Keith Primeau
Bobby Holik
SHSL Sakic/Heatly/Sundn/St.Lou 60.00 125.00
SSIR Ryan Smyth 100.00 200.00
Jason Smith
Jarome Iginla
Robyn Regehr
TLAL Marty Turco 60.00 150.00
Roberto Luongo
David Aebischer
Kari Lehtonen

2005-06 Be A Player Signatures

ONE PER PACK
GOLD PRINT RUN 10 SER.#'d SETS
GOLD NOT PRICED DUE TO SCARCITY
AA Adrian Aucoin 2.00 5.00
AB Andrew Brunette 2.00 5.00
AC Andrew Cassels 2.00 5.00
AE David Aebischer 3.00 8.00
AH Adam Hall 2.00 5.00
AL Andreas Lilja 2.00 5.00
AM Alyn McCauley 2.00 5.00
AN Dave Andreychuk 4.00 10.00
AR Andrew Raycroft 5.00 12.00
AT Alex Tanguay 4.00 10.00
AV Sean Avery 2.00 5.00
BA Matthew Barnaby 2.00 5.00
BB Bryan Berard 2.00 5.00
BD Boyd Devereaux 2.00 5.00
BE Brenden Morrow 4.00 10.00
BG Bill Guerin SP 8.00 20.00
BH Bobby Holik 2.00 5.00
BI Martin Biron 3.00 8.00
BJ Barret Jackman 2.00 5.00
BM Brendan Morrison 4.00 10.00
BN Brian Boucher 3.00 8.00
BO Bob Boughner 2.00 5.00
BR Brian Rolston 2.00 5.00
BS Brendan Shanahan 10.00 25.00
BT Brent Sopel 2.00 5.00
BW Brendan Witt 2.00 5.00
BY Bryan McCabe 2.00 5.00
CC Carlo Colaiacovo 2.00 5.00
CD Chris Drury SP 30.00 80.00
CG Craig Conroy 2.00 5.00
CP Chris Pronger 4.00 10.00
CR Craig Rivet 2.00 5.00
CS Cory Stillman 2.00 5.00
DB Daniel Briere 2.00 5.00
DC Daniel Cleary 2.00 5.00
DD Dallas Drake 2.00 5.00
DE Derian Hatcher 2.00 5.00
DI Daniel Alfredsson 5.00 12.00
DL David Legwand 3.00 8.00
DN Dan Cloutier 3.00 8.00
DO Shean Donovan 2.00 5.00
DR Dwayne Roloson 4.00 10.00
DT Mathieu Schneider 2.00 5.00
DU Dustin Brown 5.00 12.00
DY Darryl Sydor 2.00 5.00
EB Eric Brewer 2.00 5.00
EC Erik Cole 5.00 12.00
EI Eric Staal 8.00 20.00
EL Eric Lindros 8.00 20.00
ER Eric Belanger 2.00 5.00
ES Robert Esche 3.00 8.00
EW Eric Weinrich 2.00 5.00
FA Brian Rafalski 2.00 5.00
FE Ruslan Fedotenko 2.00 5.00
GI Brian Gionta 2.00 5.00
GL Martin Gelinas 2.00 5.00
GM Glen Murray 2.00 5.00
GS Garth Snow 2.00 5.00
HA Dominik Hasek 20.00 50.00
HE Bret Hedican 2.00 5.00
HF Shawn Horcoff 2.00 5.00
HO Gordie Howe SP 250.00 400.00
HT Dany Heatley 8.00 20.00
HZ Henrik Zetterberg 12.50 30.00
IG Jarome Iginla 12.00 30.00
IL Ian Laperriere 2.00 5.00
JA Jason Arnott 2.00 5.00
JB Jay Bouwmeester 5.00 12.00
JC Jonathan Cheechoo 4.00 10.00
JD Jody Shelley 2.00 5.00
JG Jean-Sebastien Giguere 4.00 10.00
JI Jim Dowd 2.00 5.00
JL Joffrey Lupul 2.00 5.00
JM John-Michael Liles 2.00 5.00
JO Jeff O'Neill 2.00 5.00
JP J-P Dumont 2.00 5.00
JS Jason Smith 2.00 5.00
JT Jocelyn Thibault 4.00 10.00
JW Justin Williams 2.00 5.00
KA Trent Klatt 2.00 5.00
KD Kris Draper 4.00 10.00
KE Kevyn Adams 2.00 5.00
KL Kari Lehtonen 8.00 20.00
KP Keith Primeau SP 8.00 20.00
KT Keith Tkachuk SP 15.00 40.00
KW Kevin Weekes 3.00 8.00
LA Robert Lang 2.00 5.00
LE Jordan Leopold 2.00 5.00
LU Luc Robitaille SP 20.00 50.00
LW Daymond Langkow 2.00 5.00
MA Brad May 2.00 5.00
MD Mathieu Dandenault 2.00 5.00
ME Mike Knuble 2.00 5.00
MF Marc-Andre Fleury 10.00 25.00
MH Marian Hossa 8.00 20.00
MI Mike Comrie 4.00 10.00
ML Martin Lapointe 2.00 5.00
MO Mattias Ohlund 2.00 5.00
MP Mark Parrish 2.00 5.00
MR Marc Denis 4.00 10.00
MS Matt Stajan 2.00 5.00
MT Martin Brodeur SP 150.00 250.00
MU Bryan Muir 2.00 5.00
MW Mattias Weinhandl 2.00 5.00
NA Markus Naslund SP 12.00 30.00
NB Nick Boynton 2.00 5.00
ND Niko Dimitrakos 2.00 5.00
NH Nathan Horton 5.00 12.00
NI Rob Niedermayer 2.00 5.00
NL Nicklas Lidstrom SP 25.00 60.00
OK Olaf Kolzig 5.00 12.00
OR Brooks Orpik 2.00 5.00
OT Steve Ott 2.00 5.00
PA Paul Martin 2.00 5.00
PB Peter Bondra 4.00 10.00
PC Patrice Bergeron 5.00 12.00
PD Pascal Dupuis 2.00 5.00
PE Mike Peca 2.00 5.00
PK Paul Kariya 12.00 30.00
PM Patrick Marleau SP 25.00 60.00
PT Pierre Turgeon 2.00 5.00
RA Rod Brind'Amour 4.00 10.00
RB Rob Blake 4.00 10.00
RC Brad Richards 5.00 12.00
RD Rick DiPietro 5.00 12.00
RF Rico Fata 2.00 5.00
RI Mike Ribeiro 3.00 8.00
RK Ryan Kesler 2.00 5.00
RL Roberto Luongo SP 25.00 60.00
RN Rick Nash 10.00 25.00
RO Gary Roberts 2.00 5.00
RR Robyn Regehr 2.00 5.00
RS Ryan Smyth 2.00 5.00
RU Tuomo Ruutu 3.00 8.00
RW Ray Whitney 2.00 5.00
RY Michael Ryder SP 8.00 20.00
SA Joe Sakic 25.00 60.00
SB Sean Burke 4.00 10.00
SC Scott Niedermayer 2.00 5.00
SD Shane Doan 2.00 5.00
SE Steve Sullivan 2.00 5.00
SG Mike Sillinger 2.00 5.00
SH Shawn McEachern 2.00 5.00
SI Steve Shields 3.00 8.00
SJ Joe Thornton 15.00 40.00
SL Martin St. Louis 4.00 10.00
SM Scott Mellanby 2.00 5.00
SN Geoff Sanderson 2.00 5.00
SO Steve Staios 2.00 5.00
SP Jason Spezza 10.00 25.00
SQ Stephane Quintal 2.00 5.00
SR Steve Rucchin 2.00 5.00
SS Sheldon Souray 2.00 5.00
SU Mats Sundin 25.00 60.00
TE Mikael Tellqvist 3.00 8.00
TH Jose Theodore 5.00 12.00
TI Mattias Timander 2.00 5.00
TL Trevor Linden 4.00 10.00
TM Todd Marchant 2.00 5.00
TN Tyson Nash 2.00 5.00
TO Steve Thomas 2.00 5.00
TP Tom Poti 2.00 5.00
TR Trent Hunter 2.00 5.00
TT Tim Taylor 2.00 5.00
TU Marty Turco 4.00 10.00
TW Todd White 2.00 5.00
VD Vincent Damphousse 2.00 5.00
VL Vincent Lecavalier 20.00 50.00
WA Scott Walker 2.00 5.00
WE Stephen Weiss 2.00 5.00
WR Wade Redden 2.00 5.00
YO Scott Young 2.00 5.00
ZE Eric Daze 2.00 5.00

2005-06 Be A Player Triple Signatures

STATED ODDS 1:90
AVS Sakic/Tanguay/Kariya SP 30.00 80.00
BSH Bondra/Spezza/Hossa SP 40.00 100.00
BUF Drury/Briere/Biron 20.00 50.00
DAL Turco/Morrow/Guerin SP 20.00 50.00
DEV Brodeur/Niedrmyr/Rafalski SP 125.00 250.00
DRL Dipietro/Raycroft/Luongo SP 30.00 80.00
FGR Fleury/Giguere/Raycroft SP 30.00 80.00
HGT Howe/Guerin/Tkachuk SP 100.00 200.00
HSN Hossa/Sundin/Naslund SP 40.00 100.00
IBM Iginla/Bergeron/Marleau SP 25.00 60.00
LBP Lidstrom/Blake/Pronger SP 30.00 80.00
LLA Luongo/Lehtnen/Aebischr SP 30.00 80.00
MTL Theodore/Ryder/Ribeiro SP 30.00 80.00
NKI Naslund/Kariya/Iginla SP 50.00 100.00
NMS Naslund/Morrison/Sopel 20.00 50.00
PAN Weiss/Horton/Bouwmeester 20.00 50.00
PDL Keith Primeau 20.00 50.00
Eric Daze
Eric Lindros
PTS Keith Primeau 30.00 80.00
Joe Thornton
Mats Sundin
SIS Joe Sakic 75.00 150.00
Jarome Iginla
Mats Sundin
SNL Mats Sundin 20.00 50.00
Markus Naslund
Nicklas Lidstrom
STL Keith Tkachuk 20.00 50.00
Chris Pronger
Dallas Drake
STS Joe Sakic 100.00 200.00
Joe Thornton
Jason Spezza
TBL Martin St. Louis 75.00 150.00
Brad Richards
Vincent Lecavalier
TGR Marty Turco 25.00 60.00
Jean-Sebastien Giguere
Andrew Raycroft
TLP Joe Thornton 75.00 150.00
Vincent Lecavalier
Keith Primeau

2005-06 Be A Player World Cup Salute

PRINT RUN 199 SER.#'d SETS
WCS1 Fredrik Modin 2.00 5.00
WCS2 Vincent Lecavalier 3.00 8.00
WCS3 Keith Tkachuk 3.00 8.00
WCS4 Joe Sakic 6.00 15.00
WCS5 Martin Havlat 2.50 6.00
WCS6 Kimmo Timonen 2.00 5.00
WCS7 Joe Thornton 5.00 12.00
WCS8 Mike Modano 3.00 8.00
WCS9 Daniel Alfredsson 2.50 6.00
WCS10 Patrik Elias 2.50 6.00
WCS11 Martin Brodeur 8.00 20.00
WCS12 Tomas Vokoun 2.50 6.00
WCS13 Miikka Kiprusoff 3.00 8.00
WCS14 Robert Esche 2.50 6.00
WCS15 Bill Guerin 2.00 5.00

2006-07 Be A Player

COMP.SET w/o SPs (170) 20.00 50.00
RC STATED PRINT RUN 999 #'d SETS
1 Dainius Zubrus .20 .50
2 Nikolai Zherdev .20 .50
3 Alexei Yashin .20 .50
4 Curtis Joseph .30 .75
5 Justin Williams .20 .50
6 Todd White .20 .50
7 Kyle Wellwood .20 .50
8 Doug Weight .20 .50
9 Cam Ward .50 1.25
10 Aaron Ward .20 .50
11 Scott Walker .20 .50
12 David Vyborny .20 .50
13 Radim Vrbata .20 .50
14 Antoine Vermette .20 .50
15 Stephane Veilleux .20 .50
16 Thomas Vanek .25 .60
17 Mike Van Ryn .20 .50
18 R.J. Umberger .20 .50
19 Marty Turco .25 .60
20 Darcy Tucker .20 .50
21 Vesa Toskala .25 .60
22 Kimmo Timonen .20 .50
23 Joe Thornton .50 1.25
24 Jose Theodore .30 .75
25 Tim Taylor .20 .50
26 Alex Tanguay .25 .60
27 Steve Sullivan .20 .50
28 Brad Stuart .20 .50
29 Martin Straka .20 .50
30 Jarret Stoll .20 .50
31 Lee Stempniak .20 .50
32 Matt Stajan .20 .50
33 Eric Staal .25 .60
34 Martin St. Louis .30 .75
35 Jason Spezza .30 .75
36 Sheldon Souray .20 .50
37 Ryan Smyth .25 .60
38 Jason Smith .20 .50
39 Chris Simon .20 .50
40 Mike Sillinger .20 .50
41 Jody Shelley .20 .50
42 Teemu Selanne .30 .75
43 Henrik Sedin .20 .50
44 Brent Seabrook .20 .50
45 Nick Schultz .20 .50
46 Marc Savard .20 .50
47 Sergei Samsonov .25 .60
48 Sami Salo .20 .50
49 Joe Sakic .60 1.50
50 Michael Ryder .25 .60
51 Tuomo Ruutu .20 .50
52 Derek Roy .20 .50
53 Dwayne Roloson .25 .60
54 Mike Richards .30 .75
55 Brad Richards .30 .75
56 Robyn Regehr .20 .50
57 Wade Redden .20 .50
58 Andrew Raycroft .25 .60
59 Brian Rafalski .20 .50
60 Petr Prucha .20 .50
61 Wayne Primeau .20 .50
62 Tom Poti .20 .50
63 Joni Pitkanen .20 .50
64 Dion Phaneuf .40 1.00
65 Andrew Peters .20 .50
66 Yanic Perreault .20 .50
67 Dustin Penner .20 .50
68 Michael Peca .20 .50
69 Mark Parrish .20 .50
70 Alexander Ovechkin 1.25 3.00
71 Steve Ott .20 .50
72 Michael Nylander .20 .50
73 Mattias Norstrom .20 .50
74 Antero Niittymaki .30 .75
75 Scott Niedermayer .20 .50
76 Markus Naslund .30 .75
77 Glen Murray .20 .50
78 Bryan Muir .20 .50
79 Brendan Morrison .20 .50
80 Steve Montador .20 .50
81 Ryan Miller .30 .75
82 Milan Michalek .20 .50
83 Andrej Meszaros .20 .50
84 Andy McDonald .20 .50
85 Jamal Mayers .20 .50
86 Patrick Marleau .25 .60
87 Andrei Markov .20 .50
88 Ryan Malone .20 .50
89 Manny Malhotra .20 .50
90 Roberto Luongo .60 1.50
91 Henrik Lundqvist .50 1.25
92 John-Michael Liles .20 .50
93 Nicklas Lidstrom .30 .75
94 Jordan Leopold .20 .50
95 Jere Lehtinen .20 .50
96 David Legwand .20 .50
97 Vincent Lecavalier .30 .75
98 Georges Laraque .20 .50
99 Andrew Ladd .20 .50
100 Chris Kunitz .20 .50
101 Slava Kozlov .20 .50
102 Alexei Kovalev .20 .50
103 Olaf Kolzig .40 1.00
104 Saku Koivu .30 .75
105 Chuck Kobasew .20 .50
106 Mike Knuble .20 .50
107 Nikolai Khabibulin .30 .75
108 Duncan Keith .40 1.00
109 Olli Jokinen .20 .50
110 Jarome Iginla .50 1.25
111 Trent Hunter .30 .75
112 Cristobal Huet .30 .75
113 Marian Hossa .25 .60
114 Shawn Horcoff .20 .50
115 Bobby Holik .20 .50
116 Chris Higgins .30 .75
117 Dany Heatley .30 .75
118 Martin Havlat .25 .60
119 Dan Hamhuis .20 .50
120 Bill Guerin .20 .50
121 Mike Green .20 .50
122 Hal Gill .20 .50
123 Martin Gerber .30 .75
124 Simon Gagne .30 .75
125 Alexander Frolov .20 .50
126 Kurtis Foster .20 .50
127 Peter Forsberg .50 1.25
128 Marc-Andre Fleury .30 .75
129 Ruslan Fedotenko .20 .50
130 Sergei Fedorov .20 .50
131 Garnet Exelby .20 .50
132 Robert Esche .25 .60
133 Steve Eminger .20 .50
134 Patrik Elias .20 .50
135 Patrick Eaves .20 .50
136 J.P. Dumont .20 .50
137 Chris Drury .25 .60
138 Shane Doan .20 .50
139 Marc Denis .25 .60
140 Craig Conroy .20 .50
141 Erik Cole .20 .50
142 Chris Clark .20 .50
143 Jonathan Cheechoo .30 .75
144 Zdeno Chara .20 .50
145 Jeff Carter .30 .75
146 Brian Campbell .20 .50
147 Mike Cammalleri .20 .50
148 Kyle Calder .20 .50
149 Brent Burns .20 .50
150 Gilbert Brule .20 .50
151 Dustin Brown .20 .50
152 Curtis Brown .20 .50
153 Rod Brind'Amour .25 .60
154 Daniel Briere .25 .60
155 Eric Brewer .20 .50
156 Dan Boyle .20 .50
157 Brad Boyes .20 .50
158 Jay Bouwmeester .20 .50
159 Pierre-Marc Bouchard .20 .50
160 Rob Blake .25 .60
161 Steve Bernier .25 .60
162 Patrice Bergeron .25 .60
163 Mark Bell .20 .50
164 Keith Ballard .20 .50
165 Sean Avery .20 .50
166 Adrian Aucoin .20 .50
167 Daniel Alfredsson .25 .60
168 Maxim Afinogenov .20 .50
169 Kevyn Adams .20 .50
170 Shawn Bates .20 .50
201 Evgeni Malkin RC 15.00 40.00
202 Phil Kessel RC 10.00 25.00
203 Luc Bourdon RC 4.00 10.00
204 Dustin Boyd RC 4.00 10.00
205 Patrick O'Sullivan RC 4.00 10.00
206 Blake Comeau RC 3.00 8.00
207 Shea Weber RC 4.00 10.00
208 Matt Carle RC 4.00 10.00
209 Loui Eriksson RC 3.00 8.00
210 Mark Stuart RC 3.00 8.00
211 Eric Fehr RC 4.00 10.00
212 Travis Zajac RC 5.00 12.00
213 Anze Kopitar RC 8.00 20.00
214 Ladislav Smid RC 3.00 8.00
215 Noah Welch RC 3.00 8.00
216 Jordan Staal RC 12.00 30.00
217 Alexander Radulov RC 8.00 20.00
218 Drew Stafford RC 4.00 10.00
219 Paul Stastny RC 12.00 30.00
220 Dave Bolland RC 6.00 15.00
221 Marek Schwarz RC 6.00 15.00
222 Ryan Potulny RC 4.00 10.00
223 Marc-Antoine Pouliot RC 4.00 10.00
224 Jarkko Immonen RC 3.00 8.00
225 Josh Hennessy RC 3.00 8.00
226 Benoit Pouliot RC 4.00 10.00
227 Nigel Dawes RC 3.00 8.00
228 Matt Lashoff RC 3.00 8.00
229 Keith Yandle RC 3.00 8.00
230 Karri Ramo RC 3.00 8.00
231 Guillaume Latendresse RC 10.00 25.00
232 Marc-Edouard Vlasic RC 3.00 8.00
233 Patrick Thoresen RC 3.00 8.00
234 Niklas Grossman RC 3.00 8.00
235 Ian White RC 3.00 8.00
236 Clarke MacArthur RC 3.00 8.00
237 Jesse Schultz RC 3.00 8.00
238 David Booth RC 3.00 8.00
239 Joe Pavelski RC 10.00 25.00
240 Martin Houle RC 4.00 10.00
241 Mikhail Grabovski RC 3.00 8.00
242 David McKee RC 4.00 10.00
243 Brandon Prust RC 3.00 8.00
244 Kristopher Letang RC 5.00 12.00
245 Shawn Belle RC 3.00 8.00

2006-07 Be A Player Autographs

STATED PRINT RUN 10 SER.#'d SETS
NOT PRICED DUE TO SCARCITY

2006-07 Be A Player Profiles

COMPLETE SET (30) 50.00 100.00
STATED PRINT RUN 499 SER.#'d SETS
PP1 Vincent Lecavalier 1.50 4.00
PP2 Thomas Vanek 1.25 3.00
PP3 Teemu Selanne 1.50 4.00
PP4 Simon Gagne 1.50 4.00
PP5 Sergei Fedorov 1.50 4.00
PP6 Scott Niedermayer 1.00 2.50
PP7 Saku Koivu 1.50 4.00
PP8 Ryan Smyth 1.25 3.00
PP9 Pierre-Marc Bouchard 1.00 2.50
PP10 Phil Kessel 3.00 8.00
PP11 Peter Forsberg 2.50 6.00
PP12 Paul Stastny 4.00 10.00
PP13 Patrice Bergeron 1.25 3.00
PP14 Nicklas Lidstrom 1.50 4.00
PP15 Markus Naslund 1.50 4.00
PP16 Marian Hossa 1.25 3.00
PP17 Marc-Andre Fleury 1.50 4.00
PP18 Jordan Staal 3.00 8.00
PP19 Jonathan Cheechoo 1.50 4.00
PP20 Joe Thornton 2.50 6.00
PP21 Joe Sakic 3.00 8.00
PP22 Jay Bouwmeester 1.00 2.50
PP23 Jarome Iginla 2.50 6.00
PP24 Guillaume Latendresse 2.50 6.00
PP25 Eric Staal 1.25 3.00
PP26 Dion Phaneuf 2.00 5.00
PP27 Dany Heatley 1.50 4.00
PP28 Daniel Alfredsson 1.25 3.00
PP29 Alexander Ovechkin 5.00 12.00
PP30 Alexander Frolov 1.00 2.50

2006-07 Be A Player Profiles Autographs

STATED PRINT RUN 5 SER.#'d SETS
NOT PRICED DUE TO SCARCITY
PP1 Vincent Lecavalier
PP2 Thomas Vanek
PP3 Teemu Selanne
PP4 Simon Gagne
PP5 Sergei Federov
PP6 Scott Niedermayer
PP7 Saku Koivu
PP8 Ryan Smyth
PP9 Pierre-Marc Bouchard
PP10 Phil Kessel
PP11 Peter Forsberg
PP12 Paul Stastny
PP13 Patrice Bergeron
PP14 Nicklas Lidstrom
PP15 Markus Naslund
PP16 Marian Hossa
PP17 Marc-Andre Fleury
PP18 Jordan Staal
PP19 Jonathan Cheechoo
PP21 Joe Sakic
PP22 Jay Bouwmeester
PP23 Jarome Iginla
PP24 Guillaume Latendresse
PP25 Eric Staal
PP26 Dion Phaneuf
PP27 Dany Heatley
PP28 Daniel Alfredsson
PP29 Alexander Ovechkin
PP30 Alexander Frolov

2006-07 Be A Player Signatures

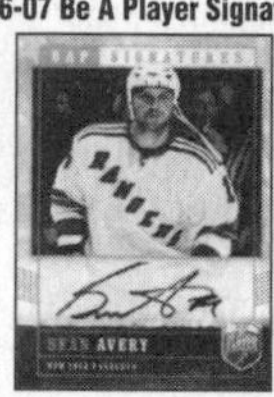

This 170-card set was released in July, 2007. The set was issued in five-card packs with a $12.99 SRP which came eight packs to a box and 15 boxes to a case.

AA Adrian Aucoin 5.00 12.00
AD Daniel Alfredsson 6.00 15.00
AF Alexander Frolov 5.00 12.00
AK Alexei Kovalev 5.00 12.00
AL Andrew Ladd 5.00 12.00
AM Andrei Markov 5.00 12.00
AN Antero Niittymaki 8.00 20.00
AO Alexander Ovechkin 30.00 80.00
AP Andrew Peters 5.00 12.00
AR Andrew Raycroft 6.00 15.00
AS Sean Avery 5.00 12.00
AT Alex Tanguay 6.00 15.00
AV Antoine Vermette 5.00 12.00
AW Aaron Ward 5.00 12.00
AY Alexei Yashin 5.00 12.00
BA Shawn Bates 5.00 12.00
BB Brad Boyes 5.00 12.00
BC Brian Campbell 5.00 12.00
BD Daniel Briere 6.00 15.00
BE Patrice Bergeron 6.00 15.00
BG Bill Guerin 5.00 12.00
BH Bobby Holik 5.00 12.00
BL Rob Blake 6.00 15.00
BM Bryan Muir 5.00 12.00
BO Dan Boyle 5.00 12.00
BR Brad Richards 8.00 20.00
BS Brad Stuart 5.00 12.00
BU Brent Burns 5.00 12.00
CA Jeff Carter 8.00 20.00
CB Curtis Brown 5.00 12.00
CC Craig Conroy 5.00 12.00
CD Chris Drury 6.00 15.00
CH Chuck Kobasew 5.00 12.00
CJ Curtis Joseph 8.00 20.00
CK Chris Kunitz 5.00 12.00
CL Chris Clark 5.00 12.00
CM Mike Cammalleri 5.00 12.00
CR Cristobal Huet 8.00 20.00
CS Chris Simon 5.00 12.00
CW Cam Ward 12.00 30.00
DA Dan Hamhuis 5.00 12.00
DB Dustin Brown 5.00 12.00
DH Dany Heatley 8.00 20.00
DK Duncan Keith 10.00 25.00
DL David Legwand 5.00 12.00
DP Dion Phaneuf 10.00 25.00
DR Derek Roy 5.00 12.00
DT Darcy Tucker 5.00 12.00
DV David Vyborny 5.00 12.00
DW Doug Weight 5.00 12.00
DZ Dainius Zubrus 5.00 12.00
EA Patrick Eaves 5.00 12.00
EB Eric Brewer 5.00 12.00
EC Erik Cole 5.00 12.00
EL Patrik Elias 5.00 12.00
EM Steve Eminger 5.00 12.00
ES Eric Staal 6.00 15.00
EX Garnet Exelby 6.00 12.00
GA Simon Gagne 8.00 20.00
GB Gilbert Brule 5.00 12.00
GE Martin Gerber 8.00 20.00
GL Georges Laraque 5.00 12.00
GM Glen Murray 5.00 12.00
HA Martin Havlat 6.00 15.00
HG Hal Gill 5.00 12.00
HI Chris Higgins 5.00 12.00
HL Henrik Lundqvist 12.00 30.00
HO Shawn Horcoff 5.00 12.00
HS Henrik Sedin 5.00 12.00
HU Trent Hunter 5.00 12.00
JA Jason Smith 5.00 12.00
JB Jay Bouwmeester 5.00 12.00
JC Jonathan Cheechoo 8.00 20.00
JD J.P. Dumont 5.00 12.00
JE Jere Lehtinen 5.00 12.00
JI Jarome Iginla 12.00 30.00
JL John-Michael Liles 5.00 12.00
JM Jamal Mayers 5.00 12.00
JO Joe Sakic 15.00 40.00
JP Joni Pitkanen 5.00 12.00
JS Jarret Stoll 5.00 12.00
JT Joe Thornton SP 100.00 200.00
JW Justin Williams 5.00 12.00
KA Kevyn Adams 5.00 12.00
KB Keith Ballard 5.00 12.00
KC Kyle Calder 5.00 12.00
KF Kurtis Foster 5.00 12.00
KN Mike Knuble 5.00 12.00
KO Saku Koivu 8.00 20.00
KT Kimmo Timonen 5.00 12.00
KW Kyle Wellwood 5.00 12.00
KZ Slava Kozlov 5.00 12.00
LE Jordan Leopold 5.00 12.00
LS Lee Stempniak 5.00 12.00
MA Manny Malhotra 5.00 12.00
MB Mark Bell 5.00 12.00
MC Andy McDonald 5.00 12.00
MD Marc Denis 6.00 15.00
MF Marc-Andre Fleury 8.00 20.00
MG Mike Green 5.00 12.00
MH Marian Hossa 6.00 15.00
MI Milan Michalek 5.00 12.00
MN Michael Nylander 5.00 12.00
MO Brendan Morrison 5.00 12.00
MP Michael Peca 5.00 12.00
MS Marc Savard 5.00 12.00
MT Marty Turco 6.00 15.00
MV Mike Van Ryn 5.00 12.00
MX Maxim Afinogenov 5.00 12.00
MZ Andrej Meszaros 5.00 12.00
NA Markus Naslund 8.00 20.00
NK Nikolai Khabibulin 8.00 20.00
NL Nicklas Lidstrom 8.00 20.00
NO Mattias Norstrom 5.00 12.00
NS Nick Schultz 5.00 12.00
NZ Nikolai Zherdev 5.00 12.00
OJ Olli Jokinen 5.00 12.00
OK Olaf Kolzig 10.00 25.00
OT Steve Ott 5.00 12.00
PA Mark Parrish 5.00 12.00
PB Pierre-Marc Bouchard 5.00 12.00
PE Dustin Penner 5.00 12.00
PF Peter Forsberg 40.00 80.00
PM Patrick Marleau 6.00 15.00
PP Petr Prucha 5.00 12.00
RA Brian Rafalski 5.00 12.00
RB Rod Brind'Amour 6.00 15.00
RD Michael Ryder 6.00 15.00
RE Robert Esche 6.00 15.00
RF Ruslan Fedotenko 5.00 12.00
RI Mike Richards 8.00 20.00
RL Roberto Luongo 40.00 80.00
RM Ryan Malone 5.00 12.00
RO Dwayne Roloson 6.00 15.00
RH Robyn Regehr 5.00 12.00
RS Ryan Smyth 6.00 15.00
RU R.J. Umberger 5.00 12.00
RV Radim Vrbata 5.00 12.00
RY Ryan Miller 8.00 20.00
SB Steve Bernier 5.00 12.00
SD Shane Doan 6.00 15.00
SE Sergei Samsonov 5.00 12.00
SF Sergei Fedorov 8.00 20.00
SH Jody Shelley 5.00 12.00
SI Mike Sillinger 5.00 12.00
SJ Matt Stajan 5.00 12.00
SK Brent Seabrook 5.00 12.00
SL Martin St. Louis 8.00 20.00
SM Steve Montador 5.00 12.00
SN Scott Niedermayer 5.00 12.00
SO Sheldon Souray 5.00 12.00
SP Jason Spezza 8.00 20.00
SS Sami Salo 5.00 12.00
ST Martin Straka 5.00 12.00
SU Steve Sullivan 5.00 12.00
TH Jose Theodore 8.00 20.00
TP Tom Poti 5.00 12.00
TR Tuomo Ruutu 5.00 12.00
TS Teemu Selanne 20.00 50.00
TT Tim Taylor 5.00 12.00
TV Thomas Vanek 6.00 15.00
TW Todd White 5.00 12.00
VE Stephane Veilleux 5.00 12.00
VL Vincent Lecavalier 8.00 20.00
VT Vesa Toskala 6.00 15.00
WA Scott Walker 5.00 12.00
WP Wayne Primeau 5.00 12.00
WR Wade Redden 5.00 12.00
YP Yanic Perreault 5.00 12.00
ZC Zdeno Chara 5.00 12.00

2006-07 Be A Player Signatures 10

STATED PRINT RUN 10 SER.#'d SETS
NOT PRICED DUE TO SCARCITY
1 Dainius Zubrus
2 Nikolai Zherdev
3 Alexei Yashin
5 Justin Williams
10 Doug Weight
11 Cam Ward
18 Thomas Vanek
21 Marty Turco
22 Darcy Tucker
23 Vesa Toskala
26 Jose Theodore
28 Alex Tanguay
32 Martin Straka
34 Lee Stempniak
35 Matt Stajan
36 Eric Staal
37 Martin St. Louis
38 Jason Spezza
39 Sheldon Souray
40 Ryan Smyth
45 Teemu Selanne
46 Henrik Sedin
49 Marc Savard
53 Joe Sakic
54 Michael Ryder
55 Tuomo Ruutu
57 Dwayne Roloson
58 Mike Richards
59 Brad Richards
62 Wade Redden
63 Andrew Raycroft
64 Brian Rafalski
65 Petr Prucha
68 Joni Pitkanen
69 Dion Phaneuf
71 Yanic Perreault
74 Mark Parrish
76 Alexander Ovechkin
81 Scott Niedermayer
82 Markus Naslund
83 Glen Murray
86 Brendan Morrison
88 Ryan Miller
89 Milan Michalek
93 Patrick Marleau
95 Ryan Malone
97 Roberto Luongo
98 Henrik Lundqvist
100 Nicklas Lidstrom
103 Jere Lehtinen
104 David Legwand
105 Vincent Lecavalier
110 Alexei Kovalev
112 Olaf Kolzig
113 Saku Koivu
117 Nikolai Khabibulin
119 Olli Jokinen
121 Jarome Iginla
123 Cristobal Huet
124 Marian Hossa
129 Dany Heatley
132 Bill Guerin
137 Martin Gerber
138 Simon Gagne
139 Alexander Frolov
141 Peter Forsberg
142 Marc-Andre Fleury
144 Sergei Federov
149 Patrik Elias
152 Chris Drury
154 Marc Denis
156 Erik Cole
158 Jonathan Cheechoo
159 Zdeno Chara
160 Jeff Carter
162 Mike Cammalleri
168 Rod Brind'Amour
169 Daniel Briere
172 Brad Boyes
173 Jay Bouwmeester
174 Pierre-Marc Bouchard
176 Rob Blake
178 Steve Bernier
179 Patrice Bergeron
185 Daniel Alfredsson
186 Maxim Afinogenov
202 Phil Kessel
203 Luc Bourdon
205 Patrick O'Sullivan
208 Matt Carle
216 Jordan Staal
219 Paul Stastny
231 Guillaume Latendresse

2006-07 Be A Player Signatures 25

*SIGS 25: .8X TO 2X
STATED PRINT RUN 25 SER.#'d SETS
3 Alexei Yashin 10.00 25.00
5 Justin Williams 10.00 25.00
8 Kyle Wellwood 10.00 25.00
10 Doug Weight 10.00 25.00
13 Scott Walker 10.00 25.00
14 David Vyborny 10.00 25.00
19 Mike Van Ryn 10.00 25.00
20 R.J. Umberger 10.00 25.00
21 Marty Turco 12.00 30.00
22 Darcy Tucker 10.00 25.00
24 Kimmo Timonen 10.00 25.00
28 Alex Tanguay 12.00 30.00
30 Steve Sullivan 10.00 25.00
31 Brad Stuart 10.00 25.00
33 Jarret Stoll 10.00 25.00
36 Eric Staal 12.00 30.00
37 Martin St. Louis 15.00 40.00
38 Jason Spezza 15.00 40.00
40 Ryan Smyth 12.00 30.00
41 Jason Smith 10.00 25.00
44 Jody Shelley 10.00 25.00
45 Teemu Selanne 40.00 100.00
47 Brent Seabrook 10.00 25.00
51 Sergei Samsonov 12.00 30.00
52 Sami Salo 10.00 25.00
53 Joe Sakic 30.00 80.00
54 Michael Ryder 12.00 30.00
56 Derek Roy 10.00 25.00
57 Dwayne Roloson 12.00 30.00
59 Brad Richards 15.00 40.00
63 Andrew Raycroft 12.00 30.00
67 Tom Poti 10.00 25.00
69 Dion Phaneuf 20.00 50.00
70 Andrew Peters 10.00 25.00
72 Dustin Penner 10.00 25.00
73 Michael Peca 10.00 25.00
76 Alexander Ovechkin 60.00 150.00
78 Michael Nylander 10.00 25.00
81 Scott Niedermayer 10.00 25.00
82 Markus Naslund 15.00 40.00
83 Glen Murray 10.00 25.00
88 Ryan Miller 15.00 40.00
91 Andy McDonald 10.00 25.00
93 Patrick Marleau 12.00 30.00
97 Roberto Luongo 75.00 150.00
98 Henrik Lundqvist 25.00 60.00
99 John-Michael Liles 10.00 25.00
100 Nicklas Lidstrom 15.00 40.00
101 Jordan Leopold 10.00 25.00
105 Vincent Lecavalier 15.00 40.00
107 Andrew Ladd 10.00 25.00
108 Chris Kunitz 10.00 25.00
109 Slava Kozlov 10.00 25.00
113 Saku Koivu 15.00 40.00
115 Chuck Kobasew 10.00 25.00
116 Mike Knuble 10.00 25.00
118 Duncan Keith 20.00 50.00
119 Olli Jokinen 10.00 25.00
121 Jarome Iginla 25.00 60.00
122 Trent Hunter 10.00 25.00
123 Cristobal Huet 15.00 40.00
124 Marian Hossa 12.00 30.00
126 Shawn Horcoff 10.00 25.00
127 Bobby Holik 10.00 25.00
128 Chris Higgins 10.00 25.00
129 Dany Heatley 15.00 40.00
132 Bill Guerin 10.00 25.00
138 Simon Gagne 15.00 40.00
141 Peter Forsberg 75.00 150.00
142 Marc-Andre Fleury 15.00 40.00
143 Ruslan Fedotenko 10.00 25.00
144 Sergei Fedorov 15.00 40.00
149 Patrik Elias 10.00 25.00
152 Chris Drury 12.00 30.00
155 Craig Conroy 10.00 25.00
157 Chris Clark 10.00 25.00
158 Jonathan Cheechoo 15.00 40.00
161 Brian Campbell 10.00 25.00
163 Kyle Calder 10.00 25.00
166 Dustin Brown 10.00 25.00
170 Eric Brewer 10.00 25.00
176 Rob Blake 12.00 30.00
179 Patrice Bergeron 12.00 30.00
185 Daniel Alfredsson 12.00 30.00
186 Maxim Afinogenov 10.00 25.00
202 Phil Kessel 30.00 80.00
207 Shea Weber 12.00 30.00
216 Jordan Staal 40.00 100.00
219 Paul Stastny 40.00 100.00
227 Nigel Dawes 10.00 25.00
231 Guillaume Latendresse 30.00 80.00
233 Patrick Thoresen 10.00 25.00

2006-07 Be A Player Signatures Duals

DAS Chris Simon / Sean Avery 6.00 15.00
DBC Rob Blake / Mike Cammalleri 8.00 20.00
DBK Patrice Bergeron / Phil Kessel 20.00 50.00
DBO Marc Savard / Glen Murray 6.00 15.00
DBP Mark Parrish / Pierre-Marc Bouchard 6.00 15.00
DBU Daniel Briere / Thomas Vanek 8.00 20.00
DBV David Vyborny / Gilbert Brule 6.00 15.00
DCA Craig Conroy / Alex Tanguay 8.00 20.00
DCB Steve Bernier / Matt Carle 8.00 20.00
DCH Brent Seabrook / Duncan Keith 12.00 30.00
DCW Aaron Ward / Zdeno Chara 6.00 15.00
DDR Chris Drury / Derek Roy 8.00 20.00
DED Jason Smith / Dwayne Roloson 8.00 20.00
DER Brian Rafalski / Patrik Elias 6.00 15.00
DEV Antoine Vermette / Patrick Eaves 6.00 15.00
DFL Nicklas Lidstrom / Peter Forsberg 15.00 40.00
DFS Marc-Andre Fleury / Jordan Staal 25.00 60.00
DFZ Nikolai Zherdev / Sergei Federov 10.00 25.00
DGC Simon Gagne / Jeff Carter 10.00 25.00
DGE Steve Eminger / Mike Green 6.00 15.00
DHK Saku Koivu / Cristobal Huet 10.00 25.00
DHM Martin Straka / Henrik Lundqvist 15.00 40.00
DHS Jason Spezza / Dany Heatley 10.00 25.00
DIH Jarome Iginla / Dany Heatley 15.00 40.00
DIP Jarome Iginla / Dion Phaneuf 15.00 40.00
DJS Jarret Stoll / Shawn Horcoff 6.00 15.00
DKH Marian Hossa / Slava Kozlov 8.00 20.00
DKR Tuomo Ruutu / Nikolai Khabibulin 10.00 25.00
DKS Sergei Samsonov / Alexei Kovalev 8.00 20.00
DLN Markus Naslund / Roberto Luongo 20.00 50.00
DLS Vincent Lecavalier / Martin St. Louis 10.00 25.00
DMB Brendan Morrison / Luc Bourdon 8.00 20.00
DMC Brian Campbell / Ryan Miller 10.00 25.00
DMG Patrick Marleau / Bill Guerin 8.00 20.00
DMK Andy McDonald / Chris Kunitz 6.00 15.00
DMS Manny Malhotra / Jody Shelley 6.00 15.00
DNA David Legwand / Steve Sullivan 6.00 15.00
DNE Robert Esche / Antero Niittymaki 10.00 25.00
DOC Alexander Ovechkin / Chris Clark 40.00 100.00
DPL Georges Laraque / Andrew Peters 6.00 15.00
DRF Brad Richards / Ruslan Fedotenko 10.00 25.00
DRH Michael Ryder / Chris Higgins 8.00 20.00
DRM Wade Redden / Andrej Meszaros 6.00 15.00
DRS Robyn Regehr / Brad Stuart 6.00 15.00
DRT Darcy Tucker / Andrew Raycroft 8.00 20.00
DRU Mike Richards / R.J. Umberger 10.00 25.00
DSA Daniel Alfredsson / Jason Spezza 10.00 25.00
DSB Rod Brind'Amour / Eric Staal 8.00 20.00
DSH Mike Sillinger / Trent Hunter 6.00 15.00
DSK Teemu Selanne / Saku Koivu 10.00 25.00
DSM Andrei Markov / Sheldon Souray 6.00 15.00
DSN Teemu Selanne / Scott Niedermayer 10.00 25.00
DSO Jody Shelley / Steve Ott 6.00 15.00
DSS Joe Sakic / Paul Stastny 25.00 60.00
DSY Alexei Yashin / Ryan Smyth 8.00 20.00
DTL Jere Lehtinen / Marty Turco 8.00 20.00
DVB Mike Van Ryn / Jay Bouwmeester 6.00 15.00
DWB Doug Weight / Brad Boyes 6.00 15.00
DWS Kyle Wellwood / Matt Stajan 6.00 15.00

2006-07 Be A Player Signatures Foursomes

STATED PRINT RUN 10 SER.#'d SETS
NOT PRICED DUE TO SCARCITY
FFLNA Markus Naslund / Nicklas Lidstrom / Peter Forsberg / Daniel Alfredsson
FIBRC Jarome Iginla / Jonathan Cheechoo / Michael Ryder / Patrice Bergeron
FLTFR Roberto Luongo / Marty Turco / Andrew Raycroft / Marc-Andre Fleury
FLTKG Olaf Kolzig / Vesa Toskala / Henrik Lundqvist / Martin Gerber
FMSRS Patrick Marleau / Brad Richards / Marc Savard / Jason Spezza
FNBRB Wade Redden / Jay Bouwmeester / Rob Blake / Scott Niedermayer
FOFKF Alexander Frolov / Alexei Kovalev / Sergei Fedorov / Alexander Ovechkin
FSKJL Teemu Selanne / Jere Lehtinen / Saku Koivu / Olli Jokinen
FSLST Joe Sakic / Vincent Lecavalier / Joe Thornton / Eric Staal
FSSLK Phil Kessel / Paul Stastny / Jordan Staal / Guillaume Latendresse

2006-07 Be A Player Signatures Trios

STATED PRINT RUN 25 SER.#'d SETS
TBKS Marc Savard / Patrice Bergeron / Phil Kessel 50.00 125.00
TCWB Shea Weber / Matt Carle / Luc Bourdon 20.00 50.00
TDBV Chris Drury / Daniel Briere / Thomas Vanek 20.00 50.00
TFCO Alexander Frolov / Mike Cammalleri / Patrick O'Sullivan 20.00 50.00
TFLS Steve Sullivan / David Legwand / Peter Forsberg 40.00 100.00
TFSM Ryan Malone / Marc-Andre Fleury / Jordan Staal 60.00 150.00
TFVB David Vyborny / Sergei Federov / Gilbert Brule
TGCR Simon Gagne / Mike Richards / Jeff Carter 25.00 60.00
THHK Cristobal Huet / Chris Higgins / Alexei Kovalev 25.00 60.00
THKH Marian Hossa / Bobby Holik / Slava Kozlov
TIPT Jarome Iginla / Alex Tanguay / Dion Phaneuf 40.00 100.00
TJBM Olli Jokinen / Jay Bouwmeester / Steve Montador
TKRL Saku Koivu / Michael Ryder / Guillaume Latendresse 50.00 125.00
TLNM Markus Naslund / Roberto Luongo / Brendan Morrison 50.00 125.00
TLRS Vincent Lecavalier / Brad Richards / Martin St. Louis 60.00 120.00
TMAR Maxim Afinogenov / Derek Roy / Ryan Miller 25.00 60.00
TOKC Olaf Kolzig / Alexander Ovechkin / Chris Clark
TRKS Tuomo Ruutu / Brent Seabrook / Nikolai Khabibulin 25.00 60.00
TRPP Michael Peca / Yanic Perreault / Andrew Raycroft 20.00 50.00
TRSH Jarret Stoll / Shawn Horcoff / Dwayne Roloson 20.00 50.00
TSAH Daniel Alfredsson / Jason Spezza / Dany Heatley
TSBC Erik Cole / Rod Brind'Amour / Eric Staal 20.00 50.00
TSNP Martin Straka / Michael Nylander / Petr Prucha 15.00 40.00
TSTJ Joe Sakic / Jose Theodore / Paul Stastny 60.00 150.00
TTBM Vesa Toskala / Milan Michalek / Steve Bernier 20.00 50.00
TTCM Patrick Marleau / Joe Thornton / Jonathan Cheechoo 40.00 100.00
TTLO Jere Lehtinen / Marty Turco / Steve Ott
TTWS Darcy Tucker / Kyle Wellwood / Matt Stajan 15.00 40.00
TWBS Doug Weight / Brad Boyes / Lee Stempniak 15.00 40.00
TYSS Alexei Yashin / Ryan Smyth / Mike Sillinger 20.00 50.00

2006-07 Be A Player Unmasked Warriors

STATED PRINT RUN 99 SER.#'d SETS
AUTO'D 1/1 VERSION ALSO EXISTS
AUTO NOT PRICED DUE TO SCARCITY
UM1 Ryan Miller 6.00 15.00
UM2 Jose Theodore 6.00 15.00
UM3 Marty Turco 5.00 12.00
UM4 Dwayne Roloson 5.00 12.00
UM5 Cristobal Huet 6.00 15.00
UM6 Henrik Lundqvist 10.00 25.00
UM7 Cam Ward 10.00 25.00
UM8 Marc-Andre Fleury 6.00 15.00
UM9 Andrew Raycroft 5.00 12.00
UM10 Roberto Luongo 12.00 30.00

2006-07 Be A Player Unmasked Warriors Autographs

STATED PRINT RUN 1 SER.#'d SET
NOT PRICED DUE TO SCARCITY

2006-07 Be A Player Up Close and Personal

STATED PRINT RUN 999 SER.#'d SETS
AUTO'D VERSION /10 EXISTS
AUTOS NOT PRICED DUE TO SCARCITY
UC1 Alex Tanguay .75 2.00
UC2 Justin Williams .60 1.50
UC3 Alexander Ovechkin 4.00 10.00
UC4 Alexei Yashin .60 1.50
UC5 Andrew Raycroft .75 2.00
UC6 Andy McDonald .60 1.50
UC7 Bill Guerin .60 1.50
UC8 Brad Richards 1.00 2.50
UC9 Brian Campbell .60 1.50
UC10 Chris Drury .75 2.00
UC11 Cristobal Huet 1.00 2.50
UC12 Dany Heatley 1.00 2.50
UC13 Darcy Tucker .60 1.50
UC14 Ryan Miller 1.00 2.50
UC15 Dion Phaneuf 1.25 3.00
UC16 Doug Weight .60 1.50
UC17 Dwayne Roloson .75 2.00
UC18 Eric Staal .75 2.00
UC19 Henrik Lundqvist 1.50 4.00
UC20 Henrik Sedin .60 1.50
UC21 Jarome Iginla 1.50 4.00
UC22 Jason Spezza 1.00 2.50
UC23 Jonathan Cheechoo 1.00 2.50
UC24 Daniel Briere .75 2.00
UC25 Joe Sakic 2.00 5.00
UC26 Joe Thornton 1.50 4.00
UC27 Lee Stempniak .60 1.50
UC28 Marc Savard .60 1.50
UC29 Marc-Andre Fleury 1.00 2.50
UC30 Marian Hossa .75 2.00
UC31 Mark Parrish .60 1.50
UC32 Markus Naslund 1.00 2.50
UC33 Martin St. Louis 1.00 2.50
UC34 Martin Straka .60 1.50
UC35 Marty Turco .75 2.00
UC36 Michael Peca .60 1.50
UC37 Michael Ryder .75 2.00
UC38 Nicklas Lidstrom 1.00 2.50
UC39 Nikolai Khabibulin 1.00 2.50
UC40 Olaf Kolzig 1.25 3.00
UC41 Martin Havlat .75 2.00
UC42 Patrice Bergeron .75 2.00
UC43 Patrick Marleau .75 2.00
UC44 Patrik Elias .60 1.50
UC45 Paul Stastny 2.50 6.00
UC46 Peter Forsberg 1.50 4.00
UC47 Rob Blake .75 2.00
UC48 Roberto Luongo 2.00 5.00
UC49 Rod Brind'Amour .75 2.00
UC50 Ryan Smyth .75 2.00
UC51 Saku Koivu 1.00 2.50
UC52 Scott Niedermayer .60 1.50
UC53 Sergei Fedorov 1.00 2.50
UC54 Simon Gagne 1.00 2.50
UC55 Kimmo Timonen .60 1.50
UC56 Teemu Selanne 1.00 2.50
UC57 Jordan Staal 2.50 6.00
UC58 Vincent Lecavalier 1.00 2.50
UC59 Wade Redden .60 1.50
UC60 Zdeno Chara .60 1.50

2006-07 Be A Player Up Close and Personal Autographs

STATED PRINT RUN 10 SER.#'d SETS
NOT PRICED DUE TO SCARCITY

2007-08 Be A Player

This set featured 360 cards with cards 1-200 as the basic veterans, 201-300 short-printed rookies serial numbered to 99 and 301-360 were released as exchange cards. Cards 301-360 featured cards with players from the 2008-09 rookie class and they were short-printed and serial numbered to 99.

COMP.SET w/o SPs (200) 20.00 50.00
RC (201-300) PRINT RUN 99 SERIAL #'d SETS
XRC (301-360) PRINT RUN 99 SERIAL #'d SETS
1 Ryan Getzlaf .25 .60
2 Jean-Sebastien Giguere .30 .75
3 Corey Perry .25 .60
4 Teemu Selanne .30 .75
5 Chris Pronger .30 .75

6 Chris Kunitz .20 .50
7 Scott Niedermayer .20 .50
8 Ilya Kovalchuk .40 1.00
9 Eric Perrin .20 .50
10 Colby Armstrong .20 .50
11 Kari Lehtonen .30 .75
12 Mark Recchi .20 .50
13 Slava Kozlov .20 .50
14 Patrice Bergeron .30 .75
15 Marc Savard .20 .50
16 Tim Thomas .40 1.00
17 Zdeno Chara .20 .50
18 Marco Sturm .20 .50
19 Phil Kessel .30 .75
20 Glen Murray .20 .50
21 Thomas Vanek .25 .60
22 Ryan Miller .30 .75
23 Derek Roy .20 .50
24 Jason Pominville .20 .50
25 Drew Stafford .25 .60
26 Steve Bernier .20 .50
27 Miikka Kiprusoff .40 1.00
28 Jarome Iginla .50 1.25
29 Daymond Langkow .20 .50
30 Dion Phaneuf .30 .75
31 Alex Tanguay .25 .60
32 Kristian Huselius .20 .50
33 Matthew Lombardi .20 .50
34 Curtis Joseph .25 .60
35 Eric Staal .30 .75
36 Rod Brind'Amour .25 .60
37 Cam Ward .30 .75
38 Justin Williams .20 .50
39 Ray Whitney .20 .50
40 Erik Cole .20 .50
41 Jason Williams .20 .50
42 Nikolai Khabibulin .30 .75
43 Patrick Sharp .20 .50
44 Brent Seabrook .20 .50
45 Robert Lang .20 .50
46 Martin Havlat .25 .60
47 Duncan Keith .30 .75
48 Joe Sakic .60 1.50
49 Jose Theodore .30 .75
50 Ryan Smyth .25 .60
51 Milan Hejduk .25 .60
52 Marek Svatos .20 .50
53 Paul Stastny .30 .75
54 Wojtek Wolski .20 .50
55 Rick Nash .30 .75
56 Gilbert Brule .20 .50
57 Pascal Leclaire .25 .60
58 Nikolai Zherdev .20 .50
59 Rostislav Klesla .20 .50
60 Michael Peca .20 .50
61 Mike Modano .30 .75
62 Brad Richards .25 .60
63 Marty Turco .30 .75
64 Mike Ribeiro .20 .50
65 Brenden Morrow .25 .60
66 Jere Lehtinen .20 .50
67 Dominik Hasek .40 1.00
68 Nicklas Lidstrom .30 .75
69 Pavel Datsyuk .30 .75
70 Chris Osgood .25 .60
71 Henrik Zetterberg .30 .75
72 Dan Cleary .25 .60
73 Tomas Holmstrom .25 .60
74 Valtteri Filppula .20 .50
75 Jarret Stoll .20 .50
76 Ales Hemsky .20 .50
77 Mathieu Garon .25 .60
78 Shawn Horcoff .20 .50
79 Dustin Penner .20 .50
80 Joni Pitkanen .20 .50
81 Dwayne Roloson .25 .60
82 Olli Jokinen .20 .50
83 Tomas Vokoun .30 .75
84 Nathan Horton .20 .50
85 David Booth .20 .50
86 Stephen Weiss .20 .50
87 Jay Bouwmeester .20 .50
88 Anze Kopitar .30 .75
89 Rob Blake .25 .60
90 Alexander Frolov .20 .50
91 Dustin Brown .20 .50
92 Mike Cammalleri .25 .60
93 Patrick O'Sullivan .25 .60
94 Marian Gaborik .40 1.00
95 Niklas Backstrom .25 .60
96 Pierre-Marc Bouchard .20 .50
97 Brian Rolston .20 .50
98 Josh Harding .25 .60
99 Mikko Koivu .20 .50
100 Saku Koivu .25 .60
101 Mark Streit .20 .50
102 Tomas Plekanec .20 .50
103 Michael Ryder .20 .50
104 Alex Kovalev .20 .50
105 Chris Higgins .25 .60
106 Andrei Markov .25 .60
107 Guillaume Latendresse .25 .60
108 Alexander Radulov .30 .75
109 Jason Arnott .20 .50
110 Chris Mason .25 .60
111 Martin Erat .20 .50
112 J.P. Dumont .20 .50
113 David Legwand .20 .50
114 Martin Brodeur .75 2.00
115 Zach Parise .25 .60
116 Patrik Elias .20 .50
117 Brian Gionta .20 .50
118 John Madden .20 .50
119 Travis Zajac .20 .50
120 Rick DiPietro .25 .60
121 Mike Comrie .20 .50
122 Bill Guerin .20 .50
123 Miroslav Satan .20 .50
124 Trent Hunter .20 .50
125 Ruslan Fedotenko .20 .50
126 Jaromir Jagr .50 1.25
127 Henrik Lundqvist .40 1.00
128 Chris Drury .25 .60
129 Scott Gomez .20 .50
130 Brendan Shanahan .30 .75
131 Michal Rozsival .20 .50
132 Sean Avery .20 .50
133 Jason Spezza .30 .75
134 Dany Heatley .40 1.00
135 Ray Emery .25 .60
136 Antoine Vermette .20 .50
137 Mike Fisher .25 .60
138 Daniel Alfredsson .25 .60
139 Wade Redden .20 .50
140 Martin Gerber .25 .60
141 Mike Richards .40 1.00
142 Martin Biron .25 .60
143 Daniel Briere .30 .75
144 Simon Gagne .30 .75
145 Mike Knuble .20 .50
146 Jeff Carter .20 .50
147 R.J. Umberger .20 .50
148 Steven Reinprecht .20 .50
149 Shane Doan .20 .50
150 Ilya Bryzgalov .30 .75
151 Ed Jovanovski .20 .50
152 Radim Vrbata .20 .50
153 Keith Ballard .20 .50
154 Petr Sykora .20 .50
155 Marc-Andre Fleury .30 .75
156 Marian Hossa .30 .75
157 Evgeni Malkin .75 2.00
158 Sergei Gonchar .20 .50
159 Ryan Malone .20 .50
160 Jordan Staal .40 1.00
161 Ryan Whitney .25 .60
162 Joe Thornton .40 1.00
163 Evgeni Nabokov .25 .60
164 Jonathan Cheechoo .25 .60
165 Milan Michalek .20 .50
166 Brian Campbell .20 .50
167 Patrick Marleau .25 .60
168 Paul Kariya .30 .75
169 Manny Legace .25 .60
170 Andy McDonald .20 .50
171 Brad Boyes .25 .60
172 Lee Stempniak .20 .50
173 Keith Tkachuk .25 .60
174 Vincent Lecavalier .30 .75
175 Mike Smith .25 .60
176 Jussi Jokinen .20 .50
177 Martin St. Louis .25 .60
178 Paul Ranger .20 .50
179 Karri Ramo .30 .75
180 Mats Sundin .30 .75
181 Vesa Toskala .25 .60
182 Alexander Steen .20 .50
183 Darcy Tucker .25 .60
184 Tomas Kaberle .20 .50
185 Nikolai Antropov .20 .50
186 Matt Stajan .20 .50
187 Jason Blake .20 .50
188 Roberto Luongo .50 1.25
189 Daniel Sedin .20 .50
190 Markus Naslund .30 .75
191 Ryan Kesler .20 .50
192 Alexander Edler .20 .50
193 Brendan Morrison .20 .50
194 Henrik Sedin .20 .50
195 Alexander Ovechkin 1.00 2.50
196 Olaf Kolzig .30 .75
197 Michael Nylander .20 .50
198 Sergei Fedorov .30 .75
199 Mike Green .20 .50
200 Alexander Semin .30 .75
201 Bobby Ryan RC 20.00 50.00
202 Drew Miller RC 5.00 12.00
203 Ryan Carter RC 6.00 15.00
204 Kent Huskins RC 5.00 12.00
205 Petteri Wirtanen RC 5.00 12.00
206 Ondrej Pavelec RC 8.00 20.00
207 Bryan Little RC 8.00 20.00
208 Brett Sterling RC 5.00 12.00
209 Tobias Enstrom RC 8.00 20.00
210 Tuukka Rask RC 12.00 30.00
211 David Krejci RC 10.00 25.00
212 Vladimir Sobotka RC 6.00 15.00
213 Milan Lucic RC 12.00 30.00
214 Matt Hunwick RC 6.00 15.00
215 Mike Weber RC 5.00 12.00
216 Patrick Kaleta RC 5.00 12.00
217 Curtis McElhinney RC 6.00 15.00
218 Matt Keetley RC 6.00 15.00
219 Casey Borer RC 5.00 12.00
220 Patrick Kane RC 75.00 150.00
221 Jack Skille RC 8.00 20.00
222 Jonathan Toews RC 75.00 150.00
223 Kris Versteeg RC 50.00 100.00
224 Petri Kontiola RC 5.00 12.00
225 Jake Dowell RC 5.00 12.00
226 David Koci RC 5.00 12.00
227 T.J. Hensick RC 6.00 15.00
228 Tyler Weiman RC 6.00 15.00
229 David Jones RC 6.00 15.00
230 Jaroslav Hlinka RC 6.00 15.00
231 Johnny Boychuk RC 5.00 12.00
232 Jared Boll RC 5.00 12.00
233 Kris Russell RC 8.00 20.00
234 Matt Niskanen RC 8.00 20.00
235 Tobias Stephan RC 6.00 15.00
236 Sam Gagner RC 30.00 60.00
237 Andrew Cogliano RC 12.00 30.00
238 Tom Gilbert RC 6.00 15.00
239 Rob Schremp RC 6.00 15.00
240 Liam Reddox RC 5.00 12.00
241 Cory Murphy RC 5.00 12.00
242 Stefan Meyer RC 5.00 12.00
243 Tanner Glass RC 5.00 12.00
244 Jack Johnson RC 8.00 20.00
245 Jonathan Bernier RC 12.00 30.00
246 Lauri Tukonen RC 5.00 12.00
247 Jonathan Quick RC 20.00 50.00
248 Matt Moulson RC 5.00 12.00
249 Brady Murray RC 5.00 12.00
250 James Sheppard RC 5.00 12.00
251 Aaron Voros RC 5.00 12.00
252 Cal Clutterbuck RC 5.00 12.00
253 Carey Price RC 75.00 150.00
254 Jaroslav Halak RC 15.00 40.00
255 Kyle Chipchura RC 8.00 20.00
256 Sergei Kostitsyn RC 15.00 40.00
257 Ryan O'Byrne RC 8.00 20.00
258 Ville Koistinen RC 5.00 12.00
259 Antti Pihlstrom RC 6.00 15.00
260 Nicklas Bergfors RC 6.00 15.00
261 David Clarkson RC 5.00 12.00
262 Andy Greene RC 5.00 12.00
263 Olli Malmivaara RC 5.00 12.00
264 Frans Nielsen RC 5.00 12.00
265 Marc Staal RC 12.00 30.00
266 Brandon Dubinsky RC 8.00 20.00
267 Ryan Callahan RC 8.00 20.00
268 Ivan Baranka RC 5.00 12.00
269 Greg Moore RC 5.00 12.00
270 Daniel Girardi RC 5.00 12.00
271 Nick Foligno RC 8.00 20.00
272 Brian Elliott RC 6.00 15.00
273 Alexander Nikulin RC 6.00 15.00
274 Steve Downie RC 6.00 15.00
275 Riley Cote RC 6.00 15.00
276 Ryan Parent RC 6.00 15.00
277 Denis Tolpeko RC 5.00 12.00
278 Peter Mueller RC 15.00 40.00
279 Martin Hanzal RC 6.00 15.00
280 Daniel Carcillo RC 6.00 15.00
281 Daniel Winnik RC 5.00 12.00
282 Craig Weller RC 5.00 12.00
283 Tyler Kennedy RC 8.00 20.00
284 Devin Setoguchi RC 10.00 25.00
285 Thomas Greiss RC 8.00 20.00
286 Torrey Mitchell RC 6.00 15.00
287 Lukas Kaspar RC 5.00 12.00
288 Tomas Plihal RC 6.00 15.00
289 Erik Johnson RC 10.00 25.00
290 David Perron RC 8.00 20.00
291 Steve Wagner RC 5.00 12.00
292 Matt Smaby RC 5.00 12.00
293 Mike Lundin RC 5.00 12.00
294 Jiri Tlusty RC 12.00 30.00
295 Anton Stralman RC 6.00 15.00
296 Mason Raymond RC 12.00 30.00
297 Jannik Hansen RC 5.00 12.00
298 Drew MacIntyre RC 6.00 15.00
299 Nicklas Backstrom RC 50.00 100.00
300 Chris Bourque RC 6.00 15.00
301 Steven Stamkos XRC 75.00 150.00
302 Michael Frolik XRC 8.00 20.00
303 Alex Pietrangelo XRC 6.00 15.00
304 Zach Bogosian XRC 15.00 40.00
305 Oscar Moller XRC 8.00 20.00
306 Colton Gillies XRC 10.00 25.00
307 Viktor Tikhonov XRC 10.00 25.00
308 Luke Schenn XRC 12.00 30.00
309 Andreas Nodl XRC 8.00 20.00
310 Blake Wheeler XRC 25.00 50.00
311 Fabian Brunnstrom XRC 12.00 30.00
312 Drew Doughty XRC 25.00 50.00
313 Kyle Okposo XRC 15.00 40.00
314 Kyle Turris XRC 15.00 40.00
315 Zach Boychuk XRC 10.00 25.00
316 Nikita Filatov XRC 12.00 30.00
317 Petr Vrana XRC 8.00 20.00
318 Luca Sbisa XRC 6.00 15.00
319 Mikkel Boedker XRC 12.00 30.00
320 Patric Hornqvist XRC 6.00 15.00
321 T.J. Oshie XRC 12.00 30.00
322 Nikolai Kulemin XRC 6.00 15.00
323 Brandon Sutter XRC 8.00 20.00
324 Derick Brassard XRC 6.00 15.00
325 James Neal XRC 12.00 30.00
326 Claude Giroux XRC 6.00 15.00
327 Vladimir Mihalik XRC 6.00 15.00
328 Patrik Berglund XRC 15.00 40.00
329 Adam Pardy XRC 6.00 15.00
330 Jonas Frogren XRC 6.00 15.00
331 Jakub Voracek XRC 8.00 20.00
332 Mark Fistric XRC 8.00 20.00
333 Marc-Andre Gragnani XRC 8.00 20.00
334 Justin Abdelkader XRC 10.00 25.00
335 Brian Boyle XRC 12.00 30.00
336 Shawn Matthias XRC 6.00 15.00
337 Lauri Korpikoski XRC 6.00 15.00
338 Robbie Earl XRC 6.00 15.00
339 Steve Mason XRC 40.00 80.00
340 Brian Lee XRC 12.00 30.00
341 Kevin Porter XRC 6.00 15.00
342 Alex Goligoski XRC 12.00 30.00
343 Ryan Jones XRC 6.00 15.00
344 Boris Valabik XRC 6.00 15.00
345 Darren Helm XRC 10.00 25.00
346 Derek Dorsett XRC 6.00 15.00
347 Wayne Simmonds XRC 12.00 30.00
348 Ben Bishop XRC 8.00 20.00
349 John Mitchell XRC 6.00 15.00
350 Jonathan Ericsson XRC 8.00 20.00
351 Tyler Plante XRC 8.00 20.00
352 Andrew Ebbett XRC 6.00 15.00
353 Tom Sestito XRC 8.00 20.00
354 Jonathan Filewich XRC 6.00 15.00
355 Ilya Zubov XRC 8.00 20.00
356 Anssi Salmela XRC 6.00 15.00
357 Dane Byers XRC 6.00 15.00
358 Adam Pineault XRC 6.00 15.00
359 Mike Iggulden XRC 8.00 20.00
360 Matt D'Agostini XRC 6.00 15.00

2007-08 Be A Player Player's Club

*PLAYER'S CLUB: 2.5X TO 6X BASE
STATED PRINT RUN 99 SERIAL #'d SETS
RCs PRINT RUN 10 SERIAL #'d SETS
PLAYER'S CLUB RCs NOT PRICED DUE TO SCARCITY

2007-08 Be A Player Player's Club Platinum

*PLATINUM: 10X TO 25X BASE
(1-200) PRINT RUN 25 SERIAL #'d SETS
(201-300) PRINT RUN 1 SERIAL #'d SET
(201-300) NOT PRICED DUE TO SCARCITY

2007-08 Be A Player Signatures

OVERALL AUTO ODDS 1 PER PACK
SAA Adrian Aucoin 4.00 10.00
SAF Andrew Ference 4.00 10.00
SAK Anze Kopitar 6.00 15.00
SAM Andrei Markov 5.00 12.00
SAO Alexander Ovechkin 40.00 80.00
SAP Andrew Peters 4.00 10.00
SAR Jason Arnott 4.00 10.00
SAS Alexander Semin 6.00 15.00
SAT Alex Tanguay 5.00 12.00
SAV Aaron Voros 4.00 10.00
SBA Nicklas Backstrom 15.00 40.00
SBB Brad Boyes 5.00 12.00
SBC Brian Campbell 4.00 10.00
SBD Daniel Briere 6.00 15.00
SBM Brendan Morrison 4.00 10.00
SBO Dan Boyle 4.00 10.00
SBP Brian Pothier 4.00 10.00
SBR Brian Rafalski 4.00 10.00
SBS Brent Seabrook 4.00 10.00
SBW Brendan Witt 4.00 10.00
SCA Mike Cammalleri 5.00 12.00
SCC Chris Clark 4.00 10.00
SCH Chris Higgins 5.00 12.00
SCI Chris Campoli 4.00 10.00
SCK Chuck Kobasew 4.00 10.00
SCL David Clarkson 4.00 10.00
SCM Chris Mason 5.00 12.00
SCN Chris Neil 4.00 10.00
SCO Mike Commodore 4.00 10.00
SCP Carey Price 20.00 50.00
SCR Chris Conner 4.00 10.00
SCS Cory Stillman 4.00 10.00
SCW Cam Ward 6.00 15.00
SCY Dan Cleary 5.00 12.00
SDA Dan Hamhuis 4.00 10.00
SDB Dustin Brown 4.00 10.00
SDC Daniel Carcillo 5.00 12.00
SDE Derian Hatcher 5.00 12.00
SDH Dominik Hasek 12.00 30.00
SDK Duncan Keith 6.00 15.00
SDM David Moss 6.00 15.00
SDO Donald Brashear 4.00 10.00
SDP Dion Phaneuf 6.00 15.00
SDR Derek Roy 4.00 10.00
SDS Daniel Sedin 4.00 10.00
SDT Darcy Tucker 5.00 12.00
SDV David Vyborny 4.00 10.00
SEC Erik Cole 4.00 10.00
SES Eric Staal 6.00 15.00
SFI Mike Fisher 5.00 12.00
SFR Alexander Frolov 4.00 10.00
SGA Simon Gagne 6.00 15.00
SGC Gregory Campbell 4.00 10.00
SGE Garnet Exelby 4.00 10.00
SHA Josh Harding 5.00 12.00
SHE Dany Heatley 8.00 20.00
SHM Martin Hanzal 5.00 12.00
SHO Marian Hossa 6.00 15.00
SHS Henrik Sedin 4.00 10.00
SHU Cristobal Huet 5.00 12.00
SIB Ilya Bryzgalov 6.00 15.00
SJB Jay Bouwmeester 4.00 10.00
SJC Jonathan Cheechoo 5.00 12.00
SJE Jeff Carter 4.00 10.00
SJH Johan Hedberg 5.00 12.00
SJI Jarome Iginla 10.00 25.00
SJJ Jack Johnson 6.00 15.00
SJL Jamie Langenbrunner 4.00 10.00
SJM Jamal Mayers 4.00 10.00
SJO Joe Thornton 12.00 30.00
SJP Jason Pominville 4.00 10.00
SJR Jarkko Ruutu 4.00 10.00
SJS Joe Sakic 25.00 50.00
SJT Jonathan Toews 25.00 60.00
SJW Jason Williams 4.00 10.00
SKB Keith Ballard 4.00 10.00
SKC Kyle Chipchura 6.00 15.00
SKD Kris Draper 5.00 12.00
SKE Tyler Kennedy 6.00 15.00
SKI Miikka Kiprusoff 8.00 20.00
SKM Kimmo Timonen 4.00 10.00
SKN Mike Knuble 4.00 10.00
SKO Saku Koivu 5.00 12.00
SKQ Kyle Quincey 4.00 10.00
SKR Kris Russell 5.00 12.00
SKS Phil Kessel 6.00 15.00
SLE Jere Lehtinen 4.00 10.00
SLJ Andreas Lilja 4.00 10.00
SLS Lee Stempniak 4.00 10.00
SLU Milan Lucic 10.00 25.00
SMA Manny Malhotra 4.00 10.00
SMC Matt Carle 4.00 10.00
SMF Marc-Andre Fleury 12.00 30.00
SMI Milan Michalek 4.00 10.00
SMK Mike Komisarek 4.00 10.00
SML Mike Lundin 4.00 10.00
SMM Mike Modano
SMN Markus Naslund 6.00 15.00
SMP Michael Peca 4.00 10.00
SMU Peter Mueller 12.00 30.00
SMY Cory Murphy 4.00 10.00
SNA Nikolai Antropov 4.00 10.00
SNB Niklas Backstrom 5.00 12.00
SNI Matt Niskanen 4.00 10.00
SNL Nicklas Lidstrom 6.00 15.00
SNS Nick Schultz 4.00 10.00
SOJ Olli Jokinen 4.00 10.00
SOK Olaf Kolzig 6.00 15.00
SOS Chris Osgood 5.00 12.00
SPA Mark Parrish 4.00 10.00
SPD David Perron 6.00 15.00
SPH Chris Phillips 4.00 10.00
SPI Pierre-Marc Bouchard 4.00 10.00
SPK Patrick Kane 25.00 60.00
SPM Patrick Marleau 5.00 12.00
SPN Paul Martin 4.00 10.00
SPR Paul Ranger 4.00 10.00
SPS Paul Stastny 6.00 15.00
SRB Rod Brind'Amour 5.00 12.00
SRD Rob Davison 4.00 10.00
SRI Mike Richards 8.00 20.00
SRK Ryan Kesler 4.00 10.00
SRL Roberto Luongo 15.00 40.00
SRN Rick Nash 6.00 15.00
SRO Rostislav Olesz 4.00 10.00
SRR Robyn Regehr 4.00 10.00
SRS Ryan Smyth 5.00 12.00
SRW Ryan Whitney 5.00 12.00
SSA Marc Savard 4.00 10.00
SSF Sergei Fedorov 12.00 30.00
SSG Sergei Gonchar 4.00 10.00
SSH James Sheppard 4.00 10.00
SSI Mike Sillinger 4.00 10.00
SSJ Matt Stajan 4.00 10.00
SSK Slava Kozlov 4.00 10.00
SSL Martin St. Louis 5.00 12.00
SSO Steve Ott 4.00 10.00
SSP Jason Spezza 6.00 15.00
SSR Steven Reinprecht 4.00 10.00
SST Jordan Staal 8.00 20.00
SSW Stephen Weiss 4.00 10.00
SSY Petr Sykora 4.00 10.00
STC Tim Connolly 4.00 10.00
STE Tobias Enstrom 6.00 15.00
STI Tim Thomas 8.00 20.00
STL Trevor Linden 5.00 12.00
STM Torrey Mitchell 5.00 12.00
STO Jordin Tootoo 5.00 12.00
STP Tomas Plekanec 4.00 10.00
STR Tuomo Ruutu 4.00 10.00
STT Tim Taylor 5.00 12.00
STV Thomas Vanek 5.00 12.00
STW Todd White 4.00 10.00
STZ Travis Zajac 4.00 10.00
SVL Vincent Lecavalier 6.00 15.00
SWA Scott Walker 4.00 10.00
SWE Shea Weber 4.00 10.00
SWH Ray Whitney 5.00 12.00
SWI Justin Williams 4.00 10.00
SWR Wade Redden 4.00 10.00
SWW Wojtek Wolski 4.00 10.00
SZP Zach Parise 5.00 12.00

2007-08 Be A Player Signatures Player's Club

This set is a parallel of the basic Be A Player Signatures set and each card is serial numbered to 15.

STATED PRINT RUN 15 SERIAL #'d SETS
NOT PRICED DUE TO SCARCITY

2007-08 Be A Player Signatures Duals

OVERALL AUTO ODDS 1 PER PACK
2SAM Jason Arnott 6.00 15.00
Chris Mason
2SBD Brent Seabrook 8.00 20.00
Duncan Keith
2SBH Josh Harding 6.00 15.00
Niklas Backstrom
2SBL Dan Boyle 5.00 12.00
Mike Lundin
2SBS Eric Staal 8.00 20.00
Rod Brind'Amour
2SCB Jeff Carter 8.00 20.00
Daniel Briere
2SCK Anze Kopitar 8.00 20.00
Mike Cammalleri
2SCR Derek Roy 5.00 12.00
Tim Connolly
2SCV Daniel Carcillo 6.00 15.00
Aaron Voros
2SCW Erik Cole 5.00 12.00
Ray Whitney
2SDC Dan Cleary 8.00 20.00
Kris Draper
2SEJ Eric Staal 12.00 30.00
Jordan Staal
2SEN Tobias Enstrom 8.00 20.00
Matt Niskanen
2SEP Zach Parise
Patrik Elias
2SFS Marc-Andre Fleury 15.00 40.00
Jordan Staal
2SGW Sergei Gonchar 6.00 15.00
Ryan Whitney
2SHO Dominik Hasek 15.00 40.00
Chris Osgood
2SHS Marian Hossa 8.00 20.00
Petr Sykora
2SIM Jarome Iginla 12.00 30.00
David Moss
2SJB Olli Jokinen 5.00 12.00
Jay Bouwmeester
2SJP Joe Sakic 30.00 60.00
Paul Stastny
2SJR Jack Johnson 8.00 20.00
Kris Russell
2SJT James Sheppard 8.00 20.00
Tyler Kennedy
2SKL Miikka Kiprusoff 30.00 60.00
Roberto Luongo
2SKR Mike Richards 10.00 25.00
Mike Knuble
2SLH Milan Lucic 12.00 30.00
Martin Hanzal
2SLS Vincent Lecavalier 8.00 20.00
Martin St. Louis
2SMC Patrick Marleau 6.00 15.00
Jonathan Cheechoo
2SMK Andrei Markov 6.00 15.00
Mike Komisarek
2SMT Tim Thomas 10.00 25.00
Glen Murray
2SNL Markus Naslund 30.00 60.00
Roberto Luongo
2SNV Rick Nash 8.00 20.00
David Vyborny
2SOT Jason Spezza 8.00 20.00
Mike Fisher
2SPP Carey Price 50.00 100.00
Tomas Plekanec
2SPV Thomas Vanek 6.00 15.00
Jason Pominville
2SRA Robyn Regehr 5.00 12.00
Adrian Aucoin
2SRC Wade Redden 5.00 12.00
Mike Commodore
2SRQ Brian Rafalski 5.00 12.00
Kyle Quincey
2SSB Lee Stempniak 6.00 15.00
Brad Boyes
2SSH Sergei Fedorov 15.00 40.00
Cristobal Huet
2SSK Marc Savard 8.00 20.00
Phil Kessel
2SSS Henrik Sedin 5.00 12.00
Daniel Sedin
2STC Joe Thornton 10.00 25.00
Brian Campbell
2STK Jonathan Toews 75.00 150.00
Patrick Kane
2STM Jonathan Toews 50.00 100.00
Peter Mueller
2SWC Brendan Witt 5.00 12.00
Chris Campoli

2007-08 Be A Player Signatures Eight Star

STATED PRINT RUN 6 SERIAL #'d SETS
NOT PRICED DUE TO SCARCITY
8SNETS Carey Price
Josh Harding
Chris Mason
Marc-Andre Fleury
Cam Ward
Cristobal Huet
Roberto Luongo
Tim Thomas
8SSTAR Joe Sakic
Vincent Lecavalier
Jarome Iginla
Joe Thornton
Rick Nash
Dany Heatley
Jonathan Toews
Eric Staal
8SWING Ryan Smyth
Rick Nash
Martin St. Louis
Justin Williams
Thomas Vanek
Alex Tanguay
Jason Arnott
Jonathan Cheechoo

2007-08 Be A Player Signatures Five Star

STATED PRINT RUN 9 SERIAL #'d SETS
NOT PRICED DUE TO SCARCITY
5SBRVSS Brad Boyes
Paul Stastny
Thomas Vanek
Mike Richards
Jordan Staal
5SCMSMK Peter Mueller
Tyler Kennedy
Torrey Mitchell
James Sheppard
David Clarkson
5SKSSTM Peter Mueller
Jordan Staal
Jonathan Toews
James Sheppard
Phil Kessel
5SMHFWP Carey Price
Marc-Andre Fleury
Cam Ward
Chris Mason
Cristobal Huet
5SOMPMH Chris Mason
Chris Osgood
Carey Price
Roberto Luongo
Josh Harding
5SSLTSS Joe Sakic
Eric Staal
Joe Thornton
Vincent Lecavalier
Jason Spezza
5SSTPKM Carey Price
Jonathan Toews
Peter Mueller
James Sheppard
Patrick Kane

2007-08 Be A Player Signatures Foursomes

STATED PRINT RUN 10 SERIAL #'d SETS
NOT PRICED DUE TO SCARCITY
4SCCCV Daniel Carcillo
Chris Conner
David Clarkson
Aaron Voros
4SCGPK Patrick Kane
Zach Parise
Tim Connolly
Brian Gionta
4SFSSH Jason Spezza
Cory Stillman
Dany Heatley
Mike Fisher
4SHFWS Marc-Andre Fleury
Marian Hossa
Jordan Staal
Ryan Whitney
4SHLDC Dominik Hasek
Nicklas Lidstrom
Dan Cleary
Kris Draper
4SIKTM Jarome Iginla
Alex Tanguay
Miikka Kiprusoff
David Moss
4SIWSC Jarome Iginla
Justin Williams
Martin St. Louis
Jonathan Cheechoo
4SKBRC Daniel Briere
Mike Richards
Mike Knuble
Jeff Carter
4SLJRR Olli Jokinen
Jere Lehtinen
Tuomo Ruutu
Jarkko Ruutu
4SLMAS Vincent Lecavalier
Patrick Marleau
Marc Savard
Jason Arnott
4SMTCC Joe Thornton
Patrick Marleau
Brian Campbell
Jonathan Cheechoo
4SNSSM Markus Naslund
Roberto Luongo
Daniel Sedin
Henrik Sedin
4SSLSS Joe Sakic
Vincent Lecavalier
Jason Spezza
Marc Savard
4SSLTK Marc Savard
Tim Thomas
Milan Lucic
Phil Kessel
4SSSSW Paul Stastny
Ryan Smyth
Joe Sakic
Wojtek Wolski
4SVSHN Thomas Vanek
Ryan Smyth
Dany Heatley
Rick Nash

2007-08 Be A Player Signatures Seven Star

STATED PRINT RUN 7 SERIAL #'d SETS
NOT PRICED DUE TO SCARCITY
7SCNTR Joe Sakic
Vincent Lecavalier
Joe Thornton
Patrick Marleau
Eric Staal
Mike Richards
Jason Spezza
7SDEF1 Nicklas Lidstrom
Duncan Keith
Brent Seabrook
Jack Johnson
Dan Boyle
Jay Bouwmeester
Mike Commodore
7SGOAL Miikka Kiprusoff
Cristobal Huet
Carey Price
Marc-Andre Fleury
Dominik Hasek
Josh Harding
Roberto Luongo
7SSWED Nicklas Lidstrom
Niklas Backstrom
Markus Naslund
Daniel Sedin
Tobias Enstrom
Johan Hedberg
Henrik Sedin

2007-08 Be A Player Signatures Six Star

STATED PRINT RUN 8 SERIAL #'d SETS
NOT PRICED DUE TO SCARCITY
6SRUS Evgeni Malkin
Alexander Ovechkin
Nikolai Zherdev
Sergei Gonchar
Andrei Markov
Ilya Bryzgalov
6SCAN1 Joe Sakic
Dany Heatley
Jarome Iginla
Wade Redden
Brian Campbell

Roberto Luongo
6SCAN2 Joe Thornton
Ryan Smyth
Martin St. Louis
Mike Commodore
Robyn Regehr
Chris Mason
6SCAN3 Jason Arnott
Dany Heatley
Rick Nash
Jay Bouwmeester
Nick Schultz
Roberto Luongo
6SYNG1 Jonathan Toews
Peter Mueller
Patrick Kane
Jack Johnson
Matt Niskanen
Carey Price
6SYNG2 Paul Stastny
Wojtek Wolski
Lee Stempniak
Brent Seabrook
Dan Boyle
Marc-Andre Fleury
6SYSTR Milan Lucic
Peter Mueller
Patrick Kane
Matt Niskanen
Tobias Enstrom
Carey Price

2007-08 Be A Player Signatures Trios

STATED PRINT RUN 25 SERIAL #'d SETS
3SASF Dany Heatley 25.00 60.00
Jason Spezza
Mike Fisher
3SBTP Jonathan Toews 100.00 200.00
Peter Mueller
Carey Price
3SCAP Daniel Carcillo 15.00 40.00
Andrew Peters
Chris Neil
3SCPV Thomas Vanek 15.00 40.00
Tim Connolly
Jason Pominville
3SCWS Justin Williams 20.00 50.00
Eric Staal
Erik Cole
3SEGP Zach Parise
Patrik Elias
Brian Gionta
3SHKS Tyler Kennedy 25.00 60.00
Marian Hossa
Jordan Staal
3SHPK Tomas Plekanec 15.00 40.00
Chris Higgins
Saku Koivu
3SIKT Alex Tanguay 30.00 80.00
Miikka Kiprusoff
Jarome Iginla
3SKBR Mike Knuble 25.00 60.00
Mike Richards
Daniel Briere
3SKPL Miikka Kiprusoff 100.00 200.00
Carey Price
Roberto Luongo
3SKSM Patrick Kane 40.00 100.00
Iorrey Mitchell
James Sheppard
3SLMH Milan Michalek 30.00 80.00
Martin Hanzal
Milan Lucic
3SMBS Jamal Mayers 15.00 40.00
Brad Boyes
Lee Stempniak
3SMHF Marc-Andre Fleury 30.00 60.00
Chris Mason
Cristobal Huet
3SNRL Kris Russell
Matt Niskanen
Mike Lundin
3SNSS Markus Naslund 20.00 50.00
Daniel Sedin
Henrik Sedin
3SPDB Rod Brind'Amour 30.00 60.00
Kris Draper
Michael Peca
3SPRC Wade Redden 12.00 30.00
Chris Phillips
Mike Commodore
3SSBH James Sheppard 15.00 40.00
Pierre-Marc Bouchard
Josh Harding
3SSHN Martin St. Louis 25.00 60.00
Rick Nash
Dany Heatley
3SSMK Marc Savard 30.00 60.00
Glen Murray
Phil Kessel
3SSSS Joe Sakic
Paul Stastny
Ryan Smyth
3SSTT Joe Sakic 100.00 200.00
Joe Thornton
Jonathan Toews
3STCM Joe Thornton 25.00 60.00
Jonathan Cheechoo
Milan Michalek

2008-09 Be A Player

COMP.SET w/o SPs (180) 25.00 60.00
STATED PRINT RUN 99 SER.#'d SETS
COMMON REDEMPTION (281-340) 12.00 30.00
1 Ryan Getzlaf .50 1.25
2 Corey Perry .40 1.00
3 Chris Pronger .30 .75
4 Teemu Selanne .40 1.00
5 Bobby Ryan .60 1.50
6 Scott Niedermayer .25 .60
7 Jean-Sebastien Giguere .40 1.00
8 Ilya Kovalchuk .50 1.25
9 Bryan Little .25 .60
10 Kari Lehtonen .25 .60
11 Slava Kozlov .25 .60
12 Todd White .25 .60
13 Patrice Bergeron .40 1.00
14 Marc Savard .25 .60
15 David Krejci .30 .75
16 Phil Kessel .40 1.00
17 Zdeno Chara .25 .60
18 Tim Thomas .40 1.00
19 Michael Ryder .30 .75
20 Derek Roy .25 .60
21 Thomas Vanek .40 1.00
22 Jason Pominville .30 .75
23 Ryan Miller .40 1.00
24 Drew Stafford .40 1.00
25 Jarome Iginla .75 2.00
26 Mike Cammalleri .40 1.00
27 Daymond Langkow .25 .60
28 Todd Bertuzzi .40 1.00
29 Dion Phaneuf .40 1.00
30 Miikka Kiprusoff .40 1.00
31 Rene Bourque .40 1.00
32 Ray Whitney .25 .60
33 Cam Ward .40 1.00
34 Eric Staal .60 1.50
35 Tuomo Ruutu .40 1.00
36 Rod Brind'Amour .30 .75
37 Sergei Samsonov .25 .60
38 Patrick Kane 1.00 2.50
39 Jonathan Toews 1.25 3.00
40 Kris Versteeg .60 1.50
41 Patrick Sharp .25 .60
42 Brian Campbell .60 1.50
43 Nikolai Khabibulin .40 1.00
44 Cristobal Huet .40 1.00
45 Paul Stastny .40 1.00
46 Milan Hejduk .30 .75
47 Ryan Smyth .30 .75
48 Wojtek Wolski .25 .60
49 Joe Sakic .60 1.50
50 Peter Budaj .30 .75
51 Rick Nash .40 1.00
52 Kristian Huselius .25 .60
53 R.J. Umberger .25 .60
54 Mike Commodore .25 .60
55 Fredrik Modin .25 .60
56 Brenden Morrow .30 .75
57 Brad Richards .30 .75
58 Mike Ribeiro .25 .60
59 Loui Eriksson .25 .60
60 Mike Modano .40 1.00
61 Marty Turco .30 .75
62 Pavel Datsyuk .40 1.00
63 Marian Hossa .60 1.50
64 Henrik Zetterberg .75 2.00
65 Nicklas Lidstrom .40 1.00
66 Tomas Holmstrom .30 .75
67 Johan Franzen .25 .60
68 Chris Osgood .40 1.00
69 Sam Gagner .60 1.50
70 Ales Hemsky .25 .60
71 Sheldon Souray .25 .60
72 Andrew Cogliano .60 1.50
73 Shawn Horcoff .25 .60
74 Dwayne Roloson .30 .75
75 Stephen Weiss .25 .60
76 David Booth .30 .75
77 Jay Bouwmeester .30 .75
78 Nathan Horton .25 .60
79 Tomas Vokoun .40 1.00
80 Anze Kopitar .40 1.00
81 Dustin Brown .25 .60
82 Alexander Frolov .25 .60
83 Patrick O'Sullivan .30 .75
84 Jarret Stoll .30 .75
85 Marek Zidlicky .25 .60
86 Mikko Koivu .40 1.00
87 Antti Miettinen .25 .60
88 Andrew Brunette .25 .60
89 Pierre-Marc Bouchard .25 .60
90 Niklas Backstrom .40 1.00
91 Robert Lang .25 .60
92 Alex Kovalev .40 1.00
93 Andrei Markov .30 .75
94 Alex Tanguay .30 .75
95 Carey Price 1.25 3.00
96 Andrei Kostitsyn .30 .75
97 Saku Koivu .40 1.00
98 J.P. Dumont .25 .60
99 Shea Weber .25 .60
100 Martin Erat .40 1.00
101 Jason Arnott .25 .60
102 Dan Ellis .25 .60
103 Martin Brodeur .75 2.00
104 Patrik Elias .25 .60
105 Zach Parise .40 1.00
106 Brian Gionta .40 1.00
107 Travis Zajac .25 .60
108 Scott Clemmensen .25 .60
109 Mark Streit .25 .60
110 Doug Weight .25 .60
111 Bill Guerin .25 .60
112 Trent Hunter .25 .60
113 Joey MacDonald .25 .60
114 Rick DiPietro .40 1.00
115 Nikolai Zherdev .25 .60
116 Scott Gomez .30 .75
117 Markus Naslund .40 1.00
118 Chris Drury .40 1.00
119 Brandon Dubinsky .30 .75
120 Henrik Lundqvist .75 2.00
121 Wade Redden .25 .60
122 Dany Heatley .50 1.25
123 Daniel Alfredsson .30 .75
124 Jason Spezza .50 1.25
125 Nick Foligno .40 1.00
126 Antoine Vermette .25 .60
127 Alex Auld .25 .60
128 Jeff Carter .40 1.00
129 Mike Richards .60 1.50
130 Simon Gagne .30 .75
131 Scott Hartnell .30 .75
132 Mike Knuble .40 1.00
133 Martin Biron .30 .75
134 Peter Mueller .50 1.25
135 Shane Doan .25 .60
136 Olli Jokinen .25 .60
137 Ed Jovanovski .25 .60
138 Martin Hanzal .30 .75
139 Ilya Bryzgalov .25 .60
140 Sidney Crosby 2.00 5.00
141 Jordan Staal .60 1.50
142 Evgeni Malkin 1.00 2.50
143 Petr Sykora .25 .60
144 Miroslav Satan .25 .60
145 Marc-Andre Fleury .40 1.00
146 Ruslan Fedotenko .25 .60
147 Joe Thornton .60 1.50
148 Devin Setoguchi .40 1.00
149 Patrick Marleau .30 .75
150 Milan Michalek .25 .60
151 Dan Boyle .30 .75
152 Jonathan Cheechoo .40 1.00
153 Evgeni Nabokov .40 1.00
154 David Backes .25 .60
155 Brad Boyes .30 .75
156 Keith Tkachuk .30 .75
157 David Perron .30 .75
158 Paul Kariya .40 1.00
159 Manny Legace .30 .75
160 Martin St. Louis .40 1.00
161 Vincent Lecavalier .40 1.00
162 Vaclav Prospal .25 .60
163 Mark Recchi .30 .75
164 Mike Smith .30 .75
165 Nik Antropov .30 .75
166 Matt Stajan .30 .75
167 Alexei Ponikarovsky .25 .60
168 Tomas Kaberle .25 .60
169 Lee Stempniak .25 .60
170 Vesa Toskala .40 1.00
171 Daniel Sedin .40 1.00
172 Henrik Sedin .40 1.00
173 Pavol Demitra .25 .60
174 Kyle Wellwood .25 .60
175 Roberto Luongo .60 1.50
176 Alexander Ovechkin 1.50 4.00
177 Nicklas Backstrom .75 2.00
178 Alexander Semin .40 1.00
179 Mike Green (Wa Capitals) .25 .60
180 Jose Theodore .40 1.00
181 Zach Bogosian RC 12.00 30.00
182 Brandon Sutter RC 8.00 20.00
183 Jakub Voracek RC 12.00 30.00
184 Fabian Brunnstrom RC 10.00 25.00
185 Drew Doughty RC 20.00 50.00
186 Colton Gillies RC 6.00 15.00
187 Josh Bailey RC 10.00 25.00
188 Kyle Okposo RC 12.00 30.00
189 Kyle Turris RC 12.00 30.00
190 Patrik Berglund RC 15.00 40.00
191 Steven Stamkos RC 60.00 120.00
192 Luke Schenn RC 20.00 50.00
193 Cory Schneider RC 12.00 30.00
194 Karl Alzner RC 10.00 25.00
195 Blake Wheeler RC 15.00 40.00
196 Zach Boychuk RC 10.00 25.00
197 Derick Brassard RC 12.00 30.00
198 James Neal RC 10.00 25.00
199 Max Pacioretty RC 15.00 40.00
200 Patric Hornqvist RC 6.00 15.00
201 Mikkel Boedker RC 10.00 25.00
202 T.J. Oshie RC 15.00 40.00
203 Nikolai Kulemin RC 6.00 15.00
204 Tim Kennedy RC 10.00 25.00
205 Nikita Filatov RC 25.00 60.00
206 Mark Fistric RC 5.00 12.00
207 Michael Frolik RC 12.00 30.00
208 Oscar Moller RC 6.00 15.00
209 Brian Lee RC 6.00 15.00
210 Claude Giroux RC 12.00 30.00
211 Alex Goligoski RC 12.00 30.00
212 Jamie McGinn RC 6.00 15.00
213 Alex Pietrangelo RC 10.00 25.00
214 Justin Pogge RC 12.00 30.00
215 Simeon Varlamov RC 50.00 100.00
216 Chris Stewart RC 8.00 20.00
217 Michal Repik RC 8.00 20.00
218 Jon Filewich RC 5.00 12.00
219 Dustin Jeffrey RC 10.00 25.00
220 Robbie Earl RC 5.00 12.00
221 Tom Cavanagh RC 5.00 12.00
222 Nathan Gerbe RC 12.00 30.00
223 Steve Mason RC 15.00 40.00
224 Brian Boyle RC 6.00 15.00
225 Ben Maxwell RC 10.00 25.00
226 Ilya Zubov RC 6.00 15.00
227 Brendan Mikkelson RC 4.00 10.00
228 Justin Abdelkader RC 12.00 30.00
229 Trevor Smith RC 5.00 12.00
230 Ty Wishart RC 6.00 15.00
231 Oskar Osala RC 15.00 40.00
232 Theo Peckham RC 6.00 15.00
233 Shawn Matthias RC 6.00 15.00
234 Tyler Plante RC 6.00 15.00
235 Kenndal McArdle RC 6.00 15.00
236 Derek Joslin RC 5.00 12.00
237 Ben Bishop RC 10.00 25.00
238 Adam Pineault RC 6.00 15.00
239 Brett Carson RC 6.00 15.00
240 Jonathan Ericsson RC 8.00 20.00
241 Trevor Lewis RC 6.00 15.00
242 Lauri Korpikoski RC 6.00 15.00
243 Ryan Stone RC 6.00 15.00
244 Boris Valabik RC 8.00 20.00
245 John Curry RC 8.00 20.00
246 Niklas Hjalmarsson RC 10.00 25.00
247 Darren Helm RC 10.00 25.00
248 Teddy Purcell RC 10.00 25.00
249 Radek Smolenak RC 8.00 20.00
250 Andrew Gordon RC 10.00 25.00
251 Josh Tordjman RC 10.00 25.00
252 Justin Peters RC 6.00 15.00
253 Tom Sestito RC 5.00 12.00
254 Matt D'Agostini RC 10.00 25.00
255 Martins Karsums RC 12.00 30.00
256 Paul Szczechura RC 8.00 20.00
257 Andrew Ebbett RC 6.00 15.00
258 Dan LaCosta RC 8.00 20.00
259 Jonas Junland RC 10.00 25.00
260 Maxsim Mayorov RC 12.00 30.00
261 Mattias Ritola RC 8.00 20.00
262 Corey Potter RC 10.00 25.00
263 Sami Lepisto RC 6.00 15.00
264 Danny Taylor RC 6.00 15.00
265 Brett Sutter RC 6.00 15.00
266 Derek Dorsett RC 8.00 20.00
267 Tim Sestito RC 5.00 12.00
268 Wayne Simmonds RC 6.00 15.00
269 Ryan Jones RC 8.00 20.00
270 Zack Smith RC 5.00 12.00
271 Luca Sbisa RC 10.00 25.00
272 Jonathon Kalinski RC 6.00 15.00
273 Viktor Tikhonov RC 6.00 15.00
274 Kevin Porter RC 5.00 12.00
275 Chris Porter RC 6.00 15.00
276 Vladimir Mihalik RC 6.00 15.00
277 Jonas Frogren RC 8.00 20.00
278 John Mitchell RC 6.00 15.00
279 Andreas Nodl RC 6.00 15.00
280 Janne Pesonen RC 5.00 12.00
281 John Tavares XRC 50.00 100.00
282 Victor Hedman XRC 15.00 40.00
283 Matt Duchene XRC 15.00 40.00
284 Jonas Gustavsson XRC 15.00 40.00
285 Oskars Bartulis XRC 8.00 20.00
286 Daniel Larsson XRC 12.00 30.00
287 Ryan O'Marra XRC 8.00 20.00
288 Mathieu Perreault XRC 6.00 15.00
289 Lars Eller XRC 8.00 20.00
290 Mathieu Carle XRC 8.00 20.00
291 Brad Marchand XRC 8.00 20.00
292 Logan Couture XRC 8.00 20.00
293 Perttu Lindgren XRC 6.00 15.00
294 Braden Holtby XRC 6.00 15.00
295 Michael Grabner XRC 10.00 25.00
296 Cody Franson XRC 6.00 15.00
297 James Reimer XRC 10.00 25.00
298 Jason Demers XRC 8.00 20.00
299 Sergei Shirokov XRC 8.00 20.00
300 Viktor Stalberg XRC 8.00 20.00
301 Benn Ferriero XRC 8.00 20.00
302 Tyler Bozak XRC 10.00 25.00
303 James van Riemsdyk XRC 12.00 30.00
304 Erik Karlsson XRC 10.00 25.00
305 Matt Gilroy XRC 8.00 20.00
306 Colin Wilson XRC 8.00 20.00
307 Alec Martinez XRC 6.00 15.00
308 Dmitry Kulikov XRC 10.00 25.00
309 Jamie Benn XRC 5.00 12.00
310 Ryan O'Reilly XRC 8.00 20.00
311 Tyler Myers XRC 8.00 20.00
312 Evander Kane XRC 12.00 30.00
313 Antti Niemi XRC 25.00 60.00
314 Frazer McLaren XRC 5.00 12.00
315 Michael Del Zotto XRC 6.00 15.00
316 Ville Leino XRC 12.00 30.00
317 Michal Neuvirth XRC 8.00 20.00
318 Matt Pelech XRC 10.00 25.00
319 Riku Helenius XRC 6.00 15.00
320 Ivan Vishnevskiy XRC 6.00 15.00
321 Jhonas Enroth XRC 6.00 15.00
322 Artem Anisimov XRC 6.00 15.00
323 Mikael Backlund XRC 8.00 20.00
324 Christian Hanson XRC 8.00 20.00
325 Yannick Weber XRC 6.00 15.00
326 T.J. Galiardi XRC 6.00 15.00
327 Spencer Machacek XRC 5.00 12.00
328 Luca Caputi XRC 12.00 30.00
329 Brian Salcido XRC 10.00 25.00
330 Tyler Ennis XRC 12.00 30.00
331 Carl Gunnarsson XRC 6.00 15.00
332 Alexander Salak XRC 8.00 20.00
333 Scott Parse XRC 5.00 12.00
334 Matt Beleskey XRC 5.00 12.00
335 Cal O'Reilly XRC 6.00 15.00
336 Taylor Chorney XRC 6.00 15.00
337 Mike Santorelli XRC 6.00 15.00
338 Peter Regin XRC 8.00 20.00
339 Kris Chucko XRC 6.00 15.00
340 John Scott XRC 5.00 12.00

2008-09 Be A Player Player's Club

STATED PRINT RUN 15 SER.#'d SETS
ROOKIE PRINT RUN 10 SER.#'d SETS
NOT PRICED DUE TO SCARCITY

2008-09 Be A Player Rookie Jerseys

STATED ODDS 1:9
STATED PRINT RUN 299 SER.#'d SETS
RJ-AP Alex Pietrangelo 6.00 15.00
RJ-BM Ben Maxwell 6.00 15.00
RJ-BS Brandon Sutter 5.00 12.00
RJ-BW Blake Wheeler 10.00 25.00
RJ-CG Colton Gillies 4.00 10.00
RJ-CS Cory Schneider 8.00 20.00
RJ-DB Derick Brassard 8.00 20.00
RJ-DD Drew Doughty 12.00 30.00
RJ-FB Fabian Brunnstrom 6.00 15.00
RJ-GI Claude Giroux 8.00 20.00
RJ-JB Josh Bailey 6.00 15.00
RJ-JN James Neal 6.00 15.00
RJ-JP Justin Pogge 8.00 20.00
RJ-JV Jakub Voracek 8.00 20.00
RJ-KA Karl Alzner 6.00 15.00
RJ-KO Kyle Okposo 8.00 20.00
RJ-KT Kyle Turris 8.00 20.00
RJ-LS Luke Schenn 12.00 30.00
RJ-MB Mikkel Boedker 6.00 15.00
RJ-MF Michael Frolik 8.00 20.00
RJ-MP Max Pacioretty 10.00 25.00
RJ-NF Nikita Filatov 15.00 40.00
RJ-NK Nikolai Kulemin 4.00 10.00
RJ-PB Patrik Berglund 10.00 25.00
RJ-SB Luca Sbisa 6.00 15.00
RJ-SM Steve Mason 15.00 40.00
RJ-SS Steven Stamkos 15.00 40.00
RJ-ST Chris Stewart 5.00 12.00
RJ-TO T.J. Oshie 10.00 25.00
RJ-VT Viktor Tikhonov 4.00 10.00
RJ-ZB Zach Bogosian 8.00 20.00

2008-09 Be A Player Signatures

STATED ODDS 1 PER PACK
S-AA Adrian Aucoin 3.00 8.00
S-AB Adam Burish 4.00 10.00
S-AE Alexander Edler 4.00 10.00
S-AF Andrew Ference 3.00 8.00
S-AK Anze Kopitar 5.00 12.00
S-AL Andreas Lilja 3.00 8.00
S-AM Andy McDonald 3.00 8.00
S-AP Andrew Peters 3.00 8.00
S-BA Bryan Allen 3.00 8.00
S-BB Brad Boyes 4.00 10.00
S-BC Brian Campbell 8.00 20.00
S-BE Patrik Berglund 12.00 30.00
S-BG Ben Guite 3.00 8.00
S-BI Kevin Bieksa 3.00 8.00
S-BJ Josh Bailey 8.00 20.00
S-BK Rob Blake 5.00 12.00
S-BL Brian Lee 5.00 12.00
S-BO David Booth 3.00 8.00
S-BR Derick Brassard 10.00 25.00
S-BS Brian Sutherby 3.00 8.00
S-BU Alexandre Burrows 4.00 10.00
S-BY Dan Boyle 4.00 10.00
S-CD Chris Drury 5.00 12.00
S-CG Colton Gillies 5.00 12.00
S-CH Cristobal Huet 5.00 12.00
S-CL David Clarkson 3.00 8.00
S-CO Chris Osgood 5.00 12.00
S-CP Corey Perry 5.00 12.00
S-CS Cory Stillman 3.00 8.00
S-DA Daniel Sedin 5.00 12.00
S-DB Dustin Boyd 3.00 8.00
S-DC Dan Cleary 5.00 12.00
S-DE Dan Ellis 3.00 8.00
S-DH Dan Hamhuis 3.00 8.00
S-DK Duncan Keith 4.00 10.00
S-DM Darren McCarty 4.00 10.00
S-DO Dominic Moore 3.00 8.00
S-DP Daniel Paille 4.00 10.00
S-DR Derek Roy 3.00 8.00
S-DU Dustin Brown 3.00 8.00
S-DV Devin Setoguchi 5.00 12.00
S-DW Doug Weight 3.00 8.00
S-EB Eric Brewer 3.00 8.00
S-EM Evgeni Malkin 25.00 60.00
S-EN Evgeni Nabokov 5.00 12.00
S-ES Eric Staal 8.00 20.00
S-FL Marc-Andre Fleury 8.00 20.00
S-FM Fredrik Modin 3.00 8.00
S-FR Alexander Frolov 3.00 8.00
S-GA Simon Gagne 4.00 10.00
S-GI Brian Gionta 5.00 12.00
S-GP George Parros 3.00 8.00
S-GU Bill Guerin 3.00 8.00
S-HA Scott Hartnell 4.00 10.00
S-HE Dany Heatley 6.00 15.00
S-HO Patric Hornqvist 5.00 12.00
S-HS Henrik Sedin 5.00 12.00
S-IB Ilya Bryzgalov 3.00 8.00
S-JA Jason Arnott 3.00 8.00
S-JB Jay Bouwmeester 4.00 10.00
S-JC Jeff Carter 5.00 12.00
S-JD J.P. Dumont 3.00 8.00
S-JF Johan Franzen 8.00 20.00
S-JH Josh Harding 4.00 10.00
S-JO John Oduya 3.00 8.00
S-JP Jason Pominville 4.00 10.00
S-JS Joe Sakic 15.00 40.00
S-JV Jakub Voracek 10.00 25.00
S-JW James Wisniewski 3.00 8.00
S-KB Keith Ballard 3.00 8.00
S-KE Ryan Kesler 3.00 8.00
S-KT Kyle Turris 10.00 25.00
S-LA Brooks Laich 4.00 10.00
S-LO Matthew Lombardi 3.00 8.00
S-LS Luca Sbisa 8.00 20.00
S-LU Brad Lukowich 3.00 8.00
S-MA Paul Martin 3.00 8.00
S-MB Martin Biron 4.00 10.00
S-MC Mike Commodore 3.00 8.00
S-MF Mike Fisher 3.00 8.00
S-MH Marian Hossa 8.00 20.00
S-MI Mikkel Boedker 8.00 20.00
S-MK Mike Komisarek 4.00 10.00
S-MM Milan Michalek 3.00 8.00
S-MN Markus Naslund 5.00 12.00
S-MO Derek Morris 3.00 8.00
S-MR Mason Raymond 3.00 8.00
S-MT Maxime Talbot 4.00 10.00
S-MU Peter Mueller 6.00 15.00
S-MV Marc-Edouard Vlasic 3.00 8.00
S-MY Manny Malhotra 3.00 8.00
S-NA Nik Antropov 4.00 10.00
S-NB Niklas Backstrom 5.00 12.00
S-NF Nick Foligno 5.00 12.00
S-NH Nathan Horton 3.00 8.00
S-NK Nikolai Kulemin 5.00 12.00
S-NL Nicklas Lidstrom 10.00 25.00
S-NS Nick Schultz 3.00 8.00
S-OJ Olli Jokinen 3.00 8.00
S-OK Kyle Okposo 10.00 25.00
S-OM Oscar Moller 5.00 12.00
S-PA Paul Kariya 8.00 20.00
S-PC Chris Phillips 3.00 8.00
S-PD David Perron 4.00 10.00
S-PE Patrik Elias 3.00 8.00
S-PH Dion Phaneuf 5.00 12.00
S-PM Patrick Marleau 4.00 10.00
S-PO Patrick O'Sullivan 4.00 10.00
S-PS Paul Stastny 5.00 12.00
S-RA Brian Rafalski 3.00 8.00
S-RB Rod Brind`Amour 4.00 10.00
S-RG Ryan Getzlaf 6.00 15.00
S-RI Mike Richards SP 75.00 150.00
S-RK Rostislav Klesla 5.00 12.00
S-RO Rostislav Olesz 3.00 8.00
S-RR Robyn Regehr 3.00 8.00
S-RS Ryan Smyth 4.00 10.00
S-RT Raffi Torres 3.00 8.00
S-RU R.J. Umberger 3.00 8.00
S-RW Ray Whitney 3.00 8.00
S-SC Sidney Crosby 75.00 150.00
S-SD Shane Doan 3.00 8.00
S-SE Brent Seabrook 4.00 10.00
S-SF Sergei Fedorov 8.00 20.00
S-SG Scott Gomez 4.00 10.00
S-SH James Sheppard 5.00 12.00
S-SI Mike Sillinger 3.00 8.00
S-SJ Jordan Staal 8.00 20.00
S-SL Luke Schenn 15.00 40.00
S-SN Scott Niedermayer 3.00 8.00
S-SP Jason Spezza 6.00 15.00
S-ST Matt Stajan 4.00 10.00
S-SU Ryan Suter 3.00 8.00
S-SW Scott Walker 3.00 8.00
S-TA Jeff Tambellini 3.00 8.00
S-TG Tim Gleason 3.00 8.00
S-TH Jose Theodore 5.00 12.00
S-TM Travis Moen 3.00 8.00
S-TN Teppo Numminen 4.00 10.00
S-TO T.J. Oshie 15.00 40.00
S-TP Tom Preissing 3.00 8.00
S-TR Tuomo Ruutu 5.00 12.00
S-TT Tim Thomas 5.00 12.00
S-TV Thomas Vanek 5.00 12.00
S-TZ Travis Zajac 3.00 8.00
S-VO Tomas Vokoun 5.00 12.00
S-WE Stephen Weiss 3.00 8.00
S-WM Willie Mitchell 3.00 8.00
S-WS Shea Weber 3.00 8.00
S-WW Wojtek Wolski 3.00 8.00
S-ZP Zach Parise 5.00 12.00
S-BRI Daniel Briere 5.00 12.00
S-BUR Brent Burns 3.00 8.00
S-MAR Andrei Markov 4.00 10.00
S-STA Marc Staal 6.00 15.00

2008-09 Be A Player Signatures Player's Club

STATED PRINT RUN 15 SER. #'d SETS
NOT PRICED DUE TO SCARCITY

2008-09 Be A Player Signatures Dual

STATED ODDS 1:8
S2-AD J.P. Dumont 5.00 12.00
Jason Arnott
S2-AK Nikolai Kulemin 8.00 20.00
Nik Antropov
S2-BB Rob Blake 8.00 20.00
Dan Boyle
S2-BH Josh Harding 8.00 20.00
Niklas Backstrom
S2-BS Rod Brind`Amour 12.00 30.00
Eric Staal
S2-BV Jakub Voracek 15.00 40.00
Derick Brassard
S2-CH Cristobal Huet 12.00 30.00
Brian Campbell
S2-FM Marc-Andre Fleury 25.00 60.00
Evgeni Malkin
S2-GB Daniel Briere 8.00 20.00
Simon Gagne
S2-GP Brian Gionta 8.00 20.00
Zach Parise
S2-HB Nathan Horton 5.00 12.00
David Booth
S2-HC Dan Cleary 15.00 40.00
Marian Hossa
S2-JK Jay Bouwmeester 6.00 15.00
Keith Ballard
S2-JP Paul Stastny 20.00 50.00
Joe Sakic
S2-KB Paul Kariya 12.00 30.00
Brad Boyes
S2-KJ Kyle Okposo 12.00 30.00
Josh Bailey
S2-LB Dustin Boyd 5.00 12.00
Matthew Lombardi
S2-ME Alexander Edler 6.00 15.00
Willie Mitchell
S2-MK Andrei Markov 6.00 15.00
Mike Komisarek
S2-MS Devin Setoguchi 8.00 20.00
Patrick Marleau
S2-MT Peter Mueller 15.00 40.00
Kyle Turris
S2-NG Ryan Getzlaf 10.00 25.00
Scott Niedermayer
S2-OK Anze Kopitar 8.00 20.00
Patrick O'Sullivan
S2-PV Thomas Vanek 8.00 20.00
Jason Pominville
S2-RC Jeff Carter 25.00 60.00
Mike Richards
S2-SG James Sheppard 8.00 20.00
Colton Gillies
S2-SH Dany Heatley 10.00 25.00
Jason Spezza
S2-SK Brent Seabrook 10.00 25.00
Duncan Keith
S2-SS Daniel Sedin 8.00 20.00
Henrik Sedin
S2-SW Shea Weber 5.00 12.00
Ryan Suter
S2-TP Patrik Berglund 20.00 50.00
T.J. Oshie
S2-WG Bill Guerin 5.00 12.00
Doug Weight

2008-09 Be A Player Signatures Four Star

STATED PRINT RUN 10 SER.#'d SETS
NOT PRICED DUE TO SCARCITY
S4-TBHF Cristobal Huet
Marc-Andre Fleury
Martin Biron
Jose Theodore

2008-09 Be A Player Signatures Six Star

STATED PRINT RUN 8 SER. #'d SETS
NOT PRICED DUE TO SCARCITY
S6DEF Brian Campbell
Scott Niedermayer
Dion Phaneuf
Jay Bouwmeester
Dan Boyle
Shea Weber

2008-09 Be A Player Signatures Trios

STATED PRINT RUN 35 SER.#'d SETS
S3-AWE Jason Arnott 12.00 30.00
Shea Weber
Dan Ellis
S3-BRC Daniel Briere 100.00 175.00
Mike Richards
Jeff Carter
S3-BSG Niklas Backstrom 20.00 50.00
James Sheppard
Colton Gillies
S3-EGP Patrik Elias 20.00 50.00
Brian Gionta
Zach Parise
S3-FMS Marc-Andre Fleury 50.00 120.00
Evgeni Malkin
Jordan Staal
S3-FSH Mike Fisher 25.00 60.00
Jason Spezza
Dany Heatley
S3-HOF Marian Hossa 30.00 80.00
Chris Osgood
Johan Franzen
S3-JDM Olli Jokinen 25.00 60.00
Shane Doan
Peter Mueller
S3-KBM Paul Kariya 20.00 50.00
Brad Boyes
Andy McDonald
S3-MNB Patrick Marleau 20.00 50.00
Evgeni Nabokov
Dan Boyle
S3-SSE Henrik Sedin 20.00 50.00
Daniel Sedin
Alexander Edler
S3-SSS Joe Sakic 30.00 80.00
Ryan Smyth
Paul Stastny
S3-TOB Jeff Tambellini 40.00 100.00
Kyle Okposo
Josh Bailey
S3-VBH Tomas Vokoun 20.00 50.00
Jay Bouwmeester
Nathan Horton
S3-WBS Ray Whitney 30.00 80.00
Rod Brind`Amour
Eric Staal

2009-10 Be A Player

COMP.SET w/o SPs (200) 25.00 50.00
RC PRINT RUN 99 SER.#'d SETS
EXCH PRINT RUN 99 SER.#'d SETS
1 Sidney Crosby 2.00 5.00
2 Joe Thornton .75 2.00
3 Jamal Mayers .25 .60
4 Ryan Getzlaf .60 1.50
5 Pierre-Marc Bouchard .30 .75
6 Eric Staal .50 1.25
7 Mikkel Boedker .30 .75
8 Daniel Sedin .50 1.25
9 Patric Hornqvist .30 .75
10 Zdeno Chara .25 .60
11 Mike Richards .75 2.00
12 Nicklas Lidstrom .50 1.25
13 Patrick Kane .75 2.00
14 Mark Stuart .25 .60
15 Oscar Moller .30 .75
16 Josh Bailey .30 .75
17 Luca Sbisa .50 1.25
18 Ethan Moreau .25 .60
19 Phil Kessel .40 1.00
20 Ondrej Pavelec .30 .75
21 Mike Sillinger .25 .60
22 Boyd Gordon .25 .60
23 Kristopher Letang .40 1.00
24 Brad Richards .30 .75
25 Nathan McIver .25 .60
26 Martin Brodeur 1.00 2.50
27 Zach Parise .40 1.00
28 Dany Heatley .75 2.00
29 Mike Cammalleri .30 .75
30 Tomas Vokoun .40 1.00
31 Scott Hartnell .25 .60
32 Roberto Luongo 1.00 2.50
33 Wojtek Wolski .25 .60
34 Ryan Callahan .25 .60
35 Aaron Voros .25 .60
36 Bobby Ryan .50 1.25
37 Nick Schultz .25 .60
38 Henrik Zetterberg .75 2.00
39 Nick Foligno .40 1.00
40 Patrick O'Sullivan .30 .75
41 Dan Hamhuis .25 .60
42 Scott Walker .25 .60
43 Eric Brewer .25 .60
44 Simon Gagne .40 1.00
45 Paul Martin .25 .60
46 Milan Lucic .40 1.00
47 Rostislav Klesla .40 1.00
48 Adrian Aucoin .25 .60
49 Ryan Kesler .30 .75
50 Brad Boyes .30 .75
51 Ryan Suter .25 .60
52 Mike Komisarek .30 .75
53 Tim Gleason .25 .60
54 Brooks Laich .30 .75
55 Dustin Brown .30 .75
56 Blake Wheeler .50 1.25
57 Ilya Bryzgalov .30 .75
58 Manny Malhotra .25 .60
59 Jason Spezza .50 1.25
60 Rich Peverley .30 .75
61 Paul Stastny .40 1.00
62 Tim Connolly .25 .60
63 Jeff Halpern .25 .60
64 Nathan Horton .25 .60
65 Kris Versteeg .50 1.25
66 Andrew Cogliano .50 1.25
67 Jonathan Quick .60 1.50
68 Nik Antropov .30 .75
69 David Perron .30 .75
70 Krys Barch .25 .60
71 Derek Roy .40 1.00

2009-10 Be A Player

72 Jordan Staal .50 1.25
73 Evgeni Malkin 1.00 2.50
74 Mark Streit .25 .60
75 Carey Price 1.00 2.50
76 Jean-Sebastien Giguere .40 1.00
77 Cal Clutterbuck .30 .75
78 Mike Modano .40 1.00
79 Jay Bouwmeester .40 1.00
80 Pavel Datsyuk .40 1.00
81 Jeff Carter .40 1.00
82 Marc Savard .25 .60
83 Luke Schenn .60 1.50
84 Patrick Marleau .40 1.00
85 R.J. Umberger .30 .75
86 Marc Staal .50 1.25
87 Drew Doughty .75 2.00
88 Erik Johnson .30 .75
89 Patrik Elias .30 .75
90 Alexandre Burrows .30 .75
91 Niklas Backstrom .40 1.00
92 David Krejci .30 .75
93 Ryan Malone .25 .60
94 J.P. Dumont .25 .60
95 Mike Commodore .25 .60
96 Daniel Alfredsson .40 1.00
97 Johan Franzen .25 .60
98 Erik Cole .25 .60
99 Peter Budaj .40 1.00
100 Bryan McCabe .25 .60
101 Jonathan Toews 1.00 2.50
102 Nikolai Kulemin .30 .75
103 Mikko Koivu .40 1.00
104 Robert Lang .25 .60
105 Tomas Plekanec .30 .75
106 Marty Turco .30 .75
107 Chris Campoli .30 .75
108 Mike Knuble .40 1.00
109 Vincent Lecavalier .50 1.25
110 Jussi Jokinen .40 1.00
111 Matt Greene .25 .60
112 Willie Mitchell .25 .60
113 Thomas Vanek .40 1.00
114 Scott Niedermayer .25 .60
115 Shea Weber .30 .75
116 Bryan Little .40 1.00
117 Pascal Leclaire .40 1.00
118 Brian Rafalski .25 .60
119 Olli Jokinen .25 .60
120 Shawn Horcoff .25 .60
121 Rene Bourque .25 .60
122 Joni Pitkanen .30 .75
123 Matt Bradley .25 .60
124 Matt Moulson .25 .60
125 Raffi Torres .25 .60
126 Miikka Kiprusoff .40 1.00
127 Shane Doan .30 .75
128 Patrice Bergeron .40 1.00
129 Scott Hannan .25 .60
130 Evgeni Nabokov .40 1.00
131 Steven Stamkos 1.00 2.50
132 Corey Perry .40 1.00
133 T.J. Oshie .60 1.50
134 Mikael Samuelsson .25 .60
135 Steve Mason .60 1.50
136 Drew Stafford .40 1.00
137 Chris Pronger .30 .75
138 Jonas Hiller .50 1.25
139 Robyn Regehr .30 .75
140 Bryan Allen .25 .60
141 Andrei Markov .30 .75
142 David Backes .30 .75
143 Derick Brassard .40 1.00
144 Tuukka Rask .50 1.25
145 Martin Havlat .30 .75
146 Mike Grier .25 .60
147 Dan Boyle .25 .60
148 Shawn Thornton .25 .60
149 Marc-Andre Fleury .40 1.00
150 Matt Stajan .30 .75
151 Daniel Briere .40 1.00
152 Maxim Afinogenov .25 .60
153 Duncan Keith .30 .75
154 Dan Cleary .40 1.00
155 Anze Kopitar .40 1.00
156 Kyle Okposo .40 1.00
157 Brent Burns .25 .60
158 Brenden Morrow .30 .75
159 Ryan Miller .40 1.00
160 Henrik Sedin .60 1.50
161 Darcy Tucker .30 .75
162 Ray Whitney .25 .60
163 Jakub Voracek .40 1.00
164 Tomas Fleischmann .25 .60
165 Braydon Coburn .25 .60
166 Saku Koivu .40 1.00
167 Adam Burish .50 1.25
168 George Parros .25 .60
169 Jarome Iginla .75 2.00
170 Brandon Sutter .40 1.00
171 Pekka Rinne .30 .75
172 Sam Gagner .50 1.25
173 Chris Drury .30 .75
174 Niklas Kronwall .30 .75
175 Dion Phaneuf .60 1.50
176 Zach Bogosian .50 1.25
177 Maxime Talbot .40 1.00
178 Daniel Winnik .25 .60
179 Scott Gomez .40 1.00
180 Cam Ward .40 1.00
181 Ilya Kovalchuk .50 1.25
182 Devin Setoguchi .30 .75
183 Mike Fisher .25 .60
184 James Neal .40 1.00
185 Ryan Smyth .40 1.00
186 Loui Eriksson .25 .60
187 Stephen Weiss .25 .60
188 Mason Raymond .25 .60
189 Jason Pominville .40 1.00
190 Teemu Selanne .40 1.00
191 Martin St. Louis .40 1.00
192 Rod Brind'Amour .30 .75
193 Brent Seabrook .30 .75
194 Ron Hainsey .25 .60
195 Milan Hejduk .40 1.00
196 Tim Thomas .40 1.00
197 David Legwand .30 .75
198 Jeff Tambellini .25 .60
199 Georges Laraque .25 .60
200 Alexander Ovechkin 1.50 4.00
201 John Tavares RC 50.00 100.00
202 Devan Dubnyk RC 8.00 20.00
203 Andrei Loktionov RC 8.00 20.00
204 Lars Eller RC 10.00 25.00
205 Tyler Eckford RC 5.00 12.00
206 Drayson Bowman RC 8.00 20.00
207 Artem Anisimov RC 8.00 20.00
208 Mikko Lehtonen RC 6.00 15.00
209 Dan Sexton RC 8.00 20.00
210 Ryan O'Reilly RC 12.00 30.00
211 Kris Chucko RC 5.00 12.00
212 Cal O'Reilly RC 6.00 15.00
213 Victor Hedman RC 12.00 30.00
214 Mike Brodeur RC 20.00 40.00
215 Carl Gunnarsson RC 10.00 25.00
216 Luca Caputi RC 8.00 20.00
217 Danny Irmen RC 5.00 12.00
218 Antti Niemi RC 20.00 50.00
219 Benn Ferriero RC 6.00 15.00
220 Jhonas Enroth RC 8.00 20.00
221 Keaton Ellerby RC 10.00 25.00
222 James Wright RC 8.00 20.00
223 Michael Del Zotto RC 12.00 30.00
224 Alexander Salak RC 6.00 15.00
225 Jonas Gustavsson RC 15.00 40.00
226 David Desharnais RC 10.00 25.00
227 Ville Leino RC 25.00 50.00
228 Riku Helenius RC 6.00 15.00
229 Braden Holtby RC 8.00 20.00
230 Joel Rechlicz RC 6.00 15.00
231 Ivan Vishnevskiy RC 8.00 20.00
232 Peter Regin RC 8.00 20.00
233 MacGregor Sharp RC 6.00 15.00
234 Michael Grabner RC 25.00 50.00
235 Alexander Sulzer RC 4.00 10.00
236 David Laliberte RC 10.00 25.00
237 Logan Couture RC 12.00 30.00
238 Vladimir Zharkov RC 6.00 15.00
239 Colin McDonald RC 6.00 15.00
240 Matt Hendricks RC 5.00 12.00
241 Brad Marchand RC 8.00 20.00
242 Taylor Chorney RC 6.00 15.00
243 T.J. Galiardi RC 8.00 20.00
244 Erik Karlsson RC 20.00 50.00
245 Perttu Lindgren RC 6.00 15.00
246 Ryan Keller RC 6.00 15.00
247 Tyler Ennis RC 15.00 40.00
248 Michael Sauer RC 5.00 12.00
249 Teemu Laakso RC 4.00 10.00
250 James van Riemsdyk RC 15.00 40.00
251 John Negrin RC 5.00 12.00
252 Ryan Stoa RC 6.00 15.00
253 Tom Wandell RC 20.00 50.00
254 Michal Neuvirth RC 25.00 50.00
255 John Carlson RC 25.00 60.00
256 Mike Santorelli RC 4.00 10.00
257 Anton Khudobin RC 6.00 15.00
258 Brian Salcido RC 5.00 12.00
259 James Reimer RC 6.00 15.00
260 Colin Wilson RC 12.00 30.00
261 Deryk Engelland RC 8.00 20.00
262 Scott Parse RC 6.00 15.00
263 Tyler Bozak RC 15.00 40.00
264 Yannick Weber RC 8.00 20.00
265 Andrew MacDonald RC 5.00 12.00
266 Matthew Corrente RC 6.00 15.00
267 Shaun Heshka RC 8.00 20.00
268 Jakub Kindl RC 8.00 20.00
269 Mark Letestu RC 6.00 15.00
270 Oskars Bartulis RC 10.00 25.00
271 Viktor Stalberg RC 10.00 25.00
272 Frazer McLaren RC 4.00 10.00
273 Jason Demers RC 5.00 12.00
274 Ryan Wilson RC 6.00 15.00
275 Evander Kane RC 15.00 40.00
276 Sergei Shirokov RC 10.00 25.00
277 Aaron Gagnon RC 4.00 10.00
278 Cody Franson RC 6.00 15.00
279 Ryan O'Marra RC 5.00 12.00
280 Mikael Backlund RC 10.00 25.00
281 Jamie Benn RC 10.00 25.00
282 Andreas Thuresson RC 5.00 12.00
283 Christian Hanson RC 8.00 20.00
284 Mathieu Carle RC 8.00 20.00
285 Phil Oreskovic RC 8.00 20.00
286 Matt Beleskey RC 6.00 15.00
287 Tyler Myers RC 25.00 60.00
288 Ryan Vesce RC 5.00 12.00
289 Bobby Sanguinetti RC 5.00 12.00
290 Mario Bliznak RC 6.00 15.00
291 Spencer Machacek RC 5.00 12.00
292 Tom Pyatt RC 8.00 20.00
293 Byron Bitz RC 5.00 12.00
294 Dmitry Kulikov RC 6.00 15.00
295 Mathieu Perreault RC 8.00 20.00
296 Chad Johnson RC 15.00 40.00
297 Daniel Larsson RC 8.00 20.00
298 Matt Pelech RC 6.00 15.00
299 Matt Gilroy RC 8.00 20.00
300 Matt Duchene RC 40.00 80.00
RED301 TBD 50.00 100.00
RED302 TBD 8.00 20.00
RED303 TBD 8.00 20.00
RED304 TBD 8.00 20.00
RED305 TBD 8.00 20.00
RED306 TBD 8.00 20.00
RED307 TBD 8.00 20.00
RED308 TBD 8.00 20.00
RED309 TBD 8.00 20.00
RED310 TBD 8.00 20.00
RED311 TBD 8.00 20.00
RED312 TBD 8.00 20.00
RED313 TBD 8.00 20.00
RED314 TBD 8.00 20.00
RED315 TBD 8.00 20.00
RED316 TBD 8.00 20.00
RED317 TBD 8.00 20.00
RED318 TBD 8.00 20.00
RED319 TBD 8.00 20.00
RED320 TBD 8.00 20.00
RED321 TBD 8.00 20.00
RED322 TBD 8.00 20.00
RED323 TBD 8.00 20.00
RED324 TBD 8.00 20.00
RED325 TBD 8.00 20.00
RED326 TBD 8.00 20.00
RED327 TBD 8.00 20.00
RED328 TBD 8.00 20.00
RED329 TBD 8.00 20.00
RED330 TBD 8.00 20.00
RED331 TBD 8.00 20.00
RED332 TBD 8.00 20.00
RED333 TBD 8.00 20.00
RED334 TBD 8.00 20.00
RED335 TBD 8.00 20.00
RED336 TBD 8.00 20.00
RED337 TBD 8.00 20.00
RED338 TBD 8.00 20.00
RED339 TBD 8.00 20.00
RED340 TBD 8.00 20.00
RED341 TBD 8.00 20.00
RED342 TBD 8.00 20.00
RED343 TBD 8.00 20.00
RED344 TBD 8.00 20.00
RED345 TBD 8.00 20.00
RED346 TBD 8.00 20.00
RED347 TBD 8.00 20.00
RED348 TBD 8.00 20.00
RED349 TBD 8.00 20.00
RED350 TBD 8.00 20.00
RED351 TBD 8.00 20.00
RED352 TBD 8.00 20.00
RED353 TBD 8.00 20.00
RED354 TBD 8.00 20.00
RED355 TBD 8.00 20.00
RED356 TBD 8.00 20.00
RED357 TBD 8.00 20.00
RED358 TBD 8.00 20.00
RED359 TBD 8.00 20.00
RED360 TBD 8.00 20.00

2009-10 Be A Player Player's Club

*SINGLES 1-200: 2.5X TO 6X BASIC
1-200 PRINT RUN 25 SER.#'d SETS
201-300 PRINT RUN 15 SER.#'d SETS
201-300 NOT PRICED DUE TO SCARCITY

2009-10 Be A Player Goalies Unmasked

COMPLETE SET (30) 60.00 120.00
STATED PRINT RUN 499 SER.#'d SETS
GU1 Martin Brodeur 5.00 12.00
GU2 Ryan Miller 2.00 5.00
GU3 Marc-Andre Fleury 2.00 5.00
GU4 Carey Price 5.00 12.00
GU5 Jose Theodore 2.00 5.00
GU6 Brian Elliott 1.50 4.00
GU7 Antero Niittymaki 2.00 5.00
GU8 Ray Emery 1.50 4.00
GU9 Tim Thomas 2.00 5.00
GU10 Henrik Lundqvist 4.00 10.00
GU11 Ondrej Pavelec 1.50 4.00
GU12 Tomas Vokoun 2.00 5.00
GU13 Dwayne Roloson 1.50 4.00
GU14 Cam Ward 2.00 5.00
GU15 Jean-Sebastien Giguere 2.00 5.00
GU16 Evgeni Nabokov 2.00 5.00
GU17 Cristobal Huet 2.00 5.00
GU18 Roberto Luongo 5.00 12.00
GU19 Jonathan Quick 3.00 8.00
GU20 Ilya Bryzgalov 1.50 4.00
GU21 Craig Anderson 1.50 4.00
GU22 Miikka Kiprusoff 2.00 5.00
GU23 Pekka Rinne 1.50 4.00
GU24 Chris Osgood 2.50 6.00
GU25 Marty Turco 1.50 4.00
GU26 Niklas Backstrom 2.00 5.00
GU27 Jonas Hiller 2.50 6.00
GU28 Chris Mason 1.50 4.00
GU29 Steve Mason 3.00 8.00
GU30 Nikolai Khabibulin 2.00 5.00

2009-10 Be A Player Meet The Rookies

COMPLETE SET (10) 40.00 80.00
STATED PRINT RUN 499 SER.#'d SETS
MR1 John Tavares 8.00 20.00
MR2 Victor Hedman 3.00 6.00
MR3 Matt Duchene 6.00 15.00
MR4 James van Riemsdyk 4.00 10.00
MR5 Mikael Backlund 2.50 6.00
MR6 Jonas Gustavsson 4.00 10.00
MR7 Colin Wilson 3.00 8.00
MR8 Logan Couture 3.00 8.00
MR9 Bobby Sanguinetti 1.25 3.00
MR10 Tyler Bozak 4.00 10.00

2009-10 Be A Player Rookie Jerseys

STATED PRINT RUN 250 SER.#'d SETS
RJAA Artem Anisimov 6.00 15.00
RJAM Andrew MacDonald 4.00 10.00
RJAN Antti Niemi 20.00 40.00
RJBA Mikael Backlund 8.00 20.00
RJBB Byron Bitz 4.00 10.00
RJBF Benn Ferriero 5.00 12.00
RJBM Brad Marchand 6.00 15.00
RJBO Tyler Bozak 10.00 25.00
RJBS Brian Salcido 4.00 10.00
RJCF Cody Franson 5.00 12.00
RJCH Christian Hanson 6.00 15.00
RJCM Colin McDonald 5.00 12.00
RJCO Cal O'Reilly 5.00 12.00
RJCW Colin Wilson 10.00 25.00
RJDD Devan Dubnyk 6.00 15.00
RJDE Michael Del Zotto 10.00 25.00
RJDI Danny Irmen 4.00 10.00
RJDK Dmitry Kulikov 5.00 12.00
RJFK Evander Kane 10.00 25.00
RJFM Frazer McLaren 3.00 8.00
RJGR Michael Grabner 6.00 15.00
RJIV Ivan Vishnevskiy 6.00 15.00
RJJB Jamie Benn 8.00 20.00
RJJD Jason Demers 4.00 10.00
RJJE Jhonas Enroth 6.00 15.00
RJJG Jonas Gustavsson 12.00 30.00
RJJK Jakub Kindl 6.00 15.00
RJJN John Negrin
RJJT John Tavares 25.00 50.00
RJJV James van Riemsdyk 12.00 30.00
RJKA Erik Karlsson 15.00 40.00
RJKE Keaton Ellerby 8.00 20.00
RJLC Luca Caputi 6.00 15.00
RJLE Lars Eller 8.00 20.00
RJLO Logan Couture 10.00 25.00
RJMB Matt Beleskey 5.00 12.00
RJMC Matthew Corrente 5.00 12.00
RJMD Matt Duchene 15.00 40.00
RJMG Matt Gilroy 6.00 15.00
RJMH Matt Hendricks
RJMN Michal Neuvirth 12.00 30.00
RJMP Matt Pelech 5.00 12.00
RJMS Mike Santorelli 3.00 8.00
RJOB Oskars Bartulis 8.00 20.00
RJOM Ryan O'Marra 4.00 10.00
RJPL Perttu Lindgren 5.00 12.00
RJPR Peter Regin 6.00 15.00
RJRH Riku Helenius 5.00 12.00
RJRO Ryan O'Reilly
RJRS Ryan Stoa 5.00 12.00
RJSA Bobby Sanguinetti 4.00 10.00
RJSM Spencer Machacek 4.00 10.00
RJSS Sergei Shirokov 8.00 20.00
RJTC Taylor Chorney 5.00 12.00
RJTG T.J. Galiardi 6.00 15.00
RJTM Tyler Myers 15.00 40.00
RJVH Victor Hedman 10.00 25.00
RJVL Ville Leino 6.00 15.00
RJVS Viktor Stalberg 8.00 20.00
RJYW Yannick Weber 6.00 15.00

2009-10 Be A Player Rookie Jerseys Autographs

RJAA Artem Anisimov 12.00 30.00
RJBO Tyler Bozak
RJCF Cody Franson 10.00 25.00
RJEK Evander Kane 15.00 40.00
RJJB Jamie Benn 15.00 40.00
RJJG Jonas Gustavsson
RJJT John Tavares
RJJV James van Riemsdyk 30.00 60.00
RJKA Erik Karlsson 30.00 80.00
RJLC Luca Caputi
RJMD Matt Duchene 40.00 80.00
RJMG Matt Gilroy 12.00 30.00
RJTM Tyler Myers
RJVH Victor Hedman 20.00 50.00

2009-10 Be A Player Rookie Patches

STATED PRINT RUN 15 SER.#'d SETS
NOT PRICED DUE TO SCARCITY

2009-10 Be A Player Sidelines

COMPLETE SET (60) 60.00 120.00
STATED ODDS 1:4
S1 Alexander Ovechkin 3.00 8.00
S2 Anze Kopitar .75 2.00
S3 Brad Richards .60 1.50
S4 Cam Ward .75 2.00
S5 Carey Price 2.00 5.00
S6 Daniel Alfredsson .75 2.00
S7 Dany Heatley 1.50 4.00
S8 Dion Phaneuf 1.25 3.00
S9 Drew Doughty 1.50 4.00
S10 Dustin Penner .50 1.25
S11 Eric Staal 1.00 2.50
S12 Evander Kane 2.00 5.00
S13 Evgeni Malkin 2.00 5.00
S14 Henrik Lundqvist 1.50 4.00
S15 Henrik Sedin 1.25 3.00
S16 Henrik Zetterberg 1.50 4.00
S17 Ilya Kovalchuk 1.00 2.50
S18 Jarome Iginla 1.50 4.00
S19 Jason Spezza 1.00 2.50
S20 Jay Bouwmeester .75 2.00
S21 Jean-Sebastien Giguere .75 2.00
S22 Jeff Carter .75 2.00
S23 Joe Thornton 1.50 4.00
S24 John Tavares 4.00 10.00
S25 Jonathan Toews 2.00 5.00
S26 Marc-Andre Fleury .75 2.00
S27 Marian Gaborik 1.25 3.00
S28 Martin Brodeur 2.00 5.00
S29 Marty Turco .60 1.50
S30 Matt Duchene 3.00 8.00
S31 Miikka Kiprusoff .75 2.00
S32 Mike Cammalleri .60 1.50
S33 Mike Green 1.50 4.00
S34 Mike Modano .75 2.00
S35 Mike Richards 1.50 4.00
S36 Mikko Koivu .75 2.00
S37 Nicklas Backstrom 1.50 4.00
S38 Nicklas Lidstrom 1.00 2.50
S39 Patrick Kane 1.50 4.00
S40 Patrick Marleau .75 2.00
S41 Paul Kariya .75 2.00
S42 Paul Stastny .75 2.00
S43 Pavel Datsyuk .75 2.00
S44 Phil Kessel .75 2.00
S45 Rick DiPietro .75 2.00
S46 Rick Nash .75 2.00
S47 Roberto Luongo 2.00 5.00
S48 Ryan Getzlaf 1.25 3.00
S49 Ryan Miller .75 2.00
S50 Sam Gagner 1.00 2.50
S51 Scott Niedermayer .50 1.25
S52 Shane Doan .60 1.50
S53 Shea Weber .60 1.50
S54 Sidney Crosby 4.00 10.00
S55 Steve Mason 1.25 3.00
S56 Steven Stamkos 2.00 5.00
S57 Thomas Vanek .75 2.00
S58 Vincent Lecavalier 1.00 2.50
S59 Zach Parise .75 2.00
S60 Zdeno Chara .50 1.25

2009-10 Be A Player Signatures

STATED ODDS 1 PER PACK
SAA Adrian Aucoin 2.50 6.00
SAB Adam Burish 5.00 12.00
SAC Andrew Cogliano
SAK Anze Kopitar 4.00 10.00
SAL Bryan Allen 2.50 6.00
SAM Andrei Markov 3.00 8.00
SAN Artem Anisimov 5.00 12.00
SAV Aaron Voros 2.50 6.00
SAX Alexandre Burrows 3.00 8.00
SBA Josh Bailey
SBB Brent Burns 2.50 6.00
SBC Braydon Coburn
SBD Martin Brodeur
SBE Jamie Benn 6.00 15.00
SBG Boyd Gordon 2.50 6.00
SBK David Backes 3.00 8.00
SBL Brooks Laich 3.00 8.00
SBM Brenden Morrow 3.00 8.00
SBN Bryan McCabe
SBO Bobby Ryan 5.00 12.00
SBR Derick Brassard 4.00 10.00
SBS Brent Seabrook 3.00 8.00
SBU Peter Budaj 4.00 10.00
SBW Blake Wheeler
SBY Brad Boyes 3.00 8.00
SBZ Tyler Bozak
SCA Chris Campoli 3.00 8.00
SCC Cal Clutterbuck
SCD Chris Drury 3.00 8.00
SCF Cody Franson 4.00 10.00
SCK David Clarkson 2.50 6.00
SCL Ryan Callahan 2.50 6.00
SCO Mike Commodore 2.50 6.00
SCP Carey Price 10.00 25.00
SCY Corey Perry 4.00 10.00
SDA Daniel Briere 4.00 10.00
SDB Dustin Brown 3.00 8.00
SDC Dan Cleary 4.00 10.00
SDD Drew Doughty
SDH Dan Hamhuis 2.50 6.00
SDK Duncan Keith
SDL David Legwand
SDM Dmitry Kulikov
SDN Dan Boyle 2.50 6.00
SDP Dion Phaneuf 10.00 25.00
SDR Derek Roy SP 12.00 30.00
SDS Daniel Sedin 5.00 12.00
SDT Darcy Tucker 3.00 8.00
SDV David Perron 3.00 8.00
SDW Daniel Winnik 2.50 6.00
SEB Eric Brewer 2.50 6.00
SEC Erik Cole 2.50 6.00
SEJ Erik Johnson
SEK Erik Karlsson 5.00 12.00
SEM Evgeni Malkin SP/1*
SES Eric Staal
SFI Mike Fisher 2.50 6.00
SGG Sam Gagner
SGI Matt Gilroy 5.00 12.00
SGL Georges Laraque 2.50 6.00
SGP George Parros 2.50 6.00
SHA Scott Hannan 2.50 6.00
SHE Milan Hejduk 4.00 10.00
SHI Jonas Hiller 5.00 12.00
SHO Shawn Horcoff
SHS Henrik Sedin 6.00 15.00
SHT Dany Heatley 8.00 20.00
SHZ Henrik Zetterberg SP 25.00 60.00
SIB Ilya Bryzgalov SP 40.00 80.00
SIK Ilya Kovalchuk
SJB Jay Bouwmeester 4.00 10.00
SJC Jeff Carter SP 12.00 30.00
SJE Jean-Sebastien Giguere
SJF Johan Franzen SP 30.00 60.00
SJG Jonas Gustavsson
SJH Jeff Halpern 2.50 6.00
SJI Jarome Iginla 15.00 40.00
SJM Jamal Mayers 2.50 6.00
SJN James Neal 4.00 10.00
SJO Joe Thornton 8.00 20.00
SJP Joni Pitkanen 3.00 8.00
SJQ Jonathan Quick
SJS Jason Spezza 15.00 40.00
SJT Jeff Tambellini 2.50 6.00
SJV Jakub Voracek 4.00 10.00
SKA Evander Kane 10.00 25.00
SKB Krys Barch 2.50 6.00
SKE Ryan Kesler 3.00 8.00
SKL Kristopher Letang 4.00 10.00
SKN Mike Knuble 4.00 10.00
SKO Mike Komisarek 3.00 8.00
SKS Phil Kessel
SKU Nikolai Kulemin 3.00 8.00
SKV Kris Versteeg
SLA Robert Lang
SLC Luca Caputi
SLS Luca Sbisa 5.00 12.00
SLU Roberto Luongo 10.00 25.00
SMA Mark Streit
SMB Mikkel Boedker 3.00 8.00
SMC Mike Cammalleri 10.00 25.00
SMD Matt Duchene 15.00 40.00
SMF Marc-Andre Fleury 8.00 20.00
SMG Matt Greene
SMH Martin Havlat
SMI Ryan Miller
SMK Mikko Koivu
SMM Manny Malhotra 2.50 6.00
SMN Matt Moulson 2.50 6.00
SMO Ethan Moreau
SMR Mike Richards SP 25.00 60.00
SMS Mike Sillinger 2.50 6.00
SMT Maxime Talbot 4.00 10.00
SMY Matt Bradley 2.50 6.00
SNB Niklas Backstrom 4.00 10.00
SNF Nick Foligno 4.00 10.00
SNH Nathan Horton
SNK Niklas Kronwall 3.00 8.00
SNL Nicklas Lidstrom 10.00 25.00
SNM Nathan McIver 2.50 6.00
SNS Nick Schultz 2.50 6.00
SOJ Olli Jokinen 2.50 6.00
SOK Kyle Okposo 4.00 10.00
SOM Oscar Moller 3.00 8.00
SOP Ondrej Pavelec 3.00 8.00
SOS Patrick O'Sullivan 3.00 8.00
SPB Patrice Bergeron 4.00 10.00
SPB Pierre-Marc Bouchard 3.00 8.00
SPD Pavel Datsyuk 15.00 40.00
SPE Patrik Elias 3.00 8.00
SPH Patric Hornqvist 3.00 8.00
SPK Patrick Kane 15.00 40.00
SPL Pascal Leclaire 4.00 10.00
SPM Paul Martin 2.50 6.00
SPO Jason Pominville 4.00 10.00
SPR Chris Pronger 8.00 20.00
SPS Paul Stastny SP 12.00 30.00
SPT Patrick Marleau 4.00 10.00
SPV Rich Peverley 3.00 8.00
SRA Mason Raymond 2.50 6.00
SRB Rene Bourque 2.50 6.00
SRC Brad Richards 3.00 8.00
SRE Peter Regin 5.00 12.00
SRF Brian Rafalski 2.50 6.00
SRG Ryan Getzlaf 6.00 15.00
SRH Ron Hainsey 2.50 6.00
SRI Pekka Rinne 3.00 8.00
SRK Rostislav Klesla 4.00 10.00
SRM Ryan Malone
SRO Ryan O'Reilly 8.00 20.00
SRR Robyn Regehr 3.00 8.00
SRS Ryan Suter SP 60.00 120.00
SRT Raffi Torres 2.50 6.00
SRU R.J. Umberger 3.00 8.00
SRY Ryan Smyth 4.00 10.00
SSA Marc Staal 5.00 12.00
SSC Luke Schenn 6.00 15.00
SSD Shane Doan 3.00 8.00
SSE Devin Setoguchi 3.00 8.00
SSG Scott Gomez 4.00 10.00
SSH Scott Hartnell 2.50 6.00
SSI Sidney Crosby 60.00 120.00
SSK Saku Koivu 4.00 10.00
SSM Steve Mason 6.00 15.00
SSR Mark Stuart 2.50 6.00
SSS Steven Stamkos
SST Martin St. Louis 4.00 10.00
SSU Brandon Sutter 4.00 10.00
SSW Shea Weber 3.00 8.00
STA John Tavares
STE Teemu Selanne
STF Tomas Fleischmann 2.50 6.00
STG Tim Gleason 2.50 6.00
STH Shawn Thornton 2.50 6.00
STJ T.J. Oshie SP 20.00 50.00
STM Tyler Myers 15.00 40.00
STP Tomas Plekanec 3.00 8.00
STT Tim Thomas 4.00 10.00
STU Marty Turco 3.00 8.00
STV Thomas Vanek 4.00 10.00
STW Jonathan Toews
STZ Travis Zajac 2.50 6.00
SVA James van Riemsdyk 10.00 25.00
SVH Victor Hedman 8.00 20.00
SVL Vincent Lecavalier 5.00 12.00
SVO Tomas Vokoun 4.00 10.00
SWE Stephen Weiss 2.50 6.00
SWK Scott Walker 3.00 8.00
SWM Willie Mitchell 3.00 8.00
SWW Wojtek Wolski 2.50 6.00
SZB Zach Bogosian 6.00 15.00
SZC Zdeno Chara SP
SZP Zach Parise 4.00 10.00

2009-10 Be A Player Signatures Player's Club

STATED PRINT RUN 10 SER.#'d SETS
NOT PRICED DUE TO SCARCITY

2009-10 Be A Player Signatures Duals

STATED ODDS 1:8
S2BB Mikkel Boedker 6.00 15.00
Ilya Bryzgalov
S2BC Daniel Briere 8.00 20.00
Jeff Carter
S2BJ Erik Johnson
Eric Brewer
S2BK Evander Kane 12.00 30.00
Zach Bogosian
S2BL Martin Brodeur
Roberto Luongo
S2BM Steve Mason 12.00 30.00
Derick Brassard
S2BW Patrice Bergeron
Blake Wheeler
S2CP Carey Price 20.00 50.00
Mike Cammalleri
S2CS Eric Staal 10.00 25.00
Erik Cole
S2CT Tim Thomas
Zdeno Chara
S2DJ Chris Drury 6.00 15.00
Olli Jokinen
S2DO Ryan O'Reilly 15.00 40.00
Matt Duchene
S2DZ Pavel Datsyuk 15.00 40.00
Henrik Zetterberg
S2FM Marc-Andre Fleury
Evgeni Malkin
S2GB Jonas Gustavsson
Tyler Bozak
S2GG Jonas Gustavsson
Jean-Sebastien Giguere
S2GP Scott Gomez 8.00 20.00
Tomas Plekanec
S2GR Ryan Getzlaf 12.00 30.00
Bobby Ryan
S2HM Victor Hedman 15.00 40.00
Tyler Myers
S2HR Mike Richards 15.00 40.00
Scott Hartnell
S2HS Milan Hejduk 8.00 20.00
Paul Stastny
S2IB Rene Bourque 15.00 40.00
Jarome Iginla
S2KB Mikko Koivu
Niklas Backstrom
S2KD Anze Kopitar
Drew Doughty
S2KE Ilya Kovalchuk
Patrik Elias
S2KP Ilya Kovalchuk
Zach Parise
S2KS Saku Koivu
Teemu Selanne
S2KV Evander Kane 20.00 50.00
James van Riemsdyk
S2LK Niklas Kronwall 10.00 25.00
Nicklas Lidstrom
S2LS Steven Stamkos
Vincent Lecavalier
S2MB Josh Bailey
Matt Moulson
S2MH Patrick Marleau 15.00 40.00
Dany Heatley
S2MT Patrick Marleau 15.00 40.00
Joe Thornton
S2NB James Neal 12.00 30.00
Jamie Benn
S2OG Sam Gagner
Patrick O'Sullivan
S2PK Phil Kessel
Dion Phaneuf
S2PM Ryan Miller
Jason Pominville
S2PO T.J. Oshie 12.00 30.00
David Perron
S2RB Robyn Regehr 8.00 20.00
Jay Bouwmeester
S2RM Brenden Morrow 6.00 15.00
Brad Richards
S2RV Derek Roy 8.00 20.00
Thomas Vanek
S2SF Jason Spezza 10.00 25.00
Nick Foligno
S2SG Marc Staal 10.00 25.00
Matt Gilroy
S2SK Duncan Keith
Brent Seabrook
S2SS Henrik Sedin 12.00 30.00
Daniel Sedin
S2SW Shea Weber 6.00 15.00
Ryan Suter
S2TD Matt Duchene
John Tavares
S2TH John Tavares
Victor Hedman
S2TK Patrick Kane
Jonathan Toews
S2WH Nathan Horton
Stephen Weiss

2009-10 Be A Player Signatures Eight Stars

STATED PRINT RUN 10 SER.#'d SETS
NOT PRICED DUE TO SCARCITY
S8DMEN Zdeno Chara
Duncan Keith
Zach Bogosian
Nicklas Lidstrom
Shea Weber
Jay Bouwmeester
Dion Phaneuf
Drew Doughty
S8FRWD Ilya Kovalchuk
Jarome Iginla
Evgeni Malkin
Dany Heatley
Pavel Datsyuk
Henrik Zetterberg
Jonathan Toews
Ryan Getzlaf
S8NETM Tim Thomas
Carey Price
Roberto Luongo
Ryan Miller
Marc-Andre Fleury
Steve Mason
Martin Brodeur
Jonas Gustavsson
S8ROOK Matt Duchene
Ryan O'Reilly
Tyler Myers
Jamie Benn
James van Riemsdyk
Victor Hedman
Evander Kane
John Tavares

2009-10 Be A Player Signatures Foursomes

STATED PRINT RUN 25 SER.#'d SETS
MOST NOT PRICED DUE TO LACK OF MARKET INFO
S41ST Matt Duchene
Evander Kane
Victor Hedman
John Tavares
S4PIM George Parros
Krys Barch
Georges Laraque
Manny Malhotra
S4CAN2 Dany Heatley
Jarome Iginla
Brenden Morrow
Ryan Getzlaf
S4CAND Chris Pronger
Shea Weber
Duncan Keith
Dan Boyle
S4CENT Evgeni Malkin
Zach Parise
Jonathan Toews
Henrik Zetterberg
S4RDEF Dmitry Kulikov
Victor Hedman
Erik Karlsson
Tyler Myers
S4SWE2 Patric Hornqvist 75.00 150.00
Johan Franzen
Niklas Kronwall
Nicklas Lidstrom
S4TCAN Roberto Luongo
Jonathan Toews
Mike Richards

Joe Thornton
S4TCZE Patrik Elias
Martin Havlat
Tomas Plekanec
Tomas Vokoun
S4TFIN Olli Jokinen
Niklas Backstrom
Saku Koivu
Teemu Selanne
S4TRUS Ilya Kovalchuk
Ilya Bryzgalov
Evgeni Malkin
Pavel Datsyuk
S4TSWE Henrik Zetterberg
Jonas Gustavsson
Daniel Sedin
Henrik Sedin
S4TUSA Phil Kessel
Zach Parise
Ryan Miller
Patrick Kane
S4USA2 Chris Drury
Ryan Malone
Ryan Kesler
Bobby Ryan
S4USAD Erik Johnson
Tim Gleason
Ryan Suter
Brian Rafalski

2009-10 Be A Player Signatures Six Stars

STATED PRINT RUN 15 SER.#'d SETS
NOT PRICED DUE TO SCARCITY
S6LW James van Riemsdyk
Dany Heatley
Thomas Vanek
Patrick Marleau
Ilya Kovalchuk
Corey Perry
S6RW Teemu Selanne
Phil Kessel
Jason Pominville
Jarome Iginla
Martin St. Louis
Patrick Kane
S6CEN Jonathan Toews
Mike Richards
Steven Stamkos
Joe Thornton
Zach Parise
Ryan Getzlaf
S6DEF Drew Doughty
Dion Phaneuf
Dan Boyle
Tyler Myers
Jay Bouwmeester
Duncan Keith
S6EUR Zdeno Chara
Nicklas Lidstrom
Henrik Zetterberg
Evgeni Malkin
Ilya Kovalchuk
Teemu Selanne
S6GOL Martin Brodeur
Jean-Sebastien Giguere
Marc-Andre Fleury
Steve Mason
Roberto Luongo
Carey Price

2009-10 Be A Player Signatures Trios

STATED ODDS 1:24
S3BLF Martin Brodeur
Roberto Luongo
Marc-Andre Fleury
S3BPO Brad Boyes 15.00 40.00
David Perron
T.J. Oshie
S3CSS Eric Staal 12.00 30.00
Brandon Sutter
Erik Cole
S3DZF Pavel Datsyuk 25.00 60.00
Henrik Zetterberg
Johan Franzen
S3EKP Zach Parise
Ilya Kovalchuk
Patrik Elias
S3GCP Tomas Plekanec 15.00 40.00
Scott Gomez
Mike Cammalleri
S3HBK Mikko Koivu
Pierre-Marc Bouchard
Martin Havlat
S3HWS Paul Stastny 10.00 25.00
Wojtek Wolski
Milan Hejduk
S3IMB Rene Bourque 20.00 50.00
Jamal Mayers
Jarome Iginla
S3LSS Martin St. Louis
Vincent Lecavalier
Steven Stamkos
S3MKH Victor Hedman 20.00 50.00
Erik Karlsson
Tyler Myers
S3MTH Joe Thornton 30.00 60.00
Dany Heatley
Patrick Marleau
S3MTQ Ryan Miller
Jonathan Quick
Tim Thomas
S3OCG Patrick O'Sullivan
Andrew Cogliano
Sam Gagner
S3OTB Josh Bailey
John Tavares
Kyle Okposo
S3PRV Thomas Vanek 10.00 25.00
Jason Pominville
Derek Roy
S3RCV Mike Richards 20.00 50.00
Jeff Carter
James van Riemsdyk
S3RMB Brad Richards 15.00 40.00
Brenden Morrow
Jamie Benn
S3SBK Anze Kopitar 10.00 25.00
Ryan Smyth
Dustin Brown
S3SKG Ryan Getzlaf
Teemu Selanne
Saku Koivu
S3SSK Ryan Kesler 15.00 40.00
Daniel Sedin
Henrik Sedin
S3TBW Patrice Bergeron
Shawn Thornton
Blake Wheeler
S3TKD Evander Kane
Matt Duchene
John Tavares
S3TKV Jonathan Toews
Patrick Kane
Kris Versteeg
S3UBV Derick Brassard 10.00 25.00
Jakub Voracek
R.J. Umberger

2002-03 BAP All-Star Edition

Released to coincide with the 2003 NHL All-Star game, this 150-card set featured players who made appearances in past all-star games. Cards 101-150 were short-printed to just 100 copies each and featured rookies.

COMP.SET w/o SP's (100) 40.00 80.00
101-150 SP/RC PRINT RUN 100 SER.#'d SETS
1 Daniel Alfredsson .25 .60
2 Tony Amonte .25 .60
2001 Denver
3 Ed Belfour .30 .75
1996 Boston
4 Rob Blake .25 .60
2002 Los Angeles
5 Peter Bondra .25 .60
1999 Tampa Bay
6 Radek Bonk .10 .25
2000 Toronto
7 Martin Brodeur .75 2.00
8 Martin Brodeur .75 2.00
9 Martin Brodeur .75 2.00
10 Valeri Bure .10 .25
2000 Toronto
11 Pavel Bure .30 .75
1997 San Jose
12 Pavel Bure .50 1.25
1997 San Jose
13 Sean Burke .25 .60
2002 Los Angeles
14 Roman Cechmanek .25 .60
2001 Denver
15 Chris Chelios .30 .75
2002 Los Angeles
16 Vincent Damphousse .10 .25
2002 Los Angeles
17 Eric Daze .25 .60
2002 Los Angeles
18 Pavol Demitra .25 .60
2000 Toronto
19 Patrik Elias .25 .60
2002 Los Angeles
20 Sergei Fedorov .50 1.25
21 Sergei Fedorov .60 1.50
1996 Boston
22 Theo Fleury .10 .25
1997 San Jose
23 Peter Forsberg .75 2.00
24 Peter Forsberg .75 2.00
1996 Boston
25 Peter Forsberg .75 2.00
1998 Vancouver
26 Simon Gagne .30 .75
2001 Denver
27 Scott Gomez .10 .25
2000 Toronto
28 Bill Guerin .25 .60
2001 Denver
29 Milan Hejduk .30 .75
2001 Denver
30 Phil Housley .10 .25
2000 Toronto
31 Brett Hull .40 1.00
32 Jarome Iginla .40 1.00
33 Arturs Irbe .25 .60
1999 Tampa Bay
34 Jaromir Jagr .50 1.25
35 Jaromir Jagr .50 1.25
1998 Vancouver
36 Jaromir Jagr .50 1.25
1996 Boston
37 Curtis Joseph .30 .75
2000 Toronto
38 Ed Jovanovski .25 .60
2002 Los Angeles
39 Tomas Kaberle .10 .25
2002 Los Angeles
40 Sami Kapanen .10 .25
2002 Los Angeles
41 Paul Kariya .30 .75
1997 San Jose
42 Paul Kariya .30 .75
2001 Denver
43 Paul Kariya .30 .75
1996 Boston
44 Nikolai Khabibulin .30 .75
2002 Los Angeles
45 Saku Koivu .30 .75
1998 Vancouver
46 Olaf Kolzig .25 .60
2000 Toronto
47 Alex Kovalev .25 .60
2001 Denver
48 John LeClair .30 .75
1997 San Jose
49 Brian Leetch .25 .60
2001 Denver
50 Brian Leetch .25 .60
1994 New York
51 Mario Lemieux 2.00 5.00
52 Mario Lemieux 2.00 5.00
53 Mario Lemieux 2.00 5.00
54 Nicklas Lidstrom .30 .75
1999 Tampa Bay
55 Nicklas Lidstrom .30 .75
2001 Denver
56 Eric Lindros .30 .75
2000 Toronto
57 Al MacInnis .25 .60
2000 Toronto
58 Mark Messier .30 .75
1994 New York
59 Mark Messier .30 .75
1996 Boston
60 Mike Modano .50 1.25
61 Mike Modano .50 1.25
62 Alexander Mogilny .25 .60
1996 Boston
63 Evgeni Nabokov .25 .60
2001 Denver
64 Markus Naslund .30 .75
2001 Denver
65 Scott Niedermayer .10 .25
1998 Vancouver
66 Owen Nolan .25 .60
2002 Los Angeles
67 Teppo Numminen .10 .25
2001 Denver
68 Chris Osgood .25 .60
1996 Boston
69 Sandis Ozolinsh .10 .25
2002 Los Angeles
70 Zigmund Palffy .25 .60
2001 Denver
71 Felix Potvin .30 .75
1996 Boston
72 Chris Pronger .25 .60
2000 Toronto
73 Mark Recchi .25 .60
2000 Toronto
74 Mike Richter .25 .60
2000 Toronto
75 Luc Robitaille .25 .60
1999 Tampa Bay
76 Jeremy Roenick .40 1.00
77 Patrick Roy 1.50 4.00
78 Patrick Roy 1.50 4.00
2001 Denver
79 Patrick Roy 1.50 4.00
1994 New York
80 Joe Sakic .60 1.50
81 Joe Sakic .60 1.50
2001 Denver
82 Tommy Salo .25 .60
2000 Toronto
83 Teemu Selanne .30 .75
2002 Los Angeles
84 Brendan Shanahan .30 .75
2002 Los Angeles
85 Brendan Shanahan .50 1.25
2000 Toronto
86 Brendan Shanahan .50 1.25
1996 Boston
87 Scott Stevens .25 .60
2000 Toronto
88 Mats Sundin .30 .75
2000 Toronto
89 Mats Sundin .30 .75
1997 San Jose
90 Darryl Sydor .10 .25
1999 Tampa Bay
91 Jose Theodore .40 1.00
92 Joe Thornton .30 .75
2002 Los Angeles
93 Keith Tkachuk .30 .75
1999 Tampa Bay
94 Ron Tugnutt .25 .60
1999 Tampa Bay
95 Roman Turek .25 .60
2000 Toronto
96 Doug Weight .25 .60
2001 Denver
97 Alexei Yashin .10 .25
1994 New York
98 Steve Yzerman 1.50 4.00
99 Steve Yzerman 1.50 4.00
100 Alexei Zhamnov .25 .60
2002 Los Angeles
101 Dany Heatley SP 6.00 15.00
102 Ilya Kovalchuk SP 6.00 15.00
103 Marian Gaborik SP 10.00 25.00
104 Marty Turco SP 5.00 12.00
105 Mike Comrie SP 5.00 12.00
106 Cody Rudkowsky RC 4.00 10.00
107 Levente Szuper RC 4.00 10.00
108 Alex Henry RC 4.00 10.00
109 Lynn Loyns RC 4.00 10.00
110 Tomi Pettinen RC 4.00 10.00
111 Micki Dupont RC 4.00 10.00
112 Shaone Morrisonn RC 6.00 15.00
113 Ryan Miller RC 40.00 80.00
114 Mikael Tellqvist RC 10.00 25.00
115 Dany Sabourin RC 6.00 15.00
116 Tim Thomas RC 10.00 25.00
117 Kurt Sauer RC 4.00 10.00
118 Kari Haakana RC 4.00 10.00
119 Lasse Pirjeta RC 4.00 10.00
120 Shawn Thornton RC 6.00 15.00
121 Curtis Sanford RC 6.00 15.00
122 Dick Tarnstrom RC 4.00 10.00
123 Radovan Somik RC 4.00 10.00
124 Martin Gerber RC 10.00 25.00
125 Dennis Seidenberg RC 4.00 10.00
126 P-M Bouchard RC 10.00 25.00
127 Alexei Smirnov RC 4.00 10.00
128 Ales Hemsky RC 30.00 80.00
129 Stephane Veilleux RC 4.00 10.00
130 Tom Koivisto RC 4.00 10.00
131 Jeff Taffe RC 4.00 10.00
132 Jordan Leopold RC 6.00 15.00
133 Stanislav Chistov RC 6.00 15.00
134 Rick Nash RC 75.00 150.00
135 Chuck Kobasew RC 10.00 25.00
136 Alexander Svitov RC 4.00 10.00
137 Carlo Colaiacovo RC 10.00 25.00
138 Jason Spezza RC 75.00 200.00
139 Henrik Zetterberg RC 75.00 125.00
140 Anton Volchenkov RC 6.00 15.00
141 Ron Hainsey RC 4.00 10.00
142 Jay Bouwmeester RC 15.00 40.00
143 Adam Hall RC 4.00 10.00
144 Steve Eminger RC 4.00 10.00
145 Mike Cammalleri RC 12.00 30.00
146 Dmitri Bykov RC 4.00 10.00
147 Ivan Majesky RC 4.00 10.00
148 Alexander Frolov RC 25.00 60.00
149 Scottie Upshall RC 10.00 25.00
150 Patrick Sharp RC 6.00 15.00

2002-03 BAP All-Star Edition Gold

PRINT RUN 1 SER.#'d SET
NOT PRICED DUE TO SCARCITY

2002-03 BAP All-Star Edition Silver

SILVER PRINT RUN 20 SER.#'d SETS
NOT PRICED DUE TO SCARCITY

2002-03 BAP All-Star Edition Bobble Heads

ONE PER BOX
STATED PRINT RUNS LISTED BELOW
1 Mario Lemieux/1066 20.00 50.00
2 Jose Theodore/1560 10.00 25.00
3 Pavel Bure/2010 10.00 25.00
4 Curtis Joseph/1031 10.00 25.00
5 Martin Brodeur/1530 12.50 30.00
6 Peter Forsberg/2031 12.50 30.00
7 Steve Yzerman/2019 12.50 30.00
8 Jaromir Jagr/2068 10.00 25.00
9 Joe Sakic/1519 10.00 25.00
10 Patrick Roy/1033 20.00 50.00

2002-03 BAP All-Star Edition He Shoots-He Scores Points

ONE PER PACK
RED.PROGRAM HAS EXPIRED
1 Brian Leetch 1 pt. .10 .25
2 Eric Lindros 1 pt. .10 .25
3 Mark Messier 1 pt. .10 .25
4 Owen Nolan 1 pt. .10 .25
5 Teemu Selanne 1 pt. .10 .25
6 Brendan Shanahan 1 pt. .10 .25
7 Mats Sundin 1 pt. .10 .25
8 Alexei Yashin 1 pt. .10 .25
9 Martin Brodeur 2 pt. .10 .25
10 Pavel Bure 2 pt. .10 .25
11 Sergei Fedorov 2 pt. .10 .25
12 Jaromir Jagr 2 pt. .10 .25
13 Curtis Joseph 2 pt. .10 .25
14 Nicklas Lidstrom 2 pt. .10 .25
15 Mike Modano 2 pt. .10 .25
16 Patrick Roy 2 pt. .10 .25
17 Joe Sakic 2 pt. .10 .25
18 Peter Forsberg 3 pt. .10 .25
19 Mario Lemieux 3 pt. .10 .25
20 Steve Yzerman 3 pt. .10 .25

2002-03 BAP All-Star Edition He Shoots-He Score Prizes

STATED PRINT RUN 20 SETS
NOT PRICED DUE TO SCARCITY
1 Tony Amonte
2 Ed Belfour
3 Martin Brodeur
4 Pavel Bure
5 Chris Chelios
6 Sergei Fedorov
7 Peter Forsberg
8 Jaromir Jagr
9 Curtis Joseph
10 Paul Kariya
11 Nikolai Khabibulin
12 John LeClair
13 Brian Leetch
14 Mario Lemieux
15 Nicklas Lidstrom
16 Eric Lindros
17 Al MacInnis
18 Mark Messier
19 Mike Modano
20 Markus Naslund
21 Owen Nolan
22 Chris Pronger
23 Mark Recchi
24 Patrick Roy
25 Joe Sakic
26 Teemu Selanne
27 Brendan Shanahan
28 Mats Sundin
29 Alexei Yashin
30 Steve Yzerman

2002-03 BAP All-Star Edition Jerseys

*MULT.COLOR SWATCH: .75X TO 1.5X HI
STAT.PRINT RUN 100 SETS
1 Daniel Alfredsson 6.00 15.00
1997 San Jose
2 Tony Amonte 6.00 15.00
2001 Denver
3 Ed Belfour 8.00 20.00
1996 Boston
4 Rob Blake 6.00 15.00
2002 Los Angeles
5 Peter Bondra 6.00 15.00
1999 Tampa Bay
6 Radek Bonk 4.00 10.00
2000 Toronto
7 Martin Brodeur 15.00 40.00
8 Martin Brodeur 15.00 40.00
9 Martin Brodeur 15.00 40.00
10 Valeri Bure 4.00 10.00
2000 Toronto
11 Pavel Bure 8.00 20.00
1997 San Jose
12 Pavel Bure 8.00 20.00
1997 San Jose
13 Sean Burke 4.00 10.00
2002 Los Angeles
14 Roman Cechmanek 4.00 10.00
2001 Denver
15 Chris Chelios 8.00 20.00
2002 Los Angeles
16 Vincent Damphousse 4.00 10.00
2002 Los Angeles
17 Eric Daze 4.00 10.00
2002 Los Angeles
18 Pavol Demitra 4.00 10.00
2000 Toronto
19 Patrik Elias 4.00 10.00
2002 Los Angeles
20 Sergei Fedorov 8.00 20.00
2002 Los Angeles
21 Sergei Fedorov 8.00 20.00
1996 Boston
22 Theo Fleury 6.00 15.00
1997 San Jose
23 Peter Forsberg 12.50 25.00
2001 Denver
24 Peter Forsberg 10.00 25.00
1996 Boston
25 Peter Forsberg 10.00 25.00
1998 Vancouver
26 Simon Gagne 8.00 20.00
2001 Denver
27 Scott Gomez 6.00 15.00
2000 Toronto
28 Bill Guerin 6.00 15.00
2001 Denver
29 Milan Hejduk 8.00 20.00
2001 Denver
30 Phil Housley 4.00 10.00
2000 Toronto
31 Brett Hull 10.00 25.00
1994 New York
32 Jarome Iginla 10.00 25.00
2002 Los Angeles
33 Arturs Irbe 6.00 15.00
1999 Tampa Bay
34 Jaromir Jagr 10.00 25.00
2000 Toronto
35 Jaromir Jagr 10.00 25.00
1998 Vancouver
36 Jaromir Jagr 10.00 25.00
1996 Boston
37 Curtis Joseph 8.00 20.00
2000 Toronto
38 Ed Jovanovski 4.00 10.00
2002 Los Angeles
39 Tomas Kaberle 4.00 10.00
2002 Los Angeles
40 Sami Kapanen 4.00 10.00
2002 Los Angeles
41 Paul Kariya 8.00 20.00
1997 San Jose
42 Paul Kariya 8.00 20.00
2001 Denver
43 Paul Kariya 8.00 20.00
1996 Boston
44 Nikolai Khabibulin 8.00 20.00
2002 Los Angeles
45 Saku Koivu 8.00 20.00
1998 Vancouver
46 Olaf Kolzig 6.00 15.00
2000 Toronto
47 Alex Kovalev 4.00 10.00
2001 Denver
48 John LeClair 6.00 15.00
1997 San Jose
49 Brian Leetch 6.00 15.00
2001 Denver
50 Brian Leetch 6.00 15.00
1994 New York
51 Mario Lemieux 20.00 50.00
52 Mario Lemieux 20.00 50.00
53 Mario Lemieux 20.00 50.00
54 Nicklas Lidstrom 8.00 20.00
1999 Tampa Bay
55 Nicklas Lidstrom 8.00 20.00
2001 Denver
56 Eric Lindros 8.00 20.00
2000 Toronto
57 Al MacInnis 6.00 15.00
2000 Toronto
58 Mark Messier 15.00 40.00
1994 New York
59 Mark Messier 15.00 40.00
1996 Boston
60 Mike Modano 8.00 20.00
61 Mike Modano 8.00 20.00
62 Alexander Mogilny 6.00 15.00
1996 Boston
63 Evgeni Nabokov 6.00 15.00
2001 Denver
64 Markus Naslund 8.00 20.00
2001 Denver
65 Scott Niedermayer 6.00 15.00
1998 Vancouver
66 Owen Nolan 6.00 15.00
2002 Los Angeles
67 Teppo Numminen 4.00 10.00
2001 Denver
68 Chris Osgood 6.00 15.00
1996 Boston
69 Sandis Ozolinsh 4.00 10.00
2002 Los Angeles
70 Zigmund Palffy 6.00 15.00
2001 Denver
71 Felix Potvin 8.00 20.00
1996 Boston
72 Chris Pronger 6.00 15.00
2000 Toronto
73 Mark Recchi 6.00 15.00
2000 Toronto
74 Mike Richter 6.00 15.00
2000 Toronto
75 Luc Robitaille 6.00 15.00
1999 Tampa Bay
76 Jeremy Roenick 10.00 25.00
2000 Toronto
77 Patrick Roy 20.00 50.00
2002 Los Angeles
78 Patrick Roy 20.00 50.00
2001 Denver
79 Patrick Roy 20.00 50.00
1994 New York
80 Joe Sakic 15.00 40.00
1998 Vancouver
81 Joe Sakic 15.00 40.00
2001 Denver
82 Tommy Salo 4.00 10.00
2000 Toronto
83 Teemu Selanne 8.00 20.00
2002 Los Angeles
84 Brendan Shanahan 8.00 20.00
2002 Los Angeles
85 Brendan Shanahan 8.00 20.00
2000 Toronto
86 Brendan Shanahan 8.00 20.00
1996 Boston
87 Scott Stevens 4.00 10.00
2000 Toronto
88 Mats Sundin 8.00 20.00
2000 Toronto
89 Mats Sundin 8.00 20.00
1997 San Jose
90 Darryl Sydor 4.00 10.00
1999 Tampa Bay
91 Jose Theodore 8.00 20.00
2002 Los Angeles
92 Joe Thornton 12.00 30.00
2002 Los Angeles
93 Keith Tkachuk 8.00 20.00
1999 Tampa Bay
94 Ron Tugnutt 4.00 10.00
1999 Tampa Bay
95 Roman Turek 4.00 10.00
2000 Toronto
96 Doug Weight 4.00 10.00
2001 Denver
97 Alexei Yashin 4.00 10.00
1994 New York
98 Steve Yzerman 15.00 40.00
99 Steve Yzerman 15.00 40.00
100 Alexei Zhamnov 4.00 10.00
2002 Los Angeles

2002-03 BAP All-Star Edition Jerseys Gold

STATED PRINT RUN 10 SETS
NOT PRICED DUE TO SCARCITY

2002-03 BAP All-Star Edition Jerseys Silver

*SILVER: .5X TO 1.25X BASIC JERSEY
STATED PRINT RUN 30 SETS

2002-03 BAP First Edition

This 440-card set contained two different subsets; "Statistical Leaders" and "Draft Picks". The draft picks cards featured different players in retail and hobby packs and are noted below with "H" or "R" suffixes. Cards 426-440 (both retail and hobby) were available by a mail-in redemption found in packs only.

COMPLETE SET (425)
CARDS 401H-425H AVAIL.HOBBY PACKS
CARDS 401R-425R AVAIL.RETAIL PACKS
CARDS 426H-440H AVAIL.BY MAIL-IN
CARDS 426R-440R AVAIL.BY MAIL-IN
1 Mario Lemieux 2.00 5.00
2 Sergei Gonchar .10 .25
3 Brian Leetch .25 .60
4 Felix Potvin .30 .75
5 Sandis Ozolinsh .10 .25
6 Steven Reinprecht .10 .25
7 Byron Dafoe .25 .60
8 Mark Bell .10 .25
9 Jeff O'Neill .10 .25
10 Sean Burke .25 .60
11 Darcy Tucker .10 .25
12 Scott Stevens .25 .60
13 David Aebischer .25 .60
14 Jocelyn Thibault .25 .60
15 Radek Bonk .10 .25
16 Milan Hejduk .30 .75
17 Zigmund Palffy .25 .60
18 Luc Robitaille .25 .60
19 Tomas Kaberle .10 .25
20 Rostislav Klesla .10 .25
21 Alexei Zhamnov .10 .25
22 Ron Francis .25 .60
23 Mike Fisher .10 .25
24 Dany Heatley .40 1.00
25 Kyle McLaren .10 .25
26 Doug Weight .25 .60
27 Henrik Sedin .10 .25
28 Roman Turek .25 .60
29 Adam Deadmarsh .10 .25
30 Sami Kapanen .10 .25
31 Sergei Samsonov .25 .60
32 Kristian Huselius .10 .25
33 Dimitri Yushkevich .10 .25
34 Patrik Elias .25 .60
35 Nick Boynton .10 .25
36 Martin Biron .25 .60
37 Brad Richards .25 .60
38 Alyn McCauley .10 .25
39 Daniel Sedin .10 .25
40 Teppo Numminen .10 .25
41 Luke Richardson .10 .25
42 Manny Fernandez .25 .60
43 Vincent Lecavalier .30 .75
44 Mattias Ohlund .10 .25
45 Milan Kraft .10 .25
46 Mike Dunham .25 .60
47 Derian Hatcher .10 .25
48 Oleg Tverdovsky .10 .25
49 Shane Doan .10 .25
50 Martin Skoula .10 .25
51 John LeClair .30 .75
52 Tommy Salo .25 .60
53 Miroslav Satan .25 .60
54 Bryan Berard .10 .25
55 Roman Cechmanek .25 .60
56 Alexei Morozov .10 .25
57 Jean-Sebastien Giguere .25 .60
58 Pierre Turgeon .25 .60
59 Martin Straka .10 .25
60 Stephane Yelle .10 .25
61 Marc Savard .10 .25
62 Sergei Zubov .10 .25
63 Jeff Friesen .10 .25
64 Daniel Briere .10 .25
65 Patrik Stefan .10 .25
66 Pavol Demitra .25 .60
67 Radek Dvorak .10 .25
68 Marty Turco .25 .60
69 Keith Tkachuk .30 .75
70 Maxim Afinogenov .10 .25
71 Mika Noronen .25 .60
72 Evgeni Nabokov .25 .60
73 Todd Bertuzzi .30 .75
74 Valeri Bure .10 .25
75 Marian Hossa .30 .75
76 J-P Dumont .10 .25
77 Niklas Sundstrom .10 .25
78 Eric Daze .25 .60
79 Brian Boucher .25 .60
80 Nikolai Khabibulin .30 .75
81 Darren McCarty .10 .25
82 Pavel Brendl .10 .25
83 Mark Recchi .25 .60
84 Dan Cloutier .25 .60
85 Manny Legace .25 .60
86 Keith Primeau .10 .25
87 Alex Tanguay .25 .60
88 Ed Jovanovski .25 .60
89 Roberto Luongo .40 1.00
90 Andreas Johansson .10 .25
91 Steve Shields .25 .60
92 Saku Koivu .30 .75
93 Chris Drury .25 .60
94 Olaf Kolzig .25 .60
95 Jan Hrdina .10 .25
96 Ivan Novoseltsev .10 .25
97 Kenny Jonsson .10 .25
98 Martin Havlat .25 .60
99 Scott Niedermayer .10 .25
100 Chris Phillips .10 .25
101 Tony Amonte .25 .60
102 Alexander Mogilny .25 .60
103 Chris Pronger .25 .60
104 Chris Gratton .10 .25
105 Sergei Fedorov .50 1.25
106 David Legwand .25 .60
107 Ron Tugnutt .25 .60
108 Steven McCarthy .10 .25
109 Brian Rolston .10 .25
110 Bobby Holik .10 .25
111 Darryl Sydor .10 .25
112 Steve Sullivan .10 .25
113 Toby Petersen .10 .25
114 Scott Gomez .10 .25
115 Adam Foote .10 .25
116 Rob Niedermayer .10 .25
117 Arturs Irbe .25 .60
118 Al MacInnis .25 .60
119 Jeff Hackett .25 .60
120 Pavel Bure .30 .75
121 Patrick Lalime .25 .60
122 Vincent Damphousse .10 .25

123 Steve Passmore .25 .60
124 Simon Gagne .30 .75
125 Shawn McEachern .10 .25
126 Bryan McCabe .10 .25
127 Jamie Storr .25 .60
128 Mike Richter .30 .75
129 Petr Sykora .10 .25
130 Trevor Kidd .25 .60
131 Jaromir Jagr .50 1.25
132 Bill Guerin .25 .60
133 Mark Messier .30 .75
134 Ilya Kovalchuk .40 1.00
135 Teemu Selanne .30 .75
136 Dominik Hasek .60 1.50
137 Mats Sundin .30 .75
138 Jose Theodore .40 1.00
139 Brendan Shanahan .30 .75
140 Daniel Alfredsson .25 .60
141 Martin Brodeur .75 2.00
142 Jarome Iginla .40 1.00
143 Peter Bondra .30 .75
144 Peter Forsberg .75 2.00
145 Curtis Joseph .30 .75
146 Alexei Yashin .10 .25
147 Patrick Roy 1.50 4.00
148 Markus Naslund .30 .75
149 Jeremy Roenick .40 1.00
150 Eric Lindros .30 .75
151 Steve Yzerman 1.50 4.00
152 Marian Gaborik .60 1.50
153 Mike Modano .50 1.25
154 Joe Sakic .60 1.50
155 Paul Kariya .30 .75
156 Owen Nolan .25 .60
157 Rob Blake .25 .60
158 Nicklas Lidstrom .30 .75
159 Joe Thornton .50 1.25
160 Mario Lemieux 2.00 5.00
161 Magnus Arvedson .10 .25
162 Chris Clark .10 .25
163 Don Sweeney .10 .25
164 Fredrik Modin .10 .25
165 Matt Cooke .10 .25
166 Rhett Warrener .10 .25
167 Tim Taylor .10 .25
168 Viktor Kozlov .10 .25
169 Michal Rozsival .10 .25
170 Mathieu Schneider .10 .25
171 Matt Cullen .10 .25
172 Vladimir Malakhov .10 .25
173 Mattias Norstrom .10 .25
174 Greg Johnson .10 .25
175 Eric Desjardins .10 .25
176 Damian Rhodes .10 .25
177 Stephane Quintal .10 .25
178 Sami Salo .10 .25
179 Craig Rivet .10 .25
180 Oleg Saprykin .10 .25
181 Chris Therien .10 .25
182 Robyn Regehr .10 .25
183 Erik Cole .10 .25
184 Ed Belfour .30 .75
185 Chris Chelios .30 .75
186 Pavel Datsyuk .30 .75
187 Mike Comrie .25 .60
188 Doug Gilmour .25 .60
189 Johan Hedberg .25 .60
190 Brett Hull .40 1.00
191 Theo Fleury .10 .25
192 Rick DiPietro .25 .60
193 Marcus Ragnarsson .10 .25
194 Mike Peca .10 .25
195 Ryan Smyth .10 .25
196 Ruslan Salei .10 .25
197 Anson Carter .25 .60
198 Eric Brewer .10 .25
199 Alexei Kovalev .25 .60
200 Gary Roberts .10 .25
201 Micki Dupont RC .10 .25
202 Pat Verbeek .10 .25
203 Dmitri Kalinin .10 .25
204 Brad Stuart .25 .60
205 Brent Johnson .25 .60
206 Todd White .10 .25
207 Andy McDonald .10 .25
208 Glen Murray .10 .25
209 Chris Osgood .25 .60
210 Tim Connolly .10 .25
211 Scott Hartnell .10 .25
212 Radim Vrbata .10 .25
213 Dmitri Khristich .10 .25
214 Brendan Morrison .25 .60
215 Matt Henderson RC .10 .25
216 Jason Allison .10 .25
217 Ray Whitney .10 .25
218 Niklas Hagman .10 .25
219 Andrew Brunette .10 .25
220 Brian Rafalski .10 .25
221 Mark Parrish .10 .25
222 Dave Andreychuk .10 .25
223 Dainius Zubrus .10 .25
224 P.J. Stock .10 .25
225 Espen Knutsen .10 .25
226 Jiri Dopita .10 .25
227 Jeff Jillson .10 .25
228 Tie Domi .25 .60
229 Milan Hnilicka .25 .60
230 Martin Lapointe .10 .25
231 Taylor Pyatt .10 .25
232 Kyle Calder .10 .25
233 Marc Denis .25 .60
234 Brenden Morrow .25 .60
235 Cliff Ronning .10 .25
236 Wade Redden .10 .25
237 Kris Beech .10 .25
238 Patrick Marleau .25 .60
239 Corey Schwab .25 .60
240 Nikita Alexeev .10 .25
241 Miikka Kiprusoff .25 .60
242 Jason Arnott .10 .25
243 Joe Nieuwendyk .25 .60
244 Adam Oates .25 .60
245 Darius Kasparaitis .10 .25
246 Mike York .10 .25
247 Donald Brashear .10 .25
248 Kevin Weekes .25 .60
249 Jaroslav Spacek .10 .25
250 Alex Auld .10 .25
251 Denis Arkhipov .10 .25
252 Cory Stillman .10 .25
253 Craig Conroy .10 .25
254 Dan Blackburn .25 .60
255 Vaclav Nedorost .25 .60
256 Ladislav Nagy .10 .25
257 Lukas Krajicek .10 .25
258 Raffi Torres .10 .25
259 Richard Zednik .10 .25
260 Brad Bombardir .10 .25
261 Ilja Bryzgalov .25 .60
262 Frederic Cassivi .10 .25
263 Geoff Sanderson .10 .25
264 Dwayne Roloson .10 .25
265 Jani Hurme .25 .60
266 Sebastien Centomo .25 .60
267 Jeff Halpern .10 .25
268 Mikael Renberg .10 .25
269 Vaclav Prospal .10 .25
270 Sylvain Blouin RC .10 .25
271 Olivier Michaud .25 .60
272 Pascal Dupuis .10 .25
273 Michael Nylander .10 .25
274 Daymond Langkow .25 .60
275 Mike Sillinger .10 .25
276 Yanic Perreault .10 .25
277 Oleg Petrov .10 .25
278 Rod Brind'Amour .25 .60
279 Scott Clemmensen .25 .60
280 Jason Smith .10 .25
281 Vladimir Orszagh .10 .25
282 Stephen Weiss .10 .25
283 Tony Hrkac .10 .25
284 Ty Conklin .25 .60
285 Ulf Dahlen .10 .25
286 Karel Pilar .10 .25
287 Krys Kolanos .10 .25
288 Marcel Hossa .10 .25
289 Martin Prusek .25 .60
290 Robert Svehla .10 .25
291 Radoslav Suchy .10 .25
292 Alexander Khavanov .10 .25
293 Andy Delmore .10 .25
294 Adrian Aucoin .10 .25
295 Bates Battaglia .10 .25
296 Jussi Markkanen .10 .25
297 Martin Erat .10 .25
298 Jim Dowd .10 .25
299 Mark Hartigan .10 .25
300 Neil Little .10 .25
301 Markus Naslund UC .40 1.00
302 Bill Guerin UC .30 .75
303 Nicklas Lidstrom UC .40 1.00
304 Sergei Fedorov UC .75 2.00
305 Mats Sundin UC .40 1.00
306 Teemu Selanne UC .40 1.00
307 Sergei Gonchar UC .12 .30
308 Brian Leetch UC .40 1.00
309 Jeremy Roenick UC .50 1.25
310 Jaromir Jagr UC .60 1.50
311 Mark Recchi UC .30 .75
312 Sandis Ozolinsh UC .12 .30
313 Jarome Iginla UC .50 1.25
314 Jose Theodore UC .50 1.25
315 Steve Yzerman UC 2.00 5.00
316 Paul Kariya UC .40 1.00
317 Eric Daze UC .30 .75
318 Ilya Kovalchuk UC .50 1.25
319 Brendan Shanahan UC .40 1.00
320 Marian Gaborik UC .75 2.00
321 Joe Sakic UC .75 2.00
322 Peter Forsberg UC 1.00 2.50
323 Mario Lemieux UC 2.50 6.00
324 Luc Robitaille UC .40 1.00
325 Eric Lindros UC .40 1.00
326 Mike Modano UC .60 1.50
327 Patrick Roy UC 2.00 5.00
328 Dominik Hasek UC .75 2.00
329 Scott Stevens UC .30 .75
330 Martin Brodeur UC 1.00 2.50
331 Keith Tkachuk UC .40 1.00
332 Rostislav Klesla UC .30 .75
333 Joe Thornton UC .60 1.50
334 Alexei Yashin UC .12 .30
335 Brett Hull UC .50 1.25
336 Olaf Kolzig UC .30 .75
337 Roberto Luongo UC .40 1.00
338 Pavel Bure UC .40 1.00
339 Chris Chelios UC .40 1.00
340 Owen Nolan UC .30 .75
341 Paul Kariya FP .40 1.00
342 Ilya Kovalchuk FP .50 1.25
343 Joe Thornton FP .60 1.50
344 Miroslav Satan FP .30 .75
345 Jarome Iginla FP .50 1.25
346 Jeff O'Neill FP .12 .30
347 Eric Daze FP .30 .75
348 Patrick Roy FP 2.00 5.00
349 Rostislav Klesla FP .30 .75
350 Mike Modano FP .60 1.50
351 Steve Yzerman FP 2.00 5.00
352 Mike Comrie FP .30 .75
353 Roberto Luongo FP .40 1.00
354 Zigmund Palffy FP .30 .75
355 Marian Gaborik FP .75 2.00
356 Jose Theodore FP .50 1.25
357 Scott Hartnell FP .12 .30
358 Martin Brodeur FP 1.00 2.50
359 Alexei Yashin FP .12 .30
360 Pavel Bure FP .40 1.00
361 Marian Hossa FP .40 1.00
362 Simon Gagne FP .40 1.00
363 Daniel Briere FP .12 .30
364 Mario Lemieux FP 2.50 6.00
365 Chris Pronger FP .30 .75
366 Owen Nolan FP .30 .75
367 Nikolai Khabibulin FP .40 1.00
368 Mats Sundin FP .40 1.00
369 Markus Naslund FP .40 1.00
370 Jaromir Jagr FP .60 1.50
371 Jarome Iginla .30 .75
Markus Naslund
Todd Bertuzzi
372 Jarome Iginla .30 .75
Mats Sundin
Glen Murray
Bill Guerin
373 Oates/Allison/Sakic .40 1.00
374 Chris Chelios .30 .75
Jeremy Roenick
Glen Murray
Simon Gagne
375 Peter Worrell .30 .75
Brad Ference
Chris Neil
376 Roy/Cechmanek/Turco .40 1.00
377 Theodore/Roy/Cech./Turco .50 1.25
378 Pavol Demitra .30 .75
Glen Murray
Mats Sundin
379 Brian Rolston .30 .75
Michael Peca
Miroslav Satan
380 Hasek/Brodeur/Nabokov .40 1.00
381 Robert Svehla .30 .75
Darius Kasparaitis
Derian Hatcher
382 Nicklas Lidstrom .30 .75
Sergei Gonchar
383 Heatley/Kovalchuk/Huselius .50 1.25
384 Kovalchuk/Heatley/Huselius .50 1.25
385 Adrian Aucoin .30 .75
Chris Pronger
Nicklas Lidstrom
386 Yanic Perreault .30 .75
Rod Brind'Amour
Ron Francis
387 Peter Bondra .30 .75
Jarome Iginla
388 Daniel Briere .30 .75
Adam Deadmarsh
Jan Hrdina
389 Patrick Roy AS 2.00 5.00
390 Chris Pronger AS .30 .75
391 Rob Blake AS .30 .75
392 Vincent Damphousse AS .30 .75
393 Owen Nolan AS .30 .75
394 Brendan Shanahan AS .60 1.50
395 Dominik Hasek AS .75 2.00
396 Nicklas Lidstrom AS .40 1.00
397 Sandis Ozolinsh AS .30 .75
398 Sergei Fedorov AS .75 2.00
399 Jaromir Jagr AS .60 1.50
400 Teemu Selanne AS .40 1.00
401H Mike Modano DP .60 1.50
401R Trevor Linden DP .12 .30
402H Jeremy Roenick DP .50 1.25
402R Mats Sundin DP .40 1.00
403H Bill Guerin DP .30 .75
403R Olaf Kolzig DP .30 .75
404H Owen Nolan DP .30 .75
404R Jaromir Jagr DP .60 1.50
405H Martin Brodeur DP 1.00 2.50
405R Eric Lindros DP .60 1.50
406H Scott Niedermayer DP .30 .75
406R Peter Forsberg DP 1.00 2.50
407H Markus Naslund DP .30 .75
407R Alexei Yashin DP .12 .30
408H Chris Pronger DP .30 .75
408R Paul Kariya DP .40 1.00
409H Jason Arnott DP .10 .25
409R Jocelyn Thibault DP .30 .75
410H Adam Deadmarsh DP .12 .30
410R Jason Allison DP .12 .30
411H Todd Bertuzzi DP .30 .75
411R Ed Jovanovski DP .30 .75
412H Jeff O'Neill DP .12 .30
412R Ryan Smyth DP .12 .30
413H Dan Cloutier DP .30 .75
413R Jarome Iginla DP .50 1.25
414H Jean-Sebastien Giguere DP .30 .75
414R Martin Biron DP .30 .75
415H Petr Sykora DP .30 .75
415R Brian Boucher DP .30 .75
416H Marc Denis DP .30 .75
416R Joe Thornton DP .60 1.50
417H Roberto Luongo DP .40 1.00
417R Eric Brewer DP .12 .30
418H Sergei Samsonov DP .30 .75
418R Marian Hossa DP .40 1.00
419H Vincent Lecavalier DP .30 .75
419R Mark Bell DP .12 .30
420H Alex Tanguay DP .40 1.00
420R Simon Gagne DP .40 1.00
421H Martin Havlat DP .30 .75
421R Rick DiPietro DP .30 .75
422H Dany Heatley DP .40 1.00
422R Marian Gaborik DP .30 .75
423H Rostislav Klesla DP .30 .75
423R Scott Hartnell DP .12 .30
424H Ilya Kovalchuk DP .50 1.25
424R Stephen Weiss DP .40 1.00
425H Dan Blackburn DP .30 .75
425R Lukas Krajicek DP .60 1.50
426H Steve Yzerman DP 6.00 15.00
426R Mario Lemieux DP 8.00 20.00
427H Gary Roberts DP .40 1.00
427R Brian Leetch DP 1.00 2.50
428H Brendan Shanahan DP 2.00 5.00
428R Pierre Turgeon DP 1.00 2.50
429H Joe Sakic DP 2.50 6.00
429R Teemu Selanne DP 2.00 5.00
430H Keith Tkachuk DP 1.25 3.00
430R H.Sedin/D.Sedin DP 2.00 5.00
431H Steve Ott DP RC 3.00 8.00
431R Brooks Orpik DP RC 2.00 5.00
432H Pascal Leclaire DP RC 3.00 8.00
432R Shaone Morrisonn DP RC 2.00 5.00
433H Alexei Smirnov DP RC 2.00 5.00
433R Ron Hainsey DP RC 2.00 5.00
434H Alexander Frolov DP RC 4.00 10.00
434R Anton Volchenkov DP RC 2.00 5.00
435H Jeff Taffe DP RC 2.00 5.00
435R Jason Spezza DP RC 6.00 15.00
436H Alexander Svitov DP RC 2.50 6.00
436R Stanislav Chistov DP RC 2.50 6.00
437H Chuck Kobasew DP RC 2.50 6.00
437R Ales Hemsky DP RC 6.00 15.00
438H Carlo Colaiacovo DP RC 2.50 6.00
438R Jay Bouwmeester DP RC 3.00 8.00
439H Rick Nash DP RC 8.00 20.00
439R Scottie Upshall DP RC 3.00 8.00
440H P-M Bouchard DP RC 4.00 10.00
440R Steve Eminger DP RC 2.00 5.00

2002-03 BAP First Edition Debut Jerseys

This 160-card set was inserted at a overall rate for memorabilia of 1:36 hobby and 1:48 retail. Each card was limited to a production run of 50 copies.

*MULT.COLOR SWATCH: .75X TO 1.5X
OVERALL MEM.ODDS 1:36 HBBY/1:48 RET.
STATED PRINT RUN 50 SETS
1 Pavel Bure 15.00 40.00
2 Patrick Roy 40.00 100.00
3 Curtis Joseph 15.00 40.00
4 Mats Sundin 15.00 40.00
5 Ed Belfour 15.00 40.00
6 Teemu Selanne 15.00 40.00
7 Martin Brodeur 25.00 60.00
8 Owen Nolan 10.00 25.00
9 Jarome Iginla 20.00 50.00
10 Steve Yzerman 30.00 80.00
11 Marian Gaborik 20.00 50.00
12 Jaromir Jagr 15.00 40.00
13 Eric Lindros 15.00 40.00
14 Ilya Kovalchuk 20.00 50.00
15 Nicklas Lidstrom 10.00 25.00
16 Paul Kariya 15.00 40.00
17 Joe Thornton 25.00 60.00
18 Mark Messier 20.00 50.00
19 Keith Tkachuk 10.00 25.00
20 Joe Sakic 20.00 50.00

2002-03 BAP First Edition He Shoots-He Score Points

ONE PER PACK
RED.PROGRAM HAS EXPIRED
1 Ron Francis 1 pt. .10 .25
2 Sergei Fedorov 1 pt. .10 .25
3 Milan Hejduk 1 pt. .10 .25
3 Saku Koivu 1 pt. .10 .25
4 Dany Heatley 1 pt. .10 .25
5 Ilya Kovalchuk 1 pt. .10 .25
7 Teemu Selanne 1 pt. .10 .25
8 Eric Lindros 1 pt. .10 .25
9 Mark Messier 1 pt. .10 .25
10 Owen Nolan 1 pt. .10 .25
11 Joe Thornton 1 pt. .10 .25
12 Pavel Bure 2 pts. .10 .25
13 Jarome Iginla 2 pts. .10 .25
14 Paul Kariya 2 pts. .10 .25
15 Joe Sakic 2 pts. .10 .25
16 Steve Yzerman 2 pts. .10 .25
17 Mike Modano 2 pts. .10 .25
18 Peter Forsberg 3 pts. .10 .25
19 Mats Sundin 3 pts. .10 .25
20 Mario Lemieux 3 pts. .10 .25

2002-03 BAP First Edition He Shoots-He Scores Prizes

PRINT RUN 20 SER. #'d SETS
NOT PRICED DUE TO SCARCITY
1 Peter Forsberg
2 Mario Lemieux
3 Mats Sundin
4 Jarome Iginla
5 Pavel Bure
6 Joe Sakic
7 Steve Yzerman
8 Paul Kariya
9 Mike Modano
10 Mark Messier
11 Milan Hejduk
12 Ron Francis
13 Saku Koivu
14 Owen Nolan
15 Joe Thornton
16 Ilya Kovalchuk
17 Dany Heatley
18 Eric Lindros
19 Teemu Selanne
20 Sergei Fedorov
21 Brendan Shanahan
22 Marian Gaborik
23 Patrick Roy
24 Martin Brodeur
25 Jose Theodore
26 Dominik Hasek
27 Jeremy Roenick
28 Jaromir Jagr
29 Keith Tkachuk
30 Markus Naslund

2002-03 BAP First Edition Jerseys

*MULT.COLOR SWATCH: .75X TO 1.5X
CARDS 1-130 AVAIL. RETAIL/HOBBY
CARDS 131-160 AVAIL.HOBBY ONLY
STATED PRINT RUN 100 SETS
1 Mario Lemieux 15.00 40.00
2 Sergei Gonchar 5.00 12.00
3 Brian Leetch 5.00 12.00
4 Felix Potvin 6.00 15.00
5 Sandis Ozolinsh 5.00 12.00
6 Steven Reinprecht 5.00 12.00
7 Byron Dafoe 5.00 12.00
8 Mark Bell 5.00 12.00
9 Jeff O'Neill 5.00 12.00
10 Sean Burke 5.00 12.00
11 Darcy Tucker 5.00 12.00
12 Scott Stevens 5.00 12.00
13 David Aebischer 5.00 12.00
14 Jocelyn Thibault 5.00 12.00
15 Radek Bonk 5.00 12.00
16 Milan Hejduk 6.00 15.00
17 Zigmund Palffy 5.00 12.00
18 Luc Robitaille 5.00 12.00
19 Tomas Kaberle 5.00 12.00
20 Rostislav Klesla 5.00 12.00
21 Alexei Zhamnov 5.00 12.00
22 Ron Francis 5.00 12.00
23 Mike Fisher 5.00 12.00
24 Dany Heatley 8.00 20.00
25 Kyle McLaren 5.00 12.00
26 Doug Weight 5.00 12.00
27 Henrik Sedin 5.00 12.00
28 Roman Turek 5.00 12.00
29 Adam Deadmarsh 5.00 12.00
30 Sami Kapanen 5.00 12.00
31 Sergei Samsonov 5.00 12.00
32 Kristian Huselius 5.00 12.00
33 Dimitri Yushkevich 5.00 12.00
34 Patrik Elias 5.00 12.00
35 Nick Boynton 5.00 12.00
36 Martin Biron 5.00 12.00
37 Brad Richards 5.00 12.00
38 Alyn McCauley 5.00 12.00
39 Daniel Sedin 5.00 12.00
40 Teppo Numminen 5.00 12.00
41 Luke Richardson 5.00 12.00
42 Manny Fernandez 5.00 12.00
43 Vincent Lecavalier 6.00 15.00
44 Mattias Ohlund 5.00 12.00
45 Milan Kraft 5.00 12.00
46 Mike Dunham 5.00 12.00
47 Derian Hatcher 5.00 12.00
48 Oleg Tverdovsky 5.00 12.00
49 Shane Doan 5.00 12.00
50 Martin Skoula 5.00 12.00
51 John LeClair 6.00 15.00
52 Tommy Salo 5.00 12.00
53 Miroslav Satan 5.00 12.00
54 Bryan Berard 5.00 12.00
55 Roman Cechmanek 5.00 12.00
56 Alexei Morozov 5.00 12.00
57 Jean-Sebastien Giguere 5.00 12.00
58 Pierre Turgeon 5.00 12.00
59 Martin Straka 5.00 12.00
60 Stephane Yelle 5.00 12.00
61 Marc Savard 5.00 12.00
62 Sergei Zubov 5.00 12.00
63 Jeff Friesen 5.00 12.00
64 Daniel Briere 5.00 12.00
65 Patrik Stefan 5.00 12.00
66 Pavol Demitra 5.00 12.00
67 Radek Dvorak 5.00 12.00
68 Marty Turco 5.00 12.00
69 Keith Tkachuk 6.00 15.00
70 Maxim Afinogenov 5.00 12.00
71 Mika Noronen 5.00 12.00
72 Evgeni Nabokov 5.00 12.00
73 Todd Bertuzzi 6.00 15.00
74 Valeri Bure 5.00 12.00
75 Marian Hossa 6.00 15.00
76 J-P Dumont 5.00 12.00
77 Niklas Sundstrom 5.00 12.00
78 Eric Daze 5.00 12.00
79 Brian Boucher 5.00 12.00
80 Nikolai Khabibulin 6.00 15.00
81 Darren McCarty 5.00 12.00
82 Pavel Brendl 5.00 12.00
83 Mark Recchi 5.00 12.00
84 Dan Cloutier 5.00 12.00
85 Manny Legace 5.00 12.00
86 Keith Primeau 5.00 12.00
87 Alex Tanguay 5.00 12.00
88 Ed Jovanovski 5.00 12.00
89 Roberto Luongo 10.00 25.00
90 Andreas Johansson 5.00 12.00
91 Steve Shields 5.00 12.00
92 Saku Koivu 6.00 15.00
93 Chris Drury 5.00 12.00
94 Olaf Kolzig 5.00 12.00
95 Jan Hrdina 5.00 12.00
96 Ivan Novoseltsev 5.00 12.00
97 Kenny Jonsson 5.00 12.00
98 Martin Havlat 5.00 12.00
99 Scott Niedermayer 5.00 12.00
100 Chris Phillips 5.00 12.00
101 Tony Amonte 5.00 12.00
102 Alexander Mogilny 5.00 12.00
103 Chris Pronger 5.00 12.00
104 Chris Gratton 5.00 12.00
105 Sergei Fedorov 8.00 20.00
106 David Legwand 5.00 12.00
107 Ron Tugnutt 5.00 12.00
108 Steven McCarthy 5.00 12.00
109 Brian Rolston 5.00 12.00
110 Bobby Holik 5.00 12.00
111 Darryl Sydor 5.00 12.00
112 Steve Sullivan 5.00 12.00
113 Toby Petersen 5.00 12.00
114 Scott Gomez 5.00 12.00
115 Adam Foote 5.00 12.00
116 Rob Niedermayer 5.00 12.00
117 Arturs Irbe 5.00 12.00
118 Al MacInnis 5.00 12.00
119 Jeff Hackett 5.00 12.00
120 Pavel Bure 6.00 15.00
121 Patrick Lalime 5.00 12.00
122 Vincent Damphousse 5.00 12.00
123 Steve Passmore 5.00 12.00
124 Simon Gagne 6.00 15.00
125 Shawn McEachern 5.00 12.00
126 Bryan McCabe 5.00 12.00
127 Jamie Storr 5.00 12.00
128 Mike Richter 6.00 15.00
129 Petr Sykora 5.00 12.00
130 Trevor Kidd 5.00 12.00
131 Jaromir Jagr 10.00 25.00
132 Bill Guerin 5.00 12.00
133 Mark Messier 6.00 15.00
134 Ilya Kovalchuk 10.00 25.00
135 Teemu Selanne 6.00 15.00
136 Dominik Hasek 15.00 40.00
137 Mats Sundin 6.00 15.00
138 Jose Theodore 10.00 25.00
139 Brendan Shanahan 6.00 15.00
140 Daniel Alfredsson 5.00 12.00
141 Martin Brodeur 15.00 40.00
142 Jarome Iginla 10.00 25.00
143 Peter Bondra 6.00 15.00
144 Peter Forsberg 15.00 40.00
145 Curtis Joseph 6.00 15.00
146 Alexei Yashin 5.00 12.00
147 Patrick Roy 20.00 50.00
148 Markus Naslund 6.00 15.00
149 Jeremy Roenick 10.00 25.00
150 Eric Lindros 6.00 15.00
151 Steve Yzerman 15.00 40.00
152 Marian Gaborik 12.50 30.00
153 Mike Modano 8.00 20.00
154 Joe Sakic 12.50 30.00
155 Paul Kariya 6.00 15.00
156 Owen Nolan 5.00 12.00
157 Rob Blake 5.00 12.00
158 Nicklas Lidstrom 6.00 15.00
159 Joe Thornton 10.00 25.00
160 Mario Lemieux 15.00 40.00

2002-03 BAP First Edition Magnificent Inserts

This 10-card set featured game-used equipment from the career of Mario Lemieux. Cards MI1-MI5 had a print run of 40 copies each and cards MI6-MI10 were limited to just 10 copies each. Cards MI6-MI10 are not priced due to scarcity.

CARDS MI1-MI5 PRINT RUN 40 SETS
CARDS MI6-MI10 PRINT RUN 10 SETS
MI6-MI10 NOT PRICED DUE TO SCARCITY
MI1 2000-01 Jersey 30.00 80.00
MI2 1985-86 Jersey 30.00 80.00
MI3 2002 All-Star Jersey 30.00 80.00
MI4 1987 Canada Cup Jersey 30.00 80.00
MI5 Dual Jersey 50.00 125.00
MI6 Number
MI7 Emblem
MI8 Triple Jersey
MI9 Quad Jersey
MI10 Complete Package

2002-03 BAP First Edition Scoring Leaders

*MULT.COLOR SWATCH: .75X TO 1.5X
STATED PRINT RUN 50.SETS
1 Paul Kariya 12.50 30.00
2 Dany Heatley 20.00 50.00
3 Sergei Samsonov 12.50 30.00
4 Jarome Iginla 15.00 40.00
5 Ron Francis 12.50 30.00
6 Eric Daze 12.50 30.00
7 Joe Sakic 20.00 50.00
8 Mike Modano 15.00 40.00
9 Brendan Shanahan 12.50 30.00
10 Patrik Elias 12.50 30.00
11 Alexei Yashin 12.50 30.00
12 Eric Lindros 12.50 30.00
13 Daniel Alfredsson 12.50 30.00
14 Jeremy Roenick 15.00 40.00
15 Alexei Kovalev 12.50 30.00
16 Owen Nolan 12.50 30.00
17 Brad Richards 12.50 30.00
18 Mats Sundin 12.50 30.00
19 Markus Naslund 12.50 30.00
20 Jaromir Jagr 15.00 40.00

1999-00 BAP Memorabilia

Released as two series, the base 300-card set was released under Be A Player Memorabilia, and the last 100-cards were released as Be A Player Memorabilia AS Update. Base cards feature color action photos and are enhanced with blue foil highlights. Gold and silver parallels of the set were also created and inserted into random packs. Gold parallels had a stated print run of 100 sets and silver parallels had a stated print run of 1000 sets. Be A Player Memorabilia was packaged in 24-pack boxes with packs containing eight cards and carried a suggested retail price of $3.29 US and $4.99 CAN.

COMPLETE SET (400) 40.00 100.00
COMP.SERIES 1 (300) 30.00 80.00
COMP.UPDATE SET (100) 8.00 20.00
COMP.UPDATE FACT.SET (100) 15.00 40.00
1 Patrik Stefan RC .25 .60
2 Glen Murray .08 .25
3 Nicklas Lidstrom .30 .75
4 Arturs Irbe .25 .60
5 Viktor Kozlov .08 .25
6 Dimitri Yushkevich .08 .25
7 Byron Ritchie RC .08 .25
8 Robert Svehla .08 .25
9 Jeremy Roenick .40 1.00
10 Ron Francis .25 .60
11 Oleg Kvasha .08 .25
12 Marian Hossa .30 .75
13 Mark Recchi .25 .60
14 Scott Mellanby .08 .25
15 Adam Graves .08 .25
16 Boris Mironov .08 .25
17 Derian Hatcher .08 .25
18 Brian Leetch .30 .75
19 Mattias Ohlund .08 .25
20 Ray Whitney .08 .25
21 Mike Richter .30 .75
22 Paul Mara .08 .25
23 Todd Bertuzzi .30 .75
24 Sergei Zubov .08 .25
25 Cliff Ronning .08 .25
26 Anson Carter .25 .60
27 Dmitri Mironov .08 .25
28 Shane Willis .08 .25
29 Shayne Corson .08 .25
30 Chris Chelios .30 .75
31 Pavel Kubina .08 .25
32 Michal Grosek .08 .25
33 Gary Suter .08 .25
34 Greg Adams .08 .25
35 Joe Thornton .50 1.25
36 Matt Higgins .08 .25
37 Chris Gratton .08 .25
38 Ray Bourque .50 1.25
39 Tommy Salo .25 .60
40 Igor Kravchuk .08 .25
41 Byron Dafoe .25 .60
42 Larry Murphy .08 .25
43 Bryan McCabe .08 .25
44 John Vanbiesbrouck .25 .60
45 Brett Hull .40 1.00
46 Christian Dube .08 .25
47 Kyle McLaren .08 .25
48 Jere Lehtinen .25 .60
49 Petr Nedved .25 .60
50 Jason Allison .08 .25
51 Brad Lukowich RC .08 .25
52 Scott Stevens .25 .60
53 Sergei Krivokrasov .08 .25
54 Olaf Kolzig .25 .60
55 Sami Kapanen .08 .25
56 Sami Salo .08 .25
57 Cory Stillman .08 .25
58 Darcy Tucker .08 .25
59 Rod Brind'Amour .25 .60
60 John Jakopin RC .08 .25
61 Martin Brodeur .75 2.00
62 Jiri Slegr .08 .25
63 Rem Murray .08 .25
64 Jason Arnott .08 .25
65 Jon Sim RC .25 .60
66 Cory Sarich .08 .25
67 Brian Rafalski RC .25 .60
68 Kevin Hatcher .08 .25
69 Ted Donato .08 .25
70 Dan LaCouture .08 .25
71 Alexei Kovalev .08 .25
72 Peter Bondra .25 .60
73 John LeClair .30 .75
74 Matthew Barnaby .08 .25
75 Adam Oates .25 .60
76 Janne Niinimaa .08 .25
77 Tom Barrasso .25 .60
78 Sergei Gonchar .08 .25
79 Alex Tanguay .25 .60
80 Jean-Luc Grand-Pierre RC .08 .25
81 Alexei Tezikov RC .25 .60
82 Doug Gilmour .08 .25
83 Sergei Brylin .08 .25

Card	Low	High
84 Ron Tugnutt	.25	.60
85 Stephane Richer	.08	.25
86 Marc Denis	.25	.60
87 Sergei Fedorov	.50	1.25
88 Brian Rolston	.08	.25
89 Chris Pronger	.25	.60
90 Dan Cloutier	.25	.60
91 Anders Eriksson	.08	.25
92 Donald Audette	.08	.25
93 Ed Jovanovski	.08	.25
94 Tony Amonte	.25	.60
95 Jamie Storr	.25	.60
96 German Titov	.08	.25
97 Eric Daze	.25	.60
98 Zigmund Palffy	.25	.60
99 Dan McGillis	.08	.25
100 Nikolai Khabibulin	.25	.60
101 Mathieu Schneider	.08	.25
102 Magnus Arvedson	.25	.60
103 Joe Sakic	.60	1.50
104 Brian Campbell RC	.08	.25
105 Wade Redden	.08	.25
106 Andrei Nikolishin	.08	.25
107 Steve Rucchin	.08	.25
108 Shawn McEachern	.08	.25
109 Alexander Karpovtsev	.08	.25
110 Miroslav Satan	.25	.60
111 Andreas Dackell	.08	.25
112 Niklas Sundstrom	.08	.25
113 Scott Niedermayer	.08	.25
114 Ken Wregget	.25	.60
115 Olli Jokinen	.25	.60
116 Vincent Lecavalier	.30	.75
117 Paul Kariya	.30	.75
118 Alexei Zhamnov	.08	.25
119 Martin Rucinsky	.08	.25
120 Daniel Cleary	.08	.25
121 Yanic Perreault	.08	.25
122 Alexei Zhitnik	.08	.25
123 Vadim Sharifijanov	.08	.25
124 Derek King	.08	.25
125 Jason Woolley	.08	.25
126 Pavel Bure	.30	.75
127 Darius Kasparaitis	.08	.25
128 Stu Barnes	.08	.25
129 Josef Beranek	.08	.25
130 Milan Hejduk	.30	.75
131 Michael Peca	.25	.60
132 Tomas Holmstrom	.08	.25
133 Patrick Marleau	.30	.75
134 Dominik Hasek	.60	1.50
135 Chris Osgood	.25	.60
136 Radek Bonk	.08	.25
137 Martin Biron	.25	.60
138 Igor Larionov	.08	.25
139 Felix Potvin	.30	.75
140 Oleg Tverdovsky	.08	.25
141 Steve Yzerman	1.50	4.00
142 Bobby Holik	.08	.25
143 Landon Wilson	.08	.25
144 Marty McInnis	.08	.25
145 Remi Royer	.08	.25
146 Brendan Morrison	.25	.60
147 Jaromir Jagr	.50	1.25
148 Steve Thomas	.08	.25
149 Rico Fata	.08	.25
150 John Madden RC	.40	1.00
151 Miroslav Guren	.08	.25
152 Jochen Hecht RC	.75	2.00
153 Gary Roberts	.08	.25
154 Patrik Elias	.25	.60
155 Al MacInnis	.25	.60
156 Jonathan Girard	.25	.60
157 Jan Hlavac	.08	.25
158 Pierre Turgeon	.25	.60
159 Matt Cullen	.08	.25
160 Trevor Letowski	.08	.25
161 Roman Turek	.25	.60
162 Luc Robitaille	.25	.60
163 Marcus Nilsson	.08	.25
164 Pavol Demitra	.25	.60
165 Fredrik Olausson	.08	.25
166 Blake Sloan	.30	.75
167 Eric Lindros	.30	.75
168 Guy Hebert	.25	.60
169 Adam Deadmarsh	.08	.25
170 Mike Leclerc	.08	.25
171 Teemu Selanne	.30	.75
172 Ty Jones	.08	.25
173 Calle Johansson	.08	.25
174 Ed Belfour	.30	.75
175 Craig MacDonald RC	.08	.25
176 Todd Harvey	.08	.25
177 Martin Straka	.08	.25
178 Mariusz Czerkawski	.08	.25
179 Grant Fuhr	.25	.60
180 Mark Parrish	.08	.25
181 Sandis Ozolinsh	.08	.25
182 Patrice Brisebois	.08	.25
183 Geoff Courtnall	.08	.25
184 Chris Drury	.25	.60
185 Saku Koivu	.30	.75
186 Teppo Numminen	.08	.25
187 Alexei Morozov	.08	.25
188 Stephane Quintal	.08	.25
189 Eric Desjardins	.25	.60
190 Pavel Patera RC	.08	.25
191 Vladimir Malakhov	.08	.25
192 Jean-Sebastien Giguere	.25	.60
193 Niclas Havelid RC	.08	.25
194 Trevor Linden	.08	.25
195 Simon Gagne	.30	.75
196 Kevin Weekes	.25	.60
197 Joe Nieuwendyk	.25	.60
198 Cameron Mann	.08	.25
199 Adam Mair RC	.25	.60
200 Kim Johnsson RC	.25	.60
201 Mikael Renberg	.25	.60
202 Curtis Joseph	.30	.75
203 Juha Lind	.08	.25
204 Doug Weight	.25	.60
205 Mats Lindgren	.08	.25
206 Marcus Ragnarsson	.08	.25
207 Igor Korolev	.08	.25
208 Claude Lemieux	.08	.25
209 Bill Hackett	.25	.60
210 Brendan Witt	.08	.25
211 Steve Kariya RC	.25	.60
212 Jarome Iginla	.40	1.00
213 Pavel Rosa	.08	.25
214 Andrei Zyuzin	.08	.25
215 Oleg Saprykin RC	.25	.60
216 Sean Burke	.25	.60
217 Mike Modano	.50	1.25
218 Phil Housley	.08	.25
219 Ryan Smyth	.08	.25
220 Daren Puppa	.25	.60
221 Aki Berg	.08	.25
222 Mike Grier	.08	.25
223 Keith Jones	.08	.25
224 Marc Savard	.08	.25
225 Bill Guerin	.25	.60
226 Theo Fleury	.08	.25
227 Shawn Heins RC	.08	.25
228 Tom Poti	.08	.25
229 Tim Connolly	.08	.25
230 Glen Wesley	.08	.25
231 Brendan Shanahan	.30	.75
232 Kenny Jonsson	.08	.25
233 Mats Sundin	.30	.75
234 Damian Rhodes	.25	.60
235 Martin Lapointe	.08	.25
236 David Legwand	.25	.60
237 Rob Niedermayer	.08	.25
238 Bill Muckalt	.08	.25
239 Valeri Bure	.08	.25
240 Manny Malhotra	.25	.60
241 Jozef Stumpel	.25	.60
242 Brad Stuart	.25	.60
243 Curtis Brown	.08	.25
244 Alexei Yashin	.08	.25
245 Owen Nolan	.25	.60
246 Shawn Bates	.08	.25
247 Jan Hrdina	.08	.25
248 Marco Sturm	.08	.25
249 Nelson Emerson	.08	.25
250 Stephane Fiset	.25	.60
251 Mike Vernon	.25	.60
252 Jason Botterill	.08	.25
253 Marty Reasoner	.25	.60
254 Roman Hamrlik	.08	.25
255 Ray Ferraro	.08	.25
256 Jamie Langenbrunner	.08	.25
257 Brian Holzinger	.08	.25
258 Andrew Brunette	.25	.60
259 Peter Forsberg	.75	2.00
260 Jyrki Lumme	.08	.25
261 Keith Primeau	.08	.25
262 Patrick Roy	1.50	4.00
263 Dmitri Nabokov	.08	.25
264 Darryl Laplante	.08	.25
265 Mark Messier	.30	.75
266 Benoit Gratton RC	.08	.25
267 Bryan Berard	.25	.60
268 Wendel Clark	.08	.25
269 Vincent Damphousse	.08	.25
270 J-P Dumont	.25	.60
271 Darryl Sydor	.08	.25
272 Darren Turcotte	.08	.25
273 Sergei Berezin	.08	.25
274 Jeff Friesen	.08	.25
275 Ville Peltonen	.08	.25
276 Rick Tocchet	.25	.60
277 Darren McCarty	.08	.25
278 Greg Johnson	.08	.25
279 Dan Smith RC	.08	.25
280 Sergei Samsonov	.25	.60
281 Petr Sykora	.08	.25
282 Dallas Drake	.08	.25
283 Steve Konowalchuk	.08	.25
284 Yan Golubovsky	.08	.25
285 Dan Boyle RC	.25	.60
286 Alexander Mogilny	.25	.60
287 Daniel Alfredsson	.25	.60
288 Steve Shields	.25	.60
289 Markus Naslund	.30	.75
290 Vyacheslav Kozlov	.30	.75
291 Keith Tkachuk	.30	.75
292 Adrian Aucoin	.08	.25
293 JocelynThibault	.25	.60
294 Kevin Stevens	.08	.25
295 John MacLean	.08	.25
296 Mike Ricci	.08	.25
297 Rob Blake	.08	.25
298 Radek Dvorak	.08	.25
299 Mike Dunham	.25	.60
300 Richard Matvichuk	.08	.25
301 Scott Gomez	.08	.25
302 Nikolai Antropov RC	.40	1.00
303 Glen Metropolit RC	.30	.75
304 Robyn Regehr	.08	.25
305 Mathieu Biron	.08	.25
306 Nathan Dempsey RC	.08	.25
307 Roberto Luongo	.40	1.00
308 Andreas Karlsson RC	.08	.25
309 Ray Bourque	.60	1.50
310 Artem Chubarov	.08	.25
311 Mike Fisher RC	.25	.60
312 Andrew Ference	.08	.25
313 Todd Reirden RC	.08	.25
314 Martin Skoula RC	.25	.60
315 Radislav Suchy RC	.08	.25
316 Joel Prpic RC	.25	.60
317 Yuri Butsayev RC	.25	.60
318 Andy Delmore RC	.25	.60
319 Steve McCarthy	.08	.25
320 Brian Holston	.08	.25
321 Dimitri Kalinin RC	.08	.25
322 Brenden Morrow	.30	.75
323 Mike Vernon	.25	.60
324 Nils Ekman RC	.08	.25
325 Felix Potvin	.30	.75
326 Jan Nemecek RC	.08	.25
327 Michael York	.08	.25
328 Evgeni Nabokov RC	2.50	6.00
329 Rick Tocchet	.08	.25
330 Vitali Vishnevsky	.08	.25
331 Francis Bouillon RC	.08	.25
332 Robert Esche RC	.75	2.00
333 Ray Giroux RC	.08	.25
334 Per Svartvadet RC	.08	.25
335 Kyle Calder RC	.40	1.00
336 Brian Boucher	.40	1.00
337 Dan Hinote RC	.25	.60
338 Darrel Scoville RC	.08	.25
339 Ivan Novoseltsev RC	.25	.60
340 Petr Schastlivy RC	.25	.60
341 Andre Savage RC	.30	.75
342 Michal Grosek	.08	.25
343 Richard Lintner RC	.08	.25
344 Tyson Nash RC	.25	.60
345 Tommy Westlund RC	.08	.25
346 Jason Krog RC	.08	.25
347 Jarkko Ruutu RC	.08	.25
348 Mike Ribeiro	.08	.25
349 Alexander Mogilny	.25	.60
350 Maxim Afinogenov	.08	.25
351 Ron Tugnutt	.25	.60
352 Jaroslav Spacek	.25	.60
353 Petr Buzek	.25	.60
354 Sami Helenius RC	.25	.60
355 Peter Schaefer	.25	.60
356 Alan Letang RC	.25	.60
357 Keith Primeau	.08	.25
358 Jay Henderson RC	.08	.25
359 Dave Tanabe	.25	.60
360 Fred Brathwaite	.25	.60
361 Chris Gratton	.25	.60
362 Maxim Balmochnykh	.25	.60
363 John Emmons	.08	.25
364 Mark Eaton RC	.25	.60
365 Kevyn Adams	.08	.25
366 Alfie Michaud RC	.25	.60
367 Chris Herperger RC	.25	.60
368 Scott Langkow	.25	.60
369 Marquis Mathieu RC	.08	.25
370 Milan Hnilicka RC	.25	.60
371 Michal Rozsival RC	.25	.60
372 Sergei Krivokrasov	.08	.25
373 Brad Chartrand RC	.08	.25
374 Ryan Bonni RC	.08	.25
375 Roman Lyashenko	.08	.25
376 Denis Hamel RC	.08	.25
377 Stephane Robidas RC	.08	.25
378 Jeff Halpern RC	.25	.60
379 Karlis Skrastins RC	.08	.25
380 Jeff Zehr RC	.08	.25
381 Brian Holzinger	.08	.25
382 Josef Beranek	.25	.60
383 Harold Druken	.25	.60
384 Doug Gilmour	.25	.60
385 Ladislav Nagy RC	.75	2.00
386 Bert Robertsson RC	.08	.25
387 Scott Fankhouser RC	.25	.60
388 Brian Willsie	.25	.60
389 Eric Boguniecki RC	.40	1.00
390 Dmitri Yakushin RC	.25	.60
391 Chris Clark RC	.25	.60
392 Paul Comrie RC	.30	.75
393 John Grahame RC	.25	.60
394 Rod Brind'Amour	.25	.60
395 Vladimir Malakhov	.08	.25
396 Jiri Fischer	.25	.60
397 Kimmo Timonen	.08	.25
398 Brad Ference	.08	.25
399 Marc Lamothe RC	.08	.25
400 Radek Dvorak	.08	.25
DT5 Dimitri Tertyshny TRIB	.30	.75
SC3 Steve Chiasson TRIB	.40	1.00

1999-00 BAP Memorabilia Gold

*VETERANS: 12X TO 30X BASIC CARDS
*ROOKIES: 8X TO 20X
STATED PRINT RUN 100 SER.#'d SETS

1999-00 BAP Memorabilia Silver

*VETERANS: 1.5X TO 4X BASIC CARDS
*ROOKIES: 1X TO 2.5X
STATED PRINT RUN 1000 SER.#'d SETS

1999-00 BAP Memorabilia Jersey

STATED ODDS 1:250
*MULT.COLOR SWATCH: 1X TO 1.5X HI
JERSEY AND STICK ODDS 1:999
*JSY EMBLEMS: .8X TO 2X BASIC JSY
JERSEY EMBLEM ODDS 1:999
*JSY NUMBERS: .8X TO 2X BASIC JSY
JERSEY NUMBERS ODDS 1:999

Card	Low	High
J1 Eric Lindros	10.00	25.00
J2 Peter Forsberg	15.00	40.00
J3 Teemu Selanne	10.00	25.00
J4 Mike Modano	12.00	30.00
J5 Mats Sundin	12.00	30.00
J6 Patrick Roy	40.00	100.00
J7 Paul Kariya	12.00	30.00
J8 Martin Brodeur	25.00	60.00
J9 Ray Bourque	15.00	40.00
J10 Mark Messier	10.00	25.00
J11 Curtis Joseph	10.00	25.00
J12 Brett Hull	12.00	30.00
J13 Al MacInnis	8.00	20.00
J14 Theo Fleury	8.00	20.00
J15 Sergei Fedorov	12.00	30.00
J16 Brian Leetch	8.00	20.00
J17 Alexei Yashin	8.00	20.00
J18 Jaromir Jagr	15.00	40.00
J19 Pavel Bure	12.00	30.00
J20 Dominik Hasek	20.00	50.00
J21 Chris Chelios	8.00	20.00
J22 John LeClair	8.00	20.00
J23 Brendan Shanahan	12.00	30.00
J24 Ed Belfour	12.00	30.00
J25 Wayne Gretzky	60.00	150.00
J26 Saku Koivu	8.00	20.00
J27 Tony Amonte	8.00	20.00
J28 Peter Bondra	8.00	20.00

1999-00 BAP Memorabilia Selects Silver

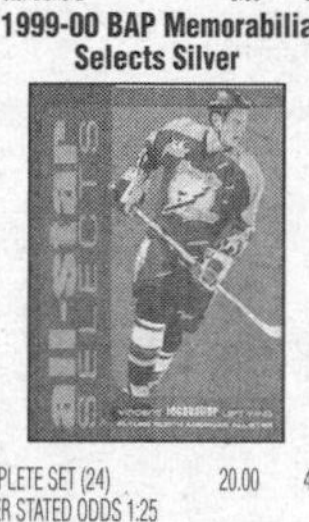

Card	Low	High
COMPLETE SET (24)	20.00	40.00
SILVER STATED ODDS 1:25		
*GOLD: 2X TO 5X SILVER		
GOLD STATED ODDS 1:250		
SL1 Peter Forsberg	2.50	6.00
SL2 Pavol Demitra	.75	2.00
SL3 Jaromir Jagr	1.50	4.00
SL4 Sandis Ozolinsh	.50	1.25
SL5 Nicklas Lidstrom	1.00	2.50
SL6 Dominik Hasek	2.00	5.00
SL7 Eric Lindros	1.00	2.50
SL8 Paul Kariya	1.00	2.50
SL9 Tony Amonte	.75	2.00
SL10 Brian Leetch	1.00	2.50
SL11 Al MacInnis	1.00	2.50
SL12 Martin Brodeur	2.50	6.00
SL13 Petr Sykora	.50	1.25
SL14 Sergei Samsonov	.75	2.00
SL15 Marian Hossa	1.00	2.50
SL16 Andrei Zyuzin	.50	1.25
SL17 Sami Salo	.50	1.25
SL18 Roman Turek	1.00	2.50
SL19 Chris Drury	.75	2.00
SL20 Vincent Lecavalier	1.00	2.50
SL21 J-P Dumont	.75	2.00
SL22 Kyle McLaren	.50	1.25
SL23 Adrian Aucoin	.50	1.25
SL24 Marc Denis	1.00	2.50

1999-00 BAP Memorabilia AS American Hobby

Randomly inserted in American hobby packs at the rate of 1:32, this 12-card set featured former NHL greats from the New York Rangers and the Boston Bruins.

Card	Low	High
COMPLETE SET (12)	15.00	30.00
STATED ODDS 1:32		
AH1 Ken Hodge	1.25	3.00
AH2 Cam Neely	2.50	6.00
AH3 Derek Sanderson	2.00	5.00
AH4 Gerry Cheevers	2.00	5.00
AH5 Johnny Bucyk	1.25	3.00
AH6 Wayne Cashman	1.25	3.00
AH7 Vic Hadfield	1.25	3.00
AH8 Andy Bathgate	1.25	3.00
AH9 Brad Park	1.25	3.00
AH10 Ed Giacomin	1.50	4.00
AH11 John Davidson	1.50	4.00
AH12 Rod Gilbert	1.25	3.00

1999-00 BAP Memorabilia AS American Hobby Autographs

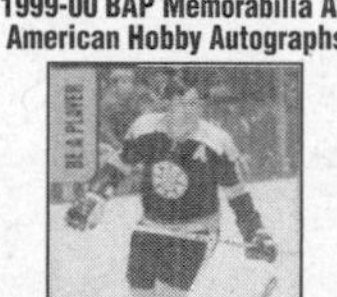

Randomly inserted in American hobby packs at the rate of 1:320, this 12 card set paralleled the base Channel Specific American insert set in an autographed version.

Card	Low	High
STATED ODDS 1:320		
AH1 Ken Hodge	15.00	40.00
AH2 Cam Neely	25.00	60.00
AH3 Derek Sanderson	25.00	60.00
AH4 Gerry Cheevers	25.00	60.00
AH5 Johnny Bucyk	15.00	40.00
AH6 Wayne Cashman	15.00	40.00
AH7 Vic Hadfield	15.00	40.00
AH8 Andy Bathgate	15.00	40.00
AH9 Brad Park	15.00	40.00
AH10 Ed Giacomin	20.00	50.00
AH11 John Davidson	20.00	50.00
AH12 Rod Gilbert	15.00	40.00

1999-00 BAP Memorabilia AS Canadian Hobby

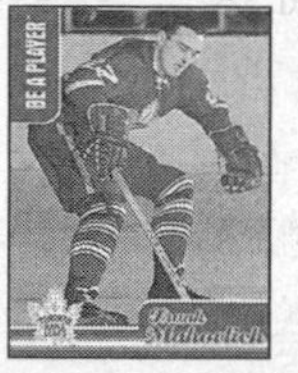

Randomly inserted in Canadian hobby packs at the rate of 1:32, this 12-card set featured former NHL greats from the Toronto Maple Leafs and the Montreal Canadians.

Card	Low	High
COMPLETE SET (12)	15.00	30.00
STATED ODDS 1:32		
CH1 Borje Salming	1.50	4.00
CH2 Dave Keon	2.00	5.00
CH3 Darryl Sittler	2.00	5.00
CH4 Frank Mahovlich	2.00	5.00
CH5 Johnny Bower	2.00	5.00
CH6 Lanny McDonald	1.25	3.00
CH7 Peter Mahovlich	1.25	3.00
CH8 Dickie Moore	1.25	3.00
CH9 John Ferguson	1.25	3.00
CH10 Larry Robinson	1.25	3.00
CH11 Yvan Cournoyer	1.25	3.00
CH12 Serge Savard	1.25	3.00

1999-00 BAP Memorabilia AS Canadian Hobby Autographs

Randomly inserted in Canadian Hobby packs at the rate of 1:320, this 12-card set paralleled the base Channel Specific Canadian insert set in an autographed version.

Card	Low	High
STATED ODDS 1:320		
CH1 Borje Salming	20.00	50.00
CH2 Dave Keon	25.00	60.00
CH3 Darryl Sittler	25.00	60.00
CH4 Frank Mahovlich	25.00	60.00
CH5 Johnny Bower	25.00	60.00
CH6 Lanny McDonald	15.00	40.00
CH7 Peter Mahovlich	15.00	40.00
CH8 Dickie Moore	15.00	40.00
CH9 John Ferguson	15.00	40.00
CH10 Larry Robinson	15.00	40.00
CH11 Yvan Cournoyer	15.00	40.00
CH12 Serge Savard	15.00	40.00

1999-00 BAP Memorabilia AS Retail

Randomly inserted in retail packs at the rate of 1:32, this 12-card set featured former NHL greats from the Chicago Blackhawks and the Detroit Red Wings.

Card	Low	High
COMPLETE SET (12)	20.00	40.00
STATED ODDS 1:32		
R1 Bobby Hull	4.00	10.00
R2 Dennis Hull	1.25	3.00
R3 Denis Savard	1.25	3.00
R4 Pierre Pilote	1.25	3.00
R5 Stan Mikita	2.50	6.00
R6 Tony Esposito	2.00	5.00
R7 Alex Delvecchio	1.50	4.00
R8 Bill Gadsby	1.25	3.00
R9 Mickey Redmond	2.00	5.00
R10 Norm Ullman	1.25	3.00
R11 Red Kelly	1.50	4.00
R12 Ted Lindsay	1.50	4.00

1999-00 BAP Memorabilia AS Retail Autographs

Randomly inserted in retail packs at the rate of 1:320, this 12-card set paralleled the base Channel Specific Retail insert set in an autographed version.

Card	Low	High
STATED ODDS 1:320		
R1 Bobby Hull	30.00	80.00
R2 Dennis Hull	20.00	40.00
R3 Denis Savard	20.00	40.00
R4 Pierre Pilote	20.00	40.00
R5 Stan Mikita	30.00	80.00
R6 Tony Esposito	30.00	80.00
R7 Alex Delvecchio	20.00	40.00
R8 Bill Gadsby	20.00	40.00
R9 Mickey Redmond	25.00	60.00
R10 Norm Ullman	20.00	40.00
R11 Red Kelly	20.00	40.00
R12 Ted Lindsay	25.00	50.00

1999-00 BAP Memorabilia AS Heritage Ruby

Randomly inserted in packs, this 24-card set featured NHL stars in their first team uniform and their current team uniform. The base set was red and sequentially numbered to 1000. Sapphire and emerald parallels were also created. Sapphire parallels were blue in color and had a stated print run of 100 sets. Emerald paral-

lels were green in color and had a stated print run of 10 sets. Emerald parallels were not priced due to scarcity.

Card	Low	High
COMPLETE SET (24)	60.00	125.00
RUBY PRINT RUN 1000 SER.#'d SETS		
*SAPPHIRE/100: 4X TO 10X RUBY/1000		
SAPPHIRE STATED PRINT RUN 100		
UNPRICED EMERALD PRINT RUN 10		
H1 Brendan Shanahan	2.00	5.00
H2 John LeClair	2.00	5.00
H3 Jeremy Roenick	2.50	6.00
H4 John Vanbiesbrouck	1.50	4.00
H5 Dominik Hasek	4.00	10.00
H6 Adam Oates	1.50	4.00
H7 Teemu Selanne	2.00	5.00
H8 Ron Francis	1.50	4.00
H9 Al MacInnis	1.50	4.00
H10 Patrick Roy	10.00	25.00
H11 Doug Gilmour	1.50	4.00
H12 Brett Hull	2.50	6.00
H13 Curtis Joseph	2.00	5.00
H14 Mark Messier	2.00	5.00
H15 Paul Coffey	2.00	5.00
H16 Byron Dafoe	2.00	5.00
H17 Ed Belfour	2.00	5.00
H18 Wayne Gretzky	12.50	30.00
H19 Pavel Bure	2.00	5.00
H20 Chris Chelios	2.00	5.00
H21 Mats Sundin	2.00	5.00
H22 Joe Nieuwendyk	1.50	4.00
H23 Pavol Demitra	1.50	4.00
H24 Grant Fuhr	2.00	5.00

1999-00 BAP Memorabilia Toronto Fall Expo

Thse cards were available only as a wrapper redemption at the 1999 Toronto Fall Expo. The cards parallel the 1999-00 Be A Player Memorabilia set but are serial numbered to 10 and are embossed with a Toronto Fall Expo logo.

UNPRICED TORONTO EXPO PRINT RUN 10

1999-00 BAP Update Double All Star Jerseys

Randomly inserted in Update Factory Sets at the rate of 1:5, this 20-card set featured player photos coupled with two swatches of game-worn jerseys.

Card	Low	High
ODDS 1:5 UPDATE FACTORY SETS		
D1 Jaromir Jagr	15.00	40.00
D2 Eric Lindros	15.00	40.00
D3 Peter Forsberg	20.00	50.00
D4 Patrick Roy	30.00	80.00
D5 Paul Kariya	15.00	40.00
D6 Mats Sundin	15.00	40.00
D7 Ray Bourque	20.00	50.00
D8 Ed Belfour	15.00	40.00
D9 Wayne Gretzky	75.00	200.00
D10 Teemu Selanne	15.00	40.00
D11 Brendan Shanahan	15.00	40.00
D12 Dominik Hasek	25.00	60.00
D13 Pavel Bure	15.00	40.00
D14 John LeClair	15.00	40.00
D15 Al MacInnis	10.00	25.00
D16 Brett Hull	15.00	40.00
D17 Brian Leetch	15.00	40.00
D18 Mark Messier	15.00	40.00
D19 Martin Brodeur	30.00	80.00
D20 Sergei Fedorov	20.00	50.00

1999-00 BAP Update Teammates Jerseys

Card	Low	High
ODDS 1:5 UPDATE FACTORY SETS		
TM1 Curtis Joseph Jeremy Roenick	12.50	30.00
TM2 Wayne Gretzky Rob Blake	40.00	100.00
TM3 Patrick Roy Mark Messier	30.00	80.00
TM4 Teemu Selanne Brett Hull	12.50	30.00
TM5 Brendan Shanahan Sergei Fedorov	20.00	50.00
TM6 Ray Bourque Brian Leetch	25.00	60.00
TM7 Eric Lindros John LeClair	12.50	30.00
TM8 Jaromir Jagr Mark Messier	20.00	50.00
TM9 Martin Brodeur Brendan Shanahan	15.00	40.00
TM10 Peter Forsberg Paul Kariya	25.00	60.00
TM11 Ed Belfour Chris Chelios	12.50	30.00
TM12 Teemu Selanne Paul Kariya	12.50	30.00
TM13 Dominik Hasek Peter Bondra	12.50	30.00
TM14 Steve Yzerman Pavel Bure	30.00	80.00
TM15 John LeClair Ray Bourque	25.00	60.00
TM16 Theo Fleury Owen Nolan	12.50	30.00
TM17 Martin Brodeur Paul Coffey	25.00	60.00
TM18 John LeClair Eric Lindros	12.50	30.00
TM19 Jaromir Jagr Pavel Bure	25.00	60.00
TM20 Dominik Hasek Nikolai Khabibulin	25.00	60.00
TM21 Patrick Roy Brian Leetch	25.00	60.00
TM22 Wayne Gretzky Mike Modano	40.00	100.00
TM23 Peter Forsberg Sandis Ozolinsh	15.00	40.00
TM24 Chris Chelios Ray Bourque	25.00	60.00
TM25 Mats Sundin Nicklas Lidstrom	12.50	30.00
TM26 Paul Kariya Mike Modano	12.50	30.00
TM27 Theo Fleury Tony Amonte	12.50	30.00
TM28 Peter Forsberg Teemu Selanne	25.00	60.00
TM29 Eric Lindros Darryl Sydor	12.50	30.00
TM30 Pavel Bure Mats Sundin	12.50	30.00
TM31 Jeremy Roenick Scott Stevens	12.50	30.00
TM32 Jaromir Jagr Olaf Kolzig	15.00	40.00
TM33 Mike Richter Tony Amonte	12.50	30.00
TM34 Chris Pronger Al MacInnis	12.50	30.00
TM35 Brendan Shanahan Martin Brodeur	20.00	50.00
TM36 Alexander Mogilny Mark Messier	12.50	30.00
TM37 Steve Yzerman Sergei Fedorov	40.00	100.00
TM38 Brendan Shanahan Sergei Fedorov	25.00	60.00
TM39 Steve Yzerman Chris Chelios	20.00	50.00
TM40 Steve Yzerman Brendan Shanahan	25.00	60.00
TM41 Mats Sundin Curtis Joseph	12.50	30.00
TM42 Peter Forsberg Patrick Roy	40.00	100.00
TM43 Peter Forsberg Joe Sakic	30.00	80.00
TM44 Joe Sakic Patrik Roy	30.00	80.00
TM45 Teemu Selanne Paul Kariya	12.50	30.00
TM46 B.Hull/M.Modano	15.00	40.00
TM47 Brett Hull Ed Belfour	12.50	30.00
TM48 E.Belfour/M.Modano	12.00	30.00
TM49 Eric Lindros John LeClair	12.50	30.00
TM50 Brian Leetch Theo Fleury	15.00	40.00

2000-01 BAP Memorabilia

Released as a 521-card base set, including two update sets, Be A Player Memorabilia cards featured full color player action shots with white borders on three sides and black lettering. Be A Player was packaged in 24-pack boxes with packs containing eight cards and carried an American SRP of $3.29 and a Canadian SRP of $4.99. A Trevor Linden Autograph redemption card was randomly inserted in series one packs. For a $20.00 donation to the Trevor Linden foundation, an autographed card was returned. Be A Player Memorabilia Update, card numbers 397-497 and inserts were issued in factory set form only. Be A Player Final Update was issued by mail redemption as a 24-card set numbered 498-521.

Card	Low	High
COMPLETE SET (521)	75.00	150.00
COMP.SER.1 (396)	60.00	120.00
COMP.UPDATE SET (101)	15.00	30.00
COMP. FINAL UPDATE SET (24)	15.00	30.00
1 Jaromir Jagr	.50	1.25
2 Scott Mellanby	.08	.25
3 Mike Fisher	.08	.25
4 Slava Kozlov	.08	.25
5 Steve Valiquette RC	.40	1.00
6 Simon Gagne	.30	.75
7 Alexei Morozov	.08	.25
8 Alexei Zhitnik	.08	.25
9 Jochen Hecht	.08	.25
10 Jamie Allison	.08	.25

11 Olli Jokinen .25 .60
12 Bobby Holik .08 .25
13 Keith Primeau .08 .25
14 Bryan McCabe .08 .25
15 Tim Connolly .08 .25
16 Marco Sturm .08 .25
17 Craig Darby .08 .25
18 Jeff Cowan RC .40 1.00
19 Brad Stuart .08 .25
20 Sean O'Donnell .08 .25
21 Mike Minard RC .40 1.00
22 Rob Blake .08 .25
23 Marek Malik .08 .25
24 Marek Posmyk .08 .25
25 Alex Tanguay .25 .60
26 Steven McCarthy .08 .25
27 Bill Guerin .25 .60
28 Ed Jovanovski .08 .25
29 Martin Skoula .08 .25
30 Jeff Hackett .25 .60
31 Vladimir Tsyplakov .08 .25
32 Sergei Zubov .08 .25
33 Damian Rhodes .25 .60
34 Brent Sopel RC .40 1.00
35 Frantisek Kaberle .08 .25
36 Michael Peca .08 .25
37 Steve Kelly .08 .25
38 Geoff Sanderson .08 .25
39 Petr Svoboda .08 .25
40 Martin Brodeur .75 2.00
41 Markus Naslund .30 .75
42 Steve Thomas .08 .25
43 Anson Carter .25 .60
44 Theo Fleury .30 .75
45 Felix Potvin .30 .75
46 Adam Deadmarsh .08 .25
47 Dave Tanabe .08 .25
48 Trevor Kidd .25 .60
49 Jeff Friesen .08 .25
50 Marc Moro RC .40 1.00
51 Luc Robitaille .25 .60
52 Mike Richter .30 .75
53 Eric Desjardins .08 .25
54 Jean-Sebastien Aubin .25 .60
55 Paul Laus .08 .25
56 Kimmo Timonen .08 .25
57 Steve Sullivan .08 .25
58 Eric Cairns .08 .25
59 Scott Stevens .25 .60
60 Andy Delmore .08 .25
61 Jeff Nielsen .08 .25
62 Mathieu Biron .08 .25
63 Juha Lind .08 .25
64 Maxim Afinogenov .08 .25
65 Guy Hebert .25 .60
66 Sergei Brylin .08 .25
67 Mike Modano .50 1.25
68 Tommy Salo .25 .60
69 Bryan Smolinski .08 .25
70 Sergei Varlamov .08 .25
71 Paul Mara .08 .25
72 Peter Forsberg .75 2.00
73 Doug Weight .25 .60
74 Peter Bondra .30 .75
75 Marc Denis .25 .60
76 Jamie Storr .25 .60
77 Alexei Kovalev .25 .60
78 Dainius Zubrus .08 .25
79 Mike Grier .08 .25
80 Olaf Kolzig .25 .60
81 Bryan Adams RC .40 1.00
82 Scott Niedermayer .08 .25
83 David Gosselin RC .40 1.00
84 Boris Mironov .08 .25
85 Kyle McLaren .08 .25
86 Steve Kariya .08 .25
87 Dimitri Yushkevich .08 .25
88 Paul Kariya .30 .75
89 Brian Leetch .30 .75
90 Jeff Daniels .08 .25
91 Brendan Morrison .25 .60
92 Brian Campbell .08 .25
93 Ray Whitney .08 .25
94 Marian Hossa .30 .75
95 Sergei Samsonov .30 .75
96 Mike York .08 .25
97 Mark Eaton .08 .25
98 Ryan VandenBussche .08 .25
99 Vladimir Malakhov .08 .25
100 Jeff Finley .08 .25
101 John Vanbiesbrouck .25 .60
102 Brad Isbister .08 .25
103 John Madden .08 .25
104 Patrick Roy 1.50 4.00
105 Radek Bonk .08 .25
106 Brett Hull .40 1.00
107 Andreas Dackell .08 .25
108 Pierre Turgeon .08 .25
109 Jason Woolley .08 .25
110 Jeff O'Neill .08 .25
111 John LeClair .30 .75
112 Darryl Sydor .08 .25
113 Ryan Smyth .08 .25
114 Curtis Joseph .30 .75
115 Gary Roberts .08 .25
116 Pavel Kubina .08 .25
117 Roman Hamrlik .08 .25
118 Sandis Ozolinsh .08 .25
119 Manny Fernandez .25 .60
120 Adam Oates .25 .60
121 Darby Hendrickson .08 .25
122 Glen Murray .08 .25
123 Jiri Slegr .08 .25
124 Steve Yzerman 1.50 4.00
125 Mats Lindgren .08 .25
126 Sergei Gonchar .08 .25
127 Joe Thornton .50 1.25
128 Petr Sykora .08 .25
129 Pavol Demitra .25 .60
130 Tyler Wright .08 .25
131 Johan Davidsson .08 .25
132 Brian Rolston .08 .25
133 Mark Messier .30 .75
134 Darcy Tucker .08 .25
135 Oleg Tverdovsky .08 .25
136 Petr Nedved .08 .25
137 Harold Druken .08 .25
138 Valeri Bure .08 .25
139 Mikael Andersson .08 .25
140 Evgeni Nabokov .25 .60
141 Janne Laukkanen .08 .25
142 Radek Dvorak .08 .25
143 Brian Boucher .30 .75
144 Eric Daze .25 .60
145 Dan Cloutier .08 .25
146 Scott Gomez .08 .25
147 Dallas Drake .08 .25
148 Shawn McEachern .08 .25
149 Joe Nieuwendyk .25 .60
150 Kenny Jonsson .08 .25
151 Saku Koivu .30 .75
152 Roman Turek .25 .60
153 Chris Gratton .08 .25
154 Steve Rucchin .08 .25
155 Teppo Numminen .08 .25
156 Jamie Langenbrunner .08 .25
157 Johnathan Aitken RC .40 1.00
158 Nikolai Antropov .08 .25
159 Stephane Fiset .08 .25
160 Manny Malhotra .08 .25
161 Pavel Bure .30 .75
162 Chris Drury .25 .60
163 Roberto Luongo .40 1.00
164 Norm Maracle .25 .60
165 Brendan Shanahan .30 .75
166 Calle Johansson .08 .25
167 Cory Stillman .08 .25
168 Jozef Stumpel .08 .25
169 Ron Tugnutt .25 .60
170 Brian Savage .08 .25
171 Viktor Kozlov .08 .25
172 Chris Simon .08 .25
173 Chris Joseph .08 .25
174 Willie Mitchell RC .40 1.00
175 Randy Robitaille .08 .25
176 Sami Kapanen .08 .25
177 Jonathan Girard .08 .25
178 Andrew Cassels .08 .25
179 Jani Hurme RC .40 1.00
180 Maxim Balmochnykh .08 .25
181 Adam Graves .08 .25
182 Steve Shields .08 .25
183 Marc Savard .08 .25
184 Zigmund Palffy .30 .75
185 Magnus Arvedson .08 .25
186 Byron Dafoe .25 .60
187 Jan Hlavac .08 .25
188 Len Barrie .08 .25
189 Jocelyn Thibault .25 .60
190 Fred Brathwaite .25 .60
191 Fredrik Modin .08 .25
192 Shane Doan .08 .25
193 Petr Mika RC .40 1.00
194 Larry Murphy .08 .25
195 Daniel Alfredsson .25 .60
196 Brenden Morrow .25 .60
197 Martin Rucinsky .08 .25
198 Michal Handzus .08 .25
199 Dominik Hasek .60 1.50
200 Rod Brind'Amour .25 .60
201 Trevor Letowski .08 .25
202 Derian Hatcher .08 .25
203 Phil Housley .08 .25
204 Martin Biron .25 .60
205 Sergei Berezin .08 .25
206 Ron Francis .25 .60
207 Cliff Ronning .08 .25
208 Robert Svehla .08 .25
209 Vincent Lecavalier .30 .75
210 Kent Manderville .08 .25
211 Andrew Brunette .08 .25
212 Chris Chelios .30 .75
213 Alexander Karpovtsev .08 .25
214 Robyn Regehr .08 .25
215 Mika Alatalo .08 .25
216 Jan Hrdina .08 .25
217 Nicklas Lidstrom .30 .75
218 Ivan Novoseltsev .08 .25
219 Alexander Mogilny .25 .60
220 Chris Pronger .25 .60
221 Paul Coffey .30 .75
222 John Grahame .25 .60
223 Jeff Farkas .08 .25
224 Eric Lindros .30 .75
225 Jorgen Jonsson .08 .25
226 Jean-Francois Labbe RC .40 1.00
227 Owen Nolan .25 .60
228 Oleg Saprykin .08 .25
229 Patrick Marleau .25 .60
230 Aaron Downey RC .40 1.00
231 Chris Osgood .25 .60
232 Mike Wilson .08 .25
233 Joe Sakic .60 1.50
234 Dieter Kochan RC .40 1.00
235 Jeremy Roenick .30 .75
236 Alexei Zhamnov .08 .25
237 Sergei Fedorov .50 1.25
238 Petr Schastlivy .08 .25
239 Milan Hejduk .30 .75
240 Patrice Brisebois .08 .25
241 Marty Reasoner .08 .25
242 Ed Belfour .30 .75
243 Vitali Vishnevsky .25 .60
244 Keith Tkachuk .30 .75
245 Petr Buzek .08 .25
246 Miroslav Satan .25 .60
247 Adam Mair .08 .25
248 Jere Karalahti .08 .25
249 Mike Dunham .25 .60
250 Mike Sillinger .08 .25
251 Andrei Skopintsev RC .40 1.00
252 Sergei Vyshedkevich .40 1.00
253 Steve Duchesne .08 .25
254 Tomas Kaberle .08 .25
255 Arturs Irbe .25 .60
256 Niklas Sundstrom .08 .25
257 Al MacInnis .25 .60
258 Mike Ribeiro .08 .25
259 Rob Niedermayer .08 .25
260 Jean-Guy Trudel RC .40 1.00
261 Martin Straka .08 .25
262 Jason Arnott .08 .25
263 David Legwand .25 .60
264 Tony Amonte .25 .60
265 Jason Allison .08 .25
266 Patrik Elias .25 .60
267 Mark Recchi .25 .60
268 Patrik Stefan .08 .25
269 Mariusz Czerkawski .08 .25
270 Vincent Damphousse .08 .25
271 Sergei Krivokrasov .08 .25
272 Teemu Selanne .30 .75
273 Patrick Lalime .25 .60
274 Nick Boynton .08 .25
275 Darren McCarty .08 .25
276 Jaroslav Spacek .08 .25
277 Chris Dingman .08 .25
278 Jarome Iginla .40 1.00
279 Andrei Zyuzin .08 .25
280 Jyrki Lumme .08 .25
281 Michal Grosek .08 .25
282 Janne Niinimaa .08 .25
283 Wade Redden .08 .25
284 Ray Bourque .60 1.50
285 Trevor Linden .08 .25
286 Ladislav Nagy .08 .25
287 Jose Theodore .40 1.00
288 Bates Battaglia .08 .25
289 Mikael Renberg .08 .25
290 Donald Audette .08 .25
291 Doug Gilmour .30 .75
292 Yanic Perreault .08 .25
293 Anders Eriksson .08 .25
294 Gary Suter .08 .25
295 Brad Ference .08 .25
296 Mats Sundin .30 .75
297 Ray Ferraro .08 .25
298 Jiri Fischer .08 .25
299 Todd Bertuzzi .30 .75
300 Derek Morris .08 .25
301 Patric Kjellberg .08 .25
302 Pat Verbeek .08 .25
303 Kip Miller .08 .25
304 Alexei Vasilyev .08 .25
305 Marcus Ragnarsson .08 .25
306 Arron Asham .08 .25
307 Sylvain Cote .08 .25
308 Vaclav Prospal .08 .25
309 Aki Berg .08 .25
310 Alexander Selivanov .08 .25
311 Wayne Primeau .08 .25
312 Brian Rafalski .08 .25
313 Jonas Hoglund .08 .25
314 Adam Foote .08 .25
315 Steve Konowalchuk .08 .25
316 Robert Dome .08 .25
317 Antti Laaksonen .08 .25
318 Mike Ricci .08 .25
319 Gino Odjick .08 .25
320 Eric Weinrich .08 .25
321 Jason Strudwick .08 .25
322 Kim Johnsson .08 .25
323 Dimitri Kalinin .08 .25
324 Daymond Langkow .08 .25
325 Todd Marchant .08 .25
326 Richard Matvichuk .08 .25
327 Travis Green .08 .25
328 Igor Larionov .25 .60
329 Mattias Ohlund .08 .25
330 Igor Kravchuk .08 .25
331 Richard Zednik .08 .25
332 Curtis Brown .08 .25
333 Krzysztof Oliwa .08 .25
334 Darius Kasparaitis .08 .25
335 Michael Nylander .08 .25
336 Stan Drulia .08 .25
337 Nelson Emerson .08 .25
338 Greg Johnson .08 .25
339 Sean Hill .08 .25
340 Keith Jones .08 .25
341 Bill Muckalt .08 .25
342 Randy McKay .08 .25
343 Stu Grimson .08 .25
344 Tyson Nash .08 .25
345 Dan Hinote .08 .25
346 Mike Rathje .08 .25
347 Brian Holzinger .08 .25
348 Eric Nickulas RC .40 1.00
349 Alexandre Daigle .08 .25
350 Jan Bulis .08 .25
351 Tom Poti .08 .25
352 Kevyn Adams .08 .25
353 Scott Thornton .08 .25
354 Sean Burke .40 1.00
355 Peter Worrell .08 .25
356 Josef Beranek .08 .25
357 Matt Cullen .08 .25
358 Sandy McCarthy .08 .25
359 Sergei Zholtok .08 .25
360 Darren Langdon .08 .25
361 Martin Lapointe .08 .25
362 Adrian Aucoin .08 .25
363 Dmitri Nabokov .08 .25
364 Jason Blake .08 .25
365 Jeff Halpern .08 .25
366 Rico Fata .08 .25
367 Dave Reid .08 .25
368 Vitali Yachmenev .08 .25
369 Hnat Domenichelli .08 .25
370 Rick Tocchet .08 .25
371 Tommy Westlund .08 .25
372 Chris Phillips .08 .25
373 Claude Lemieux .08 .25
374 Greg Adams .08 .25
375 Todd Simpson .08 .25
376 Ken Klee .08 .25
377 Andre Savage .08 .25
378 Bryan Marchment .08 .25
379 Dean McAmmond .08 .25
380 Mike Johnson .08 .25
381 Tomas Holmstrom .08 .25
382 Robert Lang .08 .25
383 Dan McGillis .08 .25
384 Jamie Rivers .08 .25
385 Dave Andreychuk .25 .60
386 Marty McInnis .08 .25
387 Sami Salo .08 .25
388 Daniel Cleary .08 .25
389 Robert Esche .08 .25
390 Aaron Gavey .08 .25
391 Andrei Nikolishin .08 .25
392 Jason Krog .08 .25
393 Stu Barnes .08 .25
394 Tomas Vokoun .08 .25
395 Peter Schaefer .08 .25
396 Daniil Markov .08 .25
397 Daniel Sedin .08 .25
398 Kris Beech .08 .25
399 Samuel Pahlsson .08 .25
400 Gary Roberts .08 .25
401 Marian Gaborik RC 2.50 6.00
402 Oleg Kvasha .08 .25
403 Martin Havlat RC 1.50 4.00
404 Roman Simicek RC .40 1.00
405 Dallas Drake .08 .25
406 Jakub Cutta RC .40 1.00
407 German Titov .08 .25
408 Jarno Kultanen RC .40 1.00
409 Sandis Ozolinsh .08 .25
410 David Vyborny .08 .25
411 Olli Jokinen .25 .60
412 Maxim Sushinski .08 .25
413 John Vanbiesbrouck .25 .60
414 Shane Hnidy RC .40 1.00
415 Milan Kraft .08 .25
416 Alexander Kharitonov RC .40 1.00
417 Andrei Nazarov .08 .25
418 Dave Andreychuk .25 .60
419 Niclas Wallin RC .40 1.00
420 Rostislav Klesla RC .60 1.50
421 Denis Shvidki .08 .25
422 Mathieu Garon .08 .25
423 Taylor Pyatt .08 .25
424 Roman Cechmanek RC .40 1.00
425 Mark Smith RC .40 1.00
426 Shayne Corson .08 .25
427 Jonas Ronnqvist RC .40 1.00
428 J-P Dumont .08 .25
429 Josef Vasicek RC .40 1.00
430 Tyler Bouck RC .40 1.00
431 Matt Schneider .08 .25
432 Andrei Markov .08 .25
433 Vladimir Malakhov .08 .25
434 Maxime Ouellet .08 .25
435 Matt Bradley .08 .25
436 Dave Manson .08 .25
437 Brad Tapper RC .40 1.00
438 Eric Boulton RC .40 1.00
439 Brent Johnson .08 .25
440 Marty Turco RC 1.50 4.00
441 Tomas Vlasak .08 .25
442 Greg Classen RC .40 1.00
443 Mark Messier .30 .75
444 Justin Williams RC 1.00 2.50
445 Sean Hill .08 .25
446 Bryan McCabe .08 .25
447 Andreas Karlsson .08 .25
448 Mika Noronen .08 .25
449 Alexander Karpovtsev .08 .25
450 Boyd Devereaux .08 .25
451 Lubomir Visnovsky RC .40 1.00
452 Scott Hartnell RC .60 1.50
453 Jason Labarbera RC .60 1.50
454 Petr Hubacek RC .40 1.00
455 Alexander Khavanov RC .40 1.00
456 Petr Svoboda RC .40 1.00
457 Tomi Kallio .08 .25
458 Mike Vernon .08 .25
459 Reto Von Arx RC .40 1.00
460 Maxim Kuznetsov .08 .25
461 Steven Reinprecht RC .40 1.00
462 Turner Stevenson .08 .25
463 Roberto Luongo .40 1.00
464 Brad Richards .08 .25
465 Bryce Salvador RC .40 1.00
466 Kevin Hatcher .08 .25
467 Paul Coffey .30 .75
468 Marty Murray .08 .25
469 Todd Fedoruk RC .40 1.00
470 Brian Swanson RC .40 1.00
471 Christian Matte .08 .25
472 Sascha Goc RC .40 1.00
473 Dale Purinton RC .40 1.00
474 Brad May .08 .25
475 Brad Brown .08 .25
476 Petteri Nummelin RC .40 1.00
477 Ruslan Fedotenko RC .60 1.50
478 Ronald Petrovicky RC .40 1.00
479 David Aebischer RC 1.00 2.50
480 Michel Riesen RC .40 1.00
481 Ladislav Benysek RC .40 1.00
482 Mark Parrish .08 .25
483 Mike Mottau .08 .25
484 Ossi Vaananen RC .40 1.00
485 Andrew Raycroft RC 1.25 3.00
486 Sylvain Cote .08 .25
487 Richard Jackman .08 .25
488 Toni Lydman .08 .25
489 Ron Tugnutt .08 .25
490 Igor Larionov .08 .25
491 Lubomir Sekeras RC .40 1.00
492 Roman Vitalik .08 .25
493 Johan Holmqvist RC .40 1.00
494 Josef Melichar RC .40 1.00
495 Sheldon Keefe .08 .25
496 Henrik Sedin .08 .25
497 Rick DiPietro RC 1.50 4.00
498 Teemu Selanne .30 .75
499 Keith Tkachuk .30 .75
500 Rob Blake .25 .60
501 Mario Lemieux 2.00 5.00
502 Johan Hedberg RC .60 1.50
503 Felix Potvin .30 .75
504 Branislav Mezei .08 .25
505 Mike Comrie RC 1.00 2.50
506 Miikka Kiprusoff .40 1.00
507 Petr Tenkrat RC .40 1.00
508 Mark Bell .08 .25
509 Steve Gainey RC .40 1.00
510 Jason Williams RC .40 1.00
511 Shawn Horcoff RC .75 2.00
512 Eric Chouinard .08 .25
513 Derek Gustafson RC .40 1.00
514 Bryan Allen .08 .25
515 Kristian Kudroc .08 .25
516 Gregg Naumenko RC .40 1.00
517 Pierre Dagenais .08 .25
518 Juraj Kolnik RC .40 1.00
519 Tomas Kloucek RC .40 1.00
520 Andreas Lilja RC .40 1.00
521 Alexei Ponikarovsky RC .40 1.00
*NNO Trevor Linden AU 15.00 25.00

2000-01 BAP Memorabilia Emerald

EMERALD STAT.PRINT RUN 10 SERIAL #'d SETS
NOT PRICED DUE TO SCARCITY

2000-01 BAP Memorabilia Ruby

*RUBY STAR: 3X TO 8X BASIC CARDS
*RUBY RC's: 1.5X TO 3X BASIC CARDS
PRINT RUN 200 SERIAL #'d SETS

2000-01 BAP Memorabilia Sapphire

*SAPPHIRE STARS: 6X TO 15X BASIC CARDS
*SAPPHIRE RC's: 5X TO 10X BASIC CARDS
PRINT RUN 100 SERIAL #'d SETS

2000-01 BAP Memorabilia Promos

This 396-card set paralleled the base series but carried the word promo on the card backs. The cards were issued as promotional materila to announce the products release. Due to the distribution method and scarcity, they were not priced.

NOT PRICED DUE TO SCARCITY

2000-01 BAP Memorabilia All-Star Tickets

Randomly seeded in packs at the rate of 1:864, this 10-card set featured swatches of All-Star Game tickets with the respective year's All-Star Game logo faded into the background.

COMPLETE SET (10) 150.00 300.00
STATED ODDS 1:864
AST1 1990 All-Star Game 12.50 30.00
AST2 1991 All-Star Game 12.50 30.00
AST3 1992 All-Star Game 12.50 30.00
AST4 1993 All-Star Game 12.50 30.00
AST5 1994 All-Star Game 12.50 30.00
AST6 1996 All-Star Game 12.50 30.00
AST7 1997 All-Star Game 12.50 30.00
AST8 1998 All-Star Game 12.50 30.00
AST9 1999 All-Star Game 12.50 30.00
AST10 2000 All-Star Game 12.50 30.00

2000-01 BAP Memorabilia Georges Vezina

Randomly inserted in packs at the rate of 1:2400, this 16-card set features today's top goalies coupled with a swatch of a Georges Vezina goalie pad. The Vezina pad used was believed to be the only one in existance.

V1 Olaf Kolzig 150.00 300.00
V2 Dominik Hasek 150.00 300.00
V3 Dominik Hasek 150.00 300.00
V4 Dominik Hasek 150.00 300.00
V5 Jim Carey 150.00 300.00
V6 Dominik Hasek 150.00 300.00
V7 Dominik Hasek 150.00 300.00
V8 Ed Belfour 150.00 300.00
V9 Patrick Roy 200.00 500.00
V10 Ed Belfour 150.00 300.00
V11 Patrick Roy 200.00 500.00
V12 Patrick Roy 200.00 500.00
V13 Grant Fuhr 150.00 300.00
V14 John Vanbiesbrouck 150.00 300.00
V15 Tom Barrasso 150.00 300.00
V16 Georges Vezina 600.00 1000.00

2000-01 BAP Memorabilia Goalie Memorabilia

Randomly inserted in packs at the rate of 1:999, this 30-card set featured swatches of goalie worn jerseys, sticks, pads and gloves. Cards G1-G11 were single player cards with two swatches of memorabilia, card numbers G12-G28 were dual player cards with two swatches of memorabilia, and card numbers G29 and G30 were triple player cards with three swatches of memorabilia.

STATED ODDS 1:999
G1 Mike Richter J/S 30.00 80.00
G2 Patrick Roy G/S 100.00 250.00
G3 Dominik Hasek G/S 60.00 150.00
G4 Ed Belfour J/S 30.00 80.00
G5 Curtis Joseph G/S 30.00 80.00
G6 Terry Sawchuk G/S 125.00 300.00
G7 Vladislav Tretiak J/G 100.00 250.00
G8 Gerry Cheevers S/P 30.00 80.00
G9 Felix Potvin G/J 30.00 80.00
G10 Frank Brimsek G/J 40.00 100.00
G11 Bernie Parent P/J 30.00 80.00
G12 Bernie Parent Jersey 40.00 100.00
Tony Esposito Jersey
G13 Johnny Bower Stick 60.00 150.00
Curtis Joseph Stick
G14 Frank Brimsek Glove 40.00 100.00
Gerry Cheevers Stick
G15 Patrick Roy Stick 125.00 300.00
Jacques Plante Glove
G16 Vlatislav Tretiak Jersey 100.00 250.00
Tony Esposito Jersey
G17 Terry Sawchuk Stick 125.00 300.00
Curtis Joseph Jersey
G18 Turk Broda Glove 40.00 100.00
Curtis Joseph Jersey
G19 Johnny Bower Glove 40.00 100.00
Turk Broda Glove
G20 Felix Potvin Glove 75.00 200.00
Curtis Joseph Glove
G21 Ed Belfour Jersey 100.00 250.00
Patrick Roy Jersey
G22 Ed Belfour Jersey 100.00 250.00
Vladislav Tretiak Jersey
G23 Terry Sawchuk Stick 150.00 400.00
Jacques Plante Glove
G24 Johnny Bower Stick 125.00 300.00
Terry Sawchuk Stick
G25 Tony Esposito Glove 40.00 100.00
Gerry Cheevers Pad
G26 Frank Brimsek Glove 40.00 100.00
Gerry Cheevers Pad
G27 Curtis Joseph Glove 40.00 100.00
Turk Broda Glove
G28 Patrick Roy Glove 200.00 500.00
Terry Sawchuk Glove
G29 Curtis Joseph Stick 125.00 300.00
Johnny Bower Stick
Terry Sawchuk Stick
G30 Gerry Cheevers Stick 75.00 200.00
Bernie Parent Stick
Tony Esposito Stick

2000-01 BAP Memorabilia Jersey

*MULT.COLOR SWATCH: 1X TO 1.5X JERSEY CARD
STATED ODDS 1:360
J1 Jeremy Roenick 10.00 25.00
J2 Mats Sundin 8.00 20.00
J3 Pavel Bure 8.00 20.00
J4 Martin Brodeur 15.00 40.00
J5 Mike Richter 8.00 20.00
J6 Brendan Shanahan 8.00 20.00
J7 Chris Pronger 8.00 20.00
J8 Al MacInnis 8.00 20.00
J9 Jaromir Jagr 12.00 30.00
J10 Olaf Kolzig 8.00 20.00
J11 Tony Amonte 8.00 20.00
J12 Scott Stevens 8.00 20.00
J13 Dominik Hasek 12.00 30.00
J14 Peter Forsberg 12.00 30.00
J15 Teemu Selanne 8.00 20.00
J16 Eric Lindros 8.00 20.00
J17 Nicklas Lidstrom 8.00 20.00
J18 Theo Fleury 8.00 20.00
J19 Darryl Sydor 8.00 20.00
J20 Mike Modano 12.00 30.00
J21 Nikolai Khabibulin 8.00 20.00
J22 Sandis Ozolinsh 8.00 20.00
J23 Mark Messier 8.00 20.00
J24 Joe Sakic 12.00 30.00
J25 Wayne Gretzky 50.00 100.00
J26 Owen Nolan 8.00 20.00
J27 Daniel Alfredsson 8.00 20.00
J28 Paul Coffey 8.00 20.00
J29 Steve Yzerman 15.00 40.00
J30 Brett Hull 12.00 30.00
J31 Paul Kariya 8.00 20.00
J32 John LeClair 8.00 20.00
J33 Ed Belfour 10.00 25.00
J34 Patrick Roy 20.00 50.00
J35 Sergei Fedorov 12.00 30.00
J36 Mark Recchi 8.00 20.00
J37 Ray Bourque 12.00 30.00
J38 Brian Leetch 8.00 20.00
J39 Rob Blake 8.00 20.00
J40 Curtis Joseph 8.00 20.00

2000-01 BAP Memorabilia Jersey Emblems

*EMBLEMS: 1X TO 2.5X JERSEY CARDS
STATED ODDS 1:999

2000-01 BAP Memorabilia Jersey Numbers

*NUMBERS: 1X TO 2.5X JERSEY CARDS
STATED ODDS 1:999

2000-01 BAP Memorabilia Jersey and Stick

*JSY/STICKS: .75X TO 1.25X JERSEY CARDS
STATED ODDS 1:999

2000-01 BAP Memorabilia Mario Lemieux Legends

Randomly inserted in packs at the rate of 1:4800, this 10-card set featured game-used memorabilia swatches from Mario Lemieux. Memorabilia combinations are listed below. The stated print run on each card was an estimated 30 sets.

STATED PRINT RUN 30 SETS
L1 1987-88 Jsy 50.00 125.00
L2 1991-92 Jsy 50.00 125.00
L3 1987 Jsy/1991 Glove 60.00 150.00
L4 1991-92 Jsy/Glove 60.00 150.00
L5 1991-92 Jsy Emblem 150.00 400.00
L6 1991-92 Jsy Number 150.00 400.00
L7 1991-92 Glove 50.00 125.00
L8 1996 AS Jsy 50.00 125.00
L9 1987 Jsy/1996 AS Jsy 60.00 150.00
L10 1991 Jsy/1996 Jsy 60.00 150.00

2000-01 BAP Memorabilia Mario Lemieux Legends Autographs

Randomly seeded in packs, this 10-card set paralleled the base Legends set enhanced with an autograph. The stated print run on each card was an estimated 6 sets.

STATED PRINT RUN 6 SETS
NOT PRICED DUE TO SCARCITY

2000-01 BAP Memorabilia Patent Power Jerseys

STATED ODDS 1:4800
PP1 M.Lemieux/W.Gretzky 250.00 600.00
PP2 P.Kariya/S.Yzerman 150.00 400.00
PP3 Pavel Bure 100.00 250.00
Jaromir Jagr
PP4 Mats Sundin 40.00 100.00
Peter Forsberg
PP5 Teemu Selanne 40.00 100.00
Brett Hull
PP6 Brendan Shanahan 40.00 100.00
John LeClair

2000-01 BAP Memorabilia Update Heritage Jerseys

Inserts were placed in the Be A Player Memorabilia Update set on top of the sealed 100 cards along with the DiPietro Rookie card. Sets contained either four random insert cards, or one memorabilia card. Memorabilia cards were inserted at approximately one in five sets. The Heritage Jersey Cards featured a gold background, full color player action photography and a swatch of a game-used jersey in the upper right hand corner of the card front. Gold parallels numbered 1/1 were also created and inserted randomly, but are not priced due to scarcity.

*MULT.COLOR SWATCH: 1X TO 2X
MEMORABILIA STATED ODDS 1:5 FACT.SETS
GOLD 1 OF 1's EXIST
H1 Mark Messier 20.00 60.00
H2 Pavel Bure 20.00 50.00
H3 Paul Coffey 15.00 40.00
H4 Mats Sundin 20.00 50.00
H5 Curtis Joseph 15.00 40.00
H6 Ed Belfour 15.00 40.00
H7 Mike Modano 25.00 60.00
H8 Brett Hull 25.00 60.00
H9 Teemu Selanne 20.00 50.00
H10 Keith Tkachuk 10.00 25.00
H11 Patrick Roy 100.00 250.00
H12 Chris Chelios 10.00 25.00
H13 Al MacInnis 10.00 25.00
H14 Theo Fleury 10.00 25.00

H15 Keith Primeau	10.00	25.00
H16 Ray Bourque	40.00	100.00
H17 Brendan Shanahan	20.00	50.00
H18 Owen Nolan	10.00	25.00
H19 Felix Potvin	20.00	50.00
H20 Trevor Linden	10.00	25.00
H21 Scott Stevens	10.00	25.00
H22 Adam Oates	10.00	25.00

2000-01 BAP Memorabilia Update Record Breakers

Inserts were placed in the Be A Player Memorabilia Update set on top of the sealed 100 cards along with the DiPietro Rookie card. Sets contained either four random insert cards, or one memorabilia card. Memorabilia cards were inserted at approximately one in five sets. This 2-card set featured full color player action photography on a white card stock with two swatches of game used memorabilia. Gold parallels numbered 1/1 were also created and inserted randomly, but are not priced due to scarcity.

MEMORABILIA STATED ODDS 1:5 FACT.SETS
GOLD 1 OF 1's EXIST

BB1 Pavel Bure Valeri Bure	50.00	125.00
RB1 Patrick Roy Terry Sawchuk	275.00	600.00

2000-01 BAP Memorabilia Update Teammates

*MULT.COLOR SWATCH:1X TO 2X
MEMORABILIA STATED ODDS 1:5 FACT.SETS
GOLD 1 OF 1's EXIST

TM1 Petr Sykora Martin Brodeur	25.00	60.00
TM2 Sergei Gonchar Adam Oates	10.00	25.00
TM3 Jaromir Jagr Mario Lemieux	40.00	100.00
TM4 Tony Amonte Bob Probert	10.00	25.00
TM5 Jeremy Roenick Keith Tkachuk	10.00	25.00
TM6 Michael Peca Dominik Hasek	10.00	25.00
TM7 Mark Messier Brian Leetch	25.00	60.00
TM8 Pavel Bure Paul Laus	10.00	25.00
TM9 Tie Domi Mats Sundin	10.00	25.00
TM10 M.Brodeur/S.Niedermayer	25.00	60.00
TM11 Kyle McLaren Byron Dafoe	10.00	25.00
TM12 Nicklas Lidstrom Chris Chelios	20.00	50.00
TM13 Darren McCarty Steve Yzerman	20.00	50.00
TM14 Darryl Sydor Ed Belfour	10.00	25.00
TM15 B.Hull/M.Modano	15.00	40.00
TM16 Brendan Shanahan Sergei Fedorov	20.00	50.00
TM17 Nicklas Lidstrom Slava Kozlov	10.00	25.00
TM18 Patrick Roy Peter Forsberg	40.00	100.00
TM19 Mike Richter Theo Fleury	10.00	25.00
TM20 Martin Straka Jaromir Jagr	10.00	25.00
TM21 Jason Arnott Scott Stevens	10.00	25.00
TM22 Brendan Shanahan Chris Osgood	10.00	25.00
TM23 Paul Kariya Guy Hebert	10.00	25.00
TM24 Curtis Joseph Mats Sundin	10.00	25.00
TM25 Tony Amonte Eric Daze	10.00	25.00
TM26 Teemu Selanne Paul Kariya	10.00	25.00
TM27 Petr Sykora Jason Arnott	10.00	25.00
TM28 Patrick Roy Joe Sakic	40.00	100.00
TM29 Steve Yzerman Sergei Fedorov	20.00	50.00
TM30 Keith Tkachuk Teppo Numminen	10.00	25.00
TM31 Scott Niedermayer Scott Stevens	10.00	25.00
TM32 Mark Messier Mike Richter	10.00	25.00
TM33 Teppo Numminen Nikolai Khabibulin	10.00	25.00
TM34 Peter Forsberg Joe Sakic	30.00	80.00
TM35 Chris Osgood Slava Kozlov	10.00	25.00
TM36 E.Belfour/M.Modano	12.50	30.00
TM37 Tie Domi Curtis Joseph	10.00	25.00
TM38 Jeremy Roenick Nikolai Khabibulin	10.00	25.00
TM39 Guy Hebert Teemu Selanne	10.00	25.00
TM40 Theo Fleury Brian Leetch	10.00	25.00

2000-01 BAP Memorabilia Update Tough Materials

*MULT.COLOR SWATCH: 1X TO 2X
MEMORABILIA STATED ODDS 1:5 FACT.SETS
GOLD 1 OF 1's EXIST

T1 Bob Probert	20.00	50.00
T2 Tie Domi	30.00	80.00
T3 Stu Grimson	25.00	60.00
T4 Eric Cairns	8.00	20.00
T5 Paul Laus	8.00	20.00
T6 Donald Brashear	15.00	40.00
T7 Rob Ray	15.00	40.00
T8 Wade Belak	8.00	20.00
T9 Kelly Chase	8.00	20.00
T10 Peter Worrell	8.00	20.00
T11 Darren McCarty	20.00	50.00
T12 Todd Simpson	8.00	20.00
T13 Krzysztof Oliwa	12.00	30.00
T14 Sandy McCarthy	8.00	20.00
T15 Brad Brown	8.00	20.00
T16 Luke Richardson	8.00	20.00
T17 Jeff Odgers	8.00	20.00
T18 Chris Dingman	8.00	20.00
T19 Enrico Ciccone	8.00	20.00
T20 Ryan VandenBussche	12.00	30.00
T21 Bob Boughner	8.00	20.00
T22 Gino Odjick	8.00	20.00
T23 Matt Johnson	8.00	20.00
T24 Jean-Luc Grand-Pierre	8.00	20.00
T25 Craig Berube	20.00	50.00
T26 Ian Laperriere	8.00	20.00

2001-02 BAP Memorabilia

Released in August 2001, this 300-card set featured color action photos on gray and black bordered card fronts.

COMP.SER.1 SET (300) 30.00 80.00
CARDS 301-500 AVAIL.IN BAP UPD.PACKS

1 Rick DiPietro	.25	.60
2 Radek Dvorak	.10	.25
3 Radek Bonk	.10	.25
4 Evgeni Nabokov	.25	.60
5 Roman Turek	.25	.60
6 Daniel Sedin	.10	.25
7 Jeff Halpern	.10	.25
8 Joe Thornton	.50	1.25
9 Maxim Afinogenov	.10	.25
10 Oleg Saprykin	.10	.25
11 Shane Willis	.10	.25
12 Jocelyn Thibault	.25	.60
13 Alex Tanguay	.25	.60
14 Brenden Morrow	.25	.60
15 Steve Yzerman	1.50	4.00
16 Anson Carter	.25	.60
17 Brad Richards	.25	.60
18 Mike York	.10	.25
19 Brian Rafalski	.10	.25
20 Maxime Ouellet	.25	.60
21 Ruslan Fedotenko	.10	.25
22 Brad Stuart	.25	.60
23 Daniel Corso	.10	.25
24 Mika Noronen	.25	.60
25 Jason Williams	.10	.25
26 Scott Stevens	.25	.60
27 Patrick Lalime	.25	.60
28 Johan Hedberg	.25	.60
29 Vincent Damphousse	.10	.25
30 Jochen Hecht	.10	.25
31 Ed Jovanovski	.25	.60
32 Jean-Sebastien Giguere	.25	.60
33 Fred Brathwaite	.25	.60
34 Arturs Irbe	.25	.60
35 Ron Tugnutt	.25	.60
36 Ed Belfour	.30	.75
37 Chris Osgood	.25	.60
38 Mike Comrie	.25	.60
39 Aaron Miller	.10	.25
40 Martin Brodeur	.75	2.00
41 Martin Havlat	.25	.60
42 Roman Cechmanek	.25	.60
43 Teppo Numminen	.10	.25
44 Milan Kraft	.10	.25
45 Pavol Demitra	.25	.60
46 Henrik Sedin	.10	.25
47 Byron Dafoe	.25	.60
48 Dave Tanabe	.10	.25
49 Chris Drury	.25	.60
50 Tommy Salo	.25	.60
51 Lubomir Visnovsky	.10	.25
52 Andrei Markov	.10	.25
53 Jason Arnott	.10	.25
54 Adam Foote	.10	.25
55 Vitali Vishnevski	.10	.25
56 Ville Nieminen	.10	.25
57 Mike Mottau	.10	.25
58 Brendan Morrison	.25	.60
59 Lee Goren	.10	.25
60 Scott Gomez	.10	.25
61 Tim Connolly	.10	.25
62 Daniel Alfredsson	.25	.60
63 Owen Nolan	.25	.60
64 Chris Pronger	.25	.60
65 Fredrik Modin	.10	.25
66 Mario Lemieux	2.00	5.00
67 Olaf Kolzig	.25	.60
68 Jeff Friesen	.10	.25
69 Patrik Stefan	.10	.25
70 Sergei Samsonov	.25	.60
71 J-P Dumont	.10	.25
72 Sandis Ozolinsh	.10	.25
73 Milan Hejduk	.30	.75
74 Sergei Zubov	.10	.25
75 Sergei Fedorov	.50	1.25
76 Janne Niinimaa	.10	.25
77 Roberto Luongo	.40	1.00
78 Felix Potvin	.30	.75
79 Petr Sykora	.10	.25
80 Petr Nedved	.10	.25
81 Shawn McEachern	.10	.25
82 Simon Gagne	.30	.75
83 Sean Burke	.25	.60
84 Al MacInnis	.25	.60
85 Vincent Lecavalier	.30	.75
86 Sergei Gonchar	.10	.25
87 Oleg Tverdovsky	.10	.25
88 Bill Guerin	.25	.60
89 Miroslav Satan	.25	.60
90 Marc Savard	.10	.25
91 Peter Forsberg	.60	1.50
92 Brett Hull	.40	1.00
93 Nicklas Lidstrom	.30	.75
94 Ryan Smyth	.10	.25
95 Luc Robitaille	.25	.60
96 Alexander Mogilny	.25	.60
97 Mark Messier	.30	.75
98 Marian Hossa	.30	.75
99 Keith Primeau	.10	.25
100 Todd Bertuzzi	.30	.75
101 Justin Williams	.10	.25
102 Ossi Vaananen	.10	.25
103 Robert Lang	.10	.25
104 Pavel Bure	.30	.75
105 Tomas Kaberle	.10	.25
106 Nikolai Antropov	.10	.25
107 Tomi Kallio	.10	.25
108 David Vyborny	.10	.25
109 Denis Shvidki	.10	.25
110 Jozef Stumpel	.10	.25
111 Dimitri Kalinin	.10	.25
112 Stephane Robidas	.10	.25
113 Scott Walker	.10	.25
114 Jamie Langenbrunner	.10	.25
115 Maxim Kuznetsov	.10	.25
116 Mike Grier	.10	.25
117 Michael Nylander	.10	.25
118 Derian Hatcher	.10	.25
119 Scott Niedermayer	.10	.25
120 Petr Schastlivy	.10	.25
121 Tomas Divisek RC	.15	.40
122 Toby Petersen	.10	.25
123 Jarkko Ruutu	.10	.25
124 Chris Chelios	.30	.75
125 Andrew Raycroft	.25	.60
126 Jason Woolley	.10	.25
127 Derek Morris	.10	.25
128 David Legwand	.25	.60
129 Jaromir Jagr	.60	1.25
130 Serge Aubin	.10	.25
131 Jere Lehtinen	.25	.60
132 Manny Legace	.25	.60
133 Patrick Roy	1.50	4.00
134 Glen Murray	.10	.25
135 Jan Bulis	.10	.25
136 Mike Dunham	.25	.60
137 Jan Hlavac	.10	.25
138 Wade Redden	.10	.25
139 Jan Hrdina	.10	.25
140 Keith Tkachuk	.30	.75
141 Yanic Perreault	.10	.25
142 Jonas Ronnqvist	.10	.25
143 John Madden	.10	.25
144 Jani Hurme	.25	.60
145 Chris Gratton	.10	.25
146 Toni Lydman	.10	.25
147 Mike Modano	.50	1.25
148 Boris Mironov	.10	.25
149 Joe Sakic	.60	1.50
150 Chris Nielsen	.10	.25
151 Marty Turco	.25	.60
152 Bryan Smolinski	.10	.25
153 Daniel Cleary	.10	.25
154 Anders Eriksson	.10	.25
155 Pierre Dagenais	.10	.25
156 Wes Walz	.10	.25
157 Brian Savage	.10	.25
158 Stu Barnes	.10	.25
159 Eric Desjardins	.10	.25
160 Juraj Kolnik	.10	.25
161 Brendan Shanahan	.30	.75
162 Karel Rachunek	.10	.25
163 Marc Denis	.25	.60
164 Martin Straka	.10	.25
165 Alexander Kharitonov	.10	.25
166 Sergei Brylin	.10	.25
167 Eric Daze	.25	.60
168 Alexei Kovalev	.25	.60
169 Jiri Slegr	.10	.25
170 Brian Rolston	.10	.25
171 Phil Housley	.10	.25
172 Josef Vasicek	.10	.25
173 Patrick Marleau	.25	.60
174 Steven Reinprecht	.10	.25
175 Gary Roberts	.10	.25
176 Darryl Sydor	.10	.25
177 Michel Riesen	.10	.25
178 Kevyn Adams	.10	.25
179 Andreas Lilja	.10	.25
180 Roman Hamrlik	.10	.25
181 Mathieu Garon	.25	.60
182 Scott Hartnell	.10	.25
183 Kenny Jonsson	.10	.25
184 Jeff Ulmer	.10	.25
185 Petr Hubacek	.10	.25
186 Jeremy Roenick	.40	1.00
187 Scott Young	.10	.25
188 Sergei Berezin	.10	.25
189 Steve Konowalchuk	.10	.25
190 Curtis Joseph	.30	.75
191 Jonathan Girard	.10	.25
192 Brian Campbell	.10	.25
193 Markus Naslund	.30	.75
194 David Aebischer	.25	.60
195 Peter Bondra	.30	.75
196 Paul Kariya	.30	.75
197 Jason Allison	.10	.25
198 Dominik Hasek	.60	1.50
199 Branislav Mezei	.10	.25
200 Peter Smrek RC	.15	.40
201 Miikka Kiprusoff	.25	.60
202 Kristian Kudroc	.10	.25
203 Kyle McLaren	.10	.25
204 Calle Johansson	.10	.25
205 Gregg Naumenko	.10	.25
206 Damian Rhodes	.25	.60
207 Willie Mitchell	.10	.25
208 Daniel Tkaczuk	.10	.25
209 Mike Ribeiro	.10	.25
210 Rostislav Klesla	.10	.25
211 Denis Arkhipov	.10	.25
212 Andy McDonald	.10	.25
213 Ivan Novoseltsev	.10	.25
214 Manny Fernandez	.25	.60
215 Reto Von Arx	.10	.25
216 Ray Bourque	.60	1.50
217 Mike Jefferson RC	.15	.40
218 Jason Chimera RC	.15	.40
219 Mattias Ohlund	.10	.25
220 Rico Fata	.10	.25
221 Brad Tapper	.10	.25
222 Mike Richter	.30	.75
223 Nick Boynton	.10	.25
224 Harold Druken	.10	.25
225 Chris Clark	.10	.25
226 Colin White	.10	.25
227 Tyler Bouck	.10	.25
228 Jesse Wallin	.10	.25
229 Jeff Hackett	.10	.25
230 Greg Classen	.10	.25
231 Adam Mair	.10	.25
232 Ivan Ciernik RC	.15	.40
233 Marc Chouinard	.10	.25
234 Chris Mason	.10	.25
235 Ronald Petrovicky	.10	.25
236 Kyle Calder	.10	.25
237 Rick Berry	.10	.25
238 Mathieu Darche RC	.15	.40
239 Theo Fleury	.10	.25
240 Mike Commodore	.10	.25
241 Michal Handzus	.10	.25
242 Bill Tibbetts RC	.15	.40
243 Cory Stillman	.10	.25
244 Valeri Bure	.10	.25
245 Matt Pettinger	.10	.25
246 Rod Brind'Amour	.25	.60
247 Pascal Dupuis RC	.15	.40
248 Martin Rucinsky	.10	.25
249 Cliff Ronning	.10	.25
250 Brad Isbister	.10	.25
251 Antti-Jussi Niemi	.10	.25
252 Mark Bell	.10	.25
253 Martin Spanhel RC	.15	.40
254 Andrew Cassels	.10	.25
255 Andrew Brunette	.10	.25
256 Ron Francis	.25	.60
257 Tony Amonte	.25	.60
258 Espen Knutsen	.10	.25
259 Viktor Kozlov	.10	.25
260 Sergei Krivokrasov	.10	.25
261 Richard Zednik	.10	.25
262 Bubba Berenzweig	.10	.25
263 Pavel Patera	.10	.25
264 Mike Johnson	.10	.25
265 Teemu Selanne	.30	.75
266 John LeClair	.30	.75
267 Adam Deadmarsh	.10	.25
268 Herbert Vasilijevs	.10	.25
269 Steven McCarthy	.10	.25
270 Mathieu Schneider	.10	.25
271 Peter Bartos	.10	.25
272 Ray Ferraro	.10	.25
273 Eric Chouinard	.10	.25
274 Marian Cisar	.10	.25
275 Jarome Iginla	.40	1.00
276 Jeff O'Neill	.10	.25
277 Steve Sullivan	.10	.25
278 Rob Blake	.25	.60
279 Geoff Sanderson	.10	.25
280 Niclas Wallin	.10	.25
281 Vitali Yeremeyev	.10	.25
282 Doug Weight	.25	.60
283 Martin Skoula	.10	.25
284 Zigmund Palffy	.25	.60
285 Marian Gaborik	.60	1.50
286 Saku Koivu	.30	.75
287 Joe Nieuwendyk	.25	.60
288 Patrik Elias	.25	.60
289 Mariusz Czerkawski	.10	.25
290 Brian Leetch	.25	.60
291 Alexei Yashin	.10	.25
292 Mark Recchi	.25	.60
293 Shane Doan	.10	.25
294 Brian Holzinger	.10	.25
295 Mikael Samuelsson RC	.15	.40
296 Pierre Turgeon	.25	.60
297 Sheldon Keefe	.10	.25
298 Mats Sundin	.30	.75
299 Bryan Allen	.10	.25
300 Adam Oates	.25	.60
301 Ilja Bryzgalov RC	1.25	3.00
302 Erik Cole RC	.15	.40
303 Pavel Datsyuk RC	1.50	4.00
304 Nikolai Khabibulin	.30	.75
305 Dan Blackburn RC	.40	1.00
306 Jeff Jillson RC	.15	.40
307 Brian Sutherby RC	.15	.40
308 Vaclav Nedorost RC	.15	.40
309 Byron Ritchie	.10	.25
310 Martin Erat RC	.15	.40
311 Vaclav Pletka RC	.15	.40
312 Karel Pilar RC	.15	.40
313 Jaroslav Obsut RC	.15	.40
314 Jason Allison	.10	.25
315 Eric Lindros	.30	.75
316 Mike Farrell RC	.15	.40
317 Doug Gilmour	.25	.60
318 Bruno St. Jacques RC	.15	.40
319 Martin Lapointe	.10	.25
320 Dan Focht RC	.15	.40
321 Ben Simon RC	.15	.40
322 Mile Peluso RC	.15	.40
323 Martin Cibak RC	.15	.40
324 Marcel Hossa RC	.15	.40
325 Chris Neil	.10	.25
326 Mark Rycroft RC	.15	.40
327 Timo Parssinen RC	.15	.40
328 Sebastien Charpentier RC	.15	.40
329 Kip Brennan RC	.15	.40
330 Christian Berglund RC	.15	.40
331 Tom Kostopoulos RC	.15	.40
332 Pat Kavanagh RC	.15	.40
333 Sebastien Centomo RC	.15	.40
334 Andrew Brunette	.10	.25
335 Toni Dahlman RC	.15	.40
336 Kamil Piros RC	.15	.40
337 Robert Schnabel RC	.15	.40
338 Radim Vrbata	.10	.25
339 Chris Osgood	.25	.60
340 Steve Montador RC	.15	.40
341 Reinhard Divis RC	.15	.40
342 Steve Moore RC	.40	1.00
343 Branko Radivojevic RC	.15	.40
344 Zdenek Kutlak RC	.15	.40
345 Jiri Dopita RC	.15	.40
346 Josef Boumedienne RC	.15	.40
347 Phil Housley	.10	.25
348 Niko Kapanen RC	.40	1.00
349 Travis Roche RC	.15	.40
350 Raffi Torres RC	.20	.50
351 Randy Robitaille	.10	.25
352 Chris Corrinet RC	.15	.40
353 Pierre Turgeon	.25	.60
354 Pavel Skrbek RC	.15	.40
355 Jeremy Roenick	.40	1.00
356 Riku Hahl RC	.15	.40
357 Stanislav Gron RC	.15	.40
358 Pasi Nurminen RC	.20	.50
359 Nick Smith RC	.15	.40
360 Shane Endicott RC	.15	.40
361 Ales Kotalik RC	1.25	3.00
362 Blake Bellefeuille RC	.15	.40
363 Jaroslav Bednar RC	.15	.40
364 Andreas Salomonsson RC	.15	.40
365 Krystofer Kolanos RC	.15	.40
366 Tim Connolly	.10	.25
367 Ivan Huml RC	.15	.40
368 Sean Avery RC	.15	.40
369 Trent Hunter RC	.75	2.00
370 Richard Scott RC	.15	.40
371 Doug Weight	.25	.60
372 Ilya Kovalchuk RC	2.50	6.00
373 Dominik Hasek	.60	1.50
374 Scott Clemmensen RC	.15	.40
375 Nikita Alexeev RC	.15	.40
376 Luc Robitaille	.25	.60
377 Mike Peca	.10	.25
378 Brett Hull	.40	1.00
379 Valeri Bure	.10	.25
380 Pavel Brendl	.10	.25
381 Jukka Hentunen RC	.15	.40
382 John Erskine RC	.15	.40
383 Nick Schultz RC	.15	.40
384 Radek Martinek RC	.15	.40
385 Dany Heatley	.40	1.00
386 Alex Auld	.10	.25
387 Tyler Arnason RC	.40	1.00
388 Ty Conklin RC	.15	.40
389 Olivier Michaud RC	.15	.40
390 Sandis Ozolinsh	.10	.25
391 Evgeny Konstantinov RC	.15	.40
392 Roman Turek	.25	.60
393 Kristian Huselius RC	.50	1.25
394 Alexei Yashin	.10	.25
395 Alexander Mogilny	.25	.60
396 Eric Meloche RC	.15	.40
397 Andy McDonald	.10	.25
398 Niklas Hagman RC	.15	.40
399 Ryan Flinn RC	.15	.40
400 Mike Weaver RC	.15	.40
401 Nolan Yonkman	.10	.25
402 Ryan Jardine	.10	.25
403 Andrej Nedorost RC	.15	.40
404 Andrej Podkonicky RC	.15	.40
405 Hnat Domenichelli	.10	.25
406 Bob Wren RC	.15	.40
407 Brad Norton RC	.15	.40
408 Brian Pothier RC	.15	.40
409 Trevor Letowski	.10	.25
410 Chris Bala RC	.15	.40
411 Tom Fitzgerald	.25	.60
412 Petr Tenkrat	.10	.25
413 Dan Snyder RC	.40	1.00
414 David Cullen RC	.15	.40
415 David Ling RC	.15	.40
416 Dean Melanson RC	.15	.40
417 Duvie Westcott RC	.15	.40
418 Eric Beaudoin RC	.15	.40
419 Marty McInnis	.10	.25
420 Francis Lessard RC	.15	.40
421 Frederic Cassivi RC	.15	.40
422 Bill Lindsay	.10	.25
423 Kim Johnsson	.10	.25
424 Daniil Markov	.10	.25
425 Guillaume Lefebvre RC	.15	.40
426 Hannes Hyvonen RC	.15	.40
427 Jeff Daw RC	.15	.40
428 Jody Shelley RC	.60	1.50
429 Joel Kwiatkowski RC	.15	.40
430 Josh Langfeld RC	.15	.40
431 Kelly Fairchild RC	.15	.40
432 Kevin Sawyer RC	.15	.40
433 Kriby Law RC	.15	.40
434 Kyle Rossiter RC	.15	.40
435 Lukas Krajicek RC	.15	.40
436 Mark Hartigan RC	.15	.40
437 Martin Prusek RC	.15	.40
438 Matt Davidson RC	.15	.40
439 Andre Roy	.10	.25
440 Chris Kelleher RC	.15	.40
441 Mike Matteucci RC	.15	.40
442 Nathan Perrott RC	.15	.40
443 Neil Little RC	.15	.40
444 Rocky Thompson RC	.15	.40
445 Ryan Tobler RC	.15	.40
446 Scott Nichol RC	.15	.40
447 Jiri Slegr	.10	.25
448 Stephen Weiss RC	.75	2.00
449 Jeff Cowan	.10	.25
450 Thomas Ziegler RC	.15	.40
451 Todd Rohloff RC	.15	.40
452 Blake Sloan	.10	.25
453 Tony Tuzzolino RC	.15	.40
454 Tony Virta RC	.15	.40
455 Adam Oates	.25	.60
456 Benoit Brunet	.10	.25
457 Benoit Hogue	.10	.25
458 Brian Savage	.10	.25
459 Cliff Ronning	.10	.25
460 Darius Kasparaitis	.10	.25
461 Dean McAmmond	.10	.25
462 Donald Brashear	.10	.25
463 Glen Murray	.10	.25
464 Jamie Allison	.10	.25
465 Jamie Langenbrunner	.10	.25
466 Jan Hlavac	.10	.25
467 Jason Arnott	.10	.25
468 Joe Nieuwendyk	.25	.60
469 Jozef Stumpel	.10	.25
470 Juha Ylonen	.10	.25
471 Kevin Weekes	.25	.60
472 Kirill Safronov	.10	.25
473 Manny Malhotra	.10	.25
474 Martin Rucinsky	.10	.25
475 Matthew Barnaby	.10	.25
476 Mike Keane	.10	.25
477 Mike York	.10	.25
478 Mikko Eloranta	.10	.25
479 Pascal Rheaume	.10	.25
480 Pavel Bure	.30	.75
481 Pierre Dagenais	.10	.25
482 Randy McKay	.10	.25
483 Ray Ferraro	.10	.25
484 Rem Murray	.10	.25
485 Rick Berry	.10	.25
486 Sean Brown	.10	.25
487 Sean Hill	.10	.25
488 Sergei Berezin	.10	.25
489 Shane Willis	.10	.25
490 Stephane Fiset	.10	.25
491 Stephane Richer	.10	.25
492 Steve Thomas	.10	.25
493 Tom Barrasso	.25	.60
494 Tom Poti	.10	.25
495 Trevor Linden	.10	.25
496 Valeri Kamensky	.10	.25
497 Ville Nieminen	.10	.25
498 Zdeno Chara	.10	.25
499 Shjon Podein	.10	.25
500 Shaun Van Allen	.10	.25

2001-02 BAP Memorabilia Emerald

STATED PRINT RUN 10 SER.#'d SETS
NOT PRICED DUE TO SCARCITY

2001-02 BAP Memorabilia Ruby

*STARS: 5X TO 12X BASIC CARDS
*RUBY RC'S: 1.5X TO 4X BASIC CARDS
STATED PRINT RUN 200 SER.#'d SETS

2001-02 BAP Memorabilia Sapphire

*STARS:8X TO 20X BASIC CARDS
*ROOKIES: 3X TO 8X BASIC CARDS
STATED PRINT RUN 100 SER.#'d SETS

2001-02 BAP Memorabilia All-Star Jerseys

*MULT.COLORS: 1X TO 1.5X BASIC CARDS
STATED PRINT RUN 98 SETS

ASJ1 Evgeni Nabokov	6.00	15.00
ASJ2 Paul Kariya	6.00	15.00
ASJ3 Zigmund Palffy	6.00	15.00
ASJ4 Milan Hejduk	6.00	15.00
ASJ5 Patrick Roy	15.00	40.00
ASJ6 Rob Blake	6.00	15.00
ASJ7 Nicklas Lidstrom	6.00	15.00
ASJ8 Martin Brodeur	12.00	30.00
ASJ9 Doug Weight	4.00	10.00
ASJ10 Bill Guerin	4.00	10.00
ASJ11 Dominik Hasek	12.50	30.00
ASJ12 Joe Sakic	12.50	30.00
ASJ13 Alexei Kovalev	4.00	10.00
ASJ14 Roman Cechmanek	4.00	10.00
ASJ15 Pavel Bure	6.00	15.00
ASJ16 Mario Lemieux	20.00	50.00
ASJ17 Ray Bourque	10.00	25.00
ASJ18 Teppo Numminen	4.00	10.00
ASJ19 Sandis Ozolinsh	4.00	10.00
ASJ20 Tony Amonte	6.00	15.00
ASJ21 Peter Forsberg	10.00	25.00
ASJ22 Brian Leetch	6.00	15.00
ASJ23 Radek Bonk	4.00	10.00
ASJ24 Theo Fleury	6.00	15.00
ASJ25 Simon Gagne	6.00	15.00
ASJ26 Valeri Bure	4.00	10.00
ASJ27 Pavol Demitra	4.00	10.00
ASJ28 Scott Gomez	6.00	15.00
ASJ29 Curtis Joseph	6.00	15.00
ASJ30 Viktor Kozlov	4.00	10.00
ASJ31 Mark Messier	8.00	20.00
ASJ32 Mike Modano	8.00	20.00
ASJ33 Owen Nolan	6.00	15.00
ASJ34 Tommy Salo	4.00	10.00
ASJ35 Roman Turek	4.00	10.00
ASJ36 Steve Yzerman	15.00	40.00
ASJ37 Jaromir Jagr	10.00	25.00
ASJ38 Mats Sundin	6.00	15.00
ASJ39 Nikolai Khabibulin	6.00	15.00
ASJ40 Markus Naslund	6.00	15.00
ASJ41 Keith Tkachuk	6.00	15.00
ASJ42 Alexei Yashin	4.00	10.00
ASJ43 Chris Pronger	6.00	15.00
ASJ44 Al MacInnis	6.00	15.00
ASJ45 Peter Bondra	4.00	10.00
ASJ46 Arturs Irbe	4.00	10.00
ASJ47 Eric Lindros	6.00	15.00
ASJ48 Teemu Selanne	6.00	15.00
ASJ49 Daniel Alfredsson	6.00	15.00
ASJ50 Brett Hull	10.00	25.00

2001-02 BAP Memorabilia All-Star Emblems

STATED PRINT RUN 10 SETS
NOT PRICED DUE TO SCARCITY

2001-02 BAP Memorabilia All-Star Numbers

STATED PRINT RUN 10 SETS
NOT PRICED DUE TO SCARCITY

2001-02 BAP Memorabilia All-Star Jersey Doubles

*MULT.COLOR: 1X TO 1.5X BASIC CARDS
STATED PRINT RUN 60 SETS

DASJ1 Paul Kariya	10.00	25.00
DASJ2 Patrick Roy	25.00	60.00
DASJ3 Rob Blake	10.00	25.00
DASJ4 Nicklas Lidstrom	10.00	25.00
DASJ5 Martin Brodeur	25.00	60.00
DASJ6 Dominik Hasek	25.00	60.00
DASJ7 Joe Sakic	20.00	50.00
DASJ8 Ray Bourque	20.00	50.00
DASJ9 Tony Amonte	10.00	25.00
DASJ10 Peter Forsberg	20.00	50.00
DASJ11 Brian Leetch	10.00	25.00
DASJ12 Theo Fleury	10.00	25.00
DASJ13 Mats Sundin	10.00	25.00
DASJ14 Pavel Bure	10.00	25.00
DASJ15 Steve Yzerman	25.00	60.00
DASJ16 Mike Modano	12.50	30.00
DASJ17 Mark Messier	10.00	25.00
DASJ18 Curtis Joseph	10.00	25.00
DASJ19 Brendan Shanahan	10.00	25.00
DASJ20 Jaromir Jagr	15.00	40.00
DASJ21 Eric Lindros	10.00	25.00
DASJ22 Mario Lemieux	30.00	80.00
DASJ23 Al MacInnis	10.00	25.00
DASJ24 John LeClair	10.00	25.00
DASJ25 Chris Pronger	10.00	25.00
DASJ26 Wayne Gretzky	75.00	200.00
DASJ27 Teemu Selanne	10.00	25.00
DASJ28 Owen Nolan	10.00	25.00
DASJ29 Alexei Yashin	10.00	25.00
DASJ30 Jeremy Roenick	12.50	30.00

2001-02 BAP Memorabilia All-Star Starting Lineup

With a print run of just 70 sets, this 12-card set featured game-worn jersey swatches from starters of the 2001 NHL All-Star Game.

*MULT.COLORS: 1X TO 1.5X BASIC CARDS
STATED PRINT RUN 70 SETS

S1 Dominik Hasek	12.50	30.00
S2 Nicklas Lidstrom	10.00	25.00
S3 Sandis Ozolinsh	10.00	25.00
S4 Milan Hejduk	10.00	25.00
S5 Peter Forsberg	15.00	40.00
S6 Pavel Bure	10.00	25.00
S7 Patrick Roy	30.00	80.00
S8 Ray Bourque	20.00	50.00
S9 Rob Blake	10.00	25.00
S10 Paul Kariya	10.00	25.00
S11 Theo Fleury	10.00	25.00
S12 Joe Sakic	20.00	50.00

2001-02 BAP Memorabilia All-Star Teammates

This 50-card set highlighted players who were teammates at either the 1994, 1996, 1997, 1998, 1999, 2000, or 2001 NHL All-Star Game. Each card carried a swatch of All-Star Game jersey from each player depicted. Each card was limited to just 80 copies.

*MULT.COLORS. 1X TO 1.5X BASIC CARDS
STATED PRINT RUN 80 SETS

AST1 Evgeni Nabokov Milan Hejduk Zigmund Palffy	12.50	30.00

AST2 Kariya/Lemieux/Gagne 30.00 80.00
AST3 Rob Blake 40.00 100.00
Patrick Roy
Joe Sakic
AST4 Martin Brodeur 20.00 50.00
Doug Weight
Brian Leetch
AST5 Roman Cechmanek 20.00 50.00
Pavel Bure
Peter Forsberg
AST6 Dominik Hasek 12.50 30.00
Alexei Kovalev
Nicklas Lidstrom
AST7 Raymond Bourque 20.00 50.00
Brian Leetch
Theo Fleury
AST8 Tony Amonte 12.50 30.00
Bill Guerin
Doug Weight
AST9 Evgeni Nabokov 15.00 40.00
Roman Cechmanek
Dominik Hasek
AST10 Paul Kariya 20.00 50.00
Joe Sakic
Theo Fleury
AST11 Peter Forsberg 20.00 50.00
Milan Hejduk
AST12 P.Roy/M.Lemieux 50.00 125.00
AST13 Raymond Bourque 20.00 50.00
Rob Blake
AST14 Pavel Bure 12.50 30.00
Valeri Bure
Viktor Kozlov
AST15 Martin Brodeur 40.00 100.00
Scott Gomez
Scott Stevens
AST16 Chris Pronger 12.50 30.00
Al MacInnis
AST17 Tony Amonte 20.00 50.00
Mike Modano
Jeremy Roenick
AST18 Olaf Kolzig 12.50 30.00
Tommy Salo
Roman Turek
AST19 Brendan Shanahan 20.00 50.00
Steve Yzerman
AST20 Mats Sundin 15.00 40.00
Tommy Salo
AST21 Jaromir Jagr 12.50 30.00
Pavel Bure
AST22 Modno/Joseph/Yzrmn 25.00 60.00
AST23 Pavel Bure 12.50 30.00
Valeri Bure
AST24 Steve Yzerman 25.00 60.00
Mark Messier
Scott Gomez
AST25 Mike Modano 12.50 30.00
Eric Lindros
AST26 Peter Forsberg 20.00 50.00
Teemu Selanne
AST27 Markus Naslund 12.50 30.00
Alexei Yashin
Peter Bondra
AST28 Dominik Hasek 15.00 40.00
Arturs Irbe
Nikolai Khabibulin
AST29 Mats Sundin 12.50 30.00
Nicklas Lidstrom
Markus Naslund
AST30 Chris Pronger 12.50 30.00
Al MacInnis
AST31 Paul Kariya 12.50 30.00
Tony Amonte
AST32 Peter Forsberg 20.00 50.00
Jaromir Jagr
AST33 Mike Modano 12.50 30.00
John LeClair
AST34 Wayne Gretzky 75.00 200.00
Mike Modano
Eric Lindros
AST35 Patrick Roy 30.00 80.00
Joe Sakic
AST36 Jaromir Jagr 25.00 60.00
Peter Forsberg
Pavel Bure
AST37 Wayne Gretzky 125.00 300.00
Patrick Roy
AST38 Bourque/Chelios/Leetch 20.00 50.00
AST39 Eric Lindros 12.50 30.00
Mark Messier
AST40 Dominik Hasek 12.50 30.00
Nikolai Khabibulin
AST41 J.Sakic/M.Modano 20.00 50.00
AST42 Dominik Hasek 15.00 40.00
Raymond Bourque
AST43 Steve Yzerman 20.00 50.00
Mats Sundin
AST44 Paul Kariya 12.50 30.00
Pavel Bure
AST45 Mats Sundin 12.50 30.00
Teemu Selanne
AST46 Brett Hull 12.50 30.00
Ed Belfour
AST47 Jaromir Jagr 12.50 30.00
Eric Lindros
AST48 Peter Forsberg 15.00 40.00
Paul Kariya
AST49 Wayne Gretzky 30.00 80.00
Curtis Joseph
AST50 Patrick Roy 25.00 60.00
Raymond Bourque

2001-02 BAP Memorabilia Country of Origin

This 60-card set featured swatches of the national flag emblem from the highlighted player's All-Star Game jersey. Cards CO41-60 were available in random packs of BAP Update and were limited to 10 copies each. Cards CO1-40 were limited to 12 copies each. The cards are not priced due to scarcity.

CO1-CO40 PRINT RUN 12 SETS
CO41-CO60 PRINT RUN 10 SETS
NOT PRICED DUE TO SCARCITY
CO1 Mario Lemieux
CO2 Eric Lindros
CO3 Theo Fleury
CO4 Paul Kariya
CO5 Joe Sakic
CO6 Ray Bourque
CO7 Al MacInnis
CO8 Rob Blake
CO9 Steve Yzerman
CO10 Patrick Roy
CO11 Martin Brodeur
CO12 Curtis Joseph
CO13 Scott Niedermayer
CO14 Bill Guerin
CO15 Mike Modano
CO16 Brian Leetch
CO17 Doug Weight
CO18 Jeremy Roenick
CO19 Tony Amonte
CO20 Keith Tkachuk
CO21 Teppo Numminen
CO22 Teemu Selanne
CO23 Dominik Hasek
CO24 Jaromir Jagr
CO25 Milan Hejduk
CO26 Radek Bonk
CO27 Roman Cechmanek
CO28 Peter Forsberg
CO29 Tommy Salo
CO30 Daniel Alfredsson
CO31 Nicklas Lidstrom
CO32 Markus Naslund
CO33 Alexei Kovalev
CO34 Pavel Bure
CO35 Alexei Yashin
CO36 Valeri Bure
CO37 Peter Bondra
CO38 Pavol Demitra
CO39 Zigmund Palffy
CO40 Sandis Ozolinsh
CO41 Patrik Elias
CO42 Sami Kapanen
CO43 Tomas Kaberle
CO44 Nikolai Khabibulin
CO45 Vincent Damphousse
CO46 Eric Daze
CO47 Jarome Iginla
CO48 Mario Lemieux
CO49 Owen Nolan
CO50 Joe Thornton
CO51 Sean Burke
CO52 Jose Theodore
CO53 Brendan Shanahan
CO54 Mats Sundin
CO55 Mark Recchi
CO56 Luc Robitaille
CO57 Ed Jovanovski
CO58 John LeClair
CO59 Sergei Fedorov
CO60 Chris Pronger

2001-02 BAP Memorabilia Draft Redemptions

Inserted randomly in packs, this 30-card set featured cards representing the top thirty draft picks in 2001. Each card was redeemable for the player it represented once that player made his NHL debut. Collectors had six months to redeem the cards once the player was available. The redemption cards themselves were hand-numbered out of 100. If by 11/1/2005, the player has still not played in the NHL, the collector has the choice of redeeming the card for others in the set or continuing to wait. Expiration dates of the redeemable cards are listed below.

STATED PRINT RUN 100 SETS
EXPIRED CARD PRINT RUNS BELOW
1 Ilya Kovalchuk/74 60.00 150.00
Expired 4/2/2002
2 Jason Spezza/55 125.00 250.00
Expired 4/24/2003
3 Alexander Svitov/52 20.00 50.00
Expired 4/10/2003
4 Stephen Weiss/55 40.00 80.00
5 Stanislav Chistov/53 15.00 40.00
6 Mikko Koivu EXCH 10.00 25.00
7 Mike Komisarek/47 25.00 60.00
Expired 8/19/2003
8 Pascal Leclaire/49 30.00 60.00
Expired 6/12/2003
9 Tuomo Ruutu/64 30.00 60.00
Expired 12/17/2003
10 Dan Blackburn/67 15.00 40.00
Expired 4/10/2002
11 Fredrik Sjostrom 10.00 25.00
Expired 4/30/2004
12 Dan Hamhuis/63 25.00 60.00
Expired 4/9/2004
13 Ales Hemsky/52 60.00 150.00
Expired 4/10/2003
14 Chuck Kobasew/50 25.00 50.00
Expired 4/10/2003
15 Carolina Hurricanes 8.00 20.00
16 R.J. Umberger EXCH 10.00 25.00
17 Carlo Colaiacovo/50 25.00 60.00
Expired 4/23/2003
18 Los Angeles Kings 8.00 20.00
19 Shaone Morrisonn/48 20.00 50.00
Expired 4/19/2003
20 Marcel Goc 10.00 25.00
21 Colby Armstrong EXCH 10.00 25.00
22 Buffalo Sabres 8.00 20.00
23 Tim Gleason/61 15.00 40.00
Expired 4/9/2004
24 Lukas Krajicek/31 25.00 60.00
Expired 10/6/2002
25 Alexander Perezhogin EXCH 10.00 25.00
26 Jason Bacashihua/46 25.00 60.00
Expired 9/5/2003
27 Jeff Woywitka EXCH 8.00 20.00
28 New Jersey Devils 8.00 20.00
29 Adam Munro 8.00 20.00
30 Dave Steckel EXCH 8.00 20.00

2001-02 BAP Memorabilia 500 Goal Scorers

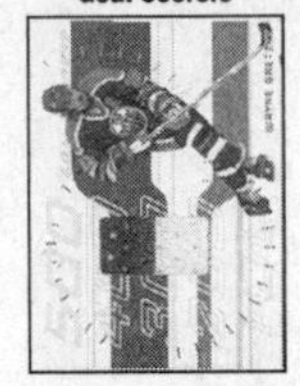

This 28-card set featured players who hit the milestone of 500 goals in their career. Each card featured an action photo of the given player alongside a game-worn swatch of his jersey on the card front. Each card was printed in quantities of 99,50,40 or 20 only. The Shanahan and Francis cards were available in random BAP Update packs only. Cards with print runs of 20 or less are not priced due to scarcity.

*MULT.COLOR: 1X TO 1.5X BASIC CARDS
STATED ODDS 1:269
NNO CARDS AVAIL.IN BAP UPD.PACKS
GS1 Wayne Gretzky/20
GS2 Gordie Howe/20
GS3 Marcel Dionne/50 20.00 50.00
GS4 Phil Esposito/40 25.00 60.00
GS5 Mike Gartner/99 10.00 25.00
GS6 Mark Messier/99 25.00 60.00
GS7 Steve Yzerman/99 30.00 80.00
GS8 Brett Hull/99 25.00 60.00
GS9 Mario Lemieux/20
GS10 Dino Ciccarelli/99 10.00 25.00
GS11 Jari Kurri/99 12.50 30.00
GS12 Luc Robitaille/99 10.00 25.00
GS13 Mike Bossy/50 10.00 25.00
GS14 Dave Andreychuk/99 10.00 25.00
GS15 Guy Lafleur/50 25.00 60.00
GS16 John Bucyk/99 10.00 25.00
GS17 Maurice Richard/20 60.00 150.00
GS18 Stan Mikita/40 25.00 60.00
GS19 Frank Mahovlich/40 25.00 60.00
GS20 Bryan Trottier/99 10.00 25.00
GS21 Dale Hawerchuk/99 10.00 25.00
GS22 Gilbert Perreault/99 15.00 40.00
GS23 Jean Beliveau/20 75.00 150.00
GS24 Pat Verbeek/99 10.00 25.00
GS25 Michel Goulet/99 10.00 25.00
GS26 Joe Mullen/99 10.00 25.00
GS27 Lanny McDonald/99 10.00 25.00
GS28 Bobby Hull/40 30.00 80.00
NNO Ron Francis/25 20.00 50.00
NNO Brendan Shanahan/25 25.00 60.00

2001-02 BAP Memorabilia Goalies Jerseys

*MULT.COLORS: 1X TO 1.5X BASIC CARDS
STATED PRINT RUN 80 SETS
GJ1 Byron Dafoe 10.00 25.00
GJ2 Dominik Hasek 15.00 40.00
GJ3 Mike Vernon 10.00 25.00
GJ4 Arturs Irbe 10.00 25.00
GJ5 Jocelyn Thibault 10.00 25.00
GJ6 Patrick Roy 20.00 50.00
GJ7 Ed Belfour 10.00 25.00
GJ8 Chris Osgood 10.00 25.00
GJ9 Johan Hedberg 10.00 25.00
GJ10 Roberto Luongo 10.00 25.00
Trevor Kid
GJ11 Jose Theodore 12.00 30.00
Jeff Hackett
GJ12 Mike Dunham 10.00 25.00
GJ13 Martin Brodeur 20.00 50.00
GJ14 Mike Richter 10.00 25.00
GJ15 Roman Cechmanek 10.00 25.00
Brian Boucher
GJ16 Jean-Sebastien Aubin 10.00 25.00
GJ17 Roman Turek 10.00 25.00
GJ18 Curtis Joseph 10.00 25.00
GJ19 Olaf Kolzig 10.00 25.00
GJ20 Felix Potvin 10.00 25.00

2001-02 BAP Memorabilia Goalie Traditions

This 42-card set featured game-worn goalie gear swatches of one, two or three goalies from the past and present. Single player cards were limited to 60 sets, two player cards were limited to 50 sets, and three player cards were limited to 20 sets. Triple player cards were not priced due to scarcity.

SNGL.STATED PRINT RUN 60 SETS
DBL.STATED PRINT RUN 50 SETS
TRPL.STATED PRINT RUN 20 SETS
TRIPLES NOT PRICED DUE TO SCARCITY
GT1 Curtis Joseph 12.50 30.00
GT2 Johnny Bower 20.00 50.00
GT3 Turk Broda 30.00 80.00
GT4 Patrick Roy 30.00 80.00
GT5 Jacques Plante 25.00 60.00
GT6 Jose Theodore 15.00 40.00
GT7 Glenn Hall 12.50 30.00
GT8 Tony Esposito 12.50 30.00
GT9 Jocelyn Thibault 12.50 30.00
GT10 Chuck Rayner 12.50 30.00
GT11 Ed Giacomin 25.00 60.00
GT12 Mike Richter 12.50 30.00
GT13 Frank Brimsek 12.50 30.00
GT14 Gerry Cheevers 12.50 30.00
GT15 Byron Dafoe 12.50 30.00
GT16 Terry Sawchuk 30.00 80.00
GT17 Glenn Hall 12.50 30.00
GT18 Chris Osgood 12.50 30.00
GT19 Curtis Joseph 40.00 100.00
Turk Broda
GT20 Curtis Joseph 40.00 100.00
Johnny Bower
GT21 Johnny Bower 20.00 50.00
Turk Broda
GT22 Terry Sawchuk 50.00 125.00
Glenn Hall
GT23 Glenn Hall 20.00 50.00
Chris Osgood
GT24 Terry Sawchuck 40.00 100.00
Chris Osgood
GT25 Glenn Hall 20.00 50.00
Jocelyn Thibault
GT26 Glenn Hall 20.00 50.00
Tony Esposito
GT27 Tony Esposito 20.00 50.00
Jocelyn Thibault
GT28 Jacques Plante 50.00 125.00
Patrick Roy
GT29 Jacques Plante 40.00 100.00
Jose Theodore
GT30 Patrick Roy 50.00 125.00
Jose Theodore
GT31 Frank Brimsek 20.00 50.00
Byron Dafoe
GT32 Frank Brimsek 20.00 50.00
Gerry Cheevers
GT33 Gerry Cheevers 20.00 50.00
Byron Dafoe
GT34 Chuck Rayner 20.00 50.00
Ed Giacomin
GT35 Chuck Rayner 20.00 50.00
Mike Richter
GT36 Ed Giacomin 20.00 50.00
Mike Richter
GT37 Curtis Joseph
Johnny Bower
Turk Broda
GT38 Terry Sawchuk
Glenn Hall
Chris Osgood
GT39 Tony Esposito
Glenn Hall
Jocelyn Thibault
GT40 Jacques Plante
Patrick Roy
Jose Theodore
GT41 Frank Brimsek
Gerry Cheevers
Bryon Dafoe
GT42 Mike Richter
Chuck Rayner
Ed Giacomin

2001-02 BAP Memorabilia He Shoots-He Scores Points

ONE PER PACK
RED.PROGRAM EXPIRED
1 Roman Cechmanek 1 pt. .20 .50
2 Martin Havlat 1 pt. .20 .50
3 Milan Hejduk 1 pt. .20 .50
4 Curtis Joseph 1 pt. .20 .50
5 Saku Koivu 1 pt. .20 .50
6 Mark Messier 1 pt. .20 .50
7 Mike Modano 1 pt. .20 .50
8 Evgeni Nabokov 1 pt. .20 .50
9 Chris Pronger 1 pt. .20 .50
10 Mats Sundin 1 pt. .20 .50
11 Martin Brodeur 2 pts. .20 .50
12 Peter Forsberg 2 pts. .20 .50
13 Paul Kariya 2 pts. .20 .50
14 Vincent Lecavalier 2 pts. .20 .50
15 Patrick Roy 2 pts. .20 .50
16 Joe Sakic 2 pts. .20 .50
17 Steve Yzerman 2 pts. .20 .50
18 Pavel Bure 3 pts. .20 .50
19 Mario Lemieux 3 pts. .20 .50
20 Teemu Selanne 3 pts. .20 .50

2001-02 BAP Memorabilia He Shoots-He Scores Prizes

STAT.PRINT RUN 20 SER.#'d SETS
NOT PRICED DUE TO SCARCITY
1 Daniel Sedin
2 Jaromir Jagr
3 Alex Tanguay
4 Steve Yzerman
5 Scott Stevens
6 Ed Belfour
7 Martin Brodeur
8 Roman Cechmanek
9 Teemu Selanne
10 Jason Arnott
11 Scott Gomez
12 Owen Nolan
13 Chris Pronger
14 Mario Lemieux
15 Olaf Kolzig
16 Patrik Stefan
17 Milan Hejduk
18 Sergei Fedorov
19 Roberto Luongo
20 Al MacInnis
21 Vincent Lecavalier
22 Peter Forsberg
23 Marian Hossa
24 Keith Primeau
25 Pavel Bure
26 Patrick Roy
27 Mike Modano
28 Joe Sakic
29 Brendan Shanahan
30 Martin Straka
31 Keith Tkachuk
32 Curtis Joseph
33 Peter Bondra
34 Ron Francis
35 Tony Amonte
36 Saku Koivu
37 Brian Leetch
38 Mark Recchi
39 Mats Sundin
40 Wayne Gretzky

2001-02 BAP Memorabilia Patented Power

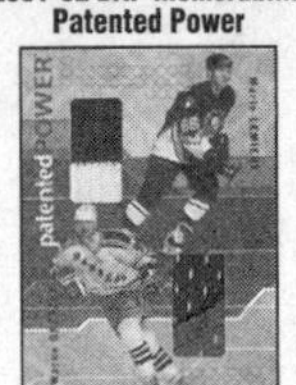

This six card set featured game-worn jersey swatches from both player's featured. Each card was limited to just 20 copies.

*MULT.COLORS: 1X TO 1.5X BASIC CARDS
STATED PRINT RUN 20 SETS
PP1 Jaromir Jagr 40.00 100.00
Mats Sundin
PP2 M.Lemieux/W.Gretzky 200.00 500.00
PP3 Pavel Bure 40.00 100.00
Milan Hejduk
PP4 Mike Modano 40.00 100.00
Chris Pronger
PP5 Paul Kariya 60.00 150.00
Jose Sakic
PP6 Peter Forsberg 75.00 200.00
Steve Yzerman

2001-02 BAP Memorabilia Rocket's Mates

This 10-card set featured game-used jersey swatches from player's who played with Hall-of-Famer Maurice "Rocket" Richard. The card fronts carried a small action photo of the featured player on the right side and a black-and-white head shot of Richard on the left. Each card was limited to 50 copies.

*MULT.COLORS: 1X TO 1.5X BASIC CARDS
STATED PRINT RUN 50 SETS
RM1 Jacques Plante 50.00 125.00
Rocket Richard
RM2 Doug Harvey 25.00 60.00
Rocket Richard
RM3 Jean Beliveau 30.00 80.00
Rocket Richard
RM4 Henri Richard 25.00 60.00
Rocket Richard
RM5 Bernie Geoffrion 30.00 80.00
RM6 Dollard St. Laurent 25.00 60.00
Rocket Richard
RM7 Elmer Lach 25.00 60.00
Rocket Richard
RM8 Dickie Moore 25.00 60.00
Rocket Richard
RM9 Butch Bouchard 25.00 60.00
Rocket Richard
RM10 Jean-Guy Talbot 25.00 60.00
Rocket Richard

2001-02 BAP Memorabilia Stanley Cup Champions

This 14-card set honored the winners of the 2001 Stanley Cup, the Colorado Avalanche. Each card carried a full-color photo of the featured player and a swatch of game-used jersey on the card front. Each card was limited to just 40 copies.

*MULT.COLORS: 1X TO 1.5X HI
STATED PRINT RUN 40 SETS
CA1 Patrick Roy 100.00 250.00
CA2 Adam Foote 15.00 40.00
CA3 Ray Bourque 75.00 200.00
CA4 Martin Skoula 15.00 40.00
CA5 Shjon Podein 15.00 40.00
CA6 Alex Tanguay 15.00 40.00
CA7 Chris Dingman 15.00 40.00
CA8 Milan Hejduk 15.00 40.00
CA9 Peter Forsberg 40.00 100.00
CA10 Joe Sakic 40.00 100.00
CA11 Eric Messier 15.00 40.00
CA12 Jon Klemm 15.00 40.00
CA13 Dave Reid 15.00 40.00
CA14 Chris Drury 15.00 40.00

2001-02 BAP Memorabilia Stanley Cup Playoffs

This 32-card set featured players who participated in the 2001 Stanley Cup Playoffs. Each card carried a full-color photo and a swatch of game-used jersey on the card front. Cards SC1-16 were limited to 95 copies each, cards SC17-24 were limited to 80, cards SC25-60 were limited to 40, and cards SC31 and 32 were limited to just 10 copies each. Cards SC31-32 are not priced due to scarcity.

*MULT.COLORS: 1X TO 1.5X BASIC CARDS
PRINT RUNS LISTED BELOW
SC31-SC32 NOT PRICED DUE TO SCARCITY
SC1 Mats Sundin/95 10.00 25.00
SC2 Daniel Alfredsson/95 10.00 25.00
SC3 Scott Stevens/95 10.00 25.00
SC4 Arturs Irbe/95 10.00 25.00
SC5 Martin Straka/95 10.00 25.00
SC6 Olaf Kolzig/95 10.00 25.00
SC7 Doug Gilmour/95 10.00 25.00
SC8 Roman Cechmanek/95 10.00 25.00
SC9 Joe Sakic/95 15.00 40.00
SC10 Daniel Sedin/95 10.00 25.00
SC11 Zigmund Palffy/95 10.00 25.00
SC12 Sergei Fedorov/95 12.50 30.00
SC13 Ed Belfour/95 10.00 25.00
SC14 Tommy Salo/95 10.00 25.00
SC15 Roman Turek/95 10.00 25.00
SC16 Owen Nolan/95 10.00 25.00
SC17 Patrick Roy/80 20.00 50.00
SC18 Luc Robitaille/80 10.00 25.00
SC19 Chris Pronger/80 10.00 25.00
SC20 Mike Modano/80 12.50 30.00
SC21 Martin Brodeur/80 20.00 50.00
SC22 Curtis Joseph/80 10.00 25.00
SC23 Dominik Hasek/80 12.50 30.00
SC24 Mario Lemieux/80 30.00 80.00
SC25 Jason Arnott/60 10.00 25.00
SC26 Johan Hedberg/60 10.00 25.00
SC27 Ray Bourque/60 15.00 40.00
SC28 Al MacInnis/60 10.00 25.00
SC29 Scott Gomez/40 10.00 25.00
SC30 Chris Drury/40 10.00 25.00
SC31 R.Bourque/10 Cup Winners
SC32 Patrick Roy/10 Conn Smythe

2002-03 BAP Memorabilia

Released in mid-November 2002, this 300-card base set featured 200 veteran cards, 30 shortprinted rookie cards and the following shortprinted subsets: Franchise Players (201-230) and the Big Deal (231-270). Shortprinted cards were inserted at a rate of one per pack. Cards 301-400 were only available via mail-in offer found in packs.

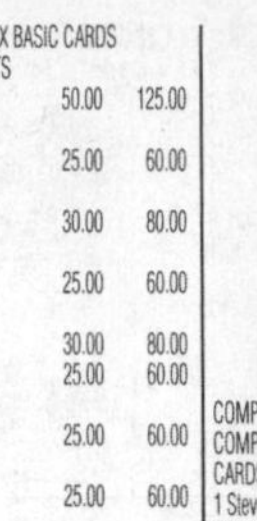

COMP.SET w/o UPDATE (300) 200.00 400.00
COMP.SET w/o SP's (200) 25.00 50.00
CARDS 301-400 AVAIL.VIA MAIL-IN
1 Steve Yzerman 1.50 4.00
2 Steve Reinprecht .10 .25
3 Jean-Sebastien Giguere .25 .60
4 Chris Simon .10 .25
5 Dany Heatley .40 1.00
6 Brendan Morrison .25 .60
7 Bill Guerin .25 .60
8 Alexander Mogilny .25 .60
9 Martin Biron .25 .60
10 Brad Richards .25 .60
11 Craig Conroy .10 .25
12 Al MacInnis .25 .60
13 Arturs Irbe .25 .60
14 Evgeni Nabokov .25 .60
15 Alexei Zhamnov .10 .25
16 Daniel Briere .10 .25
17 Alex Tanguay .25 .60
18 Milan Kraft .10 .25
19 Marc Denis .25 .60
20 Adam Oates .25 .60
21 Darryl Sydor .10 .25
22 Daniel Alfredsson .25 .60
23 Brendan Shanahan .30 .75
24 Brian Leetch .25 .60
25 Anson Carter .25 .60
26 Adrian Aucoin .10 .25
27 Kristian Huselius .10 .25
28 Jamie Langenbrunner .10 .25
29 Adam Deadmarsh .10 .25
30 Denis Arkhipov .10 .25
31 Andrew Brunette .10 .25
32 Donald Audette .10 .25
33 Rob Blake .25 .60
34 Jaromir Jagr .50 1.25
35 Felix Potvin .30 .75
36 Dan Cloutier .25 .60
37 Niklas Hagman .10 .25
38 Alyn McCauley .10 .25
39 Eric Brewer .10 .25
40 Nikolai Khabibulin .30 .75
41 Brett Hull .40 1.00
42 Brent Johnson .25 .60
43 Brenden Morrow .25 .60
44 Mike Ricci .10 .25
45 Ray Whitney .10 .25
46 Alexei Kovalev .25 .60
47 Chris Drury .25 .60
48 Daymond Langkow .25 .60
49 Eric Daze .25 .60
50 Pavel Brendl .10 .25
51 Bates Battaglia .10 .25
52 Jani Hurme .25 .60
53 Dean McAmmond .10 .25
54 Dan Blackburn .25 .60
55 Maxim Afinogenov .10 .25
56 Alexei Yashin .10 .25
57 Steve Shields .25 .60
58 Joe Nieuwendyk .25 .60
59 Frantisek Kaberle .10 .25
60 Jan Lasak .10 .25
61 Ron Francis .25 .60
62 Jeff Friesen .10 .25
63 Doug Gilmour .25 .60
64 Jeff Halpern .10 .25
65 Ilya Kovalchuk .40 1.00
66 Daniel Sedin .10 .25
67 Glen Murray .10 .25
68 Bryan McCabe .10 .25
69 Miroslav Satan .25 .60
70 Pavel Kubina .10 .25
71 Derek Morris .10 .25
72 Chris Pronger .25 .60
73 Erik Cole .10 .25
74 Owen Nolan .25 .60
75 Jocelyn Thibault .25 .60
76 Jan Hrdina .10 .25
77 Greg DeVries .10 .25
78 Krystofer Kolanos .10 .25
79 David Vyborny .10 .25
80 Jeremy Roenick .40 1.00
81 Jason Arnott .10 .25
82 Mike Leclerc .10 .25
83 Marian Hossa .30 .75
84 Chris Chelios .30 .75
85 Eric Lindros .30 .75
86 Jochen Hecht .10 .25
87 Chris Osgood .25 .60
88 Roberto Luongo .40 1.00
89 Martin Brodeur .75 2.00
90 Jaroslav Modry .10 .25
91 Martin Erat .10 .25
92 Manny Fernandez .25 .60
93 Jose Theodore .40 1.00
94 Olaf Kolzig .25 .60
95 Ed Jovanovski .25 .60
96 Sandis Ozolinsh .10 .25
97 Corey Schwab .25 .60
98 Sami Kapanen .10 .25
99 Mike Comrie .25 .60
100 Shane Willis .10 .25
101 Dominik Hasek .60 1.50
102 Jason Allison .25 .60
103 Doug Weight .25 .60
104 Marty Turco .25 .60
105 Patrick Marleau .25 .60
106 Rostislav Klesla .10 .25
107 Johan Hedberg .25 .60
108 Joe Sakic .60 1.50
109 Marian Gaborik .60 1.50

110 Sean Burke .25 .60
111 Mark Bell .10 .25
112 John LeClair .30 .75
113 Jaroslav Svoboda .10 .25
114 Todd Bertuzzi .30 .75
115 Martin Havlat .25 .60
116 Pavel Datsyuk .30 .75
117 Jarome Iginla .40 1.00
118 Mark Messier .30 .75
119 Stu Barnes .10 .25
120 Shayne Corson .10 .25
121 Mark Parrish .10 .25
122 Joe Thornton .50 1.25
123 Patrik Elias .25 .60
124 Milan Hnilicka .25 .60
125 Mike Dunham .25 .60
126 Oleg Tverdovsky .10 .25
127 Richard Zednik .10 .25
128 Peter Forsberg .75 2.00
129 Mikko Eloranta .10 .25
130 Zdeno Chara .10 .25
131 Curtis Joseph .30 .75
132 Steve Rucchin .10 .25
133 Sergei Fedorov .50 1.25
134 Josef Vasicek .10 .25
135 Ryan Smyth .10 .25
136 Scott Niedermayer .10 .25
137 Shane Doan .10 .25
138 Steve Sullivan .10 .25
139 Stephen Weiss .10 .25
140 Alexander Daigle .10 .25
141 Fred Brathwaite .25 .60
142 Peter Bondra .30 .75
143 Patrik Stefan .10 .25
144 Tony Amonte .25 .60
145 Valeri Bure .10 .25
146 Rick DiPietro .25 .60
147 Martin Straka .10 .25
148 Jeff O'Neill .10 .25
149 Milan Hejduk .30 .75
150 Kirk Maltby .10 .25
151 Mike York .10 .25
152 Scott Gomez .10 .25
153 Mike Peca .10 .25
154 Mike Richter .30 .75
155 Patrick Lalime .25 .60
156 Justin Williams .10 .25
157 Mario Lemieux 2.00 5.00
158 Kevin Weekes .25 .60
159 Scott Young .10 .25
160 Tommy Salo .25 .60
161 Steve Webb .10 .25
162 Teemu Selanne .30 .75
163 Jozef Stumpel .10 .25
164 Patrick Roy 1.50 4.00
165 Zigmund Palffy .25 .60
166 Pavel Bure .30 .75
167 Vincent Damphousse .10 .25
168 Sergei Gonchar .10 .25
169 Sergei Samsonov .25 .60
170 Luc Robitaille .25 .60
171 Scott Stevens .25 .60
172 Robert Lang .10 .25
173 Henrik Sedin .10 .25
174 Tim Connolly .10 .25
175 Pierre Turgeon .25 .60
176 Yanic Perreault .10 .25
177 Radek Bonk .10 .25
178 Keith Tkachuk .30 .75
179 Paul Kariya .30 .75
180 Mike Modano .50 1.25
181 Saku Koivu .30 .75
182 Mark Recchi .25 .60
183 Roman Turek .25 .60
184 Kris Draper .10 .25
185 Scott Hartnell .10 .25
186 Keith Primeau .10 .25
187 Vincent Lecavalier .30 .75
188 Darcy Tucker .10 .25
189 Markus Naslund .30 .75
190 Pavol Demitra .25 .60
191 Gary Roberts .10 .25
192 Rod Brind'Amour .25 .60
193 Radim Vrbata .10 .25
194 Nicklas Lidstrom .30 .75
195 Tom Poti .10 .25
196 Roman Cechmanek .25 .60
197 Scott Mellanby .10 .25
198 Mats Sundin .30 .75
199 Filip Kuba .10 .25
200 Simon Gagne .30 .75
201 Paul Kariya FP .50 1.25
202 Ilya Kovalchuk FP .60 1.50
203 Joe Thornton FP .75 2.00
204 Miroslav Satan FP .40 1.00
205 Jarome Iginla FP .60 1.50
206 Ron Francis FP .40 1.00
207 Eric Daze FP .40 1.00
208 Patrick Roy FP 2.50 6.00
209 Rostislav Klesla FP .40 1.00
210 Mike Modano FP .75 2.00
211 Steve Yzerman FP 2.50 6.00
212 Mike Comrie FP .40 1.00
213 Roberto Luongo FP .50 1.25
214 Zigmund Palffy FP .50 1.25
215 Marian Gaborik FP .40 1.00
216 Jose Theodore FP .50 1.25
217 Scott Hartnell FP .15 .40
218 Martin Brodeur FP 1.25 3.00
219 Alexei Yashin FP .30 .75
220 Pavel Bure FP .60 1.50
221 Marian Hossa FP .50 1.25
222 Simon Gagne FP .50 1.25
223 Daniel Briere FP .15 .40
224 Mario Lemieux FP 3.00 8.00
225 Chris Pronger FP .40 1.00
226 Owen Nolan FP .40 1.00
227 Nikolai Khabibulin FP .40 1.00
228 Mats Sundin FP .50 1.25
229 Markus Naslund FP .40 1.00
230 Jaromir Jagr FP .75 2.00
231 P.Forsberg/E.Lindros 1.50 4.00
232 P.Roy/J.Thibault 2.00 5.00
233 T.Sawchuk/J.Bucyk 2.00 5.00
234 J.Plante/G.Worsley 1.50 4.00
235 Chris Pronger .75 2.00
Brendan Shanahan
236 Eric Lindros .75 2.00
Pavel Brendl
237 Kris Beech .75 2.00
Jaromir Jagr
238 Ed Jovanovski .75 2.00
Pavel Bure
239 Jarome Iginla .75 2.00
Joe Nieuwendyk
240 Dominik Hasek .75 2.00
Eric Daze
241 Denis Savard .75 2.00
Chris Chelios
242 Adam Oates .75 2.00
Jason Allison
243 Dominik Hasek .75 2.00
Slava Kozlov
244 Robert Svehla .75 2.00
Dimitri Yushkevich
245 Trevor Linden .75 2.00
Todd Bertuzzi
246 Guy Lafleur .75 2.00
Sergei Zubov
247 Jason Arnott .75 2.00
Bill Guerin
248 Alexander Mogilny .75 2.00
Mike Peca
249 Brendan Shanahan .75 2.00
Keith Primeau
250 John LeClair .75 2.00
Mark Recchi
251 Rob Blake .75 2.00
Adam Deadmarsh
252 Jeremy Roenick .75 2.00
Alexei Zhamnov
253 Mike Peca .75 2.00
Tim Connolly
254 Sandis Ozolinsh .75 2.00
Owen Nolan
255 Chris Drury .75 2.00
Manny Fernandez
256 Roman Turek .75 2.00
Fred Brathwaite
257 Jason Arnott .75 2.00
Joe Nieuwendyk
258 Dave Andreychuk .75 2.00
Brian Rolston
259 Bryan Berard .75 2.00
Felix Potvin
260 Valeri Bure .75 2.00
Rob Niedermayer
261 Brian Boucher .75 2.00
Michal Handzus
262 Adam Oates .75 2.00
263 Bobby Holik .75 2.00
264 Robert Lang .75 2.00
265 Curtis Joseph .75 2.00
266 Ed Belfour .75 2.00
267 Darius Kasparaitis .75 2.00
268 Bill Guerin .75 2.00
269 Petr Sykora .75 2.00
Oleg Tverdovsky
270 Tony Amonte .75 2.00
271 P-M Bouchard RC 2.00 5.00
272 Rick Nash RC 4.00 10.00
273 Dennis Seidenberg RC 1.50 4.00
274 Jay Bouwmeester RC 2.00 5.00
275 Stanislav Chistov RC 1.50 4.00
276 Kurt Sauer RC 1.25 3.00
277 Ivan Majesky RC 1.25 3.00
278 Chuck Kobasew RC 1.25 3.00
279 Jeff Taffe RC 1.25 3.00
280 Mikael Tellqvist RC 1.25 3.00
281 Ales Hemsky RC 3.00 8.00
282 Patrick Sharp RC 1.25 3.00
283 Jordan Leopold RC 1.25 3.00
284 Dmitri Bykov RC 1.25 3.00
285 Alex Henry RC 1.25 3.00
286 Henrik Zetterberg RC 5.00 12.00
287 Alexander Frolov RC 2.00 5.00
288 Steve Eminger RC 1.25 3.00
289 Carlo Colaiacovo RC 1.50 4.00
290 Tom Koivisto RC 1.25 3.00
291 Shawn Thornton RC 1.25 3.00
292 Ron Hainsey RC 1.25 3.00
293 Martin Gerber RC 1.25 3.00
294 Adam Hall RC 1.25 3.00
295 Jason Spezza RC 4.00 10.00
296 Anton Volchenkov RC 1.25 3.00
297 Jeff Paul RC 1.25 3.00
298 Scottie Upshall RC 1.50 4.00
299 Alexander Svitov RC 1.50 4.00
300 Alexei Smirnov RC 1.25 3.00
301 Ed Belfour .30 .75
302 Ryan Bayda RC 1.25 3.00
303 Jerred Smithson RC 1.25 3.00
304 Mike Komisarek RC 3.00 8.00
305 Jarret Stoll RC 3.00 8.00
306 Radovan Somik RC 1.25 3.00
307 Rob Davison RC 1.25 3.00
308 Jason King RC 3.00 8.00
309 Tony Amonte .25 .60
310 Cam Severson RC 1.25 3.00
311 Matt Walker RC 1.25 3.00
312 Jesse Fibiger RC 1.25 3.00
313 Ray Emery RC 3.00 8.00
314 Vernon Fiddler RC 1.25 3.00
315 Alex Kovalev .25 .60
316 Marc-Andre Bergeron RC 1.25 3.00
317 Jason Elliott RC 1.25 3.00
318 Craig Andersson RC 2.50 6.00
319 Sandis Ozolinsh .10 .25
320 Ryan Miller RC 2.00 5.00
321 Chris Osgood .25 .60
322 Michael Garnett RC 1.25 3.00
323 Bobby Allen RC 1.25 3.00
324 Cristobal Huet RC 4.00 10.00
325 Curtis Murphy RC 1.25 3.00
326 Darren Haydar RC 1.25 3.00
327 Mathieu Schneider .10 .25
328 Ray Schultz RC 1.25 3.00
329 Jim Vandermeer RC 1.25 3.00
330 Miroslav Zalesak RC 1.25 3.00
331 Christian Backman RC 1.25 3.00
332 John Craighead RC 1.25 3.00
333 Doug Gilmour .25 .60
334 Dick Tarnstrom RC 1.25 3.00
335 Chad Wiseman RC 1.25 3.00
336 John Tripp RC 1.25 3.00
337 Ari Ahonen RC 1.25 3.00
338 Rickard Wallin RC 1.25 3.00
339 Jonathan Hedstrom RC 1.25 3.00
340 Daniel Briere .10 .25
341 Paul Manning RC 1.25 3.00
342 Igor Radulov RC 1.25 3.00
343 Tomas Malec RC 1.25 3.00
344 Sean McMorrow RC 1.25 3.00
345 Dany Sabourin RC 1.25 3.00
346 Steve Thomas .10 .25
347 Shaone Morrisonn RC 1.25 3.00
348 Brad DeFauw RC 1.25 3.00
349 Michael Leighton RC 2.00 5.00
350 Pascal Leclaire RC 1.50 4.00
351 Chris Schmidt RC 1.25 3.00
352 Stephane Veilleux RC 1.25 3.00
353 Jim Fahey RC 1.25 3.00
354 Konstantin Koltsov RC 1.50 4.00
355 Cody Rudkowsky RC 1.25 3.00
356 Anson Carter .25 .60
357 Francois Beauchemin RC 1.25 3.00
358 Patrick Boileau RC 1.25 3.00
359 Sylvain Blouin RC 1.25 3.00
360 Eric Bertrand RC 1.25 3.00
361 Jamie Hodson RC 1.25 3.00
362 Curtis Sanford RC 1.50 4.00
363 Ryan Kraft RC 1.25 3.00
364 Owen Nolan .25 .60
365 Niko Dimitrakos RC 1.25 3.00
366 Simon Gamache RC 1.25 3.00
367 Doug Janik RC 1.25 3.00
368 Tomas Kurka RC 1.25 3.00
369 Josh Harding RC 10.00 25.00
370 Radoslav Hecl RC 1.25 3.00
371 Kris Vernarsky RC 1.25 3.00
372 Steve Ott RC 2.50 6.00
373 Frederic Cloutier RC 1.25 3.00
374 Eric Godard RC 1.25 3.00
375 Kari Haakana RC 1.25 3.00
376 Tomi Pettinen RC 1.25 3.00
377 Brooks Orpik RC 1.25 3.00
378 Lynn Loyns RC 1.25 3.00
379 Radim Vrbata .10 .25
380 Fernando Pisani RC 1.25 3.00
381 Alexei Semenov RC 1.25 3.00
382 Burke Henry RC 1.25 3.00
383 Tim Thomas RC 1.25 3.00
384 Mike Siklenka RC 3.00 8.00
385 Lasse Pirjeta RC 1.25 3.00
386 Tomas Zizka RC 1.25 3.00
387 Tomas Surovy RC 1.25 3.00
388 Paul Gaustad RC 1.25 3.00
389 Martin Samuelsson RC 1.25 3.00
390 Matt Henderson RC 1.25 3.00
391 Mike Dunham .25 .60
392 Levente Szuper RC 1.25 3.00
393 Jared Aulin RC 1.25 3.00
394 Brandon Reid RC 1.25 3.00
395 Mike Cammalleri RC 2.00 5.00
396 Ian MacNeil RC 1.25 3.00
397 Brad Isbister .10 .25
398 Garnet Exelby RC 1.25 3.00
399 Jason Bacashihua RC 3.00 8.00
400 Sami Kapanen .10 .25

2002-03 BAP Memorabilia Emerald

EMERALD PRINT RUN 10 SER.#'d SETS
EMERALD NOT PRICED DUE TO SCARCITY

2002-03 BAP Memorabilia Ruby

*STARS: 2.5X TO 6X BASIC CARD
*SP's: .75X TO 2X
*ROOKIES: .5X TO 1.25 X
RUBY PRINT RUN 200 SER.#'d SETS

2002-03 BAP Memorabilia Sapphire

*STARS: 4X TO 10X BASIC CARDS
*SP's: 1.25X TO 3X
*ROOKIES: .75X TO 2X
SAPPHIRE PRINT RUN 100 SER.#'d SETS

2002-03 BAP Memorabilia All-Star Jerseys

This 60-card set featured swatches of all-star game-used jerseys. Each card was limited to just 90 copies each.

*MULT.COLOR: 1X TO 1.5X HI
STATED PRINT RUN 90 SETS
ASJ1 Daniel Alfredsson 6.00 15.00
ASJ2 Tony Amonte 6.00 15.00
ASJ3 Ed Belfour 6.00 15.00
ASJ4 Rob Blake 6.00 15.00
ASJ5 Peter Bondra 6.00 15.00
ASJ6 Martin Brodeur 12.50 30.00
ASJ7 Pavel Bure 6.00 15.00
ASJ8 Chris Chelios 6.00 15.00
ASJ9 Eric Daze 6.00 15.00
ASJ10 Pavol Demitra 6.00 15.00
ASJ11 Patrik Elias 6.00 15.00
ASJ12 Sergei Fedorov 10.00 25.00
ASJ13 Theo Fleury 6.00 15.00
ASJ14 Peter Forsberg 12.50 30.00
ASJ15 Simon Gagne 6.00 15.00
ASJ16 Bill Guerin 6.00 15.00
ASJ17 Dominik Hasek 12.50 30.00
ASJ18 Milan Hejduk 6.00 15.00
ASJ19 Brett Hull 12.50 30.00
ASJ20 Jarome Iginla 8.00 20.00
ASJ21 Arturs Irbe 6.00 15.00
ASJ22 Jaromir Jagr 12.50 30.00
ASJ23 Curtis Joseph 6.00 15.00
ASJ24 Ed Jovanovski 6.00 15.00
ASJ25 Paul Kariya 6.00 15.00
ASJ26 Nikolai Khabibulin 6.00 15.00
ASJ27 Saku Koivu 6.00 15.00
ASJ28 Alexei Kovalev 6.00 15.00
ASJ29 John LeClair 6.00 15.00
ASJ30 Brian Leetch 6.00 15.00
ASJ31 Mario Lemieux 15.00 40.00
ASJ32 Nicklas Lidstrom 6.00 15.00
ASJ33 Eric Lindros 6.00 15.00
ASJ34 Al MacInnis 6.00 15.00
ASJ35 Mark Messier 6.00 15.00
ASJ36 Mike Modano 8.00 20.00
ASJ37 Alexander Mogilny 6.00 15.00
ASJ38 Evgeni Nabokov 6.00 15.00
ASJ39 Markus Naslund 6.00 15.00
ASJ40 Scott Niedermayer 6.00 15.00
ASJ41 Owen Nolan 6.00 15.00
ASJ42 Felix Potvin 6.00 15.00
ASJ43 Sandis Ozolinsh 6.00 15.00
ASJ44 Zigmund Palffy 6.00 15.00
ASJ45 Chris Pronger 6.00 15.00
ASJ46 Mark Recchi 6.00 15.00
ASJ47 Mike Richter 6.00 15.00
ASJ48 Luc Robitaille 6.00 15.00
ASJ49 Jeremy Roenick 8.00 20.00
ASJ50 Patrick Roy 20.00 50.00
ASJ51 Joe Sakic 12.50 30.00
ASJ52 Teemu Selanne 6.00 15.00
ASJ53 Brendan Shanahan 6.00 15.00
ASJ54 Mats Sundin 6.00 15.00
ASJ55 Jose Theodore 8.00 20.00
ASJ56 Joe Thornton 8.00 20.00
ASJ57 Keith Tkachuk 6.00 15.00
ASJ58 Doug Weight 6.00 15.00
ASJ59 Alexei Yashin 6.00 15.00
ASJ60 Steve Yzerman 15.00 40.00

2002-03 BAP Memorabilia All-Star Emblems

PRINT RUN 10 SETS
EMBLEMS NOT PRICED DUE TO SCARCITY
ASE1 Martin Brodeur
ASE2 Pavel Bure
ASE3 Sergei Fedorov
ASE4 Peter Forsberg
ASE5 Dominik Hasek
ASE6 Brett Hull
ASE7 Jarome Iginla
ASE8 Jaromir Jagr
ASE9 Curtis Joseph
ASE10 Paul Kariya
ASE11 Brian Leetch
ASE12 Mario Lemieux
ASE13 Nicklas Lidstrom
ASE14 Eric Lindros
ASE15 Mark Messier
ASE16 Mike Modano
ASE17 Owen Nolan
ASE18 Luc Robitaille
ASE19 Patrick Roy
ASE20 Joe Sakic
ASE21 Teemu Selanne
ASE22 Brendan Shanahan
ASE23 Mats Sundin
ASE24 Jose Theodore
ASE25 Steve Yzerman

2002-03 BAP Memorabilia All-Star Numbers

PRINT RUN 10 SETS
NUMBERS NOT PRICED DUE TO SCARCITY
ASN1 Martin Brodeur
ASN2 Pavel Bure
ASN3 Sergei Fedorov
ASN4 Peter Forsberg
ASN5 Dominik Hasek
ASN6 Brett Hull
ASN7 Jarome Iginla
ASN8 Jaromir Jagr
ASN9 Curtis Joseph
ASN10 Paul Kariya
ASN11 Brian Leetch
ASN12 Mario Lemieux
ASN13 Nicklas Lidstrom
ASN14 Eric Lindros
ASN15 Mark Messier
ASN16 Mike Modano
ASN17 Owen Nolan
ASN18 Luc Robitaille
ASN19 Patrick Roy
ASN20 Joe Sakic
ASN21 Teemu Selanne
ASN22 Brendan Shanahan
ASN23 Mats Sundin
ASN24 Jose Theodore
ASN25 Steve Yzerman

2002-03 BAP Memorabilia All-Star Starting Lineup

This 12-card set featured swatches of all-star game jerseys and was limited to just 40 copies each.

*MULT.COLOR: 1X TO 1.5X HI
STATED PRINT RUN 40 SETS
AS1 Patrick Roy 60.00 150.00
AS2 Chris Pronger 20.00 50.00
AS3 Rob Blake 20.00 50.00

AS4 Vincent Damphousse 20.00 50.00
AS5 Owen Nolan 20.00 50.00
AS6 Brendan Shanahan 20.00 50.00
AS7 Dominik Hasek 30.00 80.00
AS8 Nicklas Lidstrom 20.00 50.00
AS9 Sandis Ozolinsh 20.00 50.00
AS10 Sergei Fedorov 25.00 60.00
AS11 Jaromir Jagr 30.00 80.00
AS12 Teemu Selanne 20.00 50.00

2002-03 BAP Memorabilia All-Star Teammates

STATED PRINT RUN 75 SETS
AST1 Sergei Fedorov 12.50 30.00
Teemu Selanne
AST2 Curtis Joseph 12.50 30.00
Jeremy Roenick
AST3 Patrick Roy 25.00 60.00
Mark Messier
AST4 M.Lemieux/M.Messier 30.00 80.00
AST5 Brendan Shanahan 12.50 30.00
Jaromir Jagr
AST6 Alexander Mogilny 12.50 30.00
Paul Kariya
AST7 S.Yzerman/O.Nolan 25.00 60.00
AST8 Theo Fleury 12.50 30.00
Mats Sundin
AST9 Martin Brodeur 25.00 60.00
Dominik Hasek
AST10 Pavel Bure 12.50 30.00
Peter Forsberg
AST11 Jaromir Jagr 12.50 30.00
Dominik Hasek
AST12 E.Lindros/M.Modano 12.50 30.00
AST13 Eric Lindros 12.50 30.00
Keith Tkachuk
AST14 Peter Forsberg 15.00 40.00
Dominik Hasek
AST15 Alexei Yashin 12.50 30.00
Teemu Selanne
AST16 Jaromir Jagr 12.50 30.00
Mats Sundin
AST17 S.Yzerman/J.Roenick 20.00 50.00
AST18 Martin Brodeur 25.00 60.00
Curtis Joseph
AST19 Chris Pronger 12.50 30.00
Tony Amonte
AST20 Eric Lindros 20.00 50.00
Mark Messier
AST21 Joe Sakic 12.50 30.00
Bill Guerin
AST22 M.Lemieux/P.Roy 30.00 80.00
AST23 Evgeni Nabokov 12.50 30.00
Dominik Hasek
AST24 Peter Forsberg 20.00 50.00
Pavel Bure
AST25 P.Kariya/M.Brodeur 20.00 50.00
AST26 Jose Theodore 30.00 80.00
Patrick Roy
AST27 Brendan Shanahan 12.50 30.00
Owen Nolan
AST28 J.Iginla/M.Lemieux 25.00 60.00
AST29 Jaromir Jagr 12.50 30.00
Nicklas Lidstrom
AST30 Teemu Selanne 12.50 30.00
Sergei Fedorov

2002-03 BAP Memorabilia All-Star Triple Jerseys

Limited to just 50 copies, this 20-card set featured triple swatches of jerseys from three different all-star games.

STATED PRINT RUN 50 SETS
ASTJ1 Rob Blake 12.50 30.00
ASTJ2 Martin Brodeur 30.00 80.00
ASTJ3 Pavel Bure 12.50 30.00
ASTJ4 Peter Forsberg 30.00 80.00
ASTJ5 Dominik Hasek 15.00 40.00
ASTJ6 Jaromir Jagr 15.00 40.00
ASTJ7 Paul Kariya 12.50 30.00
ASTJ8 John LeClair 12.50 30.00
ASTJ9 Brian Leetch 12.50 30.00
ASTJ10 Mario Lemieux 60.00 150.00
ASTJ11 Nicklas Lidstrom 12.50 30.00
ASTJ12 Eric Lindros 12.50 30.00
ASTJ13 Al MacInnis 12.50 30.00
ASTJ14 Mark Messier 25.00 60.00
ASTJ15 Mike Modano 15.00 40.00
ASTJ16 Owen Nolan 12.50 30.00
ASTJ17 Patrick Roy 50.00 125.00
ASTJ18 Teemu Selanne 12.50 30.00
ASTJ19 Brendan Shanahan 12.50 30.00
ASTJ20 Mats Sundin 12.50 30.00

2002-03 BAP Memorabilia Draft Redemptions

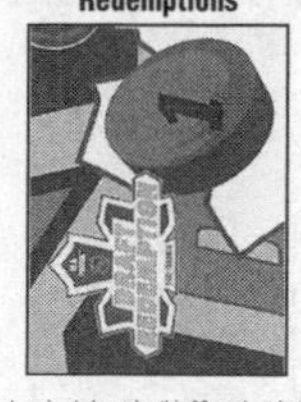

Inserted randomly in packs, this 30-card set featured cards representing the top thirty draft picks in 2002. Each card was redeemable for the player it represented once that player made his NHL debut. Collectors had six months to redeem the cards once the player was available. The redemption cards themselves were hand-numbered out of 100.

PRINT RUN 100 SER.#'d SETS
EXPIRED CARD PRINT RUNS BELOW
1 Rick Nash/67 60.00 120.00
2 Kari Lehtonen/64 40.00 80.00
3 Jay Bouwmeester/63 40.00 80.00
Expired 4/20/2003
4 Joni Pitkanen/68 25.00 60.00
Expired 4/9/2004
5 Ryan Whitney EXCH 15.00 40.00
6 Scottie Upshall/52 25.00 60.00
Expired 4/20/2003
7 Joffrey Lupul/56 30.00 60.00
Expired 4/8/2004
8 P-M Bouchard/50 25.00 60.00
Expired 4/20/2003
9 Petr Taticek 8.00 20.00
10 Eric Nystrom EXCH 6.00 15.00
11 Keith Ballard EXCH 5.00 15.00
12 Steve Eminger/51 15.00 40.00
Expired 4/20/2003
13 Alexander Semin/45 30.00 60.00
Expired 4/14/2004
14 Chris Higgins/61 25.00 60.00
Expired 4/11/2004
15 Edmonton Oilers 12.50 30.00
16 Jakub Klepis EXCH 8.00 20.00
17 Boyd Gordon/54 12.00 30.00
Expired 4/9/2004
18 Denis Grebeshkov 10.00 25.00
Expired 8/28/2004
19 Phoenix Coyotes 8.00 20.00
20 Daniel Paille 20.00 50.00
21 Anton Babchuk 10.00 25.00
Expired 7/8/2004
22 Sean Bergenheim/45 10.00 25.00
Expired 4/9/2004
23 Ben Eager 10.00 25.00
24 Alexander Steen 20.00 50.00
25 Cam Ward EXCH 15.00 40.00
26 Dallas Stars 8.00 20.00
27 San Jose Sharks 8.00 20.00
28 Colorado Avalanche 8.00 20.00
29 Hannu Toivonen EXCH 15.00 40.00
30 Jim Slater EXCH 6.00 15.00

2002-03 BAP Memorabilia Franchise Players

*MULT.COLOR: 1X TO 1.5X HI
STATED PRINT RUN 40 SETS
FP1 Paul Kariya 10.00 25.00
FP2 Ilya Kovalchuk 12.50 30.00
FP3 Joe Thornton 15.00 40.00
FP4 Miroslav Satan 10.00 25.00
FP5 Jarome Iginla 12.50 30.00
FP6 Ron Francis 10.00 25.00
FP7 Eric Daze 10.00 25.00
FP8 Patrick Roy 20.00 50.00
FP9 Rostislav Klesla 10.00 25.00
FP10 Mike Modano 12.50 30.00
FP11 Steve Yzerman 20.00 50.00
FP12 Mike Comrie 10.00 25.00
FP13 Roberto Luongo 12.50 30.00
FP14 Zigmund Palffy 10.00 25.00
FP15 Marian Gaborik 15.00 40.00
FP16 Jose Theodore 12.50 30.00
FP17 Scott Hartnell 10.00 25.00
FP18 Martin Brodeur 20.00 50.00
FP19 Alexei Yashin 10.00 25.00
FP20 Pavel Bure 10.00 25.00
FP21 Marian Hossa 10.00 25.00
FP22 Simon Gagne 10.00 25.00
FP23 Daniel Briere 10.00 25.00
FP24 Mario Lemieux 25.00 60.00
FP25 Chris Pronger 10.00 25.00
FP26 Owen Nolan 10.00 25.00
FP27 Nikolai Khabibulin 10.00 25.00
FP28 Mats Sundin 10.00 25.00
FP29 Markus Naslund 10.00 25.00
FP30 Jaromir Jagr 12.50 30.00

2002-03 BAP Memorabilia Future of the Game

*MULT.COLOR: 1X TO 1.5X HI
STATED PRINT RUN 30 SETS
FG1 Pavel Datsyuk 15.00 40.00
FG2 Dan Blackburn 15.00 40.00

FG3 Ilya Kovalchuk 20.00 50.00
FG4 Roberto Luongo 20.00 50.00
FG5 Dany Heatley 20.00 50.00
FG6 Jose Theodore 20.00 50.00
FG7 Mike Comrie 15.00 40.00
FG8 Marian Gaborik 25.00 60.00
FG9 Simon Gagne 15.00 40.00
FG10 Joe Thornton 25.00 60.00
FG11 Trent Hunter 15.00 40.00
FG12 Martin Havlat 15.00 40.00
FG13 Scott Hartnell 15.00 40.00
FG14 Kristian Huselius 15.00 40.00
FG15 Rick DiPietro 15.00 40.00
FG16 Kyle Calder 15.00 40.00
FG17 Alex Tanguay 15.00 40.00
FG18 Brad Richards 15.00 40.00
FG19 Rostislav Klesla 15.00 40.00
FG20 Justin Williams 15.00 40.00
FG21 Jason Spezza 30.00 80.00
FG22 Jay Bouwmeester 15.00 40.00

2002-03 BAP Memorabilia He Shoots-He Scores Points

COMMON CARD .10 .25
ONE PER PACK
RED.PROGRAM EXPIRED
1 Mike Modano 1 pt. .10 .25
2 Jeremy Roenick 1 pt. .10 .25
3 Owen Nolan 1 pt. .10 .25
4 Chris Pronger 1 pt. .10 .25
5 Ron Francis 1 pt. .10 .25
6 Jose Theodore 1 pt. .10 .25
7 Brendan Shanahan 1 pt. .10 .25
8 Dany Heatley 1 pt. .10 .25
9 Paul Kariya 2 pts. .10 .25
10 Pavel Bure 2 pts. .10 .25
11 Peter Forsberg 2 pts. .10 .25
12 Joe Sakic 2 pts. .10 .25
13 Dominik Hasek 2 pts. .10 .25
14 Martin Brodeur 2 pts. .10 .25
15 Eric Lindros 2 pts. .10 .25
16 Ilya Kovalchuk 2 pts. .10 .25
17 Jaromir Jagr 2 pts. .10 .25
18 Patrick Roy 3 pts. .10 .25
19 Mario Lemieux 3 pts. .10 .25
20 Steve Yzerman 3 pts. .10 .25

2002-03 BAP Memorabilia He Shoots-He Scores Prizes

PRINT RUN 20 SER.#'d SETS
NOT PRICED DUE TO SCARCITY
1 Steve Yzerman
2 Mario Lemieux
3 Patrick Roy
4 Jaromir Jagr
5 Ilya Kovalchuk
6 Eric Lindros
7 Martin Brodeur
8 Dominik Hasek
9 Joe Sakic
10 Peter Forsberg
11 Pavel Bure
12 Paul Kariya
13 Dany Heatley
14 Brendan Shanahan
15 Jose Theodore
16 Ron Francis
17 Chris Pronger
18 Owen Nolan
19 Jeremy Roenick
20 Mike Modano
21 Roberto Luongo
22 Marian Gaborik
23 Todd Bertuzzi
24 Pavel Datsyuk
25 Jarome Iginla
26 Mats Sundin
27 Mark Messier
28 Sergei Fedorov
29 Nicklas Lidstrom
30 Teemu Selanne

2002-03 BAP Memorabilia Magnificent Inserts

This 10-card set featured game-used equipment from the career of Mario Lemieux. Cards MI1-MI5 had a print run of 40 copies each and cards MI6-MI10 were limited to just 10 copies each. Cards MI6-MI10 are not priced due to scarcity.

MI1-MI5 PRINT RUN 40 SETS
MI6-MI10 PRINT RUN 10 SETS
MI6-MI10 NOT PRICED DUE TO SCARCITY
MI1 2000-01 Jersey 30.00 80.00
MI2 1985-86 Jersey 30.00 80.00
MI3 2002 All-Star Jersey 30.00 80.00
MI4 1987 Canada Cup Jersey 30.00 80.00
MI5 Dual Jersey 50.00 125.00
MI6 Number
MI7 Emblem
MI8 Triple Jersey
MI9 Quad Jersey
MI10 Complete Package

2002-03 BAP Memorabilia Magnificent Inserts Autographs

This 10-card set paralleled the base Magnificent Inserts but carried certified autographs and each card was hand numbered. Cards MI1-MI5 were serial-numbered to 15 each and cards MI6-MI10 were serial numbered out of 5.

MI1-MI5 PRINT RUN 15 SER.#'d SETS
MI6-MI10 PRINT RUN 5 SER.#'d SETS
NOT PRICED DUE TO SCARCITY

2002-03 BAP Memorabilia Mini Stanley Cups

Inserted one per hobby box, these miniature Stanley Cup replicas featured a player picture from a cup winning team on the front.

ONE PER HOBBY BOX
1 Johnny Bower 8.00 20.00
2 Tim Horton 12.00 30.00
3 Jean Beliveau 15.00 40.00
4 Lorne Worsley 8.00 20.00
5 Terry Sawchuk 12.00 30.00
6 Serge Savard 8.00 20.00
7 Henri Richard 8.00 20.00
8 Phil Esposito 8.00 20.00
9 Frank Mahovlich 8.00 20.00
10 Gerry Cheevers 8.00 20.00
11 Yvan Cournoyer 8.00 20.00
12 Bobby Clarke 8.00 20.00
13 Bernie Parent 8.00 20.00
14 Steve Shutt 8.00 20.00
15 Larry Robinson 8.00 20.00
16 Guy Lafleur 15.00 40.00
17 Guy Lapointe 8.00 20.00
18 Bryan Trottier 8.00 20.00
19 Mike Bossy 8.00 20.00
20 Denis Potvin 8.00 20.00
21 Bob Nystrom 8.00 20.00
22 Mark Messier 8.00 20.00
23 Andy Moog 8.00 20.00
24 Patrick Roy 20.00 50.00
25 Jari Kurri 15.00 40.00
26 Grant Fuhr 8.00 20.00
27 Doug Gilmour 8.00 20.00
28 Adam Graves 8.00 20.00
29 Mario Lemieux 20.00 50.00
30 Jaromir Jagr 15.00 40.00
31 John LeClair 8.00 20.00
32 Brian Leetch 8.00 20.00
33 Martin Brodeur 15.00 40.00
34 Peter Forsberg 12.00 30.00
35 Steve Yzerman 15.00 40.00
36 Nicklas Lidstrom 12.00 30.00
37 Mike Modano 12.00 30.00
38 Scott Stevens 8.00 20.00
39 Joe Sakic 12.00 30.00
40 Dominik Hasek 12.00 30.00

2002-03 BAP Memorabilia Stanley Cup Champions

This 15-card set featured swatches of game-worn jersey from the 2002 Stanley Cup Champion Detroit Red Wings. Cards were limited to just 40 copies each.

STATED PRINT RUN 40 SETS
SCC1 Jiri Fischer 15.00 40.00
SCC2 Mathieu Dandenault 15.00 40.00
SCC3 Chris Chelios 15.00 40.00
SCC4 Dominik Hasek 15.00 40.00
SCC5 Steve Yzerman 40.00 100.00
SCC6 Brendan Shanahan 15.00 40.00
SCC7 Luc Robitaille 15.00 40.00
SCC8 Nicklas Lidstrom 15.00 40.00
SCC9 Manny Legace 30.00 80.00
SCC10 Sergei Fedorov 30.00 80.00
SCC11 Darren McCarty 15.00 40.00
SCC12 Jason Williams 15.00 40.00
SCC13 Pavel Datsyuk 15.00 40.00
SCC14 Tomas Holmstrom 15.00 40.00
SCC15 Brett Hull 25.00 60.00

2002-03 BAP Memorabilia Stanley Cup Playoffs

This 32-card set featured swatches of game-worn jersey. Print runs are listed below.

*MULT.COLOR: 1X TO 1.5X HI
PRINT RUNS LISTED BELOW
LOWER PRINT RUNS NOT PRICED
DUE TO SCARCITY
SC1 Roman Cechmanek/90 8.00 20.00
SC2 Patrick Lalime/90 8.00 20.00
SC3 Gary Roberts/90 8.00 20.00
SC4 Alexei Yashin/90 8.00 20.00
SC5 Joe Thornton/90 12.50 30.00
SC6 Jose Theodore/90 15.00 40.00
SC7 Ron Francis/90 12.50 30.00
SC8 Martin Brodeur/90 20.00 50.00
SC9 Owen Nolan/90 8.00 20.00
SC10 Sean Burke/90 8.00 20.00
SC11 Felix Potvin/90 8.00 20.00
SC12 Peter Forsberg/90 15.00 40.00
SC13 Todd Bertuzzi/90 8.00 20.00
SC14 Steve Yzerman/90 20.00 50.00
SC15 Eric Daze/90 8.00 20.00
SC16 Brent Johnson/90 8.00 20.00
SC17 Teemu Selanne/60 8.00 20.00
SC18 Chris Drury/60 8.00 20.00
SC19 Alexander Mogilny/60 8.00 20.00
SC20 Daniel Alfredsson/60 8.00 20.00
SC21 Sergei Fedorov/60 15.00 40.00
SC22 Keith Tkachuk/60 12.00 30.00
SC23 Saku Koivu/60 8.00 20.00
SC24 Jeff O'Neill/60 8.00 20.00
SC25 Curtis Joseph/40 15.00 40.00
SC26 Arturs Irbe/40 10.00 25.00
SC27 Dominik Hasek/40 30.00 80.00
SC28 Patrick Roy/40 40.00 100.00
SC29 Ron Francis/30 25.00 60.00
SC30 Dominik Hasek/30 30.00 80.00
SC31 Steve Yzerman/10
SC32 Nicklas Lidstrom
Conn Smythe Winner/10

2002-03 BAP Memorabilia Teammates

STATED PRINT RUN 70 SETS
TM1 Dominik Hasek 25.00 60.00
Steve Yzerman
TM2 Sergei Fedorov 15.00 40.00
Brendan Shanahan
TM3 Luc Robitaille 12.50 30.00
Brett Hull
TM4 Joe Sakic 30.00 80.00
Peter Forsberg
TM5 Rob Blake 30.00 80.00
Patrick Roy
TM6 Pavel Bure 12.50 30.00
Eric Lindros
TM7 Brian Leetch 12.50 30.00
Mark Messier
TM8 Mats Sundin 12.50 30.00
Curtis Joseph
TM9 Jeremy Roenick 12.50 30.00
Roman Cechmanek
TM10 Mark Recchi 12.50 30.00
Simon Gagne
TM11 Jaromir Jagr 12.50 30.00
Peter Bondra
TM12 Jose Theodore 12.50 30.00
Saku Koivu
TM13 Zigmund Palffy 12.50 30.00
Felix Potvin
TM14 Martin Brodeur 12.50 30.00
Patrik Elias
TM15 Mario Lemieux 25.00 60.00
Alexei Kovalev
TM16 Chris Pronger 12.50 30.00
Al MacInnis
TM17 Doug Weight 12.50 30.00
Keith Tkachuk
TM16 Teemu Selanne 12.50 30.00
Owen Nolan
TM19 Ed Jovanovski 12.50 30.00
Markus Naslund
TM20 Jarome Iginla 12.50 30.00
Roman Turek

2003-04 BAP Memorabilia

This 250-card set came in packs as a 200-card base set including 100 veteran skaters, a 70-card Between the Pipes subset, and 30 rookies that were short-printed. Cards 201-250 were available via an online offer only for $29 US.

COMP. SET w/o UPDATE (200) 75.00 150.00
COMP.SET w/o SP's (170) 25.00 50.00
201-250 AVAIL.VIA ONLINE OFFER ONLY
1 Al MacInnis .20 .50
2 Alexei Morozov .05 .20
3 Ales Hemsky .20 .50
4 Ales Kotalik .05 .20
5 Alex Kovalev .20 .50
6 Alexander Frolov .05 .20
7 Alexander Mogilny .20 .50
8 Alexei Yashin .05 .20
9 Alexei Zhamnov .05 .20
10 Anson Carter .20 .50
11 Barret Jackman .20 .50
12 Bill Guerin .20 .50
13 Brad Richards .20 .50
14 Brad Stuart .05 .20
15 Brendan Shanahan .25 .60
16 Chris Drury .20 .50
17 Brett Hull .30 .75
18 Daniel Alfredsson .20 .50
19 Daniel Briere .05 .20
20 Dany Heatley .30 .75
21 David Legwand .20 .50
22 Daymond Langkow .20 .50
23 Derian Hatcher .05 .20
24 Doug Weight .20 .50
25 Ed Jovanovski .20 .50
26 Eric Daze .20 .50
27 Eric Lindros .25 .60
28 Geoff Sanderson .05 .20
29 Glen Murray .05 .20
30 Henrik Zetterberg .25 .60
31 Ilya Kovalchuk .30 .75
32 Jamie Langenbrunner .05 .20
33 Jarome Iginla .30 .75
34 Jaromir Jagr .40 1.00
35 Jason Allison .05 .20
36 Jason Spezza .25 .60
37 Jay Bouwmeester .05 .20
38 Jeff O'Neill .05 .20
39 Jere Lehtinen .20 .50
40 Jeremy Roenick .30 .75
41 Joe Sakic .50 1.25
42 Joe Thornton .40 1.00
43 John LeClair .25 .60
44 Keith Tkachuk .25 .60
45 Kristian Huselius .05 .20
46 Marian Gaborik .50 1.25
47 Marian Hossa .25 .60
48 Mario Lemieux 1.50 4.00
49 Mark Messier .25 .60
50 Markus Naslund .25 .60
51 Martin Havlat .20 .50
52 Martin St. Louis .20 .50
53 Mats Sundin .25 .60
54 Michael Peca .05 .20
55 Mike Comrie .20 .50
56 Mike Johnson .05 .20
57 Mike Komisarek .05 .20
58 Mike Modano .40 1.00
59 Milan Hejduk .25 .60
60 Miroslav Satan .20 .50
61 Nicklas Lidstrom .25 .60
62 Olli Jokinen .20 .50
63 Owen Nolan .20 .50
64 Pascal Dupuis .05 .20
65 Patrick Marleau .20 .50
66 Patrik Elias .20 .50
67 Patrik Stefan .05 .20
68 Paul Kariya .25 .60
69 Pavel Bure .25 .60
70 Pavol Demitra .05 .20
71 Peter Bondra .20 .50
72 Peter Forsberg .60 1.50
73 Petr Sykora .05 .20
74 Ray Whitney .05 .20
75 Richard Zednik .05 .20
76 Rick Nash .30 .75
77 Rob Blake .20 .50
78 Ron Francis .20 .50
79 Ryan Smyth .20 .50
80 Saku Koivu .25 .60
81 Sandis Ozolinsh .05 .20
82 Scott Hartnell .05 .20
83 Scott Niedermayer .05 .20
84 Scottie Upshall .05 .20
85 Sergei Fedorov .40 1.00
86 Sergei Gonchar .05 .20
87 Sergei Samsonov .20 .50
88 Sergei Zubov .05 .20
89 Simon Gagne .25 .60
90 Zdeno Chara .05 .20
91 Chuck Kobasew .05 .20
92 Steve Yzerman 1.25 3.00
93 Teemu Selanne .25 .60
94 Todd Bertuzzi .25 .60
95 Tony Amonte .20 .50
96 Vaclav Prospal .05 .20
97 Vincent Lecavalier .25 .60
98 Slava Kozlov .05 .20
99 Sylvester Flis .50 1.25
100 Zigmund Palffy .20 .50
101 Alex Auld .20 .50
102 Andrew Raycroft .20 .50
103 Ari Ahonen .20 .50
104 Brent Johnson .20 .50
105 Brian Boucher .20 .50
106 Brian Finley .20 .50
107 Byron Dafoe .20 .50
108 Chris Osgood .20 .50
109 Cristobal Huet .20 .50
110 Corey Schwab .20 .50
111 Curtis Joseph .25 .60
112 Curtis Sanford .20 .50
113 Dan Blackburn .20 .50
114 Dan Cloutier .20 .50
115 David Aebischer .20 .50
116 Dwayne Roloson .20 .50
117 Ed Belfour .25 .60
118 Evgeni Nabokov .20 .50
119 Felix Potvin .25 .60
120 Fred Brathwaite .20 .50
121 Garth Snow .20 .50
122 Jani Hurme .20 .50
123 Jason Bacashihua .20 .50
124 Jean-Sebastien Giguere .20 .50
125 Jeff Hackett .20 .50
126 Jocelyn Thibault .20 .50
127 Johan Hedberg .20 .50
128 John Grahame .20 .50
129 Jose Theodore .30 .75
130 Josh Harding .20 .50
131 Jussi Markkanen .20 .50
132 Kevin Weekes .20 .50
133 Manny Fernandez .20 .50
134 Manny Legace .20 .50
135 Marc Denis .20 .50
136 Martin Biron .20 .50
137 Martin Brodeur .60 1.50
138 Martin Gerber .20 .50
139 Martin Prusek .20 .50
140 Marty Turco .20 .50
141 Mathieu Garon .20 .50
142 Maxime Ouellet .20 .50
143 Michael Leighton .20 .50
144 Miikka Kiprusoff .20 .50
145 Mika Noronen .20 .50
146 Mikael Tellqvist .20 .50
147 Mike Dunham .20 .50
148 Nikolai Khabibulin .25 .60
149 Olaf Kolzig .20 .50
150 Pascal Leclaire .20 .50
151 Pasi Nurminen .20 .50
152 Patrick Lalime .20 .50
153 Patrick Roy 1.25 3.00
154 Ray Emery .20 .50
155 Rick DiPietro .20 .50
156 Robert Esche .20 .50
157 Roberto Luongo .30 .75
158 Roman Cechmanek .20 .50
159 Roman Turek .20 .50
160 Ron Tugnutt .20 .50
161 Ryan Miller .20 .50
162 Sean Burke .20 .50
163 Sebastien Caron .20 .50
164 Sebastien Charpentier .20 .50
165 Steve Shields .20 .50
166 Tomas Vokoun .20 .50
167 Tommy Salo .20 .50
168 Trevor Kidd .20 .50
169 Vesa Toskala .20 .50
170 Zac Bierk .20 .50
171 Tuomo Ruutu RC 1.25 3.00
172 Jordin Tootoo RC 1.25 3.00
173 Joni Pitkanen RC 1.00 2.50
174 Peter Sejna RC .50 1.25
175 Dan Hamhuis RC .75 2.00
176 Eric Staal RC 2.00 5.00
177 Dan Fritsche RC .50 1.25
178 Dustin Brown RC .50 1.25
179 Christopher Higgins RC 1.00 2.50
180 Nathan Horton RC 1.25 3.00
181 Milan Michalek RC .75 2.00
182 Boyd Gordon RC .50 1.25
183 Marc-Andre Fleury RC 2.50 6.00
184 Jeffrey Lupul RC 1.00 2.50
185 David Hale RC .50 1.25
186 Sean Bergenheim RC .50 1.25
187 Tim Gleason RC .50 1.25
188 Pavel Vorobiev RC .50 1.25
189 Paul Martin RC .50 1.25
190 Marek Svatos RC .50 1.25
191 Antoine Vermette RC .50 1.25
192 Matt Stajan RC 1.25 3.00
193 Alexander Semin RC 1.25 3.00
194 Brent Burns RC .50 1.25
195 Jiri Hudler RC .75 2.00
196 Matthew Lombardi RC .50 1.25
197 Maxim Kondratiev RC .50 1.25
198 Brent Krahn RC .50 1.25
199 Antti Miettinen RC .50 1.25
200 Patrice Bergeron RC 2.00 5.00
201 Cover Card/Checklist .05 .20
202 Marek Zidlicky XRC .60 1.50
203 John-Michael Liles XRC .60 1.50
204 Ryan Malone XRC .60 1.50
205 Tom Preissing XRC .60 1.50
206 Rastislav Stana XRC .60 1.50
207 Mike Commodore .05 .20
208 Jaromir Jagr .40 1.00
209 Fredrik Sjostrom XRC .60 1.50
210 Nikolai Zherdev XRC 1.50 4.00
211 Derek Roy XRC .60 1.50
212 Marcus Nilsson .05 .20
213 Milan Michalek XRC .60 1.50
214 Tomas Plekanec XRC 1.00 2.50
215 Mark Popovic XRC .60 1.50
216 Frederic Henry XRC .60 1.50
217 Nolan Schaefer XRC .60 1.50
218 Colton Orr XRC .60 1.50
219 Mike Smith XRC 2.00 5.00
220 Cory Stillman .05 .20
221 Carl Corazzini XRC .60 1.50
222 Eric Heffler XRC .60 1.50
223 Dimitri Afanasenkov .05 .20
224 Garth Murray .05 .20
225 Matt Ellison XRC .60 1.50
226 Ville Nieminen .05 .20
227 Brooks Laich XRC .60 1.50
228 Sergei Gonchar .05 .20
229 Fedor Tyutin XRC .60 1.50
230 Ron Francis .20 .50
231 Phil Osaer XRC .60 1.50
232 Miikka Kiprusoff .20 .50
233 Michal Barinka XRC .60 1.50
234 Brad Boyes XRC .60 1.50
235 Erik Westrum XRC .60 1.50
236 Kari Lehtonen XRC 3.00 8.00
237 Chad Alban XRC .60 1.50
238 Thomas Pock XRC .60 1.50
239 Darryl Sydor .05 .20
240 Greg Mauldin XRC .60 1.50
241 Eric Perrin XRC .60 1.50
242 Michael Ryder .05 .20
243 Esa Pirnes XRC .60 1.50
244 Matt Murley XRC .60 1.50
245 Trevor Daley XRC .60 1.50
246 Libor Pivko XRC .60 1.50
247 John Pohl XRC .60 1.50
248 Seamus Kotyk XRC .60 1.50
249 Sergei Zinovjev XRC .60 1.50
250 Joe Nieuwendyk .20 .50

2003-04 BAP Memorabilia Emerald

PRINT RUN 10 SER.#'d SETS
NOT PRICED DUE TO SCARCITY

2003-04 BAP Memorabilia Gold

AVAIL.IN BAP UPD.BOXES ONLY
PRINT RUN 1 SET
NOT PRICED DUE TO SCARCITY

2003-04 BAP Memorabilia Ruby

*STARS: 2.5X TO 6X BASIC CARDS
*ROOKIES: .5X TO 1.25X
PRINT RUN 200 SER.#'d SETS

2003-04 BAP Memorabilia Sapphire

*STARS: 4X TO 10X BASE HI
*ROOKIES : .75X TO 2X
PRINT RUN 100 SER.#'d SETS

2003-04 BAP Memorabilia All-Star Complete Jerseys

STATED PRINT RUN 10 SETS
NOT PRICED DUE TO SCARCITY
ASCJ1 Peter Forsberg
ASCJ2 Paul Kariya
ASCJ3 Patrick Roy
ASCJ4 Dany Heatley
ASCJ5 Mike Modano
ASCJ6 Joe Thornton
ASCJ7 Jose Theodore
ASCJ8 Joe Sakic
ASCJ9 Martin Brodeur
ASCJ10 Steve Yzerman

2003-04 BAP Memorabilia All-Star Emblems

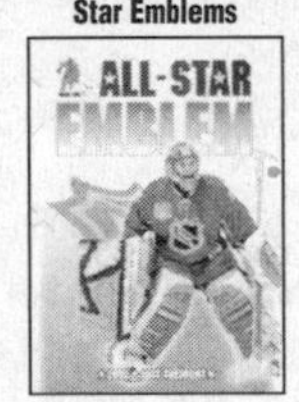

STATED PRINT RUN 10 SETS
NOT PRICED DUE TO SCARCITY
ASE1 Mike Modano
ASE2 Paul Kariya
ASE3 Nicklas Lidstrom
ASE4 Patrick Roy
ASE5 Dany Heatley
ASE6 Peter Forsberg
ASE7 Alex Kovalev
ASE8 Jaromir Jagr
ASE9 Brian Leetch
ASE10 Joe Thornton
ASE11 Brendan Shanahan
ASE12 Chris Pronger
ASE13 Jose Theodore
ASE14 Martin Brodeur
ASE15 Pavel Bure
ASE16 Joe Sakic
ASE17 Markus Naslund
ASE18 John LeClair
ASE19 Al MacInnis
ASE20 Steve Yzerman

2003-04 BAP Memorabilia All-Star Jerseys

*MULT.COLOR SWATCH: .75X TO 1.5X
STATED PRINT RUN 90 SETS
MVP CARDS PRINT RUN 10 SETS
MVP CARDS NOT PRICED DUE TO SCARCITY
ASJ1 Peter Forsberg 10.00 25.00
ASJ2 Jaromir Jagr 10.00 25.00
ASJ3 Mike Modano 8.00 20.00
ASJ4 Bill Guerin 6.00 15.00
ASJ5 Paul Kariya 6.00 15.00
ASJ6 Nicklas Lidstrom 6.00 15.00
ASJ7 Teemu Selanne 6.00 15.00
ASJ8 Patrick Roy 12.50 30.00
ASJ9 Alex Kovalev 6.00 15.00
ASJ10 Dany Heatley MVP
ASJ11 Sergei Fedorov 10.00 25.00
ASJ12 Jaromir Jagr 10.00 25.00
ASJ13 Brian Leetch 6.00 15.00
ASJ14 Joe Thornton 8.00 20.00
ASJ15 Jose Theodore 8.00 20.00
ASJ16 Brendan Shanahan 6.00 15.00
ASJ17 Patrick Roy 15.00 40.00
ASJ18 Chris Pronger 6.00 15.00
ASJ19 Nicklas Lidstrom 6.00 15.00
ASJ20 Eric Daze MVP
ASJ21 Martin Brodeur 12.50 30.00
ASJ22 Pavel Bure 6.00 15.00
ASJ23 Peter Forsberg 12.50 30.00
ASJ24 Paul Kariya 6.00 15.00
ASJ25 Brian Leetch 6.00 15.00
ASJ26 Nicklas Lidstrom 6.00 15.00
ASJ27 Markus Naslund 6.00 15.00
ASJ28 Patrick Roy 15.00 40.00
ASJ29 Joe Sakic 10.00 25.00
ASJ30 Bill Guerin MVP
ASJ31 Al MacInnis 6.00 15.00
ASJ32 Jaromir Jagr 10.00 25.00
ASJ33 John LeClair 6.00 15.00
ASJ34 Martin Brodeur 12.50 30.00
ASJ35 Mike Modano 8.00 20.00
ASJ36 Jeremy Roenick 8.00 20.00
ASJ37 Brendan Shanahan 6.00 15.00
ASJ38 Mats Sundin 6.00 15.00
ASJ39 Steve Yzerman 12.50 30.00
ASJ40 Pavel Bure MVP

2003-04 BAP Memorabilia All-Star Numbers

STATED PRINT RUN 20 SETS
NOT PRICED DUE TO SCARCITY
ASN1 Mike Modano
ASN2 Paul Kariya
ASN3 Nicklas Lidstrom
ASN4 Patrick Roy
ASN5 Dany Heatley
ASN6 Peter Forsberg
ASN7 Alex Kovalev
ASN8 Jaromir Jagr
ASN9 Brian Leetch
ASN10 Joe Thornton
ASN11 Brendan Shanahan
ASN12 Chris Pronger
ASN13 Jose Theodore
ASN14 Martin Brodeur
ASN15 Pavel Bure
ASN16 Joe Sakic
ASN17 Markus Naslund
ASN18 John LeClair
ASN19 Al MacInnis
ASN20 Steve Yzerman

2003-04 BAP Memorabilia All-Star Staring Lineup

1 Nikolai Khabibulin 8.00 20.00
2 Brian Leetch 8.00 20.00
3 Sandis Ozolinsh 8.00 20.00
4 Mario Lemieux 15.00 40.00
5 Jaromir Jagr 10.00 25.00
6 Alex Kovalev 8.00 20.00
7 Patrick Roy 15.00 40.00
8 Nicklas Lidstrom 8.00 20.00
9 Rob Blake 8.00 20.00
10 Mike Modano 10.00 25.00
11 Bill Guerin 8.00 20.00
12 Teemu Selanne 8.00 20.00

2003-04 BAP Memorabilia All-Star Teammates

STATED PRINT RUN 30 SETS
AST1 P.Forsberg/P.Roy 30.00 80.00
AST2 D.Heatley/J.Jagr 20.00 50.00
AST3 M.Modano/B.Guerin 20.00 50.00
AST4 N.Lidstrom/P.Kariya 20.00 50.00
AST5 B.Leetch/J.Thornton 25.00 60.00
AST6 J.Theodore/P.Roy 40.00 100.00
AST7 B.Shanahan/B.Leetch 20.00 50.00
AST8 M.Brodeur/P.Roy 40.00 100.00
AST9 P.Forsberg/N.Lidstrom 25.00 60.00
AST10 J.Sakic/B.Leetch 30.00 80.00

2003-04 BAP Memorabilia Brush with Greatness

This 25-card set featured artist renderings on the card fronts along with foil highlights. Foil cards were inserted at one per box. A contest entry parallel without the foil effect was also created and more plentiful. On the back of the contest cards were rules and instructions for entering a drawing for a jersey of the given player with the artist's rendering painted on the jersey. Some of the jerseys also included the player's autograph. Entry deadlines were staggered, but the last deadline was August 2004.

FOIL ODDS 1 PER BOX
COMMON CONTEST CARD .60 1.50
1 Mario Lemieux 6.00 15.00
2 Martin Brodeur 5.00 12.00
3 Marian Gaborik 4.00 10.00
4 Paul Kariya 2.00 5.00
5 Peter Forsberg 5.00 12.00
6 Jason Spezza 2.00 5.00
7 Maurice Richard 4.00 10.00
8 Jacques Plante 3.00 8.00
9 Henrik Zetterberg 2.00 5.00
10 Ed Belfour 2.00 5.00
11 Nicklas Lidstrom 2.00 5.00
12 Rick Nash 2.50 6.00
13 Bill Bariiko 2.00 5.00
14 Jean-Sebastien Giguere 2.00 5.00
15 Jose Theodore 2.00 5.00
16 Pavel Bure 2.00 5.00
17 Ilya Kovalchuk 2.50 6.00
18 Mats Sundin 2.00 5.00
19 Terry Sawchuk 3.00 8.00
20 Joe Thornton 3.00 8.00
21 Dominik Hasek 4.00 10.00
22 Joe Sakic 4.00 10.00
23 Dany Heatley 2.50 6.00
24 Steve Yzerman 5.00 12.00
25 Patrick Roy 6.00 15.00

2003-04 BAP Memorabilia Deep in the Crease

COMPLETE SET (15) 12.00 30.00
D1 Pasi Nurminen .75 2.00
Byron Dafoe
Jani Hurme
Frederic Cassivi
D2 Jocelyn Thibault .75 2.00
Michael Leighton
Craig Andersson
Steve Passmore
D3 Jose Theodore .75 2.00
Mathieu Garon
Eric Fichaud
J-F Damphousse
Oliver Michaud
D4 New Jersey Devils .75 2.00
D5 Mike Dunham .75 2.00
Dan Blackburn
Jussi Markkenen
Jason Labarbera
D6 Tomas Vokoun .75 2.00
Jan Lasek
Brian Finley
Chris Mason
D7 Jean-Sebastien Giguere .75 2.00
Martin Gerber
Ilya Bryzgalov
Gregg Naumenko
D8 Dominik Hasek 3.00 8.00
Curtis Joseph
Manny Legace
Marc Lamothe
D9 Ed Belfour 1.50 4.00
Trevor Kidd
Mikael Tellqvist
Sebastien Centomo
Jamie Hodson
D10 Dan Cloutier .75 2.00
Johan Hedberg
Alex Auld
Tyler Moss
D11 Manny Fernandez .75 2.00
Dwayne Roloson
Johan Holmqvist
Josh Harding
Frederic Cloutier
D12 Chris Osgood .75 2.00
Brent Johnson
Curtis Sanford
Reinhard Divis
Cody Rudkowsky
D13 Martin Biron .75 2.00
Mika Noronen
Ryan Miller
Tom Askey
D14 Roberto Luongo .75 2.00
Steve Shields
Simon Lajeunesse
Travis Scott
D15 Marc-Andre Fleury 2.00 5.00
Sebastien Caron
J-S Aubin
Martin Brochu

2003-04 BAP Memorabilia Draft Redemptions

Inserted randomly in packs, this 30-card set featured cards representing the top thirty draft picks in 2003. Each card was redeemable for the player it represented once that player made his NHL debut. Collectors had six months to redeem the cards once the player was

available. The redemption cards themselves were hand-numbered out of 100.

STATED PRINT RUN 100 SETS
EXPIRED CARD PRINT RUNS BELOW
1 Marc-Andre Fleury/56 75.00 150.00
Expired 6/11/2004
2 Eric Staal/51 40.00 100.00
Expired 6/11/2004
3 Nathan Horton/48 40.00 80.00
Expired 6/11/2004
4 Nikolai Zherdev/52 25.00 60.00
Expired 6/11/2004
5 Thomas Vanek EXCH 25.00 60.00
6 Milan Michalek/41 25.00 60.00
Expired 6/11/2004
7 Ryan Suter EXCH 15.00 40.00
8 Braydon Coburn EXCH 8.00 20.00
9 Dion Phaneuf EXCH 40.00 80.00
10 Andrei Kostitsyn EXCH 15.00 40.00
11 Jeff Carter EXCH 20.00 50.00
12 New York Rangers 12.50 30.00
13 Dustin Brown/43 12.50 30.00
Expired 6/11/2004
14 Brent Seabrook EXCH 10.00 25.00
15 Robert Nilsson EXCH 12.50 30.00
16 Steve Bernier EXCH 15.00 40.00
17 Zach Parise EXCH 25.00 60.00
18 Eric Fehr EXCH 15.00 40.00
19 Ryan Getzlaf EXCH 50.00 100.00
20 Brent Burns/46 25.00 60.00
Expired 6/11/2004
21 Mark Stuart EXCH 8.00 20.00
22 Edmonton Oilers 15.00 40.00
23 Ryan Kesler/40 25.00 60.00
24 Mike Richards EXCH 15.00 40.00
25 Anthony Stewart EXCH 12.50 30.00
26 Los Angeles Kings 12.50 30.00
27 Jeff Tambellini EXCH 8.00 20.00
28 Corey Perry EXCH 15.00 40.00
29 Patrick Eaves EXCH 12.00 30.00
30 St. Louis Blues 8.00 20.00

2003-04 BAP Memorabilia Future of the Game

STATED PRINT RUN 30 SETS
FG1 Scottie Upshall 10.00 25.00
FG2 Ray Emery 12.00 30.00
FG3 Rick Nash 25.00 60.00
FG4 Stanislav Chistov 10.00 25.00
FG5 Ryan Miller 15.00 40.00
FG6 Henrik Zetterberg 20.00 50.00
FG7 Alexander Frolov 10.00 25.00
FG8 Barret Jackman 10.00 25.00
FG9 Brandon Reid 10.00 25.00
FG10 Mike Komisarek 10.00 25.00
FG11 Alexei Smirnov 10.00 25.00
FG12 Steve Ott 12.00 30.00
FG13 Mike Cammalleri 10.00 25.00
FG14 Jason Spezza 25.00 60.00
FG15 Carlo Colaiacovo 10.00 25.00
FG16 Jared Aulin 10.00 25.00
FG17 Ales Hemsky 12.00 30.00
FG18 Marc-Andre Fleury 30.00 80.00
FG19 Eric Staal 25.00 60.00
FG20 Dustin Brown 10.00 25.00

2003-04 BAP Memorabilia Future Wave

STATED PRINT RUN 60 SETS
FW1 Marc-Andre Fleury 30.00 80.00
FW2 Ray Emery 12.00 30.00
FW3 David Aebischer 12.00 30.00
FW4 Rick DiPietro 12.00 30.00
FW5 Dan Blackburn 8.00 20.00
FW6 Mathieu Garon 8.00 20.00
FW7 Ryan Miller 15.00 40.00
FW8 Brian Finley 8.00 20.00
FW9 Alex Auld 8.00 20.00
FW10 Mika Noronen 8.00 20.00
FW11 Mikael Tellqvist 12.00 30.00
FW12 Andrew Raycroft 12.00 30.00

2003-04 BAP Memorabilia Gloves

STATED PRINT RUN 30 SETS
GUG1 Jean-Sebastien Giguere 15.00 40.00
GUG2 Patrick Roy 30.00 80.00
GUG3 Marty Turco 15.00 40.00
GUG4 Olaf Kolzig 15.00 40.00
GUG5 Patrick Lalime 15.00 40.00
GUG6 Jacques Plante 30.00 80.00
GUG7 Bill Durnan 15.00 40.00
GUG8 Bernie Parent 15.00 40.00
GUG9 Vladislav Tretiak 50.00 100.00
GUG10 Charlie Hodge 15.00 40.00
GUG11 Keith Tkachuk 15.00 40.00
GUG12 Mario Lemieux 30.00 80.00
GUG13 Eric Lindros 15.00 40.00
GUG14 Sergei Samsonov 15.00 40.00
GUG15 Jarome Iginla 20.00 50.00
GUG16 Wendel Clark 15.00 40.00
GUG17 Dickie Moore 15.00 40.00
GUG18 Bill Gadsby 30.00 80.00
GUG19 Bernie Geoffrion 15.00 40.00
GUG20 Eddie Shore 30.00 80.00

2003-04 BAP Memorabilia He Shoots-He Scores Points

ONE PER PACK
RED PROGRAM EXPIRED
1 Jose Theodore 1 Pt. .40 1.00
2 Jeremy Roenick 1 Pt. .40 1.00
3 Chris Pronger 1 Pt. .40 1.00
4 Markus Naslund 1 Pt. .40 1.00
5 Nicklas Lidstrom 1 Pt. .40 1.00
6 Dany Heatley 1 Pt. .40 1.00
7 Bill Guerin 1 Pt. .40 1.00
8 Pavel Bure 1 Pt. .40 1.00
9 Steve Yzerman 2 Pts. .40 1.00
10 Joe Thornton 2 Pts. .40 1.00
11 Mats Sundin 2 Pts. .40 1.00
12 Brendan Shanahan 2 Pts. .40 1.00
13 Teemu Selanne 2 Pts. .40 1.00
14 Joe Sakic 2 Pts. .40 1.00
15 Mike Modano 2 Pts. .40 1.00
16 Paul Kariya 2 Pts. .40 1.00
17 Sergei Fedorov 2 Pts. .40 1.00
18 Patrick Roy 3 Pts. .40 1.00
19 Peter Forsberg 3 Pts. .40 1.00
20 Martin Brodeur 3 Pts. .40 1.00

2003-04 BAP Memorabilia He Shoots-He Scores Prizes

PRINT RUN 20 SER.#'d SETS
NOT PRICED DUE TO SCARCITY
1 Peter Forsberg
2 Mike Modano
3 Bill Guerin
4 Paul Kariya
5 Nicklas Lidstrom
6 Teemu Selanne
7 Patrick Roy
8 Dany Heatley
9 Sergei Fedorov
10 Joe Thornton
11 Jose Theodore
12 Brendan Shanahan
13 Chris Pronger
14 Martin Brodeur
15 Pavel Bure
16 Markus Naslund
17 Joe Sakic
18 Jeremy Roenick
19 Mats Sundin
20 Steve Yzerman
21 Ed Belfour
22 Mario Lemieux
23 Jaromir Jagr
24 Curtis Joseph
25 Keith Tkachuk
26 Tony Amonte
27 Jarome Iginla
28 Eric Lindros
29 Brian Leetch
30 Milan Hejduk

2003-04 BAP Memorabilia Jersey and Stick

STATED PRINT RUN 90 SETS
SJ1 Joe Thornton 15.00 40.00
SJ2 Sergei Samsonov 8.00 20.00
SJ3 Jarome Iginla 10.00 25.00
SJ4 Ron Francis 8.00 20.00
SJ5 Jocelyn Thibault 8.00 20.00
SJ6 Mats Sundin 8.00 20.00
SJ7 Rob Blake 8.00 20.00
SJ8 Al MacInnis 8.00 20.00
SJ9 Rick Nash 15.00 40.00
SJ10 Marty Turco 8.00 20.00
SJ11 Bill Guerin 8.00 20.00
SJ12 Chris Chelios 8.00 20.00
SJ13 Luc Robitaille 8.00 20.00
SJ14 Mike Comrie 8.00 20.00
SJ15 Markus Naslund 8.00 20.00
SJ16 Roberto Luongo 10.00 25.00
SJ17 Peter Bondra 8.00 20.00
SJ18 John LeClair 8.00 20.00
SJ19 Rick DiPietro 8.00 20.00
SJ20 Tony Amonte 8.00 20.00
SJ21 Eric Lindros 8.00 20.00

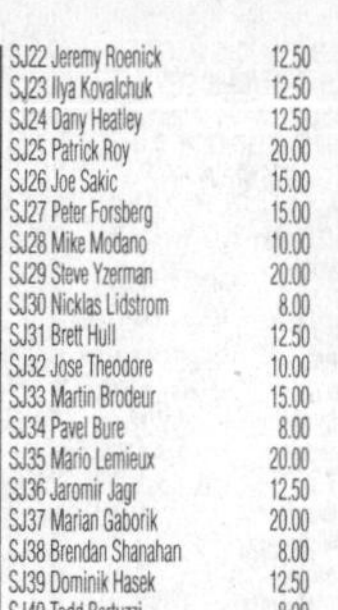

SJ22 Jeremy Roenick 12.50 30.00
SJ23 Ilya Kovalchuk 12.50 30.00
SJ24 Dany Heatley 12.50 30.00
SJ25 Patrick Roy 20.00 50.00
SJ26 Joe Sakic 15.00 40.00
SJ27 Peter Forsberg 15.00 40.00
SJ28 Mike Modano 10.00 25.00
SJ29 Steve Yzerman 20.00 50.00
SJ30 Nicklas Lidstrom 8.00 20.00
SJ31 Brett Hull 12.50 30.00
SJ32 Jose Theodore 10.00 25.00
SJ33 Martin Brodeur 15.00 40.00
SJ34 Pavel Bure 8.00 20.00
SJ35 Mario Lemieux 20.00 50.00
SJ36 Jaromir Jagr 12.50 30.00
SJ37 Marian Gaborik 20.00 50.00
SJ38 Brendan Shanahan 8.00 20.00
SJ39 Dominik Hasek 12.50 30.00
SJ40 Todd Bertuzzi 8.00 20.00

2003-04 BAP Memorabilia Jerseys

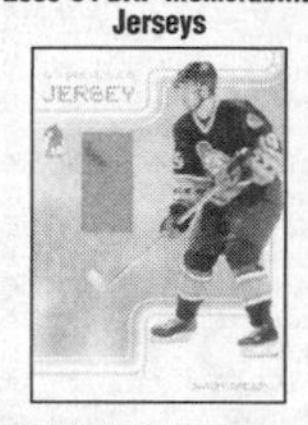

*MULT.COLOR SWATCH: .6X TO 1.5X HI
STATED PRINT RUN 90 SETS
GJ1 Joe Thornton 10.00 25.00
GJ2 Dominik Hasek 10.00 25.00
GJ3 Jarome Iginla 10.00 25.00
GJ4 Ron Francis 6.00 15.00
GJ5 Henrik Zetterberg 6.00 15.00
GJ6 Mats Sundin 6.00 15.00
GJ7 Rob Blake 6.00 15.00
GJ8 Al MacInnis 6.00 15.00
GJ9 Milan Hejduk 6.00 15.00
GJ10 Rick Nash 10.00 25.00
GJ11 Marty Turco 6.00 15.00
GJ12 Jean-Sebastien Giguere 6.00 15.00
GJ13 Jason Spezza 8.00 20.00
GJ14 Luc Robitaille 6.00 15.00
GJ15 Alexander Mogilny 6.00 15.00
GJ16 Mike Comrie 6.00 15.00
GJ17 Markus Naslund 6.00 15.00
GJ18 Roberto Luongo 10.00 25.00
GJ19 Jay Bouwmeester 6.00 15.00
GJ20 Marian Hossa 6.00 15.00
GJ21 Todd Bertuzzi 6.00 15.00
GJ22 Saku Koivu 6.00 15.00
GJ23 Curtis Joseph 6.00 15.00
GJ24 Rick DiPietro 6.00 15.00
GJ25 Ed Belfour 6.00 15.00
GJ26 Eric Lindros 6.00 15.00
GJ27 Jeremy Roenick 10.00 25.00
GJ28 Brian Leetch 6.00 15.00
GJ29 Owen Nolan 6.00 15.00
GJ30 Simon Gagne 6.00 15.00
GJ31 Brendan Shanahan 6.00 15.00
GJ32 Ilya Kovalchuk 10.00 25.00
GJ33 Dany Heatley 10.00 25.00
GJ34 Patrick Roy 15.00 40.00
GJ35 Joe Sakic 12.00 30.00
GJ36 Peter Forsberg 10.00 25.00
GJ37 Mike Modano 10.00 25.00
GJ38 Steve Yzerman 15.00 40.00
GJ39 Nicklas Lidstrom 6.00 15.00
GJ40 Brett Hull 10.00 25.00
GJ41 Jose Theodore 8.00 20.00
GJ42 Martin Brodeur 12.00 30.00
GJ43 Pavel Bure 6.00 15.00
GJ44 Mark Messier 6.00 15.00
GJ45 Mario Lemieux 15.00 40.00
GJ46 Jaromir Jagr 10.00 25.00
GJ47 Marian Gaborik 12.00 30.00
GJ48 Teemu Selanne 6.00 15.00
GJ49 Paul Kariya 6.00 15.00
GJ50 Sergei Fedorov 8.00 20.00

2003-04 BAP Memorabilia Jersey Autographs

STATED PRINT RUN 10 SETS
NOT PRICED DUE TO SCARCITY

2003-04 BAP Memorabilia Masks III

COMPLETE SET (20) 40.00 80.00
1 Jean-Sebastien Giguere 4.00 10.00
2 Roman Cechmanek 4.00 10.00
3 Dominik Hasek 6.00 15.00
4 Roberto Luongo 5.00 12.00
5 Ryan Miller 4.00 10.00
6 Sean Burke 4.00 10.00
7 Kevin Weekes 4.00 10.00
8 Mike Dunham 4.00 10.00
9 Jeff Hackett 4.00 10.00
10 Martin Prusek 4.00 10.00
11 Olaf Kolzig 4.00 10.00
12 Nikolai Khabibulin 4.00 10.00
13 Pasi Nurminen 4.00 10.00
14 Johan Hedberg 4.00 10.00
15 Marty Turco 4.00 10.00
16 Felix Potvin 4.00 10.00
17 Marc Denis 4.00 10.00
18 Marc-Andre Fleury 8.00 20.00
19 David Aebischer 4.00 10.00
20 Jocelyn Thibault 4.00 10.00

2003-04 BAP Memorabilia Masks III Gold

*GOLD: 2.5X TO 6X BASIC MASKS
STATED PRINT RUN 30 SETS

2003-04 BAP Memorabilia Masks III Silver

*SILVER: 1X TO 2.5X BASIC MASKS
PRINT RUN SERIAL 300 SETS

2003-04 BAP Memorabilia Masks III Autographs

This 16-card set paralleled the regular insert set but carried certified player autographs. Cards were limited to 10 copies each and were not priced due to scarcity.

STATED PRINT RUN 10 SETS
NOT PRICED DUE TO SCARCITY
MDA David Aebischer
MDH Mike Dunham
MFP Felix Potvin
MJH Jeff Hackett
MJT Jocelyn Thibault
MKW Kevin Weekes
MMDE Marc Denis
MMDU Mike Dunham
MMF Marc-Andre Fleury
MMT Marty Turco
MNK Nikolai Khabibulin
MOK Olaf Kolzig
MPN Pasi Nurminen
MRC Roman Cechmanek
MRL Roberto Luongo
MRM Ryan Miller

2003-04 BAP Memorabilia Masks III Memorabilia

This 20-card set paralleled the regular insert set but carried swatches of game-used memorabilia. Cards were limited to 10 copies each and were not priced due to scarcity.

STATED PRINT RUN 10 SETS
NOT PRICED DUE TO SCARCITY

2003-04 BAP Memorabilia Practice Jerseys

STATED PRINT RUN 40 SETS
PMP1 Curtis Joseph 10.00 25.00
PMP2 Martin Brodeur 15.00 40.00
PMP3 Ed Jovanovski 10.00 25.00
PMP4 Scott Niedermayer 10.00 25.00
PMP5 Al MacInnis 10.00 25.00
PMP6 Rob Blake 10.00 25.00
PMP7 Chris Pronger 10.00 25.00
PMP8 Owen Nolan 10.00 25.00
PMP9 Eric Lindros 10.00 25.00
PMP10 Paul Kariya 10.00 25.00
PMP11 Steve Yzerman 15.00 40.00
PMP12 Brendan Shanahan 10.00 25.00
PMP13 Theo Fleury 10.00 25.00
PMP14 Ryan Smyth 10.00 25.00
PMP15 Joe Nieuwendyk 10.00 25.00
PMP16 Jarome Iginla 12.50 30.00

2003-04 BAP Memorabilia Stanley Cup Champions

STATED PRINT RUN 40 SETS
SCC1 Martin Brodeur 40.00 100.00
SCC2 Jamie Langenbrunner 20.00 40.00
SCC3 Scott Gomez 20.00 40.00
SCC4 Joe Nieuwendyk 20.00 40.00
SCC5 John Madden 20.00 40.00
SCC6 Scott Niedermayer 20.00 40.00
SCC7 Jeff Friesen 20.00 40.00
SCC8 Scott Stevens 25.00 60.00
SCC9 Patrik Elias 20.00 40.00
SCC10 Corey Schwab 20.00 40.00

2003-04 BAP Memorabilia Stanley Cup Playoffs

CARDS 1-16 PRINT RUN 90 SETS
CARDS 17-24 PRINT RUN 80 SETS
CARDS 25-28 PRINT RUN 60 SETS
CARDS 29-30 PRINT RUN 20 SETS
CARDS 31-32 PRINT RUN 10 SETS
29-32 NOT PRICED DUE TO SCARCITY
SCP1 Steve Yzerman 15.00 40.00
SCP2 Jean-Sebastien Giguere 6.00 15.00

SCP3 Doug Weight 6.00 15.00
SCP4 Ed Jovanovski 6.00 15.00
SCP5 Joe Sakic 15.00 40.00
SCP6 Marian Gaborik 12.50 30.00
SCP7 Mike Modano 10.00 25.00
SCP8 Georges Laraque 6.00 15.00
SCP9 Marian Hossa 8.00 20.00
SCP10 Alexei Yashin 6.00 15.00
SCP11 Scott Niedermayer 6.00 15.00
SCP12 Jeff Hackett 6.00 15.00
SCP13 Martin St.Louis 6.00 15.00
SCP14 Jaromir Jagr 10.00 25.00
SCP15 Mark Recchi 6.00 15.00
SCP16 Alex Mogilny 6.00 15.00
SCP17 Paul Kariya 8.00 20.00
SCP18 Marty Turco 6.00 15.00
SCP19 Dwayne Roloson 6.00 15.00
SCP20 Markus Naslund 8.00 20.00
SCP21 Daniel Alfredsson 6.00 15.00
SCP22 Jeremy Roenick 10.00 25.00
SCP23 Vincent Lecavalier 8.00 20.00
SCP24 Jamie Langenbrunner 6.00 15.00
SCP25 Jean-Sebastien Giguere 6.00 15.00
SCP26 Manny Fernandez 6.00 15.00
SCP27 Jason Spezza 12.50 30.00
SCP28 John Madden 6.00 15.00
SCP29 Paul Kariya
SCP30 Martin Brodeur
SCP31 Scott Stevens Cup Winners
SCP32 Jean-Sebastien Giguere Conn Smythe

2003-04 BAP Memorabilia Super Rookies

This 12-card set was randomly inserted and featured rookies from the 2003-04 season. A silver parallel serial-numbered out of 100 and gold parallel 1/1s were also created. Prices for the silver parallel can be found by using the mutiplier below.

COMPLETE SET (12) 20.00 50.00
*SILVER: .75X TO 2X BASE HI
SILVER PRINT RUN 100 SER.#'d SETS
UNPRICED GOLD 1/1's EXIST
SR1 Tuomo Ruutu 4.00 10.00
SR2 Joffroy Lupul 0.00 0.00
SR3 Brent Burns 2.00 5.00
SR4 David Hale 2.00 5.00
SR5 Patrice Bergeron 5.00 12.00
SR6 Joni Pitkanen 3.00 8.00
SR7 Sean Bergenheim 2.00 5.00
SR8 Boyd Gordon 2.00 5.00
SR9 Eric Staal 5.00 12.00
SR10 Nathan Horton 4.00 10.00
SR11 Dustin Brown 2.00 5.00
SR12 Tim Gleason 2.00 5.00
SR13 Dan Hamhuis 2.00 5.00
SR14 Jordin Tootoo 5.00 12.00
SR15 Jiri Hudler 4.00 10.00
SR16 Marc-Andre Fleury 8.00 20.00
SR17 Christopher Higgins 3.00 8.00
SR18 Pavel Vorobiev 2.00 5.00
SR19 Alexander Semin 2.00 5.00
SR20 Brent Krahn 2.00 5.00

2003-04 BAP Memorabilia Tandems

STATED PRINT RUN 60 SETS
T1 D.Roloson/M.Fernandez 12.50 30.00
T2 P.Lalime/M.Prusek 20.00 50.00
T3 D.Hasek/M.Legace 25.00 60.00
T4 M.Biron/R.Miller 12.50 30.00
T5 M.Brodeur/C.Schwab 15.00 40.00
T6 M.Turco/R.Tugnutt 12.50 30.00
T7 J.Giguere/M.Gerber 12.50 30.00
T8 J.Theodore/M.Garon 20.00 50.00
T9 R.Luongo/J.Hurme 12.50 30.00
T10 E.Belfour/T.Kidd 15.00 40.00

2003-04 BAP Memorabilia Vintage Memorabilia

STATED PRINT RUN 15 SETS
NOT PRICED DUE TO SCARCITY
VM1 Tiny Thompson
VM2 Chuck Gardiner
VM3 Tim Horton
VM4 Gerry Cheevers
VM5 Bernie Parent
VM6 Maurice Richard
VM7 Terry Sawchuk
VM8 Newsy Lalonde

VM9 Doug Harvey
VM10 Ted Lindsay
VM11 Henri Richard
VM12 Bill Mosienko
VM13 Aurel Joliat
VM14 Alex Delvecchio
VM15 Bobby Clarke
VM16 Eddie Shore
VM17 Marcel Dionne
VM18 Jean Beliveau
VM19 Bill Durnan
VM20 George Hainsworth

2003-04 BAP Memorabilia Cleveland National

STATED PRINT RUN 10 SER.#'d SETS
NOT PRICED DUE TO SCARCITY

1999-00 BAP Millennium Prototypes

This 8-card set was issued to dealers as a promo to introduce the Be A Player Millennium brand.

COMPLETE SET (8) 4.80 12.00
1 Teemu Selanne 1.25 3.00
2 Sergei Samsonov .60 1.50
3 Mike Modano .75 2.00
4 Sergei Fedorov 1.25 3.00
5 Saku Koivu .60 1.50
6 John Vanbiesbrouck .60 1.50
7 Sergei Berezin .20 .50
8 Olaf Kolzig .60 1.50

1999-00 BAP Millennium

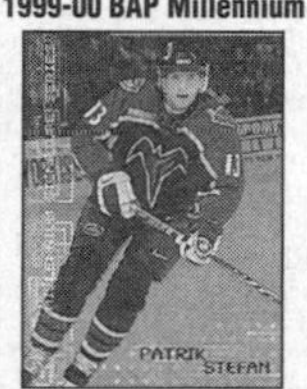

Released as a 250-card set, Be A Player Millennium featured all silver foil base cards with full color action photography. Ruby, sapphire and emerald parallels were also created and inserted randomly. Ruby parallels are red in color and have a stated print run of 1000 sets. Sapphire parallels are blue in color and have a stated print run of 100 sets. Emerald parallels are green in color and have a stated print run of 10 sets. Emerald parallels are not priced due to scarcity. Millennium was packaged in 12-pack boxes with packs containing five cards. Each pack contained one authentic autograph card. Due to a difficulty in obtaining the Jaromir Jagr Signature cards, BAP offered a special Game Jersey card to those that sent in the redemption for the autographed card. The jersey card has been added to the bottom of the checklist.

COMPLETE SET (250) 125.00 250.00
JAGR GJ ISSUED VIA EXCH.SIG. CARD
1 Paul Kariya .60 1.50
2 Teemu Selanne .60 1.50
3 Oleg Tverdovsky .25 .60
4 Niclas Havelid RC .60 1.50
5 Guy Hebert .50 1.25
6 Stu Grimson .25 .60
7 Pavel Trnka .25 .60
8 Ladislav Kohn .25 .60
9 Matt Cullen .25 .60
10 Steve Rucchin .25 .60
11 Dominic Roussel .50 1.25
12 Patrik Stefan RC .50 1.25
13 Damian Rhodes .50 1.25
14 Ray Ferraro .25 .60
15 Andrew Brunette .50 1.25
16 Johan Garpenlov .25 .60
17 Nelson Emerson .25 .60
18 Jason Botterill .25 .60
19 Kelly Buchberger .25 .60
20 Ray Bourque 1.00 2.50
21 Ken Belanger .25 .60
22 Sergei Samsonov .50 1.25
23 Byron Dafoe .50 1.25
24 Joe Thornton 1.00 2.50
25 Kyle McLaren .25 .60
26 Cameron Mann .25 .60
27 Mikko Eloranta RC .50 1.25
28 Jonathan Girard .25 .60
29 Dominik Hasek 1.25 3.00
30 Michael Peca .50 1.25
31 Erik Rasmussen .25 .60
32 Brian Campbell RC .25 .60
33 Miroslav Satan .50 1.25
34 Vaclav Varada .25 .60
35 Martin Biron .50 1.25
36 Dixon Ward .25 .60
37 Cory Sarich .25 .60
38 Grant Fuhr .50 1.25
39 Jarome Iginla .75 2.00
40 Valeri Bure .25 .60
41 Oleg Saprykin RC .50 1.25
42 Rene Corbet .25 .60
43 Cory Stillman .25 .60
44 Denis Gauthier .25 .60
45 Steve Dubinsky .25 .60
46 Rico Fata .25 .60
47 Steve Halko RC .25 .60
48 Keith Primeau .25 .60
49 Sami Kapanen .25 .60
50 Arturs Irbe .50 1.25
51 Jeff O'Neill .25 .60
52 Kent Manderville .25 .60
53 Gary Roberts .25 .60
54 Nolan Pratt .50 1.25
55 Brad Brown .25 .60
56 Tony Amonte .50 1.25
57 J-P Dumont .50 1.25
58 Anders Eriksson .25 .60
59 Bryan Muir .25 .60
60 Dean McAmmond .25 .60
61 Jocelyn Thibault .50 1.25
62 Eric Daze .50 1.25
63 Shean Donovan .25 .60
64 Scott Parker .25 .60
65 Peter Forsberg 1.00 2.50
66 Patrick Roy 2.00 5.00
67 Joe Sakic 1.25 3.00
68 Sandis Ozolinsh .25 .60
69 Chris Drury .50 1.25
70 Milan Hejduk .60 1.50
71 Shjon Podein .25 .60
72 Marc Denis .50 1.25
73 Alex Tanguay .50 1.25
74 Blake Sloan .60 1.50
75 Jamie Langenbrunner .25 .60
76 Mike Modano 1.00 2.50
77 Derian Hatcher .25 .60
78 Joe Nieuwendyk .50 1.25
79 Ed Belfour .60 1.50
80 Brad Lukowich RC .25 .60
81 Jere Lehtinen .50 1.25
82 Brett Hull .75 2.00
83 Shawn Chambers .25 .60
84 Pavel Patera RC .25 .60
85 Darryl Sydor .25 .60
86 Jiri Fischer .25 .60
87 Nicklas Lidstrom .60 1.50
88 Steve Yzerman 2.00 5.00
89 Sergei Fedorov 1.00 2.50
90 Brendan Shanahan .60 1.50
91 Chris Chelios .60 1.50
92 Aaron Ward .25 .60
93 Kirk Maltby .25 .60
94 Yuri Butsayev RC .25 .60
95 Mathieu Dandenault .25 .60
96 Doug Weight .50 1.25
97 Bill Guerin .50 1.25
98 Tom Poti .25 .60
99 Wayne Gretzky 3.00 8.00
100 Georges Laraque RC .50 1.25
101 Sean Brown .25 .60
102 Mike Grier .25 .60
103 Tommy Salo .50 1.25
104 Rem Murray .25 .60
105 Paul Comrie RC .50 1.25
106 Pavel Bure .60 1.50
107 Rob Niedermayer .25 .60
108 Oleg Kvasha .25 .60
109 Filip Kuba RC .50 1.25
110 Viktor Kozlov .25 .60
111 Radek Dvorak .25 .60
112 Ray Whitney .25 .60
113 Mark Parrish .25 .60
114 Dan Boyle RC .50 1.25
115 Marcus Nilsson .25 .60
116 Lance Pitlick .25 .60
117 Paul Laus .25 .60
118 Rob Blake .25 .60
119 Stephane Fiset .50 1.25
120 Zigmund Palffy .50 1.25
121 Donald Audette .25 .60
122 Luc Robitaille .50 1.25
123 Jamie Storr .50 1.25
124 Dan Bylsma .25 .60
125 Pavel Rosa .25 .60
126 Jason Blake RC .50 1.25
127 Mattias Norstrom .25 .60
128 Saku Koivu .60 1.50
129 Trevor Linden .25 .60
130 Arron Asham .25 .60
131 Matt Higgins .25 .60
132 Martin Rucinsky .25 .60
133 Brian Savage .25 .60
134 Jeff Hackett .50 1.25
135 Scott Thornton .25 .60
136 David Legwand .50 1.25
137 Cliff Ronning .25 .60
138 Ville Peltonen .25 .60
139 Tomas Vokoun .50 1.25
140 Sergei Krivokrasov .25 .60
141 Greg Johnson .25 .60
142 Mike Dunham .50 1.25
143 Martin Brodeur 1.50 4.00
144 Scott Niedermayer .25 .60
145 Petr Sykora .25 .60
146 Vadim Sharifijanov .25 .60
147 Denis Pederson .25 .60
148 Jason Arnott .25 .60
149 Brendan Morrison .50 1.25
150 Bobby Holik .25 .60
151 Brian Rafalski RC .60 1.50
152 Olli Jokinen .50 1.25
153 Tim Connolly .25 .60
154 Gino Odjick .25 .60
155 Zdeno Chara .25 .60
156 Kenny Jonsson .25 .60
157 Mariusz Czerkawski .25 .60
158 Kim Johnsson RC .40 1.00
159 Brian Leetch .60 1.50
160 Theo Fleury .25 .60
161 Petr Nedved .50 1.25
162 John MacLean .25 .60
163 Manny Malhotra .50 1.25
164 Jan Hlavac .25 .60
165 Valeri Kamensky .50 1.25
166 Adam Graves .25 .60
167 Michael York .25 .60
168 Mike Richter .60 1.50
169 Chris Phillips .25 .60
170 Marian Hossa .60 1.50
171 Magnus Arvedson .25 .60
172 Ron Tugnutt .50 1.25
173 Vaclav Prospal .25 .60

174 Sami Salo .25 .60
175 Jason York .25 .60
176 Shawn McEachern .25 .60
177 Rob Zamuner .25 .60
178 Eric Lindros .60 1.50
179 John LeClair .60 1.50
180 Eric Desjardins .50 1.25
181 Rod Brind'Amour .50 1.25
182 Mark Recchi .50 1.25
183 Simon Gagne .60 1.50
184 Sandy McCarthy .25 .60
185 John Vanbiesbrouck .50 1.25
186 Dan McGillis .25 .60
187 Keith Jones .25 .60
188 Keith Tkachuk .60 1.50
189 Teppo Numminen .25 .60
190 Jeremy Roenick .75 2.00
191 Nikolai Khabibulin .50 1.25
192 Deron Quint .25 .60
193 Trevor Letowski .25 .60
194 Jaromir Jagr 1.00 2.50
195 Jan Hrdina .25 .60
196 Andrew Ference .25 .60
197 Alexei Kovalev .25 .60
198 Martin Straka .25 .60
199 Kip Miller .25 .60
200 Martin Sonnenberg RC .25 .60
201 Alexei Morozov .25 .60
202 Chris Pronger .50 1.25
203 Al MacInnis .50 1.25
204 Pavol Demitra .50 1.25
205 Pierre Turgeon .50 1.25
206 Jamal Mayers .25 .60
207 Chris McAlpine .25 .60
208 Ron Sutter .25 .60
209 Mike Rathje .25 .60
210 Patrick Marleau .60 1.50
211 Jeff Friesen .25 .60
212 Niklas Sundstrom .25 .60
213 Steve Shields .50 1.25
214 Brad Stuart .50 1.25
215 Alexander Korolyuk .25 .60
216 Mike Ricci .25 .60
217 Paul Mara .25 .60
218 Fredrik Modin .25 .60
219 Dan Cloutier .50 1.25
220 Vincent Lecavalier .60 1.50
221 Pavel Kubina .25 .60
222 Chris Gratton .25 .60
223 Mike Sillinger .25 .60
224 Nikolai Antropov RC .60 1.50
225 Todd Warriner .25 .60
226 Mats Sundin .60 1.50
227 Curtis Joseph .60 1.50
228 Chris McAllister RC .25 .60
229 Bryan Berard .50 1.25
230 Tomas Kaberle .25 .60
231 Igor Korolev .25 .60
232 Sergei Berezin .25 .60
233 Artem Chubarov .25 .60
234 Ed Jovanovski .25 .60
235 Mark Messier .60 1.50
236 Bill Muckalt .25 .60
237 Brad May .25 .60
238 Adrian Aucoin .25 .60
239 Mattias Ohlund .25 .60
240 Greg Hawgood .25 .60
241 Steve Kariya RC .40 1.00
242 Markus Naslund .60 1.50
243 Alexander Mogilny .50 1.25
244 Jamie Huscroft .25 .60
245 Peter Bondra .50 1.25
246 Olaf Kolzig .50 1.25
247 Brendan Witt .25 .60
248 Adam Oates .50 1.25
249 Sergei Gonchar .25 .60
250 Jan Bulis .25 .60
NNO J.Jagr GJ Special 40.00 100.00

1999-00 BAP Millennium Emerald

UNPRICED EMERALD PRINT RUN 10

1999-00 BAP Millennium Ruby

*VETERANS: 1.5X TO 4X BASIC CARDS
*ROOKIES: 1.2X TO 3X BASIC CARDS
STATED PRINT RUN 1000 SER.#'d SETS

1999-00 BAP Millennium Sapphire

*VETERANS: 12X TO 30X BASIC CARDS
*ROOKIES: 8X TO 20X BASIC CARD
SAPPHIRE PRINT RUN 100 SER.#'d SETS

1999-00 BAP Millennium Autographs

Inserted one per pack, this 250-card set paralleled the base set with player autographs and a congratulatory note on the back. Gold parallels were also created and inserted randomly into packs. Gold SP's had a print run of 50 sets.

1 Paul Kariya SP 20.00 50.00
2 Teemu Selanne SP 12.50 30.00
3 Oleg Tverdovsky 2.50 6.00
4 Niclas Havelid 2.50 6.00
5 Guy Hebert 4.00 10.00
6 Stu Grimson 2.50 6.00
7 Pavel Trnka 2.50 6.00
8 Ladislav Kohn 2.50 6.00
9 Matt Cullen 2.50 6.00
10 Steve Rucchin 2.50 6.00
11 Dominic Roussel 2.50 6.00
12 Patrik Stefan 2.50 6.00
13 Damian Rhodes 4.00 10.00
14 Ray Ferraro 2.50 6.00
15 Andrew Brunette 2.50 6.00
16 Johan Garpenlov 2.50 6.00
17 Nelson Emerson 2.50 6.00
18 Jason Botterill 2.50 6.00
19 Kelly Buchberger 2.50 6.00
20 Ray Bourque SP 25.00 60.00
21 Ken Belanger 2.50 6.00
22 Sergei Samsonov SP 6.00 15.00
23 Byron Dafoe SP 6.00 15.00
24 Joe Thornton 8.00 20.00
25 Kyle McLaren 2.50 6.00
26 Cameron Mann 2.50 6.00
27 Mikko Eloranta 2.50 6.00
28 Jonathan Girard 2.50 6.00
29 Dominik Hasek SP 150.00 250.00
30 Michael Peca SP 6.00 15.00
31 Erik Rasmussen 2.50 6.00
32 Brian Campbell 2.50 6.00
33 Miroslav Satan 4.00 10.00
34 Vaclav Varada 2.50 6.00
35 Martin Biron 4.00 10.00
36 Dixon Ward 2.50 6.00
37 Cory Sarich 2.50 6.00
38 Grant Fuhr SP 10.00 25.00
39 Jarome Iginla 6.00 15.00
40 Valeri Bure 2.50 6.00
41 Oleg Saprykin 2.50 6.00
42 Rene Corbet 2.50 6.00
43 Cory Stillman 2.50 6.00
44 Denis Gauthier 2.50 6.00
45 Steve Dubinsky 2.50 6.00
46 Rico Fata 2.50 6.00
47 Steve Halko 2.50 6.00
48 Keith Primeau SP 6.00 15.00
49 Sami Kapanen 2.50 6.00
50 Arturs Irbe 4.00 10.00
51 Jeff O'Neill 2.50 6.00
52 Kent Manderville 2.50 6.00
53 Gary Roberts 2.50 6.00
54 Nolan Pratt 2.50 6.00
55 Brad Brown 2.50 6.00
56 Tony Amonte SP 6.00 15.00
57 J-P Dumont 2.50 6.00
58 Anders Eriksson 2.50 6.00
59 Bryan Muir 2.50 6.00
60 Dean McAmmond 2.50 6.00
61 Jocelyn Thibault 4.00 10.00
62 Eric Daze 4.00 10.00
63 Shean Donovan 2.50 6.00
64 Scott Parker 2.50 6.00
65 Peter Forsberg SP 25.00 60.00
66 Patrick Roy SP 50.00 100.00
67 Joe Sakic SP 30.00 80.00
68 Sandis Ozolinsh 2.50 6.00
69 Chris Drury 4.00 10.00
70 Milan Hejduk 5.00 12.00
71 Shjon Podein 2.50 6.00
72 Marc Denis 4.00 10.00
73 Alex Tanguay 2.50 6.00
74 Blake Sloan 2.50 6.00
75 Jamie Langenbrunner 2.50 6.00
76 Mike Modano SP 20.00 50.00
77 Derian Hatcher 2.50 6.00
78 Joe Nieuwendyk SP 6.00 15.00
79 Ed Belfour SP 20.00 50.00
80 Brad Lukowich 2.50 6.00
81 Jere Lehtinen 4.00 10.00
82 Brett Hull SP 15.00 40.00
83 Shawn Chambers 2.50 6.00
84 Pavel Patera 2.50 6.00
85 Darryl Sydor 2.50 6.00
86 Jiri Fischer 2.50 6.00
87 Nicklas Lidstrom 5.00 12.00
88 Steve Yzerman SP 40.00 100.00
89 Sergei Fedorov SP 15.00 40.00
90 Brendan Shanahan SP 10.00 25.00
91 Chris Chelios SP 10.00 25.00
92 Aaron Ward 2.50 6.00
93 Kirk Maltby 2.50 6.00
94 Yuri Butsayev 2.50 6.00
95 Mathieu Dandenault 2.50 6.00
96 Doug Weight SP 6.00 15.00
97 Bill Guerin 4.00 10.00
98 Tom Poti 2.50 6.00
99 Wayne Gretzky SP 300.00 500.00
100 Georges Laraque 5.00 12.00
101 Sean Brown 2.50 6.00
102 Mike Grier 2.50 6.00
103 Tommy Salo 4.00 10.00
104 Rem Murray 2.50 6.00
105 Paul Comrie 2.50 6.00
106 Pavel Bure SP 12.50 30.00
107 Rob Niedermayer 2.50 6.00
108 Oleg Kvasha 2.50 6.00
109 Filip Kuba 2.50 6.00
110 Viktor Kozlov 2.50 6.00
111 Radek Dvorak 2.50 6.00
112 Ray Whitney 2.50 6.00
113 Mark Parrish 2.50 6.00
114 Dan Boyle 2.50 6.00
115 Marcus Nilsson 2.50 6.00
116 Lance Pitlick 2.50 6.00
117 Paul Laus 2.50 6.00
118 Rob Blake 4.00 10.00
119 Stephane Fiset 2.50 6.00
120 Zigmund Palffy SP 6.00 15.00
121 Donald Audette 2.50 6.00
122 Luc Robitaille 4.00 10.00
123 Jamie Storr 4.00 10.00
124 Dan Bylsma 2.50 6.00
125 Pavel Rosa 2.50 6.00
126 Jason Blake 2.50 6.00
127 Mattias Norstrom 2.50 6.00
128 Saku Koivu SP 12.00 30.00
129 Trevor Linden 2.50 6.00
130 Arron Asham 2.50 6.00
131 Matt Higgins 2.50 6.00
132 Martin Rucinsky 2.50 6.00
133 Brian Savage 2.50 6.00
134 Jeff Hackett 4.00 10.00
135 Scott Thornton 2.50 6.00
136 David Legwand 4.00 10.00
137 Cliff Ronning 2.50 6.00
138 Ville Peltonen 2.50 6.00
139 Tomas Vokoun 4.00 10.00
140 Sergei Krivokrasov 2.50 6.00
141 Greg Johnson 2.50 6.00
142 Mike Dunham 4.00 10.00
143 Martin Brodeur SP 40.00 80.00
144 Scott Niedermayer SP 8.00 20.00
145 Petr Sykora 2.50 6.00
146 Vadim Sharifijanov 2.50 6.00
147 Denis Pederson 2.50 6.00
148 Jason Arnott SP 6.00 15.00
149 Brendan Morrison 4.00 10.00
150 Bobby Holik 2.50 6.00
151 Brian Rafalski 2.50 6.00
152 Olli Jokinen 4.00 10.00
153 Tim Connolly 2.50 6.00
154 Gino Odjick 2.50 6.00
155 Zdeno Chara 2.50 6.00
156 Kenny Jonsson 2.50 6.00
157 Mariusz Czerkawski 2.50 6.00
158 Kim Johnsson 2.50 6.00
159 Brian Leetch SP 12.00 30.00
160 Theo Fleury SP 8.00 20.00
161 Petr Nedved 2.50 6.00
162 John MacLean 2.50 6.00
163 Manny Malhotra 2.50 6.00
164 Jan Hlavac 2.50 6.00
165 Valeri Kamensky 2.50 6.00
166 Adam Graves 2.50 6.00
167 Michael York 2.50 6.00
168 Mike Richter SP 10.00 25.00
169 Chris Phillips 2.50 6.00
170 Marian Hossa 5.00 12.00
171 Magnus Arvedson 2.50 6.00
172 Ron Tugnutt 4.00 10.00
173 Vaclav Prospal 2.50 6.00
174 Sami Salo 2.50 6.00
175 Jason York 2.50 6.00
176 Shawn McEachern 2.50 6.00
177 Rob Zamuner 2.50 6.00
178 Eric Lindros SP 10.00 25.00
179 John LeClair SP 6.00 15.00
180 Eric Desjardins 2.50 6.00
181 Rod Brind'Amour 4.00 10.00
182 Mark Recchi 4.00 10.00
183 Simon Gagne 5.00 12.00
184 Sandy McCarthy 2.50 6.00
185 John Vanbiesbrouck SP 6.00 15.00
186 Dan McGillis 2.50 6.00
187 Keith Jones 2.50 6.00
188 Keith Tkachuk SP 6.00 15.00
189 Teppo Numminen 2.50 6.00
190 Jeremy Roenick SP 12.50 30.00
191 Nikolai Khabibulin 4.00 10.00
192 Deron Quint 2.50 6.00
193 Trevor Letowski 2.50 6.00
194 Jaromir Jagr SP 25.00 60.00
195 Jan Hrdina 2.50 6.00
196 Andrew Ference 2.50 6.00
197 Alexei Kovalev 4.00 10.00
198 Martin Straka 2.50 6.00
199 Kip Miller 2.50 6.00
200 Martin Sonnenberg 2.50 6.00
201 Alexei Morozov 2.50 6.00
202 Chris Pronger SP 6.00 15.00
203 Al MacInnis SP 6.00 15.00
204 Pavol Demitra 4.00 10.00
205 Pierre Turgeon 4.00 10.00
206 Jamal Mayers 2.50 6.00
207 Chris McAlpine 2.50 6.00
208 Ron Sutter 2.50 6.00
209 Mike Rathje 2.50 6.00
210 Patrick Marleau 4.00 10.00
211 Jeff Friesen SP 6.00 15.00
212 Niklas Sundstrom 4.00 10.00
213 Steve Shields 4.00 10.00
214 Brad Stuart 4.00 10.00
215 Alexander Korolyuk 2.50 6.00
216 Mike Ricci 2.50 6.00
217 Paul Mara 2.50 6.00
218 Fredrik Modin 2.50 6.00
219 Dan Cloutier 4.00 10.00
220 Vincent Lecavalier 5.00 12.00
221 Pavel Kubina 2.50 6.00
222 Chris Gratton SP 6.00 15.00
223 Mike Sillinger 2.50 6.00
224 Nikolai Antropov 2.50 6.00
225 Todd Warriner 2.50 6.00
226 Mats Sundin SP 15.00 40.00
227 Curtis Joseph SP 15.00 40.00
228 Chris McAllister 2.50 6.00
229 Bryan Berard SP 6.00 15.00
230 Tomas Kaberle 2.50 6.00
231 Igor Korolev 2.50 6.00
232 Sergei Berezin 2.50 6.00
233 Artem Chubarov 2.50 6.00
234 Ed Jovanovski 2.50 6.00
235 Mark Messier SP 30.00 80.00
236 Bill Muckalt 2.50 6.00
237 Brad May 2.50 6.00
238 Adrian Aucoin 2.50 6.00
239 Mattias Ohlund 2.50 6.00
240 Greg Hawgood 2.50 6.00
241 Steve Kariya 2.50 6.00
242 Markus Naslund 5.00 12.00
243 Alexander Mogilny SP 6.00 15.00
244 Jamie Huscroft 2.50 6.00
245 Peter Bondra SP 6.00 15.00
246 Olaf Kolzig SP 8.00 20.00
247 Brendan Witt 2.50 6.00
248 Adam Oates SP 8.00 20.00
249 Sergei Gonchar 2.50 6.00
250 Jan Bulis 2.50 6.00

1999-00 BAP Millennium Autographs Gold

Randomly inserted at approximately two per box, this 250-card set parallels the Signatures set in gold foil. Announced print run for the short prints in this set is 50 cards.

*GOLD: 1.2X TO 3X BASIC AUTO
*GOLD/50: .8X TO 2X BASIC AUTO
GOLD SP PRINT RUN 50 CARDS
29 Dominik Hasek SP 300.00 600.00
99 Wayne Gretzky SP 750.00 1500.00

1999-00 BAP Millennium Calder Candidates Ruby

Randomly inserted in packs, this 50-card set featured top Calder trophy prospects. Cards contained full-color action photography and were set off by a red border. Ruby versions were serial numbered 0101/1000 to 1000/1000. Sapphire and emerald parallels were also created and randomly inserted. Sapphire parallels were blue in color and had a stated print run of 100 sets. Emerald parallels were green in color and had a stated print run of 10 sets. Emerald parallels are not priced due to scarcity.

COMPLETE SET (50) 100.00 200.00
STATED PRINT RUN 1000 SETS
*SAPPHIRE/100: 1.5X TO 4X RUBY/100
SAPPHIRE PRINT RUN 100 SETS
*EMERALD/10: 4X TO 10X RUBY/10000
EMERALD STATED PRINT RUN 10
C1 Alex Tanguay 2.50 6.00
C2 Simon Gagne 3.00 8.00
C3 Kyle Calder 2.00 5.00
C4 Ryan Johnson 2.00 5.00
C5 Dave Tanabe 2.00 5.00
C6 Scott Gomez 2.00 5.00
C7 Patrik Stefan 2.00 5.00
C8 Jiri Fischer 2.00 5.00
C9 Blake Sloan 2.00 5.00
C10 Trevor Letowski 2.00 5.00
C11 Michael York 2.00 5.00
C12 Mike Ribeiro 2.00 5.00
C13 Ladislav Kohn 2.00 5.00
C14 Martin Skoula 2.00 5.00
C15 Steve Kariya 2.00 5.00
C16 Nikolai Antropov 2.00 5.00
C17 David Legwand 2.50 6.00
C18 J-P Dumont 2.00 5.00
C19 Filip Kuba 2.00 5.00
C20 Mike Fisher 2.00 5.00
C21 Tim Connolly 2.00 5.00
C22 Martin Biron 2.50 6.00
C23 Oleg Saprykin 2.00 5.00
C24 Maxim Afinogenov 2.00 5.00
C25 Petr Buzek 2.00 5.00
C26 Paul Comrie 2.00 5.00
C27 Brian Boucher 2.50 6.00
C28 Peter Schaefer 2.00 5.00
C29 Alex Tezikov 2.00 5.00
C30 Milan Hnilicka 2.50 6.00
C31 Brian Rafalski 2.00 5.00
C32 Sami Helenius 2.00 5.00
C33 Frantisek Kaberle 2.00 5.00
C34 Jochen Hecht 2.00 5.00
C35 Mathieu Biron 2.00 5.00
C36 Randy Robitaille 2.00 5.00
C37 Roberto Luongo 4.00 10.00
C38 Steve McCarthy 2.00 5.00
C39 Brad Lukowich 2.00 5.00
C40 Kim Johnsson 2.00 5.00
C41 Brad Stuart 2.00 5.00
C42 Glen Metropolit 2.00 5.00
C43 Marc Denis 2.50 6.00
C44 Robyn Regehr 2.00 5.00
C45 Per Svartvadet 2.00 5.00
C46 Jonathan Girard 2.00 5.00
C47 Mark Eaton 2.00 5.00
C48 Ivan Novoseltsev 2.00 5.00
C49 Jan Hlavac 2.00 5.00
C50 Richard Jackman 2.00 5.00

1999-00 BAP Millennium Goalie Memorabilia

STATED PRINT RUN 30 SETS
G1 Curtis Joseph 125.00 300.00
G2 Patrick Roy 200.00 400.00
G3 Grant Fuhr 60.00 150.00
G4 Garth Snow 50.00 120.00
G5 Jeff Hackett 30.00 80.00
G6 Chris Osgood 30.00 80.00
G7 Dominik Hasek 150.00 300.00
G8 Arturs Irbe 30.00 80.00

1999-00 BAP Millennium Jerseys

STATED PRINT RUN 100 SETS
*JSY NUMBER: .6X TO 1.5X BASIC JSY
JSY NUMBER PRINT RUN 30 SETS
*JSY EMBLEMS: .8X TO 2X BASIC JSY
JSY EMBLEM PRINT RUN 20 SETS
*JSY AND STICK: .5X TO 1.2X BASIC JSY
JERSEY AND STICK PRINT RUN 40
UNPRICED AUTO PRINT RUN 10
J1 Theo Fleury 8.00 20.00
J2 Brendan Shanahan 12.00 30.00
J3 Curtis Joseph 12.00 30.00
J4 Saku Koivu 12.00 30.00
J5 Dominik Hasek 25.00 60.00
J6 Al MacInnis 8.00 20.00
J7 John LeClair 12.00 30.00
J8 Teemu Selanne 12.00 30.00
J9 Wayne Gretzky 60.00 150.00
J10 Pavel Bure 12.00 30.00
J11 Mark Messier 12.00 30.00
J12 Jaromir Jagr 20.00 50.00
J13 Ray Bourque 20.00 50.00
J14 Chris Chelios 12.00 30.00
J15 Mats Sundin 12.00 30.00
J16 Paul Kariya 12.00 30.00
J17 Peter Bondra 8.00 20.00
J18 Eric Lindros 12.00 30.00
J19 Sergei Fedorov 15.00 40.00
J20 Peter Forsberg 20.00 50.00
J21 Brett Hull 12.00 30.00
J22 Tony Amonte 8.00 20.00
J23 Patrick Roy 30.00 80.00
J24 Ed Belfour 12.00 30.00
J25 Martin Brodeur 30.00 80.00
J26 Brian Leetch 8.00 20.00
J27 Mike Modano 12.00 30.00
J28 Joe Sakic 15.00 40.00
J29 Jeremy Roenick 12.00 30.00
J30 Steve Yzerman 30.00 80.00
J31 Alexander Mogilny 8.00 20.00
J32 Paul Coffey 12.00 30.00

1999-00 BAP Millennium Pearson

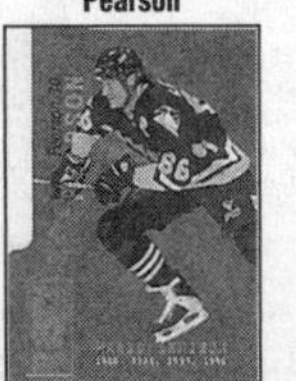

Randomly inserted in packs, this 16-card set features recipients of the Lester B. Pearson Trophy for outstanding play. Cards are foil and picture the Pearson trophy in the lower right hand corner. Stated print run for this set is 300 cards.

COMPLETE SET (16) 125.00 250.00
STATED PRINT RUN 300 SETS
P1 Jaromir Jagr 10.00 25.00
P2 Dominik Hasek 10.00 25.00
P3 Mario Lemieux 20.00 50.00
P4 Eric Lindros 2.50 6.00
P5 Sergei Fedorov 8.00 20.00
P6 Mark Messier 2.50 6.00
P7 Brett Hull 6.00 15.00
P8 Steve Yzerman 15.00 40.00
P9 Wayne Gretzky 25.00 60.00
P10 Mike Liut 2.50 6.00
P11 Marcel Dionne 4.00 10.00
P12 Guy Lafleur 5.00 12.00
P13 Bobby Orr 25.00 60.00
P14 Phil Esposito 6.00 15.00
P15 Bobby Clarke 6.00 15.00
P16 Jean Ratelle 2.50 6.00

1999-00 BAP Millennium Pearson Autographs

Randomly seeded in packs, this 16-card set parallels the base Be A Player Millennium Pearson set and is enhanced with player autographs. Players signed 30 cards each.

FIRST 30 CARDS OF PRINT RUN SIGNED
P1 Jaromir Jagr 75.00 200.00
P2 Dominik Hasek 75.00 200.00
P3 Mario Lemieux 150.00 300.00
P4 Eric Lindros 40.00 80.00
P5 Sergei Fedorov 40.00 100.00
P6 Mark Messier 75.00 200.00
P7 Brett Hull 40.00 100.00
P8 Steve Yzerman 75.00 200.00
P9 Wayne Gretzky 300.00 600.00
P10 Mike Liut 30.00 60.00
P11 Marcel Dionne 40.00 80.00
P12 Guy Lafleur 60.00 150.00
P13 Bobby Orr 400.00 600.00
P14 Phil Esposito 40.00 80.00
P15 Bobby Clarke 40.00 100.00
P16 Jean Ratelle 30.00 60.00

1999-00 BAP Millennium Players of the Decade

Randomly inserted in packs, this 10-card set features top players from the last two decades. Base cards contain full color action photography set against a blue foil background. Stated print run for this set is 1000 cards.

COMPLETE SET (10) 60.00 120.00
STATED PRINT RUN 1000 SETS
D1 Wayne Gretzky 15.00 40.00
D2 Mark Messier 3.00 8.00
D3 Patrick Roy 12.50 30.00
D4 Dominik Hasek 5.00 12.00
D5 Jaromir Jagr 4.00 10.00
D6 Eric Lindros 5.00 10.00
D7 Sergei Fedorov 5.00 12.00
D8 Brett Hull 3.00 8.00
D9 Ray Bourque 4.00 10.00
D10 Steve Yzerman 12.50 30.00

1999-00 BAP Millennium Players of the Decade Autographs

Randomly inserted in packs, this 10-card set parallels the base Players of the Decade insert set and is enhanced with player autographs. The first 90 cards in the 1000 set print run were autographed. Jagr, Hull, and Yzerman were exchange cards.

FIRST 90 CARDS OF PRINT RUN SIGNED
D1 Wayne Gretzky 125.00 300.00
D2 Mark Messier 75.00 200.00
D3 Patrick Roy 75.00 200.00
D4 Dominik Hasek 60.00 150.00
D5 Jaromir Jagr 60.00 150.00
D6 Eric Lindros 25.00 60.00
D7 Sergei Fedorov 40.00 100.00
D8 Brett Hull 30.00 80.00
D9 Ray Bourque 40.00 100.00
D10 Steve Yzerman 75.00 200.00

1999-00 BAP Millennium All-Star Fantasy

Available via wrapper redemption from the In the Game booth during the NHL All-Star Fantasy weekend in Ontario, these cards parallel the Be A Player Millennium set. Five different colors were handed out, each card was numbered to 25 and adorned with a special commemorative silver-foil stamp. Due to the limited distribution of these cards, there is not a significant amount of market data to price them, though they do have secondary market interest.

UNPRICED ALL-STAR PRINT RUN 25

1999-00 BAP Millennium Anaheim National

Available via wrapper redemption from the In the Game booth at the Anaheim National in July 2000, these cards parallel the Be A Player Millennium set.

NOT PRICED DUE TO SCARCITY

1999-00 BAP Millennium Chicago Sun-Times

Available via wrapper redemption from the In the Game booth at the Chicago Sun-Times Show in March 2000, these cards parallel the Be A Player Millennium set. A different color was available each day of the show, and each card was numbered to 10 and adorned with a special commemorative silver-foil stamp. On Friday, a ruby version was handed out, Saturday's color was sapphire and Sunday's color was gold. Due to the limited distribution of these cards, there is not a significant amount of market data to price them, though they do have secondary market interest.

UNPRICED CHICAGO SUN-TIMES PRINT RUN 10

1999-00 BAP Millennium Toronto Spring Expo

Available via wrapper redemption from the In the Game booth at the Toronto Spring Expo in May 2000, these cards parallel the Be A Player Millennium set. A different color was available each day of the show, and each card was numbered to 20 and adorned with a special commemorative silver-foil stamp. On Friday, a silver version was handed out, Saturday's color was ruby and Sunday's color was gold. Due to the limited distribution of these cards, there is not a significant amount of market data to price them, though they do have secondary market interest.

UNPRICED TORONTO EXPO PRINT RUN 20

2002 BAP NHL All-Star History

Available at the In the Game, Inc. booth during the All-Star Fantasy show, this 52-card set featured past and present players from every year of the All-Star Game. Collectors had to open a box of 2001-02 BAP product to receive one card serial-numbered out of 10. Gold 1 of 1's also were randomly available. Due to the scarcity and limited distribution of these cards, they are not priced.

PRINT RUN 10 SETS
UNPRICED GOLD 1/1'S EXIST
1 Turk Broda
2 Frank Brimsek
3 Ted Kennedy
4 Maurice Richard
5 Chuck Rayner
6 Bill Mosienko
7 Jean Beliveau
8 Doug Harvey
9 Ted Lindsay
10 Henri Richard
11 Jacques Plante
12 Glenn Hall
13 Terry Sawchuk
14 Bobby Hull
15 Johnny Bower
16 Tim Horton
17 Johnny Bucyk
18 Stan Mikita
19 Bill Gadsby
20 Gordie Howe
21 Ed Giacomin
22 Bernie Parent
23 Bobby Clarke
24 Gilbert Perreault
25 Frank Mahovlich
26 Tony Esposito
27 Denis Potvin
28 Guy Lafleur
29 Bryan Trottier
30 Lanny McDonald
31 Marcel Dionne
32 Wayne Gretzky
33 Mike Bossy
34 Mark Messier
35 Paul Coffey
36 Steve Yzerman
37 Mario Lemieux
38 Grant Fuhr
39 Patrick Roy
40 Brett Hull
41 Brian Leetch
42 Jeremy Roenick
43 Jaromir Jagr
44 Luc Robitaille
45 Joe Sakic
46 Eric Lindros
47 Paul Kariya
48 Mike Modano
49 Peter Forsberg
50 Pavel Bure
51 Milan Hejduk
52 Mats Sundin

2000-01 BAP Parkhurst 2000

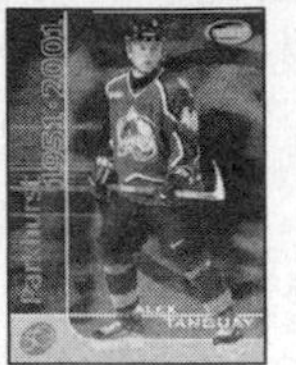

Randomly inserted in packs of Be A Player Memorabilia, Be A Player Memorabilia Update, and Be A Player Signature Series at the rate of 1:5, this 250-card set features the Parkhurst name and logo. Player action shots are framed by a green and gray border along the left and bottom of the card. Each card is enhanced with a Parkhurst 50th anniversary gold foil stamp.

COMPLETE SET (250) 50.00 125.00
COMP.SERIES 1 (100) 20.00 50.00
COMP.UPDATE SET (50) 10.00 25.00
COMP.SIG.SERIES SET (100) 20.00 50.00
STATED ODDS 1:5 SER.1/SIG.SERIES
P1 Pavel Bure .40 1.00
P2 Tony Amonte .30 .75
P3 Chris Pronger .30 .75
P4 John Madden .20 .50
P5 Kimmo Timonen .20 .50
P6 Marc Savard .20 .50
P7 Peter Forsberg .75 2.00
P8 Arturs Irbe .30 .75
P9 Mike York .20 .50
P10 Brendan Shanahan .40 1.00
P11 Simon Gagne .40 1.00
P12 Maxim Afinogenov .20 .50
P13 Joe Sakic 1.25 3.00
P14 Curtis Joseph .40 1.00
P15 Jozef Stumpel .20 .50
P16 Vitali Vishnevsky .20 .50
P17 Owen Nolan .30 .75
P18 Jan Hrdina .20 .50
P19 Brenden Morrow .30 .75
P20 Todd Bertuzzi .40 1.00
P21 Vincent Lecavalier .40 1.00
P22 Andrew Brunette .20 .50
P23 Brendan Morrison .30 .75
P24 Rod Brind'Amour .30 .75
P25 Patrik Elias .20 .50
P26 Joe Thornton 1.00 2.50
P27 Roman Turek .20 .50
P28 Fred Brathwaite .20 .50
P29 Brian Leetch .30 .75
P30 Trevor Linden .20 .50
P31 Janne Niinimaa .20 .50
P32 Nikolai Antropov .20 .50
P33 Teemu Selanne .40 1.00
P34 Calle Johansson .20 .50
P35 Boris Mironov .20 .50
P36 Eric Desjardins .20 .50
P37 Mark Parrish .20 .50
P38 Alex Tanguay .30 .75
P39 Jason Arnott .20 .50
P40 Vincent Damphousse .20 .50
P41 Dominik Hasek 1.25 3.00
P42 Teppo Numminen .20 .50
P43 Patrick Lalime .20 .50
P44 Valeri Bure .20 .50
P45 Adam Oates .30 .75
P46 Sergei Zubov .20 .50
P47 Tim Connolly .20 .50
P48 Pavel Kubina .20 .50
P49 Nicklas Lidstrom .40 1.00
P50 Mark Recchi .30 .75
P51 Chris Drury .30 .75
P52 Kyle McLaren .20 .50
P53 Steve Kariya .20 .50
P54 Scott Gomez .20 .50
P55 Rob Blake .30 .75
P56 Miroslav Satan .20 .50
P57 Cliff Ronning .20 .50
P58 Radek Dvorak .20 .50
P59 Jeff O'Neill .20 .50
P60 Dainius Zubrus .20 .50
P61 Brad Ference .20 .50
P62 Jarome Iginla .60 1.50
P63 Chris Simon .30 .75
P64 Darryl Sydor .20 .50
P65 Daniel Alfredsson .30 .75
P66 Sandis Ozolinsh .20 .50
P67 Brian Rafalski .20 .50
P68 Ryan Smyth .30 .75
P69 John LeClair .40 1.00
P70 Patrik Stefan .20 .50

P71 Patrick Marleau .30 .75
P72 Roberto Luongo .60 1.50
P73 Chris Osgood .30 .75
P74 Pierre Turgeon .30 .75
P75 Zigmund Palffy .30 .75
P76 Jeff Farkas .20 .50
P77 Milan Hejduk .40 1.00
P78 Ray Whitney .30 .75
P79 Felix Potvin .40 1.00
P80 Chris Gratton .20 .50
P81 Brad Stuart .20 .50
P82 Ron Francis .30 .75
P83 Oleg Tverdovsky .20 .50
P84 Alexei Kovalev .30 .75
P85 Sergei Fedorov .60 1.50
P86 Nick Boynton .20 .50
P87 David Legwand .20 .50
P88 Robyn Regehr .20 .50
P89 Brian Boucher .20 .50
P90 Roman Hamrlik .20 .50
P91 Jochen Hecht .20 .50
P92 Alexei Zhamnov .20 .50
P93 Olaf Kolzig .30 .75
P94 Jose Theodore .60 1.50
P95 Jeremy Roenick .60 1.50
P96 Theo Fleury .20 .50
P97 Patrick Roy 3.00 8.00
P98 Marian Hossa .40 1.00
P99 Martin Brodeur 1.50 4.00
P100 Brett Hull .60 1.50
P101 Daniel Sedin .20 .50
P102 Paul Coffey .40 1.00
P103 Ray Bourque .75 2.00
P104 Glen Murray .20 .50
P105 Mariusz Czerkawski .20 .50
P106 Jeff Friesen .20 .50
P107 Sergei Samsonov .30 .75
P108 Tyler Wright .20 .50
P109 Manny Fernandez .30 .75
P110 Mike Richter .40 1.00
P111 Pavol Demitra .20 .50
P112 Brian Rolston .20 .50
P113 Ron Tugnutt .30 .75
P114 Alexander Mogilny .30 .75
P115 Radek Bonk .20 .50
P116 Al MacInnis .30 .75
P117 J-P Dumont .20 .50
P118 Ed Belfour .60 1.50
P119 Jeff Hackett .20 .50
P120 Shawn McEachern .20 .50
P121 Dan Cloutier .20 .50
P122 Mika Noronen .20 .50
P123 Derian Hatcher .20 .50
P124 Saku Koivu .40 1.00
P125 Keith Primeau .20 .50
P126 Mats Sundin .40 1.00
P127 Damian Rhodes .20 .50
P128 Chris Chelios .40 1.00
P129 Mike Dunham .20 .50
P130 Keith Tkachuk .20 .50
P131 Steve Thomas .20 .50
P132 Phil Housley .20 .50
P133 Doug Weight .30 .75
P134 Kris Beech .20 .50
P135 Jyrki Lumme .20 .50
P136 Guy Hebert .20 .50
P137 Sami Kapanen .20 .50
P138 Trevor Kidd .20 .50
P139 Marian Gaborik 1.00 2.50
P140 Martin Straka .20 .50
P141 Ed Jovanovski .20 .50
P142 Jean-Sebastien Aubin .20 .50
P143 Viktor Kozlov .20 .50
P144 Scott Stevens .30 .75
P145 Jiri Slegr .20 .50
P146 Steve Yzerman 2.50 6.00
P147 Jocelyn Thibault .30 .75
P148 Stephane Fiset .20 .50
P149 Kenny Jonsson .20 .50
P150 Steve Shields .20 .50
P151 Paul Kariya .40 1.00
P152 Shane Willis .20 .50
P153 Martin Lapointe .20 .50
P154 Brian Savage .20 .50
P155 Alexei Yashin .20 .50
P156 Marcus Ragnarsson .20 .50
P157 Petr Tenkrat .20 .50
P158 Sandis Ozolinsh .20 .50
P159 Anson Carter .20 .50
P160 Scott Hartnell .20 .50
P161 Rick Tocchet .20 .50
P162 Brad Richards .30 .75
P163 Byron Dafoe .20 .50
P164 Marc Denis .30 .75
P165 Steve Reinprecht .20 .50
P166 Mario Lemieux 3.00 8.00
P167 Taylor Pyatt .20 .50
P168 Mike Vernon .30 .75
P169 Scott Niedermayer .20 .50
P170 Milan Kraft .20 .50
P171 Donald Audette .20 .50
P172 Steve Sullivan .20 .50
P173 Todd Marchant .20 .50
P174 Scott Walker .20 .50
P175 Daymond Langkow .20 .50
P176 Fredrik Modin .20 .50
P177 Ray Ferraro .20 .50
P178 Michael Nylander .20 .50
P179 Robert Svehla .20 .50
P180 Petr Sykora .20 .50
P181 Claude Lemieux .20 .50
P182 Sergei Berezin .20 .50
P183 Doug Gilmour .30 .75
P184 Jere Lehtinen .20 .50
P185 Maxim Sushinski .20 .50
P186 Jan Hlavac .20 .50
P187 Michal Handzus .20 .50
P188 Jamie Langenbrunner .20 .50
P189 John Vanbiesbrouck .30 .75
P190 Brent Johnson .30 .75
P191 Jason Allison .20 .50
P192 Adam Deadmarsh .20 .50
P193 Scott Mellanby .20 .50
P194 Sergei Brylin .20 .50
P195 Shane Doan .20 .50
P196 Jonas Hoglund .20 .50
P197 Bill Guerin .20 .50
P198 Espen Knutsen .20 .50
P199 Bryan Smolinski .20 .50
P200 Brad Isbister .20 .50
P201 Robert Lang .20 .50
P202 Andrew Cassels .20 .50
P203 Daniel Tkaczuk .20 .50
P204 Igor Larionov .20 .50
P205 Andrei Markov .20 .50
P206 Magnus Arvedson .20 .50
P207 Henrik Sedin .20 .50
P208 Manny Legace .20 .50
P209 Adam Graves .20 .50
P210 Marty Turco .30 .75
P211 Stu Barnes .20 .50
P212 Geoff Sanderson .20 .50
P213 Luc Robitaille .30 .75
P214 Roman Hamrlik .20 .50
P215 Jaromir Jagr 1.00 2.50
P216 Markus Naslund .40 1.00
P217 Alexei Zhitnik .20 .50
P218 Joe Nieuwendyk .30 .75
P219 Lubomir Sekeras .20 .50
P220 Petr Nedved .20 .50
P221 Dallas Drake .20 .50
P222 Sergei Gonchar .20 .50
P223 Dave Tanabe .20 .50
P224 Tommy Salo .20 .50
P225 Rick DiPietro .40 1.00
P226 Justin Williams .20 .50
P227 Dimitri Khristich .20 .50
P228 Lubomir Visnovsky .20 .50
P229 Jani Hurme .20 .50
P230 Roman Cechmanek .30 .75
P231 Cory Stillman .20 .50
P232 Mike Modano .60 1.50
P233 Scott Pellerin .20 .50
P234 Mark Messier .40 1.00
P235 Scott Young .20 .50
P236 Peter Bondra .30 .75
P237 Oleg Saprykin .20 .50
P238 Pat Verbeek .20 .50
P239 Martin Rucinsky .20 .50
P240 Martin Havlat .40 1.00
P241 Evgeni Nabokov .30 .75
P242 Tomi Kallio .20 .50
P243 Eric Daze .20 .50
P244 Roberto Luongo .60 1.50
P245 Bobby Holik .20 .50
P246 Sean Burke .20 .50
P247 Martin Biron .20 .50
P248 Mathieu Garon .30 .75
P249 Jamie Storr .20 .50
P250 Maxime Ouellet .20 .50

2006-07 Be A Player Portraits

COMP.SET w/o SPs (100) 12.00 30.00
1 Jean-Sebastien Giguere .30 .75
2 Chris Pronger .25 .60
3 Teemu Selanne .30 .75
4 Scott Niedermayer .20 .50
5 Ilya Kovalchuk .40 1.00
6 Kari Lehtonen .30 .75
7 Marian Hossa .25 .60
8 Marc Savard .20 .50
9 Brad Boyes .20 .50
10 Patrice Bergeron .25 .60
11 Hannu Toivonen .25 .60
12 Zdeno Chara .20 .50
13 Daniel Briere .25 .60
14 Chris Drury .25 .60
15 Ryan Miller .30 .75
16 Jarome Iginla .50 1.25
17 Miikka Kiprusoff .30 .75
18 Dion Phaneuf .40 1.00
19 Alex Tanguay .25 .60
20 Rod Brind'Amour .25 .60
21 Erik Cole .20 .50
22 Eric Staal .25 .60
23 Cam Ward .50 1.25
24 Nikolai Khabibulin .20 .50
25 Martin Havlat .25 .60
26 Tuomo Ruutu .20 .50
27 Marek Svatos .20 .50
28 Joe Sakic .60 1.50
29 Jose Theodore .20 .50
30 Milan Hejduk .25 .60
31 Rick Nash .30 .75
32 Pascal LeClaire .30 .75
33 Sergei Fedorov .30 .75
34 Gilbert Brule .20 .50
35 Mike Modano .30 .75
36 Marty Turco .25 .60
37 Brenden Morrow .25 .60
38 Eric Lindros .30 .75
39 Dominik Hasek .40 1.00
40 Pavel Datsyuk .30 .75
41 Nicklas Lidstrom .30 .75
42 Henrik Zetterberg .30 .75
43 Ales Hemsky .20 .50
44 Ryan Smyth .25 .60
45 Joffrey Lupul .20 .50
46 Shawn Horcoff .20 .50
47 Ed Belfour .75 2.00
48 Olli Jokinen .20 .50
49 Nathan Horton .20 .50
50 Todd Bertuzzi .25 .60
51 Rob Blake .25 .60
52 Alexander Frolov .20 .50
53 Pavol Demitra .20 .50
54 Manny Fernandez .30 .75
55 Marian Gaborik .50 1.25
56 Cristobal Huet .30 .75
57 Sergei Samsonov .25 .60
58 Saku Koivu .30 .75
59 Michael Ryder .25 .60
60 Paul Kariya .30 .75
61 Tomas Vokoun .25 .60
62 Martin Brodeur 1.00 2.50
63 Patrik Elias .20 .50
64 Brian Gionta .20 .50
65 Alexei Yashin .20 .50
66 Miroslav Satan .20 .50
67 Rick DiPietro .30 .75
68 Jaromir Jagr .50 1.25
69 Henrik Lundqvist .50 1.25
70 Brendan Shanahan .30 .75
71 Dany Heatley .30 .75
72 Jason Spezza .30 .75
73 Wade Redden .20 .50
74 Daniel Alfredsson .25 .60
75 Peter Forsberg .50 1.25
76 Antero Niittymaki .30 .75
77 Jeff Carter .30 .75
78 Simon Gagne .30 .75
79 Curtis Joseph .30 .75
80 Jeremy Roenick .30 .75
81 Shane Doan .25 .60
82 Marc-Andre Fleury .30 .75
83 Sidney Crosby 1.50 4.00
84 Joe Thornton .50 1.25
85 Patrick Marleau .25 .60
86 Jonathan Cheechoo .30 .75
87 Keith Tkachuk .25 .60
88 Doug Weight .20 .50
89 Brad Richards .30 .75
90 Vincent Lecavalier .30 .75
91 Martin St. Louis .30 .75
92 Mats Sundin .30 .75
93 Alexander Steen .25 .60
94 Michael Peca .20 .50
95 Andrew Raycroft .25 .60
96 Markus Naslund .30 .75
97 Brendan Morrison .20 .50
98 Roberto Luongo .60 1.50
99 Alexander Ovechkin 1.25 3.00
100 Olaf Kolzig .40 1.00
101 Yan Stastny RC 1.25 3.00
102 Mark Stuart RC 1.25 3.00
103 Evgeni Malkin RC 6.00 15.00
104 Patrick Thoresen RC 1.25 3.00
105 Patrick O'Sullivan RC 1.50 4.00
106 Tomas Kopecky RC 1.50 4.00
107 Marc-Antoine Pouliot RC 1.50 4.00
108 Konstantin Pushkaryov RC 1.25 3.00
109 Phil Kessel RC 4.00 10.00
110 Luc Bourdon RC 1.50 4.00
111 Shea Weber RC 1.50 4.00
112 Guillaume Latendresse RC 4.00 10.00
113 Jordan Staal RC 5.00 12.00
114 Paul Stastny RC 5.00 12.00
115 Anze Kopitar RC 3.00 8.00
116 Jarkko Immonen RC 1.25 3.00
117 Travis Zajac RC 2.00 5.00
118 Nigel Dawes RC 1.25 3.00
119 Kristopher Letang RC 2.00 5.00
120 Ryan Potulny RC 1.50 4.00
121 Ryan Shannon RC 1.25 3.00
122 Marc-Edouard Vlasic RC 1.25 3.00
123 Noah Welch RC 1.25 3.00
124 Ladislav Smid RC 1.25 3.00
125 Matt Carle RC 1.50 4.00
126 Loui Eriksson RC 1.25 3.00
127 Brendan Bell RC 1.25 3.00
128 Ian White RC 1.25 3.00
129 Jeremy Williams RC 1.25 3.00
130 Eric Fehr RC 1.50 4.00

2006-07 Be A Player Portraits First Exposures

ODDS 1 PER PACK
FEAK Andrei Kostitsyn 4.00 10.00
FEAL Andrew Ladd 3.00 8.00
FEAM Andrej Meszaros 3.00 8.00
FEAO Alexander Ovechkin 20.00 50.00
FEAP Alexander Perezhogin 3.00 8.00
FEAS Alexander Steen 4.00 10.00
FEBB Brandon Bochenski 3.00 8.00
FEBW Brad Winchester 3.00 8.00
FECB Cam Barker 3.00 8.00
FECP Corey Perry 4.00 10.00
FECW Cam Ward 8.00 20.00
FEDB Derek Boogaard 3.00 8.00
FEDP Dion Phaneuf 6.00 15.00
FEDP Daniel Paille 3.00 8.00
FEEN Eric Nystrom 3.00 8.00
FEGB Gilbert Brule 3.00 8.00
FEHL Henrik Lundqvist 8.00 20.00
FEHT Hannu Toivonen 5.00 12.00
FEJC Jeff Carter 5.00 12.00
FEJF Johan Franzen 3.00 8.00
FEJG Josh Gorges 3.00 8.00
FEJH Jim Howard 8.00 20.00
FEJJ Jussi Jokinen 3.00 8.00
FEJK Jakub Klepis 3.00 8.00
FEJT Jeff Tambellini 3.00 8.00
FEMJ Milan Jurcina 3.00 8.00
FEMK Mikko Koivu 3.00 8.00
FEMR Mike Richards 5.00 12.00
FEPB Peter Budaj 4.00 10.00
FEPN Petteri Nokelainen 3.00 8.00
FEPP Petr Prucha 3.00 8.00
FERG Ryan Getzlaf 4.00 10.00
FERO Rostislav Olesz 3.00 8.00
FERS Ryan Suter 3.00 8.00
FERU R.J. Umberger 3.00 8.00
FERW Ryan Whitney 3.00 8.00
FESC Sidney Crosby 25.00 60.00
FETV Thomas Vanek 4.00 10.00
FEVF Valtteri Filppula 3.00 8.00
FEWW Wojtek Wolski 3.00 8.00
FEYD Yann Danis 4.00 10.00
FEZP Zach Parise 4.00 10.00

2006-07 Be A Player Portraits Signature Portraits

OVERALL ODDS ONE PER PACK
SPAL Andrew Ladd 8.00 20.00
SPAO Alexander Ovechkin 50.00 120.00
SPAT Alex Tanguay 10.00 25.00
SPBB Brad Boyes 8.00 20.00
SPBG Bill Guerin 8.00 20.00
SPBH Bobby Hollik 8.00 20.00
SPBL Brian Leetch 8.00 20.00
SPBM Brenden Morrow 10.00 25.00
SPBR Brian Rolston 8.00 20.00
SPBS Brent Seabrook 8.00 20.00
SPBW Brad Winchester 8.00 20.00
SPCA Colby Armstrong 8.00 20.00
SPCB Cam Barker 8.00 20.00
SPCD Chris Drury SP 15.00 40.00
SPCH Jonathan Cheechoo 12.00 30.00
SPCW Cam Ward 20.00 50.00
SPDB Daniel Briere SP 15.00 40.00
SPDH Dany Heatley 12.00 30.00
SPDP Daniel Paille 8.00 20.00
SPDR Dwayne Roloson 10.00 25.00
SPDW Doug Weight SP 12.00 30.00
SPEJ Ed Jovanovski 8.00 20.00
SPEM Evgeni Malkin 40.00 100.00
SPEN Evgeni Nabokov 10.00 25.00
SPES Robert Esche 10.00 25.00
SPGM Glen Murray 8.00 20.00
SPHA Jeff Halpern 8.00 20.00
SPHE Milan Hejduk 10.00 25.00
SPHK Dominik Hasek 15.00 40.00
SPHL Henrik Lundqvist 20.00 50.00
SPHT Hannu Toivonen 12.00 30.00
SPJB Jay Bouwmeester SP 12.00 30.00
SPJC Jeff Carter 12.00 30.00
SPJG Jean-Sebastien Giguere SP 20.00 50.00
SPJI Jarome Iginla 20.00 50.00
SPJJ Jussi Jokinen 8.00 20.00
SPJO Joe Thornton 20.00 50.00
SPJP Joni Pitkanen 8.00 20.00
SPJS Joe Sakic 25.00 60.00
SPKB Keith Ballard 8.00 20.00
SPKL Kari Lehtonen 12.00 30.00
SPKO Mikko Koivu 8.00 20.00
SPKP Keith Primeau 8.00 20.00
SPLE John LeClair 10.00 25.00
SPLS Lee Stempniak 8.00 20.00
SPMA Marc-Andre Fleury 12.00 30.00
SPMB Mark Bell 8.00 20.00
SPMG Martin Gerber 12.00 30.00
SPMH Marian Hossa 10.00 25.00
SPMJ Milan Jurcina 8.00 20.00
SPMK Miikka Kiprusoff 12.00 30.00
SPMM Mike Modano SP 20.00 50.00
SPMN Markus Naslund 12.00 30.00
SPMO Brendan Morrison 8.00 20.00
SPMS Marek Svatos 8.00 20.00
SPMT Marty Turco 10.00 25.00
SPNH Nathan Horton 8.00 20.00
SPNK Nikolai Khabibulin SP 20.00 50.00
SPNL Nicklas Lidstrom 12.00 30.00
SPNZ Nikolai Zherdev 8.00 20.00
SPOJ Olli Jokinen SP 12.00 30.00
SPOK Olaf Kolzig 15.00 40.00
SPPB Patrice Bergeron 10.00 25.00
SPPK Paul Kariya 12.00 30.00
SPPM Patrick Marleau 10.00 25.00
SPPP Petr Prucha 8.00 20.00
SPRB Rob Blake 10.00 25.00
SPRD Mike Richards 12.00 30.00
SPRJ R.J. Umberger 8.00 20.00
SPRL Roberto Luongo 25.00 60.00
SPRM Ryan Miller 12.00 30.00
SPRN Rick Nash 12.00 30.00
SPRO Rostislav Olesz 8.00 20.00
SPRW Ryan Whitney 8.00 20.00
SPSB Steve Bernier 8.00 20.00
SPSC Sidney Crosby SP 300.00 450.00
SPSD Shane Doan 10.00 25.00
SPSF Sergei Fedorov SP 20.00 50.00
SPSG Simon Gagne SP 20.00 50.00
SPSJ Matt Stajan 8.00 20.00
SPSK Saku Koivu 12.00 30.00
SPSM Mats Sundin 12.00 30.00
SPSN Scott Niedermayer 8.00 20.00
SPSP Jason Spezza 12.00 30.00
SPSR Ryan Suter 8.00 20.00
SPSS Steve Sullivan 8.00 20.00
SPST Eric Staal 10.00 25.00
SPTP Tom Poti 8.00 20.00
SPTR Tuomo Ruutu 8.00 20.00
SPTV Thomas Vanek 10.00 25.00
SPVO Tomas Vokoun 10.00 25.00
SPWR Wade Redden 8.00 20.00
SPWW Wojtek Wolski 8.00 20.00
SPZC Zdeno Chara 8.00 20.00

2006-07 Be A Player Portraits Dual Signature Portraits

STATED ODDS 1:6
DSBB Brad Boyes / Patrice Bergeron 8.00 20.00
DSCJ Zdeno Chara / Milan Jurcina 6.00 15.00
DSCT Joe Thornton / Jonathan Cheechoo SP 40.00 80.00
DSDB Chris Drury / Daniel Briere 8.00 20.00
DSDJ Jason Spezza / Dany Heatley 10.00 25.00
DSFN Rick Nash / Sergei Fedorov 10.00 25.00
DSFW Marc-Andre Fleury / Ryan Whitney 10.00 25.00
DSGC Simon Gagne / Jeff Carter 10.00 25.00
DSGN Scott Niedermayer / Jean-Sebastien Giguere 10.00 25.00
DSHL Dominik Hasek / Nicklas Lidstrom 12.00 30.00
DSHS Milan Hejduk / Marek Svatos 8.00 20.00
DSIT Jarome Iginla / Alex Tanguay 15.00 40.00
DSJB Olli Jokinen / Jay Bouwmeester 6.00 15.00
DSKK Saku Koivu / Mikko Koivu 6.00 15.00
DSKV Paul Kariya / Tomas Vokoun 10.00 25.00
DSLN Markus Naslund / Roberto Luongo 20.00 50.00
DSLP Henrik Lundqvist / Petr Prucha 15.00 40.00
DSMT Mike Modano / Marty Turco 10.00 25.00
DSNT Tuomo Ruutu / Nikolai Khabibulin 10.00 25.00
DSOK Olaf Kolzig / Alexander Ovechkin 40.00 100.00
DSRU Mike Richards / R.J. Umberger 10.00 25.00
DSSM Joe Sakic / Mike Modano SP 50.00 100.00
DSWG Doug Weight / Bill Guerin 6.00 15.00
DSWS Eric Staal / Cam Ward 15.00 40.00

2006-07 Be A Player Portraits Quadruple Signature Portraits

PRINT RUN 10 #'d SETS
NOT PRICED DUE TO SCARCITY
[illegible] Tomas Vokoun / Marian Hossa / Dominik Hasek / Milan Hejduk
QKIHN Paul Kariya / Jarome Iginla / Dany Heatley / Rick Nash
QKKJP Saku Koivu / Olli Jokinen / Miikka Kiprusoff / Joni Pitkanen
QSSTS Joe Sakic / Joe Thornton / Jason Spezza / Eric Staal

2006-07 Be A Player Portraits Sensational Six

PRINT RUN 5 #'d SETS
NOT PRICED DUE TO SCARCITY
SS1ST Mike Modano / Mats Sundin / Joe Thornton / Rick Nash / Marc-Andre Fleury / Alexander Ovechkin
SSCON Jarome Iginla / Simon Gagne / Jason Spezza / Dany Heatley / Rick Nash / Eric Staal
SSGOL Dominik Hasek / Roberto Luongo / Jean-Sebastien Giguere / Marty Turco / Marc-Andre Fleury / Cam Ward
SSSJM Joe Sakic / Mats Sundin / Patrick Marleau / Saku Koivu / Markus Naslund / Joe Thornton
SSSTR Nicklas Lidstrom / Sergei Fedorov / Joe Sakic / Mike Modano / Mats Sundin / Dominik Hasek

2006-07 Be A Player Portraits Timeless Tens

PRINT RUN 3 #'d SETS
NOT PRICED DUE TO SCARCITY
TTCAN Joe Thornton / Jarome Iginla / Simon Gagne / Jason Spezza / Alex Tanguay / Jonathan Cheechoo / Dany Heatley / Rick Nash / Patrice Bergeron / Eric Staal
TTNET Tomas Vokoun / Dominik Hasek / Roberto Luongo / Jean-Sebastien Giguere / Evgeni Nabokov / Henrik Lundqvist / Martin Gerber / Miikka Kiprusoff / Cam Ward / Nikolai Khabibulin

2006-07 Be A Player Portraits Triple Signature Portraits

PRINT RUN 25 #'d SETS
TBOS Glen Murray / Brad Boyes / Patrice Bergeron 30.00 80.00
TBUF Chris Drury / Daniel Briere / Ryan Miller 40.00 100.00
TCGY Alex Tanguay / Miikka Kiprusoff / Jarome Iginla
TCLB Rick Nash / Nikolai Zherdev / Sergei Fedorov 40.00 100.00
TCOL Joe Sakic / Milan Hejduk / Marek Svatos 80.00 200.00
TLWF Roberto Luongo / Marc-Andre Fleury / Cam Ward 80.00 200.00
TNSS Jason Spezza / Rick Nash / Eric Staal 40.00 100.00
TOTT Dany Heatley / Wade Redden / Jason Spezza 40.00 100.00
TSJS Joe Thornton / Mark Bell / Jonathan Cheechoo 60.00 150.00
TSSM Joe Sakic / Mike Modano / Mats Sundin 80.00 200.00

2000-01 BAP Signature Series

Released in February 2001 as a 300-card set with 5 cards per pack, Be A Player Signature Series featured full color action photos on silver metallic stock with the set name on the left border and the players name in the lower right corner. Cards 251-275 were short-printed to just 1000 serial-numbered sets, and cards 276-300 were short-printed to just 500 serial-numbered sets.

COMP.SET w/o SP's (250) 50.00 100.00
SP's 251-275 PRINT RUN 1000 SER.#'d SETS
SP's 276-300 PRINT RUN 500 SER.#'d SETS
1 Doug Gilmour .50 1.25
2 Todd Reirden .30 .75
3 Mike Johnson .30 .75
4 Scott Walker .30 .75
5 Mike York .30 .75
6 Roman Turek .50 1.25
7 Sergei Zubov .30 .75
8 Brad Stuart .50 1.25
9 Michael Peca .50 1.25
10 Jyrki Lumme .30 .75
11 Steve Yzerman 3.00 8.00
12 Olaf Kolzig .50 1.25
13 Ray Bourque 1.25 3.00
14 Clarke Wilm .30 .75
15 Eric Desjardins .50 1.25
16 Rod Brind'Amour .50 1.25
17 Marc Savard .30 .75
18 Jarome Iginla .75 2.00
19 Daniel Alfredsson .50 1.25
20 Alexei Yashin .30 .75
21 Keith Tkachuk .60 1.50
22 Jaromir Jagr 1.00 2.50
23 Trevor Kidd .50 1.25
24 Alexei Kovalev .50 1.25
25 Jan Hrdina .30 .75
26 Tom Poti .30 .75
27 Jere Karalahti .30 .75
28 Janne Niinimaa .30 .75
29 Ray Whitney .30 .75
30 Nicklas Lidstrom .60 1.50
31 Martin Lapointe .30 .75
32 Matt Cullen .30 .75
33 Theo Fleury .30 .75
34 Mats Sundin .60 1.50
35 Kimmo Timonen .30 .75
36 Joe Thornton 1.00 2.50
37 Adam Graves .30 .75
38 Andrei Zyuzin .30 .75
39 Michal Handzus .30 .75
40 Jamie Storr .50 1.25
41 Teemu Selanne .60 1.50
42 Brian Rafalski .30 .75
43 Aaron Gavey .30 .75
44 Jose Theodore .75 2.00
45 Tyler Wright .30 .75
46 Alexander Mogilny .50 1.25
47 Brad Isbister .30 .75
48 Guy Hebert .50 1.25
49 Chris Simon .30 .75
50 Dominik Hasek 1.25 3.00
51 Dan Cloutier .30 .75
52 Brian Holzinger .30 .75
53 Dimitri Khristich .30 .75
54 Tyson Nash .30 .75
55 Patrick Marleau .50 1.25
56 Marty Reasoner .30 .75
57 Manny Fernandez .50 1.25
58 Brenden Morrow .50 1.25
59 Darren McCarty .30 .75
60 Milan Hejduk .60 1.50
61 Darius Kasparaitis .30 .75
62 Jere Lehtinen .50 1.25
63 Andrew Brunette .30 .75
64 Wayne Gretzky 4.00 10.00
65 Robyn Regehr .30 .75
66 Travis Green .30 .75
67 John Grahame .50 1.25
68 Mike Fisher .30 .75
69 Josef Marha .30 .75
70 Randy McKay .30 .75
71 Brett Hull .75 2.00
72 Anson Carter .50 1.25
73 Owen Nolan .50 1.25
74 Sean Burke .50 1.25
75 Mario Lemieux 4.00 10.00
76 Brian Savage .30 .75
77 Jason Ward .30 .75
78 Patrick Lalime .50 1.25
79 Glen Murray .30 .75
80 Mathieu Biron .30 .75
81 Todd Bertuzzi .60 1.50
82 Chris Drury .50 1.25
83 Maxim Afinogenov .30 .75
84 Michal Rozsival .30 .75
85 Glen Metropolit .30 .75
86 Mariusz Czerkawski .30 .75
87 Byron Dafoe .50 1.25
88 Mark Recchi .50 1.25
89 Mike Modano 1.00 2.50
90 Felix Potvin .60 1.50
91 Saku Koivu .60 1.50
92 Jay Pandolfo .30 .75
93 Todd Simpson .30 .75
94 Calle Johansson .30 .75
95 Bill Guerin .50 1.25
96 Oleg Tverdovsky .30 .75
97 Kyle McLaren .30 .75
98 Mark Messier .60 1.50
99 Chris Gratton .30 .75
100 Sergei Brylin .30 .75
101 David Legwand .50 1.25
102 Jason Allison .30 .75
103 Daniel Cleary .30 .75
104 Curtis Joseph .60 1.50
105 Sergei Fedorov 1.00 2.50
106 Jeremy Roenick .75 2.00
107 Frantisek Kaberle .30 .75
108 Chris Pronger .50 1.25
109 Martin Skoula .50 1.25
110 Jiri Slegr .30 .75
111 Trevor Letowski .30 .75
112 Colin Forbes .30 .75
113 Sergei Zholtok .30 .75
114 David Harlock .30 .75
115 Scott Stevens .50 1.25
116 Dave Tanabe .30 .75
117 Mattias Timander .30 .75
118 Stu Barnes .30 .75
119 Simon Gagne .60 1.50
120 Paul Coffey .60 1.50
121 Peter Bondra .60 1.50
122 Ed Jovanovski .50 1.25
123 J-P Dumont .30 .75
124 Pavol Demitra .50 1.25
125 Mike Vernon .50 1.25
126 Brendan Morrison .50 1.25
127 Dainius Zubrus .30 .75
128 Al MacInnis .50 1.25
129 Kevyn Adams .30 .75
130 Petr Buzek .30 .75
131 Steve Kariya .30 .75
132 Keith Primeau .30 .75
133 Kenny Jonsson .30 .75
134 Lance Pitlick .30 .75
135 Randy Robitaille .30 .75
136 Brian Rolston .30 .75
137 Alex Tanguay .50 1.25
138 Alexei Zhamnov .30 .75
139 Peter Forsberg 1.50 4.00
140 Cam Stewart .30 .75
141 Vitali Vishnevsky .30 .75
142 Tim Connolly .30 .75
143 Tie Domi .50 1.25
144 Jaroslav Modry .30 .75
145 Jarno Kultanen RC .30 .75
146 Igor Larionov .30 .75
147 Derian Hatcher .30 .75
148 Scott Niedermayer .30 .75
149 Shawn McEachern .30 .75
150 Sergei Berezin .30 .75
151 Rob Blake .50 1.25
152 Steve Thomas .30 .75
153 Ryan Smyth .30 .75
154 Petr Nedved .30 .75
155 Jochen Hecht .30 .75
156 Richard Zednik .30 .75
157 Tommy Salo .50 1.25
158 Ed Belfour .60 1.50
159 Lyle Odelein .30 .75
160 Steve Sullivan .30 .75
161 Vincent Damphousse .30 .75
162 Andy Delmore .30 .75
163 Harold Druken .30 .75
164 Martin Brodeur 1.50 4.00
165 Mike Richter .60 1.50
166 Radek Bonk .30 .75
167 Joe Sakic 1.25 3.00
168 John Vanbiesbrouck .50 1.25
169 Jeff Shantz .30 .75
170 Jean-Sebastien Aubin .50 1.25
171 Shayne Corson .30 .75

Card	Low	High
172 Jeff Friesen	.30	.75
173 Jeff Hackett	.50	1.25
174 Jozef Stumpel	.30	.75
175 Daymond Langkow	.50	1.25
176 Nikolai Antropov	.30	.75
177 Ron Tugnutt	.50	1.25
178 Viktor Kozlov	.50	1.25
179 Adam Oates	.50	1.25
180 Steve Webb	.30	.75
181 Pierre Turgeon	.50	1.25
182 Fred Brathwaite	.50	1.25
183 Martin Biron	.50	1.25
184 John LeClair	.60	1.50
185 Steve Rucchin	.30	.75
186 Patrik Elias	.50	1.25
187 Boris Mironov	.30	.75
188 Mika Alatalo	.30	.75
189 Jocelyn Thibault	.50	1.25
190 Jason York	.30	.75
191 Zigmund Palffy	.50	1.25
192 Paul Kariya	.60	1.50
193 Stu Grimson	.30	.75
194 Jeff Halpern	.30	.75
195 Scott Gomez	.30	.75
196 Tomas Vlasak	.30	.75
197 Roman Hamrlik	.30	.75
198 Radek Dvorak	.30	.75
199 Martin Straka	.30	.75
200 Martin Rucinsky	.30	.75
201 Valeri Bure	.30	.75
202 Scott Mellanby	.30	.75
203 Steve McKenna	.30	.75
204 Luc Robitaille	.50	1.25
205 Joe Nieuwendyk	.50	1.25
206 Brendan Shanahan	.60	1.50
207 Robert Lang	.30	.75
208 Todd Marchant	.30	.75
209 Doug Weight	.50	1.25
210 Andre Roy	.30	.75
211 Patrick Roy	3.00	8.00
212 Vincent Lecavalier	.60	1.50
213 Trevor Linden	.50	1.25
214 Patrik Stefan	.30	.75
215 Jan Hlavac	.30	.75
216 Ron Francis	.50	1.25
217 Brian Boucher	.60	1.50
218 Tony Hrkac	.30	.75
219 Brian Leetch	.50	1.25
220 Tony Amonte	.50	1.25
221 Nikolai Khabibulin	.50	1.25
222 Sandis Ozolinsh	.30	.75
223 Darryl Sydor	.30	.75
224 Bobby Holik	.30	.75
225 Sami Kapanen	.30	.75
226 Pavel Bure	.60	1.50
227 Steve Konowalchuk	.30	.75
228 Brent Gilchrist	.30	.75
229 Jeff O'Neill	.30	.75
230 Andre Savage	.30	.75
231 Pavel Kubina	.30	.75
232 Jason Arnott	.30	.75
233 Petr Sykora	.30	.75
234 Miroslav Satan	.50	1.25
235 Chris Osgood	.50	1.25
236 Sergei Samsonov	.50	1.25
237 Marian Hossa	.60	1.50
238 Arturs Irbe	.50	1.25
239 Josh Holden	.30	.75
240 Phil Housley	.30	.75
241 Dimitri Yushkevich	.30	.75
242 Cliff Ronning	.30	.75
243 John Madden	.30	.75
244 Jaroslav Spacek	.30	.75
245 Craig Darby	.30	.75
246 Eric Lindros	.60	1.50
247 Markus Naslund	.60	1.50
248 Sergei Gonchar	.30	.75
249 Gary Roberts	.30	.75
250 Steve Shields	.50	1.25
251 Petteri Nummelin SP RC	1.00	2.50
252 Mika Noronen SP	1.00	2.50
253 Andrew Raycroft SP RC	3.00	8.00
254 Taylor Pyatt SP	1.00	2.50
255 Toni Lydman SP	1.00	2.50
256 Matt Bradley SP	1.00	2.50
257 Petr Hubacek SP RC	1.00	2.50
258 Ossi Vaananen SP RC	1.00	2.50
259 Dimitri Kalinin SP	1.00	2.50
260 Justin Williams SP RC	3.00	8.00
261 Jeff Farkas SP	1.00	2.50
262 Brent Sopel SP RC	1.00	2.50
263 Samuel Pahlsson SP	1.00	2.50
264 Josef Vasicek SP RC	1.00	2.50
265 Shane Willis SP	1.00	2.50
266 Petr Svoboda SP RC	1.00	2.50
267 Petr Schastlivy SP	1.00	2.50
268 Roman Simicek SP RC	1.00	2.50
269 Reto Von Arx SP RC	1.00	2.50
270 Colin White SP RC	1.00	2.50
271 Lubomir Sekeras SP RC	1.00	2.50
272 Alexander Kharitonov SP RC	1.00	2.50
273 Maxim Sushinski SP	1.00	2.50
274 Sergei Vyshedkevich SP RC	1.00	2.50
275 Brad Ference SP	1.00	2.50
276 Martin Havlat SP RC	6.00	15.00
277 Maxime Ouellet SP	3.00	8.00
278 Roberto Luongo SP	4.00	10.00
279 Marian Gaborik RC	10.00	25.00
280 Daniel Sedin SP	3.00	8.00
281 Henrik Sedin SP	3.00	8.00
282 Milan Kraft SP	3.00	8.00
283 Denis Shvidki SP	3.00	8.00
284 Kris Beech SP	3.00	8.00
285 Rostislav Klesla SP RC	3.00	8.00
286 Jani Hurme SP RC	3.00	8.00
287 Oleg Saprykin SP	3.00	8.00
288 Marty Turco RC	5.00	12.00
289 Brad Richards SP	3.00	8.00
290 Steve McCarthy SP	3.00	8.00
291 Tomi Kallio SP	3.00	8.00
292 Evgeni Nabokov SP	3.00	8.00
293 Steven Reinprecht SP RC	3.00	8.00
294 Andrei Markov SP	3.00	8.00
295 Brent Johnson SP	3.00	8.00
296 Rick DiPietro SP RC	6.00	15.00
297 Roman Cechmanek SP RC	3.00	8.00
298 Daniel Tkaczuk SP	3.00	8.00
299 Mathieu Garon SP	3.00	8.00
300 Scott Hartnell SP RC	4.00	10.00

2000-01 BAP Signature Series Emerald

STAT.PRINT RUN 10 SER.#'d SETS
NOT PRICED DUE TO SCARCITY

2000-01 BAP Signature Series Ruby

*STARS: 2X TO 4X BASIC CARDS
*SP's 251-275: .3X TO .75X BASIC CARDS
*SP'S 276-300: .25X TO .5X BASIC CARDS
STAT.PRINT RUN 200 SER.#'d SETS

2000-01 BAP Signature Series Sapphire

*STARS: 4X TO 8X BASIC CARDS
*SP's 251-275: .5X TO 1X BASIC CARDS
*SP'S 276-300: .3X TO .75X
STAT.PRINT RUN 100 SER.#'d SETS

2000-01 BAP Signature Series Autographs

Randomly inserted in packs at the rate of one in one, this 250-card set paralleled the base set with player autographs.

ONE PER PACK
*GOLD AUTOS: .5X TO 1.25X HI

Card	Low	High
1 Pavel Bure SP	12.50	30.00
2 Valeri Bure SP	10.00	25.00
3 Mike Johnson	2.00	5.00
4 Rob Blake	4.00	10.00
5 Brendan Morrison	2.00	5.00
6 David Legwand	2.00	5.00
7 Dimitri Kalinin	2.00	5.00
8 Jeff Farkas	2.00	5.00
9 Brian Savage	2.00	5.00
10 Dan Cloutier	2.00	5.00
11 Tom Poti	2.00	5.00
12 Doug Gilmour SP	10.00	25.00
13 Steve Konowalchuk	2.00	5.00
14 Scott Mellanby	2.00	5.00
15 Brent Sopel	2.00	5.00
16 Ron Tugnutt SP	10.00	25.00
17 Steve Thomas	2.00	5.00
18 Dainius Zubrus	2.00	5.00
19 Jason Allison SP	10.00	25.00
20 Jason Ward	2.00	5.00
21 Brian Holzinger	2.00	5.00
22 Jere Karalahti	2.00	5.00
23 Todd Reirden	2.00	5.00
24 Brent Gilchrist	2.00	5.00
25 Steve McKenna	2.00	5.00
26 Viktor Kozlov	2.00	5.00
27 Ryan Smyth	2.00	5.00
28 Al MacInnis SP	10.00	25.00
29 Daniel Cleary	2.00	5.00
30 Patrick Lalime	2.00	5.00
31 Dimitri Khristich	2.00	5.00
32 Janne Niinimaa	2.00	5.00
33 Mike Johnson	2.00	5.00
34 Jeff O'Neill SP	10.00	25.00
35 Luc Robitaille SP	10.00	25.00
36 Adam Oates SP	10.00	25.00
37 Petr Nedved	2.00	5.00
38 Kevyn Adams	2.00	5.00
39 Curtis Joseph SP	12.50	30.00
40 Glen Murray	2.00	5.00
41 Tyson Nash	2.00	5.00
42 Ray Whitney	2.00	5.00
43 Scott Walker	2.00	5.00
44 Andre Savage	2.00	5.00
45 Joe Nieuwendyk SP	10.00	25.00
46 Steve Webb	2.00	5.00
47 Jochen Hecht	2.00	5.00
48 Petr Buzek	2.00	5.00
49 Sergei Fedorov SP	20.00	50.00
50 Mathieu Biron	2.00	5.00
51 Patrick Marleau	4.00	10.00
52 Nicklas Lidstrom SP	12.50	30.00
53 Mike York	2.00	5.00
54 Pavel Kubina	2.00	5.00
55 Brendan Shanahan SP	12.50	30.00
56 Pierre Turgeon SP	10.00	25.00
57 Richard Zednik	2.00	5.00
58 Steve Kariya	2.00	5.00
59 Jeremy Roenick SP	15.00	40.00
60 Todd Bertuzzi	4.00	10.00
61 Marty Reasoner	2.00	5.00
62 Martin Lapointe	2.00	5.00
63 Roman Turek	2.00	5.00
64 Jason Arnott SP	10.00	25.00
65 Robert Lang	2.00	5.00
66 Fred Brathwaite	2.00	5.00
67 Tommy Salo	2.00	5.00
68 Keith Primeau SP	10.00	25.00
69 Frantisek Kaberle	2.00	5.00
70 Chris Drury	4.00	10.00
71 Manny Fernandez	4.00	10.00
72 Shane Willis	2.00	5.00
73 Matt Cullen	2.00	5.00
74 Sergei Zubov	2.00	5.00
75 Petr Sykora	2.00	5.00
76 Todd Marchant	2.00	5.00
77 Martin Biron	4.00	10.00
78 Ed Belfour SP	15.00	40.00
79 Kenny Jonsson SP	10.00	25.00
80 Chris Pronger SP	10.00	25.00
81 Maxim Afinogenov	2.00	5.00
82 Brenden Morrow	4.00	10.00
83 Theo Fleury SP	10.00	25.00
84 Brad Stuart	2.00	5.00
85 Miroslav Satan	4.00	10.00
86 Doug Weight SP	10.00	25.00
87 John LeClair SP	10.00	25.00
88 Lyle Odelein	2.00	5.00
89 Lance Pitlick	2.00	5.00
90 Martin Skoula	2.00	5.00
91 Michal Rozsival	2.00	5.00
92 Darren McCarty	4.00	10.00
93 Mats Sundin SP	20.00	50.00
94 Michael Peca	2.00	5.00
95 Chris Osgood SP	10.00	25.00
96 Andre Roy	2.00	5.00
97 Steve Rucchin	2.00	5.00
98 Steve Sullivan	2.00	5.00
99 Randy Robitaille	2.00	5.00
100 Jiri Slegr	2.00	5.00
101 Glen Metropolit	2.00	5.00
102 Milan Hejduk	4.00	10.00
103 Kimmo Timonen	2.00	5.00
104 Jyrki Lumme	2.00	5.00
105 Sergei Samsonov SP	10.00	25.00
106 Patrick Roy SP	60.00	125.00
107 Patrik Elias	4.00	10.00
108 Vincent Damphousse	2.00	5.00
109 Brian Rolston	2.00	5.00
110 Peter Forsberg SP	20.00	50.00
111 Mariusz Czerkawski	2.00	5.00
112 Darius Kasparaitis	2.00	5.00
113 Joe Thornton	10.00	25.00
114 Steve Yzerman SP	40.00	100.00
115 Marian Hossa	6.00	15.00
116 Vincent Lecavalier	6.00	15.00
117 Colin White	2.00	5.00
118 Boris Mironov	2.00	5.00
119 Andy Delmore	2.00	5.00
120 Alex Tanguay	4.00	10.00
121 Colin Forbes	2.00	5.00
122 Byron Dafoe	2.00	5.00
123 Jere Lehtinen	4.00	10.00
124 Adam Graves	2.00	5.00
125 Olaf Kolzig SP	10.00	25.00
126 Arturs Irbe	2.00	5.00
127 Trevor Linden	4.00	10.00
128 Mika Alatalo	2.00	5.00
129 Harold Druken	2.00	5.00
130 Alexei Zhamnov	2.00	5.00
131 Sergei Zholtok	2.00	5.00
132 Mark Recchi SP	10.00	25.00
133 Andrew Brunette	2.00	5.00
134 Andrei Zyuzin	2.00	5.00
135 Ray Bourque SP	20.00	50.00
136 Josh Holden	2.00	5.00
137 Patrik Stefan	2.00	5.00
138 Jocelyn Thibault	4.00	10.00
139 Martin Brodeur SP	40.00	80.00
140 Trevor Letowski	2.00	5.00
141 David Harlock	2.00	5.00
142 Mike Modano SP	12.50	30.00
143 Wayne Gretzky SP	400.00	750.00
144 Michal Handzus	2.00	5.00
145 Clarke Wilm	2.00	5.00
146 Phil Housley	2.00	5.00
147 Jan Hlavac	2.00	5.00
148 Jason York	2.00	5.00
149 Mike Richter SP	12.50	30.00
150 Sergei Vyshedkevich	2.00	5.00
151 Cam Stewart	2.00	5.00
152 Scott Stevens SP	10.00	25.00
153 Felix Potvin	6.00	15.00
154 Robyn Regehr	2.00	5.00
155 Jamie Storr	2.00	5.00
156 Eric Desjardins	2.00	5.00
157 Dimitri Yushkevich	2.00	5.00
158 Ron Francis SP	10.00	25.00
159 Zigmund Palffy SP	10.00	25.00
160 Radek Bonk	2.00	5.00
161 Vitali Vishnevsky	2.00	5.00
162 Dave Tanabe	2.00	5.00
163 Saku Koivu	6.00	15.00
164 Travis Green	2.00	5.00
165 Teemu Selanne SP	15.00	40.00
166 Rod Brind'Amour	2.00	5.00
167 Cliff Ronning	2.00	5.00
168 Brian Boucher	4.00	10.00
169 Paul Kariya SP	20.00	50.00
170 Joe Sakic SP	40.00	100.00
171 Tim Connolly	2.00	5.00
172 Mattias Timander	2.00	5.00
173 Jay Pandolfo	2.00	5.00
174 John Grahame	2.00	5.00
175 Brian Rafalski	2.00	5.00
176 Marc Savard	2.00	5.00
177 John Madden	2.00	5.00
178 Tony Hrkac	2.00	5.00
179 Stu Grimson	2.00	5.00
180 John Vanbiesbrouck SP	10.00	25.00
181 Tie Domi	6.00	15.00
182 Stu Barnes	2.00	5.00
183 Todd Simpson	2.00	5.00
184 Mike Fisher	2.00	5.00
185 Aaron Gavey	2.00	5.00
186 Jarome Iginla	8.00	20.00
187 Jaroslav Spacek	2.00	5.00
188 Brian Leetch SP	12.50	30.00
189 Jeff Halpern	2.00	5.00
190 Jeff Shantz	2.00	5.00
191 Jaroslav Modry	2.00	5.00
192 Simon Gagne	6.00	15.00
193 Calle Johansson	2.00	5.00
194 Josef Marha	2.00	5.00
195 Jose Theodore	8.00	20.00
196 Daniel Alfredsson	4.00	10.00
197 Craig Darby	2.00	5.00
198 Tony Amonte SP	10.00	25.00
199 Scott Gomez	2.00	5.00
200 Jean-Sebastien Aubin	4.00	10.00
201 Jarno Kultanen	2.00	5.00
202 Paul Coffey SP	12.50	30.00
203 Bill Guerin SP	10.00	25.00
204 Roberto Luongo	8.00	20.00
205 Randy McKay	2.00	5.00
206 Tyler Wright	2.00	5.00
207 Alexei Yashin	2.00	5.00
208 Eric Lindros SP	15.00	40.00
209 Nikolai Khabibulin	6.00	15.00
210 Tomas Vlasak	2.00	5.00
211 Shayne Corson	2.00	5.00
212 Igor Larionov SP	10.00	25.00
213 Peter Bondra SP	10.00	25.00
214 Mika Noronen	2.00	5.00
215 Andrew Raycroft	8.00	20.00
216 Taylor Pyatt	2.00	5.00
217 Toni Lydman	2.00	5.00
218 Matt Bradley	2.00	5.00
219 Brad Richards	4.00	10.00
220 Steve McCarthy	2.00	5.00
221 Tomi Kallio	2.00	5.00
222 Justin Williams	2.00	5.00
223 Brad Ference	2.00	5.00
224 Steven Reinprecht	2.00	5.00
225 Samuel Pahlsson	2.00	5.00
226 Josef Vasicek	5.00	5.00
227 Jani Hurme	2.00	5.00
228 Petr Svoboda	2.00	5.00
229 Petr Schastlivy	2.00	5.00
230 Roman Simicek	2.00	5.00
231 Reto Von Arx	2.00	5.00
232 Oleg Saprykin	2.00	5.00
233 Lubomir Sekeras	2.00	5.00
234 Alexander Kharitonov	2.00	5.00
235 Maxim Sushinski	2.00	5.00
236 Andrei Markov	2.00	5.00
237 Scott Hartnell	5.00	5.00
238 Martin Havlat	4.00	10.00
239 Maxime Ouellet	2.00	5.00
240 Petteri Nummelin	2.00	5.00
241 Marian Gaborik	12.00	30.00
242 Daniel Sedin	2.00	5.00
243 Henrik Sedin	2.00	5.00
244 Milan Kraft	2.00	5.00
245 Denis Shvidki	2.00	5.00
246 Kris Beech	2.00	5.00
247 Rostislav Klesla	2.00	5.00
248 Petr Hubacek	2.00	5.00
249 Ossi Vaananen	2.00	5.00
250 Marty Turco	4.00	10.00

2000-01 BAP Signature Series Department of Defense

Randomly inserted in packs, this 20-card set featured a game-used swatch of jersey and a action player photo on a background of computer generated steel girders and rivets. Each card had a stated print run of 100 each.

*MULT.COLOR SWATCH: 1X TO 2X
STAT.PRINT RUN 100 SETS

Card	Low	High
DD1 Brian Leetch	10.00	25.00
DD2 Ray Bourque	25.00	60.00
DD3 Chris Chelios	15.00	40.00
DD4 Nicklas Lidstrom	20.00	50.00
DD5 Sandis Ozolinsh	8.00	20.00
DD6 Scott Stevens	10.00	25.00
DD7 Al MacInnis	10.00	25.00
DD8 Kyle McLaren	8.00	20.00
DD9 Kenny Jonsson	8.00	20.00
DD10 Teppo Numminen	8.00	20.00
DD11 Sergei Zubov	8.00	20.00
DD12 Scott Niedermayer	8.00	20.00
DD13 Paul Coffey	25.00	60.00
DD14 Adam Foote	8.00	20.00
DD15 Sergei Gonchar	8.00	20.00
DD16 Phil Housley	8.00	20.00
DD17 Eric Desjardins	8.00	20.00
DD18 Dimitri Yushkevich	8.00	20.00
DD19 Chris Pronger	10.00	25.00
DD20 Rob Blake	10.00	25.00

2000-01 BAP Signature Series Franchise Players

STAT.PRINT RUN 30 SETS

Card	Low	High
F1 Paul Kariya	15.00	40.00
F2 Patrik Stefan	8.00	20.00
F3 Joe Thornton	25.00	60.00
F4 Dominik Hasek	25.00	60.00
F5 Jarome Iginla	20.00	50.00
F6 Jeff O'Neill	15.00	40.00
F7 Tony Amonte	15.00	40.00
F8 Peter Forsberg	25.00	60.00
F9 Ron Tugnutt	15.00	40.00
F10 Mike Modano	20.00	40.00
F11 Steve Yzerman	50.00	125.00
F12 Doug Weight	15.00	40.00
F13 Pavel Bure	15.00	40.00
F14 Rob Blake	15.00	40.00
F15 Marian Gaborik	25.00	60.00
F16 Saku Koivu	15.00	40.00
F17 David Legwand	15.00	40.00
F18 Martin Brodeur	50.00	125.00
F19 Mariusz Czerkawski	15.00	40.00
F20 Brian Leetch	15.00	40.00
F21 Marian Hossa	15.00	40.00
F22 John LeClair	15.00	40.00
F23 Keith Tkachuk	15.00	40.00
F24 Jaromir Jagr	30.00	80.00
F25 Chris Pronger	15.00	40.00
F26 Owen Nolan	15.00	40.00
F27 Vincent Lecavalier	15.00	40.00
F28 Curtis Joseph	15.00	40.00
F29 Daniel Sedin	15.00	40.00
F30 Olaf Kolzig	15.00	40.00

2000-01 BAP Signature Series Goalie Memorabilia Autographs

Randomly inserted in packs, this 5-card set featured a game-used swatch of equipment and an autograph beside a color action photo of the player. The player's name was printed along the left border and the words "Goalie Legend" appeared on the top of each card. Each card had a stated print run of 150 sets.

STAT.PRINT RUN 150 SETS

Card	Low	High
GLS1 Gerry Cheevers	50.00	125.00
GLS2 Vladislav Tretiak	100.00	175.00
GLS3 Tony Esposito	50.00	125.00
GLS4 Johnny Bower	40.00	100.00
GLS5 Bernie Parent	50.00	125.00

2000-01 BAP Signature Series He Shoots-He Scores Points

ONE PER PACK
RED.PROGRAM HAS EXPIRED

Card	Low	High
1 P.Bure 3pts.	.20	.50
2 M.Brodeur 1pts.	.20	.50
3 T.Fleury 3pts.	.20	.50
4 P.Forsberg 1pts.	.20	.50
5 P.Forsberg 3pts.	.20	.50
6 D.Hasek 2pts.	.20	.50
7 B.Hull 2pts.	.20	.50
8 J.Jagr 3pts	.20	.50
9 C.Joseph 1pts.	.20	.50
10 P.Kariya 2pts.	.20	.50
11 M.Lemieux 3pts.	.20	.50
12 M.Messier 2pts.	.20	.50
13 M.Modano 2pts.	.20	.50
14 Z.Palffy 1pts.	.20	.50
15 L.Robitaille 2pts.	.20	.50
16 P.Roy 2pts.	.20	.50
17 J.Sakic 2pts.	.20	.50
18 B.Shanahan 1pts.	.20	.50
19 M.Sundin 1pts.	.20	.50
20 S.Yzerman 3pts.	.20	.50

2000-01 BAP Signature Series He Shoots-He Scores Prizes

STAT.PRINT RUN 20 SER.#'d SETS
NOT PRICED DUE TO SCARCITY

1 Pavel Bure
2 Milan Hejduk
3 Patrick Roy
4 Roberto Luongo
5 Alexei Yashin
6 Peter Bondra
7 Martin Brodeur
8 Steve Yzerman
9 Vincent Lecavalier
10 Mike Modano
11 Wayne Gretzky
12 Peter Forsberg
13 Mark Recchi
14 Olaf Kolzig
15 Arturs Irbe
16 Patrik Stefan
17 Al MacInnis
18 Luc Robitaille
19 Dominik Hasek
20 Curtis Joseph
21 Paul Kariya
22 Joe Sakic
23 Sergei Fedorov
24 Ed Belfour
25 Keith Tkachuk
26 Chris Pronger
27 Nicklas Lidstrom
28 Brendan Shanahan
29 Brett Hull
30 Brian Leetch
31 Mark Messier
32 Jeremy Roenick
33 Keith Primeau
34 Tony Amonte
35 Scott Gomez
36 Jason Arnott
37 Mats Sundin
38 Chris Osgood
39 Mario Lemieux
40 Jaromir Jagr

2000-01 BAP Signature Series Jersey

*MULT.COLOR SWATCH: 1X TO 2X
STAT.PRINT RUN 100 SETS

Card	Low	High
J1 Theo Fleury	10.00	25.00
J2 Brendan Shanahan	10.00	25.00
J3 Curtis Joseph	10.00	25.00
J4 Saku Koivu	10.00	25.00
J5 Dominik Hasek	20.00	50.00
J6 Al MacInnis	10.00	25.00
J7 John LeClair	10.00	25.00
J8 Teemu Selanne	10.00	25.00
J9 Scott Niedermayer	10.00	25.00
J10 Pavel Bure	10.00	25.00
J11 Mark Messier	10.00	25.00
J12 Jaromir Jagr	15.00	40.00
J13 Chris Pronger	10.00	25.00
J14 Chris Osgood	10.00	25.00
J15 Mats Sundin	10.00	25.00
J16 Paul Kariya	10.00	25.00
J17 Scott Stevens	10.00	25.00
J18 Kenny Jonsson	10.00	25.00
J19 Sergei Fedorov	12.50	30.00
J20 Peter Forsberg	15.00	40.00
J21 Brett Hull	12.50	30.00
J22 Tony Amonte	10.00	25.00
J23 Patrick Roy	30.00	80.00
J24 Ed Belfour	10.00	25.00
J25 Martin Brodeur	25.00	60.00
J26 Brian Leetch	10.00	25.00
J27 Mike Modano	12.50	30.00
J28 Jeff Friesen	10.00	25.00
J29 Jeremy Roenick	12.50	30.00
J30 Steve Yzerman	30.00	80.00
J31 Joe Sakic	20.00	50.00
J32 Mike Peca	10.00	25.00
J33 Luc Robitaille	10.00	25.00
J34 Adam Oates	10.00	25.00
J35 Valeri Bure	10.00	25.00
J36 Kyle McLaren	10.00	25.00
J37 Nicklas Lidstrom	10.00	25.00
J38 Jason Arnott	10.00	25.00
J39 Mike Richter	10.00	25.00
J40 Keith Tkachuk	10.00	25.00

2000-01 BAP Signature Series Jersey and Stick

*JSY/STICK: .5X TO 1.25X JERSEY CARDS
STAT.PRINT RUN 100 SETS

2000-01 BAP Signature Series Jersey Autographs

STAT.PRINT RUN 10 SER.#'d SETS
CARD J28 NOT RELEASED
NOT PRICED DUE TO SCARCITY

2000-01 BAP Signature Series Jersey Emblems

STAT.PRINT RUN 10 SETS
NOT PRICED DUE TO SCARCITY

2000-01 BAP Signature Series Jersey Numbers

STAT.PRINT RUN 10 SETS
NOT PRICED DUE TO SCARCITY

2000-01 BAP Signature Series Mario Lemieux Legend

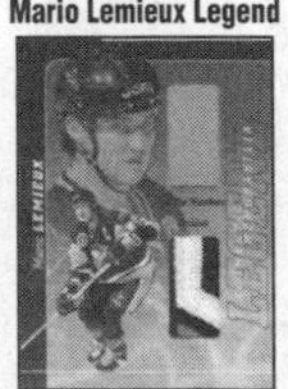

Randomly inserted in packs, this 5-card set features two swatches of game-used equipment per card, accompanied by a photo of Mario Lemieux. Each card has a stated print run of 30, but the cards are not serial numbered.

STAT.PRINT RUN 30 SETS

Card	Low	High
LM1 M.Lemieux #/EMB	250.00	500.00
LM2 M.Lemieux Jsy/GLOVE	100.00	250.00
LM3 M.Lemieux Jsy/GLOVE	100.00	250.00
LM4 M.Lemieux Jsy/Jsyy	100.00	250.00
LM5 M.Lemieux Jsy/Jsy/Jsy	250.00	500.00

2000-01 BAP Signature Series Mario Lemieux Legend Autographs

Randomly inserted in packs, this 5-card set parallels the Be A Player Signature Series Mario Lemieux Legends cards, but with an autograph on each card. Each card has a stated print run of 6, but the cards are not serial numbered.

STAT.PRINT RUN 6 SETS
NOT PRICED DUE TO SCARCITY

2000-01 BAP Signature Series Mario Lemieux Retrospective

Randomly inserted in packs, this 20-card set highlights the career of Mario Lemieux. Each card portrays a specific milestone in his career.

Card	Low	High
COMPLETE SET (20)	30.00	80.00
COMMON CARD (MLR1-MLR20)	2.00	5.00

2001-02 BAP Signature Series

This 250-card set featured full-color action photos on silver-mirrored card fronts. Cards 226-250 were available in BAP Update packs only.

Card	Low	High
COMP.SER. 1 SET (225)	100.00	200.00
CARDS 225-250 AVAIL.IN BAP UPD.PACKS		
1 Rick DiPietro	.50	1.25
2 Patrik Stefan	.30	.75
3 Hal Gill	.30	.75
4 J-P Dumont	.30	.75
5 Jarome Iginla	.75	2.00
6 Shane Willis	.30	.75
7 Chris Phillips	.30	.75
8 Rostislav Klesla	.30	.75
9 Brenden Morrow	.50	1.25
10 Manny Legace	.50	1.25
11 Anson Carter	.50	1.25
12 Roberto Luongo	.75	2.00
13 Aaron Miller	.30	.75
14 Wayne Primeau	.30	.75
15 Brian Savage	.30	.75
16 John Jakopin	.30	.75
17 Greg Johnson	.30	.75
18 Marc Chouinard	.30	.75
19 Steve Martins	.30	.75
20 Marian Hossa	.60	1.50
21 Brent Johnson	.50	1.25
22 Sean Burke	.50	1.25
23 Jan Hrdina	.30	.75
24 Evgeni Nabokov	.50	1.25
25 Adam Deadmarsh	.30	.75
26 Brad Richards	.50	1.25
27 Wade Redden	.30	.75
28 David Legwand	.50	1.25
29 Jean-Sebastien Giguere	.50	1.25
30 Ray Ferraro	.30	.75
31 Denis Hamel	.30	.75
32 Marc Savard	.30	.75
33 Craig Adams	.30	.75
34 Landon Wilson	.30	.75
35 Marc Denis	.50	1.25
36 Roman Lyashenko	.30	.75
37 Tomas Holmstrom	.30	.75
38 Mike Comrie	.50	1.25
39 Scott Hartnell	.30	.75
40 Sergei Krivokrasov	.30	.75
41 Mathieu Garon	.50	1.25
42 Denis Arkhipov	.30	.75
43 Roman Hamrlik	.30	.75
44 Mike Mottau	.30	.75
45 Shawn McEachern	.30	.75
46 Peter White	.30	.75
47 Shane Doan	.30	.75
48 Janne Laukkanen	.30	.75
49 Martin St. Louis	.50	1.25
50 Tomas Kaberle	.30	.75
51 Daniel Sedin	.30	.75
52 Jonas Ronnqvist	.30	.75
53 Damian Rhodes	.50	1.25
54 Vaclav Varada	.30	.75
55 Ronald Petrovicky	.30	.75
56 Tommy Westlund	.30	.75
57 Michael Nylander	.30	.75
58 Serge Aubin	.30	.75
59 Jiri Fischer	.30	.75
60 Shawn Horcoff	.30	.75
61 Peter Worrell	.30	.75
62 Willie Mitchell	.30	.75
63 Oleg Petrov	.30	.75
64 Scott Walker	.30	.75
65 Tomi Kallio	.30	.75
66 Jason Strudwick	.30	.75
67 Magnus Arvedson	.30	.75

68 Eric Daze .50 1.25
69 Johan Hedberg .50 1.25
70 Fredrik Modin .30 .75
71 Nathan Dempsey .30 .75
72 Henrik Sedin .30 .75
73 Mike LeClerc .30 .75
74 Hnat Domenichelli .30 .75
75 Jeff Cowan .30 .75
76 Brad Stuart .30 .75
77 Bryan Allen .30 .75
78 Wes Walz .30 .75
79 Patrick Traverse .30 .75
80 Markus Naslund .60 1.50
81 Brad Isbister .30 .75
82 Jan Hlavac .30 .75
83 Steve Sullivan .30 .75
84 Marian Gaborik 1.00 2.50
85 Kristian Kudroc .30 .75
86 Peter Schaefer .30 .75
87 Pascal Trepanier .30 .75
88 Milan Hnilicka .50 1.25
89 Dave Lowry .30 .75
90 Jamie Allison .30 .75
91 Jeff Nielsen .30 .75
92 Sheldon Souray .30 .75
93 Mike Dunham .50 1.25
94 Branislav Mezei .30 .75
95 Dale Purinton .30 .75
96 Cory Sarich .30 .75
97 Jarkko Ruutu .30 .75
98 Kyle Calder .30 .75
99 Frantisek Musil .30 .75
100 Tomas Kloucek .30 .75
101 Karel Rachunek .30 .75
102 Darcy Tucker .30 .75
103 Alex Tanguay .50 1.25
104 Patrick Lalime .50 1.25
105 Ossi Vaananen .30 .75
106 Martin Skoula .30 .75
107 Lubomir Visnovsky .30 .75
108 Richard Zednik .30 .75
109 Jani Hurme .50 1.25
110 Teppo Numminen .30 .75
111 Scott Young .30 .75
112 Robert Reichel .30 .75
113 Dave Tanabe .30 .75
114 Steven Reinprecht .30 .75
115 Ryan Smyth .30 .75
116 Jozef Stumpel .30 .75
117 Martin Rucinsky .30 .75
118 Radek Dvorak .30 .75
119 Chris Herperger .30 .75
120 Eric Weinrich .30 .75
121 Claude Lemieux .30 .75
122 Mike Ricci .30 .75
123 Cory Stillman .30 .75
124 Alyn McCauley .30 .75
125 Trevor Linden .30 .75
126 Vitali Vishnevsky .30 .75
127 Tim Connolly .30 .75
128 Oleg Saprykin .30 .75
129 Arturs Irbe .50 1.25
130 Ville Nieminen .30 .75
131 David Vyborny .30 .75
132 Janne Niinimaa .30 .75
133 Joey Tetarenko .30 .75
134 Bryan Smolinski .30 .75
135 Stacy Roest .30 .75
136 Mikael Renberg .30 .75
137 Gino Odjick .30 .75
138 Petr Sykora .30 .75
139 Alexei Yashin .30 .75
140 Martin Havlat .50 1.25
141 Rick Tocchet .30 .75
142 Daymond Langkow .30 .75
143 Kevin Stevens .30 .75
144 Patrick Marleau .50 1.25
145 Reed Low .30 .75
146 Bryan McCabe .30 .75
147 Dimitri Khristich .30 .75
148 Oleg Tverdovsky .30 .75
149 Yannick Tremblay .30 .75
150 Martin Biron .50 1.25
151 Rob Niedermayer .30 .75
152 Rod Brind'Amour .50 1.25
153 Adam Foote .30 .75
154 Geoff Sanderson .30 .75
155 Pat Verbeek .30 .75
156 Nicklas Lidstrom .60 1.50
157 Jochen Hecht .30 .75
158 Robert Svehla .30 .75
159 Mathieu Schneider .30 .75
160 Antti Laaksonen .30 .75
161 Jeff Hackett .50 1.25
162 Scott Niedermayer .30 .75
163 Sandis Ozolinsh .30 .75
164 Radek Bonk .30 .75
165 Roman Cechmanek .50 1.25
166 Mike Johnson .30 .75
167 Milan Kraft .30 .75
168 Adam Graves .30 .75
169 Pavol Demitra .50 1.25
170 Kevin Weekes .50 1.25
171 Travis Green .30 .75
172 Jeff Halpern .30 .75
173 Steve Shields .50 1.25
174 Lubos Bartecko .30 .75
175 P.J. Stock .30 .75
176 Maxim Afinogenov .30 .75
177 Derek Morris .30 .75
178 Bates Battaglia .30 .75
179 Boris Mironov .30 .75
180 David Aebischer .50 1.25
181 Espen Knutsen .30 .75
182 Darryl Sydor .30 .75
183 Igor Larionov .30 .75
184 Eric Brewer .30 .75
185 Trevor Kidd .50 1.25
186 Eric Belanger .30 .75
187 Manny Fernandez .50 1.25
188 Francois Bouillon .30 .75
189 Patrik Elias .50 1.25
190 Mariusz Czerkawski .30 .75
191 Daniel Alfredsson .50 1.25
192 Brian Boucher .50 1.25
193 Sergei Berezin .30 .75
194 Kris Beech .30 .75
195 Vincent Damphousse .30 .75
196 Fred Brathwaite .50 1.25
197 Ben Clymer .30 .75
198 Wade Belak .30 .75
199 Ed Jovanovski .50 1.25
200 Sergei Gonchar .30 .75
201 Dan Blackburn RC .75 2.00
202 Daniel Tjarnqvist .30 .75
203 Andreas Salomonsson RC 1.00 2.50
204 Vaclav Nedorost RC 1.00 2.50
205 Justin Kurtz RC 1.00 2.50
206 Jiri Dopita RC 1.00 2.50
207 Ilya Kovalchuk RC 4.00 10.00
208 Richard Jackman .30 .75
209 Scott Nichol RC 1.00 2.50
210 Brad Larsen .30 .75
211 Jason Williams .30 .75
212 Kristian Huselius RC 1.50 4.00
213 Andreas Lilja .30 .75
214 Nick Schultz RC 1.00 2.50
215 Marc Moro .30 .75
216 Scott Clemmensen RC 1.00 2.50
217 Brad Tapper .30 .75
218 Barrett Heisten .30 .75
219 Chris Neil RC 1.00 2.50
220 Pavel Brendl .30 .75
221 Miikka Kiprusoff .50 1.25
222 Jimmie Olvestad .30 .75
223 Brian Sutherby RC 1.00 2.50
224 Timo Parssinen RC 1.00 2.50
225 Sascha Goc .30 .75
226 Dany Heatley .75 2.00
227 Nick Boynton .30 .75
228 Steve Begin .30 .75
229 Erik Cole RC 1.00 2.50
230 Mark Bell .30 .75
231 Rick Berry .30 .75
232 Niko Kapanen RC 1.00 2.50
233 Pavel Datsyuk RC 2.00 5.00
234 Niklas Hagman RC 1.00 2.50
235 Jaroslav Bednar RC 1.00 2.50
236 Pascal Dupuis RC 1.00 2.50
237 Mike Ribeiro .30 .75
238 Martin Erat RC 1.00 2.50
239 Jiri Bicek .30 .75
240 Radek Martinek RC 1.00 2.50
241 Ivan Ciernik RC 1.00 2.50
242 Jesse Boulerice .30 .75
243 Krys Kolanos RC 1.00 2.50
244 Toby Petersen .30 .75
245 Jeff Jillson RC 1.00 2.50
246 Mark Rycroft RC 1.00 2.50
247 Kamil Piros RC 1.00 2.50
248 Nikita Alexeev RC 1.00 2.50
249 Stephen Peat .30 .75
250 Pierre Dagenais .30 .75

2001-02 BAP Signature Series Certified 100

This 60-card set resembled the base set, but carried a light purple background and the words "Signature Series Certified" on the card front and was numbered on the back "1 of 100". Players featured in this set were not included in the base set.

STATED PRINT RUN 100 SETS
C1 Al MacInnis 4.00 10.00
C2 Adam Oates 4.00 10.00
C3 Byron Dafoe 4.00 10.00
C4 Bill Guerin 4.00 10.00
C5 Brian Leetch 4.00 10.00
C6 Brendan Shanahan 3.00 8.00
C7 Chris Drury 4.00 10.00
C8 Chris Gratton 2.50 6.00
C9 Curtis Joseph 3.00 8.00
C10 Chris Pronger 2.50 6.00
C11 Donald Audette 2.50 6.00
C12 Doug Weight 2.50 6.00
C13 Ed Belfour 3.00 8.00
C14 Eric Lindros 3.00 8.00
C15 Jason Allison 2.50 6.00
C16 Jason Arnott 2.50 6.00
C17 John LeClair 3.00 8.00
C18 Jeff O'Neill 2.50 6.00
C19 Jeremy Roenick 3.00 8.00
C20 Joe Sakic 5.00 12.00
C21 Joe Thornton 4.00 10.00
C22 Kyle McLaren 2.50 6.00
C23 Luc Robitaille 4.00 10.00
C24 Martin Brodeur 8.00 20.00
C25 Milan Hejduk 3.00 8.00
C26 Martin Lapointe 2.50 6.00
C27 Mike Modano 4.00 10.00
C28 Mark Recchi 2.50 6.00
C29 Mats Sundin 3.00 8.00
C30 Olaf Kolzig 2.50 6.00
C31 Peter Bondra 3.00 8.00
C32 Pavel Bure 3.00 8.00
C33 Paul Kariya 3.00 8.00
C34 Pierre Turgeon 2.50 6.00
C35 Rob Blake 2.50 6.00
C36 Ron Francis 2.50 6.00
C37 Roman Turek 2.50 6.00
C38 Sergei Fedorov 4.00 10.00
C39 Scott Gomez 2.50 6.00
C40 Saku Koivu 3.00 8.00
C41 Sami Kapanen 2.50 6.00
C42 Sergei Samsonov 2.50 6.00
C43 Scott Stevens 2.50 6.00
C44 Steve Yzerman 8.00 20.00
C45 Tony Amonte 4.00 10.00
C46 Theo Fleury 2.50 6.00
C47 Teemu Selanne 3.00 8.00
C48 Tommy Salo 2.50 6.00
C49 Vincent Lecavalier 3.00 8.00
C50 Zigmund Palffy 4.00 10.00
C51 Brett Hull 3.00 8.00
C52 Dominik Hasek 5.00 12.00
C53 Jaromir Jagr 4.00 10.00
C54 Mario Lemieux 12.50 30.00
C55 Mark Messier 3.00 8.00
C56 Mike Vernon 2.50 6.00
C57 Owen Nolan 2.50 6.00
C58 Peter Forsberg 8.00 20.00
C59 Patrick Roy 8.00 20.00
C60 Wayne Gretzky 12.50 30.00

2001-02 BAP Signature Series Certified 50

This 60-card set resembled the base set, but carried a dark purple background and the words "Signature Series Certified" on the card front and is numbered on the back "1 of 50". Players featured in this set were not included in the base set.

*CERTIFIED 50 : .75X TO 2X CERTIFIED 100 BASE
STATED PRINT RUN 50 SETS

2001-02 BAP Signature Series Certified 1 of 1's

This 60-card set paralleled the base set, but carried a dark green background and the words "Signature Series Certified" on the card front and each card was numbered on the back "1 of 1".

STATED PRINT RUN 1 SET
NOT PRICED DUE TO SCARCITY

2001-02 BAP Signature Series Autographs

This 297-card set partially paralleled the base set but carried player autographs in a muted area on the card front. Card numbers that carried a "L" or "XL" prefix were short printed, but no numbers are known at this time. Cards 226-250 and numbers LTS, LPF, LSY, LSF, LTA, LJR and XLMM were available in BAP Update packs only.

ONE PER PACK
1 Rick DiPietro 6.00 15.00
2 Patrik Stefan 2.00 5.00
3 Hal Gill 2.00 5.00
4 J-P Dumont 2.00 5.00
5 Jarome Iginla 10.00 25.00
6 Shane Willis 2.00 5.00
7 Chris Phillips 2.00 5.00
8 Rostislav Klesla 2.00 5.00
9 Brenden Morrow 4.00 10.00
10 Manny Legace 4.00 10.00
11 Anson Carter SP 20.00 60.00
12 Roberto Luongo 8.00 20.00
13 Aaron Miller 2.00 5.00
14 Wayne Primeau 2.00 5.00
15 Brian Savage 2.00 5.00
16 John Jakopin 2.00 5.00
17 Greg Johnson 2.00 5.00
18 Marc Chouinard 2.00 5.00
19 Steve Martins 2.00 5.00
20 Marian Hossa 6.00 15.00
21 Brent Johnson SP 60.00 125.00
22 Sean Burke 4.00 10.00
23 Jan Hrdina 2.00 5.00
24 Evgeni Nabokov 4.00 10.00
25 Adam Deadmarsh 2.00 5.00
26 Brad Richards 4.00 10.00
27 Wade Redden 2.00 5.00
28 David Legwand 5.00 5.00
29 Jean-Sebastien Giguere 4.00 10.00
30 Ray Ferraro 2.00 5.00
31 Denis Hamel 2.00 5.00
32 Marc Savard 2.00 5.00
33 Craig Adams 2.00 5.00
34 Landon Wilson 2.00 5.00
35 Marc Denis 4.00 10.00
36 Roman Lyashenko 2.00 5.00
37 Tomas Holmstrom 2.00 5.00
38 Mike Comrie 5.00 5.00
39 Scott Hartnell 2.00 5.00
40 Sergei Krivokrasov 2.00 5.00
41 Mathieu Garon 3.00 8.00
42 Denis Arkhipov 2.00 5.00
43 Roman Hamrlik 2.00 5.00
44 Mike Mottau 2.00 5.00
45 Shawn McEachern 2.00 5.00
46 Peter White SP 60.00 150.00
47 Shane Doan 2.00 5.00
48 Janne Laukkanen 2.00 5.00
49 Martin St. Louis 10.00 25.00
50 Tomas Kaberle 2.00 5.00
51 Daniel Sedin 2.00 5.00
52 Jonas Ronnqvist 2.00 5.00
53 Damian Rhodes 3.00 8.00
54 Vaclav Varada 2.00 5.00
55 Ronald Petrovicky 2.00 5.00
56 Tommy Westlund 2.00 5.00
57 Michael Nylander 2.00 5.00
58 Serge Aubin 2.00 5.00
59 Jiri Fischer SP 40.00 100.00
60 Shawn Horcoff 2.00 5.00
61 Peter Worrell 2.00 5.00
62 Willie Mitchell 2.00 5.00
63 Oleg Petrov 2.00 5.00
64 Scott Walker 2.00 5.00
65 Tomi Kallio 2.00 5.00
66 Jason Strudwick 2.00 5.00
67 Magnus Arvedson 2.00 5.00
68 Eric Daze 5.00 12.00
69 Johan Hedberg 3.00 8.00
70 Fredrik Modin 2.00 5.00
71 Nathan Dempsey 2.00 5.00
72 Henrik Sedin 2.00 5.00
73 Mike LeClerc 2.00 5.00
74 Hnat Domenichelli 2.00 5.00
75 Jeff Cowan 2.00 5.00
76 Brad Stuart 2.00 5.00
77 Bryan Allen 2.00 5.00
78 Wes Walz 2.00 5.00
79 Patrick Traverse 2.00 5.00
80 Markus Naslund 4.00 10.00
81 Brad Isbister 2.00 5.00
82 Jan Hlavac SP 50.00 125.00
83 Steve Sullivan 2.00 5.00
84 Marian Gaborik 12.50 30.00
85 Kristian Kudroc 2.00 5.00
86 Peter Schaefer 2.00 5.00
87 Pascal Trepanier 2.00 5.00
88 Milan Hnilicka 3.00 8.00
89 Dave Lowry 2.00 5.00
90 Jamie Allison 2.00 5.00
91 Jeff Nielsen 2.00 5.00
92 Sheldon Souray 2.00 5.00
93 Mike Dunham 3.00 8.00
94 Branislav Mezei 2.00 5.00
95 Dale Purinton 2.00 5.00
96 Cory Sarich 2.00 5.00
97 Jarkko Ruutu 2.00 5.00
98 Kyle Calder 2.00 5.00
99 Frantisek Musil 2.00 5.00
100 Tomas Kloucek 2.00 5.00
101 Karel Rachunek 2.00 5.00
102 Darcy Tucker 2.00 5.00
103 Alex Tanguay 4.00 10.00
104 Patrick Lalime 3.00 8.00
105 Ossi Vaananen 2.00 5.00
106 Martin Skoula 2.00 5.00
107 Lubomir Visnovsky 2.00 5.00
108 Richard Zednik 2.00 5.00
109 Jani Hurme 3.00 8.00
110 Teppo Numminen 2.00 5.00
111 Scott Young 2.00 5.00
112 Robert Reichel 2.00 5.00
113 Dave Tanabe 2.00 5.00
114 Steven Reinprecht 2.00 5.00
115 Ryan Smyth 2.00 5.00
116 Jozef Stumpel 2.00 5.00
117 Martin Rucinsky 2.00 5.00
118 Radek Dvorak 2.00 5.00
119 Chris Herperger 2.00 5.00
120 Eric Weinrich 2.00 5.00
121 Claude Lemieux 2.00 5.00
122 Mike Ricci 2.00 5.00
123 Cory Stillman 2.00 5.00
124 Alyn McCauley 2.00 5.00
125 Trevor Linden 4.00 10.00
126 Vitaly Vishnevsky 2.00 5.00
127 Tim Connolly 2.00 5.00
128 Oleg Saprykin 2.00 5.00
129 Arturs Irbe 3.00 8.00
130 Ville Nieminen 2.00 5.00
131 David Vyborny 2.00 5.00
132 Janne Niinimaa 2.00 5.00
133 Joey Tetarenko 2.00 5.00
134 Bryan Smolinski 2.00 5.00
135 Stacy Roest 2.00 5.00
136 Mikael Renberg 2.00 5.00
137 Gino Odjick 2.00 5.00
138 Petr Sykora 2.00 5.00
139 Alexei Yashin 2.00 5.00
140 Martin Havlat 4.00 10.00
141 Rick Tocchet 2.00 5.00
142 Daymond Langkow 2.00 5.00
143 Kevin Stevens 2.00 5.00
144 Patrick Marleau 4.00 10.00
145 Reed Low 2.00 5.00
146 Bryan McCabe 2.00 5.00
147 Dimitri Khristich 2.00 5.00
148 Oleg Tverdovsky 2.00 5.00
149 Yannick Tremblay 2.00 5.00
150 Martin Biron 4.00 10.00
151 Rob Niedermayer 2.00 5.00
152 Rod Brind'Amour 4.00 10.00
153 Adam Foote 2.00 5.00
154 Geoff Sanderson 2.00 5.00
155 Pat Verbeek 2.00 5.00
156 Nicklas Lidstrom 8.00 20.00
157 Jochen Hecht 2.00 5.00
158 Robert Svehla 2.00 5.00
159 Mathieu Schneider 2.00 5.00
160 Antti Laaksonen 2.00 5.00
161 Jeff Hackett 4.00 10.00
162 Scott Niedermayer 2.00 5.00
163 Sandis Ozolinsh 2.00 5.00
164 Radek Bonk 2.00 5.00
165 Roman Cechmanek 3.00 8.00
166 Mike Johnson 2.00 5.00
167 Milan Kraft 2.00 5.00
168 Adam Graves 2.00 5.00
169 Pavol Demitra 3.00 8.00
170 Kevin Weekes 3.00 8.00
171 Travis Green 2.00 5.00
172 Jeff Halpern 2.00 5.00
173 Steve Shields 3.00 8.00
174 Lubos Bartecko 2.00 5.00
175 P.J. Stock 3.00 8.00
176 Maxim Afinogenov 2.00 5.00
177 Derek Morris 2.00 5.00
178 Bates Battaglia 2.00 5.00
179 Boris Mironov 2.00 5.00
180 David Aebischer 8.00 20.00
181 Espen Knutsen 2.00 5.00
182 Darryl Sydor 2.00 5.00
183 Igor Larionov 2.00 5.00
184 Eric Brewer 2.00 5.00
185 Trevor Kidd 3.00 8.00
186 Eric Belanger 2.00 5.00
187 Manny Fernandez 20.00 50.00
188 Francois Bouillon 2.00 5.00
189 Patrik Elias 4.00 10.00
190 Mariusz Czerkawski 2.00 5.00
191 Daniel Alfredsson 4.00 10.00
192 Brian Boucher 3.00 8.00
193 Sergei Berezin 2.00 5.00
194 Kris Beech 2.00 5.00
195 Vincent Damphousse 2.00 5.00
196 Fred Brathwaite 3.00 8.00
197 Ben Clymer 2.00 5.00
198 Wade Belak 2.00 5.00
199 Ed Jovanovski 3.00 8.00
200 Sergei Gonchar 2.00 5.00
201 Dan Blackburn 3.00 8.00
202 Daniel Tjarnqvist 2.00 5.00
203 Andreas Salomonsson 5.00 12.00
204 Vaclav Nedorost 2.00 5.00
205 Justin Kurtz 2.00 5.00
206 Jiri Dopita 2.00 5.00
207 Ilya Kovalchuk 10.00 25.00
208 Richard Jackman 2.00 5.00
209 Scott Nichol 2.00 5.00
210 Brad Larsen 2.00 5.00
211 Jason Williams 2.00 5.00
212 Kristian Huselius 2.00 5.00
213 Andreas Lilja 2.00 5.00
214 Nick Schultz 2.00 5.00
215 Marc Moro 2.00 5.00
216 Scott Clemmensen 3.00 8.00
217 Brad Tapper 2.00 5.00
218 Barrett Heisten 2.00 5.00
219 Chris Neil 2.00 5.00
220 Pavel Brendl 2.00 5.00
221 Miikka Kiprusoff 8.00 20.00
222 Jimmie Olvestad 2.00 5.00
223 Brian Sutherby 2.00 5.00
224 Timo Parssinen 2.00 5.00
225 Sascha Goc 2.00 5.00
226 Dany Heatley 10.00 25.00
227 Nick Boynton 2.00 5.00
228 Steve Begin 2.00 5.00
229 Erik Cole 2.00 5.00
230 Mark Bell 2.00 5.00
231 Rick Berry 2.00 5.00
232 Niko Kapanen 2.00 5.00
233 Pavel Datsyuk 12.50 30.00
234 Niklas Hagman 2.00 5.00
235 Jaroslav Bednar 2.00 5.00
236 Pascal Dupuis 2.00 5.00
237 Mike Ribeiro 2.00 5.00
238 Martin Erat 2.00 5.00
239 Jiri Bicek 2.00 5.00
240 Radek Martinek 2.00 5.00
241 Ivan Ciernik 2.00 5.00
242 Jesse Boulerice 2.00 5.00
243 Krystofer Kolanos 2.00 5.00
244 Toby Petersen 2.00 5.00
245 Jeff Jillson 2.00 5.00
246 Mark Rycroft 2.00 5.00
247 Kamil Piros 2.00 5.00
248 Nikita Alexeev 2.00 5.00
249 Stephen Peat 2.00 5.00
250 Pierre Dagenais 2.00 5.00
LAM Al MacInnis SP 8.00 20.00
LBD Byron Dafoe SP 10.00 25.00
LBG Bill Guerin SP 8.00 20.00
LBL Brian Leetch SP 12.50 30.00
LBS Brendan Shanahan SP 20.00 50.00
LCD Chris Drury SP 8.00 20.00
LCG Chris Gratton SP 8.00 20.00
LCP Chris Pronger SP 8.00 20.00
LDA Donald Audette SP 8.00 20.00
LDW Doug Weight SP 8.00 20.00
LEB Ed Belfour SP 20.00 50.00
LJL John LeClair SP 12.50 30.00
LJO Jeff O'Neill SP 8.00 20.00
LJR Jeremy Roenick SP 20.00 50.00
LJS Joe Sakic SP 25.00 60.00
LJT Joe Thornton SP 12.50 30.00
LKM Kyle McLaren SP 8.00 20.00
LLR Luc Robitaille SP 8.00 20.00
LMH Milan Hejduk SP 12.50 30.00
LML Martin Lapointe SP 8.00 20.00
LMR Mark Recchi SP 8.00 20.00
LOK Olaf Kolzig SP 8.00 20.00
LPK Paul Kariya SP 25.00 50.00
LPT Pierre Turgeon SP 8.00 20.00
LRB Rob Blake SP 8.00 20.00
LRF Ron Francis SP 8.00 20.00
LRT Roman Turek SP 8.00 20.00
LSF Sergei Fedorov SP 15.00 40.00
LSK Sami Kapanen SP 8.00 20.00
LSY Steve Yzerman SP 50.00 125.00
LTA Tony Amonte SP 8.00 20.00
LTS Teemu Selanne SP 12.50 30.00
LVL Vincent Lecavalier SP 12.50 30.00
LZP Zigmund Palffy SP 12.50 30.00
LJAL Jason Allison SP 8.00 20.00
LPBO Peter Bondra SP 8.00 20.00
LPBU Pavel Bure SP 12.50 30.00
LSSA Sergei Samsonov SP 8.00 20.00
LSST Scott Stevens SP 8.00 20.00
LTSA Tommy Salo SP 8.00 20.00
XLDH Dominik Hasek SP 125.00 250.00
XLML Mario Lemieux SP 250.00 500.00
XLMM Mark Messier SP 175.00 350.00
XLMV Mike Vernon SP 30.00 80.00
XLON Owen Nolan SP 40.00 100.00
XLPF Peter Forsberg SP 60.00 150.00
XLWG Wayne Gretzky SP 300.00 500.00

2001-02 BAP Signature Series Autographs Gold

This 297-card set paralleled the base autograph set but carried a gold tone card front. Gold cards were advertised as being more scarce, but no information on production numbers is known at this time.

GOLD: 1X TO 1.5X BASIC AUTO
11 Anson Carter 25.00 60.00
21 Brent Johnson 40.00 100.00
46 Peter White 25.00 60.00
59 Jiri Fischer 40.00 100.00
82 Jan Hlavac 25.00 60.00

2001-02 BAP Signature Series Department of Defense

STATED PRINT RUN 40 SETS
DD1 Rob Blake 12.50 30.00
DD2 Brian Leetch 12.50 30.00
DD3 Nicklas Lidstrom 12.50 30.00
DD4 Oleg Tverdovsky 12.50 30.00
DD5 Chris Pronger 12.50 30.00
DD6 Al MacInnis 12.50 30.00
DD7 Kyle McLaren 12.50 30.00
DD8 Sergei Gonchar 12.50 30.00
DD9 Tomas Kaberle 12.50 30.00
DD10 Sandis Ozolinsh 12.50 30.00
DD11 Darius Kasparaitis 12.50 30.00
DD12 Rostislav Klesla 12.50 30.00

2001-02 BAP Signature Series 500 Goal Scorers

This 28-card set featured game-worn jersey swatches of members of the exclusive 500-goal club. Print runs were varied and are listed below. Cards ML, MM and SY were available in random packs of BAP Update. All cards carried a S500 prefix. Cards with less than 20 copies are not priced due to scarcity.

*MULT.COLOR SWATCH: .5X TO 1.5X HI
STATED PRINT RUNS LISTED BELOW
PRINT RUNS OF 20 OR LESS NOT
PRICED DUE TO SCARCITY
UNPRICED AUTOS/10 EXIST
1 Gordie Howe/10
2 Steve Yzerman/30 75.00 150.00
3 Jean Beliveau/20
4 Frank Mahovlich/30 40.00 80.00
5 Stan Mikita/30 40.00 80.00
6 Guy Lafleur/30 25.00 60.00
7 Marcel Dionne/30 10.00 25.00
8 Bobby Hull/20
9 Phil Esposito/30 40.00 80.00
10 Mike Bossy/50 20.00 50.00
11 Luc Robitaille/30 25.00 60.00
12 Jari Kurri/90 10.00 25.00
13 Dave Andreychuk/90 10.00 25.00
14 Mike Gartner/90 10.00 25.00
15 John Bucyk/30 25.00 60.00
16 Michel Goulet/90 10.00 25.00
17 Dino Ciccarelli/90 10.00 25.00
18 Pat Verbeek/90 10.00 25.00
19 Bryan Trottier/50 10.00 25.00
20 Dale Hawerchuk/90 10.00 25.00
21 Gilbert Perreault/90 10.00 25.00
22 Joe Mullen/90 10.00 25.00
23 Lanny McDonald/90 10.00 25.00
24 Brett Hull/30 40.00 80.00
25 Mark Messier/30 60.00 120.00
26 Mario Lemieux/20
27 Maurice Richard/10
28 Ron Francis/10
29 Brendan Shanahan/10
ML Mario Lemieux/10 AU
MM Mark Messier/10 AU
SY Steve Yzerman/10 AU

2001-02 BAP Signature Series Franchise Jerseys

STATED PRINT RUN 28 SETS
FP1 Paul Kariya 12.50 30.00
FP2 Ilya Kovalchuk 20.00 50.00
FP3 Joe Thornton 15.00 40.00
FP4 Miroslav Satan 12.50 30.00
FP5 Jarome Iginla 15.00 40.00
FP6 Sami Kapanen 12.50 30.00
FP7 Tony Amonte 12.50 30.00
FP8 Joe Sakic 20.00 50.00
FP9 Rostislav Klesla 12.50 30.00
FP10 Mike Modano 15.00 40.00
FP11 Steve Yzerman 30.00 80.00
FP12 Tommy Salo 12.50 30.00
FP13 Pavel Bure 12.50 30.00
FP14 Zigmund Palffy 12.50 30.00
FP15 Marian Gaborik 25.00 60.00
FP16 Jose Theodore 15.00 40.00
FP17 David Legwand 12.50 30.00
FP18 Martin Brodeur 30.00 80.00
FP19 Eric Lindros 12.50 30.00
FP20 Alexei Yashin 12.50 30.00
FP21 Daniel Alfredsson 12.50 30.00
FP22 John LeClair 12.50 30.00
FP23 Sean Burke 12.50 30.00
FP24 Mario Lemieux 40.00 100.00
FP25 Owen Nolan 12.50 30.00
FP26 Doug Weight 12.50 30.00
FP27 Vincent Lecavalier 12.50 30.00
FP28 Mats Sundin 12.50 30.00
FP29 Markus Naslund 12.50 30.00
FP30 Jaromir Jagr 20.00 50.00

2001-02 BAP Signature Series He Shoots-He Scores Points

ONE PER PACK
RED PROGRAM HAS EXPIRED
1 Tony Amonte 1pt. .20 .50
2 Sergei Fedorov 1pt. .20 .50
3 Bill Guerin 1pt. .20 .50
4 John Leclair 1pt. .20 .50
5 Eric Lindros 1pt. .20 .50
6 Mark Messier 1 pt. .20 .50
7 Mike Modano 1pt. .20 .50
8 Luc Robitaille 1pt. .20 .50
9 Jeremy Roenick 1pt. .20 .50
10 Teemu Selanne 1pt. .20 .50
11 Mats Sundin 1pt. .20 .50
12 Pavel Bure 2 pts. .20 .50
13 Jarome Iginla 2 pts. .20 .50
14 Jaromir Jagr 2 pts. .20 .50
15 Paul Kariya 2 pts. .20 .50
16 Ilya Kovalchuk 2 pts. .20 .50
17 Brendan Shanahan 2 pts. .20 .50
18 Mario Lemieux 3 pts. .20 .50
19 Joe Sakic 3 pts. .20 .50
20 Steve Yzerman 3 pts. .20 .50

2001-02 BAP Signature Series He Shoots-He Scores Prizes

STATED PRINT RUN 20 SER.#'d SETS
NOT PRICED DUE TO SCARCITY
1 Steve Yzerman
2 Joe Sakic
3 Mario Lemieux
4 Ron Francis
5 Ilya Kovalchuk
6 Brendan Shanahan
7 Paul Kariya
8 Jaromir Jagr
9 Jarome Iginla
10 Eric Lindros
11 Mats Sundin
12 Teemu Selanne
13 Mike Modano
14 John LeClair
15 Tony Amonte
16 Luc Robitaille
17 Sergei Fedorov
18 Bill Guerin
19 Jeremy Roenick
20 Mark Messier
21 Joe Thornton
22 Sami Kapanen
23 Mark Recchi
23 Alexander Mogilny
24 Sergei Samsonov
25 Saku Koivu
26 Kristian Huselius
27 Milan Hejduk
28 Peter Forsberg
29 Chris Drury
30 Doug Weight
31 Zigmund Palffy
33 Owen Nolan
34 Daniel Alfredsson
35 Markus Naslund
36 Eric Daze
37 Keith Tkachuk
38 Alexei Yashin
39 Peter Bondra
40 Rob Blake

2001-02 BAP Signature Series International Medals

Limited to just 30 copies each, this 42-card set features game-worn jersey swatches from NHL players who participated in the 2002 Winter Olympics. The card fronts carried a color head shot photo of the featured player along with the jersey swatch under the player to appear as if it was a medal around his neck.

STATED PRINT RUN 30 SER.#'d SETS
ID1 Nikolai Khabibulin 12.50 30.00
IR2 Sergei Samsonov 12.50 30.00
IB3 Darius Kasparaitis 12.50 30.00
IB4 Alexei Yashin 12.50 30.00
IB5 Oleg Tverdovsky 12.50 30.00

IB6 Pavel Bure 12.50 30.00
IB7 Ilya Kovalchuk 15.00 40.00
IB8 Alexei Kovalev 12.50 30.00
IS1 Mike Richter 12.50 30.00
IS2 Tony Amonte 12.50 30.00
IS3 Chris Chelios 12.50 30.00
IS4 Doug Weight 12.50 30.00
IS5 John LeClair 12.50 30.00
IS6 Mike Modano 15.00 40.00
IS7 Bill Guerin 12.50 30.00
IS8 Brian Rolston 12.50 30.00
IG1 Martin Brodeur 30.00 80.00
IG2 Rob Blake 12.50 30.00
IG3 Al MacInnis 12.50 30.00
IG4 Theo Fleury 12.50 30.00
IG5 Paul Kariya 12.50 30.00
IG6 Mario Lemieux 30.00 80.00
IG7 Eric Lindros 12.50 30.00
IG8 Steve Yzerman 30.00 80.00

2001-02 BAP Signature Series Jerseys

*MULT COLOR SWATCH: .5X TO 1.5X HI
GJ1-GJ70 PRINT RUN 60 SETS
GJ71-GJ98 PRINT RUN 90 SETS
GJ71-GJ98 AVAIL.IN BAP UPD.PACKS
GJ1 Paul Kariya 10.00 25.00
GJ2 Rostislav Klesla 4.00 10.00
GJ3 Joe Thornton 12.50 30.00
GJ4 Martin Havlat 10.00 25.00
GJ5 Byron Dafoe 10.00 25.00
GJ6 Dominik Hasek 15.00 40.00
GJ7 Miroslav Satan 10.00 25.00
GJ8 Teemu Selanne 10.00 25.00
GJ9 Jarome Iginla 12.50 30.00
GJ10 Ron Francis 10.00 25.00
GJ11 Pierre Turgeon 10.00 25.00
GJ12 Tony Amonte 10.00 25.00
GJ13 Henrik Sedin 8.00 20.00
GJ14 Alex Tanguay 10.00 25.00
GJ15 Marian Gaborik 12.00 30.00
GJ16 Joe Sakic 15.00 40.00
GJ17 Patrick Roy 25.00 60.00
GJ18 Chris Drury 10.00 25.00
GJ19 Rob Blake 10.00 25.00
GJ20 Mike Modano 12.50 30.00
GJ21 Sergei Fedorov 12.50 30.00
GJ22 Nicklas Lidstrom 10.00 25.00
GJ23 Steve Yzerman 20.00 50.00
GJ24 Milan Hejduk 8.00 20.00
GJ25 Jeff O'Neill 4.00 10.00
GJ26 Luc Robitaille 10.00 25.00
GJ27 Brendan Shanahan 10.00 25.00
GJ28 Pavel Bure 10.00 25.00
GJ29 Roberto Luongo 12.50 30.00
GJ30 Zigmund Palffy 10.00 25.00
GJ31 Brian Savage 4.00 10.00
GJ32 Saku Koivu 10.00 25.00
GJ33 Scott Stevens 10.00 25.00
GJ34 Scott Gomez 8.00 20.00
GJ35 Martin Brodeur 20.00 50.00
GJ36 Jason Arnott 4.00 10.00
GJ37 Scott Niedermayer 8.00 20.00
GJ38 Eric Lindros 10.00 25.00
GJ39 Brian Leetch 10.00 25.00
GJ40 Mark Messier 10.00 25.00
GJ41 Mike Richter 10.00 25.00
GJ42 Kenny Jonsson 8.00 20.00
GJ43 Alexei Yashin 8.00 20.00
GJ44 Radek Bonk 8.00 20.00
GJ45 Ilya Kovalchuk 12.00 30.00
GJ46 Marian Hossa 10.00 25.00
GJ47 Roman Cechmanek 4.00 10.00
GJ48 Mark Recchi 10.00 25.00
GJ49 John LeClair 10.00 25.00
GJ50 Brian Boucher 10.00 25.00
GJ51 Keith Primeau 8.00 20.00
GJ52 Jeremy Roenick 12.00 30.00
GJ53 Jaromir Jagr 15.00 40.00
GJ54 Mario Lemieux 25.00 60.00
GJ55 Owen Nolan 10.00 25.00
GJ56 Doug Weight 10.00 25.00
GJ57 Chris Pronger 10.00 25.00
GJ58 Al MacInnis 10.00 25.00
GJ59 Vincent Lecavalier 10.00 25.00
GJ60 Brad Richards 10.00 25.00
GJ61 Curtis Joseph 10.00 25.00
GJ62 Mats Sundin 10.00 25.00
GJ63 Daniel Sedin 8.00 20.00
GJ64 Peter Bondra 10.00 25.00
GJ65 Adam Oates 10.00 25.00
GJ66 Olaf Kolzig 10.00 25.00
GJ67 Sergei Gonchar 8.00 20.00
GJ68 Todd Bertuzzi 10.00 25.00
GJ69 Theo Fleury 8.00 20.00
GJ70 Markus Naslund 10.00 25.00
GJ71 Alexander Mogilny 8.00 20.00
GJ72 Nikolai Khabibulin 10.00 25.00
GJ73 Ed Belfour 10.00 25.00
GJ74 Petr Sykora 4.00 10.00
GJ75 Peter Forsberg 12.00 30.00
GJ76 Patrick Lalime 8.00 20.00
GJ77 Keith Tkachuk 10.00 25.00
GJ78 Daniel Alfredsson 8.00 20.00
GJ79 Chris Chelios 10.00 25.00
GJ80 Sean Burke 4.00 10.00
GJ81 Eric Daze 4.00 10.00
GJ82 Patrik Elias 4.00 10.00
GJ83 Adam Foote 4.00 10.00
GJ84 Bill Guerin 8.00 20.00
GJ85 Jose Theodore 12.00 30.00
GJ86 Sandis Ozolinsh 4.00 10.00
GJ87 Felix Potvin 10.00 25.00
GJ88 Tommy Salo 8.00 20.00
GJ89 Martin Straka 4.00 10.00
GJ90 Jocelyn Thibault 8.00 20.00
GJ91 Pavel Bure 10.00 25.00
GJ92 Roman Turek 4.00 10.00
GJ93 Sergei Samsonov 8.00 20.00
GJ94 Dan Cloutier 8.00 20.00
GJ95 Kristian Huselius 4.00 10.00
GJ96 Arturs Irbe 8.00 20.00
GJ97 Sami Kapanen 4.00 10.00
GJ98 Evgeni Nabokov 8.00 20.00

2001-02 BAP Signature Series Jersey Autographs

This 50-card set featured autographs and game-worn jersey swatches on each card. Each card was serial-numbered out of 10. The Yzerman, Lemieux, Messier, Richter, Bonk, Roenick, Amonte, and Fedorov cards were only available in random BAP Update packs. This set is not priced due to scarcity.

STATED PRINT RUN 10 SER.#'d SETS
NOT PRICED DUE TO SCARCITY
GUAM Al MacInnis
GUAT Alex Tanguay
GUAY Alexei Yashin
GUBB Brian Boucher
GUBD Byron Dafoe
GUBL Brian Leetch
GUBR Brad Richards
GUBS Brendan Shanahan
GUBSA Brian Savage
GUCD Chris Drury
GUCP Chris Pronger
GUDH Dominik Hasek
GUDS Daniel Sedin
GUDW Doug Weight
GUHS Henrik Sedin
GUIK Ilya Kovalchuk
GUJI Jarome Iginla
GUJL John LeClair
GUJO Jeff O'Neill
GUJS Joe Sakic
GUJT Joe Thornton
GUKJ Kenny Jonsson
GUKP Keith Primeau
GULR Luc Robitaille
GUMG Marian Gaborik
GUMH Milan Hejduk
GUMHA Martin Havlat
GUMHO Marian Hossa
GUML Mario Lemieux
GUMME Mark Messier
GUMN Markus Naslund
GUMR Mike Richter
GUMS Miroslav Satan
GUNL Nicklas Lidstrom
GUOK Olaf Kolzig
GUON Owen Nolan
GUPB Pavel Bure
GUPBO Peter Bondra
GUPK Paul Kariya
GUPT Pierre Turgeon
GURB Rob Blake
GURBO Radek Bonk
GURC Roman Cechmanek
GURF Ron Francis
GURK Rostislav Klesla
GURL Roberto Luongo
GUSF Sergei Fedorov
GUSG Sergei Gonchar
GUSN Scott Niedermayer
GUSS Scott Stevens
GUSY Steve Yzerman
GUTB Todd Bertuzzi
GUTS Teemu Selanne
GUVL Vincent Lecavalier
GUZP Zigmund Palffy

2001-02 BAP Signature Series Jersey and Stick Cards

*JERSEY/STICK: .5X TO 1.25X JERSEY CARD
JERSEY/STICK PRINT RUN 60 SETS

2001-02 BAP Signature Series Emblems

STATED PRINT RUN 10 SETS
NOT PRICED DUE TO SCARCITY
GUE1 Paul Kariya
GUE2 Ilya Kovalchuk
GUE3 Joe Thornton
GUE4 Bill Guerin
GUE5 Byron Dafoe
GUE6 Dominik Hasek
GUE7 Miroslav Satan
GUE8 Teemu Selanne
GUE9 Mike Vernon
GUE10 Ron Francis
GUE11 Jarome Iginla
GUE12 Tony Amonte
GUE13 Mario Lemieux
GUE14 Peter Forsberg
GUE15 Joe Sakic
GUE16 Patrick Roy
GUE17 Chris Drury
GUE18 Brendan Shanahan
GUE19 Mike Modano
GUE20 Sergei Fedorov
GUE21 Nicklas Lidstrom
GUE22 Steve Yzerman
GUE23 Chris Pronger
GUE24 Curtis Joseph
GUE25 Doug Weight
GUE26 Pavel Bure
GUE27 Roberto Luongo
GUE28 Al MacInnis
GUE29 Jeremy Roenick
GUE30 Luc Robitaille
GUE31 Olaf Kolzig
GUE32 Peter Bondra
GUE33 Adam Oates
GUE34 Martin Brodeur
GUE35 Jason Arnott
GUE36 Eric Lindros
GUE37 Brian Leetch
GUE38 Mark Messier
GUE39 Mike Richter
GUE40 Mats Sundin
GUE41 Owen Nolan
GUE42 Alexei Yashin
GUE43 Jaromir Jagr
GUE44 Daniel Alfredsson
GUE45 Marian Hossa
GUE46 Roman Cechmanek
GUE47 Mark Recchi
GUE48 John LeClair
GUE49 Brian Boucher
GUE50 Vincent Lecavalier

2001-02 BAP Signature Series Numbers

STATED PRINT RUN 10 SETS
NOT PRICED DUE TO SCARCITY

2001-02 BAP Signature Series Teammates

STATED PRINT RUN 40 SETS
TM1 Paul Kariya 12.50 30.00
Jeff Friesen
TM2 Patrik Stefan 12.50 30.00
Ilya Kovalchuk
TM3 Bill Guerin 8.00 20.00
Byron Dafoe
TM4 Martin Biron 8.00 20.00
Miroslav Satan
TM5 Jarome Iginla 12.50 30.00
Roman Turek
TM6 Ron Francis 8.00 20.00
Sami Kapanen
TM7 Tony Amonte 8.00 20.00
Eric Daze
TM8 Joe Sakic 40.00 100.00
Patrick Roy
TM9 Chris Drury 12.50 30.00
Milan Hejduk
TM10 Mike Modano 15.00 40.00
Ed Belfour
TM11 Steve Yzerman 20.00 50.00
Brendan Shanahan
TM12 Luc Robitaille 25.00 60.00
Dominik Hasek
TM13 Pavel Bure 12.50 30.00
Roberto Luongo
TM14 Zigmund Palffy 12.50 30.00
Felix Potvin
TM15 Marian Gaborik 12.50 30.00
Manny Fernandez
TM16 Brian Savage 15.00 40.00
Jose Theodore
TM17 Jason Arnott 20.00 50.00
Martin Brodeur
TM18 Scott Niedermayer 8.00 20.00
Scott Stevens
TM19 Mark Messier 15.00 40.00
Eric Lindros
TM20 Kenny Jonsson 8.00 20.00
Alexei Yashin
TM21 Daniel Alfredsson 12.50 30.00
Patrick Lalime
TM22 Mark Recchi 12.50 30.00
Jeremy Roenick
TM23 John LeClair 8.00 20.00
Brian Boucher
TM24 Mario Lemieux 30.00 80.00
Milan Kraft
TM25 Owen Nolan 12.50 30.00
Teemu Selanne
TM26 Doug Weight 8.00 20.00
Keith Tkachuk
TM27 Vincent Lecavalier 12.50 30.00
Nikolai Khabibulin
TM28 Mats Sundin 12.50 30.00
Curtis Joseph
TM29 Daniel Sedin 12.50 30.00
Markus Naslund
TM30 Peter Bondra 25.00 60.00
Jaromir Jagr

2001-02 BAP Signature Series Vintage Autographs

This 40-card set featured autographs of retired NHL stars. Autographs were positioned beneath a full-color player photo on the card fronts. Print runs for each card are listed below. Card #VA16 was supposed to be Woody Dumart, but he passed away before he could sign, therefore that card does not exist.

STATED PRINT RUNS LISTED BELOW
CARD NUMBER VA16 NOT PRODUCED
PRINT RUNS OF 20 OR LESS NOT
PRICED DUE TO SCARCITY
VA1 Tony Esposito/60 25.00 60.00
VA2 Phil Esposito/40 30.00 80.00
VA3 Gordie Howe/20 75.00 200.00
VA4 Gordie Howe/20 75.00 200.00
VA5 Jean Beliveau/40 25.00 60.00
VA6 Jean Beliveau/40 25.00 60.00
VA7 Bobby Hull/40 20.00 50.00
Winnipeg
VA8 Bobby Hull/40 20.00 50.00
Chicago
VA9 Ted Lindsay/40 12.50 30.00
VA10 Johnny Bower/60 12.50 30.00
VA11 Milt Schmidt/80 20.00 50.00
VA12 Red Kelly/80 12.50 30.00
VA13 Glenn Hall/40 15.00 40.00
VA14 Chuck Rayner/40 20.00 50.00
VA15 Elmer Lach/80 15.00 40.00
VA17 Gerry Cheevers/40 20.00 50.00
VA18 Gump Worsley/40 30.00 80.00
VA19 Butch Bouchard/80 12.50 30.00
VA20 Henri Richard/80 12.50 30.00
VA21 Henri Richard/80 15.00 40.00
VA22 Bernie Geoffrion/80 20.00 50.00
VA23 Dollard St. Laurent/80 12.50 30.00
VA24 Dickie Moore/70 12.50 30.00
VA25 Jean-Guy Talbot/80 12.50 30.00
VA26 Bill Gadsby/80 12.50 30.00
VA27 Frank Mahovlich/40 25.00 60.00
VA28 Dino Ciccarelli/70 12.50 30.00
VA29 Jari Kurri/70 15.00 40.00
VA30 Mike Bossy/70 12.50 30.00
VA31 Johnny Bucyk/90 12.50 30.00
VA32 Michel Goulet/90 12.50 30.00
VA33 Stan Mikita/40 20.00 50.00
VA34 Bryan Trottier/70 12.50 30.00
VA35 Dale Hawerchuk/70 15.00 40.00
VA36 Gilbert Perreault/40 12.50 30.00
VA37 Marcel Dionne/40 20.00 50.00
VA38 Mike Gartner/70 12.50 30.00
VA39 Lanny McDonald/70 12.50 30.00
VA40 Guy Lafleur/40 40.00 100.00

2002-03 BAP Signature Series

Released in mid-May, this 200-card base set consisted of 177 veterans and 23 rookies.

COMPLETE SET (200) 75.00 150.00
1 Dany Heatley .50 1.25
2 Alexei Zhamnov .20 .50
3 Mike Comrie .30 .75
4 Dwayne Roloson .30 .75
5 Mike Dunham .30 .75
6 Simon Gagne .40 1.00
7 Evgeni Nabokov .30 .75
8 Bryan McCabe .20 .50
9 Todd Bertuzzi .40 1.00
10 Alex Kovalev .30 .75
11 Dave Andreychuk .20 .50
12 Daniel Alfredsson .30 .75
13 Marian Gaborik .75 2.00
14 J-S Aubin .30 .75
15 Andy McDonald .20 .50
16 Brad Richards .30 .75
17 Henrik Sedin .20 .50
18 Mark Bell .20 .50
19 Adam Deadmarsh .20 .50
20 Marc Denis .30 .75
21 Mike York .20 .50
22 Johan Hedberg .30 .75
23 Vincent Damphousse .20 .50
24 Marian Hossa .40 1.00
25 Richard Zednik .20 .50
26 Alexei Yashin .20 .50
27 Sergei Gonchar .20 .50
28 Martin Straka .20 .50
29 Ed Jovanovski .30 .75
30 Robert Lang .20 .50
31 Markus Naslund .40 1.00
32 Mike Sillinger .20 .50
33 Jamie Storr .30 .75
34 Kimmo Timonen .20 .50
35 Patrick Lalime .30 .75
36 Alyn McCauley .20 .50
37 Scott Walker .20 .50
38 Trevor Linden .30 .75
39 Ilya Kovalchuk .50 1.25
40 Jarome Iginla .50 1.25
41 Alex Tanguay .30 .75
42 Yanic Perreault .20 .50
43 Jocelyn Thibault .30 .75
44 Eric Brewer .20 .50
45 Ray Whitney .20 .50
46 Ryan Smyth .20 .50
47 Steven Reinprecht .20 .50
48 Phil Housley .20 .50
49 Milan Hnilicka .30 .75
50 Maxim Afinogenov .20 .50
51 Andrew Brunette .20 .50
52 Miroslav Satan .30 .75
53 Glen Murray .20 .50
54 Mark Parrish .20 .50
55 Daniel Sedin .20 .50
56 Brendan Morrison .30 .75
57 Brian Rafalski .20 .50
58 Dan Cloutier .30 .75
59 Espen Knutsen .20 .50
60 Radim Vrbata .20 .50
61 Patrik Stefan .20 .50
62 Eric Daze .20 .50
63 Felix Potvin .40 1.00
64 Darcy Tucker .20 .50
65 Jose Theodore .50 1.25
66 Scott Hartnell .20 .50
67 Martin Havlat .30 .75
68 Radek Bonk .20 .50
69 Patrick Marleau .30 .75
70 Andy Delmore .20 .50
71 Rostislav Klesla .20 .50
72 David Aebischer .30 .75
73 Steve Shields .30 .75
74 Stu Barnes .20 .50
75 Tim Connolly .20 .50
76 Jean-Sebastien Giguere .30 .75
77 Shane Doan .20 .50
78 Brian Rolston .20 .50
79 Shawn McEachern .20 .50
80 Martin Biron .30 .75
81 Craig Conroy .20 .50
82 Mika Noronen .20 .50
83 Brian Boucher .30 .75
84 Kyle Calder .20 .50
85 Cliff Ronning .20 .50
86 Brian Gionta .20 .50
87 Shawn Bates .20 .50
88 Michal Handzus .20 .50
89 Daniel Briere .20 .50
90 Adam Graves .20 .50
91 Martin St. Louis .30 .75
92 Ladislav Nagy .20 .50
93 Oleg Tverdovsky .20 .50
94 Pavel Brendl .20 .50
95 Alexei Morozov .20 .50
96 Daymond Langkow .20 .50
97 Krys Kolanos .20 .50
98 Sean Burke .30 .75
99 Chris Drury .30 .75
100 Steve Sullivan .20 .50
101 Paul Kariya .40 1.00
102 Peter Forsberg 1.00 2.50
103 Ron Tugnutt .30 .75
104 Manny Legace .30 .75
105 Tommy Salo .30 .75
106 Kristian Huselius .20 .50
107 Jason Allison .20 .50
108 Mariusz Czerkawski .20 .50
109 Jeff Friesen .20 .50
110 Chris Osgood .30 .75
111 Martin Prusek .30 .75
112 Steve Yzerman 1.50 4.00
113 John LeClair .40 1.00
114 Jan Hrdina .20 .50
115 Tony Amonte .30 .75
116 Teemu Selanne .40 1.00
117 Cory Stillman .20 .50
118 Nikolai Khabibulin .40 1.00
119 Mats Sundin .40 1.00
120 Olaf Kolzig .30 .75
121 Petr Sykora .20 .50
122 Joe Thornton .60 1.50
123 Roman Turek .30 .75
124 Derek Morris .20 .50
125 Bill Guerin .30 .75
126 Brendan Shanahan .40 1.00
127 Roberto Luongo .50 1.25
128 Zigmund Palffy .30 .75
129 Pavol Demitra .30 .75
130 Saku Koivu .40 1.00
131 Joe Nieuwendyk .30 .75
132 Mike Peca .20 .50
133 Petr Schastlivy .20 .50
134 Jeremy Roenick .50 1.25
135 Mario Lemieux 2.00 5.00
136 Petr Cajanek .20 .50
137 Vincent Lecavalier .40 1.00
138 Peter Bondra .30 .75
139 Brent Johnson .30 .75
140 Sergei Samsonov .30 .75
141 Joe Sakic .75 2.00
142 Brenden Morrow .30 .75
143 Arturs Irbe .30 .75
144 Chris Chelios .40 1.00
145 Sandis Ozolinsh .20 .50
146 Doug Gilmour .30 .75
147 Scott Stevens .30 .75
148 Sergei Fedorov .60 1.50
149 Keith Primeau .20 .50
150 Eric Boguniecki .20 .50
151 Shane Willis .20 .50
152 Rob Blake .30 .75
153 Luc Robitaille .30 .75
154 Pierre Turgeon .30 .75
155 Curtis Joseph .40 1.00
156 Stephen Weiss .20 .50
157 Patrik Elias .30 .75
158 Mark Recchi .30 .75
159 Al MacInnis .30 .75
160 Patrick Roy 1.50 4.00
161 Darryl Sydor .20 .50
162 Nicklas Lidstrom .40 1.00
163 Doug Weight .30 .75
164 Roman Cechmanek .30 .75
165 Marty Turco .30 .75
166 Pavel Datsyuk .40 1.00
167 Chris Pronger .30 .75
168 Scott Young .20 .50
169 Igor Larionov .20 .50
170 Keith Tkachuk .40 1.00
171 Ron Francis .30 .75
172 Dan Blackburn .30 .75
173 Jeff O'Neill .20 .50
174 Bobby Holik .20 .50
175 Erik Cole .20 .50
176 Pavel Bure .40 1.00
177 Brian Leetch .30 .75
178 Curtis Sanford RC 1.50 4.00
179 Carlo Colaiacovo RC 1.50 4.00
180 Dennis Seidenberg RC 1.50 4.00
181 Adam Hall RC 1.25 3.00
182 Ivan Majesky RC 1.25 3.00
183 Rick Nash RC 4.00 10.00
184 Alexei Smirnov RC 1.25 3.00
185 Chuck Kobasew RC 1.25 3.00
186 Ron Hainsey RC 1.25 3.00
187 Stephane Veilleux RC 1.25 3.00
188 Scottie Upshall RC 1.50 4.00
189 Lasse Pirjeta RC 1.25 3.00
190 Henrik Zetterberg RC 4.00 10.00
191 Jay Bouwmeester RC 2.00 5.00
192 Alexander Frolov RC 2.50 6.00
193 Dmitri Bykov RC 1.25 3.00
194 Stanislav Chistov RC 1.50 4.00
195 Jordan Leopold RC 1.25 3.00
196 P-M Bouchard RC 2.50 6.00
197 Mike Cammalleri RC 1.50 4.00
198 Anton Volchenkov RC 1.25 3.00
199 Lynn Loyns RC 1.25 3.00
200 Steve Eminger RC 1.25 3.00

2002-03 BAP Signature Series All-Rookie

This 12-card set featured game-worn equipment from some of the leagues most promising young players. Each card was limited to just 50 copies.

*MULT.COLOR SWATCH: .75X TO 1.5X
STATED PRINT RUN 50 SETS
AR1 Ryan Miller 15.00 40.00
AR2 Jay Bouwmeester 15.00 40.00
AR3 Dennis Seidenberg 10.00 25.00
AR4 Stephen Weiss 12.00 30.00
AR5 Marcel Hossa 12.00 30.00
AR6 Radovan Somik 10.00 25.00
AR7 Jan Lasak 10.00 25.00
AR8 Jordan Leopold 10.00 25.00
AR9 Barret Jackman 12.00 30.00
AR10 Mike Cammalleri 15.00 40.00
AR11 Henrik Zetterberg Skate 20.00 50.00
AR12 Rick Nash 20.00 50.00

2002-03 BAP Signature Series Autographs

This 200-card set paralleled the base set but carried certified autographs on the card fronts. They were inserted one per pack and short prints are designated below.

ONE PER PACK
*GOLD: .75X TO 1.25X
1 Dany Heatley 8.00 20.00
2 Alexei Zhamnov 2.00 5.00
3 Mike Comrie 4.00 10.00
4 Dwayne Roloson 4.00 10.00
5 Mike Dunham 4.00 10.00
6 Simon Gagne 6.00 15.00
7 Evgeni Nabokov 4.00 10.00
8 Bryan McCabe 2.00 5.00
9 Todd Bertuzzi 4.00 10.00
10 Alexei Kovalev 4.00 10.00
11 Dave Andreychuk 4.00 10.00
12 Daniel Alfredsson 4.00 10.00
13 Marian Gaborik 12.50 30.00
14 J-S Aubin 2.00 5.00
15 Andy McDonald 2.00 5.00
16 Brad Richards 4.00 10.00
17 Henrik Sedin 2.00 5.00
18 Mark Bell 2.00 5.00
19 Adam Deadmarsh 2.00 5.00
20 Marc Denis 4.00 10.00
21 Mike York 2.00 5.00
22 Johan Hedberg 2.00 5.00
23 Vincent Damphousse 2.00 5.00
24 Marian Hossa 6.00 15.00
25 Richard Zednik 2.00 5.00
26 Alexei Yashin 2.00 5.00
27 Sergei Gonchar 2.00 5.00
28 Martin Straka 2.00 5.00
29 Ed Jovanovski 4.00 10.00
30 Robert Lang 2.00 5.00
31 Markus Naslund 6.00 15.00
32 Mike Sillinger 2.00 5.00
33 Jamie Storr 2.00 5.00
34 Kimmo Timonen 2.00 5.00
35 Patrick Lalime 2.00 5.00
36 Alyn McCauley 2.00 5.00
37 Scott Walker 2.00 5.00
38 Trevor Linden 4.00 10.00
39 Ilya Kovalchuk 12.50 30.00
40 Jarome Iginla 8.00 20.00
41 Alex Tanguay 4.00 10.00
42 Yanic Perreault 2.00 5.00
43 Jocelyn Thibault 2.00 5.00
44 Eric Brewer 2.00 5.00
45 Ray Whitney 2.00 5.00
46 Ryan Smyth 2.00 5.00
47 Steven Reinprecht 2.00 5.00
48 Phil Housley 2.00 5.00
49 Milan Hnilicka 2.00 5.00
50 Maxim Afinogenov 2.00 5.00
51 Andrew Brunette 2.00 5.00
52 Miroslav Satan 4.00 10.00
53 Glen Murray 2.00 5.00
54 Mark Parrish 2.00 5.00
55 Daniel Sedin 2.00 5.00
56 Brendan Morrison 2.00 5.00
57 Brian Rafalski 2.00 5.00
58 Dan Cloutier 4.00 10.00
59 Espen Knutsen 2.00 5.00
60 Radim Vrbata 2.00 5.00
61 Patrik Stefan 2.00 5.00
62 Eric Daze 2.00 5.00
63 Felix Potvin 4.00 10.00
64 Darcy Tucker 2.00 5.00
65 Jose Theodore 6.00 15.00
66 Scott Hartnell 2.00 5.00
67 Martin Havlat 4.00 10.00
68 Radek Bonk 2.00 5.00
69 Patrick Marleau 4.00 10.00
70 Andy Delmore 2.00 5.00
71 Rostislav Klesla 2.00 5.00
72 David Aebischer 4.00 10.00
73 Steve Shields 2.00 5.00
74 Stu Barnes 2.00 5.00
75 Tim Connolly 2.00 5.00
76 Jean-Sebastien Giguere 6.00 15.00
77 Shane Doan 2.00 5.00
78 Brian Rolston 2.00 5.00
79 Shawn McEachern 2.00 5.00
80 Martin Biron 2.00 5.00
81 Craig Conroy 2.00 5.00
82 Mika Noronen 2.00 5.00
83 Brian Boucher 2.00 5.00
84 Kyle Calder 2.00 5.00
85 Cliff Ronning 2.00 5.00
86 Brian Gionta 2.00 5.00
87 Shawn Bates 2.00 5.00
88 Michal Handzus 2.00 5.00
89 Daniel Briere 4.00 10.00
90 Adam Graves 2.00 5.00
91 Martin St. Louis 4.00 10.00
92 Ladislav Nagy 2.00 5.00
93 Oleg Tverdovsky 2.00 5.00
94 Pavel Brendl 2.00 5.00
95 Alexei Morozov 2.00 5.00
96 Daymond Langkow 2.00 5.00
97 Krys Kolanos 2.00 5.00
98 Sean Burke 4.00 10.00
99 Chris Drury 4.00 10.00
100 Steve Sullivan 2.00 5.00
101 Paul Kariya SP 15.00 40.00
102 Peter Forsberg SP 25.00 60.00
103 Ron Tugnutt SP 8.00 20.00
104 Manny Legace 4.00 10.00
105 Tommy Salo SP 8.00 20.00
106 Kristian Huselius 2.00 5.00
107 Jason Allison SP 8.00 20.00
108 Mariusz Czerkawski 2.00 5.00
109 Jeff Friesen SP 8.00 20.00
110 Chris Osgood SP 8.00 20.00
111 Martin Prusek 2.00 5.00
112 Steve Yzerman SP 30.00 80.00
113 John LeClair SP 8.00 20.00
114 Jan Hrdina 2.00 5.00
115 Tony Amonte SP 8.00 20.00
116 Teemu Selanne SP 8.00 20.00
117 Cory Stillman 2.00 5.00
118 Nikolai Khabibulin SP 10.00 25.00
119 Mats Sundin SP 20.00 50.00
120 Olaf Kolzig SP 12.00 30.00
121 Petr Sykora 8.00 20.00
122 Joe Thornton SP 15.00 40.00
123 Roman Turek SP 8.00 20.00
124 Derek Morris SP 8.00 20.00
125 Bill Guerin SP 8.00 20.00
126 Brendan Shanahan SP 20.00 50.00
127 Roberto Luongo 8.00 20.00
128 Zigmund Palffy SP 8.00 20.00
129 Pavol Demitra SP 8.00 20.00
130 Saku Koivu SP 8.00 20.00
131 Joe Nieuwendyk SP 8.00 20.00
132 Mike Peca SP 8.00 20.00
133 Petr Schastlivy 2.00 5.00
134 Jeremy Roenick SP 15.00 40.00
135 Mario Lemieux SP 125.00 300.00
136 Petr Cajanek 2.00 5.00
137 Vincent Lecavalier SP 12.00 30.00
138 Peter Bondra SP 8.00 20.00
139 Brent Johnson SP 8.00 20.00
140 Sergei Samsonov SP 8.00 20.00
141 Joe Sakic SP 20.00 50.00
142 Brenden Morrow 4.00 10.00
143 Arturs Irbe 2.00 5.00
144 Chris Chelios SP 12.50 30.00
145 Sandis Ozolinsh 2.00 5.00
146 Doug Gilmour SP 8.00 20.00
147 Scott Stevens SP 10.00 25.00
148 Sergei Fedorov SP 12.50 30.00
149 Keith Primeau SP 8.00 20.00
150 Eric Boguniecki 2.00 5.00
151 Shane Willis 2.00 5.00
152 Rob Blake SP 8.00 20.00
153 Luc Robitaille SP 12.50 30.00
154 Pierre Turgeon SP 8.00 20.00
155 Curtis Joseph SP 12.50 30.00
156 Stephen Weiss 2.00 5.00
157 Patrik Elias SP 8.00 20.00
158 Mark Recchi SP 8.00 20.00
159 Al MacInnis SP 8.00 20.00
160 Patrick Roy SP 60.00 150.00
161 Darryl Sydor SP 8.00 20.00
162 Nicklas Lidstrom SP 15.00 40.00
163 Doug Weight SP 8.00 20.00
164 Roman Cechmanek 2.00 5.00
165 Marty Turco 4.00 10.00
166 Pavel Datsyuk 12.50 30.00
167 Chris Pronger SP 8.00 20.00
168 Scott Young 2.00 5.00
169 Igor Larionov SP 10.00 25.00
170 Keith Tkachuk SP 8.00 20.00
171 Ron Francis SP 8.00 20.00
172 Dan Blackburn 2.00 5.00
173 Jeff O'Neill SP 8.00 20.00
174 Bobby Holik SP 8.00 20.00
175 Erik Cole 2.00 5.00
176 Pavel Bure SP 8.00 20.00
177 Brian Leetch SP 8.00 20.00
178 Curtis Sanford 4.00 10.00
179 Carlo Colaiacovo 2.00 5.00
180 Dennis Seidenberg 2.00 5.00
181 Adam Hall 2.00 5.00
182 Ivan Majesky 2.00 5.00
183 Rick Nash 15.00 40.00
184 Alexei Smirnov 2.00 5.00
185 Chuck Kobasew 2.00 5.00
186 Ron Hainsey 2.00 5.00
187 Stephane Veilleux 2.00 5.00
188 Scottie Upshall 4.00 10.00
189 Lasse Pirjeta 2.00 5.00
190 Henrik Zetterberg 15.00 40.00
191 Jay Bouwmeester 6.00 15.00

192 Alexander Frolov 6.00 15.00
193 Dmitri Bykov 2.00 5.00
194 Stanislav Chistov 2.00 5.00
195 Jordan Leopold 2.00 5.00
196 P-M Bouchard 4.00 10.00
197 Mike Cammalleri 4.00 10.00
198 Anton Volchenkov 2.00 5.00
199 Lynn Loyns 2.00 5.00
200 Steve Eminger 2.00 5.00

2002-03 BAP Signature Series Autograph Buybacks 1998

Available randomly in packs of 2002-03 BAP Signature Series, these cards were older BAP autograph cards that were "bought back" by ITG and inserted into the product on a average of two per box. These cards are distinguishable by the silver foil "10th Anniversary" stamp they carry on the card fronts. Several different years are represented in this buyback series.

*BUYBACKS: .6X TO 1.5X ORIGINAL VALUES

2002-03 BAP Signature Series Autograph Buybacks 1999

*BUYBACKS: .6X TO 1.5X ORIGINAL VALUES

2002-03 BAP Signature Series Autograph Buybacks 2000

*BUYBACKS: .6X TO 1.5X ORIGINAL VALUES

2002-03 BAP Signature Series Autograph Buybacks 2001

*BUYBACKS: .6X TO 1.5X ORIGINAL VALUES

2002-03 BAP Signature Series Complete Jersey

This 10-card set featured four swatches of game-used jersey, including pieces of emblems and numbers. Cards were limited to 10 copies each and are not priced due to scarcity.

STATED PRINT RUN 10 SETS
NOT PRICED DUE TO SCARCITY
CJ1 Mario Lemieux
CJ2 Patrick Roy
CJ3 Steve Yzerman
CJ4 Paul Kariya
CJ5 Jaromir Jagr
CJ6 Marian Gaborik
CJ7 Peter Forsberg
CJ8 Pavel Bure
CJ9 Joe Sakic
CJ10 Teemu Selanne

2002-03 BAP Signature Series Defensive Wall

This 10-card set featured pieces of game-used jersey from starting defensive trios. Each card was limited to 50 copies each.

STATED PRINT RUN 50 SETS
DW1 Rob Blake 40.00 100.00
Patrick Roy
Adam Foote
DW2 Tomas Kaberle 25.00 60.00
Ed Belfour
Bryan McCabe
DW3 Eric Desjardins 15.00 40.00
Roman Cechmanek
Dennis Seidenberg
DW4 Brian Leetch 15.00 40.00
Dan Blackburn
Darius Kasparaitis
DW5 Sergei Zubov 25.00 60.00
Marty Turco
Derian Hatcher
DW6 Scott Stevens 30.00 80.00
Martin Brodeur
Scott Niedermayer
DW7 Chris Pronger 15.00 40.00
Brent Johnson
Al MacInnis
DW8 Wade Redden 15.00 40.00
Patrick Lalime
Chris Phillips
DW9 Brendan Witt 15.00 40.00
Olaf Kolzig
Sergei Gonchar
DW10 Ed Jovanovski 15.00 40.00
Dan Cloutier
Mattias Ohlund

2002-03 BAP Signature Series Famous Scraps

This 12-card set highlighted two players who have "mixed it up" at various times during their careers. Each card was limited to just 50 copies and carried pieces of jersey from each player.

STATED PRINT RUN 50 SETS
FS1 Dave Schultz 20.00 50.00
Dave Williams
FS2 Bob Probert 20.00 50.00
Wendel Clark
FS3 Ian Laperriere 20.00 50.00
Bill Guerin

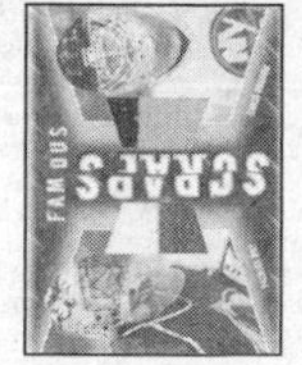

FS4 Peter Worrell 20.00 50.00
Chris Gratton
FS5 Bill Guerin 20.00 50.00
Jarome Iginla
FS6 Tie Domi 30.00 80.00
Rob Ray
FS7 Mike Comrie 20.00 50.00
Ilya Kovalchuk
FS8 Felix Potvin 20.00 50.00
Ron Hextall
FS9 Owen Nolan 20.00 50.00
Bob Probert
FS10 Patrick Roy 30.00 80.00
Chris Osgood
FS11 Donald Brashear 20.00 50.00
Georges Laraque
FS12 Matt Johnson 20.00 50.00
Sandy McCarthy

2002-03 BAP Signature Series Franchise Players

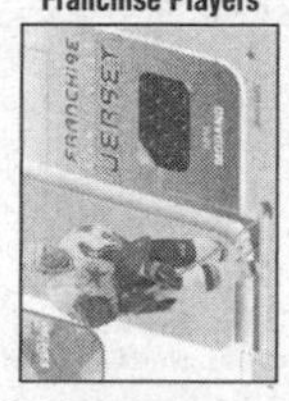

*MULT.COLOR SWATCH: .75X TO 1.5X
STATED PRINT RUN 50 SETS
FJ1 Paul Kariya 8.00 20.00
FJ2 Dany Heatley 12.50 30.00
FJ3 Joe Thornton 15.00 40.00
FJ4 Miroslav Satan 8.00 20.00
FJ5 Jarome Iginla 10.00 25.00
FJ6 Ron Francis 8.00 20.00
FJ7 Jocelyn Thibault 8.00 20.00
FJ8 Rick Nash 15.00 40.00
FJ9 Joe Sakic 15.00 40.00
FJ10 Mike Modano 12.50 30.00
FJ11 Steve Yzerman 20.00 50.00
FJ12 Mike Comrie 8.00 20.00
FJ13 Roberto Luongo 12.50 30.00
FJ14 Jason Allison 8.00 20.00
FJ15 Marian Gaborik 15.00 40.00
FJ16 Jose Theodore 8.00 20.00
FJ17 David Legwand 8.00 20.00
FJ18 Martin Brodeur 20.00 50.00
FJ19 Mike Peca 8.00 20.00
FJ20 Pavel Bure 8.00 20.00
FJ21 Marian Hossa 8.00 20.00
FJ22 Jeremy Roenick 10.00 25.00
FJ23 Daniel Briere 8.00 20.00
FJ24 Mario Lemieux 20.00 50.00
FJ25 Teemu Selanne 8.00 20.00
FJ26 Chris Pronger 8.00 20.00
FJ27 Vincent Lecavalier 8.00 20.00
FJ28 Mats Sundin 8.00 20.00
FJ29 Markus Naslund 8.00 20.00
FJ30 Jaromir Jagr 12.50 30.00

2002-03 BAP Signature Series Golf

This 100-card set was inserted one per pack and pictured players enjoying the game of golf.

COMPLETE SET (100) 50.00 100.00
ONE PER PACK
GS1 Adam Foote .50 1.25
GS2 Adam Oates .50 1.25
GS3 Adrian Aucoin .30 .75
GS4 Alex Tanguay .50 1.25
GS5 Alexander Mogilny .50 1.25
GS6 Alexei Yashin .30 .75
GS7 Alyn McCauley .30 .75
GS8 Andy McDonald .30 .75
GS9 Brian Leetch .50 1.25
GS10 Bates Battaglia .30 .75
GS11 Bobby Holik .30 .75
GS12 Brad Isbister .30 .75
GS13 Brendan Morrison .50 1.25
GS14 Arturs Irbe .50 1.25
GS15 Brian Savage .30 .75
GS16 Bryan Marchment .30 .75
GS17 Bryan McCabe .30 .75
GS18 Carlo Colaiacovo .30 .75
GS19 Chris Drury .50 1.25
GS20 Chris Gratton .30 .75
GS21 Chris Neil .30 .75
GS22 Chris Osgood .50 1.25
GS23 Chris Simon .30 .75
GS24 Curtis Joseph .60 1.50
GS25 Daniel Sedin .30 .75
GS26 Darius Kasparaitis .30 .75
GS27 Darren McCarty .30 .75
GS28 Darryl Sittler .60 1.50
GS29 David Aebischer .50 1.25
GS30 David Legwand .50 1.25
GS31 Denis Arkhipov .30 .75
GS32 Derek Morris .30 .75
GS33 Donald Brashear .30 .75
GS34 Doug Gilmour .50 1.25
GS35 Ed Belfour .60 1.50
GS36 Ed Jovanovski .50 1.25
GS37 Erik Cole .30 .75
GS38 Eric Lindros .60 1.50
GS39 Grant Fuhr .50 1.25
GS40 Jaroslav Svoboda .30 .75
GS41 Jeff O'Neill .30 .75
GS42 Jarome Iginla .75 2.00
GS43 Joe Sakic 1.25 3.00
GS44 Johan Hedberg .50 1.25
GS45 Josef Vasicek .30 .75
GS46 Jean-Sebastien Giguere .50 1.25
GS47 Kenny Jonsson .30 .75
GS48 Luc Robitaille .50 1.25
GS49 Mario Lemieux 4.00 10.00
GS50 Mark Parrish .30 .75
GS51 Martin Brodeur 1.50 4.00
GS52 Martin Erat .30 .75
GS53 Martin Skoula .30 .75
GS54 Mats Sundin .60 1.50
GS55 Matt Cooke .30 .75
GS56 Mattias Ohlund .30 .75
GS57 Mike Dunham .50 1.25
GS58 Mike Fisher .30 .75
GS59 Mike Keane .30 .75
GS60 Mike Peca .30 .75
GS61 Mike Ricci .30 .75
GS62 Milan Hejduk .60 1.50
GS63 Miroslav Satan .50 1.25
GS64 Nik Antropov .30 .75
GS65 Olaf Kolzig .50 1.25
GS66 Owen Nolan .50 1.25
GS67 Pat Verbeek .30 .75
GS68 Patrick Marleau .50 1.25
GS69 Patrick Roy 3.00 8.00
GS70 Paul Kariya .60 1.50
GS71 Peter Bondra .50 1.25
GS72 Peter Forsberg 1.50 4.00
GS73 Petr Sykora .30 .75
GS74 Radek Dvorak .30 .75
GS75 Rick DiPietro .50 1.25
GS76 Rob Blake .50 1.25
GS77 Robert Lang .30 .75
GS78 Roman Hamrlik .30 .75
GS79 Dany Heatley .50 1.25
GS80 Ron Francis .50 1.25
GS81 Ryan Smyth .30 .75
GS82 Sami Kapanen .30 .75
GS83 Scott Hartnell .30 .75
GS84 Scott Stevens .50 1.25
GS85 Scott Walker .30 .75
GS86 Stan Mikita .75 2.00
GS87 Stanislav Chistov .30 .75
GS88 Steve Konowalchuk .30 .75
GS89 Steve Rucchin .30 .75
GS90 Steve Yzerman 3.00 8.00
GS91 Stephen Peat .30 .75
GS92 Steven Reinprecht .30 .75
GS93 Teemu Selanne .60 1.50
GS94 Tie Domi .50 1.25
GS95 Todd Bertuzzi .60 1.50
GS96 Todd White .30 .75
GS97 Tom Poti .30 .75
GS98 Trent Klatt .30 .75
GS99 Trevor Kidd .50 1.25
GS100 Wade Redden .30 .75

2002-03 BAP Signature Series Jerseys

*MULT.COLOR SWATCH: .75X TO 1.5X
STATED PRINT RUN 90 SETS
SGJ1 Mario Lemieux 20.00 50.00
SGJ2 Steve Yzerman 20.00 50.00
SGJ3 Peter Forsberg 12.50 30.00
SGJ4 Patrick Roy 20.00 50.00
SGJ5 Jarome Iginla 10.00 25.00
SGJ6 Pavel Bure 8.00 20.00
SGJ7 Jaromir Jagr 10.00 25.00
SGJ8 Eric Lindros 8.00 20.00
SGJ9 Paul Kariya 8.00 20.00
SGJ10 Ilya Kovalchuk 10.00 25.00
SGJ11 Mike Modano 10.00 25.00
SGJ12 Joe Thornton 12.50 30.00
SGJ13 Jose Theodore 10.00 25.00
SGJ14 Jeremy Roenick 10.00 25.00
SGJ15 Martin Brodeur 20.00 50.00
SGJ16 Mats Sundin 8.00 20.00
SGJ17 Mark Messier 8.00 20.00
SGJ18 Alexei Yashin 6.00 15.00
SGJ19 Marian Gaborik 12.50 30.00
SGJ20 Brendan Shanahan 8.00 20.00
SGJ21 Owen Nolan 6.00 15.00
SGJ22 Joe Sakic 12.50 30.00
SGJ23 Daniel Alfredsson 6.00 15.00
SGJ24 Teemu Selanne 8.00 20.00
SGJ25 Nicklas Lidstrom 8.00 20.00
SGJ26 John LeClair 8.00 20.00
SGJ27 Keith Tkachuk 8.00 20.00
SGJ28 Brian Leetch 6.00 15.00
SGJ29 Milan Hejduk 8.00 20.00
SGJ30 Dany Heatley 10.00 25.00
SGJ31 Sergei Samsonov 6.00 15.00
SGJ32 Todd Bertuzzi 8.00 20.00
SGJ33 Markus Naslund 8.00 20.00
SGJ34 Chris Chelios 8.00 20.00
SGJ35 Rob Blake 6.00 15.00
SGJ36 Sergei Fedorov 10.00 25.00
SGJ37 Al MacInnis 6.00 15.00
SGJ38 Luc Robitaille 6.00 15.00
SGJ39 Martin Havlat 6.00 15.00
SGJ40 Ron Francis 6.00 15.00
SGJ41 Alexander Mogilny 6.00 15.00
SGJ42 Chris Pronger 6.00 15.00
SGJ43 Doug Weight 6.00 15.00
SGJ44 Zigmund Palffy 8.00 20.00
SGJ45 Peter Bondra 6.00 15.00
SGJ46 Mike Comrie 6.00 15.00
SGJ47 Pavel Datsyuk 10.00 25.00
SGJ48 Marian Hossa 8.00 20.00
SGJ49 Saku Koivu 8.00 20.00
SGJ50 Dan Blackburn 6.00 15.00
SGJ51 Steve Shields 6.00 15.00
SGJ52 Bill Guerin 6.00 15.00
SGJ53 Doug Gilmour 6.00 15.00
SGJ54 Jason Spezza 12.50 30.00
SGJ55 Jay Bouwmeester 6.00 15.00
SGJ56 Alexei Smirnov 6.00 15.00
SGJ57 Stanislav Chistov 6.00 15.00
SGJ58 Chuck Kobasew 6.00 15.00
SGJ59 Jordan Leopold 6.00 15.00
SGJ60 Niko Kapanen 6.00 15.00
SGJ61 Scottie Upshall 6.00 15.00
SGJ62 Ron Hainsey 6.00 15.00
SGJ63 Alexander Frolov 6.00 15.00
SGJ64 Mike Cammalleri 6.00 15.00
SGJ65 Dennis Seidenberg 6.00 15.00
SGJ66 Rick Nash 10.00 25.00
SGJ67 Carlo Colaiacovo 6.00 15.00
SGJ68 Marty Turco 6.00 15.00
SGJ69 Alex Kovalev 6.00 15.00
SGJ70 Vincent Lecavalier 6.00 15.00

2002-03 BAP Signature Series Jerseys Toronto Fall Expo

SGJ1 Mario Lemieux

2002-03 BAP Signature Series Jersey Autographs

PRINT RUN 10 SER.#'d SETS
NOT PRICED DUE TO SCARCITY

2002-03 BAP Signature Series Magnificent Inserts

This 10-card set featured game-used equipment from the career of Mario Lemieux. Cards MI1-MI5 had a print run of 40 copies each and cards MI6-MI10 were limited to just 10 copies each. Cards MI6-MI10 are not priced due to scarcity.

MI1-MI5 PRINT RUN 40 SETS
MI6-MI10 PRINT RUN 10 SETS
MI6-MI10 NOT PRICED DUE TO SCARCITY
MI1 2000-01 Season 30.00 80.00
MI2 1985-86 Season 30.00 80.00
MI3 2002 NHL All-Star 30.00 80.00
MI4 1987 Canada Cup 30.00 80.00
MI5 Dual Jersey 50.00 125.00
MI6 Number
MI7 Emblem
MI8 Triple Jersey
MI9 Quad Jersey
MI10 Complete Package

2002-03 BAP Signature Series Magnificent Inserts Autographs

This 10-card set paralleled the base Magnificent Inserts but carried certified autographs and each card was hand numbered. Cards MI1-MI5 were serial-numbered to 15 each and cards MI6-MI10 were serial numbered out of 5.

MI1-MI4 PRINT RUN 15 SETS
MI5-MI10 PRINT RUN 5 SETS
NOT PRICED DUE TO SCARCITY

2002-03 BAP Signature Series Phenoms

This 12-card set featured players in their 4th year in the league and included swatches of game jerseys. Cards were limited to just 40 copies each.

*MULT.COLOR SWATCH: .75X TO 1.5X
STATED PRINT RUN 40 SETS
YP1 Mike Fisher 10.00 25.00
YP2 Simon Gagne 10.00 25.00
YP3 Scott Gomez 10.00 25.00
YP4 David Legwand 10.00 25.00
YP5 Patrik Stefan 10.00 25.00

YP6 Brad Stuart 10.00 25.00
YP7 Alex Tanguay 10.00 25.00
YP8 Brent Johnson 10.00 25.00
YP9 Roberto Luongo 20.00 50.00
YP10 Evgeni Nabokov 10.00 25.00
YP11 Nik Antropov 20.00 50.00
YP12 Espen Knutsen 10.00 25.00

2002-03 BAP Signature Series Team Quads

Limited to just 10 copies each, this 20-card set featured jersey swatches from four teammates. This set is not priced due to scarcity.

STATED PRINT RUN 10 SETS
NOT PRICED DUE TO SCARCITY
TQ1 Joe Sakic
Peter Forsberg
Rob Blake
Patrick Roy
TQ2 Ed Belfour
Mats Sundin
Alexander Mogilny
Tie Domi
TQ3 Jeremy Roenick
John LeClair
Mark Recchi
Roman Cechmanek
TQ4 Eric Lindros
Brian Leetch
Pavel Bure
Dan Blackburn
TQ5 Roberto Luongo
Kristian Huselius
Jay Bouwmeester
Stephen Weiss
TQ6 Saku Koivu
Marcel Hossa
Doug Gilmour
Jose Theodore
TQ7 Scott Stevens
Scott Niedermayer
Martin Brodeur
Patrik Elias
TQ8 Mario Lemieux
Alex Kovalev
Johan Hedberg
Martin Straka
TQ9 Jaromir Jagr
Peter Bondra
Olaf Kolzig
Sergei Gonchar
TQ10 Felix Potvin
Alexander Frolov
Jason Allison
Adam Deadmarsh
TQ11 Steve Shields
Sergei Samsonov
Joe Thornton
Glen Murray
TQ12 Dany Heatley
Ilya Kovalchuk
Pasi Nurminen
Patrik Stefan
TQ13 Steve Yzerman
Sergei Fedorov
Brett Hull
Nicklas Lidstrom
TQ14 Todd Bertuzzi
Markus Naslund
Henrik Sedin
Daniel Sedin
TQ15 Keith Tkachuk
Chris Pronger
Doug Weight
Al MacInnis
TQ16 Marty Turco
Jason Arnott
Mike Modano
Bill Guerin
TQ17 Eric Brewer
Georges Laraque
Mike Comrie
Tommy Salo
TQ18 Vincent Damphousse
Teemu Selanne
Evgeni Nabokov
Owen Nolan
TQ19 Adam Oates
Paul Kariya
Jean-Sebastien Giguere
Stanislav Chistov
TQ20 Patrick Lalime
Marian Hossa
Martin Havlat
Jason Spezza

2002-03 BAP Signature Series Triple Memorabilia

STATED PRINT RUN 30 SETS
TM1 Mario Lemieux 100.00 250.00

TM2 Mats Sundin 20.00 50.00
TM3 Steve Yzerman 60.00 150.00
TM4 Joe Thornton 30.00 80.00
TM5 Eric Lindros 20.00 50.00
TM6 Patrick Roy 60.00 150.00
TM7 Brett Hull 30.00 80.00
TM8 Sergei Fedorov 30.00 80.00
TM9 Martin Brodeur 50.00 125.00
TM10 Joe Sakic 30.00 80.00

2002-03 BAP Signature Series Golf NHL All-Star FANtasy

GS1 Adam Foote
GS2 Adam Oates
GS3 Adrian Aucoin
GS4 Alex Tanguay
GS5 Alexander Mogilny
GS6 Alexei Yashin
GS7 Alyn McCauley
GS8 Andy McDonald
GS9 Brian Leetch
GS10 Bates Battaglia
GS11 Bobby Holik
GS12 Brad Isbister
GS13 Brendan Morrison
GS14 Arturs Irbe
GS15 Brian Savage
GS16 Bryan Marchment
GS17 Bryan McCabe
GS18 Carlo Colaiacovo
GS19 Chris Drury
GS20 Chris Gratton
GS21 Chris Neil
GS22 Chris Osgood
GS23 Chris Simon
GS24 Curtis Joseph
GS25 Daniel Sedin
GS26 Darius Kasparaitis
GS27 Darren McCarty
GS28 Darryl Sittler
GS29 David Aebischer
GS30 David Legwand
GS31 Denis Arkhipov
GS32 Derek Morris
GS33 Donald Brashear
GS34 Doug Gilmour
GS35 Ed Belfour
GS36 Ed Jovanovski
GS37 Erik Cole
GS38 Eric Lindros
GS39 Grant Fuhr
GS40 Jaroslav Svoboda
GS41 Jeff O'Neill
GS42 Jarome Iginla
GS43 Joe Sakic
GS44 Johan Hedberg
GS45 Josef Vasicek
GS46 Jean-Sebastien Giguere
GS47 Kenny Jonsson
GS48 Luc Robitaille
GS49 Mario Lemieux
GS50 Mark Parrish
GS51 Martin Brodeur
GS52 Martin Erat
GS53 Martin Skoula
GS54 Mats Sundin
GS55 Matt Cooke
GS56 Mattias Ohlund
GS57 Mike Dunham
GS58 Mike Fisher
GS59 Mike Keane
GS60 Mike Peca
GS61 Mike Ricci
GS62 Milan Hejduk
GS63 Miroslav Satan
GS64 Nik Antropov
GS65 Olaf Kolzig
GS66 Owen Nolan
GS67 Pat Verbeek
GS68 Patrick Marleau
GS69 Patrick Roy
GS70 Paul Kariya
GS71 Peter Bondra
GS72 Peter Forsberg
GS73 Petr Sykora
GS74 Radek Dvorak
GS75 Rick DiPietro
GS76 Rob Blake
GS77 Robert Lang
GS78 Roman Hamrlik
GS79 Roman Turek
GS80 Ron Francis
GS81 Ryan Smyth
GS82 Sami Kapanen
GS83 Scott Hartnell
GS84 Scott Stevens
GS85 Scott Walker
GS86 Stan Mikita
GS87 Stanislav Chistov
GS88 Steve Konowalchuk
GS89 Steve Rucchin
GS90 Steve Yzerman
GS91 Stephen Peat
GS92 Steven Reinprecht
GS93 Teemu Selanne
GS94 Tie Domi
GS95 Todd Bertuzzi
GS96 Todd White
GS97 Tom Poti
GS98 Trent Klatt
GS99 Trevor Kidd
GS100 Wade Redden

2000-01 BAP Ultimate Memorabilia Autographs

Be A Player Ultimate Memorabilia was released in May 2001 and boasted one memorabilia card per pack and a SRP of approximately $100 per pack. There were 5 packs in a box and 1 card per pack. This 50-card set featured certified player autographs under color action photos on silver and purple die-cut card stock. Each card in Ultimate Memorabilia was sealed in a clear plastic slab with a descriptive label at the top.

STATED PRINT RUN 90 SER.#'d SETS
GOLD AUTO STAT.PRINT RUN 10 SER.#'d SETS
GOLD NOT PRICED DUE TO SCARCITY
1 Theo Fleury 10.00 25.00
2 Brendan Shanahan 15.00 40.00
3 Curtis Joseph 15.00 40.00
4 Saku Koivu 15.00 40.00
5 Olaf Kolzig 10.00 25.00
6 Al MacInnis 10.00 25.00
7 John LeClair 15.00 40.00
8 Teemu Selanne 15.00 40.00
9 Wayne Gretzky 150.00 300.00
10 Pavel Bure 15.00 40.00
11 Mario Lemieux 100.00 250.00
12 Milan Hejduk 15.00 40.00
13 Ray Bourque 25.00 60.00
14 Daniel Alfredsson 10.00 25.00
15 Mats Sundin 20.00 50.00
16 Paul Kariya 15.00 40.00
17 Scott Gomez 10.00 25.00
18 Eric Lindros 15.00 40.00
19 Sergei Fedorov 20.00 50.00
20 Peter Forsberg 25.00 60.00
21 Vincent Lecavalier 10.00 25.00
22 Tony Amonte
23 Patrick Roy 60.00 150.00
24 Ed Belfour 15.00 40.00
25 Martin Brodeur 40.00 100.00
26 Brian Leetch 10.00 25.00
27 Mike Modano 20.00 50.00
28 Joe Sakic 40.00 100.00
29 Jeremy Roenick 15.00 40.00
30 Steve Yzerman 60.00 150.00
31 Nikolai Khabibulin 10.00 25.00
32 Roman Turek 10.00 25.00
33 Keith Primeau 10.00 25.00
34 Mike Richter 15.00 40.00
35 Patrik Stefan 10.00 25.00
36 Scott Stevens 10.00 25.00
37 Valeri Bure 10.00 25.00
38 Doug Weight 10.00 25.00
39 Nicklas Lidstrom 15.00 40.00
40 Chris Drury 10.00 25.00
41 Mike Peca 10.00 25.00
42 Chris Pronger 10.00 25.00
43 Rob Blake 10.00 25.00
44 Luc Robitaille 10.00 25.00
45 Joe Thornton 25.00 60.00
46 Jason Arnott 10.00 25.00
47 Daniel Sedin 10.00 25.00
48 Pierre Turgeon 10.00 25.00
49 Brad Stuart 10.00 25.00
50 Adam Oates 10.00 25.00

2000-01 BAP Ultimate Memorabilia Active Eight

This 8-card set featured three players on each card along with a game-used jersey swatch of each. Each card recognized the three statistical leaders in a featured category. Each card was sealed in a clear plastic slab with a descriptive label at the top. Stated print run on these cards was 30 sets.

*MULT.COLOR SWATCH: 1X TO 1.5X HI
STATED PRINT RUN 30 SERIAL #'d SETS
AE1 Messier/Yzerman/Lemieux 200.00 400.00
AE2 Messier/Yzerman/Francis 60.00 150.00
AE3 Lemieux/Hull/Bure 75.00 200.00
AE4 Mario Lemieux 125.00 250.00
Eric Lindros
Jaromir Jagr
AE5 Patrick Roy 60.00 150.00
Mike Vernon
John Vanbiesbrouck
AE6 Ed Belfour 60.00 150.00
Patrick Roy
Dominik Hasek
AE7 Martin Brodeur 60.00 150.00
Dominik Hasek
Chris Osgood
AE8 Dominik Hasek 60.00 150.00
Martin Brodeur
Guy Hebert

2000-01 BAP Ultimate Memorabilia Captain's C

This 10-card set featured a swatch of the captain's "C" patch from a game-used jersey of the featured player. The swatch was affixed in the middle of the card in the shape of the letter C. Each card was sealed in a clear

plastic slab with a descriptive label at the top. Stated print run on these cards was 5 sets. This set is not priced due to scarcity.

STATED PRINT RUN 5 SERIAL #'d SETS
NOT PRICED DUE TO SCARCITY

C1 Steve Yzerman
C2 Keith Tkachuk
C3 Mats Sundin
C4 Saku Koivu
C5 Jaromir Jagr
C6 Paul Kariya
C7 Mark Messier
C8 Joe Sakic
C9 Wayne Gretzky
C10 Mario Lemieux

2000-01 BAP Ultimate Memorabilia Dynasty Jerseys

This 20-card set featured a swatch of game-used jersey of the depicted player and commemorates that player's time with a championship team. The jersey swatch was affixed on the card in the shape of the Stanley Cup. Each card was sealed in a clear plastic slab with a descriptive label at the top. Stated print run on these cards was 50 sets.

*MULT.COLOR SWATCH:1X TO 2X BASIC CARDS
PRINT RUN 50 SERIAL #'d SETS
EMBLEM PRINT RUN 10 SER.#'d SETS
EMBLEMS NOT PRICED DUE TO SCARCITY

D1 Wayne Gretzky	150.00	300.00
D2 Mark Messier	40.00	100.00
D3 Grant Fuhr	30.00	80.00
D4 Paul Coffey	25.00	60.00
D5 Bill Ranford	30.00	80.00
D6 Mario Lemieux	100.00	200.00
D7 Paul Coffey	25.00	60.00
D8 Jaromir Jagr	40.00	100.00
D9 Tom Barrasso	25.00	60.00
D10 Ron Francis	30.00	80.00
D11 Larry Murphy	25.00	60.00
D12 Ulf Samuelsson	25.00	60.00
D13 Steve Yzerman	60.00	150.00
D14 Chris Osgood	25.00	60.00
D15 Nicklas Lidstrom	25.00	60.00
D16 Sergei Fedorov	30.00	80.00
D17 Brendan Shanahan	25.00	60.00
D18 Darren McCarty	25.00	60.00
D19 Slava Kozlov	25.00	60.00
D20 Mike Vernon	25.00	60.00

2000-01 BAP Ultimate Memorabilia Game-Used Jerseys

*MULT.COLOR SWATCH: 1X TO 2X BASIC CARDS
STATED PRINT RUN 60 SER.#'d SETS

GJ1 Theo Fleury	8.00	20.00
GJ2 Brendan Shanahan	10.00	25.00
GJ3 Curtis Joseph	10.00	25.00
GJ4 Roman Turek	10.00	25.00
GJ5 Dominik Hasek	20.00	50.00
GJ6 Al MacInnis	10.00	25.00
GJ7 John LeClair	10.00	25.00
GJ8 Teemu Selanne	10.00	25.00
GJ9 Wayne Gretzky	75.00	150.00
GJ10 Pavel Bure	10.00	25.00
GJ11 Mark Messier	10.00	25.00
GJ12 Jaromir Jagr	15.00	40.00
GJ13 Arturs Irbe	8.00	20.00
GJ14 Vincent Lecavalier	10.00	25.00
GJ15 Mats Sundin	12.50	30.00
GJ16 Paul Kariya	10.00	25.00
GJ17 Marian Hossa	10.00	25.00
GJ18 Owen Nolan	8.00	20.00
GJ19 Sergei Fedorov	12.00	30.00
GJ20 Peter Forsberg	20.00	50.00
GJ21 Brett Hull	12.50	30.00
GJ22 Tony Amonte	8.00	20.00
GJ23 Patrick Roy	50.00	125.00
GJ24 Ed Belfour	10.00	25.00
GJ25 Martin Brodeur	30.00	80.00
GJ26 Brian Leetch	8.00	20.00
GJ27 Mike Modano	15.00	40.00
GJ28 Joe Sakic	20.00	50.00
GJ29 Jeremy Roenick	12.50	30.00
GJ30 Steve Yzerman	30.00	80.00
GJ31 Jason Allison	8.00	20.00
GJ32 Milan Hejduk	10.00	25.00
GJ33 Mike Richter	10.00	25.00
GJ34 Patrik Stefan	8.00	20.00
GJ35 Kyle McLaren	8.00	20.00
GJ36 Valeri Bure	8.00	20.00
GJ37 Felix Potvin	10.00	25.00
GJ38 Chris Pronger	8.00	20.00
GJ39 Scott Stevens	8.00	20.00
GJ40 Luc Robitaille	8.00	20.00
GJ41 Roberto Luongo	15.00	40.00
GJ42 Chris Osgood	8.00	20.00
GJ43 Olaf Kolzig	8.00	20.00
GJ44 Scott Gomez	8.00	20.00
GJ45 Jason Arnott	8.00	20.00
GJ46 Rob Blake	8.00	20.00
GJ47 Keith Tkachuk	10.00	25.00
GJ48 Saku Koivu	8.00	20.00
GJ49 Alexei Yashin	8.00	20.00
GJ50 Nicklas Lidstrom	10.00	25.00

2000-01 BAP Ultimate Memorabilia Game-Used Emblems

STATED PRINT RUN 10 SERIAL #'d SETS
NOT PRICED DUE TO SCARCITY

E1 Brendan Shanahan
E2 Curtis Joseph
E3 Roman Turek
E4 Dominik Hasek
E5 John LeClair
E6 Teemu Selanne
E7 Wayne Gretzky
E8 Pavel Bure
E9 Mark Messier
E10 Jaromir Jagr
E11 Arturs Irbe
E12 Vincent Lecavalier
E13 Mats Sundin
E14 Paul Kariya
E15 Marian Hossa
E16 Owen Nolan
E17 Sergei Fedorov
E18 Peter Forsberg
E19 Brett Hull
E20 Tony Amonte
E21 Patrick Roy
E22 Ed Belfour
E23 Martin Brodeur
E24 Mike Modano
E25 Joe Sakic
E26 Steve Yzerman
E27 Jason Allison
E28 Milan Hejduk
E29 Mike Richter
E30 Patrik Stefan
E31 Chris Pronger
E32 Luc Robitaille
E33 Roberto Luongo
E34 Chris Osgood
E35 Olaf Kolzig
E36 Scott Gomez
E37 Jason Arnott
E38 Rob Blake
E39 Keith Tkachuk
E40 Alexei Yashin

2000-01 BAP Ultimate Memorabilia Game-Used In The Numbers

STATED PRINT RUN 10 SERIAL #'d SETS
NOT PRICED DUE TO SCARCITY

2000-01 BAP Ultimate Memorabilia Game-Used Sticks

*SINGLE COLOR SWATCH: .25X TO .75X
STATED PRINT RUN 90 SER.#'d SETS

GS1 Theo Fleury	8.00	20.00
GS2 Brendan Shanahan	10.00	25.00
GS3 Curtis Joseph	10.00	25.00
GS4 Roman Turek	8.00	20.00
GS5 Dominik Hasek	20.00	50.00
GS6 Al MacInnis	8.00	20.00
GS7 John LeClair	10.00	25.00
GS8 Teemu Selanne	10.00	25.00
GS9 Wayne Gretzky	50.00	125.00
GS10 Pavel Bure	10.00	25.00
GS11 Mark Messier	10.00	25.00
GS12 Jaromir Jagr	20.00	50.00
GS13 Arturs Irbe	8.00	20.00
GS14 Vincent Lecavalier	10.00	25.00
GS15 Mats Sundin	10.00	25.00
GS16 Paul Kariya	10.00	25.00
GS17 Marian Hossa	10.00	25.00
GS18 Owen Nolan	8.00	20.00
GS19 Sergei Fedorov	15.00	40.00
GS20 Peter Forsberg	20.00	50.00
GS21 Brett Hull	15.00	40.00
GS22 Tony Amonte	8.00	20.00
GS23 Patrick Roy	40.00	100.00
GS24 Ed Belfour	10.00	25.00
GS25 Martin Brodeur	30.00	80.00
GS26 Brian Leetch	10.00	25.00
GS27 Mike Modano	20.00	50.00
GS28 Joe Sakic	25.00	60.00
GS29 Jeremy Roenick	15.00	40.00
GS30 Steve Yzerman	30.00	80.00
GS31 Jason Allison	8.00	20.00
GS32 Milan Hejduk	10.00	25.00
GS33 Mike Richter	10.00	25.00
GS34 Patrik Stefan	8.00	20.00
GS35 Kyle McLaren	8.00	20.00
GS36 Valeri Bure	8.00	20.00
GS37 Felix Potvin	15.00	40.00
GS38 Chris Pronger	10.00	25.00
GS39 Scott Stevens	10.00	25.00
GS40 Luc Robitaille	10.00	25.00
GS41 Roberto Luongo	15.00	40.00
GS42 Chris Osgood	10.00	25.00
GS43 Olaf Kolzig	10.00	25.00
GS44 Scott Gomez	10.00	25.00
GS45 Jason Arnott	8.00	20.00
GS46 Rob Blake	8.00	20.00
GS47 Keith Tkachuk	10.00	25.00
GS48 Saku Koivu	10.00	25.00
GS49 Alexei Yashin	8.00	20.00
GS50 Nicklas Lidstrom	10.00	25.00

2000-01 BAP Ultimate Memorabilia Goalie Memorabilia

This 20-card set featured swatches of game-used equipment from each of the depicted goalies on the card. Each card was sealed in a clear plastic slab with a descriptive label at the top. Stated print run on these cards was 30 sets.

*MULT COLOR SWATCH:1X TO 1.5X BASIC CARDS
STATED PRINT RUN 30 SERIAL #'d SETS

GM1 Jacques Plante	75.00	200.00
Patrick Roy		
GM2 Terry Sawchuk	75.00	200.00
Patrick Roy		
GM3 Mike Vernon	25.00	60.00
Chris Osgood		
GM4 Curtis Joseph	25.00	60.00
Felix Potvin		
GM5 Tony Esposito	30.00	80.00
Ed Belfour		
GM6 Turk Broda	30.00	80.00
Johnny Bower		
GM7 Bernie Parent	25.00	60.00
Brian Boucher		
GM8 Tony Esposito	40.00	100.00
Gerry Cheevers		
GM9 Bernie Parent	50.00	125.00
Gerry Cheevers		
GM10 Jacques Plante G/J	60.00	150.00
GM11 Patrick Roy	60.00	150.00
Eddie Belfour		
GM12 Curtis Joseph	30.00	80.00
Dominik Hasek		
GM13 Roman Turek	25.00	60.00
Ed Belfour		
GM14 Martin Brodeur	60.00	150.00
Jacques Plante		
GM15 Mike Richter	25.00	60.00
John Vanbiesbrouck		
GM16 Jacques Plante G/S/J	60.00	150.00
GM17 Tony Esposito	100.00	200.00
Bernie Parent		
Vladislav Tretiak		
GM18 Frank Brimsek	50.00	125.00
Byron Dafoe		
Gerry Cheevers		
GM19 Johnny Bower	75.00	200.00
Turk Broda		
Terry Sawchuk		
GM20 Patrick Roy	200.00	350.00
Georges Vezina		
Terry Sawchuk		

2000-01 BAP Ultimate Memorabilia Goalie Memorabilia Autographed

This 5-card set featured a swatch of game-used equipment and an autograph from the depicted goalie. Each card was sealed in a clear plastic slab with a descriptive label at the top. Stated print run on these cards was 50 sets.

*MULT.COLOR SWATCH:1X TO 1.5X BASIC CARDS
STATED PRINT RUN 50 SERIAL #'d SETS

UG1 Gerry Cheevers	40.00	100.00
UG2 Vladislav Tretiak	75.00	200.00
UG3 Tony Esposito	40.00	100.00
UG4 Johnny Bower	40.00	100.00
UG5 Bernie Parent	50.00	125.00

2000-01 BAP Ultimate Memorabilia Goalie Sticks

*SINGLE COLOR STICKS: .5X TO 1X HI
STATED PRINT RUN 50 SERIAL #'d SETS

G1 Guy Hebert	12.50	30.00
G2 Damian Rhodes	12.50	30.00
G3 Byron Dafoe	12.50	30.00
G4 Dominik Hasek	15.00	40.00
G5 Mike Vernon	12.50	30.00
G6 Arturs Irbe	12.50	30.00
G7 Jocelyn Thibault	12.50	30.00
G8 Patrick Roy	50.00	125.00
G9 Marc Denis	12.50	30.00
G10 Ed Belfour	12.50	30.00
G11 Chris Osgood	12.50	30.00
G12 Tommy Salo	12.50	30.00
G13 Roberto Luongo	25.00	60.00
G14 Jamie Storr	12.50	30.00
G15 Manny Fernandez	12.50	30.00
G16 Jeff Hackett	12.50	30.00
G17 Mike Dunham	12.50	30.00
G18 Martin Brodeur	30.00	80.00
G19 John Vanbiesbrouck	12.50	30.00
G20 Mike Richter	12.50	30.00
G21 Patrick Lalime	12.50	30.00
G22 Brian Boucher	12.50	30.00
G23 Nikolai Khabibulin	12.50	30.00
G24 J-S Aubin	12.50	30.00
G25 Roman Turek	12.50	30.00
G26 Steve Shields	12.50	30.00
G27 Dan Cloutier	12.50	30.00
G28 Curtis Joseph	12.50	30.00
G29 Felix Potvin	12.50	30.00
G30 Olaf Kolzig	12.50	30.00

2000-01 BAP Ultimate Memorabilia Gordie Howe No. 9

This 3-card set featured swatches of game-used jerseys of Gordie Howe from one of the three professional teams he played for during his career. The cards carried a color action photo of Howe in the team's jersey in the forefront and the shape of the number 9 in the background with another action shot and a head shot on it. The jersey swatch was affixed in the shape of the hollow of the number 9. Each card was sealed in a clear plastic slab with a descriptive label at the top. Stated print run on these cards was 50 sets.

*MULT.COLOR SWATCH: 1X TO 1.5X BASIC CARDS
JERSEY PRINT RUN 50 SERIAL #'d SETS

COMMON JSY/AUTO	125.00	250.00
JSY/AUTO PRINT RUN 20 SER.#'d SETS		
9-1 Gordie Howe	50.00	125.00
Detroit		
9-2 Gordie Howe	50.00	125.00
New England		
9-3 Gordie Howe	50.00	125.00
Houston		

2000-01 BAP Ultimate Memorabilia Gordie Howe Retrospective Jerseys

This 7-card set featured game-used swatches of Gordie Howe's jerseys from the three teams he played for during his professional career. The cards carried a color action photo of Howe in the team's jersey in the forefront and the words "Howe Legend" in the background. Cards with one or two jersey swatches also carried larger headshots and the depicted team logo in the background. Each card was sealed in a clear plastic slab with a descriptive label at the top. Stated print run on these cards was 50 sets.

*MULT.COLOR SWATCH:1X TO 1.5X BASIC CARDS
STATED PRINT RUN 50 SERIAL #'d SETS

HL1 Gordie Howe	60.00	150.00
Detroit		
HL2 Gordie Howe	60.00	150.00
New England		
HL3 Gordie Howe	60.00	150.00
Houston		
HL4 Gordie Howe	75.00	200.00
Detroit		
New England		
HL5 Gordie Howe	75.00	200.00
Houston		
Detroit		
HL6 Gordie Howe	75.00	200.00
Houston		
New England		
HL7 Gordie Howe	100.00	250.00
Detroit		
New England		
Houston		

2000-01 BAP Ultimate Memorabilia Gordie Howe Retrospective Jerseys Autograph

This set paralleled the Be A Player Ultimate Memorabilia Gordie Howe Retrospective Jerseys set except that each card carries an autograph of Gordie Howe along with the words "Mr. Hockey" in his handwriting. Each card was sealed in a clear plastic slab with a descriptive label at the top. Stated print run on these cards was 20 sets.

*MULT.COLOR SWATCH:1X TO 1.5X BASIC CARDS
STATED PRINT RUN 20 SERIAL #'d SETS

GH1 Gordie Howe	125.00	250.00
Detroit		
GH2 Gordie Howe	125.00	250.00
New England		
GH3 Gordie Howe	125.00	250.00
Houston		
GH4 Gordie Howe	125.00	250.00
Detroit		
New England		
GH5 Gordie Howe	125.00	250.00
Houston		
Detroit		
GH6 Gordie Howe	125.00	250.00
Houston		
New England		
GH7 Gordie Howe	400.00	800.00
Detroit		
New England		
Houston		

2000-01 BAP Ultimate Memorabilia Hart Trophy

This 20-card set featured game-used jersey swatches of past winners of the Hart trophy. Each card carried a color action photo of the given player and a picture of the trophy alongside the jersey swatch. Some players

in the set have multiple cards to mirror the amount times they have won the trophy. Each card was sealed in a clear plastic slab with a descriptive label at the top. Stated print run on these cards was 30 sets.

*MULT.COLOR SWATCH:1X TO 1.5X BASIC CARDS
STATED PRINT RUN 30 SERIAL #'d SETS

H1 Chris Pronger	30.00	80.00
H2 Jaromir Jagr	40.00	100.00
H3 Dominik Hasek	40.00	100.00
H4 Dominik Hasek	40.00	100.00
H5 Mario Lemieux	60.00	150.00
H6 Eric Lindros	30.00	80.00
H7 Sergei Fedorov	30.00	80.00
H8 Mario Lemieux	60.00	150.00
H9 Mark Messier	50.00	125.00
H10 Brett Hull	40.00	100.00
H11 Mark Messier	50.00	125.00
H12 Wayne Gretzky	75.00	150.00
H13 Mario Lemieux	60.00	150.00
H14 Wayne Gretzky	75.00	150.00
H15 Wayne Gretzky	75.00	150.00
H16 Wayne Gretzky	75.00	150.00
H17 Wayne Gretzky	75.00	150.00
H18 Wayne Gretzky	75.00	150.00
H19 Wayne Gretzky	75.00	150.00
H20 Wayne Gretzky	75.00	150.00

2000-01 BAP Ultimate Memorabilia Jacques Plante Jersey Cards

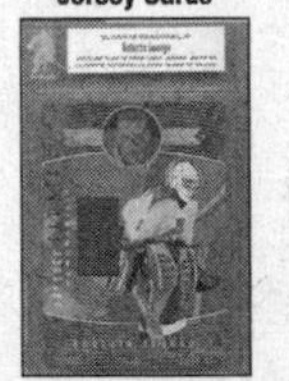

This 15-card set featured a game-used jersey swatch of goalie great Jacques Plante. Each card also carried a photo of a current day goalie and the cards are listed below based on those players. Each card was sealed in a clear plastic slab with a descriptive label at the top. Stated print run on these cards was 30 sets.

*MULT.COLOR SWATCH:1X TO 1.5X BASIC CARDS
STATED PRINT RUN 30 SERIAL #'d SETS
*SKATE CARDS: .6X TO 1.5X JSY HI
SKATE PRINT RUN 20 SER.#'d SETS

PJ1 Patrick Roy	75.00	200.00
PJ2 Ed Belfour	30.00	80.00
PJ3 Martin Brodeur	60.00	150.00
PJ4 Dominik Hasek	40.00	100.00
PJ5 Chris Osgood	30.00	80.00
PJ6 Curtis Joseph	30.00	80.00
PJ7 Tommy Salo	30.00	80.00
PJ8 Mike Richter	30.00	80.00
PJ9 Byron Dafoe	30.00	80.00
PJ10 Roberto Luongo	30.00	80.00
PJ11 Roman Turek	30.00	80.00
PJ12 Olaf Kolzig	30.00	80.00
PJ13 Felix Potvin	30.00	80.00
PJ14 Jocelyn Thibault	30.00	80.00
PJ15 Brian Boucher	30.00	80.00

2000-01 BAP Ultimate Memorabilia Journey Jerseys

This 20-card set features game-used jersey swatches of players who played for at least two different franchises during their career. Each card carries a swatch of the player's jersey for both teams depicted as well as photos of the player in each team's jersey. Each card was sealed in a clear plastic slab with a descriptive label at the top. Stated print run on these cards was 50 sets.

*MULT.COLOR SWATCH:1X TO 1.5X BASIC CARDS
PRINT RUN 50 SERIAL #'d SETS
EMBLM/NMBR PRINT RUN 10 SER.#'d SETS

JJ1 Wayne Gretzky	150.00	350.00
JJ2 Mark Messier	25.00	60.00
JJ3 Pavel Bure	20.00	50.00
JJ4 Jeff Hackett	20.00	50.00
JJ5 Mats Sundin	20.00	50.00
JJ6 Curtis Joseph	20.00	50.00
JJ7 Ed Belfour	20.00	50.00
JJ8 Mike Modano	20.00	50.00
JJ9 Brett Hull	30.00	80.00
JJ10 Teemu Selanne	20.00	50.00
JJ11 Keith Tkachuk	20.00	50.00
JJ12 Patrick Roy	125.00	300.00
JJ13 Chris Chelios	20.00	50.00
JJ14 Al MacInnis	20.00	50.00
JJ15 Theo Fleury	20.00	50.00
JJ16 Jason Allison	20.00	50.00
JJ17 Jeremy Roenick	25.00	60.00
JJ18 Brendan Shanahan	20.00	50.00
JJ19 Owen Nolan	20.00	50.00
JJ20 Felix Potvin	20.00	50.00

2000-01 BAP Ultimate Memorabilia Magnificent Ones

This 10-card set featured game-used jersey swatches from Mario Lemieux and another star player on each card. The cards carry a small headshot of Lemieux beside his jersey swatch on the right side of the card and an action shot of the other player on the left beside his jersey swatch. The words "Magnificent Ones" is printed across the top border. Each card was sealed in a clear plastic slab with a descriptive label at the top. Stated print run on these cards was 40 sets.

*MULT.COLOR SWATCH:1X TO 1.5X BASIC CARDS
STATED PRINT RUN 40 SERIAL #'d SETS
M.ONES AU STAT.PRINT RUN 6 SER.#'d SETS
M.ONES AU SIGN.BY LEMIEUX ONLY

ML1 S.Yzerman/M.Lemieux	75.00	200.00
ML2 J.Jagr/M.Lemieux	60.00	150.00
ML3 M.Brodeur/M.Lemieux	60.00	150.00
ML4 M.Messier/M.Lemieux	40.00	100.00
ML5 P.Roy/M.Lemieux	75.00	200.00
ML6 R.Bourque/M.Lemieux	60.00	150.00
ML7 R.Francis/M.Lemieux	30.00	80.00
ML8 D.Hasek/M.Lemieux	60.00	150.00
ML9 W.Gretzky/M.Lemieux	125.00	300.00
ML10 P.Coffey/M.Lemieux	30.00	80.00

2000-01 BAP Ultimate Memorabilia Maurice Richard Autographs

This 5-card set remembers one of the greats of the game, Rocket Richard. Each card features a photo of Richard and a cut autograph. The autographs were originally on 8x10 reprints of Richard's 1953-54 Parkhurst card. In the Game, Inc. obtained the autographs through a private signing with Richard. The autographs were then cut and affixed to the cards in this set as swatches. Each card was sealed in a clear plastic slab with a descriptive label at the top. Stated print run on these cards was 10 sets.

COMMON CARD (R1-R5)	300.00	500.00

STATED PRINT RUN 10 SERIAL #'d SETS

2000-01 BAP Ultimate Memorabilia NHL Records

This 10-card set recognized 10 different players who hold various NHL records. Each card featured a photo and a swatch of game-used jersey of that player. A brief explanation of the record was on the back of each card. Each card was sealed in a clear plastic slab with a descriptive label at the top. Stated print run on these cards was 30 sets.

*MULT.COLOR SWATCH:1X TO 1.5X BASIC CARDS
STATED PRINT RUN 30 SERIAL #'d SETS

R1 Terry Sawchuk	50.00	125.00
R2 Patrick Roy	60.00	150.00
R3 Tony Esposito	25.00	60.00
R4 Jacques Plante	40.00	100.00
R5 Bill Mosienko	25.00	60.00
R6 Teemu Selanne	25.00	60.00
R7 Mario Lemieux	60.00	150.00
R8 Ray Bourque	30.00	80.00
R9 Gordie Howe	40.00	100.00
R10 Wayne Gretzky	75.00	200.00

2000-01 BAP Ultimate Memorabilia Norris Trophy

This 10-card set featured game-used jersey swatches of winners of the Norris trophy. The cards carried an action photo of the given player, a picture of the Norris trophy, and a square piece of jersey. Each card was sealed in a clear plastic slab with a descriptive label at the top. Stated print run on these cards was 50 sets.

*MULT.COLOR SWATCH:1X TO 1.5X BASIC CARDS
STATED PRINT RUN 50 SER.#'d SETS

N1 Chris Pronger	20.00	50.00
N2 Al MacInnis	20.00	50.00
N3 Rob Blake	20.00	50.00
N4 Brian Leetch	20.00	50.00
N5 Chris Chelios	20.00	50.00
N6 Paul Coffey	20.00	50.00
N7 Ray Bourque	30.00	80.00
N8 Chris Chelios	20.00	50.00
N9 Brian Leetch	20.00	50.00
N10 Ray Bourque	30.00	80.00

2000-01 BAP Ultimate Memorabilia Retro-Active

This 10-card set featured a player from the past and from the present who have both won the same award. Each card carries a photo of each player along side a game-used jersey swatch of each. A photo of the shared award is in the middle of the two swatches. Each card was sealed in a clear plastic slab with a descriptive label at the top. Stated print run on these cards was 30 sets.

*MULT.COLOR SWATCH:1X TO 1.5X BASIC CARDS
STATED PRINT RUN 30 SER.#'d SETS

RA1 Gordie Howe	50.00	125.00
Chris Pronger		
RA2 Terry Sawchuk	150.00	300.00
Patrick Roy		
RA3 Tony Esposito	40.00	100.00
Mario Lemieux		
RA4 Tony Esposito	30.00	80.00
Ed Belfour		
RA5 Bernie Parent	60.00	150.00
Steve Yzerman		
RA6 Gordie Howe	125.00	300.00
Mario Lemieux		
RA7 Bill Mosienko	60.00	150.00
Paul Kariya		
RA8 Jacques Plante	125.00	300.00
Patrick Roy		
RA9 Gordie Howe	50.00	125.00
Jaromir Jagr		
RA10 Wayne Gretzky	150.00	400.00
Mark Messier		

2000-01 BAP Ultimate Memorabilia Teammates

*MULT.COLOR SWATCH: 1X TO 2X BASIC CARDS
STATED PRINT RUN 70 SER.#'d SETS

TM1 Steve Yzerman	20.00	50.00
Sergei Fedorov		
TM2 Brendan Shanahan	12.00	30.00
Slava Kozlov		
TM3 S.Yzerman/C.Chelios	20.00	50.00
TM4 S.Yzerman/B.Shanahan	30.00	80.00
TM5 Jeremy Roenick	12.00	30.00
Keith Tkachuk		
TM6 Nicklas Lidstom	15.00	40.00
Sergei Fedorov		
TM7 Nicklas Lidstrom	12.00	30.00
Chris Osgood		
TM8 Nicklas Lidstrom	15.00	40.00
Brendan Shanahan		
TM9 Chris Osgood	12.00	30.00
Sergei Fedorov		
TM10 Nikolai Khabibulin	8.00	20.00
Jeremy Roenick		
TM11 Sergei Gonchar	8.00	20.00
Adam Oates		
TM12 Curtis Joseph	12.00	30.00
Mats Sundin		
TM13 Curtis Joseph	8.00	20.00
Tie Domi		
TM14 Mats Sundin	8.00	20.00
Tie Domi		
TM15 Peter Forsberg	50.00	125.00
Patrick Roy		
TM16 Peter Forsberg	25.00	60.00
Joe Sakic		
TM17 Joe Sakic	60.00	150.00
Patrick Roy		
TM18 Boris Mironov	8.00	20.00
Tony Amonte		
TM19 Pavel Bure	8.00	20.00
Paul Laus		
TM20 Mike Peca	15.00	40.00
Dominik Hasek		
TM21 Paul Kariya	15.00	40.00
Teemu Selanne		
TM22 Teemu Selanne	8.00	20.00
Guy Hebert		
TM23 Paul Kariya	8.00	20.00
Guy Hebert		
TM24 B.Hull/M.Modano	15.00	40.00
TM25 Brett Hull	12.00	30.00
Ed Belfour		
TM26 E.Belfour/M.Modano	15.00	40.00
TM27 Sergei Zubov	8.00	20.00
Ed Belfour		
TM28 Brett Hull	8.00	20.00
Darryl Sydor		
TM29 Eric Desjardins	8.00	20.00
John LeClair		
TM30 Jason Arnott	20.00	50.00
Martin Brodeur		
TM31 S.Yzerman/M.Vernon	20.00	50.00
TM32 Brett Hull	20.00	50.00
Curtis Joseph		
TM33 Keith Tkachuk	12.00	30.00
Teemu Selanne		
TM34 Mats Sundin	12.00	30.00

Owen Nolan
TM35 Ed Belfour 12.00 30.00
Chris Chelios
TM36 Mark Messier 100.00 250.00
Wayne Gretzky
TM37 Theo Fleury 8.00 20.00
Al MacInnis
TM38 Felix Potvin 12.00 30.00
Mats Sundin
TM39 Mario Lemieux 60.00 150.00
Jaromir Jagr
TM40 Ray Bourque 20.00 50.00
Adam Oates

2001-02 BAP Ultimate Memorabilia Active Eight

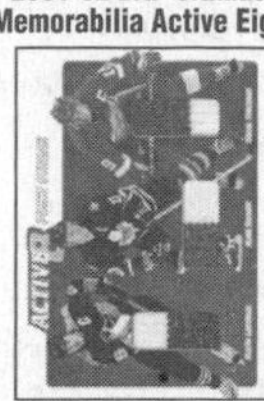

All cards in this product were graded by Beckett Grading Services and available only in graded form. Due to the various amount of grading ranges, only a median price for Mint/NmMt+ copies was assigned below.

STATED PRINT RUN 30 SER.#'d SETS
1 Kariya/Lemieux/Sakic 60.00 150.00
2 Patrick Roy 50.00 100.00
Mike Vernon
Tom Barrasso
3 Ron Francis 40.00 100.00
Mark Messier
Steve Yzerman
4 Mario Lemieux 50.00 125.00
Luc Robitaille
Jaromir Jagr
5 Messier/Hull/Lemieux 60.00 150.00
6 Teemu Selanne 40.00 100.00
Joe Nieuwendyk
Luc Robitaille
7 Mark Messier 40.00 100.00
Ron Francis
Scott Stevens
8 Mario Lemieux 40.00 100.00
Mats Sundin
Steve Yzerman

2001-02 BAP Ultimate Memorabilia All-Star History

STATED PRINT RUN 40 SER.#'d SETS
1 Turk Broda 20.00 50.00
2 Frank Brimsek 15.00 40.00
3 Ted Kennedy 15.00 40.00
4 Maurice Richard 60.00 150.00
5 Chuck Rayner 15.00 40.00
6 Bill Mosienko 15.00 40.00
7 Jean Beliveau 30.00 80.00
8 Doug Harvey 15.00 40.00
9 Ted Lindsay 15.00 40.00
10 Henri Richard 20.00 50.00
11 Jacques Plante 30.00 80.00
12 Glenn Hall 15.00 40.00
13 Terry Sawchuk 40.00 100.00
14 Bobby Hull 15.00 40.00
15 Johnny Bower 15.00 40.00
16 Tim Horton 40.00 100.00
17 Johnny Bucyk 15.00 40.00
18 Stan Mikita 15.00 40.00
19 Bill Gadsby 15.00 40.00
20 Gordie Howe 40.00 100.00
21 Ed Giacomin 15.00 40.00
22 Bernie Parent 20.00 50.00
23 Bobby Clarke 15.00 40.00
24 Gilbert Perreault 15.00 40.00
25 Frank Mahovlich 15.00 40.00
26 Tony Esposito 25.00 60.00
27 Denis Potvin 15.00 40.00
28 Guy Lafleur 25.00 60.00
29 Bryan Trottier 15.00 40.00
30 Lanny McDonald 15.00 40.00
31 Marcel Dionne 15.00 40.00
32 Wayne Gretzky 75.00 200.00
33 Mike Bossy 15.00 40.00
34 Mark Messier 15.00 40.00
35 Paul Coffey 25.00 60.00
36 Steve Yzerman 40.00 100.00
37 Mario Lemieux 40.00 100.00
38 Grant Fuhr 15.00 40.00
39 Patrick Roy 40.00 100.00
40 Brett Hull 25.00 60.00
41 Brian Leetch 15.00 40.00
42 Jeremy Roenick 20.00 50.00
43 Jaromir Jagr 25.00 60.00
44 Luc Robitaille 15.00 40.00
45 Joe Sakic 30.00 80.00
46 Eric Lindros 15.00 40.00
47 Paul Kariya 15.00 40.00
48 Mike Modano 15.00 40.00
49 Peter Forsberg 25.00 60.00
50 Pavel Bure 15.00 40.00
51 Milan Hejduk 15.00 40.00
52 Mats Sundin 15.00 40.00

2001-02 BAP Ultimate Memorabilia Autographs

PRINT RUNS LISTED BELOW
UNDER 25 NOT PRICED DUE TO SCARCITY
1 Alexei Yashin/40 15.00 40.00
2 Brian Leetch/40 25.00 60.00
3 Daniel Alfredsson/40 15.00 40.00
4 Keith Tkachuk/40 25.00 60.00
5 Milan Hejduk/40 25.00 60.00
6 Mark Recchi/40 15.00 40.00
7 Paul Kariya/40 25.00 60.00
8 Scott Stevens/40 15.00 40.00
9 Joe Sakic/40 40.00 100.00
10 Al MacInnis/30 15.00 40.00
11 Peter Bondra/40 15.00 40.00
12 John LeClair/40 25.00 60.00
13 Brendan Shanahan/40 25.00 60.00
14 Rob Blake/40 15.00 40.00
15 Luc Robitaille/40 15.00 40.00
16 Jarome Iginla/40 30.00 80.00
17 Pavel Bure/40 25.00 60.00
18 Marcel Dionne/40 15.00 40.00
19 Gordie Howe/40 50.00 125.00
20 Phil Esposito/40 15.00 40.00
21 Guy Lafleur/40 30.00 80.00
22 Gilbert Perreault/40 15.00 40.00
23 Bobby Hull/40 30.00 80.00
24 Jean Beliveau/40 25.00 60.00
25 Stan Mikita/40 30.00 80.00
26 Ted Lindsay/20
27 Frank Mahovlich/30 25.00 60.00
28 Mario Lemieux/30 100.00 250.00
29 Tony Amonte/30 15.00 40.00
30 Jeremy Roenick/30 30.00 80.00
31 Owen Nolan/40 15.00 40.00
32 Mark Messier/40 40.00 100.00
33 Steve Yzerman/40 60.00 120.00
34 Sergei Fedorov/40 30.00 80.00
35 Wayne Gretzky/30 200.00 400.00

2001-02 BAP Ultimate Memorabilia Bloodlines

STATED PRINT RUN 20 SERIAL #'d SETS
NOT PRICED DUE TO SCARCITY
1 Pavel Bure
Valeri Bure
2 Scott Niedermayer
Rob Niedermayer
3 Henri Richard
Rocket Richard
4 Peter Mahovlich
Frank Mahovlich
5 Tony Esposito
Phil Esposito
6 Brett Hull
Dennis Hull
Bobby Hull
7 Sid Abel
Brent Johnson
8 Paul Kariya
Steve Kariya

2001-02 BAP Ultimate Memorabilia Calder Trophy

STATED PRINT RUN 30 SERIAL #'d SETS
1 Evgeni Nabokov 15.00 40.00
2 Scott Gomez 10.00 40.00
3 Chris Drury 15.00 25.00
4 Sergei Samsonov 15.00 40.00
5 Bryan Berard 10.00 25.00
6 Daniel Alfredsson 10.00 25.00
7 Peter Forsberg 25.00 60.00
8 Martin Brodeur 40.00 100.00
9 Teemu Selanne 20.00 50.00
10 Pavel Bure 20.00 50.00
11 Ed Belfour 20.00 50.00
12 Tom Barrasso 15.00 40.00
13 Brian Leetch 15.00 40.00
14 Joe Nieuwendyk 15.00 40.00
15 Luc Robitaille 15.00 40.00
16 Mario Lemieux 40.00 100.00
17 Dale Hawerchuk 15.00 40.00
18 Mike Bossy 20.00 50.00
19 Bryan Trottier 15.00 40.00
20 Denis Potvin 20.00 50.00
21 Gilbert Perreault 15.00 40.00
22 Tony Esposito 20.00 50.00
23 Glenn Hall 20.00 50.00
24 Terry Sawchuk 40.00 100.00
25 Frank Brimsek 20.00 50.00

2001-02 BAP Ultimate Memorabilia Captain's C

STATED PRINT RUN 5 SETS
NOT PRICED DUE TO SCARCITY
1 Daniel Alfredsson
2 Jean Beliveau
3 Johnny Bucyk
4 Ron Francis
5 Wayne Gretzky
6 Jaromir Jagr
7 Paul Kariya
8 Brian Leetch
9 Mario Lemieux
10 Gilbert Perreault
11 Denis Potvin
12 Chris Pronger
13 Henri Richard
14 Mats Sundin
15 Steve Yzerman

2001-02 BAP Ultimate Memorabilia Complete Package

STATED PRINT RUN 10 SETS
NOT PRICED DUE TO SCARCITY
1 Wayne Gretzky
2 Tim Horton
3 Jarome Iginla
4 Curtis Joseph
5 Guy Lafleur
6 Eric Lindros
7 Jacques Plante
8 Patrick Roy
9 Terry Sawchuk
10 Mats Sundin

2001-02 BAP Ultimate Memorabilia Cornerstones

STATED PRINT RUN 20 SERIAL #'d SETS
NOT PRICED DUE TO SCARCITY
1 Ace Bailey
Johnny Bower
Lanny McDonald
Mats Sundin
2 Patrick Roy
Maurice Richard
Jean Beliveau
Guy Lafleur
3 Bobby Hull
Glenn Hall
Stan Mikita
Tony Amonte
4 Ted Lindsay
Gordie Howe
Terry Sawchuk
Steve Yzerman
5 Chuck Rayner
Ed Giacomin
Phil Esposito
Brian Leetch
6 Frank Brimsek
Johnny Bucyk
Cam Neely
Joe Thornton

2001-02 BAP Ultimate Memorabilia Decades

STATED PRINT RUN 50 SER.#'d SETS
1 Chuck Rayner 20.00 50.00
2 Frank Brimsek 20.00 50.00
3 Terry Sawchuk 40.00 100.00
4 Jacques Plante 50.00 125.00
5 Doug Harvey 20.00 50.00
6 Bill Gadsby 20.00 50.00
7 Gordie Howe 40.00 100.00
8 Ted Lindsay 20.00 50.00
9 Johnny Bower 20.00 50.00
10 Glenn Hall 20.00 50.00
11 Bobby Hull 25.00 60.00
12 Stan Mikita 20.00 50.00
13 Tony Esposito 25.00 60.00
14 Gerry Cheevers 20.00 50.00
15 Guy Lafleur 25.00 60.00
16 Bobby Clarke 20.00 50.00
17 Denis Potvin 20.00 50.00
18 Serge Savard 20.00 50.00
19 Patrick Roy 40.00 100.00
20 Grant Fuhr 20.00 50.00
21 Larry Robinson 20.00 50.00
22 Al MacInnis 20.00 50.00
23 Cam Neely 30.00 80.00
24 Mike Bossy 20.00 50.00

2001-02 BAP Ultimate Memorabilia Dynamic Duos

STATED PRINT RUN 30 SERIAL #'d SETS
1 M.Modano/W.Gretzky 50.00 125.00
2 Jaromir Jagr 20.00 50.00
John LeClair
3 Luc Robitaille 25.00 60.00
Joe Sakic
4 Milan Hejduk 25.00 60.00
Brett Hull
5 Pavel Bure 20.00 50.00
Alexei Yashin
6 Steve Yzerman 30.00 80.00
Mats Sundin
7 Paul Kariya 25.00 60.00
Peter Forsberg
8 Teemu Selanne 20.00 50.00
Brendan Shanahan
9 Mark Messier 25.00 60.00
Jarome Iginla
10 Alexander Mogilny 20.00 50.00
Mark Recchi
11 Peter Bondra 20.00 50.00
Theo Fleury
12 Jeremy Roenick 60.00 150.00
Mario Lemieux
13 Eric Lindros 25.00 60.00
Ilya Kovalchuk
14 Keith Tkachuk 20.00 50.00
Tony Amonte
15 Doug Weight 20.00 50.00
Daniel Alfredsson
10 Vincent Damphousse 20.00 50.00
Sergei Fedorov

2001-02 BAP Ultimate Memorabilia Dynasty Jerseys

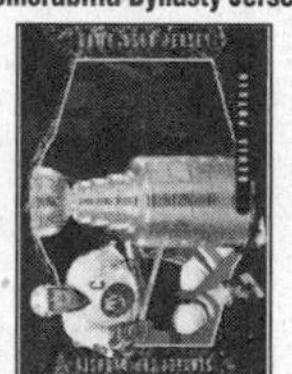

STATED PRINT RUN 50 SER.#'d SETS
1 Bill Barber 20.00 50.00
2 Mike Bossy 20.00 50.00
3 Bobby Clarke 20.00 50.00
4 Yvan Cournoyer 20.00 50.00
5 Bob Gainey 20.00 50.00
6 Guy Lafleur 25.00 60.00
7 Guy Lapointe 20.00 50.00
8 Reggie Leach 20.00 50.00
9 Bob Nystrom 20.00 50.00
10 Bernie Parent 20.00 50.00
11 Denis Potvin 20.00 50.00
12 Larry Robinson 20.00 50.00
13 Serge Savard 20.00 50.00
14 Dave Schultz 20.00 50.00
15 Steve Shutt 20.00 50.00
16 Billy Smith 20.00 50.00
17 Bryan Trottier 20.00 50.00
18 Joe Watson 20.00 50.00

2001-02 BAP Ultimate Memorabilia Dynasty Emblems

STATED PRINT RUN 10 SETS
NOT PRICED DUE TO SCARCITY

2001-02 BAP Ultimate Memorabilia Dynasty Numbers

STATED PRINT RUN 10 SETS
NOT PRICED DUE TO SCARCITY

2001-02 BAP Ultimate Memorabilia Emblems

STATED PRINT RUN 10 SERIAL #'d SETS
NOT PRICED DUE TO SCARCITY
1 Paul Kariya
2 Martin Brodeur
3 John LeClair
4 Ilya Kovalchuk
5 Bill Guerin
6 Dominik Hasek
7 Keith Tkachuk
8 Pavel Bure
9 Brian Leetch
10 Mario Lemieux
11 Mats Sundin
12 Owen Nolan
13 Mark Messier
14 Jaromir Jagr
15 Joe Sakic
16 Rob Blake
17 Brendan Shanahan
18 Eric Lindros
19 Mike Modano
20 Sergei Fedorov
21 Nicklas Lidstrom
22 Steve Yzerman
23 Teemu Selanne
24 Alexei Yashin
25 Doug Weight
26 Chris Pronger
27 Patrick Roy
28 Curtis Joseph
29 Jeremy Roenick
30 Luc Robitaille

2001-02 BAP Ultimate Memorabilia Emblem Attic

STATED PRINT RUN 5 SETS
NOT PRICED DUE TO SCARCITY
1 Jean Beliveau
2 Bobby Clarke
3 Phil Esposito
4 Wayne Gretzky
5 Glenn Hall
6 Doug Harvey
7 Gordie Howe
8 Bobby Hull
9 Guy Lafleur
10 Ted Lindsay
11 Frank Mahovlich
12 Mark Messier
13 Stan Mikita
14 Jacques Plante
15 Denis Potvin
16 Henri Richard
17 Rocket Richard
18 Larry Robinson
19 Terry Sawchuk
20 Bryan Trottier

2001-02 BAP Ultimate Memorabilia 500 Goal Scorers

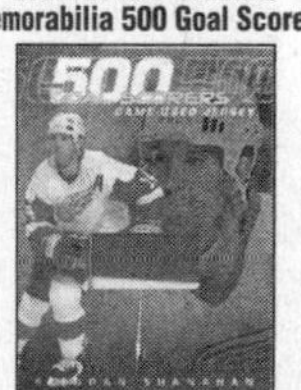

PRINT RUNS LISTED BELOW
UNDER 30 NOT PRICED DUE TO SCARCITY
1 Wayne Gretzky/10
2 Gordie Howe/10
3 Mario Lemieux/10
4 Bobby Hull/10
5 Mike Bossy/30 20.00 50.00
6 Guy Lafleur/30 30.00 80.00
7 Jean Beliveau/10
8 Stan Mikita/30 20.00 50.00
9 Marcel Dionne/30 20.00 50.00
10 Phil Esposito/30 30.00 80.00
11 Frank Mahovlich/10
12 Mark Messier/30 20.00 50.00
13 Steve Yzerman/30 75.00 200.00
14 Brett Hull/30 40.00 100.00
15 Mike Gartner/30 20.00 50.00
16 Bryan Trottier/30 20.00 50.00
17 Gilbert Perreault/30 25.00 60.00
18 Lanny McDonald/30 20.00 50.00
19 Jari Kurri/30 30.00 80.00
20 Dale Hawerchuk/30 20.00 50.00
21 Luc Robitaille/30 20.00 50.00
22 Dave Andreychuk/30 20.00 50.00
23 John Bucyk/30 25.00 60.00
24 Michel Goulet/30 20.00 50.00
25 Joe Mullen/30 20.00 50.00
26 Dino Ciccarelli/30 20.00 50.00
27 Pat Verbeek/30 20.00 50.00
28 Maurice Richard/10
29 Ron Francis/30 20.00 50.00
30 Brendan Shanahan/30 30.00 80.00

2001-02 BAP Ultimate Memorabilia 500 Goal Scorers Autographs

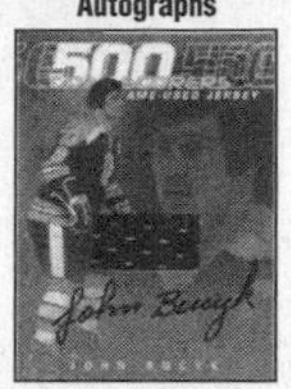

PRINT RUNS LISTED BELOW
PRINT RUNS UNDER 25 NOT PRICED
DUE TO SCARCITY
1 Bobby Hull/25 60.00 150.00
2 Bryan Trottier/15
3 Dale Hawerchuk/25 30.00 80.00
4 Dave Andreychuk/30 30.00 80.00
5 Dino Ciccarelli/30
6 Frank Mahovlich/25 40.00 100.00
7 Gilbert Perreault/15
8 Guy Lafleur/20
9 Jari Kurri/20
10 Jean Beliveau/15
11 John Bucyk/25 40.00 100.00
12 Lanny McDonald/20
13 Luc Robitaille/15
14 Marcel Dionne/25 30.00 80.00
15 Mario Lemieux/10
16 Michel Goulet/30 30.00 80.00
17 Mike Bossy/25 50.00 125.00
18 Mike Gartner/30 30.00 80.00
19 Gordie Howe/20
20 Pat Verbeek/10
21 Phil Esposito/15
22 Rocket Richard/10
23 Stan Mikita/25 30.00 80.00
24 Steve Yzerman/15
25 Joe Mullen/20

2001-02 BAP Ultimate Memorabilia 500 Goal Scorers Jerseys and Sticks

*JSY AND STICK: .5X TO 1.25X 500 GOAL JSY
STAT.PRINT RUN 40 SER.#'d SETS UNLESS
OTHERWISE NOTED
7 Jean Beliveau/40 25.00 60.00
11 Frank Mahovlich/40 25.00 60.00

2001-02 BAP Ultimate Memorabilia 500 Goal Scorers Emblems

STATED PRINT RUN 10 SETS
NOT PRICED DUE TO SCARCITY

2001-02 BAP Ultimate Memorabilia Gloves Are Off

STATED PRINT RUN 30 SER.#'d SETS
1 Rocket Richard 50.00 125.00
2 Gordie Howe 40.00 100.00
3 Mario Lemieux 40.00 100.00
4 Wayne Gretzky 75.00 200.00
5 Bill Gadsby 20.00 50.00
6 Doug Harvey 15.00 40.00
7 Ted Kennedy 20.00 50.00
8 King Clancy 40.00 100.00
9 Joe Sakic 30.00 80.00
10 Guy Lafleur 25.00 60.00
11 Eric Lindros 15.00 40.00
13 Mats Sundin 15.00 40.00
14 Al MacInnis 15.00 40.00
15 Doug Weight 15.00 40.00
16 Simon Gagne 15.00 40.00
17 Scott Niedermayer 15.00 40.00
18 Sergei Samsonov 15.00 40.00
19 Alexei Yashin 15.00 40.00
20 John LeClair 15.00 40.00
21 Sergei Fedorov 25.00 60.00
22 Chris Chelios 15.00 40.00
23 Jarome Iginla 25.00 60.00
24 Ace Bailey 30.00 80.00
25 Dickie Moore 15.00 40.00

2001-02 BAP Ultimate Memorabilia Jerseys

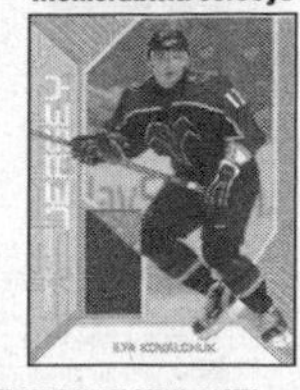

STATED PRINT RUN 50 SERIAL #'d SETS
1 Paul Kariya 12.50 30.00
2 Martin Brodeur 25.00 60.00
3 John LeClair 12.50 30.00
4 Ilya Kovalchuk 15.00 40.00
5 Bill Guerin 10.00 25.00
6 Dominik Hasek 15.00 40.00
7 Keith Tkachuk 12.50 30.00
8 Pavel Bure 12.50 30.00
9 Brian Leetch 10.00 25.00
10 Mario Lemieux 25.00 60.00
11 Mats Sundin 12.50 30.00
12 Owen Nolan 10.00 25.00
13 Mark Messier 12.50 30.00
14 Jaromir Jagr 15.00 40.00
15 Joe Sakic 20.00 50.00
16 Rob Blake 10.00 25.00
17 Brendan Shanahan 12.50 30.00
18 Eric Lindros 12.50 30.00
19 Mike Modano 15.00 40.00
20 Sergei Fedorov 15.00 40.00
21 Nicklas Lidstrom 12.50 30.00
22 Steve Yzerman 25.00 60.00
23 Teemu Selanne 12.50 30.00
24 Alexei Yashin 10.00 25.00
25 Doug Weight 10.00 25.00
26 Chris Pronger 10.00 25.00
27 Patrick Roy 25.00 60.00
28 Curtis Joseph 12.50 30.00
29 Jeremy Roenick 15.00 40.00
30 Luc Robitaille 10.00 25.00

2001-02 BAP Ultimate Memorabilia Jerseys and Sticks

*JSY/STK: .5X TO 1.25X JSY HI
STATED PRINT RUN 50 SERIAL #'d SETS

2001-02 BAP Ultimate Memorabilia Journey Jerseys

STATED PRINT RUN 50 SER.#'d SETS
1 Mark Messier 15.00 40.00
2 Curtis Joseph 15.00 40.00
3 Alexei Yashin 12.50 30.00
4 Gordie Howe 50.00 125.00
5 Felix Potvin 15.00 40.00
6 Rob Blake 12.50 30.00
7 Pavel Bure 20.00 50.00
8 Mats Sundin 15.00 40.00
9 Ed Belfour 15.00 40.00
10 Mike Modano 20.00 50.00
11 Brett Hull 20.00 50.00
12 Brendan Shanahan 15.00 40.00
13 Teemu Selanne 15.00 40.00
14 Keith Tkachuk 12.50 30.00
15 Patrick Roy 60.00 150.00
16 Luc Robitaille 15.00 40.00
17 Jeremy Roenick 20.00 50.00
18 Alexander Mogilny 12.50 30.00
19 Dominik Hasek 20.00 50.00
20 Jaromir Jagr 25.00 60.00
21 Roman Turek 12.50 30.00
22 Wayne Gretzky 150.00 350.00

2001-02 BAP Ultimate Memorabilia Journey Emblems

STATED PRINT RUN 10 SETS
NOT PRICED DUE TO SCARCITY

2001-02 BAP Ultimate Memorabilia Legend Terry Sawchuk

All cards in this product were graded by Beckett Grading Services and are available only in graded form. Cards in this 16-card set honored legendary goalie Terry Sawchuk by combining a swatch of his game-worn jersey with a swatch of game jersey from a current NHL goalie. Cards from this set were serial-numbered out of 20 on the back of the grading label. Cards were unnumbered and are listed below in checklist order.

STATED PRINT RUN 20 SER.#'d SETS
NOT PRICED DUE TO SCARCITY
1 Patrick Roy
2 Martin Brodeur
3 Dominik Hasek
4 Curtis Joseph
5 Nikolai Khabibulin
6 Johan Hedberg
7 Ed Belfour
8 Mike Richter
9 Felix Potvin
10 Tommy Salo
11 Roberto Luongo
12 Byron Dafoe
13 Jose Theodore
14 Jocelyn Thibault
15 Evgeni Nabokov
16 Olaf Kolzig

2001-02 BAP Ultimate Memorabilia Les Canadiens

STATED PRINT RUN 40 SER.#'d SETS
1 Mark Recchi 20.00 50.00
2 Yvan Cournoyer 20.00 50.00
3 Steve Shutt 20.00 50.00
4 Maurice Richard 75.00 200.00
5 Bob Gainey 25.00 60.00
6 Larry Robinson 20.00 50.00
7 Henri Richard 20.00 50.00
8 Jose Theodore 25.00 60.00
9 Saku Koivu 20.00 50.00
10 Patrick Roy 50.00 125.00
11 Jean Beliveau 30.00 80.00
12 Doug Harvey 20.00 50.00
13 Frank Mahovlich 20.00 50.00
14 Peter Mahovlich 20.00 50.00
15 Guy Lafleur 25.00 60.00
16 Serge Savard 20.00 50.00
17 Guy Lapointe 20.00 50.00
18 Jacques Plante 50.00 125.00

2001-02 BAP Ultimate Memorabilia Made to Order

Ten Made to Order redemption cards were randomly inserted into packs. Each redemption card entitled the holder to a 1 of 1 jersey card of the player they chose from a list provided by BAP.

1 Wayne Gretzky NYR
2 Wayne Gretzky Edmonton
3 Mario Lemieux Away
4 Mario Lemieux Home Left Profile
5 Mario Lemieux Home Right Profile
6 Pavel Bure
7 Marian Gaborik
NNO Redemption Card

2001-02 BAP Ultimate Memorabilia MVP

Ten MVP Winner Redemption cards were randomly inserted into packs. The redemption cards entitled the holder to a jersey card of the Hart Trophy winner for 2001-02. The cards were then graded by Beckett Grading Services and numbered out of 10.

PRINT RUN 10 CARDS
NOT PRICED DUE TO SCARCITY
1 Jose Theodore

2001-02 BAP Ultimate Memorabilia Numbers

STATED PRINT RUN 20 SERIAL #'d SETS
NOT PRICED DUE TO SCARCITY
1 Paul Kariya
2 John LeClair
3 Ilya Kovalchuk
4 Bill Guerin
5 Dominik Hasek
6 Keith Tkachuk
7 Pavel Bure
8 Brian Leetch
9 Mario Lemieux
10 Mats Sundin
11 Mark Messier
12 Joe Sakic
13 Rob Blake
14 Mike Modano
15 Sergei Fedorov
16 Martin Brodeur
17 Jaromir Jagr
18 Brendan Shanahan
19 Owen Nolan
20 Eric Lindros
21 Nicklas Lidstrom
22 Steve Yzerman
23 Teemu Selanne
24 Alexei Yashin
25 Doug Weight
26 Chris Pronger
27 Patrick Roy
28 Curtis Joseph
29 Jeremy Roenick
30 Luc Robitaille

2001-02 BAP Ultimate Memorabilia Name Plates

PRINT RUNS LISTED BELOW
1 Wayne Gretzky LA/40 100.00 200.00
2 Mario Lemieux/50 40.00 100.00
3 Paul Kariya/40 15.00 40.00
4 Pavel Bure/40 15.00 40.00
5 Mats Sundin/40 15.00 40.00
6 Mark Recchi/40 10.00 25.00
7 Dominik Hasek/40 20.00 50.00
8 Luc Robitaille/50 10.00 25.00
9 Bill Guerin/50 10.00 25.00
10 Eric Lindros/50 15.00 40.00
11 Patrick Roy/40 30.00 80.00
12 Nikolai Khabibulin/50 15.00 40.00
13 Teemu Selanne/50 15.00 40.00
14 Mark Messier/50 15.00 40.00
15 Steve Yzerman/50 30.00 80.00
16 Brian Leetch/50 10.00 25.00
17 Owen Nolan/50 10.00 25.00
18 Jarome Iginla/50 20.00 50.00
19 Gordie Howe Aeros/50 30.00 80.00
20 Roman Cechmanek/50 10.00 25.00
21 Joe Thornton/50 20.00 50.00
22 Ilya Kovalchuk/50 20.00 50.00
23 Curtis Joseph/50 15.00 40.00
24 Jeremy Roenick/50 20.00 50.00
25 Keith Tkachuk/50 15.00 40.00
26 Joe Sakic/50 20.00 50.00
27 Jaromir Jagr/50 20.00 50.00
28 Rob Blake/40 10.00 25.00
29 Mike Modano/50 20.00 50.00
30 Martin Brodeur/50 30.00 80.00
31 Nicklas Lidstrom/50 15.00 40.00
32 John LeClair/50 15.00 40.00
33 Gordie Howe NE/50 30.00 80.00
34 Chris Pronger/50 10.00 25.00
35 Sergei Fedorov/50 20.00 50.00
36 Jason Arnott/50 10.00 25.00
37 Marcel Dionne/40 10.00 25.00
38 Phil Esposito/50 20.00 50.00
39 Wayne Gretzky NYR/50 75.00 200.00
40 Doug Weight/40 10.00 25.00

2001-02 BAP Ultimate Memorabilia Playoff Records

STATED PRINT RUNS LISTED BELOW
1 Patrick Roy/50 30.00 80.00
219 Games
2 Patrick Roy/50 30.00 80.00
137 Wins
3 Larry Robinson/50 20.00 50.00
20 Years
4 Mark Messier/50 20.00 50.00
14 Goals
5 Wayne Gretzky/50 50.00 125.00
382 Points
6 Reggie Leach/50 20.00 50.00
19 Goals
7 Jari Kurri/50 25.00 60.00
12 Goals
8 Jari Kurri/50 25.00 60.00
19 Goals
9 Wayne Gretzky/50 50.00 125.00
260 Assists
10 Wayne Gretzky/10
14 Assists in a Six-Game Series
11 Wayne Gretzky/10
6 Assists in one Playoff Game
12 Wayne Gretzky/10
31 Assists
13 Wayne Gretzky/50 50.00 125.00
133 Goals
14 Wayne Gretzky/10
47 Points in 1985 Playoffs
15 Mario Lemieux/50 40.00 100.00
16 Mike Bossy/50 20.00 50.00
35 Goals
17 Mark Messier/50 20.00 50.00
236 Games
18 Wayne Gretzky/10
24 Career Playoff Game-Winning Goals
19 Joe Sakic/50 30.00 80.00
6 Goals
20 Maurice Richard/10
6 Playoff Overtime Goals

2001-02 BAP Ultimate Memorabilia Production Line

All cards in this product were graded by Beckett Grading Services and are available only in graded form. Cards from this set feature game-used jersey swatches from the legendary Production Line of the Detroit Red Wings. Each card was serial-numbered out of 20 on the back of the grading label. Cards are unnumbered and are listed below in checklist order.

STATED PRINT RUN 20 SERIAL #'d SETS
NOT PRICED DUE TO SCARCITY
1 Gordie Howe
2 Sid Abel
3 Ted Lindsay
4 Gordie Howe
Sid Abel
Ted Lindsay
5 Gordie Howe
Sid Abel
Ted Lindsay

2001-02 BAP Ultimate Memorabilia Prototypical Players

STATED PRINT RUN 40 SERIAL #'d SETS
1 Jacques Plante 60.00 150.00
Patrick Roy
2 Jacques Plante 60.00 150.00
Martin Brodeur
3 Jacques Plante 40.00 100.00
Dominik Hasek
4 Doug Harvey 25.00 60.00
Chris Pronger
5 Doug Harvey 25.00 60.00
Rob Blake
6 Doug Harvey 25.00 60.00
Nicklas Lidstrom
7 Jean Beliveau 50.00 125.00
Steve Yzerman
8 J.Beliveau/M.Lemieux 50.00 125.00
9 Jean Beliveau 40.00 100.00
Joe Sakic
10 Bobby Hull 25.00 60.00
Luc Robitaille
11 Bobby Hull 25.00 60.00
Paul Kariya
12 Bobby Hull 25.00 60.00
Brendan Shanahan
13 Gordie Howe 40.00 100.00
Jaromir Jagr
14 Gordie Howe 25.00 60.00
Pavel Bure
15 Gordie Howe 25.00 60.00
Brett Hull

2001-02 BAP Ultimate Memorabilia Retired Numbers

STATED PRINT RUN 5 SETS
NOT PRICED DUE TO SCARCITY
1 Sid Abel
2 Bill Barber
3 Jean Beliveau
4 Mike Bossy

5 Johnny Bucyk
6 Bobby Clarke
7 Marcel Dionne
8 Tony Esposito
9 Wayne Gretzky
10 Glenn Hall
11 Doug Harvey
12 Gordie Howe
13 Bobby Hull
14 Guy Lafleur
15 Ted Lindsay
16 Stan Mikita
17 Bernie Parent
18 Gilbert Perreault
19 Jacques Plante
20 Denis Potvin
21 Henri Richard
22 Rocket Richard
23 Terry Sawchuk
24 Billy Smith

2001-02 BAP Ultimate Memorabilia Retro Trophies

STATED PRINT RUN 25 SER.#'d SETS
1 Wayne Gretzky 60.00 150.00
Joe Sakic
Hart Trophy
2 Gordie Howe 40.00 100.00
Jaromir Jagr
Hart Trophy
3 Wayne Gretzky 60.00 150.00
Jaromir Jagr
Art Ross Trophy
4 W.Gretzky/M.Lemieux 75.00 200.00
5 Bobby Clarke 50.00 125.00
Mario Lemieux
Masterton Trophy
6 Mike Bossy 30.00 80.00
Joe Sakic
Lady Byng Trophy
7 Jari Kurri 25.00 60.00
Paul Kariya
Lady Byng Trophy
8 Lanny McDonald 25.00 60.00
Curtis Joseph
King Clancy Trophy
9 Terry Sawchuk 30.00 80.00
Dominik Hasek
Vezina Trophy
10 Glenn Hall 50.00 125.00
Patrick Roy
Calder Trophy
11 Terry Sawchuk 40.00 100.00
Evgeni Nabokov
Calder Trophy
12 Tony Esposito 40.00 100.00
Martin Brodeur
Calder Trophy
13 Bobby Clarke 30.00 80.00
Steve Yzerman
Selke Trophy
14 Glenn Hall 50.00 125.00
Patrick Roy
Conn Smythe Trophy
15 Bernie Parent 50.00 125.00
Patrick Roy
Conn Smythe Trophy
16 W.Gretzky/M.Lemieux 75.00 200.00
17 G.Lafleur/M.Lemieux 50.00 125.00
18 Doug Harvey 25.00 60.00
Nicklas Lidstrom
Norris Trophy
19 W.Gretzky/M.Lemieux 75.00 200.00
20 Guy Lafleur 40.00 100.00
Joe Sakic
Lester B. Pearson Award

2001-02 BAP Ultimate Memorabilia Retro Teammates

STATED PRINT RUNS LISTED BELOW
1 Beliveau/H.Richard/M.Richard/10
2 M.Richard/Plante/Harvey/10
3 Howe/Lindsay/Sawchuk/30 100.00 250.00
4 Gretzky/Messier/Coffey/10
5 Bossy/Trottier/Potvin/30 40.00 100.00
6 Clarke/Barber/Schultz/30 40.00 100.00
7 Hull/Hall/Mikita/30 75.00 150.00
8 Horton/Bower/Sawchuk/30 75.00 150.00
9 Lapointe/Savard/Mahovlich/30 40.00 100.00
10 Lafleur/Cournoyer/Beliveau/30 60.00 120.00
11 Lemieux/Coffey/Jagr/30 50.00 100.00
12 Gretzky/Leetch/Messier/30 125.00 250.00
13 Gretzky/Kurri/Robitaille/30 100.00 200.00
14 H.Richard/Harvey/M.Richard/10

2001-02 BAP Ultimate Memorabilia ROY

Ten Calder Winner Redemption cards were randomly inserted into packs.

PRINT RUN 10 SETS
NOT PRICED DUE TO SCARCITY
1 Dany Heatley

2001-02 BAP Ultimate Memorabilia Scoring Leaders

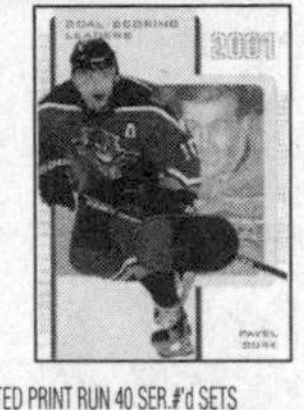

STATED PRINT RUN 40 SER.#'d SETS
1 Wayne Gretzky 1982 75.00 150.00
2 Wayne Gretzky 1983 75.00 150.00
3 Wayne Gretzky 1984 75.00 150.00
4 Wayne Gretzky 1985 75.00 150.00
5 Jari Kurri 1986 25.00 60.00
6 Wayne Gretzky 1987 75.00 150.00
7 Mario Lemieux 1988 30.00 80.00
8 Mario Lemieux 1989 30.00 80.00
9 Brett Hull 1990 15.00 40.00
10 Brett Hull 1991 15.00 40.00
11 Brett Hull 1992 15.00 40.00
12 Teemu Selanne 15.00 40.00
Alexander Mogilny
1993
13 Pavel Bure 1994 15.00 40.00
14 Peter Bondra 1995 15.00 40.00
15 Mario Lemieux 1996 30.00 80.00
16 Keith Tkachuk 1997 15.00 40.00
17 Teemu Selanne 15.00 40.00
Peter Bondra
1998
18 Teemu Selanne 1999 15.00 40.00
19 Pavel Bure 2000 15.00 40.00
20 Pavel Bure 2001 15.00 40.00
21 Jarome Iginla 2002 20.00 50.00

2001-02 BAP Ultimate Memorabilia Stanley Cup Winners

STATED PRINT RUN 50 SER.#'d SETS
1 Henri Richard 20.00 50.00
2 Jean Beliveau 30.00 80.00
3 Yvan Cournoyer 20.00 50.00
4 Red Kelly 20.00 50.00
5 Maurice Richard 75.00 200.00
6 Serge Savard 20.00 50.00
7 Jacques Plante/10
8 Johnny Bower 20.00 50.00
9 Bryan Trottier 20.00 50.00
10 Larry Robinson 20.00 50.00
11 Mark Messier 30.00 80.00
12 Jacques Laperriere 20.00 50.00
13 Doug Harvey 20.00 50.00
14 Frank Mahovlich 20.00 50.00
15 Guy Lapointe 20.00 50.00
16 Jari Kurri 25.00 60.00
17 Guy Lafleur 25.00 60.00
18 Bob Gainey 30.00 80.00
19 Grant Fuhr 20.00 50.00
20 Turk Broda/10
21 Ted Kennedy 20.00 50.00
22 Steve Shutt 20.00 50.00
23 Wayne Gretzky 75.00 200.00
24 Terry Sawchuk 40.00 100.00
25 Denis Potvin 20.00 50.00
26 Ted Lindsay 20.00 50.00
27 Billy Smith 20.00 50.00
28 Gordie Howe/10

2001-02 BAP Ultimate Memorabilia Vezina Winner

Ten Vezina Winner Redemption cards were randomly inserted into packs.

PRINT RUN 10 SETS
NOT PRICED DUE TO SCARCITY
1 Jose Theodore

2001-02 BAP Ultimate Memorabilia Waving the Flag

STATED PRINT RUN 30 SER.#'d SETS
1 Mario Lemieux 30.00 80.00
2 Joe Sakic 20.00 50.00
3 Steve Yzerman 25.00 60.00
4 Paul Kariya 15.00 40.00
5 Curtis Joseph 12.50 30.00
6 Martin Brodeur 25.00 60.00
7 Eric Lindros 12.50 30.00
8 Chris Pronger 10.00 25.00
9 Jaromir Jagr 15.00 40.00
10 Milan Hejduk 12.50 30.00
11 Dominik Hasek 20.00 50.00
12 Martin Havlat 10.00 25.00
13 Teemu Selanne 15.00 40.00
14 Jani Hurme 10.00 25.00
15 Miikka Kiprusoff 15.00 40.00
16 Sami Kapanen 10.00 25.00
17 Mats Sundin 12.50 30.00
18 Nicklas Lidstrom 12.50 30.00
19 Tommy Salo 10.00 25.00
20 Markus Naslund 12.50 30.00
21 Jeremy Roenick 15.00 40.00
22 Doug Weight 10.00 25.00
23 Tony Amonte 10.00 25.00
24 Brian Leetch 12.00 30.00
25 Mike Modano 15.00 40.00
26 Brett Hull 15.00 40.00
27 John Leclair 12.50 30.00
28 Keith Tkachuk 12.50 30.00
29 Alexei Yashin 10.00 25.00
30 Pavel Bure 12.50 30.00
31 Nikolai Khabibulin 12.50 30.00
32 Darius Kasparaitis 10.00 25.00

2002-03 BAP Ultimate Memorabilia

Released in May 2003, BAP Ultimate Memorabilia contained a graded rookie card numbered out of 250 and an encapsulated memorabilia card per pack. Rookie cards were not numbered and are listed below in checklist order. Since they were only available in graded form, raw cards were not priced.

COMPLETE SET (100)
1 P-M Bouchard
2 Rick Nash
3 Dennis Seidenberg
4 Jay Bouwmeester
5 Stanislav Chistov
6 Kurt Sauer
7 Ivan Majesky
8 Chuck Kobasew
9 Jordan Leopold
10 Steve Ott
11 Ales Hemsky
12 Patrick Sharp
13 Kari Haakana
14 Dmitri Bykov
15 Alex Henry
16 Henrik Zetterberg
17 Alexander Frolov
18 Steve Eminger
19 Scottie Upshall
20 Tom Koivisto
21 Ari Ahonen
22 Ron Hainsey
23 Martin Gerber
24 Adam Hall
25 Lasse Pirjeta
26 Anton Volchenkov
27 Jeff Paul
28 Carlo Colaiacovo
29 Alexander Svitov
30 Alexei Smirnov
31 Jeff Taffe
32 Mikael Tellqvist
33 Radovan Somik
34 Mike Komisarek
35 Chris Schmidt
36 Dick Tarnstrom
37 Ryan Bayda
38 Sylvain Blouin
39 Ray Emery
40 Stephane Veilleux
41 Curtis Sanford
42 Eric Godard
43 Pascal Leclaire
44 Patrick Boileau
45 Tim Thomas
46 Mike Cammalleri
47 Jason Spezza
48 Cody Rudkowsky
49 Darren Haydar
50 Ryan Miller
51 Brandon Reid
52 Christian Backman
53 Niko Dimitrakos
54 Garnet Exelby
55 Jason King
56 Martin Samuelsson
57 Miroslav Zalesak
58 Tomas Malec
59 Michael Garnett
60 Matt Walker
61 Shaone Morrisonn
62 Chad Wiseman
63 Michael Leighton
64 Tomas Surovy
65 Jason Bacashihua
66 Jim Vandermeer
67 Konstantin Koltsov
68 Fernando Pisani
69 Rickard Wallin
70 Brooks Orpik
71 Tomas Zizka
72 Jarret Stoll
73 Cristobal Huet
74 Levente Szuper
75 Jared Aulin
76 Simon Gamache
77 Kris Vernarsky
78 Radoslav Hecl
79 Jamie Hodson
80 Marc-Andre Bergeron
81 Mike Siklenka
82 Igor Radulov
83 Paul Manning
84 John Tripp
85 Ian MacNeil
86 Jim Fahey
87 Dany Sabourin
88 Alexei Semenov
89 Curtis Murphy
90 Jerred Smithson
91 Francois Beauchemin
92 Vernon Fiddler
93 Cam Severson
94 Burke Henry
95 Brad Defauw
96 Craig Andersson
97 Frederic Cloutier
98 Tomas Kurka
99 Jonathan Hedstrom
100 Valeri Kharlamov

2002-03 BAP Ultimate Memorabilia Active Eight

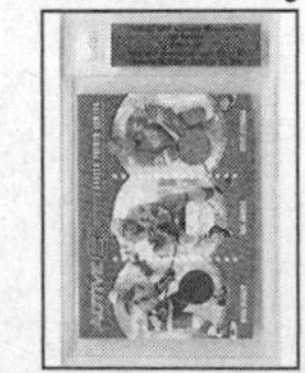

PRINT RUN 30 SER.#'d SETS
1 Messier/Francis/Yzerman 40.00 100.00
2 Lemieux/Forsberg/Oates 40.00 100.00
3 Roy/Belfour/Brodeur 100.00 250.00
4 Hull/Messier/Yzerman 40.00 100.00
5 Messier/Francis/Yzerman 40.00 100.00
6 Patrick Roy 60.00 150.00
Ed Belfour
Curtis Joseph
7 Lemieux/Sakic/Leetch 50.00 125.00
8 Lemieux/Yzerman/Oates 60.00 150.00

2002-03 BAP Ultimate Memorabilia All-Star MVP

*MULT.COLOR SWATCH: .75X TO 1.5X
PRINT RUN 40 SER.#'d SETS
1 Bill Guerin 12.50 30.00
2 Bobby Hull/1970 15.00 40.00
3 Bobby Hull/1971 15.00 40.00
4 Brett Hull 20.00 50.00
5 Dany Heatley 15.00 40.00
6 Eric Daze 12.50 30.00
7 Frank Mahovlich 15.00 40.00
8 Grant Fuhr 25.00 60.00
9 Henri Richard 12.50 30.00
10 Jean Beliveau 25.00 60.00
11 Mario Lemieux 25.00 60.00
12 Mario Lemieux 25.00 60.00
13 Mario Lemieux 25.00 60.00
14 Mark Recchi 12.50 30.00
15 Mike Bossy 12.50 30.00
16 Mike Gartner 12.50 30.00
17 Mike Richter 12.50 30.00
18 Pavel Bure 12.50 30.00
19 Peter Mahovlich 15.00 40.00
20 Reggie Leach 12.50 30.00
21 Vincent Damphousse 12.50 30.00
22 Teemu Selanne 12.50 30.00

2002-03 BAP Ultimate Memorabilia Autographs

PRINT RUN 30 SER.#'d SETS
GOLD 1 OF 1's EXIST
1 Alexander Frolov 25.00 60.00
2 Alexei Smirnov 12.50 30.00
3 Anton Volchenkov 12.50 30.00
4 Carlo Colaiacovo 12.50 30.00

5 Chuck Kobasew 12.50 30.00
6 Jay Bouwmeester 25.00 60.00
7 Jordan Leopold 12.50 30.00
8 Mike Cammalleri 12.50 30.00
9 P-M Bouchard 20.00 50.00
10 Rick Nash 40.00 80.00
11 Ron Hainsey 12.50 30.00
12 Scottie Upshall 12.50 30.00
13 Stanislav Chistov 12.50 30.00
14 Sergei Fedorov 25.00 60.00
15 Patrick Roy 100.00 250.00
16 Mario Lemieux 100.00 250.00
17 Brian Leetch 20.00 50.00
18 Dany Heatley 30.00 80.00
19 Jarome Iginla 25.00 60.00
20 Joe Sakic 50.00 125.00
21 Joe Thornton 30.00 80.00
22 Jose Theodore 25.00 60.00
23 Pavel Bure 20.00 50.00
24 Peter Forsberg 40.00 100.00
25 Saku Koivu 20.00 50.00
26 Alexander Svitov 12.50 30.00
27 Stephane Veilleux 12.50 30.00
28 Adam Hall 12.50 30.00
29 Henrik Zetterberg 40.00 100.00
30 Steve Eminger 12.50 30.00

2002-03 BAP Ultimate Memorabilia Blades of Steel

PRINT RUN 10 SER.#'d SETS
NOT PRICED DUE TO SCARCITY
1 Nels Stewart
2 Georges Vezina
3 Jean Beliveau
4 Tim Horton
5 Maurice Richard
6 Jacques Plante
7 Bill Barilko
8 Mario Lemieux
9 Aurel Joliat
10 Jarome Iginla

2002-03 BAP Ultimate Memorabilia Calder Candidates

*MULT.COLOR SWATCH: .75X TO 1.5X
PRINT RUN 40 SER.#'d SETS
1 Henrik Zetterberg 30.00 80.00
2 Niko Kapanen 12.50 30.00
3 Ron Hainsey 12.50 30.00
4 Jason Spezza 30.00 80.00
5 Anton Volchenkov 12.50 30.00
6 Ivan Huml 12.50 30.00
7 Tyler Arnason 12.50 30.00
8 Dennis Seidenberg 12.50 30.00
9 Alexander Frolov 12.50 30.00
10 Alexei Smirnov 12.50 30.00
11 Jay Bouwmeester 12.50 30.00
12 Ales Hemsky 20.00 50.00
13 Rick Nash 30.00 80.00
14 Jordan Leopold 12.50 30.00
15 Stephen Weiss 12.50 30.00
16 Ryan Miller 12.50 30.00
17 Chuck Kobasew 12.50 30.00
18 Alexander Svitov 12.50 30.00
19 Adam Hall 12.50 30.00
20 Stanislav Chistov 12.50 30.00

2002-03 BAP Ultimate Memorabilia Captains

This 8-card set featured swatches from the Captain's C on the featured player's jersey. Cards were serial-numbered to just 5 and each card was encapsulated in a clear plastic slab with a descriptive label encased at the top. This set is not priced due to scarcity. The set is unnumbered and listed below in checklist order.

PRINT RUN 5 SER.#'d SETS
NOT PRICED DUE TO SCARCITY
1 Paul Kariya
2 Mario Lemieux
3 Joe Thornton
4 Saku Koivu
5 Markus Naslund
6 Mats Sundin
7 Steve Yzerman
8 Joe Sakic

2002-03 BAP Ultimate Memorabilia Complete Package

This 10-card set featured 4 swatches of game-used memorabilia per card. Cards were serial-numbered to just 10 and each card was encapsulated in a clear plastic slab with a descriptive label encased at the top. The set is unnumbered and listed below in checklist order. This set is not priced due to scarcity.

PRINT RUN 10 SER.#'d SETS
NOT PRICED DUE TO SCARCITY
1 Curtis Joseph
2 Eric Lindros
3 Guy Lafleur
4 Jacques Plante
5 Mario Lemieux
6 Mats Sundin
7 Maurice Richard
8 Patrick Roy
9 Terry Sawchuk
10 Tim Horton

2002-03 BAP Ultimate Memorabilia Conn Smythe

*MULT.COLOR SWATCH: .75X TO 1.5X
PRINT RUN 30 SER.#'d SETS
1 Jean Beliveau/1965 30.00 80.00
2 Roger Crozier/1966 15.00 40.00
3 Glenn Hall/1968 20.00 50.00
4 Serge Savard/1969 15.00 40.00
5 Yvan Cournoyer/1973 20.00 50.00
6 Bernie Parent/1974 20.00 50.00
7 Bernie Parent/1975 20.00 50.00
8 Reggie Leach/1976 15.00 40.00
9 Guy Lafleur/1977 25.00 60.00
10 Larry Robinson/1978 15.00 40.00
11 Bryan Trottier/1980 15.00 40.00
12 Mike Bossy/1982 15.00 40.00
13 Billy Smith/1983 15.00 40.00
14 Mark Messier/1984 25.00 60.00
15 Patrick Roy/1986 40.00 100.00
16 Ron Hextall/1987 20.00 50.00
17 Al MacInnis/1989 15.00 40.00
18 Bill Ranford/1990 15.00 40.00
19 Mario Lemieux 40.00 100.00
20 Mario Lemieux 40.00 100.00
21 Patrick Roy/1993 40.00 100.00
22 Brian Leetch/1994 20.00 50.00
23 Claude Lemieux/1995 15.00 40.00
24 Joe Sakic/1996 30.00 80.00
25 Mike Vernon/1997 25.00 60.00
26 Steve Yzerman 30.00 80.00
27 Joe Nieuwendyk/1999 15.00 40.00
28 Scott Stevens/2000 15.00 40.00
29 Patrick Roy/2001 40.00 100.00
30 Nicklas Lidstrom/2002 15.00 40.00

2002-03 BAP Ultimate Memorabilia Cornerstones

This 8-card set featured swatches of game-used jerseys from 4 different players considered the greatest to play in that given city. Cards were serial-numbered to just 20 and each card was encapsulated in a clear plastic slab with a descriptive label encased at the top. The set is unnumbered and listed below in checklist order. This set is not priced due to scarcity.

PRINT RUN 20 SER.#'d SETS
NOT PRICED DUE TO SCARCITY
1 Tiny Thompson
Gerry Cheevers
Cam Neely
Joe Thornton
2 Bill Mosienko
Bobby Hull
Michel Goulet
Eric Daze
3 Ted Lindsay
Terry Sawchuk
Alex Delvecchio
Steve Yzerman
4 Aurel Joliat
Jean Beliveau
Guy Lafleur
Saku Koivu
5 Chuck Rayner
Ed Giacomin
Phil Esposito
Mark Messier
6 King Clancy
Teeder Kennedy
Lanny McDonald
Mats Sundin
7 Bernie Parent
Bobby Clarke
Eric Lindros
Simon Gagne
8 Denis Potvin
Bryan Trottier
Mike Bossy
Alexei Yashin

2002-03 BAP Ultimate Memorabilia Cup Duels

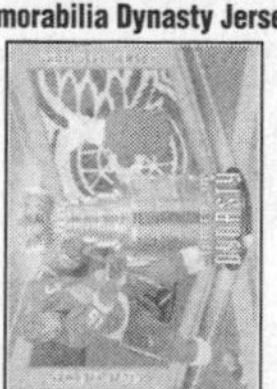

*MULT.COLOR SWATCH: .75X TO 1.5X
PRINT RUN 40 SER.#'d SETS
GOLD 1 OF 1's EXIST
1 George Hainsworth 40.00 100.00
Tiny Thompson
2 Terry Sawchuk 75.00 200.00
Jacques Plante
3 Jacques Plante 30.00 80.00
Johnny Bower
4 Glenn Hall 40.00 100.00
Terry Sawchuk
5 Johnny Bower 30.00 80.00
Terry Sawchuk
6 Roger Crozier 20.00 50.00
Gump Worsley
7 Gerry Cheevers 20.00 50.00
Ed Giacomin
8 Gilles Gilbert 20.00 50.00
Bernie Parent
9 Billy Smith 20.00 50.00
Grant Fuhr
10 Patrick Roy 30.00 80.00
Mike Vernon
11 Ron Hextall 20.00 50.00
Grant Fuhr
12 Andy Moog 20.00 50.00
Grant Fuhr
13 Patrick Roy 30.00 80.00
Mike Vernon
14 Andy Moog 20.00 50.00
Bill Ranford
15 Tom Barrasso 20.00 50.00
Ed Belfour
16 Martin Brodeur 40.00 100.00
Mike Vernon
17 John Vanbiesbrouck 40.00 100.00
Patrick Roy
18 Olaf Kolzig 20.00 50.00
Chris Osgood
19 Martin Brodeur 30.00 80.00
Ed Belfour
20 P.Roy/M.Broduer 75.00 150.00

2002-03 BAP Ultimate Memorabilia Customer Appreciation Card

This special memorabilia card was only available to collectors who held a Henrik Zetterberg autograph redemption card. The card was sent back along with the autograph card as a token of appreciation. The card was serial-numbered to just 31 copies and was sealed in a plastic card slab.

1 Henrik Zetterberg 40.00 100.00

2002-03 BAP Ultimate Memorabilia Dynamic Duos

PRINT RUN 30 SER.#'d SETS
1 M.Lemieux/J.Thornton 30.00 80.00
2 Peter Forsberg 20.00 50.00
Mats Sundin
3 I.Kovalchuk/S.Fedorov 25.00 60.00
4 S.Yzerman/D.Heatley 30.00 80.00
5 M.Modano/B.Hull 25.00 60.00
6 Brendan Shanahan 20.00 50.00
Paul Kariya
7 Joe Sakic 20.00 50.00
Eric Lindros
8 Saku Koivu 20.00 50.00
Teemu Selanne
9 J.Jagr/M.Gaborik 25.00 60.00
10 Pavel Bure 20.00 50.00
Sergei Samsonov

2002-03 BAP Ultimate Memorabilia Dynasty Jerseys

*MULT.COLOR SWATCH: .75X TO 1.5X
PRINT RUN 50 SER.#'d SETS
1 Brendan Shanahan 25.00 60.00
2 Brett Hull 30.00 80.00
3 Chris Chelios 25.00 60.00
4 Chris Osgood 20.00 50.00
5 Darren McCarty 20.00 50.00
6 Igor Larionov 20.00 50.00
7 Jiri Fischer 20.00 50.00
8 Kirk Maltby 20.00 50.00
9 Kris Draper 20.00 50.00
10 Luc Robitaille 20.00 50.00
11 Manny Legace 25.00 60.00
12 Martin Lapointe 20.00 50.00
13 Mathieu Dandenault 20.00 50.00
14 Mike Vernon 20.00 50.00
15 Nicklas Lidstrom 25.00 60.00
16 Pavel Datsyuk 25.00 60.00
17 Sergei Fedorov 25.00 60.00
18 Steve Yzerman 40.00 100.00
19 Tomas Holmstrom 20.00 50.00
20 Slava Kozlov 20.00 50.00

2002-03 BAP Ultimate Memorabilia Dynasty Emblems

PRINT RUN 10 SER.#'d SETS
NOT PRICED DUE TO SCARCITY

2002-03 BAP Ultimate Memorabilia Dynasty Numbers

PRINT RUN 10 SER.#'d SETS
NOT PRICED DUE TO SCARCITY

2002-03 BAP Ultimate Memorabilia Emblem Attic

PRINT RUN 5 SER.#'d SETS
NOT PRICED DUE TO SCARCITY.
1 George Hainsworth
2 Bernie Parent
3 Marcel Dionne
4 Gerry Cheevers
5 Frank Mahovlich
6 Roy Worters
7 Jean Beliveau
8 Doug Harvey
9 John Bucyk
10 Tony Esposito
11 Jacques Plante
12 Guy Lafleur
13 Ted Lindsay
14 Terry Sawchuk
15 Bobby Hull
16 Harry Lumley
17 Glenn Hall
18 Stan Mikita
19 Roger Crozier
20 Ed Giacomin
21 Rocket Richard
22 Frank Brimsek
23 Phil Esposito
24 Mike Bossy
25 Aurel Joliat
26 Red Kelly
27 Henri Richard
28 Bobby Clarke

2002-03 BAP Ultimate Memorabilia Emblems

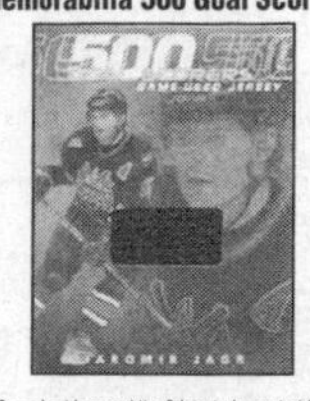

PRINT RUN 10 SER.#'d SETS
NOT PRICED DUE TO SCARCITY
GOLD 1 OF 1's EXIST
1 Mats Sundin
2 Joe Thornton
3 Steve Yzerman
4 Pavel Bure
5 Dany Heatley
6 Chris Chelios
7 Markus Naslund
8 Jaromir Jagr
9 Mario Lemieux
10 Brendan Shanahan
11 Peter Forsberg
12 Paul Kariya
13 Joe Sakic
14 Brett Hull
15 Martin Brodeur
16 Mike Comrie
17 Brian Leetch
18 Nicklas Lidstrom
19 Jeremy Roenick
20 Mike Modano
21 Patrick Roy
22 Sergei Fedorov
23 Luc Robitaille
24 John LeClair
25 Eric Lindros
26 Mark Messier
27 Saku Koivu
28 Ilya Kovalchuk
29 Marian Gaborik
30 Valeri Kharlamov

2002-03 BAP Ultimate Memorabilia Finals Showdown

This 40-card set featured jersey swatches from players who have faced off in the finals in years past. Cards were serial-numbered to just 40 and each card was encapsulated in a clear plastic slab with a descriptive label encased at the top. The set is unnumbered and listed below in checklist order.

*MULT.COLOR SWATCH: .75X TO 1.5X
PRINT RUN 40 SER.#'d SETS
1 Alex Delvecchio 20.00 50.00
Doug Harvey
2 Bernie Geoffrion 20.00 50.00
Ted Lindsay
3 Henri Richard 30.00 80.00
Tim Horton
4 Maurice Richard 40.00 100.00
Frank Mahovlich
5 Stan Mikita 30.00 80.00
Terry Sawchuk
6 Frank Mahovlich 20.00 50.00
Bobby Hull
7 Red Kelly 25.00 60.00
Terry Sawchuk
8 Tim Horton 40.00 100.00
Alex Delvecchio
9 Jean Beliveau 20.00 50.00
Glenn Hall
10 Jean Beliveau 20.00 50.00
Roger Crozier
11 Johnny Bower 20.00 50.00
John Ferguson
12 Peter Mahovlich 20.00 50.00
Bobby Hull
13 Gerry Cheevers 20.00 50.00
Rod Gilbert
14 Yvan Cournoyer 20.00 50.00
Bobby Hull
15 Bernie Parent 20.00 50.00
John Bucyk
16 Bobby Clarke 20.00 50.00
Gilbert Perreault
17 Steve Shutt 20.00 50.00
Dave Schultz
18 Guy Lapointe 20.00 50.00
Gerry Cheevers
19 Larry Robinson 20.00 50.00
Gerry Cheevers
20 Guy Lafleur 40.00 100.00
Phil Esposito
21 Billy Smith 25.00 60.00
Bobby Clarke
22 Bryan Trottier 30.00 80.00
Grant Fuhr
23 Mark Messier 20.00 50.00
Felix Potvin
24 Patrick Roy 40.00 100.00
Lanny McDonald
25 Jari Kurri 40.00 100.00
Ron Hextall
26 Kevin Lowe 20.00 50.00
Cam Neely
27 Al MacInnis 30.00 80.00
Patrick Roy
28 Mark Messier 20.00 50.00
Cam Neely
29 Mario Lemieux 50.00 125.00
Mike Modano
30 Jaromir Jagr 25.00 60.00
Jeremy Roenick
31 Patrick Roy 30.00 80.00
Luc Robitaille
32 Mark Messier 30.00 80.00
Pavel Bure
33 Martin Brodeur 40.00 100.00
Steve Yzerman
34 Patrick Roy 40.00 100.00
Rob Niedermayer
35 Steve Yzerman 50.00 125.00
Eric Lindros
36 Sergei Fedorov 20.00 50.00
Olaf Kolzig
37 Brett Hull 20.00 50.00
Mike Peca
38 Jason Arnott 20.00 50.00
Ed Belfour
39 Joe Sakic 30.00 80.00
Martin Brodeur
40 Nicklas Lidstrom 20.00 50.00
Ron Francis

2002-03 BAP Ultimate Memorabilia First Overall

This 15-card set featured players chosen first in the NHL entry draft and featured a swatch of game-worn jersey. Cards were serial-numbered to just 20 and each card was encapsulated in a clear plastic slab with a descriptive label encased at the top. The set is unnumbered and listed below in checklist order. This set is not priced due to scarcity.

PRINT RUN 20 SER.#'d SETS
NOT PRICED DUE TO SCARCITY
1 Alexandre Daigle
2 Bryan Berard
3 Chris Phillips
4 Ed Jovanovski
5 Eric Lindros
6 Ilya Kovalchuk
7 Joe Thornton
8 Mats Sundin
9 Mike Modano
10 Owen Nolan
11 Patrik Stefan
12 Rick DiPietro
13 Rick Nash
14 Roman Hamrlik
15 Vincent Lecavalier

2002-03 BAP Ultimate Memorabilia 500 Goal Scorers

This 3-card set honored the 3 latest players to hit the 500 goal mark. Cards were serial-numbered to just 30 and each card was encapsulated in a clear plastic slab with a descriptive label encased at the top. The set is unnumbered and listed below in checklist order.

*MULT.COLOR SWATCH: .75X TO 1.5X
PRINT RUN 30 SER.#'d SETS
1 Joe Nieuwendyk 15.00 40.00
2 Joe Sakic 30.00 80.00
3 Jaromir Jagr 25.00 60.00

2002-03 BAP Ultimate Memorabilia 500 Goal Scorers Jersey and Stick

This 3-card set paralleled the regular insert set but included piece of stick with the swatch of jersey. Cards were serial-numbered to just 30 and were encapsulated in a clear plastic holder with a descriptive label encased at the top. Cards were unnumbered and are listed in checklist order.

*JSY/STK: .5X TO 1.25X JERSEY
PRINT RUN 30 SER.#'d SETS

2002-03 BAP Ultimate Memorabilia 500 Goal Scorers Emblems

PRINT RUN 10 SER.#'d SETS
NOT PRICED DUE TO SCARCITY

2002-03 BAP Ultimate Memorabilia Global Dominators

This 10-card set featured game-worn jersey swatches of players who regularly represent their nation in competition. Cards were serial-numbered to just 30 and each card was encapsulated in a clear plastic slab with a descriptive label encased at the top. The set is unnumbered and listed below in checklist order. Unpriced gold one of ones were also created.

*MULT.COLOR SWATCH: .75X TO 1.5X
PRINT RUN 30 SER.#'d SETS
GOLD 1 OF 1's EXIST
1 Mario Lemieux 40.00 100.00
2 Al MacInnis 15.00 40.00
3 Rob Blake 15.00 40.00
4 Peter Forsberg 25.00 60.00
5 Igor Larionov 15.00 40.00
6 Joe Sakic 30.00 80.00
7 Steve Yzerman 40.00 100.00
8 Alexander Mogilny 15.00 40.00
9 Theo Fleury 15.00 40.00
10 Brendan Shanahan 15.00 40.00

2002-03 BAP Ultimate Memorabilia Gloves Are Off

PRINT RUN 30 SER.#'d SETS
1 Ace Bailey 40.00 100.00
2 Mario Lemieux 30.00 80.00
3 Joe Sakic 20.00 50.00
4 Aurel Joliat 40.00 100.00
5 Guy Lafleur 30.00 80.00
6 Al MacInnis 15.00 40.00
7 Dickie Moore 15.00 40.00
8 Chris Chelios 15.00 40.00
9 Sergei Fedorov 20.00 50.00
10 Eddie Shore 20.00 50.00
11 Ted Kennedy 25.00 60.00
12 Eric Lindros 15.00 40.00
13 Mats Sundin 15.00 40.00
14 Doug Harvey 20.00 50.00
15 Bill Gadsby 25.00 60.00
16 Jarome Iginla 20.00 50.00
17 Joe Thornton 20.00 50.00
18 Maurice Richard 30.00 80.00
19 Brett Hull 20.00 50.00
20 King Clancy 30.00 80.00

2002-03 BAP Ultimate Memorabilia Great Moments

This 17-card set reflected on some of the best moments in NHL history and included pieces of game-used memorabilia from the featured play. Cards were serial-numbered to just 30 unless otherwise noted below and each card was encapsulated in a clear plastic slab with a descriptive label encased at the top. The set is unnumbered and listed below in checklist order.

*MULT.COLOR SWATCH: .75X TO 1.5X
PRINT RUN 30 SER.#'d SETS/
UNLESS OTHERWISE NOTED
LOWER PRINT RUNS NOT
PRICED DUE TO SCARCITY
1 Teeder Kennedy
And Royalty
2 Eddie Shore
Ace Bailey
Shake Hands
3 Maurice Richard
Jim Henry
Shake Hands
4 Mario Lemieux 50.00 125.00
5 Darryl Sittler 50.00 125.00
10 Points In A Game
6 Bill Barilko
The Goal/10
7 Frank Brimsek 25.00 60.00
First All-Star Game
8 Teemu Selanne 25.00 60.00
Rookie Record
9 Mark Messier 25.00 60.00
Rangers First Cup
In 54 Years
10 Patrick Roy 50.00 125.00
Breaks Sawchuk's Record
11 Jacques Plante 30.00 80.00
Donning the Mask
12 Jean Beliveau 30.00 80.00
First Conn Smythe
13 Glenn Hall 25.00 60.00
500 Straight Games
14 Maurice Richard 40.00 100.00
Five Goals In Playoff Game
15 Georges Hainsworth
22 Shutouts In One Year
16 Maurice Richard 40.00 100.00
Canadiens Win 5th
Consecutive Cup
17 Bill Mosienko 25.00 60.00
Fastest Hat Trick
18 M.Richard/Fifty in Fifty 40.00 100.00
19 Terry Sawchuk 40.00 100.00
100 Shutouts
20 Stan Mikita 25.00 60.00
Second Triple Crown

2002-03 BAP Ultimate Memorabilia Hat Tricks

This 20-card set featured 3 different swatches of game-used memorabilia from the featured player. Cards were serial-numbered to just 30 and each card was encapsulated in a clear plastic slab with a descriptive label encased at the top. The set is unnumbered and listed below in checklist order.

PRINT RUN 30 SER.#'d SETS
1 Simon Gagne 20.00 50.00
2 John LeClair 20.00 50.00
3 Adam Deadmarsh 10.00 25.00
4 Jeff O'Neill 10.00 25.00
5 Keith Tkachuk 20.00 50.00
6 Joe Thornton 30.00 80.00
7 Rob Blake 10.00 25.00
8 Alexei Yashin 10.00 25.00
9 Sergei Fedorov 30.00 80.00
10 Mario Lemieux 75.00 200.00
11 Jarome Iginla 25.00 60.00
12 Doug Weight 15.00 40.00
13 Brett Hull 30.00 80.00
14 Joe Sakic 50.00 125.00
15 Sergei Samsonov 10.00 25.00
16 Al MacInnis 15.00 40.00
17 Eric Lindros 20.00 50.00
18 Steve Yzerman 60.00 150.00
19 Mats Sundin 20.00 50.00
20 Chris Chelios 20.00 50.00

2002-03 BAP Ultimate Memorabilia Jerseys

*MULT.COLOR SWATCH: .75X TO 1.5X
PRINT RUN 50 SER.#'d SETS
GOLD 1/1's EXIST
1 Bill Guerin 10.00 25.00

2 Jarome Iginla 15.00 40.00
3 Jose Theodore 15.00 40.00
4 Mario Lemieux 30.00 80.00
5 Martin Brodeur 25.00 60.00
6 Brendan Shanahan 10.00 25.00
7 Brett Hull 20.00 50.00
8 Dany Heatley 15.00 40.00
9 Ed Belfour 10.00 25.00
10 Eric Lindros 10.00 25.00
11 Ilya Kovalchuk 15.00 40.00
12 Jaromir Jagr 15.00 40.00
13 Jason Spezza 15.00 40.00
14 Jay Bouwmeester 20.00 50.00
15 Jeremy Roenick 12.50 30.00
16 Joe Sakic 15.00 40.00
17 Joe Thornton 12.50 30.00
18 John LeClair 10.00 25.00
19 Marian Gaborik 20.00 50.00
20 Marian Hossa 10.00 25.00
21 Mark Messier 10.00 25.00
22 Markus Naslund 10.00 25.00
23 Marty Turco 10.00 25.00
24 Mats Sundin 10.00 25.00
25 Mike Modano 12.50 30.00
26 Milan Hejduk 10.00 25.00
27 Nicklas Lidstrom 10.00 25.00
28 Patrick Roy 25.00 60.00
29 Paul Kariya 10.00 25.00
30 Pavel Bure 10.00 25.00
31 Peter Forsberg 25.00 60.00
32 Rick Nash 25.00 60.00
33 Saku Koivu 10.00 25.00
34 Sergei Fedorov 15.00 40.00
35 Sergei Samsonov 10.00 25.00
36 Steve Yzerman 25.00 60.00
37 Teemu Selanne 10.00 25.00
38 Todd Bertuzzi 10.00 25.00
39 Valeri Kharlamov 25.00 60.00
40 Vincent Lecavalier 10.00 25.00

2002-03 BAP Ultimate Memorabilia Jersey and Stick

*JSY/STK: .5X TO 1.25X BASIC JERSEY
PRINT RUN 50 SER.#'d SETS
GOLD 1 OF 1's EXIST
19 Roberto Luongo 15.00 40.00

2002-03 BAP Ultimate Memorabilia Journey Jerseys

This 10-card set featured swatches of game-worn jerseys from every team the given player played for. Cards were serial-numbered to just 50 and each card was encapsulated in a clear plastic slab with a descriptive label encased at the top. The set is unnumbered and listed below in checklist order. Unpriced gold one of ones were also created.

PRINT RUN 50 SER.#'d SETS
GOLD 1 OF 1's EXIST
1 Patrick Roy 50.00 125.00
2 Ed Belfour 25.00 60.00
3 Jaromir Jagr 25.00 60.00
4 Brett Hull 40.00 100.00
5 Adam Oates 20.00 50.00
6 Eric Lindros 20.00 50.00
7 Bill Guerin 20.00 50.00
8 Jeremy Roenick 25.00 60.00
9 Pavel Bure 20.00 50.00
10 Alexander Mogilny 20.00 50.00

2002-03 BAP Ultimate Memorabilia Journey Emblems

PRINT RUN 10 SER.#'d SETS
NOT PRICED DUE TO SCARCITY
GOLD 1 OF 1's EXIST

2002-03 BAP Ultimate Memorabilia Legend

This 10-card set highlighted the career of Rocket Richard. Each card carried a piece of memorabilia and dual player cards carried two pieces. Cards in this set were serial-numbered to 15 unless otherwise noted below.. This set is not priced due to scarcity.

PRINT RUN 15 SER.#'d SETS
NOT PRICED DUE TO SCARCITY
1 Maurice Richard JSY/AUTO
2 Maurice Richard GLOVE
3 Maurice Richard SKATE
4 Maurice Richard STICK
5 Maurice Richard
Complete Package
6 Maurice Richard
Doug Harvey
7 Maurice Richard
Jacques Plante
8 Maurice Richard
Jean Beliveau
9 Maurice Richard
Henri Richard
10 Maurice Richard
Complete Package Auto/5

2002-03 BAP Ultimate Memorabilia Lifetime Achievers

This 20-card set featured swatches of game-worn jerseys. Cards were serial-numbered to just 40 and each card was encapsulated in a clear plastic slab with a descriptive label encased at the top. The set is unnumbered and listed below in checklist order.

*MULT.COLOR SWATCH: .75X TO 1.5X
PRINT RUN 40 SER.#'d SETS
1 Sergei Fedorov 15.00 40.00
2 Nicklas Lidstrom 12.50 30.00
3 Brendan Shanahan 12.50 30.00
4 Ed Belfour 12.50 30.00
5 Doug Gilmour 12.50 30.00
6 Jaromir Jagr 20.00 50.00
7 Patrick Roy 30.00 80.00
8 Eric Lindros 12.50 30.00
9 Brian Leetch 12.50 30.00
10 Pavel Bure 12.50 30.00
11 Brett Hull 20.00 50.00
12 Martin Brodeur 30.00 80.00
13 Curtis Joseph 12.50 30.00
14 Mario Lemieux 30.00 80.00
15 Steve Yzerman 30.00 80.00
16 Luc Robitaille 12.50 30.00
17 Mark Messier 12.50 30.00
18 Chris Chelios 12.50 30.00
19 Ron Francis 12.50 30.00
20 Joe Sakic 25.00 60.00

2002-03 BAP Ultimate Memorabilia Made to Order

Limited to just 10 copies each, these redemption cards entitiled the holder to a special one of one memorabilia card of a player they could choose from a specific list. Exchange cards were available for single, double or triple memorabilia cards. The redemption cards and the one of ones are not priced due to scarcity.

PRINT RUN 10 SER.#'d SETS
NOT PRICED DUE TO SCARCITY

2002-03 BAP Ultimate Memorabilia Magnificent Inserts

This 10-card set featured game-used equipment from the career of Mario Lemieux. Cards 1-5 had a print run of 30 copies each and cards 6-10 were limited to just 10 copies each. Cards 6-10 are not priced due to scarcity. Each card was encapsulated in a clear plastic slab with a descriptive label encased at the top.

1-5 PRINT RUN 30 SER.#'d SETS
6-10 PRINT RUN 10 SER.#'d SETS
6-10 NOT PRICED DUE TO SCARCITY
1 1985-86 Season 50.00 125.00
2 2000-01 Season 50.00 125.00
3 2002 NHL All-Star 50.00 125.00
4 1987 Canada Cup 50.00 125.00
5 Dual Jersey 60.00 150.00
6 Number
7 Emblem
8 Triple Jersey
9 Quad Jersey
10 Complete Package

2002-03 BAP Ultimate Memorabilia Magnificent Insert Autographs

This 10-card set paralleled the basic insert set but each card also carried a certified Mario Lemieux autograph. Cards 1-5 were serial-numbered to just 15 copies each and cards 6-10 were serial-numbered to just 5 copies each. This set is not priced due to scarcity.

1-5 PRINT RUN 15 SER.#'d SETS
6-10 PRINT RUN 5 SER.#'d SETS
NOT PRICED DUE TO SCARCITY

2002-03 BAP Ultimate Memorabilia Magnificent Ones

This 10-card set featured dual swatches of jerseys from Mario Lemieux and a player he recognized as one of the best in the game. Cards were serial-numbered to just 30 and each card was encapsulated in a clear plastic slab with a descriptive label encased at the top. The set is unnumbered and listed below in checklist order.

*MULT.COLOR SWATCH: .75X TO 1.5X
PRINT RUN 30 SER.#'d SETS
1 M.Lemieux/P.Roy 75.00 200.00
2 M.Lemieux/S.Yzerman 50.00 125.00
3 M.Lemieux/J.Jagr 25.00 60.00
4 M.Lemieux/M.Modano 25.00 60.00
5 M.Lemieux/M.Brodeur 60.00 150.00
6 M.Lemieux/P.Kariya 25.00 60.00
7 M.Lemieux/J.Sakic 25.00 60.00
8 M.Lemieux/P.Forsberg 25.00 60.00
9 M.Lemieux/P.Bure 25.00 60.00
10 M.Lemieux/B.Shanahan 25.00 60.00

2002-03 BAP Ultimate Memorabilia Magnificent Ones Autographs

PRINT RUN 10 SER.#'d SETS
NOT PRICED DUE TO SCARCITY
SIGNED BY LEMIEUX ONLY

2002-03 BAP Ultimate Memorabilia MVP Winner

Limited to only 10 copies, collectors could redeem this card for a memorabilia card of Peter Forsberg, the winner of the Hart trophy.

STATED PRINT RUN 10 SER.#'d SETS
NOT PRICED DUE TO SCARCITY
1 Peter Forsberg

2002-03 BAP Ultimate Memorabilia Nameplates

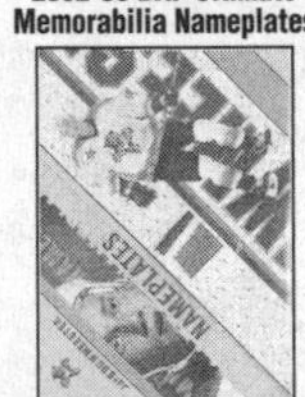

PRINT RUN 40 SER.#'d SETS
GOLD 1 OF 1's EXIST
1 Jaromir Jagr 30.00 80.00
2 Mike Modano 15.00 40.00
3 Joe Thornton 20.00 50.00
4 Nicklas Lidstrom 12.50 30.00
5 Jay Bouwmeester 10.00 25.00
6 Jason Spezza 25.00 60.00
7 Patrick Roy 40.00 100.00
8 Peter Forsberg 25.00 60.00
9 Steve Yzerman 40.00 100.00
10 Marian Hossa 12.50 30.00
11 Ilya Kovalchuk 25.00 60.00
12 Ed Belfour 12.50 30.00
13 Mario Lemieux 40.00 100.00
14 Joe Sakic 25.00 60.00
15 Marian Gaborik 30.00 80.00
16 Pavel Bure 12.50 30.00
17 Martin Brodeur 30.00 80.00
18 Markus Naslund 12.50 30.00
19 Curtis Joseph 12.50 30.00
20 Paul Kariya 12.50 30.00

2002-03 BAP Ultimate Memorabilia Number Ones

This 10-card set highlighted players who wore the jersey number one and featured a swatch of the jersey number. Cards were serial-numbered to just 10 and each card was encapsulated in a clear plastic slab with a descriptive label encased at the top. The set is unnumbered and listed below in checklist order. This set is not priced due to scarcity.

PRINT RUN 10 SER.#'d SETS
NOT PRICED DUE TO SCARCITY
1 Arturs Irbe
2 Ed Giacomin
3 Glenn Hall
4 Jacques Plante
5 Johan Hedberg
6 Roberto Luongo
7 Roger Crozier
8 Roman Turek
9 Sean Burke
10 Terry Sawchuk

2002-03 BAP Ultimate Memorabilia Numbers

PRINT RUN 10 SER.#'d SETS
NOT PRICED DUE TO SCARCITY
1 Mike Modano
2 Mario Lemieux
3 Sergei Fedorov
4 Ilya Kovalchuk
5 Patrick Roy
6 Jaromir Jagr
7 Eric Lindros
8 Peter Forsberg
9 Brendan Shanahan
10 Marian Gaborik
11 Markus Naslund
12 John LeClair
13 Saku Koivu
14 Chris Chelios
15 Dany Heatley
16 Brian Leetch
17 Mark Messier
18 Steve Yzerman
19 Pavel Bure
20 Valeri Kharlamov
21 Luc Robitaille
22 Paul Kariya
23 Brett Hull
24 Jeremy Roenick
25 Joe Sakic
26 Martin Brodeur
27 Mike Comrie
28 Joe Thornton
29 Mats Sundin
30 Nicklas Lidstrom

2002-03 BAP Ultimate Memorabilia Numerology

This 30-card set featured dual swatches of game-used jersey from the 2 featured players; who both wore the same jersey number. Cards were serial-numbered to just 40 and each card was encapsulated in a clear plastic slab with a descriptive label encased at the top. The set is unnumbered and listed below in checklist order.

*MULT.COLOR SWATCH: .75X TO 1.5X
PRINT RUN 40 SER.#'d SETS
1 Glenn Hall 15.00 40.00
Johan Hedberg
2 Terry Sawchuk 30.00 80.00
Roman Turek
3 Jacques Plante 20.00 50.00
Sean Burke
4 Bernie Parent 15.00 40.00
Roberto Luongo
5 Doug Harvey 15.00 40.00
Brian Leetch
6 Jean Beliveau 30.00 80.00
Vincent Lecavalier
7 Red Kelly 15.00 40.00
Rob Blake
8 Denis Potvin 15.00 40.00
Nicklas Lidstrom
9 Phil Esposito 30.00 80.00
Keith Tkachuk
10 Rod Gilbert 15.00 40.00
Gary Roberts
11 Maurice Richard 40.00 100.00
Paul Kariya
12 B.Hull/M.Modano 15.00 40.00
13 Johnny Bucyk 15.00 40.00
Pavel Bure
14 G.Lafleur/M.Gaborik 40.00 100.00
15 Alex Delvecchio 15.00 40.00
Ron Francis
16 Gilbert Perreault 15.00 40.00
Mark Messier
17 Yvan Cournoyer 15.00 40.00
Jarome Iginla
18 Marcel Dionne 15.00 40.00
Trevor Linden
19 Valeri Kharlamov 40.00 100.00
Ilya Kovalchuk
20 Serge Savard 15.00 40.00
Marian Hossa
21 L.Robinson/S.Yzerman 30.00 80.00
22 Bryan Trottier 15.00 40.00
Joe Sakic
23 Vladislav Tretiak 30.00 80.00
Ed Belfour
24 Stan Mikita 15.00 40.00
Peter Forsberg
25 Mike Bossy 15.00 40.00
Kristian Huselius
26 Bobby Nystrom 15.00 40.00
Milan Hejduk
27 Frank Mahovlich 15.00 40.00
Mike Peca
28 Billy Smith 15.00 40.00
Curtis Joseph
29 Grant Fuhr 40.00 100.00
Dan Blackburn
30 Tony Esposito 15.00 40.00
Marty Turco

2002-03 BAP Ultimate Memorabilia Paper Cuts Autographs

This 36-card set featured cut-signatures from some of the greatest legends in NHL history. Each card was a one-of-one and was encapsulated in a clear plastic slab with a descriptive label encased at the top. The set is unnumbered and listed below in checklist order. This set is not priced due to scarcity.

PRINT RUN 1 SET
NOT PRICED DUE TO SCARCITY
1 Harold Cotton
2 Toe Blake
3 Bun Cook
4 Bill Cook
5 Tiny Thompson
6 Ace Bailey
7 Bryan Hextall Sr.
8 Doug Harvey
9 Max Bentley
10 Harry Lumley
11 Sweeney Schriner
12 Bill Cowley
13 Flash Hollett
14 Jack Stewart
15 Bill Mosienko
16 Ebbie Goodfellow
17 Joe Primeau
18 Turk Broda
19 Busher Jackson
20 Ching Johnson
21 King Clancy
22 Terry Sawchuk
23 Neil Colville
24 Jacques Plante
25 Babe Pratt
26 Bill Barilko
27 Tim Horton
28 Hap Day
29 Sid Abel
30 Gordie Drillon
31 Harry Oliver
32 Syl Apps
33 Aurel Joliat
34 Charlie Conacher
35 Frank Boucher
36 Red Dutton

2002-03 BAP Ultimate Memorabilia Playoff Scorers

*MULT.COLOR SWATCH: .75X TO 1.5X
PRINT RUN 30 SER.#'d SETS
GOLD 1 OF 1's EXIST
1 Peter Forsberg 20.00 50.00
2 Joe Sakic 30.00 80.00
3 Brett Hull 20.00 50.00
4 Peter Forsberg 20.00 50.00
5 Steve Yzerman 30.00 80.00
6 Eric Lindros 15.00 40.00
7 Joe Sakic 30.00 80.00
8 Sergei Fedorov 20.00 50.00
9 Brian Leetch 15.00 40.00
10 Mario Lemieux 40.00 100.00
11 Mark Messier 15.00 40.00
12 Mike Bossy 25.00 60.00
13 Maurice Richard 40.00 100.00
14 Jean Beliveau 20.00 50.00
15 Brett Hull 25.00 60.00
16 Bryan Trottier 15.00 40.00
17 Mario Lemieux 40.00 100.00
18 Bobby Hull 25.00 60.00
19 Phil Esposito 30.00 80.00
20 Steve Yzerman 30.00 80.00

2002-03 BAP Ultimate Memorabilia Retro Teammates

PRINT RUN 30 SER.#'d SETS
1 Darryl Sittler 30.00 80.00

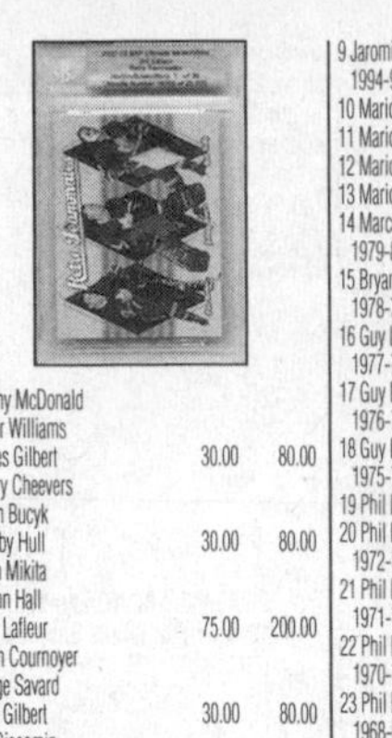

Lanny McDonald
Tiger Williams
2 Gilles Gilbert 30.00 80.00
Gerry Cheevers
John Bucyk
3 Bobby Hull 30.00 80.00
Stan Mikita
Glenn Hall
4 Guy Lafleur 75.00 200.00
Yvan Cournoyer
Serge Savard
5 Rod Gilbert 30.00 80.00
Ed Giacomin
Phil Esposito
6 Mario Lemieux 75.00 200.00
Jaromir Jagr
Ron Francis
7 Maurice Richard 75.00 200.00
JacquesPlante
Jean Beliveau
8 Tim Horton 75.00 200.00
Johnny Bower
Red Kelly
9 Dave Schultz 30.00 80.00
Bobby Clarke
Bernie Parent
10 Alex Delvecchio 30.00 80.00
Terry Sawchuk
Sid Abel

2002-03 BAP Ultimate Memorabilia Retro Trophies

*MULT.COLOR SWATCH: .75X TO 1.5X
PRINT RUN 40 SER.#'d SETS
UNLESS OTHERWISE NOTED
1 D.Heatley/M.Lemieux 40.00 100.00
2 Patrick Roy 75.00 200.00
Terry Sawchuk
3 Mike Peca 20.00 50.00
Bobby Clarke
4 Saku Koivu 20.00 50.00
Henri Richard
5 Paul Kariya 30.00 80.00
Marcel Dionne
6 Jaromir Jagr 20.00 50.00
Stan Mikita
7 S.Yzerman/J.Beliveau 25.00 60.00
8 Ed Belfour 20.00 50.00
Glenn Hall
9 M.Lemieux/H.Morenz/10
10 Jose Theodore 30.00 80.00
Jacques Plante
11 Nicklas Lidstrom 20.00 50.00
Larry Robinson
12 M.Lemieux/P.Esposito 40.00 100.00
13 Jarome Iginla 20.00 50.00
Bobby Hull
14 Mark Messier 20.00 50.00
Ron Hextall
15 Martin Brodeur 30.00 80.00
Frank Brimsek
16 Nicklas Lidstrom 20.00 50.00
Rogier Crozier
17 M.Lemieux/L.McDonald 40.00 100.00
18 Peter Forsberg 20.00 50.00
Bryan Trottier
19 Brett Hull 30.00 80.00
Bobby Hull
20 Joe Sakic 40.00 100.00
Maurice Richard

2002-03 BAP Ultimate Memorabilia Scoring Leaders

*MULT.COLOR SWATCH: .75X TO 1.5X
PRINT RUN 40 SER.#'d SETS
1 Peter Forsberg 25.00 60.00
2002-03
2 Jarome Iginla 15.00 40.00
2001-02
3 Mario Lemieux 2000-01 25.00 60.00
4 Jaromir Jagr 15.00 40.00
1999-00
5 Jaromir Jagr 15.00 40.00
1998-99
6 Jaromir Jagr 15.00 40.00
1997-98
7 Mario Lemieux 1996-97 25.00 60.00
8 Mario Lemieux 1995-96 25.00 60.00
9 Jaromir Jagr 15.00 40.00
1994-95
10 Mario Lemieux 1992-93 25.00 60.00
11 Mario Lemieux 1991-92 25.00 60.00
12 Mario Lemieux 1988-89 25.00 60.00
13 Mario Lemieux 1987-88 25.00 60.00
14 Marcel Dionne 12.50 30.00
1979-80
15 Bryan Trottier 12.50 30.00
1978-79
16 Guy Lafleur 12.50 30.00
1977-78
17 Guy Lafleur 12.50 30.00
1976-77
18 Guy Lafleur 12.50 30.00
1975-76
19 Phil Esposito 20.00 50.00
20 Phil Esposito 20.00 50.00
1972-73
21 Phil Esposito 20.00 50.00
1971-72
22 Phil Esposito 20.00 50.00
1970-71
23 Phil Esposito 20.00 50.00
1968-69
24 Stan Mikita 12.50 30.00
1967-68
25 Stan Mikita 12.50 30.00
1966-67
26 Bobby Hull 20.00 50.00
1965-66
27 Stan Mikita 12.50 30.00
1964-65
28 Stan Mikita 12.50 30.00
1963-64
29 Bobby Hull 20.00 50.00
1961-62
30 Bernie Geoffrion 12.50 30.00
1960-61
31 Bobby Hull 20.00 50.00
1959-60
32 Dickie Moore 12.50 30.00
1958-59
33 Dickie Moore 12.50 30.00
1957-58
34 Jean Beliveau 20.00 50.00
1956-57
35 Bernie Geoffrion 12.50 30.00
1955-56

2002-03 BAP Ultimate Memorabilia Seams Unbelievable

This 8-card set featured swatches of game-used jersey with the seam exposed. Cards were serial-numbered to just 10 and each card was encapsulated in a clear plastic slab with a descriptive label encased at the top. The set is unnumbered and listed below in checklist order. This set is not priced due to scarcity.

PRINT RUN 10 SER.#'d SETS
NOT PRICED DUE TO SCARCITY
1 Mario Lemieux
2 Ted Lindsay
3 Glenn Hall
4 George Hainsworth
5 Guy Lafleur
6 Gerry Cheevers
7 Bill Durnan
8 Bill Mosienko

2002-03 BAP Ultimate Memorabilia Storied Franchise

This 25-card set honored the Montreal Canadiens and featured a swatch of game-used memorabilia on the card fronts. Cards were serial-numbered to just 20 (unless otherwise noted below) and each card was encapsulated in a clear plastic slab with a descriptive label encased at the top. The set is unnumbered and listed below in checklist order. This set is not priced due to scarcity.

PRINT RUN 20 SER.#'d SETS
NOT PRICED DUE TO SCARCITY
1 Bernie Geoffrion
2 Charlie Hodge
3 Howie Morenz
4 Larry Robinson
5 Jacques Plante
6 John LeClair
7 Patrick Roy
8 Maurice Richard
9 Serge Savard
10 Bill Durnan
11 Guy Lafleur
12 Guy Lapointe
13 Lorne Worsley
14 George Hainsworth
15 Jacques Laperriere
16 Yvan Cournoyer
17 Henri Richard
18 Frank Mahovlich

19 Doug Harvey
20 Rogie Vachon
21 Steve Shutt
22 Jean Beliveau
23 Henri Richard
24 Georges Vezina/10
25 Aurel Joliat

2002-03 BAP Ultimate Memorabilia Vezina Winner

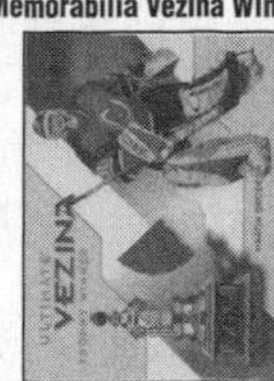

Limited to only 10 copies, collectors could redeem this card for a memorabilia card of the winner of the Vezina trophy.

PRINT RUN 10 SER.#'d SETS
NOT PRICED DUE TO SCARCITY
1 Martin Brodeur

2002-03 BAP Ultimate Memorabilia Vintage Hat Tricks

This 6-card set featured 3 pieces of game-used memorabilia from the featured player. Cards were serial-numbered to just 10 and each card was encapsulated in a clear plastic slab with a descriptive label encased at the top. The set is unnumbered and listed below in checklist order. This set is not priced due to scarcity.

PRINT RUN 10 SER.#'d SETS
NOT PRICED DUE TO SCARCITY
1 Eddie Shore
2 Aurel Joliat
3 Rocket Richard
4 Tim Horton
5 Guy Lafleur
6 Jean Beliveau

2002-03 BAP Ultimate Memorabilia Vintage Jerseys

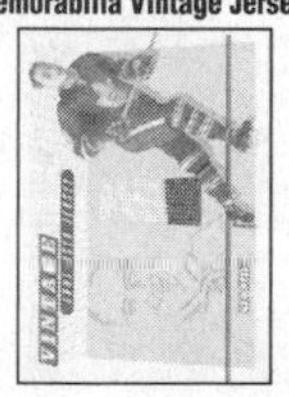

This 40-card set featured jersey swatches from past hockey greats. Cards were serial-numbered to just 40 and each card was encapsulated in a clear plastic slab with a descriptive label encased at the top. The set is unnumbered and listed below in checklist order. Unpriced gold one of one's exist.

*MULT.COLOR SWATCH: .75X TO 1.5X
PRINT RUN 40 SER.#'d SETS
UNPRICED GOLD 1 OF 1's EXIST

1 Stan Mikita	12.50	30.00
2 Alex Delvecchio	12.50	30.00
3 Aurel Joliat	30.00	80.00
4 Bernie Parent	12.50	30.00
5 Bill Barber	12.50	30.00
6 Bobby Clarke	12.50	30.00
7 Bobby Hull	12.50	30.00
8 Bryan Trottier	12.50	30.00
9 Dennis Hull	12.50	30.00
10 Doug Harvey	12.50	30.00
11 Ed Giacomin	12.50	30.00
12 Frank Brimsek	12.50	30.00
13 Frank Mahovlich	12.50	30.00
14 George Hainsworth	20.00	50.00
15 Gerry Cheevers	12.50	30.00
16 Gilbert Perreault	12.50	30.00
17 Glenn Hall	12.50	30.00
18 Guy Lafleur	12.50	30.00
19 Harry Lumley	20.00	50.00
20 Henri Richard	12.50	30.00
21 Jacques Plante	30.00	80.00
22 Jean Beliveau	25.00	60.00
23 John Bucyk	12.50	30.00
24 Lanny McDonald	12.50	30.00
25 Larry Robinson	12.50	30.00
26 Marcel Dionne	12.50	30.00
27 Maurice Richard	30.00	80.00
28 Mike Bossy	12.50	30.00
29 Peter Mahovlich	12.50	30.00
30 Phil Esposito	12.50	30.00
31 Red Kelly	20.00	50.00
32 Roger Crozier	12.50	30.00
33 Roy Worters	20.00	50.00
34 Sid Abel	12.50	30.00
35 Ted Lindsay	12.50	30.00
36 Terry Sawchuk	50.00	125.00
37 Tim Horton	30.00	80.00
38 Tony Esposito	12.50	30.00
39 Valeri Kharlamov	25.00	60.00
40 Vladislav Tretiak	40.00	100.00

2002-03 BAP Ultimate Memorabilia Vintage Jersey Autographs

PRINT RUN 10 SER.#'d SETS
NOT PRICED DUE TO SCARCITY
1 Jean Beliveau
2 John Bucyk
3 Marcel Dionne
4 Ed Giacomin
5 Glenn Hall
6 Red Kelly
7 Guy Lafleur
8 Ted Lindsay
9 Frank Mahovlich
10 Stan Mikita
11 Henri Richard
12 Bobby Hull
13 Phil Esposito

2003-04 BAP Ultimate Memorabilia Autographs

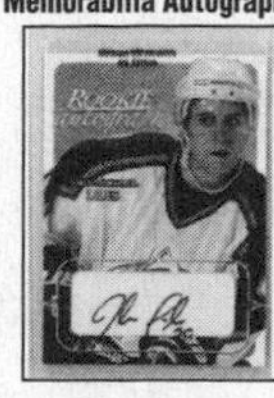

Each pack of Ultimate contained one memorabilia card that was slabbed by BGS and one unslabbed card of either an auto, gold auto, auto/jersey, auto/stick, auto/emblem or auto/number. The auto/memorabilia cards were found in sealed toploaders.

1-89 PRINT RUN 135 SER.#'d SETS
ROOKIE AU PRINT RUN 100 SER.#'d SETS
131-165 PRINT RUN 19 SER.#'d SETS

1 Alexei Kovalev	6.00	15.00
2 Shane Doan	6.00	15.00
3 Ales Hemsky	6.00	15.00
4 Ray Whitney	6.00	15.00
5 Alexander Frolov	6.00	15.00
6 Mike Peca	6.00	15.00
7 Chris Drury	6.00	15.00
8 Chris Osgood	6.00	15.00
9 Andrew Raycroft	10.00	25.00
10 Rick DiPietro	6.00	15.00
11 Chuck Kobasew	6.00	15.00
12 Vincent Lecavalier	8.00	20.00
13 Olaf Kolzig	8.00	20.00
14 Erik Cole	6.00	15.00
15 Ryan Smyth	6.00	15.00
16 Anson Carter	6.00	15.00
17 Jocelyn Thibault	6.00	15.00
18 Alexei Yashin	6.00	15.00
19 David Aebischer	6.00	15.00
20 Chris Pronger	6.00	15.00
21 Ron Francis	6.00	15.00
22 Markus Naslund	8.00	20.00
23 Tommy Salo	6.00	15.00
24 Patrick Lalime	6.00	15.00
25 Joe Nieuwendyk	6.00	15.00
26 Vincent Damphousse	6.00	15.00
27 Bill Guerin	6.00	15.00
28 Jeremy Roenick	15.00	40.00
29 Barret Jackman	6.00	15.00
30 Curtis Joseph	8.00	20.00
31 Jason Spezza	12.50	30.00
32 Sergei Fedorov	15.00	40.00
33 Gary Roberts	6.00	15.00
34 Glen Murray	6.00	15.00
35 Adam Oates	6.00	15.00
36 Felix Potvin	8.00	20.00
37 Eric Brewer	6.00	15.00
38 Jeff O'Neill	6.00	15.00
39 Tomas Vokoun	8.00	20.00
40 Olli Jokinen	6.00	15.00
41 Martin Prusek	6.00	15.00
42 Sergei Gonchar	6.00	15.00
43 Kevin Weekes	6.00	15.00
44 Roman Cechmanek	6.00	15.00
45 Scott Stevens	6.00	15.00
46 Dwayne Roloson	6.00	15.00
47 Martin Biron	6.00	15.00
48 Keith Tkachuk	6.00	15.00
49 Pasi Nurminen	6.00	15.00
50 Saku Koivu	8.00	20.00
51 David Legwand	6.00	15.00
52 Jay Bouwmeester	6.00	15.00
53 Patrik Elias	6.00	15.00
54 Zigmund Palffy	6.00	15.00
55 Tyler Arnason	6.00	15.00
56 Sergei Samsonov	6.00	15.00
57 Ryan Miller	15.00	40.00
58 Mike Dunham	6.00	15.00
59 Nikolai Khabibulin	8.00	20.00
60 Roman Turek	6.00	15.00
61 Marian Hossa	8.00	20.00
62 Marc Denis	6.00	15.00
63 Peter Bondra	10.00	25.00
64 Marty Turco	8.00	20.00
65 John LeClair	8.00	20.00
66 Johan Hedberg	6.00	15.00
67 Sean Burke	6.00	15.00
68 Ed Jovanovski	6.00	15.00
69 Tony Amonte	6.00	15.00
70 Daymond Langkow	6.00	15.00
71 Miroslav Satan	6.00	15.00
72 Jean-Sebastien Giguere	6.00	15.00
73 Evgeni Nabokov	6.00	15.00
74 Rostislav Klesla	6.00	15.00
75 Al MacInnis	6.00	15.00
76 Niko Kapanen	6.00	15.00
77 Manny Fernandez	6.00	15.00
78 Milan Hejduk	8.00	20.00
79 Doug Weight	6.00	15.00
80 Jarome Iginla	12.50	30.00
81 Martin St. Louis	8.00	20.00
82 Daniel Alfredsson	8.00	20.00
83 Marian Gaborik	12.50	30.00
84 Rob Blake	6.00	15.00
85 Dan Cloutier	6.00	15.00
86 Simon Gagne	8.00	20.00
87 Mark Recchi	6.00	15.00
88 Teemu Selanne	8.00	20.00
89 Todd Bertuzzi	8.00	20.00
90 Chris Kunitz	10.00	25.00
91 Eric Staal	60.00	120.00
92 Nathan Horton	15.00	40.00
93 Andrew Peters	10.00	25.00
94 Alexander Semin	25.00	60.00
95 Matthew Lombardi	10.00	25.00
96 Joffrey Lupul	15.00	40.00
97 John-Michael Liles	10.00	25.00
98 Jiri Hudler	12.50	30.00
99 Tuomo Ruutu	15.00	40.00
100 Anton Babchuk	10.00	25.00
101 Dan Fritsche	10.00	25.00
102 Derek Roy	12.50	30.00
103 Paul Martin	10.00	25.00
104 Pavel Vorobiev	10.00	25.00
105 Matthew Spiller	10.00	25.00
106 Patrice Bergeron	25.00	60.00
107 Chris Higgins	25.00	60.00
108 Noah Clarke	10.00	25.00
109 Nikolai Zherdev	15.00	30.00
110 Brent Burns	10.00	25.00
111 Dustin Brown	10.00	25.00
112 Michael Ryder	20.00	50.00
113 Joni Pitkanen	12.00	30.00
114 Jordin Tootoo	25.00	60.00
115 Ryan Malone	10.00	25.00
116 David Hale	10.00	25.00
117 Antti Miettinen	10.00	25.00
118 Doug Lynch	10.00	25.00
119 Tim Gleason	10.00	25.00
120 Dan Hamhuis	10.00	25.00
121 Fredrik Sjostrom	10.00	25.00
122 Kari Lehtonen	50.00	125.00
123 Marc-Andre Fleury	40.00	100.00
124 Marek Zidlicky	10.00	25.00
125 Milan Michalek	15.00	40.00
126 Matt Stajan	20.00	50.00
127 Peter Sarno	10.00	25.00
128 Antoine Vermette	10.00	25.00
129 Boyd Gordon	10.00	25.00
130 Kyle Wellwood	25.00	60.00
131 Steve Yzerman		
132 Rick Nash		
133 Roberto Luongo		
134 Joe Thornton		
135 Joe Sakic		
136 Pavel Datsyuk		
137 Martin Brodeur		
138 Mike Modano		
139 Brian Leetch		
140 Peter Forsberg		
141 Owen Nolan		
142 Brett Hull		
143 Jaromir Jagr		
144 Dominik Hasek		
145 Ilya Kovalchuk		
146 Jose Theodore		
147 Mario Lemieux		
148 Mats Sundin		
149 Eric Lindros		
150 Henrik Zetterberg		
151 Dany Heatley		
152 Nicklas Lidstrom		
153 Bobby Orr		
154 Ted Kennedy		
155 Ray Bourque		
156 Jean Beliveau		
157 Tony Esposito		
158 Patrick Roy		
159 Ted Lindsay		
160 Frank Mahovlich		
161 Guy Lafleur		
162 Henri Richard		
163 Maurice Richard		
164 Phil Esposito		
165 Johnny Bower		

2003-04 BAP Ultimate Memorabilia Autographs Gold

*GOLD 1-89: 1X TO 2.5X BASE HI
1-89 PRINT RUN 35 SER.#'d SETS
*GOLD 90-130: .6X TO 1.5X
90-130 PRINT RUN 20 SER.#'d SETS
131-165 PRINT RUN 1 SET

2003-04 BAP Ultimate Memorabilia Autographed Jerseys

10-89/PRINT RUN 30 SER.#'d SETS
91-129 PRINT RUN 20 SER.#'d SETS
91-129 NOT PRICED DUE TO SCARCITY

10 Rick DiPietro	20.00	50.00
12 Vincent Lecavalier	30.00	80.00
13 Olaf Kolzig	25.00	60.00
17 Jocelyn Thibault	20.00	50.00
19 David Aebischer	20.00	50.00
20 Chris Pronger	20.00	50.00
21 Ron Francis	20.00	50.00
22 Markus Naslund	25.00	60.00
24 Patrick Lalime	20.00	50.00
27 Bill Guerin	20.00	50.00
28 Jeremy Roenick	30.00	80.00
29 Barret Jackman	20.00	50.00
30 Curtis Joseph	25.00	60.00
31 Jason Spezza	25.00	60.00
33 Gary Roberts	20.00	50.00
39 Tomas Vokoun	20.00	50.00
48 Keith Tkachuk	25.00	60.00
50 Saku Koivu	25.00	60.00
52 Jay Bouwmeester	20.00	50.00
56 Sergei Samsonov	20.00	50.00
57 Ryan Miller	25.00	60.00
58 Mike Dunham	20.00	50.00
59 Nikolai Khabibulin	25.00	60.00
60 Roman Turek	20.00	50.00
61 Marian Hossa	25.00	60.00
62 Marc Denis	20.00	50.00
65 John LeClair	25.00	60.00
66 Johan Hedberg	20.00	50.00
68 Ed Jovanovski	20.00	50.00
69 Tony Amonte	20.00	50.00
72 Jean-Sebastien Giguere	20.00	50.00
75 Al MacInnis	20.00	50.00
77 Manny Fernandez	20.00	50.00
78 Milan Hejduk	25.00	60.00
79 Doug Weight	20.00	50.00
81 Martin St.Louis	25.00	60.00
82 Daniel Alfredsson	20.00	50.00
83 Marian Gaborik	40.00	100.00
85 Dan Cloutier	20.00	50.00
86 Simon Gagne	20.00	50.00
87 Mark Recchi	20.00	50.00
88 Teemu Selanne	30.00	80.00
89 Todd Bertuzzi	25.00	60.00
91 Eric Staal		
92 Nathan Horton		
94 Alexander Semin		
95 Matthew Lombardi		
96 Joffrey Lupul		
99 Tuomo Ruutu		
101 Dan Fritsche		
102 Derek Roy		
106 Patrice Bergeron		
107 Christopher Higgins		
109 Nikolai Zherdev		
110 Brent Burns		
111 Dustin Brown		
112 Michael Ryder		
113 Joni Pitkanen		
114 Jordin Tootoo		
115 Ryan Malone		
119 Tim Gleason		
120 Dan Hamhuis		
126 Matt Stajan		
128 Antoine Vermette		
129 Boyd Gordon		
131 Steve Yzerman	50.00	125.00
132 Rick Nash	30.00	80.00
133 Roberto Luongo	30.00	80.00
134 Joe Thornton	30.00	80.00
135 Joe Sakic	40.00	100.00
136 Pavel Datsyuk	25.00	60.00
137 Martin Brodeur	100.00	200.00
138 Mike Modano	30.00	80.00
139 Brian Leetch	25.00	60.00
140 Peter Forsberg	40.00	100.00
141 Owen Nolan	20.00	50.00
142 Brett Hull	30.00	80.00
144 Dominik Hasek	40.00	100.00
145 Ilya Kovalchuk	30.00	80.00
146 Jose Theodore	25.00	60.00
147 Mario Lemieux	75.00	200.00
148 Mats Sundin	25.00	60.00
149 Eric Lindros	25.00	60.00
150 Henrik Zetterberg	30.00	80.00
151 Dany Heatley	30.00	80.00
152 Nicklas Lidstrom	30.00	80.00
153 Bobby Orr	175.00	400.00
155 Ray Bourque	40.00	100.00
157 Tony Esposito	30.00	80.00
158 Patrick Roy	125.00	250.00
165 Johnny Bower	30.00	80.00

2003-04 BAP Ultimate Memorabilia Autographed Emblems

PRINT RUN 10 SER.#'d SETS
NOT PRICED DUE TO SCARCITY
12 Vincent Lecavalier
20 Chris Pronger
22 Markus Naslund
27 Bill Guerin
28 Jeremy Roenick
31 Jason Spezza
48 Keith Tkachuk
64 Marty Turco
65 John LeClair
78 Milan Hejduk
79 Doug Weight
81 Martin St. Louis
82 Daniel Alfredsson
83 Marian Gaborik
89 Todd Bertuzzi
91 Eric Staal
92 Nathan Horton
94 Alexander Semin
95 Matthew Lombardi
96 Joffrey Lupul
99 Tuomo Ruutu
101 Dan Fritsche
102 Derek Roy
106 Patrice Bergeron
107 Christopher Higgins
109 Nikolai Zherdev
110 Brent Burns
111 Dustin Brown
112 Michael Ryder
113 Joni Pitkanen
114 Jordin Tootoo
115 Ryan Malone
119 Tim Gleason
120 Dan Hamhuis
126 Matt Stajan
128 Antoine Vermette
129 Boyd Gordon
131 Steve Yzerman
132 Rick Nash
133 Roberto Luongo
134 Joe Thornton
135 Joe Sakic
136 Pavel Datsyuk
137 Martin Brodeur
138 Mike Modano
139 Brian Leetch
140 Peter Forsberg
141 Owen Nolan
142 Brett Hull
144 Dominik Hasek
145 Ilya Kovalchuk
146 Jose Theodore
147 Mario Lemieux
148 Mats Sundin
149 Eric Lindros
150 Henrik Zetterberg
151 Dany Heatley
152 Nicklas Lidstrom
153 Bobby Orr
155 Ray Bourque
158 Patrick Roy

2003-04 BAP Ultimate Memorabilia Autographed Numbers

PRINT RUN 20 SER.#'d SETS
NOT PRICED DUE TO SCARCITY
91 Eric Staal
92 Nathan Horton
94 Alexander Semin
95 Matthew Lombardi
96 Joffrey Lupul
99 Tuomo Ruutu
101 Dan Fritsche
102 Derek Roy
106 Patrice Bergeron
107 Christopher Higgins
109 Nikolai Zherdev
110 Brent Burns
111 Dustin Brown
112 Michael Ryder
113 Joni Pitkanen
114 Jordin Tootoo
115 Ryan Malone
119 Tim Gleason
120 Dan Hamhuis
126 Matt Stajan
128 Antoine Vermette
129 Boyd Gordon

2003-04 BAP Ultimate Memorabilia Autographed Sticks

PRINT RUN 30 SER.#'d SETS

32 Sergei Fedorov	25.00	60.00
45 Scott Stevens	40.00	100.00
56 Sergei Samsonov	15.00	40.00
86 Simon Gagne	15.00	40.00
123 Marc-Andre Fleury	30.00	80.00
131 Steve Yzerman	40.00	100.00
132 Rick Nash	30.00	80.00
134 Joe Thornton	25.00	60.00
135 Joe Sakic	30.00	80.00
136 Pavel Datsyuk	25.00	60.00
138 Mike Modano	20.00	50.00
140 Peter Forsberg	25.00	60.00
142 Brett Hull	30.00	80.00
143 Jaromir Jagr	50.00	125.00
145 Ilya Kovalchuk	30.00	80.00
147 Mario Lemieux	75.00	200.00
151 Dany Heatley	25.00	60.00
153 Bobby Orr	150.00	350.00
158 Patrick Roy	125.00	250.00
165 Johnny Bower	25.00	60.00

2003-04 BAP Ultimate Memorabilia Active Eight

PRINT RUN 30 SER.#'d SETS

1 Belfour/Brodeur/Hasek	50.00	125.00
2 Belfour/Joseph/Brodeur	50.00	125.00
3 Lemieux/Hull/Mogilny	40.00	100.00
4 Sundin/Lidstrom/Forsberg	30.00	80.00
5 Lemieux/Messier/Forsberg	50.00	125.00
6 Yzerman/Sakic/Stevens	40.00	100.00
7 Roenick/Modano/Leetch	30.00	80.00
8 Lemieux/Hull/Yzerman	50.00	125.00

2003-04 BAP Ultimate Memorabilia Always An All-Star

PRINT RUN 50 SER.#'d SETS
UNPRICED GOLD 1/1's EXIST

1 Martin Brodeur	25.00	60.00
2 Mike Modano	15.00	40.00
3 Brian Leetch	12.50	30.00
4 Brett Hull	20.00	50.00
5 Al MacInnis	12.50	30.00
6 Paul Kariya	12.50	30.00
7 Eric Lindros	12.50	30.00
8 Teemu Selanne	12.50	30.00
9 Nicklas Lidstrom	12.50	30.00
10 Sergei Fedorov	12.50	30.00
11 Patrick Roy	30.00	80.00
12 Peter Forsberg	20.00	50.00
13 Mark Messier	20.00	50.00
14 Jaromir Jagr	15.00	40.00
15 Ray Bourque	25.00	60.00
16 Mario Lemieux	40.00	100.00
17 Brendan Shanahan	12.50	30.00
18 Chris Pronger	12.50	30.00
19 Dominik Hasek	15.00	40.00
20 Mats Sundin	12.50	30.00

2003-04 BAP Ultimate Memorabilia Blades of Steel

This 7-card set featured swatches of game-used skates. Each card was limited to just 20 copies.

PRINT RUN 20 SER.#'d SETS
NOT PRICED DUE TO SCARCITY
1 Mario Lemieux
2 Henrik Zetterberg
3 Al MacInnis
4 Pavel Bure
5 Jarome Iginla
6 Raymond Bourque
7 Pavel Datsyuk

2003-04 BAP Ultimate Memorabilia Bleu,Blanc et Rouge

This 18-card set featured "cut" autographs of legendary Canadiens players. Each card was a 1/1.

PRINT RUN 1 SET
NOT PRICED DUE TO SCARCITY
1 Aurel Joliat
2 Jacques Plante
3 Sylvio Mantha
4 Newsy Lalonde
5 Johnny Gagnon
6 Toe Blake
7 Doug Harvey
8 Ken Reardon
9 Maurice Richard
10 George Hainsworth
11 Jean Beliveau
12 Guy Lafleur
13 Bill Durnan
14 Phil Watson
15 Murph Chamberlain
16 Elmer Lach
17 Dick Irvin
18 Patrick Roy

2003-04 BAP Ultimate Memorabilia Calder Candidates

PRINT RUN 50 SER.#'d SETS
UNPRICED GOLD 1/1's EXIST

1 Andrew Raycroft	10.00	25.00
2 Eric Staal	15.00	40.00
3 Michael Ryder	15.00	40.00
4 Marc-Andre Fleury	20.00	50.00
5 Ryan Malone	10.00	25.00
6 Trent Hunter	10.00	25.00
7 Patrice Bergeron	15.00	40.00
8 Joni Pitkanen	10.00	25.00
9 Matthew Lombardi	10.00	25.00
10 Nikolai Zherdev	12.00	30.00
11 Tuomo Ruutu	12.00	30.00
12 Joffrey Lupul	10.00	25.00

2003-04 BAP Ultimate Memorabilia Career Year

PRINT RUN 40 SER.#'d SETS

1 Martin Brodeur	30.00	80.00
2 Cam Neely	15.00	40.00
3 Ray Bourque	15.00	40.00
4 Patrick Roy	30.00	80.00
5 Rick Nash	20.00	50.00
6 Steve Yzerman	30.00	80.00
7 Bobby Orr	60.00	150.00
8 Mario Lemieux	40.00	100.00

2003-04 BAP Ultimate Memorabilia Complete Jersey

PRINT RUN 30 SER.#'d SETS
UNPRICED GOLD 1/1's EXIST

1 Joe Thornton	40.00	100.00
2 Mario Lemieux	100.00	250.00
3 Marian Gaborik	50.00	125.00
4 Brett Hull	40.00	100.00
5 Dany Heatley	40.00	100.00
6 Joe Sakic	60.00	150.00
7 Paul Kariya	30.00	80.00
8 Steve Yzerman	60.00	150.00
9 Rick Nash	50.00	125.00
10 Nicklas Lidstrom	30.00	80.00
11 Sergei Fedorov	40.00	100.00
12 Patrick Roy	75.00	200.00
13 Peter Forsberg	50.00	125.00
14 Henrik Zetterberg	30.00	80.00
15 Dominik Hasek	40.00	100.00
16 Martin Brodeur	75.00	150.00
17 Mike Modano	40.00	100.00
18 Brendan Shanahan	30.00	80.00
19 Ilya Kovalchuk	50.00	125.00
20 Saku Koivu	30.00	80.00

2003-04 BAP Ultimate Memorabilia Complete Package

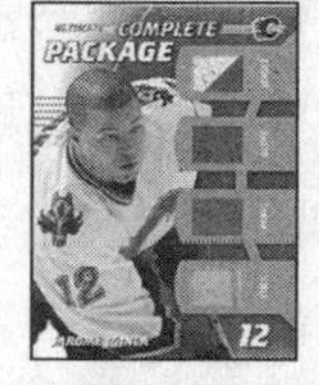

This 11-card set featured 4 different swatches per card from the featured player's equipment. Included in the memorabilia were items such as skates, jerseys, sticks, pants, socks, and pads. Cards were limited to 10 copies each.

PRINT RUN 10 SER.#'d SETS
NOT PRICED DUE TO SCARCITY
UNPRICED GOLD 1/1's EXIST
1 Mario Lemieux
2 Steve Yzerman
3 Nikolai Khabibulin
4 Al MacInnis
5 Jarome Iginla
6 Mats Sundin
7 Marty Turco
8 Eric Lindros
9 Curtis Joseph
10 José Théodore
11 David Aebischer

2003-04 BAP Ultimate Memorabilia Cornerstones

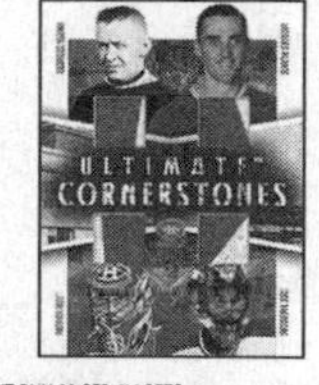

PRINT RUN 20 SER.#'d SETS
NOT PRICED DUE TO SCARCITY
1 Vezina/Plante/Roy/Theodore
2 Plante/Richard/Harvey/Beliveau
3 H.Richard/Lafleur/Robinson/Savard
4 Bower/F.Mahovlich/Kelly/Horton
5 Shore/Orr/Bourque/Thornton
6 Brimsek/Lumley/Hall/Esposito
7 Lindsay/Sawchuk/Delvecchio/Yzerman
8 Bossy/Trottier/Potvin/Smith

2003-04 BAP Ultimate Memorabilia Dynamic Duos

PRINT RUN 30 SER.#'d SETS

1 T.Selanne/S.Koivu	20.00	50.00
2 M.Sundin/P.Forsberg	20.00	50.00
3 M.Lemieux/S.Yzerman	50.00	125.00
4 J.Sakic/B.Shanahan	20.00	50.00
5 E.Lindros/P.Kariya	20.00	50.00
6 J.Roenick/K.Tkachuk	20.00	50.00
7 I.Kovalchuk/S.Fedorov	20.00	50.00
8 R.Nash/J.Thornton	20.00	50.00
9 B.Hull/M.Modano	20.00	50.00
10 M.Messier/J.Spezza	20.00	50.00

2003-04 BAP Ultimate Memorabilia Emblem Attic

PRINT RUN 5 SER.#'d SETS
NOT PRICED DUE TO SCARCITY
UNPRICED GOLD 1/1's EXIST
1 Bobby Orr
2 Johnny Bower
3 Roy Worters
4 Raymond Bourque
5 Roger Crozier
6 Frank Brimsek
7 Harry Lumley
8 Sid Abel
9 Jean Beliveau
10 Gump Worsley
11 Henri Richard
12 George Hainsworth
13 Aurel Joliat
14 Terry Sawchuk
15 Jacques Plante
16 Tony Esposito
17 Bobby Hull
18 Marcel Dionne
19 Frank Mahovlich
20 Glenn Hall

2003-04 BAP Ultimate Memorabilia Emblems

PRINT RUN 10 SER.#'d SETS
NOT PRICED DUE TO SCARCITY
UNPRICED GOLD 1/1's EXIST
1 Dany Heatley
2 Dominik Hasek
3 Ed Belfour
4 Eric Lindros
5 Henrik Zetterberg
6 Ilya Kovalchuk
7 Jarome Iginla
8 Jason Spezza
9 Joe Sakic
10 Joe Thornton
11 Jose Theodore
12 Brian Leetch
13 Marian Gaborik
14 Mario Lemieux
15 Markus Naslund
16 Martin Brodeur
17 Mats Sundin
18 Mike Modano
19 Nicklas Lidstrom
20 Paul Kariya
21 Pavel Datsyuk
22 Peter Forsberg
23 Rick Nash
24 Rob Blake
25 Roberto Luongo
26 Saku Koivu
27 Sergei Fedorov
28 Steve Yzerman
29 Todd Bertuzzi
30 Vincent Lecavalier

2003-04 BAP Ultimate Memorabilia First Trophy Winners

This 9-card set featured "cut" signatures of players who were the first to win league trophies. Cards were 1/1's.

PRINT RUN 1 SET
NOT PRICED DUE TO SCARCITY
1 Elmer Lach
2 Syl Apps
3 Frank Nighbor
4 Red Kelly
5 George Hainsworth
6 Jean Beliveau
7 Phil Esposito
8 Fred Shero
9 Jack Adams

2003-04 BAP Ultimate Memorabilia Franchise Present and Future

PRINT RUN 40 SER.#'d SETS
1 S.Fedorov/J.Lupul 15.00 40.00
2 I.Kovalchuk/D.Heatley 25.00 60.00
3 J.Thornton/P.Bergeron 20.00 50.00
4 M.Satan/D.Roy 12.00 30.00
5 J.Iginla/M.Lombardi 15.00 40.00

6 J.O'Neill/E.Staal 15.00 40.00
7 J.Thibault/T.Ruutu 12.00 30.00
8 P.Forsberg/D.Aebischer 15.00 40.00
9 R.Nash/N.Zherdev 20.00 50.00
10 M.Modano/S.Ott 15.00 40.00
11 S.Yzerman/P.Datsyuk 30.00 80.00
12 R.Smyth/A.Hemsky 12.00 30.00
13 R.Luongo/J.Bouwmeester 20.00 50.00
14 Z.Palffy/A.Frolov 15.00 40.00
15 M.Gaborik/P.Bouchard 25.00 60.00
16 J.Theodore/M.Ryder 20.00 50.00
17 D.Legwand/J.Tootoo 15.00 40.00
18 M.Brodeur/P.Martin 30.00 80.00
19 A.Yashin/R.DiPietro 15.00 40.00
20 M.Messier/F.Tyutin 20.00 50.00
21 M.Hossa/J.Spezza 15.00 40.00
22 J.LeClair/J.Pitkanen 12.00 30.00
23 S.Doan/B.Boucher 12.00 30.00
24 M.Lemieux/M.Fleury 50.00 125.00
25 C.Pronger/B.Jackman 12.00 30.00
26 E.Nabokov/J.Cheechoo 25.00 60.00
27 N.Khabibulin/V.Lecavalier 15.00 40.00
28 M.Sundin/M.Stajan 15.00 40.00
29 M.Naslund/A.Auld 15.00 40.00
30 O.Kolzig/A.Semin 15.00 40.00

2003-04 BAP Ultimate Memorabilia Gloves Are Off

PRINT RUN 25 SER.#'d SETS
1 Joe Thornton 20.00 50.00
2 Brett Hull 20.00 50.00
3 Mario Lemieux 30.00 80.00
4 Joe Sakic 20.00 50.00
5 Jarome Iginla 20.00 50.00
6 Sergei Samsonov 15.00 40.00
7 Mats Sundin 15.00 40.00
8 Eric Lindros 15.00 40.00
9 Rob Blake 15.00 40.00
10 John LeClair 15.00 40.00
11 Stan Mikita 15.00 40.00
12 Bill Gadsby 15.00 40.00
13 Aurel Joliat 25.00 60.00
14 Bernie Geoffrion 15.00 40.00
15 Dickie Moore 15.00 40.00
16 Howie Morenz 50.00 125.00
17 Doug Harvey 20.00 50.00
18 King Clancy 30.00 80.00
19 Ray Bourque 15.00 40.00
20 Eddie Shore 30.00 80.00

2003-04 BAP Ultimate Memorabilia Great Moments

COMMON CARD(1-12) 12.50 30.00
PRINT RUN 40 SER.#'d SETS
1 Bobby Orr 50.00 125.00
2 S.Mikita/B.Hull 25.00 60.00
3 Patrick Roy 30.00 80.00
4 Steve Yzerman 25.00 60.00
5 M.Messier/J.Theodore 25.00 60.00
6 Ray Bourque 15.00 40.00
7 B.Clarke/B.Barber 15.00 40.00
8 Henri Richard 12.50 30.00
9 Mike Bossy 15.00 40.00
10 Maurice Richard 30.00 80.00
11 Mark Messier 25.00 60.00
12 Cam Neely 20.00 50.00

2003-04 BAP Ultimate Memorabilia Hat Tricks

This 20-card set featured three different pieces of memorabilia. Cards were limited to 30 cards each.

PRINT RUN 30 SER.#'d SETS
1 Keith Tkachuk 15.00 40.00
2 Henrik Zetterberg 25.00 60.00
3 Alexei Yashin 12.50 30.00
4 Mats Sundin 15.00 40.00
5 Joe Thornton 25.00 60.00
6 Pavel Datsyuk 25.00 60.00
7 Joe Sakic 30.00 80.00
8 Mario Lemieux 50.00 125.00
9 Milan Hejduk 15.00 40.00
10 Eric Lindros 15.00 40.00
11 Jarome Iginla 25.00 60.00
12 Steve Yzerman 40.00 100.00
13 Sergei Samsonov 12.50 30.00
14 Brett Hull 25.00 60.00
15 Chris Chelios 15.00 40.00
16 Al MacInnis 12.50 30.00
17 Doug Weight 12.50 30.00
18 John LeClair 15.00 40.00
19 Rob Blake 12.50 30.00
20 Scott Niedermayer 15.00 40.00

2003-04 BAP Ultimate Memorabilia Heroes

PRINT RUN 30 SER.#'d SETS
UNPRICED AUTO 1/1's EXIST
1 Ilya Kovalchuk 30.00 80.00
Valeri Kharlamov
2 J.Thornton/S.Yzerman 25.00 60.00
3 Jarome Iginla 20.00 50.00
Mark Messier
4 S.Yzerman/B.Trottier 25.00 60.00
5 M.Lemieux/G.Lafleur 40.00 100.00
6 R.Nash/M.Sundin 20.00 50.00
7 Dany Heatley 20.00 50.00
Brett Hull
8 Patrick Roy 50.00 125.00
Jacques Plante
9 Terry Sawchuk 40.00 100.00
George Hainsworth
10 Jose Theodore 40.00 100.00
Patrick Roy
11 Roberto Luongo 40.00 100.00
Patrick Roy
12 Ed Belfour 30.00 80.00
Vladislav Tretiak
13 M.Brodeur/P.Roy 40.00 100.00
14 Mike Richter 20.00 50.00
Gerry Cheevers
15 Teemu Selanne 30.00 80.00
Jari Kurri
16 Alex Tanguay 25.00 60.00
Joe Sakic
17 P.Marleau/M.Lemieux 30.00 80.00
18 V.Lecavalier/S.Yzerman 25.00 60.00
19 M.St.Louis/M.Lemieux 30.00 80.00
20 Tuomo Ruutu 20.00 50.00
Peter Forsberg

2003-04 BAP Ultimate Memorabilia Hometown Heroes

PRINT RUN 50 SER.#'d SETS
UNPRICED GOLD 1/1's EXIST
1 Maurice Richard 40.00 100.00
Henri Richard
2 M.Brodeur/R.Luongo 20.00 50.00
3 Ray Bourque 20.00 50.00
Doug Harvey
4 Peter Forsberg 25.00 60.00
Markus Naslund
5 M.Gaborik/Z.Chara 15.00 40.00
6 George Hainsworth 15.00 40.00
Brad Park
7 Marcel Dionne 15.00 40.00
Yvan Cournoyer
8 Eric Staal 20.00 50.00
Alex Delvecchio
9 Frank Mahovlich 15.00 40.00
Pete Mahovlich
10 Rob Blake 15.00 40.00
Red Kelly
11 Brett Hull 15.00 40.00
Andrew Raycroft
12 Jose Theodore 25.00 60.00
Martin St.Louis
13 Joe Thornton 15.00 40.00
Eric Lindros
14 Mark Messier 15.00 40.00
Jarome Iginla
15 Bill Durnan 20.00 50.00
Conacher
16 Phil Esposito 20.00 50.00
Tony Esposito
17 Jarri Kurri 40.00 100.00
Kari Lehtonen
18 Terry Sawchuk 25.00 60.00
Bill Mosienko
19 Aurel Joliat 20.00 50.00
Denis Potvin
20 M.Bossy/M.Lemieux 40.00 100.00

2003-04 BAP Ultimate Memorabilia Jerseys

PRINT RUN 50 SER.#'d SETS
UNPRICED GOLD 1/1's EXIST
1 Paul Kariya 10.00 25.00
2 Teemu Selanne 10.00 25.00
3 Sergei Fedorov 12.50 30.00
4 Mario Lemieux 25.00 60.00
5 Dany Heatley 15.00 40.00
6 Joe Thornton 15.00 40.00
7 Steve Yzerman 25.00 60.00
8 Bill Guerin 8.00 20.00
9 Ilya Kovalchuk 15.00 40.00
10 Chris Pronger 8.00 20.00
11 Mats Sundin 10.00 25.00
12 Peter Forsberg 15.00 40.00
13 Rick Nash 12.50 30.00
14 Mike Modano 12.50 30.00
15 Martin Brodeur 25.00 60.00
16 Jason Spezza 10.00 25.00
17 Brett Hull 15.00 40.00
18 Jeremy Roenick 15.00 40.00
19 Joe Sakic 15.00 40.00
20 Ed Belfour 10.00 25.00
21 Jose Theodore 12.50 30.00
22 Roberto Luongo 12.50 30.00
23 Henrik Zetterberg 10.00 25.00
24 Dominik Hasek 12.50 30.00
25 Jarome Iginla 12.50 30.00
26 Eric Lindros 10.00 25.00
27 Keith Tkachuk 10.00 25.00
28 Marian Gaborik 15.00 40.00
29 Nicklas Lidstrom 10.00 25.00
30 John LeClair 10.00 25.00
31 Pavel Datsyuk 12.50 30.00
32 Vincent Lecavalier 10.00 25.00
33 Markus Naslund 10.00 25.00
34 Milan Hejduk 10.00 25.00
35 Todd Bertuzzi 10.00 25.00
36 Marty Turco 8.00 20.00
37 Rob Blake 8.00 20.00
38 Andrew Raycroft 12.50 30.00
39 Martin St. Louis 8.00 20.00
40 Saku Koivu 10.00 25.00

2003-04 BAP Ultimate Memorabilia Jersey and Emblems

PRINT RUN 10 SER.#'d SETS
NOT PRICED DUE TO SCARCITY
UNPRICED GOLD 1/1's EXIST
1 Alexander Mogilny
2 Bill Guerin
3 Bobby Orr
4 Brendan Shanahan
5 Brett Hull
6 Brian Leetch
7 Chris Pronger
8 Curtis Joseph
9 Dany Heatley
10 Dominik Hasek
11 Ed Belfour
12 Eric Lindros
13 Ilya Kovalchuk
14 Jarome Iginla
15 Jason Spezza
16 Jeremy Roenick
17 Joe Sakic
18 Joe Thornton
19 Jose Theodore
20 Keith Tkachuk
21 Marian Gaborik
22 Mario Lemieux
23 Markus Naslund
24 Martin Brodeur
25 Martin St. Louis
26 Marty Turco
27 Mats Sundin
28 Mike Modano
29 Nicklas Lidstrom
30 Owen Nolan
31 Patrick Roy
32 Pavel Datsyuk
33 Peter Forsberg
34 Ray Bourque
35 Rick Nash
36 Roberto Luongo
37 Sergei Fedorov
38 Sergei Samsonov
39 Steve Yzerman
40 Teemu Selanne

2003-04 BAP Ultimate Memorabilia Jersey and Numbers

PRINT RUN 10 SER.#'d SETS
NOT PRICED DUE TO SCARCITY
UNPRICED GOLD 1/1's EXIST

2003-04 BAP Ultimate Memorabilia Jersey and Stick

PRINT RUN 50 SER.#'d SETS
UNPRICED GOLD 1/1's EXIST
1 Jason Spezza 15.00 40.00
2 Brian Leetch 15.00 40.00
3 Dany Heatley 25.00 60.00
4 Mario Lemieux 40.00 100.00
5 Mats Sundin 15.00 40.00
6 Jarome Iginla 20.00 50.00
7 Mike Modano 20.00 50.00
8 Rick Nash 20.00 50.00
9 Steve Yzerman 40.00 100.00
10 Keith Tkachuk 15.00 40.00
11 Joe Thornton 25.00 60.00
12 Martin Brodeur 30.00 80.00
13 Dominik Hasek 20.00 50.00
14 Nikolai Khabibulin 15.00 40.00
15 Joe Sakic 25.00 60.00
16 Vincent Lecavalier 15.00 40.00
17 Peter Forsberg 25.00 60.00
18 Brendan Shanahan 15.00 40.00
19 Marc-Andre Fleury 30.00 80.00
20 Chris Pronger 12.50 30.00
21 Patrick Roy 40.00 100.00
22 Johnny Bower 25.00 60.00
23 Ray Bourque 20.00 50.00
24 Jacques Plante 30.00 80.00
25 Jean Beliveau 25.00 60.00
26 Gump Worsley 25.00 60.00
27 Gilbert Perreault
28 Bryan Trottier
29 Mike Bossy
30 Marcel Dionne

2003-04 BAP Ultimate Memorabilia Journey Jerseys

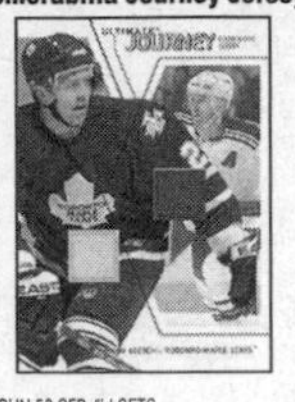

PRINT RUN 50 SER.#'d SETS
UNPRICED GOLD 1/1's EXIST
1 Sergei Fedorov 15.00 40.00
2 Paul Kariya 12.50 30.00
3 Teemu Selanne 12.50 30.00
4 Ed Belfour 15.00 40.00
5 Brian Leetch 12.50 30.00
6 Patrick Roy 40.00 100.00
7 Brett Hull 25.00 60.00
8 Mark Messier 20.00 50.00
9 Jeremy Roenick 15.00 40.00
10 Ray Bourque 25.00 60.00

2003-04 BAP Ultimate Memorabilia Journey Emblems

PRINT RUN 10 SER.#'d SETS
NOT PRICED DUE TO SCARCITY
UNPRICED GOLD 1/1's EXIST

2003-04 BAP Ultimate Memorabilia Lifetime Achievers

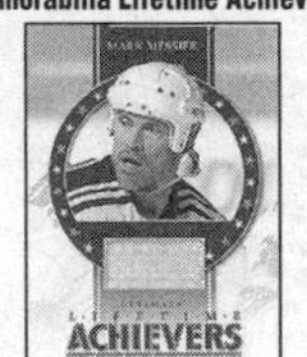

PRINT RUN 30 SER.#'d SETS
1 Mario Lemieux 30.00 80.00
2 Patrick Roy 30.00 80.00
3 Bobby Orr 50.00 125.00
4 Ray Bourque 20.00 50.00
5 Mark Messier 25.00 60.00
6 Brett Hull 15.00 40.00
7 Brian Leetch 15.00 40.00
8 Steve Yzerman 30.00 80.00

2003-04 BAP Ultimate Memorabilia Linemates

PRINT RUN 10 SER.#'d SETS
NOT PRICED DUE TO SCARCITY
1 Doug Mohns
Stan Mikita
Ken Wharram
2 John LeClair
Eric Lindros
Mikael Renberg
3 Charlie Hodge
Phil Esposito
Wayne Cashman
4 Moore/Geoffrion/Beliveau
5 Stan Mikita
Jim Pappin
Bobby Hull
6 Marcel Dionne
Charlie Simmer
Dave Taylor
7 Bryan Trottier
Clark Gillies
Mike Bossy
8 Guy Lafleur
Pete Mahovlich
Steve Shutt
9 Brett Hull
Henrik Zetterberg
Pavel Datsyuk
10 Maurice Richard
Elmer Lach
Toe Blake
11 Joe Primeau
Charlie Conacher
Busher Jackson
12 Vladimir Krutov
Igor Larionov
Sergei Makarov

2003-04 BAP Ultimate Memorabilia Lumbergraphs

This 50-card set featured "cut" signatures removed from actual autographed sticks. Each card was a 1/1.

PRINT RUN 1 SET
NOT PRICED DUE TO SCARCITY
1 Cooney Weiland
2 Woody Dumart
3 Dit Clapper
4 Bobby Bauer
5 Frank Brimsek
6 Ace Bailey
7 Lionel Conacher
8 Roy Worters
9 Charlie Conacher
10 Lorne Chabot
11 Howie Morenz
12 Black Jack Stewart
13 Sid Abel
14 Tommy Ivan
15 Boom Boom Geoffrion
16 Sweeney Schriner
17 Gordie Drillon
18 Bill Barilko
19 Syl Apps
20 Turk Broda
21 Jack Adams
22 Tim Horton
23 Toe Blake
24 Doug Harvey
25 Jacques Plante
26 Frank Selke
27 Red Horner
28 Harold Baldy Cotton
29 Hooley Smith
30 Leo Reise
31 Cy Wentworth
32 Mud Bruneteau
33 Ebbie Goodfellow
34 Elmer Lach
35 Joe Primeau
36 King Clancy
37 Cecil Hart
38 Ted Lindsay
39 Red Kelly
40 Harry Watson
41 Max Bentley
42 Bob Davidson
43 Roger Crozier
45 Frank Mahovlich
46 Babe Seibert
47 Aurel Joliat
48 George Hainsworth
49 Hap Day
50 Henri Richard
51 Maurice Richard

2003-04 BAP Ultimate Memorabilia Made to Order

RED.CARDS 10 COPIES EACH
O1 Bobby Orr Jersey
Z1 H.Zetterberg Triple Mem
Z2 H.Zetterberg Emblem
Z3 H.Zetterberg Jsy/Emblem
Z4 H.Zetterberg Comp.Jsy

2003-04 BAP Ultimate Memorabilia Magnificent Career

PRINT RUN 40 SER.#'d SETS
AUTO PRINT RUN 10 SETS
AUTOS NOT PRICED DUE TO SCARCITY
1 Mario Lemieux 30.00 80.00
A Grand Entrance
2 Mario Lemieux 30.00 80.00
Twice Is Nice
3 Mario Lemieux 30.00 80.00
A Scoring Machine
4 Mario Lemieux 30.00 80.00
A Canadian Hero
5 Mario Lemieux 30.00 80.00
A Hoard Of Hardware
6 Mario Lemieux 30.00 80.00
Farewell For Now
7 Mario Lemieux 30.00 80.00
600-Goal Man
8 Mario Lemieux 30.00 80.00
International Star
9 Mario Lemieux 30.00 80.00
1,700th Point
10 Quad Jersey 75.00 150.00

2003-04 BAP Ultimate Memorabilia Magnificent Prospects

PRINT RUN 30 SER.#'d SETS
AUTO PRINT RUN 10 SETS
AUTOS NOT PRICED DUE TO SCARCITY
AUTOS SIGNED BY LEMIEUX ONLY
1 Mario Lemieux 75.00 150.00
Marc-Andre Fleury
2 Mario Lemieux 40.00 100.00
Eric Staal
3 Mario Lemieux 40.00 100.00
Patrice Bergeron
4 Mario Lemieux 30.00 80.00
Michael Ryder
5 Mario Lemieux 40.00 100.00
Ryan Malone
6 Mario Lemieux 25.00 60.00
Tuomo Ruutu
7 Mario Lemieux 30.00 80.00
Joffrey Lupul
8 Mario Lemieux 30.00 80.00
Jordin Tootoo
9 Mario Lemieux 30.00 80.00
Andrew Raycroft
10 Mario Lemieux 30.00 80.00
Nikolai Zherdev

2003-04 BAP Ultimate Memorabilia Maple Leafs Forever

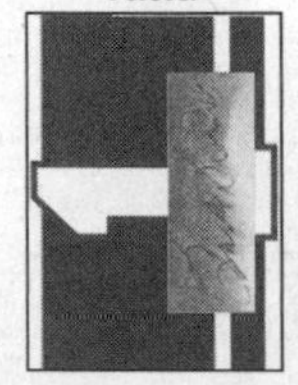

This 19-card set featured "cut" signatures from former Toronto greats on 1/1 cards.

PRINT RUN 1 SET
NOT PRICED DUE TO SCARCITY
1 Frank McCool
2 Syl Apps
3 Turk Broda
4 Babe Pratt
5 King Clancy
6 Frank Finnigan
7 Bob Davidson
8 Tim Horton
9 Harry Lumley
10 Gordie Drillon
11 Ace Bailey
12 Joe Primeau
13 Harry Watson
14 Ted Kennedy
15 Hap Day
16 Lorne Carr
17 Bill Barilko
18 Sweeney Schriner
19 Foster Hewitt

2003-04 BAP Ultimate Memorabilia Memorialized

This 14-card set featured "cut" signatures of some of hockey's pioneers on 1/1 cards.

PRINT RUN 1 SET
NOT PRICED DUE TO SCARCITY
1 Lady Byng
2 Jack Adams
3 Rocket Richard
4 Conn Smythe
5 James Norris
6 Lester Patrick
7 Frank Calder
8 Art Ross
9 Edward VIII
Prince of Wales
10 King Clancy
11 Frank J. Selke Sr.
12 Clarence Campbell
13 Laster B. Pearson
14 Cecil Hart

2003-04 BAP Ultimate Memorabilia Nameplates

PRINT RUN 40 SER.#'d SETS
UNLESS OTHERWISE NOTED
UNPRICED GOLD 1/1's EXIST
1 Sergei Fedorov 20.00 50.00
2 Dominik Hasek 20.00 50.00
3 Dany Heatley 20.00 50.00
4 Markus Naslund 12.50 30.00
5 Curtis Joseph 12.50 30.00
6 Mike Modano 15.00 40.00

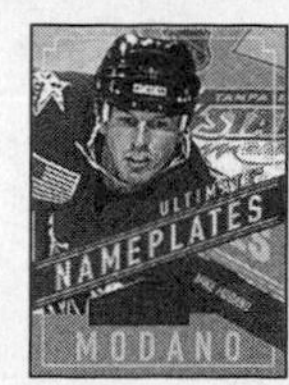

7 Paul Kariya	12.50	30.00
8 Mark Messier	25.00	60.00
9 Teemu Selanne	12.50	30.00
10 Martin Brodeur	30.00	80.00
11 Brian Leetch	15.00	40.00
12 Joe Thornton	15.00	40.00
13 Mario Lemieux	40.00	100.00
14 Steve Yzerman	25.00	60.00
15 Eric Lindros	12.50	30.00
16 Peter Forsberg	25.00	60.00
17 Zigmund Palffy	12.50	30.00
18 Jeremy Roenick	15.00	40.00
19 Chris Pronger	12.50	30.00
20 Nicklas Lidstrom	12.50	30.00
21 Mats Sundin	12.50	30.00
22 Brendan Shanahan	12.50	30.00
23 Henrik Zetterberg	15.00	40.00
24 Jose Theodore	15.00	40.00
25 Marc-Andre Fleury	25.00	60.00
26 Kari Lehtonen	25.00	60.00
27 Andrew Raycroft	20.00	50.00
28 Ray Bourque	25.00	60.00
29 Cam Neely	20.00	50.00
30 Patrick Roy/20	75.00	200.00

2003-04 BAP Ultimate Memorabilia Numbers

PRINT RUN 10 SER.#'d SETS
NOT PRICED DUE TO SCARCITY
UNPRICED GOLD 1/1's EXIST
1 Paul Kariya
2 Sergei Fedorov
3 Mario Lemieux
4 Dany Heatley
5 Joe Thornton
6 Steve Yzerman
7 Ilya Kovalchuk
8 Mats Sundin
9 Peter Forsberg
10 Rick Nash
11 Mike Modano
12 Martin Brodeur
13 Jason Spezza
14 Joe Sakic
15 Ed Belfour
16 José Théodore
17 Roberto Luongo
18 Henrik Zetterberg
19 Dominik Hasek
20 Jarome Iginla
21 Eric Lindros
22 Marian Gaborik
23 Nicklas Lidstrom
24 Pavel Datsyuk
25 Vincent Lecavalier
26 Markus Naslund
27 Todd Bertuzzi
28 Rob Blake
29 Saku Koivu
30 Patrick Roy

2003-04 BAP Ultimate Memorabilia Paper Cuts

This 19-card set featured "cut" signatures from former NHL greats on 1/1 cards.

PRINT RUN 1 SET
NOT PRICED DUE TO SCARCITY
1 Jacques Plante
2 Ace Bailey
3 Joe Primeau
4 Frank Brimsek
5 Bill Mosienko
6 Aurel Joliat
7 King Clancy
8 Toe Blake
9 Frank Patrick
10 Bill Durnan
11 Mel Hill
12 Flash Hollett
13 Foster Hewitt
14 Frank Selke
15 Gordie Drillon
16 Bill Cowley
17 Dit Clapper
18 Turk Broda
19 Terry Sawchuk
20 Red Dutton
21 Doug Harvey
22 Harry Oliver
23 Syl Apps
24 Ebbie Goodfellow
25 Mud Bruneteau
26 Muzz Patrick
27 James D. Norris
28 Bryan Hextall Sr.
29 Max Bentley
30 Charlie Conacher
31 Busher Jackson
32 Hooley Smith
33 Sweeney Schriner
34 Babe Siebert
35 Sid Abel
36 Maurice Richard
37 Art Coulter
38 Babe Pratt
39 Eddie Shore
40 Roy Worters
41 Dave Kerr
42 Bill Cook
43 Howie Morenz
44 Bill Barilko
45 Dick Irvin
46 Frank Calder
47 Lester Patrick
48 Frank Boucher
49 Lynn Patrick
50 Newsy Lalonde

2003-04 BAP Ultimate Memorabilia Perennial Powerhouse Jersey

PRINT RUN 30 SER.#'d SETS

1 Patrick Roy	30.00	80.00
2 Joe Sakic	20.00	50.00
3 Peter Forsberg	20.00	50.00
4 Ray Bourque	20.00	50.00
5 Rob Blake	12.50	30.00
6 Alex Tanguay	12.50	30.00
7 Milan Hejduk	12.50	30.00
8 David Aebischer	12.50	30.00
9 Paul Kariya	12.50	30.00
10 Teemu Selanne	12.50	30.00

2003-04 BAP Ultimate Memorabilia Perennial Powerhouse Jersey and Stick

*JSY/STK: .6X TO 1.5X JSY HI
PRINT RUN 30 SER.#'d SETS

2003-04 BAP Ultimate Memorabilia Perennial Powerhouse Emblem

PRINT RUN 10 SER.#'d SETS
NOT PRICED DUE TO SCARCITY

2003-04 BAP Ultimate Memorabilia Raised to the Rafters

This 20-card set commemorated past stars who's respective teams have retired their jersey numbers. Cards were limited to just 30 copies each.

PRINT RUN 30 SER.#'d SETS

1 Cam Neely	30.00	60.00
2 Doug Harvey	30.00	60.00
3 Mike Richter	40.00	80.00
4 Bobby Orr	150.00	250.00
5 Johnny Bower	20.00	50.00
6 Ray Bourque	30.00	60.00
7 Sid Abel	20.00	50.00
8 Ted Lindsay	20.00	40.00
9 Rod Gilbert	20.00	50.00
10 Maurice Richard	40.00	80.00
11 Jean Beliveau	40.00	80.00
12 Bobby Hull	20.00	40.00
13 Stan Mikita	20.00	40.00
14 Bobby Clarke	25.00	60.00
15 Bernie Parent	25.00	60.00
16 Jacques Plante	40.00	80.00
17 Mike Bossy	20.00	40.00
18 Marcel Dionne	20.00	40.00
19 Bryan Trottier	20.00	40.00
20 Eddie Shore	40.00	80.00

2003-04 BAP Ultimate Memorabilia Redemption Cards

This 4-card set was inserted as redemption cards redeemable for a card of the winner(s) of the Vezina, Richard, Norris and Parason awards.

PRINT RUN 10 SER.#'d SETS
NOT PRICED DUE TO SCARCITY
1 M.Brodeur/G.Vezina/Vezina
2 Scott Niedermayer
Bobby Orr
Norris Trophy
3 Martin St. Louis
Phil Esposito
Pearson Award
4 Richard/Kovy/Nash/Iginla/Richard

2003-04 BAP Ultimate Memorabilia Retro Teammates

PRINT RUN 30 SER.#'d SETS

1 Bourque/Neely/Oates	40.00	100.00
2 M.Richard/Harvey/Plante	75.00	200.00
3 Sawchuk/Lindsay/Abel	40.00	100.00
4 Messier/Richter/Leetch	75.00	200.00
5 Orr/Cheevers/Bucyk	125.00	300.00
6 Trottier/Bossy/Potvin	40.00	100.00
7 Beliveau/H.Richard/Worsley	40.00	100.00
8 Clarke/Barber/Parent	40.00	100.00
9 Sittler/McDonald/Salming	40.00	100.00
10 Shore/Thompson/Stewart	40.00	100.00

2003-04 BAP Ultimate Memorabilia Retro-Active Trophies

PRINT RUN 50 SER.#'d SETS

1 T.Lindsay/J.Iginla	15.00	40.00
2 B.Orr/P.Forsberg	40.00	100.00
3 J.Beliveau/M.Lemieux	30.00	80.00
4 R.Bourque/P.Forsberg	25.00	60.00
5 B.Orr/M.Lemieux	75.00	200.00
6 T.Sawchuk/M.Brodeur	30.00	80.00
7 R.Worters/D.Hasek	15.00	40.00
8 E.Shore/M.Messier	20.00	50.00
9 M.Richard/M.Lemieux	40.00	100.00
10 D.Harvey/N.Lidstrom	15.00	40.00
11 B.Orr/B.Leetch	40.00	100.00
12 R.Bourque/C.Pronger	15.00	40.00
13 B.Mosienko/J.Sakic	20.00	50.00
14 M.Dionne/Br.Hull	15.00	40.00
15 J.Plante/M.Brodeur	25.00	60.00
16 J.Bower/E.Belfour	15.00	40.00
17 P.Roy/J.Theodore	30.00	80.00
18 J.Beliveau/S.Yzerman	25.00	60.00
19 P.Roy/J.Sakic	30.00	80.00
20 G.Lafleur/M.Lemieux	30.00	80.00

2003-04 BAP Ultimate Memorabilia Rookie Jersey and Emblems

PRINT RUN 10 SER.#'d SETS
NOT PRICED DUE TO SCARCITY
UNPRICED GOLD 1/1's EXIST
1 Kari Lehtonen
2 Joni Pitkanen
3 Tim Gleason
4 Chris Higgins
5 Nathan Horton
6 Marek Zidlicky
7 Antti Miettinen
8 Patrice Bergeron
9 Ryan Malone
10 Matthew Lombardi
11 David Hale
12 Tuomo Ruutu
13 Derek Roy
14 Paul Martin
15 Jordin Tootoo
16 Dustin Brown
17 Antoine Vermette
18 Matt Stajan
19 Nikolai Zherdev
20 Marc-Andre Fleury
21 Fedor Tyutin
22 Niklas Kronwall
23 Eric Staal
24 Andrew Raycroft
25 Trent Hunter
26 Christian Ehrhoff
27 Alexander Semin
28 Brent Burns
29 Boyd Kane
30 Sean Bergenheim
31 Ryan Kesler
32 Peter Sejna
33 Michael Ryder
34 John-Michael Liles
35 Joffrey Lupul
36 Esa Pirnes
37 Antero Niittymaki
38 Mark Popovic
39 Patrick Leahy
40 Rastislav Stana

2003-04 BAP Ultimate Memorabilia Rookie Jersey and Numbers

PRINT RUN 10 SER.#'d SETS
NOT PRICED DUE TO SCARCITY
UNPRICED GOLD 1/1's EXIST
1 Kari Lehtonen
2 Joni Pitkanen
3 Tim Gleason
4 Christopher Higgins
5 Nathan Horton
6 Marek Zidlicky
7 Antti Miettinen
8 Patrice Bergeron
9 Ryan Malone
10 Matthew Lombardi
11 David Hale
12 Tuomo Ruutu
13 Derek Roy
14 Paul Martin
15 Jordin Tootoo
16 Dustin Brown
17 Antoine Vermette
18 Matt Stajan
19 Nikolai Zherdev
20 Marc-Andre Fleury
21 Fedor Tyutin
22 Niklas Kronwall
23 Eric Staal
24 Andrew Raycroft
25 Trent Hunter
26 Christian Ehrhoff
27 Alexander Semin
28 Brent Burns
29 Boyd Kane
30 Sean Bergenheim
31 Ryan Kesler
32 Peter Sejna
33 Michael Ryder
34 John-Michael Liles
35 Joffrey Lupul
36 Esa Pirnes
37 Antero Niittymaki
38 Mark Popovic
39 Patrick Leahy
40 Rastislav Stana

2003-04 BAP Ultimate Memorabilia Seams Unbelievable

PRINT RUN 20 SER.#'d SETS
NOT PRICED DUE TO SCARCITY
1 Mario Lemieux
2 Patrick Roy
3 Steve Yzerman
4 Bobby Orr
5 Raymond Bourque
6 Martin Brodeur
7 Ilya Kovalchuk
8 Rick Nash

2003-04 BAP Ultimate Memorabilia The Goal

This 14-card set commemorated probably the most famous goal in hockey history. Known now as "The Goal", this image of Bobby Orr flying through the air after being tripped by Noel Picard and scoring on Glenn Hall to lead the Bruins to a defeat over the Blues to win the Stanley Cup is probably one of the most recognizable in hockey. Single jersey and stick cards were limited to 35 copies. Jersey autographs were limited to 10 copies each. All other print runs are listed below.

SINGLE JSY PRINT RUN 35 SER.#'d SETS
SINGLE STK PRINT RUN 35 SER.#'d SETS
JSY AU PRINT RUN 10 SER.#'d SETS
PRINT RUNS OF 10 NOT PRICED DUE TO SCARCITY

1 Bobby Orr JSY	75.00	200.00
2 B.Orr JSY AU		
3 Noel Picard JSY	20.00	50.00
4 Glenn Hall JSY	25.00	60.00
5 B.Orr/N.Picard JSY/30	100.00	250.00
6 B.Orr/G.Hall JSY/30	125.00	250.00
7 B.Orr/G.Hall JSY AU		
8 B.Orr STK	75.00	200.00
9 G.Hall STK	25.00	60.00
10 N.Picard STK	20.00	50.00
11 Orr/Hall/Picard STK/10		
12 Orr/Hall/Picard JSY/10		
13 Orr/Hall/Picard JSY AU/10		
14 N.Picard/G.Hall JSY/29	25.00	60.00

2003-04 BAP Ultimate Memorabilia Triple Threads

PRINT RUN 40 SER.#'d SETS

1 Brodeur/Potvin/DiPietro	40.00	100.00
2 Hasek/Cloutier/Aebischer	25.00	60.00
3 Joseph/Khabibulin/Giguere	20.00	50.00
4 Belfour/Turco/Cechmanek	20.00	50.00
5 Theodore/Osgood/Luongo	25.00	60.00
6 Kolzig/Biron/Nabokov	15.00	40.00
7 Roy/Crozier/Bower	30.00	80.00
8 Sawchuk/Lumley/Plante	40.00	100.00
9 Hainsworth/Brimsek/Worters	30.00	80.00
10 Blake/Bouwmeester/Pronger	12.50	30.00
11 Lidstrom/Brewer/MacInnis	12.50	30.00
12 Leetch/Chara/Foote	15.00	40.00
13 Orr/T.Horton/Robinson	75.00	200.00
14 Harvey/Bourque/Salming	20.00	50.00
15 Sundin/Modano/Alfredsson	15.00	40.00
16 Lemieux/Hossa/Hull	40.00	100.00
17 St.Louis/Mogilny/Kovalchuk	20.00	50.00
18 Heatley/Thornton/Koivu	30.00	80.00
19 Weight/Palffy/Kariya	12.50	30.00
20 Selanne/Lindros/Tkachuk	15.00	40.00
21 Sakic/Bertuzzi/Yzerman	30.00	80.00
22 Forsberg/Amonte/Naslund	20.00	50.00
23 Nolan/Roenick/Zetterberg	15.00	40.00
24 Nash/Shanahan/Arnott	15.00	40.00
25 Gaborik/Elias/LeClair	15.00	40.00
26 Beliveau/F.Mahovlich/Bossy	25.00	60.00
27 Lindsay/H.Richard/Clarke	20.00	50.00
28 Neely/P.Esposito/McDonald	30.00	80.00
29 Bergeron/Horton/Bergenheim	25.00	60.00
30 Hunter/Gordon/Hale	12.50	30.00
31 Ruutu/Semin/Martin	15.00	40.00
32 Tootoo/Lombardi/Pitkanen	12.00	30.00
33 Staal/Ryder/Brown	30.00	80.00
34 Fleury/Zherdev/Raycroft	25.00	60.00

2003-04 BAP Ultimate Memorabilia Ultimate Captains

This 8-card set featured swatches cut from the captain's C of the featured player. Cards were limited to 5 copies each.

PRINT RUN 5 SER.#'d SETS
NOT PRICED DUE TO SCARCITY
1 Ray Bourque
2 Mike Peca
3 Chris Pronger
4 Scott Stevens
5 Vincent Lecavalier
6 Jean Beliveau
7 Mario Lemieux
8 Mario Lemieux

2003-04 BAP Ultimate Memorabilia Ultimate Defenseman

PRINT RUN 20 SER.#'d SETS
AUTO PRINT RUN 4 SER.#'d SETS
NOT PRICED DUE TO SCARCITY
1 Bobby Orr/Jersey
2 Bobby Orr/Number
3 Bobby Orr/Jersey/Stick
4 Bobby Orr/Stick
5 Bobby Orr/Skate
6 Bobby Orr/Triple Memorabilia

2003-04 BAP Ultimate Memorabilia Ultimate Forward

PRINT RUN 20 SER.#'d SETS
AUTO PRINT RUN 6 SER.#'d SETS
NOT PRICED DUE TO SCARCITY
1 Mario Lemieux/Jersey
2 Mario Lemieux/Number
3 Mario Lemieux/Jersey/Stick
4 Mario Lemieux/Glove
5 Mario Lemieux/Pants
6 Mario Lemieux/Triple Memorabilia

2003-04 BAP Ultimate Memorabilia Ultimate Goaltender

PRINT RUN 20 SER.#'d SETS
AUTO PRINT RUN 3 SER.#'d SETS
NOT PRICED DUE TO SCARCITY
1 Patrick Roy/Jersey
2 Patrick Roy/Jersey
3 Patrick Roy/Jersey/Stick
4 Patrick Roy/Number
5 Patrick Roy/Pad
6 Patrick Roy/Triple Memorabilia

2003-04 BAP Ultimate Memorabilia Vintage Blades of Steel

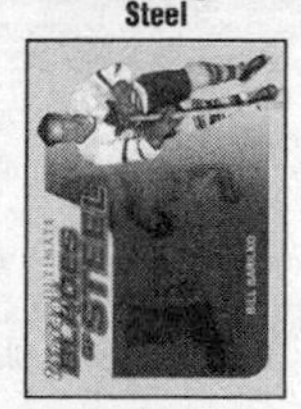

PRINT RUN 20 SER.#'d SETS
NOT PRICED DUE TO SCARCITY
1 Bill Barilko
2 Georges Vezina
3 Rocket Richard
4 Cyclone Taylor
5 Frank Patrick
6 Frank Nighbor
7 Hap Day
8 Clint Benedict
9 Elmer Lach
10 Busher Jackson
11 Eddie Shore
12 Jacques Plante
13 Toe Blake
14 Jack Adams
15 Bobby Orr
16 Tim Horton
17 Aurel Joliat
18 Nels Stewart
19 Paddy Moran
20 Jean Beliveau

2003-04 BAP Ultimate Memorabilia Vintage Complete Jersey

This 10-card set featured swatches of game-used jersey, numbers, emblems and fight straps. Cards were limited to just 10 copies each.

PRINT RUN 10 SER.#'d SETS
NOT PRICED DUE TO SCARCITY
UNPRICED GOLD 1/1's EXIST
1 Bobby Orr
2 Ray Bourque
3 Johnny Bower
4 Aurel Joliat
5 George Hainsworth
6 Roy Worters
7 Jean Beliveau
8 Bill Mosienko
9 Ted Lindsay
10 Jacques Plante

2003-04 BAP Ultimate Memorabilia Vintage Complete Package

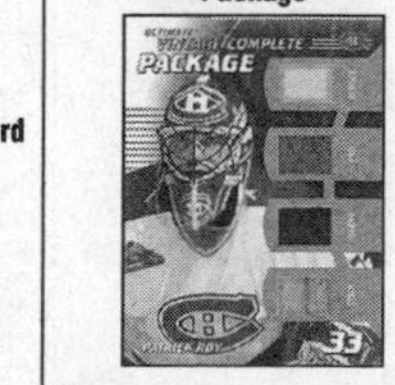

This 8-card set featured 4 different swatches per card of the featured players. Included in the memorabilia were items such as skates, jerseys, sticks, pants, socks, and pads. Cards were limited to 10 copies each.

PRINT RUN 10 SER.#'d SETS
NOT PRICED DUE TO SCARCITY
UNPRICED GOLD 1/1's EXIST
1 Terry Sawchuk
2 Jacques Plante
3 Maurice Richard
4 Ray Bourque
5 Stan Mikita
6 Patrick Roy
7 Guy Lafleur
8 Bernie Parent

2003-04 BAP Ultimate Memorabilia Vintage Hat Tricks

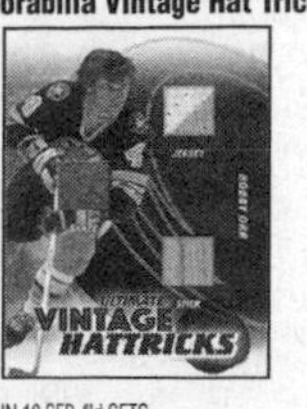

PRINT RUN 10 SER.#'d SETS
NOT PRICED DUE TO SCARCITY
1 Bobby Orr
2 Cam Neely
3 Ray Bourque
4 Eddie Shore
5 Stan Mikita
6 Aurel Joliat

2003-04 BAP Ultimate Memorabilia Vintage Jerseys

PRINT RUN 40 SER.#'d SETS
NOT PRICED DUE TO SCARCITY
UNPRICED GOLD 1/1's EXIST

1 Aurel Joliat	30.00	80.00
2 Bobby Orr	75.00	150.00
3 Doug Harvey	12.50	30.00
4 Roy Worters	20.00	50.00
5 Jacques Plante	25.00	60.00
6 Jean Beliveau	25.00	60.00
7 Johnny Bower	20.00	50.00
8 George Hainsworth	15.00	40.00
9 Frank Brimsek	15.00	40.00
10 Roger Crozier	12.50	30.00
11 Harry Lumley	20.00	50.00
12 Sid Abel	12.50	30.00
13 Bill Mosienko	12.50	30.00
14 John Bucyk	12.50	30.00
15 Ted Lindsay	12.50	30.00
16 Alex Delvecchio	12.50	30.00
17 Phil Esposito	15.00	40.00
18 Frank Mahovlich	12.50	30.00
19 Maurice Richard	30.00	80.00
20 Dennis Hull	12.50	30.00
21 Marcel Dionne	12.50	30.00
22 Terry O'Reilly	15.00	40.00
23 Vladislav Tretiak	40.00	100.00
24 Henri Richard	12.50	30.00
25 Larry Robinson	12.50	30.00
26 Mike Bossy	12.50	30.00
27 Bryan Trottier	12.50	30.00
28 Gump Worsley	12.50	30.00
29 Bobby Clarke	12.50	30.00
30 Red Kelly	15.00	40.00
31 Gilbert Perreault	12.50	30.00
32 Lanny McDonald	12.50	30.00
33 Ray Bourque	15.00	40.00
34 Ed Giacomin	15.00	40.00
35 Valeri Kharlamov	20.00	50.00
36 Stan Mikita	12.50	30.00
37 Denis Potvin	12.50	30.00
38 Bobby Hull	20.00	50.00
39 Patrick Roy	25.00	60.00
40 Cam Neely	15.00	40.00

2003-04 BAP Ultimate Memorabilia Vintage Lumber

PRINT RUN 30 SER.#'d SETS

1 Bernie Geoffrion	15.00	40.00
2 Henri Richard	20.00	50.00
3 Joe Primeau	25.00	60.00
4 Georges Vezina	100.00	250.00
5 Jean Beliveau	15.00	40.00
6 Maurice Richard	50.00	125.00
7 Tim Horton	30.00	80.00
8 Doug Harvey	15.00	40.00
9 Terry Sawchuk	30.00	80.00
10 Jacques Plante	25.00	60.00
11 Harry Lumley	20.00	50.00
12 Howie Morenz	40.00	100.00

2001-02 BAP Update

ALL BASE CARDS LISTED UNDER ORIGINAL BASE SETS

2001-02 BAP Update He Shoots-He Scores Points

Inserted one per pack, these cards carried a value of 1, 2 or 3 points. The points could be redeemed for special memorabilia cards. The cards are unnumbered and are listed below in alphabetical order by point value. Redemption cards expired May 2003.

ONE PER PACK

RED.PROGRAM HAS EXPIRED
1 Todd Bertuzzi 1 pt. .20 .50
2 Theo Fleury 1 pt. .20 .50
3 Marian Gaborik 1 pt. .20 .50
4 Bill Guerin 1 pt. .20 .50
5 Martin Havlat 1 pt. .20 .50
6 Marian Hossa 1 pt. .20 .50
7 Nicklas Lidstrom 1 pt. .20 .50
8 Alexei Yashin 1 pt. .20 .50
9 Ed Belfour 2 pts. .20 .50
10 Martin Brodeur 2 pts. .20 .50
11 Pavel Bure 2 pts. .20 .50
12 Ron Francis 2 pts. .20 .50
13 Luc Robitaille 2 pts. .20 .50
14 Jose Theodore 2 pts. .20 .50
15 Peter Forsberg 3 pts. .20 .50
16 Dominik Hasek 3 pts. .20 .50
17 Curtis Joseph 3 pts. .20 .50
18 Patrick Roy 3 pts. .20 .50

2001-02 BAP Update He Shoots-He Scores Prizes

Available only by redeeming 400 BAP Update He Shoots-He Scores points, this 40-card set featured game-used swatches of jersey and a color photo of the player. There were 14 card that resembled the Memorabilia series, 13 cards that resembled the Signature Series set and 13 cards that resembled the Parkhurst set. Each card had a stated print run of 20 serial-numbered sets and each was encased in a clear plastic slab with a descriptive label at the top. This set is unpriced due to scarcity and volatility.

STATED PRINT RUN 20 SER.#'d SETS
NOT PRICED DUE TO SCARCITY
1 Ilya Kovalchuk M
2 Patrik Elias M
3 Jose Theodore M
4 Luc Robitaille M
5 Jarome Iginla M
6 Paul Kariya M
7 Patrick Lalime M
8 Pavel Bure M
9 Markus Naslund M
10 Evgeni Nabokov M
11 Eric Lindros M
12 Jeremy Roenick M
13 Alexander Mogilny M
14 Dominik Hasek M
15 Bill Guerin S
16 Marty Turco S
17 Vincent Lecavalier S
18 Zigmund Palffy S
19 Nicklas Lidstrom S
20 Sami Kapanen S
21 Peter Forsberg S
22 Marian Hossa S
23 Alexei Yashin S
24 Ron Francis S
25 Luc Robitaille S
26 Joe Thornton S
27 Peter Bondra S
28 Roberto Luongo P
29 Theo Fleury P
30 Todd Bertuzzi P
31 Jose Theodore P
32 Marian Gaborik P
33 Pavel Bure P
34 Ed Belfour P
35 Martin Havlat P
36 Martin Brodeur P
37 Alex Tanguay P
38 Curtis Joseph P
39 Dominik Hasek P
40 Patrick Roy P

2001-02 BAP Update Heritage

Randomly inserted into packs of BAP Update, this 30-card set featured game-worn jersey swatches of the featured players affixed beside a color action photo of the player on a blue card front. Cards in this set were limited to 90 copies each.

STATED PRINT RUN 90 SETS
H1 Wayne Gretzky 30.00 80.00
H2 Curtis Joseph 10.00 25.00
H3 Felix Potvin 10.00 25.00
H4 Mark Messier 12.50 30.00
H5 Doug Gilmour 10.00 25.00
H6 Keith Tkachuk 10.00 25.00
H7 Teemu Selanne 10.00 25.00
H8 Adam Oates 10.00 25.00
H9 Pavel Bure 6.00 15.00
H10 Mats Sundin 10.00 25.00
H11 Ed Belfour 10.00 25.00
H12 Mike Modano 8.00 20.00
H13 Brett Hull 12.50 30.00
H14 Brendan Shanahan 10.00 25.00
H15 Al MacInnis 10.00 25.00
H16 Theo Fleury 6.00 15.00
H17 Ed Jovanovski 6.00 15.00
H18 Keith Primeau 6.00 15.00
H19 Patrick Roy 20.00 50.00
H20 Jeff Hackett 10.00 25.00
H21 Owen Nolan 10.00 25.00
H22 Jeremy Roenick 12.50 30.00
H23 Mark Recchi 10.00 25.00
H24 Roman Turek 10.00 25.00
H25 Alexander Mogilny 10.00 25.00
H26 Jason Allison 6.00 15.00
H27 Luc Robitaille 10.00 25.00
H28 Bill Guerin 10.00 25.00
H29 Rob Blake 10.00 25.00
H30 Gary Roberts 6.00 15.00

2001-02 BAP Update Passing the Torch

Randomly inserted into packs of BAP Update, this 6-card set featured game-worn swatches from the three players featured on each card. Two black-and-white photos flanked a smaller color photo on the card front with the jersey swatches under each photo. Cards from this set were limited to 25 copies each.

STATED PRINT RUN 25 SETS
PTT1 Johnny Bucyk 20.00 50.00
Cam Neely
Joe Thornton
PTT2 Bobby Hull 20.00 50.00
Michel Goulet
Tony Amonte
PTT3 Sid Abel 60.00 150.00
Gordie Howe
Steve Yzerman
PTT4 Rocket Richard 60.00 150.00
Guy Lafleur
Saku Koivu
PTT5 Ed Giacomin 20.00 50.00
Rod Gilbert
Brian Leetch
PTT6 King Clancy 60.00 150.00
Tim Horton
Mats Sundin

2001-02 BAP Update Rocket's Rivals

Randomly inserted into packs of BAP Update, this 10-card set featured game-worn jersey swatches of the featured player. Each card carried a black-and-white photo of Rocket Richard on the left side and a color photo of the featured player on the right. The jersey swatch was affixed in the middle. Exact print runs for each card are printed below.

STATED PRINT RUNS LISTED BELOW
LOWER PRINT RUNS NOT PRICED
DUE TO SCARCITY
RR1 Gordie Howe
Rocket Richard/10
RR2 Ted Lindsay 40.00 100.00
Rocket Richard/30
RR3 Johnny Bower 40.00 100.00
Rocket Richard/30
RR4 Terry Sawchuk 40.00 100.00
Rocket Richard/30
RR5 Frank Brimsek 20.00 50.00
Rocket Richard/40
RR6 Turk Broda
Rocket Richard/10
RR7 Bill Gadsby 20.00 50.00
Rocket Richard/30
RR8 Chuck Rayner
Rocket Richard/10
RR9 Glenn Hall 20.00 50.00
Rocket Richard/30
RR10 Bill Mosienko 40.00 100.00
Rocket Richard/40

2001-02 BAP Update Tough Customers

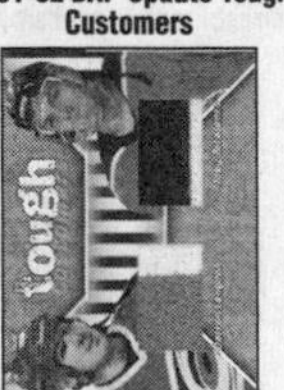

This 40-card set was randomly inserted into packs of BAP Update. Each card carried two jersey swatches from some of the league's most notorious enforcers. Jersey swatches were affixed under color photos of each player. Cards from this set were limited to 90 copies each.

*MULT.COLOR SWATCH: .75X TO 1.5X
STATED PRINT RUN 90 SETS
TC1 Dave Schultz 30.00 80.00
Tiger Williams
TC2 Bob Probert 15.00 40.00
Tie Domi
TC3 Ian Laperriere 15.00 40.00
Stu Grimson
TC4 Peter Worrell 8.00 20.00
Craig Berube
TC5 Jamal Mayers 8.00 20.00
Ken Belanger
TC6 Stu Grimson 30.00 80.00
Bob Probert
TC7 Paul Laus 8.00 20.00
Matt Johnson
TC8 Rob Ray 12.00 30.00
Chris Neil
TC9 Andrei Nazarov 8.00 20.00
Brad Brown
TC10 Joey Tetarenko 8.00 20.00
Darren Langdon
TC11 Tie Domi 12.00 30.00
Rob Ray
TC12 Krzysztof Oliwa 8.00 20.00
Peter Worrell
TC13 Luke Richardson 8.00 20.00
Jeff Odgers
TC14 P.J.Stock 8.00 20.00
Matthew Barnaby
TC15 Wade Belak 8.00 20.00
Sandy McCarthy
TC16 Donald Brashear 15.00 40.00
Georges Laraque
TC17 Andre Roy 8.00 20.00
Jeff Odgers
TC18 Andre Roy 8.00 20.00
Tie Domi
TC19 Donald Brashear 20.00 50.00
Bob Probert
TC20 Darren Langdon 8.00 20.00
Rocky Thompson
TC21 Ryan Vandenbussche 10.00 25.00
Chris Simon
TC22 Matt Johnson 8.00 20.00
Craig Berube
TC23 Scott Parker 8.00 20.00
Denny Lambert
TC24 Georges Laraque 8.00 20.00
Jeff Odgers
TC25 Luke Richardson 8.00 20.00
Wade Belak
TC26 Chris Dingman 8.00 20.00
Paul Laus
TC27 Gino Odjick 8.00 20.00
Chris Simon
TC28 Ian Laperriere 8.00 20.00
Andrei Nazarov
TC29 Georges Laraque 8.00 20.00
Paul Laus
TC30 Krzysztof Oliwa 8.00 20.00
Eric Cairns
TC31 Maurice Richard 60.00 150.00
Ted Lindsay
TC32 Gordie Howe 100.00 200.00
Stan Mikita
TC33 Denny Lambert 8.00 20.00
Andre Roy
TC34 Wendel Clark 25.00 60.00
Bob Probert
TC35 Ryan Vandenbussche 8.00 20.00
Jamal Mayers
TC36 Rocky Thompson 8.00 20.00
P.J. Stock
TC37 Scott Parker 8.00 20.00
Ken Belanger
TC38 Chris Neil 8.00 20.00
Matthew Barnaby
TC39 Chris Dingman 15.00 40.00
Sandy McCarthy
TC40 Gino Odjick 8.00 20.00
Eric Cairns

2001-02 BAP Update Travel Plans

Randomly inserted into packs of BAP Update, this 16-card set featured game-worn jersey swatches of the featured player from two different teams. Each card carried small color photos of the player in the two different uniforms alongside the two jersey swatches. Cards in this set were limited to 50 copies each.

*MULT.COLOR SWATCH: .75X TO 1.5X
STATED PRINT RUN 50 SETS
TP1 Jaromir Jagr 20.00 50.00
TP2 Dominik Hasek 20.00 50.00
TP3 Roman Turek 8.00 20.00
TP4 Teemu Selanne 12.50 30.00
TP5 Keith Tkachuk 12.50 30.00
TP6 Rob Blake 12.50 30.00
TP7 Alexander Mogilny 8.00 20.00
TP8 Luc Robitaille 12.50 30.00
TP9 Alexei Yashin 8.00 20.00
TP10 Eric Lindros 12.50 30.00
TP11 Jeremy Roenick 15.00 40.00
TP12 Doug Weight 8.00 20.00
TP13 Felix Potvin 12.50 30.00
TP14 Nikolai Khabibulin 15.00 40.00
TP15 Dave Andreychuk 8.00 20.00
TP16 Dan Cloutier 8.00 20.00

1934-44 Beehive Group I Photos

The 1934-44 Beehive photos are the first of three groups. Production was suspended in 1944 due to wartime priorities. The photos include a facsimile autograph, small script or occasionally block letters. Complete set price is not given due to an ongoing debate over what constitutes a complete set. A number of unconfirmed photos are scattered throughout the Beehive master checklist. If anyone has information to corroborate the existence of any of these cards, please forward it to Beckett Publications.

COMMON PHOTO 7.50 15.00
1 Bobby Bauer 7.50 15.00
2 Red Beattie 12.50 25.00
3 Buzz Boll
(Unconfirmed)
4 Yank Boyd 75.00 150.00
5A Frankie Brimsek 12.50 25.00
(With Net)
5B Frankie Brimsek 15.00 30.00
(Without Net)
8 Dit Clapper 10.00 20.00
9 Roy Conacher 10.00 20.00
10 Bun Cook 10.00 20.00
11 Bill Cowley 10.00 20.00
12 John Crawford 7.50 15.00
13 Woody Dumart 12.50 25.00
14 Don Gallinger 87.50 175.00
15 Ray Getliffe 15.00 30.00
17 Bep Guidolin 50.00 100.00
18 Red Hamill 15.00 30.00
19 Mel Hill 10.00 20.00
24 Pat McReavy 7.50 15.00
25 Alex Motter 15.00 30.00
26 Peggy O'Neil 10.00 20.00
29 Charlie Sands 10.00 20.00
30 Jackie Schmidt 87.50 175.00
31 Milt Schmidt 10.00 20.00
32 Jack Shewchuk 10.00 20.00
33 Eddie Shore 50.00 100.00
35 Tiny Thompson 25.00 50.00
36 Cooney Weiland 10.00 20.00
38 George Allen 12.50 25.00
39 Doug Bentley 15.00 30.00
40 Max Bentley 20.00 40.00
42 Glenn Brydson 62.50 125.00
43 Marty Burke 7.50 15.00
44 Bill Carse 7.50 15.00
45 Bob Carse 7.50 15.00
46 Lorne Chabot 25.00 50.00
47 John Chad 15.00 30.00
49 Les Cunningham 15.00 30.00
50 Cully Dahlstrom 10.00 20.00
53 Leroy Goldsworthy 12.50 25.00
54 Paul Goodman 20.00 40.00
55 Johnny Gottselig 12.50 25.00
56 Philip Hergesheimer 7.50 15.00
58 George(Wingy) Johnston 87.50 175.00
59 Alex Kaleta 15.00 30.00
60 Mike Karakas 15.00 30.00
63 Alex Levinsky 12.50 25.00
64 Sam LoPresti 25.00 50.00
65 Dave Mackay 125.00 250.00
66 Bill MacKenzie
(Unconfirmed)
67 Mush March 7.50 15.00
68 John Mariucci 25.00 50.00
69 Joe Matte 62.50 125.00
70 Red Mitchell UER 87.50 175.00
(Name misspelled
Mitchel)
72 Peter Palangio 40.00 80.00
73 Joe Papike 50.00 100.00
75 Cliff Purpur 87.50 175.00
77 Doc Romnes 25.00 50.00
78 Earl Seibert 10.00 20.00
81 Paul Thompson 15.00 30.00
83 Louis Trudel UER 20.00 40.00
(Name misspelled
Trudell)
84 Audley Tuten 87.50 175.00
85 Art Wiebe 12.50 25.00
86 Sid Abel 15.00 30.00
87 Larry Aurie 7.50 15.00
88 Marty Barry 12.50 25.00
89 Ralph Bowman 12.50 25.00
90 Adam Brown 40.00 80.00
91 Connie Brown 50.00 100.00
92 Jerry Brown 150.00 300.00
93 Mud Bruneteau 10.00 20.00
94 Eddie Bush 125.00 250.00
95 Joe Carveth 7.50 15.00
99 Les Douglas 50.00 100.00
100 Gus Biesebrecht UER 7.50 15.00
(Name misspelled
Geisebrecht)
101 Ebbie Goodfellow 10.00 20.00
102 Don Grosso 7.50 15.00
104 Syd Howe 10.00 20.00
105 Bill Jennings 40.00 80.00
106 Jack Keating 15.00 30.00
107 Pete Kelly 10.00 20.00
108 Hec Kilrea 10.00 20.00
109 Ken Kilrea 10.00 20.00
110 Wally Kilrea 10.00 20.00
111 Herb Lewis 10.00 20.00
112 Carl Liscombe 7.50 15.00
114 Douglas McCaig 40.00 80.00
115A Bucko McDonald 50.00 100.00
(Ice photo)
115B Bucko McDonald 50.00 100.00
(Dressing room photo)
116 Pat McReavy 40.00 80.00
118 Johnny Mowers 12.50 25.00
119 Jimmy Orlando 7.50 15.00
120 Gord Pettinger 20.00 40.00
121 John Sherf 20.00 40.00
123 Norm Smith 15.00 30.00
124 John Sorrell 12.50 25.00
125 Jack Stewart 20.00 40.00
128 Carl Voss 50.00 100.00
129 Eddie Wares 150.00 300.00
131 Archie Wilder 12.50 25.00
132 Douglas Young 12.50 25.00
133 Jack Adams 12.50 25.00
134 Marty Barry 200.00 400.00
135 Joe Benoit 10.00 20.00
136 Paul Bibeault 25.00 50.00
137 Toe Blake 15.00 30.00
138 Butch Bouchard 7.50 15.00
139 Claude Bourque 20.00 40.00
140 George Allan Brown 62.50 125.00
141 Walt Buswell 20.00 40.00
143 Murph Chamberlain 25.00 50.00
144 Wilf Cude 15.00 30.00
145 Bunny Dame 25.00 50.00
146 Tony DeMeres UER 7.50 15.00
(Name misspelled
Dremers)
147 Joffre Desilets 10.00 20.00
148 Gordie Drillon 350.00 700.00
149 Polly Drouin 7.50 15.00
151 Johnny Gagnon 7.50 15.00
152 Bert Gardiner 15.00 30.00
153 Ray Getliffe 40.00 80.00
154 Red Goupille 10.00 20.00
155 Tony Graboski 10.00 20.00
157 Paul Haynes 7.50 15.00
158 Gerry Heffernan 75.00 150.00
160 Roger Jenkins 30.00 60.00
161 Aurel Joliat 20.00 40.00
162 Elmer Lach 20.00 40.00
163 Leo Lamoreux UER 62.50 125.00
(Name misspelled
Camoreaux)
164 Pit Lepine 7.50 15.00
165 Rod Lorraine 15.00 30.00
166 Georges Mantha 10.00 20.00
167 Sylvio Mantha 10.00 20.00
169 Armand Mondou 7.50 15.00
170 Howie Morenz 375.00 750.00
171 Pete Morin 75.00 150.00
172 Buddy O'Connor 75.00 150.00
175 Jack Portland 7.50 15.00
176 John Quilty 12.50 25.00
177 Ken Reardon 20.00 40.00
178 Terry Reardon 50.00 100.00
179 Maurice Richard 20.00 40.00
180 Earl Robinson 200.00 400.00
181 Charlie Sands 30.00 60.00
182 Babe Siebert 20.00 40.00
183 Alex Singbush 50.00 100.00
184 Bill Summerhill 87.50 175.00
185 Louis Trudel 40.00 80.00
187 Cy Wentworth 1500.00 3000.00
188 Douglas Young 50.00 100.00
189 Bill Beveridge 30.00 60.00
190 Russ Blinco 20.00 40.00
191 Herb Cain 30.00 60.00
192 Gerry Carson UER 87.50 175.00
(Name misspelled
Jerry)
194 Alex Connell 30.00 60.00
195 Tom Cook 20.00 40.00
196 Stewart Evans 15.00 30.00
197 Bob Gracie 50.00 100.00
198 Max Kaminsky 87.50 175.00
199 Bill MacKenzie 62.50 125.00
200 Gus Marker 100.00 200.00
201 Baldy Northcott 30.00 60.00
202 Earl Robinson 25.00 50.00
203 Paul Runge 87.50 175.00
204 Gerry Shannon UER 87.50 175.00
(Name misspelled
Jerry)
206 Des Smith 20.00 40.00
207 Hooley Smith 20.00 40.00
208 Dave Trottier 50.00 100.00
209 Jimmy Ward 20.00 40.00
210 Cy Wentworth 25.00 50.00
211 Viv Allen 30.00 60.00
212 Tom Anderson 20.00 40.00
215 Bill Benson 25.00 50.00
218 Lorne Carr 25.00 50.00
219 Art Chapman 20.00 40.00
222 Red Dutton 25.00 50.00
223 Pat Egan 20.00 40.00
224 Hap Emms 40.00 80.00
225 Wilf Field 20.00 40.00
226 John Gallagher 20.00 40.00
232 Joe Jerwa 25.00 50.00
234 Jim Klein 50.00 100.00
236 Joe Krol 625.00 1250.00
237 Joe Lamb 40.00 80.00
238 Red Heron 20.00 40.00
241 Hazen McAndrew 750.00 1500.00
243 Ken Mosdell 200.00 400.00
244 Al Murray 15.00 30.00
245 John O'Flaherty 30.00 60.00
246 Chuck Rayner 100.00 200.00
247 Earl Robertson 25.00 50.00
249 Sweeny Schriner 20.00 40.00
250 Al Shields 50.00 100.00
252 Pete Slobodzian UER 30.00 60.00
(Name misspelled
Slobodian)
255 Nels Stewart 25.00 50.00
256 Fred Thurier 62.50 125.00
257 Harry Watson 112.50 225.00
258 Eddie Wiseman 15.00 30.00
259 Roy Worters 30.00 60.00
260 Ralph Wycherly 30.00 60.00
261 Frank Boucher 20.00 40.00
263 Norm Burns 50.00 100.00
265 Mac Colville 7.50 15.00
266 Neil Colville 10.00 20.00
267 Bill Cook 12.50 25.00
268 Joe Cooper 7.50 15.00
269 Art Coulter 7.50 15.00
270 Gord Davidson 30.00 60.00
271 Cecil Dillon 10.00 20.00
272 Jim Franks 100.00 200.00
273 Red Garrett 75.00 150.00
275 Ott Heller 7.50 15.00
276A Jim Henry 50.00 100.00
(Vertical photo)
276B Jim Henry 30.00 60.00
(Horizontal photo)
277 Bryan Hextall Sr. 15.00 30.00
278 Dutch Hiller 10.00 20.00
279 Ching Johnson 12.50 25.00
280 Bill Juzda 10.00 20.00
281 Butch Keeling 10.00 20.00
282 Davey Kerr 15.00 30.00
283 Bobby Kirk 50.00 100.00
284 Bob Kirkpatrick 50.00 100.00
285 Kilby MacDonald 10.00 20.00
286 Larry Molyneaux 15.00 30.00
287 John Murray Murdoch 20.00 40.00
288 Vic Myles 87.50 175.00
289 Lynn Patrick 10.00 20.00
290 Murray Patrick 7.50 15.00
291 Alf Pike 7.50 15.00
292 Babe Pratt 12.50 25.00
293 Alex Shibicky 7.50 15.00
294 Clint Smith 7.50 15.00
295 Norman Tustin 50.00 100.00
296 Grant Warwick 50.00 100.00
297 Phil Watson 7.50 15.00
298 Syl Apps Sr. 12.50 25.00
299 Murray Armstrong 7.50 15.00
300 Andy Blair 10.00 20.00
301 Buzz Boll 10.00 20.00
302 George Boothman 125.00 250.00
303 Turk Broda 12.50 25.00
304 Lorne Carr 30.00 60.00
305 Murph Chamberlain 7.50 15.00
306 Lex Chisholm 10.00 20.00
307 Jack Church 10.00 20.00
308 Francis Clancy 15.00 30.00
309 Charlie Conacher 12.50 25.00
310 Bob Copp 30.00 60.00
311 Baldy Cotton 10.00 20.00
312 Bob Davidson 7.50 15.00
313 Hap Day 7.50 15.00
314 Ernie Dickens 100.00 200.00
315 Gordie Drillon 7.50 15.00
316 Frank Finnigan 12.50 25.00
317 Jack Forsey 100.00 200.00
318 Jimmy Fowler UER 7.50 15.00
(Name misspelled Jimmie)
319 Bob Goldham 100.00 200.00
320 Hank Goldup 7.50 15.00
321 George Hainsworth 20.00 40.00
322 Reg Hamilton 7.50 15.00
323 Red Heron 10.00 20.00
324 Mel Hill 150.00 300.00
325 Frank Hoillett 7.50 15.00
326 Red Horner 10.00 20.00
327 Art Jackson 7.50 15.00
328 Harvey Jackson 7.50 15.00
329 Bingo Kampman 20.00 40.00
330 Reg Kelly 10.00 20.00
331 William Kendall 40.00 80.00
332 Hec Kilrea 25.00 50.00
333 Pete Langelle 10.00 20.00
334 Bucko McDonald 10.00 20.00
335A Norm Mann 12.50 25.00
335B Norm Mann 87.50 175.00
(Name overlaps stick)
336 Gus Marker 7.50 15.00
337 Johnny McCreedy 20.00 40.00
338 Jack McLean 50.00 100.00
339 Don Metz 7.50 15.00
340 Nick Metz 7.50 15.00
341 George Parsons 12.50 25.00
342 Bud Poile 87.50 175.00
343 Babe Pratt 125.00 250.00
344 Joe Primeau 12.50 25.00
345 Doc Romnes 25.00 50.00
346 Sweeny Schriner 15.00 30.00
347 Jack Shill 12.50 25.00
348 Wally Stanowski UER 7.50 15.00
(Name misspelled
Stanowsky)
349 Phil Stein 25.00 50.00
350A Gaye Stewart 175.00 350.00
(Home Sweater)
350B Gaye Stewart 100.00 200.00
(Away Sweater)
351 Billy Taylor 7.50 15.00
352 Rhys Thompson 200.00 400.00
353 Bill Thoms 7.50 15.00
354 1944-45 Maple Leafs 150.00 300.00
355 1937 Winnipeg Monarchs 75.00 150.00
356 Foster Hewitt 40.00 80.00
357 Wes McKnight 62.50 125.00
358A Allan Cup 30.00 60.00
(Dated on back)
358B Allan Cup 62.50 125.00
(Blank Back)
359A Lady Byng Trophy 30.00 60.00
(Dated on back)
359B Lady Byng Trophy 62.50 125.00
(Blank back)
360A Calder Trophy 30.00 60.00
(Dated on back)
360B Calder Trophy 62.50 125.00
(Blank back)
361A Hart Trophy 30.00 60.00
(Dated on back)
361B Hart Trophy 62.50 125.00
(Blank back)
362A Memorial Cup 40.00 80.00
(Dated on back)
362B Memorial Cup 75.00 150.00
(Blank back)
363A Prince of Wales Trophy 87.50 175.00
(Dated on back)
363B Prince of Wales Trophy 100.00 200.00
(Blank back)
364A Stanley Cup 30.00 60.00
(Dated on back)
364B Stanley Cup 50.00 100.00
(Blank back)
364C Stanley Cup 50.00 100.00
(Name horizontal)
365A Georges Vezina Trophy 30.00 60.00
(Dated on back)
365B Georges Vezina Trophy 62.50 125.00
(Blank back)

1944-63 Beehive Group II Photos

The 1944-63 Beehive photos are the second of three groups. Issued after World War II, this group generally had new photos and a larger script than was typical of Group I. Facsimile autographs were again featured. There are a number of unconfirmed photos that appeared on the Beehive checklist, among these are the

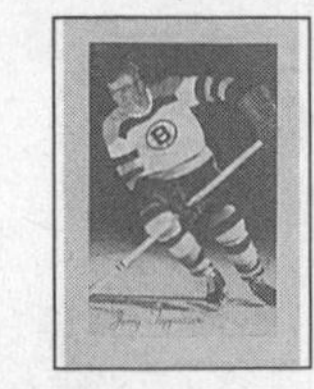

Allan and Memorial Cup trophies in either of their varieties. Because of the lack of confirmation, those cards are not listed below. Information regarding the existence of any of these unconfirmed photos can be forwarded it to Beckett Publications.

1 Bob Armstrong 5.00 10.00
2 Pete Babando 25.00 50.00
3 Ray Barry 25.00 50.00
4 Gus Bodnar 40.00 80.00
5 Leo Boivin 6.00 12.00
6 Frankie Brimsek 12.50 25.00
8 John Bucyk 7.50 15.00
9 Charlie Burns 5.00 10.00
10 Jack Caffery 30.00 60.00
11 Real Chevrefils 5.00 10.00
12A Wayne Connelly 10.00 20.00
12B Wayne Connelly 30.00 60.00
(Name overlaps skate)
14 John Crawford 10.00 20.00
15A Dave Creighton 6.00 12.00
(White sweater)
15B Dave Creighton 30.00 60.00
(Photo on ice)
16 Woody Dumart 12.50 25.00
17 Pat Egan 15.00 30.00
19 Lorne Ferguson 6.00 12.00
20 Fern Flaman 5.00 10.00
21 Bruce Gamble 6.00 12.00
22 Cal Gardner 6.00 12.00
23 Ray Gariepy 10.00 20.00
24 Jack Gelineau 12.50 25.00
25 Jean-Guy Gendron 5.00 10.00
26A Warren Godfrey 6.00 12.00
(A on sweater)
26B Warren Godfrey 30.00 60.00
(With puck)
26C Warren Godfrey 50.00 100.00
(Without puck)
27 Ed Harrison 5.00 10.00
28 Don Head 5.00 10.00
29 Andy Hebenton 7.50 15.00
30 Murray Henderson 7.50 15.00
31 Jim Henry 15.00 30.00
32 Larry Hillman 20.00 40.00
33 Pete Horeck 10.00 20.00
34 Bronco Horvath 5.00 10.00
35 Tom Johnson 6.00 12.00
36 Eddie Johnston 7.50 15.00
38 Joe Klukay 90.00 175.00
39 Edward Kryznowski 6.00 12.00
40 Orland Kurtenbach 20.00 40.00
41 Leo Labine 5.00 10.00
42 Hal Laycoe 5.00 10.00
43 Harry Lumley 7.50 15.00
44 Pentti Lund 500.00 1000.00
45 Fleming Mackell 5.00 10.00
46 Phil Maloney 10.00 20.00
47 Frank Martin 10.00 20.00
48 Jack McIntyre 10.00 20.00
49 Don McKenney 5.00 10.00
50 Dick Meissner 5.00 10.00
51 Doug Mohns 5.00 10.00
52 Murray Oliver 5.00 10.00
53 Willie O'Ree 7.50 15.00
54A John Peirson 6.00 12.00
54B Johnny Peirson 50.00 100.00
55A Cliff Pennington 10.00 20.00
(Name away from skate)
55B Cliff Pennington 50.00 100.00
(Name near skate)
56A Bob Perreault 12.50 25.00
(Name away from skate)
56B Bob Perreault 50.00 100.00
(Name overlaps skate)
57 Jim Peters 10.00 20.00
58 Dean Prentice 6.00 12.00
59 Andre Pronovost 5.00 10.00
60 Bill Quackenbush 10.00 20.00
61 Larry Regan 25.00 50.00
62 Earl Reibel 20.00 40.00
63 Paul Ronty 6.00 12.00
64 Ed Sandford 5.00 10.00
65 Terry Sawchuk 60.00 125.00
66A Don Simmons ERR 75.00 150.00
(Photo of Norm Defelice)
66B Don Simmons COR 5.00 10.00
67 Kenny Smith 6.00 12.00
68A Pat Stapleton 10.00 20.00
(Name away from skate)
68B Pat Stapleton 50.00 100.00
(Name near skate)
69 Vic Stasiuk 7.50 15.00
70 Red Sullivan 12.50 25.00
71 Jerry Toppazzini 5.00 10.00
72 Zellio Toppazzini 6.00 12.00
73 Grant Warwick 20.00 40.00
74 Tom Williams 5.00 10.00
75 Al Arbour 6.00 12.00
76 Pete Babando 10.00 20.00
77 Earl Balfour 5.00 10.00
78 Murray Balfour 5.00 10.00
79 Jim Bedard 10.00 20.00
80 Doug Bentley 12.50 25.00
81 Gus Bodnar 6.00 12.00
82 Frankie Brimsek 20.00 40.00
83 Adam Brown 10.00 20.00
84 Hank Ciesla 20.00 40.00
85 Jim Conacher 7.50 15.00
86 Pete Conacher 5.00 10.00
87 Roy Conacher 5.00 10.00
88 Joe Conn 40.00 80.00

89 Murray Costello 40.00 80.00
90 Gerry Couture 12.50 25.00
91 Al Dewsbury 6.00 12.00
92 Ernie Dickens 5.00 10.00
93 Jack Evans 5.00 10.00
94 Reggie Fleming 5.00 10.00
95 Lee Fogolin 7.50 15.00
96 Bill Gadsby 5.00 10.00
97 George Gee 6.00 12.00
98 Bob Goldham 12.50 25.00
99 Bep Guidolin 6.00 12.00
100 Glenn Hall 6.00 12.00
101 Murray Hall 15.00 30.00
102 Red Hamill 15.00 30.00
103 Billy Hay 5.00 10.00
104 Jim Henry 15.00 30.00
105 Wayne Hillman 12.50 25.00
107 Bronco Horvath 6.00 12.00
108 Fred Hucul 12.50 25.00
109A Bobby Hull 100.00 200.00
(Jersey 9)
109B Bobby Hull 15.00 30.00
(Jersey 16)
110 Lou Jankowski 12.50 25.00
111 Forbes Kennedy 25.00 50.00
112 Ted Lindsay 7.50 15.00
113 Ed Litzenberger 5.00 10.00
114 Harry Lumley 20.00 40.00
Goalie
115A Len Lunde 30.00 60.00
(Name away from stick)
115B Len Lunde 10.00 20.00
(Name overlaps stick)
116 Pat Lundy 7.50 15.00
117 Vic Lynn
(Unconfirmed)
118A Al MacNeil 20.00 40.00
(Name overlaps
stick and skate)
118B Al MacNeil 6.00 12.00
(Name overlaps stick)
119A Chico Maki 7.50 15.00
(Name away from stick)
119B Chico Maki 60.00 125.00
(Name overlaps stick)
120 Doug McCaig 12.50 25.00
121 Ab McDonald 5.00 10.00
122 Jim McFadden 20.00 40.00
124 Gerry Melnyk UER 5.00 10.00
(Name misspelled Jerry)
125 Stan Mikita 6.00 12.00
127 Gus Mortson 5.00 10.00
128 Bill Mosienko 7.50 15.00
129 Ron Murphy 5.00 10.00
130 Ralph Nattrass 12.50 25.00
131 Eric Nesterenko 5.00 10.00
132 Bert Olmstead 12.50 25.00
133 Jim Peters 20.00 40.00
134 Pierre Pilote 5.00 10.00
135 Metro Prystai 6.00 12.00
137 Clare Raglan 15.00 30.00
138A Al Rollins 50.00 100.00
(Vertical photo)
138B Al Rollins 15.00 30.00
(Horizontal photo)
139 Tod Sloan 5.00 10.00
140 Dollard St. Laurent 5.00 10.00
141 Gaye Stewart 10.00 20.00
142 Jack Stewart 20.00 40.00
143A Bob Turner 25.00 50.00
(Name away from stick)
143B Bob Turner 15.00 30.00
(Name overlaps stick)
144 Elmer Vasko 5.00 10.00
145 Kenny Wharram 5.00 10.00
146 Larry Wilson 10.00 20.00
147 Howie Young 12.50 25.00
149 Sid Abel 10.00 20.00
150 Al Arbour 20.00 40.00
151 Pete Babando 12.50 25.00
152A Doug Barkley 30.00 60.00
(Stick blade showing)
152B Doug Barkley 10.00 20.00
(No blade showing)
153 Hank Bassen 6.00 12.00
154 Stephen Black 15.00 30.00
155 Marcel Bonin 7.50 15.00
156 John Bucyk 25.00 50.00
157 John Conacher 100.00 200.00
158 Gerry Couture UER 6.00 12.00
(Name misspelled Jerry)
159 Billy Dea 12.50 25.00
160 Alex Delvecchio 5.00 10.00
162 Bill Dineen 5.00 10.00
163 Jim Enio 30.00 60.00
164 Alex Faulkner 25.00 50.00
165 Lee Fogolin 6.00 12.00
166 Val Fonteyne 5.00 10.00
167 Bill Gadsby 7.50 15.00
168 Fern Gauthier 20.00 40.00
169 George Gee 7.50 15.00
170 Fred Glover 5.00 10.00
171 Howie Glover 5.00 10.00
172 Warren Godfrey 5.00 10.00
173 Peter Goegan 5.00 10.00
174 Bob Goldham 6.00 12.00
175 Glenn Hall 40.00 80.00
176 Larry Hillman 25.00 50.00
177 Pete Horeck 20.00 40.00
178A Gordie Howe 25.00 50.00
178B Gordie Howe 40.00 80.00
(C on sweater)
179 Ron Ingram 20.00 40.00
180 Larry Jeffrey 15.00 30.00
181 Al Johnson 5.00 10.00
182 Red Kelly 5.00 10.00
183 Forbes Kennedy 5.00 10.00
184 Leo Labine 5.00 10.00
185 Tony Leswick 5.00 10.00
186 Ted Lindsay 6.00 12.00
187 Ed Litzenberger 15.00 30.00
188 Harry Lumley 12.50 25.00
189 Len Lunde 5.00 10.00
190 Parker MacDonald 5.00 10.00
191 Bruce MacGregor 5.00 10.00
192 Clare Martin 12.50 25.00
193 Jim McFadden 7.50 15.00
194 Max McNab 12.50 25.00
195 Gerry Melnyk UER 5.00 10.00
(Name misspelled Jerry)
196 Don Morrison 12.50 25.00
197 Rod Morrison 25.00 50.00
198 Gerry Odrowski 5.00 10.00
199 Murray Oliver 5.00 10.00
200 Marty Pavelich 5.00 10.00
201 Jim Peters 25.00 50.00
202 Bud Poile 75.00 150.00
203 Andre Pronovost 6.00 12.00
204 Marcel Pronovost 5.00 10.00
205 Metro Prystai 5.00 10.00
206 Bill Quackenbush 25.00 50.00
207 Earl Reibel 5.00 10.00
208 Leo Reise Jr. 6.00 12.00
209 Terry Sawchuk 20.00 40.00
210 Glen Skov 5.00 10.00
211 Floyd Smith 6.00 12.00
212A Vic Stasiuk 12.50 25.00
(Home sweater;
full stick showing)
212B Vic Stasiuk 20.00 40.00
(Home sweater;
partial stick showing)
212C Vic Stasiuk 7.50 15.00
(Away sweater)
213 Gaye Stewart 15.00 30.00
214 Jack Stewart 15.00 30.00
215 Norm Ullman 5.00 10.00
216 Johnny Wilson 5.00 10.00
217 Benny Woit 5.00 10.00
218 Howie Young 6.00 12.00
219 Larry Zeidel 12.50 25.00
220 Ralph Backstrom 5.00 10.00
221 Dave Balon 5.00 10.00
222 Jean Beliveau 10.00 20.00
223A Red Berenson 12.50 25.00
(White script)
223B Red Berenson 100.00 200.00
(Black script)
224 Marcel Bonin 5.00 10.00
225 Butch Bouchard 5.00 10.00
226 Tod Campeau 50.00 100.00
227 Joe Carveth 6.00 12.00
228 Murph Chamberlain 25.00 50.00
229 Doc Couture 20.00 40.00
230 Floyd Curry UER 5.00 10.00
(Name misspelled Currie)
231 Ian Cushenan 7.50 15.00
232 Lorne Davis 6.00 12.00
233 Eddie Dorohoy 12.50 25.00
234 Gilles Dube 30.00 60.00
235 Bill Durnan 20.00 40.00
236 Norm Dussault 12.50 25.00
237 John Ferguson 6.00 12.00
238 Bob Fillion 7.50 15.00
239 Louie Fontinato 5.00 10.00
240 Dick Gamble 10.00 20.00
241 Bernard Geoffrion 7.50 15.00
242 Phil Goyette 5.00 10.00
243 Leo Gravelle 12.50 25.00
244 John Hanna 30.00 60.00
245 Glen Harmon 10.00 20.00
246 Terry Harper 5.00 10.00
247 Doug Harvey 7.50 15.00
248 Bill Hicke 5.00 10.00
250 Bert Hirschfeld
(Unconfirmed)
251A Charlie Hodge 40.00 80.00
(White script)
251B Charlie Hodge 6.00 12.00
(Black script)
252 Tom Johnson 6.00 12.00
253 Vern Kaiser 20.00 40.00
254 Frank King 20.00 40.00
255 Elmer Lach 6.00 12.00
256 Al Langlois 5.00 10.00
257 Jacques Laperriere 5.00 10.00
258 Hal Laycoe 6.00 12.00
259 Jackie Leclair 5.00 10.00
260 Roger Leger 10.00 20.00
261 Ed Litzenberger 12.50 25.00
262 Ross Lowe 20.00 40.00
263 Al MacNeil 5.00 10.00
264 Bud MacPherson 5.00 10.00
265 Cesare Maniago 6.00 12.00
266 Don Marshall 5.00 10.00
267 Paul Masnick 5.00 10.00
268 Eddie Mazur 10.00 20.00
269 John McCormack 6.00 12.00
270 Alvin McDonald 5.00 10.00
271 Calum MacKay 6.00 12.00
272 Gerry McNeil 7.50 15.00
273 Paul Meger 10.00 20.00
274 Dickie Moore 6.00 12.00
275 Kenny Mosdell 10.00 20.00
276 Bert Olmstead 5.00 10.00
277 Gerry Plamondon 10.00 20.00
278 Jacques Plante 20.00 40.00
279 Andre Pronovost 5.00 10.00
280 Claude Provost 5.00 10.00
281 Ken Reardon 12.50 25.00
282 Billy Reay 6.00 12.00
283 Henri Richard 10.00 20.00
284 Maurice Richard 20.00 40.00
285 Rip Riopelle 15.00 30.00
286 George Robertson 50.00 100.00
287 Bobby Rousseau 5.00 10.00
288 Dollard St. Laurent 5.00 10.00
289 Jean-Guy Talbot 5.00 10.00
290A Gilles Tremblay 5.00 10.00
(Dark background)
290B Gilles Tremblay 100.00 200.00
(Light background)
291A J.C. Tremblay 5.00 10.00
(Dark background)
291B J.C. Tremblay 100.00 200.00
(Light background)
292 Bob Turner 5.00 10.00
293 Grant Warwick 20.00 40.00
294 Gump Worsley 12.50 25.00
295 Clint Albright 6.00 12.00
296A Dave Balon 12.50 25.00
(Name high on photo)
296B Dave Balon 5.00 10.00
(Name low on photo)
297A Andy Bathgate 6.00 12.00
(Home sweater)
297B Andy Bathgate 10.00 20.00
(Away sweater)
298 Max Bentley 25.00 50.00
299 Johnny Bower 25.00 50.00
300 Hy Buller 10.00 20.00
301A Larry Cahan 6.00 12.00
(Home sweater)
301B Larry Cahan 12.50 25.00
(Away sweater)
302 Bob Crystal 15.00 30.00
304 Brian Cullen 5.00 10.00
305 Ian Cushenan 5.00 10.00
306 Billy Dea 15.00 30.00
307 Frank Eddolls 5.00 10.00
308 Pat Egan 20.00 40.00
309A Jack Evans 5.00 10.00
(Name parallel to bottom)
309B Jack Evans 20.00 40.00
(Name printed diagonally)
310 Dunc Fisher 7.50 15.00
311 Louie Fontinato 5.00 10.00
312 Bill Gadsby 5.00 10.00
313 Jean-Guy Gendron 5.00 10.00
314 Rod Gilbert 6.00 12.00
315 Howie Glover 20.00 40.00
317 Phil Goyette 5.00 10.00
318 Aldo Guidolin 25.00 50.00
319 Vic Hadfield 6.00 12.00
320 Ted Hampson 5.00 10.00
321 Doug Harvey 6.00 12.00
322 Andy Hebenton 5.00 10.00
323 Camille Henry 5.00 10.00
324 Wally Hergesheimer 5.00 10.00
325 Ike Hildebrand 15.00 30.00
326 Bronco Horvath 6.00 12.00
327 Harry Howell 5.00 10.00
328A Earl Ingarfield Sr. 5.00 10.00
(Name away from stick)
328B Earl Ingarfield Sr. 12.50 25.00
(Name near stick)
329 Bing Juckes 15.00 30.00
330 Alex Kaleta 7.50 15.00
331 Stephen Kraftcheck 20.00 40.00
332 Eddie Kullman 7.50 15.00
333 Gus Kyle 6.00 12.00
334 Gord Labossiere 25.00 50.00
335 Al Langlois 5.00 10.00
336 Edgar Laprade 7.50 15.00
337 Tony Leswick 6.00 12.00
338 Danny Lewicki 5.00 10.00
339 Pentti Lund 10.00 20.00
340 Don Marshall 12.50 25.00
341 Jack McCartan 6.00 12.00
342 Bill McDonagh 12.50 25.00
343 Don McKenney 10.00 20.00
344 Jackie McLeod 10.00 20.00
345 Nick Mickoski 6.00 12.00
346 Billy Moe 7.50 15.00
348 Ron Murphy 5.00 10.00
349 Buddy O'Connor 7.50 15.00
350 Marcel Paille 50.00 100.00
351 Jacques Plante 50.00 100.00
352 Bud Poile 20.00 40.00
353 Larry Popein 5.00 10.00
354A Dean Prentice 5.00 10.00
(Home sweater)
354B Dean Prentice 7.50 15.00
(Away sweater)
355 Don Raleigh 7.50 15.00
356A Jean Ratelle ERR 25.00 50.00
(Name misspelled John)
356B Jean Ratelle COR 20.00 40.00
357 Chuck Rayner 12.50 25.00
358 Leo Reise Jr. 6.00 12.00
359 Paul Ronty 6.00 12.00
360 Ken Schinkel 5.00 10.00
361 Eddie Shack 15.00 30.00
362 Fred Shero 15.00 30.00
363 Reg Sinclair 20.00 40.00
364 Eddie Slowinski 7.50 15.00
365 Allan Stanley 5.00 10.00
366 Wally Stanowski 6.00 12.00
367 Red Sullivan 5.00 10.00
369 Gump Worsley 5.00 10.00
370 Gary Aldcorn 10.00 20.00
371 Syl Apps Sr. 90.00 175.00
372 Al Arbour 5.00 10.00
373A George Armstrong 6.00 12.00
373B George Armstrong 12.50 25.00
(Dark background)
373C George Armstrong 100.00 200.00
(Light background)
374 Bob Bailey 20.00 40.00
375 Earl Balfour 10.00 20.00
376 Bill Barilko 25.00 50.00
377 Andy Bathgate 25.00 50.00
378 Bob Baun 5.00 10.00
379 Max Bentley 12.50 25.00
380 Jack Bionda 75.00 150.00
381 Garth Boesch 6.00 12.00
382 Leo Boivin 7.50 15.00
383 Hugh Bolton 5.00 10.00
384 Johnny Bower 10.00 20.00
385 Carl Brewer 5.00 10.00
386 Turk Broda 12.50 25.00
387 Larry Cahan 7.50 15.00
388 Ray Ceresino 50.00 100.00
389 Ed Chadwick 6.00 12.00
390 Pete Conacher 50.00 100.00
391 Les Costello 20.00 40.00
392 Dave Creighton 10.00 20.00
393 Barry Cullen 12.50 25.00
394 Brian Cullen 5.00 10.00
395 Robert Dawes 12.50 25.00
396 Kent Douglas 5.00 10.00
397 Dick Duff 5.00 10.00
398 Gary Edmundson 5.00 10.00
399 Gerry Ehman 5.00 10.00
400 Bill Ezinicki 10.00 20.00
401 Fern Flaman 25.00 50.00
402 Cal Gardner 10.00 20.00
403 Ted Hampson 5.00 10.00
404 Gord Hannigan 10.00 20.00
405 Billy Harris 5.00 10.00
406 Bob Hassard 40.00 80.00
407 Larry Hillman 5.00 10.00
408 Tim Horton 12.50 25.00
409 Bronco Horvath 10.00 20.00
410 Ron Hurst 75.00 150.00
411 Gerry James UER 15.00 30.00
(Name misspelled Jerry)
412 Bill Juzda 7.50 15.00
413A Red Kelly 6.00 12.00
(Bare-headed)
413B Red Kelly 15.00 30.00
(Wearing helmet)
414 Ted Kennedy 10.00 20.00
415 Dave Keon 7.50 15.00
416 Joe Klukay 6.00 12.00
417 Stephen Kraftcheck 20.00 40.00
418 Danny Lewicki 12.50 25.00
419 Ed Litzenberger 6.00 12.00
420 Harry Lumley 12.50 25.00
421 Vic Lynn 6.00 12.00
422 Fleming MacKell 7.50 15.00
423 John MacMillan 5.00 10.00
424 Al MacNeil 10.00 20.00
425 Frank Mahovlich 12.50 25.00
426 Phil Maloney 75.00 150.00
427 Cesare Maniago 6.00 12.00
428 Frank Mathers 20.00 40.00
429 John McCormack 30.00 60.00
430 Parker MacDonald 12.50 25.00
431 Don McKenney 20.00 40.00
432 Howie Meeker 7.50 15.00
433 Don Metz 150.00 300.00
434 Nick Metz 100.00 200.00
435 Rudy Migay 5.00 10.00
436 Jim Mikol 5.00 10.00
437 Jim Morrison 5.00 10.00
438 Gus Mortson 6.00 12.00
439 Eric Nesterenko 7.50 15.00
440 Bob Nevin 5.00 10.00
441 Mike Nykoluk 25.00 50.00
442 Bert Olmstead 6.00 12.00
443 Bob Pulford 5.00 10.00
444 Marc Reaume 7.50 15.00
445 Larry Regan 5.00 10.00
446 Dave Reid 75.00 150.00
447 Al Rollins 15.00 30.00
448A Eddie Shack 150.00 300.00
(Dark background)
449 Don Simmons 6.00 12.00
450 Tod Sloan 5.00 10.00
451 Sid Smith 5.00 10.00
452 Bob Solinger 30.00 60.00
453A Allan Stanley ERR 6.00 12.00
(Name misspelled Alan;
dark background)
453B Allan Stanley COR 12.50 25.00
(Light background)
454 Wally Stanowski 200.00 400.00
455 Ron Stewart 5.00 10.00
456 Harry Taylor 20.00 40.00
457 Jim Thomson 6.00 12.00
458 Ray Timgren 7.50 15.00
459 Harry Watson 6.00 12.00
460 Johnny Wilson 5.00 10.00
461 1962-63 Maple Leafs 200.00 400.00
(Team picture)
462A Lady Byng Trophy 150.00 300.00
(Four white borders)
462B Lady Byng Trophy 60.00 125.00
(White bottom
border only)
463A Calder Memorial Trophy 150.00 300.00
(Four white borders)
463B Calder Memorial Trophy 60.00 125.00
(White bottom
border only)
464A Hart Trophy 150.00 300.00
(Four white borders)
464B Hart Trophy 60.00 125.00
(White bottom
border only)
465A James Norris 150.00 300.00
Memorial Trophy
(Four white borders)
465B James Norris 60.00 125.00
Memorial Trophy
(White bottom
border only)
466A Prince of Wales Trophy 150.00 300.00
(Four white borders)
466B Prince of Wales Trophy 60.00 125.00
(White bottom
border only)
467A Art Ross Trophy 150.00 300.00
(Four white borders)
467B Art Ross Trophy 60.00 125.00
(White bottom
border only)
468A Stanley Cup 150.00 300.00
(Four white borders)
468B Stanley Cup 60.00 125.00
(White bottom
border only)
469A Georges Vezina Trophy 150.00 300.00
(Four white borders)
469B Georges Vezina Trophy 60.00 125.00
(White bottom
border only)

1964-67 Beehive Group III Photos

The 1964-67 Beehive photo set is the third of three groups. These photos were issued by St. Lawrence Starch and measure 5 3/8" by 8". The fronts display black-and-white action poses inside a white inner border and a simulated wood-grain outer border. The player's name is displayed on an plaque in the lower wooden border. The backs are blank. A number of unconfirmed photos are part of the Beehive checklist, but have yet to be confirmed and therefore are not listed below.

1 Murray Balfour 12.50 25.00
2 Leo Boivin 6.00 12.00
3 John Bucyk 7.50 15.00
4 Wayne Connelly 75.00 150.00
5 Bob Dillabough 6.00 12.00
6 Gary Dornhoefer 7.50 15.00
7 Reggie Fleming 6.00 12.00
8 Guy Gendron 60.00 125.00
9 Warren Godfrey 150.00 300.00
10 Ted Green 6.00 12.00
11 Andy Hebenton 90.00 175.00
12 Eddie Johnston 7.50 15.00
13 Tom Johnson 7.50 15.00
14 Forbes Kennedy 10.00 20.00
15 Orland Kurtenbach 20.00 40.00
16 Bobby Leiter 6.00 12.00
17 Parker MacDonald 6.00 12.00
18 Bob McCord 10.00 20.00
19 Ab McDonald 6.00 12.00
20 Murray Oliver 6.00 12.00
21 Bernie Parent 40.00 80.00
22 Cliff Pennington 100.00 225.00
23 Bob Perreault 175.00 350.00
24 Dean Prentice 6.00 12.00
25 Ron Schock UER 6.00 12.00
(Name misspelled Shock)
26 Pat Stapleton 25.00 50.00
27 Ron Stewart 7.50 15.00
28 Ed Westfall 6.00 12.00
29 Tom Williams 6.00 12.00
30 Lou Angotti 6.00 12.00
31 Wally Boyer 6.00 12.00
32 Denis DeJordy 7.50 15.00
33 Dave Dryden 15.00 30.00
34A Phil Esposito 40.00 80.00
(Full Blade showing)
34B Phil Esposito 10.00 20.00
(Partial blade showing)
35 Glenn Hall ERR 10.00 20.00
(Name misspelled Glen)
36 Murray Hall 100.00 225.00
37 Billy Hay 6.00 12.00
38 Camille Henry 10.00 20.00
39 Wayne Hillman 75.00 150.00
40 Ken Hodge Sr. 7.50 15.00
41A Bobby Hull 100.00 225.00
41B Bobby Hull 200.00 400.00
(Home sweater;
negative reversed)
41C Bobby Hull 15.00 30.00
(Away sweater;
blade showing)
41D Bobby Hull 15.00 30.00
(Away sweater;
no blade showing)
41E Bobby Hull 200.00 400.00
(Home portrait)
41F Bobby Hull 15.00 30.00
(Promotional portrait)
42 Dennis Hull 6.00 12.00
43 Doug Jarrett 6.00 12.00
44 Len Lunde 6.00 12.00
45 Al MacNeil 6.00 12.00
46A Chico Maki 50.00 100.00
(In action)
46B Chico Maki 6.00 12.00
(Portrait)
47 John McKenzie 15.00 30.00
49 Stan Mikita 10.00 20.00
50 Doug Mohns 6.00 12.00
51A Eric Nesterenko 100.00 225.00
(Light background)
51B Eric Nesterenko 6.00 12.00
(Dark background)
52A Pierre Pilote 125.00 250.00
(Home sweater)
52B Pierre Pilote 7.50 15.00
(Away sweater)
53 Matt Ravlich 6.00 12.00
55A Fred Stanfield 75.00 150.00
55B Fred Stanfield 50.00 100.00
(Reversed negative)
56 Pat Stapleton 6.00 12.00
57 Bob Turner 125.00 250.00
58 Ed Van Impe 6.00 12.00
59 Elmer Vasko 7.50 15.00
60 Kenny Wharram 6.00 12.00
61 Doug Barkley 6.00 12.00
62 Hank Bassen 7.50 15.00
63A Andy Bathgate 6.00 12.00
(Number visible
on sleeve)
63B Andy Bathgate 6.00 12.00
(Partial number visible)
64 Gary Bergman 6.00 12.00
65 Leo Boivin 7.50 15.00
66 Roger Crozier 7.50 15.00
67A Alex Delvecchio 10.00 20.00
(Home sweater)
67B Alex Delvecchio 150.00 300.00
(Away sweater)
68 Alex Faulkner 175.00 350.00
69 Val Fonteyne 6.00 12.00
70 Bill Gadsby 6.00 12.00
71 Warren Godfrey 12.50 25.00
72 Pete Goegan 12.50 25.00
73 Murray Hall 6.00 12.00
74 Ted Hampson 6.00 12.00
75 Billy Harris 15.00 30.00
76 Paul Henderson 10.00 20.00
77A Gordie Howe 20.00 40.00
77B Gordie Howe 100.00 225.00
(C on sweater)
78 Ron Ingram 150.00 300.00
79A Larry Jeffrey 50.00 100.00
(Home sweater)
79B Larry Jeffrey 30.00 60.00
(Away sweater)
80A Eddie Joyal 12.50 25.00
80B Eddie Joyal 100.00 225.00
(Reversed negative)
81 Al Langlois 6.00 12.00
82 Ted Lindsay 10.00 20.00
83 Parker MacDonald 6.00 12.00
84A Bruce MacGregor 7.50 15.00
(Home sweater)
84B Bruce MacGregor 50.00 100.00
(Away sweater)
85 Pete Mahovlich 6.00 12.00
86 Bert Marshall 6.00 12.00
87 Pit Martin 6.00 12.00
89 Ab McDonald 6.00 12.00
90 Ron Murphy 6.00 12.00
91 Dean Prentice 6.00 12.00
92 Andre Pronovost 10.00 20.00
93 Marcel Pronovost 5.00 10.00
(Unconfirmed)
94A Floyd Smith 7.50 15.00
(Home sweater)
94B Floyd Smith 100.00 225.00
(Home sweater;
reversed negative)
94C Floyd Smith 90.00 175.00
(Away sweater)
95 Norm Ullman 10.00 20.00
96 Bob Wall 6.00 12.00
97 Ralph Backstrom 6.00 12.00
98 Dave Balon 6.00 12.00
99 Jean Beliveau 12.50 25.00
100 Red Berenson 6.00 12.00
101 Yvan Cournoyer 10.00 20.00
102 Dick Duff 7.50 15.00
103 John Ferguson 6.00 12.00
104 John Hanna 100.00 200.00
105A Terry Harper 6.00 12.00
(Posed)
105B Terry Harper 100.00 225.00
(In action)
106 Ted Harris 6.00 12.00
107 Bill Hicke 7.50 15.00
108 Charlie Hodge 10.00 20.00
109 Jacques Laperriere 6.00 12.00
110A Claude Larose 6.00 12.00
110B Claude Larose 250.00 450.00
(Reversed negative)
111 Claude Provost 6.00 12.00
112 Henri Richard 12.50 25.00
113 Maurice Richard 30.00 60.00
114 Jim Roberts 6.00 12.00
115 Bobby Rousseau 6.00 12.00
116 Jean-Guy Talbot 6.00 12.00
117A Gilles Tremblay 6.00 12.00
(Sweater 21)
117B Gilles Tremblay 50.00 100.00
(Sweater 24)
118 J.C. Tremblay 6.00 12.00
119 Gump Worsley 10.00 20.00
120 Lou Angotti 6.00 12.00
121 Arnie Brown 6.00 12.00
122 Larry Cahan 150.00 300.00
124 Reggie Fleming 6.00 12.00
125 Bernie Geoffrion 10.00 20.00
126 Ed Giacomin 12.50 25.00
127 Rod Gilbert 10.00 20.00
128 Phil Goyette 6.00 12.00
129 Vic Hadfield 7.50 15.00
131 Camille Henry 75.00 150.00
132 Bill Hicke 6.00 12.00
133 Wayne Hillman 6.00 12.00
134 Harry Howell 7.50 15.00
135 Earl Ingarfield Sr. 6.00 12.00
137 Orland Kurtenbach 10.00 20.00
138 Gord Labossiere 75.00 150.00
139 Al MacNeil 6.00 12.00
140 Cesare Maniago 10.00 20.00
141 Don Marshall 6.00 12.00
143 Jim Neilson 6.00 12.00
144 Bob Nevin 6.00 12.00
145 Marcel Paille 20.00 40.00
146 Jacques Plante 40.00 80.00
147 Jean Ratelle 12.50 25.00
148 Rod Seiling 6.00 12.00
151 George Armstrong 10.00 20.00
152 Andy Bathgate 10.00 20.00
153A Bob Baun 60.00 125.00
(Number visible)
153B Bob Baun 10.00 20.00
(No number visible)
154A Johnny Bower 90.00 175.00
(Number visible)
154B Johnny Bower 12.50 25.00
(No number visible)
155 Wally Boyer 15.00 30.00
156 John Brenneman 6.00 12.00
157 Carl Brewer 12.50 25.00
158 Turk Broda 15.00 30.00
159 Brian Conacher 6.00 12.00
160 Kent Douglas 6.00 12.00
161 Ron Ellis 6.00 12.00
162 Bruce Gamble 10.00 20.00
163A Billy Harris 50.00 100.00
(Number visible)
163B Billy Harris 100.00 225.00
(No number visible)
164 Larry Hillman 12.50 25.00
165A Tim Horton 90.00 175.00
(Number visible)
165B Tim Horton 15.00 30.00
(No number visible)
166 Bronco Horvath 90.00 175.00
167 Larry Jeffrey 15.00 30.00
168 Eddie Joyal 20.00 40.00
169 Red Kelly 10.00 20.00
170 Ted Kennedy 10.00 20.00
171A Dave Keon 75.00 150.00
(Number visible)
171B Dave Keon 12.50 25.00
(No number visible)
172 Orland Kurtenbach 7.50 20.00
173 Ed Litzenberger 10.00 20.00
174A Frank Mahovlich 90.00 175.00
(Number visible)
174B Frank Mahovlich 15.00 30.00
(No number visible)
175A Don McKenney 50.00 100.00
(Small photo)
175B Don McKenney 10.00 20.00
(Large photo)
176 Dickie Moore 10.00 20.00
177 Jim Pappin 6.00 12.00
178A Marcel Pronovost 7.50 15.00
(Blade showing)
178B Marcel Pronovost 15.00 30.00
(No Blade showing)
180A Bob Pulford 50.00 100.00
(Number visible)
180B Bob Pulford 10.00 20.00
(No number visible)
181 Terry Sawchuk 15.00 30.00
182 Brit Selby 6.00 12.00
183 Eddie Shack 12.50 25.00
184 Don Simmons 12.50 25.00
185 Allan Stanley 10.00 20.00
186 Pete Stemkowski 6.00 12.00
187A Ron Stewart 90.00 175.00
(Number visible)
187B Ron Stewart 30.00 60.00
(No number visible)
188 Mike Walton 15.00 30.00
189 Bernie Geoffrion 25.00 50.00
190 Lady Byng Trophy 60.00 125.00
191 Calder Memorial 60.00 125.00
Trophy
192 Hart Trophy 60.00 125.00
193 Prince of Wales 60.00 125.00
Trophy
194 James Norris 60.00 125.00
Memorial Trophy
195 Art Ross Trophy 60.00 125.00
196 Stanley Cup 60.00 125.00
197 Vezina Trophy 60.00 125.00

1997-98 Beehive

The Beehives set was issued in one series totaling 75 cards and was distributed in four-card packs with a suggested retail price of $4.99. This set is a revival of the 1934-67 Beehive Photos sets produced by the St. Lawrence Starch Co. of Port Credit, Ontario. This new version features color player portraits printed on 5" by 7" cards. The backs carry a black-and-white action player photos with player information and career statistics. The player information as well as a trivia question is printed in both French and English. The set contains the topical subsets: Golden Originals (57-62), and Junior League Stars (63-74).

COMPLETE SET (75) 12.00 30.00
1 Eric Lindros .25 .60
2 Teemu Selanne .25 .60
3 Brendan Shanahan .25 .60
4 Joe Sakic .60 1.50
5 John LeClair .25 .60
6 Brett Hull .30 .75
7 Jaromir Jagr .50 1.25
8 Bryan Berard .15 .40
9 Peter Forsberg .50 1.25
10 Ed Belfour .25 .60
11 Steve Yzerman 1.25 3.00
12 Curtis Joseph .25 .60
13 Saku Koivu .25 .60
14 Keith Tkachuk .25 .60
15 Pavel Bure .25 .60
16 Felix Potvin .25 .60
17 Ray Bourque .40 1.00
18 Theo Fleury .08 .25
19 Patrick Roy 1.50 4.00
20 Joe Nieuwendyk .15 .40
21 Alexei Yashin .08 .25
22 Owen Nolan .15 .40
23 Mark Recchi .15 .40
24 Dominik Hasek .60 1.50
25 Chris Chelios .25 .60
26 Mike Modano .30 .75
27 John Vanbiesbrouck .25 .60
28 Brian Leetch .25 .60
29 Dino Ciccarelli .08 .25
30 Mark Messier .25 .60
31 Paul Kariya .25 .60
32 Jocelyn Thibault .15 .40
33 Wayne Gretzky 2.00 5.00
34 Doug Weight .15 .40
35 Yanic Perreault .08 .25
36 Luc Robitaille .15 .40
37 Chris Osgood .15 .40
38 Adam Oates .15 .40
39 Mats Sundin .25 .60
40 Trevor Linden .15 .40
41 Mike Richter .25 .60
42 Zigmund Palffy .15 .40
43 Pat LaFontaine .25 .60
44 Grant Fuhr .15 .40
45 Martin Brodeur .75 2.00
46 Sergei Fedorov .30 .75

47 Doug Gilmour .15 .40
48 Daniel Alfredsson .15 .40
49 Ron Francis .15 .40
50 Geoff Sanderson .15 .40
51 Joe Thornton .60 1.50
52 Vaclav Prospal RC .25 .60
53 Patrik Elias RC 1.00 2.50
54 Mike Johnson RC .25 .60
55 Alyn McCauley .15 .40
56 Brendan Morrison RC .40 1.00
57 Johnny Bower GO .30 .75
58 John Bucyk GO .30 .75
59 Stan Mikita GO .30 .75
60 Ted Lindsay GO .30 .75
61 Maurice Richard GO 1.25 3.00
62 Andy Bathgate GO .30 .75
63 Stefan Cherneski JLS RC .15 .40
64 Craig Hillier JLS RC .25 .60
65 Daniel Tkaczuk JLS .25 .60
66 Josh Holden JLS .15 .40
67 Marian Cisar JLS RC .15 .40
68 J-P Dumont JLS RC .75 2.00
69 Roberto Luongo JLS RC 5.00 12.00
70 Aren Miller JLS RC .15 .40
71 Mathieu Garon JLS .25 .60
72 Charlie Stephens JLS RC .25 .60
73 Sergei Varlamov JLS RC .20 .50
74 Pierre Dagenais JLS RC .30 .75
75 Willie O'Ree CC RC .75 2.00
P1 Eric Lindros PROMO .08 .25
R1 Redemption .08 .25

1997-98 Beehive Authentic Autographs

Randomly inserted in packs at the rate of 1:12, this 19-card set features autographed cards of CHL stars that seem to have an outstanding chance of becoming NHL stars as well as some of the NHL's top rookies.

STATED ODDS 1:12
51 Joe Thornton 10.00 25.00
52 Vaclav Prospal 2.00 5.00
53 Patrik Elias 6.00 15.00
54 Mike Johnson 2.00 5.00
55 Alyn McCauley 3.00 8.00
56 Brendan Morrison 4.00 10.00
63 Stefan Cherneski 2.00 5.00
64 Craig Hillier 2.00 5.00
65 Daniel Tkaczuk 2.00 5.00
66 Josh Holden 2.00 5.00
67 Marian Cisar 2.00 5.00
68 J-P Dumont 4.00 10.00
69 Roberto Luongo 15.00 40.00
70 Aren Miller 2.00 5.00
71 Mathieu Garon 4.00 10.00
72 Charlie Stephens 2.00 5.00
73 Sergei Varlamov 2.00 5.00
74 Pierre Dagenais 2.00 5.00
75 Willie O'Ree 12.00 30.00

1997-98 Beehive Golden Portraits

Randomly inserted in packs at the rate of 1:3, this 75-card set is a gold-foil parallel version of the base set.

*VETS: 2X TO 5X BASIC CARDS
*ROOKIES: 1X TO 2.5X BASIC CARD
STATED ODDS 1:3

1997-98 Beehive Golden Originals Autographs

Randomly inserted in packs at the rate of 1:36, this six-card set features autographed color photos of six top retired players.

STATED ODDS 1:36
57 Johnny Bower 8.00 20.00
58 John Bucyk 8.00 20.00
59 Stan Mikita 8.00 20.00
60 Ted Lindsay 8.00 20.00
61 Maurice Richard 50.00 100.00
62 Andy Bathgate 8.00 20.00

1997-98 Beehive Team

Randomly inserted in packs at the rate of 1:11, this 25-card set features color photos of some of Hockey's best players. The backs carry player information. A Beehive Gold Team set was also produced which is a parallel version to this insert set and has an insertion rate of 1:49.

COMPLETE SET (25) 60.00 150.00

STATED ODDS 1:11
*GOLD TEAM: .8X TO 2X BASIC INSERTS
GOLD TEAM ODDS 1:49
1 Paul Kariya 2.50 6.00
2 Mark Messier 2.50 6.00
3 Mike Modano 3.00 8.00
4 Brendan Shanahan 2.50 6.00
5 John Vanbiesbrouck 1.50 4.00
6 Martin Brodeur 6.00 15.00
7 Wayne Gretzky 12.00 30.00
8 Eric Lindros 2.50 6.00
9 Peter Forsberg 4.00 10.00
10 Jaromir Jagr 4.00 10.00
11 Teemu Selanne 2.50 6.00
12 John LeClair 1.50 4.00
13 Saku Koivu 2.50 6.00
14 Brett Hull 3.00 8.00
15 Patrick Roy 10.00 25.00
16 Steve Yzerman 8.00 20.00
17 Keith Tkachuk 1.50 4.00
18 Pat LaFontaine 1.50 4.00
19 Joe Sakic 5.00 12.00
20 Patrik Elias 1.50 4.00
21 Vaclav Prospal 1.00 2.50
22 Joe Thornton 4.00 10.00
23 Sergei Samsonov 1.50 4.00
24 Alexei Morozov 1.00 2.50
25 Marco Sturm 1.00 2.50

2003-04 Beehive

This 250-card set was designed to reflect the design of the original Beehive photos with "woodgrain" borders and color player photos. The set consisted of 200 veterans and 50 short-printed rookies inserted at 1:5 packs.

COMPLETE SET (250) 100.00 200.00
COMP.SET w/o SP's (200) 12.00 30.00
RC STATED ODDS 1:5
1 Petr Sykora .08 .20
2 Martin Gerber .20 .50
3 Vaclav Prospal .08 .20
4 Jean-Sebastien Giguere .20 .50
5 Sergei Fedorov .30 .75
6 Stanislav Chistov .08 .20
7 Sandis Ozolinsh .08 .20
8 Pasi Nurminen .20 .50
9 Marc Savard .08 .20
10 Vyacheslav Kozlov .08 .20
11 Dany Heatley .30 .75
12 Ilya Kovalchuk .30 .75
13 Andrew Raycroft .20 .50
14 Glen Murray .08 .20
15 Brian Rolston .08 .20
16 Jeff Jillson .08 .20
17 Don Cherry .50 1.25
18 Nick Boynton .08 .20
19 Felix Potvin .20 .50
20 Joe Thornton .40 1.00
21 Sergei Samsonov .20 .50
22 Ales Kotalik .08 .20
23 Alexei Zhitnik .08 .20
24 Maxim Afinogenov .08 .20
25 Chris Drury .20 .50
26 Daniel Briere .08 .20
27 Martin Biron .20 .50
28 Steve Reinprecht .08 .20
29 Jamie McLennan .08 .20
30 Martin Gelinas .08 .20
31 Jarome Iginla .30 .75
32 Roman Turek .20 .50
33 Jeff O'Neill .08 .20
34 Danny Markov .08 .20
35 Erik Cole .08 .20
36 Rod Brind'Amour .08 .20
37 Jamie Storr .20 .50
38 Ron Francis .20 .50
39 Bryan Berard .08 .20
40 Eric Daze' .20 .50
41 Kyle Calder .08 .20
42 Michael Leighton .20 .50
44 Jocelyn Thibault .20 .50
45 Tyler Arnason .20 .50
46 Philippe Sauve .20 .50
47 Teemu Selanne .25 .60
48 Alex Tanguay .20 .50
49 Derek Morris .08 .20
50 Milan Hejduk .25 .60
51 Patrick Roy 1.25 3.00
52 David Aebischer .20 .50
53 Joe Sakic .50 1.25
54 Paul Kariya .25 .60
55 Peter Forsberg .60 1.50
56 Darryl Sydor .08 .20
57 Trevor Letowski .08 .20
58 Marc Denis .20 .50
59 Rick Nash .30 .75
60 Todd Marchant .08 .20
61 Brenden Morrow .20 .50
62 Jere Lehtinen .20 .50
63 Sergei Zubov .08 .20
64 Stu Barnes .08 .20
65 Teppo Numminen .08 .20
66 Bill Guerin .20 .50
67 Marty Turco .20 .50
68 Mike Modano .40 1.00
69 Gordie Howe 1.25 3.00
70 Brendan Shanahan .25 .60
71 Brett Hull .30 .75
72 Nicklas Lidstrom .25 .60
73 Dominik Hasek .50 1.00
74 Henrik Zetterberg .25 .60
75 Steve Yzerman 1.25 3.00
76 Eric Brewer .08 .20
77 Adam Oates .20 .50
78 Ryan Smyth .08 .20
79 Ales Hemsky .08 .20
80 Raffi Torres .08 .20
81 Wayne Gretzky 1.50 4.00
82 Tommy Salo .20 .50
83 Steve Shields .08 .20
84 Jay Bouwmeester .08 .20
85 Olli Jokinen .20 .50
86 Roberto Luongo .30 .75
87 Marcel Dionne .30 .75
88 Alexander Frolov .08 .20
89 Adam Deadmarsh .08 .20
90 Jason Allison .08 .20
91 Luc Robitaille .20 .50
92 Roman Cechmanek .20 .50
93 Zigmund Palffy .20 .50
94 Andrew Brunette .08 .20
95 Dwayne Roloson .20 .50
96 Pascal Dupuis .08 .20
97 Wes Walz .08 .20
98 Manny Fernandez .20 .50
99 Marian Gaborik .50 1.00
100 Pierre-Marc Bouchard .08 .20
101 Andrei Markov .08 .20
102 Guy Lafleur .60 2.50
103 Mike Ribeiro .08 .20
104 Jose Theodore .30 .75
105 Marcel Hossa .25 .60
106 Michael Ryder .08 .20
107 Saku Koivu .25 .60
108 Greg Johnson .08 .20
109 David Legwand .20 .50
110 Tomas Vokoun .20 .50
111 Jamie Langenbrunner .08 .20
112 Jeff Friesen .08 .20
113 John Madden .08 .20
114 Scott Niedermayer .08 .20
115 Martin Brodeur .60 1.50
116 Patrik Elias .08 .20
117 Scott Gomez .08 .20
118 Scott Stevens .20 .50
119 Brian Gionta .08 .20
119B Alexei Zhamnov .08 .20
120 Mariusz Czerkawski .08 .20
121 Eric Godard .08 .20
122 Jason Blake .08 .20
123 Mark Parrish .08 .20
124 Alexei Yashin .08 .20
125 Michael Peca .08 .20
126 Rick DiPietro .20 .50
127 Alex Kovalev .20 .50
128 Anson Carter .20 .50
129 Brian Leetch .20 .50
130 Petr Nedved .08 .20
131 Eric Lindros .25 .60
132 Mark Messier .25 .60
133 Mike Dunham .20 .50
134 Daniel Alfredsson .20 .50
135 Zdeno Chara .08 .20
136 Jason Spezza .25 .60
137 Marian Hossa .25 .60
138 Patrick Lalime .20 .50
139 Bobby Clarke .40 1.00
140 John LeClair .25 .60
141 Justin Williams .08 .20
142 Mark Recchi .20 .50
143 Robert Esche .20 .50
144 Tony Amonte .20 .50
145 Jeff Hackett .20 .50
146 Jeremy Roenick .30 .75
147 Simon Gagne .25 .60
148 Brian Boucher .20 .50
149 Chris Gratton .08 .20
150 David Tanabe .08 .20
151 Jan Hrdina .08 .20
152 Mike Johnson .20 .50
153 Sean Burke .20 .50
154 Brooks Orpik .08 .20
155 Konstantin Koltsov .08 .20
156 Rico Fata .08 .20
157 Sebastien Caron .20 .50
158 Mario Lemieux 1.50 4.00
159 Martin Straka .08 .20
160 Jonathan Cheechoo .10 .25
161 Kyle McLaren .08 .20
162 Niko Dimitrakos .08 .20
163 Evgeni Nabokov .20 .50
164 Patrick Marleau .20 .50
165 Vincent Damphousse .08 .20
166 Chris Pronger .20 .50
167 Reed Low .08 .20
168 Chris Osgood .20 .50
169 Doug Weight .20 .50
170 Keith Tkachuk .25 .60
171 Pavol Demitra .20 .50
172 Dave Andreychuk .20 .50
173 Martin St. Louis .20 .50
174 Nikolai Khabibulin .25 .60
175 Vincent Lecavalier .25 .60
176 Brad Richards .20 .50
177 Fredrik Modin .08 .20
178 Gary Roberts .08 .20
179 Joe Nieuwendyk .20 .50
180 Tie Domi .20 .50
181 Alexander Mogilny .20 .50
182 Ed Belfour .25 .60
183 Mats Sundin .25 .60
184 Owen Nolan .20 .50
185 Daniel Sedin .08 .20
186 Magnus Arvedson .08 .20
187 Dan Cloutier .20 .50
188 Henrik Sedin .08 .20
189 Brendan Morrison .20 .50
190 Jason King .08 .20
191 Trevor Linden .08 .20
192 Ed Jovanovski .20 .50
193 Johan Hedberg .20 .50
194 Markus Naslund .25 .60
195 Todd Bertuzzi .25 .60
196 Robert Lang .08 .20
197 Sergei Gonchar .08 .20
198 Jaromir Jagr .40 1.00
199 Olaf Kolzig .20 .50
200 Peter Bondra .20 .50
201 Joffrey Lupul RC 1.50 4.00
202 Patrice Bergeron RC 2.50 6.00
203 Niklas Kronwall RC 1.50 4.00
204 Eric Staal RC 4.00 10.00
205 Pavel Vorobiev RC 1.25 3.00
206 Tuomo Ruutu RC 1.50 4.00
207 Tomas Plekanec RC 2.00 5.00
208 Timofei Shishkanov RC 1.25 3.00
209 Tuomas Pihlman RC 1.25 3.00
210 Dan Fritsche RC 1.25 3.00
211 Antti Miettinen RC 1.25 3.00
212 Jiri Hudler RC 2.00 5.00
213 Nathan Horton RC 3.00 5.00
214 Dustin Brown RC 1.50 4.00
215 Kyle Wellwood RC 2.00 5.00
216 Mike Smith RC 2.00 5.00
217 Ryan Kesler RC 1.25 3.00
218 Fredrik Sjostrom RC 1.25 3.00
219 Chris Higgins RC 2.50 6.00
220 Dan Hamhuis RC 1.25 3.00
221 Jordin Tootoo RC 2.50 6.00
222 Carl Corazzini RC 1.25 3.00
223 Tony Martensson RC 1.25 3.00
224 Aaron Johnson RC 1.25 3.00
225 Anton Babchuk RC 1.25 3.00
226 Jozef Balej RC 1.25 3.00
227 Joni Pitkanen RC 1.50 4.00
228 Aleksander Suglobov RC 1.25 3.00
229 Marc-Andre Fleury RC 5.00 12.00
230 Nikolai Zherdev RC 1.50 4.00
231 Gavin Morgan RC 1.25 3.00
232 Milan Michalek RC 1.50 4.00
233 Peter Sejna RC 1.25 3.00
234 Matt Stajan RC 2.50 6.00
235 Maxim Kondratiev RC 1.25 3.00
236 Alexander Semin RC 4.00 10.00
237 Zbynek Michalek RC 1.25 3.00
238 Jeff Hamilton RC 1.25 3.00
239 Andrew Hutchinson RC 1.25 3.00
240 Mikhail Yakubov RC 1.25 3.00
241 Sergei Zinovjev RC 1.25 3.00
242 Noah Clarke RC 1.25 3.00
243 Tim Jackman RC 1.25 3.00
244 Jason Pominville RC 2.00 5.00
245 Tony Salmelainen RC 1.25 3.00
246 Rastislav Stana RC 1.25 3.00
247 Darryl Bootland RC 1.25 3.00
248 Trevor Daley RC 1.25 3.00
249 Peter Sarno RC 1.25 3.00
250 Nathan Smith RC 1.25 3.00

2003-04 Beehive Variations

This partial parallel set featured varying photos from the base set and could be distinguished by the lighter borders.

STATED ODDS 1:3
5 Sergei Fedorov .60 1.50
12 Ilya Kovalchuk .60 1.50
17 Don Cherry 1.00 2.50
20 Joe Thornton .75 2.00
21 Sergei Samsonov .40 1.00
25 Chris Drury .40 1.00
31 Jarome Iginla .60 1.50
35 Erik Cole .15 .40
44 Jocelyn Thibault .40 1.00
51 Patrick Roy 2.50 6.00
53 Joe Sakic 1.00 2.50
55 Peter Forsberg 1.25 3.00
59 Rick Nash .60 1.50
67 Marty Turco .40 1.00
68 Mike Modano .75 2.00
69 Gordie Howe 2.50 6.00
74 Henrik Zetterberg .50 1.25
75 Steve Yzerman 2.50 6.00
79 Ales Hemsky .15 .40
80 Raffi Torres .15 .40
81 Wayne Gretzky 3.00 8.00
86 Roberto Luongo .60 1.50
87 Marcel Dionne .60 1.50
91 Luc Robitaille .40 1.00
93 Zigmund Palffy .40 1.00
99 Marian Gaborik .75 2.00
102 Guy Lafleur 2.00 5.00
104 Jose Theodore .60 1.50
107 Saku Koivu .50 1.25
110 Tomas Vokoun .40 1.00
115 Martin Brodeur 1.25 3.00
120 Mariusz Czerkawski .15 .40
126 Rick DiPietro .40 1.00
132 Mark Messier .50 1.25
136 Jason Spezza .50 1.25
137 Marian Hossa .50 1.25
139 Bobby Clarke .75 2.00
144 Tony Amonte .40 1.00
146 Jeremy Roenick .60 1.50
153 Sean Burke .40 1.00
158 Mario Lemieux 3.00 8.00
164 Patrick Marleau .40 1.00
170 Keith Tkachuk .50 1.25
174 Nikolai Khabibulin .50 1.25
175 Vincent Lecavalier .50 1.25
182 Ed Belfour .50 1.25
183 Mats Sundin .50 1.25
190 Jason King .15 .40
195 Todd Bertuzzi .50 1.25
198 Jaromir Jagr .75 2.00

2003-04 Beehive Gold

PRINT RUN 15 SER.#'d SETS
NOT PRICED DUE TO SCARCITY

2003-04 Beehive Silver

*STARS: 3X TO 8X BASIC CARDS
*ROOKIES: 1.25X TO 3X
PRINT RUN 67 SER.#'d SETS

2003-04 Beehive Jumbos

These large box toppers were found one per box in an indivdual "jumbo" pack that carried a jumbo jersey and a jumbo base or variation card.

ONE PER BOX
1 Jean-Sebastien Giguere 1.00 2.50
2 Sergei Fedorov 1.50 4.00
3 Ilya Kovalchuk 1.50 4.00
4 Joe Thornton 2.00 5.00
5 Don Cherry 3.00 8.00
6 Ron Francis 1.00 2.50
7 Jocelyn Thibault 1.00 2.50
8 Peter Forsberg 3.00 8.00
9 Rick Nash 1.50 4.00
10 Marty Turco 1.00 2.50
11 Gordie Howe 4.00 10.00
12 Steve Yzerman 4.00 10.00
13 Roberto Luongo 1.50 4.00
14 Don Cherry 2.00 5.00
15 Marian Gaborik 2.50 6.00
16 Guy Lafleur 1.50 4.00
17 Scotty Bowman 1.50 4.00
18 Martin Brodeur 4.00 10.00
19 Jason Spezza 1.25 3.00
20 Marian Hossa 1.25 3.00
21 Jeremy Roenick 1.50 4.00
22 Mario Lemieux 5.00 12.00
23 Ed Belfour 1.25 3.00
24 Markus Naslund 1.25 3.00
25 Todd Bertuzzi 1.25 3.00

2003-04 Beehive Jumbo Variations

STATED ODDS 1:3
1 Joffrey Lupul 3.00 8.00
2 Sergei Fedorov 4.00 10.00
3 Ilya Kovalchuk 4.00 10.00
4 Joe Thornton 5.00 12.00
5 Don Cherry 8.00 20.00
6 Eric Staal 4.00 10.00
7 Tuomo Ruutu 2.50 6.00
8 Peter Forsberg 8.00 20.00
9 Rick Nash 4.00 10.00
10 Marty Turco 2.50 6.00
11 Gordie Howe 10.00 25.00
12 Jiri Hudler 4.00 10.00
13 Nathan Horton 4.00 10.00
14 Don Cherry 8.00 20.00
15 Marian Gaborik 6.00 15.00
16 Guy Lafleur 4.00 10.00
17 Scotty Bowman 4.00 10.00
18 Martin Brodeur 10.00 25.00
19 Jason Spezza 3.00 8.00
20 Marian Hossa 3.00 8.00
21 Joni Pitkanen 3.00 8.00
22 Marc-Andre Fleury 8.00 20.00
23 Ed Belfour 3.00 8.00
24 Markus Naslund 3.00 8.00
25 Todd Bertuzzi 3.00 8.00

2003-04 Beehive Jumbo Jerseys

These large box toppers were found one per box in an individual "jumbo" pack that carried a jumbo jersey and a jumbo base or variation card. Each card carried two jersey swatches.

*MULT.COLOR SWATCH: .75X TO 2X
ONE PER JUMBO PACK
BH1 Jeremy Roenick 6.00 15.00
BH2 Marty Turco 5.00 12.00
BH3 Mario Lemieux 40.00 100.00
BH4 Todd Bertuzzi 6.00 15.00
BH5 Jarome Iginla 6.00 15.00
BH6 Dominik Hasek 10.00 25.00
BH7 Chris Drury 5.00 12.00
BH8 Jose Theodore 8.00 20.00
BH9 Joe Sakic 8.00 20.00
BH10 Mike Modano 6.00 15.00
BH11 Mats Sundin 6.00 15.00
BH12 Sergei Fedorov 6.00 15.00
BH13 Keith Tkachuk 6.00 15.00
BH14 Ed Belfour 6.00 15.00
BH15 Sean Burke 5.00 12.00
BH16 Tony Amonte 5.00 12.00
BH17 Joe Thornton 8.00 20.00
BH18 Vincent Lecavalier 5.00 12.00
BH19 Roberto Luongo 8.00 20.00
BH20 Steve Yzerman 15.00 40.00
BH21 Jason Spezza 8.00 20.00
BH22 Rick Nash 8.00 20.00

2003-04 Beehive Jerseys

*MULT.COLOR SWATCH: .6X TO 1.5X
STATED ODDS 1:15
JT1 Mike Modano 5.00 12.00
JT2 Zigmund Palffy 3.00 8.00
JT3 Jason Spezza 4.00 10.00
JT4 Tony Amonte 3.00 8.00
JT5 Jeremy Roenick 5.00 12.00
JT6 Vincent Lecavalier 3.00 8.00
JT7 Marian Gaborik 8.00 20.00
JT8 Alexei Yashin 3.00 8.00
JT9 Ilya Kovalchuk 5.00 12.00
JT10 Keith Tkachuk 4.00 10.00
JT11 Markus Naslund 4.00 10.00
JT12 Bill Guerin 3.00 8.00
JT13 Brendan Shanahan 4.00 10.00
JT14 Dominik Hasek 6.00 15.00
JT15 Jose Theodore 5.00 12.00
JT16 Eric Lindros 4.00 10.00
JT17 Martin Brodeur 10.00 25.00
JT18 Patrick Lalime 3.00 8.00
JT19 Rick Nash 5.00 12.00
JT20 Ryan Smyth 3.00 8.00
JT21 Marty Turco 3.00 8.00
JT22 Roberto Luongo 5.00 12.00
JT23 Jean-Sebastien Giguere 3.00 8.00
JT24 Ed Belfour 6.00 15.00
JT25 Joe Thornton 5.00 12.00
JT26 Todd Bertuzzi 4.00 10.00
JT27 Steve Yzerman 10.00 25.00
JT28 Saku Koivu 4.00 10.00
JT29 Jarome Iginla 5.00 12.00
JT30 Chris Drury 3.00 8.00
JT31 Joe Sakic 8.00 20.00
JT32 Paul Kariya 4.00 10.00
JT33 Marian Hossa 4.00 10.00
JT34 Doug Weight 3.00 8.00
JT35 Sergei Fedorov 5.00 12.00
JT36 Mats Sundin 4.00 10.00
JT37 Mario Lemieux 12.50 30.00
JT38 Teemu Selanne 4.00 10.00
JT39 Jocelyn Thibault 4.00 10.00
JT40 Ron Francis 3.00 8.00

2003-04 Beehive Jersey Autographs

STATED ODDS 1:240
SJ1 Martin Brodeur/20
SJ2 Saku Koivu/25 40.00 100.00
SJ3 Ilya Kovalchuk/25 60.00 150.00
SJ4 Eric Lindros/25 40.00 100.00
SJ5 Patrick Roy/25 200.00 400.00
SJ6 Jason Spezza/25 50.00 100.00
SJ7 Marty Turco/25 30.00 80.00
SJ8 Jarome Iginla/30 25.00 60.00
SJ9 Wayne Gretzky/10
SJ10 Marian Hossa/50 20.00 50.00
SJ11 Gordie Howe
SJ12 Roberto Luongo/50 30.00 80.00
SJ13 Zigmund Palffy/25 15.00 40.00
SJ14 Jeremy Roenick/50 30.00 80.00
SJ15 Jose Theodore/25 40.00 100.00
SJ16 Joe Thornton/50 40.00 100.00
SJ17 David Aebischer/50 25.00 60.00
SJ18 Todd Bertuzzi/75 20.00 50.00
SJ19 Mike Comrie/75 12.50 30.00
SJ20 Marcel Hossa/75 12.50 30.00
SJ21 Markus Naslund/75 20.00 50.00
SJ22 Rick DiPietro/50 25.00 60.00
SJ23 Scott Hartnell/50 12.50 30.00
SJ24 Ales Hemsky/90 15.00 40.00
SJ25 Henrik Zetterberg/90 20.00 50.00

2003-04 Beehive Signatures

As of press time, not all cards have been verified.

STATED ODDS 1:240
KNOWN PRINT RUNS BELOW
RF1 Martin Brodeur
RF2 Patrick Roy
RF3 Jason Spezza/25 75.00 150.00
RF4 Wayne Gretzky/10
RF5 Gordie Howe/10
RF6 Jose Theodore/25 40.00 100.00
RF7 David Aebischer/25 25.00 60.00
RF8 Marian Gaborik
RF9 Jarome Iginla/25 50.00 125.00
RF10 Marian Hossa/25 25.00 60.00
RF11 Joe Thornton/100 15.00 40.00
RF12 Anson Carter/25 15.00 40.00
RF13 Chuck Kobasew/50 15.00 40.00
RF14 Roberto Luongo/25 50.00 125.00
RF15 Jeremy Roenick/25 60.00 150.00
RF16 Mike Comrie/100 8.00 20.00
RF17 Markus Naslund/100 12.50 30.00
RF18 Rick DiPietro/50 25.00 60.00
RF19 Henrik Zetterberg/100 15.00 40.00
RF20 Jared Aulin/50 12.50 30.00
RF21 Rick Nash/25 40.00 100.00
RF22 Owen Nolan/25 25.00 60.00
RF23 Marcel Hossa/50 6.00 15.00
RF24 Scott Hartnell/90 6.00 15.00
RF25 Ales Hemsky/75 6.00 15.00

2003-04 Beehive Sticks Beige Border

STATED ODDS 1:30
BE1 Jarome Iginla 5.00 12.00
BE2 Jean-Sebastien Giguere 2.50 6.00
BE3 Keith Tkachuk 4.00 10.00
BE4 Jocelyn Thibault 2.50 6.00
BE5 Martin Brodeur 10.00 25.00
BE6 Joe Sakic 8.00 20.00
BE7 Mike Modano 6.00 15.00
BE8 Johan Hedberg 2.50 6.00
BE9 Mats Sundin 4.00 10.00
BE10 Brendan Shanahan 4.00 10.00
BE11 Owen Nolan 2.50 6.00
BE12 Marc Denis 2.50 6.00
BE13 Teemu Selanne 4.00 10.00
BE14 Curtis Joseph 4.00 10.00
BE15 Patrik Stefan 2.50 6.00
BE16 Mike Comrie 2.50 6.00
BE17 Milan Hejduk 4.00 10.00
BE18 Ed Jovanovski 2.50 6.00
BE19 Luc Robitaille 2.50 6.00
BE20 Olaf Kolzig 2.50 6.00
BE21 Mika Noronen 2.50 6.00
BE22 Jeremy Roenick 6.00 15.00
BE23 Mike Dunham 2.50 6.00
BE24 Rick DiPietro 2.50 6.00
BE25 Peter Bondra 2.50 6.00
BE26 Ed Belfour 4.00 10.00
BE27 Felix Potvin 4.00 10.00
BE28 Peter Forsberg 10.00 25.00
BE29 Gordie Howe 10.00 25.00
BE30 Brian Boucher 2.50 6.00
BE31 Brett Hull 6.00 15.00
BE32 Sean Burke 2.50 6.00
BE33 Ilya Kovalchuk 6.00 15.00
BE34 Roman Cechmanek 2.50 6.00
BE35 Jaromir Jagr 6.00 15.00
BE36 David Aebischer 2.50 6.00
BE37 Dominik Hasek 8.00 20.00
BE38 Tommy Salo 2.50 6.00
BE39 Guy Lafleur 2.50 6.00
BE40 Jose Theodore 5.00 12.00
BE41 Marcel Dionne 2.50 6.00
BE42 Vincent Lecavalier 4.00 10.00

2003-04 Beehive Sticks Blue Border

STATED ODDS 1:60
BL1 Sean Burke 3.00 8.00
BL2 Zigmund Palffy 3.00 8.00
BL3 Simon Gagne 5.00 12.00
BL4 Justin Williams 3.00 8.00
BL5 Jean-Sebastien Giguere 3.00 8.00
BL6 Chris Chelios 5.00 12.00
BL7 John LeClair 5.00 12.00
BL8 Rick DiPietro 3.00 8.00
BL9 Peter Bondra 3.00 8.00
BL10 Pavel Bure 5.00 12.00
BL11 Mark Messier 5.00 12.00
BL12 Olaf Kolzig 3.00 8.00
BL13 Martin Brodeur 12.50 30.00
BL14 Felix Potvin 5.00 12.00
BL15 Owen Nolan 3.00 8.00
BL16 Patrik Stefan 3.00 8.00
BL17 Jaromir Jagr 8.00 20.00
BL18 Tommy Salo 3.00 8.00
BL19 Mark Recchi 3.00 8.00
BL20 Ed Belfour 5.00 12.00
BL21 Roman Cechmanek 3.00 8.00

2003-04 Beehive Sticks Red Border

STATED ODDS 1:60
RE1 Dominik Hasek 10.00 25.00
RE2 Brett Hull 8.00 20.00
RE3 Peter Forsberg 12.50 30.00
RE4 Jose Theodore 6.00 15.00
RE5 Marc Denis 3.00 8.00
RE6 Mike Modano 8.00 20.00

RE7 Mark Messier 6.00 15.00
RE8 Mats Sundin 5.00 12.00
RE9 Brendan Shanahan 5.00 12.00
RE10 Eric Lindros 5.00 12.00
RE11 Ron Francis 6.00 15.00
RE12 Jeremy Roenick 8.00 20.00
RE13 Ilya Kovalchuk 8.00 20.00
RE14 Martin Brodeur 12.50 30.00
RE15 Joe Sakic 10.00 25.00
RE16 Keith Tkachuk 5.00 12.00
RE17 David Aebischer 3.00 8.00
RE18 Marcel Dionne 3.00 8.00
RE19 Owen Nolan 3.00 8.00
RE20 Sergei Fedorov 8.00 20.00
RE21 Gordie Howe 12.50 30.00

2005-06 Beehive

This 250-card set was issued into the hobby in five-card (four regular and one jumbo) packs which came 15 packs to a box. Cards numbered 1-90 feature veterans in team alphabetical order while cards 91-180 feature Rookie Cards and cards 181-250 are all jumbo cards. The Rookie Cards were inserted at a stated rate of one in four.

COMP.SET w/o SP's (90) 10.00 25.00
JUMBOS 1 PER PACK
RC ODDS 1:4
1 Teemu Selanne .40 1.00
2 Joffrey Lupul .25 .60
3 Jean-Sebastien Giguere .30 .75
4 Ilya Kovalchuk .50 1.25
5 Kari Lehtonen .40 1.00
6 Marian Hossa .30 .75
7 Patrice Bergeron .40 1.00
8 Sergei Samsonov .30 .75
9 Andrew Raycroft .30 .75
10 Brian Leetch .40 1.00
11 Glen Murray .25 .60
12 Chris Drury .30 .75
13 Daniel Briere .30 .75
14 Jarome Iginla .30 .75
15 Miikka Kiprusoff .40 1.00
16 Tony Amonte .30 .75
17 Erik Cole .25 .60
18 Eric Staal .30 .75
19 Nikolai Khabibulin .40 1.00
20 Tuomo Ruutu .25 .60
21 Eric Daze .30 .75
22 Joe Sakic .75 2.00
23 Milan Hejduk .30 .75
24 Alex Tanguay .30 .75
25 Rob Blake .30 .75
26 Rick Nash .50 1.25
27 Sergei Fedorov .40 1.00
28 Mike Modano .40 1.00
29 Bill Guerin .25 .60
30 Marty Turco .30 .75
31 Steve Yzerman 1.00 2.50
32 Brendan Shanahan .40 1.00
33 Pavel Datsyuk .40 1.00
34 Nicklas Lidstrom .40 1.00
35 Ty Conklin .30 .75
36 Chris Pronger .30 .75
37 Ryan Smyth .30 .75
38 Roberto Luongo .60 1.50
39 Jay Bouwmeester .25 .60
40 Olli Jokinen .30 .75
41 Luc Robitaille .30 .75
42 Jeremy Roenick .40 1.00
43 Pavol Demitra .30 .75
44 Marian Gaborik .50 1.25
45 Dwayne Roloson .30 .75
46 Saku Koivu .40 1.00
47 Jose Theodore .40 1.00
48 Michael Ryder .30 .75
49 Mike Ribeiro .25 .60
50 Paul Kariya .40 1.00
51 Tomas Vokoun .30 .75
52 Martin Brodeur 1.00 2.50
53 Patrik Elias .30 .75
54 Scott Gomez .30 .75
55 Alexander Mogilny .30 .75
56 Miroslav Satan .25 .60
57 Alexei Yashin .25 .60
58 Rick DiPietro .30 .75
59 Jaromir Jagr .60 1.50
60 Dominik Hasek .50 1.25
61 Dany Heatley .40 1.00
62 Martin Havlat .30 .75
63 Jason Spezza .40 1.00
64 Daniel Alfredsson .30 .75
65 Peter Forsberg .60 1.50
66 Robert Esche .30 .75
67 Keith Primeau .25 .60
68 Simon Gagne .40 1.00
69 Curtis Joseph .40 1.00
70 Shane Doan .25 .60
71 Mario Lemieux 1.50 4.00
72 Mark Recchi .30 .75
73 Zigmund Palffy .30 .75
74 Joe Thornton .60 1.50
75 Patrick Marleau .30 .75
76 Jonathan Cheechoo .40 1.00
77 Evgeni Nabokov .30 .75
78 Doug Weight .30 .75
79 Keith Tkachuk .40 1.00
80 Martin St. Louis .30 .75
81 Vincent Lecavalier .40 1.00
82 Brad Richards .30 .75
83 Mats Sundin .40 1.00
84 Ed Belfour .40 1.00
85 Eric Lindros .40 1.00
86 Jason Allison .25 .60
87 Markus Naslund .40 1.00
88 Brendan Morrison .25 .60
89 Todd Bertuzzi .50 1.25
90 Olaf Kolzig .30 .75
91 Brandon Bochenski RC 1.50 4.00
92 Patrick Eaves RC 2.50 6.00
93 Derek Boogaard RC 2.00 5.00
94 Brad Richardson RC 1.50 4.00
95 Ole-Kristian Tollefsen RC 1.50 4.00
96 Dennis Wideman RC 1.50 4.00
97 Lee Stempniak RC 1.50 4.00
98 Maxim Lapierre RC 1.50 4.00
99 Andrei Kostitsyn RC 2.50 6.00
100 Rob McVicar RC 1.50 4.00
101 Sidney Crosby RC 40.00 80.00
102 Alexander Ovechkin RC 20.00 50.00
103 Jeff Carter RC 3.00 8.00
104 Corey Perry RC 3.00 8.00
105 Rostislav Olesz RC 2.00 5.00
106 Gilbert Brule RC 2.50 6.00
107 Zach Parise RC 4.00 10.00
108 Alexander Perezhogin RC 2.00 5.00
109 Hannu Toivonen RC 2.50 6.00
110 Wojtek Wolski RC 3.00 8.00
111 Jeff Woywitka RC 1.50 4.00
112 Alexander Steen RC 3.00 8.00
113 Ryan Getzlaf RC 3.00 8.00
114 Dion Phaneuf RC 6.00 15.00
115 Ryan Suter RC 2.00 5.00
116 Mike Richards RC 3.00 8.00
117 Cam Ward RC 3.00 8.00
118 Robert Nilsson RC 1.50 4.00
119 Jim Howard RC 5.00 12.00
120 Thomas Vanek RC 4.00 10.00
121 Braydon Coburn RC 1.50 4.00
122 Brent Seabrook RC 2.00 5.00
123 Peter Budaj RC 2.50 6.00
124 Yann Danis RC 2.00 4.00
125 David Leneveu RC 1.50 4.00
126 Henrik Lundqvist RC 6.00 15.00
127 Johan Franzen RC 2.00 5.00
128 Andrej Meszaros RC 1.50 4.00
129 Jussi Jokinen RC 2.50 6.00
130 Rene Bourque RC 1.50 4.00
131 Jay McClement RC 1.50 4.00
132 Keith Ballard RC 1.50 4.00
133 Evgeny Artyukhin RC 1.50 4.00
134 R.J. Umberger RC 2.00 5.00
135 Petteri Nokelainen RC 1.50 4.00
136 Petr Prucha RC 2.50 6.00
137 Ryan Whitney RC 2.00 5.00
138 Matt Foy RC 1.50 4.00
139 Ryane Clowe RC 2.00 5.00
140 Andrew Wozniewski RC 1.50 4.00
141 Maxime Talbot RC 1.50 4.00
142 Anthony Stewart RC 2.00 5.00
143 Andrew Alberts RC 1.50 4.00
144 Jakub Klepis RC 1.50 4.00
145 Mikko Koivu RC 2.50 6.00
146 Ryan Hollweg RC 1.50 4.00
147 Jim Slater RC 1.50 4.00
148 Chris Campoli RC 1.50 4.00
149 Jordan Sigalet RC 2.00 5.00
150 Steve Bernier RC 2.50 6.00
151 Tomas Fleischmann RC 1.50 4.00
152 Matt Jones RC 1.50 4.00
153 Barry Tallackson RC 2.00 5.00
154 Ben Eager RC 1.50 4.00
155 Danny Richmond RC 1.50 4.00
156 Andrew Ladd RC 2.00 5.00
157 Jeremy Colliton RC 1.50 4.00
158 Bruno Gervais RC 1.50 4.00
159 Jeff Tambellini RC 1.50 4.00
160 Gerald Coleman RC 1.50 4.00
161 Paul Ranger RC 1.50 4.00
162 Staffan Kronwall RC 1.50 4.00
163 Dustin Penner RC 2.50 6.00
164 Kyle Brodziak RC 1.50 4.00
165 Greg Jacina RC 1.50 4.00
166 Erik Christensen RC 1.50 4.00
167 Kyle Quincey RC 1.50 4.00
168 Chris Thorburn RC 1.50 4.00
169 Christoph Schubert RC 1.50 4.00
170 Dimitri Patzold RC 1.50 4.00
171 Junior Lessard RC 1.50 4.00
172 Vojtech Polak RC 1.50 4.00
173 Adam Berkhoel RC 1.50 4.00
174 Cam Barker RC 1.50 4.00
175 Kevin Dallman RC 1.50 4.00
176 Milan Jurcina RC 1.50 4.00
177 Brad Winchester RC 1.50 4.00
178 George Parros RC 1.50 4.00
179 Al Montoya RC 2.50 6.00
180 Brett Lebda RC 1.50 4.00
181 Joe Sakic 2.00 5.00
182 Alex Tanguay 1.00 2.50
183 Milan Hejduk 1.25 3.00
184 Rick Nash 1.25 3.00
185 Mike Modano 1.50 4.00
186 Bill Guerin .60 1.50
187 Steve Yzerman 2.50 6.00
188 Brendan Shanahan 1.25 3.00
189 Chris Pronger 1.00 2.50
190 Roberto Luongo 1.50 4.00
191 Jeremy Roenick 1.50 4.00
192 Luc Robitaille 1.00 2.50
193 Marian Gaborik 1.50 4.00
194 Saku Koivu 1.25 3.00
195 Jose Theodore 1.25 3.00
196 Paul Kariya 1.25 3.00
197 Martin Brodeur 2.50 6.00
198 Patrik Elias 1.00 2.50
199 Miroslav Satan .60 1.50
200 Alexei Yashin .60 1.50
201 Jaromir Jagr 1.50 4.00
202 Dominik Hasek 1.50 4.00
203 Dany Heatley 1.50 4.00
204 Jason Spezza 1.25 3.00
205 Peter Forsberg 1.50 4.00
206 Keith Primeau 1.00 2.50
207 Curtis Joseph 1.25 3.00
208 Brett Hull 1.50 4.00
209 Mario Lemieux 3.00 8.00
210 Evgeni Nabokov 1.00 2.50
211 Jonathan Cheechoo 1.25 3.00
212 Keith Tkachuk 1.25 3.00
213 Doug Weight 1.00 2.50
214 Martin St. Louis 1.00 2.50
215 Vincent Lecavalier 1.25 3.00
216 Mats Sundin 1.25 3.00
217 Ed Belfour 1.25 3.00
218 Eric Lindros 1.25 3.00
219 Markus Naslund 1.25 3.00
220 Olaf Kolzig 1.00 2.50
221 Mike Bossy 1.25 3.00
222 Wayne Cashman .60 1.50
223 Gerry Cheevers 1.00 2.50
224 Bobby Clarke 1.25 3.00
225 Phil Esposito 1.50 4.00
226 Tony Esposito 1.25 3.00
227 Grant Fuhr 1.50 4.00
228 Glenn Hall 1.25 3.00
229 Jari Kurri 1.25 3.00
230 Guy Lafleur 1.50 4.00
231 Lanny McDonald 1.00 2.50
232 Gilbert Perreault 1.25 3.00
233 Jean Beliveau 1.25 3.00
234 Johnny Bucyk 1.25 3.00
235 Gordie Howe 1.50 4.00
236 Wayne Gretzky 5.00 12.00
237 Bernie Geoffrion 1.25 3.00
238 Red Kelly .75 2.00
239 Stan Mikita 1.25 3.00
240 Bryan Trottier 1.00 2.50
241 Jean-Sebastien Giguere 1.00 2.50
242 Sergei Fedorov 1.25 3.00
243 Teemu Selanne 1.25 3.00
244 Ilya Kovalchuk 1.50 4.00
245 Marian Hossa 1.00 2.50
246 Patrice Bergeron 1.25 3.00
247 Joe Thornton 1.50 4.00
248 Jarome Iginla 1.50 4.00
249 Miikka Kiprusoff 1.25 3.00
250 Nikolai Khabibulin 1.25 3.00

2005-06 Beehive Beige

*STARS: 5X TO 12X BASE HI
*ROOKIES: 2X TO .5X
BEIGE ODDS 1:15
SKIP-NUMBERED SET
101 Sidney Crosby 20.00 50.00
102 Alexander Ovechkin 15.00 40.00

2005-06 Beehive Blue

*STARS: 4X TO 10X BASE HI
*ROOKIES: .15X TO .4X
BLUE ODDS 1:5
SKIP-NUMBERED SET
101 Sidney Crosby 25.00 60.00

2005-06 Beehive Gold

*STARS: 10X TO 25X BASE HI
*ROOKIES: 2X TO 5X
ODDS 1:240
SKIP-NUMBERED SET
101 Sidney Crosby 125.00 250.00
102 Alexander Ovechkin 60.00 120.00

2005-06 Beehive Red

*STARS: 2X TO 5X BASE HI
*ROOKIES: .10X TO .25X
ODDS 1:2
SKIP-NUMBERED SET
101 Sidney Crosby 20.00 50.00

2005-06 Beehive Rookie Jumbos

COMPLETE SET (5) 20.00 40.00
R1 Sidney Crosby 8.00 20.00
R2 Alexander Ovechkin 3.00 8.00
R3 Jeff Carter 3.00 8.00

R4 Alexander Perezhogin 1.50 4.00
R5 Corey Perry 2.00 5.00

2005-06 Beehive Matte

*STARS: 6X TO 15X BASE HI
1-100 PRINT RUN 100 SER.#'d SETS
*ROOKIES: 1.5X TO 4X
101-180 PRINT RUN 25 SER.#'d SETS
101 Sidney Crosby 500.00 1000.00

2005-06 Beehive Matted Materials

ODDS 1:7.5
MMAF Adam Foote 2.50 6.00
MMAH Ales Hemsky 5.00 12.00
MMAK Alex Kovalev 4.00 10.00
MMAR Andrew Raycroft 6.00 15.00
MMAY Alexei Yashin 5.00 12.00
MMBG Bill Guerin 5.00 12.00
MMBM Brendan Morrison 4.00 10.00
MMBR Brad Richards 6.00 15.00
MMBW Brendan Witt 5.00 12.00
MMCD Chris Drury 6.00 15.00
MMCJ Curtis Joseph 6.00 15.00
MMCO Chris Osgood 4.00 10.00
MMDA Daniel Alfredsson 6.00 15.00
MMDB Dustin Brown 5.00 12.00
MMDC Dan Cloutier 6.00 15.00
MMDE Pavol Demitra 6.00 15.00
MMDH Dany Heatley 6.00 15.00
MMDR Dwayne Roloson 6.00 15.00
MMDW Doug Weight 6.00 15.00
MMEL Eric Lindros 6.00 15.00
MMGA Mathieu Garon 6.00 15.00
MMGI Brian Gionta 2.50 6.00
MMGL Guy Lafleur 6.00 15.00
MMGM Glen Murray 5.00 12.00
MMGO Scott Gomez 6.00 15.00
MMHJ Milan Hejduk 6.00 15.00
MMHO Marian Hossa 6.00 15.00
MMHS Henrik Sedin 2.50 6.00
MMHZ Henrik Zetterberg 6.00 15.00
MMIK Ilya Kovalchuk 8.00 20.00
MMJB Jay Bouwmeester 5.00 12.00
MMJG Jean-Sebastien Giguere 6.00 15.00
MMJO Jose Theodore 5.00 12.00
MMJR Jeremy Roenick 6.00 15.00
MMJS Jason Spezza 6.00 15.00
MMJT Joe Thornton 10.00 25.00
MMJW Jason Williams 2.50 6.00
MMKP Keith Primeau 5.00 12.00
MMKT Keith Tkachuk 6.00 15.00
MMLN Ladislav Nagy 5.00 12.00
MMLR Luc Robitaille 6.00 15.00
MMLU Joffrey Lupul 5.00 12.00
MMMB Martin Brodeur 8.00 20.00
MMMC Bryan McCabe 5.00 12.00
MMMD Marc Denis 6.00 15.00
MMMF Manny Fernandez 6.00 15.00
MMMG Martin Gerber 6.00 15.00
MMMH Marcel Hossa 5.00 12.00
MMMI Milan Michalek 2.50 6.00
MMMK Miikka Kiprusoff 6.00 15.00
MMML Mario Lemieux 12.00 30.00
MMMM Mike Modano 6.00 15.00
MMMN Markus Naslund 6.00 15.00
MMMP Mark Parrish 5.00 12.00
MMMR Michael Ryder 6.00 15.00
MMMS Mats Sundin 6.00 15.00
MMMT Marty Turco 6.00 15.00
MMMW Brenden Morrow 6.00 15.00
MMNA Nik Antropov 5.00 12.00
MMNH Nathan Horton 5.00 12.00
MMNK Nikolai Khabibulin 6.00 15.00
MMOJ Olli Jokinen 6.00 15.00
MMPA Patrik Elias 6.00 15.00
MMPB Pierre-Marc Bouchard 5.00 12.00
MMPD Pavel Datsyuk 6.00 15.00
MMPE Michael Peca 5.00 12.00
MMPF Peter Forsberg 8.00 20.00
MMRB Rob Blake 6.00 15.00
MMRE Robert Esche 6.00 15.00
MMRM Ryan Miller 4.00 10.00
MMRN Rick Nash 8.00 20.00
MMSA Joe Sakic 10.00 25.00
MMSC Sidney Crosby 50.00 100.00
MMSF Sergei Fedorov 6.00 15.00
MMSG Simon Gagne 6.00 15.00
MMSK Saku Koivu 6.00 15.00
MMSL Martin St. Louis 6.00 15.00
MMSS Sergei Samsonov 6.00 15.00
MMST Matt Stajan 5.00 12.00
MMSY Steve Yzerman 8.00 20.00
MMTB Todd Bertuzzi 8.00 20.00
MMTC Ty Conklin 6.00 15.00
MMWG Wayne Gretzky 15.00 40.00

2005-06 Beehive Matted Materials Remarkable

AU 2.5X to 4X MATTED MATERIALS
PRINT RUN 50 SER.#'d SETS
RMSC Sidney Crosby 400.00 550.00

2005-06 Beehive PhotoGraphs

ODDS 1:60
PGAO Alexander Ovechkin 50.00 100.00
PGBH Bobby Hull 40.00 80.00
PGCO Corey Perry 10.00 25.00
PGCP Chris Pronger 12.00 30.00
PGDW Doug Weight 8.00 20.00
PGES Eric Staal 10.00 25.00
PGGH Gordie Howe 50.00 125.00
PGGL Guy LaFleur 30.00 80.00
PGJC Jeff Carter 12.00 30.00
PGJI Jarome Iginla 15.00 40.00
PGJS Jason Spezza 10.00 25.00
PGJT Joe Thornton 12.00 30.00
PGLA Guy Lapointe 8.00 20.00
PGMB Mike Bossy 10.00 25.00
PGMD Marcel Dionne 10.00 25.00
PGMM Mike Modano 12.00 30.00
PGMN Markus Naslund 8.00 20.00
PGMT Marty Turco 8.00 20.00
PGPE Phil Esposito SP 40.00 80.00
PGRB Ray Bourque 30.00 80.00
PGRN Rick Nash 12.00 30.00
PGSC Sidney Crosby 100.00 200.00
PGSL Martin St. Louis 8.00 20.00
PGTE Tony Esposito 15.00 40.00
PGWG Wayne Gretzky SP 200.00 300.00

2005-06 Beehive Signature Scrapbook

ODDS 1:30
SSAA Andrew Alberts 3.00 8.00
SSAM Andrej Meszaros 3.00 8.00
SSAO Alexander Ovechkin 75.00 150.00
SSAP Alexander Perezhogin 8.00 20.00
SSAR Andrew Raycroft 6.00 15.00
SSAS Anthony Stewart 8.00 20.00
SSBA Matthew Barnaby 3.00 8.00
SSBB Brandon Bochenski 3.00 8.00
SSBC Bobby Clarke 12.00 30.00
SSBE Steve Bernier 8.00 20.00
SSBM Brenden Morrow 8.00 20.00
SSBO Mike Bossy SP 20.00 50.00
SSBP Brad Park 6.00 15.00
SSBR Brad Richards 6.00 15.00
SSBS Borje Salming 8.00 20.00
SSBU Peter Budaj 6.00 15.00
SSCB Cam Barker 3.00 8.00
SSCC Chris Campoli 3.00 8.00
SSCH Jonathan Cheechoo 8.00 20.00
SSCK Chris Kunitz 5.00 12.00
SSCL Ryane Clowe 3.00 8.00
SSCN Craig Conroy 3.00 8.00
SSCO Braydon Coburn 8.00 20.00
SSCP Corey Perry 8.00 20.00
SSCS Cory Stillman 3.00 8.00
SSCW Cam Ward 15.00 40.00
SSDA Daniel Alfredsson 8.00 20.00
SSDC Don Cherry 12.00 30.00
SSDF Dan Fritsche 3.00 8.00
SSDH Dany Heatley SP 20.00 50.00
SSDI Dickie Moore 6.00 15.00
SSDK Duncan Keith 3.00 8.00
SSDL David Leneveu 8.00 20.00
SSDM Darren McCarty 6.00 15.00
SSDP Dion Phaneuf 15.00 40.00
SSDS Derek Sanderson 8.00 20.00
SSDT Dave Taylor 5.00 12.00
SSEA Patrick Eaves 6.00 15.00
SSED Eric Daze 3.00 8.00
SSFC Fred Cusick 3.00 8.00
SSFT Fedor Tjutin 3.00 8.00
SSGB Gilbert Brule 5.00 12.00
SSGH Gordie Howe SP 60.00 150.00
SSGL Guy Lafleur SP 50.00 100.00
SSGP Gilbert Perreault 10.00 25.00
SSHO Marian Hossa 6.00 15.00
SSHV Martin Havlat 8.00 20.00
SSHZ Henrik Zetterberg 10.00 25.00
SSJB Jay Bouwmeester SP 15.00 40.00
SSJC Jeff Carter 12.00 30.00
SSJF Johan Franzen 8.00 20.00
SSJH Jim Howard 15.00 40.00
SSJI Jarome Iginla SP 12.00 30.00
SSJM Jay McClement 3.00 8.00
SSJO Jeff O'Neill 3.00 8.00
SSJR Jeremy Roenick 20.00 50.00
SSJS Jason Spezza SP
SSJT Joe Thornton SP 20.00 40.00
SSJV Josef Vasicek 3.00 8.00
SSKM Ken Morrow 3.00 8.00
SSKN Kevin Nastiuk 8.00 20.00
SSKP Keith Primeau SP 8.00 20.00
SSLM Lanny McDonald 5.00 12.00
SSLR Luc Robitaille SP 30.00 80.00
SSLS Lee Stempniak 3.00 8.00
SSLU Roberto Luongo SP 25.00 60.00
SSMB Martin Brodeur SP 75.00 150.00
SSMC Mike Cammalleri 8.00 20.00
SSMD Marcel Dionne SP 20.00 50.00
SSMG Marian Gaborik SP 30.00 60.00
SSMH Marcel Hossa 3.00 8.00
SSMI Miroslav Satan 3.00 8.00
SSMJ Milan Jurcina 3.00 8.00
SSMK Mikko Koivu 8.00 20.00
SSMM Mike Modano SP 20.00 50.00
SSMN Markus Naslund SP 10.00 25.00
SSMP Michael Peca 3.00 8.00
SSMR Mike Ribeiro SP 8.00 20.00
SSMS Marco Sturm 3.00 8.00
SSMT Marty Turco 6.00 15.00
SSMU Larry Murphy 3.00 8.00
SSNH Nathan Horton 3.00 8.00
SSNK Nikolai Khabibulin 8.00 20.00
SSNY Michael Nylander 3.00 8.00
SSNZ Nikolai Zherdev 8.00 20.00
SSON Owen Nolan 5.00 12.00
SSPB Patrice Bergeron SP 10.00 25.00
SSPE Phil Esposito SP 25.00 50.00
SSPN Petteri Nokelainen 3.00 8.00
SSPP Petr Prucha 10.00 25.00
SSRB Rob Blake 8.00 20.00
SSRE Robert Esche 3.00 8.00
SSRI Michael Richards 6.00 15.00
SSRL Reggie Leach 5.00 12.00
SSRM Ryan Miller 6.00 15.00
SSRN Rick Nash SP 15.00 40.00
SSRS Ryan Smyth 10.00 25.00
SSRV Rogie Vachon 8.00 20.00
SSRW Ryan Whitney 6.00 15.00
SSRY Michael Ryder 6.00 15.00
SSSB Scotty Bowman SP 20.00 40.00
SSSC Sidney Crosby SP 200.00 350.00
SSSD Shane Doan 3.00 8.00
SSSE Brent Seabrook 3.00 8.00
SSSG Simon Gagne 10.00 25.00
SSSL Martin St. Louis SP 10.00 25.00
SSST Alexander Steen 8.00 20.00
SSSZ Sergei Zubov 3.00 8.00
SSTA Tyler Arnason 3.00 8.00
SSTB Todd Bertuzzi SP 12.00 30.00
SSTE Tony Esposito SP 20.00 40.00
SSTO Terry O'Reilly 6.00 15.00
SSTV Thomas Vanek 15.00 40.00
SSVP Vaclav Prospal 3.00 8.00
SSWC Wayne Cashman 6.00 15.00
SSYD Yann Danis 6.00 15.00
SSZC Zdeno Chara 8.00 20.00
SSZP Zach Parise 8.00 20.00

2006-07 Beehive

This 235-card set was released in April, 2007. The set was issued into the hobby in five card packs (four regular size and a jumbo card), with a $4.99 SRP, which came 15 packs to a box and 16 boxes to a case. Cards numbered 1-100 feature veterans, while cards 101-160 feature Rookie Cards and cards 161-235 feature a mix of veterans and retired greats in a 5" by 7" form.

COMPLETE SET w/o SPs (100) 10.00 25.00
5 X 7 ONE PER PACK 1.25 3.00
1 Alexander Ovechkin 1.50 4.00
2 Olaf Kolzig .50 1.25
3 Markus Naslund .40 1.00
4 Roberto Luongo .75 2.00
5 Mats Sundin .40 1.00
6 Michael Peca .25 .60
7 Alexander Steen .30 .75
8 Andrew Raycroft .30 .75
9 Vincent Lecavalier .40 1.00
10 Brad Richards .40 1.00
11 Martin St. Louis .40 1.00
12 Manny Legace .30 .75
13 Keith Tkachuk .40 1.00
14 Doug Weight .25 .60
15 Joe Thornton .60 1.50
16 Patrick Marleau .30 .75
17 Jonathan Cheechoo .40 1.00
18 Vesa Toskala .30 .75
19 Sidney Crosby 2.00 5.00
20 Mark Recchi .25 .60
21 Marc-Andre Fleury .40 1.00
22 Colby Armstrong .25 .60
23 Shane Doan .30 .75
24 Ed Jovanovski .25 .60
25 Jeremy Roenick .40 1.00
26 Owen Nolan .30 .75
27 Peter Forsberg .60 1.50
28 Simon Gagne .40 1.00
29 Jeff Carter .40 1.00
30 Joni Pitkanen .25 .60
31 Jason Spezza .40 1.00
32 Dany Heatley .40 1.00
33 Martin Gerber .40 1.00
34 Daniel Alfredsson .30 .75
35 Jaromir Jagr .60 1.50
36 Brendan Shanahan .40 1.00
37 Henrik Lundqvist .60 1.50
38 Alexei Yashin .25 .60
39 Rick DiPietro .40 1.00
40 Miroslav Satan .25 .60
41 Martin Brodeur 1.25 3.00
42 Patrik Elias .25 .60
43 Brian Gionta .25 .60
44 Paul Kariya .40 1.00
45 Tomas Vokoun .30 .75
46 Jason Arnott .25 .60
47 Saku Koivu .40 1.00
48 Cristobal Huet .40 1.00
49 Michael Ryder .30 .75
50 Alexei Kovalev .25 .60
51 Marian Gaborik .60 1.50
52 Manny Fernandez .40 1.00
53 Pavol Demitra .25 .60
54 Mark Parrish .25 .60
55 Alexander Frolov .25 .60
56 Rob Blake .30 .75
57 Ed Belfour 1.00 2.50
58 Todd Bertuzzi .30 .75
59 Olli Jokinen .25 .60
60 Ales Hemsky .25 .60
61 Jarret Stoll .25 .60
62 Ryan Smyth .30 .75
63 Joffrey Lupul .25 .60
64 Henrik Zetterberg .40 1.00
65 Dominik Hasek .50 1.25
66 Pavel Datsyuk .40 1.00
67 Nicklas Lidstrom .40 1.00
68 Mike Modano .40 1.00
69 Marty Turco .30 .75
70 Eric Lindros .40 1.00
71 Rick Nash .40 1.00
72 Pascal LeClaire .40 1.00
73 Gilbert Brule .25 .60
74 Sergei Fedorov .40 1.00
75 Joe Sakic .75 2.00
76 Milan Hejduk .30 .75
77 Jose Theodore .40 1.00
78 Marek Svatos .25 .60
79 Nikolai Khabibulin .40 1.00
80 Tuomo Ruutu .25 .60
81 Martin Havlat .30 .75
82 Eric Staal .30 .75
83 Cam Ward .60 1.50
84 Rod Brind'Amour .30 .75
85 Jarome Iginla .60 1.50
86 Miikka Kiprusoff .40 1.00
87 Alex Tanguay .30 .75
88 Dion Phaneuf .50 1.25
89 Chris Drury .30 .75
90 Ryan Miller .40 1.00
91 Patrice Bergeron .30 .75
92 Hannu Toivonen .40 1.00
93 Brad Boyes .25 .60
94 Zdeno Chara .25 .60
95 Ilya Kovalchuk .50 1.25
96 Kari Lehtonen .40 1.00
97 Marian Hossa .30 .75
98 Teemu Selanne .30 .75
99 Chris Pronger .30 .75
100 Jean-Sebastien Giguere .40 1.00
101 David McKee RC 1.50 4.00
102 Ryan Shannon RC 1.25 3.00
103 Shane O'Brien RC 1.25 3.00
104 Matt Lashoff RC 1.25 3.00
105 Phil Kessel RC 4.00 10.00
106 Mark Stuart RC 1.25 3.00
107 Yan Stastny RC 1.25 3.00
108 Clarke MacArthur RC 1.25 3.00
109 Drew Stafford RC 1.50 4.00
110 Brandon Prust RC 1.25 3.00
111 Dustin Boyd RC 1.50 4.00
112 Michael Blunden RC 1.25 3.00
113 Dave Bolland RC 2.50 6.00
114 Paul Stastny RC 5.00 12.00
115 Fredrik Norrena RC 1.25 3.00
116 Loui Eriksson RC 1.25 3.00
117 Tomas Kopecky RC 1.50 4.00
118 Stefan Liv RC 1.50 4.00
119 Jeff Drouin-Deslauriers RC 1.50 4.00
120 Alexei Mikhnov RC 1.25 3.00
121 Ladislav Smid RC 1.25 3.00
122 Patrick Thoresen RC 1.25 3.00
123 Marc-Antoine Pouliot RC 1.50 4.00
124 David Booth RC 1.25 3.00
125 Anze Kopitar RC 3.00 8.00
126 Patrick O'Sullivan RC 1.50 4.00
127 Konstantin Pushkaryov RC 1.25 3.00
128 Benoit Pouliot RC 1.50 4.00
129 Mikhail Grabovski RC 1.25 3.00
130 Guillaume Latendresse RC 4.00 10.00
131 Alexander Radulov RC 3.00 8.00
132 Shea Weber RC 1.50 4.00
133 Travis Zajac RC 2.00 5.00
134 Johnny Oduya RC 1.25 3.00
135 Blake Comeau RC 1.25 3.00
136 Nigel Dawes RC 1.25 3.00
137 Jarkko Immonen RC 1.25 3.00
138 Josh Hennessy RC 1.25 3.00
139 Kelly Guard RC 1.50 4.00
140 Martin Houle RC 1.25 3.00
141 Ryan Potulny RC 1.50 4.00
142 Enver Lisin RC 1.25 3.00
143 Keith Yandle RC 1.25 3.00
144 Evgeni Malkin RC 6.00 15.00
145 Kristopher Letang RC 2.00 5.00
146 Jordan Staal RC 5.00 12.00
147 Michel Ouellet RC 2.00 5.00
148 Noah Welch RC 1.25 3.00
149 Joe Pavelski RC 4.00 10.00
150 Marc-Edouard Vlasic RC 1.25 3.00
151 Matt Carle RC 1.50 4.00
152 Marek Schwarz RC 2.50 6.00
153 Blair Jones RC 1.25 3.00
154 Ian White RC 1.25 3.00
155 Brendan Bell RC 1.25 3.00
156 Kris Newbury RC 1.25 3.00
157 Jesse Schultz RC 1.25 3.00
158 Alexander Edler RC 1.25 3.00
159 Luc Bourdon RC 1.50 4.00
160 Eric Fehr RC 1.50 4.00
161 Alexander Ovechkin 5.00 12.00
162 Roberto Luongo 2.50 6.00
163 Markus Naslund 1.25 3.00
164 Michael Peca .75 2.00
165 Mats Sundin 1.25 3.00
166 Vincent Lecavalier 1.25 3.00
167 Joe Thornton 2.00 5.00
168 Jonathan Cheechoo 1.25 3.00
169 Sidney Crosby 6.00 15.00
170 Mario Lemieux 4.00 10.00

171 Marc-Andre Fleury 1.25 3.00
172 Jeremy Roenick 1.25 3.00
173 Shane Doan 1.00 2.50
174 Bobby Clarke 1.25 3.00
175 Peter Forsberg 2.00 5.00
176 Simon Gagne 1.25 3.00
177 Jason Spezza 1.25 3.00
178 Dany Heatley 1.25 3.00
179 Jaromir Jagr 2.00 5.00
180 Brendan Shanahan 1.25 3.00
181 Henrik Lundqvist 2.00 5.00
182 Mike Bossy 1.00 2.50
183 Billy Smith 1.50 4.00
184 Miroslav Satan .75 2.00
185 Martin Brodeur 4.00 10.00
186 Patrik Elias .75 2.00
187 Paul Kariya 1.25 3.00
188 Tomas Vokoun 1.00 2.50
189 Patrick Roy 4.00 10.00
190 Michael Ryder 1.00 2.50
191 Saku Koivu 1.25 3.00
192 Guy Lafleur 1.25 3.00
193 Marian Gaborik 2.00 5.00
194 Manny Fernandez 1.25 3.00
195 Rob Blake 1.00 2.50
196 Alexander Frolov .75 2.00
197 Luc Robitaille 1.00 2.50
198 Marcel Dionne .75 2.00
199 Ed Belfour 3.00 8.00
200 Todd Bertuzzi 1.00 2.50
201 Ryan Smyth 1.00 2.50
202 Ales Hemsky .75 2.00
203 Grant Fuhr 2.00 5.00
204 Gordie Howe 5.00 12.00
205 Henrik Zetterberg 1.25 3.00
206 Nicklas Lidstrom 1.25 3.00
207 Dominik Hasek 1.50 4.00
208 Mike Modano 1.25 3.00
209 Marty Turco 1.00 2.50
210 Eric Lindros 1.25 3.00
211 Rick Nash 1.25 3.00
212 Pascal LeClaire 1.25 3.00
213 Joe Sakic 2.50 6.00
214 Milan Hejduk 1.00 2.50
215 Jose Theodore 1.25 3.00
216 Ray Bourque 1.25 3.00
217 Bobby Hull 1.25 3.00
218 Tony Esposito 2.00 5.00
219 Martin Havlat 1.00 2.50
220 Cam Ward 2.00 5.00
221 Eric Staal 1.00 2.50
222 Jarome Iginla 2.00 5.00
223 Dion Phaneuf 1.50 4.00
224 Miikka Kiprusoff 1.25 3.00
225 Alex Tanguay 1.00 2.50
226 Chris Drury 1.00 2.50
227 Ryan Miller 1.25 3.00
228 Patrice Bergeron 1.00 2.50
229 Cam Neely 1.00 2.50
230 Brad Boyes .75 2.00
231 Bobby Orr 3.00 8.00
232 Ilya Kovalchuk 1.50 4.00
233 Kari Lehtonen 1.25 3.00
234 Teemu Selanne 1.25 3.00
235 Chris Pronger 1.00 2.50

2006-07 Beehive Blue

*STARS: 3X TO 8X BASE HI
*RCs: .3X TO .8X BASE HI
STATED ODDS 1:15
SKIP-NUMBERED SET
19 Sidney Crosby 12.00 30.00
144 Evgeni Malkin 10.00 25.00

2006-07 Beehive Gold

*GOLD (1-100): 5X TO 12X
*GOLD (101-160): 2X TO 5X
STATED ODDS 1:240
SKIP-NUMBERED SET
1 Alexander Ovechkin 20.00 50.00
3 Markus Naslund 5.00 12.00
4 Roberto Luongo 10.00 25.00
5 Mats Sundin 5.00 12.00
8 Andrew Raycroft 4.00 10.00
9 Vincent Lecavalier 5.00 12.00
11 Martin St. Louis 5.00 12.00
13 Keith Tkachuk 4.00 10.00
14 Doug Weight 3.00 8.00
15 Joe Thornton 8.00 20.00
16 Patrick Marleau 4.00 10.00
17 Jonathan Cheechoo 5.00 12.00
19 Sidney Crosby 25.00 60.00
21 Marc-Andre Fleury 5.00 12.00
23 Shane Doan 4.00 10.00
25 Jeremy Roenick 5.00 12.00
27 Peter Forsberg 8.00 20.00
28 Simon Gagne 5.00 12.00
31 Jason Spezza 5.00 12.00
32 Dany Heatley 5.00 12.00
35 Jaromir Jagr 8.00 20.00
36 Brendan Shanahan 5.00 12.00
37 Henrik Lundqvist 8.00 20.00
38 Alexei Yashin 3.00 8.00
40 Miroslav Satan 3.00 8.00
41 Martin Brodeur 15.00 40.00
42 Patrik Elias 3.00 8.00
43 Brian Gionta 3.00 8.00
44 Paul Kariya 5.00 12.00
45 Tomas Vokoun 4.00 10.00
47 Saku Koivu 5.00 12.00
49 Michael Ryder 4.00 10.00
51 Marian Gaborik 8.00 20.00
52 Manny Fernandez 5.00 12.00
55 Alexander Frolov 3.00 8.00
56 Rob Blake 4.00 10.00
57 Ed Belfour 12.00 30.00
60 Ales Hemsky 3.00 8.00
62 Ryan Smyth 4.00 10.00
64 Henrik Zetterberg 5.00 12.00
65 Dominik Hasek 6.00 15.00
66 Pavel Datsyuk 5.00 12.00
67 Nicklas Lidstrom 5.00 12.00
68 Mike Modano 5.00 12.00
69 Marty Turco 4.00 10.00
70 Eric Lindros 5.00 12.00
71 Rick Nash 5.00 12.00
74 Sergei Fedorov 5.00 12.00
75 Joe Sakic 10.00 25.00
76 Milan Hejduk 4.00 10.00
77 Jose Theodore 5.00 12.00
79 Nikolai Khabibulin 5.00 12.00
81 Martin Havlat 4.00 10.00
82 Eric Staal 4.00 10.00
83 Cam Ward 8.00 20.00
85 Jarome Iginla 8.00 20.00
86 Miikka Kiprusoff 5.00 12.00
88 Dion Phaneuf 6.00 15.00
89 Chris Drury 4.00 10.00
90 Ryan Miller 5.00 12.00
91 Patrice Bergeron 4.00 10.00
94 Zdeno Chara 3.00 8.00
95 Ilya Kovalchuk 6.00 15.00
96 Kari Lehtonen 5.00 12.00
97 Marian Hossa 4.00 10.00
98 Teemu Selanne 5.00 12.00
99 Chris Pronger 4.00 10.00
100 Jean-Sebastien Giguere 5.00 12.00
105 Phil Kessel 20.00 50.00
109 Drew Stafford 8.00 20.00
111 Dustin Boyd 8.00 20.00
114 Paul Stastny 25.00 60.00
116 Loui Eriksson 6.00 15.00
125 Anze Kopitar 15.00 40.00
126 Patrick O'Sullivan 8.00 20.00
128 Benoit Pouliot 8.00 20.00
130 Guillaume Latendresse 20.00 50.00
131 Alexander Radulov 15.00 40.00
133 Travis Zajac 10.00 25.00
144 Evgeni Malkin 30.00 80.00
146 Jordan Staal 25.00 60.00
151 Matt Carle 8.00 20.00
157 Jesse Schultz 6.00 15.00
ART Art Ross Trophy 15.00 40.00
BMT Bill Masterton Memorial 15.00 40.00
CCT Clarence Campbell Trophy 15.00 40.00
CMT Calder Memorial Trophy 15.00 40.00
CST Conn Smythe Trophy 15.00 40.00
FST Frank Selke Memorial 15.00 40.00
HMT Hart Memorial Trophy 15.00 40.00
JAA Jack Adams Award 15.00 40.00
KCT King Clancy Trophy 15.00 40.00
LBP Lester B. Pearson Award 15.00 40.00
LBT Lady Byng Trophy 15.00 40.00
LBT Lady Byng Trophy 15.00 40.00
MRT Rocket Richard Trophy 15.00 40.00
PT President's Trophy 15.00 40.00
PWT Prince of Wales Trophy 15.00 40.00
SC Stanley Cup 15.00 40.00
VT Vezina Trophy 15.00 40.00
WJT William B. Jennings Trophy 15.00 40.00

2006-07 Beehive Matte

*STARS: 5X TO 12X BASE HI
*RCs: .75X TO 2X BASE HI
PRINT RUN 100 #'d SETS
1 Alexander Ovechkin 12.00 30.00
2 Olaf Kolzig 4.00 10.00
3 Markus Naslund 3.00 8.00
4 Roberto Luongo 6.00 15.00
5 Mats Sundin 3.00 8.00
6 Michael Peca 2.00 5.00
7 Alexander Steen 2.50 6.00
8 Andrew Raycroft 2.50 6.00
9 Vincent Lecavalier 3.00 8.00
10 Brad Richards 3.00 8.00
11 Martin St. Louis 3.00 8.00
12 Manny Legace 2.50 6.00
13 Keith Tkachuk 2.50 6.00
14 Doug Weight 2.00 5.00
15 Joe Thornton 5.00 12.00
16 Patrick Marleau 2.50 6.00
17 Jonathan Cheechoo 3.00 8.00
18 Vesa Toskala 2.50 6.00
19 Sidney Crosby 15.00 40.00
20 Mark Recchi 2.00 5.00
21 Marc-Andre Fleury 3.00 8.00
22 Colby Armstrong 2.00 5.00
23 Shane Doan 2.50 6.00
24 Ed Jovanovski 2.00 5.00
25 Jeremy Roenick 3.00 8.00
26 Owen Nolan 2.50 6.00
27 Peter Forsberg 5.00 12.00
28 Simon Gagne 3.00 8.00
29 Jeff Carter 3.00 8.00
30 Joni Pitkanen 2.00 5.00
31 Jason Spezza 3.00 8.00
32 Dany Heatley 3.00 8.00
33 Martin Gerber 3.00 8.00
34 Daniel Alfredsson 2.50 6.00
35 Jaromir Jagr 5.00 12.00
36 Brendan Shanahan 3.00 8.00
37 Henrik Lundqvist 5.00 12.00
38 Alexei Yashin 3.00 8.00
39 Rick DiPietro 3.00 8.00
40 Miroslav Satan 2.00 5.00
41 Martin Brodeur 10.00 25.00
42 Patrik Elias 2.00 5.00
43 Brian Gionta 2.00 5.00
44 Paul Kariya 3.00 8.00
45 Tomas Vokoun 2.50 6.00
46 Jason Arnott 2.00 5.00
47 Saku Koivu 3.00 8.00
48 Cristobal Huet 3.00 8.00
49 Michael Ryder 2.50 6.00
50 Alexei Kovalev 2.00 5.00
51 Marian Gaborik 5.00 12.00
52 Manny Fernandez 3.00 8.00
53 Pavol Demitra 2.00 5.00
54 Mark Parrish 2.00 5.00
55 Alexander Frolov 2.00 5.00
56 Rob Blake 2.50 6.00
57 Ed Belfour 8.00 20.00
58 Todd Bertuzzi 2.50 6.00
59 Olli Jokinen 2.00 5.00
60 Ales Hemsky 2.00 5.00
61 Jarret Stoll 2.00 5.00
62 Ryan Smyth 2.00 5.00
63 Joffrey Lupul 2.00 5.00
64 Henrik Zetterberg 3.00 8.00
65 Dominik Hasek 4.00 10.00
66 Pavel Datsyuk 3.00 8.00
67 Nicklas Lidstrom 3.00 8.00
68 Mike Modano 3.00 8.00
69 Marty Turco 2.50 6.00
70 Eric Lindros 3.00 8.00
71 Rick Nash 3.00 8.00
72 Pascal LeClaire 3.00 8.00
73 Gilbert Brule 2.00 5.00
74 Sergei Fedorov 3.00 8.00
75 Joe Sakic 6.00 15.00
76 Milan Hejduk 2.50 6.00
77 Jose Theodore 3.00 8.00
78 Marek Svatos 2.00 5.00
79 Nikolai Khabibulin 3.00 8.00
80 Tuomo Ruutu 2.00 5.00
81 Martin Havlat 2.50 6.00
82 Eric Staal 2.50 6.00
83 Cam Ward 5.00 12.00
84 Rod Brind'Amour 2.50 6.00
85 Jarome Iginla 5.00 12.00
86 Miikka Kiprusoff 3.00 8.00
87 Alex Tanguay 2.50 6.00
88 Dion Phaneuf 4.00 10.00
89 Chris Drury 2.50 6.00
90 Ryan Miller 3.00 8.00
91 Patrice Bergeron 2.50 6.00
92 Hannu Toivonen 2.50 6.00
93 Brad Boyes 2.00 5.00
94 Zdeno Chara 2.00 5.00
95 Ilya Kovalchuk 4.00 10.00
96 Kari Lehtonen 3.00 8.00
97 Marian Hossa 2.50 6.00
98 Teemu Selanne 3.00 8.00
99 Chris Pronger 2.50 6.00
100 Jean-Sebastien Giguere 2.50 6.00
101 David McKee 3.00 8.00
102 Ryan Shannon 2.50 6.00
103 Shane O'Brien 2.50 6.00
104 Matt Lashoff 2.50 6.00
105 Phil Kessel 8.00 20.00
106 Mark Stuart 2.50 6.00
107 Yan Stastny 2.50 6.00
108 Clarke MacArthur 2.50 6.00
109 Drew Stafford 3.00 8.00
110 Brandon Prust 2.50 6.00
111 Dustin Boyd 3.00 8.00
112 Michael Blunden 2.50 6.00
113 Dave Bolland 5.00 12.00
114 Paul Stastny 10.00 25.00
115 Fredrik Norrena 2.50 6.00
116 Loui Eriksson 2.50 6.00
117 Tomas Kopecky 3.00 8.00
118 Stefan Liv 3.00 8.00
119 Jeff Drouin-Deslauriers 3.00 8.00
120 Alexei Mikhnov 2.50 6.00
121 Ladislav Smid 2.50 6.00
122 Patrick Thoresen 2.50 6.00
123 Marc-Antoine Pouliot 3.00 8.00
124 David Booth 2.50 6.00
125 Anze Kopitar 6.00 15.00
126 Patrick O'Sullivan 3.00 8.00
127 Konstantin Pushkaryov 2.50 6.00
128 Benoit Pouliot 3.00 8.00
129 Mikhail Grabovski 2.50 6.00
130 Guillaume Latendresse 8.00 20.00
131 Alexander Radulov 6.00 15.00
132 Shea Weber 3.00 8.00
133 Travis Zajac 4.00 10.00
134 Johnny Oduya 2.50 6.00
135 Blake Comeau 2.50 6.00
136 Nigel Dawes 2.50 6.00
137 Jarkko Immonen 2.50 6.00
138 Josh Hennessy 2.50 6.00
139 Kelly Guard 3.00 8.00
140 Martin Houle 3.00 8.00
141 Ryan Potulny 3.00 8.00
142 Enver Lisin 2.50 6.00
143 Keith Yandle 2.50 6.00
144 Evgeni Malkin 12.00 30.00
145 Kristopher Letang 4.00 10.00
146 Jordan Staal 10.00 25.00
147 Michel Ouellet 4.00 10.00
148 Noah Welch 2.50 6.00
149 Joe Pavelski 8.00 20.00
150 Marc-Edouard Vlasic 2.50 6.00
151 Matt Carle 3.00 8.00
152 Marek Schwarz 5.00 12.00
153 Blair Jones 2.50 6.00
154 Ian White 2.50 6.00
155 Brendan Bell 2.50 6.00
156 Kris Newbury 2.50 6.00
157 Jesse Schultz 2.50 6.00
158 Alexander Edler 2.50 6.00
159 Luc Bourdon 3.00 8.00
160 Eric Fehr 3.00 8.00

2006-07 Beehive Red Facsimile Signatures

*STARS: 2X TO 5X HI
*RCs: 2X TO .5X HI
STATED ODDS 1:8
SKIP-NUMBERED SET
1 Alexander Ovechkin 8.00 20.00
3 Markus Naslund 2.00 5.00
4 Roberto Luongo 4.00 10.00
5 Mats Sundin 2.00 5.00
8 Andrew Raycroft 1.50 4.00
9 Vincent Lecavalier 2.00 5.00
10 Brad Richards 2.00 5.00
11 Martin St. Louis 2.00 5.00
13 Keith Tkachuk 1.50 4.00
15 Joe Thornton 3.00 8.00
16 Patrick Marleau 1.50 4.00
17 Jonathan Cheechoo 2.00 5.00
19 Sidney Crosby 10.00 25.00
21 Marc-Andre Fleury 2.00 5.00
23 Shane Doan 1.50 4.00
24 Ed Jovanovski 1.25 3.00
25 Jeremy Roenick 2.00 5.00
26 Owen Nolan 1.50 4.00
27 Peter Forsberg 3.00 8.00
28 Simon Gagne 2.00 5.00
31 Jason Spezza 2.00 5.00
32 Dany Heatley 2.00 5.00
34 Daniel Alfredsson 1.50 4.00
35 Jaromir Jagr 3.00 8.00
36 Brendan Shanahan 2.00 5.00
37 Henrik Lundqvist 3.00 8.00
38 Alexei Yashin 1.25 3.00
40 Miroslav Satan 1.25 3.00
41 Martin Brodeur 6.00 15.00
42 Patrik Elias 1.25 3.00
43 Brian Gionta 1.25 3.00
44 Paul Kariya 2.00 5.00
45 Tomas Vokoun 1.50 4.00
47 Saku Koivu 2.00 5.00
48 Cristobal Huet 2.00 5.00
49 Michael Ryder 1.50 4.00
51 Marian Gaborik 3.00 8.00
52 Manny Fernandez 2.00 5.00
55 Alexander Frolov 1.25 3.00
56 Rob Blake 1.50 4.00
57 Ed Belfour 5.00 12.00
58 Todd Bertuzzi 1.50 4.00
59 Olli Jokinen 1.25 3.00
60 Ales Hemsky 1.25 3.00
62 Ryan Smyth 1.50 4.00
64 Henrik Zetterberg 2.00 5.00
65 Dominik Hasek 2.50 6.00
66 Pavel Datsyuk 2.00 5.00
67 Nicklas Lidstrom 2.00 5.00
68 Mike Modano 2.00 5.00
69 Marty Turco 1.50 4.00
70 Eric Lindros 2.00 5.00
71 Rick Nash 2.00 5.00
72 Pascal LeClaire 2.00 5.00
74 Sergei Fedorov 2.00 5.00
75 Joe Sakic 4.00 10.00
76 Milan Hejduk 1.50 4.00
77 Jose Theodore 2.00 5.00
79 Nikolai Khabibulin 2.00 5.00
81 Martin Havlat 1.50 4.00
82 Eric Staal 1.50 4.00
83 Cam Ward 3.00 8.00
85 Jarome Iginla 3.00 8.00
86 Miikka Kiprusoff 2.00 5.00
87 Alex Tanguay 1.50 4.00
88 Dion Phaneuf 2.50 6.00
89 Chris Drury 1.50 4.00
90 Ryan Miller 2.00 5.00
91 Patrice Bergeron 1.50 4.00
95 Ilya Kovalchuk 2.50 6.00
96 Kari Lehtonen 2.00 5.00
97 Marian Hossa 1.50 4.00
98 Teemu Selanne 2.00 5.00
99 Chris Pronger 1.50 4.00
100 Jean-Sebastien Giguere 1.50 4.00
105 Phil Kessel 5.00 12.00
109 Drew Stafford 2.00 5.00
111 Dustin Boyd 2.00 5.00
114 Paul Stastny 6.00 15.00
116 Loui Eriksson 1.50 4.00
117 Tomas Kopecky 1.50 4.00
121 Ladislav Smid 1.50 4.00
123 Marc-Antoine Pouliot 2.00 5.00
125 Anze Kopitar 4.00 10.00
126 Patrick O'Sullivan 2.00 5.00
128 Benoit Pouliot 2.00 5.00
130 Guillaume Latendresse 5.00 12.00
131 Alexander Radulov 4.00 10.00
132 Shea Weber 2.00 5.00
133 Travis Zajac 2.50 6.00
137 Nigel Dawes 1.50 4.00
138 Josh Hennessy 1.50 4.00
141 Ryan Potulny 2.00 5.00
142 Enver Lisin 1.50 4.00
144 Evgeni Malkin 8.00 20.00
146 Jordan Staal 6.00 15.00
151 Matt Carle 2.00 5.00
157 Jesse Schultz 1.50 4.00
159 Luc Bourdon 2.00 5.00
160 Eric Fehr 2.00 5.00

2006-07 Beehive Wood

*STARS: 1.5X TO 4X BASE HI
*RCs: .15X TO .4X BASE HI
STATED ODDS 1:2
SKIP-NUMBERED SET
1 Alexander Ovechkin 6.00 15.00
3 Markus Naslund 1.50 4.00
4 Roberto Luongo 3.00 8.00
5 Mats Sundin 1.50 4.00
8 Andrew Raycroft 1.25 3.00
9 Vincent Lecavalier 1.50 4.00
10 Brad Richards 1.50 4.00
11 Martin St. Louis 1.50 4.00
13 Keith Tkachuk 1.25 3.00
15 Joe Thornton 2.50 6.00
16 Patrick Marleau 1.25 3.00
17 Jonathan Cheechoo 1.50 4.00
19 Sidney Crosby 8.00 20.00
21 Marc-Andre Fleury 1.50 4.00
23 Shane Doan 1.25 3.00
24 Ed Jovanovski 1.00 2.50
25 Jeremy Roenick 1.50 4.00
26 Owen Nolan 1.25 3.00
27 Peter Forsberg 2.50 6.00
28 Simon Gagne 1.50 4.00
31 Jason Spezza 1.50 4.00
32 Dany Heatley 1.50 4.00
34 Daniel Alfredsson 1.25 3.00
35 Jaromir Jagr 2.50 6.00
36 Brendan Shanahan 1.50 4.00
37 Henrik Lundqvist 2.50 6.00
38 Alexei Yashin 1.00 2.50
40 Miroslav Satan 1.00 2.50
41 Martin Brodeur 5.00 12.00
42 Patrik Elias 1.00 2.50
43 Brian Gionta 1.00 2.50
44 Paul Kariya 1.50 4.00
45 Tomas Vokoun 1.25 3.00
47 Saku Koivu 1.50 4.00
48 Cristobal Huet 1.50 4.00
49 Michael Ryder 1.25 3.00
51 Marian Gaborik 2.50 6.00
52 Manny Fernandez 1.50 4.00
55 Alexander Frolov 1.00 2.50
56 Rob Blake 1.25 3.00
57 Ed Belfour 4.00 10.00
58 Todd Bertuzzi 1.25 3.00
59 Olli Jokinen 1.00 2.50
60 Ales Hemsky 1.00 2.50
62 Ryan Smyth 1.25 3.00
64 Henrik Zetterberg 1.50 4.00
65 Dominik Hasek 2.00 5.00
66 Pavel Datsyuk 1.50 4.00
67 Nicklas Lidstrom 1.50 4.00
68 Mike Modano 1.50 4.00
69 Marty Turco 1.25 3.00
70 Eric Lindros 1.50 4.00
71 Rick Nash 1.50 4.00
72 Pascal LeClaire 1.50 4.00
74 Sergei Fedorov 1.50 4.00
75 Joe Sakic 3.00 8.00
76 Milan Hejduk 1.25 3.00
77 Jose Theodore 1.50 4.00
79 Nikolai Khabibulin 1.50 4.00
81 Martin Havlat 1.25 3.00
82 Eric Staal 1.25 3.00
83 Cam Ward 2.50 6.00
85 Jarome Iginla 2.50 6.00
86 Miikka Kiprusoff 1.50 4.00
87 Alex Tanguay 1.25 3.00
88 Dion Phaneuf 2.00 5.00
89 Chris Drury 1.25 3.00
90 Ryan Miller 1.50 4.00
91 Patrice Bergeron 1.25 3.00
95 Ilya Kovalchuk 2.00 5.00
96 Kari Lehtonen 1.50 4.00
97 Marian Hossa 1.25 3.00
98 Teemu Selanne 1.50 4.00
99 Chris Pronger 1.25 3.00
100 Jean-Sebastien Giguere 1.50 4.00
105 Phil Kessel 3.00 8.00
109 Drew Stafford 1.50 4.00
111 Dustin Boyd 1.25 3.00
114 Paul Stastny 4.00 10.00
116 Loui Eriksson 1.00 2.50
117 Tomas Kopecky 2.00 5.00
121 Ladislav Smid 1.00 2.50
123 Marc-Antoine Pouliot 1.25 3.00
125 Anze Kopitar 2.50 6.00
126 Patrick O'Sullivan 1.25 3.00
128 Benoit Pouliot 1.25 3.00
130 Guillaume Latendresse 3.00 8.00
131 Alexander Radulov 2.50 6.00
132 Shea Weber 1.25 3.00
133 Travis Zajac 1.50 4.00
137 Nigel Dawes 1.00 2.50
138 Josh Hennessy 1.00 2.50
141 Ryan Potulny 1.25 3.00
142 Enver Lisin 1.00 2.50
144 Evgeni Malkin 5.00 12.00
146 Jordan Staal 4.00 10.00
151 Matt Carle 1.25 3.00
157 Jesse Schultz 1.00 2.50
159 Luc Bourdon 1.25 3.00
160 Eric Fehr 1.25 3.00

2006-07 Beehive 5 X 7 Black and White

STATED ODDS 1:15
SKIP-NUMBERED SET
5 Mats Sundin 2.50 6.00
17 Jonathan Cheechoo 2.50 6.00
28 Simon Gagne 2.50 6.00
45 Tomas Vokoun 2.00 5.00
47 Saku Koivu 2.50 6.00
49 Michael Ryder 2.00 5.00
51 Marian Gaborik 4.00 10.00
57 Ed Belfour 6.00 15.00
67 Nicklas Lidstrom 2.50 6.00
74 Sergei Fedorov 2.50 6.00
83 Cam Ward 4.00 10.00
85 Jarome Iginla 4.00 10.00
91 Patrice Bergeron 2.00 5.00
96 Kari Lehtonen 2.50 6.00
98 Teemu Selanne 2.50 6.00
100 Jean-Sebastien Giguere 2.50 6.00
174 Bobby Clarke 2.00 5.00
182 Mike Bossy 1.50 4.00
183 Billy Smith 2.50 6.00
192 Guy Lafleur 2.00 5.00
203 Grant Fuhr 3.00 8.00
216 Ray Bourque 2.00 5.00
217 Bobby Hull 2.00 5.00
218 Tony Esposito 3.00 8.00
229 Cam Neely 1.50 4.00

2006-07 Beehive 5 X 7 Cherry Wood

STATED ODDS 1:240
SKIP-NUMBERED SET
PT President's Trophy 12.00 30.00
SC Stanley Cup 40.00 80.00
VT Vezina Trophy 25.00 50.00
ART Art Ross Trophy 40.00 80.00
BMT Bill Masterton Trophy 12.00 30.00
CCT Campbell Trophy 12.00 30.00
CMT Calder Memorial Trophy 12.00 30.00
CST Conn Smythe Trophy 12.00 30.00
FST Selke Trophy 12.00 30.00
HMT Hart Memorial Trophy
JAA Jack Adams Award 12.00 30.00
JNT James Norris Trophy 15.00 40.00
KCT King Clancy Trophy 20.00 50.00
LBP Pearson Award 12.00 30.00
LBT Lady Byng Trophy 12.00 30.00
MRT Rocket Richard Trophy 12.00 30.00
PWT Prince of Wales Trophy 12.00 30.00
WJT William M. Jennings Trophy 12.00 30.00

2006-07 Beehive 5 X 7 Dark Wood

STATED ODDS 1:150
SKIP-NUMBERED SET
3 Markus Naslund 6.00 15.00
4 Roberto Luongo 12.00 30.00
9 Vincent Lecavalier 6.00 15.00
19 Sidney Crosby 30.00 80.00
21 Marc-Andre Fleury 6.00 15.00
31 Jason Spezza 6.00 15.00
32 Dany Heatley 6.00 15.00
36 Brendan Shanahan 6.00 15.00
37 Henrik Lundqvist 10.00 25.00
44 Paul Kariya 6.00 15.00
64 Henrik Zetterberg 6.00 15.00
68 Mike Modano 6.00 15.00
71 Rick Nash 6.00 15.00
82 Eric Staal 5.00 12.00
86 Miikka Kiprusoff 6.00 15.00
90 Ryan Miller 6.00 15.00
95 Ilya Kovalchuk 8.00 20.00
105 Phil Kessel 10.00 25.00
144 Evgeni Malkin 15.00 40.00
146 Jordan Staal 12.00 30.00
170 Mario Lemieux 15.00 40.00
189 Patrick Roy 15.00 40.00
198 Marcel Dionne 3.00 8.00
204 Gordie Howe 20.00 50.00
231 Bobby Orr 12.00 30.00

2006-07 Beehive Matted Materials

STATED ODDS 1:8
MMAE David Aebischer 5.00 12.00
MMAF Alexander Frolov 4.00 10.00
MMAH Ales Hemsky 4.00 10.00
MMAO Alexander Ovechkin 25.00 60.00
MMAS Alexander Steen 5.00 12.00
MMAT Alex Tanguay 5.00 12.00
MMBB Brad Boyes 4.00 10.00
MMBO Pierre-Marc Bouchard 4.00 10.00
MMCD Chris Drury 5.00 12.00
MMCN Cam Neely 5.00 12.00
MMCP Corey Perry 5.00 12.00
MMCS Cory Stillman 4.00 10.00
MMCW Cam Ward 10.00 25.00
MMDA Daniel Alfredsson 5.00 12.00
MMDH Dany Heatley 6.00 15.00
MMDR Dwayne Roloson 5.00 12.00
MMEB Ed Belfour 15.00 40.00
MMES Eric Staal 5.00 12.00
MMHA Martin Havlat 5.00 12.00
MMHT Hannu Toivonen 6.00 15.00
MMHZ Henrik Zetterberg 6.00 15.00
MMIK Ilya Kovalchuk 8.00 20.00
MMJB Jay Bouwmeester 4.00 10.00
MMJC Jeff Carter 6.00 15.00
MMJI Jarome Iginla 10.00 25.00
MMJJ Jaromir Jagr 10.00 25.00
MMJL Joffrey Lupul 4.00 10.00
MMJS Joe Sakic 12.00 30.00
MMJT Joe Thornton 10.00 25.00
MMLE Jere Lehtinen 4.00 10.00
MMLN Ladislav Nagy 4.00 10.00
MMMB Martin Brodeur 20.00 50.00
MMMG Marian Gaborik 10.00 25.00
MMMH Milan Hejduk 5.00 12.00
MMML Mario Lemieux SP 20.00 50.00
MMMM Mike Modano 6.00 15.00
MMMP Michael Peca 4.00 10.00
MMMS Mats Sundin 6.00 15.00
MMMT Marty Turco 5.00 12.00
MMNL Nicklas Lidstrom 6.00 15.00
MMPB Patrice Bergeron 5.00 12.00
MMPF Peter Forsberg 10.00 25.00
MMPK Paul Kariya 6.00 15.00
MMPM Patrick Marleau 5.00 12.00
MMRB Ray Bourque 6.00 15.00
MMRL Roberto Luongo 12.00 30.00
MMRM Ryan Miller 6.00 15.00
MMRN Rick Nash 6.00 15.00
MMRS Ryan Smyth 5.00 12.00
MMSA Marc Savard 4.00 10.00
MMSC Sidney Crosby SP 30.00 80.00
MMSG Scott Gomez 4.00 10.00
MMSK Saku Koivu 6.00 15.00
MMSS Sergei Samsonov 5.00 12.00
MMST Jarret Stoll 4.00 10.00
MMSV Marek Svatos 4.00 10.00
MMSZ Sergei Zubov 4.00 10.00
MMTH Tomas Holmstrom 4.00 10.00
MMTV Tomas Vokoun 5.00 12.00
MMZC Zdeno Chara 4.00 10.00

2006-07 Beehive PhotoGraphs

STATED ODDS 1:240
PGAR Andrew Raycroft 8.00 20.00
PGBO Bobby Orr SP 150.00 300.00
PGDH Dominik Hasek SP 60.00 125.00
PGES Eric Staal 8.00 20.00
PGGH Gordie Howe 75.00 125.00
PGGL Guy Lafleur 10.00 25.00
PGHE Dany Heatley 10.00 25.00
PGJI Jarome Iginla 15.00 40.00
PGJT Joe Thornton 15.00 40.00
PGKL Kari Lehtonen 10.00 25.00
PGMB Martin Brodeur 60.00 125.00
PGMG Marian Gaborik 15.00 40.00
PGML Mario Lemieux SP
PGMM Mike Modano 10.00 25.00
PGMR Michael Ryder 8.00 20.00
PGNL Nicklas Lidstrom 10.00 25.00
PGPB Patrice Bergeron 8.00 20.00
PGPR Patrick Roy 75.00 150.00
PGRB Ray Bourque 10.00 25.00
PGRL Roberto Luongo 20.00 50.00
PGRN Rick Nash 10.00 25.00
PGSC Sidney Crosby 125.00 200.00
PGTE Tony Esposito 15.00 40.00
PGVL Vincent Lecavalier 10.00 25.00
PGWG Wayne Gretzky 150.00 250.00

2006-07 Beehive Remarkable Matted Materials

STATED PRINT RUN 15 #'d SETS
NOT PRICED DUE TO SCARCITY

2006-07 Beehive Signature Scrapbook

STATED ODDS 1:15
SSAF Alexander Frolov 3.00 8.00
SSAH Ales Hemsky 3.00 8.00
SSBB Brad Boyes 3.00 8.00
SSBG Brian Gionta 3.00 8.00
SSBO Bobby Orr SP
SSCA Colby Armstrong 3.00 8.00
SSCC Chris Campoli 3.00 8.00

SSCH Chris Higgins 3.00 8.00
SSCP Chris Phillips 3.00 8.00
SSDC Don Cherry 5.00 12.00
SSDL David Leneveu 4.00 10.00
SSDR Dwayne Roloson 4.00 10.00
SSDS Darryl Sittler 3.00 8.00
SSDT Darcy Tucker 3.00 8.00
SSES Eric Staal SP 12.00 30.00
SSGE Martin Gerber 5.00 12.00
SSGH Gordie Howe SP 40.00 80.00
SSHE Milan Hejduk 4.00 10.00
SSHU Cristobal Huet 5.00 12.00
SSJA Jason Arnott 3.00 8.00
SSJB Johnny Bucyk 5.00 12.00
SSJC Jonathan Cheechoo 5.00 12.00
SSJI Jarome Iginla 8.00 20.00
SSJP Joni Pitkanen 3.00 8.00
SSJS Jarret Stoll 3.00 8.00
SSJT Jose Theodore SP 15.00 40.00
SSKD Kris Draper 3.00 8.00
SSLN Ladislav Nagy 3.00 8.00
SSMB Mike Bossy SP 12.00 30.00
SSMC Mike Cammalleri 3.00 8.00
SSMF Marc-Andre Fleury 5.00 12.00
SSMG Marian Gaborik 8.00 20.00
SSMH Martin Havlat 4.00 10.00
SSMP Michael Peca 3.00 8.00
SSMR Mike Richards 5.00 12.00
SSMS Marek Svatos 3.00 8.00
SSPA J.P. Parise 3.00 8.00
SSPB Pierre-Marc Bouchard 3.00 8.00
SSPE Patrik Elias 3.00 8.00
SSPM Patrick Marleau SP 12.00 30.00
SSPP Petr Prucha 3.00 8.00
SSPR Patrick Roy SP 125.00 250.00
SSPS Peter Stastny 3.00 8.00
SSRB Rene Bourque 3.00 8.00
SSRM Ryan Miller 5.00 12.00
SSRW Ryan Whitney 3.00 8.00
SSSA Marc Savard 3.00 8.00
SSSB Steve Bernier 3.00 8.00
SSSS Sergei Samsonov SP 12.00 30.00
SSTH Tomas Holmstrom 3.00 8.00
SSTL Ted Lindsay SP 10.00 25.00
SSTO Terry O'Reilly SP 10.00 25.00
SSVT Vesa Toskala SP 12.00 30.00
SSWG Wayne Gretzky SP 150.00 300.00

2001-02 Between the Pipes

Released in late February, this 170-card set was the first to focus exclusively on the netminders of the past and present NHL. Subsets included trophy winners and netcam photography. The last twenty cards in the set were available in BAP Update packs only. Total production for this product was limited to 800 cases.

COMPLETE SET (150) 50.00 100.00
COMP.SET w/UPDATE (170) 75.00 150.00
CARDS 151-170 AVAIL. IN BAP UPD.PACKS
1 Patrick Roy 1.50 4.00
2 Jean-Sebastien Giguere .50 1.00
3 Ron Tugnutt .50 1.00
4 Rick DiPietro .50 1.00
5 Milan Hnilicka .50 1.00
6 Jean-Sebastien Aubin .50 1.00
7 Craig Billington .50 1.00
8 Byron Dafoe .50 1.00
9 Maxime Ouellet .50 1.00
10 Ed Belfour .75 2.00
11 John Grahame .50 1.00
12 Mathieu Garon .50 1.00
13 Martin Biron .50 1.00
14 Dan Cloutier .50 1.00
15 Tomas Vokoun .50 1.00
16 Arturs Irbe .50 1.00
17 Curtis Joseph .75 2.00
18 Jocelyn Thibault .50 1.00
19 Roman Cechmanek .50 1.00
20 Miikka Kiprusoff .50 1.00
21 Olaf Kolzig .50 1.00
22 Jani Hurme .50 1.00
23 David Aebischer .50 1.00
24 Damian Rhodes .50 1.00
25 Marc Denis .50 1.00
26 Marty Turco .50 1.00
27 Evgeni Nabokov .50 1.00
28 Manny Legace .50 1.00
29 Mike Dunham .50 1.00
30 Tommy Salo .50 1.00
31 Sean Burke .50 1.00
32 Andrew Raycroft .50 1.00
33 Roberto Luongo 1.00 2.50
34 Johan Holmqvist .50 1.00
35 Felix Potvin .75 2.00
36 Martin Brodeur 1.25 3.00
37 Gregg Naumenko .50 1.00
38 Travis Scott .50 1.00
39 Manny Fernandez .50 1.00
40 Kevin Weekes .50 1.00
41 Steve Passmore .50 1.00
42 Johan Hedberg .50 1.00
43 Patrick Lalime .50 1.00
44 Jose Theodore 1.00 2.50
45 Mika Noronen .50 1.00
46 Brent Johnson .50 1.00
47 Chris Mason .50 1.00
48 Mike Fountain .50 1.00
49 Jamie McLennan .50 1.00
50 Mike Richter .75 2.00
51 Eric Fichaud .50 1.00
52 Steve Shields .50 1.00
53 Rich Parent .50 1.00
54 Mike Vernon .50 1.00
55 Jason LaBarbera .50 1.00
56 Dominik Hasek 1.25 3.00
57 Dan Blackburn RC 2.00 5.00
58 Robert Esche .50 1.00
59 Joaquin Gage .50 1.00
60 Jamie Storr .50 1.00
61 Brian Boucher .50 1.00
62 Trevor Kidd .50 1.00
63 Nikolai Khabibulin .75 2.00
64 Norm Maracle .50 1.00
65 Roman Turek .50 1.00
66 Tyler Moss .50 1.00
67 Fred Brathwaite .50 1.00
68 Garth Snow .50 1.00
69 Dieter Kochan .50 1.00
70 Bob Essensa .50 1.00
71 Kirk McLean .50 1.00
72 Chris Osgood .50 1.00
73 Jeff Hackett .50 1.00
74 Stephane Fiset .50 1.00
75 Dominic Roussel .50 1.00
76 Corey Hirsch .50 1.00
77 Vitali Yeremeyev .50 1.00
78 Tom Barrasso .50 1.00
79 Scott Clemmensen RC 1.50 4.00
80 Martin Brochu .50 1.00
81 Corey Schwab .50 1.00
82 Ty Conklin RC 1.50 4.00
83 Dwayne Roloson .50 1.00
84 Ilja Bryzgalov RC 1.50 4.00
85 Olivier Michaud RC 5.00 12.00
86 Vesa Toskala .50 1.00
87 Jussi Markkanen .50 1.00
88 Patrick Desrochers .50 1.00
89 Peter Skudra .50 1.00
90 J-F Damphousse .50 1.00
91 Mike Dunham .50 1.00
92 Mike Richter .75 2.00
93 Brian Boucher .50 1.00
94 Patrick Roy 1.50 4.00
95 Martin Biron .50 1.00
96 Jean-Sebastien Aubin .50 1.00
97 Curtis Joseph .75 2.00
98 Martin Brodeur 1.25 3.00
99 Arturs Irbe .50 1.00
100 Jeff Hackett .50 1.00
101 Ed Belfour .75 2.00
102 Jocelyn Thibault .50 1.00
103 Roman Cechmanek .50 1.00
104 Patrick Lalime .50 1.00
105 Olaf Kolzig .50 1.00
106 Byron Dafoe .50 1.00
107 Johan Hedberg .50 1.00
108 Dan Cloutier .50 1.00
109 Dominik Hasek 1.25 3.00
110 Olaf Kolzig .50 1.00
111 Patrick Roy 1.50 4.00
112 Ed Belfour .75 2.00
113 Grant Fuhr .75 2.00
114 Ron Hextall .75 2.00
115 Pelle Lindbergh 1.25 3.00
116 Tom Barrasso .75 2.00
117 Billy Smith 1.00 2.50
118 Bernie Parent .75 2.00
119 Tony Esposito 1.00 2.50
120 Gump Worsley .75 2.00
121 Glenn Hall 1.00 2.50
122 Jacques Plante 1.25 3.00
123 Johnny Bower .75 2.00
124 Terry Sawchuk 1.25 3.00
125 Harry Lumley .75 2.00
126 Bill Durnan .75 2.00
127 Turk Broda .75 2.00
128 Frank Brimsek .75 2.00
129 Tiny Thompson .75 2.00
130 George Hainsworth .75 2.00
131 Gump Worsley .75 2.00
132 Georges Vezina 1.50 4.00
133 Vladislav Tretiak 1.25 3.00
134 Tiny Thompson .75 2.00
135 Terry Sawchuk 1.25 3.00
136 Jacques Plante 1.25 3.00
137 Chuck Rayner .75 2.00
138 Bernie Parent .75 2.00
139 Harry Lumley .75 2.00
140 Glenn Hall 1.00 2.50
141 George Hainsworth .75 2.00
142 Ed Giacomin .75 2.00
143 Charlie Gardiner .75 2.00
144 Tony Esposito 1.00 2.50
145 Bill Durnan .75 2.00
146 Gerry Cheevers 1.00 2.50
147 Turk Broda .75 2.00
148 Frank Brimsek .75 2.00
149 Johnny Bower .75 2.00
150 Roy Worters .75 2.00
151 Pasi Nurminen RC 2.50 6.00
152 Alex Auld .50 1.00
153 John Vanbiesbrouck .50 1.00
154 Wade Flaherty .50 1.00
155 Kevin Weekes .50 1.00
156 Tom Barrasso .50 1.00
157 Stephane Fiset .50 1.00
158 Sebastien Centomo RC 3.00 8.00
159 Jean-Francois Labbe .50 1.00
160 Simon Lajeunesse .50 1.00
161 Frederic Cassivi RC 1.50 4.00
162 Martin Prusek RC 1.50 4.00
163 Dominik Hasek 1.25 3.00
164 David Aebischer .50 1.00
165 Dan Cloutier .50 1.00
166 Byron Dafoe .50 1.00
167 Curtis Joseph .75 2.00
168 Ed Belfour .75 2.00
169 Tommy Salo .50 1.00
170 Jose Theodore 1.00 2.50

2001-02 Between the Pipes All-Star Jerseys

Limited to just 60 copies each, this 16-card set featured goalies who played in the last several All-Star Games alongside a swatch of their jersey from the game.

STATED PRINT RUN 60 SETS

ASJ1 Ed Belfour 10.00 25.00
1996 All-Star
ASJ2 Arturs Irbe 10.00 25.00
1999 All-Star
ASJ3 Martin Brodeur 25.00 60.00
ASJ4 Roman Cechmanek 10.00 25.00
2001 All-Star
ASJ5 Dominik Hasek 15.00 40.00
1998 All-Star
ASJ6 Olaf Kolzig 10.00 25.00
2000 All-Star
ASJ7 Curtis Joseph 10.00 25.00
2000 All-Star
ASJ8 Mike Richter 10.00 25.00
2000 All-Star
ASJ9 Patrick Roy 30.00 80.00
1994 All-Star
ASJ10 Evgeni Nabokov 10.00 25.00
2001 All-Star
ASJ11 Tommy Salo 10.00 25.00
2000 All-Star
ASJ12 Curtis Joseph 10.00 25.00
1994 All-Star
ASJ13 Dominik Hasek 15.00 40.00
1997 All-Star
ASJ14 Roman Turek 10.00 25.00
2000 All-Star
ASJ15 Nikolai Khabibulin 10.00 25.00
1998 All-Star
ASJ16 Patrick Roy 30.00 80.00
2001 All-Star

2001-02 Between the Pipes Double Memorabilia

This 30-card set featured both a game-worn jersey swatch and a stick or pad swatch from the featured goalie. Each card was limited to 50 copies.

STATED PRINT RUN 50 SETS
DM1 Felix Potvin 15.00 40.00
DM2 Mike Vernon 15.00 40.00
DM3 Johan Hedberg 15.00 40.00
DM4 Olaf Kolzig 15.00 40.00
DM5 Jeff Hackett 15.00 40.00
DM6 Martin Brodeur 40.00 100.00
DM7 Mike Dunham 15.00 40.00
DM8 Trevor Kidd 15.00 40.00
DM9 Damian Rhodes 15.00 40.00
DM10 John Grahame 15.00 40.00
DM11 Roberto Luongo 20.00 50.00
DM12 Manny Legace 15.00 40.00
DM13 Evgeni Nabokov 15.00 40.00
DM14 Jose Theodore 20.00 50.00
DM15 Robert Esche 15.00 40.00
DM16 Chris Osgood 15.00 40.00
DM17 Sean Burke 15.00 40.00
DM18 Martin Biron 15.00 40.00
DM19 Jocelyn Thibault 15.00 40.00
DM20 Brian Boucher 15.00 40.00
DM21 Curtis Joseph 15.00 40.00
DM22 Roman Turek 15.00 40.00
DM23 Gerry Cheevers 15.00 40.00
DM24 Terry Sawchuk 50.00 100.00
DM25 Grant Fuhr 15.00 40.00
DM26 Bernie Parent 40.00 80.00
DM27 Ron Hextall 15.00 40.00
DM28 Gump Worsley 30.00 80.00
DM29 Tony Esposito 15.00 40.00
DM30 Ed Giacomin 15.00 40.00

2001-02 Between the Pipes Future Wave

This 10-card set featured younger goalies from around the league alongside a game-worn jersey swatch. The word "Future Wave" were printed vertically on the right border and the player's name is printed in the right bottom corner. Each card was limited to just 22 copies. The set is not priced due to scarcity.

STATED PRINT RUN 22 SETS
NOT PRICED DUE TO SCARCITY
FW1 Johan Hedberg
FW2 Martin Biron
FW3 Patrick Lalime
FW4 Roberto Luongo
FW5 Johan Holmqvist
Dan Blackburn
FW6 Dan Cloutier
FW7 Miikka Kiprusoff
Evgeni Nabokov
FW8 Brian Boucher
FW9 Mathieu Garon
FW10 Rick DiPietro

2001-02 Between the Pipes Goalie Gear

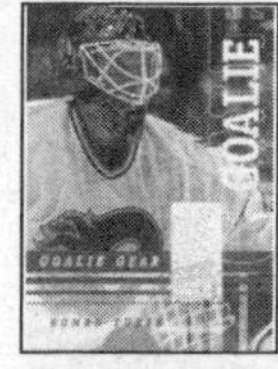

This 30-card set featured an up close color photo beside a game-used swatch of goalie pad or glove. The word "goalie" was printed vertically along the right border and the goalie's name was printed under the photo. Cards from this set were limited to just 70 copies each (unless noted differently below). Cards with fewer than 25 copies are not priced due to scarcity.

STATED PRINT RUN 70 SETS/
UNLESS OTHERWISE NOTED
PRINT RUNS OF LESS THAN 25/
NOT PRICED DUE TO SCARCITY
GG1 Felix Potvin 15.00 40.00
GG2 Jeff Hackett 10.00 25.00
GG3 Mike Vernon 10.00 25.00
GG4 Sean Burke 10.00 25.00
GG5 Johan Hedberg 10.00 25.00
GG6 Jose Theodore 15.00 40.00
GG7 Robert Esche 10.00 25.00
GG8 Dan Cloutier 10.00 25.00
GG9 Olaf Kolzig 12.50 30.00
GG10 Roberto Luongo 20.00 50.00
GG11 Manny Legace 10.00 25.00
GG12 Martin Brodeur 40.00 100.00
GG13 Marty Turco 12.50 30.00
GG14 Arturs Irbe 12.50 30.00
GG15 Damian Rhodes 10.00 25.00
GG16 Trevor Kidd 10.00 25.00
GG17 Mike Dunham 10.00 25.00
GG18 Evgeni Nabokov 12.50 30.00
GG19 Roman Turek 10.00 25.00
GG20 Brian Boucher 10.00 25.00
GG21 Jocelyn Thibault 10.00 25.00
GG22 Dominik Hasek/20
GG23 Patrick Roy/20
GG24 Curtis Joseph/20
GG25 Brent Johnson 10.00 25.00
GG26 Patrick Lalime 10.00 25.00
GG27 J-S Aubin 10.00 25.00
GG28 Martin Biron 10.00 25.00
GG29 Chris Osgood 12.50 30.00
GG30 Rick DiPietro 12.50 30.00

2001-02 Between the Pipes He Shoots-He Saves Points

Inserted one per pack, these cards carry a value of 1, 2 or 3 points. The points could be redeemed for special memorabilia cards. The cards are unnumbered and are listed below in alphabetical order by point value. The redemption program ended November 2002.

ONE PER PACK
RED.PROGRAM HAS EXPIRED
1 Brian Boucher 1pt. .20 .50
2 Sean Burke 1pt. .20 .50
3 Byron Dafoe 1pt. .20 .50
4 Nikolai Khabibulin 1pt. .20 .50
5 Olaf Kolzig 1pt. .20 .50
6 Roberto Luongo 1pt. .20 .50
7 Evgeni Nabokov 1pt. .20 .50
8 Jose Theodore 1pt. .20 .50
9 Jocelyn Thibault 1 pt. .20 .50
10 Roman Turek 1 pt. .20 .50
11 Ed Belfour 2 pts. .20 .50
12 Martin Brodeur 2 pts. .20 .50
13 Grant Fuhr 2 pts. .20 .50
14 Glenn Hall 2 pts. .20 .50
15 Jacques Plante 2 pts. .20 .50
16 Tommy Salo 2 pts. .20 .50
17 Dominik Hasek 3 pts. .20 .50
18 Curtis Joseph 3 pts. .20 .50
19 Patrick Roy 3 pts. .20 .50
20 Terry Sawchuk 3 pts. .20 .50

2001-02 Between the Pipes He Shoots-He Saves Prizes

Available only by redeeming 400 Between the Pipes He Shoots-He Saves points, this 40-card set featured game-used swatches of jersey and a color photo of the player. Each card had a stated print run of 20 serial-numbered sets and each was encased in a clear plastic slab with a descriptive label at the top. This set is unpriced due to scarcity and volatility.

STATED PRINT RUN 20 SER.#'d SETS
NOT PRICED DUE TO SCARCITY
1 Dominik Hasek
2 Ron Tugnutt
3 Mike Dunham
4 Marty Turco
5 Glenn Hall
6 Grant Fuhr
7 J-S Aubin
8 Mike Richter
9 Dan Cloutier
10 Tommy Salo
11 Roman Turek
12 Evgeni Nabokov
13 Nikolai Khabibulin
14 Patrick Lalime
15 Brian Boucher
16 Byron Dafoe
17 Olaf Kolzig
18 Jose Theodore
19 Jocelyn Thibault
20 Sean Burke
21 Felix Potvin
22 Arturs Irbe
23 Curtis Joseph
24 Jeff Hackett
25 Roman Cechmanek
26 Martin Brodeur
27 Patrick Roy
28 Manny Legace
29 Steve Shields
30 Ed Belfour
31 Martin Biron
32 Miikka Kiprusoff
33 Johan Hedberg
34 Ron Hextall
35 Manny Fernandez
36 Damian Rhodes
37 Bernie Parent
38 Billy Smith
39 Jani Hurme
40 Roberto Luongo

2001-02 Between the Pipes Jerseys

This 42-card set featured game-worn jersey swatches affixed to the right of full-color action photos on a two color background. The words "game used jersey" are printed at the card top and the player's name is printed on the right hand border. Each card was limited to 90 copies.

STATED PRINT RUN 90 SETS
*MULT.COLOR SWATCH: .5X TO 1.25X HI
GJ1 Byron Dafoe 6.00 15.00
GJ2 Dominik Hasek 15.00 40.00
GJ3 Mike Vernon 10.00 25.00
GJ4 Arturs Irbe 10.00 25.00
GJ5 Jocelyn Thibault 6.00 15.00
GJ6 Patrick Roy 25.00 60.00
GJ7 Ed Belfour 10.00 25.00
GJ8 Chris Osgood 10.00 25.00
GJ9 Johan Hedberg 6.00 15.00
GJ10 Roberto Luongo 12.50 30.00
GJ11 Jose Theodore 12.50 30.00
GJ12 Mike Dunham 6.00 15.00
GJ13 Martin Brodeur 20.00 50.00
GJ14 Mike Richter 10.00 25.00
GJ15 Roman Cechmanek 6.00 15.00
GJ16 J-S Aubin 6.00 15.00
GJ17 Roman Turek 6.00 15.00
GJ18 Curtis Joseph 10.00 25.00
GJ19 Olaf Kolzig 10.00 25.00
GJ20 Felix Potvin 10.00 25.00
GJ21 Trevor Kidd 6.00 15.00
GJ22 Tommy Salo 6.00 15.00
GJ23 Jeff Hackett 6.00 15.00
GJ24 Brian Boucher 6.00 15.00
GJ25 Dan Cloutier 6.00 15.00
GJ26 Damian Rhodes 6.00 15.00
GJ27 Ron Tugnutt 6.00 15.00
GJ28 Marty Turco 8.00 20.00
GJ29 Manny Fernandez 6.00 15.00
GJ30 Marc Denis 6.00 15.00
GJ31 Evgeni Nabokov 10.00 25.00
GJ32 Nikolai Khabibulin 10.00 25.00
GJ33 Sean Burke 6.00 15.00
GJ34 Gregg Naumenko 6.00 15.00
GJ35 Steve Shields 6.00 15.00
GJ36 Mathieu Garon 6.00 15.00
GJ37 Manny Legace 6.00 15.00
GJ38 Johan Holmqvist 6.00 15.00
GJ39 Martin Biron 6.00 15.00
GJ40 David Aebischer 6.00 25.00
GJ41 Miikka Kiprusoff 10.00 25.00
GJ42 John Grahame 6.00 15.00

2001-02 Between the Pipes Emblems

This 10-card set featured swatches of jersey emblem of the featured player. The words "game-used emblem is printed along the card top and the player's name is printed vertically along the left hand border. Each card was limited to just 20 copies. The set is not priced due to scarcity.

STATED PRINT RUN 20 SETS
NOT PRICED DUE TO SCARCITY
GUE1 Dominik Hasek
GUE2 Jocelyn Thibault
GUE3 Patrick Roy
GUE4 Johan Hedberg
GUE5 Roman Turek
GUE6 Curtis Joseph
GUE7 Olaf Kolzig
GUE8 Tommy Salo
GUE9 Brian Boucher
GUE10 Evgeni Nabokov

2001-02 Between the Pipes Jersey and Stick Cards

This 42-card set featured swatches of both game-worn jerseys and game-used sticks from the featured player. Each card was limited to 90 copies.

STATED PRINT RUN 90 SETS
GSJ1 Byron Dafoe 10.00 25.00
GSJ2 Dominik Hasek 20.00 50.00
GSJ3 Mike Vernon 10.00 25.00
GSJ4 Arturs Irbe 12.00 30.00
GSJ5 Jocelyn Thibault 10.00 25.00
GSJ6 Patrick Roy 40.00 100.00
GSJ7 Ed Belfour 12.00 30.00
GSJ8 Johan Hedberg 10.00 25.00
GSJ9 Roberto Luongo 20.00 50.00
GSJ10 Jose Theodore 12.00 30.00
GSJ11 Mike Dunham 10.00 25.00
GSJ12 Martin Brodeur 30.00 80.00
GSJ13 Mike Richter 12.00 30.00
GSJ14 Roman Cechmanek 10.00 25.00
GSJ15 J-S Aubin 10.00 25.00
GSJ16 Roman Turek 10.00 25.00
GSJ17 Curtis Joseph 12.00 30.00
GSJ18 Olaf Kolzig 12.00 30.00
GSJ19 Felix Potvin UER 12.00 30.00
GSJ20 Trevor Kidd 10.00 25.00
GSJ21 Tommy Salo 10.00 25.00
GSJ22 Jeff Hackett 10.00 25.00
GSJ23 Brian Boucher 10.00 25.00
GSJ24 Dan Cloutier 10.00 25.00
GSJ25 Manny Legace 10.00 25.00
GSJ26 Damian Rhodes 10.00 25.00
GSJ27 Martin Biron 10.00 25.00
GSJ28 Ron Tugnutt 10.00 25.00
GSJ29 Evgeni Nabokov 12.00 30.00
GSJ30 Nikolai Khabibulin 12.00 30.00
GSJ31 Sean Burke 10.00 25.00
GSJ32 Patrick Lalime 10.00 25.00
GSJ33 Steve Shields 10.00 25.00
GSJ34 Tomas Vokoun 12.00 30.00
GSJ35 Manny Fernandez 10.00 25.00
GSJ36 David Aebischer 10.00 25.00
GSJ37 Tony Esposito 30.00 80.00
GSJ38 Bernie Parent 40.00 100.00
GSJ39 Glenn Hall 40.00 100.00
GSJ40 Jacques Plante 50.00 125.00
GSJ41 Grant Fuhr 30.00 80.00
GSJ42 Terry Sawchuk 60.00 150.00

2001-02 Between the Pipes Numbers

Limited to just 20 copies each, this 10 card set featured game-worn swatches from the featured player's jersey number. The words "in the numbers" appear vertically along the right hand border and the player's name appears along the left hand border. This set is not priced due to scarcity.

STATED PRINT RUN 20 SETS
NOT PRICED DUE TO SCARCITY
ITN1 Dominik Hasek
ITN2 Jocelyn Thibault
ITN3 Patrick Roy
ITN4 Johan Hedberg
ITN5 Roman Turek
ITN6 Curtis Joseph
ITN7 Olaf Kolzig
ITN8 Tommy Salo
ITN9 Brian Boucher
ITN10 Evgeni Nabokov

2001-02 Between the Pipes Masks

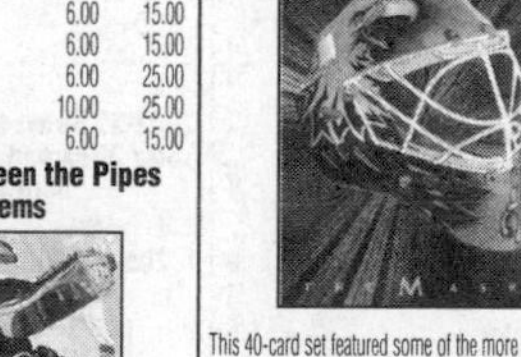

This 40-card set featured some of the more memorable goalie masks from the past and present NHL. Dufex technology was used to give the cards an overall foil effect. Cards were unnumbered and are listed below in checklist order. Cards 31-40 were available in BAP Update packs only.

COMPLETE SET (40) 100.00 200.00
CARDS 31-40 AVAIL.IN BAP UPD.PACKS
*SILVER: 1.25X TO 3X BASE HI
SILVER PRINT RUN 300 SETS
*GOLD: 3X TO 8X BASE HI
GOLD PRINT RUN 30 SETS
1 Jacques Plante 8.00 20.00
2 Curtis Joseph 5.00 12.00
3 Ed Giacomin 5.00 12.00
4 Gilles Gratton 3.00 8.00
5 Murray Bannerman 3.00 8.00
6 John Vanbiesbrouck 3.00 8.00
7 Gerry Cheevers 6.00 15.00
8 Steve Shields 3.00 8.00
9 Damian Rhodes 3.00 8.00
10 Byron Dafoe 3.00 8.00
11 Martin Biron 3.00 8.00
12 Roman Turek 3.00 8.00
13 Patrick Roy 10.00 25.00
14 Ed Belfour Red Mask 5.00 12.00
15 Manny Legace 3.00 8.00
16 Tommy Salo 3.00 8.00
17 Roberto Luongo 6.00 15.00
18 Felix Potvin 5.00 12.00
19 Manny Fernandez 3.00 8.00
20 Jose Theodore 5.00 12.00
21 Mike Dunham 3.00 8.00
22 Mike Richter 5.00 12.00
23 Patrick Lalime 3.00 8.00
24 Roman Cechmanek 3.00 8.00
25 Sean Burke 3.00 8.00
26 Johan Hedberg 3.00 8.00
27 Evgeni Nabokov 5.00 12.00
28 Brent Johnson 3.00 8.00
29 Curtis Joseph 5.00 12.00
30 Olaf Kolzig 3.00 8.00
31 Ed Belfour Gold Mask 5.00 12.00
32 Grant Fuhr 3.00 8.00
33 Brian Hayward 3.00 8.00
34 Milan Hnilicka 3.00 8.00
35 Jocelyn Thibault 3.00 8.00
36 Ron Tugnutt 3.00 8.00
37 Jeff Hackett 3.00 8.00
38 Rick DiPietro 3.00 8.00
39 Miikka Kiprusoff 3.00 8.00
40 Nikolai Khabibulin 5.00 12.00

2001-02 Between the Pipes Record Breakers

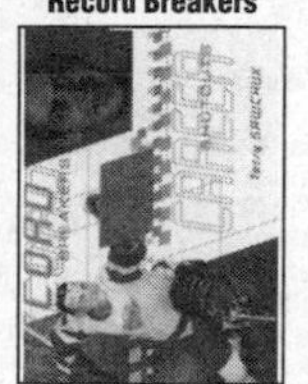

This 20-card set featured record setting goalies along side swatches of game-used jerseys. The words "Record Breakers" appeared along the top left border and the goalie's feat was printed in the bottom right border. Each card was limited to just 50 copies each.

STATED PRINT RUN 50 SETS
RB1 Patrick Roy 30.00 80.00
Most Playoff Wins
RB2 Terry Sawchuk 150.00 400.00
Martin Brodeur
Jacques Plante
Most 40 Win Seasons
RB3 Jacques Plante 30.00 80.00
Most Vezina Trophies
RB4 Martin Brodeur 40.00 100.00
RB5 Terry Sawchuk 40.00 100.00
Most Career Games
RB6 Bernie Parent 15.00 40.00
Most Wins in a Season
RB7 Tony Esposito 15.00 40.00
Most Consecutive 30 Win Seasons
RB8 Ed Belfour 15.00 40.00
Most Shutouts (Active Goalie)
RB9 Grant Fuhr 15.00 40.00
Longest Undefeated Streak by a Rookie
RB10 Patrick Roy 30.00 80.00
Most Playoff Shutouts
RB11 Patrick Roy 30.00 80.00
Most Conn Smythe Trophies
RB12 Ed Belfour 15.00 40.00
Most Consecutive Playoff Wins
RB13 Jacques Plante 30.00 80.00
Most Stanley Cup Wins
RB14 Gerry Cheevers 15.00 40.00
Longest Undefeated Streak
RB15 Terry Sawchuk 40.00 100.00
Most Career Shutouts
RB16 Patrick Roy 30.00 80.00
Most 30 Win Seasons
RB17 Patrick Roy 30.00 80.00
Most Career Wins
RB18 Chris Osgood 15.00 40.00
Best Winning Percentage
RB19 Tony Esposito 15.00 40.00
Most Shutouts by a Rookie
RB20 Glenn Hall 15.00 40.00
Most Consecutive Games Played

2001-02 Between the Pipes Tandems

This 13-card set featured goalie duos from specific teams around the league. Each card included a full-color photo of each goalie and a game-worn jersey swatch on the card front. The words "Goalie Tandems" were printed on the bottom border of each card. This set was limited to just 50 copies of each card.

STATED PRINT RUN 50 SETS
GT1 Evgeni Nabokov 30.00 80.00
Miikka Kiprusoff
GT2 Roman Cechmanek 15.00 40.00
Brian Boucher
GT3 Jose Theodore 25.00 60.00
Jeff Hackett
GT4 Roberto Luongo 15.00 40.00
Trevor Kidd
GT5 Patrick Roy 50.00 125.00
David Aebischer
GT6 Steve Shields 15.00 40.00
Jean-Sebastien Giguere
GT7 Ed Belfour 15.00 40.00
Marty Turco
GT8 Roman Turek 15.00 40.00
Mike Vernon
GT9 Dominik Hasek 15.00 40.00
Manny Legace
GT10 Byron Dafoe 15.00 40.00
John Grahame
GT11 Sean Burke 15.00 40.00
Robert Esche
GT12 Jocelyn Thibault 20.00 50.00

Steve Passmore
GT13 J-S Aubin 15.00 40.00
Johan Hedberg

2001-02 Between the Pipes Trophy Winners

This 24-card set honored goalies who have won various league awards through the years. Each card featured a color photo in the card center accompanied by a swatch of game-used jersey. On the right side of the card front the player's name and the trophy he won was printed vertically. On the left side of the card was a picture of the award itself. Each card was limited to 50 copies.

STATED PRINT RUN 40 SETS
TW1 Patrick Roy 40.00 100.00
Conn Smythe Winner
TW2 Dominik Hasek 20.00 50.00
Vezina Winner
TW3 Evgeni Nabokov 15.00 40.00
Calder Winner
TW4 Jacques Plante 40.00 100.00
Vezina Winner
TW5 Olaf Kolzig 15.00 40.00
Vezina Winner
TW6 Terry Sawchuk 60.00 150.00
Vezina Winner
TW7 Glenn Hall 15.00 40.00
Conn Smythe Winner
TW8 Billy Smith 15.00 40.00
Conn Smythe Winner
TW9 Turk Broda 15.00 40.00
Vezina Winner
TW10 Ron Hextall 15.00 40.00
Vezina Winner
TW11 Tiny Thompson 30.00 80.00
Vezina Winner
TW12 Bill Durnan 15.00 40.00
Vezina Winner
TW13 Glenn Hall 15.00 40.00
Vezina Winner
TW14 Terry Sawchuk 60.00 150.00
Calder Winner
TW15 Tony Esposito 20.00 50.00
Calder Winner
TW16 Glenn Hall 15.00 40.00
Calder Winner
TW17 Martin Brodeur 30.00 80.00
TW18 Jacques Plante 40.00 100.00
Hart Winner
TW19 Dominik Hasek 20.00 50.00
Hart Winner
TW20 Billy Smith 15.00 40.00
Vezina Winner
TW21 Bernie Parent 15.00 40.00
Conn Smythe Winner
TW22 Ed Belfour 20.00 50.00
Calder Winner
TW23 Frank Brimsek 15.00 40.00
Calder Winner
TW24 Dominik Hasek 20.00 50.00
Lester B. Pearson Award Winner

2001-02 Between the Pipes Vintage Memorabilia

This 20-card set featured game-used equipment from retired goalies. Each card carried a full color photo of the featured goalie on the right side of the card front and a larger black-and-white up close photo on the left side of the card front. The game-used swatch was affixed in the center of the two photos. Each card was limited to just 40 sets.

STATED PRINT RUN 40 SETS
VM1 Grant Fuhr 15.00 40.00
VM2 Turk Broda 25.00 60.00
VM3 Gerry Cheevers 15.00 40.00
VM4 Bernie Parent 15.00 40.00
VM5 Jacques Plante 30.00 80.00
VM6 Terry Sawchuk 50.00 125.00
VM7 Frank Brimsek 15.00 40.00
VM8 Glenn Hall 15.00 40.00
VM9 Tony Esposito 15.00 40.00
VM10 Vladislav Tretiak 60.00 150.00
VM11 Billy Smith 15.00 40.00
VM12 Johnny Bower 15.00 40.00
VM13 Georges Vezina 300.00 600.00
VM14 Ron Hextall 15.00 40.00
VM15 Ed Giacomin 15.00 40.00
VM16 Gump Worsley 25.00 60.00
VM17 Bill Durnan 15.00 40.00
VM18 Rogie Vachon 25.00 60.00
VM19 Tiny Thompson 15.00 40.00
VM20 Charlie Gardner 15.00 40.00

2002-03 Between the Pipes

This 150-card set highlighted the goal keepers, past and present, of the NHL. The set included two subsets; "enshrined", which featured retired goalies, and "home and away", which featured goalies in their home and road uniforms.

COMPLETE SET (150) 20.00 50.00
1 Patrick Roy 1.50 4.00
2 Jose Theodore .75 2.00
3 Olaf Kolzig .40 1.00
4 Roberto Luongo 1.00 2.50
5 Tommy Salo .20 .50
6 Dan Blackburn .20 .50
7 Patrick Lalime .20 .50
8 Martin Brodeur 1.25 3.00
9 Evgeni Nabokov .20 .50
10 Jani Hurme .20 .50
11 Dan Cloutier .20 .50
12 Mike Dunham .20 .50
13 Miika Kiprusoff .40 1.00
14 Rick DiPietro .40 1.00
15 Martin Biron .20 .50
16 Steve Passmore .20 .50
17 Curtis Joseph .60 1.50
18 Manny Fernandez .20 .50
19 Kevin Weekes .20 .50
20 Stephane Fiset .20 .50
21 Jocelyn Thibault .20 .50
22 David Aebischer .20 .50
23 Marty Turco .40 1.00
24 Jamie Storr .20 .50
25 Marc Denis .20 .50
26 Arturs Irbe .20 .50
27 Felix Potvin .60 1.50
28 Manny Legace .20 .50
29 Mike Richter .60 1.50
30 J-S Aubin .20 .50
31 Sean Burke .20 .50
32 Milan Hnilicka .20 .50
33 Ed Belfour .60 1.50
34 Roman Turek .20 .50
35 Frederic Cassivi .20 .50
36 Tomas Vokoun .40 1.00
37 Travis Scott .20 .50
38 Dwayne Roloson .20 .50
39 Roman Cechmanek .20 .50
40 Johan Hedberg .20 .50
41 Neil Little .20 .50
42 Jeff Hackett .20 .50
43 John Grahame .20 .50
44 Norm Maracle .20 .50
45 Ty Conklin .20 .50
46 Trevor Kidd .20 .50
47 Nikolai Khabibulin .60 1.50
48 Dieter Kochan .20 .50
49 Robert Esche .20 .50
50 Chris Osgood .20 .50
51 Jean-Sebastien Giguere .20 .50
52 Steve Shields .20 .50
53 Wade Flaherty .20 .50
54 Peter Skudra .20 .50
55 Brent Johnson .20 .50
56 Brian Boucher .20 .50
57 Garth Snow .20 .50
58 Fred Brathwaite .20 .50
59 Ron Tugnutt .20 .50
60 Craig Billington .20 .50
61 Martin Brochu .20 .50
62 Corey Schwab .20 .50
63 Tim Thomas RC 1.50 4.00
64 J-F Labbe .20 .50
65 Damian Rhodes .20 .50
66 Kevin Hodson .20 .50
67 Jamie McLennan .20 .50
68 Tyler Moss .20 .50
69 Tom Barrasso .20 .50
70 Corey Hirsch .20 .50
71 Eric Fichaud .20 .50
72 Byron Dafoe .20 .50
73 Mika Noronen .20 .50
74 Alex Auld .20 .50
75 Curtis Sanford RC .75 2.00
76 Martin Gerber RC 1.00 2.50
77 Mikael Tellqvist RC .75 2.00
78 J-M Pelletier .20 .50
79 J-F Damphousse .20 .50
80 Johan Holmqvist .20 .50
81 Mathieu Garon .20 .50
82 Martin Prusek .20 .50
83 Ilja Bryzgalov .20 .50
84 Andrew Raycroft .20 .50
85 Derek Gustafson .20 .50
86 Jason LaBarbera .20 .50
87 Marc Lamothe .20 .50
88 Scott Clemmensen .20 .50
89 Cody Rudkowsky RC .40 1.00
90 Craig Andersson RC 2.00 5.00
91 Maxime Ouellet .20 .50
92 Jan Lasak .20 .50
93 Patrick DesRochers .20 .50
94 Pasi Nurminen .20 .50
95 Sebastien Centomo .20 .50
96 Jussi Markkanen .20 .50
97 Sebastien Charpentier .20 .50
98 Reinhard Divis .20 .50
99 Simon Lajeunesse .20 .50
100 Vesa Toskala .20 .50
101 Olivier Michaud .20 .50
102 Levente Szuper RC .40 1.00
103 Philippe Sauve .20 .50
104 Dany Sabourin RC .40 1.00
105 Ryan Miller RC 2.50 6.00
106 Chris Mason .40 1.00
107 Steve Valiquette .20 .50
108 Pascal Leclaire RC 1.00 2.50
109 Jason Elliott RC .40 1.00
110 Michael Garnett RC .40 1.00
111 Tiny Thompson .60 1.50
112 Frank Brimsek .40 1.00
113 Jacques Plante 1.25 3.00
114 Terry Sawchuk 1.25 3.00
115 Georges Vezina 1.00 2.50
116 Chuck Rayner .40 1.00
117 Glenn Hall .60 1.50
118 Turk Broda .60 1.50
119 George Hainsworth .60 1.50
120 Roy Worters .60 1.50
121 Jean-Sebastien Giguere HA .20 .50
122 Milan Hnilicka HA .20 .50
123 Steve Shields HA .20 .50
124 Martin Biron HA .20 .50
125 Roman Turek HA .20 .50
126 Arturs Irbe HA .20 .50
127 Jocelyn Thibault HA .20 .50
128 Patrick Roy HA 1.50 4.00
129 Marc Denis HA .20 .50
130 Marty Turco HA .40 1.00
131 Curtis Joseph HA .60 1.50
132 Tommy Salo HA .20 .50
133 Roberto Luongo HA 1.00 2.50
134 Felix Potvin HA .60 1.50
135 Manny Fernandez HA .20 .50
136 Jose Theodore HA 1.00 2.50
137 Tomas Vokoun HA .40 1.00
138 Martin Brodeur HA 1.25 3.00
139 Chris Osgood HA .20 .50
140 Mike Richter HA .60 1.50
141 Patrick Lalime HA .20 .50
142 Roman Cechmanek HA .20 .50
143 Sean Burke HA .20 .50
144 Johan Hedberg HA .20 .50
145 Brent Johnson HA .20 .50
146 Evgeni Nabokov HA .20 .50
147 Nikolai Khabibulin HA .60 1.50
148 Ed Belfour HA .60 1.50
149 Dan Cloutier HA .20 .50
150 Olaf Kolzig HA .40 1.00

2002-03 Between the Pipes Gold

This 110-card set paralleled the first 110 cards of the base set but carried gold foil backgrounds on the card fronts. Each card was individually numbered out of 10.

GOLD PRINT RUN 10 SER.#'d SETS
NOT PRICED DUE TO SCARCITY

2002-03 Between the Pipes Silver

This 110-card set paralleled the first 110 cards of the base set but carried silver foil backgrounds on the card fronts. Each card was individually numbered out of 100.

*STARS: 3X TO 8X BASE HI
*ROOKIES: .75X TO 2X
SILVER PRINT RUN 100 SER.#'d SETS

2002-03 Between the Pipes All-Star Stick and Jersey

Limited to just 40-copies each, this 16-card set featured pieces of all-star game jerseys and sticks.

STATED PRINT RUN 40 SETS
1 Eddie Belfour 20.00 50.00
1996 Boston
2 Curtis Joseph 20.00 50.00
2000 Toronto
3 Martin Brodeur 40.00 100.00
4 Patrick Roy 50.00 125.00
1994 New York
5 Mike Richter 20.00 50.00
2000 Toronto
6 Evgeni Nabokov 20.00 50.00
2001 Denver
7 Olaf Kolzig 20.00 50.00
2000 Toronto
8 Felix Potvin 20.00 50.00
1996 Boston
9 Tommy Salo 20.00 50.00
2000 Toronto
10 Jose Theodore 25.00 60.00
2002 Los Angeles
11 Nikolai Khabibulin 20.00 50.00
2002 Los Angeles
12 Roman Turek 20.00 50.00
2000 Toronto
13 Sean Burke 20.00 50.00
2002 Los Angeles
14 Roman Cechmanek 20.00 50.00
2001 Denver
15 Arturs Irbe 20.00 50.00
1999 Tampa Bay
16 Chris Osgood 20.00 50.00
1996 Boston

2002-03 Between the Pipes All-Star Stick and Jersey Toronto Spring Expo

10 Jose Theodore

2002-03 Between the Pipes Behind the Mask

This 20-card set featured swatches of game jerseys. Cards were limited to 30 copies each.

STATED PRINT RUN 30 SETS
1 Marty Turco 15.00 40.00
2 Martin Brodeur 25.00 60.00
3 Patrick Roy 30.00 80.00
4 Roberto Luongo 20.00 50.00
5 Tommy Salo 15.00 40.00
6 Nikolai Khabibulin 15.00 40.00
7 Sean Burke 15.00 40.00
8 Patrick Lalime 15.00 40.00
9 Arturs Irbe 15.00 40.00
10 Jocelyn Thibault 15.00 40.00
11 Jose Theodore 15.00 40.00
12 Rick DiPietro 15.00 40.00
13 Marc Denis 15.00 40.00
14 Mike Dunham 15.00 40.00
15 Johan Hedberg 15.00 40.00
16 Olaf Kolzig 15.00 40.00
17 Dan Cloutier 15.00 40.00
18 Felix Potvin 15.00 40.00
19 Ed Belfour 15.00 40.00
20 Steve Shields 15.00 40.00

2002-03 Between the Pipes Blockers

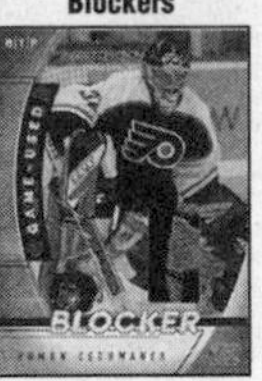

Limited to just 50 copies each, this 18-card set featured pieces of game-used goalie blockers.

*MULT.COLOR SWATCH: .75X TO 1.5X
STATED PRINT RUN 50 SETS
1 Curtis Joseph 15.00 40.00
2 Jani Hurme 10.00 25.00
3 Evgeni Nabokov 10.00 25.00
4 Felix Potvin 15.00 40.00
5 Jean-Sebastien Giguere 10.00 25.00
6 Jocelyn Thibault 10.00 25.00
7 Marty Turco 20.00 50.00
8 Mike Dunham 10.00 25.00
9 Johan Hedberg 10.00 25.00
10 Roman Cechmanek 10.00 25.00
11 Olaf Kolzig 10.00 25.00
12 Patrick Lalime 10.00 25.00
13 Roberto Luongo 12.50 30.00
14 Roman Turek 10.00 25.00
15 Nikolai Khabibulin 10.00 25.00
16 Tommy Salo 10.00 25.00
17 Trevor Kidd 10.00 25.00
18 Sean Burke 10.00 25.00

2002-03 Between the Pipes Complete Package

Limited to just 10 copies each, this 12-card set featured four pieces of game-used memorabilia. This set is not priced due to scarcity.

STATED PRINT RUN 10 SETS
NOT PRICED DUE TO SCARCITY
CP1 Patrick Roy
CP2 Curtis Joseph
CP3 Terry Sawchuk
CP4 Jacques Plante
CP5 Marty Turco
CP6 Johan Hedberg
CP7 Sean Burke
CP8 Jocelyn Thibault
CP9 Bernie Parent
CP10 Nikolai Khabibulin
CP11 Grant Fuhr
CP12 Roman Cechmanek

2002-03 Between the Pipes Double Memorabilia

This 20-card set carried dual swatches of game-used memorabillia. Each card was limited to just 40 copies each.

STATED PRINT RUN 40 SETS
1 Martin Brodeur 30.00 80.00
2 Sean Burke 12.50 30.00
3 Dan Cloutier 12.50 30.00
4 Chris Osgood 12.50 30.00
5 Jose Theodore 20.00 50.00
6 Olaf Kolzig 12.50 30.00
7 Patrick Roy 30.00 80.00
8 Tommy Salo 12.50 30.00
9 Marty Turco 12.50 30.00
10 Roman Turek 12.50 30.00
11 Mike Dunham 12.50 30.00
12 Manny Legace 12.00 30.00
13 Jocelyn Thibault 12.50 30.00
14 Nikolai Khabibulin 12.50 30.00
15 Johan Hedberg 12.50 30.00
16 Trevor Kidd 12.50 30.00
17 J-S Aubin 12.50 30.00
18 Jacques Plante 40.00 100.00
19 Terry Sawchuk 40.00 100.00
20 Roger Crozier 12.00 30.00

2002-03 Between the Pipes Emblems

Limited to 10 copies each, this 30-card set carried pieces of jersey emblems on the card fronts. This set is not priced due to scarcity.

STATED PRINT RUN 10 SETS
NOT PRICED DUE TO SCARCITY
1 Arturs Irbe
2 Miikka Kiprusoff
3 Rick DiPietro
4 Dan Blackburn
5 Dan Cloutier
6 David Aebischer
7 Evgeni Nabokov
8 Felix Potvin
9 Manny Fernandez
10 J-S Aubin
11 Jean-Sebastien Giguere
12 Jani Hurme
13 Jocelyn Thibault
14 Jose Theodore
15 Mike Dunham
16 Martin Biron
17 Johan Hedberg
18 Martin Brodeur
19 Marty Turco
20 Mika Noronen
21 Mike Richter
22 Nikolai Khabibulin
23 Olaf Kolzig
24 Patrick Lalime
25 Patrick Roy
26 Roberto Luongo
27 Roman Cechmanek
28 Roman Turek
29 Sean Burke
30 Tommy Salo

2002-03 Between the Pipes Future Wave

STATED PRINT RUN 60 SETS
1 Miikka Kiprusoff 20.00 50.00
2 Jose Theodore 20.00 50.00
3 Roberto Luongo 20.00 50.00
4 Rick DiPietro 12.00 30.00
5 Dan Blackburn 8.00 20.00
6 Mathieu Garon 8.00 20.00
7 Johan Hedberg 8.00 20.00
8 Dan Cloutier 8.00 20.00
9 Martin Biron 8.00 20.00
10 Marty Turco 12.00 30.00
11 Alex Auld 8.00 20.00
12 Brent Johnson 8.00 20.00

2002-03 Between the Pipes Goalie Autographs

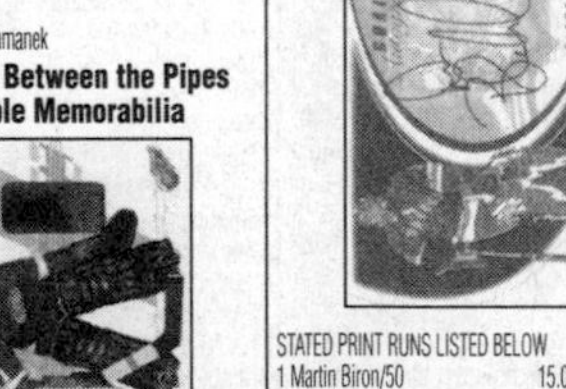

STATED PRINT RUNS LISTED BELOW
1 Martin Biron/50 15.00 40.00
2 Dan Blackburn/50 15.00 40.00
3 Sean Burke/50 15.00 40.00
4 Dan Cloutier/50 15.00 40.00
5 Marc Denis/50 15.00 40.00
6 Jean-Sebastien Giguere/50 15.00 40.00
7 Johan Hedberg/50 15.00 40.00
8 Milan Hnilicka/50 15.00 40.00
9 Arturs Irbe/50 15.00 40.00
10 Brent Johnson/50 15.00 40.00
11 Curtis Joseph/50 20.00 50.00
12 Nikolai Khabibulin/50 20.00 50.00
13 Olaf Kolzig/50 15.00 40.00
14 Patrick Lalime/50 15.00 40.00
15 Roberto Luongo/50 20.00 50.00
16 Evgeni Nabokov/50 15.00 40.00
17 Chris Osgood/50 15.00 40.00
18 Felix Potvin/50 25.00 60.00
19 Dwayne Roloson/50 15.00 40.00
20 Tommy Salo/50 15.00 40.00
21 Steve Shields/50 15.00 40.00
22 Jose Theodore/50 20.00 50.00
23 Jocelyn Thibault/50 15.00 40.00
24 Marty Turco/50 20.00 50.00
25 Roman Turek/50 15.00 40.00
26 Johnny Bower/90 15.00 40.00
27 Bernie Parent/90 15.00 40.00
28 Ed Giacomin/90 15.00 40.00
29 Gerry Cheevers/90 15.00 40.00
30 Vladislav Tretiak/90 60.00 125.00
31 Gump Worsley/40 30.00 80.00
32 Tony Esposito/90 25.00 60.00
33 John Davidson/90 15.00 40.00
34 Glenn Hall/90 15.00 40.00
35 Charlie Hodge/90 15.00 40.00
36 Rogie Vachon/90 15.00 40.00

2002-03 Between the Pipes He Shoots-He Saves Points

Inserted one per pack, these cards carried a value of 1, 2 or 3 points. The points could be redeemed for special memorabilia cards. The cards are unnumbered and are listed below in alphabetical order by point value. The redemption program ended December 31, 2003.

ONE PER PACK
RED.PROGRAM HAS EXPIRED
1 Sean Burke 1 pt. .40 1.00
2 Roman Cechmanek 1 pt. .40 1.00
3 Dan Cloutier 1 pt. .40 1.00
4 Johan Hedberg 1 pt. .40 1.00
5 Arturs Irbe 1 pt. .40 1.00
6 Patrick Lalime 1 pt. .40 1.00
7 Evgeni Nabokov 1 pt. .40 1.00
8 Felix Potvin 1 pt. .40 1.00
9 Mike Richter 1 pt. .40 1.00
10 Marty Turco 1 pt. .40 1.00
11 Roman Turek 1 pt. .40 1.00
12 Dan Blackburn 2 pt. .40 1.00
13 Nikolai Khabibulin 2 pt. .40 1.00
14 Olaf Kolzig 2 pt. .40 1.00
15 Roberto Luongo 2 pt. .40 1.00
16 Tommy Salo 2 pt. .40 1.00
17 Jocelyn Thibault 2 pt. .40 1.00
18 Martin Brodeur 3 pt. .40 1.00
19 Patrick Roy 3 pt. .40 1.00
20 Jose Theodore 3 pt. .40 1.00

2002-03 Between the Pipes He Shoots-He Saves Prizes

Available only by redeeming 400 Between the Pipes He Shoots-He Scores points, this 30-card set featured game-used swatches of jersey and a color photo of the player. Each card had a stated print run of 20 serial-numbered sets and each was encased in a clear plastic slab with a descriptive label at the top. This set is unpriced due to scarcity and volatility.

STATED PRINT RUN 20 SETS
NOT PRICED DUE TO SCARCITY
1 Patrick Roy
2 Roberto Luongo
3 Olaf Kolzig
4 Marty Turco
5 Mike Richter
6 Dan Blackburn
7 Tommy Salo
8 Sean Burke
9 Roman Cechmanek
10 Patrick Lalime
11 Roman Turek
12 Evgeni Nabokov
13 Nikolai Khabibulin
14 Johan Hedberg
15 Felix Potvin
16 Martin Brodeur
17 Arturs Irbe
18 Jocelyn Thibault
19 Dan Cloutier
20 Jose Theodore
21 Harry Lumley
22 Roy Worters
23 Roger Crozier
24 George Hainsworth
25 Tony Esposito
26 Gerry Cheevers
27 Ed Giacomin
28 Terry Sawchuk
29 Bernie Parent
30 Glenn Hall

2002-03 Between the Pipes Inspirations

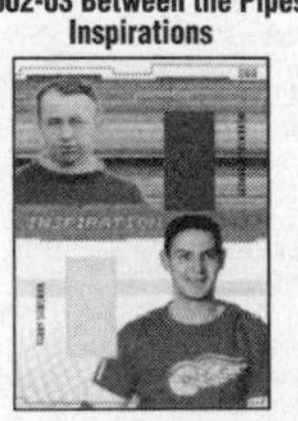

These dual jersey cards were limited to just 40 copies each.

STATED PRINT RUN 40 SETS
I1 Patrick Roy 50.00 125.00
Jacques Plante
I2 Terry Sawchuk 50.00 125.00
George Hainsworth
I3 Jose Theodore 60.00 150.00
Patrick Roy
I4 Roberto Luongo 30.00 80.00
Patrick Roy
I5 Sean Burke 25.00 60.00
Bernie Parent
I6 Eddie Belfour 40.00 100.00
Vladislav Tretiak
I7 Dan Blackburn 25.00 60.00
Curtis Joseph
I8 M.Brodeur/P.Roy 50.00 125.00
I9 Mike Richter 25.00 60.00
Gerry Cheevers
I10 Rick DiPietro 25.00 60.00
Ron Hextall

2002-03 Between the Pipes Jerseys

*MULT.COLOR SWATCH: .5X TO 1.25X
STATED PRINT RUN 90 SETS
1 Arturs Irbe 10.00 25.00
2 Miikka Kiprusoff 10.00 25.00
3 Rick DiPietro 10.00 25.00
4 Dan Blackburn 10.00 25.00
5 Dan Cloutier 10.00 25.00
6 David Aebischer 10.00 25.00
7 Evgeni Nabokov 10.00 25.00
8 Felix Potvin 10.00 25.00
9 Manny Fernandez 10.00 25.00
10 J-S Aubin 10.00 25.00
11 Jean-Sebastien Giguere 10.00 25.00
12 Jani Hurme 10.00 25.00
13 Jocelyn Thibault 10.00 25.00
14 Jose Theodore 15.00 40.00
15 Mike Dunham 10.00 25.00
16 Martin Biron 10.00 25.00
17 Johan Hedberg 10.00 25.00
18 Martin Brodeur 20.00 50.00
19 Marty Turco 10.00 25.00
20 Mika Noronen 10.00 25.00
21 Mike Richter 10.00 25.00
22 Nikolai Khabibulin 10.00 25.00
23 Olaf Kolzig 10.00 25.00
24 Patrick Lalime 10.00 25.00
25 Patrick Roy 25.00 60.00
26 Roberto Luongo 15.00 40.00
27 Roman Cechmanek 10.00 25.00
28 Roman Turek 10.00 25.00
29 Sean Burke 10.00 25.00
30 Tommy Salo 10.00 25.00
31 Maxime Ouellet 10.00 25.00
32 Ed Belfour 10.00 25.00
33 Sebastien Charpentier 10.00 25.00
34 Robert Esche 10.00 25.00
35 Curtis Sanford 10.00 25.00
36 Milan Hnilicka 10.00 25.00
37 Steve Shields 10.00 25.00
38 Tim Thomas 15.00 40.00
39 Trevor Kidd 10.00 25.00
40 Fred Brathwaite 10.00 25.00
41 Martin Prusek 10.00 25.00
42 John Grahame 10.00 25.00
43 Jamie Storr 10.00 25.00
44 Sebastien Centomo 10.00 25.00
45 Ron Tugnutt 10.00 25.00
46 Martin Gerber 10.00 25.00
47 Jussi Markkanen 10.00 25.00
48 Simon Lajeunesse 10.00 25.00
49 Reinhard Divis 10.00 25.00
50 Jeff Hackett 10.00 25.00

2002-03 Between the Pipes Masks II

Created on Dufex card stock, this 30-card set featured artist renderings of the masks made famous by the goalies who wore them.

COMPLETE SET (30) 30.00 60.00
*SILVER: 1.25X TO 3X BASE HI
SILVER PRINT RUN 300 SETS
*GOLD: 3X TO 8X BASE HI
GOLD PRINT RUN 30 SETS
1 Jean-Sebastien Giguere 2.00 5.00
2 Milan Hnilicka 2.00 5.00
3 Steve Shields 2.00 5.00
4 Martin Biron 2.00 5.00
5 Roman Turek 2.00 5.00
6 Kevin Weekes 2.00 5.00
7 Jocelyn Thibault 2.00 5.00
8 Patrick Roy 6.00 15.00
9 Marc Denis 2.00 5.00
10 Marty Turco 2.00 5.00
11 Curtis Joseph 2.50 6.00
12 Tommy Salo 2.00 5.00
13 Roberto Luongo 4.00 10.00
14 Felix Potvin 2.50 6.00
15 Manny Fernandez 2.00 5.00
16 Jose Theodore 4.00 10.00
17 Mike Dunham 2.00 5.00
18 Mike Richter 2.50 6.00
19 Rick DiPietro 2.00 5.00
20 Patrick Lalime 2.00 5.00

21 Roman Cechmanek 2.00 5.00
22 Sean Burke 2.00 5.00
23 Johan Hedberg 2.00 5.00
24 Evgeni Nabokov 2.00 5.00
25 Miikka Kiprusoff 4.00 10.00
26 Brent Johnson 2.00 5.00
27 Nikolai Khabibulin 2.50 6.00
28 Ed Belfour 2.50 6.00
29 Jeff Hackett 2.00 5.00
30 Olaf Kolzig 2.00 5.00

2002-03 Between the Pipes Nightmares

This 10-card set featured jersey swatches from NHL goalies and shooters who had a history of scoring against them. Production was limited to 60 copies each.

STATED PRINT RUN 60 SETS
GN1 DanBlackburn 15.00 40.00
Ilya Kovalchuk
GN2 M.Richter/M.Lemieux 25.00 60.00
GN3 Tommy Salo 15.00 40.00
Jaromir Jagr
GN4 F.Potvin/S.Yzerman 30.00 80.00
GN5 Stephane Fiset 12.50 30.00
Pavel Bure
GN6 Mike Richter 15.00 40.00
Jarome Iginla
GN7 Tommy Salo 12.50 30.00
Peter Forsberg
GN8 Curtis Joseph 20.00 50.00
Joe Sakic
GN9 Olaf Kolzig 12.50 30.00
Eric Lindros
GN10 Tom Barrasso 12.50 30.00
Mats Sundin

2002-03 Between the Pipes Numbers

This 30-card set partially paralleled the base jersey set but carried a piece jersey number. Each card was limited to just 10 copies each. This set is not priced due to scarcity.

STATED PRINT RUN 10 SETS
NOT PRICED DUE TO SCARCITY
1 Arturs Irbe
2 Miikka Kiprusoff
3 Rick DiPietro
4 Dan Blackburn
5 Dan Cloutier
6 David Aebischer
7 Evgeni Nabokov
8 Felix Potvin
9 Manny Fernandez
10 J-S Aubin
11 Jean-Sebastien Giguere
12 Jani Hurme
13 Jocelyn Thibault
14 Jose Theodore
15 Mike Dunham
16 Martin Biron
17 Johan Hedberg
18 Martin Brodeur
19 Marty Turco
20 Mika Noronen
21 Mike Richter
22 Nikolai Khabibulin
23 Olaf Kolzig
24 Patrick Lalime
25 Patrick Roy
26 Roberto Luongo
27 Roman Cechmanek
28 Roman Turek
29 Sean Burke
30 Tommy Salo

2002-03 Between the Pipes Pads

Limited to just 50 copies each, this 14-card set featured pieces of game-used goalie pads.

*MULT.COLOR SWATCH: .75X TO 1.5X
STAT.PRINT RUN 50 SETS
1 Martin Brodeur 30.00 80.00
2 Patrick Roy 30.00 80.00
3 Marty Turco 10.00 25.00
4 Curtis Joseph 15.00 40.00
5 Ed Belfour 15.00 40.00
6 Jose Theodore 20.00 50.00
7 Sean Burke 10.00 25.00
8 Dan Cloutier 10.00 25.00
9 Chris Osgood 10.00 25.00
10 Nikolai Khabibulin 15.00 40.00
11 J-S Aubin 10.00 25.00
12 Steve Shields 10.00 25.00
13 Mike Dunham 10.00 25.00
14 Jocelyn Thibault 10.00 25.00

2002-03 Between the Pipes Record Breakers

This 16-card memorabilia set was limited to just 40 copies each.

STATED PRINT RUN 40 SETS
1 Terry Sawchuk 30.00 80.00
Most Career Games Played
2 Patrick Roy 20.00 50.00
Most Career Playoff Games
3 George Hainsworth 20.00 50.00
4 Jacques Plante 25.00 60.00
Most Vezina Trophies
5 Patrick Roy 20.00 50.00
Most Career Wins
6 Glenn Hall 12.50 30.00
Most Consecutive Complete Games
7 Tony Esposito 12.50 30.00
Most Shutouts by a Rookie
8 Gerry Cheevers 12.50 30.00
Longest Undefeated Streak-Season
9 Martin Brodeur 30.00 80.00
10 Bernie Parent 12.50 30.00
Most Wins-Season
11 Terry Sawchuk 30.00 80.00
Most Career Shutouts
12 Patrick Roy 20.00 50.00
Most Career Playoff Wins
13 Johnny Bower 12.50 30.00
Oldest NHL Goalie
14 Ed Belfour 12.50 30.00
Most Consecutive Playoff Wins
15 Patrick Roy 20.00 50.00
Most Career 30-Win Seasons
16 Terry Sawchuk 30.00 80.00
Most Career Minutes

2002-03 Between the Pipes Stick and Jerseys

This 30-card set partially paralleled the base jersey set but also carried a piece of game-used stick. Print run was 90 copies each.

STATED PRINT RUN 90 SETS
1 Arturs Irbe 10.00 25.00
2 Miikka Kiprusoff 10.00 25.00
3 Rick DiPietro 10.00 25.00
4 Dan Blackburn 10.00 25.00
5 Dan Cloutier 10.00 25.00
6 David Aebischer 10.00 25.00
7 Evgeni Nabokov 10.00 25.00
8 Felix Potvin 10.00 25.00
9 Manny Fernandez 10.00 25.00
10 J-S Aubin 10.00 25.00
11 Jean-Sebastien Giguere 10.00 25.00
12 Jani Hurme 10.00 25.00
13 Jocelyn Thibault 10.00 25.00
14 Jose Theodore 15.00 40.00
15 Mike Dunham 10.00 25.00
16 Martin Biron 10.00 25.00
17 Johan Hedberg 10.00 25.00
18 Martin Brodeur 20.00 50.00
19 Marty Turco 10.00 25.00
20 Mika Noronen 10.00 25.00
21 Mike Richter 10.00 25.00
22 Nikolai Khabibulin 10.00 25.00
23 Olaf Kolzig 10.00 25.00
24 Patrick Lalime 10.00 25.00
25 Patrick Roy 25.00 60.00
26 Roberto Luongo 15.00 40.00
27 Roman Cechmanek 10.00 25.00
28 Roman Turek 10.00 25.00
29 Sean Burke 10.00 25.00
30 Tommy Salo 10.00 25.00

2002-03 Between the Pipes Tandems

This 20-card memorabilia set featured starting goalies and their backups. Each card was limited to 30 copies.

STATED PRINT RUN 30 SETS
1 Mike Richter 12.00 30.00
Dan Blackburn
2 Patrick Roy 50.00 100.00
David Aebischer
3 Jocelyn Thibault 12.00 30.00
Steve Passmore
4 Evgeni Nabokov 20.00 50.00
Miikka Kiprusoff
5 Patrick Lalime 12.00 30.00
Martin Prusek
6 Martin Biron 12.00 30.00
Mika Noronen
7 Johan Hedberg 12.00 30.00
J-S Aubin
8 Roman Cechmanek 12.00 30.00
Robert Esche
9 Jose Theodore 15.00 40.00
Jeff Hackett
10 Felix Potvin 15.00 40.00
Jamie Storr
11 Mike Dunham 12.00 30.00
Tomas Vokoun
12 Dan Cloutier 12.00 30.00
Alex Auld
13 Jean-Sebastien Giguere 15.00 40.00
Martin Gerber
14 Ed Belfour 20.00 50.00
Trevor Kidd
15 Brent Johnson 12.00 30.00
Fred Brathwaite
16 Chris Osgood 15.00 40.00
Rick Dipietro
17 Steve Shields 12.00 30.00
John Grahame
18 Tommy Salo 12.00 30.00
Jussi Markkanen
19 Marty Turco 15.00 40.00
Ron Tugnutt
20 Olaf Kolzig 15.00 40.00
Maxime Ouellet

2002-03 Between the Pipes Trappers

Limited to just 60 copies each, this 18-card set featured pieces of game-used goalie trappers.

*MULT.COLOR SWATCH: .75X TO 1.5X
STATED PRINT RUN 60 SETS
GT1 Vladislav Tretiak 50.00 100.00
GT2 Bill Durnan 20.00 50.00
GT3 Dan Cloutier 10.00 25.00
GT4 Byron Dafoe 10.00 25.00
GT5 Johan Hedberg 10.00 25.00
GT6 Charlie Hodge 30.00 80.00
GT7 Nikolai Khabibulin 10.00 25.00
GT8 Jacques Plante 30.00 80.00
GT9 Olaf Kolzig 12.00 30.00
GT10 Harry Lumley 10.00 25.00
GT11 Bernie Parent 25.00 60.00
GT12 Patrick Roy 40.00 100.00
GT13 Terry Sawchuk 30.00 80.00
GT14 Jocelyn Thibault 10.00 25.00
GT15 Marty Turco 12.00 30.00
GT16 Roger Crozier 15.00 40.00
GT17 Sean Burke 10.00 25.00
GT18 Grant Fuhr 20.00 50.00

2002-03 Between the Pipes Vintage Memorabilia

This 20-card memorabilia set was limited to just 20 copies per card. This set is not priced due to scarcity.

STATED PRINT RUN 20 SETS
NOT PRICED DUE TO SCARCITY
1 Johnny Bower
2 Harry Lumley
3 Roger Crozier
4 Ed Giacomin
5 Bill Durnan
6 George Hainsworth
7 Gerry Cheevers
8 Bernie Parent
9 Tony Esposito
10 Jacques Plante
11 Charlie Hodge
12 Glenn Hall
13 Roy Worters
14 Tiny Thompson
15 Charlie Gardiner
16 Terry Sawchuk
17 Frank Brimsek
18 Vladislav Tretiak
19 Bernie Parent
20 Ed Giacomin

2005 Between the Pipes

COMPLETE SET (25) 6.00 15.00
1 Johnny Bower .40 1.00
2 Turk Broda .40 1.00
3 Martin Brodeur 1.25 3.00
4 Richard Brodeur .20 .50
5 Gerry Cheevers .40 1.00
6 Tony Esposito .40 1.00
7 Grant Fuhr .40 1.00
8 Ed Giacomin .30 .75
9 Glenn Hall .30 .75
10 Ron Hextall .40 1.00
11 Charlie Hodge .20 .50
12 Mike Palmateer .30 .75
13 Bernie Parent .40 1.00
14 Jacques Plante .75 2.00
15 Bill Ranford .20 .50
16 Chico Resch .20 .50
17 Patrick Roy 1.25 3.00
18 Terry Sawchuk .75 2.00
19 Billy Smith .40 1.00
20 Jose Theodore .40 1.00
21 Tiny Thompson .40 1.00
22 Vladislav Tretiak .40 1.00
23 Rogie Vachon .30 .75
24 Georges Vezina .40 1.00
25 Gump Worsley .40 1.00

2005 Between the Pipes Autographs

COMPLETE SET (20)
RANDOM INSERTS IN BTP BOX SETS
ABP Bernie Parent 12.00 30.00
ABR Bill Ranford 6.00 15.00
ABS Billy Smith 10.00 25.00
ACH Charlie Hodge 8.00 20.00
ACR Chico Resch 6.00 15.00
AEG Ed Giacomin 10.00 25.00
AGC Gerry Cheevers 10.00 25.00
AGH Glenn Hall 10.00 25.00
AGR Grant Fuhr 10.00 25.00
AGW Gump Worsley 10.00 25.00
AJB Johnny Bower 12.00 30.00
AJT Jose Theodore 10.00 25.00
AMB Martin Brodeur 60.00 100.00
AMP Mike Palmateer 10.00 25.00
APR Patrick Roy 60.00 100.00
ARB Richard Brodeur 6.00 15.00
ARH Ron Hextall 10.00 25.00
ARV Rogie Vachon 8.00 20.00
ATO Tony Esposito 12.00 30.00
AVT Vladislav Tretiak 15.00 40.00

2005 Between the Pipes Complete Package

COMPLETE SET (7)
RANDOM INSERTS IN BTP BOX SETS
NOT PRICED DUE TO SCARCITY
CP1 Grant Fuhr
CP2 Patrick Roy
CP3 Jacques Plante
CP4 Gerry Cheevers
CP5 Terry Sawchuk
CP6 Bernie Parent
CP7 Jose Theodore

2005 Between the Pipes Double Memorabilia

COMPLETE SET (8)
PRINT RUN 40 SER. #'d SETS
DM1 Patrick Roy 20.00 50.00
DM2 Patrick Roy 20.00 50.00
DM3 Martin Brodeur 15.00 40.00
DM4 Ron Hextall 10.00 25.00
DM5 Tony Esposito 10.00 25.00
DM6 Gerry Cheevers 10.00 25.00
DM7 Vladislav Tretiak 12.00 30.00
DM8 Jose Theodore 12.00 30.00

2005 Between the Pipes Gloves

COMPLETE SET (8)
RANDOM INSERTS IN BTP BOX SETS
GUG1 Tony Esposito 10.00 25.00
GUG2 Patrick Roy 25.00 60.00
GUG3 Gilles Gilbert 10.00 25.00
GUG4 Vladislav Tretiak 15.00 40.00
GUG5 Jose Theodore 10.00 25.00
GUG6 Rogie Vachon 8.00 20.00
GUG7 Charlie Hodge 8.00 20.00
GUG8 Grant Fuhr 10.00 25.00

2005 Between the Pipes Jerseys

COMPLETE SET (12)
RANDOM INSERTS IN BTP BOX SETS
GUJ1 Patrick Roy 12.00 30.00
GUJ2 Patrick Roy 12.00 30.00
GUJ3 Martin Brodeur 12.00 30.00
GUJ4 Tony Esposito 8.00 20.00
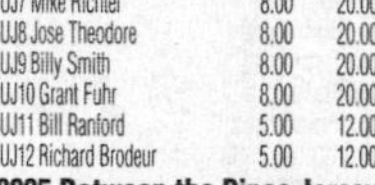
GUJ5 Vladislav Tretiak 8.00 20.00
GUJ6 Glenn Hall 8.00 20.00
GUJ7 Mike Richter 8.00 20.00
GUJ8 Jose Theodore 8.00 20.00
GUJ9 Billy Smith 8.00 20.00
GUJ10 Grant Fuhr 8.00 20.00
GUJ11 Bill Ranford 5.00 12.00
GUJ12 Richard Brodeur 5.00 12.00

2005 Between the Pipes Jersey and Sticks

COMPLETE SET (10)
RANDOM INSERTS IN BTP BOX SETS
SJ1 Patrick Roy
SJ2 Patrick Roy 20.00 50.00
SJ3 Martin Brodeur 15.00 40.00
SJ4 Ed Giacomin 10.00 25.00
SJ5 Johnny Bower 10.00 25.00
SJ6 Tony Esposito 10.00 25.00
SJ7 Mike Richter 10.00 25.00
SJ8 Ron Hextall 10.00 25.00
SJ9 Jose Theodore 10.00 25.00
SJ10 Grant Fuhr 10.00 25.00

2005 Between the Pipes Pads

COMPLETE SET (8)
PRINT RUN 20 SER. #'d SETS
GUP1 Bernie Parent 12.00 30.00
GUP2 Grant Fuhr 12.00 30.00
GUP3 Gerry Cheevers 12.00 30.00
GUP4 Ron Hextall 12.00 30.00
GUP5 Martin Brodeur 15.00 40.00
GUP6 Patrick Roy 20.00 50.00
GUP7 Jacques Plante 25.00 60.00
GUP8 Jose Theodore 12.00 30.00

2005 Between the Pipes Signed Memorabilia

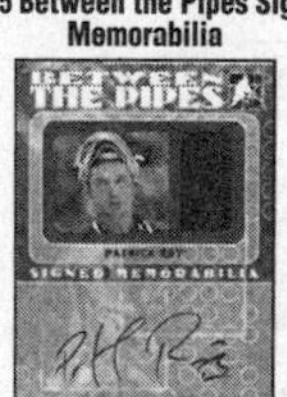

COMPLETE SET (10)
RANDOM INSERTS IN BTP BOX SETS
NOT PRICED DUE TO LACK OF MARKET INFO
SM1 Patrick Roy
SM2 Patrick Roy
SM3 Martin Brodeur
SM4 Glenn Hall
SM5 Johnny Bower
SM6 Gerry Cheevers
SM7 Ed Giacomin
SM8 Jose Theodore
SM9 Grant Fuhr
SM10 Bernie Parent

2006-07 Between The Pipes

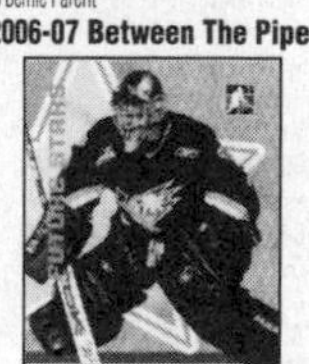

This 150-card set was released in March, 2007. The set was issued into the hobby in five-card packs with came 24 packs to a box and 24 boxes to a case. With some exceptions, the set is broken down thusly: Minor league goalies in first name Alpabetical order (1-55); current NHL goalies in 1st name alphabetical order (56-77); retired greats in 1st name alphabetical order (78-104); Current NHL goalies again in 1st name alphabetical order (105-118) and more retired goalies (107-160).

COMPLETE SET (150) 15.00 40.00
1 Al Montoya .30 .75
2 Andrew Penner .25 .60
3 Barry Brust .25 .60
4 Brent Krahn .25 .60
5 Bryan Pitton .25 .60
6 Brian Finley .25 .60
7 Carey Price 1.25 3.00
8 Chris Beckford-Tseu .30 .75
9 Corey Crawford .25 .60
10 Craig Anderson .25 .60
11 Curtis McElhinney .25 .60
12 David LeNeveu .25 .60
13 Frank Doyle .25 .60
14 Frederic Cassivi .25 .60
15 Gerald Coleman .25 .60
16 Hannu Toivonen .30 .75
17 Jaroslav Halak 1.50 4.00
18 Jason Bacashihua .25 .60
19 Jason LaBarbera .25 .60
20 Jeff Glass .25 .60
21 J-F Racine .25 .60
22 Jimmy Howard .50 1.25
23 John Murray .25 .60
24 Jonathan Bernier .75 2.00
25 Jordan Parise .50 1.25
26 Josh Harding .30 .75
27 J-P Levasseur .25 .60
28 Julien Ellis .25 .60
29 Justin Leclerc .25 .60
30 Justin Pogge .50 1.25
31 Kelly Guard .25 .60
32 Kevin Lalande .25 .60
33 Kurt Mucha .25 .60
34 Kyle Moir .25 .60
35 Leland Irving .50 1.25
36 Marek Schwarz .40 1.00
37 Martin Houle .25 .60
38 Michael Leighton .40 1.00
39 Mikael Tellqvist .30 .75
40 Mike Smith .30 .75
41 Nicola Riopel .25 .60
42 Pekka Rinne .25 .60
43 Philippe Sauve .25 .60
44 Rejean Beauchemin .25 .60
45 Ryan Daniels .25 .60
46 Stefan Liv .25 .60
47 Tobias Stephan .25 .60
48 Steve Mason .60 1.50
49 Trevor Cann .25 .60
50 Tuukka Rask .75 2.00
51 Tyler Plante .25 .60
52 Tyson Sexsmith .25 .60
53 Wade Dubielewicz .25 .60
54 Yann Danis .25 .60
55 Yutaka Fukufuji .25 .60
56 Alex Auld .25 .60
57 Antero Niittymaki .30 .75
58 Cam Ward .50 1.25
59 Cristobal Huet .30 .75
60 Peter Budaj .25 .60
61 Dominik Hasek .40 1.00
62 Dwayne Roloson .25 .60
63 Henrik Lundqvist .50 1.25
64 Ilya Bryzgalov .30 .75
65 Ed Belfour .75 2.00
66 Johan Holmqvist .30 .75
67 Kari Lehtonen .30 .75
68 Manny Fernandez .30 .75
69 Marc-Andre Fleury .30 .75
70 Martin Brodeur 1.00 2.50
71 Martin Gerber .30 .75
72 Pascal Leclaire .30 .75
73 Ray Emery .30 .75
74 Rick DiPietro .30 .75
75 Roberto Luongo .60 1.50
76 Ryan Miller .30 .75
77 Tim Thomas .30 .75
78 Andy Moog .30 .75
79 Bernie Parent .50 1.25
80 Billy Smith .40 1.00
81 Brian Hayward .25 .60
82 Charlie Hodge .40 1.00
83 Chico Resch .30 .75
84 Dan Bouchard .30 .75
85 Doug Favell .30 .75
86 Ed Giacomin .50 1.25
87 Emile Francis .30 .75
88 Felix Potvin .50 1.25
89 Gerry Cheevers .60 1.50
90 Gilles Gilbert .30 .75
91 Glenn Hall .50 1.25
92 Grant Fuhr .50 1.25
93 Gump Worsley .75 2.00
94 John Davidson .30 .75
95 Johnny Bower .50 1.25
96 Ken Wregget .25 .60
97 Mike Palmateer .30 .75
98 Patrick Roy 1.00 2.50
99 Richard Brodeur .25 .60
100 Rogie Vachon .50 1.25
101 Ron Hextall .60 1.50
102 Tom Barrasso .50 1.25
103 Tony Esposito .50 1.25
104 Vladislav Tretiak .75 2.00
105 Al Montoya .30 .75
106 Cam Ward .50 1.25
107 Carey Price 1.25 3.00
108 Grant Fuhr .50 1.25
109 Hannu Toivonen .30 .75
110 Kari Lehtonen .30 .75
111 Leland Irving .50 1.25
112 Marc-Andre Fleury .30 .75
113 Marek Schwarz .40 1.00
114 Martin Brodeur 1.00 2.50
115 Rick DiPietro .30 .75
116 Tuukka Rask .75 2.00
117 Martin Brodeur 1.00 2.50
118 Patrick Roy 1.00 2.50
119 Roberto Luongo .60 1.50
120 Marc-Andre Fleury .30 .75
121 Carey Price 1.25 3.00
122 Justin Pogge .50 1.25
123 Jeff Glass .25 .60
124 Bill Ranford .50 1.25
125 Ed Belfour .75 2.00
126 George Hainsworth .30 .75
127 Georges Vezina .50 1.25
128 Jacques Plante .50 1.25
129 Pelle Lindbergh .40 1.00
130 Roger Crozier .30 .75
131 Roy Worters .30 .75
132 Terry Sawchuk .50 1.25
133 Tiny Thompson .30 .75
134 Turk Broda .30 .75
135 Bower/Sawchuk .50 1.25
136 Parent/Favell .50 1.25
137 Smith/Resch .30 .75
138 Worsley/Vachon .50 1.25
139 Belfour/Hasek .75 2.00
140 Giacomin/Davidson .50 1.25
141 Plante/Hall .50 1.25
142 Hasek/Fuhr .50 1.25
143 Patrick Roy 1.00 2.50
144 Terry Sawchuk .50 1.25
145 Bernie Parent .50 1.25
146 George Hainsworth .30 .75
147 Glenn Hall .50 1.25
148 Grant Fuhr .50 1.25
149 Martin Brodeur 1.00 2.50
150 Gerry Cheevers .60 1.50

2006-07 Between The Pipes Aspiring

STATED PRINT RUN 50 SETS
AS01 Martin Brodeur 12.00 30.00
Cam Ward
AS02 Patrick Roy 25.00 60.00
Cristobal Huet
AS03 Dominik Hasek 10.00 25.00
Ryan Miller
AS04 Roberto Luongo 15.00 40.00
Leland Irving
AS05 Patrick Roy 30.00 80.00
Carey Price
AS06 Dominik Hasek 10.00 25.00
Marek Schwarz
AS07 Grant Fuhr 12.00 30.00
Ray Emery
AS08 Pelle Lindbergh 12.00 30.00
Henrik Lundqvist
AS09 Martin Brodeur 25.00 60.00
Jeff Glass
AS10 Patrick Roy 20.00 50.00
Jonathan Bernier

2006-07 Between The Pipes Aspiring Gold

STATED PRINT RUN 10 SETS
NOT PRICED DUE TO SCARCITY

2006-07 Between The Pipes Autographs

ODD3 1.24
AMF2 Marc-Andre Fleury SP 40.00 80.00
AAM2 Al Montoya SP 12.00 30.00
ACW2 Cam Ward SP 12.00 30.00
ACP2 Carey Price SP 75.00 150.00
AGF2 Grant Fuhr SP 12.00 30.00
AHT2 Hannu Toivonen SP 8.00 20.00
ALI2 Leland Irving SP 25.00 50.00
AMS2 Marek Schwarz SP 25.00 50.00
AMB2 Martin Brodeur SP 60.00 120.00
ARDI Rick DiPietro SP 25.00 50.00
ATR2 Tuukka Rask SP 30.00 60.00
AKL2 Kari Lehtonen SP 15.00 40.00
AAP Andrew Penner 4.00 10.00
ABF Brian Finley 4.00 10.00
AFD Frank Doyle 4.00 10.00
AJHA Jaroslav Halak 25.00 60.00
AJDL Jeff Deslauriers 4.00 10.00
AJFR J-F Racine 4.00 10.00
AJPA Jordan Parise 8.00 20.00
AJL Justin Leclerc 4.00 10.00
AKG Kelly Guard 4.00 10.00
AKMU Kurt Mucha 4.00 10.00
ANR Nicola Riopel 4.00 10.00
ATST Tobias Stephan 4.00 10.00
ATC Trevor Cann 4.00 10.00
AAM Al Montoya 5.00 12.00
ABB Barry Brust 4.00 10.00
ABK Brent Krahn 4.00 10.00
ABPI Bryan Pitton 4.00 10.00
ACP Carey Price 20.00 50.00
ACC Corey Crawford 4.00 10.00
ACA Craig Anderson 4.00 10.00
ACM Curtis McElhinney 4.00 10.00
ADD Devan Dubnyk 4.00 10.00
AFC Frederic Cassivi 4.00 10.00
AHT Hannu Toivonen 5.00 12.00
AJBA Jason Bacashihua 4.00 10.00
AJG Jeff Glass 4.00 10.00
AJH Jimmy Howard 8.00 20.00
AJM John Murray 4.00 10.00
AJBE Jonathan Bernier 12.00 30.00
AJHR Josh Harding 5.00 12.00
AJPL J-P Levasseur 4.00 10.00
AJE Julien Ellis 4.00 10.00
AJP Justin Pogge 8.00 20.00
AKLA Kevin Lalande 4.00 10.00
AKM Kyle Moir 4.00 10.00
ALI Leland Irving 8.00 20.00
AMS Marek Schwarz 6.00 15.00
AMH Martin Houle 4.00 10.00
AMSM Mike Smith 5.00 12.00
APRI Pekka Rinne 4.00 10.00
APO Philippe Sauve 4.00 10.00
ARB Rejean Beauchemin 4.00 10.00
ARD Ryan Daniels 4.00 10.00
ASL Stefan Liv 4.00 10.00

ASM Steve Mason 10.00 25.00
ATR Tuukka Rask 12.00 30.00
ATP Tyler Plante 4.00 10.00
ATS Tyson Sexsmith 4.00 10.00
AWD Wade Dubielewicz 4.00 10.00
AYD Yann Danis 4.00 10.00
ATM Thomas McCollum 4.00 10.00
AYFA Yutaka Fukufuji 40.00 80.00
AML Michael Leighton 6.00 15.00
AJLB Jason LaBarbera 4.00 10.00
ACBT Chris Beckford-Tseu 5.00 12.00
ADL David LeNeveu 4.00 10.00
AAMO Andy Moog 5.00 12.00
ABP Bernie Parent 8.00 20.00
ABS Billy Smith 6.00 15.00
ABH Brian Hayward 4.00 10.00
ACHO Charlie Hodge 6.00 15.00
ACR Chico Resch 5.00 12.00
ADB Dan Bouchard 5.00 12.00
ADF Doug Favell 5.00 12.00
AEG Ed Giacomin 8.00 20.00
AEF Emile Francis 5.00 12.00
AFP Felix Potvin 8.00 20.00
AGC Gerry Cheevers 10.00 25.00
AGG Gilles Gilbert 5.00 12.00
AGH Glenn Hall 8.00 20.00
AGF Grant Fuhr 8.00 20.00
AGW Gump Worsley 12.00 30.00
AJD John Davidson 5.00 12.00
AJB Johnny Bower 8.00 20.00
AKW Ken Wregget 4.00 10.00
AMP Mike Palmateer 5.00 12.00
APR Patrick Roy SP 60.00 120.00
ARBR Richard Brodeur 4.00 10.00
ARV Rogie Vachon 8.00 20.00
ARH Ron Hextall 10.00 25.00
ATB Tom Barrasso 8.00 20.00
ATE Tony Esposito 8.00 20.00
AVT Vladislav Tretiak 30.00 60.00
ABR Bill Ranford 8.00 20.00
AJV John Vanbiesbrouck 8.00 20.00
AAA Alex Auld 4.00 10.00
AAN Antero Niittymaki 5.00 12.00
ACW Cam Ward 8.00 20.00
ACH Cristobal Huet 5.00 12.00
ADH Dominik Hasek SP 40.00 80.00
ADR Dwayne Roloson 4.00 10.00
AEB Ed Belfour 25.00 50.00
AHL Henrik Lundqvist 15.00 40.00
AIB Ilya Bryzgalov 5.00 12.00
AJHO Johan Holmqvist 5.00 12.00
AMFR Manny Fernandez 5.00 12.00
AMF Marc-Andre Fleury SP 40.00 80.00
AMB Martin Brodeur SP 60.00 120.00
AMG Martin Gerber 5.00 12.00
APL Pascal Leclaire 5.00 12.00
ARE Ray Emery 5.00 12.00
ARL Roberto Luongo 10.00 25.00
ARM Ryan Miller 10.00 25.00
ATT Tim Thomas 5.00 12.00
AKL Kari Lehtonen 5.00 12.00
ACP3 Carey Price SP 75.00 150.00
AEB2 Ed Belfour SP 25.00 50.00
AJG2 Jeff Glass SP 8.00 20.00
AJP2 Justin Pogge SP 25.00 50.00
AMF3 Marc-Andre Fleury SP 40.00 80.00
AMB3 Martin Brodeur SP 60.00 120.00
APR2 Patrick Roy SP 60.00 120.00
ARL2 Roberto Luongo SP 40.00 80.00
AYFB Yutaka Fukufuji KANJI 125.00 200.00

2006-07 Between The Pipes Complete Jersey

STATED PRINT RUN 10 SETS
NOT PRICED DUE TO SCARCITY
CJ01 Cam Ward
CJ02 Glenn Hall
CJ03 Martin Brodeur
CJ04 Ray Emery
CJ05 Tony Esposito
CJ06 Manny Fernandez
CJ07 Marc-Andre Fleury
CJ08 Dominik Hasek
CJ09 Mike Palmateer
CJ10 Cristobal Huet
CJ11 Vladislav Tretiak
CJ12 Kari Lehtonen
CJ13 Tom Barrasso
CJ14 Roberto Luongo
CJ15 Ryan Miller
CJ16 Rogie Vachon
CJ17 Patrick Roy (MTL)
CJ18 Curtis Joseph
CJ19 Patrick Roy (COL)
CJ20 Felix Potvin

2006-07 Between The Pipes Complete Jersey Gold

STATED PRINT RUN 1 SET
NOT PRICED DUE TO SCARCITY

2006-07 Between The Pipes Complete Package

STATED PRINT RUN 10 SETS
NOT PRICED DUE TO SCARCITY
CP01 Gerry Cheevers
CP02 Grant Fuhr
CP03 Bernie Parent
CP04 Jacques Plante
CP05 Patrick Roy (MTL)
CP06 Patrick Roy (COL)
CP07 Terry Sawchuk
CP08 Marc-Andre Fleury
CP09 Martin Brodeur
CP10 Dominik Hasek

2006-07 Between The Pipes Complete Package Gold

STATED PRINT RUN 1 SET
NOT PRICED DUE TO SCARCITY

2006-07 Between The Pipes Double Jerseys

STATED PRINT RUN 40 SETS
DJ01 Al Montoya 10.00 25.00
John Davidson
DJ02 Dwayne Roloson 8.00 20.00
Manny Fernandez
DJ03 Ron Hextall 20.00 50.00
Bernie Parent
DJ04 Cam Ward 15.00 40.00
Martin Brodeur
DJ05 Cristobal Huet 25.00 60.00
Patrick Roy
DJ06 Dominik Hasek 15.00 40.00
Ryan Miller
DJ07 Dominik Hasek 15.00 40.00
Terry Sawchuk
DJ08 Ed Giacomin 25.00 60.00
Henrik Lundqvist
DJ09 Vladislav Tretiak 15.00 40.00
Vladimir Myshkin
DJ10 Gerry Cheevers 12.00 30.00
Tim Thomas
DJ11 Glenn Hall 12.00 30.00
Tony Esposito
DJ12 Grant Fuhr 15.00 40.00
Bill Ranford
DJ13 Jacques Plante 25.00 50.00
Gump Worsley
DJ14 John Davidson 12.00 30.00
Mike Richter
DJ15 Felix Potvin 15.00 40.00
Justin Pogge
DJ16 Antero Niittymaki 8.00 20.00
Kari Lehtonen
DJ17 Dan Bouchard 25.00 60.00
Patrick Roy
DJ18 Marc-Andre Fleury 15.00 40.00
Tom Barrasso
DJ19 Martin Brodeur 25.00 60.00
Terry Sawchuk
DJ20 Ilya Bryzgalov 15.00 40.00
Vladislav Tretiak
DJ21 Patrick Roy 40.00 80.00
Carey Price
DJ22 Patrick Roy 40.00 80.00
Martin Brodeur
DJ23 Ray Emery 12.00 30.00
Dominik Hasek
DJ24 Rick DiPietro 15.00 40.00
Billy Smith
DJ25 Roberto Luongo 15.00 40.00
Martin Brodeur
DJ26 Roy Worters 8.00 20.00
Frank Brimsek
DJ27 John Vanbiesbrouck 20.00 50.00
Mike Richter
DJ28 Felix Potvin 12.00 30.00
Andrew Raycroft
DJ29 Roberto Luongo 25.00 60.00
Patrick Roy

2006-07 Between The Pipes Double Jerseys Gold

STATED PRINT RUN 10 SETS
NOT PRICED DUE TO SCARCITY

2006-07 Between The Pipes Double Memorabilia

STATED PRINT RUN 40 SETS
DM01 Rogie Vachon 10.00 25.00
DM02 Martin Brodeur 20.00 50.00
DM03 Gerry Cheevers 12.00 30.00
DM04 Tony Esposito 8.00 20.00
DM05 Marc-Andre Fleury 10.00 25.00
DM06 Ed Giacomin 15.00 40.00
DM07 Dominik Hasek 12.00 30.00
DM08 Ron Hextall 15.00 40.00
DM09 Leland Irving 12.00 30.00
DM10 Roberto Luongo 15.00 40.00
DM11 Al Montoya 8.00 20.00
DM12 Bernie Parent 12.00 30.00
DM13 Jacques Plante 15.00 40.00
DM14 Patrick Roy (COL) 20.00 50.00
DM15 Patrick Roy (MTL) 20.00 50.00
DM16 Terry Sawchuk 20.00 50.00
DM17 Tiny Thompson 10.00 25.00
DM18 Hannu Toivonen 8.00 20.00
DM19 Vladislav Tretiak 15.00 40.00
DM20 Felix Potvin 15.00 40.00

2006-07 Between The Pipes Double Memorabilia Gold

STATED PRINT RUN 10 SETS
NOT PRICED DUE TO SCARCITY

2006-07 Between The Pipes Emblems

STATED PRINT RUN 10 SETS
NOT PRICED DUE TO SCARCITY
GUE01 Rogie Vachon
GUE02 Marc-Andre Fleury
GUE03 Henrik Lundqvist
GUE04 Tony Esposito
GUE05 Manny Fernandez
GUE06 Jeff Glass
GUE07 Kelly Guard
GUE08 Ron Hextall
GUE09 Kari Lehtonen
GUE10 Roberto Luongo
GUE11 Antero Niittymaki
GUE12 Billy Smith
GUE13 Mike Smith
GUE14 Hannu Toivonen
GUE15 Gump Worsley
GUE16 Tom Barrasso
GUE17 Richard Brodeur
GUE18 Barry Brust
GUE19 Dwayne Roloson
GUE20 Martin Gerber
GUE21 Jason Bacashihua
GUE22 Jonathan Bernier
GUE23 Rejean Beauchemin
GUE24 Ryan Daniels
GUE25 Yann Danis
GUE26 Curtis McElhinney
GUE27 Brian Finley
GUE28 Mathieu Garon
GUE29 Johan Holmqvist
GUE30 Mikael Tellqvist
GUE31 Pekka Rinne
GUE32 Bill Ranford
GUE33 Andrew Penner
GUE34 Corey Crawford
GUE35 Andy Moog
GUE36 Jimmy Howard
GUE37 Josh Harding
GUE38 Martin Houle
GUE39 Pascal Leclaire
GUE40 Vladislav Tretiak
GUE41 Leland Irving
GUE42 Philippe Sauve
GUE43 Brent Krahn
GUE44 Maxime Ouellet
GUE45 Grant Fuhr
GUE46 Cristobal Huet
GUE47 Ryan Miller
GUE48 Carey Price
GUE49 Terry Sawchuk
GUE50 Tim Thomas
GUE51 Justin Pogge
GUE52 Ed Giacomin
GUE53 Andrew Raycroft
GUE54 Frank Brimsek
GUE55 Glenn Hall
GUE56 Ray Emery
GUE57 J-S Aubin
GUE58 Ilya Bryzgalov
GUE59 Marek Schwarz
GUE60 Peter Budaj
GUE61 Dominik Hasek
GUE62 Curtis Joseph
GUE63 Felix Potvin
GUE64 Cam Ward
GUE65 Mike Richter
GUE66 Patrick Roy
GUE67 David LeNeveu
GUE68 Alex Auld
GUE69 Rick DiPietro
GUE70 Martin Brodeur
GUE71 Ed Belfour

2006-07 Between The Pipes Emblems Gold

STATED PRINT RUN 1 SET
NOT PRICED DUE TO SCARCITY

2006-07 Between The Pipes Emblems Autographs

STATED PRINT RUN 10 SETS
NOT PRICED DUE TO SCARCITY
GUE01 Rogie Vachon
GUE02 Marc-Andre Fleury
GUE03 Henrik Lundqvist
GUE04 Tony Esposito
GUE05 Manny Fernandez
GUE06 Jeff Glass
GUE07 Kelly Guard
GUE08 Ron Hextall
GUE10 Roberto Luongo
GUE11 Antero Niittymaki
GUE12 Billy Smith
GUE13 Mike Smith
GUE14 Hannu Toivonen
GUE15 Gump Worsley
GUE16 Tom Barrasso
GUE17 Richard Brodeur
GUE18 Barry Brust
GUE19 Dwayne Roloson
GUE20 Martin Gerber
GUE21 Jason Bacashihua
GUE22 Jonathan Bernier
GUE23 Rejean Beauchemin
GUE24 Ryan Daniels
GUE25 Yann Danis
GUE26 Curtis McElhinney
GUE27 Brian Finley
GUE29 Johan Holmqvist
GUE31 Pekka Rinne
GUE32 Bill Ranford
GUE33 Andrew Penner
GUE34 Corey Crawford
GUE35 Andy Moog
GUE36 Jimmy Howard
GUE37 Josh Harding
GUE38 Martin Houle
GUE39 Pascal Leclaire
GUE40 Vladislav Tretiak
GUE41 Leland Irving
GUE42 Philippe Sauve
GUE43 Brent Krahn
GUE45 Grant Fuhr
GUE46 Cristobal Huet
GUE47 Ryan Miller
GUE48 Carey Price
GUE50 Tim Thomas
GUE51 Justin Pogge
GUE55 Glenn Hall
GUE56 Ray Emery
GUE58 Ilya Bryzgalov
GUE59 Marek Schwarz
GUE61 Dominik Hasek
GUE63 Felix Potvin
GUE64 Cam Ward
GUE66 Patrick Roy
GUE68 Alex Auld
GUE70 Martin Brodeur
GUE71 Ed Belfour

2006-07 Between The Pipes Forgotten Franchises

COMPLETE SET (10) 12.00 30.00
ODDS 1:12 PACKS
FF01 Chuck Rayner 1.50 4.00
FF02 Hap Holmes 1.50 4.00
FF03 Alex Connell 1.50 4.00
FF04 Jake Forbes 1.50 4.00
FF05 Lorne Chabot 1.50 4.00
FF06 Earl Robertson 1.50 4.00
FF07 Clint Benedict 1.50 4.00
FF08 Wilf Cude 1.50 4.00
FF09 Roy Worters 1.50 4.00
FF10 Paddy Moran 1.50 4.00

2006-07 Between The Pipes Gloves

STATED PRINT RUN 50 SETS
GG01 Martin Brodeur 20.00 50.00
GG02 Rick DiPietro 10.00 25.00
GG03 Tony Esposito 10.00 25.00
GG04 Marc-Andre Fleury 12.00 30.00
GG05 Grant Fuhr 12.00 30.00
GG06 Ed Giacomin 20.00 50.00
GG07 Gilles Gilbert 12.00 30.00
GG08 David LeNeveu 8.00 20.00
GG09 Dominik Hasek 15.00 40.00
GG10 Charlie Hodge 10.00 25.00
GG11 Leland Irving 10.00 25.00
GG12 Curtis Joseph 12.00 30.00
GG13 Felix Potvin 15.00 40.00
GG14 Al Montoya 8.00 20.00
GG15 Jacques Plante
GG16 Patrick Roy 30.00 80.00
GG17 Hannu Toivonen 10.00 25.00
GG18 Gump Worsley 12.00 30.00
GG19 Glenn Hall

2006-07 Between The Pipes Gloves Gold

STATED PRINT RUN 10 SETS
NOT PRICED DUE TO SCARCITY

2006-07 Between The Pipes Jerseys

STATED PRINT RUN 90 SETS
GUJ01 Rogie Vachon 6.00 15.00
GUJ02 Marc-Andre Fleury 6.00 15.00
GUJ03 Henrik Lundqvist 10.00 25.00
GUJ04 Tony Esposito 6.00 15.00
GUJ05 Manny Fernandez 5.00 12.00
GUJ06 Jeff Glass 5.00 12.00
GUJ07 Kelly Guard 5.00 12.00
GUJ08 Ron Hextall 6.00 15.00
GUJ09 Kari Lehtonen 6.00 15.00
GUJ10 Roberto Luongo 10.00 25.00
GUJ11 Antero Niittymaki 5.00 12.00
GUJ12 Billy Smith 6.00 15.00
GUJ13 Mike Smith 5.00 12.00
GUJ14 Hannu Toivonen 5.00 12.00
GUJ15 Gump Worsley 6.00 15.00
GUJ16 Tom Barrasso 5.00 12.00
GUJ17 Richard Brodeur 5.00 12.00
GUJ18 Barry Brust 5.00 12.00
GUJ19 Dwayne Roloson 6.00 15.00
GUJ20 Martin Gerber 6.00 15.00
GUJ21 Jason Bacashihua 5.00 12.00
GUJ22 Jonathan Bernier 5.00 12.00
GUJ23 Rejean Beauchemin 5.00 12.00
GUJ24 Ryan Daniels 5.00 12.00
GUJ25 Yann Danis 5.00 12.00
GUJ26 Curtis McElhinney 5.00 12.00
GUJ27 Brian Finley 5.00 12.00
GUJ28 Mathieu Garon 5.00 12.00
GUJ29 Johan Holmqvist 5.00 12.00
GUJ30 Mikael Tellqvist 5.00 12.00
GUJ31 Pekka Rinne 5.00 12.00
GUJ32 Bill Ranford 6.00 15.00
GUJ33 Andrew Penner 5.00 12.00
GUJ34 Corey Crawford 5.00 12.00
GUJ35 Andy Moog 5.00 12.00
GUJ36 Jimmy Howard 5.00 12.00
GUJ37 Josh Harding 5.00 12.00
GUJ38 Martin Houle 5.00 12.00
GUJ39 Pascal Leclaire 5.00 12.00
GUJ40 Vladislav Tretiak 10.00 25.00
GUJ41 Leland Irving 5.00 12.00
GUJ42 Philippe Sauve 5.00 12.00
GUJ43 Brent Krahn 5.00 12.00
GUJ44 Maxime Ouellet 5.00 12.00
GUJ45 Grant Fuhr 10.00 25.00
GUJ46 Cristobal Huet 8.00 20.00
GUJ47 Ryan Miller 6.00 15.00
GUJ48 Carey Price 12.00 30.00
GUJ49 Terry Sawchuk 10.00 25.00
GUJ50 Tim Thomas 5.00 12.00
GUJ51 Justin Pogge 6.00 15.00
GUJ52 Ed Giacomin 10.00 25.00
GUJ53 Andrew Raycroft 5.00 12.00
GUJ54 Frank Brimsek 6.00 15.00
GUJ55 Glenn Hall 6.00 15.00
GUJ56 Ray Emery 5.00 12.00
GUJ57 J-S Aubin 5.00 12.00
GUJ58 Ilya Bryzgalov 5.00 12.00
GUJ59 Marek Schwarz 5.00 12.00
GUJ60 Peter Budaj 5.00 12.00
GUJ61 Dominik Hasek 10.00 25.00
GUJ62 Curtis Joseph 6.00 15.00
GUJ63 Felix Potvin 6.00 15.00
GUJ64 Cam Ward 6.00 15.00
GUJ65 Mike Richter 5.00 12.00
GUJ66 Patrick Roy 15.00 40.00
GUJ67 David LeNeveu 5.00 12.00
GUJ68 Alex Auld 5.00 12.00
GUJ69 Rick DiPietro 5.00 12.00
GUJ70 Martin Brodeur 12.00 30.00
GUJ71 Ed Belfour 6.00 15.00

2006-07 Between The Pipes Jerseys Gold

STATED PRINT RUN 10 SETS
NOT PRICED DUE TO SCARCITY

2006-07 Between The Pipes Jerseys Autographs

STATED PRINT RUN 10 SETS
NOT PRICED DUE TO SCARCITY
GUJ01 Rogie Vachon
GUJ02 Marc-Andre Fleury
GUJ03 Henrik Lundqvist
GUJ04 Tony Esposito
GUJ05 Manny Fernandez
GUJ06 Jeff Glass
GUJ07 Kelly Guard
GUJ08 Ron Hextall
GUJ10 Roberto Luongo
GUJ11 Antero Niittymaki
GUJ12 Billy Smith
GUJ13 Mike Smith
GUJ14 Hannu Toivonen
GUJ15 Gump Worsley
GUJ16 Tom Barrasso
GUJ17 Richard Brodeur
GUJ18 Barry Brust
GUJ19 Dwayne Roloson
GUJ20 Martin Gerber
GUJ21 Jason Bacashihua
GUJ22 Jonathan Bernier
GUJ23 Rejean Beauchemin
GUJ24 Ryan Daniels
GUJ25 Yann Danis
GUJ26 Curtis McElhinney
GUJ27 Brian Finley
GUJ29 Johan Holmqvist
GUJ31 Pekka Rinne
GUJ32 Bill Ranford
GUJ33 Andrew Penner
GUJ34 Corey Crawford
GUJ35 Andy Moog
GUJ36 Jimmy Howard
GUJ37 Josh Harding
GUJ38 Martin Houle
GUJ39 Pascal Leclaire
GUJ40 Vladislav Tretiak
GUJ41 Leland Irving
GUJ42 Philippe Sauve
GUJ43 Brent Krahn
GUJ45 Grant Fuhr
GUJ46 Cristobal Huet
GUJ47 Ryan Miller
GUJ48 Carey Price
GUJ50 Tim Thomas
GUJ51 Justin Pogge
GUJ55 Glenn Hall
GUJ56 Ray Emery
GUJ58 Ilya Bryzgalov
GUJ59 Marek Schwarz
GUJ61 Dominik Hasek
GUJ63 Felix Potvin
GUJ64 Cam Ward
GUJ66 Patrick Roy
GUJ68 Alex Auld
GUJ70 Martin Brodeur
GUJ71 Ed Belfour

2006-07 Between The Pipes Numbers

STATED PRINT RUN 10 SETS
NOT PRICED DUE TO SCARCITY
GUN01 Rogie Vachon
GUN02 Marc-Andre Fleury
GUN03 Henrik Lundqvist
GUN04 Tony Esposito
GUN05 Manny Fernandez
GUN06 Jeff Glass
GUN07 Kelly Guard
GUN08 Ron Hextall
GUN09 Kari Lehtonen
GUN10 Roberto Luongo
GUN11 Antero Niittymaki
GUN12 Billy Smith
GUN13 Mike Smith
GUN14 Hannu Toivonen
GUN15 Gump Worsley
GUN16 Tom Barrasso
GUN17 Richard Brodeur
GUN18 Barry Brust
GUN19 Dwayne Roloson
GUN20 Martin Gerber
GUN21 Jason Bacashihua
GUN22 Jonathan Bernier
GUN23 Rejean Beauchemin
GUN24 Ryan Daniels
GUN25 Yann Danis
GUN26 Curtis McElhinney
GUN27 Brian Finley
GUN28 Mathieu Garon
GUN29 Johan Holmqvist
GUN30 Mikael Tellqvist
GUN31 Pekka Rinne
GUN32 Bill Ranford
GUN33 Andrew Penner
GUN34 Corey Crawford
GUN35 Andy Moog
GUN36 Jimmy Howard
GUN37 Josh Harding
GUN38 Martin Houle
GUN39 Pascal Leclaire
GUN40 Vladislav Tretiak
GUN41 Leland Irving
GUN42 Philippe Sauve
GUN43 Brent Krahn
GUN44 Maxime Ouellet
GUN45 Grant Fuhr
GUN46 Cristobal Huet
GUN47 Ryan Miller
GUN48 Carey Price
GUN49 Terry Sawchuk
GUN50 Tim Thomas
GUN51 Justin Pogge
GUN52 Ed Giacomin
GUN53 Andrew Raycroft
GUN54 Frank Brimsek
GUN55 Glenn Hall
GUN56 Ray Emery
GUN57 J-S Aubin
GUN58 Ilya Bryzgalov
GUN59 Marek Schwarz
GUN60 Peter Budaj
GUN61 Dominik Hasek
GUN62 Curtis Joseph
GUN63 Felix Potvin
GUN64 Cam Ward
GUN65 Mike Richter
GUN66 Patrick Roy
GUN67 David LeNeveu
GUN68 Alex Auld
GUN69 Rick DiPietro
GUN70 Martin Brodeur
GUN71 Ed Belfour

2006-07 Between The Pipes Numbers Gold

STATED PRINT RUN 1 SET
NOT PRICED DUE TO SCARCITY

2006-07 Between The Pipes Numbers Autographs

STATED PRINT RUN 10 SETS
NOT PRICED DUE TO SCARCITY

2006-07 Between The Pipes Pads

STATED PRINT RUN 70 SETS
GP01 Martin Brodeur 20.00 50.00
GP02 Gerry Cheevers 8.00 20.00
GP03 Grant Fuhr 8.00 20.00
GP04 Bernie Parent 8.00 20.00
GP05 Jacques Plante 12.00 30.00
GP06 Patrick Roy 25.00 60.00
GP07 Tiny Thompson 8.00 20.00
GP08 Vladislav Tretiak 25.00 60.00
GP09 Curtis Joseph 10.00 25.00
GP10 Ron Hextall 10.00 25.00
GP11 Ed Belfour 10.00 25.00

2006-07 Between The Pipes Pads Gold

STATED PRINT RUN 10 SETS
NOT PRICED DUE TO SCARCITY

2006-07 Between The Pipes Playing For Your Country

STATED PRINT RUN 40 SETS
PC01 Jonathan Bernier 10.00 25.00
PC02 Martin Brodeur 12.00 30.00
PC03 Ilya Bryzgalov 8.00 20.00
PC04 Roberto Luongo 10.00 25.00
PC05 Tom Barrasso 10.00 25.00
PC06 Vladimir Dzurilla 8.00 20.00
PC07 Grant Fuhr 10.00 25.00
PC08 Dominik Hasek 10.00 25.00
PC09 Cristobal Huet 10.00 25.00
PC10 Marc-Andre Fleury 10.00 25.00
PC11 Carey Price 20.00 50.00
PC12 John Vanbiesbrouck 8.00 20.00
PC13 Henrik Lundqvist 10.00 25.00
PC14 Rogie Vachon 8.00 20.00
PC15 Al Montoya 8.00 20.00
PC16 Vladimir Myshkin 12.00 30.00
PC17 Antero Niittymaki 8.00 20.00
PC18 Justin Pogge 10.00 25.00
PC19 Tony Esposito 10.00 25.00
PC20 Mike Richter 8.00 20.00
PC21 Patrick Roy 20.00 50.00
PC22 Marek Schwarz 8.00 20.00
PC23 Hannu Toivonen 8.00 20.00
PC24 Vladislav Tretiak 15.00 40.00
PC25 Curtis Joseph 8.00 20.00
PC26 Kari Lehtonen 8.00 20.00

2006-07 Between The Pipes Playing For Your Country Gold

STATED PRINT RUN 10 SETS
NOT PRICED DUE TO SCARCITY

2006-07 Between The Pipes Prospect Trios

STATED PRINT RUN 40 SETS
PT01 Tim Thomas 15.00 40.00
Brian Finley
Hannu Toivonen
PT02 Pascal Leclaire
Peter Budaj
Josh Harding
PT03 Ray Emery 15.00 40.00
Jeff Glass
Kelly Guard
PT04 Antero Niittymaki 15.00 40.00
Martin Houle
Rejean Beauchemin
PT05 Curtis McElhinney 10.00 25.00
Kevin Lalande
Leland Irving
PT06 Leland Irving 15.00 40.00
Jonathan Bernier
Trevor Cann
PT07 Carey Price 15.00 40.00
Jean-Philippe Levasseur
Steve Mason
PT08 Julien Ellis 10.00 25.00
Dan LaCosta
Justin Peters
PT09 Carey Price 20.00 50.00
Kristofer Westblom
Leland Irving
PT10 Kevin Lalande 10.00 25.00
Tyler Plante
Kyle Moir
PT11 Ryan Daniels 10.00 25.00
Alexandre Vincent
Julien Ellis
PT12 Carey Price 25.00 60.00
Jonathan Boutin
Jonathan Bernier
PT13 Marc-Andre Fleury 20.00 50.00
Alex Auld
Kari Lehtonen
PT14 Jonathan Bernier 15.00 40.00
Barry Brust
Jason Labarbera
PT15 Cristobal Huet 20.00 50.00
Carey Price
Yann Danis
PT16 Chris Beckford-Tseu
Marek Schwarz
Jason Bacashihua
PT17 J-S Aubin 10.00 25.00
Gerald Coleman
Corey Crawford
PT18 Justin Pogge 15.00 40.00
Ilya Bryzgalov
Al Montoya
PT19 Billy Thompson 10.00 25.00
Jonathan Boutin
Adam Munro
PT20 David LeNeveu 10.00 25.00
Frederic Cassivi
Maxime Ouellet

2006-07 Between The Pipes Prospect Trios Gold

STATED PRINT RUN 10 SETS
NOT PRICED DUE TO SCARCITY

2006-07 Between The Pipes Roy vs. Brodeur

JSY PRINT RUN 25 SETS
PATCH PRINT RUN 10 SETS
AU PRINT RUN 10 SETS
NOT PRICED DUE TO SCARCITY
NOT PRICED DUE TO SCARCITY
RB01 Roy (MTL)/Brodeur JSY 40.00 80.00
RB02 Roy (COL)/Brodeur JSY 40.00 80.00
RB03 Roy (MTL)/Brodeur JSY 40.00 80.00
RB04 Roy (COL)/Brodeur JSY 40.00 80.00
RB05 Roy/Brodeur JSY 40.00 80.00
RB06 Roy/Brodeur JSY 40.00 80.00
RB07 Roy/Brodeur Patch/10
RB08 Roy/Brodeur Patch/10
RB09 Roy (MTL)/Brodeur AU/10
RB10 Roy (COL)/Brodeur AU/10

2006-07 Between The Pipes Roy vs. Brodeur Gold

STATED PRINT RUN 1 SET
NOT PRICED DUE TO SCARCITY

2006-07 Between The Pipes Shooting Gallery

STATED PRINT RUN 30 SETS
SG01 Vezina 250.00 400.00
Plante
Vachon
Roy
Huet
Price
SG02 Bower 125.00 250.00
Sawchuk
Palmateer
Potvin
Raycroft
Pogge
SG03 Thompson 75.00 175.00
Cheevers
Gilbert
Moog
Thomas
Toivonen
SG04 Gardiner 75.00 175.00

Francis
Brimsek
Lumley
Hall
Esposito
SG05 Giacomin 150.00 300.00
Davidson
Vanbiesbrouck
Richter
Lundqvist
Montoya
SG06 Sawchuk 150.00 300.00
Crozier
Giacomin
Vernon
Hasek
Howard
SG07 Parent 125.00 250.00
Lindbergh
Hextall
Niittymaki
Houle
Beauchemin
SG08 Tretiak 125.00 250.00
Hasek
Richter
Brodeur
Lehtonen
Lundqvist
SG09 Sawchuk 100.00 200.00
Plante
Bower
Hall
Cheevers
Giacomin
SG10 Durnan 200.00 350.00
Plante
Hall
Roy
Hasek
Brodeur

2006-07 Between The Pipes Shooting Gallery Gold

STATED PRINT RUN 10 SETS
NOT PRICED DUE TO SCARCITY

2006-07 Between The Pipes Stick and Jersey

STATED PRINT RUN 40 SETS
SJ01 Manny Fernandez 10.00 25.00
SJ02 Johnny Bower 10.00 25.00
SJ03 Martin Brodeur 20.00 40.00
SJ04 Gerry Cheevers 12.00 30.00
SJ05 John Davidson 10.00 25.00
SJ06 Rick DiPietro 15.00 40.00
SJ07 Ray Emery 10.00 25.00
SJ08 Tony Esposito 12.00 30.00
SJ09 Marc-Andre Fleury 15.00 40.00
SJ10 Grant Fuhr 12.00 30.00
SJ11 Ed Giacomin 12.00 30.00
SJ12 Glenn Hall 12.00 30.00
SJ13 Dominik Hasek 12.00 30.00
SJ14 Ron Hextall 15.00 40.00
SJ15 Cristobal Huet 12.00 30.00
SJ16 Leland Irving 12.00 30.00
SJ17 Jason LaBarbera 10.00 25.00
SJ18 Roberto Luongo 15.00 40.00
SJ19 Henrik Lundqvist 12.00 30.00
SJ20 Ryan Miller 15.00 40.00
SJ21 Al Montoya 10.00 25.00
SJ22 Antero Niittymaki 10.00 25.00
SJ23 Felix Potvin 12.00 30.00
SJ24 Bernie Parent 15.00 40.00
SJ25 Jacques Plante 25.00 60.00
SJ26 Andrew Raycroft 10.00 25.00
SJ27 Mike Richter 10.00 25.00
SJ28 Pekka Rinne 10.00 25.00
SJ29 Patrick Roy (COL) 20.00 50.00
SJ30 Patrick Roy (MTL) 25.00 60.00
SJ31 Terry Sawchuk 20.00 50.00
SJ32 Billy Smith 12.00 30.00
SJ33 Roger Crozier 10.00 25.00
SJ34 Tim Thomas 10.00 25.00
SJ35 Hannu Toivonen 10.00 25.00
SJ36 Rogie Vachon 12.00 30.00
SJ37 John Vanbiesbrouck 12.00 30.00
SJ38 Gump Worsley 12.00 30.00
SJ39 Richard Brodeur 12.00 30.00
SJ40 Tom Barrasso 12.00 30.00

2006-07 Between The Pipes Stick and Jersey Gold

STATED PRINT RUN 10 SETS
NOT PRICED DUE TO SCARCITY

2006-07 Between The Pipes Stick and Jersey Autographs

STATED PRINT RUN 10 SETS
NOT PRICED DUE TO SCARCITY
SJ01 Manny Fernandez
SJ02 Johnny Bower
SJ03 Martin Brodeur
SJ04 Gerry Cheevers
SJ05 John Davidson
SJ07 Ray Emery
SJ08 Tony Esposito
SJ09 Marc-Andre Fleury
SJ10 Grant Fuhr
SJ12 Glenn Hall
SJ13 Dominik Hasek
SJ14 Ron Hextall
SJ15 Cristobal Huet
SJ16 Leland Irving
SJ18 Roberto Luongo
SJ19 Henrik Lundqvist
SJ20 Ryan Miller
SJ21 Al Montoya
SJ22 Antero Niittymaki
SJ23 Felix Potvin
SJ24 Bernie Parent
SJ28 Pekka Rinne
SJ29 Patrick Roy (COL)
SJ30 Patrick Roy (MTL)
SJ32 Billy Smith
SJ34 Tim Thomas
SJ35 Hannu Toivonen
SJ36 Rogie Vachon
SJ38 Gump Worsley
SJ39 Richard Brodeur
SJ40 Tom Barrasso

2006-07 Between The Pipes Stick Work

STATED PRINT RUN 50 SETS
SW01 Patrick Roy 75.00 125.00
Martin Brodeur
Roberto Luongo
SW02 Roger Crozier 40.00 80.00
Dominik Hasek
Ryan Miller
SW03 Bernie Parent 40.00 80.00
Pelle Lindbergh
Ron Hextall
SW04 Gump Worsley 60.00 100.00
Patrick Roy
Cristobal Huet
SW05 Tony Esposito 30.00 60.00
Gerry Cheevers
Ed Giacomin
SW06 Johnny Bower 30.00 60.00
Mike Palmateer
Felix Potvin

2006-07 Between The Pipes Stick Work Gold

STATED PRINT RUN 10 SETS
NOT PRICED DUE TO SCARCITY

2006-07 Between The Pipes The Mask

COMPLETE SET (40) 125.00 250.00
ODDS 1:24
M01 Al Montoya 4.00 10.00
M02 Kari Lehtonen 5.00 12.00
M03 Miikka Kiprusoff 5.00 12.00
M04 Antero Niittymaki 3.00 8.00
M05 Ray Emery 3.00 8.00
M06 Andrew Raycroft 3.00 8.00
M07 Ryan Miller 5.00 12.00
M08 Martin Gerber 3.00 8.00
M09 Ken Dryden 10.00 25.00
M10 Marc-Andre Fleury 5.00 12.00
M11 Joey MacDonald 3.00 8.00
M12 Henrik Lundqvist 5.00 12.00
M13 Cam Ward 4.00 10.00
M14 Cristobal Huet 5.00 12.00
M15 Rick DiPietro 4.00 10.00
M16 Ilya Bryzgalov 3.00 8.00
M17 Jose Theodore 4.00 10.00
M18 Dominik Hasek 8.00 20.00
M19 Nikolai Khabibulin 4.00 10.00
M20 Marty Turco 4.00 10.00
M21 Marek Schwarz 4.00 10.00
M22 Patrick Roy 10.00 25.00
M23 Dominik Hasek 8.00 20.00
M24 Ed Belfour 4.00 10.00
M25 Manny Legace 3.00 8.00
M26 Curtis Joseph 4.00 10.00
M27 Hannu Toivonen 3.00 8.00
M28 Martin Biron 3.00 8.00
M29 Dan Cloutier 3.00 8.00
M30 Kevin Weekes 3.00 8.00
M31 Jimmy Howard 3.00 8.00
M32 Devan Dubnyk 3.00 8.00
M33 Mikael Tellqvist 3.00 8.00
M34 Jacques Plante 6.00 15.00
M35 Jeff Glass 3.00 8.00
M36 Henrik Lundqvist 5.00 12.00
M37 Vesa Toskala 3.00 8.00
M38 Johan Hedberg 3.00 8.00
M39 Tomas Vokoun 4.00 10.00
M40 Carey Price 10.00 25.00

2006-07 Between The Pipes The Mask Gold

STATED PRINT RUN 10 SETS
NOT PRICED DUE TO SCARCITY

2006-07 Between The Pipes The Mask Silver

*SILVER: 5X to 1.5X MASK HI
STATED PRINT RUN 100 SETS

2006-07 Between The Pipes The Mask Game-Used

STATED PRINT RUN 25 SETS
MGU01 Martin Biron 15.00 40.00
MGU02 Ilya Bryzgalov 15.00 40.00
MGU03 Rick DiPietro 25.00 50.00
MGU04 Ken Dryden 200.00 300.00
MGU05 Ray Emery 15.00 50.00
MGU06 Marc-Andre Fleury 30.00 60.00
MGU07 Dominik Hasek 40.00 80.00
MGU08 Cristobal Huet 25.00 60.00
MGU09 Miikka Kiprusoff 40.00 80.00
MGU10 Kari Lehtonen 25.00 50.00
MGU11 Henrik Lundqvist 30.00 60.00
MGU12 Ryan Miller 30.00 60.00
MGU13 Al Montoya 15.00 30.00
MGU14 Antero Niittymaki 15.00 40.00
MGU15 Jacques Plante 40.00 80.00
MGU16 Andrew Raycroft 25.00 50.00
MGU17 Patrick Roy 60.00 125.00
MGU18 Marty Turco 20.00 50.00
MGU19 Cam Ward 25.00 50.00
MGU20 Hannu Toivonen 15.00 40.00

2006-07 Between The Pipes The Mask Game-Used Gold

STATED PRINT RUN 1 SET
NOT PRICED DUE TO SCARCITY

2007-08 Between The Pipes

COMPLETE SET (100) 12.00 30.00
1 Adam Courchaine .25 .60
2 Adam Dennis .25 .60
3 Al Montoya .25 .60
4 Antoine Lafleur .25 .60
5 Braden Holtby .25 .60
6 Brian Elliott .25 .60
7 Carey Price 1.00 2.50
8 Corey Crawford .25 .60
9 Cory Schneider .40 1.00
10 Curtis McElhinney .25 .60
11 Daren Machesney .25 .60
12 Devan Dubnyk .40 1.00
13 Dustin Tokarski .25 .60
14 Erik Ersberg .50 1.25
15 Hannu Toivonen .25 .60
16 Jaroslav Halak .60 1.50
17 Jeff Deslauriers .25 .60
18 Jeff Glass .25 .60
19 Jeremy Smith .20 .50
20 Jimmy Howard .50 1.25
21 John Murray .25 .60
22 Jonas Hiller .50 1.25
23 Jonathan Bernier .50 1.25
24 Jordan Parise .30 .75
25 Jordan Sigalet .25 .60
26 Josh Tordjman .50 1.25
27 Josh Unice .30 .75
28 Justin Peters .25 .60
29 Justin Pogge .40 1.00
30 Karri Ramo .30 .75
31 Kevin Deslosses .25 .60
32 Kevin Poulin .25 .60
33 Kyle Gajewski .25 .60
34 Leland Irving .30 .75
35 Linden Rowat .30 .75
36 Marek Schwarz .25 .60
37 Matt Keetley .25 .60
38 Maxime Daigneault .25 .60
39 Michal Neuvirth .30 .75
40 Mike Murphy .25 .60
41 Ondrej Pavelec .30 .75
42 Pekka Rinne .25 .60
43 Peter Delmas .20 .50
44 Riku Helenius .25 .60
45 Robert Mayer .25 .60
46 Ryan Munce .25 .60
47 Scott Monroe .25 .60
48 Simeon Varlamov .25 .60
49 Steve Mason 2.50 6.00
50 Taylor Dakers .25 .60
51 Thomas Greiss .30 .75
52 Thomas McCollum .25 .60
53 Tobias Stephan .25 .60
54 Tomas Popperle .25 .60
55 Tomi Karhunen .25 .60
56 Torrie Jung .25 .60
57 Trevor Cann .25 .60
58 Tuukka Rask .50 1.25
59 Tyler Weiman .25 .60
60 Tyson Sexsmith .25 .60
61 Cam Ward .30 .75
62 Dan Cloutier .25 .60
63 Dominik Hasek .40 1.00
64 Jean-Sebastian Giguere .30 .75
65 Kari Lehtonen .30 .75
66 Tim Thomas .40 1.00
67 Martin Brodeur .75 2.00
68 Marty Turco .30 .75
69 Pascal Leclaire .25 .60
70 Peter Budaj .25 .60
71 Ray Emery .25 .60
72 Roberto Luongo .50 1.25
73 Ryan Miller .30 .75
74 Tomas Vokoun .30 .75
75 Terry Sawchuk .40 1.00
76 Billy Smith .30 .75
77 Felix Potvin .40 1.00
78 Glenn Hall .30 .75
79 Grant Fuhr .50 1.25
80 Gump Worsley .40 1.00
81 John Davidson .25 .60
82 Johnny Bower .30 .75
83 Mike Palmateer .30 .75
84 Patrick Roy 1.00 2.50
85 Rogie Vachon .30 .75
86 Ron Hextall .50 1.25
87 Tom Barrasso .25 .60
88 Ed Giacomin .30 .75
89 Tony Esposito .50 1.25
90 Gerry Cheevers .50 1.25
91 Joe Daley .30 .75
92 Gilles Gratton .30 .75
93 Richard Brodeur .25 .60
94 Bernie Parent .40 1.00
95 Les Binkley .25 .60
96 Ernie Wakely .25 .60
97 Michel Dion .25 .60
98 John Garrett .25 .60
99 Mike Liut .25 .60
100 Ed Mio .25 .60

2007-08 Between The Pipes Autographs

AAC Adam Courchaine 4.00 10.00
AAD Adam Dennis 4.00 10.00
AAL Antoine Lafleur 4.00 10.00
AAM Al Montoya 4.00 10.00
ABE Brian Elliott 4.00 10.00
ABH Braden Holtby 4.00 10.00
ABP Bernie Parent SP 30.00 60.00
ABS Billy Smith SP 10.00 25.00
ACC Corey Crawford 4.00 10.00
ACM Curtis McElhinney 4.00 10.00
ACO Chris Osgood SP 4.00 10.00
ACP Carey Price 30.00 60.00
ACS Corey Schneider
ACW Cam Ward 5.00 12.00
ADC Dan Cloutier 4.00 10.00
ADD Devan Dubnyk 6.00 15.00
ADH Dominik Hasek SP 20.00 50.00
ADT Dustin Tokarski 4.00 10.00
AEE Erik Ersberg 8.00 20.00
AEM Ed Mio 4.00 10.00
AEW Ernie Wakely 4.00 10.00
AFP Felix Potvin SP 20.00 50.00
AGC Gerry Cheevers SP 25.00 50.00
AGE Grant Fuhr SP
AGG Gilles Gratton 5.00 12.00
AGH Glenn Hall SP
AGW Gump Worsley SP 25.00 50.00
AHT Hannu Toivonen 4.00 10.00
AJB Johnny Bower SP
AJD Jeff Deslauriers 4.00 10.00
AJG Jeff Glass 4.00 10.00
AJH Jaroslav Halak 10.00 25.00
AJM John Murray 4.00 10.00
AJP Justin Pogge 6.00 15.00
AJS Jordan Sigalet 4.00 10.00
AJT Josh Tordjman 8.00 20.00
AJU Josh Unice 5.00 12.00
AKD Kevin Deslosses 4.00 10.00
AKG Kyle Gajewski 4.00 10.00
AKL Kari Lehtonen 5.00 12.00
AKP Kevin Poulin 4.00 10.00
AKR Karri Ramo 5.00 12.00
ALB Les Binkley 4.00 10.00
ALI Leland Irving 5.00 12.00
ALR Linden Rowat 5.00 12.00
AMB Martin Brodeur SP 20.00 50.00
AMD Michel Dion 4.00 10.00
AMG Martin Gerber SP 4.00 10.00
AMK Matt Keetley 4.00 10.00
AML Mike Liut 4.00 10.00
AMM Mike Murphy 4.00 10.00
AMN Michal Neuvirth 5.00 12.00
AMP Mike Palmateer SP 15.00 40.00
AMS Marek Schwarz 4.00 10.00
AMT Marty Turco SP 5.00 12.00
AOP Ondrej Pavelec 5.00 12.00
APB Peter Budaj 4.00 10.00
APD Peter Delmas 3.00 8.00
APL Pascal Leclaire 4.00 10.00
APR Patrick Roy SP 100.00 175.00
ARE Ray Emery SP
ARH Riku Helenius 4.00 10.00
ARL Roberto Luongo SP 30.00 60.00
ARM Ryan Miller SP 30.00 60.00
ARV Rogie Vachon SP 15.00 40.00
ASM Scott Monroe 4.00 10.00
ATB Tom Barrasso SP
ATC Trevor Cann 4.00 10.00
ATD Taylor Dakers 4.00 10.00
ATE Tony Esposito SP 15.00 40.00
ATG Thomas Greiss 5.00 12.00
ATJ Torrie Jung 4.00 10.00
ATK Tomi Karhunen 4.00 10.00
ATP Tomas Popperle 4.00 10.00
ATR Tuukka Rask 15.00 40.00
ATS Tobias Stephan 4.00 10.00
ATT Tim Thomas SP
ATV Tomas Vokoun SP 5.00 12.00
ATW Tyler Weiman 4.00 10.00
AVT Vladislav Tretiak SP 25.00 60.00
AYD Yann Danis 4.00 10.00
ADMA Drew MacIntyre 4.00 10.00
ADMA Daren Machesney 4.00 10.00
AJBE Jonathan Bernier 8.00 20.00
AJDA Joe Daley 5.00 12.00
AJGA John Garrett 4.00 10.00
AJHA Josh Harding SP 10.00 25.00
AJHI Jonas Hiller 15.00 40.00
AJHO Jimmy Howard 8.00 20.00
AJPA Jordan Parise 5.00 12.00
AJPE Justin Peters 4.00 10.00
AJSG Jean-Sebastien Giguere SP 6.00 15.00
AJSM Jeremy Smith 3.00 8.00
AMDA Maxime Daigneault 4.00 10.00
APRI Pekka Rinne 4.00 10.00
ARHE Ron Hextall SP 8.00 20.00
ARMA Robert Mayer 4.00 10.00
ARMU Ryan Munce 4.00 10.00
ASMA Steve Mason 25.00 60.00
ATMC Thomas McCollum 4.00 10.00
ATSE Tyson Sexsmith 4.00 10.00
AJDAV John Davidson SP 4.00 10.00

2007-08 Between The Pipes Complete Jersey

STATED PRINT RUN 10 SER.#'d SETS
NOT PRICED DUE TO SCARCITY
CJ01 Tuukka Rask
CJ02 Carey Price
CJ03 Al Montoya
CJ04 Justin Pogge
CJ05 Karri Ramo
CJ06 Marek Schwarz
CJ07 Tyson Sexsmith
CJ08 Trevor Cann
CJ09 Leland Irving
CJ10 Jonathan Bernier
CJ11 Patrick Roy
CJ12 Patrick Roy
CJ13 Terry Sawchuk
CJ14 Jacques Plante
CJ15 Johnny Bower
CJ16 Martin Brodeur
CJ17 Tomas Vokoun
CJ18 Dominik Hasek
CJ19 Jean-Sebastian Giguere
CJ20 Roberto Luongo
CJ21 Tobias Stephan
CJ22 Tyler Weiman
CJ23 Adam Dennis
CJ24 Pekka Rinne
CJ25 Steve Mason
CJ26 Dan Cloutier
CJ27 Ray Emery
CJ28 Ryan Miller
CJ29 Tomi Karhunen
CJ30 Peter Budaj
CJ31 Manny Fernandez
CJ32 Tony Esposito
CJ33 Thomas McCollum
CJ34 Glenn Hall
CJ35 Vladislav Tretiak
CJ36 Felix Potvin
CJ37 Bernie Parent
CJ38 Ed Giacomin
CJ39 Tom Barrasso
CJ40 Richard Brodeur

2007-08 Between The Pipes Complete Logo AHL

STATED PRINT RUN 1 SER.#'d SET
NOT PRICED DUE TO SCARCITY
AHL01 Pekka Rinne
AHL02 Tobias Stephan
AHL03 Karri Ramo
AHL04 Curtis McElhinney
AHL05 Ray Emery
AHL06 Barry Brust
AHL07 Jason LaBarbera
AHL08 Yann Danis
AHL09 Michael Leighton
AHL10 Tyler Weiman

2007-08 Between The Pipes Complete Logo CHL

STATED PRINT RUN 1 SER.#'d SET
NOT PRICED DUE TO SCARCITY
CHL01 Jeremy Smith
CHL02 Thomas McCollum
CHL03 Linden Rowat
CHL04 John Murray
CHL05 Tyson Sexsmith
CHL06 J.P. Levasseur
CHL07 Carey Price
CHL08 Trevor Cann
CHL09 Steve Mason
CHL10 Cam Ward

2007-08 Between The Pipes Emblems

STATED PRINT RUN 10 SER.#'d SETS
NOT PRICED DUE TO SCARCITY
CCE01 Adam Munro
CCE02 Barry Brust
CCE03 Brian Elliott
CCE04 Cam Ward
CCE05 Carey Price
CCE06 Corey Crawford
CCE07 David LeNeveu
CCE08 Gerald Coleman
CCE09 Jeremy Smith
CCE10 John Murray
CCE11 Jonathan Boutin
CCE12 Karri Ramo
CCE13 Kevin Nastiuk
CCE14 Leland Irving
CCE15 Linden Rowat
CCE16 Michael Leighton
CCE17 Pascal Leclaire
CCE18 Pekka Rinne
CCE19 Peter Budaj
CCE20 Ray Emery
CCE21 Roberto Luongo
CCE22 Steve Mason
CCE23 Thomas McCollum
CCE24 Trevor Cann
CCE25 Tuukka Rask
CCE26 Tyson Sexsmith
CCE27 Adam Dennis
CCE28 Curtis McElhinney
CCE29 Dan Cloutier
CCE30 Hannu Toivonen
CCE31 Jason Bacashihua
CCE32 Jonathan Bernier
CCE33 Manny Fernandez
CCE34 Marty Turco
CCE35 Patrick Roy
CCE36 Patrick Roy
CCE37 Richard Brodeur
CCE38 Ryan Miller
CCE39 Tim Thomas
CCE40 Tyler Weiman
CCE41 Dominik Hasek
CCE42 Felix Potvin
CCE43 Grant Fuhr
CCE44 Josh Harding
CCE45 Jean-Sebastian Giguere
CCE46 Kari Lehtonen
CCE47 Marek Schwarz
CCE48 Martin Brodeur
CCE49 Mike Richter
CCE50 Ron Hextall
CCE51 Ed Belfour
CCE52 Dan Bouchard
CCE53 Curtis Sanford
CCE54 Tomas Vokoun
CCE55 Philippe Sauve
CCE56 Brent Krahn
CCE57 Kevin Lalande
CCE58 Alex Auld
CCE59 Ryan Daniels
CCE60 John Vanbiesbrouck
CCE61 Mathieu Garon
CCE62 Mike Smith
CCE63 Ilya Bryzgalov
CCE64 Vladislav Tretiak

2007-08 Between The Pipes Emblems Emerald

STATED PRINT RUN 1 SER.#'d SET
NOT PRICED DUE TO SCARCITY

2007-08 Between The Pipes First Round Goalies Jerseys

STATED PRINT RUN 90 SER.#'d SETS
FRG01 Leland Irving 5.00 12.00
FRG02 John Davidson 4.00 10.00
FRG03 Jonathan Bernier 8.00 20.00
FRG04 Tuukka Rask 8.00 20.00
FRG05 Carey Price 15.00 40.00
FRG06 Marek Schwarz 4.00 10.00
FRG07 Devan Dubnyk 6.00 15.00
FRG08 Al Montoya 4.00 10.00
FRG09 Marc-Andre Fleury 5.00 12.00
FRG10 Cam Ward 5.00 12.00
FRG11 Kari Lehtonen 5.00 12.00
FRG12 Adam Munro 4.00 10.00
FRG13 Hannu Toivonen 4.00 10.00
FRG14 Pascal Leclaire 4.00 10.00
FRG15 Dan Cloutier 4.00 10.00
FRG16 Jean-Sebastian Giguere 5.00 12.00
FRG17 Roberto Luongo 8.00 20.00
FRG18 Grant Fuhr 8.00 20.00
FRG19 Tom Barrasso 4.00 10.00
FRG20 Martin Brodeur 12.00 30.00

2007-08 Between The Pipes Flashbacks

COMPLETE SET (10) 15.00 40.00
FB01 Martin Brodeur 5.00 12.00
FB02 Dominik Hasek 2.50 6.00
FB03 Ray Emery 1.50 4.00
FB04 Patrick Roy 6.00 15.00
FB05 Ryan Miller 2.00 5.00
FB06 Ed Belfour 2.00 5.00
FB07 Jean-Sebastian Giguere 2.00 5.00
FB08 Roberto Luongo 3.00 8.00
FB09 Cam Ward 2.00 5.00
FB10 Kari Lehtonen 2.00 5.00

2007-08 Between The Pipes Goaltending Traditions

COMPLETE SET (10) 20.00 50.00
GT01 Jonathan Bernier 3.00 8.00
Rogie Vachon
GT02 Carey Price 6.00 15.00
Patrick Roy
GT03 Trevor Cann 6.00 15.00
Patrick Roy
GT04 Jimmy Howard 3.00 8.00
Dominik Hasek
GT05 Leland Irving 2.00 5.00
Mike Vernon
GT06 Al Montoya 5.00 12.00
Mike Richter
GT07 Cory Schneider 3.00 8.00
Roberto Luongo
GT08 Justin Pogge 2.50 6.00
Felix Potvin
GT09 Tuukka Rask 3.00 8.00
Gerry Cheevers
GT10 Marek Schwarz 2.50 6.00
Glenn Hall

2007-08 Between The Pipes He Shoots He Saves

STATED PRINT RUN 20 SER.#'d SETS
NOT PRICED DUE TO SCARCITY
HSHS01 George Hainsworth
Roy Worters
HSHS02 Justin Pogge
Felix Potvin
HSHS03 Roberto Luongo
Richard Brodeur
HSHS04 Jimmy Howard
Chris Osgood
HSHS05 Peter Budaj
Patrick Roy
HSHS06 Ray Emery
Dominik Hasek
HSHS07 Marek Schwarz
Glenn Hall
HSHS08 Jonathan Bernier
Rogie Vachon
HSHS09 Steve Mason
Pascal Leclaire
HSHS10 Ryan Miller
Grant Fuhr
HSHS11 Carey Price
Patrick Roy
HSHS12 Mike Smith
Marty Turco
HSHS13 Dominik Hasek
Roger Crozier
HSHS14 Hannu Toivonen
Kari Lehtonen
HSHS15 Martin Brodeur
Patrick Roy
HSHS16 Jonas Hiller
Jean-Sebastien Giguere
HSHS17 Al Montoya
Ed Giacomin
HSHS18 Patrick Roy
Jacques Plante
HSHS19 Mike Richter
John Davidson
HSHS20 Marty Turco
Ed Belfour
HSHS21 Tim Thomas
Gerry Cheevers
HSHS22 Thomas McCollum
Frank Brimsek
HSHS23 John Vanbiesbrouck
Bernie Parent
HSHS24 Mathieu Garon
Grant Fuhr
HSHS25 Tomas Vokoun
Roberto Luongo
HSHS26 Ed Belfour
Tony Esposito
HSHS27 Vladimir Dzurilla
Vladislav Tretiak
HSHS28 Glenn Hall
Harry Lumley
HSHS29 Carey Price
Jacques Plante
HSHS30 Gerry Cheevers
Bernie Parent

2007-08 Between The Pipes Jerseys

STATED PRINT RUN 90 SETS
CCJ01 Adam Munro 4.00 10.00
CCJ02 Barry Brust 4.00 10.00
CCJ03 Brian Elliott 4.00 10.00
CCJ04 Cam Ward 5.00 12.00
CCJ05 Carey Price 15.00 40.00
CCJ06 Corey Crawford 4.00 10.00
CCJ07 David LeNeveu 4.00 10.00
CCJ08 Gerald Coleman 4.00 10.00
CCJ09 Jeremy Smith 3.00 8.00
CCJ10 John Murray 4.00 10.00
CCJ11 Jonathan Boutin 4.00 10.00
CCJ12 Karri Ramo 5.00 12.00
CCJ13 Kevin Nastiuk 4.00 10.00
CCJ14 Leland Irving 5.00 12.00
CCJ15 Linden Rowat 5.00 12.00
CCJ16 Michael Leighton 5.00 12.00
CCJ17 Pascal Leclaire 4.00 10.00
CCJ18 Pekka Rinne 4.00 10.00
CCJ19 Peter Budaj 4.00 10.00
CCJ20 Ray Emery 4.00 10.00
CCJ21 Roberto Luongo 8.00 20.00
CCJ22 Steve Mason 15.00 40.00
CCJ23 Thomas McCollum 4.00 10.00
CCJ24 Trevor Cann 4.00 10.00
CCJ25 Tuukka Rask 8.00 20.00
CCJ26 Tyson Sexsmith 4.00 10.00
CCJ27 Adam Dennis 4.00 10.00
CCJ28 Curtis McElhinney 4.00 10.00
CCJ29 Dan Cloutier 4.00 10.00
CCJ30 Hannu Toivonen 4.00 10.00
CCJ31 Jason Bacashihua 4.00 10.00
CCJ32 Jonathan Bernier 8.00 20.00
CCJ33 Manny Fernandez 4.00 10.00
CCJ34 Marty Turco 5.00 12.00
CCJ35 Patrick Roy (MON) 15.00 40.00
CCJ36 Patrick Roy (COL) 15.00 40.00
CCJ37 Richard Brodeur 4.00 10.00
CCJ38 Ryan Miller 5.00 12.00
CCJ39 Tim Thomas 6.00 15.00
CCJ40 Tyler Weiman 4.00 10.00
CCJ41 Dominik Hasek 6.00 15.00
CCJ42 Felix Potvin 6.00 15.00
CCJ43 Grant Fuhr 8.00 20.00
CCJ44 Josh Harding 4.00 10.00
CCJ45 Jean-Sebastian Giguere 5.00 12.00
CCJ46 Kari Lehtonen 5.00 12.00
CCJ47 Marek Schwarz 4.00 10.00
CCJ48 Martin Brodeur 12.00 30.00
CCJ49 Mike Richter 12.00 30.00
CCJ50 Ron Hextall 8.00 20.00
CCJ51 Ed Belfour 5.00 12.00
CCJ52 Dan Bouchard 4.00 10.00
CCJ53 Curtis Sanford 4.00 10.00
CCJ54 Tomas Vokoun 5.00 12.00
CCJ55 Philippe Sauve 4.00 10.00
CCJ56 Brent Krahn 4.00 10.00
CCJ57 Kevin Lalande 4.00 10.00
CCJ58 Alex Auld 4.00 10.00
CCJ59 Ryan Daniels 4.00 10.00
CCJ60 John Vanbiesbrouck 5.00 12.00
CCJ61 Mathieu Garon
CCJ62 Mike Smith 4.00 10.00
CCJ63 Ilya Bryzgalov 5.00 12.00
CCJ64 Vladislav Tretiak 4.00 10.00

2007-08 Between The Pipes Jerseys Emerald

STATED PRINT RUN 1 SER.#'d SET
NOT PRICED DUE TO SCARCITY

2007-08 Between The Pipes Net Brawlers Jerseys

STATED PRINT RUN 1 SER.#'d SET
NOT PRICED DUE TO SCARCITY
NB01 Roy vs. Vernon
NB02 Aebischer vs. Sauve
NB03 Cloutier vs. Salo
NB04 Roy vs. Osgood
NB05 Shields vs. Snow
NB06 Lalime vs. Esche

NB07 Lalime vs. Dafoe
NB08 Hextall vs. Potvin
NB09 Biron vs. Emery
NB10 Emery vs. Little

2007-08 Between The Pipes Numbers

STATED PRINT RUN 10 SER.#'d SETS
NOT PRICED DUE TO SCARCITY
CCN01 Adam Munro
CCN02 Barry Brust
CCN03 Brian Elliott
CCN04 Cam Ward
CCN05 Carey Price
CCN06 Corey Crawford
CCN07 David LeNeveu
CCN08 Gerald Coleman
CCN09 Jeremy Smith
CCN10 John Murray
CCN11 Jonathan Boulin
CCN12 Karri Ramo
CCN13 Kevin Nastiuk
CCN14 Leland Irving
CCN15 Linden Rowat
CCN16 Michael Leighton
CCN17 Pascal Leclaire
CCN18 Pekka Rinne
CCN19 Peter Budaj
CCN20 Ray Emery
CCN21 Roberto Luongo
CCN22 Steve Mason
CCN23 Thomas McCollum
CCN24 Trevor Cann
CCN25 Tuukka Rask
CCN26 Tyson Sexsmith
CCN27 Adam Dennis
CCN28 Curtis McElhinney
CCN29 Dan Cloutier
CCN30 Hannu Toivonen
CCN31 Jason Bacashihua
CCN32 Jonathan Bernier
CCN33 Manny Fernandez
CCN34 Marty Turco
CCN35 Patrick Roy
CCN36 Patrick Roy
CCN37 Richard Brodeur
CCN38 Ryan Miller
CCN39 Tim Thomas
CCN40 Tyler Weiman
CCN41 Dominik Hasek
CCN42 Felix Potvin
CCN43 Grant Fuhr
CCN44 Josh Harding
CCN45 Jean-Sebastian Giguere
CCN46 Kari Lehtonen
CCN47 Marek Schwarz
CCN48 Martin Brodeur
CCN49 Mike Richter
CCN50 Ron Hextall
CCN51 Ed Belfour
CCN52 Dan Bouchard
CCN53 Curtis Sanford
CCN54 Tomas Vokoun
CCN55 Philippe Sauve
CCN56 Brent Krahn
CCN57 Kevin Lalande
CCN58 Alex Auld
CCN59 Ryan Daniels
CCN60 John Vanbiesbrouck
CCN61 Mathieu Garon
CCN62 Mike Smith
CCN63 Ilya Bryzgalov
CCN64 Vladislav Tretiak

2007-08 Between The Pipes Numbers Emerald

STATED PRINT RUN 1 SER.#'d SET
NOT PRICED DUE TO SCARCITY

2007-08 Between The Pipes Tandem Threads

STATED PRINT RUN 90 SER.#'d SETS
TT01 Dominik Hasek 10.00 25.00
Ryan Miller
TT02 Roberto Luongo
Dan Cloutier
TT03 Felix Potvin 15.00 40.00
Justin Pogge
TT04 Patrick Roy 30.00 80.00
Carey Price
TT05 Curtis McElhinney 6.00 15.00
Leland Irving
TT06 Gerry Cheevers 10.00 25.00
Tim Thomas
TT07 Patrick Roy 20.00 40.00
Peter Budaj
TT08 Gump Worsley 12.00 30.00
Rogie Vachon
TT09 Ed Giacomin 10.00 25.00
Al Montoya
TT10 Marty Turco 6.00 15.00
Mike Smith
TT11 Patrick Roy 20.00 40.00
Martin Brodeur
TT12 Bernie Parent 20.00 40.00
Ron Hextall
TT13 Tomas Vokoun 10.00 20.00
Roberto Luongo
TT14 John Vanbiesbrouck 10.00 25.00
Mike Richter
TT15 Tony Esposito 10.00 25.00
Ed Belfour
TT16 Terry Sawchuk 10.00 25.00
Jonathan Bernier
TT17 Grant Fuhr 10.00 25.00
Mathieu Garon
TT18 Martin Gerber 6.00 15.00
Ray Emery
TT19 Cam Ward 6.00 15.00
Michael Leighton
TT20 Jean-Sebastien Giguere 6.00 15.00
Jose Theodore
Patrick Roy

2007-08 Between The Pipes The Future of Goaltending

COMPLETE SET (10) 6.00 15.00
FOG01 Carey Price 2.00 5.00
FOG02 Leland Irving .60 1.50
FOG03 Trevor Cann .50 1.25
FOG04 Tuukka Rask 1.00 2.50
FOG05 Jaroslav Halak 1.25 3.00
FOG06 Al Montoya .50 1.25
FOG07 Justin Pogge .75 2.00
FOG08 Jonathan Bernier 1.00 2.50
FOG09 Marek Schwarz .50 1.25
FOG10 Tyson Sexsmith .50 1.25

2007-08 Between The Pipes The Mask

COMPLETE SET (30) 75.00 150.00
RANDOM INSERTS IN PACKS
M1 Nikolai Khabibulin 3.00 8.00
M2 Manny Legace 2.50 6.00
M3 Dominik Hasek 4.00 10.00
M4 Carey Price 10.00 25.00
M5 Roberto Luongo 5.00 12.00
M6 Jean-Sebastian Giguere 3.00 8.00
M7 Mathieu Garon 2.50 6.00
M8 Marc-Andre Fleury 3.00 8.00
M9 Marc Denis 2.50 6.00
M10 Evgeni Nabokov 2.50 6.00
M11 Manny Fernandez 2.50 6.00
M12 Niklas Backstrom 2.50 6.00
M13 Josh Harding 2.50 6.00
M14 Miikka Kiprusoff 4.00 10.00
M15 Martin Biron 2.50 6.00
M16 Chris Mason 2.50 6.00
M17 Cam Ward 3.00 8.00
M18 Tim Thomas 4.00 10.00
M19 Marty Turco 3.00 8.00
M20 Johan Hedberg 2.50 6.00
M21 Henrik Lundqvist 4.00 10.00
M22 Martin Gerber 2.50 6.00
M23 Johan Holmqvist 2.50 6.00
M24 Pascal Leclaire 2.50 6.00
M25 Cristobal Huet 2.50 6.00
M26 David Aebischer 2.50 6.00
M27 Peter Budaj 2.50 6.00
M28 Mikael Tellqvist 2.50 6.00
M29 Ryan Miller 3.00 8.00
M30 Ty Conklin 2.50 6.00

2007-08 Between The Pipes The Mask Black

STATED PRINT RUN 1 SER.#'d SET
NOT PRICED DUE TO SCARCITY

2007-08 Between The Pipes The Mask Gold

STATED PRINT RUN 10 SER.#'d SETS
NOT PRICED DUE TO SCARCITY

2007-08 Between The Pipes The Mask Game-Used

STATED PRINT RUN 60 SETS
MGU01 Manny Legace 8.00 20.00
MGU02 Dominik Hasek 12.00 30.00
MGU03 Ryan Miller 10.00 25.00
MGU04 Roberto Luongo 20.00 50.00
MGU05 Jean-Sebastian Giguere 10.00 25.00
MGU06 Cristobal Huet 15.00 40.00
MGU07 Marc-Andre Fleury
MGU08 Evgeni Nabokov 15.00 40.00
MGU09 Miikka Kiprusoff 15.00 40.00
MGU10 Martin Biron 10.00 25.00
MGU11 Chris Mason 8.00 20.00
MGU12 Cam Ward 12.00 30.00
MGU13 Tim Thomas 10.00 25.00
MGU14 Pascal Leclaire 8.00 20.00
MGU15 Marty Turco 10.00 25.00
MGU16 Jacques Plante 20.00 50.00
MGU17 Henrik Lundqvist 12.00 30.00
MGU18 Martin Gerber 10.00 25.00
MGU19 Peter Budaj 8.00 20.00
MGU20 Carey Price 30.00 60.00

2008-09 Between The Pipes

This set was released on March 26, 2009. The base set consists of 100 cards.

COMPLETE SET (100) 12.00 30.00
1 Adam Courchaine .20 .50
2 Al Montoya .20 .50
3 Andrew Engelage .20 .50
4 Antoine Lafleur .20 .50
5 Ben Bishop .40 1.00
6 Braden Holtby .20 .50
7 Brian Elliott .20 .50
8 Simeon Varlamov 1.25 3.00
9 Chet Pickard .25 .60
10 Chris Carrozzi .20 .50
11 Corey Crawford .20 .50
12 Cory Schneider .50 1.25
13 Curtis McElhinney .20 .50
14 Daren Machesney .20 .50
15 Dustin Tokarski .25 .60
16 Erik Ersberg .25 .60
17 Jacob DeSerres .20 .50
18 Jake Allen .20 .50
19 Jaroslav Janus .20 .50
20 Jeremy Smith .20 .50
21 Jimmy Howard .20 .50
22 John Curry .30 .75
23 Jonathan Bernier .30 .75
24 Jonathan Quick .25 .60
25 Josh Unice .20 .50
26 Justin Pogge .50 1.25
27 Kevin Poulin .20 .50
28 Kurtis Mucha .20 .50
29 Kyle Gajewski .20 .50
30 Leland Irving .20 .50
31 Linden Rowat .20 .50
32 Marek Schwarz .25 .60
33 Michael Hutchinson .20 .50
34 Miika Wiikman .25 .60
35 Mike Murphy .20 .50
36 Nolan Schaefer .20 .50
37 Ondrej Pavelec .20 .50
38 Patrick Killeen .20 .50
39 Pekka Rinne .25 .60
40 Peter Delmas .25 .60
41 Raffaele D'Orso .20 .50
42 Robert Mayer .20 .50
43 Steve Mason .60 1.50
44 Steven Stanford .20 .50
45 Thomas McCollum .30 .75
46 Tobias Stephan .20 .50
47 Trevor Cann .20 .50
48 Tuukka Rask .25 .60
49 Tyler Beskorowany .20 .50
50 Tyson Sexsmith .40 1.00
51 Nicola Riopel .20 .50
52 Peter Di Salvo .20 .50
53 Jhonas Enroth .20 .50
54 Brandon Foote .20 .50
55 Alain Valiquette .20 .50
56 Jamie Tucker .20 .50
57 JP Anderson .20 .50
58 Travis Yonkman .20 .50
59 Timo Pielmeier .20 .50
60 Evgeni Nabokov .25 .60
61 Chris Osgood .25 .60
62 Jonas Hiller .25 .60
63 Carey Price .75 2.00
64 Jean-Sebastien Giguere .25 .60
65 Vesa Toskala .25 .60
66 Martin Brodeur .50 1.25
67 Niklas Backstrom .25 .60
68 Manny Fernandez .25 .60
69 Tim Thomas .25 .60
70 Olaf Kolzig .25 .60
71 Cristobal Huet .25 .60
72 Roberto Luongo .40 1.00
73 Bill Durnan .30 .75
74 Glenn Hall .20 .50
75 Gump Worsley .20 .50
76 Jacques Plante .40 1.00
77 Johnny Bower .30 .75
78 Roger Crozier .20 .50
79 Terry Sawchuk .40 1.00
80 Turk Broda .25 .60
81 Bernie Parent .25 .60
82 Rogie Vachon .25 .60
83 Dominik Hasek .40 1.00
84 Ed Belfour .30 .75
85 Gerry Cheevers .40 1.00
86 Grant Fuhr .25 .60
87 John Vanbiesbrouck .25 .60
88 Patrick Roy .75 2.00
89 Pelle Lindbergh .20 .50
90 Tony Esposito .25 .60
91 Ed Belfour .40 1.00
92 Gary Smith .20 .50
93 Gerry Desjardins .20 .50
94 Jacques Plante .40 1.00
95 Al Smith .20 .50
96 Gilles Gratton .25 .60
97 Marcel Paille .20 .50
98 George Gardner .20 .50
99 Les Binkley .20 .50
100 Ernie Wakely .25 .60

2008-09 Between The Pipes Autographs

STATED ODDS 1:12
AAA Alain Valiquette 4.00 10.00
AAC Adam Courchaine 4.00 10.00
AAE Andrew Engelage 4.00 10.00
AAL Antoine Lafleur 4.00 10.00
AAM Al Montoya 4.00 10.00
ABE Brian Elliott 4.00 10.00
ABF Brandon Foote 4.00 10.00
ABH Braden Holtby 4.00 10.00
ABP Bernie Parent SP 5.00 12.00
ACC Chris Carrozzi 4.00 10.00
ACCR Corey Crawford 4.00 10.00
ACH Cristobal Huet 5.00 12.00
ACM Curtis McElhinney 4.00 10.00
ACO Chris Osgood SP
ACP Carey Price SP 15.00 40.00
ACPI Chet Pickard 5.00 12.00
ACPR Carey Price SP 15.00 40.00
ACS Cory Schneider 10.00 25.00
ADH Dominik Hasek
ADM Daren Machesney 4.00 10.00
ADT Dustin Tokarski 5.00 12.00
AEB Ed Belfour SP
AEE Erik Ersberg 5.00 12.00
AEW Ernie Wakely 5.00 12.00
AFP Felix Potvin SP
AGC Gerry Cheevers 8.00 20.00
AGD Gerry Desjardins 4.00 10.00
AGF Grant Fuhr
AGG Gilles Gratton 5.00 12.00
AGS Gary Smith
AJA Jake Allen 4.00 10.00
AJB Jonathan Bernier 6.00 15.00
AJC John Curry 6.00 15.00
AJD Jacob DeSerres 4.00 10.00
AJH Jimmy Howard 4.00 10.00
AJHI Jonas Hiller SP 5.00 12.00
AJJ Jaroslav Janus 4.00 10.00
AJP Justin Pogge 10.00 25.00
AJPA JP Anderson 4.00 10.00
AJQ Jonathan Quick 5.00 12.00
AJS Jeremy Smith 4.00 10.00
AJSG Jean-Sebastien Giguere SP 12.00 30.00
AJT Jamie Tucker 4.00 10.00
AJU Josh Unice 4.00 10.00
AJV John Vanbiesbrouck SP
AKM Kurtis Mucha 4.00 10.00
AKP Kevin Poulin 4.00 10.00
ALB Les Binkley 8.00 20.00
ALI Leland Irving
ALR Linden Rowat 4.00 10.00
AMB Martin Brodeur SP 60.00 120.00
AMF Manny Fernandez SP 5.00 12.00
AMH Michael Hutchinson 4.00 10.00
AMM Mike Murphy 4.00 10.00
AMS Marek Schwarz
AMT Marty Turco 4.00 10.00
AMW Miika Wiikman 5.00 12.00
ANB Niklas Backstrom SP
ANS Nolan Schaefer 4.00 10.00
AOK Olaf Kolzig 5.00 12.00
AOP Ondrej Pavelec 4.00 10.00
APB Peter Budaj 4.00 10.00
APD Peter Delmas 5.00 12.00
APDI Peter Di Salvo 4.00 10.00
APK Patrick Killeen 4.00 10.00
APR Pekka Rinne 5.00 12.00
APRO Patrick Roy SP 75.00 150.00
ARD Raffaele D'Orso 4.00 10.00
ARG Ed Giacomin SP
ARL Roberto Luongo SP 20.00 50.00
ARM Robert Mayer 4.00 10.00
ARV Rogie Vachon SP 10.00 25.00
ASM Steve Mason 12.00 30.00
ASS Steven Stanford 4.00 10.00
ASV Simeon Varlamov 25.00 60.00
ATB Tyler Beskorowany 4.00 10.00
ATC Trevor Cann 4.00 10.00
ATE Tony Esposito SP 15.00 40.00
ATM Thomas McCollum 6.00 15.00
ATR Tuukka Rask 5.00 12.00
ATS Tobias Stephan 4.00 10.00
ATSE Tyson Sexsmith 8.00 20.00
ATT Tim Thomas SP 15.00 40.00
ATY Travis Yonkman 4.00 10.00
AVT Vesa Toskala SP 10.00 25.00
AVTR Vladislav Tretiak 12.00 30.00

2008-09 Between The Pipes Autothreads

STATED PRINT RUN 9 SERIAL #'d SETS
NOT PRICED DUE TO SCARCITY
ATCO Chris Osgood
ATCP Carey Price
ATDH Dominik Hasek
ATGF Grant Fuhr
ATJD John Davidson
ATJSG Jean-Sebastien Giguere
ATMB Martin Brodeur
ATMT Marty Turco
ATPR Patrick Roy
ATRL Roberto Luongo

2008-09 Between The Pipes Autothreads Gold

STATED PRINT RUN 1 SERIAL #'d SET
NOT PRICED DUE TO SCARCITY

2008-09 Between The Pipes Complete Jersey

STATED PRINT RUN 9 SERIAL #'d SETS
NOT PRICED DUE TO SCARCITY
CJ01 Martin Brodeur
CJ02 Patrick Roy
CJ03 Patrick Roy
CJ04 Chet Pickard
CJ05 Dustin Tokarski
CJ06 Carey Price
CJ07 Roberto Luongo
CJ08 Tim Thomas
CJ09 Pelle Lindbergh
CJ10 Steve Mason
CJ11 Vesa Toskala
CJ12 Olivier Roy
CJ13 Evgeni Nabokov
CJ13 Dominik Hasek

2008-09 Between The Pipes Complete Jersey Gold

STATED PRINT RUN 1 SERIAL #'d SET
NOT PRICED DUE TO SCARCITY

2008-09 Between The Pipes Complete Logo AHL

STATED PRINT RUN 1 SERIAL #'d SET
NOT PRICED DUE TO SCARCITY
AHL01 John Curry
AHL02 Daren Machesney
AHL03 Drew MacIntyre
AHL04 Jonathan Quick
AHL05 Miika Wiikman
AHL06 Corey Crawford
AHL07 Brian Elliott
AHL08 Jonas Hiller

2008-09 Between The Pipes Complete Logo CHL

STATED PRINT RUN 1 SERIAL #'d SET
NOT PRICED DUE TO SCARCITY
CHL01 Riku Helenius
CHL02 Braden Holtby
CHL03 Torrie Jung
CHL04 Kris Lazaruk
CHL05 Mike Murphy
CHL06 Chet Pickard
CHL07 Olivier Roy
CHL08 Josh Unice
CHL09 Kristofer Westblom
CHL10 Dustin Tokarski
CHL11 Peter Delmas
CHL12 Trevor Cann

2008-09 Between The Pipes Draft Day Duos

OVERALL G-U ODDS 1:20
ANNOUNCED PRINT RUN 50
DDD01 Chet Pickard 8.00 20.00
Thomas McCollum
DDD02 Trevor Cann
Tyson Sexsmith
DDD03 Jonathan Bernier 8.00 20.00
Leland Irving
DDD04 Steve Mason 15.00 40.00
Simeon Varlamov
DDD05 Carey Price 20.00 50.00
Tuukka Rask
DDD06 Al Montoya 6.00 15.00
Marek Schwarz
DDD07 Corey Crawford 5.00 12.00
Jimmy Howard
DDD08 Josh Harding 5.00 12.00
Hannu Toivonen
DDD09 Pascal Leclaire 5.00 12.00
Peter Budaj
DDD10 Philippe Sauve 5.00 12.00
Jason LaBarbera
DDD11 Roberto Luongo 10.00 25.00
Scott Clemmensen
DDD12 Jean-Sebastien Giguere 4.00 10.00
Brian Boucher
DDD13 Marty Turco
Dan Cloutier
DDD14 Grant Fuhr 6.00 15.00
Mike Vernon
DDD15 Martin Brodeur 12.00 30.00
Felix Potvin
DDD16 Mike Richter 6.00 15.00
Sean Burke
DDD17 Patrick Roy 20.00 50.00
Kirk McLean
DDD18 Dominik Hasek 10.00 25.00
Vladislav Tretiak
DDD19 Ken Wregget 6.00 15.00
Ron Hextall
DDD20 Tim Thomas 6.00 15.00
Evgeni Nabokov

2008-09 Between The Pipes Draft Day Duos Gold

STATED PRINT RUN 10 SERIAL #'d SETS
NOT PRICED DUE TO SCARCITY

2008-09 Between The Pipes Emblems

OVERALL G-U ODDS 1:20
ANNOUNCED PRINT RUN 19
NOT PRICED DUE TO SCARCITY
GUE01 Martin Brodeur
GUE02 Peter Budaj
GUE03 Corey Crawford
GUE04 John Curry
GUE05 Peter Delmas
GUE06 Brian Elliott
GUE07 Tony Esposito
GUE08 Manny Fernandez
GUE09 Jean-Sebastien Giguere
GUE10 Jaroslav Halak
GUE11 Dominik Hasek
GUE12 Riku Helenius
GUE13 Jonas Hiller
GUE14 Braden Holtby
GUE15 Tim Thomas
GUE16 Torrie Jung
GUE17 Kris Lazaruk
GUE18 Pelle Lindbergh
GUE19 Roberto Luongo
GUE20 Daren Machesney
GUE21 Steve Mason
GUE22 Cristobal Huet
GUE23 Drew MacIntyre
GUE24 Simeon Varlamov
GUE25 Mike Murphy
GUE26 Chris Osgood
GUE27 Chet Pickard
GUE28 Justin Pogge
GUE29 Felix Potvin
GUE30 Carey Price
GUE31 Jonathan Quick
GUE32 Pekka Rinne
GUE33 Olivier Roy
GUE34 Patrick Roy
GUE35 Patrick Roy
GUE36 Marek Schwarz
GUE37 Dustin Tokarski
GUE38 Vesa Toskala
GUE39 Vladislav Tretiak
GUE40 Marty Turco
GUE41 Josh Unice
GUE42 John Vanbiesbrouck
GUE43 Kristofer Westblom
GUE44 Miika Wiikman
GUE45 Evgeni Nabokov

2008-09 Between The Pipes Emblems Gold

STATED PRINT RUN 1 SERIAL #'d SET
NOT PRICED DUE TO SCARCITY

2008-09 Between The Pipes Emblems Autographs

STATED PRINT RUN 9 SERIAL #'d SETS
NOT PRICED DUE TO SCARCITY

2008-09 Between The Pipes Emblems Autographs Gold

STATED PRINT RUN 1 SER.#'d SETS
NOT PRICED DUE TO SCARCITY

2008-09 Between The Pipes Goaltending Evolution

OVERALL G-U ODDS 1:20
ANNOUNCED PRINT RUN 50
GE01 Patrick Roy 30.00 80.00
Carey Price
Jaroslav Halak
GE02 Dominik Hasek 15.00 40.00
Brian Elliott
Jeff Glass
GE03 Felix Potvin 20.00 50.00
Vesa Toskala
Justin Pogge
GE04 Gerry Cheevers 15.00 40.00
Tim Thomas
Tuukka Rask
GE05 Patrick Roy 30.00 80.00
Peter Budaj
Peter Delmas
GE06 Ed Belfour 15.00 40.00
Marty Turco
Tobias Stephan
GE07 Jacques Plante 30.00 80.00
Carey Price
Jaroslav Halak
GE08 Terry Sawchuk 15.00 40.00
Chris Osgood
Jimmy Howard
GE09 Richard Brodeur 15.00 40.00
Roberto Luongo
Julien Ellis
GE10 Terry Sawchuk 10.00 25.00
Jonathan Quick
Jonathan Bernier

2008-09 Between The Pipes Goaltending Evolution Gold

STATED PRINT RUN 10 SERIAL #'d SETS
NOT PRICED DUE TO SCARCITY

2008-09 Between The Pipes Great Moments

OVERALL G-U ODDS 1:20
ANNOUNCED PRINT RUN 40
GM01 Jacques Plante 12.00 30.00
GM02 Glenn Hall 6.00 15.00
GM03 Billy Smith 6.00 15.00
GM04 Vladislav Tretiak 6.00 15.00
GM05 Terry Sawchuk 12.00 30.00
GM06 Patrick Roy 25.00 60.00
GM07 Martin Brodeur 15.00 40.00
GM08 Clint Benedict 10.00 25.00

2008-09 Between The Pipes Great Moments Gold

STATED PRINT RUN 10 SERIAL #'d SETS
NOT PRICED DUE TO SCARCITY

2008-09 Between The Pipes Jerseys

OVERALL G-U ODDS 1:20
ANNOUNCED PRINT RUN 90 SETS
GUJ01 Martin Brodeur SP 20.00 50.00
GUJ02 Peter Budaj 6.00 15.00
GUJ03 Corey Crawford 6.00 15.00
GUJ04 John Curry 10.00 25.00
GUJ05 Peter Delmas 8.00 20.00
GUJ06 Brian Elliott 6.00 15.00
GUJ07 Tony Esposito 8.00 20.00
GUJ08 Manny Fernandez 8.00 20.00
GUJ09 Jean-Sebastien Giguere 8.00 20.00
GUJ10 Jaroslav Halak 8.00 20.00
GUJ11 Dominik Hasek 12.00 30.00
GUJ12 Riku Helenius
GUJ13 Jonas Hiller 8.00 20.00
GUJ14 Braden Holtby 6.00 15.00
GUJ15 Tim Thomas 8.00 20.00
GUJ16 Torrie Jung
GUJ17 Kris Lazaruk 8.00 20.00
GUJ18 Pelle Lindbergh SP
GUJ19 Roberto Luongo SP 15.00 40.00
GUJ20 Daren Machesney 6.00 15.00
GUJ21 Steve Mason 25.00 60.00
GUJ22 Cristobal Huet
GUJ23 Drew MacIntyre 8.00 20.00
GUJ24 Simeon Varlamov 12.00 30.00
GUJ25 Mike Murphy 6.00 15.00
GUJ26 Chris Osgood 8.00 20.00
GUJ27 Chet Pickard 8.00 20.00
GUJ28 Justin Pogge 10.00 25.00
GUJ29 Felix Potvin
GUJ30 Carey Price 25.00 60.00
GUJ31 Jonathan Quick
GUJ32 Pekka Rinne 8.00 20.00
GUJ33 Olivier Roy 8.00 20.00
GUJ34 Patrick Roy SP 25.00 60.00
GUJ35 Patrick Roy SP 25.00 60.00
GUJ36 Marek Schwarz 8.00 20.00
GUJ37 Dustin Tokarski 8.00 20.00
GUJ38 Vesa Toskala 8.00 20.00
GUJ39 Vladislav Tretiak 15.00 40.00
GUJ40 Marty Turco 6.00 15.00
GUJ41 Josh Unice 6.00 15.00
GUJ42 John Vanbiesbrouck 12.00 30.00
GUJ43 Kristofer Westblom 6.00 15.00
GUJ44 Miika Wiikman 8.00 20.00
GUJ45 Evgeni Nabokov 8.00 20.00

2008-09 Between The Pipes Jerseys Gold

STATED PRINT RUN 10 SERIAL #'d SETS
NOT PRICED DUE TO SCARCITY

2008-09 Between The Pipes Jerseys Autographs

ANNOUNCED PRINT RUN 9 SETS
NOT PRICED DUE TO SCARCITY

2008-09 Between The Pipes Jerseys Autographs Gold

STATED PRINT RUN 1 SERIAL #'d SET
NOT PRICED DUE TO SCARCITY

2008-09 Between The Pipes Masked Men

MM01 Chet Pickard 3.00 8.00
MM02 Timo Pielmeier 2.50 6.00
MM03 Carey Price 10.00 25.00
MM04 Corey Crawford 2.50 6.00
MM05 Cory Schneider 6.00 15.00
MM06 Jimmy Howard 2.50 6.00
MM07 Jonathan Bernier 4.00 10.00
MM08 Marek Schwarz 3.00 8.00
MM09 Robert Mayer 2.50 6.00
MM10 Thomas McCollum 4.00 10.00
MM11 Antoine Tardif 3.00 8.00
MM12 Gabriel Girard 2.50 6.00
MM13 Karel St. Laurent 3.00 8.00
MM14 Brent Krahn 4.00 10.00
MM15 Jean-Philippe Levasseur 4.00 10.00
MM16 Peter Delmas 3.00 8.00
MM17 Cristobal Huet 3.00 8.00
MM18 Jonas Hiller 3.00 8.00
MM19 Jean-Sebastien Giguere 3.00 8.00
MM20 Martin Brodeur 6.00 15.00
MM21 Patrick Roy 10.00 25.00
MM22 Patrick Roy 10.00 25.00
MM23 Steve Mason 10.00 25.00
MM24 Vesa Toskala 3.00 8.00
MM25 Manny Fernandez 3.00 8.00
MM26 Marty Turco 2.50 6.00
MM27 Justin Pogge 6.00 15.00
MM28 Niklas Backstrom 3.00 8.00
MM29 Olivier Roy 3.00 8.00
MM30 Tim Thomas 3.00 8.00
MM31 Travis Fullerton 2.50 6.00
MM32 Devan Dubnyk 2.50 6.00
MM33 Jacob DeSerres 2.50 6.00
MM34 Marek Benda 3.00 8.00
MM35 Nathan Dunnett 2.50 6.00
MM36 Linden Rowat 2.50 6.00
MM37 Adam Courchaine 2.50 6.00
MM38 Dustin Tokarski 3.00 8.00
MM39 Daniel Larsson 2.50 6.00
MM40 Josh Tordjman 5.00 12.00
MM41 Roberto Luongo 5.00 12.00
MM42 Brian Elliott 2.50 6.00
MM43 Trevor Cann 2.50 6.00
MM44 Ed Belfour 5.00 12.00
MM45 Felix Potvin 5.00 12.00
MM46 Dominik Hasek 5.00 12.00
MM47 Frederic Piche 2.50 6.00
MM48 Jhonas Enroth 2.50 6.00
MM49 Kurtis Mucha 2.50 6.00
MM50 Nolan Schaefer 2.50 6.00

2008-09 Between The Pipes Masked Men Gold

STATED PRINT RUN 10 SERIAL #'d SETS
NOT PRICED DUE TO SCARCITY

2008-09 Between The Pipes Numbers

ANNOUNCED PRINT RUN 19 SETS
NOT PRICED DUE TO SCARCITY
GUN01 Martin Brodeur
GUN02 Peter Budaj
GUN03 Corey Crawford
GUN04 John Curry
GUN05 Peter Delmas
GUN06 Brian Elliott
GUN07 Tony Esposito
GUN08 Manny Fernandez
GUN09 Jean-Sebastien Giguere
GUN10 Jaroslav Halak
GUN11 Dominik Hasek
GUN12 Riku Helenius
GUN13 Jonas Hiller
GUN14 Braden Holtby
GUN15 Tim Thomas
GUN16 Torrie Jung
GUN17 Kris Lazaruk
GUN18 Pelle Lindbergh
GUN19 Roberto Luongo
GUN20 Daren Machesney
GUN21 Steve Mason
GUN22 Cristobal Huet
GUN23 Drew MacIntyre
GUN24 Simeon Varlamov
GUN25 Mike Murphy
GUN26 Chris Osgood
GUN27 Chet Pickard
GUN28 Justin Pogge
GUN29 Felix Potvin
GUN30 Carey Price
GUN31 Jonathan Quick
GUN32 Pekka Rinne
GUN33 Olivier Roy
GUN34 Patrick Roy
GUN35 Patrick Roy
GUN36 Marek Schwarz
GUN37 Dustin Tokarski
GUN38 Vesa Toskala
GUN39 Vladislav Tretiak
GUN40 Marty Turco
GUN41 Josh Unice
GUN42 John Vanbiesbrouck
GUN43 Kristofer Westblom
GUN44 Miika Wiikman
GUN45 Evgeni Nabokov

2008-09 Between The Pipes Numbers Gold

STATED PRINT RUN 1 SERIAL #'d SET
NOT PRICED DUE TO SCARCITY

2008-09 Between The Pipes Numbers Autographs

ANNOUNCED PRINT RUN 9 SETS
NOT PRICED DUE TO SCARCITY

2008-09 Between The Pipes Numbers Autographs Gold

STATED PRINT RUN 1 SERIAL #'d SET
NOT PRICED DUE TO SCARCITY

2008-09 Between The Pipes Prospect Combos

ANNOUNCED PRINT RUN 90 SETS
PC01 Justin Pogge 10.00 25.00
Mike Murphy
PC02 Brian Elliott 4.00 10.00
Trevor Cann
PC03 Jimmy Howard 6.00 15.00
Thomas McCollum
PC04 Jaroslav Halak 10.00 25.00
Braden Holtby
PC05 Marek Schwarz 5.00 12.00
Kristofer Westblom
PC06 Pekka Rinne 8.00 20.00
Tyson Sexsmith
PC07 Simeon Varlamov 25.00 60.00
Nicola Riopel
PC08 Josh Harding 5.00 12.00
Dustin Tokarski
PC09 Jonathan Quick 5.00 12.00
Olivier Roy
PC10 Corey Crawford 5.00 12.00

Chet Pickard
PC11 Al Montoya 12.00 30.00
Steve Mason
PC12 Leland Irving 5.00 12.00
Kris Lazaruk

2008-09 Between The Pipes Prospect Combos Gold
STATED PRINT RUN 10 SERIAL #'d SETS
NOT PRICED DUE TO SCARCITY

2008-09 Between The Pipes Roots
ANNOUNCED PRINT RUN 9 SETS
NOT PRICED DUE TO SCARCITY

2008-09 Between The Pipes Roots Gold
STATED PRINT RUN 1 SERIAL #'d SETS
NOT PRICED DUE TO SCARCITY

2008-09 Between The Pipes Super-Sized Pads
OVERALL G-U ODDS 1:20
ANNOUNCED PRINT RUN 30 SETS
SSP01 Patrick Roy 50.00 120.00
SSP02 Patrick Roy 50.00 120.00
SSP03 Martin Brodeur 50.00 100.00
SSP04 Pelle Lindbergh 50.00 100.00
SSP05 Ed Belfour 25.00 60.00
SSP06 Gerry Cheevers 40.00 80.00
SSP07 Grant Fuhr 15.00 40.00
SSP08 Chris Osgood 25.00 60.00
SSP09 Marty Turco 20.00 50.00
SSP10 Vladislav Tretiak 60.00 120.00
SSP11 Ron Hextall 40.00 100.00
SSP12 Bernie Parent 40.00 100.00

2008-09 Between The Pipes Super-Sized Pads Gold
STATED PRINT RUN 10 SERIAL #'d SETS
NOT PRICED DUE TO SCARCITY

2008-09 Between The Pipes Super Glove
ANNOUNCED PRINT RUN 20 SETS
NOT PRICED DUE TO SCARCITY
SG01 Martin Brodeur
SG02 Peter Budaj
SG03 Rick DiPietro
SG04 Marc-Andre Fleury
SG05 Jean-Sebastien Giguere
SG06 Dominik Hasek
SG07 Miikka Kiprusoff
SG08 Chris Osgood
SG09 Felix Potvin
SG10 Jose Theodore
SG11 Jocelyn Thibault
SG12 Vesa Toskala
SG13 Marty Turco
SG14 Tomas Vokoun
SG15 Cam Ward
SG16 Roberto Luongo
SG17 Patrick Roy
SG18 Sean Burke
SG19 Olaf Kolzig
SG20 Evgeni Nabokov

2008-09 Between The Pipes Super Glove Gold
ANNOUNCED PRINT RUN 10 SETS
NOT PRICED DUE TO SCARCITY

2009-10 Between The Pipes
COMPLETE SET (150) 20.00 50.00
1 Alexander Salak .25 .60
2 Alex Stalock .20 .50
3 Anton Khudobin .25 .60
4 Ben Bishop .25 .60
5 Cedrick Desjardins .40 1.00
6 Chad Johnson .20 .50
7 Chet Pickard .30 .75
8 Cory Schneider .40 1.00
9 Daniel Larsson .30 .75
10 Devan Dubnyk .30 .75
11 Dustin Tokarski .20 .50
12 James Reimer .25 .60
13 Jhonas Enroth .30 .75
14 Joe Fallon .20 .50
15 Johan Backlund .25 .60
16 John Curry .20 .50
17 Jonathan Bernier .25 .60
18 Justin Pogge .50 1.25
19 Kevin Lalande .20 .50
20 Leland Irving .25 .60
21 Mark Dekanich .20 .50
22 Matt Climie .20 .50
23 Michal Neuvirth .60 1.50
24 Mike Brodeur .20 .50
25 Mike McKenna .20 .50
26 Mike Murphy .20 .50
27 Nathan Lawson .20 .50
28 Thomas McCollum .25 .60
29 Trevor Cann .30 .75
30 Tyler Weiman .25 .60
31 Andrew Hayes .20 .50
32 Adam Brown .20 .50
33 Adam Morrison .20 .50
34 Calvin Pickard .40 1.00
35 Darcy Kuemper .20 .50
36 Drew Owsley .20 .50
37 Garrett Zemlak .20 .50
38 James Reid .25 .60
39 Jamie Tucker .20 .50
40 Kent Simpson .20 .50
41 Linden Rowat .20 .50
42 Martin Jones .25 .60
43 Nathan Lieuwen .30 .75
44 Torrie Jung .20 .50
45 Tyler Bunz .20 .50
46 Antoine Tardif .20 .50
47 Jake Allen .30 .75
48 Kevin Poulin .30 .75
49 Louis Domingue .40 1.00
50 Marc-Antoine Gelinas .25 .60
51 Marco Cousineau .20 .50
52 Mathieu Corbeil-Theriault .20 .50
53 Matthew Dopud .20 .50
54 Maxime Clermont .20 .50
55 Mickael Audette .20 .50
56 Nathan Dunnett .20 .50
57 Nicolas Champion .20 .50
58 Olivier Roy .30 .75
59 Peter Delmas .20 .50
60 Jacob Markstrom .40 1.00
61 Brandon Maxwell .20 .50
62 Chris Carrozzi .25 .60
63 Edward Pasquale .25 .60
64 Jason Missiaen .20 .50
65 J.P. Anderson .25 .60
66 Matt Hackett .30 .75
67 Michael Houser .30 .75
68 Michael Hutchinson .30 .75
69 Patrick Killeen .20 .50
70 Peter Di Salvo .25 .60
71 Philipp Grubauer .25 .60
72 Robin Lehner .20 .50
73 Scott Stajcer .20 .50
74 Troy Passingham .20 .50
75 Tyler Beskorowany .20 .50
76 Antti Niemi .75 2.00
77 Cam Ward .25 .60
78 Carey Price .60 1.50
79 Chris Osgood .30 .75
80 Evgeni Nabokov .25 .60
81 Ilya Bryzgalov .25 .60
82 Jean-Sebastien Giguere .25 .60
83 Jaroslav Halak .25 .60
84 Jimmy Howard .30 .75
85 Jonas Hiller .30 .75
86 Josh Harding .20 .50
87 Kari Lehtonen .25 .60
88 Manny Legace .20 .50
89 Marc-Andre Fleury .25 .60
90 Martin Brodeur .60 1.50
91 Marty Turco .20 .50
92 Miikka Kiprusoff .25 .60
93 Niklas Backstrom .25 .60
94 Tuukka Rask .30 .75
95 Ondrej Pavelec .25 .60
96 Pascal Leclaire .25 .60
97 Ray Emery .20 .50
98 Rick DiPietro .20 .50
99 Roberto Luongo .60 1.50
100 Ryan Miller .25 .60
101 Scott Clemmensen .20 .50
102 Simeon Varlamov .50 1.25
103 Cristobal Huet .25 .60
104 Tim Thomas .25 .60
105 Tomas Vokoun .25 .60
106 Vesa Toskala .25 .60
107 Allan Bester .20 .50
108 Andy Moog .40 1.00
109 Bernie Parent .25 .60
110 Bill Durnan .20 .50
111 Billy Smith .40 1.00
112 Brian Hayward .25 .60
113 Bunny Larocque .20 .50
114 Dan Bouchard .40 1.00
115 Dominik Hasek .25 .60
116 Charlie Hodge .25 .60
117 Ed Giacomin .30 .75
118 Ed Johnston .30 .75
119 Felix Potvin .40 1.00
120 Gerry Cheevers .50 1.25
121 Gilles Meloche .30 .75
122 Gilles Villemure .30 .75
123 Glenn Hall .50 1.25
124 Grant Fuhr .30 .75
125 Gump Worsley .40 1.00
126 Harry Lumley .20 .50
127 Jacques Plante .40 1.00
128 Georges Vezina .40 1.00
129 Johnny Bower .30 .75
130 Mike Liut .30 .75
131 Patrick Roy .75 2.00
132 Pelle Lindbergh .30 .75
133 Pete Peeters .40 1.00
134 Richard Brodeur .25 .60
135 Rogie Vachon .40 1.00
136 Ron Hextall .50 1.25
137 Terry Sawchuk .30 .75
138 Tony Esposito .40 1.00
139 Turk Broda .25 .60
140 Vladislav Tretiak .25 .60
141 Don McLeod .25 .60
142 Pat Riggin .30 .75
143 Jim Corsi .30 .75
144 Gary Bromley .30 .75
145 George Gardner .20 .50
146 Ron Grahame .20 .50
147 Gary Inness .40 1.00
148 Mike Curran .20 .50
149 Ken Brown .20 .50
150 Wayne Rutledge .20 .50

2009-10 Between The Pipes AHL Rookies
COMPLETE SET (9) 15.00 40.00
STATED ODDS 1:8
AR01 Chad Johnson 2.00 5.00
AR02 Braden Holtby 3.00 8.00
AR03 Anton Khudobin 2.50 6.00
AR04 Dustin Tokarski 2.00 5.00
AR05 Alexander Salak 2.50 6.00
AR06 Alex Stalock 2.00 5.00
AR07 Chet Pickard 3.00 8.00
AR08 Mike Murphy 2.00 5.00
AR09 Thomas McCollum 2.50 6.00

2009-10 Between The Pipes Auto Threads Gold
STATED PRINT RUN 1 SER.#'d SET
NOT PRICED DUE TO SCARCITY

2009-10 Between The Pipes Auto Threads Silver
STATED PRINT RUN 9 SER.#'d SETS
NOT PRICED DUE TO SCARCITY

2009-10 Between The Pipes Autographs
OVERALL STATED ODDS 1:8
AAA Alex Auld SP 8.00 20.00
AAB Allan Bester SP 8.00 20.00
AAK Anton Khudobin 5.00 12.00
AAM Andy Moog 8.00 20.00
AAN Antero Niittymaki SP 10.00 25.00
AAS Alexander Salak 5.00 12.00
ABB Ben Bishop 5.00 12.00
ABH Brian Hayward 5.00 12.00
ABM Brandon Maxwell 4.00 10.00
ABP Bernie Parent SP 10.00 25.00
ABS Billy Smith 8.00 20.00
ACC Chris Carrozzi SP 10.00 25.00
ACD Cedrick Desjardins 8.00 20.00
ACH Cristobal Huet 5.00 12.00
ACJ Chad Johnson 4.00 10.00
ACO Chris Osgood 6.00 15.00
ACP Chet Pickard SP 12.00 30.00
ACS Cory Schneider 8.00 20.00
ADB Dan Bouchard 8.00 20.00
ADH Dominik Hasek SP 20.00 50.00
ADL Daniel Larsson 6.00 15.00
ADM Don McLeod 5.00 12.00
ADO Drew Owsley 4.00 10.00
ADT Dustin Tokarski SP 8.00 20.00
AEE Erik Ersberg 4.00 10.00
AEG Ed Giacomin SP 12.00 30.00
AEJ Ed Johnston 6.00 15.00
AEN Evgeni Nabokov 5.00 12.00
AEP Edward Pasquale 5.00 12.00
AFP Felix Potvin SP 15.00 40.00
AGB Gary Bromley 6.00 15.00
AGC Gerry Cheevers SP 20.00 50.00
AGF Grant Fuhr 6.00 15.00
AGH Glenn Hall SP 20.00 50.00
AGI Gary Inness 8.00 20.00
AGM Gilles Meloche 6.00 15.00
AGV Gilles Villemure 6.00 15.00
AGW Gump Worsley SP 15.00 40.00
AGZ Garrett Zemlak 4.00 10.00
AHT Hannu Toivonen 5.00 12.00
AJA Jake Allen 6.00 15.00
AJB Johan Backlund 5.00 12.00
AJC Jim Corsi 6.00 15.00
AJE Jhonas Enroth 6.00 15.00
AJG Jean-Sebastien Giguere 5.00 12.00
AJL Jason Labarbera
AJM Jason Missiaen 4.00 10.00
AJP Justin Pogge SP 20.00 50.00
AJQ Jonathan Quick 8.00 20.00
AJR James Reimer 5.00 12.00
AJT Jamie Tucker SP
AKP Kevin Poulin 6.00 15.00
AKS Kent Simpson 4.00 10.00
ALD Louis Domingue 8.00 20.00
ALI Leland Irving 5.00 12.00
ALR Linden Rowat SP
AMA Mickael Audette 4.00 10.00
AMC Matt Climie 4.00 10.00
AMG Marc-Antoine Gelinas 5.00 12.00
AMH Matt Hackett 6.00 15.00
AMJ Martin Jones 5.00 12.00
AMK Miikka Kiprusoff 5.00 12.00
AML Mike Liut 6.00 15.00
AMM Mike McKenna 4.00 10.00
AMN Michal Neuvirth 12.00 30.00
AMT Marty Turco 4.00 10.00
ANB Niklas Backstrom 5.00 12.00
ANL Nathan Lawson 4.00 10.00
AOP Ondrej Pavelec 5.00 12.00
AOR Olivier Roy 6.00 15.00
APB Peter Budaj 5.00 12.00
APD Peter Delmas 4.00 10.00
APG Philipp Grubauer 5.00 12.00
APK Patrick Killeen 4.00 10.00
APP Pete Peeters 8.00 20.00
APR Patrick Roy SP 30.00 80.00
ARB Richard Brodeur SP 10.00 25.00
ARE Ray Emery 4.00 10.00
ARG Ron Grahame 6.00 15.00
ARH Ron Hextall 10.00 25.00
ARL Robin Lehner 4.00 10.00
ARV Rogie Vachon SP 15.00 40.00
ASS Scott Stajcer 4.00 10.00
ASV Simeon Varlamov 10.00 25.00
ATB Tyler Beskorowany 4.00 10.00
ATC Trevor Cann SP 12.00 30.00
ATE Tony Esposito SP 15.00 40.00
ATM Thomas McCollum SP 10.00 25.00
ATP Troy Passingham 4.00 10.00
ATR Tuukka Rask SP 12.00 30.00
ATT Tim Thomas SP 10.00 25.00
ATV Tomas Vokoun 5.00 12.00
ATW Tyler Weiman 5.00 12.00
AVT Vesa Toskala 5.00 12.00
AAM2 Andy Moog 8.00 20.00
AAST Alex Stalock 4.00 10.00
ABH2 Brian Hayward 5.00 12.00
ABP2 Bernie Parent SP 10.00 25.00
ACHO Charlie Hodge SP 8.00 20.00
ACPI Calvin Pickard 8.00 20.00
ACPR Carey Price 15.00 40.00
ADB2 Dan Bouchard 8.00 20.00
ADH2 Dominik Hasek SP 20.00 50.00
AEG2 Ed Giacomin SP 12.00 30.00
AGB2 Gary Bromley 6.00 15.00
AGC2 Gerry Cheevers SP 20.00 50.00
AGH2 Glenn Hall SP 20.00 50.00
AGI2 Gary Inness 8.00 20.00
AGM2 Gilles Meloche 6.00 15.00
AGW2 Gump Worsley SP 15.00 40.00
AJAN J.P. Anderson SP
AJBE Jonathan Bernier 5.00 12.00
AJBO Johnny Bower SP 12.00 30.00
AJMA Jacob Markstrom 25.00 50.00
AJRE James Reid 5.00 12.00
AMBR Martin Brodeur SP 40.00 100.00
AMCL Maxime Clermont 4.00 10.00
AMCO Marco Cousineau 4.00 10.00
AMHU Michael Hutchinson 6.00 15.00
AML2 Mike Liut 6.00 15.00
ANLI Nathan Lieuwen 6.00 15.00
APDI Peter Di Salvo 5.00 12.00
APPE Pete Peeters 8.00 20.00
APR2 Pat Riggin 6.00 15.00
APRI Pat Riggin 6.00 15.00
ARB2 Richard Brodeur SP 10.00 25.00
ARLU Roberto Luongo SP 25.00 60.00
ARV2 Rogie Vachon SP 15.00 40.00
ATE2 Tony Esposito SP 15.00 40.00
AVTR Vladislav Tretiak 20.00 50.00
ACHO2 Charlie Hodge SP 8.00 20.00
AJBO2 Johnny Bower SP 12.00 30.00

2009-10 Between The Pipes Brodeur Tribute
COMPLETE SET (9) 25.00 50.00
COMMON BRODUER 3.00 8.00
OVERALL STATED ODDS 1:8

2009-10 Between The Pipes CHL Rookies
COMPLETE SET (9) 15.00 40.00
STATED ODDS 1:8
CR01 Michael Houser 3.00 8.00
CR02 Petr Mrazek 2.00 5.00
CR03 Tyson Teichmann 2.00 5.00
CR04 Brandon Anderson 2.00 5.00
CR05 Hudson Stremmel 3.00 8.00
CR06 Jordan Binnington 2.00 5.00
CR07 Guillaume Nadeau 3.00 8.00
CR08 Philippe Tremblay 2.00 5.00
CR09 Robin Gusse 2.50 6.00

2009-10 Between The Pipes Complete Jerseys Gold
STATED PRINT RUN 1 SER.#'d SET
NOT PRICED DUE TO SCARCITY

2009-10 Between The Pipes Complete Jerseys Silver
STATED PRINT RUN 9 SER.#'d SETS
NOT PRICED DUE TO SCARCITY

2009-10 Between The Pipes Complete Logo AHL
STATED PRINT RUN 1 SER.#'d SET
NOT PRICED DUE TO SCARCITY

2009-10 Between The Pipes Complete Logo CHL
STATED PRINT RUN 1 SER.#'d SET
NOT PRICED DUE TO SCARCITY

2009-10 Between The Pipes Complete Package Gold
STATED PRINT RUN 1 SER.#'d SET
NOT PRICED DUE TO SCARCITY

2009-10 Between The Pipes Complete Package Silver
STATED PRINT RUN 19 SER.#'d SETS
NOT PRICED DUE TO SCARCITY

2009-10 Between The Pipes Emblems Autographs
STATED PRINT RUN 6 SER.#'d SETS
NOT PRICED DUE TO SCARCITY

2009-10 Between The Pipes Emblems Autographs Gold
STATED PRINT RUN 1 SER.#'d SET
NOT PRICED DUE TO SCARCITY

2009-10 Between The Pipes Emblems Autographs Silver
STATED PRINT RUN 3 SER.#'d SETS
NOT PRICED DUE TO SCARCITY

2009-10 Between The Pipes Emblems Black
STATED PRINT RUN 6 SER.#'d SETS
NOT PRICED DUE TO SCARCITY

2009-10 Between The Pipes Emblems Gold
STATED PRINT RUN 1 SER.#'d SET
NOT PRICED DUE TO SCARCITY

2009-10 Between The Pipes Emblems Silver
STATED PRINT RUN 3 SER.#'d SETS
NOT PRICED DUE TO SCARCITY

2009-10 Between The Pipes Glove Save Black
STATED PRINT RUN 30 SER.#'d SETS
GS01 Cam Ward 12.00 30.00
GS02 Chris Osgood 15.00 40.00
GS03 Dominik Hasek 12.00 30.00
GS04 Ed Belfour 20.00 50.00
GS05 Evgeni Nabokov 12.00 30.00
GS06 Felix Potvin 20.00 50.00
GS07 Gerry Cheevers 25.00 60.00
GS08 Grant Fuhr 15.00 40.00
GS09 Hannu Toivonen 12.00 30.00
GS10 Jose Theodore 12.00 30.00
GS11 Jean-Sebastien Giguere 12.00 30.00
GS12 Kirk McLean 25.00 60.00
GS13 Leland Irving 12.00 30.00
GS14 Manny Fernandez 10.00 25.00
GS15 Manny Legace 10.00 25.00
GS16 Marc-Andre Fleury 12.00 30.00
GS17 Martin Brodeur 30.00 80.00
GS18 Marty Turco
GS19 Miikka Kiprusoff 12.00 30.00
GS20 Olaf Kolzig 12.00 30.00
GS21 Patrick Roy 40.00 100.00
GS22 Peter Budaj 12.00 30.00
GS23 Rick DiPietro 12.00 30.00
GS24 Roberto Luongo 30.00 80.00
GS25 Ron Hextall 25.00 60.00
GS26 Ryan Miller 25.00 50.00
GS27 Sean Burke 12.00 30.00
GS28 Tomas Vokoun 12.00 30.00
GS29 Tony Esposito 20.00 50.00
GS30 Vesa Toskala 12.00 30.00

2009-10 Between The Pipes Glove Save Gold
STATED PRINT RUN 1 SER.#'d SET
NOT PRICED DUE TO SCARCITY

2009-10 Between The Pipes Glove Save Silver
STATED PRINT RUN 9 SER.#'d SETS
NOT PRICED DUE TO SCARCITY

2009-10 Between The Pipes Gold Medal Masks
COMPLETE SET (9) 30.00 60.00
OVERALL STATED ODDS 1:8
GMM01 Tomas Vokoun 3.00 8.00
GMM02 Martin Brodeur 8.00 20.00
GMM03 Ilya Bryzgalov 2.50 6.00
GMM04 Jonas Hiller 4.00 10.00
GMM05 Miikka Kiprusoff 3.00 8.00
GMM06 Ryan Miller 3.00 8.00
GMM07 Roberto Luongo 8.00 20.00
GMM08 Jaroslav Halak 3.00 8.00
GMM09 Evgeni Nabokov 3.00 8.00

2009-10 Between The Pipes He Shoots, He Saves Gold
STATED PRINT RUN 1 SER.#'d SET
NOT PRICED DUE TO SCARCITY

2009-10 Between The Pipes He Shoots, He Saves Silver
STATED PRINT RUN 9 SER.#'d SETS
NOT PRICED DUE TO SCARCITY

2009-10 Between The Pipes Homegrown Black
STATED PRINT RUN 60 SER.#'d SETS
HG1 Martin Brodeur 15.00 40.00
HG2 Marc-Andre Fleury 15.00 40.00
HG3 Marty Turco 5.00 12.00
HG4 Roberto Luongo 15.00 40.00
HG5 Carey Price 15.00 40.00
HG6 Tomas Vokoun 6.00 15.00
HG7 Kari Lehtonen 6.00 15.00
HG8 Tuukka Rask 8.00 20.00
HG9 Miikka Kiprusoff 6.00 15.00
HG10 Niklas Backstrom 12.00 30.00
HG11 Vesa Toskala 6.00 15.00
HG12 Olaf Kolzig 6.00 15.00
HG13 Peter Budaj 6.00 15.00
HG14 Jaroslav Halak 6.00 15.00
HG15 Jacob Markstrom 15.00 40.00
HG16 Pelle Lindbergh 25.00 60.00
HG17 Evgeni Nabokov 6.00 15.00
HG18 Jonas Hiller 8.00 20.00
HG19 Tim Thomas 6.00 15.00
HG20 Rick DiPietro 6.00 15.00
HG21 Ryan Miller 15.00 40.00
HG22 Jonathan Quick 10.00 25.00
HG23 Ilya Bryzgalov 5.00 12.00
HG24 Simeon Varlamov 12.00 30.00

2009-10 Between The Pipes Homegrown Gold
STATED PRINT RUN 1 SER.#'d SET
NOT PRICED DUE TO SCARCITY

2009-10 Between The Pipes Homegrown Silver
STATED PRINT RUN 9 SER.#'d SETS
NOT PRICED DUE TO SCARCITY

2009-10 Between The Pipes International Crease Black
STATED PRINT RUN 60 SER.#'d SETS
IC01 Martin Brodeur 30.00 80.00
Roberto Luongo
Patrick Roy
IC02 Tim Thomas 25.00 60.00
Ryan Miller
Jim Craig
IC03 Jacob Markstrom 25.00 60.00
Henrik Lundqvist
Pelle Lindbergh
IC04 Miikka Kiprusoff 20.00 50.00
Kari Lehtonen
Vesa Toskala
IC05 Semyon Varlamov 15.00 40.00
Ilya Bryzgalov
Vladislav Tretiak
IC06 Ondrej Pavelec 15.00 40.00
Tomas Vokoun
Dominik Hasek

2009-10 Between The Pipes International Crease Gold
STATED PRINT RUN 1 SER.#'d SET
NOT PRICED DUE TO SCARCITY

2009-10 Between The Pipes International Crease Silver
STATED PRINT RUN 9 SER.#'d SETS
NOT PRICED DUE TO SCARCITY

2009-10 Between The Pipes Jerseys Autographs
STATED PRINT RUN 6 SER.#'d SETS
NOT PRICED DUE TO SCARCITY

2009-10 Between The Pipes Jerseys Autographs Gold
STATED PRINT RUN 1 SER.#'d SET
NOT PRICED DUE TO SCARCITY

2009-10 Between The Pipes Jerseys Autographs Silver
STATED PRINT RUN 3 SER.#'d SETS
NOT PRICED DUE TO SCARCITY

2009-10 Between The Pipes Jerseys Black
STATED PRINT RUN 130 SER.#'d SETS
M01 J.P Anderson 4.00 10.00
M02 Martin Brodeur 12.00 30.00
M03 Peter Budaj 5.00 12.00
M04 Trevor Cann 6.00 15.00
M05 Maxime Clermont 4.00 10.00
M06 John Curry 4.00 10.00
M07 Peter Delmas 4.00 10.00
M08 Cedrick Desjardins 8.00 20.00
M09 Louis Domingue
M10 Brian Elliott 4.00 10.00
M11 Andrew Engelage 10.00 25.00
M12 Marc-Andre Fleury 10.00 25.00
M13 Jean-Sebastien Giguere 8.00 20.00
M14 Jacob Markstrom 8.00 20.00
M15 Dominik Hasek 10.00 25.00
M16 Riku Helenius 5.00 12.00
M17 Braden Holtby 6.00 15.00
M18 Torrie Jung 6.00 15.00
M19 Anton Khudobin 5.00 12.00
M20 Kari Lehtonen 5.00 12.00
M21 Nathan Lieuwen 6.00 15.00
M22 Roberto Luongo 12.00 30.00
M23 Daren Machesney 4.00 10.00
M24 Drew MacIntyre 8.00 20.00
M25 Ryan Miller 8.00 20.00
M26 Mike Murphy 4.00 10.00
M27 Evgeni Nabokov 5.00 12.00
M28 Edward Pasquale 5.00 12.00
M29 Calvin Pickard 8.00 20.00
M30 Chet Pickard 6.00 15.00
M31 Felix Potvin 8.00 20.00
M32 Carey Price 12.00 30.00
M33 Jonathan Quick 8.00 20.00
M34 Nicola Riopel 4.00 10.00
M35 Olivier Roy 6.00 15.00
M36 Patrick Roy 15.00 40.00
M37 Patrick Roy 15.00 40.00
M38 Scott Stajcer 4.00 10.00
M39 Tim Thomas 5.00 12.00
M40 Dustin Tokarski 4.00 10.00
M41 Jamie Tucker 4.00 10.00
M42 Simeon Varlamov 10.00 25.00
M43 Mark Visentin 4.00 10.00
M44 Cam Ward 5.00 12.00
M45 Miika Wiikman 5.00 12.00
M46 Tony Esposito/40 8.00 20.00
M47 Bernie Parent/40 5.00 12.00
M48 Glenn Hall/40 10.00 25.00
M49 Ed Giacomin/40
M50 Ron Hextall/40

2009-10 Between The Pipes Jerseys Gold
STATED PRINT RUN 1 SER.#'d SET
NOT PRICED DUE TO SCARCITY

2009-10 Between The Pipes Jerseys Silver
STATED PRINT RUN 19 SER.#'d SETS
NOT PRICED DUE TO SCARCITY

2009-10 Between The Pipes Masked Men II
MM01 Gilles Gratton 2.00 5.00
MM02 Brian Hayward 2.50 6.00
MM03 Denis Herron 2.00 5.00
MM04 Patrick Roy 8.00 20.00
MM05 Felix Potvin 4.00 10.00
MM06 Ed Belfour 4.00 10.00
MM07 Ron Hextall 5.00 12.00
MM08 Martin Brodeur 6.00 15.00
MM09 Jimmy Howard 3.00 8.00
MM10 Evgeni Nabokov 2.50 6.00
MM11 Michael Houser 3.00 8.00
MM12 Mike McKenna 2.00 5.00
MM13 Tuukka Rask 3.00 8.00
MM14 Michal Neuvirth 6.00 15.00
MM15 Chet Pickard 3.00 8.00
MM16 James Reimer 2.50 6.00
MM17 Jean-Francois Berube 2.00 5.00
MM18 Evan Mosher 2.00 5.00
MM19 Olivier Roy 3.00 8.00
MM20 Frederic Piche 2.00 5.00
MM21 Patrick Roy 8.00 20.00
MM22 Jacques Plante 4.00 10.00
MM23 Grant Fuhr 3.00 8.00
MM24 Mark Dekanich 2.00 5.00
MM25 Chris Carrozzi 2.50 6.00
MM26 Riku Helenius 2.50 6.00
MM27 Braden Holtby 3.00 8.00
MM28 Dan LaCosta 2.00 5.00
MM29 Peter Mannino 2.50 6.00
MM30 Kevin Regan 2.50 6.00
MM31 Jeff Zatkoff 2.50 6.00
MM32 Jean-Philipp Gagnon 2.00 5.00
MM33 Tim Thomas 2.50 6.00
MM34 Miikka Kiprusoff 2.50 6.00
MM35 Roberto Luongo 6.00 15.00
MM36 Carey Price 6.00 15.00
MM37 Cristobal Huet 2.50 6.00
MM38 Ilya Bryzgalov 2.00 5.00
MM39 Scott Clemmensen 2.00 5.00
MM40 Louis Domingue 4.00 10.00
MM41 Craig Anderson 2.00 5.00
MM42 Ed Giacomin 3.00 8.00
MM43 Jason LaBarbera 2.00 5.00
MM44 Marc-Andre Fleury 2.50 6.00
MM45 Simeon Varlamov 5.00 12.00
MM46 Ryan Miller 2.50 6.00
MM47 Matthew Hackett 3.00 8.00
MM48 Chris Perugini 2.00 5.00
MM49 Cody St. Jacques 2.00 5.00
MM50 Doug Favell 2.50 6.00

2009-10 Between The Pipes Masked Men II Gold
ANNOUNCED PRINT RUN 20
NOT PRICED DUE TO SCARCITY

2009-10 Between The Pipes Mega Stars Black
STATED PRINT RUN 60 SER.#'d SETS
MS01 Patrick Roy 25.00 60.00
MS02 Felix Potvin 12.00 30.00
MS03 Chris Osgood 10.00 25.00
MS04 Ed Belfour 12.00 30.00
MS05 Martin Brodeur 20.00 50.00
MS06 Dominik Hasek 12.00 30.00
MS07 Martin Brodeur 20.00 50.00
MS08 Ed Belfour 12.00 30.00
MS09 Dominik Hasek 12.00 30.00
MS10 Patrick Roy 25.00 60.00
MS11 Arturs Irbe 12.00 30.00
MS12 Dominik Hasek 12.00 30.00
MS13 Olaf Kolzig 8.00 20.00
MS14 Martin Brodeur 20.00 50.00
MS15 Mike Richter 12.00 30.00
MS16 Tommy Salo 15.00 40.00
MS17 Dominik Hasek 12.00 30.00
MS18 Martin Brodeur 20.00 50.00
MS19 Patrick Roy 25.00 60.00
MS20 Evgeni Nabokov 8.00 20.00
MS21 Patrick Roy 25.00 60.00
MS22 Dominik Hasek 12.00 30.00
MS23 Patrick Roy 25.00 60.00
MS24 Rick DiPietro 8.00 20.00

2009-10 Between The Pipes Mega Stars Gold
STATED PRINT RUN 1 SER.#'d SET
NOT PRICED DUE TO SCARCITY

2009-10 Between The Pipes Mega Stars Silver
STATED PRINT RUN 9 SER.#'d SETS
NOT PRICED DUE TO SCARCITY

2009-10 Between The Pipes Net Brawlers
COMPLETE SET (9) 40.00 80.00
OVERALL STATED ODDS 1:8
NB01 Al Montoya 4.00 10.00
Rick DiPietro
NB02 Ty Conklin 3.00 8.00
Pasi Nurminen
NB03 Chris Osgood 12.00 30.00
Patrick Roy
NB04 Jani Hurme 6.00 15.00
Felix Potvin
NB05 Olaf Kolzig 4.00 10.00
Byron Dafoe
NB06 Tomas Vokoun 4.00 10.00
Miikka Kiprusoff
NB07 Corey Crawford 4.00 10.00
Al Montoya
NB08 Michael Leighton 5.00 12.00
Jimmy Howard
NB09 Ron Hextall 8.00 20.00
Felix Potvin

2009-10 Between The Pipes Numbers Autographs
STATED PRINT RUN 6 SER.#'d SETS
NOT PRICED DUE TO SCARCITY

2009-10 Between The Pipes Numbers Autographs Gold
STATED PRINT RUN 1 SER.#'d SET
NOT PRICED DUE TO SCARCITY

2009-10 Between The Pipes Numbers Autographs Silver
STATED PRINT RUN 3 SER.#'d SETS
NOT PRICED DUE TO SCARCITY

2009-10 Between The Pipes Numbers Black
STATED PRINT RUN 6 SER.#'d SETS
NOT PRICED DUE TO SCARCITY

2009-10 Between The Pipes Numbers Gold
STATED PRINT RUN 1 SER.#'d SET
NOT PRICED DUE TO SCARCITY

2009-10 Between The Pipes Numbers Silver
STATED PRINT RUN 3 SER.#'d SETS
NOT PRICED DUE TO SCARCITY

2009-10 Between The Pipes Origins Black
STATED PRINT RUN 40 SER.#'d SETS
O01 Gerry Cheevers 15.00 40.00
O02 Tony Esposito 12.00 30.00
O03 Bernie Parent 8.00 20.00
O04 Billy Smith 8.00 20.00
O05 Rogie Vachon 12.00 30.00
O06 Ed Belfour 12.00 30.00
O07 Miikka Kiprusoff 8.00 20.00
O08 Dominik Hasek 8.00 20.00
O09 Roberto Luongo 20.00 50.00
O10 Jean-Sebastien Giguere 8.00 20.00

2009-10 Between The Pipes Origins Gold
STATED PRINT RUN 1 SER.#'d SET
NOT PRICED DUE TO SCARCITY

2009-10 Between The Pipes Origins Silver
STATED PRINT RUN 9 SER.#'d SETS
NOT PRICED DUE TO SCARCITY

2009-10 Between The Pipes Pad Save Black
STATED PRINT RUN 60 SER.#'d SETS
PS01 David Aebischer 12.00 30.00
PS02 Ed Belfour 15.00 40.00
PS03 Brian Boucher 10.00 25.00
PS04 Martin Brodeur 25.00 60.00
PS05 Sean Burke 10.00 25.00
PS06 Gerry Cheevers 20.00 50.00
PS07 Dan Cloutier 8.00 20.00
PS08 Robert Esche 10.00 25.00
PS09 Grant Fuhr 12.00 30.00
PS10 Ron Hextall 20.00 50.00
PS11 Leland Irving 10.00 25.00
PS12 Curtis Joseph 25.00 60.00
PS13 Nikolai Khabibulin 10.00 25.00
PS14 Patrick Lalime 8.00 20.00
PS15 Pelle Lindbergh 75.00 150.00
PS16 Chris Osgood 12.00 30.00
PS17 Bernie Parent 20.00 50.00
PS18 Patrick Roy 30.00 80.00
PS19 Patrick Roy 30.00 80.00
PS20 Jose Theodore 10.00 25.00
PS21 Tim Thomas 10.00 25.00
PS22 Vladislav Tretiak 40.00 80.00
PS23 Marty Turco 8.00 20.00
PS24 Mike Vernon 12.00 30.00
PS25 Tomas Vokoun 10.00 25.00

2009-10 Between The Pipes Pad Save Gold
STATED PRINT RUN 1 SER.#'d SET
NOT PRICED DUE TO SCARCITY

2009-10 Between The Pipes Pad Save Silver
STATED PRINT RUN 9 SER.#'d SETS
NOT PRICED DUE TO SCARCITY

2009-10 Between The Pipes Roots of Goaltending
STATED PRINT RUN 1 SER.#'d SET
NOT PRICED DUE TO SCARCITY

2009-10 Between The Pipes Stick Save Black
STATED PRINT RUN 20 SER.#'d SETS
NOT PRICED DUE TO SCARCITY

2009-10 Between The Pipes Stick Save Gold

STATED PRINT RUN 1 SER.#'d SET
NOT PRICED DUE TO SCARCITY

2009-10 Between The Pipes Stick Save Silver

STATED PRINT RUN 9 SER.#'d SETS
NOT PRICED DUE TO SCARCITY

1996-97 Black Diamond

This hobby-only set was issued in one series totaling 180 cards, with three varying levels of difficulty: Single Black Diamond (1-90), Double Black Diamond (91-150), and Triple Black Diamond (151-180). Doubles were inserted 1:4 packs and Triples 1:30 packs. Packs of six cards retailed for $3.49. This set is most noteworthy because of the inlcusion of one of the most sought after RCs to date, #160 Joe Thornton. The Gretzky promo mirrors the regular issue, aside from the word SAMPLE which runs across his portrait on the card back. This set was extremely condition sensitive.

COMPLETE SET (180) 350.00 600.00
COMP.SINGLE SET (90) 10.00 25.00
91-150 DOUBLE DIAMOND ODDS 1:4
151-180 TRIPLE DIAMOND ODDS 1:30
1 Roman Turek RC .40 1.00
2 Slava Fetisov .08 .25
3 Mike Dunham .20 .50
4 Jean-Francois Fortin RC .20 .50
5 Keith Primeau .08 .25
6 Zigmund Palffy .20 .50
7 Curtis Leschyshyn .08 .25
8 Vladimir Tsyplakov RC .20 .50
9 Adam Graves .08 .25
10 Ian Laperriere .08 .25
11 Bill Lindsay .08 .25
12 Brian Leetch .40 1.00
13 Martin Lapointe .08 .25
14 Scott Barney RC .40 1.00
15 Mike Grier RC .75 2.00
16 Vladimir Konstantinov .20 .50
17 Rem Murray RC .20 .50
18 Ed Jovanovski .20 .50
19 Chris O'Sullivan .08 .25
20 Steve Rucchin .08 .25
21 Jay Pandolfo .08 .25
22 Nick Boynton RC .60 1.50
23 Greg Adams .08 .25
24 Adam Colagiacomo RC .40 1.00
25 Vincent Damphousse .08 .25
26 Shane Willis RC .60 1.50
27 Alexei Kovalev .08 .25
28 Doug Gilmour .20 .50
29 Joel Otto .08 .25
30 Donald Audette .08 .25
31 Tommy Salo .20 .50
32 Rob Ray .08 .25
33 Kris Draper .08 .25
34 Ed Belfour .40 1.00
35 Mike Richter .40 1.00
36 Nikolai Khabibulin .20 .50
37 Eric Desjardins .20 .50
38 Daniel Tkaczuk RC .40 1.00
39 Keith Jones .20 .50
40 Per Gustafsson RC .20 .50
41 Jocelyn Thibault .40 1.00
42 Mike Gartner .20 .50
43 Vitali Yachmenev .08 .25
44 Jonas Hoglund .08 .25
45 Craig Janney .08 .25
46 Daymond Langkow .20 .50
47 Mattias Timander RC .20 .50
48 Scott Young .08 .25
49 Mikael Renberg .08 .25
50 Nicklas Lidstrom .40 1.00
51 Andrei Kovalenko .08 .25
52 Adam Foote .08 .25
53 Guy Hebert .20 .50
54 Kevin Hatcher .08 .25
55 Rick Tocchet .08 .25
56 Sergei Zubov .08 .25
57 Chris Phillips .08 .25
58 Denis Savard .20 .50
59 Bernie Nicholls .08 .25
60 Jozef Stumpel .08 .25
61 Darius Kasparaitis .08 .25
62 Kelly Hrudey .20 .50
63 Marcel Cousineau RC .40 1.00
64 Brian Skrudland .08 .25
65 Byron Dafoe .20 .50
66 Ray Sheppard .08 .25
67 Chris Simon .08 .25
68 Dainius Zubrus RC .75 2.00
69 Ethan Moreau RC .40 1.00
70 Theo Fleury .08 .25
71 Damian Rhodes .20 .50
72 Kevin Dineen .08 .25
73 Kenny Jonsson .08 .25
74 Ray Ferraro .08 .25
75 Jaromir Jagr .60 1.50
76 Wayne Primeau .08 .25
77 Chris Gratton .08 .25
78 Alyn McCauley .40 1.00
79 Christian Dube .20 .50
80 Bill Ranford .20 .50
81 Adam Deadmarsh .08 .25
82 Dale Hunter .20 .50
83 Derek Plante .08 .25
84 Todd Bertuzzi .40 1.00
85 Stephane Fiset .20 .50
86 Boyd Devereaux RC .40 1.00
87 Jere Lehtinen .08 .25
88 Peter Schaefer RC 1.00 2.50
89 Alexander Mogilny .20 .50
90 Joe Juneau .20 .50
91 Alexandre Daigle .60 1.50
92 Jeff O'Neill .60 1.50
93 Todd Warriner .60 1.50
94 Sergei Berezin RC .60 1.50
95 Petr Nedved .60 1.50
96 Phil Housley .60 1.50
97 Jason Arnott 1.25 3.00
98 Sandis Ozolinsh .60 1.50
99 Mike Modano 2.00 5.00
100 Mark Messier 2.00 5.00
101 Ron Francis 1.25 3.00
102 Oleg Tverdovsky .60 1.50
103 Patrick Marleau RC 25.00 60.00
104 Brian Bellows .60 1.50
105 Eric Fichaud .60 1.50
106 Alexei Zhamnov .60 1.50
107 Wendel Clark .60 1.50
108 Dimitri Khristich .60 1.50
109 Mike Ricci .60 1.50
110 John LeClair 2.00 5.00
111 Owen Nolan 1.25 3.00
112 Bill Guerin 1.25 3.00
113 Vyacheslav Kozlov .60 1.50
114 Brendan Shanahan 2.00 5.00
115 Trevor Linden .60 1.50
116 Jose Theodore 2.00 5.00
117 Rod Brind'Amour 1.25 3.00
118 Brian Holzinger .60 1.50
119 Shayne Corson .60 1.50
120 Bryan Smolinski .60 1.50
121 Tony Granato .60 1.50
122 Mariusz Czerkawski .60 1.50
123 Andrew Cassels .60 1.50
124 Scott Stevens 1.25 3.00
125 Mike Ridley .60 1.50
126 Jamie Langenbrunner .60 1.50
127 Scott Mellanby .60 1.50
128 Grant Fuhr 1.25 3.00
129 Felix Potvin 1.25 3.00
130 Marc Denis .60 1.50
131 Corey Hirsch .60 1.50
132 Chris Osgood 1.25 3.00
133 Peter Bondra 1.25 3.00
134 Martin Brodeur 4.00 10.00
135 Pierre Turgeon 1.25 3.00
136 Pat Verbeek .60 1.50
137 Scott Niedermayer .60 1.50
138 Geoff Sanderson .60 1.50
139 Jason Dawe .60 1.50
140 Rob Niedermayer .60 1.50
141 Daniel Alfredsson 1.25 3.00
142 Jim Campbell .60 1.50
143 Roman Hamrlik .60 1.50
144 Rob Blake 1.25 3.00
145 Chris Chelios 2.00 5.00
146 Teemu Selanne .40 1.00
147 Jim Carey 1.25 3.00
148 Dino Ciccarelli .60 1.50
149 Mark Recchi 1.25 3.00
150 Chris Pronger 1.25 3.00
151 Paul Coffey 4.00 10.00
152 Adam Oates 3.00 6.00
153 Keith Tkachuk 4.00 10.00
154 Janne Niinimaa 2.00 5.00
155 Sergei Fedorov 6.00 15.00
156 Dominik Hasek 10.00 25.00
157 Eric Lindros 4.00 10.00
158 Curtis Joseph 4.00 10.00
159 Alexei Yashin 2.00 5.00
160 Joe Thornton RC 175.00 350.00
161 Bryan Berard 2.00 5.00
162 Steve Yzerman 15.00 40.00
163 Mats Sundin 5.00 12.00
164 Jarome Iginla 6.00 15.00
165 John Vanbiesbrouck 3.00 6.00
166 Mario Lemieux 20.00 50.00
167 Jeremy Roenick 8.00 20.00
168 Patrick Lalime RC 25.00 50.00
169 Joe Sakic 10.00 25.00
170 Brett Hull 5.00 12.00
171 Peter Forsberg 8.00 20.00
172 Doug Weight 3.00 6.00
173 Tony Amonte 3.00 6.00
174 Patrick Roy 20.00 50.00
175 Paul Kariya 5.00 12.00
176 Pavel Bure 5.00 12.00
177 Ray Bourque 8.00 20.00
178 Saku Koivu 5.00 12.00
179 Wade Redden 2.00 5.00
180 Wayne Gretzky 30.00 80.00
P180 Wayne Gretzky Promo 1.00 2.50

1951 Berk Ross

The 1951 Berk Ross set consists of 72 cards (each measuring approximately 2 1/16" by 2 1/2") with tinted photographs, divided evenly into four series (designated in the checklist as A, B, C and D). The cards were marketed in boxes containing two card panels, without gum, and the set includes stars of other sports as well as baseball players. The set is sometimes still found in the original packaging. Intact panels are worth 25 percent more than the sum of the individual cards. The catalog designation for this set is W532-1. In every series the first ten cards are baseball players; the set has a heavy emphasis on Yankees and Phillies players as they were in the World Series the year before. The set includes the first card of Bob Cousy as well as a card of Whitey Ford in his Rookie Card year.

COMPLETE SET (72) 900.00 1500.00
1-17 Bill Durnan Hockey 50.00 100.00
1-18 Bill Quackenbush Hockey 40.00 80.00
2-16 Jack Stewart Hockey 20.00 40.00
3-16 Sid Abel Hockey 40.00 80.00

1996-97 Black Diamond Gold

This was a gold-foil parallel to the three-tiered Upper Deck Black Diamond set. Single golds were inserted 1:15 packs, Doubles 1:46, and Triples, for which an insertion ratio was not announced, were limited to just 50 sets.

*SINGLE STARS: 3X TO 8X BASIC CARDS
*SINGLE ROOKIES: 1.2X TO 3X
1-90 SINGLE DIAMOND ODDS 1:15
*DOUBLE STARS: 1.2X TO 3X BASIC CARDS
*DOUBLE ROOKIES: .8X TO 2X
91-150 DOUBLE DIAMOND ODDS 1:46
*TRIPLE STARS: 1.5X TO 4X BASIC CARDS
*TRIPLE ROOKIES: 1.2X TO 3X
151-180 TRIPLE DIAMOND PRINT RUN 50

1996-97 Black Diamond Run for the Cup

Each card in this set was individually numbered to just 100 sets, printed on cel-chrome, and feature high profile players.

RANDOM INSERTS IN PACKS
STATED PRINT RUN 100 SERIAL #'d SETS
RC1 Wayne Gretzky 200.00 350.00
RC2 Saku Koivu 30.00 80.00
RC3 Mario Lemieux 150.00 250.00
RC4 Patrick Roy 150.00 250.00
RC5 Jaromir Jagr 30.00 80.00
RC6 John Vanbiesbrouck 15.00 40.00
RC7 Peter Forsberg 30.00 80.00
RC8 Paul Kariya 30.00 80.00
RC9 Steve Yzerman 125.00 250.00
RC10 Joe Sakic 75.00 150.00
RC11 Mark Messier 40.00 100.00
RC12 Sergei Fedorov 30.00 80.00
RC13 Mats Sundin 30.00 80.00
RC14 Pavel Bure 30.00 80.00
RC15 Ed Jovanovski 15.00 40.00
RC16 Mike Modano 30.00 80.00
RC17 Curtis Joseph 15.00 40.00
RC18 Teemu Selanne 30.00 80.00
RC19 Jarome Iginla 30.00 80.00
RC20 Eric Lindros 15.00 40.00

1997-98 Black Diamond

The 1997-98 Upper Deck Black Diamond set was issued in one series totaling 150 cards and distributed in six-card packs with a suggested retail price of $3.49. The fronts feature color action player photos reproduced on Light F/X card stock with foil treatment and one, two, three, or four Black Diamonds on the front designating its rarity. The backs carry player information and statistics.

COMPLETE SET (150) 60.00 120.00
1 Alexei Zhitnik .07 .20
2 Adam Graves .07 .20
3 Keith Primeau .07 .20
4 Mike Richter .25 .60
5 Felix Potvin .25 .60
6 Valeri Bure .07 .20
7 Mark Messier .25 .60
8 Dainius Zubrus .25 .60
9 Owen Nolan .20 .50
10 Kenny Jonsson .07 .20
11 Ron Francis .20 .50
12 Bryan Berard .07 .20
13 Eric Messier RC .20 .50
14 Paul Kariya .25 .60
15 Teemu Elomo RC .20 .50
16 Joe Nieuwendyk .07 .20
17 Scott Stevens .20 .50
18 Zigmund Palffy .20 .50
19 Brett Hull .30 .75
20 Dominik Hasek .50 1.25
21 Dino Ciccarelli .07 .20
22 Rob Niedermayer .07 .20
23 Mark Recchi .20 .50
24 Brad Isbister .07 .20
25 Timo Vertala RC .07 .20
26 Mika Noronen RC .75 2.00
27 Sandis Ozolinsh .07 .20
28 Chris Phillips .07 .20
29 Chris Chelios .25 .60
30 Jason Dawe .07 .20
31 Kirk McLean .20 .50
32 Jason Allison .07 .20
33 Brian Leetch .25 .60
34 Guy Hebert .07 .20
35 David Legwand RC 1.00 2.50
36 Pierre Hedin RC .20 .50
37 Sergei Samsonov .20 .50
38 Bill Guerin .20 .50
39 Chris Osgood .20 .50
40 Jere Lehtinen .07 .20
41 Patrick Roy 1.25 3.00
42 John Vanbiesbrouck .20 .50
43 Maxim Afinogenov RC 2.00 5.00
44 Patrik Elias RC 2.00 5.00
45 Josh Holden .07 .20
46 Saku Koivu .25 .60
47 Maxim Balmochnykh RC .40 1.00
48 Pasi Petrilainen .07 .20
49 Robert Reichel .07 .20
50 Wade Redden .07 .20
51 Richard Zednik .07 .20
52 Ty Jones RC .25 .60
53 Nikolai Khabibulin .20 .50
54 Kyle McLaren .07 .20
55 Daniel Tkaczuk .25 .60
56 Alexei Zhamnov .07 .20
57 Donald MacLean RC .07 .20
58 Dave Gagner .07 .20
59 Jeremy Roenick .30 .75
60 Ray Bourque .40 1.00
61 Rod Brind'Amour .20 .50
62 Miroslav Satan .07 .20
63 Eric Daze .20 .50
64 Mike Ricci .07 .20
65 John LeClair .25 .60
66 Bryan Marchment .07 .20
67 Henrik Petre RC .20 .50
68 John MacLean .07 .20
69 Artem Chubarov RC .20 .50
70 Doug Gilmour .20 .50
71 Marco Sturm RC 1.00 2.50
72 Jaromir Jagr .40 1.00
73 Daniel Alfredsson .20 .50
74 Daren Puppa .20 .50
75 Adam Deadmarsh .07 .20
76 Luc Robitaille .20 .50
77 Mats Sundin .25 .60
78 Dan Cloutier .07 .20
79 Manny Malhotra RC .75 2.00
80 Mike Modano .40 1.00
81 Espen Knutsen RC .75 2.00
82 Sergei Fedorov .40 1.00
83 Chris Pronger .20 .50
84 Doug Weight .20 .50
85 Dmitri Nabokov .07 .20
86 Gary Roberts .07 .20
87 Peter Bondra .20 .50
88 Robert Dome RC .07 .20
89 Jan Bulis RC .07 .20
90 Eric Brewer RC 1.25 3.00
91 Nikos Tselios RC .07 .20
92 Scott Mellanby .07 .20
93 Vitali Vishnevsky RC .40 1.00
94 Derian Hatcher .07 .20
95 Teemu Selanne .25 .60
96 Joe Sakic .50 1.25
97 Alexander Mogilny .20 .50
98 Jesse Boulerice RC .40 1.00
99 Johan Forsander RC .07 .20
100 Pierre Turgeon .20 .50
101 Tony Amonte .20 .50
102 Timo Ahmaoja RC .07 .20
103 Rob Blake .07 .20
104 Derek Morris RC .40 1.00
105 Alex Tanguay RC 4.00 10.00
106 Peter Forsberg .60 1.50
107 Shayne Corson .07 .20
108 Tyler Moss RC .20 .50
109 Adam Oates .20 .50
110 Keith Tkachuk .25 .60
111 Alexei Yashin .07 .20
112 Joe Thornton .60 1.50
113 Andy Moog .20 .50
114 Daniel Sedin RC 2.50 6.00
115 Pavel Bure .25 .60
116 Denis Shvidki RC .40 1.00
117 Jason Arnott .07 .20
118 Mike Johnson RC .40 1.00
119 Nicklas Lidstrom .25 .60
120 Mattias Ohlund .20 .50
121 Alexander Selivanov .07 .20
122 Martin Brodeur .60 1.50
123 Steve Yzerman 1.25 3.00
124 Dimitri Vlassenkov RC .20 .50
125 Jeff Farkas RC .40 1.00
126 Curtis Joseph .25 .60
127 Yanic Perreault .07 .20
128 Alyn McCauley .20 .50
129 Vyacheslav Kozlov .07 .20
130 Alexei Morozov .20 .50
131 Roberto Luongo RC 10.00 25.00
132 Jarome Iginla .30 .75
133 Pat LaFontaine .25 .60
134 Ed Belfour .25 .60
135 Toby Petersen RC .75 2.00
136 Henrik Sedin RC 3.00 8.00
137 Marcus Nilson .07 .20
138 Cameron Mann .25 .60
139 Eero Somervuori RC .20 .50
140 Patrick Marleau .40 1.00
141 Ed Jovanovski .20 .50
142 Roman Hamrlik .07 .20
143 Theo Fleury .07 .20
144 Wayne Gretzky 1.50 4.00
145 Eric Lindros .25 .60
146 Boyd Devereaux .07 .20
147 Sami Kapanen .07 .20
148 Grant Fuhr .07 .20
149 Brendan Shanahan .25 .60
150 Vincent Lecavalier RC 8.00 20.00

1997-98 Black Diamond Double Diamond

Inserted one in every pack, this 150-card set is a two black diamond parallel version of the Upper Deck Black Diamond base set.

*VETS: .75X TO 2X BASIC CARDS
*ROOKIES: .6X TO 1.5X
STATED ODDS 1:1

1997-98 Black Diamond Triple Diamond

Randomly inserted in packs at the rate of 1:3, this 150-card set is an all-gold Light F/X parallel version of the base set with three black diamonds printed on the card fronts.

*VETS: 3X TO 8X BASIC CARDS
*ROOKIES: 1.2X TO 3X
STATED ODDS 1:3

1997-98 Black Diamond Quadruple Diamond

Randomly inserted in packs, this 150-card set is an all-black Light F/X parallel version of the base set with four black diamonds printed on the card fronts. Only 50 sets were produced.

*VETS: 15X TO 40X BASIC CARDS
*ROOKIES: 4X TO 10X
STATED PRINT RUN 50 SETS
150 Vincent Lecavalier 75.00 150.00

1997-98 Black Diamond Premium Cut

Randomly inserted in packs at the rate of 1:7, this 30-card set features color action photos of top stars printed in a Light F/X card design with a single black diamond.

COMPLETE SET (30) 75.00 150.00
SINGLE DIAMOND ODDS 1:7
*DOUBLE DIAM: .6X TO 1.5X BASIC INSERTS
DOUBLE DIAMOND ODDS 1:15
*TRIPLE DIAM: 1X TO 2.5X BASIC INSERTS
TRIPLE DIAMOND ODDS 1:30
*QUAD VERTICAL: 3X TO 8X BASIC INSERTS
QUAD VERTICAL ODDS 1:180
PC1 Wayne Gretzky 12.50 30.00
PC2 Patrick Roy 10.00 25.00
PC3 Brendan Shanahan 2.00 5.00
PC4 Ray Bourque 2.00 5.00
PC5 Alexei Morozov 1.00 2.50
PC6 John LeClair 1.00 2.50
PC7 Steve Yzerman 8.00 20.00
PC8 Patrik Elias 1.00 2.50
PC9 Pavel Bure 2.00 5.00
PC10 Brian Leetch 2.00 5.00
PC11 Peter Forsberg 4.00 10.00
PC12 Marco Sturm 1.00 2.50
PC13 Eric Lindros 2.00 5.00
PC14 Keith Tkachuk 1.00 2.50
PC15 Teemu Selanne 2.00 5.00
PC16 Bryan Berard 1.00 2.50
PC17 Joe Thornton 3.00 8.00
PC18 Brett Hull 2.50 6.00
PC19 Nicklas Lidstrom 2.00 5.00
PC20 Jaromir Jagr 3.00 8.00
PC21 Vaclav Prospal 1.00 2.50
PC22 Pat LaFontaine 2.00 5.00
PC23 Mark Messier 2.00 5.00
PC24 Martin Brodeur 5.00 12.00
PC25 Mike Modano 2.50 6.00
PC26 Paul Kariya 2.00 5.00
PC27 Mike Johnson 1.00 2.50
PC28 Sergei Samsonov 1.00 2.50
PC29 Joe Sakic 4.00 10.00
PC30 Mats Sundin 2.00 5.00

1997-98 Black Diamond Premium Cut Quadruple Diamond Horizontal

This 30-card hobby only set is a special black Light F/X, embossed, horizontal, die-cut version of the regular insert set with various insertion rates. Cards #8, 10, 16, 17, 18, 19, 23, 27, 29 and 30 have an insertion rate of 1:30; #4, 5, 7, 12, 14, 15, 21, 22, 25 and 26 have a 1:90 insertion rate; #6, 9, 11, 20, 24 and 28 have a 1:2000 insertion rate; #3 and 13 have a 1:15,000 insertion rate; and #1 and 2 have a 1:30,000 insertion rate.

8/10/16/17/18/19/23/27/29/30 ODDS 1:30

4/5/7/12/14/15/21/22/25/26 ODDS 1:90
6/9/11/20/24/28 ODDS 1:2,000
3/13 ODDS 1:15,000
PC1 Wayne Gretzky 300.00 800.00
PC2 Patrick Roy 200.00 500.00
PC3 Brendan Shanahan 60.00 150.00
PC4 Ray Bourque 6.00 15.00
PC5 Alexei Morozov 5.00 12.00
PC6 John LeClair 50.00 125.00
PC7 Steve Yzerman 20.00 50.00
PC8 Patrik Elias 3.00 8.00
PC9 Pavel Bure 60.00 150.00
PC10 Brian Leetch 1.50 4.00
PC11 Peter Forsberg 60.00 150.00
PC12 Marco Sturm 8.00 20.00
PC13 Eric Lindros 60.00 150.00
PC14 Keith Tkachuk 5.00 12.00
PC15 Teemu Selanne 5.00 12.00
PC16 Bryan Berard 1.50 4.00
PC17 Joe Thornton 5.00 12.00
PC18 Brett Hull 2.50 6.00
PC19 Nicklas Lidstrom 2.00 5.00
PC20 Jaromir Jagr 50.00 125.00
PC21 Vaclav Prospal 5.00 12.00
PC22 Pat LaFontaine 5.00 12.00
PC23 Mark Messier 1.50 4.00
PC24 Martin Brodeur 50.00 125.00
PC25 Mike Modano 8.00 20.00
PC26 Paul Kariya 12.50 30.00
PC27 Mike Johnson 1.50 4.00
PC28 Sergei Samsonov 30.00 80.00
PC29 Joe Sakic 4.00 10.00
PC30 Mats Sundin 2.00 5.00

1998-99 Black Diamond

The 1998-99 Upper Deck Black Diamond set was issued in one series for a total of 120 cards and was distributed in six-card packs with a suggested retail price of $3.99. The fronts feature color action player photos reproduced on Light F/X card stock with foil treatment and one, two, three, or four Black Diamonds designating its rarity. Cards 1-90 are regular player cards with cards 91-120 displaying top prospect players and an insertion rate of 1:4 for the single diamond cards. The backs carry player information and statistics. Only 2,000 Double Diamond sets were produced, 1,000 Triple Diamond sets, and 100 Quadruple Diamond sets.

COMPLETE SET (120) 60.00 125.00
COMP.SET w/o SP's (90) 10.00 20.00
SP 91-120 STATED ODDS 1:4
1 Paul Kariya .25 .60
2 Teemu Selanne .25 .60
3 Johan Davidsson .08 .25
4 Ray Bourque .40 1.00
5 Sergei Samsonov .20 .50
6 Jason Allison .08 .25
7 Joe Thornton .40 1.00
8 Miroslav Satan .20 .50
9 Brian Holzinger .08 .25
10 Dominik Hasek .50 1.25
11 Rico Fata .08 .25
12 Jarome Iginla .30 .75
13 Theo Fleury .08 .25
14 Ron Francis .20 .50
15 Gary Roberts .08 .25
16 Keith Primeau .08 .25
17 Sami Kapanen .08 .25
18 Doug Gilmour .20 .50
19 Chris Chelios .25 .60
20 Tony Amonte .20 .50
21 Peter Forsberg .60 1.50
22 Patrick Roy 1.25 3.00
23 Joe Sakic .50 1.25
24 Chris Drury .20 .50
25 Brett Hull .30 .75
26 Ed Belfour .25 .60
27 Mike Modano .40 1.00
28 Darryl Sydor .08 .25
29 Sergei Fedorov .40 1.00
30 Steve Yzerman 1.25 3.00
31 Nicklas Lidstrom .25 .60
32 Chris Osgood .20 .50
33 Brendan Shanahan .25 .60
34 Doug Weight .20 .50
35 Bill Guerin .08 .25
36 Tom Poti .08 .25
37 Pavel Bure .25 .60
38 Mark Parrish RC 1.25 3.00
39 Rob Niedermayer .08 .25
40 Pavel Rosa RC .08 .25
41 Rob Blake .08 .25
42 Olli Jokinen .20 .50
43 Vincent Damphousse .08 .25
44 Mark Recchi .20 .50
45 Terry Ryan .08 .25
46 Saku Koivu .20 .50
47 Mike Dunham .20 .50
48 Sergei Krivokrasov .08 .25
49 Scott Stevens .20 .50
50 Martin Brodeur .60 1.50
51 Brendan Morrison .20 .50
52 Eric Brewer .08 .25
53 Zigmund Palffy .20 .50
54 Felix Potvin .25 .60
55 Wayne Gretzky 1.50 4.00
56 Brian Leetch .25 .60
57 Manny Malhotra .08 .25
58 Mike Richter .25 .60
59 Alexei Yashin .08 .25
60 Wade Redden .08 .25
61 Daniel Alfredsson .20 .50
62 Eric Lindros .25 .60
63 John LeClair .25 .60
64 John Vanbiesbrouck .20 .50
65 Rod Brind'Amour .20 .50
66 Keith Tkachuk .25 .60
67 Daniel Briere .08 .25
68 Jeremy Roenick .30 .75
69 Jaromir Jagr .40 1.00
70 German Titov .08 .25
71 Alexei Morozov .20 .50
72 Patrick Marleau .08 .25
73 Andrei Zyuzin .08 .25
74 Mike Vernon .20 .50
75 Owen Nolan .20 .50
76 Marty Reasoner .20 .50
77 Al MacInnis .20 .50
78 Chris Pronger .20 .50
79 Wendel Clark .20 .50
80 Vincent Lecavalier .60 1.50
81 Craig Janney .08 .25
82 Tomas Kaberle RC .60 1.50
83 Curtis Joseph .25 .60
84 Mats Sundin .25 .60
85 Mark Messier .25 .60
86 Bill Muckalt RC .20 .50
87 Mattias Ohlund .20 .50
88 Peter Bondra .20 .50
89 Olaf Kolzig .20 .50
90 Richard Zednik .08 .25
91 Harold Druken SP 1.25 3.00
92 Roberto Luongo SP 1.25 3.00
93 Daniel Tkaczuk SP 1.00 2.50
94 Brenden Morrow SP RC 2.00 5.00
95 Mike Van Ryn SP 1.00 2.50
96 Brian Finley SP RC 1.00 2.50
97 Jani Rita SP RC 1.25 3.00
98 Iikka Mikkola SP RC 1.25 3.00
99 Mikko Jokela SP RC 1.25 3.00
100 Tommi Santala SP RC 1.25 3.00
101 Teemu Virkkunnen SP RC 1.25 3.00
102 Arto Laatikainen SP RC 1.25 3.00
103 Kirill Safronov SP RC 1.25 3.00
104 Alexei Volkov SP RC 1.25 3.00
105 Denis Arkhipov SP RC 1.25 3.00
106 Alexander Zevakhin SP RC 1.25 3.00
107 Denis Shvidki SP 1.25 3.00
108 Maxim Afinogenov SP 1.25 3.00
109 Daniel Sedin SP 1.25 3.00
110 Henrik Sedin SP 1.25 3.00
111 Jimmie Olvestad SP RC 1.25 3.00
112 Mattias Weinhandl SP RC 1.25 3.00
113 Mathias Tjarnqvist SP RC 1.25 3.00
114 Jakob Johansson SP RC 1.25 3.00
115 David Legwand SP 1.25 3.00
116 Barrett Heisten SP RC 1.25 3.00
117 Tim Connolly SP RC 1.50 4.00
118 Andy Hilbert SP RC 1.25 3.00
119 Joe Blackburn SP RC 1.25 3.00
120 Dave Tanabe SP RC 1.25 3.00

1998-99 Black Diamond Double Diamond

Randomly inserted into packs, this 120-card set is a parallel version of the base set displaying two black diamonds on the card fronts. Only 2,000 sets were made.

*1-90 SINGLES: 2X TO 5X BASIC CARDS
*91-120 SINGLES: .6X TO 1.5X BASIC SP
STATED PRINT RUN 2000 SER.#'d SETS

1998-99 Black Diamond Triple Diamond

Randomly inserted into packs, this 120-card set is a parallel version of the base set displaying three black diamonds on the card fronts. Only 1,000 sets were made.

*1-90 TRIPLE: 3X TO 8X BASIC CARDS
*91-120 TRIPLE: 1.2X TO 3X BASIC SP
STATED PRINT RUN 1000 SER.#'d SETS

1998-99 Black Diamond Quadruple Diamond

Randomly inserted into packs, this 120-card set is a parallel version of the base set displaying four black diamonds on the card fronts. Only 100 sets were made.

*1-90 QUADS: 30X TO 60X BASIC CARDS
*91-120 QUADS: 4X TO 10X BASIC SP
STATED PRINT RUN 100 SER.#'d SETS

1998-99 Black Diamond Myriad

Randomly inserted into packs, this 30-card set features color action photos of the current top NHL's superstars. Only 1,500 serially numbered sets were produced. A limited edition parallel version of this set, Myriad 2, was produced and numbered 1 of 1.

COMPLETE SET (30)
STATED PRINT RUN 1500 SER.#'d SETS
UNPRICED MYRIAD 2 PRINT RUN 1
M1 Vincent Lecavalier 6.00 15.00
M2 John Vanbiesbrouck 2.00 5.00
M3 Paul Kariya 2.50 6.00
M4 Keith Tkachuk 2.50 6.00
M5 Mike Modano 4.00 10.00
M6 Dominik Hasek 5.00 12.00
M7 Teemu Selanne 2.50 6.00
M8 Manny Malhotra 1.00 2.50
M9 Brendan Shanahan 2.50 6.00
M10 Pavel Bure 2.50 6.00
M11 Chris Drury 2.00 5.00
M12 Curtis Joseph 2.50 6.00
M13 Joe Sakic 5.00 12.00
M14 Eric Lindros 2.50 6.00
M15 Peter Bondra 2.00 5.00
M16 Brett Hull 4.00 10.00
M17 Ray Bourque 4.00 10.00
M18 Jaromir Jagr 4.00 10.00
M19 Steve Yzerman 12.50 30.00
M20 Mark Parrish 4.00 10.00
M21 Martin Brodeur 6.00 15.00
M22 Saku Koivu 2.50 6.00
M23 Patrick Roy 12.50 30.00
M24 John LeClair 2.50 6.00
M25 Doug Gilmour 2.00 5.00
M26 Sergei Fedorov 4.00 10.00
M27 Wayne Gretzky 15.00 40.00
M28 Peter Forsberg 6.00 15.00
M29 Eric Brewer 1.00 2.50
M30 Sergei Samsonov 2.00 5.00

1998-99 Black Diamond Winning Formula Gold

Randomly inserted into hobby packs only, this 30-card set features color photos of top players and goalies. Each card is sequentially numbered to the pictured player's goals or goalie's wins multiplied times 50.

COMPLETE SET (30) 125.00 250.00
STATED PRINT RUN 800-2600
WF1 Paul Kariya/850 3.00 8.00
WF2 Teemu Selanne/2600 3.00 8.00
WF3 Sergei Samsonov/1100 2.50 6.00
WF4 Dominik Hasek/1650 6.00 15.00
WF5 Vincent Lecavalier/2200 5.00 12.00
WF6 Patrick Roy/1550 15.00 40.00
WF7 Peter Forsberg/1250 8.00 20.00
WF8 Joe Sakic/1350 5.00 12.00
WF9 Ed Belfour/1850 3.00 8.00
WF10 Brendan Shanahan/1400 3.00 8.00
WF11 Steve Yzerman/1200 20.00 50.00
WF12 Chris Osgood/1650 2.50 6.00
WF13 Curtis Joseph/1450 3.00 8.00
WF14 Manny Malhotra/800 2.50 6.00
WF15 Martin Brodeur/2150 6.00 15.00
WF16 Chris Drury/1400 2.50 6.00
WF17 Zigmund Palffy/2250 2.50 6.00
WF18 Wayne Gretzky/1150 25.00 50.00
WF19 Theo Fleury/1350 2.50 6.00
WF20 Alexei Yashin/1650 2.50 6.00
WF21 Eric Lindros/1500 3.00 8.00
WF22 John LeClair/2550 2.50 6.00
WF23 Keith Tkachuk/2000 3.00 8.00
WF24 Mark Messier/1100 3.00 8.00
WF25 Jaromir Jagr/1750 5.00 12.00
WF26 Brett Hull/1350 5.00 12.00
WF27 Mats Sundin/1650 3.00 8.00
WF28 Pavel Bure/2550 3.00 8.00
WF29 Peter Bondra/2600 2.50 6.00
WF30 Mike Modano/1050 8.00 20.00

1998-99 Black Diamond Winning Formula Platinum

Randomly inserted into packs, this 30-card set is a platinum foil parallel version of the regular Winning Formula set. Each card is numbered to the player's actual accomplishments. Scarcer cards are not priced.

STATED PRINT RUN 16-52
WF1 Paul Kariya/17
WF2 Teemu Selanne/52 50.00 100.00
WF3 Sergei Samsonov/22
WF4 Dominik Hasek/33 100.00 200.00
WF5 Vincent Lecavalier/44 100.00 200.00
WF6 Patrick Roy/31 250.00 500.00
WF7 Peter Forsberg/25
WF8 Joe Sakic/27
WF9 Ed Belfour/37 60.00 120.00
WF10 Brendan Shanahan/28
WF11 Steve Yzerman/24
WF12 Chris Osgood/33 75.00 150.00
WF13 Curtis Joseph/29
WF14 Manny Malhotra/16 25.00 60.00
WF15 Martin Brodeur/43 100.00 200.00
WF16 Chris Drury/28
WF17 Zigmund Palffy/45 60.00 120.00
WF18 Wayne Gretzky/23
WF19 Theo Fleury/27
WF20 Alexei Yashin/33 25.00 60.00
WF21 Eric Lindros/30 50.00 100.00
WF22 John LeClair/51 50.00 100.00
WF23 Keith Tkachuk/40 75.00 150.00
WF24 Mark Messier/22
WF25 Jaromir Jagr/35 60.00 150.00
WF26 Brett Hull/27
WF27 Mats Sundin/33 50.00 100.00
WF28 Pavel Bure/51 50.00 100.00
WF29 Peter Bondra/52 50.00 100.00
WF30 Mike Modano/21

1998-99 Black Diamond Year of the Great One

Randomly inserted into packs, this 99-card set features color photos of the great Wayne Gretzky. Cards 1-45 are marked with a single diamond; 46-75 display double diamonds; 76-90 show triple diamonds; and 91-99 carry quadruple diamonds. Each card is sequentially numbered to 99.

COMMON YOTG (1-99) 100.00 250.00
EACH CARD SERIAL NUMBERED TO 99

1999-00 Black Diamond

The 1999-00 Black Diamond set was released as 120-card set comprised of 90 veteran cards and 30 Diamonds in the Rough cards, short printed and inserted at one in three packs, which feature future NHL stars. Player action shots are set against a card background where the middle 2/3 is silver foil and the top and bottom are colored to match the player's team colors. Black Diamond was packaged in 24-pack boxes with 6-card packs, carried an SRP of $3.99, and was released as both hobby and retail.

COMPLETE SET (120) 60.00 150.00
COMP.SET w/o SP's (90) 20.00 50.00
SP 91-120 ODDS 1:3
1 Paul Kariya .25 .60
2 Teemu Selanne .25 .60
3 Guy Hebert .20 .50
4 Damian Rhodes .20 .50
5 Patrik Stefan RC .60 1.50
6 Dean Sylvester RC .20 .50
7 Sergei Samsonov .20 .50
8 Byron Dafoe .20 .50
9 Ray Bourque .40 1.00
10 Joe Thornton .40 1.00
11 Dominik Hasek .50 1.25
12 Michael Peca .20 .50
13 Miroslav Satan .20 .50
14 Martin Biron .20 .50
15 Oleg Saprykin RC .60 1.50
16 Valeri Bure .08 .25
17 Robyn Regehr .08 .25
18 Dave Tanabe .08 .25
19 Arturs Irbe .20 .50
20 Sami Kapanen .08 .25
21 Kyle Calder RC .20 .50
22 Tony Amonte .20 .50
23 Doug Gilmour .20 .50
24 Patrick Roy 1.25 3.00
25 Joe Sakic .50 1.25
26 Peter Forsberg .60 1.50
27 Chris Drury .20 .50
28 Milan Hejduk .25 .60
29 Mike Modano .40 1.00
30 Brett Hull .30 .75
31 Ed Belfour .25 .60
32 Jon Sim RC .20 .50
33 Nicklas Lidstrom .25 .60
34 Sergei Fedorov .40 1.00
35 Brendan Shanahan .25 .60
36 Steve Yzerman 1.25 3.00
37 Chris Osgood .20 .50
38 Paul Comrie RC .08 .25
39 Bill Guerin .08 .25
40 Doug Weight .20 .50
41 Pavel Bure .25 .60
42 Ivan Novoseltsev RC .20 .50
43 Trevor Kidd .20 .50
44 Zigmund Palffy .20 .50
45 Luc Robitaille .20 .50
46 Stephane Fiset .20 .50
47 Mike Ribeiro .08 .25
48 Saku Koivu .25 .60
49 David Legwand .20 .50
50 Robert Valicevic RC .08 .25
51 Martin Brodeur .60 1.50
52 Scott Gomez .08 .25
53 Brian Rafalski RC .20 .50
54 Tim Connolly .08 .25
55 Jorgen Jonsson RC .08 .25
56 Theo Fleury .08 .25
57 Brian Leetch .25 .60
58 Mike Richter .25 .60
59 Marian Hossa .25 .60
60 Radek Bonk .08 .25
61 Mike Fisher RC .60 1.50
62 Eric Lindros .25 .60
63 Keith Primeau .08 .25
64 John LeClair .25 .60
65 Jeremy Roenick .30 .75
66 Keith Tkachuk .25 .60
67 Mika Alatalo RC .20 .50
68 Jaromir Jagr .40 1.00
69 Martin Straka .08 .25
70 Alexei Kovalev .08 .25
71 Jochen Hecht RC .20 .50
72 Pavol Demitra .20 .50
73 Chris Pronger .20 .50
74 Patrick Marleau .20 .50
75 Owen Nolan .20 .50
76 Jeff Friesen .08 .25
77 Steve Shields .20 .50
78 Vincent Lecavalier .25 .60
79 Dan Cloutier .08 .25
80 Adam Mair RC .20 .50
81 Mike Johnson .20 .50
82 Mats Sundin .25 .60
83 Nikolai Antropov RC .75 2.00
84 Curtis Joseph .25 .60
85 Steve Kariya RC .20 .50
86 Mark Messier .25 .60
87 Alexander Mogilny .20 .50
88 Olaf Kolzig .20 .50
89 Peter Bondra .20 .50
90 Alexandre Volchkov RC .20 .50
91 Pavel Brendl SP RC 2.00 5.00
92 Jamie Lundmark SP .50 1.25
93 Kris Beech SP .50 1.25
94 Michael Zigomanis SP .50 1.25
95 Branislav Mezei SP RC .50 1.25
96 Sheldon Keefe SP RC .50 1.25
97 Brian Finley SP .50 1.25
98 Taylor Pyatt SP .50 1.25
99 Denis Shvidki SP .50 1.25
100 Barret Jackman SP .50 1.25
101 Maxime Ouellet SP .50 1.25
102 Milan Kraft SP RC 2.00 5.00
103 Brad Ralph SP RC .50 1.25
104 Alexei Volkov SP .50 1.25
105 Mathieu Chouinard SP .50 1.25
106 Mark Bell SP .50 1.25
107 Ryan Jardine SP RC .50 1.25
108 Kristian Kudroc SP RC .50 1.25
109 Norm Milley SP .50 1.25
110 Alexander Buturlin .50 1.25
111 Jaroslav Kristek SP RC .50 1.25
112 Luke Sellars SP RC .50 1.25
113 Bryan Kazarian SP RC .50 1.25
114 Brett Lysak SP RC .50 1.25
115 Andrei Shefer SP RC .50 1.25
116 Michal Sivek SP RC .50 1.25
117 Justin Papineau SP .50 1.25
118 Mattias Weinhandl SP .50 1.25
119 Daniel Sedin SP .50 1.25
120 Henrik Sedin SP .50 1.25

1999-00 Black Diamond Diamond Cut

The 90-card Diamond Cut set parallels the Black Diamond base 90-card set in a die cut version and is seeded at 1:6 packs; and the 30-card Diamond Cut Diamonds in the Rough set parallels the 30 prospect cards in a die cut version and is seeded at 1:11 packs. On the front of these parallels, the words "Diamond Cut" appear just above the player's name.

*VETERANS 1-90: 2X TO 5X BASIC CARDS
*ROOKIES 1-90: 1.2X TO 3X BASIC CARDS
1-90 STATED ODDS 1:6
*ROOKIES 91-120: .8X TO 2X BASIC CARDS
91-120 STATED ODDS 1:3

1999-00 Black Diamond Final Cut

The 90-card Final Cut set parallels the Black Diamond base 90-card set in a die cut holographic foil version and is numbered on the back out of 100; and the 30-card Final Cut Diamonds in the Rough set parallels the 30 prospect cards at the end of the set in a die cut holographic foil version and is numbered on the back out of 50. On the front of these parallels, the words "Final Cut" appear just above the player's name.

*VETERANS 1-90: 10X TO 25X BASIC CARDS
*ROOKIES 1-90: 5X TO 12X
*ROOKIES 91-120: 4X TO 10X
1-90 STATED PRINT RUN 100
91-120 SP STATED PRINT RUN 50

1999-00 Black Diamond A Piece of History

Randomly inserted in hobby packs at 1:179 and retail packs at 1:336, this 20-card set features NHL players with a single diamond-cut swatch of a game-used

stick. Hobby cards feature a red foil shift, and retail cards feature a blue foil shift. Double and triple diamond parallels of this set were also created. These parallels carry two or three swatches of memorabilia respectively. Double diamonds were seeded at 1:1008, and triple diamonds were numbered one of one. Triple diamonds not priced due to scarcity.

SINGLE STATED ODDS 1:336
*DOUBLE: .8X TO 2X SINGLE
DOUBLE ODDS 1:864 HOB, 1:1008 RET
UNPRICED TRIPLE PRINT RUN 1
BH Brett Hull 10.00 25.00
DH Dominik Hasek 10.00 25.00
EB Ed Belfour 10.00 25.00
EL Eric Lindros 10.00 25.00
GH Gordie Howe 20.00 50.00
JJ Jaromir Jagr 12.00 30.00
JL John LeClair 10.00 25.00
JS Joe Sakic 12.00 30.00
KT Keith Tkachuk 10.00 25.00
MB Martin Brodeur 20.00 50.00
MM Mike Modano 10.00 25.00
PB Pavel Bure 10.00 25.00
PF Peter Forsberg 15.00 40.00
PK Paul Kariya 10.00 25.00
PR Patrick Roy 20.00 50.00
RB Ray Bourque 10.00 25.00
SY Steve Yzerman 20.00 50.00
TC Tim Connolly 8.00 20.00
TS Teemu Selanne 10.00 25.00
WG Wayne Gretzky 30.00 80.00

1999-00 Black Diamond Diamonation

Randomly inserted in packs at 1:4, this 20-card set showcases NHL's most collectible players on a foil card with laser-etched diamonds in the background.

COMPLETE SET (20) 12.00 30.00
STATED ODDS 1:4
D1 Paul Kariya .50 1.25
D2 Patrik Stefan .75 2.00
D3 Sergei Samsonov .50 1.25
D4 Teemu Selanne .60 1.25
D5 Patrick Roy 2.50 6.00
D6 Mike Modano .75 2.00
D7 Sergei Fedorov 1.00 2.50
D8 Pavel Bure .60 1.50
D9 David Legwand .50 1.25
D10 Martin Brodeur 1.25 3.00
D11 Theo Fleury .50 1.25
D12 Eric Lindros .75 2.00
D13 Keith Tkachuk .50 1.25
D14 Jaromir Jagr .75 2.00
D15 Mats Sundin .50 1.25
D16 Steve Kariya .60 1.50
D17 Peter Bondra .50 1.25
D18 Peter Forsberg 1.25 3.00
D19 Steve Yzerman 2.50 6.00
D20 Zigmund Palffy .50 1.25

1999-00 Black Diamond Diamond Might

Randomly inserted in packs at 1:9, this 10-card set pictures NHL's toughest players set against a colored foil background.

COMPLETE SET (10) 8.00 15.00
STATED ODDS 1:9
DM1 Peter Forsberg 1.50 4.00
DM2 Brendan Shanahan 1.00 2.50
DM3 Eric Lindros 1.00 2.50
DM4 John LeClair .75 2.00
DM5 Jaromir Jagr 1.00 2.50
DM6 Keith Tkachuk .60 1.50
DM7 Teemu Selanne .60 1.50
DM8 Mats Sundin .60 1.50
DM9 Mark Messier .75 2.00
DM10 Theo Fleury .60 1.50

1999-00 Black Diamond Diamond Skills

Randomly inserted in packs at 1:24, this 10-card set features top players who make the highlight reel night after night. Action player photos on a foil-front card are set against a centered diamond background that is framed by horizontal laser-etched lines.

COMPLETE SET (10) 25.00 50.00
STATED ODDS 1:24
DS1 Teemu Selanne 1.25 3.00
DS2 Paul Kariya 3.00 8.00
DS3 Patrick Roy 6.00 15.00
DS4 Pavel Bure 1.50 4.00
DS5 Sergei Fedorov 2.50 6.00
DS6 Eric Lindros 2.00 5.00
DS7 Jaromir Jagr 2.00 5.00
DS8 Martin Brodeur 3.00 8.00
DS9 Theo Fleury 1.25 3.00
DS10 Curtis Joseph 1.25 3.00

1999-00 Black Diamond Gordie Howe Gallery

Randomly inserted in packs at 1:12, this 10-card set pays tribute to one of hockey's greatest legends. A centered picture framed by a diamond is centered on a holographic foil background. Card backs carry a "GH" prefix.

COMPLETE SET (10) 40.00 80.00
COMMON HOWE (GH1-GH10) 5.00 10.00
STATED ODDS 1:12

1999-00 Black Diamond Myriad

Randomly inserted in packs at 1:24, this 10-card set showcases 10 of the NHL's most collectible stars in action.

COMPLETE SET (10) 20.00 40.00
STATED ODDS 1:24
M1 Patrik Stefan 2.00 5.00
M2 Teemu Selanne 1.25 3.00
M3 Sergei Samsonov 1.25 3.00
M4 Joe Sakic 2.50 6.00
M5 Brett Hull 1.50 4.00
M6 Pavel Bure 1.50 4.00
M7 Steve Yzerman 6.00 15.00
M8 Jaromir Jagr 2.00 5.00
M9 Eric Lindros 2.00 5.00
M10 Paul Kariya 3.00 8.00

2000-01 Black Diamond

Released in early December 2000, Black Diamond featured a 132-card base set consisting of 82 regular issue cards and 50 short printed Precious Gems cards divided up into three tiers. Tier 1, numbers 61-75 and 112-132, were sequentially numbered to 1999, tier 2, card numbers 76-84, were sequentially numbered to 1250, and tier 3, card numbers 85-90, were sequentially numbered to 500. Cards 91-132 were only available in packs of Upper Deck Rookie Update. Base cards were all foil and have colored borders along the top and bottom of the card to match each respective player's team colors. Black Diamond was packaged in 24-pack boxes with packs containing six cards and carried a suggested retail price of $3.99.

COMPLETE SET (90) 300.00 600.00
COMP.SET w/o SP's (82) 15.00 30.00
COMP.SET w/UPD (132)
61-75, 112-132 PRINT RUN 1999 SER.#'d SETS
76-84 STAT.PRINT RUN 1250 SER.#'d SETS
85-90 STAT.PRINT RUN 500 SER.#'d SETS
CARDS 91-132 AVAIL.IN UD ROOK.UPD. PACKS
1 Paul Kariya .25 .60
2 Teemu Selanne .25 .60
3 Patrik Stefan .10 .25
4 Joe Thornton .40 1.00
5 Sergei Samsonov .20 .50
6 Dominik Hasek .50 1.25
7 Maxim Afinogenov .10 .25
8 Valeri Bure .10 .25
9 Marc Savard .10 .25
10 Ron Francis .20 .50
11 Jeff O'Neill .10 .25
12 Tony Amonte .20 .50
13 Michal Grosek .10 .25
14 Patrick Roy 1.25 3.00
15 Ray Bourque .50 1.25
16 Milan Hejduk .25 .60
17 Peter Forsberg .50 1.25
18 Brett Hull .30 .75
19 Ed Belfour .25 .60
20 Mike Modano .40 1.00
21 Brendan Shanahan .25 .60
22 Chris Osgood .20 .50
23 Steve Yzerman 1.25 3.00
24 Doug Weight .20 .50
25 Tommy Salo .20 .50
26 Pavel Bure .25 .60
27 Trevor Kidd .20 .50
28 Rob Blake .20 .50
29 Luc Robitaille .20 .50
30 Jose Theodore .30 .75
31 Saku Koivu .25 .60
32 David Legwand .20 .50
33 Martin Brodeur .60 1.50
34 Scott Gomez .10 .25
35 Scott Stevens .20 .50
36 Tim Connolly .10 .25
37 Mariusz Czerkawski .10 .25
38 Mark Messier .25 .60
39 Theo Fleury .10 .25
40 Marian Hossa .25 .60
41 Radek Bonk .10 .25
42 Brian Boucher .25 .60
43 John LeClair .25 .60
44 Simon Gagne .25 .60
45 Jeremy Roenick .30 .75
46 Keith Tkachuk .25 .60
47 Jaromir Jagr .40 1.00
48 Martin Straka UER .10 .25
(Name missing on card front)
49 Steve Shields .20 .50
50 Jeff Friesen .10 .25
51 Chris Pronger .20 .50
52 Roman Turek .20 .50
53 Vincent Lecavalier .25 .60
54 Dan Cloutier .10 .25
55 Curtis Joseph .25 .60
56 Mats Sundin .25 .60
57 Markus Naslund .25 .60
58 Felix Potvin .25 .60
59 Olaf Kolzig .20 .50
60 Jeff Halpern .10 .25
61 Matt Pettinger RC 2.00 5.00
62 Chris Nielsen RC 2.00 5.00
63 Dany Heatley RC 50.00 100.00
64 Matt Zultek RC 2.00 5.00
65 Dmitri Afanasenkov RC 2.00 5.00
66 Tyler Bouck RC 2.00 5.00
67 Jonas Andersson RC 2.00 5.00
68 Marc-Andre Thinel RC 2.00 5.00
69 Jaroslav Svoboda RC 2.00 5.00
70 Josef Vasicek RC 2.00 5.00
71 Andrew Raycroft RC 5.00 12.00
72 Juraj Kolnik RC 2.00 5.00
73 Zdenek Blatny RC 2.00 5.00
74 Sebastien Caron RC 2.00 5.00
75 Michael Ryder RC 10.00 25.00
76 Eric Nickulas RC 2.00 5.00
77 Jeff Cowan RC 2.00 5.00
78 Steven Reinprecht RC 2.00 5.00
79 David Gosselin RC 2.00 5.00
80 Colin White RC 2.00 5.00
81 Steve Valiquette RC 2.00 5.00
82 Jani Hurme RC 2.00 5.00
83 Jean-Guy Trudel RC 2.00 5.00
84 Dieter Kochan RC 2.00 5.00
85 Paul Kariya PG 10.00 25.00
86 Patrick Roy PG 15.00 40.00
87 Steve Yzerman PG 12.00 30.00
88 Pavel Bure PG 6.00 15.00
89 Martin Brodeur PG 10.00 25.00
90 Jaromir Jagr PG 8.00 20.00
91 Samuel Pahlsson .10 .25
92 Eric Boulton RC .30 .75
93 Daniel Tkaczuk .10 .25
94 Rob Shearer RC .30 .75
95 David Vyborny .10 .25
96 Tyler Bouck UD .40 1.00
97 Mike Comrie RC 4.00 10.00
98 Anson Carter .20 .50
99 Roman Simicek RC .30 .75
100 Andrei Markov .10 .25
101 Jason Arnott .10 .25
102 Mike Mottau .10 .25
103 Taylor Pyatt .10 .25
104 Alexei Yashin .10 .25
105 Todd Fedoruk RC .30 .75
106 Milan Kraft .20 .50
107 Mario Lemieux 1.50 4.00
108 Evgeni Nabokov .20 .50
109 Brad Richards .20 .50
110 Daniel Sedin .10 .25
111 Henrik Sedin .10 .25
112 Petr Tenkrat RC 2.00 5.00
113 Lee Goren RC 2.00 5.00
114 David Aebischer RC 3.00 8.00
115 Yuri Babenko RC 2.00 5.00
116 Rostislav Klesla RC 3.00 8.00
117 Marty Turco RC 4.00 10.00
118 Jason Williams RC 4.00 10.00
119 Michel Riesen RC 2.00 5.00
120 Lubomir Visnovsky RC 2.00 5.00
121 Travis Scott RC 2.00 5.00
122 Peter Bartos RC 2.00 5.00
123 Marian Gaborik RC 10.00 25.00
124 Scott Hartnell RC 2.00 5.00
125 Rick DiPietro RC 6.00 15.00
126 Vitali Yeremeyev RC 2.00 5.00
127 Martin Havlat RC 4.00 10.00
128 Roman Cechmanek RC 2.00 5.00
129 Justin Williams RC 3.00 8.00
130 Ruslan Fedotenko RC 2.00 5.00
131 Alexander Kharitonov RC 2.00 5.00
132 Alexei Ponikarovsky RC 2.00 5.00

2000-01 Black Diamond Gold

Randomly inserted in hobby packs, this 90-card set paralleled the base set enhanced with a gold stamp across the middle of the card reading "Diamond Gold." Each card was sequentially numbered to 100.

*GOLD STARS: 10X TO 25X BASIC CARD
*61-75 GOLD PG RC's: 1X TO 2X BASIC CARDS
*76-84 GOLD PG RC's: 1X TO 2X BASIC CARDS
*85-90 GOLD PG's: 1X TO 2X BASIC CARDS
GOLD STAT.PRINT RUN 100 SER.#'d SETS
63 Dany Heatley 200.00 300.00

2000-01 Black Diamond Diamonation

Randomly inserted in packs at the rate of 1:12, this nine card set features full color player action photography set against a red and silver foil background with gold foil highlights.

COMPLETE SET (9) 15.00 30.00
STATED ODDS 1:12
IG1 Paul Kariya 1.00 2.50
IG2 Patrick Roy 5.00 12.00
IG3 Sergei Fedorov 2.00 5.00
IG4 Pavel Bure 1.25 3.00
IG5 Scott Gomez 1.00 2.50
IG6 John LeClair 1.25 3.00
IG7 Jaromir Jagr 1.50 4.00
IG8 Vincent Lecavalier 1.00 2.50
IG9 Curtis Joseph 1.00 2.50

2000-01 Black Diamond Diamond Might

Randomly seeded in packs at the rate of 1:12, this nine card set features full color action photography set on an all foil card with red highlights along the card bottom in the shape of a "V." Cards have gold foil stamping highlights.

COMPLETE SET (9) 15.00 30.00
STATED ODDS 1:12
FP1 Teemu Selanne 1.25 3.00
FP2 Peter Forsberg 2.50 6.00
FP3 Ray Bourque 2.00 5.00
FP4 Mike Modano 1.50 4.00
FP5 Brendan Shanahan 1.50 4.00
FP6 Pavel Bure 1.25 3.00
FP7 Martin Brodeur 2.50 6.00
FP8 John LeClair 1.25 3.00
FP9 Jaromir Jagr 1.50 4.00

2000-01 Black Diamond Diamond Skills

Randomly inserted in packs at the rate of 1:17, this six card set features full color action photography set against a foil backdrop with cardboard borders along the top and bottom left hand corners. Cards contain gold foil stamping highlights.

COMPLETE SET (6) 20.00 40.00
STATED ODDS 1:17
IC1 Patrick Roy 6.00 15.00
IC2 Mike Modano 2.00 5.00
IC3 Steve Yzerman 6.00 15.00
IC4 Martin Brodeur 3.00 8.00
IC5 John LeClair 1.50 4.00
IC6 Jaromir Jagr 2.00 5.00

2000-01 Black Diamond Game Gear

Randomly inserted in Black Diamond packs at the rate of 1:23 and 1:30 in UD Update packs, this 32-card set features player action shots coupled with a swatch of game used memorabilia. Update cards are marked below.

STATED ODDS 1:23/1:30 UPDATE
BJV J.Vanbiesbrouck Blocker 6.00 15.00
BSB Sean Burke Blocker 6.00 15.00
BTB Tom Barrasso Blocker 6.00 15.00
BTS Tommy Salo Blocker 6.00 15.00
CJV John Vanbiesbrouck Glove 6.00 15.00
CKM Kirk McLean Glove 6.00 15.00
CSB Sean Burke Glove 6.00 15.00
CTB Tom Barrasso Glove 6.00 15.00
CTS Tommy Salo Glove 6.00 15.00
GEL Eric Lindros Glove SP 6.00 15.00
GTS Teemu Selanne Glove SP 8.00 20.00
GWG Wayne Gretzky Glove SP 40.00 100.00
LBD Byron Dafoe Pad 6.00 15.00
LCJ Curtis Joseph Pad 6.00 15.00
LDH Dominik Hasek Pad 15.00 40.00
LGF Grant Fuhr Pad 20.00 50.00
LJV John Vanbiesbrouck Pad 6.00 15.00
LMB Martin Biron Pad 6.00 15.00
LOK Olaf Kolzig Pad 6.00 15.00
LRL Roberto Luongo Pad 8.00 20.00
LSS Steve Shields Pad 6.00 15.00
SMM Mark Messier Skate SP 30.00 80.00
GDR Chris Drury Glove Upd 6.00 15.00
GFE Sergei Fedorov Glove Upd 12.50 30.00
GSA Joe Sakic Glove Upd 12.50 30.00
GTH Joe Thornton Glove Upd 12.50 30.00
GYA Alexei Yashin Glove Upd 6.00 15.00
LAU J.S. Aubin Pad 6.00 15.00
LDE Marc Denis Pad Upd 6.00 15.00
LOS Chris Osgood Pad Upd 6.00 15.00
LTU Roman Turek Pad Upd 6.00 15.00
SJA Jaromir Jagr Skate Upd 20.00 50.00

2000-01 Black Diamond Myriad

Randomly inserted in packs at the rate of 1:17, this six card set features player action photography set against a blue and silver foil background with a black and silver border along the left side of the card. Cards contain gold foil highlights.

COMPLETE SET (6) 12.00 25.00
STATED ODDS 1:17
CC1 Paul Kariya 1.50 4.00
CC2 Peter Forsberg 3.00 8.00
CC3 Pavel Bure 1.50 4.00
CC4 Scott Gomez 1.50 4.00
CC5 Jaromir Jagr 2.00 5.00
CC6 Curtis Joseph 1.50 4.00

2003-04 Black Diamond

This 198-card set consisted of four distinct tiers. Single diamond cards (1-84); double diamond cards (85-126) inserted at 1:2; triple diamond cards (127-168) inserted at 1:8 and quadruple diamond cards inserted at 1:24.

COMPLETE SET (198) 200.00 400.00
COMP.SET w/o SP's (126) 40.00 80.00
DOUBLE 85-126 ODDS 1:2
TRIPLE 127-168 ODDS 1:8
QUAD 169-198 ODDS 1:24
1 Mike York .08 .25
2 Pavel Bure .40 1.00
3 Steve Reinprecht .08 .25
4 Vincent Lecavalier .40 1.00
5 Alex Auld .08 .25
6 Eric Daze .30 .75
7 Jeff Hackett .30 .75
8 Manny Fernandez .30 .75
9 Alexei Zhamnov .08 .25
10 Bryan Marchment .08 .25
11 Jason Allison .08 .25
12 Tony Amonte .30 .75
13 David Legwand .30 .75
14 Geoff Sanderson .08 .25
15 Olaf Kolzig .30 .75
16 Vaclav Prospal .08 .25
17 Sebastien Caron .30 .75
18 Daniel Alfredsson .30 .75
19 Martin Biron .30 .75
20 Jay Bouwmeester .08 .25
21 Nikolai Khabibulin .40 1.00
22 Keith Tkachuk .40 1.00
23 Miroslav Satan .40 1.00
24 Rick DiPietro .30 .75
25 Ryan Smyth .08 .25
26 Alexander Mogilny .30 .75
27 Daniil Markov .08 .25
28 Jason Spezza .40 1.00
29 Roman Cechmanek .30 .75
30 Brendan Morrison .30 .75
31 Chris Gratton .00 .25
32 Joe Sakic .75 2.00
33 Jose Theodore .50 1.25
34 Dwayne Roloson .30 .75
35 Ed Jovanovski .30 .75
36 Peter Forsberg .75 2.00
37 Robert Esche .30 .75
38 Daniel Briere .08 .25
39 Doug Weight .30 .75
40 Mike Comrie .30 .75
41 Michael Peca .08 .25
42 Ales Kotalik .08 .25
43 Alexei Kovalev .30 .75
44 Tommy Salo .30 .75
45 Pavol Demitra .30 .75
46 Alex Tanguay .30 .75
47 Johan Hedberg .30 .75
48 Jan Hrdina .08 .25
49 Mike Komisarek .08 .25
50 Petr Sykora .08 .25
51 Ilya Kovalchuk .50 1.25
52 Mike Modano .60 1.50
53 Scottie Upshall .08 .25
54 Rico Fata .08 .25
55 Sergei Gonchar .08 .25
56 Mike Dunham .30 .75
57 Olli Jokinen .30 .75
58 Roman Turek .30 .75
59 Alexander Svitov .08 .25
60 Bill Guerin .30 .75
61 Byron Dafoe .30 .75
62 Patrick Marleau .30 .75
63 Patrik Elias .30 .75
64 Brett Hull .50 1.25
65 Marco Sturm .08 .25
66 Andrew Raycroft .30 .75
67 Scott Gomez .08 .25
68 John LeClair .40 1.00
69 Kyle Calder .08 .25
70 Pierre-Marc Bouchard .08 .25
71 Nikolai Antropov .08 .25
72 Jean-Sebastien Giguere .30 .75
73 Marc Denis .30 .75
74 Martin Straka .08 .25
75 Peter Bondra .08 .25
76 Ron Hainsey .08 .25
77 Brendan Shanahan .40 1.00
78 Evgeni Nabokov .30 .75
79 Glen Murray .08 .25
80 Martin Brodeur 1.00 2.50
81 Adam Deadmarsh .08 .25
82 Kevin Weekes .30 .75
83 Owen Nolan .30 .75
84 Zdeno Chara .08 .25
85 Andrew Cassels .40 .75
86 Simon Gagne .75 2.00
87 Derian Hatcher .40 .75
88 Mats Sundin 1.00 2.50
89 Chris Osgood .75 2.00
90 Henrik Zetterberg 1.00 2.50
91 Saku Koivu 1.00 2.50
92 Sergei Samsonov .75 2.00
93 Arron Asham .40 .75
94 Teppo Numminen .40 .75
95 Philippe Sauve .75 2.00
96 Jeff O'Neill .40 .75
97 Luc Robitaille .75 2.00
98 Marty Turco .75 2.00
99 Niko Dimitrakos .40 .75
100 Markus Naslund 1.00 2.50
101 Stephen Weiss .40 .75
102 Ed Belfour 1.00 2.50
103 Roberto Luongo 1.25 3.00
104 Eric Lindros 1.00 2.50
105 Jocelyn Thibault .75 2.00
106 Marian Hossa 1.00 2.50
107 Teemu Selanne 1.00 2.50
108 Jaromir Jagr 2.50 6.00
109 Stanislav Chistov .40 .75
110 Zigmund Palffy .75 2.00
111 P.J. Axelsson .40 .75
112 Denis Arkhipov .40 .75
113 Sean Burke .75 2.00
114 Todd Marchant .40 .75
115 Maxim Afinogenov .40 .75
116 Tomas Vokoun .75 2.00
117 Jason Blake .40 .75
118 Jordan Leopold .40 .75
119 Martin St. Louis .75 2.00
120 Pavel Datsyuk 1.00 2.50
121 Marc Savard .40 .75
122 Marian Gaborik 3.00 8.00
123 Jamie Langenbrunner .40 .75
124 Jarome Iginla 1.25 3.00
125 Al MacInnis .75 2.00
126 Nicklas Lidstrom 1.00 2.50
127 Georges Laraque 3.00 8.00
128 Justin Williams 3.00 8.00
129 Anson Carter 3.00 8.00
130 Chris Drury 3.00 8.00
131 Willie Mitchell 3.00 8.00
132 Rick Nash 4.00 10.00
133 Scott Stevens 3.00 8.00
134 Chris Pronger 3.00 8.00
135 Mario Lemieux 10.00 25.00
136 Steve Ott 3.00 8.00
137 Steve Yzerman 8.00 20.00
138 Dany Heatley 4.00 10.00
139 Ron Francis 3.00 8.00
140 Alexander Frolov 3.00 8.00
141 Tyler Arnason 3.00 8.00
142 Rob Blake 3.00 8.00
143 Patrick Lalime 3.00 8.00
144 Joe Thornton 5.00 12.00
145 David Aebischer 3.00 8.00
146 Alexei Yashin 3.00 8.00
147 Felix Potvin 3.00 8.00
148 Boyd Gordon RC 4.00 10.00
149 Tom Preissing RC 4.00 10.00
150 Brent Burns RC 4.00 10.00
151 Antoine Vermette RC 4.00 10.00
152 Antti Miettinen RC 4.00 10.00
153 Maxim Kondratiev RC 4.00 10.00
154 Christian Ehrhoff RC 4.00 10.00
155 Jiri Hudler RC 5.00 12.00
156 David Hale RC 4.00 10.00
157 Marek Svatos RC 5.00 12.00
158 Matthew Lombardi RC 4.00 10.00
159 Alexander Semin RC 10.00 25.00
160 John-Michael Liles RC 4.00 10.00
161 Dan Fritsche RC 4.00 10.00
162 Esa Pirnes RC 4.00 10.00
163 Cody McCormick RC 4.00 10.00
164 Lasse Kukkonen RC 4.00 10.00
165 Tim Gleason RC 4.00 10.00
166 Marek Zidlicky RC 4.00 10.00
167 Christoph Brandner RC 4.00 10.00
168 Sean Bergenheim RC 4.00 10.00
169 Mike Johnson 6.00 15.00
170 Erik Cole 6.00 15.00
171 Barret Jackman 6.00 15.00
172 Marcel Hossa 6.00 15.00
173 Tie Domi 6.00 15.00
174 Michael Rupp 6.00 15.00
175 Jeremy Roenick 10.00 25.00
176 Sergei Fedorov 10.00 25.00
177 Paul Kariya 8.00 20.00
178 Mike Ricci 8.00 20.00
179 Brenden Morrow 6.00 15.00
180 Dominik Hasek 10.00 25.00
181 P.J. Stock 6.00 15.00
182 Ales Hemsky 8.00 20.00
183 Todd Bertuzzi 8.00 20.00
184 Patrice Bergeron RC 10.00 25.00
185 Pavel Vorobiev RC 4.00 10.00
186 Milan Michalek RC 6.00 15.00
187 Matt Stajan RC 6.00 15.00
188 Dan Hamhuis RC 5.00 12.00
189 Jeffrey Lupul RC 6.00 15.00
190 Eric Staal RC 15.00 40.00
191 Tuomo Ruutu RC 4.00 10.00
192 Nathan Horton RC 8.00 20.00
193 Dustin Brown RC 6.00 15.00
194 Jordin Tootoo RC 8.00 20.00
195 Joni Pitkanen RC 5.00 12.00
196 Peter Sejna RC 4.00 10.00
197 Chris Higgins RC 8.00 20.00
198 Marc-Andre Fleury RC 25.00 50.00

2003-04 Black Diamond Black

This set is also referred to as the "Clarity" parallel.

NOT PRICED DUE TO SCARCITY
STATED PRINT RUN 10 SER.#'d SETS

2003-04 Black Diamond Green

This set is also referred to as the "Color" parallel.

*SINGLE STARS: 3X TO 8X BASIC CARDS
*DOUBLE STARS: 2X TO 5X
*TRIPLE STARS: 1X TO 2.5X
*TRIPLE ROOKIES: .5X TO 1.25X
*QUAD STARS: .5X TO 1.25X
*QUAD ROOKIES: .4X TO 1X
STATED PRINT RUN 100 SER.#'d SETS

2003-04 Black Diamond Red

This set is also referred to as the "Cut" parallel.

*SINGLE STARS: 5X TO 12X BASIC CARDS
*DOUBLE STARS: 3X TO 8X
*TRIPLE STARS: 1.5X TO 4X
*TRIPLE ROOKIES: .75X TO 2X
*QUAD STARS: .75X TO 2X
*QUAD ROOKIES: .5X TO 1.25X
STATED PRINT RUN 50 SER.#'d SETS

2003-04 Black Diamond Signature Gems

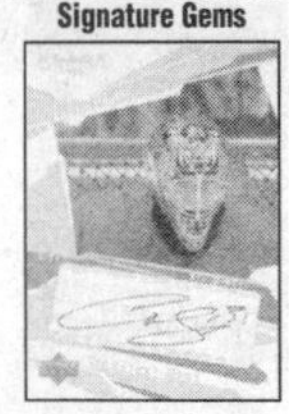

This 36-card autograph set featured certified autographs on diamond-mirrored stickers affixed to the cards.

STATED ODDS 1:48
SG1 Maxim Afinogenov 6.00 15.00
SG2 Ray Bourque 15.00 40.00
SG4 Pavel Bure 10.00 25.00
SG5 Erik Cole 6.00 15.00
SG6 Mike Comrie 6.00 15.00
SG7 Simon Gagne 6.00 15.00
SG8 Rick Nash 12.50 30.00
SG9 Wayne Gretzky 150.00 250.00
SG10 Scott Hartnell 6.00 10.00
SG11 Martin Havlat 6.00 15.00
SG12 Ilya Kovalchuk 15.00 40.00
SG13 Gordie Howe 60.00 150.00
SG14 Curtis Joseph 8.00 20.00
SG15 Alexander Svitov 6.00 15.00
SG16 John LeClair 10.00 25.00
SG17 Steve Ott 6.00 15.00
SG18 Bobby Orr 100.00 200.00
SG19 Joe Thornton 15.00 40.00
SG20 Henrik Zetterberg 10.00 25.00
SG21 Marty Turco 8.00 20.00
SG22 Marian Hossa 12.00 30.00
SG23 Patrick Roy/24 300.00 500.00
SG24 Jean-Sebastien Giguere 6.00 15.00
SG25 Marian Gaborik 15.00 40.00
SG26 Todd Bertuzzi 8.00 20.00
SG27 Jason Spezza 12.50 30.00
SG28 Jarome Iginla 15.00 40.00
SG29 Sergei Samsonov 6.00 15.00
SG30 Jose Theodore 12.50 30.00
SG31 Justin Williams 6.00 15.00
SG32 Alexander Frolov 6.00 15.00
SG33 Brooks Orpik 6.00 15.00
SG34 Kurt Sauer 6.00 15.00
SG35 Steve Yzerman 25.00 60.00
SG36 Ed Belfour 25.00 60.00
SG37 Jeff Taffe 6.00 15.00

2003-04 Black Diamond Threads

*MULT.COLOR SWATCH: .5X TO 1.25X
STATED ODDS 1:12
DTJS Jason Spezza 6.00 15.00
DTEJ Ed Jovanovski 5.00 12.00
DTRN Rick Nash 8.00 20.00
DTPK Paul Kariya 6.00 15.00
DTRL Roberto Luongo 8.00 20.00
DTAS Alexander Svitov 5.00 12.00
DTDW Doug Weight 5.00 12.00
DTAZ Alexei Zhamnov 5.00 12.00
DTBM Brenden Morrow 5.00 12.00
DTJG Jean-Sebastien Giguere 5.00 12.00
DTMO Mike Modano 8.00 20.00
DTJT Joe Thornton 8.00 20.00
DTCP Chris Pronger 5.00 12.00
DTBS Brendan Shanahan 6.00 15.00
DTKP Keith Primeau 5.00 12.00
DTML Mario Lemieux 12.50 30.00
DTTH Jocelyn Thibault 5.00 12.00
DTMN Markus Naslund 6.00 15.00
DTDU Mike Dunham 5.00 12.00
DTMB Martin Brodeur 12.50 30.00
DTMH Marian Hossa 6.00 15.00
DTMS Mats Sundin 6.00 15.00
DTMD Marc Denis 5.00 12.00
DTAF Alexander Frolov 5.00 12.00
DTPF Peter Forsberg 8.00 20.00
DTAT Alex Tanguay 5.00 12.00
DTED Eric Daze 5.00 12.00
DTMT Marty Turco 6.00 15.00
DTEL Eric Lindros 6.00 15.00
DTKC Kyle Calder 5.00 12.00
DTTE Jose Theodore 8.00 20.00
DTDA David Aebischer 5.00 12.00
DTIK Ilya Kovalchuk 8.00 20.00
DTJB Jay Bouwmeester 5.00 12.00
DTEB Ed Belfour 6.00 15.00
DTMA Maxim Afinogenov 5.00 12.00
DTSN Scott Niedermayer 5.00 12.00
DTJR Jeremy Roenick 6.00 15.00
DTDB Daniel Briere 5.00 12.00
DTMM Mark Messier 12.50 30.00
DTPB Peter Bondra 5.00 12.00
DTDH Dany Heatley 8.00 20.00

2003-04 Black Diamond Threads Green

This set is also referred to as the "Color" parallel.

*STARS: .6X TO 1.5X BASIC INSERTS
STATED PRINT RUN 99 SER.#'d SETS

2003-04 Black Diamond Threads Red

This set is also referred to as the "Cut" parallel.

*STARS: 1X TO 2.5X BASIC INSERTS
STATED PRINT RUN 50 SER.#'d SETS

2003-04 Black Diamond Threads Black

This set is also referred to as the "Clarity" parallel.

STATED PRINT RUN 10 SER.#'d SETS
NOT PRICED DUE TO SCARCITY

2005-06 Black Diamond

This 294-card set was issued both in product specific unopened and as an insert in Rookie Update packs. The unopened product had five-card packs which came 24 to a box. Those cards covered cards 1-210 while cards 211-294 were available in the Rookie Update packs. In the pack issued cards: Cards numbered 85-126 were issued at a stated rate of one in four; cards 127-168 were issued at a stated rate of one in eight and cards 169-210 were issued at a stated rate of one in 24.

COMPLETE SET
COMP.SET w/o SP's (84) 10.00 20.00
DOUBLE ODDS 1:4
TRIPLE ODDS 1:8
QUAD ODDS 1:24
1 Joffrey Lupul .15 .40
2 Steve Rucchin .15 .40
3 Riku Hahl .15 .40
4 Shawn McEachern .15 .40
5 Marc Savard .15 .40
6 Philippe Sauve .20 .50
7 Nick Boynton .15 .40
8 Martin Lapointe .15 .40
9 Maxim Afinogenov .15 .40
10 Chris Drury .20 .50
11 Mike Grier .15 .40
12 Jordan Leopold .15 .40
13 Darren McCarty .15 .40
14 Martin Gelinas .15 .40
15 Eric Staal .20 .50
16 Jeff O'Neill .15 .40
17 Erik Cole .15 .40
18 Rod Brind'Amour .15 .40
19 Jocelyn Thibault .20 .50
20 Tyler Arnason .15 .40
21 Bryan Berard .15 .40
22 Eric Daze .20 .50
23 Rob Blake .20 .50
24 Nikolai Zherdev .15 .40
25 Marc Denis .15 .40
26 Justin Williams .20 .50
27 Brenden Morrow .20 .50
28 Sergei Zubov .15 .40
29 Jere Lehtinen .20 .50
30 Henrik Zetterberg .25 .60
31 Ty Conklin .20 .50
32 Ryan Smyth .15 .40
33 Jason Smith .15 .40
34 Chris Chelios .20 .50
35 Stephen Weiss .15 .40
36 Olli Jokinen .15 .40
37 Gary Roberts .15 .40
38 Alexander Frolov .15 .40
39 Mathieu Garon .20 .50
40 Lubomir Visnovsky .15 .40
41 Dwayne Roloson .20 .50
42 Pascal Dupuis .15 .40
43 Brian Rolston .20 .50
44 Filip Kuba .15 .40
45 Richard Zednik .15 .40
46 Sheldon Souray .15 .40
47 Steve Sullivan .15 .40
48 Jordin Tootoo .15 .40
49 Tomas Vokoun .20 .50
50 Scott Walker .15 .40
51 Martin Brodeur 1.50 4.00
52 Scott Niedermayer .15 .40
53 Brian Rafalski .15 .40
54 Alexander Mogilny .20 .50
55 Bobby Holik .15 .40
56 Kevin Weekes .20 .50
57 Jamie Lundmark .15 .40
58 Michael Peca .15 .40
59 Mark Parrish .15 .40
60 Adrian Aucoin .15 .40
61 Wade Redden .15 .40
62 Zdeno Chara .15 .40
63 Simon Gagne .25 .60
64 Robert Esche .20 .50
65 Mike Comrie .15 .40
66 Shane Doan .15 .40
67 Derian Hatcher .15 .40
68 Ladislav Nagy .15 .40
69 Milan Kraft .15 .40
70 Ryan Malone .15 .40
71 Marco Sturm .15 .40
72 Brad Stuart .15 .40
73 Alyn McCauley .15 .40
74 Patrick Lalime .20 .50
75 Dustin Brown .15 .40
76 Fredrik Modin .15 .40
77 Dave Andreychuk .20 .50
78 Brian Leetch .25 .60
79 Tie Domi .20 .50
80 Ed Jovanovski .20 .50
81 Brendan Morrison .20 .50
82 Dan Cloutier .20 .50
83 Brendan Witt .15 .40
84 Martin Biron .20 .50
85 Manny Legace 1.00 2.50
86 Jean-Sebastien Giguere 1.00 2.50
87 Sergei Fedorov 1.50 4.00
88 Andrew Raycroft 1.00 2.50
89 Sergei Samsonov 1.00 2.50
90 Miroslav Satan 1.00 2.50
91 Miikka Kiprusoff 1.00 2.50
92 David Aebischer 1.00 2.50
93 Milan Hejduk 1.25 3.00
94 Marty Turco 1.00 2.50
95 Curtis Joseph 1.25 3.00
96 Nicklas Lidstrom 1.25 3.00
97 Roberto Luongo 1.00 2.50
98 Zigmund Palffy 1.00 2.50
99 Luc Robitaille 1.00 2.50
100 Mike Ribeiro 1.00 2.50
101 Michael Ryder 1.00 2.50
102 Scott Gomez 1.00 2.50
103 Patrik Elias 1.00 2.50
104 Alexei Yashin 1.00 2.50
105 Daniel Alfredsson 1.00 2.50
106 Martin Havlat 1.00 2.50
107 Tony Amonte 1.00 2.50
108 John LeClair 1.25 3.00
109 Brett Hull 1.50 4.00
110 Marc-Andre Fleury 1.00 2.50
111 Mark Recchi 1.00 2.50
112 Patrick Marleau 1.00 2.50
113 Jonathan Cheechoo 1.50 4.00
114 Chris Pronger 1.00 2.50
115 Doug Weight 1.00 2.50
116 Brad Richards 1.00 2.50
117 Glen Murray 1.00 2.50
118 Tuomo Ruutu 1.00 2.50
119 Pavol Demitra 1.00 2.50
120 David Legwand 1.00 2.50
121 Eric Lindros 1.25 3.00
122 Rick DiPietro 1.00 2.50
123 Al MacInnis 1.00 2.50
124 Joe Nieuwendyk 1.00 2.50
125 Trevor Linden 1.00 2.50
126 Olaf Kolzig 1.00 2.50
127 Dany Heatley 4.00 10.00
128 Kari Lehtonen 3.00 8.00
129 Patrice Bergeron 3.00 8.00
130 Alex Tanguay 3.00 8.00
131 Paul Kariya 3.00 8.00
132 Mike Modano 4.00 10.00
133 Bill Guerin 3.00 8.00
134 Pavel Datsyuk 3.00 8.00
135 Brendan Shanahan 3.00 8.00
136 Saku Koivu 3.00 8.00
137 Marian Hossa 3.00 8.00
138 Jason Spezza 3.00 8.00
139 Jeremy Roenick 4.00 10.00
140 Keith Primeau 3.00 8.00
141 Evgeni Nabokov 3.00 8.00
142 Vincent Lecavalier 3.00 8.00
143 Ed Belfour 3.00 8.00
144 Jason Allison 3.00 8.00
145 Markus Naslund 3.00 8.00
146 Keith Tkachuk 3.00 8.00
147 Nikolai Khabibulin 3.00 8.00
148 Andrew Alberts RC 2.50 6.00
149 Andy Wozniewski RC 2.50 6.00
150 Brandon Bochenski RC 3.00 8.00
151 Brent Seabrook RC 5.00 12.00
152 Cam Ward RC 6.00 15.00
153 Chris Campoli RC 2.50 6.00
154 David Leneveu RC 3.00 8.00
155 Duncan Keith RC 6.00 15.00
156 Henrik Lundqvist RC 10.00 25.00
157 Jay McClement RC 2.50 6.00
158 Johan Franzen RC 5.00 12.00
159 Jussi Jokinen RC 3.00 8.00
160 Keith Ballard RC 2.50 6.00
161 Kevin Dallman RC 2.50 6.00
162 Maxime Talbot RC 2.50 6.00
163 Nicklas Nordgren RC 2.50 6.00
164 Peter Budaj RC 3.00 8.00
165 Petteri Nokelainen RC 2.50 6.00
166 Rene Bourque RC 2.50 6.00
167 Jeff Woywitka RC 2.50 6.00
168 Ryan Hollweg RC 2.50 6.00
169 Ilya Kovalchuk 5.00 12.00
170 Joe Thornton 5.00 12.00
171 Jarome Iginla 5.00 12.00
172 Joe Sakic 8.00 20.00
173 Peter Forsberg 8.00 20.00
174 Rick Nash 4.00 10.00
175 Steve Yzerman 10.00 25.00
176 Marian Gaborik 5.00 12.00
177 Jose Theodore 3.00 8.00
178 Jaromir Jagr 5.00 12.00
179 Mark Messier 8.00 20.00
180 Dominik Hasek 6.00 15.00
181 Mario Lemieux 10.00 30.00
182 Martin St. Louis 4.00 10.00
183 Mats Sundin 3.00 10.00
184 Wayne Gretzky 15.00 40.00
185 Gordie Howe 8.00 20.00
186 Ray Bourque 5.00 12.00
187 Patrick Roy 10.00 30.00
188 Bryan Trottier 4.00 10.00
189 Cam Neely 4.00 10.00
190 Gilbert Brule RC 10.00 25.00
191 Alexander Ovechkin RC 60.00 120.00
192 Zach Parise RC 12.00 30.00
193 Sidney Crosby RC 125.00 250.00
194 Dion Phaneuf RC 25.00 60.00
195 Jeff Carter RC 12.00 30.00
196 Corey Perry RC 10.00 25.00
197 Thomas Vanek RC 15.00 40.00
198 Ryan Getzlaf RC 15.00 40.00
199 Mike Richards RC 10.00 25.00
200 Robert Nilsson RC 5.00 12.00
201 Alexander Steen RC 6.00 15.00
202 Rostislav Olesz RC 5.00 12.00
203 Wojtek Wolski RC 10.00 25.00
204 Ryan Suter RC 5.00 12.00
205 Hannu Toivonen RC 6.00 15.00
206 Yann Danis RC 5.00 12.00
207 Jim Howard RC 8.00 20.00
208 Andrej Meszaros RC 6.00 15.00
209 Braydon Coburn RC 4.00 10.00
210 Alexander Perezhogin RC 5.00 12.00
211 Dustin Penner RC 5.00 12.00
212 Zenon Konopka RC 2.50 6.00
213 Jim Slater RC 3.00 8.00
214 Adam Berkhoel RC 3.00 8.00
215 Jordan Sigalet RC 3.00 8.00
216 Milan Jurcina RC 2.50 6.00
217 Ben Walter RC 2.50 6.00
218 Chris Thorburn RC 2.50 6.00
219 Daniel Paille RC 2.50 6.00
220 Nathan Paetsch RC 2.50 6.00
221 Andrew Ladd RC 4.00 10.00
222 Kevin Nastiuk RC 2.50 6.00
223 Danny Richmond RC 2.50 6.00
224 Cam Barker RC 3.00 8.00
225 Corey Crawford RC 3.00 8.00
226 James Wisniewski RC 2.50 6.00
227 Brad Richardson RC 2.50 6.00
228 Vitaly Kolesnik RC 3.00 8.00
229 Ole-Kristian Tollefsen RC 2.50 6.00
230 Jaroslav Balastik RC 2.50 6.00
231 Geoff Platt RC 2.50 6.00
232 Alexandre Picard RC 2.50 6.00
233 Joakim Lindstrom RC 2.50 6.00
234 Junior Lessard RC 2.50 6.00
235 Vojtech Polak RC 2.50 6.00
236 Kyle Quincey RC 3.00 8.00
237 Valtteri Filppula RC 3.00 8.00
238 Brett Lebda RC 3.00 8.00
239 Kyle Brodziak RC 2.50 6.00
240 Brad Winchester RC 2.50 6.00
241 Danny Syvret RC 3.00 8.00
242 Matt Greene RC 2.50 6.00
243 J-F Jacques RC 2.50 6.00
244 Anthony Stewart RC 3.00 8.00
245 Rob Globke RC 2.50 6.00
246 Petr Taticek RC 2.50 6.00
247 Jeff Tambellini RC 3.00 8.00
248 Petr Kanko RC 2.50 6.00
249 George Parros RC 2.50 6.00
250 Yanick Lehoux RC 2.50 6.00
251 Richard Petiot RC 2.50 6.00
252 Mikko Koivu RC 4.00 10.00
253 Derek Boogaard RC 3.00 8.00
254 Matt Foy RC 2.50 6.00
255 Andrei Kostitsyn RC 4.00 10.00
256 Maxim Lapierre RC 2.50 6.00
257 Kevin Klein RC 2.50 6.00
258 Pekka Rinne RC 3.00 8.00
259 Barry Tallackson RC 3.00 8.00
260 Jason Ryznar RC 2.50 6.00
261 Jeremy Colliton RC 2.50 6.00
262 Bruno Gervais RC 2.50 6.00
263 Petr Prucha RC 4.00 10.00
264 Al Montoya RC 4.00 10.00
265 Christoph Schubert RC 2.50 6.00
266 Patrick Eaves RC 4.00 10.00
267 R.J. Umberger RC 4.00 10.00
268 Ben Eager RC 2.50 6.00
269 Alexandre Picard RC 2.50 6.00
270 Stefan Ruzicka RC 2.50 6.00
271 Ryan Whitney RC 3.00 8.00
272 Erik Christensen RC 3.00 8.00
273 Colby Armstrong RC 4.00 10.00
274 Steve Bernier RC 4.00 10.00
275 Dimitri Patzold RC 3.00 8.00
276 Ryane Clowe RC 2.50 6.00
277 Josh Gorges RC 2.50 6.00
278 Grant Stevenson RC 2.50 6.00
279 Lee Stempniak RC 2.50 6.00
280 Colin Hemingway RC 2.50 6.00
281 Dennis Wideman RC 2.50 6.00
282 Evgeny Artyukhin RC 2.50 6.00
283 Ryan Craig RC 2.50 6.00
284 Paul Ranger RC 2.50 6.00
285 Darren Reid RC 2.50 6.00
286 Gerald Coleman RC 3.00 8.00
287 Staffan Kronwall RC 2.50 6.00
288 Jay Harrison RC 2.50 6.00
289 Kevin Bieksa RC 2.50 6.00
290 Rob McVicar RC 3.00 8.00
291 Tomas Mojzis RC 2.50 6.00
292 Jakub Klepis RC 2.50 6.00
293 Tomas Fleischmann RC 2.50 6.00
294 Mike Green RC 5.00 12.00

2005-06 Black Diamond Emerald

COMMON SINGLE DIAMOND 8.00 20.00
*DOUBLE STARS: 4X TO 10X
*TRIPLE STARS: 1.5X TO 4X
*TRIPLE ROOKIE: 1.25X TO 3X
*QUAD STARS: .75X TO 2X
*QUAD ROOKIE: 1X TO 2.5X
PRINT RUN 25 SER.#'d SETS

2005-06 Black Diamond Gold

PRINT RUN 10 SER.#'d SETS
NOT PRICED DUE TO SCARCITY

2005-06 Black Diamond Onyx

STATED PRINT RUN 1 SET
NOT PRICED DUE TO SCARCITY

2005-06 Black Diamond Ruby

COMMON SINGLE DIAMOND (1-84) 4.00 10.00
COMMON DOUBLE DIAM. (85-126) 5.00 12.00
*TRIPLE STARS: .75X TO 2X
*TRIPLE ROOKIE: 1X TO 2.5X
*QUAD STARS: .5X TO 1.25X
*QUAD ROOKIE: .5X TO 1.25X
PRINT RUN 100 SER.#'d SETS
191 Alexander Ovechkin 175.00 300.00
193 Sidney Crosby 250.00 400.00

2005-06 Black Diamond Gemography

Overall auto odds 1:48.

STATED ODDS 1:62
GAC Anson Carter 5.00 12.00
GAV Antoine Vermette 6.00 12.00
GBA Milan Bartovic 4.00 10.00
GBB Brad Boyes 6.00 12.00
GBI Martin Biron 6.00 12.00
GCD Chris Drury 6.00 12.00
GDB Dustin Brown 5.00 12.00
GDH Dany Heatley 15.00 40.00
GEC Erik Cole 5.00 12.00
GFS Fredrik Sjostrom 4.00 10.00
GGH Gordie Howe 40.00 100.00
GHA Dominik Hasek 20.00 50.00
GHO Marcel Hossa 4.00 10.00
GIK Ilya Kovalchuk 15.00 40.00
GJC Jonathan Cheechoo 8.00 20.00
GJI Jarome Iginla 20.00 50.00
GJR Jeremy Roenick 15.00 40.00
GJT Joe Thornton 20.00 50.00
GKD Kris Draper 6.00 12.00
GLR Luc Robitaille 10.00 25.00
GMB Martin Brodeur 50.00 125.00
GMC Mike Comrie 4.00 10.00
GMF Marc-Andre Fleury 15.00 40.00
GMG Marian Gaborik 20.00 50.00
GMH Martin Havlat 6.00 12.00
GMN Markus Naslund 8.00 15.00
GMP Mark Popovic 4.00 10.00
GMR Michael Ryder 8.00 15.00
GNK Nikolai Khabibulin 8.00 15.00
GNZ Nikolai Zherdev 4.00 10.00
GPB Patrice Bergeron 6.00 15.00
GRB Ray Bourque 30.00 80.00
GRE Robert Esche 5.00 12.00
GRK Ryan Kesler 5.00 12.00
GSB Sean Bergenheim 4.00 10.00
GSL Martin St. Louis 6.00 15.00
GSP Jason Spezza 12.00 30.00
GSS Sheldon Souray 4.00 10.00
GTM Travis Moen 4.00 10.00
GTR Tuomo Ruutu 6.00 12.00
GTS Timofei Shishkanov 4.00 10.00
GWG Wayne Gretzky 200.00 300.00

2005-06 Black Diamond Gemography Emerald

*EMERALD: .6X TO 1.5X BASIC INSERTS
PRINT RUN 25 SER.#'d SETS
GWG Wayne Gretzky 150.00 300.00

2005-06 Black Diamond Gemography Gold

PRINT RUN 10 SER.#'d SETS
NOT PRICED DUE TO SCARCITY

2005-06 Black Diamond Gemography Onyx

PRINT RUN 1 SER.#'d SET
NOT PRICED DUE TO SCARCITY

2005-06 Black Diamond Gemography Ruby

*RUBY: .5X TO 1.25X BASIC INSERT
PRINT RUN 50 SER.#'d SET

2005-06 Black Diamond Jerseys

STATED ODDS 1:12
JAM Al MacInnis 4.00 10.00
JBH Brett Hull 5.00 12.00
JBO Mike Bossy 5.00 12.00
JBS Brendan Shanahan 5.00 12.00
JCC Chris Chelios 5.00 12.00
JCJ Curtis Joseph 5.00 12.00
JEB Ed Belfour 5.00 12.00
JEJ Ed Jovanovski 3.00 8.00
JGL Guy Lafleur 6.00 15.00
JHA Dominik Hasek 6.00 15.00
JJF Jeff Friesen 3.00 8.00
JJI Jarome Iginla 6.00 15.00
JJJ Jaromir Jagr 6.00 15.00
JJN Joe Nieuwendyk 3.00 8.00
JJO Jose Theodore 4.00 10.00
JJR Jeremy Roenick 5.00 12.00
JJS Joe Sakic 8.00 20.00
JJT Joe Thornton 6.00 15.00
JKP Keith Primeau 3.00 8.00
JMB Martin Brodeur 10.00 25.00
JMG Marian Gaborik 6.00 15.00
JMH Milan Hejduk 3.00 8.00
JML Mario Lemieux 15.00 40.00
JMM Mike Modano 5.00 12.00
JMS Mark Messier 8.00 20.00
JOJ Olli Jokinen 3.00 8.00
JON Owen Nolan 4.00 8.00
JPB Pavel Bure 5.00 12.00
JPE Peter Bondra 4.00 10.00
JPF Peter Forsberg 6.00 15.00
JPK Paul Kariya 5.00 12.00
JPL Patrick Lalime 3.00 8.00
JRL Roberto Luongo 6.00 15.00
JRN Rick Nash 5.00 12.00
JSF Sergei Fedorov 5.00 12.00
JSK Saku Koivu 5.00 12.00
JSL Martin St. Louis 4.00 10.00
JSU Mats Sundin 5.00 12.00
JSY Steve Yzerman 12.00 30.00
JTS Teemu Selanne 5.00 12.00
JWG Wayne Gretzky 20.00 50.00

2005-06 Black Diamond Jerseys Ruby

*RUBY: .5X TO 1.25X
PRINT RUN 100 SER.#'d SETS
JDH Dany Heatley 8.00 20.00

2005-06 Black Diamond Jersey Duals

*DUAL: 1.25X TO 3X SINGLE
PRINT RUN 25 SER.#'d SETS
DJDH Dany Heatley 12.50 30.00

2005-06 Black Diamond Jersey Triples

PRINT RUN 10 SER.#'d SETS
NOT PRICED DUE TO SCARCITY

2005-06 Black Diamond Jersey Quads

PRINT RUN 1 SET
NOT PRICED DUE TO SCARCITY

2006-07 Black Diamond

This 210-card set was issued into the hobby in five-card packs, with an $3.99 SRP, which came 24 packs to a box. Cards numbered 1-84 feature veterans in team alphabetical order while cards 85-126 also features another grouping of veterans in team alphabetical order. Cards numbered 148-168 exist in two versions, one of which is a Rookie Card and the other is a veteran player. The set concludes with more Rookie Cards from 190-210. Please note that no cards 169-189 exist in this set.

85-126 DOUBLE ODDS 1:4
TRIPLE ODDS 1:8
QUAD ODDS 1:24
CARDS 169-189 DO NOT EXIST
1 Corey Perry .40 1.00
2 Ilya Bryzgalov .50 1.25
3 Scott Niedermayer .30 .75
4 Slava Kozlov .30 .75
5 Jim Slater .15 .40
6 Hannu Toivonen .50 1.25
7 Marc Savard .30 .75
8 Zdeno Chara .30 .75
9 Glen Murray .30 .75
10 Daniel Briere .40 1.00
11 Maxim Afinogenov .30 .75
12 Thomas Vanek .40 1.00
13 Daymond Langkow .30 .75
14 Chuck Kobasew .30 .75
15 Rod Brind'Amour .40 1.00
16 Justin Williams .30 .75
17 Mike Commodore .30 .75
18 Michal Handzus .15 .40
19 Brent Seabrook .30 .75
20 Nikolai Khabibulin .50 1.25
21 Peter Budaj .40 1.00
22 Wojtek Wolski .30 .75
23 Fredrik Modin .30 .75
24 Pascal Leclaire .50 1.25
25 Bryan Berard .30 .75
26 Brenden Morrow .40 1.00
27 Sergei Zubov .30 .75
28 Jere Lehtinen .30 .75
29 Kris Draper .30 .75
30 Tomas Holmstrom .30 .75
31 Dwayne Roloson .40 1.00
32 Jarret Stoll .30 .75
33 Shawn Horcoff .30 .75
34 Fernando Pisani .30 .75
35 Olli Jokinen .30 .75
36 Nathan Horton .30 .75
37 Todd Bertuzzi .40 1.00
38 Mike Cammalleri .30 .75
39 Craig Conroy .30 .75
40 Pavol Demitra .30 .75
41 Mark Parrish .30 .75
42 Manny Fernandez .50 1.25
43 Pierre-Marc Bouchard .30 .75
44 Sergei Samsonov .40 1.00
45 Alex Kovalev .30 .75
46 Jason Arnott .30 .75
47 Steve Sullivan .30 .75
48 Scott Hartnell .15 .40
49 Scott Gomez .30 .75
50 Brian Gionta .30 .75
51 Zach Parise .40 1.00
52 Rick DiPietro .50 1.25
53 Robert Nilsson .15 .40
54 Jason Blake .30 .75
55 Petr Prucha .30 .75
56 Martin Straka .30 .75
57 Martin Gerber .50 1.25
58 Wade Redden .30 .75
59 Patrick Eaves .30 .75
60 Joni Pitkanen .30 .75
61 Mike Richards .50 1.25
62 Antero Niittymaki .50 1.25
63 Curtis Joseph .50 1.25
64 Ladislav Nagy .30 .75
65 Ed Jovanovski .30 .75
66 Colby Armstrong .30 .75
67 Ryan Whitney .30 .75
68 Ryan Malone .30 .75
69 Steve Bernier .30 .75
70 Evgeni Nabokov .40 1.00
71 Vesa Toskala .40 1.00
72 Keith Tkachuk .40 1.00
73 Bill Guerin .30 .75
74 Manny Legace .40 1.00
75 Vaclav Prospal .30 .75
76 Marc Denis .40 1.00
77 Martin St. Louis .50 1.25
78 Andrew Raycroft .40 1.00
79 Darcy Tucker .30 .75
80 Daniel Sedin .30 .75
81 Henrik Sedin .30 .75
82 Brendan Morrison .30 .75
83 Dainius Zubrus .30 .75
84 Olaf Kolzig .60 1.50
85 Teemu Selanne 3.00 8.00
86 Jean-Sebastien Giguere 3.00 8.00
87 Chris Pronger 2.50 6.00
88 Marian Hossa 2.50 6.00
89 Brad Boyes 2.00 5.00
90 Chris Drury 2.50 6.00
91 Ryan Miller 3.00 8.00
92 Alex Tanguay 2.50 6.00
93 Erik Cole 2.00 5.00
94 Tuomo Ruutu 2.00 5.00
95 Martin Havlat 2.50 6.00
96 Jose Theodore 1.50 4.00
97 Marek Svatos 1.00 2.50
98 Sergei Fedorov 1.50 4.00
99 Gilbert Brule 1.50 4.00
100 Eric Lindros 3.00 8.00
101 Marty Turco 2.50 6.00
102 Pavel Datsyuk 3.00 8.00
103 Ales Hemsky 2.00 5.00
104 Ryan Smyth 2.50 6.00
105 Jay Bouwmeester 2.00 5.00
106 Rob Blake 2.00 5.00
107 Alexander Frolov 2.00 5.00
108 Mikko Koivu 2.00 5.00
109 Cristobal Huet 3.00 8.00
110 Mike Ribeiro 2.00 5.00
111 Tomas Vokoun 2.50 6.00
112 Patrik Elias 2.00 5.00
113 Alexei Yashin 2.00 5.00
114 Miroslav Satan 2.00 5.00
115 Henrik Lundqvist 5.00 12.00
116 Daniel Alfredsson 2.50 6.00
117 Simon Gagne 3.00 8.00
118 Jeff Carter 3.00 8.00
119 Shane Doan 2.50 6.00
120 Jeremy Roenick 3.00 8.00
121 Mark Recchi 2.00 5.00
122 Patrick Marleau 2.50 6.00
123 Doug Weight 2.00 5.00
124 Brad Richards 3.00 8.00
125 Alexander Steen 2.50 6.00
126 Michael Peca 2.00 5.00
127 Kari Lehtonen 4.00 10.00
128 Patrice Bergeron 3.00 8.00
129 Miikka Kiprusoff 4.00 10.00
130 Dion Phaneuf 5.00 12.00
131 Eric Staal 3.00 8.00
132 Cam Ward 6.00 15.00
133 Milan Hejduk 3.00 8.00
134 Mike Modano 4.00 10.00
135 Henrik Zetterberg 4.00 10.00
136 Nicklas Lidstrom 4.00 10.00
137 Ed Belfour 10.00 25.00
138 Saku Koivu 4.00 10.00
139 Michael Ryder 3.00 8.00
140 Paul Kariya 4.00 10.00
141 Brendan Shanahan 4.00 10.00
142 Dany Heatley 4.00 10.00
143 Marc-Andre Fleury 4.00 10.00
144 Jonathan Cheechoo 4.00 10.00
145 Vincent Lecavalier 4.00 10.00
146 Markus Naslund 4.00 10.00
147 Roberto Luongo 8.00 20.00
148A Roman Polak RC 2.00 5.00
148B Ilya Kovalchuk 3.00 8.00
149A Joel Perrault RC 2.00 5.00
149B Ray Bourque 3.00 8.00
150A Yan Stastny RC 2.50 6.00
150B Cam Neely 3.00 8.00
151A Konstantin Pushkarev RC 2.00 5.00
151B Jarome Iginla 3.00 8.00
152A Jarkko Immonen RC 2.50 6.00
152B Joe Sakic 4.00 10.00
153A Marc-Antoine Pouliot RC 3.00 8.00
153B Patrick Roy 6.00 15.00
154A Jeremy Williams RC 2.00 5.00
154B Rick Nash 2.50 6.00
155A Michel Ouellet RC 2.50 6.00
155B Dominik Hasek 3.00 8.00
156A Tomas Kopecky RC 2.50 6.00
156B Gordie Howe 4.00 10.00
157A Keith Yandle RC 2.00 5.00
157B Wayne Gretzky 8.00 20.00
158A Marc-Edouard Vlasic RC 2.50 6.00
158B Marian Gaborik 3.00 8.00
159A Shane O'Brien RC 2.50 6.00
159B Jean Beliveau 2.50 6.00
160A Ryan Shannon RC 2.50 6.00
160B Martin Brodeur 4.00 10.00
161A John Oduya RC 2.00 5.00
161B Jaromir Jagr 3.00 8.00
162A Fredrik Norrena RC 2.50 6.00
162B Jason Spezza 3.00 8.00
163A Kristopher Letang RC 2.50 6.00
163B Peter Forsberg 3.00 8.00
164A Niklas Backstrom RC 3.00 8.00
164B Sidney Crosby 15.00 40.00
165A D.J. King RC 2.00 5.00
165B Mario Lemieux 6.00 15.00
166A Patrick Thoresen RC 2.00 5.00
166B Joe Thornton 4.00 10.00
167A Patrick Fischer RC 2.00 5.00
167B Mats Sundin 3.00 8.00
168A Mikko Lehtonen RC 2.00 5.00
168B Alexander Ovechkin 5.00 12.00
190 Mark Stuart RC 2.50 6.00
191 Eric Fehr RC 3.00 8.00
192 Ryan Potulny RC 3.00 8.00
193 Ian White RC 2.50 6.00
194 Alexei Kaigorodov RC 2.50 6.00
195 Noah Welch RC 2.50 6.00
196 Shea Weber RC 4.00 10.00
197 Enver Lisin RC 2.50 6.00
198 Matt Carle RC 3.00 8.00
199 Patrick O'Sullivan RC 5.00 12.00
200 Anze Kopitar RC 12.00 30.00
201 Travis Zajac RC 4.00 10.00
202 Phil Kessel RC 12.00 30.00
203 Guillaume Latendresse RC 10.00 25.00
204 Nigel Dawes RC 3.00 8.00
205 Jordan Staal RC 15.00 40.00
206 Paul Stastny RC 15.00 40.00
207 Luc Bourdon RC 3.00 8.00
208 Ladislav Smid RC 3.00 8.00
209 Loui Eriksson RC 3.00 8.00
210 Evgeni Malkin RC 50.00 100.00

2006-07 Black Diamond Black

STATED PRINT RUN 1/1
NOT PRICED DUE TO SCARCITY

2006-07 Black Diamond Gold

COMPLETE SET (210)
STATED PRINT RUN 10 #'d SETS
NOT PRICED DUE TO SCARCITY

2006-07 Black Diamond Ruby

COMPLETE SET (210)
STATED PRINT RUN 100 #'d SETS
1 Corey Perry 6.00 15.00
2 Ilya Bryzgalov 8.00 20.00
3 Scott Niedermayer 5.00 12.00
4 Slava Kozlov 5.00 12.00
5 Jim Slater 2.50 6.00
6 Hannu Toivonen 8.00 20.00
7 Marc Savard 5.00 12.00
8 Zdeno Chara 5.00 12.00
9 Glen Murray 5.00 12.00
10 Daniel Briere 6.00 15.00
11 Maxim Afinogenov 5.00 12.00
12 Thomas Vanek 6.00 15.00
13 Daymond Langkow 5.00 12.00
14 Chuck Kobasew 5.00 12.00
15 Rod Brind'Amour 6.00 15.00
16 Justin Williams 5.00 12.00
17 Mike Commodore 5.00 12.00
18 Michal Handzus 2.50 6.00
19 Brent Seabrook 5.00 12.00
20 Nikolai Khabibulin 8.00 20.00
21 Peter Budaj 6.00 15.00
22 Wojtek Wolski 5.00 12.00
23 Fredrik Modin 5.00 12.00
24 Pascal Leclaire 8.00 20.00
25 Bryan Berard 5.00 12.00
26 Brenden Morrow 6.00 15.00
27 Sergei Zubov 5.00 12.00
28 Jere Lehtinen 5.00 12.00
29 Kris Draper 5.00 12.00
30 Tomas Holmstrom 5.00 12.00
31 Dwayne Roloson 6.00 15.00
32 Jarret Stoll 5.00 12.00
33 Shawn Horcoff 5.00 12.00
34 Fernando Pisani 5.00 12.00
35 Olli Jokinen 5.00 12.00
36 Nathan Horton 5.00 12.00
37 Todd Bertuzzi 6.00 15.00
38 Mike Cammalleri 5.00 12.00
39 Craig Conroy 5.00 12.00
40 Pavol Demitra 5.00 12.00
41 Mark Parrish 5.00 12.00
42 Manny Fernandez 8.00 20.00
43 Pierre-Marc Bouchard 5.00 12.00
44 Sergei Samsonov 6.00 15.00
45 Alex Kovalev 5.00 12.00
46 Jason Arnott 5.00 12.00
47 Steve Sullivan 5.00 12.00
48 Scott Hartnell 2.50 6.00
49 Scott Gomez 5.00 12.00
50 Brian Gionta 5.00 12.00
51 Zach Parise 6.00 15.00
52 Rick DiPietro 8.00 20.00
53 Robert Nilsson 2.50 6.00
54 Jason Blake 5.00 12.00
55 Petr Prucha 5.00 12.00
56 Martin Straka 5.00 12.00
57 Martin Gerber 8.00 20.00
58 Wade Redden 5.00 12.00
59 Patrick Eaves 5.00 12.00
60 Joni Pitkanen 5.00 12.00
61 Mike Richards 8.00 20.00
62 Antero Niittymaki 8.00 20.00
63 Curtis Joseph 8.00 20.00
64 Ladislav Nagy 5.00 12.00
65 Ed Jovanovski 5.00 12.00
66 Colby Armstrong 5.00 12.00
67 Ryan Whitney 5.00 12.00
68 Ryan Malone 5.00 12.00
69 Steve Bernier 5.00 12.00
70 Evgeni Nabokov 6.00 15.00
71 Vesa Toskala 6.00 15.00
72 Keith Tkachuk 6.00 15.00
73 Bill Guerin 5.00 12.00
74 Manny Legace 6.00 15.00
75 Vaclav Prospal 5.00 12.00
76 Marc Denis 6.00 15.00
77 Martin St. Louis 8.00 20.00
78 Andrew Raycroft 6.00 15.00
79 Darcy Tucker 5.00 12.00
80 Daniel Sedin 5.00 12.00
81 Henrik Sedin 5.00 12.00
82 Brendan Morrison 5.00 12.00
83 Dainius Zubrus 5.00 12.00
84 Olaf Kolzig 10.00 25.00
85 Teemu Selanne 8.00 20.00
86 Jean-Sebastien Giguere 8.00 20.00
87 Chris Pronger 6.00 15.00
88 Marian Hossa 6.00 15.00
89 Brad Boyes 5.00 12.00
90 Chris Drury 6.00 15.00
91 Ryan Miller 8.00 20.00
92 Alex Tanguay 6.00 15.00
93 Erik Cole 5.00 12.00
94 Tuomo Ruutu 5.00 12.00
95 Martin Havlat 6.00 15.00
96 Jose Theodore 5.00 12.00
97 Marek Svatos 5.00 12.00
98 Sergei Fedorov 8.00 20.00
99 Gilbert Brule 5.00 12.00
100 Eric Lindros 8.00 20.00
101 Marty Turco 6.00 15.00
102 Pavel Datsyuk 8.00 20.00
103 Ales Hemsky 5.00 12.00
104 Ryan Smyth 6.00 15.00
105 Jay Bouwmeester 6.00 15.00
106 Rob Blake 6.00 15.00
107 Alexander Frolov 5.00 12.00
108 Mikko Koivu 5.00 12.00
109 Cristobal Huet 8.00 20.00
110 Mike Ribeiro 5.00 12.00
111 Tomas Vokoun 6.00 15.00
112 Patrik Elias 5.00 12.00
113 Alexei Yashin 5.00 12.00
114 Miroslav Satan 5.00 12.00
115 Henrik Lundqvist 12.00 30.00
116 Daniel Alfredsson 6.00 15.00
117 Simon Gagne 8.00 20.00
118 Jeff Carter 8.00 20.00
119 Shane Doan 6.00 15.00
120 Jeremy Roenick 8.00 20.00
121 Mark Recchi 5.00 12.00
122 Patrick Marleau 6.00 15.00
123 Doug Weight 5.00 12.00
124 Brad Richards 8.00 20.00
125 Alexander Steen 6.00 15.00
126 Michael Peca 5.00 12.00
127 Kari Lehtonen 8.00 20.00
128 Patrice Bergeron 6.00 15.00
129 Miikka Kiprusoff 8.00 20.00
130 Dion Phaneuf 10.00 25.00
131 Eric Staal 6.00 15.00
132 Cam Ward 12.00 30.00
133 Milan Hejduk 6.00 15.00
134 Mike Modano 8.00 20.00
135 Henrik Zetterberg 8.00 20.00
136 Nicklas Lidstrom 8.00 20.00
137 Ed Belfour 20.00 50.00
138 Saku Koivu 8.00 20.00
139 Michael Ryder 6.00 15.00
140 Paul Kariya 8.00 20.00
141 Brendan Shanahan 8.00 20.00
142 Dany Heatley 8.00 20.00
143 Marc-Andre Fleury 8.00 20.00
144 Jonathan Cheechoo 8.00 20.00
145 Vincent Lecavalier 8.00 20.00
146 Markus Naslund 8.00 20.00
147 Roberto Luongo 15.00 40.00
148A Roman Polak 2.50 6.00
148B Ilya Kovalchuk 10.00 25.00
149A Joel Perrault 5.00 12.00
149B Ray Bourque 8.00 20.00
150A Yan Stastny 5.00 12.00
150B Cam Neely 6.00 15.00
151A Konstantin Pushkarev 5.00 12.00
151B Jarome Iginla 12.00 30.00
152A Jarkko Immonen 5.00 12.00
152B Joe Sakic 12.00 30.00
153A Marc-Antoine Pouliot 6.00 15.00
153B Patrick Roy 15.00 40.00
154A Jeremy Williams 5.00 12.00
154B Rick Nash 8.00 20.00
155A Michel Ouellet 10.00 25.00
155B Dominik Hasek 8.00 20.00
156A Tomas Kopecky 6.00 15.00
156B Gordie Howe 10.00 25.00
157A Keith Yandle 5.00 12.00
157B Wayne Gretzky 25.00 60.00
158A Marc-Edouard Vlasic 5.00 12.00
158B Marian Gaborik 12.00 30.00
159A Shane O'Brien 5.00 12.00
159B Jean Beliveau 6.00 15.00
160A Ryan Shannon 5.00 12.00
160B Martin Brodeur 12.00 30.00
161A John Oduya 5.00 12.00
161B Jaromir Jagr 12.00 30.00
162A Fredrik Norrena 5.00 12.00
162B Jason Spezza 8.00 20.00
163A Kristopher Letang 8.00 20.00
163B Peter Forsberg 10.00 25.00
164A Niklas Backstrom 10.00 25.00
164B Sidney Crosby 60.00 100.00
165A D.J. King 2.50 6.00
165B Mario Lemieux 12.00 30.00
166A Patrick Thoresen 5.00 12.00
166B Joe Thornton 12.00 30.00
167A Patrick Fischer 2.50 6.00
167B Mats Sundin 8.00 20.00
168A Mikko Lehtonen 2.50 6.00
168B Alexander Ovechkin 20.00 50.00
190 Mark Stuart 6.00 15.00
191 Eric Fehr 8.00 20.00
192 Ryan Potulny 10.00 25.00
193 Ian White 6.00 15.00
194 Alexei Kaigorodov 6.00 15.00
195 Noah Welch 6.00 15.00
196 Shea Weber 12.00 30.00
197 Enver Lisin 6.00 15.00
198 Matt Carle 12.00 30.00
199 Patrick O'Sullivan 15.00 40.00
200 Anze Kopitar 25.00 60.00
201 Travis Zajac 10.00 25.00
202 Phil Kessel 25.00 60.00
203 Guillaume Latendresse 25.00 60.00
204 Nigel Dawes 8.00 20.00
205 Jordan Staal 40.00 80.00
206 Paul Stastny 30.00 80.00
207 Luc Bourdon 8.00 20.00
208 Ladislav Smid 8.00 20.00
209 Loui Eriksson 6.00 15.00
210 Evgeni Malkin 100.00 200.00

2006-07 Black Diamond Gemography

STATED ODDS 1:48
GAB Adam Berkhoel 3.00 8.00
GAL Andrew Ladd 3.00 8.00
GAO Alexander Ovechkin SP 125.00 250.00
GBB Brandon Bochenski 3.00 8.00
GBL Brian Leetch SP 25.00 60.00
GBM Bryan McCabe 3.00 8.00
GBW Brad Winchester 3.00 8.00
GCA Jeff Carter 6.00 15.00
GCB Cam Barker 3.00 8.00
GCK Chuck Kobasew 3.00 8.00
GCP Chris Phillips 3.00 8.00
GCS Cory Stillman 3.00 8.00
GDA David Aebischer 6.00 15.00
GDP Dion Phaneuf 8.00 20.00
GDR Danny Richmond 3.00 8.00
GDW Doug Weight 3.00 8.00
GEC Erik Christensen 4.00 10.00
GGH Gordie Howe SP 50.00 100.00
GGL Georges Laraque 3.00 8.00
GGM Glen Murray 4.00 10.00
GHA Scott Hartnell 3.00 8.00
GHZ Henrik Zetterberg SP 10.00 25.00
GJC Jonathan Cheechoo 6.00 15.00
GJG Josh Gorges 3.00 8.00
GJH Jim Howard 6.00 15.00
GJI Jarome Iginla SP 12.00 30.00
GJJ Jussi Jokinen 4.00 10.00
GJO Jeff O'Neill 3.00 8.00
GJP Joni Pitkanen SP 8.00 20.00
GJS Jim Slater 3.00 8.00
GJT Jose Theodore 8.00 20.00
GKD Kris Draper SP 10.00 25.00
GKL Kari Lehtonen SP 10.00 25.00
GKT Kimmo Timonen 8.00 20.00
GMG Marian Gaborik SP 15.00 40.00
GMH Marian Hossa SP 10.00 25.00
GMK Miikka Kiprusoff SP 15.00 40.00
GML Mario Lemieux SP 75.00 150.00
GMP Mark Parrish 3.00 8.00
GMR Mike Ribeiro 3.00 8.00
GMS Miroslav Satan 4.00 10.00
GMT Marty Turco SP 10.00 25.00
GMV Mike Van Ryn 3.00 8.00
GMZ Marek Zidlicky 3.00 8.00
GNH Nathan Horton 4.00 10.00
GPB Patrice Bergeron SP 10.00 25.00
GPM Patrick Marleau 6.00 15.00
GPP Petr Prucha 3.00 8.00
GPR Paul Ranger 3.00 8.00
GRB Rene Bourque 3.00 8.00
GRM Ryan Miller SP 10.00 25.00
GRN Rick Nash SP 20.00 50.00
GSC Sidney Crosby 100.00 175.00
GSH Shawn Horcoff 3.00 8.00
GTC Ty Conklin 6.00 15.00
GVT Vesa Toskala 6.00 15.00
GWG Wayne Gretzky SP 150.00 250.00

2006-07 Black Diamond Jerseys

STATED ODDS 1:13
JAA Arron Asham 3.00 8.00
JAF Alexander Frolov 6.00 15.00
JAH Ales Hemsky 6.00 15.00
JAK Alex Kovalev 6.00 15.00
JAL Jason Allison 3.00 8.00
JAM Andrej Meszaros 6.00 15.00
JAO Alexander Ovechkin SP 12.00 30.00
JAS Alexander Steen 4.00 10.00
JAT Alex Tanguay 4.00 10.00
JBB Brad Boyes 6.00 15.00
JBE Patrice Bergeron 5.00 12.00
JBG Bill Guerin 6.00 15.00
JBJ Barret Jackman 3.00 8.00
JBL Brian Leetch 5.00 12.00
JBM Brendan Morrison 6.00 15.00
JBO Brandon Bochenski 6.00 15.00
JBR Martin Brodeur 12.00 30.00
JBS Brad Stuart 6.00 15.00
JBU Peter Budaj 4.00 10.00
JCD Chris Drury 8.00 20.00
JCJ Curtis Joseph 5.00 12.00
JCK Chuck Kobasew 6.00 15.00
JCO Mike Comrie 6.00 15.00
JCP Corey Perry 4.00 10.00
JCW Cam Ward 5.00 12.00
JDB Donald Brashear 3.00 8.00
JDC Dan Cloutier 4.00 10.00
JDE Pavol Demitra 6.00 15.00
JDH Dan Hamhuis 6.00 15.00
JDK Duncan Keith 12.00 30.00
JDP Dion Phaneuf 6.00 15.00
JDW Doug Weight 6.00 15.00
JEA Evgeni Artyukhin 6.00 15.00
JEB Ed Belfour 5.00 12.00
JEL Eric Lindros 5.00 12.00
JGA Simon Gagne 5.00 12.00
JHE Milan Hejduk 8.00 20.00
JHZ Henrik Zetterberg 5.00 12.00
JIK Ilya Kovalchuk 8.00 20.00
JJA Jason Arnott 6.00 15.00
JJB Jay Bouwmeester 6.00 15.00
JJF Jeff Friesen 3.00 8.00
JJG Jean-Sebastien Giguere 4.00 10.00
JJH Jeff Hoggan 3.00 8.00
JJJ Jaromir Jagr 10.00 25.00
JJK Jakub Klepis 6.00 15.00
JJL Joffrey Lupul 6.00 15.00
JJN Joe Nieuwendyk 4.00 10.00
JJS Joe Sakic 10.00 25.00
JJT Joe Thornton 8.00 20.00
JKD Kris Draper 6.00 15.00
JKO Andrei Kostitsyn 8.00 20.00
JKT Keith Tkachuk 4.00 10.00
JLA Andrew Ladd 6.00 15.00
JLE Jere Lehtinen 6.00 15.00
JMA Mark Bell 6.00 15.00
JMB Martin Biron 4.00 10.00
JMC Mike Cammalleri 6.00 15.00
JMH Marian Hossa 4.00 10.00
JMI Mike Komisarek 3.00 8.00
JMJ Milan Jurcina 6.00 15.00
JMK Miikka Kiprusoff 6.00 15.00
JMM Mike Modano 5.00 12.00
JMN Markus Naslund 5.00 12.00
JMO Shaone Morrisonn 3.00 8.00
JMP Michael Peca 6.00 15.00
JMR Mark Recchi 6.00 15.00
JMS Marek Svatos 6.00 15.00
JNH Nathan Horton 6.00 15.00
JNK Nikolai Khabibulin 5.00 12.00
JPA Daniel Paille 6.00 15.00
JPB Peter Bondra 4.00 10.00
JPD Pavel Datsyuk 4.00 10.00
JPF Peter Forsberg 10.00 25.00
JPK Paul Kariya 5.00 12.00
JRB Rod Brind'Amour 4.00 10.00
JRC Ryan Craig 3.00 8.00
JRD Rick DiPietro 4.00 10.00
JRH Ryan Hollweg 3.00 8.00
JRK Rostislav Klesla 6.00 15.00
JRM Ryan Miller 5.00 12.00
JRO Rob Blake 4.00 10.00
JRU R.J. Umberger 6.00 15.00
JRY Michael Ryder 4.00 10.00
JSA Miroslav Satan 6.00 15.00
JSC Sidney Crosby SP 30.00 80.00
JSF Sergei Fedorov 5.00 12.00
JSG Scott Gomez 6.00 15.00
JSH Jody Shelley 6.00 15.00
JSM Mats Sundin 5.00 12.00
JSN Brendan Shanahan 5.00 12.00
JSS Sergei Samsonov 4.00 10.00
JST Matt Stajan 6.00 15.00
JSU Scottie Upshall 3.00 8.00
JSW Stephen Weiss 3.00 8.00
JTC Ty Conklin 4.00 10.00
JTH Tomas Holmstrom 6.00 15.00
JTP Tom Poti 6.00 15.00
JVN Ville Nieminen 3.00 8.00
JWG Wayne Gretzky 30.00 80.00

2006-07 Black Diamond Jerseys Black

COMPLETE SET (100)
STATED PRINT RUN 1/1
NOT PRICED DUE TO SCARCITY

2006-07 Black Diamond Jerseys Gold

COMPLETE SET (100)
STATED PRINT RUN 10 #'d SETS
NOT PRICED DUE TO SCARCITY

2006-07 Black Diamond Jerseys Ruby

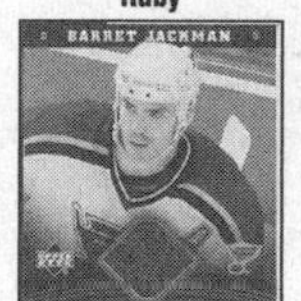

COMPLETE SET (100)
*RUBY: .5X TO 1.5X BASE HI
STATED PRINT RUN 100 SER.#'d SETS
JSC Sidney Crosby/25 75.00 175.00
JWG Wayne Gretzky/25 125.00 200.00

2006-07 Black Diamond Jerseys Black Autographs

STATED PRINT RUN 1/1
NOT PRICED DUE TO SCARCITY
JAF Alexander Frolov
JAH Ales Hemsky
JAO Alexander Ovechkin
JAT Alex Tanguay
JBB Brad Boyes
JBI Martin Biron
JBL Brian Leetch
JBO Brandon Bochenski
JCA Mike Cammalleri
JCD Chris Drury
JCK Chuck Kobasew
JDC Dan Cloutier
JDP Dion Phaneuf
JDW Doug Weight
JGO Scott Gomez
JHO Marian Hossa
JHZ Henrik Zetterberg
JIK Ilya Kovalchuk
JJB Jay Bouwmeester
JJH Jeff Hoggan
JJL Joffrey Lupul
JJT Joe Thornton
JKD Kris Draper
JKI Miikka Kiprusoff
JMB Martin Brodeur
JMH Milan Hejduk

JMN Markus Naslund
JMP Michael Peca
JMS Marek Svatos
JNH Nathan Horton
JNK Nikolai Khabibulin
JPB Patrice Bergeron
JRK Rostislav Klesla
JRM Ryan Miller
JRO Rob Blake
JRY Michael Ryder
JSA Miroslav Satan
JSC Sidney Crosby
JSS Sergei Samsonov
JSW Stephen Weiss
JWG Wayne Gretzky

2007-08 Black Diamond

COMP.SET w/o SPs (84) 15.00 40.00
DOUBLE DIAMONDS STATED ODDS 1:4
TRIPLE DIAMONDS STATED ODDS 1:8
TRIPLE DIAMONDS ROOKIE GEMS STATED ODDS 1:8
QUAD COMMONS (169-189)
QUADRUPLE DIAMONDS STATED ODDS 1:24
QUADRUPLE DIAMONDS ROOKIE GEMS ODDS 1:24
1 Scott Niedermayer .20 .50
2 Andy McDonald .20 .50
3 Bobby Holik .20 .50
4 Marc Savard .20 .50
5 Zdeno Chara .20 .50
6 Glen Murray .20 .50
7 Tim Thomas .40 1.00
8 Manny Fernandez .25 .60
9 Jason Pominville .20 .50
10 Derek Roy .20 .50
11 Daymond Langkow .20 .50
12 Matthew Lombardi .20 .50
13 Justin Williams .20 .50
14 Rod Brind'Amour .25 .60
15 Erik Cole .20 .50
16 Nikolai Khabibulin .30 .75
17 Duncan Keith .30 .75
18 Brent Seabrook .20 .50
19 Tuomo Ruutu .20 .50
20 Peter Budaj .25 .60
21 Marek Svatos .20 .50
22 Wojtek Wolski .20 .50
23 Pascal LeClaire .25 .60
24 David Vyborny .20 .50
25 Gilbert Brule .20 .50
26 Brenden Morrow .25 .60
27 Mike Ribeiro .20 .50
28 Jussi Jokinen .20 .50
29 Jere Lehtinen .20 .50
30 Tomas Holmstrom .25 .60
31 Kris Draper .20 .50
32 Jarret Stoll .20 .50
33 Shawn Horcoff .20 .50
34 Joni Pitkanen .20 .50
35 Stephen Weiss .20 .50
36 Nathan Horton .20 .50
37 Jozef Stumpel .20 .50
38 Jay Bouwmeester .20 .50
39 Mike Cammalleri .25 .60
40 Rob Blake .25 .60
41 Patrick O'Sullivan .25 .60
42 Ladislav Nagy .20 .50
43 Pierre-Marc Bouchard .20 .50
44 Pavol Demitra .20 .50
45 Brian Rolston .20 .50
46 Alexei Kovalev .20 .50
47 Chris Higgins .25 .60
48 Cristobal Huet .25 .60
49 Steve Sullivan .20 .50
50 Jason Arnott .20 .50
51 Travis Zajac .20 .50
52 Bill Guerin .20 .50
53 Scott Gomez .20 .50
54 Martin Straka .20 .50
55 Wade Redden .20 .50
56 Antoine Vermette .20 .50
57 Joffrey Lupul .20 .50
58 Mike Richards .40 1.00
59 Martin Biron .25 .60
60 Mike Knuble .20 .50
61 Ed Jovanovski .20 .50
62 David Aebischer .25 .60
63 Keith Ballard .20 .50
64 Mark Recchi .20 .50
65 Colby Armstrong .20 .50
66 Milan Michalek .20 .50
67 Steve Bernier .20 .50
68 Joe Pavelski .20 .50
69 Keith Tkachuk .25 .60
70 Lee Stempniak .20 .50
71 Brad Boyes .20 .50
72 Johan Holmqvist .25 .60
73 Marc Denis .25 .60
74 Alexander Steen .20 .50
75 Tomas Kaberle .20 .50
76 Jason Blake .20 .50
77 Henrik Sedin .20 .50
78 Daniel Sedin .20 .50
79 Brendan Morrison .20 .50
80 Mattias Ohlund .20 .50
81 Michael Nylander .20 .50
82 Alexander Semin .30 .75
83 Olaf Kolzig .30 .75
84 Viktor Kozlov .20 .50
85 Ryan Getzlaf 1.25 3.00
86 Chris Pronger 1.50 4.00
87 Phil Kessel 1.50 4.00
88 Drew Stafford 1.25 3.00
89 Alex Tanguay 1.25 3.00
90 Dion Phaneuf 1.50 4.00
91 Cam Ward 1.50 4.00
92 Martin Havlat 1.25 3.00
93 Milan Hejduk 1.25 3.00
94 Paul Stastny 1.50 4.00
95 Sergei Fedorov 1.50 4.00
96 Marty Turco 1.50 4.00
97 Nicklas Lidstrom 1.50 4.00
98 Pavel Datsyuk 1.50 4.00
99 Dwayne Roloson 1.25 3.00
100 Ales Hemsky 1.00 2.50
101 Olli Jokinen 1.00 2.50
102 Tomas Vokoun 1.50 4.00
103 Anze Kopitar 1.50 4.00
104 Alexander Frolov 1.00 2.50
105 Mikko Koivu 1.00 2.50
106 Guillaume Latendresse 1.25 3.00
107 Alexander Radulov 1.50 4.00
108 Patrik Elias 1.00 2.50
109 Brian Gionta 1.00 2.50
110 Zach Parise 1.25 3.00
111 Rick DiPietro 1.25 3.00
112 Miroslav Satan 1.00 2.50
113 Chris Drury 1.25 3.00
114 Ray Emery 1.25 3.00
115 Daniel Alfredsson 1.25 3.00
116 Daniel Briere 1.50 4.00
117 Jeff Carter 1.00 2.50
118 Shane Doan 1.00 2.50
119 Jordan Staal 2.00 5.00
120 Patrick Marleau 1.25 3.00
121 Doug Weight 1.00 2.50
122 Manny Legace 1.25 3.00
123 Brad Richards 1.25 3.00
124 Andrew Raycroft 1.25 3.00
125 Darcy Tucker 1.25 3.00
126 Markus Naslund 1.50 4.00
127 Jean-Sebastien Giguere 2.50 6.00
128 Teemu Selanne 2.50 6.00
129 Marian Hossa 2.50 6.00
130 Kari Lehtonen 2.50 6.00
131 Patrice Bergeron 2.50 6.00
132 Thomas Vanek 2.00 5.00
133 Miikka Kiprusoff 3.00 8.00
134 Rick Nash 2.50 6.00
135 Mike Modano 2.50 6.00
136 Dominik Hasek 3.00 8.00
137 Henrik Zetterberg 2.50 6.00
138 Marian Gaborik 3.00 8.00
139 Saku Koivu 2.00 5.00
140 Michael Ryder 1.50 4.00
141 Henrik Lundqvist 3.00 8.00
142 Jason Spezza 2.50 6.00
143 Simon Gagne 2.50 6.00
144 Evgeni Malkin 6.00 15.00
145 Jonathan Cheechoo 2.00 5.00
146 Paul Kariya 2.50 6.00
147 Martin St. Louis 2.00 5.00
148 Peter Kalus RC 1.50 4.00
149 Rob Schremp RC 2.00 5.00
150 Matt Smaby RC 1.50 4.00
151 Andy Greene RC 1.50 4.00
152 Drew Miller RC 1.50 4.00
153 Daniel Winnik RC 1.50 4.00
154 Frans Nielsen RC 1.50 4.00
155 Lauri Tukonen RC 1.50 4.00
156 Ryan Callahan RC 2.50 6.00
157 Jaroslav Halak RC 8.00 20.00
158 David Krejci RC 3.00 8.00
159 Mason Raymond RC 4.00 10.00
160 Curtis McElhinney RC 2.00 5.00
161 Jared Boll RC 1.50 4.00
162 Torrey Mitchell RC 2.00 5.00
163 David Perron RC 2.50 6.00
164 Milan Lucic RC 4.00 10.00
165 Jaroslav Hlinka RC 2.00 5.00
166 Brandon Dubinsky RC 2.50 6.00
167 Brian Elliott RC 2.50 6.00
168 Brett Sterling RC 1.50 4.00
169 Ilya Kovalchuk 4.00 10.00
170 Bobby Orr 12.00 30.00
171 Ryan Miller 3.00 8.00
172 Jarome Iginla 5.00 12.00
173 Eric Staal 3.00 8.00
174 Joe Sakic 6.00 15.00
175 Gordie Howe 8.00 20.00
176 Wayne Gretzky 15.00 40.00
177 Mark Messier 6.00 15.00
178 Peter Forsberg 4.00 10.00
179 Martin Brodeur 8.00 20.00
180 Jaromir Jagr 5.00 12.00
181 Dany Heatley 4.00 10.00
182 Sidney Crosby 15.00 40.00
183 Marc-Andre Fleury 3.00 8.00
184 Mario Lemieux 10.00 25.00
185 Joe Thornton 4.00 10.00
186 Vincent Lecavalier 3.00 8.00
187 Mats Sundin 3.00 8.00
188 Roberto Luongo 5.00 12.00
189 Alexander Ovechkin 10.00 25.00
190 Jack Johnson RC 6.00 15.00
191 Jonathan Toews RC 40.00 80.00
192 Bobby Ryan RC 15.00 40.00
193 Sam Gagner RC 8.00 20.00
194 Carey Price RC 40.00 80.00
195 Erik Johnson RC 8.00 20.00
196 Nicklas Bergfors RC 5.00 12.00
197 Jonathan Bernier RC 10.00 25.00
198 Nicklas Backstrom RC 12.00 30.00
199 Bryan Little RC 6.00 15.00
200 Patrick Kane RC 25.00 60.00
201 Andrew Cogliano RC 10.00 25.00
202 Marc Staal RC 10.00 25.00
203 Nick Foligno RC 6.00 15.00
204 Peter Mueller RC 12.00 30.00
205 Devin Setoguchi RC 8.00 20.00
206 Kris Russell RC 6.00 15.00
207 James Sheppard RC 4.00 10.00
208 Matt Niskanen RC 4.00 10.00
209 Kyle Chipchura RC 6.00 15.00
210 Martin Hanzal RC 5.00 12.00

2007-08 Black Diamond Gold

STATED PRINT RUN 10 SER.#'d SETS
NOT PRICED DUE TO SCARCITY

2007-08 Black Diamond Platinum

STATED PRINT RUN 1 SER.#'d SET
NOT PRICED DUE TO SCARCITY

2007-08 Black Diamond Ruby

RUBY: 5X TO 12X BASE
*DOUBLE DIAMONDS RUBY: 1.5X TO 4X BASE DOUBLE
*TRIPLE DIAMONDS RUBY: 1X TO 2.5X BASE TRIPLE
*TRIPLE DIAMONDS RUBY RCs: 1.2X TO 3X BASE
*DOUBLE DIAMONDS RUBY: .8X TO 2X BASE QUADS
*DOUBLE DIAMONDS RUBY RCs: .6X TO 1.5X BASE
STATED PRINT RUN 100 SERIAL #'d SETS
191 Jonathan Toews 100.00 200.00
194 Carey Price 100.00 200.00
198 Nicklas Backstrom 30.00 60.00
200 Patrick Kane 75.00 150.00
204 Peter Mueller 25.00 60.00

2007-08 Black Diamond Gemography

OVERALL STATED ODDS 1:48
GAF Maxim Afinogenov 3.00 8.00
GAH Ales Hemsky 3.00 8.00
GAK Andrei Kostitsyn 3.00 8.00
GAO Alexander Ovechkin SP 75.00 150.00
GAT Alex Tanguay SP
GBG Brian Gionta SP
GBL Michael Blunden 3.00 8.00
GBM Brenden Morrow 4.00 10.00
GBP Benoit Pouliot SP 15.00 40.00
GBR Martin Brodeur SP 60.00 120.00
GCA Colby Armstrong 3.00 8.00
GCB Cam Barker SP 5.00 12.00
GCH Jonathan Cheechoo 4.00 10.00
GCK Chuck Kobasew 3.00 8.00
GCO Erik Cole 3.00 8.00
GCP Corey Perry 4.00 10.00
GCT Chris Thorburn 3.00 8.00
GCW Cam Ward SP
GDB Daniel Briere 5.00 12.00
GDH Dominik Hasek SP 15.00 40.00
GDL David Leneveu 4.00 10.00
GDP Dion Phaneuf 5.00 12.00
GDR Dwayne Roloson SP 6.00 15.00
GDU Dustin Brown 3.00 8.00
GEC Erik Christensen 3.00 8.00
GEF Eric Fehr 3.00 8.00
GEM Evgeni Malkin 40.00 80.00
GEN Evgeni Nabokov 4.00 10.00
GES Eric Staal 5.00 12.00
GFO Matt Foy 3.00 8.00
GFP Fernando Pisani 3.00 8.00
GGB Gilbert Brule 3.00 8.00
GGE Martin Gerber 4.00 10.00
GGL Georges Laraque 3.00 8.00
GGO Scott Gomez 3.00 8.00
GHZ Henrik Zetterberg 5.00 12.00
GIK Ilya Kovalchuk 6.00 15.00
GJC Jeff Carter 3.00 8.00
GJH Josh Hennessy 3.00 8.00
GJI Jarome Iginla SP 25.00 60.00
GJL John-Michael Liles 3.00 8.00
GJM Jay McClement 3.00 8.00
GJP Joni Pitkanen SP 5.00 12.00
GJS Jarret Stoll 3.00 8.00
GJW Justin Williams SP 5.00 12.00
GKC Kyle Calder 3.00 8.00
GKG Kelly Guard 3.00 8.00
GKL Kristopher Letang 6.00 15.00
GKO Mikko Koivu 3.00 8.00
GKQ Kyle Quincey 3.00 8.00
GLA Guillaume Latendresse 4.00 10.00
GLE Loui Eriksson 3.00 8.00
GLN Ladislav Nagy 3.00 8.00
GMA Mario Lemieux SP
GMB Martin Biron 4.00 10.00
GMC Mike Cammalleri 4.00 10.00
GMF Marc-Andre Fleury SP 10.00 25.00
GMG Marian Gaborik SP 25.00 60.00
GMH Milan Hejduk 4.00 10.00
GMI Mike Richards 6.00 15.00
GMK Miikka Kiprusoff 6.00 15.00
GML Matt Lashoff 3.00 8.00
GMP Mark Parrish 3.00 8.00
GMR Mike Ribeiro 3.00 8.00
GMT Marty Turco 5.00 12.00
GND Nigel Dawes 3.00 8.00
GNH Nathan Horton 3.00 8.00
GPB Patrice Bergeron 5.00 12.00
GPE Patrik Elias 3.00 8.00
GPK Phil Kessel 5.00 12.00
GPM Paul Mara 3.00 8.00
GPO Patrick O'Sullivan 4.00 10.00
GPP Petr Prucha 3.00 8.00
GRB Rene Bourque SP 5.00 12.00
GRF Ruslan Fedotenko 3.00 8.00
GRI Brad Richardson 3.00 8.00
GRK Rostislav Klesla 3.00 8.00
GRM Ryan Malone 3.00 8.00
GRN Rick Nash 5.00 12.00
GSB Steve Bernier 3.00 8.00
GSC Sidney Crosby 100.00 175.00
GSG Simon Gagne 5.00 12.00
GSS Steve Sullivan 3.00 8.00
GST Mark Stuart 3.00 8.00
GSW Stephen Weiss 3.00 8.00
GTH Tomas Holmstrom 4.00 10.00
GVF Valtteri Filppula 3.00 8.00
GVT Vesa Toskala SP
GWI Jeremy Williams 3.00 8.00
GWR Wade Redden 3.00 8.00
GZC Zdeno Chara 3.00 8.00

2007-08 Black Diamond Jerseys

STATED ODDS 1:13
BDJAA Arron Asham 3.00 8.00
BDJAE David Aebischer 4.00 10.00
BDJAF Alexander Frolov 3.00 8.00
BDJAH Adam Hall 3.00 8.00
BDJAK Alexei Kovalev 3.00 8.00
BDJAM Andrei Meszaros 3.00 8.00
BDJAO Alexander Ovechkin SP 15.00 40.00
BDJAR Alexander Radulov 5.00 12.00
BDJAS Alexander Steen 3.00 8.00
BDJAT Alex Tanguay 4.00 10.00
BDJAU Alexander Auld 4.00 10.00
BDJBB Brad Boyes 4.00 10.00
BDJBE Patrice Bergeron 5.00 12.00
BDJBG Bill Guerin 3.00 8.00
BDJBI Martin Biron 4.00 10.00
BDJBJ Barret Jackman 3.00 8.00
BDJBL Jason Blake 3.00 8.00
BDJBM Brendan Morrison 3.00 8.00
BDJBO Brandon Bochenski 3.00 8.00
BDJBR Brad Richards 4.00 10.00
BDJBS Brad Stuart 3.00 8.00
BDJCD Chris Drury 4.00 10.00
BDJCH Chris Higgins 4.00 10.00
BDJCK Chuck Kobasew 3.00 8.00
BDJCO Chris Osgood 4.00 10.00
BDJCP Chris Phillips 3.00 8.00
BDJDA Daniel Alfredsson 4.00 10.00
BDJDE Pavol Demitra 3.00 8.00
BDJDH Dany Heatley SP 6.00 15.00
BDJDL David Legwand 3.00 8.00
BDJDR Dwayne Roloson 4.00 10.00
BDJDT Darcy Tucker 4.00 10.00
BDJDW Doug Weight 3.00 8.00
BDJEB Ed Belfour 5.00 12.00
BDJEJ Ed Jovanovski 3.00 8.00
BDJEN Evgeni Nabokov 4.00 10.00
BDJES Eric Staal 5.00 12.00
BDJFP Fernando Pisani 3.00 8.00
BDJGE Martin Gerber 4.00 10.00
BDJGM Glen Murray 3.00 8.00
BDJHA Dominik Hasek SP 6.00 15.00
BDJHE Milan Hejduk 4.00 10.00
BDJHM Martin Havlat 4.00 10.00
BDJHS Henrik Sedin 3.00 8.00
BDJHT Hannu Toivonen 4.00 10.00
BDJIK Ilya Kovalchuk 6.00 15.00
BDJJA Jason Arnott 3.00 8.00
BDJJB Jay Bouwmeester 3.00 8.00
BDJJC Jeff Carter 3.00 8.00
BDJJG Jean-Sebastien Giguere 5.00 12.00
BDJJI Jarome Iginla 8.00 20.00
BDJJJ Jaromir Jagr 8.00 20.00
BDJJL Jere Lehtinen 3.00 8.00
BDJJO Jonathan Cheechoo 4.00 10.00
BDJJS Jarret Stoll 3.00 8.00
BDJJT Joe Thornton 6.00 15.00
BDJJU Jussi Jokinen 3.00 8.00
BDJJW Jason Williams 3.00 8.00
BDJKC Kyle Calder 3.00 8.00
BDJKT Keith Tkachuk 4.00 10.00
BDJLU Joffrey Lupul 3.00 8.00
BDJMA Martin Brodeur 12.00 30.00
BDJMB Mark Bell 3.00 8.00
BDJMC Bryan McCabe 3.00 8.00
BDJMD Marc Denis 4.00 10.00
BDJMF Manny Fernandez 4.00 10.00
BDJMG Marian Gaborik SP 6.00 15.00
BDJMH Marian Hossa 5.00 12.00
BDJMI Michael Peca 3.00 8.00
BDJMJ Milan Jurcina 3.00 8.00
BDJML Manny Legace 4.00 10.00
BDJMM Milan Michalek 3.00 8.00
BDJMN Markus Naslund 3.00 8.00
BDJMO Brenden Morrow 4.00 10.00
BDJMP Mark Parrish 3.00 8.00
BDJMR Mike Ribeiro 3.00 8.00
BDJMS Marc Savard 3.00 8.00
BDJMT Marty Turco 5.00 12.00
BDJNL Nicklas Lidstrom 5.00 12.00
BDJNZ Nikolai Zherdev 3.00 8.00
BDJOH Mattias Ohlund 3.00 8.00
BDJOJ Olli Jokinen 3.00 8.00
BDJPB Pierre-Marc Bouchard 3.00 8.00
BDJPC Corey Perry 4.00 10.00
BDJPD Pavel Datsyuk SP 5.00 12.00
BDJPE Patrik Elias 3.00 8.00
BDJPF Peter Forsberg 6.00 15.00
BDJPM Patrick Marleau 4.00 10.00
BDJRA Andrew Raycroft 4.00 10.00
BDJRL Roberto Luongo 8.00 20.00
BDJRM Ryan Miller 5.00 12.00
BDJRN Rick Nash SP 5.00 12.00
BDJSA Joe Sakic 10.00 25.00
BDJSC Sidney Crosby SP 25.00 60.00
BDJSG Simon Gagne 5.00 12.00
BDJSH Brendan Shanahan 5.00 12.00
BDJSP Jason Spezza SP 5.00 12.00
BDJSU Mats Sundin 5.00 12.00
BDJTH Jose Theodore 5.00 12.00
BDJWI Justin Williams 3.00 8.00

2007-08 Black Diamond Jerseys Ruby Dual

*RUBY DUAL: .5X TO 1.2X
STATED PRINT RUN 100 SER.#'d SETS

2007-08 Black Diamond Jerseys Gold Triple

*GOLD TRIPLE: 1X TO 2.5X
STATED PRINT RUN 25 SER.#'d SETS

2007-08 Black Diamond Jerseys Black Quad

STATED PRINT RUN 10 SER.#'d SETS
NOT PRICED DUE TO SCARCITY

2007-08 Black Diamond Run for the Cup

STATED ODDS 1:288
CUP1 Jean-Sebastien Giguere 12.00 30.00
CUP2 Ilya Kovalchuk 15.00 40.00
CUP3 Thomas Vanek 10.00 25.00
CUP4 Jarome Iginla 20.00 50.00
CUP5 Eric Staal 12.00 30.00
CUP6 Joe Sakic 25.00 60.00
CUP7 Mike Modano 12.00 30.00
CUP8 Henrik Zetterberg 12.00 30.00
CUP9 Ales Hemsky 8.00 20.00
CUP10 Marian Gaborik 15.00 40.00
CUP11 Saku Koivu 10.00 25.00
CUP12 Martin Brodeur 30.00 80.00
CUP13 Jaromir Jagr 20.00 50.00
CUP14 Dany Heatley 15.00 40.00
CUP15 Sidney Crosby 60.00 150.00
CUP16 Joe Thornton 15.00 40.00
CUP17 Paul Kariya 12.00 30.00
CUP18 Vincent Lecavalier 12.00 30.00
CUP19 Mats Sundin 12.00 30.00
CUP20 Roberto Luongo 20.00 50.00
CUP21 Alexander Ovechkin 40.00 100.00

2008-09 Black Diamond

This set was released on December 17, 2008. The base set consists of 210 cards. Cards 1-147 and 169-189 feature veterans, and cards 148-168 as well as 190-210 are rookies

Comp.Set W/O SP's 10.00 25.00
(190-210) STATED ODDS 1:
1 Bobby Ryan .40 1.00
2 Corey Perry .25 .60
3 Bryan Little .15 .40
4 Marco Sturm .15 .40
5 Patrice Bergeron .25 .60
6 Tim Thomas .25 .60
7 Zdeno Chara .15 .40
8 Jason Pominville .20 .50
9 Daymond Langkow .15 .40
10 Mike Cammalleri .25 .60
11 Justin Williams .15 .40
12 Ray Whitney .15 .40
13 Rod Brind'Amour .20 .50
14 Brian Campbell .40 1.00
15 Cristobal Huet .25 .60
16 Dustin Byfuglien .20 .50
17 Darcy Tucker .20 .50
18 Marek Svatos .15 .40
19 Wojtek Wolski .15 .40
20 Pascal Leclaire .20 .50
21 Brenden Morrow .20 .50
22 Sean Avery .20 .50
23 Sergei Zubov .15 .40
24 Valtteri Filppula .15 .40
25 Dan Cleary .25 .60
26 Johan Franzen .25 .60
27 Niklas Kronwall .20 .50
28 Dustin Penner .15 .40
29 Dwayne Roloson .20 .50
30 Erik Cole .15 .40
31 Gilbert Brule .25 .60
32 Mathieu Garon .25 .60
33 Andrew Cogliano .40 1.00
34 Jay Bouwmeester .20 .50
35 Dustin Brown .15 .40
36 Jack Johnson .20 .50
37 Josh Harding .20 .50
38 Pierre-Marc Bouchard .15 .40
39 Alex Kovalev .25 .60
40 Jaroslav Halak .25 .60
41 Andrei Markov .20 .50
42 Guillaume Latendresse .20 .50
43 Sergei Kostitsyn .25 .60
44 Tomas Plekanec .15 .40
45 Dan Ellis .15 .40
46 Brian Gionta .25 .60
47 Brian Rolston .15 .40
48 Patrik Elias .15 .40
49 Bill Guerin .15 .40
50 Mark Streit .15 .40
51 Mike Comrie .15 .40
52 Brendan Shanahan .25 .60
53 Chris Drury .25 .60
54 Marc Staal .30 .75
55 Nikolai Zherdev .15 .40
56 Scott Gomez .20 .50
57 Wade Redden .15 .40
58 Antoine Vermette .15 .40
59 Martin Gerber .20 .50
60 Jeff Carter .25 .60
61 Mike Knuble .25 .60
62 Scott Hartnell .20 .50
63 Daniel Carcillo .15 .40
64 Ed Jovanovski .15 .40
65 Ilya Bryzgalov .15 .40
66 Sergei Gonchar .25 .60
67 Milan Michalek .15 .40
68 Patrick Marleau .20 .50
69 Andy McDonald .15 .40
70 Brad Boyes .20 .50
71 Manny Legace .20 .50
72 Paul Kariya .25 .60
73 Radim Vrbata .15 .40
74 Ryan Malone .15 .40
75 Vaclav Prospal .15 .40
76 Jason Blake .15 .40
77 Nikolai Antropov .15 .40
78 Tomas Kaberle .15 .40
79 Kevin Bieksa .15 .40
80 Mattias Ohlund .15 .40
81 Alexander Semin .25 .60
82 Jose Theodore .25 .60
83 Michael Nylander .15 .40
84 Mike Green .20 .50
85 Chris Pronger .20 .50
86 Teemu Selanne .25 .60
87 Kari Lehtonen .15 .40
88 Marc Savard .15 .40
89 Derek Roy .15 .40
90 Cam Ward .25 .60
91 Patrick Kane .60 1.50
92 Patrick Sharp .15 .40
93 Milan Hejduk .20 .50
94 Brad Richards .20 .50
95 Marty Turco .20 .50
96 Mike Ribeiro .15 .40
97 Mike Modano .25 .60
98 Chris Osgood .25 .60
99 Ales Hemsky .15 .40
100 Shawn Horcoff .15 .40
101 Nathan Horton .15 .40
102 Tomas Vokoun .25 .60
103 Anze Kopitar .25 .60
104 Alexander Frolov .15 .40
105 Niklas Backstrom .25 .60
106 Andrei Kostitsyn .20 .50
107 Sam Gagner .40 1.00
108 Jason Arnott .15 .40
109 J.P. Dumont .15 .40
110 Zach Parise .25 .60
111 Rick DiPietro .25 .60
112 Markus Naslund .25 .60
113 Simon Gagne .20 .50
114 Daniel Briere .25 .60
115 Mike Richards .40 1.00
116 Martin Biron .20 .50
117 Shane Doan .15 .40
118 Peter Mueller .30 .75
119 Olli Jokinen .15 .40
120 Jordan Staal .40 1.00
121 Evgeni Nabokov .25 .60
122 Jonathan Cheechoo .25 .60
123 Erik Johnson .30 .75
124 Vesa Toskala .25 .60
125 Daniel Sedin .25 .60
126 Henrik Sedin .25 .60
127 Ryan Getzlaf .30 .75
128 Jean-Sebastien Giguere .25 .60
129 Ryan Miller .25 .60
130 Thomas Vanek .25 .60
131 Dion Phaneuf .25 .60
132 Miikka Kiprusoff .25 .60
133 Eric Staal .40 1.00
134 Jonathan Toews .75 2.00
135 Peter Forsberg .40 1.00
136 Paul Stastny .25 .60
137 Rick Nash .25 .60
138 Marian Hossa .40 1.00
139 Pavel Datsyuk .25 .60
140 Nicklas Lidstrom .25 .60
141 Marian Gaborik .40 1.00
142 Saku Koivu .25 .60
143 Dany Heatley .30 .75
144 Jason Spezza .30 .75
145 Daniel Alfredsson .20 .50
146 Martin St. Louis .25 .60
147 Nicklas Backstrom .50 1.25
148 Viktor Tikhonov RC 3.00 8.00
149 Steve Mason RC 8.00 20.00
150 Mark Fistric RC 2.50 6.00
151 Justin Abdelkader RC 6.00 15.00
152 Mattias Ritola RC 4.00 10.00
153 Darren Helm RC 5.00 12.00
154 Claude Giroux RC 6.00 15.00
155 Tom Sestito RC 2.50 6.00
156 Shawn Matthias RC 3.00 8.00
157 Luca Sbisa RC 5.00 12.00
158 Oscar Moller RC 3.00 8.00
159 Erik Ersberg RC 3.00 8.00
160 Patric Hornqvist RC 3.00 8.00
161 Brian Lee RC 3.00 8.00
162 Ilya Zubov RC 3.00 8.00
163 Alex Goligoski RC 6.00 15.00
164 Jon Filewich RC 2.50 6.00
165 Vladimir Mihalik RC 3.00 8.00
166 Nikolai Kulemin RC 3.00 8.00
167 Robbie Earl RC 2.50 6.00
168 Mike Brown RC 4.00 10.00
169 Ilya Kovalchuk 5.00 12.00
170 Bobby Orr 12.00 30.00
171 Jarome Iginla 8.00 20.00
172 Joe Sakic 6.00 15.00
173 Gordie Howe 15.00 40.00
174 Henrik Zetterberg 8.00 20.00
175 Wayne Gretzky 20.00 50.00
176 Mark Messier 8.00 20.00
177 Patrick Roy 12.00 30.00
178 Carey Price 12.00 30.00
179 Martin Brodeur 8.00 20.00
180 Henrik Lundqvist 8.00 20.00
181 Mario Lemieux 10.00 25.00
182 Sidney Crosby 20.00 50.00
183 Evgeni Malkin 10.00 25.00
184 Marc-Andre Fleury 4.00 10.00
185 Joe Thornton 6.00 15.00
186 Vincent Lecavalier 4.00 10.00
187 Mats Sundin 4.00 10.00
188 Roberto Luongo 6.00 15.00
189 Alexander Ovechkin 15.00 40.00
190 Zach Bogosian RC 10.00 25.00
191 Blake Wheeler RC 12.00 30.00
192 Brandon Sutter RC 6.00 15.00
193 Jakub Voracek RC 10.00 25.00
194 Derick Brassard RC 10.00 25.00
195 James Neal RC 8.00 20.00
196 Michael Frolik RC 10.00 25.00
197 Drew Doughty RC 15.00 40.00
198 Colton Gillies RC 8.00 20.00
199 Kyle Okposo RC 10.00 25.00
200 Lauri Korpikoski RC 5.00 12.00
201 Fabian Brunnstrom RC 8.00 20.00
202 Zach Boychuk RC 8.00 20.00
203 Mikkel Boedker RC 8.00 20.00
204 Kyle Turris RC 10.00 25.00
205 Nikita Filatov RC 20.00 50.00
206 Alex Pietrangelo RC 8.00 20.00
207 T.J. Oshie RC 12.00 30.00
208 Patrik Berglund RC 12.00 30.00
209 Steven Stamkos RC 25.00 60.00
210 Luke Schenn RC 15.00 40.00

2008-09 Black Diamond Onyx

STATED PRINT RUN 1 SERIAL #'d SET
NOT PRICED DUE TO SCARCITY

2008-09 Black Diamond Gold

STATED PRINT RUN 10 SERIAL #'d SETS
NOT PRICED DUE TO SCARCITY

2008-09 Black Diamond Gemography

STATED ODDS 1:
GAC Andrew Cogliano
GAO Alexander Ovechkin
GAT Alex Tanguay
GBA Cam Barker
GBB Brendan Bell 4.00 10.00
GBC Blake Comeau 4.00 10.00
GBD Brandon Dubinsky 8.00 20.00
GBE Jonathan Bernier 8.00 20.00

GBO Brad Boyes 5.00 12.00
GBR Bobby Ryan 10.00 25.00
GCA Ryan Carter 4.00 10.00
GCB Casey Borer 6.00 15.00
GCD Chris Drury 6.00 15.00
GCK Chris Kunitz 4.00 10.00
GCO Corey Perry 6.00 15.00
GCP Chris Phillips 4.00 10.00
GDC Dan Cleary 6.00 15.00
GDG Daniel Girardi
GDH Dany Heatley
GDM Drew Miller 6.00 15.00
GDP Daniel Paille
GDS Daniel Sedin 6.00 15.00
GDU Dustin Penner 4.00 10.00
GEJ Erik Johnson 8.00 20.00
GHA Josh Harding
GHS Henrik Sedin 6.00 15.00
GJB Jay Bouwmeester 5.00 12.00
GJG Jean-Sebastien Giguere 6.00 15.00
GJH Jannik Hansen
GJI Jarome Iginla
GJL John-Michael Liles 4.00 10.00
GJO Johnny Boychuk 4.00 10.00
GJS Jordan Staal
GJT Joe Thornton
GJW Justin Williams 4.00 10.00
GKD Kris Draper
GKE Phil Kessel
GKQ Kyle Quincey
GLE Loui Eriksson
GLK Lukas Kaspar
GLT Lauri Tukonen
GMA Drew MacIntyre 6.00 15.00
GMB Martin Biron 5.00 12.00
GMC Marco Sturm 4.00 10.00
GMG Martin Gerber 5.00 12.00
GMH Michal Handzus 4.00 10.00
GMK Mike Knuble 6.00 15.00
GML Milan Lucic 12.00 30.00
GMM Mark Mancari 5.00 12.00
GMN Markus Naslund 6.00 15.00
GMO Mike Modano
GMP Marc-Antoine Pouliot 6.00 15.00
GMR Mason Raymond 4.00 10.00
GMS Matt Stajan 5.00 12.00
GNB Nicklas Bergfors
GNI Nicklas Backstrom 12.00 30.00
GNW Noah Welch
GNZ Nikolai Zherdev 4.00 10.00
GPB Pierre-Marc Bouchard 4.00 10.00
GPE Rod Pelley 4.00 10.00
GPJ Jason Pominville 5.00 12.00
GPK Patrick Kane 30.00 60.00
GPO Ryan Potulny 4.00 10.00
GPR Carey Price 20.00 50.00
GPS Paul Stastny 20.00 50.00
GRC Ryane Clowe 4.00 10.00
GRG Ryan Getzlaf
GRI Mike Richards 10.00 25.00
GRK Rostislav Klesla
GRO Rob Schremp
GRP Rich Peverley 4.00 10.00
GRS Ryan Smyth 5.00 12.00
GSC Sidney Crosby 100.00 200.00
GSE Devin Setoguchi 6.00 15.00
GSM Stefan Meyer 4.00 10.00
GST Drew Stafford 6.00 15.00
GSW Stephen Weiss 4.00 10.00
GSZ Marek Schwarz 6.00 15.00
GTG Tom Gilbert 4.00 10.00
GTH Tomas Holmstrom
GTI Jussi Timonen
GTK Tyler Kennedy
GTL Jiri Tlusty 6.00 15.00
GTP Tomas Plihal 5.00 12.00
GTV Thomas Vanek
GTZ Travis Zajac 4.00 10.00

2008-09 Black Diamond Jerseys Quad

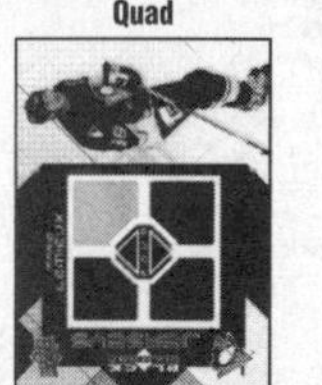

STATED ODDS 1:
BDJAK Anze Kopitar 6.00 15.00
BDJAM Andrej Meszaros 4.00 10.00
BDJAO Alexander Ovechkin 25.00 60.00
BDJAR Andrew Raycroft 6.00 15.00
BDJAS Alexander Semin
BDJBB Brad Boyes 5.00 12.00
BDJBD Brandon Dubinsky 5.00 12.00
BDJBG Brian Gionta 6.00 15.00
BDJBM Brenden Morrow 5.00 12.00
BDJBO Brandon Bochenski 5.00 12.00
BDJBR Brad Richardson 6.00 15.00
BDJBW Brendan Witt 4.00 10.00
BDJCA Jeff Carter 6.00 15.00
BDJCC Chris Chelios 8.00 20.00
BDJCD Chris Drury 6.00 15.00
BDJCH Chris Higgins 4.00 10.00
BDJCK Chuck Kobasew 4.00 10.00
BDJCW Cam Ward 6.00 15.00
BDJDA Daniel Alfredsson 5.00 12.00
BDJDB Daniel Briere 6.00 15.00
BDJDH Dany Heatley 8.00 20.00
BDJDP Dion Phaneuf 6.00 15.00
BDJDR Dwayne Roloson 5.00 12.00
BDJDT Darcy Tucker 5.00 12.00
BDJDW Doug Weight 4.00 10.00
BDJEC Erik Cole 4.00 10.00
BDJEF Eric Fehr 5.00 12.00
BDJEJ Ed Jovanovski 4.00 10.00
BDJEN Evgeni Nabokov 6.00 15.00
BDJES Eric Staal 10.00 25.00
BDJGB Gilbert Brule 6.00 15.00
BDJGE Martin Gerber 5.00 12.00
BDJGL Guillaume Latendresse 5.00 12.00
BDJGU Bill Guerin 4.00 10.00
BDJHL Henrik Lundqvist 12.00 30.00
BDJHZ Henrik Zetterberg 12.00 30.00
BDJIK Ilya Kovalchuk 8.00 20.00
BDJIW Ian White 4.00 10.00
BDJJA Jason Arnott 4.00 10.00
BDJJB Jay Bouwmeester 5.00 12.00
BDJJC Jonathan Cheechoo 6.00 15.00
BDJJG Jean-Sebastien Giguere 6.00 15.00
BDJJI Jarome Iginla 12.00 30.00
BDJJM John-Michael Liles 4.00 10.00
BDJJP Joni Pitkanen 4.00 10.00
BDJJS Joe Sakic 10.00 25.00
BDJJT Joe Thornton 10.00 25.00
BDJKL Kari Lehtonen 4.00 10.00
BDJKO Alex Kovalev 6.00 15.00
BDJLE Manny Legace 5.00 12.00
BDJLS Lee Stempniak 4.00 10.00
BDJMA Mark Stuart 4.00 10.00
BDJMB Martin Brodeur 12.00 30.00
BDJMC Mike Cammalleri 6.00 15.00
BDJMF Manny Fernandez 6.00 15.00
BDJMG Marian Gaborik 10.00 25.00
BDJMI Milan Michalek 4.00 10.00
BDJML Mario Lemieux 15.00 40.00
BDJMM Mark Messier 12.00 30.00
BDJMN Markus Naslund 6.00 15.00
BDJMO Mike Modano 6.00 15.00
BDJMR Michael Ryder 5.00 12.00
BDJMS Martin St. Louis 6.00 15.00
BDJMU Joe Mullen 6.00 15.00
BDJMV Andrei Markov 5.00 12.00
BDJMZ Marek Zidlicky 4.00 10.00
BDJNZ Nikolai Zherdev 4.00 10.00
BDJOJ Olli Jokinen 4.00 10.00
BDJPB Patrice Bergeron 6.00 15.00
BDJPD Pavel Datsyuk 6.00 15.00
BDJPF Peter Forsberg 10.00 25.00
BDJPI Pierre-Marc Bouchard 4.00 10.00
BDJPK Paul Kariya 6.00 15.00
BDJPL Pascal Leclaire 5.00 12.00
BDJPR Patrick Roy 20.00 50.00
BDJPS Paul Stastny 6.00 15.00
BDJRD Rick DiPietro 6.00 15.00
BDJRE Mark Recchi 5.00 12.00
BDJRI Mike Richards 10.00 25.00
BDJRJ R.J. Umberger 4.00 10.00
BDJRL Roberto Luongo 10.00 25.00
BDJRN Rick Nash 6.00 15.00
BDJSA Marc Savard 4.00 10.00
BDJSC Sidney Crosby 30.00 80.00
BDJSG Simon Gagne 5.00 12.00
BDJSH Jody Shelley 4.00 10.00
BDJSP Jason Spezza 8.00 20.00
BDJST Alexander Steen 6.00 15.00
BDJSU Mats Sundin 6.00 15.00
BDJSW Shea Weber 4.00 10.00
BDJTE Jose Theodore 6.00 15.00
BDJTK Keith Tkachuk 5.00 12.00
BDJTP Tomas Plekanec 4.00 10.00
BDJTS Teemu Selanne 6.00 15.00
BDJTT Tim Thomas 6.00 15.00
BDJTV Thomas Vanek 6.00 15.00
BDJWG Wayne Gretzky 30.00 80.00
BDJZP Zach Parise 6.00 15.00

2008-09 Black Diamond Jerseys Quad Gold

*GOLD: .6X TO 1.5X BASE
STATED PRINT RUN 25 SERIAL #'d SETS

2008-09 Black Diamond Jerseys Quad Onyx

STATED PRINT RUN 10 SERIAL #'d SETS
NOT PRICED DUE TO SCARCITY

2008-09 Black Diamond Jerseys Quad Ruby

*RUBY: .5X TO 1.2X BASE
STATED PRINT RUN 100 SERIAL #'d SETS

2008-09 Black Diamond Premier Die-Cut

STATED ODDS 1:1,015
PDC1 Scott Niedermayer 5.00 12.00
PDC2 Marian Hossa 12.00 30.00
PDC3 Jason Spezza 10.00 25.00
PDC4 Daniel Alfredsson 6.00 15.00
PDC5 Ryan Getzlaf 10.00 25.00
PDC6 Chris Pronger 6.00 15.00
PDC7 Ryan Malone 5.00 12.00
PDC8 Brenden Morrow 6.00 15.00
PDC9 Mike Ribeiro 5.00 12.00
PDC10 Alex Kovalev 8.00 20.00
PDC11 Alexander Frolov 5.00 12.00
PDC12 Mike Richards 12.00 30.00
PDC13 Daniel Briere 8.00 20.00
PDC14 Peter Mueller 10.00 25.00
PDC15 Shane Doan 5.00 12.00
PDC16 Olli Jokinen 5.00 12.00
PDC17 Henrik Sedin 8.00 20.00
PDC18 Daniel Sedin 8.00 20.00
PDC19 Patrick Marleau 6.00 15.00
PDC20 J.P. Dumont 5.00 12.00
PDC21 Zach Parise 8.00 20.00
PDC22 Andrew Cogliano 12.00 30.00
PDC23 Brad Richards 6.00 15.00
PDC24 Chris Drury 8.00 20.00
PDC25 Chris Osgood 8.00 20.00
PDC26 Dany Heatley 10.00 25.00
PDC27 Dion Phaneuf 8.00 20.00
PDC28 Eric Staal 12.00 30.00
PDC29 Henrik Lundqvist 15.00 40.00
PDC30 Jean-Sebastien Giguere 8.00 20.00
PDC31 Jonathan Cheechoo 8.00 20.00
PDC32 Marc-Andre Fleury 8.00 20.00
PDC33 Marian Gaborik 12.00 30.00
PDC34 Martin St. Louis 8.00 20.00
PDC35 Nicklas Lidstrom 8.00 20.00
PDC36 Patrik Elias 5.00 12.00
PDC37 Paul Stastny 8.00 20.00
PDC38 Rick Nash 8.00 20.00
PDC39 Roberto Luongo 12.00 30.00
PDC40 Ryan Miller 8.00 20.00
PDC41 Sam Gagner 12.00 30.00
PDC42 Thomas Vanek 8.00 20.00
PDC43 Carey Price 25.00 60.00
PDC44 Evgeni Malkin 20.00 50.00
PDC45 Henrik Zetterberg 15.00 40.00
PDC46 Ilya Kovalchuk 10.00 25.00
PDC47 Jarome Iginla 15.00 40.00
PDC48 Joe Thornton 12.00 30.00
PDC49 Jonathan Toews 25.00 60.00
PDC50 Mark Messier 15.00 40.00
PDC51 Martin Brodeur 15.00 40.00
PDC52 Nicklas Backstrom 15.00 40.00
PDC53 Patrick Kane 20.00 50.00
PDC54 Patrick Roy 25.00 60.00
PDC55 Alexander Ovechkin 30.00 80.00
PDC56 Bobby Orr 25.00 60.00
PDC57 Gordie Howe 30.00 80.00
PDC58 Mario Lemieux 20.00 50.00
PDC59 Sidney Crosby 40.00 100.00
PDC60 Wayne Gretzky 40.00 100.00

2008-09 Black Diamond Run for the Cup

STATED PRINT RUN 100 SERIAL #'d SETS

2009-10 Black Diamond

COMP.SET w/o SPs (90) 15.00 40.00
1 Jonas Hiller .30 .75
2 Sean Avery .20 .50
3 Peter Mueller .30 .75
4 Alexander Frolov .20 .50
5 Phil Kessel .25 .60
6 Mikhail Grabovski .20 .50
7 Teemu Selanne .25 .60
8 Justin Abdelkader .25 .60
9 Daniel Sedin .30 .75
10 Brent Burns .15 .40
11 Sheldon Souray .15 .40
12 Scott Gomez .25 .60
13 Evgeni Nabokov .25 .60
14 Joe Pavelski .15 .40
15 Kyle Turris .30 .75
16 Martin Havlat .20 .50
17 Andrew Cogliano .30 .75
18 Marian Gaborik .40 1.00
19 Darren Helm .30 .75
20 Niklas Kronwall .20 .50
21 Ryan Suter .15 .40
22 Mike Knuble .25 .60
23 Shea Weber .20 .50
24 Simeon Varlamov .50 1.25
25 Chris Kunitz .25 .60
26 Nik Antropov .20 .50
27 Mikkel Boedker .25 .60
28 Ryan Malone .15 .40
29 Ilya Bryzgalov .20 .50
30 Drew Doughty .50 1.25
31 Tim Thomas .25 .60
32 Andrei Kostitsyn .20 .50
33 Paul Kariya .25 .60
34 Sam Gagner .30 .75
35 Patrik Elias .20 .50
36 Devin Setoguchi .20 .50
37 Scott Hartnell .15 .40
38 Derek Roy .25 .60
39 Brian Campbell .20 .50
40 Derick Brassard .25 .60
41 Todd White .15 .40
42 Jack Johnson .20 .50
43 Milan Hejduk .25 .60
44 Andrei Markov .20 .50
45 Marc Savard .25 .60
46 Jean-Sebastien Giguere .25 .60
47 Chris Mason .20 .50
48 Niklas Backstrom .25 .60
49 Jussi Jokinen .20 .50
50 Steve Ott .15 .40
51 Jonathan Cheechoo .25 .60
52 Pekka Rinne .20 .50
53 Ian Laperriere .15 .40
54 Steve Mason .40 1.00
55 Kari Lehtonen .25 .60
56 Zdeno Chara .15 .40
57 Matt Stajan .20 .50
58 Dan Ellis .15 .40
59 Antti Miettinen .15 .40
60 Brian Gionta .25 .60
61 Sergei Gonchar .15 .40
62 Ryan Kesler .20 .50
63 Rene Bourque .15 .40
64 R.J. Umberger .20 .50
65 Alex Kovalev .25 .60
66 Tomas Kaberle .15 .40
67 Jaroslav Halak .25 .60
68 Chris Pronger .20 .50
69 David Booth .15 .40
70 Valtteri Filppula .25 .60
71 Henrik Sedin .40 1.00
72 Erik Cole .15 .40
73 Mike Ribeiro .15 .40
74 Daniel Carcillo .25 .60
75 Jamie Langenbrunner .15 .40
76 Jason Pominville .25 .60
77 Patrick Sharp .20 .50
78 Mike Cammalleri .25 .60
79 Jakub Voracek .25 .60
80 Scott Niedermayer .15 .40
81 David Krejci .20 .50
82 Marian Hossa .40 1.00
83 Dustin Penner .15 .40
84 Tomas Vokoun .25 .60
85 Nikolai Khabibulin .25 .60
86 Loui Eriksson .15 .40
87 Rob Blake .25 .60
88 Martin St. Louis .25 .60
89 Ethan Moreau .15 .40
90 Dan Boyle .15 .40
91 Ales Hemsky .25 .60
92 Johan Franzen .25 .60
93 Ryan Smyth .40 1.00
94 Pascal Leclaire .40 1.00
95 Simon Gagne .40 1.00
96 Brenden Morrow .30 .75
97 Vincent Lecavalier .50 1.25
98 Mikko Koivu .40 1.00
99 Jean Beliveau .60 1.50
100 Zach Parise .40 1.00
101 Patrick Marleau .40 1.00
102 Luc Robitaille .40 1.00
103 Paul Stastny .40 1.00
104 Chris Drury .30 .75
105 Doug Gilmour .40 1.00
106 Bobby Ryan .50 1.25
107 Shane Doan .30 .75
108 Corey Perry .40 1.00
109 Jason Arnott .25 .60
110 Henrik Lundqvist .75 2.00
111 Milan Lucic .40 1.00
112 Ryan Getzlaf .60 1.50
113 Anze Kopitar .40 1.00
114 Guy Carbonneau .60 1.50
115 Mats Sundin .40 1.00
116 Jason Spezza .50 1.25
117 Olli Jokinen .25 .60
118 Ryan Miller .40 1.00
119 Mike Green .75 2.00
120 Marty Turco .30 .75
121 Rogie Vachon .60 1.50
122 Alexandre Burrows .30 .75
123 Alexander Semin .40 1.00
124 Johnny Bucyk .60 1.50
125 Daniel Alfredsson .40 1.00
126 Brendan Shanahan .40 1.00
127 J.P. Dumont .25 .60
128 Clark Gillies .40 1.00
129 Dion Phaneuf .60 1.50
130 David Backes .30 .75
131 Eric Staal .50 1.25
132 Luke Schenn .60 1.50
133 Bob Bourne .30 .75
134 Pavel Datsyuk .40 1.00
135 Cam Ward .40 1.00
136 Dale Hawerchuk 1.00 2.50
137 Stan Mikita 1.50 4.00
138 Jeff Carter 1.00 2.50
139 Ilya Kovalchuk 1.25 3.00
140 Steven Stamkos 2.50 6.00
141 Dany Heatley 2.00 5.00
142 Carey Price 2.50 6.00
143 Henrik Zetterberg 2.00 5.00
144 Mike Richards 2.00 5.00
145 Harry Howell .75 2.00
146 Rick Nash 1.00 2.50
147 Gilbert Perreault 1.00 2.50
148 Patrick Kane 2.00 5.00
149 Joe Thornton 2.00 5.00
150 Miikka Kiprusoff 1.00 2.50
151 Jordan Staal 1.25 3.00
152 Tony Esposito 1.50 4.00
153 Nicklas Lidstrom 1.25 3.00
154 Nicklas Backstrom 2.00 5.00
155 Thomas Vanek 1.00 2.50
156 Phil Esposito 2.00 5.00
157 Marc-Andre Fleury 1.00 2.50
158 Brian Salcido RC 2.00 5.00
159 Luca Caputi RC 3.00 8.00
160 Yannick Weber RC 3.00 8.00
161 Kris Chucko RC 2.00 5.00
162 Riku Helenius RC 2.50 6.00
163 Ivan Vishnevskiy RC 3.00 8.00
164 T.J. Galiardi RC 3.00 8.00
165 Benn Ferriero RC 2.50 6.00
166 Cody Franson RC 2.50 6.00
167 Byron Bitz RC 2.00 5.00
168 Taylor Chorney RC 2.50 6.00
169 John Negrin RC 2.00 5.00
170 Jesse Joensuu RC 3.00 8.00
171 Cal O'Reilly RC 2.50 6.00
172 Spencer Machacek RC 2.00 5.00
173 Christian Hanson RC 3.00 8.00
174 Matt Beleskey RC 2.50 6.00
175 Jay Rosehill RC 1.50 4.00
176 Michael Sauer RC 2.00 5.00
177 Michael Grabner RC 3.00 8.00
178 Dmitry Kulikov RC 2.50 6.00
179 Alec Martinez RC 1.50 4.00
180 Matt Hendricks RC 2.00 5.00
181 Peter Stastny 3.00 8.00
182 Bobby Hull 8.00 20.00
183 Joe Sakic 6.00 15.00
184 Jarome Iginla 6.00 15.00
185 Don Cherry 3.00 8.00
186 Roberto Luongo 8.00 20.00
187 Jonathan Toews 8.00 20.00
188 Jari Kurri 3.00 8.00
189 Evgeni Malkin 8.00 20.00
190 Scotty Bowman 3.00 8.00
191 Martin Brodeur 8.00 20.00
192 Ray Bourque 5.00 12.00
193 Steve Yzerman 10.00 25.00
194 Sidney Crosby 15.00 40.00
195 Alexander Ovechkin 12.00 30.00
196 Bobby Orr 12.00 30.00
197 Mark Messier 6.00 15.00
198 Patrick Roy 10.00 25.00
199 Mario Lemieux 8.00 20.00
200 Gordie Howe 12.00 30.00
201 Wayne Gretzky 15.00 40.00
202 Tyler Bozak RC 10.00 25.00
203 Michael Del Zotto RC 8.00 20.00
204 Colin Wilson RC 6.00 15.00
205 Tyler Myers RC 15.00 40.00
206 Jamie Benn RC 6.00 15.00
207 Erik Karlsson RC 12.00 30.00
208 Viktor Stalberg RC 6.00 15.00
209 Matt Gilroy RC 5.00 12.00
210 Antti Niemi RC 12.00 30.00
211 Jhonas Enroth RC 5.00 12.00
212 Artem Anisimov RC 5.00 12.00
213 Ryan O'Reilly RC 8.00 20.00
214 Mikael Backlund RC 6.00 15.00
215 Ville Leino RC 5.00 12.00
216 Jonas Gustavsson RC 15.00 40.00
217 Sergei Shirokov RC 6.00 15.00
218 Victor Hedman RC 8.00 20.00
219 Evander Kane RC 10.00 25.00
220 James Van Riemsdyk RC 10.00 25.00
221 Matt Duchene RC 15.00 40.00
222 John Tavares RC 40.00 80.00

2009-10 Black Diamond Gold

STATED PRINT RUN 10 SER.#'d SETS
NOT PRICED DUE TO SCARCITY

2009-10 Black Diamond Onyx

STATED PRINT RUN 1 SER.#'d SET
NOT PRICED DUE TO SCARCITY

2009-10 Black Diamond Ruby

*RUBY SINGLE DIAMOND: 10X TO 25X BASE
*RUBY DOUBLE DIAMOND: 6X TO 15X BASE
*RUBY TRIPLE DIAMOND: 5X TO 12X BASE
*RUBY TRIPLE D ROOKIES: 1X TO 2.5X BASE
*RUBY QUAD DIAMOND: .8X TO 2X BASE
*RUBY QUAD D ROOKIES: .5X TO 1.2X BASE
STATED PRINT RUN 100 SER.#'d SETS
210 Antti Niemi 25.00 50.00
216 Jonas Gustavsson 30.00 60.00
222 John Tavares 125.00 250.00

2009-10 Black Diamond Gemography

GAE Andrew Ebbett 5.00 12.00
GAF Alexander Frolov 5.00 12.00
GAM Al MacInnis
GAO Adam Oates 6.00 15.00
GAT Alex Tanguay 5.00 12.00
GBB Brian Boyle 5.00 12.00
GBD Brandon Dubinsky 5.00 12.00
GBE Brendan Bell 4.00 10.00
GBM Bryan McCabe 5.00 12.00
GBO Bobby Orr 175.00 300.00
GBW Blake Wheeler 8.00 20.00
GCP Carey Price 15.00 40.00
GDB David Backes 5.00 12.00
GDD Drew Doughty 12.00 30.00
GDH Darren Helm 8.00 20.00
GDL Dan LaCosta 5.00 12.00
GDU J.P. Dumont 4.00 10.00
GEL Patrik Elias
GEM Evgeni Malkin 50.00 100.00
GFL Marc-Andre Fleury 15.00 40.00
GFR Mark Fraser 4.00 10.00
GGH Gordie Howe 100.00 200.00
GHZ Henrik Zetterberg
GJA Jason Arnott 4.00 10.00
GJD Jeff Drouin-Deslauriers 4.00 10.00
GJE Jonathan Ericsson 6.00 15.00
GJG Jean-Sebastien Giguere 6.00 15.00
GJI Jarome Iginla 12.00 30.00
GJK Jari Kurri 6.00 15.00
GJO Joel Perrault 4.00 10.00
GJT Jiri Tlusty 6.00 15.00
GKN Patrick Kane 30.00 60.00
GKT Kyle Turris 8.00 20.00
GMD Matt D'Agostini 8.00 20.00
GMF Mark Fistric 4.00 10.00
GMH Michal Handzus 4.00 10.00
GMP Michael Peca 5.00 12.00
GMR Mattias Ritola 5.00 12.00
GMS Miroslav Satan 4.00 10.00
GNG Nathan Gerbe 8.00 20.00
GNK Nikolai Khabibulin 6.00 15.00
GNW Noah Welch 4.00 10.00
GOV Alexander Ovechkin 75.00 150.00
GPA Max Pacioretty 6.00 15.00
GPJ Joni Pitkanen 5.00 12.00
GPK Phil Kessel
GPO Marc-Antoine Pouliot 5.00 12.00
GPR Patrick Roy 100.00 200.00
GRC Ryane Clowe 4.00 10.00
GRK Rostislav Klesla 6.00 15.00
GRP Rich Peverley 5.00 12.00
GSC Sidney Crosby 100.00 200.00
GSM Stefan Meyer 5.00 12.00
GSS Steven Stamkos 15.00 40.00
GTO Jonathan Toews 15.00 40.00
GTV Thomas Vanek 6.00 15.00
GTZ Travis Zajac 4.00 10.00
GWG Wayne Gretzky
GYZ Steve Yzerman
GZB Zach Bogosian 8.00 20.00

2009-10 Black Diamond Hardware Heroes

COMPLETE SET (42) 500.00 1000.00
STATED PRINT RUN 100 SER.#'d SETS
HH1 Patrick Kane 10.00 25.00
HH2 Evgeni Malkin 12.00 30.00
HH3 Dale Hawerchuk 5.00 12.00
HH4 Peter Stastny 5.00 12.00
HH5 Luc Robitaille 5.00 12.00
HH6 Mike Bossy 5.00 12.00
HH7 Gilbert Perreault 5.00 12.00
HH8 Steve Mason 8.00 20.00
HH9 Evgeni Malkin 12.00 30.00
HH10 Henrik Zetterberg 10.00 25.00
HH11 Steve Yzerman 15.00 40.00
HH12 Brad Richards 4.00 10.00
HH13 Wayne Gretzky 25.00 60.00
HH14 Wayne Gretzky 25.00 60.00
HH15 Mario Lemieux 12.00 30.00
HH16 Mark Messier 10.00 25.00
HH17 Mark Messier 10.00 25.00
HH18 Joe Sakic 10.00 25.00
HH19 Sidney Crosby 25.00 60.00
HH20 Phil Esposito 10.00 25.00
HH21 Gordie Howe 20.00 50.00
HH22 Bobby Hull 12.00 30.00
HH23 Stan Mikita 8.00 20.00
HH24 Bobby Clarke 8.00 20.00
HH25 Alexander Ovechkin 20.00 50.00
HH26 Steve Yzerman 15.00 40.00
HH27 Jarome Iginla 10.00 25.00
HH28 Sidney Crosby 25.00 60.00
HH29 Bobby Orr 20.00 50.00
HH30 Nicklas Lidstrom 6.00 15.00
HH31 Ray Bourque 8.00 20.00
HH32 Brian Leetch 5.00 12.00
HH33 Zdeno Chara 3.00 8.00
HH34 Pavel Datsyuk 5.00 12.00
HH35 Martin Brodeur 12.00 30.00
HH36 Patrick Roy 15.00 40.00
HH37 Ron Hextall 10.00 25.00
HH38 Grant Fuhr 6.00 15.00
HH39 Miikka Kiprusoff 5.00 12.00
HH40 Jose Theodore 5.00 12.00
HH41 Teemu Selanne 5.00 12.00
HH42 Tim Thomas 5.00 12.00

2009-10 Black Diamond Horizontal

*HORIZ: .5X TO 1.2X DIE-CUTS
STATED ODDS 1:48

2009-10 Black Diamond Horizontal Perimeter Die-Cut

STATED ODDS 1:12
BD1 Ilya Kovalchuk 3.00 8.00
BD2 Steven Stamkos 4.00 10.00
BD3 Carey Price 6.00 15.00
BD4 Henrik Zetterberg 5.00 12.00
BD5 Patrick Kane 5.00 12.00
BD6 Joe Thornton 5.00 12.00
BD7 Miikka Kiprusoff 2.50 6.00
BD8 Nicklas Lidstrom 3.00 8.00
BD9 Phil Esposito 5.00 12.00
BD10 Peter Stastny 2.50 6.00
BD11 Bobby Hull 5.00 12.00
BD12 Joe Sakic 5.00 12.00
BD13 Jarome Iginla 5.00 12.00
BD14 Don Cherry 2.50 6.00
BD15 Roberto Luongo 5.00 12.00
BD16 Jonathan Toews 5.00 12.00
BD17 Jari Kurri 2.50 6.00
BD18 Evgeni Malkin 5.00 12.00
BD19 Scotty Bowman 2.50 6.00
BD20 Ray Bourque 4.00 10.00
BD21 Martin Brodeur SP 8.00 20.00
BD22 Steve Yzerman SP 12.00 30.00
BD23 Sidney Crosby SP 20.00 50.00
BD24 Alexander Ovechkin SP 15.00 40.00
BD25 Bobby Orr SP 15.00 40.00
BD26 Mark Messier SP 5.00 12.00
BD27 Patrick Roy SP 15.00 40.00
BD28 Mario Lemieux SP 10.00 25.00
BD29 Gordie Howe SP 10.00 25.00
BD30 Wayne Gretzky SP 25.00 60.00

2009-10 Black Diamond Jerseys Quad

QJAF Alexander Frolov 5.00 12.00
QJAK Anze Kopitar 6.00 15.00
QJAO Alexander Ovechkin 20.00 50.00
QJBD Brandon Dubinsky 5.00 12.00
QJBR Derick Brassard 6.00 15.00
QJCH Cristobal Huet 6.00 15.00
QJCP Carey Price 15.00 40.00
QJDB David Booth 4.00 10.00
QJDD Drew Doughty 12.00 30.00
QJDH Dale Hawerchuk 6.00 15.00
QJDP David Perron 5.00 12.00
QJDS Drew Stafford 6.00 15.00
QJDU Dustin Brown
QJEM Evgeni Malkin 15.00 40.00
QJFB Francis Bouillon 4.00 10.00
QJGA Glenn Anderson 6.00 15.00
QJJB Jay Bouwmeester 6.00 15.00
QJJL Jordan Leopold 4.00 10.00
QJJP Jason Pominville 6.00 15.00
QJJT Jeff Tambellini 4.00 10.00
QJJV Jakub Voracek 6.00 15.00
QJKA Sami Kapanen 4.00 10.00
QJLM Lanny McDonald 6.00 15.00
QJMB Martin Brodeur 15.00 40.00
QJMH Marian Hossa 10.00 25.00
QJMK Mike Komisarek 5.00 12.00
QJMS Marc Staal 8.00 20.00
QJNH Nathan Horton 4.00 10.00
QJPH Dion Phaneuf 10.00 25.00
QJPK Patrick Kane
QJPO Patrick O'Sullivan 5.00 12.00
QJPS Patrick Sharp 5.00 12.00
QJRD Rick DiPietro 6.00 15.00
QJRM Ryan Miller 6.00 15.00
QJRN Rick Nash 6.00 15.00
QJSC Sidney Crosby 25.00 60.00
QJSD Shane Doan 5.00 12.00
QJSG Simon Gagne 6.00 15.00
QJSK Saku Koivu 6.00 15.00
QJSS Steve Shutt 6.00 15.00
QJST Jordan Staal 8.00 20.00
QJSW Shea Weber 5.00 12.00
QJTO Jonathan Toews 15.00 40.00
QJTV Thomas Vanek 6.00 15.00
QJVL Vincent Lecavalier 8.00 20.00
QJVO Tomas Vokoun 6.00 15.00
QJWE Stephen Weiss 4.00 10.00
QJWR Wade Redden
QJZB Zach Bogosian 8.00 20.00
QJZP Zach Parise 6.00 15.00

2009-10 Black Diamond Jerseys Quad Gold

*SINGLES: .6X TO 1.5X BASIC INSERTS
STATED PRINT RUN 25 SER.#'d SETS

2009-10 Black Diamond Jerseys Quad Onyx

STATED PRINT RUN 10 SER.#'d SETS
NOT PRICED DUE TO SCARCITY

2009-10 Black Diamond Jerseys Quad Onyx Autographs

STATED PRINT RUN 5 SER.#'d SETS
NOT PRICED DUE TO SCARCITY
QJAF Alexander Frolov
QJAK Anze Kopitar
QJAO Alexander Ovechkin
QJBD Brandon Dubinsky
QJBR Derick Brassard
QJCH Cristobal Huet
QJCP Carey Price
QJDB David Booth
QJDD Drew Doughty
QJDH Dale Hawerchuk
QJDP David Perron
QJDS Drew Stafford
QJDU Dustin Brown
QJEM Evgeni Malkin
QJGA Glenn Anderson
QJJP Jason Pominville
QJJV Jakub Voracek
QJLM Lanny McDonald
QJMB Martin Brodeur
QJMH Marian Hossa
QJMS Marc Staal
QJNH Nathan Horton
QJPH Dion Phaneuf
QJPK Patrick Kane
QJPO Patrick O'Sullivan
QJRM Ryan Miller
QJRN Rick Nash
QJSC Sidney Crosby
QJSD Shane Doan
QJSG Simon Gagne
QJSK Saku Koivu
QJSS Steve Shutt
QJST Jordan Staal
QJSW Shea Weber
QJTO Jonathan Toews
QJTV Thomas Vanek
QJVL Vincent Lecavalier
QJVO Tomas Vokoun
QJWE Stephen Weiss
QJZB Zach Bogosian

2009-10 Black Diamond Jerseys Quad Ruby

*SINGLES: .5X TO 1.2X BASIC INSERTS
STATED PRINT RUN 50 SER.#'d SETS

1968-69 Blackhawks Team Issue

This 8-card set measures approximately 4" by 6".

COMPLETE SET (8) 25.00 50.00
1 Dennis Hull 4.00 8.00
2 Doug Jarrett 2.50 5.00
3 Chico Maki 3.00 6.00
4 Gilles Marotte 2.50 5.00
5 Stan Mikita 10.00 20.00
6 Jim Pappin 2.50 5.00
7 Pat Stapleton 2.50 5.00
8 Ken Wharram 3.00 6.00

1970-71 Blackhawks Postcards

This 14-card set measures approximately 4" by 6". T

COMPLETE SET (14) 25.00 50.00
1 Lou Angotti 1.50 3.00
2 Bryan Campbell 1.50 3.00
3 Bobby Hull 10.00 20.00
Bill Wirtz OWN
Stan Mikita
4 Dennis Hull 3.00 6.00
5 Tommy Ivan GM 1.50 3.00
Billy Reay CO
6 Doug Jarrett 1.50 3.00
7 Keith Magnuson 2.50 5.00
8 Pit Martin 1.50 3.00
9 Stan Mikita 5.00 10.00
10 Eric Nesterenko 2.50 5.00
11 Jim Pappin 2.00 4.00
12 Allan Pinder 1.50 3.00
13 Paul Shmyr 1.50 3.00
14 Bill White 2.00 4.00

1979-80 Blackhawks Postcards

COMPLETE SET (21) 12.50 25.00
1 Keith Brown .50 1.00
2 J.P. Bordeleau .50 1.00
3 Ted Bulley .50 1.00
4 Alain Daigle .50 1.00
5 Tony Esposito 3.00 6.00
6 Greg Fox .50 1.00
7 Tim Higgins .50 1.00
8 Reggie Kerr .50 1.00
9 Cliff Koroll .50 1.00
10 Tom Lysiak .50 1.00
11 Keith Magnuson 1.00 2.00
12 John Marks .50 1.00
13 Stan Mikita 4.00 8.00
14 Grant Mulvey 1.00 2.00
15 Bob Murray 1.00 2.00
16 Mike O'Connell .50 1.00
17 Rich Preston .50 1.00
18 Bob Pulford 1.00 2.00
19 Terry Ruskowski .50 1.00
20 Mike Veisor .50 1.00
21 Doug Wilson 2.00 4.00

1980-81 Blackhawks Postcards

These postcard-size cards measure approximately 4" by 6".

COMPLETE SET (16) 12.50 25.00
1 Keith Brown .75 2.00
2 Greg Fox .40 1.00
3 Dave Hutchison .40 1.00
4 Cliff Koroll ACO .40 1.00
5 Keith Magnuson CO .60 1.50
6 Peter Marsh .60 1.50
7 Grant Mulvey .60 1.50
8 Rich Preston .40 1.00
9 Florent Robidoux .40 1.00
10 Terry Ruskowski .60 1.50
11 Denis Savard 2.50 5.00
12 Al Secord .75 2.00
13 Ron Sedlbauer .40 1.00
14 Glen Sharpley .40 1.00
15 Darryl Sutter .75 2.00
16 Miles Zaharko .40 1.00

1980-81 Blackhawks White Border

These 14 blank-backed photos measure approximately 5 1/2" by 8 1/2".

COMPLETE SET (14) 10.00 20.00
1 Murray Bannerman .60 1.50
2 J.P. Bordeleau .40 1.00
3 Keith Brown .75 2.00
4 Tony Esposito 2.50 5.00
5 Greg Fox .40 1.00
6 Tim Higgins .40 1.00
7 Doug Lecuyer .40 1.00
8 John Marks .40 1.00
9 Grant Mulvey .60 1.50
10 Rich Preston .40 1.00
11 Terry Ruskowski .60 1.50
12 Denis Savard 2.50 5.00
13 Darryl Sutter .75 2.00
14 Tim Trimper .40 1.00

1981-82 Blackhawks Borderless Postcards

These 28 postcards measure approximately 3 1/2" by 5 1/2".

COMPLETE SET (28) 12.00 30.00
1 Murray Bannerman .60 1.50
2 Keith Brown .60 1.50
3 Ted Bulley .30 .75
4 Doug Crossman .60 1.50
5 Jerome Dupont .30 .75
6 Tony Esposito 2.00 5.00
7 Greg Fox .30 .75
8 Bill Gardner .30 .75
9 Tim Higgins .30 .75
10 Dave Hutchison .30 .75
11 Reg Kerr .30 .75
12 Cliff Koroll ACO .30 .75
13 Tom Lysiak .60 1.50
14 Keith Magnuson CO .60 1.50
15 John Marks .30 .75
16 Peter Marsh .30 .75
17 Grant Mulvey .30 .75
18 Bob Murray .30 .75
19 Rick Paterson .30 .75
20 Rich Preston .30 .75
21 Bob Pulford GM .60 1.50
22 Terry Ruskowski .30 .75
23 Denis Savard 2.00 5.00
24 Al Secord .75 2.00
25 Glen Sharpley .30 .75
26 Darryl Sutter .75 2.00
27 Toni Tanti .75 2.00
28 Doug Wilson 1.25 3.00

1981-82 Blackhawks Brown Background

These 17 postcards measure approximately 4" by 6".

COMPLETE SET (17) 10.00 25.00
1 Keith Brown .75 2.00
2 Greg Fox .40 1.00
3 Dave Hutchison .40 1.00
4 Cliff Koroll ACO .40 1.00
5 Keith Magnuson CO .75 2.00
6 Peter Marsh .75 2.00
7 Grant Mulvey .75 2.00
8 Bob Pulford GM/CO 1.25 3.00
9 Rich Preston .40 1.00
10 Florent Robidoux .40 1.00
11 Terry Ruskowski .75 2.00
12 Denis Savard 3.00 8.00
13 Al Secord .75 2.00
14 Ron Sedlbauer .40 1.00
15 Glen Sharpley .40 1.00
16 Darryl Sutter 1.25 3.00
17 Miles Zaharko .40 1.00

1982-83 Blackhawks Postcards

COMPLETE SET (23) 12.00 30.00
1 Murray Bannerman .50 1.25
2 Keith Brown .50 1.25
3 Doug Crossman .40 1.00
4 Dennis Cyr .30 .75
5 Tony Esposito 1.50 4.00
6 Dave Feamster .30 .75
7 Bill Gardner .30 .75
8 Greg Fox .30 .75
9 Tim Higgins .30 .75
10 Steve Larmer 2.00 5.00
11 Steve Ludzik .60 1.50
12 Tom Lysiak .50 1.25
13 Peter Marsh .30 .75
14 Grant Mulvey .30 .75
15 Bob Murray .30 .75
16 Troy Murray .40 1.00
17 Rick Paterson .30 .75
18 Rich Preston .30 .75
19 Denis Savard 1.50 4.00
20 Al Secord .75 2.00
21 Darryl Sutter .60 1.50
22 Orval Tessier CO .40 1.00
23 Doug Wilson 1.00 2.50

1983-84 Blackhawks Postcards

These 27 postcards measure approximately 3 1/2" by 5 1/2".

COMPLETE SET (27) 14.00 35.00
1 Murray Bannerman .60 1.50
2 Keith Brown .40 1.00
3 Denis Cyr .30 .75
4 Jerome Dupont .30 .75
5 Tony Esposito 1.50 4.00
6 Dave Feamster .30 .75
7 Curt Fraser .40 1.00
8 Bill Gardner .30 .75
9 Bob Janecyk .60 1.50
10 Cliff Koroll ACO .20 .50
11 Steve Larmer 3.00 8.00
12 Steve Ludzik .60 1.50
13 Tom Lysiak .60 1.50
14 Peter Marsh .30 .75
15 Bob Murray .30 .75
16 Troy Murray .60 1.50
17 Jack O'Callahan .30 .75
18 Rick Paterson .30 .75
19 Rich Preston .30 .75
20 Denis Savard 1.50 4.00
21 Al Secord .75 2.00
22 Darryl Sutter .75 2.00
23 Orval Tessier CO .20 .50
24 Behn Wilson .30 .75
25 Doug Wilson 1.00 2.50
26 Ken Yaremchuk .30 .75
27 Title Card .20 .50

1985-86 Blackhawks Team Issue

COMPLETE SET (26) 20.00 40.00
1 Steve Larmer 1.25 3.00
2 Keith Brown .75 2.00
3 Cliff Koroll .40 1.00
4 Roger Neilson .40 1.00
5 Bob Pulford .40 1.00
6 Behn Wilson .75 2.00
7 Jerome Dupont .75 2.00
8 Rick Paterson .40 1.00
9 Al Secord 1.25 3.00
10 Marc Bergevin .40 1.00
11 Darryl Sutter 1.25 3.00
12 Murray Bannerman .75 2.00
13 Bruce Cassidy .40 1.00
14 Bill Watson .40 1.00
15 Curt Fraser .40 1.00
16 Warren Skorodenski .75 2.00
17 Troy Murray .40 1.00
18 Bill Gardner .40 1.00
19 Ken Yaremchuk .40 1.00
20 Steve Ludzik .40 1.00
21 Jack O'Callahan .75 2.00
22 Tom Lysiak .40 1.00
23 Bob Murray .40 1.00
24 Ed Olczyk .75 2.00
25 Denis Savard 1.25 3.00
26 Doug Wilson 1.25 3.00

1986-87 Blackhawks Coke

The cards measure approximately 3 1/2" by 6 1/2".

COMPLETE SET (24) 8.00 20.00
1 Murray Bannerman .40 1.00
2 Marc Bergevin .30 .75
3 Keith Brown .30 .75
4 Dave Donnelly .30 .75
5 Curt Fraser .30 .75
6 Steve Larmer 1.25 3.00
7 Steve Ludzik .30 .75
8 Dave Manson .60 1.50
9 Bob Murray .30 .75
10 Troy Murray .30 .75
11 Gary Nylund .30 .75
12 Jack O'Callahan .30 .75
13 Ed Olczyk .40 1.00
14 Rick Paterson .30 .75
15 Wayne Presley .30 .75
16 Rich Preston .30 .75
17 Bob Sauve .40 1.00
18 Denis Savard 1.25 3.00
19 Al Secord .40 1.00
20 Mike Stapleton .30 .75
21 Darryl Sutter .40 1.00
22 Bill Watson .30 .75
23 Behn Wilson .30 .75
24 Doug Wilson .60 1.50

1987-88 Blackhawks Coke

The cards measure approximately 3 1/2" by 6 1/2".

COMPLETE SET (30) 8.00 20.00
1 Murray Bannerman .40 1.00
2 Marc Bergevin .30 .75
3 Keith Brown .30 .75
4 Glen Cochrane .30 .75
5 Curt Fraser .30 .75
6 Steve Larmer 1.00 2.50
7 Mark LaVarre .30 .75
8 Steve Ludzik .30 .75
9 Dave Manson .60 1.50
10 Bob Mason .40 1.00
11 Bob McGill .30 .75
12 Bob Murdoch CO .30 .75
13 Bob Murray .30 .75
14 Troy Murray .40 1.00
15 Brian Noonan .30 .75
16 Gary Nylund .30 .75
17 Darren Pang .60 1.50
18 Wayne Presley .30 .75
19 Everett Sanipass .30 .75
20 Denis Savard 1.00 2.50
21 Mike Stapleton .30 .75
22 Darryl Sutter CO .30 .75
23 Duane Sutter .40 1.00
24 Steve Thomas .50 1.25
25 Wayne Thomas CO .30 .75
26 Rick Vaive .40 1.00
27 Dan Vincelette .30 .75
28 Bill Watson .30 .75
29 Behn Wilson .30 .75
30 Doug Wilson .60 1.50

1988-89 Blackhawks Coke

The cards measure approximately 3 1/2" by 6 1/2".

COMPLETE SET (25) 8.00 20.00
1 Ed Belfour 4.00 10.00
2 Keith Brown .20 .50
3 Bruce Cassidy .20 .50
4 Mike Eagles .20 .50
5 Dirk Graham .40 1.00
6 Mike Hudson .20 .50
7 Mike Keenan CO .60 1.50
8 Steve Larmer .60 1.50
9 Dave Manson .40 1.00
10 Jacques Martin CO .08 .25
11 Bob McGill .20 .50
12 E.J. McGuire CO .08 .25
13 Troy Murray .40 1.00
14 Brian Noonan .20 .50
15 Darren Pang .30 .75
16 Wayne Presley .20 .50
17 Everett Sanipass .20 .50
18 Denis Savard .75 2.00
19 Duane Sutter .30 .75
20 Steve Thomas .40 1.00
21 Rick Vaive .30 .75
22 Dan Vincelette .20 .50
23 Jimmy Waite .30 .75
24 Doug Wilson .40 1.00
25 Trent Yawney .20 .50

1989-90 Blackhawks Coke

This 27-card set was issued in a photo album consisting of five unperforated sheets measuring approximately 12" by 12". The first four sheets have six players each, while the last sheet features the three coaches.

COMPLETE SET (27) 8.00 20.00
1 Denis Savard .75 2.00
2 Troy Murray .30 .75
3 Steve Larmer .60 1.50
4 Doug Wilson .60 1.50
5 Bob Murray .20 .50
6 Jeremy Roenick 3.00 8.00
7 Duane Sutter .30 .75
8 Greg Gilbert .20 .50
9 Trent Yawney .20 .50
10 Bob McGill .20 .50
11 Jacques Cloutier .30 .75
12 Bob Bassen .20 .50
13 Steve Thomas .40 1.00
14 Adam Creighton .30 .75
15 Wayne Van Dorp .30 .75
16 Dirk Graham .40 1.00
17 Mike Hudson .20 .50
18 Al Secord .30 .75
19 Alain Chevrier .30 .75
20 Wayne Presley .20 .50
21 Steve Konroyd .20 .50
22 Everett Sanipass .20 .50
23 Keith Brown .20 .50
24 Dave Manson .40 1.00
25 Mike Keenan CO .40 1.00
26 E.J. McGuire CO .08 .25
27 Jacques Martin CO .08 .25

1990-91 Blackhawks Coke

This 28-card set was issued in a photo album consisting of five unperforated sheets measuring approximately 11 3/4" by 12 1/4".

COMPLETE SET (28) 8.00 20.00
1 Dirk Graham .30 .75
2 Troy Murray .30 .75
3 Steve Larmer .40 1.00
4 Doug Wilson .40 1.00
5 Chris Chelios 1.00 2.50
6 Jeremy Roenick 2.00 5.00
7 Steve Thomas .30 .75
8 Greg Gilbert .20 .50
9 Trent Yawney .20 .50
10 Bob McGill .20 .50
11 Jacques Cloutier .25 .60
12 Jocelyn Lemieux .20 .50
13 Michel Goulet .40 1.00
14 Adam Creighton .25 .60
15 Mike McNeill .20 .50
16 Ed Belfour 2.50 6.00
17 Mike Hudson .20 .50
18 Greg Millen .20 .50
19 Stu Grimson .20 .50
20 Wayne Presley .20 .50
21 Steve Konroyd .20 .50
22 Mike Peluso .20 .50
23 Keith Brown .20 .50
24 Dave Manson .30 .75
25 Mike Keenan CO .30 .75
26 Darryl Sutter CO .30 .75
27 E.J. McGuire CO .08 .25
28 Vladislav Tretiak CO 1.00 2.50

1991-92 Blackhawks Coke

This photo album measured approximately 11 5/8" by 12 1/4".

COMPLETE SET (28) 8.00 20.00
1 Ed Belfour 1.25 3.00
2 Keith Brown .20 .50
3 Rod Buskas .20 .50
4 Chris Chelios .75 2.00
5 Karl Dykhuis .20 .50
6 Greg Gilbert .20 .50
7 Michel Goulet .30 .75
8 Dirk Graham .30 .75
9 Stu Grimson .40 1.00
10 Mike Hudson .20 .50
11 Mike Keenan GM/CO .40 1.00
12 Steve Konroyd .20 .50
13 Frantisek Kucera .20 .50
14 Steve Larmer .40 1.00
15 Brad Lauer .20 .50
16 Jocelyn Lemieux .20 .50
17 Bryan Marchment .20 .50
18 Dave McDowall CO .08 .25
19 Brian Noonan .20 .50
20 Mike Peluso .20 .50
21 Rich Preston CO .08 .25
22 Jeremy Roenick 1.25 3.00
23 Steve Smith .30 .75
24 Mike Stapleton .30 .75
25 Brent Sutter .30 .75
26 Darryl Sutter CO .30 .75
27 John Tonelli .30 .75
28 Jimmy Waite .30 .75

1992-93 Blackhawks Coke

COMPLETE SET (20) 10.00 25.00
1 Adam Bennett .30 .75
2 Cam Russell .30 .75
3 Christian Ruuttu .30 .75
4 Stu Grimson .75 2.00
5 Brent Sutter .75 2.00
6 Dave Christian .40 1.00
7 Mike Hudson .30 .75
8 Rob Brown .30 .75
9 Steve Larmer .75 2.00
10 Bryan Marchment .30 .75
11 Igor Kravchuk .30 .75
12 Paul Baxter .30 .75
13 Vladislav Tretiak .75 2.00
14 Rich Preston .30 .75
15 Darryl Sutter .75 2.00
16 Keith Brown .30 .75
17 Bob Pulford .30 .75
18 Jimmy Waite .40 1.00
19 Ed Belfour 1.25 3.00
20 Jeremy Roenick 1.25 3.00

1993-94 Blackhawks Coke

This team photo album measured approximately 11 1/2" by 12 1/4". Each of the four glossy pages features two rows with three player cards per row; the final six player cards are printed on the inside of the back cover.

COMPLETE SET (30) 6.00 15.00
1 Joe Murphy .30 .75
2 Chris Chelios .75 2.00
3 Rich Sutter .20 .50
4 Frantisek Kucera .20 .50
5 Jeff Shantz .20 .50
6 Brian Noonan .20 .50
7 Michel Goulet .30 .75
8 Jeremy Roenick .75 2.00
9 Dave Christian .20 .50
10 Patrick Poulin .20 .50
11 Brent Sutter .20 .50
12 Cam Russell .20 .50
13 Stephane Matteau .20 .50
14 Ed Belfour 1.00 2.50
15 Neil Wilkinson .20 .50
16 Eric Weinrich .20 .50
17 Christian Ruuttu .20 .50
18 Kevin Todd .20 .50
19 Jeff Hackett .40 1.00
20 Steve Smith .25 .60
21 Jocelyn Lemieux .20 .50
22 Keith Carney .20 .50
23 Troy Murray .20 .50
24 Darin Kimble .20 .50
25 Dirk Graham .30 .75
26 Bob Pulford GM .20 .50
27 Darryl Sutter CO .20 .50
28 Paul Baxter ACO .08 .25
29 Rich Preston ACO .08 .25
30 Phil Myre ACO .08 .25

1994-95 Blackhawks Coke

These cards are more like oversized photos, and came complete with an album.

COMPLETE SET(21) 6.00 15.00
1 Tony Amonte .75 2.00
2 Ed Belfour 1.00 2.50
3 Keith Carney .20 .50
4 Chris Chelios .75 2.00
5 Dirk Graham .30 .75
6 Brent Grieve .20 .50
7 Jeff Hackett .40 1.00
8 Roger Johansson .20 .50
9 Darin Kimble .20 .50
10 Sergei Krivokrasov .20 .50
11 Joe Murphy .20 .50
12 Bernie Nicholls .40 1.00
13 Patrick Poulin .20 .50
14 Bob Probert .40 1.00
15 Cam Russell .20 .50
16 Jeff Shantz .20 .50
17 Steve Smith .20 .50
18 Greg Smyth .20 .50
19 Gary Suter .30 .75
20 Brent Sutter .20 .50
21 Eric Weinrich .20 .50

1995-96 Blackhawks Coke

COMPLETE SET (19) 6.00 15.00
1 Tony Amonte .75 2.00
2 Ed Belfour 1.00 2.50
3 Keith Carney .20 .50
4 Chris Chelios .75 2.00
5 Murray Craven .20 .50
6 Jim Cummins .20 .50
7 Eric Daze .40 1.00
8 Jeff Hackett .40 1.00
9 Sergei Krivokrasov .20 .50
10 Joe Murphy .20 .50
11 Bernie Nicholls .40 1.00
12 Bob Probert .40 1.00
13 Cam Russell .20 .50
14 Denis Savard .40 1.00
15 Jeff Shantz .20 .50
16 Steve Smith .20 .50
17 Gary Suter .20 .50
18 Brent Sutter .20 .50
19 Eric Weinrich .20 .50

1998 Blackhawks Legends

Made and distributed by Pizza Hut in 1998, these cards feature rounded corners, and full color photos on the front.

COMPLETE SET (5) 4.80 12.00
1 Tony Esposito 1.25 3.00
2 Glenn Hall 1.25 3.00
3 Bobby Hull 2.00 5.00
4 Steve Larmer .60 1.50
5 Denis Savard .60 1.50

1998-99 Blackhawks Chicago Sun-Times

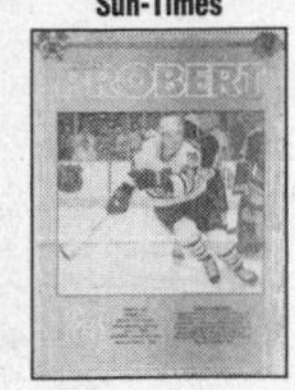

These full-page color player profiles ran in the Chicago Sun-Times during the 1998-99 season. Each page contains a action photo along with player stats and career highlights. The pages are unnumbered and are listed below in alphabetical order.

COMPLETE SET 3.00 8.00
1 Chris Chelios 1.25 3.00
2 Mark Fitzpatrick .40 1.00
3 Doug Gilmour .75 2.00
4 Christian Laflamme .40 1.00
5 Bob Probert 1.25 3.00
6 Jocelyn Thibault .40 1.00

1999-00 Blackhawks Chicago Sun-Times

These full-page color player profiles ran in the Chicago Sun-Times during the 1999-2000 season. Each page contains a action photo along with player stats and career highlights. The pages are unnumbered and are listed below in alphabetical order.

COMPLETE SET (12) 4.00 10.00
1 Tony Amonte .75 2.00
2 Brad Brown .40 1.00
3 Mark Janssens .40 1.00
4 Jean-Yves Leroux .40 1.00
5 Dave Manson .40 1.00
6 Bryan McCabe .40 1.00
7 Boris Mironov .40 1.00
8 Michael Nylander .40 1.00
9 Doug Zmolek .40 1.00
10 Denis Savard .40 1.00
Trent Yawney
Lorne Molliken
Bob Pulford
11 Team photo .40 1.00

1999-00 Blackhawks Lineup Cards

These 8X10 items were inserted in the first 4,000 copies of each Blackhawks game program.

COMPLETE SET (10) 8.00 20.00
1 Tony Amonte 1.50 4.00
2 Brad Brown .40 1.00
3 Eric Daze 1.25 3.00
4 Doug Gilmour 1.50 4.00
5 Dean McAmmond .40 1.00
6 Bryan McCabe .40 1.00
7 Boris Mironov .40 1.00
8 Steve Sullivan .75 2.00
9 Jocelyn Thibault 1.25 3.00
10 Alexei Zhamnov .40 1.00

2002-03 Blackhawks Postcards

These are standard postcard size and feature blank backs. Please forward additional information to hockeymag@beckett.com

COMPLETE SET (7)
1 Eric Daze .40 1.00
2 Steve Poapst .40 1.00
3 Jason Strudwick .40 1.00
4 Brian Sutter CO .40 1.00
5 Jocelyn Thibault .75 2.00
6 Ryan Vandenbussche .40 1.00
7 Alexei Zhamnov .40 1.00

2003-04 Blackhawks Postcards

COMPLETE SET (31) 10.00 25.00
1 Craig Andersson .40 1.00
2 Tyler Arnason .30 .75
3 Anton Babchuk .20 .50
4 Mark Bell .40 1.00
5 Kyle Calder .40 1.00
6 Eric Daze .40 1.00
7 Nathan Dempsey .20 .50
8 Alexander Karpovtsev .20 .50
9 Igor Korolev .20 .50
10 Lasse Kukkonen .20 .50
11 Michael Leighton .40 1.00
12 Al MacAdam ACO .02 .10
13 Steve McCarthy .20 .50
14 Brett McLean .20 .50
15 Travis Moen .20 .50
16 Scott Nichol .20 .50
17 Ville Nieminen .20 .50
18 Steve Passmore .40 1.00
19 Steve Poapst .20 .50
20 Deron Quint .20 .50
21 Igor Radulov .40 1.00
22 Tuomo Ruutu 2.00 5.00
23 Denis Savard ACO .30 .75
24 Jason Strudwick .20 .50
25 Steve Sullivan .40 1.00
26 Brent Sutter CO .10 .25
27 Jocelyn Thibault .75 2.00
28 Vladislav Tretiak ACO .40 1.00
29 Ryan VandenBussche .20 .50
30 Pavel Vorobiev .20 .50
31 Alexei Zhamnov .20 .50

2006-07 Blackhawks Postcards

COMPLETE SET (23) 10.00 20.00
1 Adrian Aucoin .40 1.00
2 Denis Arkhipov .40 1.00
3 Jeff Hamilton .40 1.00
4 Martin Lapointe .40 1.00
5 Tony Salmelainen .40 1.00
6 Jassen Cullimore .40 1.00
7 Martin Havlat .60 1.50
8 Patrick Sharp .40 1.00
9 Michael Holmqvist .40 1.00
10 Brent Seabrook .40 1.00
11 Rene Bourque .40 1.00
12 Jim Vandermeer .40 1.00
13 Duncan Keith .40 1.00
14 Nikolai Khabibulin .75 2.00
15 Michal Handzus .40 1.00
16 Tuomo Ruutu .75 2.00
17 Radim Vrbata .40 1.00
18 Brian Boucher .60 1.50
19 Bryan Smolinski .40 1.00
20 Lasse Kukkonen .40 1.00
21 Denis Savard CO .75 2.00
22 Mark Hardy CO .20 .50
23 Stephane Waite ACO .20 .50

2006-07 Blackhawks Postcards Glossy

We have no pricing information on this set. It is believed that there are other singles not yet catalogued. Please forward any additional information to hockeymag@beckett.com.

1 Troy Brouwer
2 Peter Bondra
3 James Wisniewski
4 Karl Stewart
5 Ryan Stewart CO

2007-08 Blackhawks Team Issue

COMPLETE SET (28) 8.00 20.00
1 Kevyn Adams .30 .75
2 Rene Bourque .30 .75
3 Adam Burish .30 .75
4 Martin Havlat .30 .75
5 Magnus Johansson .30 .75
6 Patrick Kane 1.50 4.00
7 Duncan Keith .30 .75
8 Nikolai Khabibulin .40 1.00
9 David Koci .75 2.00
10 Patrick Lalime .40 1.00
11 Robert Lang .30 .75
12 Martin Lapointe .30 .75
13 Yanic Perreault .30 .75
14 Danny Richmond .30 .75
15 Tuomo Ruutu .40 1.00
16 Sergei Samsonov .30 .75
17 Brent Seabrook .30 .75
18 Patrick Sharp .30 .75
19 Brent Sopel .30 .75
20 Jonathan Toews 1.50 4.00
21 Jason Williams .30 .75
22 James Wisniewski .30 .75
23 Andrei Zyuzin .30 .75
24 Denis Savard HC .30 .75
25 Mark Hardy AC .10 .25
26 Ryan Stewart AC .10 .25
27 John Torchetti AC .10 .25
28 Stephane Waite CO .10 .25

1993 Bleachers 23K Manon Rheaume

This four-card standard-size set featured 23 Karat gold borders. The production run was reportedly 10,000 numbered sets and 1,500 uncut numbered strips.

COMPLETE SET (4) 2.00 5.00

1996 Bleachers Lemieux

This one-card set featured an embossed image of Mario Lemieux on a 23 Karat all-gold sculptured card. The card was packaged in a clear acrylic holder along with a Certificate of Authenticity inside a collectible foil-stamped box. Only 10,000 of the card were produced and are serially numbered.

1 Mario Lemieux 2.00 5.00

2001-02 Blizzak Kim St-Pierre

This single card was issued as a promotional premium with the purchase of a set of Bridgestone Blizzak tires in the province of Quebec during the winter of 2001-02. The card features a photo of Canadian National Women's team goalie St-Pierre wearing a Bridgestone jersey on the front, and features personal and statistical data on the back in French. It is believed that 2,000 of these cards were produced, but less than 500 were actually given out in the promotion.

NNO Kim St-Pierre 2.00 5.00

2001-02 Blue Jackets Donatos Pizza

Sponsored by Donatos Pizza, this 24-card set was issued in sheets containing 6 cards, a pizza coupon and a merchandise coupon.

COMPLETE SET (24) 5.00 12.00
1 Geoff Sanderson .20 .50
2 Grant Marshall .20 .50
3 Serge Aubin .20 .50
4 Robert Kron .20 .50
5 Blake Sloan .20 .50
6 Mattias Timander .20 .50
7 Tyler Wright .20 .50
8 Espen Knutsen .40 1.00
9 Rostislav Klesla .40 1.00
10 Kevin Dineen .20 .50
11 Deron Quint .20 .50
12 Ron Tugnutt .40 1.00
13 Marc Denis .40 1.00
14 David Vyborny .20 .50
15 Lyle Odelein .20 .50
16 Jean-Luc Grand-Pierre .20 .50
17 Radim Bicanek .20 .50
18 Geoff Sanderson .20 .50
19 Ron Tugnutt .40 1.00
20 Ray Whitney .20 .50
21 Mike Sillinger .20 .50
22 Chris Nielsen .20 .50
23 Jamie Pushor .20 .50
24 Jamie Heward .20 .50

1971-72 Blues Postcards

This 30-card set measures approximately 3 1/2" by 5 1/2".

COMPLETE SET (30) 35.00 70.00
1 Al Arbour CO 2.50 5.00
2 John Arbour 1.00 2.00
3 Curt Bennett 1.00 2.00
4 Chris Bordeleau 1.00 2.00
5 Carl Brewer 1.50 3.00
6 Jacques Caron 1.00 2.00
7 Terry Crisp 2.00 4.00
8 Andre Dupont 1.50 3.00
9 Jack Egers 1.00 2.00
10 Larry Hornung 1.00 2.00
11 Brian Lavender 1.00 2.00
11 Mike Murphy 1.00 2.00
12 Gerry Odrowski 1.00 2.00
12 Gordon Marchant ATR .50 1.00
Alex McPherson ATR
13 Bill McCreary AGM .50 1.00
14 Danny O'Shea 1.00 2.00
15 Mike Parizeau 1.00 2.00
16 Noel Picard 1.50 3.00
17 Barclay Plager 2.00 4.00
18 Bill Plager 1.50 3.00
19 Bob Plager 2.00 4.00
20 Phil Roberto 1.50 3.00
21 Gary Sabourin 1.00 2.00
22 Jim Shires 1.00 2.00
23 Frank St. Marseille 1.50 3.00
24 Floyd Thomson 1.00 2.00
25 Garry Unger 2.50 5.00
26 Garry Unger action 2.50 5.00
27 Ernie Wakely 1.50 3.00
28 Tom Woodcock TR .50 1.00

1972-73 Blues White Border

Printed on thin white stock, this set of 22 photos measures approximately 6 7/8" by 8 3/4".

COMPLETE SET (22) 30.00 60.00
1 Jacques Caron 1.50 3.00
2 Steve Durbano 2.00 4.00
3 Jack Egers 1.50 3.00
4 Chris Evans 1.50 3.00
5 Jean Hamel 1.50 3.00
6 Fran Huck 1.50 3.00
7 Brent Hughes 1.50 3.00
8 Bob Johnson 2.00 4.00
9 Mike Lampman 1.50 3.00
10 Bob McCord 1.50 3.00
11 Wayne Merrick 2.00 4.00
12 Mike Murphy 1.50 3.00
13 Danny O'Shea 1.50 3.00
14 Barclay Plager 2.50 5.00
15 Bob Plager 2.50 5.00
16 Pierre Plante 1.50 3.00

17 Phil Roberto	2.00	4.00
18 Gary Sabourin	1.50	3.00
19 Wayne Stephenson	2.50	5.00
20 Jean-Guy Talbot CO	1.50	3.00
21 Floyd Thomson	1.50	3.00
22 Garry Unger	2.50	5.00
AC1 Garry Unger	2.50	5.00
AC2 Phil Roberto	2.00	4.00

1973-74 Blues White Border

Printed on thin white stock, this set of 24 photos measures approximately 6 7/8" by 8 3/4". The set is dated by the Glen Sather photo; 1973-74 was his only season with the team.

COMPLETE SET (24)	25.00	50.00
1 Lou Angotti	.75	1.50
2 Don Awrey	.75	1.50
3 John Davidson	2.50	5.00
4 Ab Demarco	.75	1.50
5 Steve Durbano	.75	1.50
6 Chris Evans	.75	1.50
7 Larry Giroux	.75	1.50
8 Jean Hamel	.75	1.50
9 Nick Harbaruk	.75	1.50
10 J.Bob Kelly	1.00	2.00
11 Mike Lampman	.75	1.50
12 Wayne Merrick	.75	1.50
13 Barclay Plager	2.00	4.00
14 Bob Plager	2.00	4.00
15 Pierre Plante	1.50	3.00
16 Phil Roberto	2.50	5.00
17 Gary Sabourin	.75	1.50
18 Glen Sather	2.00	4.00
19 Wayne Stephenson	2.00	4.00
20 Jean-Guy Talbot CO	.75	1.50
21 Floyd Thomson	.75	1.50
22 Garry Unger	1.25	2.50
23 Garry Unger action	1.25	2.50
24 Team Photo	1.50	3.00
(1972-73 team)		

1978-79 Blues Postcards

This 21-postcard set of the St. Louis Blues measures approximately 3 1/2" by 5 1/2".

COMPLETE SET (24)	15.00	30.00
1 Wayne Babych	1.00	2.00
2 Curt Bennett	1.00	2.00
3 Harvey Bennett	.50	1.00
4 Red Berenson	1.50	3.00
5 Blue Angels	1.00	2.00
6 Jack Brownschidle	1.00	2.00
7 Mike Crombeen	.50	1.00
8 Tony Currie	.50	1.00
9 Fanvan	.10	.25
10 Bernie Federko	2.00	4.00
11 Barry Gibbs	.50	1.00
12 Larry Giroux	.50	1.00
13 Inge Hammarstrom	1.00	2.00
14 Neil Labatte	.50	1.00
15 Bob Murdoch	.50	1.00
16 Phil Myre	1.00	2.00
17 Larry Patey	.50	1.00
18 Barclay Plager CO	1.00	2.00
19 Rick Shinske	.50	1.00
20 John Smrke	.50	1.00
21 Ed Staniowski	.50	1.00
22 Bob Stewart	.50	1.00
23 Brian Sutter	2.00	4.00
24 Garry Unger	1.50	3.00

1987-88 Blues Team Photos

The 20 team photos in this set each measure approximately 8 1/2" by 11".

COMPLETE SET (20)	6.00	15.00
1 1967-68 Team Photo	.60	1.50
2 1968-69 Team Photo	.40	1.00
3 1969-70 Team Photo	.40	1.00
4 1970-71 Team Photo	.40	1.00
5 1971-72 Team Photo	.40	1.00
6 1972-73 Team Photo	.40	1.00
7 1973-74 Team Photo	.40	1.00
8 1974-75 Team Photo	.40	1.00
9 1975-76 Team Photo	.40	1.00
10 1976-77 Team Photo	.40	1.00
11 1977-78 Team Photo	.40	1.00
12 1978-79 Team Photo	.40	1.00
13 1979-80 Team Photo	.40	1.00
14 1980-81 Team Photo	.40	1.00
15 1981-82 Team Photo	.40	1.00
16 1982-83 Team Photo	.40	1.00
17 1983-84 Team Photo	.40	1.00
18 1984-85 Team Photo	.40	1.00
19 1985-86 Team Photo	.40	1.00
20 1986-87 Team Photo	.40	1.00

1987-88 Blues Kodak

The 1987-88 St. Louis Blues Team Photo Album was sponsored by Kodak in conjunction with KMOX Radio. The set consists of three large sheets, each measuring approximately 11" by 8 1/4" and joined together to form one continuous sheet.

COMPLETE SET (26)	12.00	30.00
1 Brian Benning	.40	1.00
2 Tim Bothwell	.30	.75
3 Charlie Bourgeois	.30	.75
4 Paul Cavallini	.40	1.00
5 Gino Cavallini	.40	1.00
6 Michael Dark	.30	.75
7 Doug Evans	.30	.75
8 Todd Ewen	.60	1.50
9 Bernie Federko	1.25	3.00
10 Ron Flockhart	.30	.75
11 Doug Gilmour	2.50	6.00
12 Gaston Gingras	.30	.75
13 Tony Hrkac	.40	1.00
14 Mark Hunter	.40	1.00
15 Jocelyn Lemieux	.30	.75
16 Tony McKegney	.40	1.00
17 Rick Meagher	.40	1.00
18 Greg Millen	.60	1.50
19 Robert Nordmark	.30	.75
20 Greg Paslawski	.30	.75
21 Herb Raglan	.30	.75
22 Rob Ramage	.40	1.00
23 Cliff Ronning	1.00	2.50
24 Brian Sutter	.60	1.50
25 Perry Turnbull	.30	.75
26 Rick Wamsley	.60	1.50

1987-88 Blues Team Issue

This 24-card set measures 3 1/2" by 5 1/2".

COMPLETE SET (24)	14.00	35.00
1 Brian Benning	.40	1.00
2 Mike Bullard	.75	2.00
3 Gino Cavallini	.40	1.00
4 Paul Cavallini	.40	1.00
5 Craig Coxe	.30	.75
6 Robert Dirk	.30	.75
7 Doug Evans	.30	.75
8 Todd Ewen	.60	1.50
9 Bernie Federko	1.25	3.00
10 Gaston Gingras	.30	.75
11 Tony Hrkac	.40	1.00
12 Brett Hull	6.00	15.00
13 Tony McKegney	.40	1.00
14 Rick Meagher	.40	1.00
15 Greg Millen	.60	1.50
16 Sergio Momesso	.30	.75
17 Greg Paslawski	.30	.75
18 Herb Raglan	.30	.75
19 Dave Richter	.30	.75
20 Vincent Riendeau	.40	1.00
21 Gordie Roberts	.40	1.00
22 Brian Sutter	.60	1.50
23 Tom Tilley	.30	.75
24 Steve Tuttle	.30	.75

1988-89 Blues Kodak

The 1988-89 St. Louis Blues Team Photo Album was sponsored by Kodak. It consists of three large sheets, each measuring approximately 11" by 8 1/4" and joined together to form one continuous sheet.

COMPLETE SET (25)	10.00	25.00
1 Brian Benning	.30	.75
2 Tim Bothwell	.30	.75
3 Gino Cavallini	.30	.75
4 Paul Cavallini	.30	.75
5 Craig Coxe	.30	.75
6 Doug Evans	.30	.75
7 Todd Ewen	.40	1.00
8 Bernie Federko	.75	2.00
9 Gaston Gingras	.30	.75
10 Tony Hrkac	.40	1.00
11 Brett Hull	5.00	12.00
12 Mike Lalor	.30	.75
13 Tony McKegney	.40	1.00
14 Rick Meagher	.30	.75
15 Greg Millen	.40	1.00
16 Sergio Momesso	.30	.75
17 Greg Paslawski	.30	.75
18 Herb Raglan	.30	.75
19 Vincent Riendeau	.40	1.00
20 Dave Richter	.30	.75
21 Gordie Roberts	.30	.75
22 Cliff Ronning	.75	2.00
23 Tom Tilley	.30	.75
24 Steve Tuttle	.30	.75
25 Peter Zezel	.40	1.00

1988-89 Blues Team Issue

This 24-card set measures approximately 3 1/2" by 5 1/4".

COMPLETE SET (24)	10.00	25.00
1 Brian Benning	.30	.75
2 Mike Bullard	.60	1.50
3 Gino Cavallini	.30	.75
4 Paul Cavallini	.30	.75
5 Craig Coxe	.30	.75
6 Robert Dirk	.30	.75
7 Doug Evans	.30	.75
8 Todd Ewen	.40	1.00
9 Bernie Federko	.75	2.00
10 Gaston Gingras	.30	.75
11 Tony Hrkac	.40	1.00
12 Brett Hull	5.00	12.00
13 Tony McKegney	.40	1.00
14 Rick Meagher	.30	.75
15 Greg Millen	.40	1.00
16 Sergio Momesso	.30	.75
17 Greg Paslawski	.30	.75
18 Herb Raglan	.30	.75
19 Dave Richter	.30	.75
20 Vincent Riendeau	.40	1.00
21 Gordie Roberts	.30	.75
22 Brian Sutter CO	.40	1.00
23 Tom Tilley	.30	.75
24 Steve Tuttle	.30	.75

1989-90 Blues Kodak

This 25-card set of St. Louis Blues measures approximately 2 3/8" by 3 1/2" and has a portrait shot of the player surrounded by yellow borders. The set was supposedly passed out to the first 15,000 ticket-holders at the Blues vs. Buffalo Sabres game on February 27th.

COMPLETE SET (25)	10.00	25.00
1 Pat Jablonski	.40	1.00
4 Gordie Roberts	.20	.50
6 Tony Twist	.60	1.50
9 Peter Zezel	.30	.75
10 Dave Lowry	.20	.50
12 Adam Oates	1.25	3.00
14 Paul Cavallini	.20	.50
15 Paul MacLean	.30	.75
16 Brett Hull	2.00	5.00
17 Gino Cavallini	.20	.50
19 Rod Brind'Amour	1.25	3.00
20 Tom Tilley	.20	.50
21 Jeff Brown	.40	1.00
22 Rick Meagher	.20	.50
23 Adrien Plavsic	.20	.50
25 Herb Raglan	.20	.50
26 Mike Lalor	.20	.50
27 Sergio Momesso	.20	.50
30 Vincent Riendeau	.40	1.00
31 Curtis Joseph	4.00	10.00
35 Steve Tuttle	.20	.50
38 Dominic Lavoie	.20	.50
39 Kelly Chase	.20	.50
40 Dave Thomlinson	.20	.50
NNO Brian Sutter CO	.30	.75

1990-91 Blues Kodak

This 25-card standard-size set was sponsored by Kodak in conjunction with KMOX Radio.

COMPLETE SET (25)	10.00	25.00
1 Bob Bassen	.20	.50
2 Rod Brind'Amour	1.25	3.00
3 Jeff Brown	.30	.75
4 David Bruce	.20	.50
5 Gino Cavallini	.20	.50
6 Paul Cavallini	.20	.50
7 Geoff Courtnall	.40	1.00
8 Robert Dirk	.20	.50
9 Glen Featherstone	.20	.50
10 Brett Hull	2.00	5.00
11 Curtis Joseph	1.25	3.00
12 Dave Lowry	.20	.50
13 Paul MacLean	.20	.50
14 Mario Marois	.20	.50
15 Rick Meagher	.20	.50
16 Sergio Momesso	.20	.50
17 Adam Oates	1.25	3.00
18 Vincent Riendeau	.30	.75
19 Cliff Ronning	.50	1.25
20 Harold Snepsts	.40	1.00
21 Scott Stevens	.60	1.50
22 Brian Sutter CO	.20	.50
23 Rich Sutter	.20	.50
24 Steve Tuttle	.20	.50
25 Ron Wilson	.20	.50

1991-92 Blues Postcards

This 22-card set measures approximately 3 1/2" by 5 1/2".

COMPLETE SET (22)	8.00	20.00
1 Murray Baron	.20	.50
2 Bob Bassen	.20	.50
3 Jeff Brown	.40	1.00
4 Garth Butcher	.30	.75
5 Gino Cavallini	.20	.50
6 Paul Cavallini	.20	.50
7 Kelly Chase	.25	.60
8 Dave Christian	.30	.75
9 Nelson Emerson	.30	.75
10 Brett Hull	1.50	4.00
11 Pat Jablonski	.30	.75
12 Curtis Joseph	1.25	3.00
13 Darin Kimble	.20	.50
14 Dave Lowry	.20	.50
15 Michel Mongeau	.20	.50
16 Adam Oates	.75	2.00
17 Rob Robinson	.20	.50
18 Brendan Shanahan	1.50	4.00
19 Rich Sutter	.30	.75
20 Ron Sutter	.30	.75
21 Ron Wilson	.20	.50
22 Rick Zombo	.20	.50

1992-93 Blues UD Best of the Blues

This 28-card standard-size set, subtitled "Best of the Blues" was distributed at McDonald's restaurants of St. Louis and Metro East and showcases St. Louis Blues' players from the past 25 years.

COMPLETE SET (28)	12.00	30.00
1 Glenn Hall	1.25	3.00
2 Doug Gilmour	1.25	3.00
3 Al Arbour	.40	1.00
4 Mike Liut	.40	1.00
5 Blake Dunlop	.20	.50
6 Noel Picard	.20	.50
7 Bob Plagor	.40	1.00
8 Ab McDonald	.20	.50
9 Curtis Joseph	2.00	5.00
10 Wayne Babych	.20	.50
11 Red Berenson	.40	1.00
12 Brett Hull	1.50	4.00
13 Bob Gassoff	.40	1.00
14 Bernie Federko	.40	1.00
15 Gary Sabourin	.20	.50
16 Joe Mullen	.40	1.00
17 Adam Oates	.75	2.00
18 Jorgen Pettersson	.20	.50
19 Frank St. Marseille	.30	.75
20 Scott Stevens	.60	1.50
21 Rob Ramage	.40	1.00
22 Jacques Plante	1.25	3.00
23 Rick Meagher	.20	.50
24 Barclay Plager	.40	1.00
25 Brian Sutter	.40	1.00
26 Perry Turnbull	.20	.50
27 Garry Unger	.40	1.00
28 Checklist SP	2.00	5.00
NNO Brett Hull AU	60.00	150.00

1996-97 Blues Dispatch 30th Anniversary

This set was created by the St. Louis Post-Dispatch to commemorate the 30th anniversary of the Blues joining the NHL.

COMPLETE SET (5)	4.00	10.00
1 Grant Fuhr	.75	2.00
2 Brett Hull	1.50	4.00
3 Al MacInnis	.75	2.00
4 Chris Pronger	.75	2.00
5 Tony Twist	.75	2.00

1999-00 Blues Taco Bell

Released by In the Game in conjunction with Taco Bell, this 24-card set features the 1999-2000 St. Louis Blues on four different six card sheets with a Taco Bell coupon.

COMPLETE SET (24)	6.00	15.00
1 Marc Bergevin	.08	.25
2 Jochen Hecht	.20	.50
3 Jamie McLennan	.20	.50
4 Pierre Turgeon	.30	.75
5 Scott Young	.20	.50
6 Dave Ellett	.08	.25
7 Lubos Bartecko	.08	.25
8 Pavol Demitra	.40	1.00
9 Michal Handzus	.20	.50
10 Jeff Finley	.08	.25
11 Ricard Persson	.08	.25
12 Bob Bassen	.08	.25
13 Craig Conroy	.08	.25
14 Mike Eastwood	.08	.25
15 Scott Pellerin	.08	.25
16 Chris Pronger	1.25	3.00
17 Todd Reirden	.08	.25
18 Roman Turek	.30	.75
19 Kelly Chase	.20	.50
20 Al MacInnis	.75	2.00
21 Jamal Mayers	.20	.50
22 Pascal Rheaume	.08	.25
23 Tyson Nash	.75	2.00
24 Stephane Richer	.08	.25

2002-03 Blues Magnets

These magnets were handed out at home games throughout the 2002-03 season. Please forward any further information to us at hockeymag@beckett.com.

COMPLETE SET (?)		
1 Pavol Demitra	2.00	5.00
2 Martin Rucinsky	1.25	3.00
3 Doug Weight	2.00	5.00

2002-03 Blues Team Issue

This set was handed out at a home game during the 2002-03 season. The cards came attached in a large foldout format.

COMPLETE SET (24)	8.00	20.00
1 Fred Brathwaite	.30	.75
2 Petr Cajanek	.20	.50
3 Daniel Corso	.20	.50
4 Pavol Demitra	.40	1.00
5 Dallas Drake	.20	.50
6 Mike Eastwood	.20	.50
7 Jeff Finley	.20	.50
8 Barret Jackman	.80	2.00
9 Brent Johnson	.40	1.00
10 Alexander Khavanov	.20	.50
11 Tom Koivisto	.20	.50
12 Christian Laflamme	.20	.50
13 Reed Low	.20	.50
14 Al MacInnis	.60	1.50
15 Jamal Mayers	.30	.75
16 Scott Mellanby	.20	.50
17 Tyson Nash	.40	1.00
18 Shjon Podein	.20	.50
19 Chris Pronger	.60	1.50
20 Bryce Salvador	.20	.50
21 Cory Stillman	.20	.50
22 Keith Tkachuk	.80	2.00
23 Mike Van Ryn	.20	.50
24 Doug Weight	.60	1.50

2005-06 Blues Team Set

1 Christian Backman
2 Eric Boguniecki
3 Eric Brewer
4 Petr Cajanek
5 Aaron Downey
6 Dallas Drake
7 Jeff Hoggan
8 Barret Jackman
9 Ryan Johnson
10 Patrick LaLime
11 Jamal Mayers
12 Dean McAmmond
13 Jay McClement
14 Mark Rycroft
15 Bryce Salvador
16 Curtis Sanford
17 Mike Sillinger
18 Lee Stempniak
19 Keith Tkachuk
20 Matt Walker
21 Doug Weight
22 Eric Weinrich
23 Dennis Wideman
24 Scott Young

1938 Bocnal Tobacco Luminous

Cards measure 1 3/8 x 2 1/2 and feature white design on a black background. They are meant to glow in the dark. Produced for Newgent Cigarettes in London.

19 Field Hockey	15.00	30.00
20 Ice Hockey	25.00	50.00

1990-91 Bowman

The 1990-91 Bowman set contains 264 standard-size cards.

COMPLETE SET (264)	6.00	15.00
COMP.FACT.SET (264)	8.00	20.00
1 Jeremy Roenick RC	.50	1.25
2 Doug Wilson	.01	.05
3 Greg Millen	.01	.05
4 Steve Thomas	.02	.10
5 Steve Larmer	.02	.10
6 Denis Savard	.02	.10
7 Ed Belfour RC	.75	2.00
8 Dirk Graham	.01	.05
9 Adam Creighton	.01	.05
10 Keith Brown	.01	.05
11 Jacques Cloutier RC	.01	.05
12 Al Secord	.01	.05
13 Troy Murray	.01	.05
14 Kelly Chase RC	.01	.05
15 Dave Lowry RC	.01	.05
16 Adam Oates	.02	.10
17 Sergio Momesso RC	.02	.10
18 Paul MacLean	.01	.05
19 Peter Zezel	.01	.05
20 Vincent Riendeau RC	.02	.10
21 Dave Thomlinson RC	.01	.05
22 Paul Cavallini	.01	.05
23 Rod Brind'Amour RC	.40	1.00
24 Brett Hull	.25	.60
25 Jeff Brown	.01	.05
26 Dominic Lavoie RC	.01	.05
27 Andy Brickley	.01	.05
28 Bob Sweeney	.01	.05
29 Cam Neely	.08	.25
30 Bob Carpenter	.01	.05
31 Ray Bourque	.15	.40
32 Rejean Lemelin	.02	.10
33 Craig Janney	.02	.10
34 Bob Beers RC	.02	.10
35 Andy Moog	.08	.25
36 Dave Poulin	.01	.05
37 Brian Propp	.01	.05
38 John Byce RC	.01	.05
39 John Carter RC	.01	.05
40 Dave Christian	.01	.05
41 Shayne Corson	.02	.10
42 Chris Chelios	.08	.25
43 Mike McPhee	.01	.05
44 Guy Carbonneau	.02	.10
45 Stephane Richer	.02	.10
46 Petr Svoboda	.01	.05
Chris Chelios actually pictured		
47 Russ Courtnall	.01	.05
48 Sylvain Lefebvre RC	.01	.05
49 Brian Skrudland	.01	.05
50 Patrick Roy	.50	1.25
51 Bobby Smith	.02	.10
52 Mathieu Schneider RC	.08	.25
53 Stephan Lebeau RC	.02	.10
54 Petri Skriko	.01	.05
55 Jim Sandlak	.01	.05
56 Doug Lidster	.01	.05
57 Kirk McLean	.02	.10
58 Brian Bradley	.01	.05
59 Greg Adams	.01	.05
60 Paul Reinhart	.01	.05
61 Trevor Linden	.02	.10
62 Adrien Plavsic	.01	.05
63 Igor Larionov RC	.20	.50
64 Steve Bozek	.01	.05
65 Dan Quinn	.01	.05
66 Mike Liut	.02	.10
67 Nick Kypreos RC	.01	.05
68 Michal Pivonka RC	.02	.10
69 Dino Ciccarelli	.02	.10
70 Kevin Hatcher	.01	.05
71 Dale Hunter	.01	.05
72 Don Beaupre	.02	.10
73 Geoff Courtnall	.01	.05
74 Rob Murray RC	.01	.05
75 Calle Johansson	.01	.05
76 Kelly Miller	.01	.05
77 Mike Ridley	.01	.05
78 Alan May RC	.01	.05
79 Bob Brooke	.01	.05
80 Slava Fetisov RC	.08	.25
81 Sylvain Turgeon	.01	.05
82 Kirk Muller	.01	.05
83 John MacLean	.02	.10
84 Jon Morris RC	.01	.05
85 Brendan Shanahan	.08	.25
86 Peter Stastny	.02	.10
87 Bruce Driver	.01	.05
88 Neil Brady RC	.01	.05
89 Patrik Sundstrom	.01	.05
90 Eric Weinrich RC	.08	.25
91 Joe Nieuwendyk	.02	.10
92 Sergei Makarov RC	.08	.25
93 Al MacInnis	.02	.10
94 Mike Vernon	.02	.10
95 Gary Roberts	.02	.10
96 Doug Gilmour	.02	.10
97 Joe Mullen	.02	.10
98 Rick Wamsley	.02	.10
99 Joel Otto	.01	.05
100 Paul Ranheim RC	.02	.10
101 Gary Suter	.01	.05
102 Theo Fleury	.01	.05
103 Sergei Priakin RC	.01	.05
104 Tony Horacek RC	.01	.05
105 Ron Hextall	.02	.10
106 Gord Murphy RC	.02	.10
107 Pelle Eklund	.01	.05
108 Rick Tocchet	.02	.10
109 Murray Craven	.01	.05
110 Doug Sulliman	.01	.05
111 Kjell Samuelsson	.01	.05
112 Ilkka Sinisalo	.01	.05
113 Keith Acton	.01	.05
114 Mike Bullard	.01	.05
115 Doug Crossman	.01	.05
116 Tom Fitzgerald	.01	.05
117 Don Maloney	.01	.05
118 Alan Kerr	.01	.05
119 Mark Fitzpatrick RC	.08	.25
120 Hubie McDonough RC	.01	.05
121 Randy Wood	.01	.05
122 Jeff Norton	.01	.05
123 Pat LaFontaine	.08	.25
124 Pat Flatley	.01	.05
125 Joe Reekie RC	.01	.05
126 Brent Sutter	.01	.05
127 David Volek	.01	.05
128 Shawn Cronin RC	.01	.05
129 Dale Hawerchuk	.02	.10
130 Brent Ashton	.01	.05
131 Bob Essensa RC	.20	.50
132 Dave Ellett	.01	.05
133 Thomas Steen	.01	.05
134 Doug Smail	.01	.05
135 Fredrik Olausson	.01	.05
136 Dave McLlwain	.01	.05
137 Pat Elynuik RC	.01	.05
138 Teppo Numminen RC	.02	.10
139 Paul Fenton	.01	.05
140 Tony Granato	.01	.05
141 Tomas Sandstrom	.01	.05
142 Rob Blake RC	.25	.60
143 Wayne Gretzky	.60	1.50
144 Kelly Hrudey	.02	.10
145 Mike Krushelnyski	.01	.05
146 Steve Duchesne	.01	.05
147 Steve Kasper	.01	.05
148 John Tonelli	.01	.05
149 Dave Taylor	.02	.10
150 Larry Robinson	.02	.10
151 Todd Elik RC	.01	.05
152 Luc Robitaille	.02	.10
153 Al Iafrate	.02	.10
154 Allan Bester	.02	.10
155 Gary Leeman	.01	.05
156 Mark Osborne	.01	.05
157 Tom Fergus	.01	.05
158 Brad Marsh	.01	.05
159 Wendel Clark	.02	.10
160 Daniel Marois	.01	.05
161 Ed Olczyk	.01	.05
162 Rob Ramage	.01	.05
163 Vincent Damphousse	.01	.05
164 Lou Franceschetti RC	.01	.05
165 Paul Gillis	.01	.05
166 Craig Wolanin RC	.01	.05
167 Marc Fortier	.01	.05
168 Tony McKegney	.01	.05
169 Joe Sakic	.30	.75
170 Michel Petit	.01	.05
171 Scott Gordon RC	.01	.05
172 Tony Hrkac	.01	.05
173 Bryan Fogarty RC	.01	.05
174 Mike Hough	.01	.05
175 Claude Loiselle RC	.01	.05
176 Ulf Dahlen	.01	.05
177 Larry Murphy	.02	.10
178 Neal Broten	.02	.10
179 Don Barber	.01	.05
180 Shawn Chambers	.01	.05
181 Clark Donatelli RC	.01	.05
182 Brian Bellows	.01	.05
183 Jon Casey	.02	.10
184 Neil Wilkinson RC	.01	.05
185 Aaron Broten	.01	.05
186 Dave Gagner	.02	.10
187 Basil McRae	.01	.05
188 Mike Modano RC	.60	1.50
189 Grant Fuhr	.08	.25
190 Martin Gelinas RC	.10	.30
191 Jari Kurri	.08	.25
192 Geoff Smith RC	.01	.05
193 Craig MacTavish	.01	.05
194 Esa Tikkanen	.01	.05
195 Glenn Anderson	.02	.10
196 Joe Murphy RC	.02	.10
197 Petr Klima	.01	.05
198 Kevin Lowe	.01	.05
199 Mark Messier	.08	.25
200 Steve Smith	.01	.05
201 Craig Simpson	.01	.05
202 Rob Brown	.01	.05
203 Wendell Young RC	.02	.10
204 Mario Lemieux	.60	1.50
205 Phil Bourque	.01	.05
206 Mark Recchi RC	.40	1.00
207 Zarley Zalapski	.01	.05
208 Kevin Stevens RC	.08	.25
209 Tom Barrasso	.02	.10
210 John Cullen	.01	.05
211 Paul Coffey	.08	.25
212 Bob Errey	.01	.05
213 Tony Tanti	.01	.05
214 Carey Wilson	.01	.05
215A Brian Leetch ERR	.25	.60
(Name spelled eetch)		
215B Brian Leetch COR	.10	.30
216 Darren Turcotte RC	.02	.10
217 Brian Mullen	.01	.05
218 Mike Richter RC	.40	1.00
219 Troy Mallette RC	.01	.05
220 Mike Gartner	.02	.10
221 Bernie Nicholls	.02	.10
222 John Vanbiesbrouck	.02	.10
223 John Ogrodnick	.01	.05
224 Paul Broten	.01	.05
225 James Patrick	.01	.05
226 Mark Janssens RC	.01	.05
227 Randy McKay RC	.01	.05
228 Marc Habscheid	.01	.05
229 Jimmy Carson	.01	.05
230 Yves Racine RC	.02	.10
231 Dave Barr	.01	.05
232 Shawn Burr	.01	.05
233 Steve Yzerman	.40	1.00
234 Steve Chiasson	.01	.05
235 Daniel Shank RC	.01	.05
236 John Chabot	.01	.05
237 Gerard Gallant	.01	.05
238 Bernie Federko	.01	.05
239 Phil Housley	.02	.10
240 Alexander Mogilny RC	.50	1.25
241 Pierre Turgeon	.08	.25
242 Daren Puppa	.02	.10
243 Scott Arniel	.01	.05
244 Christian Ruuttu	.01	.05
245 Doug Bodger	.01	.05
246 Dave Andreychuk	.02	.10
247 Mike Foligno	.01	.05
248 Dean Kennedy RC	.01	.05
249 Dave Snuggerud	.01	.05
250 Rick Vaive	.01	.05
251 Todd Krygier RC	.01	.05
252 Adam Burt RC	.01	.05
253 Scott Young	.01	.05
254 Ron Francis	.02	.10
255 Peter Sidorkiewicz	.02	.10
256 Dave Babych	.01	.05
257 Pat Verbeek	.01	.05
258 Ray Ferraro	.01	.05
259 Chris Govedaris RC	.01	.05
260 Brad Shaw RC	.01	.05
261 Kevin Dineen	.01	.05
262 Dean Evason	.01	.05
263 Checklist 1-132	.01	.05
264 Checklist 133-264	.01	.05

1990-91 Bowman Tiffany

Parallel to base set, Topps only produced 3000 sets. Cards can be distinguished by a glossy coating not found on regular issued cards.

COMPLETE SET (264)	60.00	125.00
*VETS: 10X TO 25X BASIC CARDS		
*ROOKIES: 4X TO 10X BASIC CARDS		

1990-91 Bowman Hat Tricks

This 22-card standard size set was issued as an insert in the 1990-91 Bowman hockey wax packs. This set honored the 14 players (1-14) who scored three or more goals (a hat trick) in a game at least twice during the 1989-90 regular season and the eight players (15-22) who performed the feat during the 1990 NHL playoffs. The fronts of the cards have a glossy sheen to them while the backs talk about the hat tricks of the players. There are two Mike Gartner cards as he had hat tricks for two different teams.

COMPLETE SET (22)	2.50	6.00
*TIFFANY: 4X TO 10X BASIC INSERTS		
1 Brett Hull	.25	.60
2 Mario Lemieux	1.00	2.50
3 Rob Brown	.05	.15
4 Mark Messier	.25	.60
5 Steve Yzerman	.60	1.50
6 Vincent Damphousse	.15	.40
7 Kevin Dineen	.05	.15
8 Mike Gartner	.15	.40
9 Pat LaFontaine	.20	.50
10 Gary Leeman	.05	.15
11 Stephane Richer	.15	.40
12 Luc Robitaille	.15	.40
13 Steve Thomas	.15	.40
14 Rick Tocchet	.15	.40
15 Dino Ciccarelli	.15	.40
16 John Druce	.05	.15
17 Mike Gartner	.15	.40
18 Tony Granato	.05	.15
19 Jari Kurri	.15	.40
20 Bernie Nicholls	.15	.40
21 Tomas Sandstrom	.15	.40
22 Dave Taylor	.05	.15

1991-92 Bowman

The 1991-92 Bowman hockey set contains 429 standard-size cards. On a white card face, the fronts display color action player photos enclosed by blue and tan border stripes. The player's name appears in a purple stripe below the picture. The backs are colorful (displaying blue, green, and red fading to yellow sections) and present biography and statistics (career and for the 1990-91 season). The season statistics are broken down to show the player's performance against each NHL team. The cards are numbered on the back and checklisted below according to teams. The only Rookie Card worthy of note is John LeClair.

COMPLETE SET (429)	5.00	12.00
COMP.FACT.SET (429)	6.00	15.00
1 John Cullen	.01	.05
2 Todd Krygier	.01	.05
3 Kay Whitmore	.02	.10
4 Terry Yake	.01	.05
5 Randy Ladouceur	.01	.05
6 Kevin Dineen	.01	.05
7 Jim McKenzie	.01	.05
8 Brad Shaw	.01	.05
9 Mark Hunter	.01	.05
10 Dean Evason	.01	.05
11 Mikael Andersson	.01	.05
12 Pat Verbeek	.01	.05
13 Peter Sidorkiewicz	.02	.10
14 Mike Tomlak	.01	.05
15 Zarley Zalapski	.01	.05

16 Rob Brown .01 .05
17 Sylvain Cote .01 .05
18 Bobby Holik .02 .10
19 Daryl Reaugh .02 .10
20 Paul Cyr .01 .05
21 Doug Bodger .01 .05
22 Dave Andreychuk .02 .10
23 Clint Malarchuk .02 .10
24 Darrin Shannon .01 .05
25 Christian Ruuttu .01 .05
26 Uwe Krupp .01 .05
27 Pierre Turgeon .02 .10
28 Kevin Haller RC .01 .05
29 Dave Snuggerud .01 .05
30 Alexander Mogilny .07 .20
31 Dale Hawerchuk .02 .10
32 Mike Ramsey .01 .05
33 Darcy Wakaluk RC .02 .10
34 Tony Tanti .01 .05
35 Jay Wells .01 .05
36 Mikko Makela .01 .05
37 Daren Puppa .02 .10
38 Benoit Hogue .01 .05
39 Rick Vaive .01 .05
40 Grant Ledyard .01 .05
41 Steve Yzerman HT .15 .40
42 Steve Yzerman .40 1.00
43 Shawn Burr .01 .05
44 Yves Racine .01 .05
45 Johan Garpenlov .01 .05
46 Keith Primeau .01 .05
47 Tim Cheveldae .02 .10
48 Brad McCrimmon .01 .05
49 Dave Barr .01 .05
50 Sergei Fedorov .10 .30
51 Brent Fedyk .01 .05
52 Jimmy Carson .01 .05
53 Paul Ysebaert .01 .05
54 Rick Zombo .01 .05
55 Bob Probert .02 .10
56 Gerard Gallant .01 .05
57 Kevin Miller .01 .05
58 Randy Moller .01 .05
59 Kris King .01 .05
60 Corey Millen RC .01 .05
61 Brian Mullen .01 .05
62 Darren Turcotte .01 .05
63 Ray Sheppard .01 .05
64 David Shaw .01 .05
65 Troy Mallette .01 .05
66 James Patrick .01 .05
67 Mark Janssens .01 .05
68 John Vanbiesbrouck .02 .10
69 Joey Kocur .02 .10
70 Mike Richter .07 .20
71 John Ogrodnick .01 .05
72 Kelly Kisio .01 .05
73 Normand Rochefort .01 .05
74 Mike Gartner .02 .10
75 Brian Leetch .07 .20
76 Bernie Nicholls .02 .10
77 Jan Erixon .01 .05
78 Larry Murphy .02 .10
79 Joe Mullen .02 .10
80 Tom Barrasso .02 .10
81 Paul Coffey .07 .20
82 Jiri Hrdina .01 .05
83 Mark Recchi .07 .20
84 Randy Gilhen .01 .05
85 Bob Errey .01 .05
86 Scott Young .01 .05
87 Mario Lemieux .50 1.25
88 Ulf Samuelsson .01 .05
89 Frank Pietrangelo .01 .05
90 Ron Francis .02 .10
91 Paul Stanton .01 .05
92 Kevin Stevens .01 .05
93 Bryan Trottier .07 .20
94 Phil Bourque .01 .05
95 Jaromir Jagr .10 .30
96 Petr Klima HT .01 .05
97 Adam Graves .02 .10
98 Esa Tikkanen .01 .05
99 Norm Maciver RC .01 .05
100 Craig MacTavish .01 .05
101 Bill Ranford .02 .10
102 Martin Gelinas .01 .05
103 Charlie Huddy .01 .05
104 Petr Klima .01 .05
105 Ken Linseman .01 .05
106 Steve Smith .01 .05
107 Craig Simpson .01 .05
108 Chris Joseph .01 .05
109 Joe Murphy .01 .05
110 Jeff Beukeboom .01 .05
111 Grant Fuhr .07 .20
112 Geoff Smith .01 .05
113 Anatoli Semenov .01 .05
114 Mark Messier .07 .20
115 Kevin Lowe .02 .10
116 Glenn Anderson .02 .10
117 Bobby Smith .02 .10
118 Doug Smail .01 .05
119 Jon Casey .02 .10
120 Gaetan Duchesne .01 .05
121 Neal Broten .02 .10
122 Brian Hayward .02 .10
123 Brian Propp .01 .05
124 Mark Tinordi .01 .05
125 Mike Modano .15 .40
126 Marc Bureau .01 .05
127 Ulf Dahlen .01 .05
128 Chris Dahlquist .01 .05
129 Brian Bellows .01 .05
130 Mike Craig .01 .05
131 Dave Gagner .01 .05
132 Brian Glynn .01 .05
133 Joe Sakic .15 .40
134 Owen Nolan .07 .20
135 Everett Sanipass .01 .05
136 Jamie Baker RC .01 .05
137 Mats Sundin .07 .20
138 Craig Wolanin .01 .05
139 Kip Miller .01 .05
140 Steven Finn .01 .05
141 Tony Hrkac .01 .05
142 Curtis Leschyshyn .01 .05
143 Mike McNeil .01 .05
144 Mike Hough .01 .05
145 Alexei Gusarov RC .02 .10
146 Jacques Cloutier .02 .10
147 Shawn Anderson .01 .05
148 Stephane Morin .01 .05
149 Bryan Fogarty .01 .05
150 Scott Pearson .01 .05
151 Ron Tugnutt .02 .10
152 Randy Velischek .01 .05
153 David Reid .01 .05
154 Rob Ramage .01 .05
155 Dave Hannan .01 .05
156 Wendel Clark .02 .10
157 Peter Ing .02 .10
158 Michel Petit .01 .05
159 Brian Bradley .01 .05
160 Rob Cimetta .01 .05
161 Gary Leeman .01 .05
162 Aaron Broten .01 .05
163 Dave Ellett .01 .05
164 Peter Zezel .01 .05
165 Daniel Marois .01 .05
166 Mike Krushelnyski .01 .05
167 Luke Richardson .01 .05
168 Scott Thornton .01 .05
169 Mike Foligno .01 .05
170 Vincent Damphousse .01 .05
171 Todd Gill .01 .05
172 Kevin Maguire .01 .05
173 Wayne Gretzky HT .30 .75
174 Tomas Sandstrom HT .01 .05
175 John Tonelli .01 .05
176 Wayne Gretzky .50 1.25
177 Larry Robinson .02 .10
178 Jay Miller .01 .05
179 Tomas Sandstrom .01 .05
180 John McIntyre .01 .05
181 Brad Jones .01 .05
182 Rob Blake .02 .10
183 Kelly Hrudey .02 .10
184 Marty McSorley .01 .05
185 Todd Elik .01 .05
186 Dave Taylor .02 .10
187 Steve Kasper .01 .05
188 Luc Robitaille .02 .10
189 Bob Kudelski .01 .05
190 Daniel Berthiaume .02 .10
191 Steve Duchesne .01 .05
192 Tony Granato .01 .05
193 Bob Essensa .02 .10
194 Phil Sykes .01 .05
195 Paul MacDermid .01 .05
196 Dave McLlwain .01 .05
197 Phil Housley .02 .10
198 Pat Elynuik .01 .05
199 Randy Carlyle .01 .05
200 Thomas Steen .01 .05
201 Teppo Numminen .01 .05
202 Danton Cole .01 .05
203 Doug Evans .01 .05
204 Ed Olczyk .01 .05
205 Moe Mantha .01 .05
206 Scott Arniel .01 .05
207 Rick Tabaracci .02 .10
208 Bryan Marchment RC .02 .10
209 Mark Osborne .01 .05
210 Fredrik Olausson .01 .05
211 Brent Ashton .01 .05
212 Ray Ferraro .01 .05
213 Mark Fitzpatrick .02 .10
214 Hubie McDonough .01 .05
215 Joe Reekie .01 .05
216 Bill Berg .01 .05
217 Wayne McBean .01 .05
218 Pat Flatley .01 .05
219 Jeff Hackett .02 .10
220 Derek King .01 .05
221 Craig Ludwig .01 .05
222 Pat LaFontaine .07 .20
223 David Volek .01 .05
224 Glenn Healy .02 .10
225 Jeff Norton .01 .05
226 Brent Sutter .01 .05
227 Randy Wood .01 .05
228 Gary Nylund .01 .05
229 Dave Chyzowski .01 .05
230 Rick Tocchet .02 .10
231 Ken Wregget .02 .10
232 Terry Carkner .01 .05
233 Martin Hostak .01 .05
234 Ron Hextall .02 .10
235 Gord Murphy .01 .05
236 Scott Mellanby .01 .05
237 Pete Peeters .02 .10
238 Ron Sutter .01 .05
239 Murray Craven .01 .05
240 Kjell Samuelsson .01 .05
241 Pelle Eklund .01 .05
242 Mark Pederson .01 .05
243 Murray Baron .01 .05
244 Keith Acton .01 .05
245 Derrick Smith .01 .05
246 Mike Ricci .07 .20
247 Dale Kushner .01 .05
248 Normand Lacombe .01 .05
249 Theo Fleury HT .01 .05
250 Sergei Makarov HT .01 .05
251 Paul Ranheim .01 .05
252 Joe Nieuwendyk .02 .10
253 Mike Vernon .02 .10
254 Gary Suter .01 .05
255 Doug Gilmour .02 .10
256 Paul Fenton .01 .05
257 Roger Johansson .01 .05
258 Stephane Matteau .01 .05
259 Frank Musil .01 .05
260 Joel Otto .01 .05
261 Tim Sweeney .01 .05
262 Al MacInnis .02 .10
263 Gary Roberts .02 .10
264 Sergei Makarov .01 .05
265 Carey Wilson .01 .05
266 Ric Nattress .01 .05
267 Robert Reichel .01 .05
268 Rick Wamsley .02 .10
269 Brian MacLellan .01 .05
270 Theo Fleury .01 .05
271 Claude Lemieux .01 .05
272 John MacLean .02 .10
273 Slava Fetisov .02 .10
274 Kirk Muller .01 .05
275 Sean Burke .02 .10
276 Alexei Kasatonov .01 .05
277 Claude Lemieux .01 .05
278 Eric Weinrich .01 .05
279 Patrik Sundstrom .01 .05
280 Zdeno Ciger .01 .05
281 Bruce Driver .01 .05
282 Laurie Boschman .01 .05
283 Chris Terreri .02 .10
284 Ken Daneyko .01 .05
285 Doug Brown .01 .05
286 Jon Morris .01 .05
287 Peter Stastny .02 .10
288 Brendan Shanahan .07 .20
289 John MacLean .02 .10
290 Mike Liut .02 .10
291 Michal Pivonka .01 .05
292 Kelly Miller .01 .05
293 John Druce .01 .05
294 Calle Johansson .01 .05
295 Alan May .01 .05
296 Kevin Hatcher .02 .10
297 Tim Bergland .01 .05
298 Mikhail Tatarinov .01 .05
299 Peter Bondra .02 .10
300 Al Iafrate .02 .10
301 Nick Kypreos .01 .05
302 Dino Ciccarelli .02 .10
303 Dale Hunter .01 .05
304 Don Beaupre .02 .10
305 Jim Hrivnak .02 .10
306 Stephen Leach .01 .05
307 Dimitri Khristich .01 .05
308 Mike Ridley .01 .05
309 Sergio Momesso .01 .05
310 Kirk McLean .02 .10
311 Greg Adams .01 .05
312 Adrien Plavsic .01 .05
313 Cliff Ronning .01 .05
314 Garry Valk .01 .05
315 Troy Gamble .02 .10
316 Gino Odjick .01 .05
317 Doug Lidster .01 .05
318 Geoff Courtnall .02 .10
319 Tom Kurvers .01 .05
320 Robert Kron .01 .05
321 Jyrki Lumme .01 .05
322 Jay Mazur .01 .05
323 Dave Capuano .01 .05
324 Petr Nedved .02 .10
325 Steve Bozek .01 .05
326 Igor Larionov .01 .05
327 Trevor Linden .02 .10
328 Shayne Corson .01 .05
329 Eric Desjardins .02 .10
330 Stephane Richer .02 .10
331 Brian Skrudland .01 .05
332 Sylvain Lefebvre .01 .05
333 Stephan Lebeau .01 .05
334 Mike Keane .01 .05
335 Patrick Roy .40 1.00
336 Brent Gilchrist .01 .05
337 Andre Racicot RC .02 .10
338 Guy Carbonneau .02 .10
339 Mike McPhee .01 .05
340 Andrew Cassels .01 .05
341 Petr Svoboda .01 .05
342 Denis Savard .02 .10
343 Mathieu Schneider .02 .10
344 John LeClair RC .50 1.25
345 Tom Chorske .01 .05
346 Russ Courtnall .01 .05
347 Ken Hodge Jr. HT .01 .05
348 Cam Neely HT .02 .10
349 Randy Burridge .01 .05
350 Glen Wesley .01 .05
351 Chris Nilan .01 .05
352 Jeff Lazaro .01 .05
353 Wes Walz .01 .05
354 Rejean Lemelin .02 .10
355 Craig Janney .02 .10
356 Ray Bourque .10 .30
357 Bob Sweeney .01 .05
358 Dave Christian .01 .05
359 Dave Poulin .01 .05
360 Garry Galley .01 .05
361 Andy Moog .07 .20
362 Ken Hodge Jr. .01 .05
363 Jim Wiemer .01 .05
364 Petri Skriko .01 .05
365 Don Sweeney .01 .05
366 Cam Neely .07 .20
367 Brett Hull HT .07 .20
368 Gino Cavallini .01 .05
369 Scott Stevens .02 .10
370 Rich Sutter .01 .05
371 Glen Featherstone .01 .05
372 Vincent Riendeau .02 .10
373 Dave Lowry .01 .05
374 Rod Brind'Amour .07 .20
375 Brett Hull .08 .25
376 Dan Quinn .01 .05
377 Tom Tilley .01 .05
378 Paul Cavallini .01 .05
379 Bob Bassen .01 .05
380 Mario Marois .01 .05
381 Darin Kimble .01 .05
382 Ron Wilson .01 .05
383 Garth Butcher .01 .05
384 Adam Oates .02 .10
385 Jeff Brown .01 .05
386 Jeremy Roenick HT .07 .20
387 Tony McKegney .01 .05
388 Troy Murray .01 .05
389 Dave Manson .01 .05
390 Ed Belfour .07 .20
391 Steve Thomas .01 .05
392 Michel Goulet .02 .10
393 Trent Yawney .01 .05
394 Adam Creighton .01 .05
395 Steve Larmer .02 .10
396 Jimmy Waite .02 .10
397 Dirk Graham .01 .05
398 Chris Chelios .07 .20
399 Mike Hudson .01 .05
400 Doug Wilson .02 .10
401 Greg Gilbert .01 .05
402 Wayne Presley .01 .05
403 Jeremy Roenick .07 .20
404 Frantisek Kucera .01 .05
405 Blackhawks/North Stars .01 .05
406 Blues/Red Wings .01 .05
407 Flames/Oilers .01 .05
408 Penguins/Devils .01 .05
409 Rangers/Capitals .01 .05
410 Bruins/Whalers .01 .05
411 Canadiens/Sabres .01 .05
412 Kings/Canucks .01 .05
413 Penguins/Capitals .01 .05
414 Bruins/Canadiens .01 .05
415 North Stars/Blues .01 .05
416 Kings/Oilers .01 .05
417 North Stars/Oilers .01 .05
418 Bruins/Penguins .01 .05
419 Game 1 Cup Finals .02 .10
420 Game 2 Cup Finals .02 .10
421 Game 3 Cup Finals .02 .10
422 Game 4 Cup Finals .02 .10
423 Game 5 Cup Finals .02 .10
424 Game 6 Cup Finals .02 .10
425 Mario Lemieux Smythe .10 .30
426 Checklist 1-108 .01 .05
427 Checklist 109-216 .01 .05
428 Checklist 217-324 .01 .05
429 Checklist 325-429 .01 .05

1992-93 Bowman

The 1992-93 Bowman hockey set contains 442 standard-size cards. Reportedly only 2,000 16-box wax cases were produced. One of 45 gold-foil engraved cards was inserted in each 15-card pack. These gold-foil cards feature 44 All-Stars (Campbell Conference on cards 199-220 and Wales Conference on cards 222-243) and a special card commemorating Mario Lemieux as the winner of the Conn Smythe trophy (440). The 18 gold-foil All-Stars that were single printed are listed in the checklist below as SP. The basic card fronts feature color action player photos with white borders. A magenta bar at the top left corner carries the Bowman "B". A gradated turquoise bar at the bottom right displays the player's name. The backs have a burlap-textured background and carry a close-up photo, a yellow and white statistics box presenting the player's performance vs. other teams, and biography. The only noteworthy Rookie Card in the set is Guy Hebert. There are a number of non glossy Eric Lindros (No. 442) cards on the market. These are unauthorized releases and should be avoided by collectors.

COMPLETE SET (442) 100.00 200.00
FOIL ODDS 1:15
BEWARE NON-GLOSS LINDROS
1 Wayne Gretzky 2.50 6.00
2 Mike Krushelnyski .08 .25
3 Ray Bourque .75 2.00
4 Keith Brown .08 .25
5 Bob Sweeney .08 .25
6 Dave Christian .08 .25
7 Frantisek Kucera .08 .25
8 John LeClair .50 1.25
9 Jamie Macoun .08 .25
10 Bob Carpenter .08 .25
11 Garry Galley .08 .25
12 Bob Kudelski .08 .25
13 Doug Bodger .08 .25
14 Craig Janney .20 .50
15 Glen Wesley .08 .25
16 Daren Puppa .20 .50
17 Andy Brickley .08 .25
18 Steve Konroyd .08 .25
19 Dave Poulin .08 .25
20 Phil Housley .20 .50
21 Kevin Todd .08 .25
22 Tomas Sandstrom .20 .50
23 Pierre Turgeon .20 .50
24 Steve Smith .08 .25
25 Ray Sheppard .08 .25
26 Stu Barnes .08 .25
27 Grant Ledyard .08 .25
28 Benoit Hogue .08 .25
29 Randy Burridge .08 .25
30 Clint Malarchuk .20 .50
31 Steve Duchesne .08 .25
32 Guy Hebert RC 1.50 4.00
33 Steve Kasper .08 .25
34 Alexander Mogilny .20 .50
35 Marty McSorley .08 .25
36 Doug Weight .60 1.50
37 Dave Taylor .20 .50
38 Guy Carbonneau .20 .50
39 Brian Benning .08 .25
40 Nelson Emerson .08 .25
41 Craig Wolanin .08 .25
42 Kelly Hrudey .20 .50
43 Chris Chelios .50 1.25
44 Dave Andreychuk .20 .50
45 Russ Courtnall .08 .25
46 Stephane Richer .20 .50
47 Petr Svoboda .08 .25
48 Barry Pederson .08 .25
49 Claude Lemieux .08 .25
50 Tony Granato .08 .25
51 Al MacInnis .20 .50
52 Luciano Borsato .08 .25
53 Sergei Makarov .08 .25
54 Bobby Smith .20 .50
55 Gary Suter .08 .25
56 Tom Draper .08 .25
57 Corry Millen .08 .25
58 Joe Mullen .20 .50
59 Joe Nieuwendyk .20 .50
60 Brian Hayward .20 .50
61 Steve Larmer .20 .50
62 Cam Neely .50 1.25
63 Ric Nattress .08 .25
64 Denis Savard .20 .50
65 Gerald Diduck .08 .25
66 Pat Jablonski .20 .50
67 Brad McCrimmon .08 .25
68 Dirk Graham .08 .25
69 Joel Otto .08 .25
70 Luc Robitaille .20 .50
71 Dana Murzyn .08 .25
72 Jocelyn Lemieux .08 .25
73 Mike Hudson .08 .25
74 Patrick Roy 2.00 5.00
75 Doug Wilson .20 .50
76 Wayne Presley .08 .25
77 Felix Potvin .50 1.25
78 Jeremy Roenick .50 1.25
79 Andy Moog .50 1.25
80 Joey Kocur .20 .50
81 Neal Broten .20 .50
82 Shayne Corson .08 .25
83 Doug Gilmour .20 .50
84 Rob Zettler .08 .25
85 Bob Probert .20 .50
86 Mike Vernon .20 .50
87 Rick Zombo .08 .25
88 Adam Creighton .08 .25
89 Mike McPhee .08 .25
90 Ed Belfour .50 1.25
91 Steve Chiasson .08 .25
92 Dominic Roussel .20 .50
93 Troy Murray .08 .25
94 Jari Kurri .50 1.25
95 Geoff Smith .08 .25
96 Paul Ranheim .08 .25
97 Rick Wamsley .20 .50
98 Brian Noonan .08 .25
99 Kevin Lowe .20 .50
100 Josef Beranek .08 .25
101 Michel Petit .08 .25
102 Craig Billington .20 .50
103 Steve Yzerman 1.50 4.00
104 Glenn Anderson .08 .25
105 Perry Berezan .08 .25
106 Bill Ranford .20 .50
107 Randy Ladouceur .08 .25
108 Jimmy Carson .08 .25
109 Gary Roberts .08 .25
110 Checklist 1-110 .08 .25
111 Brad Shaw .08 .25
112 Pat Verbeek .08 .25
113 Mark Messier .50 1.25
114 Grant Fuhr .50 1.25
115 Sylvain Cote .08 .25
116 Mike Sullivan .08 .25
117 Steve Thomas .20 .50
118 Craig MacTavish .08 .25
119 Dave Babych .08 .25
120 Jim Waite .20 .50
121 Kevin Dineen .08 .25
122 Shawn Burr .08 .25
123 Ron Francis .20 .50
124 Garth Butcher .08 .25
125 Jarmo Myllys .08 .25
126 Doug Brown .08 .25
127 James Patrick .08 .25
128 Ray Ferraro .08 .25
129 Terry Carkner .08 .25
130 John MacLean .20 .50
131 Randy Velischek .08 .25
132 John Vanbiesbrouck .20 .50
133 Dean Evason .08 .25
134 Patrick Flatley .08 .25
135 Petr Klima .08 .25
136 Geoff Sanderson .20 .50
137 Joe Reekie .08 .25
138 Kirk Muller .08 .25
139 Brian Mullen .08 .25
140 Daniel Berthiaume .20 .50
141 David Shaw .08 .25
142 Pat LaFontaine .50 1.25
143 Ulf Dahlen .08 .25
144 Esa Tikkanen .08 .25
145 Slava Fetisov .08 .25
146 Mike Gartner .20 .50
147 Brent Sutter .08 .25
148 Darcy Wakaluk .20 .50
149 Brian Leetch .50 1.25
150 Craig Simpson .08 .25
151 Mike Modano .60 1.50
152 Bryan Trottier .20 .50
153 Larry Murphy .20 .50
154 Pavel Bure .50 1.25
155 Kay Whitmore .20 .50
156 Darren Turcotte .08 .25
157 Frank Musil .08 .25
158 Mikael Andersson .08 .25
159 Rick Tocchet .20 .50
160 Scott Stevens .20 .50
161 Bernie Nicholls .20 .50
162 Peter Sidorkiewicz .20 .50
163 Scott Mellanby .08 .25
164 Alexander Semak .08 .25
165 Kjell Samuelsson .08 .25
166 Kelly Kisio .08 .25
167 Sylvain Turgeon .08 .25
168 Rob Brown .08 .25
169 Gerard Gallant .08 .25
170 Jyrki Lumme .08 .25
171 Dave Gagner .20 .50
172 Tony Tanti .08 .25
173 Zarley Zalapski .08 .25
174 Joe Murphy .08 .25
175 Ron Sutter .08 .25
176 Dino Ciccarelli .20 .50
177 Jim Johnson .08 .25
178 Mike Hough .08 .25
179 Pelle Eklund .08 .25
180 John Druce .08 .25
181 Paul Coffey .50 1.25
182 Ken Wregget .20 .50
183 Brendan Shanahan .50 1.25
184 Keith Acton .08 .25
185 Steven Finn .08 .25
186 Brett Hull .75 2.00
187 Rollie Melanson .20 .50
188 Derek King .08 .25
189 Mario Lemieux 2.00 5.00
190 Mathieu Schneider .08 .25
191 Claude Vilgrain .08 .25
192 Gary Leeman .08 .25
193 Paul Cavallini .08 .25
194 John Cullen .08 .25
195 Ron Hextall .20 .50
196 David Volek .08 .25
197 Gordie Roberts .08 .25
198 Dale Craigwell .08 .25
199 Ed Belfour 2.00 5.00
FOIL
200 Brian Bellows 2.00 5.00
FOIL SP
201 Chris Chelios .60 1.50
FOIL
202 Tim Cheveldae 2.00 5.00
FOIL SP
203A Vincent Damphousse .50 1.25
FOIL ERR
(Team name missing
on card back)
203B Vincent Damphousse .50 1.25
FOIL COR
204 Dave Ellett .40 1.00
FOIL
205 Sergei Fedorov 6.00 15.00
FOIL SP
206 Theo Fleury 1.50 4.00
FOIL
207 Wayne Gretzky 6.00 15.00
FOIL
208 Phil Housley .60 1.50
FOIL
209 Brett Hull 2.00 5.00
FOIL
210 Trevor Linden 2.00 5.00
FOIL SP
211 Al MacInnis 2.00 5.00
FOIL SP
212 Kirk McLean 2.00 5.00
FOIL SP
213 Adam Oates .50 1.25
FOIL
214 Gary Roberts 2.00 5.00
FOIL SP
215 Larry Robinson .40 1.00
FOIL
216 Luc Robitaille .50 1.25
FOIL
217 Jeremy Roenick 6.00 15.00
FOIL SP
218 Mark Tinordi .40 1.00
FOIL
219 Doug Wilson .50 1.25
FOIL
220 Steve Yzerman 4.00 10.00
FOIL
221 Checklist 111-220 .08 .25
222 Don Beaupre 2.00 5.00
FOIL SP
223 Ray Bourque 2.00 5.00
FOIL SP
224 Rod Brind'Amour UER 2.00 5.00
FOIL SP
(Apostrophe in last
name is missing)
225 Randy Burridge 2.00 5.00
FOIL SP
226 Paul Coffey 2.50 6.00
FOIL SP
227 John Cullen 2.00 5.00
FOIL SP
228 Eric Desjardins 2.00 5.00
FOIL SP
229 Ray Ferraro 2.00 5.00
FOIL SP
230 Kevin Hatcher .50 1.25
FOIL
231 Jaromir Jagr 1.50 4.00
FOIL
232 Brian Leetch 2.50 6.00
FOIL SP
233 Mario Lemieux 4.00 10.00
FOIL
234 Mark Messier .60 1.50
FOIL
235 Alexander Mogilny .60 1.50
FOIL
236 Kirk Muller .60 1.50
FOIL
237 Owen Nolan .60 1.50
FOIL
238 Mike Richter .60 1.50
FOIL
239 Patrick Roy 4.00 10.00
FOIL
240 Joe Sakic 8.00 20.00
FOIL SP
241 Kevin Stevens .50 1.25
FOIL
242 Scott Stevens .40 1.00
FOIL
243 Brian Trottier 2.50 6.00
FOIL SP
244 Joe Sakic 1.25 3.00
245 Daniel Marois .08 .25
246 Randy Wood .08 .25
247 Jeff Brown .08 .25
248 Peter Bondra .20 .50
249 Peter Stastny .20 .50
250 Tom Barrasso .20 .50
251 Al Iafrate .20 .50
252 James Black .08 .25
253 Jan Erixon .08 .25
254 Brian Lawton .08 .25
255 Luke Richardson .08 .25
256 Rich Sutter .08 .25
257 Jeff Chychrun .08 .25
258 Adam Oates .20 .50
259 Tom Kurvers .08 .25
260 Brian Bellows .08 .25
261 Trevor Linden .20 .50
262 Vincent Riendeau .20 .50
263 Peter Zezel .08 .25
264 Rich Pilon .08 .25
265 Paul Broten .08 .25
266 Gaetan Duchesne .08 .25
267 Doug Lidster .08 .25
268 Rod Brind'Amour .20 .50
269 Jon Casey .20 .50
270 Pat Elynuik .08 .25
271 Kevin Hatcher .08 .25
272 Brian Propp .08 .25
273 Tom Fergus .08 .25
274 Steve Weeks .20 .50
275 Calle Johansson .08 .25
276 Russ Romaniuk .08 .25
277 Greg Paslawski .08 .25
278 Ed Olczyk .08 .25
279 Rod Langway .08 .25
280 Murray Craven .08 .25
281 Guy Larose .08 .25
282 Paul MacDermid .08 .25
283 Brian Bradley .08 .25
284 Paul Stanton .08 .25
285 Kirk McLean .20 .50
286 Andrei Lomakin .08 .25
287 Randy Carlyle .08 .25
288 Donald Audette .08 .25
289 Dan Quinn .08 .25
290 Mike Keane .08 .25
291 Dave Ellett .08 .25
292 Joe Juneau UER .20 .50
(Card back says shoots
right& should be left)
293 Phil Bourque .08 .25
294 Michal Pivonka .08 .25
295 Fredrik Olausson .08 .25
296 Randy McKay .08 .25
297 Don Beaupre .20 .50
298 Steve Leach .08 .25
299 Teppo Numminen .08 .25
300 Slava Kozlov .20 .50
301 Kevin Haller .08 .25
302 Jaromir Jagr .75 2.00
303 Dale Hunter .20 .50
304 Bob Errey .08 .25
305 Nicklas Lidstrom .75 2.00
306 Bob Essensa .20 .50
307 Sylvain Lefebvre .08 .25
308 Dale Hawerchuk .20 .50
309 Dave Snuggerud .08 .25
310 Michel Goulet .20 .50
311 Eric Desjardins .20 .50
312 Thomas Steen .08 .25
313 Scott Niedermayer .08 .25
314 Mark Recchi .20 .50
315 Gord Murphy .08 .25
316 Sergio Momesso .08 .25
317 Todd Elik .08 .25
318 Louie DeBrusk .08 .25
319 Mike Lalor .08 .25
320 Jamie Leach .08 .25
321 Darryl Sydor .08 .25
322 Brent Gilchrist .08 .25
323 Alexei Kasatonov .08 .25
324 Rick Tabaracci .20 .50
325 Wendel Clark .20 .50
326 Vladimir Konstantinov .50 1.25
327 Randy Gilhen .08 .25
328 Owen Nolan .20 .50
329 Vincent Damphousse .08 .25
330 Checklist 221-331 .08 .25
331 Yves Racine .08 .25
332 Jacques Cloutier .20 .50
333 Greg Adams .08 .25
334 Mike Craig .08 .25
335 Curtis Leschyshyn .08 .25
336 John McIntyre .08 .25
337 Stephane Quintal .08 .25
338 Kelly Miller .08 .25
339 Dave Manson .08 .25
340 Stephane Matteau .08 .25
341 Christian Ruuttu .08 .25
342 Mike Donnelly .08 .25
343 Eric Weinrich .08 .25
344 Mats Sundin .50 1.25
345 Geoff Courtnall .08 .25
346 Stephan Lebeau .08 .25
347 Jeff Beukeboom .08 .25
348 Jeff Hackett .20 .50
349 Uwe Krupp .08 .25
350 Igor Larionov .08 .25
351 Ulf Samuelsson .08 .25
352 Marty McInnis .08 .25
353 Peter Ahola .08 .25
354 Mike Richter .50 1.25
355 Theo Fleury .08 .25
356 Dan Lambert .08 .25
357 Brent Ashton .08 .25
358 David Bruce .08 .25
359 Chris Dahlquist .08 .25
360 Mike Ridley .08 .25
361 Pat Falloon .08 .25
362 Doug Smail .08 .25
363 Adrien Plavsic .08 .25
364 Ron Wilson .08 .25

365 Derian Hatcher .08 .25
366 Kevin Stevens .08 .25
367 Rob Blake .50 1.25
368 Curtis Joseph .50 1.25
369 Tom Fitzgerald .08 .25
370 Dave Lowry .08 .25
371 J.J. Daigneault .08 .25
372 Jim Hrivnak .20 .50
373 Adam Graves .08 .25
374 Brad May .08 .25
375 Todd Gill .08 .25
376 Paul Ysebaert .08 .25
377 David Williams RC .08 .25
378 Bob Bassen .08 .25
379 Brian Glynn .08 .25
380 Kris King .08 .25
381 Rob Pearson .08 .25
382 Marc Bureau .08 .25
383 Jim Paek .08 .25
384 Tomas Forslund .08 .25
385 Darrin Shannon .08 .25
386 Chris Terreri .20 .50
387 Andrew Cassels .08 .25
388 Jay More .08 .25
389 Tony Amonte .20 .50
390 Mark Pederson .08 .25
391 Kevin Miller .08 .25
392 Igor Ulanov .08 .25
393 Kelly Buchberger .08 .25
394 Mark Fitzpatrick .20 .50
395 Mikhail Tatarinov .08 .25
396 Petr Nedved .20 .50
397 Jeff Odgers .08 .25
398 Stephane Fiset .20 .50
399 Mark Tinordi .08 .25
400 Johan Garpenlov .08 .25
401 Robert Reichel .08 .25
402 Don Sweeney UER .08 .25
(Back photo actually Bob Sweeney)
403 Rob DiMaio .08 .25
404 Bill Lindsay RC .08 .25
405 Steph Beauregard .20 .50
406 Mike Ricci .20 .50
407 Bobby Holik .20 .50
408 Igor Kravchuk .08 .25
409 Murray Baron .08 .25
410 Troy Gamble .20 .50
411 Cliff Ronning .08 .25
412 Jeff Reese .08 .25
413 Robert Kron .08 .25
414 Benoit Brunet .08 .25
415 Shawn McEachern .08 .25
416 Sergei Fedorov .75 2.00
417 Joe Sacco .08 .25
418 Bryan Marchment .08 .25
419 John LeBlanc RC .08 .25
420 Tim Cheveldae .20 .50
421 Claude LaPointe .08 .25
422 Ken Sutton .08 .25
423 Anatoli Semenov .08 .25
424 Mike McNeil .08 .25
425 Norm Maciver .08 .25
426 Sergei Nemchinov .08 .25
427 Dimitri Khristich .08 .25
428 Dominik Hasek 1.25 3.00
429 Bob McGill .08 .25
430 Valeri Zelepukin .08 .25
431 Vladimir Ruzicka .08 .25
432 Valeri Kamensky .08 .25
433 Pat MacLeod .08 .25
434 Glenn Healy .20 .50
435 Patrice Brisebois .08 .25
436 James Baker .08 .25
437 Michel Picard .08 .25
438 Scott Lachance UER .08 .25
(Back photo actually Brad Turner)
439 Gilbert Dionne .08 .25
440 Mario Lemieux 4.00 10.00
Smythe FOIL
441 Checklist 332-441 .08 .25
442 Eric Lindros UER .50 1.25
(Acquired 6-30-92 not 6-20-92 as in bio)

1995-96 Bowman

The 1995-96 Bowman set - the first hockey release under that name by the Topps company since 1992-93 - was issued in one series totaling 165 cards. The 9-card packs had a suggested retail price of $2.00. The highlight of the set is an extended Rookies subset (91-165). Rookie Cards in the set include Daniel Alfredsson and Petr Sykora. The Cool Trade redemption offer expired on October 15, 1996.

COMPLETE SET (165) 12.50 25.00
1 Wayne Gretzky .75 2.00
2 Ray Bourque .20 .50
3 Craig Janney .02 .10
4 Andrew Cassels .02 .10
5 Alexander Mogilny .05 .15
6 Pierre Turgeon .05 .15
7 Dave Andreychuk .05 .15
8 Mark Messier .10 .30
9 Igor Korolev .02 .10
10 Tomas Sandstrom .02 .10
11 Shayne Corson .02 .10
12 Chris Chelios .10 .30
13 Claude Lemieux .02 .10
14 Stephane Richer .05 .15
15 Patrick Roy .60 1.50
16 Al MacInnis .05 .15
17 Cam Neely .10 .30
18 Doug Gilmour .05 .15
19 Steve Thomas .05 .15
20 Jeremy Roenick .15 .40
21 Steve Yzerman .60 1.50
22 Petr Klima .02 .10
23 Luc Robitaille .05 .15
24 Bill Ranford .05 .15
25 Grant Fuhr .10 .30
26 Sean Burke .05 .15
27 John MacLean .05 .15
28 Brendan Shanahan .10 .30
29 Pat LaFontaine .10 .30
30 John Vanbiesbrouck .05 .15
31 Ron Francis .05 .15
32 Brian Leetch .05 .15
33 Dave Gagner .05 .15
34 Larry Murphy .05 .15
35 Mike Modano .20 .50
36 Rick Tocchet .05 .15
37 Scott Mellanby .02 .10
38 Ron Hextall .05 .15
39 Joe Juneau .02 .10
40 Mario Lemieux .60 1.50
41 Paul Coffey .10 .30
42 Joe Sakic .25 .60
43 Brett Hull .15 .40
44 Adam Oates .05 .15
45 Wendel Clark .05 .15
46 Trevor Linden .05 .15
47 Tom Barrasso .05 .15
48 Kevin Hatcher .02 .10
49 Mats Sundin .10 .30
50 Scott Stevens .05 .15
51 Mark Recchi .05 .15
52 Theo Fleury .02 .10
53 Ed Belfour .10 .30
54 Adam Graves .02 .10
55 Peter Bondra .05 .15
56 Dominik Hasek .25 .60
57 Jaromir Jagr .20 .50
58 Owen Nolan .05 .15
59 Kevin Stevens .02 .10
60 Alexei Zhamnov .05 .15
61 Dimitri Khristich .02 .10
62 Chris Pronger .10 .30
63 John LeClair .10 .30
64 Scott Niedermayer .10 .30
65 Pavel Bure .10 .30
66 Chris Osgood .05 .15
67 Geoff Sanderson .02 .10
68 Doug Weight .05 .15
69 Keith Tkachuk .10 .30
70 Martin Brodeur .30 .75
71 Eric Lindros .10 .30
72 Martin Straka .02 .10
73 Alexander Selivanov .02 .10
74 Jim Carey .05 .15
75 Teemu Selanne .10 .30
76 Rob Niedermayer .05 .15
77 Vyacheslav Kozlov .05 .15
78 Todd Harvey .05 .15
79 Felix Potvin .10 .30
80 Sergei Fedorov .15 .40
81 Mathieu Schneider .02 .10
82 Roman Hamrlik .05 .15
83 Mikael Renberg .05 .15
84 Jeff Friesen .02 .10
85 Peter Forsberg .30 .75
86 Kenny Jonsson .02 .10
87 Brian Savage .02 .10
88 Oleg Tverdovsky .02 .10
89 Nikolai Khabibulin .05 .15
90 Paul Kariya .10 .30
91 Zdenek Nedved .02 .10
92 Darren Langdon RC .02 .10
93 Lonny Bohonos RC .02 .10
94 Mike Wilson .02 .10
95 Landon Wilson RC .02 .10
96 Bryan McCabe .02 .10
97 Byron Dafoe .05 .15
98 Denny Lambert .02 .10
99 Craig Mills .02 .10
100 Ed Jovanovski .10 .30
101 Jason Bonsignore .02 .10
102 Clayton Beddoes UER .02 .10
back reads Bleddoes
103 Jamie Pushor .02 .10
104 Drew Bannister .02 .10
105 Ed Ward .02 .10
106 Todd Warriner .02 .10
107 Deron Quint .02 .10
108 Rhett Warrener .02 .10
109 Marko Kiprusoff .02 .10
110 Daniel Alfredsson RC .75 2.00
111 Marcus Ragnarsson UER RC .05 .15
Spelled Ragnarasson
112 Miroslav Satan RC .75 2.00
113 Niklas Sundstrom .05 .15
114 Mathieu Dandenault .02 .10
115 Vitali Yachmenev .02 .10
116 Petr Sykora RC .75 2.00
117 Antti Tormanen .02 .10
118 Jeff O'Neill .02 .10
119 David Nemirovsky RC .02 .10
120 Jason Doig .02 .10
121 Aaron Gavey .02 .10
122 Ladislav Kohn .02 .10
123 Richard Park .02 .10
124 Stephane Yelle .02 .10
125 Eric Daze .05 .15
126 Niclas Andersson .02 .10
127 Brendan Witt .02 .10
128 Jamie Storr .05 .15
129 Darby Hendrickson .02 .10
130 Radek Dvorak RC .20 .50
131 Cory Stillman .02 .10
132 Jamie Rivers .02 .10
133 Ville Peltonen .02 .10
134 Peter Ferraro .02 .10
135 Trent McCleary RC .02 .10
136 Chris Wells .02 .10
137 Chad Kilger RC .02 .10
138 Denis Pederson .02 .10
139 Roman Vopat .02 .10
140 Shean Donovan .02 .10
141 Alex Stojanov .02 .10
142 Mark Kolesar .02 .10
143 Scott Walker RC .02 .10
144 Dave Roche RC .02 .10
145 Corey Hirsch .05 .15
146 Aki Berg .02 .10
147 Stefan Ustorf .02 .10
148 Saku Koivu .10 .30
149 Shane Doan RC .30 .75
150 Jere Lehtinen .05 .15
151 Kyle McLaren RC .02 .10
152 Marty Murray .02 .10
153 Sean Pronger RC .02 .10
154 Joaquin Gage RC .02 .10
155 Eric Fichaud .05 .15
156 Todd Bertuzzi RC 1.25 3.00
157 Wayne Primeau .02 .10
158 Scott Bailey .02 .10
159 Viktor Kozlov .05 .15
160 Valeri Bure .02 .10
161 Dody Wood .02 .10
162 Grant Marshall .02 .10
163 Ken Klee RC .02 .10
164 Corey Schwab RC .20 .50
165 Brian Holzinger RC .10 .30

1995-96 Bowman Foil

The 1995-96 Bowman All-Foil set is a 165-card parallel of the regular version. The cards, which were inserted one per pack, feature a stylish metallicized front, while the backs remain the same as the basic cards.

*VETS: 3X TO 8X BASIC CARDS
*ROOKIES: 1.2X TO 3X BASIC CARDS
ONE PER PACK

1995-96 Bowman Draft Prospects

Inserted one in every pack, this 40-card set features the players who participated in the first annual 1996 CHL Draft Prospects game in Toronto. Fourteen of the players pictured went on to become first-round selections in the 1996 NHL entry draft.

COMPLETE SET (40) 4.00 10.00
ONE PER PACK
P1 Johnathan Aitken .08 .25
P2 Chris Allen .08 .25
P3 Matt Bradley .08 .25
P4 Daniel Briere 1.00 2.50
P5 Jeff Brown .08 .25
P6 Jan Bulis .08 .25
P7 Daniel Corso .08 .25
P8 Luke Curtin .08 .25
P9 Matthieu Descoteaux .08 .25
P10 Boyd Devereaux .08 .25
P11 Jason Doyle .08 .25
P12 Etienne Drapeau .08 .25
P13 J-P Dumont .40 1.00
P14 Mathieu Garon .40 1.00
P15 Josh Green .08 .25
P16 Chris Hajt .08 .25
P17 Matt Higgins .08 .25
P18 Craig Hillier .08 .25
P19 Josh Holden .08 .25
P20 Dan Focht .08 .25
P21 Henry Kuster .08 .25
P22 Francis Larivee .08 .25
P23 Mario Larocque .08 .25
P24 Wes Mason .08 .25
P25 Francois Methot .08 .25
P26 Geoff Peters .08 .25
P27 Randy Petruk .08 .25
P28 Chris Phillips .40 1.00
P29 Boris Protsenko .08 .25
P30 Remi Royer .08 .25
P31 Cory Sarich .08 .25
P32 Jaroslav Svejkovsky .08 .25
P33 Curtis Tipler .08 .25
P34 Darren Van Oene .08 .25
P35 Jesse Wallin .08 .25
P36 Kurt Walsh .08 .25
P37 Lance Ward .08 .25
P38 Steve Wasylko .08 .25
P39 Trevor Wasyluk .08 .25
P40 Jon Zukiwsky .08 .25

1995-96 Bowman Bowman's Best

Randomly inserted in packs at a rate of 1:12, this 30-card set is dedicated to the finest stars and up'n'comers in the NHL. A refractor parallel to this set was also created and inserted at a rate of 1:36.

COMPLETE SET (30) 40.00 100.00
STATED ODDS 1:12
*REFRACTOR: 1X TO 2.5X BASIC INSERTS
BB1 Peter Forsberg 3.00 8.00
BB2 Teemu Selanne 1.50 4.00
BB3 Eric Lindros 1.50 4.00
BB4 Scott Stevens .75 2.00
BB5 Wayne Gretzky 8.00 20.00
BB6 Mark Messier 1.50 4.00
BB7 Jaromir Jagr 2.50 6.00
BB8 Martin Brodeur 4.00 10.00
BB9 Alexander Mogilny .75 2.00
BB10 Mario Lemieux 6.00 15.00
BB11 Joe Sakic 3.00 8.00
BB12 Sergei Fedorov 2.00 5.00
BB13 Pavel Bure 1.50 4.00
BB14 Brian Leetch .75 2.00
BB15 Paul Kariya 1.50 4.00
BB16 Daniel Alfredsson 2.00 5.00
BB17 Saku Koivu 1.50 4.00
BB18 Eric Daze .40 1.00
BB19 Ed Jovanovski 1.50 4.00
BB20 Vitali Yachmenev .40 1.00
BB21 Niklas Sundstrom .40 1.00
BB22 Radek Dvorak .40 1.00
BB23 Byron Dafoe .75 2.00
BB24 Shane Doan 1.50 4.00
BB25 Chad Kilger .40 1.00
BB26 Jeff O'Neill .40 1.00
BB27 Cory Stillman .40 1.00
BB28 Valeri Bure .40 1.00
BB29 Marcus Ragnarsson .40 1.00
BB30 Todd Bertuzzi 2.00 5.00

1998-99 Bowman's Best

This 150-card set was distributed in six-card packs with a suggested retail price of $5. The set features color action photos of 100 key veterans printed on cards with a gold design and 35 top NHL rookies and 14 CHL stars showcased on silver-designed cards. The cards are all printed on thick 26-pt. stock. The backs carry player information and career statistics.

COMPLETE SET (150) 50.00 125.00
COMP.SET w/o SP's (100) 10.00 25.00
1 Steve Yzerman 1.50 4.00
2 Paul Kariya .30 .75
3 Wayne Gretzky 2.00 5.00
4 Jaromir Jagr .50 1.25
5 Mark Messier .30 .75
6 Keith Tkachuk .30 .75
7 John LeClair .30 .75
8 Martin Brodeur .75 2.00
9 Rob Blake .25 .60
10 Brett Hull .40 1.00
11 Dominik Hasek .60 1.50
12 Peter Forsberg .75 2.00
13 Doug Gilmour .25 .60
14 Vincent Damphousse .08 .25
15 Zigmund Palffy .25 .60
16 Daniel Alfredsson .25 .60
17 Mike Vernon .25 .60
18 Chris Pronger .25 .60
19 Wendel Clark .25 .60
20 Curtis Joseph .30 .75
21 Peter Bondra .25 .60
22 Grant Fuhr .25 .60
23 Nikolai Khabibulin .25 .60
24 Kevin Hatcher .08 .25
25 Brian Leetch .30 .75
26 Patrik Elias .25 .60
27 Chris Osgood .25 .60
28 Patrick Roy 1.50 4.00
29 Chris Chelios .30 .75
30 Trevor Kidd .08 .25
31 Theo Fleury .08 .25
32 Michael Peca .08 .25
33 Ray Bourque .50 1.25
34 Ed Belfour .30 .75
35 Sergei Fedorov .50 1.25
36 Adrian Aucoin .08 .25
37 Alexei Yashin .08 .25
38 Rick Tocchet .25 .60
39 Mats Sundin .30 .75
40 Alexander Mogilny .25 .60
41 Jeff Friesen .08 .25
42 Eric Lindros .30 .75
43 Mike Richter .30 .75
44 Saku Koivu .30 .75
45 Teemu Selanne .30 .75
46 Doug Weight .25 .60
47 Nicklas Lidstrom .30 .75
48 Mike Modano .50 1.25
49 Joe Sakic .60 1.50
50 Ron Francis .25 .60
51 Jason Allison .08 .25
52 Brendan Shanahan .30 .75
53 Bobby Holik .08 .25
54 Damian Rhodes .25 .60
55 Jeremy Roenick .40 1.00
56 Tom Barrasso .08 .25
57 Al MacInnis .25 .60
58 Pavel Bure .30 .75
59 Olaf Kolzig .25 .60
60 Patrick Marleau .08 .25
61 Cliff Ronning .08 .25
62 Joe Nieuwendyk .25 .60
63 Jeff Hackett .25 .60
64 Keith Primeau .08 .25
65 Jarome Iginla .40 1.00
66 Sergei Samsonov .25 .60
67 Rod Brind'Amour .25 .60
68 Dino Ciccarelli .25 .60
69 Ryan Smyth .25 .60
70 Owen Nolan .25 .60
71 Mike Johnson .08 .25
72 Adam Oates .25 .60
73 Mattias Ohlund .25 .60
74 Jamie Heward RC .08 .25
75 Mike Dunham .25 .60
76 Jere Lehtinen .25 .60
77 Tony Amonte .25 .60
78 Derek Morris .08 .25
79 Darren McCarty .08 .25
80 Bryan Berard .25 .60
81 Adam Graves .08 .25
82 John Vanbiesbrouck .25 .60
83 Marco Sturm .08 .25
84 Joe Thornton .50 1.25
85 Wade Redden .08 .25
86 Pierre Turgeon .25 .60
87 Bill Ranford .25 .60
88 Alexei Zhitnik .08 .25
89 Valeri Kamensky .08 .25
90 Dean McAmmond .08 .25
91 Jozef Stumpel .25 .60
92 Jocelyn Thibault .25 .60
93 Joe Juneau .25 .60
94 Craig Janney .25 .60
95 Robert Reichel .25 .60
96 Mark Recchi .25 .60
97 Sami Kapanen .08 .25
98 Shayne Corson .08 .25
99 Scott Niedermayer .08 .25
100 Trevor Linden .25 .60
101 Olli Jokinen SP 1.25 3.00
102 Chris Drury SP 2.00 5.00
103 Daniel Cleary SP 1.00 2.50
104 Yan Golubovsky SP RC 1.25 3.00
105 Brendan Morrison SP 1.25 3.00
106 Manny Malhotra SP 1.00 2.50
107 Marian Hossa SP 1.25 3.00
108 Daniel Briere SP 1.00 2.50
109 Vincent Lecavalier SP 1.50 4.00
110 Milan Hejduk SP RC 3.00 8.00
111 Tom Poti SP 1.00 2.50
112 Mike Maneluk SP RC 1.25 3.00
113 Marty Reasoner SP 1.00 2.50
114 Rico Fata SP 1.00 2.50
115 Eric Brewer SP 1.00 2.50
116 Dan Cloutier SP 1.00 2.50
117 Mike Leclerc SP 1.00 2.50
118 Dimitri Tertyshny SP RC 1.00 2.50
119 Josh Green SP RC 1.50 4.00
120 Mark Parrish SP RC 1.50 4.00
121 Jamie Wright SP 1.00 2.50
122 Fred Lindquist SP RC 1.00 2.50
123 Daniil Markov SP RC 1.00 2.50
124 Bill Muckalt SP RC 1.25 3.00
125 Johan Davidsson SP 1.00 2.50
126 Oleg Kvasha SP RC 1.25 3.00
127 Cameron Mann SP 1.00 2.50
128 Pascal Trepanier SP RC 1.00 2.50
129 Clarke Wilm SP RC 1.00 2.50
130 Alain Nasreddine SP RC 1.00 2.50
131 Bryan Helmer SP RC 1.00 2.50
132 Michal Handzus SP RC 1.50 4.00
133 Pavel Kubina SP RC 1.25 3.00
134 Zdeno Chara SP 1.00 2.50
135 Matt Higgins SP RC 1.00 2.50
136 David Legwand SP 1.50 4.00
137 Brad Stuart SP RC 2.00 5.00
138 Mark Bell SP RC 2.00 5.00
139 Eric Chouinard SP 1.00 2.50
140 Simon Gagne SP 1.50 4.00
141 Ramzi Abid SP RC 2.00 5.00
142 Sergei Varlamov SP 1.25 3.00
143 Mike Ribeiro SP 1.00 2.50
144 Derrick Walser SP RC 1.00 2.50
145 Mathieu Garon SP 1.00 2.50
146 Daniel Tkaczuk SP 1.00 2.50
147 Jeff Heerema SP RC 1.50 4.00
148 Sebastien Roger SP RC 1.00 2.50
149 Bret DeCecco SP 1.00 2.50
150 Checklist SP 1.25 3.00

1998-99 Bowman's Best Refractors

Randomly inserted in packs at the rate of 1:52, this 150-card set is a refractive parallel version of the base set. Only 400 of each card were produced and sequentially numbered.

*1-100 REFRACTOR: 8X TO 20X BASIC CARDS
*101-150 REFRACTOR: 3X TO 6X BASIC SP
REFRACTOR STATED ODDS 1:387

1998-99 Bowman's Best Atomic Refractors

Randomly inserted into packs at the rate of 1:1549, this 150-card set is a parallel version of the base set and is similar in design. The difference is seen in the special sparkling refractive sheen of the cards. Only 100 of each card was produced and sequentially numbered.

*1-100 ATOMIC REF: 20X TO 50X BASIC CARDS
*101-150 ATOMIC REF: 6X TO 15X BASIC SP
ATOMIC REFRACTOR/100 ODDS 1:1549
ATOMIC REF PRINT RUN 100 SER.#'d SETS
1 Steve Yzerman 40.00 100.00
3 Wayne Gretzky 60.00 150.00
28 Patrick Roy 40.00 100.00

1998-99 Bowman's Best Autographs

Randomly inserted in packs at the rate of 1:97, this 20-card set displays autographed color photos of five rookie and five veteran players each featured in two different photos. Both versions of the rookies carry silver backgrounds, with gold backgrounds for the veterans. Each card is stamped with the Topps "Certified Autograph Issue" logo.

STATED ODDS 1:97
*REFRACTOR: .8X TO 2X BASIC AUTO
REFRACTOR STATED ODDS 1:516
*ATOMIC REF: 1.5X TO 4X BASIC AUTO
ATOMIC REFRACTOR ODDS 1:1549
A1A Dominik Hasek 15.00 40.00
A1B Dominik Hasek 15.00 40.00
A2A Jaromir Jagr 15.00 40.00
A2B Jaromir Jagr 15.00 40.00
A3A Peter Bondra 6.00 15.00
A3B Peter Bondra 6.00 15.00
A4A Sergei Fedorov 15.00 40.00
A4B Sergei Fedorov 15.00 40.00
A5A Ray Bourque 20.00 50.00
A5B Ray Bourque 20.00 50.00
A6A Bill Muckalt 3.00 8.00
A6B Bill Muckalt 3.00 8.00
A7A Brendan Morrison 6.00 15.00
A7B Brendan Morrison 6.00 15.00
A8A Chris Drury 6.00 15.00
A8B Chris Drury 6.00 15.00
A9A Mark Parrish 3.00 8.00
A9B Mark Parrish 3.00 8.00
A10A Manny Malhotra 3.00 8.00
A10B Manny Malhotra 3.00 8.00

1998-99 Bowman's Best Mirror Image Fusion

Randomly inserted in packs at the rate of 1:12, this 20-card set features color action photos of Western and Eastern Conference players printed on die-cut, double-sided cards. Each card features a veteran on one side and a rising star on the other and can be married to its die-cut counterpart from the opposite conference.

COMPLETE SET (20) 60.00 125.00
STATED ODDS 1:12
*REFRACTOR/100: 4X TO 10X BASIC INSERTS
REFRACTOR/100 STATED ODDS 1:387
REFRACTOR PRINT RUN 100 SER.#'d SETS
*ATOMIC REF/25: 12X TO 30X BASIC INSERTS
ATOMIC REFRACTOR/25 ODDS 1:1549
ATOMIC REF.PRINT RUN 25 SER.#'d SETS
F1 John LeClair 2.00 5.00
Bates Battaglia
F2 Paul Kariya 2.00 5.00
Mike LeClerc
F3 Jaromir Jagr 4.00 10.00
Mark Parrish
F4 Teemu Selanne 2.00 5.00
Frederik Lindquist
F5 Eric Lindros 2.00 5.00
Vicent Lecavalier
F6 Peter Forsberg 5.00 12.00
Olli Jokinen
F7 Brian Leetch 1.25 3.00
Daniil Markov
F8 Nicklas Lidstrom 2.00 5.00
Yan Golubovsky
F9 Dominik Hasek 4.00 10.00
Dan Cloutier
F10 Patrick Roy 8.00 20.00
Tyler Moss
F11 Sergei Samsonov 1.25 3.00
Mike Watt
F12 Keith Tkachuk 2.50 6.00
Jamie Wright
F13 Peter Bondra 2.50 6.00
Marian Hossa
F14 Pavel Bure 2.00 5.00
Bill Muckalt
F15 Wayne Gretzky 12.00 30.00
Brendan Morrison
F16 Sergei Fedorov 3.00 8.00
Marty Reasoner
F17 Ray Bourque 3.00 8.00
Eric Brewer
F18 Chris Pronger 1.25 3.00
Tom Poti
F19 Martin Brodeur 5.00 12.00
Jose Theodore
F20 Chris Osgood 1.25 3.00
Jamie Storr

1998-99 Bowman's Best Performers

Randomly inserted in packs at the rate of 1:12, this 10-card set features action color photos of top young stars and rookies.

COMPLETE SET (10) 10.00 25.00
STATED ODDS 1:12
*REFRACTOR/200: 4X TO 10X BASIC INSERTS
REFRACTOR/200 STATED ODDS 1:387
REFRACTOR PRINT RUN 200 SER.#'d SETS
*ATOMIC REF/50: 10X TO 25X BASIC INSERTS
ATOMIC REFRACTOR/50 ODDS 1:1549
ATOMTC REFRACTOR PRINT RUN 50
BP1 Mike Johnson .75 2.00
BP2 Sergei Samsonov 1.25 3.00
BP3 Patrik Elias .75 2.00
BP4 Patrick Marleau 1.25 3.00
BP5 Mattias Ohlund .75 2.00
BP6 Manny Malhotra .75 2.00
BP7 Chris Drury .75 2.00
BP8 Daniel Briere 1.25 3.00
BP9 Brendan Morrison .75 2.00
BP10 Vincent Lecavalier 4.00 10.00

1998-99 Bowman's Best Scotty Bowman's Best

Randomly inserted into packs at the rate of 1:6, this 11-card set features color photos of ten of the best present day players in the NHL according to Scotty Bowman who is one of the greatest coaches of all time. Card #11 is a card of the coach himself and 100 of these cards were autographed with an insertion rate of 1:7,745.

COMPLETE SET (11) 25.00 50.00
STATED ODDS 1:6
*REFRACT/200: 3X TO 8X BASIC INSERTS
REFRACTOR/200 STATED ODDS 1:704
REFRACTOR PRINT RUN 200 SER.#'d SETS
*ATOMIC REF/50: 10X TO 20X BASIC INSERTS
ATOMIC REFRACTOR/50 ODDS 1:2816
ATOMIC REF PRINT RUN 50 SER.#'d SETS
SB1 Dominik Hasek 2.50 6.00
SB2 Martin Brodeur 3.00 8.00
SB3 Chris Osgood 1.25 3.00
SB4 Nicklas Lidstrom 1.25 3.00
SB5 Eric Lindros 1.25 3.00
SB6 Jaromir Jagr 2.00 5.00
SB7 Steve Yzerman 6.00 15.00
SB8 Peter Forsberg 3.00 8.00
SB9 Paul Kariya 1.25 3.00
SB10 Ray Bourque 2.00 5.00
SB11 Scotty Bowman 1.25 3.00
SB11S Scotty Bowman AU 40.00 100.00

2001-02 Bowman YoungStars

Released in late May, this 165-card set carried an SRP of $3.00. Card fronts carried gold foil accents and black borders on full-color action photos. The Topps/NHL Young Stars logo appeared in the bottom left hand corner.

COMPLETE SET (165) 75.00 150.00
1 Patrick Roy 2.50 6.00
2 Brett Hull .60 1.50
3 Mario Lemieux 3.00 8.00
4 Jaromir Jagr .75 2.00
5 Mats Sundin .50 1.25
6 Mike Modano .75 2.00
7 Jarome Iginla .60 1.50
8 Jason Allison .20 .50

9 Mike Richter .50 1.25
10 Chris Pronger .40 1.00
11 Patrik Elias .40 1.00
12 Tommy Salo .40 1.00
13 Tony Amonte .40 1.00
14 Joe Thornton .75 2.00
15 Joe Sakic 1.00 2.50
16 Pavel Bure .50 1.25
17 Teemu Selanne .50 1.25
18 Markus Naslund .50 1.25
19 Nikolai Khabibulin .50 1.25
20 Paul Kariya .50 1.25
21 Dominik Hasek 1.00 2.50
22 Ron Francis .40 1.00
23 Ray Ferraro .20 .50
24 Miroslav Satan .40 1.00
25 Milan Hejduk .50 1.25
26 Jose Theodore .60 1.50
27 Daniel Alfredsson .40 1.00
28 Michael Peca .20 .50
29 Keith Primeau .20 .50
30 Doug Weight .40 1.00
31 Sean Burke .40 1.00
32 Adam Oates .40 1.00
33 Brian Rolston .20 .50
34 Rob Blake .40 1.00
35 Steve Yzerman 2.50 6.00
36 Eric Lindros .50 1.25
37 Keith Tkachuk .50 1.25
38 Dan Cloutier .40 1.00
39 Chris Osgood .40 1.00
40 Zigmund Palffy .40 1.00
41 Jocelyn Thibault .40 1.00
42 Roman Turek .40 1.00
43 Ed Belfour .50 1.25
44 Adam Deadmarsh .20 .50
45 Marian Hossa .50 1.25
46 Owen Nolan .40 1.00
47 Curtis Joseph .50 1.25
48 Peter Bondra .40 1.00
49 Jeremy Roenick .60 1.50
50 Brendan Shanahan .50 1.25
51 Eric Daze .40 1.00
52 J-P Dumont .20 .50
53 Bill Guerin .40 1.00
54 Jukka Hentunen RC .75 2.00
55 Brian Leetch .40 1.00
56 Alexei Kovalev .40 1.00
57 Olaf Kolzig .40 1.00
58 Mike York .20 .50
59 Felix Potvin .50 1.25
60 Pierre Turgeon .40 1.00
61 Luc Robitaille .40 1.00
62 Sami Kapanen .20 .50
63 Byron Dafoe .40 1.00
64 Ryan Smyth .20 .50
65 John LeClair .50 1.25
66 Pavol Demitra .40 1.00
67 Alexei Yashin .20 .50
68 Vincent Lecavalier .50 1.25
69 Chris Drury .40 1.00
70 Mike Dunham .40 1.00
71 Patrick Lalime .40 1.00
72 Derek Morris .20 .50
73 Peter Forsberg 1.25 3.00
74 Sergei Fedorov .75 2.00
75 Mark Parrish .20 .50
76 Simon Gagne .50 1.25
77 Jeff O'Neill .20 .50
78 Alexander Mogilny .40 1.00
79 Johan Hedberg .40 1.00
80 Martin Brodeur 1.25 3.00
81 Claude Lemieux .20 .50
82 Mark Messier .50 1.25
83 Nicklas Lidstrom .50 1.25
84 Stu Barnes .20 .50
85 Steve Sullivan .20 .50
86 Jeff Friesen .20 .50
87 Brent Johnson .40 1.00
88 Marc Denis .40 1.00
89 Jason Arnott .20 .50
90 Brendan Morrison .40 1.00
91 Jere Lehtinen .40 1.00
92 Craig Conroy .20 .50
93 Petr Sykora .20 .50
94 Gary Roberts .20 .50
95 Saku Koivu .50 1.25
96 Scott Stevens .40 1.00
97 Radek Bonk .20 .50
98 Roman Cechmanek .40 1.00
99 Robert Lang .20 .50
100 Tom Barrasso .40 1.00
101 Yanic Perreault .20 .50
102 Joe Nieuwendyk .40 1.00
103 Al MacInnis .40 1.00
104 Vincent Damphousse .20 .50
105 Anson Carter .40 1.00
106 Sergei Samsonov .40 1.00
107 Theo Fleury .20 .50
108 Mark Recchi .40 1.00
109 Marco Sturm .20 .50
110 Jiri Dopita RC .75 2.00
111 Tim Connolly .20 .50
112 Mike Fisher .20 .50
113 Alex Tanguay .40 1.00
114 Christian Berglund RC .75 2.00
115 Olivier Michaud RC 1.25 3.00
116 John Erskine RC .75 2.00
117 Mikael Samuelsson RC .75 2.00
118 Radek Martinek RC .75 2.00
119 Mark Rycroft RC .75 2.00
120 Mike Ribeiro .20 .50
121 Vaclav Pletka RC .75 2.00
122 Toni Dahlman RC .75 2.00
123 Brian Sutherby RC .75 2.00
124 Karel Rachunek .75 2.00
125 Robyn Regehr .75 2.00
126 Martin Erat RC .75 2.00
127 Nick Boynton .75 2.00
128 Nick Schultz RC .75 2.00
129 Timo Parssinen RC .75 2.00
130 Jaroslav Bednar RC .75 2.00
131 Roberto Luongo .60 1.50
132 Pascal Dupuis RC .75 2.00
133 Dave Tanabe .20 .50
134 Dany Heatley .60 1.50
135 Jeff Jillson RC .75 2.00
136 Marian Gaborik 1.00 2.50
137 Radim Vrbata .20 .50
138 Andrew Ference .20 .50
139 Rostislav Klesla .20 .50
140 Dan Blackburn RC .60 1.50
141 Andy Hilbert .20 .50
142 Martin Havlat .40 1.00
143 Niko Kapanen RC .75 2.00
144 Brenden Morrow .40 1.00
145 Scott Hartnell .20 .50
146 Raffi Torres RC 1.00 2.50
147 Vaclav Nedorost RC .75 2.00
148 Krys Kolanos RC .75 2.00
149 Kyle Calder .20 .50
150 Niklas Hagman RC .75 2.00
151 Brian Gionta .20 .50
152 Kristian Huselius RC .75 2.00
153 Mike Comrie .40 1.00
154 Ty Conklin RC .75 2.00
155 Justin Williams .20 .50
156 Erik Cole RC .75 2.00
157 Nikita Alexeev RC .75 2.00
158 Paul Mara .20 .50
159 Ilya Kovalchuk RC 4.00 10.00
160 David Legwand .40 1.00
161 Ilja Bryzgalov RC .75 2.00
162 Brad Richards .40 1.00
163 Evgeni Nabokov .40 1.00
164 Kris Beech .20 .50
165 Pavel Datsyuk RC 3.00 8.00

2001-02 Bowman YoungStars Gold

This 165-card set paralleled the base set, but card fronts had a gold glitter effect added. Each card was serial-numbered out of 250.

*GOLD: 1.5X TO 4X BASIC CARD
STATED PRINT RUN 250 SER.#'d SETS

2001-02 Bowman YoungStars Ice Cubed

This 165-card set paralleled the base set, but the card stock was approximately 3 times thicker and the card fronts were high gloss. These cards were inserted into every pack that did not contain a memorabilia card to prevent pack searching.

*ICE CUBED: .5X TO 1.25X BASIC CARD
ONE PER NON-MEMORABILIA PACK

2001-02 Bowman YoungStars Autographs

This 23-card set featured certified autographs of players who participated in the 2002 Topps/NHL Young Stars Game. All cards carried a YSA prefix.

STATED ODDS 1:478
ALL CARDS CARRY YSA PREFIX
AF Andrew Ference 10.00 25.00
BM Brenden Morrow 15.00 40.00
BR Brad Richards 25.00 60.00
DB Dan Blackburn 10.00 25.00
DH Dany Heatley 25.00 60.00
DL David Legwand 10.00 25.00
DT Dave Tanabe 10.00 25.00
IK Ilya Kovalchuk 30.00 80.00
JW Justin Williams 10.00 25.00
KC Kyle Calder 10.00 25.00
KH Kristian Huselius 10.00 25.00
KR Karel Rachunek 10.00 25.00
MC Mike Comrie 10.00 25.00
MF Mike Fisher 10.00 25.00
MG Marian Gaborik 25.00 60.00
MR Mike Ribeiro 10.00 25.00
NB Nick Boynton 10.00 25.00
PD Pavel Datsyuk 25.00 60.00
PM Paul Mara 10.00 25.00
RL Roberto Luongo 20.00 50.00
RR Robyn Regehr 10.00 25.00
SH Scott Hartnell 10.00 25.00
TC Tim Connolly 10.00 25.00

2001-02 Bowman YoungStars Autographed Puck Redemptions

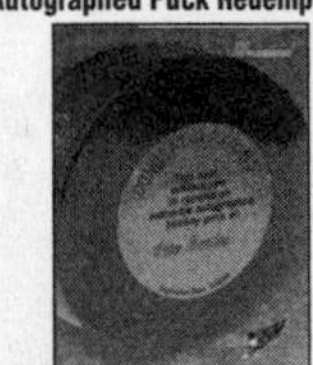

Inserted at overall odds of 1:186, this set of redemption cards entitled the holder to an autographed team logo puck. Redemption cards expired 5/30/03. The Ilya Kovalchuk redemption card was inserted at odds of 1:1978.

COMMON EXPIRED CARD .20 .50
OVERALL ODDS 1:186
ALL CARDS HAVE EXPIRED

2001-02 Bowman YoungStars Relics

This 69-card set featured swatches of jerseys and sticks used in the 2002 Topps/NHL Young Stars Game. Jersey swatches were inserted at a rate of one in six. Stick swatches were inserted at a rate of 1:193. Combo cards with both jersey and stick swatches were serial-numbered out of 25. All cards carried a FF prefix.

JERSEY STATED ODDS 1:6
STICK STATED ODDS 1:193
JSY/STK PRINT RUN 25 SER.#'d SETS
ALL CARDS CARRY FF PREFIX
JAF Andrew Ference 2.00 5.00
JBM Brenden Morrow 3.00 8.00
JBR Brad Richards 3.00 8.00
JDB Dan Blackburn 2.00 5.00
JDH Dany Heatley 4.00 10.00
JDL David Legwand 2.00 5.00
JDT Dave Tanabe 2.00 5.00
JIK Ilya Kovalchuk 6.00 15.00
JJW Justin Williams 2.00 5.00
JKC Kyle Calder 2.00 5.00
JKH Kristian Huselius 2.00 5.00
JKR Karel Rachunek 2.00 5.00
JMC Mike Comrie 2.00 5.00
JMF Mike Fisher 2.00 5.00
JMG Marian Gaborik 12.00 30.00
JMR Mike Ribeiro 2.00 5.00
JNB Nick Boynton 2.00 5.00
JPD Pavel Datsyuk 4.00 10.00
JPM Paul Mara 2.00 5.00
JRL Roberto Luongo 4.00 10.00
JRR Robyn Regehr 2.00 5.00
JSH Scott Hartnell 2.00 5.00
JTC Tim Connolly 2.00 5.00
SAF Andrew Ference 8.00 20.00
SBM Brenden Morrow 10.00 25.00
SBR Brad Richards 8.00 20.00
SDB Dan Blackburn 8.00 20.00
SDH Dany Heatley 10.00 25.00
SDL David Legwand 8.00 20.00
SDT Dave Tanabe 8.00 20.00
SIK Ilya Kovalchuk 20.00 50.00
SJW Justin Williams 10.00 25.00
SKC Kyle Calder 8.00 20.00
SKH Kristian Huselius 8.00 20.00
SKR Karel Rachunek 8.00 20.00
SMC Mike Comrie 8.00 20.00
SMF Mike Fisher 8.00 20.00
SMG Marian Gaborik 15.00 40.00
SMR Mike Ribeiro 8.00 20.00
SNB Nick Boynton 8.00 20.00
SPD Pavel Datsyuk 10.00 25.00
SPM Paul Mara 8.00 20.00
SRL Roberto Luongo 10.00 25.00
SRR Robyn Regehr 8.00 20.00
SSH Scott Hartnell 8.00 20.00
STC Tim Connolly 8.00 20.00
DSAF Andrew Ference 15.00 40.00
DSBM Brenden Morrow 15.00 40.00
DSBR Brad Richards 25.00 60.00
DSDB Dan Blackburn 25.00 60.00
DSDH Dany Heatley 50.00 125.00
DSDL David Legwand 12.00 30.00
DSDT Dave Tanabe 15.00 40.00
DSIK Ilya Kovalchuk 75.00 200.00
DSJW Justin Williams 15.00 40.00
DSKC Kyle Calder 15.00 40.00
DSKH Kristian Huselius 15.00 40.00
DSKR Karel Rachunek 15.00 40.00
DSMC Mike Comrie 25.00 60.00
DSMF Mike Fisher 15.00 40.00
DSMG Marian Gaborik 50.00 125.00
DSMR Mike Ribeiro 25.00 60.00
DSNB Nick Boynton 15.00 40.00
DSPD Pavel Datsyuk 50.00 125.00
DSPM Paul Mara 15.00 40.00
DSRL Roberto Luongo 40.00 100.00
DSRR Robyn Regehr 15.00 40.00
DSSH Scott Hartnell 15.00 40.00
DSTC Tim Connolly 15.00 40.00

2001-02 Bowman YoungStars Rivals

This 11-card set featured dual game-worn swatches from players who participated in the 2002 Topps Young Stars game. Each card was serial-numbered out of 250. All cards carried a FF prefix.

STATED PRINT RUN 250 SER.#'d SETS
ALL CARDS CARRY FF PREFIX
R1 Roberto Luongo 15.00 40.00
Dan Blackburn
R2 Karel Rachunek 12.00 30.00
Brad Richards
R3 Andrew Ference 10.00 25.00
Dave Tanabe
R4 Nick Boynton 12.00 30.00
Robyn Regehr
R5 M.Gaborik/I.Kovalchuk 20.00 50.00
R6 M.Comrie/D.Heatley 15.00 40.00
R7 Mike Ribeiro 10.00 25.00
Justin Williams
R8 Tim Connolly 10.00 25.00
David Legwand
R9 Mike Fisher 15.00 40.00
Pavel Datsyuk
R10 Scott Hartnell 12.00 30.00
Brenden Morrow
R11 Kristian Huselius 10.00 25.00
Kyle Calder

2002 Bowman Toronto Spring Expo

This 10-card set was part of a wrapper redemption program at the Topps booth during the 2002 Toronto Spring Expo. A total of 500 sets were made available, with the first 300 including a card autographed by top prospect Ilya Kovalchuk. The remaining 200 sets included a non-signed Kovalchuk card.

COMPLETE SET (10) 10.00 25.00
1 Ilya Kovalchuk 6.00 15.00
1B Ilya Kovalchuk AU 20.00 50.00
2 Curtis Joseph .80 2.00
3 Pavel Datsyuk 2.00 5.00
4 Jose Theodore .80 2.00
5 Jarome Iginla .40 1.00
6 Martin Brodeur .80 2.00
7 Patrick Roy 1.20 3.00
8 Dany Heatley 1.20 3.00
9 Dan Blackburn 1.20 3.00
10 Mats Sundin .40 1.00

2002-03 Bowman YoungStars

Released in April 2003, this 165-card set featured color action photos on black-bordered card fronts. The set highlighted the annual Topps YoungStars game held on All-Star weekend.

COMPLETE SET (165) 20.00 50.00
1 Nicklas Lidstrom .30 .75
2 Martin Brodeur 1.00 2.50
3 Tony Amonte .20 .50
4 Todd Bertuzzi .30 .75
5 Joe Thornton .60 1.50
6 Ron Francis .20 .50
7 Paul Kariya .30 .75
8 Eric Lindros .30 .75
9 John LeClair .30 .75
10 Doug Weight .20 .50
11 Jaromir Jagr .60 1.50
12 Mats Sundin .30 .75
13 Saku Koivu .30 .75
14 Peter Forsberg .60 1.50
15 Alexei Yashin .10 .25
16 Mike Modano .40 1.00
17 Chris Drury .20 .50
18 Ryan Smyth .10 .25
19 Tomas Vokoun .20 .50
20 Marian Hossa .30 .75
21 Owen Nolan .20 .50
22 Vincent Lecavalier .30 .75
23 Jocelyn Thibault .20 .50
24 Marc Denis .20 .50
25 Roberto Luongo .40 1.00
26 Mario Lemieux 1.50 4.00
27 Keith Tkachuk .30 .75
28 Radek Bonk .10 .25
29 Bill Guerin .20 .50
30 Jason Allison .10 .25
31 Jeff O'Neill .10 .25
32 Alexei Zhamnov .10 .25
33 Scott Stevens .20 .50
34 Mark Recchi .20 .50
35 Alexander Mogilny .20 .50
36 Olaf Kolzig .20 .50
37 Sean Burke .20 .50
38 Brett Hull .40 1.00
39 Andrew Cassels .10 .25
40 Jarome Iginla .40 1.00
41 Joe Sakic .75 2.00
42 Brian Leetch .20 .50
43 Simon Gagne .30 .75
44 Dan Cloutier .20 .50
45 Brian Rolston .10 .25
46 Milan Hejduk .30 .75
47 Steve Yzerman 1.25 3.00
48 Martin Havlat .20 .50
49 Alexei Kovalev .20 .50
50 Pavol Demitra .20 .50
51 Mark Parrish .10 .25
52 Felix Potvin .30 .75
53 Brenden Morrow .20 .50
54 Steve Sullivan .10 .25
55 Patrick Roy 1.50 4.00
56 Manny Fernandez .20 .50
57 Vincent Damphousse .10 .25
58 Michael Peca .10 .25
59 Anson Carter .20 .50
60 Kevin Weekes .10 .25
61 Peter Bondra .20 .50
62 Brad Richards .20 .50
63 Johan Hedberg .20 .50
64 Olli Jokinen .20 .50
65 Miroslav Satan .20 .50
66 Petr Sykora .10 .25
67 Al MacInnis .20 .50
68 Markus Naslund .30 .75
69 Mark Messier .30 .75
70 Rob Blake .20 .50
71 Sergei Samsonov .20 .50
72 Jose Theodore .30 .75
73 Eric Boguniecki .10 .25
74 Nikolai Khabibulin .30 .75
75 Marco Sturm .10 .25
76 Patrick Lalime .20 .50
77 Jeremy Roenick .40 1.00
78 John Madden .10 .25
79 Steve Rucchin .10 .25
80 Jere Lehtinen .20 .50
81 Stu Barnes .10 .25
82 Roman Turek .20 .50
83 Curtis Joseph .30 .75
84 Evgeni Nabokov .20 .50
85 Daniel Alfredsson .20 .50
86 Brendan Morrison .20 .50
87 Roman Cechmanek .20 .50
88 Chris Osgood .20 .50
89 Tommy Salo .20 .50
90 Craig Conroy .10 .25
91 Zigmund Palffy .20 .50
92 Pavel Bure .30 .75
93 Brent Johnson .20 .50
94 Ed Belfour .30 .75
95 Shane Doan .10 .25
96 David Legwand .20 .50
97 Sergei Fedorov .40 1.00
98 Jason Arnott .10 .25
99 Keith Primeau .10 .25
100 Martin St. Louis .20 .50
101 Teemu Selanne .30 .75
102 Patrik Elias .20 .50
103 Ray Whitney .10 .25
104 Brendan Shanahan .30 .75
105 Taylor Pyatt .10 .25
106 Niklas Hagman .10 .25
107 Henrik Tallinder .10 .25
108 Rostislav Klesla .10 .25
109 David Aebischer .20 .50
110 Marcel Hossa .30 .75
111 Pavel Brendl .10 .25
112 Ossi Vaananen .10 .25
113 Erik Cole .10 .25
114 Marian Gaborik .60 1.50
115 Alexander Svitov RC .40 1.00
116 Stanislav Chistov RC .40 1.00
117 Jordan Leopold RC .40 1.00
118 Ryan Miller RC 2.50 6.00
119 Kurt Sauer RC .40 1.00
120 Jonathan Cheechoo .10 .25
121 Radovan Somik RC .40 1.00
122 Anton Volchenkov RC .40 1.00
123 Pavel Datsyuk .30 .75
124 Alexander Frolov RC .75 2.00
125 Steve Ott RC .75 2.00
126 Jason Spezza RC 2.50 6.00
127 Barret Jackman .20 .50
128 Steve Eminger RC .40 1.00
129 Pascal Dupuis .10 .25
130 Brian Sutherby .10 .25
131 Dan Blackburn .20 .50
132 Ron Hainsey RC .40 1.00
133 Jay Bouwmeester RC .75 2.00
134 Adam Hall RC .40 1.00
135 Mike Comrie .20 .50
136 Nick Schultz .10 .25
137 Henrik Zetterberg RC 2.50 6.00
138 Radim Vrbata .10 .25
139 Jaroslav Svoboda .10 .25
140 Tyler Arnason .20 .50
141 Dany Heatley .40 1.00
142 Ivan Huml .10 .25
143 Kristian Huselius .10 .25
144 Martin Gerber RC .60 1.50
145 Tom Koivisto RC .40 1.00
146 Mikael Tellqvist RC .40 1.00
147 Dennis Seidenberg RC .40 1.00
148 Mike Cammalleri RC .75 2.00
149 Niko Kapanen .10 .25
150 Shawn Thornton RC .40 1.00
151 Alexei Smirnov RC .40 1.00
152 Jamie Lundmark .10 .25
153 Shawn Horcoff .10 .25
154 Branko Radivojevic .10 .25
155 Rick Nash RC 2.50 6.00
156 Mattias Weinhandl .10 .25
157 Stephen Weiss .10 .25
158 Dmitri Bykov RC .40 1.00
159 Ales Hemsky RC 1.00 2.50
160 Chuck Kobasew RC .60 1.50
161 P-M Bouchard RC .60 1.50
162 Scottie Upshall RC .60 1.50
163 Patrick Sharp RC .40 1.00
164 Derrick Walser .10 .25
165 Ilya Kovalchuk .40 1.00
NNO Jerry Walsh .02 .10
Honorary Eqmt. Mgr.

2002-03 Bowman YoungStars Gold

Inserted at 1:11, this 165-card set paralleled the base ste but carried a gold "glitter" effect on the card fronts. Each card was serial-numbered out of 250 on the card back.

*STARS: 1.5X TO 4X BASE HI
*ROOKIES: .75X TO 2X
STATED ODDS 1:11
STATED PRINT RUN 250 SER.#'d SETS

2002-03 Bowman YoungStars Silver

Inserted one per non-memorabilia pack, this 165-card set paralleled the base set but carried a silver "glitter" effect on the card fronts.

*STARS: .5X TO1.25X BASIC CARD
*ROOKIES: .3X TO .75X
ONE PER PACK

2002-03 Bowman YoungStars Autographs

Inserted at 1:333, this 27-card set featured certified autographs of players who competed in the annual Topps YoungStars game.

STATED ODDS 1:333
STATED PRINT RUN 50 SER.#'d SETS
AF Alexander Frolov 25.00 60.00
AH Adam Hall 15.00 40.00
AS Alexander Svitov 15.00 40.00
AV Anton Volchenkov 15.00 40.00
BJ Barret Jackman 15.00 20.00
BR Branko Radivojevic 15.00 40.00
BS Brian Sutherby 15.00 40.00
DA David Aebischer 25.00 60.00
DS Dennis Seidenberg 15.00 40.00
HT Henrik Tallinder 15.00 40.00
JB Jay Bouwmeester 30.00 80.00
JL Jordan Leopold 15.00 40.00
MH Marcel Hossa 15.00 40.00
MW Mattias Weinhandl 15.00 40.00
NH Niklas Hagman 15.00 40.00
NK Niko Kapanen 15.00 40.00
NS Nick Schultz 15.00 40.00
OV Ossi Vaananen 15.00 40.00
PB Pavel Brendl 15.00 40.00
RK Rostislav Klesla 15.00 40.00
RM Ryan Miller 40.00 100.00
RN Rick Nash 40.00 100.00
SC Stanislav Chistov 15.00 40.00
SH Shawn Horcoff 15.00 40.00
SW Stephen Weiss 15.00 40.00
TA Tyler Arnason 20.00 50.00
TP Taylor Pyatt 15.00 40.00

2002-03 Bowman YoungStars Autograph Puck Redemptions

Inserted at 1:3262, this 28-card set entitled the bearer to an autographed puck of the featured player. Though the cards were not serial-numbered, it was announced that each player signed 10 pucks each.

STATED ODDS 1:3263
STATED PRINT RUN 10 SETS
NOT PRICED DUE TO SCARCITY
1 Rick Nash
2 Niko Kapanen
3 Shawn Horcoff
4 Marcel Hossa
5 Henrik Tallinder
6 Nick Schultz
7 Adam Hall
8 Brian Sutherby
9 Alexander Frolov
10 Alexander Svitov
11 Anton Volchenkov
12 Barrett Jackman
13 Branko Radivojevec
14 Brian Sutherby
15 David Aebischer
16 Dennis Seidenberg
17 Jay Bouwmeester
18 Jordan Leopold
19 Mattias Weinhandl
20 Ossi Vaananen
21 Niklas Hagman
22 Pavel Brendl
23 Rostislav Klesla
24 Ryan Miller
25 Stanislav Chistov
26 Stephen Weiss
27 Taylor Pyatt
28 Tyler Arnason

2002-03 Bowman YoungStars Jerseys

Inserted at 1:7, this 27-card set featured a swatch of player jersey worn during the annual Topps YoungStars game. All cards carried a "FFJ" prefix on the card back.

*MULT.COLOR SWATCH: .75X TO 1.5X HI
STATED ODDS 1:7
AF Alexander Frolov 4.00 10.00
AH Adam Hall 3.00 8.00
AS Alexander Svitov 3.00 8.00
AV Anton Volchenkov 3.00 8.00
BJ Barret Jackman 3.00 8.00
BR Branko Radivojevic 3.00 8.00
BS Brian Sutherby 3.00 8.00
DA David Aebischer 4.00 10.00
DS Dennis Seidenberg 3.00 8.00
HT Henrik Tallinder 3.00 8.00
JB Jay Bouwmeester 5.00 12.00
JL Jordan Leopold 3.00 8.00
MH Marcel Hossa 3.00 8.00
MW Mattias Weinhandl 3.00 8.00
NH Niklas Hagman 3.00 8.00
NK Niko Kapanen 3.00 8.00
NS Nick Schultz 3.00 8.00
OV Ossi Vaananen 3.00 8.00
PB Pavel Brendl 3.00 8.00
RK Rostislav Klesla 3.00 8.00
RM Ryan Miller 5.00 12.00
RN Rick Nash 8.00 20.00
SC Stanislav Chistov 3.00 8.00
SH Shawn Horcoff 3.00 8.00
SW Stephen Weiss 3.00 8.00
TA Tyler Arnason 3.00 8.00
TP Taylor Pyatt 3.00 8.00

2002-03 Bowman YoungStars Patches

Inserted at 1:333, this 27-card set paralleled the basic jersey set but the jersey swatch was replaced with a patch variation. All cards carried "FFP" prefix on the card back.

STATED ODDS 1:333
STATED PRINT RUN 50 SER.#'d SETS

2002-03 Bowman YoungStars Double Stuff

Inserted at 1:667, this 27-card set paralleled the basic jersey set but also included a piece of game-used stick. All cards carried a "FFDS" prefix on the card back.

STATED ODDS 1:667
STATED PRINT RUN 25 SER.#'d SETS

2002-03 Bowman YoungStars Triple Stuff

Inserted at 1:1203, this 27-card set paralleled the basic jersey set but also included a piece of game-used stick and a swatch of jersey patch. All cards carried a "FFTS" prefix on the card back and were serial-numbered out of 10. The cards are not priced due to scarcity.

STATED ODDS 1:1203
STATED PRINT RUN 10 SER.#'d SETS
NOT PRICED DUE TO SCARCITY

2002-03 Bowman YoungStars MVP Puck Relic

Inserted at 1:1340, this 1-card set featured a piece of puck used during the Topps YoungStars game during the 2003 NHL All-Star weekend. The card front pictured the game MVP, Brian Sutherby and Topps representative J.Peter Sawkins. Each card was serial-numbered out of 100.

STATED ODDS 1:1340
STATED PRINT RUN 100 SER.#'d SETS
1 Brian Sutherby 20.00 50.00

2002-03 Bowman YoungStars Rivals

Inserted at 1:139, this 13-card set featured game-worn jersey swatches of the two players pictured. All cards carry a "FFR" prefix on the card backs and were serial-numbered out of 250.

*MULT.COLOR SWATCH: .5X TO 1.25X HI
STATED ODDS 1:139
STATED PRINT RUN 250 SER.#'d SETS
AFAS Alexander Frolov / Alexander Svitov 8.00 20.00
AHMW Adam Hall / Mattias Weinhandl 8.00 20.00
BJDS Barret Jackman / Dennis Seidenberg 8.00 20.00
BRPB Branko Radivojevic / Pavel Brendl 8.00 20.00
DARM David Aebischer / Ryan Miller 10.00 25.00
JLTP Jordan Leopold / Taylor Pyatt 8.00 20.00
NKMH Niko Kapanen / Marcel Hossa 8.00 20.00
NSNH Nick Schultz / Niklas Hagman 8.00 20.00
OVHT Ossi Vaananen / Henrik Tallinder 8.00 20.00
RKAV Rostislav Klesla / Anton Volchenkov 8.00 20.00
RNJB R.Nash/J.Bouwmeester 10.00 25.00
SCSW Stanislav Chistov / Stephen Weiss 8.00 20.00
TABS Tyler Arnason / Brian Sutherby 8.00 20.00

2002-03 Bowman YoungStars Rivals Patches

Inserted at 1:3446, this 13-card set paralleled the basic Rivals set but each card carried two swatches of jersey patch on the card front. Each card was serial-numbered out of 10, and the cards are not priced due to scarcity.

STATED ODDS 1:3446
STATED PRINT RUN 10 SER.#'d SETS
NOT PRICED DUE TO SCARCITY

2002-03 Bowman YoungStars Sticks

Inserted at 1:167, this 27-card set featured pieces of game-used sticks from the annual Topps YoungStars game. Each card carried a "FFS" prefix on the card back.

STATED ODDS 1:167
AF Alexander Frolov 12.50 30.00
AH Adam Hall 8.00 20.00
AS Alexander Svitov 8.00 20.00
AV Anton Volchenkov 8.00 20.00
BJ Barret Jackman 8.00 20.00
BR Branko Radivojevic 8.00 20.00
BS Brian Sutherby 8.00 20.00
DA David Aebischer 15.00 40.00
DS Dennis Seidenberg 8.00 20.00
HI Henrik Tallinder 8.00 20.00
JB Jay Bouwmeester 12.50 30.00
JL Jordan Leopold 10.00 25.00
MH Marcel Hossa 8.00 20.00
MW Mattias Weinhandl 8.00 20.00
NH Niklas Hagman 8.00 20.00
NK Niko Kapanen 8.00 20.00
NS Nick Schultz 8.00 20.00
OV Ossi Vaananen 8.00 20.00
PB Pavel Brendl 8.00 20.00
RK Rostislav Klesla 8.00 20.00
RM Ryan Miller 15.00 40.00
RN Rick Nash 25.00 60.00
SC Stanislav Chistov 10.00 25.00
SH Shawn Horcoff 8.00 20.00
SW Stephen Weiss 8.00 20.00
TA Tyler Arnason 8.00 20.00
TP Taylor Pyatt 8.00 20.00

2003-04 Bowman

2003-04 Bowman/Bowman Chrome was packaged as one product consisting of two distinct brands.

COMP.SET w/o SP's (110) 20.00 40.00
1 Rick Nash .30 .75
2 Brian Leetch .20 .50
3 Pasi Nurminen .20 .50
4 Vincent Lecavalier .25 .60
5 Nicklas Lidstrom .25 .60
6 Barret Jackman .20 .50
7 Stanislav Chistov .12 .30
8 Patrick Marleau .20 .50
9 Paul Kariya .25 .60
10 Joe Thornton .40 1.00
11 Daniel Alfredsson .20 .50
12 Bill Guerin .20 .50
13 Tyler Arnason .20 .50
14 Dwayne Roloson .20 .50
15 Dany Heatley .30 .75
16 Brett Hull .30 .75
17 Ilya Kovalchuk .30 .75
18 Marian Hossa .25 .60
19 Joe Sakic .50 1.25
20 Henrik Zetterberg .25 .60
21 Peter Forsberg .60 1.50
22 Ales Kotalik .12 .30
23 Jamie Lundmark .12 .30
24 Brian Sutherby .12 .30
25 Patrik Elias .20 .50
26 Tomas Vokoun .20 .50
27 Jeremy Roenick .25 .60
28 Alexander Svitov .12 .30
29 Josef Vasicek .12 .30
30 Martin Brodeur .60 1.50
31 Chuck Kobasew .12 .30
32 Kyle Calder .12 .30
33 Daymond Langkow .20 .50
34 Marc Denis .20 .50
35 Sergei Samsonov .20 .50
36 Chris Pronger .20 .50
37 Sebastien Caron .20 .50
38 Markus Naslund .25 .60
39 Dominik Hasek .50 1.25
40 Alex Kovalev .20 .50
41 Roman Turek .20 .50
42 Petr Sykora .20 .50
43 Niko Kapanen .12 .30
44 Todd Bertuzzi .25 .60
45 Aleksey Morozov .12 .30
46 Ed Belfour .25 .60
47 David Aebischer .20 .50
48 Mike Johnson .12 .30
49 Jose Theodore .30 .75
50 Marian Gaborik .50 1.25
51 Evgeni Nabokov .20 .50
52 Eric Brewer .12 .30
53 Chris Osgood .20 .50
54 Sergei Gonchar .12 .30
55 Michael Rupp .12 .30
56 Olaf Kolzig .20 .50
57 Jan Bulis .12 .30
58 Dan Cloutier .20 .50
59 Nik Antropov .12 .30
60 Roberto Luongo .30 .75
61 Ales Hemsky .20 .50
62 Robert Esche .20 .50
63 Adam Hall .12 .30
64 Chris Drury .20 .50
65 Alyn McCauley .12 .30
66 Mario Lemieux .75 2.00
67 Pierre-Marc Bouchard .20 .50
68 Jaromir Jagr .40 1.00
69 Alexei Yashin .12 .30
70 Patrick Lalime .20 .50
71 Miroslav Satan .20 .50
72 Michael Peca .12 .30
73 Ziggy Palffy .20 .50
74 Jason Spezza .25 .60
75 Jay Bouwmeester .12 .30
76 Tommy Salo .20 .50
77 Simon Gagne .25 .60
78 Nick Schultz .12 .30
79 Scott Stevens .20 .50
80 Jarome Iginla .30 .75
81 Roman Cechmanek .20 .50
82 Alexander Mogilny .20 .50
83 Ron Francis .20 .50
84 Mike Dunham .20 .50
85 Glen Murray .12 .30
86 Rick DiPietro .20 .50
87 David Legwand .20 .50
88 Nikolai Khabibulin .25 .60
89 Mike Comrie .20 .50
90 Marty Turco .20 .50
91 Sergei Fedorov .30 .75
92 Brian Boucher .20 .50
93 Kristian Huselius .12 .30
94 Saku Koivu .25 .60
95 Justin Papineau .12 .30
96 Martin Biron .20 .50
97 Derian Hatcher .12 .30
98 Martin St. Louis .20 .50
99 Mike Modano .40 1.00
100 Jean-Sebastien Giguere .20 .50
101 Pavol Demitra .12 .30
102 Olli Jokinen .20 .50
103 Kevin Weekes .20 .50
104 Steve Shields .20 .50
105 Mats Sundin .25 .60
106 Artem Chubarov .12 .30
107 Alexander Frolov .12 .30
108 Jocelyn Thibault .20 .50
109 Martin Havlat .20 .50
110 Milan Hejduk .25 .60
111 Nathan Horton RC 2.50 6.00
112 Joffrey Lupul RC 1.50 4.00
113 Tuomo Ruutu RC 1.50 4.00
114 Jiri Hudler RC 1.50 4.00
115 Marek Svatos RC 4.00 10.00
116 Milan Michalek RC 1.25 3.00
117 Maxim Kondratiev RC 1.25 3.00
118 Dan Hamhuis RC 1.25 3.00
119 Boyd Gordon RC 1.25 3.00
120 Eric Staal RC 8.00 20.00
121 Dan Fritsche RC 1.25 3.00
122 Matthew Spiller RC 1.25 3.00
123 Ryan Malone RC 1.50 4.00
124 Cody McCormick RC 1.25 3.00
125 Tom Preissing RC 1.25 3.00
126 Dominic Moore RC 1.25 3.00
127 Matthew Lombardi RC 1.25 3.00
128 Chris Higgins RC 2.00 5.00
129 Pavel Vorobiev RC 1.25 3.00
130 Wade Brookbank RC 1.25 3.00
131 Tim Gleason RC 1.25 3.00
132 Matt Murley RC 1.25 3.00
133 Andrew Peters RC 1.25 3.00
134 Gregory Campbell RC 1.25 3.00
135 John-Michael Liles RC 1.25 3.00
136 Sergei Zinovjev RC 1.25 3.00
137 Alexander Semin RC 2.50 6.00
138 Lasse Kukkonen RC 1.25 3.00
139 Marek Zidlicky RC 1.25 3.00
140 Tony Salmelainen RC 1.25 3.00
141 Travis Moen RC 1.25 3.00
142 Nikolai Zherdev RC 2.00 5.00
143 Paul Martin RC 1.25 3.00
144 Peter Sarno RC 1.25 3.00
145 David Hale RC 1.25 3.00
146 Dustin Brown RC 1.25 3.00
147 Matt Stajan AU RC 10.00 25.00
148 Peter Sejna AU RC 6.00 15.00
149 S.Bergenheim AU RC 6.00 15.00
150 Antti Miettinen AU RC 6.00 15.00
151 Patrice Bergeron AU RC 20.00 50.00
152 Marc-Andre Fleury AU RC 20.00 50.00
153 Antoine Vermette AU RC 6.00 15.00
154 Jordin Tootoo AU RC 10.00 25.00
155 Rick Mrozik AU RC 6.00 15.00
156 Joni Pitkanen AU RC 10.00 25.00

2003-04 Bowman Gold

*STARS: 2.5X TO 6X BASE HI
*ROOKIES 111-146: .2X TO .5X
*ROOKIES 147-156: .08X TO .2X
ONE PER PACK

2003-04 Bowman Future Fabrics

*MULT.COLOR SWATCH: .75X TO 1.5X
STATED ODDS 1:178
FFMW Mattias Weinhandl 3.00 8.00
FFJL Jordan Leopold 3.00 8.00
FFRM Ryan Miller 8.00 20.00
FFNH Niklas Hagman 3.00 8.00
FFAS Alexander Svitov 3.00 8.00
FFKH Kristian Huselius 3.00 8.00
FFNK Niko Kapanen 3.00 8.00
FFAH Adam Hall 3.00 8.00
FFSHO Shawn Horcoff 3.00 8.00
FFJB Jay Bouwmeester 3.00 8.00
FFDB Dan Blackburn 4.00 10.00
FFBS Brian Sutherby 3.00 8.00
FFJS Jason Spezza 8.00 20.00
FFSH Scott Hartnell 3.00 8.00
FFJLU Jamie Lundmark 3.00 8.00
FFDA David Aebischer 5.00 12.00
FFTA Tyler Arnason 3.00 8.00
FFAF Alexander Frolov 5.00 12.00
FFBJ Barret Jackman 3.00 8.00
FFSC Stanislav Chistov 3.00 8.00

2003-04 Bowman Future Fabric Patches

STATED ODDS 1:437
PRINT RUN 20 SER.#'d SETS
NOT PRICED DUE TO SCRACITY

2003-04 Bowman Future Rivals

*MULT.COLOR SWATCH .75X TO 1.5X
STATED ODDS 1:187
AK T.Arnason/N.Kapanen 4.00 10.00
AT D.Aebischer/M.Turco 8.00 20.00
CH S.Chistov/M.Hejduk 4.00 10.00
CI M.Comrie/J.Iginla 8.00 20.00
GH M.Gaborik/D.Heatley 12.00 30.00
HD M.Hejduk/P.Datsyuk 10.00 25.00
HG K.Huselius/S.Gagne 4.00 10.00
HH S.Horcoff/A.Hall 4.00 10.00
JF B.Jackman/A.Frolov 4.00 10.00
KD N.Kapanen/P.Datsyuk 6.00 15.00
LK V. Lecavalier/I.Kovalchuk 10.00 25.00
LT P.Lalime/J.Theodore 6.00 15.00
ML R.Miller/R.Luongo 10.00 25.00
MM P.Marleau/B.Morrison 6.00 15.00
NC R.Nash/S.Chistov 10.00 25.00
NG R.Nash/M.Gaborik 12.00 30.00
RS B.Richards/B.Sutherby 6.00 15.00
SH J.Spezza/N.Hagman 8.00 20.00
WL M. Weinhandl/J.Lundmark 4.00 10.00

2003-04 Bowman Future Rivals Patches

STATED ODDS 1:450
PRINT RUN 20 SER.#'d SETS
NOT PRICED DUE TO SCARCITY

2003-04 Bowman Goal to Goal

This 9-card set featured swatches of game-worn jerseys of both players featured along with a piece of all-star goal net.

STATED ODDS 1:299
AY D.Alfredsson/A.Yashin 12.00 30.00
GC M.Gaborik/S.Chistov 15.00 40.00
HG D.Heatley/B.Guerin 12.00 30.00
JH J.Jagr/M.Hejduk 20.00 50.00
KN N.Kapanen/R.Nash 15.00 40.00
MN M.Modano/M.Naslund 15.00 40.00
SG J.Spezza/S.Gagne 15.00 40.00
SI M.Satan/J.Iginla 12.00 30.00
TK J.Thornton/I.Kovalchuk 25.00 60.00

2003-04 Bowman Premier Performance

*MULT.COLOR SWATCH: .75X TO 1.5X
STATED ODDS 1:28
PPMS Marek Svatos 10.00 25.00
PPPS Peter Sejna 2.50 6.00
PPDH Dan Hamhuis 2.50 6.00
PPJL Joffrey Lupul 3.00 8.00
PPAV Antoine Vermette 2.50 6.00
PPSB Sean Bergenheim 2.50 6.00
PPAM Antti Miettinen 2.50 6.00
PPJP Joni Pitkanen 2.50 6.00
PPNH Nathan Horton 4.00 10.00
PPMSTO Matt Stajan 4.00 10.00

2003-04 Bowman Premier Performance Patches

*PATCHES: .75X TO 2X JSY HI
PRINT RUN 50 SER.#'d SETS

2003-04 Bowman Signs of the Future

STATED ODDS 1:81
SOFES Eric Staal 8.00 20.00
SOFRN Rick Nash 10.00 25.00
SOFMAF Marc-Andre Fleury 15.00 40.00
SOFMS Matt Stajan 8.00 20.00
SOFMZ Miroslav Zalesak 4.00 10.00
SOFPMB Pierre-Marc Bouchard 5.00 12.00
SOFAM Antti Miettinen 4.00 10.00
SOFPS Peter Sejna 4.00 10.00
SOFAV Antoine Vermette 4.00 10.00

2003-04 Bowman Chrome

2003-04 Bowman/Bowman Chrome was packaged as one product consisting of two distinct brands.

COMP.SET w/o SP's (110) 30.00 60.00
RC AUTO PRINT RUN 250 SER.#'d SETS
1 Rick Nash .50 1.25
2 Brian Leetch .30 .75
3 Pasi Nurminen .30 .75
4 Vincent Lecavalier .40 1.00
5 Nicklas Lidstrom .40 1.00
6 Barret Jackman .30 .75
7 Stanislav Chistov .20 .50
8 Patrick Marleau .30 .75
9 Paul Kariya .40 1.00
10 Joe Thornton .60 1.50
11 Daniel Alfredsson .30 .75
12 Bill Guerin .30 .75
13 Tyler Arnason .30 .75
14 Dwayne Roloson .30 .75
15 Dany Heatley .50 1.25
16 Brett Hull .50 1.25
17 Ilya Kovalchuk .50 1.25
18 Marian Hossa .40 1.00
19 Joe Sakic .75 2.00
20 Henrik Zetterberg .40 1.00
21 Peter Forsberg 1.00 2.50
22 Ales Kotalik .20 .50
23 Jamie Lundmark .20 .50
24 Brian Sutherby .20 .50
25 Patrik Elias .30 .75
26 Tomas Vokoun .30 .75
27 Jeremy Roenick .50 1.25
28 Alexander Svitov .20 .50
29 Josef Vasicek .20 .50
30 Martin Brodeur 1.00 2.50
31 Chuck Kobasew .20 .50
32 Kyle Calder .20 .50
33 Daymond Langkow .30 .75
34 Marc Denis .30 .75
35 Sergei Samsonov .30 .75
36 Chris Pronger .30 .75
37 Sebastien Caron .30 .75
38 Markus Naslund .40 1.00
39 Dominik Hasek .75 2.00
40 Alex Kovalev .30 .75
41 Roman Turek .30 .75
42 Petr Sykora .30 .75
43 Niko Kapanen .20 .50
44 Todd Bertuzzi .40 1.00
45 Aleksey Morozov .20 .50
46 Ed Belfour .40 1.00
47 David Aebischer .30 .75
48 Mike Johnson .20 .50
49 Jose Theodore .50 1.25
50 Marian Gaborik .75 2.00
51 Evgeni Nabokov .30 .75
52 Eric Brewer .20 .50
53 Chris Osgood .30 .75
54 Sergei Gonchar .20 .50
55 Michael Rupp .20 .50
56 Olaf Kolzig .30 .75
57 Jan Bulis .20 .50
58 Dan Cloutier .30 .75
59 Nik Antropov .20 .50
60 Roberto Luongo .50 1.25
61 Ales Hemsky .30 .75
62 Robert Esche .30 .75
63 Adam Hall .20 .50
64 Chris Drury .30 .75
65 Alyn McCauley .20 .50
66 Mario Lemieux 1.25 3.00
67 Pierre-Marc Bouchard .30 .75
68 Jaromir Jagr .60 1.50
69 Alexei Yashin .20 .50
70 Patrick Lalime .30 .75
71 Miroslav Satan .30 .75
72 Michael Peca .20 .50
73 Ziggy Palffy .30 .75
74 Jason Spezza .40 1.00
75 Jay Bouwmeester .20 .50
76 Tommy Salo .30 .75
77 Simon Gagne .40 1.00
78 Nick Schultz .20 .50
79 Scott Stevens .30 .75
80 Jarome Iginla .50 1.25
81 Roman Cechmanek .30 .75
82 Alexander Mogilny .30 .75
83 Ron Francis .30 .75
84 Mike Dunham .30 .75
85 Glen Murray .20 .50
86 Rick DiPietro .30 .75
87 David Legwand .30 .75
88 Nikolai Khabibulin .40 1.00
89 Mike Comrie .30 .75
90 Marty Turco .30 .75
91 Sergei Fedorov .50 1.25
92 Brian Boucher .30 .75
93 Kristian Huselius .20 .50
94 Saku Koivu .40 1.00
95 Justin Papineau .20 .50
96 Martin Biron .30 .75
97 Derian Hatcher .20 .50
98 Martin St. Louis .30 .75
99 Mike Modano .60 1.50
100 Jean-Sebastien Giguere .30 .75
101 Pavol Demitra .20 .50
102 Olli Jokinen .30 .75
103 Kevin Weekes .30 .75
104 Steve Shields .30 .75
105 Mats Sundin .40 1.00
106 Artem Chubarov .20 .50
107 Alexander Frolov .20 .50
108 Jocelyn Thibault .30 .75
109 Martin Havlat .30 .75
110 Milan Hejduk .40 1.00
111 Nathan Horton RC 3.00 8.00
112 Joffrey Lupul RC 2.00 5.00
113 Tuomo Ruutu RC 2.00 5.00
114 Jiri Hudler RC 2.00 5.00
115 Marek Svatos RC 3.00 8.00
116 Milan Michalek RC 1.50 4.00
117 Maxim Kondratiev RC 1.50 4.00
118 Dan Hamhuis RC 1.50 4.00
119 Boyd Gordon RC 1.50 4.00
120 Eric Staal RC 10.00 25.00
121 Dan Fritsche RC 1.50 4.00
122 Matthew Spiller RC 1.50 4.00
123 Ryan Malone RC 1.50 4.00
124 Cody McCormick RC 1.50 4.00
125 Tom Preissing RC 1.50 4.00
126 Dominic Moore RC 1.50 4.00
127 Matthew Lombardi RC 2.00 5.00
128 Chris Higgins RC 3.00 8.00
129 Pavel Vorobiev RC 1.50 4.00
130 Wade Brookbank RC 1.50 4.00
131 Tim Gleason RC 1.50 4.00
132 Matt Murley RC 1.50 4.00
133 Andrew Peters RC 1.50 4.00
134 Gregory Campbell RC 1.50 4.00
135 John-Michael Liles RC 1.50 4.00
136 Sergei Zinovjev RC 1.50 4.00
137 Alexander Semin RC 3.00 8.00
138 Lasse Kukkonen RC 1.50 4.00
139 Marek Zidlicky RC 1.50 4.00
140 Tony Salmelainen RC 1.50 4.00
141 Travis Moen RC 1.50 4.00
142 Nikolai Zherdev RC 2.00 5.00
143 Paul Martin RC 1.50 4.00
144 Peter Sarno RC 1.50 4.00
145 David Hale RC 1.50 4.00
146 Dustin Brown RC 1.50 4.00
147 Matt Stajan AU RC 15.00 40.00
148 Peter Sejna AU RC 8.00 20.00
149 Sean Bergenheim AU RC 8.00 20.00
150 Antti Miettinen AU RC 8.00 20.00
151 Patrice Bergeron AU RC 30.00 80.00
152 Marc-Andre Fleury AU RC 40.00 100.00
153 Antoine Vermette AU RC 8.00 20.00
154 Jordin Tootoo AU RC 15.00 40.00
155 Rick Mrozik AU RC 8.00 20.00
156 Joni Pitkanen AU RC 10.00 25.00

2003-04 Bowman Chrome Refractors

*STARS: 3X TO 8X BASE HI
*ROOKIES 111-146: .6X TO 1.5X
1-146 PRINT RUN 300 SER.#'d SETS
*ROOKIE AU: .5X TO 1.25X
ROOKIE AU PRINT RUN 50 SER.#'d SETS
152 Marc-Andre Fleury 50.00 120.00

2003-04 Bowman Chrome Gold Refractors

*STARS: 6X TO 15X
*ROOKIES 111-146: 1.25X TO 3X

2003-04 Bowman Chrome Xfractors

*STARS: 4X TO 10X BASE HI
*ROOKIES 111-146: .75X TO 2X
CARDS 1-146 PRINT RUN 150 SER.#'d SETS
*ROOKIES AU: .6X TO 1.5X
ROOKIE AU PRINT RUN 25 SER.#'d SETS
152 Marc-Andre Fleury AU 75.00 200.00

1938-39 Bruins Garden Magazine Supplement

These large (8 X 10") photos were printed on very thin, sepia-toned stock and inserted in game programs issued at the Boston Gardens. Any additional information would be appreciated.

COMPLETE SET (9) 350.00 700.00
1 Red Beattie 20.00 40.00
2 Walter Galbraith 20.00 40.00
3 Lionel Hitchman 40.00 80.00
4 Joseph Lamb 20.00 40.00
5 Harry Oliver 20.00 40.00
6 Art Ross 75.00 150.00
7 Eddie Shore 125.00 250.00
8 Nels Stewart 40.00 80.00
9 Tiny Thompson 50.00 100.00

1955-56 Bruins Photos

These black and white photos measure approximately 6" x 8" and were distributed in an envelope bearing the Bruins logo.

COMPLETE SET (17) 100.00 200.00
1 Bob Armstrong 5.00 10.00
2 Marcel Bonin 5.00 10.00
3 Leo Boivin 7.50 15.00
4 Real Chevrefils 5.00 10.00
5 Fern Flaman 7.50 15.00
6 Cal Gardner 2.50 5.00
7 Lionel Heinrich 2.50 5.00
8 Leo Labine 7.50 15.00
9 Hal Laycoe 5.00 10.00
10 Fleming Mackell 5.00 10.00
11 Don McKenney 5.00 10.00
12 Doug Mohns 7.50 15.00
13 Bill Quackenbush 7.50 15.00
14 Johnny Peirson 5.00 10.00
15 Terry Sawchuk 25.00 50.00
16 Vic Stasiuk 5.00 10.00
17 Jerry Toppazzini 5.00 10.00
NNO Envelope 10.00 20.00

1957-58 Bruins Photos

This 14-card set measures approximately 6 5/8" by 8 1/8".

COMPLETE SET (20) 100.00 200.00
1 Bob Armstrong 5.00 10.00
2 Jack Bionda 2.50 5.00
3 Leo Boivin 5.00 10.00
4 Johnny Bucyk 25.00 50.00
5 Real Chevrefils 4.00 8.00
6 Fern Flaman 6.00 12.00
7 Jean-Guy Gendron 5.00 10.00
8 Larry Hillman 5.00 10.00
9 Bronco Horvath 6.00 12.00
10 Norm Johnson 6.00 12.00
11 Leo Labine 5.00 10.00
12 Fleming Mackell 4.00 8.00
13 Don McKenney 4.00 8.00
14 Doug Mohns 6.00 12.00
15 Jim Morrison 2.50 5.00
16 Johnny Peirson 2.50 5.00
17 Larry Regan 2.50 5.00
18 Milt Schmidt CO 10.00 20.00
19 Vic Stasiuk 6.00 12.00
20 Jerry Toppazzini 2.50 5.00

1958-59 Bruins Photos

These 6X8 photos were issued by the team.

COMPLETE SET (15) 75.00 150.00
1 Bob Armstrong 5.00 10.00
2 Johnny Bucyk 15.00 30.00
3 Real Chevrefils 5.00 10.00
4 Fern Flaman 6.00 12.00
5 Jean-Guy Gendron 5.00 10.00
6 Larry Hillman 5.00 10.00
7 Leo Labine 5.00 10.00
8 Fleming MacKell 5.00 10.00
9 Don McKenney 5.00 10.00
10 Jim Morrison 5.00 10.00
11 Larry Regan 5.00 10.00
12 Dutch Reibel 5.00 10.00
13 Don Simmons 10.00 20.00
14 Vic Stasiuk 5.00 10.00
15 Jerry Toppazzini 5.00 10.00

1970-71 Bruins Postcards

Cards are standard postcard size and were issued in a binder with perforations.

COMPLETE SET (21) 75.00 150.00
1 Team Photo 2.50 5.00
2 Ed Johnston 2.50 5.00
3 Gerry Cheevers 7.50 15.00
4 Wayne Cashman 2.50 5.00
5 Garnet Bailey 5.00 10.00
6 Don Marcotte 1.50 3.00
7 John Bucyk 5.00 10.00
8 Wayne Carleton 1.50 3.00
9 Reggie Leach 4.00 8.00
10 Ken Hodge 2.50 5.00
11 Ed Westfall 2.00 4.00
12 John McKenzie 2.00 4.00
13 Phil Esposito 10.00 20.00
14 Fred Stanfield 1.50 3.00
15 Derek Sanderson 5.00 10.00
16 Bobby Orr 25.00 50.00
17 Dallas Smith 2.00 4.00
18 Rick Smith 1.50 3.00
19 Ted Green 2.00 4.00
20 Don Awrey 1.50 3.00
21 Tom Johnson CO 2.00 4.00

1970-71 Bruins Team Issue

This set of 18 team-issue photos commemorates the Boston Bruins as 1970 Stanley Cup Champions. The set was issued in two different photo packs of nine photos each. The photos measure approximately 6" by 8".

COMPLETE SET (18) 50.00 100.00
1 Garnet Bailey 5.00 10.00
2 Johnny Bucyk 5.00 10.00
3 Gary Doak 2.00 4.00
4 Phil Esposito 10.00 20.00
5 Ed Johnston 2.50 5.00
6 Don Marcotte 1.50 3.00
7 Derek Sanderson 5.00 10.00
8 Dallas Smith 2.00 4.00
9 Ed Westfall 2.00 4.00
10 Don Awrey 1.50 3.00
11 Wayne Carleton 1.50 3.00
12 Wayne Cashman 2.50 5.00
13 Gerry Cheevers 7.50 15.00
14 Ken Hodge 2.50 5.00
15 John McKenzie 2.00 4.00
16 Bobby Orr 25.00 50.00
17 Rick Smith 1.50 3.00
18 Fred Stanfield 1.50 3.00

1971-72 Bruins Postcards

Originally issued in booklet form, these 20 photo cards measure 3 1/2" by 5 1/2". The cards have perforated tops that allow them to be detached from the yellow booklet, which bears the Bruins logo and crossed hockey sticks on its front.

COMPLETE SET (20) 50.00 100.00
1 Ed Johnston 2.00 4.00
2 Bobby Orr 20.00 40.00
3 Teddy Green 1.50 3.00
4 Phil Esposito 10.00 20.00
5 Ken Hodge 2.00 4.00
6 John Bucyk 4.00 8.00
7 Rick Smith 1.00 2.00
8 Mike Walton 1.50 3.00
9 Wayne Cashman 2.00 4.00
10 Ace Bailey 5.00 10.00
11 Derek Sanderson 4.00 8.00
12 Fred Stanfield 1.00 2.00
13 Ed Westfall 1.50 3.00
14 John McKenzie 1.50 3.00
15 Dallas Smith 1.00 2.00
16 Don Marcotte 1.00 2.00
17 Garry Peters 1.00 2.00
18 Don Awrey 1.00 2.00
19 Reggie Leach 2.00 4.00
20 Gerry Cheevers 5.00 10.00

1983-84 Bruins Team Issue

This 17-card set measures approximately 3 1/8" by 4 1/8".

COMPLETE SET (17) 10.00 25.00
1 Ray Bourque 4.00 10.00
2 Bruce Crowder .40 1.00
3 Keith Crowder .60 1.50
4 Luc Dufour .40 1.00
5 Tom Fergus .40 1.00
6 Randy Hillier .40 1.00
7 Steve Kasper .60 1.50
8 Gord Kluzak .60 1.50
9 Mike Krushelnycki .40 1.00
10 Peter McNab .60 1.50
11 Rick Middleton 1.25 3.00
12 Mike Milbury .60 1.50
13 Mike O'Connell .60 1.50
14 Terry O'Reilly .75 2.00
15 Brad Palmer .40 1.00
16 Barry Pederson .60 1.50
17 Pete Peeters .75 2.00

1984-85 Bruins Postcards

This set features 20 postcard-size issues of the Bruins. It is believed they were issued as giveaways at player signing appearances.

COMPLETE SET (20) 12.00 30.00
1 Ray Bourque 3.00 8.00
2 Lyndon Byers 1.25 3.00
3 Geoff Courtnall .75 2.00
4 Keith Crowder .60 1.50
5 Tom Fergus .40 1.00
6 Mike Gillis .40 1.00
7 Steve Kasper .60 1.50
8 Doug Keans .60 1.50
9 Gord Kluzak .60 1.50
10 Ken Linseman .60 1.50
11 Nevin Markwart .60 1.50
12 Rick Middleton 1.25 3.00
13 Mike Milbury .60 1.50
14 Mike O'Connell .40 1.00
15 Terry O'Reilly 1.25 3.00
16 Barry Pederson .60 1.50
17 Pete Peeters .75 2.00
18 Charlie Simmer .60 1.50
19 Lou Sleigher .60 1.50
20 Mats Thelin .40 1.00

1988-89 Bruins Sports Action

This 24-card set measures the standard size and was issued by Sports Action.

COMPLETE SET (24) 6.00 15.00
1 Ray Bourque

2 Randy Burridge .15 .40
3 Lyndon Byers .40 1.00
4 Keith Crowder .20 .50
5 Craig Janney .20 .50
6 Bob Joyce .08 .25
7 Steve Kasper .20 .50
8 Gord Kluzak .20 .50
9 Reed Larson .08 .25
10 Rejean Lemelin .30 .75
11 Ken Linseman .20 .50
12 Tom McCarthy .08 .25
13 Rick Middleton .60 1.50
14 Jay Miller .40 1.00
15 Andy Moog .60 1.50
16 Cam Neely 1.00 2.50
17 Terry O'Reilly CO .20 .50
18 Allen Pederson .08 .25
19 Willi Plett .08 .25
20 Bob Sweeney .08 .25
21 Michael Thelven .08 .25
22 Glen Wesley .20 .50
23 Bob Joyce .20 .50
Craig Janney
24 Dynamic Duo .75 2.00
Ray Bourque
Cam Neely

1988-89 Bruins Postcards

This 20-postcard set of the Boston Bruins was produced by Sports Action Marketing.

COMPLETE SET (20) 8.00 20.00
1 Ray Bourque 1.50 4.00
2 Andy Brickley .20 .50
3 John Carter .20 .50
4 Garry Galley .30 .75
5 Craig Janney .60 1.50
6 Greg Johnston .20 .50
7 Bob Joyce .20 .50
8 Steve Kasper .30 .75
9 Gord Kluzak .30 .75
10 Rejean Lemelin .40 1.00
11 Ken Linseman .30 .75
12 Rick Middleton .60 1.50
13 Andy Moog 1.00 2.50
14 Cam Neely 1.50 4.00
15 Bill O'Dwyer .20 .50
16 Allen Pedersen .20 .50
17 Stephane Quintal .20 .50
18 Bob Sweeney .20 .50
19 Michael Thelven .20 .50
20 Glen Wesley .40 1.00

1989-90 Bruins Sports Action

This standard sized 24-card set was issued by Sports Action.

COMPLETE SET (24) 4.80 12.00
1 Ray Bourque .75 2.00
2 Andy Brickley .20 .50
3 Randy Burridge .20 .50
4 Lyndon Byers .20 .50
5 Bob Carpenter .20 .50
6 John Carter .20 .50
7 Rob Cimetta .20 .50
8 Garry Galley .30 .75
9 Bob Gould .20 .50
10 Greg Hawgood .20 .50
11 Craig Janney .30 .75
12 Bob Joyce .20 .50
13 Rejean Lemelin .30 .75
14 Ken Linseman .20 .50
15 Andy Moog .40 1.00
16 Nevin Markwart .20 .50
17 Cam Neely .60 1.50
18 Allen Pedersen .20 .50
19 Stephane Quintal .20 .50
20 Bob Sweeney .20 .50
21 Michael Thelven .20 .50
22 Glen Wesley .30 .75
23 Bruins Top 10 Scorers .40 1.00
24 Stanley Cup Champions .40 1.00

1989-90 Bruins Sports Action Update

This 12-card standard-size set was issued by Sports Action.

COMPLETE SET (12) 3.00 8.00
1 Ray Bourque .75 2.00
2 Dave Christian .30 .75
3 Peter Douris .20 .50
4 Gord Kluzak .30 .75
5 Brian Lawton .20 .50
6 Mike Millar .20 .50
7 Dave Poulin .20 .50
8 Brian Propp .30 .75
9 Don Sweeney .30 .75
10 Graeme Townshend .20 .50
11 Jim Wiemer .20 .50
12 Bruins Leaders .75 2.00
Ray Bourque
Rejean Lemelin
Cam Neely

1990-91 Bruins Sports Action

The Markwart and Quintal cards were reportedly only issued in the first print run of 400 24-card sets. In the second and larger print run, these cards were replaced by Byers and Hodge. Consequently, the Markwart and Quintal cards are more difficult to find than the Byers and Hodge cards.

COMPLETE SET (26) 8.00 20.00
1 Bob Beers .20 .50
2 Ray Bourque 1.25 3.00
3 Andy Brickley .20 .50
4 Randy Burridge .25 .60
5 John Byce .20 .50
6 Lyndon Byers .30 .75
7 Bob Carpenter .20 .50
8 John Carter .20 .50
9 Dave Christian .25 .60
10 Peter Douris .20 .50
11 Garry Galley .20 .50
12 Ken Hodge Jr. .20 .50
13 Craig Janney .30 .75
14 Rejean Lemelin .30 .75
15 Nevin Markwart SP 1.25 3.00
16 Andy Moog .60 1.50
17 Cam Neely .75 2.00
18 Chris Nilan .25 .60
19 Allen Pedersen .25 .60
20 Dave Poulin .25 .60
21 Stephane Quintal SP 1.25 3.00
22 Bob Sweeney .20 .50
23 Don Sweeney .25 .60
24 Wes Walz .20 .50
25 Glen Wesley .30 .75
26 Rejean Lemelin .40 1.00
Andy Moog

1991-92 Bruins Sports Action

This 24-card standard-size set was issued by Sports Action.

COMPLETE SET (24) 4.80 12.00
1 Brent Ashton .15 .40
2 Bob Beers .15 .40
3 Daniel Berthiaume .20 .50
4 Ray Bourque 1.00 2.50
5 Bob Carpenter .15 .40
6 Peter Douris .08 .25
7 Glen Featherstone .08 .25
8 Ken Hodge Jr. .08 .25
9 Jeff Lazaro .08 .25
10 Stephen Leach .15 .40
11 Andy Moog .40 1.00
12 Gord Murphy .08 .25
13 Cam Neely .75 2.00
14 Adam Oates .40 1.00
15 Dave Poulin .20 .50
16 David Reid .15 .40
17 Vladimir Ruzicka .15 .40
18 Bob Sweeney .15 .40
19 Don Sweeney .15 .40
20 Jim Vesey .08 .25
21 Glen Wesley .15 .40
22 Jim Wiemer .08 .25
23 Chris Winnes .08 .25
24 The Big Three .60 1.50
Andy Moog
Ray Bourque
Cam Neely

1991-92 Bruins Sports Action Legends

COMPLETE SET (36) 6.00 15.00
1 Bob Armstrong .08 .25
2 Leo Boivin .15 .40
3 Ray Bourque .75 2.00
4 Frank Brimsek .30 .75
5 Johnny Bucyk .40 1.00
6 Wayne Cashman .08 .25
7 Gerry Cheevers .40 1.00
8 Dit Clapper .30 .75
9 Bill Cowley .08 .25
10 Phil Esposito .50 1.25
11 Fernie Flaman .15 .40
12 Mel Hill .15 .40
Bill Cowley
Roy Conacher
13 Lionel Hitchman .15 .40
14 Fleming Mackell .08 .25
15 Don Marcotte .08 .25
16 Don McKenney .08 .25
17 Rick Middleton .20 .50
18 Doug Mohns .08 .25
19 Terry O'Reilly .15 .40
20 Bobby Orr 1.25 3.00
21 Brad Park .30 .75
22 John Peirson .08 .25
23 Bill Quackenbush .20 .50
24 Jean Ratelle .30 .75
25 Art Ross CO/GM .20 .50
26 Ed Sandford .08 .25
27 Terry Sawchuk .60 1.50
28 Milt Schmidt .40 1.00
29 Milt Schmidt .20 .50
Cooney Weiland
Bill Cowley
30 Eddie Shore .40 1.00
31 Harry Sinden CO/GM .20 .50
and President
32 Tiny Thompson .15 .40
33 Cooney Weiland .15 .40
34 Ed Westfall .08 .25
35 Bruins Defense .20 .50
1955-56
Bill Quackenbush
Fern Flaman
Terry Sawchuk
Bob Armstrong
Leo Boivin
36 The Kraut Line .30 .75
Milt Schmidt
Woody Dumart
Bobby Bauer

1992-93 Bruins Postcards

This set measures approximately 3 1/2" by 5 1/2".

COMPLETE SET (12) 4.00 10.00
1 Ray Bourque 1.25 3.00
2 Ted Donato .20 .50
3 Joe Juneau .30 .75
4 Dimitri Kvartalnov .20 .50
5 Stephen Leach .20 .50
6 Andy Moog .75 2.00
7 Adam Oates .75 2.00
8 Dave Poulin .30 .75
9 Gordie Roberts .20 .50
10 Vladimir Ruzicka .20 .50
11 Don Sweeney .30 .75
12 Glen Wesley .30 .75

1998 Bruins Alumni

Released for sale at the Fleet Center, this 35-card set features Boston Bruins from the past. The sets were sold for $18, and each set contained one autographed card.

COMPLETE SET (35) 8.00 20.00
1 Reggie Lemelin .20 .50
2 Harry Sinden .08 .25
3 Jim Craig .20 .50
4 Bobby Orr 2.00 5.00
5 Ferny Flaman .20 .50
6 Bob Beers .08 .25
7 Ken Hodge .20 .50
8 Cam Neely 1.25 3.00
9 John Bucyk .40 1.00
10 Jean Ratelle .20 .50
11 Bob Miller .02 .10
12 Ed Sandford .02 .10
13 Ken Linseman .20 .50
14 Woody Dumart .20 .50
15 Milt Schmidt .30 .75
16 Derek Sanderson .40 1.00
17 Fred Stanfield .08 .25
18 Garnet Bailey .75 2.00
19 John McKenzie .20 .50
20 Dallas Smith .08 .25
21 Don Marcotte .08 .25
22 Brad Park .30 .75
23 Matt Glennon .02 .10
24 Terry O'Reilly .40 1.00
25 Gary Doak .08 .25
26 Don Awrey .08 .25
27 Billy O'Dwyer .02 .10
28 Dave Hynes .02 .10
29 Tom Songin .02 .10
30 Gerry Cheevers .40 1.00
31 Don McKenney .08 .25
32 Frank Simonetti .02 .10
33 Bronco Horvath .08 .25
34 Doug Mohns .08 .25
35 Header Card .04 .01

1998 Bruins Alumni Autographs

One autographed card was inserted in each set of 1998 Boston Bruins Alumni. Since so many sets would need to be purchase to complete a set, it's quite possible that no complete sets exist. The autographs of Bobby Orr and Cam Neely have not yet been confirmed, and so prices are not listed (nor are they included in the complete set value). If you can confirm either of these cards, please write to hockeymag@beckett.com. The Ace Bailey card is believed to be his only certified autographed single. Bailey was killed in the 9/11 plane hijackings.

COMPLETE SET (35) 120.00 300.00
1 Reggie Lemelin 4.00 10.00
2 Harry Sinden 4.00 10.00
3 Jim Craig 6.00 15.00
4 Bobby Orr
5 Ferny Flaman 2.00 5.00
6 Bob Beers .75 2.00
7 Ken Hodge 3.00 8.00
8 Cam Neely
9 John Bucyk 10.00 25.00
10 Jean Ratelle 8.00 20.00
11 Bob Miller .40 1.00
12 Ed Sandford .40 1.00
13 Ken Linseman 2.00 5.00
14 Woody Dumart 15.00 40.00
15 Milt Schmidt 10.00 25.00
16 Derek Sanderson 15.00 40.00
17 Fred Stanfield 1.25 3.00
18 Garnet Bailey 15.00 40.00
19 John McKenzie 3.00 8.00
20 Dallas Smith 4.00 10.00
21 Don Marcotte 1.25 3.00
22 Brad Park 6.00 15.00
23 Matt Glennon .40 1.00
24 Terry O'Reilly 15.00 40.00
25 Gary Doak 1.25 3.00
26 Don Awrey 1.25 3.00
27 Billy O'Dwyer .40 1.00
28 Dave Hynes .40 1.00
29 Tom Songin .40 1.00
30 Gerry Cheevers 10.00 25.00
31 Don McKenney 1.25 3.00
32 Frank Simonetti .40 1.00
33 Bronco Horvath 4.00 10.00
34 Doug Mohns 2.00 5.00
35 Header Card .40 1.00

1999-00 Bruins Season Ticket Offer

This two card set was mailed to Bruins season ticket holders in an effort to bolster the renewal rate. The cards were perforated at the end of the offer. They are regular card stock and, because of the nature of distribution, are extremely rare in the hobby.

COMPLETE SET (2) 25.00 60.00
1 Joe Thornton 20.00 50.00
2 Sergei Samsonov 6.00 15.00

2002-03 Bruins Team Issue

These oversized (4X6) player photos feature action photos on the front and blank backs. They were distributed through the Bruins marketing department and were used mainly for autograph signings.

COMPLETE SET (8) 6.00 15.00
1 Blades MASCOT .20 .50
2 Nick Boynton .40 1.00
3 Hal Gill .40 1.00
4 Glen Murray .75 2.00
5 Brian Rolston .75 2.00
6 Sergei Samsonov 1.25 3.00
7 P.J. Stock 1.25 3.00
8 Joe Thornton 2.00 5.00

2003-04 Bruins Team Issue

These oversized,very thin cards were available only in singles form at team events or through by-mail requests. It's possible that the checklist not complete. Send additional info to hockeymag@beckett.com

COMPLETE SET (14) 8.00 20.00
1 Nick Boynton .40 1.00
2 Hal Gill .40 1.00
3 Mike Knuble .40 1.00
4 Martin Lapointe .60 1.50
5 Dan McGillis .40 1.00
6 Glen Murray .60 1.50
7 Sean O'Donnell .40 1.00
8 Felix Potvin .40 1.00
9 Andrew Raycroft 1.25 3.00
10 Sergei Samsonov 1.25 3.00
11 Mike Sullivan CO .10 .25
12 Joe Thornton 2.00 5.00
13 Blades MASCOT .10 .25
14 Team photo .40 1.00

2005-06 Bruins Boston Globe

Produced by Upper Deck, this set was distributed in two unperforated sheets with the purchase of a Sunday Boston Globe newspaper on consecutive weekends in late 2005.

COMPLETE SET (24) 8.00 20.00
1 Glen Murray .20 .50
2 Hannu Toivonen 1.00 2.50
3 Andrew Alberts .20 .50
4 Hal Gill .20 .50
5 Tom Fitzgerald .20 .50
6 Milan Jurcina .20 .50
7 Brad Boyes .30 .75
8 David Tanabe .20 .50
9 Wayne Primeau .20 .50
10 Brad Stuart .20 .50
11 Alexei Zhamnov .20 .50
12 Brian Leetch .75 2.00
13 Patrice Bergeron .75 2.00
14 Marco Sturm .20 .50
15 Nick Boynton .20 .50
16 Brad Isbister .20 .50
17 Sergei Samsonov .40 1.00
18 Pat Leahy .20 .50
19 Andrew Raycroft .40 1.00
20 Tim Thomas .75 2.00
21 Travis Green .20 .50
22 Josh Langfeld .20 .50
23 Dan LaCouture .20 .50
24 P.J. Axelsson .20 .50

1911-12 C55

The C55 Hockey set, probably issued during the 1911-12 season, contains 45 numbered cards. Being one of the early Canadian cigarette cards, the issuer of this set is unknown, although there is speculation that it may have been Imperial Tobacco. These small cards measure approximately 1 1/2" by 2 1/2". The line drawing, color portrait on the front of the card is framed by two hockey sticks. The number of the card appears on both the front and back as does the player's name. The players in the set were members of the NHA: Quebec Bulldogs, Ottawa Senators, Montreal Canadiens, Montreal Wanderers, and Renfrew Millionaires. This set is prized highly by collectors but is the easiest of the three early sets (C55, C56, or C57) to find. The complete set price includes either variety of the Small variation.

COMPLETE SET (45) 7500.00 15000.00
1 Paddy Moran 300.00 600.00
2 Joe Hall RC 250.00 500.00
3 Barney Holden 100.00 200.00
4 Joe Malone RC 500.00 1000.00
5 Ed Oatman RC 100.00 200.00
6 Tom Dunderdale 150.00 300.00
7 Ken Mallen RC 100.00 200.00
8 Jack MacDonald RC 100.00 200.00
9 Fred Lake 100.00 200.00
10 Albert Kerr RC 100.00 250.00
11 Marty Walsh 150.00 300.00
12 Hamby Shore RC 100.00 200.00
13 Alex Currie RC 100.00 200.00
14 Bruce Ridpath 150.00 300.00
15 Bruce Stuart 150.00 300.00
16 Percy Lesueur 150.00 300.00
17 Jack Darragh RC 200.00 400.00
18 Steve Vair RC 100.00 200.00
19 Don Smith RC 100.00 200.00
20 Cyclone Taylor 750.00 1500.00
21 Bert Lindsay RC 125.00 250.00
22 H.L. Gilmour RC 150.00 300.00
23 Bobby Rowe RC 100.00 200.00
24 Sprague Cleghorn RC 250.00 500.00
25 Odie Cleghorn RC 150.00 300.00
26 Skene Ronan RC 100.00 200.00
27A Walter Smaill RC 350.00 700.00
(Right hand on stick)
27B Walter Smaill RC 400.00 800.00
(Right hand on hip)
28 Ernest(Moose) Johnson 200.00 400.00
29 Jack Marshall 150.00 300.00
30 Harry Hyland 125.00 250.00
31 Art Ross 750.00 1500.00
32 Riley Hern 150.00 300.00
33 Gordon Roberts 200.00 400.00
34 Frank Glass 100.00 200.00
35 Ernest Russell 200.00 400.00
36 James Gardner RC 150.00 300.00
37 Art Bernier 100.00 200.00
38 Georges Vezina RC 3000.00 6000.00
39 Henri Dallaire RC 100.00 200.00
40 R.(Rocket) Power RC 150.00 300.00
41 Didier(Pit) Pitre 150.00 300.00
42 Newsy Lalonde 750.00 1500.00
43 Eugene Payan RC 100.00 200.00
44 George Poulin RC 100.00 200.00
45 Jack Laviolette 200.00 400.00

1910-11 C56

One of the first hockey sets to appear (circa 1910-11), this full-color set of unknown origin (although there is speculation that the issuer was Imperial Tobacco) features 36 cards. The card numbering appears in the upper left part of the front of the card. These small cards measure approximately 1 1/2" by 2 5/8". The player's name and affiliation appear at the bottom within the border. The backs feature the player's name and career affiliations below crossed hockey sticks, a puck and the words "Hockey Series."

COMPLETE SET (36) 5000.00 10000.00
1 Frank Patrick RC 300.00 600.00
2 Percy Lesueur RC 300.00 500.00
3 Gordon Roberts RC 150.00 300.00
4 Barney Holden RC 100.00 200.00
5 Frank Glass RC 100.00 200.00
6 Edgar Dey RC 100.00 200.00
7 Marty Walsh RC 150.00 300.00
8 Art Ross RC 500.00 1000.00
9 Angus Campbell RC 125.00 250.00
10 Harry Hyland RC 175.00 350.00
11 Herb Clark RC 75.00 150.00
12 Art Ross RC 500.00 1000.00
13 Ed Decary RC 75.00 150.00
14 Tom Dunderdale RC 200.00 400.00
15 Cyclone Taylor RC 500.00 1000.00
16 Joseph Cattarinich RC 100.00 200.00
17 Bruce Stuart RC 175.00 350.00
18 Nick Bawlf RC 75.00 150.00
19 Jim Jones RC 100.00 200.00
20 Ernest Russell RC 175.00 350.00
21 Jack Laviolette RC 125.00 250.00
22 Riley Hern RC 150.00 300.00
23 Didier Pitre RC 150.00 300.00
24 Skinner Poulin RC 75.00 150.00
25 Art Bernier RC 75.00 150.00
26 Lester Patrick RC 400.00 700.00
27 Fred Lake RC 75.00 150.00
28 Paddy Moran RC 300.00 600.00
29 C.Toms RC 75.00 150.00
30 Ernest Johnson RC 275.00 550.00
31 Horace Gaul RC 75.00 150.00
32 Harold McNamara RC 75.00 150.00
33 Jack Marshall RC 125.00 250.00
34 Bruce Ridpath RC 75.00 150.00
35 Jack Marshall RC 125.00 250.00
36 Newsy Lalonde RC 500.00 1000.00

1912-13 C57

This set of 50 black and white cards was produced circa 1912-13. These small cards measure approximately 1 1/2" by 2 1/2". The player's name and affiliation are printed on both the front and back. The card number appears on the back only with the words "Series of 50." Although the origin of the set is unknown, it is safe to assume that the producer who issued the C56 series issued this as well, as the backs of the cards are quite similar. A brief career outline in English is contained on the back. This set is considered to be the toughest to find of the three early hockey sets.

COMPLETE SET (50) 12000.00 20000.00
1 Georges Vezina 2500.00 5000.00
2 Punch Broadbent RC 350.00 600.00
3 Clint Benedict RC 350.00 600.00
4 A. Atchinson RC 150.00 300.00
5 Tom Dunderdale 200.00 400.00
6 Art Bernier 150.00 300.00
7 G.(Henri) Dallaire 150.00 300.00
8 George Poulin 150.00 300.00
9 Eugene Payan 150.00 300.00
10 Steve Vair 150.00 300.00
11 Bobby Rowe 150.00 300.00
12 Don Smith 150.00 300.00
13 Bert Lindsay 150.00 300.00
14 Skene Ronan 150.00 300.00
15 Sprague Cleghorn 350.00 600.00
16 Joe Hall 200.00 400.00
17 Jack MacDonald 150.00 300.00
18 Paddy Moran 300.00 500.00
19 Harry Hyland 150.00 300.00
20 Art Ross 700.00 1200.00
21 Frank Glass 150.00 300.00
22 Walter Smaill 150.00 300.00
23 Gordon Roberts 150.00 300.00
24 James Gardner 200.00 400.00
25 Ernest(Moose) Johnson 200.00 400.00
26 Ernie Russell 200.00 400.00
27 Percy Lesueur 300.00 500.00
28 Bruce Ridpath 150.00 300.00
29 Jack Darragh 200.00 400.00
30 Hamby Shore 150.00 300.00
31 Fred Lake 150.00 300.00
32 Alex Currie 150.00 300.00
33 Albert Kerr 150.00 300.00
34 Eddie Gerard RC 200.00 400.00
35 Carl Kendall RC 150.00 300.00
36 Jack Fournier RC 150.00 300.00
37 Goldie Prodgers RC 200.00 400.00
38 Jack Marks RC 150.00 300.00
39 George Broughton RC 150.00 300.00
40 Arthur Boyce RC 150.00 300.00
41 Lester Patrick 500.00 1000.00
42 Joe Dennison RC 150.00 300.00
43 Cyclone Taylor 700.00 1200.00
44 Newsy Lalonde 700.00 1200.00
45 Didier(Pit) Pitre 150.00 300.00
46 Jack Laviolette 150.00 300.00
47 Ed Oatman 150.00 300.00
48 Joe Malone 500.00 1000.00
49 Marty Walsh 300.00 600.00
50 Odie Cleghorn 400.00 1000.00

1912 C61 Lacrosse

This set, produced by Imperial Tobacco, features prominent lacrosse stars of the day, but is included in this book because it features several prominent hockey players of the day, including Newsy Lalonde, Jack Laviolette and Clint Benedict.

1 Charlie Querrie 150.00 400.00
2 Dolly Durkin 60.00 150.00
3 Fred Rowntree 60.00 150.00
4 Fred Graydon 60.00 150.00
5 Kid Kinsman 60.00 150.00
6 Al Dade 60.00 150.00
7 Jimmy Hogan 60.00 150.00
8 A. Kenna 60.00 150.00
9 W. O'Kane 60.00 150.00
10 F. Scott 60.00 150.00
11 Newsy Lalonde 500.00 800.00
12 Mickey Ion 100.00 200.00
13 Mag MacGregor 60.00 150.00
14 Dot Phelan 60.00 150.00
15 Spike Griffiths 60.00 150.00
16 Whitey Eastwood 60.00 150.00
17 Red McCarthy 60.00 150.00
18 Jack Shea 60.00 150.00
19 Clint Benedict 250.00 500.00
20 Bobby Pringle 60.00 150.00
21 A. Ranson 60.00 150.00
22 Lawrence Degray 60.00 150.00
23 Francis Cummings 60.00 150.00
24 Fred Degan 60.00 150.00
25 Don Cameron 60.00 150.00
26 James Gifford 60.00 150.00
27 Archie Hall 60.00 150.00
28 W. Turnbull 60.00 150.00
29 Punk Wintermute 60.00 150.00
30 Tom Gifford 60.00 150.00
31 O. Secours 60.00 150.00
32 Dr. Lachapelle 60.00 150.00
33 Joe Cattarinich 100.00 200.00
34 Dare Devil Gauthier 60.00 150.00
35 Jack Laviolette 100.00 200.00
36 George Roberts 60.00 150.00
37 Steve Rochford 60.00 150.00
38 Henry Scott 60.00 150.00
39 J. McIlwane 60.00 150.00
40 Nick Neville 60.00 150.00
41 P.J. Brennan 60.00 150.00
42 Howie McIntyre 60.00 150.00
43 Gus Dillon 60.00 150.00
44 J. Barry 60.00 150.00
45 Johnny Howard 60.00 150.00
46 Eddie Powers 60.00 150.00
47 Art Warwick 60.00 150.00
48 Ernie Menary 60.00 150.00
49 Georgie Kalls 60.00 150.00
50 Fred Slagg 60.00 150.00

1924-25 C144 Champ's Cigarettes

This unnumbered 60-card set was issued during the 1924-25 season by Champ's Cigarettes. There is a brief biography on the card back written in English. The cards are sepia tone and measure approximately 1 1/2" by 2 1/2". Since the cards are unnumbered, they are checklisted in alphabetical order by subject.

COMPLETE SET (60) 10000.00 20000.00
1 Jack Adams 150.00 250.00
2 Lloyd Andrews RC 125.00 200.00
3 Clint Benedict 250.00 400.00
4 Louis Berlinquette RC 125.00 200.00
5 Eddie Bouchard 125.00 200.00
6 Billy Boucher 150.00 250.00
7 Bob Boucher RC 125.00 200.00
8 Punch Broadbent 200.00 350.00
9 Billy Burch 200.00 350.00
10 Dutch Cain RC 125.00 200.00
11 Earl Campbell RC 125.00 200.00
12 George Carroll RC 125.00 200.00
13 King Clancy 1000.00 1750.00
14 Odie Cleghorn 150.00 250.00
15 Sprague Cleghorn 250.00 400.00
16 Alex Connell RC 250.00 400.00
17 Carson Cooper RC 125.00 200.00
18 Bert Corbeau 150.00 250.00
19 Billy Coutu 125.00 200.00
20 Clarence Day RC 250.00 400.00
21 Cy Denneny 200.00 350.00
22 Charles A. Dinsmore RC 125.00 200.00
23 Babe Dye 200.00 350.00
24 Frank Finnigan RC 200.00 350.00
25 Vernon Forbes 125.00 200.00
26 Norman Fowler RC 150.00 250.00
27 Red Green 125.00 200.00
28 Shorty Green 200.00 350.00
29 Curly Headley RC 125.00 200.00
30 Jim Herberts RC 125.00 200.00
31 Fred Hitchman RC 125.00 200.00
32 Albert Holway RC 125.00 200.00
33 Stan Jackson 125.00 200.00
34 Aurel Joliat 800.00 1400.00
35 Louis C. Langlois RC 125.00 200.00
36 Fred Lowrey RC 125.00 200.00
37 Sylvio Mantha 200.00 350.00
38 Albert McCaffrey RC 125.00 200.00
39 Robert McKinnon RC 125.00 200.00
40 Herbie Mitchell RC 125.00 200.00
41 Howie Morenz 2000.00 3500.00
42 Dunc Munro RC 150.00 250.00
43 Gerald J.M. Munro RC 125.00 200.00
44 Frank Nighbor 250.00 400.00
45 Reg Noble 200.00 350.00
46 Mickey O'Leary RC 125.00 200.00
47 Goldie Prodgers 125.00 200.00
48 Ken Randall 125.00 200.00
49 George Redding RC 125.00 200.00
50 John Ross Roach 150.00 250.00
51 Mickey Roach 125.00 200.00
52 Sam Rothschild RC 125.00 200.00
53 Werner Schnarr RC 125.00 200.00
54 Ganton Scott RC 125.00 200.00
55 Alf Skinner RC 125.00 200.00
56 Hooley Smith RC 200.00 350.00
57 Chris Speyers RC 125.00 200.00
58 Jesse Spring 125.00 200.00
59 The Stanley Cup 350.00 600.00
60 Georges Vezina 1200.00 2000.00

1930 Campbell's Soup

Measures approximately 2" x 7" and is black and white. Lower portion of card features a Campbell's slogan. The player pictured is unidentified.

COMPLETE SET (1) 50.00 100.00
NNO Hockey Player 50.00 100.00

1994-95 Canada Games NHL POGS

Produced by Canada Games Company Limited, this set includes 376 POGS and 8 checklist cards. Each POG measures 1 5/8" in diameter; the checklist cards measure 2 3/8" by 3 1/2". Each cello pack featured 5 POGS and one checklist card; also one in every five packs contained a bonus kini. The fronts display color action head shots framed by foil and color geometric designs. The team name, player's name, and his position are printed on the fronts. In black on white, the backs carry biography, 1993-94 season statistics, NHL totals, and various logos. The POGS are numbered on the back.

COMPLETE SET (376) 40.00 100.00
1 Kini-Kings .20 .50
2 Kini-Rangers .20 .50
3 Kini-Penguins .20 .50
4 Kini-Stars .20 .50
5 Kini-Senators .20 .50
6 Kini-Jets .20 .50
7 Kini-Canucks .20 .50
8 Kini-Capitals .20 .50
9 Kini-Ducks .20 .50
10 Kini-Bruins .20 .50
11 Kini-Sabres .20 .50
12 Kini-Flames .20 .50
13 Kini-Blackhawks .20 .50
14 Kini-Red Wings .20 .50
15 Kini-Oilers .20 .50
16 Kini-Panthers .20 .50
17 Kini-Whalers .20 .50
18 Kini-Canadiens .20 .50
19 Kini-Devils .20 .50
20 Kini-Islanders .20 .50
21 Kini-Flyers .20 .50
22 Kini-Nordiques .20 .50
23 Kini-Sharks .20 .50
24 Kini-Blues .20 .50
25 Kini-Lightning .20 .50
26 Kini-Leafs .20 .50
27 Cliff Ronning .02 .10
28 Bob Corkum .02 .10
29 Joe Sacco .02 .10
30 Peter Douris .02 .10
31 Shaun Van Allen .02 .10
32 Stephan Lebeau .02 .10
33 Stu Grimson .02 .10
34 Tim Sweeney .02 .10
35 Adam Oates .08 .25
36 Al Iafrate .05 .15
37 Alexei Kasatonov .02 .10
38 Bryan Smolinski .08 .25
39 Cam Neely .30 .75
40 Don Sweeney .02 .10
41 Glen Murray .02 .10
42 Ray Bourque .40 1.00
43 Ted Donato .02 .10
44 Alexander Mogilny .40 1.00
45 Doug Gilmour .40 1.00
46 Dale Hawerchuk .02 .10
47 Derek Plante .08 .25
48 Donald Audette .08 .25
49 Doug Bodger .02 .10
50 Pat LaFontaine .20 .50
51 Randy Wood .02 .10
52 Richard Smehlik .02 .10
53 Yuri Khmylev .02 .10
54 Theo Fleury .30 .75
55 Kelly Kisio .02 .10
56 Joe Nieuwendyk .08 .25
57 Michael Nylander .02 .10
58 Joel Otto .02 .10
59 James Patrick .02 .10
60 Robert Reichel .08 .25
61 Gary Roberts .08 .25
62 Wes Walz .02 .10
63 Ulf Dahlen .02 .10
64 Zarley Zalapski .02 .10
65 Tony Amonte .30 .75
66 Dirk Graham .02 .10
67 Joe Murphy .05 .15
68 Bernie Nicholls .08 .25
69 Patrick Poulin .02 .10
70 Jeremy Roenick .40 1.00
71 Christian Ruuttu .02 .10
72 Brent Sutter .02 .10
73 Chris Chelios .60 1.50
74 Steve Smith .02 .10
75 Gary Suter .02 .10
76 Neal Broten .05 .15
77 Russ Courtnall .02 .10
78 Dean Evason .02 .10
79 Dave Gagner .05 .15
80 Mike McPhee .02 .10
81 Mike Modano .30 .75
82 Paul Cavallini .02 .10
83 Derian Hatcher .02 .10
84 Grant Ledyard .02 .10
85 Mark Tinordi .02 .10

86 Dino Ciccarelli .15 .40
87 Sergei Fedorov 1.25 3.00
88 Slava Kozlov .08 .25
89 Darren McCarty .08 .25
90 Keith Primeau .08 .25
91 Ray Sheppard .08 .25
92 Steve Yzerman 2.00 5.00
93 Paul Coffey .40 1.00
94 Vladimir Konstantinov .02 .10
95 Nicklas Lidstrom .15 .40
96 Greg Adams .02 .10
97 Jason Arnott .30 .75
98 Kelly Buchberger .02 .10
99 Shayne Corson .02 .10
100 Scott Pearson .02 .10
101 Doug Weight .20 .50
102 Boris Mironov .08 .25
103 Fredrik Olausson .02 .10
104 Stu Barnes .02 .10
105 Bob Kudelski .02 .10
106 Andrei Lomakin .02 .10
107 Dave Lowry .02 .10
108 Scott Mellanby .08 .25
109 Rob Niedermayer .20 .50
110 Brian Skrudland .02 .10
111 Brian Benning .02 .10
112 Gord Murphy .02 .10
113 Andrew Cassels .02 .10
114 Robert Kron .02 .10
115 Jocelyn Lemieux .02 .10
116 Paul Ranheim .02 .10
117 Geoff Sanderson .20 .50
118 Jim Sandlak .02 .10
119 Darren Turcotte .02 .10
120 Pat Verbeek .08 .25
121 Chris Pronger .15 .40
122 Pat Conacher .02 .10
123 Mike Donnelly .04 .10
124 John Druce .02 .10
125 Tony Granato .05 .15
126 Wayne Gretzky 4.00 10.00
127 Jari Kurri .08 .25
128 Warren Rychel .02 .10
129 Rob Blake .07 .20
130 Marty McSorley .08 .25
131 Alexei Zhitnik .02 .10
132 Brian Bellows .02 .10
133 Vince Damphousse .20 .50
134 Gilbert Dionne .02 .10
135 Mike Keane .02 .10
136 John LeClair 1.00 2.50
137 Kirk Muller .08 .25
138 Oleg Petrov .02 .10
139 Eric Desjardins .02 .10
140 Lyle Odelein .02 .10
141 Peter Popovic .02 .10
142 Mathieu Schneider .02 .10
143 Trent Klatt .02 .10
144 Bobby Holik .02 .10
145 Claude Lemieux .15 .40
146 John MacLean .07 .20
147 Corey Millen .02 .10
148 Stephane Richer .05 .15
149 Valeri Zelepukin .02 .10
150 Bruce Driver .02 .10
151 Gino Odjick .02 .10
152 Scott Stevens .08 .25
153 Brad Dalgarno .02 .10
154 Ray Ferraro .02 .10
155 Pat Flatley .02 .10
156 Travis Green .05 .15
157 Derek King .02 .10
158 Marty McInnis .02 .10
159 Steve Thomas .08 .25
160 Pierre Turgeon .20 .50
161 Darius Kasparaitis .02 .10
162 Vladimir Malakhov .02 .10
163 Alexei Kovalev .08 .25
164 Steve Larmer .08 .25
165 Stephane Matteau .02 .10
166 Mark Messier .75 2.00
167 Sergei Nemchinov .02 .10
168 Brian Noonan .02 .10
169 Petr Nedved .08 .25
170 Brian Leetch .60 1.50
171 Kevin Lowe .02 .10
172 Sergei Zubov .02 .10
173 Sylvain Turgeon .02 .10
174 Alexei Yashin .20 .50
175 Norm Maciver .02 .10
176 Brad Shaw .02 .10
177 Brent Fedyk .02 .10
178 Mark Lamb .02 .10
179 Don McSween .02 .10
180 Mark Recchi .20 .50
181 Mikael Renberg .30 .75
182 Garry Galley .02 .10
183 Ron Francis .20 .50
184 Jaromir Jagr 2.00 5.00
185 Mario Lemieux 3.00 8.00
186 Shawn McEachern .02 .10
187 Joe Mullen .07 .20
188 Tomas Sandstrom .05 .15
189 Kevin Stevens .07 .20
190 Martin Straka .02 .10
191 Larry Murphy .08 .25
192 Kjell Samuelsson .02 .10
193 Ulf Samuelsson .02 .10
194 Wendel Clark .15 .40
195 Valeri Kamensky .15 .40
196 Andrei Kovalenko .02 .10
197 Owen Nolan .20 .50
198 Mike Ricci .02 .10
199 Joe Sakic 1.25 3.00
200 Scott Young .02 .10
201 Uwe Krupp .02 .10
202 Curtis Leschyshyn .02 .10
203 Brett Hull .75 2.00
204 Craig Janney .08 .25
205 Kevin Miller .02 .10
206 Vitali Prokhorov .02 .10
207 Brendan Shanahan 1.25 3.00
208 Peter Stastny .08 .25
209 Esa Tikkanen .07 .20
210 Steve Duchesne .02 .10
211 Gaetan Duchesne .02 .10
212 Todd Elik .02 .10
213 Pogman .20 .50
214 Pat Falloon .02 .10
215 Johan Garpenlov .02 .10
216 Igor Larionov .08 .25
217 Sergei Makarov .05 .15
218 Jeff Norton .02 .10
219 Sandis Ozolinsh .20 .50
220 Mikael Andersson .02 .10
221 Brian Bradley .08 .25
222 Danton Cole .02 .10
223 Chris Gratton .20 .50
224 Petr Klima .02 .10
225 Denis Savard .08 .25
226 John Tucker .02 .10
227 Shawn Chambers .02 .10
228 Chris Joseph .02 .10
229 Dave Andreychuk .08 .25
230 Nikolai Borschevsky .02 .10
231 Mike Craig .02 .10
232 Mike Eastwood .02 .10
233 Mike Gartner .20 .50
234 Doug Gilmour .40 1.00
235 Kent Manderville .02 .10
236 Mike Ridley .02 .10
237 Mats Sundin .30 .75
238 Dave Ellett .02 .10
239 Todd Gill .02 .10
240 Jamie Macoun .02 .10
241 Dmitri Mironov .02 .10
242 Peter Bondra .40 1.00
243 Randy Burridge .02 .10
244 Dale Hunter .02 .10
245 Joe Juneau .15 .40
246 Dmitri Khristich .08 .25
247 Kelly Miller .02 .10
248 Michal Pivonka .02 .10
249 Sylvain Cote .02 .10
250 Tie Domi .20 .50
251 Dallas Drake .02 .10
252 Nelson Emerson .02 .10
253 Teemu Selanne 1.25 3.00
254 Darrin Shannon .02 .10
255 Thomas Steen .02 .10
256 Keith Tkachuk .60 1.50
257 Dave Manson .02 .10
258 Stephane Quintal .02 .10
259 Adam Graves AS .08 .25
260 Brian Leetch AS .40 1.00
261 John Vanbiesbrouck AS .60 1.50
262 Scott Stevens AS .08 .25
263 Ray Bourque AS .40 1.00
264 Al MacInnis AS .08 .25
265 Brendan Shanahan AS 1.25 3.00
266 Pavel Bure AS 1.50 4.00
267 Sergei Fedorov AS 1.25 3.00
268 Wayne Gretzky AS 4.00 10.00
269 Guy Hebert .20 .50
270 Kirk McLean .20 .50
271 John Blue .08 .25
272 Vincent Riendeau .08 .25
273 Grant Fuhr .20 .50
274 Dominik Hasek 1.25 3.00
275 Trevor Kidd .15 .40
276 Ed Belfour .60 1.50
277 Andy Moog .20 .50
278 Mike Vernon .20 .50
279 Bill Ranford .20 .50
280 John Vanbiesbrouck 1.00 2.50
281 Sean Burke .20 .50
282 Kelly Hrudey .20 .50
283 Patrick Roy 3.00 8.00
284 Martin Brodeur 1.50 4.00
285 Chris Terreri .05 .15
286 Jamie McLennan .07 .20
287 Glenn Healy .08 .25
288 Mike Richter .60 1.50
289 Craig Billington .08 .25
290 Dominic Roussel .07 .20
291 Tom Barrasso .08 .25
292 Stephane Fiset .08 .25
293 Curtis Joseph .75 2.00
294 Arturs Irbe .40 1.00
295 Daren Puppa .20 .50
296 Felix Potvin .60 1.50
297 Tim Cheveldae .08 .25
298 Don Beaupre .08 .25
299 Rick Tabaracci .07 .20
300 Anaheim Mighty Ducks .15 .40
301 Boston Bruins .15 .40
302 Buffalo Sabres .02 .10
303 Calgary Flames .02 .10
304 Chicago Blackhawks .08 .25
305 Dallas Stars .02 .10
306 Detroit Red Wings .15 .40
307 Edmonton Oilers .02 .10
308 Florida Panthers .02 .10
309 Hartford Whalers .02 .10
310 Los Angeles Kings .15 .40
311 Montreal Canadiens .15 .40
312 New Jersey Devils .02 .10
313 Jeff Brown .02 .10
314 New York Rangers .15 .40
315 Ottawa Senators .02 .10
316 Philadelphia Flyers .02 .10
317 Pittsburgh Penguins .02 .10
318 Quebec Nordiques .02 .10
319 St. Louis Blues .02 .10
320 San Jose Sharks .08 .25
321 Tampa Bay Lightning .02 .10
322 Toronto Maple Leafs .08 .25
323 Vancouver Canucks .02 .10
324 Washington Capitals .02 .10
325 Winnipeg Jets .02 .10
326 Martin Brodeur AW 1.50 4.00
327 Brian Leetch AW .40 1.00
328 Cam Neely AW .30 .75
329 Geoff Courtnall .02 .10
330 Pogman .20 .50
331 Sergei Fedorov AW 1.25 3.00
332 Dominik Hasek AW 1.25 3.00
333 Dominik Hasek 1.25 3.00
Grant Fuhr AW
334 Brian Leetch .40 1.00
335 Martin Gelinas .07 .20
336 Cam Neely .20 .50
337 Mike Richter .60 1.50
338 Luke Richardson .02 .10
339 Jyrki Lumme .02 .10
340 Nathan Lafayette .02 .10
341 Pavel Bure 1.00 2.50
342 Sergio Momesso .02 .10
343 Trevor Linden .20 .50
344 Tie Domi .15 .40
345 Scott Stevens .08 .25
346 Teppo Numminen .02 .10
347 Anatoli Semenov .02 .10
348 Steve Heinze .02 .10
349 Tom Chorske .02 .10
350 Bill Guerin .07 .20
351 Scott Niedermayer .08 .25
352 Adam Graves .08 .25
353 Alexandre Daigle .20 .50
354 Troy Mallette .02 .10
355 Dave McLlwain .02 .10
356 Josef Beranek .02 .10
357 Kevin Dineen .02 .10
358 Eric Lindros 1.50 4.00
359 Bob Rouse .02 .10
360 Sergei Fedorov AW 1.25 3.00
361 Bob Errey .02 .10
362 Brad May .02 .10
363 Kevin Hatcher .02 .10
364 New York Islanders .02 .10
365 Randy Ladouceur .02 .10
366 Bobby Dollas .02 .10
367 Igor Kravchuk .02 .10
368 Jesse Belanger .02 .10
369 Pogman .20 .50
370 Gary Valk .02 .10
371 Pogman .20 .50
372 Ron Hextall .20 .50
373 Rod Brind'Amour .20 .50
374 Benoit Hogue .02 .10
375 Alexei Zhamnov .08 .25
376 Pavel Bure AW 1.50 4.00
NNO Checklist 1-47 .02 .10
NNO Checklist 48-94 .02 .10
NNO Checklist 95-141 .02 .10
NNO Checklist 142-188 .02 .10
NNO Checklist 189-235 .02 .10
NNO Checklist 236-282 .02 .10
NNO Checklist 283-329 .02 .10
NNO Checklist 330-376 .02 .10

1995-96 Canada Games NHL POGS

This set of 296 POGS was produced by Canada Games. The POGS were distributed in packs of five, with every fifth pack containing a bonus Kini. These Kinis are listed at the end of the checklist with a K-prefix. They do not picture the trophy mentioned. The POGS themselves feature a colorful action shot of the player, while the backs feature abbreviated stats.

COMPLETE SET (296) 32.00 80.00
1 Wayne Gretzky 2.50 6.00
2 Mario Lemieux 2.00 5.00
3 Cam Neely .40 1.00
4 Ray Bourque .75 2.00
5 Patrick Roy 1.50 4.00
6 Mark Messier .50 1.25
7 Brett Hull .50 1.25
8 Grant Fuhr .30 .75
9 Eric Lindros 1.00 2.50
10 John LeClair .60 1.50
11 Jaromir Jagr 1.25 3.00
12 Chris Chelios .40 1.00
13 Paul Coffey .40 1.00
14 Dominik Hasek .75 2.00
15 Alexei Zhamnov .30 .75
16 Keith Tkachuk .40 1.00
17 Theo Fleury .40 1.00
18 Ray Bourque .75 2.00
19 Larry Murphy .30 .75
20 Ed Belfour .40 1.00
21 Pavel Bure 1.00 2.50
22 Doug Gilmour .40 1.00
23 Brett Hull .50 1.25
24 Mark Messier .50 1.25
25 Cam Neely .40 1.00
26 Jeremy Roenick .40 1.00
27 Patrick Roy 1.50 4.00
28 Jim Carey .30 .75
29 Peter Forsberg 1.00 2.50
30 Jeff Friesen .02 .10
31 Kenny Jonsson .30 .75
32 Paul Kariya 1.25 3.00
33 Ian Laperriere .02 .10
34 David Oliver .02 .10
35 Kyle McLaren .30 .75
36 Ray Bourque .50 1.25
37 Alexei Kasatonov .02 .10
38 Blaine Lacher .30 .75
39 Brian Holzinger .30 .75
40 Derek Plante .02 .10
41 Mike Peca .02 .10
42 Pat LaFontaine .40 1.00
43 Jason Dawe .02 .10
44 Brad May .02 .10
45 Yuri Khmylev .02 .10
46 Garry Galley .02 .10
47 Alexei Zhitnik .02 .10
48 Dominik Hasek .75 2.00
49 Joe Nieuwendyk .30 .75
50 German Titov .02 .10
51 Cory Stillman .02 .10
52 Theo Fleury .40 1.00
53 Paul Kruse .02 .10
54 Michael Nylander .02 .10
55 Gary Roberts .02 .10
56 Phil Housley .02 .10
57 Steve Chiasson .02 .10
58 Zarley Zalapski .02 .10
59 Ron Stern .02 .10
60 Trevor Kidd .30 .75
61 Jeremy Roenick .40 1.00
62 Denis Savard .40 1.00
63 Tony Amonte .40 1.00
64 Bernie Nicholls .02 .10
65 Sergei Krivokrasov .02 .10
66 Joe Murphy .02 .10
67 Patrick Poulin .02 .10
68 Bob Probert .30 .75
69 Gary Suter .02 .10
70 Chris Chelios .40 1.00
71 Ed Belfour .40 1.00
72 Joe Sakic .75 2.00
73 Mike Ricci .02 .10
74 Valeri Kamensky .30 .75
75 Andrei Kovalenko .02 .10
76 Owen Nolan .30 .75
77 Peter Forsberg 1.00 2.50
78 Scott Young .02 .10
79 Uwe Krupp .02 .10
80 Curtis Leschyshyn .02 .10
81 Adam Deadmarsh .30 .75
82 Stephane Fiset .30 .75
83 Bob Bassen .02 .10
84 Corey Millen .02 .10
85 Mike Modano .50 1.25
86 Dave Gagner .30 .75
87 Mike Donnelly .02 .10
88 Trent Klatt .02 .10
89 Kevin Hatcher .02 .10
90 Grant Ledyard .02 .10
91 Greg Adams .02 .10
92 Andy Moog .30 .75
93 Keith Primeau .30 .75
94 Kris Draper .02 .10
95 Sergei Fedorov .75 2.00
96 Steve Yzerman 1.25 3.00
97 Vyacheslav Kozlov .02 .10
98 Ray Sheppard .30 .75
99 Dino Ciccarelli .30 .75
100 Slava Fetisov .02 .10
101 Nicklas Lidstrom .40 1.00
102 Paul Coffey .40 1.00
103 Darren McCarty .30 .75
104 Mike Vernon .30 .75
105 Doug Weight .30 .75
106 Jason Arnott .30 .75
107 Todd Marchant .02 .10
108 David Oliver .02 .10
109 Igor Kravchuk .02 .10
110 Jiri Slegr .02 .10
111 Kelly Buchberger .02 .10
112 Scott Thornton .02 .10
113 Bill Ranford .30 .75
114 Jesse Belanger .02 .10
115 Stu Barnes .02 .10
116 Scott Mellanby .30 .75
117 Bill Lindsay .02 .10
118 Dave Lowry .02 .10
119 Gaetan Duchesne .02 .10
120 Johan Garpenlov .02 .10
121 Paul Laus .02 .10
122 Gord Murphy .02 .10
123 John Vanbiesbrouck .40 1.00
124 Andrew Cassels .02 .10
125 Geoff Sanderson .30 .75
126 Brendan Shanahan .75 2.00
127 Paul Ranheim .02 .10
128 Steven Rice .02 .10
129 Frantisek Kucera .02 .10
130 Glen Wesley .02 .10
131 Sean Burke .30 .75
132 Wayne Gretzky 2.50 6.00
133 Dimitri Khristich .02 .10
134 Jari Kurri .30 .75
135 John Druce .02 .10
136 Pat Conacher .02 .10
137 Rick Tocchet .30 .75
138 Rob Blake .30 .75
139 Tony Granato .02 .10
140 Marty McSorley .30 .75
141 Darryl Sydor .30 .75
142 Eric Lacroix .02 .10
143 Kelly Hrudey .30 .75
144 Brian Savage .02 .10
145 Pierre Turgeon .30 .75
146 Benoit Brunet .02 .10
147 Valeri Bure .30 .75
148 Vincent Damphousse .30 .75
149 Mike Keane .02 .10
150 Mark Recchi .30 .75
151 Vladimir Malakhov .02 .10
152 Patrice Brisebois .02 .10
153 J.J. Daigneault .02 .10
154 Yves Racine .02 .10
155 Patrick Roy 1.50 4.00
156 Bob Carpenter .02 .10
157 Neal Broten .02 .10
158 Steve Thomas .30 .75
159 Bobby Holik .30 .75
160 John MacLean .30 .75
161 Mike Peluso .02 .10
162 Randy McKay .02 .10
163 Stephane Richer .30 .75
164 Scott Niedermayer .30 .75
165 Scott Stevens .30 .75
166 Bill Guerin .30 .75
167 Martin Brodeur 1.00 2.50
168 Kirk Muller .30 .75
169 Zigmund Palffy .40 1.00
170 Travis Green .02 .10
171 Brett Lindros .02 .10
172 Derek King .02 .10
173 Pat Flatley .02 .10
174 Wendel Clark .30 .75
175 Bryan McCabe .02 .10
176 Mathieu Schneider .02 .10
177 Eric Fichaud .30 .75
178 Ray Ferraro .02 .10
179 Adam Graves .30 .75
180 Mark Messier .50 1.25
181 Sergei Nemchinov .02 .10
182 Pat Verbeek .30 .75
183 Luc Robitaille .30 .75
184 Alexei Kovalev .30 .75
185 Jeff Beukeboom .02 .10
186 Brian Leetch .40 1.00
187 Ulf Samuelsson .02 .10
188 Alexander Karpovtsev .02 .10
189 Mike Richter .40 1.00
190 Alexandre Daigle .30 .75
191 Alexei Yashin .30 .75
192 Dan Quinn .02 .10
193 Martin Straka .02 .10
194 Radek Bonk .02 .10
195 Pavol Demitra .30 .75
196 Steve Duchesne .30 .75
197 Chris Dahlquist .02 .10
198 Sean Hill .02 .10
199 Stanislav Neckar .02 .10
200 Don Beaupre .30 .75
201 Eric Lindros 1.00 2.50
202 Rod Brind'Amour .30 .75
203 Shjon Podein .02 .10
204 Brent Fedyk .02 .10
205 Joel Otto .02 .10
206 John LeClair .60 1.50
207 Kevin Dineen .02 .10
208 Petr Svoboda .02 .10
209 Eric Desjardins .02 .10
210 Ron Hextall .30 .75
211 Mario Lemieux 2.00 5.00
212 Petr Nedved .30 .75
213 Bryan Smolinski .30 .75
214 Tomas Sandstrom .30 .75
215 Ron Francis .30 .75
216 Jaromir Jagr 1.25 3.00
217 Sergei Zubov .02 .10
218 Drake Berehowsky .02 .10
219 Dmitri Mironov .02 .10
220 Ken Wregget .30 .75
221 Tom Barrasso .30 .75
222 Igor Larionov .30 .75
223 Jeff Friesen .30 .75
224 Kevin Miller .02 .10
225 Ray Whitney .02 .10
226 Craig Janney .30 .75
227 Pat Falloon .02 .10
228 Ulf Dahlen .02 .10
229 Viktor Kozlov .02 .10
230 Michal Sykora .02 .10
231 Sandis Ozolinsh .30 .75
232 Jamie Baker .02 .10
233 Arturs Irbe .30 .75
234 Adam Creighton .02 .10
235 Ian Laperriere .02 .10
236 Brett Hull .50 1.25
237 Brian Noonan .02 .10
238 Dale Hawerchuk .30 .75
239 Esa Tikkanen .30 .75
240 Geoff Courtnall .02 .10
241 Shayne Corson .02 .10
242 Al MacInnis .30 .75
243 Chris Pronger .30 .75
244 Jeff Norton .02 .10
245 Grant Fuhr .30 .75
246 Brian Bradley .30 .75
247 Chris Gratton .30 .75
248 John Cullen .02 .10
249 John Tucker .02 .10
250 Paul Ysebaert .02 .10
251 Petr Klima .02 .10
252 Alexander Selivanov .02 .10
253 Brian Bellows .02 .10
254 Enrico Ciccone .02 .10
255 Roman Hamrlik .30 .75
256 Daren Puppa .30 .75
257 Doug Gilmour .40 1.00
258 Benoit Hogue .02 .10
259 Mats Sundin .40 1.00
260 Dave Andreychuk .30 .75
261 Mike Gartner .30 .75
262 Randy Wood .02 .10
263 Tie Domi .30 .75
264 Dave Ellett .02 .10
265 Todd Gill .02 .10
266 Larry Murphy .30 .75
267 Kenny Jonsson .30 .75
268 Felix Potvin .40 1.00
269 Cliff Ronning .30 .75
270 Mike Ridley .02 .10
271 Trevor Linden .30 .75
272 Alexander Mogilny .30 .75
273 Martin Gelinas .30 .75
274 Pavel Bure .75 2.00
275 Russ Courtnall .02 .10
276 Jeff Brown .02 .10
277 Jyrki Lumme .02 .10
278 Kirk McLean .30 .75
279 Steve Konowalchuk .02 .10
280 Kelly Miller .02 .10
281 Peter Bondra .40 1.00
282 Keith Jones .02 .10
283 Joe Juneau .30 .75
284 Mark Tinordi .02 .10
285 Calle Johansson .02 .10
286 Sergei Gonchar .02 .10
287 Jim Carey .30 .75
288 Dallas Drake .02 .10
289 Alexei Zhamnov .30 .75
290 Mike Eastwood .02 .10
291 Igor Korolev .02 .10
292 Teemu Selanne .75 2.00
293 Keith Tkachuk .40 1.00
294 Teppo Numminen .02 .10
295 Dave Manson .02 .10
296 Tim Cheveldae .30 .75
K1 Lester B. Pearson .30 .75
K2 Art Ross .30 .75
K3 Bill Masterton .30 .75
K4 Calder .30 .75
K5 Clarence S. Campbell .30 .75
K6 Conn Smythe .30 .75
K7 Frank J. Selke .30 .75
K8 Hart .30 .75
K9 Jack Adams .30 .75
K10 James Norris .30 .75
K11 King Clancy .30 .75
K12 Lady Byng .30 .75
K13 Prince of Wales .30 .75
K14 Stanley Cup .30 .75
K15 Vezina .30 .75
K16 William M. Jennings .30 .75

1983 Canadian National Juniors

This 21-card set features Canada's 1983 National Junior Team. The cards measure approximately 3 1/2" by 5" and feature on the fronts either color posed action shots or close-up photos, shot against a blue background. On a red card face, the photos are enclosed by white borders, and the upper right corner of the picture is cut off to allow space for the team logo. The backs are blank and the unnumbered cards are checklisted below in alphabetical order. The set includes early cards of Mario Lemieux, Steve Yzerman, Mike Vernon, Dave Andreychuk, and Pat Verbeek. Three other players on the team who were not at the photo session and therefore not represented in the set are Paul Boutillier, Marc Habscheid, and Brad Shaw. A large team card (approximately 5" by 10 1/4") featuring all the players (except Marc Habscheid) and coaches was also produced. A two-thirds size (measuring approximately 5" by 7 1/4") team card entitled Celebration '82 with Troy Murray holding the Championship Plate as well as a (7 1/4" by 10 1/4") '82 team card were also produced. These special oversized cards are not typically included as part of the complete set as listed and valued below.

COMPLETE SET (21) 60.00 150.00
1 Dave Andreychuk 3.00 8.00
2 Joe Cirella .75 2.00
3 Paul Cyr .40 1.00
4 Dale Derkatch .40 1.00
5 Mike Eagles .40 1.00
6 Pat Flatley UER .75 2.00
(Misspelled Flately)
7 Mario Gosselin .75 2.00
8 Gary Leeman .75 2.00
9 Mario Lemieux 30.00 80.00
10 Mark Morrison .40 1.00
11 James Patrick .75 2.00
12 Mike Sands .60 1.50
13 Gord Sherven .40 1.00
14 Tony Tanti .75 2.00
15 Larry Trader .40 1.00
16 Sylvain Turgeon .60 1.50
17 Pat Verbeek 3.00 8.00
18 Mike Vernon 3.00 8.00
19 Steve Yzerman 25.00 60.00
20 Checklist Card .20 .50
21 Title Card .20 .50
NNO Team Card 3.00 8.00
(Regular size)
NNO Large Team Card 4.00 10.00
NNO Team Card '82 2.00 5.00
NNO Celebration '82 2.00 5.00
(Troy Murray)

2003 Canada Post

Released in early 2003, this 24-card set, produced by Pacific Trading Cards, featured actual Canada Post stamps on the cards. Packs were sold exclusively at Canada Post offices and contained six cards.

COMPLETE SET (24) 30.00 75.00
1 Wayne Gretzky 4.00 10.00
2 Gordie Howe 3.20 8.00
3 Maurice Richard 1.60 5.00
4 Doug Harvey 1.20 3.00
5 Bobby Orr 4.00 10.00
6 Jacques Plante 2.40 5.00
7 Jean Beliveau 2.40 5.00
8 Terry Sawchuk 2.40 5.00
9 Eddie Shore 2.00 5.00
10 Denis Potvin 1.20 3.00
11 Bobby Hull 2.00 5.00
12 Syl Apps 1.20 3.00
13 Tim Horton 1.60 4.00
14 Guy Lafleur 1.60 4.00
15 Howie Morenz 1.20 4.00
16 Glenn Hall 1.20 5.00
17 Red Kelly 1.20 3.00
18 Phil Esposito 1.60 4.00
19 Frank Mahovlich 1.20 3.00
20 Ray Bourque 1.60 4.00
21 Serge Savard 1.20 3.00
22 Stan Mikita 1.20 3.00
23 Mike Bossy 1.20 3.00
24 Bill Durnan 1.20 4.00

2003 Canada Post Autographs

These autographed versions of the Canada Post cards were randomly inserted into packs. Each player signed just 100 cards. We were unable to confirm enough sales of any of these singles to provide accurate pricing, so we are simply checklisting them below.

COMPLETE SET (4) 200.00 350.00
7 Jean Beliveau 40.00 100.00
11 Bobby Hull 40.00 100.00
14 Guy Lafleur 40.00 100.00
16 Glenn Hall 30.00 80.00

2004 Canada Post

This 6-card set, produced by Pacific Trading Cards, updated the 2003 set and featured actual Canada Post stamps on the cards. Packs were sold exclusively at Canada Post offices.

COMPLETE SET (6) 6.00 15.00
25 Johnny Bower 1.50 4.00
26 Marcel Dionne 1.25 3.00
27 Ted Lindsay 1.25 3.00
28 Brad Park 1.25 3.00
29 Larry Robinson 1.25 3.00
30 Milt Schmidt 1.25 3.00

2004 Canada Post Autographs

Randomly inserted in Canada Post packs, found only at Canada Post outlets, at a rate of about 1:9 packs. Limited to 300 serial numbered sets.

COMPLETE SET (6) 150.00 250.00
PRINT RUN 300 SER.#'d SETS
1 Johnny Bower 25.00 50.00
2 Marcel Dionne 20.00 40.00
3 Larry Robinson 20.00 50.00
4 Milt Schmidt 20.00 50.00
5 Ted Lindsay 25.00 60.00
6 Brad Park 20.00 50.00

2005 Canada Post

This 6-card set, produced by Pacific Trading Cards, updated further the set that featured actual Canada Post stamps on the cards. Packs were sold exclusively at Canada Post offices.

COMPLETE SET (6) 6.00 15.00
31 Henri Richard 1.25 3.00
32 Grant Fuhr 1.25 3.00
33 Allan Stanley 1.25 3.00
34 Pierre Pilote 1.25 3.00
35 Bryan Trottier 1.25 3.00
36 John Bucyk 1.25 3.00

2005 Canada Post Autographs

This 6-card set was randomly inserted in Canada Post packs, found only at Canada Post outlets, at a rate of about 1:10 packs.

COMPLETE SET (6) 125.00 200.00
31 Henri Richard 15.00 40.00
32 Grant Fuhr 15.00 40.00
33 Allan Stanley 15.00 40.00
34 Pierre Pilote 15.00 40.00
35 Bryan Trottier 15.00 40.00
36 John Bucyk 15.00 40.00

2004 Canadian Women's World Championship Team

This oversized (3 3/4 by 5 1/4) series features players who competed for Team Canada at the 2004 World Women's Championships in Halifax. It's believed they were sold in set form at the event. The cards are unnumbered and so are listed in alphabetical order.

COMPLETE SET (22) 25.00
1 Dana Antal .40 1.00
2 Gillian Apps .60 1.50
3 Kelly Bechard .40 1.00
4 Jennifer Botterill .40 1.00
5 Therese Brisson .40 1.00
6 Cassie Campbell 1.25 3.00
7 Delaney Collins .40 1.00
8 Gillian Ferrari .40 1.00
9 Danielle Goyette .40 1.00
10 Jayna Hefford .75 2.00
11 Becky Kellar .40 1.00
12 Gina Kingsbury .40 1.00
13 Charline Labonte 1.25 3.00
14 Caroline Ouellette .40 1.00
15 Cherie Piper .40 1.00
16 Cheryl Pounder .40 1.00
17 Sami Jo Small .75 2.00
18 Colleen Sostorics .40 1.00
19 Kim St-Pierre .75 2.00
20 Vicky Sunohara .75 2.00
21 Sarah Vaillancourt .40 1.00
22 Hayley Wickenheiser 1.25 3.00

1964-65 Canadiens Postcards

This 24-postcard set features the Montreal Canadiens. The standard-size postcards feature action, black and white photography on the front, with the player's autograph stamped on in blue ink. The backs are blank. The set is noteworthy for including collectibles of HOFers Yvan Cournoyer and Rogatien Vachon before their RCs were issued.

COMPLETE SET (24) 100.00 200.00
1 Ralph Backstrom 2.50 5.00
2 Jean Beliveau 12.50 25.00
3 Toe Blake 5.00 10.00
4 Yvan Cournoyer 15.00 30.00
5 Dick Duff 2.50 5.00
6 John Ferguson 5.00 10.00
7 Donny Grant 2.50 5.00
8 Terry Harper 2.50 5.00
9 Ted Harris 2.50 5.00
10 Jacques Laperriere 4.00 8.00
11 Claude Larose 2.50 5.00
12 Jacques Lemaire 10.00 20.00

13 Garry Monahan 2.50 5.00
14 Claude Provost 2.50 5.00
15 Mickey Redmond 10.00 20.00
16 Henri Richard 7.50 15.00
17 Bobby Rousseau 2.50 5.00
18 Serge Savard 5.00 10.00
19 Gilles Tremblay 2.50 5.00
20 J.C. Tremblay 2.50 5.00
21 Carol Vadnais 1.50 3.00
22 Rogatien Vachon 15.00 30.00
23 Bryan Watson 1.50 3.00
24 Gump Worsley 5.00 10.00

1965-66 Canadiens Steinberg Glasses

This set of plastic glasses honoring members of the Montreal Canadiens were issued in the mid 1960's. As they are unnumbered, we are sequencing them in alphabetical order.

COMPLETE SET (12) 75.00 150.00
1 Ralph Backstrom 5.00 10.00
2 Jean Beliveau 15.00 30.00
3 John Ferguson 7.50 15.00
4 Charlie Hodge 7.50 15.00
5 Jacques Laperriere 5.00 10.00
6 Claude Provost 5.00 10.00
7 Henri Richard 10.00 20.00
8 Bob Rousseau 5.00 10.00
9 Jean Guy Talbot 5.00 10.00
10 Gilles Tremblay 5.00 10.00
11 J.C. Trembley 6.00 12.00
12 Gump Worsley 10.00 20.00

1966-67 Canadiens IGA

The 1966-67 Canadiens IGA set apparently is comprised of 10 small, postage stamp sized (3/4" by 3/4") cards which likely were part of a larger coupon book. With no attention to date on the card, it has been set by the Gilles Tremblay issue. The cards feature a head shot on a pinkish-red background. If anyone knows of other cards in this set, please forward the information to Beckett Publications.

COMPLETE SET (10) 150.00 300.00
1 J.C. Tremblay 15.00 30.00
2 Ralph Backstrom 15.00 30.00
3 Dick Duff 15.00 30.00
4 Ted Harris 12.50 25.00
5 Claude Larose 12.50 25.00
6 Bobby Rousseau 15.00 30.00
7 Terry Harper 15.00 30.00
8 Gilles Tremblay 12.50 25.00
9 John Ferguson 15.00 30.00
10 Gump Worsley 40.00 80.00

1967-68 Canadiens IGA

The 1967-68 IGA Montreal Canadiens set includes 23 color cards measuring approximately 1 5/8" by 1 7/8". The cards are unnumbered other than by jersey number which is how they are listed below. The cards were part of a game involving numerous prizes. The card backs contain no personal information about the player (only information about the IGA game) and are written in French and English. The set features early cards of Jacques Lemaire and Rogatien Vachon in their Rookie Card year as well as Serge Savard two years prior to his Rookie Card year.

COMPLETE SET (30) 325.00 650.00
1 Gump Worsley 25.00 50.00
2 Jacques Laperriere 15.00 30.00
3 J.C. Tremblay 12.50 25.00
4 Jean Beliveau 40.00 80.00
5 Gilles Tremblay 10.00 20.00
6 Ralph Backstrom 10.00 20.00
8 Dick Duff 12.50 25.00
10 Ted Harris 10.00 20.00
11 Claude Larose 10.00 20.00
12 Yvan Cournoyer 20.00 40.00
14 Claude Provost 10.00 20.00
15 Bobby Rousseau 10.00 20.00
16 Henri Richard 25.00 50.00
17 Carol Vadnais 10.00 20.00
18 Serge Savard 25.00 50.00
19 Terry Harper 12.50 25.00
20 Garry Monahan 10.00 20.00
22 John Ferguson 12.50 25.00
23 Danny Grant 12.50 25.00
24 Mickey Redmond 20.00 40.00
25 Jacques Lemaire 30.00 60.00
30 Rogatien Vachon 40.00 80.00
NNO Toe Blake CO 15.00 30.00

1968-69 Canadiens IGA

The 1968-69 IGA Montreal Canadiens set includes 19 color cards measuring approximately 1 1/4" by 2 1/4". The cards are unnumbered other than by jersey number which is how they are listed below. The cards were part of a game involving numerous prizes. The card backs contain no personal information about the player (only information about the IGA game) and are written in French and English.

COMPLETE SET (30) 300.00 600.00
1 Gump Worsley 30.00 60.00
2 Jacques Laperriere 15.00 30.00
3 J.C. Tremblay 12.50 25.00
4 Jean Beliveau 40.00 80.00
5 Gilles Tremblay 10.00 20.00
6 Ralph Backstrom 12.50 25.00
8 Dick Duff 12.50 25.00
10 Ted Harris 10.00 20.00
12 Yvan Cournoyer 25.00 50.00
14 Claude Provost 10.00 20.00
15 Bobby Rousseau 12.50 25.00
16 Henri Richard 25.00 50.00
18 Serge Savard 20.00 40.00
19 Terry Harper 12.50 25.00
20 Garry Monahan 10.00 20.00
22 John Ferguson 10.00 20.00
24 Mickey Redmond 20.00 40.00
25 Jacques Lemaire 30.00 60.00
30 Rogatien Vachon 30.00 60.00

1968-69 Canadiens Postcards BW

This 20-card set of black and white postcards features full-bleed posed player photos with facsimile autographs in white. This set marks the last year the Canadiens' organization issued black and white postcards. The cards are unnumbered and checklisted below in alphabetical order. Serge Savard appears in this set prior to his Rookie Card year.

COMPLETE SET (20) 40.00 80.00
1 Ralph Backstrom 1.50 3.00
2 Jean Beliveau 7.50 15.00
3 Yvan Cournoyer 4.00 8.00
4 Dick Duff 1.50 3.00
5 John Ferguson 2.50 5.00
6 Terry Harper 1.50 3.00
7 Ted Harris 1.25 2.50
8 Jacques Laperriere 2.00 4.00
9 Jacques Lemaire 5.00 10.00
10 Garry Monahan 1.25 2.50
11 Claude Provost 1.25 2.50
12 Mickey Redmond 4.00 8.00
13 Henri Richard 4.00 8.00
14 Bobby Rousseau 1.50 3.00
15 Claude Ruel CO 1.25 2.50
16 Serge Savard 4.00 8.00
17 Gilles Tremblay 1.25 2.50
18 J.C. Tremblay 1.50 3.00
19 Rogatien Vachon 5.00 10.00
20 Gump Worsley 5.00 10.00

1969-71 Canadiens Postcards Color

This 31-card set of postcards features full-bleed posed color player photos with facsimile autographs in black across the bottom of the pictures. These postcards were also issued without facsimile autographs. For the 1969-70, 1970-71, and 1971-72 seasons, many of the same postcards were issued. The cards are unnumbered and checklisted below in alphabetical order.

COMPLETE SET (31) 50.00 100.00
1 Ralph Backstrom 1.50 3.00
2 Jean Beliveau 6.00 12.00
3 Chris Bordeleau 1.25 2.50
4 Pierre Bouchard 1.25 2.50
5 Guy Charron 1.25 2.50
6 Bill Collins 1.25 2.50
7 Yvan Cournoyer 4.00 8.00
8 John Ferguson 2.00 4.00
9 Terry Harper 1.50 3.00
10 Ted Harris 1.25 2.50
11 Rejean Houle 2.00 4.00
12 Jacques Laperriere 2.00 4.00
13 Guy Lapointe 3.00 6.00
14 Claude Larose 1.25 2.50
15 Jacques Lemaire 4.00 8.00
16 Al MacNeil CO 1.25 2.50
17 Frank Mahovlich 4.00 8.00
18 Peter Mahovlich 3.00 6.00
19 Phil Myre 2.00 4.00
20 Larry Pleau 1.50 3.00
21 Claude Provost 1.50 3.00
22 Mickey Redmond 4.00 8.00
23 Henri Richard 4.00 8.00
24 Phil Roberto 1.25 2.50
25 Jim Roberts 1.25 2.50
26 Bobby Rousseau 1.50 3.00
27 Claude Ruel CO 1.25 2.50
28 Serge Savard 4.00 8.00
29 Marc Tardif 1.50 3.00
30 J.C. Tremblay 1.50 3.00
31 Rogatien Vachon 5.00 10.00

1970-72 Canadiens Pins

This 22-pin set features members of the Montreal Canadiens. Each pin measures approximately 1 3/4" in diameter and has a black and white picture of the player. With the exception of Guy Lafleur, Frank Mahovlich, and Claude Ruel, who are pictured from the waist up, the other pictures are full body shots. The player's name appears below the picture. The pins are made of metal and have a metal clasp on the back. The pins are undated; since Bobby Rousseau's last season with the Canadiens was 1969-70 and 1971-72 was Ken Dryden, Guy Lafleur, and Frank Mahovlich's first season with Montreal, we have assigned 1970-72 to the set, meaning the set was likely issued over a period of years and may, in fact, comprise two distinct sets entirely.

COMPLETE SET (22) 75.00 150.00
1 Jean Beliveau 10.00 20.00
2 Yvan Cournoyer 4.00 8.00
3 Ken Dryden 20.00 40.00
4 John Ferguson 2.50 5.00
5 Terry Harper 2.00 4.00
6 Guy Lafleur 12.50 25.00
7 Jacques Laperriere 2.50 5.00
8 Guy Lapointe 2.50 5.00
9 Jacques Lemaire 4.00 8.00
10 Frank Mahovlich 5.00 10.00
11 Peter Mahovlich 2.50 5.00
12 Henri Richard 4.00 8.00
13 Bobby Rousseau 2.50 5.00
14 Claude Ruel CO 1.50 3.00
15 Serge Savard 2.50 5.00
16 J.C. Tremblay 2.00 4.00
17 Rogatien Vachon 4.00 8.00
18 Ted Harris 2.50 5.00
19 Claude Provost 2.50 5.00
20 Mickey Redmond 3.00 6.00
21 Ralph Backstrom 2.50 5.00
22 Gump Worsley 5.00 10.00

1971-72 Canadiens Postcards

This 25-card set of postcards features full-bleed posed color player photos with facsimile autographs in black across the pictures. For the 1969-70, 1970-71, and 1971-72 seasons, many of the same poses were issued. The cards are unnumbered and checklisted below in alphabetical order. The key cards in the set are Ken Dryden and Guy Lafleur appearing in their Rookie Card year. Also noteworthy is Coach Scotty Bowman's first card.

COMPLETE SET (25) 75.00 150.00
1 Pierre Bouchard .75 1.50
2 Scotty Bowman CO 4.00 8.00
3 Yvan Cournoyer 4.00 8.00
4 Denis DeJordy 1.50 3.00
5 Ken Dryden 20.00 40.00
6 Terry Harper 1.00 2.00
7 Dale Hoganson .75 1.50
8 Rejean Houle 1.00 2.00
9 Guy Lafleur 15.00 30.00
10 Jacques Laperriere 2.00 4.00
11 Guy Lapointe 2.00 4.00
12 Claude Larose .75 1.50
13 Jacques Lemaire 4.00 8.00
14 Frank Mahovlich 4.00 8.00
15 Peter Mahovlich 1.50 3.00
16 Phil Myre 1.50 3.00
17 Larry Pleau 1.00 2.00
18 Henri Richard 4.00 8.00
19 Phil Roberto .75 1.50
20 Jim Roberts .75 1.50
21 Leon Rochefort .75 1.50
22 Serge Savard 2.00 4.00
23 Marc Tardif 1.25 2.50
24 J.C. Tremblay 1.25 2.50
25 Rogatien Vachon 4.00 8.00

1972-73 Canadiens Postcards

This 22-card set features white bordered posed color player photos with pale green backgrounds. A facsimile autograph appears across the picture. The words "Pro Star Promotions, Inc." are printed in the border at the bottom. The Scotty Bowman card is the same as in the 1971-72 set. The cards are unnumbered and checklisted below in alphabetical order. The card of Steve Shutt predates his Rookie Card by two years.

COMPLETE SET (22) 62.50 125.00
1 Chuck Arnason 1.00 2.00
2 Pierre Bouchard 1.50 3.00
3 Scotty Bowman CO 5.00 10.00
4 Yvan Cournoyer 2.50 5.00
5 Ken Dryden 17.50 35.00
6 Rejean Houle 1.50 3.00
7 Guy Lafleur 10.00 20.00
8 Jacques Laperriere 2.00 4.00
9 Guy Lapointe 2.00 4.00
10 Claude Larose 1.00 2.00
11 Chuck Lefley 1.00 2.00
12 Jacques Lemaire 2.50 5.00
13 Frank Mahovlich 2.50 5.00
14 Peter Mahovlich 2.00 4.00
15 Bob Murdoch 1.00 2.00
16 Michel Plasse 2.00 4.00
17 Henri Richard 2.50 5.00
18 Jim Roberts 1.00 2.00
19 Serge Savard 2.00 4.00
20 Steve Shutt 4.00 8.00
21 Marc Tardif 1.50 3.00
22 Murray Wilson 1.00 2.00

1972 Canadiens Great West Life Prints

Cards measure 11" x 14" and were produced by Great West Life Insurance Company. Backs are blank. Cards are unnumbered and checklisted below in alphabetical order.

COMPLETE SET (6) 50.00 100.00
1 Pierre Bouchard 5.00 10.00
2 Yvan Cournoyer 5.00 10.00
3 Ken Dryden 20.00 40.00
4 Pete Mahovlich 5.00 10.00
5 Guy Lafleur 12.50 25.00
6 Steve Shutt 5.00 10.00

1973-74 Canadiens Postcards

This 24-card set features full-bleed color action player photos. The player's name, number and a facsimile autograph are printed on the back. Reportedly distribution problems limited sales to the public. The cards are unnumbered and checklisted below in alphabetical order. The card of Bob Gainey predates his Rookie Card by one year.

COMPLETE SET (24) 40.00 80.00
1 Jean Beliveau 6.00 12.00
(Portrait)
2 Pierre Bouchard .75 1.50
3 Scotty Bowman CO 3.00 6.00
4 Yvan Cournoyer 2.50 5.00
5 Bob Gainey 4.00 8.00
6 Dave Gardner .75 1.50
7 Guy Lafleur 5.00 10.00
8 Yvon Lambert .75 1.50
9 Jacques Laperriere 1.25 2.50
10 Guy Lapointe 1.25 2.50
11 Michel Larocque 1.50 3.00
12 Claude Larose SP 2.50 5.00
13 Chuck Lefley .75 1.50
14 Jacques Lemaire 1.50 3.00
15 Frank Mahovlich 2.50 5.00
16 Peter Mahovlich 1.25 2.50
17 Michel Plasse SP 2.50 5.00
18 Henri Richard 2.50 5.00
19 Jim Roberts SP 2.50 5.00
20 Larry Robinson 5.00 10.00
21 Serge Savard 1.25 2.50
22 Steve Shutt 2.50 5.00
23 Wayne Thomas 1.25 2.50
24 Murray Wilson SP 2.50 5.00

1974-75 Canadiens Postcards

This 27-card set features full-bleed color photos of players seated on a bench in the forum. The cards were issued with and without facsimile autographs. Claude Larose (13) and Chuck Lefley (14) went to St. Louis mid-season resulting in limited distribution of their cards. The Mario Tremblay card (25) was issued only without a facsimile autograph. The cards are unnumbered and checklisted below in alphabetical order.

COMPLETE SET (27) 37.50 75.00
1 Pierre Bouchard .75 1.50
2 Scotty Bowman CO 2.00 4.00
3 Rick Chartraw .75 1.50
4 Yvan Cournoyer 2.00 4.00
5 Ken Dryden 6.00 12.00
6 Bob Gainey 4.00 8.00
7 Glenn Goldup .75 1.50
8 Guy Lafleur 4.00 8.00
9 Yvon Lambert .75 1.50
10 Jacques Laperriere 1.00 2.00
11 Guy Lapointe 1.50 3.00
12 Michel Larocque 1.00 2.00
13 Claude Larose SP 1.50 3.00
14 Chuck Lefley SP 1.50 3.00
15 Jacques Lemaire 2.00 4.00
16 Peter Mahovlich 1.00 2.00
17 Henri Richard 2.00 4.00
18 Doug Risebrough 1.00 2.00
19 Jim Roberts SP 1.50 3.00
20 Larry Robinson 4.00 8.00
21 Glen Sather 1.50 3.00
22 Serge Savard 1.00 2.00
23 Steve Shutt 2.00 4.00
24 Wayne Thomas 1.00 2.00
25 Mario Tremblay 1.00 2.00
26 John Van Boxmeer .75 1.50
27 Murray Wilson SP 1.50 3.00

1975-76 Canadiens Postcards

This 20-card set features posed color photos of players on ice. A facsimile autograph appears in a white bottom border. The cards are unnumbered and checklisted below in alphabetical order. The Doug Jarvis card predates his Rookie Card by one year.

COMPLETE SET (20) 25.00 50.00
1 Don Awrey .75 1.50
2 Pierre Bouchard .75 1.50
3 Scotty Bowman CO 2.00 4.00
4 Yvan Cournoyer 2.00 4.00
5 Ken Dryden 6.00 12.00
6 Bob Gainey 2.00 4.00
7 Doug Jarvis 2.00 4.00
8 Guy Lafleur 4.00 8.00
9 Yvon Lambert .75 1.50
10 Guy Lapointe 1.25 2.50
11 Michel Larocque 1.00 2.00
12 Jacques Lemaire 2.00 4.00
13 Peter Mahovlich 1.00 2.00
14 Doug Risebrough .75 1.50
15 Jim Roberts .75 1.50
16 Larry Robinson 3.00 6.00
17 Serge Savard 1.25 2.50
18 Steve Shutt 2.00 4.00
19 Mario Tremblay 1.00 2.00
20 Murray Wilson .75 1.50

1976-77 Canadiens Postcards

This 23-card set features posed color photos of players seated in front of a light blue studio background. A facsimile autograph appears in a white bottom border. The cards are unnumbered and checklisted below in alphabetical order.

COMPLETE SET (23) 25.00 50.00
1 Pierre Bouchard .75 1.50
2 Scotty Bowman CO 2.00 4.00
3 Rick Chartraw .75 1.50
4 Yvan Cournoyer 1.50 3.00
5 Ken Dryden 5.00 10.00
6 Bob Gainey 2.00 4.00
7 Rejean Houle .75 1.50
8 Doug Jarvis 1.00 2.00
9 Guy Lafleur 4.00 8.00
10 Yvon Lambert .75 1.50
11 Guy Lapointe 1.00 2.00
12 Michel Larocque 1.25 2.50
13 Jacques Lemaire 1.50 3.00
14 Peter Mahovlich 1.00 2.00
15 Bill Nyrop .75 1.50
16 Doug Risebrough .75 1.50
17 Jim Roberts .75 1.50
18 Larry Robinson 2.50 5.00
19 Claude Ruel CO .50 1.00
20 Serge Savard 1.00 2.00
21 Steve Shutt 1.50 3.00
22 Mario Tremblay 1.00 2.00
23 Murray Wilson .75 1.50

1977-78 Canadiens Postcards

This 25-card set features posed action color photos of players on the ice. A facsimile autograph appears in a white bottom border. New players were photographed from the shoulders up. Many of the cards are the same as in the 1975-76 set. The cards are unnumbered and checklisted below in alphabetical order.

COMPLETE SET (25) 25.00 50.00
1 Pierre Bouchard .50 1.00
2 Scotty Bowman CO 1.50 3.00
3 Rick Chartraw .50 1.00
4 Yvan Cournoyer 1.50 3.00
5 Ken Dryden 4.50 9.00
6 Brian Engblom .75 1.50
7 Bob Gainey 1.50 3.00
8 Rejean Houle .50 1.00
9 Doug Jarvis .75 1.50
10 Guy Lafleur 3.00 6.00
11 Yvon Lambert .50 1.00
12 Guy Lapointe 1.00 2.00
13 Michel Larocque .75 1.50
14 Pierre Larouche 1.00 2.00
15 Jacques Lemaire 1.25 2.50
16 Gilles Lupien .50 1.00
17 Pierre Mondou .50 1.00
18 Bill Nyrop .50 1.00
19 Doug Risebrough .50 1.00
20 Larry Robinson 2.00 4.00
21 Claude Ruel CO .50 1.00
22 Serge Savard 1.00 2.00
23 Steve Shutt 1.50 3.00
24 Mario Tremblay .75 1.50
25 Murray Wilson .50 1.00

1978-79 Canadiens Postcards

This 26-card set features posed color player photos taken from the shoulders up. All the pictures have a red background except for Ruel and Cournoyer who are shown against blue. A facsimile autograph appears in a white bottom border. The cards are unnumbered and checklisted below in alphabetical order. The key card in the set is Rod Langway, appearing two years before his Rookie Card.

COMPLETE SET (26) 25.00 50.00
1 Scotty Bowman CO 1.50 3.00
2 Rick Chartraw .50 1.00
3 Cam Connor .50 1.00
4 Yvan Cournoyer 1.50 3.00
5 Ken Dryden 4.00 8.00
6 Brian Engblom .50 1.00
7 Bob Gainey 1.50 3.00
8 Rejean Houle .50 1.00
9 Pat Hughes .50 1.00
10 Doug Jarvis .75 1.50
11 Guy Lafleur 3.00 6.00
12 Yvon Lambert .50 1.00
13 Rod Langway 2.00 4.00
14 Guy Lapointe 1.00 2.00
15 Michel Larocque .75 1.50
16 Pierre Larouche 1.00 2.00
17 Jacques Lemaire 1.25 2.50
18 Gilles Lupien .50 1.00
19 Pierre Mondou .50 1.00
20 Mark Napier .50 1.00
21 Doug Risebrough .50 1.00
22 Larry Robinson 2.00 4.00
23 Claude Ruel CO .50 1.00
24 Serge Savard 1.00 2.00
25 Steve Shutt 1.50 3.00
26 Mario Tremblay .50 1.00

1979-80 Canadiens Postcards

This 25-card set features posed color player photos taken from the waist up. All the pictures have a red background except for Ruel who is shown against blue. A facsimile autograph appears in a white bottom border. Several cards are the same as the 1978-79 issue. Bernie Geoffrion's card was not distributed after he resigned as coach on December 12, 1980. Richard Sevigny's card received limited distribution because of late issue. The cards are unnumbered and checklisted below in alphabetical order. The cards measure approximately 3 1/2" by 5 1/2" and the backs are blank.

COMPLETE SET (25) 20.00 40.00
1 Rick Chartraw .50 1.00
2 Normand Dupont .50 1.00
3 Brian Engblom .50 1.00
4 Bob Gainey 1.50 3.00
5 Bernie Geoffrion CO SP 2.50 5.00
6 Danny Geoffrion .50 1.00
7 Denis Herron .75 1.50
8 Rejean Houle .50 1.00
9 Doug Jarvis .50 1.00
10 Guy Lafleur 2.50 5.00
11 Yvon Lambert .50 1.00
12 Rod Langway 1.00 2.00
13 Guy Lapointe 1.00 2.00
14 Michel Larocque .75 1.50
15 Pierre Larouche 1.00 2.00
16 Gilles Lupien .50 1.00
17 Pierre Mondou .50 1.00
18 Mark Napier .75 1.50
19 Doug Risebrough .75 1.50
20 Larry Robinson 1.50 3.00
21 Claude Ruel CO .50 1.00
22 Serge Savard .75 1.50
23 Richard Sevigny SP 2.50 5.00
24 Steve Shutt 1.00 2.00
25 Mario Tremblay .75 1.50

1980-81 Canadiens Postcards

This 26-card set features posed color player photos taken from the waist up against a blue background. A facsimile autograph appears in a white bottom border. The cards are unnumbered and checklisted below in alphabetical order. The cards measure approximately 3 1/2" by 5 1/2" and the backs are blank.

COMPLETE SET (26) 17.50 35.00
1 Keith Acton .60 1.50
2 Bill Baker .40 1.00
3 Rick Chartraw .40 1.00
4 Brian Engblom .40 1.00
5 Bob Gainey .75 2.00
6 Gaston Gingras .40 1.00
7 Denis Herron .75 2.00
8 Rejean Houle .60 1.50
9 Doug Jarvis .40 1.00
10 Guy Lafleur 2.50 5.00
11 Yvon Lambert .40 1.00
12 Rod Langway .60 1.50
13 Guy Lapointe .75 2.00
14 Michel Larocque .75 2.00
15 Pierre Larouche .60 1.50
16 Pierre Mondou .40 1.00
17 Mark Napier .40 1.00
18 Chris Nilan .75 2.00
19 Doug Risebrough .40 1.00
20 Larry Robinson 1.25 3.00
21 Claude Ruel CO .40 1.00
22 Serge Savard .60 1.50
23 Richard Sevigny .40 1.00
24 Steve Shutt .75 2.00
25 Mario Tremblay .60 1.50
26 Doug Wickenheiser .40 1.00

1981-82 Canadiens Postcards

This 28-card set features posed color player photos taken from the waist up against a blue or blue-white background. A facsimile autograph appears in a white bottom border. Many cards are the same as in the 1980-81 set. The Gilbert Delorme card was short-printed. The cards are unnumbered and checklisted below in alphabetical order.

COMPLETE SET (28) 14.00 35.00
1 Team Photo 1.25 3.00
2 Keith Acton .40 1.00
3 Bob Berry CO .30 .75
4 Jeff Brubaker .30 .75
5 Gilbert Delorme SP 1.50 4.00
6 Brian Engblom .30 .75
7 Bob Gainey .75 2.00
8 Gaston Gingras .30 .75
9 Denis Herron .50 1.25
10 Rejean Houle .40 1.00
11 Mark Hunter .30 .75
12 Doug Jarvis .30 .75
13 Guy Lafleur 2.00 5.00
14 Rod Langway .60 1.50
15 Jacques Laperriere .60 1.50
16 Guy Lapointe .60 1.50
17 Craig Laughlin .30 .75
18 Pierre Mondou .30 .75
19 Mark Napier .40 1.00
20 Chris Nilan .40 1.00
21 Robert Picard .30 .75
22 Doug Risebrough .30 .75
23 Larry Robinson 1.25 3.00
24 Richard Sevigny .50 1.25
25 Steve Shutt .75 2.00
26 Mario Tremblay .40 1.00
27 Rick Wamsley .50 1.25
28 Doug Wickenheiser .30 .75

1982-83 Canadiens Postcards

This 28-card set features posed color player photos taken from the waist up against a blue background. A facsimile autograph appears in a white bottom panel. Many photos are the same as in the 1980-81 and 1981-82 sets. Player information, jersey number, and the team logo are on the back. The Richard card has the same style but it is not originally part of the set; it was issued in 1983. The Root card was issued late in the year and thus was limited in its distribution. Some color variations appear in the Gainey and Picard cards. The cards are unnumbered and checklisted below in alphabetical order. Notable cards in the set include Guy Carbonneau and Mats Naslund appearing the year before their Rookie Card.

COMPLETE SET (28) 12.00 30.00
1 Keith Acton .30 .75
2 Bob Berry CO .30 .75
3 Guy Carbonneau 1.50 4.00
4 Dan Daoust .30 .75
5 Gilbert Delorme .30 .75
6 Bob Gainey .75 2.00
7 Gaston Gingras .30 .75
8 Rick Green .30 .75
9 Rejean Houle .30 .75
10 Mark Hunter .30 .75
11 Guy Lafleur 2.00 5.00
12 Jacques Laperriere .40 1.00
13 Craig Ludwig .60 1.50
14 Pierre Mondou .30 .75
15 Mark Napier .40 1.00
16 Mats Naslund 1.25 3.00
17 Ric Nattress .30 .75
18 Chris Nilan .40 1.00
19 Robert Picard .30 .75
20 Henri Richard 1.25 3.00
21 Larry Robinson 1.25 3.00
22 Bill Root SP .75 2.00
23 Richard Sevigny .50 1.25
24 Steve Shutt .75 2.00
25 Mario Tremblay .40 1.00
26 Ryan Walter .40 1.00
27 Rick Wamsley .50 1.25
28 Doug Wickenheiser .30 .75

1982-83 Canadiens Steinberg

This 24-card set was sponsored by Steinberg and the Montreal Canadiens Hockey Club as the "Follow the Play" promotion. The cards were issued in a small vinyl photo album with one card per binder and measure approximately 3 1/2" by 4 15/16". For a few of the players, the biography on the card back is written in French; those players are so noted in the checklist below. We have checklisted the cards below in alphabetical order.

COMPLETE SET (24) 10.00 25.00
1 Keith Acton .20 .50
2 Guy Carbonneau 1.25 3.00
3 Gilbert Delorme .20 .50
(French bio)
4 Bob Gainey .60 1.50
5 Rick Green .20 .50
6 Mark Hunter .20 .50
7 Rejean Houle .20 .50
8 Guy Lafleur 1.50 4.00
9 Craig Ludwig .40 1.00
10 Pierre Mondou .20 .50
11 Mark Napier .30 .75
12 Mats Naslund .75 2.00
13 Ric Nattress .20 .50
(French bio)
14 Chris Nilan .30 .75
15 Robert Picard .20 .50
16 Larry Robinson .75 2.00
17 Bill Root .20 .50
18 Richard Sevigny .40 1.00
19 Steve Shutt .60 1.50
20 Mario Tremblay .30 .75
21 Ryan Walter .30 .75
22 Rick Wamsley .40 1.00
(French bio)
23 Doug Wickenheiser .20 .50
24 Title Card .50 1.25
Team photo (Canadiens celebrating on ice)
xx Vinyl Card Album 2.00 5.00

1983-84 Canadiens Postcards

This 33-card set features color photos of players posed on the ice. A facsimile autograph appears at the bottom. Player information, jersey number, and the team logo are on the back. The team continued to issue cards throughout the season, so several card were distributed on a limited basis. The Laperriere card (number 14) is the same card as in the 1982-83 set. The Delorme and Wickenheiser cards were not issued as part of the set because of trade. Issued in 1984, the Beliveau card was not part of the team set but has the same style. The cards are unnumbered and checklisted below in alphabetical order. The key card in the set is Chris Chelios appearing the year before his Rookie Card.

COMPLETE SET (33) 16.00 40.00
1 Jean Beliveau 1.25 3.00
2 Bob Berry CO .30 .75
3 Guy Carbonneau .75 2.00
4 Kent Carlson .30 .75
5 John Chabot .30 .75
6 Chris Chelios 4.00 10.00
7 Gilbert Delorme SP 1.25 3.00
8 Bob Gainey .60 1.50
9 Rick Green .30 .75
10 Jean Hamel .30 .75
11 Mark Hunter .30 .75
12 Guy Lafleur 1.50 4.00
13 Jacques Lemaire .60 1.50
14 Jacques Laperriere .40 1.00
(Action shot)
15 Jacques Laperriere .40 1.00
(Head shot)
16 Craig Ludwig .40 1.00
17 Pierre Mondou .30 .75
18 Mats Naslund .75 2.00
19 Ric Nattress .30 .75
20 Chris Nilan .40 1.00
21 Steve Penney .40 1.00
22 Jacques Plante 1.25 3.00
23 Larry Robinson 1.00 2.50
24 Bill Root .30 .75
25 Richard Sevigny .40 1.00
26 Steve Shutt .60 1.50
27 Bobby Smith .60 1.50
28 Mario Tremblay .40 1.00
29 Alfie Turcotte .30 .75
30 Perry Turnbull .30 .75
31 Ryan Walter .30 .75
32 Rick Wamsley .50 1.25
33 Doug Wickenheiser SP 1.25 3.00

1984-85 Canadiens Postcards

This 31-card set features color photos of players posed on the ice. A facsimile autograph appears at the bottom. Player information, jersey number, and the team logo are on the back. Many cards are the same as in the 1983-84 set. The cards are unnumbered and checklisted below in alphabetical order.

COMPLETE SET (31) 12.00 30.00
1 Guy Carbonneau .60 1.50
(Action on ice& foot raised& with puck)
2 Guy Carbonneau .60 1.50
(Still& both feet on ice& no puck)
3 Kent Carlson .30 .75
4 Chris Chelios 2.50 6.00
Same card as 1983-84, but with autograph on front
5 Lucien Deblois .30 .75
6 Ron Flockhart .30 .75
7 Bob Gainey .60 1.50
8 Rick Green .30 .75
9 Jean Hamel .30 .75
10 Mark Hunter .30 .75
11 Tom Kurvers .30 .75
12 Guy Lafleur 1.50 4.00
13 Jacques Laperriere .40 1.00
14 Jacques Lemaire .60 1.50
15 Craig Ludwig .40 1.00
16 Mike McPhee .60 1.50
17 Pierre Mondou .30 .75
18 Mats Naslund .75 2.00
19 Ric Nattress .30 .75
20 Chris Nilan .40 1.00
21 Steve Penney .40 1.00
(Same card as 1983-84)
22 Steve Penney .40 1.00
23 Jean Perron .30 .75
24 Larry Robinson 1.00 2.50
25 Bobby Smith .60 1.50
26 Doug Soetaert .40 1.00
27 Petr Svoboda .60 1.50
28 Mario Tremblay .30 .75
29 Alfie Turcotte .30 .75
(Same card as 1983-84)
30 Alfie Turcotte .30 .75
(Autograph on front)
31 Ryan Walter .40 1.00

1985-86 Canadiens Placemats

Sponsored by Pepsi-Cola and 7-Up, this set of seven placemats was issued to commemorate the Montreal Canadiens as the 1984-85 Division Champions. Each placemat measures approximately 11" by 17". On an yellow-orange background with a white border, the front carries a painted portrait, action shot and a facsimile autograph of two different players. Player name, position, and number, date and place of birth, and career statistics in French and English are also found on the front. The sponsors' logos appear in the upper right corner. The backs feature a red-and-white plaid design. The placemats are unnumbered. One placemat shows portraits of all twelve players with their facsimile autographs.

COMPLETE SET (7) 8.00 20.00
1 Bob Gainey 1.50 4.00
Guy Carbonneau
2 Mats Naslund .75 2.00
Tom Kurvers
3 Chris Nilan .75 2.00
Petr Svoboda
4 Steve Penney 2.00 5.00
Chris Chelios
5 Larry Robinson 1.50 4.00
Serge Boisvert
6 Mario Tremblay .75 2.00
Bobby Smith
7 Hockey Stars 2.00 5.00
Steve Penney
Chris Chelios
Larry Robinson
Serge Boisvert
Mario Tremblay
Bobby Smith
Mats Naslund
Tom Kurvers
Bob Gainey
Guy Carbonneau

Chris Nilan
Petr Svoboda

1985-86 Canadiens Postcards

This 40-card set features color photos of players posed in red uniforms against a white background. A facsimile autograph appears on a red diagonal line in the lower right corner on most cards. However, there is some variation in the autograph location. Player information and the team logo are on the back. Several cards (1, 2, 3, 11, 14, 17, 19) were issued late in the season. The cards are unnumbered and checklisted below in alphabetical order. The key card in this set is Patrick Roy, which pre-dates his Rookie Card by one year. Other notable early cards include Claude Lemieux, Stephane Richer, and Brian Skrudland.

Card		
COMPLETE SET (40)	24.00	60.00
1 Serge Boisvert SP (No red line or autograph)	.60	1.50
2 Serge Boisvert SP (Portrait)	.60	1.50
3 Randy Bucyk SP (No red line or autograph)	.60	1.50
4 Guy Carbonneau	.40	1.00
5 Chris Chelios	1.50	4.00
6 Kjell Dahlin (J in autograph on stick)	.20	.50
7 Kjell Dahlin (E in autograph on stick)	.20	.50
8 Lucien Deblois	.20	.50
9 Bob Gainey (B in autograph on stick)	.60	1.50
10 Bob Gainey (G in autograph on stick)	.60	1.50
11 Gaston Gingras SP	.60	1.50
12 Rick Green (No letters on stick)	.20	.50
13 Rick Green (C in autograph on stick)	.20	.50
14 John Kordic SP (No red line or autograph)	2.00	5.00
15 Tom Kurvers	.20	.50
16 Mike Lalor	.20	.50
17 Claude Lemieux SP (No red line or autograph)	3.00	8.00
18 Craig Ludwig	.30	.75
19 David Maley SP (No red line or autograph)	.60	1.50
20 Mike McPhee	.40	1.00
21 Sergio Momesso	.30	.75
22 Mats Naslund	.60	1.50
23 Chris Nilan (Dot from i in Nilan touching toe)	.30	.75
24 Chris Nilan (Dot from i in Nilan away from toe)	.30	.75
25 Steve Penney	.30	.75
26 Jean Perron (Portrait)	.20	.50
27 Stephane Richer	.75	2.00
28 Larry Robinson	1.00	2.50
29 Steve Rooney (Loop in R through skate toe)	.20	.50
30 Steve Rooney (Loop in R through skate laces)	.20	.50
31 Patrick Roy	10.00	25.00
32 Brian Skrudland	.75	2.00
33 Bobby Smith (B in autograph touching stick)	.40	1.00
34 Bobby Smith (O in autograph on stick)	.40	1.00
35 Doug Soetaert (T at end of name by pad)	.30	.75
36 Doug Soetaert (T at end of name away from pad)	.30	.75
37 Petr Svoboda	.30	.75
38 Mario Tremblay (T in autograph touching blade)	.30	.75
39 Mario Tremblay (T in autograph away from blade)	.30	.75
40 Ryan Walter	.30	.75

1985-86 Canadiens Provigo

This 25-sticker set of the Montreal Canadiens was produced by Provigo. The puffy (Styrofoam-backed) stickers measure approximately 1 1/8" by 2 1/4" and feature a color head and shoulders photo of the player, with the player's number and name bordered by star-studded banners across the bottom of the picture. The Canadiens' logo is superimposed over the banner at its right end. The backs are blank. We have checklisted them below in alphabetical order, with the uniform number to the right of the player's name. The 25 stickers were to be attached to a cardboard poster. The poster measures approximately 20" by 11" and has 25 white spaces designated for the stickers on a red background. At the center is a picture of a goalie mask, with the Canadiens' logo above and slightly to the right. The back of the poster has a checklist, stripes in the team's colors, and two team logos. The set features early cards of Stephane Richer and Patrick Roy pre-dating their actual Rookie Cards.

Card		
COMPLETE SET (25)	10.00	40.00
1 Guy Carbonneau 21	.50	1.25
2 Chris Chelios 24	1.50	4.00
3 Kjell Dahlin 20	.20	.50
4 Lucien Deblois 27	.20	.50
5 Bob Gainey 23	.60	1.50
6 Rick Green 5	.20	.50
7 Tom Kurvers 18	.20	.50
8 Mike Lalor 38	.20	.50
9 Craig Ludwig 17	.30	.75
10 Mike McPhee 35	.40	1.00
11 Sergio Momesso 36	.30	.75
12 Mats Naslund 26	.60	1.50
13 Chris Nilan 30	.30	.75
14 Steve Penney 37	.30	.75
15 Jean Perron CO	.20	.50
16 Stephane Richer 44	.75	2.00
17 Larry Robinson 19	1.00	2.50
18 Steve Rooney 28	.20	.50
19 Patrick Roy 33	10.00	25.00
20 Brian Skrudland 39	.75	2.00
21 Bobby Smith 15	.40	1.00
22 Doug Soetaert 1	.30	.75
23 Petr Svoboda 25	.30	.75
24 Mario Tremblay 14	.30	.75
25 Ryan Walter 11	.30	.75
NNO Provigo Poster	2.00	5.00

1986-87 Canadiens Postcards

Each of the 25 cards in this set measures approximately 3 3/8" by 5 1/2". The front features a color posed photo (without borders) of the player. The information on the back has a diagonal orientation and is printed in the Canadiens' team colors read and blue. At the top on the back appears the Canadiens' logo, followed by the player's name, his signature, and brief biographical information (in French and English). Notably, the Shayne Corson card in this set pre-dates his RC by three years.

Card		
COMPLETE SET (25)	14.00	35.00
1 Guy Carbonneau 21	.40	1.00
2 Chris Chelios 24	1.25	3.00
3 Shayne Corson 34	.75	2.00
4 Kjell Dahlin 20	.20	.50
5 Bob Gainey 23	.40	1.00
6 Rick Green 5	.20	.50
7 Brian Hayward 1	.40	1.00
8 John Kordic 31	.60	1.50
9 Mike Lalor 38	.20	.50
10 Jacques Laperriere ACO	.30	.75
11 Claude Lemieux	1.50	4.00
12 Craig Ludwig 17	.20	.50
13 Mike McPhee 35	.30	.75
14 Sergio Momesso 36	.20	.50
15 Mats Naslund 26	.40	1.00
16 Chris Nilan 30	.30	.75
17 Jean Perron CO	.20	.50
18 Stephane Richer 44	.75	2.00
19 Larry Robinson 19	.75	2.00
20 Patrick Roy 33	6.00	15.00
21 Scott Sandelin 3	.20	.50
22 Brian Skrudland 39	.60	1.50
23 Bobby Smith 15	.30	.75
24 Petr Svoboda 25	.20	.50
25 Ryan Walter 11	.30	.75
26 Serge Savard		
27 Larry Trader		
28 Francois Allaire		

1987 Canadiens Kodak

Little is known about this set. It is believed that the cards below represent a partial checklist for what likely was a promotional giveaway. Any additional information may be forwarded to hockeymag@beckett.com.

Card		
COMPLETE SET (7)	2.50	6.00
1 Guy Carbonneau	.40	1.00
2 Bob Gainey	.50	1.25
3 Mike McPhee	.30	.75
4 Mats Naslund	.40	1.00
5 Chris Nilan	.30	.75
6 Larry Robinson	.75	2.00
7 Bobby Smith	.30	.75

1987-88 Canadiens Postcards

This 35-card set is in the postcard size format, with each card measuring approximately 3 1/2" by 5 1/2". The fronts feature full-bleed posed color action shots. In a diagonal format at the top of the back appears the team logo, followed by the player's name, his signature, and brief biographical information (in French and English). The cards are unnumbered and checklisted below in alphabetical order. There are two versions of the Stephane Richer postcard (#23); both are included in the complete set price.

Card		
COMPLETE SET (35)	12.00	30.00
1 Francois Allaire ACO	.08	.25
2 Guy Carbonneau	.40	1.00
3 Jose Charbonneau	.20	.50
4 Chris Chelios	1.00	2.50
5 Shayne Corson	.40	1.00
6 Kjell Dahlin	.20	.50
7 Bob Gainey	.50	1.25
8 Rick Green	.20	.50
9 Gaston Gingras	.20	.50
10 Brian Hayward	.30	.75
11 John Kordic	.60	1.50
12 Mike Lalor	.20	.50
13 Jacques Laperriere ACO	.20	.50
14 Claude Lemieux	1.25	3.00
15 Craig Ludwig	.20	.50
16 David Maley	.20	.50
17 Mike McPhee	.30	.75
18 Sergio Momesso	.20	.50
19 Claude Mouton ANN	.08	.25
20 Mats Naslund	.40	1.00
21 Chris Nilan	.30	.75
22 Jean Perron CO	.08	.25
23A Stephane Richer (With moustache)	.60	1.50
23B Stephane Richer (No moustache)	.60	1.50
24 Larry Robinson	.75	2.00
25 Steve Rooney	.20	.50
26 Patrick Roy	6.00	15.00
27 Scott Sandelin	.20	.50
28 Serge Savard DIR	.30	.75
29 Brian Skrudland	.50	1.25
30 Bobby Smith	.30	.75
31 Petr Svoboda	.20	.50
32 Gilles Thibaudeau	.20	.50
33 Larry Trader	.20	.50
34 Ryan Walter	.30	.75

1987-88 Canadiens Vachon Stickers

Featuring the Montreal Canadiens, this set consists of 28 panels, each measuring approximately 2 7/8" by 5 9/16". Each panel is made up of five stickers, two that measure approximately 1 1/2" by 2 5/8", and three that measure approximately 1" by 1 11/16". The larger stickers carry color action player photos or team pictures. The smaller ones are close-ups of players or action shots. The stickers appear in a variety of combinations on the panels, with one panel showing small player shots and another panel carrying the same player shots but with different action photos. All told, 88 different stickers were printed. The back of the panel explains in French and English that albums are available for 49 cents at participating supermarkets and at "Les Canadiens" souvenir boutiques, and that collectors can send in 2.00 to Super Series Vachon and receive the album through the mail. The first six stickers can be pieced together to form a composite team photo. The stickers are numbered on the front.

Card		
COMPLETE SET (88)	16.00	40.00
1 Canadiens Team Photo (Top left)	.08	.25
2 Canadiens Team Photo (Top middle)	.08	.25
3 Canadiens Team Photo (Top right)	.08	.25
4 Canadiens Team Photo (Bottom left)	.08	.25
5 Canadiens Team Photo (Bottom middle)	.08	.25
6 Canadiens Team Photo (Bottom right)	.08	.25
7 Jean Perron CO	.08	.25
8 Jacques Laperriere ACO	.08	.25
9 Francois Allaire ACO	.08	.25
10 Jean Perron CO	.08	.25
11 Jacques Laperriere	.08	.25
12 Bob Gainey	.30	.75
13 Bob Gainey	.30	.75
14 Guy Carbonneau	.15	.40
15 Guy Carbonneau	.15	.40
16 Guy Carbonneau	.15	.40
17 Michael McPhee	.15	.40
18 Bob Gainey	.30	.75
19 Chris Nilan	.15	.40
20 Chris Nilan	.15	.40
21 Guy Carbonneau	.15	.40
22 Mike Lalor	.08	.25
23 Patrick Roy and Guy Carbonneau	1.50	4.00
24 Ryan Walter	.08	.25
25 Ryan Walter	.08	.25
26 Bobby Smith	.15	.40
27 Mats Naslund	.15	.40
28 Bobby Smith	.15	.40
29 Mike McPhee	.15	.40
30 Bobby Smith	.15	.40
31 Claude Lemieux	.75	2.00
32 Brian Skrudland	.08	.25
33 Craig Ludwig	.15	.40
34 Brian Skrudland	.15	.40
35 Craig Ludwig	.08	.25
36 Brian Skrudland	.15	.40
37 Mike McPhee	.15	.40
38 Mike McPhee	.15	.40
39 Kjell Dahlin	.08	.25
40 Kjell Dahlin	.08	.25
41 Bobby Smith	.15	.40
42 Patrick Roy	2.00	5.00
43 Patrick Roy	2.00	5.00
44 Larry Trader	.08	.25
45 Mats Naslund	.20	.50
46 Mats Naslund	.20	.50
47 Mats Naslund	.20	.50
48 Mats Naslund	.20	.50
49 Shayne Corson	.20	.50
50 Shayne Corson	.20	.50
51 Stephane Richer	.20	.50
52 Stephane Richer	.20	.50
53 Bob Gainey	.30	.75
54 Stephane Richer	.20	.50
55 Sergio Momesso	.08	.25
56 Sergio Momesso	.08	.25
57 John Kordic	.40	1.00
58 John Kordic	.40	1.00
59 Mike Lalor	.08	.25
60 Mike Lalor	.08	.25
61 Brian Hayward	.15	.40
62 Guy Carbonneau	.15	.40
63 Guy Carbonneau	.15	.40
64 Brian Hayward	.15	.40
65 Rick Green	.08	.25
66 Rick Green	.08	.25
67 Brian Hayward	.15	.40
68 Rick Green	.08	.25
69 Patrick Roy	2.00	5.00
70 Rick Green	.08	.25
71 Patrick Roy	2.00	5.00
72 Larry Robinson	.40	1.00
73 Larry Robinson	.40	1.00
74 Patrick Roy	2.00	5.00
75 Petr Svoboda	.08	.25
76 Patrick Roy	2.00	5.00
77 Petr Svoboda	.08	.25
78 Chris Chelios	.60	1.50
79 Chris Chelios	.60	1.50
80 Craig Ludwig	.15	.40
81 Craig Ludwig	.15	.40
82 Chris Chelios	.60	1.50
83 Chris Chelios	.60	1.50
84 Brian Hayward	.15	.40
85 Craig Ludwig	.15	.40
86 Bobby Smith	.15	.40
87 Mats Naslund	.15	.40
88 Bob Gainey	.30	.75
xx Sticker Album	2.00	5.00

1988-89 Canadiens Postcards

This 30-card, team-issued set measures approximately 3 1/2" by 5 1/2" and features full-bleed color player photos. The players are posed on the ice against a white background. The coaches' cards feature color portraits against a black background. The backs are white and show the team name and logo in large red letters at the top. The player's name, number, and biography are printed in blue. A facsimile autograph at the bottom rounds out the back. The cards are unnumbered and checklisted below in alphabetical order.

Card		
COMPLETE SET (30)	10.00	25.00
1 Francois Allaire ACO	.08	.25
2 Pat Burns CO	.40	1.00
3 Guy Carbonneau	.40	1.00
4 Jose Charbonneau	.20	.50
5 Chris Chelios	.75	2.00
6 Ronald Corey PRES	.08	.25
7 Shayne Corson	.40	1.00
8 Russ Courtnall	.40	1.00
9 Eric Desjardins	.60	1.50
10 Bob Gainey	.40	1.00
11 Brent Gilchrist	.30	.75
12 Rick Green	.20	.50
13 Brian Hayward	.30	.75
14 Mike Keane	.40	1.00
15 Mike Lalor	.20	.50
16 Jacques Laperriere ACO	.20	.50
17 Claude Lemieux	.60	1.50
18 Craig Ludwig	.30	.75
19 Steven Martinson	.20	.50
20 Mike McPhee	.30	.75
21 Mats Naslund	.40	1.00
22 Stephane Richer	.40	1.00
23 Larry Robinson	.75	2.00
24 Patrick Roy	4.00	10.00
25 Serge Savard DIR	.40	1.00
26 Brian Skrudland	.40	1.00
27 Bobby Smith	.30	.75
28 Petr Svoboda	.20	.50
30 Ryan Walter	.20	.50
39 Gilles Thibaudeau	.20	.50

1989-90 Canadiens Kraft

This 24-card set of Montreal Canadiens was sponsored by Le Journal de Montreal and Kraft Foods. The cards were issued as two four-card insert sheets in Les Canadiens magazine. The cards measure approximately 3 3/4" by 5 7/16". The front features a posed color photo of the player on white card stock. The cards are unnumbered and hence are listed below in alphabetical order.

Card		
COMPLETE SET (24)	10.00	25.00
1 Pat Burns CO	.40	1.00
2 Guy Carbonneau	.40	1.00
3 Chris Chelios	1.00	2.50
4 Shayne Corson	.60	1.50
5 Russ Courtnall	.30	.75
6 J.J. Daigneault	.30	.75
7 Eric Desjardins	.40	1.00
8 Todd Ewen	.30	.75
9 Brent Gilchrist	.30	.75
10 Brian Hayward	.30	.75
11 Mike Keane	.40	1.00
12 Stephan Lebeau	.50	1.25
13 Sylvain Lefebvre	.30	.75
14 Claude Lemieux	.75	2.00
15 Craig Ludwig	.40	1.00
16 Mike McPhee	.40	1.00
17 Mats Naslund	.60	1.50
18 Stephane Richer	.60	1.50
19 Patrick Roy	3.00	8.00
20 Mathieu Schneider	.60	1.50
21 Brian Skrudland	.30	.75
22 Bobby Smith	.30	.75
23 Petr Svoboda	.30	.75
24 Ryan Walter	.30	.75

1989-90 Canadiens Postcards

This 32-card set measures approximately 3 7/16" by 5 7/16" and features borderless color player photos. The players are posed on the ice against a white background. The coaches' cards feature color portraits against a black background. The backs are white and carry the team name and logo in large red letters at the top. The player's name, jersey number, and biography are printed in blue. A facsimile autograph at the bottom rounds out the back. The cards are unnumbered and checklisted below in alphabetical order.

Card		
COMPLETE SET (32)	10.00	25.00
1 Francois Allaire ACO	.08	.25
2 Pat Burns CO	.40	1.00
3 Guy Carbonneau	.30	.75
4 Chris Chelios	.60	1.50
5 Tom Chorske	.20	.50
6 Ronald Corey PR	.08	.25
7 Shayne Corson	.40	1.00
8 Russ Courtnall	.40	1.00
9 Jean-Jacques Daigneault	.20	.50
10 Eric Desjardins	.40	1.00
11 Martin Desjardins	.20	.50
12 Donald Dufresne	.20	.50
13 Brent Gilchrist	.30	.75
14 Brian Hayward	.30	.75
15 Mike Keane	.30	.75
16 Jacques Laperriere ACO	.20	.50
17 Stephan Lebeau	.30	.75
18 Sylvain Lefebvre	.40	1.00
19 Claude Lemieux	.40	1.00
20 Jocelyn Lemieux	.20	.50
21 Craig Ludwig	.20	.50
22 Jyrki Lumme	.40	1.00
23 Steven Martinson	.20	.50
24 Mike McPhee	.30	.75
25 Mats Naslund	.40	1.00
26 Stephane Richer	.40	1.00
27 Patrick Roy	2.50	6.00
28 Serge Savard DIR	.20	.50
29 Brian Skrudland	.40	1.00
30 Bobby Smith	.30	.75
31 Petr Svoboda	.30	.75
32 Ryan Walter	.20	.50

1989-90 Canadiens Provigo Figurines

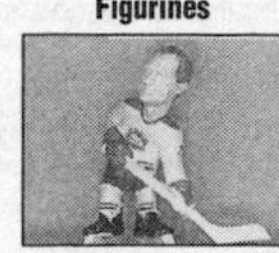

These 13 plastic figurines of the 1989-90 Canadiens are approximately 3" tall and show the players in their white home jerseys, wearing skates and holding white hockey sticks. The players' names and uniform numbers appear on their jersey backs. The figurines are numbered on the backs of the hockey sticks. The original issue price for these figurines was 1.99 Canadian. The figurines were distributed in a package with a coupon booklet.

Card		
COMPLETE SET (13)	28.00	70.00
6 Russ Courtnall	1.50	4.00
15 Bobby Smith	1.50	4.00
17 Craig Ludwig	1.25	3.00
21 Guy Carbonneau	1.50	4.00
23 Bob Gainey	2.00	5.00
24 Chris Chelios	3.00	8.00
25 Petr Svoboda	1.25	3.00
26 Mats Naslund	2.00	5.00
27 Shayne Corson	2.00	5.00
33 Patrick Roy	10.00	25.00
35 Mike McPhee	1.25	3.00
39 Brian Skrudland	1.50	4.00
44 Stephane Richer	2.00	5.00

1990-91 Canadiens Postcards

This 33-card set measures approximately 3 1/2" by 5 1/2" and features borderless color player photos. The players are posed on the ice against a white background. The coaches' cards feature color portraits against a black background. The backs are white and carry the team name and logo in large red letters at the top. The player's name, jersey number, and biography are printed in blue. A facsimile autograph at the bottom rounds out the back. The cards are unnumbered and checklisted below in alphabetical order.

Card		
COMPLETE SET (33)	10.00	25.00
1 Francois Allaire ACO	.08	.25
2 Jean-Claude Bergeron	.30	.75
3 Benoit Brunet	.20	.50
4 Pat Burns CO	.30	.75
5 Guy Carbonneau	.30	.75
6 Andrew Cassels	.30	.75
7 Tom Chorske	.20	.50
8 Ronald Corey PR	.08	.25
9 Shayne Corson	.40	1.00
10 Russ Courtnall	.30	.75
11 Jean-Jacques Daigneault	.20	.50
12 Eric Desjardins	.40	1.00
13 Gerald Diduck	.20	.50
14 Donald Dufresne	.20	.50
15 Todd Ewen	.25	.60
16 Brent Gilchrist	.30	.75
17 Mike Keane	.30	.75
18 Jacques Laperriere ACO	.30	.75
19 Stephan Lebeau	.20	.50
20 Sylvain Lefebvre	.30	.75
21 Mike McPhee	.30	.75
22 Lyle Odelein	.40	1.00
23 Mark Pederson	.20	.50
24 Stephane Richer	.30	.75
25 Patrick Roy	2.50	6.00
26 Denis Savard	.60	1.50
27 Serge Savard DIR	.30	.75
28 Mathieu Schneider	.40	1.00
29 Brian Skrudland	.40	1.00
30 Petr Svoboda	.30	.75
31 Charles Thiffault ACO	.08	.25
32 Sylvain Turgeon	.20	.50
33 Ryan Walter	.20	.50

1991 Canadiens Panini Team Stickers

This 32-sticker set was issued in a plastic bag that contained two 16-sticker sheets (approximately 9" by 12") and a foldout poster, "Super Poster - Hockey 91", on which the stickers could be affixed. The players' names appear only on the poster, not on the stickers. Each sticker measures about 2 1/8" by 2 7/8" and features a color player action shot on its white-bordered front. The back of the white sticker sheet is lined off into 16 panels, each carrying the logos for Panini, the NHL, and the NHLPA, as well as the same number that appears on the front of the sticker. Every Canadian NHL team was featured in this promotion. Each team set was available by mail-order from Panini Canada Ltd. for 2.99 plus 50 cents for shipping and handling.

Card		
COMPLETE SET (32)	2.00	5.00
1 Jean-Claude Bergeron	.02	.10
2 Guy Carbonneau	.02	.10
3 Andrew Cassels	.05	.15
4 Tom Chorske	.01	.05
5 Shayne Corson	.05	.15
6 Russ Courtnall	.05	.15
7 Jean-Jacques Daigneault	.02	.10
8 Eric Desjardins	.02	.10
9 Gerald Diduck	.01	.05
10 Donald Dufresne	.01	.05
11 Todd Ewen	.01	.05
12 Brent Gilchrist	.02	.10
13 Mike Keane	.02	.10
14 Stephan Lebeau	.02	.10
15 Sylvain Lefebvre	.02	.10
16 Mike McPhee	.02	.10
17 Mark Pederson	.01	.05
18 Stephane Richer	.08	.25
19 Patrick Roy	1.00	2.50
20 Denis Savard	.15	.40
21 Mathieu Schneider	.02	.10
22 Brian Skrudland	.02	.10
23 Petr Svoboda	.02	.10
24 Ryan Walter	.02	.10
A Team Logo Left Side	.05	.15
B Team Logo Right Side	.05	.15
C Canadiens in Action Upper Left Corner	.05	.15
D Canadiens in Action Lower Left Corner	.05	.15
E Game Action Upper Right Corner	.05	.15
F Game Action Lower Right Corner	.05	.15
G Patrick Roy	.75	2.00
H Game Action	.08	.25

1991-92 Canadiens Postcards

This 31-card team-issued set measures approximately 3 1/2" by 5 1/2". The fronts feature full-bleed color photos, with the players posed in front of a white background. The backs are white and show the team name in large red letters at the top. The player's name, number, and biography (in French and English) are printed in blue. A facsimile autograph at the bottom rounds out the back. The cards are unnumbered and checklisted below in alphabetical order.

Card		
COMPLETE SET (31)	10.00	25.00
1 Francois Allaire ACO	.08	.25
2 Patrice Brisebois	.30	.75
3 Pat Burns CO	.30	.75
4 Guy Carbonneau	.30	.75
5 Ronald Corey PRES	.08	.25
6 Shayne Corson	.40	1.00
7 Alain Cote	.20	.50
8 Russ Courtnall	.40	1.00
9 Jean-Jacques Daigneault	.20	.50
10 Eric Desjardins	.30	.75
11 Donald Dufresne	.20	.50
12 Todd Ewen	.20	.50
13 Brent Gilchrist	.30	.75
14 Mike Keane	.30	.75
15 Jacques Laperriere ACO	.20	.50
16 Stephan Lebeau	.20	.50
17 John LeClair	2.50	6.00
18 Sylvain Lefebvre	.30	.75
19 Mike McPhee	.30	.75
20 Kirk Muller	.40	1.00
21 Lyle Odelein	.30	.75
22 Andre Racicot	.30	.75
23 Mario Roberge	.20	.50
24 Patrick Roy	2.00	5.00
25 Denis Savard	.40	1.00
26 Serge Savard DIR	.30	.75
27 Mathieu Schneider	.30	.75
28 Brian Skrudland	.30	.75
29 Petr Svoboda	.20	.50
30 Charles Thiffault ACO	.08	.25
31 Sylvain Turgeon	.20	.50
32 Roland Melanson		

1992-93 Canadiens Postcards

This 27-card team-issued set measures 3 1/2" by 5 1/2" and features full-bleed glossy color player photos. The players are posed on the ice against a white background. The backs are white and show the team name in large red letters at the top. The player's name, number, and biography are printed in blue. A facsimile autograph at the bottom rounds out the back. The cards are unnumbered and checklisted below in alphabetical order.

Card		
COMPLETE SET (27)	7.20	18.00
1 Brian Bellows	.30	.75
2 Patrice Brisebois	.20	.50
3 Benoit Brunet	.20	.50
4 Guy Carbonneau	.30	.75
5 Jean-Jacques Daigneault	.20	.50
6 Vincent Damphousse	.40	1.00
7 Eric Desjardins	.30	.75
8 Jacques Demers CO	.30	.75
9 Gilbert Dionne	.20	.50
10 Donald Dufresne	.20	.50
11 Todd Ewen	.20	.50
12 Kevin Haller	.20	.50
13 Sean Hill	.20	.50
14 Mike Keane	.30	.75
15 Patric Kjellberg	.20	.50
16 Stephan Lebeau	.20	.50
17 John LeClair	1.25	3.00
18 Kirk Muller	.40	1.00
19 Lyle Odelein	.30	.75
20 Oleg Petrov	.30	.75
21 Andre Racicot	.25	.60
22 Mario Roberge	.20	.50
23 Ed Ronan	.20	.50
24 Patrick Roy	1.50	4.00
25 Denis Savard	.40	1.00
26 Mathieu Schneider	.30	.75
27 Brian Skrudland	.30	.75

1993-94 Canadiens Molson

Measuring approximately 8" by 10 1/2", this ten-card set was sponsored by Molson and was apparently distributed in conjunction with certain games throughout the season. The fronts feature full-bleed posed color photos. The photos are accented by a red line on the top and each side; at the bottom, a blue stripe carries the player's name and his uniform number. Inside a white outer border and a fading team color-coded inner border, the backs present team line-ups in English and French for the Canadiens and the respective visiting team. The cards are unnumbered and checklisted below in alphabetical order.

Card		
COMPLETE SET (10)	20.00	50.00
1 Brian Bellows	2.50	6.00
2 Benoit Brunet	2.00	5.00
3 Guy Carbonneau	2.50	6.00
4 Vincent Damphousse	4.00	10.00
5 Jean-Jacques Daigneault	3.00	8.00
6 Kevin Haller	2.00	5.00
7 Mike Keane	2.50	6.00
8 Kirk Muller	2.50	6.00
9 Peter Popovic	2.00	5.00
10 Mathieu Schneider	2.50	6.00

1993-94 Canadiens Postcards

This 26-card, team-issued set measures approximately 3 1/2" by 5 1/2" and features full-bleed glossy color player photos. The players are posed on the ice against a white background. The bilingual (French and English) backs are white and show the team name in large red letters at the top. The player's name, number, and biography are printed in blue. A facsimile autograph at the bottom rounds out the back. The cards are unnumbered and checklisted below in alphabetical order.

Card		
COMPLETE SET (26)	8.00	20.00
1 Brian Bellows	.30	.75
2 Patrice Brisebois	.25	.60
3 Benoit Brunet	.20	.50
4 Guy Carbonneau	.30	.75
5 Jean-Jacques Daigneault	.20	.50
6 Vincent Damphousse	.40	1.00
7 Jacques Demers CO	.20	.50
8 Eric Desjardins	.30	.75
9 Gilbert Dionne	.20	.50
10 Paul DiPietro	.20	.50
11 Kevin Haller	.20	.50
12 Mike Keane	.25	.60
13 Stephan Lebeau	.20	.50
14 John LeClair	1.00	2.50
15 Gary Leeman	.20	.50
16 Kirk Muller	.30	.75
17 Lyle Odelein	.30	.75
18 Peter Popovic	.20	.50
19 Andre Racicot	.25	.60
20 Rob Ramage	.20	.50
21 Mario Roberge	.20	.50
22 Ed Ronan	.20	.50
23 Patrick Roy	2.00	5.00
24 Mathieu Schneider	.30	.75
25 Pierre Sevigny	.20	.50
26 Ron Wilson	.20	.50

1994-95 Canadiens Postcards

This 27-card set measures approximately 3 1/2" by 5 1/2" and features borderless color player photos. The players are posed on the ice against a white background. The backs are white and carry the team name and logo in large red letters at the top. The player's name, jersey number, and biography are printed in blue. A facsimile autograph at the bottom rounds out the back. The cards are unnumbered and checklisted below in alphabetical order.

Card		
COMPLETE SET (27)	6.00	15.00
1 Brian Bellows	.30	.75
2 Donald Brashear	.20	.50
3 Patrice Brisebois	.20	.50
4 Benoit Brunet	.20	.50
5 J.J Daigneault	.20	.50
6 Vincent Damphousse	.30	.75
7 Jacques Demers CO	.20	.50
8 Eric Desjardins	.30	.75
9 Gilbert Dionne	.20	.50
10 Paul DiPietro	.20	.50
11 Gerry Fleming	.20	.50
12 Bryan Fogarty	.20	.50
13 Mike Keane	.20	.50
14 John LeClair	.75	2.00
15 Jim Montgomery	.20	.50
16 Kirk Muller	.30	.75
17 Lyle Odelein	.30	.75
18 Oleg Petrov	.20	.50
19 Peter Popovic	.20	.50
20 Yves Racine	.20	.50
21 Ed Ronan	.20	.50
22 Patrick Roy	1.50	4.00
23 Brian Savage	.30	.75
24 Mathieu Schneider	.30	.75
25 Pierre Sevigny	.20	.50
26 Turner Stevenson	.20	.50
27 Ron Tugnutt	.40	1.00

1995-96 Canadiens Postcards

This 20-card set measures approximately 3 1/2" by 5 1/2" and features borderless color player photos. The players are posed on the ice against a white background. The backs are white and carry the team name and logo in large red letters at the top. The player's name, jersey number, and biography are printed in blue. A facsimile autograph at the bottom rounds out the back. The cards are unnumbered and checklisted below in alphabetical order.

Card		
COMPLETE SET (20)	6.00	15.00
1 Donald Brashear	.20	.50
2 Patrice Brisebois	.20	.50
3 Benoit Brunet	.20	.50
4 Valeri Bure	.20	.50
5 Marc Bureau	.20	.50
6 Vincent Damphousse	.40	1.00
7 Mike Keane	.25	.60
8 Saku Koivu	1.50	4.00
9 Vladimir Malakhov	.20	.50
10 Lyle Odelein	.20	.50
11 Oleg Petrov	.20	.50
12 Peter Popovic	.20	.50
13 Stephane Quintal	.20	.50
14 Yves Racine	.20	.50
15 Mark Recchi	.40	1.00
16 Patrick Roy	1.50	4.00
17 Brian Savage	.25	.60
18 Turner Stevenson	.20	.50
19 Mario Tremblay CO	.20	.50
20 Pierre Turgeon	.40	1.00

1995-96 Canadiens Sheets

These 12 sheets were inserted in Montreal Canadiens game programs during the 1995-96 season. The fronts of the 8 1/2" by 11" sheets feature black and white photos of Montreal players in construction gear, while the backs feature lineups for that evening's match. There are reports that the Bure sheet is the toughest to find; hence a premium has been attached. The cards are dated, but unnumbered, and thus have been checklisted alphabetically below.

Card		
COMPLETE SET (12)	48.00	120.00
1 Valeri Bure	8.00	20.00
2 Benoit Brunet	4.00	10.00
3 Peter Popovic	4.00	10.00
4 Saku Koivu	6.00	15.00
5 Turner Stevenson	4.00	10.00
6 Mark Recchi	5.00	12.00
7 Vladimir Malakhov	4.00	10.00
8 Stephane Quintal	4.00	10.00
9 Brian Savage	4.00	10.00

10 Patrice Brisebois 4.00 10.00
11 Vincent Damphousse 5.00 12.00
12 Pierre Turgeon 5.00 12.00

1996-97 Canadiens Postcards

This 33-card postcard set was produced by the team for distribution in set form through the club store, or as autographable handouts by the players. They are standard postcard size and feature full-bleed color photos on the front. The backs include biographical information. The unnumbered cards are listed below alphabetically.

COMPLETE SET (33) 8.00 20.00
1 Murray Baron .20 .50
2 Sebastien Bordeleau .20 .50
3 Patrice Brisebois .20 .50
4 Benoit Brunet .20 .50
5 Valeri Bure .20 .50
6 Marc Bureau .20 .50
7 Ronald Corey PRES .20 .50
8 Shayne Corson .40 1.00
9 Yvan Cournoyer .60 1.50
10 Jassen Cullimore .20 .50
11 Vincent Damphousse .40 1.00
12 Rejean Houle .20 .50
13 Pat Jablonski .30 .75
14 Saku Koivu 1.25 3.00
15 Jacques Laperriere .30 .75
16 Vladimir Malakhov .20 .50
17 Dave Manson .20 .50
18 Chris Murray .20 .50
19 Peter Popovic .20 .50
20 Stephane Quintal .20 .50
21 Mark Recchi .40 1.00
22 Stephane Richer .40 1.00
23 Craig Rivet .20 .50
24 Martin Rucinsky .30 .75
25 Brian Savage .30 .75
26 Steve Shutt .30 .75
27 Turner Stevenson .20 .50
28 Jose Theodore 4.00 10.00
29 Jocelyn Thibault .75 2.00
30 Scott Thornton .20 .50
31 Mario Tremblay .20 .50
32 Darcy Tucker .40 1.00
33 David Wilkie .20 .50

1996-97 Canadiens Sheets

These large (8.5" X 11") sheets were distributed one per issue of the Montreal Canadiens game program during the exhibition and regular season. The fronts are dominated by a posed head shot, with a smaller action photo superimposed. The player's name and sweater number also appear. The back features the lineups for both teams from that evening's contest, as well as the logo of sponsor Molson Export. Unnumbered, the set is listed below in alphabetical order.

COMPLETE SET (28) 40.00 100.00
1 Patrice Brisebois 1.25 3.00
2 Benoit Brunet 1.25 3.00
3 Valeri Bure 1.50 4.00
4 Marc Bureau 1.25 3.00
5 Shayne Corson 1.50 4.00
6 Jassen Cullimore 1.25 3.00
7 Vincent Damphousse 2.00 5.00
8 Rory Fitzpatrick 1.25 3.00
9 Saku Koivu 4.00 10.00
10 Vladimir Malakhov 1.25 3.00
11 Dave Manson 1.50 4.00
12 Chris Murray 1.25 3.00
13 Peter Popovic 1.25 3.00
14 Stephane Quintal 1.25 3.00
15 Mark Recchi 2.00 5.00
16 Stephane Richer 1.50 4.00
17 Craig Rivet 1.25 3.00
18 Martin Rucinsky 1.50 4.00
19 Brian Savage 1.50 4.00
20 Turner Stevenson 1.25 3.00
21 Jose Theodore 8.00 20.00
22 Jocelyn Thibault 3.00 8.00
23 Scott Thornton 1.25 3.00
24 Darcy Tucker 1.50 4.00
25 Pierre Turgeon 2.00 5.00
26 David Wilkie 1.25 3.00
27 Centre Molson First Anniversary .40 1.00
28 Canadiens Line-up 1.25 3.00

1997-98 Canadiens Postcards

This 26-card set was produced by the team and measures the standard postcard size. The fronts feature color player photos. The backs carry player information. The cards are unnumbered and checklisted below in alphabetical order.

COMPLETE SET (26) 6.00 15.00
1 Sebastien Bordeleau .20 .50
2 Patrice Brisebois .20 .50
3 Benoit Brunet .20 .50
4 Valeri Bure .20 .50
5 Marc Bureau .20 .50
6 Brett Clark .20 .50
7 Shayne Corson .40 1.00
8 Jassen Cullimore .20 .50
9 Vincent Damphousse .40 1.00
10 Saku Koivu 1.25 3.00
11 Vladimir Malakhov .20 .50
12 Dave Manson .20 .50
13 Andy Moog .40 1.00
14 Peter Popovic .20 .50
15 Stephane Quintal .20 .50
16 Mark Recchi .30 .75
17 Stephane Richer .40 1.00
18 Craig Rivet .20 .50
19 Martin Rucinsky .30 .75
20 Brian Savage .30 .75
21 Turner Stevenson .20 .50
22 Jocelyn Thibault .40 1.00
23 Scott Thornton .20 .50
24 Darcy Tucker .20 .50
25 Alain Vigneault .20 .50
26 David Wilkie .20 .50

1998-99 Canadiens Team Issue

This 26-card set pictures the 1998-99 Montreal Canadiens team on 3.5X5.5" cards. Each card back contains a facsimile signature of the respective player. Cards are numbered alphabetically.

COMPLETE SET (26) 4.00 15.00
1 Benoit Brunet .20 .50
2 Brett Clark .20 .50
3 Shayne Corson .20 .50
4 Vincent Damphousse .40 1.00
5 Jeff Hackett .40 1.00
6 Matt Higgins .20 .50
7 Jonas Hoglund .20 .50
8 Eric Houde .20 .50
9 Saku Koivu .75 2.00
10 Vladimir Malakhov .20 .50
11 Trent McCleary .20 .50
12 Dave Morissette .20 .50
13 Alain Nasreddine .20 .50
14 Patrick Poulin .20 .50
15 Stephane Quintal .20 .50
16 Marc Recchi .30 .75
17 Craig Rivet .20 .50
18 Martin Rucinsky .20 .50
19 Brian Savage .30 .75
20 Turner Stevenson .20 .50
21 Jose Theodore 1.25 3.00
22 Scott Thornton .20 .50
23 Igor Ulanov .20 .50
24 Alain Vigneault .20 .50
25 Eric Weinrich .20 .50
26 Sergei Zholtok .20 .50

2000-01 Canadiens Postcards

This set features the Canadiens of the NHL. These postcard-like collectibles were issued by the team to each player to be used for autograph signing sessions. Sets were also available directly through the team.

COMPLETE SET (34) 8.00 20.00
1 Francois Bouillon .20 .50
2 Andrei Bashkirov .20 .50
3 Mathieu Garon .60 1.50
4 Karl Dykhuis .20 .50
5 Xavier Delisle .20 .50
6 Patrice Brisebois .20 .50
7 Benoit Brunet .20 .50
8 Jose Theodore 1.20 3.00
9 Craig Darby .20 .50
10 Eric Chouinard .30 .75
11 Jeff Hackett .40 1.00
12 Chad Kilger .20 .50
13 Jim Campbell .20 .50
14 Christian Laflamme .20 .50
15 Eric Landry .20 .50
16 Juha Lind .20 .50
17 Trevor Linden .40 1.00
18 Andrei Markov .20 .50
19 Gino Odjick .30 .75
20 Patrick Poulin .20 .50
21 Oleg Petrov .20 .50
22 Craig Rivet .20 .50
23 Stephane Robidas .20 .50
24 Martin Rucinsky .20 .50
25 Brian Savage .40 1.00
26 Sheldon Souray .20 .50
27 Saku Koivu .60 1.50
28 Johan Witehall .20 .50
29 Eric Weinrich .20 .50
30 Dainius Zubrus .20 .50
31 Michel Therrien CO .10 .25
32 Guy Carbonneau CO .40 1.00
33 Rick Green CO .10 .25
34 Andre Savard GM .20 .50

2001-02 Canadiens Postcards

This set is a postcard-sized issue capturing the members of the 2001-02 Canadiens. The cards were available at team appearances in singles form. They were not believed to be issued in set form. The cards are unnumbered and are listed in alphabetical order.

COMPLETE SET (32) 9.78 24.44
1 Donald Audette .30 .75
2 Shaun Van Allen .30 .75
3 Patrice Brisebois .30 .75
4 Benoit Brunet .30 .75
5 Jan Bulis .30 .75
6 Andreas Dackell .30 .75
7 Karl Dykhuis .30 .75
8 Mathieu Garon .60 1.50
9 Doug Gilmour .80 2.00
10 Jeff Hackett .60 1.50
11 Joe Juneau .30 .75
12 Chad Kilger .30 .75
13 Saku Koivu .80 2.00
14 Gino Odjick .30 .75
15 Yanic Perreault .30 .75
16 Oleg Petrov .30 .75
17 Patrick Poulin .30 .75
18 Stephane Quintal .30 .75
19 Mike Ribeiro .40 1.00
20 Craig Rivet .30 .75
21 Stephane Robidas .30 .75
22 Martin Rucinsky .30 .75
23 Jose Theodore 1.20 3.00
24 Brian Savage .30 .75
25 Reid Simpson .30 .75
26 Sheldon Souray .30 .75
27 Patrick Traverse .30 .75
28 Richard Zednik .30 .75
29 Michel Therrien HCO .10 .25
30 Guy Carbonneau CO .30 .75
31 Rick Green CO .10 .25
32 Roland Melanson CO .20 .50

2002 Canadiens AGF

These four cards were distributed as a complete set inside a single package that was distributed as a promotional giveaway by Quebec-based mutual fund firm AGF. The cards mimic OPC designs from the 1970s, and feature each player involved in a typical post-retirement activity such as golfing and fishing. Although it is believed they were issued in 2002, that has not been confirmed.

COMPLETE SET (4) 2.00 5.00
NNO Henri Richard .80 2.00
NNO Yvan Cournoyer .80 2.00
NNO Rejean Houle .40 1.00
NNO Steve Shutt .80 2.00

2002-03 Canadiens le Journal de Montreal

1 Stephane Quintal
2 Oleg Petrov
3 Donald Audette
4 Mariusz Czerkawski
5 Patrice Brisebois
6 Saku Koivu
7 Andreas Dackell
8 Joe Juneau
9 Mike Ribeiro
10 Yanic Perreault
11 Andrei Markov
12 Jose Theodore
13 Jan Bulis
14 Karl Dykhuis
15 Bill Lindsay
16 Doug Gilmour
17 Richard Zednik
18 Ron Hainsey
19 Randy McKay
20 Sheldon Souray
21 Jeff Hackett
22 Patrick Traverse
23 Chad Kilger
24 Craig Rivet

2002-03 Canadiens Postcards

This postcard sized set resembled many of the Canadiens issues of the past with color action photos on the fronts and the player/coach's name, position, birthday, and birth place on the back in both French and English. A facsimile autograph adorned the card backs as well. Cards measured approximately 3 1/2 X 5 1/2.

COMPLETE SET (31) 7.20 18.00
1 Stephane Quintal .20 .50
2 Saku Koivu .80 2.00
3 Oleg Petrov .20 .50
4 Richard Zednik .20 .50
5 Randy McKay .20 .50
6 Bill Lindsay .20 .50
7 Andreas Dackell .20 .50
8 Chad Kilger .20 .50
9 Sylvain Blouin .20 .50
10 Mariusz Czerkawski .20 .50
11 Karl Dykhuis .20 .50
12 Mathieu Garon .40 1.00
13 Jeff Hackett .40 1.00
14 Jan Bulis .20 .50
15 Patrice Brisebois .20 .50
16 Sheldon Souray .20 .50
17 Craig Rivet .20 .50
18 Patrick Traverse .20 .50
19 Jose Theodore .80 2.00
20 Ron Hainsey .60 1.50
21 Mike Ribeiro .20 .50
22 Andrei Markov .20 .50
23 Donald Audette .20 .50
24 Joe Juneau .20 .50
25 Doug Gilmour .40 1.00
26 Yanic Perreault .20 .50
27 Michel Therrien HCO .04 .10
28 Guy Charron ACO .04 .10
29 Rick Green ACO .04 .10
30 Clement Jodoin ACO .04 .10
31 Roland Melanson ACO .10 .25

2003-04 Canadiens Postcards

Team-issued cards feature a blurred player image on the front, with player name, number, facsimile autograph and bio info in French and English on the back.

COMPLETE SET (30) 10.00 25.00
1 Donald Audette .20 .50
2 Steve Begin .20 .50
3 Francois Bouillon .20 .50
4 Patrice Brisebois .20 .50
5 Jan Bulis .20 .50
6 Andreas Dackell .20 .50
7 Karl Dykhuis .20 .50
8 Bob Gainey GM .20 .50
9 Mathieu Garon .40 1.00
10 Ron Hainsey .20 .50
11 Chris Higgins 1.00 2.50
12 Marcel Hossa .40 1.00
13 Claude Julien CO .10 .25
14 Joe Juneau .20 .50
15 Chad Kilger .20 .50
16 Saku Koivu .75 2.00
17 Mike Komisarek .40 1.00
18 Darren Langdon .40 1.00
19 Andrei Markov .20 .50
20 Yanic Perreault .20 .50
21 Stephane Quintal .20 .50
22 Mike Ribeiro .40 1.00
23 Craig Rivet .20 .50
24 Michael Ryder 1.25 3.00
25 Sheldon Souray .40 1.00
26 Niklas Sundstrom .20 .50
27 Jose Theodore 1.25 3.00
28 Jason Ward .20 .50
29 Richard Zednik .20 .50
30 Team Photo .20 .50

2005-06 Canadiens Team Issue

COMPLETE SET (25) 15.00 30.00
1 Steve Begin .40 1.00
2 Radek Bonk .40 1.00
3 Francis Bouillon .40 1.00
4 Jan Bulis .40 1.00
5 Pierre Dagenais .40 1.00
6 Mathieu Dandenault .40 1.00
7 Yann Danis .60 1.50
8 Chris Higgins .40 1.00
9 Cristobal Huet 1.00 2.50
10 Raitis Ivanans .75 2.00
11 Saku Koivu .75 2.00
12 Mike Komisarek .40 1.00
13 Alexei Kovalev .40 1.00
14 Andrei Markov .40 1.00
15 Alexander Perezhogin .40 1.00
16 Tomas Plekanec .40 1.00
17 Mike Ribeiro .40 1.00
18 Craig Rivet .40 1.00
19 Michael Ryder .75 2.00
20 Sheldon Souray .40 1.00
21 Mark Streit .40 1.00
22 Niklas Sundstrom .40 1.00
23 Jose Theodore 1.00 2.50
24 Richard Zednik .40 1.00
25 Youppi MASCOT .10 .25

2006-07 Canadiens Postcards

1 David Aebischer .60 1.50
2 Cristobal Huet .75 2.00
3 Steve Begin .40 1.00
4 Radek Bonk .40 1.00
5 Francis Bouillon .40 1.00
6 Mathieu Dandenault .40 1.00
7 Aaron Downey .60 1.50
8 Christopher Higgins .60 1.50
9 Mike Johnson .40 1.00
10 Mike Komisarek .40 1.00
11 Alex Kovalev .40 1.00
12 Guillaume Latendresse 1.25 3.00
13 Andrei Markov .40 1.00
14 Garth Murray .40 1.00
15 Janne Niinimaa .40 1.00
16 Alexander Perezhogin .40 1.00
17 Tomas Plekanec .40 1.00
18 Craig Rivet .40 1.00
19 Michael Ryder .60 1.50
20 Mark Streit .75 2.00
21 Sheldon Souray .40 1.00
22 Sergei Samsonov .40 1.00
23 Team Photo .40 1.00
24 Youppi MASCOT .10 .25

2007-08 Canadiens Postcards

1 Saku Koivu .40 1.00
2 Carey Price 1.50 4.00
3 Josh Gorges .30 .75
4 Mike Komisarek .30 .75
5 Andrei Kostitsyn .30 .75
6 Christopher Higgins .40 1.00
7 Kyle Chipchura .50 1.25
8 Steve Begin .30 .75
9 Alex Kovalev .30 .75
10 Guillaume Latendresse .40 1.00
11 Francis Bouillon .30 .75
12 Tomas Plekanec .30 .75
13 Mikhail Grabovski .40 1.00
14 Mark Streit .30 .75
15 Michael Ryder .30 .75
16 Roman Hamrlik .30 .75
17 Maxim Lapierre .30 .75
18 Andrei Markov .40 1.00
19 Garth Murray .30 .75
20 Bryan Smolinski .30 .75
21 Mathieu Dandenault .30 .75
22 Tom Kostopoulos .30 .75
23 Patrice Brisebois .30 .75
24 Cristobal Huet .40 1.00

2007-08 Canadiens Team Issue

COMPLETE SET (25) 10.00 25.00
1 Steve Begin .30 .75
2 Francis Bouillon .30 .75
3 Patrice Brisebois .30 .75
4 Kyle Chipchura .50 1.25
5 Mathieu Dandenault .30 .75
6 Josh Gorges .30 .75
7 Mikhail Grabovski .40 1.00
8 Roman Hamrlik .30 .75
9 Christopher Higgins .40 1.00
10 Cristobal Huet .40 1.00
11 Saku Koivu .40 1.00
12 Mike Komisarek .30 .75
13 Andrei Kostitsyn .30 .75
14 Tom Kostopoulos .30 .75
15 Alex Kovalev .30 .75
16 Maxim Lapierre .30 .75
17 Guillaume Latendresse .40 1.00
18 Andrei Markov .40 1.00
19 Garth Murray .30 .75
20 Tomas Plekanec .30 .75
21 Carey Price 1.50 4.00
22 Michael Ryder .30 .75
23 Bryan Smolinski .30 .75
24 Mark Streit .30 .75
25 Youppi MASCOT .30 .75

1970-71 Canucks Royal Bank

This 20-card set of Vancouver Canucks was sponsored by Royal Bank, whose company logo appears at the lower left corner on the front. The set is subtitled Royal Bank Leo's Leaders Canucks Player of the Week. The black and white posed player photos measure approximately 5" by 7" and have white borders. The player's signature is inscribed across the bottom of the picture, and the backs are blank. The cards are unnumbered and checklisted below in alphabetical order.

COMPLETE SET (20) 30.00 60.00
1 Andre Boudrias 2.00 4.00
2 Mike Corrigan 1.50 3.00
3 Ray Cullen 2.50 5.00
4 Gary Doak 1.50 3.00
5 George Gardner 1.50 3.00
6 Murray Hall 1.50 3.00
7 Charlie Hodge 4.00 8.00
8 Danny Johnson 1.50 3.00
9 Orland Kurtenbach 2.50 5.00
10 Wayne Maki 1.50 3.00
11 Rosaire Paiement 2.00 4.00
12 Paul Popiel 2.00 4.00
13 Pat Quinn 4.00 8.00
14 Marc Reaume 1.50 3.00
15 Darryl Sly 1.50 3.00
16 Dale Tallon 2.50 5.00
17 Ted Taylor 1.50 3.00
18 Barry Wilkins 1.50 3.00
19 Dunc Wilson 2.50 5.00
20 Jim Wiste 1.50 3.00

1971-72 Canucks Royal Bank

This 20-card set of Vancouver Canucks was sponsored by Royal Bank, whose company logo appears at the lower left corner on the front. The set is subtitled Royal Bank Leo's Leaders Canucks Player of the Week. The black and white posed player photos measure approximately 5" by 7" and have white borders. The player's signature is inscribed across the bottom of the picture, and the backs are blank. The cards are numbered by week of issue. Card number 10 is unknown and may have never been issued.

COMPLETE SET (20) 25.00 50.00
1 Bobby Lalonde 1.00 2.00
2 Mike Corrigan 1.00 2.00
3 Murray Hall 1.00 2.00
4 Jocelyn Guevremont 2.00 4.00
5 Pat Quinn 3.00 6.00
6 Orland Kurtenbach 2.00 4.00
7 Paul Popiel 2.00 4.00
8 Ron Ward 1.00 2.00
9 Rosaire Paiement 1.50 3.00
11 Dale Tallon 2.00 4.00
12 Bobby Schmautz 2.00 4.00
13 Dennis Kearns 1.00 2.00
14 Barry Wilkins 1.00 2.00
15 Dunc Wilson 2.50 5.00
16 Andre Boudrias 2.00 4.00
17 Ted Taylor 1.50 3.00
18 George Gardner 1.00 2.00
19 John Schella 1.00 2.00
20 Wayne Maki 1.50 3.00
21 Gary Doak 1.00 2.00

1972-73 Canucks Nalley's

This six-card set was available on the backs of specially marked Nalley's Triple Pak Potato Chips boxes. The back yellow panel has a 6 3/4" by 5 3/8" (approximately) action shot of a Canuck player beside the goalie and net. One player card is superimposed over the lower left corner of this large action photo. The card is framed by a thin perforated line; if the card were cut out, it would measure about 3" by 3 3/4". The front features a close-up posed color player photo (from the waste up) with white borders. The player's name and position appear in white bottom border. The backs are blank. At the bottom of each back panel are miniature blue-tinted versions of all six player cards. The cards are unnumbered and checklisted below in alphabetical order.

COMPLETE SET (6) 62.50 125.00
1 Andre Boudrias 10.00 20.00
2 George Gardner 10.00 20.00
3 Wayne Maki 12.50 25.00
4 Rosaire Paiement 12.50 25.00
5 Pat Quinn 20.00 40.00
6 Barry Wilkins 10.00 20.00

1972-73 Canucks Royal Bank

This 21-card set of Vancouver Canucks was sponsored by Royal Bank, whose company logo appears at the lower left corner on the front. The set is subtitled Leo's Leaders Canucks Player of the Week. These colorful full body player photos measure approximately 5" by 7" and have white borders. The background of the photos ranges from light blue to royal blue. The player's facsimile signature is inscribed across the bottom of the picture, and the backs are blank. The cards are unnumbered on the front and checklisted below in alphabetical order.

COMPLETE SET (21) 20.00 40.00
1 Dave Balon 1.50 3.00
2 Gregg Boddy 1.00 2.00
3 Larry Bolonchuk 1.00 2.00
4 Andre Boudrias 1.00 2.00
5 Ed Dyck 1.00 2.00
6 Jocelyn Guevremont 1.50 3.00
7 James Hargreaves 1.00 2.00
8 Dennis Kearns 1.00 2.00
9 Orland Kurtenbach 1.50 3.00
10 Bobby Lalonde 1.00 2.00
11 Richard Lemieux 1.00 2.00
12 Don Lever 1.50 3.00
13 Wayne Maki 1.50 3.00
14 Bryan McSheffrey 1.00 2.00
15 Gerry O'Flaherty 1.00 2.00
16 Bobby Schmautz 1.50 3.00
17 Dale Tallon 1.50 3.00
18 Don Tannahill 1.00 2.00
19 Barry Wilkins 1.00 2.00
20 Dunc Wilson 1.50 3.00
21 John Wright 1.00 2.00

1973-74 Canucks Royal Bank

This 21-card set of Vancouver Canucks was sponsored by Royal Bank, whose company logo appears at the lower left corner on the front. The set is subtitled Royal Leaders Canucks Player of the Week. These colorful full body player photos measure approximately 5" by 7" and have white borders. The background of the photos ranges from yellowish green to green. The player's facsimile signature is inscribed across the bottom of the picture, and the backs are blank. The cards are unnumbered on the front and checklisted below in alphabetical order.

COMPLETE SET (21) 20.00 40.00
1 Paulin Bordeleau 1.00 2.00
2 Andre Boudrias 1.00 2.00
3 Jacques Caron 1.00 2.00
4 Bob Dailey 1.00 2.00
5 Dave Dunn 1.00 2.00
6 Jocelyn Guevremont 1.50 3.00
7 Dennis Kearns 1.00 2.00
8 Jerry Korab 1.00 2.00
9 Orland Kurtenbach 2.00 4.00
10 Bobby Lalonde 1.00 2.00
11 Richard Lemieux 1.00 2.00
12 Don Lever 1.50 3.00
13 Bill McCreary 1.00 2.00
14 Bryan McSheffrey 1.00 2.00
15 Gerry O'Flaherty 1.00 2.00
16 Bobby Schmautz 2.00 4.00
17 Gary Smith 2.00 4.00
18 Don Tannahill 1.00 2.00
19 Dennis Ververgaert 1.50 3.00
20 Barry Wilkins 1.00 2.00
21 John Wright 1.00 2.00

1974-75 Canucks Royal Bank

This 20-card set of Vancouver Canucks was sponsored by Royal Bank, whose company logo appears at the lower left corner on the front. The set is subtitled Royal Leaders Player of the Week. These colorful head and shoulders player photos are presented on a white background with a thin black border. The cards measure approximately 5" by 7", have white borders, and are printed on glossy paper. The player's facsimile signature is inscribed across the bottom of the picture, and the backs are blank. The cards are unnumbered on the front and checklisted below in alphabetical order.

COMPLETE SET (20) 20.00 40.00
1 Gregg Boddy 1.00 2.00
2 Paulin Bordeleau 1.50 3.00
3 Andre Boudrias 1.50 3.00
4 Bob Dailey 1.00 2.00
5 Ab DeMarco 1.00 2.00
6 John Gould 1.00 2.00
7 John Grisdale 1.00 2.00
8 Dennis Kearns 1.00 2.00
9 Bobby Lalonde 1.00 2.00
10 Don Lever 1.50 3.00
11 Ken Lockett 1.00 2.00
12 Gerry Meehan 1.50 3.00
13 Garry Monahan 1.00 2.00
14 Chris Oddleifson 1.00 2.00
15 Gerry O'Flaherty 1.00 2.00
16 Tracy Pratt 1.00 2.00
17 Mike Robitaille 1.00 2.00
18 Leon Rochefort 1.00 2.00
19 Gary Smith 1.50 3.00
20 Dennis Ververgaert 1.50 3.00

1975-76 Canucks Royal Bank

This 22-card set of Vancouver Canucks was sponsored by Royal Bank, whose company logo appears at the lower left corner on the front. The set is subtitled Royal Leaders Player of the Week. The cards measure approximately 4 3/4" by 7 1/4" and are printed on glossy paper. The fronts feature a color head and shoulders shot of the player on white background with a thin black border. The player's facsimile autograph appears below the picture. The backs are blank. The cards are unnumbered and we have checklisted them below in alphabetical order.

COMPLETE SET (22) 20.00 40.00
1 Rick Blight 1.00 2.00
2 Gregg Boddy 1.00 2.00
3 Paulin Bordeleau 1.00 2.00
4 Andre Boudrias 1.00 2.00
5 Bob Dailey 1.00 2.00
6 Ab DeMarco 1.00 2.00
7 John Gould 1.00 2.00
8 John Grisdale 1.00 2.00
9 Dennis Kearns 1.00 2.00
10 Bobby Lalonde 1.00 2.00
11 Don Lever 1.50 3.00
12 Ken Lockett 1.00 2.00
13 Garry Monahan 1.00 2.00
14 Bob Murray 1.00 2.00
15 Chris Oddleifson 1.00 2.00
16 Gerry O'Flaherty 1.00 2.00
17 Tracy Pratt 1.00 2.00
18 Mike Robitaille 1.00 2.00
19 Ron Sedlbauer 1.00 2.00
20 Gary Smith 1.50 3.00
21 Harold Snepsts 3.00 6.00
22 Dennis Ververgaert 1.50 3.00

1976-77 Canucks Royal Bank

This 23-card set of Vancouver Canucks was sponsored by Royal Bank, whose company logo appears at the lower left corner on the front. The set is subtitled Royal Leaders Player of the Week. The cards measure approximately 4 3/4" by 7 1/4" and are printed on glossy paper. The fronts feature a color head and shoulders shot of the player on white background with a thin black border. The player's facsimile autograph appears below the picture. The backs are blank. The cards are unnumbered and we have checklisted them below in alphabetical order.

COMPLETE SET (23) 20.00 40.00
1 Rick Blight 1.00 2.00
2 Bob Dailey 1.00 2.00
3 Dave Fortier 1.00 2.00
4 Brad Gassoff 1.00 2.00
5 John Gould 1.00 2.00
6 John Grisdale 1.00 2.00
7 Dennis Kearns 1.00 2.00
8 Bobby Lalonde 1.00 2.00
9 Don Lever 1.50 3.00
10 Cesare Maniago 2.00 4.00
11 Garry Monahan 1.00 2.00
12 Bob Murray 1.00 2.00
13 Chris Oddleifson 1.00 2.00
14 Gerry O'Flaherty 1.00 2.00
15 Curt Ridley 1.00 2.00
16 Mike Robitaille 1.00 2.00
17 Ron Sedlbauer 1.00 2.00
18 Harold Snepsts 2.50 5.00
19 Andy Spruce 1.00 2.00
20 Ralph Stewart 1.00 2.00
21 Dennis Ververgaert 1.50 3.00
22 Mike Walton 1.50 3.00
23 Jim Wiley 1.50 3.00

1977-78 Canucks Canada Dry Cans

This extremely scarce set features the Canucks of the NHL. Each specially-marked regular sized ginger ale can sold in the Vancouver area for a limited time featured a headshot of a player on the back side. Unopened cans sell for a premium of 100 percent.

COMPLETE SET (16) 20.00 40.00
1 Rick Blight 1.00 2.00
2 Brad Gassoff 1.00 2.00
3 Jere Gillis 1.00 2.00
4 Larry Goodenough 1.00 2.00
5 Hilliard Graves 1.00 2.00
6 Dennis Kearns 1.00 2.00
7 Don Lever 1.00 2.00
8 Cesare Maniago 2.50 5.00
9 Jack McIlhargey 1.00 2.00
10 Garry Monahan 1.00 2.00
11 Chris Oddleifson 1.00 2.00
12 Curt Ridley 1.00 2.00
13 Derek Sanderson 2.50 5.00
14 Harold Snepsts 2.00 4.00
15 Mike Walton 1.00 2.00
16 Dennis Ververgaert 1.00 2.00

1977-78 Canucks Royal Bank

This 21-card set of Vancouver Canucks was sponsored by Royal Bank, whose company logo appears at the lower left corner on the front. The set is subtitled Royal Leaders Player of the Week. The cards measure approximately 4 1/4" by 5 1/2" and are printed on thin cardboard stock. The fronts feature a color head and shoulders shot of the player on white background with a thin black border. The player's facsimile autograph appears below the picture. The backs are blank. The cards are unnumbered; they are checklisted below in alphabetical order.

COMPLETE SET (21) 20.00 40.00
1 Rick Blight 1.00 2.00
2 Larry Carriere 1.00 2.00
3 Rob Flockhart 1.00 2.00
4 Brad Gassoff 1.00 2.00
5 Jere Gillis 1.00 2.00
6 Larry Goodenough 1.00 2.00
7 Hilliard Graves 1.00 2.00
8 John Grisdale 1.00 2.00
9 Dennis Kearns 1.00 2.00
10 Don Lever 1.50 3.00
11 Cesare Maniago 2.00 4.00
12 Bob Manno 1.00 2.00
13 Jack McIlhargey 1.00 2.00
14 Garry Monahan 1.00 2.00
15 Chris Oddleifson 1.00 2.00
16 Gerry O'Flaherty 1.00 2.00
17 Curt Ridley 1.50 3.00
18 Ron Sedlbauer 1.00 2.00
19 Harold Snepsts 2.00 4.00
20 Dennis Ververgaert 1.50 3.00
21 Mike Walton 1.00 2.00

1978-79 Canucks Royal Bank

This 23-card set of Vancouver Canucks was sponsored by Royal Bank, whose company logo appears at the upper left corner on the front. The cards measure approximately 4 1/4" by 5 1/2" and are printed on thin cardboard stock. The fronts feature a color head and shoulders shot of the player on white background with a thin blue border. The player's facsimile autograph and the team logo appear above the picture. The backs present biographical and statistical information. The cards are unnumbered; they are checklisted below in alphabetical order.

COMPLETE SET (23) 20.00 40.00
1 Rick Blight .75 1.50
2 Gary Bromley 1.00 2.00
3 Bill Derlago .75 1.50
4 Roland Eriksson .75 1.50
5 Curt Fraser 1.00 2.00
6 Jere Gillis .75 1.50
7 Thomas Gradin 2.00 4.00
8 Hilliard Graves .75 1.50
9 John Grisdale .75 1.50
10 Glen Hanlon 1.25 2.50
11 Randy Holt .75 1.50
12 Dennis Kearns .75 1.50
13 Don Lever 1.00 2.00
14 Lars Lindgren .75 1.50
15 Bob Manno .75 1.50
16 Pit Martin 1.00 2.00
17 Jack McIlhargey .75 1.50
18 Chris Oddleifson .75 1.50
19 Ron Sedlbauer .75 1.50
20 Stan Smyl 2.00 4.00
21 Harold Snepsts 2.00 4.00
22 Dennis Ververgaert 1.00 2.00
23 Lars Zetterstrom .75 1.50

1979-80 Canucks Royal Bank

This 22-card set features posed color player photos from the shoulders up of the Vancouver Canucks. There are actually two different sets with the same value, a team-issued (no reference to Royal Bank) blank back set and a Royal Bank set; the card pictures (and values) are the same in both versions of the set. The sponsor name appears in black print at the card top, with the words "Player of the Week 1979/80" immediately below. The cards measure approximately 4 1/4" by 5 1/2". The front features a color head shot with a blue background and black and white borders. The player's jersey number, facsimile autograph, and team logo appear in the bottom white border. Since this is an unnumbered set, the cards are listed alphabetically. The Royal Bank backs carry biography, career summary, and complete statistical information (season by season, regular schedule, and playoffs).

COMPLETE SET (22)	15.00	30.00
1 Brent Ashton	1.00	2.00
2 Rick Blight	.75	1.50
3 Gary Bromley	1.00	2.00
4 Drew Callander	.75	1.50
5 Bill Derlago	1.00	2.00
6 Curt Fraser	1.00	2.00
7 Jere Gillis	.75	1.50
8 Thomas Gradin	1.50	3.00
9 Glen Hanlon	1.25	2.50
10 John Hughes	.75	1.50
11 Dennis Kearns	.75	1.50
12 Don Lever	1.00	2.00
13 Lars Lindgren	.75	1.50
14 Bob Manno	.75	1.50
15 Kevin McCarthy	.75	1.50
16 Jack McIlhargey	.75	1.50
17 Chris Oddleifson	.75	1.50
18 Curt Ridley	.75	1.50
19 Ron Sedlbauer	.75	1.50
20 Stan Smyl	1.50	3.00
21 Harold Snepsts	1.50	3.00
22 Rick Vaive	1.25	2.50

1980-81 Canucks Silverwood Dairies

This 24-card set of Vancouver Canucks was sponsored by Silverwood Dairies. The cards measure approximately 2 1/2" by 3 1/2" individually but were issued as perforated panels of three. The cards are checklisted below in alphabetical order.

COMPLETE SET (24)	20.00	40.00
1 Brent Ashton	.75	2.00
2 Ivan Boldirev	.75	2.00
3 Per-Olov Brasar	.60	1.50
4 Richard Brodeur	1.50	4.00
5 Gary Bromley	.75	2.00
6 Jerry Butler	.60	1.50
7 Colin Campbell	1.00	2.50
8 Curt Fraser	.75	2.00
9 Thomas Gradin	1.00	2.50
10 Glen Hanlon	1.00	2.50
11 Dennis Kearns	.60	1.50
12 Rick Lanz	.60	1.50
13 Lars Lindgren	.60	1.50
14 Dave Logan	.60	1.50
15 Gary Lupul	.60	1.50
16 Bob Manno	.60	1.50
17 Kevin McCarthy	.60	1.50
18 Gerry Minor	.60	1.50
19 Kevin Primeau	.60	1.50
20 Darcy Rota	.60	1.50
21 Stan Smyl	1.25	3.00
22 Harold Snepsts	1.25	3.00
23 Bobby Schmautz	.60	1.50
24 Dave(Tiger) Williams	1.50	4.00

1980-81 Canucks Team Issue

This 22-card set measures approximately 3 3/4" by 4 7/8" and features posed color head and shoulder player photos against a light blue-gray background. The pictures have rounded corners and are enclosed by thick black and thin red border stripes. The player's name, uniform number, position, and the team logo appear in the thicker bottom border. A facsimile autograph runs vertically to the left of the player's head. The backs are blank.

COMPLETE SET (22)	15.00	30.00
1 Brent Ashton	.75	2.00
2 Ivan Boldirev	.75	2.00
3 Per-Olov Brasar	.60	1.50
4 Richard Brodeur	1.50	4.00
5 Gary Bromley	.75	2.00
6 Jerry Butler	.60	1.50
7 Colin Campbell	1.00	2.50
8 Curt Fraser	.75	2.00
9 Thomas Gradin	1.00	2.50
10 Glen Hanlon	1.00	2.50
11 Dennis Kearns	.60	1.50
12 Rick Lanz	.60	1.50
13 Lars Lindgren	.60	1.50
14 Dave Logan	.60	1.50
15 Gary Lupul	.60	1.50
16 Kevin McCarthy	.60	1.50
17 Gerry Minor	.60	1.50
18 Darcy Rota	.60	1.50
19 Bobby Schmautz	.60	1.50
20 Stan Smyl	1.25	3.00
21 Harold Snepsts	1.25	3.00
22 Tiger Williams	1.50	4.00

1981-82 Canucks Silverwood Dairies

This 24-card set of Vancouver Canucks was sponsored by Silverwood Dairies, and the sponsor's name and logo appear at the top of the card face. The cards measure approximately 2 7/16" by 4 1/16" and feature a color action player photo, with the team logo superimposed at the lower right corner of the picture. The cards are unnumbered and so are checklisted in alphabetical order.

COMPLETE SET (24)	10.00	25.00
1 Per-Olov Brasar	.40	1.00
2 Richard Brodeur	1.00	2.50
3 Ivan Boldirev	.50	1.25
4 Jiri Bubla	.40	1.00
5 Jerry Butler	.40	1.00
6 Colin Campbell	.60	1.50
7 Marc Crawford	.75	2.00
8 Anders Eldebrink	.40	1.00
9 Curt Fraser	.40	1.00
10 Thomas Gradin	.75	2.00
11 Doug Halward	.40	1.00
12 Glen Hanlon	.60	1.50
12 Darcy Rota	.40	1.00
13 Ivan Hlinka	.40	1.00
13 Stan Smyl	1.00	2.50
14 Rick Lanz	.40	1.00
15 Lars Lindgren	.40	1.00
16 Blair MacDonald	.40	1.00
17 Gerry Minor	.40	1.00
18 Gary Lupul	.40	1.00
22 Kevin McCarthy	.40	1.00
24 Lars Molin	.40	1.00
24 Dave(Tiger) Williams	1.00	2.50
25 Harold Snepsts	1.00	2.50

1981-82 Canucks Team Issue

This 20-card set measures approximately 3 3/4" by 4 7/8" and features posed color head and shoulder player photos against a blue background. The pictures have rounded corners and are enclosed by thick black and thin red border stripes. The player's name, uniform number, position, and the team logo appear in the thicker bottom border. A facsimile autograph runs vertically to the left of the player's head. The backs are blank. The card of Richard Brodeur is the same one used in the 1980-81 team-issued set.

COMPLETE SET (20)	8.00	20.00
1 Ivan Boldirev	.60	1.50
2 Per-Olov Brasar	.40	1.00
3 Richard Brodeur	1.00	2.50
4 Jiri Bubla	.40	1.00
5 Jerry Butler	.40	1.00
6 Colin Campbell	1.00	2.50
7 Anders Eldebrink	.40	1.00
8 Curt Fraser	.60	1.50
9 Thomas Gradin	.75	2.00
10 Doug Halward	.40	1.00
11 Glen Hanlon	.60	1.50
12 Rick Lanz	.40	1.00
13 Gary Lupul	.40	1.00
14 Blair MacDonald	.40	1.00
15 Kevin McCarthy	.40	1.00
16 Gerry Minor	.40	1.00
17 Lars Molin	.40	1.00
18 Darcy Rota	.40	1.00
19 Stan Smyl	.75	2.00
20 Tiger Williams	1.00	2.50

1982-83 Canucks Team Issue

This 23-card set of the Vancouver Canucks was issued in three panels of six cards each with a fourth panel having five cards because the team photo fills the space of two player cards. The cards measure approximately 3 3/4" by 4 7/8". The fronts feature a color posed photo of the player with rounded corners and surrounded by a thick black and a thin red border. The player's name, position, jersey number and team logo appear below the photo in a wide black border. The horizontal backs carry the player's name, position, jersey number, biographical and statistical information. The cards are unnumbered and checklisted below in alphabetical order.

COMPLETE SET (23)	8.00	20.00
1 Ivan Boldirev	.40	1.00
2 Richard Brodeur	1.00	2.50
3 Jiri Bubla	.30	.75
4 Garth Butcher	.40	1.00
5 Ron Delorme	.30	.75
6 Ken Ellacott	.30	.75
7 Curt Fraser	.30	.75
8 Thomas Gradin	.60	1.50
9 Doug Halward	.30	.75
10 Ivan Hlinka	.30	.75
11 Hick Lanz	.30	.75
12 Moe Lemay	.30	.75
13 Lars Lindgren	.30	.75
14 Kevin McCarthy	.30	.75
15 Gerry Minor	.30	.75
16 Lars Molin	.30	.75
17 Jim Nill	.30	.75
18 Darcy Rota	.30	.75
19 Stan Smyl	.60	1.50
20 Harold Snepsts	1.00	2.50
21 Patrik Sundstrom	.75	2.00
22 Dave Williams	.75	2.00
23 Team Photo	.30	.75

1983-84 Canucks Team Issue

This 23-card set of Vancouver Canucks was issued in three panels of six cards each, with the fourth panel having 5 cards (the team photo card fills the space of two player cards). The player cards measure approximately 3 11/16" by 4 5/8". The front features a color posed photo (with rounded corners) of the player, surrounded by a thick black and a thin red border. The Canucks' logo and player information appear below the picture. The back has biographical and statistical information in a horizontal format. We have checklisted the names below in alphabetical order, with the uniform number to the right of the name.

COMPLETE SET (23)	10.00	25.00
1 Richard Brodeur 35	.75	2.00
2 Jiri Bubla 29	.20	.50
3 Garth Butcher 5	.40	1.00
4 Marc Crawford 28	.40	1.00
5 Ron Delorme 19	.20	.50
6 John Garrett 31	.40	1.00
7 Jere Gillis 4	.20	.50
8 Thomas Gradin 23	.60	1.50
9 Doug Halward 2	.20	.50
10 Mark Kirton 16	.20	.50
11 Rick Lanz 4	.20	.50
12 Gary Lupul 7	.20	.50
13 Kevin McCarthy 25	.20	.50
14 Lars Molin 26	.20	.50
15 Jim Nill 8	.20	.50
16 Michel Petit 3	.40	1.00
17 Darcy Rota 18	.20	.50
18 Stan Smyl 12	.60	1.50
19 Harold Snepsts 27	.75	2.00
20 Patrik Sundstrom 17	.60	1.50
21 Tony Tanti 9	.60	1.50
22 Dave(Tiger) Williams 22	.75	2.00
23 Team Photo	.40	1.00

1984-85 Canucks Team Issue

This 26-card set of Vancouver Canucks was issued in four six-card panels plus a larger team photo card and an Air Canucks advertisement card (the latter two measure approximately 4 5/8" by 7"). The player cards measure 3 5/16" by 4 1/4". The key card in the set is Cam Neely appearing in his Rookie Card year. The cards are unnumbered and checklisted below in alphabetical order.

COMPLETE SET (26)	10.00	25.00
1 Neil Belland	.20	.50
2 Richard Brodeur	.60	1.50
3 Jiri Bubla	.20	.50
4 Garth Butcher	.30	.75
5 Frank Caprice	.30	.75
6 J.J. Daigneault	.30	.75
7 Ron Delorme	.20	.50
8 John Garrett	.40	1.00
9 Thomas Gradin	.60	1.50
10 Taylor Hall	.20	.50
11 Doug Halward	.20	.50
12 Rick Lanz	.20	.50
13 Moe Lemay	.20	.50
14 Doug Lidster	.30	.75
15 Gary Lupul	.20	.50
16 Al MacAdam	.20	.50
17 Peter McNab	.30	.75
18 Cam Neely	4.00	10.00
19 Michel Petit	.30	.75
20 Darcy Rota	.20	.50
21 Petri Skriko	.40	1.00
22 Stan Smyl	.40	1.00
23 Patrik Sundstrom	.40	1.00
24 Tony Tanti	.40	1.00
25 Team Photo (Large size)	.60	1.50
26 Air Canucks (Advertisment)	.08	.25

1985-86 Canucks Team Issue

This 25-card set of Vancouver Canucks was issued in four panels of six cards each, with a separate team photo card. The player cards measure approximately 3 3/8" by 4 1/4". The team photo measures approximately 7" by 4 5/8". The fronts feature color posed player photos (with rounded corners) surrounded by thick black and thin red borders. The Canucks' logo and player information appear below the picture. The backs are blank. The cards are unnumbered and checklisted below in alphabetical order.

COMPLETE SET (25)	7.20	18.00
1 Richard Brodeur	.60	1.50
2 Jiri Bubla	.20	.50
3 Garth Butcher	.30	.75
4 Frank Caprice	.30	.75
5 Glen Cochrane	.20	.50
6 Craig Coxe	.20	.50
7 J.J. Daigneault	.30	.75
8 Thomas Gradin	.40	1.00
9 Taylor Hall	.20	.50
10 Doug Halward	.20	.50
11 Jean-Marc Lanthier	.20	.50
12 Rick Lanz	.20	.50
13 Moe Lemay	.20	.50
14 Doug Lidster	.30	.75
15 Dave Lowry	.20	.50
16 Gary Lupul	.20	.50
17 Cam Neely	3.00	8.00
18 Brent Peterson	.20	.50
19 Jim Sandlak	.30	.75
20 Petri Skriko	.40	1.00
21 Stan Smyl	.40	1.00
22 Patrik Sundstrom	.40	1.00
23 Steve Tambellini	.20	.50
24 Tony Tanti	.40	1.00
25 Team Photo (Large size)	1.25	3.00

1986-87 Canucks Team Issue

This 24-card set of Vancouver Canucks was issued in four panels of six cards each; after perforation, the cards measure the standard size (2 1/2" by 3 1/2"). The front design has color head and shoulder shots with white borders. Below the picture the player's name and number appear between two team logos. The horizontally oriented backs have biography and career statistics. The cards are unnumbered and checklisted below in alphabetical order, with the uniform number after the name.

COMPLETE SET (24)	4.80	12.00
1 Richard Brodeur 35	.60	1.50
2 Garth Butcher 5	.30	.75
3 Frank Caprice 30	.30	.75
4 Glen Cochrane 29	.20	.50
5 Craig Coxe 32	.20	.50
6 Taylor Hall 8	.20	.50
7 Stu Kulak 16	.20	.50
8 Moe Lemay 14	.20	.50
9 Dave Lowry 22	.20	.50
10 Brad Maxwell 27	.20	.50
11 Petri Skriko 26	.30	.75
12 Barry Pederson 7	.40	1.00
13 Rick Lanz 4	.20	.50
14 Doug Lidster 3	.30	.75
15 Brent Peterson 10	.20	.50
16 Michel Petit 24	.30	.75
17 Dave Richter 6	.20	.50
18 Stan Smyl 12	.40	1.00
19 Jim Sandlak 33	.20	.50
20 Patrik Sundstrom 17	.40	1.00
21 Rich Sutter 15	.20	.50
22 Steve Tambellini 20	.20	.50
23 Tony Tanti 9	.40	1.00
24 Wendell Young 1	.40	1.00

1987-88 Canucks Shell Oil

This 24-card set of Vancouver Canucks was sponsored by Shell Oil and released only in British Columbia. It was issued as eight different three-card panels, with the cards measuring the standard size, 2 1/2" by 3 1/2", after perforation. The cards were distributed as a promotion for Shell Oil, with one panel set per week given out at participating Shell stations. Included with the cards was a coupon offering a 5.00 discount on tickets to the Canucks games. The front features a color head and shoulders shot of the player, with the Canucks' logo superimposed at the upper left hand corner of the picture. The player's name, position, and the "Formula Shell" logo appear below the picture. The back has biographical and career information on the player. The cards are unnumbered and checklisted below in alphabetical order. Kirk McLean's card predates his Rookie Card by two years.

COMPLETE SET (24)	3.00	8.00
1 Greg Adams	.30	.75
2 Jim Benning	.08	.25
3 Randy Boyd	.08	.25
4 Richard Brodeur	.40	1.00
5 David Bruce	.08	.25
6 Garth Butcher	.08	.25
7 Frank Caprice	.15	.40
8 Craig Coxe	.08	.25
9 Willie Huber	.08	.25
10 Doug Lidster	.20	.50
11 Dave Lowry	.08	.25
12 Kirk McLean	1.00	2.50
13 Larry Melnyk	.08	.25
14 Barry Pederson	.20	.50
15 Dave Richter	.08	.25
16 Jim Sandlak	.08	.25
17 Dave Saunders	.08	.25
18 Petri Skriko	.20	.50
19 Stan Smyl	.30	.75
20 Daryl Stanley	.08	.25
21 Rich Sutter	.08	.25
22 Steve Tambellini	.08	.25
23 Tony Tanti	.30	.75
24 Doug Wickenheiser	.08	.25

1988-89 Canucks Mohawk

This 24-card standard-size set of Vancouver Canucks was sponsored by Mohawk and issued in six panels of four cards each. The cards feature on the front a color head and shoulders shot of the player on while card stock. The Canucks' and Mohawk logos appear at the bottom of the card. The player's name, position, and number are given in black lettering running the bottom to top on the left side of the picture. The backs are blank. We have checklisted the cards below in alphabetical order, with the player's number to the right of his name. The cards of Trevor Linden and Kirk McLean's predate their Rookie Cards by one year.

COMPLETE SET (24)	6.00	15.00
1 Greg Adams 8	.40	1.00
2 Jim Benning 4	.20	.50
3 Ken Berry 18	.20	.50
4 Randy Boyd 29	.20	.50
5 Steve Bozek 14	.20	.50
6 Brian Bradley 10	.60	1.50
7 David Bruce 25	.20	.50
8 Garth Butcher 5	.20	.50
9 Kevan Guy 2	.20	.50
10 Doug Lidster 3	.20	.50
11 Trevor Linden 16	2.00	5.00
12 Kirk McLean 1	1.25	3.00
13 Larry Melnyk 24	.20	.50
14 Robert Nordmark 6	.20	.50
15 Barry Pederson 7	.30	.75
16 Paul Reinhart 23	.30	.75
17 Jim Sandlak 19	.20	.50
18 Petri Skriko 26	.30	.75
19 Stan Smyl 12	.30	.75
20 Harold Snepsts 27	.60	1.50
21 Ronnie Stern 20	.20	.50
22 Rich Sutter 15	.20	.50
23 Tony Tanti 9	.30	.75
24 Steve Weeks 31	.30	.75

1989-90 Canucks Mohawk

This 24-card standard-size set was sponsored by Mohawk to commemorate the Vancouver Canucks' 20th year in the NHL and was issued in six panels of four cards each. The cards feature a color head and shoulders shot of the player on white card stock. The Canucks' and Mohawk logos appear at the bottom of the card, and the Canucks' logo has the number "2" before it joining with the circular shape of the logo to suggest "20." The player's name, position, and number are given in black lettering running the bottom to top on the left side of the picture. The backs are blank. We have checklisted the cards below in alphabetical order, with the player's number to the right of his name.

COMPLETE SET (24)	6.00	15.00
1 Greg Adams 8	.30	.75
2 Jim Benning 4	.20	.50
3 Steve Bozek 14	.20	.50
4 Brian Bradley 10	.40	1.00
5 Garth Butcher 5	.20	.50
6 Craig Coxe 22	.20	.50
7 Vladimir Krutov 17	.40	1.00
8 Igor Larionov 18	.75	2.00
9 Doug Lidster 3	.20	.50
10 Trevor Linden 16	1.50	4.00
11 Kirk McLean 1	.75	2.00
12 Larry Melnyk 24	.20	.50
13 Robert Nordmark 6	.20	.50
14 Barry Pederson 7	.30	.75
15 Paul Reinhart 23	.30	.75
16 Jim Sandlak 19	.20	.50
17 Petri Skriko 26	.30	.75
18 Doug Smith	.20	.50
19 Stan Smyl 12	.40	1.00
20 Harold Snepsts 27	.40	1.00
21 Daryl Stanley 29	.20	.50
22 Rich Sutter 15	.20	.50
23 Tony Tanti 9	.30	.75
24 Steve Weeks 31	.30	.75

1990-91 Canucks Mohawk

This 29-card set of Vancouver Canucks was sponsored by Mohawk and issued in panels. After perforation, the cards measure the standard size. The front features color mug shots of the players, with thin red borders on a white card face. The player's name and position appear in black lettering above the picture, while the team logo in the lower right corner rounds out the card face. The horizontally oriented backs have biographical information and statistics (regular season and playoff). The cards are unnumbered and checklisted below in alphabetical order.

COMPLETE SET (29)	6.00	15.00
1 Greg Adams	.30	.75
2 Jim Agnew	.20	.50
3 Steve Bozek	.20	.50
4 Garth Butcher	.20	.50
5 Dave Capuano	.20	.50
6 Craig Coxe	.20	.50
7 Gerald Diduck	.20	.50
8 Troy Gamble	.30	.75
9 Don Gibson	.20	.50
10 Kevan Guy	.20	.50
11 Robert Kron	.20	.50
12 Tom Kurvers	.20	.50
13 Igor Larionov	.60	1.50
14 Doug Lidster	.20	.50
15 Trevor Linden	.75	2.00
16 Jyrki Lumme	.30	.75
17 Jay Mazur	.20	.50
18 Andrew McBain	.20	.50
19 Kirk McLean	.60	1.50
20 Rob Murphy	.20	.50
21 Petr Nedved	.60	1.50
22 Robert Nordmark	.20	.50
23 Gino Odjick	.30	.75
24 Adrien Plavsic	.20	.50
25 Dan Quinn	.20	.50
26 Jim Sandlak	.20	.50
27 Stan Smyl	.30	.75
28 Ronnie Stern	.20	.50
29 Garry Valk	.20	.50

1990-91 Canucks Molson

This set features large (approximately 8" by 10") glossy color close-up photos of Canucks, who were honored as the Molson Canadian Player of the Month. The photos are enclosed by a gold border. The player's name appears in the bottom gold border. At the bottom center is a picture of the Molson Cup. The team logo and a Molson logo in the lower corners round out the front. The backs are blank, and the unnumbered photos are checklisted below in alphabetical order.

COMPLETE SET (6)	16.00	40.00
1 Brian Bradley	2.00	5.00
2 Troy Gamble	2.00	5.00
3 Doug Lidster	2.00	5.00
4 Trevor Linden	4.00	10.00
5 Kirk McLean (Facing right)	3.00	8.00
6 Kirk McLean (Facing front)	3.00	8.00

1991 Canucks Panini Team Stickers

This 32-sticker set was issued in a plastic bag that contained two 16-sticker sheets (approximately 9" by 12") and a foldout poster, "Super Poster - Hockey 91", on which the stickers could be affixed. The players' names appear only on the poster, not on the stickers. Each sticker measures about 2 1/8" by 2 7/8" and features a color player action shot on its white-bordered front. The back of the white sticker sheet is lined off into 16 panels, each carrying the logos for Panini, the NHL, and the NHLPA, as well as the same number that appears on the front of the sticker. Every Canadian NHL team was featured in this promotion. Each team set was available by mail-order from Panini Canada Ltd. for 2.99 plus 50 cents for shipping and handling.

COMPLETE SET (32)	1.50	4.00
1 Greg Adams	.02	.10
2 Jim Agnew	.01	.05
3 Steve Bozek	.01	.05
4 Brian Bradley	.07	.20
5 Garth Butcher	.01	.05
6 Dave Capuano	.01	.05
7 Craig Coxe	.01	.05
8 Troy Gamble	.02	.10
9 Kevan Guy	.01	.05
10 Robert Kron	.01	.05
11 Igor Larionov	.08	.25
12 Doug Lidster	.02	.10
13 Trevor Linden	.20	.50
14 Jyrki Lumme	.02	.10
15 Andrew McBain	.01	.05
16 Rob Murphy	.01	.05
17 Petr Nedved	.20	.50
18 Robert Nordmark	.01	.05
19 Adrien Plavsic	.01	.05
20 Dan Quinn	.02	.10
21 Jim Sandlak	.01	.05
22 Petri Skriko	.02	.10
23 Stan Smyl	.07	.20
24 Ronnie Stern	.01	.05
A Team Logo Left Side	.05	.15
B Team Logo Right Side	.05	.15
C Canucks in Action Upper Left Corner	.05	.15
D Canucks in Action Lower Left Corner	.05	.15
E Game Action Upper Right Corner	.05	.15
F Game Action Lower Right Corner	.05	.15
G Kirk McLean	.20	.50
H Trevor Linden	.20	.50

1991-92 Canucks Autograph Cards

These autograph cards, each measuring approximately 3 3/4" by 8 1/2", were issued by the team with a large white area at the bottom for the players to sign. The front features a glossy color close-up photo, with the year and the team logo in the white border above the picture. In cursive lettering, the player's name and number appear below the picture, with his position printed in block lettering. The unnumbered cards are blank on the back and checklisted below in alphabetical order.

COMPLETE SET (23)	10.00	25.00
1 Greg Adams	.40	1.00
2 Pavel Bure	3.00	8.00
3 Dave Babych	.40	1.00
4 Geoff Courtnall	.40	1.00
5 Gerald Diduck	.20	.50
6 Robert Dirk	.20	.50
7 Troy Gamble	.30	.75
8 Randy Gregg	.20	.50
9 Robert Kron	.20	.50
10 Igor Larionov	.60	1.50
11 Doug Lidster	.20	.50
12 Trevor Linden	1.00	2.50
13 Jyrki Lumme	.30	.75
14 Kirk McLean	1.25	3.00
15 Sergio Momesso	.20	.50
16 Rob Murphy	.20	.50
17 Dana Murzyn	.20	.50
18 Petr Nedved	1.25	3.00
19 Gino Odjick	.30	.75
20 Adrien Plavsic	.20	.50
21 Cliff Ronning	.60	1.50
22 Jim Sandlak	.20	.50
23 Ryan Walter	.20	.50
24 Garry Valk	.20	.50

1991-92 Canucks Molson

This set features large (approximately 8" by 10") glossy color close-up photos of Canucks, who were honored as the Molson Canadian Player of the Month or Player of the Year. The photos are enclosed by white, red, and blue border stripes. A gold leaf appear above the picture, while a gold plaque identifying the player appears below the picture. The team logo and a Molson logo appear in the lower corners. The backs are blank, and the unnumbered photos are checklisted below in alphabetical order.

COMPLETE SET (7)	20.00	50.00
1 Greg Adams	1.50	4.00
2 Pavel Bure (White uniform)	6.00	15.00
3 Pavel Bure POY (Black uniform)	6.00	15.00
4 Igor Larionov	2.50	6.00
5 Trevor Linden	3.00	8.00
6 Kirk McLean	3.00	8.00
7 Cliff Ronning	2.00	5.00

1991-92 Canucks Team Issue 8x10

This set features 8" by 10" glossy color close-up photos of the Vancouver Canucks. The photos are enclosed by a thin black border. In cursive lettering, the player's name and number appear below the picture, with his position printed in block lettering. The team logo in the lower left corner completes the front. The backs carry a black and white head shot, biography, 1990-91 season summary, career highlights, personal information, and complete statistics. The cards are unnumbered and checklisted below in alphabetical order.

COMPLETE SET (23)	30.00	75.00
1 Greg Adams	1.50	4.00
2 Pavel Bure	6.00	15.00
3 Dave Babych	1.25	3.00
4 Geoff Courtnall	1.50	4.00
5 Gerald Diduck	1.25	3.00
6 Robert Dirk	1.25	3.00
7 Troy Gamble	1.50	4.00
8 Randy Gregg	1.25	3.00
9 Robert Kron	1.25	3.00
10 Igor Larionov	1.50	4.00
11 Doug Lidster	1.25	3.00
12 Trevor Linden	2.00	5.00
13 Jyrki Lumme	1.25	3.00
14 Kirk McLean	2.00	5.00
15 Sergio Momesso	1.25	3.00
16 Rob Murphy	1.25	3.00
17 Dana Murzyn	1.25	3.00
18 Petr Nedved	2.00	5.00
19 Gino Odjick	1.50	4.00
20 Adrien Plavsic	1.25	3.00
21 Cliff Ronning	2.00	5.00
22 Jim Sandlak	1.25	3.00
23 Ryan Walter	1.25	3.00

1992-93 Canucks Road Trip Art

Dubbed "Road Trip Art Cards," this set of 25 approximately 4 3/4" by 7" player portraits was available only at Subway and Payless stores. Each week for six weeks, a set of four player portraits was released at a suggested price of 2.29 per pack. Also there was a tab inside each package and one could win a pair of 1993-94 season tickets, autographed Road Trip prints, limited edition Road Trip prints, Road Trip puzzles, and Road Trip coloring books. The photos are black-and-white and picture the Canuck players dressed in western garb. A gold foil facsimile autograph is printed near the bottom. The backs carry the player's name in a wide red stripe at the top. Humorous text in the form of player quotes rests against a white background along with the team logo and the words "Road Trip." A bright yellow stripe accents the bottom of the card and contains manufacturer information. The portraits are listed below in alphabetical order with the week issued denoted.

COMPLETE SET (25)	6.00	15.00
1 Greg Adams W1	.30	.75
2 Shawn Antoski W5	.20	.50
3 Dave Babych W5	.30	.75
4 Pavel Bure W3	2.00	5.00
5 Geoff Courtnall W5	.30	.75
6 Gerald Diduck W4	.20	.50
7 Robert Dirk W5	.20	.50
8 Tom Fergus W3	.20	.50
9 Robert Kron W2	.20	.50
10 Doug Lidster W2	.20	.50
11 Trevor Linden W1	.60	1.50
12 Jyrki Lumme W1	.30	.75
13 Kirk McLean W2	.60	1.50
14 Sergio Momesso W2	.20	.50
15 Dana Murzyn W3	.20	.50
16 Petr Nedved W2	.60	1.50
17 Gino Odjick W4	.40	1.00
18 Adrien Plavsic W6	.20	.50
19 Cliff Ronning W6	.30	.75
20 Jim Sandlak W6	.20	.50
21 Jiri Slegr W1	.20	.50
22 Garry Valk W4	.20	.50
23 Ryan Walter W5	.20	.50
24 Dixon Ward W3	.20	.50
25 Kay Whitmore W6	.30	.75

1994-95 Canucks Program Inserts

Measuring approximately 8" by 10 1/2", these program inserts feature the 1994-95 Vancouver Canucks. The fronts have color action player shots with white borders. The player's name, number and position appear on the fronts, along with the words "Canucks Collector Series" in a bar at the top. The backs are blank. The inserts are unnumbered and checklisted below in alphabetical order.

COMPLETE SET (22)	32.00	80.00
1 Greg Adams	1.50	4.00
2 Shawn Antoski	1.50	4.00
3 Dave Babych	1.50	4.00
4 Jeff Brown	1.50	4.00
5 Pavel Bure	4.00	10.00
6 Geoff Courtnall	1.50	4.00
7 Gerald Diduck	1.50	4.00
8 Robert Dirk	1.50	4.00
9 Martin Gelinas	1.50	4.00
10 Brian Glynn	1.50	4.00
11 Tim Hunter	1.50	4.00
12 Nathan LaFayette	1.50	4.00
13 Trevor Linden	2.00	5.00
14 Jyrki Lumme	1.50	4.00
15 Kirk McLean	2.00	5.00
16 Dana Murzyn	1.50	4.00
17 Gino Odjick	1.50	4.00
18 Adrien Plavsic	1.50	4.00
19 Cliff Ronning	1.50	4.00
20 Jiri Slegr	1.50	4.00
21 Dixon Ward	1.50	4.00
22 Kay Whitmore	2.00	5.00

1995-96 Canucks Building the Dream Art

This 18-card set of the Vancouver Canucks features 5" by 7" borderless black-and-white player photos in construction worker poses with gold facsimile autographs at the bottom. The backs carry player information. This set continues the tradition begun in 1992-93 with the Canucks Road Trip Art set.

COMPLETE SET (18)	6.00	15.00
1 Kirk McLean	.40	1.00
2 Kay Whitmore	.25	.60
3 Bret Hedican	.20	.50
4 Tim Hunter	.20	.50
5 Dana Murzyn	.20	.50
6 Jyrki Lumme	.25	.60
7 Cliff Ronning	.30	.75
8 Jeff Brown	.30	.75
9 Martin Gelinas	.40	1.00
10 Pavel Bure	2.00	5.00
11 Jiri Slegr	.20	.50
12 Sergio Momesso	.20	.50
13 Gino Odjick	.40	1.00
14 Geoff Courtnall	.20	.50
15 John McIntyre	.20	.50
16 Trevor Linden	.75	2.00
17 Mike Peca	.40	1.00
18 Dave Babych	.20	.50

1996-97 Canucks Postcards

This extremely attractive, 27-postcard set was produced by the Canucks and sponsored by IGA grocery stores as a promotional giveaway. The highly stylized fronts have an action color photo with the team name above, and a row of team logos to the right. Immediately below the photo is a strip for autographing. The backs are blank. As the postcards are unnumbered, they are listed according to their sweater number, which is displayed on the lower right hand front corner.

COMPLETE SET (27)	6.00	15.00
1 Kirk McLean	.30	.75
3 Bret Hedican	.08	.25
4 Mark Wotton	.08	.25
5 Dana Murzyn	.08	.25
6 Adrian Aucoin	.08	.25
7 David Roberts	.08	.25
8 Donald Brashear	.08	.25
9 Russ Courtnall	.20	.50
10 Esa Tikkanen	.20	.50
16 Trevor Linden	.30	.75
17 Mike Ridley	.20	.50
18 Troy Crowder	.08	.25
19 Markus Naslund	.20	.50
20 Alexander Semak	.08	.25
21 Jyrki Lumme	.20	.50
23 Martin Gelinas	.30	.75
24 Scott Walker	.20	.50
26 Mike Sillinger	.08	.25
27 Leif Rohlin	.08	.25
29 Gino Odjick	.30	.75
30 Mike Fountain	.20	.50
31 Corey Hirsch	.30	.75
32 Chris Joseph	.08	.25
44 Dave Babych	.20	.50
89 Alexander Mogilny	.60	1.50
96 Pavel Bure	1.50	4.00
NNO Team Photo	.20	.50

2001-02 Canucks Postcards

This is not belived to be the complete checklist

COMPLETE SET (11)	4.00	10.00
1 Todd Bertuzzi	.40	1.00
2 Murray Baron	.40	1.00
3 Artem Chubarov	.40	1.00
4 Dan Cloutier	.60	1.50
5 Matt Cooke	.40	1.00
6 Ed Jovanovski	.60	1.50
7 Scott Lachance	.40	1.00
8 Trevor Linden	.75	2.00
9 Brendan Morrison	.60	1.50
10 Markus Naslund	.60	1.50
11 Peter Skudra	.40	1.00

2002-03 Canucks Team Issue

These singles were offered at team appearances. The checklist is believed to be incomplete. If you have additional information, contact us at hockeymag@beckett.com.

COMPLETE SET (?)		
1 Murray Baron		1.00
2 Todd Bertuzzi		5.00
3 Dan Cloutier		3.00
4 Matt Cooke		3.00
5 Artem Chubarov		
6 Ed Jovanovski		3.00
7 Trent Klatt		
8 Trevor Linden		3.00
9 Marek Malik		
10 Brendan Morrison		3.00
11 Markus Naslund		5.00
12 Mattias Ohlund		1.00
13 Sami Salo		
14 Daniel Sedin		3.00
15 Henrik Sedin		3.00

2003-04 Canucks Postcards

COMPLETE SET (28)		18.00
1 Bryan Allen		.50
2 Magnus Arvedson		.50
3 Todd Bertuzzi		1.00
4 Brian Burke GM		.10
5 Artem Chubarov		.50
6 Dan Cloutier		1.00
7 Matt Cooke		1.00
8 Marc Crawford CO		.25
9 Johan Hedberg		.50
10 Mike Johnston ACO		.10
11 Ed Jovanovski		1.00
12 Mike Keane		.50
13 Jason King		.50
14 Trevor Linden		1.00
15 Mats Lindgren		.50
16 Marek Malik		.50
17 Brad May		.50
18 Jack McIlhargey ACO		.10
19 Brendan Morrison		1.00
20 Markus Naslund		2.00
21 Mattias Ohlund		.50
22 Jarkko Ruutu		.50
23 Sami Salo		.50
24 Daniel Sedin		1.00
25 Henrik Sedin		1.00
26 Jiri Slegr		.50
27 Brent Sopel		.50
28 Finn MASCOT		.10

2003-04 Canucks Sav-on-Foods

Created by Pacific Trading Cards, this 24-card set featured players from the Vancouver Canucks and were sold exclusively at Sav-on-Foods stores. Cards were sold in 4-card packs for an SRP of $2.99. Autographs of Markus Naslund, Todd Bertuzzi and Brendan Morrison were also randomly inserted. Because of lack of market information, they are unpriced.

COMPLETE SET (30)	6.00	15.00
1 Trevor Linden	.60	1.50
2 Johan Hedberg	.20	.50
3 Mike Keane	.20	.50
4 Todd Bertuzzi Brendan Morrison Markus Naslund	.40	1.00
5 Markus Naslund	.60	1.50
6 Daniel Sedin	.40	1.00
7 Marek Malik	.20	.50
8 Brad May	.20	.50
9 Brendan Morrison	.20	.50
10 Mattias Ohlund	.20	.50
11 Magnus Arvedson	.20	.50
12 Bryan Allen	.20	.50
13 Jason King	.20	.50
14 Henrik Sedin	.40	1.00
15 Brent Sopel	.20	.50
16 Ed Jovanovski Dan Cloutier Mattias Ohlund	.40	1.00
17 Dan Cloutier	.40	1.00
18 Artem Chubarov	.20	.50
19 Jarkko Ruutu	.20	.50
20 Daniel Sedin Henrik Sedin Jason King	.40	1.00
21 Ed Jovanovski	.40	1.00
22 Todd Bertuzzi	.40	1.00
23 Matt Cooke	.40	1.00
24 Sami Salo	.20	.50
NNO Todd Bertuzzi AU		
NNO Markus Naslund AU		
NNO Brendan Morrison AU		

2006-07 Canucks Postcards

COMPLETE SET (25)	15.00	25.00
1 Kevin Bieksa	.60	1.50
2 Luc Bourdon	.40	1.00
3 Jan Bulis	.40	1.00
4 Alexandre Burrows	.40	1.00
5 Marc Chouinard	.40	1.00
6 Matt Cooke	.60	1.50
7 Rory Fitzpatrick	.40	1.00
8 Josh Green	.40	1.00
9 Ryan Kesler	.40	1.00
10 Lukas Krajicek	.40	1.00
11 Trevor Linden	.75	2.00
12 Roberto Luongo	1.25	3.00
13 Willie Mitchell	.40	1.00
14 Brendan Morrison	.40	1.00
15 Markus Naslund	.75	2.00
16 Mattias Ohlund	.40	1.00
17 Taylor Pyatt	.40	1.00
18 Dany Sabourin	.40	1.00
19 Sami Salo	.40	1.00
20 Tommi Santala	.40	1.00
21 Daniel Sedin	.75	2.00
22 Henrik Sedin	.75	2.00
23 Alain Vigneault CO	.10	.25
24 Fin MASCOT	.10	.25
25 Logo Card	.10	.25

2007-08 Canucks Team Issue

COMPLETE SET (21)	5.00	12.00
1 Logo Card	.30	.75
2 Kevin Bieksa	.30	.75
3 Alex Burrows	.30	.75
4 Jeff Cowan	.30	.75
5 Matt Cooke	.30	.75
6 Brad Isbister	.30	.75
7 Ryan Kesler	.30	.75
8 Lukas Krajicek	.30	.75
9 Trevor Linden	.40	1.00
10 Roberto Luongo	.75	2.00
11 Willie Mitchell	.30	.75
12 Aaron Miller	.30	.75
13 Brendan Morrison	.30	.75
14 Markus Naslund	.50	1.25
15 Mattias Ohlund	.30	.75
16 Taylor Pyatt	.30	.75
17 Byron Ritchie	.30	.75
18 Sami Salo	.30	.75
19 Daniel Sedin	.30	.75
20 Henrik Sedin	.30	.75
21 Curtis Sanford	.40	1.00

1974-75 Capitals White Borders

This 25-card set measures approximately 5" by 7" is printed on very thin paper stock. The fronts have black-and-white player portraits with white borders. The player's name and the team logo appear under the photo. The backs are blank. The cards are unnumbered and checklisted below in alphabetical order.

COMPLETE SET (25)	30.00	60.00
1 John Adams	1.00	2.00
2 Jim Anderson CO	1.00	2.00
3 Ron Anderson	1.00	2.00
4 Steve Atkinson	1.00	2.00
5 Michel Belhumeur	2.00	4.00
6 Mike Bloom	1.00	2.00
7 Gord Brooks	1.00	2.00
8 Bruce Cowick	1.00	2.00
9 Denis Dupere	1.00	2.00
10 Jack Egers	1.00	2.00
11 Jim Hrycuik	1.00	2.00
12 Greg Joly	1.50	3.00
13 Dave Kryskow	1.00	2.00
14 Yvon Labre	1.50	3.00
15 Pete Laframboise	1.00	2.00
16 Bill Lesuk	1.00	2.00
17 Ron Low	2.00	4.00
18 Joe Lundrigan	1.00	2.00
19 Mike Marson	1.50	3.00
20 Bill Mikkelson	1.00	2.00
21 Doug Mohns	2.00	4.00
22 Andre Peloffy	1.00	2.00
23 Milt Schmidt GM	2.50	5.00
24 Gord Smith	1.00	2.00
25 Tom Williams	1.50	3.00

1978-79 Capitals Team Issue

This set features the Capitals of the NHL. The oversized cards feature black and white head shots on thin paper stock. It is believed they were issued as a set to fans who requested them by mail.

COMPLETE SET (18)	7.50	15.00
1 Michel Bergeron	.75	1.50
2 Greg Carroll	.50	1.00
3 Guy Charron	.50	1.00
4 Rolf Edberg	.50	1.00
5 Rick Green	.50	1.00
6 Gordie Lane	.50	1.00
7 Mark Lofthouse	.50	1.00
8 Jack Lynch	.50	1.00
9 Dennis Maruk	.75	1.50
10 Paul Mulvey	.50	1.00
11 Robert Picard	.50	1.00
12 Bill Riley	.50	1.00
13 Tom Rowe	.50	1.00
14 Bob Sirois	.50	1.00
15 Gord Smith	.50	1.00
16 Leif Svensson	.75	1.50
17 Ryan Walter	.75	1.50
18 Bernie Wolf	.50	1.00

1979-80 Capitals Team Issue

This set features the Capitals of the NHL. The oversized cards feature black and white head shots on thin paper stock. It is believed they were issued as a set to fans who requested them by mail.

COMPLETE SET (23)	20.00	40.00
1 Pierre Bouchard	.50	1.00
2 Guy Charron	.50	1.00
3 Rolf Edberg	.50	1.00
4 Mike Gartner	12.50	25.00
5 Rick Green	.50	1.00
6 Bengt Gustafsson	.75	1.50
7 Dennis Hextall	.75	1.50
8 Gary Inness	.50	1.00
9 Yvon Labre	.50	1.00
10 Antero Lehtonen	.50	1.00
11 Mark Lofthouse	.50	1.00
12 Paul McKinnon	.50	1.00
13 Dennis Maruk	.75	1.50
14 Paul Mulvey	.50	1.00
15 Robert Picard	.75	1.50
16 Greg Polis	.50	1.00
17 Errol Rausse	.50	1.00
18 Tom Rowe	.50	1.00
19 Peter Scamurra	.50	1.00
20 Bob Sirois	.50	1.00
21 Wayne Stephenson	.50	1.00
22 Leif Svensson	.75	1.50
23 Ryan Walter	.50	1.00

1981-82 Capitals Team Issue

This 21-card set measures approximately 5" by 7". The fronts have black-and-white player portraits with white borders. The player's name, position, jersey number, and the team logo appear under the photo. The backs are blank. The cards are unnumbered and checklisted below in alphabetical order.

COMPLETE SET (21)	12.00	30.00
1 Timo Blomqvist	.40	1.00
2 Bobby Carpenter	1.25	3.00
3 Glen Currie	.40	1.00
4 Gaetan Duchesne	.60	1.50
5 Mike Gartner	4.00	10.00
6 Rick Green	.60	1.50
7 Randy Holt	.40	1.00
8 Wes Jarvis	.40	1.00
9 Al Jensen	.60	1.50
10 Dennis Maruk	1.25	3.00
11 Terry Murray	.40	1.00
12 Lee Norwood	.40	1.00
13 Mike Palmateer	1.25	3.00
14 Dave Parro	.60	1.50
15 Torrie Robertson	.60	1.50
16 Greg Theberge	.40	1.00
17 Chris Valentine	.40	1.00
18 Darren Veitch	.40	1.00
20 Howard Walker	.40	1.00
21 Ryan Walter	.75	2.00

1982-83 Capitals Team Issue

This 25-card set measures approximately 5" by 7". The fronts have black-and-white player portraits with white borders. The player's name, position, jersey number, and the team logo appear under the photo. The backs are blank. The cards are unnumbered and checklisted below in alphabetical order. The card of Scott Stevens appears one year before his Rookie Card.

COMPLETE SET (25)	16.00	40.00
1 Timo Blomqvist	.40	1.00
2 Ted Bulley	.40	1.00
3 Bobby Carpenter	.75	2.00
4 Glen Currie	.40	1.00
5 Brian Engblom	.60	1.50
6 Mike Gartner	3.00	8.00
7 Bob Gould	.40	1.00
8 Bengt Gustafsson	.75	2.00
9 Alan Haworth	.40	1.00
10 Randy Holt	.40	1.00
11 Ken Houston	.40	1.00
12 Doug Jarvis	.75	2.00
13 Rod Langway	1.50	4.00
14 Craig Laughlin	.40	1.00
15 Dennis Maruk	.75	2.00
16 Bryan Murray CO	.40	1.00
17 Terry Murray ACO	.40	1.00
18 Lee Norwood	.40	1.00
19 Milan Novy	.40	1.00
20 Dave Parro	.60	1.50
21 David Poile GM	.40	1.00
22 Pat Riggin	1.00	2.50
23 Scott Stevens	4.00	10.00
24 Chris Valentine	.40	1.00
25 Darren Veitch	.40	1.00

1984-85 Capitals Pizza Hut

These cards of Washington Capitals were given out to members of the Junior Capitals Club and measure approximately 4 1/2" by 6". The front features a color action photo of the player, with three blue stripes on the picture. The back has a small head shot of the player and his career statistics. The cards are unnumbered and hence are listed below alphabetically by player name.

COMPLETE SET (15)	14.00	35.00
1 Bob Carpenter	.75	2.00
2 Dave Christian	1.00	2.50
3 Glen Currie	.60	1.50
4 Gaetan Duchesne	.60	1.50
5 Mike Gartner	3.00	8.00
6 Bob Gould	.60	1.50
7 Bengt Gustafsson	.75	2.00
8 Alan Haworth	.60	1.50
9 Doug Jarvis	.75	2.00
10 Al Jensen	.75	2.00
11 Rod Langway	1.25	3.00
12 Craig Laughlin	.60	1.50
13 Larry Murphy	2.00	5.00
14 Pat Riggin	.75	2.00
15 Scott Stevens	3.00	8.00

1985-86 Capitals Pizza Hut

These cards of Washington Capitals were mailed three at a time to members of the Junior Capitals Club and measure approximately 4 1/2" by 6". The front features a color action photo of the player, with three red stripes on the picture. The back has a small head shot of the player and his career statistics. When Doug Jarvis, Pat Riggin, and Darren Veitch were traded, supposedly their cards were pulled and never mailed to club members. It is alleged that these cards were destroyed and only a few were kept. Consequently, these player cards are scarce.

COMPLETE SET (15)	14.00	35.00
1 Bob Carpenter	.75	2.00
2 Dave Christian	1.00	2.50
3 Gaetan Duchesne	.60	1.50
4 Mike Gartner	2.50	6.00
5 Bob Gould	.60	1.50
6 Bengt Gustafsson	.75	2.00
7 Alan Haworth	.60	1.50
8 Doug Jarvis SP	1.50	4.00
9 Al Jensen	.75	2.00
10 Rod Langway	1.25	3.00
11 Craig Laughlin	.60	1.50
12 Larry Murphy	2.00	5.00
13 Pat Riggin SP	2.00	5.00
14 Scott Stevens	2.50	6.00
15 Darren Veitch SP	1.50	4.00

1986-87 Capitals Kodak

The 1986-87 Washington Capitals Team Photo Album was sponsored by Kodak. It consists of three large sheets joined together to form one continuous sheet. The first panel has a team photo measuring approximately 10" by 8". The second and third panels consist of player cards; after perforation, they measure approximately 2" by 2 5/8". The cards feature color posed photos, with player information below. The cards are unnumbered and we have checklisted them below in alphabetical order. Kevin Hatcher's card predates his Rookie Card by one year.

COMPLETE SET (26)	12.00	30.00
1 Greg Adams	.60	1.50
2 John Barrett	.30	.75
3 John Blum	.30	.75
4 Dave Christian	.40	1.00
5 Bob Crawford	.30	.75
6 Gaetan Duchesne	.30	.75
7 Lou Franceschetti	.30	.75
8 Mike Gartner	1.50	4.00
9 Bob Gould	.30	.75
10 Jeff Greenlaw	.30	.75
11 Kevin Hatcher	.75	2.00
12 Alan Haworth	.30	.75
13 David A. Jensen	.30	.75
14 Rod Langway	.75	2.00
15 Craig Laughlin	.30	.75
16 Bob Mason	.40	1.00
17 Kelly Miller	.40	1.00
18 Larry Murphy	1.00	2.50
19 Bryan Murray CO	.30	.75
20 Pete Peeters	.75	2.00
21 Michal Pivonka	1.25	3.00
22 Mike Ridley	.75	2.00
23 Gary Sampson	.30	.75
24 Greg Smith	.30	.75
25 Scott Stevens	1.50	4.00
26 Large Team Photo	.75	2.00

1986-87 Capitals Police

This 24-card police set features players of the Washington Capitals. The cards measure approximately 2 5/8" by 3 3/4" and were issued in two-card panels. The front has a color action photo on white card stock, with player information and the Capitals' logo below the picture. Inside a thin black border the back features a hockey tip ("Caps Tips"), an anti-crime tip, and logos of sponsoring police agencies. The cards are unnumbered and we have checklisted them below in alphabetical order, with the jersey number to the right of the player's name. Kevin Hatcher's card predates his Rookie Card by one year.

COMPLETE SET (24)	6.00	15.00
1 Greg Adams 22	.40	1.00
2 John Barrett 6	.20	.50
3 Bob Carpenter 10	.20	.50
4 Dave Christian 27	.30	.75
5 Yvon Corriveau 26	.20	.50
6 Gaetan Duchesne 14	.20	.50
7 Lou Franceschetti 32	.20	.50
8 Mike Gartner 11	1.25	3.00
9 Bob Gould 23	.20	.50
10 Kevin Hatcher 4	.60	1.50
11 Alan Haworth 15	.20	.50
12 Al Jensen 35	.25	.60
13 David A. Jensen 9	.20	.50
14 Rod Langway 5	.60	1.50
15 Craig Laughlin 18	.20	.50
16 Stephen Leach 21	.30	.75
17 Larry Murphy 8	.75	2.00
18 Bryan Murray CO	.20	.50
19 Pete Peeters 1	.60	1.50
20 Jorgen Pettersson 12	.20	.50
21 Michal Pivonka 17	.75	2.00
22 David Poile VP/GM	.20	.50
23 Greg Smith 19	.20	.50
24 Scott Stevens 3	1.25	3.00

1987-88 Capitals Kodak

The 1987-88 Washington Capitals Team Photo Album was sponsored by Kodak. It consists of three large sheets, each measuring approximately 11" by 8 1/4" and joined together to form one continuous sheet. The first panel has a team photo, with the players' names listed according to rows below the picture. While the second panel presents three rows of five cards each, the third panel presents two rows of five cards, with five Kodak coupons completing the left over portion of the panel. After perforation, the cards measure approximately 2 3/16" by 2 15/16". They feature color-posed photos bordered in red, with player information below the picture. The Capitals' logo and a picture of a Kodak film box complete the card face. The back has biographical and statistical information in a horizontal format. The cards are checklisted below by sweater number.

COMPLETE SET (26)	8.00	20.00
1 Pete Peeters	.40	1.00
2 Garry Galley	.40	1.00
3 Scott Stevens	.75	2.00
4 Kevin Hatcher	.75	2.00
5 Rod Langway	.40	1.00
6 John Barrett	.20	.50
8 Larry Murphy	.60	1.50
10 Kelly Miller	.30	.75
11 Mike Gartner	1.00	2.50
12 Peter Sundstrom	.30	.75
16 Bengt Gustafsson	.30	.75
17 Mike Ridley	.60	1.50
18 Craig Laughlin	.20	.50
19 Greg Smith	.20	.50
20 Michal Pivonka	.60	1.50
22 Greg Adams	.40	1.00
23 Bob Gould	.20	.50
25 Lou Franceschetti	.20	.50
27 Dave Christian	.40	1.00
29 Ed Kastelic	.20	.50
30 Clint Malarchuk	.40	1.00
32 Dale Hunter	.60	1.50
34 Bill Houlder	.30	.75
xx Bryan Murray CO	.20	.50
XX Team Photo	.20	.50
xx David Poile VP/GM	.20	.50

1987-88 Capitals Team Issue

This 23-card set measures 5 1/4" by 8". The fronts feature autographed color action photos. The backs carry a head shot, biography, 1986-87 recap, career highlights, personal information and complete statistics with the player's name, position and jersey number at the top. The cards are unnumbered and checklisted below in alphabetical order.

COMPLETE SET (23)	10.00	25.00
1 Greg Adams	.50	1.25
2 John Barrett	.30	.75
3 Dave Christian	.50	1.25
4 Lou Franceschetti	.30	.75
5 Garry Galley	.60	1.50
6 Mike Gartner	1.25	3.00
7 Bob Gould	.30	.75
8 Bengt Gustafsson	.40	1.00
9 Kevin Hatcher	1.25	3.00
10 Dale Hunter	.75	2.00
11 David Jensen	.30	.75
12 Ed Kastelic	.30	.75
13 Rod Langway	.50	1.25
14 Craig Laughlin	.30	.75
15 Clint Malarchuk	.50	1.25
16 Kelly Miller	.40	1.00
17 Larry Murphy	.75	2.00
18 Pete Peeters	.60	1.50
19 Michal Pivonka	.75	2.00
20 Mike Ridley	.75	2.00
21 Greg Smith	.30	.75
22 Scott Stevens	1.00	2.50
23 Peter Sundstrom	.40	1.00

1988-89 Capitals Borderless

Measuring approximately 5" by 7", this 21-card set features the 1988-89 Washington Capitals. The fronts have borderless color action player photos. The backs carry player biography and statistics, season and career highlights, and short personal information. The cards are unnumbered and checklisted below in alphabetical order.

COMPLETE SET (21)	6.00	15.00
1 Dave Christian	.40	1.00
2 Yvon Corriveau	.30	.75
3 Geoff Courtnall	.75	2.00
4 Lou Franceschetti	.30	.75
5 Mike Gartner	.75	2.00
6 Bob Gould	.30	.75
7 Bengt Gustafsson	.40	1.00
8 Kevin Hatcher	.60	1.50
9 Dale Hunter	.60	1.50
10 Rod Langway	.60	1.50
11 Stephen Leach	.30	.75
12 Grant Ledyard	.30	.75
13 Clint Malarchuk	.40	1.00
14 Kelly Miller	.30	.75
15 Larry Murphy	.60	1.50
16 Pete Peeters	.40	1.00
17 Michal Pivonka	.75	2.00
18 Mike Ridley	.60	1.50
19 Neil Sheehy	.30	.75
20 Scott Stevens	.75	2.00
21 Peter Sundstrom	.40	1.00

1988-89 Capitals Smokey

This 24-card safety set features players of the Washington Capitals. The cards measure approximately 2 5/8" by 3 3/4" and were issued in two-card panels. The front has a color action photo on white card stock, with player information and logos below the picture. Inside a thin black border the back features a hockey tip ("Caps Tips") and a fire prevention cartoon starring Smokey. The cards are unnumbered and we have checklisted them below in alphabetical order, with the sweater number to the right of the player's name. Geoff Courtnall's card predates his Rookie Card by a year.

COMPLETE SET (24)	6.00	15.00
1 Dave Christian 27	.30	.75
2 Yvon Corriveau 26	.20	.50
3 Geoff Courtnall 14	.60	1.50
4 Lou Franceschetti 25	.20	.50
5 Mike Gartner 11	.60	1.50
6 Bob Gould 23	.20	.50
7 Bengt Gustafsson 16	.30	.75
8 Kevin Hatcher 4	.40	1.00
9 Dale Hunter 32	.40	1.00
10 Rod Langway 5	.40	1.00
11 Stephen Leach 21	.20	.50
12 Grant Ledyard 6	.20	.50
13 Clint Malarchuk 30	.30	.75
14 Kelly Miller 10	.20	.50
15 Larry Murphy 8	.40	1.00
16 Bryan Murray CO	.30	.75
17 Pete Peeters 1	.30	.75
18 Michal Pivonka 20	.60	1.50
19 David Poile VP/GM	.20	.50
20 Mike Ridley 17	.40	1.00
21 Neil Sheehy 15	.20	.50
22 Scott Stevens 3	.60	1.50
23 Peter Sundstrom 12	.30	.75
24 Title Card Smokey the Bear	.20	.50

1989-90 Capitals Kodak

The 1989-90 Washington Capitals Team Photo Album was co-sponsored by Kodak and W. Bell and Co. It consists of three large sheets, each measuring approximately 11" by 8 1/4" and joined together to form one continuous sheet. The first panel has a large blue square designated for autographs. While the second panel presents three rows of five cards each, the third panel presents two rows of five cards, with Kodak advertisements completing the left over portion of the panel. After perforation, the cards measure approximately 2 3/16" by 2 1/2". They feature color action photos bordered in red, with player information below the picture. The Capitals' logo and a picture of a Kodak film box complete the card face. The back has biographical and statistical information in a horizontal format. The cards are checklisted below by sweater number.

COMPLETE SET (25)	8.00	20.00
1 Mike Liut	.40	1.00
3 Scott Stevens	.75	2.00
4 Kevin Hatcher	.60	1.50
5 Rod Langway	.60	1.50
6 Calle Johansson	.40	1.00
8 Bob Rouse	.30	.75
10 Kelly Miller	.40	1.00
11 Tim Bergland	.30	.75
12 John Tucker	.30	.75
14 Geoff Courtnall	.60	1.50
15 Neil Sheehy	.30	.75
16 Alan May	.30	.75
17 Mike Ridley	.40	1.00
19 John Druce	.30	.75
20 Michal Pivonka	.40	1.00
21 Stephen Leach	.30	.75
22 Dino Ciccarelli	.75	2.00
26 Steve Maltais	.30	.75
27 Bob Joyce	.30	.75
29 Scot Kleinendorst	.30	.75
32 Dale Hunter	.60	1.50
33 Don Beaupre	.40	1.00
xx Rob Laird ACO	.20	.50
xx Terry Murray CO	.20	.50
xx David Poile VP/GM	.20	.50

1989-90 Capitals Team Issue

This 23-card set measures approximately 5" by 7". The fronts feature full-bleed, posed color photos with the player's jersey as a background. The backs are blank. The cards are unnumbered and checklisted below in alphabetical order.

COMPLETE SET (23)	7.20	18.00
1 Don Beaupre	.30	.75
2 Dave Christian	.30	.75
3 Dino Ciccarelli	.60	1.50
4 Yvon Corriveau	.20	.50
5 Geoff Courtnall	.40	1.00
6 Kevin Hatcher	.40	1.00
7 Bill Houlder	.30	.75
8 Dale Hunter	.40	1.00
9 Calle Johansson	.30	.75
10 Dimitri Khristich	.60	1.50
11 Scot Kleinendorst	.20	.50
12 Nick Kypreos	.20	.50
13 Rod Langway	.40	1.00
14 Stephen Leach	.20	.50
15 Bob Mason	.30	.75
16 Alan May	.20	.50
17 Kelly Miller	.30	.75
18 Michal Pivonka	.30	.75
19 Mike Ridley	.30	.75
20 Bob Rouse	.20	.50
21 Neil Sheehy	.20	.50
22 Scott Stevens	.60	1.50
23 Doug Wickenheiser	.20	.50

1990-91 Capitals Kodak

The 1990-91 Washington Capitals Team Photo Album was sponsored by Kodak. It consists of three large sheets joined together to form one continuous sheet. The first panel has a team photo measuring approximately 10" by 8". The second and third panels consist of player cards; after perforation, they measure approximately 2" by 2 5/8". The cards feature color posed photos, with player information below. The cards are unnumbered and we have checklisted them below in alphabetical order.

COMPLETE SET (25)	6.00	15.00
1 Don Beaupre	.40	1.00
2 Tim Bergland	.20	.50
3 Peter Bondra	2.00	5.00
4 Dino Ciccarelli	.40	1.00
5 John Druce	.20	.50
6 Kevin Hatcher	.40	1.00
7 Dale Hunter	.40	1.00
8 Al Iafrate	.60	1.50
9 Calle Johansson	.30	.75
10 Dimitri Khristich	.40	1.00
11 Nick Kypreos	.20	.50
12 Mike Lalor	.20	.50
13 Rod Langway	.40	1.00
14 Stephen Leach	.20	.50
15 Mike Liut	.40	1.00
16 Alan May	.20	.50
17 Kelly Miller	.20	.50
18 Terry Murray CO	.08	.25
19 John Perpich	.20	.50
20 Michal Pivonka	.40	1.00
21 David Poile VP/GM	.08	.25
22 Mike Ridley	.40	1.00
23 Ken Sabourin	.20	.50
24 Mikhail Tatarinov	.20	.50
25 Dave Tippett	.20	.50

1990-91 Capitals Postcards

This 5 x 7 set features full color photos on the front and a blank back. Cards are unnumbered and checklisted below in alphabetical order.

COMPLETE SET (22)	8.00	20.00
1 Don Beaupre	.40	1.00
2 Tim Bergland	.20	.50
3 Peter Bondra	2.00	5.00
4 Dino Ciccarelli	.40	1.00
5 John Druce	.20	.50
6 Kevin Hatcher	.40	1.00
7 Jim Hrivnak	.25	.60
8 Dale Hunter	.40	1.00
9 Al Iafrate	.60	1.50
10 Calle Johansson	.30	.75
11 Nick Kypreos	.20	.50
12 Mike Lalor	.20	.50
13 Rod Langway	.40	1.00
14 Steve Leach	.20	.50
15 Mike Liut	.40	1.00
16 Alan May	.20	.50
17 Kelly Miller	.20	.50
18 Rob Murray	.20	.50
19 Michal Pivonka	.40	1.00
20 Mike Ridley	.40	1.00
21 Neil Sheehy	.20	.50
22 Dave Tippett	.20	.50

1990-91 Capitals Smokey

This fire safety set contains 22 cards and features members of the Washington Capitals. The cards measure approximately 2 1/2" by 3 3/4" and were issued in two-card panels. The front has a color action photo of the player, with player information below the picture between the Smokey the Bear and team logos. The back includes %%Caps Tips– and a fire prevention message from Smokey.

COMPLETE SET (22)	4.80	12.00
1 Don Beaupre	.30	.75
2 Tim Bergland	.15	.40
3 Peter Bondra	1.50	4.00
4 Dino Ciccarelli	.40	1.00
5 John Druce	.15	.40
6 Kevin Hatcher	.30	.75
7 Jim Hrivnak	.20	.50
8 Dale Hunter	.30	.75
9 Calle Johansson	.20	.50
10 Nick Kypreos	.15	.40
11 Mike Lalor	.15	.40
12 Rod Langway	.30	.75
13 Stephen Leach	.20	.50
14 Mike Liut	.40	1.00
15 Alan May	.15	.40
16 Kelly Miller	.15	.40
17 Rob Murray	.15	.40
18 Michal Pivonka	.40	1.00
19 Mike Ridley	.30	.75
20 Neil Sheehy	.15	.40
21 Mikhail Tatarinov	.15	.40
22 Dave Tippett	.15	.40

1991-92 Capitals Junior 5x7

This 25-card set measures approximately 5" by 7" and features full-bleed glossy action photos; in small black type across the bottom, the uniform number, name, and position are burned in. The backs are blank.

COMPLETE SET (25)	7.20	18.00
1 Don Beaupre	.40	1.00
2 Tim Bergland	.20	.50
3 Peter Bondra	1.50	4.00
4 Randy Burridge	.30	.75
5 Shawn Chambers	.20	.50
6 Dino Ciccarelli	.60	1.50
7 Sylvain Cote	.30	.75
8 John Druce	.20	.50
9 Jeff Greenlaw	.20	.50
10 Kevin Hatcher	.60	1.50
11 Dale Hunter	.60	1.50
12 Al Iafrate	.60	1.50
13 Calle Johansson	.30	.75
14 Dimitri Khristich	.60	1.50
15 Todd Krygier	.20	.50
16 Nick Kypreos	.20	.50
17 Mike Lalor	.20	.50
18 Rod Langway	.40	1.00
19 Mike Liut	.40	1.00
20 Alan May	.20	.50
21 Kelly Miller	.20	.50
22 Michal Pivonka	.60	1.50
23 Mike Ridley	.40	1.00
24 Ken Sabourin	.20	.50
25 Dave Tippett	.20	.50

1991-92 Capitals Kodak

The 1991-92 Washington Capitals Team Photo Album was sponsored by Kodak. It consists of three large sheets joined together to form one continuous sheet. The first panel measures approximately 11" by 8," and it has blank space allotted for autographs. The second panel carries three rows with five player cards each; after perforation, they measure approximately 2 3/16" by 2 3/4." The third panel has two rows with five player cards each, and a final row consisting of two Kodak coupons. The cards feature color head shots, with player information, team logo, and a picture of a Kodak film box below. In a horizontal format, the backs have biographical and statistical information. Though the cards are unnumbered, they are arranged in alphabetical order by players' last names and checklisted below accordingly.

COMPLETE SET (25)	4.80	12.00
1 Don Beaupre	.30	.75
2 Tim Bergland	.15	.40
3 Peter Bondra	1.00	2.50
4 Randy Burridge	.20	.50
5 Shawn Chambers	.15	.40
6 Dino Ciccarelli	.40	1.00
7 Sylvain Cote	.20	.50
8 John Druce	.15	.40
9 Kevin Hatcher	.30	.75
10 Jim Hrivnak	.20	.50
11 Dale Hunter	.30	.75
12 Al Iafrate	.40	1.00
13 Calle Johansson	.20	.50
14 Dimitri Khristich	.40	1.00
15 Todd Krygier	.15	.40
16 Nick Kypreos	.15	.40
17 Rod Langway	.30	.75
18 Mike Liut	.30	.75
19 Paul MacDermid	.15	.40
20 Alan May	.15	.40
21 Kelly Miller	.15	.40
22 Michal Pivonka	.40	1.00
23 Mike Ridley	.30	.75
24 Brad Schlegel	.15	.40
25 Dave Tippett	.15	.40

1992-93 Capitals Kodak

The 1992-93 Washington Capitals Team Photo Album was sponsored by Kodak. It consists of three 8 1/4" by 11" sheets joined together to form one continuous sheet. The first panel has a slot for collecting autographs. The second and third panels consist of player cards; after perforation, they measure approximately 2 3/16" by 2 3/4". The fronts feature color action player photos with white borders. Player information and the team logo are printed in the bottom white border. The horizontal backs carry biography and complete statistical information. Though the cards are unnumbered, they are arranged alphabetically on the sheet and checklisted below accordingly.

COMPLETE SET (25)	6.00	15.00

1 Shawn Anderson .20 .50
2 Don Beaupre .40 1.00
3 Peter Bondra 1.00 2.50
4 Randy Burridge .25 .60
5 Bobby Carpenter .25 .60
6 Paul Cavallini .20 .50
7 Sylvain Cote .20 .50
8 Pat Elynuik .20 .50
9 Kevin Hatcher .30 .75
10 Jim Hrivnak .25 .60
11 Dale Hunter .40 1.00
12 Al Iafrate .40 1.00
13 Calle Johansson .25 .60
14 Keith Jones .25 .60
15 Dimitri Khristich .40 1.00
16 Steve Konowalchuk .30 .75
17 Todd Krygier .20 .50
18 Rod Langway .30 .75
19 Paul MacDermid .20 .50
20 Alan May .20 .50
21 Kelly Miller .20 .50
22 Michal Pivonka .40 1.00
23 Mike Ridley .30 .75
24 Reggie Savage .20 .50
25 Jason Woolley .25 .60

1995-96 Capitals Team Issue

This 28-card set was given away as a premium in complete sheet form at a game late in the '95-96 season. The cards -- which feature the Caps in their new sweaters -- are perforated to be removed. As the cards are unnumbered, they are listed below in alphabetical order.

COMPLETE SET (28) 4.80 12.00
1 Jason Allison .60 1.50
2 Craig Berube .15 .40
3 Peter Bondra 1.25 3.00
4 Jim Carey .20 .50
5 Sylvain Cote .15 .40
6 Mike Eagles .15 .40
7 Martin Gendron .15 .40
8 Sergei Gonchar .15 .40
9 Dale Hunter .30 .75
10 Calle Johansson .20 .50
11 Jim Johnson .15 .40
12 Keith Jones .20 .50
13 Joe Juneau .30 .75
14 Kevin Kaminski .15 .40
15 Ken Klee .15 .40
16 Olaf Kolzig .60 1.50
17 Steve Konowalchuk .30 .75
18 Kelly Miller .15 .40
19 Jeff Nelson .15 .40
20 Pat Peake .15 .40
21 Michal Pivonka .20 .50
22 Joe Reekie .15 .40
23 Jim Schoenfeld CO .08 .25
24 Slapshot Mascot .02 .10
25 Slapshot Mascot .02 .10
26 Mark Tinordi .15 .40
27 Stefan Ustorf .15 .40
28 Brendan Witt .20 .50

1998-99 Capitals Kids and Cops

This set features the Capitals of the NHL. These slightly oversized singles were given out to kids by local police officers. A completed set could be turned in at local police stations for a "special gift." If anyone knows what that gift was, we'd love to hear about it.

COMPLETE SET (7) 4.00 10.00
1 Olaf Kolzig 1.25 3.00
2 Peter Bondra 1.25 3.00
3 Adam Oates .75 2.00
4 Dale Hunter .75 2.00
5 Calle Johansson .40 1.00
6 Steve Konowalchuk .40 1.00
7 Slapshot MAS .40 1.00

2002-03 Capitals Team Issue

Checklist is incomplete. We are looking for additional information on this set.

COMPLETE SET (?)
1 Peter Bondra .60 1.50
2 Jason Doig .40 1.00
3 Sergei Gonchar .40 1.00
4 Jaromir Jagr 1.25 3.00
5 Olaf Kolzig 1.25 3.00
6 Steve Konowalchuk .40 1.00
7 Robert Lang .40 1.00
8 Brendan Witt .40 1.00
9 Dainius Zubrus .40 1.00

1949 Carrera Ltd Sports Series

Cards feature blank backs, and come from a multi-sport series of 50 cards. Each card was cutout of a tobacco pack. The Anning single recently was discovered by collector Barry Chreptyk. Based on the numbering, it's possible there may be other hockey players in the set.

44 Les Anning 35.00
46 Duke Campbell 17.50 35.00

1934-35 CCM Brown Border Photos

These lovely oversized (11 X 9) photos were issued as premiums inside boxes of CCM skates. One such premium was included per box. The photos showed teams of the day and thus are highly prized by today's collectors. They are rarely seen in high grade and when offered, typically bring prices well above those listed below. Since the photos are unnumbered, they are listed below in alphabetical order.

COMPLETE SET (12) 500.00 1000.00
1 Boston Bruins 50.00 100.00
2 Chicago Blackhawks 50.00 100.00
3 Detroit Red Wings 50.00 100.00
4 Montreal Canadiens 62.50 125.00
5 Montreal Maroons 62.50 125.00
6 New York Americans 62.50 125.00
7 New York Rangers 50.00 100.00
8 Toronto Maple Leafs 50.00 100.00
9 All-Star Game 75.00 150.00
10 Allan Cup Champs, Moncton 25.00 50.00
11 Can-Am Champs, Providence 30.00 60.00
12 Memorial Cup Champs, St. Mike's 25.00 50.00

1935-36 CCM Green Border Photos

Like the previous year's offering, singles from this set were offered as a premium with the purchase of a new pair of CCM skates. This season, however, individual players were offered, along with teams. As they are unnumbered, they are listed below in alphabetical order.

COMPLETE SET (10) 375.00 750.00
1 Boston Cubs (Can-Am champs) 25.00 50.00
2 Boston Bruins 62.50 125.00
3 Halifax (Allan Cup) 25.00 50.00
4 Montreal Maroons 75.00 150.00
5 Toronto Maple Leafs 62.50 125.00
6 Winnipeg (Memorial Cup) 25.00 50.00
7 Frank Boucher 37.50 75.00
8 Lorne Chabot 50.00 100.00
9 Charlie Conacher 50.00 100.00
10 Foster Hewitt 37.50 75.00

2008 Celebrity Cuts

COMPLETE SET (100) 125.00 200.00
STATED PRINT RUN 499 SERIAL #'d SETS
67 Patrick Roy 3.00 8.00
89 Tony Esposito 1.50 4.00

2008 Celebrity Cuts Century Silver

*SILVER: .6X TO 1.5X BASIC
RANDOM INSERTS IN PACKS
STATED PRINT RUN 50 SERIAL #'d SETS

2008 Celebrity Cuts Century Gold

*GOLD: .75X TO 2X BASIC
RANDOM INSERTS IN PACKS
STATED PRINT RUN 25 SERIAL #'d SETS

2008 Celebrity Cuts Century Platinum

RANDOM INSERTS IN PACKS
STATED PRINT RUN 1 SERIAL #'d SET
NO PRICING DUE TO SCARCITY

2008 Celebrity Cuts Century Material

RANDOM INSERTS IN PACKS
PRINT RUNS B/WN 5-100 COPIES
NO PRICING ON QTY OF 5
67 Patrick Roy/100 6.00 15.00
89 Tony Esposito/100 4.00 10.00

2008 Celebrity Cuts Century Material Combo

RANDOM INSERTS IN PACKS
PRINT RUNS B/WN 5-50 COPIES PER
NO PRICING ON QTY OF 10 OR LESS
67 Patrick Roy/50 8.00 20.00
89 Tony Esposito/50 6.00 15.00

2008 Celebrity Cuts Century Material Combo Prime

RANDOM INSERTS IN PACKS
PRINT RUNS B/WN 1-10 COPIES PER
NO PRICING DUE TO SCARCITY

2008 Celebrity Cuts Century Signature Gold

RANDOM INSERTS IN PACKS
PRINT RUNS B/WN 1-200 COPIES PER
NO PRICING ON QTY OF 14 OR LESS
67 Patrick Roy/75 30.00 60.00
89 Tony Esposito/50 10.00 25.00

2008 Celebrity Cuts Century Signature Platinum

RANDOM INSERTS IN PACKS
STATED PRINT RUN 1 SERIAL #'d SET
NO PRICING DUE TO SCARCITY

2008 Celebrity Cuts Century Signature Material

RANDOM INSERTS IN PACKS
PRINT RUNS B/WN 1-50 COPIES PER
NO PRICING ON QTY OF 14 OR LESS
67 Patrick Roy/50 40.00 80.00
89 Tony Esposito/50 10.00 25.00

2008 Celebrity Cuts Century Signature Material Prime

RANDOM INSERTS IN PACKS
PRINT RUNS B/WN 1-50 COPIES PER
NO PRICING ON QTY OF 10 OR LESS
67 Patrick Roy/2

2008 Celebrity Cuts Century Signature Material Combo

RANDOM INSERTS IN PACKS
PRINT RUNS B/WN 1-10 COPIES PER
NO PRICING DUE TO SCARCITY
67 Patrick Roy/10
89 Tony Esposito/10

2008 Celebrity Cuts Century Signature Material Combo Prime

RANDOM INSERTS IN PACKS
PRINT RUNS B/WN 1-25 COPIES PER
NO PRICING ON QTY OF 10 OR LESS
67 Patrick Roy/1

1936 Champion Postcards

The set is in the same format as the 1936 Triumph set and was issued in the same manner as the Triumph set, except as an insert in "Boys" magazine published weekly in Great Britain. Three cards were issued in the first week of the promotion in "The Champion" and then one per week in "Boys" magazine. The cards are sepia toned and are postcard size, measuring approximately 3 1/2" by 5 1/2". The set is subtitled "Stars of the Ice Rinks". The cards are unnumbered and hence presented in alphabetical order. The date mentioned below is the issue date as noted on the card back in Canadian style, day/month/year.

COMPLETE SET (10) 875.00 1750.00
1 Marty Barry 10/1/00 40.00 80.00
2 Harold(Mush) March 8/2/36 40.00 80.00
3 Reg(Hooley) Smith 18/1/36 87.50 175.00
4 Sweeney Schriner 22/2/36 87.50 175.00
5 King Clancy 18/1/36 250.00 500.00
6 Bill Cook 1/2/36 100.00 200.00
7 Pep Kelly 25/1/36 40.00 80.00
8 Aurel Joliat 15/2/36 225.00 450.00
9 Charles Conacher 29/2/36 200.00 400.00
10 Fred(Bun) Cook 7/3/36 100.00 200.00

1963-65 Chex Photos

The 1963-65 Chex Photos measure approximately 5" by 7". This unnumbered set depicts players from four NHL teams, Chicago Blackhawks, Detroit Red Wings, Toronto Maple Leafs, and Montreal Canadiens. These blank-backed, stiff-cardboard photos are thought to have been issued during the 1963-64 (Canadiens and Maple Leafs) and 1964-65 (Blackhawks, Red Wings, and Canadiens again) seasons. Since these photo cards are unnumbered, they are ordered and numbered below alphabetically according to the player's name. There is rumored to be a Denis DeJordy in this set. The complete set price below includes both varieties of Beliveau and Rousseau.

COMPLETE SET (60) 1000.00 2000.00
1 George Armstrong 20.00 40.00
2 Ralph Backstrom 10.00 20.00
3 Dave Balon 7.50 15.00
4 Bob Baun 12.50 25.00
5A Jean Beliveau (Looking ahead) 50.00 100.00
5B Jean Beliveau (Looking left) 50.00 100.00
6 Red Berenson 10.00 20.00
7 Toe Blake CO 15.00 30.00
8 Johnny Bower 25.00 50.00
9 Alex Delvecchio 20.00 40.00
10 Kent Douglas 7.50 15.00
11 Dick Duff 10.00 20.00
12 Phil Esposito 75.00 150.00
13 John Ferguson 12.50 25.00
14 Bill Gadsby 15.00 30.00
15 Jean Gauthier 7.50 15.00
16 BoomBoom Geoffrion 30.00 60.00
17 Glenn Hall 25.00 50.00
18 Terry Harper 10.00 20.00
19 Billy Harris 7.50 15.00
20 Bill(Red) Hay 7.50 15.00
21 Paul Henderson 20.00 40.00
22 Bill Hicke 7.50 15.00
23 Wayne Hillman 7.50 15.00
24 Charlie Hodge 12.50 25.00
25 Tim Horton 50.00 100.00
26 Gordie Howe 112.50 225.00
27 Bobby Hull 100.00 200.00
28 Punch Imlach CO 10.00 20.00
29 Red Kelly 20.00 40.00
30 Dave Keon 30.00 60.00
31 Jacques Laperriere 12.50 25.00
32 Ed Litzenberger 7.50 15.00
33 Parker MacDonald 7.50 15.00
34 Bruce MacGregor 7.50 15.00
35 Frank Mahovlich 30.00 60.00
36 Chico Maki 10.00 20.00
37 Pit Martin 10.00 20.00
38 John MacMillan 7.50 15.00
39 Stan Mikita 30.00 60.00
40 Bob Nevin 7.50 15.00
41 Pierre Pilote 12.50 25.00
42 Marcel Pronovost 15.00 30.00
43 Claude Provost 7.50 15.00
44 Bob Pulford 15.00 30.00
45 Marc Reaume 7.50 15.00
46 Henri Richard 30.00 60.00
47A Bobby Rousseau 10.00 20.00
47B Bob Rousseau 15.00 30.00
48 Eddie Shack 20.00 40.00
49 Don Simmons 10.00 20.00
50 Allan Stanley 15.00 30.00
51 Ron Stewart 7.50 15.00
52 Jean-Guy Talbot 10.00 20.00
53 Gilles Tremblay 7.50 15.00
54 J.C. Tremblay 10.00 20.00
55 Norm Ullman 20.00 40.00
56 Elmer(Moose) Vasko 7.50 15.00
57 Ken Wharram 10.00 20.00
58 Gump Worsley 25.00 50.00

1992-93 Clark Candy Mario Lemieux

Issued by Clark Candy, this three-card set features three different color player photos of the Pittsburgh Penguins' Mario Lemieux. One card was inserted in each Bun candy bar pack. Each card measures approximately 3" by 3" and has a facsimile autograph in black inscribed across the picture. The pictures have black borders, and a gold stripe carrying the team logo cuts across the bottom of the card. The backs present biographical information, career summary, honors and awards, or career playing record. Only card number 3 listed below has a black-and-white close-up photo on its back. The cards are unnumbered and checklisted below in alphabetical order. There are reports that Lemieux may have signed some cards for insertion; to date, these rumors remain unsubstantiated.

COMPLETE SET (3) 2.50 6.00
COMMON CARD (1-3) 1.00 2.50

1972-73 Cleveland Crusaders WHA

This 15-card set measures 8 1/2" x 11" and features a black and white head shot on the front along with a facsimile autograph, and a Cleveland Crusaders color logo in the lower left corner. Featured portraits were done by Charles Linnett. The cards are unnumbered and checklisted below in alphabetical order.

COMPLETE SET (15) 25.00 50.00
1 Ron Buchanan 2.00 4.00
2 Ray Clearwater 2.00 4.00
3 Bob Dillabough 2.00 4.00
4 Grant Erickson 2.00 4.00
5 Ted Hodgson 2.00 4.00
6 Ralph Hoplavouri 2.00 4.00
7 Bill Horton 2.00 4.00
8 Gary Jarrett 2.00 4.00
9 Skip Krake 2.00 4.00
10 Wayne Muloin 2.00 4.00
11 Bill Needham CO 2.00 4.00
12 Rick Pumple 2.50 5.00
13 Paul Shmyr 2.00 4.00
14 Robert Whidden 2.00 4.00
15 Jim Wiste 2.50 5.00

1964-65 Coca-Cola Caps

The 1964-65 Coca-Cola Caps set contains 108 bottle caps measuring approximately 1 1/8" in diameter. The caps feature a black and white picture on the tops, and are unnumbered except for uniform numbers (which is listed to the right of the player's name in the checklist below). These caps were issued with both Coke and Sprite. Because Sprite was sold in lesser quantities than Coke, those caps tend to be harder to find. As such, some dealers charge a slight premium for those caps. There are also rumored to be French variations for both the Coke and the Sprite caps, making a total of four possible ways to put the set together. While no transactions have been reported for these French versions, it's fair to assume that their scarcity alone might earn them a slight premium over the prices listed below. The set numbering below is by teams and numerically within teams as follows: Boston Bruins (1-18), Chicago Blackhawks (19-36), Detroit Red Wings (37-54), Montreal Canadiens (55-72, New York Rangers (73-90), and Toronto Maple Leafs (91-108). A plastic holder (in the shape of a rink) was also available for holding and displaying the caps; the holder is not included in the complete set price below.

COMPLETE SET (108) 375.00 750.00
1 Ed Johnston 1 2.50 5.00
2 Bob McCord 4 1.50 3.00
3 Ted Green 6 2.00 4.00
4 Orland Kurtenbach 7 2.00 4.00
5 Gary Dornhoefer 8 2.00 4.00
6 Johnny Bucyk 9 5.00 10.00
7 Tom Johnson 10 2.00 4.00
8 Tom Williams 11 1.50 3.00
9 Murray Balfour 12 1.50 3.00
10 Forbes Kennedy 14 1.50 3.00
11 Murray Oliver 16 1.50 3.00
12 Dean Prentice 17 2.00 4.00
13 Ed Westfall 18 2.00 4.00
14 Reg Fleming 19 1.50 3.00
15 Leo Boivin 20 2.00 4.00
16 Ab McDonald 21 1.50 3.00
17 Ron Schock 23 1.50 3.00
18 Bob Leiter 24 1.50 3.00
19 Glenn Hall 1 6.00 12.00
20 Doug Mohns 2 2.00 4.00
21 Pierre Pilote 3 2.50 5.00
22 Elmer Vasko 4 1.50 3.00
23 Fred Stanfield 6 1.50 3.00
24 Phil Esposito 7 20.00 40.00
25 Bobby Hull 9 25.00 50.00
26 Bill(Red) Hay 11 1.25 2.50
27 John Brenneman 12 1.25 2.50
28 Doug Robinson 14 1.50 3.00
29 Eric Nesterenko 15 2.00 4.00
30 Chico Maki 16 1.50 3.00
31 Ken Wharram 17 1.50 3.00
32 John McKenzie 18 1.50 3.00
33 Al MacNeil 19 1.50 3.00
34 Wayne Hillman 20 1.50 3.00
35 Stan Mikita 21 7.50 15.00
36 Denis DeJordy 30 1.50 3.00
37 Roger Crozier 1 2.00 4.00
38 Albert Langlois 2 1.50 3.00
39 Marcel Pronovost 3 2.00 4.00
40 Bill Gadsby 4 2.00 4.00
41 Doug Barkley 5 1.50 3.00
42 Norm Ullman 7 4.00 8.00
43 Pit Martin 9 1.50 3.00
44 Gordie Howe 9 30.00 60.00
45A Gordie Howe 10 40.00 80.00
45B Alex Delvecchio 10 15.00 30.00
46 Ron Murphy 12 1.50 3.00
47 Larry Jeffrey 14 1.50 3.00
48 Ted Lindsay 15 5.00 10.00
49 Bruce MacGregor 16 1.50 3.00
50 Floyd Smith 17 1.50 3.00
51 Gary Bergman 18 1.50 3.00
52 Paul Henderson 19 3.00 6.00
53 Parker MacDonald 20 1.50 3.00
54 Eddie Joyal 21 1.50 3.00
55 Charlie Hodge 1 2.00 4.00
56 Jacques Laperriere 2 2.00 4.00
57 J.C. Tremblay 3 2.00 4.00
58 Jean Beliveau 4 10.00 20.00
59 Ralph Backstrom 6 2.00 4.00
60 Bill Hicke 8 1.50 3.00
61 Ted Harris 10 1.50 3.00
62 Claude Larose 11 1.50 3.00
63 Yvan Cournoyer 12 7.50 15.00
64 Claude Provost 14 1.50 3.00
65 Bobby Rousseau 15 2.00 4.00
66 Henri Richard 16 6.00 12.00
67 Jean-Guy Talbot 17 2.00 4.00
68 Terry Harper 19 2.00 4.00
69 Dave Balon 20 1.50 3.00
70 Gilles Tremblay 21 1.50 3.00
71 John Ferguson 22 2.50 5.00
72 Jim Roberts 26 1.50 3.00
73 Jacques Plante 1 10.00 20.00
74 Harry Howell 3 2.00 4.00
75 Arnie Brown 4 1.50 3.00
76 Don Johns 6 1.50 3.00
77 Rod Gilbert 7 4.00 8.00
78 Bob Nevin 8 1.50 3.00
79 Dick Duff 9 2.00 4.00
80 Earl Ingarfield 10 1.50 3.00
81 Vic Hadfield 11 2.00 4.00
82 Jim Mikol 12 1.50 3.00
83 Val Fonteyne 14 1.50 3.00
84 Jim Neilson 15 1.50 3.00
85 Rod Seiling 16 1.50 3.00
86 Lou Angotti 17 1.50 3.00
87 Phil Goyette 20 1.50 3.00
88 Camille Henry 21 2.00 4.00
89 Don Marshall 22 2.00 4.00
90 Marcel Paille 23 2.00 4.00
91 Johnny Bower 1 5.00 10.00
92 Carl Brewer 2 2.00 4.00
93 Red Kelly 4 5.00 10.00
94 Tim Horton 7 7.50 15.00
95 George Armstrong 9 4.00 8.00
96 Andy Bathgate 10 4.00 8.00
97 Ron Ellis 11 2.00 4.00
98 Ralph Stewart 12 1.50 3.00
99 Dave Keon 14 4.00 8.00
100 Dickie Moore 16 2.50 5.00
101 Don McKenney 17 1.50 3.00
102 Kent Douglas 19 1.50 3.00
103 Bob Pulford 20 2.50 5.00
104 Bob Baun 21 2.50 5.00
105 Eddie Shack 23 4.00 8.00
106 Terry Sawchuk 24 10.00 20.00
107 Allan Stanley 26 2.50 5.00
108 Frank Mahovlich 6.00 12.00
xx Cap Holder (Plastic Rink) 50.00 100.00

1965-66 Coca-Cola

This set contains 108 unnumbered black and white cards featuring 18 players from each of the six NHL teams. The cards were issued in perforated team panels of 18 cards. The cards are priced below as perforated cards; the value of unperforated strips is approximately 20-30 percent more than the sum of the individual prices. The cards are approximately 2 3/4" by 3 1/2" and have bi-lingual (French and English) write-ups on the card backs. An album to hold the cards was available from the company on a mail-order basis. It retails in the $50-$75 range in Near Mint. The set numbering below is by teams and numerically within teams as follows: Boston Bruins (1-18), Chicago Blackhawks (19-36), Detroit Red Wings (37-54), Montreal Canadiens (55-72, New York Rangers (73-90), and Toronto Maple Leafs (91-108).

COMPLETE SET (108) 250.00 500.00
1 Gerry Cheevers 15.00 30.00
2 Albert Langlois .75 1.50
3 Ted Green 1.00 2.00
4 Ron Stewart .75 1.50
5 Bob Woytowich .75 1.50
6 Johnny Bucyk 3.00 6.00
7 Tom Williams .75 1.50
8 Forbes Kennedy .75 1.50
9 Murray Oliver .75 1.50
10 Dean Prentice 1.00 2.00
11 Ed Westfall 1.00 2.00
12 Reg Fleming .75 1.50
13 Leo Boivin 1.50 3.00
14 Parker MacDonald .75 1.50
15 Bob Dillabough .75 1.50
16 Barry Ashbee 2.50 5.00
17 Don Awrey .75 1.50
18 Bernie Parent 15.00 30.00
19 Glenn Hall 5.00 10.00
20 Doug Mohns 1.00 2.00
21 Pierre Pilote 1.50 3.00
22 Elmer Vasko .75 1.50
23 Matt Ravlich .75 1.50
24 Fred Stanfield .75 1.50
25 Phil Esposito 20.00 40.00
26 Bobby Hull 20.00 40.00
27 Dennis Hull 2.50 5.00
28 Bill(Red) Hay 1.00 2.00
29 Ken Hodge 1.50 3.00
30 Eric Nesterenko 1.00 2.00
31 Chico Maki 1.00 2.00
32 Ken Wharram 1.00 2.00
33 Al MacNeil .75 1.50
34 Doug Jarrett .75 1.50
35 Stan Mikita 6.00 12.00
36 Dave Dryden 1.25 2.50
37 Roger Crozier 1.50 3.00
38 Warren Godfrey .75 1.50
39 Bert Marshall .75 1.50
40 Bill Gadsby 1.50 3.00
41 Doug Barkley .75 1.50
42 Norm Ullman 2.00 4.00
43 Gordie Howe 30.00 60.00
44 Alex Delvecchio 2.50 5.00
45 Val Fonteyne .75 1.50
46 Ron Murphy .75 1.50
47 Billy Harris .75 1.50
48 Bruce MacGregor .75 1.50
49 Floyd Smith .75 1.50
50 Paul Henderson 4.00 8.00
51 Andy Bathgate 1.75 3.50
52 Ab McDonald .75 1.50
53 Gary Bergman .75 1.50
54 Hank Bassen 1.25 2.50
55 Charlie Hodge 1.50 3.00
56 Jacques Laperriere 1.50 3.00
57 Jean-Claude Tremblay 1.00 2.00
58 Jean Beliveau 7.50 15.00
59 Ralph Backstrom 1.00 2.00
60 Dick Duff 1.25 2.50
61 Ted Harris 1.00 2.00
62 Claude Larose .75 1.50
63 Yvan Cournoyer 10.00 20.00
64 Claude Provost 1.00 2.00
65 Bobby Rousseau 1.00 2.00
66 Henri Richard 5.00 10.00
67 Jean-Guy Talbot 1.25 2.50
68 Terry Harper 1.00 2.00
69 Gilles Tremblay .75 1.50
70 John Ferguson 1.25 2.50
71 Jim Roberts .75 1.50
72 Gump Worsley 5.00 10.00
73 Ed Giacomin 12.50 25.00
74 Wayne Hillman .75 1.50
75 Harry Howell 2.00 4.00
76 Arnie Brown .75 1.50
77 Doug Robinson .75 1.50
78 Mike McMahon .75 1.50
79 Rod Gilbert 2.50 5.00
80 Bob Nevin .75 1.50
81 Earl Ingarfield .75 1.50
82 Vic Hadfield 1.25 2.50
83 Bill Hicke .75 1.50
84 John McKenzie 1.00 2.00
85 Jim Neilson .75 1.50
86 Jean Ratelle 2.50 5.00
87 Phil Goyette .75 1.50
88 Garry Peters .75 1.50
89 Don Marshall .75 1.50
90 Don Simmons 1.25 2.50
91 Johnny Bower 5.00 10.00
92 Marcel Pronovost 2.00 4.00
93 Red Kelly 2.50 5.00
94 Tim Horton 7.50 15.00
95 Ron Ellis 1.00 2.00
96 George Armstrong 2.00 4.00
97 Brit Selby .75 1.50
98 Pete Stemkowski .75 1.50
99 Dave Keon 5.00 10.00
100 Mike Walton 1.00 2.00
101 Kent Douglas .75 1.50
102 Bob Pulford 2.00 4.00
103 Bob Baun 2.00 4.00
104 Eddie Shack 2.50 5.00
105 Orland Kurtenbach 1.00 2.00
106 Allan Stanley 1.50 3.00
107 Frank Mahovlich 5.00 10.00
108 Terry Sawchuk 10.00 20.00
NNO Album 40.00 80.00

1965-66 Coca-Cola Booklets

These four "How To Play" booklets are illustrated with cartoon-like drawings, each measure approximately 4 7/8" by 3 1/2", and are printed on newsprint. Booklets A and B have yellow covers, while booklets C and D have blue covers. The 31-page booklets could be obtained through a mail-in offer. Under bottle caps of Coke or Sprite (marked with a hockey stick) were cork liners bearing the name of the player who wrote a booklet. To receive a booklet, the collector had to send in ten cork liners (with name of the player whose booklet was desired), ten cents, and the correct answer to a trivia question. Issued by Coca-Cola to promote hockey among the school-aged, they are designed in comic book fashion showing correct positions and moves for goalie, forward (both defensive and offensive), and defensemen. They are authored by the hockey players listed below. They are lettered rather than numbered and we have checklisted them below accordingly. The booklets were available in both English and French.

COMPLETE SET (4) 75.00 150.00
A Johnny Bower How To Play Goal 25.00 50.00
B Dave Keon How To Play Forward (Defensive) 25.00 50.00
C Jacques Laperriere How To Play Defence 12.50 25.00
D Henri Richard How To Play Forward (Offensive) 25.00 50.00

1977-78 Coca-Cola

Each of these mini-cards measures approximately 1 3/8" by 1 3/8". The fronts feature a color "mug shot" of the player, with his name given above the picture. Red and blue lines form the borders on the sides of the picture. The year 1978, the city from which the team hails, and the Coke logo appear below the picture. Inside a black border (with rounded corners) the back has basic biographical information. These unnumbered cards are listed alphabetically below.

COMPLETE SET (30) 62.50 300.00
1 Syl Apps .75 3.00
2 Dave Burrows .75 3.00
3 Bobby Clarke 6.00 25.00
4 Yvan Cournoyer 2.50 10.00
5 John Davidson 1.50 10.00
6 Marcel Dionne 4.00 15.00
7 Doug Favell 1.25 5.00
8 Rod Gilbert 1.50 10.00
9 Brian Glennie .75 3.00
10 Butch Goring .75 3.00
11 Lorne Henning .75 3.00
12 Cliff Koroll .75 3.00
13 Guy Lapointe 1.50 5.00
14 Dave Maloney .75 3.00
15 Pit Martin .75 3.00
16 Lou Nanne .75 3.00
17 Bobby Orr 30.00 125.00
18 Brad Park 2.50 10.00
19 Craig Ramsay .75 3.00
20 Larry Robinson 5.00 20.00
21 Jim Rutherford 1.25 5.00
22 Don Saleski .75 3.00
23 Steve Shutt 2.50 8.00
24 Darryl Sittler 4.00 20.00
25 Billy Smith 3.00 10.00
26 Bob Stewart .75 3.00
27 Rogatien Vachon 2.50 10.00
28 Jimmy Watson .75 3.00
29 Joe Watson .75 3.00
30 Ed Westfall .75 3.00

1994 Coca-Cola Wayne Gretzky Cups

Standing approximately 6" high, these full color cups featuring an image of Wayne along with a biographical fact from the appropriate year. Set may be incomplete and we welcome any additional information you may have.

COMPLETE SET (5) 8.00 20.00
COMMON CUP 1.50 4.00

1994 Coke/Mac's Milk Gretzky POGs

This 18-disc set features POGs measuring approximately 1 5/8" in diameter. These cards were offered through Mac's Milk stores in Canada (primarily Ontario); they were available at the store counter with the purchase of any Coke bottled product from May through middle of June of 1994. Inside a gold-foil holographic border, the fronts feature action color player photos with the words "The Great One" printed in black letters above the photo and a Coca-Cola Future Stars emblem at the bottom. The backs feature Gretzky's most prolific records and accomplishments.

COMPLETE SET (18) 6.00 15.00
COMMON POG (1-18) .40 1.00

1970-71 Colgate Stamps

The 1970-71 Colgate Stamps set includes 93 small color stamps measuring approximately 1" by 1 1/4". The set was distributed in three sheets of 31. Sheet one featured centers (numbered 1-31) and was available with the giant size of toothpaste, sheet two featured wings (numbered 32-62) and was available with the family size of toothpaste, and sheet three featured goalies and defensemen (numbered 63-93) and was available with king and super size toothpaste. The cards are priced below as individual stamps; the value of a complete sheet would be approximately 20 percent more than the sum of the individual stamp prices. Colgate also issued three calendars so that brushers could stick a stamp on each day for brushing regularly. These calendars retail in the $5-$10 range. The cards were numbered in a star in the upper left corner of the card face.

COMPLETE SET (93) 100.00 200.00
1 Walt McKechnie .50 1.00
2 Bob Pulford 1.50 3.00
3 Mike Walton .50 1.00
4 Alex Delvecchio 2.50 5.00
5 Tom Williams .50 1.00
6 Derek Sanderson 5.00 10.00
7 Garry Unger 1.00 2.00
8 Lou Angotti .50 1.00
9 Ted Hampson .50 1.00
10 Phil Goyette .50 1.00
11 Juha Widing .50 1.00
12 Norm Ullman 2.00 4.00
13 Garry Monahan .50 1.00
14 Henri Richard 2.50 5.00
15 Ray Cullen .50 1.00
16 Danny O'Shea .50 1.00
17 Marc Tardif .75 1.50
18 Jude Drouin .50 1.00
19 Charlie Burns .50 1.00
20 Gerry Meehan .75 1.50
21 Ralph Backstrom .75 1.50
22 Frank St.Marseille .50 1.00
23 Orland Kurtenbach .50 1.00
24 Red Berenson 1.00 2.00
25 Jean Ratelle 2.00 4.00
26 Syl Apps .75 1.50
27 Don Marshall .50 1.00
28 Gilbert Perreault 5.00 10.00
29 Andre Lacroix .75 1.50
30 Jacques Lemaire 1.50 3.00
31 Pit Martin .75 1.50
32 Dennis Hull .75 1.50
33 Dave Balon .50 1.00
34 Keith McCreary .50 1.00
35 Bobby Rousseau .75 1.50
36 Danny Grant .75 1.50
37 Brit Selby .50 1.00
38 Bob Nevin .50 1.00
39 Rosaire Paiement .50 1.00
40 Gary Dornhoefer 1.00 2.00
41 Eddie Shack 2.00 4.00
42 Ron Schock .50 1.00
43 Jim Pappin .50 1.00
44 Mickey Redmond 1.50 3.00
45 Vic Hadfield .75 1.50
46 Johnny Bucyk 2.00 4.00
47 Gordie Howe 12.00 30.00
48 Ron Anderson .50 1.00
49 Gary Jarrett .50 1.00
50 Jean Pronovost .75 1.50
51 Simon Nolet .50 1.00
52 Bill Goldsworthy .75 1.50
53 Rod Gilbert 2.00 4.00
54 Ron Ellis .75 1.50
55 Mike Byers .50 1.00
56 Norm Ferguson .50 1.00
57 Gary Sabourin .50 1.00
58 Tim Ecclestone .50 1.00
59 John McKenzie .50 1.00
60 Yvan Cournoyer 2.00 4.00
61 Ken Schinkel .50 1.00
62 Ken Hodge 1.00 2.00
63 Cesare Maniago 1.50 3.00
64 J.C. Tremblay .75 1.50
65 Gilles Marotte .50 1.00
66 Bob Baun 1.00 2.00
67 Gerry Desjardins 1.00 2.00
68 Charlie Hodge 1.50 3.00
69 Matt Ravlich .50 1.00
70 Ed Giacomin 3.00 6.00
71 Gerry Cheevers 4.00 8.00
72 Pat Quinn .75 1.50
73 Gary Bergman .50 1.00
74 Serge Savard 1.00 2.00
75 Les Binkley 1.00 2.00
76 Arnie Brown .50 1.00
77 Pat Stapleton .50 1.00
78 Ed Van Impe .50 1.00
79 Jim Dorey .50 1.00
80 Dave Dryden 1.50 3.00
81 Dale Tallon .75 1.50
82 Bruce Gamble 1.50 3.00
83 Roger Crozier 1.50 3.00
84 Denis DeJordy 1.50 3.00
85 Rogatien Vachon 2.00 4.00
86 Carol Vadnais .50 1.00
87 Bobby Orr 20.00 50.00
88 Noel Picard .50 1.00
89 Gilles Villemure 1.50 3.00
90 Gary Smith 1.50 3.00
91 Doug Favell 1.50 3.00
92 Ernie Wakely 1.50 3.00
93 Bernie Parent 5.00 10.00
NNO Stamp Calendar Sheet 5.00 10.00

1971-72 Colgate Heads

The 16 hockey collectibles in this set measure approximately 1 1/4" in height with a base of 7/8" and are made out of cream-colored or beige plastic. The promotion lasted approximately five months during the winter of 1972. The busts were issued in series of four in the various sizes of Colgate Toothpaste. The player's last name is found only on the back of the base of the head. The Ullmann error is not included in the complete set price below. The heads are unnumbered and checklisted below in alphabetical order.

COMPLETE SET (16) 100.00 200.00
1 Yvon Cournoyer 3.00 8.00
2 Marcel Dionne UER 6.00 15.00
3 Ken Dryden 8.00 20.00
4 Paul Henderson 2.50 6.00
5 Guy Lafleur 8.00 20.00
6 Frank Mahovlich 4.00 10.00
7 Richard Martin SP 15.00 30.00
8 Bobby Orr 20.00 40.00
9 Brad Park SP 20.00 40.00
10 Jacques Plante 6.00 15.00
11 Jean Ratelle 3.00 8.00
12 Derek Sanderson 6.00 15.00
13 Dale Tallon 2.00 5.00
14 Walt Tkaczuk 2.00 4.00
15A Norm Ullman ERR 4.00 10.00
15B Norm Ullman COR 10.00 25.00
16 Garry Unger 2.00 5.00

1995-96 Collector's Choice

This 396 card standard-size set was issued in 12-card packs with a suggested retail price of 99 cents per pack. The design is similar to the 1995 Collector Choice issues in baseball, basketball and football. Each card features a photo framed by white borders. The player's name and team is identified in the lower right-hand corner. The backs contain another photograph, biographical information and statistics. The last 70 cards of the set are dedicated to the following subsets: 1995 European Junior Championship (325-354), What's Your Game? (355-369), and Hardware Heroes (370-394). Rookie Cards in this set include Teemu Riihijarvi and Marcus Nilsson. In addition, a 15-card set was available only to collectors who redeemed through the mail a Young Guns Trade card, which was inserted at a rate of 1:34 packs. The cards were intended to "complete" the Collector's Choice set by including several of the top rookies of 1995-96, and thus bear the same design and continue the numbering from that set.

COMPLETE SET (396) 10.00 20.00
1 Wayne Gretzky .60 1.50
2 Darius Kasparaitis .01 .05
3 Scott Niedermayer .01 .05
4 Brendan Shanahan .08 .25
5 Doug Gilmour .02 .10
6 Lyle Odelein .01 .05
7 Dave Gagner .01 .05
8 Gary Suter .01 .05
9 Sandis Ozolinsh .01 .05
10 Sergei Zubov .01 .05
11 Don Beaupre .02 .10
12 Bill Lindsay .01 .05
13 David Oliver .01 .05
14 Bob Corkum .01 .05
15 German Titov .01 .05
16 Jari Kurri .08 .25
17 Cliff Ronning .01 .05
18 Paul Coffey .08 .25
19 Ian Laperriere .01 .05
20 Dave Andreychuk .02 .10
21 Andrei Nikolishin .01 .05
22 Blaine Lacher .02 .10
23 Yuri Khmylev .01 .05
24 Darren Turcotte .01 .05
25 Joe Mullen .02 .10
26 Peter Forsberg .25 .60
27 Paul Ysebaert .01 .05
28 Tommy Soderstrom .02 .10
29 Rod Brind'Amour .02 .10
30 Jim Carey .02 .10
31 Geoff Courtnall .01 .05
32 Slava Kozlov .02 .10
33 Ray Ferraro .01 .05
34 John MacLean .02 .10
35 Benoit Brunet .01 .05
36 Trent Klatt .01 .05
37 Chris Chelios .08 .25
38 Tom Pederson .01 .05
39 Pat Elynuik .01 .05
40 Rob Niedermayer .02 .10
41 Jason Arnott .01 .05
42 Patrik Carnback .01 .05
43 Steve Chiasson .01 .05
44 Marty McSorley .01 .05
45 Pavel Bure .08 .25
46 Glenn Anderson .08 .25
47 Doug Brown .01 .05
48 Mike Ridley .01 .05
49 Alexei Zhamnov .02 .10
50 Mariusz Czerkawski .01 .05
51 Derek Plante .01 .05
52 Andrew Cassels .01 .05
53 Tom Barrasso .02 .10
54 Andrei Kovalenko .01 .05
55 Pat Verbeek .01 .05
56 Alexander Semak .01 .05
57 Eric Lindros .08 .25
58 Peter Bondra .02 .10
59 Marty McInnis .01 .05
60 Bill Guerin .02 .10
61 Patrice Brisebois .01 .05
62 Andy Moog .08 .25
63 Eric Weinrich .01 .05
64 Arturs Irbe .02 .10
65 Sean Hill .01 .05
66 Jesse Belanger .01 .05
67 Bryan Marchment .01 .05
68 Joe Sacco .01 .05
69 Trevor Kidd .02 .10
70 Dan Quinn .01 .05
71 Kirk McLean .02 .10
72 Benoit Hogue .01 .05
73 Garry Galley .01 .05
74 Randy Wood .01 .05
75 Nikolai Khabibulin .02 .10
76 Ted Donato .01 .05
77 Doug Bodger .01 .05
78 Paul Ranheim .01 .05
79 Ulf Samuelsson .01 .05
80 Uwe Krupp .01 .05
81 Oleg Tverdovsky .01 .05
82 Kelly Miller .01 .05
83 Darryl Sydor .02 .10
84 Brian Bellows .01 .05
85 Jeremy Roenick .10 .30
86 Phil Bourque .01 .05
87 Louie DeBrusk .01 .05
88 Joel Otto .01 .05
89 Dino Ciccarelli .02 .10
90 Mats Sundin .08 .25
91 Don Sweeney .01 .05
92 Roman Hamrlik .02 .10
93 Petr Svoboda .01 .05
94 Zigmund Palffy .02 .10
95 Patrick Roy .40 1.00
96 Sergei Krivokrasov .01 .05
97 Wade Flaherty RC .02 .10
98 Fredrik Olausson .01 .05
99 Sergio Momesso .01 .05
100 Mike Vernon .02 .10
101 Todd Gill .01 .05
102 Cam Neely .08 .25
103 Wendel Clark .02 .10
104 John Tucker .01 .05
105 Eric Desjardins .02 .10
106 Ed Olczyk .01 .05
107 Bob Beers .01 .05
108 Mark Recchi .02 .10
109 Ed Belfour .08 .25
110 Radek Bonk .01 .05
111 Cory Stillman .01 .05
112 Jeff Norton .01 .05
113 Terry Carkner .01 .05
114 Felix Potvin .08 .25
115 Alexei Kasatonov .01 .05
116 Sergio Momesso .01 .05
117 Daren Puppa .02 .10
118 Joe Juneau .01 .05
119 Valeri Bure .01 .05
120 Murray Craven .01 .05
121 Marko Tuomainen .01 .05
122 Trevor Linden .02 .10
123 Zarley Zalapski .01 .05
124 Jeff Shantz .01 .05
125 Sergio Momesso .01 .05
126 Jamie Huscroft .01 .05
127 Jaromir Jagr .15 .40
128 Brian Bradley .01 .05
129 Brett Lindros .01 .05
130 Calle Johansson .01 .05
131 Pierre Turgeon .02 .10
132 Denis Savard .02 .10
133 Joe Nieuwendyk .02 .10
134 Petr Klima .01 .05
135 John Druce .01 .05
136 Chris Osgood .02 .10
137 Kenny Jonsson .01 .05
138 Jocelyn Lemieux .01 .05
139 Tomas Sandstrom .01 .05
140 Chris Gratton .01 .05
141 Mark Tinordi .01 .05
142 Kirk Muller .01 .05
143 Vladimir Malakhov .01 .05
144 Jiri Slegr .01 .05
145 Shawn McEachern .01 .05
146 Shayne Corson .01 .05
147 Kelly Hrudey .02 .10
148 Sergei Fedorov .10 .30
149 Mike Gartner .02 .10
150 Stephane Fiset .02 .10
151 Larry Murphy .02 .10
152 Enrico Ciccone .01 .05
153 Mike Keane .01 .05
154 Steve Larmer .02 .10
155 Dale Hunter .02 .10
156 Joe Murphy .01 .05
157 Pat LaFontaine .08 .25
158 Rob Gaudreau .01 .05
159 Paul Kariya .08 .25
160 Rob Blake .02 .10
161 Keith Primeau .01 .05
162 Dave Ellett .01 .05
163 Alexander Mogilny .02 .10
164 Luc Robitaille .02 .10
165 Alexander Selivanov .01 .05
166 Keith Jones .02 .10
167 Turner Stevenson .01 .05
168 Keith Tkachuk .08 .25
169 Bernie Nicholls .01 .05
170 Stanislav Neckar .01 .05
171 Scott Mellanby .01 .05
172 Doug Weight .02 .10
173 Shaun Van Allen .01 .05
174 Gary Roberts .01 .05
175 Robert Lang .01 .05
176 Martin Gelinas .01 .05
177 Ray Sheppard .01 .05
178 Bryan Smolinski .01 .05
179 Wayne Presley .01 .05
180 Jimmy Carson .01 .05
181 John Cullen .01 .05
182 Mikael Andersson .01 .05
183 Dimitri Khristich .01 .05
184 Chris Therien .01 .05
185 Bobby Holik .01 .05
186 Kevin Hatcher .01 .05
187 Patrick Poulin .01 .05
188 Pat Falloon .01 .05
189 Alexei Yashin .01 .05
190 Gord Murphy .01 .05
191 Kirk Maltby .02 .10
192 Dave Karpa .01 .05
193 Kelly Kisio .01 .05
194 Tony Granato .01 .05
195 Al Iafrate .02 .10
196 Nelson Emerson .01 .05
197 Adam Oates .02 .10
198 Rob Ray .08 .25
199 Sean Burke .02 .10
200 Ron Francis .02 .10
201 Theo Fleury .01 .05
202 Patrick Flatley .01 .05
203 Ron Hextall .02 .10
204 Martin Brodeur .25 .60
205 Mike Kennedy RC .01 .05
206 Tony Amonte .01 .05
207 Sergei Makarov .01 .05
208 Alexandre Daigle .01 .05
209 Stu Barnes .01 .05
210 Todd Marchant .01 .05
211 Valeri Karpov .01 .05
212 Phil Housley .02 .10
213 Jamie Storr .02 .10
214 Brett Hull .10 .30
215 Kris King .01 .05
216 Ray Bourque .15 .40
217 Donald Audette .01 .05
218 Steven Rice .01 .05
219 Kevin Stevens .01 .05
220 Mark Messier .08 .25
221 Valeri Kamensky .02 .10
222 Mikael Renberg .02 .10
223 Scott Stevens .02 .10
224 Derian Hatcher .01 .05
225 Ray Whitney .02 .10
226 Bob Kudelski .01 .05
227 Mikhail Shtalenkov .01 .05
228 Nicklas Lidstrom .08 .25
229 Adam Creighton .01 .05
230 Dave Manson .01 .05
231 Craig Simpson .01 .05
232 Chris Pronger .08 .25
233 Adrien Plavsic .01 .05
234 Alexei Kovalev .01 .05
235 Tommy Salo RC .40 1.00
236 Patrik Juhlin .01 .05
237 Tom Chorske .01 .05
238 Mike Modano .15 .40
239 Igor Larionov .01 .05
240 Johan Garpenlov .01 .05
241 Todd Krygier .01 .05
242 Tie Domi .02 .10
243 Bill Houlder .01 .05
244 Teemu Selanne .08 .25
245 Dale Hawerchuk .08 .25
246 Bill Ranford .02 .10
247 Brian Leetch .02 .10
248 Steve Thomas .02 .10
249 Dimitri Yushkevich .01 .05
250 Stephane Richer .02 .10
251 Todd Harvey .02 .10
252 Viktor Kozlov .02 .10
253 John Vanbiesbrouck .02 .10
254 Rick Tocchet .02 .10
255 Bret Hedican .01 .05
256 Mario Lemieux .50 1.25
257 Igor Korolev .01 .05
258 Dominik Hasek .20 .50
259 Owen Nolan .02 .10
260 Michal Pivonka .01 .05
261 John LeClair .08 .25
262 Claude Lemieux .01 .05
263 Mike Donnelly .01 .05
264 Craig Janney .01 .05
265 Milos Holan .01 .05
266 Steve Yzerman .50 1.25
267 Russ Courtnall .01 .05
268 Esa Tikkanen .01 .05
269 Dallas Drake .01 .05
270 Norm Maciver .01 .05
271 Scott Young .01 .05
272 Glenn Healy .02 .10
273 Brian Rolston .01 .05
274 Corey Millen .01 .05
275 Kevin Miller .01 .05
276 Eric LaCroix .01 .05
277 Adam Graves .01 .05
278 Christian Ruuttu .01 .05
279 Steve Duchesne .01 .05
280 Stephane Quintal .01 .05
281 Brent Gretzky .01 .05
282 Mike Ricci .02 .10
283 Sergei Nemchinov .01 .05
284 Sylvain Cote .01 .05
285 Neal Broten .02 .10
286 Greg Adams .01 .05
287 Guy Hebert .02 .10
288 Joe Sakic .20 .50
289 Bobby Dollas .01 .05
290 Gino Odjick .01 .05
291 Curtis Joseph .08 .25
292 Teppo Numminen .01 .05
293 Geoff Sanderson .01 .05
294 Adam Deadmarsh .01 .05
295 Kevin Haller .01 .05
296 Sergei Brylin .01 .05
297 Ulf Dahlen .01 .05
298 Robert Kron .01 .05
299 Dave Lowry .01 .05
300 Nikolai Borschevsky .01 .05
301 Jeff Brown .01 .05
302 Guy Carbonneau .08 .25
303 Alexei Zhitnik .01 .05
304 Frantisek Kucera .01 .05
305 Curtis Leschyshyn .01 .05
306 Mike Richter .08 .25
307 Dean Evason .01 .05
308 Jozef Stumpel .01 .05
309 Jeff Friesen .01 .05
310 Kelly Buchberger .01 .05
311 Michael Nylander .01 .05
312 Josef Beranek .01 .05
313 Al MacInnis .02 .10
314 Ken Wregget .02 .10
315 Glen Wesley .01 .05
316 Jocelyn Thibault .08 .25
317 Jeff Beukeboom .01 .05
318 Steve Konowalchuk .01 .05
319 Tim Cheveldae .02 .10
320 Vincent Damphousse .01 .05
321 Mats Naslund .01 .05
322 Mathieu Schneider .01 .05
323 Petr Nedved .02 .10
324 Brent Fedyk .01 .05
325 Jussi Tie RC .02 .10
326 Mikko Markkanen RC .02 .10
327 Timo Hakanen RC .02 .10
328 Sami Salonen RC .02 .10
329 Juha Viinikainen RC .02 .10
330 Jani Riihinen RC .02 .10
331 Teemu Riihijarvi RC .02 .10
332 Jaako Niskavaara RC .02 .10
333 Miika Elomo .02 .10
334 Tomi Kallio RC .40 1.00
335 Vesa Toskala RC .02 .10
336 Tuomas Reijonen RC .02 .10
337 Aki Berg RC .01 .05
338 Tomi Hirvonen RC .02 .10
339 Jussi Salminen RC .02 .10
340 Andreas Sjolund RC .02 .10
341 Johan Ramstedt RC .01 .05
342 Bjorn Danielsson RC .02 .10
343 Per Gustavsson RC .02 .10
344 Niklas Anger RC .02 .10
345 Marcus Nilsson RC .08 .25
346 Per Anton Lundstrom RC .02 .10
347 Henrik Rehnberg RC .02 .10
348 Robert Borgqvist RC .02 .10
349 Ted Christensen RC .02 .10
350 Samuel Phalsson RC .01 .05
351 Fredrik Loven RC .01 .05
352 Patrik Wallenberg RC .02 .10
353 Jan Labraaten RC .02 .10
354 Peter Wallin RC .01 .05
355 Cam Neely WYG .08 .25
356 Keith Tkachuk WYG .08 .25
357 Chris Gratton WYG .01 .05
358 Adam Graves WYG .01 .05
359 Doug Gilmour WYG .02 .10
360 Adam Deadmarsh WYG .01 .05
361 Wayne Gretzky WYG .08 .25
362 Joe Sakic WYG .08 .25
363 Paul Kariya WYG .08 .25
364 Brett Hull WYG .08 .25
365 Sergei Fedorov WYG .08 .25
366 Brian Rolston WYG .01 .05
367 Dominik Hasek WYG .08 .25
368 John Vanbiesbrouck WYG .02 .10
369 Jim Carey WYG .01 .05
370 Paul Kariya HH .08 .25
371 Peter Forsberg HH .08 .25
372 Jeff Friesen HH .01 .05
373 Kenny Jonsson HH .01 .05
374 Chris Therien HH .01 .05
375 Jim Carey HH .01 .05
376 John LeClair HH .08 .25
377 Eric Lindros HH .08 .25
378 Jaromir Jagr HH .08 .25
379 Paul Coffey HH .08 .25
380 Chris Chelios HH .08 .25
381 Dominik Hasek HH .08 .25
382 Keith Tkachuk HH .08 .25
383 Alexei Zhamnov HH .02 .10
384 Theo Fleury HH .01 .05
385 Ray Bourque HH .08 .25
386 Larry Murphy HH .02 .10
387 Ed Belfour HH .08 .25
388 Eric Lindros HH .08 .25
389 Jaromir Jagr HH .08 .25
390 Paul Coffey HH .08 .25
391 Peter Forsberg HH .08 .25
392 Claude Lemieux HH .01 .05
393 Ron Francis HH .02 .10
394 Dominik Hasek HH .08 .25
395 Checklist/Gretzky .08 .25
396 Checklist/Gretzky .08 .25
397 Saku Koivu YG 1.25 3.00
398 Radek Dvorak YG .08 .25
399 Ed Jovanovski YG .08 .25
400 Brendan Witt YG .08 .25
401 Jeff O'Neill YG .08 .25
402 Daymond Langkow YG .08 .25
403 Shane Doan RC 1.25 3.00
404 Bryan McCabe YG .08 .25
405 Marty Murray YG .08 .25
406 Daniel Alfredsson YG 1.00 2.50
407 Jason Doig YG .08 .25
408 Niklas Sundstrom YG .08 .25
409 Vitali Yachmenev YG .08 .25
410 Aki Berg YG .08 .25
411 Eric Daze YG .40 1.00

1995-96 Collector's Choice Player's Club

Issued one per pack, this 396 card standard-size set is a parallel to the regular Collector's Choice issue. These cards have silver borders and the words "Players Club" are printed vertically on the left side of the card in silver-foil.

COMPLETE SET (396) 60.00 100.00
*VETS: 4X TO 10X BASIC CARDS
*ROOKIES: 1.5X TO 4X BASIC CARDS

1995-96 Collector's Choice Player's Club Platinum

This 396-card standard size set is a parallel to the regular Collector's Choice set. Issued a rate of 1:34 packs, these cards are printed on silver-foil paper stock. Although difficult to pull from packs, many of the cards came over from Europe, where they were readily available from collectors clubs. This added supply dampened demand somewhat for these cards in North America.

*VETS: 30X TO 80X BASIC CARDS
*ROOKIES: 15X TO 40X BASIC CARDS

1995-96 Collector's Choice Crash the Game Silver

Consisting of 90 cards, this interactive set featured 30 players. Each player had three cards with different dates on the front. If the player scored a goal on either of the dates, the card with the corresponding date could be redeemed for a special 30-card set. Randomly inserted in packs, these cards came in silver (1:5 packs) and gold (1:34 packs) foil versions. The words "silver" or "gold" were in their respective color foil at bottom left and the date was also printed in foil. There are also several parallels of this set, including gold and silver redeemed winner sets, and gold and silver bonus cards awarded of the redeemed player along with the gold or silver set. Because not every player had a winning card, however, the gold and silver bonus sets are considered complete at 23 cards each. It should be noted however that a few copies of the bonus cards have been confirmed to exist of the seven players that did not have winning cards. Also, several erroneous variation cards have been reported featuring game dates on which that player's team did not play. These cards appear to be in short supply, but do not demand exorbitant premiums. To differentiate between each of the player's three insert cards, they are numbered here with A, B and C suffixes. The expiration date for redeeming cards was July 1st, 1996.

COMPLETE SET (90) 40.00 80.00
*GOLD STARS: 1.5X TO 4X BASIC CARDS
*EXCHANGE CARDS: .1X TO .25X BASIC CARDS
*GOLD EXCH.CARDS: .4X TO .8X BASIC CARDS
*BONUS CARDS: 1X TO 2X BASIC CARDS
*GOLD BONUS CARDS: 2.5X TO 5X BASIC CARDS
BONUS NOT PRICED: 3/4/17/18/20/22/27
C1A Pavel Bure 10/12/95 .30 .75
C1B Pavel Bure 12/17/95 .30 .75
C1C Pavel Bure 3/23/96 .30 .75
C2A Sergei Fedorov 10/19/95 .50 1.25
C2B Sergei Fedorov 12/31/95 .50 1.25
C2C Sergei Fedorov 3/12/96 .50 1.25
C3A Wayne Gretzky 10/7/95 2.00 5.00
C3B Wayne Gretzky 12/31/95 2.00 5.00
C3C Wayne Gretzky 2/10/96 2.00 5.00
C4A Eric Lindros 11/12/95 .30 .75
C4B Eric Lindros 1/3/96 .30 .75
C4C Eric Lindros 3/3/96 .30 .75
C5A Brett Hull 10/10/95 .50 1.25
C5B Brett Hull 12/9/95 .50 1.25
C5C Brett Hull 3/24/96 .50 1.25
C6A Mark Messier 11/8/95 .30 .75
C6B Mark Messier 1/22/96 .30 .75
C6C Mark Messier 3/31/96 .30 .75
C7A Jaromir Jagr 10/14/95 .50 1.25
C7B Jaromir Jagr 12/17/95 .50 1.25
C7C Jaromir Jagr 3/5/96 .50 1.25
C8A Alexei Zhamnov 10/9/95 .25 .60
C8B Alexei Zhamnov 12/28/95 .25 .60
C8C Alexei Zhamnov 2/21/96 .25 .60
C9A Joe Sakic 10/6/95 .60 1.50
C9B Joe Sakic 12/9/95 .60 1.50
C9C Joe Sakic 2/3/96 .60 1.50
C10A Paul Kariya 10/18/95 .30 .75
C10B Paul Kariya 12/19/95 .30 .75
C10C Paul Kariya 3/17/96 .30 .75
C11A Theo Fleury 10/27/95 .20 .50
C11B Theo Fleury 12/11/95 .20 .50
C11C Theo Fleury 2/6/96 .20 .50
C12A Owen Nolan 11/1/95 .25 .60
C12B Owen Nolan 1/4/96 .25 .60
C12C Owen Nolan 3/17/96 .25 .60
C13A Peter Bondra 10/13/95 .25 .60
C13B Peter Bondra 12/2/95 .25 .60
C13C Peter Bondra 3/12/96 .25 .60
C14A Cam Neely 11/7/95 .30 .75
C14B Cam Neely 1/11/96 .30 .75
C14C Cam Neely 3/23/96 .30 .75
C15A Pierre Turgeon 10/25/95 .25 .60
C15B Pierre Turgeon 12/23/95 .25 .60
C15C Pierre Turgeon 2/21/96 .25 .60
C16A Mike Modano 11/1/95 .60 1.50
C16B Mike Modano 1/5/96 .60 1.50
C16C Mike Modano 2/22/96 .60 1.50
C17A Bernie Nicholls 10/10/95 .20 .50
C17B Bernie Nicholls 12/15/95 .20 .50
C17C Bernie Nicholls 3/24/96 .20 .50
C18A Alexei Yashin 11/4/95 .20 .50
C18B Alexie Yashin 12/23/95 .20 .50
C18C Alexei Yashin 3/21/96 .20 .50
C19A Jason Arnott 10/27/95 .20 .50
C19B Jason Arnott 12/18/95 .20 .50
C19C Jason Arnott 2/28/96 .20 .50
C20A Peter Forsberg 11/22/95 .75 2.00
C20B Peter Forsberg 2/15/96 .75 2.00
C20C Peter Forsberg 3/27/96 .75 2.00
C21A Doug Gilmour 10/17/95 .25 .60
C21B Doug Gilmour 12/16/95 .25 .60
C21C Doug Gilmour 2/18/96 .25 .60
C22A Geoff Sanderson 10/11/95 .20 .50
C22B Geoff Sanderson 12/18/95 .20 .50
C22C Geoff Sanderson 3/6/96 .20 .50
C23A John LeClair 10/15/95 .30 .75
C23B John LeClair 12/16/95 .30 .75
C23C John LeClair 2/19/96 .30 .75
C24A Ray Bourque 10/11/95 .20 .50
C24B Ray Bourque 12/16/95 .20 .50
C24C Ray Bourque 2/6/96 .20 .50
C25A Mario Lemieux 11/1/95 1.50 4.00
C25B Mario Lemieux 12/1/95 1.50 4.00
C25C Mario Lemieux 2/6/96 1.50 4.00
C26A Steve Yzerman 11/7/95 1.50 4.00
C26B Steve Yzerman 1/24/96 1.50 4.00
C26C Steve Yzerman 2/27/96 1.50 4.00
C27A Pat LaFontaine 10/20/95 .30 .75
C27B Pat LaFontaine 12/27/95 .30 .75
C27C Pat LaFontaine 2/17/96 .30 .75
C28A Claude Lemieux 10/7/95 .20 .50
C28B Claude Lemieux 12/15/95 .20 .50
C28C Claude Lemieux 2/10/96 .20 .50
C29A Paul Coffey 10/15/95 .30 .75
C29B Paul Coffey 12/5/95 .30 .75
C29C Paul Coffey 2/13/96 .30 .75
C30A Mats Sundin 11/7/95 .30 .75
C30B Mats Sundin 1/3/96 .30 .75
C30C Mats Sundin 3/15/96 .30 .75

1996-97 Collector's Choice

The '96-97 Collector's Choice set was issued in one series totaling 348 cards. The 12-card packs retailed for $.99 each. The set contains three subsets: Scotty Bowman's Winning Formula (289-308), Three-Star Selection (309-336) and Captain Tomorrow (337-346). Fifteen additional Young Guns cards (numbered 349-363) were available via mail in exchange for the randomly inserted Young Guns Trade card (1:35 packs). They are not considered part of the complete set, but are listed below as they are numbered consecutively to the regular set. The Gretzky 4 X 6 cards were received when redeeming winning trivia cards from the Meet the Stars contest.

COMPLETE SET (348) 8.00 20.00
1 Paul Kariya .08 .25
2 Teemu Selanne .08 .25
3 Steve Rucchin .01 .05
4 Mikhail Shtalenkov .01 .05
5 Guy Hebert .02 .10
6 Shaun Van Allen .01 .05
7 Anatoli Semenov .01 .05
8 J.F. Jomphe RC .01 .05
9 Alex Hicks .01 .05
10 Roman Oksiuta .01 .05
11 Todd Ewen .01 .05
12 Adam Oates .02 .10
13 Ray Bourque .15 .40
14 Don Sweeney .01 .05
15 Kyle McLaren .01 .05
16 Cam Neely .08 .25
17 Bill Ranford .02 .10
18 Rick Tocchet .02 .10
19 Ted Donato .01 .05
20 Shawn McEachern .01 .05
21 Jon Rohloff .01 .05
22 Joe Mullen .02 .10
23 Pat LaFontaine .08 .25
24 Brian Holzinger .02 .10
25 Wayne Primeau .01 .05
26 Alexei Zhitnik .01 .05
27 Derek Plante .01 .05
28 Randy Burridge .01 .05
29 Brad May .02 .10
30 Dominik Hasek .20 .50
31 Jason Dawe .01 .05
32 Mike Peca .01 .05
33 Matthew Barnaby .02 .10
34 Trevor Kidd .02 .10
35 Theo Fleury .01 .05
36 Cale Hulse .01 .05
37 Bob Sweeney .01 .05
38 Michael Nylander .01 .05
39 German Titov .01 .05
40 Cory Stillman .01 .05
41 Zarley Zalapski .01 .05
42 Jocelyn Lemieux .01 .05
43 Sandy McCarthy .01 .05
44 Gary Roberts .01 .05
45 Eric Daze .02 .10
46 Jeremy Roenick .10 .30
47 Chris Chelios .08 .25
48 Joe Murphy .01 .05
49 Tony Amonte .02 .10
50 Bernie Nicholls .01 .05
51 Eric Weinrich .01 .05
52 Gary Suter .01 .05
53 Jeff Shantz .01 .05
54 Jeff Hackett .02 .10
55 Ed Belfour .08 .25
56 Uwe Krupp .01 .05
57 Claude Lemieux .01 .05
58 Adam Deadmarsh .01 .05
59 Stephane Fiset .02 .10
60 Sandis Ozolinsh .01 .05
61 Stephane Yelle .01 .05
62 Valeri Kamensky .02 .10
63 Peter Forsberg .25 .60
64 Joe Sakic .20 .50
65 Patrick Roy .50 1.25
66 Chris Simon .01 .05
67 Todd Harvey .01 .05
68 Joe Nieuwendyk .02 .10
69 Mike Modano .15 .40
70 Derian Hatcher .01 .05
71 Kevin Hatcher .01 .05
72 Benoit Hogue .01 .05
73 Guy Carbonneau .01 .05
74 Jamie Langenbrunner .01 .05
75 Jere Lehtinen .01 .05
76 Craig Ludwig .01 .05
77 Grant Marshall .01 .05
78 Greg Johnson .01 .05
79 Steve Yzerman .40 1.00
80 Sergei Fedorov .10 .30
81 Vyacheslav Kozlov .01 .05
82 Vladimir Konstantinov .02 .10
83 Igor Larionov .01 .05
84 Chris Osgood .02 .10
85 Paul Coffey .08 .25
86 Nicklas Lidstrom .08 .25
87 Keith Primeau .01 .05
88 Dino Ciccarelli .02 .10
89 Darren McCarty .01 .05
90 Curtis Joseph .08 .25
91 Doug Weight .02 .10
92 Jason Arnott .01 .05
93 Mariusz Czerkawski .01 .05
94 Kelly Buchberger .01 .05
95 Zdeno Ciger .01 .05
96 David Oliver .01 .05
97 Todd Marchant .01 .05
98 Miroslav Satan .01 .05
99 Bryan Marchment .01 .05
100 Louie DeBrusk .01 .05
101 John Vanbiesbrouck .02 .10
102 Scott Mellanby .02 .10
103 Rob Niedermayer .02 .10
104 Robert Svehla .01 .05
105 Ed Jovanovski .02 .10
106 Johan Garpenlov .01 .05
107 Jody Hull .01 .05
108 Bill Lindsay .01 .05
109 Terry Carkner .01 .05
110 Stu Barnes .01 .05
111 Ray Sheppard .02 .10
112 Brendan Shanahan .08 .25
113 Geoff Sanderson .02 .10
114 Andrei Nikolishin .01 .05
115 Andrew Cassels .01 .05
116 Nelson Emerson .01 .05
117 Jason Muzzatti .02 .10
118 Marek Malik .01 .05
119 Sean Burke .02 .10
120 Jeff Brown .01 .05
121 Jeff O'Neill .01 .05
122 Kelly Chase .01 .05
123 Dimitri Khristich .01 .05
124 Kevin Stevens .01 .05
125 Vitali Yachmenev .01 .05
126 Yanic Perreault .01 .05
127 Kevin Todd .01 .05
128 Aki Berg .01 .05
129 Craig Johnson .01 .05
130 Mattias Norstrom .01 .05
131 Ray Ferraro .01 .05
132 Steven Finn .01 .05
133 Pierre Turgeon .02 .10
134 Saku Koivu .08 .25
135 Mark Recchi .02 .10
136 Jocelyn Thibault .08 .25
137 Andrei Kovalenko .01 .05
138 Vincent Damphousse .01 .05
139 Vladimir Malakhov .01 .05
140 Brian Savage .01 .05
141 Valeri Bure .01 .05
142 Patrice Brisebois .01 .05
143 Martin Rucinsky .01 .05
144 Martin Brodeur .25 .60
145 Steve Thomas .01 .05
146 Bill Guerin .01 .05
147 Petr Sykora .01 .05
148 Scott Stevens .02 .10
149 Scott Niedermayer .01 .05
150 Phil Housley .02 .10
151 Brian Rolston .01 .05
152 Neal Broten .02 .10
153 Dave Andreychuk .02 .10
154 Randy McKay .01 .05
155 Eric Fichaud .02 .10
156 Zigmund Palffy .02 .10
157 Travis Green .02 .10
158 Darby Hendrickson .01 .05
159 Kenny Jonsson .01 .05
160 Marty McInnis .01 .05
161 Bryan McCabe .01 .05
162 Darius Kasparaitis .01 .05
163 Alexander Semak .01 .05
164 Todd Bertuzzi .08 .25
165 Niclas Andersson .01 .05
166 Mark Messier .08 .25
167 Mike Richter .08 .25
168 Niklas Sundstrom .01 .05
169 Brian Leetch .08 .25
170 Wayne Gretzky .75 2.00
171 Luc Robitaille .02 .10
172 Marty McSorley .01 .05
173 Jari Kurri .02 .10
174 Adam Graves .01 .05
175 Sergei Nemchinov .01 .05
176 Alexei Kovalev .01 .05
177 Daniel Alfredsson .02 .10
178 Randy Cunneyworth .01 .05
179 Alexei Yashin .01 .05
180 Alexandre Daigle .01 .05
181 Radek Bonk .01 .05
182 Steve Duchesne .01 .05
183 Ted Drury .01 .05
184 Antti Tormanen .01 .05
185 Stan Neckar .01 .05
186 Damian Rhodes .02 .10
187 Janne Laukkanen .01 .05
188 Eric Lindros .08 .25
189 Mikael Renberg .02 .10
190 John LeClair .08 .25
191 Ron Hextall .02 .10

192 Rod Brind'Amour .02 .10
193 Joel Otto .01 .05
194 Pat Falloon .01 .05
195 Eric Desjardins .02 .10
196 Dale Hawerchuk .02 .10
197 Chris Therien .01 .05
198 Dan Quinn .01 .05
199 Oleg Tverdovsky .02 .10
200 Chad Kilger .01 .05
201 Keith Tkachuk .08 .25
202 Igor Korolev .01 .05
203 Alexei Zhamnov .02 .10
204 Nikolai Khabibulin .02 .10
205 Shane Doan .01 .05
206 Deron Quint .01 .05
207 Craig Janney .02 .10
208 Norm Maciver .01 .05
209 Teppo Numminen .01 .05
210 Mario Lemieux .50 1.25
211 Jaromir Jagr .15 .40
212 Ron Francis .02 .10
213 Tom Barrasso .02 .10
214 Sergei Zubov .01 .05
215 Tomas Sandstrom .01 .05
216 Joe Dziedzic .01 .05
217 Richard Park .01 .05
218 Bryan Smolinski .01 .05
219 Petr Nedved .02 .10
220 Ken Wregget .02 .10
221 Dmitri Mironov .01 .05
222 Peter Zezel .01 .05
223 Brett Hull .10 .30
224 Grant Fuhr .02 .10
225 Shayne Corson .01 .05
226 Chris Pronger .02 .10
227 Craig MacTavish .01 .05
228 Al MacInnis .02 .10
229 Geoff Courtnall .01 .05
230 Stephane Matteau .01 .05
231 Tony Twist .01 .05
232 Brian Noonan .01 .05
233 Owen Nolan .02 .10
234 Shean Donovan .01 .05
235 Darren Turcotte .01 .05
236 Marcus Ragnarsson .01 .05
237 Viktor Kozlov UER .01 .05
(has Slava Kozlov's stats)
238 Jeff Friesen .01 .05
239 Chris Terreri .02 .10
240 Ray Whitney .01 .05
241 Ville Peltonen .01 .05
242 Andrei Nazarov .01 .05
243 Ulf Dahlen .01 .05
244 Roman Hamrlik .02 .10
245 Chris Gratton .02 .10
246 Petr Klima .01 .05
247 Daren Puppa .02 .10
248 Rob Zamuner .01 .05
249 Aaron Gavey .01 .05
250 Brian Bradley .01 .05
251 Paul Ysebaert .01 .05
252 Igor Ulanov .01 .05
253 Alexander Selivanov .01 .05
254 Shawn Burr .01 .05
255 Mats Sundin .08 .25
256 Doug Gilmour .02 .10
257 Felix Potvin .08 .25
258 Wendel Clark .02 .10
259 Kirk Muller .01 .05
260 Dave Gagner .02 .10
261 Tie Domi .02 .10
262 Mathieu Schneider .01 .05
263 Dimitri Yushkevich .01 .05
264 Don Beaupre .02 .10
265 Larry Murphy .02 .10
266 Pavel Bure .08 .25
267 Alexander Mogilny .02 .10
268 Trevor Linden .02 .10
269 Jyrki Lumme .01 .05
270 Cliff Ronning .01 .05
271 Kirk McLean .02 .10
272 Corey Hirsch .02 .10
273 Esa Tikkanen .01 .05
274 Gino Odjick .01 .05
275 Markus Naslund .08 .25
276 Russ Courtnall .01 .05
277 Joe Juneau .01 .05
278 Jim Carey .08 .25
279 Peter Bondra .02 .10
280 Michal Pivonka .01 .05
281 Steve Konowalchuk .01 .05
282 Pat Peake .01 .05
283 Brendan Witt .01 .05
284 Stefan Ustorf .01 .05
285 Keith Jones .01 .05
286 Sergei Gonchar .01 .05
287 Sylvain Cote .01 .05
288 Dale Hunter .01 .05
289 Paul Kariya SB .08 .25
290 Wayne Gretzky SB .08 .25
291 Eric Lindros SB .08 .25
292 Steve Yzerman SB .08 .25
293 Mario Lemieux SB .08 .25
294 Jaromir Jagr SB .08 .25
295 Keith Tkachuk SB .08 .25
296 Mark Messier SB .08 .25
297 Jeremy Roenick SB .10 .30
298 Peter Forsberg SB .08 .25
299 Joe Sakic SB .08 .25
300 Theo Fleury SB .01 .05
301 Chris Chelios SB .08 .25
302 Vlad Konstantinov SB .01 .05
303 Brian Leetch SB .08 .25
304 Ray Bourque SB .08 .25
305 Scott Stevens SB .02 .10
306 Martin Brodeur SB .08 .25
307 Patrick Roy SB .08 .25
308 Scotty Bowman .02 .10
309 Paul Kariya .01 .05
Teemu Selanne
Guy Hebert
310 Adam Oates .02 .10
Ray Bourque
Cam Neely
311 Pat LaFontaine .02 .10
Alexei Zhitnik
Dominik Hasek
312 Theo Fleury .02 .10
Michael Nylander
Trevor Kidd
313 Jeremy Roenick .02 .10
Chris Chelios
Eric Daze
314 Joe Sakic .30 .75
Patrick Roy
Peter Forsberg
315 Mike Modano .02 .10
Joe Nieuwendyk
Todd Harvey
316 Sergei Fedorov .08 .25
Vladimir Konstantinov
Paul Coffey
317 Doug Weight .10 .30
Jason Arnott
Curtis Joseph
318 Ed Jovanovski .02 .10
John Vanbiesbrouck
Rob Niedermayer
319 Brendan Shanahan .02 .10
Geoff Sanderson
Sean Burke
320 Vitali Yachmenev .01 .05
Dimitri Khristich
Ray Ferraro
321 Jocelyn Thibault .08 .25
Pierre Turgeon
Saku Koivu
322 Martin Brodeur .02 .10
Steve Thomas
Scott Stevens
323 Todd Bertuzzi .02 .10
Eric Fichaud
Zigmund Palffy
324 Brian Leetch .08 .25
Adam Graves
Mike Richter
325 Alexander Daigle .01 .05
Alexei Yashin
Damian Rhodes
326 Ron Hextall .02 .10
John LeClair
Mikael Renberg
327 Alexei Zhamnov .02 .10
Keith Tkachuk
Oleg Tverdovsky
328 Jaromir Jagr .08 .25
Petr Nedved
Ron Francis
329 Wayne Gretzky .40 1.00
Brett Hull
Al MacInnis
330 Owen Nolan .02 .10
Darren Turcotte
Chris Terreri
331 Roman Hamrlik .02 .10
Chris Gratton
Darren Puppa
332 Doug Gilmour .02 .10
Felix Potvin
Mats Sundin
333 Alexander Mogilny .02 .10
Pavel Bure
Trevor Linden
334 Jim Carey .02 .10
Joe Juneau
Peter Bondra
335 Mario Lemieux .08 .25
Mark Messier
Eric Lindros
336 Wayne Gretzky .40 1.00
Teemu Selanne
Joe Sakic
337 Chad Kilger .01 .05
338 Todd Bertuzzi .08 .25
339 Petr Sykora .01 .05
340 Ed Jovanovski .02 .10
341 Kyle McLaren .01 .05
342 Brian Holzinger .02 .10
343 Jeff O'Neill .01 .05
344 Daniel Alfredsson .02 .10
345 Brendan Witt .01 .05
346 Daymond Langkow .02 .10
347 Checklist .01 .05
348 Checklist .01 .05
349 Jarome Iginla YG .75 2.00
350 Sergei Berezin YG .20 .50
351 Jose Theodore YG .75 2.00
352 Rem Murray YG .08 .25
353 Daniel Goneau YG .08 .25
354 Ethan Moreau YG .08 .25
355 Jonas Hoglund YG .08 .25
356 Anders Eriksson YG .08 .25
357 Christian Dube YG .08 .25
358 Roman Turek YG .20 .50
359 Bryan Berard YG .08 .25
360 Jim Campbell YG .08 .25
361 Janne Niinimaa YG .08 .25
362 Wade Redden YG .20 .50
363 Marc Denis YG .20 .50
P222 Wayne Gretzky PROMO 2.00 5.00
NNO1 Wayne Gretzky '79-80 2.50 6.00
Meet the Stars 4X6
NNO2 Wayne Gretzky 802 2.50 6.00
Meet the Stars 4X6

1996-97 Collector's Choice Jumbos 5x7

These 5 X 7 cards were inserted as box toppers.

COMPLETE SET (5) 3.00 8.00
1 Theo Fleury .75 2.00
2 Curtis Joseph 1.00 2.50
3 Jose Theodore 1.00 2.50
4 Wade Redden .40 1.00
5 Mats Sundin 1.00 2.50

1996-97 Collector's Choice MVP

This set consists of 45 of the NHL's top stars and rookies. Silver versions are found one per pack, while the tougher gold parallel version is found 1:35 packs. These cards can be differentiated by the color of the foil on the left-hand border. The card fronts feature a color action photo with abbreviation "MVP" appearing in either silver or gold (depending on the version) at the bottom of the card. Values for the gold cards can be determined by utilizing the multiplier below.

COMPLETE SET (45) 10.00 25.00
*GOLD: 2.5X TO 6X BASIC INSERTS
UD1 Wayne Gretzky 2.00 5.00
UD2 Ron Francis .08 .25
UD3 Peter Forsberg .60 1.50
UD4 Alexander Mogilny .08 .25
UD5 Joe Sakic .50 1.25
UD6 Claude Lemieux .05 .15
UD7 Teemu Selanne .25 .60
UD8 John LeClair .25 .60
UD9 Doug Weight .08 .25
UD10 Paul Kariya .25 .60
UD11 Theo Fleury .05 .15
UD12 John Vanbiesbrouck .08 .25
UD13 Sergei Fedorov .30 .75
UD14 Steve Yzerman 1.25 3.00
UD15 Adam Oates .08 .25
UD16 Keith Tkachuk .25 .60
UD17 Mike Modano .40 1.00
UD18 Jeremy Roenick .30 .75
UD19 Patrick Roy 1.25 3.00
UD20 Felix Potvin .25 .60
UD21 Martin Brodeur .60 1.50
UD22 Pavel Bure .25 .60
UD23 Peter Bondra .08 .25
UD24 Zigmund Palffy .08 .25
UD25 Roman Hamrlik .08 .25
UD26 Brendan Shanahan .25 .60
UD27 Ray Bourque .40 1.00
UD28 Paul Coffey .25 .60
UD29 Brett Hull .30 .75
UD30 Brian Leetch .25 .60
UD31 Chris Chelios .25 .60
UD32 Vitali Yachmenev .05 .15
UD33 Nicklas Lidstrom .25 .60
UD34 Ed Jovanovski .08 .25
UD35 Sandis Ozolinsh .05 .15
UD36 Scott Stevens .08 .25
UD37 Eric Daze .08 .25
UD38 Saku Koivu .25 .60
UD39 Daniel Alfredsson .08 .25
UD40 Pat LaFontaine .25 .60
UD41 Cam Neely .25 .60
UD42 Owen Nolan .08 .25
UD43 Jaromir Jagr .40 1.00
UD44 Mats Sundin .25 .60
UD45 Doug Gilmour .08 .25

1996-97 Collector's Choice Stick'Ums

This unusual set consists of 30 stickers, the first 25 of which feature the NHL's top players. The remaining stickers feature a variety of hockey-oriented doo-daddery. These stickers were randomly inserted at 1:3 packs.

COMPLETE SET (30) 10.00 20.00
S1 Wayne Gretzky 2.50 6.00
S2 Brett Hull .40 1.00
S3 Peter Forsberg .75 2.00
S4 Patrick Roy 1.50 4.00
S5 Cam Neely .30 .75
S6 Jeremy Roenick .40 1.00
S7 Mario Lemieux 1.50 4.00
S8 Jaromir Jagr .50 1.25
S9 Eric Lindros .30 .75
S10 Mark Messier .30 .75
S11 Felix Potvin .30 .75
S12 Brendan Shanahan .30 .75
S13 Teemu Selanne .30 .75
S14 Paul Kariya .30 .75
S15 Mike Modano .50 1.25
S16 Pavel Bure .30 .75
S17 Jim Carey .30 .75
S18 Roman Hamrlik .10 .30
S19 Pierre Turgeon .10 .30
S20 Theo Fleury .05 .15
S21 Pat LaFontaine .30 .75
S22 Steve Yzerman 1.50 4.00
S23 Sergei Fedorov .40 1.00
S24 Martin Brodeur .75 2.00
S25 Owen Nolan .10 .30
S26 Ice Machine .05 .15
S27 Champions .05 .15
S28 Slap Shot .05 .15
S29 Stripes .05 .15
S30 Goal .05 .15

1996-97 Collector's Choice Crash the Game Silver

This interactive set features 30 NHL stars on a total of 88 cards. 28 players appear on 3 variations each, while two (Joe Sakic and Adam Oates) are featured on but two by virtue of an error by Upper Deck. Randomly inserted in packs, these cards come in silver (1:5 packs) and gold (1:44 packs) foil versions. If the player scored a goal against the team featured on his card, the winning card could be redeemed for a special exchange card. There are two versions of this set as well. Both versions feature the same design and photos, but they are different from the Crash cards for which they were redeemed. Furthermore, the gold versions of the exchange cards were die-cut. To differentiate between each of the player's three insert cards, they are numbered here with A, B and C suffixes. These suffixes do not appear on the cards themselves. The expiration date for these cards was July 1, 1997.

COMPLETE SET (88) 40.00 80.00
*GOLD: 1.25X TO 3X BASIC INSERTS
*EXCH.STARS: 1.25X TO 3X BASIC INSERTS
*GOLD EXCH: 4X TO 10X BASIC INSERTS
ONE EXCH.CARD VIA MAIL PER WINNER
EXCH.CARDS 20 AND 25 NOT ISSUED
C1A Wayne Gretzky 2.00 5.00
C1B Wayne Gretzky 2.00 5.00
C1C Wayne Gretzky 2.00 5.00
C2A Doug Gilmour .25 .60
C2B Doug Gilmour .25 .60
C2C Doug Gilmour .25 .60
C3A Alexander Mogilny .25 .60
C3B Alexander Mogilny .25 .60
C3C Alexander Mogilny .25 .60
C4A Peter Bondra .25 .60
C4B Peter Bondra .25 .60
C4C Peter Bondra .25 .60
C5A Mario Lemieux 1.50 4.00
C5B Mario Lemieux 1.50 4.00
C5C Mario Lemieux 1.50 4.00
C6A Jaromir Jagr .50 1.25
C6B Jaromir Jagr .50 1.25
C6C Jaromir Jagr .50 1.25
C7A Joe Sakic .60 1.50
C7B Joe Sakic .60 1.50
C7C Joe Sakic .60 1.50
C8A Vitali Yachmenev .20 .50
C8B Vitali Yachmenev .20 .50
C8C Vitali Yachmenev .20 .50
C9A Doug Weight .25 .60
C9B Doug Weight .25 .60
C9C Doug Weight .25 .60
C10A Steve Yzerman 1.50 4.00
C10B Steve Yzerman 1.50 4.00
C10C Steve Yzerman 1.50 4.00
C11A Alexei Zhamnov .20 .50
C11B Alexei Zhamnov .20 .50
C11C Alexei Zhamnov .20 .50
C12A John LeClair .30 .75
C12B John LeClair .30 .75
C12C John LeClair .30 .75
C13A Daniel Alfredsson .25 .60
C13B Daniel Alfredsson .25 .60
C13C Daniel Alfredsson .25 .60
C14A Brendan Shanahan .50 1.25
C14B Brendan Shanahan .50 1.25
C14C Brendan Shanahan .50 1.25
C15A Saku Koivu .30 .75
C15B Saku Koivu .30 .75
C15C Saku Koivu .30 .75
C16A Steve Thomas .20 .50
C16B Steve Thomas .20 .50
C16C Steve Thomas .20 .50
C17A Pavel Bure .30 .75
C17B Pavel Bure .50 1.25
C17C Pavel Bure .50 1.25
C18A Slava Kozlov .20 .50
C18B Slava Kozlov .20 .50
C18C Slava Kozlov .20 .50
C19A Teemu Selanne .30 .75
C19B Teemu Selanne .30 .75
C19C Teemu Selanne .30 .75
C20A Eric Daze .20 .50
C20B Eric Daze .20 .50
C20C Eric Daze .20 .50
C21A Adam Oates .25 .60
C21B Adam Oates .25 .60
C22A Ray Bourque .50 1.25
C22B Ray Bourque .50 1.25
C22C Ray Bourque .50 1.25
C23A Jason Arnott .20 .50
C23B Jason Arnott .20 .50
C23C Jason Arnott .20 .50
C24A Paul Kariya .30 .75
C24B Paul Kariya .30 .75
C24C Paul Kariya .30 .75
C25A Mikael Renberg .20 .50
C25B Mikael Renberg .20 .50
C25C Mikael Renberg .20 .50
C26A Keith Tkachuk .30 .75
C26B Keith Tkachuk .30 .75
C26C Keith Tkachuk .30 .75
C27A Brian Leetch .25 .60
C27B Brian Leetch .25 .60
C27C Brian Leetch .25 .60
C28A Eric Lindros .30 .75
C28B Eric Lindros .50 1.25
C28C Eric Lindros .50 1.25
C29A Mats Sundin .30 .75
C29B Mats Sundin .30 .75
C29C Mats Sundin .30 .75
C30A Mark Messier .40 1.00
C30B Mark Messier .40 1.00
C30C Mark Messier .40 1.00

1996-97 Collector's Choice Jumbos

The ten cards in this set were issued one per special retail box of Collector's Choice. The cards are identical in every way to their corresponding regular version, except for the size; these cards measure 4 X 6 inches.

COMPLETE SET (10) 10.00 25.00
13 Ray Bourque .75 2.00
23 Pat LaFontaine .50 1.25
35 Theo Fleury .60 1.50
62 Valeri Kamensky .50 1.25
69 Mike Modano .75 2.00
84 Chris Osgood .60 1.50
133 Pierre Turgeon .50 1.25
170 Wayne Gretzky 4.00 10.00
244 Roman Hamrlik .40 1.00
257 Felix Potvin .50 1.25

1996-97 Collector's Choice Jumbos Bi-Way

These eight oversized (4 by 6 inches) cards mirrored the regular edition Collector's Choice cards, save for the numbering on the back. The cards were inserted one per box sold through the Bi-Way discount chain in Canada.

COMPLETE SET (8) 6.00 15.00
1 Wayne Gretzky 4.00 10.00
2 Theo Fleury .60 1.50
3 Jason Arnott .50 1.25
4 Saku Koivu .60 1.50
5 Pierre Turgeon .50 1.25
6 Daniel Alfredsson .50 1.25
7 Felix Potvin .50 1.25
8 Alexander Mogilny .50 1.25

1997-98 Collector's Choice

This 320-card set features color photos of approximately ten players from each of the NHL's 26 teams and was distributed in 14-card packs with a suggested retail price of $1.29. The set contains 275 regular player cards and two subsets: National Heroes (36 cards) which includes some of the most talented junior players, and Chippy's Checklist (9 cards) which highlights nine of the mascot's favorite players on the set's checklist cards. The cards are dual numbered and are checklisted in team order alphabetized by city.

COMPLETE SET (320) 8.00 20.00
1 Guy Hebert .08 .25
2 Sean Pronger .02 .10
3 Dmitri Mironov .02 .10
4 Darren Van Impe .02 .10
5 Joe Sacco .02 .10
6 Ted Drury .02 .10
7 Steve Rucchin .02 .10
8 Teemu Selanne .10 .30
9 Paul Kariya .10 .30
10 Jari Kurri .08 .25
11 Kevin Todd .02 .10
12 Ray Bourque .20 .50
13 Anson Carter .08 .25
14 Ted Donato .02 .10
15 Kyle McLaren .02 .10
16 Jason Allison .02 .10
17 Jim Carey .08 .25
18 Jozef Stumpel .08 .25
19 Jean-Yves Roy .02 .10
20 Steve Heinze .02 .10
21 Sheldon Kennedy .02 .10
22 Dominik Hasek .25 .60
23 Rob Ray .02 .10
24 Derek Plante .02 .10
25 Brian Holzinger .02 .10
26 Mike Peca .02 .10
27 Matthew Barnaby .02 .10
28 Donald Audette .02 .10
29 Alexei Zhitnik .02 .10
30 Garry Galley .02 .10
31 Pat LaFontaine .10 .30
32 Jason Dawe .02 .10
33 Hnat Domenichelli .02 .10
34 Jarome Iginla .15 .40
35 Chris O'Sullivan .02 .10
36 Todd Simpson .02 .10
37 Trevor Kidd .08 .25
38 Dave Gagner .02 .10
39 German Titov .08 .25
40 Theo Fleury .02 .10
41 Dwayne Roloson .02 .10
42 Marty McInnis .02 .10
43 Jonas Hoglund .02 .10
44 Tony Amonte .08 .25
45 Gary Suter .02 .10
46 Chris Chelios .10 .30
47 Jeff Hackett .08 .25
48 Ulf Dahlen .02 .10
49 Bob Probert .02 .10
50 Kevin Miller .02 .10
51 Ethan Moreau .02 .10
52 Eric Weinrich .02 .10
53 Eric Daze .08 .25
54 Peter Forsberg .30 .75
55 Joe Sakic .25 .60
56 Patrick Roy .60 1.50
57 Adam Deadmarsh .02 .10
58 Valeri Kamensky .08 .25
59 Keith Jones .02 .10
60 Sandis Ozolinsh .02 .10
61 Mike Ricci .02 .10
62 Claude Lemieux .02 .10
63 Mike Keane .02 .10
64 Adam Foote .02 .10
65 Mike Modano .20 .50
66 Pat Verbeek .02 .10
67 Andy Moog .08 .25
68 Joe Nieuwendyk .08 .25
69 Jamie Langenbrunner .02 .10
70 Derian Hatcher .02 .10
71 Greg Adams .02 .10
72 Darryl Sydor .02 .10
73 Dave Reid .02 .10
74 Jere Lehtinen .02 .10
75 Todd Harvey .02 .10
76 Brendan Shanahan .10 .30
77 Mike Vernon .08 .25
78 Steve Yzerman .60 1.50
79 Sergei Fedorov .20 .50
80 Chris Osgood .08 .25
81 Nicklas Lidstrom .10 .30
82 Vladimir Konstantinov .08 .25
83 Darren McCarty .02 .10
84 Kirk Maltby .02 .10
85 Vyacheslav Kozlov .02 .10
86 Martin Lapointe .02 .10
87 Doug Weight .08 .25
88 Mike Grier .02 .10
89 Curtis Joseph .10 .30
90 Andrei Kovalenko .02 .10
91 Rem Murray .02 .10
92 Ryan Smyth .08 .25
93 Mariusz Czerkawski .02 .10
94 Drew Bannister .02 .10
95 Jason Arnott .02 .10
96 Luke Richardson .02 .10
97 Dean McAmmond .02 .10
98 Kirk Muller .02 .10
99 Ray Sheppard .02 .10
100 Scott Mellanby .02 .10
101 Ed Jovanovski .08 .25
102 John Vanbiesbrouck .08 .25
103 Radek Dvorak .02 .10
104 Robert Svehla .02 .10
105 Rob Niedermayer .02 .10
106 Dave Nemirovsky .02 .10
107 Steve Washburn .02 .10
108 Bill Lindsay .02 .10
109 Kevin Dineen .02 .10
110 Keith Primeau .02 .10
111 Sean Burke .08 .25
112 Derek King .02 .10
113 Andrew Cassels .02 .10
114 Glen Wesley .02 .10
115 Nelson Emerson .02 .10
116 Geoff Sanderson .08 .25
117 Jeff O'Neill .02 .10
118 Kent Manderville .02 .10
119 Dimitri Khristich .02 .10
120 Ian Laperriere .02 .10
121 Aki Berg .02 .10
122 Vladimir Tsyplakov .02 .10
123 Vitali Yachmenev .02 .10
124 Roman Vopat .02 .10
125 Rob Blake .08 .25
126 Jan Vopat .02 .10
127 Jeff Shevalier RC .02 .10
128 Byron Dafoe .08 .25
129 Saku Koivu .10 .30
130 Vincent Damphousse .02 .10
131 Brian Savage .02 .10
132 Valeri Bure .02 .10
133 Mark Recchi .08 .25
134 Jocelyn Thibault .08 .25
135 Jose Theodore .15 .40
136 Dave Manson .02 .10
137 Shayne Corson .02 .10
138 Stephane Richer .02 .10
139 Doug Gilmour .08 .25
140 Scott Stevens .08 .25
141 Martin Brodeur .30 .75
142 Dave Andreychuk .02 .10
143 Bobby Holik .02 .10
144 Brian Rolston .02 .10
145 Jay Pandolfo .02 .10
146 John MacLean .02 .10
147 Bill Guerin .08 .25
148 Scott Niedermayer .02 .10
149 Denis Pederson .02 .10
150 Zigmund Palffy .08 .25
151 Robert Reichel .02 .10
152 Bryan Smolinski .02 .10
153 Eric Fichaud .08 .25
154 Todd Bertuzzi .10 .30
155 Bryan Berard .08 .25
156 Niklas Andersson .02 .10
157 Bryan McCabe .02 .10
158 Tommy Salo .08 .25
159 Kenny Jonsson .02 .10
160 Travis Green .02 .10
161 Mike Richter .10 .30
162 Brian Leetch .10 .30
163 Adam Graves .02 .10
164 Vladimir Vorobiev RC .02 .10
165 Niklas Sundstrom .02 .10
166 Russ Courtnall .02 .10
167 Wayne Gretzky .75 2.00
168 Mark Messier .10 .30
169 Alexander Karpovtsev .02 .10
170 Luc Robitaille .08 .25
171 Ulf Samuelsson .02 .10
172 Daniel Alfredsson .08 .25
173 Alexei Yashin .02 .10
174 Alexandre Daigle .02 .10
175 Andreas Dackell .02 .10
176 Wade Redden .02 .10
177 Sergei Zholtok .02 .10
178 Damian Rhodes .08 .25
179 Steve Duchesne .02 .10
180 Shawn McEachern .02 .10
181 Ron Tugnutt .08 .25
182 John LeClair .10 .30
183 Janne Niinimaa .08 .25
184 Mikael Renberg .08 .25
185 Vaclav Prospal RC .10 .30
186 Eric Lindros .10 .30
187 Dainius Zubrus .10 .30
188 Ron Hextall .08 .25
189 Paul Coffey .10 .30
190 Dale Hawerchuk .08 .25
191 Trent Klatt .02 .10
192 Rod Brind'Amour .08 .25
193 Nikolai Khabibulin .08 .25
194 Keith Tkachuk .10 .30
195 Jeremy Roenick .15 .40
196 Mike Gartner .08 .25
197 Dallas Drake .02 .10
198 Oleg Tverdovsky .02 .10
199 Cliff Ronning .02 .10
200 Teppo Numminen .02 .10
201 Craig Janney .02 .10
202 Deron Quint .02 .10
203 Jason Wooley .02 .10
204 Ron Francis .08 .25
205 Jaromir Jagr .20 .50
206 Greg Johnson .02 .10
207 Kevin Hatcher .02 .10
208 Patrick Lalime .08 .25
209 Petr Nedved .08 .25
210 Ken Wregget .08 .25
211 Darius Kasparaitis .02 .10
212 Stu Barnes .02 .10
213 Joe Dziedzic .02 .10
214 Owen Nolan .08 .25
215 Jeff Friesen .02 .10
216 Ed Belfour .10 .30
217 Viktor Kozlov .02 .10
218 Tony Granato .02 .10
219 Darren Turcotte .02 .10
220 Stephen Guolla RC .02 .10
221 Marty McSorley .02 .10
222 Marcus Ragnarsson .02 .10
223 Al Iafrate .02 .10
224 Brett Hull .15 .40
225 Grant Fuhr .08 .25
226 Pierre Turgeon .08 .25
227 Geoff Courtnall .02 .10
228 Jim Campbell .02 .10
229 Harry York .02 .10
230 Tony Twist .08 .25
231 Joe Murphy .02 .10
232 Pavol Demitra .08 .25
233 Chris Pronger .08 .25
234 Al MacInnis .08 .25
235 Daren Puppa .08 .25
236 Chris Gratton .08 .25
237 Dino Ciccarelli .02 .10
238 Rob Zamuner .02 .10
239 Igor Ulanov .02 .10
240 Roman Hamrlik .02 .10
241 Alexander Selivanov .02 .10
242 Patrick Poulin .02 .10
243 Daymond Langkow .08 .25
244 Corey Schwab .08 .25
245 Mats Sundin .10 .30
246 Wendel Clark .08 .25
247 Sergei Berezin .02 .10
248 Steve Sullivan .02 .10
249 Fredrik Modin .02 .10
250 Darby Hendrickson .02 .10
251 Jason Podollan .02 .10
252 Felix Potvin .10 .30
253 Tie Domi .08 .25
254 Todd Warriner .02 .10
255 Pavel Bure .10 .30
256 Alexander Mogilny .08 .25
257 Martin Gelinas .02 .10
258 Corey Hirsch .08 .25
259 Trevor Linden .08 .25
260 Mike Sillinger .02 .10
261 Markus Naslund .10 .30
262 Jyrki Lumme .02 .10
263 Gino Odjick .02 .10
264 Mike Ridley .02 .10
265 Dave Roberts .02 .10
266 Adam Oates .08 .25
267 Bill Ranford .08 .25
268 Joe Juneau .08 .25
269 Chris Simon .02 .10
270 Peter Bondra .08 .25
271 Dale Hunter .02 .10
272 Jaroslav Svejkovski .08 .25
273 Sergei Gonchar .02 .10
274 Steve Konowalchuk .02 .10
275 Phil Housley .02 .10
276 Angela James RC .40 1.00
277 Nancy Drolet RC .02 .10
278 Lesley Reddon RC .40 1.00
279 Hayley Wickenheiser RC 1.00 2.50
280 Vicky Sunohara RC .60 1.50
281 Cassie Campbell RC .75 2.00
282 Geraldine Heaney RC .02 .10
283 Judy Diduck RC .02 .10
284 France St. Louis RC .02 .10
285 Danielle Goyette RC .02 .10
286 Therese Brisson RC .02 .10
287 Stacey Wilson RC .02 .10
288 Danielle Dube RC .02 .10
289 Jayna Hefford RC .60 1.50
290 Luce Letendre RC .02 .10
291 Lori Dupuis RC .02 .10
292 Rebecca Fahey RC .02 .10
293 Fiona Smith RC .02 .10
294 Laura Schuler RC .02 .10
295 Karen Nystrom RC .02 .10
296 Joe Thornton .30 .75
297 Peter Schaefer .20 .50
298 Daniel Tkaczuk .15 .40
299 Alyn McCauley .08 .25
300 Shane Willis .02 .10
301 Chris Phillips .02 .10
302 Marc Denis .08 .25
303 Jason Ward .02 .10
304 Patrick Marleau .20 .50
305 Brad Isbister .02 .10
306 Cameron Mann .15 .40
307 Daniel Cleary .08 .25
308 Brad Larsen .02 .10
309 Nick Boynton .08 .25
310 Scott Barney .08 .25
311 Boyd Devereaux .02 .10
312 Wayne Gretzky CL .10 .30
313 Steve Yzerman CL .10 .30
314 Jaromir Jagr CL .10 .30
315 Jarome Iginla CL .10 .30
316 Patrick Roy CL .10 .30
317 John Vanbiesbrouck CL .08 .25
318 Paul Kariya CL .10 .30
319 Doug Weight CL .02 .10
320 Mats Sundin CL .08 .25

1997-98 Collector's Choice Blow-Ups

Very little is known about this oversized set that consisted of 5 cards other than the two mentioned below. Cards were numbered "X of 5" on the card backs.

1 Wayne Gretzky 4.00 10.00
2 Tony Amonte 1.00 2.50

1997-98 Collector's Choice Crash the Game

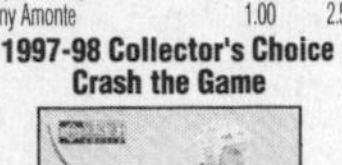

Randomly inserted in packs at the rate of 1:5, this 90-card set features color player photos. If the pictured player scores against the designated team, the card could be redeemed for a special high quality redemption card of that player (expired 7/1/1998).

COMPLETE SET (90) 15.00 30.00
COMP.EXCH.SET (30) 25.00 50.00
*EXCH: 2X TO 4X BASIC INSERTS
C1A Wayne Gretzky 1.50 4.00
C1B Wayne Gretzky 1.50 4.00
C1C Wayne Gretzky 1.50 4.00
C2A Mike Modano .40 1.00
C2B Mike Modano .40 1.00
C2C Mike Modano .40 1.00
C3A Doug Weight .25 .60
C3B Doug Weight .25 .60
C3C Doug Weight .25 .60
C4A Brendan Shanahan .25 .60
C4B Brendan Shanahan .75 2.00
C4C Brendan Shanahan .75 2.00
C5A Ray Sheppard .15 .40
C5B Ray Sheppard .15 .40
C5C Ray Sheppard PHO 1.50 4.00
C6A Keith Primeau .15 .40
C6B Keith Primeau .15 .40
C6C Keith Primeau .15 .40
C7A Ray Bourque CHI L .40 1.00
C7B Ray Bourque .40 1.00
C7C Ray Bourque .40 1.00
C8A Teemu Selanne .25 .60
C8B Teemu Selanne .25 .60
C8C Teemu Selanne .25 .60
C9A Paul Kariya .25 .60
C9B Paul Kariya .25 .60
C9C Paul Kariya TB .25 .60
C10A Tony Amonte .20 .50
C10B Tony Amonte .20 .50
C10C Tony Amonte .20 .50
C11A Saku Koivu .40 1.00
C11B Saku Koivu .40 1.00
C11C Saku Koivu .40 1.00
C12A Donald Audette .15 .40
C12B Donald Audette .15 .40
C12C Donald Audette .15 .40
C13A Doug Gilmour .40 1.00
C13B Doug Gilmour STL .40 1.00
C13C Doug Gilmour .40 1.00
C14A Theo Fleury .25 .60
C14B Theo Fleury FLO .25 .60
C14C Theo Fleury .25 .60
C15A Alexei Yashin COL .15 .40
C15B Alexei Yashin .15 .40
C15C Alexei Yashin .15 .40
C16A Zigmund Palffy .50 1.25
C16B Zigmund Palffy .50 1.25
C16C Zigmund Palffy .50 1.25
C17A Dimitri Khristich .25 .60
C17B Dimitri Khristich .25 .60
C17C Dimitri Khristich .25 .60
C18A Joe Sakic 1.00 2.50
C18B Joe Sakic 1.00 2.50
C18C Joe Sakic 1.00 2.50
C19A Steve Yzerman 2.00 5.00
C19B Steve Yzerman 2.00 5.00
C19C Steve Yzerman 2.00 5.00
C20A Eric Lindros .25 .60
C20B Eric Lindros .40 1.00
C20C Eric Lindros .40 1.00
C21A Peter Forsberg FLO .60 1.50
C21B Peter Forsberg .60 1.50
C21C Peter Forsberg .60 1.50
C22A Dino Ciccarelli .15 .40
C22B Dino Ciccarelli .15 .40
C22C Dino Ciccarelli .15 .40
C23A Mats Sundin .25 .60
C23B Mats Sundin .25 .60
C23C Mats Sundin .25 .60
C24A Pavel Bure .25 .60
C24B Pavel Bure .40 1.00
C24C Pavel Bure .40 1.00
C25A Peter Bondra CHI .25 .60
C25B Peter Bondra .25 .60
C25C Peter Bondra .25 .60
C26A Brett Hull .30 .75
C26B Brett Hull .30 .75
C26C Brett Hull .30 .75
C27A Keith Tkachuk BOS .30 .75
C27B Keith Tkachuk .30 .75
C27C Keith Tkachuk .30 .75
C28A Jaromir Jagr .40 1.00
C28B Jaromir Jagr .40 1.00
C28C Jaromir Jagr .40 1.00
C29A Jarome Iginla .30 .75
C29B Jarome Iginla .30 .75
C29C Jarome Iginla .30 .75
C30A Owen Nolan .15 .40
C30B Owen Nolan .15 .40
C30C Owen Nolan NYI L .15 .40

1997-98 Collector's Choice Magic Men

Randomly inserted in Canadian packs at the rate of 1:32, this 10-card set features five color photos each of Wayne Gretzky and Patrick Roy.

COMMON GRETZKY (MM1-MM5) 5.00 10.00
COMMON ROY (MM6-MM10) 3.00 8.00

1997-98 Collector's Choice Star Quest

This 90-card, four-tier insert set features color photos of some of the top NHL Superstars printed using the hobby's top technology. The 45 cards in Tier One (SQ1-SQ45) were randomly inserted one in every pack; the 20 cards in Tier Two (SQ45-SQ65) were randomly inserted 1:21 packs; the 15 cards of Tier Three (SQ66-SQ80) were randomly inserted 1:71 packs; the 10 cards of Tier Four were randomly inserted 1:145 packs.

COMPLETE SET (90) 125.00 250.00
COMP.SERIES 1 (45) 3.00 8.00
SQ1 Bryan Berard .15 .40
SQ2 Robert Svehla .07 .20
SQ3 Petr Nedved .15 .40
SQ4 Steve Sullivan .07 .20
SQ5 Nicklas Lidstrom .20 .50
SQ6 Wade Redden .07 .20
SQ7 Jason Arnott .07 .20
SQ8 Martin Gelinas .07 .20
SQ9 Mikael Renberg .07 .20
SQ10 Jeff Friesen .07 .20
SQ11 Chris Chelios .20 .50
SQ12 Jarome Iginla .25 .60
SQ13 Vyacheslav Kozlov .07 .20
SQ14 Brian Holzinger .07 .20
SQ15 Eric Daze .15 .40
SQ16 Pat Verbeek .07 .20
SQ17 Jozef Stumpel .15 .40
SQ18 Rob Niedermayer .15 .40
SQ19 Sergei Fedorov .30 .75
SQ20 Brian Leetch .20 .50
SQ21 Bill Guerin .07 .20
SQ22 Dino Ciccarelli .07 .20
SQ23 Adam Oates .15 .40
SQ24 Mike Grier .07 .20
SQ25 Alexandre Daigle .07 .20
SQ26 Janne Niinimaa .15 .40
SQ27 Dimitri Khristich .07 .20
SQ28 Oleg Tverdovsky .07 .20
SQ29 Felix Potvin .20 .50
SQ30 Mike Richter .20 .50
SQ31 Curtis Joseph .20 .50
SQ32 Vincent Damphousse .07 .20
SQ33 Vladimir Konstantinov .15 .40
SQ34 Andy Moog .15 .40
SQ35 Nikolai Khabibulin .15 .40
SQ36 Ed Belfour .20 .50
SQ37 Scott Mellanby .07 .20
SQ38 Sandis Ozolinsh .07 .20
SQ39 Travis Green .07 .20
SQ40 Patrick Lalime .15 .40
SQ41 Niklas Sundstrom .07 .20
SQ42 Guy Hebert .15 .40
SQ43 Vitali Yachmenev .07 .20
SQ44 Roman Hamrlik .07 .20
SQ45 Adam Deadmarsh .07 .20
SQ46 Alexei Zhamnov .60 1.50
SQ47 Saku Koivu 1.25 3.00
SQ48 Sergei Berezin 1.00 2.50
SQ49 Mark Messier 1.25 3.00
SQ50 Martin Brodeur 3.00 8.00
SQ51 Daniel Alfredsson 1.00 2.50
SQ52 John LeClair 1.25 3.00
SQ53 Mike Vernon 1.00 2.50
SQ54 Ron Francis 1.00 2.50
SQ55 Keith Primeau .60 1.50
SQ56 Pierre Turgeon 1.00 2.50
SQ57 Jim Carey 1.00 2.50
SQ58 Peter Bondra 1.00 2.50
SQ59 Pavel Bure 1.25 3.00
SQ60 Ray Sheppard .60 1.50
SQ61 Chris Gratton 1.00 2.50
SQ62 Derek Plante .60 1.50
SQ63 Joe Sakic 2.50 6.00
SQ64 Theo Fleury .60 1.50
SQ65 Tony Amonte 1.00 2.50
SQ66 Zigmund Palffy 2.00 5.00
SQ67 Steve Yzerman 10.00 25.00
SQ68 Doug Weight 2.00 5.00
SQ69 Alexander Mogilny 2.00 5.00
SQ70 Doug Gilmour 2.50 5.00
SQ71 Peter Forsberg 6.00 15.00
SQ72 Alexei Yashin 2.00 5.00
SQ73 Geoff Sanderson 2.00 5.00
SQ74 Brendan Shanahan 2.50 6.00
SQ75 Mark Recchi 2.00 5.00
SQ76 Brett Hull 3.00 8.00
SQ77 Ray Bourque 4.00 10.00
SQ78 Owen Nolan 2.00 5.00
SQ79 Jeremy Roenick 3.00 8.00
SQ80 Teemu Selanne 2.50 6.00
SQ81 Dominik Hasek 6.00 15.00
SQ82 Mike Modano 4.00 10.00
SQ83 Mats Sundin 4.00 10.00
SQ84 John Vanbiesbrouck 4.00 10.00
SQ85 Paul Kariya 3.00 8.00
SQ86 Patrick Roy 10.00 25.00
SQ87 Keith Tkachuk 4.00 10.00
SQ88 Eric Lindros 4.00 10.00
SQ89 Jaromir Jagr 6.00 15.00
SQ90 Wayne Gretzky 15.00 40.00

1997-98 Collector's Choice Stick 'Ums

Randomly inserted in packs at the rate of 1:3, this 30-card set features color action player photos printed on re-stickable stickers that stick anywhere.

COMPLETE SET (30) 15.00 30.00
S1 Wayne Gretzky 2.50 5.00
S2 John Vanbiesbrouck .25 .60
S3 Martin Brodeur .75 2.00
S4 Rob Blake .25 .60
S5 Saku Koivu .30 .75
S6 Curtis Joseph .30 .75
S7 Chris Chelios .30 .75
S8 Mike Modano .50 1.25
S9 Paul Kariya .30 .75
S10 Eric Lindros .30 .75
S11 Daniel Alfredsson .25 .60
S12 Jarome Iginla .40 1.00
S13 Jeremy Roenick .40 1.00
S14 Brendan Shanahan .30 .75
S15 Jaromir Jagr .50 1.25
S16 Zigmund Palffy .25 .60
S17 Mats Sundin .30 .75
S18 Teemu Selanne .30 .75
S19 Joe Sakic .60 1.50
S20 Ed Belfour .30 .75
S21 Peter Forsberg .75 2.00
S22 Dino Ciccarelli .25 .60
S23 Patrick Roy 1.50 4.00
S24 Doug Gilmour .25 .60
S25 Pavel Bure .30 .75
S26 Brett Hull .40 1.00
S27 Ray Bourque .50 1.25
S28 Adam Oates .25 .60
S29 Steve Yzerman 1.50 4.00
S30 Dominik Hasek .60 1.50

1997-98 Collector's Choice World Domination

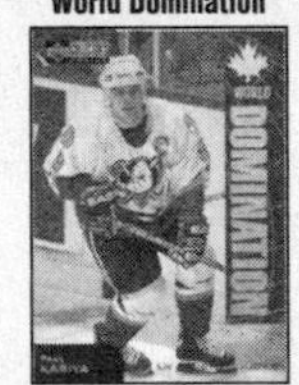

Randomly inserted in Canadian packs at the rate of 1:4, this 20-card set features color photos of top players. The backs carry player information.

COMPLETE SET (20) 25.00 50.00
W1 Wayne Gretzky 5.00 12.00
W2 Mark Messier .75 2.00
W3 Steve Yzerman 4.00 10.00
W4 Brendan Shanahan .75 2.00
W5 Paul Kariya .75 2.00
W6 Joe Sakic 1.50 4.00
W7 Eric Lindros .75 2.00
W8 Rod Brind'Amour .60 1.50
W9 Keith Primeau .60 1.50
W10 Trevor Linden .60 1.50
W11 Theo Fleury .60 1.50
W12 Scott Niedermeyer .60 1.50
W13 Rob Blake .60 1.50
W14 Chris Pronger .60 1.50
W15 Eric Desjardins .60 1.50
W16 Adam Foote .60 1.50
W17 Scott Stevens .60 1.50
W18 Patrick Roy 4.00 10.00
W19 Curtis Joseph .75 2.00
W20 Martin Brodeur 2.00 5.00

2008-09 Collector's Choice

This set was released on February 24, 2009. The base set consists of 300 cards. Cards 201-250 consist of rookies.

COMPLETE SET (300) 30.00 60.00
COMP.SET w/o SPs (200) 12.00 30.00
RC STATED ODDS 1:2
3S STATED PRINT RUN 1:5
CC STATED ODDS 1:5
1 Ales Hemsky .12 .30
2 Ales Kotalik .12 .30
3 Alex Kovalev .20 .50
4 Alex Tanguay .15 .40
5 Alexander Edler .15 .40
6 Alexander Frolov .12 .30
7 Alexander Ovechkin .75 2.00
8 Alexander Semin .20 .50
9 Alexander Steen .20 .50
10 Andrei Kostitsyn .15 .40
11 Andrew Cogliano .30 .75
12 Anze Kopitar .20 .50
13 Bill Guerin .12 .30
14 Brad Boyes .15 .40
15 Brad Richards .15 .40
16 Brendan Morrison .12 .30
17 Aaron Voros .12 .30
18 Brenden Morrow .15 .40
19 Brian Campbell .30 .75
20 Brian Gionta .20 .50
21 Brian Rolston .12 .30
22 Cam Ward .20 .50
23 Carey Price .60 1.50
24 Chris Drury .20 .50
25 Chris Higgins .12 .30
26 Chris Kunitz .12 .30
27 Chris Osgood .20 .50
28 Chris Pronger .15 .40
29 Colby Armstrong .12 .30
30 Corey Perry .20 .50
31 Cristobal Huet .20 .50
32 Dan Boyle .15 .40
33 Dan Cleary .20 .50
34 Dan Ellis .12 .30
35 Daniel Alfredsson .15 .40
36 Daniel Briere .20 .50
37 Daniel Carcillo .12 .30
38 Daniel Sedin .20 .50
39 Dany Heatley .25 .60
40 Darcy Tucker .15 .40
41 David Booth .12 .30
42 David Clarkson .12 .30
43 David Legwand .15 .40
44 Daymond Langkow .12 .30
45 Derek Roy .12 .30
46 Dion Phaneuf .20 .50
47 Doug Weight .12 .30
48 Drew Stafford .20 .50
49 Duncan Keith .15 .40
50 Dustin Brown .12 .30
51 Dustin Penner .12 .30
52 Dwayne Roloson .15 .40
53 Ed Jovanovski .12 .30
54 Eric Staal .30 .75
55 Erik Cole .12 .30
56 Erik Johnson .25 .60
57 Evgeni Malkin .50 1.25
58 Evgeni Nabokov .20 .50
59 George Parros .12 .30
60 Gilbert Brule .20 .50
61 Chuck Kobasew .12 .30
62 Guillaume Latendresse .15 .40
63 Henrik Lundqvist .40 1.00
64 Henrik Sedin .20 .50
65 Henrik Zetterberg .40 1.00
66 Ilya Bryzgalov .12 .30
67 Ilya Kovalchuk .25 .60
68 J.P. Dumont .12 .30
69 Jack Johnson .15 .40
70 Jarome Iginla .40 1.00
71 Jarret Stoll .15 .40
72 Jason Arnott .12 .30
73 Jason LaBarbera .15 .40
74 Jason Pominville .15 .40
75 Jason Spezza .25 .60
76 Jay Bouwmeester .15 .40
77 Jean-Sebastien Giguere .20 .50
78 Jeff Carter .20 .50
79 Jere Lehtinen .12 .30
80 Joe Sakic .30 .75
81 Joe Thornton .30 .75
82 Johan Franzen .20 .50
83 Johan Hedberg .15 .40
84 Jaroslav Halak .20 .50
85 Jonathan Cheechoo .20 .50
86 Jonathan Toews .60 1.50
87 Jordan Staal .30 .75
88 Josh Harding .15 .40
89 Jussi Jokinen .12 .30
90 Justin Williams .12 .30
91 Kari Lehtonen .12 .30
92 Keith Tkachuk .15 .40
93 Kristian Huselius .12 .30
94 Lee Stempniak .12 .30
95 Manny Legace .15 .40
96 Marc Savard .12 .30
97 Marc Staal .25 .60
98 Marc-Andre Fleury .20 .50
99 Marek Zidlicky .12 .30
100 Marian Gaborik .30 .75
101 Marian Hossa .30 .75
102 Markus Naslund .20 .50
103 Martin Biron .15 .40
104 Martin Brodeur .40 1.00
105 Martin Erat .20 .50
106 Martin Gerber .15 .40
107 Martin Hanzal .15 .40
108 Martin Havlat .15 .40
109 Martin St. Louis .20 .50
110 Marty Turco .15 .40
111 Mats Sundin .20 .50
112 Matt Stajan .15 .40
113 Matthew Lombardi .12 .30
114 Michael Peca .15 .40
115 Michael Ryder .15 .40
116 Michal Rozsival .12 .30
117 Miikka Kiprusoff .20 .50
118 Mike Cammalleri .20 .50
119 Mike Comrie .12 .30
120 Mike Knuble .20 .50
121 Mike Modano .20 .50
122 Mike Ribeiro .12 .30
123 Mike Richards .30 .75
124 Mike Smith .15 .40
125 Mikko Koivu .20 .50
126 Milan Hejduk .15 .40
127 Milan Lucic .40 1.00
128 Milan Michalek .12 .30
129 Miroslav Satan .12 .30
130 Nathan Horton .12 .30
131 Nicklas Backstrom .40 1.00
132 Nicklas Lidstrom .20 .50
133 Niklas Backstrom .20 .50
134 Nikolai Antropov .15 .40
135 Nikolai Khabibulin .20 .50
136 Nikolai Zherdev .12 .30
137 Olli Jokinen .12 .30
138 Pascal Leclaire .15 .40
139 Patrice Bergeron .20 .50
140 Patrick Kane .50 1.25
141 Patrick Marleau .15 .40
142 Patrick O'Sullivan .15 .40
143 Patrick Sharp .12 .30
144 Patrik Elias .12 .30
145 Paul Kariya .20 .50
146 Paul Ranger .12 .30
147 Paul Stastny .20 .50
148 Pavel Datsyuk .20 .50
149 Peter Budaj .15 .40
150 Peter Forsberg .30 .75
151 Peter Mueller .25 .60
152 Phil Kessel .20 .50
153 Pierre-Marc Bouchard .12 .30
154 R.J. Umberger .12 .30
155 Radim Vrbata .12 .30
156 Ray Whitney .12 .30
157 Rick DiPietro .20 .50
158 Rick Nash .20 .50
159 Robert Lang .12 .30
160 Roberto Luongo .30 .75
161 Rod Brind'Amour .15 .40
162 Ryan Getzlaf .25 .60
163 Ryan Kesler .12 .30
164 Ryan Malone .12 .30
165 Ryan Miller .20 .50
166 Ryan Smyth .15 .40
167 Ryan Suter .12 .30
168 Saku Koivu .20 .50
169 Sam Gagner .30 .75
170 Scott Gomez .15 .40
171 Scott Niedermayer .12 .30
172 Sergei Fedorov .30 .75
173 Sergei Zubov .12 .30
174 Shane Doan .12 .30
175 Shawn Horcoff .12 .30
176 Shea Weber .12 .30
177 Sidney Crosby 1.00 2.50
178 Simon Gagne .15 .40
179 Slava Kozlov .12 .30
180 Stephen Weiss .12 .30
181 Steve Bernier .12 .30
182 Teemu Selanne .20 .50
183 Thomas Vanek .20 .50
184 Tim Thomas .20 .50
185 Tobias Enstrom .20 .50
186 Todd White .12 .30
187 Tomas Holmstrom .15 .40
188 Tomas Kaberle .12 .30
189 Tomas Vokoun .20 .50
190 Travis Zajac .12 .30
191 Trent Hunter .12 .30
192 Ty Conklin .15 .40
193 Vaclav Prospal .12 .30
194 Valtteri Filppula .12 .30
195 Vesa Toskala .20 .50
196 Vincent Lecavalier .20 .50
197 Wade Redden .12 .30
198 Wojtek Wolski .12 .30
199 Zach Parise .20 .50
200 Zdeno Chara .12 .30
201 Justin Abdelkader RC 1.25 3.00
202 Patrik Berglund RC 1.50 4.00
203 Mikkel Boedker RC 1.00 2.50
204 Zach Bogosian RC 1.25 3.00
205 Zach Boychuk RC 1.00 2.50
206 Derick Brassard RC 1.25 3.00
207 Fabian Brunnstrom RC 1.00 2.50
208 Matt D'Agostini RC 1.00 2.50
209 Drew Doughty RC 2.00 5.00
210 Robbie Earl RC .50 1.25
211 Andrew Ebbett RC .60 1.50
212 Jonathan Ericsson RC 1.00 2.50
213 Erik Ersberg RC .60 1.50
214 Nikita Filatov RC 2.50 6.00
215 Michael Frolik RC 1.25 3.00
216 Colton Gillies RC .60 1.50
217 Claude Giroux RC 1.25 3.00
218 Alex Goligoski RC 1.25 3.00
219 Darren Helm RC 1.00 2.50
220 Patric Hornqvist RC .60 1.50
221 Josh Bailey RC 1.00 2.50
222 Ryan Jones RC .75 2.00
223 Lauri Korpikoski RC .60 1.50
224 Nikolai Kulemin RC .60 1.50
225 Brian Lee RC .60 1.50
226 Shawn Matthias RC .60 1.50
227 Vladimir Mihalik RC .60 1.50
228 Oscar Moller RC .60 1.50
229 James Neal RC 1.00 2.50
230 Andreas Nodl RC .60 1.50
231 Kyle Okposo RC 1.25 3.00
232 T.J. Oshie RC 1.50 4.00
233 Nathan Oystrick RC .60 1.50
234 Alex Pietrangelo RC 1.00 2.50
235 Kevin Porter RC .50 1.25
236 Teddy Purcell RC .60 1.50
237 Tim Ramholt RC .50 1.25
238 Mattias Ritola RC .75 2.00
239 Luca Sbisa RC 1.00 2.50
240 Luke Schenn RC 2.00 5.00
241 Tom Sestito RC .50 1.25
242 Steven Stamkos RC 5.00 12.00
243 Brandon Sutter RC .75 2.00
244 Viktor Tikhonov RC .60 1.50
245 Kyle Turris RC 1.25 3.00
246 Boris Valabik RC .75 2.00
247 Jakub Voracek RC 1.25 3.00
248 Petr Vrana RC .75 2.00
249 Blake Wheeler RC 1.50 4.00
250 Ilya Zubov RC .60 1.50
251 Ryan Getzlaf 1.00 2.50
Jean-Sebastien Giguere
Chris Pronger
252 Ilya Kovalchuk 1.00 2.50
Kari Lehtonen
Bryan Little
253 Marc Savard .75 2.00
Tim Thomas
Zdeno Chara
254 Thomas Vanek .75 2.00
Ryan Miller
Derek Roy
255 Jarome Iginla 1.50 4.00
Miikka Kiprusoff
Dion Phaneuf
256 Eric Staal 1.25 3.00
Cam Ward
Ray Whitney
257 Jonathan Toews 2.50 6.00
Cristobal Huet
Patrick Kane
258 Joe Sakic 1.25 3.00
Peter Budaj
Paul Stastny
259 Rick Nash .75 2.00
Pascal Leclaire
Kristian Huselius
260 Brenden Morrow .60 1.50
Marty Turco
Brad Richards
261 Henrik Zetterberg 1.50 4.00
Chris Osgood
Pavel Datsyuk
262 Ales Hemsky .75 2.00
Mathieu Garon
Shawn Horcoff
263 Nathan Horton .75 2.00
Tomas Vokoun
David Booth
264 Anze Kopitar .75 2.00
Jason LaBarbera
Alexander Frolov
265 Marian Gaborik 1.25 3.00
Niklas Backstrom
Brent Burns
266 Saku Koivu 2.50 6.00
Carey Price
Alex Kovalev
267 J.P. Dumont .50 1.25
Dan Ellis
Jason Arnott
268 Zach Parise 1.50 4.00
Martin Brodeur
Patrik Elias
269 Mike Comrie .75 2.00
Rick DiPietro
Mark Streit
270 Markus Naslund 1.50 4.00
Henrik Lundqvist
Chris Drury
271 Dany Heatley 1.00 2.50
Martin Gerber
Jason Spezza
272 Mike Richards 1.25 3.00
Martin Biron
Jeff Carter
273 Shane Doan .50 1.25
Ilya Bryzgalov
Olli Jokinen
274 Sidney Crosby 4.00 10.00
Marc-Andre Fleury
Evgeni Malkin
275 Joe Thornton 1.25 3.00
Evgeni Nabokov
Jonathan Cheechoo
276 Paul Kariya .75 2.00
Manny Legace
Brad Boyes
277 Vincent Lecavalier .75 2.00
Mike Smith
Martin St. Louis
278 Nik Antropov .75 2.00
Vesa Toskala
Tomas Kaberle
279 Daniel Sedin 1.25 3.00
Roberto Luongo
Henrik Sedin
280 Alexander Ovechkin 3.00 8.00
Jose Theodore
Mike Green
281 Alexander Ovechkin 3.00 8.00
282 Brenden Morrow .60 1.50
283 Chris Pronger .60 1.50
284 Daniel Carcillo .50 1.25
285 Dion Phaneuf .75 2.00
286 Dustin Brown .50 1.25
287 Ed Jovanovski .50 1.25
288 Eric Staal 1.25 3.00
289 Henrik Lundqvist 1.50 4.00
290 Henrik Zetterberg 1.50 4.00
291 Ilya Kovalchuk 1.00 2.50
292 Jonathan Toews 2.50 6.00
293 Martin Brodeur 1.50 4.00
294 Rick Nash .75 2.00
295 Roberto Luongo 1.25 3.00
296 Ryan Getzlaf 1.00 2.50
297 Sidney Crosby 4.00 10.00
298 Vincent Lecavalier .75 2.00
299 Wade Redden .50 1.25
300 Zdeno Chara .50 1.25

2008-09 Collector's Choice Prime Reserve Gold

*GOLD (1-200): 5X TO 12X BASIC CARDS
*GOLD (201-250): 1.2X TO 3X BASIC CARDS
*GOLD (251-300): 1X TO 2.5X BASIC CARDS
STATED ODDS 1:24

2008-09 Collector's Choice Reserve Silver

COMPLETE SET (300) 50.00 100.00
*SINGLES (1-200): .6X TO 2X BASIC CARDS
*SINGLES (201-250): 1X TO 2.5X BASIC CARDS
*SINGLES (251-300): .6X TO 1.5X BASIC CARDS
STATED ODDS 1 PER PACK

2008-09 Collector's Choice Cup Quest

COMPLETE SET (90) 50.00 100.00
FIRST ROUND STATED ODDS 1:10
SECOND ROUND STATED ODDS 1:14
SEMI-FINALS STATED ODDS 1:16
FINALS STATED ODDS 1:16
OVERALL STATED ODDS 1:6
CQ1 Ales Hemsky FR .40 1.00
CQ2 Brian Rafalski FR .40 1.00
CQ3 Brian Rolston FR .40 1.00
CQ4 Corey Perry FR .60 1.50
CQ5 Cristobal Huet FR .60 1.50
CQ6 Daniel Sedin FR .60 1.50
CQ7 David Booth FR .40 1.00
CQ8 Derek Roy FR .40 1.00
CQ9 Ed Jovanovski FR .40 1.00
CQ10 J.P. Dumont FR .40 1.00
CQ11 Jason Arnott FR .40 1.00
CQ12 Jeff Carter FR .60 1.50
CQ13 Jere Lehtinen FR .40 1.00
CQ14 Jordan Staal FR 1.00 2.50
CQ15 Kari Lehtonen FR .40 1.00
CQ16 Manny Legace FR .50 1.25
CQ17 Johan Franzen FR .40 1.00
CQ18 Mark Streit FR .40 1.00
CQ19 Martin Biron FR .50 1.25
CQ20 Martin Gerber FR .50 1.25
CQ21 Mike Green FR .40 1.00
CQ22 Milan Hejduk FR .50 1.25
CQ23 Nathan Horton FR .40 1.00
CQ24 Niklas Backstrom FR .60 1.50
CQ25 Pascal Leclaire FR .50 1.25
CQ26 Pavol Demitra FR .40 1.00
CQ27 Rob Blake FR .60 1.50
CQ28 Rod Brind'Amour FR .50 1.25
CQ29 Ryan Malone FR .40 1.00
CQ30 Scott Gomez FR .50 1.25
CQ31 Todd Bertuzzi FR .60 1.50
CQ32 Tomas Holmstrom FR .50 1.25
CQ33 Tomas Kaberle FR .40 1.00
CQ34 Vesa Toskala FR .60 1.50
CQ35 Zdeno Chara FR .40 1.00
CQ36 Alex Kovalev SR .75 2.00
CQ37 Andrew Cogliano SR 1.25 3.00
CQ38 Anze Kopitar SR .75 2.00
CQ39 Brenden Morrow SR .60 1.50
CQ40 Carey Price SR 2.50 6.00
CQ41 Chris Drury SR .75 2.00
CQ42 Chris Osgood SR .75 2.00
CQ43 Henrik Lundqvist SR 1.50 4.00
CQ44 Henrik Sedin SR .75 2.00
CQ45 Jason Spezza SR 1.00 2.50
CQ46 Joe Sakic SR 1.25 3.00
CQ47 Jonathan Toews SR 2.50 6.00
CQ48 Miikka Kiprusoff SR .75 2.00
CQ49 Mike Ribeiro SR .50 1.25
CQ50 Mikko Koivu SR .75 2.00
CQ51 Nicklas Backstrom SR 1.50 4.00
CQ52 Olli Jokinen SR .50 1.25
CQ53 Patrick Kane SR 2.00 5.00
CQ54 Peter Mueller SR 1.00 2.50
CQ55 Ryan Miller SR .75 2.00
CQ56 Sam Gagner SR 1.25 3.00
CQ57 Shawn Horcoff SR .50 1.25
CQ58 Thomas Vanek SR .75 2.00
CQ59 Wade Redden SR .50 1.25
CQ60 Zach Parise SR .75 2.00
CQ61 Daniel Alfredsson SF .75 2.00
CQ62 Dany Heatley SF 1.25 3.00
CQ63 Dion Phaneuf SF 1.00 2.50
CQ64 Evgeni Nabokov SF 1.00 2.50
CQ65 Jean-Sebastien Giguere SF 1.00 2.50
CQ66 Jonathan Cheechoo SF 1.00 2.50
CQ67 Marc-Andre Fleury SF 1.00 2.50
CQ68 Marian Gaborik SF 1.50 4.00
CQ69 Marian Hossa SF 1.50 4.00
CQ70 Markus Naslund SF 1.00 2.50
CQ71 Martin St. Louis SF 1.00 2.50
CQ72 Mats Sundin SF 1.00 2.50
CQ73 Mike Modano SF 1.00 2.50
CQ74 Nicklas Lidstrom SF 1.00 2.50
CQ75 Paul Stastny SF 1.00 2.50
CQ76 Pavel Datsyuk SF 1.00 2.50
CQ77 Rick Nash SF .60 1.50
CQ78 Ryan Getzlaf SF 1.25 3.00
CQ79 Saku Koivu SF 1.00 2.50
CQ80 Shane Doan SF .60 1.50
CQ81 Alexander Ovechkin F 6.00 15.00
CQ82 Sidney Crosby F 8.00 20.00
CQ83 Evgeni Malkin F 4.00 10.00
CQ84 Jarome Iginla F 3.00 8.00
CQ85 Vincent Lecavalier F 1.50 4.00
CQ86 Roberto Luongo F 2.50 6.00
CQ87 Henrik Zetterberg F 3.00 8.00
CQ88 Ilya Kovalchuk F 2.00 5.00
CQ89 Joe Thornton F 2.50 6.00
CQ90 Martin Brodeur F 3.00 8.00

2008-09 Collector's Choice Stick-Ums

COMPLETE SET (30) 25.00 60.00
STATED ODDS 1:18
UMS1 Alexander Ovechkin 2.50 6.00
UMS2 Anze Kopitar .60 1.50
UMS3 Carey Price 2.00 5.00
UMS4 Dany Heatley .75 2.00
UMS5 Evgeni Malkin 1.50 4.00
UMS6 Henrik Lundqvist 1.25 3.00
UMS7 Henrik Zetterberg 1.25 3.00
UMS8 Ilya Kovalchuk .75 2.00
UMS9 Jarome Iginla 1.25 3.00
UMS10 Jean-Sebastien Giguere .60 1.50
UMS11 Joe Sakic 1.00 2.50
UMS12 Joe Thornton 1.00 2.50
UMS13 Jonathan Toews 2.00 5.00
UMS14 Marc-Andre Fleury .60 1.50
UMS15 Marian Gaborik 1.00 2.50
UMS16 Martin Brodeur 1.25 3.00
UMS17 Martin St. Louis .60 1.50
UMS18 Marty Turco .50 1.25
UMS19 Mike Modano .60 1.50
UMS20 Mike Richards 1.00 2.50
UMS21 Nicklas Backstrom 1.25 3.00
UMS22 Nicklas Lidstrom .60 1.50
UMS23 Patrick Kane 1.50 4.00
UMS24 Paul Stastny .60 1.50
UMS25 Pavel Datsyuk .60 1.50
UMS26 Rick Nash .60 1.50
UMS27 Roberto Luongo 1.00 2.50
UMS28 Ryan Miller .60 1.50
UMS29 Sidney Crosby 3.00 8.00
UMS30 Vincent Lecavalier .60 1.50

2009-10 Collector's Choice

COMP.SET w/o SPS (200) 15.00 40.00
1 Rick DiPietro .20 .50
2 Kyle Okposo .20 .50
3 Josh Bailey .15 .40
4 Mark Streit .12 .30
5 Doug Weight .12 .30
6 Trent Hunter .12 .30
7 Vincent Lecavalier .25 .60
8 Steven Stamkos .50 1.25
9 Ryan Malone .12 .30
10 Mike Smith .15 .40
11 Vaclav Prospal .12 .30
12 Martin St. Louis .20 .50
13 Paul Stastny .20 .50
14 Peter Budaj .20 .50
15 John-Michael Liles .15 .40
16 Milan Hejduk .20 .50
17 Marek Svatos .12 .30
18 Wojtek Wolski .12 .30
19 Chris Stewart .20 .50
20 Ilya Kovalchuk .25 .60
21 Todd White .12 .30
22 Bryan Little .20 .50
23 Kari Lehtonen .20 .50
24 Colby Armstrong .12 .30
25 Zach Bogosian .25 .60
26 Anze Kopitar .20 .50
27 Dustin Brown .15 .40
28 Jonathan Quick .30 .75
29 Alexander Frolov .15 .40
30 Drew Doughty .40 1.00
31 Ryan Smyth .20 .50
32 Peter Mueller .25 .60
33 Shane Doan .15 .40
34 Scottie Upshall .12 .30
35 Ilya Bryzgalov .15 .40
36 Keith Yandle .12 .30
37 Matthew Lombardi .12 .30
38 Nikolai Kulemin .15 .40
39 Mike Komisarek .15 .40
40 Vesa Toskala .20 .50
41 Matt Stajan .15 .40
42 Tomas Kaberle .12 .30
43 Mikhail Grabovski .15 .40
44 Luke Schenn .30 .75
45 Marty Turco .15 .40
46 James Neal .20 .50
47 Mike Ribeiro .12 .30
48 Steve Ott .12 .30
49 Brad Richards .15 .40
50 Loui Eriksson .12 .30
51 Mike Modano .20 .50
52 Jason Spezza .25 .60
53 Jarkko Ruutu .12 .30
54 Filip Kuba .12 .30
55 Daniel Alfredsson .20 .50
56 Alex Kovalev .20 .50
57 Nick Foligno .20 .50
58 Dany Heatley .40 1.00
59 Ales Hemsky .15 .40
60 Patrick O'Sullivan .15 .40
61 Nikolai Khabibulin .20 .50
62 Sheldon Souray .12 .30
63 Shawn Horcoff .12 .30
64 Andrew Cogliano .25 .60
65 Sam Gagner .25 .60
66 Pekka Rinne .15 .40
67 Jason Arnott .12 .30
68 Shea Weber .15 .40
69 Jordin Tootoo .20 .50
70 Ryan Suter .12 .30
71 J.P. Dumont .12 .30
72 Mikko Koivu .20 .50
73 Martin Havlat .15 .40
74 Niklas Backstrom .20 .50
75 Marek Zidlicky .12 .30
76 Pierre-Marc Bouchard .15 .40
77 Andrew Brunette .12 .30
78 Thomas Vanek .20 .50
79 Tim Connolly .12 .30
80 Derek Roy .20 .50
81 Ryan Miller .20 .50
82 Jason Pominville .20 .50
83 Drew Stafford .20 .50
84 Clarke MacArthur .12 .30
85 Stephen Weiss .12 .30
86 Michael Frolik .15 .40
87 Keith Ballard .12 .30
88 David Booth .12 .30
89 Nathan Horton .12 .30
90 Tomas Vokoun .20 .50
91 Ryan Getzlaf .30 .75
92 Scott Niedermayer .12 .30
93 Corey Perry .20 .50
94 Saku Koivu .20 .50
95 Teemu Selanne .20 .50
96 Bobby Ryan .25 .60
97 Steve Mason .30 .75
98 Rick Nash .20 .50
99 Jakub Voracek .20 .50
100 Kris Russell .20 .50
101 R.J. Umberger .15 .40
102 Derick Brassard .20 .50
103 Paul Kariya .20 .50
104 David Perron .15 .40
105 T.J. Oshie .30 .75
106 Brad Boyes .15 .40
107 Andy McDonald .12 .30
108 David Backes .15 .40
109 Chris Mason .15 .40
110 Carey Price .50 1.25
111 Andrei Markov .15 .40
112 Scott Gomez .15 .40
113 Mike Cammalleri .15 .40
114 Tomas Plekanec .15 .40
115 Maxim Lapierre .12 .30
116 Andrei Kostitsyn .15 .40
117 Chris Drury .15 .40
118 Brandon Dubinsky .15 .40
119 Henrik Lundqvist .40 1.00
120 Marc Staal .25 .60
121 Sean Avery .15 .40
122 Chris Higgins .12 .30
123 Marian Gaborik .30 .75
124 Olli Jokinen .12 .30
125 Dion Phaneuf .30 .75
126 Jay Bouwmeester .20 .50
127 Craig Conroy .12 .30
128 Miikka Kiprusoff .20 .50
129 Daymond Langkow .12 .30
130 Jarome Iginla .40 1.00
131 Mike Richards .40 1.00
132 Claude Giroux .40 1.00
133 Braydon Coburn .12 .30
134 Jeff Carter .20 .50
135 Simon Gagne .20 .50
136 Chris Pronger .15 .40
137 Daniel Briere .20 .50
138 Roberto Luongo .50 1.25
139 Henrik Sedin .30 .75
140 Kyle Wellwood .12 .30
141 Alexander Edler .12 .30
142 Ryan Kesler .15 .40
143 Daniel Sedin .25 .60
144 Mason Raymond .12 .30
145 Patrik Elias .15 .40
146 Paul Martin .12 .30
147 Martin Brodeur .50 1.25
148 Zach Parise .20 .50
149 Travis Zajac .12 .30
150 Jamie Langenbrunner .12 .30
151 David Clarkson .12 .30
152 Alexander Ovechkin .75 2.00
153 Simeon Varlamov .40 1.00
154 Tomas Fleischmann .12 .30
155 Alexander Semin .20 .50
156 Nicklas Backstrom .40 1.00
157 Brooks Laich .15 .40
158 Mike Green .40 1.00
159 Tim Thomas .20 .50
160 Michael Ryder .15 .40
161 Marc Savard .12 .30
162 David Krejci .15 .40
163 Phil Kessel .20 .50
164 Zdeno Chara .12 .30
165 Patrice Bergeron .20 .50
166 Joe Thornton .40 1.00
167 Ryane Clowe .12 .30
168 Dan Boyle .12 .30
169 Joe Pavelski .12 .30
170 Patrick Marleau .20 .50
171 Evgeni Nabokov .20 .50
172 Devin Setoguchi .15 .40
173 Eric Staal .25 .60
174 Jussi Jokinen .20 .50
175 Rod Brind'Amour .15 .40
176 Tuomo Ruutu .12 .30
177 Sergei Samsonov .12 .30
178 Ray Whitney .12 .30
179 Cam Ward .20 .50
180 Patrick Kane .40 1.00
181 Brian Campbell .15 .40
182 Kris Versteeg .25 .60
183 Marian Hossa .30 .75
184 Cristobal Huet .20 .50
185 Patrick Sharp .15 .40
186 Jonathan Toews .50 1.25
187 Sidney Crosby 1.00 2.50
188 Maxime Talbot .20 .50
189 Marc-Andre Fleury .20 .50
190 Evgeni Malkin .50 1.25
191 Sergei Gonchar .12 .30
192 Kristopher Letang .20 .50
193 Jordan Staal .25 .60
194 Henrik Zetterberg .40 1.00
195 Dan Cleary .25 .60
196 Chris Osgood .25 .60
197 Pavel Datsyuk .20 .50
198 Valtteri Filppula .20 .50
199 Niklas Kronwall .15 .40
200 Nicklas Lidstrom .25 .60
201 Saku Koivu 1.00 2.50
Bobby Ryan
Ryan Getzlaf
202 Bryan Little .75 2.00
Kari Lehtonen
Ilya Kovalchuk
203 Tim Thomas .60 1.50
Marc Savard
Zdeno Chara
204 Ryan Miller .60 1.50
Derek Roy
Thomas Vanek
205 Jarome Iginla 1.00 2.50
Miikka Kiprusoff
Dion Phaneuf
206 Eric Staal .75 2.00
Cam Ward
Ray Whitney
207 Patrick Sharp 1.50 4.00
Patrick Kane
Jonathan Toews
208 Milan Hejduk .60 1.50
Paul Stastny
Wojtek Wolski
209 Derick Brassard 1.00 2.50
Steve Mason
Rick Nash
210 Marty Turco .50 1.25
Loui Eriksson
Mike Ribeiro
211 Henrik Zetterberg 1.25 3.00
Nicklas Lidstrom
Pavel Datsyuk
212 Sam Gagner .75 2.00
Sheldon Souray
Ales Hemsky
213 David Booth .60 1.50
Tomas Vokoun
Stephen Weiss
214 Alexander Frolov 1.25 3.00
Anze Kopitar
Drew Doughty
215 Mikko Koivu .60 1.50
Niklas Backstrom
Owen Nolan
216 Scott Gomez 1.50 4.00
Andrei Markov
Carey Price
217 Jason Arnott .50 1.25
Shea Weber
Pekka Rinne
218 Martin Brodeur 1.50 4.00
Zach Parise
Patrik Elias
219 Mark Streit .60 1.50
Kyle Okposo
Doug Weight
220 Marian Gaborik 1.25 3.00
Henrik Lundqvist
Chris Drury
221 Jason Spezza .75 2.00
Alex Kovalev
Daniel Alfredsson
222 Chris Pronger 1.25 3.00
Jeff Carter
Mike Richards
223 Shane Doan .75 2.00
Ilya Bryzgalov
Peter Mueller
224 Sidney Crosby 3.00 8.00
Evgeni Malkin
Marc-Andre Fleury
225 Evgeni Nabokov 1.25 3.00
Joe Thornton
Patrick Marleau
226 Brad Boyes .50 1.25
Chris Mason
David Perron
227 Martin St. Louis 1.50 4.00
Vincent Lecavalier
Steven Stamkos
228 Luke Schenn 1.00 2.50
Phil Kessel
Vesa Toskala
229 Roberto Luongo 1.50 4.00
Henrik Sedin
Daniel Sedin
230 Nicklas Backstrom 2.50 6.00
Mike Green
Alexander Ovechkin
231 Brian Salcido RC .60 1.50
232 Matt Beleskey RC .75 2.00
233 Spencer Machacek RC .60 1.50
234 Evander Kane RC 2.00 5.00
235 Brad Marchand RC 1.00 2.50
236 Byron Bitz RC .60 1.50
237 Jhonas Enroth RC 1.00 2.50
238 Tyler Myers RC 3.00 8.00
239 Chris Butler RC .75 2.00
240 Riley Armstrong RC .60 1.50
241 Mikael Backlund RC 1.25 3.00
242 Kris Chucko RC .60 1.50
243 Matt Pelech RC .75 2.00
244 John Negrin RC .60 1.50
245 Jakub Petruzalek RC .75 2.00
246 Antti Niemi RC 2.50 6.00
247 Chris Durno RC .60 1.50
248 T.J. Galiardi RC 1.00 2.50
249 Ray Macias RC .75 2.00
250 Matt Hendricks RC .60 1.50
251 Matt Duchene RC 3.00 8.00
252 Ryan O'Reilly RC 1.50 4.00
253 Ivan Vishnevskiy RC 1.00 2.50
254 Tom Wandell RC 2.50 6.00
255 Jamie Benn RC 1.25 3.00
256 Ville Leino RC 1.00 2.50
257 Taylor Chorney RC .75 2.00
258 Dmitry Kulikov RC .75 2.00
259 Davis Drewiske RC .75 2.00
260 Alec Martinez RC .50 1.25
261 Jaime Sifers RC .60 1.50
262 Mathieu Carle RC 1.00 2.50
263 Yannick Weber RC 1.00 2.50
264 Cal O'Reilly RC .75 2.00
265 Alexander Sulzer RC .50 1.25
266 Mike Santorelli RC .50 1.25
267 Colin Wilson RC 1.25 3.00
268 Teemu Laakso RC .50 1.25
269 Cody Franson RC .75 2.00
270 Jesse Joensuu RC 1.00 2.50
271 Andrew MacDonald RC .60 1.50
272 Joel Rechlicz RC .75 2.00
273 John Tavares RC 8.00 20.00
274 Michael Sauer RC .60 1.50
275 Artem Anisimov RC 1.00 2.50
276 Matt Gilroy RC 1.00 2.50
277 Michael Del Zotto RC 1.50 4.00
278 Peter Regin RC 1.00 2.50
279 Erik Karlsson RC 2.50 6.00
280 James Van Riemsdyk RC 2.00 5.00
281 Mika Pyorala RC .75 2.00
282 David Schlemko RC .60 1.50
283 Luca Caputi RC 1.00 2.50
284 Jason Demers RC .60 1.50
285 Benn Ferriero RC .75 2.00
286 Frazer McLaren RC .50 1.25
287 Steven Zalewski RC .75 2.00
288 Logan Couture RC 1.50 4.00
289 Kevin Quick RC .50 1.25
290 Riku Helenius RC .75 2.00
291 James Wright RC 1.00 2.50
292 Victor Hedman RC 1.50 4.00
293 Christian Hanson RC 1.00 2.50
294 Viktor Stalberg RC 1.25 3.00
295 Tyler Bozak RC 2.00 5.00
296 Jonas Gustavsson RC 5.00 12.00
297 Sergei Shirokov RC 1.25 3.00
298 Guillaume Desbiens RC .75 2.00
299 Michael Grabner RC 1.00 2.50
300 Michal Neuvirth RC 2.00 5.00

2009-10 Collector's Choice Reserve

*SINGLES 1-200: .8X TO 2X BASIC
*SINGLES 201-230: .6X TO 1.5X BASIC
*ROOKIES 231-300: .6X TO 1.5X BASIC
OVERALL STATED ODDS 1 PER PACK

2009-10 Collector's Choice Reserve Prime

*SINGLES 1-200: 5X TO 12X BASIC
*SINGLES 201-230: 2X TO 5X BASIC
*SINGLES 231-300: 2X TO 5X BASIC
OVERALL ODDS 1:36

2009-10 Collector's Choice Badge of Honor Tattoos

COMPLETE SET (30) 4.00 10.00
STATED ODDS 1:6
BH1 Anaheim Ducks .20 .50
BH2 Atlanta Thrashers .20 .50
BH3 Boston Bruins .20 .50
BH4 Buffalo Sabres .20 .50
BH5 Calgary Flames .20 .50
BH6 Carolina Hurricanes .20 .50
BH7 Chicago Blackhawks .20 .50
BH8 Colorado Avalanche .20 .50
BH9 Columbus Blue Jackets .20 .50
BH10 Dallas Stars .20 .50
BH11 Detroit Red Wings .20 .50
BH12 Edmonton Oilers .20 .50
BH13 Florida Panthers .20 .50
BH14 Los Angeles Kings .20 .50
BH15 Minnesota Wild .20 .50
BH16 Montreal Canadiens .20 .50
BH17 Nashville Predators .20 .50
BH18 New Jersey Devils .20 .50
BH19 New York Islanders .20 .50
BH20 New York Rangers .20 .50
BH21 Ottawa Senators .20 .50
BH22 Philadelphia Flyers .20 .50
BH23 Phoenix Coyotes .20 .50
BH24 Pittsburgh Penguins .20 .50
BH25 San Jose Sharks .20 .50
BH26 St. Louis Blues .20 .50
BH27 Tampa Bay Lightning .20 .50
BH28 Toronto Maple Leafs .20 .50
BH29 Vancouver Canucks .20 .50
BH30 Washington Capitals .20 .50

2009-10 Collector's Choice Cup Quest

COMPLETE SET (80) 150.00 300.00
F STATED PRINT RUN 100 SER.#'d SETS
OVERALL STATED ODDS 1:9
CQ1 Chris Pronger FR .50 1.25
CQ2 Patrice Bergeron FR .60 1.50
CQ3 Dion Phaneuf FR 1.00 2.50
CQ4 Dany Heatley FR 1.25 3.00
CQ5 Marty Turco FR .50 1.25
CQ6 Nicklas Lidstrom FR .75 2.00
CQ7 Ales Hemsky FR .50 1.25
CQ8 Tomas Vokoun FR .60 1.50
CQ9 Anze Kopitar FR .60 1.50
CQ10 Owen Nolan FR .60 1.50
CQ11 Shea Weber FR .50 1.25
CQ12 Doug Weight FR .40 1.00
CQ13 Rick DiPietro FR .60 1.50
CQ14 Chris Drury FR .50 1.25
CQ15 Patrick Marleau FR .60 1.50
CQ16 Simon Gagne FR .60 1.50
CQ17 Shane Doan FR .50 1.25
CQ18 Devin Setoguchi FR .50 1.25
CQ19 David Perron FR .50 1.25
CQ20 Matt Stajan FR .60 1.50
CQ21 Mike Green FR 1.25 3.00
CQ22 Zdeno Chara FR .40 1.00
CQ23 Brian Campbell FR .50 1.25
CQ24 Brad Richards FR .50 1.25
CQ25 Andrew Cogliano FR .75 2.00
CQ26 David Booth FR .40 1.00
CQ27 Pekka Rinne FR .50 1.25
CQ28 Peter Mueller FR .75 2.00
CQ29 Paul Kariya FR .60 1.50
CQ30 Ryan Kesler FR .50 1.25
CQ31 Mikko Koivu SR .75 2.00
CQ32 Jeff Carter SR .75 2.00
CQ33 Jordan Staal SR 1.00 2.50
CQ34 Jason Spezza SR 1.00 2.50
CQ35 Nicklas Backstrom SR 1.50 4.00
CQ36 Marian Gaborik SR 1.25 3.00
CQ37 Bobby Ryan SR 1.00 2.50
CQ38 Phil Kessel SR .75 2.00
CQ39 Ryan Miller SR .75 2.00
CQ40 Miikka Kiprusoff SR .75 2.00
CQ41 Eric Staal SR 1.00 2.50
CQ42 Rick Nash SR .75 2.00
CQ43 Steve Mason SR 1.25 3.00
CQ44 Mike Modano SR .75 2.00
CQ45 Pavel Datsyuk SR .75 2.00
CQ46 Sam Gagner SR 1.00 2.50
CQ47 Drew Doughty SR 1.50 4.00
CQ48 Zach Parise SR .75 2.00
CQ49 Henrik Lundqvist SR 1.50 4.00
CQ50 Paul Stastny SR .75 2.00
CQ51 Mike Richards SR 1.50 4.00
CQ52 Marc-Andre Fleury SR .75 2.00
CQ53 Teemu Selanne SR .75 2.00
CQ54 Martin St. Louis SR .75 2.00
CQ55 Luke Schenn SR 1.25 3.00
CQ56 Ryan Getzlaf SR 1.25 3.00
CQ57 Thomas Vanek SR .75 2.00
CQ58 Cam Ward SR .75 2.00
CQ59 Steven Stamkos SR 2.00 5.00
CQ60 Saku Koivu SR .75 2.00
CQ61 Ilya Kovalchuk TR 1.25 3.00
CQ62 Jarome Iginla TR 2.50 6.00
CQ63 Jonathan Toews TR 3.00 8.00
CQ64 Joe Thornton TR 2.50 6.00
CQ65 Henrik Zetterberg TR 2.50 6.00
CQ66 Carey Price TR 3.00 8.00
CQ67 Evgeni Malkin TR 3.00 8.00
CQ68 Vincent Lecavalier TR 1.50 4.00
CQ69 Roberto Luongo TR 3.00 8.00
CQ70 Patrick Kane TR 2.50 6.00
CQ71 Martin Brodeur F/100 12.00 30.00
CQ72 Sidney Crosby F/100 25.00 60.00
CQ73 Alexander Ovechkin F/100 20.00 50.00
CQ74 Wayne Gretzky F/100 25.00 60.00
CQ75 Bobby Orr F/100 20.00 50.00
CQ76 Gordie Howe F/100 20.00 50.00
CQ77 Mario Lemieux F/100 12.00 30.00
CQ78 Steve Yzerman F/100 15.00 40.00
CQ79 Patrick Roy F/100 15.00 40.00
CQ80 Mark Messier F/100 10.00 25.00

2009-10 Collector's Choice Stick-Ums

COMPLETE SET (30) 12.00 30.00
STATED ODDS 1:4
SU1 Ilya Kovalchuk .50 1.25
SU2 Phil Kessel .40 1.00
SU3 Ryan Miller .40 1.00
SU4 Jarome Iginla .75 2.00
SU5 Eric Staal .50 1.25
SU6 Patrick Kane .75 2.00
SU7 Jonathan Toews 1.00 2.50
SU8 Paul Stastny .40 1.00
SU9 Rick Nash .40 1.00
SU10 Henrik Zetterberg .75 2.00
SU11 Pavel Datsyuk .40 1.00
SU12 Drew Doughty .75 2.00
SU13 Carey Price 1.00 2.50
SU14 Shea Weber .30 .75
SU15 Martin Brodeur 1.00 2.50
SU16 Zach Parise .40 1.00
SU17 Henrik Lundqvist .75 2.00
SU18 Daniel Alfredsson .40 1.00
SU19 Jason Spezza .50 1.25
SU20 Jeff Carter .40 1.00
SU21 Mike Richards .75 2.00
SU22 Sidney Crosby 2.00 5.00
SU23 Evgeni Malkin 1.00 2.50
SU24 Marc-Andre Fleury .40 1.00
SU25 Joe Thornton .75 2.00
SU26 Vincent Lecavalier .50 1.25
SU27 Luke Schenn .60 1.50
SU28 Roberto Luongo 1.00 2.50
SU29 Alexander Ovechkin 1.50 4.00
SU30 Mike Green .75 2.00

2009-10 Collector's Choice Warriors of Ice

COMPLETE SET (6) 4.00 10.00
STATED ODDS 1:6
W1 Alexander Ovechkin 1.50 4.00
W2 Henrik Zetterberg .75 2.00
W3 Jarome Iginla .75 2.00
W4 Martin Brodeur 1.00 2.50
W5 Sidney Crosby 2.00 5.00
W6 Zdeno Chara .25 .60

1996-97 Coyotes Coca-Cola

This set features the Coyotes of the NHL. The postcard-sized set was issued for autograph sessions and other personal appearances by team players. There are multiple versions of the cards of some players. These cards features different front photos, but identical backs.

COMPLETE SET (37) 10.00 25.00
1 Bob Corkum .20 .50
2 Shane Doan .60 1.50
3 Dallas Drake .20 .50
4 Dallas Eakins .20 .50
5 Mike Eastwood .20 .50
6 Jeff Finley .20 .50
7 Mike Gartner .30 .75
8 Mike Gartner .30 .75
9 Mike Hudson .20 .50
10 Craig Janney .20 .50
11 Jim Johnson .20 .50
12 Nikolai Khabibulin .60 1.50
13 Nikolai Khabibulin .60 1.50
14 Chad Kilger .20 .50
15 Kris King .20 .50
16 Kris King .20 .50
17 Igor Korolev .20 .50
18 Norm Maciver .20 .50
19 Dave Manson .20 .50
20 Brad McCrimmon .20 .50
21 Jim McKenzie .20 .50
22 Teppo Numminen .30 .75
23 Deron Quint .20 .50
24 Jeremy Roenick .75 2.00
25 Jeremy Roenick .75 2.00
26 Jeremy Roenick .75 2.00
27 Cliff Ronning .20 .50
28 Darrin Shannon .20 .50
29 Mike Stapleton .20 .50
30 Keith Tkachuk .75 2.00
31 Keith Tkachuk .75 2.00
32 Oleg Tverdovsky .20 .50
33 Darcy Wakaluk .25 .60
34 Paul MacLean CO .08 .25
34 Zinetula Bilyaletinov CO .08 .25
34 Don Hay CO .08 .25
36 Team Photo .20 .50

2001-02 Coyotes Team Issue

This set features the Phoenix Coyotes. This set was given away a few cards at a time at various home games, as well as at player autograph appearances. The oversized cards measure approximately 3 X 6. It is believed the checklist is complete, but due to the nature of the distribution, there may be other singles out there. If you discover one, please contact us at hockeymag@beckett.com.

COMPLETE SET (22) 10.00 25.00
1 Drake Berehowsky .40 1.00
2 Sergei Berezin .40 1.00
3 Daniel Briere .80 2.00
4 Sean Burke .80 2.00
5 Shane Doan .80 2.00
6 Robert Esche .80 2.00
7 Michal Handzus .40 1.00
8 Mike Johnson .40 1.00
9 Krys Kolanos 1.20 3.00
10 Daymond Langkow .80 2.00
11 Claude Lemieux .40 1.00
12 Paul Mara .40 1.00
13 Daniil Markov .40 1.00
14 Brad May .40 1.00
15 Ladislav Nagy .40 1.00
16 Teppo Numminen .40 1.00
17 Denis Pederson .40 1.00
18 Todd Simpson .40 1.00
19 Radoslav Suchy .40 1.00
20 Mike Sullivan .40 1.00
21 Ossi Vaananen .60 1.50
22 Landon Wilson .40 1.00

2002-03 Coyotes Team Issue

Cards were issued by the team in an unknown fashion. Cards are oversized (3X6), unnumbered and are blank backed.

COMPLETE SET (25) 15.00 30.00
1 Header .10 .25
2 Todd Simpson .40 1.00
3 Ossi Vaananen .40 1.00
4 Drake Berehowsky .40 1.00
5 Deron Quint .40 1.00
6 Daymond Langkow .60 1.50
7 Mike Johnson .40 1.00
8 Radoslav Suchy .40 1.00
9 Kelly Buchberger .40 1.00
10 Ladislav Nagy .75 2.00
11 Shane Doan .75 2.00
12 Paul Mara .40 1.00
13 Teppo Numminen .40 1.00
14 Landon Wilson .40 1.00
15 Branko Radivojevic .60 1.50
16 Brian Boucher .60 1.50
17 Krys Kolanos .40 1.00
18 Andrei Nazarov .40 1.00
19 Brian Savage .40 1.00
20 Danny Markov .40 1.00
21 Sean Burke .75 2.00
22 Benoit Allaire ACO .10 .25
23 Pat Conacher ACO .10 .25
24 Rick Bowness ACO .10 .25
25 Bob Francis CO .10 .25
26 Scott Pellerin .40 1.00
27 Paul Ranheim .40 1.00
28 Zac Bierk .60 1.50
29 Tony Amonte .75 2.00
30 Charlie Simmer ANN .20 .50
31 Curt Keilback ANN .10 .25
32 Ramzi Abid .40 1.00
33 Dan Focht .40 1.00
34 Daniel Briere .75 2.00
35 Brad May .40 1.00

2003-04 Coyotes Postcards

This checklist may be incomplete. Send additional info to hockeymag@beckett.com.

COMPLETE SET (27) 10.00 20.00
1 Zac Bierk .40 1.00
2 Brian Boucher .30 .75
3 Sean Burke .40 1.00
4 Daniel Cleary .20 .50
5 Shane Doan 1.00 2.50
6 Brad Ference .20 .50
7 Dave Tanabe .20 .50
8 Jan Hrdina .20 .50
9 Cale Hulse .20 .50
10 Mike Johnson .20 .50
11 Krystofer Kolanos .20 .50
12 Daymond Langkow .30 .75
13 Paul Mara .20 .50
14 Ladislav Nagy .60 1.50
15 Tyson Nash .40 1.00
16 Andrei Nazarov .20 .50
17 Ivan Novoseltsev .20 .50
18 Branko Radivojevic .40 1.00
19 Brian Savage .20 .50
20 Mike Sillinger .20 .50
21 Fredrik Sjostrom .30 .75
22 Matthew Spiller .20 .50
23 Radoslav Suchy .20 .50
24 Jeff Taffe .20 .50
25 Dave Tanabe .20 .50
26 Ossi Vaananen .20 .50
27 Landon Wilson .20 .50

1924-25 Crescent Falcon-Tigers

The 1924-25 Crescent Ice Cream Falcon-Tigers set contains 13 black and white cards measuring approximately 1 9/16" by 2 3/8". The back has the card number (at the top) and two offers: 1) a brick of ice cream to any person bringing to the Crescent Ice Cream plant any 14 Crescent Hockey Pictures bearing consecutive numbers; and 2) a hockey stick to anyone bringing to the ice cream plant three sets of Crescent Hockey Pictures bearing consecutive numbers from 1-14. The complete set price below does not include the unknown card 6, which is believed to have been short printed.

COMPLETE SET (13) 1200.00 2400.00
1 Bill Cockburn 112.50 225.00
2 Wally Byron 100.00 200.00
3 Wally Fridfinson 100.00 200.00
4 Murray Murdoch 125.00 250.00
5 Oliver Redpath 100.00 200.00
7 Ward McVey 100.00 200.00
8 Tote Mitchell 100.00 200.00
9 Lorne Carrol 100.00 200.00
10 Tony Wise 100.00 200.00
11 Johnny Myres 100.00 200.00
12 Gordon McKenzie 100.00 200.00
13 Harry Neal 112.50 225.00
14 Blake Watson 112.50 225.00

1923-24 Crescent Selkirks

The 1923-24 Crescent Ice Cream set contains 14 cards measuring approximately 1 9/16" by 2 3/8". The set features the Selkirks hockey club and was produced by Crescent Ice Cream of Winnipeg, Manitoba. The front shows a black and white head and shoulders shot of the player, with the team name written in a crescent over the player's head. At the bottom of the picture, the player's name and position appear in white lettering in a black stripe. The back has the card number (at the top) and two offers: 1) a brick of ice cream to any person bringing to the Crescent Ice Cream plant any 14 Crescent Hockey Pictures bearing consecutive numbers; and 2) a hockey stick to anyone bringing to the ice cream plant three sets of Crescent Hockey Pictures bearing consecutive numbers from 1-14. The complete set price below does not include the unknown card number 6.

COMPLETE SET (13) 600.00 1200.00
1 Cliff O'Meara 62.50 125.00
2 Leo Benard 50.00 100.00
3 Pete Speirs 50.00 100.00
4 Howard Brandon 50.00 100.00
5 George A. Clark 50.00 100.00
7 Cecil Browne 50.00 100.00
8 Jack Connelly 50.00 100.00
9 Charlie Gardiner 100.00 200.00
10 Ward Turvey 50.00 100.00
11 Connie Johanneson 50.00 100.00
12 Frank Woodall 50.00 100.00
13 Harold McMunn 50.00 100.00
14 Connie Neil 62.50 125.00

1924-25 Crescent Selkirks

The 1924-25 Crescent Ice Cream Selkirks set contains 14 black and white cards measuring approximately 1 9/16" by 2 3/8". The back has the card number (at the top) and two offers: 1) a brick of ice cream to any person bringing to the Crescent Ice Cream plant any 14 Crescent Hockey Pictures bearing consecutive numbers; and 2) a hockey stick to anyone bringing to the ice cream plant three sets of Crescent Hockey Pictures bearing consecutive numbers from 1-14.

COMPLETE SET (14) 850.00 1700.00
1 Howard Brandon 50.00 100.00
2 Jack Hughes 50.00 100.00
3 Tony Baril 50.00 100.00
4 Bill Bowman 50.00 100.00
5 W. Roberts 50.00 100.00
6 Cecil Browne SP 375.00 750.00
7 Errol Gillis 50.00 100.00
8 Selkirks Team 100.00 200.00
On The Ice
9 Fred Comfort 50.00 100.00
10 Cliff O'Meara 50.00 100.00
11 Leo Benard 50.00 100.00
12 Pete Speirs 50.00 100.00
13 Peter Meurer 50.00 100.00
14 Bill Borland 50.00 100.00

1997-98 Crown Royale

The 1997-98 Pacific Crown Royale set was issued in one series totalling 144 cards and was distributed in four-card packs. The fronts features color player images printed on an all-die-cut crown format. The backs carry player information

COMPLETE SET (144) 40.00 100.00
1 Guy Hebert .40 1.00
2 Paul Kariya .60 1.50
3 Steve Rucchin .20 .50
4 Tomas Sandstrom .20 .50
5 Teemu Selanne .60 1.50
6 Jason Allison .20 .50
7 Ray Bourque 1.00 2.50
8 Anson Carter .40 1.00
9 Byron Dafoe .40 1.00
10 Ted Donato .20 .50
11 Joe Thornton 1.50 4.00
12 Jason Dawe .20 .50
13 Michal Grosek .20 .50
14 Dominik Hasek 1.25 3.00
15 Michael Peca .20 .50
16 Miroslav Satan .20 .50
17 Chris Dingman RC .20 .50
18 Theo Fleury .20 .50
19 Jarome Iginla .75 2.00
20 Tyler Moss RC .20 .50
21 Cory Stillman .20 .50
22 Kevin Dineen .20 .50
23 Nelson Emerson .20 .50
24 Trevor Kidd .40 1.00
25 Keith Primeau .20 .50
26 Geoff Sanderson .20 .50
27 Tony Amonte .40 1.00
28 Chris Chelios .60 1.50
29 Eric Daze .20 .50
30 Jeff Hackett .40 1.00
31 Chris Terreri .40 1.00
32 Adam Deadmarsh .20 .50
33 Peter Forsberg 1.00 2.50
34 Valeri Kamensky .20 .50
35 Jari Kurri .40 1.00
36 Claude Lemieux .20 .50
37 Patrick Roy 2.00 5.00
38 Joe Sakic 1.25 3.00
39 Ed Belfour .60 1.50
40 Derian Hatcher .20 .50
41 Mike Modano 1.00 2.50
42 Joe Nieuwendyk .40 1.00
43 Pat Verbeek .20 .50
44 Sergei Zubov .20 .50
45 Sergei Fedorov 1.00 2.50
46 Vyacheslav Kozlov .20 .50
47 Nicklas Lidstrom .60 1.50
48 Darren McCarty .20 .50
49 Chris Osgood .40 1.00
50 Brendan Shanahan .60 1.50
51 Steve Yzerman 2.00 5.00
52 Jason Arnott .20 .50
53 Curtis Joseph .60 1.50

54 Ryan Smyth .40 1.00
55 Doug Weight .40 1.00
56 Dave Gagner .20 .50
57 Ed Jovanovski .40 1.00
58 Viktor Kozlov .20 .50
59 Scott Mellanby .20 .50
60 John Vanbiesbrouck .40 1.00
61 Kevin Weekes RC .60 1.50
62 Rob Blake .40 1.00
63 Donald MacLean .20 .50
64 Yanic Perreault .20 .50
65 Luc Robitaille .40 1.00
66 Jozef Stumpel .20 .50
67 Shayne Corson .20 .50
68 Vincent Damphousse .20 .50
69 Saku Koivu .60 1.50
70 Andy Moog .40 1.00
71 Mark Recchi .40 1.00
72 Stephane Richer .20 .50
73 Martin Brodeur 1.50 4.00
74 Patrik Elias RC 1.25 3.00
75 Doug Gilmour .40 1.00
76 Bobby Holik .20 .50
77 Scott Stevens .40 1.00
78 Bryan Berard .20 .50
79 Zigmund Palffy .40 1.00
80 Robert Reichel .20 .50
81 Tommy Salo .40 1.00
82 Bryan Smolinski .20 .50
83 Adam Graves .20 .50
84 Wayne Gretzky 3.00 8.00
85 Pat LaFontaine .60 1.50
86 Brian Leetch .60 1.50
87 Mike Richter .60 1.50
88 Niklas Sundstrom .20 .50
89 Daniel Alfredsson .40 1.00
90 Alexandre Daigle .20 .50
91 Shawn McEachern .20 .50
92 Chris Phillips .20 .50
93 Ron Tugnutt .40 1.00
94 Alexei Yashin .20 .50
95 Rod Brind'Amour .40 1.00
96 Chris Gratton .20 .50
97 Ron Hextall .40 1.00
98 John LeClair .60 1.50
99 Eric Lindros .60 1.50
100 Vaclav Prospal RC .60 1.50
101 Dainius Zubrus .60 1.50
102 Mike Gartner .40 1.00
103 Brad Isbister .20 .50
104 Nikolai Khabibulin .40 1.00
105 Jeremy Roenick .75 2.00
106 Cliff Ronning .20 .50
107 Keith Tkachuk .60 1.50
108 Tom Barrasso .40 1.00
109 Ron Francis .40 1.00
110 Jaromir Jagr 1.00 2.50
111 Alexei Morozov .20 .50
112 Ed Olczyk .20 .50
113 Jim Campbell .20 .50
114 Pavol Demitra .40 1.00
115 Steve Duchesne .20 .50
116 Grant Fuhr .40 1.00
117 Brett Hull .75 2.00
118 Pierre Turgeon .40 1.00
119 Jeff Friesen .20 .50
120 Patrick Marleau .60 1.50
121 Owen Nolan .40 1.00
122 Marco Sturm RC 1.00 2.50
123 Mike Vernon .40 1.00
124 Dino Ciccarelli .20 .50
125 Roman Hamrlik .20 .50
126 Daren Puppa .40 1.00
127 Paul Ysebaert .20 .50
128 Sergei Berezin .20 .50
129 Wendel Clark .40 1.00
130 Alyn McCauley .20 .50
131 Felix Potvin .60 1.50
132 Mats Sundin .60 1.50
133 Pavel Bure .60 1.50
134 Martin Gelinas .20 .50
135 Trevor Linden .40 1.00
136 Mark Messier .60 1.50
137 Alexander Mogilny .40 1.00
138 Peter Bondra .40 1.00
139 Dale Hunter .20 .50
140 Joe Juneau .20 .50
141 Olaf Kolzig .40 1.00
142 Adam Oates .40 1.00
143 Jaroslav Svejkovsky .20 .50
144 Richard Zednik .20 .50

1997-98 Crown Royale Emerald Green

Randomly inserted in Canadian packs only at the rate of 4:25, this 144-card set is a parallel version of the base set with green foil highlights.

*VETS: 1.2X TO 3X BASIC CARDS
*ROOKIES: .8X TO 2X BASIC CARDS

1997-98 Crown Royale Ice Blue

Randomly inserted in packs at the rate of 1:25, this 144-card set is a parallel version of the base set with blue foil highlights.

*VETS: 2.5X TO 6X BSIC CARDS
*ROOKIES: 2X TO 5X BASIC CARDS

1997-98 Crown Royale Silver

Randomly inserted in U.S. packs only at the rate of 4:25, this 144-card set is a parallel version of the base set with silver foil highlights.

*VETS: 1.2X TO 3X BASIC CARDS
*ROOKIES: .8X TO 2X BASIC CARDS

1997-98 Crown Royale Blades of Steel Die-Cuts

Randomly inserted in packs at the rate of 1:49, this 20-card set features color images of top NHL players on a laser-cut and die-cut skate background.

COMPLETE SET (20) 50.00 125.00
1 Paul Kariya 2.00 5.00
2 Teemu Selanne 2.00 5.00
3 Joe Thornton 4.00 10.00
4 Chris Chelios 1.50 4.00
5 Peter Forsberg 4.00 10.00
6 Patrick Roy 10.00 25.00
7 Mike Modano 2.50 6.00
8 Sergei Fedorov 2.50 6.00
9 Brendan Shanahan 2.00 5.00
10 Steve Yzerman 8.00 20.00
11 Ryan Smyth 1.50 4.00
12 Saku Koivu 2.00 5.00
13 Bryan Berard .75 2.00
14 Wayne Gretzky 12.00 30.00
15 Brian Leetch 1.50 4.00
16 Eric Lindros 2.00 5.00
17 Jaromir Jagr 4.00 10.00
18 Brett Hull 2.50 6.00
19 Pavel Bure 2.00 5.00
20 Mark Messier 2.50 6.00

1997-98 Crown Royale Cramer's Choice Jumbos

Inserted one per box, this ten-card set features top NHL Hockey players as chosen by Pacific President and CEO, Michael Cramer. The fronts display a color action player cut-out on a pyramid die-cut shaped background printed on a premium-sized card.

COMPLETE SET (10) 15.00 40.00
*GOLD: 1.5X TO 4X BASIC CARDS
UNPRICED CRAMER SIGNED #'d TO 10
1 Paul Kariya 1.50 4.00
2 Teemu Selanne 1.25 3.00
3 Joe Thornton 2.50 6.00
4 Peter Forsberg 1.50 4.00
5 Patrick Roy 3.00 8.00
6 Steve Yzerman 2.50 6.00
7 Wayne Gretzky 4.00 10.00
8 Eric Lindros 1.25 3.00
9 Jaromir Jagr 1.50 4.00
10 Pavel Bure 1.25 3.00

1997-98 Crown Royale Freeze Out Die-Cuts

Randomly inserted in packs at the rate of 1:25, this 20-card set features color action photos of top goalies on a background of shattering ice and printed on a die-cut card.

COMPLETE SET (20) 30.00 80.00
1 Guy Hebert 1.00 2.50
2 Byron Dafoe 1.00 2.50
3 Dominik Hasek 4.00 10.00
4 Tyler Moss 1.00 2.50
5 Patrick Roy 10.00 25.00
6 Ed Belfour 2.00 5.00
7 Chris Osgood 1.00 2.50
8 Curtis Joseph 2.00 5.00
9 John Vanbiesbrouck 2.00 5.00
10 Andy Moog 2.00 5.00
11 Martin Brodeur 6.00 15.00
12 Mike Richter 2.00 5.00
13 Ron Hextall 2.00 5.00
14 Garth Snow 1.00 2.50
15 Nikolai Khabibulin 2.00 5.00
16 Tom Barrasso 1.00 2.50
17 Grant Fuhr 2.00 5.00
18 Mike Vernon 2.00 5.00
19 Felix Potvin 2.00 5.00
20 Olaf Kolzig 2.00 5.00

1997-98 Crown Royale Hat Tricks Die-Cuts

Randomly inserted in packs at the rate of 1:25, this 20-card set features color photos of top NHL scorers printed on a hat-shaped die-cut card.

COMPLETE SET (20) 40.00 100.00
1 Paul Kariya 2.50 6.00
2 Teemu Selanne 2.50 6.00
3 Joe Thornton 4.00 10.00
4 Peter Forsberg 4.00 10.00
5 Joe Sakic 5.00 12.00
6 Mike Modano 4.00 10.00
7 Brendan Shanahan 2.50 6.00
8 Steve Yzerman 6.00 15.00
9 Ryan Smyth 1.50 4.00
10 Zigmund Palffy 1.50 4.00
11 Wayne Gretzky 10.00 25.00
12 John LeClair 1.50 4.00
13 Eric Lindros 2.00 5.00
14 Keith Tkachuk 1.50 4.00
15 Jaromir Jagr 4.00 10.00
16 Brett Hull 3.00 8.00
17 Mats Sundin 2.00 5.00
18 Pavel Bure 2.00 5.00
19 Mark Messier 2.00 5.00
20 Peter Bondra 1.50 4.00

1997-98 Crown Royale Lamplighters Cel-Fusion Die-Cuts

Randomly inserted in packs at the rate of 1:73, this 20-card set features color photos of the NHL's top goal scorers with a net and goal light as background and printed on a die-cut cel-fusion card.

COMPLETE SET (20) 60.00 150.00
1 Paul Kariya 2.00 5.00
2 Teemu Selanne 2.00 5.00
3 Joe Thornton 6.00 15.00
4 Michael Peca 1.00 2.50
5 Peter Forsberg 6.00 15.00
6 Joe Sakic 8.00 20.00
7 Mike Modano 4.00 10.00
8 Brendan Shanahan 2.00 5.00
9 Steve Yzerman 12.00 30.00
10 Saku Koivu 2.00 5.00
11 Wayne Gretzky 20.00 50.00
12 Pat LaFontaine 1.00 2.50
13 John LeClair 1.00 2.50
14 Eric Lindros 2.00 5.00
15 Dainius Zubrus 1.00 2.50
16 Keith Tkachuk 2.00 5.00
17 Jaromir Jagr 6.00 15.00
18 Brett Hull 2.00 5.00
19 Pavel Bure 2.00 5.00
20 Mark Messier 4.00 10.00

1998-99 Crown Royale

The 1998-99 Pacific Crown Royale set was issued in one series totaling 144 cards and was distributed in six-card packs with a suggested retail price of $5.99. The set features color action player photos printed on cards with silver and gold foil highlights, dual etching and a die-cut crown as background.

COMPLETE SET (144) 30.00 80.00
1 Travis Green .20 .50
2 Guy Hebert .30 .75
3 Paul Kariya .40 1.00
4 Tomas Sandstrom .20 .50
5 Teemu Selanne .40 1.00
6 Jason Allison .20 .50
7 Ray Bourque 1.00 2.50
8 Byron Dafoe .30 .75
9 Dimitri Khristich .20 .50
10 Sergei Samsonov .30 .75
11 Matthew Barnaby .20 .50
12 Michal Grosek .20 .50
13 Dominik Hasek 1.25 3.00
14 Michael Peca .20 .50
15 Miroslav Satan .20 .50
16 Andrew Cassels .20 .50
17 Rico Fata .20 .50
18 Theo Fleury .20 .50
19 Jarome Iginla .75 2.00
20 Martin St. Louis RC 4.00 10.00
21 Ken Wregget .30 .75
22 Ron Francis .30 .75
23 Arturs Irbe .30 .75
24 Sami Kapanen .20 .50
25 Trevor Kidd .30 .75
26 Keith Primeau .20 .50
27 Tony Amonte .30 .75
28 Chris Chelios .40 1.00
29 Eric Daze .20 .50
30 Doug Gilmour .30 .75
31 Jocelyn Thibault .30 .75
32 Chris Drury .30 .75
33 Peter Forsberg 1.25 3.00
34 Milan Hejduk RC 2.00 5.00
35 Patrick Roy 2.50 6.00
36 Joe Sakic 1.25 3.00
37 Ed Belfour .40 1.00
38 Brett Hull .40 1.00
39 Jamie Langenbrunner .20 .50
40 Jere Lehtinen .30 .75
41 Mike Modano 1.00 2.50
42 Joe Nieuwendyk .30 .75
43 Darryl Sydor .20 .50
44 Sergei Fedorov 1.00 2.50
45 Nicklas Lidstrom .40 1.00
46 Darren McCarty .20 .50
47 Chris Osgood .30 .75
48 Brendan Shanahan .40 1.00
49 Steve Yzerman 2.50 6.00
50 Bob Essensa .30 .75
51 Bill Guerin .30 .75
52 Janne Niinimaa .20 .50
53 Tom Poti .20 .50
54 Ryan Smyth .20 .50
55 Doug Weight .30 .75
56 Sean Burke .30 .75
57 Dino Ciccarelli .20 .50
58 Ed Jovanovski .20 .50
59 Viktor Kozlov .20 .50
60 Oleg Kvasha RC .40 1.00
61 Mark Parrish RC .75 2.00
62 Rob Blake .30 .75
63 Manny Legace .40 1.00
64 Yanic Perreault .20 .50
65 Luc Robitaille .30 .75
66 Jozef Stumpel .50 1.25
67 Shayne Corson .20 .50
68 Vincent Damphousse .20 .50
69 Jeff Hackett .30 .75
70 Saku Koivu .40 1.00
71 Mark Recchi .30 .75
72 Andrew Brunette .50 1.25
73 Mike Dunham .30 .75
74 Tom Fitzgerald .20 .50
75 Greg Johnson .20 .50
76 Sergei Krivokrasov .20 .50
77 Jason Arnott .20 .50
78 Martin Brodeur 1.50 4.00
79 Patrik Elias .30 .75
80 Bobby Holik .20 .50
81 Brendan Morrison .30 .75
82 Bryan Berard .20 .50
83 Trevor Linden .30 .75
84 Zigmund Palffy .30 .75
85 Robert Reichel .20 .50
86 Tommy Salo .30 .75
87 Adam Graves .20 .50
88 Wayne Gretzky 3.00 8.00
89 Brian Leetch .40 1.00
90 Manny Malhotra .20 .50
91 Mike Richter .40 1.00
92 Daniel Alfredsson .30 .75
93 Igor Kravchuk .20 .50
94 Shawn McEachern .20 .50
95 Damian Rhodes .30 .75
96 Alexei Yashin .20 .50
97 Rod Brind'Amour .30 .75
98 Ron Hextall .30 .75
99 John LeClair .40 1.00
100 Eric Lindros .40 1.00
101 John Vanbiesbrouck .30 .75
102 Dainius Zubrus .20 .50
103 Nikolai Khabibulin .30 .75
104 Jeremy Roenick .75 2.00
105 Keith Tkachuk .40 1.00
106 Rick Tocchet .30 .75
107 Oleg Tverdovsky .20 .50
108 Tom Barrasso .30 .75
109 Jan Hrdina RC .40 1.00
110 Jaromir Jagr 1.00 2.50
111 Alexei Morozov .20 .50
112 German Titov .20 .50
113 Jim Campbell .20 .50
114 Grant Fuhr .30 .75
115 Al MacInnis .30 .75
116 Chris Pronger .30 .75
117 Pierre Turgeon .30 .75
118 Jeff Friesen .20 .50
119 Patrick Marleau .20 .50
120 Owen Nolan .30 .75
121 Marco Sturm .20 .50
122 Mike Vernon .30 .75
123 Wendel Clark .30 .75
124 Vincent Lecavalier 1.25 3.00
125 Bill Ranford .30 .75
126 Stephane Richer .30 .75
127 Rob Zamuner .20 .50
128 Sergei Berezin .20 .50
129 Tie Domi .30 .75
130 Mike Johnson .20 .50
131 Curtis Joseph .40 1.00
132 Mats Sundin .40 1.00
133 Donald Brashear .20 .50
134 Pavel Bure .40 1.00
135 Mark Messier .40 1.00
136 Alexander Mogilny .30 .75
137 Bill Muckalt RC .20 .50
138 Mattias Ohlund .20 .50
139 Garth Snow .30 .75
140 Peter Bondra .20 .50
141 Matthew Herr RC .20 .50
142 Joe Juneau .30 .75
143 Olaf Kolzig .30 .75
144 Adam Oates .30 .75

1998-99 Crown Royale Limited Series

Randomly inserted into packs, this 144-card set is a limited parallel edition of the base set printed on 24-point card stock. Only 99 serial-numbered sets were produced.

*VETERANS: 3X TO 8X BASIC CARDS
*ROOKIES: 2.5X TO 6X BASIC CARDS
STATED PRINT RUN 99 SER.#'d SETS

1998-99 Crown Royale Cramer's Choice Jumbos

Inserted one per box, this 10-card set features color action cut-outs of top NHL players as chosen by Pacific President and CEO, Michael Cramer, printed on premium-sized, dual-foiled, die-cut pyramid-shaped cards. Six different serial-numbered parallel sets were also produced: 35 serial-numbered dark blue foil sets, 30 serial-numbered green foil sets, 25 serial-numbered red foil sets, 20 serial-numbered light blue foil sets, 10 serial-numbered gold foil sets, and 1 serial-numbered purple foil set.

COMPLETE SET (10) 20.00 40.00
*DARK BLUE/35: 10X TO 25X BASIC INSERTS
*GOLD/10: 20X TO 50X BASIC INSERTS
*GREEN/30: 10X TO 25X BASIC INSERTS
*LT.BLUE/20: 15X TO 40X BASIC INSERTS
*RED/25: 10X TO 25X BASIC INSERTS
UNPRICED PURPLE PRINT RUN 1
1 Paul Kariya 1.25 3.00
2 Teemu Selanne 1.25 3.00
3 Dominik Hasek 2.00 5.00
4 Peter Forsberg 2.50 6.00
5 Patrick Roy 3.00 8.00
6 Steve Yzerman 3.00 8.00
7 Martin Brodeur 3.00 8.00
8 Wayne Gretzky 4.00 10.00
9 Eric Lindros 1.25 3.00
10 Jaromir Jagr 1.50 4.00

1998-99 Crown Royale Living Legends

Randomly inserted in hobby packs at the rate of 1:73, this 10-card set features color action photos of some of the NHL's all-time great players. Only 375 serial-numbered sets were produced.

COMPLETE SET (10) 100.00 200.00
STATED ODDS 1:73
1 Paul Kariya 12.50 30.00
2 Teemu Selanne 8.00 20.00
3 Dominik Hasek 8.00 20.00
4 Peter Forsberg 10.00 25.00
5 Patrick Roy 20.00 50.00
6 Steve Yzerman 12.50 30.00
7 Martin Brodeur 10.00 25.00
8 Wayne Gretzky 25.00 60.00
9 Eric Lindros 8.00 20.00
10 Jaromir Jagr 25.00 60.00

1998-99 Crown Royale Master Performers

Randomly inserted in hobby packs at the rate of 2:25, this 20-card set features color action photos of some of the most popular players printed on fully foiled, etched cards.

COMPLETE SET (20) 40.00 100.00
STATED ODDS 2:25
1 Paul Kariya 2.00 5.00
2 Teemu Selanne 2.00 5.00
3 Dominik Hasek 4.00 10.00
4 Peter Forsberg 3.00 8.00
5 Patrick Roy 8.00 20.00
6 Joe Sakic 4.00 10.00
7 Brett Hull 2.50 6.00
8 Mike Modano 3.00 8.00
9 Sergei Fedorov 2.50 6.00
10 Brendan Shanahan 2.00 5.00
11 Steve Yzerman 6.00 15.00
12 Saku Koivu 2.00 5.00
13 Martin Brodeur 5.00 12.00
14 Wayne Gretzky 10.00 25.00
15 John LeClair 1.50 4.00
16 Eric Lindros 2.00 5.00
17 Jaromir Jagr 3.00 8.00
18 Mats Sundin 2.00 5.00
19 Mark Messier 2.00 5.00
20 Peter Bondra 1.50 4.00

1998-99 Crown Royale Pillars of the Game

Inserted one at the bottom of every pack, this 25-card set features color action photos of popular players with a hockey puck in the background and printed on holographic gold foil cards.

COMPLETE SET (25) 10.00 20.00
STATED ODDS 1:1
1 Teemu Selanne .30 .75
2 Ray Bourque .50 1.25
3 Michael Peca .25 .60
4 Theo Fleury .25 .60
5 Chris Chelios .30 .75
6 Doug Gilmour .25 .60
7 Patrick Roy 1.50 4.00
8 Joe Sakic .60 1.50
9 Ed Belfour .30 .75
10 Brett Hull .40 1.00
11 Mike Modano .50 1.25
12 Sergei Fedorov .50 1.25
13 Brendan Shanahan .30 .75
14 Steve Yzerman 1.50 4.00
15 Saku Koivu .30 .75
16 Martin Brodeur .75 2.00
17 John LeClair .30 .75
18 Eric Lindros .30 .75
19 John Vanbiesbrouck .25 .60
20 Keith Tkachuk .30 .75
21 Jaromir Jagr .50 1.25
22 Curtis Joseph .30 .75
23 Mats Sundin .30 .75
24 Mark Messier .30 .75
25 Peter Bondra .25 .60

1998-99 Crown Royale Pivotal Players

Inserted one at the top of every pack, this 25-card set features color action photos of top stars and rookies printed on holographic silver foil cards.

COMPLETE SET (25) 10.00 20.00
STATED ODDS 1:1
1 Paul Kariya .30 .75
2 Dominik Hasek .60 1.50
3 Michael Peca .25 .60
4 Peter Forsberg .75 2.00
5 Joe Sakic .60 1.50
6 Brett Hull .40 1.00
7 Mike Modano .50 1.25
8 Sergei Fedorov .50 1.25
9 Chris Osgood .25 .60
10 Brendan Shanahan .25 .60
11 Ryan Smyth .25 .60
12 Mark Parrish .40 1.00
13 Saku Koivu .30 .75
14 Martin Brodeur .75 2.00
15 Trevor Linden .25 .60
16 Wayne Gretzky 2.00 5.00
17 Alexei Yashin .25 .60
18 John LeClair .30 .75
19 John Vanbiesbrouck .25 .60
20 Keith Tkachuk .30 .75
21 Vincent Lecavalier .75 2.00
22 Mats Sundin .30 .75
23 Mark Messier .30 .75
24 Peter Bondra .25 .60
25 Olaf Kolzig .25 .60

1998-99 Crown Royale Rookie Class

Randomly inserted in packs at the rate of 1:25, this 10-card set features color action photos of top rookies printed on full-foil designed cards.

COMPLETE SET (10) 15.00 40.00
1 Chris Drury 2.00 5.00
2 Milan Hejduk 2.00 5.00
3 Mark Parrish 1.25 3.00
4 Manny Legace 2.00 5.00
5 Brendan Morrison 1.25 3.00
6 Manny Malhotra 1.25 3.00
7 Daniel Briere 2.00 5.00
8 Vincent Lecavalier 4.00 10.00
9 Tomas Kaberle 1.25 3.00
10 Bill Muckalt 1.25 3.00

1999-00 Crown Royale

The 1999-00 Pacific Crown Royale set was issued in one series totaling 144 cards and was distributed in six-card packs with a suggested retail price of $5.99. The set features color action player photos printed on cards with silver and gold foil highlights, dual etching and a die-cut crown as background.

COMPLETE SET (144) 40.00 100.00
1 Guy Hebert .30 .75
2 Paul Kariya 1.25 3.00
3 Steve Rucchin .20 .50
4 Teemu Selanne .60 1.50
5 Andrew Brunette .20 .50
6 Scott Fankhouser RC 1.25 3.00
7 Andreas Karlsson RC .75 2.00
8 Damian Rhodes .20 .50
9 Patrik Stefan SP RC 1.00 2.50
10 Jason Allison .20 .50
11 Ray Bourque 1.00 2.50
12 Byron Dafoe .30 .75
13 Mikko Eloranta RC .20 .50
14 Sergei Samsonov .30 .75
15 Joe Thornton 1.00 2.50
16 Maxim Afinogenov SP .75 2.00
17 Martin Biron SP .75 2.00
18 Dominik Hasek 1.25 3.00
19 Michael Peca .20 .50
20 Miroslav Satan .30 .75
21 Valeri Bure .20 .50
22 Grant Fuhr .30 .75
23 Jarome Iginla .75 2.00
24 Robyn Regehr SP .75 2.00
25 Oleg Saprykin SP RC 1.00 2.50
26 Ron Francis .30 .75
27 Arturs Irbe .30 .75
28 Sami Kapanen .20 .50
29 Jeff O'Neill .20 .50
30 Tony Amonte .30 .75
31 Kyle Calder SP RC 1.00 2.50
32 Eric Daze .20 .50
33 Doug Gilmour .30 .75
34 Jocelyn Thibault .30 .75
35 Marc Denis SP .75 2.00
36 Chris Drury .30 .75
37 Peter Forsberg 1.25 3.00
38 Milan Hejduk .60 1.50
39 Patrick Roy 2.50 6.00
40 Joe Sakic 1.25 3.00
41 Alex Tanguay SP 1.50 4.00
42 Ed Belfour .60 1.50
43 Ryan Christie RC .75 2.00
44 Brett Hull .75 2.00
45 Jere Lehtinen .30 .75
46 Mike Modano 1.00 2.50
47 Joe Nieuwendyk .30 .75
48 Chris Chelios .60 1.50
49 Sergei Fedorov 1.00 2.50
50 Nicklas Lidstrom .60 1.50
51 Chris Osgood .30 .75
52 Brendan Shanahan .60 1.50
53 Steve Yzerman 2.50 6.00
54 Bill Guerin .30 .75
55 Tommy Salo .30 .75
56 Alexander Selivanov .20 .50
57 Ryan Smyth .30 .75
58 Doug Weight .30 .75
59 Pavel Bure .60 1.50
60 Trevor Kidd .30 .75
61 Ivan Novoseltsev SP RC 1.00 2.50
62 Ray Whitney .20 .50
63 Mike Vernon .30 .75
64 Rob Blake .30 .75
65 Stephane Fiset .30 .75
66 Zigmund Palffy .30 .75
67 Luc Robitaille .30 .75
68 Brian Smolinski .20 .50
69 Jeff Hackett .30 .75
70 Saku Koivu .60 1.50
71 Trevor Linden .20 .50
72 Brian Savage .20 .50
73 Jose Theodore .75 2.00
74 Mike Dunham .30 .75
75 Sergei Krivokrasov .20 .50
76 David Legwand SP .75 2.00
77 Cliff Ronning .20 .50
78 Martin Brodeur 1.50 4.00
79 Patrik Elias .30 .75
80 Scott Gomez SP .75 2.00
81 Bobby Holik .20 .50
82 Claude Lemieux .20 .50
83 Petr Sykora .20 .50
84 Tim Connolly SP .75 2.00
85 Mariusz Czerkawski .20 .50
86 Brad Isbister .20 .50
87 Kenny Jonsson .20 .50
88 Roberto Luongo SP .75 2.00
89 Theo Fleury .20 .50
90 Milan Hnilicka RC 1.25 3.00
91 Brian Leetch .60 1.50
92 Mike Richter .60 1.50
93 Michael York SP .75 2.00
94 Daniel Alfredsson .30 .75
95 Radek Bonk .20 .50
96 Mike Fisher SP RC .75 2.00
97 Marian Hossa .60 1.50
98 Joe Juneau .20 .50
99 Ron Tugnutt .30 .75
100 Alexei Yashin .20 .50
101 Simon Gagne SP 1.50 4.00
102 John LeClair .30 .75
103 Eric Lindros .60 1.50
104 Keith Primeau .20 .50
105 Mark Recchi .30 .75
106 John Vanbiesbrouck .30 .75
107 Travis Green .20 .50
108 Nikolai Khabibulin .30 .75
109 Jeremy Roenick .75 2.00
110 Keith Tkachuk .60 1.50
111 Tom Barrasso .30 .75
112 Jaromir Jagr 1.00 2.50
113 Alexei Kovalev .20 .50
114 Robert Lang .20 .50
115 Pavol Demitra .30 .75
116 Jochen Hecht SP RC 1.50 4.00
117 Al MacInnis .30 .75
118 Ladislav Nagy RC 1.50 4.00
119 Chris Pronger .30 .75
120 Roman Turek .20 .50
121 Pierre Turgeon .30 .75
122 Vincent Damphousse .20 .50
123 Jeff Friesen .20 .50
124 Patrick Marleau .30 .75
125 Owen Nolan .30 .75
126 Steve Shields .30 .75
127 Dan Cloutier .20 .50
128 Chris Gratton .20 .50
129 Vincent Lecavalier .60 1.50
130 Mike Sillinger .20 .50
131 Nikolai Antropov SP RC 1.25 3.00
132 Sergei Berezin .20 .50
133 Tie Domi .30 .75

134 Curtis Joseph .60 1.50
135 Mats Sundin .60 1.50
136 Steve Kariya SP RC 1.25 3.00
137 Mark Messier .60 1.50
138 Markus Naslund .60 1.50
139 Peter Schaefer SP .75 2.00
140 Garth Snow .30 .75
141 Peter Bondra .30 .75
142 Jan Bulis .20 .50
143 Olaf Kolzig .30 .75
144 Adam Oates .30 .75

1999-00 Crown Royale Limited Series

Randomly inserted in packs, This 144-card parallel set features the base card with a red foil Limited Series logo and box with the serial number in the lower front right corner. This set is serial numbered out of 99.

*LIMITED SER/99: 5X TO 12X BASIC CARDS
*LIMITED SER/99: 3X TO 8X BASIC SP

1999-00 Crown Royale Premiere Date

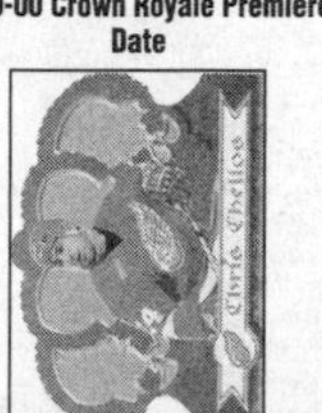

Randomly inserted in packs, This 144-card parallel set features the base card with a gold foil Premier Date logo and box with the serial number in the lower front right corner. This set is serial numbered out of 73.

*PREM.DATE/73: 6X TO 15X BASIC CARDS
*PREM.DATE/73: 4X TO 10X BASIC SP

1999-00 Crown Royale Prospects Parallel

Randomly inserted at 1:24 packs, this 23-card parallel set showcases the prospect cards with a gold foil box on the bottom right-front corner of the card. This set is skip-numbered. The cards are serial numbered out of 450.

*PROSPECT PAR: 1.2X TO 3X BASIC CARDS

1999-00 Crown Royale Card-Supials

Randomly inserted in packs at 2:25, this 25-card set was issued in two versions. The large version features player action-shots with a rainbow holo-foil border and a cut on the back where a Card-Supials Mini card is inserted. The Mini's may or may not match the large card.

COMP.LARGE SET (20) 20.00 50.00
1 Paul Kariya 1.00 2.50
2 Teemu Selanne 1.00 2.50
3 Patrik Stefan 1.50 4.00
4 Joe Thornton 1.25 3.00
5 Dominik Hasek 2.00 5.00
6 Peter Forsberg 1.50 4.00
7 Patrick Roy 4.00 10.00
8 Alex Tanguay 1.00 2.50
9 Mike Modano 1.50 4.00
10 Brendan Shanahan 1.00 2.50
11 Steve Yzerman 3.00 8.00
12 Pave Bure 1.00 2.50
13 Martin Brodeur 2.50 6.00
14 Scott Gomez 1.00 2.50
15 Roberto Luongo 1.50 4.00
16 Eric Lindros 1.00 2.50
17 John Vanbiesbrouck 1.00 2.50
18 Jaromir Jagr 1.50 4.00
19 Mats Sundin 1.00 2.50
20 Steve Kariya 1.50 4.00

1999-00 Crown Royale Century 21

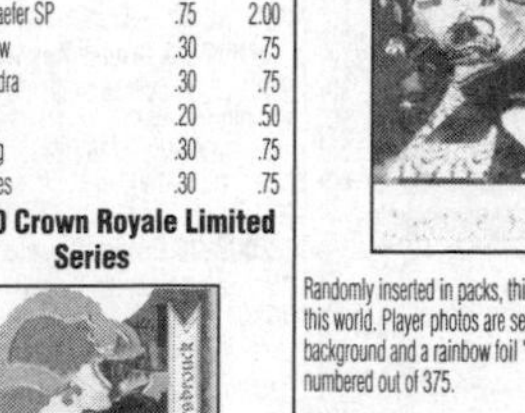

Randomly inserted in packs, this 10-card set is out of this world. Player photos are set against an outer-space background and a rainbow foil "21." Each card is serial numbered out of 375.

COMPLETE SET (10) 30.00 60.00
1 Paul Kariya 3.00 8.00
2 Patrik Stefan .75 2.00
3 Chris Drury 2.00 5.00
4 Peter Forsberg 5.00 12.00
5 Pave Bure 3.00 8.00
6 Scott Gomez 1.25 3.00
7 Roberto Luongo 4.00 10.00
8 Marian Hossa 2.00 5.00
9 Jaromir Jagr 5.00 12.00
10 Vincent Lecavalier 3.00 8.00

1999-00 Crown Royale Cramer's Choice Jumbos

Inserted one per box, this 10-card set features color action cut-outs of top NHL players as chosen by Pacific President and CEO, Michael Cramer, printed on premium sized, dual-foiled, die-cut pyramid-shaped cards. Six different serial-numbered parallel sets were also produced: 35 serial-numbered dark blue foil sets, 30 serial-numbered green foil sets, 25 serial-numbered red foil sets, 20 serial-numbered light blue foil sets, 10 serial-numbered gold foil sets, and 1 serial-numbered purple foil set. Purple and gold parallels are not priced due to scarcity.

COMPLETE SET (10) 15.00 30.00
*DARK BLUE/35: 5X TO 12X BASIC INSERTS
*GREEN/30: 5X TO 12X BASIC INSERTS
*LIGHT BLUE/20: 6X TO 15X BASIC INSERTS
*RED/25: 6X TO 15X BASIC INSERTS
UNPRICED PURPLE PRINT RUN 1
1 Paul Kariya 1.00 2.50
2 Teemu Selanne 1.00 2.50
3 Peter Forsberg 2.00 5.00
4 Patrick Roy 3.00 8.00
5 Mike Modano 1.25 3.00
6 Steve Yzerman 3.00 8.00
7 Pave Bure 1.00 2.50
8 Martin Brodeur 3.00 8.00
9 Eric Lindros 1.00 2.50
10 Jaromir Jagr 1.25 3.00

1999-00 Crown Royale Gold Crown Die-Cuts Jumbos

Inserted at six in 10 boxes, this 6-card jumbo set is an enhanced version of the base cards. The jumbos are vertical instead of horizontal, and feature rainbow foil on the die-cut crown background. Each card is serial numbered out of 960.

COMPLETE SET (6) 25.00 50.00
1 Teemu Selanne 3.00 8.00
2 Dominik Hasek 3.00 8.00
3 Patrick Roy 8.00 20.00
4 Steve Yzerman 8.00 20.00
5 Martin Brodeur 4.00 10.00
6 John LeClair 2.00 5.00

1999-00 Crown Royale Ice Elite

Inserted in packs at a rate of 1:1, this 25-card set silhouettes 25 of the NHL's most exciting players against a blue-ice background. A parallel of this set was also created and randomly inserted. The parallel was numbered to just 10.

COMPLETE SET (25) 10.00 20.00
UNPRICED PARALLEL PRINT RUN 10
1 Paul Kariya .30 .75
2 Teemu Selanne .30 .75
3 Joe Thornton .50 1.25
4 Dominik Hasek .60 1.50
5 Tony Amonte .25 .60
6 Milan Hejduk .30 .75
7 Patrick Roy 1.50 4.00
8 Joe Sakic .60 1.50
9 Ed Belfour .30 .75
10 Brett Hull .40 1.00
11 Brendan Shanahan .30 .75
12 Steve Yzerman 1.50 4.00
13 Luc Robitaille .25 .60
14 Trevor Linden .25 .60
15 David Legwand .25 .60
16 Martin Brodeur .75 2.00
17 Theo Fleury .25 .60
18 Marian Hossa .30 .75
19 John LeClair .30 .75
20 Mark Recchi .25 .60
21 Jeremy Roenick .40 1.00
22 Owen Nolan .25 .60
23 Vincent Lecavalier .30 .75
24 Curtis Joseph .30 .75
25 Steve Kariya .25 .60

1999-00 Crown Royale International Glory

Inserted in packs at a rate of one in one, this 25-card set places 25 of the NHL's top players in action to the background of their home country's flag. A parallel of this set was also created and randomly inserted in packs. The parallel was numbered to just 20.

COMPLETE SET (25) 10.00 20.00
*PARALLEL/20: 60X TO 150X BASIC INSERTS
1 Teemu Selanne .30 .75
2 Patrik Stefan .25 .60
3 Dominik Hasek .60 1.50
4 Arturs Irbe .25 .60
5 Chris Drury .25 .60
6 Peter Forsberg .75 2.00
7 Patrick Roy 1.50 4.00
8 Mike Modano .50 1.25
9 Sergei Fedorov .50 1.25
10 Brendan Shanahan .30 .75
11 Pave Bure .30 .75
12 Zigmund Palffy .25 .60
13 Saku Koivu .30 .75
14 Martin Brodeur .75 2.00
15 Scott Gomez .25 .60
16 Theo Fleury .25 .60
17 Simon Gagne .30 .75
18 Eric Lindros .30 .75
19 John Vanbiesbrouck .30 .75
20 Keith Tkachuk .30 .75
21 Jaromir Jagr .50 1.25
22 Pavol Demitra .25 .60
23 Jochen Hecht .25 .60
24 Jeff Friesen .25 .60
25 Mats Sundin .30 .75

1999-00 Crown Royale Team Captain Die-Cuts

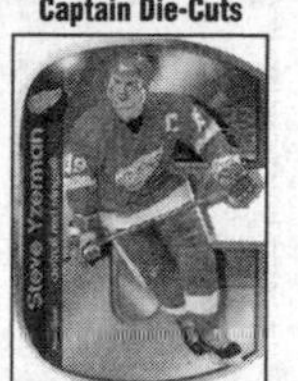

Randomly inserted in packs at 1:25, this 10-card set showcases hockey's most respected team captains. Player action shots are set against a die-cut "C" background.

COMPLETE SET (10) 25.00 50.00
1 Paul Kariya 4.00 10.00
2 Ray Bourque 2.50 6.00
3 Joe Sakic 3.00 8.00
4 Steve Yzerman 8.00 20.00
5 Eric Lindros 2.50 6.00
6 Keith Tkachuk 1.50 4.00
7 Jaromir Jagr 2.50 6.00
8 Owen Nolan 1.25 3.00
9 Mats Sundin 1.50 4.00
10 Mark Messier 2.50 6.00

2000-01 Crown Royale

The 2000-01 Crown Royale set was issued in March 2001. The 6-card packs carried an SRP of $6.99. The set was issued as one series totaling 144 cards of which the last 35 were sequentially numbered to 400. The set features color action player photos printed on cards with silver and gold foil highlights, dual etching and a die-cut crown as background.

COMP. SET w/o SP's (108) 15.00 40.00
1 Guy Hebert .30 .75
2 Paul Kariya .60 1.50
3 Teemu Selanne .60 1.50
4 Donald Audette .20 .50
5 Andrew Brunette .20 .50
6 Damian Rhodes .20 .50
7 Patrik Stefan .20 .50
8 Jason Allison .20 .50
9 Byron Dafoe .30 .75
10 Bill Guerin .30 .75
11 Sergei Samsonov .30 .75
12 Joe Thornton 1.00 2.50
13 Doug Gilmour .30 .75
14 Chris Gratton .20 .50
15 Dominik Hasek 1.25 3.00
16 Michael Peca .20 .50
17 Valeri Bure .20 .50
18 Jarome Iginla .75 2.00
19 Marc Savard .20 .50
20 Ron Francis .30 .75
21 Arturs Irbe .30 .75
22 Sami Kapanen .20 .50
23 Tony Amonte .30 .75
24 Jocelyn Thibault .30 .75
25 Alexei Zhamnov .20 .50
26 Ray Bourque 1.00 2.50
27 Chris Drury .30 .75
28 Peter Forsberg 1.00 2.50
29 Milan Hejduk .30 .75
30 Patrick Roy 2.00 5.00
31 Joe Sakic 1.25 3.00
32 Geoff Sanderson .20 .50
33 Ron Tugnutt .30 .75
34 Ed Belfour .40 1.00
35 Brett Hull .60 1.50
36 Mike Modano 1.00 2.50
37 Joe Nieuwendyk .30 .75
38 Sergei Fedorov .60 1.50
39 Chris Osgood .30 .75
40 Brendan Shanahan .60 1.50
41 Steve Yzerman 1.50 4.00
42 Tommy Salo .30 .75
43 Ryan Smyth .20 .50
44 Doug Weight .30 .75
45 Pavel Bure .60 1.50
46 Rob Niedermayer .30 .75
47 Ray Whitney .20 .50
48 Stephane Fiset .20 .50
49 Zigmund Palffy .30 .75
50 Luc Robitaille .30 .75
51 Jamie Storr .30 .75
52 Jim Dowd .20 .50
53 Jamie McLennan .20 .50
54 Scott Pellerin .20 .50
55 Saku Koivu .60 1.50
56 Martin Rucinsky .20 .50
57 Brian Savage .20 .50
58 Jose Theodore .75 2.00
59 Mike Dunham .20 .50
60 David Legwand .20 .50
61 Vitali Yachmenev .20 .50
62 Martin Brodeur 1.50 4.00
63 Patrik Elias .30 .75
64 Scott Gomez .20 .50
65 Alexei Mogilny .30 .75
66 Tim Connolly .20 .50
67 Brad Isbister .20 .50
68 John Vanbiesbrouck .30 .75
69 Theo Fleury .20 .50
70 Brian Leetch .30 .75
71 Mark Messier .60 1.50
72 Mike Richter .40 1.00
73 Daniel Alfredsson .30 .75
74 Radek Bonk .20 .50
75 Marian Hossa .40 1.00
76 Patrick Lalime .30 .75
77 Alexei Yashin .20 .50
78 Brian Boucher .30 .75
79 Simon Gagne .40 1.00
80 John LeClair .40 1.00
81 Eric Lindros .60 1.50
82 Sean Burke .30 .75
83 Shane Doan .20 .50
84 Jeremy Roenick .75 2.00
85 Keith Tkachuk .40 1.00
86 Jaromir Jagr 1.00 2.50
87 Mario Lemieux 2.00 5.00
88 Martin Straka .20 .50
89 Chris Pronger .30 .75
90 Roman Turek .30 .75
91 Pierre Turgeon .30 .75
92 Scott Young .20 .50
93 Patrick Marleau .30 .75
94 Owen Nolan .30 .75
95 Steve Shields .30 .75
96 Vincent Lecavalier .40 1.00
97 Fredrik Modin .20 .50
98 Kevin Weekes .20 .50
99 Sergei Berezin .20 .50
100 Curtis Joseph .40 1.00
101 Gary Roberts .20 .50
102 Mats Sundin .60 1.50
103 Andrew Cassels .20 .50
104 Markus Naslund .40 1.00
105 Felix Potvin .40 1.00
106 Peter Bondra .40 1.00
107 Olaf Kolzig .30 .75
108 Adam Oates .30 .75
109 Samuel Pahlsson SP 1.50 4.00
110 Tomi Kallio SP 1.50 4.00
111 Andrew Raycroft RC 4.00 10.00
112 Eric Boulton RC 1.50 4.00
113 Dimitri Kalinin SP 1.50 4.00
114 Oleg Saprykin SP 1.50 4.00
115 Josef Vasicek RC 1.50 4.00
116 Shane Willis SP 1.50 4.00
117 Steven McCarthy SP 1.50 4.00
118 David Aebischer RC 6.00 15.00
119 Serge Aubin RC 1.50 4.00
120 Marc Denis SP 1.50 4.00
121 David Vyborny SP 1.50 4.00
122 Marty Turco RC 6.00 15.00
123 Roberto Luongo SP 6.00 15.00
124 Ivan Novoseltsev SP 1.50 4.00
125 Denis Shvidki SP 1.50 4.00
126 Steven Reinprecht RC 1.50 4.00
127 Marian Gaborik RC 12.00 30.00
128 Filip Kuba SP 1.50 4.00
129 Andrei Markov SP 1.50 4.00
130 Scott Hartnell RC 3.00 8.00
131 Colin White RC 1.50 4.00
132 Rick DiPietro RC 8.00 20.00
133 Taylor Pyatt SP 1.50 4.00
134 Martin Havlat RC 4.00 10.00
135 Jani Hurme RC 1.50 4.00
136 Justin Williams RC 3.00 8.00
137 Robert Esche SP 1.50 4.00
138 Milan Kraft SP 1.50 4.00
139 Brent Johnson SP 1.50 4.00
140 Evgeni Nabokov SP 3.00 8.00
141 Sheldon Keele SP 1.50 4.00
142 Brad Richards SP 3.00 8.00
143 Daniel Sedin SP 1.50 4.00
144 Henrik Sedin SP 1.50 4.00

2000-01 Crown Royale Ice Blue

This set paralleled the first 108 cards of the base set.

*STARS: 10X TO 20X BASIC CARDS
PRINT RUN 75 SER.#'d SETS

2000-01 Crown Royale Limited Series

This set paralleled the first 108 cards of the base set.The cards look the same as the base set except for silver foil in place of the gold and a serial number to 25 on the card front.

*STARS: 15X TO 30X BASIC CARDS

2000-01 Crown Royale Premiere Date

This set paralleled the first 108 cards of the base set.

*STARS: 10X TO 20X BASIC CARDS

2000-01 Crown Royale Red

Randomly inserted in retail packs, this 108-card set parallels the base set with red foil highlights.

*RED: 1X TO 2X BASIC CARD
RANDOM INSERTS IN RETAIL PACKS

2000-01 Crown Royale 21st Century Rookies

This 25-card set was inserted at the stated rate of 1:1. The set features color action photos of each player on a mostly green background accompanied by the players name, position, and team.

COMPLETE SET (25) 10.00 25.00
1 Tomi Kallio .20 .50
2 Andrew Raycroft 1.25 3.00
3 Eric Boulton .20 .50
4 Oleg Saprykin .20 .50
5 Shane Willis .20 .50
6 Steven McCarthy .20 .50
7 David Aebischer 1.25 3.00
8 Marc Denis .75 2.00
9 Marty Turco 1.25 3.00
10 Roberto Luongo 1.25 3.00
11 Steven Reinprecht .20 .50
12 Marian Gaborik 2.00 5.00
13 Andrei Markov .20 .50
14 Colin White .20 .50
15 Rick DiPietro 1.25 3.00
16 Taylor Pyatt .20 .50
17 Martin Havlat 1.25 3.00
18 Jani Hurme .20 .50
19 Justin Williams .75 2.00
20 Milan Kraft .20 .50
21 Brent Johnson .20 .50
22 Evgeni Nabokov .75 2.00
23 Brad Richards .75 2.00
24 Daniel Sedin .20 .50
25 Henrik Sedin .20 .50

2000-01 Crown Royale Game-Worn Jerseys

Randomly inserted in packs, this 25-card set featured game-used jersey swatches and full-color player photographs on a mostly gray background. Please note that the cards have different print runs which are player specific. They are listed below, following the player's name.

*MULT.COLOR SWATCH:1X TO 2X HI COL.
1 Byron Dafoe/602 3.00 8.00
2 Valeri Bure/599 3.00 8.00
3 Rico Fata/596 3.00 8.00
4 Phil Housley/599 3.00 8.00
5 Marc Savard/597 3.00 8.00
6 Peter Forsberg/624 6.00 15.00
7 Ed Belfour/608 4.00 10.00
8 Brett Hull/591 5.00 12.00
9 Jamie Langenbrunner/599 3.00 8.00
10 Grant Marshall/593 3.00 8.00
11 Mike Modano/587 5.00 12.00
12 Joe Nieuwendyk/597 3.00 8.00
13 Chris Chelios/1157 4.00 10.00
14 Chris Osgood/502 3.00 8.00
15 Brendan Shanahan/781 4.00 10.00
16 Patric Kjellberg/594 3.00 8.00
17 Mike Richter/596 4.00 10.00
18 Alexei Yashin/946 3.00 8.00
19 Eric Desjardins/594 3.00 8.00
20 John LeClair/594 4.00 10.00
21 Jyrki Lumme/592 3.00 8.00
22 Michal Rozsival/591 3.00 8.00
23 Martin Straka/581 3.00 8.00
24 Mats Sundin/343 4.00 10.00
25 Felix Potvin/585 4.00 10.00

2000-01 Crown Royale Game-Worn Jersey Patches

This randomly inserted set paralleled the Crown Royale Game-Worn Jerseys set, but each card carries a swatch of jersey patch. Please note that the cards have different print runs which are player specific. They are listed below, following the player's name.

1 Byron Dafoe/141 15.00 40.00
2 Valeri Bure/145 10.00 25.00
3 Rico Fata/144 10.00 25.00
4 Phil Housley/144 10.00 25.00
5 Marc Savard/144 10.00 25.00
6 Peter Forsberg/141 20.00 50.00
7 Ed Belfour/145 20.00 50.00
8 Brett Hull/144 15.00 40.00
9 Jamie Langenbrunner/143 10.00 25.00
10 Grant Marshall/144 10.00 25.00
11 Mike Modano/143 20.00 50.00
12 Joe Nieuwendyk/142 15.00 40.00
13 Chris Chelios/192 20.00 50.00
14 Chris Osgood/143 15.00 40.00
15 Brendan Shanahan/163 20.00 50.00
16 Patric Kjellberg/136 10.00 25.00
17 Mike Richter/135 20.00 50.00
18 Alexei Yashin/283 10.00 25.00
19 Eric Desjardins/145 10.00 25.00
20 John LeClair/144 10.00 25.00
21 Jyrki Lumme/144 10.00 25.00
22 Michal Rozsival/144 10.00 25.00
23 Martin Straka/144 10.00 25.00
24 Mats Sundin/104 20.00 50.00
25 Felix Potvin/144 20.00 50.00

2000-01 Crown Royale Premium-Sized Game-Worn Jerseys

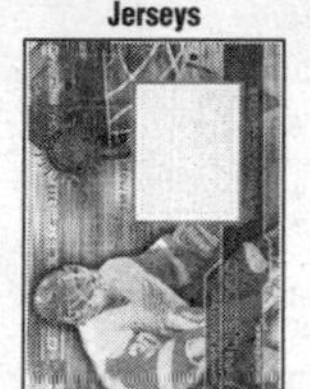

This 25-card set was inserted one per hobby box. Individual cards measured 3 1/2" x 5" and carry a premium-sized jersey swatch that measured 1 1/2" x 2". Each card also carried a color action photo of each player, and the back describes when the jersey was worn. Please note that the cards have different print runs which are player specific. They are listed below, following the player's name.

*MULT.COLOR SWATCH: 1X TO 2X HI COL.
1 Byron Dafoe/343 10.00 25.00
2 Valeri Bure/349 6.00 15.00
3 Rico Fata/343 6.00 15.00
4 Phil Housley/344 6.00 15.00
5 Marc Savard/343 6.00 15.00
6 Peter Forsberg/95 25.00 60.00
7 Ed Belfour/352 10.00 25.00
8 Brett Hull/317 15.00 40.00
9 Jamie Langenbrunner/338 6.00 15.00
10 Grant Marshall/342 6.00 15.00
11 Mike Modano/320 15.00 40.00
12 Joe Nieuwendyk/333 8.00 20.00
13 Chris Chelios/94 15.00 40.00
14 Chris Osgood/351 8.00 20.00
15 Brendan Shanahan/96 10.00 25.00
16 Patric Kjellberg/327 6.00 15.00
17 Mike Richter/346 10.00 25.00
18 Alexei Yashin/345 6.00 15.00
19 Eric Desjardins/349 6.00 15.00
20 John LeClair/330 6.00 15.00
21 Jyrki Lumme/338 6.00 15.00
22 Michal Rozsival/357 6.00 15.00
23 Martin Straka/334 6.00 15.00
25 Felix Potvin/345 10.00 25.00

2000-01 Crown Royale Game-Worn Jersey Redemptions

This 11-card set was inserted into random packs as redemption cards only. It was substituted into the product at the last minute in place of the Crown Royale Road To The Gold insert set. The cards are serial numbered to 475 unless noted differently below.

1 Stu Barnes 10.00 25.00
2 Jarome Iginla 12.50 30.00
3 Joe Sakic 20.00 50.00
4 David Legwand 10.00 25.00
5 Scott Niedermayer 10.00 25.00
6 Theo Fleury 10.00 25.00
7 Daniel Alfredsson 10.00 25.00
8 Jeremy Roenick 12.50 30.00
9 Jaromir Jagr 15.00 40.00
10 Curtis Joseph 10.00 25.00
11 Mario Lemieux/100 40.00 100.00

2000-01 Crown Royale Jewels of the Crown

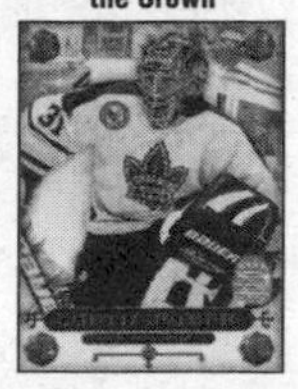

Inserted at a rate of 1:1, this 25-card set features full-color action photos of top stars on front with computer-generated purple jewels in each corner.

COMPLETE SET (25) 20.00 40.00
1 Paul Kariya .60 1.50
2 Teemu Selanne .60 1.50
3 Patrik Stefan .40 1.00
4 Jason Allison .40 1.00
5 Joe Thornton 1.00 2.50
6 Dominik Hasek 1.25 3.00
7 Ray Bourque 1.25 3.00
8 Peter Forsberg 1.50 4.00
9 Patrick Roy 3.00 8.00
10 Joe Sakic 1.25 3.00
11 Brett Hull .75 2.00
12 Mike Modano 1.00 2.50
13 Brendan Shanahan 1.00 2.50
14 Steve Yzerman 3.00 8.00
15 Doug Weight .40 1.00
16 Pavel Bure .75 2.00
17 Martin Brodeur 1.50 4.00
18 Mark Messier .75 2.00
19 John LeClair .75 2.00
20 Eric Lindros 1.00 2.50
21 Jaromir Jagr 1.00 2.50
22 Mario Lemieux 4.00 10.00
23 Vincent Lecavalier .60 1.50
24 Curtis Joseph .60 1.50
25 Mats Sundin .60 1.50

2000-01 Crown Royale Landmarks

Randomly inserted in packs, this 10-card set features color action photos in the forefront and the skyline of the depicted player's team city in the background. Each card was serial numbered out of 102.

COMPLETE SET (10) 75.00 150.00
1 Paul Kariya 6.00 15.00
2 Dominik Hasek 10.00 25.00
3 Peter Forsberg 12.50 30.00
4 Patrick Roy 25.00 60.00
5 Steve Yzerman 25.00 60.00
6 Pavel Bure 6.00 15.00
7 Martin Brodeur 12.50 30.00
8 Jaromir Jagr 8.00 20.00
9 Mario Lemieux 30.00 80.00
10 Curtis Joseph 6.00 15.00

2000-01 Crown Royale Now Playing

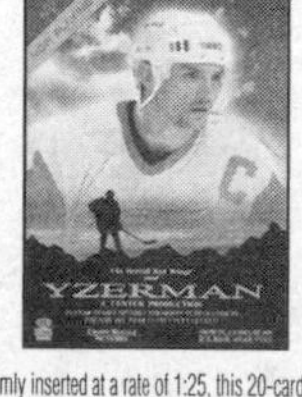

Randomly inserted at a rate of 1:25, this 20-card set features a movie poster look, that carries a large color player photo over a small silhouette. The words "Now Playing" run diagonally in the left hand corner, and the player's name in bold is at the bottom above mock movie credits.

COMPLETE SET (20) 50.00 100.00
1 Paul Kariya 1.50 4.00
2 Teemu Selanne 1.50 4.00
3 Jason Allison 1.25 3.00
4 Ray Bourque 3.00 8.00
5 Peter Forsberg 3.00 8.00
6 Patrick Roy 8.00 20.00
7 Brett Hull 2.00 5.00
8 Steve Yzerman 6.00 15.00
9 Pavel Bure 2.00 5.00
10 Marian Gaborik 4.00 10.00
11 Martin Brodeur 4.00 10.00
12 Theo Fleury 1.25 3.00
13 John LeClair 1.50 4.00
14 Jaromir Jagr 2.50 6.00
15 Mario Lemieux 8.00 20.00
16 Vincent Lecavalier 1.50 4.00
17 Curtis Joseph 1.50 4.00
18 Mats Sundin 1.50 4.00
19 Daniel Sedin 1.25 3.00
20 Henrik Sedin 1.25 3.00

2001 Crown Royale Calder Collection Gold Edition

Available only through a mail-in offer, this 8-card set used the Crown Royale die-cut design to highlight several young players considered to be contenders for the Calder trophy. Each card was highlighted with gold foil. The set cost $39.95 US and each card was serial-numbered out of 1000. The offers were found in packs of 2000-01 Pacific products.

COMPLETE SET (8) 24.00 60.00
1 Evgeni Nabokov 6.00 15.00
2 Daniel Sedin 2.40 6.00
3 Henrik Sedin 1.60 4.00
4 Marian Gaborik 6.00 15.00
5 Rick DiPietro 4.80 12.00
6 Martin Havlat 6.00 15.00
7 Brad Richards 2.40 6.00
8 David Aebischer 4.00 10.00

2001 Crown Royale Calder Collection All-Star Edition

This 8-card set was produced by Pacific as a wrapper redemption for the 2001 All-Star Fan Fest. Base cards feature full color player portrait photos on a silver and maroon crown die-cut card. Each card is sequentially numbered to 2,001.

COMPLETE SET (8) 20.00 50.00
C1 David Aebischer 3.20 8.00
C2 Marian Gaborik 4.00 10.00
C3 Rick DiPietro 3.20 8.00
C4 Martin Havlat 4.00 10.00
C5 Evgeni Nabokov 3.20 8.00
C6 Brad Richards 1.60 4.00
C7 Daniel Sedin 1.60 4.00
C8 Henrik Sedin 1.20 3.00

2001-02 Crown Royale

Released in both hobby and retail channels, this 180-card set featured die-cut base cards and 35 short printed rookies with a crown style die-cut. Rookies were serial-numbered out of 267. Hobby versions were enhanced with gold foil, retail versions with green foil. Hobby packs carried a SRP $5.99 for a 3-card pack. Retail packs included 5 cards.

COMP.SET w/o SP's (144) 30.00 80.00
1 Matt Cullen .20 .50
2 Jeff Friesen .20 .50
3 Jean-Sebastien Giguere .30 .75
4 Paul Kariya .60 1.00
5 Ray Ferraro .20 .50
6 Dany Heatley .75 2.00
7 Milan Hnilicka .30 .75
8 Patrik Stefan .20 .50
9 Byron Dafoe .30 .75
10 Glen Murray .20 .50
11 Brian Rolston .20 .50
12 Sergei Samsonov .30 .75
13 Joe Thornton 1.00 2.50
14 Stu Barnes .20 .50
15 Martin Biron .30 .75
16 Tim Connolly .20 .50
17 J-P Dumont .20 .50
18 Miroslav Satan .30 .75
19 Craig Conroy .20 .50
20 Jarome Iginla .75 2.00
21 Dean McAmmond .20 .50
22 Derek Morris .20 .50
23 Marc Savard .20 .50
24 Roman Turek .20 .50
25 Ron Francis .30 .75
26 Arturs Irbe .30 .75
27 Sami Kapanen .20 .50
28 Jeff O'Neill .20 .50
29 Tony Amonte .30 .75
30 Mark Bell .20 .50
31 Kyle Calder .20 .50
32 Eric Daze .20 .50
33 Steve Sullivan .20 .50
34 Jocelyn Thibault .30 .75
35 Rob Blake .30 .75
36 Chris Drury .30 .75
37 Peter Forsberg 1.50 2.50
38 Milan Hejduk .30 .75
39 Patrick Roy 4.00 5.00
40 Joe Sakic 1.25 2.50
41 Alexei Tanguay .30 .75
42 Marc Denis .30 .75
43 Rostislav Klesla .20 .50
44 Geoff Sanderson .20 .50
45 Ron Tugnutt .30 .75
46 Ed Belfour .60 1.00
47 Jere Lehtinen .30 .75
48 Mike Modano 1.00 2.50
49 Joe Nieuwendyk .30 .75
50 Pierre Turgeon .30 .75
51 Sergei Fedorov 1.00 2.50
52 Dominik Hasek 1.25 2.50
53 Brett Hull .75 1.00
54 Nicklas Lidstrom .60 1.00
55 Luc Robitaille .30 .75
56 Brendan Shanahan .60 1.00
57 Steve Yzerman 3.00 4.00
58 Anson Carter .20 .50
59 Daniel Cleary .20 .50
60 Mike Comrie .20 .50
61 Tommy Salo .30 .75
62 Ryan Smyth .30 .75
63 Pavel Bure .60 1.00
64 Viktor Kozlov .20 .50
65 Roberto Luongo .75 2.00
66 Jason Allison .20 .50
67 Adam Deadmarsh .20 .50
68 Steve Heinze .20 .50
69 Zigmund Palffy .30 .75
70 Felix Potvin .60 1.00
71 Andrew Brunette .20 .50
72 Jim Dowd .20 .50
73 Manny Fernandez .30 .75
74 Marian Gaborik 1.25 2.50
75 Doug Gilmour .30 .75
76 Jeff Hackett .20 .50
77 Yanic Perreault .20 .50
78 Brian Savage .20 .50
79 Jose Theodore .75 2.00
80 Mike Dunham .30 .75
81 David Legwand .20 .50
82 Cliff Ronning .20 .50
83 Scott Walker .20 .50
84 Jason Arnott .20 .50
85 Martin Brodeur 1.50 3.00
86 Patrik Elias .30 .75
87 Scott Stevens .30 .75
88 Petr Sykora .20 .50
89 Rick DiPietro .30 .75
90 Chris Osgood .30 .75
91 Mark Parrish .20 .50
92 Mike Peca .20 .50
93 Alexei Yashin .20 .50
94 Theo Fleury .20 .50
95 Brian Leetch .30 .75
96 Eric Lindros .60 1.00
97 Mark Messier .60 1.00
98 Mike Richter .60 1.00
99 Daniel Alfredsson .30 .75
100 Martin Havlat .30 .75
101 Marian Hossa .60 1.00
102 Patrick Lalime .30 .75
103 Todd White .20 .50
104 Brian Boucher .20 .50
105 Roman Cechmanek .20 .50
106 Simon Gagne .60 1.00
107 John LeClair .30 .75
108 Mark Recchi .30 .75
109 Jeremy Roenick .75 2.00
110 Daniel Briere .20 .50
111 Sean Burke .30 .75
112 Shane Doan .20 .50
113 Claude Lemieux .20 .50
114 Johan Hedberg .30 .75
115 Alexei Kovalev .30 .75
116 Roberto Lang .20 .50
117 Mario Lemieux 2.50 6.00
118 Pavol Demitra .30 .75
119 Brent Johnson .30 .75
120 Chris Pronger .30 .75
121 Keith Tkachuk .60 1.00
122 Doug Weight .30 .75
123 Vincent Damphousse .20 .50
124 Evgeni Nabokov .30 .75
125 Owen Nolan .30 .75
126 Teemu Selanne .60 1.00
127 Nikolai Khabibulin .60 1.00
128 Vincent Lecavalier .60 1.00
129 Brad Richards .30 .75
130 Martin St. Louis .30 .75
131 Curtis Joseph .60 1.00
132 Alexander Mogilny .30 .75
133 Gary Roberts .30 .75
134 Mats Sundin .60 1.00
135 Darcy Tucker .20 .50
136 Dan Cloutier .30 .75
137 Brendan Morrison .30 .75
138 Markus Naslund .30 .75
139 Daniel Sedin .20 .50
140 Henrik Sedin .20 .50
141 Peter Bondra .60 1.00
142 Jaromir Jagr 1.00 2.50
143 Olaf Kolzig .30 .75
144 Adam Oates .30 .75
145 Ilja Bryzgalov RC 6.00 15.00
146 Timo Parssinen RC 4.00 10.00
147 Ilya Kovalchuk RC 50.00 100.00
148 Brian Pothier RC 4.00 10.00
149 Jukka Hentunen RC 4.00 10.00
150 Erik Cole RC 6.00 15.00
151 Vaclav Nedorost RC 4.00 10.00
152 Brian Gionta SP 4.00 10.00
153 Mathieu Darche RC 4.00 10.00
154 Jody Shelley RC 8.00 20.00
155 Martin Spanhel RC 4.00 10.00
156 Niko Kapanen RC 4.00 10.00
157 Pavel Datsyuk RC 40.00 80.00
158 Jason Chimera RC 4.00 10.00
159 Ty Conklin RC 4.00 10.00
160 Jussi Markkanen SP 4.00 10.00
161 Niklas Hagman RC 4.00 10.00
162 Kristian Huselius RC 8.00 20.00
163 Jaroslav Bednar RC 4.00 10.00
164 David Cullen RC 4.00 10.00
165 Pascal Dupuis RC 4.00 10.00
166 Nick Schultz RC 4.00 10.00
167 Martin Erat RC 6.00 15.00
168 Andreas Salomonsson RC 4.00 10.00
169 Radek Martinek RC 4.00 10.00
170 Raffi Torres RC 8.00 20.00
171 Dan Blackburn RC 4.00 10.00
172 Chris Neil RC 6.00 15.00
173 Jiri Dopita RC 4.00 10.00
174 Krystofer Kolanos RC 4.00 10.00
175 Billy Tibbetts RC 4.00 10.00
176 Mark Rycroft RC 4.00 10.00
177 Jeff Jillson RC 4.00 10.00
178 Nikita Alexeev RC 4.00 10.00
179 Chris Corrinet RC 4.00 10.00
180 Brian Sutherby RC 4.00 10.00

2001-02 Crown Royale Blue

This 144-card set paralleled the base set not including the SP's, but carried blue foil in place of the green and were serial-numbered out of 89. These cards were found in retail packs only at a stated rate of 2:25.

BLUE: 5X TO 12X BASIC CARD

2001-02 Crown Royale Premiere Date

This 144-card set paralleled the base set not including the SP's, but carried a premiere date stamp and were serial-numbered out of 60. These cards were found in hobby packs only at a stated rate of 1:25.

PREM.DATE: 4X TO 10X BASIC CARD

2001-02 Crown Royale Red

This 144-card set paralleled the base set not including the SP's, but carried red foil in place of the gold and were serial-numbered out of 35. These cards were found in hobby packs only at a stated rate of 1:49.

RED: 5X TO 12X BASIC CARD

2001-02 Crown Royale All-Star Honors

COMPLETE SET (1-20) 60.00 125.00
STATED ODDS 1:49 HOBBY/1:97 RETAIL
1 Paul Kariya 2.00 5.00
2 Roman Turek 1.50 4.00
3 Rob Blake 1.50 4.00
4 Patrick Roy 10.00 25.00
5 Joe Sakic 4.00 10.00
6 Mike Modano 3.00 8.00
7 Dominik Hasek 4.00 10.00
8 Brett Hull 2.50 6.00
9 Brendan Shanahan 3.00 8.00
10 Steve Yzerman 10.00 25.00
11 Pavel Bure 3.00 8.00
12 Martin Brodeur 5.00 12.00
13 Patrik Elias 1.50 4.00
14 Alexei Yashin 1.50 4.00
15 Eric Lindros 3.00 8.00
16 Mark Messier 2.50 6.00
17 Mario Lemieux 12.50 30.00
18 Doug Weight 1.50 4.00
19 Curtis Joseph 2.00 5.00
20 Mats Sundin 2.00 5.00

2001-02 Crown Royale Crowning Achievement

COMPLETE SET (20) 25.00 60.00
CARDS 1-10 INSERTED IN RETAIL PACKS
CARDS 11-20 INSERTED IN HOBBY PACKS
STATED ODDS 1:25
1 Dany Heatley 2.00 5.00
2 Ilya Kovalchuk 8.00 10.00
3 Mark Bell .75 2.00
4 Rostislav Klesla .75 2.00
5 Kristian Huselius .75 2.00
6 Martin Erat .75 2.00
7 Rick Dipietro 1.25 3.00
8 Dan Blackburn .75 2.00
9 Krystofer Kolanos .75 2.00
10 Johan Hedberg .75 2.00
11 Jarome Iginla 2.50 6.00
12 Patrick Roy 6.00 15.00
13 Joe Sakic 2.00 5.00
14 Dominik Hasek 2.50 6.00
15 Steve Yzerman 4.00 10.00
16 Pavel Bure 1.25 3.00
17 Martin Brodeur 3.00 8.00
18 Eric Lindros 1.25 3.00
19 Mario Lemieux 6.00 15.00
20 Jaromir Jagr 2.00 5.00

2001-02 Crown Royale Jewels of the Crown

COMPLETE SET (1-30) 40.00 100.00
STATED ODDS 1:25 HOBBY/RETAIL
1 Paul Kariya 1.00 2.50
2 Joe Thornton 2.00 5.00
3 Jarome Iginla 1.50 4.00
4 Roman Turek .75 2.00
5 Jeff O'Neill .75 2.00
6 Peter Forsberg 2.00 5.00
7 Patrick Roy 6.00 15.00
8 Joe Sakic 2.50 6.00
9 Mike Modano 1.50 4.00
10 Dominik Hasek 2.50 6.00
11 Brendan Shanahan 1.25 3.00
12 Steve Yzerman 4.00 10.00
13 Ryan Smyth .75 2.00
14 Pavel Bure 1.25 3.00
15 Jason Allison .75 2.00
16 Marian Gaborik 2.00 5.00
17 Saku Koivu 1.00 2.50
18 Martin Brodeur 3.00 8.00
19 Patrik Elias .75 2.00
20 Alexei Yashin .75 2.00
21 Eric Lindros 1.25 3.00
22 Mark Messier 1.50 4.00
23 Marian Hossa 1.00 2.50
24 Jeremy Roenick 1.25 3.00
25 Mario Lemieux 6.00 15.00
26 Keith Tkachuk 1.00 2.50
27 Teemu Selanne 1.00 2.50
28 Curtis Joseph 1.00 2.50
29 Mats Sundin 1.00 2.50
30 Jaromir Jagr 2.00 5.00

2001-02 Crown Royale Legendary Heroes

Inserted at a stated rate of 1:48 hobby boxes and 1:60 retail boxes, this 10-card set featured both a small full body photo on the left side of the card front and a larger head shot in the center under the players number. Each card was serial-numbered out of 31.

1 Paul Kariya 20.00 50.00
2 Patrick Roy 40.00 100.00
3 Dominik Hasek 12.50 30.00
4 Steve Yzerman 40.00 100.00
5 Martin Brodeur 20.00 50.00
6 Eric Lindros 12.50 30.00
7 Mark Messier 10.00 25.00
8 Mario Lemieux 50.00 125.00
9 Curtis Joseph 10.00 25.00
10 Jaromir Jagr 15.00 40.00

2001-02 Crown Royale Rookie Royalty

COMPLETE SET (1-20) 20.00 50.00
STATED ODDS 1:49 HOBBY/1:97 RETAIL
1 Dany Heatley 4.00 10.00
2 Ilya Kovalchuk 8.00 20.00
3 Erik Cole 1.25 3.00
4 Mark Bell .75 2.00
5 Vaclav Nedorost .75 2.00
6 Brian Willsie .75 2.00
7 Rostislav Klesla .75 2.00
8 Pavel Datsyuk 6.00 15.00
9 Ty Conklin .75 2.00
10 Kristian Huselius .75 2.00
11 Jaroslav Bednar .75 2.00
12 Martin Erat .75 2.00
13 Rick Dipietro 2.00 5.00
14 Dan Blackburn .75 2.00
15 Krystofer Kolanos .75 2.00
16 Kris Beech .75 2.00
17 Johan Hedberg .75 2.00
18 Toby Petersen .75 2.00
19 Jeff Jillson .75 2.00
20 Nikita Alexeev .75 2.00

2001-02 Crown Royale Triple Threads

Inserted at a rate of 2:25 hobby and 1:97 retail, this 20-card set featured three swatches of game-used sweaters from the players featured. The swatches were affixed beside a small color photo of each player and arranged vertically.

1 Paul Kariya 10.00 25.00
Steve Rucchin
Oleg Tverdovsky
2 Craig Conroy 5.00 12.00
Marc Savard
Roman Turek
3 Sergei Samsonov 5.00 12.00
Valeri Bure
Sergei Zubov
4 Jean-Sebastien Giguere 12.00 30.00
Jonas Hiller
Scott Niedermayer
5 J-P Dumont 5.00 12.00
Richard Smehlik
Alexei Zhitnik
6 Kyle Calder 5.00 12.00
Matthieu Dandenault
Eric Daze
7 Joe Sakic 10.00 25.00
Patrick Roy
Greg DeVries
8 Dallas Stars 10.00 25.00
9 Jarome Iginla 8.00 20.00
Jochen Hecht
Andrew Cassels
10 Tom Fitzgerald 5.00 12.00
Cliff Ronning
Vitali Yachmenev
11 Steve Yzerman 15.00 40.00
Joe Sakic
Eric Lindros
12 Saku Koivu 8.00 20.00
Mats Sundin
Roman Turek
13 Scott Niedermayer 5.00 12.00
Chris Terreri
Manny Malhotra
14 Mariusz Czerkawski 5.00 12.00
Mats Lindgren
Mika Alatalo
15 Petr Nedved 8.00 20.00
Mike Richter
Theo Fleury
16 Mike Dunham 5.00 12.00
Scott Walker
Tom Fitzgerald
17 Mario Lemieux 15.00 40.00
Martin Straka
Alexei Kovalev
18 Scott Young 5.00 12.00
Jamie McLennan
Mike Eastwood
19 Cory Stillman 5.00 12.00
Jochen Hecht
Pierre Turgeon
20 Peter Bondra 8.00 20.00
Jaromir Jagr
Martin Straka

2001 Crown Royale Toronto Expo Rookie Collection

This set was issued by Pacific in a wrapper redemption program at the Toronto Spring Expo, May 4-6, 2001. The set features top rookies on the Crown Royale base card design with a blue background. Each card is serial numbered out of 499.

COMPLETE SET (8) 32.00 80.00
G1 Marty Turco 4.80 12.00
G2 Mike Comrie 10.00 25.00
G3 Rick DiPietro 6.00 15.00
G4 Martin Havlat 8.00 20.00
G5 Roman Cechmanek 4.00 10.00
G6 Brent Johnson 3.20 8.00
G7 Evgeni Nabokov 4.00 10.00
G8 Brad Richards 4.00 10.00

2002-03 Crown Royale

This 140-card set contained 100 veteran base cards and 40 shortprinted rookie cards that were inserted at 1:2 and serial-numbered to 2299 copies each.

COMPLETE SET (140) 75.00 150.00
COMP.SET w/o SP's (100) 40.00 80.00
1 Jean-Sebastien Giguere .50 1.25
2 Paul Kariya .60 1.50
3 Adam Oates .50 1.25
4 Dany Heatley .75 2.00
5 Ilya Kovalchuk .75 2.00
6 Glen Murray .30 .75
7 Sergei Samsonov .50 1.25
8 Steve Shields .50 1.25
9 Joe Thornton 1.00 2.50
10 Martin Biron .50 1.25
11 Chris Gratton .30 .75
12 Miroslav Satan .50 1.25
13 Chris Drury .50 1.25
14 Jarome Iginla .75 2.00
15 Roman Turek .50 1.25
16 Rod Brind'Amour .50 1.25
17 Ron Francis .50 1.25
18 Arturs Irbe .50 1.25
19 Jeff O'Neill .30 .75
20 Eric Daze .50 1.25
21 Jocelyn Thibault .50 1.25
22 Alexei Zhamnov .30 .75
23 Peter Forsberg 1.50 4.00
24 Milan Hejduk .60 1.50
25 Patrick Roy 3.00 8.00
26 Joe Sakic 1.25 3.00
27 Andrew Cassels .30 .75
28 Marc Denis .50 1.25
29 Bill Guerin .50 1.25
30 Mike Modano 1.00 2.50
31 Marty Turco .50 1.25
32 Sergei Fedorov 1.00 2.50
33 Brett Hull .75 2.00
34 Curtis Joseph .60 1.50
35 Nicklas Lidstrom .60 1.50
36 Brendan Shanahan .60 1.50
37 Steve Yzerman 3.00 8.00
38 Anson Carter .50 1.25
39 Mike Comrie .50 1.25
40 Tommy Salo .50 1.25
41 Ryan Smyth .30 .75
42 Kristian Huselius .30 .75
43 Roberto Luongo .75 2.00
44 Jason Allison .30 .75
45 Zigmund Palffy .50 1.25
46 Felix Potvin .50 1.25
47 Manny Fernandez .50 1.25
48 Marian Gaborik 1.25 3.00
49 Bill Muckalt .30 .75
50 Jeff Hackett .50 1.25
51 Saku Koivu .60 1.50
52 Jose Theodore .75 2.00
53 Richard Zednik .30 .75
54 David Legwand .50 1.25
55 Tomas Vokoun .50 1.25
56 Martin Brodeur 1.50 4.00
57 Patrik Elias .50 1.25
58 Scott Gomez .30 .75
59 Joe Nieuwendyk .50 1.25
60 Chris Osgood .50 1.25
61 Michael Peca .30 .75
62 Alexei Yashin .30 .75
63 Pavel Bure .60 1.50
64 Eric Lindros .60 1.50
65 Mike Richter .60 1.50
66 Daniel Alfredsson .50 1.25
67 Marian Hossa .60 1.50
68 Patrick Lalime .50 1.25
69 Roman Cechmanek .50 1.25
70 Simon Gagne .60 1.50
71 John LeClair .60 1.50
72 Jeremy Roenick .75 2.00
73 Tony Amonte .50 1.25
74 Daniel Briere .30 .75
75 Sean Burke .50 1.25
76 Johan Hedberg .50 1.25
77 Alexei Kovalev .50 1.25
78 Mario Lemieux 4.00 10.00
79 Alexei Morozov .30 .75
80 Pavol Demitra .50 1.25
81 Brent Johnson .50 1.25
82 Keith Tkachuk .60 1.50
83 Doug Weight .50 1.25
84 Vincent Damphousse .30 .75
85 Evgeni Nabokov .50 1.25
86 Teemu Selanne .60 1.50
87 Nikolai Khabibulin .60 1.50
88 Vincent Lecavalier .60 1.50
89 Martin St. Louis .50 1.25
90 Ed Belfour .60 1.50
91 Trevor Kidd .50 1.25
92 Alexander Mogilny .50 1.25
93 Mats Sundin .60 1.50
94 Todd Bertuzzi .60 1.50
95 Dan Cloutier .50 1.25
96 Brendan Morrison .50 1.25
97 Markus Naslund .60 1.50
98 Peter Bondra .50 1.25
99 Jaromir Jagr 1.00 2.50
100 Olaf Kolzig .50 1.25
101 Stanislav Chistov RC 2.00 5.00
102 Martin Gerber RC 1.50 4.00
103 Alexei Smirnov RC 1.50 4.00
104 Tim Thomas RC 2.50 6.00
105 Ryan Miller RC 4.00 10.00
106 Chuck Kobasew RC 1.50 4.00
107 Jordan Leopold RC 1.50 4.00
108 Pascal Leclaire RC 1.50 4.00
109 Rick Nash RC 8.00 20.00
110 Lasse Pirjeta RC 1.50 4.00
111 Steve Ott RC 2.50 6.00
112 Dmitri Bykov RC 1.50 4.00
113 Henrik Zetterberg RC 4.00 10.00
114 Ales Hemsky RC 4.00 10.00
115 Jay Bouwmeester RC 2.50 6.00
116 Ivan Majesky RC 1.50 4.00
117 Mike Cammalleri RC 2.00 5.00
118 Alexander Frolov RC 2.50 6.00
119 P-M Bouchard RC 2.50 6.00
120 Stephane Veilleux RC 1.50 4.00
121 Kyle Wanvig SP 1.50 4.00
122 Sylvain Blouin RC 1.50 4.00
123 Ron Hainsey RC 1.50 4.00
124 Adam Hall RC 1.50 4.00
125 Scottie Upshall RC 2.50 6.00
126 Ray Schultz RC 1.50 4.00
127 Jason Spezza RC 6.00 15.00
128 Anton Volchenkov RC 1.50 4.00
129 Dennis Seidenberg RC 1.50 4.00
130 Patrick Sharp RC 1.50 4.00
131 Radovan Somik RC 1.50 4.00
132 Jeff Taffe RC 1.50 4.00
133 Dick Tarnstrom RC 1.50 4.00
134 Tom Koivisto RC 1.50 4.00
135 Curtis Sanford RC 2.00 5.00
136 Lynn Loyns RC 1.50 4.00
137 Alexander Svitov RC 1.50 4.00
138 Carlo Colaiacovo RC 1.50 4.00
139 Steve Eminger RC 1.50 4.00
140 Alex Henry RC 1.50 4.00

2002-03 Crown Royale Blue

*STARS: X TO X BASIC CARDS
BLUE VETERAN ODDS 1:2 RETAIL PACKS
*ROOKIES (101-140): .75X TO 2X
ROOKIE PRINT RUN 350 SER.#'d SETS

2002-03 Crown Royale Purple

This 40-card hobby only set paralleled the last 40 cards of the base set but carried purple foil highlights. These cards were inserted at 1:5 and were serial-numbered out of 799.

*PURPLE: .3X TO .75X BASIC CARDS

2002-03 Crown Royale Red

*STARS: .75X TO 2X BASIC CARDS
RED VETERANS ODDS 1:4
*ROOKIES (101-140): .5X TO 1.25X
RED ROOKIE ODDS 1:12
RED ROOKIE PRINT RUN 350 SER.#'d SETS

2002-03 Crown Royale Retail

This 140-card set resembled the Hobby version but each card was highlighted with silver foil accents. Cards 101-140 were inserted at 1:7 packs.

*STARS: SAME VALUE AS HOBBY
*SP's: .3X TO .75X HOBBY HI

2002-03 Crown Royale Jerseys

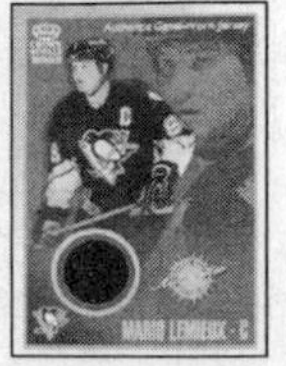

*MULT.COLOR SWATCH: .75X TO 1.5X
STATED ODDS 2:23 HBBY/1:25 RETAIL
1 Dany Heatley/755 6.00 15.00
2 Ilya Kovalchuk/762 8.00 20.00
3 Joe Sakic/513 10.00 25.00
4 Geoff Sanderson/758 5.00 12.00
5 Marty Turco/763 5.00 12.00
6 Mike Comrie/762 5.00 12.00
7 Valeri Bure/760 5.00 12.00
8 Zigmund Palffy/512 5.00 12.00
9 Jose Theodore/513 6.00 15.00
10 Martin Brodeur 12.50 30.00
11 Patrik Elias/503 5.00 12.00
12 Mike Peca/762 5.00 12.00
13 Brian Leetch/762 5.00 12.00
14 Martin Havlat/757 5.00 12.00
15 Jeremy Roenick/746 6.00 15.00
16 Mario Lemieux 12.50 30.00
17 Alexei Morozov/753 5.00 12.00
18 Chris Pronger/763 5.00 12.00
19 Sergei Varlamov 5.00 12.00
20 Owen Nolan/513 5.00 12.00
21 Fredrik Modin/759 5.00 12.00
22 Alexander Mogilny/762 5.00 12.00
23 Markus Naslund/754 5.00 12.00
24 Peter Bondra/761 5.00 12.00
25 Jaromir Jagr/763 10.00 25.00

2002-03 Crown Royale Jerseys Gold

*GOLD: .75X TO 2X BASIC JERSEYS
STATED PRINT RUN 25 SER.#'d SETS

2002-03 Crown Royale Dual Patches

Inserted as box toppers in hobby boxes, this 23-card set featured dual pieces of jersey patches. Print runs are listed below.

1 Dany Heatley 30.00 80.00
Ilya Kovalchuk/63
2 Martin Biron 12.50 30.00
J-P Dumont/273
3 Rod Brind'Amour 12.50 30.00
Erik Cole
4 Alexei Zhamnov 12.50 30.00
Steve Sullivan/209
5 Patrick Roy 60.00 125.00
Peter Forsberg SP
6 Joe Sakic 15.00 40.00
Alex Tanguay/228
7 Geoff Sanderson 12.50 30.00
Rostislav Klesla/403
8 M.Modano/P.Turgeon SP 15.00 40.00
9 Sergei Fedorov 12.50 30.00
Luc Robitaille/117
10 Tommy Salo 12.50 30.00
Ryan Smyth/188
11 Valeri Bure 12.50 30.00
Kristian Huselius/403
12 Adam Deadmarsh 12.50 30.00
Bryan Smolinski/403
13 M.Gaborik/M.Fernandez 25.00 60.00
14 Martin Brodeur 20.00 50.00
Patrik Elias/153
15 Michael Peca 12.50 30.00
Alexei Yashin/253
16 Brian Leetch 15.00 40.00
Mike Richter/213
17 M.Lemieux/A.Morozov 25.00 60.00
18 Alexei Kovalev 20.00 50.00
Martin Straka/403
19 Evgeni Nabokov 15.00 40.00
Patrick Marleau/163
20 Nikolai Khabibulin 20.00 40.00
Brad Richards/303
21 Alexander Mogilny 12.50 30.00
Darcy Tucker/203
22 Daniel Sedin 12.50 30.00
Henrik Sedin/243

23 Peter Bondra 12.50 30.00
Olaf Kolzig/347

2002-03 Crown Royale Coats of Armor

COMPLETE SET (10) 20.00 40.00
STATED ODDS 1:8 HBBY/1:25 RETAIL
1 Patrick Roy 4.00 10.00
2 Marty Turco .60 1.50
3 Curtis Joseph .75 2.00
4 Roberto Luongo 1.00 2.50
5 Jose Theodore 1.00 2.50
6 Martin Brodeur 2.00 5.00
7 Mike Richter .75 2.00
8 Patrick Lalime .60 1.50
9 Nikolai Khabibulin .75 2.00
10 Ed Belfour .75 2.00

2002-03 Crown Royale Lords of the Rink

COMPLETE SET (20) 30.00 60.00
STATED ODDS 1:5
1 Paul Kariya .75 2.00
2 Dany Heatley 1.00 2.50
3 Ilya Kovalchuk 1.00 2.50
4 Joe Thornton 1.25 3.00
5 Jarome Iginla 1.00 2.50
6 Peter Forsberg 2.00 5.00
7 Joe Sakic 1.50 4.00
8 Mike Modano 1.25 3.00
9 Brendan Shanahan 1.25 3.00
10 Steve Yzerman 4.00 10.00
11 Zigmund Palffy .60 1.50
12 Marian Gaborik 1.50 4.00
13 Saku Koivu .75 2.00
14 Pavel Bure 1.00 2.50
15 Eric Lindros .75 2.00
16 Mario Lemieux 5.00 12.00
17 Teemu Selanne .75 2.00
18 Vincent Lecavalier .75 2.00
19 Mats Sundin .75 2.00
20 Jaromir Jagr 1.25 3.00

2002-03 Crown Royale Rookie Royalty

COMPLETE SET (20) 12.00 25.00
STATED ODDS 1:5 HBBY/1:13 RETAIL
1 Stanislav Chistov .75 2.00
2 Martin Gerber .75 2.00
3 Alexei Smirnov .75 2.00
4 Ivan Huml .75 2.00
5 Chuck Kobasew .75 2.00
6 Tyler Arnason .75 2.00
7 Rick Nash 1.50 4.00
8 Dmitri Bykov .75 2.00
9 Henrik Zetterberg 1.50 4.00
10 Ales Hemsky .75 2.00
11 Jay Bouwmeester .75 2.00
12 Stephen Weiss .75 2.00
13 Alexander Frolov .75 2.00
14 Scottie Upshall .75 2.00
15 Justin Mapletoft .75 2.00
16 Jamie Lundmark .75 2.00
17 Jason Spezza 1.50 4.00
18 Petr Cajanek .75 2.00
19 Jonathan Cheechoo .75 2.00
20 Alexander Svitov .75 2.00

2002-03 Crown Royale Royal Portraits

STATED ODDS 1:45 HBBY/1:97 RETAIL
1 Paul Kariya 2.50 6.00
2 Ilya Kovalchuk 3.00 8.00
3 Patrick Roy 10.00 [illegible]
4 Joe Sakic 5.00 12.00
5 Rick Nash 15.00 40.00
6 Steve Yzerman 12.50 30.00
7 Martin Brodeur 6.00 15.00
8 Jason Spezza 12.50 30.00
9 Mario Lemieux 15.00 40.00
10 Jaromir Jagr 4.00 10.00

2003-04 Crown Royale

This 136-card die-cut set consisted of 100 veteran cards and 36 rookie cards short-printed to 575 serial-numbered copies each.

COMPLETE SET (136)
COMP.SET w/o SP's (100) 20.00 50.00
1 Sergei Fedorov .60 1.50
2 Martin Gerber .30 .75
3 Jean-Sebastien Giguere .30 .75
4 Ilya Kovalchuk .60 1.50
5 Pasi Nurminen .30 .75
6 Marc Savard .20 .50
7 Glen Murray .20 .50
8 Felix Potvin .50 1.25
9 Joe Thornton .75 2.00
10 Martin Biron .30 .75
11 J-P Dumont .20 .50
12 Taylor Pyatt .20 .50
13 Jarome Iginla .60 1.50
14 Chuck Kobasew .20 .50
15 Roman Turek .30 .75
16 Erik Cole .20 .50
17 Jeff O'Neill .30 .75
18 Kevin Weekes .30 .75
19 Tyler Arnason .30 .75
20 Brett McLean .20 .50
21 Jocelyn Thibault .30 .75
22 David Aebischer .30 .75
23 Peter Forsberg 1.00 2.50
24 Milan Hejduk .30 .75
25 Paul Kariya .50 1.25
26 Joe Sakic 1.00 2.50
27 Philippe Sauve .30 .75
28 Marc Denis .30 .75
29 Todd Marchant .20 .50
30 Rick Nash .60 1.50
31 Jason Arnott .20 .50
32 Bill Guerin .30 .75
33 Mike Modano .75 2.00
34 Marty Turco .30 .75
35 Dominik Hasek 1.00 2.50
36 Nicklas Lidstrom .50 1.25
37 Brendan Shanahan .50 1.25
38 Ray Whitney .20 .50
39 Steve Yzerman 1.50 4.00
40 Georges Laraque .20 .50
41 Tommy Salo .30 .75
42 Ryan Smyth .20 .50
43 Jay Bouwmeester .20 .50
44 Olli Jokinen .20 .50
45 Roberto Luongo .60 1.50
46 Jason Allison .20 .50
47 Roman Cechmanek .30 .75
48 Ziggy Palffy .30 .75
49 Luc Robitaille .30 .75
50 Pierre-Marc Bouchard .20 .50
51 Marian Gaborik .75 2.00
52 Dwayne Roloson .30 .75
53 Mathieu Garon .20 .50
54 Saku Koivu .50 1.25
55 Mike Ribeiro .20 .50
56 Jose Theodore .50 1.25
57 Scottie Upshall .20 .50
58 Tomas Vokoun .30 .75
59 Martin Brodeur 1.25 3.00
60 Patrik Elias .30 .75
61 Jeff Friesen .20 .50
62 Scott Gomez .20 .50
63 Mariusz Czerkawski .20 .50
64 Jason Blake .20 .50
65 Rick DiPietro .30 .75
66 Mike Dunham .30 .75
67 Alex Kovalev .30 .75
68 Mark Messier .50 1.25
69 Daniel Alfredsson .30 .75
70 Marian Hossa .50 1.25
71 Patrick Lalime .30 .75
72 Jason Spezza .50 1.25
73 Jeff Hackett .30 .75
74 Mark Recchi .30 .75
75 Jeremy Roenick .50 1.25
76 Justin Williams .20 .50
77 Sean Burke .30 .75
78 Ladislav Nagy .20 .50
79 Rico Fata .20 .50
80 Mario Lemieux 2.00 5.00
81 Chris Osgood .30 .75
82 Chris Pronger .30 .75
83 Keith Tkachuk .30 .75
84 Doug Weight .30 .75
85 Jonathan Cheechoo .30 .75
86 Alyn McCauley .20 .50
87 Evgeni Nabokov .30 .75
88 Nikolai Khabibulin .50 1.25
89 Vincent Lecavalier .50 1.25
90 Brad Richards .30 .75
91 Martin St. Louis .30 .75
92 Ed Belfour .30 .75
93 Alexander Mogilny .30 .75
94 Owen Nolan .30 .75
95 Mats Sundin .50 1.25
96 Todd Bertuzzi .50 1.25
97 Jason King .20 .50
98 Markus Naslund .30 .75
99 Jaromir Jagr .60 1.50
100 Olaf Kolzig .30 .75
101 Garrett Burnett RC 1.50 4.00
102 Joffrey Lupul RC 2.00 5.00
103 Patrice Bergeron RC 6.00 15.00
104 Sergei Zinovjev RC 1.50 4.00
105 Brent Krahn RC 1.50 4.00
106 Matthew Lombardi RC 1.50 4.00
107 Eric Staal RC 6.00 15.00
108 Tuomo Ruutu RC 2.50 6.00
109 Pavel Vorobiev RC 1.50 4.00
110 John-Michael Liles RC 1.50 4.00
111 Cody McCormick RC 1.50 4.00
112 Dan Fritsche RC 1.50 4.00
113 Nikolai Zherdev RC 2.50 6.00
114 Trevor Daley RC 1.50 4.00
115 Antti Miettinen RC 1.50 4.00
116 Jiri Hudler RC 2.00 5.00
117 Gregory Campbell RC 1.50 4.00
118 Nathan Horton RC 3.00 8.00
119 Dustin Brown RC 1.50 4.00
120 Tim Gleason RC 1.50 4.00
121 Brent Burns RC 1.50 4.00
122 Christopher Higgins RC 4.00 10.00
123 Dan Hamhuis RC 1.50 4.00
124 Jordin Tootoo RC 2.50 6.00
125 Marek Zidlicky RC 1.50 4.00
126 Paul Martin RC 1.50 4.00
127 Sean Bergenheim RC 1.50 4.00
128 Antoine Vermette RC 1.50 4.00
129 Joni Pitkanen RC 1.50 4.00
130 Matthew Spiller RC 1.50 4.00
131 Marc-Andre Fleury RC 10.00 25.00
132 Peter Sejna RC 1.50 4.00
133 Milan Michalek RC 2.00 5.00
134 Tom Preissing RC 1.50 4.00
135 Matt Stajan RC 2.50 6.00
136 Boyd Gordon RC 1.50 4.00

2003-04 Crown Royale Blue

*STARS: 1.25X TO 3X BASE HI
STATED PRINT RUN 850 SER.#'d SETS

2003-04 Crown Royale Red

STATED PRINT RUN 5 SER.#'d SETS
NOT PRICED DUE TO SCARCITY

2003-04 Crown Royale Retail

The retail version of this product carried silver foil highlights. Rookies in the retail set were serial-numbered out of 899.

*STARS: SAME VALUE HOBBY
*RCs: .3X TO .75X
RC PRINT RUN 899 SER.#'d SETS

2003-04 Crown Royale Gauntlet of Glory

COMPLETE SET (20) 10.00 20.00
STATED ODDS 1:6
1 Jean-Sebastien Giguere .50 1.25
2 Pasi Nurminen .50 1.25
3 Felix Potvin .60 1.50
4 Martin Biron .50 1.25
5 Jocelyn Thibault .50 1.25
6 David Aebischer .50 1.25
7 Marc Denis .50 1.25
8 Marty Turco .50 1.25
9 Dominik Hasek 1.25 3.00
10 Roberto Luongo .75 2.00
11 Jose Theodore .75 2.00
12 Martin Brodeur 1.50 4.00
13 Rick DiPietro .50 1.25
14 Patrick Lalime .50 1.25
15 Sean Burke .50 1.25
16 Marc-Andre Fleury 1.50 4.00
17 Evgeni Nabokov .50 1.25
18 Nikolai Khabibulin .60 1.50
19 Ed Belfour .60 1.50
20 Dan Cloutier .50 1.25

2003-04 Crown Royale Global Conquest

STATED ODDS 1:11
1 M.Brodeur/M.Lemieux 2.00 5.00
2 Dominik Hasek .75 2.00
Jaromir Jagr
3 Teemu Selanne .60 1.50
Saku Koivu
4 Olaf Kolzig .60 1.50
Marco Sturm
5 Evgeni Nabokov .60 1.50
Nik Antropov
6 Sergei Fedorov 1.25 3.00
Ilya Kovalchuk
7 M.Gaborik/M.Hossa 1.00 2.50
8 Markus Naslund 1.25 3.00
Peter Forsberg
9 David Aebischer .60 1.50
Martin Gerber
10 Mike Modano .60 1.50
Jeremy Roenick

2003-04 Crown Royale Jerseys

STATED ODDS 3:20
1 Sergei Fedorov 4.00 10.00
2 Ilya Kovalchuk 5.00 12.00
3 Joe Thornton 5.00 12.00
4 Ryan Miller 3.00 8.00
5 Matthew Lombardi 2.00 5.00
6 Peter Forsberg 6.00 15.00
7 Teemu Selanne 3.00 8.00
8 Mike Modano 4.00 10.00
9 Steve Yzerman 8.00 20.00
10 Ales Hemsky 2.50 6.00
11 Jay Bouwmeester 2.00 5.00
12 Nathan Horton 4.00 10.00
13 Saku Koivu 3.00 8.00
14 Martin Brodeur 8.00 20.00
15 Rick DiPietro 2.50 6.00
16 Eric Lindros 3.00 8.00
17 Jason Spezza 6.00 15.00
18 Antoine Vermette 2.00 5.00
19 Jeremy Roenick 4.00 10.00
20 Mario Lemieux 10.00 25.00
21 Barret Jackman 2.00 5.00
22 Vincent Lecavalier 3.00 8.00
23 Ed Belfour 3.00 8.00
24 Owen Nolan 2.50 6.00
25 Markus Naslund 3.00 8.00

2003-04 Crown Royale Patches

*PATCHES: .75X TO 2X JERSEY CARDS
STATED ODDS 1:20
20 Mario Lemieux/25 50.00 125.00

2003-04 Crown Royale Lords of the Rink

COMPLETE SET (24) 15.00 40.00
STATED ODDS 1:6
1 Sergei Fedorov .75 2.00
2 Ilya Kovalchuk .75 2.00
3 Joe Thornton 1.00 2.50
4 Eric Staal .50 1.25
5 Peter Forsberg 1.50 4.00
6 Milan Hejduk .60 1.50
7 Paul Kariya .60 1.50
8 Joe Sakic 1.25 3.00
9 Rick Nash .75 2.00
10 Mike Modano 1.00 2.50
11 Steve Yzerman 2.00 5.00
12 Henrik Zetterberg .60 1.50
13 Jay Bouwmeester .50 1.25
14 Ziggy Palffy .50 1.25
15 Marian Hossa .60 1.50
16 Jason Spezza .60 1.50
17 Jeremy Roenick .60 1.50
18 Mario Lemieux 2.50 6.00
19 Keith Tkachuk .60 1.50
20 Vincent Lecavalier .50 1.25
21 Mats Sundin .60 1.50
22 Todd Bertuzzi .60 1.50
23 Markus Naslund .60 1.50
24 Jaromir Jagr .75 2.00

2003-04 Crown Royale Royal Portraits

COMPLETE SET (10) 12.50 25.00
STATED ODDS 1:11
1 Joffrey Lupul 1.00 2.50
2 Patrice Bergeron 2.00 5.00
3 Eric Staal 2.00 5.00
4 Jiri Hudler 1.00 2.50
5 Nathan Horton 1.50 4.00
6 Jordin Tootoo 1.50 4.00
7 Joni Pitkanen 1.00 2.50
8 Marc-Andre Fleury 3.00 8.00
9 Milan Michalek 1.00 2.50
10 Matt Stajan 1.50 4.00

1970-71 Dad's Cookies

The 1970-71 Dad's Cookies set contains 144 unnumbered color cards. Each card measures approximately 1 7/8" by 5 3/8". Each player is pictured on the front dressed in an "NHL Players" emblazoned jersey. The fronts contain player statistics for the 1969-70 season and for his career. The backs, in both English and French, are the same for all cards. The backs contain an ad for these cards and Dad's Cookies, a special offer for an NHL Players Association decal and a 1969 NHL Players Association copyright line.

COMPLETE SET (144) 100.00 200.00
1 Lou Angotti .75 1.50
2 Don Awrey .50 1.00
3 Bob Baun .75 1.50
4 Jean Beliveau 4.00 8.00
5 Red Berenson .75 1.50
6 Gary Bergman .50 1.00
7 Les Binkley 1.00 2.00
8 Andre Boudrias .50 1.00
9 Wally Boyer .50 1.00
10 Arnie Brown .50 1.00
11 Johnny Bucyk 1.50 3.00
12 Charlie Burns .50 1.00
13 Larry Cahan .50 1.00
14 Gerry Cheevers 2.50 5.00
15 Bobby Clarke 6.00 12.00
16 Wayne Connelly .50 1.00
17 Yvan Cournoyer 1.50 3.00
18 Roger Crozier 1.00 2.00
19 Ray Cullen .50 1.00
20 Denis DeJordy 1.00 2.00
21 Alex Delvecchio 1.50 3.00
22 Bob Dillabough .50 1.00
23 Gary Doak .50 1.00
24 Gary Dornhoefer 1.00 2.00
25 Dick Duff .75 1.50
26 Tim Ecclestone .50 1.00
27 Roy Edwards 1.00 2.00
28 Gerry Ehman .50 1.00
29 Ron Ellis .75 1.50
30 Phil Esposito 5.00 10.00
31 Tony Esposito 5.00 10.00
32 Doug Favell 1.00 2.00
33 John Ferguson .75 1.50
34 Norm Ferguson .50 1.00
35 Reg Fleming .50 1.00
36 Bill Flett .50 1.00
37 Bruce Gamble 1.00 2.00
38 Jean-Guy Gendron .50 1.00
39 Ed Giacomin 2.00 4.00
40 Rod Gilbert 1.00 2.00
41 Bill Goldsworthy .75 1.50
42 Phil Goyette .50 1.00
43 Danny Grant .75 1.50
44 Ted Green .75 1.50
45 Vic Hadfield .75 1.50
46 Al Hamilton .50 1.00
47 Ted Hampson .50 1.00
48 Terry Harper .50 1.00
49 Ted Harris .50 1.00
50 Paul Henderson 1.50 3.00
51 Bryan Hextall .50 1.00
52 Bill Hicke .50 1.00
53 Larry Hillman .50 1.00
54 Wayne Hillman .50 1.00
55 Charlie Hodge 1.25 2.50
56 Ken Hodge .75 1.50
57 Gordie Howe 10.00 20.00
58 Harry Howell 1.00 2.00
59 Bobby Hull 7.50 15.00
60 Dennis Hull .75 1.50
61 Earl Ingarfield .50 1.00
62 Doug Jarrett .50 1.00
63 Gary Jarrett .50 1.00
64 Ed Johnston 1.00 2.00
65 Dave Keon 1.50 3.00
66 Skip Krake .50 1.00
67 Orland Kurtenbach .75 1.50
68 Andre Lacroix .75 1.50
69 Jacques Laperriere .75 1.50
70 Jacques Lemaire 1.50 3.00
71 Rick Ley .50 1.00
72 Bruce MacGregor .50 1.00
73 Keith Magnuson .75 1.50
74 Frank Mahovlich 2.00 4.00
75 Chico Maki .50 1.00
76 Gilles Marotte .50 1.00
77 Bert Marshall .50 1.00
78 Don Marshall .50 1.00
79 Pit Martin .75 1.50
80 Keith McCreary .50 1.00
81 Ab McDonald .50 1.00
82 Jim McKenny .75 1.50
83 John McKenzie .75 1.50
84 Mike McMahon .50 1.00
85 Larry Mickey .50 1.00
86 Stan Mikita 2.50 5.00
87 Doug Mohns .50 1.00
88 Wayne Muloin .50 1.00
89 Jim Neilson .50 1.00
90 Bob Nevin .50 1.00
91 Murray Oliver .50 1.00
92 Bobby Orr 20.00 40.00
93 Danny O'Shea .50 1.00
94 Rosaire Paiement .50 1.00
95 Bernie Parent 2.50 5.00
96 Jean-Paul Parise .50 1.00
97 Brad Park 1.50 3.00
98 Mike Pelyk .50 1.00
99 Gilbert Perreault 2.00 4.00
100 Noel Picard .75 1.50
101 Barclay Plager .75 1.50
102 Jacques Plante 5.00 10.00
103 Tracy Pratt .50 1.00
104 Dean Prentice .50 1.00
105 Jean Pronovost .75 1.50
106 Bob Pulford .75 1.50
107 Pat Quinn 1.00 2.00
108 Jean Ratelle 1.00 2.00
109 Matt Ravlich .50 1.00
110 Mickey Redmond 1.00 2.00
111 Henri Richard 2.00 4.00
112 Jim Roberts .50 1.00
113 Dale Rolfe .50 1.00
114 Bobby Rousseau .50 1.00
115 Gary Sabourin .50 1.00
116 Derek Sanderson 2.50 5.00
117 Glen Sather 1.50 3.00
118 Serge Savard 1.00 2.00
119 Ken Schinkel .50 1.00
120 Rod Seiling .50 1.00
121 Brit Selby .50 1.00
122 Eddie Shack 1.50 3.00
123 Floyd Smith .50 1.00
124 Fred Stanfield .50 1.00
125 Pat Stapleton .50 1.00
126 Frank St.Marseille .50 1.00
127 Dale Tallon .50 1.00
128 Walt Tkaczuk .50 1.00
129 J.C. Tremblay .50 1.00
130 Norm Ullman .75 1.50
131 Garry Unger .75 1.50
132 Rogatien Vachon 1.50 3.00
133 Carol Vadnais .50 1.00
134 Ed Van Impe .50 1.00
135 Bob Wall .50 1.00
136 Mike Walton .50 1.00
137 Bryan Watson .50 1.00
138 Joe Watson .50 1.00
139 Tom Webster .50 1.00
140 Juha Widing 1.00 2.00
141 Tom Williams .50 1.00
142 Jim Wiste .50 1.00
143 Gump Worsley 2.50 5.00
144 Bob Woytowich .75 1.50

1983-84 Devils Postcards

This set is the first confirmed to feature the franchise transferred from Colorado to New Jersey. The color postcards feature action photos and were issued by the team as promotional items at player appearances.

COMPLETE SET (25) 10.00 25.00
1 Mike Antonovich .20 .50
2 Mel Bridgman .30 .75
3 Aaron Broten .20 .50
4 Murray Brumwell .30 .75
5 Dave Cameron .30 .75
6 Rich Chernomaz .20 .50
7 Joe Cirella .30 .75
8 Ken Daneyko .60 1.50
9 Larry Floyd .20 .50
10 Paul Gagne .20 .50
11 Mike Kitchen .30 .75
12 Jeff Larmer .30 .75
13 Don Lever .20 .50
14 Dave Lewis .20 .50
15 Bob Lorimer .20 .50
16 Ron Low .30 .75
17 Jan Ludvig .20 .50
18 John Maclean 2.50 6.00
19 Bob MacMillan .30 .75
20 Hector Marini .20 .50
21 Rick Meagher .20 .50
22 Grant Mulvey .30 .75
23 Glenn Resch .60 1.50
24 Phil Russell .20 .50
25 Pat Verbeek 2.50 6.00

1984-85 Devils Postcards

This 25-card set of New Jersey Devils features on the front borderless color photos of the players, with two team logos (in green and red) in the white stripe below the picture. The cards measure approximately 3 1/4" by 6 1/8" and are in the postcard type format. On the left half of the back appear a black and white head shot of the player, basic player information, and the Devils' team logo. The cards are checklisted below according to uniform number. The side panel of the package of Colgate Dental Cream listed the checklist of the complete set. The cards of John MacLean and Kirk Muller predate their Rookie Cards.

COMPLETE SET (25) 8.00 20.00
1 Chico Resch .75 2.00
2 Joe Cirella .30 .75
4 Bob Lorimer .20 .50
5 Phil Russell .20 .50
8 Dave Pichette .20 .50
9 Don Lever .30 .75
10 Aaron Broten .20 .50
12 Pat Verbeek 2.00 5.00
14 Rich Chernomaz .20 .50
15 John MacLean 1.50 4.00
16 Rick Meagher .20 .50
17 Paul Gagne .20 .50
18 Mel Bridgman .30 .75
19 Rich Preston .20 .50
20 Tim Higgins .20 .50
21 Bob Hoffmeyer .20 .50
22 Doug Sulliman .20 .50
23 Bruce Driver .40 1.00
25 Dave Lewis .20 .50
27 Kirk Muller 2.00 5.00
28 Uli Hiemer .20 .50
29 Jan Ludvig .20 .50
30 Ron Low .30 .75
33 Hannu Kamppuri .30 .75
NNO Doug Carpenter CO .20 .50

1985-86 Devils Postcards

This ten-card set of New Jersey Devils features on the front borderless color player photos. The cards measure approximately 3 5/8" by 5 1/2" and are in the postcard format. The horizontal backs are divided in half by a thin black line and have the year, biographical information, home town, and a career highlight at the upper left corner. The cards are unnumbered and checklisted below in alphabetical order. Key cards in the set are Kirk Muller in his Rookie Card year and Craig Billington prior to his Rookie Card year.

COMPLETE SET (10) 5.60 14.00
1 Greg Adams .60 1.50
2 Perry Anderson .40 1.00
3 Craig Billington .75 2.00
4 Alain Chevrier .60 1.50
5 Paul Gagne .40 1.00
6 Mark Johnson .40 1.00
7 Kirk Muller 1.50 4.00
8 Chico Resch 1.00 2.50
9 Randy Velischek .40 1.00
10 Craig Wolanin .40 1.00

1986-87 Devils Police

This 20-card set was jointly sponsored by the New Jersey Devils, S.O.B.E.R., Howard Bank, and Independent Insurance Agents of Bergen County. Logos for these sponsors appear on the bottom of the card back. The front features a color action photo of the player, with the Devils' and NHL logos superimposed over the top corners of the picture. A thin black line and a green line serves as the inner and outer borders respectively; the area in between is yellow, with printing in the team's colors red and black. In addition to sponsors' logos, the back has biographical information, an anti-drug message, and career statistics. We have checklisted the cards below in alphabetical order, with uniform number to the right of the player's name.

COMPLETE SET (20) 12.00 30.00
1 Greg Adams 24 .60 1.50
2 Perry Anderson 25 .40 1.00
3 Timo Blomqvist 5 .40 1.00
4 Andy Brickley 26 .40 1.00
5 Mel Bridgman 18 .60 1.50
6 Aaron Broten 10 .40 1.00
7 Alain Chevrier 30 .60 1.50
8 Joe Cirella 2 .60 1.50
9 Ken Daneyko 3 .60 1.50
10 Bruce Driver 23 .75 2.00
11 Uli Hiemer 28 .40 1.00
12 Mark Johnson 12 .60 1.50
13 Jan Ludvig 29 .40 1.00
14 John MacLean 15 1.50 4.00
15 Peter McNab 7 .60 1.50
16 Kirk Muller 9 2.00 5.00
17 Doug Sulliman 22 .40 1.00
18 Randy Velischek 27 .40 1.00
19 Pat Verbeek 2.00 5.00
20 Craig Wolanin 6 .40 1.00

1988-89 Devils Caretta

This 30-card set has color action photos of the New Jersey Devils on the front, with a thin black border on white card stock. The cards measure approximately 2 7/8" by 4 1/4". The team name and logo on the top are printed in green and red; the text below the picture, giving player name, uniform number, and position, is printed in black. The horizontally oriented back has career statistics, a team logo, and a Caretta Trucking logo. We have checklisted the cards below in alphabetical order. Brendan Shanahan appears in his Rookie Card year.

COMPLETE SET (30) 10.00 25.00
1 Perry Anderson 25 .20 .50
2 Bob Bellemore CO .20 .50
3 Aaron Broten 10 .20 .50
4 Doug Brown 24 .20 .50
5 Sean Burke 1 1.25 3.00
6 Anders Carlsson 20 .20 .50
7 Joe Cirella 2 .20 .50
8 Pat Conacher 32 .20 .50
9 Ken Daneyko 3 .30 .75
10 Bruce Driver 23 .30 .75
11 Bob Hoffmeyer CO .20 .50
12 Jamie Huscroft 4 .20 .50
13 Mark Johnson 12 .30 .75
14 Jim Korn 14 .20 .50
15 Tom Kurvers 5 .20 .50
16 Lou Lamoriello P/GM .08 .25
17 Claude Loiselle 19 .20 .50
18 John MacLean 15 .75 2.00
19 David Maley 8 .20 .50
20 Doug McKay CO .08 .25
21 Kirk Muller 9 .75 2.00
22 Jack O'Callahan 7 .20 .50
23 Steve Rooney 18 .20 .50
24 Bob Sauve 28 .30 .75
25 Jim Schoenfeld CO .40 1.00
26 Brendan Shanahan 11 6.00 15.00
27 Patrik Sundstrom 17 .30 .75
28 Randy Velischek 27 .20 .50
29 Pat Verbeek 16 .75 2.00
30 Craig Wolanin 6 .20 .50

1989-90 Devils Caretta

This 29-card set has color action photos of the New Jersey Devils on the front, with a thin red border on white card stock. The team name and logo on the top are printed in green and red; the text below the picture, giving player name, uniform number, and position, is printed in black. The horizontal back provides brief biographical information and career statistics, a black-and-white picture and a Caretta Trucking logo. (The set also was issued without the trucking logo.) The cards measure approximately 2 7/8" by 4 1/4". These unnumbered cards are checklisted below alphabetically with sweater number noted to the right.

COMPLETE SET (29) 8.00 20.00
1 Tommy Albelin 26 .20 .50
2 Bob Bellemore CO .08 .25
3 Neil Brady 19 .20 .50
4 Aaron Broten 10 .20 .50
5 Doug Brown 24 .20 .50
6 Sean Burke 1 .75 2.00
7 Pat Conacher 32 .20 .50
8 John Cunniff CO .08 .25
9 Ken Daneyko 3 .20 .50
10 Bruce Driver 23 .40 1.00
11 Slava Fetisov 2 .75 2.00
12 Mark Johnson 12 .20 .50
13 Jim Korn 14 .20 .50
14 Lou Lamoriello P/GM .08 .25
15 John MacLean 15 .60 1.50
16 David Maley 8 .20 .50
17 Kirk Muller 9 .75 2.00
18 Janne Ojanen 22 .20 .50
19 Walt Poddubny 21 .20 .50
20 Reijo Ruotsalainen 29 .20 .50
21 Brendan Shanahan 11 2.00 5.00
22 Sergei Starikov 4 .20 .50
23 Patrik Sundstrom 17 .20 .50
24 Peter Sundstrom 20 .20 .50
25 Chris Terreri 31 .40 1.00
26 Sylvain Turgeon 16 .20 .50
27 Randy Velischek 27 .20 .50
28 Eric Weinrich 7 .20 .50
29 Craig Wolanin 6 .20 .50

1990-91 Devils Team Issue

This set contains 30 standard-size cards and features members of the New Jersey Devils. The front has a color photo of the player, with the team logo in the upper left corner. The back has statistical information. These cards are unnumbered and are checklisted below in alphabetical order.

COMPLETE SET (30) 6.00 15.00

1 Tommy Albelin .15 .40
2 Laurie Boschman .15 .40
3 Doug Brown .20 .50
4 Sean Burke .60 1.50
5 Tim Burke .15 .40
6 Zdeno Ciger .20 .50
7 Pat Conacher .15 .40
8 Troy Crowder .20 .50
9 John Cunniff CO .08 .25
10 Ken Daneyko .30 .75
11 Bruce Driver .20 .50
12 Slava Fetisov .30 .75
13 Alexei Kasatonov .20 .50
14 Lou Lamoriello P/GM .08 .25
15 Claude Lemieux .40 1.00
16 David Maley .15 .40
17 John MacLean .40 1.00
18 Jon Morris .15 .40
19 Kirk Muller .60 1.50
20 Lee Norwood .15 .40
21 Myles O'Connor .15 .40
22 Walt Poddubny .20 .50
23 Brendan Shanahan 2.00 5.00
24 Peter Stastny .60 1.50
25 Alan Stewart .15 .40
26 Warren Strelow .15 .40
27 Doug Sulliman .15 .40
28 Patrik Sundstrom .20 .50
29 Chris Terreri .20 .50
30 Eric Weinrich .20 .50

1991-92 Devils Teams Carvel

This ten-card set features team photos of the ten Devils teams from 1982-83 through 1991-92. The cards have a coupon for Carvel Ice Cream with an entry form for the "Shoot to Win" contest. The backs list all the players who are pictured and the statistical leaders from that particular year. The cards are unnumbered and measure approximately 2 1/2" by 6" with coupon. One card was issued per spectator at certain home games during the 1991-92 season.

COMPLETE SET (10) 8.00 20.00
1 1982-83 Devils Team 1.25 3.00
2 1983-84 Devils Team 1.00 2.50
3 1984-85 Devils Team 1.00 2.50
4 1985-86 Devils Team 1.00 2.50
5 1986-87 Devils Team 1.00 2.50
6 1987-88 Devils Team 1.00 2.50
7 1988-89 Devils Team 1.00 2.50
8 1989-90 Devils Team 1.00 2.50
9 1990-91 Devils Team 1.00 2.50
10 1991-92 Devils Team 1.00 2.50

1996-97 Devils Team Issue

This attractive team-issued set is complete at 30-cards. It was apparently issued as a premium at a game sometime during the '96-97 season and was sponsored by Sharp Electronics. The fronts feature action color photos surrounded by a red border. The player's name and number appear at the top, while his position and team logo grace the bottom. The backs include a black and white head shot as well as comprehensive statistics.

COMPLETE SET (30) 12.00 30.00
1 Mike Dunham .75 2.00
3 Ken Daneyko .20 .50
4 Scott Stevens .30 .75
10 Denis Pederson .30 .75
11 Steve Sullivan .40 1.00
12 Bill Guerin .75 2.00
14 Brian Rolston .30 .75
15 John MacLean .30 .75
16 Bobby Holik .30 .75
17 Petr Sykora .75 2.00
18 Sergei Brylin .20 .50
19 Bob Carpenter .08 .25
20 Jay Pandolfo .20 .50
21 Randy McKay .30 .75
22 Patrik Elias 4.00 10.00
23 Dave Andreychuk .20 .50
24 Lyle Odelein .20 .50
25 Valeri Zelepukin .08 .25
26 Jason Smith .20 .50
27 Scott Niedermayer .40 1.00
28 Kevin Dean .08 .25
29 Shawn Chambers .08 .25
30 Martin Brodeur 2.00 5.00
32 Steve Thomas .20 .50
33 Reid Simpson .08 .25
NNO Jacques Lemaire CO .20 .50
NNO John J. McMullen CH .02 .10
NNO Robbie Ftorek ACO .08 .25
NNO Jacques Caron ACO .02 .10
NNO Lou Lamoriello GM .02 .10

1997-98 Devils Team Issue

This set features the Devils of the NHL. The cards were sponsored by Zebra Pens and were given away as a promotion at a single home game.

COMPLETE SET (32) 8.00 20.00
1 Mike Dunham .40 1.00
2 Sheldon Souray .15 .40
3 Ken Daneyko .15 .40
4 Scott Stevens .30 .75
5 Ken Sutton .15 .40
6 Brad Bombardir .15 .40
7 Vlastimil Kroupa .15 .40
8 Denis Pederson .15 .40
9 Bill Guerin .40 1.00
10 John MacLean .15 .40
11 Bobby Holik .20 .50
12 Petr Sykora .40 1.00
13 Sergei Brylin .15 .40
14 Bobby Carpenter .15 .40
15 Jay Pandolfo .15 .40
16 Randy McKay .20 .50
17 Scott Daniels .15 .40
18 Dave Andreychuk .20 .50
19 Lyle Odelein .15 .40
20 Valeri Zelepukin .15 .40
21 Patrik Elias 1.25 3.00
22 Kevin Dean .15 .40
23 Krzysztof Oliwa .30 .75
24 Martin Brodeur 1.25 3.00
25 Steve Thomas .20 .50
26 Reid Simpson .15 .40
27 Doug Gilmour .40 1.00
28 Jacques Lemaire CO .08 .25
29 Robbie Ftorek CO .02 .10
30 Jacques Caron CO .02 .10
31 Lou Lamoriello PRES .02 .10
32 John McMullen CHAIR .02 .10

1998-99 Devils Team Issue

COMPLETE SET (30) 20.00
1 Dave Andreychuk .30 .75
2 Jason Arnott .30 .75
3 Brad Bombardir .20 .50
4 Martin Brodeur 2.00 5.00
5 Sergei Brylin .20 .50
6 Jacques Caron ACO .02 .10
7 Bob Carpenter ACO .02 .10
8 Ken Daneyko .20 .50
9 Kevin Dean .20 .50
10 Patrik Elias .40 1.00
11 Slava Fetisov CO .08 .25
12 Robbie Ftorek HCO .02 .10
13 Bobby Holik .20 .50
14 Sasha Lakovic .20 .50
15 Lou Lamoriello GM .02 .10
16 John Madden .40 1.00
17 Randy McKay .20 .50
18 John McMullen OWN .02 .10
19 Brendan Morrison .40 1.00
20 Scott Niedermayer .30 .75
21 Lyle Odelein .20 .50
22 Krzysztof Oliwa .40 1.00
23 Jay Pandolfo .30 .75
24 Denis Pederson .20 .50
25 Brian Rolston .30 .75
26 Vadim Sharifijanov .20 .50
27 Sheldon Souray .20 .50
28 Scott Stevens .40 1.00
29 Petr Sykora .40 1.00
30 Chris Terreri .30 .75

1999-00 Devils Team Issue

This set features the Devils of the NHL. The set is believed to have been issued as a promotional giveaway and was sponsored by PSEG Energy.

COMPLETE SET (31) 8.00 20.00
1 Scott Stevens .30 .75
2 Sheldon Souray .15 .40
3 Ken Daneyko .15 .40
4 Brad Bombardir .15 .40
5 Vadim Sharifijanov .15 .40
6 Brendan Morrison .40 1.00
7 John Madden .40 1.00
8 Sergei Nemchinov .15 .40
9 Bobby Holik .20 .50
10 Petr Sykora .40 1.00
11 Sergei Brylin .15 .40
12 Denis Pederson .15 .40
13 Jay Pandolfo .15 .40
14 Randy McKay .20 .50
15 Claude Lemieux .30 .75
16 Scott Gomez .40 1.00
17 Lyle Odelein .15 .40
18 Jason Arnott .30 .75
19 Patrik Elias .60 1.50
20 Scott Niedermayer .30 .75
21 Brian Rafalski .20 .50
22 Krzysztof Oliwa .40 1.00
23 Martin Brodeur 1.50 4.00
24 Chris Terreri .20 .50
25 Robbie Ftorek CO .15 .40
26 Slava Fetisov CO .20 .50
27 Larry Robinson CO .20 .50
28 Jacques Caron CO .02 .10
29 Lou Lamoriello GM .02 .10
30 Dr. John J. McMullen .02 .10
31 PSEG Energy .02 .10

2000-01 Devils Team Issue

This set was issued as a promotional giveaway at a single home game early in the season.

COMPLETE SET (30) 10.00 25.00
1 Jason Arnott .40 1.00
2 Martin Brodeur 2.00 5.00
3 Sergei Brylin .20 .50
4 Mike Commodore .30 .75
5 Ken Daneyko .20 .50
6 Patrik Elias .80 2.00
7 Sascha Goc .20 .50
8 Scott Gomez .40 1.00
9 Bobby Holik .30 .75
10 Steve Kelly .20 .50
11 John Madden .80 2.00
12 Randy McKay .30 .75
13 Jim McKenzie .20 .50
14 Alexander Mogilny .30 .75
15 Sergei Nemchinov .20 .50
16 Scott Niedermayer .40 1.00
17 Jay Pandolfo .20 .50
18 Brian Rafalski .20 .50
19 Scott Stevens .40 1.00
20 Turner Stevenson .20 .50
21 Ken Sutton .20 .50
22 Petr Sykora .80 2.00
23 Chris Terreri .30 .75
24 Colin White .30 .75
25 Larry Robinson CO .20 .50
26 Slava Fetisov ACO .20 .50
27 Kurt Kleinendorst ACO .04 .10
28 Jacques Caron ACO .04 .10
29 Lou Lamoriello GM .04 .10
30 2000 Stanley Cup Champions .20 .50

2001-02 Devils Team Issue

This set features the Devils of the NHL. The set was sponsored by Model's and was issued as a promotional giveaway at a home game early in the 2001-02 season.

COMPLETE SET (25) 8.00 20.00
1 Jason Arnott .40 1.00
2 Martin Brodeur 2.00 5.00
3 Sergei Brylin .20 .50
4 Jacques Caron ACO .04 .11
5 Pierre Dagenais .20 .50
6 Patrik Elias .80 2.00
7 Slava Fetisov ACO .20 .50
8 Scott Gomez .40 1.00
9 Bobby Holik .31 .78
10 Lou Lamoriello GM .04 .11
11 Jay Leach ACO .04 .11
12 John Madden .40 1.00
13 Randy McKay .31 .78
14 Jim McKenzie .20 .50
15 Sergei Nemchinov .20 .50
16 Scott Niedermayer .40 1.00
17 Devil Mascot .04 .11
18 Jay Pandolfo .20 .50
19 Brian Rafalski .20 .50
20 Larry Robinson CO .20 .50
21 Andreas Salomonsson .80 2.00
22 Scott Stevens 1.00
23 Turner Stevenson .20 .50
24 Petr Sykora .80 2.00
NNO Title Card .04 .11

2002-03 Devils Team Issue

Issued by the team at a game late in 2002, this 30-card set featured color photos on the card fronts and blank backs. The cards were unnumbered and are listed below by jersey number.

COMPLETE SET (30)
1 Ken Daneyko .10 .40
2 Scott Stevens .30 1.00
3 Colin White .10 .40
4 Tommy Albelin .10 .40
5 Steve Guolla .10 .40
6 Jiri Bicek .10 .50
7 Craig Darby .10 .40
8 Oleg Tverdovsky .10 .40
9 John Madden .30 1.00
10 Jeff Friesen .20 .75
11 Brian Gionta .30 1.00
12 Jamie Langenbrunner .20 .75
13 Christian Berglund .10 .40
14 Sergei Brylin .10 .40
15 Jim McKenzie .10 .40
16 Jay Pandolfo .10 .40
17 Scott Gomez .20 .75
18 Turner Stevenson .10 .40
19 Joe Nieuwendyk .30 1.00
20 Patrik Elias .20 .75
21 Scott Niedermayer .30 1.00
22 Brian Rafalski .10 .50
23 Martin Brodeur 2.00 5.00
24 Corey Schwab .20 .75
25 Lou Lamoriello GM .04 .10
26 Pat Burns HCO .04 .10
27 Bobby Carpenter ACO .04 .10
28 John MacLean ACO .04 .10
29 Jacques Caron CO .04 .10
30 Mascot .04 .10

2003-04 Devils Team Issue

This team set was sponsored by Verizon and handed out at a home game during the 2003-04 season. They are listed below by player number.

2 Sean Brown .20 .50
4 Scott Stevens .30 .75
5 Colin White .20 .50
6 Tommy Albelin .20 .50
7 Paul Martin .40 1.00
8 Igor Larionov .30 .75
10 Erik Rasmussen .20 .50
11 John Madden .40 1.00
12 Jeff Friesen .30 .75
14 Brian Gionta .75 2.00
15 Jamie Langenbrunner .30 .75
16 Mike Rupp .20 .50
17 Christian Berglund .20 .50
18 Sergei Brylin .20 .50
20 Jay Pandolfo .20 .50
23 Scott Gomez .40 1.00
24 Turner Stevenson .20 .50
25 David Hale .20 .50
26 Patrik Elias .40 1.00
27 Scott Niedermayer .40 1.00
28 Brian Rafalski .20 .50
29 Grant Marshall .20 .50
30 Martin Brodeur 5.00
35 Corey Schwab .30 .75
40 Scott Clemmensen .30 .75
41 Lou Lamoriello GM .02 .10
42 Pat Burns HCO .02 .10
43 Bob Carpenter ACO .02 .10
44 John MacLean ACO .02 .10
45 Jacques Laperiere ACO .02 .10
46 Jacques Caron ACO .02 .10
47 Mascot .02 .10

2005-06 Devils Team Issue

COMPLETE SET (30) 10.00 20.00
1 N.J. Devil MASCOT .02 .10
2 Jacques Caron ACO .02 .10
3 John MacLean ACO .02 .10
4 Jacques Laperriere ACO .02 .10
5 Larry Robinson CO .02 .10
6 Lou Lamoriello GM .02 .10
7 Alexander Mogilny .30 .75
8 Scott Clemmensen .30 .75
9 Ari Ahonen .30 .75
10 Martin Brodeur 2.00 5.00
11 Grant Marshall .20 .50
12 Brian Rafalski .20 .50
13 Patrik Elias .30 .75
14 David Hale .20 .50
15 Richard Matvichuk .20 .50
16 Scott Gomez .30 .75
17 Viktor Kozlov .20 .50
18 Jay Pandolfo .20 .50
19 Sergei Brylin .20 .50
20 Darren Langdon .30 .75
21 Jamie Langenbrunner .20 .50
22 Brain Gionta .40 1.00
23 John Madden .20 .50
24 Erik Rasmussen .20 .50
25 Zach Parise 2.00 5.00
26 Sean Brown .20 .50
27 Paul Martin .20 .50
28 Dan McGillis .20 .50
29 Colin White .20 .50
30 Vladimir Malakhov .20 .50

2006-07 Devils Team Set

COMPLETE SET (41) 10.00 25.00
1 Martin Brodeur 2.00 5.00
2 Alex Brooks .20 .50
3 Sergei Brylin .20 .50
4 Scott Clemmensen .20 .50
5 Jim Dowd .20 .50
6 Patrik Elias .30 .75
7 Brian Gionta .40 1.00
8 Scott Gomez .40 1.00
9 David Hale .20 .50
10 Cam Janssen .40 1.00
11 Dan LaCouture .20 .50
12 Jamie Langenbrunner .20 .50
13 Brad Lukowich .20 .50
14 John Madden .20 .50
15 Paul Martin .20 .50
16 Richard Matvichuk .20 .50
17 Alexander Mogilny .30 .75
18 Johnny Oduya .20 .50
19 Jay Pandolfo .20 .50
20 Zach Parise .75 2.00
21 Brian Rafalski .20 .50
22 Erik Rasmussen .20 .50
23 Mike Rupp .20 .50
24 Barry Tallackson .20 .50
25 Colin White .20 .50
26 Jason Wiemer .20 .50
27 Travis Zajac .40 1.00
28 Lou Lamoriello GM .10 .25
29 Claude Julien CO .10 .25
30 Jacques Laperriere ACO .10 .25
31 John MacLean ACO .10 .25
32 Jacques Caron ACO .10 .25
33 Mel Bridgman .20 .50
34 Bruce Driver .20 .50
35 Patrik Elias .30 .75
36 Don Lever .20 .50
37 Kirk Muller .20 .50
38 Scott Niedermayer .30 .75
39 Scott Stevens .30 .75
40 Ken Daneyko .20 .50
41 Scott Stevens .30 .75

1934-35 Diamond Matchbooks Silver

Covers from this first hockey matchbook issue generally feature color action shots with a silver background and green and black vertical bars on the cover's left side. "The Diamond Match Co., NYC" imprint appears on a double line below the striker. These matchbooks usually were issued in twin-packs through cigar and drug stores of the day. Complete matchbooks carry a 50 percent premium over the prices listed below.

COMPLETE SET (60) 1500.00 2400.00
1 Taffy Abel 15.00 25.00
2 Marty Barry 15.00 25.00
3 Red Beattie 15.00 25.00
4 Frank Boucher 25.00 40.00
5 Doug Brennan 15.00 25.00
6 Bill Brydge 15.00 25.00
7 Eddie Burke 35.00 50.00
8 Marty Burke 15.00 25.00
9 Gerald Carson 15.00 25.00
10 Lorne Chabot 35.00 50.00
11 Art Chapman 15.00 25.00
12 Dit Clapper 50.00 80.00
13 Lionel Conacher 50.00 80.00
14 Red Conn 15.00 25.00
15 Bill Cook 35.00 50.00
16 Bun Cook 35.00 50.00
17 Thomas Cook 18.00 30.00
18 Rosario Lolo Couture 15.00 25.00
19 Bob Davie 15.00 25.00
20 Cecil Dillon 15.00 25.00
21 Duke Dutkowski 15.00 25.00
22 Red Dutton 25.00 40.00
23 Johnny Gagnon 15.00 25.00
24 Chuck Gardiner 35.00 50.00
25 Johnny Gottselig 15.00 25.00
26 Robert Gracie 15.00 25.00
27 Lloyd Gross 15.00 25.00
28 Ott Heller 15.00 25.00
29 Normie Himes 15.00 25.00
30 Lionel Hitchman 35.00 50.00
31 Red Jackson 15.00 25.00
32 Roger Jenkins 15.00 25.00
33 Aurel Joliat 50.00 80.00
34 Butch Keeling 15.00 25.00
35 William Kendall 15.00 25.00
36 Jim Klein 15.00 25.00
37 Joe Lamb 15.00 25.00
38 Wildor Larochelle 18.00 30.00
39 Pit Lepine 15.00 25.00
40 Jack Leswick 15.00 25.00
41 Georges Mantha 35.00 50.00
42 Sylvio Mantha 35.00 50.00
43 Harold Mush March 18.00 30.00
44 Ronnie Martin 15.00 25.00
45 Rabbitt McVeigh 15.00 25.00
46 Howie Morenz 200.00 350.00
47 Murray Murdoch 15.00 25.00
48 Harold Oliver 25.00 40.00
49 George Patterson 15.00 25.00
50 Hal Picketts 15.00 25.00
51 Victor Ripley 15.00 25.00
52 Doc Romnes 15.00 25.00
53 Johnny Sheppard 15.00 25.00
54 Eddie Shore 75.00 125.00
55 Art Somers 15.00 25.00
56 Chris Speyers 15.00 25.00
57 Nelson Stewart 35.00 50.00
58 Tiny Thompson 50.00 80.00
59 Louis Trudel 15.00 25.00
60 Roy Worters 35.00 50.00

1935-36 Diamond Matchbooks Tan 1

The reverse of these tan-colored covers feature a brief player history with the player's name and team affiliation or position appearing at the top. "The Diamond Match Co., NYC" imprint appears below the striker on a single line. Complete matchbooks carry a 50 percent premium over the prices below. A matchbook of Joe Starke is reported to exist, but we cannot officially confirm that at this point in time.

COMPLETE SET (69) 1100.00 1800.00
1 Andy Aitkenhead 15.00 25.00
2 Vern Ayres 15.00 25.00
3 Bill Beveridge 18.00 30.00
4 Ralph Bowman 15.00 25.00
5 Bill Brydge 15.00 25.00
6 Glenn Brydson 15.00 25.00
7 Eddie Burke 18.00 30.00
8 Marty Burke 15.00 25.00
9 Lorne Carr 15.00 25.00
10 Gerald Carson 15.00 25.00
11 Lorne Chabot 25.00 40.00
12 Art Chapman 15.00 25.00
13 Red Conn 15.00 25.00
14 Bert Connoly 15.00 25.00
15 Bun Cook 25.00 40.00
16 Tommy Cook 15.00 25.00
17 Art Coulter 15.00 25.00
18 Lolo Couture 15.00 25.00
19 Bill Cowley 18.00 30.00
20 Wilf Cude 18.00 30.00
21 Mervin Dutton 18.00 30.00
22 Frank Finnigan 15.00 25.00
23 Irv Frew 15.00 25.00
24 LeRoy Goldsworthy 15.00 25.00
25 Johnny Gottselig 15.00 25.00
26 Bob Gracie 15.00 25.00
27 Ott Heller 15.00 25.00
28 Normie Himes 15.00 25.00
29 Syd Howe 25.00 40.00
30 Roger Jenkins 15.00 25.00
31 Ching Johnson 30.00 50.00
32 Aurel Joliat 35.00 60.00
33 Max Kaminsky 15.00 25.00
34 Butch Keeling 15.00 25.00
35 Bill Kendall 15.00 25.00
36 Lloyd Klein 15.00 25.00
37 Joe Lamb 15.00 25.00
38 Wildor Larochelle 15.00 25.00
39 Pit Lepine 15.00 25.00
40 Norman Locking 15.00 25.00
41 Georges Mantha 25.00 40.00
42 Sylvio Mantha 25.00 40.00
43 Harold March 15.00 25.00
44 Charlie Mason 15.00 25.00
45 Donnie McFadyen 15.00 25.00
46 Jack McGill 15.00 25.00
47 Rabbit McVeigh 15.00 25.00
48 Armand Mondou 15.00 25.00
49 Howie Morenz 180.00 300.00
50 Murray Murdoch 15.00 25.00
51 Al Murray 15.00 25.00
52 Harry Oliver 25.00 40.00
53 Jean Pusie 15.00 25.00
54 Paul Marcel Raymond 15.00 25.00
55 Jack Riley 15.00 25.00
56 Vic Ripley 15.00 25.00
57 Desse Roche 15.00 25.00
58 Earl Roche 15.00 25.00
59 Doc Romnes 15.00 25.00
60 Sweeney Schriner 30.00 50.00
61 Earl Seibert 25.00 40.00
62 Gerald Shannon 15.00 25.00
63 Alex Smith 15.00 25.00
64 Joe Starke 15.00 25.00
recently confirmed
65 Nels Stewart 30.00 50.00
66 Paul Thompson 15.00 25.00
67 Louis Trudel 15.00 25.00
68 Carl Voss 15.00 25.00
69 Art Wiebe 15.00 25.00
70 Roy Worters 25.00 40.00

1935-36 Diamond Matchbooks Tan 2

The Type 2 covers are similar to the Type 1 tan-bordered set except that the player's position or team affiliation information has been omitted from the reverse side. "The Diamond Match Co., NYC" imprint appears in a single line. As complete matchbooks are fairly scarce, they carry a premium of 50 percent over the prices below.

COMPLETE SET (63) 1100.00 1800.00
1 Tommy Anderson 15.00 25.00
2 Vern Ayres 15.00 25.00
3 Frank Boucher 25.00 40.00
4 Frank Boucher 25.00 40.00
5 Bill Brydge 15.00 25.00
6 Marty Burke 15.00 25.00
7 Lorne Carr 15.00 25.00
8 Lorne Chabot 25.00 40.00
9 Art Chapman 15.00 25.00
10 Bert Connolly 15.00 25.00
11 Bill Cook 25.00 40.00
12 Bill Cook 25.00 40.00
13 Bun Cook 25.00 40.00
14 Tommy Cook 15.00 25.00
15 Art Coulter 15.00 25.00
16 Lolo Couture 15.00 25.00
17 Wilf Cude 25.00 40.00
18 Cecil Dillon 15.00 25.00
19 Cecil Dillon 15.00 25.00
20 Red Dutton 25.00 40.00
21 Hap Emms 25.00 40.00
22 Irv Frew 15.00 25.00
23 Johnny Gagnon 15.00 25.00
24 Leroy Goldsworthy 15.00 25.00
25 Johnny Gottselig 15.00 25.00
26 Paul Haynes 15.00 25.00
27 Ott Heller 15.00 25.00
28 Irving Jaffee 15.00 25.00
recently confirmed
29 Joe Jerwa 15.00 25.00
30 Ching Johnson 25.00 40.00
31 Aurel Joliat 30.00 50.00
32 Butch Keeling 15.00 25.00
33 William Kendall 15.00 25.00
34 Davey Kerr 25.00 40.00
35 Lloyd Klein 15.00 25.00
36 Wildor Larochelle 15.00 25.00
37 Pit Lepine 15.00 25.00
38 Arthur Lesieur 15.00 25.00
39 Alex Levinsky 15.00 25.00
40 Alex Levinsky 15.00 25.00
41 Norm Locking 15.00 25.00
42 Georges Mantha 25.00 40.00
43 Sylvio Mantha 25.00 40.00
44 Mush Marsh 15.00 25.00
45 Charlie Mason 15.00 25.00
46 Donnie McFadyen 15.00 25.00
47 Jack McGill 15.00 25.00
48 Armand Mondou 15.00 25.00
49 Howie Morenz 180.00 300.00
50 Murray Murdoch 15.00 25.00
51 Al Murray 15.00 25.00
52 Harry Oliver 25.00 40.00
53 Eddie Ouellette 15.00 25.00
54 Lynn Patrick 25.00 40.00
55 Lynn Patrick 25.00 40.00
56 Paul Runge 15.00 25.00
57 Sweeney Schriner 25.00 40.00
58 Art Somers 15.00 25.00
59 Harold Starr 15.00 25.00
recently confirmed
60 Nels Stewart 30.00 50.00
61 Paul Thompson 15.00 25.00
62 Louis Trudel 15.00 25.00
63 Carl Voss 15.00 25.00
64 Art Wiebe 25.00 40.00
65 Roy Worters 25.00 40.00

1935-36 Diamond Matchbooks Tan 3

The Type 3 matchbook covers are almost identical to the Type 2 covers except that the manufacturer's imprint "Made In The USA/The Diamond Match Co. NYC" is a double line designation. Complete matchbooks are rarely scarce and carry a 50 percent premium over the prices below.

COMPLETE SET (60) 950.00 1600.00
1 Tommy Anderson 15.00 25.00
2 Vern Ayres 15.00 25.00
3 Frank Boucher 18.00 30.00
4 Bill Brydge 15.00 25.00
5 Marty Burke 15.00 25.00
6 Walter Buswell 15.00 25.00
7 Lorne Carr 15.00 25.00
8 Lorne Chabot 25.00 40.00
9 Art Chapman 15.00 25.00
10 Bert Connolly 15.00 25.00
11 Bill Cook 25.00 40.00
12 Bun Cook 25.00 40.00
13 Tommy Cook 18.00 30.00
14 Art Coulter 15.00 25.00
15 Lolo Couture 15.00 25.00
16 Wilf Cude 18.00 30.00
17 Cecil Dillon 15.00 25.00
18 Red Dutton 18.00 30.00
19 Hap Emms 18.00 30.00
20 Irvin Frew 15.00 25.00
21 Johnny Gagnon 15.00 25.00
22 Leroy Goldsworthy 15.00 25.00
23 Johnny Gottselig 15.00 25.00
24 Paul Haynes 15.00 25.00
25 Ott Heller 15.00 25.00
26 Joe Jerwa 15.00 25.00
27 Ching Johnson 25.00 40.00
28 Aurel Joliat 30.00 50.00
29 Mike Karakas 18.00 30.00
30 Butch Keeling 18.00 30.00
31 Dave Kerr 18.00 30.00
32 Lloyd Klein 15.00 25.00
33 Wildor Larochelle 18.00 30.00
34 Pit Lepine 15.00 25.00
35 Arthur Lesieur 15.00 25.00
36 Alex Levinsky 18.00 30.00
37 Norman Locking 15.00 25.00
38 George Mantha 25.00 40.00
39 Sylvio Mantha 25.00 40.00
40 Harold Mush March 18.00 30.00
41 Charlie Mason 15.00 25.00
42 Charlie Mason 15.00 25.00
43 Donnie McFadyen 15.00 25.00
44 Jack McGill 15.00 25.00
45 Armand Mondou 15.00 25.00
46 Howie Morenz 180.00 300.00
47 Murray Murdoch 15.00 25.00
48 Al Murray 15.00 25.00
49 Harry Oliver 25.00 40.00
50 Eddie Ouellette 15.00 25.00
51 Lynn Patrick 25.00 40.00
52 Paul Runge 15.00 25.00
53 Sweeney Schriner 25.00 40.00
54 Harold Starr 15.00 25.00
recently confirmed
55 Nels Stewart 30.00 50.00
56 Paul Thompson 15.00 25.00
57 Louis Trudel 15.00 25.00
58 Carl Voss 18.00 30.00
59 Art Wiebe 18.00 30.00
60 Roy Worters 18.00 30.00

1935-36 Diamond Matchbooks Tan 4

This tan-bordered issue is comprised only of Chicago Blackhawks players. The set is similar to Type 1 in that the player's team name appears between the player's name and bio on the reverse. The "Made in USA/The Diamond Match Co., NYC" imprint appears on two lines. Complete matchbooks carry a 50 percent premium.

COMPLETE SET (15) 180.00 300.00
1 Andy Blair 15.00 25.00
2 Glenn Brydson 15.00 25.00
3 Marty Burke 15.00 25.00
4 Tommy Cook 18.00 30.00
5 Johnny Gottselig 15.00 25.00
6 Harold Jackson 15.00 25.00
7 Mike Karakas 18.00 30.00
8 Wildor Larochelle 18.00 30.00
9 Alex Levinsky 18.00 30.00
10 Clem Loughlin 15.00 25.00
11 Harold March 18.00 30.00
12 Earl Seibert 25.00 40.00
13 Paul Thompson 15.00 25.00
14 Louis Trudel 15.00 25.00
15 Art Wiebe 18.00 30.00

1935-36 Diamond Matchbooks Tan 5

This tan-bordered set features only players from the Chicago Blackhawks. This is the hardest match cover issue to distinguish. The difference is that the team name is not featured between the player's name and his bio on the reverse. Complete matchbooks carry a 50 percent premium over the prices listed below.

COMPLETE SET (14) 125.00 200.00
1 Glenn Brydson 15.00 25.00
2 Marty Burke 15.00 25.00
3 Tommy Cook 15.00 25.00
4 Cully Dahlstrom 15.00 25.00
5 Johnny Gottselig 15.00 25.00
6 Vic Heyliger 15.00 25.00
7 Mike Karakas 15.00 25.00
8 Alex Levinsky 15.00 25.00
9 Harold March 15.00 25.00
10 Earl Seibert 15.00 25.00
11 William J. Stewart 15.00 25.00
12 Paul Thompson 15.00 25.00
13 Louis Trudel 15.00 25.00
14 Art Wiebe 15.00 25.00

1937 Diamond Matchbooks Tan 6

This 14-matchbook set is actually a reissue of the Type 5 Blackhawks set, and was released one year later. The only difference between the two series is that the reissued matchbooks have black match tips while the Type 5 issue has tan match tips. Complete matchbooks carry a 50 percent premium over the prices listed below.

COMPLETE SET (14) 150.00 250.00
1 Glenn Brydson 15.00 25.00
2 Martin A. Burke 15.00 25.00
3 Tom Cook 15.00 25.00
4 Cully Dahlstrom 15.00 25.00
5 Johnny Gottselig 15.00 25.00
6 Vic Heyliger 15.00 25.00
7 Mike Karakas 15.00 25.00
8 Alex Levinsky 15.00 25.00
9 Harold March 15.00 25.00
10 Earl Seibert 18.00 30.00
11 William J. Stewart 15.00 25.00
12 Paul Thompson 15.00 25.00
13 Louis Trudel 15.00 25.00
14 Art Wiebe 15.00 25.00

1972-83 Dimanche/Derniere Heure *

The blank-backed photo sheets in this multi-sport set measure approximately 8 1/2" by 11" and feature white-bordered color sports star photos from Dimanche Derniere Heure, a Montreal newspaper. The player's name, position and biographical information appear within the lower white margin. All text is in French. A white vinyl album was available for storing the photo sheets. Printed on the album's spine are the words, "Mes Vedettes du Sport" (My Stars of Sport). The photos are unnumbered and are checklisted below in alphabetical order according to sport or team as follows: Montreal Expos baseball players (1-117; National League baseball players (118-130); Montreal Canadiens hockey players (131-177); wrestlers (178-202); prize fighters (203-204); auto racing drivers (250-208); women's golf (209); Patof the circus clown (210); and CFL (211-278).

131 Chuck Arnason .78 1.56
132 Jean Beliveau VP 2.50 5.00
133 Pierre Bouchard .78 1.56
(Action)
134 Pierre Bouchard .78 1.56
(Posed)
135 Scotty Bowman CO 2.50 5.00
136 Yvan Cournoyer 2.50 5.00
(Action)
137 Yvan Cournoyer 2.50 5.00
(Posed)
138 Ken Dryden 5.00 10.00
139 Bob Gainey 2.50 5.00
140 Dale Hoganson .78 1.56
141 Rejean Houle 1.00 2.00
142 Guy Lafleur 5.00 10.00

Card		
(Action)		
143 Guy Lafleur (Posed)	5.00	10.00
144 Yvon Lambert	1.00	2.00
145 Jacques Laperriere (Action)	2.50	5.00
146 Jacques Laperriere (Posed)	2.50	5.00
147 Guy Lapointe (Action)	2.50	5.00
148 Guy Lapointe (Posed)	2.50	5.00
149 Michel Larocque	1.22	2.44
150 Claude Larose (Action)	1.00	2.00
151 Claude Larose (Posed)	1.00	2.00
152 Chuck Lefley (Action)	.78	1.56
153 Chuck Lefley (Posed)	.78	1.56
154 Jacques Lemaire (Action)	2.50	5.00
155 Jacques Lemaire (Posed)	2.50	5.00
156 Frank Mahovlich (Action)	3.00	6.00
157 Frank Mahovlich (Posed)	3.00	6.00
158 Pete Mahovlich (Action)	1.50	3.00
159 Pete Mahovlich (Posed)	1.50	3.00
160 Bob J. Murdoch	.78	1.56
161 Michel Plasse (Action)	1.22	2.44
162 Michel Plasse (Posed)	1.22	2.44
163 Henri Richard (Action)	3.00	6.00
164 Henri Richard (Posed)	3.00	6.00
165 Jim Roberts (Action)	1.00	2.00
166 Jim Roberts (Posed)	1.00	2.00
167 Larry Robinson (Action)	3.00	6.00
168 Larry Robinson (Posed)	3.00	6.00
169 Serge Savard (Action)	2.50	5.00
170 Serge Savard (Posed)	2.50	5.00
171 Steve Shutt (Action)	2.50	5.00
172 Steve Shutt (Posed)	2.50	5.00
173 Marc Tardif	1.00	2.00
174 Wayne Thomas (Action)	.78	1.56
175 Wayne Thomas (Posed)	1.00	2.00
176 Murray Wilson (Action)	.78	1.56
177 Murray Wilson (Posed)	.78	1.56

1992 Disney Mighty Ducks Movie

Issued to promote the Walt Disney movie "The Mighty Ducks", this eight-card set measures approximately 3 1/2" by 6" and is designed in the postcard format. Each card is perforated; the left portion, measuring the standard size, displays a full-bleed color photo, while the right portion is a solid neon color with a box for the stamp at the upper right. The back of the trading card portion has a brief player profile, while the other portion has an advertisement for the movie. The cards are unnumbered and checklisted below in alphabetical order. The character's name in the movie is given on the continuation line.

Card		
COMPLETE SET (8)	16.00	40.00
1 Brandon Adams Jesse	2.00	5.00
2 Emilio Estevez Coach Bombay	2.50	6.00
3 Joshua Jackson Charlie	3.00	8.00
4 Marguerite Moreau Connie	2.00	5.00
5 Elden Ratliff Fulton	2.00	5.00
6 Shaun Weiss Goldberg	2.00	5.00
7 Rollerblading in Shopping Mall	2.00	5.00
8 Team Photo	2.00	5.00

1925 Dominion Chocolates

This set consisted of 120 multi-sport cards, 32 of which were hockey. The cards were black and white and measured approx. 3" x 1 1/4".

COMMON CARD	200.00
13 Granite Club Olympic Champs	200.00
28 North Ontario Team	200.00
35 Peterborough Team	200.00
49 Owen Sound Jrs.	200.00
55 E.J. Collett	200.00
56 Hughie J. Fox	200.00
57 Dunc Munro	200.00
58 M.Rutherford	200.00
59 Beattie Ramsay	200.00
60 Bert McCaffrey	200.00
61 Soo Greyhounds	200.00
68 J.P. Aggatts	200.00
69 Hooley Smith	350.00
70 J.Cameron	200.00
81 William Fraser	200.00
82 Vernon Forbes	200.00
83 Shorty Green	300.00
84 Red Green	200.00
86 Jack Langtry	200.00
89 Billy Coutu	200.00
92 Jack Hughes	200.00
95 Edouard Lalonde	500.00
101 Bill Brydge	200.00
103 Cecil Browne	200.00
106 Red Porter	200.00
112 North Bay Team	200.00
113 Ross Somerville	200.00
114 Harry Watson	250.00
117 Odie Cleghorn UER First Name Spelled Ogie	200.00
118 Lionel Conacher	500.00
119 Aurel Joliat	800.00
120 Georges Vezina	1500.00

1993-94 Donruss

These 510 standard-size cards feature borderless color player action shots on their fronts. The player's name appears in gold foil within a team-color-coded stripe near the bottom. His team logo rests in a lower corner. The backs, some of which are horizontal, carry another borderless color player action shot. The player's name, team, position, and biography are shown within a black rectangle on the left. His statistics appear in ghosted strips below or alongside. Production of the Update set (401-510) was limited to 4,000 cases. Rookie Cards include Jason Arnott, Chris Osgood, Jocelyn Thibault and German Titov.

Card		
COMPLETE SET (510)	8.00	20.00
COMP.SERIES 1 (400)	5.00	15.00
COMP.UPDATE SET (110)	2.00	5.00
1 Steven King	.02	.10
2 Joe Sacco	.02	.10
3 Anatoli Semenov	.02	.10
4 Terry Yake	.02	.10
5 Alexei Kasatonov	.02	.10
6 Patrik Carnback RC	.02	.10
7 Sean Hill	.02	.10
8 Bill Houlder	.02	.10
9 Todd Ewen	.02	.10
10 Bob Corkum	.02	.10
11 Tim Sweeney	.02	.10
12 Ron Tugnutt	.05	.15
13 Guy Hebert	.05	.15
14 Shaun Van Allen	.02	.10
15 Stu Grimson	.02	.10
16 Jon Casey	.05	.15
17 Dan Marois	.02	.10
18 Adam Oates	.05	.15
19 Glen Wesley	.02	.10
20 Cam Stewart RC	.02	.10
21 Don Sweeney	.02	.10
22 Glen Murray	.02	.10
23 Jozef Stumpel	.02	.10
24 Ray Bourque	.20	.50
25 Ted Donato	.02	.10
26 Joe Juneau	.05	.15
27 Dmitri Kvartalnov	.02	.10
28 Steve Leach	.02	.10
29 Cam Neely	.10	.30
30 Bryan Smolinski	.02	.10
31 Craig Simpson	.02	.10
32 Donald Audette	.02	.10
33 Doug Bodger	.02	.10
34 Grant Fuhr	.05	.15
35 Dale Hawerchuk	.05	.15
36 Yuri Khmylev	.02	.10
37 Pat LaFontaine	.10	.30
38 Brad May	.05	.15
39 Alexander Mogilny	.05	.15
40 Richard Smehlik	.02	.10
41 Petr Svoboda	.02	.10
42 Matthew Barnaby	.05	.15
43 Sergei Petrenko	.02	.10
44 Mark Astley RC	.02	.10
45 Derek Plante RC	.02	.10
46 Theo Fleury	.02	.10
47 Al MacInnis	.05	.15
48 Joe Nieuwendyk	.05	.15
49 Joel Otto	.02	.10
50 Paul Ranheim	.02	.10
51 Robert Reichel	.02	.10
52 Gary Roberts	.02	.10
53 Gary Suter	.02	.10
54 Mike Vernon	.05	.15
55 Kelly Kisio	.02	.10
56 German Titov RC	.02	.10
57 Wes Walz	.02	.10
58 Ted Drury	.02	.10
59 Sandy McCarthy	.02	.10
60 Vesa Viitakoski RC	.02	.10
61 Jeff Hackett	.05	.15
62 Neil Wilkinson	.02	.10
63 Dirk Graham	.02	.10
64 Ed Belfour	.10	.30
65 Chris Chelios	.10	.30
66 Joe Murphy	.02	.10
67 Jeremy Roenick	.15	.40
68 Steve Smith	.02	.10
69 Brent Sutter	.02	.10
70 Steve Dubinsky RC	.02	.10
71 Michel Goulet	.05	.15
72 Christian Ruuttu	.02	.10
73 Bryan Marchment	.02	.10
74 Sergei Krivokrasov	.02	.10
75 Jeff Shantz RC	.02	.10
76 Mike Modano	.20	.50
77 Derian Hatcher	.02	.10
78 Ulf Dahlen	.02	.10
79 Mark Tinordi	.02	.10
80 Russ Courtnall	.02	.10
81 Mike Craig	.02	.10
82 Trent Klatt	.02	.10
83 Dave Gagner	.05	.15
84 Chris Tancill	.02	.10
85 James Black	.02	.10
86 Dean Evason	.02	.10
87 Andy Moog	.05	.15
88 Paul Cavallini	.02	.10
89 Grant Ledyard	.02	.10
90 Jarkko Varvio	.02	.10
91 Slava Kozlov	.05	.15
92 Mike Sillinger	.02	.10
93 Aaron Ward RC	.02	.10
94 Greg Johnson	.02	.10
95 Steve Yzerman	.60	1.50
96 Tim Cheveldae	.05	.15
97 Steve Chiasson	.02	.10
98 Dino Ciccarelli	.05	.15
99 Paul Coffey	.10	.30
100 Dallas Drake RC	.02	.10
101 Sergei Fedorov	.20	.50
102 Nicklas Lidstrom	.10	.30
103 Darren McCarty RC	.25	.60
104 Bob Probert	.05	.15
105 Ray Sheppard	.05	.15
106 Scott Pearson	.02	.10
107 Steven Rice	.02	.10
108 Louie DeBrusk	.02	.10
109 Dave Manson	.02	.10
110 Dean McAmmond	.02	.10
111 Roman Oksiuta RC	.02	.10
112 Geoff Smith	.02	.10
113 Zdeno Ciger	.02	.10
114 Shayne Corson	.02	.10
115 Luke Richardson	.02	.10
116 Igor Kravchuk	.02	.10
117 Bill Ranford	.05	.15
118 Doug Weight	.05	.15
119 Fred Brathwaite RC	.25	.60
120 Jason Arnott RC	.60	1.50
121 Tom Fitzgerald	.02	.10
122 Mike Hough	.02	.10
123 Jesse Belanger	.02	.10
124 Brian Skrudland	.02	.10
125 Dave Lowry	.02	.10
126 Scott Mellanby	.05	.15
127 Evgeny Davydov	.02	.10
128 Andrei Lomakin	.02	.10
129 Brian Benning	.02	.10
130 Scott Levins RC	.02	.10
131 Gord Murphy	.02	.10
132 John Vanbiesbrouck	.05	.15
133 Mark Fitzpatrick	.05	.15
134 Rob Niedermayer	.05	.15
135 Alexander Godynyuk	.02	.10
136 Eric Weinrich	.02	.10
137 Mark Greig	.02	.10
138 Jim Sandlak	.02	.10
139 Adam Burt	.02	.10
140 Nick Kypreos	.02	.10
141 Sean Burke	.05	.15
142 Andrew Cassels	.02	.10
143 Robert Kron	.02	.10
144 Michael Nylander	.02	.10
145 Robert Petrovicky	.02	.10
146 Patrick Poulin	.02	.10
147 Geoff Sanderson	.05	.15
148 Pat Verbeek	.02	.10
149 Zarley Zalapski	.02	.10
150 Chris Pronger	.15	.40
151 Jari Kurri	.10	.30
152 Wayne Gretzky	.75	2.00
153 Pat Conacher	.02	.10
154 Shawn McEachern	.02	.10
155 Mike Donnelly	.02	.10
156 Warren Rychel	.02	.10
157 Gary Shuchuk	.02	.10
158 Rob Blake	.05	.15
159 Jimmy Carson	.02	.10
160 Tony Granato	.02	.10
161 Kelly Hrudey	.05	.15
162 Luc Robitaille	.05	.15
163 Tomas Sandstrom	.02	.10
164 Darryl Sydor	.02	.10
165 Alexei Zhitnik	.02	.10
166 Benoit Brunet	.02	.10
167 Lyle Odelein	.02	.10
168 Kevin Haller	.02	.10
169 Pierre Sevigny	.02	.10
170 Brian Bellows	.02	.10
171 Patrice Brisebois	.02	.10
172 Vincent Damphousse	.02	.10
173 Eric Desjardins	.05	.15
174 Gilbert Dionne	.02	.10
175 Stephan Lebeau	.02	.10
176 John LeClair	.10	.30
177 Kirk Muller	.02	.10
178 Patrick Roy	.60	1.50
179 Mathieu Schneider	.02	.10
180 Peter Popovic RC	.02	.10
181 Corey Millen	.02	.10
182 Jason Smith RC	.02	.10
183 Bobby Holik	.02	.10
184 John MacLean	.05	.15
185 Bruce Driver	.02	.10
186 Bill Guerin	.02	.10
187 Claude Lemieux	.02	.10
188 Bernie Nicholls	.02	.10
189 Scott Niedermayer	.02	.10
190 Stephane Richer	.05	.15
191 Alexander Semak	.02	.10
192 Scott Stevens	.05	.15
193 Valeri Zelepukin	.02	.10
194 Chris Terreri	.05	.15
195 Martin Brodeur	.40	1.00
196 Ron Hextall	.05	.15
197 Brad Dalgarno	.02	.10
198 Ray Ferraro	.02	.10
199 Patrick Flatley	.02	.10
200 Travis Green	.05	.15
201 Benoit Hogue	.02	.10
202 Steve Junker RC	.02	.10
203 Darius Kasparaitis	.02	.10
204 Derek King	.02	.10
205 Uwe Krupp	.02	.10
206 Scott Lachance	.02	.10
207 Vladimir Malakhov	.02	.10
208 Steve Thomas	.02	.10
209 Pierre Turgeon	.05	.15
210 Scott Scissons	.02	.10
211 Glenn Healy	.05	.15
212 Alexander Karpovtsev	.02	.10
213 James Patrick	.02	.10
214 Sergei Nemchinov	.02	.10
215 Esa Tikkanen	.02	.10
216 Corey Hirsch	.05	.15
217 Tony Amonte	.05	.15
218 Mike Gartner	.05	.15
219 Adam Graves	.02	.10
220 Alexei Kovalev	.05	.15
221 Brian Leetch	.10	.30
222 Mark Messier	.10	.30
223 Mike Richter	.10	.30
224 Darren Turcotte	.02	.10
225 Sergei Zubov	.02	.10
226 Craig Billington	.05	.15
227 Troy Mallette	.02	.10
228 Vladimir Ruzicka	.02	.10
229 Darrin Madeley RC	.02	.10
230 Mark Lamb	.02	.10
231 Dave Archibald	.02	.10
232 Bob Kudelski	.02	.10
233 Norm Maciver	.02	.10
234 Brad Shaw	.02	.10
235 Sylvain Turgeon	.02	.10
236 Brian Glynn	.02	.10
237 Alexandre Daigle	.02	.10
238 Alexei Yashin	.02	.10
239 Dimitri Filimonov	.02	.10
240 Pavol Demitra	.05	.15
241 Jason Bowen	.02	.10
242 Eric Lindros	.10	.30
243 Dominic Roussel	.05	.15
244 Milos Holan RC	.02	.10
245 Greg Hawgood	.02	.10
246 Yves Racine	.02	.10
247 Josef Beranek	.02	.10
248 Rod Brind'Amour	.05	.15
249 Kevin Dineen	.02	.10
250 Pelle Eklund	.02	.10
251 Garry Galley	.02	.10
252 Mark Recchi	.05	.15
253 Tommy Soderstrom	.05	.15
254 Dimitri Yushkevich	.02	.10
255 Mikael Renberg	.10	.30
256 Marty McSorley	.02	.10
257 Joe Mullen	.05	.15
258 Doug Brown	.02	.10
259 Kjell Samuelsson	.02	.10
260 Tom Barrasso	.05	.15
261 Ron Francis	.05	.15
262 Mario Lemieux	.60	1.50
263 Larry Murphy	.05	.15
264 Ulf Samuelsson	.02	.10
265 Kevin Stevens	.02	.10
266 Martin Straka	.02	.10
267 Rick Tocchet	.05	.15
268 Bryan Trottier	.05	.15
269 Markus Naslund	.10	.30
270 Jaromir Jagr	.20	.50
271 Martin Gelinas	.02	.10
272 Adam Foote	.02	.10
273 Curtis Leschyshyn	.02	.10
274 Stephane Fiset	.05	.15
275 Jocelyn Thibault RC	.40	1.00
276 Steve Duchesne	.02	.10
277 Valeri Kamensky	.05	.15
278 Andrei Kovalenko	.02	.10
279 Owen Nolan	.05	.15
280 Mike Ricci	.02	.10
281 Martin Rucinsky	.02	.10
282 Joe Sakic	.25	.60
283 Mats Sundin	.10	.30
284 Scott Young	.02	.10
285 Claude Lapointe	.02	.10
286 Brett Hull	.15	.40
287 Vitali Karamnov	.02	.10
288 Ron Sutter	.02	.10
289 Garth Butcher	.02	.10
290 Vitali Prokhorov	.02	.10
291 Bret Hedican	.02	.10
292 Tony Hrkac	.02	.10
293 Jeff Brown	.02	.10
294 Phil Housley	.05	.15
295 Craig Janney	.05	.15
296 Curtis Joseph	.10	.30
297 Igor Korolev	.02	.10
298 Kevin Miller	.02	.10
299 Brendan Shanahan	.10	.30
300 Jim Montgomery RC	.02	.10
301 Gaetan Duchesne	.02	.10
302 Jimmy Waite	.05	.15
303 Jeff Norton	.02	.10
304 Sergei Makarov	.02	.10
305 Igor Larionov	.02	.10
306 Mike Lalor	.02	.10
307 Michal Sykora RC	.02	.10
308 Pat Falloon	.02	.10
309 Johan Garpenlov	.02	.10
310 Rob Gaudreau RC	.02	.10
311 Arturs Irbe	.05	.15
312 Sandis Ozolinsh	.02	.10
313 Doug Zmolek	.02	.10
314 Mike Rathje	.02	.10
315 Vlastimil Kroupa RC	.02	.10
316 Daren Puppa	.05	.15
317 Petr Klima	.02	.10
318 Brent Gretzky RC	.02	.10
319 Denis Savard	.05	.15
320 Garard Gallant	.02	.10
321 Joe Reekie	.02	.10
322 Mikael Andersson	.02	.10
323 Bill McDougall RC	.02	.10
324 Brian Bradley	.02	.10
325 Shawn Chambers	.02	.10
326 Adam Creighton	.02	.10
327 Roman Hamrlik	.05	.15
328 John Tucker	.02	.10
329 Rob Zamuner	.02	.10
330 Chris Gratton	.05	.15
331 Sylvain Lefebvre	.02	.10
332 Nikolai Borschevsky	.02	.10
333 Bob Rouse	.02	.10
334 John Cullen	.02	.10
335 Todd Gill	.02	.10
336 Drake Berehowsky	.02	.10
337 Wendel Clark	.05	.15
338 Peter Zezel	.02	.10
339 Rob Pearson	.02	.10
340 Glenn Anderson	.05	.15
341 Doug Gilmour	.05	.15
342 Dave Andreychuk	.05	.15
343 Felix Potvin	.10	.30
344 David Ellett	.02	.10
345 Alexei Kudashov RC	.02	.10
346 Gino Odjick	.02	.10
347 Jyrki Lumme	.02	.10
348 Dana Murzyn	.02	.10
349 Sergio Momesso	.02	.10
350 Greg Adams	.02	.10
351 Pavel Bure	.10	.30
352 Geoff Courtnall	.02	.10
353 Murray Craven	.02	.10
354 Trevor Linden	.05	.15
355 Kirk McLean	.05	.15
356 Petr Nedved	.05	.15
357 Cliff Ronning	.02	.10
358 Jiri Slegr	.02	.10
359 Kay Whitmore	.05	.15
360 Gerald Diduck	.02	.10
361 Pat Peake	.02	.10
362 Dave Poulin	.02	.10
363 Rick Tabaracci	.05	.15
364 Jason Woolley	.02	.10
365 Kelly Miller	.02	.10
366 Peter Bondra	.05	.15
367 Sylvain Cote	.02	.10
368 Pat Elynuik	.02	.10
369 Kevin Hatcher	.02	.10
370 Dale Hunter	.02	.10
371 Al Iafrate	.02	.10
372 Calle Johansson	.02	.10
373 Dimitri Khristich	.02	.10
374 Michal Pivonka	.02	.10
375 Mike Ridley	.02	.10
376 Paul Ysebaert	.02	.10
377 Stu Barnes	.02	.10
378 Sergei Bautin	.02	.10
379 Kris King	.02	.10
380 Alexei Zhamnov	.05	.15
381 Tie Domi	.05	.15
382 Bob Essensa	.05	.15
383 Nelson Emerson	.02	.10
384 Boris Mironov	.02	.10
385 Teppo Numminen	.02	.10
386 Fredrik Olausson	.02	.10
387 Teemu Selanne	.10	.30
388 Darrin Shannon	.02	.10
389 Thomas Steen	.02	.10
390 Keith Tkachuk	.10	.30
391 Opening Night Panthers	.30	.75
392 Opening Night-Ducks	.30	.75
393 Alexandre Daigle Chris Pronger Chris Gratton	.05	.15
394 Teemu Selanne Joe Juneau RB	.15	.40
395 Wayne Gretzky Luc Robitaille	.30	.75
396 Inserts Checklist	.02	.10
397 Atlantic Div. Checklist	.02	.10
398 Northeast Div. Checklist	.02	.10
399 Central Div. Checklist	.02	.10
400 Pacific Div. Checklist	.02	.10
401 Garry Valk	.02	.10
402 Al Iarante	.02	.10
403 David Reid	.02	.10
404 Jason Dawe	.02	.10
405 Craig Muni	.02	.10
406 Dan Keczmer RC	.02	.10
407 Michael Nylander	.02	.10
408 James Patrick	.02	.10
409 Andrei Trefilov	.02	.10
410 Zarley Zalapski	.02	.10
411 Tony Amonte	.05	.15
412 Keith Carney	.02	.10
413 Randy Cunneyworth	.02	.10
414 Ivan Droppa RC	.02	.10
415 Gary Suter	.02	.10
416 Eric Weinrich	.02	.10
417 Paul Ysebaert	.02	.10
418 Richard Matvichuk	.02	.10
419 Alan May	.02	.10
420 Darcy Wakaluk	.05	.15
421 Micah Aivazoff RC	.02	.10
422 Terry Carkner	.02	.10
423 Kris Draper	.02	.10
424 Chris Osgood RC	.60	1.50
425 Keith Primeau	.02	.10
426 Bob Beers	.02	.10
427 Ilya Byakin RC	.02	.10
428 Kirk Maltby RC	.02	.10
429 Boris Mironov	.02	.10
430 Fredrik Olausson	.02	.10
431 Peter White RC	.02	.10
432 Stu Barnes	.02	.10
433 Mike Foligno	.02	.10
434 Bob Kudelski	.02	.10
435 Geoff Smith	.02	.10
436 Igor Chibirev RC	.02	.10
437 Ted Drury	.02	.10
438 Alexander Godynyuk	.02	.10
439 Frank Kucera	.02	.10
440 Jocelyn Lemieux	.02	.10
441 Brian Propp	.02	.10
442 Paul Ranheim	.02	.10
443 Jeff Reese	.02	.10
444 Kevin Smyth RC	.02	.10
445 Jim Storm RC	.02	.10
446 Phil Crowe RC	.02	.10
447 Marty McSorley	.02	.10
448 Keith Redmond RC	.02	.10
449 Dixon Ward	.02	.10
450 Guy Carbonneau	.02	.10
451 Mike Keane	.02	.10
452 Oleg Petrov	.02	.10
453 Ron Tugnutt	.05	.15
454 Randy McKay	.02	.10
455 Jaroslav Modry RC	.02	.10
456 Yan Kaminsky	.02	.10
457 Marty McInnis	.02	.10
458 Jamie McLennan RC	.05	.15
459 Zigmund Palffy	.05	.15
460 Glenn Anderson	.05	.15
461 Steve Larmer	.05	.15
462 Craig MacTavish	.02	.10
463 Stephane Matteau	.02	.10
464 Brian Noonan	.02	.10
465 Mattias Norstrom RC	.02	.10
466 Scott Levins	.02	.10
467 Derek Mayer RC	.02	.10
468 Andy Schneider RC	.02	.10
469 Todd Hlushko RC	.02	.10
470 Stewart Malgunas RC	.02	.10
471 Justin Duberman RC	.02	.10
472 Ladislav Karabin RC	.02	.10
473 Shawn McEachern	.02	.10
474 Ed Patterson RC	.02	.10
475 Tomas Sandstrom	.02	.10
476 Bob Bassen	.02	.10
477 Garth Butcher	.02	.10
478 Iain Fraser RC	.02	.10
479 Mike McKee RC	.02	.10
480 Dwayne Norris RC	.02	.10
481 Garth Snow RC	.15	.40
482 Ron Sutter	.02	.10
483 Kelly Chase	.02	.10
484 Steve Duchesne	.02	.10
485 Daniel Laperrire	.02	.10
486 Petr Nedved	.05	.15
487 Peter Stastny	.05	.15
488 Ulf Dahlen	.02	.10
489 Todd Elik	.02	.10
490 Andrei Nazarov RC	.02	.10
491 Danton Cole	.02	.10
492 Chris Joseph	.02	.10
493 Chris LiPuma RC	.02	.10
494 Mike Gartner	.05	.15
495 Mark Greig	.02	.10
496 David Harlock	.02	.10
497 Matt Martin RC	.02	.10
498 Shawn Antoski	.02	.10
499 Jeff Brown	.02	.10
500 Jimmy Carson	.02	.10
501 Martin Gelinas	.02	.10
502 Yevgeny Namestnikov RC	.02	.10
503 Randy Burridge	.02	.10
504 Joe Juneau	.05	.15
505 Kevin Kaminski RC	.02	.10
506 Arto Blomsten	.02	.10
507 Tim Cheveldae	.05	.15
508 Dallas Drake	.02	.10
509 Dave Manson	.02	.10
510 Update Checklist	.02	.10

1993-94 Donruss Elite Inserts

These 15 cards feature on their fronts color player photos framed by diamond-shaped starburst designs set within dark marbleized inner borders and prismatic foil outer borders. The player's name appears within the lower prismatic foil margin. The back carries the player's name, career highlights, and a color head shot, all set on a dark marbleized background framed by a silver border. The 10 first-series Elite cards (1-10) were random inserts in '93-94 Donruss Series 1 packs. The five Elite Update cards (U1-U5) were randomly inserted in Donruss Update packs. All Elite cards are individually numbered on the back and have a production limited to 10,000 of each.

Card		
COMPLETE SET (10)	30.00	60.00
1 Mario Lemieux	5.00	12.00
2 Alexandre Daigle	1.25	3.00
3 Teemu Selanne	1.25	3.00
4 Eric Lindros	1.25	3.00
5 Brett Hull	2.00	5.00
6 Jeremy Roenick	1.50	4.00
7 Doug Gilmour	1.25	3.00
8 Alexander Mogilny	1.25	3.00
9 Patrick Roy	5.00	12.00
10 Wayne Gretzky	6.00	15.00
U1 Mikael Renberg	1.25	3.00
U2 Sergei Fedorov	1.50	4.00
U3 Felix Potvin	1.25	3.00
U4 Cam Neely	1.25	3.00
U5 Alexei Yashin	1.25	3.00

1993-94 Donruss Ice Kings

Randomly inserted in Series 1 packs, these 10 cards feature on their fronts borderless color player drawings by noted sports artist Dick Perez. The player's name, his team's logo, and the year, 1994, appear within a blue banner near the bottom. The blue-bordered back carries the player's career highlights on a ghosted representation of a hockey rink. The cards are numbered on the back as "X of 10."

Card		
COMPLETE SET (10)	12.50	25.00
1 Patrick Roy	2.00	5.00
2 Pat LaFontaine	.40	1.00
3 Jaromir Jagr	.60	1.50
4 Wayne Gretzky	2.50	6.00
5 Chris Chelios	.40	1.00
6 Felix Potvin	.40	1.00
7 Mario Lemieux	2.00	5.00
8 Pavel Bure	.40	1.00
9 Eric Lindros	.40	1.00
10 Teemu Selanne	.40	1.00

1993-94 Donruss Rated Rookies

Randomly inserted in Series 1 packs, these 15 cards have borderless fronts that feature color player action shots on motion streaked backgrounds. The player's name appears at the top. On its right side, the black horizontal back carries a color player action cutout superposed upon his team's logo. Biography and career highlights are shown alongside on the left. The cards are numbered on the back as "X of 15."

Card		
COMPLETE SET (15)	6.00	15.00
1 Alexandre Daigle	.20	.50
2 Chris Gratton	.30	.75
3 Chris Pronger	.75	2.00
4 Rob Niedermayer	.30	.75
5 Mikael Renberg	.30	.75
6 Jarkko Varvio	.20	.50
7 Alexei Yashin	.20	.50
8 Markus Naslund	.60	1.50
9 Boris Mironov	.20	.50
10 Martin Brodeur	2.00	5.00
11 Jocelyn Thibault	.60	1.50
12 Jason Arnott	.75	2.00
13 Jim Montgomery	.20	.50
14 Ted Drury	.20	.50
15 Roman Oksiuta	.20	.50

1993-94 Donruss Special Print

Randomly inserted in Series 1 packs, these 26 cards feature on their fronts color player action shots that are borderless, except at the bottom, where the black edge carries the player's name in white cursive lettering. The prismatic foil set logo rests in a lower corner. The words "Special Print 1 of 20,000" appear in prismatic foil across the top.The cards are numbered, or rather lettered (A-Z), on the back. Two additional unnumbered special print cards (Robitaille WC and Lemieux EC) could be found at the rate of 1:360 packs.

Card		
COMPLETE SET (26)	30.00	80.00
A Ron Tugnutt	.60	1.50
B Adam Oates	.60	1.50
C Alexander Mogilny	.60	1.50
D Theo Fleury	.40	1.00
E Jeremy Roenick	1.50	4.00
F Mike Modano	1.50	4.00
G Steve Yzerman	4.00	10.00
H Jason Arnott	.60	1.50
I Rob Niedermayer	.60	1.50
J Chris Pronger	1.50	4.00
K Wayne Gretzky	6.00	15.00
L Patrick Roy	5.00	12.00
M Scott Niedermayer	.40	1.00
N Pierre Turgeon	.60	1.50
O Mark Messier	1.25	3.00
P Alexandre Daigle	.40	1.00
Q Eric Lindros	1.25	3.00
R Mario Lemieux	5.00	12.00
S Mats Sundin	1.25	3.00
T Pat Falloon	.40	1.00
U Brett Hull	1.50	4.00
V Chris Gratton	.60	1.50
W Felix Potvin	1.25	3.00
X Pavel Bure	1.25	3.00
Y Al Iafrate	.40	1.00
Z Teemu Selanne	1.25	3.00
NNO Luc Robitaille WC	1.50	4.00
NNO Mario Lemieux EC	5.00	12.00

1993-94 Donruss Team Canada

One of these 22 (or one of the 22 Team USA) cards were inserted in every 1993-94 Donruss Update pack. The front of each card features a player action cutout set on a red metallic background highlighted by a world map. The player's name appears at the upper left. The horizontal back carries a color player action shot on the right side. Below the photo are the player's statistics from his 1994 World Junior Championships play. On the left side are the player's name, position, biography, and NHL status. The cards are numbered on the back as "X of 22." The unnumbered checklist car

ries the 22 Team Canada cards, as well as the 22 Team USA cards.

COMPLETE SET (22) 5.00 10.00
1 Jason Allison .40 1.00
2 Chris Armstrong .20 .50
3 Drew Bannister .20 .50
4 Jason Botterill .20 .50
5 Joel Bouchard .20 .50
6 Curtis Bowen .20 .50
7 Anson Carter .60 1.50
8 Brandon Convery .20 .50
9 Yannick Dube .20 .50
10 Manny Fernandez .75 2.00
11 Jeff Friesen .20 .50
12 Aaron Gavey .20 .50
13 Martin Gendron .20 .50
14 Rick Girard .20 .50
15 Todd Harvey .40 1.00
16 Bryan McCabe .40 1.00
17 Marty Murray .20 .50
18 Mike Peca .60 1.50
19 Nick Stajduhar .20 .50
20 Jamie Storr .40 1.00
21 Brent Tully .20 .50
22 Brendan Witt .40 1.00
NNO WJC Checklist .20 .50

1993-94 Donruss Team USA

One of these 22 (or one of the 22 Team Canada) cards were inserted in every 1993-94 Donruss Update pack. The front of each card features a player action cutout set on a blue metallic background highlighted by a world map. The player's name appears at the upper left. The horizontal back carries a color player action shot on the right side. Below the photo are the player's statistics from his 1994 World Junior Championships play. On the left side are the player's name, position, biography, and NHL status. The cards are numbered on the back as "X of 22." The unnumbered checklist carries the 22 Team Canada cards, as well as the 22 Team USA cards.

COMPLETE SET (22) 3.00 8.00
1 Kevyn Adams .20 .50
2 Jason Bonsignore .20 .50
3 Andy Brink .20 .50
4 Jon Coleman .20 .50
5 Adam Deadmarsh .20 .50
6 Aaron Ellis .20 .50
7 John Emmons .20 .50
8 Ashlin Halfnight .20 .50
9 Kevin Hilton .20 .50
10 Jason Karmanos .20 .50
11 Toby Kvalevog .20 .50
12 Bob Lachance .20 .50
13 Jamie Langenbrunner .40 1.00
14 Jason McBain .20 .50
15 Chris O'Sullivan .20 .50
16 Jay Pandolfo .20 .50
17 Richard Park .20 .50
18 Deron Quint .20 .50
19 Ryan Sittler .20 .50
20 Blake Sloan .20 .50
21 John Varga .20 .50
22 David Wilkie .20 .50
NNO WJC Checklist .20 .50

1994-95 Donruss

This 330-card standard-size set was issued in one series. Cards were issued in 12-card hobby packs and 18-card jumbo packs. Fronts feature a near full-bleed design, other than the bottom right corner which displays player name, set name, and position stamped in a silver foil sunburst design. This silver foil area is very difficult to read. Backs feature two additional photos, team logo, and single season stats. Rookie Cards in the set include Mariusz Czerkawski, Mikhail Shtalenkov and John Gruden.

COMPLETE SET (330) 6.00 15.00
1 Steve Yzerman .60 1.50
2 Paul Ysebaert .02 .10
3 Doug Weight .05 .15
4 Trevor Kidd .05 .15
5 Mario Lemieux .60 1.50
6 Andrei Kovalenko .02 .10
7 Arturs Irbe .05 .15
8 Doug Gilmour .05 .15
9 Mark Messier .10 .30
10 Milos Holan .02 .10
11 Kevin Miller .02 .10
12 Felix Potvin .10 .30
13 Josef Beranek .02 .10
14 Mikael Andersson .02 .10
15 Stephane Matteau .02 .10
16 Todd Simon RC .02 .10
17 Darcy Wakaluk .05 .15
18 Kelly Buchberger .02 .10
19 Pavel Bure .10 .30
20 Dave Lowry .02 .10
21 Bryan Smolinski .02 .10
22 Kirk McLean .05 .15
23 Pierre Turgeon .05 .15
24 Martin Brodeur .30 .75
25 Jason Arnott .02 .10
26 Steve Dubinsky .02 .10
27 Larry Murphy .05 .15
28 Craig Janney .05 .15
29 Patrik Carnback .02 .10
30 Derek King .02 .10
31 Peter Bondra .05 .15
32 Jason Bowen .02 .10
33 Maxim Bets .02 .10
34 Matt Martin .02 .10
35 Jeff Hackett .05 .15
36 Kevin Dineen .02 .10
37 Trent Klatt .02 .10
38 Joe Murphy .02 .10
39 Sandy McCarthy .02 .10
40 Brian Bradley .02 .10
41 Scott Lachance .02 .10
42 Scott Mellanby .05 .15
43 Adam Graves .02 .10
44 Dale Hawerchuk .05 .15
45 Owen Nolan .05 .15
46 Keith Primeau .02 .10
47 Jim Dowd .02 .10
48 Dan Plante RC .02 .10
49 Rick Tabaracci .05 .15
50 Geoff Courtnall .02 .10
51 Markus Naslund .10 .30
52 Kelly Miller .02 .10
53 Kirk Maltby .02 .10
54 Paul Coffey .10 .30
55 Gord Murphy .02 .10
56 Joe Nieuwendyk .05 .15
57 Ulf Dahlen .02 .10
58 Dmitri Mironov .02 .10
59 Kevin Smyth .02 .10
60 Tie Domi .05 .15
61 Oleg Petrov .02 .10
62 Bill Guerin .05 .15
63 Alexei Yashin .02 .10
64 Joe Sacco .02 .10
65 Aris Brimanis RC .02 .10
66 Randy Burridge .02 .10
67 Neal Broten .05 .15
68 Ray Bourque .20 .50
69 Ron Tugnutt .05 .15
70 Darryl Sydor .02 .10
71 Jocelyn Thibault .10 .30
72 Shawn Chambers .02 .10
73 Alexei Zhamnov .05 .15
74 Michael Nylander .02 .10
75 Travis Green .05 .15
76 Brad May .02 .10
77 Geoff Sanderson .05 .15
78 Derek Plante .02 .10
79 Stephane Richer .05 .15
80 Rod Brind'Amour .05 .15
81 Guy Hebert .05 .15
82 Claude Lemieux .02 .10
83 Pat Falloon .02 .10
84 Alexei Kudashov .02 .10
85 Andrei Lomakin .02 .10
86 Dino Ciccarelli .05 .15
87 John Tucker .02 .10
88 Jamie McLennan .05 .15
89 Peter Taglianetti .02 .10
90 Bobby Holik .02 .10
91 Sergei Krivokrasov .02 .10
92 Alexander Mogilny .05 .15
93 Jari Kurri .05 .15
94 Dominik Hasek .30 .75
95 Shawn McEachern .02 .10
96 Bob Corkum .02 .10
97 Dimitri Filimonov .02 .10
98 John LeClair .10 .30
99 Theo Fleury .02 .10
100 Daren Puppa .05 .15
101 Greg Adams .02 .10
102 Joel Otto .02 .10
103 Sergei Makarov .05 .15
104 Mike Ricci .02 .10
105 Sylvain Turgeon .02 .10
106 Igor Larionov .02 .10
107 Tony Amonte .05 .15
108 Andy Moog .10 .30
109 Jeff Brown .02 .10
110 Checklist 1-83 .02 .10
111 Mike Gartner .05 .15
112 Craig Simpson .02 .10
113 Rob Niedermayer .05 .15
114 Robert Kron .02 .10
115 Jason York RC .02 .10
116 Valeri Kamensky .05 .15
117 Ray Whitney .02 .10
118 Chris Chelios .10 .30
119 Scott Levins .02 .10
120 Sandis Ozolinsh .02 .10
121 Mark Recchi .05 .15
122 Ron Francis .05 .15
123 Dean McAmmond .02 .10
124 Jerry Yake .02 .10
125 Sergei Nemchinov .02 .10
126 Vitali Prokhorov .02 .10
127 Wayne Gretzky .75 2.00
128 Roman Hamrlik .05 .15
129 Jarkko Varvio .02 .10
130 Brian Skrudland .02 .10
131 Murray Craven .02 .10
132 Jeff Norton .02 .10
133 Pavol Demitra .05 .15
134 Mike Keane .02 .10
135 Paul Cavallini .02 .10
136 Richard Smehlik .02 .10
137 Eric Lindros .10 .30
138 Mariusz Czerkawski RC .10 .30
139 Darrin Shannon .02 .10
140 Brian Noonan .02 .10
141 Joe Sakic .25 .60
142 Steve Thomas .02 .10
143 Gary Roberts .02 .10
144 Patrick Poulin .02 .10
145 Tony Granato .02 .10
146 Donald Brashear RC .02 .10
147 Ron Hextall .05 .15
148 Corey Millen .02 .10
149 Dale Hunter .02 .10
150 Greg Johnson .02 .10
151 John MacLean .05 .15
152 Brian Leetch .10 .30
153 Sylvain Cote .02 .10
154 Thomas Steen .02 .10
155 Ted Donato .02 .10
156 Nathan Lafayette .02 .10
157 Kelly Chase .02 .10
158 Sean Burke .05 .15
159 Jaromir Jagr .20 .50
160 Checklist 84-166 .02 .10
161 Scott Niedermayer .02 .10
162 Ray Ferraro .02 .10
163 Todd Elik .02 .10
164 Dave Gagner .05 .15
165 Mike Richter .10 .30
166 Garry Galley .02 .10
167 Russ Courtnall .02 .10
168 Marty McSorley .02 .10
169 Robert Reichel .02 .10
170 Mike Rathje .02 .10
171 Bill Ranford .05 .15
172 Danton Cole .02 .10
173 Sergei Fedorov .20 .50
174 Brendan Shanahan .10 .30
175 Byron Dafoe RC .40 1.00
176 John Vanbiesbrouck .05 .15
177 Eric Desjardins .05 .15
178 Andrew Cassels .02 .10
179 John Gruden RC .02 .10
180 Slava Kozlov .05 .15
181 Trevor Linden .05 .15
182 Kris Draper .02 .10
183 Steve Smith .02 .10
184 Andre Faust .02 .10
185 James Patrick .02 .10
186 Ted Drury .02 .10
187 Dan Laperriere .02 .10
188 Benoit Hogue .02 .10
189 Chris Gratton .02 .10
190 Jyrki Lumme .02 .10
191 Peter Stastny .05 .15
192 Keith Tkachuk .10 .30
193 Mike Modano .20 .50
194 Nicklas Lidstrom .10 .30
195 Pierre Sevigny .02 .10
196 Scott Pearson .02 .10
197 Jaroslav Modry .02 .10
198 Garry Valk .02 .10
199 Kevin Hatcher .02 .10
200 Denis Tsygurov RC .02 .10
201 Paul Laus .02 .10
202 Alexander Godynyuk .02 .10
203 Brian Bellows .02 .10
204 Michal Sykora .02 .10
205 Al Iafrate .02 .10
206 Mark Tinordi .02 .10
207 Kelly Hrudey .05 .15
208 Tom Barrasso .05 .15
209 Craig Billington .05 .15
210 Teemu Selanne .10 .30
211 Alexandre Daigle .02 .10
212 Grant Fuhr .05 .15
213 Doug Brown .02 .10
214 Tim Sweeney .02 .10
215 Chris Pronger .10 .30
216 Alexei Gusarov .02 .10
217 Gary Suter .02 .10
218 Boris Mironov .02 .10
219 Sergei Zubov .02 .10
220 Checklist 167-249 .02 .10
221 Shayne Corson .02 .10
222 Jeremy Roenick .15 .40
223 John Druce .02 .10
224 Martin Straka .02 .10
225 Stephane Fiset .05 .15
226 Vincent Damphousse .02 .10
227 Bob Kudelski .02 .10
228 German Titov .02 .10
229 Kevin Stevens .02 .10
230 Dave Ellett .02 .10
231 Steve Larmer .05 .15
232 Glen Wesley .02 .10
233 Mathieu Schneider .02 .10
234 Stephan Lebeau .02 .10
235 Mark Fitzpatrick .05 .15
236 Mikael Renberg .05 .15
237 Darren McCarty .02 .10
238 Todd Nelson .02 .10
239 Igor Korolev .02 .10
240 Warren Rychel .02 .10
241 Gino Odjick .02 .10
242 Dave Manson .02 .10
243 Calle Johansson .02 .10
244 Andrei Trefilov .02 .10
245 Jason Dawe .02 .10
246 Glen Murray .02 .10
247 Jeff Shantz .02 .10
248 Zarley Zalapski .02 .10
249 Petr Klima .02 .10
250 Patrice Brisebois .02 .10
251 Chris Osgood .20 .50
252 Darius Kasparaitis .02 .10
253 Chris Joseph .02 .10
254 Glenn Anderson .05 .15
255 Kirk Muller .02 .10
256 Jason Smith .02 .10
257 Bob Bassen .02 .10
258 Joe Juneau .05 .15
259 Igor Kravchuk .02 .10
260 John Lilley .02 .10
261 Philippe Bozon .02 .10
262 Scott Stevens .05 .15
263 Dominic Roussel .05 .15
264 Dimitri Khristich .02 .10
265 Ed Patterson .02 .10
266 Mike Peca .02 .10
267 Teppo Numminen .02 .10
268 Alexei Kovalev .05 .15
269 Cam Neely .10 .30
270 Iain Fraser .02 .10
271 Tomas Sandstrom .02 .10
272 Lyle Odelein .02 .10
273 Norm Maciver .02 .10
274 Zdeno Ciger .02 .10
275 Ed Belfour .10 .30
276 Brian Savage .02 .10
277 Vlastimil Kroupa .02 .10
278 Cliff Ronning .02 .10
279 Alexei Zhitnik .02 .10
280 Jim Storm .02 .10
281 Don Sweeney .02 .10
282 Mike Donnelly .02 .10
283 Glenn Healy .05 .15
284 Denis Savard .05 .15
285 Chris Terreri .05 .15
286 Darren Turcotte .02 .10
287 Curtis Joseph .10 .30
288 Ken Baumgartner .02 .10
289 Matthew Barnaby .05 .15
290 Brent Sutter .02 .10
291 Valeri Zelepukin .02 .10
292 Michal Pivonka .02 .10
293 Ray Sheppard .05 .15
294 Jiri Slegr .02 .10
295 Vesa Viitakoski .02 .10
296 Ulf Samuelsson .02 .10
297 Nelson Emerson .02 .10
298 John Slaney .02 .10
299 Pat Verbeek .02 .10
300 Pat LaFontaine .10 .30
301 Johan Garpenlov .02 .10
302 Eric Weinrich .02 .10
303 Richard Matvichuk .02 .10
304 Steve Duchesne .02 .10
305 Donald Audette .02 .10
306 Stu Barnes .02 .10
307 Vladimir Malakhov .02 .10
308 Dimitri Yushkevich .02 .10
309 David Sacco .02 .10
310 Scott Young .02 .10
311 Marty McInnis .02 .10
312 Grant Ledyard .02 .10
313 Peter Popovic .20 .50
314 Mikhail Shtalenkov RC .02 .10
315 Dave McLlwain .02 .10
316 Cam Stewart .02 .10
317 Derian Hatcher .02 .10
318 Pat Peake .02 .10
319 Wes Walz .02 .10
320 Fred Brathwaite .05 .15
321 Jesse Belanger .02 .10
322 Jozef Stumpel .02 .10
323 Dave Andreychuk .05 .15
324 Yuri Khmylev .02 .10
325 Tim Cheveldae .05 .15
326 Anatoli Semenov .02 .10
327 Alexander Karpovtsev .02 .10
328 Patrick Roy .60 1.50
329 Troy Mallette .02 .10
330 Checklist 250-330 .02 .10

1994-95 Donruss Dominators

The eight cards in this set were randomly inserted in Donruss product at the rate of 1:36 packs. Each card features head shots of three players, grouped by position and conference, over a silver foil set logo. Individual photos appear on the back with statistical information. Cards are numbered "X of 8."

COMPLETE SET (8) 30.00 60.00
1 Eric Lindros 3.00 8.00
Mario Lemieux
Mark Messier
2 Brian Leetch 4.00 10.00
Ray Bourque
Scott Stevens
3 Patrick Roy 6.00 15.00
Dominik Hasek
John Vanbiesbrouck
4 Cam Neely 2.00 5.00
Jaromir Jagr
Mikael Renberg
5 Sergei Fedorov 8.00 20.00
Jeremy Roenick
Wayne Gretzky
6 Chris Chelios 2.00 5.00
Paul Coffey
Al MacInnis
7 Arturs Irbe 2.00 5.00
Ed Belfour
Felix Potvin
8 Brett Hull 3.00 8.00
Pavel Bure
Teemu Selanne

1994-95 Donruss Elite Inserts

This ten-card standard-size set was issued in Donruss product at the rate of 1:72 packs. The design features a silver border with a deckle edge cut and rounded corners surrounding an action player photo. The set title tops the photo, with team logo, player name and team name below it. Card backs feature a small photo and personal information. Each card is individually numbered out of 10,000 on the back.

COMPLETE SET (10) 30.00 60.00
1 Jason Arnott .40 1.00
2 Martin Brodeur 3.00 8.00
3 Pavel Bure 1.25 3.00
4 Sergei Fedorov 2.00 5.00
5 Wayne Gretzky 8.00 20.00
6 Mario Lemieux 6.00 15.00
7 Eric Lindros 1.25 3.00
8 Felix Potvin 1.25 3.00
9 Jeremy Roenick 1.50 4.00
10 Patrick Roy 6.00 15.00

1994-95 Donruss Ice Masters

This ten-card set was produced in the style of previous Diamond King sets in baseball, featuring the renderings of artist Dick Perez. The cards were randomly inserted at the rate of 1:18 packs. A foil logo and player name are stamped in silver foil on the front. Backs are black and have a brief paragraph of information. Cards are numbered "X of 10."

COMPLETE SET (10) 8.00 15.00
1 Ed Belfour .50 1.25
2 Sergei Fedorov .75 2.00
3 Doug Gilmour .25 .60
4 Wayne Gretzky 3.00 8.00
5 Mario Lemieux 2.50 6.00
6 Eric Lindros .50 1.25
7 Mark Messier .50 1.25
8 Mike Modano .75 2.00
9 Luc Robitaille .25 .60
10 John Vanbiesbrouck .25 .60

1994-95 Donruss Masked Marvels

The ten cards in this set of NHL goalies were randomly inserted at a rate of 1:18 packs. The card fronts display a small action photo to the left and a holographic facial image printed in a silver foil disc at right. Cards are numbered X of 10 on the back. These cards feature a removable clear plastic coating on the front which is designed to protect the hologram from scratches. A white sticker reading "Remove Protective Coating" covers a small segment of each card front. Prices below reflect values for cards with the coating intact; collectors are free to preserve their cards with or without this coating.

COMPLETE SET (10) 15.00 30.00
1 Ed Belfour 1.00 2.50
2 Martin Brodeur 2.50 6.00
3 Dominik Hasek 2.00 5.00
4 Arturs Irbe .75 2.00
5 Curtis Joseph 1.25 3.00
6 Kirk McLean .75 2.00
7 Felix Potvin 1.00 2.50
8 Mike Richter 1.00 2.50
9 Patrick Roy 5.00 12.00
10 John Vanbiesbrouck 1.00 2.50

1995-96 Donruss

These 390 standard-size cards represent the first and second series of the 1995-96 Donruss issue. The fronts feature borderless color action player photos. The player's name and team is identified on the bottom of the card. The borderless backs carry a color action photo with seasonal and career stats as an inset on the right side. Rookie Cards include Daniel Alfredsson and Daymond Langkow.

COMPLETE SET (390) 15.00 30.00
COMP.SERIES 1 (205) 9.00 18.00
COMP.SERIES 2 (185) 6.00 12.00
1 Eric Lindros .10 .30
2 Steve Larmer .05 .15
3 Oleg Tverdovsky .02 .10
4 Vladimir Malakhov .02 .10
5 Ian Laperriere .02 .10
6 Chris Marinucci RC .02 .10
7 Nelson Emerson .02 .10
8 David Oliver .02 .10
9 Felix Potvin .10 .30
10 Manny Fernandez .10 .30
11 Jason Wiemer .02 .10
12 Dale Hunter .05 .15
13 Wayne Gretzky .75 2.00
14 Todd Gill .02 .10
15 Radim Bicanek .02 .10
16 Kirk McLean .05 .15
17 Esa Tikkanen .02 .10
18 Yuri Khmylev .02 .10
19 Peter Bondra .05 .15
20 Brian Savage .02 .10
21 Mariusz Czerkawski .02 .10
22 Rob Blake .05 .15
23 Chris Osgood .05 .15
24 Bernie Nicholls .02 .10
25 Doug Weight .05 .15
26 Shaun Van Allen .02 .10
27 Jeremy Roenick .15 .40
28 Sean Burke .05 .15
29 Pat Verbeek .02 .10
30 Dino Ciccarelli .05 .15
31 Trevor Kidd .05 .15
32 Steve Thomas .02 .10
33 Dominik Hasek .25 .60
34 Sandis Ozolinsh .02 .10
35 Bill Guerin .05 .15
36 Scott Young .02 .10
37 Scott Mellanby .02 .10
38 Joe Mullen .05 .15
39 Steve Larouche RC .02 .10
40 Joe Nieuwendyk .05 .15
41 Rick Tocchet .05 .15
42 Keith Primeau .02 .10
43 Darren Turcotte .02 .10
44 Jason Arnott .02 .10
45 Brantt Myhres RC .02 .10
46 Murray Craven .02 .10
47 Martin Gendron .02 .10
48 Mark Recchi .05 .15
49 Uwe Krupp .02 .10
50 Alexei Zhitnik .02 .10
51 Rob Niedermayer .05 .15
52 Sergei Brylin .02 .10
53 Mats Naslund .02 .10
54 Glenn Healy .05 .15
55 Mathieu Schneider .02 .10
56 Marko Tuomainen .02 .10
57 Paul Kariya .10 .30
58 Dave Gagner .02 .10
59 Mike Richter .10 .30
60 Patrik Juhlin .02 .10
61 Pierre Turgeon .05 .15
62 Mike Modano .20 .50
63 Chris Pronger .10 .30
64 Chris Joseph .02 .10
65 Peter Forsberg .30 .75
66 Roman Oksiuta .02 .10
67 Jamie Storr .05 .15
68 Brett Hull .15 .40
69 Steve Chiasson .02 .10
70 Benoit Hogue .02 .10
71 Guy Hebert .05 .15
72 Chris Therien .02 .10
73 Darryl Sydor .05 .15
74 Phil Housley .05 .15
75 Jason Allison .02 .10
76 Richard Smehlik .02 .10
77 Shean Donovan .02 .10
78 Keith Tkachuk .10 .30
79 Cliff Ronning .02 .10
80 Mikael Renberg .05 .15
81 Steven Rice .02 .10
82 Adam Graves .02 .10
83 Nicklas Lidstrom .10 .30
84 Daren Puppa .05 .15
85 Todd Warriner .02 .10
86 Jon Rohloff .02 .10
87 Patrice Tardif .02 .10
88 John MacLean .05 .15
89 Ulf Samuelsson .02 .10
90 Alexander Selivanov .02 .10
91 Chris Chelios .10 .30
92 Ulf Dahlen .02 .10
93 Brad May .02 .10
94 Ron Francis .05 .15
95 Kevin Hatcher .02 .10
96 Steve Yzerman .60 1.50
97 Jocelyn Thibault .10 .30
98 Dave Andreychuk .05 .15
99 Gary Suter .02 .10
100 Teemu Selanne .10 .30
101 Don Sweeney .02 .10
102 Valeri Bure .02 .10
103 Todd Harvey .05 .15
104 Luc Robitaille .05 .15
105 Scott Niedermayer .02 .10
106 John Vanbiesbrouck .05 .15
107 Alexei Yashin .02 .10
108 Ed Belfour .10 .30
109 Jyrki Lumme .02 .10
110 Petr Klima .02 .10
111 Tony Granato .02 .10
112 Bob Corkum .02 .10
113 Chris McAlpine RC .02 .10
114 John LeClair .10 .30
115 Kenny Jonsson .02 .10
116 Garry Galley .02 .10
117 Jeff Norton .02 .10
118 Tomas Sandstrom .02 .10
119 Paul Coffey .10 .30
120 Mike Ricci .05 .15
121 Tony Amonte .05 .15
122 Chris Gratton .02 .10
123 Blaine Lacher .05 .15
124 Andrei Nikolishin .02 .10
125 Michal Grosek .02 .10
126 Shawn Chambers .02 .10
127 Ray Bourque .20 .50
128 Jeff Nelson .02 .10
129 Kirk Muller .02 .10
130 Sergei Zubov .02 .10
131 Stanislav Neckar .02 .10
132 Stu Barnes .02 .10
133 Jari Kurri .10 .30
134 Slava Kozlov .05 .15
135 Curtis Joseph .10 .30
136 Joe Juneau .02 .10
137 Craig Janney .02 .10
138 Bryan Smolinski .02 .10
139 Brian Bradley .02 .10
140 Steve Rucchin .05 .15
141 Donald Audette .02 .10
142 Jaromir Jagr .20 .50
143 Mike Torchia RC .05 .15
144 Ray Ferraro .02 .10
145 Adam Deadmarsh .02 .10
146 Joe Murphy .02 .10
147 Ron Hextall .05 .15
148 Andrew Cassels .02 .10
149 Martin Brodeur .30 .75
150 Marek Malik .02 .10
151 Eric Desjardins .05 .15
152 Cory Stillman .02 .10
153 Owen Nolan .05 .15
154 Randy Wood .02 .10
155 Alexei Zhamnov .05 .15
156 John Cullen .02 .10
157 Zdenek Nedved .02 .10
158 Greg Adams .02 .10
159 Kelly Miller .02 .10
160 Alexandre Daigle .02 .10
161 Gord Murphy .02 .10
162 Jeff Friesen .02 .10
163 Scott Stevens .05 .15
164 Denis Chasse .02 .10
165 Cam Neely .10 .30
166 Magnus Svensson RC .02 .10
167 Joe Sakic .25 .60
168 Kevin Brown .02 .10
169 Craig Conroy RC .02 .10
170 Pavel Bure .10 .30
171 Viktor Kozlov .05 .15
172 Pat LaFontaine .10 .30
173 Sergei Gonchar .02 .10
174 Brett Lindros .02 .10
175 Jassen Cullimore .02 .10
176 Mats Sundin .10 .30
177 Zarley Zalapski .02 .10
178 Stephane Richer .05 .15
179 Steve Smith .02 .10
180 Brendan Shanahan .10 .30
181 Brian Leetch .05 .15
182 Ken Wregget .05 .15
183 Jeff Brown .02 .10
184 Darby Hendrickson .02 .10
185 Nikolai Khabibulin .05 .15
186 Glen Wesley .02 .10
187 Andrei Nazarov .02 .10
188 Rod Brind'Amour .05 .15
189 Jim Carey .05 .15
190 Derek Plante .02 .10
191 Valeri Karpov .02 .10
192 Mike Kennedy RC .02 .10
193 Wendel Clark .05 .15
194 Radek Bonk .02 .10
195 Jozef Stumpel .02 .10
196 Tommy Salo RC .40 1.00
197 Michal Pivonka .02 .10
198 Ray Sheppard .02 .10
199 Russ Courtnall .02 .10
200 Todd Marchant .02 .10
201 Geoff Sanderson .02 .10
202 Vincent Damphousse .02 .10
203 Sergei Krivokrasov .02 .10
204 Jesse Belanger .02 .10
205 Al MacInnis .05 .15
206 Philippe DeRouville .02 .10
207 Mike Eastwood .02 .10
208 Travis Green .05 .15
209 Jeff Shantz .02 .10
210 Shane Doan RC .30 .75
211 Mike Sullivan .02 .10
212 Kevin Dineen .02 .10
213 Pat Falloon .02 .10
214 Rick Tabaracci .05 .15
215 Kelly Hrudey .05 .15
216 Alexei Kovalev .02 .10
217 Matt Johnson .02 .10
218 Turner Stevenson .02 .10
219 Mike Sillinger .02 .10
220 Bobby Holik .02 .10
221 Kevin Stevens .02 .10
222 Dave Lowry .02 .10
223 Martin Gelinas .02 .10
224 Darren Langdon RC .02 .10
225 Tie Domi .05 .15
226 Doug Bodger .02 .10
227 Patrick Flatley .02 .10
228 Anders Myrvold RC .02 .10
229 German Titov .02 .10
230 Pat Peake .02 .10
231 Robert Kron .02 .10
232 Mike Donnelly .02 .10
233 Denis Savard .05 .15
234 Mathieu Dandenault RC .02 .10
235 Joe Dziedzic .02 .10
236 Valeri Kamensky .05 .15
237 Joaquin Gage RC .02 .10
238 Geoff Courtnall .02 .10
239 Arturs Irbe .05 .15
240 Dan Quinn .02 .10
241 J.C. Bergeron .02 .10
242 Brian Noonan .02 .10
243 Ulf Samuelsson .02 .10

244 Jeff O'Neill .02 .10
245 Sandy Moger RC .02 .10
246 Don Beaupre .05 .15
247 Bob Probert .05 .15
248 Mattias Norstrom .02 .10
249 Jason Bonsignore .02 .10
250 Mike Ridley .02 .10
251 Joe Mullen .05 .15
252 Petr Nedved .05 .15
253 Jason Doig .02 .10
254 Olaf Kolzig .05 .15
255 Mark Tinordi .02 .10
256 Roman Hamrlik .05 .15
257 Denis Pederson .02 .10
258 Paul Ysebaert .02 .10
259 Neal Broten .05 .15
260 Jason Woolley .02 .10
261 Teppo Numminen .02 .10
262 Scott Thornton .02 .10
263 Ted Donato .02 .10
264 Marcus Ragnarsson RC .05 .15
265 Dimitri Khristich .02 .10
266 Mike Peca .05 .15
267 Dominic Roussel .05 .15
268 Owen Nolan .05 .15
269 Patrick Poulin .02 .10
270 Mario Lemieux .60 1.50
271 Mark Messier .10 .30
272 Slava Fetisov .02 .10
273 Andrei Trefilov .02 .10
274 Damian Rhodes .05 .15
275 Alexander Mogilny .05 .15
276 Ray Sheppard .02 .10
277 Radek Dvorak RC .20 .50
278 Steve Duchesne .02 .10
279 Jason Smith RC .02 .10
280 Wade Flaherty RC .05 .15
281 Lyle Odelein .02 .10
282 Keith Jones .05 .15
283 Saku Koivu .10 .30
284 Marty Murray .02 .10
285 Sergei Fedorov .15 .40
286 Brian Rolston .02 .10
287 Dave Roche RC .02 .10
288 Sylvain Lefebvre .02 .10
289 Theo Fleury .02 .10
290 Andy Moog .10 .30
291 Tom Barrasso .05 .15
292 Craig Mills RC .02 .10
293 Mike Gartner .05 .15
294 Stefan Ustorf .02 .10
295 Darren Turcotte .02 .10
296 Steve Konowalchuk .02 .10
297 Ray Ferraro .02 .10
298 Brian Holzinger RC .02 .10
299 Daniel Alfredsson RC .30 .75
300 Derek King .02 .10
301 Mark Fitzpatrick .05 .15
302 Joe Sacco .02 .10
303 Scott Walker RC .02 .10
304 Ricard Persson RC .02 .10
305 Mike Rathje .02 .10
306 Petr Svoboda .02 .10
307 Roman Vopat RC .02 .10
308 Ray Whitney .05 .15
309 Calle Johansson .02 .10
310 Grant Fuhr .10 .30
311 John Tucker .02 .10
312 Anatoli Semenov .02 .10
313 Darren McCarty .02 .10
314 Stephane Quintal .02 .10
315 Jason Dawe .02 .10
316 Zigmund Palffy .05 .15
317 Dave Manson .02 .10
318 Vitali Yachmenev .02 .10
319 Chris Pronger .10 .30
320 Valeri Zelepukin .02 .10
321 Ryan Smyth .05 .15
322 Johan Garpenlov .02 .10
323 Bill Ranford .05 .15
324 Daymond Langkow RC .20 .50
325 Aki Berg RC .05 .15
326 Derian Hatcher .02 .10
327 Bryan Smolinski .02 .10
328 Michel Picard .02 .10
329 Alek Stojanov .02 .10
330 Trent Klatt .02 .10
331 Richard Park .02 .10
332 Jere Lehtinen .05 .15
333 Bryan McCabe .02 .10
334 Kyle McLaren RC .02 .10
335 Todd Krygier .02 .10
336 Adam Creighton .02 .10
337 Jamie Pushor .02 .10
338 Patrick Roy .60 1.50
339 Milos Holan .02 .10
340 Dave Ellett .02 .10
341 Brian Bellows .02 .10
342 Jamie Rivers .02 .10
343 Claude Lemieux .02 .10
344 Leif Rohlin RC .02 .10
345 Eric Daze .05 .15
346 Todd Bertuzzi RC .50 1.25
347 Antti Tormanen RC .02 .10
348 Luc Robitaille .05 .15
349 Tim Taylor RC .02 .10
350 Stephane Yelle RC .02 .10
351 Marko Kiprusoff .02 .10
352 Igor Korolev .02 .10
353 Scott Lachance .02 .10
354 Marty McSorley .02 .10
355 Joel Otto .02 .10
356 Josef Beranek .02 .10
357 Sergei Zubov .02 .10
358 Rhett Warrener RC .02 .10
359 Jimmy Carson .02 .10
360 Zdeno Ciger .02 .10
361 Brendan Witt .02 .10
362 Byron Dafoe .05 .15
363 Steve Thomas .05 .15
364 Deron Quint .02 .10
365 Nelson Emerson .02 .10
366 Larry Murphy .05 .15
367 Benoit Brunet .02 .10
368 Kjell Samuelsson .02 .10
369 Aaron Gavey .02 .10
370 Robert Svehla RC .02 .10
371 Rene Corbet .02 .10
372 Gary Roberts .02 .10
373 Shawn McEachern .02 .10
374 Andrei Kovalenko .02 .10
375 Yanic Perreault .02 .10
376 Shayne Corson .02 .10
377 Brendan Shanahan .10 .30
378 Sergei Nemchinov .02 .10
379 Chad Kilger RC .02 .10
380 Sergio Momesso .02 .10
381 Craig Billington .05 .15
382 Niklas Sundstrom .05 .15
383 Matthew Barnaby .10 .30
384 Dale Hawerchuk .10 .30
385 Trevor Linden .05 .15
386 Adam Oates .05 .15
387 Dimitri Yushkevich .02 .10
388 Todd Elik .02 .10
389 Wendel Clark .05 .15
390 Stephane Fiset .05 .15
NNO Checklist Card 1 .05 .15
NNO Checklist Card 2 .05 .15
NNO Checklist Card 3 .05 .15
NNO Checklist Card 4 .05 .15
NNO Checklist Card 5 .05 .15
NNO Checklist Card 6 .05 .15
NNO Checklist Card 7 .05 .15
NNO Checklist Card 8 .05 .15

1995-96 Donruss Between The Pipes

Shaped like a goal and outlined in red foil, these ten cards were randomly inserted in series 1 (1-5) and 2 (6-10) packs at a rate of 1:36. The goaltender is pictured within the goal with a solid blue background. The backs feature a brief write-up and career statistics.

COMPLETE SET (10) 25.00 60.00
COMPLETE SERIES 1 (5) 12.00 30.00
COMPLETE SERIES 2 (5) 12.00 30.00
1 Blaine Lacher 2.00 5.00
2 Dominik Hasek 4.00 10.00
3 Mike Vernon 2.00 5.00
4 Trevor Kidd 2.00 5.00
5 Martin Brodeur 5.00 12.00
6 Jim Carey 2.00 5.00
7 Patrick Roy 10.00 25.00
8 Sean Burke 2.00 5.00
9 Felix Potvin 3.00 8.00
10 Ed Belfour 3.00 8.00

1995-96 Donruss Canadian World Junior Team

These 22 standard-size cards were randomly inserted into series 1 (1-11) and series 2 (12-22) packs at a rate of 1:2. These cards honor players who represented Canada in the 1995 World Junior Championships. Large player photographs are superimposed on a maple leaf design. The backs feature two player photos. One is an inset photo in a maple leaf and the other on the left side is a black-and-white image. Information about the player is located in the upper left corner while his National Junior Team career stats are printed on the right side of the card. The cards are numbered "X of 22" in the upper right-hand corner.

COMPLETE SET (22) 5.00 12.00
COMP.SERIES 1 (11) 2.00 5.00
COMP.SERIES 2 (11) 3.00 8.00
1 Jamie Storr .60 1.50
2 Dan Cloutier .20 .50
3 Nolan Baumgartner .20 .50
4 Chad Allen .20 .50
5 Wade Redden .20 .50
6 Ed Jovanovski .60 1.50
7 Jamie Rivers .20 .50
8 Bryan McCabe .60 1.50
9 Lee Sorochan .20 .50
10 Marty Murray .20 .50
11 Larry Courville .20 .50
12 Jason Allison .20 .50
13 Darcy Tucker .20 .50
14 Jeff O'Neill .20 .50
15 Eric Daze .60 1.50
16 Alexandre Daigle .20 .50
17 Todd Harvey .60 1.50
18 Jason Botterill .20 .50
19 Shean Donovan .20 .50
20 Denis Pederson .20 .50
21 Jeff Friesen .20 .50
22 Ryan Smyth .40 1.00

1995-96 Donruss Dominators

The eight cards in this set were randomly inserted in series two hobby packs only at a rate of 1:36. Each features three of the top players at each position from each conference. The cards are individually numbered on the backs out of 5,000.

COMPLETE SET (8) 20.00 40.00
1 Peter Forsberg 4.00 10.00
Eric Lindros
Mario Lemieux
2 John LeClair 4.00 10.00
Mikael Renberg
Jaromir Jagr
3 Sergei Zubov 1.50 4.00
Ray Bourque
Brian Leetch
4 Jim Carey 3.00 8.00
Martin Brodeur
Dominik Hasek
5 Doug Gilmour 4.00 10.00
Wayne Gretzky
Sergei Fedorov
6 Brett Hull 2.00 5.00
Paul Kariya
Pavel Bure
7 Paul Coffey 1.50 4.00
Chris Chelios
Al MacInnis
8 Felix Potvin 4.00 10.00
Ed Belfour
Trevor Kidd

1995-96 Donruss Elite Inserts

These ten standard-size cards were randomly inserted into first (1-5) and second series (6-10) Donruss at a rate of 1:116 and 1:47 packs respectively. Each card is sequentially numbered out of 10,000. The fronts feature blue holographic foil, layered with copper foil which emphasize the player's name and team logo. The word "Elite" is noted in the upper right-hand corner. The card backs are printed in metallic copper and metallic blue ink silhouetting the player's image. There is a brief blurb about the player on the left side of the card. The cards are numbered "X" of 10 in the upper right corner.

COMPLETE SET (10) 25.00 50.00
1 Alexei Zhamnov .60 1.50
2 Joe Sakic 2.50 6.00
3 Mikael Renberg .60 1.50
4 Sergei Fedorov 1.50 4.00
5 Paul Coffey 1.25 3.00
6 Paul Kariya 1.25 3.00
7 Wayne Gretzky 8.00 20.00
8 Eric Lindros 1.25 3.00
9 Mario Lemieux 6.00 15.00
10 Jaromir Jagr 2.00 5.00

1995-96 Donruss Igniters

These 10 standard-size cards were randomly inserted in Series 1 hobby packs. The horizontally-oriented cards feature the player's photo superimposed against the word "Igniters". His name and team are identified on the bottom of the card. The backs are individually numbered out of 5,000.

COMPLETE SET (10) 15.00 30.00
1 Adam Oates 1.25 3.00
2 Paul Coffey 1.50 4.00
3 Doug Gilmour 1.25 3.00
4 Pierre Turgeon 1.25 3.00
5 Mark Messier 1.50 4.00
6 Alexei Zhamnov 1.25 3.00
7 Jeremy Roenick 2.00 5.00
8 Steve Yzerman 6.00 15.00
9 Joe Nieuwendyk 1.25 3.00
10 Ron Francis 1.25 3.00

1995-96 Donruss Marksmen

The eight cards in this set were randomly inserted into series one Donruss retail packs only at a rate of 1:24. The cards showcase the top eight goal scorers of the 1994-95 season.

COMPLETE SET (8) 6.00 12.00
1 Peter Bondra .75 2.00
2 Owen Nolan .75 2.00
3 Eric Lindros .75 2.00
4 Ray Sheppard .75 2.00
5 Jaromir Jagr 1.25 3.00
6 Theo Fleury .75 2.00
7 Brett Hull 1.00 2.50
8 Brendan Shanahan .75 2.00

1995-96 Donruss Pro Pointers

Inserted one per series two pack, these twenty cards feature hockey tips from top players born in the United States (1-10) and Canada (11-20).

COMPLETE SET (20) 3.00 6.00
1 Jeremy Roenick USA .20 .50
2 Pat LaFontaine USA .15 .40
3 Jason Bonsignore USA .02 .10
4 Chris Chelios USA .15 .40
5 Brian Leetch USA .07 .20
6 Brett Hull USA .20 .50
7 Keith Tkachuk USA .15 .40
8 Mike Modano USA .25 .60
9 Brian Rolston USA .02 .10
10 Darren Turcotte USA .02 .10
11 Jeff Friesen CAN .02 .10
12 Theo Fleury CAN .02 .10
13 Eric Lindros CAN .15 .40
14 Mario Lemieux .75 2.00
15 Jamie Storr CAN .07 .20
16 Trevor Kidd CAN .07 .20
17 Chris Pronger CAN .15 .40
18 Brendan Witt CAN .02 .10
19 Paul Kariya CAN .15 .40
20 Todd Harvey CAN .07 .20

1995-96 Donruss Rated Rookies

Randomly inserted at a rate of 1:24 series two retail packs, this 16-card set features a plethora of players who made their NHL debuts in the 1995-96 season.

COMPLETE SET (16) 15.00 40.00
1 Saku Koivu 4.00 10.00
2 Todd Bertuzzi 2.00 5.00
3 Niklas Sundstrom .75 2.00
4 Jeff O'Neill .75 2.00
5 Zdenek Nedved .75 2.00
6 Eric Daze .75 2.00
7 Chad Kilger .75 2.00
8 Shane Doan .75 2.00
9 Vitali Yachmenev .75 2.00
10 Radek Dvorak .75 2.00
11 Marty Murray .75 2.00
12 Cory Stillman .75 2.00
13 Marcus Ragnarsson .75 2.00
14 Daniel Alfredsson 2.00 5.00
15 Antti Tormanen .75 2.00
16 Petr Sykora 1.50 4.00

1995-96 Donruss Rookie Team

These nine standard-size cards featuring leading rookies from the 1994-95 season were issued in first series packs (1:12). The borderless fronts feature the player's photo blending into various colors which represent his team's color pattern. The player's name and team identification are located on the bottom. The horizontal back features a close-up player photo, along with a brief note. The cards are numbered on the upper right as "X" of 9.

COMPLETE SET (9) 3.00 6.00
1 Jim Carey .20 .50
2 Peter Forsberg 1.00 2.50
3 Paul Kariya .40 1.00
4 David Oliver .10 .30
5 Blaine Lacher .20 .50
6 Oleg Tverdovsky .10 .30
7 Jeff Friesen .10 .30
8 Todd Marchant .10 .30
9 Todd Harvey .20 .50

1996-97 Donruss

The 1996-97 Donruss set was issued in one series totaling 240 cards. The 10-card packs retailed for $1.89 each. Card fronts feature a borderless color action photo along with player name at the top and team name and logo at the bottom. Card backs feature another color action photo, along with stats and biographical information. Key Rookie Cards include Ethan Moreau and Kevin Hodson.

COMPLETE SET (240) 6.00 15.00
1 Joe Sakic .20 .50
2 Jeremy Roenick .10 .30
3 Kirk McLean .02 .10
4 Zarley Zalapski .01 .05
5 Jyrki Lumme .01 .05
6 Owen Nolan .02 .10
7 Luc Robitaille .02 .10
8 Bob Probert .02 .10
9 Ken Baumgartner .01 .05
10 Rick Tabaracci .02 .10
11 Alexei Zhitnik .01 .05
12 Al MacInnis .02 .10
13 Brian Leetch .08 .25
14 Valeri Kamensky .02 .10
15 Todd Gill .01 .05
16 Mark Messier .08 .25
17 Pierre Turgeon .02 .10
18 Mathieu Schneider .01 .05
19 Vyacheslav Kozlov .01 .05
20 Milos Holan .01 .05
21 Yanic Perreault .01 .05
22 Mike Modano .15 .40
23 Claude Lemieux .01 .05
24 Rob Niedermayer .02 .10
25 Eric Desjardins .02 .10
26 Alexander Semak .01 .05
27 Mark Recchi .02 .10
28 Slava Fetisov .01 .05
29 Kevin Hatcher .01 .05
30 Mats Sundin .08 .25
31 Jeff Reese .02 .10
32 Alexander Selivanov .01 .05
33 Jim Carey .08 .25
34 Daren Puppa .02 .10
35 Vincent Damphousse .01 .05
36 John LeClair .08 .25
37 Jon Casey .02 .10
38 Chris Terreri .02 .10
39 Larry Murphy .02 .10
40 Geoff Sanderson .02 .10
41 Adam Oates .02 .10
42 Sandy McCarthy .01 .05
43 Jaromir Jagr .15 .40
44 Roman Oksiuta .01 .05
45 Zigmund Palffy .02 .10
46 Doug Gilmour .02 .10
47 Cliff Ronning .01 .05
48 Curtis Leschyshyn .01 .05
49 Scott Mellanby .02 .10
50 Sergei Fedorov .10 .30
51 Denis Savard .02 .10
52 Mike Vernon .02 .10
53 Todd Marchant .01 .05
54 Geoff Courtnall .01 .05
55 Shayne Corson .01 .05
56 Dimitri Khristich .01 .05
57 Scott Stevens .02 .10
58 German Titov .01 .05
59 Darren Turcotte .01 .05
60 Michal Pivonka .01 .05
61 Ron Hextall .02 .10
62 Ed Belfour .08 .25
63 Chris Pronger .02 .10
64 Brian Bellows .01 .05
65 Pavel Bure .08 .25
66 Adam Graves .01 .05
67 Tom Barrasso .02 .10
68 Stu Barnes .01 .05
69 Norm Maciver .01 .05
70 Jesse Belanger .01 .05
71 Chris Chelios .08 .25
72 Tommy Soderstrom .02 .10
73 Nelson Emerson .01 .05
74 Kenny Jonsson .01 .05
75 Bill Lindsay .01 .05
76 Petr Nedved .02 .10
77 Robert Svehla .01 .05
78 Tomas Sandstrom .01 .05
79 Jeff Friesen .01 .05
80 Tony Amonte .02 .10
81 Sylvain Lefebvre .01 .05
82 Greg Adams .01 .05
83 Vladimir Konstantinov .02 .10
84 Roman Hamrlik .02 .10
85 Doug Weight .02 .10
86 Shaun Van Allen .01 .05
87 Bill Ranford .02 .10
88 Jeff Hackett .02 .10
89 Alexei Zhamnov .02 .10
90 Dale Hawerchuk .02 .10
91 Sergei Zubov .01 .05
92 Dan Quinn .01 .05
93 Wayne Gretzky .75 2.00
94 Todd Harvey .01 .05
95 Chris Osgood .02 .10
96 Felix Potvin .08 .25
97 Richard Matvichuk .01 .05
98 Wendel Clark .02 .10
99 Bryan Smolinski .01 .05
100 Rob Blake .02 .10
101 Jocelyn Thibault .08 .25
102 Trevor Linden .02 .10
103 Craig MacTavish .01 .05
104 Sandis Ozolinsh .01 .05
105 Oleg Tverdovsky .01 .05
106 Garry Galley .01 .05
107 Derek Plante .01 .05
108 Stephane Richer .02 .10
109 Dave Andreychuk .02 .10
110 Curtis Joseph .08 .25
111 Greg Johnson .01 .05
112 Patrick Roy .50 1.25
113 Pat LaFontaine .08 .25
114 Uwe Krupp .01 .05
115 Ulf Dahlen .01 .05
116 Brian Bradley .01 .05
117 Grant Fuhr .02 .10
118 Brian Skrudland .01 .05
119 Nicklas Lidstrom .08 .25
120 Steve Chiasson .01 .05
121 Sean Burke .02 .10
122 Rick Tocchet .02 .10
123 Martin Rucinsky .01 .05
124 Alexei Yashin .01 .05
125 Mikael Renberg .02 .10
126 Teppo Numminen .01 .05
127 Randy Burridge .01 .05
128 Radek Bonk .01 .05
129 Scott Young .01 .05
130 Gary Suter .01 .05
131 Mario Lemieux .50 1.25
132 Ray Bourque .15 .40
133 Martin Gelinas .01 .05
134 Keith Tkachuk .08 .25
135 Benoit Hogue .01 .05
136 Ken Wregget .02 .10
137 Eric Lindros .08 .25
138 Keith Primeau .01 .05
139 Peter Forsberg .25 .60
140 Paul Coffey .08 .25
141 Mike Ridley .01 .05
142 Paul Kariya .08 .25
143 Jason Arnott .01 .05
144 Joe Murphy .01 .05
145 Adam Deadmarsh .01 .05
146 John MacLean .02 .10
147 Peter Bondra .02 .10
148 Martin Brodeur .25 .60
149 Ron Francis .02 .10
150 Dino Ciccarelli .02 .10
151 Joe Juneau .02 .10
152 Matthew Barnaby .02 .10
153 Mark Tinordi .01 .05
154 Craig Janney .02 .10
155 Rod Brind'Amour .02 .10
156 Damian Rhodes .01 .05
157 Teemu Selanne .08 .25
158 James Patrick .01 .05
159 Theo Fleury .01 .05
160 Trevor Kidd .02 .10
161 Kirk Muller .01 .05
162 Andrew Cassels .01 .05
163 Brent Fedyk .01 .05
164 Guy Hebert .02 .10
165 Jason Dawe .01 .05
166 Andy Moog .02 .10
167 Igor Larionov .01 .05
168 Brian Savage .01 .05
169 Kris Draper .01 .05
170 Dave Gagner .02 .10
171 Steve Yzerman .50 1.25
172 Nikolai Khabibulin .02 .10
173 Chris Gratton .01 .05
174 Dave Lowery .01 .05
175 Travis Green .02 .10
176 Alexei Kovalev .01 .05
177 Mike Ricci .01 .05
178 Brendan Shanahan .08 .25
179 Corey Hirsch .02 .10
180 Bill Guerin .01 .05
181 Alexander Mogilny .02 .10
182 Steve Duchesne .01 .05
183 Ray Ferraro .01 .05
184 Mike Richter .08 .25
185 Yuri Khmylev .01 .05
186 Stephane Fiset .02 .10
187 John Vanbiesbrouck .02 .10
188 Scott Niedermayer .01 .05
189 Brad May .02 .10
190 Shawn McEachern .01 .05
191 Joe Mullen .02 .10
192 Dominik Hasek .20 .50
193 Steve Thomas .01 .05
194 Russ Courtnall .01 .05
195 Joe Nieuwendyk .02 .10
196 Petr Klima .01 .05
197 Brett Hull .10 .30
198 Bernie Nicholls .01 .05
199 Dale Hunter .01 .05
200 Pat Verbeek .01 .05
201 Phil Housley .02 .10
202 Todd Krygier .01 .05
203 Zdeno Ciger .01 .05
204 Alexandre Daigle .01 .05
205 Cam Neely .08 .25
206 Mike Gartner .02 .10
207 Garth Snow .02 .10
208 Pat Falloon .01 .05
209 Kelly Hrudey .02 .10
210 Ray Sheppard .02 .10
211 Ted Donato .01 .05
212 Glenn Healy .02 .10
213 Radek Dvorak .01 .05
214 Niclas Andersson .01 .05
215 Miroslav Satan .01 .05
216 Roman Vopat .01 .05
217 Bryan McCabe .01 .05
218 Jamie Langenbrunner .01 .05
219 Kyle McLaren .01 .05
220 Stephane Yelle .01 .05
221 Byron Dafoe .02 .10
222 Grant Marshall .01 .05
223 Ryan Smyth .08 .25
224 Ville Peltonen .01 .05
225 Deron Quint .01 .05
226 Brian Holzinger .02 .10
227 Jose Theodore .10 .30
228 Ethan Moreau RC .08 .25
229 Steve Sullivan RC .20 .50
230 Kevin Hodson RC .08 .25
231 Cory Stillman .01 .05
232 Ralph Intranuovo .01 .05
233 Vitali Yachmenev .01 .05
234 Marcus Ragnarsson .01 .05
235 Nolan Baumgartner .01 .05
236 Chad Kilger .01 .05
237 Niklas Sundstrom .01 .05
238 Paul Coffey CL (1-120) .08 .25
239 Doug Gilmour CL (121-240) .08 .25
240 Steve Yzerman CL (inserts) .10 .30

1996-97 Donruss Press Proofs

This 240-card standard size set is a parallel issue to the regular Donruss set. A cut-out star in the upper right-hand corner, along with the words "First 2,000 Printed, Press Proof" printed above the set logo, along the bottom distinguish these cards from their regular counterparts.

*SINGLES: 4X TO 10X BASIC CARDS

1996-97 Donruss Between the Pipes

This standard-size set features 10 of the NHL's top netminders. These cards are found only in retail packs and are serially numbered to 4,000.

COMPLETE SET (10) 15.00 40.00
1 Patrick Roy 6.00 15.00
2 Martin Brodeur 3.00 8.00
3 Jim Carey 1.25 3.00
4 John Vanbiesbrouck 2.00 5.00
5 Chris Osgood 2.00 5.00
6 Ed Belfour 2.00 5.00
7 Jocelyn Thibault 1.25 3.00
8 Curtis Joseph 2.00 5.00
9 Nikolai Khabibulin 2.00 5.00
10 Felix Potvin 2.00 5.00

1996-97 Donruss Dominators

The ten cards in this set were randomly inserted in hobby packs at indeterminable odds and feature three of the top players at each position. These cards are serially numbered to 5,000 and printed on laminated holographic foil stock.

COMPLETE SET (10) 20.00 40.00
1 Jim Carey 1.50 4.00
Martin Brodeur
John Vanbiesbrouck
2 Nikolai Khabibulin 1.50 4.00
Chris Osgood
Jocelyn Thibault
3 Chris Chelios 2.00 5.00
Paul Coffey
Ray Bourque
4 Mario Lemieux 4.00 10.00
Jaromir Jagr
Ron Francis
5 Eric Lindros 4.00 10.00
Wayne Gretzky
Jason Arnott
6 Doug Gilmour 1.50 4.00
Wendel Clark
Pierre Turgeon
7 Alexander Mogilny 1.50 4.00
Pavel Bure
Trevor Linden
8 Paul Kariya 1.50 4.00
Teemu Selanne
Keith Tkachuk
9 Mike Modano 1.50 4.00
Jeremy Roenick
Sergei Fedorov
10 Eric Daze 1.50 4.00
Saku Koivu
Ed Jovanovski

1996-97 Donruss Elite Inserts

These ten standard-size cards were randomly inserted into all varieties of packs. The basic version of the set has silver borders with cards serially numbered to 10,000. The tougher-to-find gold parallel version features, naturally enough, gold borders with serial numbering to 2,000.

COMPLETE SET (10) 15.00 40.00
*GOLD: 1.2X TO 3X BASIC INSERTS
1 Pavel Bure 1.25 3.00
2 Wayne Gretzky 8.00 20.00
3 Doug Weight 1.25 3.00
4 Brett Hull 2.00 5.00
5 Mark Messier 1.25 3.00
6 Brendan Shanahan 1.25 3.00
7 Joe Sakic 2.50 6.00
8 Sergei Fedorov 1.50 4.00
9 Eric Lindros 1.25 3.00
10 Patrick Roy 6.00 15.00

1996-97 Donruss Go Top Shelf

This 10-card set was distributed only through magazine packs, with each card numbered out of 2,000.

COMPLETE SET (10) 20.00 50.00
1 Mario Lemieux 8.00 20.00
2 Teemu Selanne 2.00 5.00
3 Joe Sakic 4.00 10.00
4 Alexander Mogilny 1.25 3.00
5 Jaromir Jagr 3.00 8.00
6 Brett Hull 2.50 6.00
7 Mike Modano 2.50 6.00
8 Paul Kariya 2.00 5.00
9 Eric Lindros 2.00 5.00
10 Peter Forsberg 3.00 8.00

1996-97 Donruss Hit List

This set features 20 of the NHL's top bangers and crashers. Individually numbered to 10,000, these cards feature an internal die-cut with a color photo, and the player's name and position in silver foil on the front.

COMPLETE SET (20) 10.00 25.00
1 Eric Lindros .75 2.00
2 Wendel Clark .40 1.00
3 Ed Jovanovski .20 .50
4 Jeremy Roenick 1.50 4.00
5 Doug Weight .40 1.00
6 Chris Chelios .75 2.00
7 Brendan Shanahan .75 2.00
8 Mark Messier 1.25 3.00
9 Scott Stevens .20 .50
10 Keith Tkachuk .60 1.50
11 Trevor Linden .60 1.50
12 Eric Daze .20 .50
13 John LeClair .60 1.50
14 Peter Forsberg 2.00 5.00
15 Doug Gilmour .60 1.50
16 Roman Hamrlik .20 .50
17 Owen Nolan .20 .50
18 Claude Lemieux .20 .50
19 Saku Koivu .75 2.00
20 Theo Fleury .20 .50
P1 Eric Lindros PROMO .40 1.00

1996-97 Donruss Rated Rookies

This set features ten top young superstars. A press proof version of these cards exists, though quantity of production is unknown. They are fairly easy to distinguish by virtue of their gold foil finish.

COMPLETE SET (10)	8.00	20.00
*PRESS PROOF: 4X TO 10X BASIC INSERTS		
1 Eric Daze	.75	2.00
2 Petr Sykora	.75	2.00
3 Valeri Bure	.75	2.00
4 Jere Lehtinen	.75	2.00
5 Jeff O'Neill	.75	2.00
6 Saku Koivu	1.50	4.00
7 Ed Jovanovski	.75	2.00
8 Eric Fichaud	.75	2.00
9 Todd Bertuzzi	1.50	4.00
10 Daniel Alfredsson	1.50	4.00

1997-98 Donruss

The 1997-98 Donruss set was issued in one series totaling 230 cards and distributed in 10-card packs. The fronts featured color action player photos. The backs carried player information.

COMPLETE SET (230)	10.00	25.00
1 Peter Forsberg	.30	.75
2 Steve Yzerman	.60	1.50
3 Eric Lindros	.10	.30
4 Mark Messier	.10	.30
5 Patrick Roy	.60	1.50
6 Jeremy Roenick	.15	.40
7 Paul Kariya	.10	.30
8 Valeri Bure	.02	.10
9 Dominik Hasek	.25	.60
10 Doug Gilmour	.07	.20
11 Garth Snow	.07	.20
12 Todd Bertuzzi	.10	.30
13 Chris Osgood	.07	.20
14 Jarome Iginla	.15	.40
15 Lonny Bohonos	.02	.10
16 Jeff O'Neill	.02	.10
17 Daniel Alfredsson	.07	.20
18 Daymond Langkow	.07	.20
19 Alexei Yashin	.02	.10
20 Byron Dafoe	.07	.20
21 Mike Peca	.02	.10
22 Jim Carey	.07	.20
23 Pat Verbeek	.02	.10
24 Terry Ryan	.02	.10
25 Adam Oates	.07	.20
26 Kevin Hatcher	.02	.10
27 Ken Wregget	.07	.20
28 Pierre Turgeon	.07	.20
29 John LeClair	.10	.30
30 Jere Lehtinen	.02	.10
31 Jamie Storr	.07	.20
32 Doug Weight	.07	.20
33 Tommy Salo	.07	.20
34 Bernie Nicholls	.02	.10
35 Jocelyn Thibault	.07	.20
36 Dale Hawerchuk UER front Dave	.07	.20
37 Chris Chelios	.10	.30
38 Kirk Muller	.02	.10
39 Steve Sullivan	.02	.10
40 Andy Moog	.07	.20
41 Martin Gelinas	.02	.10
42 Shayne Corson	.02	.10
43 Curtis Joseph	.10	.30
44 Donald Audette	.02	.10
45 Rick Tocchet	.07	.20
46 Craig Janney	.02	.10
47 Geoff Courtnall	.02	.10
48 Wade Redden	.02	.10
49 Steve Rucchin	.02	.10
50 Ethan Moreau	.02	.10
51 Steve Shields RC	.20	.50
52 Jamie Pushor	.02	.10
53 Saku Koivu	.10	.30
54 Oleg Tverdovsky	.02	.10
55 Jeff Friesen	.02	.10
56 Chris Gratton	.07	.20
57 Wendel Clark	.07	.20
58 John Vanbiesbrouck	.07	.20
59 Trevor Kidd	.07	.20
60 Sandis Ozolinsh	.02	.10
61 Dave Andreychuk	.02	.10
62 Travis Green	.02	.10
63 Paul Coffey	.10	.30
64 Roman Turek	.07	.20
65 Vladimir Konstantinov	.07	.20
66 Ray Bourque	.20	.50
67 Wayne Primeau	.02	.10
68 Todd Harvey	.02	.10
69 Derek King	.02	.10
70 Adam Graves	.02	.10
71 Brett Hull	.15	.40
72 Scott Niedermayer	.02	.10
73 Mike Vernon	.07	.20
74 Brian Holzinger	.02	.10
75 Dainius Zubrus	.10	.30
76 Patrick Lalime	.07	.20
77 Corey Schwab	.07	.20
78 Alexandre Daigle	.02	.10
79 Geoff Sanderson	.07	.20
80 Dave Gagner	.02	.10
81 Jose Theodore	.15	.40
82 Sergei Fedorov	.20	.50
83 Keith Tkachuk	.10	.30
84 Owen Nolan	.07	.20
85 Brandon Convery	.02	.10
86 Trevor Linden	.07	.20
87 Landon Wilson	.02	.10
88 Claude Lemieux	.02	.10
89 Dimitri Khristich	.02	.10
90 Luc Robitaille	.07	.20
91 Todd Warriner	.02	.10
92 Kelly Hrudey	.07	.20
93 Mike Dunham	.07	.20
94 Mike Grier	.02	.10
95 Joe Juneau	.07	.20
96 Alexei Zhamnov	.02	.10
97 Jamie Langenbrunner	.02	.10
98 Sean Pronger	.02	.10
99 Janne Niinimaa	.07	.20
100 Chris Pronger	.07	.20
101 Ray Sheppard	.02	.10
102 Tony Amonte	.07	.20
103 Ron Tugnutt	.07	.20
104 Mike Modano	.20	.50
105 Dan Trebil	.02	.10
106 Alexander Mogilny	.07	.20
107 Darren McCarty	.02	.10
108 Ted Donato	.02	.10
109 Brian Savage	.02	.10
110 Mike Gartner	.07	.20
111 Jim Campbell	.02	.10
112 Roman Hamrlik	.02	.10
113 Andreas Dackell	.02	.10
114 Ron Hextall	.07	.20
115 Steve Washburn	.02	.10
116 Jeff Hackett	.07	.20
117 Joe Sakic	.25	.60
118 Anson Carter	.07	.20
119 Vyacheslav Kozlov	.02	.10
120 Nikolai Khabibulin	.07	.20
121 Tony Granato	.02	.10
122 Al MacInnis	.07	.20
123 Daren Puppa	.07	.20
124 Mike Richter	.10	.30
125 Zigmund Palffy	.07	.20
126 Martin Brodeur	.30	.75
127 Rem Murray	.02	.10
128 Sean Burke	.07	.20
129 Aki Berg	.02	.10
130 Dmitri Mironov	.02	.10
131 Jamie Allison	.02	.10
132 Valeri Kamensky	.07	.20
133 Pat LaFontaine	.10	.30
134 Jozef Stumpel	.07	.20
135 Peter Bondra	.07	.20
136 Mark Recchi	.07	.20
137 Ron Francis	.07	.20
138 Harry York	.02	.10
139 Mats Sundin	.10	.30
140 Bobby Holik	.02	.10
141 Eric Desjardins	.07	.20
142 Scott Lachance	.02	.10
143 Wayne Gretzky	.75	2.00
144 Ed Jovanovski	.07	.20
145 Jason Arnott	.02	.10
146 Andrew Cassels	.02	.10
147 Roman Vopat	.02	.10
148 Dwayne Roloson	.02	.10
149 Derek Plante	.02	.10
150 Phil Housley	.02	.10
151 Mikael Renberg	.07	.20
152 Petr Nedved	.07	.20
153 Grant Fuhr	.07	.20
154 Felix Potvin	.10	.30
155 John MacLean	.02	.10
156 Brian Leetch	.10	.30
157 Rod Brind'Amour	.07	.20
158 Ryan Smyth	.07	.20
159 Teemu Selanne	.10	.30
160 Theo Fleury	.02	.10
161 Adam Deadmarsh	.02	.10
162 Corey Hirsch	.07	.20
163 Bryan Berard	.07	.20
164 Ed Belfour	.10	.30
165 Sergei Berezin	.02	.10
166 Damian Rhodes	.07	.20
167 Guy Hebert	.07	.20
168 Derian Hatcher	.02	.10
169 Jonas Hoglund	.02	.10
170 Matthew Barnaby	.02	.10
171 Scott Mellanby	.02	.10
172 Bill Ranford	.07	.20
173 Vincent Damphousse	.02	.10
174 Anders Eriksson	.02	.10
175 Chad Kilger	.02	.10
176 Darren Turcotte	.02	.10
177 Dino Ciccarelli	.02	.10
178 Niklas Sundstrom	.02	.10
179 Stephane Fiset	.07	.20
180 Mike Ricci	.02	.10
181 Brendan Shanahan	.10	.30
182 Darcy Tucker	.02	.10
183 Eric Fichaud	.07	.20
184 Todd Marchant	.02	.10
185 Keith Primeau	.02	.10
186 Joe Nieuwendyk	.07	.20
187 Pavel Bure	.10	.30
188 Jaromir Jagr	.20	.50
189 Kirk McLean	.07	.20
190 Daniel Goneau	.02	.10
191 Rob Niedermayer	.02	.10
192 Eric Daze	.07	.20
193 Richard Matvichuk	.02	.10
194 Scott Stevens	.07	.20
195 Dale Hunter	.02	.10
196 Hnat Domenichelli	.02	.10
197 Philippe DeRouville	.02	.10
198 Marcel Cousineau	.07	.20
199 Kevin Hodson	.07	.20
200 Jean-Sebastien Giguere	.07	.20
201 Paxton Schafer RC	.07	.20
202 Marc Denis	.07	.20
203 Frank Banham RC	.02	.10
204 Vadim Sharifijanov	.02	.10
205 Paul Healey RC	.02	.10
206 D.J. Smith RC	.02	.10
207 Christian Matte RC	.02	.10
208 Sean Brown RC	.02	.10
209 Tomas Vokoun RC	.60	1.50
210 Vladimir Vorobiev RC	.02	.10
211 Jean-Yves Leroux RC	.02	.10
212 Domenic Pittis RC	.02	.10
213 Derek Wilkinson RC	.02	.10
214 Jason Holland	.02	.10
215 Pascal Rheaume RC	.02	.10
216 Steve Kelly RC	.02	.10
217 Vaclav Varada	.02	.10
218 Mike Fountain	.02	.10
219 Vaclav Prospal RC	.10	.30
220 Jaroslav Svejkovsky	.07	.20
221 Marty Murray	.02	.10
222 Wade Belak RC	.07	.20
223 Jamal Mayers RC	.02	.10
224 Shayne Toporowski RC	.02	.10
225 Mike Knuble RC	.07	.20
226 Jarome Iginla CL (1-60)	.10	.30
227 Keith Tkachuk CL (61-120)	.07	.20
228 Adam Oates CL (121-180)	.02	.10
229 John LeClair CL (181-230)	.10	.30
230 Brian Leetch CL (inserts)	.07	.20

1997-98 Donruss Press Proofs Silver

Randomly inserted in packs, this 230-card set was a parallel to the Donruss base set and featured a full foil card stock with silver foil accents. Only 2000 of this set were produced.

*VETS: 8X TO 20X BASIC CARDS
*ROOKIES: 4X TO 10X BASIC CARDS

1997-98 Donruss Press Proofs Gold

Randomly inserted in packs, this 230-card set was a parallel to the Donruss base set and featured a unique die cut design with gold foil stamping. Only 500 of this set were produced and were sequentially numbered.

*VETS: 15X TO 40X BASIC CARDS
*ROOKIES: 8X TO 20X BASIC CARDS

1997-98 Donruss Between The Pipes

Randomly inserted in hobby packs only, this 10-card set featured color photos of the league's top defensive players printed on an etched, full foil card stock with foil stamped accents. Only 3000 of this set were produced and were sequentially numbered.

COMPLETE SET (10)	50.00	125.00
1 Patrick Roy	15.00	40.00
2 Martin Brodeur	12.00	30.00
3 John Vanbiesbrouck	4.00	10.00
4 Dominik Hasek	10.00	20.00
5 Chris Osgood	4.00	10.00
6 Jose Theodore	4.00	10.00
7 Garth Snow	4.00	10.00
8 Curtis Joseph	5.00	12.00
9 Felix Potvin	5.00	12.00
10 Jocelyn Thibault	4.00	10.00

1997-98 Donruss Elite Inserts

Randomly inserted in packs, this 12-card set featured color photos of the league's most dominant superstars printed on card stock utilizing a double treatment of gold and holographic gold foils. Only 2500 of each card were produced and were sequentially numbered.

COMPLETE SET (12)	30.00	60.00
1 Wayne Gretzky	8.00	20.00
2 Jaromir Jagr	2.00	5.00
3 Eric Lindros	1.25	3.00
4 Paul Kariya	1.25	3.00
5 Patrick Roy	6.00	15.00
6 Steve Yzerman	5.00	12.00
7 Peter Forsberg	3.00	8.00
8 John Vanbiesbrouck	.75	2.00
9 Brendan Shanahan	1.25	3.00
10 Martin Brodeur	3.00	8.00
11 Dominik Hasek	2.50	6.00
12 Teemu Selanne	1.25	3.00
13P Martin Brodeur PROMO	2.00	5.00

1997-98 Donruss Line 2 Line

Randomly inserted in packs, this 24-card fractured insert set contained three levels of scarcity with each level printed on foil card stocks. Level one was "Red Line" which featured color photos of 12 players with red foil enhancements and each card sequentially numbered to 4000; Level two was "Blue Line" which featured color photos of eight players with blue foil enhancements and each sequentially numbered to 2000; Level three was "Gold Line" which featured color photos of four players with each sequentially numbered to 1000. The first 250 of each Line two card featured a unique die-cut design.

COMPLETE SET (24)	100.00	200.00
*RED DIE CUT: 2X TO 5X BASIC RED		
*BLUE DIE CUT: 1.2X TO 3X BASIC BLUE		
*GOLD DIE CUT: 1X TO 2.5X BASIC GOLD		
1 Wayne Gretzky G	20.00	50.00
2 Teemu Selanne R	4.00	10.00
3 Brian Leetch B	4.00	10.00
4 Peter Forsberg R	8.00	20.00
5 Steve Yzerman R	12.00	30.00
6 Oleg Tverdovsky B	1.25	3.00
7 Doug Gilmour R	1.50	4.00
8 Eric Lindros G	3.00	8.00
9 Bryan Berard B	2.50	6.00
10 Brendan Shanahan R	1.50	4.00
11 Pavel Bure R	3.00	8.00
12 Joe Sakic R	6.00	15.00
13 Chris Chelios B	5.00	12.00
14 Mike Modano R	5.00	12.00
15 Paul Coffey B	5.00	12.00
16 Jaromir Jagr G	10.00	25.00
17 Jarome Iginla R	4.00	10.00
18 Brett Hull R	4.00	10.00
19 Wade Redden B	2.50	6.00
20 Paul Kariya G	10.00	25.00
21 Ray Bourque B	7.50	15.00
22 Ryan Smyth R	1.50	4.00
23 Mark Messier R	3.00	8.00
24 Sandis Ozolinsh B	1.25	3.00
P4 Peter Forsberg PROMO	8.00	20.00
P5 Steve Yzerman PROMO	10.00	25.00

1997-98 Donruss Rated Rookies

Randomly inserted in packs, this 10-card set featured color action photos of the hottest young rookie prospects printed on a background with the letters "RR." A "Medalist" parallel was also created and printed on foil card stock accented with both gold foil and silver holographic foil treatments.

COMPLETE SET (10)	6.00	15.00
*MEDALIST: 1.5X TO 4X BASIC INSERTS		
1 Tomas Vokoun	2.00	5.00
2 Paxton Schafer	.40	1.00
3 Vaclav Prospal	.75	2.00
4 Marc Denis	.75	2.00
5 Domenic Pittis	.40	1.00
6 Christian Matte	.40	1.00
7 Marcel Cousineau	.40	1.00
8 Steve Kelly	.40	1.00
9 Jaroslav Svejkovsky	.40	1.00
10 Jean-Sebastien Giguere	2.00	5.00

1997-98 Donruss Red Alert

Randomly inserted in retail packs only, this 10-card set featured color photos of the league's top goal scorers printed on thick plastic card stock, die cut in the shape of a goal light and highlighted with red holographic foil treatments. Only 5,000 of the set were produced and were sequentially numbered.

COMPLETE SET (10)	40.00	80.00
1 Adam Deadmarsh	2.00	5.00
2 Ryan Smyth	4.00	10.00
3 Sergei Fedorov	6.00	15.00
4 Keith Tkachuk	4.00	10.00
5 Brett Hull	6.00	15.00
6 Pavel Bure	6.00	15.00
7 John LeClair	2.00	5.00
8 Zigmund Palffy	4.00	10.00
9 Mats Sundin	4.00	10.00
10 Peter Bondra	4.00	10.00

1996-97 Donruss Canadian Ice

This 150-card set was issued eight cards per pack with a suggested retail price of $2.99. While these sets were initially made for distribution to Canada, a large amount of the product was shipped to the United States. Card fronts featured a full color action photo with the player's name and team appearing near the bottom of the card. Key rookies in this set included Mike Grier, Kevin Hodson, Ethan Moreau, and Dainius Zubrus.

COMPLETE SET (150)	10.00	25.00
1 Jaromir Jagr	.30	.75
2 Jocelyn Thibault	.20	.50
3 Paul Kariya	.20	.50
4 Derian Hatcher	.02	.10
5 Wayne Gretzky	1.00	2.50
6 Peter Forsberg	.30	.75
7 Eric Lindros	.20	.50
8 Adam Oates	.08	.25
9 Paul Coffey	.20	.50
10 Chris Osgood	.08	.25
11 Pat LaFontaine	.20	.50
12 Mats Sundin	.20	.50
13 Rob Niedermayer	.08	.25
14 Doug Weight	.08	.25
15 Al MacInnis	.08	.25
16 Damian Rhodes	.08	.25
17 Stephane Fiset	.08	.25
18 Mike Gartner	.08	.25
19 Patrick Roy	.60	1.50
20 Eric Daze	.08	.25
21 Ray Bourque	.30	.75
22 Keith Tkachuk	.20	.50
23 Mark Recchi	.08	.25
24 Peter Bondra	.08	.25
25 Mike Modano	.25	.60
26 Mike Richter	.20	.50
27 Keith Primeau	.02	.10
28 Todd Bertuzzi	.20	.50
29 Wendel Clark	.08	.25
30 Scott Young	.02	.10
31 Mario Lemieux	.60	1.50
32 Valeri Kamensky	.08	.25
33 Kirk McLean	.08	.25
34 Daniel Alfredsson	.08	.25
35 Ed Jovanovski	.08	.25
36 Kelly Hrudey	.08	.25
37 Trevor Kidd	.08	.25
38 Joe Juneau	.02	.10
39 Steve Yzerman	.50	1.25
40 Saku Koivu	.20	.50
41 Alexei Kovalev	.02	.10
42 Rob Blake	.08	.25
43 Shayne Corson	.02	.10
44 Roman Hamrlik	.08	.25
45 Stephane Yelle	.02	.10
46 Martin Brodeur	.40	1.00
47 Kirk Muller	.02	.10
48 Pat Verbeek	.02	.10
49 Jari Kurri	.08	.25
50 Michal Pivonka	.02	.10
51 Ron Hextall	.08	.25
52 Trevor Linden	.08	.25
53 Vincent Damphousse	.02	.10
54 Owen Nolan	.08	.25
55 Sergei Fedorov	.25	.60
56 Chris Chelios	.20	.50
57 Jeremy Roenick	.25	.60
58 Zigmund Palffy	.20	.50
59 Pavel Bure	.20	.50
60 Dominik Hasek	.40	1.00
61 Alexei Yashin	.02	.10
62 Chris Gratton	.08	.25
63 Joe Nieuwendyk	.08	.25
64 Luc Robitaille	.08	.25
65 Brett Hull	.25	.60
66 Sean Burke	.08	.25
67 Felix Potvin	.20	.50
68 Jason Arnott	.02	.10
69 Valeri Bure	.02	.10
70 Tom Barrasso	.08	.25
71 Vyacheslav Kozlov	.02	.10
72 Petr Sykora	.02	.10
73 Corey Hirsch	.08	.25
74 Joe Sakic	.40	1.00
75 Bill Ranford	.08	.25
76 Yanic Perreault	.02	.10
77 Mikael Renberg	.08	.25
78 Theo Fleury	.08	.25
79 Jim Carey	.08	.25
80 Vitali Yachmenev	.02	.10
81 Martin Rucinsky	.02	.10
82 Jeff O'Neill	.02	.10
83 Marcus Ragnarsson	.02	.10
84 John Vanbiesbrouck	.20	.50
85 Teemu Selanne	.20	.50
86 Larry Murphy	.08	.25
87 Mark Messier	.20	.50
88 Alexei Zhamnov	.08	.25
89 Ryan Smyth	.20	.50
90 Andy Moog	.08	.25
91 Alexander Mogilny	.08	.25
92 Kris Draper	.02	.10
93 Ron Francis	.08	.25
94 Mike Vernon	.08	.25
95 Nikolai Khabibulin	.08	.25
96 Mariusz Czerkawski	.02	.10
97 Mathieu Schneider	.02	.10
98 Stephane Richer	.08	.25
99 Mike Ricci	.02	.10
100 John LeClair	.20	.50
101 Brendan Shanahan	.20	.50
102 Daren Puppa	.08	.25
103 Scott Stevens	.08	.25
104 Alexandre Daigle	.02	.10
105 Dimitri Khristich	.02	.10
106 Bernie Nicholls	.02	.10
107 Scott Mellanby	.08	.25
108 Brian Leetch	.20	.50
109 Grant Fuhr	.08	.25
110 Pierre Turgeon	.08	.25
111 Jere Lehtinen	.02	.10
112 Doug Gilmour	.08	.25
113 Ed Belfour	.20	.50
114 Geoff Sanderson	.08	.25
115 Claude Lemieux	.02	.10
116 Curtis Joseph	.20	.50
117 Igor Larionov	.02	.10
118 Jamie Pushor	.02	.10
119 Sergei Berezin RC	.20	.50
120 Eric Fichaud	.08	.25
121 Wade Redden	.02	.10
122 Hnat Domenichelli	.02	.10
123 Rem Murray RC	.02	.10
124 Jarome Iginla	.25	.60
125 Richard Zednik RC	.25	.60
126 Daniel Goneau RC	.02	.10
127 Ethan Moreau RC	.20	.50
128 Janne Niinimaa	.20	.50
129 Tomas Holmstrom RC	.60	1.50
130 Fredrik Modin RC	.30	.75
131 Bryan Berard	.20	.50
132 Jim Campbell	.02	.10
133 Chris O'Sullivan	.02	.10
134 Andreas Dackell RC	.02	.10
135 Daymond Langkow	.08	.25
136 Kevin Hodson RC	.20	.50
137 Jamie Langenbrunner	.02	.10
138 Mattias Timander RC	.02	.10
139 Tuomas Gronman	.02	.10
140 Jonas Hoglund	.02	.10
141 Mike Grier RC	.40	1.00
142 Terry Ryan RC	.02	.10
143 Darcy Tucker	.02	.10
144 Brandon Convery	.02	.10
145 Anders Eriksson	.02	.10
146 Christian Dube	.02	.10
147 Dainius Zubrus RC	.50	1.25
148 Grant Fuhr CL	.02	.10
149 Paul Coffey CL	.08	.25
150 Ray Bourque CL	.08	.25

1996-97 Donruss Canadian Ice Gold Press Proofs

This 150-card set was the tougher of two parallels to the base set. Production of these cards were limited to 150 sets, a fact which is noted on the card. The words Canadian Gold appeared on the top of the card, and a gold foil treatment was used to enhance the appearance.

*VETS: 12X TO 30X BASIC CARDS
*ROOKIES: 6X TO 15X BASIC CARDS

1996-97 Donruss Canadian Ice Red Press Proofs

This 150-card set was the easier of two parallels to the base set. Production of these cards was limited to 750 sets, a fact noted on the card. The fronts featured silver and red foil enhancements, along with the words Canadian Red.

*VETS: 6X TO 15X BASIC CARDS
*ROOKIES: 3X TO 8X

1996-97 Donruss Canadian Ice Les Gardiens

This bronze foil set featured 10 of the NHL's top netminders, each of whom were born in Quebec. A full-color portrait of each player adorned the card fronts, along with the skyline of Montreal in the background. The player's name and team were printed in gold foil along the bottom of these cards. Each card was serially numbered out of 1,500.

COMPLETE SET (10)	25.00	60.00
1 Patrick Roy	10.00	25.00
2 Jocelyn Thibault	2.00	5.00
3 Felix Potvin	3.00	8.00
4 Martin Brodeur	6.00	15.00
5 Stephane Fiset	2.00	5.00
6 Eric Fichaud	2.00	5.00
7 Dominic Roussel	2.00	5.00
8 Emmanuel Fernandez	2.00	5.00
9 Martin Biron	2.00	5.00
10 Jose Theodore	4.00	10.00

1996-97 Donruss Canadian Ice Mario Lemieux Scrapbook

This 25-card set was made as a tribute to Mario Lemieux. Each card depicted a different highlight from the storied career of the Penguins' great. Only 1,966 individually numbered copies of each card were produced. Mario also hand signed a number of these cards, and there were two distinct versions of this card. The first, numbered out of 1200, was randomly inserted into packs. The second, numbered out of 500, was available in a framed version of the set available directly through an in-pack offer from Donruss.

COMPLETE SET (25)	100.00	200.00
COMMON CARD (1-25)	4.00	10.00
NNO1 M.Lemieux AU/500	100.00	250.00
NNO2 M.Lemieux AU/1200	30.00	80.00

1996-97 Donruss Canadian Ice O Canada

This 16-card set featured some of the top players born in Canada. Card fronts contained a color action photo, with the Canadian flag in the background. Each card had die-cut corners and featured gold and red foil printing. Just 2,000 individually numbered copies of each of these cards were produced.

COMPLETE SET (16)	40.00	100.00
1 Joe Sakic	6.00	15.00
2 Paul Kariya	2.50	6.00
3 Mark Messier	2.50	6.00
4 Jarome Iginla	3.00	8.00
5 Theo Fleury	.75	2.00
6 Ed Belfour	2.50	6.00
7 Wayne Gretzky	25.00	40.00
8 Chris Gratton	.75	2.00
9 Doug Gilmour	2.00	5.00
10 Kirk Muller	.75	2.00
11 Eric Lindros	2.50	6.00
12 Brendan Shanahan	2.50	6.00
13 Mario Lemieux	10.00	25.00
14 Eric Daze	.75	2.00
15 Geoff Sanderson	.75	2.00
16 Terry Ryan	.75	2.00

1997-98 Donruss Canadian Ice

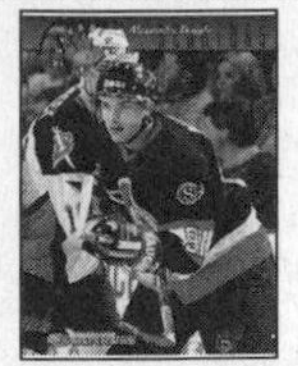

The 1997-98 Donruss Canadian Ice set was issued in one series totaling 150 cards and distributed in eight-card packs. The fronts featured color action player photos. The backs carryed player information.

COMPLETE SET (150)	15.00	30.00
1 Patrick Roy	1.00	2.50
2 Paul Kariya	.20	.50
3 Eric Lindros	.20	.50
4 Steve Yzerman	1.00	2.50
5 Wayne Gretzky	1.25	3.00
6 Peter Forsberg	.50	1.25
7 John Vanbiesbrouck	.08	.25
8 Jaromir Jagr	.30	.75
9 Jim Campbell	.02	.10
10 Dominik Hasek	.40	1.00
11 Ray Bourque	.30	.75
12 Jarome Iginla	.25	.60
13 Mike Modano	.30	.75
14 Ed Jovanovski	.08	.25
15 Jocelyn Thibault	.08	.25
16 Keith Tkachuk	.20	.50
17 Brett Hull	.25	.60
18 Pavel Bure	.20	.50
19 Saku Koivu	.20	.50
20 Curtis Joseph	.20	.50
21 Eric Daze	.08	.25
22 Keith Primeau	.02	.10
23 Theo Fleury	.02	.10
24 Pierre Turgeon	.08	.25
25 Peter Bondra	.08	.25
26 Ed Belfour	.20	.50
27 Pat Verbeek	.02	.10
28 Chris Osgood	.08	.25
29 Ray Sheppard	.02	.10
30 Stephane Fiset	.08	.25
31 Wade Redden	.02	.10
32 Trevor Linden	.08	.25
33 Zigmund Palffy	.08	.25
34 Tony Amonte	.08	.25
35 Derek Plante	.02	.10
36 Jonas Hoglund	.02	.10
37 Guy Hebert	.08	.25
38 Garth Snow	.08	.25
39 Chris Gratton	.08	.25
40 Mats Sundin	.20	.50
41 Geoff Sanderson	.08	.25
42 Martin Brodeur	.50	1.25
43 Jozef Stumpel	.08	.25
44 Ron Francis	.08	.25
45 Alexander Mogilny	.08	.25
46 Bill Ranford	.08	.25
47 Kirk Muller	.02	.10
48 Ron Hextall	.08	.25
49 Doug Gilmour	.08	.25
50 Mark Messier	.20	.50
51 Joe Nieuwendyk	.08	.25
52 Ryan Smyth	.08	.25
53 Mark Recchi	.08	.25
54 Mike Gartner	.08	.25
55 Al MacInnis	.08	.25
56 Felix Potvin	.20	.50
57 Rob Blake	.08	.25
58 Dimitri Khristich	.02	.10
59 Jim Carey	.08	.25
60 Trevor Kidd	.08	.25
61 Martin Gelinas	.02	.10
62 Oleg Tverdovsky	.02	.10
63 Ron Tugnutt	.08	.25
64 Paul Coffey	.20	.50
65 Travis Green	.02	.10
66 Andrew Cassels	.02	.10
67 Brendan Shanahan	.20	.50
68 Luc Robitaille	.08	.25
69 Pat LaFontaine	.20	.50
70 Daymond Langkow	.08	.25
71 Petr Nedved	.08	.25
72 Sergei Fedorov	.30	.75
73 Anson Carter	.08	.25
74 Teemu Selanne	.20	.50
75 Nikolai Khabibulin	.08	.25
76 Ken Wregget	.08	.25
77 Dino Ciccarelli	.02	.10
78 Adam Oates	.08	.25
79 Kirk McLean	.08	.25
80 Wendel Clark	.08	.25
81 Jeff Friesen	.02	.10
82 Valeri Kamensky	.08	.25
83 Ethan Moreau	.02	.10
84 Matthew Barnaby	.02	.10
85 Andy Moog	.08	.25
86 Doug Weight	.08	.25
87 Mike Dunham	.08	.25
88 Brian Leetch	.20	.50
89 Mike Peca	.02	.10
90 Chris Pronger	.08	.25
91 Alexei Zhamnov	.02	.10
92 Bryan Berard	.08	.25
93 John LeClair	.20	.50
94 Steve Sullivan	.02	.10
95 Grant Fuhr	.08	.25

96 Mikael Renberg .08 .25
97 Adam Graves .02 .10
98 Ray Ferraro .02 .10
99 Sean Burke .08 .25
100 Jeremy Roenick .25 .60
101 Jeff Hackett .08 .25
102 Joe Sakic .40 1.00
103 Jamie Langenbrunner .02 .10
104 Stephane Richer .02 .10
105 Dave Andreychuk .02 .10
106 Tommy Salo .08 .25
107 Mike Richter .20 .50
108 Owen Nolan .08 .25
109 Corey Hirsch .08 .25
110 Daren Puppa .08 .25
111 Darcy Tucker .02 .10
112 Daniel Alfredsson .08 .25
113 Rod Brind'Amour .08 .25
114 Scott Stevens .08 .25
115 Vincent Damphousse .02 .10
116 Mathieu Schneider .02 .10
117 Jason Arnott .02 .10
118 Mike Vernon .08 .25
119 Sandis Ozolinsh .02 .10
120 Chris Chelios .20 .50
121 Mike Grier .02 .10
122 Alexandre Daigle .02 .10
123 Roman Hamrlik .02 .10
124 Derian Hatcher .02 .10
125 Damian Rhodes .08 .25
126 Adam Deadmarsh .02 .10
127 Alexei Yashin .02 .10
128 Terry Ryan .02 .10
129 Jeff Ware .02 .10
130 Steve Kelly .02 .10
131 Hnat Domenichelli .02 .10
132 Steve Shields RC .30 .75
133 Paxton Schafer RC .08 .25
134 Vadim Sharifijanov .02 .10
135 Vaclav Prospal RC .20 .50
136 Mike Fountain .02 .10
137 Christian Matte RC .02 .10
138 Tomas Vokoun RC .60 1.50
139 Vladimir Vorobiev RC .02 .10
140 Domenic Pittis RC .02 .10
141 Vaclav Varada .02 .10
142 D.J. Smith RC .02 .10
143 Jaroslav Svejkovsky .08 .25
144 Jason Holland .02 .10
145 Marc Denis .08 .25
146 Jean-Sebastien Giguere .08 .25
147 Marcel Cousineau .08 .25
148 Dave Andreychuk CL (1-75) .02 .10
149 Mike Gartner CL (76-150) .02 .10
150 Stanley Cup .02 .10
Team Picture CL (inserts)

1997-98 Donruss Canadian Ice Dominion Series

This 150-card set was a parallel to the base set and was similar in design. Only 150 of each card were produced. Serial numbered and non-serial numbered cards carry the same value.

*VETS: 8X TO 20X BASIC CARDS
*ROOKIES: 4X TO 10X BASIC CARDS

1997-98 Donruss Canadian Ice Provincial Series

This 150-card set was a parallel to the base set and was similar in design. Only 750 of each card were produced, and were sequentially numbered.

*VETS: 5X TO 12X BASIC CARDS
*ROOKIES: 1X TO 2.5X BASIC CARDS

1997-98 Donruss Canadian Ice Les Gardiens

Randomly inserted in packs, this 12-card set featured color photos honoring great goaltenders from Quebec printed on micro-etched foil board. Only 1500 of each card were produced and were sequentially numbered.

COMPLETE SET (12) 30.00 80.00
*PROMOS: 4X TO 1X BASIC INSERTS
1 Patrick Roy 12.00 30.00
2 Felix Potvin 4.00 10.00
3 Martin Brodeur 8.00 20.00
4 Jean-Sebastien Giguere 4.00 10.00
5 Stephane Fiset 2.00 5.00
6 Jose Theodore 4.00 10.00
7 Jocelyn Thibault 2.00 5.00
8 Eric Fichaud 2.00 5.00
9 Patrick Lalime 2.00 5.00
10 Marcel Cousineau 2.00 5.00
11 Philippe DeRouville 2.00 5.00
12 Marc Denis 2.00 5.00

1997-98 Donruss Canadian Ice National Pride

Randomly inserted in packs, this 30-card set featured color photos of the most prominent native Canadian players printed on a die cut plastic card in the shape of a maple leaf and with gold foil highlights.

COMPLETE SET (30) 75.00 150.00
1 Wayne Gretzky 20.00 50.00
2 Mark Messier 3.00 8.00
3 Paul Kariya 3.00 8.00
4 Steve Yzerman 15.00 40.00
5 Brendan Shanahan 3.00 8.00
6 Chris Osgood 1.50 4.00
7 Adam Oates 1.50 4.00
8 Eric Lindros 3.00 8.00
9 Doug Gilmour 1.50 4.00
10 Ryan Smyth 1.50 4.00
11 Ray Bourque 5.00 12.00
12 Jason Arnott 1.00 2.50
13 Jarome Iginla 4.00 10.00
14 Geoff Sanderson 1.50 4.00
15 Alexandre Daigle 1.00 2.50
16 Trevor Linden 1.50 4.00
17 Joe Sakic 6.00 15.00
18 Mark Recchi 1.50 4.00
19 Theo Fleury 1.00 2.50
20 Ron Francis 1.50 4.00
21 Daymond Langkow 1.50 4.00
22 Ed Belfour 3.00 8.00
23 Paul Coffey 3.00 8.00
24 Pierre Turgeon 1.50 4.00
25 Claude Lemieux 1.00 2.50
26 Ron Hextall 1.50 4.00
27 Curtis Joseph 3.00 8.00
28 Mike Vernon 1.50 4.00
29 Vincent Damphousse 1.00 2.50
30 Owen Nolan 1.50 4.00

1997-98 Donruss Canadian Ice Stanley Cup Scrapbook

Randomly inserted in packs, this 33-card set was a fractured chase set which features color photos of players from each round of the 1997 Stanley Cup Playoffs. Only 2000 of the 16 Quarterfinals cards were produced and were sequentially numbered; 1500 of the eight sequentially numbered Conference Semifinals cards were produced; 1000 of the six sequentially numbered Conference Finals cards were produced; 750 of the two sequentially numbered Stanley Cup Finals cards were produced; only 250 of the one Stanley Cup Champions cards were produced and were sequentially numbered. Mike Vernon and Eric Lindros each autographed 750 of the Stanley Cup Finals cards, and Brendan Shanahan autographed 250 of the Stanley Cup Champions cards. A framed version of this set serial numbered to 500 was also available through a mail-in offer in packs. The cards were a parallel to the base set except that the words "Canadian Collectors Set" appeared at the top of the card. Sets were available intially for $500 through this offer.

*FRAMED/500: .5X TO 1.2X BASIC INSERTS
FRAMED/500 ISSUED VIA MAIL REDEMPTION
1 Mike Modano Q 4.00 10.00
2 Curtis Joseph Q 4.00 10.00
3 Joe Sakic Q 8.00 20.00
4 Chris Chelios Q 2.50 6.00
5 Chris Osgood Q 2.50 6.00
6 Brett Hull Q 4.00 10.00
7 Jeremy Roenick Q 4.00 10.00
8 Teemu Selanne Q 4.00 10.00
9 Jaromir Jagr Q 6.00 15.00
10 Garth Snow Q 2.00 5.00
11 Alexei Yashin Q 2.00 5.00
12 Steve Shields Q 2.00 5.00
13 Doug Gilmour Q 3.00 8.00
14 Jose Theodore Q 4.00 10.00
15 Mike Richter Q 2.50 6.00
16 John Vanbiesbrouck Q 2.50 6.00
17 Ryan Smyth CS 2.50 6.00
18 Peter Forsberg CS 8.00 20.00
19 Steve Yzerman CS 12.00 30.00
20 Paul Kariya CS 4.00 10.00
21 Janne Niinimaa CS 2.00 5.00
22 Dominik Hasek CS 8.00 20.00
23 Mark Messier CS 4.00 10.00
24 Martin Brodeur CS 12.50 30.00
25 Slava Kozlov CF 2.50 6.00
26 Sergei Fedorov CF 8.00 20.00
27 Patrick Roy CF 15.00 40.00
28 Wayne Gretzky CF 25.00 60.00
29 John LeClair CF 2.50 6.00
30 Paul Coffey CF 4.00 10.00
31 Mike Vernon AU/750 10.00 25.00
32 Eric Lindros AU/750 20.00 50.00
33 Brendan Shanahan AU/250 50.00 100.00

1995-96 Donruss Elite

This 110-card super premium set was the last mainstream release of the 1995-96 card season. The product was distributed by Pinnacle Brands, which purchased Donruss and all of its sports licenses just prior to the set's debut. The eight-card packs had a suggested retail of $2.99. The Cool Trade Exchange card was randomly inserted 1:48 packs, although there were numerous reports of collectors finding up to eight copies per box. When found, it could be redeemed for parallel versions of the four Donruss Elite cards found in the NHL Cool Trade wrapper redemption set. This offer expired on September 30, 1996. Rookie Cards include Daniel Alfredsson, Todd Bertuzzi, Radek Dvorak, Chad Kilger and Shane Doan.

COMPLETE SET (110) 10.00 25.00
1 Jocelyn Thibault .20 .50
2 Nicklas Lidstrom .20 .50
3 Brendan Shanahan .20 .50
4 Kenny Jonsson .05 .15
5 Doug Weight .08 .25
6 Oleg Tverdovsky .05 .15
7 Brett Hull .25 .60
8 Larry Murphy .08 .25
9 Ray Bourque .30 .75
10 Adam Graves .05 .15
11 Gary Suter .05 .15
12 Bill Ranford .08 .25
13 Zigmund Palffy .08 .25
14 Cam Neely .20 .50
15 Al MacInnis .08 .25
16 Joe Sakic .40 1.00
17 Kevin Hatcher .05 .15
18 Alexander Mogilny .08 .25
19 Radek Dvorak RC .30 .75
20 Ed Belfour .20 .50
21 Jeff O'Neill .05 .15
22 Valeri Kamensky .08 .25
23 John MacLean .08 .25
24 Zdeno Ciger .05 .15
25 Daniel Alfredsson RC .50 1.25
26 Owen Nolan .08 .25
27 Wendel Clark .08 .25
28 Brian Savage .05 .15
29 Alexei Zhamnov .08 .25
30 Dominik Hasek .40 1.00
31 Paul Kariya .20 .50
32 Mike Modano .30 .75
33 Craig Janney .05 .15
34 Todd Harvey .08 .25
35 Jaromir Jagr .30 .75
36 Roman Hamrlik .08 .25
37 Sergei Zubov .05 .15
38 Marcus Ragnarsson RC .08 .25
39 Peter Forsberg .50 1.25
40 Ron Francis .08 .25
41 German Titov .05 .15
42 Grant Fuhr .20 .50
43 Martin Brodeur .50 1.25
44 Claude Lemieux .05 .15
45 Trevor Linden .08 .25
46 Mark Messier .20 .50
47 Jeremy Roenick .25 .60
48 Peter Bondra .08 .25
49 Donald Audette .05 .15
50 Joe Nieuwendyk .08 .25
51 Mario Lemieux CL .30 .75
52 Vitali Yachmenev .05 .15
53 Sergei Fedorov .30 .75
54 Kirk Muller .05 .15
55 Chad Kilger RC .05 .15
56 John LeClair .20 .50
57 Todd Bertuzzi RC .75 2.00
58 Wayne Gretzky 1.25 3.00
59 Curtis Joseph .20 .50
60 Niklas Sundstrom .08 .25
61 Chris Chelios .20 .50
62 Radek Bonk .05 .15
63 Eric Daze .08 .25
64 Patrick Roy 1.00 2.50
65 Rob Niedermayer .08 .25
66 Mario Lemieux 1.00 2.50
67 Saku Koivu .20 .50
68 Ed Jovanovski .20 .50
69 Jim Carey .08 .25
70 Scott Stevens .08 .25
71 Steve Thomas .08 .25
72 Mats Sundin .20 .50
73 Teemu Selanne .20 .50
74 Tomas Sandstrom .05 .15
75 Pat LaFontaine .20 .50
76 Pat Verbeek .05 .15
77 Pavel Bure .20 .50
78 Jeff Brown .05 .15
79 Alexei Yashin .05 .15
80 Adam Oates .08 .25
81 Keith Tkachuk .20 .50
82 Brian Bradley .05 .15
83 John Vanbiesbrouck .08 .25
84 Alexander Selivanov .08 .25
85 Paul Coffey .20 .50
86 Scott Mellanby .08 .25
87 Slava Kozlov .08 .25
88 Eric Lindros .20 .50
89 Deron Quint .05 .15
90 Pierre Turgeon .08 .25
91 Rod Brind'Amour .08 .25
92 Doug Gilmour .08 .25
93 Sandis Ozolinsh .05 .15
94 Mikael Renberg .08 .25
95 Kevin Stevens .05 .15
96 Vincent Damphousse .05 .15
97 Felix Potvin .20 .50
98 Brian Leetch .08 .25
99 Steve Yzerman 1.00 2.50
100 Dale Hawerchuk .20 .50
101 Jason Arnott .05 .15
102 Ray Sheppard .05 .15
103 Mark Recchi .08 .25
104 Joe Juneau .05 .15
105 Luc Robitaille .08 .25
106 Theo Fleury .05 .15
107 Sean Burke .08 .25
108 Ron Hextall .08 .25
109 Shane Doan RC .50 1.25
110 Eric Lindros CL .08 .25
NNO Cool Trade Exchange .05 .15

1995-96 Donruss Elite Die Cuts

This die-cut set paralleled the main Donruss Elite set. The first 500 cards off the press had the die-cut pattern. Interestingly, boxes from early in the production run contained cards intended to be die-cut which weren't. These cards are differentiated from regular issue cards by a curved pattern which runs across the top of the cards just above the photo. Although some collectors speculated that these cards were in shorter supply than the regular die-cuts, that was not verified by the company, and unsubstantiated by market evidence.

*DIE CUT VETS: 12X TO 30X BASIC CARDS
*DIE CUT ROOKIES: 4X TO 10X

1995-96 Donruss Elite Die Cuts Uncut

These cards are discernible from regular issue cards by a curved pattern which runs across the top of the cards just above the photo. Although some collectors speculate that these cards are in shorter supply than the regular die-cuts, that was not verified by the company, and unsubstantiated by market evidence.

*UNCUT VETS: 10X TO 25X BASIC CARDS
*UNCUT ROOKIES: 5X TO 12X
RANDOM INSERTS IN PACKS

1995-96 Donruss Elite Cutting Edge

This 15-card insert set celebrated the top performers of the 1995-96 season. The cards were printed and embossed on laminated polycarbonate material that simulated brushed steel. Each card was serially numbered out of 2,500. The cards were randomly inserted at a rate of 1:32 packs.

COMPLETE SET (15) 25.00 60.00
1 Eric Lindros 2.00 5.00
2 Mario Lemieux 5.00 12.00
3 Wayne Gretzky 8.00 20.00
4 Peter Forsberg 3.00 8.00
5 Paul Kariya 2.00 5.00
6 Jaromir Jagr 3.00 8.00
7 Alexander Mogilny 1.00 2.50
8 Mark Messier 2.00 5.00
9 Sergei Fedorov 2.00 5.00
10 Pierre Turgeon 1.00 2.50
11 Mats Sundin 2.00 5.00
12 Brett Hull 2.00 5.00
13 Paul Coffey 1.00 2.50
14 Jeremy Roenick 2.00 5.00
15 Teemu Selanne 2.00 5.00

1995-96 Donruss Elite Lemieux/Lindros Series

These two seven-card sets recognized two of the most dominating players in the game, Eric Lindros and Mario Lemieux, who also happened to be Donruss spokesmen. The cards were printed on gold holographic foil, with the Lindros cards serially numbered up to 1,088 and the Lemieux cards to 1,066. The seventh card in each series was autographed, giving it a considerably higher value. The seven cards were inserted at a rate of 1:160. There also was a card signed by both Lindros and Lemieux, which was not considered part of either complete set. Both this card and the Lemieux autograph were available only through redemption cards; Lemieux was unable to sign them in time for random insertion. The dual signed card was limited to 500 copies and was inserted in 1:2400 packs. The Lindros cards were assigned an E suffix for cataloguing purposes only.

COMP.LEMIEUX SET (7) 125.00 300.00
COMMON LEMIEUX (1-6) 15.00 40.00
COMP.LINDROS SET (7) 75.00 200.00
COMMON LINDROS (1-6) 10.00 25.00
7 Mario Lemieux AU 50.00 100.00
7E Eric Lindros AU 30.00 80.00
NNO Mario Lemieux AU/500 100.00 200.00
Eric Lindros AU

1995-96 Donruss Elite Painted Warriors

This ten card insert set focused on top goalies and their brightly painted headgear. Each card was printed on clear plastic and then die-cut around the face mask. The cards were individually numbered out of 2,500. The cards were inserted at a rate of 1:48 packs.

COMPLETE SET (10) 15.00 30.00
1 Patrick Roy 3.00 8.00
2 Felix Potvin .75 2.00
3 Martin Brodeur 2.50 6.00
4 Ed Belfour .75 2.00
5 Guy Hebert .75 2.00
6 John Vanbiesbrouck .75 2.00
7 Jocelyn Thibault .75 2.00
8 Ron Hextall .75 2.00
9 Grant Fuhr .75 2.00
10 Jim Carey .75 2.00
P3 Martin Brodeur PROMO 2.50 6.00
P4 Ed Belfour PROMO 2.50 6.00
P9 Grant Fuhr PROMO 2.50 6.00

1995-96 Donruss Elite Rookies

The fifteen cards in this set -- inserted 1:16 packs -- highlighted the top rookies of the 1995-96 season. The cards were printed on an icy silver foil background and detailed with gold trim. The cards were individually numbered out of 5,000.

COMPLETE SET (15) 15.00 40.00
1 Eric Daze 1.00 2.50
2 Vitali Yachmenev 1.00 2.50
3 Daniel Alfredsson 2.00 5.00
4 Todd Bertuzzi 2.00 5.00
5 Byron Dafoe 1.00 2.50
6 Eric Fichaud 1.00 2.50
7 Marcus Ragnarsson 1.00 2.50
8 Saku Koivu 3.00 8.00
9 Chad Kilger 1.00 2.50
10 Radek Dvorak 1.00 2.50
11 Ed Jovanovski 2.00 5.00
12 Jeff O'Neill 2.00 5.00
13 Shane Doan 2.00 5.00
14 Niklas Sundstrom 1.00 2.50
15 Kyle McLaren 1.00 2.50

1995-96 Donruss Elite World Juniors

This 44-card insert set featured the top Canadian and US players from the 1996 World Junior Championships. The cards were printed on canvas stock that simulated the flag of the player's home country. Each card was individually numbered out of 1,000. The cards were inserted 1:30 packs.

COMPLETE SET (44) 125.00 200.00
1 Marc Denis 3.00 8.00
2 Jose Theodore 5.00 12.00
3 Chad Allan 2.00 5.00
4 Nolan Baumgartner 2.00 5.00
5 Denis Gauthier 2.00 5.00
6 Jason Holland 2.00 5.00
7 Chris Phillips 3.00 8.00
8 Wade Redden 4.00 10.00
9 Rhett Warrener 2.00 5.00
10 Jason Botterill 2.00 5.00
11 Curtis Brown 2.00 5.00
12 Hnat Domenichelli 2.00 5.00
13 Christian Dube 2.00 5.00
14 Robb Gordon 2.00 5.00
15 Jarome Iginla 10.00 25.00
16 Daymond Langkow 3.00 8.00
17 Brad Larsen 2.00 5.00
18 Alyn McCauley 2.00 5.00
19 Craig Mills 2.00 5.00
20 Jason Podollan 2.00 5.00
21 Mike Watt 2.00 5.00
22 Jamie Wright 2.00 5.00
23 Brian Boucher 3.00 8.00
24 Marc Magliarditi 2.00 5.00
25 Bryan Berard 2.00 5.00
26 Chris Bogas 2.00 5.00
27 Ben Clymer 2.00 5.00
28 Jeff Kealty 2.00 5.00
29 Mike McBain 2.00 5.00
30 Jeremiah McCarthy 2.00 5.00
31 Tom Poti 2.00 5.00
32 Reg Berg 2.00 5.00
33 Matt Cullen 3.00 8.00
34 Chris Drury 6.00 15.00
35 Jeff Farkas 2.00 5.00
36 Casey Hankinson 2.00 5.00
37 Matt Herr 2.00 5.00
38 Mark Parrish 3.00 8.00
39 Erik Rasmussen 2.00 5.00
40 Marty Reasoner 2.00 5.00
41 Wyatt Smith 2.00 5.00
42 Brian Swanson 2.00 5.00
43 Mike Sylvia 2.00 5.00
44 Mike York 3.00 8.00

1996-97 Donruss Elite

The 1996-97 Donruss Elite set was issued in one series totalling 150 cards. Packs contained eight cards for a suggested retail price of $3.99, and were distributed as a hobby-only product. Card fronts featured a color action photo with a foil background. A 20-card rookie subset was found at the end of the set (#128-147). Key rookies included Sergei Berezin, Patrick Lalime, Ethan Moreau, and Dainius Zubrus.

COMPLETE SET (150) 12.50 25.00
1 Paul Kariya .25 .60
2 Ron Hextall .10 .30
3 Andy Moog .10 .30
4 Brett Hull .30 .75
5 Felix Potvin .25 .60
6 Jocelyn Thibault .25 .60
7 Eric Lindros .25 .60
8 Jaromir Jagr .40 1.00
9 Sergei Fedorov .30 .75
10 Wayne Gretzky 1.50 4.00
11 Peter Bondra .10 .30
12 Peter Forsberg .60 1.50
13 Stephane Fiset .10 .30
14 Owen Nolan .10 .30
15 Rob Niedermayer .10 .30
16 Martin Brodeur .60 1.50
17 Ray Bourque .40 1.00
18 Todd Bertuzzi .25 .60
19 Jim Carey .25 .60
20 Chris Chelios .25 .60
21 Chris Osgood .10 .30
22 Mark Messier .25 .60
23 Roman Hamrlik .10 .30
24 Kevin Hatcher .05 .15
25 Doug Weight .10 .30
26 Mark Recchi .10 .30
27 Jeremy Roenick .30 .75
28 Derian Hatcher .05 .15
29 Grant Fuhr .10 .30
30 Scott Stevens .10 .30
31 Adam Oates .10 .30
32 Scott Mellanby .10 .30
33 Mikael Renberg .10 .30
34 Corey Hirsch .10 .30
35 Michal Pivonka .05 .15
36 Stephane Richer .10 .30
37 Dominik Hasek .50 1.25
38 Steve Yzerman 1.25 3.00
39 Jeff O'Neill .05 .15
40 Ron Francis .10 .30
41 Alexei Yashin .05 .15
42 Pat Verbeek .05 .15
43 Geoff Courtnall .05 .15
44 Doug Gilmour .10 .30
45 Trevor Kidd .10 .30
46 Jason Arnott .05 .15
47 Niklas Sundstrom .05 .15
48 Rob Blake .10 .30
49 Nikolai Khabibulin .10 .30
50 Igor Larionov .05 .15
51 Sean Burke .10 .30
52 Zigmund Palffy .10 .30
53 Jeff Friesen .05 .15
54 Theo Fleury .05 .15
55 Mats Sundin .25 .60
56 Alexander Mogilny .10 .30
57 John LeClair .25 .60
58 Shayne Corson .05 .15
59 Teemu Selanne .25 .60
60 Kelly Hrudey .10 .30
61 Keith Tkachuk .25 .60
62 Joe Nieuwendyk .10 .30
63 Tom Barrasso .10 .30
64 Aaron Gavey .05 .15
65 Alexei Zhamnov .05 .15
66 Patrick Roy 1.25 3.00
67 Al MacInnis .10 .30
68 Trevor Linden .10 .30
69 Bill Guerin .05 .15
70 Dimitri Khristich .05 .15
71 Eric Daze .10 .30
72 Paul Coffey .25 .60
73 Keith Primeau .05 .15
74 John Vanbiesbrouck .10 .30
75 Bernie Nicholls .05 .15
76 Yanic Perreault .05 .15
77 Jere Lehtinen .05 .15
78 Luc Robitaille .10 .30
79 Todd Gill .05 .15
80 Saku Koivu .25 .60
81 Vyacheslav Kozlov .05 .15
82 Ed Jovanovski .10 .30
83 Brendan Witt .05 .15
84 Alexandre Daigle .05 .15
85 Jari Kurri .10 .30
86 Mike Vernon .10 .30
87 Jeff Beukeboom .05 .15
88 Mathieu Schneider .05 .15
89 Niklas Andersson .05 .15
90 Joe Juneau .05 .15
91 Ed Belfour .25 .60
92 Curtis Joseph .25 .60
93 Rod Brind'Amour .10 .30
94 Vitali Yachmenev .05 .15
95 Alexander Selivanov .05 .15
96 Mike Richter .25 .60
97 Bill Ranford .10 .30
98 Wendel Clark .10 .30
99 Slava Fetisov .05 .15
100 Daniel Alfredsson .10 .30
101 Pat LaFontaine .25 .60
102 Joe Murphy .05 .15
103 Pavel Bure .25 .60
104 Craig Janney .10 .30
105 Radek Dvorak .05 .15
106 Cory Stillman .05 .15
107 Adam Graves .05 .15
108 Aki Berg .05 .15
109 Mario Lemieux 1.25 3.00
110 Claude Lemieux .05 .15
111 Sergei Zubov .05 .15
112 Pierre Turgeon .10 .30
113 Damian Rhodes .10 .30
114 Daren Puppa .10 .30
115 Alexei Zhitnik .05 .15
116 Mike Modano .40 1.00
117 Kenny Jonsson .05 .15
118 Valeri Kamensky .10 .30
119 Valeri Bure .05 .15
120 Joe Sakic .50 1.25
121 Kirk McLean .10 .30
122 Petr Sykora .05 .15
123 Mike Gartner .10 .30
124 Ryan Smyth .25 .60
125 Brian Leetch .25 .60
126 Brendan Shanahan .25 .60
127 Geoff Sanderson .10 .30
128 Corey Schwab .10 .30
129 Anders Eriksson .05 .15
130 Harry York RC .25 .60
131 Jarome Iginla .30 .75
132 Eric Fichaud .10 .30
133 Patrick Lalime RC 1.25 3.00
134 Daymond Langkow .10 .30
135 Mattias Timander RC .05 .15
136 Ethan Moreau RC .25 .60
137 Christian Dube .05 .15
138 Sergei Berezin RC .50 1.25
139 Jose Theodore .30 .75
140 Wade Redden .05 .15
141 Dainius Zubrus RC .40 1.00
142 Jim Campbell .05 .15
143 Daniel Goneau RC .10 .30
144 Jamie Langenbrunner .06 .15
145 Rem Murray RC .05 .15
146 Jonas Hoglund .05 .15
147 Bryan Berard .25 .60
148 Chris Osgood CL (1-75) .10 .30
149 Eric Lindros CL (76-150) .25 .60
150 Jason Arnott CL (inserts) .05 .15

1996-97 Donruss Elite Die Cut Stars

This die-cut set paralleled the main Donruss Elite set. Card fronts featured a die-cut, silver-poly laminate foil to distinguish them from their base counterparts.

*VETS: 4X TO 10X BASIC CARDS
*ROOKIES: 2X TO 5X
RANDOM INSERTS IN PACKS

1996-97 Donruss Elite Aspirations

This set featured twenty-five of the NHL's top rookies and young superstars. Each card was serially numbered out of 3,000. Card fronts featured a color action photo with blue and silver foil surrounding the photo.

COMPLETE SET (25) 12.00 30.00
1 Eric Daze .40 1.00
2 Daniel Alfredsson 2.00 5.00
3 Petr Sykora .40 1.00
4 Todd Bertuzzi .75 2.00
5 Saku Koivu 2.00 5.00
6 Ed Jovanovski .75 2.00
7 Jim Campbell .40 1.00
8 Valeri Bure .40 1.00
9 Jeff O'Neill .40 1.00
10 Jere Lehtinen .75 2.00
11 Terry Ryan .40 1.00
12 Jonas Hoglund .40 1.00
13 Daymond Langkow .40 1.00
14 Eric Fichaud .40 1.00
15 Dainius Zubrus .40 1.00
16 Janne Niinimaa .40 1.00
17 Sergei Berezin .40 1.00
18 Daniel Goneau .40 1.00
19 Jarome Iginla 4.00 10.00
20 Ethan Moreau .40 1.00
21 Jamie Langenbrunner .40 1.00
22 Rem Murray .40 1.00
23 Bryan Berard .40 1.00
24 Wade Redden .40 1.00
25 Christian Dube .40 1.00

1996-97 Donruss Elite Hart to Hart

This special insert set was issued in two parts, one featuring Eric Lindros and the other featuring Mario Lemieux. Each set contained six cards. The Lindros set was serial numbered to 1,996 sets, with the first 188 signed by Lindros. The Lemieux set was serial numbered to 1,995 sets, with the first 166 signed by Lemieux. In addition, Donruss also included a dual autograph of Lemieux and Lindros, serial numbered to just 500. The prefixes listed below for the autographs are for checklisting purposes only.

COMPLETE LEMIEUX SET (6) 75.00 125.00
COMMON LEMIEUX 12.50 25.00
COMMON LEMIEUX AU 25.00 60.00
LEMIEUX PRINT RUN 1995 SER.#'d SETS
COMPLETE LINDROS SET (6) 40.00 80.00
COMMON LINDROS 6.00 15.00
COMMON LINDROS AU 30.00 80.00
LINDROS PRINT RUN 1996 SER.#'d SETS
ELML Eric Lindros 50.00 125.00
Mario Lemieux AU

1996-97 Donruss Elite Painted Warriors

This 10-card insert set focused on top goalies and their brightly painted headgear. Each card was printed on clear plastic and then die-cut around the mask. The cards were individually numbered out of 2,500.

COMPLETE SET (10) 30.00 80.00
1 Patrick Roy 10.00 25.00
2 Mike Richter 4.00 10.00
3 Jim Carey 2.00 5.00
4 John Vanbiesbrouck 4.00 10.00
5 Jocelyn Thibault 2.00 5.00
6 Felix Potvin 4.00 10.00
7 Ed Belfour 4.00 10.00
8 Martin Brodeur 6.00 15.00
9 Nikolai Khabibulin 4.00 10.00
10 Stephane Fiset 2.00 5.00

1996-97 Donruss Elite Painted Warriors Promos

These cards mirrored the regular versions except in the serial number box on the back, where the number read PROMO/2500. The Brodeur was the most readily available of these cards.

COMPLETE SET (10) 30.00 75.00
P1 Patrick Roy 6.00 12.00
P2 Mike Richter 6.00 12.00
P3 Jim Carey 6.00 12.00
P4 John Vanbiesbrouck 6.00 12.00
P5 Jocelyn Thibault 6.00 12.00
P6 Felix Potvin 6.00 12.00
P7 Ed Belfour 6.00 12.00

P8 Martin Brodeur 6.00 12.00
P9 Nikolai Khabibulin 6.00 12.00
P10 Stephane Fiset 6.00 12.00

1996-97 Donruss Elite Perspective

This 12-card set focused on the NHL's veteran stars. Card fronts featured a die-cut, micro-etched, foil design. Each card was individually numbered out of 500.

COMPLETE SET (12) 40.00 100.00
1 Wayne Gretzky 15.00 40.00
2 Mark Messier 3.00 8.00
3 Steve Yzerman 10.00 25.00
4 Mario Lemieux 12.00 30.00
5 Paul Coffey 2.00 5.00
6 Doug Gilmour 2.00 5.00
7 Brendan Shanahan 3.00 8.00
8 Jaromir Jagr 5.00 12.00
9 Brett Hull 4.00 10.00
10 Pat LaFontaine 2.00 5.00
11 Chris Chelios 2.00 5.00
12 Grant Fuhr 2.00 5.00

1996-97 Donruss Elite Status

This 12-card set took an up-close look at some of the NHL's top players who were in the prime of their careers. Card fronts were foil laminate and featured a full-color photo. Each card was serially numbered out of 750.

COMPLETE SET (12) 25.00 60.00
1 Pavel Bure 2.50 6.00
2 Keith Tkachuk 2.50 6.00
3 Sergei Fedorov 3.00 8.00
4 Doug Weight 1.25 3.00
5 Paul Kariya 2.50 6.00
6 Owen Nolan 1.25 3.00
7 Peter Forsberg 6.00 15.00
8 Eric Lindros 2.50 6.00
9 Alexander Mogilny 1.25 3.00
10 Teemu Selanne 2.50 6.00
11 Joe Sakic 5.00 12.00
12 Jeremy Roenick 3.00 8.00

1997-98 Donruss Elite

The 1997-98 Donruss Elite hobby exclusive set was issued in one series totaling 150 cards and was distributed in five-card packs with a suggested retail price of $3.99. The fronts featured color player photos printed on thick foil card stock. The backs carried player information. The set contained the topical subset: Elite Generations (115-144).

COMPLETE SET (150) 15.00 40.00
1 Peter Forsberg .60 1.50
2 Mike Modano .40 1.00
3 John Vanbiesbrouck .20 .50
4 Pavel Bure .25 .60
5 Mark Messier .25 .60
6 Joe Thornton .60 1.50
7 Paul Kariya .25 .60
8 Martin Brodeur .60 1.50
9 Wayne Gretzky 1.50 4.00
10 Eric Lindros .25 .60
11 Jaromir Jagr .40 1.00
12 Brett Hull .30 .75
13 Jarome Iginla .30 .75
14 Patrick Roy 1.25 3.00
15 Steve Yzerman 1.25 3.00
16 Sergei Samsonov .20 .50
17 Teemu Selanne .25 .60
18 Brendan Shanahan .25 .60
19 Curtis Joseph .25 .60
20 Saku Koivu .25 .60
21 Ray Bourque .40 1.00
22 Jaroslav Svejkovsky .20 .50
23 Keith Primeau .07 .20
24 Alexandre Daigle .07 .20
25 Vyacheslav Kozlov .07 .20
26 Jozef Stumpel .20 .50
27 Alexei Yashin .20 .50
28 Marian Hossa RC 2.00 5.00
29 Bryan Berard .20 .50
30 Dominik Hasek .50 1.25
31 Chris Chelios .25 .60
32 Derian Hatcher .07 .20
33 Ed Jovanovski .20 .50
34 Zigmund Palffy .20 .50
35 Ron Hextall .20 .50
36 Daymond Langkow .20 .50
37 Daniel Cleary .20 .50
38 Alyn McCauley .20 .50
39 Sean Burke .20 .50
40 Brian Leetch .25 .60
41 Joe Juneau .20 .50
42 Damian Rhodes .20 .50
43 Dino Ciccarelli .07 .20
44 Valeri Kamensky .20 .50
45 Guy Hebert .20 .50
46 Brad Isbister .07 .20
47 Adam Graves .07 .20
48 Andrew Cassels .07 .20
49 Joe Sakic .50 1.25
50 Dainius Zubrus .25 .60
51 Roberto Luongo RC 2.50 6.00
52 Ethan Moreau .07 .20
53 Chris Osgood .20 .50
54 Stephane Fiset .07 .20
55 Sergei Berezin .07 .20
56 Mike Richter .25 .60
57 Valeri Bure .07 .20
58 Mats Sundin .25 .60
59 Mike Dunham .20 .50
60 Byron Dafoe .20 .50
61 Joe Nieuwendyk .20 .50
62 Mike Grier .07 .20
63 Paul Coffey .25 .60
64 Chris Phillips .07 .20
65 Patrik Elias RC 1.00 2.50
66 Andy Moog .20 .50
67 Geoff Sanderson .20 .50
68 Jere Lehtinen .07 .20
69 Alexander Mogilny .20 .50
70 Ryan Smyth .20 .50
71 John LeClair .25 .60
72 Olli Jokinen RC .75 2.00
73 Doug Gilmour .20 .50
74 Theo Fleury .07 .20
75 Adam Deadmarsh .07 .20
76 Scott Mellanby .07 .20
77 Jeremy Roenick .30 .75
78 Jim Campbell .07 .20
79 Daren Puppa .20 .50
80 Vaclav Prospal RC .25 .60
81 Vincent Damphousse .07 .20
82 Derek Plante .07 .20
83 Sandis Ozolinsh .07 .20
84 Darren McCarty .07 .20
85 Luc Robitaille .20 .50
86 Wade Redden .07 .20
87 Eric Fichaud .20 .50
88 Jocelyn Thibault .20 .50
89 Trevor Linden .20 .50
90 Boyd Devereaux .07 .20
91 Chris Gratton .20 .50
92 Janne Niinimaa .20 .50
93 Jeff Friesen .07 .20
94 Roman Hamrlik .07 .20
95 Jason Arnott .07 .20
96 Sergei Fedorov .40 1.00
97 Tony Amonte .20 .50
98 Mattias Ohlund .20 .50
99 Patrick Marleau .40 1.00
100 Felix Potvin .25 .60
101 Tommy Salo .20 .50
102 Ed Belfour .25 .60
103 Doug Weight .20 .50
104 Daniel Alfredsson .20 .50
105 Pierre Turgeon .20 .50
106 Espen Knutsen RC .30 .75
107 Trevor Kidd .20 .50
108 Alexei Morozov .20 .50
109 Oleg Tverdovsky .07 .20
110 Grant Fuhr .20 .50
111 Pat LaFontaine .25 .60
112 Keith Tkachuk .25 .60
113 Ron Francis .20 .50
114 Derek Morris RC .30 .75
115 Joe Sakic G .25 .60
116 Brian Leetch G .25 .60
117 Alyn McCauley G .07 .20
118 Pavel Bure G .15 .40
119 Eric Lindros G .20 .50
120 Teemu Selanne G .25 .60
121 Jarome Iginla G .30 .75
122 Steve Yzerman G .60 1.50
123 Daniel Cleary G .07 .20
124 Bryan Berard G .07 .20
125 Jaromir Jagr G .20 .50
126 John Vanbiesbrouck G .20 .50
127 Mark Messier G .15 .40
128 Patrick Marleau G .20 .50
129 Mike Modano G .25 .60
130 Zigmund Palffy G .25 .60
131 Felix Potvin G .25 .60
132 Derek Morris G .07 .20
133 Brendan Shanahan G .20 .50
134 Sergei Samsonov G .20 .50
135 Dainius Zubrus G .25 .60
136 Paul Kariya G .25 .60
137 Martin Brodeur G .30 .75
138 Joe Thornton G .30 .75
139 Mattias Ohlund G .07 .20
140 Ryan Smyth G .07 .20
141 Jaroslav Svejkovsky G .07 .20
142 Patrick Roy G .60 1.50
143 Wayne Gretzky G .75 2.00
144 Espen Knutsen G .07 .20
145 Patrick Marleau CL .25 .60
146 Pat Lafontaine CL .07 .20
147 Mike Gartner CL .07 .20
148 Joe Thornton CL .30 .75
149 Teemu Selanne CL .25 .60
150 Mark Messier CL .20 .50

1997-98 Donruss Elite Aspirations

Randomly inserted in packs, this 150-card set was a die-cut parallel version of the base set printed on foil board. Each card was numbered 1 of 750.

*VETS: 4X TO 10X BASIC CARDS
*ROOKIES: 2X TO 5X BASIC CARDS

1997-98 Donruss Elite Status

Randomly inserted in packs, this 150-card set was a die-cut parallel version of the base set printed on holo-foil board. Each card was sequentially numbered to 100.

*VETS: 20X TO 50X BASIC CARDS
*ROOKIES: 8X TO 20X BASIC CARDS

1997-98 Donruss Elite Back to the Future

Randomly inserted in packs, this eight-card set featured color player photos printed on double-sided cards. One side displayed a veteran star or Hockey HOF member while the other side highlighted a younger talent. The first 100 of each card was autographed by both of the featured players.

COMPLETE SET (8) 30.00 60.00
1 Eric Lindros 3.00 8.00
Joe Thornton
2 Jocelyn Thibault 3.00 8.00
Marc Denis
3 Teemu Selanne 3.00 8.00
Patrick Marleau
4 Jaromir Jagr 4.00 10.00
Daniel Cleary
5 Sergei Fedorov 5.00 12.00
Peter Forsberg
6 Brett Hull 4.00 10.00
Bobby Hull
7 Martin Brodeur 5.00 12.00
Roberto Luongo
8 Gordie Howe 6.00 15.00
Steve Yzerman

1997-98 Donruss Elite Back to the Future Autographs

Randomly inserted in packs, this eight-card set was a parallel to the regular Back to the Future insert set and consisted of the first 100 cards of the regular set autographed by both players.

1 Eric Lindros 40.00 100.00
Joe Thornton
2 Jocelyn Thibault 40.00 100.00
Marc Denis
3 Teemu Selanne 40.00 100.00
Patrick Marleau
4 Jaromir Jagr 40.00 100.00
Daniel Cleary
5 Sergei Fedorov 75.00 200.00
Peter Forsberg
6 Brett Hull 75.00 200.00
Bobby Hull
7 Martin Brodeur 150.00 300.00
Roberto Luongo
8 Gordie Howe 150.00 400.00
Steve Yzerman

1997-98 Donruss Elite Craftsmen

Randomly inserted in packs, this 30-card set featured color photos of top players printed on full foil board and micro-etched. The cards were sequentially numbered to 2,500.

COMPLETE SET (30) 75.00 150.00
*MASTER/100: 2X TO 5X BASIC INSERTS
MASTER CRAFTSMEN PRINT RUN 100
1 John Vanbiesbrouck 1.00 2.50
2 Eric Lindros 1.50 4.00
3 Joe Sakic 3.00 8.00
4 Mark Messier 2.00 5.00
5 Jaroslav Svejkovsky 1.00 2.50
6 Dominik Hasek 3.00 8.00
7 Chris Osgood 1.00 2.50
8 Martin Brodeur 4.00 10.00
9 Sergei Fedorov 2.00 5.00
10 Daniel Cleary 1.00 2.50
11 Patrick Marleau 1.25 3.00
12 Sergei Samsonov 1.25 3.00
13 Felix Potvin 1.50 4.00
14 Patrick Roy 8.00 20.00
15 Teemu Selanne 1.50 4.00
16 Steve Yzerman 8.00 20.00
17 Jarome Iginla 2.00 5.00
18 Mike Modano 2.50 6.00
19 Wayne Gretzky 10.00 25.00
20 Pavel Bure 1.50 4.00
21 Ryan Smyth 1.25 3.00
22 Paul Kariya 1.50 4.00
23 Peter Forsberg 4.00 10.00
24 Joe Thornton 2.50 6.00
25 Jaromir Jagr 2.50 6.00
26 Bryan Berard 1.00 2.50
27 Brendan Shanahan 1.50 4.00
28 Keith Tkachuk 1.50 4.00
29 Curtis Joseph 1.50 4.00
30 Brian Leetch 1.00 2.50

1997-98 Donruss Elite Prime Numbers

Randomly inserted in packs, this 36-card set featured color photos of 12 top stars with a number in the background. Each star appeared on three cards which, when linked together in the right order, displayed a significant career statistic. Each card in the set was sequentially numbered to the career statistic and that number followed the player's name below.

STATED PRINT RUN 7-530
SERIAL #'d UNDER 20 NOT PRICED
1A Peter Forsberg 2/54 30.00 80.00
1B Peter Forsberg 5/204 8.00 20.00
1C Peter Forsberg 4/250 8.00 20.00
2A Patrick Roy 3/49 50.00 125.00
2B Patrick Roy 4/309 12.50 30.00
2C Patrick Roy 9/340 12.50 30.00
3A Mark Messier 2/95 8.00 20.00
3B Mark Messier 9/205 4.00 10.00
3C Mark Messier 5/290 4.00 10.00
4A Eric Lindros 4/36 15.00 40.00
4B Eric Lindros 3/406 4.00 10.00
4C Eric Lindros 6/430 4.00 10.00
5A Paul Kariya 2/46 30.00 80.00
5B Paul Kariya 4/206 8.00 20.00
5C Paul Kariya 6/240 4.00 10.00
6A Jaromir Jagr 2/66 20.00 50.00
6B Jaromir Jagr 6/206 10.00 25.00
6C Jaromir Jagr 6/260 10.00 25.00
7A Teemu Selanne 2/37 15.00 40.00
7B Teemu Selanne 3/207 4.00 10.00
7C Teemu Selanne 7/230 4.00 10.00
8A John Vanbiesbrouck 2/88 6.00 15.00
8B John Vanbiesbrouck 8/208 4.00 10.00
8C John Vanbiesbrouck 8/280 4.00 10.00
9A Brendan Shanahan 3/35 12.50 30.00
9B Brendan Shanahan 3/305 4.00 10.00
9C Brendan Shanahan 5/330 4.00 10.00
10A Steve Yzerman 5/39 60.00 150.00
10B Steve Yzerman 3/509 12.50 30.00
10C Steve Yzerman 9/530 12.50 30.00
11A Joe Sakic 3/7
11B Joe Sakic 0/307 6.00 15.00
11C Joe Sakic 7/300 6.00 15.00
12A Pavel Bure 3/88 8.00 20.00
12B Pavel Bure 8/308 4.00 10.00
12C Pavel Bure 8/380 4.00 10.00

1997-98 Donruss Elite Prime Numbers Die-Cuts

Randomly inserted in packs, this 36-card set was a die-cut parallel version of the regular Prime Numbers set. How many of each card was produced depended on the specified statistical number the card represented. Print runs of less than 10 not priced due to scarcity.

1A Peter Forsberg 2 (200) 12.50 30.00
1B Peter Forsberg 5 (50) 50.00 125.00
1C Peter Forsberg 4 (4)
2A Patrick Roy 3 (300) 15.00 40.00
2B Patrick Roy 4 (40) 60.00 150.00
2C Patrick Roy 9 (9)
3A Mark Messier 2 (200) 8.00 20.00
3B Mark Messier 9 (90) 12.50 30.00
3C Mark Messier 5 (5)
4A Eric Lindros 4 (400) 8.00 20.00
4B Eric Lindros 3 (30) 20.00 50.00
4C Eric Lindros 6 (6)
5A Paul Kariya 2 (200) 12.50 30.00
5B Paul Kariya 4 (40) 50.00 125.00
5C Paul Kariya 6 (6)
6A Jaromir Jagr 2 (200) 10.00 25.00
6B Jaromir Jagr 6 (60) 30.00 80.00
6C Jaromir Jagr 6 (6)
7A Teemu Selanne 2 (200) 8.00 20.00
7B Teemu Selanne 3 (30) 15.00 40.00
7C Teemu Selanne 7 (7)
8A John Vanbiesbrouck 2 (200) 8.00 20.00
8B John Vanbiesbrouck 8 (80) 12.50 30.00
8C John Vanbiesbrouck 8 (8)
9A Brendan Shanahan 3 (300) 8.00 20.00
9B Brendan Shanahan 3 (30) 20.00 50.00
9C Brendan Shanahan 5 (5)
10A Steve Yzerman 5 (500) 15.00 40.00
10B Steve Yzerman 3 (30) 60.00 150.00
10C Steve Yzerman 9 (9)
11A Joe Sakic 3 (300) 10.00 25.00
11C Joe Sakic 7 (7)
12A Pavel Bure 3 (300) 8.00 20.00
12B Pavel Bure 8 (80) 12.50 30.00
12C Pavel Bure 8 (8)

1998-99 Donruss Elite Promos

These cards were issued in the summer of 1998 in anticipation of an upcoming Donruss Elite hockey product. Prior to the release of the full set, Donruss went out of business. No regular cards from this set exist. Each card is marked PROMO/2500 on the back, although it is believed that far fewer than 2,500 copies were produced of each, with some probably limited to 100 or less. Some were believed to be easier to acquire than others, including the Sergei Samsonov and Dominik Hasek issue.

1 John LeClair 10.00 25.00
2 Brett Hull 6.00 15.00
3 Saku Koivu 4.00 10.00
4 Mark Messier 10.00 25.00
5 Keith Tkachuk 6.00 15.00
6 Teemu Selanne 15.00 40.00
7 Sergei Samsonov 2.00 5.00
8 Pavel Bure 15.00 40.00
9 Brendan Shanahan 10.00 25.00
10 Dominik Hasek 2.00 5.00
11 Joe Thornton 20.00 50.00
12 Joe Sakic 20.00 50.00
13 Martin Brodeur 10.00 25.00
14 Peter Forsberg 20.00 50.00
15 Steve Yzerman 40.00 100.00
16 Patrick Roy 40.00 100.00
17 Jaromir Jagr 10.00 25.00
18 Paul Kariya 20.00 50.00
19 Eric Lindros 15.00 40.00
20 Wayne Gretzky 40.00 125.00

1997-98 Donruss Limited

This 200-card set was distributed in five-card packs with a suggested retail price of $4.99 and featured full-bleed player photographs printed on double-sided cards. The set contained the following subsets: Counterparts, which displayed photos of two superstar players connected by their positions utilizing a Poly-Chromium print technology; Double Team, which featured two formidable teammates back-to-back; Star Factor, which highlighted the top stars using a different photo of the same star on each side; and Unlimited Potential/Talent, which combined a photo of a young rookie on one side and a veteran star's photo on the other.

COMPLETE SET (200) 150.00 400.00
COMP.COUNTERPART.SET (100) 10.00 25.00
1 Brendan Shanahan .25 .60
Harry York C
2 Peter Forsberg RC .60 1.50
Michael Knuble C
3 Chris Osgood .25 .60
Kirk McLean C
4 Wayne Gretzky S 20.00 50.00
5 John Vanbiesbrouck 1.00 2.50
Ed Jovanovski D
6 Paul Coffey .25 .60
Darryl Sydor C
7 Pavel Bure .25 .60
Valeri Bure C
8 Sergei Berezin 2.00 5.00
Jaromir Jagr U
9 Saku Koivu .15 .40
Mats Sundin C
10 Trevor Kidd .08 .25
Corey Hirsch C
11 Teemu Selanne S 2.50 6.00
12 Zigmund Palffy .08 .25
Radek Bonk C
13 Mats Sundin 1.00 2.50
Sergei Berezin D
14 Jim Carey .08 .25
Bill Ranford C
15 John LeClair .08 .25
Claude Lemieux C
16 Janne Niinimaa 1.50 4.00
Chris Chelios U
17 Kevin Hodson 1.00 2.50
Michael Knuble D
18 Adam Graves .08 .25
Keith Jones C
19 M.Modano/T.Linden C .40 1.00
20 Brett Hull S 4.00 10.00
21 Derian Hatcher .08 .25
Kevin Hatcher C
22 Daniel Alfredsson .08 .25
Dave Andreychuk C
23 Steve Shields 1.00 2.50
Vaclav Varada D
24 Theo Fleury .08 .25
Geoff Courtnall C
25 Mark Messier .25 .60
Dino Ciccarelli C
26 Ryan Smyth S 2.00 5.00
27 Mike Grier 1.00 2.50
Jason Arnott D
28 Ed Belfour .25 .60
Andy Moog C
29 Jarome Iginla/Ed Belfour/Martin St. Louis/Jean-Sebastien Giguere/Jose Theodore
/Manny Legace 2.00 5.00
30 Eric Lindros .25 .60
Todd Bertuzzi C
31 Daymond Langkow .08 .25
David Roberts C
32 Mike Richter .15 .40
Grant Fuhr C
33 Adam Oates 1.00 2.50
Jaroslav Svejkovsky D
34 Saku Koivu 1.00 2.50
Darcy Tucker D
35 Paul Kariya S 2.50 6.00
36 Joe Sakic .50 1.25
Bernie Nicholls C
37 Ed Jovanovski RC .08 .25
D.J.Smith C
38 Vaclav Prospal 1.50 4.00
Brendan Shanahan U
39 Mike Peca .08 .25
Marty Murray C
40 Mike Gartner .08 .25
Wendel Clark C
41 Steve Yzerman S 12.00 30.00
42 M.Modano/R.Turek D 1.50 4.00
43 Joe Nieuwendyk .08 .25
Jarome Iginla C
44 Patrick Roy 1.25 3.00
Jocelyn Thibault C
45 Hnat Domenichelli .08 .25
Andrew Cassels C
46 Christian Dube .08 .25
Steve Sullivan C
47 Marc Denis 1.00 2.50
Valeri Kamensky D
48 Peter Forsberg S 6.00 15.00
49 Derek Plante .08 .25
Todd Harvey C
50 Mike Grier 2.50 6.00
Eric Lindros U
51 Brett Hull 1.25 3.00
Jim Campbell D
52 Mark Recchi .08 .25
Landon Wilson C
53 Darcy Tucker RC .08 .25
Pascal Rheaume C
54 Chris O'Sullivan .08 .25
Anders Eriksson C
55 Jaromir Jagr S 6.00 15.00
56 Paul Kariya 1.00 2.50
Teemu Selanne D
57 Felix Potvin .25 .60
Damian Rhodes C
58 Brian Holzinger .08 .25
Mike Ricci C
59 Eric Fichaud 1.00 2.50
Travis Green D
60 Ethan Moreau .08 .25
John MacLean C
61 Joe Juneau .08 .25
Jeff O'Neill C
62 John Vanbiesbrouck S 2.00 5.00
63 Byron Dafoe RC .08 .25
Steve Shields C
64 Mikael Renberg .08 .25
Niklas Sundstrom C
65 Ryan Smyth .08 .25
Eric Daze C
66 Doug Gilmour 1.00 2.50
Pascal Rheaume D
67 Jim Campbell .08 .25
Craig Janney C
68 Alexander Mogilny .08 .25
Mathew Barnaby C
69 Alexei Yashin S 2.00 5.00
70 Bryan Berard 1.50 4.00
Brian Leetch U
71 Alexei Yashin .08 .25
Brain Savage C
72 Jeff Friesen .08 .25
Darren McCarty C
73 Dimitri Khristich .08 .25
Chad Kilger C
74 Martin Brodeur 2.50 6.00
Dave Andreychuk D
75 Luc Robitaille .08 .25
Pat Verbeek C
76 Dominik Hasek .50 1.25
Jamie Storr C
77 Felix Potvin S 2.50 6.00
78 Mike Dunham 1.00 2.50
Vadim Sharifijanov D
79 Jason Arnott .08 .25
Rob Niedermayer C
80 Eric Desjardins .08 .25
Chris Phillips C
81 Curtis Joseph .25 .60
Jose Theodore C
82 Doug Gilmour .08 .25
Rod Brind'Amour C
83 Keith Tkachuk .25 .60
Rick Tocchet C
84 Mark Messier S 2.50 6.00
85 Chris Pronger .08 .25
Aki Berg C
86 Marcel Cousineau 2.50 6.00
Dominik Hasek U
87 Ethan Moreau 1.00 2.50
Chris Chelios D
88 Jonas Hoglund .08 .25
Rob Zamuner C
89 Ron Hextall .08 .25
Kevin Hodson C
90 John LeClair S 2.50 6.00
91 Vaclav Prospal RC .25 .60
Viktor Kozlov C
92 Ray Bourque 2.50 6.00
Joe Thornton D
93 Oleg Tverdovsky .08 .25
Sergei Zubov C
94 Ethan Moreau 1.50 4.00
John LeClair U
95 Adam Deadmarsh S 2.00 5.00
96 Jaroslav Svejkovsky .08 .25
Jozef Stumpel C
97 Wayne Gretzky 6.00 15.00
Vladimir Vorobiev D
98 Sergei Fedorov S 3.00 8.00
99 Jim Campbell 1.50 4.00
Ryan Smyth U
100 Vaclav Prospal 1.00 2.50
Paul Coffey D
101 Wayne Primeau .08 .25
Sean Pronger C
102 Jean Giguere .08 .25
Felix Potvin U
103 Curtis Joseph S 2.50 6.00
104 Pavel Bure 1.00 2.50
Alexander Mogilny D
105 Jeremy Roenick .25 .60
Tony Amonte C
106 Sandis Ozolinsh .08 .25
Kirk McLaren C
107 Anson Carter .08 .25
Steve Kelly C
108 Paul Coffey S 2.00 5.00
109 Dainius Zubrus 2.50 6.00
Peter Forsberg U
110 Travis Green .08 .25
Scott Mellanby C
111 Pat LaFontaine .08 .25
Valeri Kamensky C
112 Adam Oates S 2.00 5.00
113 John Vanbiesbrouck .08 .25
Roman Turek C
114 Jarome Iginla 4.00 10.00
Paul Kariya U
115 Steve Yzerman 4.00 10.00
Chris Osgood D
116 Marcel Cousineau .60 1.50
Steve Sullivan D
117 Owen Nolan .08 .25
Steve Rucchin C
118 Donald Audette .08 .25
Ted Donato C
119 Geoff Sanderson .75 2.00
Sean Burke D
120 Jeremy Roenick S 4.00 10.00
121 Vladimir Vorobiev RC .08 .25
Andreas Johansson
122 Alexander Mogilny S 2.00 5.00
123 Jocelyn Thibault 1.00 2.50
Terry Ryan D
124 Eric Fichaud .08 .25
Nikolai Khabibulin C
125 Ray Bourque RC .50 1.25
Eric Messier C
126 Sergei Fedorov .30 .75
Keith Primeau C
127 Marc Denis 4.00 10.00
Martin Brodeur U
128 Mats Sundin S 2.50 6.00
129 Peter Bondra .08 .25
Roman Vopat C
130 Tommy Salo .08 .25
Corey Schwab C
131 Sergei Samsonov 1.00 2.50
Jim Carey D
132 Adam Deadmarsh 2.00 5.00
Joe Sakic D
133 Daymond Langkow 1.50 4.00
Keith Tkachuk U
134 Mike Richter S 2.50 6.00
135 Geoff Sanderson .08 .25
Jere Lehtinen C
136 Janne Niinimaa .08 .25
Jamie Pushor C
137 Andreas Dackell .08 .25
Vincent Damphousse C
138 Keith Tkachuk S 2.00 5.00
139 Ray Bourque S 4.00 10.00
140 Keith Tkachuk 1.25 3.00
Jeremy Roenick D
141 Rem Murray .08 .25
Ray Sheppard C
142 Peter Schaefer .08 .25
Patrick Lalime C
143 Jaroslav Svejkovsky 2.00 5.00
Teemu Selanne U
144 Todd Marchant .08 .25
Tony Granato C
145 Sandis Ozolinsh S 1.50 4.00
146 Roman Hamrlik .25 .60
Nicklas Lidstrom C
147 Dominik Hasek S 6.00 15.00
148 Chris Gratton .08 .25
Daniel Goneau C
149 Martin Brodeur S 8.00 20.00
150 Martin Brodeur .60 1.50
Stephane Fiset C
151 Jose Theodore 8.00 20.00
Patrick Roy U
152 Jose Theodore 1.00 2.50
Mark Recchi D
153 Pavel Bure S 2.50 6.00
154 Sergei Berezin .08 .25
Denis Pederson C
155 Doug Gilmour S 2.00 5.00
156 Peter Nedved .08 .25
Kirk Muller C
157 Theo Fleury S 2.00 5.00
158 Harry York 1.00 2.50
Pierre Turgeon D
159 Andreas Johansson 1.00 2.50
Patrick Lalime D
160 Marcel Cousineau .08 .25
Jeff Hackett C
161 Adam Deadmarsh .08 .25
Alexandre Daigle C
162 Adam Oates .08 .25
Todd Warriner C
163 Zigmund Palffy S 1.50 4.00
164 Ed Belfour S 2.50 6.00
165 Saku Koivu 6.00 15.00
Steve Yzerman U
166 Chris Chelios .25 .60
Scott Lachance C
167 Jamie Langenbrunner .08 .25
Brandon Convery C
168 Janne Niinimaa .75 2.00
John LeClair D
169 Brendan Shanahan S 2.50 6.00
170 Darren Puppa .08 .25
Garth Snow C
171 Chris Osgood S 2.00 5.00
172 Pierre Turgeon .08 .25
Shane Corson C
173 Doug Weight .75 2.00
Rem Murray D

174 Eric Fichaud 1.50 4.00
Curtis Joseph U
175 Chris Chelios S 2.00 5.00
176 Wade Redden .08 .25
Scott Stevens C
177 Jarome Iginla 1.00 2.50
Theo Fleury D
178 Vaclav Varada .08 .25
Igor Larionov C
179 Brian Leetch S 2.00 5.00
180 Stephane Fiset 1.00 2.50
Roman Vopat D
181 Zigmund Palffy 1.00 2.50
Bryan Berard D
182 Bryan Berard 1.00 2.50
Brian Leetch D
183 Eric Lindros S 2.50 6.00
184 Derek Plante .60 1.50
Brian Holzinger D
185 Brett Hull .30 .75
Martin Gelinas C
186 Daniel Alfredsson 1.00 2.50
Damian Rhodes D
187 Joe Thornton 4.00 10.00
Mark Messier U
188 Mike Vernon .08 .25
Ken Wregget C
189 Alexei Yashin .60 1.50
Wade Redden D
190 Joe Sakic S 8.00 20.00
191 Doug Weight .08 .25
Darren Turcotte C
192 Daymond Langkow .08 .25
Darren Puppa C
193 Mike Modano S 4.00 10.00
194 Sean Burke .08 .25
Mike Dunham C
195 Dainius Zubrus .08 .25
Sebastien Bordeleau C
196 Owen Nolan .75 2.00
Jeff Friesen D
197 Vladimir Vorobiev 2.00 5.00
Sergei Fedorov U
198 Patrick Roy S 15.00 40.00
199 Mike Grier .08 .25
Ron Francis C
200 Patrick Marleau 10.00 25.00
Wayne Gretzky U
P183 Eric Lindros PROMO .40 1.00

1997-98 Donruss Limited Exposure

Randomly inserted in packs, this 200-card set was a parallel to the base set and featured holographic polychromium technology on both sides. The set was designated by an exclusive "Limited Exposure" stamp. Donruss announced that 25 or fewer sets of the Star Factor cards and 40 or less Unlimited cards were produced.

*COUNTERPARTS: 5X TO 10X BASIC CARDS
*DOUBLE TEAM: 5X TO 10X BASIC CARDS
*STAR FACTOR: 2.5X TO 6X BASIC CARDS
*UNLIMITED: 2X TO 5X BASIC CARDS

1997-98 Donruss Limited Fabric of the Game

Randomly inserted in packs, this 72-card partial multi-fractured set featured color player photos distinguished by using three different technologies, each of which represented a different statistical category: Embossed Canvas (Wins), Leather (Goals), and Wood (Assists). Five more levels crossed the sections and were sequentially numbered: Legendary Material (numbered to 100), Hall of Fame Material (numbered to 250), Superstar Material (numbered to 500), Star Material (numbered to 750), and Major Material (numbered to 1000).

ALL MATERIAL TYPES EQUAL VALUE
1 Wayne Gretzky HF 40.00 100.00
2 Martin Brodeur S 6.00 15.00
3 Dainius Zubrus M 1.00 2.50
4 Joe Sakic SS 8.00 20.00
5 Joe Sakic HF 12.00 30.00
6 Sergei Fedorov S 3.00 8.00
7 John Vanbiesbrouck HF 6.00 15.00
8 Saku Koivu M 2.50 6.00
9 Jean-Sebastien Giguere M 2.50 6.00
10 Paul Kariya S 3.00 8.00
11 Mike Richter SS 4.00 10.00
12 Paul Coffey L 10.00 25.00
13 Brendan Shanahan L 20.00 50.00
14 Jaromir Jagr SS 6.00 15.00
15 Felix Potvin SS 4.00 10.00
16 Mats Sundin SS 4.00 10.00
17 Mike Vernon HF 6.00 15.00
18 Keith Tkachuk S 2.00 5.00
19 Doug Gilmour HF 6.00 15.00
20 Patrick Roy L 60.00 150.00
21 Sergei Samsonov M 2.50 6.00
22 Mike Grier M 1.00 2.50
23 Curtis Joseph SS 3.00 8.00
24 Zigmund Palffy S 2.00 5.00
25 Chris Osgood S 2.00 5.00
26 Mats Sundin S 3.00 8.00
27 Kelly Hrudey HF 6.00 15.00
28 Brett Hull L 25.00 60.00
29 Ray Bourque HF 10.00 25.00
30 Nikolai Khabibulin S 2.00 5.00
31 Bryan Berard M 1.00 2.50
32 Jaroslav Svejkovsky M 1.00 2.50
33 Ed Belfour SS 4.00 10.00
34 Wayne Gretzky L 75.00 200.00
35 Jeremy Roenick SS 5.00 12.00
36 Andy Moog L 10.00 25.00
37 Eric Lindros S 3.00 8.00
38 Brett Hull SS 5.00 12.00
39 Marcel Cousineau M 1.00 2.50
40 Paul Kariya M 2.50 6.00
41 Mike Dunham M 1.00 2.50
42 Chris Phillips M 1.00 2.50
43 Teemu Selanne SS 4.00 10.00
44 Mark Messier L 25.00 60.00
45 Grant Fuhr L 15.00 40.00
46 Daniel Alfredsson M 1.50 4.00
47 Marc Denis M 1.00 2.50
48 Daymond Langkow M 1.00 2.50
49 Steve Yzerman HF 25.00 60.00
50 Ryan Smyth S 2.00 5.00
51 Alexander Mogilny HF 6.00 15.00
52 Ron Hextall HF 6.00 15.00
53 Brendan Shanahan S 3.00 8.00
54 Jim Carey S 2.00 5.00
55 Eric Lindros S 3.00 8.00
56 Eric Fichaud M 1.00 2.50
57 Sergei Berezin M 1.00 2.50
58 Chris Chelios HF 6.00 15.00
59 Mark Messier HF 10.00 25.00
60 Damian Rhodes M 2.50 6.00
61 Jarome Iginla M 3.00 8.00
62 Jocelyn Thibault S 2.00 5.00
63 John LeClair S 2.00 5.00
64 Brian Leetch SS 4.00 10.00
65 Dominik Hasek S 6.00 15.00
66 Pavel Bure SS 4.00 10.00
67 Mike Modano S 4.00 10.00
68 Daniel Cleary M 1.00 2.50
69 Janne Niinimaa M 1.00 2.50
70 Steve Yzerman L 40.00 100.00
71 Jose Theodore M 3.00 6.00
72 Peter Forsberg S 5.00 12.00

1997-98 Donruss Preferred

The 1997-98 Donruss Preferred set was issued in one series totaling 200 cards and distributed in five-card packs inside collectible tins. The set featured color player photos on an all micro-etched foil board card with bronze, silver, gold, and platinum finishes.

COMPLETE SET (200) 400.00 800.00
COMP.BRONZE SET (100) 12.50 30.00
1 Dominik Hasek G 8.00 20.00
2 Peter Forsberg G 10.00 25.00
3 Brendan Shanahan P 8.00 20.00
4 Wayne Gretzky P 25.00 60.00
5 Eric Lindros P 8.00 20.00
6 Keith Tkachuk G 4.00 10.00
7 Mark Messier P 8.00 20.00
8 Mike Modano G 6.00 15.00
9 John Vanbiesbrouck P 8.00 20.00
10 Paul Kariya P 8.00 20.00
11 Saku Koivu G 4.00 10.00
12 Paul Coffey B .25 .60
13 Joe Juneau B .20 .50
14 Jeff Friesen S .75 2.00
15 Brett Hull G 5.00 12.00
16 Martin Brodeur G 10.00 25.00
17 Jarome Iginla G 5.00 12.00
18 Keith Primeau S .75 2.00
19 Ed Jovanovski B .20 .50
20 Jamie Langenbrunner B .08 .25
21 Derian Hatcher S .75 2.00
22 Brian Leetch G 4.00 10.00
23 Daymond Langkow S 1.50 4.00
24 Ray Bourque S 3.00 8.00
25 Pavel Bure G 2.50 6.00
26 Janne Niinimaa S 1.50 4.00
27 Jamie Storr S 1.50 4.00
28 Darcy Tucker B .08 .25
29 Anson Carter B .20 .50
30 Jeff O'Neill B .08 .25
31 Jason Arnott G 1.50 4.00
32 Tommy Salo B .20 .50
33 Petr Nedved B .20 .50
34 Mike Peca B .20 .50
35 Ethan Moreau S .75 2.00
36 Ray Sheppard B .20 .50
37 Damian Rhodes B .20 .50
38 Mats Sundin S 2.00 5.00
39 Alexander Mogilny G 3.00 8.00
40 Mike Dunham S 1.50 4.00
41 Steve Yzerman P 20.00 50.00
42 Alexei Yashin S .75 2.00
43 Jim Carey S 1.50 4.00
44 Mike Grier S .75 2.00
45 Steve Rucchin B .08 .25
46 Mark Recchi S .75 2.00
47 Mike Gartner B .20 .50
48 Alexandre Daigle S 1.50 4.00
49 Eric Fichaud G 3.00 8.00
50 Harry York B .08 .25
51 Dino Ciccarelli B .20 .50
52 Bill Ranford B .20 .50
53 Adam Deadmarsh G 1.50 4.00
54 Ed Belfour B .25 .60
55 Jozef Stumpel S 1.50 4.00
56 Rem Murray B .08 .25
57 Pat Verbeek B .08 .25
58 Pat LaFontaine S 1.50 4.00
59 Dainius Zubrus S 1.50 4.00
60 Grant Fuhr B .20 .50
61 Rob Niedermayer B .20 .50
62 Brian Savage B .08 .25
63 Gary Roberts B .08 .25
64 Tony Amonte B .20 .50
65 Jere Lehtinen B .20 .50
66 Dave Andreychuk B .20 .50
67 Rod Brind'Amour B .20 .50
68 Mikael Renberg B .20 .50
69 Doug Gilmour S 1.50 4.00
70 Kevin Hatcher B .08 .25
71 Byron Dafoe B .20 .50
72 Derek Plante S .75 2.00
73 Trevor Kidd B .20 .50
74 Doug Weight S 1.50 4.00
75 Valeri Bure B .08 .25
76 John LeClair G 4.00 10.00
77 Sergei Berezin B .20 .50
78 Peter Bondra S 1.50 4.00
79 Bryan Berard G 3.00 8.00
80 Steve Shields B RC .25 .60
81 Chris Osgood G 3.00 8.00
82 Mike Vernon B .20 .50
83 Martin Gelinas B .20 .50
84 Curtis Joseph S 2.00 5.00
85 Geoff Sanderson S 1.50 4.00
86 Patrick Roy P 20.00 50.00
87 Jocelyn Thibault G 3.00 8.00
88 Jeremy Roenick S 2.50 6.00
89 Trevor Linden B .20 .50
90 Daniel Alfredsson S 1.50 4.00
91 Sergei Zubov B .08 .25
92 Dimitri Khristich S .75 2.00
93 Brian Holzinger B .08 .25
94 Andrew Cassels B .08 .25
95 Teemu Selanne G 4.00 10.00
96 Ron Hextall B .20 .50
97 Wade Redden B .08 .25
98 Jim Campbell B .08 .25
99 Felix Potvin G 4.00 10.00
100 Adam Oates S 1.50 4.00
101 Nikolai Khabibulin B .20 .50
102 Jose Theodore S 2.50 6.00
103 Sandis Ozolinsh S .75 2.00
104 Sean Burke B .20 .50
105 Vaclav Prospal G RC 3.00 8.00
106 Zigmund Palffy G 3.00 8.00
107 Kyle McLaren B .08 .25
108 Owen Nolan S 1.50 4.00
109 Chris Pronger S 1.50 4.00
110 Daren Puppa B .20 .50
111 Garth Snow B .20 .50
112 Aki Berg B .08 .25
113 Andy Moog B .20 .50
114 Darren McCarty B .08 .25
115 Joe Nieuwendyk B .20 .50
116 Eric Daze S 1.50 4.00
117 Pierre Turgeon S 1.50 4.00
118 Ken Wregget B .20 .50
119 Ryan Smyth G 3.00 8.00
120 Kirk Muller B .08 .25
121 Luc Robitaille B .20 .50
122 Sergei Fedorov G 6.00 15.00
123 Sean Pronger B .08 .25
124 Mike Richter B 2.00 5.00
125 Jaromir Jagr P 10.00 25.00
126 Claude Lemieux B .08 .25
127 Chris Chelios S 2.00 5.00
128 Joe Sakic P 12.50 30.00
129 Guy Hebert S 1.50 4.00
130 Chris Gratton S 1.50 4.00
131 Steve Sullivan B .08 .25
132 Al MacInnis B .20 .50
133 Adam Graves S .75 2.00
134 Vyacheslav Kozlov B .08 .25
135 Scott Mellanby S .75 2.00
136 Stephane Fiset B .20 .50
137 Oleg Tverdovsky S .75 2.00
138 Theo Fleury S .75 2.00
139 Jeff Hackett B .20 .50
140 Vincent Damphousse B .08 .25
141 Roman Hamrlik S .75 2.00
142 Ron Francis S 1.50 4.00
143 Scott Lachance B .08 .25
144 Todd Harvey B .08 .25
145 Marc Denis S 1.50 4.00
146 Jaroslav Svejkovsky G 3.00 8.00
147 Olli Jokinen S RC 6.00 15.00
148 Sergei Samsonov G 3.00 8.00
149 Chris Phillips G 1.50 4.00
150 Patrick Marleau G 8.00 20.00
151 Joe Thornton G 10.00 25.00
152 Daniel Cleary S 1.50 4.00
153 Alyn McCauley G 3.00 8.00
154 Brad Isbister S .75 2.00
155 Alexei Morozov S 2.00 5.00
156 Shawn Bates B RC .08 .25
157 Jean-Yves Leroux B RC .08 .25
158 Marcel Cousineau B .20 .50
159 Vaclav Varada B .08 .25
160 Jean-Sebastien Giguere S 1.50 4.00
161 Espen Knutsen B RC .75 2.00
162 Marian Hossa S RC 15.00 30.00
163 Robert Dome B RC .08 .25
164 Juha Lind B RC .08 .25
165 Sergei Fedorov NT B .40 1.00
166 Jarome Iginla NT B .30 .75
167 Jaroslav Svejkovsky NT B .20 .50
168 Patrick Roy NT S 10.00 25.00
169 Dominik Hasek NT B .50 1.25
170 Alexander Mogilny NT B .20 .50
171 Chris Chelios NT B .25 .60
172 Wayne Gretzky NT S 12.50 30.00
173 Peter Forsberg NT B .60 1.50
174 Ray Bourque NT B .40 1.00
175 Joe Sakic NT S 4.00 10.00
176 Mike Modano NT B .25 .60
177 Mark Messier NT B .25 .60
178 Teemu Selanne NT B .25 .60
179 Steve Yzerman NT S 10.00 25.00
180 Eric Lindros NT S 2.00 5.00
181 Doug Weight NT B .20 .50
182 John Vanbiesbrouck NT B .20 .50
183 Paul Kariya NT S 2.00 5.00
184 Brendan Shanahan NT S 2.00 5.00
185 Martin Brodeur NT B .60 1.50
186 Bryan Berard NT B .20 .50
187 Marc Denis NT B .20 .50
188 Brian Leetch NT B .25 .60
189 Ryan Smyth NT S 2.00 5.00
190 Dainius Zubrus NT B .20 .50
191 Keith Tkachuk NT B .25 .60
192 Jaromir Jagr NT S 3.00 8.00
193 Brett Hull NT B .30 .75
194 Pavel Bure NT B .25 .60
195 Sergei Samsonov B .20 .50
196 Olli Jokinen B .40 1.00
197 Chris Phillips B .20 .50
198 Patrick Marleau B .50 1.25
199 Daniel Cleary B .20 .50
200 Joe Thornton B .75 2.00

1997-98 Donruss Preferred Cut to the Chase

Randomly inserted in packs, this 200-card set was a die-cut parallel version of the base set. Each card featured a background of bronze, silver gold, or platinum.

*BRONZE VETS: 4X TO 10X BASIC CARDS
*BRONZE ROOKIES: 2X TO 5X
*SILVER VETS: 1.5X TO 4X BASIC CARDS
*SILVER ROOKIES: 1X TO 2.5X
*GOLD: 1.2X TO 3X BASIC CARDS
*PLATINUM: 1X TO 2.5X BASIC CARDS
162 Marian Hossa S 60.00 100.00

1997-98 Donruss Preferred Color Guard

Randomly inserted in packs, this 18-card set featured color images of top puckstoppers printed on die-cut plastic cards with the player's team colors in the background. The set was sequentially numbered to 1500.

*PROMOS: .6X TO 1.5X BASIC INSERTS
1 Patrick Roy 15.00 40.00
2 Martin Brodeur 10.00 25.00
3 Curtis Joseph 3.00 8.00
4 John Vanbiesbrouck 3.00 8.00
5 Felix Potvin 3.00 8.00
6 Dominik Hasek 6.00 15.00
7 Chris Osgood 3.00 8.00
8 Eric Fichaud 2.00 5.00
9 Jocelyn Thibault 2.00 5.00
10 Marc Denis 2.00 5.00
11 Jose Theodore 5.00 12.00
12 Mike Vernon 3.00 8.00
13 Jim Carey 2.00 5.00
14 Ron Hextall 3.00 8.00
15 Mike Richter 3.00 8.00
16 Ed Belfour 3.00 8.00
17 Mike Dunham 2.00 5.00
18 Damian Rhodes 2.00 5.00

1997-98 Donruss Preferred Line of the Times

Randomly inserted in packs, this 24-card set featured color photos of star players printed on die-cut cards and utilizing micro-etching technology. Three cards were made to be placed side by side to form one interactive card which spelled out a particular word in the background. The set was sequentially numbered to 2500.

COMPLETE SET (24) 125.00 250.00
*PROMO: .3X TO .8X BASIC INSERTS
1A Ryan Smyth 3.00 8.00
1B Sergei Fedorov 6.00 15.00
1C Jaromir Jagr 6.00 15.00
2A Eric Lindros 4.00 10.00
2B Joe Thornton 6.00 15.00
2C Brendan Shanahan 4.00 10.00
3A John LeClair 4.00 10.00
3B Keith Tkachuk 4.00 10.00
3C Brett Hull 5.00 12.00
4A Pavel Bure 4.00 10.00
4B Sergei Samsonov 3.00 8.00
4C Paul Kariya 4.00 10.00
5A Mike Modano 6.00 15.00
5B Teemu Selanne 4.00 10.00
5C Patrick Marleau 4.00 10.00
6A Wayne Gretzky 25.00 60.00
6B Steve Yzerman 20.00 50.00
6C Daniel Cleary 2.50 6.00
7A Jarome Iginla 5.00 12.00
7B Peter Forsberg 10.00 25.00
7C Mark Messier 4.00 10.00
8A Joe Sakic 8.00 20.00
8B Jaroslav Svejkovsky 3.00 8.00
8C Dainius Zubrus 3.00 8.00

1997-98 Donruss Preferred Precious Metals

Randomly inserted in packs, this 15-card set was a partial parallel version of the base set. The cards were printed on card stock consisting of 1 gram of real gold or platinum. Only 100 of each card was produced.

1 Brendan Shanahan P 60.00 150.00
2 Joe Thornton G 60.00 150.00
3 Wayne Gretzky P 200.00 400.00
4 Mark Messier P 75.00 175.00
5 Patrick Roy P 150.00 300.00
6 Martin Brodeur G 100.00 250.00

7 Eric Lindros P 40.00 100.00
8 Paul Kariya P 40.00 100.00
9 Teemu Selanne G 40.00 100.00
10 Jaromir Jagr P 60.00 150.00
11 Joe Sakic P 75.00 200.00
12 Peter Forsberg G 100.00 200.00
13 John Vanbiesbrouck P 30.00 80.00
14 Steve Yzerman P 100.00 250.00
15 Sergei Samsonov G 30.00 80.00

1997-98 Donruss Preferred Tin Packs

This 24-tin set features color images printed on special tin containers of the NHL players who played in the 1998 Winter Olympic Games on either the Canadian or United States teams. The larger US tin outer boxes are highlighted in blue and limited to 499 serial numbered sets, and the Canadian version is highlighted in red and also limited to 499 sets. There was also a gold version of these tin packs which were originally slated to be included in boxes, but was later available only through the manufacturer. Golds were limited to 499 serial numbered sets. Prices below refer to opened packs.

COMPLETE SET (24) 8.00 20.00
*GOLD PACK/499: 4X TO 10X BASIC TIN
*BLUE BOX/499: 2.5X TO 6X BASIC TIN
*RED PACK: .4X TO 1X BASIC TIN
*RED BOX/499: 2.5X TO 6X BASIC TIN
1 Eric Lindros .25 .60
2 Paul Kariya .50 1.25
3 Wayne Gretzky 1.00 2.50
4 Teemu Selanne .30 .75
5 Patrick Roy .75 2.00
6 John Vanbiesbrouck .25 .60
7 Mike Modano .25 .60
8 Joe Sakic .30 .75
9 Peter Forsberg .40 1.00
10 Martin Brodeur .40 1.00
11 Sergei Samsonov .40 1.00
12 Brendan Shanahan .25 .60
13 Steve Yzerman .60 1.50
14 Jaromir Jagr .40 1.00
15 Mark Messier .20 .50
16 Joe Thornton .40 1.00
17 Pavel Bure .40 1.00
18 Brett Hull .20 .50
19 Brendan Shanahan MC .25 .60
20 Jaromir Jagr MC .40 1.00
21 Eric Lindros MC .25 .60
22 Paul Kariya MC .50 1.25
23 Wayne Gretzky MC 1.00 2.50
24 Patrick Roy MC .75 2.00

1997-98 Donruss Preferred Tin Packs Double Wide

These packages contained five Donruss Preferred cards, but are considered collectibles themselves by virture of the pair of players pictured on the front.

COMPLETE SET (12) 10.00 25.00
1 Wayne Gretzky 1.25 3.00
Joe Thornton
2 Paul Kariya .50 1.25
Brett Hull
3 Eric Lindros .50 1.25
Joe Sakic
4 Teemu Selanne .60 1.50
Peter Forsberg
5 Pavel Bure .60 1.50
Mike Modano
6 Sergei Samsonov 1.50 4.00
Steve Yzerman
7 Jaromir Jagr .50 1.25
Brendan Shanahan
8 Mark Messier .40 1.00
John Vanbiesbrouck
9 Patrick Roy 1.25 3.00
Martin Brodeur
10 Brendan Shanahan .40 1.00
Eric Lindros
11 Jaromir Jagr 1.00 2.50
Paul Kariya
12 Wayne Gretzky 1.50 4.00
Patrick Roy

1997-98 Donruss Priority

The 1997-98 Donruss Priority hobby only set was issued in one series totaling 220 cards and was distributed in two-types of five-card packs, postcard and stamp packs, with a suggested retail price of $4.99. Postcard packs had a 5" by 7" horizontal format and contained only even numbered cards from the set. The odd numbered cards were twice as scarce and could be found only in the stamp packs. The fronts featured color action player photos printed with foil treatments, while the backs carried player information. The set contained the topical subset: 1st Class Package (185-214). The set was released towards the end of the 97-98 NHL season.

COMPLETE SET (220) 25.00 50.00
1 Patrick Roy SP 1.25 3.00
2 Eric Lindros .20 .50
3 Keith Tkachuk SP .15 .40
4 Steve Yzerman .75 2.00
5 John Vanbiesbrouck SP .25 .60
6 Teemu Selanne .20 .50
7 Martin Brodeur SP .60 1.50
8 Peter Forsberg .40 1.00
9 Brett Hull SP .30 .75
10 Wayne Gretzky 1.00 2.50
11 Mike Modano SP .40 1.00
12 Sergei Fedorov .25 .60
13 Paul Kariya SP .60 1.50
14 Saku Koivu .20 .50
15 Pavel Bure SP .25 .60
16 Mark Messier .20 .50
17 Joe Sakic SP .50 1.25
18 Jaromir Jagr .25 .60
19 Brendan Shanahan SP .25 .60
20 Ray Bourque .25 .60
21 Daymond Langkow SP .10 .30
22 Alexandre Daigle .07 .20
23 Dainius Zubrus SP .10 .30
24 Ryan Smyth .10 .30
25 Derek Plante SP .10 .30
26 Eric Daze .10 .30
27 Ed Jovanovski SP .10 .30
28 Sergei Berezin .07 .20
29 Roman Turek SP .15 .40
30 Derian Hatcher .07 .20
31 Jarome Iginla SP .25 .60
32 Luc Robitaille .10 .30
33 Rod Brind'Amour SP .15 .40
34 Mathieu Schneider .07 .20
35 Olaf Kolzig SP .15 .40
36 Nikolai Khabibulin .10 .30
37 Scott Niedermayer SP .10 .30
38 Keith Primeau .07 .20
39 Dimitri Khristich SP .10 .30
40 Eric Fichaud .10 .30
41 Pierre Turgeon SP .15 .40
42 Kevin Stevens .07 .20
43 Nicklas Lidstrom SP .10 .30
44 Sean Burke .10 .30
45 Sandis Ozolinsh SP .10 .30
46 Owen Nolan .10 .30
47 Peter Bondra SP .25 .60
48 Ron Hextall .10 .30
49 Rob Blake SP .10 .30
50 Geoff Sanderson .10 .30
51 Sergei Zubov SP .10 .30
52 Doug Gilmour .10 .30
53 Oleg Tverdovsky SP .10 .30
54 Bryan Berard .07 .20
55 Bill Ranford SP .15 .40
56 Mats Sundin .20 .50
57 Damian Rhodes SP .15 .40
58 Zigmund Palffy .10 .30
59 Mike Grier SP .10 .30
60 Jozef Stumpel .10 .30
61 Mark Recchi SP .10 .30
62 Alexei Zhamnov .07 .20
63 Jere Lehtinen SP .10 .30
64 Andrew Cassels .07 .20
65 Kevin Hodson SP .15 .40
66 Dino Ciccarelli .10 .30
67 Niklas Sundstrom SP .10 .30
68 Jeff Hackett .10 .30
69 Brian Holzinger SP .15 .40
70 Jeff Friesen .07 .20
71 Ed Belfour SP .25 .60
72 Wayne Primeau .07 .20
73 Sami Kapanen SP .10 .30
74 Brian Leetch .10 .30
75 Mikael Renberg SP .15 .40
76 Ron Tugnutt .10 .30
77 Ron Francis SP .15 .40
78 Jocelyn Thibault .10 .30
79 Jamie Langenbrunner SP .10 .30
80 Dominik Hasek .30 .75
81 Chris Osgood SP .15 .40
82 Grant Fuhr .10 .30
83 Adam Graves SP .10 .30
84 Janne Niinimaa .10 .30
85 Kelly Hrudey SP .15 .40
86 Mike Dunham .10 .30
87 Valeri Kamensky SP .15 .40
88 Cory Stillman .07 .20
89 Anson Carter SP .10 .30
90 Igor Larionov .07 .20
91 Chris Pronger SP .15 .40
92 Steve Sullivan .07 .20
93 Mike Gartner SP .15 .40
94 Jim Campbell .10 .30
95 Valeri Bure SP .10 .30
96 Stephane Fiset .10 .30
97 Jason Arnott SP .10 .30
98 Trevor Kidd .10 .30
99 Chris Chelios SP .25 .60
100 Kevin Hatcher .07 .20
101 Felix Potvin SP .25 .60
102 Travis Green .07 .20
103 Dave Gagner SP .10 .30
104 Byron Dafoe .10 .30
105 Rick Tabaracci SP .15 .40
106 Gary Roberts .07 .20
107 Mike Ricci SP .10 .30
108 Andy Moog .10 .30
109 Sean Pronger SP .10 .30
110 Paul Coffey .10 .30
111 Trevor Linden SP .15 .40
112 Rob Zamuner .07 .20
113 Daniel Alfredsson SP .15 .40
114 Ray Sheppard .10 .30
115 Steve Shields SP RC .40 1.00
116 Ethan Moreau .07 .20
117 Tomas Sandstrom SP .10 .30
118 Chris Gratton .10 .30
119 Alexander Mogilny SP .15 .40
120 Roman Hamrlik .07 .20
121 Tommy Salo SP .15 .40
122 Jason Allison .07 .20
123 Curtis Joseph SP .25 .60
124 Guy Hebert .10 .30
125 Jeff O'Neill SP .10 .30
126 Donald Audette .07 .20
127 Claude Lemieux SP .10 .30
128 Brian Savage .07 .20
129 Scott Mellanby SP .10 .30
130 Vyacheslav Kozlov .10 .30
131 Wade Redden SP .10 .30
132 John LeClair .20 .50
133 Jeremy Roenick SP .25 .60
134 Andreas Johansson .07 .20
135 Nelson Emerson SP .10 .30
136 Daren Puppa .10 .30
137 Joe Juneau SP .15 .40
138 Garth Snow .10 .30
139 Tom Barrasso SP .15 .40
140 Joe Nieuwendyk .10 .30
141 Theo Fleury SP .10 .30
142 Yanic Perreault .07 .20
143 Mike Richter SP .25 .60
144 Al MacInnis .10 .30
145 Mike Peca SP .15 .40
146 Darren McCarty .07 .20
147 Alexei Yashin SP .10 .30
148 Rick Tocchet .10 .30
149 Adam Oates SP .15 .40
150 Wendel Clark .07 .20
151 Tony Amonte SP .15 .40
152 Dave Andreychuk .07 .20
153 Jamie Storr SP .15 .40
154 Craig Janney .10 .30
155 Todd Bertuzzi SP .10 .30
156 Harry York .07 .20
157 Todd Harvey SP .10 .30
158 Bobby Holik .07 .20
159 Mike Vernon SP .15 .40
160 Pat LaFontaine .10 .30
161 Doug Weight SP .15 .40
162 Kirk McLean .10 .30
163 Adam Deadmarsh SP .10 .30
164 Vincent Damphousse .07 .20
165 Vaclav Prospal SP RC .15 .40
166 Daniel Cleary .10 .30
167 Jaroslav Svejkovsky SP .15 .40
168 Marco Sturm RC .20 .50
169 Robert Dome SP RC .10 .30
170 Patrik Elias RC .50 1.25
171 Mattias Ohlund SP .15 .40
172 Espen Knutsen RC .20 .50
173 Joe Thornton SP .60 1.50
174 Jan Bulis RC .07 .20
175 Patrick Marleau SP .40 1.00
176 Brad Isbister .07 .20
177 Kevin Weekes SP RC 1.00 2.50
178 Sergei Samsonov .10 .30
179 Tyler Moss RC SP .10 .30
180 Chris Phillips .07 .20
181 Alyn McCauley SP .10 .30
182 Derek Morris RC .10 .30
183 Alexei Morozov SP .15 .40
184 Boyd Devereaux .07 .20
185 Peter Forsberg SP .15 .40
186 Brendan Shanahan .10 .30
187 Teemu Selanne SP .15 .40
188 Eric Lindros .10 .30
189 Mark Messier SP .15 .40
190 Vaclav Prospal .10 .30
191 Jarome Iginla SP .25 .60
192 Mike Modano .10 .30
193 John Vanbiesbrouck SP .15 .40
194 Bryan Berard .07 .20
195 Patrick Marleau SP .15 .40
196 Martin Brodeur .10 .30
197 Patrick Roy SP .15 .40
198 Felix Potvin .20 .50
199 Wayne Gretzky SP 1.50 4.00
200 Sergei Samsonov .10 .30
201 Ryan Smyth SP .15 .40
202 Keith Tkachuk .20 .50
203 Chris Osgood SP .15 .40
204 Paul Kariya .10 .30
205 John LeClair SP .25 .60
206 Alyn McCauley .10 .30
207 Joe Thornton SP .40 1.00
208 Joe Sakic .10 .30
209 Steve Yzerman SP 1.25 3.00
210 Saku Koivu .20 .50
211 Pavel Bure SP .15 .40
212 Zigmund Palffy .10 .30
213 Alexei Yashin SP .10 .30
214 Sergei Fedorov .10 .30
215 Joe Thornton CL SP .40 1.00
216 Patrick Marleau CL .10 .30
217 Daniel Cleary CL SP .10 .30
218 Sergei Samsonov CL .10 .30
219 Jaroslav Svejkovsky CL SP .10 .30
220 Alyn McCauley CL .07 .20

1997-98 Donruss Priority Stamp of Approval

This 220-card set was a parallel to the base set. Each card was randomly inserted into packs and was serial numbered out of 100. Card design featured a deckle edge similar to a postage stamp, and design front was different from that of the base set.

*EVEN CARD #: 20X TO 50X BASIC CARDS
*ODD CARD #: 15X TO 40X BASIC CARDS

1997-98 Donruss Priority Direct Deposit

Randomly inserted in packs, this 30-card set featured color action photos of top goal scorers printed on swirled-look foil board with micro etching. The cards were sequentially numbered to just 3,000.

COMPLETE SET (30) 100.00 200.00
*PROMOS: .3X TO .8X BASIC INSERTS
1 Brendan Shanahan 2.50 6.00
2 Steve Yzerman 8.00 20.00
3 Pavel Bure 2.50 6.00
4 Jaromir Jagr 4.00 10.00
5 Ryan Smyth 1.50 4.00
6 Sergei Samsonov 1.50 4.00
7 Mark Messier 2.50 6.00
8 Wayne Gretzky 10.00 25.00
9 Jarome Iginla 3.00 8.00
10 Peter Forsberg 6.00 15.00
11 Joe Sakic 5.00 12.00
12 Sergei Fedorov 4.00 10.00
13 Mike Modano 4.00 10.00
14 Paul Kariya 2.50 6.00
15 Teemu Selanne 2.50 6.00
16 Eric Lindros 2.50 6.00
17 Keith Tkachuk 2.50 6.00
18 Patrick Marleau 1.50 4.00
19 Jaroslav Svejkovsky 1.50 4.00
20 Alyn McCauley 1.50 4.00
21 Saku Koivu 2.50 6.00
22 Zigmund Palffy 1.50 4.00
23 Brett Hull 3.00 8.00
24 Patrik Elias 2.50 6.00
25 Joe Thornton 6.00 15.00
26 Espen Knutsen 1.50 4.00
27 Daniel Alfredsson 2.00 5.00
28 John LeClair 2.50 6.00
29 Dainius Zubrus 1.50 4.00
30 Jason Arnott 1.50 4.00

1997-98 Donruss Priority Postcards

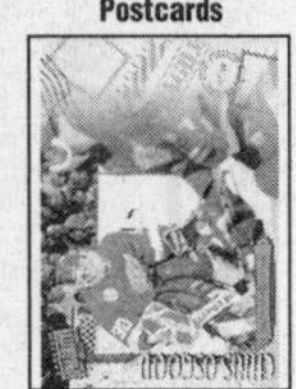

Inserted one per large pack, this 36-card set featured standard postcard sized cards.

COMPLETE SET (36) 25.00 50.00
*OPEN.DAY/1000: 2X TO 5X BASIC INSERTS
OPENING DAY PRINT RUN 1000 SETS
1 Patrick Roy 2.50 6.00
2 Brendan Shanahan .50 1.25
3 Steve Yzerman 2.50 6.00
4 Jaromir Jagr .75 2.00
5 Pavel Bure .50 1.25
6 Mark Messier .50 1.25
7 Wayne Gretzky 3.00 8.00
8 Eric Lindros .50 1.25
9 Joe Sakic 1.00 2.50
10 Peter Forsberg 1.25 3.00
11 John Vanbiesbrouck .40 1.00
12 Mike Modano .75 2.00
13 Paul Kariya .50 1.25
14 Teemu Selanne .50 1.25
15 Sergei Fedorov .75 2.00
16 Joe Thornton 1.25 3.00
17 Sergei Samsonov .40 1.00
18 Patrick Marleau .75 2.00
19 Ryan Smyth .40 1.00
20 Jarome Iginla .60 1.50
21 John LeClair .50 1.25
22 Brian Leetch .50 1.25
23 Chris Chelios .50 1.25
24 Martin Brodeur 1.25 3.00
25 Bryan Berard .40 1.00
26 Keith Tkachuk .50 1.25
27 Saku Koivu .50 1.25
28 Brett Hull .60 1.50
29 Felix Potvin .50 1.25
30 Chris Osgood .40 1.00
31 Dominik Hasek 1.00 2.50
32 Zigmund Palffy .40 1.00
33 Jeremy Roenick .60 1.50
34 Dainius Zubrus .40 1.00
35 Ray Bourque .75 2.00
36 Jocelyn Thibault .40 1.00

1997-98 Donruss Priority Postmaster Generals

Randomly inserted in packs, this 20-card set featured color photos of top goalies printed on all-foil board with foil stamping. Only 1,500 of each card were produced and sequentially numbered.

COMPLETE SET (20) 40.00 80.00
*PROMO: .3X TO .8X BASIC INSERTS
1 Patrick Roy 12.00 30.00
2 John Vanbiesbrouck 2.00 5.00
3 Felix Potvin 3.00 8.00
4 Curtis Joseph 3.00 8.00
5 Mike Richter 2.00 5.00
6 Jocelyn Thibault 1.00 2.50
7 Ed Belfour 2.00 5.00
8 Chris Osgood 2.00 5.00
9 Ron Hextall 2.00 5.00
10 Martin Brodeur 8.00 20.00
11 Mike Vernon 2.00 5.00
12 Eric Fichaud 1.00 2.50
13 Dominik Hasek 6.00 15.00
14 Byron Dafoe 1.00 2.50
15 Tommy Salo 1.00 2.50
16 Garth Snow 1.00 2.50
17 Tom Barrasso 1.00 2.50
18 Marc Denis 1.00 2.50
19 Grant Fuhr 2.00 5.00
20 Guy Hebert 1.00 2.50

1997-98 Donruss Priority Stamps

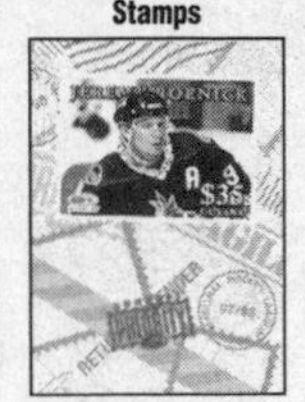

Randomly inserted one per small pack, this 36-card set featured color photos of top NHL players printed on real currency stamps. Printed in the country of Grenada, each stamp came protected in a stamp holder card. Bronze, silver, and gold parallel versions of this set were also produced with an insertion rate of 1:6.

COMPLETE SET (36) 20.00 40.00
*BRONZE: .8X TO 2X BASIC INSERTS
*SILVER: 1.5X TO 4X BASIC INSERTS
*GOLD: 3X TO 8X BASIC INSERTS
1 Patrick Roy 2.50 6.00
2 Brendan Shanahan .50 1.25
3 Steve Yzerman 2.50 6.00
4 Jaromir Jagr .75 2.00
5 Pavel Bure .50 1.25
6 Mark Messier .50 1.25
7 Wayne Gretzky 3.00 8.00
8 Eric Lindros .50 1.25
9 Joe Sakic 1.00 2.50
10 Peter Forsberg 1.25 3.00
11 John Vanbiesbrouck .40 1.00
12 Mike Modano .75 2.00
13 Paul Kariya .50 1.25
14 Teemu Selanne .50 1.25
15 Sergei Fedorov .75 2.00
16 Joe Thornton 1.25 3.00
17 Sergei Samsonov .40 1.00
18 Patrick Marleau .75 2.00
19 Ryan Smyth .40 1.00
20 Jarome Iginla .60 1.50
21 John LeClair .50 1.25
22 Brian Leetch .40 1.00
23 Chris Chelios .50 1.25
24 Martin Brodeur 1.25 3.00
25 Bryan Berard .40 1.00
26 Keith Tkachuk .50 1.25
27 Saku Koivu .50 1.25
28 Brett Hull .60 1.50
29 Felix Potvin .50 1.25
30 Chris Osgood .40 1.00
31 Dominik Hasek 1.00 2.50
32 Zigmund Palffy .40 1.00
33 Jeremy Roenick .60 1.50
34 Dainius Zubrus .40 1.00
35 Ray Bourque .75 2.00
36 Jocelyn Thibault .40 1.00

2008 Donruss Sports Legends

This set was released on December 10, 2008. The base set consists of 144 cards and features cards of players from various sports.

COMPLETE SET (144)
11 Patrick Roy 1.00 2.50
17 Ray Bourque .75 2.00
24 Norm Ullman .50 1.25
34 Bill Gadsby .50 1.25
54 Gerry Cheevers .40 1.00
58 Pierre Pilote .60 1.50
66 Brad Park .60 1.50
84 Alex Delvecchio .60 1.50
91 Phil Esposito .60 1.50
103 Mike Bossy .60 1.50
111 Paul Coffey .60 1.50
126 Tony Esposito .50 1.25
132 Pat LaFontaine .60 1.50

2008 Donruss Sports Legends Mirror Red

*RED/250: 1.5X TO 4X BASIC CARDS
STATED PRINT RUN 250 SER.#'d SETS

2008 Donruss Sports Legends Mirror Blue

*BLUE/100: 2X TO 5X BASIC CARDS
STATED PRINT RUN 100 SER.#'d SETS

2008 Donruss Sports Legends Mirror Gold

*GOLD/25: 3X TO 8X BASIC CARDS
STATED PRINT RUN 25 SER.#'d SETS

2008 Donruss Sports Legends Mirror Emerald

UNPRICED MIRROR EMERALD PRINT RUN 5

2008 Donruss Sports Legends Mirror Black

UNPRICED MIRROR BLACK PRINT RUN 1

2008 Donruss Sports Legends Certified Cuts

STATED PRINT RUN 1-100
SERIAL #'d TO 1 NOT PRICED
5 Alex Delvecchio 10.00 25.00
Fats/100

2008 Donruss Sports Legends Museum Collection

SILVER PRINT RUN 1000 SER.#'d SETS
*GOLD/100: .6X TO 1.5X SILVER/1000
GOLD PRINT RUN 100 SER.#'d SETS
3 Ray Bourque 2.00 5.00
35 Mike Bossy 1.50 4.00

2008 Donruss Sports Legends Museum Collection Signatures

STATED PRINT RUN 1-250
SERIAL #'d UNDER 25 NOT PRICED
3 Ray Bourque/50 20.00 40.00
35 Mike Bossy/100 6.00 15.00

2008 Donruss Sports Legends Signature Connection Combos

STATED PRINT RUN 25-100
13 Bill Gadsby 20.00 40.00
Pierre Pilote/100
15 Phil Esposito 20.00 40.00
Gerry Cheevers/100

2008 Donruss Sports Legends Signatures Mirror Red

*MIRROR RED: .3X TO .8X MIRROR BLUE
MIRROR RED PRINT RUN 25-1370
17 Ray Bourque/25 20.00 50.00
24 Norm Ullman/714 4.00 10.00
34 Bill Gadsby/564 4.00 10.00
54 Gerry Cheevers/568 4.00 10.00
58 Pierre Pilote/539 4.00 10.00
66 Brad Park/269 3.00 8.00
84 Alex Delvecchio/563 4.00 10.00
91 Phil Esposito/109 10.00 25.00
103 Mike Bossy/269 8.00 20.00
111 Paul Coffey/25 10.00 25.00
126 Tony Esposito/93 10.00 25.00
132 Pat LaFontaine/290 6.00 15.00

2008 Donruss Sports Legends Signatures Mirror Blue

MIRROR BLUE PRINT RUN 2-250
SERIAL #'d UNDER 10 NOT PRICED
UNPRICED MIRROR EMERALD PRINT RUN 1-5
UNPRICED MIRROR BLACK PRINT RUN 1
17 Ray Bourque/25 20.00 50.00
24 Norm Ullman/250 5.00 12.00
34 Bill Gadsby/250 5.00 12.00
54 Gerry Cheevers/250 5.00 12.00
58 Pierre Pilote/250 5.00 12.00
66 Brad Park/50 4.00 10.00
84 Alex Delvecchio/250 5.00 12.00
91 Phil Esposito/25 12.00 30.00
103 Mike Bossy/50 10.00 25.00
111 Paul Coffey/25 10.00 25.00
126 Tony Esposito/25 12.00 30.00
132 Pat LaFontaine/100 8.00 20.00

2008 Donruss Sports Legends Signatures Mirror Gold

MIRROR GOLD PRINT RUN 4-25
SERIAL #'d UNDER 10 NOT PRICED
11 Patrick Roy/5
17 Ray Bourque/10 25.00 60.00
24 Norm Ullman/25 8.00 20.00
34 Bill Gadsby/25 8.00 20.00
54 Gerry Cheevers/25 8.00 20.00
58 Pierre Pilote/25 8.00 20.00
66 Brad Park/25 5.00 12.00
84 Alex Delvecchio/25 6.00 15.00
91 Phil Esposito/10 15.00 40.00
103 Mike Bossy/25 12.00 30.00
111 Paul Coffey/10 12.00 30.00
126 Tony Esposito/15 15.00 40.00
132 Pat LaFontaine/25 10.00 25.00

2008 Donruss Sports Legends Materials Mirror Red

MIRROR RED PRINT RUN 10-500
SERIAL #'d UNDER 25 NOT PRICED
*GOLD/25: .8X TO 2X MIRROR RED
UNPRICED MIRROR EMERALD PRINT RUN 1-5
UNPRICED MIRROR BLACK PRINT RUN 1
11 Patrick Roy Jsy/500 6.00 15.00
24 Norm Ullman Jsy/250 4.00 10.00
34 Bill Gadsby Jsy/500 3.00 8.00
58 Pierre Pilote Jsy/500 4.00 10.00
126 Tony Esposito Jsy/250 4.00 10.00

2008 Donruss Sports Legends Materials Mirror Blue

*MIRROR BLUE: .5X TO 1.2X MIRROR RED
MIRROR BLUE PRINT RUN 5-250
SERIAL #'d UNDER 15 NOT PRICED

2008 Donruss Sports Legends Materials Mirror Gold

*GOLD/25: .8X TO 2X MIRROR RED
GOLD PRINT RUN 1-25 SER.#'d SETS
SERIAL #'d UNDER 20 NOT PRICED

1993-94 Ducks Milk Caps

This set of six milk caps measured approximately 1 1/2" in diameter and featuresdthe Mighty Ducks of Anaheim. The fronts showed a color player headshot set against a teal green background with a neon yellow stripe. The player's name appeared at the bottom, along with the production figures "One of 15,000". The backs were solid white. The milk caps were numbered on the front.

COMPLETE SET (6) 2.00 5.00
1 Tim Sweeney .40 1.00
2 Bobby Dollas .40 1.00
3 Stu Grimson .60 1.50
4 Terry Yake .40 1.00
5 Bob Corkum .40 1.00
NNO Inaugural Season .40 1.00
First Win

1994-95 Ducks Carl's Jr.

The 28-card standard-size set was sponsored by Carl's Jr. The fronts featured a color action player photo on a back ground with a purple border. The player's name and team logo was at the left. The backs carried a head shot of the player, biographical information, statistics, and jersey number. The sponsor name and logo was at the bottom with a saying against drug use.

COMPLETE SET (28) 6.00 15.00
1 Patrik Carnback .08 .25
2 Bob Corkum .08 .25
3 Robert Dirk .08 .25
4 Bobby Dollas .08 .25
5 Peter Douris .08 .25
6 Todd Ewen .20 .50
7 Shaun Van Allen .08 .25
8 Garry Valk .08 .25
9 Guy Hebert .60 1.50
10 Paul Kariya 4.00 10.00
11 Valeri Karpov .08 .25
12 Steven King .08 .25
13 Todd Krygier .08 .25
14 Tom Kurvers .08 .25
15 Randy Ladouceur .08 .25
16 Stephan Lebeau .20 .50
17 John Lilley .08 .25
18 Don McSween .08 .25
19 Steve Rucchin .30 .75
20 David Sacco .08 .25
21 Joe Sacco .08 .25
22 Mikhail Shtalenkov .30 .75
23 Jim Thomson .08 .25
24 Oleg Tverdovsky .30 .75
25 David Williams .08 .25
26 Wild Wing (Mascot) .08 .25
27 Carl Karcher .01
(Sponsor Owner)
28 Happy Star .01
(Sponsor Logo)

1995-96 Ducks Team Issue

These five oversized (5" X 7") black and white photos pictured members of the '95-96 Mighty Ducks of Anaheim. The cards featured a posed head shot, with the player's name and a pair of team logos along the bottom. The backs were blank. The photos were unnumbered, and were listed below alphabetically. It's highly unlikely that the checklist was complete as listed below. Additional information would be appreciated and can be forwarded to Beckett Publications.

COMPLETE SET (5) 1.25 3.00
1 Bobby Dollas .20 .50
2 David Karpa .20 .50
3 Steve Rucchin .30 .75
4 Mikhail Shtalenkov .30 .75
5 Garry Valk .20 .50

1996-97 Ducks Team Issue

This unique 26-card set was produced by Up Front Sports and sponsored by Southland Micro Systems. The first twenty cards in the set followed the standard design of action photo on the front and stats on the back. Cards 21-24, however, were die-cut pop-up cards. Reports indicated that the Garry Valk destroyed or pulled since he was traded before the set's release. It's non known how many copies may still exist, but the card has been confirmed.

COMPLETE SET (26) 8.00 20.00
1 Mikhail Shtalenkov .20 .50
2 Bobby Dollas .15 .40
3 Roman Oksiuta .15 .40
4 Kevin Todd .15 .40
5 Ted Drury .15 .40
6 Joe Sacco .15 .40
7 Dmitri Mironov .20 .50
8 Warren Rychel .20 .50
10 Shawn Antoski .15 .40
11 Steve Rucchin .20 .50
12 Ken Baumgartner .15 .40
13 Brian Bellows .15 .40
14 Nikolai Tsulygin .15 .40
15 Jason Marshall .15 .40
16 Darren Van Impe .15 .40
17 David Karpa .15 .40
18 Wild Wing .02 .10
19 J.F. Jomphe .15 .40
20 Sean Pronger .15 .40
21 Guy Hebert .60 1.50
22 Paul Kariya 2.50 6.00
23 Jari Kurri .75 2.00
24 Teemu Selanne 1.50 4.00
25 Southland .01
26 Southland .01
27 Ron Wilson CO .08 .25

2002-03 Ducks Team Issue

The singles in this odd size set were distributed at promotional events. The set listing below is not complete. If you can confirm others, please contact us at hockeymag@beckett.com.

COMPLETE SET (?)
1 Adam Oates .40 1.00
1 Dan Bylsma .20 .50
2 Jean-Sebastien Giguere 1.25 3.00
3 Paul Kariya 1.25 3.00
4 Ruslan Salei .20 .50
5 Petr Sykora .20 .50
6 Vitaly Vishnevski .20 .50

2005-06 Ducks Team Issue

COMPLETE SET (22) 6.00 15.00
1 Kip Brennan .20 .50
2 Ilya Bryzgalov .30 .75
3 Keith Carney .20 .50
4 Joe DiPenta .30 .75
5 Todd Fedoruk .20 .50
6 Ryan Getzlaf .75 2.00
7 Jean-Sebastien Giguere .40 1.00
8 Jonathan Hedstrom .20 .50
9 Joffrey Lupul .40 1.00
10 Jason Marshall .20 .50
11 Andy McDonald .20 .50
12 Travis Moen .20 .50
13 Rob Niedermayer .20 .50
14 Scott Niedermayer .20 .50
15 Sandis Ozolinsh .20 .50
16 Samuel Pahlsson .20 .50
17 Corey Perry .75 2.00
18 Ruslan Salei .20 .50
19 Teemu Selanne .75 2.00
20 Petr Sykora .20 .50
21 Vitali Vishnevsky .20 .50
22 Randy Carlyle HC .02 .10

1992-93 Durivage Panini

This 50-card standard-size set showcased hockey stars who were born in Quebec. The cards, which were inserted in loaves of bread, featured color, action player photos set on a gold plaque design. The player's name appeared below the photo on the plaque. The words "Les Grands Hockeyeurs Quebecois" were printed in red at the top of the card. The backs had a ghosted black-and-white player photo with biography and career summary printed in French over the picture. The Patrick Roy signed card was randomly inserted. It is believed he signed 500 copies, although that has not been confirmed.

COMPLETE SET (50) 8.00 20.00
1 Guy Carbonneau .08 .25
2 Lucien Deblois .07 .20
3 Benoit Hogue .07 .20
4 Steve Kasper .07 .20
5 Mike Krushelnyski .07 .20
6 Claude Lapointe .07 .20
7 Stephan Lebeau .07 .20
8 Mario Lemieux 1.50 4.00
9 Stephane Morin .07 .20
10 Denis Savard .08 .25
11 Pierre Turgeon .08 .25
12 Kevin Dineen .07 .20
13 Gord Donnelly .07 .20
14 Claude Lemieux .08 .25
15 Jocelyn Lemieux .07 .20
16 Daniel Marois .07 .20
17 Scott Mellanby .07 .20
18 Stephane Richer .08 .25
19 Benoit Brunet .08 .25
20 Vincent Damphousse .08 .25
21 Gilbert Dionne .08 .25
22 Gaetan Duchesne .07 .20
23 Bob Errey .07 .20
24 Michel Goulet .08 .25
25 Mike Hough .07 .20
26 Sergio Momesso .07 .20
27 Mario Roberge .07 .20
28 Luc Robitaille .10 .30
29 Sylvain Turgeon .07 .20
30 Marc Bergevin .07 .20
31 Ray Bourque .50 1.25
32 Patrice Brisebois .07 .20
33 Jeff Chychrun .07 .20
34 Sylvain Cote .07 .20
35 J.J. Daigneault .07 .20
36 Eric Desjardins .08 .25
37 Gord Dineen .07 .20
38 Steve Duchesne .07 .20
39 Donald Dufresne .07 .20
40 Steven Finn .07 .20
41 Garry Galley .07 .20
42 Kevin Lowe .08 .25
43 Michel Petit .07 .20
44 Normand Rochefort .07 .20
45 Randy Velischek .07 .20
46 Jacques Cloutier .08 .25
47 Stephane Fiset .10 .30
48 Rejean Lemelin .08 .25
49 Andre Racicot .08 .25
50 Patrick Roy 3.00 8.00
NNO Patrick Roy AU 50.00 125.00

1993-94 Durivage Score

These 50 standard-size white-bordered cards featured color player action shots "mounted" on golden plaque designs. The player's name and hometown appeared within a black stripe below the photo. All the players in the set were from the province of Quebec. His team's logo appeared further below. The white-bordered back carried a color player action photo on the right and, on the left, bilingual biography and statistics. Cards 1-6 belonged to a "Special Edition" subset and had gold-foil highlights on their fronts. The cards were numbered on the back as "X of 50."

COMPLETE SET (50) 12.00 30.00
1 Alexandre Daigle .30 .75
2 Pierre Sevigny .10 .30
3 Jocelyn Thibault .50 1.25
4 Philippe Boucher .10 .30
5 Martin Brodeur 1.50 4.00
New Jers
6 Martin Lapointe .40 1.00
7 Patrice Brisebois .40 1.00
8 Benoit Brunet .10 .30
9 Guy Carbonneau .40 1.00
10 Jean-Jacques Daigneault .10 .30
11 Vincent Damphousse .40 1.00
12 Eric Desjardins .40 1.00
13 Gilbert Dionne .10 .30
14 Stephan Lebeau .40 1.00
15 Andre Racicot .40 1.00
16 Mario Roberge .10 .30
17 Patrick Roy 3.00 8.00
18 Jacques Cloutier .40 1.00
19 Alain Cote .10 .30
20 Steven Finn .10 .30
21 Stephane Fiset .30 .75
22 Martin Gelinas .10 .30
23 Reggie Savage .10 .30
24 Claude Lapointe .10 .30
25 Denis Savard .50 1.25
26 Ray Bourque .75 2.00
27 Joe Juneau .30 .75
28 Ron Stern .10 .30
29 Benoit Hogue .40 1.00
30 Pierre Turgeon .50 1.25
31 Mike Krushelnyski .10 .30
32 Felix Potvin .50 1.25
33 Sergio Momesso .10 .30
34 Yves Racine .10 .30
35 Sylvain Cote .10 .30
36 Sylvain Turgeon .10 .30
37 Kevin Dineen .40 1.00
38 Garry Galley .40 1.00
39 Dominic Roussel .40 1.00
40 Gaetan Duchesne .10 .30
41 Luc Robitaille .50 1.25
42 Michel Goulet .50 1.25
43 Jocelyn Lemieux .10 .30
44 Stephane Matteau .10 .30
45 Mike Hough .10 .30
46 Scott Mellanby .50 1.25
47 Claude Lemieux .30 .75
48 Stephane Richer .50 1.25
49 Jimmy Waite .10 .30
50 Patrick Poulin .40 1.00
NNO Patrick Roy AU 75.00 200.00
NNO Jocelyn Thibault AU 40.00 100.00

1996-97 Duracell All-Cherry Team

This 22-card set was available in three-card packs with the purchase of specially-marked packages of Duracell batteries in English-speaking Canada and was produced by Pinnacle Brands. The players featured in the set were chosen by CBC commentator and fashion doyenne Don Cherry. The card fronts featured a color action photo, along with manufacturer logos. The backs included a brief resume. Interestingly, the player's stats could only be revealed by pressing a trio of heat-sensitive strips. There were rumored to be short printed cards in the set, but no confirmation of this has become available.

COMPLETE SET (22) 8.00 20.00
DC1 Paul Coffey .30 .75
DC2 Lyle Odelein .08 .25
DC3 Joe Sakic .50 1.25
DC4 Curtis Joseph .40 1.00
DC5 Brett Hull .40 1.00
DC6 Eric Lindros .60 1.50
DC7 Doug Gilmour .30 .75
DC8 Chris Chelios .30 .75
DC9 Marty McSorley .08 .25
DC10 Kirk Muller .08 .25
DC11 Trevor Linden .08 .25
DC12 Brendan Shanahan .60 1.50
DC13 Tie Domi .20 .50
DC14 Rick Tocchet .08 .25
DC15 Steve Yzerman 1.25 3.00
DC16 Scott Stevens .08 .25
DC17 Patrick Roy 1.50 4.00
DC18 Keith Tkachuk .30 .75
DC19 Owen Nolan .20 .50
DC20 Dale Hunter .08 .25
DC21 Don Cherry .40 1.00
DC22 Don Cherry .40 1.00

1996-97 Duracell L'Equipe Beliveau

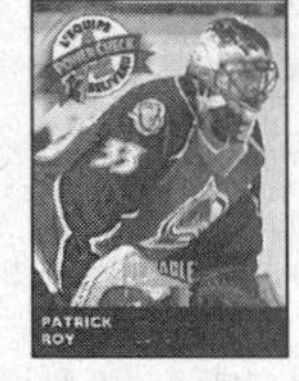

This 22-card set was available in 3-card packs with specially marked packages of Duracell batteries in French-speaking Canada. The set was produced by Pinnacle. The design was the same as that of the All-Cherry team cards, save for the different logo in the upper left corner of the front; also the text on the back of these cards is French. As the team was selected by former Habs great Jean Beliveau, the player composition was slightly different, with a notable increase in the francophone content. As this series was produced in more limited quantities than the Cherry set, the French version of the singles which appear in both sets carry a slight premium.

COMPLETE SET (22) 14.00 35.00
JB1 Paul Coffey .40 1.00
JB2 Lyle Odelein .08 .25
JB3 Joe Sakic 1.00 2.50
JB4 Eric Daze .30 .75
JB5 Brett Hull .75 2.00
JB6 Martin Brodeur 1.25 3.00
JB7 Doug Gilmour .60 1.50
JB8 Peter Forsberg 1.25 3.00
JB9 Mike Gartner .20 .50
JB10 Saku Koivu .60 1.50
JB11 Trevor Linden .08 .25
JB12 Felix Potvin .40 1.00
JB13 Mats Sundin .40 1.00
JB14 Pierre Turgeon .20 .50
JB15 Vincent Damphousse .08 .25
JB16 Scott Stevens .08 .25
JB17 Patrick Roy 2.00 5.00
JB18 Keith Tkachuk .60 1.50
JB19 Ray Bourque .75 2.00
JB20 Paul Kariya 1.25 3.00
JB21 Jean Beliveau .40 1.00
JB22 Jean Beliveau .40 1.00

2003-04 Duracell

These cards were issued as a mail-in premium with the purchase of Duracell batteries in Canada.

COMPLETE SET (15) 20.00
1 Jean-Sebastien Giguere .40 1.00
2 Patrick Lalime .20 .50
3 Curtis Joseph .75 2.00
4 Marty Turco .40 1.00
5 Ed Belfour .75 2.00
6 Sean Burke .20 .50
7 Roberto Luongo .75 2.00
8 Jose Theodore .75 2.00
9 Olaf Kolzig .20 .50
10 Martin Brodeur 1.25 3.00
11 Mike Richter .20 .50
12 Dan Blackburn .20 .50
13 Patrick Roy 1.50 4.00
14 Dwayne Roloson .20 .50
15 Dan Cloutier .20 .50

1994 EA Sports

This 225-card boxed set was issued by Electronic Arts Sports as a premium with packages of its NHLPA '94 video game. Two cards were included with each game. In addition, an order form for a complete set was found inside the game box; the original price was 24.95 direct. The fronts were white with action player photos that had airbrushed edges. The team logo appeared in the upper left corner with the player's name printed on a black bar across the bottom edge. The player's position was on a team color-coded stripe above the player's name. The borderless backs displayed a head shot in the upper left corner with player performance rating below. A brief biography and career summary appeared to the right.

COMPLETE SET (225) 30.00 75.00
1 Alexei Kasatonov .01 .05
2 Randy Ladouceur .01 .05
3 Terry Yake .01 .05
4 Troy Loney .01 .05
5 Anatoli Semenov .01 .05
6 Guy Hebert .05 .15
7 Ray Bourque 1.25 3.00
8 Don Sweeney .01 .05
9 Adam Oates .20 .50
10 Joe Juneau .15 .40
11 Cam Neely .40 1.00
12 Andy Moog .08 .25
13 Doug Bodger .01 .05
14 Petr Svoboda .01 .05
15 Pat LaFontaine .20 .50
16 Dale Hawerchuk .08 .25
17 Alexander Mogilny .20 .50
18 Grant Fuhr .08 .25
19 Gary Suter .01 .05
20 Al MacInnis .05 .15
21 Joe Nieuwendyk .05 .15
22 Gary Roberts .05 .15
23 Theo Fleury .08 .25
24 Mike Vernon .05 .15
25 Chris Chelios .40 1.00
26 Steve Smith .01 .05
27 Jeremy Roenick .60 1.50
28 Michel Goulet .05 .15
29 Steve Larmer .05 .15
30 Ed Belfour .60 1.50
31 Mark Tinordi .01 .05
32 Tommy Sjodin .01 .05
33 Mike Modano .75 2.00
34 Dave Gagner .05 .15
35 Russ Courtnall .05 .15
36 Jon Casey .05 .15
37 Paul Coffey .40 1.00
38 Steve Chiasson .01 .05
39 Steve Yzerman 2.50 6.00
40 Sergei Fedorov 1.25 3.00
41 Dino Ciccarelli .05 .15
42 Tim Cheveldae .05 .15
43 Dave Manson .01 .05
44 Igor Kravchuk .01 .05
45 Doug Weight .08 .25
46 Shayne Corson .05 .15
47 Petr Klima .01 .05
48 Bill Ranford .05 .15
49 Joe Cirella .01 .05
50 Gord Murphy .01 .05
51 Brian Skrudland .01 .05
52 Andrei Lomakin .01 .05
53 Scott Mellanby .05 .15
54 John Vanbiesbrouck .40 1.00
55 Zarley Zalapski .01 .05
56 Eric Weinrich .01 .05
57 Andrew Cassels .01 .05
58 Geoff Sanderson .05 .15
59 Pat Verbeek .05 .15
60 Sean Burke .05 .15
61 Rob Blake .05 .15
62 Marty McSorley .05 .15
63 Wayne Gretzky 4.00 10.00
64 Luc Robitaille .20 .50
65 Tomas Sandstrom .05 .15
66 Kelly Hrudey .05 .15
67 Eric Desjardins .05 .15
68 Mathieu Schneider .05 .15
69 Kirk Muller .05 .15
70 Vincent Damphousse .08 .25
71 Brian Bellows .01 .05
72 Patrick Roy 3.00 8.00
73 Scott Stevens .05 .15
74 Slava Fetisov .05 .15
75 Alexander Semak .01 .05
76 Stephane Richer .05 .15
77 Claude Lemieux .08 .25
78 Chris Terreri .05 .15
79 Vladimir Malakhov .01 .05
80 Darius Kasparaitis .01 .05
81 Pierre Turgeon .20 .50
82 Steve Thomas .05 .15
83 Benoit Hogue .01 .05
84 Glenn Healy .01 .05
85 Brian Leetch .40 1.00
86 James Patrick .01 .05
87 Mark Messier .75 2.00
88 Designer Tip .01 .05
89 Mike Gartner .05 .15
90 Mike Richter .40 1.00
91 Norm Maciver .01 .05
92 Brad Shaw .01 .05

93 Jamie Baker .01 .05
94 Sylvain Turgeon .01 .05
95 Bob Kudelski .01 .05
96 Peter Sidorkiewicz .01 .05
97 Garry Galley .01 .05
98 Dimitri Yushkevich .01 .05
99 Eric Lindros 1.50 4.00
100 Rod Brind'Amour .05 .15
101 Mark Recchi .20 .50
102 Tommy Soderstrom .01 .05
103 Larry Murphy .08 .25
104 Ulf Samuelsson .01 .05
105 Mario Lemieux 3.00 8.00
106 Kevin Stevens .05 .15
107 Jaromir Jagr 2.00 5.00
108 Tom Barrasso .08 .25
109 Steve Duchesne .05 .15
110 Curtis Leschyshyn .01 .05
111 Mats Sundin .40 1.00
112 Joe Sakic 1.25 3.00
113 Owen Nolan .20 .50
114 Ron Hextall .08 .25
115 Doug Wilson .05 .15
116 Neil Wilkinson .01 .05
117 Kelly Kisio .01 .05
118 Johan Garpenlov .01 .05
119 Pat Falloon .05 .15
120 Arturs Irbe .15 .40
121 Jeff Brown .05 .15
122 Garth Butcher .05 .15
123 Craig Janney .05 .15
124 Brendan Shanahan .75 2.00
125 Brett Hull .75 2.00
126 Curtis Joseph .75 2.00
127 Bob Beers .01 .05
128 Roman Hamrlik .08 .25
129 Brian Bradley .05 .15
130 Mikael Andersson .01 .05
131 Chris Kontos .01 .05
132 Wendell Young .01 .05
133 Todd Gill .01 .05
134 Dave Ellett .01 .05
135 Doug Gilmour .40 1.00
136 Dave Andreychuk .05 .15
137 Nikolai Borschevsky .01 .05
138 Felix Potvin .40 1.00
139 Jyrki Lumme .01 .05
140 Doug Lidster .01 .05
141 Cliff Ronning .05 .15
142 Geoff Courtnall .05 .15
143 Pavel Bure 1.50 4.00
144 Kirk McLean .05 .15
145 Phil Housley .05 .15
146 Teppo Numminen .01 .05
147 Alexei Zhamnov .05 .15
148 Thomas Steen .01 .05
149 Teemu Selanne 1.25 3.00
150 Bob Essensa .05 .15
151 Kevin Hatcher .01 .05
152 Al Iafrate .05 .15
153 Mike Ridley .01 .05
154 Dimitri Khristich .01 .05
155 Peter Bondra .08 .25
156 Don Beaupre .01 .05
157 All Stars East CL .05 .15
158 All Stars West CL .05 .15
159 Mighty Ducks Team CL .08 .25
160 Bruins Team CL .08 .25
161 Sabres Team CL .05 .15
162 Flames Team CL .05 .15
163 Blackhawks Team CL .08 .25
164 Red Wings Team CL .08 .25
165 Oilers Team CL .05 .15
166 Panthers Team CL .05 .15
167 Whalers Team CL .05 .15
168 Kings Team CL .08 .25
169 Stars Team CL .05 .15
170 Canadiens Team CL .08 .25
171 Devils Team CL .05 .15
172 Islanders Team CL .05 .15
173 Rangers Team CL .08 .25
174 Senators Team CL .05 .15
175 Flyers Team CL .05 .15
176 Penguins Team CL .05 .15
177 Nordiques Team CL .05 .15
178 Sharks Team CL .08 .25
179 Blues Team CL .05 .15
180 Lightning Team CL .05 .15
181 Leafs Team CL .08 .25
182 Canucks Team CL .05 .15
183 Capitals Team CL .05 .15
184 Jets Team CL .05 .15
185 Ray Bourque SL .08 .25
186 Chris Chelios SL .08 .25
187 Ed Belfour SL .40 1.00
188 Adam Oates SL .08 .25
189 Skill Leaders Shot Accu 1.50 4.00
190 Al Iafrate SL .05 .15
191 Alexander Mogilny SL .20 .50
192 Wayne Gretzky SL 2.00 5.00
193 New Feature .01 .05
194 Derian Hatcher .01 .05
195 Dmitri Kvartalnov .01 .05
196 Randy Wood .01 .05
197 Gord Murphy .01 .05
198 New Feature .01 .05
199 Ducks/Panthers Team Logo .08 .25
200 Luc Robitaille .08 .25
201 Terry Yake .01 .05
202 Mark Fitzpatrick .01 .05
203 Brad Shaw .01 .05
204 NHL Logos .01 .05
205 Jyrki Lumme .01 .05
206 Peter Sidorkiewicz .01 .05
207 Gord Murphy .01 .05
208 Slava Fetisov .01 .05
209 Stephan LeBeau .01 .05
210 Gord Murphy .01 .05
211 Dominik Hasek 1.25 3.00
212 Cam Neely .40 1.00
213 Designer Tips .01 .05
214 Designer Tips .01 .05
215 Designer Tips .01 .05
216 Designer Tips .01 .05
217 Designer Tips .01 .05
218 Designer Tips .01 .05
219 Designer Tips .01 .05
220 Designer Tips .01 .05
221 Designer Tips .01 .05
222 Designer Tips .01 .05
223 Designer Tips .01 .05
224 Designer Tips .01 .05
225 Designer Tips .01 .05

2001 EA Sports

This 9-card set was inserted one-card-per-game in EA Sports' NHL 2002 video game and was produced by Upper Deck. A Gold parallel was also produced and inserted randomly. An autographed Mario Lemieux card has also been rumored to exist, but no verification of that has been made.

COMPLETE SET (9)
*GOLD: 2X TO 5 X BASIC CARD
1 Mario Lemieux 4.00 15.00
2 Mario Lemieux 4.00 15.00
3 Owen Nolan .40 1.00
4 Jere Lehtinen .08 1.00
5 Martin Rucinsky .20 .50
6 Chris Pronger .40 1.00
7 Markus Naslund .40 2.00
8 Peter Forsberg 1.60 6.00
9 Steve Yzerman 3.20 12.00

1964-67 Eaton's Sports Adviser

Issued between 1964 and 1967, these cards were used as promotional material by Eaton's of Canada.

NNO Gordie Howe All-Star uniform 10.00 25.00
NNO Gordie Howe standing 10.00 25.00
NNO Gordie Howe action 10.00 25.00

1962-63 El Producto Discs

The six discs in this set measured approximately 3" in diameter. They were issued as a strip of six connected in a fragile manner and were in full color. The discs were unnumbered and checklisted below in alphabetical order. The set in unperforated form is valued 25 percent greater than the value below.

COMPLETE SET (6) 150.00 300.00
1 Jean Beliveau 30.00 60.00
2 Glenn Hall 25.00 50.00
3 Gordie Howe 75.00 150.00
4 Dave Keon 30.00 60.00
5 Frank Mahovlich 25.00 50.00
6 Henri Richard 25.00 50.00

1995-96 Emotion Promo Strip

This 6" by 3" strip was distributed by Skybox to introduce its Emotion line of cards. The front featured two cards of Jeremy Roenick of the Chicago Blackhawks: his basic Emotion issue and his X-Cited insert. They were identical to the regularly issued cards, save for the word sample found in the back upper right corner. They were separated by a white bar with the sponsor logo horizontally printed in gold and date cards premier in black.

1 Jeremy Roenick .40 1.00

1995-96 Emotion

This 200-card high end set was released in 8-card packs with an SRP of $4.99. The set was distinguished by its use of an "emotional" term to describe the action on the card face. The Jeremy Roenick SkyMotion card was obtainable in exchange for three wrappers and $25. The unique card featured three seconds of actual game footage. The offer for this card expired on June 30, 1996.

COMPLETE SET (200) 20.00 40.00
1 Bobby Dollas .05 .15
2 Guy Hebert .10 .30
3 Paul Kariya .20 .50
4 Oleg Tverdovsky .05 .15
5 Shaun Van Allen .05 .15
6 Ray Bourque .30 .75
7 Al Iafrate .10 .30
8 Blaine Lacher .10 .30
9 Joe Mullen .10 .30
10 Cam Neely .20 .50
11 Adam Oates .10 .30
12 Kevin Stevens .05 .15
13 Don Sweeney .05 .15
14 Donald Audette .05 .15
15 Garry Galley .05 .15
16 Dominik Hasek .40 1.00
17 Brian Holzinger RC .20 .50
18 Pat LaFontaine .20 .50
19 Alexei Zhitnik .05 .15
20 Steve Chiasson .05 .15
21 Theo Fleury .05 .15
22 Phil Housley .10 .30
23 Trevor Kidd .10 .30
24 Joe Nieuwendyk .10 .30
25 Gary Roberts .05 .15
26 Zarley Zalapski .05 .15
27 Ed Belfour .20 .50
28 Chris Chelios .20 .50
29 Sergei Krivokrasov .05 .15
30 Joe Murphy .05 .15
31 Bernie Nicholls .05 .15
32 Patrick Poulin .05 .15
33 Jeremy Roenick .25 .60
34 Gary Suter .05 .15
35 Rene Corbet .05 .15
36 Peter Forsberg .50 1.25
37 Valeri Kamensky .10 .30
38 Uwe Krupp .05 .15
39 Curtis Leschyshyn .05 .15
40 Owen Nolan .10 .30
41 Mike Ricci .10 .30
42 Joe Sakic .40 1.00
43 Jocelyn Thibault .20 .50
44 Bob Bassen .05 .15
45 Dave Gagner .05 .15
46 Todd Harvey .10 .30
47 Derian Hatcher .05 .15
48 Kevin Hatcher .05 .15
49 Mike Modano .30 .75
50 Andy Moog .20 .50
51 Dino Ciccarelli .10 .30
52 Paul Coffey .20 .50
53 Sergei Fedorov .30 .75
54 Vladimir Konstantinov .10 .30
55 Slava Kozlov .10 .30
56 Nicklas Lidstrom .20 .50
57 Keith Primeau .05 .15
58 Ray Sheppard .05 .15
59 Mike Vernon .10 .30
60 Steve Yzerman 1.00 2.50
61 Jason Arnott .05 .15
62 Curtis Joseph .20 .50
63 Igor Kravchuk .05 .15
64 Todd Marchant .05 .15
65 David Oliver .05 .15
66 Bill Ranford .10 .30
67 Doug Weight .10 .30
68 Stu Barnes .05 .15
69 Jesse Belanger .05 .15
70 Gord Murphy .05 .15
71 Magnus Svensson RC .05 .15
72 John Vanbiesbrouck .10 .30
73 Sean Burke .10 .30
74 Andrew Cassels .05 .15
75 Frantisek Kucera .05 .15
76 Andrei Nikolishin .05 .15
77 Geoff Sanderson .05 .15
78 Brendan Shanahan .20 .50
79 Darren Turcotte .05 .15
80 Rob Blake .10 .30
81 Wayne Gretzky 1.50 4.00
82 Dimitri Khristich .05 .15
83 Jari Kurri .20 .50
84 Jamie Storr .10 .30
85 Darryl Sydor .10 .30
86 Rick Tocchet .10 .30
87 Vincent Damphousse .05 .15
88 Vladimir Malakhov .05 .15
89 Stephane Quintal .05 .15
90 Mark Recchi .10 .30
91 Patrick Roy 1.00 2.50
92 Brian Savage .05 .15
93 Pierre Turgeon .10 .30
94 Martin Brodeur .50 1.25
95 Neal Broten .10 .30
96 Shawn Chambers .05 .15
97 Claude Lemieux .05 .15
98 John MacLean .10 .30
99 Randy McKay .05 .15
100 Scott Niedermayer .05 .15
101 Stephane Richer .10 .30
102 Scott Stevens .10 .30
103 Todd Bertuzzi RC 1.00 2.50
104 Patrick Flatley .05 .15
105 Brett Lindros .05 .15
106 Kirk Muller .05 .15
107 Tommy Salo RC .75 2.00
108 Mathieu Schneider .05 .15
109 Alexander Semak .05 .15
110 Dennis Vaske .05 .15
111 Ray Ferraro .05 .15
112 Adam Graves .05 .15
113 Alexei Kovalev .05 .15
114 Steve Larmer .10 .30
115 Brian Leetch .10 .30
116 Mark Messier .20 .50
117 Mike Richter .20 .50
118 Luc Robitaille .10 .30
119 Ulf Samuelsson .05 .15
120 Pat Verbeek .05 .15
121 Don Beaupre .05 .15
122 Radek Bonk .05 .15
123 Alexandre Daigle .05 .15
124 Steve Duchesne .05 .15
125 Steve Larouche .05 .15
126 Dan Quinn .05 .15
127 Martin Straka .05 .15
128 Alexei Yashin .05 .15
129 Rod Brind'Amour .10 .30
130 Eric Desjardins .10 .30
131 Ron Hextall .10 .30
132 John LeClair .20 .50
133 Eric Lindros .20 .50
134 Mikael Renberg .10 .30
135 Chris Therien .05 .15
136 Ron Francis .10 .30
137 Jaromir Jagr .30 .75
138 Mario Lemieux 1.00 2.50
139 Dmitri Mironov .05 .15
140 Petr Nedved .10 .30
141 Tomas Sandstrom .05 .15
142 Bryan Smolinski .05 .15
143 Ken Wregget .10 .30
144 Sergei Zubov .05 .15
145 Shayne Corson .05 .15
146 Geoff Courtnall .05 .15
147 Dale Hawerchuk .20 .50
148 Brett Hull .25 .60
149 Ian Laperriere .05 .15
150 Al MacInnis .10 .30
151 Chris Pronger .20 .50
152 David Roberts .05 .15
153 Esa Tikkanen .05 .15
154 Ulf Dahlen .05 .15
155 Jeff Friesen .05 .15
156 Arturs Irbe .10 .30
157 Craig Janney .05 .15
158 Sergei Makarov .05 .15
159 Sandis Ozolinsh .05 .15
160 Mike Rathje .05 .15
161 Ray Whitney .10 .30
162 Brian Bradley .05 .15
163 Chris Gratton .05 .15
164 Roman Hamrlik .10 .30
165 Petr Klima .05 .15
166 Daren Puppa .10 .30
167 Paul Ysebaert .05 .15
168 Dave Andreychuk .10 .30
169 Mike Gartner .10 .30
170 Todd Gill .05 .15
171 Doug Gilmour .10 .30
172 Kenny Jonsson .05 .15
173 Larry Murphy .10 .30
174 Felix Potvin .20 .50
175 Mats Sundin .20 .50
176 Josef Beranek .05 .15
177 Jeff Brown .05 .15
178 Pavel Bure .20 .50
179 Russ Courtnall .05 .15
180 Trevor Linden .10 .30
181 Kirk McLean .10 .30
182 Alexander Mogilny .10 .30
183 Roman Oksiuta .05 .15
184 Mike Ridley .05 .15
185 Jason Allison .05 .15
186 Jim Carey .10 .30
187 Sergei Gonchar .05 .15
188 Dale Hunter .10 .30
189 Calle Johansson .05 .15
190 Joe Juneau .05 .15
191 Joe Reekie .05 .15
192 Nelson Emerson .05 .15
193 Nikolai Khabibulin .10 .30
194 Dave Manson .05 .15
195 Teppo Numminen .05 .15
196 Teemu Selanne .20 .50
197 Keith Tkachuk .20 .50
198 Alexei Zhamnov .10 .30
199 Checklist #1 .05 .15
200 Checklist #2 .05 .15
NNO Roenick SkyMotion Exch. 2.50 5.00
NNO J.Roenick SkyMotion 15.00 30.00

1995-96 Emotion generatioNext

This ten-card set took a look at those players thought to be the stars of tomorrow. The cards, which featured a player bust over a fiery metallic foil background were inserted at a rate of 1:10 packs. The cards were numbered "X of 10" on the back.

COMPLETE SET (10) 8.00 15.00
1 Brian Holzinger 1.00 2.50
2 Eric Daze .60 1.50
3 Jason Bonsignore .30 .75
4 Jamie Storr .60 1.50
5 Tommy Salo 2.00 5.00
6 Brendan Witt .30 .75
7 Saku Koivu 1.00 2.50
8 Todd Bertuzzi 3.00 8.00
9 Ed Jovanovski .30 .75
10 Chad Kilger .30 .75

1995-96 Emotion Ntense Power

This ten-card set highlighted the game's top power forwards. Utilizing a design element similar to the previous set using this name, the cards featured a cut-out player photo over a swirling foil background. The cards were randomly inserted 1:30 packs, and were numbered "X of 10" on the back.

COMPLETE SET (10) 10.00 20.00
1 Cam Neely 1.50 4.00
2 Keith Primeau .50 1.25
3 Mark Messier 1.50 4.00
4 Eric Lindros 1.50 4.00
5 Mikael Renberg 1.00 2.50
6 Owen Nolan 1.00 2.50
7 Brendan Shanahan 1.50 4.00
8 Kevin Stevens .50 1.25
9 Keith Tkachuk 1.50 4.00
10 Rick Tocchet 1.00 2.50

1995-96 Emotion Xcel

This ten-card set featured the top ten players in the league as chosen by the Fleer staff. The cards were issued randomly in packs at the rate of 1:72 packs. It was apparent, however, that a significant quantity of these cards entered the market through non-pack distribution, making them significantly easier to acquire than the long pack odds would suggest.

COMPLETE SET (10) 30.00 60.00
1 Adam Oates .75 2.00
2 Jeremy Roenick 2.00 5.00
3 Sergei Fedorov 2.00 5.00
4 Wayne Gretzky 10.00 25.00
5 Alexei Yashin .60 1.50
6 Eric Lindros 1.25 3.00
7 Ron Francis .75 2.00
8 Mario Lemieux 8.00 20.00
9 Joe Sakic 3.00 8.00
10 Alexei Zhamnov .60 1.50

1995-96 Emotion Xcited

This twenty-card set was the easiest pull from this issue, randomly inserted 1:3 packs. The set included many of the top offensive players in the game.

COMPLETE SET (20) 15.00 30.00
1 Theo Fleury .20 .50
2 Jeremy Roenick .75 2.00
3 Mike Modano 1.00 2.50
4 Sergei Fedorov 1.00 2.50
5 Wayne Gretzky 5.00 12.00
6 Brian Leetch .40 1.00
7 Alexei Yashin .20 .50
8 Brett Hull .75 2.00
9 Jaromir Jagr 1.00 2.50
10 Mario Lemieux 3.00 8.00
11 Ron Francis .40 1.00
12 Keith Primeau .20 .50
13 Joe Sakic 1.25 3.00
14 Peter Forsberg 1.50 4.00
15 Paul Kariya .60 1.50
16 Pavel Bure .60 1.50
17 Alexei Zhamnov .40 1.00
18 Martin Brodeur 1.50 4.00
19 Jim Carey .40 1.00
20 Chris Chelios .60 1.50

1992-93 Enor Mark Messier

One card from this ten-card standard-size set was included in each specially marked package of Enor Progard Plus sports card pages. The cards featured color player photos with silver borders. A red stripe that ran along the right edge and top of the photo accented the card face and provided a backdrop for the player's name, which was printed in white and blue. The horizontal back showed a close-up player photo that overlaped a red border stripe similar to the one on the front and a pale blue panel. The red stripe contained the player's name. The blue panel containsedplayer information. A black vertical bar ran along the left edge of the panel and contained biographical information.

COMPLETE SET (10) 2.00 5.00
COMMON MESSIER (1-10) .20 .50

1969-73 Equitable Sports Hall of Fame

Little is known about these miniature prints beyond the confirmed checklist. Additional information can be forwarded to hockeymag@beckett.com.

COMPLETE SET (6) 62.50 125.00
1 Phil Esposito 10.00 20.00
2 Bernie Geoffrion 10.00 20.00
3 Gordie Howe 25.00 50.00
4 Ching Johnson 7.50 15.00
5 Stan Mikita 10.00 20.00
6 Maurice Richard 12.50 25.00

1970-71 Esso Power Players

The 1970-71 Esso Power Players set included 252 color stamps measuring approximately 1 1/2" by 2". The stamps were issued in six-stamp sheets and given away free with a minimum purchase of $3 of Esso gasoline. There were 18 stamps for each of the 14 teams then in the NHL. The stamps were unnumbered except for jersey (uniform) number. The set was issued with an album, which could be found in either a soft or hard bound version. The hard cover album supposedly had extra pages with additional players. The stamps and albums were available in both French and English language versions. The set was numbered below numerically within each team as follows: Montreal Canadiens (1-18), Toronto Maple Leafs (19-36), Vancouver Canucks (37-54), Boston Bruins (55-72), Buffalo Sabres (73-90), California Golden Seals (91-108), Chicago Blackhawks (109-126), Detroit Red Wings (127-144), Los Angeles Kings (145-162), Minnesota North Stars (163-180), New York Rangers (181-198), Philadelphia Flyers (199-216), Pittsburgh Penguins (217-234), and St. Louis Blues (235-252). Supposedly there were 59 stamps which are tougher to find than the others. The short-printed stamps were apparently those players who were pre-printed into the soft-cover album and hence not included in the first stamp printing.

COMPLETE SET (252) 125.00 250.00
1 Rogatien Vachon 1 1.50 3.00
2 Jacques Laperriere 2 .38 .75
3 J.C. Tremblay 3 .25 .50
4 Jean Beliveau 4 4.00 8.00
5 Guy Lapointe 5 .50 1.00
6 Fran Huck 6 .20 .40
7 Bill Collins 10 .20 .40
8 Marc Tardif 11 .25 .50
9 Yvan Cournoyer 12 .75 1.50
10 Claude Larose 15 .20 .40
11 Henri Richard 16 2.00 4.00
12 Serge Savard 18 .38 .75
13 Terry Harper 19 .25 .50
14 Pete Mahovlich 20 .38 .75
15 John Ferguson 22 .50 1.00
16 Mickey Redmond 24 .63 1.25
17 Jacques Lemaire 25 .63 1.25
18 Phil Myre 30 .50 1.00
19 Jacques Plante 1 4.00 8.00
20 Rick Ley 2 .25 .50
21 Mike Pelyk 4 .20 .40
22 Ron Ellis 6 .25 .50
23 Jim Dorey 8 .20 .40
24 Norm Ullman 9 1.00 2.00
25 Guy Trottier 11 .20 .40
26 Jim Harrison 12 .20 .40
27 Dave Keon 14 1.00 2.00
28 Mike Walton 16 .25 .50
29 Jim McKenny 18 .20 .40
30 Paul Henderson 19 .50 1.00
31 Garry Monahan 20 SP .50 1.00
32 Bob Baun 21 .38 .75
33 Bill MacMillan 23 .20 .40
34 Brian Glennie 24 .20 .40
35 Darryl Sittler 27 5.00 10.00
36 Bruce Gamble 30 .50 1.00
37 Charlie Hodge 1 .63 1.25
38 Gary Doak 2 .20 .40
39 Pat Quinn 3 .38 .75
40 Barry Wilkins 4 .20 .40
41 Darryl Sly 5 SP .50 1.00
42 Marc Reaume 6 .20 .40
43 Andre Boudrias 7 .20 .40
44 Danny Johnson 8 .20 .40
45 Ray Cullen 10 SP .50 1.00
46 Wayne Maki 11 .20 .40
47 Mike Corrigan 12 .20 .40
48 Rosaire Paiement 15 .20 .40
49 Paul Popiel 18 SP .38 .75
50 Dale Tallon 19 .25 .50
51 Murray Hall 23 SP .50 1.00
52 Len Lunde 24 .20 .40
53 Orland Kurtenbach 25 .25 .50
54 Dunc Wilson 30 SP .50 1.00
55 Ed Johnston 1 .50 1.00
56 Bobby Orr 4 12.50 25.00
57 Ted Green 6 .25 .50
58 Phil Esposito 7 2.50 5.00
59 Ken Hodge 8 .38 .75
60 Johnny Bucyk 9 1.00 2.00
61 Rick Smith 10 SP .50 1.00
62 Wayne Carleton 11 SP .50 1.00
63 Wayne Cashman 12 SP .75 1.50
64 Garnet Bailey 14 .20 .40
65 Derek Sanderson 16 2.00 4.00
66 Fred Stanfield 17 SP .50 1.00
67 Ed Westfall 18 .25 .50
68 John McKenzie 19 .20 .40
69 Dallas Smith 20 .20 .40
70 Don Marcotte 21 .20 .40
71 Don Awrey 26 SP .50 1.00
72 Gerry Cheevers 30 1.50 3.00
73 Roger Crozier 1 .75 1.50
74 Jim Watson 2 .25 .50
75 Tracy Pratt 3 .20 .40
76 Doug Barrie 5 SP .50 1.00
77 Al Hamilton 6 .25 .50
78 Cliff Schmautz 7 SP .50 1.00
79 Reg Fleming 9 .20 .40
80 Phil Goyette 10 .20 .40
81 Gilbert Perreault 11 2.50 5.00
82 Skip Krake 12 .20 .40
83 Gerry Meehan 15 .25 .50
84 Ron Anderson 16 .20 .40
85 Floyd Smith 17 SP .50 1.00
86 Steve Atkinson 19 .20 .40
87 Paul Andrea 21 SP .50 1.00
88 Don Marshall 22 .20 .40
89 Eddie Shack 23 SP 1.50 3.00
90 Larry Keenan 26 .20 .40
91 Gary Smith 1 .50 1.00
92 Doug Roberts 2 .20 .40
93 Harry Howell 3 .63 1.25
94 Wayne Muloin 4 .20 .40
95 Carol Vadnais 5 .20 .40
96 Dick Mattiussi 6 .20 .40
97 Earl Ingarfield 7 .20 .40
98 Gerry Ehman 8 .20 .40
99 Bill Hicke 9 .20 .40
100 Ted Hampson 10 .20 .40
101 Gary Jarrett 12 .20 .40
102 Joe Hardy 14 SP .50 1.00
103 Tony Featherstone 16 SP .50 1.00
104 Gary Croteau 18 .20 .40
105 Ernie Hicke 20 SP .50 1.00
106 Ron Stackhouse 21 .20 .40
107 Dennis Hextall 22 SP .75 1.50
108 Bob Sneddon 30 SP .50 1.00
109 Gerry Desjardins 1 SP .75 1.50
110 Bill White 2 .25 .50
111 Keith Magnuson 3 .50 1.00
112 Doug Jarrett 4 SP .50 1.00
113 Lou Angotti 6 .20 .40
114 Pit Martin 7 .25 .50
115 Jim Pappin 8 .20 .40
116 Bobby Hull 9 5.00 10.00
117 Dennis Hull 10 SP 1.00 2.00
118 Doug Mohns 11 .25 .50
119 Pat Stapleton 12 .25 .50
120 Bryan Campbell 14 SP .50 1.00
121 Eric Nesterenko 15 .25 .50
122 Chico Maki 16 .25 .50
123 Gerry Pinder 18 .20 .40
124 Cliff Koroll 20 .20 .40
125 Stan Mikita 21 3.00 6.00
126 Tony Esposito 35 3.00 6.00
127 Jim Rutherford 1 SP 1.00 2.00
128 Gary Bergman 2 .25 .50
129 Dale Rolfe 3 .20 .40
130 Larry Brown 4 SP .50 1.00
131 Serge Lajeunesse 5 .20 .40
132 Garry Unger 7 .38 .75
133 Tom Webster 8 .25 .50
134 Gordie Howe 9 7.50 15.00
135 Alex Delvecchio 10 1.00 2.00
136 Don Luce 11 SP .50 1.00
137 Bruce MacGregor 12 .20 .40
138 Nick Libett 14 .25 .50
139 Al Karlander 15 .20 .40
140 Ron Harris 16 .20 .40
141 Wayne Connelly 17 SP .50 1.00
142 Billy Dea 21 SP .50 1.00
143 Frank Mahovlich 27 2.00 4.00
144 Roy Edwards 30 .38 .75
145 Jack Norris 1 .20 .40
146 Dale Hoganson 2 .20 .40
147 Larry Cahan 3 .20 .40
148 Gilles Marotte 4 SP .50 1.00
149 Noel Price 5 SP .50 1.00
150 Paul Curtis 6 SP .50 1.00
151 Ross Lonsberry 8 .20 .40
152 Gord Labossiere 9 .20 .40
153 Doug Robinson 11 SP .50 1.00
154 Larry Mickey 12 .20 .40
155 Juha Widing 15 .20 .40
156 Eddie Joyal 16 .20 .40
157 Bill Flett 17 .20 .40
158 Bob Berry 18 .25 .50
159 Bob Pulford 20 .38 .75
160 Matt Ravlich 21 .20 .40
161 Mike Byers 24 SP .50 1.00
162 Denis DeJordy 30 .50 1.00
163 Gump Worsley 1 2.00 4.00
164 Barry Gibbs 2 SP .50 1.00
165 Fred Barrett 3 .20 .40
166 Ted Harris 4 .20 .40
167 Danny O'Shea 7 .20 .40
168 Bill Goldsworthy 8 .25 .50
169 Charlie Burns 9 .20 .40
170 Murray Oliver 10 .20 .40
171 Jean-Paul Parise 11 .20 .40
172 Tom Williams 12 SP .50 1.00
173 Bobby Rousseau 15 .25 .50
174 Buster Harvey 18 SP .50 1.00
175 Tom Reid 20 SP .50 1.00
176 Danny Grant 21 .25 .50
177 Walt McKechnie 22 .20 .40
178 Lou Nanne 23 .25 .50
179 Danny Lawson 24 SP .50 1.00
180 Cesare Maniago 30 .50 1.00
181 Ed Giacomin 1 1.50 3.00
182 Brad Park 2 2.50 5.00
183 Tim Horton 3 2.50 5.00
184 Arnie Brown 4 .20 .40
185 Rod Gilbert 7 .75 1.50
186 Bob Nevin 8 .20 .40
187 Bill Fairbairn 10 SP .50 1.00
188 Vic Hadfield 11 .25 .50
189 Ron Stewart 12 .20 .40
190 Jim Neilson 15 .25 .50
191 Rod Seiling 16 SP .50 1.00
192 Dave Balon 17 SP .50 1.00
193 Walt Tkaczuk 18 .25 .50
194 Jean Ratelle 19 .75 1.50
195 Jack Egers 20 .20 .40
196 Pete Stemkowski 21 SP .50 1.00
197 Ted Irvine 27 .20 .40
198 Gilles Villemure 30 .50 1.00
199 Doug Favell 1 .75 1.50
200 Ed Van Impe 2 .20 .40
201 Larry Hillman 3 .20 .40
202 Barry Ashbee 4 .38 .75
203 Wayne Hillman 6 SP .50 1.00
204 Andre Lacroix 7 .25 .50
205 Lew Morrison 8 .20 .40
206 Bob Kelly 9 SP .50 1.00
207 Jean-Guy Gendron 11 .20 .40
208 Gary Dornhoefer 12 .38 .75
209 Joe Watson 14 .20 .40
210 Garry Peters 15 SP .50 1.00
211 Bobby Clarke 16 5.00 10.00
212 Earl Heiskala 19 SP .50 1.00
213 Jim Johnson 20 .20 .40
214 Serge Bernier 21 .20 .40
215 Larry Hale 23 SP .50 1.00
216 Bernie Parent 30 2.50 5.00
217 Al Smith 1 .38 .75
218 Duane Rupp 2 .20 .40
219 Bob Woytowich 3 .20 .40
220 Bob Blackburn 4 .20 .40
221 Bryan Watson 5 SP .50 1.00
222 Dunc McCallum 6 .25 .50
223 Bryan Hextall 7 .25 .50
224 Andy Bathgate 9 SP 1.25 2.50
225 Keith McCreary 10 SP .50 1.00
226 Nick Harbaruk 11 .20 .40
227 Ken Schinkel 12 .20 .40
228 Glen Sather 16 SP 1.25 2.50
229 Ron Schock 17 .20 .40
230 Wally Boyer 18 .20 .40
231 Jean Pronovost 19 .25 .50
232 Dean Prentice 20 .25 .50
233 Jim Morrison 27 .20 .40
234 Les Binkley 30 SP .75 1.50
235 Glenn Hall 1 2.00 4.00
236 Bob Wall 2 .20 .40
237 Noel Picard 4 .20 .40
238 Bob Plager 5 .25 .50
239 Jim Roberts 6 .25 .50
240 Red Berenson 7 .25 .50
241 Barclay Plager 8 .25 .50
242 Frank St.Marseille 9 .20 .40
243 George Morrison 10 SP .50 1.00
244 Gary Sabourin 11 .20 .40
245 Terry Crisp 12 SP 1.00 2.00
246 Tim Ecclestone 14 .20 .40
247 Bill McCreary 15 .20 .40
248 Brit Selby 18 SP .50 1.00
249 Jim Lorentz 19 SP .50 1.00
250 Ab McDonald 20 .20 .40
251 Chris Bordeleau 21 SP .50 1.00
252 Ernie Wakely 31 .50 1.00
xx Soft Cover Album 7.50 15.00
xx Hard Cover Album 25.00 50.00

1983-84 Esso

The 1983-84 Esso set contained 21 color cards measuring approximately 4 1/2" by 3" although the player photo portion of the card was only 2" by 3". There were actually two different sets, one in French and one in English. The cards were actually part of a lottery-type game where 5000.00 cash could be won instantly via a scratch-off. The card backs contained information about the contest on the back of the contest portion and player statistics on the back of the player photo portion of the card. The cards were numbered and hence they are checklisted below alphabetically. There was very little difference in availability of the English set as opposed to the French set; however there seemed to be a slight premium on the French set over the English set of about 20 percent over the prices listed below.

COMPLETE SET (21) 6.00 15.00
1 Glenn Anderson .40 1.00
2 John Anderson .20 .50
3 Dave Babych .20 .50
4 Richard Brodeur .40 1.00

5 Paul Coffey 1.50 4.00
6 Bill Derlago .20 .50
7 Bob Gainey .60 1.50
8 Michel Goulet .40 1.00
9 Dale Hawerchuk .75 2.00
10 Dale Hunter .30 .75
11 Morris Lukowich .20 .50
12 Lanny McDonald .60 1.50
13 Mark Messier 2.00 5.00
14 Jim Peplinski .20 .50
15 Paul Reinhart .20 .50
16 Larry Robinson .50 1.25
17 Stan Smyl .30 .75
18 Harold Snepsts .30 .75
19 Marc Tardif .20 .50
20 Mario Tremblay .20 .50
21 Rick Vaive .30 .75

1988-89 Esso All-Stars

The 1988-89 Esso All-Stars set contained 48 color cards (actually adhesive-backed "stickers") measuring approximately 2 1/8" by 3 1/4". The fronts featured borderless color action photos with facsimile autographs. The backs had complete checklists for the whole set. The players depicted included hockey greats from the past and present. The cards (stickers) were unnumbered and hence are checklisted below in alphabetical order. There was a 32-page album (8 1/2" by 11") available in either English or French, which was intended to hold the stickers. In fact each album already contained five pasted-in cards, Ed Giacomin, Al MacInnis, Rick Middleton, Bernie Parent, and Pierre Pilote. The cards were distributed in Canada in packs of six with a purchase of gasoline at participating Esso service stations. The complete set price below includes the album.

COMPLETE SET (48) 6.00 15.00
1 Jean Beliveau .30 .75
2 Mike Bossy .30 .75
3 Ray Bourque .30 .75
4 Johnny Bower .15 .40
5 Bobby Clarke .20 .50
6 Paul Coffey .30 .75
7 Yvan Cournoyer .08 .25
8 Marcel Dionne .15 .40
9 Ken Dryden .40 1.00
10 Phil Esposito .30 .75
11 Tony Esposito .20 .50
12 Grant Fuhr .15 .40
13 Clark Gillies .07 .20
14 Michel Goulet .08 .25
15 Wayne Gretzky 1.50 4.00
16 Dale Hawerchuk .08 .25
17 Ron Hextall .15 .40
18 Gordie Howe .60 1.50
19 Mark Howe .07 .20
20 Bobby Hull .30 .75
21 Tim Kerr .07 .20
22 Jari Kurri .08 .25
23 Guy Lafleur .30 .75
24 Rod Langway .07 .20
25 Jacques Laperriere .07 .20
26 Guy Lapointe .08 .25
27 Mario Lemieux 1.00 2.50
28 Frank Mahovlich .20 .50
29 Lanny McDonald .08 .25
30 Mark Messier .40 1.00
31 Stan Mikita .20 .50
32 Mats Naslund .07 .20
33 Bobby Orr .75 2.00
34 Brad Park .08 .25
35 Gilbert Perreault .08 .25
36 Denis Potvin .08 .25
37 Larry Robinson .08 .25
38 Luc Robitaille .20 .50
39 Borje Salming .07 .20
40 Denis Savard .08 .25
41 Serge Savard .08 .25
42 Steve Shutt .08 .25
43 Darryl Sittler .08 .25
44 Billy Smith .08 .25
45 John Tonelli .07 .20
46 Bryan Trottier .08 .25
47 Norm Ullman .08 .25
48 Gump Worsley .20 .50
xx Album 1.25 3.00

1997-98 Esso Olympic Hockey Heroes

These oversized cards featured color action photos on the front, along with biographical information on the back. Each player was pictured in his or her respective Olympic uniform. The set was available in six series from Esso gas stations and comes complete with a black binder.

COMPLETE SET (60) 12.00 30.00
*FRENCH VERSION: 1X TO 1.5X BASIC CARDS
1 Header Card .02 .10
2 Olympic Hockey History .02 .10
3 CBC Broadcast Guide .02 .10
4 Olympic Hockey Bracket .02 .10
5 Team Canada .02 .10
6 Eric Lindros .75 2.00
7 Joe Sakic .60 1.50
8 Trevor Linden .15 .40
9 Paul Kariya .75 2.00
10 Brendan Shanahan .40 1.00
11 Rod Brind'Amour .15 .40
12 Theo Fleury .15 .40
13 Eric Desjardins .08 .25
14 Scott Niedermayer .08 .25
15 Chris Pronger .15 .40
16 Rob Blake .08 .25
17 Patrick Roy 1.00 2.50
18 Curtis Joseph .20 .50
19 Keith Primeau .15 .40
20 Mark Messier .30 .75
21 Adam Foote .08 .25
22 Team USA .02 .10
23 Keith Tkachuk .25 .60
24 Mike Modano .20 .50
25 John LeClair .30 .75
26 Doug Weight .15 .40
27 Brett Hull .25 .60
28 Jeremy Roenick .20 .50
29 Brian Leetch .20 .50
30 Chris Chelios .20 .50
31 Kevin Hatcher .08 .25
32 Derian Hatcher .08 .25
33 Mike Richter .20 .50
34 John Vanbiesbrouck .40 1.00
35 Team Russia .02 .10
36 Sergei Fedorov .40 1.00
37 Alexei Yashin .15 .40
38 Pavel Bure .40 1.00
39 Alexander Mogilny .15 .40
40 Nikolai Khabibulin .15 .40
41 Team Sweden .02 .10
42 Mats Sundin .20 .50
43 Peter Forsberg .60 1.50
44 Daniel Alfredsson .15 .40
45 Nicklas Lidstrom .15 .40
46 Kenny Jonsson .08 .25
47 Team Finland .02 .10
48 Saku Koivu .40 1.00
49 Esa Tikkanen .15 .40
50 Teemu Selanne .40 1.00
51 Team Czech Republic .02 .10
52 Jaromir Jagr .60 1.50
53 Roman Hamrlik .15 .40
54 Dominik Hasek .40 1.00
55 Women's Team Canada .02 .10
56 Nancy Drolet .20 .50
57 Geraldine Heaney .20 .50
58 Hayley Wickenheiser .20 .50
59 Cassie Campbell .20 .50
60 Stacy Wilson .20 .50
NNO E.Lindros AU 40.00 100.00

2001-02 eTopps

The 2001-02 eTopps cards were issued via Topps' website and initially sold exclusively on eBay's eTopps Trade Floor. Owner's of the cards could hold the cards on account with Topps and freely trade those cards similar to shares of stock. They also could pay a fee to take actual delivery of their cards, but most are still held on account with Topps. The production quantity of each card is listed beside the player's name. Prices below are derived from sales on the eTopps trading floor on ebay.

1 Joe Sakic/782
2 Paul Kariya/1032
3 Curtis Joseph/714
4 Brendan Shanahan/2000
5 Patrick Elias/859
6 Evgeni Nabokov/549
7 Johan Hedberg/574
8 Patrick Roy/938
9 John LeClair/494
10 Martin Brodeur/663
11 Teemu Selanne/784
12 Mike Modano/559
13 Martin Havlat/510
14 Roberto Luongo/747
15 Peter Forsberg/598
16 Steve Yzerman/796
17 Pavel Bure/896
18 Mark Messier/618
19 Mike Comrie/809
20 Mats Sundin/717
21 Owen Nolan/457
22 Ed Belfour/730
23 Mario Lemieux/1116
24 Keith Tkachuk/751
25 Milan Hejduk/532
26 Rick Dipietro/579
27 Roman Cechmanek/511
28 Sergei Fedorov/710
29 Vincent Lecavalier/550
30 Eric Lindros/634
31 Ilya Kovalchuk/2513
32 Zigmund Palffy/550
33 Dominik Hasek/753
34 Jaromir Jagr/569
35 Doug Weight/521

2002-03 eTopps

The 2002-03 eTopps cards were issued via Topps' website and initially sold exclusively on eBay's eTopps Trade Floor. Owner's of the cards could hold the cards on account with Topps and freely trade those cards similar to shares of stock. They also could pay a fee to take actual delivery of their cards, but most are still

held on account with Topps. Prices below are derived from sales on the eTopps trading floor on ebay. Production numbers are listed below.

1 Jarome Iginla/1668
2 Pavel Bure/1475
3 Patrick Roy/1500
4 Mats Sundin/1320
5 Jaromir Jagr/1500
6 Martin Brodeur/1459
7 Jose Theodore/1181
8 Nicklas Lidstrom/1551
9 Joe Sakic/1162
10 Ilya Kovalchuk/1500
11 Mike Modano/922
12 Sergei Fedorov/1583
13 Pavel Datsyuk/1500
14 Saku Koivu/1276
15 Peter Forsberg/1240
16 Dany Heatley/2580
17 Erik Cole/1952
18 Mario Lemieux/2000
19 Eric Lindros/1243
20 Patrik Elias/1500
21 Steve Yzerman/1000
22 Michael Peca/837
23 Todd Bertuzzi/2000
24 Evgeni Nabokov/925
25 Paul Kariya/971
26 Peter Bondra/1102
27 Chris Pronger/1147
28 Alexei Yashin/1133
29 Daniel Alfredsson/840
30 Teemu Selanne/949
31 Brendan Shanahan/1078
32 Brett Hull/1739
33 Ron Francis/1063
34 Simon Gagne/1500
35 Marty Turco/1500
36 Roberto Luongo/918
37 Joe Thornton/1500
38 Mike Comrie/1196
39 Rick Nash/3000
40 Stanislav Chistov/2000
41 Henrik Zetterberg/3000
42 Ales Hemsky/2000
43 Jay Bouwmeester/3000
44 Alexei Smirnov/2000
45 Chuck Kobasew/2000
46 P-M Bouchard/2000
47 Jason Spezza/2000
48 Alexander Svitov/2000
49 Marian Gaborik/2000
50 Jeremy Roenick/1145
51 Olli Jokinen/1260
52 Marian Hossa/1500
53 Markus Naslund/2000
54 Ryan Miller/2000
55 Martin St. Louis/1489
56 Jocelyn Thibault/930

2003-04 eTopps

The 2003-04 eTopps cards were issued via Topps' website and initially sold exclusively on eBay's eTopps Trade Floor. Owner's of the cards could hold the cards on account with Topps and freely trade those cards similar to shares of stock. They also could pay a fee to take actual delivery of their cards, but most are still held on account with Topps. Since most do not trade hands as physical cards, we've simply listed the check-liProduction numbers are listed below. Prices below are derived from sales on the eTopps trading floor on ebay.

1 Pasi Nurminen/757
2 Al MacInnis/871
3 Daniel Briere/743
4 Jordan Leopold/861
5 Tyler Arnason/920
6 Niko Kapanen/780
7 Kristian Huselius/797
8 Jamie Langenbrunner/756
10 Jean-Sebastien Giguere/693
11 Mario Lemieux/1000
12 Patrick Lalime/832
13 Milan Hejduk/841
14 Rick DiPietro/749
15 Owen Nolan/839
16 Dany Heatley/698
17 Mattias Weinhandl/774
18 Brendan Morrison/687
19 Paul Kariya/767
20 Zigmund Palffy/636
21 Marian Gaborik/872
22 Sergei Fedorov/706
23 Tony Amonte/558
24 Roberto Luongo/674
26 Saku Koivu/651
27 Todd Bertuzzi/868
28 Patrik Elias/804
29 Jeremy Roenick/1000
30 Marian Hossa/839
31 Brad Richards/1000
32 Joe Thornton/1123
33 Peter Forsberg/1000
34 Daymond Langkow/644
35 Ed Jovanovski/873
36 Martin Brodeur/1000
37 Jarome Iginla/913
38 Jaromir Jagr/792
39 Rick Nash/1035
40 Teemu Selanne/769
41 Patrice Bergeron/1500
42 Peter Sejna/838
43 Matthew Stajan/1000
44 Eric Staal/1500
45 Nathan Horton/1000
46 Joffrey Lupul/886
47 Tuomo Ruutu/1462
48 Jordin Tootoo/990
49 Dustin Brown/918
50 Marc-Andre Fleury/2000
51 Patrick Marleau/932
52 Joni Pitkanen/1000
53 Pavel Datsyuk/1000
54 Brian Leetch/1000
55 Chris Chelios/896
56 Andrew Raycroft/1500

1948-52 Exhibits Canadian

These cards measured approximately 3 1/4" by 5 1/4" and were issued on heavy cardboard stock. The cards showed full-bleed photos with the player's name burned in toward the bottom. The hockey exhibit cards were generally considered more scarce than their baseball exhibit counterparts. Since the cards were unnumbered, the set is arranged below alphabetically within teams as follows: Montreal (1-27), Toronto (28-42), Detroit (43-46), Boston (47-48), Chicago (49-50), and New York (51). The set closes with an Action subset (52-65).

COMPLETE SET (65) 750.00 1500.00
1 Reggie Abbott 6.00 12.00
2 Jean Beliveau 37.50 75.00
3 Jean Beliveau (Aces' captain) 50.00 100.00
4 Toe Blake 20.00 40.00
5 Butch Bouchard 10.00 20.00
6 Bob Fillion 6.00 12.00
7 Dick Gamble 7.50 15.00
8 Bernie Geoffrion 25.00 50.00
9 Doug Harvey 20.00 40.00
10 Tom Johnson 10.00 20.00
11 Elmer Lach 20.00 40.00
12 Hal Laycoe 6.00 12.00
13 Jacques Locas 6.00 12.00
14 Bud McPherson 6.00 12.00
15 Paul Masnick 6.00 12.00
16 Gerry McNeil 20.00 40.00
17 Paul Meger 6.00 12.00
18 Dickie Moore 20.00 40.00
19 Ken Mosdell 6.00 12.00
20 Bert Olmstead 10.00 20.00
21 Ken Reardon 12.50 25.00
22 Billy Reay 7.50 15.00
23 Maurice Richard (Stick on ice) 50.00 100.00
24 Maurice Richard (Stairs in back ground) 50.00 100.00
25 Dollard St.Laurent 7.50 15.00
26 Grant Warwick 6.00 12.00
27 Floyd Curry 7.50 15.00
28 Bill Barilko 20.00 40.00
29 Turk Broda 20.00 40.00
30 Cal Gardner 10.00 20.00
31 Bill Juzda 6.00 12.00
32 Ted Kennedy 20.00 40.00
33 Joe Klukay 6.00 12.00
34 Fleming Mackell 6.00 12.00
35 Howie Meeker 15.00 30.00
36 Gus Mortson 6.00 12.00
37 Al Rollins 12.50 25.00
38 Sid Smith 7.50 15.00
39 Tod Sloan 6.00 12.00
40 Ray Timgren 6.00 12.00
41 Jim Thomson 6.00 12.00
42 Max Bentley 12.50 25.00
43 Sid Abel 10.00 20.00
44 Gordie Howe 62.50 125.00
45 Ted Lindsay 25.00 50.00
46 Harry Lumley 20.00 40.00
47 Jack Gelineau 6.00 12.00
48 Paul Ronty 6.00 12.00
49 Doug Bentley 12.50 25.00
50 Roy Conacher 7.50 15.00
51 Chuck Rayner 12.50 25.00
52 Boston vs. Montreal (In front of net; 23 of Boston visible) 10.00 20.00
53 Detroit vs. New York (Howe and Ranger on goal line on ice) 30.00 60.00
54 Montreal vs. Toronto (Richard shooting puck past Toronto goalie) 30.00 60.00
55 New York vs. Montreal (Richard is on goalie) 30.00 60.00
56 New York vs. Montreal (Open net; 9 of Rangers on ice) 10.00 20.00
57 Montreal vs. Boston (Ref and several players in front of Boston goal) 10.00 20.00
58 Detroit vs. Montreal (Two Canadiens in front of Detroit goalie) 10.00 20.00
59 Chicago vs. Montreal (5 Blackhawks and 2 Canadiens on ice in front of goalie) 10.00 20.00
60 New York vs. Montreal (Richard and Elmer Lach in front of Ranger and Rayner) 25.00 50.00
61 Chicago vs. Montreal (5 Geoffrion shooting at Chicago goalie) 15.00 30.00
62 Detroit vs. Montreal (Sawchuk saves against 8) 20.00 40.00
63 Detroit vs. Montreal (Canadiens score) 10.00 20.00
64 Toronto vs. Montreal (Canadiens score) 10.00 20.00
65 Chicago vs. Montreal (Canadiens score) 10.00 20.00

1995-96 Fanfest Phil Esposito

This five-card set was sponsored by the five licensed card companies (Donruss, Fleer/Skybox, Pinnacle, Topps, and Upper Deck) who each produced one card for distribution at the 1996 All-Star Game Fanfest, which was held in Boston. The fronts featured color action photos of Phil Esposito in designs unique to each manufacturer. The backs carried information about the legendary Bruin great.

COMPLETE SET (5) 8.00 20.00
COMMON ESPO (1-5) 2.50 6.00

2008-09 Fathead Tradeables

COMPLETE SET (30) 40.00 100.00
1 Ales Hemsky .60 1.50
2 Alexander Ovechkin 4.00 10.00
3 Anze Kopitar 1.00 2.50
4 Carey Price 3.00 8.00
5 Daniel Alfredsson .75 2.00
6 Eric Staal 1.50 4.00
7 Henrik Lundqvist 2.00 5.00
8 Henrik Zetterberg 2.00 5.00
9 Ilya Kovalchuk 1.25 3.00
10 Jarome Iginla 2.00 5.00
11 Jason Arnott .60 1.50
12 Joe Sakic 1.50 4.00
13 Joe Thornton 1.50 4.00
14 Jonathan Toews 3.00 8.00
15 Luke Schenn 3.00 8.00
16 Martin Brodeur 2.00 5.00
17 Mike Modano 1.00 2.50
18 Mike Richards 1.50 4.00
19 Mikko Koivu 1.00 2.50
20 Nathan Horton .60 1.50
21 Paul Kariya 1.00 2.50
22 Rick DiPietro 1.00 2.50
23 Rick Nash 1.00 2.50
24 Roberto Luongo 1.50 4.00
25 Ryan Getzlaf 1.25 3.00
26 Ryan Miller 1.00 2.50
27 Shane Doan .60 1.50
28 Sidney Crosby 5.00 12.00
29 Vincent Lecavalier 1.00 2.50
30 Zdeno Chara .60 1.50

1994-95 Finest

This 165-card super-premium set was issued in seven-card packs, in 24-pack boxes. The cards featured a blue marbleized foil border with a centered player photo. The player's last name only, along with the Finest logo, dominated the top of the front. The card fronts also featured a clear protective peel-off coating which was designed to prevent scratches and other damage to the card. Values below reflect unpeeled cards, although hobby opinions on whether to leave the coating intact or remove it vary. Collectors are advised to make a decision based on their own preference. Card backs had player photos, brief stats, and a recap of that player's finest moment. Card numbers 5, 56, 68, and 99 had wrong photos and player names on the back. These were corrected only in the '94-95 Finest Super Team Stanley Cup Winner Redemption set. A World Junior players subset was included (112-165). Rookie cards in the set included Bryan Berard, Radek Bonk, Eric Daze, Miikka Elomo, Eric Fichaud, Sean Haggerty, Ed Jovanovski, Ryan Smyth, Jeff O'Neill and Wade Redden.

COMPLETE SET (165) 30.00 80.00
1 Peter Forsberg .75 2.00
2 Oleg Tverdovsky .50 1.25
3 Radek Bonk RC .30 .75
4 Brian Rolston .10 .30
5 Kenny Jonsson UER .10 .30
6 Patrik Juhlin RC .30 .75
7 Paul Kariya .50 1.25
8 Janne Laukkanen .10 .30
9 Brett Lindros .10 .30
10 Andrei Nikolishin .10 .30
11 Jeff Friesen .10 .30
12 Jamie Storr .20 .50
13 Chris Therien .10 .30
14 Alexander Cherbayev .10 .30
15 Kevin Brown RC .10 .30
16 Mark Messier .50 1.25
17 Kevin Hatcher .10 .30
18 Scott Stevens .20 .50
19 Keith Tkachuk .50 1.25
20 Guy Hebert .20 .50
21 Jason Arnott .10 .30
22 Cam Neely .50 1.25
23 Adam Graves .10 .30
24 Pavel Bure .50 1.25
25 Mark Tinordi .10 .30
26 Felix Potvin .50 1.25
27 Nikolai Khabibulin .20 .50
28 Theo Fleury .10 .30
29 Curtis Joseph .50 1.25
30 Patrick Roy 1.25 3.00
31 Adam Deadmarsh .10 .30
32 Pat Falloon .10 .30
33 Jaromir Jagr .75 2.00
34 Chris Chelios .50 1.25
35 Ray Bourque .75 2.00
36 Mike Vernon .20 .50
37 Steve Thomas .10 .30
38 Eric Lindros .50 1.25
39 Dave Andreychuk .20 .50
40 John Vanbiesbrouck .20 .50
41 Wayne Gretzky 2.00 5.00
42 Brett Hull .75 2.00
43 Dominik Hasek .75 2.00
44 Kirk Muller .10 .30
45 Rob Blake .20 .50
46 Viktor Kozlov .10 .30
47 Todd Harvey .10 .30
48 Valeri Bure .10 .30
49 Brian Leetch .50 1.25
50 Ray Sheppard .20 .50
51 Ed Belfour .50 1.25
52 Rick Tocchet .20 .50
53 Daren Puppa .20 .50
54 Russ Courtnall .10 .30
55 Jason Allison .10 .30
56 Alexei Yashin UER .10 .30
57 Sandis Ozolinsh .10 .30
58 Chris Gratton .10 .30
59 Mike Peca .10 .30
60 Glen Wesley .10 .30
61 Kirk McLean .20 .50
62 Chris Pronger .50 1.25
63 Steve Larmer .20 .50
64 Michal Grosek RC .20 .50
65 Sergei Fedorov .60 1.50
66 Stu Barnes .10 .30
67 Adam Oates .20 .50
68 Paul Coffey UER .50 1.25
69 Joe Sakic .75 2.00
70 Pat LaFontaine .50 1.25
71 Martin Brodeur 1.00 2.50
72 Bob Corkum .10 .30
73 Jeremy Roenick .50 1.25
74 Shayne Corson .10 .30
75 German Titov .10 .30
76 Teemu Selanne .50 1.25
77 Eric Fichaud RC .30 .75
78 Pierre Turgeon .20 .50
79 Alexander Selivanov RC .30 .75
80 Kevin Stevens .10 .30
81 Jari Kurri .20 .50
82 Gary Roberts .10 .30
83 Geoff Courtnall .10 .30
84 Steve Yzerman 1.25 3.00
85 Rod Brind'Amour .20 .50
86 Mike Richter .50 1.25
87 Bernie Nicholls .20 .50
88 Alexandre Daigle .10 .30
89 Luc Robitaille .20 .50
90 John MacLean .20 .50
91 Phil Housley .20 .50
92 Brendan Shanahan .50 1.25
93 Joe Juneau .20 .50
94 Stephane Richer .20 .50
95 Blaine Lacher RC .30 .75
96 Mike Gartner .20 .50
97 Rene Corbet .10 .30
98 Vincent Damphousse .10 .30
99 Alexander Mogilny UER .20 .50
100 Doug Gilmour .20 .50
101 Petr Nedved .20 .50
102 Alexei Zhamnov .20 .50
103 Wendel Clark .20 .50
104 Arturs Irbe .20 .50
105 Brian Bellows .10 .30
106 Mike Modano .75 2.00
107 Ravil Gusmanov RC .20 .50
108 Geoff Sanderson .20 .50
109 Mark Recchi .20 .50
110 Mats Sundin .50 1.25
111 Pavol Demitra .20 .50
112 Richard Park .10 .30
113 Doug Bonner RC .30 .75
114 Bryan Berard RC .30 .75
115 Rory Fitzpatrick RC .60 1.50
116 Deron Quint .10 .30
117 Jason Bonsignore .10 .30
118 Adam Deadmarsh .10 .30
119 Sean Haggerty RC .30 .75
120 Jamie Langenbrunner .10 .30
121 Jeff Mitchell RC .30 .75
122 Antti Aalto RC .30 .75
123 Tommi Rajamaki RC .30 .75
124 J. Markkanen RC UER .75 2.00
125 Miikka Kiprusoff RC 12.50 30.00
126 Jere Karalahti RC .30 .75
127 Petri Kokko RC .30 .75
128 Janne Niinimaa .50 1.25
129 Kimmo Timonen .20 .50
130 Martti Jarventie RC .30 .75
131 Mikko Helisten RC .30 .75
132 Niko Halttunen RC .30 .75
133 Tommi Miettinen .20 .50
134 Miska Kangasniemi RC .30 .75
135 Veli-Pekka Nutikka RC .30 .75
136 Jani Hassinen RC .30 .75
137 Timo Salonen RC .30 .75
138 Tommi Sova RC .30 .75
139 Toni Makiaho RC .30 .75
140 Tommi Hamalainen RC .30 .75
141 Juha Vuorivirta RC .30 .75
142 Jussi Tarvainen RC .30 .75
143 Miikka Elomo RC .30 .75
144 Jason Botterill .10 .30
145 Dan Cloutier RC .60 1.50
146 Jamie Storr .20 .50
147 Chad Allan RC .30 .75
148 Nolan Baumgartner RC .20 .50
149 Ed Jovanovski RC .30 .75
150 Bryan McCabe .10 .30
151 Wade Redden RC .30 .75
152 Jamie Rivers RC .30 .75
153 Lee Sorochan RC .30 .75
154 Jason Allison .10 .30
155 Alexandre Daigle .10 .30
156 Larry Courville RC .30 .75
157 Eric Daze RC .30 .75
158 Shean Donovan RC .30 .75
159 Jeff Friesen .10 .30
160 Todd Harvey .10 .30
161 Marty Murray .10 .30
162 Jeff O'Neill RC .30 .75
163 Denis Pederson RC .38 .75
164 Darcy Tucker RC .30 .75
165 Ryan Smyth RC 1.00 2.50

1994-95 Finest Super Team Winners

This 165-card set was awarded to collectors who redeemed the winning New Jersey Devils team card. The cards were the same as the regular Finest cards save for the Super Team Winner embossed logo.

COMPLETE SET (165) 50.00 100.00
*SUPER TEAM: 1.2X TO 3X BASIC CARDS
125 Miikka Kiprusoff WJC 30.00 80.00

1994-95 Finest Refractors

The cards in this set were parallel to the Finest set. They were randomly inserted at the rate of 1:12 packs. These cards appeared identical to the regular issue; careful examination in the proper light revealed a reflective, rainbow-like sheen to the foil on the front. If in doubt, we recommend comparing to other cards from the set; in this setting, a refractor truly stands out. These cards also came with the clear protective peel-off coating. Multipliers can be found in the header below to determine value for these.

*VETS: 4X TO 10X BASIC CARDS
*ROOKIES: 2.5X TO 6X BASIC CARDS
125 Miikka Kiprusoff WJC 25.00 60.00

1994-95 Finest Bowman's Best

This 45-card set was randomly inserted in Finest packs at the rate of 1:4. Card fronts featured a cut-out player photo over a blue or red hi-tech half moon background utilizing the Finest printing technology. The first twenty cards in the set feature NHL veterans. The second twenty consists of NHL rookies. The last five cards pair a star veteran and a top rookie in a horizontal format. The card fronts have the clear protective peel-off coating. The backs of the first forty cards have brief text information outlining the player's strong points, and a small portrait photo. The final five cards simply feature text comparing the two players. Cards are numbered with a B (1-20) prefix for veterans, R (1-20) for rookies, and X (21-25) for dual player cards.

COMPLETE SET (45) 30.00 80.00
*B1-B20 REF: 3X TO 8X BASIC INSERTS
*R1-R20 REF: 2X TO 5X BASIC INSERTS
*X21-X25 REF: 1.5X TO 4X BASIC INSERTS
B1 Ray Bourque 2.00 5.00
B2 Mark Messier 1.50 4.00
B3 Cam Neely 1.50 4.00
B4 Theo Fleury 1.25 3.00
B5 Jeremy Roenick 2.00 5.00
B6 Mike Modano 2.00 5.00
B7 Sergei Fedorov 2.00 5.00
B8 John Vanbiesbrouck 1.25 3.00
B9 Pierre Turgeon .40 1.00
B10 Kirk Muller .40 1.00
B11 Pavel Bure 2.00 5.00
B12 Brian Leetch 1.25 3.00
B13 Mike Richter 1.25 3.00
B14 Teemu Selanne 1.25 3.00
B15 Brett Hull 1.50 4.00
B16 Eric Lindros 1.25 3.00
B17 Keith Tkachuk 1.25 3.00
B18 Joe Sakic 3.00 8.00
B19 Doug Gilmour 1.25 3.00
B20 Jaromir Jagr 2.00 5.00
R1 Paul Kariya 1.25 3.00
R2 Oleg Tverdovsky .40 1.00
R3 Blaine Lacher .40 1.00
R4 Todd Harvey .40 1.00
R5 Roman Oksiuta .40 1.00
R6 David Oliver .40 1.00
R7 Jamie Storr .40 1.00
R8 Brian Savage .40 1.00
R9 Brian Rolston .40 1.00
R10 Brett Lindros .40 1.00
R11 Radek Bonk .40 1.00
R12 Peter Forsberg 2.00 5.00
R13 Adam Deadmarsh .40 1.00
R14 Jeff Friesen .40 1.00
R15 Denis Chasse .40 1.00
R16 Jason Wiemer .40 1.00
R17 Alexander Selivanov .40 1.00
R18 Kenny Jonsson .40 1.00
R19 Todd Marchant .40 1.00
R20 Mariusz Czerkawski .40 1.00
X21 Theo Fleury / Paul Kariya 1.25 3.00
X22 Doug Gilmour 2.00 5.00

Peter Forsberg
X23 Joe Sakic 1.25 3.00
Radek Bonk
X24 Brian Leetch 1.25 3.00
Oleg Tverdovsky
X25 Cam Neely 1.25 3.00
Jason Wiemer

1994-95 Finest Division's Finest Clear Cut

The 20 cards in this set were randomly inserted in Finest packs at the rate of 1:12.

COMPLETE SET (20) 25.00 60.00
1 Patrick Roy 5.00 12.00
2 Ray Bourque 2.00 5.00
3 Adam Oates .60 1.50
4 Luc Robitaille .60 1.50
5 Mark Recchi .60 1.50
6 Mike Richter 1.25 3.00
7 Scott Stevens .60 1.50
8 Eric Lindros 1.25 3.00
9 Adam Graves .40 1.00
10 Stephane Richer .60 1.50
11 Ed Belfour 1.25 3.00
12 Al MacInnis .60 1.50
13 Sergei Fedorov 2.00 5.00
14 Brendan Shanahan 1.25 3.00
15 Brett Hull 2.00 5.00
16 Arturs Irbe .60 1.50
17 Sandis Ozolinsh .40 1.00
18 Wayne Gretzky 8.00 20.00
19 Gary Roberts .40 1.00
20 Pavel Bure 1.25 3.00

1994-95 Finest Ring Leaders

This 20-card set was comprised of players who have earned at least two Stanley Cup rings. Unlike other Finest cards, these did not come with a peel-off coating.

COMPLETE SET (20) 30.00 80.00
STATED ODDS 1:24
1 Mark Messier 3.00 8.00
2 Kevin Lowe 1.00 2.50
3 Jari Kurri 3.00 8.00
4 Grant Fuhr 2.00 5.00
5 Wayne Gretzky 12.00 30.00
6 Paul Coffey 2.00 5.00
7 Craig Simpson 1.00 2.50
8 Craig MacTavish 1.00 2.50
9 Jeff Beukeboom 1.00 2.50
10 Joe Mullen 1.00 2.50
11 Marty McSorley 1.00 2.50
12 Steve Smith 1.00 2.50
13 Kevin Stevens 1.00 2.50
14 Patrick Roy 6.00 15.00
15 Jaromir Jagr 4.00 10.00
16 Ron Francis 2.00 5.00
17 Bill Ranford 2.00 5.00
18 Larry Murphy 1.00 2.50
19 Tom Barrasso 2.00 5.00
20 Adam Graves 1.00 2.50

1995-96 Finest

The 1995-96 Finest set was issued in one series totaling 191 cards. The 6-card hobby packs had an SRP of $5.00 each. The players were featured across three themes: Finest Rookies, Finest Performers and Finest Defenders. Within those themes, cards were produced in different quantities: some players were common, some uncommon and some rare. The breakdown for the player selection of common (bronze), uncommon (silver) and rare (gold) cards was supposedly random with no consideration given to the status of each player in the set, although many of the gold cards did feature upper-echelon stars. Odds of finding an uncommon silver card were 1:4 packs, while golds were found 1:24 packs.

COMPLETE SET (191) 150.00 300.00
1 Eric Lindros B .40 1.00
2 Ray Bourque G 8.00 20.00
3 Eric Daze B .20 .50
4 Craig Janney S 1.00 2.50
5 Wayne Gretzky B 2.00 5.00
6 Dave Andreychuk B .20 .50
7 Phil Housley B .08 .25
8 Mike Gartner B .20 .50
9 Cam Neely B .40 1.00
10 Brett Hull B .60 1.50
11 Daren Puppa S 1.50 4.00
12 Tomas Sandstrom S 1.00 2.50
13 Patrick Roy G 15.00 40.00
14 Steve Thomas B .08 .25
15 Joe Sakic B .75 2.00
16 Ray Sheppard S 1.00 2.50
17 Steve Duchesne B .08 .25
18 Shayne Corson S 1.00 2.50
19 Chris Chelios G 5.00 12.00
20 John Vanbiesbrouck B .20 .50
21 Randy Burridge B .08 .25
22 Shane Doan B RC 1.00 2.50
23 Brian Savage B .08 .25
24 Luc Robitaille B .20 .50
25 Jeremy Roenick G 8.00 20.00
26 Peter Forsberg B 1.00 2.50
27 Jeff Friesen S 1.00 2.50
28 Aaron Gavey S 1.00 2.50
29 Kenny Jonsson S 1.00 2.50
30 Theo Fleury G 5.00 12.00
31 Dave Gagner S 1.00 2.50
32 Alexander Selivanov S 1.00 2.50
33 Scott Stevens B .20 .50
34 Valeri Bure B .08 .25
35 Teemu Selanne G 6.00 15.00
36 Ray Ferraro S 1.00 2.50
37 Sylvain Cote S 1.00 2.50
38 John MacLean B .08 .25
39 Brendan Shanahan B .40 1.00
40 Pat LaFontaine B .08 .25
41 Brian Leetch G 5.00 12.00
42 Larry Murphy B .20 .50
43 Adam Oates B .20 .50
44 Rod Brind'Amour B .20 .50
45 Martin Brodeur G 10.00 25.00
46 Pierre Turgeon B .08 .25
47 Claude Lemieux B .08 .25
48 Al MacInnis S 1.50 4.00
49 Geoff Courtnall S 1.00 2.50
50 Mark Messier B .40 1.00
51 Bill Ranford B .08 .25
52 Vincent Damphousse S 1.00 2.50
53 Jere Lehtinen B .08 .25
54 Bryan McCabe S 1.00 2.50
55 Doug Gilmour G 4.00 10.00
56 Mathieu Schneider S 1.00 2.50
57 Igor Larionov S 1.00 2.50
58 Joe Murphy S 1.00 2.50
59 Niklas Sundstrom B .08 .25
60 John LeClair B .40 1.00
61 Cory Stillman B .08 .25
62 David Oliver B .08 .25
63 Nikolai Khabibulin B .40 1.00
64 Steve Rucchin B .08 .25
65 Brendan Shanahan S 2.00 5.00
66 Jim Carey B .20 .50
67 Brian Holzinger S RC 1.00 2.50
68 Stu Barnes S 1.00 2.50
69 Nicklas Lidstrom B .40 1.00
70 Jaromir Jagr B .60 1.50
71 Donald Audette S 1.00 2.50
72 Dominik Hasek B .75 2.00
73 Peter Bondra S 1.50 4.00
74 Andrew Cassels B .08 .25
75 Pavel Bure B .40 1.00
76 Marcus Ragnarsson B RC .20 .50
77 Ray Bourque S 3.00 8.00
78 Alexei Zhamnov B .08 .25
79 Travis Green S 1.00 2.50
80 Joe Sakic B .75 2.00
81 Chad Kilger B RC .08 .25
82 Bill Guerin S 1.00 2.50
83 Vyacheslav Kozlov B .08 .25
84 Igor Korolev S 1.00 2.50
85 Saku Koivu G 4.00 10.00
86 Ron Hextall B .20 .50
87 Wendel Clark S 1.00 2.50
88 Eric Lindros G 6.00 15.00
89 Richard Park B .08 .25
90 Dominik Hasek S 4.00 10.00
91 Shawn McEachern B .08 .25
92 Martin Straka S 1.00 2.50
93 Roman Hamrlik B .08 .25
94 Roman Oksiuta S 1.00 2.50
95 Sergei Fedorov B .60 1.50
96 Jeff O'Neill S 1.00 2.50
97 Todd Harvey S 1.00 2.50
98 Rob Niedermayer B .08 .25
99 Mark Messier G 6.00 15.00
100 Peter Forsberg G 8.00 20.00
101 Deron Quint B .08 .25
102 Nelson Emerson S 1.00 2.50
103 Scott Niedermayer B .08 .25
104 Doug Weight S 1.50 4.00
105 Felix Potvin B .40 1.00
106 Brendan Witt B .08 .25
107 Zdeno Ciger B .08 .25
108 Ed Belfour S 2.00 5.00
109 Jody Hull B .08 .25
110 Cam Neely S 2.00 5.00
111 Kyle McLaren B RC .08 .25
112 Petr Klima S 1.00 2.50
113 Grant Fuhr B .20 .50
114 Todd Krygier B .08 .25
115 Brian Leetch B .20 .50
116 Daniel Alfredsson S RC 6.00 15.00
117 Zigmund Palffy B .20 .50
118 Antti Tormanen B .08 .25
119 Mark Recchi B .20 .50
120 Mikael Renberg B .08 .25
121 Chris Chelios B .40 1.00
122 Guy Hebert B .20 .50
123 Keith Tkachuk G 6.00 15.00
124 Joe Juneau S 1.00 2.50
125 Radek Dvorak S RC 1.50 4.00
126 Gary Suter B .08 .25
127 Ron Francis B .20 .50
128 Mike Modano G 8.00 20.00
129 Tom Barrasso B .20 .50
130 Pat LaFontaine B .20 .50
131 Pat Verbeek B .08 .25
132 Sean Burke S 1.50 4.00
133 Rick Tocchet B .08 .25
134 Petr Sykora B RC .75 2.00
135 Felix Potvin B .40 1.00
136 Scott Mellanby B .08 .25
137 Paul Coffey B .40 1.00
138 Aki Berg G RC 4.00 10.00
139 Jason Arnott B .08 .25
140 Alexander Mogilny G 4.00 10.00
141 Sandis Ozolinsh B .08 .25
142 Owen Nolan S 1.50 4.00
143 Brian Bradley B .08 .25
144 Trevor Linden B .08 .25
145 Patrick Roy B 1.50 4.00
146 Todd Bertuzzi B RC 1.50 4.00
147 Michal Pivonka B .08 .25
148 Kevin Hatcher S 1.00 2.50
149 Chris Terreri B .20 .50
150 Mario Lemieux B 1.50 4.00
151 Alexei Yashin S 1.00 2.50
152 Scott Stevens S 1.00 2.50
153 Dale Hawerchuk B .08 .25
154 Markus Naslund B .40 1.00
155 Teemu Selanne B .40 1.00
156 Darcy Wakaluk S 1.00 2.50
157 Vitali Yachmenev B .08 .25
158 Jason Dawe B .08 .25
159 Chris Osgood B .20 .50
160 Alexander Mogilny B .20 .50
161 Kirk McLean S 1.00 2.50
162 Steve Yzerman G 12.00 30.00
163 Shean Donovan B .08 .25
164 Valeri Kamensky S 1.00 2.50
165 Paul Kariya B .40 1.00
166 Dimitri Khristich S 1.00 2.50
167 Teppo Numminen B .08 .25
168 Joe Nieuwendyk S 1.50 4.00
169 Mike Richter S 2.00 5.00
170 Doug Gilmour B .20 .50
171 Sergei Zubov B .08 .25
172 Michael Nylander B .08 .25
173 Geoff Sanderson B .08 .25
174 Eric Desjardins S 1.00 2.50
175 Jeremy Roenick B .50 1.25
176 Ed Jovanovski G 4.00 10.00
177 Mats Sundin B .40 1.00
178 Martin Brodeur B 1.00 2.50
179 John LeClair G 5.00 12.00
180 Wayne Gretzky G 20.00 50.00
181 Theo Fleury B .08 .25
182 Pierre Turgeon S 1.00 2.50
183 Robert Svehla B RC .08 .25
184 Brett Hull G 6.00 15.00
185 Jaromir Jagr G 8.00 20.00
186 Sergei Fedorov B .60 1.50
187 Pavel Bure G 6.00 15.00
188 John Vanbiesbrouck B .20 .50
189 Paul Kariya B .40 1.00
190 Mario Lemieux G 15.00 40.00
191 Checklist UER G 4.00 10.00

1995-96 Finest Refractors

The 1995-96 Finest Refractors set was issued as a parallel to the Finest set. Mirroring it's three levels of difficulty, the cards were inserted at varying rates. Common refractors could be found 1:12 packs. Uncommon refractors were 1:48, while the rare refractors were hidden 1:288 packs. It is believed there were less than 150 rare refractors, less than 450 uncommon and less than 1,000 common refractors available.

*BRONZE VETS: 3X TO 8X BASIC CARDS
*BRONZE ROOKIES: 2.5X TO 6X
*SILVER VETS: 2X TO 5X BASIC CARDS
*SILVER ROOKIES: 1.2X TO 3X
*GOLD VETS: .8X TO 2X BASIC CARDS

1998-99 Finest

The 1998-99 Finest set was issued in one series totaling 150 cards and was distributed in six-card packs with a suggested retail price of $5. The fronts featured color action player photos printed on 29-pt. stock and identified by a different graphic according to the player's position. The backs carried player information and career statistics.

COMPLETE SET (150) 30.00 60.00
1 Teemu Selanne .30 .75
2 Theo Fleury .10 .30
3 Ed Belfour .30 .75
4 Dominik Hasek .60 1.50
5 Dino Ciccarelli .25 .60
6 Peter Forsberg .75 2.00
7 Rob Blake .25 .60
8 Martin Gelinas .10 .30
9 Vincent Damphousse .10 .30
10 Doug Brown .10 .30
11 Dave Andreychuk .25 .60
12 Bill Guerin .25 .60
13 Daniel Alfredsson .25 .60
14 Dainius Zubrus .10 .30
15 Nikolai Khabibulin .25 .60
16 Sergei Nemchinov .10 .30
17 Rod Brind'Amour .25 .60
18 Patrick Marleau .10 .30
19 Brett Hull .40 1.00
20 Rob Zamuner .10 .30
21 Anson Carter .25 .60
22 Chris Pronger .25 .60
23 Owen Nolan .25 .60
24 Alexandre Daigle .10 .30
25 Darius Kasparaitis .10 .30
26 Steve Rucchin .10 .30
27 Grant Fuhr .25 .60
28 Mike Sillinger .10 .30
29 Tony Amonte .25 .60
30 Jeremy Roenick .40 1.00
31 Garry Galley .10 .30
32 Jeff Friesen .10 .30
33 Alexei Zhitnik .10 .30
34 Sergei Fedorov .50 1.25
35 Martin Brodeur .75 2.00
36 Curtis Joseph .30 .75
37 Mike Johnson .10 .30
38 Mattias Ohlund .25 .60
39 Derian Hatcher .10 .30
40 Zigmund Palffy .25 .60
41 Rob Niedermayer .10 .30
42 Keith Primeau .10 .30
43 Valeri Kamensky .10 .30
44 Cliff Ronning .10 .30
45 Saku Koivu .30 .75
46 Jiri Slegr .10 .30
47 Igor Korolev .10 .30
48 Sergei Samsonov .25 .60
49 Vaclav Prospal .10 .30
50 Ron Francis .25 .60
51 John LeClair .30 .75
52 Peter Bondra .25 .60
53 Matt Cullen .10 .30
54 Doug Gilmour .25 .60
55 John Vanbiesbrouck .25 .60
56 Kevin Stevens .25 .60
57 Vladimir Malakhov .10 .30
58 Guy Hebert .25 .60
59 Patrik Elias .25 .60
60 Boris Mironov .10 .30
61 Rob DiMaio .10 .30
62 Pavol Demitra .25 .60
63 Michael Nylander .10 .30
64 Wayne Gretzky 2.00 5.00
65 Miroslav Satan .10 .30
66 Eric Daze .25 .60
67 Jozef Stumpel .25 .60
68 Mark Messier .30 .75
69 Pat Verbeek .10 .30
70 Felix Potvin .30 .75
71 Ethan Moreau .10 .30
72 Steve Yzerman 1.50 4.00
73 Paul Ysebaert .10 .30
74 Jaromir Jagr .50 1.25
75 Mike Modano .50 1.25
76 Chris Osgood .25 .60
77 Robert Svehla .10 .30
78 Joe Juneau .25 .60
79 Adam Deadmarsh .10 .30
80 Keith Tkachuk .30 .75
81 Mark Recchi .25 .60
82 Andrew Cassels .10 .30
83 Mike Hough .10 .30
84 Rem Murray .10 .30
85 Trevor Kidd .25 .60
86 Jeff Hackett .25 .60
87 Mikael Renberg .25 .60
88 Al MacInnis .25 .60
89 Mike Richter .30 .75
90 Markus Naslund .30 .75
91 Joe Sakic .60 1.50
92 Michael Peca .10 .30
93 Scott Thornton .10 .30
94 Vyacheslav Kozlov .25 .60
95 Bobby Holik .10 .30
96 Alexei Yashin .10 .30
97 Robert Kron .10 .30
98 Adam Oates .25 .60
99 Chris Simon .10 .30
100 Paul Kariya .30 .75
101 Ray Bourque .50 1.25
102 Eric Desjardins .25 .60
103 Glen Murray .10 .30
104 Oleg Tverdovsky .10 .30
105 Pavel Bure .30 .75
106 Mats Sundin .30 .75
107 Bryan Berard .25 .60
108 Janne Niinimaa .10 .30
109 Wade Redden .10 .30
110 Trevor Linden .25 .60
111 Jarome Iginla .40 1.00
112 Joe Nieuwendyk .25 .60
113 Alexei Kovalev .25 .60
114 Dave Gagner .10 .30
115 Dimitri Yushkevich .10 .30
116 Sandis Ozolinsh .10 .30
117 Dimitri Khristich .10 .30
118 Jim Campbell .10 .30
119 Nicklas Lidstrom .30 .75
120 Scott Niedermayer .10 .30
121 Niklas Sundstrom .10 .30
122 Karl Dykhuis .10 .30
123 Brendan Shanahan .30 .75
124 Sandy McCarthy .10 .30
125 Pierre Turgeon .25 .60
126 Olaf Kolzig .25 .60
127 Chris Chelios .30 .75
128 Luc Robitaille .25 .60
129 Alexander Mogilny .25 .60
130 Sami Kapanen .10 .30
131 Stu Barnes .10 .30
132 Scott Stevens .25 .60
133 Doug Weight .25 .60
134 Alexei Zhamnov .10 .30
135 Mike Vernon .25 .60
136 Derek Morris .10 .30
137 Brian Leetch .30 .75
138 Ray Whitney .10 .30
139 Chris Gratton .25 .60
140 Patrick Roy 1.50 4.00
141 Jason Allison .10 .30
142 Tom Barrasso .25 .60
143 Derek Plante .10 .30
144 Denis Pederson .10 .30
145 Mike Ricci .10 .30
146 Damian Rhodes .25 .60
147 Marco Sturm .10 .30
148 Darryl Sydor .10 .30
149 Eric Lindros .30 .75
150 Checklist .10 .30

1998-99 Finest No Protectors

Randomly inserted into packs at the rate of 1:4, this 150-card set was a parallel to the base set without the Finest Protector.

*NO PROTECTOR: 1.2X TO 3X BASIC CARDS

1998-99 Finest No Protectors Refractors

Randomly inserted into packs at the rate of 1:24, this 150-card set was a parallel to the regular refractor set without the Finest protector.

*NO PROT REF: 4X TO 10X BASIC CARDS
STATED ODDS 1:24

1998-99 Finest Refractors

Randomly inserted into packs at the rate of 1:12, this 150-card set was a parallel to the base set and was distinguished by the refractive quality of the card.

COMPLETE SET (150) 120.00 300.00
*REFRACTORS: 2X TO 5X BASIC CARDS

1998-99 Finest Centurion

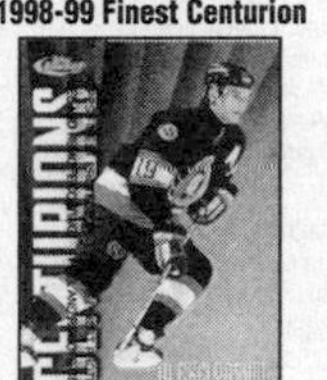

Randomly inserted into packs at the rate of 1:72, this 20-card set featured color action photos of rising NHL stars. Only 500 serial-numbered sets were produced. A refractor parallel was also produced and inserted at a rate of 1:477. Each refractor was serial numbered out of 75.

COMPLETE SET (20) 75.00 150.00
STATED PRINT RUN 500 SER.#'d SETS
*REFRACTOR/75: 2X TO 4X BASIC INSERTS
REFRACTOR/75 STATED ODDS 1:477
REFRACTOR PRINT RUN 75 SER.#'d SETS
C1 Patrik Elias 5.00 12.00
C2 Bryan Berard 5.00 12.00
C3 Chris Osgood 3.00 8.00
C4 Saku Koivu 6.00 15.00
C5 Alexei Yashin 3.00 8.00
C6 Zigmund Palffy 3.00 8.00
C7 Peter Forsberg 15.00 40.00
C8 Jason Allison 3.00 8.00
C9 Wade Redden 3.00 8.00
C10 Paul Kariya 6.00 15.00
C11 Martin Brodeur 15.00 40.00
C12 Patrick Marleau 3.00 8.00
C13 Jaromir Jagr 10.00 25.00
C14 Mattias Ohlund 5.00 12.00
C15 Teemu Selanne 6.00 15.00
C16 Mike Johnson 5.00 12.00
C17 Joe Thornton 8.00 20.00
C18 Jocelyn Thibault 5.00 12.00
C19 Daniel Alfredsson 5.00 12.00
C20 Sergei Samsonov 5.00 12.00

1998-99 Finest Double Sided Mystery Finest

Randomly inserted into packs at the rate of 1:36, this 50-card set featured color action photos of 20 players printed on double-sided cards with one of three other players on the back or the same player on both sides. The opaque Finest Protector had to be peeled off in order to view the card. A refractor parallel was also produced and randomly inserted at a rate of 1:144.

COMPLETE SET (50) 250.00 500.00
*REFRACTORS: .8X TO 2X BASIC INSERTS
REFRACTOR STATED ODDS 1:144
M1 Jaromir Jagr 10.00 25.00
Wayne Gretzky
M2 Jaromir Jagr 5.00 12.00
Dominik Hasek
M3 Jaromir Jagr 5.00 12.00
Eric Lindros
M4 Jaromir Jagr 5.00 12.00
Jaromir Jagr
M5 Dominik Hasek 12.50 30.00
Wayne Gretzky
M6 Dominik Hasek 5.00 12.00
Eric Lindros
M7 Dominik Hasek 5.00 12.00
Dominik Hasek
M8 Wayne Gretzky 12.50 30.00
Eric Lindros
M9 Wayne Gretzky 20.00 50.00
Wayne Gretzky
M10 Eric Lindros 5.00 12.00
Eric Lindros
M11 Paul Kariya 5.00 12.00
Teemu Selanne
M12 Paul Kariya 5.00 12.00
Ray Bourque
M13 Paul Kariya 5.00 12.00
Sergei Samsonov
M14 Paul Kariya 5.00 12.00
Paul Kariya
M15 Teemu Selanne 5.00 12.00
Ray Bourque
M16 Teemu Selanne 5.00 12.00
Sergei Samsonov
M17 Teemu Selanne 5.00 12.00
Teemu Selanne
M18 Ray Bourque 5.00 12.00
Sergei Samsonov
M19 Ray Bourque 5.00 12.00
Ray Bourque
M20 Sergei Samsonov 5.00 12.00
Sergei Samsonov
M21 Martin Brodeur 10.00 25.00
Peter Forsberg
M22 M.Brodeur/P.Roy 10.00 25.00
M23 Martin Brodeur 8.00 20.00
Joe Sakic
M24 Martin Brodeur 8.00 20.00
Martin Brodeur
M25 Peter Forsberg 12.50 30.00
Patrick Roy
M26 Peter Forsberg 10.00 25.00
Joe Sakic
M27 Peter Forsberg 10.00 25.00
Peter Forsberg
M28 Patrick Roy 12.50 30.00
Joe Sakic
M29 Patrick Roy 15.00 40.00
Patrick Roy
M30 Joe Sakic 5.00 12.00
Joe Sakic
M31 M.Modano/S.Yzerman 12.50 30.00
M32 Mike Modano 8.00 20.00
Sergei Fedorov
M33 Mike Modano 8.00 20.00
Brendan Shanahan
M34 Mike Modano 5.00 12.00
Mike Modano
M35 Steve Yzerman 8.00 20.00
Sergei Fedorov
M36 Steve Yzerman 8.00 20.00
Brendan Shanahan
M37 S.Yzerman/S.Yzerman 15.00 40.00
M38 Sergei Fedorov 5.00 12.00
Brendan Shanahan
M39 Sergei Fedorov 5.00 12.00
Sergei Fedorov
M40 Brendan Shanahan 5.00 12.00
Brendan Shanahan
M41 Mark Messier 5.00 12.00
John Leclair
M42 Mark Messier 5.00 12.00
Keith Tkachuk
M43 Mark Messier 5.00 12.00
Pavel Bure
M44 Mark Messier 5.00 12.00
Mark Messier
M45 John Leclair 5.00 12.00
Keith Tkachuk
M46 John Leclair 5.00 12.00
Pavel Bure
M47 John Leclair 5.00 12.00
John Leclair
M48 Pavel Bure 5.00 12.00
Keith Tkachuk
M49 Pavel Bure 5.00 10.00
Pavel Bure
M50 Keith Tkachuk 5.00 12.00
Keith Tkachuk

1998-99 Finest Futures Finest

Randomly inserted into packs at the rate of 1:72, this 20-card set featured color action photos of hard-charging NHL prospects and CHL players. Only 500 serial-numbered sets were produced. A refractor parallel was also produced and randomly inserted at a rate of 1:238. Refractors were serial numbered to 150.

COMPLETE SET (20) 40.00 80.00
*REFRACTOR/150: .6X TO 1.5X BASIC INSERTS
REFRACTOR/150 ODDS 1:238
REFRACTOR PRINT RUN 150 SER.#'d SETS
F1 David Legwand 2.00 5.00
F2 Manny Malhotra 2.00 5.00
F3 Vincent Lecavalier 6.00 15.00
F4 Brad Stuart 2.00 5.00
F5 Bryan Allen 2.00 5.00
F6 Rico Fata 2.00 5.00
F7 Mark Bell 2.00 5.00
F8 Michael Rupp 2.00 5.00
F9 Jeff Heerema 2.00 5.00
F10 Alex Tanguay 5.00 10.00
F11 Patrick Desrochers 2.00 5.00
F12 Mathieu Chouinard 2.00 5.00
F13 Eric Chouinard 2.00 5.00
F14 Martin Skoula 2.00 5.00
F15 Robyn Regehr 2.00 5.00
F16 Marian Hossa 6.00 15.00
F17 Daniel Cleary 2.00 5.00
F18 Olli Jokinen 2.00 5.00
F19 Brendan Morrison 2.00 5.00
F20 Erik Rasmussen 2.00 5.00

1998-99 Finest Oversize

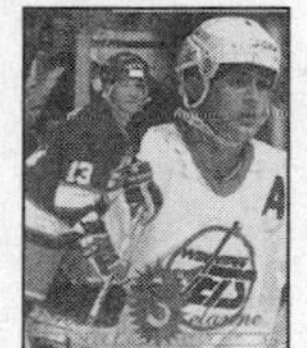

Inserted one per hobby box, this seven-card set featured color action photos of top NHL players printed on oversized cards measuring approximately 3 1/4" by 4 9/16". A refractor parallel was also produced and inserted at a rate of 1 in 6 boxes.

COMPLETE SET (7) 15.00 30.00
*REFRACTORS: 1.2X TO 3X BASIC INSERTS
REFRACTOR ODDS ONE PER 6 BOXES
1 Teemu Selanne 1.50 4.00
2 Dominik Hasek 1.50 4.00
3 Martin Brodeur 2.00 5.00
4 Wayne Gretzky 5.00 12.00
5 Steve Yzerman 4.00 10.00
6 Jaromir Jagr 1.25 3.00
7 Eric Lindros 1.50 4.00

1998-99 Finest Promos

This six-card set featured color action player photos printed on an embossed card with faint skating marks in the background. The fronts were covered with the Finest Protector film. The backs carried another player photos, biographical information, and season and career statistics. The cards were numbered with a "PP" prefix on the backs.

COMPLETE SET (6) 2.00 5.00
PP1 Scott Stevens .20 .50
PP2 Michael Nylander .20 .50
PP3 Brendan Shanahan .60 1.50
PP4 Trevor Kidd .30 .75
PP5 Bill Guerin .40 1.00
PP6 Brian Leetch .40 1.00

1998-99 Finest Red Lighters

Randomly inserted in packs at the rate of 1:24, this 20-card set featured color action photos of top NHL scorers printed on die-cut chromium cards. A refractor parallel was also created and inserted at 1:72.

COMPLETE SET (20) 40.00 80.00
*REFRACTORS: .8X TO 2X BASIC INSERTS
REFRACTOR STATED ODDS 1:72
R1 Jaromir Jagr 2.50 6.00
R2 Mike Modano 2.50 6.00
R3 Paul Kariya 1.25 3.00
R4 Pavel Bure 1.25 3.00
R5 Peter Bondra 1.50 4.00
R6 Sergei Fedorov 2.00 5.00
R7 Steve Yzerman 6.00 15.00
R8 Teemu Selanne 1.25 3.00
R9 Wayne Gretzky 8.00 20.00
R10 Brendan Shanahan 1.25 3.00
R11 Eric Lindros 1.25 3.00
R12 Alexei Yashin 1.25 3.00
R13 Jason Allison 1.25 3.00
R14 Joe Nieuwendyk 1.50 4.00
R15 Joe Sakic 3.00 8.00
R16 John Leclair 1.25 3.00
R17 Keith Tkachuk 1.25 3.00
R18 Mark Messier 1.25 3.00
R19 Mats Sundin 1.25 3.00
R20 Zigmund Palffy 1.50 4.00

1994-95 Flair

This 225-card super premium set was issued in 10-card packs with a suggested retail price of $3.99. The cards featured a full-bleed design with dual action photos on the front and gold foil printing. The card stock was thicker than any basic issue. Yearly stats appeared on back in silver, printed over one more photo. The cards were arranged alphabetically within teams. Rookie cards in this set included Mariusz Czerkawski, David Oliver, Eric Fichaud and Jason Wiemer. To prevent tampering or searching, Fleer employed an innovative packaging design: the packs are actually a cello-wrapped, two-piece silver foil box, with the cards inside wrapped again in a sealed cello pouch.

COMPLETE SET (225) 25.00 50.00
1 Bob Corkum .07 .20
2 Bobby Dollas .07 .20
3 Guy Hebert .15 .40
4 Paul Kariya .30 .75
5 Anatoli Semenov .07 .20

6 Tim Sweeney	.07	.20
7 Garry Valk	.07	.20
8 Ray Bourque	.50	1.25
9 Mariusz Czerkawski RC	.40	1.00
10 Al Iafrate	.07	.20
11 Cam Neely	.30	.75
12 Adam Oates	.15	.40
13 Vincent Riendeau	.15	.40
14 Don Sweeney	.07	.20
15 Donald Audette	.07	.20
16 Doug Bodger	.07	.20
17 Dominik Hasek	.75	2.00
18 Dale Hawerchuk	.15	.40
19 Pat LaFontaine	.30	.75
20 Alexander Mogilny	.15	.40
21 Craig Muni	.07	.20
22 Richard Smehlik	.07	.20
23 Denis Tsygurov RC	.07	.20
24 Theo Fleury	.07	.20
25 Trevor Kidd	.15	.40
26 James Patrick	.07	.20
27 Robert Reichel	.07	.20
28 Gary Roberts	.07	.20
29 German Titov	.07	.20
30 Zarley Zalapski	.07	.20
31 Ed Belfour	.30	.75
32 Chris Chelios	.30	.75
33 Dirk Graham	.07	.20
34 Joe Murphy	.07	.20
35 Bernie Nicholls	.15	.40
36 Jeremy Roenick	.40	1.00
37 Steve Smith	.07	.20
38 Gary Suter	.07	.20
39 Neal Broten	.15	.40
40 Russ Courtnall	.07	.20
41 Todd Harvey	.07	.20
42 Grant Ledyard	.07	.20
43 Mike Modano	.50	1.25
44 Andy Moog	.30	.75
45 Mark Tinordi	.07	.20
46 Dino Ciccarelli	.15	.40
47 Paul Coffey	.30	.75
48 Sergei Fedorov	.50	1.25
49 Vladimir Konstantinov	.15	.40
50 Slava Kozlov	.15	.40
51 Keith Primeau	.07	.20
52 Ray Sheppard	.15	.40
53 Mike Vernon	.15	.40
54 Jason York RC	.07	.20
55 Steve Yzerman	1.50	4.00
56 Jason Arnott	.07	.20
57 Shayne Corson	.07	.20
58 Igor Kravchuk	.07	.20
59 Dean McAmmond	.07	.20
60 David Oliver RC	.07	.20
61 Bill Ranford	.15	.40
62 Doug Weight	.15	.40
63 Jesse Belanger	.07	.20
64 Bob Kudelski	.07	.20
65 Scott Mellanby	.15	.40
66 Gord Murphy	.07	.20
67 Rob Niedermayer	.15	.40
68 Brian Skrudland	.07	.20
69 John Vanbiesbrouck	.15	.40
70 Sean Burke	.15	.40
71 Andrew Cassels	.07	.20
72 Alexander Godynyuk	.07	.20
73 Chris Pronger	.30	.75
74 Geoff Sanderson	.15	.40
75 Darren Turcotte	.07	.20
76 Pat Verbeek	.07	.20
77 Rob Blake	.15	.40
78 Mike Donnelly	.07	.20
79 Wayne Gretzky	2.00	5.00
80 Kelly Hrudey	.15	.40
81 Jari Kurri	.15	.40
82 Marty McSorley	.07	.20
83 Rick Tocchet	.15	.40
84 Brian Bellows	.07	.20
85 Patrice Brisebois	.07	.20
86 Valeri Bure	.07	.20
87 Vincent Damphousse	.07	.20
88 Eric Desjardins	.15	.40
89 Kirk Muller	.07	.20
90 Oleg Petrov	.07	.20
91 Patrick Roy	1.50	4.00
92 Martin Brodeur	.75	2.00
93 David Emma	.07	.20
94 Bill Guerin	.15	.40
95 John MacLean	.15	.40
96 Scott Niedermayer	.07	.20
97 Stephane Richer	.15	.40
98 Brian Rolston	.07	.20
99 Alexander Semak	.07	.20
100 Scott Stevens	.15	.40
101 Valeri Zelepukin	.07	.20
102 Patrick Flatley	.07	.20
103 Derek King	.07	.20
104 Brett Lindros	.07	.20
105 Vladimir Malakhov	.07	.20
106 Marty McInnis	.07	.20
107 Jamie McLennan	.15	.40
108 Steve Thomas	.07	.20
109 Pierre Turgeon	.15	.40
110 Jeff Beukeboom	.07	.20
111 Adam Graves	.07	.20
112 Alexei Kovalev	.15	.40
113 Steve Larmer	.15	.40
114 Brian Leetch	.30	.75
115 Mark Messier	.30	.75
116 Sergei Nemchinov	.07	.20
117 Mike Richter	.30	.75
118 Sergei Zubov	.07	.20
119 Craig Billington	.15	.40
120 Alexandre Daigle	.07	.20
121 Sean Hill	.07	.20
122 Norm Maciver	.07	.20
123 Dave McLlwain	.07	.20
124 Alexei Yashin	.07	.20
125 Vladislav Boulin RC	.07	.20
126 Rod Brind'Amour	.15	.40
127 Ron Hextall	.15	.40
128 Patrik Juhlin RC	.07	.20
129 Eric Lindros	.30	.75
130 Mark Recchi	.15	.40
131 Mikael Renberg	.15	.40
132 Chris Therien	.07	.20
133 Tom Barrasso	.15	.40
134 Ron Francis	.15	.40
135 Mario Lemieux	1.50	4.00
136 Shawn McEachern	.07	.20
137 Larry Murphy	.15	.40
138 Luc Robitaille	.15	.40
139 Ulf Samuelsson	.07	.20
140 Kevin Stevens	.07	.20
141 Martin Straka	.07	.20
142 Wendel Clark	.15	.40
143 Rene Corbet	.07	.20
144 Adam Deadmarsh	.07	.20
145 Stephane Fiset	.15	.40
146 Peter Forsberg	1.00	2.50
147 Valeri Kamensky	.15	.40
148 Janne Laukkanen	.07	.20
149 Sylvain Lefebvre	.07	.20
150 Mike Ricci	.07	.20
151 Joe Sakic	.60	1.50
152 Steve Duchesne	.07	.20
153 Brett Hull	.40	1.00
154 Craig Janney	.15	.40
155 Craig Johnson	.07	.20
156 Curtis Joseph	.30	.75
157 Al MacInnis	.15	.40
158 Brendan Shanahan	.30	.75
159 Peter Stastny	.15	.40
160 Esa Tikkanen	.07	.20
161 Ulf Dahlen	.07	.20
162 Todd Elik	.07	.20
163 Pat Falloon	.07	.20
164 Jeff Friesen	.07	.20
165 Johan Garpenlov	.07	.20
166 Arturs Irbe	.15	.40
167 Sergei Makarov	.07	.20
168 Jeff Norton	.07	.20
169 Sandis Ozolinsh	.07	.20
170 Brian Bradley	.07	.20
171 Shawn Chambers	.07	.20
172 Aaron Gavey	.07	.20
173 Chris Gratton	.07	.20
174 Petr Klima	.07	.20
175 Daren Puppa	.15	.40
176 Jason Wiemer RC	.07	.20
177 Dave Andreychuk	.15	.40
178 Dave Ellett	.07	.20
179 Eric Fichaud RC	.15	.40
180 Mike Gartner	.15	.40
181 Doug Gilmour	.15	.40
182 Kenny Jonsson	.07	.20
183 Dmitri Mironov	.07	.20
184 Felix Potvin	.30	.75
185 Mike Ridley	.07	.20
186 Mats Sundin	.30	.75
187 Greg Adams	.07	.20
188 Jeff Brown	.07	.20
189 Pavel Bure	.30	.75
190 Nathan Lafayette	.07	.20
191 Trevor Linden	.15	.40
192 Jyrki Lumme	.07	.20
193 Kirk McLean	.15	.40
194 Cliff Ronning	.07	.20
195 Jason Allison	.07	.20
196 Peter Bondra	.15	.40
197 Randy Burridge	.07	.20
198 Sylvain Cote	.07	.20
199 Dale Hunter	.07	.20
200 Joe Juneau	.15	.40
201 Dimitri Khristich	.07	.20
202 Todd Nelson	.07	.20
203 Pat Peake	.07	.20
204 Rick Tabaracci	.15	.40
205 Tim Cheveldae	.15	.40
206 Dallas Drake	.07	.20
207 Dave Manson	.07	.20
208 Teppo Numminen	.07	.20
209 Teemu Selanne	.30	.75
210 Darrin Shannon	.07	.20
211 Keith Tkachuk	.30	.75
212 Alexei Zhamnov	.15	.40
213 Sergei Fedorov	.30	.75
214 Sergei Fedorov	.30	.75
215 Sergei Fedorov	.30	.75
216 Sergei Fedorov	.30	.75
217 Sergei Fedorov	.30	.75
218 Sergei Fedorov	.30	.75
219 Sergei Fedorov	.30	.75
220 Sergei Fedorov	.30	.75
221 Sergei Fedorov	.30	.75
222 Sergei Fedorov	.30	.75
223 Checklist	.07	.20
224 Checklist	.07	.20
225 Checklist	.07	.20

1994-95 Flair Center Spotlight

The 10 cards in this set, which highlighted some of the league's top centers, were randomly inserted in Flair product at the rate of 1:4 packs. The cards featured an action shot with two spotlights defining the background. Backs featured another action photo, along with a player profile. The cards were numbered on the back as "X of 10".

COMPLETE SET (10)	10.00	20.00
1 Jason Arnott	.15	.40
2 Sergei Fedorov	1.00	2.50
3 Doug Gilmour	.30	.75
4 Wayne Gretzky	4.00	10.00
5 Pat LaFontaine	.60	1.50
6 Mario Lemieux	3.00	8.00
7 Eric Lindros	.60	1.50
8 Mark Messier	.60	1.50
9 Mike Modano	1.00	2.50
10 Jeremy Roenick	.75	2.00

1994-95 Flair Hot Numbers

The ten cards in this set, which highlight some of the game's deadliest snipers, were randomly inserted in Flair product at the rate of 1:16 packs. The cards featured an action shot over a black background featuring a scribble of neon colors. The player, team, and set name appeared vertically along the left border of the card. Card backs had a similar style as the front and are numbered as "X of 10".

COMPLETE SET (10)	20.00	40.00
1 Pavel Bure	.75	2.00
2 Wayne Gretzky	5.00	12.00
3 Dominik Hasek	2.00	5.00
4 Brett Hull	1.00	2.50
5 Mario Lemieux	4.00	10.00
6 Adam Oates	.40	1.00
7 Luc Robitaille	.40	1.00
8 Patrick Roy	4.00	10.00
9 Brendan Shanahan	.75	2.00
10 Steve Yzerman	4.00	10.00

1994-95 Flair Scoring Power

This 10-card standard-size set was inserted in packs at a rate of 1:8. The fronts had a color action photo on the right side and the player's name and the word "Power" going down the left side in silver-foil. The background consisted of many multi-color lines scrawled about. The backs has a color photo with player information and the player's name and "Scoring Power" in silver-foil at the top. The background was similar to the front and they are numbered "X of 10" at the bottom.

COMPLETE SET (10)	6.00	12.00
1 Pavel Bure	.75	2.00
2 Alexandre Daigle	.20	.50
3 Sergei Fedorov	1.25	3.00
4 Alexei Kovalev	.40	1.00
5 Brian Leetch	.75	2.00
6 Eric Lindros	.75	2.00
7 Mike Modano	1.25	3.00
8 Alexander Mogilny	.40	1.00
9 Jeremy Roenick	1.00	2.50
10 Alexei Yashin	.20	.50

1996-97 Flair

The 1996-97 Flair set was issued in one series totaling 125 cards. The set contained the Wave of the Future subset (101-125). Although numbered as part of the set, these cards were short printed and inserted at a rate of 1:4 packs. Card fronts featured a color action photo, and a background portrait of the player. Card backs contained a color action photo and statistics. Cards were distributed in four-card packs and carried a suggested retail price of $3.99. Key rookies include Sergei Berezin, Mike Grier, Patrick Lalime, Ethan Moreau and Dainius Zubrus.

COMPLETE SET (125)	40.00	80.00
COMP.BASE SET (100)	20.00	40.00
1 Guy Hebert	.20	.50
2 Paul Kariya	.30	.75
3 Teemu Selanne	.30	.75
4 Ray Bourque	.50	1.25
5 Adam Oates	.20	.50
6 Bill Ranford	.20	.50
7 Jozef Stumpel	.08	.25
8 Dominik Hasek	.60	1.50
9 Pat LaFontaine	.30	.75
10 Alexei Zhitnik	.08	.25
11 Theo Fleury	.08	.25
12 Dave Gagner	.20	.50
13 Trevor Kidd	.20	.50
14 Tony Amonte	.20	.50
15 Chris Chelios	.30	.75
16 Eric Daze	.20	.50
17 Alexei Zhamnov	.20	.50
18 Peter Forsberg	.75	2.00
19 Sandis Ozolinsh	.08	.25
20 Patrick Roy	1.50	4.00
21 Joe Sakic	.60	1.50
22 Derian Hatcher	.08	.25
23 Mike Modano	.50	1.25
24 Andy Moog	.20	.50
25 Pat Verbeek	.08	.25
26 Sergei Fedorov	.50	1.25
27 Slava Fetisov	.08	.25
28 Nicklas Lidstrom	.30	.75
29 Chris Osgood	.20	.50
30 Brendan Shanahan	.30	.75
31 Steve Yzerman	1.50	4.00
32 Jason Arnott	.08	.25
33 Curtis Joseph	.30	.75
34 Boris Mironov	.08	.25
35 Ryan Smyth	.30	.75
36 Doug Weight	.20	.50
37 Ed Jovanovski	.20	.50
38 Ray Sheppard	.20	.50
39 Robert Svehla	.08	.25
40 John Vanbiesbrouck	.20	.50
41 Andrew Cassels	.08	.25
42 Jason Muzzatti	.20	.50
43 Keith Primeau	.08	.25
44 Geoff Sanderson	.20	.50
45 Rob Blake	.20	.50
46 Dimitri Khristich	.08	.25
47 Vincent Damphousse	.08	.25
48 Saku Koivu	.30	.75
49 Mark Recchi	.30	.75
50 Martin Rucinsky	.08	.25
51 Jocelyn Thibault	.30	.75
52 Martin Brodeur	.75	2.00
53 Bill Guerin	.08	.25
54 Scott Stevens	.20	.50
55 Scott Lachance	.08	.25
56 Zigmund Palffy	.20	.50
57 Tommy Salo	.20	.50
58 Bryan Smolinski	.08	.25
59 Wayne Gretzky	2.50	5.00
60 Brian Leetch	.30	.75
61 Mark Messier	.30	.75
62 Mike Richter	.30	.75
63 Daniel Alfredsson	.20	.50
64 Damian Rhodes	.20	.50
65 Alexei Yashin	.08	.25
66 Paul Coffey	.30	.75
67 Dale Hawerchuk	.20	.50
68 Ron Hextall	.20	.50
69 John LeClair	.30	.75
70 Eric Lindros	.30	.75
71 Nikolai Khabibulin	.20	.50
72 Jeremy Roenick	.40	1.00
73 Keith Tkachuk	.30	.75
74 Oleg Tverdovsky	.20	.50
75 Ron Francis	.20	.50
76 Kevin Hatcher	.08	.25
77 Jaromir Jagr	.50	1.25
78 Mario Lemieux	1.50	4.00
79 Petr Nedved	.20	.50
80 Grant Fuhr	.20	.50
81 Brett Hull	.40	1.00
82 Al MacInnis	.20	.50
83 Ed Belfour	.30	.75
84 Tony Granato	.08	.25
85 Owen Nolan	.20	.50
86 Dino Ciccarelli	.20	.50
87 John Cullen	.08	.25
88 Roman Hamrlik	.20	.50
89 Wendel Clark	.20	.50
90 Doug Gilmour	.20	.50
91 Felix Potvin	.30	.75
92 Mats Sundin	.30	.75
93 Pavel Bure	.30	.75
94 Corey Hirsch	.20	.50
95 Trevor Linden	.20	.50
96 Alexander Mogilny	.20	.50
97 Peter Bondra	.20	.50
98 Jim Carey	.30	.75
99 Dale Hunter	.08	.25
100 Chris Simon	.08	.25
101 Mattias Timander RC	.30	.75
102 Vaclav Varada RC	.30	.75
103 Jarome Iginla SP	.40	1.00
104 Ethan Moreau RC	.75	2.00
105 Jamie Langenbrunner SP	.30	.75
106 Roman Turek RC	.75	2.00
107 Tomas Holmstrom RC	.75	2.00
108 Kevin Hodson RC	.75	2.00
109 Mats Lindgren SP	.30	.75
110 Mike Grier SP RC	1.00	2.50
111 Rem Murray RC	.75	2.00
112 Jose Theodore SP	2.00	5.00
113 David Wilkie SP	.30	.75
114 Bryan Berard SP	.30	.75
115 Eric Fichaud SP	.30	.75
116 Daniel Goneau RC	.75	2.00
117 Andreas Dackell RC	.75	2.00
118 Wade Redden SP	.30	.75
119 Dainius Zubrus RC	.75	2.00
120 Janne Niinimaa SP	.30	.75
121 Patrick Lalime RC	2.00	5.00
122 Harry York RC SP	.75	2.00
123 Jim Campbell SP	.30	.75
124 Sergei Berezin RC	.75	2.00
125 Jaro. Svejkovsky RC	.75	2.00

1996-97 Flair Blue Ice

This 125-card set paralleled the basic Flair set. The cards were randomly inserted in packs at a rate of 1:20, though many dealers suggested they were harder to obtain than the odds suggest. Each card was serial numbered to 250, and card fronts carried a blue foil background along with the words BLUE ICE. No complete set price is listed below due to the extremely short print run of the set, and the lack of market activity in complete set form. Values can be determined by applying the multipliers below to the prices for the corresponding regular card.

*VETS: 8X TO 20X BASIC CARDS
*SPs: 1.5X TO 3X

1996-97 Flair Center Ice Spotlight

This set featured ten of the NHL's top players. Card fronts featured a color action photo, with purple, red and yellow spotlights highlighting the background. The cards were randomly inserted in packs at a rate of 1:30.

COMPLETE SET (10)	15.00	40.00
1 Pavel Bure	1.50	4.00
2 Sergei Fedorov	2.00	5.00
3 Peter Forsberg	2.00	5.00
4 Brett Hull	2.00	5.00
5 Jaromir Jagr	2.50	6.00
6 Paul Kariya	1.50	4.00
7 Joe Sakic	3.00	8.00
8 Teemu Selanne	1.50	4.00
9 Mats Sundin	1.50	4.00
10 Steve Yzerman	6.00	15.00

1996-97 Flair Hot Gloves

This insert set focused on twelve of the NHL's best netminders. Card fronts featured a color action photo with the mesh of a goalie glove in the background. Card backs contained a player photo and biographical information. Each card was die-cut and randomly inserted in packs at a rate of 1:40.

COMPLETE SET (12)	40.00	100.00
1 Ed Belfour	4.00	10.00
2 Martin Brodeur	10.00	25.00
3 Jim Carey	2.00	5.00
4 Dominik Hasek	6.00	15.00
5 Curtis Joseph	4.00	10.00
6 Patrick Lalime	2.00	5.00
7 Chris Osgood	4.00	10.00
8 Felix Potvin	4.00	10.00
9 Mike Richter	4.00	10.00
10 Patrick Roy	15.00	40.00
11 Jocelyn Thibault	2.00	5.00
12 John Vanbiesbrouck	4.00	10.00

1996-97 Flair Hot Numbers

This 10-card insert set featured NHL superstars who wear double numbers on their jerseys. Card fronts featured a color photo with an orange/red background and their jersey number along the top of the card. The cards were randomly inserted in packs at a rate of 1:72.

COMPLETE SET (10)	25.00	50.00
1 Ray Bourque	2.50	6.00
2 Paul Coffey	1.50	4.00
3 Eric Daze	1.00	2.50
4 Wayne Gretzky	10.00	25.00
5 Ed Jovanovski	1.00	2.50
6 Saku Koivu	1.50	4.00
7 Mario Lemieux	8.00	20.00
8 Eric Lindros	1.50	4.00
9 Mark Messier	1.50	4.00
10 Owen Nolan	1.00	2.50

1996-97 Flair Now And Then

Each card in this set featured three players who share a common bond. They are pictured in their rookie seasons on the front, while the back gave an up-to-date look. The cards were randomly inserted in packs at a rate of 1:400.

COMPLETE SET (3)	40.00	100.00
1 Wayne Gretzky	25.00	60.00
Mark Messier		
Mike Gartner		
2 Mario Lemieux	15.00	40.00
Patrick Roy		
Kirk Muller		
3 Eric Lindros	10.00	25.00
Peter Forsberg		
Scott Niedermayer		

2006-07 Flair Showcase

This 300-card set was issued to the hobby in five-card packs, with an $4.99 SRP, which came 18 packs to a box and 16 boxes to a case. This set was broken into several levels with cards from what was called the press and lower level being inserted into packs at a stated rate of one in six and cards from the private box and executive level being inserted at a stated rate of one in 18. A cards of Evgeni Malkin was issued as a redemption at the Toronto Sportscard and Memorabilia Expo. Cards numbered 301-330 were inserted into update dealer packs available through hobby dealers.

MALKIN AVAIL. AS EXPO REDEMPTION		
COMMON UPDATE RC	1.50	4.00
SEMISTAR UPDATE RC	2.50	6.00
UPD. RCs AVAIL IN UPDATE DEALER PACKS		
1 Jean-Sebastien Giguere	.50	1.25
2 Teemu Selanne	.60	1.50
3 Corey Perry	.50	1.25
4 Scott Niedermayer	.30	.75
5 Jeffrey Lupul	.30	.75
6 Ilya Kovalchuk	.75	2.00
7 Marian Hossa	.50	1.25
8 Kari Lehtonen	.60	1.50
9 Patrice Bergeron	.60	1.50
10 Marc Savard	.30	.75
11 Brad Boyes	.30	.75
12 Mark Stuart RC	.60	2.00
13 Chris Drury	.30	.75
14 Ryan Miller	.60	1.50
15 Thomas Vanek	.30	.75
16 Jarome Iginla	.75	2.00
17 Miikka Kiprusoff	.75	2.00
18 Dion Phaneuf	.75	2.00
19 Eric Staal	.50	1.25
20 Cam Ward	.60	1.50
21 Justin Williams	.30	.75
22 Erik Cole	.30	.75
23 Doug Weight	.30	.75
24 Nikolai Khabibulin	.60	1.50
25 Tuomo Ruutu	.30	.75
26 Dustin Byfuglien RC	2.50	6.00
27 Milan Hejduk	.50	1.25
28 Alex Tanguay	.50	1.25
29 Jose Theodore	.75	2.00
30 Marek Svatos	.30	.75
31 Rob Blake	.50	1.25
32 Rick Nash	.75	2.00
33 Sergei Fedorov	.60	1.50
34 Mike Modano	.75	2.00
35 Marty Turco	.50	1.25
36 Brenden Morrow	.30	.75
37 Jere Lehtinen	.30	.75
38 Steve Yzerman	2.00	5.00
39 Tomas Kopecky RC	1.25	3.00
40 Henrik Zetterberg	.50	1.25
41 Pavel Datsyuk	.50	1.25
42 Tomas Holmstrom	.30	.75
43 Kris Draper	.30	.75
44 M-A Pouliot RC	1.00	3.00
45 Ales Hemsky	.30	.75
46 Roberto Luongo	.75	2.00
47 Olli Jokinen	.30	.75
48 Konstantin Pushkarev RC	.60	2.00
49 Jeremy Roenick	.75	2.00
50 Alexander Frolov	.30	.75
51 Marian Gaborik	1.25	3.00
52 Manny Fernandez	.50	1.25
53 Saku Koivu	.60	1.50
54 Michael Ryder	.50	1.25
55 Mike Ribeiro	.30	.75
56 Cristobal Huet	.50	1.25
57 Paul Kariya	.60	1.50
58 Tomas Vokoun	.50	1.25
59 Shea Weber RC	.75	2.00
60 Patrik Elias	.30	.75
61 Masi Marjamaki RC	.60	1.50
62 Alexei Yashin	.30	.75
63 Rick DiPietro	.50	1.25
64 Miroslav Satan	.30	.75
65 Henrik Lundqvist	.75	2.00
66 Jarkko Immonen RC	.75	1.50
67 Daniel Alfredsson	.50	1.25
68 Martin Gerber	.50	1.25
69 Jason Spezza	.60	1.50
70 Dany Heatley	.75	2.00
71 Martin Havlat	.50	1.25
72 Zdeno Chara	.30	.75
73 Simon Gagne	.60	1.50
74 Ryan Potulny RC	.75	2.00
75 Jeff Carter	.50	1.25
76 Peter Forsberg	1.25	3.00
77 Shane Doan	.30	.75
78 Ladislav Nagy	.30	.75
79 Curtis Joseph	.60	1.50
80 Marc-Andre Fleury	.60	1.50
81 Noah Welch RC	1.00	1.50
82 Matt Carle RC	1.00	2.50
83 Evgeni Nabokov	.50	1.25
84 Jonathan Cheechoo	.50	1.25
85 Patrick Marleau	.50	1.25
86 Keith Tkachuk	.60	1.50
87 Vincent Lecavalier	.60	1.50
88 Martin St. Louis	.50	1.25
89 Brad Richards	.50	1.25
90 Ian White RC	.75	1.50
91 Ben Ondrus RC	.60	1.50
92 Eric Lindros	.60	1.50
93 Alexander Steen	.50	1.25
94 Jeremy Williams RC	.60	2.00
95 Todd Bertuzzi	.50	1.25
96 Markus Naslund	.60	1.50
97 Ed Jovanovski	.30	.75
98 Eric Fehr RC	.75	2.00
99 Alexander Ovechkin	2.50	6.00
100 Olaf Kolzig	.60	1.50
101 Teemu Selanne	.60	1.50
102 Scott Niedermayer	.30	.75
103 Corey Perry	.50	1.25
104 Marian Hossa	.50	1.25
105 Kari Lehtonen	.60	1.50
106 Yan Stastny RC	.75	1.50
107 Glen Murray	.30	.75
108 Brian Leetch	.60	1.50
109 Brad Boyes	.30	.75
110 Chris Drury	.30	.75
111 Ryan Miller	.60	1.50
112 Thomas Vanek	.30	.75
113 Dion Phaneuf	.75	2.00
114 Erik Cole	.30	.75
115 Cam Ward	.60	1.50
116 Mark Recchi	.30	.75
117 Nikolai Khabibulin	.60	1.50
118 Tuomo Ruutu	.30	.75
119 Rob Blake	.50	1.25
120 Milan Hejduk	.50	1.25
121 Marek Svatos	.30	.75
122 Sergei Fedorov	.60	1.50
123 Brenden Morrow	.30	.75
124 Marty Turco	.50	1.25
125 Tomas Kopecky RC	1.25	3.00
126 Pavel Datsyuk	.50	1.25
127 Henrik Zetterberg	.50	1.25
128 M-A Pouliot RC	1.25	2.50
129 Ales Hemsky	.30	.75
130 Olli Jokinen	.30	.75
131 Konstantin Pushkarev RC	.60	2.00
132 Luc Robitaille	.50	1.25
133 Jeremy Roenick	.75	2.00
134 Alexander Frolov	.30	.75
135 Marian Gaborik	1.25	3.00
136 Michael Ryder	.50	1.25
137 Shea Weber RC	.75	2.00
138 Paul Kariya	.60	1.50
139 Tomas Vokoun	.50	1.25
140 Patrik Elias	.30	.75
141 Alexei Yashin	.30	.75
142 Rick DiPietro	.50	1.25
143 Miroslav Satan	.30	.75
144 Henrik Lundqvist	.75	2.00
145 Billy Thompson RC	.75	1.50
146 Filip Novak RC	.40	1.50
147 Daniel Alfredsson	.50	1.25
148 Zdeno Chara	.30	.75
149 Martin Havlat	.50	1.25
150 Simon Gagne	.60	1.50
151 Keith Primeau	.30	.75
152 Jeff Carter	.50	1.25
153 Shane Doan	.30	.75
154 Ladislav Nagy	.30	.75
155 Curtis Joseph	.60	1.50
156 Noah Welch RC	.60	2.50
157 Marc-Andre Fleury	.60	1.50
158 Evgeni Nabokov	.50	1.25
159 Jonathan Cheechoo	.50	1.25
160 Patrick Marleau	.50	1.25
161 Keith Tkachuk	.60	1.50
162 Brad Richards	.50	1.25
163 Ben Ondrus RC	.60	2.00
164 Brendan Bell RC	.75	1.50
165 Ian White RC	.60	2.00
166 Eric Lindros	.60	1.50
167 Todd Bertuzzi	.50	1.25
168 Ed Jovanovski	.30	.75
169 Eric Fehr RC	.75	2.00
170 Olaf Kolzig	.60	1.50
171 Jean-Sebastien Giguere	.50	1.25
172 Ilya Kovalchuk	.75	2.00
173 Patrice Bergeron	.60	1.50
174 Jarome Iginla	.75	2.00
175 Miikka Kiprusoff	.60	2.00
176 Eric Staal	.60	1.50
177 Joe Sakic	1.25	3.00
178 Jose Theodore	.75	1.50
179 Alex Tanguay	.50	1.25
180 Rick Nash	.60	2.00
181 Mike Modano	.75	1.50
182 Steve Yzerman	2.00	5.00
183 Brendan Shanahan	.60	1.50
184 Chris Pronger	.50	1.25
185 Roberto Luongo	.75	2.00
186 Saku Koivu	.60	1.50
187 Martin Brodeur	2.00	5.00
188 Jaromir Jagr	1.00	2.50
189 Jason Spezza	.60	1.50
190 Dany Heatley	.75	2.00
191 Martin Gerber	.50	1.25
192 Peter Forsberg	1.50	4.00
193 Sidney Crosby	5.00	12.00
194 Joe Thornton	1.00	2.50
195 Vincent Lecavalier	.60	1.50
196 Martin St. Louis	.50	1.25
197 Mats Sundin	.60	1.50
198 Andrew Raycroft	.50	1.25
199 Markus Naslund	.60	1.50
200 Alexander Ovechkin	3.00	8.00
201 Jean-Sebastien Giguere	1.25	3.00
202 Teemu Selanne	1.50	4.00
203 Kari Lehtonen	1.50	4.00
204 Marian Hossa	1.25	3.00
205 Ilya Kovalchuk	2.00	5.00
206 Ray Bourque	2.00	5.00
207 Patrice Bergeron	1.50	4.00
208 Brian Leetch	1.50	4.00
209 Chris Drury	.75	2.00
210 Ryan Miller	1.50	4.00
211 Jarome Iginla	2.00	5.00
212 Miikka Kiprusoff	2.00	5.00
213 Dion Phaneuf	1.50	4.00
214 Eric Staal	1.50	4.00
215 Cam Ward	1.50	4.00
216 Rod Brind'Amour	.75	2.00
217 Nikolai Khabibulin	1.25	3.00
218 Joe Sakic	3.00	8.00
219 Alex Tanguay	.75	2.00
220 Milan Hejduk	.75	2.00
221 Jose Theodore	1.50	4.00
222 Marek Svatos	.75	2.00
223 Rick Nash	2.00	5.00
224 Sergei Fedorov	1.25	3.00
225 Mike Modano	2.00	5.00
226 Marty Turco	1.25	3.00
227 Brenden Morrow	.75	2.00
228 Steve Yzerman	4.00	10.00
229 Gordie Howe	2.50	6.00
230 Brendan Shanahan	2.00	5.00
231 Henrik Zetterberg	1.25	3.00
232 Pavel Datsyuk	1.25	3.00
233 Chris Pronger	1.25	3.00
234 Roberto Luongo	3.00	8.00
235 Olli Jokinen	1.50	4.00
236 Luc Robitaille	2.00	5.00
237 Jeremy Roenick	2.00	5.00
238 Marian Gaborik	4.00	10.00
239 Saku Koivu	2.00	5.00
240 Patrick Roy	15.00	40.00
241 Michael Ryder	2.00	5.00
242 Paul Kariya	3.00	8.00
243 Martin Brodeur	8.00	20.00
244 Patrik Elias	2.00	5.00
245 Alexei Yashin	2.00	5.00
246 Rick DiPietro	2.00	5.00
247 Jaromir Jagr	6.00	15.00
248 Henrik Lundqvist	4.00	10.00
249 Martin Gerber	2.00	5.00
250 Dany Heatley	4.00	10.00
251 Jason Spezza	2.50	6.00
252 Daniel Alfredsson	2.00	5.00
253 Peter Forsberg	6.00	15.00
254 Simon Gagne	2.00	5.00
255 Shane Doan	2.00	5.00
256 Mario Lemieux	12.00	30.00
257 Sidney Crosby	15.00	40.00
258 Marc-Andre Fleury	3.00	8.00
259 Evgeni Nabokov	2.50	6.00
260 Joe Thornton	4.00	10.00
261 Jonathan Cheechoo	2.50	6.00
262 Vincent Lecavalier	3.00	8.00
263 Martin St. Louis	2.50	6.00

264 Brad Richards 2.50 6.00
265 Andrew Raycroft 2.50 6.00
266 Mats Sundin 2.50 6.00
267 Markus Naslund 2.50 6.00
268 Todd Bertuzzi 2.50 6.00
269 Alexander Ovechkin 8.00 20.00
270 Olaf Kolzig 2.50 6.00
271 Jean-Sebastien Giguere 2.50 6.00
272 Ilya Kovalchuk 6.00 15.00
273 Ray Bourque 6.00 15.00
274 Jarome Iginla 8.00 20.00
275 Miikka Kiprusoff 6.00 15.00
276 Eric Staal 6.00 15.00
277 Joe Sakic 10.00 25.00
278 Rick Nash 8.00 20.00
279 Mike Modano 6.00 15.00
280 Steve Yzerman 12.00 30.00
281 Gordie Howe 8.00 20.00
282 Henrik Zetterberg 6.00 15.00
283 Roberto Luongo 8.00 20.00
284 Saku Koivu 6.00 15.00
285 Patrick Roy 12.00 30.00
286 Paul Kariya 6.00 15.00
287 Martin Brodeur 10.00 25.00
288 Jaromir Jagr 8.00 20.00
289 Daniel Alfredsson 5.00 12.00
290 Dany Heatley 8.00 20.00
291 Jason Spezza 6.00 15.00
292 Peter Forsberg 10.00 25.00
293 Mario Lemieux 15.00 40.00
294 Sidney Crosby 25.00 60.00
295 Joe Thornton 10.00 25.00
296 Vincent Lecavalier 8.00 20.00
297 Andrew Raycroft 5.00 12.00
298 Mats Sundin 6.00 15.00
299 Markus Naslund 8.00 20.00
300 Alexander Ovechkin 15.00 40.00
301 Ryan Shannon RC 3.00 8.00
302 David McKee RC 4.00 10.00
303 Phil Kessel RC 4.00 10.00
304 Matt Lashoff RC 3.00 8.00
305 Drew Stafford RC 3.00 8.00
306 Clarke MacArthur RC 3.00 8.00
307 Dustin Boyd RC 4.00 10.00
308 Brandon Prust RC 3.00 8.00
309 Dave Bolland RC 6.00 15.00
310 Paul Stastny RC 5.00 12.00
311 Loui Eriksson RC 3.00 8.00
312 Ladislav Smid RC 3.00 8.00
313 Patrick O'Sullivan RC 3.00 8.00
314 Anze Kopitar RC 4.00 10.00
315 Benoit Pouliot RC 4.00 10.00
316 Guillaume Latendresse RC 3.00 8.00
317 Alexander Radulov RC 3.00 8.00
318 Travis Zajac RC 5.00 12.00
319 Nigel Dawes RC 3.00 8.00
320 Josh Hennessy RC 3.00 8.00
321 Enver Lisin RC 3.00 8.00
322 Evgeni Malkin RC 12.00 30.00
323 Jordan Staal RC 6.00 15.00
324 Kristopher Letang RC 5.00 12.00
325 Marc-Edouard Vlasic RC 3.00 8.00
326 Joe Pavelski RC 10.00 25.00
327 Marek Schwarz RC 6.00 15.00
328 Karri Ramo RC 3.00 8.00
329 Luc Bourdon RC 4.00 10.00
330 Jesse Schultz RC 3.00 8.00
FF301 Evgeni Malkin 15.00 40.00

2006-07 Flair Showcase Parallel

1-100: 1.5X TO 3X HI COLUMN

2006-07 Flair Showcase Hot Gloves

STATED ODDS 1:72
HG1 Jean-Sebastien Giguere 6.00 15.00
HG2 Kari Lehtonen 6.00 15.00
HG3 Hannu Toivonen 6.00 15.00
HG4 Ryan Miller 10.00 25.00
HG5 Miikka Kiprusoff 10.00 25.00
HG6 Martin Gerber 10.00 25.00
HG7 Nikolai Khabibulin 10.00 25.00
HG8 Jose Theodore 10.00 25.00
HG9 Marc Denis 6.00 15.00
HG10 Marty Turco 10.00 25.00
HG11 Cam Ward 6.00 15.00
HG12 Dwayne Roloson 6.00 15.00
HG13 Roberto Luongo 12.00 30.00
HG14 Mathieu Garon 6.00 15.00
HG15 Manny Fernandez 6.00 15.00
HG16 Cristobal Huet 8.00 20.00
HG17 Tomas Vokoun 6.00 15.00
HG18 Martin Brodeur 15.00 40.00
HG19 Rick DiPietro 6.00 15.00
HG20 Henrik Lundqvist 10.00 25.00
HG21 Pascal Leclaire 8.00 20.00
HG22 Antero Niittymaki 6.00 15.00
HG23 Curtis Joseph 6.00 15.00
HG24 Marc-Andre Fleury 12.00 30.00
HG25 Evgeni Nabokov 6.00 15.00
HG26 Curtis Sanford 6.00 15.00
HG27 Vesa Toskala 6.00 15.00
HG28 Andrew Raycroft 6.00 15.00
HG29 Alex Auld 6.00 15.00
HG30 Olaf Kolzig 10.00 25.00

2006-07 Flair Showcase Hot Numbers

STATED ODDS 1:180
HN1 Teemu Selanne 8.00 20.00
HN2 Kari Lehtonen 8.00 20.00
HN3 Ray Bourque 8.00 20.00
HN4 Miikka Kiprusoff 10.00 25.00
HN5 Jarome Iginla 10.00 25.00
HN6 Martin Gerber 8.00 20.00
HN7 Eric Staal 8.00 20.00
HN8 Nikolai Khabibulin 10.00 25.00
HN9 Alex Tanguay 12.00 30.00
HN10 Jose Theodore 8.00 20.00
HN11 Joe Sakic 15.00 40.00
HN12 Milan Hejduk 6.00 15.00
HN13 Rick Nash 8.00 20.00
HN14 Sergei Fedorov 8.00 20.00
HN15 Mike Modano 8.00 20.00
HN16 Henrik Zetterberg 6.00 15.00
HN17 Gordie Howe 10.00 25.00
HN18 Brendan Shanahan 6.00 15.00
HN19 Steve Yzerman 15.00 40.00
HN20 Ales Hemsky 6.00 15.00
HN21 Jeremy Roenick 6.00 15.00
HN22 Luc Robitaille 8.00 20.00
HN23 Marian Gaborik 10.00 25.00
HN24 Patrick Roy 20.00 50.00
HN25 Michael Ryder 6.00 15.00
HN26 Saku Koivu 6.00 15.00
HN27 Martin Brodeur 15.00 40.00
HN28 Alexei Yashin 6.00 15.00
HN29 Jaromir Jagr 12.00 30.00
HN30 Dominik Hasek 10.00 25.00
HN31 Dany Heatley 10.00 25.00
HN32 Peter Forsberg 10.00 25.00
HN33 Sidney Crosby 30.00 60.00
HN34 Mario Lemieux 15.00 40.00
HN35 Joe Thornton 10.00 25.00
HN36 Vincent Lecavalier 8.00 20.00
HN37 Martin St. Louis 6.00 15.00
HN38 Mats Sundin 8.00 20.00
HN39 Eric Lindros 8.00 20.00
HN40 Todd Bertuzzi 6.00 15.00
HN41 Markus Naslund 6.00 15.00
HN42 Alexander Ovechkin 12.00 30.00

2006-07 Flair Showcase Hot Numbers Parallel

#'d to JERSEY NUMBER
PRINT RUNS UNDER 24 NOT LISTED
HN1 Teemu Selanne
HN2 Kari Lehtonen 25.00 60.00
HN3 Ray Bourque 15.00 40.00
HN4 Miikka Kiprusoff 25.00 60.00
HN5 Jarome Iginla
HN6 Martin Gerber 40.00 80.00
HN7 Eric Staal
HN8 Nikolai Khabibulin 12.00 30.00
HN9 Alex Tanguay
HN10 Jose Theodore 12.00 30.00
HN11 Joe Sakic
HN12 Milan Hejduk
HN13 Rick Nash 12.00 30.00
HN14 Sergei Fedorov 12.00 30.00
HN15 Mike Modano
HN16 Henrik Zetterberg 15.00 40.00
HN17 Gordie Howe
HN18 Brendan Shanahan
HN19 Steve Yzerman
HN20 Ales Hemsky 8.00 20.00
HN21 Jeremy Roenick 12.00 30.00
HN22 Luc Robitaille
HN23 Marian Gaborik
HN24 Patrick Roy 50.00 100.00
HN25 Michael Ryder 8.00 20.00
HN26 Saku Koivu
HN27 Martin Brodeur 25.00 80.00
HN28 Alexei Yashin 8.00 20.00
HN29 Jaromir Jagr 15.00 40.00
HN30 Dominik Hasek 20.00 50.00
HN31 Dany Heatley 15.00 30.00
HN32 Peter Forsberg
HN33 Sidney Crosby 40.00 80.00
HN34 Mario Lemieux 25.00 60.00
HN35 Joe Thornton
HN36 Vincent Lecavalier
HN37 Martin St. Louis 20.00 50.00
HN38 Mats Sundin
HN39 Eric Lindros 12.00 30.00
HN40 Todd Bertuzzi 8.00 20.00
HN41 Markus Naslund
HN42 Alexander Ovechkin

2006-07 Flair Showcase Inks

STATED ODDS 1:18
IAF Alexander Frolov 4.00 10.00
IAH Ales Hemsky 6.00 15.00
IAL Andrew Ladd 4.00 10.00
IAM Andy McDonald 4.00 10.00
IAN Antero Niittymaki 12.00 30.00
IAO Alexander Ovechkin SP 50.00 100.00
IBB Brad Boyes 6.00 15.00
IBE Ben Eager 4.00 10.00
IBG Brian Gionta 6.00 15.00
IBI Martin Biron 6.00 15.00
IBL Brian Leetch 6.00 15.00
IBR Brenden Morrow 6.00 15.00
ICD Chris Drury 4.00 10.00
ICH Cristobal Huet 10.00 25.00
ICK Chris Kunitz 4.00 10.00
IDA David Aebischer 6.00 15.00
IDB Daniel Briere 10.00 25.00
IDC Dan Cloutier 4.00 10.00
IDK Duncan Keith 4.00 10.00
IDL David Leneveu 4.00 10.00
IDP Dion Phaneuf 10.00 25.00
IDR Dwayne Roloson 6.00 15.00
IDU Dustin Brown 4.00 10.00
IED Eric Daze 4.00 10.00
IEN Evgeni Nabokov 6.00 15.00
IFP Fernando Pisani 4.00 10.00
IHA Michal Handzus 4.00 10.00
IHE Dany Heatley
IHJ Milan Hejduk 6.00 15.00
IHO Marcel Hossa 5.00 12.00
IHZ Henrik Zetterberg 15.00 40.00
IIK Ilya Kovalchuk SP 15.00 40.00
IJC Jonathan Cheechoo 6.00 15.00
IJI Jarome Iginla 12.00 30.00
IJL Jeffrey Lupul 6.00 15.00
IJO Jeff O'Neill 4.00 10.00
IJP Joni Pitkanen 4.00 10.00
IJR Jeremy Roenick SP 15.00 40.00
IJT Jose Theodore 6.00 15.00
IKD Kris Draper 4.00 10.00
IKE Ryan Kesler 4.00 10.00
IKI Miikka Kiprusoff 10.00 25.00
IKL Kari Lehtonen 6.00 15.00
IKO Chuck Kobasew 4.00 10.00
ILR Luc Robitaille 10.00 25.00
ILX Mario Lemieux SP 100.00 200.00
IMA Maxim Afinogenov 5.00 12.00
IMB Martin Brodeur SP 50.00 100.00
IMC Mike Cammalleri 4.00 10.00
IMF Marc-Andre Fleury 12.00 30.00
IMG Marian Gaborik 12.00 30.00
IMH Martin Havlat 6.00 15.00
IMI Ryan Miller 8.00 20.00
IML Manny Legace 6.00 15.00
IMM Milan Michalek 6.00 15.00
IMN Markus Naslund 6.00 15.00
IMO Brendan Morrison 4.00 10.00
IMP Mark Parrish 4.00 10.00
IMR Mike Richards 8.00 20.00
IMS Marc Savard 4.00 10.00
IMT Marty Turco SP 10.00 25.00
INA Nikolai Antropov 4.00 10.00
IOJ Olli Jokinen 4.00 10.00
IOK Olaf Kolzig 8.00 20.00
IPA Jay McClement 4.00 10.00
IPB Pierre-Marc Bouchard 4.00 10.00
IPM Patrick Marleau SP 6.00 15.00
IRB Rob Blake 4.00 10.00
IRF Ruslan Fedotenko 4.00 10.00
IRI Mike Ribeiro 4.00 10.00
IRM Ryan Malone 4.00 10.00
IRS Ryan Smyth 6.00 15.00
IRY Michael Ryder 6.00 15.00
ISA Miroslav Satan 4.00 10.00
ISC Sidney Crosby SP 125.00 250.00
ISG Scott Gomez 4.00 10.00
ISH Shawn Horcoff 6.00 15.00
ISS Sergei Samsonov SP 6.00 15.00
ISV Marek Svatos SP 12.00 30.00
ITB Todd Bertuzzi SP 15.00 40.00
ITC Ty Conklin 4.00 10.00
ITE Mikael Tellqvist 6.00 15.00
ITH Joe Thornton SP 20.00 50.00
ITV Tomas Vokoun 8.00 20.00
IVL Vincent Lecavalier 12.00 30.00
IWH Wade Hedden 4.00 10.00

2006-07 Flair Showcase Stitches

STATED ODDS 1:9
SSAH Ales Hemsky 3.00 8.00
SSAK Alex Kovalev 3.00 8.00
SSAO Alexander Ovechkin 10.00 25.00
SSAT Alex Tanguay 3.00 8.00
SSBG Bill Guerin 3.00 8.00
SSBL Rob Blake 3.00 8.00
SSBM Brenden Morrow 4.00 10.00
SSBO Radek Bonk 3.00 8.00
SSBR Martin Brodeur 8.00 20.00
SSBS Brad Stuart 3.00 8.00
SSCA Carlo Colaiacovo 3.00 8.00
SSCC Chris Chelios 4.00 10.00
SSCD Chris Drury 3.00 8.00
SSCO Chris Osgood 4.00 10.00
SSCP Chris Pronger 4.00 10.00
SSDA Daniel Alfredsson 4.00 10.00
SSDB Donald Brashear 3.00 8.00
SSDC Dan Cloutier 3.00 8.00
SSDE Pavol Demitra 3.00 8.00
SSDH Dan Hamhuis 3.00 8.00
SSDL David Legwand 3.00 8.00
SSDM Darren McCarty 3.00 8.00
SSDR Dwayne Roloson 4.00 10.00
SSEB Ed Belfour 4.00 10.00
SSED Eric Daze 3.00 8.00
SSEL Eric Lindros 4.00 10.00
SSEN Evgeni Nabokov 4.00 10.00
SSES Eric Staal 4.00 10.00
SSFP Fernando Pisani 3.00 8.00
SSGA Mathieu Garon 4.00 10.00
SSGM Glen Murray 3.00 8.00
SSGR Gary Roberts 3.00 8.00
SSHO Marcel Hossa 3.00 8.00
SSJA Jason Arnott 3.00 8.00
SSJB Jay Bouwmeester 3.00 8.00
SSJC Jonathan Cheechoo 3.00 8.00
SSJG Jean-Sebastien Giguere 4.00 10.00
SSJI Jarome Iginla 6.00 15.00
SSJJ Jaromir Jagr 6.00 15.00
SSJL Joffrey Lupul 3.00 8.00
SSJO Joe Thornton 6.00 15.00
SSJR Jeremy Roenick 4.00 10.00
SSJS Jason Spezza 4.00 10.00
SSJT Jose Theodore 4.00 10.00
SSJW Justin Williams 3.00 8.00
SSKP Keith Primeau 3.00 8.00
SSKT Keith Tkachuk 3.00 8.00
SSLE Jere Lehtinen 3.00 8.00
SSLM Mario Lemieux 10.00 25.00
SSLN Ladislav Nagy 3.00 8.00
SSLU Jamie Lundmark 3.00 8.00
SSMA Marian Gaborik 6.00 15.00
SSMB Martin Biron 4.00 10.00
SSMC Bryan McCabe 3.00 8.00
SSMG Martin Gerber 4.00 10.00
SSMH Marian Hossa 4.00 10.00
SSMK Miikka Kiprusoff 4.00 10.00
SSML Manny Legace 3.00 8.00
SSMM Mike Modano 5.00 12.00
SSMN Markus Naslund 4.00 10.00
SSMO Brendan Morrison 3.00 8.00
SSMP Michael Peca 3.00 8.00
SSMR Mike Ribeiro 3.00 8.00
SSMS Marek Svatos 4.00 10.00
SSNA Nikolai Antropov 3.00 8.00
SSOH Mattias Ohlund 3.00 8.00
SSOJ Olli Jokinen 3.00 8.00
SSPA Mark Parrish 3.00 8.00
SSPB Pierre-Marc Bouchard 3.00 8.00
SSPD Pavel Datsyuk 4.00 10.00
SSPE Patrik Elias 3.00 8.00
SSPF Peter Forsberg 6.00 15.00
SSRA Brian Rafalski 3.00 8.00
SSRB Rod Brind'Amour 3.00 8.00
SSRE Robert Esche 4.00 10.00
SSRL Robert Lang 3.00 8.00
SSRM Ryan Miller 4.00 10.00
SSRR Robyn Regehr 3.00 8.00
SSRT Raffi Torres 3.00 8.00
SSRY Michael Ryder 3.00 8.00
SSRZ Richard Zednik 3.00 8.00
SSSA Miroslav Satan 3.00 8.00
SSSC Sidney Crosby 20.00 50.00
SSSG Simon Gagne 4.00 10.00
SSSK Sami Kapanen 3.00 8.00
SSSM Matt Stajan 4.00 10.00
SSSN Scott Niedermayer 3.00 8.00
SSST Martin Straka 3.00 8.00
SSSU Mats Sundin 4.00 10.00
SSSW Stephen Weiss 3.00 8.00
SSSY Steve Yzerman 8.00 20.00
SSTA Tony Amonte 3.00 8.00
SSTC Ty Conklin 4.00 10.00
SSTH Tomas Holmstrom 3.00 8.00
SSTL Trevor Linden 4.00 10.00
SSTR Tuomo Ruutu 4.00 10.00
SSTS Teemu Selanne 4.00 10.00
SSWI Jason Williams 3.00 8.00
SSWR Wade Redden 3.00 8.00
SSZC Zdeno Chara 3.00 8.00

2006-07 Flair Showcase Wave of the Future

STATED ODDS 1:6
WF1 Joffrey Lupul 1.00 2.50
WF2 Kari Lehtonen 1.50 4.00
WF3 Ilya Kovalchuk 2.00 5.00
WF4 Patrice Bergeron 1.50 4.00
WF5 Brad Boyes 1.00 2.50
WF6 Ryan Miller 1.50 4.00
WF7 Dion Phaneuf 2.00 5.00
WF8 Eric Staal 1.50 4.00
WF9 Tuomo Ruutu 1.00 2.50
WF10 Marek Svatos 1.00 2.50
WF11 Rick Nash 1.50 4.00
WF12 Jussi Jokinen 1.00 2.50
WF13 Henrik Zetterberg 1.50 4.00
WF14 Ales Hemsky 1.00 2.50
WF15 Jarret Stoll 1.00 2.50
WF16 Nathan Horton 1.00 2.50
WF17 Dustin Brown 1.00 2.50
WF18 Alexander Frolov 1.00 2.50
WF19 Marian Gaborik 2.00 5.00
WF20 Mikko Koivu 1.00 2.50
WF21 Corey Perry 1.50 4.00
WF22 Thomas Vanek 1.50 4.00
WF23 Michael Ryder 1.50 4.00
WF24 Chris Higgins 1.00 2.50
WF25 Zach Parise 1.00 2.50
WF26 Rick DiPietro 1.50 4.00
WF27 Henrik Lundqvist 1.50 4.00
WF28 Petr Prucha 1.00 2.50
WF29 Jason Spezza 1.50 4.00
WF30 Dany Heatley 2.00 5.00
WF31 Martin Havlat 1.50 4.00
WF32 Jeff Carter 1.50 4.00
WF33 Joni Pitkanen 1.00 2.50
WF34 Mike Richards 1.50 4.00
WF35 Sidney Crosby 8.00 20.00
WF36 Marc-Andre Fleury 2.00 5.00
WF37 Steve Bernier 1.00 2.50
WF38 Alexander Steen 1.50 4.00
WF39 Kyle Wellwood 1.00 2.50
WF40 Andrew Raycroft 1.50 4.00
WF41 Ryan Kesler 1.00 2.50
WF42 Alexander Ovechkin 3.00 8.00

1972-73 Flames Postcards

This 20-card set of the Atlanta Flames measured 3 1/2" by 5 1/2". The fronts featured color action player photos with a white border. The player's autograph was across the bottom of the photo. The backs were blank. The cards were unnumbered and checklisted below in alphabetical order.

COMPLETE SET (20) 30.00 60.00
1 Curt Bennett 1.00 2.00
2 Dan Bouchard 2.50 5.00
3 Rey Comeau 1.00 2.00
4 BoomBoom Geoffrion CO 5.00 10.00
5 Bob Leiter 1.00 2.00
6 Kerry Ketter 1.00 2.00
7 Billy MacMillan 1.00 2.00
8 Randy Manery 1.00 2.00
9 Keith McCreary 1.00 2.00
10 Lew Morrison 1.00 2.00
11 Phil Myre 3.00 6.00
12 Bob Paradise 1.00 2.00
13 Noel Picard 1.00 2.00
14 Bill Plager 1.50 3.00
15 Noel Price 1.50 3.00
16 Pat Quinn 2.50 5.00
17 Jacques Richard 1.50 3.00
18 Leon Rochefort 1.00 2.00
19 Larry Romanchych 1.00 2.00
20 John Stewart 1.00 2.00

1978-79 Flames Majik Market

This 20 card set was issued during the 1978-79 season and features members of the Atlanta Flames. The front had an action shot as well as a facsimile autograph. The back had the player's name, uniform number and some personal statistics. At the bottom, sponsors "Coca-Cola Bottling" and radio station WTLA are credited. Pat Ribble, who was traded during the season, was the most difficult card to obtain and is listed as an SP. We have checklisted this set by the uniform number.

COMPLETE SET (19) 15.00 30.00
1 Rejean Lemelin 1.50 3.00
2 Greg Fox .50 1.00
3 Pat Ribble SP 5.00 10.00
5 Brad Marsh 2.00 4.00
6 Ken Houston .50 1.00
7 Bobby LaLonde .50 1.00
8 David Shand .50 1.00
9 Jean Pronovost .75 1.50
10 Bill Clement 1.50 3.00
11 Bob MacMillan .50 1.00
12 Tom Lysiak 1.00 2.00
15 Rod Seiling .50 1.00
16 Guy Chouinard 1.00 2.00
19 Ed Kea .50 1.00
20 Bob Murdoch .75 1.50
24 Harold Phillipoff .50 1.00
25 Willi Plett 1.00 2.00
27 Eric Vail 1.00 2.00
30 Daniel Bouchard 1.50 3.00

1979-80 Flames Postcards

This 20-card set was sponsored by the Atlanta Coca-Cola Bottling Company, Winn Dixie, and radio station WLTA-100. The set was in the postcard format, with each card measuring approximately 3 1/2" by 5 1/2". The fronts featured full-bleed color action shots; a facsimile autograph was inscribed across the lower portion of the pictures. The backs carried the player's name, uniform number, biography, and sponsor logos. The cards were unnumbered and checklisted below in alphabetical order.

COMPLETE SET (20) 15.00 30.00
1 Curt Bennett .50 1.00
2 Dan Bouchard 1.50 3.00
3 Guy Chouinard 1.00 2.00
4 Bill Clement 2.00 4.00
5 Jim Craig 2.50 5.00
6 Ken Houston .50 1.00
7 Don Lever .50 1.00
8 Bob MacMillan .50 1.00
9 Brad Marsh 2.50 5.00
10 Bob Murdoch .50 1.00
11 Kent Nilsson 2.50 5.00
12 Willi Plett 1.25 2.50
13 Jean Pronovost .75 1.50
14 Pekka Rautakallio .50 1.00
15 Paul Reinhart .75 1.50
16 Pat Riggin 1.25 2.50
17 Phil Russell .50 1.00
18 David Shand .50 1.00
19 Garry Unger 1.50 3.00
20 Eric Vail .75 1.50

1979-80 Flames Team Issue

Cards measured 3 3/4 x 5 1/4 and featured black and white action photos on the front along with a facsimile signature. Backs were blank. Cards were unnumbered and checklisted below in alphabetical order.

COMPLETE SET (22) 20.00 40.00
1 Curt Bennett .50 1.00
2 Ivan Boldirev .50 1.00
3 Dan Bouchard 1.50 3.00
4 Guy Chouinard 1.00 2.00
5 Bill Clement 1.00 2.50
6 Jim Craig 2.00 4.00
7 Ken Houston .50 1.00
8 Brad Marsh 1.50 3.00
9 Bob MacMillan .50 1.00
10 Al MacNeil .50 1.00
11 Bob Murdoch .75 1.50
12 Kent Nilsson 2.00 4.00
13 Willi Plett 1.00 2.00
14 Jean Pronovost .75 1.50
15 Pekka Rautakallio .50 1.00
16 Paul Reinhart .75 1.50
17 Pat Riggin 1.00 2.00
18 Darcy Rota .50 1.00
19 Phil Russell .50 1.00
20 David Shand .50 1.00
21 Garry Unger 1.25 2.50
22 Eric Vail 1.00 2.00

1980-81 Flames Postcards

This 24-postcard set measured approximately 3 3/4" by 5". The fronts featured borderless posed color player photos. The backs were blank. The cards were unnumbered and checklisted below in alphabetical order.

COMPLETE SET (24) 20.00 40.00
1 Daniel Bouchard 1.25 3.00
2 Guy Chouinard .75 2.00
3 Bill Clement .75 2.00
4 Denis Cyr .40 1.00
5 Randy Holt .40 1.00
6 Ken Houston .40 1.00
7 Rejean Lemelin 2.50 5.00
8 Kevin Lavallee .40 1.00
9 Don Lever .40 1.00
10 Bob MacMillan .40 1.00
11 Bob Murdoch .40 1.00
12 Brad Marsh 1.00 2.50
13 Kent Nilsson 1.50 4.00
14 Willi Plett .60 1.50
15 Jim Peplinski 1.00 2.50
16 Pekka Rautakallio .75 2.00
17 Paul Reinhart 1.00 2.50
18 Pat Riggin .75 2.00
19 Phil Russell .40 1.00
20 Brad Smith .40 1.00
21 Jay Soleway .40 1.00
22 Eric Vail .60 1.50
23 Bert Wilson .40 1.00
24 Team Photo .60 1.50

1981-82 Flames Postcards

This 20-postcard set measured approximately 3 3/4" by 5". The fronts featured borderless posed color player photos. The backs were blank. The cards are unnumbered and checklisted below in alphabetical order.

COMPLETE SET (20) 10.00 25.00
1 Charlie Bourgeois .30 .75
2 Mel Bridgman .40 1.00
3 Guy Chouinard .60 1.50
4 Bill Clement .60 1.50
5 Denis Cyr .30 .75
6 Jamie Hislop .30 .75
7 Ken Houston .30 .75
8 Steve Konroyd .30 .75
9 Dan Labraaten .30 .75
10 Kevin Lavallee .30 .75
11 Rejean Lemelin 1.25 3.00
12 Lanny McDonald 1.25 3.00
13 Gary McAdam .30 .75
14 Bob Murdoch .40 1.00
15 Jim Peplinski .75 2.00
16 Willi Plett .60 1.50
17 Pekka Rautakallio .40 1.00
18 Paul Reinhart .60 1.50
19 Pat Riggin .60 1.50
20 Phil Russell .30 .75

1982-83 Flames Dollars

These six cards, measuring approximately 3" by 5" and perforated on each end, were issued with "Hockey Dollars" or what may be better described as silver-colored coins. Each coin (measuring approximately 1 1/4" in diameter) displayed an engraving of the player's face on the obverse and the team logo on the reverse. The card fronts were gray with tan lettering. They had the player's name, number, year, team logo, and a picture of the coin. In a horizontal format, the backs carried biography, career highlights, and career statistics. The cards were numbered on the back in the upper right corner. The prices below refer to the coin-card combination intact.

COMPLETE SET (6) 10.00 25.00
1 Mel Bridgman 1.50 4.00
2 Don Edwards 1.50 4.00
3 Lanny McDonald DP 3.00 8.00
4 Kent Nilsson 2.50 6.00
5 Jim Peplinski 1.50 4.00
6 Paul Reinhart 2.00 5.00

1985-86 Flames Red Rooster

This 30-card set of Calgary Flames was sponsored by Red Rooster Food Stores, Old Dutch Potato Chips, and Post Cereals. The player cards could be collected from any Red Rooster Food Stores. The cards measured approximately 2 3/4" by 3 5/8" and featured on the front a color posed head shot (with rounded corners) of the player, with a facsimile autograph in white ink in the lower right-hand corner of the picture. The player's name, uniform number, the Calgary Flames' logo, and a hockey tip appeared below the picture. The back had biographical and statistical information on the top portion, while the bottom has sponsor advertisements and the anti-crime slogan "Support Crime Stoppers." The set included two different cards of Lanny McDonald and Doug Risebrough. Al MacInnis appeared in his Rookie Card year whereas Mike Vernon's appearance predated his Rookie Card by two years.

COMPLETE SET (30) 10.00 25.00
1 Paul Baxter .15 .40
2 Ed Beers .15 .40
3 Perry Berezan .15 .40
4 Charlie Bourgeois .15 .40
5 Steve Bozek .15 .40
6 Gino Cavallini .15 .40
7 Marc D'Amour .20 .50
8 Tim Hunter .40 1.00
9 Bob Johnson CO 1.00 2.50
10 Steve Konroyd .15 .40
11 Richard Kromm .15 .40
12 Rejean Lemelin .40 1.00
13 Hakan Loob .40 1.00
14 Lanny McDonald .75 2.00
15 Lanny McDonald .75 2.00
16 Al MacInnis 2.50 6.00
17 Jamie Macoun .20 .50
18 Bob Murdoch CO .15 .40
19 Joel Otto .60 1.50
20 Pierre Page CO .20 .50
21 Colin Patterson .15 .40
22 Jim Peplinski .30 .75
23 Dan Quinn .20 .50
24 Paul Reinhart .30 .75
25 Doug Risebrough .15 .40
26 Doug Risebrough .15 .40
27 Neil Sheehy .15 .40
28 Gary Suter .40 1.00
29 Mike Vernon 2.50 6.00
(No facsimile autograph on card front)
30 Carey Wilson .15 .40

1986-87 Flames Red Rooster

This 30-card set of Calgary Flames was sponsored by Red Rooster Food Stores in conjunction with Old Dutch Potato Chips. The player cards could be collected from any Red Rooster Food Stores. The cards measured approximately 2 3/4" by 3 5/8" and featured a color posed photo (with rounded corners) of the player, with a facsimile autograph in blue ink across the bottom of the picture. The player's name, uniform number, the Calgary Flames' logo, and a hockey tip appeared below the picture. The back had biographical and statistical information on the top portion, while the bottom had sponsor advertisements and the anti-crime slogan "Support Crime Stoppers." The set included two different cards of Lanny McDonald, Joe Mullen, and Paul Reinhart. Gary Roberts' card predated his Rookie Card year by three years.

COMPLETE SET (30) 8.00 20.00
1 Paul Baxter .20 .50
2 Perry Berezan .20 .50
3 Steve Bozek .20 .50
4 Brian Bradley .40 1.00
5 Brian Engblom .20 .50
6 Nick Fotiu .20 .50
7 Tim Hunter .30 .75
8 Bob Johnson CO .75 2.00
9 Rejean Lemelin .40 1.00
10 Hakan Loob .40 1.00
11 Al MacInnis 1.25 3.00
12 Jamie Macoun .20 .50
13 Lanny McDonald .60 1.50
14 Lanny McDonald .60 1.50
15 Joe Mullen .60 1.50
16 Joe Mullen .60 1.50
17 Bob Murdoch CO .20 .50
18 Joel Otto .40 1.00
19 Pierre Page CO .20 .50
20 Colin Patterson .20 .50
21 Jim Peplinski .20 .50
22 Paul Reinhart .20 .50
23 Paul Reinhart .20 .50
24 Doug Risebrough .20 .50
25 Gary Roberts 1.50 4.00
26 Neil Sheehy .20 .50
27 Gary Suter .30 .75
28 John Tonelli .30 .75
29 Mike Vernon 1.25 3.00
30 Carey Wilson .20 .50

1987-88 Flames Red Rooster

This 30-card set of Calgary Flames was sponsored by Red Rooster Food Stores, and the player cards could be collected from any of these stores. The cards measured 2 11/16" by 3 9/16" and featured on the front a color posed head-and-shoulders shot (with rounded corners) of the player, with a facsimile autograph in blue ink across the bottom of the picture. The player's name, uniform number, the Calgary Flames' logo, and a hockey tip appeared below the picture. The back had biographical and statistical information on the top portion, while the bottom had a sponsor advertisement and the anti-crime slogan "Support Crime Stoppers." The set included two different cards of Hakan Loob, Lanny McDonald, and Joe Nieuwendyk. The Brett Hull and Joe Nieuwendyk cards were the key cards in the set since they pre-dated their O-Pee-Chee and Topps Rookie Cards by one year.

COMPLETE SET (30) 20.00 50.00
1 Perry Berezan .15 .40
2 Steve Bozek .15 .40
3 Mike Bullard .20 .50
4 Shane Churla .30 .75
5 Terry Crisp CO .15 .40
6 Doug Dadswell .20 .50
7 Brian Glynn .15 .40
8 Brett Hull 12.00 30.00
9 Tim Hunter .20 .50
10 Hakan Loob .30 .75
11 Hakan Loob .30 .75
12 Al MacInnis .75 2.00
13 Brad McCrimmon .20 .50
14 Lanny McDonald .40 1.00
15 Lanny McDonald .40 1.00
16 Joe Mullen .40 1.00
17 Dana Murzyn .15 .40
18 Ric Nattress .15 .40
19 Joe Nieuwendyk 2.50 6.00
20 Joe Nieuwendyk 2.50 6.00
21 Joel Otto .30 .75
22 Pierre Page CO .15 .40
23 Colin Patterson .15 .40
24 Jim Peplinski .20 .50
25 Paul Reinhart .20 .50
26 Doug Risebrough CO .15 .40
27 Gary Roberts .75 2.00
28 Gary Suter .30 .75
29 John Tonelli .20 .50
30 Mike Vernon .75 2.00

1990-91 Flames IGA/McGavin's

This 30-card standard size set was sponsored by IGA food stores in conjunction with McGavin's, a distributor of bread and other products in Alberta. Protected by a cello pack, one card was inserted in bread loaves distributed by McGavin's to IGA stores in Calgary and Edmonton. Calgary consumers received a Flames' card, while Edmonton consumers received an Oilers' card. Checklist and coaches cards were not inserted in the loaves but were included on five hundred individually numbered and uncut sheets not offered to the general public. The cards were printed on thin card stock. The fronts had posed color player photos, with a border that shaded from red to orange and back to red. The player's name was printed in the bottom border, and his uniform number was printed in a circle in the upper left corner of each picture. The horizontally oriented backs featured biographical information, with year-by-year statistics presented in a pink rectangle. Sponsor logos at the bottom round ed out the back. The cards were unnumbered and checklisted below in alphabetical order.

Card	Low	High
COMPLETE SET (30)	14.00	35.00
1 Paul Baxter CO SP	1.25	3.00
2 Guy Charron CO SP	1.50	4.00
3 Theo Fleury	2.00	5.00
4 Doug Gilmour	2.00	5.00
5 Jiri Hrdina	.20	.50
6 Mark Hunter	.20	.50
7 Tim Hunter	.40	1.00
8 Roger Johansson	.20	.50
9 Al MacInnis	.75	2.00
10 Brian MacLellan	.20	.50
11 Jamie Macoun	.30	.75
12 Sergei Makarov	.60	1.50
13 Sergei Makarov (Calder Trophy Winner) and Al MacInnis (NHL First AS Team& Defence 1989-90)	.60	1.50
14 Stephane Matteau	.30	.75
15 Dana Murzyn	.20	.50
16 Frantisek Musil	.20	.50
17 Ric Nattress	.20	.50
18 Joe Nieuwendyk	1.25	3.00
19 Joel Otto	.40	1.00
20 Colin Patterson	.20	.50
21 Sergei Priakin	.20	.50
22 Paul Ranheim	.30	.75
23 Robert Reichel	.60	1.50
24 Doug Risebrough SP CO/GM	1.25	3.00
25 Gary Roberts	.75	2.00
26 Gary Suter	.40	1.00
27 Tim Sweeney	.20	.50
28 Mike Vernon	.75	2.00
29 Rick Wamsley	.40	1.00
30 Checklist Card SP	1.25	3.00

1991 Flames Panini Team Stickers

This 32-sticker set was issued in a plastic bag that contained two 16-sticker sheets (approximately 9" by 12") and a foldout poster, "Super Poster - Hockey 91", on which the stickers could be affixed. The players' names appeared only on the poster, not on the stickers. Each sticker measured about 2 1/8" by 2 7/8" and featured a color player action shot on its white-bordered front. The back of the white sticker sheet was lined off into 16 panels, each carried the logos for Panini, the NHL, and the NHLPA, as well as the same number that appears on the front of the sticker. Every Canadian NHL team was featured in this promotion. Each team set was available by mail-order from Panini Canada Ltd. for 2.99 plus 50 cents for shipping and handling.

Card	Low	High
COMPLETE SET (32)	1.50	4.00
1 Theo Fleury	.30	.75
2 Doug Gilmour	.30	.75
3 Jiri Hrdina	.01	.05
4 Mark Hunter	.01	.05
5 Tim Hunter	.02	.10
6 Roger Johansson	.01	.05
7 Al MacInnis	.15	.40
8 Brian MacLellan	.01	.05
9 Jamie Macoun	.01	.05
10 Sergei Makarov	.08	.25
11 Stephane Matteau	.01	.05
12 Dana Murzyn	.01	.05
13 Ric Nattress	.01	.05
14 Joe Nieuwendyk	.15	.40
15 Joel Otto	.05	.15
16 Colin Patterson	.01	.05
17 Sergei Priakin	.01	.05
18 Paul Ranheim	.02	.10
19 Gary Roberts	.15	.40
20 Ken Sabourin	.01	.05
21 Gary Suter	.02	.10
22 Tim Sweeney	.01	.05
23 Mike Vernon	.15	.40
24 Rick Wamsley	.02	.10
A Team Logo Left Side	.01	.05
B Team Logo Right Side	.01	.05
C Flames' Time Out Upper Left Corner	.01	.05
D Flames' Time Out Lower Left Corner	.01	.05
E Flames' Time Out Upper Right Corner	.01	.05
F Flames' Time Out Lower Right Corner	.01	.05
G Joel Otto Roger Johansson	.02	.10
H Gary Suter	.02	.10

1991-92 Flames IGA

This 30-card standard-size set of Calgary Flames was sponsored by IGA food stores and included manufacturers' discount coupons. One pack of cards was distributed in Calgary and Edmonton IGA stores with any grocery purchase of 10.00 or more. The cards were printed on thin card stock. The fronts had posed color action photos bordered in red. The player's name was printed vertically in the wider left border, and his uniform number and the team name appeared at the bottom of the picture. In black print on a white background, the backs presented biography and statistics (regular season and playoff). Packs were kept under the cash drawer, and therefore many of the cards were creased. Each pack contained three Oilers and two Flames cards. The checklist and coaches cards for both teams were not included in the packs but were available on a very limited basis through an uncut team sheet offer. Also the Osiecki card seemed to be in short supply, either because of short printing or short distribution. The cards were unnumbered and checklisted below in alphabetical order, with the coaches cards listed after the players.

Card	Low	High
COMPLETE SET (30)	10.00	25.00
1 Theo Fleury	1.00	2.50
2 Tomas Forslund	.15	.40
3 Doug Gilmour	1.00	2.50
4 Marc Habscheid	.15	.40
5 Tim Hunter	.25	.60
6 Jim Kyte	.15	.40
7 Al MacInnis	.40	1.00
8 Jamie Macoun	.15	.40
9 Sergei Makarov	.40	1.00
10 Stephane Matteau	.15	.40
11 Frantisek Musil	.15	.40
12 Ric Nattress	.15	.40
13 Joe Nieuwendyk	.50	1.25
14 Mark Osiecki	.75	2.00
15 Joel Otto	.25	.60
16 Paul Ranheim	.15	.40
17 Robert Reichel	.30	.75
18 Gary Roberts	.40	1.00
19 Neil Sheehy	.15	.40
20 Martin Simard	.15	.40
21 Ronnie Stern	.15	.40
22 Gary Suter	.30	.75
23 Tim Sweeney	.15	.40
24 Mike Vernon	.40	1.00
25 Rick Wamsley	.30	.75
26 Carey Wilson	.15	.40
27 Paul Baxter CO SP	1.00	2.50
28 Guy Charron CO SP	1.00	2.50
29 Doug Risebrough CO SP	1.00	2.50
30 Checklist Card SP	1.00	2.50

1992-93 Flames IGA

Sponsored by IGA food stores, the 30 standard-size cards comprising this Special Edition Collector Series set featured color player action shots on their fronts. Each photo was trimmed with a black line and offset flush with the thin white border on the right, which surrounds the card. On the remaining three sides, the picture was edged with a gray and white netlike pattern. The player's name appeard in the upper right and the Flames logo rested in the lower left. The back carried the player's name at the top, with his position, uniform number, biography, and stat table set within a reddish-gray screened background. The Flames logo in the upper right rounded out the card.

Card	Low	High
COMPLETE SET (30)	8.00	20.00
1 Checklist	.02	.10
2 Craig Berube	.20	.50
3 Gary Leeman	.15	.40
4 Joel Otto	.30	.75
5 Robert Reichel	.40	1.00
6 Gary Roberts	.40	1.00
7 Greg Smyth	.15	.40
8 Gary Suter	.30	.75
9 Jeff Reese	.25	.60
10 Mike Vernon	.40	1.00
11 Carey Wilson	.15	.40
12 Trent Yawney	.15	.40
13 Michel Petit	.15	.40
14 Paul Ranheim	.15	.40
15 Sergei Makarov	.40	1.00
16 Frantisek Musil	.15	.40
17 Joe Nieuwendyk	.75	2.00
18 Alexander Godynyuk	.15	.40
19 Roger Johansson	.15	.40
20 Theo Fleury	1.00	2.50
21 Chris Lindberg	.15	.40
22 Al MacInnis	.60	1.50
23 Kevin Dahl	.15	.40
24 Chris Dahlquist	.15	.40
25 Ronnie Stern	.20	.50
26 Dave King CO	.15	.40
27 Guy Charron CO	.02	.10
28 Slavomir Lener CO	.02	.10
29 Jamie Hislop CO	.02	.10
30 Franchise History	.02	.10

1997-98 Flames Collector's Photos

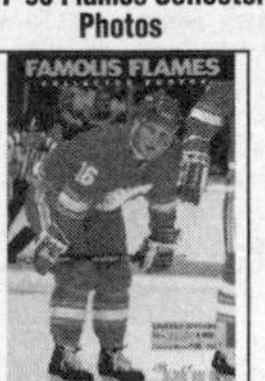

COMPLETE SET (20)
COMMON CARD (1-20)
1 Mike Vernon
2 Theoren Fleury
3 Trevor Kidd
4 Aaron Gavey
5 Mike Peluso
6 Derek Morris
7 Brian Sutter
8 Ron Stern
9 Joe Nieuwendyk
10 Andrew Cassels
11 Joel Otto
12 Todd Simpson
13 Lanny McDonald
14 Marty McInnis
15 Dave Gagner
16 Brett Hull
17 Cale Hulse
18 Doug Gilmour
19 Sandy McCarthy
20 Tim Hunter

1994-95 Fleer

This set was issued in a single 250-card series. Cards were issued in 12-card hobby and 18-card jumbo packs. There were four different card front designs, one unique to each of the NHL's divisions. Each card front had personal information in varying positions on the card. The card backs were all similar as they featured two photos, the player's name and expanded statistics. Rookie Cards included Mariusz Czerkawski, Blaine Lacher, David Oliver, Radek Bonk and Jim Carey.

Card	Low	High
COMPLETE SET (250)	8.00	20.00
1 Patrik Carnback	.02	.10
2 Bob Corkum	.02	.10
3 Paul Kariya	.10	.30
4 Valeri Karpov RC	.02	.10
5 Tom Kurvers	.02	.10
6 John Lilley	.02	.10
7 Mikhail Shtalenkov RC	.02	.10
8 Oleg Tverdovsky	.05	.15
9 Ray Bourque	.20	.50
10 Mariusz Czerkawski RC	.10	.30
11 John Gruden RC	.02	.10
12 Al Iafrate	.02	.10
13 Blaine Lacher RC	.05	.15
14 Mats Naslund	.02	.10
15 Cam Neely	.10	.30
16 Adam Oates	.05	.15
17 Bryan Smolinski	.02	.10
18 Don Sweeney	.02	.10
19 Donald Audette	.02	.10
20 Dominik Hasek	.25	.60
21 Dale Hawerchuk	.05	.15
22 Yuri Khmylev	.02	.10
23 Pat LaFontaine	.10	.30
24 Brad May	.02	.10
25 Alexander Mogilny	.05	.15
26 Derek Plante	.02	.10
27 Richard Smehlik	.02	.10
28 Steve Chiasson	.02	.10
29 Theo Fleury	.02	.10
30 Phil Housley	.05	.15
31 Trevor Kidd	.05	.15
32 Joe Nieuwendyk	.05	.15
33 James Patrick	.02	.10
34 Robert Reichel	.02	.10
35 Gary Roberts	.02	.10
36 German Titov	.02	.10
37 Tony Amonte	.02	.10
38 Ed Belfour	.10	.30
39 Chris Chelios	.10	.30
40 Dirk Graham	.02	.10
41 Sergei Krivokrasov	.02	.10
42 Joe Murphy	.02	.10
43 Bernie Nicholls	.05	.15
44 Patrick Poulin	.02	.10
45 Jeremy Roenick	.15	.40
46 Steve Smith	.02	.10
47 Gary Suter	.02	.10
48 Russ Courtnall	.02	.10
49 Dave Gagner	.05	.15
50 Brent Gilchrist	.02	.10
51 Todd Harvey	.02	.10
52 Derian Hatcher	.02	.10
53 Kevin Hatcher	.02	.10
54 Mike Kennedy RC	.02	.10
55 Mike Modano	.05	.15
56 Andy Moog	.10	.30
57 Dino Ciccarelli	.05	.15
58 Paul Coffey	.10	.30
59 Sergei Fedorov	.15	.40
60 Vladimir Konstantinov	.05	.15
61 Slava Kozlov	.05	.15
62 Nicklas Lidstrom	.10	.30
63 Chris Osgood	.20	.50
64 Keith Primeau	.05	.15
65 Ray Sheppard	.05	.15
66 Mike Vernon	.05	.15
67 Steve Yzerman	.60	1.50
68 Jason Arnott	.02	.10
69 Shayne Corson	.02	.10
70 Igor Kravchuk	.02	.10
71 Todd Marchant	.02	.10
72 Roman Oksiuta	.02	.10
73 Fredrik Olausson	.02	.10
74 David Oliver RC	.02	.10
75 Bill Ranford	.05	.15
76 Stu Barnes	.02	.10
77 Jesse Belanger	.02	.10
78 Keith Brown	.02	.10
79 Bob Kudelski	.02	.10
80 Scott Mellanby	.05	.15
81 Gord Murphy	.02	.10
82 Rob Niedermayer	.05	.15
83 John Vanbiesbrouck	.05	.15
84 Sean Burke	.05	.15
85 Jimmy Carson	.02	.10
86 Andrew Cassels	.02	.10
87 Andrei Nikolishin	.02	.10
88 Chris Pronger	.10	.30
89 Geoff Sanderson	.05	.15
90 Darren Turcotte	.02	.10
91 Pat Verbeek	.02	.10
92 Glen Wesley	.02	.10
93 Rob Blake	.05	.15
94 Wayne Gretzky	.75	2.00
95 Kelly Hrudey	.05	.15
96 Jari Kurri	.05	.15
97 Eric Lacroix	.02	.10
98 Marty McSorley	.02	.10
99 Jamie Storr	.05	.15
100 Rick Tocchet	.05	.15
101 Brian Bellows	.02	.10
102 Patrice Brisebois	.02	.10
103 Vincent Damphousse	.02	.10
104 Kirk Muller	.02	.10
105 Lyle Odelein	.02	.10
106 Mark Recchi	.05	.15
107 Patrick Roy	.60	1.50
108 Brian Savage	.02	.10
109 Mathieu Schneider	.02	.10
110 Turner Stevenson	.02	.10
111 Martin Brodeur	.30	.75
112 Bill Guerin	.05	.15
113 Claude Lemieux	.02	.10
114 John MacLean	.05	.15
115 Scott Niedermayer	.02	.10
116 Stephane Richer	.05	.15
117 Brian Rolston	.02	.10
118 Alexander Semak	.02	.10
119 Scott Stevens	.05	.15
120 Ray Ferraro	.02	.10
121 Patrick Flatley	.02	.10
122 Darius Kasparaitis	.02	.10
123 Derek King	.02	.10
124 Scott Lachance	.02	.10
125 Brett Lindros	.02	.10
126 Vladimir Malakhov	.02	.10
127 Jamie McLennan	.05	.15
128 Zigmund Palffy	.05	.15
129 Steve Thomas	.02	.10
130 Pierre Turgeon	.05	.15
131 Jeff Beukeboom	.02	.10
132 Adam Graves	.05	.15
133 Alexei Kovalev	.05	.15
134 Steve Larmer	.05	.15
135 Brian Leetch	.10	.30
136 Mark Messier	.10	.30
137 Petr Nedved	.05	.15
138 Sergei Nemchinov	.02	.10
139 Mike Richter	.10	.30
140 Sergei Zubov	.02	.10
141 Don Beaupre	.05	.15
142 Radek Bonk RC	.10	.30
143 Alexandre Daigle	.02	.10
144 Pavol Demitra	.02	.10
145 Pat Elynuik	.02	.10
146 Rob Gaudreau	.02	.10
147 Sean Hill	.02	.10
148 Sylvain Turgeon	.02	.10
149 Alexei Yashin	.02	.10
150 Rod Brind'Amour	.05	.15
151 Eric Desjardins	.05	.15
152 Gilbert Dionne	.02	.10
153 Garry Galley	.02	.10
154 Ron Hextall	.05	.15
155 Patrik Juhlin RC	.02	.10
156 John LeClair	.10	.30
157 Eric Lindros	.10	.30
158 Mikael Renberg	.05	.15
159 Chris Therien	.02	.10
160 Dimitri Yushkevich	.02	.10
161 Len Barrie	.02	.10
162 Ron Francis	.05	.15
163 Jaromir Jagr	.20	.50
164 Shawn McEachern	.02	.10
165 Joe Mullen	.05	.15
166 Larry Murphy	.05	.15
167 Luc Robitaille	.05	.15
168 Ulf Samuelsson	.02	.10
169 Tomas Sandstrom	.02	.10
170 Kevin Stevens	.02	.10
171 Martin Straka	.02	.10
172 Ken Wregget	.05	.15
173 Wendel Clark	.05	.15
174 Adam Deadmarsh	.02	.10
175 Stephane Fiset	.05	.15
176 Peter Forsberg	.40	1.00
177 Valeri Kamensky	.05	.15
178 Andrei Kovalenko	.02	.10
179 Uwe Krupp	.02	.10
180 Sylvain Lefebvre	.02	.10
181 Owen Nolan	.05	.15
182 Mike Ricci	.02	.10
183 Joe Sakic	.25	.60
184 Denis Chasse RC	.02	.10
185 Adam Creighton	.02	.10
186 Steve Duchesne	.02	.10
187 Brett Hull	.15	.40
188 Curtis Joseph	.10	.30
189 Ian Laperriere RC	.02	.10
190 Al MacInnis	.05	.15
191 Brendan Shanahan	.10	.30
192 Patrice Tardif RC	.02	.10
193 Esa Tikkanen	.02	.10
194 Ulf Dahlen	.02	.10
195 Pat Falloon	.02	.10
196 Jeff Friesen	.02	.10
197 Arturs Irbe	.05	.15
198 Sergei Makarov	.02	.10
199 Andrei Nazarov	.02	.10
200 Sandis Ozolinsh	.02	.10
201 Michal Sykora	.02	.10
202 Ray Whitney	.02	.10
203 Brian Bradley	.02	.10
204 Shawn Chambers	.02	.10
205 Eric Charron	.02	.10
206 Chris Gratton	.02	.10
207 Roman Hamrlik	.05	.15
208 Petr Klima	.02	.10
209 Daren Puppa	.05	.15
210 Alexander Selivanov RC	.02	.10
211 Jason Wiemer RC	.02	.10
212 Dave Andreychuk	.05	.15
213 Dave Ellett	.02	.10
214 Mike Gartner	.05	.15
215 Doug Gilmour	.05	.15
216 Kenny Jonsson	.02	.10
217 Dmitri Mironov	.02	.10
218 Felix Potvin	.10	.30
219 Mike Ridley	.02	.10
220 Mats Sundin	.10	.30
221 Josef Beranek	.02	.10
222 Jeff Brown	.02	.10
223 Pavel Bure	.10	.30
224 Geoff Courtnall	.02	.10
225 Trevor Linden	.05	.15
226 Jyrki Lumme	.02	.10
227 Kirk McLean	.05	.15
228 Gino Odjick	.02	.10
229 Mike Peca	.02	.10
230 Cliff Ronning	.02	.10
231 Jason Allison	.02	.10
232 Peter Bondra	.05	.15
233 Jim Carey RC	.10	.30
234 Sylvain Cote	.02	.10
235 Dale Hunter	.02	.10
236 Joe Juneau	.05	.15
237 Dimitri Khristich	.02	.10
238 Pat Peake	.02	.10
239 Mark Tinordi	.02	.10
240 Nelson Emerson	.02	.10
241 Michal Grosek	.02	.10
242 Nikolai Khabibulin	.05	.15
243 Dave Manson	.02	.10
244 Stephane Quintal	.02	.10
245 Teemu Selanne	.10	.30
246 Keith Tkachuk	.10	.30
247 Alexei Zhamnov	.05	.15
248 Checklist	.02	.10
249 Checklist	.02	.10
250 Checklist	.02	.10

1994-95 Fleer Franchise Futures

The 10-card set was randomly inserted at a rate of 1:7 12-card hobby packs. The set featured young stars of the NHL in action photos positioned over the card title. The background was in the color of the team. The back had a photo and player information.

Card	Low	High
COMPLETE SET (10)	5.00	10.00
1 Jason Arnott	.40	1.00
2 Rob Blake	.60	1.50
3 Adam Graves	.40	1.00
4 Arturs Irbe	.60	1.50
5 Joe Juneau	.60	1.50
6 Sandis Ozolinsh	.40	1.00
7 Mikael Renberg	.60	1.50
8 Keith Tkachuk	1.25	3.00
9 Alexei Yashin	.40	1.00
10 Sergei Zubov	.40	1.00

1994-95 Fleer Headliners

This 10-card set was randomly inserted in packs at the rate of 1:4. The set featured the superstars of the league in a borderless design. The word "Headliner", the player's name and team were printed in silver foil on the lower portion of the card front. A photo and informative text were on the back.

Card	Low	High
COMPLETE SET (10)	8.00	15.00
1 Pavel Bure	.60	1.50
2 Sergei Fedorov	.75	2.00
3 Doug Gilmour	.30	.75
4 Wayne Gretzky	4.00	10.00
5 Brian Leetch	.60	1.50
6 Eric Lindros	.60	1.50
7 Mark Messier	.60	1.50
8 Cam Neely	.60	1.50
9 Mark Recchi	.30	.75
10 Brendan Shanahan	.60	1.50

1994-95 Fleer Netminders

The easiest of the Fleer insert sets, this 10-card set was found at the rate of 1:2 packs. The set featured the top goalies in the league in a silhouetted design. The word "Netminder" and the player's name were printed in gold foil on the front side portion of the card front. A portrait photo and player information were on the back.

Card	Low	High
COMPLETE SET (10)	3.00	8.00
1 Ed Belfour	.30	.75
2 Martin Brodeur	.75	2.00
3 Dominik Hasek	.60	1.50
4 Arturs Irbe	.15	.40
5 Curtis Joseph	.30	.75
6 Kirk McLean	.15	.40
7 Felix Potvin	.30	.75
8 Mike Richter	.30	.75
9 Patrick Roy	1.50	4.00
10 John Vanbiesbrouck	.15	.40

1994-95 Fleer Rookie Sensations

This 10-card set was randomly inserted at a rate of 1:7 jumbo retail packs. The set featured the top first-year stars of the league over a water-splashed design. The phrase "Rookie Sensation" along with the player's name were printed in silver foil in the center portion of the card front. A photo and text information were on the back.

Card	Low	High
COMPLETE SET (10)	10.00	25.00
1 Radek Bonk	.75	2.00
2 Peter Forsberg	4.00	10.00
3 Jeff Friesen	.75	2.00
4 Todd Harvey	.75	2.00
5 Paul Kariya	2.50	6.00
6 Blaine Lacher	.75	2.00
7 Brett Lindros	.75	2.00
8 Mike Peca	.75	2.00
9 Jamie Storr	.75	2.00
10 Oleg Tverdovsky	.75	2.00

1994-95 Fleer Slapshot Artists

The most difficult of the Fleer inserts, the ten cards in this set were inserted at the rate of 1:12 packs. The cards featured a silhouetted player photo surrounded by three smaller cut-out versions of the same photo. The background was in the team's color. The back had the player's photo and career information.

Card	Low	High
COMPLETE SET (10)	10.00	20.00
1 Wendel Clark	.75	2.00
2 Brett Hull	2.00	5.00
3 Al Iafrate	.50	1.25
4 Jaromir Jagr	2.50	6.00
5 Al MacInnis	.75	2.00
6 Mike Modano	.75	2.00
7 Stephane Richer	.75	2.00
8 Jeremy Roenick	2.00	5.00
9 Geoff Sanderson	.75	2.00
10 Steve Thomas	.50	1.25

1996-97 Fleer Promo Sheet

This sheet, which featured samples of John LeClair and Peter Ferraro regular cards, as well as a John LeClair Art Ross insert card, contained product and release date information for '96-97 Fleer. The cards were unnumbered, and would bear perforation marks if removed, distinguishing them from their regular counterparts. They are listed below as they appear on the sheet.

Card	Low	High
COMPLETE SET (3)	.40	1.00
1 John LeClair	.08	.25
2 John LeClair Art Ross insert	.30	.75
3 Peter Ferraro	.02	.10

1996-97 Fleer

This 150-card set was released in one series in 10-card packs for both the hobby and retail markets with an SRP of $1.49. Although rarely delving past first-line players, the set boasted a strong player selection. All major stars were represented, among them Wayne Gretzky's first card in a New York Rangers sweater. The only Rookie Card of note was Martin Biron.

Card	Low	High
COMPLETE SET (150)	7.50	15.00
1 Guy Hebert	.05	.15
2 Paul Kariya	.10	.30
3 Teemu Selanne	.10	.30
4 Ray Bourque	.20	.50
5 Kyle McLaren	.02	.10
6 Adam Oates	.05	.15
7 Bill Ranford	.05	.15
8 Rick Tocchet	.05	.15
9 Jason Dawe	.02	.10
10 Dominik Hasek	.25	.60
11 Pat LaFontaine	.10	.30
12 Theo Fleury	.02	.10
13 Trevor Kidd	.05	.15
14 German Titov	.02	.10
15 Ed Belfour	.10	.30
16 Chris Chelios	.10	.30
17 Eric Daze	.05	.15
18 Jeremy Roenick	.15	.40
19 Gary Suter	.02	.10
20 Peter Forsberg	.30	.75
21 Valeri Kamensky	.05	.15
22 Claude Lemieux	.02	.10
23 Sandis Ozolinsh	.02	.10
24 Patrick Roy	.60	1.50
25 Joe Sakic	.25	.60
26 Derian Hatcher	.02	.10
27 Mike Modano	.20	.50
28 Sergei Zubov	.02	.10
29 Paul Coffey	.10	.30
30 Sergei Fedorov	.15	.40
31 Vladimir Konstantinov	.05	.15
32 Slava Kozlov	.05	.15
33 Chris Osgood	.05	.15
34 Keith Primeau	.05	.15
35 Steve Yzerman	.60	1.50
36 Jason Arnott	.02	.10
37 Curtis Joseph	.10	.30
38 Doug Weight	.05	.15
39 Ed Jovanovski	.05	.15
40 Scott Mellanby	.05	.15
41 Rob Niedermayer	.05	.15
42 Ray Sheppard	.05	.15
43 Robert Svehla	.02	.10
44 John Vanbiesbrouck	.05	.15
45 Sean Burke	.05	.15
46 Andrew Cassels	.05	.15
47 Geoff Sanderson	.05	.15
48 Brendan Shanahan	.10	.30
49 Ray Ferraro	.02	.10
50 Dimitri Khristich	.02	.10
51 Vitali Yachmenev	.02	.10
52 Valeri Bure	.02	.10
53 Vincent Damphousse	.02	.10
54 Saku Koivu	.10	.30
55 Mark Recchi	.05	.15
56 Jocelyn Thibault	.10	.30
57 Pierre Turgeon	.05	.15
58 Martin Brodeur	.30	.75
59 Phil Housley	.05	.15
60 Scott Niedermayer	.02	.10
61 Scott Stevens	.05	.15
62 Steve Thomas	.05	.15
63 Todd Bertuzzi	.10	.30
64 Travis Green	.05	.15
65 Kenny Jonsson	.02	.10
66 Zigmund Palffy	.05	.15
67 Adam Graves	.02	.10
68 Wayne Gretzky	.75	2.00
69 Alexei Kovalev	.02	.10
70 Brian Leetch	.10	.30
71 Mark Messier	.10	.30
72 Niklas Sundstrom	.02	.10
73 Daniel Alfredsson	.05	.15
74 Radek Bonk	.02	.10
75 Steve Duchesne	.02	.10
76 Damian Rhodes	.05	.15
77 Alexei Yashin	.02	.10
78 Rod Brind'Amour	.05	.15
79 Eric Desjardins	.05	.15
80 Ron Hextall	.05	.15
81 John LeClair	.10	.30
82 Eric Lindros	.10	.30
83 Mikael Renberg	.05	.15
84 Tom Barrasso	.05	.15
85 Ron Francis	.05	.15
86 Jaromir Jagr	.20	.50
87 Mario Lemieux	.60	1.50
88 Petr Nedved	.05	.15
89 Bryan Smolinski	.02	.10
90 Nikolai Khabibulin	.05	.15
91 Teppo Numminen	.02	.10
92 Keith Tkachuk	.10	.30
93 Oleg Tverdovsky	.05	.15
94 Alexei Zhamnov	.02	.10
95 Shayne Corson	.02	.10
96 Grant Fuhr	.05	.15
97 Brett Hull	.15	.40
98 Al MacInnis	.05	.15
99 Chris Pronger	.05	.15
100 Owen Nolan	.05	.15
101 Marcus Ragnarsson	.02	.10
102 Chris Terreri	.05	.15
103 Brian Bradley	.02	.10
104 Roman Hamrlik	.05	.15
105 Daren Puppa	.05	.15
106 Alexander Selivanov	.02	.10
107 Doug Gilmour	.05	.15
108 Larry Murphy	.05	.15
109 Felix Potvin	.10	.30
110 Mats Sundin	.10	.30
111 Pavel Bure	.10	.30
112 Trevor Linden	.05	.15
113 Kirk McLean	.05	.15
114 Alexander Mogilny	.05	.15
115 Peter Bondra	.05	.15
116 Jim Carey	.10	.30
117 Sergei Gonchar	.02	.10
118 Joe Juneau	.02	.10
119 Michal Pivonka	.02	.10
120 Brendan Witt	.02	.10
121 Nolan Baumgartner	.02	.10
122 Martin Biron RC	1.00	2.50
123 Jason Bonsignore	.02	.10
124 Andrew Brunette RC	.20	.50
125 Jason Doig	.02	.10
126 Peter Ferraro	.02	.10
127 Eric Fichaud	.05	.15
128 Ladislav Kohn RC	.02	.10
129 Jamie Langenbrunner	.02	.10
130 Daymond Langkow	.05	.15
131 Jay McKee RC	.02	.10
132 Wayne Primeau RC	.02	.10
133 Jamie Storr RC	.05	.15
134 Jose Theodore	.15	.40
135 Roman Vopat RC	.02	.10
136 Rookie Scoring Leaders Daniel Alfredsson Valeri Bure Eric Daze Saku Koivu	.05	.15
137 Points Leaders Ron Francis Jaromir Jagr Mario Lemieux Joe Sakic	.10	.30
138 Goals Leaders Peter Bondra Jaromir Jagr Mario Lemieux Alexander Mogilny	.05	.15
139 Assists Leaders Peter Forsberg Ron Francis Jaromir Jagr Mario Lemieux	.10	.30
140 Defensive Points Leaders Ray Bourque Chris Chelios Paul Coffey Brian Leetch	.10	.30
141 Mario Lemieux Jaromir Jagr Paul Kariya Keith Tkachuk	.10	.30
142 Jaromir Jagr Sergei Fedorov John LeClair Claude Lemieux	.02	.10
143 Plus/Minus Leaders Sergei Federov Slava Fetisov Vladimir Konstantinov Petr Nedved	.02	.10
144 Goals Against Avg. Ldrs. Jim Carey Ron Hextall Chris Osgood Mike Vernon	.05	.15

145 Games Won Leaders .05 .15
Martin Brodeur
Jim Carey
Ron Hextall
Chris Osgood
146 Shutouts Leaders .05 .15
Martin Brodeur
Jim Carey
Chris Osgood
Daren Puppa
147 Dominik Hasek .05 .15
Daren Puppa
Jeff Hackett
Guy Hebert
148 Checklist (1-72) .02 .10
149 Checklist (73-150) .02 .10
150 Checklist (Inserts) .02 .10

1996-97 Fleer Art Ross

Randomly inserted in packs at a rate of 1:6, this 25-card set featured players in contention for the Art Ross trophy as the league's leading scorer.

COMPLETE SET (25) 20.00 50.00
1 Pavel Bure .60 1.50
2 Sergei Fedorov .75 2.00
3 Theo Fleury .20 .50
4 Peter Forsberg 1.50 4.00
5 Ron Francis .30 .75
6 Wayne Gretzky 5.00 10.00
7 Brett Hull .75 2.00
8 Jaromir Jagr 1.00 2.50
9 Valeri Kamensky .30 .75
10 Paul Kariya .60 1.50
11 Pat LaFontaine .60 1.50
12 John LeClair .60 1.50
13 Mario Lemieux 4.00 8.00
14 Eric Lindros .60 1.50
15 Mark Messier .60 1.50
16 Alexander Mogilny .30 .75
17 Petr Nedved .30 .75
18 Adam Oates .30 .75
19 Jeremy Roenick .75 2.00
20 Joe Sakic 1.25 3.00
21 Teemu Selanne .60 1.50
22 Keith Tkachuk .60 1.50
23 Pierre Turgeon .30 .75
24 Doug Weight .30 .75
25 Steve Yzerman 4.00 8.00

1996-97 Fleer Calder Candidates

Randomly inserted in packs at a rate of 1:96, this 10-card set featured up-and-comers poised to make a run at the Calder trophy, which is awarded to the NHL's rookie of the year.

COMPLETE SET (10) 8.00 20.00
1 Andrew Brunette .75 2.00
2 Jason Doig .75 2.00
3 Peter Ferraro .75 2.00
4 Eric Fichaud .75 2.00
5 Ladislav Kohn .75 2.00
6 Jamie Langenbrunner 1.25 3.00
7 Daymond Langkow 1.25 3.00
8 Jamie Storr .75 2.00
9 Jose Theodore 3.00 8.00
10 Roman Vopat .75 2.00

1996-97 Fleer Norris

Randomly inserted in retail packs only at a rate of 1:36, this 10-card set featured veteran rearguards in contention for recognition as the game's top blueliner.

COMPLETE SET (10) 15.00 40.00
1 Ray Bourque 6.00 15.00
2 Chris Chelios 4.00 10.00
3 Paul Coffey 4.00 10.00
4 Eric Desjardins 1.25 3.00
5 Phil Housley 1.25 3.00
6 Vladimir Konstantinov 2.50 6.00
7 Brian Leetch 4.00 10.00
8 Teppo Numminen 1.25 3.00
9 Larry Murphy 1.25 3.00
10 Sandis Ozolinsh 1.25 3.00

1996-97 Fleer Pearson

Randomly inserted in packs at a rate of 1:144, this 10-card set was the most difficult to come by of this year's Fleer offering, and also the most star-studded. Gracing this set were ten top stars worthy of consideration for the NHLPA MVP award.

COMPLETE SET (10) 50.00 125.00
1 Pavel Bure 3.00 8.00
2 Sergei Fedorov 3.00 8.00
3 Peter Forsberg 5.00 12.00
4 Wayne Gretzky 15.00 40.00
5 Jaromir Jagr 5.00 12.00
6 Paul Kariya 3.00 8.00
7 Mario Lemieux 10.00 25.00
8 Eric Lindros 3.00 8.00
9 Patrick Roy 10.00 25.00
10 Joe Sakic 6.00 15.00

1996-97 Fleer Rookie Sensations

Randomly inserted in hobby packs only at a rate of 1:20, this 10-card set featured some of the top rookie attractions of the '95-96 campaign.

COMPLETE SET (10) 6.00 15.00
1 Daniel Alfredsson .75 2.00
2 Todd Bertuzzi .75 2.00
3 Valeri Bure .40 1.00
4 Eric Daze .40 1.00
5 Sergei Gonchar .40 1.00
6 Ed Jovanovski .40 1.00
7 Saku Koivu .75 2.00
8 Marcus Ragnarsson .40 1.00
9 Petr Sykora .40 1.00
10 Vitali Yachmenev .40 1.00

1996-97 Fleer Vezina

Randomly inserted in packs at a rate of 1:60, this set featured ten netminders who are perennial favorites to win the Vezina award.

COMPLETE SET (10) 50.00 100.00
1 Ed Belfour 4.00 10.00
2 Sean Burke 3.00 8.00
3 Jim Carey 4.00 10.00
4 Dominik Hasek 8.00 20.00
5 Ron Hextall 3.00 8.00
6 Chris Osgood 4.00 10.00
7 Felix Potvin 4.00 10.00
8 Daren Puppa 3.00 8.00
9 Patrick Roy 15.00 40.00
10 John Vanbiesbrouck 4.00 10.00

1996-97 Fleer Picks

This 90-card set was a joint venture with Topps and was skip-numbered. All cards in this set had even numbers, while the Topps Picks set had the odds. The cards were issued in seven-card packs with a suggested retail price of $.99. The two card companies held a fantasy-style draft with each picking 56 forwards, 28 defensemen and six goaltenders to be included in their half of the set. The fronts featured color action player photos in a bordered design with the backs displaying projected stats for the 1996-97 season.

COMPLETE SET (92) 4.00 10.00
2 Joe Sakic .20 .50
4 Eric Lindros .08 .25
6 Paul Kariya .08 .25
8 Wayne Gretzky 1.50 4.00
10 Chris Osgood .02 .10
12 Brian Leetch .08 .25
14 Ray Bourque .15 .40
16 Ron Francis .02 .10
18 Keith Tkachuk .08 .25
20 Paul Coffey .08 .25
22 Phil Housley .02 .10
24 Theo Fleury .01 .05
26 Sergei Zubov .01 .05
28 Adam Oates .02 .10
30 John LeClair .08 .25
32 Pierre Turgeon .02 .10
34 Nicklas Lidstrom .08 .25
36 Vincent Damphousse .01 .05
38 Pat LaFontaine .08 .25
40 Brendan Shanahan .08 .25
42 Robert Svehla .01 .05
44 Peter Bondra .02 .10
46 Mikael Renberg .02 .10
48 Alexei Yashin .01 .05
50 Zigmund Palffy .02 .10
52 Larry Murphy .02 .10
54 Rod Brind'Amour .02 .10
56 Alexei Zhamnov .02 .10
58 Jason Arnott .01 .05
60 Craig Janney .02 .10
62 Jason Woolley .01 .05
64 Jeff Brown .01 .05
66 Tomas Sandstrom .01 .05
68 Doug Gilmour .02 .10
70 Travis Green .02 .10
72 Teppo Numminen .01 .05
74 Petr Sykora .01 .05
76 Saku Koivu .08 .25
78 Daniel Alfredsson .02 .10
80 Ron Hextall .02 .10
82 Jocelyn Thibault .08 .25
84 Mike Richter .08 .25
86 Nikolai Khabibulin .02 .10
88 John Vanbiesbrouck .02 .10
90 Adam Graves .02 .10
92 Kenny Jonsson .01 .05
94 Jyrki Lumme .01 .05
96 Zdeno Ciger .01 .05
98 Ed Jovanovski .02 .10
100 Greg Johnson .01 .05
102 Pat Falloon .01 .05
104 Andrew Cassels .01 .05
106 German Titov .01 .05
108 Joe Juneau .01 .05
110 Igor Larionov .01 .05
112 Norm Maciver .01 .05
114 Chris Pronger .02 .10
116 Scott Niedermayer .01 .05
118 Vladimir Malakhov .01 .05
120 Dale Hawerchuk .02 .10
122 Jason Dawe .01 .05
124 Valeri Bure .01 .05
126 Marcus Ragnarsson .01 .05
128 Stephane Richer .02 .10
130 Wendel Clark .02 .10
132 Bryan Smolinski .01 .05
134 Dimitri Khristich .01 .05
136 Benoit Hogue .01 .05
138 Kirk Muller .01 .05
140 Peter Ferraro .01 .05
142 Vitali Yachmenev .01 .05
144 Jere Lehtinen .01 .05
146 Brandon Convery .01 .05
148 Darcy Tucker .01 .05
150 Curtis Brown .01 .05
152 Alexei Zhitnik .01 .05
154 John Slaney .01 .05
156 Bruce Driver .01 .05
158 Jeff O'Neill .01 .05
160 Patrice Brisebois .01 .05
162 Gord Murphy .01 .05
164 Doug Bodger .01 .05
166 Marty McSorley .01 .05
168 Nolan Baumgartner .01 .05
170 Mike Gartner .02 .10
172 Andrei Nikolishin .01 .05
174 Alexei Yegorov RC .01 .05
176 Dave Reid .01 .05
178 Marty Murray .01 .05
180 Anders Eriksson .01 .05
182 Checklist (2-180) .01 .05
184 Checklist (inserts) .01 .05

1996-97 Fleer Picks Captain's Choice

Randomly inserted in packs at a rate of 1:360, this set featured ten top team captains. The fronts carried borderless color action player photos while the backs displayed player information.

COMPLETE SET (10) 50.00 100.00
1 Eric Lindros 2.00 5.00
2 Steve Yzerman 10.00 25.00
3 Mario Lemieux 12.00 30.00
4 Wayne Gretzky 20.00 50.00
5 Mark Messier 3.00 8.00
6 Joe Sakic 6.00 15.00
7 Keith Tkachuk 2.00 5.00
8 Doug Gilmour 2.50 6.00
9 Trevor Linden 2.00 5.00
10 Brendan Shanahan 2.50 6.00

1996-97 Fleer Picks Dream Lines

Randomly inserted in packs at a rate of 1:70, this 10-card set featured three star players sharing some connection on each card.

COMPLETE SET (10) 40.00 80.00
1 Wayne Gretzky 15.00 40.00
Mario Lemieux
Eric Lindros
2 Jeremy Roenick 2.00 5.00
Chris Chelios
Mike Richter
3 Daniel Alfredsson 4.00 10.00
Peter Forsberg
Martin Brodeur
4 Sergei Fedorov 3.00 8.00
Alexander Mogilny
Pavel Bure
5 Teemu Selanne 2.00 5.00
Paul Kariya
Keith Tkachuk
6 Jaromir Jagr 3.00 8.00
Dominik Hasek
Roman Hamrlik
7 John LeClair 3.00 8.00
Brendan Shanahan
Mike Modano
8 Patrick Roy 12.00 30.00
Ed Belfour
John Vanbiesbrouck
9 Joe Sakic 3.00 8.00
Valeri Kamensky
Sandis Ozolinsh
10 Brett Hull 2.00 5.00
Pat Verbeek
Pat LaFontaine

1996-97 Fleer Picks Fabulous 50

Inserted one in every pack, this 50-card set featured color action photos of the best players in the NHL. The nature of this set allowed Fleer to include players they were unable to select in the draft, thus giving a more complete feel to the entire product.

COMPLETE SET (50) 12.50 30.00
1 Daniel Alfredsson .20 .50
2 Peter Bondra .20 .50
3 Ray Bourque .50 1.25
4 Martin Brodeur .75 2.00
5 Pavel Bure .30 .75
6 Jim Carey .30 .75
7 Chris Chelios .30 .75
8 Paul Coffey .30 .75
9 Eric Daze .20 .50
10 Sergei Fedorov .40 1.00
11 Theo Fleury .07 .20
12 Peter Forsberg .75 2.00
13 Ron Francis .20 .50
14 Sergei Gonchar .20 .50
15 Wayne Gretzky 2.00 5.00
16 Roman Hamrlik .20 .50
17 Kevin Hatcher .07 .20
18 Ron Hextall .07 .20
19 Brett Hull .40 1.00
20 Jaromir Jagr .50 1.25
21 Ed Jovanovski .20 .50
22 Valeri Kamensky .07 .20
23 Paul Kariya .30 .75
24 John LeClair .30 .75
25 Brian Leetch .30 .75
26 Mario Lemieux 1.50 4.00
27 Trevor Linden .07 .20
28 Eric Lindros .30 .75
29 Mark Messier .30 .75
30 Mike Modano .50 1.25
31 Alexander Mogilny .20 .50
32 Petr Nedved .07 .20
33 Joe Nieuwendyk .07 .20
34 Owen Nolan .20 .50
35 Adam Oates .07 .20
36 Chris Osgood .20 .50
37 Sandis Ozolinsh .07 .20
38 Zigmund Palffy .20 .50
39 Jeremy Roenick .40 1.00
40 Patrick Roy 1.50 4.00
41 Joe Sakic .60 1.50
42 Teemu Selanne .30 .75
43 Brendan Shanahan .30 .75
44 Keith Tkachuk .30 .75
45 Pierre Turgeon .07 .20
46 John Vanbiesbrouck .20 .50
47 Doug Weight .07 .20
48 Alexei Yashin .07 .20
49 Steve Yzerman 1.50 4.00
50 Alexei Zhamnov .20 .50

1996-97 Fleer Picks Fantasy Force

Randomly inserted in packs at a rate of 1:50, this 10-card set featured color action photos of ten of the league's most valuable assets to fantasy league owners.

COMPLETE SET (10) 25.00 60.00
1 John LeClair 1.25 3.00
2 Chris Osgood 1.25 3.00
3 Ron Hextall 1.25 3.00
4 Eric Daze .75 2.00
5 Jaromir Jagr 4.00 10.00
6 Brett Hull 2.00 5.00
7 Ron Francis 1.25 3.00
8 Martin Brodeur 6.00 15.00
9 Sergei Fedorov 3.00 8.00
10 Petr Nedved .75 2.00

1996-97 Fleer Picks Jagged Edge

Randomly inserted in packs at a rate of 1:18, this 20-card set featured color action photos of players with a propensity for the dramatic.

COMPLETE SET (20) 12.00 30.00
1 Daniel Alfredsson 1.25 3.00
2 Theo Fleury .75 2.00
3 Alexander Mogilny 1.25 3.00
4 Doug Weight .75 2.00
5 Alexei Yashin .75 2.00
6 Paul Kariya 1.50 4.00
7 Saku Koivu 1.50 4.00
8 Sandis Ozolinsh .40 1.00
9 Petr Nedved .40 1.00
10 Jeremy Roenick 2.00 5.00
11 Mike Modano 2.00 5.00
12 Jim Carey .40 1.00
13 Ed Jovanovski .40 1.00
14 Alexei Zhamnov .40 1.00
15 Adam Oates .75 2.00
16 Ron Francis .75 2.00
17 Brian Leetch 1.50 4.00
18 Paul Coffey 1.50 4.00
19 Eric Daze .40 1.00
20 Zigmund Palffy .75 2.00

2006-07 Fleer

This 230-card set was released into the hobby in 10-card packs, with a $1.59 SRP, which came 36 packs to a box. Cards numbered 1-200 feature veterans in team alphabetical order while cards 201-230 feature NHL rookies.

COMPLETE SET w/o SPs (200) 6.00 15.00
COMPLETE SET (230) 40.00 80.00
1 Jean-Sebastien Giguere .25 .60
2 Andy McDonald .15 .40
3 Teemu Selanne .25 .60
4 Scott Niedermayer .15 .40
5 Chris Pronger .20 .50
6 Ilya Bryzgalov .25 .60
7 Ryan Getzlaf .20 .50
8 Corey Perry .20 .50
9 Jim Slater .07 .20
10 Ilya Kovalchuk .30 .75
11 Kari Lehtonen .25 .60
12 Marian Hossa .20 .50
13 Bobby Holik .15 .40
14 Slava Kozlov .15 .40
15 Patrice Bergeron .20 .50
16 Hannu Toivonen .25 .60
17 Brad Boyes .15 .40
18 Zdeno Chara .15 .40
19 Marco Sturm .15 .40
20 Glen Murray .15 .40
21 Marc Savard .15 .40
22 Maxim Afinogenov .15 .40
23 Chris Drury .20 .50
24 Ryan Miller .25 .60
25 Ales Kotalik .15 .40
26 Thomas Vanek .20 .50
27 Daniel Briere .20 .50
28 Jaroslav Spacek .07 .20
29 Jarome Iginla .40 1.00
30 Miikka Kiprusoff .25 .60
31 Daymond Langkow .15 .40
32 Dion Phaneuf .30 .75
33 Chuck Kobasew .15 .40
34 Alex Tanguay .20 .50
35 Eric Staal .20 .50
36 Justin Williams .15 .40
37 Cam Ward .40 1.00
38 Cory Stillman .15 .40
39 Rod Brind'Amour .20 .50
40 Mike Commodore .15 .40
41 Erik Cole .15 .40
42 Andrew Ladd .15 .40
43 Michal Handzus .07 .20
44 Tuomo Ruutu .15 .40
45 Nikolai Khabibulin .25 .60
46 Martin Havlat .20 .50
47 Rene Bourque .15 .40
48 Brent Seabrook .15 .40
49 Joe Sakic .50 1.25
50 Wojtek Wolski .15 .40
51 Milan Hejduk .20 .50
52 Marek Svatos .15 .40
53 Jose Theodore .25 .60
54 Pierre Turgeon .15 .40
55 Peter Budaj .20 .50
56 Sergei Fedorov .25 .60
57 Fredrik Modin .15 .40
58 Rick Nash .25 .60
59 Pascal Leclaire .25 .60
60 Bryan Berard .15 .40
61 David Vyborny .15 .40
62 Mike Modano .25 .60
63 Marty Turco .20 .50
64 Brenden Morrow .20 .50
65 Eric Lindros .25 .60
66 Jussi Jokinen .15 .40
67 Jere Lehtinen .15 .40
68 Sergei Zubov .15 .40
69 Pavel Datsyuk .25 .60
70 Tomas Holmstrom .15 .40
71 Henrik Zetterberg .25 .60
72 Nicklas Lidstrom .25 .60
73 Dominik Hasek .30 .75
74 Robert Lang .07 .20
75 Kris Draper .15 .40
76 Ales Hemsky .15 .40
77 Jeffrey Lupul .15 .40
78 Dwayne Roloson .20 .50
79 Ryan Smyth .20 .50
80 Jarret Stoll .15 .40
81 Shawn Horcoff .15 .40
82 Fernando Pisani .15 .40
83 Todd Bertuzzi .20 .50
84 Nathan Horton .15 .40
85 Jay Bouwmeester .15 .40
86 Olli Jokinen .15 .40
87 Joe Nieuwendyk .15 .40
88 Ed Belfour .60 1.50
89 Alexander Frolov .15 .40
90 Mike Cammalleri .15 .40
91 Mathieu Garon .20 .50
92 Lubomir Visnovsky .15 .40
93 Craig Conroy .15 .40
94 Rob Blake .20 .50
95 Pavol Demitra .15 .40
96 Brian Rolston .15 .40
97 Manny Fernandez .25 .60
98 Marian Gaborik .40 1.00
99 Pierre-Marc Bouchard .15 .40
100 Mikko Koivu .15 .40
101 Mark Parrish .15 .40
102 Cristobal Huet .25 .60
103 Saku Koivu .25 .60
104 Alex Kovalev .15 .40
105 Michael Ryder .20 .50
106 Mike Ribeiro .15 .40
107 Chris Higgins .15 .40
108 David Aebischer .20 .50
109 Paul Kariya .25 .60
110 Steve Sullivan .15 .40
111 Tomas Vokoun .20 .50
112 David Legwand .15 .40
113 Jason Arnott .15 .40
114 Scott Hartnell .07 .20
115 Martin Brodeur .75 2.00
116 Patrik Elias .15 .40
117 Brian Gionta .15 .40
118 Brian Rafalski .15 .40
119 Scott Gomez .15 .40
120 Zach Parise .20 .50
121 Alexei Yashin .15 .40
122 Jason Blake .15 .40
123 Rick DiPietro .25 .60
124 Miroslav Satan .15 .40
125 Trent Hunter .15 .40
126 Mike Sillinger .15 .40
127 Jaromir Jagr .40 1.00
128 Henrik Lundqvist .40 1.00
129 Martin Straka .15 .40
130 Brendan Shanahan .25 .60
131 Petr Prucha .15 .40
132 Matt Cullen .15 .40
133 Martin Gerber .25 .60
134 Antoine Vermette .15 .40
135 Daniel Alfredsson .25 .60
136 Jason Spezza .25 .60
137 Dany Heatley .25 .60
138 Wade Redden .15 .40
139 Patrick Eaves .15 .40
140 Ray Emery .25 .60
141 Simon Gagne .25 .60
142 Antero Niittymaki .25 .60
143 Peter Forsberg .40 1.00
144 Keith Primeau .15 .40
145 Jeff Carter .25 .60
146 Joni Pitkanen .15 .40
147 R.J. Umberger .15 .40
148 Shane Doan .20 .50
149 Curtis Joseph .25 .60
150 Ladislav Nagy .15 .40
151 Mike Comrie .15 .40
152 Jeremy Roenick .25 .60
153 Ed Jovanovski .15 .40
154 Sidney Crosby 1.25 3.00
155 Ryan Malone .15 .40
156 Colby Armstrong .15 .40
157 Marc-Andre Fleury .25 .60
158 Sergei Gonchar .07 .20
159 John LeClair .20 .50
160 Patrick Marleau .20 .50
161 Jonathan Cheechoo .25 .60
162 Vesa Toskala .20 .50
163 Joe Thornton .40 1.00
164 Evgeni Nabokov .20 .50
165 Steve Bernier .15 .40
166 Keith Tkachuk .20 .50
167 Manny Legace .20 .50
168 Doug Weight .15 .40
169 Petr Cajanek .15 .40
170 Lee Stempniak .15 .40
171 Bill Guerin .15 .40
172 Vincent Lecavalier .25 .60
173 Martin St. Louis .25 .60
174 Marc Dénis .25 .60
175 Brad Richards .25 .60
176 Vaclav Prospal .15 .40
177 Ryan Craig .07 .20
178 Ruslan Fedotenko .15 .40
179 Mats Sundin .25 .60
180 Michael Peca .15 .40
181 Kyle Wellwood .15 .40
182 Bryan McCabe .15 .40
183 Alexander Steen .20 .50
184 Andrew Raycroft .15 .40
185 Darcy Tucker .15 .40
186 Tomas Kaberle .15 .40
187 Roberto Luongo .50 1.25
188 Markus Naslund .25 .60
189 Daniel Sedin .15 .40
190 Henrik Sedin .15 .40
191 Mattias Ohlund .15 .40
192 Brendan Morrison .15 .40
193 Willie Mitchell .07 .20
194 Ryan Kesler .15 .40
195 Alexander Ovechkin 1.00 2.50
196 Olaf Kolzig .30 .75
197 Dainius Zubrus .15 .40
198 Brent Johnson .12 .30
199 Chris Clark .15 .40
200 Richard Zednik .07 .20
201 Shea Weber RC 1.00 2.50
202 Noah Welch RC 1.50 4.00
203 Eric Fehr RC 1.00 2.50
204 Mark Stuart RC 1.00 2.50
205 Matt Carle RC 1.00 2.50
206 Jarkko Immonen RC .75 2.00
207 Michel Ouellet RC 1.00 2.50
208 Konstantin Pushkarev RC 1.50 4.00
209 Marc-Antoine Pouliot RC 1.00 2.50
210 Ian White RC 1.50 4.00
211 Filip Novak RC 1.50 4.00
212 Tomas Kopecky RC 1.00 2.50
213 Billy Thompson RC .75 2.00
214 Dustin Byfuglien RC 3.00 8.00
215 Yan Stastny RC 1.00 2.50
216 Ben Ondrus RC 1.50 4.00
217 Brendan Bell RC 1.50 4.00
218 Steve Regier RC 1.50 4.00
219 Erik Reitz RC 1.50 4.00
220 Joel Perrault RC 1.50 4.00
221 Bill Thomas RC 1.50 4.00
222 Carsen Germyn RC .75 2.00
223 Rob Collins RC 1.50 4.00
224 Frank Doyle RC .75 2.00
225 Dan Jancevski RC 1.50 4.00
226 David Liffiton RC 1.60 4.00
227 Matt Koalska RC 1.50 4.00
228 Ryan Potulny RC 1.00 2.50
229 Ryan Caldwell RC 1.50 4.00
230 David Printz RC 1.50 4.00

2006-07 Fleer Oversized

COMPLETE SET (14) 12.00 30.00
15 Patrice Bergeron 1.00 2.50
30 Miikka Kiprusoff 1.25 3.00
35 Eric Staal 1.00 2.50
49 Joe Sakic 2.50 6.00
71 Henrik Zetterberg 1.25 3.00
103 Saku Koivu 1.25 3.00
115 Martin Brodeur 2.50 6.00
127 Jaromir Jagr 2.00 5.00
137 Dany Heatley 1.25 3.00
143 Peter Forsberg 1.50 4.00
154 Sidney Crosby 4.00 10.00
163 Joe Thornton 2.00 5.00
179 Mats Sundin 1.25 3.00
195 Alexander Ovechkin 3.00 8.00

2006-07 Fleer Tiffany

COMMONS 1.50 4.00
STARS 6X TO 15X
STATED ODDS (1-200) 1:36
201-230 NOT YET PRICED/ SCARCITY
STATED ODDS (201-230) 1:360
154 Sidney Crosby 12.00 30.00
195 Alexander Ovechkin 8.00 20.00

2006-07 Fleer Fabricology

STATED ODDS 1:40
FAA Ari Ahonen 2.50 6.00
FAF Alexander Frolov 2.50 6.00
FAH Adam Hall 2.50 6.00
FAK Alex Kovalev 2.50 6.00
FAM Andrej Meszaros 2.50 6.00
FAO Alexander Ovechkin SP 15.00 40.00
FAR Andrew Raycroft 3.00 8.00
FAU Alex Auld 3.00 8.00
FBG Bill Guerin 2.50 6.00
FBJ Barret Jackman 2.50 6.00
FBM Brendan Morrison 2.50 6.00
FBO Jay Bouwmeester 2.50 6.00
FBR Brian Rolston 2.50 6.00
FBS Brad Stuart 2.50 6.00
FBT Barry Tallackson 2.50 6.00
FCC Chris Chelios 3.00 8.00
FCD Chris Drury 3.00 8.00
FCO Chris Osgood 4.00 10.00
FCP Chris Pronger 3.00 8.00
FDB Donald Brashear 2.50 6.00
FDE Pavol Demitra 2.50 6.00
FDH Dan Hamhuis 2.50 6.00
FDL David Legwand 2.50 6.00
FDM Dominic Moore 2.50 6.00
FDS Daniel Sedin 2.50 6.00
FDW Doug Weight 2.50 6.00
FEB Ed Belfour SP 8.00 20.00
FED Eric Daze 2.50 6.00
FEL Eric Lindros 4.00 10.00
FEP Patrik Elias 2.50 6.00
FGA Mathieu Garon 3.00 8.00
FGR Gary Roberts 2.50 6.00
FHO Marian Hossa 3.00 8.00
FIK Ilya Kovalchuk 6.00 15.00
FJA Jason Arnott 2.50 6.00
FJB Jason Bacashihua 3.00 8.00
FJG Jean-Sebastien Giguere 3.00 8.00
FJJ Jaromir Jagr 6.00 15.00
FJL Jamie Lundmark 2.50 6.00
FJR Jeremy Roenick 4.00 10.00
FJS Jason Spezza 4.00 10.00
FJT Joe Thornton 6.00 15.00
FJW Justin Williams 2.50 6.00
FKL Kari Lehtonen 4.00 10.00
FKO Mike Komisarek 2.50 6.00
FKP Keith Primeau 2.50 6.00
FKT Keith Tkachuk 3.00 8.00
FLE Jere Lehtinen 3.00 8.00
FMA Martin Brodeur 8.00 20.00
FMB Martin Biron 3.00 8.00
FMC Bryan McCabe 2.50 6.00
FMG Marian Gaborik 5.00 12.00
FMH Marcel Hossa 2.50 6.00
FMK Miikka Kiprusoff 4.00 10.00
FMM Mike Modano 5.00 12.00
FMN Markus Naslund 3.00 8.00
FMO Mathias Ohlund 2.50 6.00
FMP Mark Parrish 2.50 6.00
FMS Martin Straka 2.50 6.00
FMT Marty Turco 4.00 10.00
FNA Nikolai Antropov 2.50 6.00
FNO Mika Noronen 3.00 8.00
FOJ Olli Jokinen 2.50 6.00
FOK Olaf Kolzig 4.00 10.00
FPA Patrik Stefan 2.50 6.00
FPB Peter Bondra 3.00 8.00
FPD Pavel Datsyuk 4.00 10.00
FPE Michael Peca 2.50 6.00
FPF Peter Forsberg 6.00 15.00
FPL Patrick Lalime 3.00 8.00
FPM Patrick Marleau 3.00 8.00
FPS Patrick Sharp 4.00 10.00
FPT Pierre Turgeon 2.50 6.00
FRB Rob Blake 2.50 6.00
FRE Robert Esche 3.00 8.00
FRF Ruslan Fedotenko 2.50 6.00
FRH Ryan Hollweg 2.50 6.00
FRK Rostislav Klesla 2.50 6.00
FRL Robert Lang 2.50 6.00
FRM Ryan Miller 4.00 10.00
FRN Rob Niedermayer 2.50 6.00
FRO Rod Brind'Amour 2.50 6.00
FRT Raffi Torres 3.00 8.00
FSA Philippe Sauve 3.00 8.00
FSC Sidney Crosby SP 30.00 80.00
FSF Sergei Fedorov 6.00 15.00
FSG Simon Gagne 3.00 8.00
FSK Sami Kapanen 2.50 6.00
FSN Scott Niedermayer 2.50 6.00
FSS Sergei Samsonov 3.00 8.00
FST Matt Stajan 2.50 6.00
FSW Stephen Weiss 2.50 6.00
FTC Tim Connolly 2.50 6.00
FTH Tomas Holmstrom 3.00 8.00
FTO Jordin Tootoo 4.00 10.00
FTP Tom Poti 2.50 6.00
FTR Tuomo Ruutu 3.00 8.00
FTS Teemu Selanne 4.00 10.00
FTY Ty Conklin 3.00 8.00
FZC Zdeno Chara 2.50 6.00

2006-07 Fleer Hockey Headliners

COMPLETE SET (25) 10.00 25.00
STATED ODDS 1:4
HL1 Sidney Crosby 2.50 6.00
HL2 Alexander Ovechkin 1.00 2.50
HL3 Teemu Selanne .30 .75
HL4 Cam Ward .30 .75
HL5 Luc Robitaille .25 .60
HL6 Mario Lemieux 1.50 4.00
HL7 Joe Thornton .50 1.25
HL8 Ilya Kovalchuk .40 1.00

HL9 Daniel Alfredsson .25 .60
HL10 Henrik Lundqvist .40 1.00
HL11 Brian Leetch .30 .75
HL12 Pierre Turgeon .15 .40
HL13 Fernando Pisani .15 .40
HL14 Alexander Ovechkin 1.00 2.50
HL15 Sidney Crosby 2.50 6.00
HL16 Alexander Ovechkin 1.00 2.50
HL17 Dany Heatley .40 1.00
HL18 Martin Havlat .25 .60
HL19 Dion Phaneuf .40 1.00
HL20 Miikka Kiprusoff .30 .75
HL21 Jaromir Jagr .50 1.25
HL22 Jonathan Cheechoo .30 .75
HL23 Martin Brodeur 1.00 2.50
HL24 Ilya Bryzgalov .25 .60
HL25 Marek Svatos .15 .40

2006-07 Fleer Netminders

COMPLETE SET (25) 8.00 20.00
STATED ODDS 1:4
N1 Ilya Bryzgalov .75 2.00
N2 Kari Lehtonen .75 2.00
N3 Ryan Miller .75 2.00
N4 Dominik Hasek 1.00 2.50
N5 Miikka Kiprusoff .75 2.00
N6 Cam Ward 1.25 3.00
N7 Nikolai Khabibulin .75 2.00
N8 Jose Theodore .75 2.00
N9 Marty Turco .75 2.00
N10 Dwayne Roloson .60 1.50
N11 Roberto Luongo 1.50 4.00
N12 Manny Fernandez .75 2.00
N13 Cristobal Huet 1.00 2.50
N14 Tomas Vokoun .75 2.00
N15 Martin Brodeur 2.00 5.00
N16 Rick DiPietro .75 2.00
N17 Henrik Lundqvist 1.25 3.00
N18 Martin Gerber .75 2.00
N19 Antero Niittymaki .75 2.00
N20 Curtis Joseph .75 2.00
N21 Marc-Andre Fleury 1.00 2.50
N22 Andrew Raycroft .60 1.50
N23 Vesa Toskala .60 1.50
N24 Olaf Kolzig 1.00 2.50
N25 Marc Denis .60 1.50

2006-07 Fleer Signing Day

STATED ODDS 1:432
SDAA Adrian Aucoin 6.00 15.00
SDAF Alexander Frolov 6.00 15.00
SDAH Ales Hemsky 10.00 25.00
SDAO Alexander Ovechkin SP 250.00 350.00
SDBA Matthew Barnaby 6.00 15.00
SDBB Brad Boyes 6.00 15.00
SDBI Martin Biron 10.00 25.00
SDBL Brian Leetch 20.00 50.00
SDBR Dustin Brown 6.00 15.00
SDBS Brent Seabrook 8.00 20.00
SDCD Chris Drury 6.00 15.00
SDCK Chuck Kobasew 6.00 15.00
SDCP Chris Phillips 6.00 15.00
SDCW Cam Ward 12.00 30.00
SDDA David Aebischer 10.00 25.00
SDDB Daniel Briere 15.00 40.00
SDDP Dion Phaneuf 15.00 40.00
SDDR Dwayne Roloson 10.00 25.00
SDEA Evgeni Artyukhin 6.00 15.00
SDGL Georges Laraque 12.00 30.00
SDHO Marcel Hossa 6.00 15.00
SDJC Jonathan Cheechoo 10.00 25.00
SDJF Johan Franzen 6.00 15.00
SDJH Jeff Halpern 8.00 20.00
SDJI Jarome Iginla SP
SDJT Jose Theodore 12.00 30.00
SDKC Kyle Calder 6.00 15.00
SDKD Kris Draper 6.00 15.00
SDKI Miikka Kiprusoff SP
SDMB Martin Brodeur SP
SDMG Marian Gaborik SP
SDMH Milan Hejduk 10.00 25.00
SDMJ Milan Jurcina 6.00 15.00
SDMK Mikko Koivu 10.00 25.00
SDMR Mike Ribeiro 6.00 15.00
SDMS Marc Savard 6.00 15.00
SDMT Mikael Tellqvist 10.00 25.00
SDPB Peter Budaj 10.00 25.00
SDPN Petteri Nokelainen 6.00 15.00
SDRB Rob Blake 8.00 20.00
SDRF Ruslan Fedotenko 6.00 15.00
SDRG Ryan Getzlaf 12.00 30.00
SDRI Raitis Ivanans 6.00 15.00
SDRO Rostislav Olesz 6.00 15.00
SDRS Ryan Suter 6.00 15.00
SDRY Michael Ryder 8.00 20.00
SDSC Sidney Crosby 125.00 250.00
SDSG Scott Gomez 6.00 15.00
SDSH Scott Hartnell 6.00 15.00
SDTA Jeff Tambellini 6.00 15.00
SDTC Ty Conklin 8.00 20.00
SDTH Joe Thornton SP
SDTV Thomas Vanek 12.00 30.00
SDVL Vincent Lecavalier SP

2006-07 Fleer Speed Machines

COMPLETE SET (25) 6.00 15.00
STATED ODDS 1:4
SM1 Scott Niedermayer .30 .75
SM2 Teemu Selanne .50 1.25
SM3 Ilya Kovalchuk .60 1.50
SM4 Marian Hossa .40 1.00
SM5 Erik Cole .30 .75
SM6 Chris Drury .40 1.00
SM7 Alex Tanguay .40 1.00
SM8 Joe Sakic 1.00 2.50
SM9 Sergei Fedorov .50 1.25
SM10 Bill Guerin .30 .75
SM11 Mike Modano .50 1.25
SM12 Pavel Datsyuk .50 1.25
SM13 Jay Bouwmeester .30 .75
SM14 Marian Gaborik .75 2.00
SM15 Alex Kovalev .30 .75
SM16 Paul Kariya .50 1.25
SM17 Miroslav Satan .30 .75
SM18 Dany Heatley .50 1.25
SM19 Sami Kapanen .15 .40
SM20 Simon Gagne .50 1.25
SM21 Patrick Marleau .40 1.00
SM22 Martin St. Louis .50 1.25
SM23 Mats Sundin .50 1.25
SM24 Markus Naslund .50 1.25
SM25 Alexander Ovechkin 2.00 5.00

2006-07 Fleer Total O

COMPLETE SET (25) 8.00 20.00
STATED ODDS 1:4
O1 Ilya Kovalchuk .60 1.50
O2 Patrice Bergeron .40 1.00
O3 Jarome Iginla .75 2.00
O4 Eric Staal .40 1.00
O5 Joe Sakic 1.00 2.50
O6 Rick Nash .50 1.25
O7 Mike Modano .50 1.25
O8 Pavel Datsyuk .50 1.25
O9 Henrik Zetterberg .50 1.25
O10 Ales Hemsky .30 .75
O11 Olli Jokinen .30 .75
O12 Saku Koivu .50 1.25
O13 Paul Kariya .50 1.25
O14 Patrik Elias .30 .75
O15 Jaromir Jagr .75 2.00
O16 Dany Heatley .50 1.25
O17 Daniel Alfredsson .40 1.00
O18 Jason Spezza .50 1.25
O19 Peter Forsberg .75 2.00
O20 Sidney Crosby 2.50 6.00
O21 Joe Thornton .75 2.00
O22 Jonathan Cheechoo .50 1.25
O23 Mats Sundin .50 1.25
O24 Markus Naslund .50 1.25
O25 Alexander Ovechkin 2.00 5.00

2001-02 Fleer Legacy

Released in mid-March 2002, this 64-card set was carried an SRP of $4.99 for a 4 card pack. Cards 1-8 resembled the design of Ultra and were short printed to 2002 copies each. Cards 9-64 were a horizontal design featuring color photos on a white card front.

COMPLETE SET (64) 40.00 80.00
1 Mario Lemieux SP 5.00 12.00
2 Bobby Hull SP 2.50 6.00
3 Guy Lafleur SP 2.00 5.00
4 Phil Esposito SP 2.50 6.00
5 Cam Neely SP 2.00 5.00
6 Jean Beliveau SP 1.50 4.00
7 Bryan Trottier SP 1.50 4.00
8 Jari Kurri SP 2.00 5.00
9 Jean Beliveau .30 .75
10 Bob Nystrom .12 .30
11 Phil Esposito .50 1.25
12 Bobby Hull .50 1.25
13 Guy Lafleur .40 1.00
14 Gilbert Perreault .12 .30
15 Henri Richard .30 .75
16 Marcel Dionne .30 .75
17 Tony Esposito .40 1.00
18 Clark Gillies .12 .30
19 Grant Fuhr .25 .60
20 Brad Park .25 .60
21 Frank Mahovlich .30 .75
22 John Bucyk .12 .30
23 Billy Smith .25 .60
24 Ulf Samuelsson .12 .30
25 Mario Lemieux 1.25 3.00
26 Rod Gilbert .30 .75
27 Basil McRae .12 .30
28 Dave Semenko .12 .30
29 Neal Broten .12 .30
30 Terry Sawchuk .50 1.25
31 Dino Ciccarelli .12 .30
32 Mike Bossy .30 .75
33 Borje Salming .25 .60
34 Stan Mikita .40 1.00
35 Ted Lindsay .30 .75
36 Gerry Cheevers .40 1.00
37 Michel Goulet .12 .30
38 Red Kelly .30 .75
39 Bobby Clarke .30 .75
40 Todd Ewen .12 .30
41 Denis Potvin .25 .60
42 Paul Henderson .12 .30
43 Butch Goring .25 .60
44 Nick Fotiu .12 .30
45 Denis Savard .25 .60
46 Larry Robinson .25 .60
47 Joe Kocur .40 1.00
48 Bernie Parent .30 .75
49 Mike Liut .25 .60
50 Bernie Geoffrion .30 .75
51 Tony Twist .12 .30
52 Bryan Trottier .25 .60
53 Cam Neely .30 .75
54 Brent Sutter .12 .30
55 Dave Schultz .25 .60
56 Terry O'Reilly .12 .30
57 Jari Kurri .25 .60
58 Lanny McDonald .12 .30
59 Mike Gartner .12 .30
60 Alex Delvecchio .30 .75
61 Ron Hextall .40 1.00
62 Darryl Sittler .30 .75
63 Dale Hunter .12 .30
64 John Vanbiesbrouck .25 .60

2001-02 Fleer Legacy Ultimate

This set paralleled the entire base set and carried a serial-numbering to 202. Gold replaced the white on the card front backgrounds.

*STARS: 4X TO 10X BASIC CARD
*SP's: 1.25X TO 3X BASIC SP's

2001-02 Fleer Legacy In the Corners

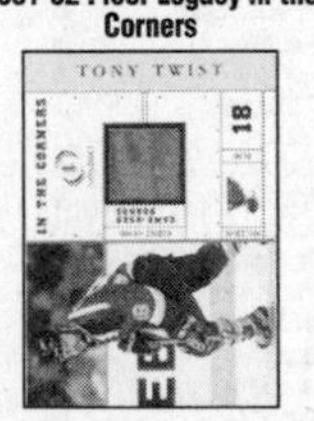

Inserted at stated rates of 1:24 hobby and 1:36 retail, this 12-card set features pieces of dasher boards from Joe Louis Arena. Card fronts carry a color photo of the featured player on the left, the player's name vertically on the right and a postage stamp-sized board piece in the center. Card backs carry a congratulatory message. Cards are unnumbered and are listed below in checklist order.

1 Dino Ciccarelli 5.00 12.00
2 Jari Kurri 6.00 15.00
3 Guy Lafleur 6.00 15.00
4 Mario Lemieux 10.00 25.00
5 Lanny McDonald 5.00 12.00
6 Cam Neely 5.00 12.00
7 Denis Potvin 5.00 12.00
8 Larry Robinson 5.00 12.00
9 Borje Salming 5.00 12.00
10 Darryl Sittler 5.00 12.00
11 Billy Smith 5.00 12.00
12 Tony Twist 5.00 12.00

2001-02 Fleer Legacy Memorabilia

Inserted at stated odds of 1:24 hobby and 1:36 retail, this 25-card set featured game-used swatches of jersey or sticks. Card fronts carry a color photo on the left side and the memorabilia piece on the left. Jersey cards had the words "Tailor Made" printed under the jersey swatch and the swatch was postage stamp sized. Stick cards had the words "Hockey Kings" above the dime-sized stick piece. Card backs carried a congratulatory message. Cards are unnumbered and listed below in checklist order.

*MULT.COLOR SWATCH: .5X TO 1.25X HI
1 Dino Ciccarelli 6.00 15.00
2 Tony Esposito JSY 8.00 20.00
3 Michel Goulet 6.00 15.00
4 Guy Lafleur 8.00 20.00
5 Mario Lemieux JSY 10.00 25.00
6 Larry Robinson 6.00 15.00
7 Borje Salming 6.00 15.00
8 Denis Savard 6.00 15.00
9 Jean Beliveau 8.00 20.00
10 Marcel Dionne 5.00 12.00
11 Tony Esposito 6.00 15.00
12 Phil Esposito 10.00 25.00
13 Mike Gartner 6.00 15.00
14 Bobby Hull 12.50 30.00
15 Guy Lafleur 6.00 15.00
16 Mario Lemieux STK 12.50 30.00
17 Stan Mikita 10.00 25.00
18 Cam Neely 10.00 25.00
19 Brad Park 6.00 15.00
20 Gilbert Perreault 6.00 15.00
21 Henri Richard 6.00 15.00
22 Terry Sawchuk 20.00 50.00
23 Darryl Sittler 8.00 20.00
24 Bryan Trottier 6.00 15.00
25 John Vanbiesbrouck 6.00 15.00

2001-02 Fleer Legacy Memorabilia Autographs

This 9-card set paralleled the stick cards in the memorabilia set but also carried the player's autograph under the stick piece. All cards in the checklist were only available as redemption cards out of packs. Cards were serial-numbered out of 100 each. Redemption cards expired March 2003.

1 Jean Beliveau 20.00 50.00
2 Phil Esposito 25.00 60.00
3 Bobby Hull 30.00 80.00
4 Guy Lafleur 20.00 50.00
5 Mario Lemieux 50.00 125.00
6 Stan Mikita 20.00 50.00
7 Darryl Sittler 20.00 50.00
8 Bryan Trottier 15.00 40.00

2002 Fleer Lemieux All-Star Fantasy

Available as a wrapper redemption from the Fleer booth at the NHL All-Star Game in LA, this special Mario Lemieux card was limited to 10,000 copies.

1 Mario Lemieux 2.00 5.00

2002-03 Fleer Throwbacks

This 91-card set featured players from the past and featured a few former players first main stream card. Card #92 was not available in packs, and was only available via redemption at the 2003 NHL All-Star Block Party.

COMPLETE SET (91) 20.00 40.00
1 Terry O'Reilly .40 1.00
2 Barry Beck .20 .50
3 Bobby Clarke .30 .75
4 Mike Foligno .20 .50
5 Danny Gare .20 .50
6 Clark Gillies .20 .50
7 Bernie Federko .20 .50
8 Dale Hunter .20 .50
9 Kris King .20 .50
10 Ted Lindsay .40 1.00
11 Tie Domi .20 .50
12 Rob Ramage .20 .50
13 Jim Schoenfeld .20 .50
14 Steve Smith .20 .50
15 Harold Snepsts .20 .50
16 Rod Langway .20 .50
17 Denis Potvin .20 .50
18 John Bucyk .25 .60
19 Dirk Graham .20 .50
20 Lanny McDonald .20 .50
21 Stan Smyl .20 .50
22 Andre Dupont .20 .50
23 Todd Ewen .20 .50
24 George McPhee .20 .50
25 Paul Baxter .20 .50
26 Keith Magnuson .20 .50
27 Kevin Kaminski .20 .50
28 Mike Peluso .20 .50
29 Dave Semenko .20 .50
30 David Maley .20 .50
31 Jeff Beukeboom .20 .50
32 Dave Brown .20 .50
33 Troy Crowder .20 .50
34 Bobby Hull .50 1.25
35 Dan Maloney .20 .50
36 Jimmy Mann .20 .50
37 Rudy Poeschek .20 .50
38 John Wensink .20 .50
39 Kim Clackson .20 .50
40 Jay Wells .20 .50
41 Glen Cochrane RC .30 .75
42 Alan May .20 .50
43 Willi Plett .20 .50
44 Kevin McClelland .20 .50
45 Jim Cummins .20 .50
46 Basil McRae .20 .50
47 Ron Delorme .20 .50
48 John Ferguson .20 .50
49 Gord Donnelly .20 .50
50 Nick Kypreos .20 .50
51 Larry Playfair .20 .50
52 Marty McSorley .20 .50
53 Tim Hunter .20 .50
54 Billy Smith .25 .60
55 Laurie Boschman .20 .50
56 Wayne Cashman .20 .50
57 Link Gaetz .20 .50
58 Darin Kimble .20 .50
59 Bob Nystrom .25 .60
60 Ronnie Stern .20 .50
61 Ken Baumgartner .20 .50
62 Ken Linseman .20 .50
63 Kelly Chase .20 .50
64 Bob Gassoff .20 .50
65 Joey Kocur .20 .50
66 Chris Nilan .20 .50
67 Dave Schultz .20 .50
68 Tony Twist .20 .50
69 Enrico Ciccone .20 .50
70 Jay Miller .20 .50
71 Phil Russell .20 .50
72 Bryan Watson .20 .50
73 Paul Holmgren .20 .50
74 Garth Butcher .20 .50
75 Al Iafrate .20 .50
76 Barclay Plager .20 .50
77 Brent Severyn .20 .50
78 Ron Hextall .25 .60
79 Shane Churla .20 .50
80 Dino Ciccarelli .20 .50
81 Cam Neely .40 1.00
82 Ulf Samuelsson .20 .50
83 Mick Vukota .20 .50
84 Garry Howatt .20 .50
85 Gary Rissling RC .30 .75
86 Behn Wilson .20 .50
87 Jack Carlson RC .30 .75
88 Bob Bassen .20 .50
89 Curt Brackenbury .20 .50
90 Mario Roberge .20 .50
91 Serge Roberge RC .30 .75
92 Bob Probert 5.00 12.00

2002-03 Fleer Throwbacks Gold

*GOLD: 2X TO 5X BASIC CARDS
STATED ODDS 1:1

2002-03 Fleer Throwbacks Platinum

*PLATINUM: 6X TO 15X BASIC CARDS
STAT.PRINT RUN 50 SER.#'d SETS

2002-03 Fleer Throwbacks Autographs

This 23-card set featured certified player autographs and was inserted at a rate of 1:144.

1 Terry O'Reilly 15.00 40.00
2 Bobby Clarke 15.00 40.00
3 Clark Gillies 8.00 20.00
4 Dale Hunter 8.00 20.00
5 Ted Lindsay 25.00 60.00
6 Tie Domi 15.00 40.00
7 Jim Schoenfeld 15.00 40.00
8 Denis Potvin 8.00 20.00
9 Todd Ewen 8.00 20.00
10 Kevin Kaminski 8.00 20.00
11 Bob Probert 100.00 250.00
12 Dave Brown 12.50 30.00
13 Bobby Hull 40.00 100.00
14 Basil McRae 15.00 40.00
15 Larry Playfair 8.00 20.00
16 Marty McSorley 20.00 50.00
17 Billy Smith 40.00 100.00
18 Bob Nystrom 8.00 20.00
19 Ken Baumgartner 8.00 20.00
20 Kelly Chase 8.00 20.00
21 Joey Kocur 15.00 40.00
22 Dave Schultz 10.00 25.00
23 Tony Twist 25.00 60.00

2002-03 Fleer Throwbacks Drop the Gloves

Serial-numbered to 200 copies each, this 5-card set featured pieces of game-used gloves. Cards were not numbered and are listed below in checklist order.

1 Bob Probert 40.00 100.00
2 Ron Hextall 20.00 50.00
3 Tony Twist 12.50 30.00
4 Marty McSorley 8.00 20.00
5 Jim Cummins 8.00 20.00

2002-03 Fleer Throwbacks Scraps

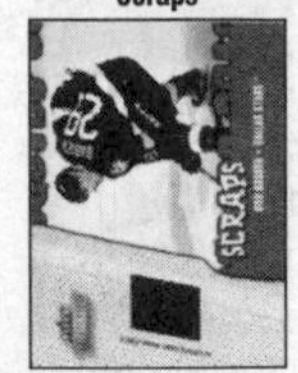

Inserted at 1:25, this 8-card set featured pieces of game jerseys. Cards were not numbered and are listed below in checklist order.

1 Basil McRae 5.00 12.00
2 Enrico Ciccone 5.00 12.00
3 Bob Bassen 6.00 15.00
4 Joey Kocur 6.00 15.00
5 Clark Gillies 5.00 12.00
6 Marty McSorley 5.00 12.00
7 Tony Twist 5.00 12.00
8 Dale Hunter 5.00 12.00

2002-03 Fleer Throwbacks Tie Downs

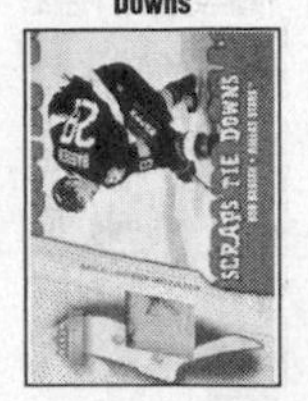

This 8-card set paralleled the basic jersey set but featured swatches of jersey tie-downs. Each card was serial-numbered out of 50.

1 Basil McRae 20.00 50.00
2 Enrico Ciccone 20.00 50.00
3 Bob Bassen 25.00 60.00
4 Joey Kocur 25.00 60.00
5 Clark Gillies 20.00 50.00
6 Marty McSorley 20.00 50.00
7 Tony Twist 20.00 50.00
8 Dale Hunter 20.00 50.00

2002-03 Fleer Throwbacks Squaring Off

COMPLETE SET (9) 15.00 30.00
STATED ODDS 1:24
1 Bob Probert 2.50 6.00
Joey Kocur
2 Dave Schultz 1.50 4.00
Clark Gillies
3 Cam Neely 2.00 5.00
Ulf Samuelsson
4 Terry O'Reilly 1.50 4.00
Jim Schoenfeld
5 Barry Beck 1.50 4.00
Denis Potvin
6 Bobby Clarke 1.50 4.00
Dale Hunter
7 Tony Twist 2.50 6.00
Marty McSorley
8 Dave Brown 2.50 6.00
Dave Schultz
9 Ron Hextall 1.50 4.00
Billy Smith

2002-03 Fleer Throwbacks Squaring Off Memorabilia

This 8-card set was inserted at 1:48 and paralleled the basic insert set but carried dual memorabilia swatches.

1 Bob Probert JSY 10.00 25.00
Joey Kocur STK
2 Dave Schultz JSY 6.00 15.00
Clark Gillies JSY
3 Cam Neely JSY 8.00 20.00
Ulf Samuelsson JSY
4 Terry O'Reilly JSY 6.00 15.00
Jim Schoenfeld JSY
5 Barry Beck JSY 6.00 15.00
Denis Potvin JSY
6 Bobby Clarke STK 6.00 15.00
Dale Hunter JSY
7 Tony Twist JSY 10.00 25.00
Marty McSorley JSY
8 Dave Brown JSY 10.00 25.00
Dave Schultz JSY

2002-03 Fleer Throwbacks Stickwork

Cards are not numbered and are listed below in checklist order.

1 Kelly Chase 5.00 12.00
2 Dale Hunter 5.00 12.00
3 Curt Brackenbury 5.00 12.00
4 Todd Ewen 5.00 12.00
5 Jim Cummins 6.00 15.00
6 Rudy Poeschek 5.00 12.00
7 Jay Wells 5.00 12.00
8 Enrico Ciccone 5.00 12.00
9 Marty McSorley 15.00 40.00
10 Bobby Hull 8.00 20.00
11 Cam Neely 6.00 15.00
12 Bobby Clarke 8.00 20.00
13 Bob Probert 8.00 20.00

1994 Fleury Hockey Tips

Titled "Theoren Fleury Hockey School Tip of the Week," this 14-card set measured the standard size. The lavender-bordered fronts had color action photos illustrating each hockey tip. The backs carried the "Tip of the Week" in black lettering followed by discussion. The cards were numbered on both sides.

COMPLETE SET (14) 2.00 5.00
COMMON CARD (1-14) .20 .50

1970-71 Flyers Postcards

This 12-card, team-issued set measured 3 1/2" by 5 1/2" and was in the postcard format. The fronts featured full-bleed color photos, with the players posed on ice at the skating rink. A facsimile autograph was inscribed across the bottom. The white backs carried player information and team logo across the top. The cards were unnumbered and checklisted below in alphabetical order.

COMPLETE SET (12) 20.00 40.00
1 Barry Ashbee 3.00 6.00
2 Gary Dornhoefer 3.00 6.00
3 Warren Elliott 1.00 2.00
Frank Leurs
4 Doug Favell 3.00 6.00
5 Earl Heiskala 1.50 3.00
6 Larry Hillman 2.50 5.00
7 Andre Lacroix 2.50 5.00
8 Lew Morrison 1.50 3.00
9 Simon Nolet 2.00 4.00
10 Garry Peters 1.50 3.00
11 Vic Stasiuk CO 1.50 3.00
12 George Swarbrick 1.50 3.00

1972 Flyers Mighty Milk

These seven panels, which were issued on the sides of half gallon cartons of Mighty Milk, featured members of the Philadelphia Flyers. After cutting, the panels measured approximately 3 5/8" by 7 1/2". All lettering and the portrait itself were in blue. Inside a frame with rounded corners, each panel displayed a portrait of the player and a player profile. The words "Philadelphia Hockey Star" and the player's name appeared above the frame, while an advertisement for Mighty Milk and another for TV Channel 29 appeared immediately below. The backs were blank. The panels were unnumbered and checklisted below in alphabetical order.

COMPLETE SET (8) 87.50 175.00
1 Serge Bernier 7.50 15.00
2 Bobby Clarke 40.00 80.00
3 Gary Dornhoefer 10.00 20.00
4 Doug Favell 15.00 30.00
5 Jean-Guy Gendron 7.50 15.00
6 Bob Kelly
7 Bill Lesuk 7.50 15.00
8 Ed Van Impe 10.00 20.00

1973-74 Flyers Linnett

These oversize cards were produce by Charles Linnett Studios. Cards were done in black and white and featured a facsimile signature. Original price per piece was only 50 cents. Cards measure 8 1/2 x 11. They were unnumbered and checklisted below in alphabetical order.

COMPLETE SET (1-18) 40.00 80.00
1 Barry Ashbee 1.50 3.00
2 Bill Barber 5.00 10.00
3 Tom Bladon 1.50 3.00
4 Bob Clarke 5.00 10.00
5 Bill Clement 3.00 6.00
6 Terry Crisp 2.50 5.00
7 Bill Flett 2.00 4.00
8 Bob Kelly 1.50 3.00
9 Orest Kindrachuk 1.50 3.00
10 Ross Lonsberry 1.50 3.00
11 Rick MacLeish 2.00 4.00
12 Simon Nolet 2.00 4.00
13 Bernard Parent 5.00 10.00
14 Don Saleski 1.50 3.00
15 Dave Schultz 3.00 6.00
16 Ed Van Impe 1.50 3.00
17 Jimmy Watson 2.00 4.00
18 Joe Watson 2.00 4.00

1983-84 Flyers J.C. Penney

Sponsored by J.C. Penney, this 22-card set measured approximately 4" by 6". The fronts featured color posed action shots of the players on ice. Beneath the picture were the team name, logo, player's name, and the phrase "Compliments of J.C. Penney Stores in the Delaware Valley." The backs were blank. The cards were unnumbered and checklisted below in alphabetical order.

COMPLETE SET (22) 14.00 35.00

1 Ray Allison	.40	1.00
2 Bill Barber	.75	2.00
3 Frank Bathe	.40	1.00
4 Lindsay Carson	.40	1.00
5 Bobby Clarke	2.00	5.00
6 Glen Cochrane	.40	1.00
7 Doug Crossman	.60	1.50
8 Miroslav Dvorak	.40	1.00
9 Thomas Eriksson	.40	1.00
10 Bob Froese	.60	1.50
11 Randy Holt	.40	1.00
12 Mark Howe	.75	2.00
13 Tim Kerr	.75	2.00
14 Pelle Lindbergh	5.00	12.00
15 Brad Marsh	.60	1.50
16 Brad McCrimmon	.60	1.50
17 Dave Poulin	.60	1.50
18 Brian Propp	.75	2.00
19 Ilkka Sinisalo	.60	1.50
20 Darryl Sittler	1.50	4.00
21 Rich Sutter	.40	1.00
22 Ron Sutter	.40	1.00

1985-86 Flyers Postcards

This 31 card set featured action photos on the front, and came complete with player name, number and statistics.

COMPLETE SET (31)	10.00	25.00
1 Bill Barber	.40	1.00
2 Dave Brown	.30	.75
3 Lindsay Carson	.20	.50
4 Bob Clarke	.75	2.00
5 Murray Craven	.20	.50
6 Pat Croce	.08	.25
7 Doug Crossman	.20	.50
8 Per-Erik Eklund	.20	.50
9 Thomas Eriksson	.20	.50
10 Bob Froese	.30	.75
11 Len Hachborn	.08	.25
12 Paul Holmgren	.20	.50
13 Ed Hospodar	.20	.50
14 Mark Howe	.30	.75
15 Mike Keenan	.40	1.00
16 Tim Kerr	.30	.75
17 Pelle Lindbergh	3.00	8.00
18 Brad Marsh	.20	.50
19 Brad McCrimmon	.30	.75
20 E.J. McGuire CO	.08	.25
21 Bernie Parent CO	.40	1.00
22 Joe Paterson	.08	.25
23 Dave Poulin	.20	.50
24 Brian Propp	.40	1.00
25 Ilkka Sinisalo	.20	.50
26 Derrick Smith	.20	.50
27 Rich Sutter	.20	.50
28 Ron Sutter	.20	.50
29 Rick Tocchet	2.50	6.00
30 Peter Zezel	.75	2.00
31 Team Photo	.75	2.00

1986-87 Flyers Postcards

This 29-card set of Philadelphia Flyers featured full-bleed, color action and posed photos. The cards measured approximately 4 1/8" by 6" and were in a postcard format. A player's autograph facsimile was printed on the front. A diagonal black stripe cut across the lower portion of the picture. Within the black stripe appeared narrow orange stripes, the Flyers logo, and player information. The horizontal white backs carried career statistics and biography on the left, and the postcard format mailing address space on the right. The cards were unnumbered and checklisted below in alphabetical order.

COMPLETE SET (29)	10.00	25.00
1 Bill Barber CO	.40	1.00
2 Dave Brown	.30	.75
3 Lindsay Carson	.20	.50
4 Murray Craven	.20	.50
5 Pat Croce TR	.08	.25
6 Doug Crossman	.20	.50
7 Jean-Jacques Daigneault	.20	.50
8 Pelle Eklund	.30	.75
9 Ron Hextall	1.50	4.00
10 Paul Holmgren CO	.20	.50
11 Ed Hospodar	.20	.50
12 Mark Howe	.60	1.50
13 Mike Keenan CO	.40	1.00
14 Tim Kerr	.60	1.50
15 Brad Marsh	.20	.50
16 Brad McCrimmon	.30	.75
17 E.J. McGuire CO	.08	.25
18 Scott Mellanby	.60	1.50
19 Bernie Parent CO	.40	1.00
20 Dave Poulin	.30	.75
21 Brian Propp	.40	1.00
22 Glenn Resch	.40	1.00
23 Ilkka Sinisalo	.20	.50
24 Derrick Smith	.20	.50
25 Daryl Stanley	.20	.50
26 Ron Sutter	.20	.50
27 Rick Tocchet	2.00	5.00
28 Peter Zezel	.40	1.00
29 Team Photo	.75	2.00

1989-90 Flyers Postcards

This 29-card set measured 4 1/8" by 6" and was in the postcard format. The fronts featured full-bleed color action player photos. A team color-coded (black with thin orange stripes) diagonal stripe cut across the bottom portion and carried the team logo, biographical information, and jersey number. The white horizontal backs carried the team logo, biography, and career summary. The cards were unnumbered and checklisted below in alphabetical order.

COMPLETE SET (29)	8.00	20.00
1 Keith Acton	.20	.50
2 Craig Berube	.20	.50
3 Mike Bullard	.20	.50
4 Terry Carkner	.20	.50
5 Jeff Chychrun	.20	.50
6 Bob Clarke VP/GM	.75	2.00
7 Murray Craven	.20	.50
8 Mike Eaves ACO	.08	.25
9 Pelle Eklund	.30	.75
10 Ron Hextall	.75	2.00
11 Paul Holmgren CO	.20	.50
12 Mark Howe	.40	1.00
13 Kerry Huffman	.20	.50
14 Tim Kerr	.40	1.00
15 Scott Mellanby	.40	1.00
16 Gord Murphy	.20	.50
17 Andy Murray ACO	.08	.25
18 Pete Peeters	.40	1.00
19 Dave Poulin	.40	1.00
20 Brian Propp	.40	1.00
21 Kjell Samuelsson	.40	1.00
22 Ilkka Sinisalo	.20	.50
23 Derrick Smith	.20	.50
24 Doug Sulliman	.20	.50
25 Ron Sutter	.20	.50
26 Rick Tocchet	.75	2.00
27 Jay Wells	.20	.50
28 Ken Wregget	.75	2.00
29 Team Photo	.75	2.00

1990-91 Flyers Postcards

This 26-card set was issued by the Philadelphia Flyers. Each card measured approximately 4 1/8" by 6". The fronts displayed full-bleed color action photos. A team color-coded (black with thin orange stripes) diagonal stripe cut across the bottom portion and carried the team logo, biographical information, and jersey number. The horizontal backs were postcard design and, on the left, presented biography, statistics, and notes. The cards were unnumbered and checklisted below in alphabetical order.

COMPLETE SET (26)	6.00	15.00
1 Keith Acton	.30	.75
2 Murray Baron	.20	.50
3 Craig Berube	.20	.50
4 Terry Carkner	.20	.50
5 Jeff Chychrun	.20	.50
6 Murray Craven	.30	.75
7 Pelle Eklund	.30	.75
8 Ron Hextall	.60	1.50
9 Tony Horacek	.20	.50
10 Martin Hostak	.20	.50
11 Mark Howe	.40	1.00
12 Kerry Huffman	.20	.50
13 Tim Kerr	.40	1.00
14 Dale Kushner	.20	.50
15 Norman Lacombe	.20	.50
16 Jiri Latal	.20	.50
17 Scott Mellanby	.40	1.00
18 Gord Murphy	.20	.50
19 Pete Peeters	.30	.75
20 Mike Ricci	.60	1.50
21 Kjell Samuelsson	.30	.75
22 Derrick Smith	.20	.50
23 Ron Sutter	.20	.60
24 Rick Tocchet	.75	2.00
25 Ken Wregget	.30	.75
26 Team Photo	.75	2.00

1991-92 Flyers J.C. Penney

This 26-card set was issued by the Flyers in conjunction with J.C. Penney Stores and Lee. Each card measured approximately 4 1/8" by 6". The fronts displayed full-bleed color action photos. A team color-coded (black with thin orange stripes) diagonal stripe cut across the bottom portion and carried the team logo, biographical information, and jersey number. The horizontal backs were postcard design and, on the left, presented biography, statistics, and notes. The cards were unnumbered and checklisted below in alphabetical order.

COMPLETE SET (26)	6.00	15.00
1 Keith Acton	.30	.75
2 Rod Brind'Amour	.60	1.50
3 Dave Brown	.30	.75
4 Terry Carkner	.20	.50
5 Kimbi Daniels	.20	.50
6 Kevin Dineen	.40	1.00
7 Steve Duchesne	.30	.75
8 Pelle Eklund	.20	.50
9 Corey Foster	.20	.50
10 Ron Hextall	.60	1.50
11 Tony Horacek	.20	.50
12 Mark Howe	.40	1.00
13 Kerry Huffman	.20	.50
14 Brad Jones	.20	.50
15 Steve Kasper UER	.20	.50
(Misspelled Kaspar		
on front)		
16 Dan Kordic	.20	.50
17 Jiri Latal	.20	.50
18 Andrei Lomakin	.20	.50
19 Gord Murphy	.20	.50
20 Mark Pederson	.20	.50
21 Dan Quinn	.20	.50
22 Mike Ricci	.40	1.00
23 Kjell Samuelsson	.25	.60
24 Rick Tocchet	.60	1.50
25 Ken Wregget	.40	1.00
26 Team Photo	.60	1.50

1992-93 Flyers J.C. Penney

This 23-card set was sponsored by J.C. Penney Stores and Lee in the Delaware Valley. The cards measured approximately 4 1/8" by 6" and featured color, action player photos with facsimile autographs near the bottom of each picture. A gray border stripe across the bottom carried the team logo, player's name, position, and jersey number. The horizontal backs displayed biographical information, statistics, and career notes within a postcard-type format. The cards were unnumbered and checklisted below in alphabetical order.

COMPLETE SET (23)	8.00	20.00
1 Keith Acton	.25	.60
2 Stephane Beauregard	.25	.60
3 Brian Benning	.20	.50
4 Rod Brind'Amour	.60	1.50
5 Claude Boivin	.20	.50
6 Dave Brown	.30	.75
7 Terry Carkner	.20	.50
8 Shawn Cronin	.20	.50
9 Kevin Dineen	.30	.75
10 Pelle Eklund	.20	.50
11 Doug Evans	.20	.50
12 Brent Fedyk	.20	.50
13 Garry Galley	.30	.75
14 Gord Hynes	.20	.50
15 Eric Lindros	4.00	10.00
16 Andrei Lomakin	.20	.50
17 Ryan McGill	.20	.50
18 Ric Nattress	.20	.50
19 Greg Paslawski	.20	.50
20 Mark Recchi	.75	2.00
21 Dominic Roussel	.30	.75
22 Dimitri Yushkevich	.20	.50
23 Team Photo	.60	1.50

1992-93 Flyers Upper Deck Sheets

The 44 commemorative sheets in this set were distributed individually in game programs at Philadelphia Flyers home games during the 1992-93 season in Flyer magazine. The sheets measured approximately 8 1/2" by 11" and featured color, posed and action, player photos with orange and white borders. A black bar with an orange accent stripe above it carried either the player's name or a picture title. On sheets with a title, the player's name was printed on the photo in either orange or white lettering. A black diamond design was printed with the individual sheet number and the production run. The backs displayed the game date and teams playing. All sheets were the Flyers versus another NHL team. The roster and management of each team was also given. The sheets are unnumbered and checklisted below in chronological order. There was a second team photo issued March 13th. Due to a violent winter storm, only a few thousand spectators made it to the Spectrum. Play was halted when a severe wind blew out a few windows in the concourse area causing debris to scatter out into the seats. The sheets were distributed again during the make-up game on April 1.

COMPLETE SET (44)	100.00	250.00
1 Quebec Nordiques	2.00	5.00
Sept. 19& 1992 (4&500)		
Kevin Dineen		
2 New Jersey Devils	1.25	3.00
Sept. 24& 1992 (4&500)		
Brian Benning		
3 Washington Capitals	3.00	8.00
Oct. 3& 1992 (4&500)		
Mark Recchi		
4 New Jersey Devils	1.50	4.00
Oct. 9& 1992 (7&500)		
Keith Acton		
5 New York Islanders	3.00	8.00
Oct. 15& 1992 (4&500)		
Rod Brind'Amour		
6 Winnipeg Jets	1.50	4.00
Oct. 18& 1992 (4&500)		
Dave Brown		
7 Vancouver Canucks	2.00	5.00
Oct. 22& 1992 (4&500)		
Dominic Roussel		
8 Montreal Canadiens	1.25	3.00
Oct. 24& 1992 (4&500)		
Gord Hynes		
9 St. Louis Blues	1.25	3.00
Nov. 7& 1992 (4&500)		
Claude Boivin		
10 New York Islanders	1.25	3.00
Nov. 12& 1992 (4&500)		
Dimitri Yushkevich		
11 Ottawa Senators	15.00	40.00
Nov. 15& 1992 (5&500)		
Eric Lindros		
12 New York Rangers	1.50	4.00
Nov. 19& 1992 (4&500)		
Steve Kasper		
13A Buffalo Sabres	5.00	12.00
Nov. 22& 1992 (4&500)		
1992-93 Team Picture		
13B Buffalo Sabres	4.00	10.00
Nov. 22& 1992		
1992-93 Team Picture		
(Pizza Hut logo on front		
and Citation Graphics		
Ad on back)		
14 New York Islanders	1.25	3.00
Nov. 27& 1992 (5&500)		
Greg Paslawski		
15 Quebec Nordiques	1.50	4.00
Dec. 3& 1992 (4&500)		
Terry Carkner		
16 Boston Bruins	1.25	3.00
Dec. 6& 1992 (4&500)		
Shawn Cronin		
17 Washington Capitals	1.25	3.00
Dec. 12& 1992 (4&500)		
Brent Fedyk		
18 Pittsburgh Penguins	1.50	4.00
Dec. 17& 1992 (4&500)		
Garry Galley		
19 Chicago Blackhawks	1.25	3.00
Dec. 19& 1992 (5&000)		
Andrei Lomakin		
20 Pittsburgh Penguins	2.00	5.00
Dec. 23& 1992 (5&500)		
Bill and Kevin Dineen		
21 Washington Capitals	1.50	4.00
Jan. 7& 1993 (4&500)		
Stephane Beauregard		
22 New York Rangers	0.00	0.00
Jan. 9& 1993 (6&000)		
Mark Recchi		
23 Edmonton Oilers	1.25	3.00
Jan. 10& 1993 (5&000)		
Ryan McGill		
24 Calgary Flames	1.25	3.00
Jan. 14& 1993 (6&500)		
Doug Evans		
25 Detroit Red Wings	2.00	5.00
Jan. 17& 1993 (5&000)		
The Captains		
Kevin Dineen		
Keith Acton		
Terry Carkner		
26 Boston Bruins	1.25	3.00
Jan. 21& 1993 (5&000)		
Ric Nattress		
27 Hartford Whalers	3.00	8.00
Jan. 24& 1993 (5&000)		
Rod Brind'Amour		
28 Buffalo Sabres	2.00	5.00
Jan. 26& 1993 (5&000)		
Tommy Soderstrom		
29 Quebec Nordiques	1.50	4.00
Jan. 28& 1993 (5&000)		
Pelle Eklund		
30 Ottawa Senators	1.50	4.00
Feb. 9& 1993 (5&000)		
Dave Brown		
31 Montreal Canadiens	10.00	25.00
Feb. 11& 1993 (5&500)		
The Rookies		
Tommy Soderstrom		
Dimitri Yushkevich		
Dominic Roussel		
Ryan McGill		
Eric Lindros		
32 New Jersey Devils	1.25	3.00
Feb. 14& 1993 (5&000)		
Josef Beranek		
33 New Jersey Devils	1.25	3.00
Feb. 25& 1993 (6&000)		
Greg Paslawski		
34 New York Islanders	1.50	4.00
Feb. 27& 1993 (5&000)		
The Coaches		
Craig Hartsburg		
Bill Dineen		
Ken Hitchcock		
35 Pittsburgh Penguins	1.50	4.00
Mar. 2& 1993 (5&000)		
Keith Acton		
36 Washington Capitals	3.00	8.00
Mar. 11& 1993 (5&500)		
NHL All-Star		
Mark Recchi		
37A Los Angeles Kings	1.50	4.00
Mar. 13& 1993 (5&000)		
Garry Galley		
37B Los Angeles Kings	3.00	8.00
Make-up Game		
1992-93 Team Picture		
38 Minnesota North Stars	1.50	4.00
Mar. 16& 1993 (5&000)		
Terry Carkner		
39 New Jersey Devils	2.00	5.00
Mar. 21& 1993 (5&000)		
Dominic Roussel		
40 San Jose Sharks	1.25	3.00
Mar. 25& 1993 (5&000)		
Greg Hawgood		
41 Tampa Bay Lightning	1.25	3.00
Apr. 3& 1993 (5&500)		
Viacheslav Butsayev		
42 Toronto Maple Leafs	10.00	25.00
Apr. 4& 1993 (6&000)		
Crazy 8's		
Mark Recchi		
Eric Lindros		
Brent Fedyk		
43 Washington Capitals	2.00	5.00
Apr. 8& 1993 (5&500)		
European Style		
Andrei Lomakin		
Dimitri Yushkevich		
Viacheslav Butsayev		
44 New York Rangers	4.00	10.00
Apr. 12& 1993 (5&500)		
Hockey Hall of Famers		
Bob Clarke		
Ed Snider		
Bill Barber		
Bernie Parent		
Keith Allen		

1993-94 Flyers J.C. Penney

This 24-card set was issued by the Flyers as a promotional item at a home game, and was sponsored by JC Penney. These collectibles were postcard sized, featured full color action photos on the front, and player data on the back. The cards were unnumbered, and were checklisted below in alphabetical order.

COMPLETE SET (24)	8.00	20.00
1 Josef Beranek	.30	.75
2 Claude Boivin	.20	.50
3 Jason Bowen	.20	.50
4 Rod Brind'Amour	.60	1.50
5 Slava Butsayev	.20	.50
6 Dave Brown	.30	.75
7 Al Conroy	.20	.50
8 Kevin Dineen	.30	.75
9 Pelle Eklund	.20	.50
10 Brent Fedyk	.20	.50
11 Jeff Finley	.20	.50
12 Garry Galley	.30	.75
13 Eric Lindros	3.00	8.00
14 Stewart Malgunas	.20	.50
15 Ryan McGill	.20	.50
16 Rob Ramage	.20	.50
17 Mark Recchi	.75	2.00
18 Mikael Renberg	.60	1.50
19 Dominic Roussel	.30	.75
20 Yves Racine	.20	.50
21 Tommy Soderstrom	.30	.75
22 Dave Tippett	.20	.50
23 Dimitri Yuskevich	.20	.50
NNO Team Photo	.40	1.00

1993-94 Flyers Lineup Sheets

The 44 commemorative sheets in this set were distributed individually in game programs at Philadelphia Flyers home games during the 1993-94 season in Flyer magazine. The sheets measured approximately 8 1/2" by 11" and featured color, posed and action, player photos with orange and white borders. The sheets are listed below by player in alphabetical order.

COMPLETE SET (43)	50.00	125.00
1 Josef Beranek	1.00	2.50
2 Claude Boivin	1.00	2.50
3 Jason Bowen	1.00	2.50
4 Rod Brind'Amour	2.00	5.00
5 Rod Brind'Amour	2.00	5.00
6 Dave Brown	2.00	5.00
7 Slava Butsayev	1.00	2.50
8 Terry Carkner	1.00	2.50
9 Al Conroy	1.00	2.50
10 Kevin Dineen	1.00	2.50
11 Kevin Dineen	1.00	2.50
12 Pelle Eklund	1.00	2.50
13 Andre Faust	1.00	2.50
14 Brent Fedyk	1.00	2.50
15 Brent Fedyk	1.00	2.50
16 Jeff Finley	1.00	2.50
17 Garry Galley	1.00	2.50
18 Greg Hawgood	1.00	2.50
19 Tim Kerr	2.00	5.00
20 Mark Lamb	1.00	2.50
21 Eric Lindros	4.00	10.00
22 Eric Lindros	4.00	10.00
23 Eric Lindros	4.00	10.00
24 Stewart Malgunas	1.00	2.50
25 Ryan McGill	1.00	2.50
26 Yves Racine	1.00	2.50
27 Rob Ramage	1.00	2.50
28 Mark Recchi	2.00	5.00
29 Mark Recchi	2.00	5.00
30 Mikael Renberg	1.00	2.50
31 Dominic Roussel	1.50	4.00
32 Dominic Roussel	1.50	4.00
33 Dave Tippett	1.00	2.50
34 Dmitri Yushkevich	1.00	2.50
35 Dmitri Yushkevich	1.00	2.50
36 Rob Zettler	1.00	2.50
37 The Coaches	1.00	2.50
38 Team Photo	1.00	2.50
39 Team Photo	1.00	2.50
40 Renberg, Bowen, Malgunas	1.00	2.50
41 The Captains	2.00	5.00
42 Recchi, Lindros, Galley	2.00	5.00
43 Flyers and their Fans	1.00	2.50

1996-97 Flyers Postcards

This attractive 24-card set was produced late in the '96-97 season by the club. The standard-sized postcards featured an action photo on the front, along with the player's name, position and jersey number. The back contained a remarkably thorough stats package, including career numbers, awards and transaction info. Unnumbered, the cards are listed below in alphabetical order.

COMPLETE SET (24)	6.00	15.00
1 Team Photo	.20	.50
2 Rod Brind'Amour	.30	.75
3 Paul Coffey	.40	1.00
4 Scott Daniels	.08	.25
5 Eric Desjardins	.15	.40
6 John Druce	.08	.25
7 Karl Dykhuis	.08	.25
8 Pat Falloon	.08	.25
9 Dale Hawerchuk	.30	.75
10 Ron Hextall	.30	.75
11 Trent Klatt	.08	.25
12 Dan Kordic	.08	.25
13 Daniel Lacroix	.08	.25
14 John LeClair	.75	2.00
15 Eric Lindros	2.00	5.00
16 Janne Niinimaa	.60	1.50
17 Joel Otto	.08	.25
18 Shjon Podein	.08	.25
19 Mikael Renberg	.30	.75
20 Kjell Samuelsson	.08	.25
21 Garth Snow	.20	.50
22 Petr Svoboda	.08	.25
23 Chris Therien	.08	.25
24 Dainius Zubrus	.75	2.00

1997 Flyers Phone Cards

These phone cards produced by Comcast, were available only in the Philadelphia area. Each card was worth 15-minutes of long distance.

COMPLETE SET (4)	3.00	8.00
1 Alexandre Daigle	.40	1.00
2 Chris Gratton	.40	1.00
3 John LeClair	1.25	3.00
4 Eric Lindros	2.00	5.00

2001-02 Flyers Postcards

This 30-card set featured full-color action photos bordered by team colors and logos. Each card measured approximately 4" X 6". The set was unnumbered and is listed below in alphabetical order.

COMPLETE SET (30)	9.78	24.44
1 Brian Boucher	1.00	2.50
2 Donald Brashear	.30	.75
3 Roman Cechmanek	.40	1.00
4 Eric Desjardins	.20	.50
5 Jiri Dopita	.40	1.00
6 Todd Fedoruk	.30	.75
7 Ruslan Fedotenko	.30	.75
8 Simon Gagne	1.20	3.00
9 Kim Johnsson	.20	.50
10 Kent Manderville	.20	.50
11 John LeClair	.80	2.00
12 Chris McAllister	.20	.50
13 Dan McGillis	.20	.50
14 Marty Murray	.20	.50
15 Keith Primeau	.40	1.00
16 Paul Ranheim	.20	.50
17 Mark Recchi	.40	1.00
18 Luke Richardson	.20	.50
19 Jeremy Roenick	.80	2.00
20 Chris Therien	.20	.50
21 Rick Tocchet	.30	.75
22 Eric Weinrich	.20	.50
23 Justin Williams	.40	1.00
24 Flyers Team Photo	.40	1.00
25 Bill Barber	.10	.25
Mike Stothers		
E.J. McGuire		
26 Broadcasters	.04	.10
27 Bob Clarke GM	.30	.75
28 Ron Hextall ACO	.30	.75
29 Phantoms Team Photo	.20	.50
30 Phlex MASCOT	.10	.25

2002-03 Flyers Postcards

COMPLETE SET (24)	8.00	20.00
1 Eric Weinrich	.30	.75
2 Kim Johnsson	.30	.75
3 Mark Recchi	.40	1.00
4 John LeClair	.40	1.00
5 Simon Gagne	.60	1.50
6 Justin Williams	.30	.75
7 Paul Ranheim	.30	.75
8 Radovan Somik	.30	.75
9 Chris McAllister	.30	.75
10 Keith Primeau	.40	1.00
11 Chris Therien	.30	.75
12 Michal Handzus	.30	.75
13 Todd Fedoruk	.40	1.00
14 Roman Cechmanek	.40	1.00
15 Dennis Seidenberg	.30	.75
16 Eric Desjardins	.30	.75
17 Marty Murray	.30	.75
18 Robert Esche	.40	1.00
19 Pavel Brendl	.30	.75
20 Donald Brashear	.30	.75
21 Jeremy Roenick	.75	2.00
22 The Coaches	.10	.25
23 Team Card	.20	.50
24 Philadelphia Phantoms	.20	.50

2003-04 Flyers Program Inserts

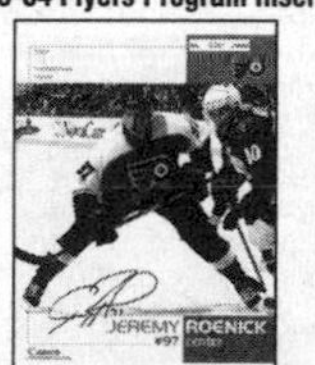

Inserted into individual game programs, these sheets measure approximately 8 1/2" x 11" and each sheet was individually serial-numbered at the top. The checklist below is incomplete. If you have any further info on this set, please forward it to hockeymag@beckett.com.

1 Jeremy Roenick	2.00	5.00
2 Joni Pitkanen	1.25	3.00
3 Tony Amonte	1.50	4.00
4 Robert Esche	1.50	4.00
5 Danny Markov	1.25	3.00
6 Keith Primeau	1.50	4.00

2003-04 Flyers Postcards

This 24-card set was produced by the team and available through the team website and appearances.

COMPLETE SET (24)	8.00	20.00
1 Tony Amonte	.40	1.00
2 Donald Brashear	.40	1.00
3 Mike Comrie	.40	1.00
4 Eric Desjardins	.20	.50
5 Robert Esche	.40	1.00
6 Todd Fedoruk	.40	1.00
7 Simon Gagne	.40	1.00
8 Jeff Hackett	.30	.75
9 Michal Handzus	.20	.50
10 Kim Johnsson	.20	.50
11 Sami Kapanen	.20	.50
12 Claude Lapointe	.20	.50
13 John LeClair	.40	1.00
14 Danny Markov	.20	.50
15 Joni Pitkanen	.40	1.00
16 Keith Primeau	.40	1.00
17 Marcus Ragnarsson	.20	.50
18 Mark Recchi	.40	1.00
19 Jeremy Roenick	.75	2.00
20 Radovan Somik	.20	.50
21 Chris Therien	.20	.50
22 Jim Vandermeer	.20	.50
23 Eric Weinrich	.20	.50
24 Coaches	.10	.25

2005-06 Flyers Team Issue

COMPLETE SET (25)	8.00	15.00
1 Philadelphia Flyers CL	.01	.01
2 Donald Brashear	.30	.75
3 Jeff Carter	2.00	5.00
4 Eric Desjardins	.20	.50
5 Robert Esche	.30	.75
6 Peter Forsberg	.75	2.00
7 Simon Gagne	.40	1.00
8 Michal Handzus	.20	.50
9 Derian Hatcher	.20	.50
10 Kim Johnsson	.20	.50
11 Sami Kapanen	.20	.50
12 Mike Knuble	.20	.50
13 Antero Niittymaki	.75	2.00
14 Joni Pitkanen	.40	1.00
15 Keith Primeau	.20	.50
16 Branko Radivojevic	.20	.50
17 Mike Rathje	.20	.50
18 Mike Richards	.40	1.00
19 Brian Savage	.20	.50
20 Dennis Seidenberg	.20	.50
21 Patrick Sharp	.20	.50
22 Jonathan Sim	.20	.50
23 Turner Stevenson	.20	.50
24 Chris Therien	.20	.50
25 R.J. Umberger	.40	1.00

2006-07 Flyers Postcards

COMPLETE SET (23)	10.00	25.00
1 Derian Hatcher	.40	1.00
2 Mike Rathje	.40	1.00
3 Randy Jones	.40	1.00
4 Geoff Sanderson	.40	1.00
5 Scottie Upshall	.40	1.00
6 Simon Gagne	.75	2.00
7 Jeff Carter	.75	2.00
8 Mike Richards	.75	2.00
9 Kyle Calder	.40	1.00
10 R.J. Umberger	.40	1.00
11 Mike Knuble	.40	1.00
12 Denis Gauthier	.40	1.00
13 Sami Kapanen	.40	1.00
14 Dmitry Afanasenkov	.40	1.00
15 Todd Fedoruk	.75	2.00
16 Antero Niittymaki	.60	1.50
17 Robert Esche	.60	1.50
18 Joni Pitkanen	.40	1.00
19 Alexandre Picard	.40	1.00
20 Michael Leighton	.60	1.50
21 Ben Eager	.40	1.00
22 Mike York	.40	1.00
23 Alexei Zhitnik	.40	1.00

1971-72 Frito-Lay

This ten-card set featured members of the Toronto Maple Leafs and Montreal Canadiens. Since the cards were unnumbered, they had been listed below in alphabetical order within team, Montreal (1-5) and Toronto (6-10). The cards were paper thin, each measuring approximately 1 1/2" by 2".

COMPLETE SET (10)	50.00	100.00
1 Yvan Cournoyer	4.00	8.00
2 Ken Dryden	25.00	50.00
3 Frank Mahovlich	5.00	10.00
4 Henri Richard	5.00	10.00
5 J.C. Tremblay	2.00	4.00
6 Bobby Baun	2.00	4.00
7 Ron Ellis	2.00	4.00
8 Paul Henderson	3.00	6.00
9 Jacques Plante	10.00	20.00
10 Norm Ullman	3.00	6.00

1988-89 Frito-Lay Stickers

The 1988-89 Frito-Lay Hockey Stickers set included 42 small (1 3/8" by 1 3/4") stickers. The fronts were dominated by color photos, but also had each player's name and uniform number. The stickers were distributed in sealed plastic, and packaged one per special Frito-Lay snack bag. Reportedly distribution was via 35 million bags of Ruffles, O'Gradys, Dulac, Lays, Doritos, Fritos, Tostitos, Cheetos, and Chester Popcorn -- each containing one of the 42 players in the set. Since they were actually stickers, there was very little information on the backing. The checklist below also gave the player's uniform number as listed on each card. A poster was also available from the company by sending in 2.00 and one UPC symbol from any Frito-Lay product.

COMPLETE SET (42)	12.00	30.00
1 Mario Lemieux 66	2.50	6.00
2 Bryan Trottier 19	.20	.50
3 Steve Yzerman 19	1.50	4.00
4 Bernie Federko 24	.15	.40
5 Brian Bellows 23	.15	.40
6 Denis Savard 18	.20	.50
7 Neal Broten 7	.15	.40
8 Doug Gilmour 9	.60	1.50
9 Dale Hawerchuk 10	.20	.50
10 Luc Robitaille 20	.60	1.50
11 Ed Olczyk 16	.08	.25
12 Andrew McBain 20	.08	.25
13 Mike Gartner 11	.20	.50
14 Pat LaFontaine 16	.40	1.00
15 Scott Stevens 3	.20	.50
16 Ray Bourque 77	.75	2.00
17 Cam Neely 8	.60	1.50
18 Mike Foligno 17	.08	.25
19 Tom Barrasso 30	.20	.50
20 Ron Francis 10	.30	.75
21 Peter Stastny 26	.20	.50
22 Michel Goulet 16	.20	.50
23 Bernie Nicholls 9	.20	.50
24 Paul Coffey 77	.60	1.50
25 Mats Naslund 26	.15	.40
26 Glenn Anderson 9	.20	.50
27 Dave Poulin 20	.08	.25
28 Kevin Dineen 11	.08	.25
29 Wendel Clark 17	.30	.75
30 James Patrick 3	.08	.25

31 Al MacInnis 2 .30 .75
32 Troy Murray 19 .08 .25
33 Kirk Muller 9 .20 .50
34 Marcel Dionne 16 .20 .50
35 Mark Messier 11 .75 2.00
36 Joe Nieuwendyk 25 .60 1.50
37 Ron Hextall 27 .30 .75
38 Sean Burke 1 .20 .50
39 Barry Pederson 7 .08 .25
40 Stephane Richer 44 .20 .50
41 Bob Probert 24 .60 1.50
42 Tony Tanti 9 .08 .25
NNO Set Poster 1.25 3.00

1996-97 Frosted Flakes Masks

One of these 7 cards was inserted into specially marked boxes of Frosted Flakes in Canada early in the season. These unique die-cut cards featured a net design and a goalie mask, which could be popped up on display in front of the net. Just two of the cards featured the actual faces and mask designs of individual goalies (#1-2). Cards 3-6 featured generic masks with the design of the team logo, while the seventh featured a Tony the Tiger mask. The complete set was available by mail for $2.50 plus three proofs of purchase.

COMPLETE SET (7) 8.00 20.00
1 Felix Potvin 1.25 3.00
2 Curtis Joseph 2.00 5.00
3 Montreal Canadiens 1.25 3.00
4 Ottawa Senators 1.25 3.00
5 Calgary Flames 1.25 3.00
6 Vancouver Canucks 1.25 3.00
7 Tony the Tiger 1.25 3.00

1991-92 Future Trends Canada '72 Promos

This standard-size three-card set was issued to promote the release of Future Trends' Team Canada '72 set. To commemorate Team Canada of 1972, 7200 of each promotional card were offered for sale at Canada's Hudson Bay Stores. The fronts featured full-bleed black-and-white action shots from a game between Team Canada and the Soviet team. The card title appeared in white lettering within a red stripe across the bottom of the picture. The '72 Hockey Canada logo appeared in the lower right. Except for their horizontal orientation, the backs were similar to the fronts, with full-bleed black-and-white photos, white lettering within a red stripe at the bottom, and logo in the lower right. The cards were unnumbered and checklisted below in alphabetical order by title. These promos were issued in English and French versions.

COMPLETE SET (3) 7.20 18.00
1 The Goal 3.00 8.00
The Scoreboard
2 The Leader 4.00 10.00
Phil Esposito
3 The Legend 2.50 6.00
The Kid

1991-92 Future Trends Canada '72

Future Trends Experience Ltd. produced this 101-card standard-size set to celebrate the 20th anniversary of the 1972 Summit Series between the Soviets and the Canadians. The cards were available initially only at the Bay and were sold in ten-card foil packs with no factory sets. The 70 players of the Canadian and Russian teams were represented, and 30 additional special cards captured unforgettable moments from the series. Between one and two special cards, signed in gold paint pen by living Canadian players, were randomly inserted into each foil case. Only one non-Canadian, Vladislav Tretiak, signed cards. Supposedly each of the signers signed only 750 cards for insertion and distribution within the packs. These cards were specially coated with a swirl pattern over the autograph. Reportedly, The Bay also issued 2500 autographed sets without the special coating, but we have no confirmation of this at this time. The cards featured on the fronts borderless black-and-white, action or posed pictures. A white, red, and gold stripe cut across the bottom of the card face and intersected the '72 Hockey Canada logo at the lower right corner. The backs carried additional photos, biographical information, series statistics, sportswriters' editorial comments, and/or player quotes. Card number 40 featured Phil Esposito's September 8, 1972, address to the nation. The card number appeared in a blue oblong design within the bottom red stripe on both sides. The '72 Hockey Canada logo also appeared in the lower right corner of the back. The set was issued in both an English and a French version. The production quantities were reportedly 9,000 English and 1,000 French 12-box cases. Also released were 1972 uncut sheet sets. Signed cards generally commanded 100 to 250 times the values below.

COMPLETE SET (101) 2.50 6.00
1 In The Beginning .05 .15
2 The Backyard Rink .01 .05
3 It Didn't Take Long .01 .05
4 The Patriarch .05 .15
Anatoli Tarasov
5 More Hours a Day .20 .50
Vladislav Tretiak
6 Coming Out Party .05 .15
7 Never In Doubt .01 .05
8 Team Canada .08 .25
9 Pat Stapleton .01 .05
10 Vsevolod Bobrov .01 .05
11 Vladislav Tretiak .20 .50
12 Faceoff .01 .05
Game 1& Montreal (9/2/72)
13 30 Seconds .02 .10
Game 1& Montreal (9/2/72)
14 Yevgeny Zimin .01 .05
15 Bill White .01 .05
16 7-3 .01 .05
Game 1 Statistics
17 Don Awrey .01 .05
18 Mickey Redmond .07 .20
19 Alexander Gusev .05 .15
20 Alexander Maltsev .08 .25
21 Rod Seiling .01 .05
22 Dale Tallon .01 .05
23 Coming Back .01 .05
Game 2& Toronto (9/4/72)
24 Unforgettable .01 .05
Game 2 Statistics
25 Wayne Cashman .05 .15
26 Frank Mahovlich .08 .25
27 Peter Mahovlich .01 .05
28 Vyacheslav Solodukhin .05 .15
Alexander Sidelnikov
29 Yuri Shatalov .05 .15
30 Brothers .05 .15
Frank Mahovlich
Peter Mahovlich
31 The Goalies .20 .50
32 Alexander Bodunov .01 .05
33 All Even .01 .05
Game 3 Statistics
34 Yuri Blinov .01 .05
35 Jocelyn Guevremont .01 .05
36 Vic Hadfield .01 .05
37 Yuri Lebedev .01 .05
38 Yevgeny Poladiev .05 .15
Vyacheslav Starshinov
39 Disaster .01 .05
Game 4 Statistics
40 Address to The Nation .08 .25
Phil Esposito
41 Victor Kuzkin .01 .05
42 Vladimir Lutchenko .08 .25
43 Boris Mikhailov .15 .40
44 Grace Under Pressure .01 .05
Game 5& Moscow (9/22/72)
45 Afraid to Lose .01 .05
46 Ready To Win .01 .05
Game 5 Statistics
47 Vladimir Vikulov .01 .05
48 Red Berenson .01 .05
49 Richard Martin .01 .05
50 Alexander Martynyuk .01 .05
51 Gilbert Perreault .08 .25
52 Vladimir Petrov .15 .40
53 Serge Savard .05 .15
54 Vladimir Shadrin .01 .05
55 DA DA KA-NA-DA .01 .05
Game 6& Moscow (9/24/72)
56 One Step Back .01 .05
Game 6 Statistics
57 Bobby Clarke .15 .40
58 Valeri Kharlamov .20 .50
59 Alexander Volchkov .05 .15
60 Standing Guard .05 .15
61 Stan Mikita .15 .40
62 One More To Go .01 .05
Game 7 Statistics
Moscow (9/26/72)
63 The Winner .01 .05
64 The Fans Go Wild .01 .05
65 Alexander Ragulin .05 .15
66 Jean Ratelle .05 .15
67 Gennady Tsygankov .05 .15
68 Valeri Vasiliev .15 .40
69 International Dialogue .01 .05
70 Series Stars .15 .40
Phil Esposito
Alexander Yakushev
71 Series Stars .15 .40
Borje Salming
Paul Henderson
Vladislav Tretiak
72 No Solitudes .01 .05
Game 8& Moscow (9/28/72)
The Telegrams
73 2-2 .01 .05
Game 8& Moscow (9/28/72)
74 Rod Gilbert .05 .15
75 Yevgeny Mishakov .05 .15
76 Ron Ellis .01 .05
77 5-4 .01 .05
78 Different Games .01 .05
Game 8& Moscow (9/28/72)
Interlude
79 Bill Goldsworthy .01 .05
80 The Huddle .01 .05
81 The Moment .20 .50
82 Yvan Cournoyer .08 .25
83 Yuri Liapkin .01 .05
84 Phil Esposito .15 .40
85 Ken Dryden .20 .50
86 Peace .01 .05
Game 8 Statistics
87 Gary Bergman .01 .05
88 Brian Glennie .01 .05
89 Dennis Hull .01 .05
90 Vyacheslav Anisin .01 .05
91 Marcel Dionne .08 .25
92 Guy Lapointe .05 .15
93 Ed Johnston .02 .10
94 Harry Sinden GM .01 .05
95 Brad Park .08 .25
96 Tony Esposito .08 .25
97 Alexander Yakushev .15 .40
98 Paul Henderson .20 .50
99 J.P. Parise .01 .05
100 Valeri Kharlamov .20 .50
Alex Kharlamov on back
101 Checklist .05 .15

1992 Future Trends '76 Canada Cup

This 100-card, standard-size set was produced by The Future Trends Experience Ltd. and licensed by Hockey Canada. Commemorating the 1976 Canada Cup, the card numbering picked up where the '72 Team Canada set left off by tracing the growth of international hockey. According to the company the production run was 50,000 numbered display boxes. Randomly inserted in the packs were 3,750 gold-foil stamped signature cards; five players (Bobby Orr, Bobby Hull, Rogatien Vachon, Darryl Sittler, and Bobby Clarke) signed 750 cards each. These cards are valued generally 75 to 100 times the values below. A Tretiak card serial-numbered out of 1976 is also known to exist. The cards featured vertical and horizontal color action and posed player and team photos. Some shots were of game action with several players pictured. The bottom of each was accented by red and gold border stripes with a red Canada Cup logo in the right corner. Most cards were bordered in white, but some were bordered on the top by the national flags of the various teams in the set. The horizontal backs carried the same flag pattern ghosted behind information about the pictured player or team. A color photo of the players or player was displayed to the right of the copy. Red and gold border stripes similar to the front appeared below. Topical subsets featured are '72 Retrospective (102-106), 1974 Russian team vs. WHA (107-110), a 6-card training camp subset (111-116), MVPs (184-190), and the first ever Canada Cup All-Star Team (195-200). The cards were numbered on the back. An 8 1/2" by 11" sheet was also issued; it has an artist's color painting of the players on the front and a checklist on its back.

COMPLETE SET (100) 3.00 8.00
102 Phil Esposito .15 .40
103 Vladislav Tretiak .20 .50
104 Bobby Orr .30 .75
105 Paul Henderson .05 .15
The Goal
106 Alexander Yakushev .05 .15
107 Bobby Hull .20 .50
108 Valeri Kharlamov .15 .40
109 Gerry Cheevers .08 .25
Vladislav Tretiak
110 Bobby Hull .20 .50
Vladislav Tretiak
111 Soviet on-ice workout .02 .10
112 Czech on-ice workout .01 .05
113 Finn on-ice workout .01 .05
114 Swedes take the ice .01 .05
115 USA on-ice workout .02 .10
116 Darryl Sittler .08 .25
117 Serge Savard .05 .15
118 Team Finland .01 .05
119 Team Sweden .01 .05
120 Team Czechoslavakia .01 .05
121 Soviets .05 .15
122 Team USA .05 .15
123 Team Canada .05 .15
124 The Opening Barrage .01 .05
125 Richard Martin .01 .05
126 Bobby Orr .30 .75
127 Sweden vs. USA .01 .05
128 Ivan Hlinka .01 .05
129 CSSR 5 - CCCP 3 .01 .05
130 Helmut Balderis .05 .15
131 Peter Stastny .07 .20
132 Valeri Vasiliev .05 .15
133 Out of Contention .01 .05
134 Standing Alone .01 .05
135 The Miracle On Ice .01 .05
136 Josef Augusta .01 .05
137 A Soviet Rout .01 .05
138 Vicktor Zhluktov .02 .10
139 Bobby Hull .15 .40
Phil Esposito
Marcel Dionne
140 Bob Gainey .05 .15
141 Anders Hedberg .05 .15
142 Bobby Hull .20 .50
143 Ulf Nilsson .05 .15
144 Sergei Kapustin .05 .15
145 Borje Salming .05 .15
146 Well Enough To Win .01 .05
147 Biggest Upset .01 .05
148 Matti Hagman .01 .05
149 Unbeatable .01 .05
150 Boris Alexandrov .05 .15
151 A Goal Tending Duel .02 .10
152 Vladimir Dzurilla .02 .10
153 Phil Esposito .15 .40
154 Rogatien Vachon .05 .15
155 Milan Novy .01 .05
156 Vladimir Martinec .02 .10
157 Good For Hockey .01 .05
158 Bill Nyrop .01 .05
159 Pride .01 .05
160 Another Summit .01 .05
161 Alexander Maltsev .05 .15
162 Gilbert Perreault .08 .25
163 Vladislav Tretiak .20 .50
163A Vladislav Tretiak AU
164 Vladimir Vikulov .02 .10
165 Canada Cup Final .01 .05
Game 1
166 Not There Yet .01 .05
167 Fast and Furious .01 .05
168 4 - 3 .01 .05
4 - 4
169 Bill Barber .05 .15
170 The Grapevine .02 .10
171 Guy Lapointe .05 .15
172 Reggie Leach .01 .05
173 Sittler's Goal .08 .25
174 Lanny McDonald .08 .25
175 Darryl Sittler .08 .25
176 The Canada Cup .05 .15
177 Bobby Clarke .08 .25
178 Last Time for No. 9 .08 .25
179 Marcel Dionne .08 .25
180 Peter Mahovlich .01 .05
181 Denis Potvin .08 .25
182 Larry Robinson .08 .25
183 Steve Shutt .05 .15
184 Bobby Orr .30 .75
Tournament MVP
185 Rogatien Vachon .05 .15
186 Milan Novy .02 .10
187 Matti Hagman .01 .05
188 Borje Salming .05 .15
189 Robbie Ftorek .01 .05
190 Alexander Maltsev .05 .15
191 Canada Final Series .01 .05
192 Canada Series Totals .01 .05
193 CSSR Final Series .01 .05
194 CSSR Series Totals .01 .05
195 Rogatien Vachon AS .05 .15
196 Bobby Orr AS .30 .75
197 Borje Salming AS .05 .15
198 Milan Novy AS .01 .05
199 Darryl Sittler AS .05 .15
200 Alexander Maltsev AS .05 .15
201 Canada Cup Checklist .02 .10
NNO Checklist Sheet .75 2.00
(8 1/2~ by 11~; artist rendition on front)

1992 Gartlan USA Wayne Gretzky

1 Wayne Gretzky

1997 Gatorade Stickers

This set was issued as a promotional giveaway with the purchase of a Gatorade beverage in Canada. The stickers featured head shots and a brief note of interest about the player. They were distributed in six sheets, with four players appearing on each sheet.

COMPLETE SET (6) 8.00 20.00
1 Daniel Alfredsson
2 Vincent Damphousse
3 Tie Domi
4 Grant Fuhr
5 Bill Guerin
6 Jarome Iginla
7 Jaromir Jagr
8 Paul Kariya
9 Saku Koivu
10 Eric Lindros
11 Mark Messier
12 Mike Modano
13 Alexander Mogilny
14 Joe Nieuwendyk
15 Chris Pronger
16 Mark Recchi
17 Luc Robitaille
18 Patrick Roy
19 Joe Sakic
20 Teemu Selanne
21 Mats Sundin
22 Jose Theodore
23 Ron Tugnutt
24 Doug Weight
PAN1 Daniel Alfredsson .40 1.00
Vincent Damphousse
Bill Guerin
Jarome Iginla
PAN2 Saku Koivu
Eric Lindros
Mark Messier
Mike Modano
PAN3 Alexander Mogilny .60 1.50
Jose Theodore
Ron Tugnutt
Doug Weight
PAN4 Joe Nieuwendyk .60 1.50
Chris Pronger
Mark Recchi
Luc Robitaille
PAN5 Tie Domi 2.00 5.00
Grant Fuhr
Jaromir Jagr
Paul Kariya
PAN6 Patrick Roy 4.00 10.00
Joe Sakic
Teemu Selanne
Mats Sundin

2006-07 Gatorade

COMPLETE SET (91) 60.00 100.00
1 Miikka Kiprusoff 1.50 4.00
2 Dion Phaneuf 2.00 5.00
3 Jarome Iginla 2.00 5.00
4 Alex Tanguay 1.25 3.00
5 Daymond Langkow .75 2.00
6 Matthew Lombardi .75 2.00
7 Chuck Kobasew .40 1.00
8 Kristian Huselius .40 1.00
9 Roman Hamrlik .40 1.00
10 Stephane Yelle .40 1.00
11 Tony Amonte .40 1.00
12 Robyn Regehr .40 1.00
13 Jeff Friesen .40 1.00
14 Marcus Nilson .40 1.00
15 Andrew Ference .40 1.00
16 Petr Sykora .40 1.00
17 Ales Hemsky 1.25 3.00
18 Joffrey Lupul .75 2.00
19 Dwayne Roloson .75 2.00
20 Ryan Smyth 1.25 3.00
21 Jarret Stoll .75 2.00
22 Patrick Thoresen .75 2.00
23 Raffi Torres .75 2.00
24 Fernando Pisani .75 2.00
25 Shawn Horcoff .75 2.00
26 Marc-Andre Bergeron .40 1.00
27 Jason Smith .40 1.00
28 Ladislav Smid .40 1.00
29 Steve Staios .40 1.00
30 Jussi Markkanen .60 1.50
31 Saku Koivu 2.00 5.00
32 Chris Higgins .75 2.00
33 Sheldon Souray .40 1.00
34 Andrei Markov .40 1.00
35 Michael Ryder .75 2.00
36 Cristobal Huet 1.50 4.00
37 David Aebischer .75 2.00
38 Alex Kovalev .40 1.00
39 Mike Johnson .40 1.00
40 Alexander Perezhogin .40 1.00
41 Guillaume Latendresse 2.00 5.00
42 Radek Bonk .40 1.00
43 Sergei Samsonov .75 2.00
44 Tomas Plekanec .75 2.00
45 Michael Komisarek .75 2.00
46 Jason Spezza 1.25 3.00
47 Dany Heatley 1.50 4.00
48 Joe Corvo .40 1.00
49 Daniel Alfredsson 1.25 3.00
50 Martin Gerber .75 2.00
51 Ray Emery 1.25 3.00
52 Antoine Vermette .40 1.00
53 Patrick Eaves .40 1.00
54 Dean McAmmond .40 1.00
55 Mike Fisher .75 2.00
56 Chris Neil .75 2.00
57 Wade Redden .75 2.00
58 Chris Phillips .75 2.00
59 Andrej Meszaros .75 2.00
60 Chris Kelly .40 1.00
61 Mats Sundin 1.25 3.00
62 Alexander Steen 1.25 3.00
63 Darcy Tucker 1.25 3.00
64 Kyle Wellwood .75 2.00
65 Andrew Raycroft .75 2.00
66 Bryan McCabe .75 2.00
67 Tomas Kaberle .75 2.00
68 Jeff O'Neill .40 1.00
69 Alexei Ponikarovsky .40 1.00
70 Ian White .40 1.00
71 Michael Peca .75 2.00
72 Chad Kilger .40 1.00
73 Hal Gill .40 1.00
74 Matt Stajan .75 2.00
75 Pavel Kubina .40 1.00
76 Markus Naslund .75 2.00
77 Roberto Luongo 2.00 5.00
78 Daniel Sedin .75 2.00
79 Henrik Sedin .75 2.00
80 Brendan Morrison .40 1.00
81 Sami Salo .40 1.00
82 Jan Bulis .40 1.00
83 Taylor Pyatt .40 1.00
84 Mattias Ohlund .40 1.00
85 Lukas Krajicek .40 1.00
86 Trevor Linden 1.25 3.00
87 Ryan Kesler .40 1.00
88 Matt Cooke .40 1.00
89 Willie Mitchell .40 1.00
90 Kevin Bieksa .75 2.00
91 Sidney Crosby SP 25.00 60.00

1967-68 General Mills

Little is known about this recently catalogued five-card set, save for it measured approximately 2 5/16" by 2 13/16" and featured color player photos in a white border. It appeared the cards were cut-outs from boxes of General Mills cereal, as a full box back picturing Harry Howell with a checklist listing these cards was known to exist. Further information would be appreciated. The backs are blank. The cards are unnumbered and checklisted below in alphabetical order.

COMPLETE SET (5) 500.00 1000.00
1 Jean Beliveau 75.00 150.00
2 Gordie Howe 150.00 300.00
3 Harry Howell 40.00 80.00
4 Stan Mikita 62.50 125.00
5 Bobby Orr 250.00 500.00

1991-92 Gillette

This 48-card standard-size set, sponsored by Gillette, featured players from the old four divisions of the NHL: Smythe (1-10), Norris (11-20), Adams (21-30), and Patrick (31-40). Each ten-card pack came with a trivia card and a checklist card. To receive one ten-card pack, collectors were required to send to Gillette of Canada one UPC symbol from any Canadian Gillette product, the dated receipt with purchase price circled, and 2.00 for shipping and handling. The entire set could be obtained by sending in three UPC symbols plus 5.00. Reportedly just 30,000 sets were produced, and the offer expired on August 28, 1992. On a black card face, the fronts carried a color action photo enclosed by a gold border. The title "Gillette Series" appeard in gold lettering at the top, while the player's name appeard at the bottom between the 75th NHL Anniversary logo and the team logo. Some of the cards had the words "Rookie Card" in the bottom gold border (numbers 3, 10, 20, 30, 40). In a horizontal format, the backs had biography and statistics (1987-91) in English and French, as well as a color head shot. The player cards were numbered on the back. Although the backs of the four unnumbered checklist cards were identical (each one lists all 40 cards), a different division name appeard on the front of each checklist card: Smythe, Norris, Adams, and Patrick. The fronts of each of the four unnumbered trivia card were identical, while their backs featured two different questions and answers.

COMPLETE SET (48) 10.00 25.00
1 Luc Robitaille .20 .50
2 Esa Tikkanen .08 .25
3 Pat Falloon .05 .15
4 Theo Fleury .30 .75
5 Trevor Linden .20 .50
6 Rob Blake .20 .50
7 Al MacInnis .20 .50
8 Bob Essensa .20 .50
9 Bill Ranford .20 .50
10 Pavel Bure .75 2.00
11 Wendel Clark .20 .50
12 Sergei Fedorov .60 1.50
13 Jeremy Roenick .30 .75
14 Brett Hull .40 1.00
15 Mike Modano .40 1.00
16 Chris Chelios .30 .75
17 Dave Ellett .05 .15
18 Ed Belfour .30 .75
19 Grant Fuhr .20 .50
20 Martin Lapointe .05 .15
21 Kirk Muller .08 .25
22 Joe Sakic .60 1.50
23 Pat LaFontaine .20 .50
24 Pat Verbeek .20 .50
25 Owen Nolan .20 .50
26 Ray Bourque .40 1.00
27 Eric Desjardins .08 .25
28 Patrick Roy 1.50 4.00
29 Andy Moog .20 .50
30 Valeri Kamensky .20 .50
31 Mark Messier .40 1.00
32 Mike Ricci .20 .50
33 Mario Lemieux 1.50 4.00
34 Jaromir Jagr 1.00 2.50
35 Pierre Turgeon .20 .50
36 Kevin Hatcher .05 .15
37 Paul Coffey .30 .75
38 Chris Terreri .08 .25
39 Mike Richter .30 .75
40 Kevin Todd .05 .15
NNO Smythe Checklist .02 .10
NNO Smythe Trivia .02 .10
NNO Norris Checklist .02 .10
NNO Adams Trivia .02 .10
NNO Patrick Trivia .02 .10
NNO Patrick Checklist .02 .10
NNO Norris Trivia .02 .10
NNO Adams Checklist .02 .10

2001-02 Greats of the Game

Released in mid-October 2001, this set carried an SRP of $5.99 for a 5-card pack. The 89-card set featured past greats of the NHL with color and black-and-white photos on white background card fronts.

COMPLETE SET (89) 15.00 30.00
1 Gordie Howe 1.00 2.50
2 Glenn Hall .30 .75
3 Jean Beliveau .30 .75
4 Bob Nystrom .20 .50
5 Phil Esposito .50 1.25
6 Dennis Maruk .20 .50
7 Bobby Hull .50 1.25
8 Guy Lafleur .40 1.00
9 Gilbert Perreault .20 .50
10 John Davidson .25 .60
11 Peter Stastny .25 .60
12 Steve Shutt .20 .50
13 Henri Richard .30 .75
14 Johnny Bower .30 .75
15 Barry Beck .20 .50
16 Marcel Dionne .30 .75
17 Billy Smith .25 .60
18 Dale Hunter .20 .50
19 Tony Esposito .40 1.00
20 Guy Lapointe .20 .50
21 Ed Giacomin .30 .75
22 Denis Savard .25 .60
23 Rod Gilbert .30 .75
24 Steve Larmer .20 .50
25 Yvan Cournoyer .30 .75
26 Ulf Nilsson .20 .50
27 Jean Ratelle .20 .50
28 Dino Ciccarelli .20 .50
29 Bryan Trottier .25 .60
30 Tim Horton .25 .60
31 Stan Mikita .40 1.00
32 Glenn Anderson .20 .50
33 Bobby Clarke .30 .75
34 Wendel Clark .25 .60
35 Reggie Leach .20 .50
36 Terry Sawchuk .50 1.25
37 Bernie Geoffrion .30 .75
38 Bill Barber .20 .50
39 Tiger Williams .25 .60
40 Alex Delvecchio .30 .75
41 Bernie Parent .25 .60
42 Paul Henderson .20 .50
43 Norm Ullman .20 .50
44 Larry Robinson .25 .60
45 Dave Schultz .25 .60
46 John Ogrodnick .20 .50
47 Rick MacLeish .20 .50
48 Richard Brodeur .25 .60
49 Rick Martin .20 .50
50 Bobby Smith .20 .50
51 Denis Potvin .25 .60
52 Darryl Sittler .30 .75
53 Lanny McDonald .30 .75
54 Brian Bellows .20 .50
55 Frank Mahovlich .30 .75
56 Cam Neely .25 .60
57 Grant Fuhr .25 .60
58 Harry Howell .20 .50
59 Michel Goulet .20 .50
60 Gerry Cheevers .40 1.00
61 Dave Taylor .20 .50
62 Clark Gillies .20 .50
63 Bernie Federko .20 .50
64 Chico Resch .25 .60
65 Andy Bathgate .30 .75
66 Jacques Lemaire .25 .60
67 Ken Hodge .20 .50
68 Rogie Vachon .30 .75
69 Brian Sutter .25 .60
70 Rick Middleton .20 .50
71 Neal Broten .20 .50
72 Mike Bossy .30 .75
73 Borje Salming .25 .60
74 Ted Lindsay .25 .60
75 Mike Gartner .20 .50
76 John Bucyk .20 .50
77 Brad Park .25 .60
78 Red Kelly .30 .75
79 Joe Mullen .20 .50
80 Terry O'Reilly .20 .50
81 Mario Lemieux 1.00 2.50
82 Butch Goring .25 .60
83 Mike Liut .25 .60
84 Marcel Pronovost .20 .50
85 Serge Savard .30 .75
86 Jari Kurri .25 .60
87 Rick Kehoe .20 .50
88 Gump Worsley .30 .75
89 Kent Nilsson .20 .50

2001-02 Greats of the Game Retro Collection

This 13-card set featured both color and vintage black-and-white action photos on the card fronts with colored foil at each top corner and along the card bottom. The players name was printed on the bottom of the card front, and the card backs carried a player bio and league stats.

COMPLETE SET (13) 15.00 30.00
1 Gordie Howe 2.50 6.00
2 Jean Beliveau 1.00 2.50
3 Phil Esposito 1.25 3.00
4 Bobby Hull 1.25 3.00
5 Guy LaFleur 1.00 2.50
6 Peter Stastny .60 1.50
7 Henri Richard .60 1.50
8 Marcel Dionne .75 2.00
9 Bryan Trottier .60 1.50
10 Bobby Clarke .75 2.00
11 Terry Sawchuk 1.25 3.00
12 Mario Lemieux 3.00 8.00
13 Tony Esposito 1.00 2.50

2001-02 Greats of the Game Autographs

Inserted at a rate of 1:12 hobby and 1:120 retail, this set paralleled the base set but the featured player's autograph on the front bottom of the card. Card backs carried a congratulatory message and a statement of authenticity. Cards #30, 36, and 88 were not produced. Most players signed between 400-475 cards except those marked as SP below. Short prints were reported to be less than 200 copies each.

1 Gordie Howe SP 125.00 250.00
2 Glenn Hall SP 25.00 60.00
3 Jean Beliveau SP 30.00 60.00
4 Bob Nystrom 8.00 20.00
5 Phil Esposito SP 25.00 60.00
6 Dennis Maruk 8.00 20.00
7 Bobby Hull SP 30.00 80.00
8 Guy Lafleur SP 20.00 50.00
9 Gilbert Perreault 8.00 20.00
10 John Davidson 8.00 20.00
11 Peter Stastny SP 20.00 50.00
12 Steve Shutt 8.00 20.00
13 Henri Richard SP 25.00 60.00
14 Johnny Bower 8.00 20.00
15 Barry Beck 8.00 20.00
16 Marcel Dionne SP 20.00 50.00
17 Billy Smith 8.00 20.00
18 Dale Hunter 8.00 20.00
19 Tony Esposito 12.00 30.00
20 Guy LaPointe 8.00 20.00
21 Ed Giacomin 10.00 25.00
22 Denis Savard 8.00 20.00
23 Rod Gilbert 15.00 30.00
24 Steve Larmer 8.00 20.00
25 Yvan Cournoyer 8.00 20.00
26 Ulf Nilsson 8.00 20.00
27 Jean Ratelle 8.00 20.00
28 Dino Ciccarelli 10.00 25.00
29 Bryan Trottier SP 15.00 40.00
31 Stan Mikita SP 25.00 60.00
32 Glenn Anderson 8.00 20.00
33 Bobby Clarke SP 25.00 60.00
34 Wendel Clark 15.00 40.00
35 Reggie Leach 8.00 20.00
37 Bernie Geoffrion 15.00 40.00
38 Bill Barber 8.00 20.00
39 Tiger Williams 8.00 20.00
40 Alex Delvecchio SP 12.00 30.00
41 Bernie Parent 12.00 30.00
42 Paul Henderson SP 30.00 80.00

Card	Low	High
43 Norm Ullman	8.00	20.00
44 Larry Robinson	8.00	20.00
45 Dave Schultz	8.00	20.00
46 John Ogrodnick	8.00	20.00
47 Rick MacLeish	8.00	20.00
48 Richard Brodeur	8.00	20.00
49 Rick Martin	8.00	20.00
50 Bobby Smith	8.00	20.00
51 Denis Potvin	8.00	20.00
52 Darryl Sittler	8.00	20.00
53 Lanny McDonald	8.00	20.00
54 Brian Bellows	8.00	20.00
55 Frank Mahovlich	8.00	20.00
56 Cam Neely SP	30.00	60.00
57 Grant Fuhr	10.00	25.00
58 Harry Howell	8.00	20.00
59 Michel Goulet	8.00	20.00
60 Gerry Cheevers	12.00	30.00
61 Dave Taylor	8.00	20.00
62 Clark Gillies	8.00	20.00
63 Bernie Federko	8.00	20.00
64 Chico Resch	15.00	30.00
65 Andy Bathgate	8.00	20.00
66 Jacques Lemaire	8.00	20.00
67 Ken Hodge	8.00	20.00
68 Rogie Vachon	8.00	20.00
69 Brian Sutter	8.00	20.00
70 Rick Middleton	8.00	20.00
71 Neal Broten	8.00	20.00
72 Mike Bossy SP	20.00	50.00
73 Borje Salming	8.00	20.00
74 Ted Lindsay SP	20.00	50.00
75 Mike Gartner SP	15.00	40.00
76 John Bucyk	12.00	30.00
77 Brad Park	8.00	20.00
78 Red Kelly	8.00	20.00
79 Joe Mullen	8.00	20.00
80 Terry O'Reilly	8.00	20.00
81 Mario Lemieux	60.00	120.00
82 Butch Goring	8.00	20.00
83 Mike Liut	8.00	20.00
84 Marcel Pronovost	8.00	20.00
85 Serge Savard	8.00	20.00
86 Jari Kurri	8.00	20.00
87 Rick Kehoe	8.00	20.00
89 Kent Nilsson	8.00	20.00
NNO Rod Langway	8.00	20.00

2001-02 Greats of the Game Board Certified

Inserted at a rate of 1:24 hobby and 1:17 retail packs, this 5-card set featured a swatch of the boards from Joe Louis Arena in Detroit. The card fronts carried a full color photo of the featured player and the board swatch. The card backs carried a congratulatory message and authenticity statement. Cards were not numbered and are listed below in alphabetical order.

Card	Low	High
1 Mike Bossy	3.00	8.00
2 Guy LaFleur	3.00	8.00
3 Mario Lemieux	10.00	25.00
4 Cam Neely	3.00	8.00
5 Peter Stastny	3.00	8.00

2001-02 Greats of the Game Jerseys

Inserted at a rate of 1:30 hobby packs, this 8-card set featured a swatch of game-worn jersey from the featured player on the card front accompanied by a full color photo of the player trimmed in the team's colors. Card backs carried a congratulatory message and a statement of authenticity. Cards were not numbered and are listed below in alphabetical order. The Patrick Roy, long believed to have been pulled from circulation, has shown up in large numbers recently as a result of the Fleer inventory liquidation. The prices are reflective of this widespread availability.

*MULT.COLOR SWATCH: .75X TO 2X HI

Card	Low	High
1 Dino Ciccarelli	6.00	15.00
2 Tony Esposito	8.00	20.00
3 Michel Goulet	6.00	15.00
4 Guy Lafleur	10.00	25.00
5 Larry Robinson	8.00	20.00
6 Borje Salming	6.00	15.00
7 Glen Sather	6.00	15.00
8 Denis Savard	6.00	15.00
9 Patrick Roy	15.00	40.00

2001-02 Greats of the Game Patches Gold

This 0-card set paralleled the basic jersey set but featured a patch swatch on the card front. Each card was serial-numbered out of 50. The card backs carried a congratulatory message and authenticity statement. These cards were hobby exclusive.

*GOLD PATCH: 1.25X TO 3X BASIC JERSEY CARD

2001-02 Greats of the Game Sticks

Inserted at a rate of 1:84 hobby and 1:400 retail, this 11-card set featured pieces of game-used sticks of the featured players on the card fronts. The card backs carried a congratulatory message and authenticity statement.

Card	Low	High
1 Marcel Dionne	10.00	25.00
2 Phil Esposito	12.50	30.00
3 Tony Esposito	15.00	40.00
4 Gordie Howe	25.00	60.00
5 Bobby Hull	15.00	40.00
6 Cam Neely	10.00	25.00
7 Willie O'Ree	12.50	30.00
8 Brad Park	10.00	25.00
9 Henri Richard	10.00	25.00
10 Terry Sawchuk	25.00	60.00
11 Darryl Sittler	10.00	25.00

1983 Hall of Fame Postcards

These postcard-sized (approximately 4" by 6") cards were distributed by complete sub-series. The set was complete at 15 series totaling 240 members of the Hockey Hall of Fame. Cards were listed alphabetically within each sub-series in the checklist below. The cards in this imperial postcard-sized set featured full-color art work by Carlton McDiarmid. The set was produced by the Hockey Hall of Fame, McDiarmid, and Cartophilium. The postcard backs contained the player's name and the year he was elected to the Hockey Hall of Fame. Career milestones or significant accomplishments of the player were listed in both French and English.

Card	Low	High
COMPLETE SET (240)	140.00	350.00
A1 Sid Abel	.75	2.00
A2 Punch Broadbent	.40	1.00
A3 Clarence Campbell	.40	1.00
A4 Neil Colville	.40	1.00
A5 Charlie Conacher	1.25	3.00
A6 Mervyn(Red) Dutton	.40	1.00
A7 Foster Hewitt	1.25	3.00
A8 Fred Hume	.40	1.00
A9 Mickey Ion	.40	1.00
A10 Ernest(Moose) Johnson	.40	1.00
A11 Bill Mosienko	.40	1.00
A12 Maurice Richard	6.00	15.00
A13 Barney Stanley	.40	1.00
A14 Lord Stanley	.75	2.00
A15 Cyclone Taylor	1.00	2.50
A16 Tiny Thompson	1.25	3.00
B1 Dan Bain	.40	1.00
B2 Hobey Baker	.75	2.00
B3 Frank Calder	.40	1.00
B4 Frank Foyston	.40	1.00
B5 James Hendy	.40	1.00
B6 Gordie Howe	6.00	15.00
B7 Harry Lumley	1.25	3.00
B8 Reg Noble	.40	1.00
B9 Frank Patrick	.40	1.00
B10 Harvey Pulford	.40	1.00
B11 Ken Reardon	.60	1.50
B12 Bullet Joe Simpson	.60	1.50
B13 Conn Smythe	.75	2.00
B14 Red Storey	.40	1.00
B15 Lloyd Turner	.40	1.00
B16 Georges Vezina	3.00	8.00
C1 Jean Beliveau	3.00	8.00
C2 Max Bentley	.60	1.50
C3 King Clancy	1.25	3.00
C4 Babe Dye	.40	1.00
C5 Ebbie Goodfellow	.40	1.00
C6 Charles Hay	.40	1.00
C7 Percy Lesueur	.60	1.50
C8 Tommy Lockhart	.40	1.00
C9 Jack Marshall	.40	1.00
C10 Lester Patrick	.75	2.00
C11 Bill Quackenbush	.60	1.50
C12 Frank Selke	.60	1.50
C13 Cooper Smeaton	.40	1.00
C14 Hooley Smith	.40	1.00
C15 Capt.J.T.Sutherland	.40	1.00
C16 Fred Whitcroft	.40	1.00
D1 Charles F. Adams	.40	1.00
D2 Russell Bowie	.40	1.00
D3 Frank Frederickson	.40	1.00
D4 Billy Gilmour	.40	1.00
D5 Ching Johnson	.60	1.50
D6 Tom Johnson	.60	1.50
D7 Aurel Joliat	1.50	4.00
D8 Duke Keats	.40	1.00
D9 Red Kelly	1.25	3.00
D10 Frank McGee	.40	1.00
D11 James D. Norris	.60	1.50
D12 Philip D. Ross	.40	1.00
D13 Terry Sawchuk	3.00	8.00
D14 Babe Siebert	.60	1.50
D15 Anatoli V. Tarasov	.60	1.50
D16 Roy Worters	.75	2.00
E1 T. Franklin Ahearn	.40	1.00
E2 Harold E. Ballard	.75	2.00
E3 Billy Burch	.40	1.00
E4 Bill Chadwick	.40	1.00
E5 Sprague Cleghorn	.75	2.00
E6 Rusty Crawford	.40	1.00
E7 Alex Delvecchio	1.25	3.00
E8 George S. Dudley	.40	1.00
E9 Ted Kennedy	.75	2.00
E10 Newsy Lalonde	1.00	2.50
E11 Billy McGimsie	.40	1.00
E12 Frank Nighbor	.60	1.50
E13 Bobby Orr	6.00	15.00
E14 Sen. Donat Raymond	.40	1.00
E15 Art Ross	1.00	2.50
E16 Jack Walker	.40	1.00
F1 Doug Bentley	.60	1.50
F2 Walter A. Brown	.40	1.00
F3 Dit Clapper	1.00	2.50
F4 Hap Day	.40	1.00
F5 Frank Dilio	.40	1.00
F6 Bobby Hewitson	.40	1.00
F7 Harry Howell	.40	1.00
F8 Paul Loicq	.40	1.00
F9 Sylvio Mantha	.60	1.50
F10 Jacques Plante	3.00	8.00
F11 George Richardson	.40	1.00
F12 Nels Stewart	.75	2.00
F13 Hod Stuart	.40	1.00
F14 Harry Trihey	.40	1.00
F15 Marty Walsh	.40	1.00
F16 Arthur M. Wirtz	.40	1.00
G1 Toe Blake	1.25	3.00
G2 Frank Boucher	.60	1.50
G3 Turk Broda	1.50	4.00
G4 Harry Cameron	.40	1.00
G5 Leo Dandurand	.40	1.00
G6 Joe Hall	.40	1.00
G7 George Hay	.40	1.00
G8 William A. Hewitt	.40	1.00
G9 Bouse Hutton	.40	1.00
G10 Dick Irvin	.75	2.00
G11 Henri Richard	1.25	3.00
G12 John Ross Robertson	.40	1.00
G13 Frank D. Smith	.40	1.00
G14 Allan Stanley	.40	1.00
G15 Norm Ullman	.40	1.00
G16 Harry Watson	.40	1.00
H1 Clint Benedict	1.25	3.00
H2 Dickie Boon	.40	1.00
H3 Gordie Drillon	.60	1.50
H4 Bill Gadsby	.40	1.00
H5 Rod Gilbert	.40	1.00
H6 Moose Goheen	.40	1.00
H7 Tommy Gorman	.40	1.00
H8 Glenn Hall	1.25	3.00
H9 Red Horner	.40	1.00
H10 Gen.J.R.Kilpatrick	.40	1.00
H11 Robert Lebel	.40	1.00
H12 Howie Morenz	3.00	8.00
H13 Fred Scanlan	.40	1.00
H14 Tommy Smith	.40	1.00
H15 Fred C. Waghorne	.40	1.00
H16 Cooney Weiland	.75	2.00
I1 Weston Adams	.40	1.00
I2 Sir Montagu Allan	.40	1.00
I3 Frank Brimsek	1.25	3.00
I4 Angus Campbell	.40	1.00
I5 Bill Cook	.75	2.00
I6 Tom Dunderdale	.40	1.00
I7 Emile Francis	.40	1.00
I8 Charlie Gardiner	.60	1.50
I9 Elmer Lach	.60	1.50
I10 Frank Mahovlich	1.25	3.00
I11 Didier Pitre	.40	1.00
I12 Joe Primeau	1.25	3.00
I13 Frank Rankin	.40	1.00
I14 Ernie Russell	.40	1.00
I15 Thayer Tutt	.40	1.00
I16 Harry Westwick	.40	1.00
J1 Jack Adams	.40	1.00
J2 Bunny Ahearne	.40	1.00
J3 J.P. Bickell	.40	1.00
J4 Johnny Bucyk	.60	1.50
J5 Art Coulter	.40	1.00
J6 C.G. Drinkwater	.40	1.00
J7 George Hainsworth	1.25	3.00
J8 Tim Horton	2.00	5.00
J9 Maj. F. McLaughlin	.40	1.00
J10 Dickie Moore	.75	2.00
J11 Pierre Pilote	.40	1.00
J12 Claude C. Robinson	.40	1.00
J13 Sweeney Schriner	.40	1.00
J14 Oliver Seibert	.40	1.00
J15 Alfred Smith	.40	1.00
J16 Phat Wilson	.60	1.50
K1 Yvan Cournoyer	.60	1.50
K2 Scotty Davidson	.40	1.00
K3 Cy Denneny	.60	1.50
K4 Bill Durnan	1.00	2.50
K5 Shorty Green	.40	1.00
K6 Riley Hern	.40	1.00
K7 Bryan Hextall Sr.	.40	1.00
K8 Bill Jennings	.40	1.00
K9 Gordon W. Juckes	.40	1.00
K10 Paddy Moran	.60	1.50
K11 James Norris	.40	1.00
K12 Harry Oliver	.40	1.00
K13 Sam Pollock	.40	1.00
K14 Marcel Pronovost	.40	1.00
K15 Jack Ruttan	.40	1.00
K16 Earl Seibert	.40	1.00
L1 Buck Boucher	.40	1.00
L2 George V. Brown	.40	1.00
L3 Arthur F. Farrell	.40	1.00
L4 Herb Gardiner	.40	1.00
L5 Si Griffis	.40	1.00
L6 Hap Holmes	.40	1.00
L7 Harry Hyland	.40	1.00
L8 Tommy Ivan	.40	1.00
L9 Jack Laviolette	.40	1.00
L10 Ted Lindsay	1.25	3.00
L11 Francis Nelson	.40	1.00
L12 William M. Northey	.40	1.00
L13 Babe Pratt	.40	1.00
L14 Chuck Rayner	.75	2.00
L15 Milt Rodden	.40	1.00
L16 Milt Schmidt	1.00	2.50
M1 Butch Bouchard	.60	1.50
M2 Jack Butterfield	.40	1.00
M3 Joseph Cattarinich	.40	1.00
M4 Alex Connell	.75	2.00
M5 Bill Cowley	.60	1.50
M6 Chaucer Elliott	.40	1.00
M7 Jimmy Gardner	.40	1.00
M8 Boom Boom Geoffrion	1.50	4.00
M9 Tom Hooper	.40	1.00
M10 Syd Howe	.40	1.00
M11 Harvey(Busher)Jackson	.60	1.50
M12 Al Leader	.40	1.00
M13 Steamer Maxwell	.40	1.00
M14 Blair Russell	.40	1.00
M15 William W. Wirtz	.40	1.00
M16 Gump Worsley	1.25	3.00
N1 George Armstrong	.75	2.00
N2 Ace Bailey	1.25	3.00
N3 Jack Darragh	.40	1.00
N4 Ken Dryden	3.00	8.00
N5 Eddie Gerard	.40	1.00
N6 Jack Gibson	.40	1.00
N7 Hugh Lehman	.40	1.00
N8 Mickey MacKay	.40	1.00
N9 Joe Malone	1.25	3.00
N10 Bruce A. Norris	.40	1.00
N11 J. Ambrose O'Brien	.40	1.00
N12 Lynn Patrick	.60	1.50
N13 Tommy Phillips	.40	1.00
N14 Allan W. Pickard	.40	1.00
N15 Jack Stewart	.40	1.00
N16 Frank Udvari	.40	1.00
O1 Syl Apps	.75	2.00
O2 John G. Ashley	.40	1.00
O3 Marty Barry	.40	1.00
O4 Andy Bathgate	.60	1.50
O5 Johnny Bower	1.25	3.00
O6 Frank Buckland	.40	1.00
O7 Jimmy Dunn	.40	1.00
O8 Michael Grant	.40	1.00
O9 Doug Harvey	1.25	3.00
O10 George McNamara	.40	1.00
O11 Stan Mikita	1.25	3.00
O12 Sen.H.de M. Molson	.40	1.00
O13 Gordon Roberts	.40	1.00
O14 Eddie Shore	3.00	8.00
O15 Bruce Stuart	.40	1.00
O16 Carl P. Voss	.40	1.00
NNO Binder	.40	1.00

1985-87 Hall of Fame

This 261-card standard-size set was basically two different sets but the second set was merely a reissue of the first Hall of Fame set done two years before, adding the new inductees since that time. The only difference in the first 240 cards in this later 1987 set and the prior set was the different copyright year at the bottom of each reverse in this set. Note however that the copyright line for the 1985 set confusingly showed a 1983 copyright date (apparently referring back to the post card set) vertically printed on the card back. One exception was Gordie Howe; his career was so long that his season-by-season statistics filled up the entire card back leaving no room for a copyright line. The set featured members of the Hockey Hall of Fame portrayed by the artwork of Carlton McDiarmid. Backs were written in both French and English. The set was originally sold in the Canadian Sears 1985 Christmas Catalog.

Card	Low	High
COMPLETE SET (261)	40.00	100.00
1 Maurice Richard	3.00	8.00
2 Sid Abel	.30	.75
3 Punch Broadbent	.15	.40
4 Clarence S. Campbell	.15	.40
5 Neil Colville	.15	.40
6 Charlie Conacher	.40	1.00
7 Morvyn(Rod) Dutton	.16	.40
8 Foster W. Hewitt	.40	1.00
9 Mickey Ion	.15	.40
10 Ernest(Moose) Johnson	.15	.40
11 Bill Mosienko	.15	.40
12 Russell Stanley	.15	.40
13 Lord Stanley	.30	.75
14 Cyclone Taylor	.30	.75
15 Tiny Thompson	.30	.75
16 Gordie Howe	3.00	8.00
17 Hobey Baker	.30	.75
18 Frank Calder	.15	.40
19 Jim Hendy	.15	.40
20 Frank Foyston	.15	.40
21 Harry Lumley	.40	1.00
22 Reg Noble	.15	.40
23 Frank A. Patrick	.15	.40
24 Harvey Pulford	.15	.40
25 Ken Reardon	.20	.50
26 Bullet Joe Simpson	.20	.50
27 Conn Smythe	.30	.75
28 Red Storey	.15	.40
29 Lloyd Turner	.15	.40
30 Georges Vezina	1.00	2.50
31 Jean Beliveau	1.00	2.50
32 Max Bentley	.20	.50
33 King Clancy	.40	1.00
34 Babe Dye	.15	.40
35 Ebbie Goodfellow	.15	.40
36 Charles Hay	.15	.40
37 Percy Lesueur	.20	.50
38 Tommy Lockhart	.15	.40
39 Jack Marshall	.15	.40
40 Lester Patrick	.30	.75
41 Frank Selke	.20	.50
42 J. Cooper Smeaton	.15	.40
43 Hooley Smith	.15	.40
44 Capt.J.T. Sutherland	.15	.40
45 Fred Whitcroft	.15	.40
46 Terry Sawchuk	1.50	4.00
47 Charles F. Adams	.15	.40
48 Russell Bowie	.15	.40
49 Frank Fredrickson	.15	.40
50 Billy Gilmour	.15	.40
51 Ching Johnson	.20	.50
52 Tom Johnson	.30	.75
53 Aurel Joliat	.60	1.50
54 Duke Keats	.15	.40
55 Red Kelly	.40	1.00
56 Frank McGee	.15	.40
57 James D. Norris	.15	.40
58 Philip D. Ross	.15	.40
59 Babe Siebert	.20	.50
60 Roy Worters	.30	.75
61 Bobby Orr	3.00	8.00
62 T. Franklin Ahearn	.15	.40
63 Harold E. Ballard	.30	.75
64 Billy Burch	.15	.40
65 Bill Chadwick	.15	.40
66 Sprague Cleghorn	.30	.75
67 Rusty Crawford	.15	.40
68 George S. Dudley	.15	.40
69 Teeder Kennedy	.30	.75
70 Newsy Lalonde	.40	1.00
71 Billy McGimsie	.15	.40
72 Frank Nighbor	.20	.50
73 Sen. Donat Raymond	.15	.40
74 Art Ross	.40	1.00
75 Jack Walker	.15	.40
76 Jacques Plante	1.50	4.00
77 Doug Bentley	.20	.50
78 Walter A. Brown	.15	.40
79 Dit Clapper	.40	1.00
80 Hap Day	.15	.40
81 Frank Dilio	.15	.40
82 Bobby Hewitson	.15	.40
83 Harry Howell	.15	.40
84 Sylvio Mantha	.20	.50
85 George Richardson	.15	.40
86 Nels Stewart	.30	.75
87 Hod Stuart	.15	.40
88 Harry Trihey	.15	.40
89 Marty Walsh	.15	.40
90 Arthur M. Wirtz	.15	.40
91 Henri Richard	.60	1.50
92 Toe Blake	.40	1.00
93 Frank Boucher	.20	.50
94 Turk Broda	.60	1.50
95 Harry Cameron	.15	.40
96 Leo J.V. Dandurand	.15	.40
97 Joe Hall	.15	.40
98 George W. Hay	.15	.40
99 William A. Hewitt	.15	.40
100 Bouse Hutton	.15	.40
101 Dick Irvin	.20	.50
102 John Ross Robertson	.15	.40
103 Frank D. Smith	.15	.40
104 Norm Ullman	.15	.40
105 Moose Watson	.15	.40
106 Howie Morenz	1.00	2.50
107 Clint Benedict	.40	1.00
108 Dickie Boon	.15	.40
109 Gordon Drillon	.20	.50
110 Bill Gadsby	.15	.40
111 Rod Gilbert	.15	.40
112 Moose Goheen	.15	.40
113 Tommy Gorman	.15	.40
114 Glenn Hall	.40	1.00
115 Red Horner	.15	.40
116 Gen.J.R. Kilpatrick	.15	.40
117 Robert Lebel	.15	.40
118 Fred Scanlan	.15	.40
119 Fred C. Waghorne	.15	.40
120 Cooney Weiland	.30	.75
121 Frank Mahovlich	.40	1.00
122 Weston Adams Sr.	.15	.40
123 Sir Montagu Allan	.15	.40
124 Frank Brimsek	.40	1.00
125 Angus D. Campbell	.15	.40
126 Bill Cook	.30	.75
127 Tom Dunderdale	.15	.40
128 Chuck Gardiner	.15	.40
129 Elmer Lach	.20	.50
130 Didier Pitre	.15	.40
131 Joe Primeau	.40	1.00
132 Frank Rankin	.15	.40
133 Ernie Russell	.15	.40
134 W. Thayer Tutt	.15	.40
135 Harry Westwick	.15	.40
136 Yvan Cournoyer	.20	.50
137 Scotty Davidson	.15	.40
138 Cy Denneny	.20	.50
139 Bill Durnan	.40	1.00
140 Shorty Green	.15	.40
141 Bryan Hextall Sr.	.15	.40
142 Bill Jennings	.15	.40
143 Gordon W. Juckes	.15	.40
144 Paddy Moran	.20	.50
145 James Norris	.15	.40
146 Harold Oliver	.15	.40
147 Sam Pollock	.15	.40
148 Marcel Pronovost	.15	.40
149 Jack Ruttan	.15	.40
150 Earl W. Seibert	.15	.40
151 Ted Lindsay	.40	1.00
152 George V. Brown	.15	.40
153 Arthur F. Farrell	.15	.40
154 Herb Gardiner	.15	.40
155 Si Griffis	.15	.40
156 Hap Holmes	.15	.40
157 Harry Hyland	.15	.40
158 Tommy Ivan	.15	.40
159 Jack Laviolette	.15	.40
160 Francis Nelson	.15	.40
161 William M. Northey	.15	.40
162 Babe Pratt	.15	.40
163 Chuck Rayner	.30	.75
164 Mike Rodden	.15	.40
165 Milt Schmidt	.40	1.00
166 Boom Boom Geoffrion	.60	1.50
167 Jack Butterfield	.15	.40
168 Joseph Cattarinich	.15	.40
169 Alex Connell	.30	.75
170 Bill Cowley	.20	.50
171 Chaucer Eliott	.15	.40
172 Jimmy Gardner	.15	.40
173 Tom Hooper	.15	.40
174 Syd Howe	.15	.40
175 Harvey(Busher) Jackson	.20	.50
176 Al Leader	.15	.40
177 Steamer Maxwell	.15	.40
178 Blair Russell	.15	.40
179 William W. Wirtz	.15	.40
180 Gump Worsley	.40	1.00
181 Johnny Bucyk	.20	.50
182 Jack Adams	.15	.40
183 Bunny Ahearne	.15	.40
184 J.P. Bickell	.15	.40
185 Art Coulter	.15	.40
186 C.G. Drinkwater	.15	.40
187 George Hainsworth	.40	1.00
188 Tim Horton	1.00	2.50
189 Maj.F. McLaughlin	.15	.40
190 Dickie Moore	.30	.75
191 Pierre Pilote	.15	.40
192 Claude C. Robinson	.15	.40
193 Oliver L. Seibert	.15	.40
194 Alfred E. Smith	.15	.40
195 Phat Wilson	.15	.40
196 Ken Dryden	1.50	4.00
197 George Armstrong	.30	.75
198 Ace Bailey	.40	1.00
199 Jack Darragh	.15	.40
200 Eddie Gerard	.15	.40
201 Jack Gibson	.15	.40
202 Hugh Lehman	.15	.40
203 Mickey MacKay	.15	.40
204 Joe Malone	.30	.75
205 Bruce A. Norris	.15	.40
206 J.Ambrose O'Brien	.15	.40
207 Lynn Patrick	.20	.50
208 Tommy Phillips	.15	.40
209 Allan W. Pickard	.15	.40
210 Jack Stewart	.15	.40
211 Johnny Bower	.40	1.00
212 Syl Apps	.30	.75
213 John G. Ashley	.15	.40
214 Marty Barry	.15	.40
215 Andy Bathgate	.20	.50
216 Frank Buckland	.15	.40
217 Jimmy Dunn	.15	.40
218 Michael Grant	.15	.40
219 Doug Harvey	.40	1.00
220 George McNamara	.15	.40
221 Sen.H.deM. Molson	.15	.40
222 Gordon Roberts	.15	.40
223 Eddie Shore	1.00	2.50
224 Bruce Stuart	.15	.40
225 Carl P. Voss	.15	.40
226 Stan Mikita	.40	1.00
227 Dan Bain	.15	.40
228 Butch Bouchard	.20	.50
229 Buck Boucher	.15	.40
230 Alex Delvecchio	.40	1.00
231 Emile P. Francis	.15	.40
232 Riley Hern	.15	.40
233 Fred J. Hume	.15	.40
234 Paul Loicq	.15	.40
235 Bill Quackenbush	.20	.50
236 Sweeney Schriner	.15	.40
237 Tommy Smith	.15	.40
238 Allan Stanley	.15	.40
239 Anatoli V. Tarasov	.20	.50
240 Frank Udvari	.15	.40
241 Harry Sinden	.30	.75
242 Bobby Hull	1.50	4.00
243 Punch Imlach	.25	.60
244 Phil Esposito	.75	2.00
245 Jacques Lemaire	.30	.75
246 Bernie Parent	.40	1.00
247 Rudy Pilous	.25	.60
248 Bert Olmstead	.25	.60
249 Jean Ratelle	.40	1.00
250 Gerry Cheevers	.40	1.00
251 William Hanley	.25	.60
252 Leo Boivin	.25	.60
253 Jake Milford	.25	.60
254 John Mariucci	.25	.60
255 Dave Keon	.40	1.00
256 Serge Savard	.25	.60
257 John A. Ziegler Jr.	.25	.60
258 Bobby Clarke	.60	1.50
259 Ed Giacomin	.40	1.00
260 Jacques Laperriere	.25	.60
261 Matt Pavelich	.25	.60

1992-93 Hall of Fame Legends

The Hockey Hall of Fame in association with the Diamond Connection and the Sports Gallery of Art produced this 18-card set as the first of three series to be released each year. Over a four year period, all members and builders of Hockey's Hall of Fame will have been featured. Production was limited to 10,000 numbered sets, and buyers retained exclusive rights to their assigned number throughout the duration of the project. Issued in a cardboard box, the cards measured approximately 3 1/2" by 5 1/2" and featured the work of noted sports artist Doug West. The front displayed a color reproduction of the artist's original painting. The back had a parchment background with navy blue borders and included biographical information, a player profile, career statistics, each team played for, and the years played. A registration form and an ownership transfer form were included with each set. The card number and set serial number are in the lower right corner.

Card	Low	High
COMPLETE SET (36)	60.00	150.00
1 Harry Lumley	2.00	5.00
2 Conn Smythe CO	1.50	4.00
3 Maurice Richard	6.00	15.00
4 Bobby Orr	8.00	20.00
5 Bernie Geoffrion	2.50	6.00
6 Hobey Baker	2.00	5.00
7 Phil Esposito	2.50	6.00
8 King Clancy	2.50	6.00
9 Gordie Howe	6.00	15.00
10 Emile Francis	1.50	4.00
11 Jacques Plante	3.00	8.00
12 Sid Abel	1.50	4.00
13 Foster Hewitt	2.00	5.00
14 Charlie Conacher	2.00	5.00
15 Stan Mikita	2.50	6.00
16 Bobby Clarke	2.00	5.00
17 Norm Ullman	1.50	4.00
18 Lord Stanley of Preston	2.00	5.00
19 Ted Lindsay	2.00	5.00
20 Duke Keats	1.50	4.00
21 Jack Adams	1.50	4.00
22 Bill Mosienko	1.50	4.00
23 Johnny Bower	2.00	5.00
24 Tim Horton	3.00	8.00
25 Punch Imlach	1.50	4.00
26 Georges Vezina	4.00	10.00
27 Earl Seibert	1.50	4.00
28 Bryan Hextall Sr.	1.50	4.00
29 Babe Pratt	1.50	4.00
30 Gump Worsley	2.00	5.00
31 Ed Giacomin	2.00	5.00
32 Ace Bailey	2.00	5.00
33 Harry Sinden	1.50	4.00
34 Lanny McDonald	2.00	5.00
35 Tommy Ivan	1.50	4.00
36 Frank Calder	1.50	4.00

1994 Hall of Fame Tickets

Measuring approximately 2 5/16" by 3 1/2", each of these tickets admitted one to the Hockey Hall of Fame in Toronto. Each ticket was printed on thin cardboard stock and featured a full-bleed photo on its front. On a background that shades from blue to white, the horizontal backs carried the Hall of Fame's street address, a description of the front picture, founding sponsors' logos, and a barcode. The tickets were numbered on the back.

Card	Low	High
COMPLETE SET (12)	18.00	45.00
1 Stanley Cup	1.50	4.00
2 O'Brien Trophy	1.25	3.00
3 Dan Bain Artifacts	1.25	3.00
4 Art Ross Artifacts	1.50	4.00
5 Ace Bailey Artifacts	1.50	4.00
6 Clint Benedict Artifacts	2.00	5.00
7 Howie Morenz Artifacts	3.00	8.00
8 Roy Worters Artifacts	1.50	4.00
9 Andy Bathgate Artifacts	1.25	3.00
10 Jacques Plante Artifacts	3.00	8.00
11 Terry Sawchuk Artifacts	3.00	8.00
12 Milt Schmidt Artifacts	1.50	4.00

1998 Hall of Fame Medallions

Issued only in Canada, these medallions were mounted on a clear plastic holder and featured statistical and biographical information on the back.

Card	Low	High
COMPLETE SET (2)	6.00	15.00
1 Michel Goulet	3.00	8.00
2 Peter Stastny	4.00	8.00

1914 Happy Christmas Postcard

Full color postcard that measures 3 1/2 x 5 1/2. Front featured a young lady with a hockey stick and the words Happy Christmas in the lower right-hand corner. Small print on card back said Series 259 F.

Card	Low	High
NNO Happy Christmas	10.00	20.00

1999 Hasbro Starting Lineup Cards

These cards were packaged along with plastic figurines in the Hasbro Starting Lineup product. Because these packages often were left intact, it could be difficult to obtain these singles. This set was produced by Upper Deck.

Card	Low	High
COMPLETE SET (17)	10.00	25.00
1 Mike Dunham	.40	1.00
2 Peter Forsberg	.60	1.50
3 Wayne Gretzky	2.00	5.00
4 Jeff Hackett	.60	1.50
5 Dominik Hasek	.60	1.50
6 Jaromir Jagr	.60	1.50
7 Curtis Joseph	.75	2.00
8 Paul Kariya	.60	1.50
9 Nikolai Khabibulin	.40	1.00
10 Olaf Kolzig	.40	1.00
11 Nicklas Lidstrom	.75	2.00
12 Eric Lindros	.60	1.50
13 Mike Modano	.40	1.00
14 Keith Primeau	.40	1.00
15 Chris Pronger	.40	1.00
16 Sergei Samsonov	.75	2.00
17 Steve Yzerman	1.25	3.00

1975-76 Heroes Stand-Ups

These 31 "Hockey Heroes Autographed Pin-up/Stand-Up Sportrophies" featured NHL players from five different teams. The stand-ups came in two different sizes. The Bruins and Flyers stand-ups were approximately 15 1/2" by 8/3/4", while the Islanders stand-ups were approximately 13 1/2" by 7 1/2" and were issued three to a strip. The stand-ups were made of laminated cardboard, and the yellow frame is decorated with red stars. Each stand-up featured a color action shot of the player. A facsimile autograph was inscribed across the bottom of the stand-up. The stand-ups were unnumbered and checklisted below alphabetically according to and within teams as follows: Boston Bruins (1-7), Montreal Canadiens (8-13), New York Islanders (14-19), Philadelphia Flyers (20-25), and Toronto Maple Leafs (26-31).

Card	Low	High
COMPLETE SET (31)	125.00	250.00
1 Gerry Cheevers	6.00	12.00
2 Terry O'Reilly	3.00	6.00
3 Bobby Orr	25.00	50.00
4 Brad Park	4.00	8.00
5 Jean Ratelle	4.00	8.00
6 Andre Savard	2.50	5.00
7 Gregg Sheppard	2.50	5.00
8 Yvan Cournoyer	4.00	8.00
9 Guy Lafleur	10.00	20.00
10 Jacques Lemaire	4.00	8.00
11 Peter Mahovlich	2.50	5.00
12 Doug Risebrough	2.50	5.00
13 Larry Robinson	6.00	12.00
14 Billy Harris	2.50	5.00
15 Gerry Hart	2.50	5.00
16 Denis Potvin	6.00	12.00
17 Glenn Resch	4.00	8.00
18 Bryan Trottier	6.00	12.00
19 Ed Westfall	2.50	5.00
20 Bill Barber	4.00	8.00
21 Bobby Clarke	6.00	12.00
22 Reggie Leach	2.50	5.00
23 Rick MacLeish	2.50	5.00
24 Bernie Parent	6.00	12.00
25 Dave Schultz	4.00	8.00
26 Lanny McDonald	4.00	8.00
27 Borje Salming	3.00	6.00
28 Darryl Sittler	4.00	8.00
29 Wayne Thomas	3.00	6.00
30 Errol Thompson	2.50	5.00
31 Dave(Tiger) Williams	4.00	8.00

1992-93 High Liner Stanley Cup

National Sea Products Ltd., producer and manufacturer of High Liner brand fish products, produced a 28-card, standard-size set to celebrate the Centennial of the Stanley Cup (1893-1993). Specially marked packages of High Liner frozen fish products contained two cards. Collectors could also order additional cards by clipping the order form from the box, checking the cards desired, and sending it in with six UPC symbols from any High Liner brand product plus 3.99. The form limited requests to one card request per card number. The fronts featured full-bleed black-and-white and color team pictures of Stanley Cup champions. The pale blue, horizontal backs presented a French and English summary of the championship season and a list of the players pictured. A darker blue stripe across the top displayed the Stanley Cup logo and the set name in French and English. The team name and the year they won the Stanley Cup appeared in the lower left corner.

COMPLETE SET (28)	16.00	40.00
1 Montreal AAA	.40	1.00
2 Winnipeg Victorias	.40	1.00
3 Montreal Victorias	.40	1.00
4 Montreal Shamrocks	.40	1.00
5 Ottawa Silver Seven	.40	1.00
6 Kenora Thistles	.40	1.00
7 Montreal Wanderers	1.00	2.50
8 Quebec Bulldogs	.40	1.00
9 Toronto Blueshirts	1.00	2.50
10 Vancouver Millionaires	1.00	2.50
11 Seattle Metropolitans	1.00	2.50
12 Toronto Arenas	1.00	2.50
13 Toronto St. Patricks	1.00	2.50
14 Victoria Cougars	.40	1.00
15 Ottawa Senators	.40	1.00
16 Montreal Maroons	1.00	2.50
17 New York Rangers	.40	1.00
18 Detroit Red Wings	1.25	3.00
19 Montreal Canadiens	1.50	4.00
20 Chicago Blackhawks	.40	1.00
21 Toronto Maple Leafs	1.25	3.00
22 Boston Bruins	1.25	3.00
23 Philadelphia Flyers	.40	1.00
24 New York Islanders	.40	1.00
25 Edmonton Oilers	2.00	5.00
26 Calgary Flames	.40	1.00
27 Pittsburgh Penguins	1.00	2.50
28 Checklist Card	.40	1.00

1993-94 High Liner Greatest Goalies

National Sea Products Ltd., producer and manufacturer of High Liner brand fish products, produced a 15-card, standard-size set of the Greatest Goalies of the NHL, a follow-up to High Liner's 28-card 1992-93 Stanley Cup Centennial set. Specially marked packages of High Liner frozen fish products contained one card. Collectors could also order the complete set through a mail-in offer as outlined on the inside of the specially marked High Liner packages. The set was made from white card stock and was primarily devoted to goalies that have won the Vezina Trophy, the NHL's top annual award for goaltenders. The fronts featured white-bordered color player action shots, with the player's name, team and, season printed in white within a blue band at the bottom. The logo, with Greatest Goalies printed in French and English, appeared in the lower left. The white back had a color posed player head shot in the upper left, with the player's name in orange lettering alongside to the right. A biography, stat table, and career highlights were printed in English and French. The High Liner, NHLPA, and NHL logos on the bottom rounded out the card.

COMPLETE SET (15)	8.00	20.00
1 Patrick Roy	3.00	8.00
2 Ed Belfour	.60	1.50
3 Grant Fuhr	.40	1.00
4 Ron Hextall	.40	1.00
5 John Vanbiesbrouck	.40	1.00
6 Tom Barrasso	.40	1.00
7 Bernie Parent	.40	1.00
8 Tony Esposito	.60	1.50
9 Johnny Bower	.60	1.50
10 Jacques Plante	1.00	2.50
11 Terry Sawchuk	1.00	2.50
12 Bill Durnan	.40	1.00
13 Felix Potvin	.60	1.50
14 The Evolution of the Goalie Mask	1.00	2.50
15 Vezina Trophy Checklist	.40	1.00

1992 High-5 Previews

These six cards featured color action player photos with the player's name and position printed above the photo. The backs carried another color player photo, with the player's name and career highlights on a white panel. The words "Preview Sample" appeared in the top left corner. The cards were numbered on the back with a "P" prefix. Bourque and Belfour were produced in larger quantities. The cards were originally distributed as promo items at the 1992 National which led to extremely high values. In 1996, an additional supply of these cards was inserted into boxes of Collector's Edge Future Legends product in three-card sleeves. The additional quantities severely dampened demand. A signed version of the Belfour card also was included as a random insert in these packs, and as a promotional giveaway direct from Collector's Edge. This card was serially numbered out of 1500.

COMPLETE SET (6)	48.00	120.00
P1 Ray Bourque DP	2.00	5.00
P2 Mario Lemieux Pittsburg	4.00	10.00
P3 Wayne Gretzky	20.00	50.00
P4 Mark Messier	4.00	10.00
P5 Mario Lemieux	15.00	40.00
P6 Ed Belfour AU/1500	20.00	50.00
P6 Ed Belfour DP	1.50	4.00

1997 Highland Mint Legends Mint-Cards

The Highland Mint Legends Collection featured NHL greats in a Highland Mint designed Mint-Card and was processed in the same way as the regular Highland Mint series. These standard-sized bronze ingots were enclosed in a plastic display holder case. Silver versions of these cards were produced as well. Since these cards are unnumbered, they are listed below in alphabetical order.

Card	Low	High
1 Gordie Howe 95/S/1000	75.00	225.00
2 Gordie Howe 95/B/5000	20.00	50.00
3 Bobby Orr 95/S/1000	75.00	225.00
4 Bobby Orr 95/B/5000	20.00	50.00

1997 Highland Mint Magnum Series Medallions

Measuring 2 1/2" in diameter and encased in a 6" by 5" velvet box, these larger medallions commemorated the Colorado Avalanche's Stanley Cup Championship. The relief on these medallions are 10 times greater than the regular medallions.

Card	Low	High
1 Colorado Avalanche S/250	150.00	200.00
2 Colorado Avalanche B/1000	25.00	60.00

1997 Highland Mint Mint-Cards Pinnacle/Score

These Highland Mint cards were exact replicas of Pinnacle or Score brand cards. The silver and bronze cards contained 4.25 ounces of metal; the gold cards were 24-karat gold-plated on silver. Each card was individually numbered, packaged in a Lucite display holder and accompanied by a certificate of authenticity. The production mintage according to Highland Mint is listed below.

Card	Low	High
1 Martin Brodeur 95/S/250	75.00	225.00
2 Martin Brodeur 95/B/1500	25.00	60.00
3 Alexandre Daigle 94/S/250	75.00	200.00
4 Alexandre Daigle 94/B/1500	20.00	50.00
5 Jaromir Jagr 94/S/500	75.00	200.00
6 Jaromir Jagr 94/B/2500	25.00	60.00
7 Paul Kariya 94/S/250	75.00	225.00
8 Paul Kariya 94/B/1500	25.00	60.00
9 Pat LaFontaine 93/S/250	75.00	225.00
10 Pat LaFontaine 93/B/1500	20.00	50.00
11 Cam Neely 95/S/250	75.00	225.00
12 Cam Neely 95/B/1500	20.00	50.00
13 Jeremy Roenick 94/S/500	75.00	225.00
14 Jeremy Roenick 94/B/2500	20.00	50.00

1997 Highland Mint Mint-Cards Topps

These cards, from the Highland Mint, measured 2 1/2" by 3 1/2", and were exact reproductions of Topps hockey cards. The cards were packaged in a Lucite display case within a numbered album. Each card came with a sequentially numbered Certificate of Authenticity. The cards featured future heroes, current, and past stars. When the Highland Mint/Topps relationship ended in 1994, the remaining unsold stock was destroyed; the final available mintage according to Highland Mint is listed below. The cards are checklisted below alphabetically.

Card	Low	High
1 Ray Bourque 80/S/128	100.00	250.00
2 Ray Bourque 80/B/634	25.00	60.00
3 Pavel Bure 92/S/414	75.00	225.00
4 Pavel Bure 92/B/1519	20.00	50.00
5 Sergei Fedorov 91/S/208	100.00	250.00
6 Sergei Fedorov 91/B/914	25.00	60.00
7 Doug Gilmour 85/S/101	100.00	250.00
8 Doug Gilmour 85/B/461	20.00	50.00
9 Wayne Gretzky 79/S/1000	200.00	500.00
10 Wayne Gretzky 79/B/5000	60.00	140.00
11 Bobby Hull 95/S/500	75.00	225.00
12 Bobby Hull 95/B/2500	20.00	50.00
13 Brett Hull 88/S/500	75.00	225.00
14 Brett Hull 88/B/1202	20.00	50.00
15 Mario Lemieux 85/S/999	250.00	325.00
16 Mario Lemieux 85/B/3557	25.00	60.00
17 Eric Lindros 92/S/694	100.00	250.00
18 Eric Lindros 92/B/2668	25.00	60.00
19 Mark Messier 84/S/280	75.00	225.00
20 Mark Messier 84/B/1034	20.00	50.00
21 Felix Potvin 92/S/210	75.00	225.00
22 Felix Potvin 92/B/902	20.00	50.00
23 Patrick Roy 86/S/500	100.00	250.00
24 Patrick Roy 86/B/1986	25.00	60.00
25 Teemu Selanne 92/S/131	75.00	225.00
26 Teemu Selanne 92/B/537	20.00	50.00
27 Steve Yzerman 84/S/233	75.00	225.00
28 Steve Yzerman 84/B/926	30.00	75.00

1997 Highland Mint Mint-Coins

Each medallion weighed one-troy ounce and was individually numbered. The fronts featured a player likeness as well as name, uniform number, and signature. The backs displayed the team logo and statistics. The suggested retail prices for silver ranged from $19.95 to $24.95. The medallions were packaged in a hard plastic capsule and a velvet jewelry box. The Gold-Signature series medallions were two-tone silver medallions with gold plating in selected areas. Packaged in a box with a special foil certificate of authenticity, the front featured the player's likeness, name, uniform number and signature, while the back carried the NHLPA logo. The suggested retail price was $49.95.

Card	Low	High
1 Ray Bourque S/5000	10.00	20.00
2 Pavel Bure S/5000	10.00	20.00
3 Sergei Fedorov S/5000	10.00	25.00
4 Brett Hull S/5000	10.00	20.00
5 Jaromir Jagr S/5000	10.00	25.00
6 Mario Lemieux Gold Sig./1000	25.00	60.00
7 Mario Lemieux S/5000	10.00	25.00
8 Mario Lemieux B/25000	5.00	12.00
9 Eric Lindros Gold Sig./1000	25.00	60.00
10 Eric Lindros S/5000	10.00	25.00
11 Bobby Orr S/5000	10.00	25.00
12 B.Orr/R.Bourque S/500	20.00	50.00
13 Chris Osgood S/5000	10.00	20.00
14 Patrick Roy S/5000	10.00	25.00
15 Teemu Selanne S/5000	10.00	20.00
16 J.Vanbiesbrouck S/5000	10.00	25.00
17 Steve Yzerman S/5000	10.00	20.00

1997 Highland Mint Sandblast Mint-Cards

These Highland Mint cards were metal replicas of already issued Pinnacle cards. All these standard size replicas contained approximately 4.25 ounces of metal and featured a "sandblast" background that accents the shiny surface of the player's likeness. Suggested retail was 60.00 for bronze and 250.00 for silver. Each card included a certificate of authenticity, and was packaged in a numbered album and a three-piece Lucite display. The cards were checklisted below alphabetically; the final mintage figures for each card are also listed.

Card	Low	High
1 Mario Lemieux 96/S/250	100.00	250.00
2 Mario Lemieux 96/B/1500	25.00	60.00

1994 Hockey Wit

Seventh in a series of "WIT" trivia games, this Hockey Wit card set featured 108 standard-size cards and included hockey players of the past and present. The fronts featured full-bleed color action player photos, with the player's name inside a blue box with a gold-foil border and the words "Hockey Wit". On a white background, the backs carried a small color headshot, player biography and trivia questions and answers. Inserted in each master case of 72 games was a bonus card which collectors could redeem for one of 500 limited edition sets of uncut flat sheets. The production run was reportedly limited to 30,000 sets, and a portion of the proceeds from the sale benefited amateur hockey in Canada and the United States. The set included 21 Hall of Famers. The collector who answers all the questions on the backs achieved a perfect score of 801, the total number of goals scored in the NHL by Gordie Howe. The cards were numbered on the back at the lower right corner.

COMPLETE SET (108)	8.00	20.00
1 Mike Richter	.07	.20
2 Tony Amonte	.07	.20
3 Patrick Roy	1.25	3.00
4 Craig Janney	.02	.10
5 Adam Oates	.07	.20
6 Geoff Sanderson	.07	.20
7 Pavel Bure	.60	1.50
8 Steve Duchesne	.02	.10
9 Gordie Howe	.75	2.00
10 Brad Park	.07	.20
11 Brian Bellows	.02	.10
12 Chris Chelios	.20	.50
13 Bill Barber	.07	.20
14 Gump Worsley	.07	.20
15 The Stanley Cup	.07	.20
16 Maurice Richard	.20	.50
17 Kevin Hatcher	.02	.10
18 Ed Belfour	.20	.50
19 Kirk Muller	.07	.20
20 Kevin Stevens	.07	.20
21 Dave Taylor	.02	.10
22 Dale Hawerchuk	.08	.25
23 Jean Beliveau	.08	.25
24 Rogatien Vachon	.07	.20
25 Tom Barrasso	.07	.20
26 Rod Langway	.02	.10
27 Pierre Turgeon	.08	.25
28 Derek King	.02	.10
29 Brendan Shanahan	.40	1.00
30 Darren Turcotte	.02	.10
31 Chris Terreri	.02	.10
32 Tony Granato	.02	.10
33 Michel Goulet	.02	.10
34 Felix Potvin	.08	.25
35 Curtis Joseph	.30	.75
36 Cam Neely	.08	.25
37 Borje Salming	.07	.20
38 Denis Savard	.07	.20
39 Stan Mikita	.08	.25
40 Grant Fuhr	.07	.20
41 Gary Suter	.02	.10
42 Serge Savard	.02	.10
43 Steve Larmer	.07	.20
44 Bryan Trottier	.08	.25
45 Mike Vernon	.07	.20
46 Paul Coffey	.08	.25
47 Bernie Federko	.02	.10
48 Larry Murphy	.07	.20
49 Scotty Bowman CO	.08	.25
50 Glenn Anderson	.02	.10
51 Mats Sundin	.20	.50
52 Henri Richard	.08	.25
53 Ron Francis	.08	.25
54 Scott Niedermayer	.07	.20
55 Teemu Selanne	.40	1.00
56 Frank Mahovlich	.08	.25
57 Owen Nolan	.07	.20
58 Rick Tocchet	.07	.20
59 Rod Brind'Amour	.07	.20
60 Mike Modano	.08	.25
61 Doug Gilmour	.08	.25
62 Jimmy Carson	.02	.10
63 Mike Keane	.02	.10
64 Bernie Nicholls	.07	.20
65 Scott Stevens	.07	.20
66 Mario Lemieux Pittsburg	1.25	3.00
67 Keith Primeau	.08	.25
68 Bobby Carpenter	.02	.10
69 Sergei Fedorov	.40	1.00
70 Peter Stastny	.07	.20
71 Brian Leetch	.08	.25
72 Vincent Damphousse	.07	.20
73 Darryl Sitter	.07	.20
74 Al Iafrate	.07	.20
75 Alexander Mogilny	.07	.20
76 Bill Ranford	.08	.25
77 Ray Bourque	.30	.75
78 Joey Mullen	.02	.10
79 Mike Ricci	.07	.20
80 Bobby Clarke	.08	.25
81 Gerry Cheevers	.07	.20
82 Joe Nieuwendyk	.07	.20
83 Terry Sawchuk	.08	.25
84 Ray Ferraro	.02	.10
85 Lanny McDonald	.07	.20
86 Adam Graves	.07	.20
87 Tomas Sandstrom	.02	.10
88 Eric Lindros	.60	1.50
89 Jari Kurri	.08	.25
90 Al MacInnis	.07	.20
91 Alexandre Daigle	.02	.10
92 Larry Robinson	.08	.25
93 Kelly Hrudey	.07	.20
94 Theo Fleury	.08	.25
95 Billy Smith	.07	.20
96 Luc Robitaille	.08	.25
97 Brett Hull	.30	.75
98 Pat Falloon	.07	.20
99 Wayne Gretzky	1.50	4.00
100 Joe Sakic	.40	1.00
101 Phil Housley	.07	.20
102 Mark Messier	.20	.50
103 Jeremy Roenick	.08	.25
104 Mark Recchi	.08	.25
105 Pat LaFontaine	.08	.25
106 Trevor Linden	.07	.20
107 Jaromir Jagr	.75	2.00
108 Steve Yzerman	.75	2.00

1996-97 Hockey Greats Coins

This 25-coin set featured one coin and checklist card per pack. Each box -- with a suggested retail price of $149.95 contained 80 packs. The coins were silver in color, about the size of a half dollar and featured a bust of the player on the obverse. A Collectors Album also was available for $5.49. The Chris Chelios coin (#4) was believed to be short printed, and thus earns the sizable premium noted below. A gold parallel version of the set existed as well. These coins were inserted at a rate of 1:150 packs. The gold coins are valued at 15 to 25 times the prices below, except for the Chelios, which goes for 3 to 5 times.

COMPLETE SET (25)	30.00	75.00
*GOLD: 15X TO 25X BASIC COIN		
1 Ed Belfour	.60	1.50
2 Ray Bourque	.75	2.00
3 Pavel Bure	1.25	3.00
4 Chris Chelios	6.00	15.00
5 Vincent Damphousse	.40	1.00
6 Sergei Fedorov	1.25	3.00
7 Theo Fleury	.60	1.50
8 Doug Gilmour	.60	1.50
9 Wayne Gretzky	4.00	10.00
10 Brett Hull	.75	2.00
11 Jaromir Jagr	1.50	4.00
12 Paul Kariya	1.50	4.00
13 Mario Lemieux	3.00	8.00
14 Eric Lindros	1.25	3.00
15 Mark Messier	.75	2.00
16 Alexander Mogilny	.40	1.00
17 Jeremy Roenick	.60	1.50
18 Patrick Roy	3.00	8.00
19 Joe Sakic	1.25	3.00
20 Steve Yzerman	2.00	5.00
21 Sergei Berezin	.40	1.00
22 Jim Campbell	.20	.50
23 Jarome Iginla	.60	1.50
24 Rem Murray	.20	.50
25 David Wilkie	.20	.50
NNO Album	2.00	5.00

1924-25 Holland Creameries

The 1924-25 Holland Creameries set contained ten black and white cards measuring approximately 1 1/2" by 3". The front had a black and white head and shoulders shot of the player, in an oval-shaped black frame on white card stock. The words %%Holland Hockey Competition- appeared above the picture, with the player's name and position below. The cards were numbered in the lower left corner on the front. The horizontally formatted card back had an offer to exchange one complete collection of ten players for either a brick of ice cream or three Holland Banquets. Supposedly the difficult card in the set was Connie Neil, marked as SP in the checklist below.

COMPLETE SET (10)	1000.00	1500.00
1 Wally Fridfinson	60.00	150.00
2 Harold McMunn	60.00	150.00
3 Art Somers	60.00	150.00
4 Frank Woodall	60.00	150.00
5 Frank Fredrickson	125.00	300.00
6 Bobby Benson	60.00	150.00
7 Harry Neal	60.00	150.00
8 Wally Byron	60.00	150.00
9 Connie Neil SP	300.00	500.00
10 J. Austman	60.00	150.00

2005-06 Hot Prospects

This 276-card set was released in the hobby in five-card packs which came 15 packs to a box and 12 boxes to a case. Cards numbered 1-100 feature veterans in team alphabetical order while cards 101-276 are all Rookie Cards. The Rookie Cards were issued in several groupings: Cards 101-186; Cards 187-216 were signed and cards 217-276 were issued both a signature and a player-worn jersey swatch. The cards numbeed 101-186 were issued to a stated print run of 1999 serial numbered sets, cards 187-216 were issued to a stated print run of 999 serial numbered sets and 217-276 were issued to a stated print run of 199 to 349 serial numbered sets.

COMPLETE SET w/o SPs (100)	8.00	20.00
UNIQUE SWATCHES MAY EARN SUBSTANTIAL PREMIUM		
1 Joffrey Lupul	.20	.50
2 Jean-Sebastien Giguere	.25	.60
3 Teemu Selanne	.30	.75
4 Marian Hossa	.25	.60
5 Ilya Kovalchuk	.40	1.00
6 Kari Lehtonen	.30	.75
7 Patrice Bergeron	.30	.75
8 Brian Leetch	.30	.75
9 Andrew Raycroft	.25	.60
10 Glen Murray	.20	.50
11 Ryan Miller	.15	.40
12 Chris Drury	.25	.60
13 Tim Connolly	.10	.25
14 Jarome Iginla	.25	.60
15 Miikka Kiprusoff	.30	.75
16 Mark Recchi	.25	.60
17 Eric Staal	.25	.60
18 Martin Gerber	.25	.60
19 Doug Weight	.25	.60
20 Erik Cole	.20	.50
21 Nikolai Khabibulin	.30	.75
22 Tuomo Ruutu	.20	.50
23 Joe Sakic	.60	1.50
24 Marek Svatos	.10	.25
25 Milan Hejduk	.30	.75
26 Alex Tanguay	.25	.60
27 Jose Theodore	.30	.75
28 Sergei Fedorov	.30	.75
29 Rick Nash	.40	1.00
30 Mike Modano	.30	.75
31 Marty Turco	.25	.60
32 Brenden Morrow	.25	.60
33 Steve Yzerman	.75	2.00
34 Brendan Shanahan	.30	.75
35 Pavel Datsyuk	.30	.75
36 Henrik Zetterberg	.30	.75
37 Nicklas Lidstrom	.30	.75
38 Chris Pronger	.25	.60
39 Shawn Horcoff	.10	.25
40 Ryan Smyth	.25	.60
41 Ales Hemsky	.20	.50
42 Olli Jokinen	.20	.60
43 Roberto Luongo	.50	1.25
44 Nathan Horton	.20	.50
45 Alexander Frolov	.25	.60
46 Luc Robitaille	.25	.60
47 Pavol Demitra	.25	.60
48 Jeremy Roenick	.30	.75
49 Marian Gaborik	.40	1.00
50 Manny Fernandez	.25	.60
51 David Aebischer	.25	.60
52 Saku Koivu	.30	.75
53 Michael Ryder	.25	.60
54 Mike Ribeiro	.25	.50
55 Paul Kariya	.30	.75
56 Tomas Vokoun	.25	.60
57 Steve Sullivan	.20	.50
58 Martin Brodeur	.75	2.00
59 Patrik Elias	.25	.60
60 Brian Gionta	.10	.25
61 Scott Gomez	.25	.60
62 Alexei Yashin	.20	.50
63 Rick DiPietro	.25	.60
64 Miroslav Satan	.20	.50
65 Jaromir Jagr	.50	1.25
66 Martin Straka	.10	.25
67 Jason Spezza	.30	.75
68 Dominik Hasek	.40	1.00
69 Daniel Alfredsson	.25	.60
70 Dany Heatley	.30	.75
71 Peter Forsberg	.50	1.25
72 Simon Gagne	.30	.75
73 Keith Primeau	.20	.50
74 Antero Niittymaki	.15	.40
75 Curtis Joseph	.30	.75
76 Shane Doan	.20	.50
77 Ladislav Nagy	.20	.50
78 Mario Lemieux	1.25	3.00
79 Marc-Andre Fleury	.25	.60
80 Sergei Gonchar	.10	.25
81 Ryan Malone	.20	.50
82 Joe Thornton	.50	1.25
83 Patrick Marleau	.25	.60
84 Evgeni Nabokov	.25	.60
85 Jonathan Cheechoo	.30	.75
86 Barret Jackman	.20	.50
87 Keith Tkachuk	.30	.75
88 Vincent Lecavalier	.30	.75
89 Brad Richards	.25	.60
90 Vaclav Prospal	.10	.25
91 Martin St. Louis	.25	.60
92 Mats Sundin	.30	.75
93 Ed Belfour	.30	.75
94 Bryan McCabe	.20	.50
95 Eric Lindros	.30	.75
96 Markus Naslund	.30	.75
97 Alexander Auld	.10	.25
98 Todd Bertuzzi	.40	1.00
99 Brendan Morrison	.20	.50
100 Olaf Kolzig	.25	.60
101 Dustin Penner RC	3.00	8.00
102 Zenon Konopka RC	1.50	4.00
103 Michael Wall RC	2.00	5.00
104 Brian Eklund RC	2.00	5.00
105 Jay Leach RC	1.50	4.00
106 Eric Healey RC	1.50	4.00
107 Ben Guite RC	1.50	4.00
108 Nathan Paetsch RC	1.50	4.00
109 Jiri Novotny RC	1.50	4.00
110 Richie Regehr RC	1.50	4.00
111 Mark Giordano RC	1.50	4.00
112 Chad Larose RC	1.50	4.00
113 Keith Aucoin RC	1.50	4.00
114 David Gove RC	1.50	4.00
115 Cam Barker RC	2.50	6.00
116 Corey Crawford RC	2.00	5.00
117 Martin St. Pierre RC	1.50	4.00
118 Mark Cullen RC	1.50	4.00
119 James Wisniewski RC	1.50	4.00
120 Vitaly Kolesnik RC	2.00	5.00
121 Steven Goertzen RC	1.50	4.00
122 Joakim Lindstrom RC	1.50	4.00
123 Andrew Penner RC	1.50	4.00
124 Geoff Platt RC	1.50	4.00
125 Junior Lessard RC	1.50	4.00
126 Vojtech Polak RC	1.50	4.00
127 Kyle Brodziak RC	3.00	8.00
128 Matt Greene RC	1.50	4.00
129 Danny Syvret RC	1.50	4.00
130 Adam Hauser RC	2.50	6.00
131 Jean-Francois Jacques RC	1.50	4.00
132 Mathieu Roy RC		
133 Petr Taticek RC	1.50	4.00
134 Greg Jacina RC	1.50	4.00
135 Rob Globke RC	1.50	4.00
136 Yanick Lehoux RC	1.50	4.00
137 Petr Kanko RC	2.00	5.00
138 Jeff Giuliano RC	1.50	4.00
139 Matt Ryan RC	1.50	4.00
140 Connor James RC	1.50	4.00
141 Richard Petiot RC	1.50	4.00
142 Jean-Philippe Cote RC	1.50	4.00
143 Mark Streit RC	3.00	8.00
144 Jonathan Ferland RC	1.50	4.00
145 Kevin Klein RC	1.50	4.00
146 Pekka Rinne RC	2.00	5.00
147 Greg Zanon RC	1.50	4.00
148 Jason Ryznar RC	1.50	4.00
149 Cam Janssen RC	1.50	4.00
150 Bruno Gervais RC	1.50	4.00
151 Kevin Colley RC	1.50	4.00
152 Petr Prucha RC	5.00	12.00
153 Brandon Bochenski RC	3.00	8.00
154 Brian McGrattan RC	3.00	8.00
155 Stefan Ruzicka RC	1.50	4.00
156 Wade Skolney RC	3.00	8.00
157 Ryan Ready RC	1.50	4.00
158 Josh Gratton RC	1.50	4.00
159 Alexandre Picard RC	1.50	4.00
160 Matt Jones RC	1.50	4.00
161 Colby Armstrong RC	4.00	10.00
162 Doug Murray RC	1.50	4.00
163 Grant Stevenson RC	1.50	4.00
164 Dennis Wideman RC	1.50	4.00
165 Andy Roach RC	3.00	8.00
166 Colin Hemingway RC	1.50	4.00
167 Chris Beckford-Tseu RC	2.50	6.00
168 Jon DiSalvatore RC	1.50	4.00
169 Mike Glumac RC	1.50	4.00
170 Gerald Coleman RC	2.00	5.00
171 Nick Tarnasky RC	1.50	4.00
172 Paul Ranger RC	3.00	8.00
173 Darren Reid RC	1.50	4.00
174 Doug O'Brien RC	1.50	4.00
175 Chris Holt RC	3.00	8.00
176 Jay Harrison RC	1.50	4.00
177 Staffan Kronwall RC	1.50	4.00
178 Tomas Mojzis RC	1.50	4.00
179 Rob McVicar RC	2.00	5.00
180 Rick Rypien RC	1.50	4.00
181 Alexandre Burrows RC	1.50	4.00
182 Prestin Ryan RC	1.50	4.00
183 Mike Green RC	5.00	12.00
184 David Steckel RC	1.50	4.00
185 Joey Tenute RC	1.50	4.00
186 Louis Robitaille RC	2.50	6.00
187 Jim Slater AU RC	6.00	15.00
188 Adam Berkhoel AU RC	6.00	15.00
189 Jordan Sigalet AU RC	4.00	10.00
190 Ben Walter AU RC	3.00	8.00
191 Chris Thorburn AU RC	3.00	8.00
192 Niklas Nordgren AU RC	6.00	15.00
193 Danny Richmond AU RC	3.00	8.00
194 Rene Bourque AU RC	6.00	15.00
195 Duncan Keith AU RC	12.00	30.00
196 Jaroslav Balastik AU RC	6.00	15.00
197 Ole-Kristian Tollefsen AU RC	3.00	8.00
198 Alexandre Picard AU RC	4.00	10.00
199 Brett Lebda AU RC	6.00	15.00
200 Kyle Quincey AU RC	3.00	8.00
201 George Parros AU RC	6.00	15.00
202 Matt Foy AU RC	6.00	15.00
203 Derek Boogaard AU RC	6.00	15.00
204 Maxim Lapierre AU RC	3.00	8.00
205 Chris Campoli AU RC	6.00	15.00
206 Ryan Hollweg AU RC	6.00	15.00
207 Patrick Eaves AU RC	6.00	15.00
208 Christoph Schubert AU RC	3.00	8.00
209 Erik Christensen AU RC	4.00	10.00
210 Dimitri Patzold AU RC	4.00	10.00
211 Josh Gorges AU RC	6.00	15.00
212 Ryane Clowe AU RC	3.00	8.00
213 Jay McClement AU RC	6.00	15.00
214 Lee Stempniak AU RC	4.00	10.00
215 Kevin Dallman AU RC	6.00	15.00
216 Andrew Wozniewski AU RC	6.00	15.00
217 Corey Perry JSY AU RC	30.00	80.00
218 Ryan Getzlaf JSY AU RC	50.00	100.00
219 Braydon Coburn JSY AU RC	12.00	30.00
220 Andrew Alberts JSY AU RC	10.00	25.00
221 Hannu Toivonen JSY AU RC	15.00	40.00
222 Milan Jurcina JSY AU RC	10.00	25.00
223 Daniel Paille JSY AU RC	12.00	30.00
224 Thomas Vanek JSY AU RC	30.00	80.00
225 Eric Nystrom JSY AU RC	10.00	25.00
226 Andrew Ladd JSY AU RC	12.00	30.00
227 Cam Ward JSY AU RC	20.00	50.00
228 Kevin Nastiuk JSY AU RC	12.00	30.00
229 Brent Seabrook JSY AU RC	15.00	40.00
230 Brad Richardson JSY AU RC	12.00	30.00
231 Peter Budaj JSY AU RC	15.00	40.00
232 Wojtek Wolski JSY AU RC	25.00	60.00
233 Gilbert Brule JSY AU RC	30.00	80.00
234 Jussi Jokinen JSY AU RC	15.00	40.00
235 Jim Howard JSY AU RC	20.00	50.00
236 Johan Franzen JSY AU RC	25.00	50.00
237 Valtteri Filppula AU RC	15.00	40.00
238 Brad Winchester JSY AU RC	10.00	25.00
239 Anthony Stewart JSY AU RC	12.00	30.00
240 Rostislav Olesz JSY AU RC	15.00	40.00
241 Jeff Tambellini JSY AU RC	10.00	25.00
242 Mikko Koivu JSY AU RC	20.00	50.00
243 Alexander Perezhogin JSY AU RC	10.00	25.00
244 Andrei Kostitsyn JSY AU RC	60.00	120.00
245 Yann Danis JSY AU RC	15.00	40.00
246 Raitis Ivanans JSY AU RC	10.00	25.00
247 Ryan Suter JSY AU RC	12.00	30.00
248 Barry Tallackson JSY AU RC	10.00	25.00
249 Zach Parise JSY AU RC	75.00	125.00
250 Jeremy Colliton JSY AU RC	10.00	25.00
251 Petteri Nokelainen JSY AU RC	10.00	25.00
252 Robert Nilsson JSY AU RC	10.00	25.00
253 Al Montoya JSY AU RC	15.00	40.00
254 Henrik Lundqvist JSY AU RC	100.00	200.00
255 Andrej Meszaros JSY AU RC	12.00	30.00
256 Ben Eager JSY AU RC	10.00	25.00
257 Jeff Carter JSY AU RC	40.00	100.00
258 Mike Richards JSY AU RC	40.00	100.00
259 R.J. Umberger JSY AU RC	15.00	40.00
260 David LeNeveu JSY AU RC	12.00	30.00
261 Keith Ballard JSY AU RC	10.00	25.00
262 Maxime Talbot JSY AU RC	12.00	30.00
263 Ryan Whitney JSY AU RC	25.00	60.00
264 Steve Bernier AU RC	10.00	25.00
265 Jeff Hoggan JSY AU RC	10.00	25.00
266 Jeff Woywitka JSY AU RC	12.00	30.00
267 Timo Helbling JSY AU RC	10.00	20.00
268 Evgeny Artyukhin JSY AU RC	12.00	30.00
269 Ryan Craig JSY AU RC	12.00	30.00
270 Alexander Steen JSY AU RC	30.00	80.00
271 Kevin Bieksa JSY AU RC	12.00	30.00
272 Jakub Klepis JSY AU RC	12.00	30.00
273 Tomas Fleischmann JSY AU RC	12.00	30.00
274 Dion Phaneuf JSY AU RC	100.00	200.00
275 Alexander Ovechkin JSY AU RC	350.00	500.00
276 Sidney Crosby JSY AU RC	750.00	1000.00

2005-06 Hot Prospects Autographed Patch Variation

STATED PRINT RUN 5 SETS
NOT PRICED DUE TO SCARCITY

2005-06 Hot Prospects Autographed Patch Variation Gold

STATED PRINT RUN 1/1
NOT PRICED DUE TO SCARCITY

2005-06 Hot Prospects En Fuego

STATED PRINT RUN 1/1
NOT PRICED DUE TO SCARCITY

2005-06 Hot Prospects Hot Materials

STATED ODDS 1:8		
HMAA Andrew Alberts	2.00	5.00
HMAH Adam Hall	2.00	5.00
HMAK Andrei Kostitsyn	2.50	6.00
HMAL Andrew Ladd	2.50	6.00
HMAM Andrej Meszaros	2.00	5.00
HMAO Alexander Ovechkin	8.00	20.00
HMAP Alexander Perezhogin	2.50	6.00
HMAS Anthony Stewart	2.50	6.00
HMBC Braydon Coburn	2.50	6.00
HMBE Ben Eager	2.00	5.00
HMBG Bill Guerin	2.00	5.00
HMBI Kevin Bieksa	2.00	5.00
HMBR Brad Richardson	2.00	5.00
HMBS Brent Seabrook	3.00	8.00
HMBT Barry Tallackson	2.00	5.00
HMBW Brad Winchester	2.00	5.00
HMCA Carlo Colaiacovo	2.00	5.00
HMCC Chris Campoli	2.00	5.00
HMCO Jeremy Colliton	2.00	5.00
HMCP Corey Perry	3.00	8.00
HMCS Christoph Schubert	2.00	5.00
HMCT Chris Thorburn	2.00	5.00
HMCW Cam Ward	3.00	8.00
HMDB Derek Boogaard	2.50	6.00
HMDH Dan Hamhuis	2.00	5.00
HMDK Duncan Keith	4.00	10.00
HMDL David Legwand	2.50	6.00
HMDP Dimitri Patzold	2.50	6.00
HMDR Danny Richmond	2.00	5.00
HMEA Evgeny Artyukhin	2.00	5.00
HMEC Erik Christensen	2.50	6.00
HMEN Eric Nystrom	2.50	6.00
HMFP Fernando Pisani	2.00	5.00
HMGB Gilbert Brule	2.50	6.00
HMGP George Parros	2.00	5.00
HMHL Henrik Lundqvist	5.00	12.00
HMHT Hannu Toivonen	2.50	6.00
HMJB Jaroslav Balastik	2.00	5.00
HMJC Jeff Carter	3.00	8.00
HMJF Johan Franzen	2.00	5.00
HMJH Jim Howard	4.00	10.00
HMJJ Jussi Jokinen	2.50	6.00
HMJK Jakub Klepis	2.00	5.00
HMJS Jim Slater	2.50	6.00
HMJT Jeff Tambellini	2.00	5.00
IIMJW Jeff Woywitka	2.00	5.00
HMKB Keith Ballard	2.00	5.00
HMKD Kevin Dallman	2.00	5.00
HMKI Jason King	2.00	5.00
HMKN Kevin Nastiuk	2.50	6.00
HMKQ Kyle Quincey	2.00	5.00
HMLE David Leneveu	2.50	6.00

HMLS Lee Stempniak 2.50 6.00
HMMC Mike Cammalleri 2.00 5.00
HMMF Matt Foy 2.00 5.00
HMMG Martin Gerber 2.50 6.00
HMMJ Milan Jurcina 2.00 5.00
HMMK Mikko Koivu 2.50 6.00
HMML Maxim Lapierre 2.00 5.00
HMMO Al Montoya 2.50 6.00
HMMR Mike Richards 2.50 6.00
HMMT Maxime Talbot 2.00 5.00
HMNN Niklas Nordgren 2.00 5.00
HMOT Ole-Kristian Tollefsen 2.00 5.00
HMPA Daniel Paille 2.00 5.00
HMPB Peter Budaj 2.50 6.00
HMPH Dion Phaneuf 5.00 12.00
HMPN Petteri Nokelainen 2.00 5.00
HMPS Patrik Stefan 2.00 5.00
HMRC Ryan Craig 2.00 5.00
HMRG Ryan Getzlaf 4.00 10.00
HMRI Raitis Ivanans 2.00 5.00
HMRN Robert Nilsson 2.50 6.00
HMRO Rostislav Olesz 2.50 6.00
HMRS Ryan Suter 2.50 6.00
HMRU R.J. Umberger 2.50 6.00
HMRW Ryan Whitney 2.50 6.00
HMSA Philippe Sauve 2.50 6.00
HMSB Steve Bernier 2.50 6.00
HMSC Sidney Crosby 20.00 50.00
HMSI Jordan Sigalet 2.50 6.00
HMST Alexander Steen 2.50 6.00
HMTF Tomas Fleischmann 2.50 6.00
HMTH Timo Helbling 2.00 5.00
HMTV Thomas Vanek 4.00 10.00
HMVF Valtteri Filppula 2.00 5.00
HMWI Brendan Witt 2.00 5.00
HMWW Wojtek Wolski 3.00 8.00
HMYD Yann Danis 2.50 6.00
HMZP Zach Parise 3.00 8.00

2005-06 Hot Prospects Red Hot

*RED: 5X TO 12X BASE HI
*RED RC/1999: .75X TO 2X BASE HI
1-186 PRINT RUN: 100 SETS
217-276 PRINT RUN: 50 SETS
SKIP-NUMBERED SET
216 Andrew Wozniewski AU 8.00 20.00
217 Corey Perry JSY AU 25.00 60.00
218 Ryan Getzlaf JSY AU 40.00 100.00
219 Braydon Coburn JSY AU 8.00 20.00
220 Andrew Alberts JSY AU 8.00 20.00
221 Hannu Toivonen JSY AU 20.00 40.00
222 Milan Jurcina JSY AU 8.00 20.00
224 Thomas Vanek JSY AU 60.00 150.00
225 Eric Nystrom JSY AU 8.00 20.00
226 Andrew Ladd JSY AU 15.00 30.00
227 Cam Ward JSY AU 30.00 80.00
228 Kevin Nastiuk JSY AU 8.00 20.00
229 Brent Seabrook JSY AU 10.00 25.00
230 Brad Richardson JSY AU 8.00 20.00
231 Peter Budaj JSY AU 20.00 40.00
232 Wojtek Wolski JSY AU 50.00 100.00
234 Jussi Jokinen JSY AU 20.00 50.00
235 Jim Howard JSY AU 30.00 80.00
236 Johan Franzen JSY AU 8.00 20.00
238 Brad Winchester JSY AU 8.00 20.00
239 Anthony Stewart JSY AU 8.00 20.00
240 Rostislav Olesz JSY AU 10.00 25.00
241 Jeff Tambellini JSY AU 8.00 20.00
242 Mikko Koivu JSY AU 15.00 30.00
243 Alexander Perezhogin JSY AU 8.00 20.00
244 Andrei Kostitsyn JSY AU 25.00 60.00
245 Yann Danis JSY AU 10.00 25.00
246 Raitis Ivanans JSY AU 8.00 20.00
247 Ryan Suter JSY AU 10.00 25.00
248 Barry Tallackson JSY AU 8.00 20.00
249 Zach Parise JSY AU 40.00 100.00
250 Jeremy Colliton JSY AU 8.00 20.00
251 Petteri Nokelainen JSY AU 8.00 20.00
252 Robert Nilsson JSY AU 8.00 20.00
253 Al Montoya JSY AU 20.00 40.00
254 Henrik Lundqvist JSY AU 75.00 175.00
255 Andrej Meszaros JSY AU 8.00 20.00
256 Ben Eager JSY AU 8.00 20.00
257 Jeff Carter JSY AU 40.00 100.00
258 Mike Richards JSY AU 50.00 100.00
259 R.J. Umberger JSY AU 10.00 25.00
260 David Leneveu JSY AU 8.00 20.00
261 Keith Ballard JSY AU 15.00 30.00
262 Maxime Talbot JSY AU 8.00 20.00
263 Ryan Whitney JSY AU 20.00 40.00
264 Jeff Hoggan JSY AU 8.00 20.00
265 Jeff Woywitka JSY AU 8.00 20.00
267 Timo Helbling JSY AU 8.00 20.00
268 Evgeny Artyukhin JSY AU 8.00 20.00
269 Ryan Craig JSY AU 20.00 50.00
270 Alexander Steen JSY AU 30.00 60.00
271 Kevin Bieksa JSY AU 8.00 20.00
272 Jakub Klepis JSY AU 15.00 30.00
273 Tomas Fleischmann JSY AU 15.00 30.00
274 Dion Phaneuf JSY AU 75.00 175.00
275 Alexander Ovechkin JSY AU 175.00 300.00
276 Sidney Crosby JSY AU 500.00 750.00

2005-06 Hot Prospects White Hot

STATED PRINT RUN: 10 SETS
NOT PRICED DUE TO SCARCITY

2006-07 Hot Prospects

This 202-card set was released in March 2007. The set was issued into the hobby in five-card packs with a $6.99 SRP which came 15 packs to a box and 12 boxes to a case. Cards numbered 1-100 feature veterans while the rest of the set are all Rookie Cards. Cards numbered 101-139 feature both a player-worn swatch and an autograph and were issued to a stated print run of 599 serial numbered sets while cards numbered 140-142 also have player-worn swatches and an autograph and were issued to a stated print run of 199 serial numbered sets. Cards numbered 143-202 were issued to a stated print run of 1999 serial numbered sets

1 Chris Pronger .40 1.00
2 Jean-Sebastien Giguere .50 1.25
3 Teemu Selanne .50 1.25
4 Ilya Kovalchuk .60 1.50
5 Marian Hossa .40 1.00
6 Kari Lehtonen .50 1.25
7 Patrice Bergeron .40 1.00
8 Hannu Toivonen .50 1.25
9 Zdeno Chara .30 .75
10 Brad Boyes .30 .75
11 Ryan Miller .50 1.25
12 Thomas Vanek .40 1.00
13 Daniel Briere .40 1.00
14 Maxim Afinogenov .30 .75
15 Jarome Iginla .75 2.00
16 Dion Phaneuf .60 1.50
17 Alex Tanguay .40 1.00
18 Miikka Kiprusoff .50 1.25
19 Eric Staal .40 1.00
20 Cam Ward .75 2.00
21 Rod Brind'Amour .40 1.00
22 Tuomo Ruutu .30 .75
23 Nikolai Khabibulin .50 1.25
24 Martin Havlat .40 1.00
25 Joe Sakic 1.00 2.50
26 Jose Theodore .50 1.25
27 Milan Hejduk .40 1.00
28 Marek Svatos .30 .75
29 Rick Nash .50 1.25
30 Sergei Fedorov .50 1.25
31 Pascal LeClaire .50 1.25
32 Nikolai Zherdev .30 .75
33 Mike Modano .50 1.25
34 Eric Lindros .50 1.25
35 Marty Turco .40 1.00
36 Pavel Datsyuk .50 1.25
37 Dominik Hasek .60 1.50
38 Nicklas Lidstrom .50 1.25
39 Henrik Zetterberg .50 1.25
40 Ryan Smyth .40 1.00
41 Ales Hemsky .30 .75
42 Dwayne Roloson .40 1.00
43 Ed Belfour 1.25 3.00
44 Todd Bertuzzi .40 1.00
45 Olli Jokinen .30 .75
46 Rob Blake .40 1.00
47 Alexander Frolov .30 .75
48 Marian Gaborik .75 2.00
49 Manny Fernandez .50 1.25
50 Pavol Demitra .30 .75
51 Saku Koivu .50 1.25
52 Cristobal Huet .50 1.25
53 Michael Ryder .40 1.00
54 David Aebischer .30 .75
55 Paul Kariya .50 1.25
56 Tomas Vokoun .40 1.00
57 Martin Brodeur 1.50 4.00
58 Patrik Elias .30 .75
59 Brian Gionta .30 .75
60 Rick DiPietro .50 1.25
61 Alexei Yashin .30 .75
62 Miroslav Satan .30 .75
63 Jaromir Jagr .75 2.00
64 Brendan Shanahan .50 1.25
65 Henrik Lundqvist .75 2.00
66 Daniel Alfredsson .50 1.25
67 Jason Spezza .50 1.25
68 Dany Heatley .50 1.25
69 Martin Gerber .50 1.25
70 Peter Forsberg .75 2.00
71 Simon Gagne .50 1.25
72 Jeff Carter .50 1.25
73 Antero Niittymaki .50 1.25
74 Shane Doan .40 1.00
75 Jeremy Roenick .50 1.25
76 Curtis Joseph .50 1.25
77 Sidney Crosby 2.50 6.00
78 Marc-Andre Fleury .50 1.25
79 Mark Recchi .30 .75
80 Doug Weight .30 .75
81 Manny Legace .40 1.00
82 Keith Tkachuk .40 1.00
83 Joe Thornton .75 2.00
84 Jonathan Cheechoo .50 1.25
85 Patrick Marleau .40 1.00
86 Vesa Toskala .40 1.00
87 Vincent Lecavalier .50 1.25
88 Brad Richards .50 1.25
89 Martin St. Louis .50 1.25
90 Mats Sundin .50 1.25
91 Andrew Raycroft .40 1.00
92 Alexander Steen .40 1.00
93 Darcy Tucker .30 .75
94 Roberto Luongo 1.00 2.50
95 Markus Naslund .50 1.25
96 Daniel Sedin .30 .75
97 Henrik Sedin .30 .75
98 Alexander Ovechkin 2.00 5.00
99 Olaf Kolzig .60 1.50
100 Alexander Semin .25 .60
101 Ryan Shannon JSY AU RC 15.00 40.00
102 Shane O'Brien JSY AU RC 15.00 40.00
103 Yan Stastny JSY AU RC 15.00 40.00
104 Mark Stuart JSY AU RC 15.00 40.00
105 Drew Stafford JSY AU RC 30.00 80.00
106 Dustin Boyd JSY AU RC 20.00 50.00
107 Dustin Byfuglien JSY AU RC 30.00 80.00
108 Paul Stastny JSY AU RC 40.00 80.00
109 Fredrik Norrena JSY AU RC 15.00 40.00
110 Filip Novak JSY AU RC 15.00 40.00
111 Loui Eriksson JSY AU RC 15.00 40.00
112 Tomas Kopecky JSY AU RC 20.00 50.00
113 M-A Pouliot JSY AU RC 20.00 50.00
114 Ladislav Smid JSY AU RC 15.00 40.00
115 Patrick Thoresen JSY AU RC 15.00 40.00
116 Patrick O'Sullivan JSY AU RC 20.00 50.00
117 Anze Kopitar JSY AU RC 25.00 60.00
118 K. Pushkaryov JSY AU RC 15.00 40.00
119 G. Latendresse JSY AU RC 20.00 50.00
120 Shea Weber JSY AU RC 20.00 50.00
121 Alexander Radulov JSY AU RC 25.00 60.00
122 Travis Zajac JSY AU RC 20.00 50.00
123 Jarkko Immonen JSY AU RC 15.00 40.00
124 Nigel Dawes JSY AU RC 15.00 40.00
125 Ryan Potulny JSY AU RC 20.00 50.00
126 Benoit Pouliot JSY AU RC 20.00 50.00
127 Keith Yandle JSY AU RC 15.00 40.00
128 Noah Welch JSY AU RC 15.00 40.00
129 Kristopher Letang JSY AU RC 25.00 60.00
130 Michel Ouellet JSY AU RC 25.00 60.00
131 Matt Carle JSY AU RC 20.00 50.00
132 M-E Vlasic JSY AU RC 15.00 40.00
133 Marek Schwarz JSY AU RC 30.00 80.00
134 Roman Polak JSY AU RC 8.00 20.00
135 Ben Ondrus JSY AU RC 15.00 40.00
136 Brendan Bell JSY AU RC 15.00 40.00
137 Ian White JSY AU RC 15.00 40.00
138 Jeremy Williams JSY AU RC 15.00 40.00
139 Eric Fehr JSY AU RC 20.00 50.00
140 Jordan Staal JSY/199 AU RC 50.00 100.00
141 Phil Kessel JSY/199 AU RC 40.00 100.00
142 Evgeni Malkin JSY/199 AU RC 150.00 250.00
143 David McKee RC 4.00 10.00
144 Mike Brown RC 2.50 6.00
145 Matt Lashoff RC 3.00 8.00
146 Nate Thompson RC 1.50 4.00
147 Mike Card RC 1.50 4.00
148 Adam Dennis RC 1.50 4.00
149 Michael Funk RC 1.50 4.00
150 Michael Ryan RC 1.50 4.00
151 Brandon Prust RC 3.00 8.00
152 Adam Burish RC 1.50 4.00
153 Michael Blunden RC 3.00 8.00
154 Dave Bolland RC 6.00 15.00
155 Stefan Liv RC 4.00 10.00
156 Alexei Mikhnov RC 3.00 8.00
157 Jan Hejda RC 1.50 4.00
158 Jeff Drouin-Deslauriers RC 4.00 10.00
159 Drew Larman RC 1.50 4.00
160 Janis Sprukts RC 3.00 8.00
161 David Booth RC 3.00 8.00
162 Peter Harrold RC 1.50 4.00
163 Benoit Pouliot RC 4.00 10.00
164 Niklas Backstrom RC 3.00 8.00
165 Miroslav Kopriva RC 3.00 8.00
166 Mikko Lehtonen RC 1.50 4.00
167 John Oduya RC 3.00 8.00
168 Alex Brooks RC 1.50 4.00
169 Kelly Guard RC 4.00 10.00
170 Martin Houle RC 4.00 10.00
171 Jussi Timonen RC 1.50 4.00
172 Lars Jonsson RC 1.50 4.00
173 Triston Grant RC 1.50 4.00
174 Bill Thomas RC 3.00 8.00
175 Patrick Fischer RC 1.50 4.00
176 Joe Pavelski RC 10.00 25.00
177 D.J. King RC 1.50 4.00
178 Blair Jones RC 3.00 8.00
179 Jean-Francois Racine RC 4.00 10.00
180 Nathan McIver RC 1.50 4.00
181 Alexander Edler RC 3.00 8.00
182 Luc Bourdon RC 4.00 10.00
183 Patrick Coulombe RC 1.50 4.00
184 Jesse Schultz RC 3.00 8.00
185 Kyle Cumiskey RC 1.50 4.00
186 David Backes RC 2.50 6.00
187 Mikhail Grabovski RC 3.00 8.00
188 Daren Machesney RC 3.00 8.00
189 Enver Lisin RC 3.00 8.00
190 Tim Brent RC 1.50 4.00
191 Blake Comeau RC 3.00 8.00
192 Barry Brust RC 4.00 10.00
193 Karri Ramo RC 3.00 8.00
194 Kris Newbury RC 3.00 8.00
195 Kamil Kreps RC 1.50 4.00
196 Derek Meech RC 3.00 8.00
197 Andrej Sekera RC 1.50 4.00
198 Clarke MacArthur RC 3.00 8.00
199 Josh Hennessy RC 3.00 8.00
200 Niklas Grossman RC 3.00 8.00
201 Joel Perrault RC 3.00 8.00
202 Troy Brouwer RC 2.50 6.00

2006-07 Hot Prospects Red Hot

*1-100: 5X TO 12X BASE HI
PRINT RUN 100 #'d SETS (1-100/143-180)
PRINT RUN 25 #'d SETS (101-142)
101-142 NOT PRICED DUE TO SCARCITY
AU RCs: 1.5X TO 3X BASE HI
NON-AU RCs: .75X TO 1.5X BASE HI
1 Chris Pronger JSY 5.00 12.00
2 Jean-Sebastien Giguere JSY 6.00 15.00
3 Teemu Selanne JSY 6.00 15.00
4 Ilya Kovalchuk JSY 8.00 20.00
5 Marian Hossa JSY 5.00 12.00
6 Kari Lehtonen JSY 6.00 15.00
7 Patrice Bergeron JSY 5.00 12.00
8 Hannu Toivonen JSY 6.00 15.00
9 Zdeno Chara JSY 4.00 10.00
10 Brad Boyes JSY 4.00 10.00
11 Ryan Miller JSY 6.00 15.00
13 Daniel Briere JSY 5.00 12.00
14 Maxim Afinogenov JSY 4.00 10.00
15 Jarome Iginla JSY 10.00 25.00
16 Dion Phaneuf JSY 8.00 20.00
17 Alex Tanguay JSY 5.00 12.00
18 Miikka Kiprusoff JSY 6.00 15.00
19 Eric Staal JSY 5.00 12.00
20 Cam Ward JSY 10.00 25.00
21 Rod Brind'Amour JSY 5.00 12.00
22 Tuomo Ruutu JSY 4.00 10.00
23 Nikolai Khabibulin JSY 6.00 15.00
24 Martin Havlat JSY 5.00 12.00
25 Joe Sakic JSY 12.00 30.00
26 Jose Theodore JSY 6.00 15.00
27 Milan Hejduk JSY 5.00 12.00
28 Marek Svatos JSY 4.00 10.00
29 Rick Nash JSY 6.00 15.00
30 Sergei Fedorov JSY 6.00 15.00
31 Pascal LeClaire JSY 6.00 15.00
32 Nikolai Zherdev JSY 4.00 10.00
33 Mike Modano JSY 6.00 15.00
34 Eric Lindros JSY 6.00 15.00
35 Marty Turco JSY 5.00 12.00
36 Pavel Datsyuk JSY 6.00 15.00
37 Dominik Hasek JSY 8.00 20.00
38 Nicklas Lidstrom JSY 6.00 15.00
39 Henrik Zetterberg JSY 6.00 15.00
40 Ryan Smyth JSY 5.00 12.00
41 Ales Hemsky JSY 4.00 10.00
42 Dwayne Roloson JSY 5.00 12.00
43 Ed Belfour JSY 15.00 40.00
44 Todd Bertuzzi JSY 5.00 12.00
45 Olli Jokinen JSY 4.00 10.00
46 Rob Blake JSY 5.00 12.00
47 Alexander Frolov JSY 4.00 10.00
48 Marian Gaborik JSY 10.00 25.00
49 Manny Fernandez JSY 6.00 15.00
50 Pavol Demitra JSY 4.00 10.00
51 Saku Koivu JSY 6.00 15.00
52 Cristobal Huet JSY 6.00 15.00
53 Michael Ryder JSY 5.00 12.00
54 David Aebischer JSY 5.00 12.00
55 Paul Kariya JSY 6.00 15.00
56 Tomas Vokoun JSY 5.00 12.00
57 Martin Brodeur JSY 20.00 50.00
58 Patrik Elias JSY 4.00 10.00
59 Brian Gionta JSY 4.00 10.00
60 Rick DiPietro JSY 6.00 15.00
61 Alexei Yashin JSY 4.00 10.00
62 Miroslav Satan JSY 4.00 10.00
63 Jaromir Jagr JSY 10.00 25.00
64 Brendan Shanahan JSY 6.00 15.00
65 Henrik Lundqvist JSY 10.00 25.00
66 Daniel Alfredsson JSY 5.00 12.00
67 Jason Spezza JSY 6.00 15.00
68 Dany Heatley JSY 6.00 15.00
69 Martin Gerber JSY 6.00 15.00
70 Peter Forsberg JSY 10.00 25.00
71 Simon Gagne JSY 6.00 15.00
72 Joni Pitkanen JSY 4.00 10.00
73 Antero Niittymaki JSY 6.00 15.00
74 Shane Doan JSY 5.00 12.00
75 Jeremy Roenick JSY 6.00 15.00
76 Curtis Joseph JSY 6.00 15.00
77 Sidney Crosby JSY 20.00 50.00
79 Mark Recchi JSY 4.00 10.00
80 Doug Weight JSY 4.00 10.00
81 Manny Legace JSY 5.00 12.00
82 Keith Tkachuk JSY 5.00 12.00
83 Joe Thornton JSY 10.00 25.00
84 Jonathan Cheechoo JSY 6.00 15.00
85 Patrick Marleau JSY 5.00 12.00
86 Evgeni Nabokov JSY 5.00 12.00
87 Vincent Lecavalier JSY 8.00 15.00
88 Brad Richards JSY 6.00 15.00
89 Martin St. Louis JSY 6.00 15.00
90 Mats Sundin JSY 6.00 15.00
91 Andrew Raycroft JSY 5.00 12.00
92 Alexander Steen JSY 5.00 12.00
93 Darcy Tucker JSY 4.00 10.00
94 Roberto Luongo JSY 12.00 30.00
95 Markus Naslund JSY 6.00 15.00
96 Daniel Sedin JSY 4.00 10.00
97 Henrik Sedin JSY 4.00 10.00
98 Alexander Ovechkin JSY 25.00 60.00
99 Olaf Kolzig JSY 8.00 20.00
101 Ryan Shannon JSY AU
102 Shane O'Brien JSY AU
103 Yan Stastny JSY AU
104 Mark Stuart JSY AU
105 Drew Stafford JSY AU
106 Dustin Boyd JSY AU
107 Dustin Byfuglien JSY AU 30.00 60.00
108 Paul Stastny JSY AU
109 Fredrik Norrena JSY AU
110 Filip Novak JSY AU
111 Loui Eriksson JSY AU
112 Tomas Kopecky JSY AU
113 Marc-Antoine Pouliot JSY AU
114 Ladislav Smid JSY AU
115 Patrick Thoresen JSY AU
116 Patrick O'Sullivan JSY AU
117 Anze Kopitar JSY AU
118 Konstantin Pushkaryov JSY AU
119 Guillaume Latendresse JSY AU
120 Shea Weber JSY AU
121 Alexander Radulov JSY AU
122 Travis Zajac JSY AU
123 Jarkko Immonen JSY AU
124 Nigel Dawes JSY AU
125 Ryan Potulny JSY AU
126 Benoit Pouliot JSY AU
127 Keith Yandle JSY AU
128 Noah Welch JSY AU
129 Kristopher Letang JSY AU
130 Michel Ouellet JSY AU
131 Matt Carle JSY AU
132 Marc-Edouard Vlasic JSY AU
133 Marek Schwarz JSY AU
134 Roman Polak JSY AU
135 Ben Ondrus JSY AU
136 Brendan Bell JSY AU
137 Ian White JSY AU
138 Jeremy Williams JSY AU
139 Eric Fehr JSY AU
140 Jordan Staal JSY AU
141 Phil Kessel JSY AU
142 Evgeni Malkin JSY AU
143 David McKee 4.00 10.00
144 Mike Brown AU 5.00 12.00
145 Matt Lashoff AU 6.00 15.00
146 Nate Thompson AU 5.00 12.00
147 Mike Card AU 5.00 12.00
148 Adam Dennis AU 6.00 15.00
149 Michael Funk 2.50 6.00
150 Michael Ryan 2.50 6.00
151 Brandon Prust AU 5.00 12.00
152 Adam Burish AU 5.00 12.00
153 Michael Blunden AU 5.00 12.00
154 Dave Bolland AU 6.00 15.00
155 Stefan Liv 4.00 10.00
156 Alexei Mikhnov AU 5.00 12.00
157 Jan Hejda 2.50 6.00
158 Jeff Drouin-Deslauriers AU 5.00 12.00
159 Drew Larman AU 5.00 12.00
160 Janis Sprukts AU 5.00 12.00
161 David Booth 2.50 6.00
162 Peter Harrold 2.50 6.00
163 Shawn Belle 2.50 6.00
164 Niklas Backstrom 5.00 12.00
165 Miroslav Kopriva 2.50 6.00
166 Mikko Lehtonen 2.50 6.00
167 John Oduya 2.50 6.00
168 Alex Brooks AU 5.00 12.00
169 Kelly Guard AU 5.00 12.00
170 Martin Houle 2.50 6.00
171 Jussi Timonen 2.50 6.00
172 Lars Jonsson 2.50 6.00
173 Triston Grant 2.50 6.00
174 Bill Thomas 2.50 6.00
175 Patrick Fischer 2.50 6.00
176 Joe Pavelski 5.00 12.00
177 D.J. King 2.50 6.00
178 Blair Jones 2.50 6.00
179 Jean-Francois Racine AU 5.00 12.00
180 Nathan McIver AU 5.00 12.00
181 Alexander Edler AU 5.00 12.00
182 Luc Bourdon AU 5.00 12.00
183 Patrick Coulombe 2.50 6.00
184 Jesse Schultz 2.50 6.00

2006-07 Hot Prospects White Hot

PRINT RUN 10 #'d SETS (1-99, 143-184)
PRINT RUN 1/1 (101-142)
NOT PRICED DUE TO SCARCITY

2006-07 Hot Prospects Hot Materials

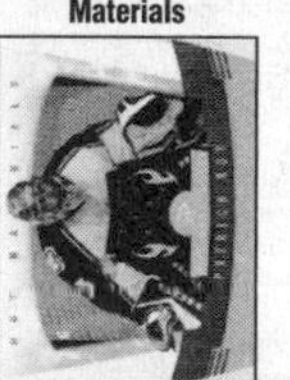

ODDS 1:8
HMAE David Aebischer 2.50 6.00
HMAK Anze Kopitar 4.00 10.00
HMAO Alexander Ovechkin SP 8.00 20.00
HMAS Alexander Steen SP 3.00 8.00
HMBB Brandon Bochenski 1.50 4.00
HMBE Brendan Bell 1.50 4.00
HMBM Brenden Morrow 2.50 6.00
HMBO Ben Ondrus 1.50 4.00
HMBR Brad Boyes 1.50 4.00
HMBS Brendan Shanahan 3.00 8.00
HMBT Billy Thompson 1.50 4.00
HMCD Chris Drury 3.00 8.00
HMCJ Curtis Joseph 3.00 8.00
HMCP Corey Perry 2.50 6.00
HMCS Curtis Sanford 2.50 6.00
HMCW Cam Ward 3.00 8.00
HMDA Daniel Alfredsson 2.50 6.00
HMDH Dominik Hasek SP 5.00 12.00
HMDP Dion Phaneuf 3.00 8.00
HMDS Drew Stafford 2.50 6.00
HMEB Ed Belfour 3.00 8.00
HMEF Eric Fehr 2.50 6.00
HMEM Evgeni Malkin 10.00 25.00
HMES Eric Staal 3.00 8.00
HMGL Guillaume Latendresse 3.00 8.00
HMGM Glen Murray 1.50 4.00
HMGR Gary Roberts 1.50 4.00
HMHA Martin Havlat 2.50 6.00
HMHE Dany Heatley SP 4.00 10.00
HMHJ Milan Hejduk 2.50 8.00
HMHS Henrik Sedin 1.50 4.00
HMHT Hannu Toivonen 2.50 6.00
HMIG Jarome Iginla 4.00 10.00
HMIK Ilya Kovalchuk 4.00 10.00
HMIW Ian White 1.50 4.00
HMJB Jay Bouwmeester 1.50 4.00
HMJC Jeff Carter 3.00 6.00
HMJD J.P. Dumont 1.50 4.00
HMJI Jarkko Immonen 1.50 4.00
HMJJ Jaromir Jagr 5.00 12.00
HMJL Jere Lehtinen 1.50 4.00
HMJP Joni Pitkanen 1.50 4.00
HMJS Jarret Stoll 1.50 4.00
HMJT Joe Thornton 5.00 12.00
HMKL Kristopher Letang 2.50 6.00
HMKP Konstantin Pushkaryov 1.50 4.00
HMKY Keith Yandle 1.50 4.00
HMLB Luc Bourdon 2.50 6.00
HMLE Loui Eriksson 1.50 4.00
HMLS Ladislav Smid 1.50 4.00
HMLU Joffrey Lupul 1.50 4.00
HMMB Martin Brodeur 6.00 15.00
HMMC Matt Carle 2.50 6.00
HMMG Marian Gaborik 4.00 10.00
HMMH Marian Hossa 2.50 6.00
HMMI Mike Grier 1.50 4.00
HMML Mario Lemieux 10.00 25.00
HMMM Mike Modano 3.00 8.00
HMMN Markus Naslund 3.00 8.00
HMMP Marc-Antoine Pouliot 2.50 6.00
HMMR Mark Recchi 1.50 4.00
HMMS Mark Stuart 1.50 4.00
HMMV Marc-Edouard Vlasic 1.50 4.00
HMND Nigel Dawes 1.50 4.00
HMNL Nicklas Lidstrom 3.00 8.00
HMNW Noah Welch 1.50 4.00
HMOK Olaf Kolzig 3.00 8.00
HMOS Patrick O'Sullivan 1.50 4.00
HMPA Patrick Thoresen 2.50 6.00
HMPB Patrice Bergeron 3.00 8.00
HMPE Michael Peca 1.50 4.00
HMPF Peter Forsberg 4.00 10.00
HMPK Phil Kessel 4.00 10.00
HMPM Patrick Marleau 2.50 6.00
HMPR Patrick Roy 10.00 25.00
HMPS Paul Stastny 3.00 8.00
HMPT Pierre Turgeon 1.50 4.00
HMRE Robert Esche 2.50 6.00
HMRI Brad Richards 2.50 6.00
HMRL Roberto Luongo 4.00 10.00
HMRN Rick Nash 3.00 8.00
HMRY Michael Ryder 2.50 6.00
HMSA Joe Sakic 5.00 12.00
HMSC Sidney Crosby SP 20.00 50.00
HMSD Shane Doan 1.50 4.00
HMSK Saku Koivu 3.00 8.00
HMSO Shane O'Brien 1.50 4.00
HMSP Jason Spezza 3.00 8.00
HMSS Sergei Samsonov 2.50 6.00
HMST Jordan Staal 6.00 15.00
HMSU Mats Sundin 3.00 8.00
HMSW Shea Weber 2.50 6.00
HMTH Tomas Holmstrom 1.50 4.00
HMTP Tom Poti 1.50 4.00
HMTS Teemu Selanne 3.00 8.00
HMTT Tim Thomas 2.50 6.00
HMTV Tomas Vokoun 2.50 6.00
HMTZ Travis Zajac 3.00 8.00
HMZC Zdeno Chara 1.50 4.00

2006-07 Hot Prospects Hot Materials Red Hot

RED HOT: .6X TO 1.5X HOT MATERIALS
PRINT RUN 100 #'d SETS

2006-07 Hot Prospects Hot Materials White Hot

PRINT RUN 10 #'d SETS
NOT PRICED DUE TO SCARCITY

2006-07 Hot Prospects Hotagraphs

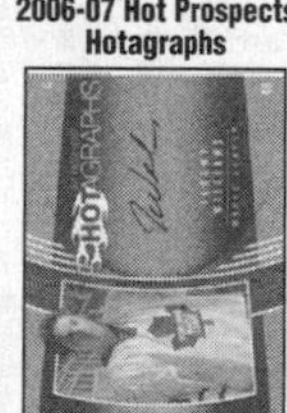

1 HOT PACK PER 180 PACKS
5 HOTAGRAPHS PER HOT PACK
HAF Alexander Frolov 8.00 20.00
HAK Anze Kopitar 20.00 50.00
HAR Andrew Raycroft 10.00 25.00
HBB Brendan Bell 6.00 15.00
HBE Patrice Bergeron 10.00 25.00
HBI Martin Biron 10.00 25.00
HBM Brenden Morrow 10.00 25.00
HBO Ben Ondrus 6.00 15.00
HBP Benoit Pouliot 12.00 30.00
HBR Brad Boyes 6.00 15.00
HBT Barry Tallackson 3.00 8.00
HCA Mike Cammalleri 6.00 15.00
HCH Chris Higgins 6.00 15.00
HCK Chris Kunitz 6.00 15.00
HCP Chris Phillips 6.00 15.00
HDA David Aebischer 10.00 25.00
HDK Duncan Keith 12.00 30.00
HDL David Leneveu 10.00 25.00
HDR Dwayne Roloson 10.00 25.00
HEF Eric Fehr 12.00 30.00
HEM Evgeni Malkin 75.00 150.00
HES Eric Staal 10.00 25.00
HFL Marc-Andre Fleury 15.00 40.00
HFN Filip Novak 6.00 15.00
HFP Fernando Pisani 8.00 20.00
HGB Gilbert Brule 8.00 20.00
HGL Guillaume Latendresse 20.00 50.00
HHA Martin Havlat 10.00 25.00
HHO Tomas Holmstrom 10.00 25.00
HHU Cristobal Huet 12.00 30.00
HIG Jarome Iginla 30.00 80.00
HIK Ilya Kovalchuk 15.00 40.00
HIW Ian White 6.00 15.00
HJB Jaroslav Balastik 3.00 8.00
HJC Jeff Carter 12.00 30.00
HJI Jarkko Immonen 8.00 20.00
HJL John-Michael Liles 6.00 15.00
HJO Jonathan Cheechoo 12.00 30.00
HJP Joni Pitkanen 6.00 15.00
HJS Jarret Stoll 6.00 15.00
HJT Joe Thornton 25.00 60.00
HJW Jeremy Williams 8.00 20.00
HKB Keith Ballard 6.00 15.00
HKC Kyle Calder 6.00 15.00
HKE Kevin Bieksa 3.00 8.00
HKL Kari Lehtonen 12.00 30.00
HKO Chuck Kobasew 6.00 15.00
HLE Loui Eriksson 6.00 15.00
HLN Ladislav Nagy 6.00 15.00
HLS Ladislav Smid 6.00 15.00
HMA Mark Stuart 6.00 15.00
HMB Martin Brodeur 40.00 100.00
HMC Matt Carle 10.00 25.00
HMF Matt Foy 4.00 10.00
HMH Marcel Hossa 4.00 10.00
HMI Michal Handzus 3.00 8.00
HML Mario Lemieux SP
HMM Masi Marjamaki 6.00 15.00
HMO Michel Ouellet 12.00 30.00
HMP Marc-Antoine Pouliot 8.00 20.00
HMR Michael Ryder 8.00 20.00
HMS Marek Svatos 6.00 15.00
HMV Mike Van Ryn 6.00 15.00
HND Nigel Dawes 6.00 15.00
HNW Noah Welch 6.00 15.00
HNZ Nikolai Zherdev 6.00 15.00
HOT Ole-Kristian Tollefsen 3.00 8.00
HPA Patrik Elias 6.00 15.00
HPB Pierre-Marc Bouchard 6.00 15.00
HPE Michael Peca 6.00 15.00
HPK Phil Kessel 25.00 60.00
HPM Paul Mara 3.00 8.00
HPO Patrick O'Sullivan 15.00 40.00
HPP Petr Prucha 8.00 20.00
HPR Paul Ranger 3.00 8.00
HPS Paul Stastny 25.00 60.00
HRA Alexander Radulov 12.00 30.00
HRB Keith Yandle 6.00 15.00
HRE Robert Esche 10.00 25.00
HRK Rostislav Klesla 6.00 15.00
HRL Roberto Luongo 50.00 125.00
HRM Ryan Malone 6.00 15.00
HRP Roman Polak 3.00 8.00
HRS Ryan Shannon 6.00 15.00
HRY Ryan Potulny 10.00 25.00
HSC Sidney Crosby 75.00 150.00
HSG Scott Gomez 6.00 15.00
HSO Shane O'Brien 6.00 15.00
HST Jordan Staal 40.00 100.00
HSW Shea Weber 10.00 25.00
HTH Trent Hunter 6.00 15.00
HTK Tomas Kopecky 10.00 25.00
HTZ Travis Zajac 10.00 25.00
HVF Valtteri Filppula 12.00 30.00
HVL Vincent Lecavalier 20.00 50.00
HYS Yan Stastny 6.00 15.00
HZC Zdeno Chara 8.00 20.00

2007-08 Hot Prospects

COMP.SET w/o SP's (100) 15.00 40.00
HC STATED PRINT RUN 999 SERIAL #'d SETS
PP RC STATED PRINT RUNS 999 SERIAL #'d SETS
PP JSY AU RC STATED PRINT RUNS 399 SERIAL #'d SETS
PP JSY AU RC SP STATED PRINT RUN 199 SERIAL #'d SETS
1 Ales Hemsky .20 .50
2 Alex Tanguay .25 .60
3 Alexander Frolov .20 .50
4 Alexander Ovechkin 1.00 2.50
5 Alexander Radulov .30 .75
6 Alexander Semin .30 .75
7 Alexander Steen .20 .50
8 Anze Kopitar .30 .75
9 Bill Guerin .20 .50
10 Brad Richards .25 .60
11 Brendan Shanahan .30 .75
12 Brian Gionta .20 .50
13 Cam Ward .30 .75
14 Chris Drury .25 .60
15 Chris Mason .25 .60
16 Corey Perry .25 .60
17 Cristobal Huet .25 .60
18 Daniel Alfredsson .25 .60
19 Daniel Briere .30 .75
20 Daniel Sedin .20 .50
21 Dany Heatley .40 1.00
22 Darcy Tucker .25 .60
23 David Vyborny .20 .50
24 Dion Phaneuf .30 .75
25 Dominik Hasek .40 1.00
26 Doug Weight .20 .50
27 Drew Stafford .25 .60
28 Dwayne Roloson .25 .60
29 Eric Staal .30 .75
30 Evgeni Malkin .75 2.00
31 Guillaume Latendresse .25 .60
32 Henrik Lundqvist .40 1.00
33 Henrik Sedin .20 .50
34 Henrik Zetterberg .30 .75
35 Ilya Kovalchuk .40 1.00
36 Jarome Iginla .50 1.25
37 Jaromir Jagr .50 1.25
38 Jason Spezza .30 .75
39 Jean-Sebastien Giguere .30 .75
40 Jeff Carter .20 .50
41 Joe Sakic .60 1.50
42 Joe Thornton .40 1.00
43 Jonathan Cheechoo .25 .60
44 Joni Pitkanen .20 .50
45 Jordan Staal .40 1.00

46 Justin Williams	.20	.50
47 Kari Lehtonen	.30	.75
48 Keith Tkachuk	.25	.60
49 Marc Savard	.20	.50
50 Marc-Andre Fleury	.30	.75
51 Marian Gaborik	.40	1.00
52 Marian Hossa	.30	.75
53 Markus Naslund	.30	.75
54 Martin Brodeur	.75	2.00
55 Tuomo Ruutu	.20	.50
56 Martin St. Louis	.25	.60
57 Marty Turco	.30	.75
58 Mats Sundin	.30	.75
59 Michael Ryder	.20	.50
60 Miikka Kiprusoff	.40	1.00
61 Mike Modano	.30	.75
62 Mike Ribeiro	.20	.50
63 Mikko Koivu	.20	.50
64 Milan Hejduk	.25	.60
65 Miroslav Satan	.20	.50
66 Nathan Horton	.20	.50
67 Nicklas Lidstrom	.30	.75
68 Niklas Backstrom	.25	.60
69 Nikolai Khabibulin	.30	.75
70 Olaf Kolzig	.30	.75
71 Olli Jokinen	.20	.50
72 Patrice Bergeron	.30	.75
73 Patrick Marleau	.25	.60
74 Patrik Elias	.20	.50
75 Paul Kariya	.30	.75
76 Paul Stastny	.30	.75
77 Pavel Datsyuk	.30	.75
78 Phil Kessel	.30	.75
79 Ray Emery	.25	.60
80 Rick DiPietro	.25	.60
81 Rick Nash	.30	.75
82 Rob Blake	.25	.60
83 Roberto Luongo	.50	1.25
84 Ryan Getzlaf	.25	.60
85 Ryan Miller	.30	.75
86 Ryan Smyth	.25	.60
87 Saku Koivu	.25	.60
88 Chris Pronger	.30	.75
89 Sergei Fedorov	.30	.75
90 Sergei Samsonov	.20	.50
91 Shane Doan	.20	.50
92 Sidney Crosby	1.50	4.00
93 Simon Gagne	.30	.75
94 Steve Bernier	.20	.50
95 Jason Arnott	.20	.50
96 Thomas Vanek	.25	.60
97 Tomas Vokoun	.30	.75
98 Vesa Toskala	.25	.60
99 Vincent Lecavalier	.30	.75
100 Zach Parise	.25	.60
101 Alexander Ovechkin HC	5.00	12.00
102 Alexander Radulov HC	1.50	4.00
103 Alexander Semin HC	1.50	4.00
104 Anze Kopitar HC	1.50	4.00
105 Bobby Orr HC	6.00	15.00
106 Brendan Shanahan HC	1.50	4.00
107 Cam Ward HC	1.50	4.00
108 Daniel Briere HC	1.50	4.00
109 Dany Heatley HC	2.00	5.00
110 Dominik Hasek HC	2.00	5.00
111 Dwayne Roloson HC	1.25	3.00
112 Eric Staal HC	1.50	4.00
113 Evgeni Malkin HC	4.00	10.00
114 Gordie Howe HC	4.00	10.00
115 Henrik Lundqvist HC	2.00	5.00
116 Henrik Zetterberg HC	1.50	4.00
117 Ilya Kovalchuk HC	2.00	5.00
118 Jarome Iginla HC	2.50	6.00
119 Jaromir Jagr HC	2.50	6.00
120 Jason Spezza HC	1.50	4.00
121 Jean-Sebastien Giguere HC	1.50	4.00
122 Joe Sakic HC	3.00	8.00
123 Joe Thornton HC	2.00	5.00
124 Jonathan Cheechoo HC	1.25	3.00
125 Kari Lehtonen HC	1.50	4.00
126 Marc-Andre Fleury HC	1.50	4.00
127 Marian Gaborik HC	2.00	5.00
128 Marian Hossa HC	1.50	4.00
129 Mario Lemieux HC	5.00	12.00
130 Mark Messier HC	3.00	8.00
131 Markus Naslund HC	1.50	4.00
132 Martin Brodeur HC	4.00	10.00
133 Martin Havlat HC	1.25	3.00
134 Martin St. Louis HC	1.25	3.00
135 Marty Turco HC	1.50	4.00
136 Mats Sundin HC	1.50	4.00
137 Michael Ryder HC	1.00	2.50
138 Miikka Kiprusoff HC	2.00	5.00
139 Mike Modano HC	1.50	4.00
140 Nicklas Lidstrom HC	1.50	4.00
141 Patrice Bergeron HC	1.50	4.00
142 Patrick Marleau HC	1.25	3.00
143 Paul Kariya HC	1.50	4.00
144 Paul Stastny HC	1.50	4.00
145 Phil Kessel HC	1.50	4.00
146 Rick DiPietro HC	1.25	3.00
147 Rick Nash HC	1.50	4.00
148 Roberto Luongo HC	2.50	6.00
149 Ryan Getzlaf HC	1.25	3.00
150 Ryan Miller HC	1.50	4.00
151 Saku Koivu HC	1.25	3.00
152 Scott Niedermayer HC	1.00	2.50
153 Shane Doan HC	1.00	2.50
154 Sidney Crosby HC	8.00	20.00
155 Simon Gagne HC	1.50	4.00
156 Thomas Vanek HC	1.25	3.00
157 Tomas Vokoun HC	1.50	4.00
158 Vincent Lecavalier HC	1.50	4.00
159 Mark Recchi HC	1.00	2.50
160 Zach Parise HC	1.25	3.00
161 Mike Weber PP RC	2.50	6.00
162 Tyler Kennedy PP RC	4.00	10.00
163 Bryan Young PP RC	2.50	6.00
164 Cal Clutterbuck PP RC	2.50	6.00
165 Curtis Glencross PP RC	2.50	6.00
166 Daniel Carcillo PP RC	3.00	8.00
167 Magnus Johansson PP RC	2.50	6.00
168 Marc Methot PP RC	2.50	6.00
169 David Clarkson PP RC	2.50	6.00
170 Drew Fata PP RC	2.50	6.00
171 Duncan Milroy PP RC	2.50	6.00
172 Tobias Enstrom PP RC	4.00	10.00
173 Chris Bourque PP RC	3.00	8.00
174 Jeff Finger PP RC	2.50	6.00
175 Jeff Schultz PP RC	2.50	6.00
176 Joel Lundqvist PP RC	2.50	6.00
177 John Zeiler PP RC	2.50	6.00
178 Cory Murphy PP RC	2.50	6.00
179 Kent Huskins PP RC	2.50	6.00
180 Mark Fraser PP RC	2.50	6.00
181 Mark Mancari PP RC	3.00	8.00
182 Martin Lojek PP RC	2.50	6.00
183 Matt Keetley PP RC	3.00	8.00
184 Steve Wagner PP RC	2.50	6.00
185 Nathan Guenin PP RC	2.50	6.00
186 Ryan Carter PP RC	3.00	8.00
187 Petteri Wirtanen PP RC	2.50	6.00
188 Rod Pelley PP RC	2.50	6.00
189 David Moss PP RC	4.00	10.00
190 Matt Ellis PP RC	2.50	6.00
191 Sebastien Bisaillon PP RC	2.50	6.00
192 Daniel Winnik PP RC	2.50	6.00
193 Craig Weller PP RC	2.50	6.00
194 Tomas Plihal PP RC	3.00	8.00
195 Riley Cote PP RC	3.00	8.00
196 Brady Murray PP RC	2.50	6.00
197 Tomas Popperle PP RC	3.00	8.00
198 Tom Gilbert PP RC	3.00	8.00
199 Denis Tolpeko PP RC	2.50	6.00
200 Zach Stortini PP RC	2.50	6.00
201 Bobby Ryan PP JSY AU RC	50.00	120.00
202 Sam Gagner PP JSY AU RC	25.00	60.00
203 Nicklas Bergfors PP JSY AU RC	15.00	40.00
204 Jonathan Bernier PP JSY AU RC	30.00	80.00
205 Bryan Little PP JSY AU RC	20.00	50.00
206 Kris Russell PP JSY AU RC	20.00	50.00
207 Matt Niskanen PP JSY AU RC	12.00	30.00
208 Andrew Cogliano PP JSY AU RC	30.00	80.00
209 Nick Foligno PP JSY AU RC	20.00	50.00
210 Brett Sterling PP JSY AU RC	12.00	30.00
211 Martin Hanzal PP JSY AU RC	15.00	40.00
212 Jaroslav Hlinka PP JSY AU RC	15.00	40.00
213 Matt Smaby PP JSY AU RC	12.00	30.00
214 Petr Kalus PP JSY AU RC	12.00	30.00
215 Andy Greene PP JSY AU RC	12.00	30.00
216 Frans Nielsen PP JSY AU RC	12.00	30.00
217 Rob Schremp PP JSY AU RC	15.00	40.00
218 James Sheppard PP JSY AU RC	12.00	30.00
219 Kyle Chipchura PP JSY AU RC	20.00	50.00
220 Ryan Parent PP JSY AU RC	15.00	40.00
221 David Krejci PP JSY AU RC	25.00	60.00
222 Lauri Tukonen PP JSY AU RC	12.00	30.00
223 Tuukka Rask PP JSY AU RC	30.00	80.00
224 Mason Raymond PP JSY AU RC	30.00	80.00
225 Brandon Dubinsky PP JSY AU RC	20.00	50.00
226 Curtis McElhinney PP JSY AU RC	15.00	40.00
227 Brian Elliott PP JSY AU RC	15.00	40.00
228 Drew Miller PP JSY AU RC	12.00	30.00
229 Ryan Callahan PP JSY AU RC	20.00	50.00
230 Ondrej Pavelec PP JSY AU RC	20.00	50.00
231 Ville Koistinen PP JSY AU RC	12.00	30.00
232 Torrey Mitchell PP JSY AU RC	15.00	40.00
233 David Perron PP JSY AU RC	20.00	50.00
234 Jonathan Sigalet PP JSY AU RC	12.00	30.00
235 Jannik Hansen PP JSY AU RC	12.00	30.00
236 Jaroslav Halak PP JSY AU RC	40.00	100.00
237 Devin Setoguchi PP JSY AU RC	25.00	60.00
238 Milan Lucic PP JSY AU RC	30.00	80.00
239 Lukas Kaspar PP JSY AU RC	12.00	30.00
240 Tyler Weiman PP JSY AU RC	15.00	40.00
241 Tobias Stephan PP JSY AU RC	15.00	40.00
242 Daniel Girardi PP JSY AU RC	12.00	30.00
243 Stefan Meyer PP JSY AU RC	12.00	30.00
244 Jared Boll PP JSY AU RC	12.00	30.00
245 Jiri Tlusty PP JSY AU RC	30.00	80.00
246 Jonas Hiller PP JSY AU RC	30.00	80.00
247 T.J. Hensick PP JSY AU RC	15.00	40.00
248 Anton Stralman PP JSY AU RC	15.00	40.00
249 Jonathan Toews PP JSY AU SP/199 RC	100.00	200.00
250 Carey Price PP JSY AU SP/199 RC	125.00	250.00
251 Peter Mueller PP JSY AU SP/199 RC	50.00	100.00
252 Patrick Kane PP JSY AU SP/199 RC	100.00	200.00
253 Marc Staal PP JSY AU SP/199 RC	50.00	100.00
254 Nicklas Backstrom PP JSY AU SP/199 RC	75.00	150.00
255 Erik Johnson PP JSY AU SP/199 RC	50.00	100.00
256 Jack Johnson PP JSY AU SP/199 RC	50.00	100.00

2007-08 Hot Prospects Red Hot

*RED HOT JSY (1-100): 8X TO 20X
1-100 STATED PRINT RUN 100 SER.#'d SETS
*RED HOT HC (101-160): .5X TO 1.2X
(101-160) PRINT RUN 100 SER.#'d SETS
*RED HOT PP (161-200): .5X TO 1.2X
(1-200) PRINT RUN 100 SER.#'d SETS
*RED HOT PP JSY AU (201-248): .5X TO 1.2X
201-256 STATED PRINT RUN 25 SERIAL #'d SETS

249 Jonathan Toews JSY AU	125.00	250.00
250 Carey Price JSY AU	150.00	300.00
251 Peter Mueller JSY AU	60.00	120.00
252 Patrick Kane JSY AU	125.00	250.00
253 Marc Staal JSY AU	60.00	120.00
254 Nicklas Backstrom JSY AU	100.00	200.00
255 Erik Johnson JSY AU	60.00	120.00
256 Jack Johnson JSY AU	60.00	120.00

2007-08 Hot Prospects White Hot

1-160 STATED PRINT RUN 10 SER.#'d SETS
161-200 STATED PRINT RUN 10 SERIAL #'d SETS
201-256 STATED PRINT RUN 1 SERIAL #'d SET
NOT PRICED DUE TO SCARCITY

2007-08 Hot Prospects Hot Materials

STATED ODDS 1:8

HMAG Andy Greene	3.00	8.00
HMAK Alex Kovalev	3.00	8.00
HMAM Andrej Meszaros	3.00	8.00
HMAO Alexander Ovechkin	15.00	40.00
HMAR Alexander Radulov	5.00	12.00
HMAS Alexander Steen	3.00	8.00
HMBB Brad Boyes	4.00	10.00
HMBD Brandon Dubinsky	5.00	12.00
HMBE Bryan Berard	3.00	8.00
HMBG Bill Guerin	3.00	8.00
HMBJ Barret Jackman	3.00	8.00
HMBL Brendan Bell	3.00	8.00
HMBM Brendan Morrison	3.00	8.00
HMBO Brandon Bochenski	3.00	8.00
HMBR Brenden Morrow	4.00	10.00
HMBS Brad Stuart	3.00	8.00
HMCA Matt Carle	3.00	8.00
HMCH Jonathan Cheechoo	4.00	10.00
HMCK Chuck Kobasew	3.00	8.00
HMCM Mike Cammalleri	4.00	10.00
HMCS Curtis Sanford	4.00	10.00
HMCW Cam Ward	5.00	12.00
HMDA David Aebischer	4.00	10.00
HMDB Dustin Brown	3.00	8.00
HMDH Dany Heatley	6.00	15.00
HMDK David Krejci	6.00	15.00
HMDL David Legwand	3.00	8.00
HMDM Drew Miller	3.00	8.00
HMDO Dominik Hasek	6.00	15.00
HMDP Daniel Paille	3.00	8.00
HMDR Dwayne Roloson	4.00	10.00
HMDU Duncan Keith	5.00	12.00
HMDW Doug Weight	3.00	8.00
HMEC Erik Cole	3.00	8.00
HMES Eric Staal	5.00	12.00
HMFN Frans Nielsen	3.00	8.00
HMGB Gilbert Brule	3.00	8.00
HMGE Martin Gerber	4.00	10.00
HMGI Brian Gionta	3.00	8.00
HMHA Jannik Hansen	3.00	8.00
HMHS Henrik Sedin	3.00	8.00
HMIK Ilya Kovalchuk	6.00	15.00
HMIW Ian White	3.00	8.00
HMJA Jaromir Jagr	8.00	20.00
HMJB Jay Bouwmeester	3.00	8.00
HMJC Jeff Carter	3.00	8.00
HMJH Jaroslav Halak	10.00	25.00
HMJI Jarome Iginla	8.00	20.00
HMJJ Jack Johnson	5.00	12.00
HMJL Jere Lehtinen	3.00	8.00
HMJO Jussi Jokinen	3.00	8.00
HMJP Joni Pitkanen	3.00	8.00
HMJS Jonathan Sigalet	3.00	8.00
HMJT Joe Thornton	6.00	15.00
HMJW Justin Williams	3.00	8.00
HMKE Phil Kessel	5.00	12.00
HMKL Kari Lehtonen	5.00	12.00
HMKT Keith Tkachuk	4.00	10.00
HMLE Jordan Leopold	3.00	8.00
HMLT Lauri Tukonen	3.00	8.00
HMLU Joffrey Lupul	3.00	8.00
HMMA Marc Savard	3.00	8.00
HMMB Martin Brodeur	12.00	30.00
HMMC Bryan McCabe	3.00	8.00
HMMF Manny Fernandez	4.00	10.00
HMMG Marian Gaborik	6.00	15.00
HMMH Marian Hossa	5.00	12.00
HMMI Milan Michalek	3.00	8.00
HMMK Mikko Koivu	3.00	8.00
HMMM Marc Methot	3.00	8.00
HMMN Markus Naslund	5.00	12.00
HMMO Mike Modano	5.00	12.00
HMMR Mike Richards	6.00	15.00
HMMS Matt Stajan	3.00	8.00
HMMT Marty Turco	5.00	12.00
HMNH Nathan Horton	3.00	8.00
HMNL Nicklas Lidstrom	5.00	12.00
HMPB Patrice Bergeron	5.00	12.00
HMPF Peter Forsberg	6.00	15.00
HMPK Petr Kalus	3.00	8.00
HMPL Pascal Leclaire	4.00	10.00
HMRA Andrew Raycroft	4.00	10.00
HMRC Ryan Callahan	5.00	12.00
HMRE Mark Recchi	3.00	8.00
HMRP Ryan Parent	4.00	10.00
HMRS Rob Schremp	4.00	10.00
HMRY Michael Ryder	3.00	8.00
HMSA Joe Sakic	10.00	25.00
HMSB Steve Bernier	3.00	8.00
HMSC Sidney Crosby	25.00	60.00
HMSE Brent Seabrook	3.00	8.00
HMSH Brendan Shanahan	5.00	12.00
HMSL Martin St. Louis	4.00	10.00
HMSM Ryan Smyth	4.00	10.00
HMSP Jason Spezza	5.00	12.00
HMST Jarret Stoll	3.00	8.00
HMSV Marek Svatos	3.00	8.00
HMTR Tuomo Ruutu	3.00	8.00
HMVL Vincent Lecavalier	5.00	12.00

2007-08 Hot Prospects Hot Materials Red Hot

*RED HOT: .5X TO 1.2X HOT MATERIALS
STATED PRINT RUN 100 SER.#'d SETS

2007-08 Hot Prospects Hot Materials White Hot

STATED PRINT RUN 10 SER.#'d SETS
NOT PRICED DUE TO SCARCITY

1995-96 Hoyle Eastern Playing Cards

COMPLETE SET (54)	8.00	20.00
1 Eric Lindros	.20	.50
2 Peter Bondra	.20	.50
3 Radek Bonk	.08	.25
4 Ray Bourque	.40	1.00
5 Brian Bradley	.08	.25
6 Rod Brind'Amour	.20	.50
7 Martin Brodeur	.75	2.00
8 Wendel Clark	.40	1.00
9 Alexandre Daigle	.08	.25
10 Vincent Damphousse	.08	.25
11 Ray Ferraro	.08	.25
12 Stephane Fiset	.20	.50
13 Peter Forsberg	.60	1.50
14 Joe Sakic	.75	2.00
15 Mikael Renberg	.08	.25
16 Stephane Richer	.08	.25
17 Mike Richter	.40	1.00
18 Luc Robitaille	.40	1.00
19 Geoff Sanderson	.08	.25
20 Bryan Smolinski	.08	.25
21 Kevin Stevens	.08	.25
22 Scott Stevens	.08	.25
23 Steve Thomas	.08	.25
24 Darren Turcotte	.08	.25
25 John Vanbiesbrouck	.20	.50
26 New Jersey Devils Cup Winners	.08	.25
27 Patrick Roy	1.25	3.00
28 Chris Gratton	.08	.25
29 Adam Graves	.08	.25
30 Dominik Hasek	.60	1.50
31 Ron Hextall	.40	1.00
32 Jaromir Jagr	.60	1.50
33 Joe Juneau	.08	.25
34 Dimitri Khristich	.08	.25
35 Petr Klima	.08	.25
36 Bob Kudelski	.08	.25
37 Scott Lachance	.08	.25
38 Pat Lafontaine	.08	.25
39 John Leclair	.08	.25
40 Mark Messier	.40	1.00
41 Brian Leetch	.20	.50
42 Alexander Mogilny	.20	.50
43 Kirk Muller	.08	.25
44 Cam Neely	.40	1.00
45 Rob Niedermayer	.08	.25
46 Scott Niedermayer	.20	.50
47 Owen Nolan	.08	.25
48 Adam Oates	.08	.25
49 Michal Pivonka	.08	.25
50 Derek Plante	.08	.25
51 Chris Pronger	.20	.50
52 Mark Recchi	.20	.50
53 Sergei Zubov	.08	.25
54 Alexei Yashin	.08	.25

1995-96 Hoyle Western Playing Cards

COMPLETE SET (54)	8.00	20.00
1 Jeremy Roenick	.40	1.00
2 Dave Andreychuk	.08	.25
3 Jason Arnott	.08	.25
4 Ed Belfour	.40	1.00
5 Rob Blake	.20	.50
6 Jeff Brown	.08	.25
7 Patrick Carnback	.08	.25
8 Chris Chelios	.30	.75
9 Tim Cheveldae	.20	.50
10 Paul Coffey	.30	.75
11 Shayne Corson	.08	.25
12 Geoff Courtnall	.08	.25
13 Russ Courtnall	.08	.25
14 Wayne Gretzky	2.00	5.00
15 Joe Sacco	.08	.25
16 Denis Savard	.20	.50
17 Teemu Selanne	.40	1.00
18 Brendan Shanahan	.40	1.00
19 Ray Sheppard	.08	.25
20 Mats Sundin	.40	1.00
21 Esa Tikkanen	.08	.25
22 German Titov	.08	.25
23 Keith Tkachuk	.20	.50
24 Rick Tocchet	.08	.25
25 Doug Weight	.08	.25
26 Detroit Red Wings Team Photo	.08	.25
27 Sergei Fedorov	.40	1.00
28 Ulf Dahlen	.08	.25
29 Pat Falloon	.08	.25
30 Theoren Fleury	.20	.50
31 Doug Gilmour	.40	1.00
32 Todd Harvey	.08	.25
33 Kevin Hatcher	.08	.25
34 Guy Hebert	.20	.50
35 Phil Housley	.08	.25
36 Brett Hull	.60	1.50
37 Arturs Irbe	.20	.50
38 Curtis Joseph	.40	1.00
39 Paul Kariya	.40	1.00
40 Pavel Bure	.30	.75
41 Jari Kurri	.30	.75
42 Igor Larionov	.08	.25
43 Nicklas Lidstrom	.20	.50
44 Trevor Linden	.40	1.00
45 Marty McSorley	.08	.25
46 Mike Modano	.40	1.00
47 Bernie Nicholls	.08	.25
48 Joe Nieuwendyk	.20	.50
49 David Oliver	.08	.25
50 Felix Potvin	.40	1.00
51 Bill Ranford	.20	.50
52 Gary Roberts	.08	.25
53 Steve Yzerman	1.25	3.00
54 Alexei Zhamnov	.08	.25

1975-76 Houston Aeros WHA

Little was known about this rare WHA issue. The checklist was confirmed and as the cards are unnumbered, they are listed below in alphabetical order. Any additional information can be forwarded to hockeymag@beckett.com.

COMPLETE SET (19)	40.00	80.00
1 Ron Grahame	2.00	4.00
2 Larry Hale	1.00	2.00
3 Murray Hall	1.50	3.00
4 Gordie Howe	15.00	30.00
5 Mark Howe	5.00	10.00
6 Marty Howe	4.00	8.00
7 Andre Hinse	1.00	2.00
8 Frank Hughes	1.00	2.00
9 Glen Irwin	1.00	2.00
10 Gord Labossiere	1.50	3.00
11 Don Larway	1.00	2.00
12 Larry Lund	1.50	3.00
13 Paul Popeil	1.50	3.00
14 Rich Preston	1.50	3.00
15 Terry Ruskowski	1.50	3.00
16 Wayne Rutledge	2.00	4.00
17 John Schella	1.00	2.00
18 Ted Taylor	1.00	2.00
19 John Tonelli	5.00	10.00

1992-93 Humpty Dumpty I

This 26-card set was sponsored by Humpty Dumpty Foods Ltd., a snack food company located in Eastern Canada and owned by Borden Inc. This promotion consisted of one cello-wrapped (approximately) 1 7/16" by 1 15/16" mini-hockey card, which was inserted into specially marked bags of Humpty Dumpty Chips and Snacks. Two series of cards were produced, and complete sets could be obtained only by collecting the cards through the promotion. The promotion lasted from October 1992 to March 1993. A total of 11,000,000 series I cards were produced, or 423,077 of each card, and they were evenly distributed between Ontario, Quebec, and the Atlantic provinces. The fronts displayed glossy color action photos, with the team logo superimposed toward the bottom of the picture. On a white panel framed by gray, the back presented 1991-92 season statistics and biography in French and English. The cards were unnumbered and checklisted below in alphabetical order.

COMPLETE SET (26)	8.00	20.00
1 Ray Bourque	.40	1.00
2 Rod Brind'Amour	.20	.50
3 Chris Chelios	.30	.75
4 Wendel Clark	.20	.50
5 Gilbert Dionne	.08	.25
6 Pat Falloon	.15	.40
7 Ray Ferraro	.15	.40
8 Theo Fleury	.30	.75
9 Grant Fuhr	.20	.50
10 Wayne Gretzky	2.00	5.00
11 Kevin Hatcher	.08	.25
12 Valeri Kamensky	.20	.50
13 Mike Keane	.08	.25
14 Brian Leetch	.30	.75
15 Kirk McLean	.20	.50
16 Alexander Mogilny	.25	.60
17 Troy Murray	.08	.25
18 Patrick Roy	1.50	4.00
19 Joe Sakic	.60	1.50
20 Brendan Shanahan	.60	1.50
21 Kevin Stevens	.15	.40
22 Scott Stevens	.20	.50
23 Mark Tinordi	.08	.25
24 Steve Yzerman	1.00	2.50
25 Zarley Zalapski	.08	.25
26 Checklist	.20	.50

1992-93 Humpty Dumpty II

This 26-card set was sponsored by Humpty Dumpty Foods Ltd., a snack food company located in Eastern Canada and owned by Borden Inc. This promotion consisted of one cello-wrapped approximately 1 7/16" by 1 15/16" mini-hockey card randomly inserted into specially marked bags of Humpty Dumpty Chips and Snacks. Two series of cards were produced, and complete sets could be obtained only by collecting the cards through the promotion. The promotion lasted from October 1992 to March 1993. A total of 18,000,000 series II cards were produced, or 692,307 of each card, and they were evenly distributed between Ontario, Quebec, and the Atlantic provinces. The fronts displayed glossy color action photos, with the team logo superimposed toward the bottom of the picture. On a white panel framed by beige, the back presented 1991-92 season statistics and biography in French and English. The cards were unnumbered and checklisted below in alphabetical order.

COMPLETE SET (26)	8.00	20.00
1 Drake Berehowsky	.08	.25
2 Shayne Corson	.15	.40
3 Russ Courtnall	.15	.40
4 Dave Ellett	.08	.25
5 Sergei Fedorov	.60	1.50
6 Dave Gagner	.15	.40
7 Doug Gilmour	.30	.75
8 Phil Housley	.15	.40
9 Brett Hull	.40	1.00
10 Jaromir Jagr	1.00	2.50
11 Pat LaFontaine	.20	.50
12 Mario Lemieux	1.50	4.00
13 Trevor Linden	.15	.40
14 Al MacInnis	.20	.50
15 Mark Messier	.40	1.00
16 Cam Neely	.30	.75
17 Owen Nolan	.20	.50
18 Bill Ranford	.20	.50
19 Luc Robitaille	.25	.60
20 Jeremy Roenick	.30	.75
21 Mats Sundin	.30	.75
22 Chris Terreri	.15	.40
23 Steve Thomas	.15	.40
24 Pat Verbeek	.15	.40
25 Neil Wilkinson	.08	.25
26 Checklist	.20	.50

1997-98 Hurricanes Team Issue

The set was issued by the team as a promotional giveaway. The cards were unnumbered and checklisted below in alphabetical order.

COMPLETE SET (28)	4.80	12.00
1 Jeff Brown	.08	.25
2 Sean Burke	.40	1.00
3 Adam Burt	.08	.25
4 Steve Chiasson	.08	.25
5 Enrico Ciccone	.08	.25
6 Kevin Dineen	.10	.30
7 Nelson Emerson	.10	.30
8 Martin Gelinas	.10	.30
9 Stu Grimson	.10	.30
10 Steve Halko	.08	.25
11 Kevin Haller	.08	.25
12 Sean Hill	.08	.25
13 Sami Kapanen	1.25	3.00
14 Trevor Kidd	.40	1.00
15 Robert Kron	.10	.30
16 Steve Leach	.08	.25
17 Curtis Leschyshyn	.08	.25
18 Kent Manderville	.08	.25
19 Jeff O'Neill	.08	.25
20 Nolan Pratt	.08	.25
21 Keith Primeau	.60	1.50
22 Paul Ranheim	.08	.25
23 Steven Rice	.10	.30
24 Gary Roberts	.10	.30
25 Geoff Sanderson	.20	.50
26 Glen Wesley	.10	.30
27 Paul Maurice Tom Webster Randy Ladouceur CO	.07	.20
28 Stormy the Mascot	.02	.10

1998-99 Hurricanes Team Issue

This set featured the Hurricanes of the NHL. The post-card-sized singles were issued at autograph signings and other promotional ventures. Other singles may exist as well; information on these can be forwarded to hockeymag@beckett.com.

COMPLETE SET (25)	12.00	30.00
1 Arturs Irbe	.75	2.00
2 Glen Wesley	.40	1.00
3 Steve Chiasson	.40	1.00
4 Nolan Pratt	.40	1.00
5 Marek Malik	.40	1.00
6 Adam Burt	.40	1.00
7 Curtis Leschyshyn	.40	1.00
8 Gary Roberts	.40	1.00
9 Kevin Dineen	.40	1.00
10 Bates Battaglia	.60	1.50
11 Steven Halko	.40	1.00
12 Byron Ritchie	.40	1.00
13 Ron Francis	1.25	3.00
14 Sean Hill	.40	1.00
15 Martin Gelinas	.40	1.00
16 Sami Kapanen	.75	2.00
17 Ray Sheppard	.40	1.00
18 Paul Ranheim	.40	1.00
19 Dave Karpa	.40	1.00
20 Trevor Kidd	.60	1.50
21 Kent Manderville	.40	1.00
22 Mike Rucinski	.40	1.00
23 Keith Primeau	.60	1.50
24 Jeff O'Neill	.75	2.00
25 Stormy MASCOT	.08	.25

2002-03 Hurricanes Postcards

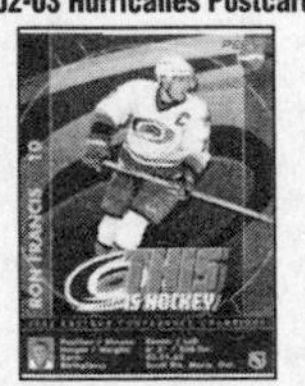

These 3X5 blank backed cards feature a photo, stats and player ID on the front. They were issued as promotional items at team events. The checklist is not complete -- if you can confirm others, please write us at hockeymag@beckett.com.

COMPLETE SET (?)		
1 Rod Brind'Amour		1.50
2 Erik Cole		1.50
3 Ron Francis		1.50
4 Arturs Irbe		2.00
5 Jeff O'Neill		1.00
6 Kevin Weekes		1.50
7 Glen Wesley		1.00

2003-04 Hurricanes Postcards

These oversized cards were issued by the team and sponsored by Pepsi.

COMPLETE SET (24)	10.00	25.00
1 Craig Adams	.30	.75
2 Kevyn Adams	.30	.75
3 Ryan Bayda	.30	.75
4 Bob Boughner	.30	.75
5 Jesse Boulerice	.30	.75
6 Pavel Brendl	.30	.75
7 Rod Brind'Amour	.60	1.50
8 Erik Cole	.40	1.00
9 Ron Francis	.60	1.50
10 Bret Hedican	.30	.75
11 Sean Hill	.30	.75
12 Kevin McCarthy	.30	.75
13 Marty Murray	.30	.75
14 Jeff O'Neill	.40	1.00
15 Eric Staal	2.00	5.00
16 Bruno St. Jacques	.30	.75
17 Jamie Storr	.40	1.00
18 Jaroslav Svoboda	.30	.75
19 Josef Vasicek	.30	.75
20 Radim Vrbata	.30	.75
21 Niclas Wallin	.30	.75
22 Aaron Ward	.30	.75
23 Kevin Weekes	.40	1.00
24 Glen Wesley	.30	.75

2006-07 Hurricanes Postcards

COMPLETE SET (28)	15.00	25.00
1 Logo Card	.10	.25
2 Craig Adams	.40	1.00
3 Kevyn Adams	.40	1.00
4 Anton Babchuk	.40	1.00
5 Eric Belanger	.40	1.00
6 Rod Brind'Amour	.75	2.00
7 Erik Cole	1.00	2.50
8 Mike Commodore	.40	1.00
9 Jeff Daniels ACO	.10	.25
10 Tim Gleason	.40	1.00
11 John Grahame	.60	1.50
12 Bret Hedican	.40	1.00
13 Andrew Hutchinson	.40	1.00
14 Frantisek Kaberle	.40	1.00
15 Andrew Ladd	.40	1.00
16 Chad Larose	.40	1.00
17 Peter Laviolette CO	.20	.50
18 Trevor Letowski	.40	1.00
19 Kevin McCarthy ACO	.10	.25
20 Eric Staal	1.25	3.00
21 Cory Stillman	.40	1.00
22 David Tanabe	.40	1.00
23 Scott Walker	.40	1.00
24 Niclas Wallin	.40	1.00
25 Cam Ward	.75	2.00
26 Glen Wesley	.40	1.00
27 Ray Whitney	.40	1.00
28 Justin Williams	.75	2.00

1995-96 Imperial Stickers

This set of 136 stickers was released in five-sticker packs (plus one stick of tasty gum!) late in the 1995-96 season. The stickers measured the standard size and featured color player photos and name on the front, and playing information on the back. Collation of this product was extremely poor, making set building somewhat arduous.

COMPLETE SET (136)	14.00	35.00
1 Ducks Logo	.20	.50
2 Paul Kariya	.75	2.00
3 Chad Kilger	.20	.50
4 Oleg Tverdovsky	.20	.50
5 Bruins Logo	.20	.50
6 Ray Bourque	.60	1.50
7 Cam Neely	.25	.60
8 Adam Oates	.25	.60
9 Kevin Stevens	.20	.50
10 Sabres Logo	.20	.50
11 Pat LaFontaine	.25	.60
12 Dominik Hasek	.40	1.00
13 Alexei Zhitnik	.01	.05
14 Flames Logo	.20	.50
15 Theo Fleury	.20	.50
16 Phil Housley	.20	.50
17 Trevor Kidd	.20	.50
18 Joe Nieuwendyk	.20	.50
19 Zarley Zalapski	.01	.05
20 Blackhawks Logo	.20	.50
21 Jeremy Roenick	.20	.50
22 Chris Chelios	.20	.50
23 Ed Belfour	.25	.60
24 Joe Murphy	.20	.50
25 Patrick Poulin	.01	.05
26 Avalanche Logo	.20	.50
27 Joe Sakic	.60	1.50
28 Peter Forsberg	.60	1.50
29 Sandis Ozolinsh	.20	.50
30 Mike Ricci	.02	.10
31 Valeri Kamensky	.20	.50

32 Stars Logo .20 .50
33 Mike Modano .30 .75
34 Kevin Hatcher .01 .05
35 Andy Moog .20 .50
36 Red Wings Logo .20 .50
37 Steve Yzerman 1.25 3.00
38 Sergei Fedorov .40 1.00
39 Paul Coffey .20 .50
40 Keith Primeau .02 .10
41 Nicklas Lidstrom .25 .60
42 Oilers Logo .20 .50
43 Doug Weight .20 .50
44 Jason Arnott .20 .50
45 Bill Ranford .20 .50
46 Panthers Logo .20 .50
47 John Vanbiesbrouck .20 .50
48 Stu Barnes .20 .50
49 Scott Mellanby .02 .10
50 Rob Niedermayer .20 .50
51 Whalers Logo .20 .50
52 Brendan Shanahan .40 1.00
53 Geoff Sanderson .20 .50
54 Sean Burke .02 .10
55 Jeff O'Neill .02 .10
56 Kings Logo .20 .50
57 Wayne Gretzky 2.00 5.00
58 Rob Blake .20 .50
59 Rick Tocchet .20 .50
60 Dimitri Khristich .01 .05
61 Kelly Hrudey .20 .50
62 Canadiens Logo .20 .50
63 Pierre Turgeon .20 .50
64 Mark Recchi .20 .50
65 Saku Koivu .20 .50
66 Patrick Roy 1.50 4.00
67 Vincent Damphousse .20 .50
68 Devils Logo .20 .50
69 Stephane Richer .01 .05
70 Martin Brodeur .60 1.50
71 Scott Niedermayer .20 .50
72 Scott Stevens .20 .50
73 Islander Logo .20 .50
74 Kirk Muller .02 .10
75 Mathieu Schneider .01 .05
76 Derek King .20 .50
77 Wendel Clark .01 .05
78 Ranger Logo .20 .50
79 Brian Leetch .20 .50
80 Mark Messier .30 .75
81 Alexei Kovalev .20 .50
82 Luc Robitaille .20 .50
83 Mike Richter .20 .50
84 Senators Logo .20 .50
85 Dan Quinn .01 .05
86 Alexandre Daigle .02 .10
87 Steve Duchesne .01 .05
88 Radek Bonk .02 .10
89 Flyers Logo .20 .50
90 Eric Lindros .75 2.00
91 Mikael Renberg .20 .50
92 John LeClair .40 1.00
93 Eric Desjardins .20 .50
94 Rod Brind'Amour .20 .50
95 Penguins Logo .20 .50
96 Jaromir Jagr .75 2.00
97 Mario Lemieux 1.50 4.00
98 Ron Francis .20 .50
99 Sergei Zubov .02 .10
100 Blues Logo .20 .50
101 Brett Hull .30 .75
102 Al MacInnis .20 .50
103 Dale Hawerchuk .20 .50
104 Chris Pronger .20 .50
105 Sharks Logo .20 .50
106 Craig Janney .02 .10
107 Pat Falloon .01 .05
108 Arturs Irbe .20 .50
109 Ulf Dahlen .01 .05
110 Owen Nolan .20 .50
111 Lightning Logo .20 .50
112 Roman Hamrlik .20 .50
113 Brian Bradley .20 .50
114 Chris Gratton .20 .50
115 Brian Bellows .01 .05
116 Maple Leafs Logo .20 .50
117 Doug Gilmour .20 .50
118 Mats Sundin .20 .50
119 Dave Andreychuk .20 .50
120 Felix Potvin .20 .50
121 Larry Murphy .20 .50
122 Canucks Logo .20 .50
123 Pavel Bure .60 1.50
124 Alexander Mogilny .20 .50
125 Trevor Linden .20 .50
126 Jeff Brown .01 .05
127 Kirk McLean .20 .50
128 Capitals Logo .20 .50
129 Joe Juneau .20 .50
130 Peter Bondra .20 .50
131 Jim Carey .20 .50
132 Calle Johansson .01 .05
133 Jets Logo .20 .50
134 Teemu Selanne .40 1.00
135 Alexei Zhamnov .20 .50
136 Keith Tkachuk .25 .60

1995-96 Imperial Stickers Die Cut Superstars

These die-cut stickers were randomly inserted in packs at indeterminate odds. They featured player images over a starburst background. Backs were blank.

COMPLETE SET (25) 12.00 30.00
1 Pierre Turgeon .20 .50
2 Patrick Roy 1.50 4.00
3 Pat LaFontaine .20 .50
4 Joe Sakic .60 1.50
5 Paul Coffey .30 .75
6 Ray Bourque .40 1.00
7 Brian Leetch .30 .75
8 Joe Juneau .15 .40
9 Jeremy Roenick .30 .75
10 Chris Chelios .30 .75
11 Brett Hull .40 1.00
12 Paul Kariya 1.25 3.00
13 Jason Arnott .15 .40
14 Pavel Bure .75 2.00
15 Steve Duchesne .20 .50
16 Martin Brodeur .75 2.00
17 Eric Lindros 1.00 2.50
18 Mikael Renberg .20 .50
19 Felix Potvin .25 .60
20 Roman Hamrlik .15 .40
21 Wayne Gretzky 2.00 5.00
22 Brendan Shanahan .60 1.50
23 Jaromir Jagr 1.00 2.50
24 Mario Lemieux 1.50 4.00
25 Steve Yzerman 1.00 2.50

1927 Imperial Tobacco

Card was black and white and measured approximately 1 1/2 x 2 1/2.

NNO Montreal Victorias 25.00 50.00

1929 Imperial Tobacco

Card is black and white and measured approximately 2 1/2 x 3.

NNO Ice Hockey 20.00 40.00

2003-04 ITG Action

ITG Action was the largest set of the year consisiting of 600 veteran cards found in packs and 74 update cards available via various redemptions. Cards 601-616 were available via redemption cards found in hobby boxes. Cards 617-624 were available only in factory sets and cards 625-674 were available via an online only purchase. Print runs for cards 601-624 are listed below.

COMP.SET w/o UPDATE (600) 75.00 150.00
1 Joe Thornton .50 1.25
2 Dany Heatley .40 1.00
3 Ales Kotalik .10 .25
4 Steve Montador .10 .25
5 Dan Bylsma .10 .25
6 Andrew Ference .10 .25
7 Andy Hilbert .10 .25
8 Andy McDonald .10 .25
9 Bob Boughner .10 .25
10 Brad Tapper .10 .25
11 Brian Campbell .10 .25
12 Brian Rolston .10 .25
13 Daniel Tjarnqvist .10 .25
14 Glen Murray .10 .25
15 Byron Dafoe .25 .60
16 Bryan Berard .10 .25
17 Alexei Zhitnik .10 .25
18 Craig Conroy .10 .25
19 Curtis Brown .10 .25
20 Dan McGillis .10 .25
21 Dan Snyder .10 .25
22 Daniel Briere .10 .25
23 Chris Clark .10 .25
24 Frantisek Kaberle .10 .25
25 Adam Oates .25 .60
26 Denis Gauthier .10 .25
27 Dimitri Kalinin .10 .25
28 Martin Lapointe .10 .25
29 Keith Carney .10 .25
30 Garnet Exelby .10 .25
31 Dean McAmmond .10 .25
32 Hal Gill .10 .25
33 Henrik Tallinder .10 .25
34 Ilya Kovalchuk .40 1.00
35 Ivan Huml .10 .25
36 J-P Dumont .10 .25
37 Alexei Smirnov .10 .25
38 Jarome Iginla .40 1.00
39 Jason Krog .10 .25
40 Jay McKee .10 .25
41 Jean-Sebastien Giguere .25 .60
42 Krzysztof Oliwa .10 .25
43 Jeff Odgers .10 .25
44 Jochen Hecht .10 .25
45 Joe DiPenta RC .30 .75
46 Adam Mair .10 .25
47 Jonathan Girard .10 .25
48 Jordan Leopold .10 .25
49 Andrew Raycroft .25 .60
50 Kamil Piros .10 .25
51 Eric Boulton .10 .25
52 Kurt Sauer .10 .25
53 Lubos Bartecko .10 .25
54 Marc Chouinard .10 .25
55 Marc Savard .10 .25
56 Martin Biron .25 .60
57 Martin Gelinas .10 .25
58 Martin Gerber .25 .60
59 Chuck Kobasew .10 .25
60 Martin Samuelsson .10 .25
61 Jamie McLennan .10 .25
62 Mika Noronen .10 .25
63 Mike Knuble .10 .25
64 Mike Leclerc .10 .25
65 Pasi Nurminen .25 .60
66 Miroslav Satan .10 .25
67 Nick Boynton .10 .25
68 Nicklas Havelid .10 .25
69 Oleg Saprykin .10 .25
70 Milan Bartovic RC .30 .75
71 P.J. Stock .10 .25
72 Roman Turek .25 .60
73 Patrik Stefan .10 .25
74 Maxim Afinogenov .10 .25
75 Petr Sykora .10 .25
76 Rick Mrozik RC .10 .25
77 Rob Niedermayer .10 .25
78 Robyn Regehr .10 .25
79 P.J. Axelsson .10 .25
80 Ruslan Salei .10 .25
81 Ryan Miller .25 .60
82 Sandis Ozolinsh .10 .25
83 Blake Sloan .10 .25
84 Tim Connolly .10 .25
85 Shaone Morrisonn .10 .25
86 Shawn McEachern .10 .25
87 Shean Donovan .10 .25
88 Simon Gamache .10 .25
89 Stanislav Chistov .10 .25
90 Stephane Yelle .10 .25
91 Steve Rucchin .10 .25
92 Steve Shields .25 .60
93 Steve Thomas .10 .25
94 Taylor Pyatt .10 .25
95 Yannick Tremblay .10 .25
96 Toni Lydman .10 .25
97 Tony Hrkac .10 .25
98 Vitali Vishnevsky .10 .25
99 Slava Kozlov .10 .25
100 Sergei Samsonov .25 .60
101 Riku Hahl .10 .25
102 Tyler Wright .10 .25
103 Tyler Arnason .25 .60
104 Tomas Kurka .10 .25
105 Theo Fleury .10 .25
106 Stu Barnes .10 .25
107 Steve Sullivan .10 .25
108 Paul Kariya .30 .75
109 Steve Poapst .10 .25
110 Steve Ott .10 .25
111 Steve McCarthy .10 .25
112 Sergei Zubov .10 .25
113 Serge Aubin .10 .25
114 Niko Kapanen .10 .25
115 Pascal Leclaire .25 .60
116 Patrick Roy 1.50 4.00
117 Pavel Brendl .10 .25
118 Peter Forsberg .75 2.00
119 Philippe Boucher .10 .25
120 Radim Vrbata .10 .25
121 Ray Whitney .10 .25
122 Richard Matvichuk .10 .25
123 Rick Nash .40 1.00
124 Sami Helenius .10 .25
125 Rob Blake .25 .60
126 Rob DiMaio .10 .25
127 Rod Brind'Amour .25 .60
128 Chris McAllister .10 .25
129 Ron Tugnutt .25 .60
130 Rostislav Klesla .10 .25
131 Ryan Bayda .10 .25
132 Ryan VandenBussche .10 .25
133 Ron Francis .25 .60
134 Charlie Stephens .10 .25
135 Scott Young .10 .25
136 Sean Hill .10 .25
137 Sean Pronger .10 .25
138 Nathan Dempsey .10 .25
139 Jason Bacashihua .25 .60
140 Jason Strudwick .10 .25
141 Jeff O'Neill .10 .25
142 Jere Lehtinen .25 .60
143 Alexander Karpovtsev .10 .25
144 Jody Shelley .10 .25
145 Alex Tanguay .25 .60
146 John Erskine .10 .25
147 Jon Klemm .10 .25
148 Josef Vasicek .10 .25
149 Kent McDonell RC .30 .75
150 Kevyn Adams .10 .25
151 Kyle Calder .10 .25
152 Lasse Pirjeta .10 .25
153 Manny Malhotra .10 .25
154 Marc Denis .25 .60
155 Mark Bell .10 .25
156 Martin Skoula .10 .25
157 Marty Turco .25 .60
158 Matt Davidson .10 .25
159 Michael Leighton .25 .60
160 Kevin Weekes .25 .60
161 Luke Richardson .10 .25
162 Mike Keane .10 .25
163 Mike Modano .50 1.25
164 Scott Lachance .10 .25
165 Mike Zigomanis .10 .25
166 Milan Hejduk .30 .75
167 Jason Arnott .10 .25
168 Jaroslav Svoboda .10 .25
169 Jaroslav Spacek .10 .25
170 Aaron Ward .10 .25
171 Alexei Zhamnov .10 .25
172 Teemu Selanne .30 .75
173 Jan Hlavac .10 .25
174 Duvie Westcott .10 .25
175 Erik Cole .10 .25
176 Philippe Sauve .25 .60
177 Eric Daze .10 .25
178 Derrick Walser .10 .25
179 Aaron Downey .10 .25
180 Derek Morris .10 .25
181 David Vyborny .10 .25
182 Craig Andersson .10 .25
183 Patrick DesRochers .10 .25
184 David Aebischer .25 .60
185 Stephane Robidas .10 .25
186 Dan Hinote .10 .25
187 Craig Adams .10 .25
188 Burke Henry .10 .25
189 Bret Hedican .10 .25
190 Brenden Morrow .25 .60
191 Brad DeFauw .10 .25
192 Bill Guerin .25 .60
193 Bates Battaglia .10 .25
194 Andrew Cassels .10 .25
195 Adam Foote .10 .25
196 Geoff Sanderson .10 .25
197 Jocelyn Thibault .25 .60
198 Joe Sakic .60 1.50
199 Espen Knutsen .10 .25
200 Igor Radulov .10 .25
201 Jason Smith .10 .25
202 Dominik Hasek .60 1.50
203 Sean Avery .10 .25
204 Steve Staios .10 .25
205 Kirk Maltby .10 .25
206 Denis Shvidki .10 .25
207 Sergei Fedorov .50 1.25
208 Sergei Zholtok .10 .25
209 Shawn Horcoff .10 .25
210 Stephen Weiss .10 .25
211 Steve Yzerman 1.50 4.00
212 Brad Chartrand .10 .25
213 Brad Isbister .10 .25
214 Valeri Bure .10 .25
215 Brendan Shanahan .30 .75
216 Ryan Smyth .10 .25
217 Chris Chelios .30 .75
218 Cliff Ronning .10 .25
219 Curtis Joseph .30 .75
220 Darcy Hordichuk .10 .25
221 Darren McCarty .10 .25
222 Eric Brewer .10 .25
223 Derek Armstrong .10 .25
224 Dwayne Roloson .25 .60
225 Eric Belanger .10 .25
226 Brett Hull .40 1.00
227 Joe Corvo .10 .25
228 Ethan Moreau .10 .25
229 Felix Potvin .30 .75
230 Fernando Pisani .10 .25
231 Filip Kuba .10 .25
232 Georges Laraque .10 .25
233 Henrik Zetterberg .30 .75
234 Ian Laperriere .10 .25
235 Igor Larionov .10 .25
236 Mattias Norstrom .10 .25
237 Ivan Novoseltsev .10 .25
238 Jamie Storr .25 .60
239 Jani Hurme .25 .60
240 Jani Rita .10 .25
241 Willie Mitchell .10 .25
242 Jaroslav Bednar .10 .25
243 Jaroslav Modry .10 .25
244 Lubomir Sekeras .10 .25
245 Lubomir Visnovsky .10 .25
246 Manny Fernandez .25 .60
247 Jared Aulin .10 .25
248 Marcus Nilson .10 .25
249 Ales Hemsky .25 .60
250 Igor Ulanov .10 .25
251 Alexei Semenov .10 .25
252 Mathieu Schneider .10 .25
253 Matt Cullen .10 .25
254 Andrew Brunette .10 .25
255 Viktor Kozlov .10 .25
256 Mike Comrie .25 .60
257 Brad Bombardir .10 .25
258 Scott Ferguson .10 .25
259 Tomas Holmstrom .10 .25
260 Tomas Zizka .10 .25
261 Manny Legace .25 .60
262 Jon Sim .10 .25
263 Wes Walz .10 .25
264 Jay Bouwmeester .10 .25
265 Zigmund Palffy .25 .60
266 Andreas Lilja .10 .25
267 Pascal Dupuis .10 .25
268 Alexander Frolov .10 .25
269 Tommy Salo .25 .60
270 Antti Laaksonen .10 .25
271 Mike Cammalleri .10 .25
272 Bill Muckalt .10 .25
273 Mike York .10 .25
274 Nick Schultz .10 .25
275 Nicklas Lidstrom .30 .75
276 Andrei Zyuzin .10 .25
277 Adam Deadmarsh .10 .25
278 Olli Jokinen .25 .60
279 Pavel Datsyuk .30 .75
280 Jason Chimera .10 .25
281 Kristian Huselius .10 .25
282 Jarret Stoll .10 .25
283 Jason Allison .10 .25
284 Richard Park .10 .25
285 Marty Reasoner .10 .25
286 Mathieu Biron .25 .60
287 Jason Woolley .10 .25
288 Pavel Trnka .10 .25
289 Jim Dowd .10 .25
290 Kris Draper .10 .25
291 Peter Worrell .10 .25
292 P-M Bouchard .10 .25
293 Radek Dvorak .10 .25
294 Matt Johnson .10 .25
295 Aaron Miller .10 .25
296 Mathieu Dandenault .10 .25
297 Marian Gaborik .60 1.50
298 Roberto Luongo .40 1.00
299 Jason Williams .10 .25
300 Niklas Hagman .10 .25
301 Jamie Langenbrunner .10 .25
302 Greg Johnson .10 .25
303 Alexei Kovalev .25 .60
304 Ron Hainsey .10 .25
305 Ari Ahonen .25 .60
306 Mark Parrish .10 .25
307 Andrei Markov .10 .25
308 Jason York .10 .25
309 Jason Wiemer .10 .25
310 Mark Messier .30 .75
311 Joe Juneau .10 .25
312 Colin White .10 .25
313 Mike Dunham .25 .60
314 Brian Finley .25 .60
315 Jeff Friesen .10 .25
316 Boris Mironov .10 .25
317 Brian Rafalski .10 .25
318 Chad Kilger .10 .25
319 Arron Asham .10 .25
320 Corey Schwab .25 .60
321 Craig Rivet .10 .25
322 Dale Purinton .10 .25
323 John Madden .10 .25
324 Bill Houlder .10 .25
325 Denis Arkhipov .10 .25
326 Bobby Holik .10 .25
327 Jay Pandolfo .10 .25
328 Adam Hall .10 .25
329 Adrian Aucoin .10 .25
330 Michael Rupp .10 .25
331 Donald Audette .10 .25
332 Brian Gionta .10 .25
333 Jan Bulis .10 .25
334 Jamie Lundmark .10 .25
335 Jason Ward .10 .25
336 Anson Carter .25 .60
337 Grant Marshall .10 .25
338 Garth Snow .25 .60
339 Eric Lindros .30 .75
340 Dusan Salficky RC .30 .75
341 Darius Kasparaitis .10 .25
342 Patrik Elias .25 .60
343 David Legwand .25 .60
344 Brian Leetch .25 .60
345 Jason Blake .10 .25
346 Kimmo Timonen .10 .25
347 Dan Blackburn .25 .60
348 Jose Theodore .40 1.00
349 Justin Mapletoft .10 .25
350 Vernon Fiddler .10 .25
351 Ken Daneyko .10 .25
352 Martin Erat .10 .25
353 Janne Niinimaa .10 .25
354 Marcel Hossa .10 .25
355 Scott Niedermayer .10 .25
356 Petr Nedved .10 .25
357 Martin Brodeur .75 2.00
358 Rick DiPietro .25 .60
359 Mathieu Garon .25 .60
360 Vladimir Malakhov .10 .25
361 Mike Ribeiro .10 .25
362 Michael Peca .10 .25
363 Andreas Dackell .10 .25
364 Scott Stevens .25 .60
365 Dave Scatchard .10 .25
366 Mike Richter .30 .75
367 Niklas Sundstrom .10 .25
368 Oleg Petrov .10 .25
369 Alexei Yashin .10 .25
370 Darren Haydar .10 .25
371 Patrice Brisebois .10 .25
372 Scott Walker .10 .25
373 Pavel Bure .30 .75
374 Yanic Perreault .10 .25
375 Vladimir Orszagh .10 .25
376 Kenny Jonsson .10 .25
377 Vitali Yachmenev .10 .25
378 Turner Stevenson .10 .25
379 Trent Hunter .10 .25
380 Tomas Vokoun .25 .60
381 Tom Poti .10 .25
382 Shawn Bates .10 .25
383 Sergei Brylin .10 .25
384 Scottie Upshall .10 .25
385 Mattias Weinhandl .10 .25
386 Joe Nieuwendyk .25 .60
387 Mike Komisarek .10 .25
388 Matthew Barnaby .10 .25
389 Scott Gomez .10 .25
390 Sandy McCarthy .10 .25
391 Saku Koivu .30 .75
392 Ronald Petrovicky .10 .25
393 Scott Hartnell .10 .25
394 Roman Hamrlik .10 .25
395 Andreas Johansson .10 .25
396 Richard Zednik .10 .25
397 Rem Murray .10 .25
398 Randy Robitaille .10 .25
399 Randy McKay .10 .25
400 Oleg Kvasha .10 .25
401 Steve McKenna .10 .25
402 Radoslav Suchy .10 .25
403 Wayne Primeau .10 .25
404 Wade Redden .10 .25
405 Vincent Damphousse .10 .25
406 Sebastien Caron .25 .60
407 Vaclav Varada .10 .25
408 Tony Amonte .25 .60
409 Tomas Surovy .10 .25
410 Sami Kapanen .10 .25
411 Mike Ricci .10 .25
412 Alexei Morozov .10 .25
413 Miroslav Zalesak .10 .25
414 Mark Recchi .25 .60
415 Patrick Marleau .25 .60
416 Robert Esche .25 .60
417 Brooks Orpik .10 .25
418 Ville Nieminen .10 .25
419 Mike Rathje .10 .25
420 Michal Rozsival .10 .25
421 Todd Harvey .10 .25
422 Zdeno Chara .10 .25
423 Scott Hannan .10 .25
424 Rob Ray .10 .25
425 Zac Bierk .25 .60
426 Vesa Toskala .25 .60
427 Todd White .10 .25
428 Eric Meloche .10 .25
429 Niko Dimitrakos .10 .25
430 Patrick Lalime .25 .60
431 Simon Gagne .30 .75
432 Sean Burke .25 .60
433 John LeClair .30 .75
434 Petr Schastlivy .10 .25
435 Scott Thornton .10 .25
436 Radek Bonk .10 .25
437 Rico Fata .10 .25
438 Mike Johnson .25 .60
439 Mike Fisher .10 .25
440 Radovan Somik .10 .25
441 Peter Schaefer .10 .25
442 Michal Handzus .10 .25
443 Landon Wilson .10 .25
444 Jonathan Cheechoo .12 .30
445 Mario Lemieux 2.00 5.00
446 Martin Havlat .25 .60
447 Mark Smith .10 .25
448 Kris Booth .10 .25
449 Keith Primeau .25 .60
450 Marian Hossa .30 .75
451 Marcus Ragnarsson .10 .25
452 Martin Straka .10 .25
453 Kim Johnsson .10 .25
454 Milan Kraft .10 .25
455 Martin Prusek .10 .25
456 Krys Kolanos .10 .25
457 Kyle McLaren .10 .25
458 Ladislav Nagy .10 .25
459 Claude Lapointe .10 .25
460 Magnus Arvedson .10 .25
461 Marco Sturm .10 .25
462 Karel Rachunek .10 .25
463 Justin Williams .10 .25
464 Evgeni Nabokov .25 .60
465 Mathias Johansson .10 .25
466 Eric Desjardins .10 .25
467 Daniel Alfredsson .25 .60
468 Chris Therien .10 .25
469 Jeremy Roenick .40 1.00
470 Jeff Taffe .10 .25
471 Johan Hedberg .25 .60
472 Dimitri Yushkevich .10 .25
473 Shane Doan .10 .25
474 Paul Mara .10 .25
475 Eric Weinrich .10 .25
476 Jim Fahey .10 .25
477 Konstantin Koltsov .10 .25
478 Jason Jaspers .10 .25
479 Jason Spezza .30 .75
480 J-S Aubin .10 .25
481 Deron Quint .10 .25
482 Dennis Seidenberg .10 .25
483 Daymond Langkow .10 .25
484 Kelly Buchberger .10 .25
485 Michal Sivek .10 .25
486 Donald Brashear .10 .25
487 Chris Phillips .10 .25
488 Chris Gratton .10 .25
489 Bryan Smolinski .10 .25
490 Guillaume Lefebvre .10 .25
491 Brian Savage .10 .25
492 Alyn McCauley .10 .25
493 Andrei Nazarov .10 .25
494 Anton Volchenkov .10 .25
495 Brad Ference .10 .25
496 Brad Stuart .10 .25
497 Branko Radivojevic .10 .25
498 Brian Boucher .25 .60
499 Dick Tarnstrom .10 .25
500 Adam Graves .10 .25
501 Al MacInnis .25 .60
502 Scott Mellanby .10 .25
503 Matt Stajan RC 3.00 8.00
504 Andre Roy .10 .25
505 Alexander Mogilny .25 .60
506 Barret Jackman .10 .25
507 Nik Antropov .10 .25
508 Ben Clymer .10 .25
509 Maxime Ouellet .25 .60
510 Trevor Kidd .25 .60
511 Brad Richards .25 .60
512 Todd Bertuzzi .30 .75
513 Wade Belak .10 .25
514 Brian Sutherby .10 .25
515 Fedor Fedorov .10 .25
516 Cory Sarich .10 .25
517 Brent Sopel .10 .25
518 Chris Pronger .10 .25
519 Brendan Morrison .25 .60
520 Sebastien Charpentier .25 .60
521 Alexander Svitov .10 .25
522 Calle Johansson .10 .25
523 Bryan McCabe .10 .25
524 Bryan Allen .10 .25
525 Bryce Salvador .10 .25
526 Dainius Zubrus .10 .25
527 Dallas Drake .10 .25
528 Dan Boyle .10 .25
529 Dan Cloutier .25 .60
530 Ken Klee .10 .25
531 Keith Tkachuk .30 .75
532 Brandon Reid .10 .25
533 Sergei Berezin .10 .25
534 Alex Auld .10 .25
535 Jaromir Jagr .50 1.25
536 Markus Naslund .30 .75
537 Jamal Mayers .10 .25
538 Ivan Ciernik .10 .25
539 Marek Malik .10 .25
540 Karel Pilar .10 .25
541 Fredrik Modin .10 .25
542 Gary Roberts .10 .25
543 Eric Boguniecki .10 .25
544 Henrik Sedin .10 .25
545 Ed Belfour .30 .75
546 Doug Weight .25 .60
547 Carlo Colaiacovo .10 .25
548 Peter Sejna RC 2.00 5.00
549 Michael Nylander .10 .25
550 Daniel Sedin .10 .25
551 Kip Miller .10 .25
552 Robert Reichel .10 .25
553 Olaf Kolzig .25 .60
554 Reed Low .10 .25
555 Mikael Renberg .10 .25
556 Mike Grier .10 .25
557 Owen Nolan .25 .60
558 Nikolai Khabibulin .30 .75
559 Brad May .10 .25
560 Nikita Alexeev .10 .25
561 Sami Salo .10 .25
562 Martin St. Louis .25 .60
563 Brendan Witt .10 .25
564 Martin Rucinsky .10 .25
565 Mattias Ohlund .10 .25
566 Doug Gilmour .25 .60
567 Matt Cooke .10 .25
568 Dave Andreychuk .10 .25
569 Robert Lang .10 .25
570 Alexander Khavanov .10 .25
571 Tie Domi .25 .60
572 Ruslan Fedotenko .10 .25
573 Robert Svehla .10 .25
574 Tim Taylor .10 .25
575 Brent Johnson .25 .60
576 Brad Lukowich .10 .25
577 Sergei Gonchar .10 .25
578 Sheldon Keefe .10 .25
579 Steve Eminger .10 .25
580 Tomas Kaberle .10 .25
581 Steve Konowalchuk .10 .25
582 Chris Osgood .25 .60
583 Trevor Linden .10 .25
584 Travis Green .10 .25
585 Steve Martins .10 .25
586 John Grahame .25 .60
587 Darcy Tucker .10 .25
588 Jassen Cullimore .10 .25
589 Peter Bondra .25 .60
590 Pavol Demitra .25 .60
591 Nolan Pratt .10 .25
592 Jeff Halpern .10 .25
593 Vincent Lecavalier .30 .75
594 Petr Cajanek .10 .25
595 Chris Dingman .10 .25
596 Artem Chubarov .10 .25
597 Curtis Sanford .10 .25
598 Ed Jovanovski .25 .60
599 Mats Sundin .30 .75
600 Jarkko Ruutu .10 .25
601 Marc-Andre Fleury RC/321 20.00 50.00
602 Eric Staal RC/340 10.00 25.00
603 Tuomo Ruutu RC/299 4.00 10.00
604 Joni Pitkanen RC/316 6.00 15.00
605 Dustin Brown RC/287 4.00 10.00
606 Alexander Semin RC/291 12.00 30.00
607 Boyd Gordon RC/268 4.00 10.00
608 Pavel Vorobiev RC/203 4.00 10.00
609 Dan Hamhuis RC/286 6.00 15.00
610 Marek Zidlicky RC/308 4.00 10.00
611 Brent Burns RC/270 6.00 15.00
612 Cody McCormick RC/271 4.00 10.00
613 Antoine Vermette RC/280 4.00 10.00
614 Sean Bergenheim RC/291 4.00 10.00
615 Ryan Malone RC/310 8.00 20.00
616 Peter Sarno RC/284 4.00 10.00
617 Nathan Horton XRC/301 8.00 20.00
618 Joffrey Lupul XRC/306 8.00 20.00
619 Jordin Tootoo XRC/302 8.00 20.00
620 Patrice Bergeron XRC/299 10.00 25.00
621 Jiri Hudler XRC/291 8.00 20.00
622 Chris Higgins XRC/297 10.00 25.00
623 Maxim Kondratiev XRC/293 5.00 12.00
624 Brent Krahn XRC/283 5.00 12.00
625 Cover Card/Checklist .10 .25
626 Kari Lehtonen XRC 3.00 8.00
627 Dan Fritsche XRC .60 1.50
628 Tim Gleason XRC .60 1.50
629 Derek Roy XRC .60 1.50
630 Matthew Lombardi XRC .60 1.50
631 John-Michael Liles XRC .60 1.50
632 Brian Leetch .25 .60
633 Michael Ryder .10 .25
634 Karl Stewart XRC .60 1.50
635 Jed Ortmeyer XRC .60 1.50
636 Dominic Moore XRC .60 1.50
637 Andrew Allen XRC .60 1.50
638 Ryan Kesler XRC .60 1.50
639 Tony Salmelainen XRC .60 1.50
640 Mikhail Yakubov XRC .60 1.50
641 Nathan Robinson XRC .60 1.50
642 Chris Simon .10 .25
643 Jeff Hamilton XRC .60 1.50
644 Nikolai Zherdev XRC 2.00 5.00
645 Steve Sullivan .10 .25
646 Niklas Kronwall XRC 2.00 5.00
647 Joey MacDonald XRC .60 1.50
648 Antero Niittymaki XRC 4.00 10.00
649 Noah Clarke XRC .60 1.50
650 Tim Jackman XRC .60 1.50
651 Timofei Shishkanov XRC .60 1.50
652 Marek Svatos XRC 4.00 10.00
653 Sergei Fedorov .50 1.25
654 Aleksander Suglobov XRC .60 1.50
655 Darryl Bootland XRC 2.00 5.00
656 Andrew Peters XRC 2.00 5.00
657 Anton Babchuk XRC .60 1.50
658 Kyle Wellwood XRC 2.00 5.00
659 Chris Kunitz XRC .60 1.50
660 Jozef Balej XRC .60 1.50
661 Christian Ehrhoff XRC .60 1.50
662 Dan Ellis XRC .60 1.50
663 Robert Lang .10 .25
664 Thomas Pihlman XRC .60 1.50
665 Andy Chiodo XRC .60 1.50
666 Adam Munro XRC .60 1.50
667 Denis Grebeshkov XRC .60 1.50
668 Matt Underhill XRC .60 1.50
669 Brad Boyes XRC 2.50 6.00
670 Paul Martin XRC .60 1.50
671 Matthew Yeats XRC .60 1.50
672 Alexei Zhamnov .10 .25
673 Wade Dubielewicz XRC .60 1.50
674 Miikka Kiprusoff .25 .60

2003-04 ITG Action Center of Attention

COMPLETE SET (10) 20.00 40.00
STATED ODDS 1:46
CA1 Mario Lemieux 5.00 12.00
CA2 Steve Yzerman 4.00 10.00
CA3 Joe Sakic 2.50 6.00
CA4 Peter Forsberg 3.00 8.00
CA5 Todd Bertuzzi 1.25 3.00
CA6 Joe Thornton 2.00 5.00
CA7 Sergei Fedorov 1.50 4.00
CA8 Mike Modano 2.00 5.00

CA9 Jason Spezza 2.00 5.00
CA10 Mats Sundin 1.25 3.00

2003-04 ITG Action First Time All-Star

COMPLETE SET (10) 8.00 15.00
STATED ODDS 1:38
FT1 Marian Gaborik 2.00 5.00
FT2 Dany Heatley 1.25 3.00
FT3 Marty Turco .75 2.00
FT4 Todd Bertuzzi .75 2.00
FT5 Olli Jokinen .75 2.00
FT6 Vincent Lecavalier .75 2.00
FT7 Patrick Lalime .75 2.00
FT8 Glen Murray .75 2.00
FT9 Martin St-Louis .75 2.00
FT10 Jocelyn Thibault .75 2.00

2003-04 ITG Action Highlight Reel

COMPLETE SET (12) 20.00 40.00
STATED ODDS 1:38
HR1 Jean-Sebastien Giguere .75 2.00
HR2 Patrick Roy 3.00 8.00
HR3 Martin Brodeur 2.50 6.00
HR4 Mario Lemieux 4.00 10.00
HR5 Dany Heatley 1.00 2.50
HR6 Joe Sakic 2.00 5.00
HR7 Joe Nieuwendyk .75 2.00
HR8 Jaromir Jagr 1.25 3.00
HR9 Brett Hull 1.00 2.50
HR10 Rick Nash 1.00 2.50
HR11 Marty Turco .75 2.00
HR12 Marian Gaborik 1.50 4.00

2003-04 ITG Action Homeboys

COMPLETE SET (14) 15.00 30.00
STATED ODDS 1:24
HB1 Markus Naslund 1.50 4.00
Peter Forsberg
HB2 Ron Francis .75 2.00
Marty Turco
HB3 Z.Chara/M.Gaborik .75 2.00
HB4 Mike Comrie .75 2.00
Scott Niedermayer
HB5 Mark Messier .75 2.00
Jarome Iginla
HB6 Doug Gilmour .75 2.00
Kirk Muller
HB7 Eric Lindros 1.00 2.50
Joe Thornton
HB8 Nikolai Khabibulin .75 2.00
Alexei Yashin
HB9 Jani Hurme .75 2.00
Saku Koivu
HB10 M.Brodeur/M.Lemieux 5.00 12.00
HB11 Bates Battaglia .75 2.00
Chris Chelios
HB12 Stephen Weiss .75 2.00
Anson Carter
HB13 Jean-Sebastien Giguere .75 2.00
Roberto Luongo
HB14 Pavel Bure .75 2.00
Sergei Samsonov

2003-04 ITG Action Jerseys

This 270-card memorabilia set was tiered by color. Ruby cards (M1-M90) were serial-numbered to 500 each. Sapphire (M91-M120) were serial-numbered to 300 each. Emerald cards (M121-150) were serial-numbered to 200 sets. Bronze (M151-M180) were serial-numbered to 100. Silver (M181-M200) were serial-numbered to 50 each. Gold cards (M201-M220) were 1/1's and are not priced due to scarcity. Quad jerseys (M221-M240) were serial-numbered to 50 each. Cards M240-M270 were only available in factory sets and were limited to 100 each.

M1 Nik Antropov 4.00 10.00
M2 Jason Arnott 4.00 10.00
M3 Jared Aulin 4.00 10.00
M4 Mark Bell 4.00 10.00
M5 Bryan Berard 4.00 10.00
M6 Martin Biron 4.00 10.00
M7 Radek Bonk 4.00 10.00
M8 Nick Boynton 4.00 10.00
M9 Donald Brashear 4.00 10.00
M10 Eric Brewer 4.00 10.00
M11 Sergei Brylin 4.00 10.00
M12 Mike Cammalleri 4.00 10.00
M13 Dan Cloutier 4.00 10.00
M14 Carlo Colaiacovo 4.00 10.00
M15 Tim Connolly 4.00 10.00
M16 Byron Dafoe 4.00 10.00
M17 Adam Deadmarsh 4.00 10.00
M18 Shane Doan 4.00 10.00
M19 Tie Domi 4.00 10.00
M20 J-P Dumont 4.00 10.00
M21 Robert Esche 4.00 10.00
M22 Mike Fisher 4.00 10.00
M23 Adam Foote 4.00 10.00
M24 Martin Gerber 6.00 15.00
M25 Scott Gomez 4.00 10.00
M26 John Grahame 6.00 15.00
M27 Jeff Hackett 6.00 15.00
M28 Ron Hainsey 4.00 10.00
M29 Scott Hartnell 4.00 10.00
M30 Derian Hatcher 4.00 10.00
M31 Bobby Holik 4.00 10.00
M32 Marcel Hossa 4.00 10.00
M33 Ivan Huml 4.00 10.00
M34 Barret Jackman 6.00 15.00
M35 Brent Johnson 6.00 15.00
M36 Ed Jovanovski 6.00 15.00
M37 Tomas Kaberle 4.00 10.00
M38 Niko Kapanen 4.00 10.00
M39 Sami Kapanen 4.00 10.00
M40 Darius Kasparaitis 4.00 10.00
M41 Rostislav Klesla 4.00 10.00
M42 Chuck Kobasew 4.00 10.00
M43 Vyacheslav Kozlov 4.00 10.00
M44 Georges Laraque 6.00 15.00
M45 Igor Larionov 4.00 10.00
M46 Manny Legace 4.00 10.00
M47 David Legwand 4.00 10.00
M48 Jordan Leopold 4.00 10.00
M49 Trevor Linden 4.00 10.00
M50 John Madden 4.00 10.00
M51 Patrick Marleau 6.00 15.00
M52 Aleksey Morozov 4.00 10.00
M53 Derek Morris 4.00 10.00
M54 Brendan Morrison 6.00 15.00
M55 Brenden Morrow 6.00 15.00
M56 Rob Niedermayer 4.00 10.00
M57 Scott Niedermayer 4.00 10.00
M58 Joe Nieuwendyk 6.00 15.00
M59 Mika Noronen 4.00 10.00
M60 Pasi Nurminen 4.00 10.00
M61 Sandis Ozolinsh 4.00 10.00
M62 Yanic Perreault 4.00 10.00
M63 Chris Phillips 4.00 10.00
M64 Tom Poti 4.00 10.00
M65 Keith Primeau 4.00 10.00
M66 Branko Radivojevic 4.00 10.00
M67 Brian Rafalski 4.00 10.00
M68 Wade Redden 4.00 10.00
M69 Brandon Reid 4.00 10.00
M70 Steven Reinprecht 4.00 10.00
M71 Mike Richter 8.00 20.00
M72 Brian Rolston 4.00 10.00
M73 Miroslav Satan 4.00 10.00
M74 Kevin Sawyer 4.00 10.00
M75 Nick Schultz 4.00 10.00
M76 Daniel Sedin 4.00 10.00
M77 Henrik Sedin 4.00 10.00
M78 Alexei Smirnov 4.00 10.00
M79 Ryan Smyth 4.00 10.00
M80 Garth Snow 4.00 10.00
M81 Radovan Somik 4.00 10.00
M82 Martin Straka 4.00 10.00
M83 Alexander Svitov 4.00 10.00
M84 Darryl Sydor 4.00 10.00
M85 Roman Turek 6.00 15.00
M86 Pierre Turgeon 4.00 10.00
M87 Scottie Upshall 4.00 10.00
M88 Anton Volchenkov 4.00 10.00
M89 Peter Worrell 4.00 10.00
M90 Scott Young 5.00 10.00
M91 David Aebischer 6.00 15.00
M92 Jason Allison 6.00 15.00
M93 Tyler Arnason 6.00 15.00
M94 Dan Blackburn 6.00 15.00
M95 Daniel Briere 6.00 15.00
M96 Sean Burke 6.00 15.00
M97 Roman Cechmanek 6.00 15.00
M98 Erik Cole 6.00 15.00
M99 Vincent Damphousse 6.00 15.00
M100 Pavol Demitra 6.00 15.00
M101 Marc Denis 6.00 15.00
M102 Chris Drury 6.00 15.00
M103 Mike Dunham 6.00 15.00
M104 Manny Fernandez 6.00 15.00
M105 Simon Gagne 10.00 25.00
M106 Mathieu Garon 6.00 15.00
M107 Sergei Gonchar 6.00 15.00
M108 Johan Hedberg 6.00 15.00
M109 Ales Hemsky 6.00 15.00
M110 Kristian Huselius 6.00 15.00
M111 Jamie Langenbrunner 6.00 15.00
M112 Felix Potvin 10.00 25.00
M113 Brad Richards 6.00 15.00
M114 Dwayne Roloson 10.00 25.00
M115 Patrik Stefan 6.00 15.00
M116 Scott Stevens 6.00 15.00
M117 Alex Tanguay 6.00 15.00
M118 Kevin Weekes 6.00 15.00
M119 Stephen Weiss 6.00 15.00
M120 Sergei Zubov 6.00 15.00
M121 Daniel Alfredsson 8.00 20.00
M122 Tony Amonte 8.00 20.00
M123 Peter Bondra 8.00 20.00
M124 Chris Chelios 10.00 25.00
M125 Stanislav Chistov 8.00 20.00
M126 Pavel Datsyuk 12.50 30.00
M127 Eric Daze 8.00 20.00
M128 Patrik Elias 8.00 20.00
M129 Alexander Frolov 8.00 20.00
M130 Doug Gilmour 8.00 20.00
M131 Martin Havlat 8.00 20.00
M132 Olli Jokinen 8.00 20.00
M133 Nikolai Khabibulin 10.00 25.00
M134 Olaf Kolzig 8.00 20.00
M135 Patrick Lalime 8.00 20.00
M136 Vincent Lecavalier 10.00 25.00
M137 Ryan Miller 8.00 20.00
M138 Glen Murray 8.00 20.00
M139 Evgeni Nabokov 8.00 20.00
M140 Adam Oates 8.00 20.00
M141 Zigmund Palffy 8.00 20.00
M142 Mike Peca 8.00 20.00
M143 Chris Pronger 8.00 20.00
M144 Mark Recchi 8.00 20.00
M145 Gary Roberts 8.00 20.00
M146 Tommy Salo 8.00 20.00
M147 Martin St-Louis 8.00 20.00
M148 Keith Tkachuk 10.00 25.00
M149 Doug Weight 8.00 20.00
M150 Alexei Yashin 8.00 20.00
M151 Ed Belfour 12.50 30.00
M152 Todd Bertuzzi 12.50 30.00
M153 Rob Blake 10.00 25.00
M154 Jay Bouwmeester 10.00 25.00
M155 Mike Comrie 10.00 25.00
M156 Rick DiPietro 10.00 25.00
M157 Ron Francis 10.00 25.00
M158 Bill Guerin 10.00 25.00
M159 Milan Hejduk 12.50 30.00
M160 Marian Hossa 12.50 30.00
M161 Jarome Iginla 15.00 40.00
M162 Saku Koivu 12.50 30.00
M163 John LeClair 12.50 30.00
M164 Brian Leetch 10.00 25.00
M165 Eric Lindros 12.50 30.00
M166 Roberto Luongo 15.00 40.00
M167 Al MacInnis 10.00 25.00
M168 Mark Messier 15.00 40.00
M169 Alexander Mogilny 10.00 25.00
M170 Rick Nash 12.00 30.00
M171 Markus Naslund 12.50 30.00
M172 Owen Nolan 10.00 25.00
M173 Luc Robitaille 10.00 25.00
M174 Jeremy Roenick 15.00 40.00
M175 Sergei Samsonov 12.50 30.00
M176 Brendan Shanahan 12.50 30.00
M177 Jason Spezza 12.50 30.00
M178 Mats Sundin 12.50 30.00
M179 Jocelyn Thibault 10.00 25.00
M180 Marty Turco 8.00 20.00
M181 Martin Brodeur 30.00 80.00
M182 Pavel Bure 12.50 30.00
M183 Sergei Fedorov 20.00 50.00
M184 Peter Forsberg 15.00 40.00
M185 Marian Gaborik 15.00 40.00
M186 Jean-Sebastien Giguere 12.50 30.00
M187 Dany Heatley 20.00 50.00
M188 Brett Hull 20.00 50.00
M189 Jaromir Jagr 20.00 50.00
M190 Paul Kariya 12.50 30.00
M191 Ilya Kovalchuk 20.00 50.00
M192 Mario Lemieux 30.00 80.00
M193 Nicklas Lidstrom 12.50 30.00
M194 Mike Modano 15.00 40.00
M195 Patrick Roy 25.00 60.00
M196 Joe Sakic 20.00 50.00
M197 Dominik Hasek 15.00 40.00
M198 Jose Theodore 10.00 25.00
M199 Joe Thornton 15.00 40.00
M200 Steve Yzerman 30.00 80.00
M201 Martin Brodeur
M202 Pavel Bure
M203 Sergei Fedorov
M204 Peter Forsberg
M205 Marian Gaborik
M206 Jean-Sebastien Giguere
M207 Dany Heatley
M208 Brett Hull
M209 Jaromir Jagr
M210 Paul Kariya
M211 Ilya Kovalchuk
M212 Mario Lemieux
M213 Nicklas Lidstrom
M214 Mike Modano
M215 Patrick Roy
M216 Joe Sakic
M217 Dominik Hasek
M218 Jose Theodore
M219 Joe Thornton
M220 Steve Yzerman
M221 Gig/Chistv/Kriya/Sykra 20.00 50.00
M222 Brdur/Elias/Stens/Maddn 20.00 50.00
M223 Belfr/Sndin/Mgilny/Noln 30.00 80.00
M224 LeClr/Rnick/Amnte/Ggne 40.00 100.00
M225 Berrd/Smsnv/Thrntn/Mrry 20.00 50.00
M226 Hull/Yze/Hasek/Fedrv 40.00 100.00
M227 Roy/Frsbrg/Sakic/Hduk 40.00 100.00
M228 Turco/Mdno/Guerin/Mrrow 20.00 50.00
M229 Blckbrn/Bure/Mess/Lndros. 30.00 80.00
M230 Lalime/Hssa/Spzza/Hvlat 60.00 150.00
M231 Thiblt/Daze/Sllinv/Arnson 15.00 40.00
M232 Miller/Satn/Afingnv/Briere 25.00 60.00
M233 Salo/Comrie/Smith/Laraque 20.00 50.00
M234 Heat/Kvlchuk/Dfoe/Stfan 20.00 50.00
M235 Osgd/Jkmn/Prngr/Mclnns 20.00 50.00
M236 Klzig/Jagr/Bndra/Grnger 20.00 50.00
M237 Lmieux/Hdbrg/Strka/Mrzv 40.00 100.00
M238 Clotier/Brtzzi/Nslnd/Jovo 20.00 50.00
M239 Vkun/Hartnll/Lgwnd/Upshll 20.00 50.00
M240 Theodre/Koivu/Garn/Hnsy 30.00 80.00
M241 Jean-Sebastien Giguere 10.00 25.00
M242 Dany Heatley 12.50 30.00
M243 Joe Thornton 12.50 30.00
M244 Miroslav Satan 10.00 25.00
M245 Jarome Iginla 15.00 40.00
M246 Ron Francis 10.00 25.00
M247 Jocelyn Thibault 10.00 25.00
M248 Patrick Roy 20.00 50.00
M249 Rick Nash 12.00 30.00
M250 Mike Modano 12.50 30.00
M251 Steve Yzerman 20.00 50.00
M252 Mike Comrie 10.00 25.00
M253 Roberto Luongo 15.00 40.00
M254 Zigmund Palffy 10.00 25.00
M255 Marian Gaborik 15.00 40.00
M256 Jose Theodore 15.00 40.00
M257 David Legwand 10.00 25.00
M258 Martin Brodeur 20.00 50.00
M259 Alexei Yashin 10.00 25.00
M260 Pavel Bure 12.50 30.00
M261 Marian Hossa 12.50 30.00
M262 Jeremy Roenick 12.50 30.00
M263 Sean Burke 10.00 25.00
M264 Mario Lemieux 40.00 100.00
M265 Chris Pronger 10.00 25.00
M266 Evgeni Nabokov 10.00 25.00
M267 Vincent Lecavalier 12.50 30.00
M268 Mats Sundin 12.50 30.00
M269 Markus Naslund 12.50 30.00
M270 Jaromir Jagr 12.50 30.00

2003-04 ITG Action League Leaders

COMPLETE SET (10) 12.50 25.00
STATED ODDS 1:29
L1 Peter Forsberg 2.50 6.00
Milan Hejduk
L2 Milan Hejduk .60 1.50
L3 Peter Forsberg 2.00 5.00
L4 Peter Forsberg 2.00 5.00
L5 Marty Turco .60 1.50
L6 Henrik Zetterberg .60 1.50
L7 Martin Brodeur 1.50 4.00
L8 Martin Brodeur 1.50 4.00
L9 Markus Naslund .60 1.50
L10 Dany Heatley .75 2.00

2003-04 ITG Action Oh Canada

COMPLETE SET 25.00 50.00
STATED ODDS 1:21
OC1 Mario Lemieux 4.00 10.00
OC2 Patrick Roy 3.00 8.00
OC3 Steve Yzerman 3.00 8.00
OC4 Martin Brodeur 2.50 6.00
OC5 Paul Kariya .75 2.00
OC6 Joe Sakic 2.00 5.00
OC7 Mark Messier .75 2.00
OC8 Jean-Sebastien Giguere .75 2.00
OC9 Jason Spezza 1.00 2.50
OC10 Dany Heatley 1.00 2.50
OC11 Curtis Joseph .75 2.00
OC12 Ed Belfour .75 2.00
OC13 Brendan Shanahan .75 2.00
OC14 Joe Thornton 1.00 2.50

2003-04 ITG Action Trophy Winners

STATED ODDS 1:64
TW1 Peter Forsberg 3.00 8.00
TW2 Martin Brodeur 3.00 8.00
TW3 Nicklas Lidstrom 1.50 4.00
TW4 Barret Jackman 1.50 4.00
TW5 Markus Naslund 1.50 4.00
TW6 Peter Forsberg 3.00 8.00

2004 ITG NHL All-Star FANtasy All-Star History Jerseys

Available only in "Super Boxes" produced by ITG for the 2004 NHL All-Star FANtasy, this 54-card set featured jerseys of players who represented the All-Star game from 1947 to the present. Cards SB1-SB21 were limited to 10 copies each; cards SB22-SB41 were limited to 20 copies each and cards SB42-SB54 were limited to 30 copies each. Cards under 30 were not priced due to scarcity.

SB1 Turk Broda
SB2 Frank Brimsek
SB3 Ted Kennedy
SB4 Maurice Richard
SB5 Chuck Rayner
SB6 Bill Mosienko
SB7 Jean Beliveau
SB8 Doug Harvey
SB9 Ted Lindsay
SB10 Henri Richard
SB11 Jacques Plante
SB12 Glenn Hall
SB13 Terry Sawchuk
SB14 Bobby Hull
SB15 Johnny Bower
SB16 Tim Horton
SB17 John Bucyk
SB18 Stan Mikita
SB19 Bill Gadsby
SB20 Ed Giacomin
SB21 Bobby Orr
SB22 Bernie Parent
SB23 Bobby Clarke
SB24 Gilbert Perreault
SB25 Frank Mahovlich
SB26 Tony Esposito
SB27 Denis Potvin
SB28 Guy Lafleur
SB29 Bryan Trottier
SB30 Lanny McDonald
SB31 Marcel Dionne
SB32 Bill Barber
SB33 Mike Bossy
SB34 Mark Messier
SB35 Ray Bourque
SB36 Steve Yzerman
SB37 Mario Lemieux
SB38 Grant Fuhr
SB39 Patrick Roy
SB40 Brett Hull
SB41 Brian Leetch
SB42 Jeremy Roenick 12.50 30.00
SB43 Jaromir Jagr 12.50 30.00
SB44 Luc Robitaille 12.50 30.00
SB45 Joe Sakic 15.00 40.00
SB46 Eric Lindros 12.50 30.00
SB47 Paul Kariya 15.00 40.00
SB48 Mike Modano 12.50 30.00
SB49 Peter Forsberg 20.00 50.00
SB50 Pavel Bure 12.50 30.00
SB51 Milan Hejduk 12.50 30.00
SB52 Mats Sundin 12.50 30.00
SB53 Marian Gaborik 15.00 40.00
SB54 Ilya Kovalchuk 12.50 30.00

2004 ITG All-Star FANtasy Hall Minnesota

This 10-card set was only available in "Super Boxes" produced by ITG booth for the 2004 NHL All-Star Fantasy. Each card was limited to 100 copies each.

COMPLETE SET (10) 75.00 125.00
1 Mike Gartner 4.00 10.00
2 Derian Hatcher 4.00 10.00
3 Mike Modano 12.00 30.00
4 Jordan Leopold 4.00 10.00
5 Manny Fernandez 6.00 15.00
6 Dwayne Roloson 6.00 15.00
7 Marian Gaborik 20.00 50.00
8 Pierre-Marc Bouchard 6.00 15.00
9 Gump Worsley 12.00 30.00
10 Dino Ciccarelli 4.00 10.00

2008-09 ITG Bleu Blanc et Rouge

This set was released on January 23, 2009. The base set consists of 40 cards.

STATED PRINT RUN 20 SERIAL #'d SETS
NOT PRICED DUE TO SCARCITY
1 Alex Tanguay
2 Bernie Geoffrion
3 Bobby Rousseau
4 Bobby Smith
5 Carey Price
6 Charlie Hodge
7 Chris Chelios
8 Denis Savard
9 Dick Duff
10 Dickie Moore
11 Dollard St. Laurent
12 Doug Gilmour
13 Doug Harvey
14 Frank Mahovlich
15 Guillaume Latendresse
16 Gump Worsley
17 Guy Carbonneau
18 Guy Lafleur
19 Guy Lapointe
20 Henri Richard
21 J.C. Tremblay
22 Jacques Laperriere
23 Jacques Lemaire
24 Jacques Plante
25 Jean Beliveau
26 Jean Guy Talbot
27 Cristobal Huet
28 Larry Robinson
29 Mats Naslund
30 Patrick Roy
31 Pete Mahovlich
32 Phil Goyette
33 Ralph Backstrom
34 Rogie Vachon
35 Saku Koivu
36 Serge Savard
37 Stephane Richer
38 Steve Shutt
39 Terry Harper
40 Yvan Cournoyer

2008-09 ITG Bleu Blanc et Rouge Rouge

STATED PRINT RUN 5 SERIAL #'d SETS
NOT PRICED DUE TO SCARCITY

2008-09 ITG Bleu Blanc et Rouge All Century Team

STATED PRINT RUN 9 SERIAL #'d SETS
NOT PRICED DUE TO SCARCITY
1 Jacques Plante
Doug Harvey
Serge Savard
Guy Lafleur
Jean Beliveau
Maurice Richard
2 Ken Dryden
Larry Robinson
Guy Lapointe
Saku Koivu
Henri Richard
Bernie Geoffrion

2008-09 ITG Bleu Blanc et Rouge All Century Team Rouge

STATED PRINT RUN 1 SERIAL #'d SET
NOT PRICED DUE TO SCARCITY

2008-09 ITG Bleu Blanc et Rouge Autographs

STATED PRINT RUN 40 SERIAL #'d SETS
AAT Alex Tanguay/19 15.00 40.00
ABR Bobby Rousseau/40 10.00 25.00
ABS Bobby Smith/40 10.00 25.00
ABSA Brian Savage/25 12.00 30.00
ACC Chris Chelios/25 25.00 60.00
ACH Charlie Hodge/40 12.00 30.00
ACHU Cristobal Huet/25 20.00 50.00
ACP1 Carey Price/25 50.00 100.00
ACP2 Carey Price/25 50.00 100.00
ADD Dick Duff/40 15.00 40.00
ADG Doug Gilmour/40 20.00 50.00
ADM1 Dickie Moore/40 12.00 30.00
ADM2 Dickie Moore/25 15.00 40.00
AEB Emile Bouchard/40 25.00 60.00
AEL1 Elmer Lach/40 25.00 60.00
AEL2 Elmer Lach/40 25.00 60.00
AGC Guy Carbonneau/40 20.00 50.00
AGL1 Guy Lafleur/19 20.00 50.00
AGL2 Guy Lafleur/19 20.00 50.00
AGLA Guy Lapointe/40 12.00 30.00
AGLAT Guillaume Latendresse/25 15.00 40.00
AHR1 Henri Richard/19 25.00 60.00
AHR2 Henri Richard/19 25.00 60.00
AJB1 Jean Beliveau/19 30.00 80.00
AJB2 Jean Beliveau/19 30.00 80.00
AJGT1 Jean Guy Talbot/25 15.00 40.00
AJGT2 Jean Guy Talbot/25 15.00 40.00
AJL1 Jacques Laperriere/40 25.00 60.00
AJL2 Jacques Laperriere/25 30.00 80.00
AJLE Jacques Lemaire/40 10.00 25.00
ALR1 Larry Robinson/25 20.00 50.00
ALR2 Larry Robinson/25 20.00 50.00
AMD Mathieu Dandenault/40 15.00 40.00
AMN Mats Naslund/40 12.00 30.00
AMT Marc Tardif/40 12.00 30.00
AMTR Mario Tremblay/40 20.00 50.00
APG1 Phil Goyette/25 15.00 40.00
APG2 Phil Goyette/25 15.00 40.00
APM Pete Mahovlich/40 20.00 50.00
APR1 Patrick Roy/19 60.00 150.00
APR2 Patrick Roy/19 60.00 150.00
ARV Rogie Vachon/25 20.00 50.00
ARW Ryan Walter/40 10.00 25.00
ASD Denis Savard/40 15.00 40.00
ASK1 Saku Koivu/19 20.00 50.00
ASK2 Saku Koivu/19 20.00 50.00
ASQ Stephane Quintal/25 12.00 30.00
ASR Stephane Richer/40 12.00 30.00
ASS1 Serge Savard/25 30.00 80.00
ASS2 Serge Savard/25 30.00 80.00
ASSH1 Steve Shutt/25 20.00 50.00
ASSH2 Steve Shutt/25 20.00 50.00
AYC1 Yvan Cournoyer/40 20.00 50.00
AYC2 Yvan Cournoyer/25 25.00 60.00
AYL Yvon Lambert/40 15.00 40.00

2008-09 ITG Bleu Blanc et Rouge Autographs Rouge

STATED PRINT RUN 1-10 SERIAL #'d SETS
NOT PRICED DUE TO SCARCITY

2008-09 ITG Bleu Blanc et Rouge Autographs Plus Emblem

STATED PRINT RUN 9 SERIAL #'d SETS
NOT PRICED DUE TO SCARCITY
APBS Bobby Smith
APBSA Brian Savage
APCC Chris Chelios
APCP Carey Price
APDG Doug Gilmour
APDS Denis Savard
APGC Guy Carbonneau
APGL Guy Lapointe
APGLAF Guy Lafleur
APGLS Guillaume Latendresse
APHR Henri Richard
APJB Jean Beliveau
APJL Jacques Laperriere
APLR Larry Robinson
APMD Mathieu Dandenault
APMN Mats Naslund
APPM Pete Mahovlich
APPR Patrick Roy
APRV Rogie Vachon
APSK Saku Koivu
APSS Steve Shutt
APSSA Serge Savard
APYC Yvan Cournoyer

2008-09 ITG Bleu Blanc et Rouge Autographs Plus Emblem Rouge

STATED PRINT RUN 1 SERIAL #'d SET
NOT PRICED DUE TO SCARCITY

2008-09 ITG Bleu Blanc et Rouge Autographs Plus Glove

STATED PRINT RUN 9 SERIAL #'d SETS
NOT PRICED DUE TO SCARCITY
APGLAF Guy Lafleur
APPR Patrick Roy
APRV Rogie Vachon

2008-09 ITG Bleu Blanc et Rouge Autographs Plus Glove Rouge

STATED PRINT RUN 1 SERIAL #'d SET
NOT PRICED DUE TO SCARCITY

2008-09 ITG Bleu Blanc et Rouge Autographs Plus Jersey

STATED PRINT RUN 19 SERIAL #'d SETS
NOT PRICED DUE TO SCARCITY
APBS Bobby Smith
APBSA Brian Savage
APCC Chris Chelios
APCP Carey Price
APDG Doug Gilmour
APDS Denis Savard
APGC Guy Carbonneau
APGL Guy Lapointe
APGLAF Guy Lafleur
APGLS Guillaume Latendresse
APHR Henri Richard
APJB Jean Beliveau
APJL Jacques Laperriere
APLR Larry Robinson
APMD Mathieu Dandenault
APMN Mats Naslund
APPM Pete Mahovlich
APPR Patrick Roy
APRV Rogie Vachon
APSK Saku Koivu
APSS Steve Shutt
APSSA Serge Savard
APYC Yvan Cournoyer

2008-09 ITG Bleu Blanc et Rouge Autographs Plus Jersey Rouge

STATED PRINT RUN 1 SERIAL #'d SET
NOT PRICED DUE TO SCARCITY

2008-09 ITG Bleu Blanc et Rouge Autographs Plus Number Rouge

STATED PRINT RUN 1 SERIAL #'d SET
NOT PRICED DUE TO SCARCITY

2008-09 ITG Bleu Blanc et Rouge Autographs Plus Pad

STATED PRINT RUN 9 SERIAL #'d SETS
NOT PRICED DUE TO SCARCITY
APPR Patrick Roy

2008-09 ITG Bleu Blanc et Rouge Autographs Plus Pad Rouge

STATED PRINT RUN 1 SERIAL #'d SET
NOT PRICED DUE TO SCARCITY

2008-09 ITG Bleu Blanc et Rouge Autographs Plus Pants

STATED PRINT RUN 9 SERIAL #'d SETS
NOT PRICED DUE TO SCARCITY
APGLAF Guy Lafleur

2008-09 ITG Bleu Blanc et Rouge Autographs Plus Pants Rouge

STATED PRINT RUN 1 SERIAL #'d SET1
NOT PRICED DUE TO SCARCITY

2008-09 ITG Bleu Blanc et Rouge Autographs Plus Skate

STATED PRINT RUN 9 SERIAL #'d SETS
NOT PRICED DUE TO SCARCITY
APEL Elmer Lach
APJB Jean Beliveau

2008-09 ITG Bleu Blanc et Rouge Autographs Plus Skate Rouge

STATED PRINT RUN 1 SERIAL #'d SETS
NOT PRICED DUE TO SCARCITY

2008-09 ITG Bleu Blanc et Rouge Autographs Plus Stick

STATED PRINT RUN 9 SERIAL #'d SETS
NOT PRICED DUE TO SCARCITY
APPR Patrick Roy

2008-09 ITG Bleu Blanc et Rouge Autographs Plus Stick Rouge

STATED PRINT RUN 1 SERIAL #'d SET
NOT PRICED DUE TO SCARCITY

2008-09 ITG Bleu Blanc et Rouge Autothreads

STATED PRINT RUN 9 SERIAL #'d SETS
NOT PRICED DUE TO SCARCITY
1 Carey Price
2 Patrick Roy
3 Guillaume Latendresse
4 Jean Beliveau
5 Saku Koivu
6 Denis Savard
7 Doug Gilmour
8 Guy Carbonneau
9 Jacques Laperriere
10 Larry Robinson
11 Steve Shutt
12 Bobby Smith
13 Serge Savard
14 Pete Mahovlich

2008-09 ITG Bleu Blanc et Rouge Autothreads Rouge

STATED PRINT RUN 1 SERIAL #'d SET
NOT PRICED DUE TO SCARCITY

2008-09 ITG Bleu Blanc et Rouge Captains

STATED PRINT RUN 9 SERIAL #'d SETS
NOT PRICED DUE TO SCARCITY
1 Toe Blake
2 Bill Durnan
3 Maurice Richard
4 Doug Harvey
5 Jean Beliveau
6 Henri Richard
7 Yvan Cournoyer
8 Serge Savard
9 Chris Chelios
10 Guy Carbonneau
11 Kirk Muller
12 Saku Koivu

2008-09 ITG Bleu Blanc et Rouge Captains Rouge

STATED PRINT RUN 1 SERIAL #'d SET
NOT PRICED DUE TO SCARCITY

2008-09 ITG Bleu Blanc et Rouge Complete Jersey

STATED PRINT RUN 9 SERIAL #'d SETS
NOT PRICED DUE TO SCARCITY
1 Carey Price
2 Patrick Roy

3 Saku Koivu
4 Guillaume Latendresse
5 Guy Lafleur
6 Larry Robinson
7 Maurice Richard

2008-09 ITG Bleu Blanc et Rouge Complete Package

STATED PRINT RUN 9 SERIAL #'d SETS
NOT PRICED DUE TO SCARCITY
1 Jacques Plante
2 Patrick Roy
3 Jean Beliveau
4 Maurice Richard
5 Guy Lafleur

2008-09 ITG Bleu Blanc et Rouge Complete Package Rouge

STATED PRINT RUN 1 SERIAL #'d SET
NOT PRICED DUE TO SCARCITY

2008-09 ITG Bleu Blanc et Rouge Decades

STATED PRINT RUN 9 SERIAL #'d SETS
NOT PRICED DUE TO SCARCITY
1 Maurice Richard
Toe Blake
Elmer Lach
Bill Durnan 1940s
2 Henri Richard
Doug Harvey
Jacques Plante
Jean Beliveau 1950s
3 Charlie Hodge
Henri Richard
Jacques Laperriere
Jean Beliveau 1960s
4 Yvan Cournoyer
Larry Robinson
Guy Lafleur
Steve Shutt 1970s
5 Patrick Roy
Chris Chelios
Bobby Smith
Mats Naslund 1980s
6 Patrick Roy
Saku Koivu
Brian Savage
Denis Savard 1990s
7 Carey Price
Saku Koivu
Guillaume Latendresse
Mathieu Dandenault 2000s

2008-09 ITG Bleu Blanc et Rouge Decades Rouge

STATED PRINT RUN 1 SERIAL #'d SET
NOT PRICED DUE TO SCARCITY

2008-09 ITG Bleu Blanc et Rouge Enshrined

STATED PRINT RUN 9 SERIAL #'d SETS
NOT PRICED DUE TO SCARCITY
1 Bob Gainey
2 Doug Harvey
3 Frank Mahovlich
4 Gump Worsley
5 Guy Lafleur
6 Henri Richard
7 Jacques Laperriere
8 Jacques Plante
9 Jean Beliveau
10 Ken Dryden
11 Larry Robinson
12 Patrick Roy
13 Serge Savard
14 Steve Shutt
15 Yvan Cournoyer
16 Maurice Richard

2008-09 ITG Bleu Blanc et Rouge Enshrined Rouge

STATED PRINT RUN 1 SERIAL #'d SET
NOT PRICED DUE TO SCARCITY

2008-09 ITG Bleu Blanc et Rouge Game Used Stick

STATED PRINT RUN 9 SERIAL #'d SETS
NOT PRICED DUE TO SCARCITY
1 Patrick Roy
2 Benoit Brunet
3 Bob Gainey
4 Bobby Smith
5 Vincent Damphousse
6 Denis Savard
7 Gilbert Dionne
8 Jesse Belanger
9 Kjell Dahlin
10 Mario Roberge
11 Mathieu Schneider
12 Mark Bureau
13 Mike Keane
14 Paul DiPietro
15 Pierre Mondou
16 Rejean Houle
17 Rick Green
18 Ryan Walter
19 Saku Koivu
20 Sergio Momesso
21 Pat Jablonski
22 Chris Chelios
23 Jose Theodore
24 Stephane Richer
25 Turner Stevenson
26 Patrice Brisebois
27 Martin Rucinsky
28 Lyle Odelein
29 Mathieu Garon
30 Steve Shutt

2008-09 ITG Bleu Blanc et Rouge Game Used Stick Rouge

STATED PRINT RUN 1 SERIAL #'d SET
NOT PRICED DUE TO SCARCITY

2008-09 ITG Bleu Blanc et Rouge Gardiens de But

STATED PRINT RUN 9 SERIAL #'d SETS
NOT PRICED DUE TO SCARCITY
1 Jacques Plante
2 Ken Dryden
3 George Hainsworth
4 Gump Worsley
5 Patrick Roy
6 Jose Theodore
7 Carey Price
8 Bill Durnan
9 Rogie Vachon
10 Cristobal Huet

2008-09 ITG Bleu Blanc et Rouge Gardiens de But Rouge

STATED PRINT RUN 1 SERIAL #'d SET
NOT PRICED DUE TO SCARCITY

2008-09 ITG Bleu Blanc et Rouge Greatest Moments

STATED PRINT RUN 9 SERIAL #'d SETS
NOT PRICED DUE TO SCARCITY
1 Richard Riots
2 Morenz Funeral
3 Patrick Roy's Last Game
4 Jacques Plante Dons A Mask
5 Five Cups In A Row
6 Jean Beliveau Joins The Canadiens

2008-09 ITG Bleu Blanc et Rouge Greatest Moments Rouge

STATED PRINT RUN 1 SERIAL #'d SET
NOT PRICED DUE TO SCARCITY

2008-09 ITG Bleu Blanc et Rouge King Sized Memorabilia

STATED PRINT RUN 9 SERIAL #'d SETS
NOT PRICED DUE TO SCARCITY
1 Bob Gainey
2 Carey Price
3 Doug Gilmour
4 Guillaume Latendresse
5 Henri Richard
6 Jean Beliveau
7 John Ferguson
8 Ken Dryden
9 Patrick Roy
10 Saku Koivu

2008-09 ITG Bleu Blanc et Rouge King Sized Memorabilia Rouge

STATED PRINT RUN 1 SERIAL #'d SET
NOT PRICED DUE TO SCARCITY

2008-09 ITG Bleu Blanc et Rouge Nameplates

STATED PRINT RUN 3-11 SERIAL #'d SETS
NOT PRICED DUE TO SCARCITY
1 Patrick Roy/3
2 Claude Lemieux/7
3 Doug Gilmour/7
4 Stephane Quintal/7
5 Guillaume Latendresse/11
6 Brian Savage/6
7 Jose Theodore/8
8 Craig Rivet/5
9 Steve Shutt/5
10 Guy Carbonneau/10
11 Denis Savard/6

2008-09 ITG Bleu Blanc et Rouge Paper Cuts

STATED PRINT RUN 1 SERIAL #'d SET
NOT PRICED DUE TO SCARCITY
1 Walter Buswell
2 Joe Carveth
3 Murph Chamberlain
4 Wilf Cude
5 Floyd Curry
6 Ken Dryden
7 Bill Durnan
8 Frank Eddols
9 LeRoy Goldsworthy
10 Glen Harmon
11 Doug Harvey
12 Tom Johnson
13 Pit Lepine
14 Gerry McNeil
15 Jack Portland
16 Ken Reardon
17 Maurice Richard
18 Cy Wentworth
19 Bernie Geoffrion
20 Ray Getliffe

2008-09 ITG Bleu Blanc et Rouge Quad Memorabilia

STATED PRINT RUN 9 SERIAL #'d SETS
NOT PRICED DUE TO SCARCITY
1 Jacques Plante
Bill Durnan
Gump Worsley
George Hainsworth
2 Carey Price
Patrick Roy
Ken Dryden
Jose Theodore
3 Larry Robinson
Guy Lapointe
Craig Rivet
Chris Chelios
4 Doug Harvey
Serge Savard
Jacques Laperriere
Mike Komisarek
5 Guy Lafleur
Markus Naslund
John Ferguson
Guilliam Latendresse
6 Maurice Richard
Steve Shutt
Mark Recchi
Bob Gainey
7 Jean Beliveau
Doug Gilmour
Saku Koivu
Denis Savard
8 Henri Richard
Gilbert Perreault
Chris Higgins
Frank Mahovlich

2008-09 ITG Bleu Blanc et Rouge Quad Memorabilia Rouge

STATED PRINT RUN 1 SERIAL #'d SET
NOT PRICED DUE TO SCARCITY

2008-09 ITG Bleu Blanc et Rouge Raised to the Rafters

STATED PRINT RUN 9 SERIAL #'d SETS
NOT PRICED DUE TO SCARCITY
1 Howie Morenz
2 Maurice Richard
3 Jean Beliveau
4 Henri Richard
5 Guy Lafleur
6 Doug Harvey
7 Jacques Plante
8 Dickie Moore
9 Yvan Cournoyer
10 Bernard Geoffrion
11 Serge Savard
12 Ken Dryden
13 Larry Robinson
14 Bob Gainey
15 Patrick Roy

2008-09 ITG Bleu Blanc et Rouge Raised to the Rafters Rouge

STATED PRINT RUN 1 SERIAL #'d SET
NOT PRICED DUE TO SCARCITY

2008-09 ITG Bleu Blanc et Rouge Records

STATED PRINT RUN 9 SERIAL #'d SETS
NOT PRICED DUE TO SCARCITY
1 Henri Richard
2 Maurice Richard
3 Guy Lafleur
4 Guy Lafleur
5 Newsy Lalonde
6 George Hainsworth
7 Larry Robinson
8 Patrick Roy
9 Jacques Plante
10 Steve Shutt
Guy Lafleur

2008-09 ITG Bleu Blanc et Rouge Records Rouge

STATED PRINT RUN 1 SERIAL #'d SET
NOT PRICED DUE TO SCARCITY

2008-09 ITG Bleu Blanc et Rouge Scoring Leaders

STATED PRINT RUN 9 SERIAL #'d SETS
NOT PRICED DUE TO SCARCITY
1 Guy LafLeur
2 Jean Beliveau
3 Henri Richard
4 Maurice Richard
5 Larry Robinson
6 Yvan Cournoyer
7 Jacques Lemaire
8 Steve Shutt
9 Bernie Geoffrion
10 Elmer Lach

2008-09 ITG Bleu Blanc et Rouge Scoring Leaders Rouge

STATED PRINT RUN 1 SERIAL #'d SET
NOT PRICED DUE TO SCARCITY

2008-09 ITG Bleu Blanc et Rouge Snap Shots

STATED PRINT RUN 1 SERIAL #'d SET
NOT PRICED DUE TO SCARCITY
1 Pete Mahovlich
2 Saku Koivu
3 Patrick Roy
4 Alexei Kovalev
5 Guy Lafleur
6 Larry Robinson
7 Carey Price
8 Alex Tanguay
9 Elmer Lach
10 Steve Shutt

2008-09 ITG Bleu Blanc et Rouge Stick Rack

STATED PRINT RUN 1 SERIAL #'d SET
NOT PRICED DUE TO SCARCITY
1 Patrick Roy
2 Benoit Brunet
3 Bob Gainey
4 Bobby Smith
5 Vincent Damphousse
6 Denis Savard
7 Gilbert Dionne
8 Jesse Belanger
9 Kjell Dahlin
10 Mario Roberge
11 Mathieu Schneider
12 Mark Bureau
13 Mike Keane
14 Paul DiPietro
15 Pierre Mondou
16 Rejean Houle
17 Rick Green
18 Ryan Walter
19 Saku Koivu
20 Sergio Momesso
21 Pat Jablonski
22 Chris Chelios
23 Jose Theodore
24 Stephane Richer
25 Turner Stevenson
26 Patrice Brisebois
27 Martin Rucinsky
28 Lyle Odelein
29 Mathieu Garon
30 Steve Shutt

2008-09 ITG Bleu Blanc et Rouge The Cup

STATED PRINT RUN 9 SERIAL #'d SETS
NOT PRICED DUE TO SCARCITY
1 Newsy Lalonde
2 Aurel Joliat
3 Howie Morenz
4 George Hainsworth
5 Maurice Richard
6 Bill Durnan
7 Elmer Lach
8 Jean Beliveau
9 Doug Harvey
10 Henri Richard
11 Jacques Plante
12 Dickie Moore
13 Gump Worsley
14 Jacques Laperriere
15 Serge Savard
16 Rogie Vachon
17 Frank Mahovlich
18 Guy Lapointe
19 Yvan Cournoyer
20 Guy Lafleur
21 Larry Robinson
22 Steve Shutt
23 Chris Chelios
24 Patrick Roy

2008-09 ITG Bleu Blanc et Rouge The Cup Rouge

STATED PRINT RUN 1 SERIAL #'d SET
NOT PRICED DUE TO SCARCITY

2008-09 ITG Bleu Blanc et Rouge Vintage

STATED PRINT RUN 35 SERIAL #'d SETS
1 Armand Mondou 6.00 15.00
2 Aurel Joliat 10.00 25.00
3 Babe Siebert 8.00 20.00
4 Albert Leduc 8.00 20.00
5 Bill Boucher 6.00 15.00
6 Bill Durnan 12.00 30.00
7 Cecil Hart 6.00 15.00
8 Didier Pitre 6.00 15.00
9 Elmer Lach 15.00 40.00
10 Pit Lepine 12.00 30.00
11 George Hainsworth 15.00 40.00
12 Georges Vezina 20.00 50.00
13 Herb Gardiner 6.00 15.00
14 Howie Morenz 6.00 15.00
15 Jack Laviolette 8.00 20.00
16 Joe Malone 8.00 20.00
17 Johnny Gagnon 6.00 15.00
18 Lorne Chabot 6.00 15.00
19 Maurice Richard 20.00 50.00
20 Newsy Lalonde 8.00 20.00
21 Paul Haynes 6.00 15.00
22 Sprague Cleghorn 15.00 40.00
23 Sylvio Mantha 12.00 30.00
24 Toe Blake 6.00 15.00
25 Wilf Cude 12.00 30.00

2008-09 ITG Bleu Blanc et Rouge Vintage Rouge

STATED PRINT RUN 5 SERIAL #'d SETS
NOT PRICED DUE TO SCARCITY

2004-05 ITG Franchises Canadian

This 150-card set was the first release in the Franchise trio produced by In the Game. The set focused on vintage players from Canadian clubs.

COMPLETE SET (150) 20.00 40.00
1 Dan Bouchard .30 .75
2 Phil Housley .20 .50
3 Reggie Lemelin .30 .75
4 Hakan Loob .20 .50
5 Jamie Macoun .20 .50
6 Kent Nilsson .20 .50
7 Joel Otto .20 .50
8 Jim Peplinski .20 .50
9 Paul Ranheim .20 .50
10 Mark Hunter .20 .50
11 Doug Gilmour .30 .75
12 Joe Mullen .30 .75
13 Lanny McDonald .30 .75
14 Paul Reinhart .20 .50
15 Gary Suter .20 .50
16 Guy Chouinard .20 .50
17 Grant Fuhr .40 1.00
18 Bernie Nicholls .20 .50
19 Andy Moog .30 .75
20 Esa Tikkanen .20 .50
21 Dave Semenko .20 .50
22 Mark Napier .20 .50
23 Bill Ranford .30 .75
24 Paul Coffey .40 1.00
25 Glenn Anderson .20 .50
26 Kent Nilsson .20 .50
27 Jari Kurri .50 1.25
28 Randy Gregg .20 .50
29 Charlie Huddy .20 .50
30 Dave Hunter .20 .50
31 Mike Krushelnyski .20 .50
32 Ed Mio .30 .75
33 Garry Unger .20 .50
34 Lee Fogolin .20 .50
35 Billy Burch .20 .50
36 Goldie Prodgers .20 .50
37 Rocket Richard .75 2.00
38 Henri Richard .40 1.00
39 Jean Beliveau .50 1.25
40 Jacques Plante .60 1.50
41 Doug Harvey .30 .75
42 Howie Morenz .30 .75
43 Bernie Geoffrion .40 1.00
44 Georges Vezina .60 1.50
45 Gump Worsley .40 1.00
46 Rogie Vachon .40 1.00
47 John Ferguson .20 .50
48 Guy Lafleur .50 1.25
49 Dickie Moore .40 1.00
50 Larry Robinson .30 .75
51 Serge Savard .40 1.00
52 Yvan Cournoyer .40 1.00
53 Toe Blake .40 1.00
54 Butch Bouchard .30 .75
55 Steve Shutt .40 1.00
56 Jacques Lemaire .40 1.00
57 Frank Mahovlich .40 1.00
58 Georges Hainsworth .30 .75
59 Patrick Roy .75 2.00
60 Guy Lapointe .30 .75
61 Elmer Lach .20 .50
62 Jacques Laperriere .30 .75
63 Aurel Joliat .40 1.00
64 Bill Durnan .20 .50
65 Nels Stewart .20 .50
66 Clint Benedict .30 .75
67 Hooley Smith .20 .50
68 Art Ross .30 .75
69 Cy Denneny .20 .50
70 Frank Finnigan .20 .50
71 Joe Malone .30 .75
72 Harry Mummery RC .60 1.50
73 Andre Savard .20 .50
74 Marian Stastny .20 .50
75 Marc Tardif .20 .50
76 Peter Stastny .30 .75
77 Dan Bouchard .30 .75
78 Michel Goulet .30 .75
79 Dale Hunter .20 .50
80 Real Cloutier .20 .50
81 Robbie Ftorek .20 .50
82 Mike Hough .20 .50
83 Anton Stastny .20 .50
84 Jack Adams .30 .75
85 Reg Noble .20 .50
86 Ken Randall .20 .50
87 Red Kelly .40 1.00
88 Teeder Kennedy .20 .50
89 Frank Mahovlich .40 1.00
90 Dick Duff .30 .75
91 Bob Pulford .30 .75
92 Ace Bailey .30 .75
93 Sid Smith .20 .50
94 Johnny Bower .40 1.00
95 Bob Nevin .30 .75
96 Bob Baun .30 .75
97 Jim McKenny .20 .50
98 Mike Palmateer .30 .75
99 Frank McCool RC .60 1.50
100 Lanny McDonald .30 .75
101 Tiger Williams .30 .75
102 Darryl Sittler .40 1.00
103 Borje Salming .30 .75
104 Ian Turnbull .20 .50
105 King Clancy .30 .75
106 Joe Primeau .20 .50
107 Turk Broda .40 1.00
108 Howie Meeker .20 .50
109 Rick Vaive .20 .50
110 Tim Horton .40 1.00
111 Wendel Clark .30 .75
112 Doug Gilmour .30 .75
113 Bill Barilko RC 1.25 3.00
114 Red Horner .20 .50
115 Babe Dye .20 .50
116 Hap Day .30 .75
117 Tiger Williams .30 .75
118 Harold Snepsts .20 .50
119 Richard Brodeur .30 .75
120 Stan Smyl .20 .50
121 Cam Neely .40 1.00
122 Dennis Kearns .20 .50
123 Brian Bradley .20 .50
124 Jack McIlhargey .20 .50
125 Andre Boudrias .20 .50
126 Gary Smith .30 .75
127 Gino Odjick .20 .50
128 Kirk McLean .20 .50
129 Darcy Rota .20 .50
130 Garth Butcher .20 .50
131 Ron Delorme .20 .50
132 Thomas Gradin .20 .50
133 Dale Tallon .20 .50
134 Don Lever .20 .50
135 Bobby Hull .60 1.50
136 Laurie Boschman .20 .50
137 Bob Essensa .30 .75
138 Jimmy Mann .20 .50
139 Randy Carlyle .20 .50
140 Dale Hawerchuck .20 .50
141 Thomas Steen .20 .50
142 Darrin Shannon .20 .50
143 Doug Smail .20 .50
144 Mario Marois .20 .50
145 Morris Lukowich .20 .50
146 Jim Kyte .20 .50
147 Dave Ellett .20 .50
148 Dave Babych .20 .50
149 Tim Watters .20 .50
150 Paul MacLean .20 .50

2004-05 ITG Franchises Canadian Autographs

STATED ODDS 1:10
AM2 Andy Moog 8.00 20.00
AS2 Allan Stanley 15.00 40.00
BB2 Bobby Baun 15.00 40.00
BG Bernie Geoffrion 20.00 50.00
BH2 Bobby Hull SP 40.00 80.00
BN2 Bob Nevin 8.00 20.00
BR Bill Ranford 5.00 12.00
BS Borje Salming SP 25.00 60.00
CN2 Cam Neely SP 20.00 50.00
DB2 Dan Bouchard 8.00 20.00
Calgary
DB3 Dan Bouchard 8.00 20.00
Quebec
DD Dick Duff 15.00 40.00
DG2 Doug Gilmour 20.00 50.00
DK Dennis Kearns 5.00 12.00
DM2 Dickie Moore 15.00 40.00
DS2 Darryl Sittler SP 25.00 60.00
EL Elmer Lach SP 20.00 50.00
EM Ed Mio 5.00 12.00
FM2 Frank Mahovlich SP 25.00 50.00
Toronto
FM3 Frank Mahovlich SP 25.00 50.00
Montreal
GA Glenn Anderson 5.00 12.00
GB Garth Butcher 5.00 12.00
GF Grant Fuhr SP 20.00 50.00
GL Guy Lafleur SP 30.00 80.00
GO Gino Odjick 5.00 12.00
GS Gary Suter 5.00 12.00
GU2 Garry Unger 5.00 12.00
GW3 Gump Worsley 15.00 40.00
HM Howie Meeker 20.00 50.00
HR Henri Richard SP 12.00 30.00
HS Harold Snepsts 5.00 12.00
IT Ian Turnbull 5.00 12.00
JB Johnny Bower 20.00 50.00
JF John Ferguson 5.00 12.00
JK Jari Kurri SP 12.50 30.00
JL Jacques Laperriere 10.00 25.00
KN Kent Nilsson 5.00 12.00
LF Lee Fogolin 8.00 20.00
LM2 Lanny McDonald SP 25.00 60.00
Calgary
LM3 Lanny McDonald SP 25.00 60.00
Montreal
MG2 Michel Goulet 12.00 30.00
MM Mario Marois 5.00 12.00
MN Mark Napier 5.00 12.00
MP Mike Palmateer 25.00 60.00
MT Marc Tardiff 5.00 12.00
PC1 Paul Coffey SP 25.00 60.00
PH2 Phil Housley 5.00 12.00
PR2 Patrick Roy 100.00 250.00
RC2 Randy Carlyle 8.00 20.00
RD Ron Delorme 5.00 12.00
RV2 Rogie Vachon 12.00 30.00
TG Thomas Gradin 5.00 12.00
TK Teeder Kennedy 20.00 50.00
TW1 Tiger Williams 12.00 30.00
Toronto
TW2 Tiger Williams SP 12.00 30.00
Montreal
YC Yvan Cournoyer 12.00 30.00
ABO Andre Boudrias 5.00 12.00
ASV Andre Savard 5.00 12.00
BBO Butch Bouchard 12.00 30.00
BES Bob Essensa 5.00 12.00
BPL Bob Pulford 8.00 20.00
CHU Charlie Huddy 5.00 12.00
DBB Dave Babych 5.00 12.00
DEL Dave Ellett 5.00 12.00
DHA Dale Hawerchuk 20.00 50.00
DHU2 Dale Hunter 5.00 12.00
DLV Don Lever 15.00 40.00
DRO Darcy Rota 5.00 12.00
DSE Dave Semenko 8.00 20.00
DSH Darrin Shannon 5.00 12.00
DSM Doug Smail 5.00 12.00
DTL Dale Tallon 5.00 12.00
DVH Dave Hunter 5.00 12.00
GCH Guy Chouinard 5.00 12.00
GLP Guy Lapointe 8.00 20.00
JBE Jean Beliveau SP 25.00 50.00
JKY Jim Kyte 8.00 20.00
JLE Jacques Lemaire 8.00 20.00
JMC Jamie Macoun 5.00 12.00
JMIO Jack McIlhargey 5.00 12.00
JMK Jim McKenny 5.00 12.00
JMN Jimmy Mann 5.00 12.00
JOT Joel Otto 5.00 12.00
JPE Jim Peplinski 5.00 12.00
KML Kirk McLean 5.00 12.00
LBH Laurie Boschman 5.00 12.00
MKR Mike Krushelnyski 5.00 12.00
MLU Morris Lukowich 5.00 12.00
MST Marian Stastny 5.00 12.00
PML Paul MacLean 5.00 12.00
PRA Paul Ranheim 5.00 12.00
PRE Paul Reinhart 5.00 12.00
RBR Richard Brodeur 8.00 20.00
RCL Real Cloutier 5.00 12.00
RFT Robbie Ftorek 5.00 12.00
RGR Randy Gregg 5.00 12.00
RHO Red Horner SP 100.00 200.00
RLM Reggie Lemelin 5.00 12.00
RVA Rick Vaive 15.00 40.00
SSH Steve Shutt 8.00 20.00
SSM Stan Smyl 5.00 12.00
SSV Serge Savard 5.00 12.00
TWA Tim Watters 5.00 12.00
WCL2 Wendel Clark 20.00 50.00

2004-05 ITG Franchises Canadian Barn Burners

PRINT RUN 50 SETS
GOLD PRINT RUN 20 SETS
GOLD NOT PRICED DUE TO SCARCITY
BB1 Lanny McDonald 12.50 30.00
BB2 Darryl Sittler 12.50 30.00
BB3 Jean Beliveau 15.00 40.00
BB4 Rick Vaive 12.50 30.00
BB5 Paul Coffey 15.00 40.00
BB6 Henri Richard 12.50 30.00
BB7 Jacques Plante 25.00 60.00
BB8 Rocket Richard 50.00 125.00

2004-05 ITG Franchises Canadian Boxtoppers

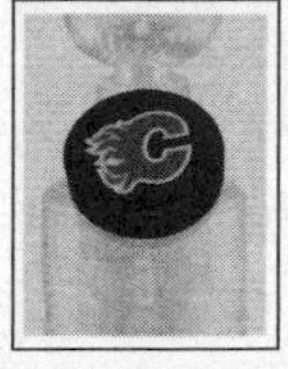

This 25-card set of jumbo boxtoppers were inserted at 1 per box and depicted the various Canadian clubs' logos through the years.

TH1 Calgary Flames/Original 2.00 5.00
TH2 Calgary Flames/Horse 2.00 5.00
TH3 Calgary Flames 2.00 5.00
TH4 Edmonton Oilers/Original 2.00 5.00
TH5 Edmonton Oilers 2.00 5.00
TH6 Edmonton Oilers/25th Ann. 2.00 5.00
TH7 Hamilton Tigers 2.00 5.00
TH8 Montreal Canadiens 2.00 5.00
TH9 Montreal Maroons 2.00 5.00
TH10 Montreal Wanderers 2.00 5.00
TH11 Ottawa Senators/Original 2.00 5.00
TH12 Ottawa Senators 2.00 5.00
TH13 Quebec Bulldogs 2.00 5.00
TH14 Quebec Nordiques 2.00 5.00
TH15 Toronto Arenas 2.00 5.00
TH16 Toronto Maple Leafs/Original 2.00 5.00
TH17 Toronto Maple Leafs/1950s 2.00 5.00
TH18 Toronto Maple Leafs/1960s 2.00 5.00
TH19 Toronto Maple Leafs 2.00 5.00
TH20 Toronto St. Patricks 2.00 5.00
TH21 Vancouver Canucks/original 2.00 5.00
TH22 Vancouver Canucks/1980s 2.00 5.00
TH23 Vancouver Canucks 2.00 5.00
TH24 Winnipeg Jets/1980s 2.00 5.00
TH25 Winnipeg Jets/1990s 2.00 5.00

2004-05 ITG Franchises Canadian Complete Jerseys

PRINT RUN 10 SETS
NOT PRICED DUE TO SCARCITY
GOLD 1/1'S EXIST
CJ1 Jacques Plante
CJ2 Jean Beliveau
CJ3 Patrick Roy
CJ4 Grant Fuhr
CJ5 Wendel Clark
CJ6 Glenn Anderson
CJ7 Richard Brodeur
CJ8 Phil Housley
CJ9 Paul Coffey
CJ10 Jari Kurri

2004-05 ITG Franchises Canadian Double Memorabilia

PRINT RUN 60 SETS
GOLD PRINT RUN 20 SETS
GOLD NOT PRICED DUE TO SCARCITY
DM1 George Hainsworth 25.00 60.00
DM2 Jean Beliveau 25.00 60.00
DM3 Johnny Bower 25.00 60.00
DM4 Georges Vezina 100.00 200.00
DM5 Patrick Roy 30.00 80.00
DM6 Aurel Joliat 25.00 60.00
DM7 Jacques Plante 30.00 80.00
DM8 Howie Morenz 60.00 125.00
DM9 Gump Worsley 15.00 40.00
DM10 Guy Lafleur 25.00 60.00
DM11 Wendel Clark 20.00 50.00
DM12 Grant Fuhr 15.00 40.00
DM13 Bernie Geoffrion 15.00 40.00
DM14 Tim Horton 40.00 100.00
DM15 Frank Mahovlich 15.00 40.00
DM16 Joe Mullen 15.00 40.00
DM17 Henri Richard 15.00 40.00
DM18 Jari Kurri 15.00 40.00
DM19 Glenn Anderson 15.00 40.00
DM20 Paul Coffey 15.00 40.00
DM21 Phil Housley 15.00 40.00
DM22 Doug Gilmour 15.00 40.00

2004-05 ITG Franchises Canadian Double Memorabilia Autographs

PRINT RUN 10 SETS
NOT PRICED DUE TO SCARCITY
DM2 Jean Beliveau

DM3 Johnny Bower
DM5 Patrick Roy
DM10 Guy Lafleur
DM11 Wendel Clark
DM12 Grant Fuhr
DM15 Frank Mahovlich
DM17 Henri Richard
DM18 Jari Kurri
DM20 Paul Coffey

2004-05 ITG Franchises Canadian Forever Rivals

PRINT RUN 50 SETS
GOLD PRINT RUN 20 SETS
GOLD NOT PRICED DUE TO SCARCITY
FR1 Johnny Bower 50.00 125.00
Jacques Plante
FR2 Red Kelly 30.00 80.00
Jean Beliveau
FR3 Grant Fuhr 20.00 50.00
Mike Vernon
FR4 B.Salming/G.Lafleur 25.00 60.00
FR5 Paul Coffey 15.00 40.00
Joe Mullen
FR6 Jari Kurri 25.00 60.00
Hakan Loob
FR7 Darryl Sittler 15.00 40.00
Larry Robinson
FR8 Wendel Clark 50.00 125.00
Patrick Roy
FR9 Tim Horton 40.00 100.00
Henri Richard
FR10 Lanny McDonald 15.00 40.00
Steve Shutt

2004-05 ITG Franchises Canadian Goalie Gear

PRINT RUN 70 SETS
GOLD PRINT RUN 20 SETS
GOLD NOT PRICED DUE TO SCARCITY
GG1 Bill Durnan 10.00 25.00
GG2 Johnny Bower 15.00 40.00
GG3 Patrick Roy 20.00 50.00
GG4 Grant Fuhr 15.00 40.00
GG5 Jacques Plante 20.00 50.00
GG6 Gump Worsley 15.00 40.00
GG7 Mike Vernon 15.00 40.00
GG8 Dan Bouchard 10.00 25.00
GG9 Bill Ranford 10.00 25.00
GG10 Richard Brodeur 12.50 30.00

2004-05 ITG Franchises Canadian Goalie Gear Autographs

PRINT RUN 10 SETS
NOT PRICED DUE TO SCARCITY
GG2 Johnny Bower
GG3 Patrick Roy
GG4 Grant Fuhr
GG6 Gump Worsley
GG9 Bill Ranford
GG10 Richard Brodeur

2004-05 ITG Franchises Canadian Memorabilia

PRINT RUN 70 SETS
GOLD PRINT RUN 20 SETS
GOLD NOT PRICED DUE TO SCARCITY
SM1 Jacques Plante 20.00 50.00
SM2 Henri Richard 12.50 30.00
SM3 Jean Beliveau 15.00 40.00
SM4 Larry Robinson 8.00 20.00
SM5 Patrick Roy 20.00 50.00
SM6 Paul Coffey 12.50 30.00
SM7 Grant Fuhr 12.50 30.00
SM8 Yvan Cournoyer 8.00 20.00
SM9 Lanny McDonald 8.00 20.00
SM10 Guy Lapointe 8.00 20.00
SM11 Serge Savard 8.00 20.00
SM12 Gump Worsley 8.00 20.00
SM13 Guy Lafleur 12.50 30.00
SM14 Borje Salming 8.00 20.00
SM15 Joe Mullen 8.00 20.00
SM17 Steve Shutt 8.00 20.00
SM18 Wendel Clark 12.50 30.00
SM19 Frank Mahovlich 12.50 30.00
SM20 Glenn Anderson 8.00 20.00
SM21 John Ferguson 8.00 20.00
SM22 Richard Brodeur 8.00 20.00
SM23 Tim Horton 20.00 50.00
SM24 Jari Kurri 12.50 30.00
SM25 Jacques Laperriere 8.00 20.00
SM26 Newsy Lalonde 15.00 40.00
SM27 Phil Housley 8.00 20.00
SM28 Bernie Geoffrion 12.50 30.00
SM29 Aurel Joliat 20.00 50.00
SM30 Doug Gilmour 12.50 30.00
SM31 Rick Vaive 8.00 20.00
SM32 Hakan Loob 8.00 20.00

2004-05 ITG Franchises Canadian Memorabilia Autographs

PRINT RUN 10 SETS
NOT PRICED DUE TO SCARCITY
SM2 Henri Richard
SM3 Jean Beliveau
SM5 Patrick Roy
SM6 Paul Coffey
SM7 Grant Fuhr
SM8 Yvan Cournoyer
SM9 Lanny McDonald
SM10 Guy Lapointe
SM11 Serge Savard
SM12 Gump Worsley
SM13 Guy Lafleur
SM14 Borje Salming
SM17 Steve Shutt
SM18 Wendel Clark
SM19 Frank Mahovlich
SM22 Richard Brodeur
SM24 Jari Kurri
SM30 Doug Gilmour

2004-05 ITG Franchises Canadian Original Sticks

PRINT RUN 70 SETS
GOLD PRINT RUN 20 SETS
GOLD NOT PRICED DUE TO SCARCITY
OS1 Jean Beliveau 12.50 30.00
OS2 Paul Coffey 8.00 20.00
OS3 Guy Lafleur 12.50 30.00
OS4 Lanny McDonald 6.00 15.00
OS5 Guy Lapointe 6.00 15.00
OS6 Larry Robinson 6.00 15.00
OS7 Steve Shutt 6.00 15.00
OS8 Patrick Roy 15.00 40.00
OS9 Rogie Vachon 8.00 20.00
OS10 Denis Savard 6.00 15.00
OS11 Jacques Plante 15.00 40.00
OS12 Dale Hawerchuk 8.00 20.00
OS13 Phil Housley 6.00 15.00
OS14 Doug Gilmour 15.00 40.00
OS15 Jari Kurri 10.00 25.00
OS16 Glenn Anderson 6.00 15.00

2004-05 ITG Franchises Canadian Original Sticks Autographs

PRINT RUN 10 SETS
NOT PRICED DUE TO SCARCITY
OS1 Jean Beliveau
OS2 Paul Coffey
OS3 Guy Lafleur
OS4 Lanny McDonald
OS5 Guy Lapointe
OS7 Steve Shutt
OS8 Patrick Roy
OS12 Dale Hawerchuk

2004-05 ITG Franchises Canadian Teammates

PRINT RUN 60 SETS
GOLD PRINT RUN 20 SETS
GOLD NOT PRICED DUE TO SCARCITY
TM1 George Hainsworth 25.00 60.00
Aurel Joliat
TM2 Glenn Anderson 15.00 40.00
Jari Kurri
TM3 Mike Vernon 12.50 30.00
Phil Housley
TM4 Jean Beliveau 20.00 50.00
Jacques Plante
TM5 Lanny McDonald 20.00 50.00
Darryl Sittler
TM6 G.Fuhr/P.Coffey 15.00 40.00
TM7 Guy Lapointe 12.50 30.00
Larry Robinson
TM8 Patrick Roy 30.00 80.00
Denis Savard
TM9 Henri Richard 20.00 50.00
Gump Worsley
TM10 Doug Gilmour 20.00 50.00
Wendel Clark

2004-05 ITG Franchises Canadian Triple Memorabilia

PRINT RUN 20 SETS
GOLD PRINT RUN 5 SETS
AUTO PRINT RUN 10 SETS
NOT PRICED DUE TO SCARCITY
TM1 Patrick Roy

TM2 Maurice Richard
TM3 Guy Lafleur
TM4 Jacques Plante
TM5 Aurel Joliat
TM6 Tim Horton
TM7 Jean Beliveau
TM8 Grant Fuhr
TM9 Johnny Bower
TM10 Wendel Clark

2004-05 ITG Franchises Canadian Triple Memorabilia Autographs

PRINT RUN 10 SETS
NOT PRICED DUE TO SCARCITY
TM1 Patrick Roy
TM3 Guy Lafleur
TM7 Jean Beliveau
TM8 Grant Fuhr
TM9 Johnny Bower
TM10 Wendel Clark

2004-05 ITG Franchises Canadian Trophy Winners

PRINT RUN 70 SETS
GOLD PRINT RUN 20 SETS
GOLD NOT PRICED DUE TO SCARCITY
TW1 Guy Lafleur 12.50 30.00
TW2 Jacques Plante 25.00 60.00
TW3 Gump Worsley 12.50 30.00
TW4 Patrick Roy 20.00 50.00
TW5 Larry Robinson 8.00 20.00
TW6 Paul Coffey 12.50 30.00
TW7 Bill Ranford 8.00 20.00
TW8 Jean Beliveau 15.00 40.00
TW9 Doug Gilmour 12.50 30.00
TW10 Henri Richard 12.50 30.00

2004-05 ITG Franchises He Shoots-He Scores Prizes

PRINT RUN 20 SER.#'d SETS
NOT PRICED DUE TO SCARCITY
1 Joe Mullen
2 Grant Fuhr
3 Jari Kurri
4 Rocket Richard
5 Henri Richard
6 Jean Beliveau
7 Jacques Plante
8 Gump Worsley
9 Guy Lafleur
10 Larry Robinson
11 Yvan Cournoyer
12 Patrick Roy
13 Frank Mahovlich
14 Johnny Bower
15 Lanny McDonald
16 Darryl Sittler
17 Richard Brodeur
18 Bobby Hull
19 Stan Mikita
20 Tony Esposito
21 Denis Savard
22 Patrick Roy
23 Ray Bourque
24 Ted Lindsay
25 Steve Yzerman
26 Alex Delvecchio
27 Marcel Dionne
28 Mario Lemieux
29 Glenn Hall
30 Michel Goulet
31 Roger Crozier
32 Rogie Vachon
33 Paul Coffey
34 Ray Bourque
35 John Bucyk
36 Gerry Cheevers
37 Phil Esposito
38 Ed Giacomin
39 Jean Ratelle
40 Bryan Trottier
41 Mike Bossy
42 Denis Potvin
43 Billy Smith
44 Bobby Clarke
45 Bill Barber
46 Bernie Parent
47 Gilbert Perreault
48 Cam Neely
49 Roy Worters
50 Pelle Lindbergh

2004-05 ITG Franchises Update

Available only online, this 50-card set rounded out the Franchises product run. Each update set contained included a memorabilia card or autograph card also.

COMPLETE SET (50) 12.00 25.00
451 Jari Kurri .40 1.00
452 Bill Quackenbush .20 .50
453 Jean Ratelle .40 1.00
454 Lionel Hitchman .20 .50
455 Terry Sawchuk .60 1.50
456 Grant Fuhr .40 1.00
457 Bill Clement .20 .50
458 Paul Coffey .40 1.00
459 Dick Irvin .20 .50
460 Pierre Pilote .40 1.00
461 Mike Karakas .20 .50
462 Tom Lysiak .20 .50
463 Andy Moog .30 .75
464 Marcel Dionne .40 1.00
465 Borje Salming .30 .75
466 Johnny Bucyk .40 1.00
467 Norm Smith .20 .50
468 Marty McSorley .20 .50
469 Dave Keon .20 .50
470 Rick MacLeish .20 .50
471 Steve Shutt .20 .50
472 Billy Smith .30 .75
473 Neal Broten .20 .50
474 Guy Carbonneau .30 .75
475 Peter Mahovlich .20 .50
476 Tony Esposito .40 1.00
477 Rod Langway .20 .50
478 Newsy Lalonde .50 1.25
479 Pat Verbeek .20 .50
480 Joe Simpson .20 .50
481 Wendel Clark .30 .75
482 Marcel Dionne .40 1.00
483 Frank Boucher .20 .50
484 Johnny Bower .40 1.00
485 Don Beaupre .20 .50
486 Brad Marsh .20 .50
487 Darryl Sittler .40 1.00

Available only online, this 50-card set rounded out the Franchises product run. Each update set contained included a memorabilia card or autograph card also.

488 Barry Ashbee .20 .50
489 Michel Briere .20 .50
490 Guy Lafleur .50 1.25
491 Brian Sutter .20 .50
492 Denis Savard .40 1.00
493 Terry Sawchuk .60 1.50
494 Syl Apps .20 .50
495 Marcel Pronovost .30 .75
496 Dave Keon .20 .50
497 Garth Boesch .20 .50
498 Rick Vaive .20 .50
499 Dino Ciccarelli .20 .50
500 Serge Savard .40 1.00

2004-05 ITG Franchises Update Autographs

ONE AUTO OR MEM.CARD PER SET
AA Al Arbour 6.00 15.00
CK Cliff Koroll 6.00 15.00
DC2 Dino Ciccarelli 12.50 30.00
ET Esa Tikkanen 8.00 20.00
HL Hakan Loob 6.00 15.00
JG John Garrett 6.00 15.00
KW Ken Wregget 6.00 15.00
PF Pat Falloon 6.00 15.00
PV1 Pat Verbeek SP 8.00 20.00
TR Tom Reid 6.00 15.00
TS Thomas Steen 6.00 15.00
ALX Andre Lacroix 6.00 15.00
DKN1 Dave Keon Har. SP 30.00 80.00
DKN2 Dave Keon TML SP 50.00 125.00
JPA Jim Pappin 6.00 15.00
MBU Mike Bullard 6.00 15.00
PBR Pat Price 6.00 15.00
RBA Ralph Backstrom 6.00 15.00
RLY Rick Ley 6.00 15.00

2004-05 ITG Franchises Update Complete Jerseys

PRINT RUN 10 SETS
GOLD PRINT RUN 1 SET
NOT PRICED DUE TO SCARCITY
UCJ1 Larry Robinson
UCJ2 Dan Bouchard
UCJ3 Hakan Loob
UCJ4 Dino Ciccarelli
UCJ5 Dale Hawerchuk
UCJ6 Mike Bossy

2004-05 ITG Franchises Update Double Memorabilia

PRINT RUN 60 SETS
GOLD PRINT RUN 20 SETS
GOLD NOT PRICED DUE TO SCARCITY
UDM1 Pat Lafontaine 15.00 40.00
UDM2 Bill Durnan 20.00 50.00
UDM3 Frank Brimsek 15.00 40.00
UDM4 Billy Smith 12.50 30.00

2004-05 ITG Franchises Update Exceptions

PRINT RUN 25 SETS
GOLD PRINT RUN 5 SETS
GOLD NOT PRICED DUE TO SCARCITY
1 Howie Morenz

2004-05 ITG Franchises Update Goalie Gear

PRINT RUN 60 SETS
GOLD PRINT RUN 20 SETS
GOLD NOT PRICED DUE TO SCARCITY
UGG1 Jacques Plante 20.00 50.00
UGG2 Terry Sawchuk 15.00 40.00
UGG3 Mike Richter 12.50 30.00
UGG4 John Vanbiesbrouck 12.50 30.00

2004-05 ITG Franchises Update Linemates

PRINT RUN 10 SETS
GOLD PRINT RUN 1 SET
NOT PRICED DUE TO SCARCITY
UL1 Joe Primeau/Charlie Conacher/Busher Jackson
UL2 Elmer Lach/Toe Blake/Rocket Richard
UL3 Clark Gillies/Bryan Trottier/Mike Bossy
UL4 Guy Lafleur/Pete Mahovlich/Steve Shutt
UL5 Moore/Geoffrion/Beliveau

2004-05 ITG Franchises Update Memorabilia

PRINT RUN 70 SETS
GOLD PRINT RUN 20 SETS
GOLD NOT PRICED DUE TO SCARCITY
USM1 Patrick Roy 15.00 40.00
USM2 Mario Lemieux 15.00 40.00
USM3 Steve Yzerman 12.50 30.00
USM4 Frank Brimsek 8.00 20.00
USM5 Gary Dornhoefer 8.00 20.00
USM6 Rick MacLeish 8.00 20.00
USM7 Pelle Lindbergh 25.00 60.00
USM8 Marcel Dionne 8.00 20.00

2004-05 ITG Franchises Update Memorabilia Autographs

PRINT RUN 10 SETS
NOT PRICED DUE TO SCARCITY
WSMDC Dino Ciccarelli

2004-05 ITG Franchises Update Original Sticks

PRINT RUN 70 SETS
GOLD PRINT RUN 20 SETS
GOLD NOT PRICED DUE TO SCARCITY
UOS1 Doug Harvey 8.00 20.00
UOS2 Dave Keon 12.50 30.00
UOS3 Bill Durnan 6.00 15.00
UOS4 Terry Sawchuk 15.00 40.00
UOS5 Wayne Cashman 6.00 15.00
UOS6 Phil Esposito 12.50 30.00
UOS7 Mark Howe 6.00 15.00
UOS8 Clark Gillies 6.00 15.00
UOS9 Howie Morenz 15.00 40.00
UOS10 Bob Davidson 6.00 15.00

2004-05 ITG Franchises Update Original Sticks Autographs

PRINT RUN 10 SETS
NOT PRICED DUE TO SCARCITY
UOSDK Dave Keon

2004-05 ITG Franchises Update Teammates

PRINT RUN 60 SETS
GOLD PRINT RUN 20 SETS
GOLD NOT PRICED DUE TO SCARCITY
UTM1 Gilles Gilbert/Gerry Cheevers 15.00 40.00
UTM2 Marcel Dionne/Charlie Simmer 12.50 30.00
UTM3 Dave Keon/Red Kelly 15.00 40.00

2004-05 ITG Franchises Update Trophy Winners

PRINT RUN 70 SETS
GOLD PRINT RUN 20 SETS
GOLD NOT PRICED DUE TO SCARCITY
UTW1 Mario Lemieux 15.00 40.00
UTW2 Steve Yzerman 12.50 30.00
UTW3 Dave Keon 15.00 40.00
UTW4 John Vanbiesbrouck 8.00 20.00

2004-05 ITG Franchises US East

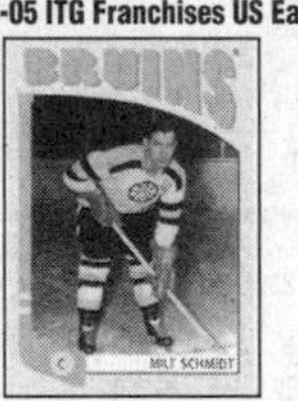

The last in the series issued in pack form, Franchises US East focused on the history of clubs from the eastern United States. Numbering picked up where US West left ended.

COMPLETE SET (150) 25.00 50.00
301 Tom Lysiak .20 .50
302 Bob MacMillan .20 .50
303 Guy Chouinard .20 .50
304 Pat Quinn .50 1.25
305 Eric Vail .20 .50
306 Dan Bouchard .30 .75
307 Curt Bennett .20 .50
308 Phil Myre .30 .75
309 Milt Schmidt .50 1.25
310 Woody Dumart .30 .75
311 Gerry Cheevers .60 1.50
312 Brad Park .30 .75
313 Jacques Plante .60 1.50
314 Johnny Bucyk .40 1.00
315 Terry O'Reilly .20 .50
316 Derek Sanderson .20 .50
317 Phil Esposito .75 2.00
318 Wayne Cashman .20 .50
319 Frank Brimsek .30 .75
320 Wayne Carleton .20 .50
321 Gilles Gilbert .30 .75
322 Bronco Horvath .20 .50
323 Eddie Shore .40 1.00
324 Bill Cowley .20 .50
325 Don Marcotte .20 .50
326 Cam Neely .40 1.00
327 Ray Bourque .75 2.00
328 Andy Moog .30 .75
329 Pete Peeters .30 .75
330 Bobby Bauer .20 .50
331 Tiny Thompson .30 .75
332 Don Awrey .20 .50
333 Rogie Vachon .40 1.00
334 Dit Clapper .30 .75
335 Rick Middleton .30 .75
336 Chuck Rayner .30 .75
337 Mel Hill .20 .50
338 Rick Martin .20 .50
339 Pat LaFontaine .20 .50
340 Sean McKenna RC .20 .50
341 Gilbert Perreault .40 1.00
342 Mike Foligno .20 .50
343 Don Edwards .30 .75
344 Danny Gare .20 .50
345 Phil Housley .20 .50
346 Larry Playfair .20 .50
347 Don Luce .20 .50
348 Tim Horton .40 1.00
349 Roger Crozier .30 .75
350 John Vanbiesbrouck .30 .75
351 Mike Hough .20 .50
352 Bobby Hull .75 2.00
353 Dave Babych .20 .50
354 Tiger Williams .30 .75
355 Mark Howe .20 .50
356 Mike Liut .20 .50
357 Chico Resch .30 .75
358 Bob Carpenter .20 .50
359 Doug Gilmour .40 1.00
360 Chris Terreri .30 .75
361 Kirk Muller .20 .50
362 John MacLean .20 .50
363 Don Lever .20 .50
364 Bruce Driver .20 .50
365 Red Dutton .20 .50
366 Ching Johnson .20 .50
367 Roy Worters .30 .75
368 Sweeney Schriner .20 .50
369 Mike Bossy .40 1.00
370 Billy Smith .30 .75
371 Denis Potvin .30 .75
372 Butch Goring .30 .75
373 Clark Gillies .20 .50
374 Bryan Trottier .30 .75
375 Chico Resch .30 .75
376 Pat LaFontaine .20 .50
377 Garry Howatt .20 .50
378 Bob Bourne .20 .50
379 Bob Nystrom .20 .50
380 J.P. Parise .20 .50
381 Edgar Laprade .20 .50
382 Nick Fotiu .20 .50
383 Rod Gilbert .40 1.00
384 Ed Giacomin .40 1.00
385 Brad Park .30 .75
386 Jean Ratelle .40 1.00
387 John Davidson .30 .75
388 Barry Beck .20 .50
389 Gump Worsley .40 1.00
390 Ron Duguay .20 .50
391 Andy Bathgate .40 1.00
392 Harry Howell .30 .75
393 Phil Esposito .75 2.00
394 Bob Nevin .20 .50
395 Bill Cook .20 .50
396 Allan Stanley .40 1.00
397 Bernie Geoffrion .40 1.00
398 Red Garrett RC .20 .50
399 Don Marshall .20 .50
400 Ron Greschner .20 .50
401 Mike Richter .40 1.00
402 Doug Harvey .20 .50
403 Don Murdoch .20 .50
404 Red Sullivan .20 .50
405 Camille Henry .20 .50
406 Terry Sawchuk .60 1.50
407 Fred Shero .20 .50
408 Red Berenson .20 .50
409 Jim Neilson .20 .50
410 Vic Hadfield .20 .50
411 Bobby Clarke .40 1.00
412 Dave Schultz .30 .75
413 Joe Watson .20 .50
414 Bernie Parent .40 1.00
415 Ron Hextall .30 .75
416 Reggie Leach .20 .50
417 Bill Barber .20 .50
418 Gary Dornhoefer .20 .50
419 Don Saleski .20 .50
420 Bill Clement .20 .50
421 Orest Kindrachuk .20 .50
422 Pelle Lindbergh .30 .75
423 Bobby Taylor .20 .50
424 Mark Howe .20 .50
425 Tom Bladon .20 .50
426 Doug Favell .20 .50
427 Mel Bridgman .20 .50
428 Andre Dupont .20 .50
429 Bob Kelly .20 .50
430 Tim Kerr .20 .50
431 Brad Marsh .20 .50
432 Brian Propp .20 .50
433 Rick MacLeish .20 .50
434 Paul Holmgren .20 .50
435 Keith Acton .20 .50
436 Syd Howe .20 .50
437 Brian Bradley .20 .50
438 Wendel Clark .30 .75
439 Dino Ciccarelli .20 .50
440 Daren Puppa .20 .50
441 Larry Murphy .20 .50
442 Bob Mason RC .20 .50
443 Yvon Labre .20 .50
444 Dennis Maruk .20 .50
445 Dale Hunter .20 .50
446 Al Iafrate .20 .50
447 Rod Langway .20 .50
448 Ryan Walter .20 .50
449 Mike Palmateer .20 .50
450 Don Beaupre .30 .75

2004-05 ITG Franchises US East Autographs

STATED ODDS 1:16
ABSM Billy Smith 12.50 30.00
ABNY Bob Nystrom 5.00 12.00
ADMR Don Marshall 5.00 12.00
ABPA Bernie Parent 20.00 50.00
AJBU Johnny Bucyk 8.00 20.00
ACBN Curt Bennett 5.00 12.00
ARMA Rick Martin 5.00 12.00
ADBR Don Beaupre 5.00 12.00
ADMA Don Marcotte 5.00 12.00
AWCA Wayne Carleton 5.00 12.00
ARDU Ron Duguay 5.00 12.00
ABHV Bronco Horvath 8.00 20.00
ARLN Rod Langway 5.00 12.00
APHO Paul Holmgren 5.00 12.00
AMHO Mike Hough 5.00 12.00
ATLY Tom Lysiak 5.00 12.00
AMBO Mike Bossy 8.00 20.00
ABBA Bill Barber 10.00 25.00
ABTA Bobby Taylor 5.00 12.00
ABMM Bob MacMillan 5.00 12.00
ADOS Don Saleski 5.00 12.00
ADMU Don Murdoch 5.00 12.00
AGHO Garry Howatt 5.00 12.00
ASMK Sean McKenna 5.00 12.00
ABPR Brian Propp 8.00 20.00
ABBN Bob Bourne 5.00 12.00
ABCA Bobby Carpenter 5.00 12.00
ARGI Rod Gilbert 15.00 40.00
ATKR Tim Kerr 5.00 12.00
ADGA Danny Gare 8.00 20.00
ARSU Red Sullivan 5.00 12.00
APMY Phil Myre 8.00 20.00
ADLU Don Luce 8.00 20.00
ATBL Tom Bladon 5.00 12.00
ABBR Brian Bradley 5.00 12.00
AADU Andre Dupont 5.00 12.00
AWCL Wendel Clark SP 20.00 50.00
ABMS Bob Mason 5.00 12.00
ABDR Bruce Driver 5.00 12.00
ADPU Daren Puppa 5.00 12.00
ABCL Bill Clement 8.00 20.00
AJMA John MacLean 5.00 12.00
ARMI Rick Middleton 5.00 12.00
ADMK1 Dennis Maruk 5.00 12.00
APPE1 Pete Peeters 8.00 20.00
ABBK1 Barry Beck 5.00 12.00
ADSA1 Derek Sanderson 10.00 25.00
ADHU1 Dale Hunter 5.00 12.00
ADSC1 Dave Schultz 12.50 30.00
ALMU2 Larry Murphy 8.00 20.00
ABGO2 Butch Goring 5.00 12.00
APPE2 Pete Peeters 8.00 20.00
AAB Andy Bathgate 8.00 20.00
AAM1 Andy Moog 10.00 25.00
ABC Bobby Clarke 15.00 40.00
ABK Bob Kelly 8.00 20.00
ABM Brad Marsh 5.00 12.00
ABN1 Bob Nevin 10.00 25.00
ABP1 Brad Park BOS SP 20.00 50.00
ABP2 Brad Park NYR SP 15.00 40.00
ABT Bryan Trottier 10.00 25.00
ACG Clark Gillies 8.00 20.00
ACN1 Cam Neely SP 25.00 60.00
ACR2 Chico Resch 10.00 25.00
ACR3 Chico Resch 8.00 20.00
ACT Chris Terreri 5.00 12.00
ADA Don Awrey 5.00 12.00
ADB1 Dan Bouchard 10.00 25.00
ADC1 Dino Ciccarelli SP
ADE Don Edwards 8.00 20.00
ADF1 Doug Favell 5.00 12.00
ADP Denis Potvin 8.00 20.00
AEG1 Ed Giacomin 15.00 40.00
AEV Eric Vail 5.00 12.00
AGC Gerry Cheevers SP 30.00 80.00
AGD Gary Dornhoefer 5.00 12.00
AGG Gilles Gilbert 10.00 25.00
AGP Gilbert Perreault 15.00 40.00
AGW1 Gump Worsley 15.00 40.00
AHH Harry Howell 5.00 12.00
AIA Al Iafrate 5.00 12.00
AJD John Davidson 5.00 12.00
AJN Jim Neilson 5.00 12.00
AJR Jean Ratelle 8.00 20.00
AJV John Vanbiesbrouck 5.00 12.00
AJW1 Joe Watson 5.00 12.00
AKM2 Kirk Muller 5.00 12.00
ALA Lou Angotti 8.00 20.00
ALP Larry Playfair 5.00 12.00
AMF Mike Foligno 8.00 20.00
AMH Mark Howe 5.00 12.00
ANF Nick Fotiu 5.00 12.00
AOK Orest Kindrachuk 5.00 12.00
APC2 Paul Coffey SP 25.00 60.00
APE1 Phil Esposito BOS SP 25.00 60.00
APE2 Phil Esposito NYR SP 20.00 50.00
APH1 Phil Housley 5.00 12.00
APL1 Pat LaFontaine BUF SP 40.00 100.00
APL2 Pat LaFontaine NYI SP 40.00 100.00
APQ Pat Quinn 8.00 20.00
APV2 Pat Verbeek 5.00 12.00
ARB1 Ray Bourque SP 60.00 125.00
ARG Ron Greschner 5.00 12.00
ARH Ron Hextall 12.50 30.00
ARL Reggie Leach 10.00 25.00
ARM Rick MacLeish 8.00 20.00
ARW Ryan Walter 5.00 12.00
ATO Terry O'Reilly 8.00 20.00
AWC Wayne Cashman 5.00 12.00
AYL Yvon Labre 5.00 12.00

2004-05 ITG Franchises US East Barn Burners

PRINT RUN 50 SETS
GOLD PRINT RUN 20 SETS
GOLD NOT PRICED DUE TO SCARCITY
EBB1 Jean Ratelle 8.00 20.00
EBB2 Mike Bossy 8.00 20.00
EBB3 Denis Potvin 8.00 20.00
EBB4 Gerry Cheevers 12.50 30.00
EBB5 Reggie Leach 8.00 20.00
EBB6 Ray Bourque 15.00 40.00
EBB7 Billy Smith 8.00 20.00
EBB8 Cam Neely 20.00 50.00
EBB9 Pat LaFontaine 15.00 40.00
EBB10 Mike Richter 10.00 25.00

2004-05 ITG Franchises US East Boxtoppers

COMPLETE SET (25) 40.00 80.00
ONE PER BOX
TH51 Atlanta Flames 2.00 5.00
TH52 Atlanta Thrashers 2.00 5.00
TH53 Atlanta Thrashers Alt 2.00 5.00
TH54 Boston Bruins Orig 2.00 5.00
TH55 Boston Bruins 2.00 5.00
TH56 Boston Bruins Alt 2.00 5.00
TH57 Brooklyn Americans 2.00 5.00
TH58 Buffalo Sabres Orig 2.00 5.00
TH59 Buffalo Sabres 2.00 5.00
TH60 Carolina Hurricanes 2.00 5.00
TH61 Florida Panthers 2.00 5.00
TH62 Hartford Whalers 2.00 5.00
TH63 Nashville Predators 2.00 5.00
TH64 Nashville Predators Alt 2.00 5.00
TH65 New Jersey Devils 2.00 5.00
TH66 New York Americans 2.00 5.00
TH67 New York Islanders 2.00 5.00
TH68 New York Islanders Fish 2.00 5.00
TH69 New York Rangers 2.00 5.00
TH70 New York Rangers Liberty 2.00 5.00
TH71 Philadelphia Flyers 2.00 5.00
TH72 Philadelphia Quakers 2.00 5.00
TH73 Tampa Bay Lightning 2.00 5.00
TH74 Washington Capitals Orig 2.00 5.00
TH75 Washington Capitals 2.00 5.00

2004-05 ITG Franchises US East Complete Jerseys

PRINT RUN 10 SETS
NOT PRICED DUE TO SCARCITY
UNPRICED GOLD 1/1's EXIST
ECJ1 Ray Bourque
ECJ2 Paul Coffey
ECJ3 Bill Barber
ECJ4 Gilbert Perreault
ECJ5 Cam Neely
ECJ6 Brad Park
ECJ7 Denis Potvin
ECJ8 Dale Hawerchuk
ECJ9 Terry O'Reilly
ECJ10 Bobby Clarke

2004-05 ITG Franchises US East Double Memorabilia

PRINT RUN 60 SETS
GOLD PRINT RUN 20 SETS
GOLD NOT PRICED DUE TO SCARCITY
EDM1 Eddie Shore 20.00 50.00
EDM2 Bobby Clarke 12.50 30.00
EDM3 Gerry Cheevers 15.00 40.00
EDM4 Cam Neely 25.00 60.00
EDM5 Bernie Parent 20.00 50.00
EDM6 Tiny Thompson 20.00 50.00
EDM7 Ray Bourque 15.00 40.00
EDM8 Ron Hextall 30.00 80.00
EDM9 Ed Giacomin 25.00 60.00
EDM10 Gilles Gilbert 15.00 40.00
EDM11 Bryan Trottier 10.00 25.00
EDM12 Mike Bossy 10.00 25.00
EDM13 Gilbert Perreault 15.00 40.00
EDM14 Denis Potvin 10.00 25.00
EDM15 Bill Barber 10.00 25.00
EDM16 Terry O'Reilly 10.00 25.00
EDM17 Reggie Leach 10.00 25.00
EDM18 Bob Nystrom 10.00 25.00
EDM19 Pelle Lindbergh 30.00 80.00
EDM20 Phil Esposito 20.00 50.00
EDM21 Rick Middleton 12.50 30.00
EDM22 Mike Richter 12.50 30.00

2004-05 ITG Franchises US East Double Memorabilia Autographs

PRINT RUN 10 SETS
NOT PRICED DUE TO SCARCITY
EDMTO Terry O'Reilly
EDMBB Bill Barber
EDMRH Ron Hextall
EDMRB Ray Bourque
EDMCN Cam Neely
EDMBT Bryan Trottier
EDMBP Bernie Parent
EDMPE Phil Esposito
EDMDP Denis Potvin
EDMMB Mike Bossy
EDMBN Bob Nystrom
EDMBC Bobby Clarke
EDMRM Rick Middleton
EDMGG Gilles Gilbert
EDMGC Gerry Cheevers
EDMGP Gilbert Perreault
EDMEG Ed Giacomin

2004-05 ITG Franchises US East Forever Rivals

PRINT RUN 50 SETS
GOLD PRINT RUN 20 SETS
GOLD NOT PRICED DUE TO SCARCITY
EFR1 Phil Esposito/Brad Park 15.00 40.00
EFR2 Mike Bossy/Rick Middleton 12.50 30.00
EFR3 G.Perreault/B. Clarke 12.50 30.00
EFR4 Cam Neely/Pat LaFontaine 15.00 40.00
EFR5 Gerry Cheevers/Bernie Parent 30.00 75.00
EFR6 Ray Bourque/Denis Potvin 15.00 40.00

2004-05 ITG Franchises US East Goalie Gear

GOLD PRINT RUN 20 SETS
GOLD NOT PRICED DUE TO SCARCITY
EGG1 Gerry Cheevers 12.50 30.00
EGG2 Billy Smith 12.50 30.00
EGG3 Tiny Thompson 15.00 40.00
EGG4 Bernie Parent 15.00 40.00
EGG5 Pelle Lindbergh 20.00 50.00
EGG6 Ed Giacomin 20.00 50.00
EGG7 Andy Moog 12.50 30.00
EGG8 Gilles Gilbert 12.50 30.00

2004-05 ITG Franchises US East Goalie Gear Autographs

PRINT RUN 10 SETS
NOT PRICED DUE TO SCARCITY
EGGGC Gerry Cheevers
EGGBS Billy Smith
EGGBP Bernie Parent
EGGEG Ed Giacomin
EGGGG Gilles Gilbert

2004-05 ITG Franchises US East Memorabilia

PRINT RUN 70 SETS
GOLD PRINT RUN 20 SETS
GOLD NOT PRICED DUE TO SCARCITY
ESM1 Eddie Shore 15.00 40.00
ESM2 Bobby Clarke 8.00 20.00
ESM3 Ray Bourque 15.00 40.00
ESM4 Reggie Leach 8.00 20.00
ESM5 Gerry Cheevers 12.50 30.00
ESM6 Ron Hextall 20.00 50.00
ESM7 Paul Coffey 12.50 30.00
ESM8 Cam Neely 20.00 50.00
ESM9 Gilbert Perreault 12.50 30.00
ESM10 Brad Park 8.00 20.00
ESM11 Billy Smith 8.00 20.00
ESM12 Dave Schultz 15.00 40.00
ESM13 Denis Potvin 8.00 20.00
ESM14 Bill Barber 8.00 20.00
ESM15 Tiny Thompson 15.00 40.00
ESM16 Mike Bossy 8.00 20.00
ESM17 Bryan Trottier 8.00 20.00
ESM18 Gilles Gilbert 12.50 30.00
ESM19 Phil Esposito 15.00 40.00
ESM20 Roy Worters 12.50 30.00
ESM21 Ed Giacomin 20.00 50.00
ESM22 Terry O'Reilly 8.00 20.00
ESM23 Rick Middleton 10.00 25.00
ESM24 Doug Gilmour 8.00 20.00
ESM25 Dale Hawerchuk 12.50 30.00
ESM26 Kirk McLean 8.00 20.00
ESM27 Andy Moog 12.50 30.00
ESM28 Bob Nystrom 8.00 20.00
ESM29 Bernie Parent 15.00 40.00
ESM30 Jean Ratelle 8.00 20.00
ESM31 Pat Verbeek 8.00 20.00
ESM32 John Vanbiesbrouck 10.00 25.00
ESM33 Pat LaFontaine 15.00 40.00
ESM34 Mike Richter 10.00 25.00

2004-05 ITG Franchises US East Memorabilia Autographs

PRINT RUN 10 SETS
NOT PRICED DUE TO SCARCITY
ESMBC Bobby Clarke
ESMBP Bernie Parent
ESMRB Ray Bourque
ESMGC Gerry Cheevers
ESMBN Bob Nystrom
ESMDS Dave Schultz
ESMBT Bryan Trottier
ESMMB Mike Bossy
ESMCN Cam Neely
ESMJR Jean Ratelle
ESMDP Denis Potvin
ESMRH Ron Hextall
ESMPE Phil Esposito
ESMRM Rick Middleton
ESMGG Gilles Gilbert
ESMGP Gilbert Perreault
ESMTO Terry O'Reilly
ESMEG Ed Giacomin
ESMBS Billy Smith
ESMBP Brad Park
ESMBB Bill Barber
ESMPV Pat Verbeek
ESMPL Pat LaFontaine

2004-05 ITG Franchises US East Original Sticks

PRINT RUN 70 SETS
GOLD PRINT RUN 20 SETS
GOLD NOT PRICED DUE TO SCARCITY
EOS1 Cam Neely 12.50 30.00
EOS2 Larry Murphy 6.00 15.00
EOS3 Bobby Clarke 6.00 15.00
EOS4 Ron Duguay 8.00 20.00
EOS5 Phil Esposito 12.50 30.00
EOS6 Vic Hadfield 6.00 15.00
EOS7 Reggie Leach 6.00 15.00
EOS8 Pelle Lindbergh 20.00 50.00
EOS9 Ray Bourque 12.50 30.00
EOS10 Bob Nystrom 6.00 15.00
EOS11 Terry O'Reilly 6.00 15.00
EOS12 Denis Potvin 6.00 15.00
EOS13 Bill Barber 6.00 15.00
EOS14 Ed Giacomin 15.00 40.00
EOS15 Ron Hextall 15.00 40.00
EOS16 Bernie Parent 12.50 30.00
EOS17 Gerry Cheevers 10.00 25.00
EOS18 Johnny Bucyk 6.00 15.00
EOS19 Rick Middleton 8.00 20.00
EOS20 John Davidson 6.00 15.00

2004-05 ITG Franchises US East Original Sticks Autographs

PRINT RUN 10 SETS
NOT PRICED DUE TO SCARCITY
EOSBP Bernie Parent
EOSTO Terry O'Reilly
EOSPE Phil Esposito
EOSBC Bobby Clarke
EOSGC Gerry Cheevers
EOSRH Ron Hextall
EOSRD Ron Duguay
EOSBB Bill Barber
EOSRM Rick Middleton
EOSBN Bob Nystrom
EOSCN Cam Neely
EOSJB John Bucyk
EOSDP Denis Potvin
EOSEG Ed Giacomin
EOSRB Ray Bourque

2004-05 ITG Franchises US East Teammates

PRINT RUN 60 SETS
GOLD PRINT RUN 20 SETS
GOLD NOT PRICED DUE TO SCARCITY
ETM1 T.Thompson/E.Shore 30.00 80.00
ETM2 Mike Bossy/Bryan Trottier 15.00 40.00
ETM3 Bobby Clarke/Bill Barber 12.50 30.00
ETM4 Ray Bourque/Cam Neely 20.00 50.00
ETM5 Brad Park/Rick Middleton 12.50 30.00
ETM6 R.Leach/D.Schultz 15.00 40.00
ETM7 Bob Nystrom/Denis Potvin 12.50 30.00
ETM8 Gerry Cheevers/Terry O'Reilly 12.50 30.00

2004-05 ITG Franchises US East Triple Memorabilia

PRINT RUN 20 SETS
GOLD PRINT RUN 5 SETS
NOT PRICED DUE TO SCARCITY
ETM1 Gerry Cheevers
ETM2 Bernie Parent
ETM3 Eddie Shore
ETM4 Ray Bourque
ETM5 Cam Neely
ETM6 Ron Hextall
ETM7 Ed Giacomin

2004-05 ITG Franchises US East Triple Memorabilia Autographs

PRINT RUN 10 SETS
NOT PRICED DUE TO SCARCITY
ETMEG Ed Giacomin
ETMCN Cam Neely
ETMGC Gerry Cheevers
ETMRH Ron Hextall
ETMRB Ray Bourque
ETPBP Bernie Parent

2004-05 ITG Franchises US East Trophy Winners

PRINT RUN 70 SETS
GOLD PRINT RUN 20 SETS
GOLD NOT PRICED DUE TO SCARCITY
ETW1 Eddie Shore 12.50 30.00
ETW2 Bobby Clarke 8.00 20.00
ETW3 Mike Bossy 8.00 20.00
ETW4 Bryan Trottier 8.00 20.00
ETW5 Ray Bourque 15.00 40.00
ETW6 Reggie Leach 8.00 20.00
ETW7 Ron Hextall 20.00 50.00
ETW8 Denis Potvin 8.00 20.00
ETW9 Bernie Parent 15.00 40.00
ETW10 Pelle Lindbergh 20.00 50.00

2004-05 ITG Franchises US West

The second product of the series, Franchises US West focused on the history of clubs in the western United States. Numbering picked up where Franchises Canadian ended.

COMPLETE SET (150) 20.00 40.00
151 Guy Hebert .30 .75
152 Wayne Carleton .20 .50
153 Gary Sabourin .20 .50
154 Gilles Meloche .30 .75
155 Gary Smith .30 .75
156 Bob Stewart .20 .50
157 Reggie Leach .20 .50
158 Glenn Hall .40 1.00
159 Bobby Hull .60 1.50
160 Dennis Hull .30 .75
161 Stan Mikita .50 1.25
162 Bill White .20 .50
163 Tony Esposito .50 1.25
164 Pat Stapleton .20 .50
165 Moose Vasko .20 .50
166 Bill Mosienko .40 1.00
167 Michel Goulet .30 .75
168 Dirk Graham .20 .50
169 Doug Bentley .20 .50
170 Max Bentley .20 .50
171 Phil Esposito .75 2.00
172 Charlie Gardiner .30 .75
173 Lou Angotti .20 .50
174 Denis Savard .40 1.00
175 Murray Bannerman .30 .75
176 Cliff Koroll .20 .50
177 Johnny Gottselig .20 .50
178 Al MacAdam .20 .50
179 Dennis Maruk .20 .50
180 Greg Smith .20 .50
181 Dave Gardner .20 .50
182 Gilles Meloche .20 .50
183 Patrick Roy .75 2.00
184 Ray Bourque .60 1.50
185 Barry Beck .20 .50
186 Chico Resch .30 .75
187 Joe Watson .20 .50
188 Wilf Paiement .20 .50
189 Doug Favell .20 .50
190 Lanny McDonald .30 .75
191 Bob MacMillan .20 .50
192 Jack Valiquette .20 .50
193 Guy Carbonneau .30 .75
194 Kirk Muller .20 .50
195 Neal Broten .20 .50
196 Craig Ludwig .20 .50
197 Frank Foyston RC .50 1.25
198 Carson Cooper .20 .50
199 Ebbie Goodfellow .30 .75
200 Herb Lewis .20 .50
201 Frank Mahovlich .40 1.00
202 Peter Mahovlich .20 .50
203 Ted Lindsay .40 1.00
204 Red Kelly .40 1.00
205 Ed Giacomin .30 .75
206 Roger Crozier .30 .75
207 Henry Boucha .20 .50
208 Reed Larson .20 .50
209 Vladimir Konstantinov .20 .50
210 Steve Yzerman .75 2.00
211 Glenn Hall .40 1.00
212 Sid Abel .40 1.00
213 Terry Sawchuk .50 1.25
214 Alex Delvecchio .40 1.00
215 Mud Bruneteau .20 .50
216 Mark Howe .20 .50
217 Harry Lumley .30 .75
218 Bruce MacGregor .20 .50
219 Jack Stewart .20 .50
220 Darryl Sittler .40 1.00
221 John Ogrodnick .20 .50
222 Norm Ullman .20 .50
223 Alex Faulkner .20 .50
224 Marcel Pronovost .30 .75
225 Joe Kocur .20 .50
226 Wilf Paiement .20 .50
227 Denis Herron .30 .75
228 Henry Boucha .30 .75
229 Gary Croteau .20 .50
230 Marcel Dionne .40 1.00
231 Charlie Simmer .20 .50
232 Dave Taylor .20 .50
233 Terry Sawchuk .50 1.25
234 Grant Fuhr .40 1.00
235 Rogie Vachon .40 1.00
236 Mike Murphy .20 .50
237 Bob Pulford .30 .75
238 Butch Goring .30 .75
239 Larry Robinson .30 .75
240 Jari Kurri .40 1.00
241 Bernie Nicholls .20 .50
242 Larry Murphy .20 .50
243 Bill Masterton RC 1.25 3.00
244 Bobby Smith .20 .50
245 J.P. Parise .20 .50
246 Gump Worsley .40 1.00
247 Cesare Maniago .30 .75
248 Keith Acton .20 .50
249 Fred Barrett .20 .50
250 Brian Bellows .20 .50
251 Don Beaupre .20 .50
252 Dino Ciccarelli .30 .75
253 Lou Nanne .20 .50
254 Dave Gagner .20 .50
255 Bill Goldsworthy .20 .50
256 Danny Grant .20 .50
257 Craig Hartsburg .20 .50
258 Basil McRae .20 .50
259 Bob Baun .30 .75
260 Bill Hicke .20 .50
261 Carol Vadnais .20 .50
262 Ted Hampson .20 .50
263 Charlie Hodge .20 .50
264 Kent Douglas .20 .50
265 Harry Howell .20 .50
266 Darrin Shannon .20 .50
267 Mario Lemieux 1.00 2.50
268 Greg Malone .20 .50
269 Rick Kehoe .20 .50
270 Les Binkley .30 .75
271 Randy Carlyle .20 .50
272 Lowell MacDonald .20 .50
273 Paul Coffey .40 1.00
274 Kevin Stevens .20 .50
275 Syl Apps Jr. .20 .50
276 Dave Schultz .20 .50
277 Pierre Larouche .20 .50
278 Tim Horton .40 1.00
279 Mike Bullard .20 .50
280 Lionel Conacher .20 .50
281 Odie Cleghorn .20 .50
282 Roy Worters .30 .75
283 Red Berenson .20 .50
284 Mark Hunter .20 .50
285 Glenn Hall .40 1.00
286 Dickie Moore .40 1.00
287 Derek Sanderson .20 .50
288 Wayne Babych .20 .50
289 Bernie Federko .20 .50
290 Doug Harvey .30 .75
291 Jacques Plante .50 1.25
292 Garry Unger .20 .50
293 Doug Gilmour .30 .75
294 Joe Mullen .30 .75
295 Mike Liut .30 .75
296 Frank Finnigan .20 .50
297 Syd Howe .20 .50
298 Brian Hayward .20 .50
299 Kelly Kisio .20 .50
300 Pat Falloon .20 .50

2004-05 ITG Franchises US West Autographs

STATED ODDS 1:16
ABHA Brian Hayward 5.00 12.00
AMHU Mark Hunter 5.00 12.00
AMLE Mario Lemieux 75.00 150.00
ACHA Craig Hartsburg 5.00 12.00
AGHE Guy Hebert 10.00 25.00
ARLA Reed Larson 5.00 12.00
ARKE Rick Kehoe 5.00 12.00
ABHI Bill Hicke 5.00 12.00
AGAS Gary Smith 10.00 25.00
ALMD Lowell MacDonald 5.00 12.00
AJKO Joey Kocur 5.00 12.00
ARBE Red Berenson 5.00 12.00
APLA Pierre Larouche 5.00 12.00
AGCR Gary Croteau 5.00 12.00
AJPP J.P. Parise 5.00 12.00
ADTA Dave Taylor 5.00 12.00
AMPR Marcel Pronovost 10.00 25.00
AMIM Mike Murphy 5.00 12.00
ADVG Dave Gardner 5.00 12.00
ADGR Danny Grant 5.00 12.00
AAMA Al MacAdam 5.00 12.00
ADHE Denis Herron 5.00 12.00
AGCA Guy Carbonneau 5.00 12.00
AGMA Greg Malone 5.00 12.00
ATHA Ted Hampson 5.00 12.00
ABMC Basil McRae 5.00 12.00
AJOG John Ogrodnick 5.00 12.00
ABNI Bernie Nicholls 5.00 12.00
ACLU Craig Ludwig 5.00 12.00
ABST Bob Stewart 5.00 12.00
ABBE Brian Bellows 5.00 12.00
AGRS Greg Smith 5.00 12.00
ADGH Dirk Graham 5.00 12.00
AGSB Gary Sabourin 5.00 12.00
ABMG Bruce MacGregor 5.00 12.00
ABSH Bobby Smith 5.00 12.00
AJVA Jack Valiquette 5.00 12.00
ADSV Denis Savard 15.00 40.00
ADGG Dave Gagner 5.00 12.00
ALMU1 Larry Murphy 8.00 20.00
ABG01 Butch Goring 5.00 12.00
AGME1 Gilles Meloche 10.00 25.00
AGME2 Gilles Meloche 10.00 25.00
ADMK2 Dennis Maruk 5.00 12.00
ABBK2 Barry Beck 5.00 12.00
AAD Alex Delvecchio SP 30.00 80.00
AAF Alex Faulkner 15.00 40.00
ABB1 Bobby Baun 10.00 25.00
ABF Bernie Federko 10.00 25.00
ABH1 Bobby Hull SP 40.00 100.00
ABW Bill White 5.00 12.00
ACH Charlie Hodge 5.00 12.00
ACM Cesare Maniago 10.00 25.00
ACR1 Chico Resch 8.00 20.00
ACS Charlie Simmer 5.00 12.00
ACV Carol Vadnais 5.00 12.00
ADF1 Doug Favell 5.00 12.00
ADG1 Doug Gilmour SP 15.00 40.00
ADH Dennis Hull 10.00 25.00
ADM1 Dickie Moore 15.00 40.00
ADS1 Darryl Sittler 20.00 50.00
AEG2 Ed Giacomin SP 40.00 100.00
AFB Fred Barrett 5.00 12.00
AFM1 Frank Mahovlich SP 30.00 80.00
AGH1 Glenn Hall SP 20.00 50.00
AGH2 Glenn Hall SP 20.00 50.00
AGH3 Glenn Hall SP 20.00 50.00
AGU Garry Unger 5.00 12.00
AGW2 Gump Worsley SP 20.00 50.00
AHB Henry Boucha 5.00 12.00
AJM2 Joe Mullen 10.00 25.00
AKA Keith Acton 5.00 12.00
AKD Kent Douglas 5.00 12.00
AKK Kelly Kisio 5.00 12.00
AKM1 Kirk Muller 5.00 12.00
AKS Kevin Stevens 5.00 12.00
ALB Les Binkley 10.00 25.00
ALM1 Lanny McDonald SP 20.00 50.00
ALN Lou Nanne 5.00 12.00
ALR1 Larry Robinson 10.00 25.00
AMBN Murray Bannerman 10.00 25.00
AMD Marcel Dionne SP 15.00 40.00
AMG1 Michel Goulet 10.00 25.00
AML Mike Liut 10.00 25.00
ANB Neal Broten 5.00 12.00
ANU Norm Ullman 5.00 12.00
APC3 Paul Coffey SP 40.00 100.00
APE3 Phil Esposito SP 30.00 80.00
APR1 Patrick Roy SP 125.00 250.00
APS Pat Stapleton 5.00 12.00
ARB2 Ray Bourque SP 30.00 75.00
ARC1 Randy Carlyle 10.00 25.00
ARK Red Kelly 15.00 40.00
ARV1 Rogie Vachon 15.00 40.00
ASA Syl Apps Jr 5.00 12.00
ASM Stan Mikita SP 15.00 40.00
ASY Steve Yzerman SP 60.00 150.00
ATE Tony Esposito SP 15.00 40.00
ATL Ted Lindsay SP 15.00 40.00
AWB Wayne Babych 5.00 12.00
AWP1 Wilf Paiement 5.00 12.00
AWP2 Wilf Paiement 5.00 12.00

2004-05 ITG Franchises US West Barn Burners

PRINT RUN 50 SETS
WBB1 Mario Lemieux 20.00 50.00
WBB2 Bill Mosienko 10.00 25.00
WBB3 Ray Bourque 15.00 40.00
WBB4 Garry Unger 10.00 25.00
WBB5 Patrick Roy 15.00 40.00
WBB6 Marcel Dionne 10.00 25.00
WBB7 Ted Lindsay 12.50 30.00
WBB8 Bobby Hull 12.50 30.00
WBB9 Steve Yzerman 20.00 50.00
WBB10 Glenn Hall 12.50 30.00

2004-05 ITG Franchises US West Boxtoppers

COMPLETE SET (25) 40.00 80.00
ONE PER BOX
TH26 Mighty Ducks of Anaheim 2.00 5.00
TH27 California Golden Seals 2.00 5.00
TH28 Chicago Blackhawks 1930's 2.00 5.00
TH29 Chicago Blackhawks 2.00 5.00
TH30 Cleveland Barons 2.00 5.00
TH31 Colorado Avalanche 2.00 5.00
TH32 Colorado Rockies 2.00 5.00
TH33 Columbus Blue Jackets 2.00 5.00
TH34 Dallas Stars 2.00 5.00
TH35 Detroit Cougars 2.00 5.00
TH36 Detroit Falcons 2.00 5.00
TH37 Detroit Red Wings 2.00 5.00
TH38 Kansas City Scouts 2.00 5.00
TH39 Los Angeles Kings Original 2.00 5.00
TH40 Los Angeles Kings 2.00 5.00
TH41 Minnesota North Stars 2.00 5.00
TH42 Minnesota Wild 2.00 5.00
TH43 Oakland Seals 2.00 5.00
TH44 Phoenix Coyotes 2.00 5.00
TH45 Pittsburgh Penguins Original 2.00 5.00
TH46 Pittsburgh Penguins 2.00 5.00
TH47 Pittsburgh Pirates 2.00 5.00
TH48 St. Louis Blues 2.00 5.00
TH49 St. Louis Eagles 2.00 5.00
TH50 San Jose Sharks 2.00 5.00

2004-05 ITG Franchises US West Complete Jerseys

PRINT RUN 10 SETS
NOT PRICED DUE TO SCARCITY
UNPRICED GOLD 1/1's EXIST
WCJ1 Ray Bourque
WCJ2 Jari Kurri
WCJ3 Paul Coffey
WCJ4 Stan Mikita
WCJ5 Steve Yzerman
WCJ6 Patrick Roy
WCJ7 Mario Lemieux
WCJ8 Norm Ullman

2004-05 ITG Franchises US West Double Memorabilia

PRINT RUN 60 SETS
GOLD PRINT RUN 20 SETS
GOLD NOT PRICED DUE TO SCARCITY
WDM1 Bill Mosienko 12.50 30.00
WDM2 Harry Lumley 15.00 40.00
WDM3 Dino Ciccarelli 12.50 30.00
WDM4 Marcel Dionne 12.50 30.00
WDM5 Frank Brimsek 12.50 30.00
WDM6 Patrick Roy 20.00 50.00
WDM7 Ray Bourque 15.00 40.00
WDM8 Glenn Hall 15.00 40.00
WDM9 Jari Kurri 12.50 30.00
WDM10 Mario Lemieux 30.00 80.00
WDM11 Stan Mikita 12.50 30.00
WDM12 Bobby Hull 12.50 30.00
WDM13 Steve Yzerman 20.00 50.00
WDM14 Tony Esposito 12.50 30.00
WDM15 Terry Sawchuk 20.00 50.00
WDM16 Norm Ullman 12.50 30.00
WDM17 Garry Unger 12.50 30.00
WDM18 Michel Goulet 12.50 30.00
WDM19 Roger Crozier 12.50 30.00

2004-05 ITG Franchises US West Double Memorabilia Autographs

PRINT RUN 10 SETS
NOT PRICED DUE TO SCARCITY
WDMBH Bobby Hull
WDMGH Glenn Hall
WDMMD Marcel Dionne
WDMML Mario Lemieux
WDMPR Patrick Roy
WDMRB Ray Bourque
WDMSM Stan Mikita
WDMSY Steve Yzerman
WDMTE Tony Esposito

2004-05 ITG Franchises US West Forever Rivals

PRINT RUN 50 SETS
WFR1 P.Roy/S.Yzerman 25.00 60.00
WFR2 Bill Mosienko/Sid Abel 12.50 30.00
WFR3 Ted Lindsay/Harry Lumley 15.00 40.00
WFR4 Alex Delvecchio/Stan Mikita 20.00 50.00
WFR5 B.Hull/T.Sawchuk 30.00 80.00

2004-05 ITG Franchises US West Goalie Gear

COMMON CARD (WGG1-WGG6) 10.00 25.00
PRINT RUN 60 SETS
WGG1 Roger Crozier 10.00 25.00
WGG2 Tony Esposito 12.50 30.00
WGG3 Charlie Gardiner 10.00 25.00
WGG4 Patrick Roy 15.00 40.00
WGG5 Frank Brimsek 12.50 30.00
WGG6 Glenn Hall 12.50 30.00

2004-05 ITG Franchises US West Memorabilia

PRINT RUN 70 SETS
WSM1 Bill Mosienko 8.00 20.00
WSM2 Roger Crozier 8.00 20.00
WSM3 Ted Lindsay 10.00 25.00
WSM4 Harry Lumley 10.00 25.00
WSM5 Dino Ciccarelli 8.00 20.00
WSM6 Alex Delvecchio 8.00 20.00
WSM7 Marcel Dionne 8.00 20.00
WSM8 Frank Brimsek 10.00 25.00
WSM9 Patrick Roy 15.00 40.00
WSM10 Ray Bourque 12.50 30.00
WSM11 Charlie Gardiner 10.00 25.00
WSM12 Glenn Hall 10.00 25.00
WSM13 Jari Kurri 12.50 30.00
WSM14 Mario Lemieux 12.50 30.00
WSM15 Stan Mikita 8.00 20.00
WSM16 Sid Abel 8.00 20.00
WSM17 Bobby Hull 12.50 30.00
WSM18 Craig Hartsburg 8.00 20.00
WSM19 Paul Coffey 12.50 30.00
WSM20 Grant Fuhr 10.00 25.00
WSM21 Steve Yzerman 12.50 30.00
WSM22 Tony Esposito 10.00 25.00
WSM23 Bill Gadsby 8.00 20.00
WSM24 Michel Goulet 8.00 20.00
WSM25 Dennis Hull 8.00 20.00
WSM26 Terry Sawchuk 15.00 40.00
WSM27 Norm Ullman 8.00 20.00
WSM28 Steve Yzerman 12.50 30.00
WSM29 Patrick Roy 15.00 40.00
WSM30 Mario Lemieux 15.00 40.00
WSM31 Garry Unger 8.00 20.00
WSM32 Larry Murphy 8.00 20.00
WSM33 Mike Vernon 12.50 30.00

2004-05 ITG Franchises US West Memorabilia Edmonton Expo '05

WSM14 Mario Lemieux

2004-05 ITG Franchises US West Original Sticks

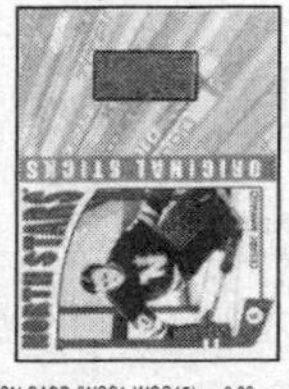

COMMON CARD (WOS1-WOS15) 6.00 15.00
PRINT RUN 70 SETS
WOS1 Patrick Roy 15.00 40.00
WOS2 Harry Lumley 10.00 25.00
WOS3 Steve Yzerman 12.50 30.00
WOS4 Glenn Hall 8.00 20.00
WOS5 Jari Kurri 10.00 25.00
WOS6 Garry Unger 6.00 15.00
WOS7 Stan Mikita 6.00 15.00
WOS8 Ray Bourque 12.50 30.00
WOS9 Roger Crozier 6.00 15.00
WOS10 Marcel Dionne 6.00 15.00
WOS11 Tony Esposito 8.00 20.00
WOS12 Denis Savard 6.00 15.00
WOS13 Mario Lemieux 15.00 40.00
WOS14 Cesare Maniago 6.00 15.00
WOS15 Charlie Simmer 6.00 15.00

2004-05 ITG Franchises US West Teammates

PRINT RUN 60 SETS
WTM1 Sid Abel/Ted Lindsay 20.00 50.00
WTM2 Stan Mikita/Bobby Hull 15.00 40.00
WTM3 Garry Unger/Glenn Hall 12.50 30.00
WTM4 Patrick Roy/Ray Bourque 20.00 50.00
WTM5 M.Lemieux/P.Coffey 20.00 50.00
WTM6 Bill Gadsby/Norm Ullman 12.50 30.00
WTM7 Michel Goulet/Denis Savard 12.50 30.00
WTM8 Steve Yzerman/Dino Ciccarelli 20.00 50.00
WTM9 Tony Esposito/Dennis Hull 12.50 30.00
WTM10 Terry Sawchuk/Alex Delvecchio 25.00 60.00

2004-05 ITG Franchises US West Triple Memorabilia

WTM1 Roger Crozier
WTM2 Harry Lumley
WTM3 Marcel Dionne
WTM4 Patrick Roy
WTM5 Ray Bourque
WTM6 Glenn Hall
WTM7 Steve Yzerman
WTM8 Mario Lemieux
WTM9 Stan Mikita
WTM10 Tony Esposito

2004-05 ITG Franchises US West Trophy Winners

PRINT RUN 70 SETS
WTW1 Stan Mikita 8.00 20.00
WTW2 Mario Lemieux 12.50 30.00
WTW3 Bobby Hull 10.00 25.00
WTW4 Ted Lindsay 10.00 25.00
WTW5 Marcel Dionne 8.00 20.00
WTW6 Roger Crozier 8.00 20.00
WTW7 Glenn Hall 10.00 25.00
WTW8 Patrick Roy 15.00 40.00
WTW9 Steve Yzerman 12.50 30.00
WTW10 Charlie Gardiner 12.50 30.00

2006 ITG Going For Gold

COMPLETE SET (25) 4.00 10.00
1 Charline Labonte .40 1.00
2 Kim St. Pierre .40 1.00
3 Gillian Ferrari .20 .50
4 Becky Kellar .20 .50
5 Carla MacLeod .20 .50
6 Caroline Ouellette .20 .50
7 Cheryl Pounder .20 .50
8 Colleen Sostorics .20 .50
9 Meghan Agosta .20 .50
10 Gillian Apps .20 .50
11 Jennifer Botterill .20 .50
12 Cassie Campbell .40 1.00
13 Danielle Goyette .20 .50
14 Jayna Hefford .40 1.00
15 Gina Kingsbury .20 .50
16 Cherie Piper .20 .50
17 Vicky Sunohara .20 .50
18 Sarah Vaillancourt .20 .50
19 Katie Weatherston .20 .50
20 Hayley Wickenheiser .75 2.00
21 Sami Jo Small .40 1.00
22 Delaney Collins .20 .50
23 France St. Louis .20 .50

24 Stacy Wilson .20 .50
25 Checklist .02 .10

2006 ITG Going For Gold Autographs

ONE AU OR GJ PER BOX SET
AA Meghan Agosta 10.00 25.00
AAP Gillian Apps 15.00 40.00
AB Jennifer Botterill 10.00 25.00
AC Cassie Campbell 25.00 60.00
ACO Delaney Collins 10.00 25.00
AF Gillian Ferrari 10.00 25.00
AG Danielle Goyette 10.00 25.00
AH Jayna Hefford 15.00 40.00
AK Becky Kellar 10.00 25.00
AKI Gina Kingsbury 10.00 25.00
AL Charline Labonte 15.00 40.00
AM Carla MacLeod 10.00 25.00
AO Caroline Ouellette 10.00 25.00
AP Cherie Piper 10.00 25.00
APO Cheryl Pounder 10.00 25.00
AS Colleen Sostorics 10.00 25.00
ASM Sami Jo Small 15.00 40.00
AST Kim St. Pierre 15.00 40.00
ASTL France St. Louis 10.00 25.00
ASU Vicky Sunohara 10.00 25.00
AV Sarah Vaillancourt 10.00 25.00
AW Katie Weatherston 10.00 25.00
AWI Hayley Wickenheiser 25.00 60.00
AWIL Stacy Wilson 10.00 25.00

2006 ITG Going For Gold Jerseys

ONE GJ OR AU PER BOXED SET
GUJ01 Charline Labonte 15.00 40.00
GUJ02 Kim St. Pierre 12.00 30.00
GUJ03 Gillian Ferrari 10.00 25.00
GUJ04 Becky Kellar 10.00 25.00
GUJ05 Carla MacLeod 10.00 25.00
GUJ06 Caroline Ouellette 10.00 25.00
GUJ07 Cheryl Pounder 10.00 25.00
GUJ08 Colleen Sostorics 10.00 25.00
GUJ09 Meghan Agosta 10.00 25.00
GUJ10 Gillian Apps 10.00 25.00
GUJ11 Jennifer Botterill 10.00 25.00
GUJ12 Cassie Campbell 20.00 50.00
GUJ13 Danielle Goyette 10.00 25.00
GUJ14 Jayna Hefford 15.00 40.00
GUJ15 Gina Kingsbury 10.00 25.00
GUJ16 Cherie Piper 10.00 25.00
GUJ17 Vicky Sunohara 10.00 25.00
GUJ18 Sarah Vaillancourt 10.00 25.00
GUJ19 Katie Weatherston 10.00 25.00
GUJ20 Hayley Wickenheiser 15.00 40.00
GUJ21 Sami Jo Small 15.00 40.00
GUJ22 Delaney Collins 10.00 25.00

2007 ITG Going For Gold World Juniors

COMPLETE SET (30) 10.00 25.00
1 Carey Price 2.00 5.00
2 Leland Irving .40 1.00
3 Karl Alzner .30 .75
4 Ryan Parent .20 .50
5 Kristopher Letang .30 .75
6 Luc Bourdon .30 .75
7 Kris Russell .20 .50
8 Marc Staal .30 .75
9 Cody Franson .20 .50
10 Steve Downie .40 1.00
11 Andrew Cogliano .30 .75
12 Marc-Andre Cliché .20 .50
13 Kenndal McArdle .20 .50
14 Darren Helm .30 .75
15 Brad Marchand .20 .50
16 James Neal .20 .50
17 Bryan Little .30 .75
18 Daniel Bertram .20 .50
19 Ryan O'Marra .20 .50
20 Tom Pyatt .20 .50
21 Jonathan Toews 1.25 3.00
22 Sam Gagner .75 2.00
23 Eric Lindros .40 1.00
24 Roberto Luongo .60 1.50
25 Jason Spezza .40 1.00
26 Dion Phaneuf .40 1.00
27 Marc-Andre Fleury .60 1.50
28 Joe Thornton .60 1.50
29 Justin Pogge .40 1.00
30 Checklist .02 .10

2007 ITG Going For Gold World Juniors Autographs

1 Carey Price 40.00 80.00
2 Leland Irving 15.00 40.00
3 Karl Alzner 10.00 25.00
4 Ryan Parent 10.00 25.00
5 Kristopher Letang 10.00 25.00
6 Luc Bourdon 10.00 25.00
7 Kris Russell 8.00 20.00
8 Marc Staal 8.00 20.00
9 Cody Franson 6.00 15.00
10 Steve Downie 12.00 30.00
11 Andrew Cogliano 8.00 20.00
12 Marc-Andre Cliché 6.00 15.00
13 Kenndal McArdle 8.00 20.00
14 Darren Helm 8.00 20.00
15 Brad Marchand 6.00 15.00
16 James Neal 6.00 15.00
17 Bryan Little 8.00 20.00
18 Daniel Bertram 6.00 15.00
19 Ryan O'Marra 6.00 15.00
20 Tom Pyatt 6.00 15.00
21 Jonathan Toews 20.00 50.00
22 Sam Gagner 20.00 50.00
23 Eric Lindros 10.00 25.00
24 Roberto Luongo 15.00 40.00
25 Jason Spezza 10.00 25.00
26 Dion Phaneuf 10.00 25.00
27 Marc-Andre Fleury 15.00 40.00
28 Joe Thornton 12.00 30.00
29 Justin Pogge 12.00 30.00

2007 ITG Going For Gold World Juniors Emblems

STATED PRINT RUN 20 SETS
GUE1 Carey Price 30.00 80.00
GUE2 Leland Irving 25.00 60.00
GUE3 Karl Alzner 20.00 50.00
GUE4 Ryan Parent 20.00 50.00
GUE5 Kristopher Letang 15.00 40.00
GUE6 Luc Bourdon 20.00 50.00
GUE7 Kris Russell 20.00 50.00
GUE8 Marc Staal 15.00 40.00
GUE9 Cody Franson 15.00 40.00
GUE10 Steve Downie 25.00 60.00
GUE11 Andrew Cogliano 25.00 60.00
GUE12 Marc-Andre Cliché 15.00 40.00
GUE13 Kenndal McArdle 15.00 40.00
GUE14 Darren Helm 15.00 40.00
GUE15 Brad Marchand 15.00 40.00
GUE16 James Neal 15.00 40.00
GUE17 Bryan Little 15.00 40.00
GUE18 Daniel Bertram 15.00 40.00
GUE19 Ryan O'Marra 15.00 40.00
GUE20 Tom Pyatt 15.00 40.00
GUE21 Jonathan Toews 30.00 80.00
GUE22 Sam Gagner 25.00 60.00
GUE23 Dion Phaneuf
GUE24 Roberto Luongo 90.00 150.00
GUE25 Jason Spezza
GUE26 Justin Pogge
GUE27 Marc-Andre Fleury
GUE28 Dany Heatley

2007 ITG Going For Gold World Juniors Jerseys

GUJ1 Carey Price 20.00 50.00
GUJ2 Leland Irving 12.00 30.00
GUJ3 Karl Alzner 10.00 25.00
GUJ4 Ryan Parent 8.00 20.00
GUJ5 Kristopher Letang 8.00 20.00
GUJ6 Luc Bourdon 10.00 25.00
GUJ7 Kris Russell 8.00 20.00
GUJ8 Marc Staal 8.00 20.00
GUJ9 Cody Franson 8.00 20.00
GUJ10 Steve Downie 10.00 25.00
GUJ11 Andrew Cogliano 10.00 25.00
GUJ12 Marc-Andre Cliché 8.00 20.00
GUJ13 Kenndal McArdle 8.00 20.00
GUJ14 Darren Helm 8.00 20.00
GUJ15 Brad Marchand 8.00 20.00
GUJ16 James Neal 8.00 20.00
GUJ17 Bryan Little 10.00 25.00
GUJ18 Daniel Bertram 8.00 20.00
GUJ19 Ryan O'Marra 8.00 20.00
GUJ20 Tom Pyatt 8.00 20.00
GUJ21 Jonathan Toews 12.00 30.00
GUJ22 Sam Gagner 12.00 30.00
GUJ23 Dion Phaneuf
GUJ24 Roberto Luongo
GUJ25 Jason Spezza
GUJ26 Justin Pogge
GUJ27 Marc-Andre Fleury
GUJ28 Dany Heatley

2007 ITG Going For Gold World Juniors Numbers

STATED PRINT RUN 20 COPIES
GUN1 Carey Price 30.00 80.00
GUN2 Leland Irving 25.00 60.00
GUN3 Karl Alzner 20.00 50.00
GUN4 Ryan Parent 20.00 50.00
GUN5 Kristopher Letang 15.00 40.00
GUN6 Luc Bourdon 20.00 50.00
GUN7 Kris Russell 20.00 50.00
GUN8 Marc Staal 15.00 40.00
GUN9 Cody Franson 15.00 40.00
GUN10 Steve Downie 25.00 60.00
GUN11 Andrew Cogliano 20.00 50.00
GUN12 Marc-Andre Cliché 15.00 40.00
GUN13 Kenndal McArdle 15.00 40.00
GUN14 Darren Helm 15.00 40.00
GUN15 Brad Marchand 15.00 40.00
GUN16 James Neal 15.00 40.00
GUN17 Bryan Little 15.00 40.00
GUN18 Daniel Bertram 15.00 40.00
GUN19 Ryan O'Marra 15.00 40.00
GUN20 Tom Pyatt 15.00 40.00
GUN21 Jonathan Toews 30.00 80.00
GUN22 Sam Gagner 25.00 60.00

2004-05 ITG Heroes and Prospects

Released in Novemeber 2004 in the wake of the NHL lockout, this 180-card set focused on top minor league prospects, top juniors and retired greats as well as Russian star Alexander Ovechkin. Heroes and Prospects was available as a hobby product that featured 2 autographs and 1 memorabilia card per box (on average) and also as an arena reatail version with no memorabilia and tougher odds on autographs.

COMPLETE SET (230) 30.00 80.00
COMP.SET w/o UPDATE(180) 25.00 60.00
COMP. UPDATE SET (50) 10.00 20.00
1 Cory Pecker .20 .50
2 Hannu Toivonen .40 1.00
3 Duncan Keith .20 .50
4 Jiri Novotny .20 .50
5 Carlo Colaiacovo .20 .50
6 Igor Knyazev .20 .50
7 Pascal Leclaire .30 .75
8 Brad Boyes .20 .50
9 Duncan Milroy .20 .50
10 Jeff Woywitka .20 .50
11 Peter Budaj .20 .50
12 Timofei Shishkanov .20 .50
13 Brandon Nolan .20 .50
14 Denis Grebeshkov .20 .50
15 Danny Groulx .20 .50
16 Martin Kariya .40 1.00
17 Greg Watson .20 .50
18 Tomas Kopecky .20 .50
19 Petr Taticek .20 .50
20 Filip Novak .20 .50
21 Matt Foy .20 .50
22 Adam Hauser .20 .50
23 Yanick Lehoux .20 .50
24 Kari Lehtonen .40 1.00
25 Marcel Goc .20 .50
26 Scottie Upshall .20 .50
27 David LeNeveu .30 .75
28 Kiel McLeod .20 .50
29 Jean-Marc Pelletier .20 .50
30 Colby Armstrong .20 .50
31 Adrian Foster .20 .50
32 Victor Uchevatov .20 .50
33 Jay McClement .20 .50
34 Marc-Andre Fleury 1.00 2.50
35 Kirill Koltsov .20 .50
36 Alexandre Giroux .20 .50
37 Rastislav Stana .20 .50
38 Ryan Miller .40 1.00
39 Mike Glumac .20 .50
40 Chris Kunitz .20 .50
41 Martin Podlesak .20 .50
42 Michel Ouellet .20 .50
43 Ryan Kesler .20 .50
44 Garrett Stafford .20 .50
45 Ray Emery .30 .75
46 Fedor Tjutin .20 .50
47 Jozef Balej .30 .75
48 Antero Niittymaki .60 1.50
49 Tom Lawson .20 .50
50 Grant Stevenson .20 .50
51 Adam Berti .20 .50
52 Alexandre Picard .40 1.00
53 Andrew Ladd .40 1.00
54 Anthony Stewart .40 1.00
55 Bobby Ryan .60 1.50
56 Boris Valabik .20 .50
57 Braydon Coburn .30 .75
58 Brent Seabrook .30 .75
59 Bryan Bickell .20 .50
60 Bryan Little .40 1.00
61 Cam Barker .40 1.00
62 Cam Ward .40 1.00
63 Chris Campoli .20 .50
64 Corey Locke .20 .50
65 Corey Perry .75 2.00
66 Andy Rogers .20 .50
67 Dan Paille .30 .75
68 David Bolland .30 .75
69 David Shantz .30 .75
70 Dennis Wideman .20 .50
71 Devan Dubnyk .30 .75
72 Dion Phaneuf 1.00 2.50
73 Doug O'Brien .20 .50
74 Eric Fehr .30 .75
75 Eric Himelfarb .20 .50
76 Gilbert Brule .60 1.50
77 James Wisniewski .20 .50
78 Jeff Carter .75 2.00
79 Jeff Drouin-Deslauriers .30 .75
80 Jeff Glass .40 1.00
81 Jeff Schultz .20 .50
82 Josh Gorges .20 .50
83 Julien Ellis-Plante .40 1.00
84 Justin Peters .20 .50
85 Kelly Guard .40 1.00
86 Kevin Klein .20 .50
87 Kyle Chipchura .40 1.00
88 Liam Reddox .20 .50
89 Marc Staal .40 1.00
90 Marc-Antoine Pouliot .30 .75
91 Martin Houle .30 .75
92 Martin St. Pierre .20 .50
93 Matt Lashoff .30 .75
94 Maxime Daigneault .30 .75
95 Mike Green .20 .50
96 Mike Richards .40 1.00
97 Paulo Colaiacovo .20 .50
98 Patrick O'Sullivan .40 1.00
99 Philippe Roberge .20 .50
100 Robbie Schremp .60 1.50
101 Ryan Garlock .20 .50
102 Ryan Getzlaf .60 1.50
103 Shawn Belle .20 .50
104 Sidney Crosby 8.00 20.00
105 Stefan Ruzicka .30 .75
106 Steve Bernier .40 1.00
107 Tim Brent .20 .50
108 Tomas Fleischmann .20 .50
109 Vaclav Meidl .20 .50
110 Wojtek Wolski .60 1.50
111 Stephen Weiss .30 .75
112 Fredrik Sjostrom .20 .50
113 Alexander Svitov .20 .50
114 Anton Babchuk .20 .50
115 Jason Spezza .40 1.00
116 Alexander Ovechkin 3.00 8.00
117 Alexander Ovechkin 3.00 8.00
118 Alexander Ovechkin 3.00 8.00
119 Alexander Ovechkin 3.00 8.00
120 Marc-Andre Fleury .75 2.00
121 Marc-Andre Fleury .75 2.00
122 Marc-Andre Fleury .75 2.00
123 Tim Horton .40 1.00
124 Frank Mahovlich .40 1.00
125 Gilbert Perreault .30 .75
126 Ed Giacomin .20 .50
127 Jean Ratelle .20 .50
128 Marcel Dionne .30 .75
129 Milt Schmidt .20 .50
130 Phil Esposito .40 1.00
131 Bernie Parent .40 1.00
132 Serge Savard .30 .75
133 Stan Mikita .30 .75
134 Tony Esposito .40 1.00
135 Vic Hadfield .20 .50
136 Wayne Cashman .20 .50
137 Yvan Cournoyer .40 1.00
138 Johnny Bower .40 1.00
139 Bill Barber .20 .50
140 Bobby Hull .60 1.50
141 Denis Potvin .30 .75
142 Gerry Cheevers .30 .75
143 Guy Lafleur .40 1.00
144 Larry Robinson .30 .75
145 Rogie Vachon .40 1.00
146 Steve Shutt .20 .50
147 Ted Lindsay .40 1.00
148 Red Kelly .40 1.00
149 Wendel Clark .30 .75
150 Ray Bourque .40 1.00
151 Cam Neely .40 1.00
152 Glenn Hall .40 1.00
153 Jean Beliveau .40 1.00
154 Grant Fuhr .40 1.00
155 Andy Bathgate .30 .75
156 Gump Worsley .40 1.00
157 Henri Richard .40 1.00
158 Mike Bossy .30 .75
159 Johnny Bucyk .20 .50
160 Elmer Lach .20 .50
161 Vladislav Tretiak .30 .75
162 Lanny McDonald .30 .75
163 Guy Lapointe .30 .75
164 Jacques Plante .60 1.50
165 Terry Sawchuk .60 1.50
166 Rocket Richard .75 2.00
167 Doug Harvey .30 .75
168 Howie Morenz .30 .75
169 Bill Barilko .30 .75
170 Brad Park .20 .50
171 Bobby Orr 1.00 2.50
172 Mario Lemieux .75 2.00
173 Paul Coffey .40 1.00
174 Patrick Roy .75 2.00
175 Bobby Clarke .40 1.00
176 Georges Vezina .60 1.50
177 Alex Delvecchio .40 1.00
178 Toe Blake .40 1.00
179 Sid Abel .40 1.00
180 Woody Dumart .30 .75
181 Jason King .20 .50
182 Yann Danis .30 .75
183 Zach Parise .60 1.50
184 Dan Hamhuis .40 1.00
185 Thomas Vanek .75 2.00
186 Mikko Koivu .40 1.00
187 Ryan Whitney .40 1.00
188 Jakub Klepis .20 .50
189 Ben Eager .20 .50
190 Kyle Wellwood .40 1.00
191 Jiri Hudler .40 1.00
192 Aaron Voros .20 .50
193 Eric Staal .60 1.50
194 Jay Bouwmeester .20 .50
195 Patrice Bergeron .60 1.50
196 Peter Sarno .20 .50
197 Mike Cammalleri .30 .75
198 Derek Roy .40 1.00
199 R.J. Umberger .40 1.00
200 Junior Lessard .20 .50
201 Rene Vydareny .20 .50
202 Alexander Ovechkin 3.00 8.00
203 Dylan Hunter .20 .50
204 Alexandre Vincent .30 .75
205 Kevin Nastiuk .30 .75
206 Evan McGrath .20 .50
207 Alex Bourret .20 .50
208 Andrej Meszaros .20 .50
209 Benoit Pouliot .20 .50
210 Dany Roussin .20 .50
211 Jeremy Colliton .20 .50
212 Danny Syvret .20 .50
213 Jonathan Boutin .30 .75
214 Ryan Stone .40 1.00
215 Jordan Staal 1.00 2.50
216 Marek Zagrapan .20 .50
217 Clarke MacArthur .30 .75
218 John Hughes .20 .50
219 Alexander Radulov .75 2.00
220 Colin Fraser .20 .50
221 Jakub Petruzalek .20 .50
222 Sidney Crosby 10.00 25.00
223 Nigel Dawes .40 1.00
224 Luc Bourdon .40 1.00
225 Devin Setoguchi .30 .75
226 Carey Price 3.00 8.00
227 Daren Machesney .30 .75
228 Corey Crawford .30 .75
229 Marek Schwarz .30 .75
230 Gerald Coleman .30 .75
NNO Roy/Ovechkin/Crosby/Fleury CL 2.00 5.00

2004-05 ITG Heroes and Prospects Aspiring

STATED PRINT RUN 50 SETS
1 M. Lemieux/S.Crosby 100.00 200.00
2 M.Lemieux/A.Ovechkin 75.00 200.00
3 Patrick Roy/Marc-Andre Fleury 40.00 100.00
4 Patrick Roy/Kari Lehtonen 40.00 100.00
5 Ray Bourque/Dion Phaneuf 30.00 80.00
6 Cam Neely/Alexander Ovechkin 50.00 125.00
7 Mike Bossy/Mike Richards 20.00 50.00
8 Frank Mahovlich/Patrick O'Sullivan 20.00 50.00
9 Phil Esposito/Brad Boyes 20.00 50.00
10 Grant Fuhr/Devan Dubnyk 30.00 80.00
11 Bobby Clarke/Jeff Carter 25.00 60.00
12 Jacques Plante/Julien Ellis-Plante 15.00 40.00
13 Gilbert Perreault/Sidney Crosby 75.00 200.00
14 Stan Mikita/Corey Perry 15.00 40.00
15 Jean Beliveau/Corey Locke 15.00 40.00
16 Gerry Cheevers/David LeNeveu 15.00 40.00

2004-05 ITG Heroes and Prospects Autographs

Inserted on an average of 2 per hobby box, this 160-card set featured certified autographs of young prospects and retired greats. Odds for retail arena boxes were not given. Cards with "U" prefix available in Update sets only, please note that card backs do not carry the "U" prefix, they are for checklisting only.

STATED ODDS 2 PER HOBBY BOX
U PREFIX IN H&P UPDATE SETS ONLY
AB Adam Berti 4.00 10.00
AD Alex Delvecchio 10.00 25.00
AF Adrian Foster 4.00 10.00
AG Alexandre Giroux 4.00 10.00
AH Adam Hauser 4.00 10.00
AL Andrew Ladd 10.00 25.00
AO1 Alexander Ovechkin 75.00 150.00
AO2 Alexander Ovechkin 75.00 150.00
AO3 Alexander Ovechkin 75.00 150.00
AO4 Alexander Ovechkin 75.00 150.00
AP Alexandre Picard 8.00 20.00
AR Andy Rogers 4.00 10.00
AS Anthony Stewart 8.00 20.00
BB Brad Boyes 4.00 10.00
BC Braydon Coburn 8.00 20.00
BH Bobby Hull 25.00 60.00
BL Bryan Little 6.00 15.00
BN Brandon Nolan 4.00 10.00
BO Bobby Orr 75.00 200.00
BP Bernie Parent 10.00 25.00
BR Bobby Ryan 8.00 25.00
BS Brent Seabrook 4.00 10.00
BV Boris Valabik 4.00 10.00
CA Colby Armstrong 8.00 20.00
CB Cam Barker 8.00 20.00
CC Carlo Colaiacovo 4.00 10.00
CK Chris Kunitz 4.00 10.00
CL Corey Locke 4.00 10.00
CN Cam Neely 12.00 30.00
CP Cory Pecker 4.00 10.00
CW Cam Ward 10.00 25.00
DB David Bolland 4.00 10.00
DD Devan Dubnyk 6.00 15.00
DG Denis Grebeshkov 4.00 10.00
DK Duncan Keith 4.00 10.00
DL David LeNeveu 4.00 10.00
DM Duncan Milroy 4.00 10.00
DO Doug O'Brien 4.00 10.00
DP Dan Paille 4.00 10.00
DS David Shantz 4.00 10.00
DW Dennis Wideman 4.00 10.00
EF Eric Fehr 8.00 20.00
EG Ed Giacomin 15.00 40.00
EH Eric Himelfarb 6.00 15.00
EL Elmer Lach 10.00 25.00
FM Frank Mahovlich 8.00 20.00
FN Filip Novak 4.00 10.00
FS Fredrik Sjostrom 4.00 10.00
FT Fedor Tjutin 6.00 15.00
GB Gilbert Brule 10.00 25.00
GC Gerry Cheevers 8.00 20.00
GF Grant Fuhr 10.00 25.00
GH Glenn Hall 10.00 25.00
GL Guy Lafleur 10.00 25.00
GP Gilbert Perreault 10.00 25.00
GS Garrett Stafford 6.00 15.00
GW Greg Watson 4.00 10.00
HR Henri Richard 10.00 25.00
HT Hannu Toivonen 6.00 15.00
JB Jozef Balej 6.00 15.00
JC Jeff Carter 15.00 40.00
JD Jeff Drouin-Deslauriers 6.00 15.00
JE Julien Ellis-Plante 6.00 15.00
JG Jeff Glass 8.00 20.00
JM Jay McClement 4.00 10.00
JN Jiri Novotny 4.00 10.00
JP Jean-Marc Pelletier 4.00 10.00
JR Jean Ratelle 8.00 20.00
JS Jeff Schultz 4.00 10.00
JW Jeff Woywitka 6.00 15.00
KC Kyle Chipchura 8.00 20.00
KG Kelly Guard 8.00 20.00
KM Kiel McLeod 4.00 10.00
LM Lanny McDonald 8.00 20.00
LR Liam Reddox 4.00 10.00
LW Lorne Worsley 10.00 25.00
MC Marcel Goc 8.00 20.00
MF1 Marc-Andre Fleury 20.00 40.00
MF2 Marc-Andre Fleury 20.00 40.00
MF3 Marc-Andre Fleury 20.00 40.00
MF4 Marc-Andre Fleury 20.00 40.00
MH Martin Houle 6.00 15.00
MK Martin Kariya 8.00 20.00
ML Matt Lashoff 4.00 10.00
MO Michel Ouellet 6.00 15.00
MP Martin Podlesak 4.00 10.00
MR Mike Richards 15.00 40.00
MS Marc Staal 12.00 30.00
PB Peter Budaj 4.00 10.00
PC Paulo Colaiacovo 4.00 10.00
PE Phil Esposito 12.50 30.00
PL Pascal Leclaire 4.00 10.00
PO Patrick O'Sullivan 10.00 25.00
PR Philippe Roberge 4.00 10.00
PT Petr Taticek 4.00 10.00
RB Ray Bourque 15.00 40.00
RE Ray Emery 4.00 10.00
RG Ryan Garlock 4.00 10.00
RK Ryan Kesler 4.00 10.00
RM Ryan Miller 10.00 25.00
RV Rogie Vachon 8.00 20.00
SB Shawn Belle 6.00 15.00
SC Sidney Crosby 150.00 350.00
SM Stan Mikita 8.00 20.00
SR Stefan Ruzicka 4.00 10.00
SS Serge Savard 10.00 25.00
SU Scottie Upshall 4.00 10.00
TB Tim Brent 4.00 10.00
TE Tony Esposito 15.00 40.00
TF Tomas Fleischmann 4.00 10.00
TK Tomas Kopecky 4.00 10.00
TL Tom Lawson 4.00 10.00
TS Timofei Shishkanov 4.00 10.00
VH Vic Hadfield 8.00 20.00
VM Vaclav Meidl 4.00 10.00
VT Vladislav Tretiak 15.00 40.00
VU Victor Uchevatov 4.00 10.00
WC Wayne Cashman 6.00 15.00
WW Wojtek Wolski 12.00 30.00
YC Yvan Cournoyer 10.00 25.00
YL Yanick Lehoux 4.00 10.00
ABA Andy Bathgate 8.00 20.00
BBA Bill Barber 6.00 15.00
BBI Bryan Bickell 4.00 10.00
BCL Bobby Clarke 12.00 30.00
BPA Brad Park 6.00 15.00
CCA Chris Campoli 4.00 10.00
CPE Corey Perry 15.00 40.00
DGR Danny Groulx 4.00 10.00
DPH Dion Phaneuf 30.00 80.00
DPO Denis Potvin 10.00 25.00
GLA Guy Lapointe 8.00 20.00
GST Grant Stevenson 4.00 10.00
JBE Jean Beliveau 12.00 30.00
JBO Johnny Bower 8.00 20.00
JBU Johnny Bucyk 6.00 15.00
JGO Josh Gorges 4.00 10.00
JPE Justin Peters 6.00 15.00
JWI James Wisniewski 4.00 10.00
KKL Kevin Klein 4.00 10.00
LRO Larry Robinson 8.00 20.00
MBO Mike Bossy 6.00 15.00
MDI Marcel Dionne 10.00 25.00
MFO Matt Foy 4.00 10.00
MGL Mike Glumac 4.00 10.00
MGR Mike Green 4.00 10.00
MLE Mario Lemieux 30.00 80.00
MPO Marc-Antoine Pouliot 8.00 20.00
MSC Milt Schmidt 8.00 20.00
MSP Martin St. Pierre 4.00 10.00
PCO Paul Coffey 10.00 25.00
PRO Patrick Roy 60.00 125.00
RGE Ryan Getzlaf 30.00 60.00
RKE Red Kelly 6.00 15.00
RSC Robbie Schremp 10.00 25.00
SBE Steve Bernier 8.00 20.00
SSH Steve Shutt 8.00 20.00
TLI Ted Lindsay 8.00 20.00
WCL Wendel Clark 10.00 25.00
UMKO Mikko Koivu 6.00 15.00
UPBE Patrice Bergeron 10.00 25.00
UPSR Peter Sarno 6.00 15.00
UMCA Mike Cammalleri 4.00 10.00
UJBW Jay Bouwmeester 6.00 15.00
UAN Antero Niittymaki 10.00 25.00
UDH Dan Hamhuis 4.00 10.00
UDR Derek Roy 6.00 15.00
UES Eric Staal 10.00 25.00
UJH Jiri Hudler 8.00 20.00
UKW Kyle Wellwood 12.00 30.00
UMD Maxime Daigneault 4.00 10.00
URS Rastislav Stana 6.00 15.00
URV Rene Vydareny 4.00 10.00
URW Ryan Whitney 4.00 10.00
USC2 Sidney Crosby 150.00 350.00
USW Stephen Weiss 4.00 10.00
UTV Thomas Vanek 15.00 40.00
UZP Zach Parise 15.00 40.00
ABAB Anton Babchuk 4.00 10.00

2004-05 ITG Heroes and Prospects Combos

Cards 15-18 only available randomly in sets of ITG Heroes and Prospects Update.

CARDS 15-18 AVAIL. H&P UPDATE ONLY
CARDS 1-14 PRINT RUN 50 SETS
1 Marc-Andre Fleury/Kari Lehtonen 30.00 80.00
2 Sidney Crosby/Michel Ouellet 75.00 200.00
3 Devan Dubnyk/Ryan Miller 12.50 30.00
4 R.Getzlaf/B.Boyes 25.00 60.00
5 Brent Seabrook/Garrett Stafford 6.00 15.00
6 Dave Bolland/Kiel McLeod 6.00 15.00
7 Marc-Antoine Pouliot/Tomas Kopecky 8.00 20.00
8 Corey Perry/Scottie Upshall 15.00 40.00
9 Julien Ellis-Plante/Pascal Leclaire 12.50 30.00
10 Jeff Carter/Ray Emery 12.50 30.00
11 Patrick O'Sullivan/Ryan Kesler 12.50 30.00
12 Mike Richards/Mike Green 15.00 40.00
13 Kyle Chipchura/Corey Locke 12.50 30.00
14 Braydon Coburn/Carlo Colaiacovo 15.00 40.00
15 Sidney Crosby/Alexander Ovechkin 150.00 300.00
16 S.Crosby/A.Ovechkin Emblms/20
17 S.Crosby/A.Ovechkin Nmbrs
18 S.Crosby/A.Ovechkin Gloves

2004-05 ITG Heroes and Prospects Complete Emblems

This 30-card memorabilia set featured the entire CHL emblem from the back of player jerseys. Each card was a 1/1.

STATED PRINT RUN 1 SET
NOT PRICED DUE TO SCARCITY
1 Devan Dubnyk
2 Mike Green
3 Corey Perry
4 Corey Locke
5 Kyle Chipchura
6 Mike Richards
7 Brent Seabrook
8 Eric Fehr
9 Anthony Stewart
10 Wojtek Wolski
11 Sidney Crosby
12 Marc-Andre Fleury
13 Colby Armstrong
14 Danny Groulx
15 Michael Garnett
16 Ryan Getzlaf
17 Adrian Foster
18 Eric Healey
19 Tomas Kopecky
20 David LeNeveu
21 Yanick Lehoux
22 Martin Podlesak
23 Matt Foy
24 Kiel McLeod
25 Michel Ouellet
26 Garrett Stafford
27 Grant Stevenson
28 Garth Murray
29 Peter Budaj
30 Brad Boyes

2004-05 ITG Heroes and Prospects Emblems

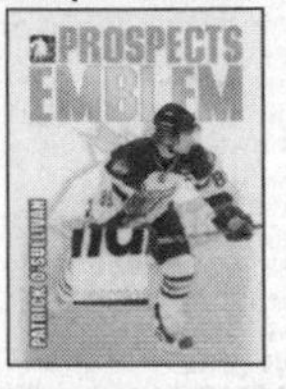

Cards 59-66 were only available randomly in the ITG Heroes and Prospects Update sets.

*EMBLEMS: X TO X BASIC JERSEYS
1-58 PRINT RUN 30 SETS
59-66 PRINT RUN 20 SETS
1-58 GOLD PRINT RUN 10 SETS
59-66 GOLD PRINT RUN 5 SETS
UNDER 25 NOT PRICED DUE TO SCARCITY

2004-05 ITG Heroes and Prospects First Overall

TRIPLE PRINT RUN 20 SETS
COMP.JSY/PKG. PRINT RUN 10 SETS
NOT PRICED DUE TO SCARCITY
1 Alexander Ovechkin/Triple Memorabilia/20
2 Alexander Ovechkin/Complete Jersey/10
3 Alexander Ovechkin/Complete Package/10

2004-05 ITG Heroes and Prospects Gloves

Available only in random sets of ITG Heroes and Prospects Update.

AVAIL. IN UPD.PACKS ONLY
PRINT RUN 50 SETS
GOLD PRINT RUN 10 SETS
GOLD NORT PRICED DUE TO SCARCITY
1 Sidney Crosby 60.00 150.00
SC Sidney Crosby AU

2004-05 ITG Heroes and Prospects He Shoots-He Scores Prizes

STATED PRINT RUN 20 SETS
NOT PRICED DUE TO SCARCITY
1 Marc-Andre Fleury/Kari Lehtonen
2 Sidney Crosby/Alexander Ovechkin
3 Marc-Andre Fleury/Patrick Roy
4 S.Crosby/M. Lemieux
5 Kari Lehtonen/Grant Fuhr
6 Alexander Ovechkin/Marcel Dionne
7 Sidney Crosby/Marc-Andre Fleury
8 Alexander Ovechkin/Eric Fehr
9 Kari Lehtonen/Michael Garnett
10 Ryan Getzlaf/Corey Perry
11 Brad Boyes/Andrew Raycroft
12 Brent Seabrook/David Bolland
13 Wojtek Wolski/Peter Budaj
14 Alexandre Picard/Pascal Leclaire
15 Tomas Kopecky/Danny Groulx
16 Devan Dubnyk/Marc-Antoine Pouliot
17 Anthony Stewart/Stephen Weiss
18 Patrick O'Sullivan/Matt Foy
19 Kyle Chipchura/Corey Locke
20 Scottie Upshall/Timofei Shishkanov
21 Adrian Foster/Ari Ahonen
22 Trent Hunter/Rick DiPietro
23 Fedor Tyutin/Garth Murray
24 Jason Spezza/Ray Emery
25 Jeff Carter/Mike Richards
26 David LeNeveu/Kiel McLeod
27 Grant Stevenson/Garrett Stafford
28 John Pohl/Jason Bacashihua
29 Carlo Colaiacovo/Mikael Tellqvist
30 Brandon Reid/Alex Auld
31 Yanick Lehoux/Denis Grebeshkov
32 Ryan Miller/Mika Noronen
33 Julien Ellis-Plante/Ryan Kesler
34 Maxime Ouellet/Rastislav Stana
35 Colby Armstrong/Michel Ouellet

36 Michael Ryder/Ron Hainsey
37 Jean-Marc Pelletier/Martin Podlesak
38 Ilja Bryzgalov/Mark Popovic
39 Martin Prusek/Julien Vauclair
40 Dion Phaneuf/Braydon Coburn

2004-05 ITG Heroes and Prospects Hero Memorabilia

STATED PRINT RUN 30 SETS
UNLESS OTHERWISE NOTED
1 Tony Esposito 8.00 20.00
2 Stan Mikita 8.00 20.00
3 Gump Worsley/10
4 Ray Bourque 12.50 30.00
5 Phil Esposito 15.00 40.00
6 Patrick Roy 50.00 125.00
7 Mike Bossy 15.00 40.00
8 Marcel Dionne 8.00 20.00
9 Larry Robinson 8.00 20.00
10 Johnny Bower 12.50 30.00
11 Jean Beliveau 25.00 60.00
12 Jacques Plante 25.00 60.00
13 Henri Richard 8.00 20.00
14 Mario Lemieux 40.00 100.00
15 Gilbert Perreault 12.50 30.00
16 Gerry Cheevers 15.00 40.00
17 Ed Giacomin 15.00 40.00
18 Denis Potvin 8.00 20.00
19 Cam Neely 40.00 100.00
20 Frank Mahovlich/10
21 Alex Delvecchio 15.00 40.00
22 Rogie Vachon 15.00 40.00
23 Serge Savard 15.00 40.00
24 Guy Lapointe 12.50 30.00
25 Bill Barber 12.50 30.00
26 Grant Fuhr
27 Ted Lindsay 25.00 60.00
28 Paul Coffey 15.00 40.00
29 Doug Harvey/10
30 Bobby Orr

2004-05 ITG Heroes and Prospects Jersey Autographs

STATED PRINT RUN 5 SETS
NOT PRICED DUE TO SCARCITY
1 Jiri Novotny
2 Marc-Andre Fleury
3 Corey Perry
4 Jeff Carter
5 Kari Lehtonen
6 David LeNeveu
7 Colby Armstrong
8 Adrian Foster
9 Ryan Miller
10 Grant Stevenson
11 Garrett Stafford
12 Michel Ouellet
13 Ray Emery
14 Fedor Tjutin
15 Brad Boyes
16 Marc-Andre Fleury
17 Eric Healey
18 Devan Dubnyk
19 Alexandre Picard
20 Patrick O'Sullivan
21 Corey Locke
22 Kyle Chipchura
23 Jean-Marc Pelletier
24 Mike Richards
25 Michael Ryder
26 Carlo Colaiacovo
37 Denis Grebeshkov
40 Kiel McLeod
41 Chris Kunitz
42 Timofei Shishkanov
43 Peter Budaj
44 Danny Groulx
45 Brent Seabrook
46 Dion Phaneuf
47 Eric Fehr
48 Yanick Lehoux
49 Ryan Getzlaf
50 Matt Foy
51 Marc-Antoine Pouliot
52 Tomas Kopecky
53 David Bolland
54 Wojtek Wolski
55 Sidney Crosby
56 Anthony Stewart
57 Alexander Ovechkin
58 Scottie Upshall

2004-05 ITG Heroes and Prospects Jerseys

Cards 59-66 were only available randomly in the ITG Heroes and Prospects Update sets.

*SINGLE COLOR SWATCH: .25X TO .75X
CARDS 59-66 AVAIL. H&P UPDATE ONLY
STATED PRINT RUN 90 SETS
GOLD PRINT RUN 10 SETS
GOLD NOT PRICED DUE TO SCARCITY
1 Jiri Novotny 4.00 10.00

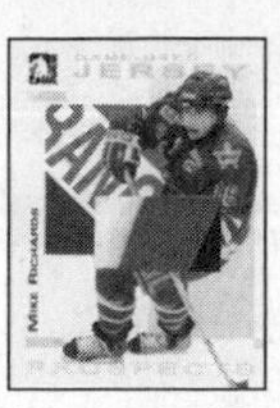

2 Marc-Andre Fleury 15.00 40.00
3 Corey Perry 15.00 40.00
4 Jeff Carter 20.00 50.00
5 Kari Lehtonen 20.00 50.00
6 David LeNeveu 8.00 20.00
7 Colby Armstrong 12.00 30.00
8 Adrian Foster 4.00 10.00
9 Ryan Miller 10.00 25.00
10 Grant Stevenson 4.00 10.00
11 Garrett Stafford 4.00 10.00
12 Michel Ouellet 8.00 20.00
13 Ray Emery 6.00 15.00
14 Fedor Tjutin 4.00 10.00
15 Brad Boyes 6.00 15.00
16 Marc-Andre Fleury 15.00 40.00
17 Eric Healey 8.00 20.00
18 Devan Dubnyk 4.00 10.00
19 Alexandre Picard 10.00 25.00
20 Patrick O'Sullivan 10.00 25.00
21 Corey Locke 6.00 15.00
22 Kyle Chipchura 8.00 20.00
23 Jean-Marc Pelletier 8.00 20.00
24 Mike Richards 15.00 40.00
25 Michael Ryder 12.50 30.00
26 Carlo Colaiacovo 4.00 10.00
27 Garth Murray 4.00 10.00
28 John Pohl 4.00 10.00
29 Mark Popovic 4.00 10.00
30 Trent Hunter 6.00 15.00
31 Ron Hainsey 4.00 10.00
32 Tony Salmelainen 4.00 10.00
33 Jason Spezza 10.00 25.00
34 Fedor Fedorov 8.00 20.00
35 Denis Shvidki 4.00 10.00
36 Andrew Hutchinson 4.00 10.00
37 Denis Grebeshkov 4.00 10.00
38 Julien Vauclair 6.00 15.00
39 Brandon Reid 4.00 10.00
40 Kiel McLeod 4.00 10.00
41 Chris Kunitz 4.00 10.00
42 Timofei Shishkanov 4.00 10.00
43 Peter Budaj 4.00 10.00
44 Danny Groulx 4.00 10.00
45 Brent Seabrook 12.50 30.00
46 Dion Phaneuf 15.00 40.00
47 Eric Fehr 8.00 20.00
48 Yanick Lehoux 4.00 10.00
49 Ryan Getzlaf 15.00 40.00
50 Matt Foy 4.00 10.00
51 Marc-Antoine Pouliot 6.00 15.00
52 Tomas Kopecky 4.00 10.00
53 David Bolland 4.00 10.00
54 Wojtek Wolski 8.00 20.00
55 Sidney Crosby 75.00 150.00
56 Anthony Stewart 8.00 20.00
57 Alexander Ovechkin 40.00 100.00
58 Scottie Upshall 4.00 10.00
59 Alexander Ovechkin 40.00 100.00
61 Patrice Bergeron 8.00 20.00
62 Robbie Schremp 10.00 25.00
63 Ryan Whitney 6.00 15.00
64 Danny Syvret 6.00 15.00
65 Dany Roussin 4.00 10.00
66 Wojtek Wolski 8.00 20.00

2004-05 ITG Heroes and Prospects National Pride

STATED PRINT RUN 50 SETS
1 Sidney Crosby 100.00 200.00
2 Jeff Carter 20.00 50.00
3 Jason Spezza 15.00 40.00
4 Alexander Ovechkin 40.00 100.00
5 Marc-Andre Fleury 25.00 60.00
6 Mike Richards 15.00 40.00
7 Kari Lehtonen 25.00 60.00
8 Patrick O'Sullivan 15.00 40.00

2004-05 ITG Heroes and Prospects Net Prospects

STATED PRINT RUN 60 SETS
GOLD PRINT RUN 20 SETS
GOLD NOT PRICED DUE TO SCARCITY
1 Kari Lehtonen 25.00 50.00
2 Marc-Andre Fleury 25.00 50.00
3 Andrew Raycroft 12.00 30.00
4 Rick DiPietro 6.00 15.00
5 Ilja Bryzgalov 6.00 15.00
6 Antero Niittymaki 12.00 30.00
7 Ryan Miller 12.00 30.00
8 Jason Bacashihua 10.00 25.00
9 Rastislav Stana 6.00 15.00
10 Philippe Sauve 6.00 15.00
11 Ray Emery 10.00 25.00
12 Ari Ahonen 6.00 15.00
13 Alex Auld 10.00 25.00
14 David LeNeveu 10.00 25.00
15 Neil Little 6.00 15.00
16 Tim Thomas 6.00 15.00
17 Devan Dubnyk 10.00 25.00
18 Jean-Marc Pelletier 6.00 15.00
19 Mathieu Garon 10.00 25.00
20 Marc-Andre Fleury 25.00 50.00
21 Michael Garnett 6.00 15.00
22 Sebastien Centomo 6.00 15.00
23 Peter Budaj 6.00 15.00
24 Sebastien Charpentier 6.00 15.00
25 Martin Prusek 6.00 15.00
26 Pascal Leclaire 10.00 25.00
27 Mikael Tellqvist 10.00 25.00
28 Reinhard Divis 6.00 15.00
29 Phil Osaer 6.00 15.00
30 Maxime Ouellet 6.00 15.00
31 Mika Noronen 6.00 15.00
32 Julien Ellis-Plante 10.00 25.00

2004-05 ITG Heroes and Prospects Numbers

Cards 59-66 were only available randomly in the ITG Heroes and Prospects Update sets.

*NUMBERS: X TO X BASIC JERSEYS
1-58 PRINT RUN 25 SETS
59-66 PRINT RUN 10 SETS
1-58 GOLD PRINT RUN 10 SETS
59-66 GOLD PRINT RUN 5 SETS
UNDER 25 NOT PRICED DUE TO SCARCITY

2004-05 ITG Heroes and Prospects Numbers Gold

STATED PRINT RUN 5 SETS
NOT PRICED DUE TO SCARCITY

2004-05 ITG Heroes and Prospects Top Prospects

1 Wojtek Wolski 1.25 3.00
2 David Shantz .75 2.00
3 Adam Berti .75 2.00
4 Cam Barker 1.25 3.00
5 Dave Bolland .75 2.00
6 Jeff Schultz .75 2.00
7 Alexandre Picard 1.25 3.00
8 Julien Ellis-Plante .75 2.00
9 Vaclav Meidl .75 2.00
10 Eric Fehr .75 2.00
11 Robbie Schremp 1.25 3.00
12 Andrew Ladd 1.25 3.00
13 Devan Dubnyk .75 2.00
14 Boris Valabik .75 2.00
15 Justin Peters .75 2.00
16 Mike Green .75 2.00
17 Bryan Bickell .75 2.00
18 Marc-Andre Fleury 2.00 5.00
19 Anthony Stewart 1.25 3.00
20 Ryan Getzlaf 1.25 3.00

2005-06 ITG Heroes and Prospects

This 430-card set was released in two series. Each series had five-card packs which came 24 packs to a box and 24 boxes to a case. This set features a mix of retired greats and players yet to make their NHL debut.

COMPLETE SET (430) 40.00 100.00
COMP.SERIES 1 SET(180) 15.00 40.00
COMP.SERIES 2 SET (200) 15.00 40.00
COMP. UPDATE SET (50) 10.00 20.00
1 Martin Brodeur .60 1.50
2 Bobby Hull .40 1.00
3 Glenn Hall .40 1.00
4 Harry Howell .30 .75
5 Doug Gilmour .30 .75
6 Phil Esposito .40 1.00
7 Red Kelly .40 1.00
8 Cam Neely .40 1.00
9 Jean Beliveau .40 1.00
10 Johnny Bower .40 1.00
11 Milt Schmidt .20 .50
12 Jose Theodore .40 1.00
13 Ray Bourque .40 1.00
14 Dave Keon .40 1.00
15 Henri Richard .30 .75
16 Marcel Dionne .30 .75
17 Paul Henderson .30 .75
18 Wendel Clark .30 .75
19 Steve Yzerman .75 2.00
20 Vladislav Tretiak .30 .75
21 Brett Hull .40 1.00
22 Mike Bossy .30 .75
23 Tony Esposito .40 1.00
24 Bobby Clarke .40 1.00
25 Brian Leetch .40 1.00
26 Guy Lafleur .40 1.00
27 Grant Fuhr .40 1.00
28 Pat LaFontaine .20 .50
29 Jean Ratelle .20 .50
30 Bernie Parent .40 1.00
31 Ed Giacomin .30 .75
32 Darryl Sittler .40 1.00
33 Patrick Roy .75 2.00
34 Dino Ciccarelli .20 .50
35 Frank Mahovlich .40 1.00
36 Stan Mikita .30 .75
37 Neal Broten .20 .50
38 Ted Lindsay .30 .75
39 Derek Sanderson .20 .50
40 Mario Lemieux .75 2.00
41 Cam Ward .40 1.00
42 Brandon Bochenski .20 .50
43 Steve Ott .20 .50
44 Kevin Bieksa .20 .50
45 Ryane Clowe .20 .50
46 Jason Spezza .40 1.00
47 Adam Hauser .20 .50
48 Derek Roy .30 .75
49 R.J. Umberger .30 .75
50 Alex Auld .30 .75
51 Joey MacDonald .30 .75
52 Denis Hamel .20 .50
53 Yann Danis .30 .75
54 Brent Burns .20 .50
55 Josh Harding .30 .75
56 Jason LaBarbera .30 .75
57 Antero Niittymaki .40 1.00
58 Mike Egener .20 .50
59 Thomas Vanek .40 1.00
60 Rene Bourque .30 .75
61 Brad Boyes .30 .75
62 Kari Lehtonen .40 1.00
63 Jeff Carter .60 1.50
64 Ryan Kesler .30 .75
65 Cam Barker .30 .75
66 Ray Emery .30 .75
67 Michel Ouellet .20 .50
68 Andrew Hutchinson .20 .50
69 Mike Richards .40 1.00
70 Yanick Lehoux .20 .50
71 Lawrence Nycholat .20 .50
72 Jay Bouwmeester .20 .50
73 Ryan Whitney .30 .75
74 Zach Parise .40 1.00
75 Jordin Tootoo .40 1.00
76 Joni Pitkanen .30 .75
77 Chris Bourque .30 .75
78 Mikko Koivu .40 1.00
79 Eric Nystrom .20 .50
80 Mathieu Garon .30 .75
81 Patrice Bergeron .40 1.00
82 Eric Staal .60 1.50
83 Dustin Brown .30 .75
84 Marc-Andre Fleury .60 1.50
85 Marek Svatos .30 .75
86 Steve Eminger .20 .50
87 Andy Hilbert .20 .50
88 Chris Campoli .20 .50
89 Pascal Leclaire .30 .75
90 Anton Volchenkov .20 .50
91 Corey Locke .20 .50
92 Ryan Miller .40 1.00
93 Mike Cammalleri .20 .50
94 Simon Gamache .20 .50
95 Chuck Kobasew .30 .75
96 Christian Ehrhoff .20 .50
97 Hannu Toivonen .40 1.00
98 Mike Zigomanis .20 .50
99 Niklas Kronwall .20 .50
100 Patrick Sharp .20 .50
101 Ryan Suter .30 .75
102 Michael Leighton .30 .75
103 Denis Grebeshkov .20 .50
104 Dan Hamhuis .20 .50
105 Sidney Crosby 3.00 8.00
106 Alexander Svitov .20 .50
107 Al Montoya .40 1.00
108 Carlo Colaiacovo .20 .50
109 Alexander Ovechkin 1.50 4.00
110 Evgeni Malkin 2.00 5.00
111 John Tavares 6.00 15.00
112 Bobby Ryan .40 1.00
113 Steve Downie .60 1.50
114 Adam McQuaid .20 .50
115 Robbie Schremp .60 1.50
116 Jordan Staal .75 2.00
117 Matt Lashoff .30 .75
118 Ryan O'Marra .40 1.00
119 James Neal .20 .50
120 Bryan Little .30 .75
121 David Bolland .30 .75
122 Evan McGrath .30 .75
123 Kevin Lalande .20 .50
124 Radek Smolenak .40 1.00
125 Marc Staal .60 1.50
126 Michael Blunden .20 .50
127 Tom Pyatt .20 .50
128 Daren Machesney .30 .75
129 Evan Brophey .20 .50
130 Jakub Kindl .20 .50
131 Ryan Parent .30 .75
132 Daniel Ryder .20 .50
133 Matt Pelech .20 .50
134 Benoit Pouliot .40 1.00
135 Derick Brassard .60 1.50
136 Brad Marchand .20 .50
137 Alexander Radulov .75 2.00
138 Marc-Andre Cliche .30 .75
139 Luc Bourdon .30 .75
140 David Krejci .20 .50
141 Marek Zagrapan .20 .50
142 Chad Denny .20 .50
143 James Sheppard .30 .75
144 Jean-Philippe Levasseur .30 .75
145 Alex Bourret .20 .50
146 Kristopher Letang .30 .75
147 Pier-Olivier Pelletier .30 .75
148 Jean-Philippe Paquet .20 .50
149 Marc-Edouard Vlasic .40 1.00
150 Nicolas Blanchard .20 .50
151 Guillaume Latendresse .60 1.50
152 Jonathan Bernier .75 2.00
153 Oskars Bartulis .20 .50
154 Corey Perry .40 1.00
155 Alexandre Vincent .20 .50
156 Marc-Andre Gragnani .20 .50
157 Carey Price 1.25 3.00
158 Brett Sutter .20 .50
159 Angelo Esposito 2.00 5.00
160 Devin Setoguchi .30 .75
161 Shea Weber .20 .50
162 Tyler Plante .20 .50
163 Kris Russell .20 .50
164 Gilbert Brule .60 1.50
165 Brendan Mikkelson .20 .50
166 Dustin Kohn .20 .50
167 Chris Durand .20 .50
168 Kristofer Westblom .20 .50
169 Blair Jones .20 .50
170 Raymond Macias .20 .50
171 Michael Sauer .20 .50
172 Brodie Dupont .20 .50
173 Ben Maxwell .20 .50
174 Kenndal McArdle .20 .50
175 Matt Kassian .20 .50
176 J.D. Watt .20 .50
177 Scott Jackson .20 .50
178 Devan Dubnyk .30 .75
179 Tyler Mosienko .20 .50
180 Cody Bass .20 .50
181 Martin Brodeur .50 1.25
182 Ray Bourque .40 1.00
183 Steve Yzerman .50 1.25
184 Dany Heatley .40 1.00
185 Herb Carnegie .75 2.00
186 Jim Craig .40 1.00
187 Gilbert Perreault .25 .60
188 Ron Hextall .20 .50
189 Gerry Cheevers .30 .75
190 Yvan Cournoyer .30 .75
191 Larry Robinson .20 .50
192 Borje Salming .20 .50
193 Ted Kennedy .20 .50
194 Rod Gilbert .20 .50
195 Patrick Roy .75 2.00
196 Mario Lemieux .75 2.00
197 Eric Lindros .50 1.25
198 Ilya Kovalchuk .50 1.25
199 Tod Sloan .20 .50
200 Mark Howe .20 .50
201 Erik Westrum .20 .50
202 Chris Madden .20 .50
203 Alexandre Picard .40 1.00
204 Jeff Tambellini .20 .50
205 Marc-Antoine Pouliot .30 .75
206 Brian Finley .20 .50
207 Sean Bergenheim .20 .50
208 Ryan Shannon .20 .50
209 Clarke MacArthur .20 .50
210 Nicklas Bergfors .30 .75
211 Noah Welch .20 .50
212 Mark Hartigan .20 .50
213 Dan DaSilva .20 .50
214 Eric Fehr .20 .50
215 Shawn Belle .30 .75
216 Joey Tenute .20 .50
217 Maxime Ouellet .20 .50
218 Yan Stastny .40 1.00
219 Petr Taticek .20 .50
220 Ladislav Smid .20 .50
221 Curtis Sanford .30 .75
222 Erik Christensen .20 .50
223 Tyler Redenbach .20 .50
224 Roman Voloshenko .20 .50
225 Dustin Penner .40 1.00
226 Rejean Beauchemin .20 .50
227 Martin St. Pierre .20 .50
228 Tim Gleason .20 .50
229 Drent Krahn .20 .50
230 Jason Pominville .30 .75
231 Andrei Kostitsyn .30 .75
232 Steve Gainey .20 .50
233 Pekka Rinne .20 .50
234 Nigel Dawes .20 .50
235 Braydon Coburn .30 .75
236 Corey Crawford .30 .75
237 Ryan Stone .40 1.00
238 Jeremy Colliton .20 .50
239 Ron Hainsey .20 .50
240 Nolan Schaefer .20 .50
241 Jason Bacashihua .30 .75
242 Geoff Platt .20 .50
243 Chad Larose .20 .50
244 Drew MacIntyre .20 .50
245 Peter Sejna .20 .50
246 Ryan Vesce .20 .50
247 Brian Pothier .20 .50
248 Colin Murphy .20 .50
249 Curtis McElhinney .20 .50
250 Mike Glumac .20 .50
251 Lauri Tukonen .20 .50
252 Nathan Marsters .20 .50
253 Matt Ellison .20 .50
254 Kurtis Foster .20 .50
255 Jean-Francois Jacques .20 .50
256 Dmitri Patzold .30 .75
257 John Pohl .20 .50
258 Alexander Perezhogin .20 .50
259 Nathan Paetsch .20 .50
260 Kelly Guard .20 .50
261 Andrew Wozniewski .20 .50
262 Tomi Maki .20 .50
263 Tomas Plekanec .30 .75
264 Noah Clarke .20 .50
265 Steve Bernier .40 1.00
266 Gerald Coleman .30 .75
267 Jiri Hudler .40 1.00
268 Daniel Carcillo .20 .50
269 Bruno Gervais .20 .50
270 Dany Sabourin .20 .50
271 Junior Lessard .20 .50
272 Thomas Pock .20 .50
273 Andy Chiodo .30 .75
274 Vitaly Kolesnik .20 .50
275 Patrick Eaves .20 .50
276 Petr Prucha .40 1.00
277 Henrik Lundqvist .75 2.00
278 Evgeni Malkin 2.00 5.00
279 Alexander Ovechkin 1.50 4.00
280 Nick Foligno .20 .50
281 Chris Stewart .20 .50
282 Ryan MacDonald .20 .50
283 Liam Reddox .20 .50
284 Tyler Kennedy .20 .50
285 Dylan Hunter .20 .50
286 Bob Sanguinetti .20 .50
287 Dan LaCosta .30 .75
288 Derek Joslin .20 .50
289 Ryan Daniels .20 .50
290 Sergei Kostitsyn .20 .50
291 Jonathan D'Aversa .20 .50
292 Cory Emmerton .20 .50
293 Dan Turple .20 .50
294 John de Gray .20 .50
295 Bobby Hughes .20 .50
296 Rafael Rotter .20 .50
297 Justin Garay .20 .50
298 Marek Horsky .20 .50
299 Joe Ryan .20 .50
300 Ondrej Pavelec .20 .50
301 Olivier Latendresse .20 .50
302 Maxime Boisclair .20 .50
303 Mathieu Roy .40 1.00
304 Ryan Hillier .20 .50
305 Stanislav Lascek .20 .50
306 Julien Ellis .40 1.00
307 Mathieu Carle .20 .50
308 Alex Grant .20 .50
309 David Desharnais .20 .50
310 Bryce Swan .20 .50
311 Jeff Schultz .20 .50
312 Zach Hamill .20 .50
313 A.J. Thelen .20 .50
314 Brandon Sutter .75 2.00
315 Brady Calla .20 .50
316 Troy Brouwer .20 .50
317 Mark Fistric .20 .50
318 Codey Burki .20 .50
319 Kevin Armstrong .20 .50
320 Michael Funk .20 .50
321 Ty Wishart .20 .50
322 Dustin Boyd .20 .50
323 Peter Mueller .60 1.50
324 Wacey Rabbit .30 .75
325 Andy Rogers .20 .50
326 Leland Irving .60 1.50
327 Logan Stephenson .20 .50
328 Kyle Chipchura .40 1.00
329 Ryan White .20 .50
330 Blake Comeau .20 .50
331 Justin Pogge .75 2.00
332 Corey Perry .40 1.00
333 Ryan Getzlaf .40 1.00
334 Dion Phaneuf .75 2.00
335 Cam Ward .40 1.00
336 Mike Richards .40 1.00
337 Sidney Crosby 3.00 8.00
338 Mario Lemieux .75 2.00
339 Guy Lafleur .20 .50
340 Jeff Carter .60 1.50
341 Eric Lindros .50 1.25
342 Jose Theodore .50 1.25
343 Mike Cammalleri .20 .50
344 Jason Spezza .60 1.50
345 Patrick Roy .75 2.00
346 Brett Hull .30 .75
347 Ron Hextall .20 .50
348 Kari Lehtonen .60 1.50
349 Keith Ballard .20 .50
350 Greg Hogeboom .20 .50
351 Hugh Jessiman .20 .50
352 Chris Beckford-Tseu .40 1.00
353 Mike Brodeur .20 .50
354 Andy Franck .20 .50
355 Brett Jaeger .20 .50
356 D'Arcy McConvey .20 .50
357 Chris Durno .20 .50
358 Rosario Ruggeri .20 .50
359 Garett Bembridge .20 .50
360 Mike Morrison .20 .50
361 Sidney Crosby 3.00 8.00
362 Alexander Ovechkin 1.50 4.00
363 Marek Svatos .20 .50
364 Mike Richards .40 1.00
365 Jeff Carter 1.00 2.50
366 Eric Nystrom .50 1.25
367 Evgeni Malkin 2.00 5.00
368 Ray Emery
369 Thomas Vanek 1.00 2.50
370 Eric Staal .30 .75
371 John Tavares 2.00 5.00
372 Bobby Ryan .60 1.50
373 Angelo Esposito 1.50 4.00
374 Al Montoya 1.00 2.50
375 Patrick O'Sullivan .30 .75
376 Dion Phaneuf 2.00 5.00
377 Corey Perry .40 1.00
378 Henrik Lundqvist 2.00 5.00
379 Andrew Ladd .30 .75
380 Wojtek Wolski .60 1.50
381 Staffan Kronwall .20 .50
382 Ben Walter .30 .75
383 Jamie Holden .20 .50
384 Danny Richmond .20 .50
385 Tomas Fleischmann .20 .50
386 Alexandre Picard .30 .75
387 Jeff Glass .40 1.00
388 Josh Hennessy .20 .50
389 Brad Winchester .30 .75
390 Richie Regehr .20 .50
391 Alexandre Burrows .20 .50
392 Robert Nilsson .30 .75
393 Mark Stuart .30 .75
394 Filip Novak .20 .50
395 Stefan Ruzicka .20 .50
396 Loui Eriksson .30 .75
397 Jay McClement .20 .50
398 Ryan Callahan .20 .50
399 Ben Shutron .20 .50
400 Logan Couture .60 1.50
401 Adam Dennis .20 .50
402 Justin Donati .20 .50
403 Luch Aquino .20 .50
404 John Armstrong .20 .50
405 Matt Beleskey .20 .50
406 Jamie McGinn .20 .50
407 Matthew Corrente .20 .50
408 Theo Peckham .20 .50
409 Mike Weber .20 .50
410 Cal Clutterbuck .30 .75
411 Jean-Christophe Blanchard .20 .50
412 Francois Bouchard .20 .50
413 Claude Giroux .40 1.00
414 Ilya Ejov .20 .50
415 Benjamin Breault .20 .50
416 Keith Yandle .20 .50
417 Ivan Vishnevskiy .20 .50
418 Ondrej Fiala .20 .50
419 Michael Grabner .40 1.00
420 Riley Holzapfel .20 .50
421 Lukas Bohunicky .20 .50
422 Tysen Dowzak .20 .50
423 Colton Yellow Horn .40 1.00
424 Dustin Slade .20 .50
425 Bud Holloway .20 .50
426 David Ruzicka .20 .50
427 Marek Schwarz .30 .75
428 Michael Frolik .60 1.50
429 Cristobal Huet .40 1.00
430 Ray Emery .30 .75

2005-06 ITG Heroes and Prospects AHL Grads

PRINT RUN 70 SETS
GOLD PRINT RUN 10 SETS
GOLD NOT PRICED DUE TO SCARCITY
AG1 Jason Spezza 6.00 15.00
AG2 Brett Hull 6.00 15.00
AG3 Patrick Roy 15.00 40.00
AG4 Kari Lehtonen 8.00 20.00
AG5 Keith Ballard 3.00 8.00
AG6 Jose Theodore 6.00 15.00
AG7 Ron Hextall 6.00 15.00
AG8 Mike Cammalleri 4.00 10.00
AG9 Cam Ward 8.00 20.00

2005-06 ITG Heroes and Prospects Aspiring

PRINT RUN 50 SETS
ASP1 P.Roy/C.Price 40.00 80.00
ASP2 M.Lemieux/E.Malkin 50.00 125.00
ASP3 D.Keon/P.O'Sullivan 15.00 40.00
ASP4 B.Mosienko/T.Mosienko 10.00 25.00
ASP5 P.Coffey/J.Pitkanen 10.00 25.00
ASP6 C.Neely/P.Bergeron 15.00 40.00
ASP7 M.Bossy/R.Schremp 10.00 25.00
ASP8 P.LaFontaine/B.Ryan 10.00 25.00
ASP9 R.Bourque/S.Weber 15.00 40.00
ASP10 B.Parent/A.Niittymaki 15.00 40.00
ASP11 M.Dionne/D.Brown 10.00 25.00
ASP12 B.Clarke/J.Carter 20.00 50.00
ASP13 G.Lafleur/G.Latendresse 15.00 40.00
ASP14 J.Beliveau/P.Bouchard 15.00 40.00
ASP15 D.Sittler/E.Staal 15.00 40.00
ASP16 B.Hull/J.Spezza 20.00 50.00
ASP17 S.Yzerman/B.Pouliot 20.00 50.00
ASP18 M.Brodeur/M.Fleury 25.00 60.00
ASP19 M.Lemieux/S.Crosby 100.00 200.00
ASP20 Mario Lemieux 60.00 150.00
Alexander Ovechkin

2005-06 ITG Heroes and Prospects Autographs

DUAL PRINT RUN 15 SETS
DUALS NOT PRICED DUE TO SCARCITY
ARSC Robbie Schremp 10.00 25.00
AAA Alex Auld 6.00 15.00
AAB Alex Bourret 5.00 12.00
AAH Adam Hauser 5.00 12.00
AAM Al Montoya 10.00 25.00
AAN Antero Niittymaki 8.00 20.00
AAO Alexander Ovechkin 75.00 150.00
AAR Alexander Radulov 20.00 50.00
AAS Alexander Svitov 4.00 10.00

AAV Anton Volchenkov 4.00 10.00
ABB Brad Boyes 4.00 10.00
ABD Brodie Dupont 4.00 10.00
ABJ Blair Jones 4.00 10.00
ABL Brian Leetch 6.00 15.00
ABP Benoit Pouliot 6.00 15.00
ABR Bobby Ryan 12.00 30.00
ABS Brett Sutter 5.00 12.00
ACB Cam Barker 6.00 15.00
ACC Chris Campoli 4.00 10.00
ACD Chad Denny 4.00 10.00
ACK Chuck Kobasew 4.00 10.00
ACL Corey Locke 4.00 10.00
ACN Cam Neely 12.50 30.00
ACP Carey Price 60.00 125.00
ACW Cam Ward 15.00 40.00
ADB David Bolland 4.00 10.00
ADC Dino Ciccarelli 4.00 10.00
ADD Devan Dubnyk 6.00 15.00
ADG Denis Grebeshkov 4.00 10.00
ADH Denis Hamel 4.00 10.00
ADK Dave Keon 25.00 60.00
ADR Daniel Ryder 4.00 10.00
ADS Darryl Sittler 8.00 20.00
AEB Evan Brophey 4.00 10.00
AEG Ed Giacomin 12.00 30.00
AEM Evan McGrath 4.00 10.00
AEN Eric Nystrom 4.00 10.00
AES Eric Staal 12.00 30.00
AFM Frank Mahovlich 8.00 20.00
AGB Gilbert Brule 10.00 25.00
AGF Grant Fuhr 8.00 20.00
AGH Glenn Hall 10.00 25.00
AGL Guillaume Latendresse 15.00 40.00
AHH Harry Howell 5.00 12.00
AHR Henri Richard 10.00 25.00
AHT Hannu Toivonen 10.00 25.00
AJB Jean Beliveau 12.50 30.00
AJC Jeff Carter 15.00 40.00
AJD John de Gray 6.00 15.00
AJH Josh Harding 8.00 20.00
AJK Jakub Kindl 4.00 10.00
AJM Joey MacDonald 6.00 15.00
AJN James Neal 5.00 12.00
AJR Jean Ratelle 8.00 20.00
AJT John Tavares 150.00 250.00
AKR Kris Russell 5.00 12.00
AKW Kristofer Westblom 4.00 10.00
ALB Luc Bourdon 8.00 20.00
ALN Lawrence Nycholat 4.00 10.00
AMB Martin Brodeur 40.00 80.00
AMC Mike Cammalleri 5.00 12.00
AMD Marcel Dionne 6.00 15.00
AME Mike Egener 4.00 10.00
AMG Mathieu Garon 6.00 15.00
AMK Mikko Koivu 8.00 20.00
AML Mario Lemieux 40.00 100.00
AMO Michel Ouellet 6.00 15.00
AMP Matt Pelech 4.00 10.00
AMR Mike Richards 10.00 25.00
AMZ Marek Zagrapan 4.00 10.00
ANB Neal Broten 6.00 15.00
AOB Oksars Bartulis 4.00 10.00
APE Phil Esposito
APH Paul Henderson 6.00 15.00
APL Pascal Leclaire 5.00 12.00
APR Patrick Roy 40.00 100.00
APS Patrick Sharp 5.00 12.00
ARB Raymond Bourque 15.00 40.00
ARC Ryane Clowe 5.00 12.00
ARE Ray Emery 6.00 15.00
ARK Red Kelly 6.00 15.00
ARM Raymond Macias 4.00 10.00
ARO Ryan O'Marra 5.00 12.00
ARP Ryan Parent 5.00 12.00
ARS Radek Smolenak 6.00 15.00
ASC Sidney Crosby 100.00 200.00
ASD Steve Downie 10.00 25.00
ASE Steve Eminger 6.00 15.00
ASG Simon Gamache 4.00 10.00
ASJ Scott Jackson 4.00 10.00
ASM Stan Mikita 8.00 20.00
ASO Steve Ott 5.00 12.00
ASW Shea Weber 6.00 15.00
ASY Steve Yzerman 30.00 80.00
ATE Tony Esposito 8.00 20.00
ATL Ted Lindsay 6.00 15.00
ATM Tyler Mosienko 4.00 10.00
ATP Tom Pyatt 4.00 10.00
ATV Thomas Vanek 15.00 30.00
AVT Vladislav Tretiak 15.00 40.00
AWC Wendel Clark 10.00 25.00
AYD Yann Danis 6.00 15.00
AYL Yanick Lehoux 4.00 10.00
AZP Zach Parise 8.00 20.00
AAHI Andy Hilbert 4.00 10.00
AAHU Andrew Hutchinson 4.00 10.00
AAMQ Adam McQuaid 4.00 10.00
AAVI Alexandre Vincent 4.00 10.00
ABBO Brandon Bochenski 5.00 12.00
ABBU Brent Burns 5.00 12.00
ABCL Bobby Clarke 12.50 30.00
ABLI Bryan Little 8.00 20.00
ABMA Brad Marchand 5.00 12.00
ABMI Brendan Mikkelson 4.00 10.00
ABMX Ben Maxwell 4.00 10.00
ABOH Bobby Hull 15.00 40.00
ABPA Bernie Parent 12.50 30.00
ABRH Brett Hull 15.00 40.00
ACBA Cody Bass 6.00 15.00
ACBO Chris Bourque 8.00 20.00
ACCO Carlo Colaiacovo 4.00 10.00
ACDU Chris Durand 4.00 10.00
ACEO Christian Ehrhoff 4.00 10.00
ACPE Corey Perry 10.00 25.00
ADBN Dustin Brown 6.00 15.00
ADBR Derick Brassard 8.00 20.00
ADGI Doug Gilmour 6.00 15.00
ADHA Dan Hamhuis 5.00 12.00
ADKO Dustin Kohn 5.00 12.00
ADKR David Kreici 5.00 12.00
ADMA Daren Machesney 4.00 10.00
ADRY Derek Roy 6.00 15.00
ADSA Derek Sanderson 6.00 15.00
ADSE Devin Setoguchi 6.00 15.00
AEMA Evgeni Malkin 75.00 150.00
AGLF Guy Lafleur 8.00 20.00
AJBE Jonathan Bernier 10.00 25.00
AJBO Jay Bouwmeester 8.00 20.00
AJBW Johnny Bower 8.00 20.00
AJDW J.D. Watt 4.00 10.00
AJLB Jason LaBarbera 4.00 10.00
AJPI Joni Pitkanen 4.00 10.00
AJPL Jean-Philippe Levasseur 4.00 10.00
AJPP Jean-Philippe Paquet 4.00 10.00
AJSH James Sheppard 6.00 15.00
AJST Jordan Staal 30.00 80.00
AJTH Jose Theodore
AJTO Jordin Tootoo 8.00 20.00
AKBI Kevin Bieksa 5.00 12.00
AKLA Kevin Lalande 4.00 10.00
AKLT Kristopher Letang 6.00 15.00
AKMC Kenndal McArdle 5.00 12.00
AMAC Marc-Andre Cliche 4.00 10.00
AMAF Marc-Andre Fleury 10.00 25.00
AMAG Marc-Andre Gragnani 4.00 10.00
AMBL Michael Blunden 5.00 12.00
AMBO Mike Bossy 6.00 15.00
AMEV Marc-Edouard Vlasic 8.00 20.00
AMKA Matt Kassian 4.00 10.00
AMLF Matt Lashoff 5.00 12.00
AMLN Michael Leighton 5.00 12.00
AMSH Milt Schmidt 6.00 15.00
AMSR Michael Sauer 4.00 10.00
AMST Marc Staal 10.00 25.00
AMSV Marek Svatos 8.00 20.00
AMZI Mike Zigomanis 4.00 10.00
ANBL Nicolas Blanchard 4.00 10.00
APBR Patrice Bergeron 8.00 20.00
APLF Pat LaFontaine 8.00 20.00
APOP Pier-Olivier Pelletier 4.00 10.00
ARBQ Rene Bourque 4.00 10.00
ARJU R.J. Umberger 5.00 12.00
ARKS Ryan Kesler 5.00 12.00
ARMI Ryan Miller 12.50 30.00
ARSU Ryan Suter 8.00 20.00
ATPL Tyler Plante 4.00 10.00
DABB Chris Bourque
Ray Bourque
DABC Gilbert Brule
Bobby Clarke
DABF Martin Brodeur
Marc-Andre Fleury
DABL Jay Bouwmeester
Brian Leetch
DABO Patrice Bergeron
Alexander Ovechkin
DACR Jeff Carter
Mike Richards
DADF Devan Dubnyk
Grant Fuhr
DADT Yann Danis
Jose Theodore
DAHH Brett Hull
Bobby Hull
DALL Guillaume Latendresse
Guy Lafleur
DAML Evgeni Malkin
Mario Lemieux
DAMO Evgeni Malkin
Alexander Ovechkin
DAPM Zach Parise
Frank Mahovlich
DAPR Carey Price
Patrick Roy
DARL Bobby Ryan
Pat LaFontaine
DASY Eric Staal
Steve Yzerman

2005-06 ITG Heroes and Prospects Autographs Series II

DUAL SIG PRINT RUN 15 SETS
DUAL NOT PRICED DUE TO SCARCITY
AC Andy Chiodo 6.00 15.00
AF Andy Franck 4.00 10.00
AG Alex Grant 6.00 15.00
AK Andrei Kostitsyn 8.00 20.00
AL Andrew Ladd 6.00 15.00
AP Alexandre Picard 8.00 20.00
AW Andrew Wozniewski 4.00 10.00
BC Braydon Coburn 6.00 15.00
BF Brian Finley 4.00 10.00
BG Bruno Gervais 4.00 10.00
BK Brent Krahn 6.00 15.00
CM Clarke MacArthur 4.00 10.00
CS Chris Stewart 5.00 12.00
DJ Derek Joslin 4.00 10.00
DL Dan LaCosta 4.00 10.00
DP Dion Phaneuf 20.00 50.00
DT Dan Turple 4.00 10.00
EF Eric Fehr 8.00 20.00
EL Eric Lindros 15.00 40.00
EW Erik Westrum 4.00 10.00
GC Gerry Cheevers 10.00 25.00
GP Gilbert Perreault 10.00 25.00
HC Herb Carnegie 30.00 60.00
HJ Hugh Jessiman 4.00 10.00
HL Henrik Lundqvist 20.00 50.00
IK Ilya Kovalchuk 12.00 30.00
JB Bobby Hughes 4.00 10.00
JE Julien Ellis-Plante 6.00 15.00
JG Justin Garay 6.00 15.00
JL Junior Lessard 6.00 15.00
KA Kevin Armstrong 4.00 10.00
KB Keith Ballard 5.00 12.00
KC Kyle Chipchura 6.00 15.00
KF Kurtis Foster 4.00 10.00
KG Kelly Guard 5.00 12.00
LI Leland Irving 8.00 20.00
LR Larry Robinson 6.00 15.00
LS Ladislav Smid 4.00 10.00
LT Lauri Tukonen 4.00 10.00
MH Mark Howe 8.00 20.00
MM Mike Morrison 6.00 15.00
NC Noah Clarke 4.00 10.00
ND Nigel Dawes 5.00 12.00
NF Nick Foligno 5.00 12.00
NM Nathan Marsters 4.00 10.00
NP Nathan Paetsch 4.00 10.00
NS Nolan Schaefer 4.00 10.00
NW Noah Welch 8.00 20.00
OL Olivier Latendresse 6.00 15.00
OP Ondrej Pavelec 4.00 10.00
PM Peter Mueller 10.00 25.00
PP Petr Prucha 15.00 40.00
PT Petr Taticek 4.00 10.00
RD Ryan Daniels 4.00 10.00
RG Ryan Getzlaf 10.00 25.00
RH Ron Hextall 20.00 50.00
RR Rosario Ruggeri 4.00 10.00
RV Roman Voloshenko 6.00 15.00
SB Sean Bergenheim 4.00 10.00
SL Stanislav Lascek 4.00 10.00
TB Troy Brouwer 4.00 10.00
TG Tim Gleason 4.00 10.00
TK Tyler Kennedy 4.00 10.00
TR Tyler Redenbach 4.00 10.00
TS Tod Sloan 4.00 10.00
TW Ty Wishart 4.00 10.00
VK Vitaly Kolesnik 5.00 12.00
WR Wacey Rabbit 6.00 15.00
YC Yvan Cournoyer 8.00 20.00
YS Yan Stastny 4.00 10.00
ZH Zach Hamill 6.00 15.00
AE2 Angelo Esposito 75.00 150.00
AJT A.J. Thelen 4.00 10.00
AM2 Al Montoya 8.00 20.00
AO2 Alexander Ovechkin 50.00 125.00
AO3 Alexander Ovechkin 50.00 125.00
APR Alexander Perezhogin 10.00 25.00
ARG Andy Rogers 4.00 10.00
BCA Brady Calla 4.00 10.00
BCO Blake Comeau 5.00 12.00
BJG Brett Jaeger 4.00 10.00
BJS Borje Salming 10.00 25.00
BPO Brian Pothier 4.00 10.00
BR2 Bobby Ryan 12.00 30.00
BSG Bob Sanguinetti 10.00 25.00
BSU Brandon Sutter 8.00 20.00
BSW Bryce Swan 4.00 10.00
CBK Codey Burki 4.00 10.00
CCR Corey Crawford 5.00 12.00
CDR Chris Durno 4.00 10.00
CEM Cory Emmerton 4.00 10.00
CLR Chad Larose 4.00 10.00
CMD Chris Madden 4.00 10.00
CME Curtis McElhinney 4.00 10.00
CMU Colin Murphy 4.00 10.00
CP2 Corey Perry 8.00 20.00
CP3 Corey Perry 10.00 25.00
CSA Curtis Sanford 8.00 20.00
CW2 Cam Ward 10.00 25.00
DBO Dustin Boyd 6.00 15.00
DCA Daniel Carcillo 4.00 10.00
DDE David Desharnais 4.00 10.00
DDS Dan DaSilva 4.00 10.00
DHE Dany Heatley 10.00 25.00
DHU Dylan Hunter 5.00 12.00
DMC D'Arcy McConvey 4.00 10.00
DMI Drew MacIntyre 4.00 10.00
DP2 Dion Phaneuf 20.00 50.00
DPE Dustin Penner 6.00 15.00
DPZ Dmitri Patzold 5.00 12.00
DSB Dany Sabourin 4.00 10.00
EL2 Eric Lindros 15.00 40.00
EN2 Eric Nystrom 5.00 12.00
ES2 Eric Staal 15.00 40.00
GBE Garrett Bembridge 4.00 10.00
GCL Gerald Coleman 5.00 12.00
GHO Greg Hogeboom 4.00 10.00
GPL Geoff Platt 4.00 10.00
HL2 Henrik Lundqvist 40.00 100.00
JBC Jason Bacashihua 6.00 15.00
JC2 Jeff Carter 15.00 40.00
JC3 Jeff Carter 15.00 40.00
JCO Jeremy Colliton 6.00 15.00
JCR Jim Craig 10.00 25.00
JDA Jonathan D'Aversa 4.00 10.00
JFJ Jean-Francois Jacques 4.00 10.00
JHU Jiri Hudler 6.00 15.00
JOP John Pohl 6.00 15.00
JPG Justin Pogge 30.00 80.00
JPO Jason Pominville 8.00 20.00
JRY Joe Ryan 4.00 10.00
JSC Jeff Schultz 4.00 10.00
JT2 John Tavares 100.00 200.00
JTA Jeff Tambellini 6.00 15.00
JTE Joey Tenute 4.00 10.00
KL2 Kari Lehtonen 12.00 30.00
LRD Liam Reddox 4.00 10.00
LST Logan Stephenson 4.00 10.00
MAP Marc-Antoine Pouliot 8.00 20.00
MB2 Martin Brodeur 40.00 80.00
MBR Mike Brodeur 6.00 15.00
MC2 Mike Cammalleri 5.00 12.00
MCL Mathieu Carle 4.00 10.00
MEL Matt Ellison 4.00 10.00
MFI Mark Fistric 4.00 10.00
MFU Michael Funk 4.00 10.00
MGL Mike Glumac 4.00 10.00
MHA Mark Hartigan 6.00 15.00
MHO Mareк Horsky 4.00 10.00
ML2 Mario Lemieux 40.00 100.00
ML3 Mario Lemieux 40.00 100.00
MR2 Mike Richards 10.00 25.00
MR3 Mike Richards 10.00 25.00
MRY Mathieu Roy 6.00 15.00
MSP Martin St. Pierre 4.00 10.00
MXB Maxime Boisclair 6.00 15.00
MXO Maxime Ouellet 4.00 10.00
NBG Nicklas Bergfors 6.00 15.00
POS Patrick O'Sullivan 8.00 20.00
PR2 Patrick Roy 40.00 100.00
PR3 Patrick Roy 40.00 80.00
PRI Pekka Rinne 5.00 12.00
PSJ Peter Sejna 4.00 10.00
RB2 Ray Bourque 25.00 60.00
RBE Rejean Beauchemin 5.00 12.00
RE2 Ray Emery 6.00 15.00
RGI Rod Gilbert 6.00 15.00
RH2 Ron Hextall 10.00 25.00
RHA Ron Hainsey 6.00 15.00
RHI Ryan Hillier 4.00 10.00
RMC Ryan MacDonald 5.00 12.00
RRO Rafael Rotter 4.00 10.00
RSH Ryan Shannon 4.00 10.00
RST Ryan Stone 4.00 10.00
RVE Ryan Vesce 4.00 10.00
RWH Ryan White 4.00 10.00
SBE Shawn Belle 4.00 10.00
SBR Steve Bernier 8.00 20.00
SC2 Sidney Crosby 75.00 150.00
SC3 Sidney Crosby 75.00 150.00
SGA Steve Gainey 4.00 10.00
SKO Sergei Kostitsyn 6.00 15.00
SY2 Steve Yzerman 40.00 80.00
TKE Ted Kennedy 6.00 15.00
TMK Tomi Maki 4.00 10.00
TPC Tomas Plekanec 4.00 10.00
TPK Thomas Pock 4.00 10.00
TV2 Thomas Vanek 12.00 30.00
BRH2 Brett Hull 12.00 30.00
EMA2 Evgeni Malkin 75.00 200.00
EMA3 Evgeni Malkin 75.00 200.00
GLF2 Guy Lafleur 10.00 25.00
JTH2 Jose Theodore 8.00 20.00
MSV2 Marek Svatos 5.00 12.00
BP Martin Brodeur
Justin Pogge
CM2 Jim Craig
Al Montoya
HK Dany Heatley
Ilya Kovalchuk
LN Henrik Lundqvist
Antero Niittymaki
LT2 Eric Lindros
John Tavares
PL Petr Prucha
Henrik Lundqvist
RP Larry Robinson
Dion Phaneuf
RT Patrick Roy
Jose Theodore
YC2 Jim Craig
Vladislav Tretiak

2005-06 ITG Heroes and Prospects Autographs Update

ONE PER UPDATE BOX
AAE Angelo Esposito SP 75.00 200.00
AFB Francois Bouchard 3.00 8.00
AFN Filip Novak 3.00 8.00
AMF Michael Frolik SP 25.00 60.00
AOF Ondrej Fiala 3.00 8.00
ARN Robert Nilsson 4.00 10.00
ASK Staffan Kronwall 3.00 8.00
ATD Tysen Dowzak 3.00 8.00
ATF Tomas Fleischmann 4.00 10.00
ABSH Ben Shutron 3.00 8.00
ACBT Chris Beckford-Tseu 15.00 40.00
ACHT Cristobal Huet SP
ADRI Danny Richmond 3.00 8.00
ADRU David Ruzicka SP
AJGL Jeff Glass 5.00 12.00
AJHO Jamie Holden 3.00 8.00
AMCO Matthew Corrente 4.00 10.00
AMKS Mark Stuart 4.00 10.00
AMSZ Marek Schwarz SP 15.00 30.00
ARE3 Ray Emery SP 6.00 15.00
ARRG Richie Regehr 3.00 8.00
DAET John Tavares 125.00 250.00
Angelo Esposito

2005-06 ITG Heroes and Prospects CHL Grads

PRINT RUN 70 SETS
GOLD PRINT RUN 10 SETS
GOLD NOT PRICED DUE TO SCARCITY
CG1 Marc-Antoine Pouliot 6.00 15.00
CG2 Gilbert Brule 10.00 25.00
CG3 Jeff Carter 12.00 30.00
CG4 Mike Richards 6.00 15.00
CG5 Mario Lemieux 20.00 50.00
CG6 Patrick Roy 15.00 40.00
CG7 Steve Yzerman 15.00 40.00
CG8 Guy Lafleur 10.00 25.00
CG9 Dion Phaneuf 15.00 40.00
CG10 Ryan Getzlaf 10.00 25.00
CG11 Corey Perry 8.00 20.00
CG12 Ray Bourque 10.00 25.00
CG13 Grant Fuhr 10.00 25.00
CG14 Martin Brodeur 12.00 30.00
CG15 Eric Fehr 6.00 15.00
CG16 Sidney Crosby 25.00 60.00

2005-06 ITG Heroes and Prospects Complete Jerseys

PRINT RUN 10 SETS
NOT PRICED DUE TO SCARCITY
UNPRICED GOLD 1/1's EXIST
CJ1 Al Montoya
CJ2 Gilbert Brule
CJ3 David Bolland
CJ4 Zach Parise
CJ5 Mike Richards
CJ6 Jeff Carter
CJ7 Shawn Belle
CJ8 Chris Bourque
CJ9 John Tavares
CJ10 Carey Price
CJ11 Robbie Schremp
CJ12 Bryan Little
CJ13 Pierre-Marc Bouchard
CJ14 Alexander Ovechkin
CJ15 Corey Perry
CJ16 Antero Niittymaki
CJ17 Mikko Koivu
CJ18 Bobby Ryan
CJ19 Jason Spezza
CJ20 Cam Ward
CJ21 Guillaume Latendresse
CJ22 Marc-Andre Fleury
CJ23 Patrice Bergeron
CJ24 Evgeni Malkin
CJ25 Sidney Crosby
CJ26 Eric Staal
CJ27 Thomas Vanek
CJ28 Brad Boyes
CJ29 Sean Bergenheim
CJ30 Alexander Perezhogin
CJ31 Dion Phaneuf
CJ32 Jay Bouwmeester
CJ33 Marc Staal
CJ34 Benoit Pouliot
CJ35 Gerald Coleman
CJ36 Rejean Beauchemin
CJ37 Justin Pogge
CJ38 Patrick Eaves
CJ39 Jeff Tambellini
CJ40 Chris Campoli

2005-06 ITG Heroes and Prospects Complete Logos

STATED PRINT RUN 1 SET
NOT PRICED DUE TO SCARCITY
AHL1 Mikko Koivu
AHL2 Brandon Bochenski
AHL3 Pavel Vorobiev
AHL4 Pascal Leclaire
AHL5 Brian Sutherby
AHL6 Andy Hilbert
AHL7 Brent Burns
AHL8 Boyd Gordon
AHL9 Jason LaBarbera
AHL10 Denis Hamel
AHL11 Ryan Whitney
AHL12 Lawrence Nycholat
AHL13 Brad Boyes
AHL14 Patrick Eaves
AHL15 Adam Munro
AHL16 Al Montoya
AHL17 Brent Krahn
AHL18 Jeff Tambellini
AHL19 Dennis Wideman
AHL20 Yan Stastny
AHL21 Chris Bourque
AHL22 Keith Ballard
AHL23 Matt Ellison
AHL24 Chris Beckford-Tseu
CHL1 Bobby Ryan
CHL2 Guillaume Latendresse
CHL3 Devin Setoguchi
CHL4 Chris Durand
CHL5 Kenndal McArdle
CHL6 Benoit Pouliot
CHL7 Carey Price
CHL8 Shea Weber
CHL9 Marek Zagrapan
CHL10 Marc Staal
CHL11 Eric Staal
CHL12 Gilbert Brule
CHL13 Dany Roussin
CHL14 Alexandre Vincent
CHL15 David Bolland
CHL16 John Tavares
CHL17 Luc Bourdon
CHL18 Blake Comeau
CHL19 Kristofer Westblom
CHL20 Robbie Schremp
CHL21 Tyler Mosienko
CHL22 Patrick O'Sullivan
CHL23 Gerald Coleman
CHL24 Justin Pogge
CHL25 Marc-Andre Fleury
ECHL1 Mike Brodeur

2005-06 ITG Heroes and Prospects Emblems

*EMBLEMS: .75X TO 2X JSY HI
PRINT RUN 30 SETS
GOLD PRINT RUN 10 SETS
GOLD NOT PRICED DUE TO SCARCITY
GUE36 Carey Price 40.00 100.00
GUE49 Evgeni Malkin 100.00 200.00
GUE53 Sidney Crosby 150.00 300.00
GUE54 Alexander Ovechkin 75.00 200.00
GUE65 John Tavares 75.00 200.00
GUE89 Evgeni Malkin 100.00 200.00
GUE90 Sidney Crosby 125.00 250.00
GUE91 Alexander Ovechkin 75.00 200.00
GUE98 Carey Price 40.00 100.00

2005-06 ITG Heroes and Prospects Future Teammates

PRINT RUN 30 SETS
FT1 P.Bouchard/M.Koivu 10.00 25.00
FT2 J.Pitkanen/A.Niittymaki 10.00 25.00
FT3 C.Perry/R.Getzlaf 15.00 40.00
FT4 M.Fleury/M.Lemieux 50.00 125.00
FT5 J.Spezza/B.Bochenski 20.00 50.00
FT6 C.Ward/E.Staal 20.00 50.00
FT7 D.Keon/F.Mahovlich 20.00 50.00
FT8 P.Roy/R.Bourque 25.00 60.00
FT9 P.LaFontaine/G.Fuhr 15.00 40.00
FT10 P.Bergeron/B.Boyes 15.00 40.00
FT11 R.Bourque/C.Neely 20.00 50.00
FT12 B.Hull/G.Hall 20.00 50.00
FT13 S.Crosby/E.Malkin 125.00 200.00
FT14 Alexander Ovechkin 50.00 100.00
Eric Fehr

2005-06 ITG Heroes and Prospects He Shoots-He Scores Prizes

PRINT RUN 20 SER.#'d SETS
NOT PRICED DUE TO SCARCITY
1 Sidney Crosby
Mario Lemieux
2 Guillaume Latendresse
Guy Lafleur
3 Kari Lehtonen
Martin Brodeur
4 Dion Phaneuf
Ray Bourque
5 Jose Theodore
Patrick Roy
6 Evgeni Malkin
Alexander Ovechkin
7 Benoit Pouliot
Steve Yzerman
8 Alexander Ovechkin
Mario Lemieux
9 Jay Bouwmeester
Brian Leetch
10 Carey Price
Jose Theodore
11 Evgeni Malkin
Mario Lemieux
12 Tyler Mosienko
Bill Mosienko
13 Eric Staal
Marc Staal
14 Brett Hull
Bobby Hull
15 Danny Syvret
Dan Fritsche
16 Corey Perry
David Bolland
17 Kristofer Westblom
Blake Comeau
18 Bobby Ryan
Ryan Getzlaf
19 Kari Lehtonen
Alexander Ovechkin
20 Patrice Bergeron
Brad Boyes
21 Derek Roy
Ryan Miller
22 Brent Krahn
Dion Phaneuf
23 Cam Ward
Eric Staal
24 Brent Seabrook
Pavel Vorobiev
25 Wojtek Wolski
Marek Svatos
26 Pascal Leclaire
Dan Fritsche
27 Marc-Antoine Pouliot
Rob Schremp
28 Jay Bouwmeester
Anthony Stewart
29 Jason LaBarbera
Mike Cammalleri
30 Mikko Koivu
Patrick O'Sullivan
31 Kyle Chipchura
Guillaume Latendresse
32 Scottie Upshall
Dan Hamhuis
33 Brandon Bochenski
Jason Spezza
34 Antero Niittymaki
Joni Pitkanen
35 Jeff Carter
Mike Richards
36 Sidney Crosby
Evgeni Malkin
37 Marc-Andre Fleury
Ryan Whitney
38 Sidney Crosby
Carlo Colaiacovo
39 Ryan Kesler
Alex Auld
40 Alexander Ovechkin
Eric Fehr
41 Alexander Ovechkin
Alexander Radulov
42 Mario Lemieux
Evgeni Malkin
43 Steve Yzerman
John Tavares
44 Patrick Roy
Angelo Esposito
45 Mark Messier
Steve Downie
46 Frank Mahovlich
Benoit Pouliot
47 Martin Brodeur
Carey Price
48 Jaromir Jagr
Michael Frolik
49 Terry Sawchuk
Leland Irving
50 Maurice Richard
John Tavares
51 Alexander Ovechkin
Dion Phaneuf
52 Mario Lemieux
Jordan Staal
53 Steve Yzerman
Patrick O'Sullivan
54 Patrick Roy
Corey Crawford
55 Mark Messier
Peter Mueller
56 Tim Horton
Marc Staal
57 Martin Brodeur
Marek Schwarz
58 Jaromir Jagr
Jiri Tlusty
59 Brett Hull
Ryan Getzlaf
60 Johnny Bower
Justin Pogge

2005-06 ITG Heroes and Prospects Hero Memorabilia

HM1-HM20 PRINT RUN 50 SETS
HM21-HM41 PRINT RUN 30 SETS
HM42-56 PRINT RUN 60 SETS
HM1 Mario Lemieux 30.00 80.00
HM2 Ray Bourque 10.00 25.00
HM3 Cam Neely 6.00 15.00
HM4 Doug Gilmour 6.00 15.00
HM5 Wendel Clark 6.00 15.00
HM6 Stan Mikita 6.00 15.00
HM7 Pat LaFontaine 6.00 15.00
HM8 Patrick Roy 20.00 50.00
HM9 Dino Ciccarelli 6.00 15.00
HM10 Ed Giacomin 12.50 30.00
HM11 Vladislav Tretiak 15.00 40.00
HM12 Brad Park 6.00 15.00
HM13 Brett Hull 8.00 20.00
HM14 Brian Leetch 6.00 15.00
HM15 Martin Brodeur 25.00 60.00
HM16 Steve Yzerman 12.50 30.00
HM17 Jose Theodore 8.00 20.00
HM18 Bobby Hull 10.00 25.00
HM19 Jean Beliveau 20.00 50.00
HM20 Guy Lafleur 10.00 25.00
HM21 Frank Mahovlich 8.00 20.00
HM22 Grant Fuhr 12.00 30.00
HM23 Glenn Hall 6.00 15.00
HM24 Gerry Cheevers 15.00 40.00
HM25 Marcel Dionne 6.00 15.00
HM26 Phil Esposito 12.50 30.00
HM27 Valeri Kharlamov 20.00 50.00
HM28 Tony Esposito 8.00 20.00
HM29 Bobby Clarke 10.00 25.00
HM30 Eddie Shore 8.00 20.00
HM31 Bernie Parent 10.00 25.00
HM32 Mike Bossy 12.50 30.00
HM33 Jean Ratelle 15.00 40.00
HM34 Gump Worsley 12.00 30.00
HM35 Darryl Sittler 8.00 20.00
HM36 Jacques Plante 35.00 60.00
HM37 Steve Shutt 8.00 20.00
HM38 Ted Lindsay 8.00 20.00
HM39 Red Kelly 8.00 20.00
HM40 Johnny Bower 12.50 30.00
HM41 Dave Keon 15.00 40.00
HM42 Borje Salming 15.00 40.00
HM43 Lanny McDonald 6.00 15.00
HM44 Rod Gilbert 6.00 15.00
HM45 Eric Lindros 6.00 15.00
HM46 Ilya Kovalchuk 10.00 25.00
HM47 Dany Heatley 10.00 25.00
HM48 George Hainsworth 30.00 80.00
HM49 Bill Barber 6.00 15.00
HM50 Serge Savard 6.00 15.00
HM51 Guy Lapointe 6.00 15.00
HM52 Yvan Cournoyer 6.00 15.00
HM53 Denis Potvin 10.00 25.00
HM54 Larry Robinson 6.00 15.00
HM55 Rogie Vachon 6.00 15.00
HM56 Mark Howe 6.00 15.00

2005-06 ITG Heroes and Prospects Hero Memorabilia Dual

PRINT RUN 30 SETS
HDM1 Bill Mosienko 8.00 20.00
HDM2 Brett Hull 15.00 40.00
HDM3 Wendel Clark 12.50 30.00
HDM4 Patrick Roy 25.00 60.00
HDM5 Ray Bourque 15.00 40.00
HDM6 Cam Neely 10.00 25.00
HDM7 Doug Gilmour 8.00 20.00
HDM8 Steve Yzerman 25.00 60.00
HDM9 Brian Leetch 10.00 25.00
HDM10 Grant Fuhr 15.00 40.00
HDM11 Jose Theodore 10.00 25.00
HDM12 Guy Lafleur 10.00 25.00
HDM13 Dave Keon 8.00 20.00
HDM14 Mario Lemieux 25.00 60.00
HDM15 Bobby Hull 12.50 30.00
HDM16 Stan Mikita 8.00 20.00
HDM17 Ron Hextall 12.50 30.00

2005-06 ITG Heroes and Prospects Jerseys

PRINT RUN 100 SETS
GOLD PRINT RUN 10 SETS
GOLD NOT PRICED DUE TO SCARCITY
GUJ1 Bobby Ryan 10.00 20.00
GUJ2 Brian Sutherby 4.00 10.00
GUJ3 Jay Bouwmeester 8.00 20.00
GUJ4 Denis Hamel 6.00 15.00
GUJ5 Andy Hilbert 6.00 15.00
GUJ6 Mike Cammalleri 6.00 15.00
GUJ7 Mikko Koivu 6.00 15.00
GUJ8 Boyd Gordon 4.00 10.00
GUJ9 Brad Boyes 6.00 15.00

Card	Low	High
GUJ10 Ryan Kesler	4.00	10.00
GUJ11 Joni Pitkanen	6.00	15.00
GUJ12 Pascal Leclaire	4.00	10.00
GUJ13 Derek Roy	6.00	15.00
GUJ14 Ryan Whitney	8.00	20.00
GUJ15 Jason Spezza	8.00	20.00
GUJ16 Eric Staal	8.00	20.00
GUJ17 Dustin Brown	4.00	10.00
GUJ18 Chuck Kobasew	6.00	15.00
GUJ19 Ray Emery	6.00	15.00
GUJ20 Jason LaBarbera	4.00	10.00
GUJ21 Michel Ouellet	8.00	20.00
GUJ22 Antero Niittymaki	8.00	20.00
GUJ23 Cam Ward	8.00	20.00
GUJ24 Marc-Andre Fleury	10.00	25.00
GUJ25 Devin Setoguchi	6.00	15.00
GUJ26 Shea Weber	6.00	15.00
GUJ27 Chris Durand	4.00	10.00
GUJ28 Guillaume Latendresse	10.00	25.00
GUJ29 Brandon Bochenski	4.00	10.00
GUJ30 Pavel Vorobiev	4.00	10.00
GUJ31 P-M Bouchard	4.00	10.00
GUJ32 Patrice Bergeron	8.00	20.00
GUJ33 Kenndal McArdle	4.00	10.00
GUJ34 Patrick O'Sullivan	8.00	20.00
GUJ35 Marek Zagrapan	6.00	15.00
GUJ36 Carey Price	6.00	15.00
GUJ37 Corey Crawford	4.00	10.00
GUJ38 Rob Schremp	8.00	20.00
GUJ39 Lee Goren	4.00	10.00
GUJ40 Tyler Mosienko	4.00	10.00
GUJ41 Brent Burns	4.00	10.00
GUJ42 Travis Roche	4.00	10.00
GUJ43 Kristofer Westblom	4.00	10.00
GUJ44 Lawrence Nycholat	4.00	10.00
GUJ45 Wojtek Wolski	8.00	20.00
GUJ46 Mathieu Garon	4.00	10.00
GUJ47 Adam Munro	4.00	10.00
GUJ48 Blake Comeau	4.00	10.00
GUJ49 Evgeni Malkin	50.00	80.00
GUJ50 Benoit Pouliot	4.00	10.00
GUJ51 Gerald Coleman	4.00	10.00
GUJ52 Marc Staal	8.00	20.00
GUJ53 Sidney Crosby	50.00	80.00
GUJ54 Alexander Ovechkin	40.00	60.00
GUJ55 Al Montoya	8.00	20.00
GUJ56 Gilbert Brule	8.00	20.00
GUJ57 David Bolland	4.00	10.00
GUJ58 Zach Parise	8.00	20.00
GUJ59 Mike Richards	8.00	20.00
GUJ60 Jeff Carter	12.00	30.00
GUJ61 Jeff Tambellini	6.00	15.00
GUJ62 Chris Campoli	4.00	10.00
GUJ63 Shawn Belle	4.00	10.00
GUJ64 Chris Bourque	8.00	20.00
GUJ65 John Tavares	25.00	50.00
GUJ66 Tim Thomas	8.00	20.00
GUJ67 Justin Pogge	25.00	40.00
GUJ68 Bryan Little	10.00	25.00
GUJ69 Patrick Eaves	6.00	15.00
GUJ70 Brett Sutter	4.00	10.00
GUJ71 Yan Stastny	6.00	15.00
GUJ72 Gerald Coleman	4.00	10.00
GUJ73 Rejean Beauchemin	6.00	15.00
GUJ74 Chris Beckford-Tseu	6.00	15.00
GUJ75 Luc Bourdon	8.00	20.00
GUJ76 Matt Ellison	4.00	10.00
GUJ77 Brian Pothier	4.00	10.00
GUJ78 Alexandre Vincent	4.00	10.00
GUJ79 Corey Perry	8.00	20.00
GUJ80 Anthony Stewart	4.00	10.00
GUJ81 Ryan Getzlaf	8.00	20.00
GUJ82 Eric Fehr	6.00	15.00
GUJ83 Keith Ballard	4.00	10.00
GUJ84 Marc-Antoine Pouliot	6.00	15.00
GUJ85 Julien Ellis-Plante	8.00	20.00
GUJ86 Dany Roussin	4.00	10.00
GUJ87 Eric Nystrom	8.00	20.00
GUJ88 Brent Krahn	6.00	15.00
GUJ89 Evgeni Malkin	50.00	80.00
GUJ90 Sidney Crosby	50.00	80.00
GUJ91 Alexander Ovechkin	40.00	60.00
GUJ92 Maxime Ouellet	8.00	20.00
GUJ93 Carlo Colaiacovo	4.00	10.00
GUJ94 Henrik Lundqvist	15.00	30.00
GUJ95 Alexander Perezhogin	8.00	20.00
GUJ96 Sean Bergenheim	4.00	10.00
GUJ97 Kari Lehtonen	8.00	20.00
GUJ98 Jason Bacashihua	8.00	20.00
GUJ99 Jordin Tootoo	8.00	20.00
GUJ100 Marek Svatos	8.00	20.00
GUJ101 Dennis Wideman	4.00	10.00
GUJ102 Colby Armstrong	6.00	15.00
GUJ103 Mike Brodeur	4.00	10.00
GUJ104 Matt Foy	4.00	10.00
GUJ105 Grant Stevenson	4.00	10.00
GUJ106 Ari Ahonen	6.00	15.00
GUJ107 Andrew Ladd	6.00	15.00
GUJ108 Adam Hauser	6.00	15.00
GUJ109 Dion Phaneuf	12.00	30.00
GUJ110 Jeff Schultz	4.00	10.00
GUJ111 Petr Prucha	10.00	20.00
GUJ112 Alexander Mogilny	6.00	15.00
GUJ113 Devan Dubnyk	10.00	20.00
GUJ114 Thomas Vanek	10.00	20.00
GUJ115 Carey Price	8.00	20.00
GUJ116 Tom Pyatt	4.00	10.00

2005-06 ITG Heroes and Prospects Making the Bigs

PRINT RUN 40 SETS

Card	Low	High
MTB1 [illegible]	10.00	[illegible]
MTB2 Jason Spezza	10.00	25.00
MTB3 P-M Bouchard	5.00	12.00
MTB4 Brian Sutherby	5.00	12.00
MTB5 Eric Staal	10.00	25.00
MTB6 Boyd Gordon	5.00	12.00
MTB7 Alexander Ovechkin	30.00	80.00
MTB8 Ray Emery	8.00	20.00
MTB9 Derek Roy	8.00	20.00
MTB10 Maxime Ouellet	5.00	12.00
MTB11 Dustin Brown	5.00	12.00
MTB12 Scottie Upshall	5.00	12.00
MTB13 Guillaume Latendresse	10.00	25.00
MTB14 Mike Richards	6.00	15.00
MTB15 Jeff Carter	12.00	30.00
MTB16 Gerald Coleman	5.00	12.00

2005-06 ITG Heroes and Prospects Measuring Up

PRINT RUN 60 SETS
GOLD PRINT RUN 10 SETS
GOLD NOT PRICED DUE TO SCARCITY

Card	Low	High
MU1 Cam Ward / Patrick Roy	15.00	40.00
MU2 Jason LaBarbera / Patrick Roy	15.00	40.00
MU3 Julien Ellis-Plante / Patrick Roy	15.00	40.00
MU4 Jason Bacashihua / Patrick Roy	15.00	40.00
MU5 Alex Auld / Patrick Roy	15.00	40.00
MU6 Scott Clemmensen / Patrick Roy	15.00	40.00
MU7 Maxime Ouellet / Patrick Roy	15.00	40.00
MU8 Brent Krahn / Patrick Roy	15.00	40.00
MU9 Henrik Lundqvist / Patrick Roy	30.00	80.00
MU10 Ryan Miller / Patrick Roy	30.00	80.00
MU11 Antero Niittymaki / Patrick Roy	20.00	40.00
MU12 Marc-Andre Fleury / Patrick Roy	15.00	40.00
MU13 Gerald Coleman / Patrick Roy	15.00	40.00
MU14 Devan Dubnyk / Patrick Roy	15.00	40.00
MU15 Rejean Beauchemin / Patrick Roy	15.00	40.00
MU16 Kelly Guard / Patrick Roy	15.00	40.00
MU17 Carey Price / Patrick Roy	20.00	50.00
MU18 Al Montoya / Patrick Roy	15.00	40.00
MU19 Justin Pogge / Patrick Roy	20.00	50.00
MU20 Kari Lehtonen / Patrick Roy	20.00	50.00

2005-06 ITG Heroes and Prospects Memorial Cup

Card	Low	High
COMPLETE SET	8.00	20.00

2005-06 ITG Heroes and Prospects Nameplates

PRINT RUN 20 SETS
NOT PRICED DUE TO SCARCITY
UNPRICED GOLD 1/1's EXIST

2005-06 ITG Heroes and Prospects National Pride

NPR1-12/22-41 PRINT RUN 60 SETS
NPR13-21 PRIN RUN 20 SETS
NPR12-21 NOT PRICED DUE TO SCARCITY

Card	Low	High
NPR1 Kari Lehtonen	6.00	15.00
NPR2 Marc-Andre Fleury	8.00	20.00
NPR3 Dany Roussin	4.00	10.00
NPR4 Jason Spezza	8.00	20.00
NPR5 Jay Bouwmeester	4.00	10.00
NPR6 Dion Phaneuf	15.00	40.00
NPR7 P-M Bouchard	4.00	10.00
NPR8 Mikko Koivu	4.00	10.00
NPR9 Mike Cammalleri	4.00	10.00
NPR10 Evgeni Malkin	30.00	80.00
NPR11 Sidney Crosby	40.00	100.00
NPR12 Alexander Ovechkin	30.00	80.00
NPR13 Tony Esposito		
NPR14 Darryl Sittler		
NPR15 Patrick Roy		
NPR16 Bobby Clarke		
NPR17 Martin Brodeur		
NPR18 Brett Hull		
NPR19 Steve Yzerman		
NPR20 Brian Leetch		
NPR21 Pat LaFontaine		
NPR22 Pelle Lindbergh	15.00	40.00
NPR23 Phil Esposito	8.00	20.00
NPR24 Lanny McDonald	4.00	10.00
NPR25 Dany Heatley	8.00	20.00
NPR26 Borje Salming	6.00	15.00
NPR27 Eric Lindros	[illegible]	[illegible]
NPR28 Gilbert Perreault	6.00	15.00
NPR29 Gerry Cheevers	8.00	20.00
NPR30 Larry Robinson	6.00	15.00
NPR31 Ilya Kovalchuk	12.00	30.00
NPR32 Justin Pogge	20.00	50.00
NPR33 Alexander Ovechkin	30.00	80.00
NPR34 Bobby Ryan	8.00	20.00
NPR35 Evgeni Malkin	30.00	80.00
NPR36 Sidney Crosby	40.00	100.00
NPR37 Corey Perry	8.00	20.00
NPR38 Jeff Carter	10.00	25.00
NPR39 Mike Richards	6.00	15.00
NPR40 Al Montoya	6.00	15.00
NPR41 Anthony Stewart	4.00	10.00

2005-06 ITG Heroes and Prospects Net Prospects

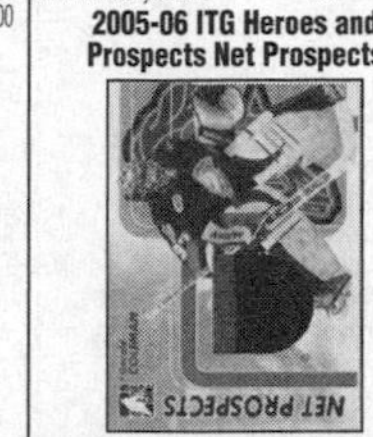

PRINT RUN 80 SETS
GOLD PRINT RUN 10 SETS
GOLD NOT PRICED DUE TO SCARCITY

Card	Low	High
NP1 Kari Lehtonen	8.00	20.00
NP2 Marc-Andre Fleury	8.00	20.00
NP3 Antero Niittymaki	8.00	20.00
NP4 Adam Hauser	4.00	10.00
NP5 Mathieu Garon	4.00	10.00
NP6 Pascal Leclaire	4.00	10.00
NP7 Ray Emery	6.00	15.00
NP8 Adam Munro	4.00	10.00
NP9 Cam Ward	8.00	20.00
NP10 Jason LaBarbera	4.00	10.00
NP11 Ryan Miller	8.00	20.00
NP12 Brent Krahn	4.00	10.00
NP13 Alex Auld	6.00	15.00
NP14 Devan Dubnyk	4.00	10.00
NP15 Carey Price	6.00	15.00
NP16 Kyle Moir	4.00	10.00
NP17 Corey Crawford	4.00	10.00
NP18 Kevin Nastiuk	4.00	10.00
NP19 Jonathan Boutin	4.00	10.00
NP20 Gerald Coleman	6.00	15.00
NP21 Kristofer Westblom	4.00	10.00

2005-06 ITG Heroes and Prospects Net Prospects Dual

PRINT RUN 80 SETS
GOLD PRINT RUN 10 SETS
GOLD NOT PRICED DUE TO SCARCITY

Card	Low	High
NPD1 Maxime Ouellet / Alex Auld	8.00	20.00
NPD2 Adam Hauser / Jason LaBarbera	8.00	20.00
NPD3 Antero Niittymaki / Rejean Beauchemin	8.00	20.00
NPD4 Kristofer Westblom / Gerald Coleman	8.00	20.00
NPD5 Al Montoya / Pascal Leclaire	15.00	40.00
NPD6 Brent Krahn / Cam Ward	8.00	20.00
NPD7 Kari Lehtonen / Marc-Andre Fleury	20.00	50.00
NPD8 Devan Dubnyk / Justin Pogge	15.00	40.00
NPD9 Chris Beckford-Tseu / Mike Brodeur	8.00	20.00
NPD10 Carey Price / Julien Ellis-Plante	8.00	20.00

2005-06 ITG Heroes and Prospects Numbers

*NUMBERS: .75X TO 2X JSY HI
PRINT RUN 30 SETS
GOLD PRINT RUN 10 SETS
GOLD NOT PRICED DUE TO SCARCITY

Card	Low	High
GUN49 Evgeni Malkin	100.00	200.00
GUN53 Sidney Crosby	100.00	250.00
GUN54 Alexander Ovechkin	75.00	200.00
GUN89 Evgeni Malkin	100.00	200.00
GUN90 Sidney Crosby	100.00	200.00
GUN91 Alexander Ovechkin	75.00	200.00

2005-06 ITG Heroes and Prospects Oh Canada

STATED PRINT RUN 50 #'d SETS

Card	Low	High
OC1 Liam Reddox	8.00	20.00
OC2 Julien Ellis-Plante	8.00	20.00
OC3 Cody Bass	8.00	20.00
OC4 Derick Brassard	8.00	20.00
OC5 Ryan O'Marra	8.00	20.00
OC6 Kristopher Letang	10.00	25.00
OC7 David Bolland	8.00	20.00
OC8 Benoit Pouliot	10.00	25.00
OC9 Blake Comeau	8.00	20.00
OC10 Ryan Parent	10.00	25.00
OC11 Dustin Boyd	10.00	25.00
OC12 Steve Downie	10.00	25.00
OC13 Kyle Chipchura	8.00	20.00
OC14 Justin Peters	8.00	20.00
OC15 Dustin Kohn	8.00	20.00
OC16 Justin Keller	8.00	20.00
OC17 Dan LaCosta	8.00	20.00

2005-06 ITG Heroes and Prospects Shooting Stars

Card	Low	High
COMPLETE SET (12)	8.00	15.00
AS1 Jason LaBarbera	.75	2.00

Card	Low	High
AS2 Lawrence Nycholat	.40	1.00
AS3 Dennis Wideman	.40	1.00
AS4 Jason Spezza	.75	2.00
AS5 Mike Cammalleri	.75	2.00
AS6 Michel Ouellet	.40	1.00
AS7 Kari Lehtonen	2.00	5.00
AS8 Niklas Kronwall	.75	2.00
AS9 Joni Pitkanen	.75	2.00
AS10 Zach Parise	.75	2.00
AS11 Andy Hilbert	.40	1.00
AS12 Dustin Brown	1.00	2.00

2005-06 ITG Heroes and Prospects Team Cherry

Card	Low	High
TC1 Ty Wishart	2.00	5.00
TC2 Mike Weber	2.00	5.00
TC3 Chris Stewart	2.00	5.00
TC4 Joe Ryan	2.00	5.00
TC5 Theo Peckham	2.00	5.00
TC6 Peter Mueller	3.00	8.00
TC7 Jamie McGinn	2.00	5.00
TC8 Ben Maxwell	2.00	5.00
TC9 Bobby Hughes	2.00	5.00
TC10 Ryan Hillier	2.00	5.00
TC11 Nick Foligno	2.00	5.00
TC12 John de Gray	2.00	5.00
TC13 Cal Clutterbuck	2.00	5.00
TC14 Mathieu Carle	2.00	5.00
TC15 Brady Calla	2.00	5.00
TC16 Derick Brassard	2.50	6.00
TC17 Francois Bouchard	2.00	5.00
TC18 Jonathan Bernier	2.50	6.00
TC19 Matt Beleskey	2.00	5.00
TC20 Kevin Armstrong	2.00	5.00

2005-06 ITG Heroes and Prospects Team Orr

Card	Low	High
TO1 John Armstrong	2.00	5.00
TO2 Lukas Bohunicky	2.00	5.00
TO3 Benjamin Breault	2.00	5.00
TO4 Codey Burki	2.00	5.00
TO5 Matthew Corrente	2.00	5.00
TO6 Ryan Daniels	2.00	5.00
TO7 Tysen Dowzak	2.00	5.00
TO8 Cory Emmerton	2.00	5.00
TO9 Ondrej Fiala	2.00	5.00
TO10 Claude Giroux	2.50	6.00
TO11 Michael Grabner	2.50	6.00
TO12 Riley Holzapfel	2.00	5.00
TO13 Leland Irving	2.50	6.00
TO14 Bryan Little	3.00	8.00
TO15 Bob Sanguinetti	2.00	5.00
TO16 James Sheppard	2.00	5.00
TO17 Ben Shutron	2.00	5.00
TO18 Jordan Staal	3.00	8.00
TO19 Yvan Vishnevskiy	2.00	5.00
TO20 Ryan White	2.00	5.00

2006-07 ITG Heroes and Prospects

The final 50-cards in this set were issued as a factory set by ITG. Those factory sets included either an autograph or a game-used memorabilia card.

Card	Low	High
COMPLETE SET (150)	20.00	50.00
COMPLETE UPDATE SET (50)	10.00	20.00
1 Elmer Lach	.20	.50
2 Milt Schmidt	.20	.50
3 Brian Leetch	.30	.75
4 Peter Stastny	.20	.50
5 Mark Messier	.40	1.00
6 Willie O'Ree	.30	.75
7 Bryan Trottier	.20	.50
8 Jaromir Jagr	.40	1.00
9 Mario Lemieux	.75	2.00
10 Luc Robitaille	.30	.75
11 Dick Duff	.20	.50
12 Ron Francis	.20	.50
13 Guy Lafleur	.40	1.00
14 Patrick Roy	.75	2.00
15 Martin Brodeur	.60	1.50
16 Tim Thomas	.30	.75
17 Cristobal Huet	.40	1.00
18 Jeff Carter	.30	.75
19 Marc-Andre Fleury	.40	1.00
20 Billy Smith	.30	.75
21 Johnny Bower	.30	.75
22 Antero Niittymaki	.30	.75
23 Brad Boyes	.30	.75
24 Sidney Crosby	2.00	5.00
25 Cam Ward	.40	1.00
26 Kyle Wellwood	.20	.50
27 Jason Spezza	.30	.75
28 Wendel Clark	.30	.75
29 Denis Potvin	.20	.50
30 Bobby Clarke	.30	.75
31 Tony Voce	.20	.50
32 Martin Houle	.30	.75
33 Brendan Bell	.20	.50
34 Eric Fehr	.20	.50
35 Carsen Germyn	.20	.50
36 Yann Danis	.30	.75
37 Roman Voloshenko	.20	.50
38 Tomas Kopecky	.30	.75
39 Ben Ondrus	.20	.50
40 Nathan Marsters	.20	.50
41 Marc-Antoine Pouliot	.30	.75
42 Konstantin Pushkarev	.20	.50
43 Ian White	.20	.50
44 Jeremy Williams	.20	.50
45 Noah Welch	.20	.50
46 Rick Rypien	.20	.50
47 Lauri Tukonen	.20	.50
48 Danny Syvret	.20	.50
49 Mark Giordano	.20	.50
50 Andrew Penner	.20	.50
51 Aleksander Suglobov	.20	.50
52 David LeNeveu	.20	.50
53 Doug O'Brien	.20	.50
54 Martin St. Pierre	.20	.50
55 Dan Fritsche	.30	.75
56 Connor James	.20	.50
57 Dustin Penner	.30	.75
58 Ryan Vesce	.20	.50
59 Colby Genoway	.20	.50
60 Ben Walter	.20	.50
61 Richie Regehr	.20	.50
62 Trevor Gillies	.30	.75
63 Mark Hartigan	.20	.50
64 Garett Bembridge	.20	.50
65 Ladislav Smid	.20	.50
66 Braydon Coburn	.30	.75
67 Jeremy Colliton	.20	.50
68 Nathan Paetsch	.20	.50
69 Pavel Vorobiev	.20	.50
70 Matt Jones	.20	.50
71 Corey Locke	.20	.50
72 Corey Crawford	.30	.75
73 Erik Westrum	.20	.50
74 Patrick O'Sullivan	.30	.75
75 Jeff Tambellini	.20	.50
76 Al Montoya	.20	.50
77 Mathew Spiller	.20	.50
78 Nigel Dawes	.20	.50
79 Ryan Shannon	.20	.50
80 John Tavares / Steven Stamkos / Drew Doughty	4.00	10.00
81 Angelo Esposito	1.00	2.50
82 John Tavares	2.00	5.00
83 Jordan Staal	1.00	2.50
84 Derick Brassard	.40	1.00
85 Peter Mueller	.60	1.50
86 Bryan Little	.40	1.00
87 James Sheppard	.40	1.00
88 Cory Emmerton	.30	.75
89 Bob Sanguinetti	.20	.50
90 Ondrej Fiala	.20	.50
91 Logan Couture	.30	.75
92 Ty Wishart	.20	.50
93 Ryan Hillier	.20	.50
94 Jared Staal	1.00	2.50
95 Bobby Hughes	.20	.50
96 Brady Calla	.20	.50
97 Joe Ryan	.20	.50
98 Ivan Vishnevskiy	.20	.50
99 Gilbert Brule	.30	.75
100 Bud Holloway	.20	.50
101 Ben Maxwell	.20	.50
102 Matt Beleskey	.20	.50
103 John Armstrong	.20	.50
104 Michael Grabner	.30	.75
105 Oskar Osala	.20	.50
106 Jamie McGinn	.20	.50
107 Luke Lynes	.20	.50
108 Drew Doughty	.40	1.00
109 Alex Bourret	.30	.75
110 Chris Stewart	.30	.75
111 Jonathan Bernier	.75	2.00
112 Leland Irving	.60	1.50
113 Claude Giroux	.30	.75
114 Ryan Daniels	.20	.50
115 Nick Foligno	.30	.75
116 Matthew Corrente	.20	.50
117 Francois Bouchard	.20	.50
118 Brandon Sutter	.60	1.50
119 Michael Del Zotto	1.50	4.00
120 Sergei Kostitsyn	.60	1.50
121 Corey Syvret	.20	.50
122 Steve Downie	.40	1.00
123 Brett Sutter	.20	.50
124 Shawn Matthais	.20	.50
125 Alexander Radulov	.60	1.50
126 Guillaume Latendresse	1.00	2.50
127 Ryan White	.20	.50
128 Luc Bourdon	.30	.75
129 Colton Gillies	.20	.50
130 Marc Staal	.30	.75
131 Anze Kopitar	1.00	2.50
132 Jiri Tlusty	.60	1.50
133 Yuri Alexandrov	.20	.50
134 Tuukka Rask	1.25	3.00
135 Evgeni Malkin	1.25	3.00
136 Phil Kessel	.75	2.00
137 Alexander Vasyunov	.20	.50
138 Michael Frolik	.40	1.00
139 John Tavares	3.00	8.00
140 Justin Pogge	1.00	2.50
141 Jonathan Bernier	.75	2.00
142 Brandon Sutter	.60	1.50
143 Luc Bourdon	.75	2.00
144 Steve Downie	.60	1.50
145 Kristopher Letang	.40	1.00
146 Ryan Parent	.60	1.50
147 Sidney Crosby	2.00	5.00
148 Marc Staal	.60	1.50
149 Guillaume Latendresse	1.00	2.50
150 Tom Pyatt	.40	1.00
151 Joe Pavelski	.30	.75
152 Chris Harrington	.20	.50
153 Bill Thomas	.20	.50
154 Loui Eriksson	.30	.75
155 Benoit Pouliot	.30	.75
156 Eric Nystrom	.30	.75
157 Bryan Bickell	.20	.50
158 Nicklas Bergfors	.20	.50
159 Hugh Jessiman	.20	.50
160 Jiri Hudler	.30	.75
161 Alexander Radulov	.40	1.00
162 Mike Green	.20	.50
163 Staffan Kronwall	.20	.50
164 Drew Miller	.40	1.00
165 Brett Sterling	.20	.50
166 Jeff Taffe	.20	.50
167 Geoff Platt	.20	.50
168 Blake Comeau	.20	.50
169 Ryan Carter	.20	.50
170 Drew Stafford	.60	1.50
171 Petr Kalus	.40	1.00
172 Josh Hennessy	.30	.75
173 Rob Schremp	.30	.75
174 Janis Sprukts	.20	.50
175 Patrick Kane	6.00	15.00
176 Bobby Ryan	.20	.50
177 Devin Setoguchi	.30	.75
178 Michael Frolik	.40	1.00
179 Brodie Dupont	.20	.50
180 Tom Pyatt	.20	.50
181 Kenndal McArdle	.20	.50
182 Michael Caruso	.20	.50
183 James Neal	.30	.75
184 Ben Shutron	.20	.50
185 Marc-Andre Cliché	.20	.50
186 Felix Schutz	.20	.50
187 Cody Bass	.20	.50
188 Dustin Kohn	.20	.50
189 Marc-Edouard Vlasic	.30	.75
190 Dan Ryder	.20	.50
191 Mathieu Carle	.20	.50
192 Justin Azevedo	.20	.50
193 Kristofer Letang	.30	.75
194 Kris Russell	.30	.75
195 Patrick McNeill	.20	.50
196 Marc-Andre Gragnani	.20	.50
197 Cody Franson	.20	.50
198 Cal Clutterbuck	.20	.50
199 Jakub Voracek	.40	1.00
200 Sam Gagner	1.50	4.00

2006-07 ITG Heroes and Prospects Toronto Spring Expo

19 Marc-Andre Fleury

2006-07 ITG Heroes and Prospects AHL All-Star Emblems

*EMBLEMS: 1X TO 2.5X JERSEY HI
STATED PRINT RUN 30 SETS
GOLD VERSION /10 EXISTS
GOLD NOT PRICED DUE TO SCARCITY

2006-07 ITG Heroes and Prospects AHL All-Star Jerseys

STATED PRINT RUN 80 SETS
GOLD VERSION /10 EXISTS
GOLD NOT PRICED DUE TO SCARCITY

Card	Low	High
AJ01 Jeff Tambellini	4.00	10.00
AJ02 Martin St. Pierre	4.00	10.00
AJ03 Jiri Hudler	6.00	15.00
AJ04 John Pohl	6.00	15.00
AJ05 Yann Danis	6.00	15.00
AJ06 Patrick O'Sullivan	6.00	15.00
AJ07 Denis Hamel	6.00	15.00
AJ08 Keith Ballard	4.00	10.00
AJ09 Denis Shvidki	4.00	10.00
AJ10 Rick DiPietro	6.00	15.00
AJ11 Phillipe Sauve	6.00	15.00
AJ12 Kyle Wellwood	6.00	15.00

2006-07 ITG Heroes and Prospects AHL All-Star Numbers

*NUMBERS: 1X TO 2.5 X JERSEY HI
STATED PRINT RUN 30 SETS
GOLD VERSION /10 EXISTS
GOLD NOT PRICED DUE TO SCARCITY

2006-07 ITG Heroes and Prospects AHL Shooting Stars

Card	Low	High
COMPLETE SET (12)	6.00	15.00
AS01 Pekka Rinne	.75	2.00
AS02 Sven Butenschon	.40	1.00
AS03 Noah Welch	.75	2.00
AS04 Jiri Hudler	.75	2.00
AS05 John Pohl	.75	2.00
AS06 Erik Westrum	.75	2.00
AS07 Wade Flaherty	.75	2.00
AS08 Nathan Paetsch	.40	1.00
AS09 John Slaney	.40	1.00
AS10 Jimmy Roy	.40	1.00
AS11 Kirby Law	.40	1.00
AS12 Eric Fehr	.75	2.00

2006-07 ITG Heroes and Prospects Autographs

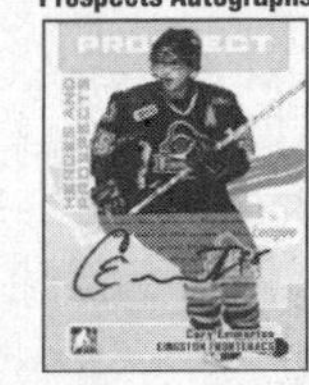

STATED ODDS 1:14

Card	Low	High
AAB Alex Bourret	5.00	12.00
AAE Angelo Esposito	40.00	80.00
AAK Anze Kopitar	25.00	50.00
AAN Antero Niittymaki	8.00	20.00
AAP Andrew Penner	5.00	12.00
AAR Alexander Radulov	15.00	40.00
AAS Aleksander Suglobov	4.00	10.00
AAV Alexander Vasyunov	5.00	12.00
ABB Brendan Bell	4.00	10.00
ABC Bobby Clarke	10.00	25.00
ABD Brodie Dupont	4.00	10.00
ABH Bobby Hughes	4.00	10.00
ABL Brian Leetch		
ABM Ben Maxwell	4.00	10.00
ABO Ben Ondrus	4.00	10.00
ABP Benoit Pouliot	5.00	12.00
ABR Bobby Ryan	4.00	10.00
ABT Bill Thomas	4.00	10.00
ABW Ben Walter	4.00	10.00
ACB Cody Bass	4.00	10.00
ACC Corey Crawford	5.00	12.00
ACE Cory Emmerton	5.00	12.00
ACF Cody Franson	4.00	10.00
ACG Carsen Germyn	4.00	10.00
ACH Cristobal Huet	15.00	40.00
ACJ Connor James	4.00	10.00
ACL Corey Locke	4.00	10.00
ACS Chris Stewart	5.00	12.00
ACW Cam Ward	10.00	25.00
ADB Derick Brassard	6.00	15.00
ADD Dick Duff	8.00	20.00
ADF Dan Fritsche	5.00	12.00
ADK Dustin Kohn	4.00	10.00
ADL David LeNeveu	6.00	15.00
ADM Drew Miller		
ADO Doug O'Brien	4.00	10.00
ADP Denis Potvin	6.00	15.00
ADR Dan Ryder	4.00	10.00
ADS Drew Stafford	8.00	20.00
AEF Eric Fehr	6.00	15.00
AEL Elmer Lach	10.00	25.00
AEM Evgeni Malkin	75.00	150.00
AEN Eric Nystrom	4.00	10.00
AEW Erik Westrum	6.00	15.00
AFB Francois Bouchard	4.00	10.00
AFS Felix Schutz	4.00	10.00
AGB Garett Bembridge	4.00	10.00
AGP Geoff Platt	4.00	10.00
AHJ Hugh Jessiman	4.00	10.00
AIV Ivan Vishnevskiy	5.00	12.00
AIW Ian White	5.00	12.00
AJA John Armstrong	4.00	10.00
AJC Jeremy Colliton	4.00	10.00
AJH Jiri Hudler	4.00	10.00
AJJ Jaromir Jagr		
AJM Jamie McGinn	4.00	10.00
AJN James Neal	4.00	10.00
AJP Justin Pogge	20.00	50.00
AJR Joe Ryan	5.00	12.00
AJS Jason Spezza	10.00	25.00
AJV Jakub Voracek	25.00	60.00
AJW Jeremy Williams	5.00	12.00
AKL Kristopher Letang	5.00	12.00
AKM Kenndal McArdle	4.00	10.00
AKP Konstantin Pushkarev	4.00	10.00
AKR Kris Russell	5.00	12.00
AKW Kyle Wellwood	6.00	15.00
ALC Logan Couture	8.00	20.00
ALE Loui Eriksson	4.00	10.00
ALI Leland Irving	10.00	25.00
ALL Luke Lynes	4.00	10.00
ALR Luc Robitaille	12.00	30.00
ALS Ladislav Smid	5.00	12.00
ALT Lauri Tukonen	5.00	12.00
AMB Martin Brodeur	25.00	60.00
AMC Matthew Corrente	4.00	10.00
AMF Michael Frolik	10.00	25.00
AMG Mike Green	4.00	10.00
AMH Martin Houle	6.00	15.00
AMJ Matt Jones	5.00	12.00
AML Mario Lemieux		
AMM Mark Messier	30.00	80.00
ANB Nicklas Bergfors	4.00	10.00
AND Nigel Dawes	5.00	12.00
ANF Nick Foligno	5.00	12.00
ANM Nathan Marsters	5.00	12.00
ANP Nathan Paetsch	4.00	10.00
ANW Noah Welch	5.00	12.00
AOF Ondrej Fiala	4.00	10.00
AOO Oskar Osala	4.00	10.00
APK Phil Kessel	12.00	30.00
APM Peter Mueller	6.00	15.00
APR Patrick Roy	50.00	100.00
APS Peter Stastny	[illegible]	[illegible]
APV Pavel Vorobiev	4.00	10.00
ARC Ryan Carter	4.00	10.00
ARF Ron Francis		

ARH Ryan Hillier 4.00 10.00
ARP Ryan Parent 8.00 20.00
ARR Rick Rypien 4.00 10.00
ARS Ryan Shannon 5.00 12.00
ARV Roman Voloshenko 5.00 12.00
ARW Ryan White 5.00 12.00
ASG Sam Gagner 40.00 100.00
ASK Sergei Kostitsyn 12.00 30.00
ASM Shawn Matthais 4.00 10.00
ASS Steven Stamkos 60.00 120.00
ATG Trevor Gillies 4.00 10.00
ATK Tomas Kopecky 4.00 10.00
ATP Tom Pyatt 6.00 15.00
ATR Tuukka Rask 15.00 40.00
ATT Tim Thomas 6.00 15.00
ATV Tony Voce 4.00 10.00
ATW Ty Wishart 4.00 10.00
AWC Wendel Clark 8.00 20.00
AWO Willie O'Ree 12.00 30.00
AYA Yuri Alexandrov 4.00 10.00
AYD Yann Danis 5.00 12.00
AAMO Al Montoya 8.00 20.00
AAR2 Alexander Radulov 10.00 25.00
ABBI Bryan Bickell 4.00 10.00
ABBO Brad Boyes 6.00 15.00
ABCA Brady Calla 4.00 10.00
ABCM Blake Comeau 4.00 10.00
ABCO Braydon Coburn 6.00 15.00
ABHO Bud Holloway 4.00 10.00
ABLI Bryan Little 6.00 15.00
ABRS Brett Sutter 4.00 10.00
ABS1 Brandon Sutter 8.00 20.00
ABS2 Brandon Sutter 8.00 20.00
ABSA Bob Sanguinetti 4.00 10.00
ABSH Ben Shutron 4.00 10.00
ABSM Billy Smith 8.00 20.00
ABST Brett Sterling 4.00 10.00
ABTR Bryan Trottier 8.00 20.00
ACCL Cal Clutterbuck 4.00 10.00
ACGE Colby Genoway 4.00 10.00
ACGI Colton Gillies 6.00 15.00
ACGR Claude Giroux 6.00 15.00
ACHA Chris Harrington 4.00 10.00
ACSV Corey Syvret 4.00 10.00
ADDO Drew Doughty 5.00 12.00
ADPE Dustin Penner 6.00 15.00
ADSE Devin Setoguchi 6.00 15.00
ADSV Danny Syvret 5.00 12.00
AGBR Gilbert Brule 6.00 15.00
AGLF Guy Lafleur 12.00 30.00
AJAS Jared Staal 15.00 40.00
AJAZ Justin Azevedo 4.00 10.00
AJB1 Jonathan Bernier 10.00 25.00
AJB2 Jonathan Bernier 10.00 25.00
AJBO Johnny Bower 6.00 15.00
AJCA Jeff Carter 6.00 15.00
AJHE Josh Hennessy 4.00 10.00
AJPV Joe Pavelski 6.00 15.00
AJSH James Sheppard 5.00 12.00
AJSP Janis Sprukts 4.00 10.00
AJST Jordan Staal 20.00 50.00
AJT1 John Tavares 60.00 120.00
AJT2 John Tavares 60.00 120.00
AJTA Jeff Tambellini 4.00 10.00
AJTF Jeff Taffe 4.00 10.00
AJTL Jiri Tlusty 10.00 25.00
AKL2 Kristopher Letang 5.00 12.00
ALB1 Luc Bourdon 6.00 15.00
ALB2 Luc Bourdon 6.00 15.00
AMAC Marc-Andre Cliché 4.00 10.00
AMAF Marc-Andre Fleury 10.00 25.00
AMAG Marc-Andre Gragnani 4.00 10.00
AMAP Marc-Antoine Pouliot 6.00 15.00
AMBL Matt Beleskey 4.00 10.00
AMCA Michael Caruso 4.00 10.00
AMCR Mathieu Carle 5.00 12.00
AMDZ Michael Del Zotto 12.00 30.00
AMEV Marc-Edouard Vlasic 5.00 12.00
AMF2 Michael Frolik 4.00 10.00
AMGI Mark Giordano 4.00 10.00
AMGR Michael Grabner 6.00 15.00
AMHA Mark Hartigan 4.00 10.00
AMS1 Marc Staal 10.00 25.00
AMS2 Marc Staal 10.00 25.00
AMSC Milt Schmidt 8.00 20.00
AMSP Matthew Spiller 4.00 10.00
AMST Martin St. Pierre 4.00 10.00
APKA Petr Kalus 4.00 10.00
APKN Patrick Kane 100.00 200.00
APMC Patrick McNeill 4.00 10.00
APOS Patrick O'Sullivan 8.00 20.00
ARDA Ryan Daniels 4.00 10.00
ARRG Richie Regehr 4.00 10.00
ARSC Rob Schremp
ARVE Ryan Vesce 4.00 10.00
ASC1 Sidney Crosby 60.00 100.00
ASC2 Sidney Crosby 60.00 100.00
ASD1 Steve Downie 8.00 20.00
ASD2 Steve Downie 8.00 20.00
ASKR Staffan Kronwall 4.00 10.00
ATP2 Tom Pyatt 4.00 10.00

2006-07 ITG Heroes and Prospects Calder Cup Champions

COMPLETE SET (13) 20.00 50.00
COMMONS 2.00 5.00
CC01 Frederic Cassivi 2.50 6.00
CC02 Tomas Fleischmann 2.00 5.00
CC03 Mike Green 2.00 5.00
CC04 Kris Beech 2.00 5.00
CC05 Brooks Laich 2.00 5.00
CC06 Graham Mink 3.00 8.00
CC07 Boyd Gordon 2.00 5.00
CC08 Dave Steckel 2.00 5.00
CC09 Lawrence Nycholat 2.50 6.00
CC10 Boyd Kane 2.00 5.00
CC11 Joey Tenute 2.50 6.00
CC12 Jeff Schultz 2.00 5.00
CC13 Eric Fehr 2.00 5.00

2006-07 ITG Heroes and Prospects CHL Top Prospects

STATED PRINT RUN 100 SETS
GOLD VERSION /10 EXISTS
GOLD NOT PRICED DUE TO SCARCITY
TP01 Ben Shutron 10.00 25.00
TP02 Claude Giroux 10.00 25.00
TP03 Francois Bouchard 10.00 25.00
TP04 Ivan Visnevskiy 10.00 25.00
TP05 Corey Perry 12.00 30.00
TP06 Mike Richards 12.00 30.00
TP07 Bob Sanguinetti 10.00 25.00
TP08 Derick Brassard 12.00 30.00
TP09 James Sheppard 12.00 30.00
TP10 Jonathan Bernier 12.00 30.00
TP11 Jordan Staal 25.00 60.00
TP12 Matthew Corrente 10.00 25.00
TP13 Ryan Daniels 10.00 25.00
TP14 Tysen Dowzak 10.00 25.00
TP15 Ben Maxwell 10.00 25.00
TP16 Carey Price 12.00 30.00
TP17 Eric Fehr 10.00 25.00
TP18 Julien Ellis 12.00 30.00
TP19 Eric Staal 15.00 40.00

2006-07 ITG Heroes and Prospects Class of 2006

COMPLETE SET (13) 10.00 25.00
STATED ODDS 1:24
CL01 Jordan Staal 2.00 5.00
CL02 Phil Kessel 1.50 4.00
CL03 Derick Brassard 1.25 3.00
CL04 Peter Mueller 1.25 3.00
CL05 James Sheppard 1.25 3.00
CL06 Michael Frolik 1.25 3.00
CL07 Jonathan Bernier 1.25 3.00
CL08 Bryan Little 1.25 3.00
CL09 Michael Grabner .75 2.00
CL10 Ty Wishart .75 2.00
CL11 Chris Stewart .75 2.00
CL12 Bob Sanguinetti .75 2.00
CL13 Claude Giroux .75 2.00

2006-07 ITG Heroes and Prospects Complete AHL Logos

STATED PRINT RUN 1/1
NOT PRICED DUE TO SCARCITY
AHL01 Cam Ward
AHL02 Alexandre Picard
AHL03 Yann Danis
AHL04 Ian White
AHL05 Dustin Penner
AHL06 Jimmy Howard
AHL07 Ryan Miller
AHL08 Jay Bouwmeester
AHL09 Nigel Dawes
AHL10 Martin Houle
AHL11 Jiri Hudler
AHL12 Alexander Radulov
AHL13 Drew Stafford
AHL14 Rob Schremp

2006-07 ITG Heroes and Prospects Complete CHL Logos

STATED PRINT RUN 1/1
NOT PRICED DUE TO SCARCITY
CHL01 Jordan Staal
CHL02 Claude Giroux
CHL03 Angelo Esposito
CHL04 James Sheppard
CHL05 Derick Brassard
CHL06 Peter Mueller
CHL07 Cal Clutterbuck
CHL08 Marc Staal
CHL09 Benoit Pouliot
CHL10 Jonathan Bernier
CHL11 John Tavares
CHL12 Carey Price
CHL13 Angelo Esposito
CHL14 Jakub Voracek
CHL15 Adam Perry
CHL16 Sam Gagner

2006-07 ITG Heroes and Prospects Complete Jerseys

PRINT RUN 10 SER. #'d SETS
GOLD VERSION /1 EXISTS
GOLD NOT PRICED DUE TO SCARCITY
NOT PRICED DUE TO SCARCITY
CJ01 Angelo Esposito
CJ02 John Tavares
CJ03 Leland Irving
CJ04 Marek Schwarz
CJ05 Sidney Crosby
CJ06 Phil Kessel
CJ07 Jordan Staal
CJ08 Michael Frolik
CJ09 Cam Ward
CJ10 Ryan Miller
CJ11 Corey Perry
CJ12 Jiri Tlusty
CJ13 Peter Mueller
CJ14 Marc Staal
CJ15 Alexander Radulov
CJ16 Drew Stafford
CJ17 Justin Pogge
CJ18 Benoit Pouliot

2006-07 ITG Heroes and Prospects Double Memorabilia

STATED PRINT RUN 30 SETS
DM01 Jordan Staal 20.00 40.00
DM02 Mario Lemieux 30.00 60.00
DM03 Sidney Crosby 30.00 80.00
DM04 Martin Brodeur 20.00 50.00
DM05 Patrick Roy 30.00 60.00
DM06 Mark Messier 20.00 40.00
DM07 Joe Sakic 20.00 50.00
DM08 John Tavares 25.00 60.00
DM09 Roberto Luongo 15.00 40.00
DM10 Sam Gagner 15.00 40.00

2006-07 ITG Heroes and Prospects Emblems

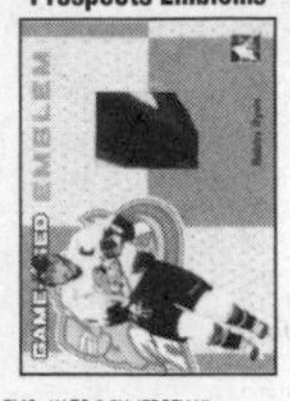

*EMBLEMS: 1X TO 2.5X JERSEY HI
STATED PRINT RUN 30 SETS
GOLD VERSION /10 EXISTS
GOLD NOT PRICED DUE TO SCARCITY

2006-07 ITG Heroes and Prospects Heroes Memorabilia

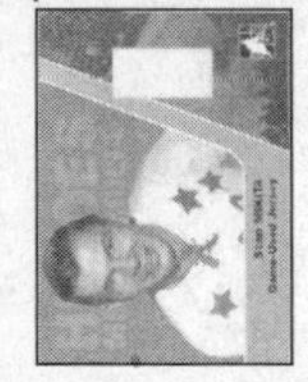

HM01 Luc Robitaille 10.00 25.00
HM02 Billy Smith 10.00 25.00
HM03 Steve Yzerman 25.00 60.00
HM04 Ron Francis 10.00 25.00
HM05 Martin Brodeur 20.00 50.00
HM06 Patrick Roy 25.00 60.00
HM07 Jaromir Jagr 12.00 30.00
HM08 Mark Messier 12.00 30.00
HM09 Brian Leetch 10.00 25.00
HM10 Dave Keon 12.00 30.00
HM11 Milt Schmidt 12.00 30.00
HM12 Jacques Plante 20.00 50.00
HM13 Bobby Hull 15.00 40.00
HM14 Frank Mahovlich 12.00 30.00
HM15 Jean Beliveau 20.00 50.00
HM16 Red Kelly 12.00 30.00
HM17 Stan Mikita 15.00 40.00
HM18 Tim Horton 20.00 50.00
HM19 Terry Sawchuk 20.00 50.00
HM20 Johnny Bower 12.00 30.00
HM21 Joe Sakic 15.00 40.00
HM22 Ed Belfour 10.00 25.00
HM23 Joe Thornton 12.00 30.00
HM24 Roberto Luongo 12.00 30.00
HM25 Nicklas Lidstrom 12.00 30.00
HM26 Manny Fernandez 10.00 25.00

2006-07 ITG Heroes and Prospects Jerseys

STATED PRINT RUN 100 SETS
GOLD VERSION /10 EXISTS
GOLD NOT PRICED DUE TO SCARCITY
GUJ01 Marek Schwarz 6.00 15.00
GUJ02 David Ruzicka 4.00 10.00
GUJ03 Jimmy Howard 8.00 20.00
GUJ04 Daniel Girardi 4.00 10.00
GUJ05 Mike Green 4.00 10.00
GUJ06 Nigel Dawes 4.00 10.00
GUJ07 Curtis McElhinney 6.00 15.00
GUJ08 Mike Smith 6.00 15.00
GUJ09 Corey Locke 4.00 10.00
GUJ10 Yann Danis 6.00 15.00
GUJ11 Tomi Maki 4.00 10.00
GUJ12 Erik Christensen 6.00 15.00
GUJ13 Maxime Talbot 6.00 15.00
GUJ14 Tony Voce 4.00 10.00
GUJ15 Josh Harding 6.00 15.00
GUJ16 Ian White 4.00 10.00
GUJ17 Jarkko Immonen 4.00 10.00
GUJ18 Ryan Getzlaf 8.00 20.00
GUJ19 Jeremy Colliton 4.00 10.00
GUJ20 Fernando Pisani 6.00 15.00
GUJ21 Noah Welch 4.00 10.00
GUJ22 Billy Thompson 6.00 15.00
GUJ23 Staffan Kronwall 4.00 10.00
GUJ24 Darryl Bootland 4.00 10.00
GUJ25 Dustin Penner 6.00 15.00
GUJ26 Paul Ranger 4.00 10.00
GUJ27 Alexandre Picard 6.00 15.00
GUJ28 Daniel Paille 4.00 10.00
GUJ29 Andy Rogers 4.00 10.00
GUJ30 Tysen Dowzak 4.00 10.00
GUJ31 Jamie McGinn 4.00 10.00
GUJ32 Ryan Callahan 4.00 10.00
GUJ33 Angelo Esposito 15.00 30.00
GUJ34 John Tavares 25.00 50.00
GUJ35 Tim Thomas 8.00 20.00
GUJ36 Bud Holloway 4.00 10.00
GUJ37 Kevin Lalande 4.00 10.00
GUJ38 Leland Irving 6.00 15.00
GUJ39 Peter Mueller 6.00 15.00
GUJ40 Marc Staal 6.00 15.00
GUJ41 Benoit Pouliot 6.00 15.00
GUJ42 Wojtek Wolski 8.00 20.00
GUJ43 Bryan Little 8.00 20.00
GUJ44 Ben Shutron 4.00 10.00
GUJ45 Ryan O'Marra 4.00 10.00
GUJ46 Adam Perry 4.00 10.00
GUJ47 James Sheppard 6.00 15.00
GUJ48 Nicholas Drazeovic 4.00 10.00
GUJ49 Bobby Ryan 8.00 20.00
GUJ50 Tyler Plante 4.00 10.00
GUJ51 Matt Corrente 4.00 10.00
GUJ52 Ondrej Fiala 6.00 15.00
GUJ53 J-S Aubin 6.00 15.00
GUJ54 Ryan Vesce 4.00 10.00
GUJ55 Petr Taticek 4.00 10.00
GUJ56 Ben Walter 4.00 10.00
GUJ57 Andrew Penner 6.00 15.00
GUJ58 Francois Beauchemin 6.00 15.00
GUJ59 Cristobal Huet 8.00 20.00
GUJ60 Jay Bouwmeester 6.00 15.00
GUJ61 Phil Kessel 10.00 25.00
GUJ62 Petr Kalus 6.00 15.00
GUJ63 Drew Stafford 12.00 30.00
GUJ64 Alexander Radulov 12.00 30.00
GUJ65 Jiri Hudler 6.00 15.00
GUJ66 Cory Emmerton 4.00 10.00
GUJ67 Loui Eriksson 4.00 10.00
GUJ68 Bobby Ryan 6.00 15.00
GUJ69 Jakub Voracek 12.00 30.00
GUJ70 Sam Gagner 12.00 30.00
GUJ71 Michael Grabner 6.00 15.00
GUJ72 Rob Schremp 10.00 25.00
GUJ73 Cal Clutterbuck 4.00 10.00

2006-07 ITG Heroes and Prospects Making The Bigs

STATED PRINT RUN 70 SETS
GOLD VERSION /10 EXISTS
GOLD NOT PRICED DUE TO SCARCITY
MTB01 Wojtek Wolski 10.00 25.00
MTB02 Tim Gleason 5.00 12.00
MTB03 Cam Ward 12.00 30.00
MTB04 Ryan Miller 10.00 25.00
MTB05 Mike Glumac 5.00 12.00
MTB06 Pascal Leclaire 6.00 15.00
MTB07 Ryan Getzlaf 10.00 25.00
MTB08 Eric Nystrom 5.00 12.00
MTB09 Ray Emery 6.00 15.00
MTB10 Eric Staal 10.00 25.00
MTB11 Marc-Antoine Pouliot 6.00 15.00
MTB12 Alexander Ovechkin 15.00 40.00

2006-07 ITG Heroes and Prospects Memorial Cup Champions

COMPLETE SET (12) 8.00 20.00
MC01 Cedrick Desjardins .75 2.00
MC02 Joe Ryan .60 1.50
MC03 Brent Aubin .60 1.50
MC04 Jordan LaVallee .60 1.50
MC05 Andrew Andricopoulos .60 1.50
MC06 Marc-Edouard Vlasic 1.25 3.00
MC07 Mathieu Melanson .60 1.50
MC08 Michal Sersen .60 1.50
MC09 Angelo Esposito 2.50 6.00
MC10 Maxime Lacroix .60 1.50
MC11 Alexander Radulov 2.00 5.00
MC12 Patrick Roy 3.00 8.00

2006-07 ITG Heroes and Prospects National Pride

STATED PRINT RUN 80 SETS
GOLD VERSION /10 ALSO EXISTS
GOLD NOT PRICED DUE TO SCARCITY
NP01 Logan Stephenson 4.00 10.00
NP02 Sidney Crosby 20.00 50.00
NP03 Frederik Cabana 4.00 10.00
NP04 Alex Bourret 4.00 10.00
NP05 Tom Pyatt 4.00 10.00
NP06 Marc-Andre Gragnani 4.00 10.00
NP07 Olivier Latendresse 4.00 10.00
NP08 Marc Staal 8.00 20.00
NP09 Tyler Kennedy 4.00 10.00
NP10 Stephane Goulet 4.00 10.00
NP11 Devin Setoguchi 8.00 20.00
NP12 Benoit Pouliot 8.00 20.00
NP13 Jeff Schultz 4.00 10.00
NP14 Wacey Rabbit 6.00 15.00
NP15 Patrick McNeill 4.00 10.00
NP16 Steve Downie 10.00 25.00
NP17 Blake Comeau 6.00 15.00
NP18 Dustin Boyd 6.00 15.00
NP19 Kyle Chipchura 6.00 15.00
NP20 Carey Price 15.00 40.00
NP21 Marc Staal 8.00 20.00
NP22 Sam Gagner 10.00 25.00
NP23 Steve Downie 10.00 25.00

2006-07 ITG Heroes and Prospects Net Prospects

STATED PRINT RUN 70 SETS
GOLD VERSION /10 EXISTS
GOLD NOT PRICED DUE TO SCARCITY
NPR01 Leland Irving 8.00 20.00
NPR02 Marek Schwarz 6.00 15.00
NPR03 Jimmy Howard 8.00 20.00
NPR04 Cam Ward 12.00 30.00
NPR05 Cristobal Huet 12.00 30.00
NPR06 Ryan Miller 10.00 25.00
NPR07 Ray Emery 6.00 15.00
NPR08 Justin Pogge 12.00 30.00
NPR09 Carey Price 12.00 30.00
NPR10 Jonathan Bernier 6.00 15.00
NPR11 Hannu Toivonen 8.00 20.00
NPR12 Thomas McCollum 6.00 15.00
NPR13 Justin Pogge 12.00 30.00
NPR14 Mike Smith 6.00 15.00

2006-07 ITG Heroes and Prospects Numbers

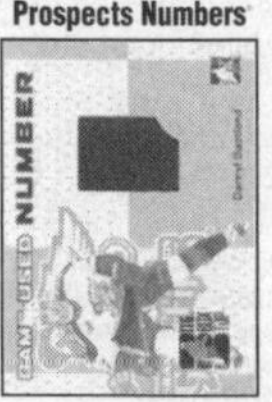

*NUMBERS: 1X TO 2.5X JERSEY HI
STATED PRINT RUN 30 SETS
GOLD VERSION /10 EXISTS
GOLD NOT PRICED DUE TO SCARCITY

2006-07 ITG Heroes and Prospects Quad Emblems

STATED PRINT RUN 10 SETS
GOLD VERSION /1 EXISTS
NOT PRICED DUE TO SCARCITY
GOLD NOT PRICED DUE TO SCARCITY
QE01 Bryan Little
Jordan Staal
Chris Stewart
Ben Maxwell
QE02 Sidney Crosby
John Tavares
Angelo Esposito
Brandon Sutter
QE03 Marc Staal
Dion Phaneuf
Luc Bourdon
Shea Weber
QE04 Marc-Andre Fleury
Cam Ward
Kari Lehtonen
Ryan Miller
QE05 Sidney Crosby
Gilbert Brule
Bobby Ryan
Steve Downie
QE06 Alexander Ovechkin
Henrik Lundqvist
Petr Prucha
Evgeni Malkin
QE07 Rob Schremp
Wojtek Wolski
Corey Perry
Benoit Pouliot
QE08 Tyler Plante
Carey Price
Devan Dubnyk
Justin Pogge
QE09 Marek Svatos
Ray Emery
Andrew Ladd
Antero Niittymaki
QE10 Mike Richards
Thomas Vanek
Ryan Getzlaf
Eric Staal
QE11 Stafford
Radulov
Pouliot
Schremp
QE12 Voracek
Esposito
Hamill
Alzner
QE13 Gagner
Kane
Couture
Cann
QE14 Brodeur
Luongo
Belfour
Roy
QE15 Tavares
Price
Esposito
Voracek
QE16 Staal
Kopitar
Brule
Kessel

2006-07 ITG Heroes and Prospects Sticks and Jerseys

STATED PRINT RUN 100 SETS
GOLD VERSION /10 EXISTS
GOLD NOT PRICED DUE TO SCARCITY
SJ01 Eric Staal 12.00 30.00
SJ02 John Tavares
SJ03 Patrice Bergeron 12.00 30.00
SJ04 Alexander Ovechkin 25.00 60.00
SJ05 Peter Mueller 12.00 30.00
SJ06 Brady Calla 20.00
SJ07 Leland Irving 12.00 30.00
SJ08 Ondrej Fiala 8.00 20.00
SJ09 Ryan Miller 15.00 40.00
SJ10 Sidney Crosby 40.00 100.00
SJ11 Antero Niittymaki 12.00 30.00
SJ12 Jason Spezza 8.00 20.00
SJ13 Petr Prucha 20.00
SJ14 Henrik Lundqvist 15.00 40.00
SJ15 Al Montoya 12.00 30.00
SJ16 Dion Phaneuf 15.00 40.00
SJ17 Marek Svatos 8.00 20.00
SJ18 Hannu Toivonen 12.00 30.00
SJ19 Ray Emery 8.00 20.00
SJ20 Brad Boyes 8.00 20.00

2006-07 ITG Heroes and Prospects Triple Memorabilia

STATED PRINT RUN 50 SETS
GOLD VERSION /10 EXISTS
GOLD NOT PRICED DUE TO SCARCITY
TM01 Mark Messier 40.00 80.00
Grant Fuhr
Jari Kurri
TM02 Patrick Roy 60.00 125.00
Martin Brodeur
Bernie Parent
TM03 Alexander Ovechkin 60.00 125.00
Evgeni Malkin
Ilya Kovalchuk
TM04 Sidney Crosby 100.00 200.00
Evgeni Malkin
Mario Lemieux
TM05 Leland Irving 25.00 60.00
Carey Price
Justin Pogge
TM06 Guillaume Latendresse 20.00 50.00
Alexander Radulov
Luc Bourdon
TM07 Corey Perry 25.00 60.00
Bobby Ryan
Ryan Getzlaf
TM08 Eric Staal 25.00 60.00
Marc Staal
Jordan Staal
TM09 Radulov 20.00 50.00
Stafford
Pouliot
TM10 Sakic 30.00 80.00
Thornton
Jagr
TM11 Esposito 15.00 40.00
Gagner
Alzner
TM12 Belfour 15.00 40.00
Luongo
Fernandez

2007-08 ITG Heroes and Prospects

COMP.SET w/o SP's (100) 15.00 30.00
COMP.UPDATE SET (50) 10.00 25.00
1 Joe Sakic .75 2.00
2 Ed Belfour .40 1.00
3 Mike Modano .40 1.00
4 Vincent Lecavalier .40 1.00
5 Chris Pronger .40 1.00
6 Jean-Sebastien Giguere .40 1.00
7 Dominik Hasek .50 1.25
8 Roberto Luongo .60 1.50
9 Joe Thornton .50 1.25
10 Keith Tkachuk .30 .75
11 Dave Keon .30 .75
12 Alexei Cherepanov .40 1.00
13 Tuukka Rask .60 1.50
14 Ilya Zubov .30 .75
15 Simeon Varlamov .30 .75
16 Jack Skille .40 1.00
17 Adam Dennis .30 .75
18 Ryan Callahan .40 1.00
19 Justin Pogge .50 1.25
20 Nathan Oystrick .25 .60
21 Benoit Pouliot .25 .60
22 Andrew Ebbett .25 .60
23 Matt Moulson .25 .60
24 Bobby Ryan 1.00 2.50
25 Cal Clutterbuck .25 .60
26 Matt D'Agostini .25 .60
27 Kyle Wilson .25 .60
28 Keith Yandle .25 .60
29 Bob Sanguinetti .25 .60
30 T.J. Kemp .25 .60
31 Cal O'Reilly .50 1.25
32 Marek Zagrapan .25 .60
33 Jannik Hansen .25 .60
34 Danny Irmen .25 .60
35 Marek Schwarz .30 .75
36 Alex Bourret .30 .75
37 David Krejci .50 1.25
38 Brett Sterling .25 .60
39 Tobias Stephan .30 .75
40 Mikhail Grabovski .30 .75
41 Carey Price 1.25 3.00
42 Tyler Weiman .30 .75
43 Rich Peverley .25 .60
44 Jordan Caron .25 .60
45 Claude Giroux .25 .60
46 T.J. Brennan .25 .60
47 Francois Bouchard .25 .60
48 Maxime Tanguay .25 .60
49 Antoine Lafleur .30 .75
50 Yann Sauve .30 .75
51 Jonathan Bernier .60 1.50
52 Olivier Fortier .25 .60
53 Jean-Simon Allard .25 .60
54 Brad Marchand .40 1.00
55 Alex Grant .25 .60
56 Kevin Armstrong .25 .60
57 Colten Teubert .25 .60
58 Jusso Puustinen .30 .75
59 Riley Holzapfel .30 .75
60 Codey Burki .25 .60
61 Milan Lucic .60 1.50
62 Luke Schenn .50 1.25
63 Dana Tyrell .30 .75
64 Kyle Beach .30 .75
65 Zach Boychuk .40 1.00
66 Mark Santorelli .25 .60
67 Justin McCrae .25 .60
68 Ryan White .30 .75
69 Cass Mappin .25 .60
70 Leland Irving .40 1.00
71 Scott Jackson .25 .60
72 Jesse Dudas .25 .60
73 Graham Potuer .25 .60
74 John Tavares 1.50 4.00
75 Matt Caria .25 .60
76 Josh Godfrey .25 .60
77 P.K. Subban .75 2.00
78 Jamie McGinn .25 .60
79 Cody Hodgson .40 1.00
80 Steve Mason 1.25 3.00
81 Drew Doughty .60 1.50
82 Cory Emmerton .30 .75
83 Ryan O'Reilly .25 .60
84 Dale Mitchell .25 .60
85 Steven Stamkos .75 2.00
86 Thomas McCollum .30 .75
87 Matt Duchene .25 .60
88 Michael Del Zotto .40 1.00
89 Alex Pietrangelo .25 .60
90 Zack Torquato .25 .60
91 Jordan Staal .50 1.25
Trevor Cann
92 Darryl Sittler .50 1.25
Sam Gagner
93 Alex Delvecchio 1.50 4.00
John Tavares
94 Guy Lafleur 1.00 2.50
Angel Esposito
95 Denis Potvin .40 1.00
Logan Couture
96 Joe Thornton .60 1.50
Jiri Tlusty
97 Joe Sakic .75 2.00
Kyle Moir
98 Wendel Clark .40 1.00
Colton Gillies
99 Roberto Luongo .60 1.50
Brad Marchand
100 Vincent Lecavalier .40 1.00
Jordan Caron
101 Thomas Hickey TP JSY 12.00 30.00
102 Logan MacMillan TP JSY 6.00 15.00
103 Akim Aliu TP JSY 12.00 30.00
104 Linden Rowat TP JSY 10.00 25.00
105 Zach Hamill TP JSY 6.00 15.00
106 Nick Ross TP JSY 6.00 15.00
107 Jakub Voracek TP JSY 8.00 20.00
108 Ruslan Bashkirov TP JSY 6.00 15.00
109 John Negrin TP JSY 8.00 20.00
110 Sam Gagner TP JSY 12.00 30.00
111 Stefan Legein TP JSY 6.00 15.00
112 Jeremy Smith TP JSY 6.00 15.00
113 Nick Palmieri TP JSY 6.00 15.00
114 David Skokan TP JSY 6.00 15.00
115 Logan Couture TP JSY 10.00 25.00
116 Drayson Bowman TP JSY 6.00 15.00
117 Alex Plante TP JSY 6.00 15.00
118 Eric Doyle TP JSY 6.00 15.00
119 Keaton Ellerby TP JSY 6.00 15.00
120 Brandon Sutter TP JSY 8.00 20.00
121 Trevor Cann TP JSY 8.00 20.00
122 Keven Veilleux TP JSY 6.00 15.00
123 Karl Alzner TP JSY 8.00 20.00
124 Michal Repik TP JSY 12.00 30.00
125 Angelo Esposito TP JSY 15.00 40.00
126 Taylor Ellington TP JSY 6.00 15.00
127 Brett MacLean TP JSY 6.00 15.00
128 Tyson Sexsmith TP JSY 8.00 20.00
129 Mark Katic TP JSY 6.00 15.00
130 Jonathon Blum TP JSY 6.00 15.00
131 Bryan Cameron TP JSY 6.00 15.00
132 Colton Gillies TP JSY 10.00 25.00
133 Brett Sonne TP JSY 6.00 15.00
134 David Stich TP JSY 6.00 15.00
135 Patrick Kane TP JSY 40.00 100.00
136 Kevin Marshall TP JSY 6.00 15.00
137 Oscar Moller TP JSY 8.00 20.00
138 Maxim Gratchev TP JSY 6.00 15.00
139 Carey Price TP JSY 30.00 80.00
140 Jordan Staal TP JSY 12.00 30.00
141 Kyle Okposo .30 .75
142 Teddy Purcell .30 .75

143 Alex Goligoski .60 1.50
144 T.J. Hensick .40 1.00
145 Brian Lee .60 1.50
146 Derick Brassard .30 .75
147 Darryl Boyce .50 1.25
148 Jonathan Matsumoto .30 .75
149 John Curry .50 1.25
150 Alexander Nikulin .40 1.00
151 Cody Franson .60 1.50
152 Chris Stewart .30 .75
153 Jaroslav Halak 1.00 2.50
154 Kyle Greentree .30 .75
155 Jerome Samson .40 1.00
156 Brian Boyle .60 1.50
157 Julian Talbot .30 .75
158 Devin Setoguchi .60 1.50
159 Michael Grabner .40 1.00
160 Steve Downie .40 1.00
161 Chris Doyle .50 1.25
162 Mikhail Stefanovich .30 .75
163 Joel Champagne .50 1.25
164 Maxime Sauve .50 1.25
165 Kelsey Tessier .40 1.00
166 Philippe Cornet .30 .75
167 Tomas Knotek .30 .75
168 Nicolas Deschamps .30 .75
169 Jordan Eberle .30 .75
170 Chet Pickard .30 .75
171 Mitch Wahl .50 1.25
172 Colby Robak .30 .75
173 James Wright .30 .75
174 Tyler Ennis .50 1.25
175 Geordie Wudrick .30 .75
176 Kruise Reddick .30 .75
177 Mitch Fadden .50 1.25
178 Tyler Myers 1.00 2.50
179 Luca Sbisa .30 .75
180 Shawn Matthias .30 .75
181 Patrick Maroon .50 1.25
182 Zach Bogosian .75 2.00
183 Mikkel Boedker .60 1.50
184 Jared Staal .50 1.25
185 Luca Caputi .60 1.50
186 Jamie Arniel .30 .75
187 Taylor Hall .50 1.25
188 Josh Bailey .30 .75
189 Tyler Cuma .30 .75
190 Phil McRae .30 .75

2007-08 ITG Heroes and Prospects Autographs

STATED ODDS 1:24
AAA Akim Aliu 6.00 15.00
AAC Alexei Cherepanov 5.00 12.00
AAD Adam Dennis 4.00 10.00
AAE Angelo Esposito 8.00 20.00
AAEB Andrew Ebbett 3.00 8.00
AAG Alex Grant 3.00 8.00
AAL Antoine Lafleur 4.00 10.00
AAO Alexander Ovechkin 40.00 80.00
AAP Alex Pietrangelo 3.00 8.00
ABB Brian Boyle 6.00 15.00
ABC Blake Comeau 3.00 8.00
ABLI Bryan Little 4.00 10.00
ABM Brad Marchand 5.00 12.00
ABP Benoit Pouliot 3.00 8.00
ABR Bobby Ryan 12.00 30.00
ABS Brandon Sutter 4.00 10.00
ABST Brett Sterling 3.00 8.00
ACB Codey Burki 3.00 8.00
ACC Cal Clutterbuck 3.00 8.00
ACD Chris Doyle 5.00 12.00
ACE Cory Emmerton 4.00 10.00
ACF Cody Franson 6.00 15.00
ACG Claude Giroux 3.00 8.00
ACH Cody Hodgson 5.00 12.00
ACM Curtis McElhinney 4.00 10.00
ACMA Cass Mappin 3.00 8.00
ACO Cal O'Reilly 6.00 15.00
ACP Chris Pronger
ACP Chet Pickard
ACPR Carey Price 30.00 80.00
ACS Chris Stewart
ACT Colten Teubert 3.00 8.00
ADB Derick Brassard 3.00 8.00
ADB Darryl Boyce 5.00 12.00
ADD Drew Doughty 8.00 20.00
ADH Dominik Hasek
ADI Danny Irmen 3.00 8.00
ADK Dave Keon
ADM Dale Mitchell 3.00 8.00
ADS Drew Stafford 4.00 10.00
ADS Devin Setoguchi 6.00 15.00
ADT Dana Tyrell 4.00 10.00
AEB Ed Belfour
AFB Francois Bouchard 3.00 8.00
AGP Graham Potuer 3.00 8.00
AGW Geordie Wudrick
AJB Josh Bailey 15.00 40.00
AJB Jonathan Bernier
AJC Joel Champagne 5.00 12.00
AJC Jordan Caron 3.00 8.00
AJDU Jesse Dudas 3.00 8.00
AJE Jordan Eberle 3.00 8.00
AJG Josh Godfrey 3.00 8.00
AJH Jaroslav Halak 10.00 25.00
AJHA Jannik Hansen 3.00 8.00
AJM Jonathan Matsumoto
AJM Jamie McGinn 3.00 8.00
AJMC Justin McCrae 3.00 8.00
AJOC Joe Sakic 40.00 80.00
AJP Justin Pogge
AJPU Jusso Puustinen 4.00 10.00
AJPV Joe Pavelski 3.00 8.00
AJS Jerome Samson 4.00 10.00
AJS Jordan Sigalet 4.00 10.00
AJSA Jean-Simon Allard 3.00 8.00
AJSG Jean-Sebastien Giguere
AJSH James Sheppard 3.00 8.00
AJSK Jack Skille 5.00 12.00
AJSM Jeremy Smith 3.00 8.00
AJST Jordan Staal 6.00 15.00
AJT John Tavares 50.00
AJTH Joe Thornton 6.00 15.00
AKA Kevin Armstrong 3.00 8.00
AKAL Karl Alzner 4.00 10.00
AKB Kyle Beach 4.00 10.00
AKO Kyle Okposo 15.00 40.00
AKT Kelsey Tessier 4.00 10.00
AKT Keith Tkachuk 4.00 10.00
AKW Kyle Wilson 3.00 8.00
AKY Keith Yandle 3.00 8.00
ALC Luca Caputi
ALI Leland Irving 5.00 12.00
ALR Linden Rowat 5.00 12.00
ALS Luke Schenn 6.00 15.00
AMB Mikael Boedker 6.00 15.00
AMC Matt Caria 3.00 8.00
AMD Matt Duchene 3.00 8.00
AMDA Matt D'Agostini 3.00 8.00
AMDZ Michael Del Zotto 15.00 40.00
AMF Mitch Fadden 5.00 12.00
AMG Mikhail Grabovski 4.00 10.00
AMG Michael Grabner
AMM Matt Moulson 3.00 8.00
AMMO Mike Modano 5.00 12.00
AMN Michal Neuvirth 5.00 12.00
AMS Marek Schwarz 4.00 10.00
AMT Maxime Tanguay 3.00 8.00
AMW Mitch Wahl 5.00 12.00
AMZ Marek Zagrapan 3.00 8.00
AND Nicolas Deschamps
AOF Olivier Fortier 3.00 8.00
APD Peter Delmas 3.00 8.00
APK Patrick Kane 40.00 80.00
APKS P.K. Subban 12.00 30.00
APMU Peter Mueller 10.00 25.00
APO Patrick O'Sullivan 4.00 10.00
ARC Ryan Callahan 5.00 12.00
ARH Riley Holzapfel 4.00 10.00
ARL Roberto Luongo 40.00 80.00
ARO Ryan O'Reilly 3.00 8.00
ARP Rich Peverley 3.00 8.00
ARS Rob Schremp 4.00 10.00
ARW Ryan White 4.00 10.00
ASD Steve Downie
ASG Sam Gagner 6.00 15.00
ASJ Scott Jackson 3.00 8.00
ASM Shawn Matthias 3.00 8.00
ASM Shawn Matthias 3.00 8.00
ASMA Steve Mason 15.00 40.00
ASMU Scott Munroe 3.00 8.00
ASS Steven Stamkos 50.00 100.00
ATC Trevor Cann 4.00 10.00
ATH Thomas Hickey 6.00 15.00
ATJB T.J. Brennan 3.00 8.00
ATJK T.J. Kemp 3.00 8.00
ATK Tomas Knotek 3.00 8.00
ATM Thomas McCollum 4.00 10.00
ATP Teddy Purcell 3.00 8.00
ATR Tuukka Rask 8.00 20.00
ATS Tobias Stephan 4.00 10.00
ATSE Tyson Sexsmith 4.00 10.00
AVL Vincent Lecavalier 5.00 12.00
AYS Yann Sauve 4.00 10.00
AZB Zach Bogosian 15.00 40.00
AZB Zach Boychuk 5.00 12.00
AZT Zack Torquato 3.00 8.00

2007-08 ITG Heroes and Prospects Calder Cup Champions

COMPLETE SET (9) 5.00 12.00
STATED ODDS 1:12
CC01 Corey Locke .60 1.50
CC02 Kyle Chipchura 1.00 2.50
CC03 Dan Jancevski .60 1.50
CC04 Matt D'Agostini .60 1.50
CC05 Maxime Lapierre .60 1.50
CC06 Mikhail Grabovski .75 2.00
CC07 Ajay Baines .60 1.50
CC08 Andre Benoit .60 1.50
CC09 Carey Price 3.00 8.00

2007-08 ITG Heroes and Prospects Canada and Russia Challenge

STATED PRINT RUN 50 SETS
CR01 Logan Couture 6.00 15.00
CR02 John Tavares 25.00 60.00
CR03 Drew Doughty 10.00 25.00
CR04 Sam Gagner 8.00 20.00
CR05 Bryan Little 5.00 12.00
CR06 Steve Mason 20.00 50.00
CR07 Chris Stewart 4.00 10.00
CR08 Francois Bouchard 4.00 10.00
CR09 Jean-Philippe Levasseur 4.00 10.00
CR10 Angelo Esposito 10.00 25.00
CR11 Claude Giroux 4.00 10.00
CR12 Yann Sauve 5.00 12.00
CR13 Brad Marchand 6.00 15.00
CR14 Karl Alzner 5.00 12.00
CR15 Keaton Ellerby 4.00 10.00
CR16 Colton Gillies 6.00 15.00
CR17 Zach Hamill 4.00 10.00
CR18 Carey Price 20.00 50.00
CR19 Kris Russell 5.00 12.00
CR20 Brandon Sutter 5.00 12.00

2007-08 ITG Heroes and Prospects Canada and Russia Challenge Gold

STATED PRINT RUN 10 SER.#'d SETS
NOT PRICED DUE TO SCARCITY

2007-08 ITG Heroes and Prospects Complete Jerseys

STATED PRINT RUN 9 SER.#'d SETS
NOT PRICED DUE TO SCARCITY
CJ01 Alexei Cherepanov
CJ02 Tuukka Rask
CJ03 John Tavares
CJ04 Angelo Esposito
CJ05 Sam Gagner
CJ06 Patrick Kane
CJ07 Steven Stamkos
CJ08 Justin Pogge
CJ09 Drew Stafford
CJ10 Carey Price
CJ11 Drew Doughty
CJ12 Kyle Okposo
CJ13 Zach Bogosian
CJ14 Cody Hodgson

2007-08 ITG Heroes and Prospects Complete Jerseys Gold

STATED PRINT RUN 1 SER.#'d SET
NOT PRICED DUE TO SCARCITY

2007-08 ITG Heroes and Prospects Complete Logos

STATED PRINT 1 SER.#'d SET
NOT PRICED DUE TO SCARCITY
AHL01 Ryan Callahan
AHL02 Justin Pogge
AHL03 Patrick O'Sullivan
AHL04 Adam Dennis
AHL05 Marek Schwarz
AHL06 David Krejci
AHL07 Jiri Tlusty
AHL08 Marc-Antoine Pouliot
AHL09 Andrew Ebbett
AHL10 Carey Price
CHL01 Logan Couture
CHL02 Thomas Hickey
CHL03 Patrick Kane
CHL04 Trevor Cann
CHL05 Brandon Sutter
CHL06 Stefan Legein
CHL07 Michael Del Zotto
CHL08 Francois Bouchard
CHL09 Zach Hamill
CHL10 Karl Alzner

2007-08 ITG Heroes and Prospects Double Memorabilia

STATED PRINT RUN 20 SER.#'d SETS
DM01 Patrick Kane 30.00 00.00
Sam Gagner
DM02 Brandon Sutter 15.00 30.00
Brett Sutter
DM03 John Tavares 30.00 60.00
Steven Stamkos
DM04 Angelo Esposito 20.00 40.00
Claude Giroux
DM05 Bobby Ryan 20.00 40.00
Benoit Pouliot
DM06 Justin Pogge 30.00 60.00
Carey Price

2007-08 ITG Heroes and Prospects Double Memorabilia Gold

STATED PRINT RUN 10 SER.#'d SETS
NOT PRICED DUE TO SCARCITY

2007-08 ITG Heroes and Prospects Emblems

*EMBLEMS: 1X TO 2.5X JERSEYS
STATED PRINT RUN 30 SERIAL #'d SETS
GUE02 Tuukka Rask 20.00 50.00
GUE04 John Tavares 50.00 120.00
GUE09 Marc Staal 20.00 50.00
GUE10 Sam Gagner 15.00 40.00
GUE13 Peter Mueller 25.00 60.00
GUE18 Patrick Kane 50.00 120.00
GUE27 Steven Stamkos 25.00 60.00
GUE36 Justin Pogge 15.00 40.00
GUE38 Carey Price 40.00 100.00
GUE39 Jiri Tlusty 20.00 50.00
GUE48 Jimmy Howard 20.00 50.00
GUE55 Thomas Hickey 15.00 40.00
GUE59 David Krejci 15.00 40.00
GUE60 Jonathan Bernier 20.00 50.00
GUE61 Kyle Okposo
GUE63 Luke Schenn 15.00 40.00
GUE64 Jonas Hiller
GUE05 Steve Mason 40.00 100.00
GUE66 Devin Setoguchi
GUE68 Zach Bogosian 20.00 50.00
GUE69 Cody Hodgson

2007-08 ITG Heroes and Prospects Gloves Are Off

STATED PRINT RUN 70 SERIAL #'d SETS
GO01 Patrick Kane 20.00 50.00
GO02 Angelo Esposito 15.00 40.00
GO03 Keaton Ellerby 6.00 15.00
GO04 Drew Doughty 15.00 40.00
GO05 Luc Bourdon 8.00 20.00
GO06 Marc Staal 15.00 40.00
GO07 Karl Alzner 8.00 20.00
GO08 Jordan Staal 12.00 30.00
GO09 James Sheppard 6.00 15.00
GO10 Sam Gagner 12.00 30.00
GO11 Bryan Little 8.00 20.00
GO12 Peter Mueller 20.00 50.00
GO13 Devin Setoguchi 12.00 30.00
GO14 Zach Hamill 6.00 15.00
GO15 Benoit Pouliot 6.00 15.00
GO16 Steve Downie 8.00 20.00

2007-08 ITG Heroes and Prospects Gloves Are Off Gold

STATED PRINT RUN 10 SER.#'d SETS
NOT PRICED DUE TO SCARCITY

2007-08 ITG Heroes and Prospects He Shoots He Scores

STATED PRINT RUN 20 SERIAL #'d SETS
NOT PRICED DUE TO SCARCITY
HSHS1 Patrick Kane
HSHS2 Marc Staal
HSHS3 Brandon Sutter
HSHS4 Colton Gillies
HSHS5 Sam Gagner
HSHS6 Logan Couture
HSHS7 Peter Mueller
HSHS8 Thomas Hickey
HSHS9 Jakub Voracek
HSHS10 Keaton Ellerby
HSHS11 Jonathan Bernier
HSHS12 Zach Hamill
HSHS13 Angelo Esposito
HSHS14 Karl Alzner
HSHS15 Leland Irving
HSHS16 Michael Frolik
HSHS17 Alexander Radulov
HSHS18 Carey Price
HSHS19 Drew Stafford
HSHS20 Bobby Ryan
HSHS21 Al Montoya
HSHS22 Jiri Tlusty
HSHS23 Tuukka Rask
HSHS24 Rob Schremp
HSHS25 Marek Schwarz
HSHS26 Benoit Pouliot
HSHS27 Alexei Cherepanov
HSHS28 John Tavares
HSHS29 Drew Doughty
HSHS30 Steven Stamkos
HSHS31 Dany Heatley
HSHS32 Jaromir Jagr
HSHS33 Jordan Staal
HSHS34 Kari Lehtonen
HSHS35 Alexander Ovechkin
HSHS36 Vincent Lecavalier
HSHS37 Ilya Kovalchuk
HSHS38 Joe Sakic
HSHS39 Roberto Luongo
HSHS40 Mike Modano

2007-08 ITG Heroes and Prospects Heroes Memorabilia

STATED PRINT RUN 30 SETS
HM01 Chris Pronger 8.00 20.00
HM02 Vincent Lecavalier 8.00 20.00
HM03 Roberto Luongo 12.00 30.00
HM04 Dominik Hasek 10.00 25.00
HM05 Joe Thornton 10.00 25.00
HM06 Dany Heatley 10.00 25.00
HM07 Joe Sakic 15.00 40.00
HM08 Mike Modano 8.00 20.00
HM09 Ilya Kovalchuk 10.00 25.00
HM10 Dave Keon 6.00 15.00
HM11 Peter Forsberg 10.00 25.00
HM12 Mats Sundin 8.00 20.00

2007-08 ITG Heroes and Prospects Jerseys

STATED PRINT RUN 130 SER.#'d SETS
STATED PRINT RUN 130 SER.#'d SETS
GUJ01 Alexei Cherepanov 5.00 12.00
GUJ02 Tuukka Rask 8.00 20.00
GUJ03 Jack Skille 5.00 12.00
GUJ04 John Tavares 20.00 50.00
GUJ05 Karl Alzner 4.00 10.00
GUJ06 Brandon Sutter 4.00 10.00
GUJ07 Angelo Esposito 8.00 20.00
GUJ08 Zach Hamill 3.00 8.00
GUJ09 Marc Staal 8.00 20.00
GUJ10 Sam Gagner 6.00 15.00
GUJ11 Leland Irving 5.00 12.00
GUJ12 Steve Downie 4.00 10.00
GUJ13 Peter Mueller 10.00 25.00
GUJ14 Thomas McCollum 4.00 10.00
GUJ15 Luc Bourdon 4.00 10.00
GUJ16 Cal Clutterbuck 3.00 8.00
GUJ17 Keaton Ellerby 3.00 8.00
GUJ18 Patrick Kane 20.00 50.00
GUJ19 Bryan Cameron 3.00 8.00
GUJ20 Claude Giroux 3.00 8.00
GUJ21 Drew Doughty 8.00 20.00
GUJ22 Michael Del Zotto 5.00 12.00
GUJ23 Trevor Cann 4.00 10.00
GUJ24 Michael Frolik 4.00 10.00
GUJ25 Trevor Lewis 4.00 10.00
GUJ26 James Sheppard 3.00 8.00
GUJ27 Steven Stamkos 10.00 25.00
GUJ28 Alexander Radulov 5.00 12.00
GUJ29 Marc-Antoine Pouliot 3.00 8.00
GUJ30 Ryan Callahan 5.00 12.00
GUJ31 Cody Bass 4.00 10.00
GUJ32 Benoit Pouliot 3.00 8.00
GUJ33 Rob Schremp 4.00 10.00
GUJ34 Marek Schwarz 4.00 10.00
GUJ35 Andrew Ebbett 3.00 8.00
GUJ36 Justin Pogge 6.00 15.00
GUJ37 Drew Stafford 4.00 10.00
GUJ38 Carey Price 15.00 40.00
GUJ39 Jiri Tlusty 8.00 20.00
GUJ40 Jeff Glass 4.00 10.00
GUJ41 Adam Dennis 4.00 10.00
GUJ42 Tobias Stephan 4.00 10.00
GUJ43 Josh Hennessy 3.00 8.00
GUJ44 Nigel Dawes 3.00 8.00
GUJ45 Loui Eriksson 3.00 8.00
GUJ46 Martin Houle 3.00 8.00
GUJ47 Jon Filewich 3.00 8.00
GUJ48 Jimmy Howard 8.00 20.00
GUJ49 Keith Aucoin 3.00 8.00
GUJ50 Bryan Little 4.00 10.00
GUJ51 Kevin Klein 3.00 8.00
GUJ52 Tyler Weiman 4.00 10.00
GUJ53 Stefan Legein 3.00 8.00
GUJ54 Michael Grabner 4.00 10.00
GUJ55 Thomas Hickey 6.00 15.00
GUJ56 David LeNeveu 4.00 10.00
GUJ57 Keith Yandle 3.00 8.00
GUJ58 Mikhail Grabovski 4.00 10.00
GUJ59 David Krejci 6.00 15.00
GUJ60 Jonathan Bernier 8.00 20.00
GUJ61 Kyle Okposo 4.00 10.00
GUJ62 Alex Pietrangelo 4.00 10.00
GUJ63 Luke Schenn 8.00 20.00
GUJ64 Jonas Hiller 10.00 25.00
GUJ65 Steve Mason 20.00 50.00
GUJ66 Devin Setoguchi 8.00 20.00
GUJ67 Brett MacLean 4.00 10.00
GUJ68 Zach Bogosian 10.00 25.00
GUJ69 Cody Hodgson 6.00 15.00

2007-08 ITG Heroes and Prospects John Tavares Firsts

COMPLETE SET (9) 25.00 60.00
COMMON CARD 4.00 10.00
STATED ODDS 1:14
JT01 John Tavares First Overall 4.00 10.00
JT02 John Tavares First Game 4.00 10.00
JT03 John Tavares First Goal 4.00 10.00
JT04 John Tavares First Multi-Point Game 4.00 10.00
JT05 John Tavares First Assist 4.00 10.00
JT06 John Tavares First Hat Trick 4.00 10.00
JT07 John Tavares First ADT Canada /Russia Challenge 4.00 10.00
JT08 John Tavares First OHL All-Star Classic 4.00 10.00
JT09 John Tavares First Playoff Game 4.00 10.00

2007-08 ITG Heroes and Prospects Memorial Cup Champions

COMPLETE SET (9) 8.00 20.00
STATED ODDS 1:14 ARENA PACKS
MC01 Spencer Machacek 1.00 2.50
MC02 Kenndal McArdle 1.00 2.50
MC03 Michal Repik 2.00 5.00
MC04 Milan Lucic 2.50 6.00
MC05 Brendan Mikkelson 1.00 2.50
MC06 Cody Franson 2.00 5.00
MC07 Jonathan Blum 1.00 2.50
MC08 A.J. Thelen 1.00 2.50
MC09 Tyson Sexsmith 1.25 3.00

2007-08 ITG Heroes and Prospects My Country My Team

STATED PRINT RUN 50 SETS
MCT01 John Tavares 30.00 80.00
MCT02 Marc Staal 12.00 30.00
MCT03 Ty Wishart 5.00 12.00
MCT04 Ryan O'Marra 5.00 12.00
MCT05 Angelo Esposito 12.00 30.00
MCT06 Bryan Little 6.00 15.00
MCT07 Leland Irving
MCT08 Carey Price 25.00 60.00
MCT09 Joe Sakic 15.00 40.00
MCT10 Martin Brodeur 20.00 50.00

2007-08 ITG Heroes and Prospects My Country My Team Gold

STATED PRINT RUN 10 SER.#'d SETS
NOT PRICED DUE TO SCARCITY

2007-08 ITG Heroes and Prospects Net Prospects

STATED PRINT RUN 90 SETS
NP01 Carey Price
NP02 Adam Dennis 5.00 12.00
NP03 Justin Pogge 8.00 20.00
NP04 Tobias Stephan 5.00 12.00
NP05 Jeremy Smith 4.00 10.00
NP06 Thomas McCollum 5.00 12.00
NP07 Steve Mason 20.00 50.00
NP08 Trevor Cann 5.00 12.00
NP09 Tyson Sexsmith 5.00 12.00
NP10 Jonathan Bernier 10.00 25.00
NP11 Leland Irving 6.00 15.00
NP12 Tuukka Rask 10.00 25.00
NP13 Jonas Hiller
NP14 Chet Pickard

2007-08 ITG Heroes and Prospects Net Prospects Gold

STATED PRINT RUN 10 SER.#'d SETS
NOT PRICED DUE TO SCARCITY

2007-08 ITG Heroes and Prospects Numbers

STATED PRINT RUN 20 SETS
GUN01 Alexei Cherepanov 15.00 40.00
GUN02 Tuukka Rask 25.00 60.00
GUN03 Jack Skille 15.00 40.00
GUN04 John Tavares 60.00 150.00
GUN05 Karl Alzner 12.00 30.00
GUN06 Brandon Sutter 12.00 30.00
GUN07 Angelo Esposito 25.00 60.00
GUN08 Zach Hamill 10.00 25.00
GUN09 Marc Staal 25.00 60.00
GUN10 Sam Gagner 20.00 50.00
GUN11 Leland Irving 15.00 40.00
GUN12 Steve Downie 12.00 30.00
GUN13 Peter Mueller 30.00 80.00
GUN14 Thomas McCollum 12.00 30.00
GUN15 Luc Bourdon 12.00 30.00
GUN16 Cal Clutterbuck 10.00 25.00
GUN17 Keaton Ellerby 10.00 25.00
GUN18 Patrick Kane 60.00 150.00
GUN19 Bryan Cameron 10.00 25.00
GUN20 Claude Giroux 10.00 25.00
GUN21 Drew Doughty 25.00 60.00
GUN22 Michael Del Zotto 15.00 40.00
GUN23 Trevor Cann 12.00 30.00
GUN24 Michael Frolik 12.00 30.00
GUN25 Trevor Lewis 12.00 30.00
GUN26 James Sheppard 10.00 25.00
GUN27 Steven Stamkos 30.00 80.00
GUN28 Alexander Radulov 15.00 40.00
GUN29 Marc-Antoine Pouliot 10.00 25.00
GUN30 Ryan Callahan 15.00 40.00
GUN31 Cody Bass 12.00 30.00
GUN32 Benoit Pouliot 10.00 25.00
GUN33 Rob Schremp 12.00 30.00
GUN34 Marek Schwarz 12.00 30.00
GUN35 Andrew Ebbett 10.00 25.00
GUN36 Justin Pogge 20.00 50.00
GUN37 Drew Stafford 12.00 30.00
GUN38 Carey Price 50.00 120.00
GUN39 Jiri Tlusty 25.00 60.00
GUN40 Jeff Glass 12.00 30.00
GUN41 Adam Dennis 12.00 30.00
GUN42 Tobias Stephan 12.00 30.00
GUN43 Josh Hennessy 10.00 25.00
GUN44 Nigel Dawes 10.00 25.00
GUN45 Loui Eriksson 10.00 25.00
GUN46 Martin Houle 10.00 25.00
GUN47 Jon Filewich 10.00 25.00
GUN48 Jimmy Howard 25.00 60.00
GUN49 Keith Aucoin 10.00 25.00
GUN50 Bryan Little 12.00 30.00
GUN51 Kevin Klein 10.00 25.00
GUN52 Tyler Weiman 12.00 30.00
GUN53 Stefan Legein 10.00 25.00
GUN54 Michael Grabner 12.00 30.00
GUN55 Thomas Hickey 20.00 50.00
GUN56 David LeNeveu 12.00 30.00
GUN57 Keith Yandle 10.00 25.00
GUN58 Mikhail Grabovski 12.00 30.00
GUN59 David Krejci 20.00 50.00
GUN60 Jonathan Bernier 25.00 60.00
GUN61 Kyle Okposo
GUN62 Alex Pietrangelo
GUN63 Luke Schenn
GUN64 Jonas Hiller 25.00 60.00
GUN65 Steve Mason
GUN66 Devin Setoguchi 20.00 50.00
GUN67 Brett MacLean 10.00 25.00
GUN68 Zach Bogosian 25.00 60.00
GUN69 Cody Hodgson

2007-08 ITG Heroes and Prospects Quad Emblems

STATED PRINT RUN 9 SER.#'d SETS
NOT PRICED DUE TO SCARCITY
QE01 John Tavares
Steven Stamkos
Patrick Kane
Sam Gagner
QE02 Jakub Voracek
Angelo Esposito
Claude Giroux
James Sheppard
QE03 Karl Alzner
Peter Mueller
Zach Hamill
Thomas Hickey
QE04 Drew Stafford
Patrick O'Sullivan
Ryan Callahan
Alexander Radulov
QE05 Carey Price
Justin Pogge
Marek Schwarz
Al Montoya
QE06 John Tavares
Tuukka Rask
Patrick Kane
Alexei Cherepanov
QE07 Patrick Roy
Martin Brodeur
Dominik Hasek
Roberto Luongo
QE08 Joe Sakic
Mike Modano
Joe Thornton
Vincent Lecavalier
QE09 Alexander Radulov
Jaromir Jagr
Ilya Kovalchuk
Alexander Ovechkin
QE10 Steve Downie
John Tavares
Carey Price
Kristopher Letang

2007-08 ITG Heroes and Prospects Quad Emblems Gold

STATED PRINT RUN 1 SER.#'d SET
NOT PRICED DUE TO SCARCITY

2007-08 ITG Heroes and Prospects Triple Memorabilia

STATED PRINT RUN 20 SERIAL #'d SETS
TM01 Al Montoya 50.00 100.00
Justin Pogge
Carey Price
TM02 Karl Alzner 15.00 30.00
Brandon Sutter
Colton Gillies
TM03 John Tavares 50.00 80.00
Drew Doughty
Steven Stamkos
TM04 Jakub Voracek 25.00 50.00
Angelo Esposito
James Sheppard
TM05 Drew Stafford 25.00 50.00
Patrick O'Sullivan
Alexander Radulov
TM06 Eric Staal 30.00 60.00
Marc Staal
Jordan Staal

2007-08 ITG Heroes and Prospects Triple Memorabilia Gold

STATED PRINT RUN 10 SER.#'d SETS
NOT PRICED DUE TO SCARCITY

2008-09 ITG Heroes and Prospects

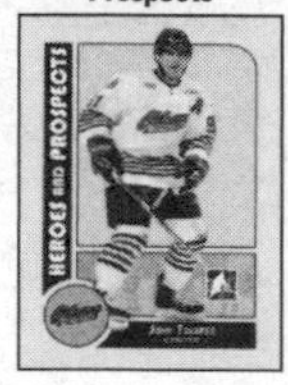

This set was released on December 17, 2008. The base set consists of 100 cards.

COMPLETE SET (100) 15.00 40.00
COMP.UPD.SET (50) 12.00 30.00
1 Mats Sundin .25 .60
2 Peter Forsberg .40 1.00
3 Pavel Datsyuk .25 .60
4 Ryan Getzlaf .30 .75
5 Alexander Ovechkin 1.00 2.50
6 Teemu Selanne .25 .60
7 Chris Osgood .25 .60
8 Fabian Brunnstrom .40 1.00
9 Ville Leino .50 1.25
10 Victor Hedman 1.00 2.50
11 Alex Goligoski .50 1.25
12 Alexander Nikulin .15 .40
13 Benoit Pouliot .15 .40
14 Blake Comeau .15 .40
15 Brendan Mikkelson .15 .40
16 Brian Boyle .25 .60
17 Brian Lee .25 .60
18 Bryan Little .15 .40
19 Chris Collins .15 .40
20 Chris Stewart .30 .75
21 Cody Franson .20 .50
22 Darren Helm .40 1.00
23 Derick Brassard .50 1.25
24 Devin Setoguchi .25 .60
25 Jack Skille .20 .50
26 Max Pacioretty .60 1.50
27 Jiri Tlusty .25 .60
28 Julian Talbot .15 .40
29 Kyle Greentree .30 .75
30 Kyle Okposo .50 1.25
31 Marc-Andre Gragnani .20 .50
32 Michael Grabner .15 .40
33 Mike Santorelli .20 .50
34 Nick Foligno .25 .60
35 Rob Schremp .20 .50
36 Ryan Parent .15 .40
37 Sergei Kostitsyn .25 .60
38 Justin Pogge .50 1.25
39 Teddy Purcell .25 .60
40 Vladimir Mihalik .25 .60
41 Alex Pietrangelo .40 1.00
42 Brett MacLean .15 .40
43 Cody Hodgson .15 .40
44 Drew Doughty .75 2.00
45 Greg Nemisz .15 .40
46 Jamie Arniel .15 .40
47 Jared Staal .40 1.00
48 John Tavares .75 2.00
49 Joshua Bailey .15 .40
50 Justin Azevedo .15 .40
51 Matt Duchene .15 .40
52 John McFarland .15 .40
53 Michael Del Zotto .20 .50
54 Mikkel Roedker .40 1.00
55 P.K. Subban .50 1.25
56 John Carlson .15 .40
57 Ryan O'Reilly .15 .40
58 Taylor Hall .15 .40

59 Steven Stamkos 2.00 5.00
60 Tyler Cuma .15 .40
61 Zach Bogosian .50 1.25
62 Brandon Sutter .30 .75
63 Brayden Schenn .25 .60
64 Colton Gillies .25 .60
65 Drayson Bowman .15 .40
66 Geordie Wudrick .15 .40
67 Jared Cowen .25 .60
68 Jonathon Blum .50 1.25
69 Jordan Eberle .15 .40
70 Jyri Niemi .15 .40
71 Karl Alzner .40 1.00
72 Keaton Ellerby .15 .40
73 Kyle Beach .15 .40
74 Luke Schenn .75 2.00
75 Landon Ferraro .15 .40
76 Mitch Wahl .15 .40
77 Nick Ross .15 .40
78 Oscar Moller .25 .60
79 T.J. Galiardi .15 .40
80 Thomas Hickey .30 .75
81 Tyler Ennis .15 .40
82 Zach Hamill .15 .40
83 Zach Boychuk .40 1.00
84 Angelo Esposito .40 1.00
85 Claude Giroux .50 1.25
86 Danick Paquette .15 .40
87 Francois Bouchard .15 .40
88 Philippe Cornet .15 .40
89 Jakub Voracek .50 1.25
90 Joel Champagne .15 .40
91 Kelsey Tessier .15 .40
92 Keven Veilleux .15 .40
93 Logan MacMillan .15 .40
94 Marco Scandella .15 .40
95 Mathieu Perreault .30 .75
96 Mikhail Stefanovich .15 .40
97 Nicolas Deschamps .15 .40
98 Patrice Cormier .15 .40
99 Stefan Chaput .15 .40
100 Yann Sauve .15 .40
101 Nikita Filatov 1.00 2.50
102 Chris Minard .25 .60
103 Justin Abdelkader .50 1.25
104 Oskar Osala .60 1.50
105 David Desharnais .15 .40
106 Mattias Karlsson .15 .40
107 Brad Marchand .20 .50
108 Bob Sanguinetti .20 .50
109 Chad Kolarik .15 .40
110 Simeon Varlamov 1.25 3.00
111 Luca Caputi .40 1.00
112 Michal Repik .30 .75
113 Mark Dekanich .15 .40
114 Zack Smith .20 .50
115 Jeff Frazee .15 .40
116 Tim Kennedy .40 1.00
117 Patrick Maroon .25 .60
118 Ben Maxwell .40 1.00
119 Viatcheslav Voynov .25 .60
120 Nathan Gerbe .50 1.25
121 Simon Despres .25 .60
122 Andrej Nestrasil .25 .60
123 Charles-Olivier Roussel .25 .60
124 Christopher DiDomenico .25 .60
125 David Gilbert .15 .40
126 Dmitry Kulikov .30 .75
127 Jordan Caron .25 .60
128 Olivier Roy .25 .60
129 Keith Aulie .15 .40
130 Colten Teubert .25 .60
131 Carter Ashton .20 .50
132 Brett Sonne .15 .40
133 Tyler Myers .15 .40
134 Scott Glennie .25 .60
135 Levko Koper .25 .60
136 Cody Eakin .15 .40
137 Jamie Benn .15 .40
138 Stefan Elliott .15 .40
139 Jimmy Bubnick .15 .40
140 Evander Kane .60 1.50
141 Peter Holland .15 .40
142 Evgeny Grachev .15 .40
143 Edward Pasquale .15 .40
144 Stefan Della Rovere .15 .40
145 Nazem Kadri .25 .60
146 Zack Kassian .50 1.25
147 Calvin de Haan .15 .40
148 Michael Latta .15 .40
149 Ryan Ellis .50 1.25
150 John Tavares .75 2.00

2008-09 ITG Heroes and Prospects ADT Canada/Russia Challenge Emblems

STATED PRINT RUN 19 SERIAL #'d SETS
NOT PRICED DUE TO SCARCITY

2008-09 ITG Heroes and Prospects ADT Canada/Russia Challenge Emblems Gold

STATED PRINT RUN 1 SERIAL #'d SET
NOT PRICED DUE TO SCARCITY

2008-09 ITG Heroes and Prospects ADT Canada/Russia Challenge Jerseys

STATED PRINT RUN 29 SERIAL #'d SETS
CRJ01 John Tavares 15.00 40.00
CRJ02 Alex Pietrangelo 8.00 20.00
CRJ03 Karl Alzner
CRJ04 Steven Stamkos
CRJ05 Luke Schenn 15.00 40.00
CRJ06 Shawn Matthias
CRJ07 Steve Mason 12.00 30.00
CRJ08 Brett MacLean
CRJ09 Thomas Hickey 6.00 15.00
CRJ10 Michael Del Zotto

2008-09 ITG Heroes and Prospects ADT Canada/Russia Challenge Jerseys Gold

STATED PRINT RUN 1 SERIAL #'d SET
NOT PRICED DUE TO SCARCITY

2008-09 ITG Heroes and Prospects ADT Canada/Russia Challenge Numbers

STATED PRINT RUN 19 SERIAL #'d SETS
NOT PRICED DUE TO SCARCITY

2008-09 ITG Heroes and Prospects ADT Canada/Russia Challenge Numbers Gold

STATED PRINT RUN 1 SERIAL #'d SET
NOT PRICED DUE TO SCARCITY

2008-09 ITG Heroes and Prospects Autographs

AAP Alex Pietrangelo 10.00 25.00
AAN Alexander Nikulin 4.00 10.00
AAO Alexander Ovechkin SP
AAE Angelo Esposito 10.00 25.00
ABP Benoit Pouliot 4.00 10.00
ABR Bobby Ryan 10.00 25.00
ABMAR2 Brad Marchand 5.00 12.00
ABSU Brandon Sutter 8.00 20.00
ABSC Brayden Schenn 6.00 15.00
ABMI Brendan Mikkelson 4.00 10.00
ABMA Brett MacLean 4.00 10.00
ABB Brian Boyle 6.00 15.00
ABLE Brian Lee 6.00 15.00
ABLI Bryan Little 4.00 10.00
ACD Chris Doyle 5.00 12.00
ACO Chris Osgood SP 12.00 30.00
ACS Chris Stewart 8.00 20.00
ACG Claude Giroux 12.00 30.00
ACF Cody Franson 5.00 12.00
ACH Cody Hodgson 4.00 10.00
ADH Darren Helm 10.00 25.00
ADB Derick Brassard 12.00 30.00
ADS Devin Setoguchi 6.00 15.00
ADD Drew Doughty 20.00 50.00
AFB Fabian Brunnstrom SP 10.00 25.00
AGW Geordie Wudrick 4.00 10.00
AGB Gilbert Brule 6.00 15.00
AIV Ivan Vishnevskiy 4.00 10.00
AJV Jakub Voracek 12.00 30.00
AJN James Neal 10.00 25.00
AJAR Jamie Arniel 4.00 10.00
AJCO Jared Cowen 6.00 15.00
AJST Jared Staal 10.00 25.00
AJSA Jerome Samson 4.00 10.00
AJT Jiri Tlusty 6.00 15.00
AJCH Joel Champagne 4.00 10.00
AJTAV John Tavares 50.00 100.00
AJM Jonathan Matsumoto 4.00 10.00
AJBL Jonathon Blum 12.00 30.00
AJE Jordan Eberle 20.00 50.00
AJBA Joshua Bailey 4.00 10.00
AJAZ Justin Azevedo 4.00 10.00
AJN Jyri Niemi 4.00 10.00
AKA Karl Alzner 10.00 25.00
AKE Keaton Ellerby 4.00 10.00
AKT Kelsey Tessier 4.00 10.00
AKV Keven Veilleux 4.00 10.00
AKL Kristopher Letang 4.00 10.00
AKO Kyle Okposo 12.00 30.00
ALC Logan Couture 4.00 10.00
ALM Logan MacMillan 4.00 10.00
ALC2 Luca Caputi 4.00 10.00
AMAG Marc-Andre Gragnani 5.00 12.00
AMSA Mark Santorelli 4.00 10.00
AMSU Mats Sundin SP 20.00 50.00
AMD Matt Duchene 4.00 10.00
AML Matt Lashoff 4.00 10.00
AMDZ Michael Del Zotto 5.00 12.00
AMFR Michael Frolik 12.00 30.00
AMG Michael Grabner 4.00 10.00
AMB Mikkel Boedker 10.00 25.00
AMFA Mitch Fadden 4.00 10.00
AMW Mitch Wahl 4.00 10.00
ANR Nick Ross 4.00 10.00
AND Nicolas Deschamps 4.00 10.00
AMO Oscar Moller 6.00 15.00
APKS P.K. Subban 12.00 30.00
APD Pavel Datsyuk SP 25.00 60.00
APF Peter Forsberg SP
ARS Rob Schremp 5.00 12.00
ARG Ryan Getzlaf SP
ARP Ryan Parent 4.00 10.00
ASMAT Shawn Matthias 6.00 15.00
ASMA Spencer Machacek 4.00 10.00
ASST Steven Stamkos 40.00 100.00
ATH Taylor Hall 50.00 100.00
ATP Teddy Purcell 6.00 15.00
ATS Teemu Selanne SP 15.00 40.00
ATH Thomas Hickey 8.00 20.00
ATW Ty Wishart 6.00 15.00
ATE Tyler Ennis 4.00 10.00
AVH Victor Hedman 50.00 100.00
AVL Ville Leino 12.00 30.00
AYS Yann Sauve 4.00 10.00
AZBOG Zach Bogosian 12.00 30.00
AZH Zach Hamill 4.00 10.00
AZBOY Zack Boychuk 10.00 25.00
AANE Andrej Nestrasil 6.00 15.00
ABMAR Brad Marchand 5.00 12.00
ABS Bob Sanguinetti 5.00 12.00
ABMAX Ben Maxwell 10.00 25.00
ACA Carter Ashton 5.00 12.00
ACE Cody Eakin 4.00 10.00
ACDH Calvin de Haan 4.00 10.00
ACR Charles-Olivier Roussel 6.00 15.00
ADG David Gilbert 4.00 10.00
ADK Dmitry Kulikov 8.00 20.00
AEK Evander Kane 15.00 40.00
AEP Edward Pasquale 4.00 10.00
AJBU Jimmy Bubnick 4.00 10.00
AJCA Jordan Caron 6.00 15.00
AJTAV2 John Tavares 50.00 100.00
AJTAV3 John Tavares 50.00 100.00
ALC Luca Caputi 10.00 25.00
ALK Levko Koper 6.00 15.00
AMLA Michael Latta 4.00 10.00
AMR Michal Repik 8.00 20.00
ANK Nazem Kadri 6.00 15.00
AOO Oskar Osala
AOR Olivier Roy
APH Peter Holland 4.00 10.00
ARE Ryan Ellis 12.00 30.00
ASD Simon Despres 6.00 15.00
ASE Stefan Elliott 4.00 10.00
ASG Scott Glennie 6.00 15.00
ASV Simeon Varlamov 30.00 80.00
AZK Zack Kassian 12.00 30.00

2008-09 ITG Heroes and Prospects Calder Cup Winners

COMPLETE SET (13) 20.00 50.00
1 Jason Krog 5.00 12.00
2 Darren Haydar 2.50 6.00
3 Joel Kwiatkowski 2.50 6.00
4 Brian Fahey 2.50 6.00
5 Steve Martins 2.50 6.00
6 Brett Sterling 3.00 8.00
7 Jesse Shultz 2.50 6.00
8 Joe Motzko 2.50 6.00
9 Nathan Oystrick 4.00 10.00
10 Jordan LaVallee 4.00 10.00
11 Boris Valabik 5.00 12.00
12 Bryan Little 2.50 6.00
13 Ondrej Pavelec 3.00 8.00

2008-09 ITG Heroes and Prospects Complete Jerseys

STATED PRINT RUN 9 SERIAL #'d SETS
NOT PRICED DUE TO SCARCITY

2008-09 ITG Heroes and Prospects Complete Jerseys Gold

NOT PRICED DUE TO SCARCITY

2008-09 ITG Heroes and Prospects Complete Logos

STATED PRINT RUN 1 SERIAL #'d SET
NOT PRICED DUE TO SCARCITY

2008-09 ITG Heroes and Prospects Draft Picks

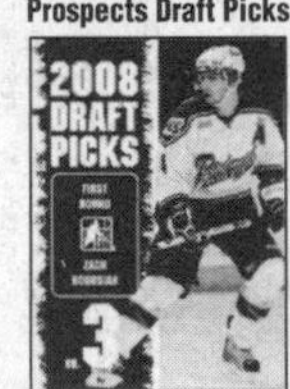

COMPLETE SET (20) 15.00 40.00
1 Steven Stamkos 8.00 20.00
2 Drew Doughty 3.00 8.00
3 Zach Bogosian 2.00 5.00
4 Alex Pietrangelo 1.50 4.00
5 Luke Schenn 3.00 8.00
6 Mikkel Boedker 1.50 4.00
7 Joshua Bailey .60 1.50
8 Cody Hodgson .60 1.50
9 Kyle Beach .60 1.50
10 Tyler Myers .60 1.50
11 Tyler Ennis .60 1.50
12 Zach Boychuk 1.50 4.00
13 Chet Pickard 1.00 2.50
14 Michael Del Zotto .75 2.00
15 Jordan Eberle .60 1.50
16 Thomas McCollum 1.25 3.00
17 Philip McRae .60 1.50
18 Nicolas Deschamps .60 1.50
19 Mitch Wahl .60 1.50
20 Jared Staal 1.50 4.00

2008-09 ITG Heroes and Prospects Emblems

STATED PRINT RUN 9 SERIAL #'d SETS
NOT PRICED DUE TO SCARCITY

2008-09 ITG Heroes and Prospects Emblems Gold

NOT PRICED DUE TO SCARCITY

2008-09 ITG Heroes and Prospects Emblems Autographs

STATED PRINT RUN 9 SERIAL #'d SETS
NOT PRICED DUE TO SCARCITY

2008-09 ITG Heroes and Prospects Emblems Autographs Gold

NOT PRICED DUE TO SCARCITY

2008-09 ITG Heroes and Prospects Gloves Are Off Memorabilia Autographs

STATED PRINT RUN 9 SERIAL #'d SETS
NOT PRICED DUE TO SCARCITY

2008-09 ITG Heroes and Prospects Gloves Are Off Memorabilia Autographs Gold

NOT PRICED DUE TO SCARCITY

2008-09 ITG Heroes and Prospects Hero and Prospect Memorabilia

STATED PRINT RUN 50 SERIAL #'d SETS
HP01 Patrick Roy 60.00 120.00
Carey Price
HP02 Alexander Ovechkin 20.00 50.00
Sergei Kostitsyn
HP03 Martin Brodeur 20.00 50.00
Jonathan Bernier
HP04 Jaromir Jagr 15.00 40.00
Jiri Tlusty
HP05 Mario Lemieux 50.00 100.00
Marc-Andre Gragnani
HP06 Cam Neely 25.00 60.00
John Tavares
HP07 Vincent Lecavalier 20.00 50.00
Steven Stamkos
HP08 Marian Gaborik 25.00 60.00
Jakub Voracek
HP09 Bobby Clarke 12.00 30.00
Steve Downie
HP10 Joe Sakic 20.00 50.00
Karl Alzner

2008-09 ITG Heroes and Prospects Hero and Prospect Memorabilia Gold

STATED PRINT RUN 10 SERIAL #'d SETS
NOT PRICED DUE TO SCARCITY

2008-09 ITG Heroes and Prospects Heroes Memorabilia

STATED PRINT RUN 60 SERIAL #'d SETS
HM01 Mats Sundin 8.00 20.00
HM02 Peter Forsberg 12.00 30.00
HM03 Pavel Datsyuk 8.00 20.00
HM04 Ryan Getzlaf 10.00 25.00
HM05 Alexander Ovechkin 30.00 80.00
HM06 Teemu Selanne 8.00 20.00
HM07 Chris Osgood 8.00 20.00

2008-09 ITG Heroes and Prospects Heroes Memorabilia Gold

STATED PRINT RUN 10 SERIAL #'d SETS
NOT PRICED DUE TO SCARCITY

2008-09 ITG Heroes and Prospects Heroes Memorabilia Autographs

STATED PRINT RUN 9 SERIAL #'d SETS
NOT PRICED DUE TO SCARCITY

2008-09 ITG Heroes and Prospects Heroes Memorabilia Autographs Gold

NOT PRICED DUE TO SCARCITY

2008-09 ITG Heroes and Prospects How Swede It Is Memorabilia Combos Autographs

STATED PRINT RUN 9 SERIAL #'d SETS
NOT PRICED DUE TO SCARCITY

2008-09 ITG Heroes and Prospects How Swede It Is Memorabilia Combos Autographs Gold

NOT PRICED DUE TO SCARCITY

2008-09 ITG Heroes and Prospects Jerseys

STATED PRINT RUN 100 SERIAL #'d SETS
GUJ01 Bryan Little 3.00 8.00
GUJ02 Blake Comeau 3.00 8.00
GUJ03 Benoit Pouliot 3.00 8.00
GUJ04 Matt Duchene 3.00 8.00
GUJ05 Chris Collins 3.00 8.00
GUJ06 Chris Stewart 6.00 15.00
GUJ07 Nick Foligno 5.00 12.00
GUJ08 Brian Lee 5.00 12.00
GUJ09 Stephen Dixon 4.00 10.00
GUJ10 Cody Hodgson 3.00 8.00
GUJ11 Joshua Bailey 3.00 8.00
GUJ12 Michael Del Zotto 4.00 10.00
GUJ13 Steven Stamkos 15.00 40.00
GUJ14 Brandon Sutter 6.00 15.00
GUJ15 Colton Gillies 5.00 12.00
GUJ16 Keaton Ellerby 3.00 8.00
GUJ17 Karl Alzner 8.00 20.00
GUJ18 Jakub Voracek 10.00 25.00
GUJ19 Logan MacMillan 3.00 8.00
GUJ20 Carey Price 15.00 40.00
GUJ21 P.K. Subban 10.00 25.00
GUJ22 Patrick Maroon 5.00 12.00
GUJ23 Keven Veilleux 3.00 8.00
GUJ24 Mark Katic 3.00 8.00
GUJ25 Kyle DeCoste 4.00 10.00
GUJ26 John Tavares 15.00 40.00
GUJ27 Mikhail Grabovski 8.00 20.00
GUJ28 Marc Staal 6.00 15.00
GUJ29 Marc-Andre Gragnani 4.00 10.00
GUJ30 Bobby Hughes 3.00 8.00
GUJ31 Alexander Nikulin 3.00 8.00
GUJ32 Brendan Mikkelson 3.00 8.00
GUJ33 Cody Franson 4.00 10.00
GUJ34 Devin Setoguchi 5.00 12.00
GUJ35 Gilbert Brule 5.00 12.00
GUJ36 James Neal 8.00 20.00
GUJ37 Jerome Samson 3.00 8.00
GUJ38 Jiri Tlusty 5.00 12.00
GUJ39 Julian Talbot 3.00 8.00
GUJ40 Kristopher Letang 3.00 8.00
GUJ41 Kyle Greentree 6.00 15.00
GUJ42 Matt Lashoff 3.00 8.00
GUJ43 Mike Santorelli 4.00 10.00
GUJ44 Sergei Kostitsyn 5.00 12.00
GUJ45 Vladimir Mihalik 5.00 12.00

2008-09 ITG Heroes and Prospects Jerseys Gold

STATED PRINT RUN 10 SERIAL #'d SETS
NOT PRICED DUE TO SCARCITY

2008-09 ITG Heroes and Prospects Jerseys Autographs

STATED PRINT RUN 19 SERIAL #'d SETS
NOT PRICED DUE TO SCARCITY

2008-09 ITG Heroes and Prospects Jerseys Autographs Gold

NOT PRICED DUE TO SCARCITY

2008-09 ITG Heroes and Prospects Memorial Cup Winners

COMPLETE SET (12) 15.00 40.00
1 Mitch Wahl 2.50 6.00
2 Chris Bruton 2.50 6.00
3 Jared Cowen 4.00 10.00
4 Levko Koper 4.00 10.00
5 Dustin Tokarski 4.00 10.00
6 Drayson Bowman 2.50 6.00
7 Justin Falk 2.50 6.00
8 Trevor Glass 2.50 6.00
9 Ondrej Roman 2.50 6.00
10 Judd Blackwater 2.50 6.00
11 Justin McCrae 2.50 6.00
12 Jared Spurgeon 2.50 6.00

2008-09 ITG Heroes and Prospects Numbers

STATED PRINT RUN 9 SERIAL #'d SETS
NOT PRICED DUE TO SCARCITY

2008-09 ITG Heroes and Prospects Numbers Gold

NOT PRICED DUE TO SCARCITY

2008-09 ITG Heroes and Prospects Numbers Autographs

STATED PRINT RUN 9 SERIAL #'d SETS
NOT PRICED DUE TO SCARCITY

2008-09 ITG Heroes and Prospects Numbers Autographs Gold

NOT PRICED DUE TO SCARCITY

2008-09 ITG Heroes and Prospects Prospect Combos Memorabilia

STATED PRINT RUN 60 SERIAL #'d SETS
PC01 Kristopher Letang 15.00 40.00
John Tavares
PC02 James Neal 15.00 40.00
Steven Stamkos
PC03 Matt Lashoff 12.00 30.00
Drew Doughty
PC04 Justin Pogge 20.00 50.00
Steve Mason
PC05 Marc-Andre Gragnani 15.00 40.00
Michael Del Zotto
PC06 Gilbert Brule 8.00 20.00
Brandon Sutter
PC07 Cody Franson 8.00 20.00
P.K. Subban
PC08 Jiri Tlusty
Luke Schenn
PC09 Sergei Kostitsyn
Alex Plante
PC10 Alexander Nikulin 8.00 20.00
Mikkel Boedker

2008-09 ITG Heroes and Prospects Prospect Combos Memorabilia Gold

STATED PRINT RUN 10 SERIAL #'d SETS
NOT PRICED DUE TO SCARCITY

2008-09 ITG Heroes and Prospects Selects Memorabilia

STATED PRINT RUN 9 SERIAL #'d SETS
NOT PRICED DUE TO SCARCITY

2008-09 ITG Heroes and Prospects Selects Memorabilia Gold

STATED PRINT RUN 1 SERIAL #'d SET
NOT PRICED DUE TO SCARCITY

2008-09 ITG Heroes and Prospects Top Prospects Emblems

STATED PRINT RUN 9 SERIAL #'d SETS
NOT PRICED DUE TO SCARCITY

2008-09 ITG Heroes and Prospects Top Prospects Emblems Gold

NOT PRICED DUE TO SCARCITY

2008-09 ITG Heroes and Prospects Top Prospects Jerseys

STATED PRINT RUN
TPJ01 Akim Aliu 4.00 10.00
TPJ02 Trevor Cann 5.00 12.00
TPJ03 Keaton Ellerby 4.00 10.00
TPJ04 Angelo Esposito 10.00 25.00
TPJ05 Sam Gagner 10.00 25.00
TPJ06 Zach Hamill 4.00 10.00
TPJ07 Thomas Hickey
TPJ08 Patrick Kane
TPJ09 Brandon Sutter 8.00 20.00
TPJ10 Jakub Voracek 12.00 30.00
TPJ11 Jonathon Blum 12.00 30.00
TPJ12 Alex Pietrangelo 10.00 25.00
TPJ13 Jared Staal 10.00 25.00
TPJ14 Joshua Bailey 4.00 10.00
TPJ15 Michael Del Zotto 5.00 12.00
TPJ16 Drew Doughty
TPJ17 Logan MacMillan 4.00 10.00
TPJ18 Colton Gillies 6.00 15.00
TPJ19 Zach Boychuk 10.00 25.00
TPJ20 Zach Bogosian 12.00 30.00

2008-09 ITG Heroes and Prospects Top Prospects Jerseys Gold

STATED PRINT RUN 10 SERIAL #'d SETS
NOT PRICED DUE TO SCARCITY

2008-09 ITG Heroes and Prospects Top Prospects Numbers

STATED PRINT RUN 9 SERIAL #'d SETS
NOT PRICED DUE TO SCARCITY

2008-09 ITG Heroes and Prospects Top Prospects Numbers Gold

NOT PRICED DUE TO SCARCITY

2009-10 ITG Heroes and Prospects

COMPLETE SET (150) 15.00 40.00
1 Elmer Lach .50 1.25
2 Ted Lindsay .25 .60
3 Larry Kwong .60 1.50
4 Ted Kennedy .40 1.00
5 Oliver Ekman-Larsson .20 .50
6 Jacob Josefson .15 .40
7 Dmitry Kulikov .25 .60
8 Mikkel Boedker .20 .50
9 Kevin Bieksa .15 .40
10 Jay Bouwmeester .25 .60
11 Mike Cammalleri .20 .50
12 David Backes .20 .50
13 Kyle Okposo .25 .60
14 Kristopher Letang .25 .60
15 Ryan Getzlaf .40 1.00
16 Eric Staal .30 .75
17 Jason Spezza .30 .75
18 Maxime Talbot .25 .60
19 Devin Setoguchi .20 .50
20 Jason Pominville .25 .60
21 Zach Parise .25 .60
22 Matt Stajan .20 .50
23 Shea Weber .20 .50
24 Jhonas Enroth .30 .75
25 Mattias Karlsson .15 .40
26 Yannick Weber .30 .75
27 Justin Abdelkader .25 .60
28 Ben Maxwell .40 1.00
29 Shawn Matthias .25 .60
30 Bobby Sanguinetti .20 .50
31 Michal Neuvirth .60 1.50
32 Brad Marchand .30 .75
33 Brandon Sutter .25 .60
34 Maxsim Mayorov .20 .50
35 Nathan Gerbe .30 .75
36 Karl Alzner .25 .60
37 Artem Anisimov .30 .75
38 Justin Azevedo .15 .40
39 Nathan Lawson .20 .50
40 Matt Beaudoin .15 .40
41 Jonathan Bernier .25 .60
42 Kevin Porter .15 .40
43 David Desharnais .40 1.00
44 Zack Smith .15 .40
45 Chad Kolarik .15 .40
46 Cory Schneider .40 1.00
47 Byron Bitz .20 .50
48 Tim Kennedy .25 .60
49 Tuukka Rask .30 .75
50 Patrick Maroon .15 .40
51 Kyle Turris .30 .75
52 Cody Franson .25 .60
53 Luca Caputi .30 .75
54 Mikko Lehtonen .25 .60
55 Nikita Filatov .50 1.25
56 Max Pacioretty .25 .60
57 Michal Repik .20 .50
58 Spencer Machacek .20 .50
59 Angelo Esposito .20 .50
60 Andrei Loktionov .30 .75
61 Jonathon Blum .20 .50
62 Christian Hanson .30 .75
63 Viktor Stalberg .40 1.00
64 PK Subban .40 1.00
65 Thomas Hickey .15 .40
66 Tyler Ennis .60 1.50
67 Zach Boychuk .30 .75
68 Lars Eller .40 1.00
69 Brayden Schenn .50 1.25
70 Scott Glennie .20 .50
71 Jared Cowen .25 .60
72 Evander Kane .60 1.50
73 Matt Duchene 1.00 2.50
74 Peter Holland .15 .40
75 Zack Kassian .25 .60
76 Calvin de Haan .15 .40
77 Ryan Ellis .20 .50
78 Nazem Kadri .40 1.00
79 Ryan O'Reilly .50 1.25
80 Matthew Hackett .30 .75
81 Tyler Seguin .50 1.25
82 Shawn Lalonde .20 .50
83 Taylor Beck .15 .40
84 Michael Latta .15 .40
85 Taylor Doherty .15 .40
86 John McFarland .25 .60
87 Ryan Spooner .20 .50
88 Tyler Toffoli .15 .40
89 Erik Gudbranson .25 .60
90 Cody Hodgson .25 .60
91 Jesse Blacker .20 .50
92 Ethan Werek .15 .40
93 Edward Pasquale .25 .60
94 Joey Hishon .25 .60
95 Taylor Hall 2.00 5.00
96 Cam Fowler .40 1.00
97 Cameron Gaunce .15 .40
98 Ryan Bourque .25 .60
99 Jake Allen .30 .75
100 Simon Despres .25 .60
101 Brandon Gormley .40 1.00
102 Nicolas Deschamps .20 .50
103 Marco Scandella .15 .40
104 Benjamin Casavant .15 .40
105 Charles-Olivier Roussel .25 .60
106 Luke Adam .20 .50
107 Kirill Kabanov .30 .75
108 Peter Delmas .20 .50
109 Mathieu Brodeur .20 .50
110 Jordan Caron .15 .40
111 Dave Labrecque .15 .40
112 Olivier Roy .30 .75
113 Eric Gelinas .15 .40
114 Chris Doyle .15 .40
115 Kelsey Tessier .15 .40
116 Philippe Paradis .30 .75
117 Nicolas Deslauriers .15 .40
118 Gleason Fournier .15 .40
119 Andrej Nestrasil .15 .40
120 Louis Domingue .40 1.00
121 Ryan Howse .15 .40
122 Brayden McNabb .15 .40
123 Quinton Howden .25 .60
124 Carter Ashton .20 .50
125 Jimmy Bubnick .15 .40
126 Stefan Elliott .20 .50
127 Nathan Lieuwen .30 .75
128 Tyson Barrie .20 .50
129 Landon Ferraro .20 .50
130 Jordan Eberle .50 1.25
131 Travis Hamonic .15 .40
132 Martin Jones .25 .60
133 Calvin Pickard .40 1.00
134 Adam Morrison .20 .50
135 Brandon McMillan .15 .40
136 Brandon Kozun .20 .50
137 Brett Ponich .15 .40
138 Colby Robak .15 .40
139 Brett Connolly .25 .60
140 Cody Eakin .20 .50
141 Stanislav Galiev .30 .75
142 Daniel Catenacci .20 .50
143 Brandon Maxwell .20 .50
144 Matt Puempel .20 .50
145 Ivan Telegin .15 .40
146 Olivier Archambault .20 .50
147 Brent Andrews .15 .40
148 Alexander Burmistrov .20 .50
149 Ryan Nugent-Hopkins .30 .75
150 Shane McColgan .25 .60

2009-10 ITG Heroes and Prospects AHL All Star Legends

COMPLETE SET (20) 40.00 100.00
AS01 Tuukka Rask 4.00 10.00
AS02 Bobby Ryan 4.00 10.00
AS03 Drew Stafford 3.00 8.00
AS04 Dustin Byfuglien 2.50 6.00
AS05 Jaroslav Halak 3.00 8.00
AS06 Pekka Rinne 2.50 6.00
AS07 Mike Keane 2.00 5.00
AS08 Patrick O'Sullivan 2.50 6.00
AS09 Zach Parise 3.00 8.00
AS10 Jason Spezza 4.00 10.00
AS11 Mikko Koivu 3.00 8.00
AS12 Ryan Miller 3.00 8.00
AS13 Jay Bouwmeester 3.00 8.00
AS14 Mike Cammalleri 2.50 6.00
AS15 Eric Staal 4.00 10.00
AS16 Patrice Bergeron 3.00 8.00
AS17 Brad Boyes 2.50 6.00
AS18 Miikka Kiprusoff 3.00 8.00
AS19 Kari Lehtonen 3.00 8.00
AS20 Jason LaBarbera 2.50 6.00

2009-10 ITG Heroes and Prospects AHL Grad Jerseys

STATED PRINT RUN 30 SER.#'d SETS
AG01 Blake Comeau 4.00 10.00
AG02 Corey Perry
AG03 David Krejci
AG04 Devin Setoguchi 5.00 12.00
AG05 Jay Bouwmeester
AG06 Jeff Carter 6.00 15.00
AG07 Kari Lehtonen
AG08 Kyle Okposo 6.00 15.00
AG09 Carey Price
AG10 Marc-Andre Fleury 15.00 40.00
AG11 Mike Green
AG12 Pascal Leclaire 6.00 15.00
AG13 Ryan Callahan
AG14 Ryan Getzlaf 10.00 25.00
AG15 Ryan Miller
AG16 Tim Thomas 6.00 15.00

2009-10 ITG Heroes and Prospects AHL Grad Jerseys Gold

STATED PRINT RUN 10 SER.#'d SETS
NOT PRICED DUE TO SCARCITY

2009-10 ITG Heroes and Prospects Autographs

AAB Alex Bourret 4.00 10.00
AAE Angelo Esposito 5.00 12.00
AAL Andrei Loktionov 8.00 20.00
AAN Andrej Nestrasil 4.00 10.00
ABA Brent Andrews 4.00 10.00
ABB Byron Bitz 5.00 12.00
ABC Brett Connolly 6.00 15.00
ABG Brandon Gormley 10.00 25.00

ABH Bobby Hull 15.00 40.00
ABK Brandon Kozun 5.00 12.00
ABM Brad Marchand 8.00 20.00
ABP Benoit Pouliot 4.00 10.00
ABS Bobby Sanguinetti 5.00 12.00
ACA Carter Ashton 5.00 12.00
ACC Cal Clutterbuck 5.00 12.00
ACF Cody Franson 6.00 15.00
ACG Claude Giroux 12.00 30.00
ACH Christian Hanson 8.00 20.00
ACK Chuck Kobasew 4.00 10.00
ACR Charles-Olivier Roussel 6.00 15.00
ACS Cory Schneider 10.00 25.00
ADC Daniel Catenacci 5.00 12.00
ADK Dmitry Kulikov
ADS Devin Setoguchi 5.00 12.00
AEG2 Erik Gudbranson 6.00 15.00
AEG Erik Gudbranson 6.00 15.00
AEK Evander Kane 15.00 40.00
AEL Elmer Lach 12.00 30.00
AES Eric Staal 8.00 20.00
AEW Ethan Werek 4.00 10.00
AGB Gilbert Brule 8.00 20.00
AIL Igor Larionov
AIT Ivan Telegin 4.00 10.00
AJA Justin Azevedo 4.00 10.00
AJB Jonathan Bernier 6.00 15.00
AJC Jeff Carter 6.00 15.00
AJE Jordan Eberle 30.00 60.00
AJH Joey Hishon 6.00 15.00
AJJ Jacob Josefson 4.00 10.00
AJM John McFarland 6.00 15.00
AKA Karl Alzner 6.00 15.00
AKM Kenndal McArdle 5.00 12.00
AKO Kyle Okposo 6.00 15.00
AKT Kyle Turris 8.00 20.00
AKV Keven Veilleux 4.00 10.00
ALA Luke Adam 5.00 12.00
ALC Luca Caputi 8.00 20.00
ALD Louis Domingue 10.00 25.00
ALE Lars Eller 10.00 25.00
ALF Landon Ferraro 5.00 12.00
ALK Larry Kwong 15.00 40.00
AMB Mikkel Boedker 5.00 12.00
AMC Mike Cammalleri 5.00 12.00
AMD Matt Duchene 25.00 60.00
AMH Matthew Hackett 8.00 20.00
AMJ Martin Jones 6.00 15.00
AML Michael Latta 4.00 10.00
AMM Maxsim Mayorov 5.00 12.00
AMN Michal Neuvirth 15.00 40.00
AMP Max Pacioretty 6.00 15.00
AMR Michal Repik 5.00 12.00
AMS Marco Scandella 4.00 10.00
AMW Mike Weber
AND Nicolas Deschamps 5.00 12.00
ANK Nazem Kadri 25.00 50.00
ANL Nathan Lawson 5.00 12.00
ANP Nick Petrecki 6.00 15.00
AOA Olivier Archambault 5.00 12.00
AOR Olivier Roy 8.00 20.00
APH Peter Holland 4.00 10.00
APP Philippe Paradis 8.00 20.00
AQH Quinton Howden 6.00 15.00
ARB Raphael Bussieres 4.00 10.00
ARG Ryan Getzlaf 10.00 25.00
ARO Ryan O'Reilly 12.00 30.00
ARS Ryan Spooner 5.00 12.00
ASD Simon Despres 6.00 15.00
ASE Stefan Elliott 5.00 12.00
ASG Scott Glennie 5.00 12.00
ASL Shawn Lalonde 5.00 12.00
ASM Spencer Machacek 5.00 12.00
ATB Tyler Bozak 15.00 40.00
ATD Taylor Doherty 4.00 10.00
ATE Tyler Ennis 15.00 40.00
ATH Thomas Hickey 4.00 10.00
ATH2 Taylor Hall 25.00 60.00
ATK Ted Kennedy 25.00 50.00
ATL Ted Lindsay 6.00 15.00
ATP Tom Pyatt 8.00 20.00
ATS Tyler Seguin 50.00 100.00
ATS2 Tyler Seguin 50.00 100.00
ATT Tyler Toffoli 4.00 10.00
ATW Tyler Weiman 6.00 15.00
AVS Viktor Stalberg 10.00 25.00
AYW Yannick Weber 8.00 20.00
AZK Zack Kassian 6.00 15.00
AZP Zach Parise 6.00 15.00
ABMA Brandon Maxwell 5.00 12.00
ABMC Brandon McMillan 4.00 10.00
ABSC Brayden Schenn 12.00 30.00
ABSU Brandon Sutter 6.00 15.00
ACDH Calvin de Haan 4.00 10.00
ACFO Cam Fowler 20.00 40.00
ACGA Cameron Gaunce 4.00 10.00
ACRO Colby Robak 4.00 10.00
AJAL Jake Allen 8.00 20.00
AJBE Jean Beliveau 40.00 80.00
AJBL Jonathan Blum 5.00 12.00
AJBU Jimmy Bubnick 4.00 10.00
AJCA Jordan Caron 4.00 10.00
AJCO Jared Cowen 20.00 40.00
ALCO Logan Couture 12.00 30.00
AMBE Matt Beaudoin 4.00 10.00
AMPU Matt Puempel 5.00 12.00
AOEL Oliver Ekman-Larsson 5.00 12.00
ARNH Ryan Nugent-Hopkins 8.00 20.00
ASGA Stanislav Galiev 8.00 20.00
ASMA Shawn Matthias 6.00 15.00
ASMC Shane McColgan 6.00 15.00
ATBA Tyson Barrie 5.00 12.00
ATBE Taylor Beck 4.00 10.00
ATHA Taylor Hall 50.00 100.00

2009-10 ITG Heroes and Prospects Calder Cup Winners

COMPLETE SET (18) 60.00 120.00
CC01 Michal Neuvirth 10.00 25.00
CC02 Alexandre Giroux 5.00 12.00
CC03 Keith Aucoin 5.00 12.00
CC04 Chris Bourque 4.00 10.00
CC05 Graham Mink 4.00 10.00
CC06 Staffan Kronwall 3.00 8.00
CC07 Andrew Gordon 3.00 8.00
CC08 Oskar Osala 4.00 10.00
CC09 Mathieu Perreault 5.00 12.00
CC10 Karl Alzner 4.00 10.00
CC11 Francois Bouchard 4.00 10.00
CC12 John Carlson 8.00 20.00
CC13 Tyler Sloan 4.00 10.00
CC14 Kyle Wilson 2.50 6.00
CC15 Bryan Helmer 4.00 10.00
CC16 Steve Pinizzotto 3.00 8.00
CC17 Quintin Laing 3.00 8.00
CC18 Jay Beagle 4.00 10.00

2009-10 ITG Heroes and Prospects Class of 2010

COMPLETE SET (15)
C01 Taylor Hall 15.00 40.00
C02 Kirill Kabanov 5.00 12.00
C03 John McFarland 4.00 10.00
C04 Cam Fowler 6.00 15.00
C05 Tyler Seguin 8.00 20.00
C06 Joey Hishon 4.00 10.00
C07 Erik Gudbranson 4.00 10.00
C08 Brett Connolly 4.00 10.00
C09 Brandon Gormley 6.00 15.00
C10 Stanislav Galiev 5.00 12.00
C11 Quinton Howden 4.00 10.00
C12 Jeffery Skinner 6.00 15.00
C13 Mark Pysyk 3.00 8.00
C14 Alexander Burmistrov 3.00 8.00
C15 Vladimir Tarasenko 4.00 10.00

2009-10 ITG Heroes and Prospects Complete Jersey

STATED PRINT RUN 9 SER.#'d SETS
NOT PRICED DUE TO SCARCITY
CJ01 Taylor Hall
CJ02 Cody Hodgson
CJ03 Brayden Schenn
CJ04 Jordan Eberle
CJ05 Tyler Myers
CJ06 Matt Duchene
CJ07 Karl Alzner
CJ08 Brandon Sutter
CJ09 Brian Lee
CJ10 Cody Franson
CJ11 Tyler Seguin
CJ12 Nazem Kadri

2009-10 ITG Heroes and Prospects Complete Jersey Gold

STATED PRINT RUN 1 SER.#'d SET
NOT PRICED DUE TO SCARCITY

2009-10 ITG Heroes and Prospects Complete Logos AHL

STATED PRINT RUN 1 SER.#'d SET
NOT PRICED DUE TO SCARCITY

2009-10 ITG Heroes and Prospects Complete Logos CHL

STATED PRINT RUN 1 SER.#'d SET
NOT PRICED DUE TO SCARCITY

2009-10 ITG Heroes and Prospects Double Patch

STATED PRINT RUN 9 SER.#'d SETS
NOT PRICED DUE TO SCARCITY

2009-10 ITG Heroes and Prospects Double Patch Gold

STATED PRINT RUN 1 SER.#'d SET
NOT PRICED DUE TO SCARCITY

2009-10 ITG Heroes and Prospects Enforcers

COMPLETE SET (10) 30.00 60.00
E01 Matt Clackson 4.00 10.00
E02 Jeremy Yablonski 5.00 12.00
E03 Justin Soryal 4.00 10.00
E04 Trevor Gillies 4.00 10.00
E05 Kip Brennan 4.00 10.00
E06 Wade Brookbank 3.00 8.00
E07 Tim Spencer 3.00 8.00
E08 Brodie Dupont 3.00 8.00
E09 Jesse Boulerice 5.00 12.00
E10 Brett Henley 4.00 10.00

2009-10 ITG Heroes and Prospects Game Used Emblems

STATED PRINT RUN 6 SER.#'d SETS
NOT PRICED DUE TO SCARCITY

2009-10 ITG Heroes and Prospects Game Used Emblems Gold

STATED PRINT RUN 1 SER.#'d SET
NOT PRICED DUE TO SCARCITY

2009-10 ITG Heroes and Prospects Game Used Emblems Silver

STATED PRINT RUN 3 SER.#'d SETS
NOT PRICED DUE TO SCARCITY

2009-10 ITG Heroes and Prospects Game Used Emblems Autographs

STATED PRINT RUN 6 SER.#'d SETS
NOT PRICED DUE TO SCARCITY

2009-10 ITG Heroes and Prospects Game Used Emblems Autographs Gold

STATED PRINT RUN 1 SER.#'d SET
NOT PRICED DUE TO SCARCITY

2009-10 ITG Heroes and Prospects Game Used Emblems Autographs Silver

STATED PRINT RUN 3 SER.#'d SETS
NOT PRICED DUE TO SCARCITY

2009-10 ITG Heroes and Prospects Game Used Jerseys

STATED PRINT RUN 100 SER.#'d SETS
M01 Leland Irving 6.00 15.00
M02 Brandon Sutter
M03 Brian Lee 6.00 15.00
M04 Cody Hodgson 6.00 15.00
M05 Matt Duchene 20.00 50.00
M06 Brayden Schenn
M07 Scott Glennie 5.00 12.00
M08 Mark Katic 4.00 10.00
M09 Michael Latta
M10 Peter Holland 4.00 10.00
M11 Sergei Kostitsyn 6.00 15.00
M12 Karl Alzner 6.00 15.00
M13 Tyler Myers 25.00 60.00
M14 Tyson Barrie 5.00 12.00
M15 Phillippe Paradis 8.00 20.00
M16 Chris Stewart 6.00 15.00
M17 Jonathan Bernier
M18 James Neal
M19 Chet Pickard 8.00 20.00
M20 Jonathan Blum
M21 Calvin de Haan 4.00 10.00
M22 Joey Hishon 6.00 15.00
M23 Ben Duffy
M24 Zack Kassian 6.00 15.00
M25 Tyler Seguin 12.00 30.00
M26 Riley Boychuk
M27 Brett Connolly 6.00 15.00
M28 Mikhail Stefanovich 4.00 10.00
M29 Alex Petrovic 4.00 10.00
M30 Landon Ferraro 5.00 12.00
M31 Jordan Weal
M32 Patrice Cormier
M33 Carter Ashton 5.00 12.00
M34 Michal Repik 5.00 12.00
M35 Andrej Nestrasil
M36 Stefan Elliott 5.00 12.00
M37 Jared Cowen 6.00 15.00
M38 Jared Staal 5.00 12.00
M39 Cody Eakin 5.00 12.00
M40 Brandon Gormley
M41 Evander Kane 15.00 40.00
M42 Keven Veilleux 4.00 10.00
M43 Ryan Ellis 5.00 12.00
M44 Taylor Hall 25.00 60.00
M45 Erik Gudbranson

2009-10 ITG Heroes and Prospects Game Used Jerseys Gold

STATED PRINT RUN 10 SER.#'d SETS
NOT PRICED DUE TO SCARCITY

2009-10 ITG Heroes and Prospects Game Used Jerseys Silver

*SINGLES: .5X TO 1.2X BASIC INSERTS
STATED PRINT RUN 40 SER.#'d SETS

2009-10 ITG Heroes and Prospects Game Used Jerseys Autographs

STATED PRINT RUN 6 SER.#'d SETS
NOT PRICED DUE TO SCARCITY

2009-10 ITG Heroes and Prospects Game Used Jerseys Autographs Gold

STATED PRINT RUN 1 SER.#'d SET
NOT PRICED DUE TO SCARCITY

2009-10 ITG Heroes and Prospects Game Used Jerseys Autographs Silver

STATED PRINT RUN 3 SER.#'d SETS
NOT PRICED DUE TO SCARCITY

2009-10 ITG Heroes and Prospects Game Used Numbers

STATED PRINT RUN 6 SER.#'d SETS
NOT PRICED DUE TO SCARCITY

2009-10 ITG Heroes and Prospects Game Used Numbers Gold

STATED PRINT RUN 1 SER.#'d SET
NOT PRICED DUE TO SCARCITY

2009-10 ITG Heroes and Prospects Game Used Numbers Silver

STATED PRINT RUN 3 SER.#'d SETS
NOT PRICED DUE TO SCARCITY

2009-10 ITG Heroes and Prospects Game Used Numbers Autographs

STATED PRINT RUN 6 SER.#'d SETS
NOT PRICED DUE TO SCARCITY

2009-10 ITG Heroes and Prospects Game Used Numbers Autographs Gold

STATED PRINT RUN 1 SER.#'d SET
NOT PRICED DUE TO SCARCITY

2009-10 ITG Heroes and Prospects Game Used Numbers Autographs Silver

STATED PRINT RUN 3 SER.#'d SETS
NOT PRICED DUE TO SCARCITY

2009-10 ITG Heroes and Prospects Gloves Are Off

STATED PRINT RUN 40 SER.#'d SETS
GA001 Angelo Esposito 8.00 20.00
GA002 Bob Sanguinetti 8.00 20.00
GA003 Cody Hodgson 10.00 25.00
GA004 Bryan Little
GA005 Devin Setoguchi 8.00 20.00
GA006 Karl Alzner 10.00 25.00
GA007 Zach Hamill
GA008 Marc-Andre Gragnani 10.00 25.00

2009-10 ITG Heroes and Prospects Gloves Are Off Gold

STATED PRINT RUN 10 SER.#'d SETS
NOT PRICED DUE TO SCARCITY

2009-10 ITG Heroes and Prospect Hero and Prospect Jerseys

STATED PRINT RUN 30 SER.#'d SETS
HP01 Patrick Roy
Carey Price
HP02 Martin Brodeur 25.00 60.00
Jonathan Bernier
HP03 Ilya Kovalchuk 12.00 30.00
Angelo Esposito
HP04 Mario Lemieux 30.00 80.00
Taylor Hall
HP05 Cam Neely 15.00 40.00
Milan Lucic
HP06 Miikka Kiprusoff 10.00 25.00
Leland Irving
HP07 Joe Sakic 25.00 60.00
Matt Duchene
HP08 Larry Robinson
P.K. Subban

2009-10 ITG Heroes and Prospects Hero and Prospect Jerseys Gold

STATED PRINT RUN 10 SER.#'d SETS
NOT PRICED DUE TO SCARCITY

2009-10 ITG Heroes and Prospects Heroes Game Used Jerseys

STATED PRINT RUN 9 SER.#'d SETS
NOT PRICED DUE TO SCARCITY

2009-10 ITG Heroes and Prospects Heroes Game Used Jerseys Gold

STATED PRINT RUN 1 SER.#'d SET
NOT PRICED DUE TO SCARCITY

2009-10 ITG Heroes and Prospects Heroes Game Used Jerseys Autographs

STATED PRINT RUN 9 SER.#'d SETS
NOT PRICED DUE TO SCARCITY

2009-10 ITG Heroes and Prospects Heroes Game Used Jerseys Autographs Gold

STATED PRINT RUN 1 SER.#'d SET
NOT PRICED DUE TO SCARCITY

2009-10 ITG Heroes and Prospects Memorial Cup Winners

COMPLETE SET (18) 50.00 100.00
MC01 Taylor Hall 10.00 25.00
MC02 Greg Nemisz 2.00 5.00
MC03 Scott Timmins 4.00 10.00
MC04 Dale Mitchell 4.00 10.00
MC05 Ryan Ellis 2.00 5.00
MC06 Jesse Blacker 2.00 5.00
MC07 Andrei Loktionov 3.00 8.00
MC08 Rob Kwiet 1.50 4.00
MC09 Eric Wellwood 3.00 8.00
MC10 Ben Shutron 2.00 5.00
MC11 Lane MacDermid 2.50 6.00
MC12 Adam Henrique 2.50 6.00
MC13 Justin Shugg 1.50 4.00
MC14 Mark Cundari 4.00 10.00
MC15 Andrew Engelage 5.00 12.00
MC16 Harry Young 4.00 10.00
MC17 Conor O'Donnell 2.00 5.00
MC18 Austin Watson 4.00 10.00

2009-10 ITG Heroes and Prospects Prospect Combos Jerseys

STATED PRINT RUN 40 SER.#'d SETS
PC01 Ryan Ellis
P.K. Subban
PC02 Evander Kane 20.00 50.00
Angelo Esposito
PC03 Cody Hodgson 15.00 40.00
Logan Couture
PC04 Brayden Schenn
Zach Boychuk
PC05 Taylor Hall 10.00 25.00
Brad Marchand
PC06 Olivier Roy 10.00 25.00
Jonathan Bernier
PC07 Calvin de Haan
Thomas Hickey
PC08 Jake Allen 10.00 25.00
Thomas McCollum

2009-10 ITG Heroes and Prospects Prospect Combos Jerseys Gold

STATED PRINT RUN 10 SER.#'d SETS
NOT PRICED DUE TO SCARCITY

2009-10 ITG Heroes and Prospects Real Heroes

COMPLETE SET (24) 75.00 150.00
RH01 Woody Dumart 2.50 6.00
RH02 Milt Schmidt 3.00 8.00
RH03 Gordie Drillon 4.00 10.00
RH04 Ken Reardon 4.00 10.00
RH05 Sid Abel 4.00 10.00
RH06 Turk Broda 4.00 10.00
RH07 Hobey Baker 3.00 8.00
RH08 Frank Brimsek 3.00 8.00
RH09 Syl Apps 4.00 10.00
RH10 Conn Smythe 4.00 10.00
RH11 Red Garrett 2.50 6.00
RH12 Joe Turner 2.50 6.00
RH13 Bobby Bauer 5.00 12.00
RH14 Frank McGee 4.00 10.00
RH15 Howie Meeker 5.00 12.00
RH16 Johnny Bower 5.00 12.00
RH17 Frank Frederickson 2.50 6.00
RH18 Bob Carse 3.00 8.00
RH19 Alex Shibicky 4.00 10.00
RH20 Lynn Patrick 6.00 15.00
RH21 Max Bentley 2.50 6.00
RH22 Neil Colville 2.50 6.00
RH23 Chuck Rayner 3.00 8.00
RH24 Roy Conacher 4.00 10.00

2009-10 ITG Heroes and Prospects Selects Jerseys

STATED PRINT RUN 19 SER.#'d SETS
NOT PRICED DUE TO SCARCITY

2009-10 ITG Heroes and Prospects Selects Jerseys Gold

STATED PRINT RUN 1 SER.#'d SET
NOT PRICED DUE TO SCARCITY

2009-10 ITG Heroes and Prospects Subway Series Emblems

STATED PRINT RUN 6 SER.#'d SETS
NOT PRICED DUE TO SCARCITY

2009-10 ITG Heroes and Prospects Subway Series Emblems Gold

STATED PRINT RUN 1 SER.#'d SETS
NOT PRICED DUE TO SCARCITY

2009-10 ITG Heroes and Prospects Subway Series Emblems Silver

STATED PRINT RUN 3 SER.#'d SETS
NOT PRICED DUE TO SCARCITY

2009-10 ITG Heroes and Prospects Subway Series Emblems Autographs

STATED PRINT RUN 6 SER.#'d SETS
NOT PRICED DUE TO SCARCITY

2009-10 ITG Heroes and Prospects Subway Series Emblems Autographs Gold

STATED PRINT RUN 1 SER.#'d SET
NOT PRICED DUE TO SCARCITY

2009-10 ITG Heroes and Prospects Subway Series Emblems Autographs Silver

STATED PRINT RUN 3 SER.#'d SETS
NOT PRICED DUE TO SCARCITY

2009-10 ITG Heroes and Prospects Subway Series Jerseys

STATED PRINT RUN 60 SER.#'d SETS
CRM34 Karl Alzner 6.00 15.00
CRM35 P.K. Subban
CRM36 Brandon Sutter
SSM01 Jake Allen 8.00 20.00
SSM02 Maxime Clermont 5.00 12.00
SSM03 Louis Domingue 10.00 25.00
SSM04 Olivier Roy 8.00 20.00
SSM05 Simon Despres 6.00 15.00
SSM06 Brandon Gormley
SSM07 Charles-Olivier Roussel 6.00 15.00
SSM08 Yann Sauve
SSM09 Jordan Caron
SSM10 Patrice Cormier 8.00 20.00
SSM11 Michael Kirkpatrick 4.00 10.00
SSM12 Philippe Paradis 8.00 20.00
SSM13 Taylor Hall 25.00 60.00
SSM14 Nazem Kadri 10.00 25.00
SSM15 Peter Holland
SSM16 Jeff Skinner
SSM17 Michael Hutchinson 8.00 20.00
SSM18 Erik Gudbranson 6.00 15.00
SSM19 Stefan Della Rovere 6.00 15.00
SSM20 Tyler Toffoli 4.00 10.00
SSM21 Colten Teubert 4.00 10.00
SSM22 Zack Kassian
SSM23 Scott Glennie 5.00 12.00
SSM24 Brayden Schenn 12.00 30.00
SSM25 Brent Raedeke
SSM26 Linden Vey 4.00 10.00
SSM27 Jordan Eberle 12.00 30.00
SSM28 Brendan Shinnimin
SSM29 Mark Pysyk
SSM30 Jared Cowen 6.00 15.00
SSM31 Martin Jones
SSM32 Calvin Pickard
SSM33 Brett Ponich

2009-10 ITG Heroes and Prospects Subway Series Jerseys Gold

STATED PRINT RUN 10 SER.#'d SETS
NOT PRICED DUE TO SCARCITY

2009-10 ITG Heroes and Prospects Subway Series Jerseys Silver

*SINGLES: .5X TO 1.2X BASIC INSERTS
STATED PRINT RUN 30 SER.#'d SETS

2009-10 ITG Heroes and Prospects Subway Series Jerseys Autographs

STATED PRINT RUN 6 SER.#'d SETS
NOT PRICED DUE TO SCARCITY

2009-10 ITG Heroes and Prospects Subway Series Jerseys Autographs Gold

STATED PRINT RUN 1 SER.#'d SET
NOT PRICED DUE TO SCARCITY

2009-10 ITG Heroes and Prospects Subway Series Jerseys Autographs Silver

STATED PRINT RUN 3 SER.#'d SETS
NOT PRICED DUE TO SCARCITY

2009-10 ITG Heroes and Prospects Subway Series Numbers

STATED PRINT RUN 6 SER.#'d SETS
NOT PRICED DUE TO SCARCITY

2009-10 ITG Heroes and Prospects Subway Series Numbers Gold

STATED PRINT RUN 1 SER.#'d SET
NOT PRICED DUE TO SCARCITY

2009-10 ITG Heroes and Prospects Subway Series Numbers Silver

STATED PRINT RUN 3 SER.#'d SETS
NOT PRICED DUE TO SCARCITY

2009-10 ITG Heroes and Prospects Subway Series Numbers Autographs

STATED PRINT RUN 6 SER.#'d SETS
NOT PRICED DUE TO SCARCITY

2009-10 ITG Heroes and Prospects Subway Series Numbers Autographs Gold

STATED PRINT RUN 1 SER.#'d SET
NOT PRICED DUE TO SCARCITY

2009-10 ITG Heroes and Prospects Subway Series Numbers Autographs Silver

STATED PRINT RUN 3 SER.#'d SETS
NOT PRICED DUE TO SCARCITY

2009-10 ITG Heroes and Prospects Top Prospects Game Used Emblems

STATED PRINT RUN 6 SER.#'d SETS
NOT PRICED DUE TO SCARCITY

2009-10 ITG Heroes and Prospects Top Prospects Game Used Emblems Gold

STATED PRINT RUN 1 SER.#'d SET
NOT PRICED DUE TO SCARCITY

2009-10 ITG Heroes and Prospects Top Prospects Game Used Emblems Silver

STATED PRINT RUN 3 SER.#'d SETS
NOT PRICED DUE TO SCARCITY

2009-10 ITG Heroes and Prospects Top Prospects Game Used Emblems Autographs

STATED PRINT RUN 6 SER.#'d SETS
NOT PRICED DUE TO SCARCITY

2009-10 ITG Heroes and Prospects Top Prospects Game Used Emblems Autographs Gold

STATED PRINT RUN 1 SER.#'d SET
NOT PRICED DUE TO SCARCITY

2009-10 ITG Heroes and Prospects Top Prospects Game Used Emblems Autographs Silver

STATED PRINT RUN 3 SER.#'d SETS
NOT PRICED DUE TO SCARCITY

2009-10 ITG Heroes and Prospects Top Prospects Game Used Jerseys

STATED PRINT RUN 60 SER.#'d SETS
JM01 Bobby Hughes 4.00 10.00
JM02 Brayden Schenn
JM03 Calvin de Haan
JM04 Carter Ashton
JM05 Chet Pickard
JM06 Chris Stewart
JM07 Colten Teubert
JM08 Corey Perry 6.00 15.00
JM09 Dmitry Kulikov 6.00 15.00
JM10 Ethan Werek 4.00 10.00
JM11 Evander Kane
JM12 Greg Nemisz 5.00 12.00
JM13 Jamie Arniel 5.00 12.00
JM14 Jared Cowen 6.00 15.00
JM15 Jared Staal 5.00 12.00
JM16 Jimmy Bubnick 4.00 10.00
JM17 Jordan Caron
JM18 Jordan Eberle 12.00 30.00
JM19 Landon Ferraro 5.00 12.00
JM20 Luca Sbisa 8.00 20.00
JM21 Marcus Foligno
JM22 Matt Duchene 20.00 50.00
JM23 Maxime Sauve 4.00 10.00
JM24 Nazem Kadri 10.00 25.00
JM25 Nicholas Deschamps
JM26 Olivier Roy
JM27 Peter Delmas
JM28 Ryan Ellis 5.00 12.00
JM29 Ryan Getzlaf
JM30 Scott Glennie
JM31 Simon Despres
JM32 Stefan Elliott 5.00 12.00
JM33 Thomas McCollum
JM34 Tyler Cuma 4.00 10.00
JM35 Zach Boychuk 8.00 20.00
JM36 Zack Kassian

2009-10 ITG Heroes and Prospects Top Prospects Game Used Jerseys Gold

STATED PRINT RUN 10 SER.#'d SETS
NOT PRICED DUE TO SCARCITY

2009-10 ITG Heroes and Prospects Top Prospects Game Used Jerseys Silver

*SINGLES: .5X TO 1.2X BASIC INSERTS
STATED PRINT RUN 30 SER.#'d SETS
JM00 Dmitry Kulikov 8.00 20.00

2009-10 ITG Heroes and Prospects Top Prospects Game Used Jerseys Autographs

STATED PRINT RUN 6 SER.#'d SETS
NOT PRICED DUE TO SCARCITY

2009-10 ITG Heroes and Prospects Top Prospects Game Used Jerseys Autographs Gold

STATED PRINT RUN 1 SER.#'d SET
NOT PRICED DUE TO SCARCITY

2009-10 ITG Heroes and Prospects Top Prospects Game Used Jerseys Autographs Silver

STATED PRINT RUN 3 SER.#'d SETS
NOT PRICED DUE TO SCARCITY

2009-10 ITG Heroes and Prospects Top Prospects Game Used Numbers

STATED PRINT RUN 6 SER.#'d SETS
NOT PRICED DUE TO SCARCITY

2009-10 ITG Heroes and Prospects Top Prospects Game Used Numbers Silver

STATED PRINT RUN 3 SER.#'d SETS
NOT PRICED DUE TO SCARCITY

2006-07 ITG International Ice

1 Vladislav Tretiak 2.00 5.00
2 Bobby Hull 1.50 4.00
3 Bobby Clarke 1.25 3.00
4 Raymond Bourque 2.00 5.00
5 Paul Coffey 1.00 2.50
6 Pat LaFontaine .75 2.00
7 Brett Hull 1.25 3.00
8 Steve Yzerman 3.00 8.00
9 Marek Schwarz 1.00 2.50
10 Sidney Crosby 6.00 15.00
11 Gerry Cheevers 1.00 2.50
12 Phil Esposito 1.25 3.00
13 Marcel Dionne 1.25 3.00
14 Grant Fuhr 1.50 4.00
15 Jaromir Jagr 2.00 5.00
16 Antero Niittymaki 1.00 2.50
17 Mario Lemieux 4.00 10.00
18 Henrik Lundqvist 2.00 5.00
19 Alexander Yakushev 1.00 2.50
20 Michel Goulet .75 2.00
21 Paul Coffey 1.00 2.50
22 Darryl Sittler 1.25 3.00
23 Stan Mikita 1.25 3.00
24 Borje Salming 1.00 2.50
25 Vladislav Tretiak 2.00 5.00
26 Steve Yzerman 3.00 8.00
27 Dale Hawerchuk .75 2.00
28 Martin Brodeur 2.50 6.00
29 Ilya Bryzgalov 1.25 3.00
30 Bobby Ryan 1.25 3.00
31 Tony Esposito 1.25 3.00
32 Jari Kurri 1.25 3.00
33 Larry Robinson 1.00 2.50
34 Doug Gilmour 1.25 3.00
35 Mike Richter 1.00 2.50
36 Brett Hull 1.25 3.00
37 Michael Frolik 1.00 2.50
38 Cristobal Huet 1.25 3.00
39 Phil Esposito 1.25 3.00
40 Valeri Vasilyev .75 2.00
41 Borje Salming 1.00 2.50
42 Glenn Anderson .75 2.00
43 Raymond Bourque 2.00 5.00
44 Luc Robitaille 1.00 2.50
45 Pat LaFontaine .75 2.00
46 Petr Prucha 1.00 2.50
47 Steve Shutt .75 2.00
48 Larry Robinson 1.00 2.50
49 Mats Naslund .75 2.00
50 Dale Hawerchuk .75 2.00
51 Pat LaFontaine .75 2.00
52 Jaromir Jagr 2.00 5.00
53 John Tavares 4.00 10.00
54 Tuukka Rask 2.00 5.00
55 Anders Hedberg .75 2.00
56 John Vanbiesbrouck 1.00 2.50
57 Larry Murphy .75 2.00
58 Jari Kurri 1.25 3.00
59 Alexander Ovechkin 3.00 8.00
60 Mike Bossy 1.00 2.50
61 Valeri Kharlamov 1.50 4.00
62 Rick Ley .75 2.00
63 Guy Lafleur 2.00 5.00
64 Tony Esposito 1.25 3.00
65 Kent Nilsson .75 2.00
66 Paul Coffey 1.00 2.50
67 Bill Ranford 1.25 3.00
68 Nicklas Lidstrom 1.25 3.00
69 Evgeni Malkin 3.00 8.00
70 Alexander Radulov 2.00 5.00
71 Borje Salming 1.00 2.50
72 Michel Goulet .75 2.00
73 Thomas Steen .75 2.00
74 Denis Potvin 1.00 2.50
75 Larry Robinson 1.00 2.50
76 Mark Howe .75 2.00
77 Wayne Cashman .75 2.00
78 Marcel Dionne 1.25 3.00
79 Neal Broten .75 2.00
80 Grant Fuhr 1.50 4.00
81 Jari Kurri 1.25 3.00
82 Brian Leetch 1.25 3.00
83 Jim Craig 1.00 2.50
84 Al Montoya 1.00 2.50
85 Mark Messier 1.25 3.00
86 Esa Tikkanen .75 2.00
87 Glenn Anderson .75 2.00
88 Brian Bellows .75 2.00
89 Ulf Nilsson .75 2.00
90 Gilbert Perreault 1.25 3.00
91 Peter Mahovlich .75 2.00
92 Peter Stastny .75 2.00
93 Igor Larionov .75 2.00
94 Mark Messier 1.25 3.00
95 Vladimir Krutov .75 2.00
96 Mats Naslund .75 2.00
97 Mike Richter 1.00 2.50
98 Martin Brodeur 2.50 6.00
99 Justin Pogge 1.50 4.00
100 Paul Coffey 1.00 2.50
101 Paul Henderson 1.25 3.00
102 Mark Messier 1.25 3.00
103 Gilbert Perreault 1.25 3.00
104 Pelle Lindbergh 1.25 3.00
105 Bill Barber .75 2.00
106 Andre Lacroix .75 2.00
107 J.P. Parise .75 2.00
108 Brad Park 1.00 2.50
109 Alex Auld 1.00 2.50
110 Phil Kessel 2.00 5.00
111 Yan Stastny .75 2.00
112 Steve Larmer .75 2.00
113 Mats Naslund .75 2.00
114 Rod Langway .75 2.00
115 Peter Stastny .75 2.00
116 Bryan Trottier 1.00 2.50
117 Bobby Hull 1.50 4.00
118 Frank Mahovlich 1.25 3.00
119 Guy Lapointe .75 2.00
120 Danny Gare .75 2.00
121 Guy Lafleur 1.50 4.00
122 Rick Middleton 1.00 2.50
123 Larry Murphy .75 2.00
124 Jeff Glass 1.00 2.50
125 Chris Chelios 1.00 2.50

126 Ryan Malone .75 2.00
127 Marc-Andre Fleury 1.25 3.00
128 Patrick Roy 4.00 10.00
129 Paul Henderson 1.25 3.00
130 Marcel Dionne 1.25 3.00
131 Serge Savard .75 2.00
132 Gilbert Perreault 1.25 3.00
133 Raymond Bourque 2.00 5.00
134 Phil Housley .75 2.00
135 Rogie Vachon 1.25 3.00
136 Vladimir Myshkin .75 2.00
137 Bobby Clarke 1.25 3.00
138 Robbie Schremp 1.25 3.00
139 Peter Mahovlich .75 2.00
140 Mike Bossy 1.00 2.50
141 Esa Tikkanen .75 2.00
142 Chris Chelios 1.00 2.50
143 Serge Savard .75 2.00
144 Lanny McDonald 1.00 2.50
145 Ilya Kovalchuk 2.00 5.00
146 Jason Spezza 1.25 3.00
147 Ryan Miller 1.25 3.00
148 Denis Potvin 1.00 2.50
149 Peter Mueller 1.50 4.00
150 Yvan Cournoyer 1.25 3.00
151 Ladislav Smid .75 2.00
152 Chris Bourque 1.25 3.00
153 Ralph Backstrom .75 2.00
154 Henrik Zetterberg 1.25 3.00
155 Angelo Esposito 2.00 5.00
156 Alexei Kasatonov .75 2.00
157 Ed Olczyk .75 2.00
158 Mark Messier 2.00 5.00
159 Andrei Markov .75 2.00
160 A.Ovechkin/E.Malkin 3.00 8.00

2006-07 ITG International Ice Gold

STATED PRINT RUN 10 SETS
NOT PRICED DUE TO SCARCITY

2006-07 ITG International Ice Autographs

STATED ODDS 1:1
AAA Alex Auld 4.00 10.00
AAE Angelo Esposito SP 25.00 50.00
AAH Anders Hedberg 4.00 10.00
AAK Alexei Kasatonov 4.00 10.00
AAL Andre Lacroix 4.00 10.00
AAM Al Montoya 6.00 15.00
AAN Antero Niittymaki 6.00 15.00
AAO Alexander Ovechkin SP 30.00 60.00
AAR Alexander Radulov SP 15.00 40.00
AAY Alexander Yakushev 10.00 25.00
ABB Brian Bellows 4.00 10.00
ABC Bobby Clarke 10.00 25.00
ABH Bobby Hull SP 15.00 40.00
ABL Brian Leetch SP 15.00 40.00
ABP Brad Park 8.00 20.00
ABR Bill Ranford 6.00 15.00
ABS Borje Salming 6.00 15.00
ABT Bryan Trottier 12.00 30.00
ACB Chris Bourque 6.00 15.00
ACC Chris Chelios 8.00 20.00
ACH Cristobal Huet 10.00 25.00
ADG Doug Gilmour 8.00 20.00
ADH Dale Hawerchuk 6.00 15.00
ADP Denis Potvin 6.00 15.00
ADS Darryl Sittler 10.00 25.00
AEM Evgeni Malkin SP 100.00 200.00
AEO Ed Olczyk 4.00 10.00
AET Esa Tikkanen 6.00 15.00
AFM Frank Mahovlich SP 20.00 40.00
AGA Glenn Anderson 6.00 15.00
AGC Gerry Cheevers 10.00 25.00
AGF Grant Fuhr 8.00 20.00
AGL Guy Lafleur 15.00 40.00
AGP Gilbert Perreault 8.00 20.00
AHL Henrik Lundqvist 10.00 25.00
AHZ Henrik Zetterberg SP 25.00 50.00
AIB Ilya Bryzgalov 6.00 15.00
AIK Ilya Kovalchuk SP 25.00 50.00
AIL Igor Larionov 8.00 20.00
AJC Jim Craig 15.00 40.00
AJG Jeff Glass 6.00 15.00
AJJ Jaromir Jagr SP 25.00 50.00
AJK Jari Kurri 6.00 15.00
AJP Justin Pogge 15.00 40.00
AJS Jason Spezza SP 15.00 40.00
AJT John Tavares SP 75.00 150.00
AJV John Vanbiesbrouck 6.00 15.00
AKN Kent Nilsson 4.00 10.00
ALM Larry Murphy 4.00 10.00
ALR Larry Robinson 8.00 20.00
ALS Ladislav Smid 4.00 10.00
AMB Martin Brodeur SP 60.00 100.00
AMD Marcel Dionne 10.00 25.00
AMF Michael Frolik 8.00 20.00
AMG Michel Goulet 4.00 10.00
AMH Mark Howe 4.00 10.00
AML Mario Lemieux SP 100.00 175.00
AMM Mark Messier SP 40.00 100.00
AMN Mats Naslund 6.00 15.00
AMS Marek Schwarz 6.00 15.00
ANB Neal Broten 6.00 15.00
ANL Nicklas Lidstrom SP 8.00 20.00
AOM Alexander Ovechkin 300.00 450.00
Evgeni Malkin/10
APC Paul Coffey SP 15.00 40.00
APE Phil Esposito SP 20.00 50.00
APH Paul Henderson 8.00 20.00
APK Phil Kessel 20.00 40.00
APL Pat LaFontaine SP 12.00 30.00
APM Peter Mahovlich 8.00 20.00
APP Petr Prucha 8.00 20.00
APR Patrick Roy 40.00 100.00
APS Peter Stastny 6.00 15.00
ARB Raymond Bourque SP 30.00 80.00
ARL Rick Ley 4.00 10.00
ARM Rick Middleton 6.00 15.00
ARS Robbie Schremp 6.00 15.00
ARV Rogie Vachon 6.00 15.00
ASC Sidney Crosby SP 100.00 200.00
ASL Steve Larmer 4.00 10.00
ASM Stan Mikita 10.00 25.00
ASS Steve Shutt
ASY Steve Yzerman SP 40.00 100.00
ATE Tony Esposito SP 25.00 50.00
ATR Tuukka Rask 25.00 50.00
ATS Thomas Steen 4.00 10.00
AUN Ulf Nilsson 4.00 10.00
AVK Vladimir Krutov 10.00 25.00
AVM Vladimir Myshkin 8.00 20.00
AVT Vladislav Tretiak 20.00 50.00
AVV Valeri Vasilyev 6.00 15.00
AWC Wayne Cashman 4.00 10.00
AYC Yvan Cournoyer 12.00 30.00
AYS Yan Stastny 4.00 10.00
AAMK Andrei Markov 4.00 10.00
ABBR Bill Barber 4.00 10.00
ABC2 Bobby Clarke 10.00 25.00
ABH2 Bobby Hull SP 15.00 40.00
ABHU Brett Hull SP 40.00 80.00
ABRY Bobby Ryan 6.00 15.00
ABS2 Borje Salming 6.00 15.00
ABS3 Borje Salming 6.00 15.00
ACC2 Chris Chelios 8.00 20.00
ADGR Danny Gare 4.00 10.00
ADH2 Dale Hawerchuk 6.00 15.00
ADP2 Denis Potvin 6.00 15.00
AET2 Esa Tikkanen 6.00 15.00
AGA2 Glenn Anderson 6.00 15.00
AGF2 Grant Fuhr 8.00 20.00
AGL2 Guy Lafleur 15.00 40.00
AGLP Guy Lapointe 4.00 10.00
AGP2 Gilbert Perreault 8.00 20.00
AGP3 Gilbert Perreault 8.00 20.00
AJJ2 Jaromir Jagr SP 20.00 50.00
AJK2 Jari Kurri 6.00 15.00
AJK3 Jari Kurri 6.00 15.00
AJPP J.P. Parise 4.00 10.00
ALM2 Larry Murphy 4.00 10.00
ALMC Lanny McDonald 6.00 15.00
ALR2 Larry Robinson 8.00 20.00
ALR3 Larry Robinson 8.00 20.00
ALRO Luc Robitaille SP 20.00 50.00
AMAF Marc-Andre Fleury 20.00 40.00
AMB2 Martin Brodeur SP 60.00 100.00
AMBO Mike Bossy 6.00 15.00
AMD2 Marcel Dionne 10.00 25.00
AMD3 Marcel Dionne 10.00 25.00
AMG2 Michel Goulet 4.00 10.00
AMM2 Mark Messier SP 40.00 80.00
AMM3 Mark Messier SP 40.00 80.00
AMM4 Mark Messier SP 40.00 80.00
AMN2 Mats Naslund 6.00 15.00
AMN3 Mats Naslund 6.00 15.00
APC2 Paul Coffey SP 15.00 40.00
APC3 Paul Coffey SP 15.00 40.00
APC4 Paul Coffey SP 15.00 40.00
APE2 Phil Esposito SP 20.00 50.00
APH2 Paul Henderson 8.00 20.00
APHO Phil Housley 4.00 10.00
APL2 Pat LaFontaine SP 12.00 30.00
APL3 Pat LaFontaine SP 12.00 30.00
APM2 Peter Mahovlich 8.00 20.00
APMU Peter Mueller 6.00 15.00
APS2 Peter Stastny 6.00 15.00
ARB2 Raymond Bourque SP 30.00 80.00
ARB3 Raymond Bourque SP 30.00 80.00
ARBA Ralph Backstrom 4.00 10.00
ARLW Rod Langway 6.00 15.00
ARMI Ryan Miller 12.00 30.00
ARML Ryan Malone 4.00 10.00
ASSV Serge Savard 4.00 10.00
ASY2 Steve Yzerman SP 40.00 100.00
ATE2 Tony Esposito SP 20.00 40.00
AVT2 Vladislav Tretiak 20.00 50.00
ABHU2 Brett Hull SP 40.00 80.00
AMBO2 Mike Bossy 6.00 15.00
ASSV2 Serge Savard 4.00 10.00

2006-07 ITG International Ice Best of the Best

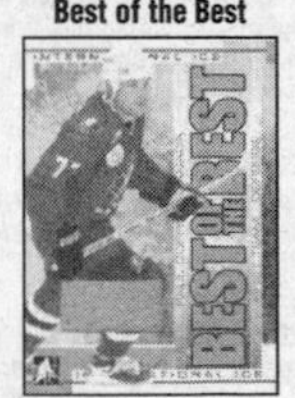

STATED PRINT RUN 60 SETS
GOLD VERSION /10 ALSO EXISTS
GOLD NOT PRICED DUE TO SCARCITY
BB01 Vladislav Tretiak 12.00 30.00
BB02 Brian Leetch 6.00 15.00
BB03 Paul Coffey 6.00 15.00
BB04 Mark Messier 10.00 25.00
BB05 Valeri Kharlamov 12.00 30.00
BB06 Mario Lemieux 20.00 50.00
BB07 Martin Brodeur 12.00 30.00
BB08 Raymond Bourque 8.00 20.00
BB09 Nicklas Lidstrom 6.00 15.00
BB10 Phil Esposito 6.00 15.00
BB11 Jaromir Jagr 10.00 25.00
BB12 Bobby Hull 10.00 25.00

2006-07 ITG International Ice Canadian Dream Team

STATED PRINT RUN 60 SETS
GOLD VERSION / 10 ALSO EXISTS
GOLD NOT PRICED DUE TO SCARCITY
DT01 Bobby Hull 10.00 25.00
DT02 Mark Messier 10.00 25.00
DT03 Martin Brodeur 12.00 30.00
DT04 Bobby Clarke 10.00 25.00
DT05 Phil Esposito 8.00 20.00

DT06 Darryl Sittler 8.00 20.00
DT07 Raymond Bourque 10.00 25.00
DT08 Mario Lemieux 20.00 50.00
DT09 Grant Fuhr 10.00 25.00
DT10 Paul Coffey 8.00 20.00
DT11 Sidney Crosby 25.00 60.00
DT12 John Tavares 12.00 30.00

2006-07 ITG International Ice Complete Jersey

STATED PRINT RUN 10 SETS
GOLD 1/1 VERSION ALSO EXISTS
NOT PRICED DUE TO SCARCITY
GOLD NOT PRICED DUE TO SCARCITY
CJ01 John Tavares
CJ02 Justin Pogge
CJ03 Martin Brodeur
CJ04 Sidney Crosby
CJ05 Jay Bouwmeester
CJ06 Steve Yzerman
CJ07 Mario Lemieux
CJ08 Alexander Ovechkin
CJ09 Evgeni Malkin
CJ10 Michael Frolik
CJ11 Henrik Lundqvist
CJ12 Petr Prucha
CJ13 Jaromir Jagr
CJ14 Brett Hull
CJ15 Brian Leetch
CJ16 Nicklas Lidstrom
CJ17 Patrick Roy
CJ18 Jari Kurri
CJ19 Mark Messier
CJ20 Vladimir Dzurilla

2006-07 ITG International Ice Cornerstones

STATED PRINT RUN 20 SETS
GOLD 1/1 VERSION ALSO EXISTS
GOLD NOT PRICED DUE TO SCARCITY
NOT PRICED DUE TO SCARCITY
IC01 Yzerman
Esposito
Lemieux
Crosby
IC02 Kharlamov
Tretiak
Malkin
Ovechkin
IC03 Lidstrom
Naslund
Salming
Lundqvist
IC04 Niittymaki
Kurri
Tikkanen
Kiprusoff
IC05 Stastny
Frolik
Prucha
Jagr
IC06 Leetch
LaFontaine
Richter
Hull
IC07 Kharlamov
Tretiak
Vasiliev
Mikhailov
IC08 Esposito
Vanbiesbrouck
Richter
Montoya
IC09 Vachon
Cheevers
Brodeur
Roy
IC10 Tretiak
Myshkin
Mylnikov
Bryzgalov
IC11 Crosby
Tavares
Spezza
Heatley
IC12 Potvin
Robinson
Coffey
Bourque

2006-07 ITG International Ice Double Memorabilia

STATED PRINT RUN 20 SETS
GOLD 1/1 VERSION ALSO EXISTS
GOLD NOT PRICED DUE TO SCARCITY
DM01 Eric Lindros 10.00 25.00
DM02 Patrick Roy 30.00 80.00
DM03 Martin Brodeur 25.00 50.00
DM04 Alexander Ovechkin 30.00 60.00
DM05 Sidney Crosby 40.00 80.00
DM06 Mario Lemieux 30.00 80.00

2006-07 ITG International Ice Emblem Autographs

STATED PRINT RUN 10 SETS
GOLD 1/1 VERSION ALSO EXISTS
GOLD NOT PRICED DUE TO SCARCITY
NOT PRICED DUE TO SCARCITY
GUE01 Brett Hull
GUE02 Alexander Yakushev
GUE04 Vladislav Tretiak
GUE06 Nicklas Lidstrom
GUE08 Michel Goulet
GUE09 Jason Spezza
GUE11 John Tavares
GUE12 Martin Brodeur
GUE13 Sidney Crosby
GUE15 Steve Yzerman
GUE20 Gilbert Perreault
GUE21 Phil Esposito
GUE22 Ilya Bryzgalov
GUE23 Jaromir Jagr
GUE25 Borje Salming
GUE26 Mats Naslund
GUE27 Brian Leetch
GUE28 Pat LaFontaine
GUE29 Jari Kurri
GUE30 Peter Stastny
GUE33 Bobby Clarke
GUE34 Marcel Dionne
GUE35 Darryl Sittler
GUE36 Eric Lindros
GUE38 Patrick Roy/1
GUE40 Ilya Kovalchuk

2006-07 ITG International Ice Emblems

STATED PRINT RUN 10 SETS
GOLD 1/1 VERSION ALSO EXISTS
NOT PRICED DUE TO SCARCITY
GOLD NOT PRICED DUE TO SCARCITY
GUE01 Brett Hull
GUE02 Alexander Yakushev
GUE03 Vladimir Krutov
GUE04 Vladislav Tretiak
GUE05 Valeri Kharlamov
GUE06 Nicklas Lidstrom
GUE07 Vladimir Myshkin
GUE08 Michel Goulet
GUE09 Jason Spezza
GUE10 Jay Bouwmeester
GUE11 John Tavares
GUE12 Martin Brodeur
GUE13 Sidney Crosby
GUE14 Dale Hawerchuk
GUE15 Steve Yzerman
GUE16 Mike Bossy
GUE17 Patrice Bergeron
GUE18 Sergei Mylnikov
GUE19 Mario Lemieux
GUE20 Gilbert Perreault
GUE21 Phil Esposito
GUE22 Ilya Bryzgalov
GUE23 Jaromir Jagr
GUE24 Vladimir Dzurilla
GUE25 Borje Salming
GUE26 Mats Naslund
GUE27 Brian Leetch
GUE28 Pat LaFontaine
GUE29 Jari Kurri
GUE30 Peter Stastny
GUE31 Danny Gare
GUE33 Bobby Clarke
GUE34 Marcel Dionne
GUE35 Darryl Sittler
GUE36 Eric Lindros
GUE37 Boris Mikhailov
GUE38 Patrick Roy
GUE39 Chris Chelios
GUE40 Ilya Kovalchuk

2006-07 ITG International Ice Goaltending Glory

STATED PRINT RUN 60 SETS
GOLD VERSION /10 ALSO EXISTS
GOLD NOT PRICED DUE TO SCARCITY
GG01 Tony Esposito 10.00 25.00
GG02 Grant Fuhr 10.00 25.00
GG03 Martin Brodeur 12.00 30.00
GG04 Justin Pogge 10.00 25.00
GG05 Henrik Lundqvist 12.00 30.00
GG06 Mike Richter 8.00 20.00
GG07 Pelle Lindbergh 12.00 30.00
GG08 Vladimir Dzurilla 6.00 15.00
GG09 Jonathan Bernier 6.00 15.00
GG10 Rogie Vachon 6.00 15.00
GG11 Bill Ranford 10.00 25.00
GG12 Antero Niittymaki 6.00 15.00
GG13 Cristobal Huet 10.00 25.00
GG14 John Vanbiesbrouck 8.00 20.00
GG15 Vladislav Tretiak 12.00 30.00
GG16 Vladimir Myshkin 6.00 15.00
GG17 Ilya Bryzgalov 6.00 15.00
GG18 Al Montoya 6.00 15.00
GG19 Gerry Cheevers 10.00 25.00
GG20 Sergei Mylnikov 8.00 20.00
GG21 Patrick Roy 20.00 50.00
GG22 Miikka Kiprusoff 10.00 25.00

2006-07 ITG International Ice Greatest Moments

STATED PRINT RUN 50 SETS
GOLD VERSION /10 ALSO EXISTS
GOLD NOT PRICED DUE TO SCARCITY
GM01 Russian Upset 15.00 40.00
GM02 Esposito's Speech 8.00 20.00
GM03 Cournoyer's Assist 8.00 20.00
GM04 Hull Gets His Chance 10.00 25.00
GM05 Sittler's Goal 10.00 25.00
GM06 Swapping Sweaters 8.00 20.00
GM07 1984 Comeback 12.00 30.00
GM08 Lemieux's Big Moment 20.00 50.00
GM09 American Victory 8.00 20.00
GM10 World Junior Gold 25.00 60.00

2006-07 ITG International Ice Hockey Passport

STATED PRINT RUN 60 SETS
GOLD VERSION /10 ALSO EXISTS
GOLD NOT PRICED DUE TO SCARCITY
HP01 Jaromir Jagr 10.00 25.00
HP02 Vladislav Tretiak 12.00 30.00
HP03 Valeri Kharlamov 12.00 30.00
HP04 Bobby Hull 10.00 25.00
HP05 Martin Brodeur 12.00 30.00
HP06 Borje Salming 8.00 20.00
HP07 Jari Kurri 10.00 25.00
HP08 Mark Messier 10.00 25.00
HP09 Brett Hull 10.00 25.00
HP10 Mario Lemieux 20.00 50.00
HP11 Henrik Lundqvist 8.00 20.00
HP12 Sidney Crosby 25.00 60.00

2006-07 ITG International Ice International Rivals

STATED PRINT RUN 50 SETS
GOLD VERSION /10 ALSO EXISTS
GOLD NOT PRICED DUE TO SCARCITY
IR01 Tony Esposito 20.00 40.00
Vladislav Tretiak
IR02 Alexander Maltsev 12.00 30.00
Phil Esposito
IR03 Frank Mahovlich 8.00 20.00
Alexander Yakushev
IR04 Valeri Kharlamov 15.00 40.00
Gerry Cheevers
IR05 Darryl Sittler 10.00 25.00
Vladimir Dzurilla
IR06 Peter Stastny 8.00 20.00
Bobby Hull
IR07 Grant Fuhr 10.00 25.00
Sergei Mylnikov
IR08 Raymond Bourque 8.00 20.00
Mats Naslund
IR09 Mike Bossy 8.00 20.00
Jari Kurri
IR10 Guy LaFleur 10.00 25.00
Borje Salming
IR11 Vladimir Krutov 25.00 50.00
Mario Lemieux
IR12 Steve Yzerman 15.00 40.00
Pat LaFontaine
IR13 Michel Goulet 6.00 15.00
Vladimir Myshkin
IR14 Pat LaFontaine 6.00 15.00
Bill Ranford
IR15 Jaromir Jagr 12.00 30.00
Igor Larionov
IR16 Mark Messier 10.00 25.00
Brett Hull
IR17 Martin Brodeur 12.00 30.00
Mike Richter
IR18 Sidney Crosby 20.00 50.00
Al Montoya
IR19 Evgeni Malkin 30.00 60.00
Justin Pogge
IR20 Paul Coffey 6.00 15.00
Chris Chelios

2006-07 ITG International Ice Jersey Autographs

STATED PRINT RUN 10 SETS
GOLD 1/1 VERSION EXISTS
GOLD NOT PRICED DUE TO SCARCITY
NOT PRICED DUE TO SCARCITY

2006-07 ITG International Ice Jerseys

STATED PRINT RUN 100 SETS
GOLD VERSION /10 ALSO EXISTS
GOLD NOT PRICED DUE TO SCARCITY
GUJ01 Brett Hull 6.00 15.00
GUJ02 Alexander Yakushev 8.00 20.00
GUJ03 Vladimir Krutov 8.00 20.00
GUJ04 Vladislav Tretiak 12.00 30.00
GUJ05 Valeri Kharlamov 12.00 30.00
GUJ06 Nicklas Lidstrom 5.00 12.00
GUJ07 Vladimir Myshkin 5.00 12.00
GUJ08 Michel Goulet 5.00 12.00
GUJ09 Jason Spezza 6.00 15.00
GUJ10 Jay Bouwmeester 5.00 12.00
GUJ11 John Tavares 15.00 40.00
GUJ12 Martin Brodeur 10.00 25.00
GUJ13 Sidney Crosby 25.00 60.00
GUJ14 Dale Hawerchuk 5.00 12.00
GUJ15 Steve Yzerman 10.00 25.00
GUJ16 Mike Bossy 5.00 12.00
GUJ17 Patrice Bergeron 5.00 12.00
GUJ18 Sergei Mylnikov 6.00 15.00
GUJ19 Mario Lemieux 15.00 40.00
GUJ20 Gilbert Perreault 5.00 12.00
GUJ21 Phil Esposito 8.00 20.00
GUJ22 Ilya Bryzgalov 5.00 12.00
GUJ23 Jaromir Jagr 10.00 25.00
GUJ24 Vladimir Dzurilla 8.00 20.00
GUJ25 Borje Salming 5.00 12.00
GUJ26 Mats Naslund 5.00 12.00
GUJ27 Brian Leetch 5.00 12.00
GUJ28 Pat LaFontaine 5.00 12.00
GUJ29 Jari Kurri 6.00 15.00
GUJ30 Peter Stastny 5.00 12.00
GUJ31 Danny Gare 5.00 12.00
GUJ33 Bobby Clarke 8.00 20.00
GUJ34 Marcel Dionne 5.00 12.00
GUJ35 Darryl Sittler 8.00 20.00
GUJ36 Eric Lindros 6.00 15.00
GUJ37 Boris Mikhailov 10.00 25.00
GUJ38 Patrick Roy 15.00 40.00
GUJ39 Chris Chelios 5.00 12.00
GUJ40 Ilya Kovalchuk 6.00 15.00

2006-07 ITG International Ice My Country My Team

STATED PRINT RUN 60 SETS
GOLD VERSION /10 ALSO EXISTS
GOLD NOT PRICED DUE TO SCARCITY
MC1 Chris Chelios 6.00 15.00
MC2 Jaromir Jagr 10.00 25.00
MC3 Steve Yzerman 15.00 40.00
MC4 Brett Hull 10.00 25.00
MC5 Pat LaFontaine 4.00 10.00
MC7 Steve Shutt 4.00 10.00
MC8 Gilbert Perreault 6.00 15.00
MC9 Michel Goulet 4.00 10.00
MC10 Patrick Roy 15.00 40.00
MC11 Jason Spezza 6.00 15.00
MC12 Jay Bouwmeester 4.00 10.00
MC13 Mike Bossy 6.00 15.00
MC14 Phil Esposito 8.00 20.00
MC15 Mario Lemieux 20.00 50.00
MC16 Mats Naslund 4.00 10.00
MC17 Borje Salming 6.00 15.00
MC18 Jari Kurri 6.00 15.00
MC19 Dale Hawerchuk 4.00 10.00
MC20 Bobby Clarke 8.00 20.00
MC21 Eric Lindros 6.00 15.00
MC22 Ilya Bryzgalov 4.00 10.00
MC23 Marcel Dionne 6.00 15.00
MC24 Darryl Sittler 6.00 15.00
MC25 John Tavares 12.00 30.00
MC26 Martin Brodeur 12.00 30.00

2006-07 ITG International Ice Numbers

STATED PRINT RUN 10 SETS
GOLD 1/1 VERSION ALSO EXISTS
NOT PRICED DUE TO SCARCITY
GOLD NOT PRICED DUE TO SCARCITY
GUN01 Brett Hull
GUN02 Alexander Yakushev
GUN03 Vladimir Krutov
GUN04 Vladislav Tretiak
GUN05 Valeri Kharlamov
GUN06 Nicklas Lidstrom
GUN07 Vladimir Myshkin
GUN08 Michel Goulet
GUN09 Jason Spezza
GUN10 Jay Bouwmeester
GUN11 John Tavares
GUN12 Martin Brodeur
GUN13 Sidney Crosby
GUN14 Dale Hawerchuk
GUN15 Steve Yzerman
GUN16 Mike Bossy
GUN17 Patrice Bergeron
GUN18 Sergei Mylnikov
GUN19 Mario Lemieux
GUN20 Gilbert Perreault
GUN21 Phil Esposito
GUN22 Ilya Bryzgalov
GUN23 Jaromir Jagr
GUN24 Vladimir Dzurilla
GUN25 Borje Salming
GUN26 Mats Naslund
GUN27 Brian Leetch
GUN28 Pat LaFontaine
GUN29 Jari Kurri
GUN30 Peter Stastny
GUN31 Danny Gare
GUN33 Bobby Clarke
GUN34 Marcel Dionne
GUN35 Darryl Sittler
GUN36 Eric Lindros
GUN37 Boris Mikhailov
GUN38 Patrick Roy
GUN39 Chris Chelios
GUN40 Ilya Kovalchuk

2006-07 ITG International Ice Numbers Autographs

STATED PRINT RUN 10 SETS
GOLD 1/1 VERSION ALSO EXISTS
GOLD NOT PRICED DUE TO SCARCITY
NOT PRICED DUE TO SCARCITY
GUN01 Brett Hull
GUN02 Alexander Yakushev
GUN04 Vladislav Tretiak
GUN06 Nicklas Lidstrom
GUN08 Michel Goulet
GUN09 Jason Spezza
GUN11 John Tavares
GUN12 Martin Brodeur
GUN13 Sidney Crosby
GUN15 Steve Yzerman
GUN20 Gilbert Perreault
GUN21 Phil Esposito
GUN22 Ilya Bryzgalov
GUN23 Jaromir Jagr
GUN25 Borje Salming
GUN26 Mats Naslund
GUN27 Brian Leetch
GUN28 Pat LaFontaine
GUN29 Jari Kurri
GUN30 Peter Stastny
GUN33 Bobby Clarke
GUN34 Marcel Dionne
GUN35 Darryl Sittler
GUN36 Eric Lindros
GUN38 Patrick Roy
GUN40 Ilya Kovalchuk

2006-07 ITG International Ice Passing The Torch

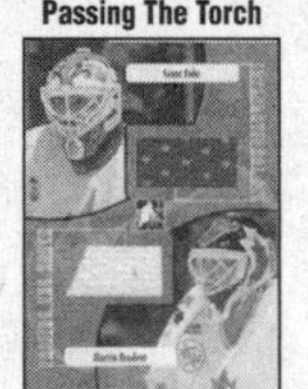

STATED PRINT RUN 60 SETS
GOLD VERSION /10 EXISTS
GOLD NOT PRICED DUE TO SCARCITY
PTT1 Tony Esposito 12.00 30.00
Grant Fuhr
PTT2 Grant Fuhr 15.00 40.00
Martin Brodeur
PTT3 Martin Brodeur 15.00 30.00
Justin Pogge
PTT4 Mike Richter 8.00 20.00
Al Montoya
PTT5 Sergei Mylnikov 6.00 15.00
Ilya Bryzgalov
PTT6 Miikka Kiprusoff 12.00 30.00
Antero Niittymaki
PTT7 Vladimir Dzurilla 10.00 25.00
Marek Schwarz
PTT8 Vladislav Tretiak 15.00 40.00
Vladimir Myshkin
PTT9 Phil Esposito 12.00 30.00
Mark Messier
PTT10 Mario Lemieux 30.00 80.00
Sidney Crosby
PTT11 Peter Stastny 12.00 30.00
Jaromir Jagr
PTT12 Valeri Kharlamov 10.00 25.00
Ilya Kovalchuk
PTT13 Alexander Yakushev 12.00 30.00
Evgeni Malkin
PTT14 Borje Salming 8.00 20.00
Nicklas Lidstrom
PTT15 Igor Larionov 20.00 40.00
Alexander Ovechkin
PTT16 Jaromir Jagr 10.00 25.00
Michael Frolik

2006-07 ITG International Ice Quad Patch

STATED PRINT RUN 6 SETS
GOLD 1/1 VERSION ALSO EXISTS
GOLD NOT PRICED DUE TO SCARCITY
NOT PRICED DUE TO SCARCITY
QP02 Hull
LaFontaine
Leetch
Chelios
QP03 Esposito
Vachon

Brodeur
Fuhr
QP04 Tretiak
Myshkin
Bryzgalov
Mylnikov
QP05 Lemieux
Messier
Bourque
Yzerman
QP06 Ovechkin
Kovalchuk
Malkin
Radulov

2006-07 ITG International Ice Stick and Jersey

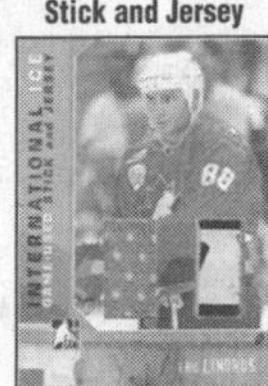

STATED PRINT RUN 90 SETS
GOLD VERSION /10 EXISTS
GOLD NOT PRICED DUE TO SCARCITY

SJ01 Mario Lemieux 25.00 50.00
SJ02 Mark Messier 10.00 25.00
SJ03 Raymond Bourque 10.00 25.00
SJ04 Steve Yzerman 15.00 40.00
SJ05 Brian Leetch 8.00 20.00
SJ06 Sidney Crosby 25.00 60.00
SJ07 Alexander Ovechkin 15.00 40.00
SJ08 Patrick Roy 20.00 50.00
SJ09 Henrik Lundqvist 8.00 20.00
SJ10 Eric Lindros 8.00 20.00
SJ11 Peter Stastny 8.00 20.00
SJ12 Mike Richter 10.00 25.00
SJ13 Bobby Clarke 10.00 25.00
SJ14 Phil Esposito 10.00 25.00
SJ15 Brett Hull 10.00 25.00
SJ16 Jaromir Jagr 12.00 30.00
SJ17 Jason Spezza 8.00 20.00
SJ18 Jari Kurri 10.00 25.00
SJ19 Martin Brodeur 15.00 40.00
SJ20 Guy Lafleur 20.00 50.00
SJ21 Gilbert Perreault 8.00 20.00
SJ22 Igor Larionov 8.00 20.00
SJ23 Vladimir Krutov 8.00 20.00
SJ24 Chris Chelios 8.00 20.00
SJ25 Henrik Zetterberg 10.00 25.00
SJ26 Nicklas Lidstrom 8.00 20.00
SJ27 Marcel Dionne 8.00 20.00
SJ28 Cristobal Huet 12.00 30.00

2006-07 ITG International Ice Teammates

STATED PRINT RUN 70 SETS
GOLD VERSION /10 ALSO EXISTS
GOLD NOT PRICED DUE TO SCARCITY

IT01 Phil Esposito 15.00 40.00
Tony Esposito
IT02 Mario Lemieux 20.00 50.00
Mark Messier
IT03 Darryl Sittler 8.00 20.00
Lanny McDonald
IT04 Marcel Dionne 8.00 20.00
Gilbert Perreault
IT05 Mike Bossy 10.00 25.00
Guy Lafleur
IT06 Raymond Bourque 10.00 25.00
Rick Middleton
IT07 Steve Yzerman 12.00 30.00
Paul Coffey
IT08 Eric Lindros 10.00 25.00
Mark Messier
IT09 Mario Lemieux 25.00 60.00
Martin Brodeur
IT10 Sidney Crosby 25.00 60.00
Dion Phaneuf
IT11 Gerry Cheevers 10.00 25.00
Bobby Hull
IT12 Mike Richter 8.00 20.00
Brian Leetch
IT13 Brett Hull 10.00 25.00
Chris Chelios
IT14 John Vanbiesbrouck 8.00 20.00
Pat LaFontaine
IT15 Mats Naslund 8.00 20.00
Borje Salming
IT16 Nicklas Lidstrom 10.00 25.00
Henrik Lundqvist
IT17 Igor Larionov 10.00 25.00
Vladimir Krutov
IT18 Vladislav Tretiak 15.00 40.00
Alexander Yakushev
IT19 Valeri Kharlamov 15.00 40.00
Alexander Maltsev
IT20 Peter Stastny 10.00 25.00
Vladimir Dzurilla
IT21 Alexander Ovechkin 20.00 50.00
Evgeni Malkin
IT22 Frank Mahovlich 8.00 20.00
Peter Mahovlich

2006-07 ITG International Ice Triple Memorabilia

STATED PRINT RUN 9 SETS
GOLD 1/1 VERSION ALSO EXISTS
NOT PRICED DUE TO SCARCITY
GOLD NOT PRICED DUE TO SCARCITY

TM01 Vachon
Dzurilla
Sittler
TM02 Cournoyer
Tretiak
Esposito
TM03 Kharlamov
Yakushev
Mikhailov
TM04 Bergeron
Crosby
Perry
TM05 Lemieux
Messier
Yzerman
TM06 Jagr
Ovechkin
Brodeur
TM07 Krutov
Larionov
Makarov
TM08 Lundqvist
Niittymaki
Pogge

2007-08 ITG O Canada

This 100 card set was issued into the hobby in five-card packs which came 24 packs to a box and 24 boxes to a case.This set honored players who participated in series in which any version of a Canadian National Team (Senior, Junior or Women) competed.

COMPLETE SET (100) 10.00 25.00
1 Alex Grant .12 .30
2 Angelo Esposito .30 .75
3 Braden Holtby .15 .40
4 Brandon Sutter .15 .40
5 Colton Gillies .20 .50
6 Dion Knelsen .12 .30
7 Drew Doughty .30 .75
8 Eric Doyle .12 .30
9 Jamie Arniel .12 .30
10 John Negrin .15 .40
11 Kyle Turris .60 1.50
12 Logan Couture .20 .50
13 Luke Schenn .25 .60
14 Mark Katic .12 .30
15 Olivier Fortier .12 .30
16 Steven Stamkos .40 1.00
17 Trevor Cann .15 .40
18 Yann Sauve .15 .40
19 Yves Bastien .12 .30
20 Zachary Boychuk .20 .50
21 Zack Torquato .12 .30
22 Carla MacLeod .20 .50
23 Caroline Ouellette .20 .50
24 Charline Labonte .30 .75
25 Cheryl Pounder .20 .50
26 Colleen Sostorics .20 .50
27 Danielle Goyette .25 .60
28 Delaney Collins .20 .50
29 Gillian Apps .25 .60
30 Gillian Ferrari .20 .50
31 Gina Kingsbury .20 .50
32 Hayley Wickenheiser .50 1.25
33 Jayna Hefford .25 .60
34 Jennifer Botterill .20 .50
35 Katie Weatherston .20 .50
36 Kelly Bechard .20 .50
37 Kim St. Pierre .60 1.50
38 Meghan Agosta .25 .60
39 Sarah Vaillancourt .20 .50
40 Tessa Bonhomme .20 .50
41 Vicky Sunohara .25 .60
42 Karl Alzner .15 .40
43 Daniel Bertram .12 .30
44 Luc Bourdon .15 .40
45 Marc-Andre Cliché .12 .30
46 Andrew Cogliano .30 .75
47 Steve Downie .15 .40
48 Cody Franson .25 .60
49 Sam Gagner .25 .60
50 Darren Helm .20 .50
51 Leland Irving .20 .50
52 Kristopher Letang .25 .60
53 Bryan Little .15 .40
54 Brad Marchand .20 .50
55 Kenndal McArdle .12 .30
56 James Neal .25 .60
57 Ryan O'Marra .12 .30
58 Ryan Parent .15 .40
59 Carey Price .60 1.50
60 Tom Pyatt .25 .60
61 Kris Russell .15 .40
62 Marc Staal .20 .50
63 Jonathan Toews .75 2.00
64 Martin Brodeur .50 1.25
65 Marc-Andre Fleury .20 .50
66 Vincent Lecavalier .20 .50
67 Chris Pronger .20 .50
68 Eric Lindros .20 .50
69 Roberto Luongo .30 .75
70 Dion Phaneuf .20 .50
71 Justin Pogge .25 .60
72 Joe Sakic .40 1.00
73 Jason Spezza .20 .50
74 Patrick Roy .60 1.50
75 Jordan Staal .25 .60
76 Joe Thornton .25 .60
77 Dany Heatley .25 .60
78 Steve Yzerman .60 1.50
79 Cassie Campbell .75 2.00
80 Manon Rheaume .75 2.00
81 Angelo Esposito .40 1.00
Steven Stamkos
82 Danielle Goyette .25 .60
Vicky Sunohara
83 Hayley Wickenheiser .50 1.25
Jennifer Botterill
84 Karl Alzner .30 .75
Marc Staal
85 Steve Downie .75 2.00
Jonathan Toews
86 Carey Price .60 1.50
Leland Irving
87 Kristopher Letang .25 .60
Luc Bourdon
88 Sam Gagner .25 .60
Bryan Little
89 Charline Labonte .60 1.50
Kim St. Pierre
90 Cassie Campbell .75 2.00
Manon Rheaume
91 Jaromir Jagr .30 .75
92 Henrik Zetterberg .20 .50
93 Alexei Cherepanov .20 .50
94 Dominik Hasek .25 .60
95 Mike Modano .20 .50
96 Bill Guerin .12 .30
97 Alexander Ovechkin .60 1.50
98 Vladislav Tretiak .15 .40
99 Chris Chelios .12 .30
100 Jari Kurri .20 .50

2007-08 ITG O Canada Autographs

AAC Andrew Cogliano 8.00 20.00
AACH Alexei Cherepanov SP 12.00 30.00
AAE Angelo Esposito 8.00 20.00
AAG Alex Grant 3.00 8.00
AAO Alexander Ovechkin SP 40.00 100.00
ABG Bill Guerin SP 8.00 20.00
ABH Braden Holtby 4.00 10.00
ABL Bryan Little 4.00 10.00
ABM Brad Marchand 5.00 12.00
ABS Brandon Sutter 4.00 10.00
ACC Cassie Campbell 20.00 50.00
ACF Cody Franson 6.00 15.00
ACG Colton Gillies 5.00 12.00
ACL Charline Labonte 8.00 20.00
ACM Carla MacLeod 5.00 12.00
ACO Caroline Ouellette 5.00 12.00
ACP Carey Price 60.00
ACPD Cheryl Pounder 5.00 12.00
ACPR Chris Pronger SP 12.00 30.00
ACS Colleen Sostorics 5.00 12.00
ADB Daniel Bertram 3.00 8.00
ADC Delaney Collins 5.00 12.00
ADD Drew Doughty 8.00 20.00
ADG Danielle Goyette 6.00 15.00
ADH Darren Helm 5.00 12.00
ADHA Dominik Hasek SP 15.00 40.00
ADK Dion Knelsen 3.00 8.00
ADP Dion Phaneuf SP
AED Eric Doyle 3.00 8.00
AGA Gillian Apps 6.00 15.00
AGF Gillian Ferrari 5.00 12.00
AGK Gina Kingsbury 5.00 12.00
AHW Hayley Wickenheiser 12.00 30.00
AJA Jamie Arniel 3.00 8.00
AJB Jennifer Botterill 5.00 12.00
AJH Jayna Hefford 6.00 15.00
AJJ Jaromir Jagr SP 20.00 50.00
AJK Jari Kurri SP 12.00 30.00
AJN James Neal 6.00 15.00
AJNE John Negrin 4.00 10.00
AJP Justin Pogge SP
AJS Joe Sakic SP
AJSP Jason Spezza SP
AJST Jordan Staal SP 15.00 40.00
AJT Jonathan Toews 60.00 120.00
AJTA John Tavares SP 50.00 120.00
AJTH Joe Thornton SP 15.00 40.00
AKA Karl Alzner 4.00 10.00
AKB Kelly Bechard 5.00 12.00
AKL Kristopher Letang 6.00 15.00
AKMA Kenndal McArdle 3.00 8.00
AKR Kris Russell 4.00 10.00
AKS Kim St. Pierre 15.00 40.00
AKT Kyle Turris 15.00 40.00
AKW Katie Weatherston 5.00 12.00
ALB Luc Bourdon 4.00 10.00
ALC Logan Couture 5.00 12.00
ALI Leland Irving 5.00 12.00
ALS Luke Schenn 6.00 15.00
AMAC Meghan Agosta 6.00 15.00
AMAC Marc-Andre Cliché 3.00 8.00
AMAF Marc-Andre Fleury SP 12.00 30.00
AMB Martin Brodeur SP 30.00 80.00
AMK Mark Katic 3.00 8.00
AMM Mike Modano SP 12.00 30.00
AMR Manon Rheaume 20.00 50.00
AMS Marc Staal 8.00 20.00
AOF Olivier Fortier 3.00 8.00
ARL Roberto Luongo SP
ARO Ryan O'Marra 3.00 8.00
ARP Ryan Parent 4.00 10.00
ASD Steve Downie 4.00 10.00
ASG Sam Gagner 6.00 15.00
ASS Steven Stamkos 40.00 80.00
ASV Sarah Vaillancourt 5.00 12.00
ASY Steve Yzerman SP 40.00 100.00
ATB Tessa Bonhomme 5.00 12.00
ATC Trevor Cann 4.00 10.00
ATP Tom Pyatt 6.00 15.00
AVL Vincent Lecavalier SP 12.00 30.00
AVS Vicky Sunohara 6.00 15.00
AVT Vladislav Tretiak SP 60.00 120.00
AYB Yves Bastien 3.00 8.00
AYS Yann Sauve 4.00 10.00
AZB Zachary Boychuk 5.00 12.00
AZT Zack Torquato 3.00 8.00

2007-08 ITG O Canada Complete Jerseys

STATED PRINT RUN 10 SER.#'d SETS
NOT PRICED DUE TO SCARCITY

CJ01 Hayley Wickenheiser
CJ02 Cassie Campbell
CJ03 Vicky Sunohara
CJ04 Kim St. Pierre
CJ05 Carey Price
CJ06 Steve Downie
CJ07 Jonathan Toews
CJ08 Sam Gagner
CJ09 Karl Alzner
CJ10 Logan Couture
CJ11 Kyle Turris
CJ12 Steven Stamkos
CJ13 Angelo Esposito
CJ14 Brandon Sutter
CJ15 Chris Pronger
CJ16 Joe Sakic
CJ17 Roberto Luongo
CJ18 Joe Thornton
CJ19 Martin Brodeur
CJ20 Vincent Lecavalier

2007-08 ITG O Canada Dual Jerseys

STATED PRINT RUN 50 SETS

DJ01 Charline Labonte 25.00 60.00
Kim St. Pierre
DJ02 Vicky Sunohara 10.00 25.00
Danielle Goyette
DJ03 Hayley Wickenheiser 20.00 50.00
Jennifer Botterill
DJ04 Jayna Hefford 10.00 25.00
Caroline Ouellette
DJ05 Charline Labonte 25.00 60.00
Carey Price
DJ06 Kyle Turris 25.00 60.00
Colton Gillies
DJ07 Angelo Esposito 8.00 20.00
Logan Couture
DJ08 Steven Stamkos 15.00 40.00
Brandon Sutter
DJ09 Drew Doughty 12.00 30.00
Yann Sauve
DJ10 Trevor Cann 6.00 15.00
Braden Holtby
DJ11 Jonathan Toews 30.00 80.00
Daniel Bertram
DJ12 Sam Gagner 10.00 25.00
Steve Downie
DJ13 Karl Alzner 6.00 15.00
Luc Bourdon
DJ14 Kristopher Letang 10.00 25.00
Kris Russell
DJ15 Carey Price 25.00 60.00
Leland Irving
DJ16 Danielle Goyette 10.00 25.00
Steve Downie
DJ17 Vicky Sunohara 15.00 40.00
Steven Stamkos
DJ18 Jennifer Botterill 30.00 80.00
Jonathan Toews
DJ19 Hayley Wickenheiser 25.00 60.00
Kyle Turris

2007-08 ITG O Canada Emblems

STATED PRINT RUN 20 SER.#'d SETS
NOT PRICED DUE TO SCARCITY

GUE01 Alex Grant
GUE02 Angelo Esposito
GUE03 Braden Holtby
GUE04 Brandon Sutter
GUE05 Colton Gillies
GUE06 Dion Knelsen
GUE07 Drew Doughty
GUE08 Eric Doyle
GUE09 Jamie Arniel
GUE10 John Negrin
GUE11 Keven Veilleux
GUE12 Kyle Turris
GUE13 Logan Couture
GUE14 Luke Schenn
GUE15 Mark Katic
GUE16 Olivier Fortier
GUE17 Steven Stamkos
GUE18 Trevor Cann
GUE19 Yann Sauve
GUE20 Yves Bastien
GUE21 Zachary Boychuk
GUE22 Zack Torquato
GUE23 Carla MacLeod
GUE24 Caroline Ouellette
GUE25 Charline Labonte
GUE26 Cheryl Pounder
GUE27 Colleen Sostorics
GUE28 Danielle Goyette
GUE29 Delaney Collins
GUE30 Gillian Apps
GUE31 Gillian Ferrari
GUE32 Gina Kingsbury
GUE33 Hayley Wickenheiser
GUE34 Jayna Hefford
GUE35 Jennifer Botterill
GUE36 Katie Weatherston
GUE37 Kelly Bechard
GUE38 Kim St. Pierre
GUE39 Meghan Agosta
GUE40 Sarah Vaillancourt
GUE41 Tessa Bonhomme
GUE42 Vicky Sunohara
GUE43 Karl Alzner
GUE44 Daniel Bertram
GUE45 Luc Bourdon
GUE46 Marc-Andre Cliché
GUE47 Andrew Cogliano
GUE48 Steve Downie
GUE49 Cody Franson
GUE50 Sam Gagner
GUE51 Darren Helm
GUE52 Leland Irving
GUE53 Kristopher Letang
GUE54 Bryan Little
GUE55 Brad Marchand
GUE56 Kenndal McArdle
GUE57 James Neal
GUE58 Ryan O'Marra
GUE59 Ryan Parent
GUE60 Carey Price
GUE61 Tom Pyatt
GUE62 Kris Russell
GUE63 Marc Staal
GUE64 Jonathan Toews
GUE65 Cassie Campbell
GUE66 Vincent Lecavalier
GUE67 Roberto Luongo
GUE68 John Tavares
GUE69 Joe Thornton
GUE70 Jason Spezza
GUE71 Joe Sakic
GUE73 Dany Heatley
GUE74 Eric Lindros
GUE75 Chris Pronger
GUE77 Steve Yzerman
GUE78 Martin Brodeur

2007-08 ITG O Canada Emblems Autographs

STATED PRINT RUN 10 SER.#'d SETS
NOT PRICED DUE TO SCARCITY

2007-08 ITG O Canada Formidable Foes Jerseys

STATED PRINT RUN 50 SETS

FF01 Dominik Hasek 20.00 50.00
Patrick Roy
FF02 Jaromir Jagr 12.00 30.00
Joe Sakic
FF03 Kari Lehtonen 6.00 15.00
Dwayne Roloson
FF04 Keith Tkachuk 6.00 15.00
Eric Lindros
FF05 Mike Modano 6.00 15.00
Vincent Lecavalier
FF06 Chris Chelios 6.00 15.00
Chris Pronger
FF07 Henrik Zetterberg 8.00 20.00
Joe Thornton
FF08 Mike Richter 15.00 40.00
Martin Brodeur
FF09 Alexander Ovechkin 20.00 50.00
Dion Phaneuf
FF10 Vladislav Tretiak 15.00 40.00
Paul Henderson
FF11 Valeri Kharlamov 6.00 15.00
Bobby Clarke
FF12 Borje Salming 8.00 20.00
Larry Robinson
FF13 Jari Kurri 6.00 15.00
Mike Bossy
FF14 Brett Hull 20.00 50.00
Steve Yzerman
FF15 Phil Housley 8.00 20.00
Raymond Bourque
FF16 Peter Stastny 15.00 40.00
Guy Lafleur
FF17 Brian Leetch 6.00 15.00
Paul Coffey
FF18 Pat LaFontaine 5.00 12.00
Luc Robitaille
FF19 Alexander Yakushev 10.00 25.00
Phil Esposito
FF20 Mats Naslund 5.00 12.00
Michel Goulet

2007-08 ITG O Canada He Shoots He Scores

STATED PRINT RUN 20 SER.#'d SETS
NOT PRICED DUE TO SCARCITY

HSHS01 Angelo Esposito
HSHS02 Marc Staal
HSHS03 Cassie Campbell
HSHS04 Sam Gagner
HSHS05 Carey Price
HSHS06 Vincent Lecavalier
HSHS07 Brandon Sutter
HSHS08 Raymond Bourque
HSHS09 Roberto Luongo
HSHS10 Hayley Wickenheiser
HSHS11 Bryan Little
HSHS12 John Tavares
HSHS13 Drew Doughty
HSHS14 Dominik Hasek
HSHS15 Joe Thornton
HSHS16 Jonathan Toews
HSHS17 Kristopher Letang
HSHS18 Patrick Roy
HSHS19 Kyle Turris
HSHS20 Jaromir Jagr
HSHS21 Joe Sakic
HSHS22 Mike Modano
HSHS23 Brett Hull
HSHS24 Dany Heatley
HSHS25 Andrew Cogliano
HSHS26 Kim St-Pierre
HSHS27 Chris Pronger
HSHS28 Steven Stamkos
HSHS29 Steve Downie
HSHS30 Martin Brodeur

2007-08 ITG O Canada International Goalies Jerseys

STATED PRINT RUN 50 SETS

IG01 Mike Richter 12.00 30.00
IG02 Vladislav Tretiak 12.00 30.00
IG03 Cristobal Huet 4.00 10.00
IG04 Dominik Hasek 6.00 15.00
IG05 Tom Barrasso 4.00 10.00
IG06 Tony Esposito 8.00 20.00
IG07 John Vanbiesbrouck 5.00 12.00
IG08 Vladimir Dzurilla 5.00 12.00
IG09 Tuukka Rask 8.00 20.00
IG10 Kari Lehtonen 5.00 12.00

2007-08 ITG O Canada Jerseys

STATED PRINT RUN 100 SER.#'d SETS

GUJ01 Alex Grant 3.00 8.00
GUJ02 Angelo Esposito 8.00 20.00
GUJ03 Braden Holtby 4.00 10.00
GUJ04 Brandon Sutter 4.00 10.00
GUJ05 Colton Gillies 5.00 12.00
GUJ06 Dion Knelsen 3.00 8.00
GUJ07 Drew Doughty 8.00 20.00
GUJ08 Eric Doyle 3.00 8.00
GUJ09 Jamie Arniel 3.00 8.00
GUJ10 John Negrin 4.00 10.00
GUJ11 Keven Veilleux 3.00 8.00
GUJ12 Kyle Turris 15.00 40.00
GUJ13 Logan Couture 5.00 12.00
GUJ14 Luke Schenn 6.00 15.00
GUJ15 Mark Katic 3.00 8.00
GUJ16 Olivier Fortier 3.00 8.00
GUJ17 Steven Stamkos 10.00 25.00
GUJ18 Trevor Cann 4.00 10.00
GUJ19 Yann Sauve 4.00 10.00
GUJ20 Yves Bastien 3.00 8.00
GUJ21 Zachary Boychuk 5.00 12.00
GUJ22 Zack Torquato 3.00 8.00
GUJ23 Carla MacLeod 5.00 12.00
GUJ24 Caroline Ouellette 5.00 12.00
GUJ25 Charline Labonte 8.00 20.00
GUJ26 Cheryl Pounder 5.00 12.00
GUJ27 Colleen Sostorics 5.00 12.00
GUJ28 Danielle Goyette 6.00 15.00
GUJ29 Delaney Collins 5.00 12.00
GUJ30 Gillian Apps 6.00 15.00
GUJ31 Gillian Ferrari 5.00 12.00
GUJ32 Gina Kingsbury 5.00 12.00
GUJ33 Hayley Wickenheiser 12.00 30.00
GUJ34 Jayna Hefford 6.00 15.00
GUJ35 Jennifer Botterill 5.00 12.00
GUJ36 Katie Weatherston 5.00 12.00
GUJ37 Kelly Bechard 5.00 12.00
GUJ38 Kim St. Pierre 15.00 40.00
GUJ39 Meghan Agosta 6.00 15.00
GUJ40 Sarah Vaillancourt 5.00 12.00
GUJ41 Tessa Bonhomme 5.00 12.00
GUJ42 Vicky Sunohara 6.00 15.00
GUJ43 Karl Alzner 4.00 10.00
GUJ44 Daniel Bertram 3.00 8.00
GUJ45 Luc Bourdon 4.00 10.00
GUJ46 Marc-Andre Cliché 3.00 8.00
GUJ47 Andrew Cogliano 8.00 20.00
GUJ48 Steve Downie 4.00 10.00
GUJ49 Cody Franson 6.00 15.00
GUJ50 Sam Gagner 6.00 15.00
GUJ51 Darren Helm 5.00 12.00
GUJ52 Leland Irving 5.00 12.00
GUJ53 Kristopher Letang 6.00 15.00
GUJ54 Bryan Little 4.00 10.00
GUJ55 Brad Marchand 5.00 12.00
GUJ56 Kenndal McArdle 3.00 8.00
GUJ57 James Neal 6.00 15.00
GUJ58 Ryan O'Marra 3.00 8.00
GUJ59 Ryan Parent 4.00 10.00
GUJ60 Carey Price 15.00 40.00
GUJ61 Tom Pyatt 6.00 15.00
GUJ62 Kris Russell 4.00 10.00
GUJ63 Marc Staal 8.00 20.00
GUJ64 Jonathan Toews 20.00 50.00
GUJ65 Cassie Campbell 20.00 50.00
GUJ66 Vincent Lecavalier 5.00 12.00
GUJ67 Roberto Luongo 8.00 20.00
GUJ68 John Tavares 20.00 50.00
GUJ69 Joe Thornton 6.00 15.00
GUJ70 Jason Spezza 5.00 12.00
GUJ71 Joe Sakic 10.00 25.00
GUJ73 Dany Heatley 6.00 15.00
GUJ74 Eric Lindros 5.00 12.00
GUJ75 Chris Pronger 5.00 12.00
GUJ77 Steve Yzerman 15.00 40.00
GUJ78 Martin Brodeur 12.00 30.00
GUJ79 Marc-Andre Fleury 5.00 12.00
GUJ80 Dion Phaneuf 5.00 12.00

2007-08 ITG O Canada Numbers

STATED PRINT RUN 10 SER.#'d SETS
NOT PRICED DUE TO SCARCITY

GUN01 Alex Grant
GUN02 Angelo Esposito
GUN03 Braden Holtby
GUN04 Brandon Sutter
GUN05 Colton Gillies
GUN06 Dion Knelsen
GUN07 Drew Doughty
GUN08 Eric Doyle
GUN09 Jamie Arniel
GUN10 John Negrin
GUN11 Keven Veilleux
GUN12 Kyle Turris
GUN13 Logan Couture
GUN14 Luke Schenn
GUN15 Mark Katic
GUN16 Olivier Fortier
GUN17 Steven Stamkos
GUN18 Trevor Cann
GUN19 Yann Sauve
GUN20 Yves Bastien
GUN21 Zachary Boychuk
GUN22 Zack Torquato
GUN23 Carla MacLeod
GUN24 Caroline Ouellette
GUN25 Charline Labonte
GUN26 Cheryl Pounder
GUN27 Colleen Sostorics
GUN28 Danielle Goyette
GUN29 Delaney Collins
GUN30 Gillian Apps
GUN31 Gillian Ferrari
GUN32 Gina Kingsbury
GUN33 Hayley Wickenheiser
GUN34 Jayna Hefford
GUN35 Jennifer Botterill
GUN36 Katie Weatherston
GUN37 Kelly Bechard
GUN38 Kim St. Pierre
GUN39 Meghan Agosta
GUN40 Sarah Vaillancourt
GUN41 Tessa Bonhomme
GUN42 Vicky Sunohara
GUN43 Karl Alzner
GUN44 Daniel Bertram
GUN45 Luc Bourdon
GUN46 Marc-Andre Cliché
GUN47 Andrew Cogliano
GUN48 Steve Downie
GUN49 Cody Franson
GUN50 Sam Gagner
GUN51 Darren Helm
GUN52 Leland Irving
GUN53 Kristopher Letang
GUN54 Bryan Little
GUN55 Brad Marchand
GUN56 Kenndal McArdle
GUN57 James Neal
GUN58 Ryan O'Marra
GUN59 Ryan Parent
GUN60 Carey Price
GUN61 Tom Pyatt
GUN62 Kris Russell
GUN63 Marc Staal
GUN64 Jonathan Toews
GUN65 Cassie Campbell
GUN66 Vincent Lecavalier
GUN67 Roberto Luongo
GUN68 John Tavares
GUN69 Joe Thornton
GUN70 Jason Spezza
GUN71 Joe Sakic
GUN73 Dany Heatley
GUN74 Eric Lindros
GUN75 Chris Pronger
GUN77 Steve Yzerman
GUN78 Martin Brodeur

2005 ITG Passing the Torch

Available only in ITG Super Boxes available for the 2005 Chicago Sportsfest, this 30-card set honored the two greatest goalies in recent history. Each box contained one set and two memorabilia cards or one memorabilia card and one dual signed card.

COMPLETE SET (25) 8.00 20.00
1 Checklist .40 1.00
2 Martin Brodeur .40 1.00
Rookie Season
3 Martin Brodeur .40 1.00
Calder Trophy
4 Martin Brodeur .40 1.00
First Stanley Cup
5 Martin Brodeur .40 1.00
First Vezina Trophy
6 Martin Brodeur .40 1.00
First NHL All-Star Game
7 Martin Brodeur .40 1.00
400th Career Win
8 Martin Brodeur .40 1.00
50th Career Shutout
9 Martin Brodeur .40 1.00
Winning Streak
10 Martin Brodeur .40 1.00
International Experience
11 Martin Brodeur .40 1.00
Patrick Roy NHL Dreams
12 Martin Brodeur .40 1.00
Patrick Roy Immediate Impact
13 Martin Brodeur .40 1.00
Patrick Roy First Cup
14 Martin Brodeur .40 1.00
Patrick Roy Best of the Best
15 Martin Brodeur .40 1.00
Patrick Roy Among the Stars

16 Martin Brodeur .40 1.00
Patrick Roy Passing the Torch
17 Patrick Roy .40 1.00
Rookie Season
18 Patrick Roy .40 1.00
First Stanley Cup and Conn Smythe Trophy
19 Patrick Roy .40 1.00
First NHL All-Star Game
20 Patrick Roy .40 1.00
First Vezina Trophy
21 Patrick Roy .40 1.00
Traded to Colorado
22 Patrick Roy .40 1.00
First Stanley Cup in Colorado
23 Patrick Roy .40 1.00
Most Career Playoff Wins
24 Patrick Roy .40 1.00
Most Career Wins
25 Patrick Roy .40 1.00
Retirement

2005 ITG Passing the Torch Autographs

This dual-autograph card was available randomly in ITG Super boxes, they were limited to just ten copies.

NOT PRICED DUE TO SCARCITY
PTT1 M.Brodeur/P.Roy

2005 ITG Passing the Torch Memorabilia

Available only in ITG Super Boxes during the 2005 National Convention, this 31-card set featured game-used memorabilia of Patrick Roy and Martin Brodeur. Cards were limited to just 100 copies each unless marked differently below.

UNDER 25 NOT PRICED DUE TO SCARCITY
PTT1 Martin Brodeur NJ 12.00 30.00
PTT2 Martin Brodeur AS 12.00 30.00
PTT3 Martin Brodeur AS 12.00 30.00
PTT4 Martin Brodeur AS 12.00 30.00
PTT5 Martin Brodeur Pad 12.00 30.00
PTT6 Martin Brodeur Stk 12.00 30.00
PTT7 Patrick Roy MTL 12.00 30.00
PTT8 Patrick Roy COL 12.00 30.00
PTT9 Patrick Roy AS 12.00 30.00
PTT10 Patrick Roy AS 12.00 30.00
PTT11 Patrick Roy AS 12.00 30.00
PTT12 Patrick Roy Glove 12.00 30.00
PTT13 Patrick Roy Pad 12.00 30.00
PTT14 Patrick Roy Stk 12.00 30.00
PTT15 M.Brodeur/P.Roy MTL J/J 15.00 40.00
PTT16 M.Brodeur/P.Roy AVS J/J 15.00 40.00
PTT17 M.Brodeur/P.Roy AS J/J 15.00 40.00
PTT18 M.Brodeur/P.Roy Dual Pad 15.00 40.00
PTT19 M.Brodeur/P.Roy S/S 15.00 40.00
PTT20 Martin Brodeur Jsy/Stk 15.00 40.00
PTT21 Patrick Roy Jsy/Stk MTL 15.00 40.00
PTT22 Patrick Roy Jsy/Stk COL 15.00 40.00
PTT23 M.Brodeur/P.Roy MTL Emblms/20
PTT24 M.Brodeur/P.Roy COL Emblms/20
PTT25 Martin Brodeur Nmbr/30 40.00 100.00
PTT26 Martin Brodeur Emblm/30
PTT27 Patrick Roy Nmbr MTL/33 50.00 125.00
PTT28 Patrick Roy Emblm MTL/33 50.00 125.00
PTT29 Patrick Roy Nmbr COL/33 40.00 100.00
PTT30 Patrick Roy Emblm COL/33 40.00 100.00
NNO Checklist

2005 ITG Passing the Torch Memorabilia Autographs

This 24-card set partially paralleled the basic Passing the Torch set but also carried certified autographs. Each card was limited to just 10 copies.

PTT1A Martin Brodeur NJ
PTT2A Martin Brodeur AS
PTT3A Martin Brodeur AS
PTT4A Martin Brodeur AS
PTT5A Martin Brodeur Pad
PTT6A Martin Brodeur Stk
PTT7A Patrick Roy MTL
PTT8A Patrick Roy COL
PTT9A Patrick Roy AS
PTT10A Patrick Roy AS
PTT11A Patrick Roy AS
PTT12A Patrick Roy Glove
PTT13A Patrick Roy Pad
PTT14A Patrick Roy Stk
PTT20A Martin Brodeur Jsy/Stk
PTT21A Patrick Roy Jsy/Stk MTL
PTT22A Patrick Roy Jsy/Stk COL
PTT25A Martin Brodeur Nmbr
PTT26A Martin Brodeur Emblm
PTT27A Patrick Roy Nmbr MTL
PTT28A Patrick Roy Emblm MTL
PTT29A Patrick Roy Nmbr COL
PTT30A Patrick Roy Emblm COL
NNO Checklist

2005 ITG Sidney Crosby Series

COMPLETE SET (25) 15.00 40.00
COMMON CARD (1-25) 1.00 2.50

2005 ITG Sidney Crosby Series Gold

COMMON GOLD (1-25) 8.00 20.00
PRINT RUN 87 SETS

2005 ITG Sidney Crosby Series Autographs

COMMON AUTO (1-25) 75.00 150.00
PRINT RUN 35 SETS
EMERALD 1/1'S EXIST
ONE PER BOX SET

2005 ITG Sidney Crosby Series Autographs Emerald

STATED PRINT RUN 1 SER.#'d SET
NOT PRICED DUE TO SCARCITY

2005 ITG Sidney Crosby Series Memorabilia

PRINT RUN 87 SETS UNLESS OTHERWISE NOTED BELOW
UNDER 25 NOT PRICED DUE TO SCARCITY
SCM1 Sidney Crosby 75.00 200.00
Mario Lemieux Jsys
SCM2 Sidney Crosby
Mario Lemieux Emblems
SCM3 Sidney Crosby
Mario Lemieux Nmbrs
SCM4 Sidney Crosby
Mario Lemieux Gloves
SCM5 Sidney Crosby 60.00 150.00
Marc-Andre Fleury Jsys
SCM6 Sidney Crosby
Marc-Andre Fleury Emblems
SCM7 Sidney Crosby
Marc-Andre Fleury Nmbrs
SCM8 Sidney Crosby
Evgeni Malkin Nmbrs
SCM9 Sidney Crosby 75.00 200.00
Evgeni Malkin Jsys
SCM10 Sidney Crosby
Evgeni Malkin Emblems
SCM11 Sidney Crosby 40.00 100.00
CHL Canada-Russia Challenge Jsy
SCM12 Sidney Crosby 40.00 100.00
2004 World Juniors Jsy
SCM13 Sidney Crosby 50.00 125.00
CHL Canada-Russia Challenge Stick & Jersey
SCM14 Sidney Crosby 50.00 125.00
2004 World Juniors Stick & Jersey
SCM15 Sidney Crosby
Glove
SCM16 Sidney Crosby
CHL Canada-Russia Challenge Emblem
SCM17 Sidney Crosby
2004 World Juniors Emblem
SCM18 Sidney Crosby 100.00 200.00
Triple Memorabilia
SCM19 Sidney Crosby 60.00 150.00
Glove & Jersey
SCM20 Sidney Crosby 50.00 125.00
Dual Jsy

2005 ITG Sidney Crosby Series Signed Memorabilia

PRINT RUN 25 SETS
CAM1 Sidney Crosby 200.00 400.00
2003 CHL Canada-Russia Challenge Jsy
CAM2 Sidney Crosby 200.00 400.00
2004 Team Canada World Junior Jsy
CAM3 Sidney Crosby 200.00 400.00
Game-Used Glove
CAM4 Sidney Crosby 200.00 400.00
Game-Used Stick

2007-08 ITG Superlative Autographs Silver

OVERALL AU ODDS 3 PER PACK
AAO Alexander Ovechkin 40.00 80.00
ABC Bobby Clarke 20.00 40.00
ABH Brett Hull 15.00 40.00
ABL Brian Leetch 10.00 25.00
ABOH Bobby Hull 15.00 40.00
ABP Bernie Parent 12.00 30.00
ACC Chris Chelios 20.00 40.00
ACN Cam Neely 10.00 25.00
ACO Chris Osgood 12.50 30.00
ACP Chris Pronger 10.00 25.00
ADH Dany Heatley 12.00 30.00
ADH Dominik Hasek 20.00 40.00
ADK Dave Keon 15.00 30.00
ADP Denis Potvin 8.00 20.00
AEG Ed Giacomin 10.00 25.00
AFM Frank Mahovlich 15.00 40.00
AGF Grant Fuhr 15.00 40.00
AGH Glenn Hall 12.00 30.00
AGL Guy Lafleur 20.00 40.00
AHR Henri Richard 15.00 40.00
AIK Ilya Kovalchuk 12.00 30.00
AJB Jean Beliveau 15.00 40.00
AJBO Johnny Bower 10.00 25.00
AJJ Jaromir Jagr 25.00 50.00
AJSG Jean-Sebastien Giguere 8.00 20.00
AJSK Joe Sakic 30.00 60.00
AJT Joe Thornton 12.50 30.00
AMB Martin Brodeur 40.00 80.00
AMD Marcel Dionne 8.00 20.00
AMG Marian Gaborik 12.00 30.00
AML Mario Lemieux 50.00 100.00
AMM Mike Modano 10.00 25.00
AMS Milt Schmidt 10.00 25.00
AMSL Martin St-Louis 8.00 20.00
AMT Marty Turco 10.00 25.00
ANL Nicklas Lidstrom 10.00 25.00
APC Paul Coffey 10.00 25.00
APD Pavel Datsyuk 20.00 40.00
APE Phil Esposito 20.00 40.00
APR Patrick Roy 50.00 100.00
ARB Raymond Bourque 30.00 60.00
ARE Ray Emery 8.00 20.00
ARK Red Kelly 10.00 25.00
ARL Roberto Luongo 20.00 40.00
ASM Stan Mikita 15.00 40.00
ATE Tony Esposito 15.00 40.00
ATL Ted Lindsay 12.50 30.00
AVL Vincent Lecavalier 12.50 30.00
AVT Vladislav Tretiak 20.00 40.00
AJSN Scott Niedermayer 6.00 15.00

2007-08 ITG Superlative Jerseys Autographs Silver

STATED PRINT RUN 50 SERIAL #'d SETS
AJAO Alexander Ovechkin 75.00 150.00
AJBC Bobby Clarke 12.00 30.00
AJBH Brett Hull 20.00 50.00
AJBL Brian Leetch 12.00 30.00
AJBOH Bobby Hull 20.00 50.00
AJBP Bernie Parent 15.00 40.00
AJCC Chris Chelios 12.50 30.00
AJCN Cam Neely 12.00 30.00
AJCO Chris Osgood 12.50 30.00
AJCP Chris Pronger 12.00 30.00
AJDH Dominik Hasek 15.00 40.00
AJDH Dany Heatley 12.50 30.00
AJDK Dave Keon 15.00 40.00
AJDP Denis Potvin 10.00 25.00
AJEG Ed Giacomin 12.00 30.00
AJFM Frank Mahovlich 15.00 40.00
AJGF Grant Fuhr 12.50 30.00
AJGH Glenn Hall 15.00 40.00
AJGL Guy Lafleur 25.00 50.00
AJHR Henri Richard 20.00 50.00
AJIK Ilya Kovalchuk 15.00 40.00
AJJB Jean Beliveau 20.00 50.00
AJBO Johnny Bower 25.00 50.00
AJJJ Jaromir Jagr 40.00 80.00
AJSG Jean-Sebastien Giguere 15.00 40.00
AJSK Joe Sakic 40.00 80.00
AJJT Joe Thornton 15.00 40.00
AJMB Martin Brodeur 40.00 80.00
AJMD Marcel Dionne 8.00 20.00
AJMG Marian Gaborik 15.00 40.00
AJML Mario Lemieux 60.00 120.00
AJMM Mike Modano 12.00 30.00
AJMS Milt Schmidt 15.00 40.00
AJMSL Martin St-Louis 10.00 25.00
AJMT Marty Turco 12.00 30.00
AJNL Nicklas Lidstrom 15.00 40.00
AJPC Paul Coffey 12.00 30.00
AJPD Pavel Datsyuk 15.00 40.00
AJPE Phil Esposito 20.00 50.00
AJPR Patrick Roy 50.00 100.00
AJRB Raymond Bourque 25.00 50.00
AJRE Ray Emery 10.00 25.00
AJRK Red Kelly 10.00 25.00
AJRL Roberto Luongo 20.00 50.00
AJSM Stan Mikita 12.50 30.00
AJSN Scott Niedermayer 10.00 25.00
AJTE Tony Esposito 20.00 50.00
AJTL Ted Lindsay 12.50 30.00
AJVL Vincent Lecavalier 12.00 30.00
AJVT Vladislav Tretiak 40.00 80.00

2007-08 ITG Superlative Jerseys Silver

STATED PRINT RUN 30 SERIAL #'d SETS
GUJ01 Jean Beliveau 15.00 40.00
GUJ02 Raymond Bourque Boston 12.00 30.00
GUJ03 Raymond Bourque Colorado 15.00 40.00
GUJ04 Martin Brodeur 25.00 50.00
GUJ05 Gerry Cheevers 15.00 40.00
GUJ06 Chris Chelios 6.00 15.00
GUJ07 Alexei Cherepanov 10.00 25.00
GUJ08 Bobby Clarke 15.00 40.00
GUJ09 Paul Coffey 12.00 30.00
GUJ10 Marcel Dionne 10.00 25.00
GUJ11 Ray Emery 8.00 20.00
GUJ12 Angelo Esposito 15.00 40.00
GUJ13 Phil Esposito 15.00 40.00
GUJ14 Tony Esposito 10.00 25.00
GUJ15 Grant Fuhr 12.50 30.00
GUJ16 Jaromir Jagr Pittsburgh 15.00 40.00
GUJ17 Ed Giacomin 10.00 25.00
GUJ18 Glenn Hall 12.00 30.00
GUJ19 Dominik Hasek 10.00 25.00
GUJ20 Dany Heatley
GUJ21 Bobby Hull 15.00 40.00
GUJ22 Brett Hull Dallas 15.00 40.00
GUJ23 Brett Hull Detroit 15.00 40.00
GUJ24 Jaromir Jagr New York 15.00 40.00
GUJ25 Dave Keon 8.00 20.00
GUJ26 Ilya Kovalchuk 15.00 40.00
GUJ27 Guy Lafleur 12.00 30.00
GUJ28 Pat LaFontaine 8.00 20.00
GUJ29 Vincent Lecavalier 10.00 25.00
GUJ30 Brian Leetch 10.00 25.00
GUJ31 Joe Thornton San Jose 12.00 30.00
GUJ32 Ted Lindsay 10.00 25.00
GUJ33 Roberto Luongo Vancouver 15.00 40.00
GUJ34 Roberto Luongo Florida 15.00 40.00
GUJ35 Frank Mahovlich 15.00 40.00
GUJ36 Stan Mikita 8.00 20.00
GUJ37 Mike Modano 10.00 25.00
GUJ38 Cam Neely 10.00 25.00
GUJ39 Alexander Ovechkin 30.00 60.00
GUJ40 Denis Potvin 8.00 20.00
GUJ41 Felix Potvin 15.00 40.00
GUJ42 Carey Price 30.00 60.00
GUJ43 Chris Pronger 10.00 25.00
GUJ44 Tuukka Rask 25.00 50.00
GUJ45 Henri Richard 12.00 30.00
GUJ46 Maurice Richard 50.00 100.00
GUJ47 Patrick Roy Montreal 25.00 50.00
GUJ48 Patrick Roy Colorado 25.00 50.00
GUJ49 Joe Sakic 15.00 40.00
GUJ50 Milt Schmidt 8.00 20.00
GUJ51 Jari Kurri 20.00 40.00
GUJ52 John Tavares 30.00 60.00
GUJ53 Joe Thornton Boston 10.00 25.00
GUJ54 Vladislav Tretiak 25.00 50.00
GUJ55 Marty Turco 10.00 25.00
GUJ56 Mario Lemieux 25.00 50.00
GUJ57 Pavel Datsyuk 15.00 40.00
GUJ58 Mats Sundin 15.00 40.00
GUJ59 Steven Stamkos 25.00 50.00
GUJ60 Ed Belfour 12.00 30.00
GUJ61 Markus Naslund 10.00 25.00
GUJ62 Paul Stastny 10.00 25.00
GUJ63 Doug Gilmour
GUJ64 Marc Staal 15.00 40.00
GUJ65 Sam Gagner 12.00 30.00
GUJ66 Jordan Staal 12.00 30.00
GUJ67 Bill Barber 6.00 15.00
GUJ68 Martin St. Louis 8.00 20.00
GUJ69 Scott Niedermayer 6.00 15.00
GUJ70 Lanny McDonald 10.00 25.00
GUJ71 Borje Salming 10.00 25.00
GUJ72 Darryl Sittler 8.00 20.00
GUJ73 Marian Gaborik 12.00 30.00
GUJ74 Jean-Sebastien Giguere 10.00 25.00
GUJ75 Paul Kariya 10.00 25.00

2007-08 ITG Superlative Patches Silver

STATED PRINT RUN 30 SERIAL #'d SETS
SP01 Alexander Ovechkin 30.00 60.00
SP02 Alexei Cherepanov 12.00 30.00
SP03 Angelo Esposito 20.00 50.00
SP04 Bobby Clarke 15.00 40.00
SP05 Bobby Hull 20.00 50.00
SP06 Borje Salming 15.00 40.00
SP07 Brett Hull Dallas 15.00 40.00
SP08 Brett Hull Detroit 15.00 40.00
SP09 Brian Leetch 12.00 30.00
SP10 Cam Neely 12.00 30.00
SP11 Carey Price 40.00 80.00
SP12 Chris Chelios 12.00 30.00
SP13 Chris Osgood 15.00 40.00
SP14 Chris Pronger 12.00 30.00
SP15 Dany Heatley 15.00 40.00
SP16 Darryl Sittler 10.00 25.00
SP17 Dave Keon 12.00 30.00
SP18 Denis Potvin 15.00 40.00
SP19 Dominik Hasek 12.00 30.00
SP20 Doug Gilmour 10.00 25.00
SP21 Ed Belfour 12.00 30.00
SP22 Felix Potvin 15.00 40.00
SP23 Frank Mahovlich 15.00 40.00
SP24 Glenn Hall
SP25 Guy Lafleur 20.00 50.00
SP26 Henri Richard 20.00 50.00
SP27 Ilya Kovalchuk 15.00 40.00
SP28 Jari Kurri 30.00 60.00
SP29 Jaromir Jagr Pittsburgh 30.00 60.00
SP30 Jaromir Jagr New York 30.00 60.00
SP31 Jean Beliveau 20.00 50.00
SP32 Joe Sakic 20.00 50.00
SP33 Joe Thornton San Jose 15.00 40.00
SP34 Joe Thornton Boston 20.00 50.00
SP35 John Tavares 30.00 60.00
SP36 Jordan Staal 15.00 40.00
SP37 Jean-Sebastien Giguere 15.00 40.00
SP38 Lanny McDonald 10.00 25.00
SP39 Marc Staal 12.00 30.00
SP40 Marcel Dionne 10.00 25.00
SP41 Marian Gaborik 15.00 40.00
SP42 Mario Lemieux 30.00 60.00
SP43 Markus Naslund 12.00 30.00
SP44 Martin Brodeur 30.00 60.00
SP45 Martin St. Louis 10.00 25.00
SP46 Marty Turco 12.00 30.00
SP47 Mats Sundin 20.00 50.00
SP48 Mike Modano 12.00 30.00
SP49 Milt Schmidt 15.00 40.00
SP50 Pat LaFontaine 20.00 50.00
SP51 Patrick Roy Montreal 40.00 80.00
SP52 Patrick Roy Colorado 40.00 80.00
SP53 Paul Coffey 12.00 30.00
SP54 Paul Stastny 15.00 40.00
SP55 Pavel Datsyuk 15.00 40.00
SP56 Phil Esposito 20.00 50.00
SP57 Ray Emery 10.00 25.00
SP58 Raymond Bourque Boston 20.00 50.00
SP59 Raymond Bourque Colorado 20.00 50.00
SP60 Roberto Luongo Vancouver 20.00 50.00
SP61 Roberto Luongo Florida 20.00 50.00
SP62 Sam Gagner 12.00 30.00
SP63 Scott Niedermayer 10.00 25.00
SP64 Stan Mikita 12.00 30.00
SP65 Vladislav Tretiak 30.00 60.00
SP66 Steven Stamkos 40.00 80.00
SP67 Tony Esposito 30.00 60.00
SP68 Tuukka Rask 40.00 80.00
SP69 Vincent Lecavalier 12.00 30.00
SP70 Larry Robinson 12.00 30.00
SP71 Grant Fuhr Edmonton 20.00 50.00
SP72 Gilbert Perreault 12.00 30.00
SP73 Jean Ratelle 15.00 40.00
SP74 Peter Forsberg 20.00 50.00
SP75 Paul Kariya 12.00 30.00

2007-08 ITG Superlative Prospects Jerseys Autographs Silver

STATED PRINT RUN 50 SERIAL #'d SETS
SPAB Alex Bourret 8.00 20.00
SPACO Andrew Cogliano 15.00 40.00
SPAE Angelo Esposito 15.00 40.00
SPAP Alex Pietrangelo 15.00 40.00
SPAS Alexander Semin 20.00 50.00
SPBB Brian Boyle 15.00 40.00
SPBL Bryan Little 12.00 30.00
SPBLE Brian Lee 10.00 25.00
SPBM Brett MacLean 10.00 25.00
SPBS Brandon Sutter 12.00 30.00
SPCF Cody Franson 10.00 25.00
SPCG Colton Gillies 10.00 25.00
SPCGI Claude Giroux 25.00 50.00
SPCPR Carey Price 75.00 150.00
SPDD Drew Doughty 25.00 50.00
SPDP Dustin Penner 12.00 30.00
SPDS Devin Setoguchi 12.00 30.00
SPGB Gilbert Brule 15.00 40.00
SPJBL Jonathan Blum 12.00 30.00
SPJH Jonas Hiller 15.00 40.00
SPJS Jordan Staal 20.00 40.00
SPJSK Jack Skille 12.00 30.00
SPJT John Tavares 75.00 150.00
SPJTL Jiri Tlusty 15.00 40.00
SPKA Karl Alzner 25.00 50.00
SPKE Keaton Ellerby 12.00 30.00
SPKM Kenndal McArdle 8.00 20.00
SPKR Kris Russell 10.00 25.00
SPLB Luc Bourdon 12.00 30.00
SPLC Logan Couture 8.00 20.00
SPLI Leland Irving 10.00 25.00
SPMC Matthew Corrente 8.00 20.00
SPMDZ Michael Del Zotto 10.00 25.00
SPMF Michael Frolik 8.00 20.00
SPMG Michael Grabner 10.00 25.00
SPML Matt Lashoff 8.00 20.00
SPMS Marc Staal 15.00 40.00
SPOM Oscar Moller 12.00 30.00
SPPM Peter Mueller 25.00 50.00
SPPS Paul Stastny 15.00 40.00
SPRP Ryan Parent 15.00 40.00
SPSD Steve Downie 12.00 30.00
SPSG Sam Gagner 25.00 50.00
SPSM Steve Mason 15.00 40.00
SPSS Steven Stamkos 50.00 100.00
SPTH Thomas Hickey 12.00 30.00
SPTM Thomas McCollum 10.00 25.00
SPTP Tom Pyatt 8.00 20.00
SPTR Tuukka Rask 25.00 50.00
SPTW Ty Wishart 8.00 20.00

2009-10 ITG Superlative Autographs

STATED PRINT RUN 50 SER.#'d SETS
AAK Anze Kopitar 10.00 25.00
AAO Alexander Ovechkin 40.00 100.00
AAS Alexander Semin 10.00 25.00
ACC Chris Chelios 12.00 30.00
ACP Carey Price 25.00 60.00
ADB Daniel Briere 10.00 25.00
ADG Doug Gilmour 10.00 25.00
ADH Dominik Hasek 10.00 25.00
AEN Evgeni Nabokov 10.00 25.00
AGL Guy Lafleur 15.00 40.00
AIK Ilya Kovalchuk 12.00 30.00
AJB Jean Beliveau 15.00 40.00
AJJ Jaromir Jagr 15.00 40.00
AJS Joe Sakic 20.00 50.00
AJT Joe Thornton 20.00 50.00
ALR Larry Robinson 12.00 30.00
AMB Martin Brodeur 40.00 80.00
AMG Mike Green 20.00 50.00
AMK Mikko Koivu 15.00 30.00
AML Mario Lemieux 40.00 100.00
AMM Mike Modano 10.00 25.00
AMS Martin St. Louis 10.00 25.00
ANL Nicklas Lidstrom 12.00 30.00
APM Patrick Marleau 10.00 25.00
APR Patrick Roy 40.00 100.00
ARB Rob Blake 10.00 25.00
ARG Ryan Getzlaf 15.00 40.00
ARL Roberto Luongo 25.00 60.00
ASF Sergei Fedorov 20.00 50.00
ASK Saku Koivu 10.00 25.00
ASN Scott Niedermayer 6.00 15.00
ATS Teemu Selanne 10.00 25.00
ATT Tim Thomas 10.00 25.00
AMGA Marian Gaborik 15.00 40.00
APRO Patrick Roy 40.00 100.00
ARBO Ray Bourque 15.00 40.00

2009-10 ITG Superlative AutoThreads Gold

STATED PRINT RUN 1 SER.#'d SET
NOT PRICED DUE TO SCARCITY

2009-10 ITG Superlative AutoThreads Silver

STATED PRINT RUN 9 SER.#'d SETS
NOT PRICED DUE TO SCARCITY

2009-10 ITG Superlative Complete Jersey Gold

STATED PRINT RUN 1 SER.#'d SET
NOT PRICED DUE TO SCARCITY

2009-10 ITG Superlative Complete Jersey Silver

STATED PRINT RUN 9 SER.#'d SETS
NOT PRICED DUE TO SCARCITY

2009-10 ITG Superlative Complete Package Gold

STATED PRINT RUN 1 SER.#'d SET
NOT PRICED DUE TO SCARCITY

2009-10 ITG Superlative Complete Package Silver

STATED PRINT RUN 9 SER.#'d SETS
NOT PRICED DUE TO SCARCITY

2009-10 ITG Superlative Famous Fabrics 500 Goal Scorers Jerseys Gold

STATED PRINT RUN 1 SER.#'d SET
NOT PRICED DUE TO SCARCITY

2009-10 ITG Superlative Famous Fabrics 500 Goal Scorers Jerseys Silver

STATED PRINT RUN 9 SER.#'d SETS
NOT PRICED DUE TO SCARCITY

2009-10 ITG Superlative Famous Fabrics 500 Goal Scorers Sticks Gold

STATED PRINT RUN 1 SER.#'d SET
NOT PRICED DUE TO SCARCITY

2009-10 ITG Superlative Famous Fabrics 500 Goal Scorers Sticks Silver

STATED PRINT RUN 9 SER.#'d SETS
NOT PRICED DUE TO SCARCITY

2009-10 ITG Superlative Famous Fabrics All Star Gold

STATED PRINT RUN 1 SER.#'d SET
NOT PRICED DUE TO SCARCITY

2009-10 ITG Superlative Famous Fabrics All Star Quads Gold

STATED PRINT RUN 1 SER.#'d SET
NOT PRICED DUE TO SCARCITY

2009-10 ITG Superlative Famous Fabrics All Star Quads Silver

STATED PRINT RUN 9 SER.#'d SETS
NOT PRICED DUE TO SCARCITY

2009-10 ITG Superlative Famous Fabrics All Star Silver

STATED PRINT RUN 9 SER.#'d SETS
NOT PRICED DUE TO SCARCITY

2009-10 ITG Superlative Famous Fabrics Complete Career Gold

STATED PRINT RUN 1 SER.#'d SET
NOT PRICED DUE TO SCARCITY

2009-10 ITG Superlative Famous Fabrics Complete Career Silver

STATED PRINT RUN 9 SER.#'d SETS
NOT PRICED DUE TO SCARCITY

2009-10 ITG Superlative Famous Fabrics Emblem

STATED PRINT RUN 1 SER.#'d SET
NOT PRICED DUE TO SCARCITY

2009-10 ITG Superlative Famous Fabrics Famous Lines Gold

STATED PRINT RUN 1 SER.#'d SET
NOT PRICED DUE TO SCARCITY

2009-10 ITG Superlative Famous Fabrics Famous Lines Silver

STATED PRINT RUN 9 SER.#'d SETS
NOT PRICED DUE TO SCARCITY

2009-10 ITG Superlative Famous Fabrics First Goal Jerseys Gold

STATED PRINT RUN 1 SER.#'d SET
NOT PRICED DUE TO SCARCITY

2009-10 ITG Superlative Famous Fabrics First Goal Jerseys Silver

STATED PRINT RUN 9 SER.#'d SETS
NOT PRICED DUE TO SCARCITY

2009-10 ITG Superlative Famous Fabrics History of the Conn Smyth Gold

STATED PRINT RUN 1 SER.#'d SET
NOT PRICED DUE TO SCARCITY

2009-10 ITG Superlative Famous Fabrics History of the Conn Smyth Silver

STATED PRINT RUN 9 SER.#'d SETS
NOT PRICED DUE TO SCARCITY

2009-10 ITG Superlative Famous Fabrics Stickwork Gold

STATED PRINT RUN 1 SER.#'d SET
NOT PRICED DUE TO SCARCITY

2009-10 ITG Superlative Famous Fabrics Stickwork Silver

STATED PRINT RUN 9 SER.#'d SETS
NOT PRICED DUE TO SCARCITY

2009-10 ITG Superlative Famous Fabrics Superlative Leader

STATED PRINT RUN 1 SER.#'d SET
NOT PRICED DUE TO SCARCITY

2009-10 ITG Superlative Famous Fabrics Superlative Numbers

STATED PRINT RUN 1 SER.#'d SET
NOT PRICED DUE TO SCARCITY

2009-10 ITG Superlative Famous Fabrics Superlative Tag

STATED PRINT RUN 1 SER.#'d SET
NOT PRICED DUE TO SCARCITY

2009-10 ITG Superlative Famous Fabrics Trophy Case Gold

STATED PRINT RUN 1 SER.#'d SET
NOT PRICED DUE TO SCARCITY

2009-10 ITG Superlative Famous Fabrics Trophy Case Silver

STATED PRINT RUN 9 SER.#'d SETS
NOT PRICED DUE TO SCARCITY

2009-10 ITG Superlative Game Used Jerseys Gold

STATED PRINT RUN 9 SER.#'d SETS
NOT PRICED DUE TO SCARCITY

2009-10 ITG Superlative Game Used Jerseys Onyx

STATED PRINT RUN 1 SER.#'d SET
NOT PRICED DUE TO SCARCITY

2009-10 ITG Superlative Game Used Jerseys Silver

STATED PRINT RUN 30 SER.#'d SETS
GUJ01 Alexander Ovechkin/40 30.00 80.00
GUJ02 John Tavares 30.00 80.00
GUJ03 Corey Perry 8.00 20.00
GUJ04 Jean-Sebastien Giguere 15.00 40.00
GUJ05 Ryan Getzlaf 12.00 30.00
GUJ06 Scott Niedermayer 8.00 20.00
GUJ07 Teemu Selanne 8.00 20.00
GUJ08 Ilya Kovalchuk 10.00 25.00
GUJ09 Kari Lehtonen 8.00 20.00
GUJ10 Ray Bourque 12.00 30.00
GUJ11 Milan Lucic 8.00 20.00
GUJ12 Tim Thomas 8.00 20.00
GUJ13 Gilbert Perreault 8.00 20.00
GUJ14 Ryan Miller 15.00 40.00
GUJ15 Miikka Kiprusoff 8.00 20.00
GUJ16 Cam Ward 8.00 20.00
GUJ17 Chris Chelios 10.00 25.00
GUJ18 Denis Savard 8.00 20.00
GUJ19 Ray Bourque 12.00 30.00
GUJ20 Joe Sakic 15.00 40.00
GUJ21 Patrick Roy 25.00 60.00
GUJ22 Rob Blake 8.00 20.00
GUJ23 Brenden Morrow 6.00 15.00
GUJ24 Brett Hull 15.00 40.00
GUJ25 Ed Belfour 12.00 30.00
GUJ26 Marty Turco 6.00 15.00
GUJ27 Mike Modano 8.00 20.00
GUJ28 Dominik Hasek 8.00 20.00
GUJ29 Nicklas Lidstrom 10.00 25.00
GUJ30 Sergei Fedorov 15.00 40.00
GUJ31 Nazem Kadri 12.00 30.00
GUJ32 Anze Kopitar 8.00 20.00
GUJ33 Luc Robitaille 8.00 20.00
GUJ34 Marcel Dionne 10.00 25.00
GUJ35 Rob Blake 8.00 20.00
GUJ36 Marian Gaborik 12.00 30.00
GUJ37 Carey Price 20.00 50.00
GUJ38 Eric Staal 10.00 25.00
GUJ39 Mats Sundin 8.00 20.00
GUJ40 Patrick Roy 25.00 60.00
GUJ41 Saku Koivu 8.00 20.00
GUJ42 Martin Brodeur 20.00 50.00
GUJ43 Scott Niedermayer 8.00 20.00
GUJ44 Ilya Kovalchuk 10.00 25.00
GUJ45 Marian Gaborik 12.00 30.00
GUJ46 Dominik Hasek 8.00 20.00
GUJ47 Dale Hawerchuk 8.00 20.00
GUJ48 Daniel Briere 8.00 20.00
GUJ49 Jaromir Jagr 12.00 30.00
GUJ50 Marc-Andre Fleury 12.00 30.00
GUJ51 Mario Lemieux 20.00 50.00
GUJ52 Tyler Seguin 15.00 40.00
GUJ53 Patrick Marleau 8.00 20.00
GUJ54 Doug Gilmour 8.00 20.00
GUJ55 Martin St. Louis 8.00 20.00
GUJ56 Mike Green 15.00 40.00
GUJ57 Alexander Semin 8.00 20.00
GUJ58 Jaromir Jagr 12.00 30.00
GUJ59 Taylor Hall 30.00 80.00
GUJ60 Teemu Selanne 8.00 20.00
GUJ61 Dave Keon SP/15
GUJ62 Larry Robinson SP/15
GUJ63 Milt Schmidt SP/15
GUJ64 Stan Mikita SP/15
GUJ65 Tony Esposito SP/15

2009-10 ITG Superlative Game Used Patches Gold

STATED PRINT RUN 9 SER.#'d SETS
NOT PRICED DUE TO SCARCITY

2009-10 ITG Superlative Game Used Patches Silver

*SINGLES: .5X TO 1.2X BASIC INSERTS
STATED PRINT RUN 30 SER.#'d SETS
SP02 John Tavares 75.00 150.00

2009-10 ITG Superlative Get Real 2

STATED PRINT RUN 1 SER.#'d SET
NOT PRICED DUE TO SCARCITY

2009-10 ITG Superlative Goalie Gold

STATED PRINT RUN 1 SER.#'d SET
NOT PRICED DUE TO SCARCITY

2009-10 ITG Superlative Goalie Silver

STATED PRINT RUN 9 SER.#'d SETS
NOT PRICED DUE TO SCARCITY

2009-10 ITG Superlative How Swede It Is Gold

STATED PRINT RUN 1 SER.#'d SET
NOT PRICED DUE TO SCARCITY

2009-10 ITG Superlative How Swede It Is Silver

STATED PRINT RUN 9 SER.#'d SETS
NOT PRICED DUE TO SCARCITY

2009-10 ITG Superlative International Ice Gold

STATED PRINT RUN 1 SER.#'d SET
NOT PRICED DUE TO SCARCITY

2009-10 ITG Superlative International Ice Silver

STATED PRINT RUN 9 SER.#'d SETS
NOT PRICED DUE TO SCARCITY

2009-10 ITG Superlative Jerseys Autographs Gold

STATED PRINT RUN 9 SER.#'d SETS
NOT PRICED DUE TO SCARCITY

2009-10 ITG Superlative Jerseys Autographs Silver

STATED PRINT RUN 50 SER.#'d SETS
AJAK Anze Kopitar 12.00 30.00
AJAO Alexander Ovechkin 40.00 80.00
AJAS Alexander Semin 20.00 50.00
AJCC Chris Chelios 15.00 40.00
AJCP Carey Price 20.00 50.00
AJDB Daniel Briere 12.00 30.00
AJDG Doug Gilmour 12.00 30.00
AJDH Dominik Hasek 15.00 40.00
AJEN Evgeni Nabokov 15.00 40.00
AJGL Guy Lafleur 20.00 50.00
AJIK Ilya Kovalchuk 15.00 40.00
AJJB Jean Beliveau 20.00 50.00
AJJJ Jaromir Jagr 25.00 60.00
AJJS Joe Sakic 25.00 60.00
AJJT Joe Thornton 15.00 40.00
AJLR Larry Robinson 10.00 25.00
AJMB Martin Brodeur 25.00 60.00
AJMG Mike Green 20.00 50.00
AJMK Mikko Koivu 12.00 30.00
AJML Mario Lemieux 40.00 80.00
AJMM Mike Modano 15.00 40.00
AJMS Martin St. Louis 10.00 25.00
AJNL Nicklas Lidstrom 15.00 40.00
AJPM Patrick Marleau 12.00 30.00
AJPR Patrick Roy 60.00 120.00
AJRG Ryan Getzlaf 10.00 25.00
AJRL Roberto Luongo 20.00 50.00
AJSF Sergei Fedorov 20.00 50.00
AJSK Saku Koivu 15.00 40.00
AJSN Scott Niedermayer 10.00 25.00
AJTS Teemu Selanne 15.00 40.00
AJTT Tim Thomas 12.00 30.00
AJMGA2 Marian Gaborik 15.00 40.00
AJMGA Marian Gaborik 15.00 40.00
AJPRO Patrick Roy 40.00 80.00
AJRBO Ray Bourque 20.00 50.00

2009-10 ITG Superlative Jumbo Emblem Gold

STATED PRINT RUN 1 SER.#'d SET
NOT PRICED DUE TO SCARCITY

2009-10 ITG Superlative Jumbo Emblem Silver

STATED PRINT RUN 9 SER.#'d SETS
NOT PRICED DUE TO SCARCITY

2009-10 ITG Superlative Jumbo Number Gold

STATED PRINT RUN 1 SER.#'d SET
NOT PRICED DUE TO SCARCITY

2009-10 ITG Superlative Jumbo Number Silver

STATED PRINT RUN 9 SER.#'d SETS
NOT PRICED DUE TO SCARCITY

2009-10 ITG Superlative Monogram

STATED PRINT RUN 1 SER.#'d SET
NOT PRICED DUE TO SCARCITY

2009-10 ITG Superlative Nameplates

STATED PRINT RUN 1 SER.#'d SET
NOT PRICED DUE TO SCARCITY

2009-10 ITG Superlative Nicknames Gold

STATED PRINT RUN 1 SER.#'d SET
NOT PRICED DUE TO SCARCITY

2009-10 ITG Superlative Nicknames Silver

STATED PRINT RUN 9 SER.#'d SETS
NOT PRICED DUE TO SCARCITY

2009-10 ITG Superlative Paper Cuts
STATED PRINT RUN 1 SER.#'d SETS
NOT PRICED DUE TO SCARCITY

2009-10 ITG Superlative Past, Present and Future Gold
STATED PRINT RUN 1 SER.#'d SET
NOT PRICED DUE TO SCARCITY

2009-10 ITG Superlative Past, Present and Future Silver
STATED PRINT RUN 9 SER.#'d SETS
NOT PRICED DUE TO SCARCITY

2009-10 ITG Superlative Patches Autographs
STATED PRINT RUN 9 SER.#'d SETS
NOT PRICED DUE TO SCARCITY

2009-10 ITG Superlative Player Quad Emblems Gold
STATED PRINT RUN 1 SER.#'d SET
NOT PRICED DUE TO SCARCITY

2009-10 ITG Superlative Player Quad Emblems Silver
STATED PRINT RUN 9 SER.#'d SETS
NOT PRICED DUE TO SCARCITY

2009-10 ITG Superlative Player Quad Jerseys Gold
STATED PRINT RUN 1 SER.#'d SET
NOT PRICED DUE TO SCARCITY

2009-10 ITG Superlative Player Quad Jerseys Silver
STATED PRINT RUN 9 SER.#'d SETS
NOT PRICED DUE TO SCARCITY

2009-10 ITG Superlative Player Quad Numbers Gold
STATED PRINT RUN 1 SER.#'d SET
NOT PRICED DUE TO SCARCITY

2009-10 ITG Superlative Player Quad Numbers Silver
STATED PRINT RUN 9 SER.#'d SETS
NOT PRICED DUE TO SCARCITY

2009-10 ITG Superlative Player Sticks Gold
STATED PRINT RUN 9 SER.#'d SETS
NOT PRICED DUE TO SCARCITY

2009-10 ITG Superlative Player Sticks Silver
STATED PRINT RUN 9 SER.#'d SETS
NOT PRICED DUE TO SCARCITY

2009-10 ITG Superlative Plus Emblem Autographs
STATED PRINT RUN 9 SER.#'d SETS
NOT PRICED DUE TO SCARCITY

2009-10 ITG Superlative Plus Glove Autographs
STATED PRINT RUN 9 SER.#'d SETS
NOT PRICED DUE TO SCARCITY

2009-10 ITG Superlative Plus Number Autographs
STATED PRINT RUN 9 SER.#'d SETS
NOT PRICED DUE TO SCARCITY

2009-10 ITG Superlative Plus Pads Autographs
STATED PRINT RUN 9 SER.#'d SETS
NOT PRICED DUE TO SCARCITY

2009-10 ITG Superlative Plus Pants Autographs
STATED PRINT RUN 9 SER.#'d SETS
NOT PRICED DUE TO SCARCITY

2009-10 ITG Superlative Plus Skate Autographs
STATED PRINT RUN 9 SER.#'d SETS
NOT PRICED DUE TO SCARCITY

2009-10 ITG Superlative Plus Sock Autographs
STATED PRINT RUN 9 SER.#'d SETS
NOT PRICED DUE TO SCARCITY

2009-10 ITG Superlative Plus Stick Autographs
STATED PRINT RUN 9 SER.#'d SETS
NOT PRICED DUE TO SCARCITY

2009-10 ITG Superlative Prospect Autographs Gold
STATED PRINT RUN 10 SER.#'d SETS
NOT PRICED DUE TO SCARCITY

2009-10 ITG Superlative Prospect Autographs Silver
STATED PRINT RUN 40 SER.#'d SETS

PABS Brayden Schenn	15.00	40.00
PACH Cody Hodgson	30.00	60.00
PACP Chet Pickard	15.00	40.00
PADH Darren Helm	10.00	25.00
PADT Dana Tyrell	8.00	20.00
PAEK Evander Kane	15.00	40.00
PAFB Fabian Brunnstrom	8.00	20.00
PAJC Jared Cowen	8.00	20.00
PAJE Jordan Eberle	25.00	60.00
PAJT John Tavares	40.00	80.00
PAKA Karl Alzner	8.00	20.00
PAMB Mikkel Boedker	8.00	20.00
PAMD Matt Duchene	30.00	60.00
PANK Nazem Kadri	20.00	50.00
PARN Ryan Nugent-Hopkins	15.00	40.00
PASV Semyon Varlamov	25.00	60.00
PATH Taylor Hall	50.00	100.00
PATS Tyler Seguiin	50.00	100.00
PAVH Victor Hedman	10.00	25.00
PAZB Zach Boychuk	10.00	25.00
PATHI Thomas Hickey	15.00	40.00

2009-10 ITG Superlative Prospect Jerseys Autographs Gold
STATED PRINT RUN 10 SER.#'d SETS
NOT PRICED DUE TO SCARCITY

2009-10 ITG Superlative Prospect Jerseys Autographs Silver
STATED PRINT RUN 40 SER.#'d SETS

PAJBS Brayden Schenn	20.00	50.00
PAJCH Cody Hodgson	30.00	60.00
PAJCP Chet Pickard	20.00	50.00
PAJDH Darren Helm	12.00	30.00
PAJDT Dana Tyrell	10.00	25.00
PAJEK Evander Kane	20.00	50.00
PAJFB Fabian Brunnstrom	10.00	25.00
PAJJC Jared Cowen	12.00	30.00
PAJJE Jordan Eberle	40.00	80.00
PAJJT John Tavares	60.00	120.00
PAJKA Karl Alzner	10.00	25.00
PAJMB Mikkel Boedker	10.00	25.00
PAJMD Matt Duchene	30.00	60.00
PAJNK Nazem Kadri	30.00	60.00
PAJSV Semyon Varlamov	40.00	80.00
PAJTH Taylor Hall	60.00	120.00
PAJTS Tyler Seguiin	60.00	120.00
PAJVH Victor Hedman	12.00	30.00
PAJZB Zach Boychuk	12.00	30.00
PAJRNH Ryan Nugent-Hopkins	20.00	50.00
PAJTHI Thomas Hickey	20.00	50.00

2009-10 ITG Superlative Prospects Jerseys Triples Gold
STATED PRINT RUN 1 SER.#'d SETS
NOT PRICED DUE TO SCARCITY

2009-10 ITG Superlative Prospects Jerseys Triples Silver
STATED PRINT RUN 9 SER.#'d SETS
NOT PRICED DUE TO SCARCITY

2009-10 ITG Superlative Prospect Patches Autographs
STATED PRINT RUN 9 SER.#'d SETS
NOT PRICED DUE TO SCARCITY

2009-10 ITG Superlative Prospect Plus Emblem Autographs
STATED PRINT RUN 9 SER.#'d SETS
NOT PRICED DUE TO SCARCITY

2009-10 ITG Superlative Prospect Plus Glove Autographs
STATED PRINT RUN 9 SER.#'d SETS
NOT PRICED DUE TO SCARCITY

2009-10 ITG Superlative Prospect Plus Number Autographs
STATED PRINT RUN 9 SER.#'d SETS
NOT PRICED DUE TO SCARCITY

2009-10 ITG Superlative Prospect Plus Pants Autographs
STATED PRINT RUN 9 SER.#'d SETS
NOT PRICED DUE TO SCARCITY

2009-10 ITG Superlative Prospect Plus Sock Autographs
STATED PRINT RUN 9 SER.#'d SETS
NOT PRICED DUE TO SCARCITY

2009-10 ITG Superlative Prospect Plus Stick Autographs
STATED PRINT RUN 9 SER.#'d SETS
NOT PRICED DUE TO SCARCITY

2009-10 ITG Superlative Quad Patches Gold
STATED PRINT RUN 1 SER.#'d SET
NOT PRICED DUE TO SCARCITY

2009-10 ITG Superlative Quad Patches Silver
STATED PRINT RUN 9 SER.#'d SETS
NOT PRICED DUE TO SCARCITY

2009-10 ITG Superlative Ring Leaders Gold
STATED PRINT RUN 1 SER.#'d SET
NOT PRICED DUE TO SCARCITY

2009-10 ITG Superlative Ring Leaders Silver
STATED PRINT RUN 9 SER.#'d SETS
NOT PRICED DUE TO SCARCITY

2009-10 ITG Superlative Seasons Gold
STATED PRINT RUN 1 SER.#'d SET
NOT PRICED DUE TO SCARCITY

2009-10 ITG Superlative Seasons Silver
STATED PRINT RUN 9 SER.#'d SETS
NOT PRICED DUE TO SCARCITY

2009-10 ITG Superlative Starting Lineup Gold
STATED PRINT RUN 1 SER.#'d SET
NOT PRICED DUE TO SCARCITY

2009-10 ITG Superlative Starting Lineup Silver
STATED PRINT RUN 9 SER.#'d SETS
NOT PRICED DUE TO SCARCITY

2009-10 ITG Superlative Stick Rack 2
STATED PRINT RUN 1 SER.#'d SET
NOT PRICED DUE TO SCARCITY

2003-04 ITG Toronto Fall Expo Forever Rivals
This 10-card set was a bonus available in "Super Boxes" available from In the Game, Inc. during the 2003 Toronto Fall Expo. Cards were limited to 100 copies each.

FR1 Mats Sundin Saku Koivu	6.00	15.00
FR2 Doug Gilmour Patrick Roy	8.00	20.00
FR3 Wendel Clark Chris Chelios	6.00	15.00
FR4 Rick Vaive Guy Lafleur	8.00	20.00
FR5 Lanny McDonald Larry Robinson	6.00	15.00
FR6 Darryl Sittler Yvan Cournoyer	6.00	15.00
FR7 Johnny Bower Jacques Plante	8.00	20.00
FR8 Tim Horton Doug Harvey	6.00	15.00
FR9 Ted Kennedy Maurice Richard	6.00	15.00
FR10 George Hainsworth Howie Morenz	6.00	15.00

2003-04 ITG Toronto Fall Expo Jerseys
This 30-card set was a bonus inside "Super Boxes" available from In the Game, Inc. during the 2003 Toronto Fall Expo. Cards FE1-FE20 were limited to 40 copies while cards FE21-FE30 were limited to 20 copies and are unpriced due to scarcity.

COMMON JERSEY	10.00	25.00
FE1 Pavel Datsyuk	12.50	30.00
FE2 Vincent Lecavalier	12.50	30.00
FE3 Jay Bouwmeester	10.00	25.00
FE4 Saku Koivu	12.50	30.00
FE5 Roberto Luongo	12.50	30.00
FE6 Rick Nash	12.50	30.00
FE7 Owen Nolan	10.00	25.00
FE8 Brendan Shanahan	12.50	30.00
FE9 Jason Spezza	10.00	25.00
FE10 Mats Sundin	12.50	30.00
FE11 Marty Turco	10.00	25.00
FE12 Henrik Zetterberg	12.50	30.00
FE13 Nicklas Lidstrom	12.50	30.00
FE14 Pavel Bure	12.50	30.00
FE15 Jose Theodore	12.50	30.00
FE16 Joe Thornton	15.00	40.00
FE17 Jaromir Jagr	15.00	40.00
FE18 Ilya Kovalchuk	15.00	40.00
FE19 Mike Modano	15.00	40.00
FE20 Brett Hull	15.00	40.00
FE21 Ed Belfour		
FE22 Jean-Sebastien Giguere		
FE23 Dany Heatley		
FE24 Mario Lemieux		
FE25 Patrick Roy		
FE26 Joe Sakic		
FE27 Peter Forsberg		
FE28 Marian Gaborik		
FE29 Martin Brodeur		
FE30 Steve Yzerman		

2003-04 ITG Toronto Spring Expo Class of 2004

Inserted one in each "Super Box" available at the Toronto Spring Expo, this 10 -card set featured promising prospects. Each card was limited to 100 copies each.

1 Eric Staal Tuomo Ruutu	6.00	15.00
2 Marc-Andre Fleury Matt Lombardi	8.00	20.00
3 Ryan Malone Joffrey Lupul	6.00	15.00
4 Matt Stajan Dustin Brown	6.00	15.00
5 Patrice Bergeron Jiri Hudler	6.00	15.00
6 Fedor Tyutin Anton Babchuk	6.00	15.00
7 Derek Roy Nikolai Zherdev	8.00	20.00
8 Nathan Horton Jordin Tootoo	6.00	15.00
9 Joni Pitkanen Dan Hamhuis	6.00	15.00
10 Kari Lehtonen Adam Munro	10.00	25.00

2005-06 ITG Toronto Fall Expo Jerseys
FE05 Steve Yzerman/20

2005 ITG Tough Customers

COMPLETE SET (25)	6.00	15.00
BG Bill Goldthorpe	.40	1.00
BM Basil McRae	.20	.50
BP Bob Probert	.40	1.00
CN Cam Neely	.75	2.00
DB Donald Brashear	.20	.50
DH Dale Hunter	.20	.50
DM Dan Maloney	.20	.50
DS Dave Schultz	.40	1.00
ES Eddie Shack	.40	1.00
FB Frank Bialowas	.40	1.00
GO Gino Odjick	.20	.50
JF John Ferguson	.20	.50
JK Joey Kocur	.20	.50
JM Jimmy Mann	.20	.50
KC Kelly Chase	.20	.50
LF Lou Fontinato	.20	.50
LG Link Gaetz	.20	.50
SG Stu Grimson	.20	.50
SJ Stan Jonathan	.40	1.00
TL Ted Lindsay	.40	1.00
TO Terry O'Reilly	.40	1.00
TW Tiger Williams	.40	1.00
WC Wendel Clark	.40	1.00
CNI Chris Nilan	.20	.50
DSE Dave Semenko	.20	.50

2005 ITG Tough Customers Autographs

BG Bill Goldthorpe	4.00	10.00
BM Basil McRae	4.00	10.00
BP Bob Probert	10.00	25.00
CN Chris Nilan	4.00	10.00
DB Donald Brashear	4.00	10.00
DH Dale Hunter	4.00	10.00
DM Dan Maloney	4.00	10.00
DS Dave Schultz	8.00	20.00
ES Eddie Shack	8.00	20.00
FB Frank Bialowas	8.00	20.00
GO Gino Odjick	4.00	10.00
JK Joey Kocur	4.00	10.00
JM Jimmy Mann	4.00	10.00
KC Kelly Chase	6.00	15.00
LF Lou Fontinato	6.00	15.00
LG Link Gaetz	4.00	10.00
SG Stu Grimson	4.00	10.00
SJ Stan Jonathan	8.00	20.00
TL Ted Lindsay	6.00	15.00
TO Terry O'Reilly	10.00	25.00
TW Tiger Williams	8.00	20.00
WC Wendel Clark	10.00	25.00

2005 ITG Tough Customers Complete Jerseys
NOT PRICED DUE TO SCARCITY
BG Bill Goldthorpe
BP Bob Probert
DB Donald Brashear
FB Frank Bialowas
KC Kelly Chase
SG Stu Grimson
TO Terry O'reilly
WC Wendel Clark

2005 ITG Tough Customers Double Memorabilia

BP Bob Probert	10.00	25.00
CN Cam Neely	12.00	30.00
DB Donald Brashear	8.00	20.00
SG Stu Grimson	8.00	20.00
TO Terry O'Reilly	12.00	30.00
WC Wendel Clark	12.00	30.00

2005 ITG Tough Customers Emblem and Numbers
NOT PRICED DUE TO SCARCITY
BG Bill Goldthorpe
BP Bob Probert
DB Donald Brashear
DM Dan Maloney
FB Frank Bialowas
GO Gino Odjick
KC Kelly Chase
SG Stu Grimson

2005 ITG Tough Customers Famous Battles Autographs

BB Donald Brashear Frank Bialowas	12.00	30.00
GP Stu Grimson Bob Probert	15.00	40.00
HN Dale Hunter Chris Nilan	12.00	30.00
PC Bob Probert Wendel Clark	20.00	50.00
SO Dave Schultz Terry O'Reilly	15.00	40.00
WS Tiger Williams Dave Schultz	12.00	30.00

2005 ITG Tough Customers Jerseys

BG Bill Goldthorpe	3.00	8.00
BP Bob Probert	6.00	15.00
DB Donald Brashear	3.00	8.00
DM Dan Maloney	3.00	8.00
DS Dave Schultz	5.00	12.00
FB Frank Bialowas	4.00	10.00
GO Gino Odjick	3.00	8.00
JF John Ferguson	5.00	12.00
KC Kelly Chase	3.00	8.00
SG Stu Grimson	3.00	8.00
SJ Stan Jonathan	4.00	10.00
TO Terry O'Reilly	5.00	12.00
TW Tiger Williams	5.00	12.00
WC Wendel Clark	5.00	12.00

2005 ITG Tough Customers Signed Memorabilia

BG Bill Goldthorpe	10.00	25.00
BP Bob Probert	15.00	40.00
CN Cam Neely	15.00	40.00
DB Donald Brashear	10.00	25.00
DM Dan Maloney	10.00	25.00
DS Dave Schultz	12.00	30.00
FB Frank Bialowas	10.00	25.00
GO Gino Odjick	10.00	25.00
KC Kelly Chase	10.00	25.00
SG Stu Grimson	10.00	25.00
TW Tiger Williams	12.00	30.00
WC Wendel Clark	15.00	40.00

2005 ITG Tough Customers Stickwork

BP Bob Probert	10.00	25.00
CN Cam Neely	10.00	25.00
DH Dale Hunter	6.00	15.00
DS Dave Semenko	6.00	15.00
SG Stu Grimson	6.00	15.00
SJ Stan Jonathan	8.00	20.00
CNI Chris Nilan	6.00	15.00

2004-05 ITG Ultimate Memorabilia
ITG's fifth installment of Ultimate Memorabilia contained one autograph card, one memorabilia card and one base card or "Archives" 1/1 card per pack. Base cards were limited to 45 copies each. Every card was encased in a Beckett slab.

PRINT RUN 45 SER.#'d SETS
UNPRICED GOLD 1/1's EXIST

1 Bun Cook	6.00	15.00
2 Doug Harvey	6.00	15.00
3 Butch Bouchard	6.00	15.00
4 Bill Barilko	20.00	50.00
5 Jean Ratelle	10.00	25.00
6 Phil Esposito	12.00	30.00
7 Ted Lindsay	10.00	25.00
8 Gordie Drillon	6.00	15.00
9 Johnny Bucyk	6.00	15.00
10 Bobby Hull	12.00	30.00
11 Ted Lindsay	10.00	25.00
12 Bill Gadsby	6.00	15.00
13 Busher Jackson	6.00	15.00
14 Aurel Joliat	12.00	30.00
15 John Davidson	12.00	30.00
16 Billy Smith	10.00	25.00
17 Bill Cook	10.00	25.00
18 Bill Cowley	10.00	25.00
19 Babe Pratt	10.00	25.00
20 Ed Giacomin	10.00	25.00
21 Neil Colville	6.00	15.00
22 Foster Hewitt	10.00	25.00
23 Georges Vezina	20.00	50.00
24 King Clancy	10.00	25.00
25 Red Dutton	6.00	15.00
26 Cyclone Taylor	30.00	80.00
27 Dale Hawerchuk	6.00	15.00
28 Norm Ullman	10.00	25.00
29 Harry Howell	12.00	30.00
30 Stan Mikita	12.00	30.00
31 Borje Salming	10.00	25.00
32 Ching Johnson	12.00	30.00
33 Harry Lumley	12.00	30.00
34 Bernie Geoffrion	12.00	30.00
35 Ted Kennedy	12.00	30.00
36 Howie Morenz	12.00	30.00
37 Ace Bailey	12.00	30.00
38 Bill Ranford	6.00	15.00
39 Charlie Gardiner	10.00	25.00
40 Rod Gilbert	10.00	25.00
41 Syl Apps	10.00	25.00
42 Ed Giacomin	10.00	25.00
43 Norm Ullman	10.00	25.00
44 Guy Lafleur	12.00	30.00
45 Andy Bathgate	10.00	25.00
46 Max Bentley	10.00	25.00
47 Steve Shutt	10.00	25.00
48 Bobby Hull	12.00	30.00
49 Denis Potvin	10.00	25.00
50 Dit Clapper	10.00	25.00
51 Phil Esposito	12.00	30.00
52 Hap Day	10.00	25.00
53 Henri Richard	12.00	30.00
54 Bernie Geoffrion	12.00	30.00
55 Marcel Pronovost	10.00	25.00
56 Bill Gadsby	6.00	15.00
57 Jean-Guy Talbot	6.00	15.00
58 Pelle Lindbergh	12.00	30.00
59 Marcel Dionne	10.00	25.00
60 Allan Stanley	10.00	25.00
61 Frank Brimsek	12.00	30.00
62 Alex Delvecchio	12.00	30.00
63 Chuck Rayner	10.00	25.00
64 Frank Brimsek	12.00	30.00
65 Ebbie Goodfellow	10.00	25.00
66 Newsy Lalonde	12.00	30.00
67 Jean Ratelle	10.00	25.00
68 Bryan Hextall	6.00	15.00
69 Bobby Bauer	6.00	15.00
70 Red Horner	12.00	30.00
71 Lord Stanley	6.00	15.00
72 Phil Esposito	12.00	30.00
73 Jacques Laperriere	10.00	25.00
74 Ken Wharram	6.00	15.00
75 Dickie Moore	10.00	25.00
76 Harry Lumley	12.00	30.00
77 Charlie Conacher	10.00	25.00
78 Elmer Lach	10.00	25.00
79 Terry Sawchuk	12.00	30.00
80 George Hainsworth	12.00	30.00
81 Red Kelly	12.00	30.00
82 Joe Primeau	12.00	30.00
83 Eddie Shore	12.00	30.00
84 Pierre Pilote	10.00	25.00
85 Lester Patrick	10.00	25.00
86 Ken Reardon	10.00	25.00
87 Bobby Baun	10.00	25.00
88 Jack Stewart	10.00	25.00
89 Doug Gilmour	12.00	30.00
90 Frank Boucher	6.00	15.00
91 Red Kelly	12.00	30.00
92 Joe Mullen	6.00	15.00
93 John Ferguson	12.00	30.00
94 Allan Stanley	10.00	25.00
95 Bill Mosienko	10.00	25.00
96 Milt Schmidt	12.00	30.00
97 Sweeney Schriner	10.00	25.00
98 Marcel Dionne	10.00	25.00
99 Bill Durnan	12.00	30.00
100 Babe Siebert	10.00	25.00
101 Brad Park	10.00	25.00
102 Cam Neely	12.00	30.00
103 Derek Sanderson	12.00	30.00
104 Gerry Cheevers	12.00	30.00
105 Milt Schmidt	12.00	30.00
106 Ray Bourque	12.00	30.00
107 Terry O'Reilly	10.00	25.00
108 Tiny Thompson	12.00	30.00
109 Wayne Cashman	10.00	25.00
110 Woody Dumart	10.00	25.00
111 Terry Sawchuk	12.00	30.00
112 Gilbert Perreault	12.00	30.00
113 Grant Fuhr	12.00	30.00
114 Pat LaFontaine	6.00	15.00
115 Rick Martin	6.00	15.00
116 Roger Crozier	12.00	30.00
117 Lanny McDonald	12.00	30.00
118 Denis Savard	12.00	30.00
119 Doug Bentley	10.00	25.00
120 Glenn Hall	12.00	30.00
121 Roy Conacher	10.00	25.00
122 Tony Esposito	12.00	30.00
123 Howie Morenz	12.00	30.00
124 Patrick Roy	30.00	80.00
125 Ray Bourque	12.00	30.00
126 Brad Park	10.00	25.00
127 Darryl Sittler	12.00	30.00
128 Dino Ciccarelli	6.00	15.00
129 Glenn Hall	12.00	30.00
130 Paul Coffey	10.00	25.00
131 Roger Crozier	12.00	30.00
132 Tiny Thompson	12.00	30.00
133 Sid Abel	10.00	25.00
134 Steve Yzerman	20.00	50.00
135 Syd Howe	10.00	25.00
136 Frank Mahovlich	12.00	30.00
137 Vladimir Konstantinov	10.00	25.00
138 Sid Abel	10.00	25.00
139 Grant Fuhr	12.00	30.00
140 Jari Kurri	10.00	25.00
141 Paul Coffey	10.00	25.00
142 Jari Kurri	10.00	25.00
143 Larry Robinson	10.00	25.00
144 Rogie Vachon	10.00	25.00
145 Dino Ciccarelli	6.00	15.00
146 Gump Worsley	12.00	30.00
147 Denis Savard	12.00	30.00
148 Frank Mahovlich	12.00	30.00
149 Gump Worsley	12.00	30.00
150 Guy Lapointe	6.00	15.00
151 Jacques Lemaire	10.00	25.00
152 Jacques Plante	12.00	30.00
153 Jean Beliveau	20.00	50.00
154 Larry Robinson	10.00	25.00
155 Maurice Richard	25.00	60.00
156 Patrick Roy	30.00	80.00
157 Rogie Vachon	10.00	25.00
158 Serge Savard	10.00	25.00
159 Toe Blake	10.00	25.00
160 Toe Blake	10.00	25.00
161 Lionel Conacher	10.00	25.00
162 Art Ross	10.00	25.00
163 Lady Byng	10.00	25.00
164 Roy Worters	10.00	25.00
165 Al Arbour	6.00	15.00
166 Bryan Trottier	10.00	25.00
167 Clark Gillies	10.00	25.00
168 Mike Bossy	12.00	30.00
169 Brad Park	10.00	25.00
170 Gump Worsley	12.00	30.00
171 Guy Lafleur	12.00	30.00
172 Vic Hadfield	10.00	25.00
173 Jacques Plante	12.00	30.00
174 Bernie Parent	12.00	30.00
175 Bill Barber	6.00	15.00
176 Bobby Clarke	12.00	30.00
177 Fred Shero	6.00	15.00
178 Bryan Trottier	10.00	25.00
179 Larry Murphy	6.00	15.00
180 Mario Lemieux	30.00	80.00
181 Paul Coffey	10.00	25.00
182 Hobey Baker	6.00	15.00
183 Guy Lafleur	12.00	30.00
184 Michel Goulet	6.00	15.00
185 Glenn Hall	12.00	30.00
186 Jack Adams	10.00	25.00
187 Al Arbour	6.00	15.00
188 Andy Bathgate	10.00	25.00
189 Darryl Sittler	12.00	30.00
190 Frank Mahovlich	12.00	30.00
191 Jacques Plante	12.00	30.00
192 Johnny Bower	10.00	25.00
193 Lanny McDonald	12.00	30.00
194 Terry Sawchuk	12.00	30.00
195 Tim Horton	12.00	30.00
196 Turk Broda	6.00	15.00
197 Wendel Clark	12.00	30.00
198 Valeri Kharlamov	12.00	30.00
199 Cam Neely	12.00	30.00
200 Roger Neilson	6.00	15.00

2004-05 ITG Ultimate Memorabilia Gold
PRINT RUN 1 SER.#'d SET
NOT PRICED DUE TO SCARCITY

2004-05 ITG Ultimate Memorabilia Archives 1st Edition
The Archives sets were all 1/1 cards from past Ultimate releases that carried new backs and were slabbed in Beckett cases.

NOT PRICED DUE TO SCARCITY
1 Mike Richter/Emblem
2 Steve Yzerman
Emblem
3 Patrick Roy/Emblem
4 Mike Richter/In The Numbers
5 Steve Yzerman
In The Numbers
6 Patrick Roy/In The Numbers
7 Patrick Roy/Journey Jersey
8 Steve Yzerman
Gold Autograph
9 Patrick Roy/Gold Autograph
10 Patrick Roy/Jacques Plante Memorabilia
11 Mike Richter/Jacques Plante Memorabilia
12 Ray Bourque/NHL Records
13 Jacques Plante/NHL Records
14 Tony Esposito/NHL Records
15 Steve Yzerman/Mike Vernon
Teammates
16 Mike Richter/Jersey
17 Steve Yzerman
Jersey
18 Vernon/Roy/Vanbiesbrouck/Active 8
19 Patrick Roy/Jersey
20 Plante/Roy/RetroActive Trophy
21 Parent/Yzerman
RetroActive Trophy
22 Esposito/Lemieux
RetroActive Trophy
23 Paul Coffey-Det/Dynasty Emblem
24 Bill Ranford/Dynasty Emblem
25 Paul Coffey-Edm/Dynasty Emblem
26 Grant Fuhr/Dynasty Emblem
27 Mario Lemieux 1988
Hart Trophy Jersey
28 Mario Lemieux 1993
Hart Trophy Jersey
29 Ray Bourque/Norris Trophy Jersey
30 Lemieux/Coffey
The Magnificent Ones
31 Lemieux/Bourque
The Magnificent Ones
32 Lemieux/Roy
The Magnificent Ones
33 Richter/Vanbiesbrouck/Goalie Collection
34 T. Esposito/Cheevers/Goalie Collection
35 Roy/Plante/Goalie Collection
36 Steve Yzerman
Dynasty Game Jersey
37 Mike Vernon/Dynasty Game Jersey

2004-05 ITG Ultimate Memorabilia Archives 2nd Edition
ALL CARDS 1/1's
NOT PRICED DUE TO SCARCITY
1 Guy Lafleur/Gloves Are Off
2 Ace Bailey/Gloves Are Off
3 Rocket Richard/Gloves Are Off
4 Doug Harvey/Gloves Are Off
5 Ted Kennedy/Gloves Are Off
6 King Clancy/Gloves Are Off
7 Mario Lemieux/Gloves Are Off
8 Patrick Roy/In The Numbers
9 Steve Yzerman/In The Numbers
10 Mario Lemieux/Emblem
11 Steve Yzerman/Emblem
12 Patrick Roy/Emblem
13 Jacques Plante/Patrick Roy/Prototypical Players
14 Jean Beliveau/Mario Lemieux/Prototypical Players
15 Jean Beliveau/Steve Yzerman/Prototypical Players
16 Terry Sawchuk/Patrick Roy/Be A Player Legend
17 Terry Sawchuk/Mike Richter/Be A Player Legend
18 Mario Lemieux/Waving The Flag
19 Steve Yzerman/Waving The Flag
20 Turk Broda/All-Star History
21 Frank Brimsek/All-Star History
22 Ted Kennedy/All-Star History
23 Rocket Richard/All-Star History
24 Chuck Rayner/All-Star History
25 Bill Mosienko/All-Star History
26 Jean Beliveau/All-Star History
27 Doug Harvey/All-Star History
28 Ted Lindsay/All-Star History
29 Henri Richard/All-Star History
30 Jacques Plante/All-Star History
31 Glenn Hall/All-Star History
32 Terry Sawchuk/All-Star History
33 Bobby Hull/All-Star History
34 Johnny Bower/All-Star History
35 Johnny Bucyk/All-Star History
36 Tim Horton/All-Star History
37 Stan Mikita/All-Star History
38 Bill Gadsby/All-Star History
39 Ed Giacomin/All-Star History
40 Bernie Parent/All-Star History
41 Bobby Clarke/All-Star History
42 Gilbert Perreault/All-Star History
43 Frank Mahovlich/All-Star History
44 Tony Esposito/All-Star History
45 Guy Lafleur/All-Star History
46 Bryan Trottier/All-Star History
47 Lanny McDonald/All-Star History
48 Mike Bossy/All-Star History
49 Steve Yzerman/All-Star History
50 Mario Lemieux/All-Star History
51 Patrick Roy/All-Star History
52 Bobby Hull/500 Goal Scorers S&J
53 Henri Richard/Rocket Richard/Bloodlines
54 Tony Esposito/Phil Esposito/Bloodlines
55 Glenn Hall/Calder Trophy
56 Tony Esposito/Calder Trophy
57 Mario Lemieux/Calder Trophy
58 Dale Hawerchuk/Calder Trophy
59 Mike Bossy/Calder Trophy
60 Bryan Trottier/Calder Trophy
61 Denis Potvin/Calder Trophy
62 Gilbert Perreault/Calder Trophy
63 Terry Sawchuk/Calder Trophy
64 Ted Lindsay/Production Line
65 Sid Abel/Production Line
66 Bobby Clarke/Players of the Decade
67 Frank Brimsek/Players of the Decade
68 Chuck Rayner/Players of the Decade
69 Serge Savard/Players of the Decade
70 Jacques Plante/Players of the Decade
71 Steve Yzerman/Stick and Jersey
72 Patrick Roy/Stick and Jersey
73 Steve Yzerman/Nameplates
74 Patrick Roy/Nameplates
75 Phil Esposito/Nameplates
76 Steve Yzerman/Autograph Gold

77 Joe Watson/Dynasty Jersey
78 Bill Barber/Dynasty Jersey
79 Dave Schultz/Dynasty Jersey
80 Guy Lapointe/Dynasty Jersey
81 Serge Savard/Dynasty Jersey
82 Guy Lafleur/Dynasty Jersey
83 Steve Shutt/Dynasty Jersey
84 Larry Robinson/Dynasty Jersey
85 Billy Smith/Dynasty Jersey
86 Bob Nystrom/Dynasty Jersey
87 Mike Bossy/Dynasty Jersey
88 Dave Schultz/Dynasty In The Numbers
89 Bernie Parent/Dynasty In The Numbers
90 Bob Clarke/Dynasty In The Numbers
91 Reggie Leach/Dynasty In The Numbers
92 Joe Watson/Dynasty In The Numbers
93 Mike Bossy/Dynasty In The Numbers
94 Billy Smith/Dynasty In The Numbers
95 Bryan Trottier/Dynasty In The Numbers
96 Bob Nystrom/Dynasty In The Numbers
97 Yvan Cournoyer/Dynasty In The Numbers
98 Larry Robinson/Dynasty In The Numbers
99 Steve Shutt/Dynasty In The Numbers
100 Guy Lafleur/Dynasty In The Numbers
101 Serge Savard/Dynasty In The Numbers
102 Reggie Leach/Dynasty Emblem
103 Joe Watson/Dynasty Emblem
104 Bob Clarke/Dynasty Emblem
105 Bernie Parent/Dynasty Emblem
106 Dave Schultz/Dynasty Emblem
107 Yvan Cournoyer/Dynasty Emblem
108 Larry Robinson/Dynasty Emblem
109 Steve Shutt/Dynasty Emblem
110 Serge Savard/Dynasty Emblem
111 Mike Bossy/Dynasty Emblem
112 Billy Smith/Dynasty Emblem
113 Bryan Trottier/Dynasty Emblem
114 Bob Nystrom/Dynasty Emblem
115 Rocket Richard/500 Goal Scorers Autograph
116 Jean Beliveau/500 Goal Scorers Jersey
117 Bobby Hull/500 Goal Scorers Jersey
118 Guy Lafleur/500 Goal Scorers Jersey
119 Marcel Dionne/500 Goal Scorers Jersey
120 Phil Esposito/500 Goal Scorers Jersey
121 Lanny McDonald/500 Goal Scorers Jersey
122 Bryan Trottier/500 Goal Scorers Jersey
123 Stan Mikita/500 Goal Scorers Jersey
124 Gilbert Perreault/500 Goal Scorers Jersey
125 Mike Bossy/500 Goal Scorers Jersey
126 John Bucyk/500 Goal Scorers Jersey
127 Steve Yzerman/500 Goal Scorers Emblem
128 Bryan Trottier/500 Goal Scorers Emblem
129 Marcel Dionne/500 Goal Scorers Emblem
130 Mario Lemieux/500 Goal Scorers Emblem
131 Joe Mullen/500 Goal Scorers Emblem
132 Dino Ciccarelli/500 Goal Scorers Emblem
133 Jari Kurri/500 Goal Scorers Emblem
134 Joe Mullen/500 Goal Scorers S&J
135 Rocket Richard/500 Goal Scorers S&J
136 Dino Ciccarelli/500 Goal Scorers S&J
137 Stan Mikita/Players Of The Decade
138 Rocket Richard/Stanley Cup Playoff Records
139 Patrick Roy/Stanley Cup Playoff Records
140 Mario Lemieux/Stanley Cup Playoff Records
141 Mike Bossy/Stanley Cup Playoff Records
142 Reggie Leach/Stanley Cup Playoff Records
143 Jari Kurri/Stanley Cup Playoff Records
144 Peter Mahovlich/Les Canadiens
145 Guy lafleur/Les Canadiens
146 Guy Lapointe/Les Canadiens
147 Serge Savard/Les Canadiens
148 Frank Mahovlich/Les Canadiens
149 Patrick Roy
Les Canadiens
150 Jean Beliveau/Les Canadiens
151 Yvan Cournoyer/Les Canadiens
152 Steve Shutt/Les Canadiens
153 Rocket Richard/Les Canadiens
154 Larry Robinson/Les Canadiens
155 Henri Richard/Les Canadiens
156 Doug Harvey/Les Canadiens
157 Cournoyer/Beliveau/Lafleur/Retro Teammates
158 Bossy/Trottier/Potvin/Retro Teammates
159 M.Richard/Harvey/H.Richard/Retro Teammates
160 Hall/Mikita/Hull/Retro Teammates
161 Sawchuk/Horton/Bower/Retro Teammates
162 Mahovlich/Savard/Lapointe/Retro Teammates
163 Barber/Schultz/Clarke/Retro Teammates
164 Plante/Richard/Harvey/Retro Teammates
165 Mario Lemieux/Nameplates
166 Lafleur/Lemieux/Retro-Active Trophies
167 Hall/Roy/Retro-Active Trophies
168 Clarke/Yzerman/Retro-Active Trophies
169 Parent/Roy/Retro-Active Trophies
170 Clarke/Lemieux/Retro-Active Trophies
171 Roy/Beliveau/Richard/Lafleur/Cornerstones
172 Bill Gadsby/Players Of The Decade
173 Doug Harvey/Players Of The Decade
174 Terry Sawchuk/Players Of The Decade
175 Larry Robinson/Players Of The Decade
176 Ted Lindsay/Players Of The Decade
177 Patrick Roy/Players Of The Decade
178 Grant Fuhr/Players Of The Decade
179 Denis Potvin/Players Of The Decade
180 Guy Lafleur/Players Of The Decade
181 Mike Bossy/Players Of The Decade
182 Tony Esposito/Players Of The Decade
183 Can Neely/Players Of The Decade
184 Gerry Cheevers/Players Of The Decade
185 Jacques Plante/Complete Package
186 Guy Lafleur/Complete Package
187 Patrick Roy/Complete Package
188 Terry Sawchuk/Complete Package
189 Guy Lafleur/Retired Numbers
190 Rocket Richard/Retired Numbers
191 Gilbert Perreault/Retired Numbers
192 John Bucyk/Retired Numbers
193 Bobby Hull/Retired Numbers
194 Glenn Hall/Retired Numbers
195 Tony Esposito/Retired Numbers
196 Stan Mikita/Retired Numbers
197 Terry Sawchuk/Retired Numbers
198 Ted Lindsay/Retired Numbers
199 Jacques Plante/Retired Numbers
200 Marcel Dionne/Retired Numbers
201 Jean Beliveau/Retired Numbers
202 Doug Harvey/Retired Numbers
203 Henri Richard/Retired Numbers
204 Bill Barber/Retired Numbers
205 Mike Bossy/Retired Numbers
206 Denis Potvin/Retired Numbers
207 Billy Smith/Retired Numbers
208 Bernie Parent/Retired Numbers
209 Bobby Clarke/Retired Numbers
210 Sid Abel/Retired Numbers
211 Mario Lemieux/Ultimate Captains
212 Jean Beliveau/Ultimate Captains
213 Henri Richard/Ultimate Captains
214 Gilbert Perreault/Ultimate Captains
215 Johnny Bucyk/Ultimate Captains
216 Phil Esposito/Emblem Attic
217 Denis Potvin/Emblem Attic
218 Bryan Trottier/Emblem Attic
219 Stan Mikita/Emblem Attic
220 Bobby Hull/Emblem Attic
221 Henri Richard/Emblem Attic
222 Ted Lindsay/Emblem Attic
223 Jean Beliveau/Emblem Attic
224 Glenn Hall/Emblem Attic
225 Rocket Richard/Emblem Attic
226 Terry Sawchuk/Emblem Attic
227 Jacques Plante/Emblem Attic
228 Doug Harvey/Emblem Attic
229 Frank Mahovlich/Emblem Attic
230 Larry Robinson/Emblem Attic
231 Doug Harvey/Stanley Cup Winners
232 Denis Potvin/Stanley Cup Winners
233 Jean Beliveau/Stanley Cup Winners
234 Rocket Richard/Stanley Cup Winners
235 Terry Sawchuk/Stanley Cup Winners
236 Larry Robinson/Stanley Cup Winners
237 Jacques Laperriere/Stanley Cup Winners
238 Henri Richard/Stanley Cup Winners
239 Turk Broda/Stanley Cup Winners
240 Steve Shutt/Stanley Cup Winners
241 Yvan Cournoyer/Stanley Cup Winners
242 Ted Kennedy/Stanley Cup Winners
243 Grant Fuhr/Stanley Cup Winners

2004-05 ITG Ultimate Memorabilia Archives 3rd Edition

ALL CARDS 1/1's
NOT PRICED DUE TO SCARCITY
1 Henri Richard/Storied Franchise
2 Georges Vezina/Storied Franchise
3 Rocket Richard/Storied Franchise
4 Bill Durnan/Storied Franchise
5 Bernie Geoffrion/Storied Franchise
6 Charlie Hodge/Storied Franchise
7 Frank Mahovlich/Storied Franchise
8 Patrick Roy/Storied Franchise
9 Mario Lemieux/Ultimate Captains
10 Tim Horton/Complete Package
11 Mario Lemieux/Complete Package
12 Guy Lafleur/Complete Package
13 Jacques Plante/Complete Package
14 Terry Sawchuk/Complete Package
15 Patrick Roy/Complete Package
16 Rocket Richard/Complete Package
17 Roger Crozier/Gump Worsley/Stanley Cup Duels
18 Andy Moog/Bill Ranford/Stanley Cup Duels
19 Mario Lemieux/Blades of Steel
20 Georges Vezina/Blades of Steel
21 Jacques Plante/Blades of Steel
22 Tim Horton/Blades of Steel
23 Rocket Richard/Blades of Steel
24 Aurel Joliat/Blades of Steel
25 Bill Barilko/Blades of Steel
26 Nels Stewart/Blades of Steel
27 Jean Beliveau/Blades of Steel
28 Patrick Roy/Jersey
29 Mario Lemieux/Hat Tricks
30 Mario Lemieux/Nameplates
31 Patrick Roy/Lifetime Achievers
32 Mario Lemieux/Lifetime Achievers
33 Steve Yzerman/Lifetime Achievers
34 Aurel Joliat/Vintage Hat Tricks
35 Eddie Shore/Vintage Hat Tricks
36 Patrick Roy/Journey Emblem
37 Mario Lemieux/Magnificent Inserts (Complete Package)
38 Mario Lemieux/Magnificent Inserts (Quad Jersey)
40 Patrick Roy/Silver Autograph
41 Steve Yzerman/In The Numbers
42 Patrick Roy/In The Numbers
43 Mario Lemieux/In The Numbers
44 Steve Yzerman/Emblem
45 Patrick Roy/Emblem
46 Mario Lemieux/Emblem
47 Mario Lemieux/Stick and Jersey
48 Steve Yzerman/Stick and Jersey
49 Reggie Leach/All-Star MVP
50 Mike Richter/All-Star MVP
51 M. Richard/H.Richard/Be Player Legend
52 M. Richard/Harvey/Be Player Legend
53 M.Richard/Jean Beliveau/Be Player Legend
54 M.Richard/Jacques Plante/Be Player Legend
55 Mario Lemieux/Seams Unbelievable
56 Bill Mosienko/Seams Unbelievable
57 Ted Lindsay/Seams Unbelievable
58 Glenn Hall/Seams Unbelievable
59 George Hainsworth/Seams Unbelievable
60 Guy Lafleur/Seams Unbelievable
61 Gerry Cheevers/Seams Unbelievable
62 Jean Beliveau/Conn Smythe Trophy Winner
63 Roger Crozier/Conn Smythe Trophy Winner
64 Glenn Hall/Conn Smythe Trophy Winner
65 Serge Savard/Conn Smythe Trophy Winner
66 Yvan Cournoyer/Conn Smythe Trophy Winner
67 Bernie Parent/Conn Smythe Trophy Winner
68 Guy Lafleur/Conn Smythe Trophy Winner
69 Larry Robinson/Conn Smythe Trophy Winner
70 Bryan Trottier/Conn Smythe Trophy Winner
71 Mike Bossy/Conn Smythe Trophy Winner
72 Billy Smith/Conn Smythe Trophy Winner
73 Patrick Roy/Conn Smythe Trophy Winner
74 Ron Hextall/Conn Smythe Trophy Winner
75 Bill Ranford/Conn Smythe Trophy Winner
76 Mario Lemieux/Conn Smythe Trophy Winner
77 Patrick Roy/Conn Smythe Trophy Winner
78 Mike Vernon/Conn Smythe Trophy Winner
79 Steve Yzerman/Conn Smythe Trophy Winner
80 Patrick Roy/Conn Smythe Trophy Winner
81 Patrick Roy/Terry Sawchuk/Retro-Active Trophies
82 Mario Lemieux/Phil Esposito/Retro-Active Trophies
83 Steve Yzerman/Jean Beliveau/Retro-Active Trophies
84 Mario Lemieux/Lanny McDonald/Retro-Active Trophies
85 Aurel Joliat/Emblem Attic
86 Harry Lumley/Emblem Attic
87 Ted Lindsay/Emblem Attic
88 Tony Esposito/Emblem Attic
89 George Hainsworth/Emblem Attic
90 Roy Worters/Emblem Attic
91 Jean Beliveau/Emblem Attic
92 Red Kelly/Emblem Attic
93 Frank Brimsek/Emblem Attic
94 Roger Crozier/Emblem Attic
95 Glenn Hall/Emblem Attic
96 Terry Sawchuk/Emblem Attic
97 Jacques Plante/Emblem Attic
98 Frank Mahovlich/Emblem Attic
99 Doug Harvey/Emblem Attic
100 Henri Richard/Emblem Attic
101 Phil Esposito/Emblem Attic
102 Ed Giacomin/Emblem Attic
103 Stan Mikita/Emblem Attic
104 Bobby Hull/Emblem Attic
105 Guy Lafleur/Emblem Attic
106 Marcel Dionne/Emblem Attic
107 Gerry Cheevers/Emblem Attic
108 John Bucyk/Emblem Attic
109 Bobby Clarke/Emblem Attic
110 Glenn Hall/Number Ones
110 Mike Bossy/Emblem Attic
111 Jacques Plante/Number Ones
112 Roger Crozier/Number Ones
113 Ed Giacomin/Number Ones
114 Steve Yzerman/Jersey
115 Valeri Kharlamov/Jersey
116 Guy Lafleur/Vintage Hat Tricks
117 Marcel Dionne/NHL Scoring Leaders
118 Rocket Richard/Vintage Hat Tricks
119 Tim Horton/Vintage Hat Tricks
120 Jean Beliveau/Vintage Hat Tricks
121 Mario Lemieux/Howie Morenz/Retro-Active Trophies
122 Mario Lemieux/Playoff Scorers
123 Steve Yzerman/Playoff Scorers(67 goals)
124 Steve Yzerman/Playoff Scorers(97-98)
125 Bobby Hull/Playoff Scorers
126 Bryan Trottier/Playoff Scorers
127 Phil Esposito/Playoff Scorers
128 Jean Beliveau/Playoff Scorers
129 Rocket Richard/Playoff Scorers
130 Mario Lemieux/Playoff Scorers
131 Mike Bossy/Playoff Scorers
132 Larry Robinson/Numerology
133 Gilbert/Cheevers/Bucyk/Retro Teammates
134 Sittler/McDonald/Williams/Retro Teammates
135 Hull/Mikita/Hall/Retro Teammates
136 Delvecchio/Sawchuk/Abel/Retro Teammates
137 M.Richard/Plante/Beliveau/Retro Teammates
138 Schultz/Clarke/Parent/Retro Teammates
139 Gilbert/Giacomin/Esposito/Retro Teammates
140 Lafleur/Cournoyer/Savard/Retro Teammates
141 Horton/Bower/Kelly/Retro Teammates
142 Mario Lemieux/NHL Scoring Leaders
143 Mario Lemieux/NHL Scoring Leaders
144 Mario Lemieux/NHL Scoring Leaders
145 Phil Esposito/NHL Scoring Leaders
146 Tony Esposito/Vintage Jersey
147 Ed Giacomin/Vintage Jersey
148 George Hainsworth/Vintage Jersey
149 Glenn Hall
Vintage Jersey
150 Doug Harvey/Vintage Jersey
151 Tim Horton/Vintage Jersey
152 Bobby Hull/Vintage Jersey
153 Henri Richard/Vintage Jersey
154 Aurel Joliat/Vintage Jersey
155 Jacques Plante/Vintage Jersey
156 Red Kelly/Vintage Jersey
157 Dennis Hull/Vintage Jersey
158 Rocket Richard/Vintage Jersey
159 Larry Robinson/Vintage Jersey
160 Aurel Joliat/Storied Franchise
161 Terry Sawchuk/Vintage Jersey
162 Vladislav Tretiak/Vintage Jersey
163 Bryan Trottier/Vintage Jersey
164 Roy Worters/Vintage Jersey
165 Terry Sawchuk/Number Ones
166 Howie Morenz/Storied Franchise
167 George Hainsworth/Storied Franchise
168 Doug Harvey/Storied Franchise
169 Henri Richard/Storied Franchise
170 Jean Beliveau/Storied Franchise
171 Jacques Plante/Storied Franchise
172 Lorne Worsley/Storied Franchise
173 Jacques Laperriere/Storied Franchise
174 Serge Savard/Storied Franchise
175 Rogie Vachon/Storied Franchise
176 Yvan Cournoyer/Storied Franchise
177 Steve Shutt/Storied Franchise
178 Larry Robinson/Storied Franchise
179 Guy Lafleur/Storied Franchise
180 Guy Lapointe/Storied Franchise
181 Rocket Richard/Be A Player Legend
182 Steve Yzerman/Dynasty Jersey
183 Steve Yzerman/Dynasty Numbers
184 Mike Vernon/Dynasty Numbers
185 Steve Yzerman/Dynasty Emblem
186 Mike Vernon/Dynasty Emblem
187 Rocket Richard/Be A Player Legend Autograph
188 Rocket Richard/Be A Player Legend Autograph
189 Rocket Richard/Be A Player Legend Autograph
190 Rocket Richard/Be A Player Legend Autograph
191 Rocket Richard/Be A Player Legend Autograph
192 Guy Lafleur/Vintage Jersey
193 Ted Lindsay/Vintage Jersey
194 Harry Lumley/Vintage Jersey
195 Frank Mahovlich/Vintage Jersey
196 Peter Mahovlich/Vintage Jersey
197 Lanny McDonald/Vintage Jersey
198 Stan Mikita/Vintage Jersey
199 Bernie Parent/Vintage Jersey
200 Gilbert Perreault/Vintage Jersey
201 Sid Abel/Vintage Jersey
202 Bill Barber/Vintage Jersey
203 Mike Bossy/Vintage Jersey
204 Frank Brimsek/Vintage Jersey
205 John Bucyk/Vintage Jersey
206 Gerry Cheevers/Vintage Jersey
207 Bobby Clarke/Vintage Jersey
208 Roger Crozier/Vintage Jersey
209 Alex Delvecchio/Vintage Jersey
210 Marcel Dionne/Vintage Jersey
211 Phil Esposito/Vintage Jersey
212 Mario Lemieux/NHL Scoring Leaders
213 Bryan Trottier/NHL Scoring Leaders
214 Mario Lemieux/NHL Scoring Leaders
215 Phil Esposito/NHL Scoring Leaders
216 Bobby Hull/NHL Scoring Leaders
217 Bernie Geoffrion/NHL Scoring Leaders
218 Jean Beliveau/NHL Scoring Leaders
219 Phil Esposito/NHL Scoring Leaders
220 Phil Esposito/NHL Scoring Leaders
221 Phil Esposito/NHL Scoring Leaders
222 Stan Mikita/NHL Scoring Leaders
223 Stan Mikita/NHL Scoring Leaders
224 Bobby Hull/NHL Scoring Leaders
225 Guy Lafleur/NHL Scoring Leaders
226 Stan Mikita/NHL Scoring Leaders
227 Guy Lafleur/NHL Scoring Leaders
228 Dickie Moore/NHL Scoring Leaders
229 Bernie Geoffrion/NHL Scoring Leaders
230 Dickie Moore/NHL Scoring Leaders
231 Stan Mikita/NHL Scoring Leaders
232 Bobby Hull/NHL Scoring Leaders
233 Guy Lafleur/NHL Scoring Leaders
234 Mario Lemieux/NHL Scoring Leaders
235 Lindsay/Delvecchio/Sawchuk/Yzerman/Cornerstones
236 Bernie Parent/Conn Smythe Trophy Winners
237 Reggie Leach/Conn Smythe Trophy Winners
238 Mario Lemieux/Conn Smythe Trophy Winners
239 Steve Yzerman/Hat Tricks
240 Frank Mahovlich/All-Star MVP
241 Jean Beliveau/Vintage Jersey
242 Henri Richard/All-Star MVP
243 Bobby Hull/All-Star MVP
244 Bobby Hull/All-Star MVP
245 Peter Mahovlich/All-Star MVP
246 Mike Bossy/All-Star MVP
247 Grant Fuhr/All-Star MVP
248 Mario Lemieux/All-Star MVP
249 Mario Lemieux/All-Star MVP
250 Mario Lemieux/All-Star MVP
251 Mario Lemieux/Autograph Silver
252 Mike Vernon/Dynasty Jersey
253 Valeri Kharlamov/Vintage Jersey
254 Delvecchio/Harvey/Final Showdown
255 Geoffrion/Lindsay/Final Showdown
256 H. Richard/Horton/Final Showdown
257 Mikita/Sawchuk/Final Showdown
258 M. Richard/F. Mahovlich/Final Showdown
259 Mario Lemieux/Global Dominators
260 F.Mahovlich/B.Hull/Final Showdown
261 Horton/Delvecchio/Final Showdown
262 Beliveau/Hall/Final Showdown
263 Beliveau/Crozier/Final Showdown
264 Bower/Ferguson/Final Showdown
265 Mahovlich/Hull/Final Showdown
266 Cheevers/Gilbert/Final Showdown
267 Cournoyer/D.Hull/Final Showdown
268 Clarke/Perreault/Final Showdown
269 Parent/Bucyk/Final Showdown
270 Steve Yzerman/Global Dominators
271 King Clancy/Gloves Are Off
272 Eddie Shore/Gloves Are Off
273 Ted Kennedy/Gloves Are Off
274 Mario Lemieux/Gloves Are Off
275 Ace Bailey/Gloves Are Off
276 Rocket Richard/Gloves Are Off
277 Guy Lafleur/Gloves Are Off
278 Dickie Moore/Gloves Are Off
279 Aurel Joliat/Gloves Are Off
280 Bill Gadsby/Gloves Are Off
281 Doug Harvey/Gloves Are Off
282 Patrick Roy/Stick and Jersey
283 Valeri Kharlamov/In The Numbers
284 Patrick Roy/Journey Jersey
285 Trottier/Fuhr/Final Showdown
286 Roy/McDonald/Final Showdown
287 Shutt/Schultz/Final Showdown
288 Lapointe/Cheevers/Final Showdown
289 Robinson/Cheevers/Final Showdown
290 Kurri/Hextall/Final Showdown
291 Mario Lemieux/Magnificent Insert(International)
292 Mario Lemieux/Magnificent Insert(All-Star)
293 Mario Lemieux/Magnificent Insert(85-86)
294 Mario Lemieux/Magnificent Insert (00/01)
295 Mario Lemieux/Magnificent Insert(85-86/00-01)

2004-05 ITG Ultimate Memorabilia Archives 4th Edition

ALL CARDS 1/1's
NOT PRICED DUE TO SCARCITY
1 Patrick Roy/Perennial Powerhouse Emblem
2 Ray Bourque/Perennial Powerhouse Emblem
3 Ray Bourque/Perennial Powerhouse Stick&Jersey
4 Patrick Roy/Perennial Powerhouse Stick&Jersey
5 Patrick Roy/Perennial Powerhouse Jersey
6 Ray Bourque/Perennial Powerhouse Jersey
7 Mario Lemieux/Always An All-Star
8 Ray Bourque/Always An All-Star
9 Patrick Roy/Always An All-Star
10 Steve Yzerman/Hattricks
11 Mario Lemieux/Hattricks
12 Patrick Roy/In The Numbers
13 Mario Lemieux/In The Numbers
14 Steve Yzerman/Emblem
15 Mario Lemieux/Emblem
16 Steve Yzerman/Jersey and Emblem
17 Patrick Roy/Jersey and Emblem
18 Mario Lemieux/Jersey and Emblem
19 Ray Bourque/Lifetime Achievers
20 Patrick Roy/Lifetime Achievers
21 Mario Lemieux/Lifetime Achievers
22 Steve Yzerman/Lifetime Achievers
23 Mario Lemieux/Jersey
24 Steve Yzerman/Jersey
25 Ray Bourque/Stick and Jersey
26 Gump Worsley/Stick and Jersey
27 Jean Beliveau/Stick and Jersey
28 Mario Lemieux/Stick and Jersey
29 Mike Bossy/Stick and Jersey
30 Bryan Trottier/Stick and Jersey
31 Patrick Roy/Stick and Jersey
32 Jacques Plante/Stick and Jersey
33 Gilbert Perreault/Stick and Jersey
34 Marcel Dionne/Stick and Jersey
35 Johnny Bower/Stick and Jersey
36 Steve Yzerman/Stick and Jersey
37 Aurel Joliat/Vintage Complete Jersey
38 George Hainsworth/Vintage Complete Jersey
39 Jean Beliveau/Vintage Complete Jersey
39 Mario Lemieux/Magnificent Inserts Numbers
40 Bill Mosienko/Vintage Complete Jersey
41 Ray Bourque/Vintage Complete Jersey
42 Ted Lindsay/Vintage Complete Jersey
43 Steve Yzerman/Complete Jersey
44 Patrick Roy/Complete Jersey
45 Mario Lemieux/Complete Jersey
46 Mario Lemieux/Steve Yzerman/Dynamic Duos
47 Steve Yzerman/Seams Unbelievable
48 Patrick Roy/Seams Unbelievable
49 Ray Bourque/Seams Unbelievable
50 Mario Lemieux/Seams Unbelievable
51 Ray Bourque/Emblem Attic
52 Roger Crozier/Emblem Attic
53 Roy Worters/Emblem Attic
54 Gump Worsley/Emblem Attic
55 Jean Beliveau/Emblem Attic
56 Terry Sawchuk/Emblem Attic
57 Sid Abel/Emblem Attic
58 Aurel Joliat/Emblem Attic
59 Tony Esposito/Emblem Attic
60 Bobby Hull/Emblem Attic
61 Marcel Dionne/Emblem Attic
62 Glenn Hall/Emblem Attic
63 Frank Mahovlich/Emblem Attic
64 Jacques Plante/Emblem Attic
65 Henri Richard/Emblem Attic
66 George Hainsworth/Emblem Attic
67 Mario Lemieux/Ultimate Forward (Number)
68 Mario Lemieux/Ultimate Forward (Jersey)
69 Mario Lemieux/Ultimate Forward (Triple)
70 Mario Lemieux/Ultimate Forward (Glove)
71 Mario Lemieux/Ultimate Forward(pants)
72 Mario Lemieux/Ultimate Forward (Jersey/Stick)
73 Patrick Roy/Ultimate Goaltender(Jersey/Stick)
74 Patrick Roy/Ultimate Goaltender(Triple)
75 Patrick Roy/Ultimate Goaltender(Number)
76 Patrick Roy/Ultimate Goaltender(pad)
77 Patrick Roy/Ultimate Goaltender(Col. Jersey)
78 Patrick Roy/Ultimate Goaltender(MTL Jersey)
79 Mario Lemieux/Ultimate Captains(vintage)
80 Mario Lemieux/Ultimate Captains(current)
81 Stan Mikita/Vintage Hattricks
82 Jean Beliveau/Vintage Lumber
83 Georges Vezina/Vintage Lumber
84 Henri Richard/Vintage Lumber
85 Bernie Geoffrion/Vintage Lumber
86 Howie Morenz/Vintage Lumber
87 Joe Primeau/Vintage Lumber
88 Doug Harvey/Vintage Lumber
89 Harry Lumley/Vintage Lumber
90 Rocket Richard/Vintage Lumber
91 Mario Lemieux/Magnificent Career(Grand Entrance)
92 Mario Lemieux/Magnificent Career(Hoard of Hardware)
93 Mario Lemieux/Magnificent Career(Scoring Machine)
94 Mario Lemieux/Magnificent Career(Canadian Hero)
95 Mario Lemieux/Magnificent Career(1,700th point)
96 Mario Lemieux/Magnificent Career(Twice is Nice)
97 Mario Lemieux/Magnificent Career(International Star)
98 Mario Lemieux/Magnificent Career(Farewell for Now)
99 Mario Lemieux/Magnificent Career(Quad)
100 Trottier/Yzerman/Ultimate Heroes
101 Plante/Roy/Ultimate Heroes
102 Lafleur/Lemieux/Ultimate Heroes
103 Cheevers/Richter/Ultimate Heroes
104 Hainsworth/Sawchuk/Ultimate Heroes
105 Bobby Clarke/Raised To The Rafters
106 Bernie Parent/Raised To The Rafters
107 Ted Lindsay/Raised To The Rafters
108 Sid Abel/Raised To The Rafters
109 Eddie Shore/Raised To The Rafters
110 Ray Bourque/Raised To The Rafters
111 Cam Neely/Raised To The Rafters
112 Doug Harvey/Raised To The Rafters
113 Jacques Plante/Raised To The Rafters
114 Stan Mikita/Raised To The Rafters
115 Bobby Hull/Raised To The Rafters
116 Mike Bossy/Raised To The Rafters
117 Rod Gilbert/Raised To The Rafters
118 Rocket Richard/Raised To The Rafters
119 Jean Beliveau/Raised To The Rafters
120 Bryan Trottier/Raised To The Rafters
121 Mike Bossy/Raised To The Rafters
122 Marcel Dionne/Raised To The Rafters
123 Johnny Bower/Raised To The Rafters
124 Bobby Clarke/Vintage Jersey
125 Red Kelly/Vintage Jersey
126 Gilbert Perreault/Vintage Jersey
127 Gump Worsley/Vintage Jersey
128 Terry O'Reilly/Vintage Jersey
129 Denis Potvin/Vintage Jersey
130 Stan Mikita/Vintage Jersey
131 Valeri Kharlamov/Vintage Jersey
132 Ed Giacomin/Vintage Jersey
133 Alex Delvecchio/Vintage Jersey
134 Doug Harvey/Vintage Jersey
135 Lanny McDonald/Vintage Jersey
136 Patrick Roy/Vintage Jersey
137 Bobby Hull/Vintage Jersey
138 Dennis Hull/Vintage Jersey
139 Marcel Dionne/Vintage Jersey
140 Bryan Trottier/Vintage Jersey
141 Mike Bossy/Vintage Jersey
142 Henri Richard/Vintage Jersey
143 Aurel Joliat/Vintage Jersey
144 John Bucyk/Vintage Jersey
145 Ray Bourque/Vintage Jersey
146 Larry Robinson/Vintage Jersey
147 Rocket Richard/Vintage Jersey
148 Roger Crozier
Vintage Jersey
149 Sid Abel/Vintage Jersey
150 Frank Brimsek/Vintage Jersey
151 George Hainsworth/Vintage Jersey
152 Frank Mahovlich/Vintage Jersey
153 Ted Lindsay/Vintage Jersey
154 Harry Lumley/Vintage Jersey
155 Roy Worters/Vintage Jersey
156 Bill Mosienko/Vintage Jersey
157 Jean Beliveau/Vintage Jersey
158 Jacques Plante/Vintage Jersey
159 Vladislav Tretiak/Vintage Jersey
160 Cam Neely/Vintage Jersey
161 Ray Bourque/Ultimate Career Year
162 Cam Neely/Ultimate Career Year
163 Steve Yzerman/Ultimate Career Year
164 Mario Lemieux/Ultimate Career Year
165 Hainsworth/Worters/Brimsek/Triple Thread
166 Lindsay/Clarke/H.Richard/Triple Thread
167 Harvey/Salming/Bourque/Triple Thread
168 Neely/McDonald/P.Esposito/Triple Thread
169 Roy/Bower/Crozier/Triple Thread
170 Lafleur/Mahovlich/Shutt/Ultimate Linemates
171 Primeau/Conacher/Jackson/Ultimate Linemates
172 Simmer/Dionne/Taylor/Ultimate Linemates
173 Trottier/Gillies/Bossy/Ultimate Linemates
174 M.Richard/Lach/Blake/Ultimate Linemates
175 Moore/Geoffrion/Beliveau/Ultimate Linemates
176 Mario Lemieux/Guy Lafleur/Retro-Active Trophies
177 Mario Lemieux/Jean Beliveau/Retro-Active Trophies
178 Mario Lemieux/M. Richard/Retro-Active Trophies
179 Bower/Mahovlich/Kelly/Horton/Cornerstones
180 Richard/Robinson/Lafleur/Savard/Cornerstones
181 Plante/Richard/Harvey/Beliveau/Cornerstones
182 Brimsek/Lumley/Esposito/Hall/Cornerstones
183 Lindsay/Sawchuk/Delvecchio/Yzerman/Cornerstones
184 Bossy/Trottier/Potvin/Smith/Cornerstones
185 Patrick Roy/Journey Jersey
186 Ray Bourque/Journey Jersey
187 Patrick Roy/Journey Emblem
188 Ray Bourque/Journey Emblem
189 Mario Lemieux/Blades of Steel
190 Ray Bourque/Blades of Steel
191 Steve Yzerman/Great Moments in Hockey
192 Cam Neely/Great Moments in Hockey
193 Patrick Roy/Great Moments in Hockey
194 Mikita/Hull/Great Moments in Hockey
195 Clarke/Barber/Great Moments in Hockey
196 Mike Bossy/Great Moments in Hockey
197 Ray Bourque/Great Moments in Hockey
198 Henri Richard/Great Moments in Hockey
199 Mario Lemieux/Jersey and Number
200 Patrick Roy/Jersey and Number
201 Ray Bourque/Jersey and Number
202 Steve Yzerman/Jersey and Number
203 Steve Yzerman/Nameplates
204 Mario Lemieux/Nameplates
205 Patrick Roy/Nameplates
206 Ray Bourque/Nameplates
207 Cam Neely/Nameplates
208 Sawchuk/Lindsay/Abel/Retro Teammates
209 Sittler/Salming/McDonald/Retro Teammates
210 Clarke/Barber/Parent/Retro Teammates
211 Richard/Harvey/Plante/Retro Teammates
212 Shore/Thompson/Stewart/Retro Teammates
213 Trottier/Bossy/Potvin/Retro Teammates
214 Beliveau/Richard/Worsley/Retro Teammates
215 Conacher/Joliat/Hometown Heroes
216 P.Mahovlich/F.Mahovlich/Hometown Heroes
217 T.Esposito/P.Esposito/Hometown Heroes
218 Bossy/Lemieux/Hometown Heroes
219 Sawchuk/Mosienko/Hometown Heroes
220 Potvin/Joliat/Hometown Heroes
221 Harvey/Bourque/Hometown Heroes
222 Cournoyer/Dionne/Hometown Heroes
223 Park/Hainsworth/Hometown Heroes
224 M.Richard/H.Richard/Hometown Heroes

2004-05 ITG Ultimate Memorabilia Art Ross Trophy

PRINT RUN 25 SER.#'d SETS

1 Mario Lemieux	25.00	60.00
2 Jean Beliveau	15.00	40.00
3 Bobby Hull	15.00	40.00
4 Stan Mikita	12.50	30.00
5 Bryan Trottier	12.50	30.00
6 Phil Esposito	12.50	30.00
7 Ted Lindsay	12.50	30.00
8 Guy Lafleur	20.00	50.00

2004-05 ITG Ultimate Memorabilia Auto Threads

STATED PRINT RUN 10 SETS
NOT PRICED DUE TO SCARCITY
1 Patrick Roy MTL
2 Glenn Hall
3 Paul Coffey
4 Ted Lindsay
5 Larry Robinson
6 Alex Delvecchio
7 Denis Savard
8 Marcel Dionne
9 Ray Bourque COL
10 Phil Esposito
11 Patrick Roy COL
12 Ed Giacomin
13 Ray Bourque BOS
14 Stan Mikita
15 Henri Richard
16 Jean Beliveau
17 Bobby Clarke
18 Ron Hextall
19 Cam Neely
20 Brad Park
21 Denis Potvin
22 Jean Ratelle
23 Bernie Parent
24 Bill Barber
25 Gilbert Perreault
26 Doug Gilmour
27 Grant Fuhr
28 Johnny Bower
29 Wendel Clark

2004-05 ITG Ultimate Memorabilia Autographs

STATED PRINT RUN 60 SETS

1 Henri Richard	20.00	50.00
2 Larry Robinson	20.00	50.00
3 Marcel Dionne	20.00	50.00
4 Ray Bourque COL	20.00	50.00
5 Guy Lapointe	15.00	40.00
6 Cam Neely	20.00	50.00
7 Patrick Roy COL	50.00	125.00
8 Ray Bourque BOS	25.00	60.00
9 Ed Giacomin	20.00	50.00
10 Wendel Clark	25.00	60.00
11 Stan Mikita	20.00	50.00
12 Alex Delvecchio	20.00	50.00
13 Marcel Pronovost	15.00	40.00
14 Paul Coffey	15.00	40.00
15 Patrick Roy MTL	60.00	150.00
16 Glenn Hall	20.00	50.00
17 Cam Neely	20.00	50.00
18 Marcel Dionne	15.00	40.00
19 Joe Mullen	15.00	40.00
20 Phil Esposito	25.00	60.00
21 Denis Savard	15.00	40.00
22 Glenn Hall	20.00	50.00
23 Tony Esposito	25.00	60.00
24 Bobby Hull	30.00	80.00
25 Phil Esposito	20.00	50.00
26 Jean Beliveau	30.00	80.00
27 Bobby Hull	25.00	60.00
28 Steve Yzerman	40.00	100.00
29 Terry O'Reilly	15.00	40.00
30 Denis Potvin	20.00	50.00
31 Harry Howell	20.00	50.00
32 Dino Ciccarelli	15.00	40.00
33 Gilbert Perreault	20.00	50.00
34 Mark Howe	15.00	40.00
35 Bobby Clarke	20.00	50.00
36 Brad Park NYR	20.00	50.00
37 Ron Hextall	30.00	80.00
38 Jean Ratelle	15.00	40.00
39 John Bucyk	15.00	40.00
40 Bernie Parent	25.00	60.00
41 Billy Smith	20.00	50.00
42 Brad Park BOS	20.00	50.00
43 Bryan Trottier	20.00	50.00
44 Mike Bossy	25.00	60.00
45 Bill Barber	15.00	40.00
46 Gerry Cheevers	25.00	60.00
47 Pat LaFontaine	15.00	40.00
48 Johnny Bower	20.00	50.00
49 Doug Gilmour	25.00	60.00
50 Glenn Anderson	20.00	50.00
51 Bill Gadsby	15.00	40.00
52 Pierre Pilote	20.00	50.00
53 Grant Fuhr	20.00	50.00
54 Mario Lemieux	50.00	125.00
55 Butch Bouchard	15.00	40.00
56 Chuck Rayner	25.00	60.00
57 Elmer Lach	20.00	50.00
58 Frank Brimsek	60.00	150.00
59 Harry Lumley	25.00	60.00
60 Harry Watson	40.00	100.00
61 Howie Meeker	20.00	50.00
62 Rocket Richard	150.00	300.00
63 Milt Schmidt	15.00	40.00
64 Red Horner	75.00	175.00
65 Red Kelly	20.00	50.00
66 Sid Abel	30.00	80.00
67 Ted Kennedy	30.00	80.00
68 Ted Lindsay	20.00	50.00
69 Woody Dumart	25.00	60.00

2004-05 ITG Ultimate Memorabilia Autographs Gold

STATED PRINT RUN 10 SETS
NOT PRICED DUE TO SCARCITY

2004-05 ITG Ultimate Memorabilia Beantown's Best

This set featured "cut" signatures of past greats and was limited to one set.

PRINT RUN 1 SER.#'d SET
NOT PRICED DUE TO SCARCITY
1 Dit Clapper
2 Milt Schmidt
3 Flash Hollett
4 Frank Brimsek
5 Tiny Thompson
6 Eddie Shore
7 Bill Cowley

2004-05 ITG Ultimate Memorabilia Blades of Steel

STATED PRINT RUN 25 SETS
UNLESS OTHERWISE NOTED
CARDS UNDER 25 NOT PRICED
DUE TO SCARCITY
1 Bill Barilko 60.00 150.00
2 Rocket Richard 75.00 200.00
3 Cyclone Taylor 100.00 250.00
4 Jacques Plante 40.00 100.00
5 Hap Day 30.00 80.00
6 Elmer Lach 25.00 60.00
7 Eddie Shore 50.00 125.00
8 Nels Stewart 30.00 80.00
9 Tim Horton 30.00 80.00
10 Toe Blake 30.00 80.00
11 Busher Jackson 30.00 80.00
12 Jean Beliveau 40.00 100.00
13 Mario Lemieux 30.00 80.00
14 Clint Benedict 30.00 80.00
15 Joe Primeau 25.00 60.00
16 Paddy Moran 30.00 80.00
17 Dit Clapper 40.00 100.00
18 Georges Vezina/10
19 Frank Patrick/10
20 Frank Nighbor/10
21 Aurel Joliat/10

2004-05 ITG Ultimate Memorabilia Bleu Blanc et Rouge

This set featured "cut" signatures of past greats and was limited to one set.

PRINT RUN 1 SER.#'d SET
NOT PRICED DUE TO SCARCITY
1 Rocket Richard
2 Bill Durnan
3 Sprague Cleghorn
4 Doug Harvey
5 Toe Blake
6 Sylvio Mantha
7 Jacques Plante
8 George Hainsworth
9 Frank Selke

2004-05 ITG Ultimate Memorabilia Broad Street Bullies Jerseys

PRINT RUN 25 SER.#'d SETS
AUTO PRINT RUN 10 SER.#'d SETS
AUTOS NOT PRICED DUE TO SCARCITY
1 Bobby Clarke 25.00 60.00
2 Bill Barber 15.00 40.00
3 Bernie Parent 20.00 50.00
4 Dave Schultz 25.00 60.00
5 Rick MacLeish 15.00 40.00
6 Reggie Leach 15.00 40.00
7 Gary Dornhoefer 15.00 40.00
8 Joe Watson 15.00 40.00

2004-05 ITG Ultimate Memorabilia Broad Street Bullies Emblems

PRINT RUN 10 SER.#'d SETS
AUTO PRINT RUN 10 SER.#'d SETS
NOT PRICED DUE TO SCARCITY

2004-05 ITG Ultimate Memorabilia Broad Street Bullies Emblem Autographs

PRINT RUN 10 SER.#'d SETS
NOT PRICED DUE TO SCARCITY

2004-05 ITG Ultimate Memorabilia Broad Street Bullies Numbers

PRINT RUN 10 SER.#'d SETS
AUTO PRINT RUN 10 SETS
NOT PRICED DUE TO SCARCITY

2004-05 ITG Ultimate Memorabilia Broad Street Bullies Number Autographs

PRINT RUN 10 SER.#'d SETS
NOT PRICED DUE TO SCARCITY
1 Bobby Clarke
2 Bill Barber
3 Bernie Parent
4 Dave Schultz
5 Rick MacLeish
6 Reggie Leach
7 Gary Dornhoefer
8 Joe Watson

2004-05 ITG Ultimate Memorabilia Broadway Blueshirts

This set featured "cut" signatures of past greats and was limited to one set.

PRINT RUN 1 SER.#'d SET
NOT PRICED DUE TO SCARCITY
1 Lester Patrick
2 Frank Boucher
3 Bun Cook
4 Bill Cook
5 Bryan Hextall
6 Chuck Rayner
7 Doug Harvey
8 Ching Johnson
9 Ott Heller

2004-05 ITG Ultimate Memorabilia Calder Trophy

PRINT RUN 25 SER.#'d SETS
1 Mario Lemieux 30.00 80.00
2 Mike Bossy 15.00 40.00
3 Bryan Trottier 12.50 30.00
4 Gilbert Perreault 20.00 50.00
5 Terry Sawchuk 25.00 60.00
6 Glenn Hall 12.50 30.00
7 Ray Bourque 15.00 40.00
8 Denis Potvin 10.00 25.00

2004-05 ITG Ultimate Memorabilia Changing the Game

PRINT RUN 25 SER.#'d SETS
1 Phil Esposito 12.50 30.00
2 Patrick Roy 40.00 100.00
3 Mario Lemieux 40.00 100.00
4 Ted Lindsay 12.50 30.00
5 Bobby Hull 15.00 40.00
6 Jacques Plante 30.00 80.00
7 Rocket Richard 40.00 100.00
8 Borje Salming 15.00 40.00
9 Steve Yzerman 25.00 60.00
10 Howie Morenz 30.00 80.00
11 Eddie Shore 30.00 80.00
12 Doug Harvey 15.00 40.00

2004-05 ITG Ultimate Memorabilia Chitown Immortals

This set featured "cut" signatures of past greats and was limited to one set.

PRINT RUN 1 SER.#'d SET
NOT PRICED DUE TO SCARCITY
1 Bill Mosienko
2 Clint Smith
3 Mush March
4 Max Bentley
5 Tommy Ivan
6 Harry Lumley
7 Earl Seibert

2004-05 ITG Ultimate Memorabilia Complete Jerseys

PRINT RUN 10 SER.#'d SETS
NOT PRICED DUE TO SCARCITY
1 Paul Coffey
2 Sid Abel
3 Johnny Bower
4 Ray Bourque
5 Cam Neely
6 Brad Park
7 Aurel Joliat
8 Jean Beliveau
9 Patrick Roy
10 Alex Delvecchio
11 Harry Lumley
12 Jacques Plante
13 Steve Yzerman
14 Frank Brimsek

2004-05 ITG Ultimate Memorabilia Complete Logo

PRINT RUN 1 SER.#'d SET
NOT PRICED DUE TO SCARCITY
1 Ray Bourque/Boston
2 Ray Bourque/Colorado
3 Ray Bourque/AS 2001
4 Ray Bourque/AS 1998
5 Dino Ciccarelli
6 Wendel Clark
7 Paul Coffey
8 Grant Fuhr
9 Doug Gilmour/Buffalo
10 Doug Gilmour/Montreal
11 Doug Gilmour/Toronto
12 Ron Hextall
13 Jari Kurri
14 Mario Lemieux
15 Mario Lemieux AS 2002
16 Mario Lemieux AS 2001
17 Larry Murphy
18 Andy Moog
19 Bill Ranford
20 Mike Richter
21 Patrick Roy/Colorado
22 Patrick Roy/Montreal
23 Patrick Roy/AS 2002
24 Patrick Roy/AS 2001
25 Patrick Roy/AS 1994
26 Patrick Roy/AS 2003
27 Steve Yzerman
28 Steve Yzerman AS 2000
29 Dale Hawerchuk
30 Cam Neely
31 Michel Goulet
32 Phil Housley

2004-05 ITG Ultimate Memorabilia Complete Package

PRINT RUN 10 SER.#'d SETS
NOT PRICED DUE TO SCARCITY
1 Bobby Hull
2 Terry Sawchuk
3 Guy Lafleur
4 Mario Lemieux
5 Jacques Plante
6 Bernie Parent
7 Rocket Richard
8 Patrick Roy
9 Ray Bourque
10 Cam Neely
11 Stan Mikita
12 Steve Yzerman
13 Tim Horton
14 Johnny Bower

2004-05 ITG Ultimate Memorabilia Conn Smythe Trophy

PRINT RUN 25 SER.#'d SETS
1 Jean Beliveau 15.00 40.00
2 Patrick Roy 40.00 100.00
3 Steve Yzerman 30.00 80.00
4 Mario Lemieux 40.00 100.00
5 Mike Bossy 12.50 30.00
6 Bryan Trottier 12.50 30.00
7 Glenn Hall 12.50 30.00
8 Guy Lafleur 20.00 50.00

2004-05 ITG Ultimate Memorabilia Cornerstones

PRINT RUN 10 SER.#'d SETS
NOT PRICED DUE TO SCARCITY
UNPRICED GOLD 1/1'S EXIST
1 Lindsay/Sawchuk/Delvecchio/Yzerman
2 Stan Mikita/Bobby Hull/Tony Esposito/Denis Savard
3 Tim Horton/Hap Day/King Clancy/Borje Salming
4 Howie Morenz/Rocket Richard/Jean Beliveau/Guy-Lafleur
5 Ray Bourque/Johnny Bucyk/Phil Esposito/Eddie Shore
6 Ed Giacomin/Mike Richter/Rod Gilbert/Phil Esposito
7 Gilmour/Sittler/Bailey/Kennedy
8 Bernie Parent/Bobby Clarke/Ron Hextall/Pelle Lindbergh
9 Billy Smith/Denis Potvin/Mike Bossy/Bryan Trottier
10 Patrick Roy/Georges Vezina/George Hainsworth/Jacques Plante

2004-05 ITG Ultimate Memorabilia Country of Origin

PRINT RUN 25 SER.#'d SETS
GOLD PRINT RUN 5 SER.#'d SETS
GOLD NOT PRICED DUE TO SCARCITY
1 Pelle Lindbergh 30.00 80.00
2 Gilbert Perreault 20.00 50.00
3 Bobby Hull 20.00 50.00
4 Mario Lemieux 60.00 150.00
5 Jari Kurri 20.00 50.00
6 Valeri Kharlamov 25.00 60.00
7 Steve Yzerman 40.00 100.00
8 Patrick Roy 60.00 150.00
9 Mike Bossy 15.00 40.00
10 Phil Esposito 20.00 50.00
11 Joe Mullen 15.00 40.00
12 Lanny McDonald 15.00 40.00
13 Ray Bourque 20.00 50.00
14 Tony Esposito 20.00 50.00
15 Yvan Cournoyer 15.00 40.00
16 Denis Potvin 15.00 40.00
17 Bobby Clarke 15.00 40.00
18 Paul Coffey 15.00 40.00
19 Larry Robinson 15.00 40.00
20 Guy Lafleur 25.00 60.00

2004-05 ITG Ultimate Memorabilia Day In History

PRINT RUN 25 SER.#'d SETS
GOLD PRINT RUN 5 SER.#'d SETS
GOLD NOT PRICED DUE TO SCARCITY
1 Henri Richard/Steve Yzerman 25.00 60.00
2 Mike Bossy/Reggie Leach 15.00 40.00
3 Ted Lindsay/Mike Vernon 20.00 50.00
4 F.Brimsek/F.Mahovlich 20.00 50.00
5 Grant Fuhr/Billy Smith 15.00 40.00
6 Jean Beliveau/Ray Bourque 25.00 60.00
7 G.Hall/S.Yzerman 30.00 80.00
8 Doug Gilmour/Mike Bossy 15.00 40.00
9 D.Hawerchuk/S.Yzerman 25.00 60.00
10 George Hainsworth/Rocket Richard 30.00 80.00
11 Bill Barber/Jacques Plante 15.00 40.00
12 G.Perreault/B.Geoffrion 15.00 40.00
13 Elmer Lach/Patrick Roy 50.00 125.00
14 Bill Mosienko/Rocket Richard 30.00 80.00
15 George Hainsworth/Phil Esposito 25.00 60.00
16 Stan Mikita/Terry Sawchuk 15.00 40.00
17 Marcel Dionne/Doug Gilmour 25.00 60.00
18 Bo.Hull/S.Yzerman 30.00 80.00
19 Clint Benedict/Billy Smith 15.00 40.00
20 Darryl Sittler/Tim Horton 25.00 60.00
21 Patrick Roy/Jari Kurri 50.00 125.00
22 B.Barilko/S.Yzerman 40.00 100.00
23 Johnny Bucyk/Rocket Richard 30.00 80.00
24 Paul Coffey/Bobby Hull 15.00 40.00
25 Mike Bossy/Darryl Sittler 15.00 40.00
26 Bobby Hull/Mike Vernon 15.00 40.00
27 Paul Coffey/Ray Bourque 25.00 60.00
28 Bobby Hull/Darryl Sittler 15.00 40.00
29 Denis Potvin/Bobby Clarke 15.00 40.00
30 Bernie Parent/Larry Robinson 15.00 40.00
31 Denis Potvin/Tony Esposito 15.00 40.00
32 M.Lemieux/T.Broda 30.00 80.00
33 Doug Harvey/Bill Durnan 15.00 40.00
34 Bryan Trottier/Toe Blake 15.00 40.00
35 Terry Sawchuk/Charlie Conacher 25.00 60.00
36 Clint Benedict/Patrick Roy 30.00 80.00
37 Charlie Conacher/Jean Beliveau 15.00 40.00
38 Ace Bailey/Marcel Dionne 20.00 50.00
39 Michel Goulet/Dicke Moore 15.00 40.00
40 Stan Mikita/Elmer Lach 15.00 40.00
41 J.Ratelle/M.Lemieux 30.00 80.00
42 Phil Esposito/Frank Mahovlich 25.00 60.00
43 Dale Hawerchuk/Ray Bourque 20.00 50.00
44 Phil Esposito/Johnny Bucyk 15.00 40.00
45 Terry Sawchuk/Guy Lafleur 30.00 80.00
46 Turk Broda/Rod Gilbert 15.00 40.00
47 Paul Coffey/Joe Mullen 15.00 40.00
48 Tony Esposito/Guy Lafleur 15.00 40.00
49 Paul Coffey/Bernie Parent 15.00 40.00
50 M.Lemieux/J.Bower 30.00 80.00

2004-05 ITG Ultimate Memorabilia Emblem Attic

PRINT RUN 5 SER.#'d SETS
NOT PRICED DUE TO SCARCITY
UNPRICED GOLD 1/1'S EXIST
1 Jacques Plante
2 Jean Beliveau
3 Bobby Hull
4 Glenn Hall
5 Phil Esposito
6 Johnny Bower
7 Roy Worters
8 Aurel Joliat

2004-05 ITG Ultimate Memorabilia Gloves are Off

PRINT RUN 25 SER.#'d SETS
UNLESS OTHERWISE NOTED
CARDS UNDER 25 NOT PRICED
DUE TO SCARCITY
1 Ray Bourque 15.00 40.00
2 Cam Neely 25.00 60.00
3 Steve Yzerman 30.00 80.00
4 Mario Lemieux 40.00 100.00
5 Patrick Roy 40.00 100.00
6 Dale Hawerchuk 25.00 60.00
7 Pelle Lindbergh 30.00 80.00
8 Charlie Conacher 25.00 60.00
9 Bill Durnan/10
10 Rocket Richard/10
11 Doug Harvey/10
12 King Clancy/10
13 George Hainsworth/10
14 Ace Bailey/10

2004-05 ITG Ultimate Memorabilia Goalie Gear

PRINT RUN 15 SER.#'d SETS
NOT PRICED DUE TO SCARCITY
1 Gump Worsley
2 Jacques Plante
3 George Hainsworth
4 Tiny Thompson
5 Gerry Cheevers
6 Ron Hextall
7 Frank Brimsek
8 Roger Crozier
9 Harry Lumley
10 Bernie Parent
11 Glenn Hall
12 Patrick Roy
13 Tony Esposito
14 Ed Giacomin
15 Pelle Lindbergh
16 Terry Sawchuk
17 Bill Durnan
18 Johnny Bower
19 Billy Smith
20 Georges Vezina

2004-05 ITG Ultimate Memorabilia Hart Trophy

PRINT RUN 25 SER.#'d SETS
1 Mario Lemieux 40.00 100.00
2 Rocket Richard 40.00 100.00
3 Jacques Plante 20.00 50.00
4 Stan Mikita 12.50 30.00
5 Guy Lafleur 15.00 40.00
6 Bobby Hull 20.00 50.00
7 Phil Esposito 12.50 30.00
8 Howie Morenz 30.00 80.00

2004-05 ITG Ultimate Memorabilia Heroes Mario Lemieux

PRINT RUN 25 SER.#'d SETS
1 Rookie Season 30.00 80.00
2 Five Goals, Five Ways 30.00 80.00
3 First Cup 30.00 80.00
4 M.Lemieux/P.Coffey 25.00 60.00
5 M.Lemieux/L.Murphy 25.00 60.00
6 M.Lemieux/B.Trottier 30.00 80.00
7 All-Star Career 30.00 80.00
8 International Play AU 75.00 150.00
9 Short-Handed Goals AU 75.00 150.00
10 Points in Playoff Game AU 75.00 150.00

2004-05 ITG Ultimate Memorabilia Heroes Patrick Roy

1-7 PRINT RUN 25 SER.#'d SETS
AUTO PRINT RUN 10 SER.#'d SETS
AUTOS NOT PRICED DUE TO SCARCITY
1 Patrick Roy/Rookie Season 40.00 100.00
2 Patrick Roy/First Conn Smythe Trophy 40.00 100.00
3 Patrick Roy/First Cup 40.00 100.00
4 P.Roy/L.Robinson 40.00 100.00
5 Patrick Roy/Ray Bourque 40.00 100.00
6 Patrick Roy/All-Star Career 40.00 100.00
7 Patrick Roy/International Play 40.00 100.00
8 Patrick Roy
Most Career Playoff Wins AU
9 Patrick Roy
Most Career Wins AU
10 Patrick Roy
Most Career Games AU

2004-05 ITG Ultimate Memorabilia Heroes Steve Yzerman

PRINT RUN 25 SER.#'d SETS
1 Rookie Season 25.00 60.00
2 First Cup 25.00 60.00
3 Team Points Record 25.00 60.00
4 S.Yzerman/D.Sittler 25.00 60.00
5 S.Yzerman/P.Coffey 25.00 60.00
6 S.Yzerman/D.Ciccarelli 25.00 60.00
7 All-Star Career 25.00 60.00
8 International Play 25.00 60.00
9 Youngest All-Star AU 75.00 150.00
10 Longest Captaincy AU 75.00 150.00

2004-05 ITG Ultimate Memorabilia Holy Grail

This card featured a cut signature of Lord Stanley of Preston, for whom the Stanley Cup is named.

PRINT RUN 1 SER.#'d SET
NOT PRICED DUE TO SCARCITY
1 Lord Stanley

2004-05 ITG Ultimate Memorabilia Jerseys

PRINT RUN 25 SER.#'d SETS
1 Ray Bourque 15.00 40.00
2 Patrick Roy 50.00 125.00
3 Aurel Joliat 30.00 80.00
4 Paul Coffey 15.00 40.00
5 George Hainsworth 20.00 50.00
6 Mario Lemieux 30.00 80.00
7 Red Kelly 15.00 40.00
8 Terry Sawchuk 25.00 60.00
9 Jean Beliveau 20.00 50.00
10 Rocket Richard 50.00 100.00
11 Steve Yzerman 25.00 60.00
12 Roy Worters 20.00 50.00
13 Frank Brimsek 12.50 30.00
14 Phil Esposito 12.50 30.00
15 Norm Ullman 12.50 30.00
16 Sid Abel 12.50 30.00
17 Ted Lindsay 12.50 30.00

2004-05 ITG Ultimate Memorabilia Jerseys Gold

PRINT RUN 5 SER.#'d SETS
NOT PRICED DUE TO SCARCITY

2004-05 ITG Ultimate Memorabilia Jersey Autographs

PRINT RUN 40 SER.#'d SETS
GOLD PRINT RUN 10 SER.#'d SETS
NOT PRICED DUE TOP SCARCITY
2 Steve Yzerman 75.00 150.00
3 Jean Beliveau 40.00 100.00
5 Paul Coffey 20.00 50.00
6 Guy Lapointe 15.00 40.00
7 Pat LaFontaine 20.00 50.00
8 Guy Lafleur 30.00 80.00
10 Jari Kurri 25.00 60.00
11 Bobby Hull 30.00 80.00
13 Bernie Parent 25.00 60.00
14 Patrick Roy COL 100.00 200.00
15 Gerry Cheevers 20.00 50.00
16 Brad Park 20.00 50.00
17 Gilbert Perreault 15.00 40.00
20 Cam Neely 25.00 60.00
21 Patrick Roy MTL 150.00 300.00
26 Grant Fuhr 25.00 60.00
27 Ed Giacomin 20.00 50.00
28 Johnny Bower 25.00 60.00
30 Ted Lindsay 20.00 50.00
31 Mario Lemieux 75.00 150.00
32 Frank Mahovlich 25.00 60.00
33 Denis Potvin 20.00 50.00
34 Stan Mikita 15.00 40.00
36 Red Kelly 25.00 60.00
37 Lanny McDonald 20.00 50.00
38 Phil Esposito 25.00 60.00
39 Darryl Sittler 25.00 60.00
40 Denis Savard 20.00 50.00
42 Tony Esposito 25.00 60.00
43 Wendel Clark 25.00 60.00
44 Doug Gilmour 25.00 60.00
46 Bobby Clarke 20.00 50.00
47 Henri Richard 15.00 40.00
48 Johnny Bucyk 15.00 40.00
50 Ray Bourque 30.00 80.00
51 Alex Delvecchio 15.00 40.00
52 Gump Worsley 20.00 50.00

2004-05 ITG Ultimate Memorabilia Jersey and Sticks

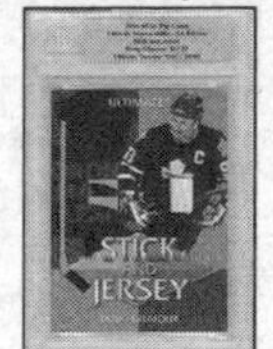

PRINT RUN 25 SER.#'d SETS
GOLD PRINT RUN 5 SER.#'d SETS
GOLD NOT PRICED DUE TO SCARCITY
1 Doug Harvey 15.00 40.00
2 Denis Potvin 12.50 30.00
3 Ray Bourque 20.00 50.00
4 Paul Coffey 20.00 50.00
5 Brad Park 12.50 30.00
6 Mike Bossy 15.00 40.00
7 Jean Beliveau 20.00 50.00
8 Steve Yzerman 30.00 80.00
9 Phil Esposito 20.00 50.00
10 Marcel Dionne 12.50 30.00
11 Bobby Hull 20.00 50.00
12 Doug Gilmour 25.00 60.00
13 Mario Lemieux 40.00 100.00
14 Guy Lafleur 25.00 60.00
15 Cam Neely 25.00 60.00
16 Patrick Roy 60.00 150.00
17 Grant Fuhr 20.00 50.00
18 Johnny Bower 20.00 50.00
19 Jacques Plante 30.00 80.00
20 Harry Lumley 12.50 30.00

2004-05 ITG Ultimate Memorabilia Made to Order

In the Ultimate tradition, the Made to Order set was limited to 10 copies each of cards redeemable for special 1/1 memorabilia cards. Special autograph Made to Order cards were also randomly available and limited to 1 copy each.

PRINT RUN 10 SER.#'d SETS
AUTO PRINT RUN 1 SER.#'d SET
NOT PRICED DUE TO SCARCITY
1 Single
2 Single/Auto

3 Double
4 Double/Auto
5 Triple
6 Triple/Auto
7 Dual Player
8 Triple Player
9 Complete Jersey
10 Complete Package

2004-05 ITG Ultimate Memorabilia Maple Leafs Forever

This set featured "cut" signatures of past greats and was limited to one set.

PRINT RUN 1 SER.#'d SET
NOT PRICED DUE TO SCARCITY
1 Syl Apps
2 Bill Barilko
3 Turk Broda
4 Joe Primeau
5 King Clancy
6 Conn Smythe
7 Tim Horton
8 Charlie Conacher
9 Ace Bailey
10 Busher Jackson
11 Gordie Drillon
12 Baldy Cotton

2004-05 ITG Ultimate Memorabilia Marvelous Maroons

This set featured "cut" signatures of past greats and was limited to one set.

PRINT RUN 1 SER.#'d SET
NOT PRICED DUE TO SCARCITY
1 Hooley Smith
2 Baldy Northcott
3 Babe Siebert
4 Cy Wentworth
5 Carl Voss
6 Red Dutton

2004-05 ITG Ultimate Memorabilia Motown Heroes

This set featured "cut" signatures of past greats and was limited to one set.

PRINT RUN 1 SER.#'d SET
NOT PRICED DUE TO SCARCITY
1 Johnny Mowers
2 Ebbie Goodfellow
3 Mud Bruneteau
4 Syd Howe
5 Terry Sawchuk
6 Jack Stewart
7 Sid Abel
8 Jimmy Orlando
9 Harry Lumley

2004-05 ITG Ultimate Memorabilia Nicknames

PRINT RUN 25 SER.#'d SETS
1 Stan Mikita 25.00 60.00
2 Rocket Richard 60.00 120.00
3 Toe Blake 30.00 80.00
4 Jacques Plante 25.00 60.00
5 Mario Lemieux 60.00 120.00
6 Terry Sawchuk 30.00 80.00
7 Steve Yzerman 25.00 60.00
8 Glenn Hall 15.00 40.00
9 Larry Robinson 15.00 40.00
10 Bernie Geoffrion Clv 20.00 40.00
11 Henri Richard 15.00 40.00
12 Jean Beliveau 20.00 50.00
13 Johnny Bower 25.00 60.00
14 Ted Kennedy
15 Doug Gilmour 25.00 60.00
16 Ace Bailey 30.00 80.00
17 Nels Stewart 30.00 80.00
18 Tony Esposito 20.00 50.00
19 Frank Mahovlich 15.00 40.00
20 Gump Worsley 25.00 60.00
21 Marcel Dionne
22 Frank Brimsek 25.00 60.00
23 Ted Lindsay 15.00 40.00
24 Gerry Cheevers 50.00 100.00
25 Patrick Roy 75.00 150.00
26 Cyclone Taylor 250.00 350.00
27 Howie Morenz 50.00 100.00
28 Bobby Hull 20.00 50.00
29 Guy Lafleur 25.00 60.00
30 Georges Vezina 125.00 200.00

2004-05 ITG Ultimate Memorabilia Nickname Autographs

PRINT RUN 10 SER.#'d SETS
NOT PRICED DUE TO SCARCITY
1 Doug Gilmour
2 Mario Lemieux
3 Steve Yzerman
4 Ted Kennedy
5 Larry Robinson
6 Gerry Cheevers
7 Ted Lindsay
8 Guy Lafleur
9 Frank Mahovlich
10 Stan Mikita
11 Gump Worsley
12 Jean Beliveau
13 Johnny Bower
14 Glenn Hall
15 Henri Richard
16 Patrick Roy

2004-05 ITG Ultimate Memorabilia Norris Trophy

PRINT RUN 25 SER.#'d SETS
1 Ray Bourque 25.00 60.00
2 Larry Robinson 15.00 40.00
3 Doug Harvey 15.00 40.00
4 Jacques Laperriere 10.00 25.00
5 Paul Coffey 15.00 40.00
6 Denis Potvin 10.00 25.00

2004-05 ITG Ultimate Memorabilia Original Six

PRINT RUN 6 SER.#'d SETS
NOT PRICED DUE TO SCARCITY
1 Stan Mikita/Guy Lafleur/Johnny Bower /Ray Bourque/Terry Sawchuk/Ed Giacomin
2 Bobby Hull/Jean Beliveau/Tim Horton/Terry O'Reilly / Ted Lindsay/Rod Gilbert
3 Mosienko/Worsley/Salming/Gilbert/Yzerman/Gadsby
4 Dennis Hull/George Hainsworth/Doug Gilmour /Eddie Shore/Alex Delvecchio/Mike Richter
5 Michel Goulet/Patrick Roy/Doug Gilmour /Cam Neely/Sid Abel/Mike Richter
6 Chuck Gardiner/JacquesPlante/Wendel Clark /Tiny Thompson/Mike Vernon/Gump Worsley
7 Frank Brimsek/Yvon Cournoyer/Rick Vaive /Andy Moog/Bill Gadsby/Jean Ratelle
8 Harry Lumley/Doug Harvey/Dunc Williams /Brad Park/Dino Ciccarelli/Terry Sawchuk
9 Glenn Hall/John Ferguson/Teeder Kennedy /Johnny Bucyk/Ted Lindsay/Doug Harvey
10 Harry Lumley/Dickie Moore/Darryl Sittler /Brad Park/Bill Gadsby/Jean Ratelle
11 Tony Esposito/Guy Lapointe/Darryl Sittler /Rick Middleton/Glenn Hall/Marcel Dionne
12 Phil Esposito/Newsy Lalonde/Charlie Conacher /Frank Brimsek/Sid Abel/Tony Esposito
13 Bill Mosienko/Charlie Hodge/Bill Barilko /Ray Bourque/Roger Crozier/Ed Giacomin
14 Bobby Hull/Henri Richard/Turk Broda /Cam Neely/Alex Delvecchio/Jacques Plante
15 Savard/Roy/Broda/Esposito/Yzerman/Dionne
16 Glenn Hall/Rocket Richard/Frank Mahovlich /Gerry Cheevers/Norm Ullman/Phil Esposito
17 Michel Goulet/Georges Vezina/Red Kelly /Phil Esposito/Terry Sawchuk/Rod Gilbert
18 Frank Brimsek/Rocket Richard/Lanny McDonald /Gerry Cheevers/Dino Ciccarelli/John Davidson
19 Denis Savard/Larry Robinson/Lanny McDonald /Tiny Thompson/Roger Crozier/John Davidson
20 Stan Mikita/Aurel Joliat/Bill Barilko /Eddie Shore/Norm Ullman/Chuck Rayner

2004-05 ITG Ultimate Memorabilia Paper Cuts

This set featured "cut" signatures of past greats and legendary figures in hockey. It was limited to one set.

PRINT RUN 1 SER.#'d SET
NOT PRICED DUE TO SCARCITY
1 Lord Stanley
2 Red Dutton
3 Sweeney Schriner
4 Aurel Joliat
5 Toe Blake
6 Bill Barilko
7 Joe Primeau
8 Jack Stewart
9 Doug Harvey
10 Turk Broda
11 Frank Calder
12 Eddie Shore
13 Frank Selke
14 Cy Wentworth
15 Baldy Northcott
16 Tim Horton
17 Dit Clapper
18 Lady Byng
19 Carl Voss
20 Fred Shero
21 Frank Boucher
22 Cecil Hart
23 Bullet Joe Simpson

2004-05 ITG Ultimate Memorabilia Paper Cuts Memorabilia

This set featured "cut" signatures and memorabilia of past greats and important figures in hockey. It was limited to one set.

PRINT RUN 1 SER.#'d SET
NOT PRICED DUE TO SCARCITY
1 Bill Barilko
2 Doug Harvey
3 Maurice Richard
4 Eddie Shore
5 Newsy Lalonde
6 Jack Adams
7 Aurel Joliat
8 Jacques Plante
9 Toe Blake
10 Hap Day
11 Tim Horton
12 Dit Clapper
13 Howie Morenz
14 Turk Broda
15 Bill Mosienko
16 Frank Brimsek
17 King Clancy
18 Ace Bailey
19 Chuck Rayner
20 Harry Lumley
21 George Hainsworth
22 Charlie Conacher
23 Busher Jackson
24 Nels Stewart

2004-05 ITG Ultimate Memorabilia Raised to the Rafters

PRINT RUN 25 SER.#'d SETS
1 Patrick Roy 60.00 125.00
2 Jacques Plante 30.00 80.00
3 Ray Bourque 20.00 50.00
4 Johnny Bower 20.00 50.00
5 Doug Harvey 20.00 50.00
6 Stan Mikita 20.00 50.00
7 Bobby Hull 20.00 50.00
8 Jean Beliveau 25.00 60.00
9 Bobby Clarke 25.00 60.00
10 Jari Kurri 25.00 60.00

2004-05 ITG Ultimate Memorabilia Retro Teammates

PRINT RUN 25 SER.#'d SETS
1 Ray Bourque/Cam Neely/Rick Middleton /Andy Moog 60.00 120.00
2 Rocket Richard/Henri Richard/Doug Harvey /Jacques Plante 125.00 250.00
3 Stan Mikita/Denis Hull/Glenn Hall /Bobby Hull 60.00 120.00
4 Darryl Sittler/Lanny McDonald/Borje Salming /Tiger Williams 75.00 150.00
5 Bryan Trottier/Mike Bossy/Denis Potvin /Billy Smith 50.00 100.00
6 Sid Abel/Alex Delvecchio/Ted Lindsay /Terry Sawchuk 60.00 120.00
7 Eddie Shore/Tiny Thompson/Nels Stewart /Dit Clapper 100.00 200.00
8 Paul Coffey/Grant Fuhr/Glenn Anderson /Jarri Kurri 125.00 200.00
9 Guy Lafleur/Steve Shutt/Larry Robinson /Denis Savard 125.00 250.00
10 Bailey/Day/Clancy/Primeau 100.00 200.00
11 Bill Barber/Bernie Parent/Bobby Clarke /Reggie Leach 100.00 200.00
12 Jean Ratelle/Ed Giacomin/Brad Park /Rod Gilbert 60.00 120.00
13 Johnny Bucyk/Phil Esposito/Gerry Cheevers /Wayne Cashman 60.00 120.00
14 Terry O'Reilly/Brad Park/Ray Bourque /Gilles Gilbert 60.00 120.00
15 Jean Beliveau/Gump Worsley/Yvan Cournoyer /Jacques Laperriere 60.00 120.00

2004-05 ITG Ultimate Memorabilia Seams Unbelievable

PRINT RUN 25 SER.#'d SETS
1 Mario Lemieux 40.00 100.00
2 Steve Yzerman 25.00 60.00
3 Patrick Roy 50.00 125.00
4 Mike Bossy 15.00 40.00
5 Bryan Trottier 15.00 40.00
6 Charlie Gardiner 25.00 60.00
7 Rocket Richard 75.00 200.00
8 Darryl Sittler 25.00 60.00
9 Ray Bourque 25.00 60.00
10 Roy Worters 25.00 60.00

2004-05 ITG Ultimate Memorabilia Stick Autographs

PRINT RUN 40 SER.#'d SETS
UNLESS OTHERWISE NOTED
GOLD PRINT RUN 10 SER.#'d SETS
1 Michel Goulet 12.50 30.00
2 Mike Bossy 12.50 30.00
3 Cam Neely 25.00 60.00
4 Phil Esposito 25.00 60.00
5 Ray Bourque 25.00 60.00
6 Dale Hawerchuk 12.50 30.00
7 Tony Esposito 20.00 50.00
8 Mario Lemieux 60.00 150.00
9 Guy Lapointe 12.50 30.00
10 Marcel Dionne 12.50 30.00
11 Henri Richard 15.00 40.00
12 Larry Robinson 12.50 30.00
13 Gerry Cheevers 20.00 50.00
14 Bobby Hull 30.00 80.00
15 Bryan Trottier 12.50 30.00
16 Dino Ciccarelli 12.50 30.00
17 Gump Worsley 30.00 80.00
18 Guy Lafleur 25.00 60.00
19 Johnny Bower 25.00 60.00
20 Pat LaFontaine 12.50 30.00
21 Steve Yzerman 50.00 125.00
22 Terry O'Reilly 12.50 30.00
23 Bernie Geoffrion/30 30.00 80.00
24 Bill Barber/30 12.50 30.00
25 Bobby Clarke/30 25.00 60.00
26 Frank Mahovlich/30 25.00 60.00
27 Gilbert Perreault/30 25.00 60.00
28 Johnny Bucyk/30 20.00 50.00
29 Paul Coffey/30 25.00 60.00
30 Stan Mikita/30 25.00 60.00
31 Jean Beliveau/30 60.00 125.00
32 Jari Kurri 20.00 50.00
33 Bernie Parent 20.00 50.00
34 Alex Delvecchio 20.00 50.00
35 John Ferguson 12.50 30.00
36 Joe Mullen 12.50 30.00
37 Brad Park 20.00 50.00
38 Wendel Clark 20.00 50.00
39 Doug Gilmour 20.00 50.00
40 Yvan Cournoyer 12.50 30.00
41 Billy Smith 12.50 30.00
42 Ed Giacomin 12.50 30.00
43 Denis Savard/30 20.00 50.00
44 Grant Fuhr/30 30.00 80.00
45 Darryl Sittler/30 30.00 80.00

2004-05 ITG Ultimate Memorabilia Triple Threads

PRINT RUN 25 SER.#'d SETS

2004-05 ITG Ultimate Memorabilia Vezina Trophy

PRINT RUN 25 SER.#'d SETS
1 Jacques Plante 25.00 60.00
2 Terry Sawchuk 25.00 60.00
3 Pelle Lindbergh 40.00 100.00
4 George Hainsworth 25.00 60.00
5 Bernie Parent 30.00 80.00
6 Patrick Roy 60.00 150.00
7 Grant Fuhr 25.00 60.00
8 Tony Esposito 25.00 60.00

2004-05 ITG Ultimate Memorabilia Vintage Lumber

PRINT RUN 15 SER.#'d SETS
NOT PRICED DUE TO SCARCITY
1 Harry Lumley
2 Bill Durnan
3 Glenn Hall
4 Johnny Bucyk
5 Stan Mikita
6 Bobby Hull
7 Howie Morenz
8 Rocket Richard
9 Jean Beliveau
10 Doug Harvey
11 Joe Primeau
12 Bob Davidson
13 Bernie Geoffrion
14 Jacques Plante
15 Terry Sawchuk
16 Georges Vezina/12

2005-06 ITG Ultimate Memorabilia Level 1

PRINT RUN 9 SER.#'d SETS
NOT PRICED DUE TO SCARCITY

2005-06 ITG Ultimate Memorabilia Level 2

PRINT RUN 45 COPIES
1 Alex Delvecchio 6.00 15.00
2 Alexander Ovechkin 20.00 50.00
3 Alexander Yakushev 6.00 15.00
4 Antero Niittymaki 6.00 15.00
5 Aurel Joliat 6.00 15.00
6 Bernie Geoffrion 8.00 20.00
7 Bernie Parent 6.00 15.00
8 Bill Barilko 12.00 30.00
9 Bill Durnan 6.00 15.00
10 Billy Smith 6.00 15.00
11 Bobby Clarke 8.00 20.00
12 Bobby Hull 10.00 25.00
13 Borje Salming 6.00 15.00
14 Brett Hull 8.00 20.00
15 Brian Leetch 5.00 12.00
16 Cam Neely 6.00 15.00
17 Charlie Conacher 6.00 15.00
18 Charlie Gardiner 5.00 12.00
19 Corey Perry 6.00 15.00
20 Cyclone Taylor 20.00 50.00
21 Dany Heatley 6.00 15.00
22 Darryl Sittler 5.00 12.00
23 Dave Keon 8.00 20.00
24 Denis Potvin 6.00 15.00
25 Dion Phaneuf 8.00 20.00
26 Dit Clapper 6.00 15.00
27 Doug Gilmour 6.00 15.00
28 Doug Harvey 6.00 15.00
29 Ed Giacomin 6.00 15.00
30 Eddie Shack 6.00 15.00
31 Eddie Shore 6.00 15.00
32 Elmer Lach 6.00 15.00
33 Eric Lindros 8.00 20.00
34 Evgeni Malkin 20.00 50.00
35 Frank Brimsek 6.00 15.00
36 Frank Mahovlich 6.00 15.00
37 Frank McGee 6.00 15.00
38 Frank Nighbor 6.00 15.00
39 George Hainsworth 6.00 15.00
40 Georges Vezina 8.00 20.00
41 Gerry Cheevers 6.00 15.00
42 Gilbert Perreault 6.00 15.00
43 Glenn Hall 6.00 15.00
44 Grant Fuhr 6.00 15.00
45 Gump Worsley 6.00 15.00
46 Guy Lafleur 6.00 15.00
47 Henri Richard 6.00 15.00
48 Henrik Lundqvist 8.00 20.00
49 Howie Meeker 5.00 12.00
50 Howie Morenz 8.00 20.00
51 Ilya Kovalchuk 6.00 15.00
52 Jacques Plante 8.00 20.00
53 Jari Kurri 8.00 20.00
54 Jean Beliveau 6.00 15.00
55 Jim Craig 6.00 15.00
56 Joe Malone 6.00 15.00
57 Johnny Bower 4.00 10.00
58 Johnny Bucyk 4.00 10.00
59 Jose Theodore 6.00 15.00
60 King Clancy 6.00 15.00
61 Lanny McDonald 6.00 15.00
62 Larry Robinson 6.00 15.00
63 Lester Patrick 4.00 10.00
64 Lionel Conacher 6.00 15.00
65 Lord Stanley 5.00 12.00
66 Marcel Dionne 5.00 12.00
67 Mario Lemieux 12.00 30.00
68 Martin Brodeur 10.00 25.00
69 Maurice Richard 8.00 20.00
70 Mike Bossy 6.00 15.00
71 Mike Richards 6.00 15.00
72 Milt Schmidt 4.00 10.00
73 Nels Stewart 6.00 15.00
74 Newsy Lalonde 6.00 15.00
75 Pat LaFontaine 5.00 12.00
76 Patrick Roy 12.00 30.00
77 Paul Coffey 6.00 15.00
78 Paul Henderson 5.00 12.00
79 Pelle Lindbergh 8.00 20.00
80 Petr Prucha 6.00 15.00
81 Phil Esposito 6.00 15.00
82 Raymond Bourque 8.00 20.00
83 Red Kelly 4.00 10.00
84 Rogie Vachon 4.00 10.00
85 Ron Hextall 6.00 15.00
86 Sid Abel 6.00 15.00
87 Sidney Crosby 40.00 100.00
88 Stan Mikita 6.00 15.00
89 Steve Yzerman 10.00 25.00
90 Ted Kennedy 6.00 15.00
91 Ted Lindsay 6.00 15.00
92 Terry Sawchuk 8.00 20.00
93 Tim Horton 8.00 20.00
94 Tiny Thompson 6.00 15.00
95 Toe Blake 6.00 15.00
96 Tony Esposito 6.00 15.00
97 Turk Broda 6.00 15.00
98 Valeri Kharlamov 6.00 15.00
99 Vladislav Tretiak 8.00 20.00
100 Yvan Cournoyer 5.00 12.00

2005-06 ITG Ultimate Memorabilia Level 3

PRINT RUN 40 SER. #'d SETS
SAME PRICE AS LEVEL 2

2005-06 ITG Ultimate Memorabilia Level 4

PRINT RUN 30 SER. #'d SETS
*STARS: .5X to 1.5X LEVEL 2 HI

2005-06 ITG Ultimate Memorabilia Level 5

PRINT RUN 1/1
NOT PRICED DUE TO SCARCITY

2005-06 ITG Ultimate Memorabilia Alexander The Gr8

PRINT RUNS VARY
PRINT RUNS UNDER 25 NOT PRICED DUE TO SCARCITY
GOLD 1/1 VERSION ALSO EXISTS
GOLD NOT PRICED DUE TO SCARCITY
1 Alexander Ovechkin/25 50.00 100.00
2 Alexander Ovechkin/25 50.00 100.00
3 Alexander Ovechkin/25 50.00 100.00
4 Alexander Ovechkin/15
5 Alexander Ovechkin/10
6 Alexander Ovechkin/10
7 Alexander Ovechkin/10
8 Alexander Ovechkin/7

2005-06 ITG Ultimate Memorabilia Amazing Amerks Autos

COMPLETE SET (6)
PRINT RUN 1/1
NOT PRICED DUE TO SCARCITY
1 Bullet Joe Simpson
2 Lorne Carr
3 Roy Worters
4 Red Dutton
5 Sweeney Schriner
6 Harry Oliver

2005-06 ITG Ultimate Memorabilia Beantown's Best Autos

COMPLETE SET (4)
PRINT RUN 1/1
NOT PRICED DUE TO SCARCITY
1 Dit Clapper
2 Eddie Shore
3 Paul Ronty
4 Woody Dumart

2005-06 ITG Ultimate Memorabilia Blades of Steel

PRINT RUN 25 SER. #'d SETS
1/1 GOLD VERSION ALSO EXISTS
GOLD NOT PRICED DUE TO SCARCITY
1 Alexander Ovechkin 60.00 125.00
2 Mario Lemieux 30.00 80.00
3 Ray Bourque 20.00 50.00
4 Joe Primeau 15.00 40.00
5 Elmer Lach 15.00 40.00
6 Jack Adams 20.00 50.00
7 Nels Stewart 20.00 50.00
8 Tim Horton 25.00 60.00
9 Toe Blake 20.00 50.00
10 Frank Nighbor 20.00 50.00
11 Aurel Joliat 40.00 100.00
12 Dit Clapper 20.00 50.00
13 Eddie Shore 20.00 50.00
14 Jean Beliveau 40.00 80.00
15 Georges Vezina 75.00 125.00
16 Jacques Plante 20.00 50.00
17 Cyclone Taylor 450.00 600.00
18 Clint Benedict 20.00 50.00
19 Maurice Richard 30.00 80.00
20 Bill Barilko 30.00 80.00

2005-06 ITG Ultimate Memorabilia Bleu Blanc et Rouge Autos

PRINT RUN 1/1
NOT PRICED DUE TO SCARCITY
1 Jacques Plante
2 Bill Durnan
3 George Hainsworth
4 Howie Morenz
5 Maurice Richard
6 Kenny Reardon
7 Doug Harvey
8 Buddy O'Connor
9 Art Lesieur
10 Toe Blake
11 Sylvio Mantha
12 Armand Mondou
13 Johnny Gagnon
14 Pit Lepine

2005-06 ITG Ultimate Memorabilia Broadway Blueshirts Autos

PRINT RUN 1/1
NOT PRICED DUE TO SCARCITY
1 Buddy O'Connor
2 Frank Eddolls
3 Alex Shibicky
4 Lester Patrick
5 Ott Heller
6 Bun Cook
7 Frank Boucher
8 Bill Cook
9 Lynn Patrick
10 Clint Smith
11 Bryan Hextall Sr.
12 Neil Colville

2005-06 ITG Ultimate Memorabilia Builders Autos

PRINT RUN 1/1
NOT PRICED DUE TO SCARCITY
1 Frank Selke
2 Dick Irvin
3 Frank Calder
4 James D. Norris
5 Conn Smythe
6 Punch Imlach
7 Clarence Campbell

2005-06 ITG Ultimate Memorabilia Chi-Town Immortals Autos

PRINT RUN 1/1
NOT PRICED DUE TO SCARCITY
1 Bill Mosienko
2 Marty Burke
3 Alex Levinsky
4 Doug Bentley
5 Johnny Gottselig
6 Mush March

2005-06 ITG Ultimate Memorabilia Complete Jersey

PRINT RUN 10 SER. #'d SETS
NOT PRICED DUE TO SCARCITY
GOLD 1/1 VERSION EXISTS
GOLD NOT PRICED DUE TO SCARCITY
1 Ron Hextall
2 Evgeni Malkin
3 Alexander Ovechkin
4 Sidney Crosby
5 Dion Phaneuf
6 Wendel Clark
7 Frank Mahovlich
8 Jose Theodore
9 Eric Lindros
10 Brian Leetch
11 Martin Brodeur
12 Brett Hull
13 Terry Sawchuk
14 Darryl Sittler
15 Marcel Dionne
16 Doug Gilmour
17 Larry Robinson
18 Cam Neely
19 Steve Yzerman
20 Mario Lemieux
21 Raymond Bourque
22 Patrick Roy
23 Dave Keon
24 Bobby Hull
25 Lanny McDonald
26 Ilya Kovalchuk

2005-06 ITG Ultimate Memorabilia Complete Package

PRINT RUN 10 SER. #'d SETS
NOT PRICED DUE TO SCARCITY
GOLD 1/1 VERSION EXISTS
GOLD NOT PRICED DUE TO SCARCITY
1 Bobby Hull
2 Stan Mikita
3 Tim Horton
4 Jacques Plante
5 Eddie Shore
6 Jean Beliveau
7 Terry Sawchuk
8 Guy Lafleur
9 Jose Theodore
10 Eric Lindros
11 Ron Hextall
12 Maurice Richard
13 Cam Neely
14 Raymond Bourque

15 Patrick Roy
16 Alexander Ovechkin
17 Bernie Parent
18 Mario Lemieux
19 Steve Yzerman

2005-06 ITG Ultimate Memorabilia Cornerstones Jerseys

PRINT RUN 10 SER. #'d SETS
NOT PRICED DUE TO SCARCITY
GOLD 1/1 VERSION EXISTS
GOLD NOT PRICED DUE TO SCARCITY
1 Charlie Gardiner
Bill Mosienko
Bobby Hull
Stan Mikita
2 Eddie Shore
Johnny Bucyk
Phil Esposito
Ray Bourque
3 Bill Durnan
Jacques Plante
Patrick Roy
Jose Theodore
4 Sid Abel
Ted Lindsay
Alex Delvecchio
Steve Yzerman
5 Charlie Conacher
Dave Keon
Darryl Sittler
Doug Gilmour
6 Rod Gilbert
Ed Giacomin
Brian Leetch
Henrik Lundqvist
7 Paul Coffey
Glen Anderson
Jari Kurri
Grant Fuhr
8 Billy Smith
Denis Potvin
Bryan Trottier
Mike Bossy
9 Howie Morenz
Maurice Richard
Jean Beliveau
Guy Lafleur
10 Bobby Clarke
Bernie Parent
Mark Howe
Ron Hextall

2005-06 ITG Ultimate Memorabilia Decades Jerseys

PRINT RUN 10 SER. #'d SETS
NOT PRICED DUE TO SCARCITY
GOLD 1/1 VERSION EXISTS
GOLD NOT PRICED DUE TO SCARCITY
1 Eddie Shore
Frank Brimsek
Johnny Bucyk
Phil Esposito
Brad Park
Ray Bou
2 Sid Abel
Ted Lindsay
Norm Ullman
Roger Crozier
Alex Delvecchio
Steve Y
3 Toe Blake
Maurice Richard
Jean Beliveau
Jacques Plante
Guy Lafleur
Lar
4 Eddie Shore
Dit Clapper
Doug Harvey
Tim Horton
Serge Savard
Ray Bourqu
5 George Hainsworth
Harry Lumley
Jacques Plante
Glenn Hall
Bernie Parent
6 Charlie Conacher
Ted Kennedy
Tim Horton
Dave Keon
Darryl Sittler
Wende
7 Howie Morenz
Chuck Rayner
Bill Gadsby
Ed Giacomin
Rod Gilbert
John Van
8 Charlie Gardiner
Frank Brimsek
Gump Worsley
Johnny Bower
Tony Esposito

2005-06 ITG Ultimate Memorabilia Double Autos

PRINT RUN 34 SER #'d SETS
GOLD 1/1 VERSION EXISTS
GOLD NOT PRICED DUE TO SCARCITY
1 Dion Phaneuf 30.00 60.00
Brian Leetch
2 Patrick Roy 50.00 125.00
Angelo Esposito
3 Phil Esposito 25.00 50.00
Gerry Cheevers
4 Paul Henderson 25.00 60.00
Vladislav Tretiak
5 Antero Niittymaki 25.00 50.00
Bernie Parent
6 Martin Brodeur 75.00 200.00
Patrick Roy
7 Dave Keon 30.00 60.00
Ted Kennedy
8 Mario Lemieux 75.00 125.00
Jean Beliveau
9 Henrik Lundqvist 30.00 60.00
Ed Giacomin
10 Steve Yzerman 40.00 80.00
Ted Lindsay
11 Borje Salming 20.00 40.00
Larry Robinson
12 Alexander Ovechkin 100.00 200.00
Evgeni Malkin
13 Glenn Hall 25.00 50.00
Tony Esposito
14 Mario Lemieux 75.00 125.00
Ron Francis
15 Tony Esposito 25.00 50.00
Phil Esposito
16 Milt Schmidt 20.00 40.00
Elmer Lach
17 Cristobal Huet 50.00 125.00
Patrick Roy
18 Paul Coffey 25.00 50.00
Grant Fuhr
19 Dany Heatley 20.00 40.00
Ilya Kovalchuk
20 Yvan Cournoyer
Paul Henderson

2005-06 ITG Ultimate Memorabilia Double Memorabilia

PRINT RUN 25 SER. #'d SETS
NOT PRICED DUE TO SCARCITY
GOLD 1/1 VERSION EXISTS
GOLD NOT PRICED DUE TO SCARCITY
1 Martin Brodeur
2 Eric Lindros
3 Vladislav Tretiak
4 Patrick Roy
5 Guy Lafleur
6 Stan Mikita
7 Brett Hull
8 Cam Neely
9 Marcel Dionne
10 Bernie Parent
11 Borje Salming
12 Jose Theodore
13 Dave Keon
14 Paul Coffey
15 Raymond Bourque
16 Steve Yzerman
17 Mario Lemieux
18 Jacques Plante
19 Eddie Shore
20 Bobby Hull
21 Bobby Clarke
22 Grant Fuhr
23 Sidney Crosby
24 Alexander Ovechkin
25 Tony Esposito

2005-06 ITG Ultimate Memorabilia Double Memorabilia Autos

PRINT RUN 34 SER. #'d SETS
GOLD 1/1 VERSION EXISTS
GOLD NOT PRICED DUE TO SCARCITY
1 Alexander Ovechkin 125.00 200.00
Evgeni Malkin
2 Martin Brodeur 125.00 250.00
Patrick Roy
3 Phil Esposito 40.00 80.00
Gerry Cheevers
4 Dion Phaneuf 30.00 75.00
Brian Leetch
5 Henrik Lundqvist 30.00 75.00
Ed Giacomin
6 Steve Yzerman 50.00 125.00
Ted Lindsay
7 Dave Keon 25.00 60.00
Ted Kennedy
8 Mario Lemieux 50.00 125.00
Jean Beliveau
9 Antero Niittymaki 25.00 60.00
Bernie Parent
10 Tony Esposito 40.00 80.00
Phil Esposito
11 Paul Coffey 20.00 50.00
Grant Fuhr
12 Glenn Hall 25.00 60.00
Tony Esposito
13 Pat LaFontaine 25.00 60.00
Gilbert Perreault
14 Darryl Sittler 25.00 50.00
Lanny McDonald
15 Frank Mahovlich 40.00 80.00
Henri Richard
16 Ron Hextall
Bernie Parent
17 Bobby Hull 30.00 75.00
Stan Mikita
18 Vladislav Tretiak 50.00 100.00
Yvan Cournoyer
19 Doug Gilmour 25.00 60.00
Wendel Clark
20 Mike Bossy 25.00 60.00
Guy Lafleur

2005-06 ITG Ultimate Memorabilia Emblem Attic

PRINT RUN 5 SER. #'d SETS
NOT PRICED DUE TO SCARCITY
GOLD 1/1 VERSION EXISTS
GOLD NOT PRICED DUE TO SCARCITY
1 Frank Mahovlich
2 Henri Richard
3 Ed Giacomin
4 Gump Worsley
5 Norm Ullman
6 George Hainsworth
7 Aurel Joliat
8 Roy Worters
9 Johnny Bower
10 Frank Brimsek
11 Stan Mikita
12 Terry Sawchuk
13 Doug Harvey
14 Sid Abel
15 Dave Keon
16 Harry Lumley
17 Bobby Hull
18 Jean Beliveau
19 Glenn Hall
20 Jacques Plante

2005-06 ITG Ultimate Memorabilia Emblems

PRINT RUN 10 SER. #'d SETS
NOT PRICED DUE TO SCARCITY
GOLD 1/1 VERSION EXISTS
GOLD NOT PRICED DUE TO SCARCITY
1 Sidney Crosby
2 Alexander Ovechkin
3 Evgeni Malkin
4 Al Montoya
5 Darryl Sittler
6 Dave Keon
7 Rod Gilbert
8 Jean Beliveau
9 Frank Mahovlich
10 Pat LaFontaine
11 Bobby Hull
12 Brett Hull
13 Mike Bossy
14 Marcel Dionne
15 Ron Hextall
16 Cam Neely
17 Doug Gilmour
18 Stan Mikita
19 Mario Lemieux
20 Patrick Roy MON
21 Raymond Bourque
22 Patrick Roy COL
23 Martin Brodeur
24 Brian Leetch
25 Steve Yzerman
26 Jose Theodore
27 Wendel Clark
28 Denis Potvin
29 Lanny McDonald

2005-06 ITG Ultimate Memorabilia First Overall Jerseys

PRINT RUN 25 SER. #'d SETS
GOLD 1/1 VERSION EXISTS
GOLD NOT PRICED DUE TO SCARCITY
1 Gilbert Perreault 20.00 40.00
2 Guy Lafleur 25.00 50.00
3 Denis Potvin 20.00 40.00
4 Dale Hawerchuk 20.00 40.00
5 Mario Lemieux 40.00 80.00
6 Wendel Clark 20.00 40.00
7 Marc-Andre Fleury 20.00 50.00
8 Alexander Ovechkin 40.00 80.00
9 Sidney Crosby 75.00 150.00

2005-06 ITG Ultimate Memorabilia First Rounders Jerseys

PRINT RUN 25 SER. #'d SETS
GOLD 1/1 VERSION EXISTS
GOLD NOT PRICED DUE TO SCARCITY
1 Mario Lemieux 50.00 100.00
Gilbert Perreault
Guy Lafleur
Dale Hawerchuk
2 Marc-Andre Fleury 100.00 200.00
Mario Lemieux
Sidney Crosby
Evgeni Malkin
3 Grant Fuhr 40.00 80.00
Brian Leetch
Steve Yzerman
Denis Savard
4 Marcel Dionne 40.00 80.00
Guy Lafleur
Mike Bossy
Darryl Sittler
5 Martin Brodeur 40.00 80.00
Kari Lehtonen
Al Montoya
Marc-Andre Fleury
6 Mario Lemieux 100.00 200.00
Sidney Crosby
Evgeni Malkin
Alexander Ovechkin
7 Cam Neely 40.00 80.00
Dion Phaneuf
Ryan Getzlaf
Cam Ward
8 Ray Bourque 40.00 80.00
Brian Leetch
Dion Phaneuf
Joni Pitkanen
9 Ray Bourque 50.00 100.00
Michel Goulet
Dale Hawerchuk
Mario Lemieux
10 Steve Yzerman 50.00 100.00
Alexander Ovechkin
Corey Perry
Mike Richards

2005-06 ITG Ultimate Memorabilia Future Stars Autos

PRINT RUN 40 SER #'d SETS
GOLD PRINT RUN 10 SER #'d SETS
GOLD NOT PRICED DUE TO SCARCITY
1 Marc-Andre Fleury 20.00 50.00
2 Henrik Lundqvist 20.00 50.00
3 Marek Svatos 8.00 20.00
4 Ray Emery 12.00 30.00
5 Cam Ward 15.00 40.00
6 Sidney Crosby 100.00 175.00
7 Alexander Ovechkin 50.00 100.00
8 Evgeni Malkin 60.00 125.00
9 Cristobal Huet 15.00 40.00
10 Thomas Vanek 15.00 40.00
11 Al Montoya 10.00 25.00
12 Dion Phaneuf 20.00 50.00
13 Ryan Getzlaf 12.00 30.00
14 Marek Schwarz 8.00 20.00
15 David Ruzicka 8.00 20.00
16 Jason LaBarbera 8.00 20.00
17 Mike Richards 15.00 40.00
18 Petr Prucha 12.00 30.00
19 Angelo Esposito 20.00 50.00
20 Michael Frolik 12.00 30.00
21 Eric Nystrom 8.00 20.00
22 Antero Niittymaki 12.00 30.00

2005-06 ITG Ultimate Memorabilia Future Stars Jerseys

PRINT RUN 25 SER. #'d SETS
GOLD PRINT RUN 10 SER. #'d SETS
GOLD NOT PRICED DUE TO SCARCITY
1 Marc-Andre Fleury 30.00 60.00
2 Henrik Lundqvist 30.00 60.00
3 Marek Svatos 20.00 40.00
4 Ray Emery 20.00 40.00
5 Cam Ward 25.00 50.00
6 Sidney Crosby 60.00 150.00
7 Alexander Ovechkin 40.00 100.00
8 Evgeni Malkin 60.00 150.00
9 Antero Niittymaki 20.00 40.00
10 Thomas Vanek 20.00 40.00
11 Al Montoya
12 Dion Phaneuf 30.00 60.00
13 Ryan Getzlaf 20.00 40.00
14 Corey Perry
15 Marek Schwarz 10.00 25.00
16 David Ruzicka 10.00 25.00
17 Jason LaBarbera 10.00 25.00
18 Mike Richards 20.00 40.00
19 Petr Prucha 25.00 50.00

2005-06 ITG Ultimate Memorabilia Future Stars Memorabilia Autos

PRINT RUN 40 SER #'d SETS
GOLD PRINT RUN 10 SER #'d SETS
GOLD NOT PRICED DUE TO SCARCITY
1 Marc-Andre Fleury 20.00 40.00
2 Henrik Lundqvist 30.00 60.00
3 Marek Svatos 10.00 25.00
4 Ray Emery 10.00 25.00
5 Cam Ward 12.00 30.00
6 Sidney Crosby 125.00 200.00
7 Alexander Ovechkin 75.00 125.00
8 Evgeni Malkin 75.00 200.00
9 Antero Niittymaki 12.00 30.00
10 Thomas Vanek 25.00 50.00
11 Al Montoya 12.00 30.00
12 Dion Phaneuf 30.00 60.00
13 Ryan Getzlaf 12.00 30.00
14 Marek Schwarz 12.00 30.00
15 David Ruzicka 10.00 25.00
16 Jason LaBarbera 10.00 25.00
17 Mike Richards 12.00 30.00
18 Petr Prucha 12.00 30.00

2005-06 ITG Ultimate Memorabilia Gloves Are Off

PRINT RUN 25 SER. #'d SETS
GOLD 1/1 VERSION EXISTS
GOLD NOT PRICED DUE TO SCARCITY
1 Sidney Crosby 60.00 125.00
2 Alexander Ovechkin 40.00 80.00
3 Mario Lemieux 40.00 80.00
4 Paul Coffey 20.00 40.00
5 Maurice Richard 50.00 100.00
6 Steve Yzerman 30.00 60.00
7 Raymond Bourque 25.00 50.00
8 Patrick Roy 40.00 80.00
9 Cam Neely 25.00 50.00
10 Brett Hull 25.00 50.00
11 King Clancy 20.00 40.00
12 Glenn Hall 20.00 40.00
13 Jacques Plante 30.00 60.00
14 Ace Bailey 20.00 40.00
15 Charlie Conacher 20.00 40.00
16 Bill Durnan 20.00 40.00
17 Stan Mikita 20.00 40.00
18 Eddie Shore 25.00 50.00
19 Howie Morenz 40.00 80.00
20 Aurel Joliat 20.00 40.00

2005-06 ITG Ultimate Memorabilia Goalie Gear

PRINT RUN 25 SER. #'d SETS
GOLD 1/1 VERSION EXISTS
GOLD NOT PRICED DUE TO SCARCITY
1 Bernie Parent 20.00 50.00
2 Bill Durnan 20.00 50.00
3 Billy Smith 20.00 50.00
4 Ed Giacomin 20.00 50.00
5 Frank Brimsek 20.00 50.00
6 George Hainsworth 25.00 60.00
7 Gerry Cheevers 20.00 50.00
8 Glenn Hall 20.00 50.00
9 Gump Worsley 20.00 50.00
10 Harry Lumley 15.00 30.00
11 Jacques Plante 40.00 80.00
12 Johnny Bower 20.00 50.00
13 Martin Brodeur 25.00 60.00
14 Patrick Roy MON 50.00 100.00
15 Patrick Roy COL 30.00 80.00
16 Pelle Lindbergh 25.00 60.00
17 Jose Theodore 15.00 40.00
18 Ron Hextall 20.00 50.00
19 Tiny Thompson 20.00 50.00
20 Tony Esposito 20.00 50.00

2005-06 ITG Ultimate Memorabilia In The Numbers

PRINT RUN 10 SER. #'d SETS
NOT PRICED DUE TO SCARCITY
GOLD 1/1 VERSION EXISTS
GOLD NOT PRICED DUE TO SCARCITY

2005-06 ITG Ultimate Memorabilia Jersey and Emblem

PRINT RUN 10 SER. #'d SETS
NOT PRICED DUE TO SCARCITY
GOLD 1/1 VERSION EXISTS
GOLD NOT PRICED DUE TO SCARCITY
1 Jari Kurri
2 Guy Lafleur
3 Ron Hextall
4 Jose Theodore
5 Steve Yzerman
6 Brian Leetch
7 Martin Brodeur
8 Patrick Roy MON
9 Patrick Roy COL
10 Raymond Bourque
11 Cam Neely
12 Mario Lemieux
13 Wendel Clark
14 Denis Potvin
15 Lanny McDonald
16 Marcel Dionne
17 Mike Bossy
18 Brett Hull
19 Bobby Hull
20 Pat LaFontaine
21 Frank Mahovlich
22 Sidney Crosby
23 Alexander Ovechkin
24 Evgeni Malkin
25 Al Montoya
26 Darryl Sittler
27 Dave Keon
28 Rod Gilbert
29 Jean Beliveau

2005-06 ITG Ultimate Memorabilia Jersey Autos

PRINT RUN 50 SER #'d SETS
GOLD PRINT RUN 10 SER #'d SETS
GOLD NOT PRICED DUE TO SCARCITY
1 Martin Brodeur 40.00 80.00
2 Marcel Dionne 12.00 30.00
3 Bobby Clarke 20.00 40.00
4 Phil Esposito 20.00 40.00
5 Tony Esposito 20.00 40.00
6 Ed Giacomin 20.00 40.00
7 Rod Gilbert 12.00 30.00
8 Doug Gilmour 12.00 30.00
9 Glenn Hall 20.00 40.00
10 Dany Heatley 20.00 40.00
11 Bobby Hull 25.00 50.00
12 Brett Hull
13 Dave Keon 25.00 50.00
14 Ilya Kovalchuk 25.00 50.00
15 Guy Lafleur 20.00 40.00
16 Brian Leetch 12.00 30.00
17 Mario Lemieux 50.00 100.00
18 Eric Lindros 20.00 40.00
19 Frank Mahovlich 20.00 40.00
20 Stan Mikita 20.00 40.00
21 Jean Beliveau 25.00 50.00
22 Gilbert Perreault 20.00 40.00
23 Henri Richard 20.00 40.00
24 Larry Robinson 12.00 30.00
25 Patrick Roy 50.00 100.00
26 Borje Salming 20.00 40.00
27 Jose Theodore 25.00 50.00
28 Vladislav Tretiak 40.00 80.00
29 Gump Worsley 20.00 40.00
30 Steve Yzerman 50.00 100.00
31 Wendel Clark 20.00 40.00
32 Brad Park 12.00 30.00
33 Denis Potvin 12.00 30.00
34 Lanny McDonald 12.00 30.00
35 Terry O'Reilly 12.00 30.00
36 Alexander Ovechkin 75.00 125.00
37 Sidney Crosby 125.00 200.00
38 Henrik Lundqvist 40.00 80.00
39 Marek Svatos 20.00 40.00
40 Antero Niittymaki 20.00 40.00

2005-06 ITG Ultimate Memorabilia Jerseys

PRINT RUN 25 SER. #'d SETS
GOLD 1/1 VERSION EXISTS
GOLD NOT PRICED DUE TO SCARCITY
1 Alexander Ovechkin 40.00 80.00
2 Bernie Parent 15.00 30.00
3 Bobby Clarke 20.00 40.00
4 Bobby Hull 15.00 40.00
5 Brett Hull 15.00 30.00
6 Brian Leetch 15.00 30.00
7 Bryan Trottier 15.00 30.00
8 Cam Neely 15.00 30.00
9 Darryl Sittler 15.00 30.00
10 Dave Keon 20.00 40.00
11 Denis Potvin 15.00 30.00
12 Doug Gilmour 15.00 30.00
13 Evgeni Malkin 40.00 80.00
14 Frank Mahovlich 15.00 30.00
15 Gilbert Perreault 20.00 40.00
16 Guy Lafleur 20.00 40.00
17 Henri Richard 15.00 30.00
18 Jacques Plante 25.00 50.00
19 Jari Kurri 25.00 50.00
20 Jean Beliveau 20.00 40.00
21 Jose Theodore 20.00 40.00
22 Lanny McDonald 20.00 40.00
23 Marcel Dionne 15.00 30.00
24 Mario Lemieux 40.00 80.00
25 Martin Brodeur 25.00 50.00
26 Mike Bossy 15.00 30.00
27 Pat LaFontaine 15.00 30.00
28 Patrick Roy
29 Paul Coffey 15.00 30.00
30 Phil Esposito 15.00 30.00
31 Raymond Bourque 20.00 40.00
32 Rod Gilbert 15.00 30.00
33 Ron Hextall 20.00 50.00
34 Sidney Crosby 60.00 125.00
35 Stan Mikita 20.00 40.00
36 Steve Yzerman 30.00 60.00
37 Terry Sawchuk
38 Tony Esposito 15.00 30.00
39 Wendel Clark 15.00 30.00

2005-06 ITG Ultimate Memorabilia Lumbergraphs

PRINT RUN 1/1
NOT PRICED DUE TO SCARCITY
1 George Hainsworth
2 Cecil Hart
3 Terry Sawchuk
4 Red Horner
5 Joe Primeau
6 Bill Barilko
7 Maurice Richard
8 Lester Patrick
9 Turk Broda
10 Lorne Chabot
11 Jack Adams
12 Babe Siebert

2005-06 ITG Ultimate Memorabilia Maple Leafs Forever Autos

PRINT RUN 1/1
NOT PRICED DUE TO SCARCITY
1 King Clancy
2 Red Horner
3 Syl Apps
4 Max Bentley
5 Turk Broda
6 Baldy Cotton
7 Alex Levinsky
8 Foster Hewitt
9 Busher Jackson
10 George Hainsworth
11 Flash Hollett
12 Charlie Conacher

2005-06 ITG Ultimate Memorabilia Marvelous Maroons Autos

PRINT RUN 1/1
NOT PRICED DUE TO SCARCITY
1 Russell Blinco
2 Herb Cain
3 Dave Trottier
4 Baldy Northcott
5 Gus Marker
6 Dave Kerr
7 Alex Connell
8 Lionel Conacher
9 Hooley Smith
10 Cy Wentworth

2005-06 ITG Ultimate Memorabilia Motown Heroes Autos

PRINT RUN 1/1
NOT PRICED DUE TO SCARCITY
1 Jimmy Orlando
2 Sid Abel
3 Ebbie Goodfellow
4 Jack Adams
5 Harry Lumley
6 Larry Aurie

2005-06 ITG Ultimate Memorabilia Paper Cut Autos

PRINT RUN 1/1
NOT PRICED DUE TO SCARCITY
1 Howie Morenz
2 Ace Bailey
3 King Clancy
4 George Hainsworth
5 Bullet Joe Simpson
6 Lionel Conacher
7 Lorne Chabot
8 Bill Barilko
9 Hap Day

2005-06 ITG Ultimate Memorabilia Passing the Torch Jerseys

COMMON CARD 30.00 60.00
PRINT RUN 25 SER. #'d SETS
GOLD 1/1 VERSION EXISTS
GOLD NOT PRICED DUE TO SCARCITY
1 Maurice Richard 150.00 250.00
Mario Lemieux
Sidney Crosby
2 Jacques Plante 90.00 150.00
Patrick Roy
Jose Theodore
3 Alexander Kharlamov/Vladimir Krutov/Alexander Ovechkin 40.00 80.00
4 Terry Sawchuk 60.00 100.00
Grant Fuhr
Martin Brodeur
5 Tiny Thompson 40.00 80.00
Gerry Cheevers
Gilles Gilbert
6 Eddie Shore 60.00 100.00
Brad Park
Ray Bourque
7 Johnny Bower 75.00 125.00
Gerry Cheevers
Patrick Roy
8 Doug Harvey 30.00 60.00
Serge Savard
Larry Robinson
9 Roy Worters 30.00 60.00
Ed Giacomin
Mike Richter
10 Ted Lindsay 60.00 100.00
Alex Delvecchio
Steve Yzerman
11 Bill Mosienko 30.00 80.00
Stan Mikita
Denis Savard
12 Bobby Hull 40.00 80.00
Dennis Hull
Brett Hull
13 Aurel Joliat 60.00 100.00
Jean Believeau
Guy Lafleur
14 Charlie Gardiner 40.00 80.00
Glenn Hall
Tony Esposito
15 Bernie Parent 50.00 100.00
Pelle Lindbergh
Ron Hextall
16 Tim Horton 40.00 80.00
Borje Salming
Brian Leetch
17 John Ferguson 40.00 80.00
Dave Schultz
Bob Probert
18 Patrick Roy 75.00 125.00
Martin Brodeur
Marc-Andre Fleury
19 Dave Keon 30.00 60.00
Bryan Trottier
Doug Gilmour
20 Gilbert Perreault 30.00 60.00
Pat LaFontaine
Thomas Vanek

2005-06 ITG Ultimate Memorabilia Quadruple Paper Cuts Autos

PRINT RUN 1/1
NOT PRICED DUE TO SCARCITY
1 Bill Cowley
Frank Brimsek
Mel Hill
Harry Oliver
2 Al Rollins
Tommy Ivan
Lionel Conacher
Earl Seibert
3 Jack Stewart
Harry Lumley
Sid Abel
Mud Bruneteau
4 Toe Blake
Bernie Geoffrion
Doug Harvey
Jacques Plante
5 Frank Boucher
Bryan Hextall Sr.
Bun Cook
Chuck Rayner
6 King Clancy
Ace Bailey
Red Horner
Hap Day

2005-06 ITG Ultimate Memorabilia R.O.Y. Autos

PRINT RUN 39 SER #'d SETS
GOLD 1/1 VERSION EXISTS
GOLD NOT PRICED DUE TO SCARCITY
1 Brian Leetch 20.00 40.00
2 Denis Potvin 15.00 30.00
3 Thomas Vanek 20.00 40.00
4 Cam Ward 20.00 40.00
5 Dion Phaneuf 30.00 60.00
6 Sidney Crosby 125.00 250.00
7 Mike Richards 15.00 30.00
8 Henrik Lundqvist 25.00 50.00
9 Petr Prucha 10.00 25.00
10 Jason LaBarbera 10.00 25.00
11 Dany Heatley 20.00 40.00
12 Dave Keon 25.00 50.00
13 Tony Esposito 20.00 40.00
14 Martin Brodeur 40.00 80.00
15 Marek Svatos 15.00 30.00
16 Gilbert Perreault 15.00 30.00
17 Raymond Bourque 25.00 50.00
18 Mario Lemieux 60.00 125.00
19 Antero Niittymaki 15.00 30.00
20 Alexander Ovechkin 60.00 120.00

2005-06 ITG Ultimate Memorabilia R.O.Y. Emblems

PRINT RUN 10 SER. #'d SETS
NOT PRICED DUE TO SCARCITY
GOLD 1/1 VERSION EXISTS
GOLD NOT PRICED DUE TO SCARCITY
1 Dave Keon
2 Tony Esposito
3 Gilbert Perreault
4 Raymond Bourque
5 Mario Lemieux
6 Brian Leetch
7 Martin Brodeur
8 Dany Heatley
9 Alexander Ovechkin
10 Sidney Crosby
11 Henrik Lundqvist
12 Dion Phaneuf
13 Petr Prucha
14 Marek Svatos
15 Thomas Vanek

2005-06 ITG Ultimate Memorabilia R.O.Y. Jerseys

PRINT RUN 25 SER. #'d SETS
NOT PRICED DUE TO SCARCITY
GOLD 1/1 VERSION EXISTS
GOLD NOT PRICED DUE TO SCARCITY
1 Dave Keon
2 Tony Esposito
3 Gilbert Perreault
4 Raymond Bourque
5 Mario Lemieux
6 Brian Leetch
7 Martin Brodeur
8 Dany Heatley
9 Alexander Ovechkin
10 Sidney Crosby
11 Henrik Lundqvist
12 Dion Phaneuf
13 Petr Prucha
14 Marek Svatos
15 Thomas Vanek

2005-06 ITG Ultimate Memorabilia R.O.Y. Numbers

PRINT RUN 10 SER. #'d SETS
NOT PRICED DUE TO SCARCITY
GOLD 1/1 VERSION EXISTS
GOLD NOT PRICED DUE TO SCARCITY

1 Dave Keon
2 Tony Esposito
3 Gilbert Perreault
4 Raymond Bourque
5 Mario Lemieux
6 Brian Leetch
7 Martin Brodeur
8 Dany Heatley
9 Alexander Ovechkin
10 Sidney Crosby
11 Henrik Lundqvist
12 Dion Phaneuf
13 Petr Prucha
14 Marek Svatos
15 Thomas Vanek

2005-06 ITG Ultimate Memorabilia Raised to the Rafters

PRINT RUN 25 SER. #'d SETS
NOT PRICED DUE TO SCARCITY
GOLD 1/1 VERSION EXISTS
GOLD NOT PRICED DUE TO SCARCITY
1 Mario Lemieux
2 Henri Richard
3 Grant Fuhr
4 Bobby Clarke
5 Darryl Sittler
6 Mike Bossy
7 Pat LaFontaine
8 Gilbert Perreault
9 Bernie Parent
10 Denis Potvin
11 Alex Delvecchio
12 Yvan Cournoyer
13 Lanny McDonald
14 Tim Horton
15 Patrick Roy
16 Raymond Bourque
17 Cam Neely
18 Stan Mikita
19 Bobby Hull
20 Jean Beliveau

2005-06 ITG Ultimate Memorabilia Record Breakers Jerseys

PRINT RUN 25 SER. #'d SETS
NOT PRICED DUE TO SCARCITY
GOLD 1/1 VERSION EXISTS
GOLD NOT PRICED DUE TO SCARCITY
1 Newsy Lalonde
Reggie Leach
2 Bobby Hull
Phil Esposito
3 Elmer Lach
Ted Lindsay
4 Jean Beliveau
Stan Mikita
5 Bill Mosienko
Dale Hawerchuk
6 Patrick Roy
Martin Brodeur
7 Bobby Hull
Steve Shutt
8 Guy Lafleur
Mike Bossy
9 Jari Kurri
Brett Hull
10 Darryl Sittler
Bryan Trottier
11 George Hainsworth
Terry Sawchuk
12 Terry Sawchuk
Patrick Roy
13 Grant Fuhr
Patrick Roy
14 Terry Sawchuk
Bernie Parent
15 Tony Esposito
Patrick Roy
16 Stan Mikita
Phil Esposito
17 Nels Stewart
Maurice Richard
18 Paul Coffey
Raymond Bourque
19 Dave Schultz
Tiger Williams
20 Denis Potvin
Paul Coffey

2005-06 ITG Ultimate Memorabilia Retro Teammates Jerseys

PRINT RUN 25 SER. #'d SETS
GOLD 1/1 VERSION EXISTS
GOLD NOT PRICED DUE TO SCARCITY
1 Mike Bossy 15.00 30.00
Bryan Trottier
2 Eddie Shore 20.00 40.00
Tiny Thompson
3 Billy Smith 20.00 40.00
Denis Potvin
4 Ted Lindsay 15.00 30.00
Sid Abel
5 Paul Coffey 30.00 75.00
Mario Lemieux
6 Jari Kurri 25.00 50.00
Grant Fuhr
7 George Hainsworth 25.00 50.00
Aurel Joliat
8 Bobby Clarke 20.00 40.00
Bernie Parent
9 Darryl Sittler 15.00 30.00
Borje Salming
10 Jean Beliveau 20.00 40.00
Frank Mahovlich
11 Doug Gilmour 20.00 40.00
Wendel Clark
12 Henri Richard 20.00 40.00
Frank Mahovlich
13 Guy Lafleur 20.00 40.00
Yvan Cournoyer
14 Patrick Roy 30.00 60.00
Larry Robinson
15 Jean Beliveau 40.00 80.00
Doug Harvey
16 Steve Shutt 20.00 40.00
Guy Lafleur
17 Gerry Cheevers 15.00 30.00
Terry O'Reilly
18 Patrick Roy 30.00 60.00
Raymond Bourque
19 Cam Neely 20.00 50.00
Raymond Bourque
20 Tim Horton
Red Kelly
21 Jean Ratelle 15.00 30.00
Ed Giacomin
22 Phil Esposito
Rod Gilbert
23 Tony Esposito 15.00 30.00
Denis Savard
24 Alex Delvecchio 15.00 30.00
Norm Ullman
25 Dino Ciccarelli 20.00 50.00
Steve Yzerman
26 Michel Goulet 15.00 30.00
Denis Savard
27 Stan Mikita
Bobby Hull
28 Bill Mosienko 15.00 30.00
Harry Lumley
29 Mike Richter 15.00 30.00
Brian Leetch
30 Valeri Kharlamov
Vladislav Tretiak

2005-06 ITG Ultimate Memorabilia Seams Unbelievable

PRINT RUN 15 SER. #'d SETS
NOT PRICED DUE TO SCARCITY
GOLD 1/1 VERSION EXISTS
GOLD NOT PRICED DUE TO SCARCITY
1 Mario Lemieux
2 Patrick Roy
3 Raymond Bourque
4 Steve Yzerman
5 Martin Brodeur
6 Henri Richard
7 Glenn Hall
8 Eric Lindros
9 Tony Esposito
10 Ron Hextall
11 Alexander Ovechkin
12 Phil Esposito
13 Bobby Hull
14 Lanny McDonald
15 Gerry Cheevers
16 Pat LaFontaine
17 Frank Mahovlich
18 Valeri Kharlamov
19 Brian Leetch
20 Borje Salming

2005-06 ITG Ultimate Memorabilia Sextuple Autos

PRINT RUN 1/1
NOT PRICED DUE TO SCARCITY
1 Gerry Cheevers
Patrick Roy
Martin Brodeur
Johnny Bower
Gump Worsley
To
2 Dion Phaneuf
Corey Perry
Mike Richards
Henrik Lundqvist
Alexander Ovech
3 Eric Lindros
Ilya Kovalchuk
Dany Heatley
Mario Lemieux
Steve Yzerman
B
4 Frank Mahovlich
Bobby Hull
Stan Mikita
Jean Beliveau
Henri Richard
Dav
5 Marcel Dionne
Mike Bossy
Darryl Sittler
Guy Lafleur
Bobby Clarke
Phil

2005-06 ITG Ultimate Memorabilia Stick Autos

COMMON CARD 15.00 30.00
PRINT RUN 50 SER #'d SETS
GOLD PRINT RUN 10 SER. #'d SETS
GOLD NOT PRICED DUE TO SCARCITY
1 Jean Beliveau 25.00 50.00
2 Raymond Bourque 25.00 50.00
3 Martin Brodeur 40.00 80.00
4 Marcel Dionne 15.00 30.00
5 Phil Esposito 20.00 40.00
6 Grant Fuhr 25.00 50.00
7 Gerry Cheevers 20.00 40.00
8 Glenn Hall 20.00 40.00
9 Dany Heatley 20.00 40.00
10 Ron Francis 20.00 40.00
11 Red Kelly 25.00 50.00
12 Dave Keon 20.00 40.00
13 Ilya Kovalchuk 25.00 50.00
14 Vladimir Krutov 20.00 40.00
15 Guy Lafleur 20.00 40.00
16 Brian Leetch 15.00 30.00
17 Mario Lemieux 50.00 100.00
18 Eric Lindros 20.00 40.00
19 Petr Prucha 20.00 40.00
20 Cam Neely 25.00 50.00
21 Bernie Parent 15.00 30.00
22 Gilbert Perreault 20.00 40.00
23 Jose Theodore 15.00 40.00
24 Gump Worsley 20.00 40.00
25 Steve Yzerman 40.00 80.00
26 Marek Svatos 20.00 40.00
27 Paul Coffey 15.00 30.00
28 Bill Barber 15.00 30.00
29 Marc-Andre Fleury 25.00 50.00
30 Alexander Ovechkin 75.00 125.00
31 Sidney Crosby 125.00 250.00
32 Ed Giacomin 20.00 40.00
33 Antero Niittymaki 20.00 40.00
34 Frank Mahovlich 20.00 40.00
35 Patrick Roy 50.00 100.00
36 Wendel Clark 15.00 30.00
37 Denis Potvin 15.00 30.00
38 Doug Gilmour 20.00 40.00
39 Lanny McDonald 20.00 40.00
40 Stan Mikita 15.00 30.00

2005-06 ITG Ultimate Memorabilia Sticks and Jerseys

PRINT RUN 25 SER. #'d SETS
GOLD 1/1 VERSION EXISTS
GOLD NOT PRICED DUE TO SCARCITY
1 Mario Lemieux 30.00 60.00
2 Steve Yzerman 30.00 60.00
3 Ilya Kovalchuk 12.00 30.00
4 Phil Esposito 12.00 30.00
5 Eric Lindros 12.00 30.00
6 Alexander Ovechkin 30.00 60.00
7 Sidney Crosby 60.00 100.00
8 Doug Harvey 15.00 40.00
9 Dany Heatley 12.00 30.00
10 Jean Beliveau 15.00 40.00
11 Guy Lafleur 12.00 30.00
12 Pat LaFontaine 12.00 30.00
13 Jari Kurri 12.00 30.00
14 Red Kelly 12.00 30.00
15 Lanny McDonald 12.00 30.00
16 Cam Neely 12.00 30.00
17 Mark Howe 12.00 30.00
18 Paul Coffey 12.00 30.00
19 Denis Potvin 12.00 30.00
20 Steve Shutt 12.00 30.00
21 Gump Worsley 12.00 30.00
22 Roger Crozier 12.00 30.00
23 Ed Giacomin 12.00 30.00
24 Grant Fuhr 12.00 30.00
25 Marc-Andre Fleury 15.00 40.00
26 Tony Esposito 15.00 40.00
27 Patrick Roy
28 Martin Brodeur 25.00 50.00
29 Ron Hextall 12.00 30.00
30 Jacques Plante 15.00 40.00

2005-06 ITG Ultimate Memorabilia The Holy Grail Auto

PRINT RUN 1/1
NOT PRICED DUE TO SCARCITY
1 Lord Stanley of Preston

2005-06 ITG Ultimate Memorabilia Three Stars of the Game Jerseys

PRINT RUN 25 SER. #'d SETS
GOLD 1/1 VERSION EXISTS
GOLD NOT PRICED DUE TO SCARCITY
1 Eddie Shore 20.00 50.00
Tiny Thompson
Aurel Joliat
2 Doug Harvey 20.00 50.00
Ted Kennedy
Bill Durnan
3 Frank Brimsek 20.00 50.00
Bill Mosienko
Sid Abel
4 Jacques Plante
Ted Lindsay
Henri Richard
5 Bernie Geoffrion 20.00 50.00
Dickie Moore
Tim Horton
6 Frank Mahovlich 20.00 50.00
Bobby Hull
Red Kelly
7 Alex Delvecchio 20.00 50.00
Dave Keon
Norm Ullman
8 Gump Worsley 30.00 60.00
Jean Beliveau
Johnny Bower
9 Roger Crozier 20.00 50.00
Glenn Hall
Stan Mikita
10 Jean Ratelle 20.00 50.00
Ed Giacomin
Johnny Bucyk
11 Guy Lafleur 20.00 50.00
Steve Shutt
Gerry Cheevers
12 Terry O'Reilly 20.00 50.00
Tony Esposito
Brad Park
13 Darryl Sittler 20.00 50.00
Serge Savard
Yvon Cournoyer
14 Phil Esposito 20.00 50.00
Bob Nystrom
Rod Gilbert
15 Gilbert Perreault 20.00 50.00
Bobby Clarke
Reggie Leach
16 Billy Smith 20.00 50.00
Glen Anderson
Bryan Trottier
17 Jari Kurri 50.00
Lanny McDonald
Grant Fuhr
18 Patrick Roy 30.00 60.00
Larry Robinson
Rick Middleton
19 Tiger Williams 20.00 50.00
Marcel Dionne
Richard Brodeur
20 Denis Potvin 20.00 50.00
Pat Verbeek
Mike Bossy
21 Borje Salming 20.00 50.00
Denis Savard
Rick Vaive
22 Steve Yzerman 30.00 60.00
Doug Gilmour
Wendel Clark
23 Mike Richter 20.00 50.00
Kirk McLean
Brian Leetch
24 Ray Bourque 75.00 125.00
Martin Brodeur
Patrick Roy
25 Dion Phaneuf 100.00 200.00
Sidney Crosby
Alexander Ovechkin

2005-06 ITG Ultimate Memorabilia Trifecta Autos

PRINT RUN 18 SER. #'d SETS
NOT PRICED DUE TO SCARCITY
GOLD 1/1 VERSION EXISTS
GOLD NOT PRICED DUE TO SCARCITY
1 Bobby Hull
2 Dave Keon
3 Bernie Parent
4 Jean Beliveau
5 Martin Brodeur
6 Sidney Crosby
7 Mario Lemieux
8 Steve Yzerman
9 Patrick Roy
10 Alexander Ovechkin

2005-06 ITG Ultimate Memorabilia Triple Autos

PRINT RUN 9 SER. #'d SETS
NOT PRICED DUE TO SCARCITY
GOLD 1/1 VERSION EXISTS
GOLD NOT PRICED DUE TO SCARCITY
1 Bobby Hull
Stan Mikita
Glenn Hall
2 Bobby Clarke
Bill Barber
Bernie Parent
3 Kari Lehtonen
Cam Ward
Christobal Huet
4 Vladislav Tretiak
Alexander Yakushev
Vladimir Krutov
5 Dave Keon
Ted Kennedy
Doug Gilmour
6 Darryl Sittler
Lanny McDonald
Borje Salming
7 Dany Heatley
Ilya Kovalchuk
Alexander Ovechkin
8 Guy Lafleur
Jean Beliveau
Henri Richard
9 Martin Brodeur
Patrick Roy
Jose Theodore
10 Phil Esposito
Tony Esposito
Angelo Esposito
11 Cam Neely
Ray Bourque
Terry O'Reilly
12 Paul Henderson
Phil Esposito
Vladislav Tretiak
13 Marc-Andre Fleury
Christobal Huet
Henrik Lundqvist
14 Marek Svatos
Dion Phaneuf
Alexander Ovechkin
15 Henrik Lundqvist
Ed Giacomin
Gump Worsley
16 Brian Leetch
Jim Craig
Pat LaFontaine
17 Mario Lemieux
Jean Beliveau
Marcel Dionne
18 Alexander Ovechkin
Evgeni Malkin
Ilya Kovalchuk
19 Denis Potvin
Brad Park
Larry Robinson
20 Brett Hull
Steve Yzerman
Ted Lindsay

2005-06 ITG Ultimate Memorabilia Triple Threads Jerseys

PRINT RUN 25 SER. #'d SETS
GOLD 1/1 VERSION EXISTS
GOLD NOT PRICED DUE TO SCARCITY
1 Alexander Ovechkin 75.00 175.00
Sidney Crosby
Evgeni Malkin
2 Martin Brodeur 60.00 100.00
Patrick Roy
Marc-Andre Fleury
3 Steve Yzerman 60.00 100.00
Mario Lemieux
Cam Neely
4 Billy Smith 25.00 60.00
Ron Hextall
Grant Fuhr
5 Ray Bourque 25.00 60.00
Larry Robinson
Denis Potvin
6 Bobby Hull 25.00 60.00
Frank Mahovlich
Norm Ullman
7 Henri Richard 25.00 60.00
Dave Keon
Stan Mikita
8 Johnny Bower 40.00 80.00
Glenn Hall
Jacques Plante
9 Bernie Parent 40.00 80.00
Gerry Cheevers
Tony Esposito
10 Guy Lafleur 25.00 60.00
Marcel Dionne
Gilbert Perreault

2005-06 ITG Ultimate Memorabilia Ultimate Autos

PRINT RUN 50 SER #'d SETS
GOLD PRINT RUN 10 SER. #'d SETS
GOLD NOT PRICED DUE TO SCARCITY
1 Steve Yzerman 25.00 60.00
2 Gump Worsley 20.00 40.00
3 Valeri Vasilyev 15.00 30.00
4 Vladislav Tretiak 25.00 50.00
5 Darryl Sittler 15.00 30.00
6 Tod Sloan 10.00 25.00
7 Milt Schmidt 15.00 30.00
8 Borje Salming 20.00 40.00
9 Patrick Roy 40.00 100.00
10 Larry Robinson 10.00 25.00
11 Henri Richard 15.00 30.00
12 Jean Ratelle 10.00 25.00
13 Gilbert Perreault 15.00 30.00
14 Bernie Parent 20.00 40.00
15 Cam Neely 20.00 40.00
16 Stan Mikita 15.00 30.00
17 Frank Mahovlich 15.00 30.00
18 Ted Lindsay
19 Eric Lindros 20.00 40.00
20 Mario Lemieux 60.00 120.00
21 Brian Leetch 10.00 25.00
22 Pat LaFontaine 15.00 30.00
23 Guy Lafleur 20.00 40.00
24 Elmer Lach 20.00 40.00
25 Vladimir Krutov
26 Alexander Yakushev 20.00 40.00
27 Dave Keon 20.00 40.00
28 Ted Kennedy 10.00 25.00
29 Red Kelly 10.00 25.00
30 Brett Hull 20.00 40.00
31 Bobby Hull 20.00 40.00
32 Paul Henderson 10.00 25.00
33 Dany Heatley 15.00 30.00
34 Glenn Hall 15.00 30.00
35 Doug Gilmour 20.00 40.00
36 Rod Gilbert 10.00 25.00
37 Ed Giacomin 10.00 25.00
38 Grant Fuhr 25.00 50.00
39 Tony Esposito 15.00 30.00
40 Phil Esposito 15.00 30.00
41 Bobby Clarke 15.00 30.00
42 Marcel Dionne 10.00 25.00
43 Paul Coffey 20.00 40.00
44 Jim Craig 25.00 50.00
45 Yvan Cournoyer 15.00 30.00
46 Gerry Cheevers 20.00 40.00
47 Martin Brodeur 30.00 80.00
48 Raymond Bourque 20.00 40.00
49 Mike Bossy 15.00 30.00
50 Jean Beliveau 25.00 50.00

2005-06 ITG Ultimate Memorabilia Ultimate Hero Double Jerseys

PRINT RUN 20 SER. #'d SETS
NOT PRICED DUE TO SCARCITY
GOLD 1/1 VERSION EXISTS
GOLD NOT PRICED DUE TO SCARCITY
1 Terry Sawchuk
2 Maurice Richard
3 Jacques Plante
4 Dave Keon
5 Mario Lemieux
6 Patrick Roy
7 Martin Brodeur
8 Steve Yzerman

2005-06 ITG Ultimate Memorabilia Ultimate Hero Single Jerseys

PRINT RUN 20 SER. #'d SETS
NOT PRICED DUE TO SCARCITY
GOLD 1/1 VERSION EXISTS
GOLD NOT PRICED DUE TO SCARCITY
1 Terry Sawchuk
2 Maurice Richard
3 Jacques Plante
4 Dave Keon
5 Mario Lemieux
6 Patrick Roy
7 Martin Brodeur
8 Steve Yzerman

2005-06 ITG Ultimate Memorabilia Ultimate Hero Triple Jerseys

PRINT RUN 25 SER. #'d SETS
NOT PRICED DUE TO SCARCITY
GOLD 1/1 VERSION EXISTS
GOLD NOT PRICED DUE TO SCARCITY
1 Terry Sawchuk
2 Maurice Richard
3 Jacques Plante
4 Dave Keon
5 Mario Lemieux
6 Patrick Roy
7 Martin Brodeur
8 Steve Yzerman

2005-06 ITG Ultimate Memorabilia Vintage Lumber

PRINT RUN 25 SER. #'d SETS
GOLD 1/1 VERSION EXISTS
GOLD NOT PRICED DUE TO SCARCITY
1 Howie Morenz 50.00 100.00
2 Georges Vezina 60.00 125.00
3 Jacques Plante 25.00 60.00
4 Henri Richard 15.00 40.00
5 Maurice Richard 60.00 120.00
6 Terry Sawchuk 60.00 120.00
7 Bernie Geoffrion 15.00 40.00
8 Joe Primeau 15.00 40.00
9 Red Kelly 15.00 40.00
10 Doug Harvey 15.00 40.00
11 Stan Mikita 20.00 50.00
12 Johnny Bucyk 15.00 40.00
13 Glenn Hall 20.00 50.00
14 Bill Durnan 15.00 40.00
15 Jean Beliveau 20.00 50.00
16 Bobby Hull 60.00 120.00
17 Harry Lumley 20.00 50.00
18 Ed Giacomin 15.00 40.00
19 Dave Keon 25.00 60.00
20 Alex Delvecchio 15.00 40.00
21 Turk Broda 15.00 40.00
22 Tim Horton 25.00 60.00
23 Bob Davidson 12.00 30.00
24 Frank Mahovlich 15.00 40.00
25 Phil Esposito 15.00 40.00
26 Emile Francis 15.00 40.00
27 King Clancy 25.00 60.00
28 Bill Barilko 40.00 80.00
29 Gump Worsley 15.00 40.00
30 Roger Crozier 12.00 30.00

2006-07 ITG Ultimate Memorabilia

1 Ace Bailey 4.00 10.00
2 Al Montoya 3.00 8.00
3 Alex Connell 5.00 12.00
4 Alex Delvecchio 4.00 10.00
5 Alexander Ovechkin 8.00 20.00
6 Anders Hedberg 3.00 8.00
7 Angelo Esposito 8.00 20.00
8 Antero Niittymaki 3.00 8.00
9 Art Ross 4.00 10.00
10 Aurel Joliat 5.00 12.00
11 Babe Pratt 4.00 10.00
12 Bernie Geoffrion 5.00 12.00
13 Bernie Parent 4.00 10.00
14 Bill Barber 3.00 8.00
15 Bill Barilko 4.00 10.00
16 Bill Durnan 4.00 10.00
17 Bobby Clarke 4.00 10.00
18 Bobby Hull 5.00 12.00
19 Borje Salming 4.00 10.00
20 Brad Park 3.00 8.00
21 Brett Hull 5.00 12.00
22 Brian Leetch 4.00 10.00
23 Bryan Trottier 4.00 10.00
24 Butch Bouchard 3.00 8.00
25 Cam Neely 5.00 12.00
26 Cam Ward 5.00 12.00
27 Charlie Conacher 4.00 10.00
28 Charlie Gardiner 3.00 8.00
29 Ching Johnson 3.00 8.00
30 Chris Chelios 5.00 12.00
31 Clarence Campbell 3.00 8.00
32 Conn Smythe 3.00 8.00
33 Cristobal Huet 5.00 12.00
34 Cyclone Taylor 15.00 40.00
35 Dany Heatley 6.00 15.00
36 Darryl Sittler 5.00 12.00
37 Dave Keon 6.00 15.00
38 Dave Schultz 3.00 8.00
39 Denis Potvin 4.00 10.00
40 Dion Phaneuf 6.00 15.00
41 Dominik Hasek 6.00 15.00
42 Doug Gilmour 5.00 12.00
43 Ed Belfour 4.00 10.00
44 Ed Giacomin 4.00 10.00
45 Ed Olczyk 3.00 8.00
46 Eddie Shore 4.00 10.00
47 Eric Staal 3.00 8.00
48 Evgeni Malkin 8.00 20.00
49 Foster Hewitt 3.00 8.00
50 Frank Calder 3.00 8.00
51 Frank Mahovlich 4.00 10.00
52 George Hainsworth 6.00 15.00
53 Georges Vezina 6.00 15.00
54 Gerry Cheevers 5.00 12.00
55 Gilbert Brule 3.00 8.00
56 Gilbert Perreault 5.00 12.00
57 Glenn Hall 5.00 12.00
58 Grant Fuhr 6.00 15.00
59 Gump Worsley 4.00 10.00
60 Guy Lafleur 5.00 12.00
61 Guy Lapointe 3.00 8.00
62 Hap Day 3.00 8.00
63 Henri Richard 4.00 10.00
64 Henrik Lundqvist 6.00 15.00
65 Henrik Zetterberg 5.00 12.00
66 Herb Carnegie 15.00 40.00
67 Hobey Baker 4.00 10.00
68 Howie Morenz 6.00 15.00
69 Igor Larionov 3.00 8.00
70 Jack Adams 3.00 8.00
71 Jacques Plante 6.00 15.00
72 Jari Kurri 5.00 12.00
73 Jaromir Jagr 6.00 15.00
74 Jason Spezza 5.00 12.00
75 Jean Beliveau 5.00 12.00
76 Jean Ratelle 3.00 8.00
77 Joe Malone 4.00 10.00
78 Joe Sakic 8.00 20.00
79 Joe Thornton 8.00 20.00
80 John Bucyk 4.00 10.00
81 John Tavares 10.00 25.00
82 Johnny Bower 5.00 12.00
83 Jordan Staal 6.00 15.00
84 Kari Lehtonen 4.00 10.00
85 Lady Byng 3.00 8.00
86 Lanny McDonald 4.00 10.00
87 Larry Robinson 4.00 10.00
88 Lester Patrick 3.00 8.00
89 Lionel Conacher 3.00 8.00
90 Ilya Kovalchuk 6.00 15.00
91 Lord Stanley 4.00 10.00
92 Luc Robitaille 5.00 12.00
93 Lynn Patrick 3.00 8.00
94 Marc-Andre Fleury 5.00 12.00
95 Marcel Dionne 4.00 10.00
96 Mario Lemieux 10.00 25.00
97 Mark Messier 5.00 12.00
98 Martin Brodeur 8.00 20.00
99 Marty Turco 3.00 8.00
100 Mats Naslund 4.00 10.00
101 Maurice Richard 6.00 15.00
102 Max Bentley 4.00 10.00
103 Michel Goulet 3.00 8.00
104 Mike Bossy 5.00 12.00
105 Mike Modano 5.00 12.00
106 Milt Schmidt 4.00 10.00
107 Newsy Lalonde 5.00 12.00
108 Nicklas Lidstrom 4.00 10.00
109 Pat LaFontaine 4.00 10.00
110 Patrick Roy Colorado 10.00 25.00
111 Patrick Roy Montreal 12.00 30.00
112 Paul Coffey 4.00 10.00
113 Paul Henderson 3.00 8.00
114 Pelle Lindbergh 5.00 12.00
115 Peter Stastny 3.00 8.00
116 Phil Esposito 5.00 12.00
117 Phil Kessel 5.00 12.00
118 Punch Imlach 3.00 8.00
119 Raymond Bourque 6.00 15.00
120 Red Kelly 3.00 8.00
121 Roberto Luongo 6.00 15.00
122 Rod Gilbert 3.00 8.00
123 Rogie Vachon 4.00 10.00
124 Ron Francis 4.00 10.00
125 Ron Hextall 4.00 10.00
126 Ryan Miller 4.00 10.00
127 Scotty Bowman 5.00 12.00
128 Serge Savard 4.00 10.00
129 Sid Abel 3.00 8.00
130 Stan Mikita 5.00 12.00
131 Steve Shutt 3.00 8.00
132 Steve Yzerman 10.00 25.00
133 Syl Apps 4.00 10.00
134 Ted Kennedy 4.00 10.00
135 Ted Lindsay 4.00 10.00
136 Terry Sawchuk 6.00 15.00
137 Tiger Williams 5.00 12.00
138 Tim Horton 5.00 12.00
139 Tiny Thompson 5.00 12.00
140 Toe Blake 3.00 8.00
141 Tom Barrasso 4.00 10.00
142 Tommy Ivan 3.00 8.00
143 Tony Esposito 5.00 12.00
144 Turk Broda 4.00 10.00
145 Ulf Nilsson 3.00 8.00
146 Valeri Kharlamov 5.00 12.00
147 Vladislav Tretiak 6.00 15.00
148 Wendel Clark 4.00 10.00
149 Willie O'Ree 3.00 8.00
150 Yvan Cournoyer 4.00 10.00

2006-07 ITG Ultimate Memorabilia Artist Proof

STATED PRINT RUN 10 #'d SETS
NOT PRICED DUE TO SCARCITY

2006-07 ITG Ultimate Memorabilia Amazing Amerks Autos

STATED PRINT RUN 1 SER.#'d SET
NOT PRICED DUE TO SCARCITY
1 Nels Stewart
2 Ching Johnson
3 Dave Schriner
4 Lorne Carr
5 Art Chapman
6 Hooley Smith
7 Hap Day
8 Earl Robertson

2006-07 ITG Ultimate Memorabilia Autos

STATED PRINT RUN 50 SER.#'d SETS
1 Bill Barber 10.00 25.00
2 Jean Beliveau 20.00 50.00
3 Martin Brodeur 25.00 60.00
4 Chris Chelios 10.00 25.00
5 Wendel Clark 12.00 30.00
6 Paul Coffey 12.00 30.00
7 Bobby Clarke 12.00 30.00
8 Alex Delvecchio 10.00 25.00
9 Marcel Dionne 10.00 25.00
10 Angelo Esposito 30.00 60.00
11 Phil Esposito 20.00 50.00
12 Tony Esposito 15.00 40.00
13 Doug Gilmour 12.00 30.00
14 Michel Goulet 12.00 30.00
15 Glenn Hall 15.00 40.00
16 Bobby Hull 15.00 40.00
17 Brett Hull 15.00 40.00
18 Jaromir Jagr 20.00 50.00
19 Dave Keon 20.00 50.00
20 Jari Kurri 20.00 50.00
21 Guy Lafleur 15.00 40.00
22 Pat LaFontaine 12.00 30.00
23 Lanny McDonald 10.00 25.00
24 Ted Lindsay 10.00 25.00
25 Mark Messier 40.00 100.00
26 Stan Mikita 15.00 40.00
27 Cam Neely 12.00 30.00
28 Brad Park 10.00 25.00
29 Gilbert Perreault 12.00 30.00
30 Larry Robinson 10.00 25.00
31 Darryl Sittler 15.00 40.00
32 Vladislav Tretiak 25.00 60.00
33 Bryan Trottier 10.00 25.00
34 Rogie Vachon 12.00 30.00
35 Gump Worsley 15.00 40.00
36 Denis Potvin 12.00 30.00
37 Ray Emery 10.00 25.00
38 Marc-Andre Fleury 12.00 30.00
39 Dominik Hasek 20.00 50.00
40 Dany Heatley 15.00 40.00
41 Cristobal Huet 12.00 30.00
42 Ilya Kovalchuk 20.00 50.00

43 Brian Leetch 12.00 30.00
44 Kari Lehtonen 12.00 30.00
45 Nicklas Lidstrom 15.00 40.00
46 Henrik Lundqvist 20.00 50.00
47 Roberto Luongo 20.00 50.00
48 Frank Mahovlich 15.00 40.00
49 Mike Modano 15.00 40.00
50 Alexander Ovechkin 30.00 60.00
51 Dion Phaneuf 15.00 40.00
52 Petr Prucha 10.00 25.00
53 Henri Richard 10.00 25.00
54 Patrick Roy 50.00 125.00
55 Joe Sakic 25.00 60.00
56 Eric Staal 12.00 30.00
57 John Tavares 75.00 175.00
58 Joe Thornton 20.00 50.00
59 Marty Turco 12.00 30.00
60 Cam Ward 10.00 25.00
61 Steve Yzerman 40.00 80.00
62 Henrik Zetterberg 15.00 40.00
63 Ed Belfour 15.00 40.00
64 Ryan Miller 15.00 40.00
65 Boris Mikhailov 10.00 25.00
66 Bernie Parent 15.00 40.00
67 Paul Henderson 10.00 25.00
68 Felix Potvin 20.00 50.00
69 Jason Spezza 12.00 30.00
70 Vincent Lecavalier 15.00 40.00
71 Thomas Vanek 15.00 40.00
72 Maurice Richard/30 250.00 400.00

2006-07 ITG Ultimate Memorabilia Autos Gold

STATED PRINT RUN 10 SER.#'d SETS
NOT PRICED DUE TO SCARCITY

2006-07 ITG Ultimate Memorabilia Autos Dual

STATED PRINT RUN 40 SER.#'d SETS
1 Jaromir Jagr 60.00 150.00
Mario Lemieux
2 Steve Yzerman 40.00 80.00
Ted Lindsay
3 Martin Brodeur 75.00 175.00
Patrick Roy
4 Eric Staal 25.00 50.00
Jordan Staal
5 Phil Kessel 20.00 50.00
Phil Esposito
6 Nicklas Lidstrom 25.00 60.00
Henrik Zetterberg
7 Alexander Ovechkin 40.00 80.00
Joe Thornton
8 Mark Messier 75.00 150.00
John Tavares
9 Vladislav Tretiak 30.00 80.00
Paul Henderson
10 Mike Modano 25.00 60.00
Doug Gilmour
11 Ilya Kovalchuk 20.00 50.00
Kari Lehtonen
12 Roberto Luongo 30.00 80.00
Dominik Hasek

2006-07 ITG Ultimate Memorabilia Autos Dual Gold

STATED PRINT RUN 1 SER.#'d SET
NOT PRICED DUE TO SCARCITY

2006-07 ITG Ultimate Memorabilia Autos Triple

STATED PRINT RUN 10 SER.#'d SETS
NOT PRICED DUE TO SCARCITY
1 Bourque
Thornton
Esposito
2 Lidstrom
Yzerman
Zetterberg
3 Henderson
Tretiak
Cournoyer
4 Brodeur
Roy
Hasek
5 Roy
Sakic
Wolski
6 Staal
Staal
Staal
7 Jagr
Kovalchuk
Ovechkin
8 Lemieux
Yzerman
Modano
9 Sittler
Keon
Kennedy
10 Tavares
Esposito
Cherepanov

2006-07 ITG Ultimate Memorabilia Autos Triple Gold

STATED PRINT RUN 1 SER.#'d SET
NOT PRICED DUE TO SCARCITY

2006-07 ITG Ultimate Memorabilia Beantown's Best Autos

STATED PRINT RUN 1 SER.#'d SET
NOT PRICED DUE TO SCARCITY
1 Dit Clapper
2 Tiny Thompson
3 Eddie Shore
4 Cooney Weiland
5 Lionel Hitchman
6 Art Ross
7 Bobby Bauer
8 Woody Dumart

2006-07 ITG Ultimate Memorabilia Blades of Steel

STATED PRINT RUN 25 SER.#'d SETS
1 Elmer Lach 20.00 50.00
2 Aurel Joliat 20.00 50.00
3 Busher Jackson 25.00 60.00
4 Clint Benedict 25.00 60.00
5 Darryl Sittler 15.00 40.00
6 Dave Keon 15.00 40.00
7 Dit Clapper 20.00 50.00
8 Doug Gilmour 12.00 30.00
9 Eddie Shore 20.00 50.00
10 Jaromir Jagr 15.00 40.00
11 Frank Nighbor 15.00 40.00
12 Frank Patrick 25.00 60.00
13 Gilbert Perreault 12.00 30.00
14 Hap Day 20.00 50.00
15 Henrik Zetterberg 12.00 30.00
16 Jack Adams 15.00 40.00
17 Jacques Plante 25.00 60.00
18 Jean Beliveau 20.00 50.00
19 Joe Thornton 15.00 40.00
20 Johnny Bucyk
21 Keith Tkachuk 10.00 25.00
22 King Clancy 20.00 50.00
23 Luc Robitaille 12.00 30.00
24 Mario Lemieux 25.00 60.00
25 Nels Stewart 15.00 40.00
26 Paddy Moran 25.00 60.00
27 Paul Coffey 10.00 25.00
28 Phil Esposito 12.00 30.00
29 Stan Mikita 10.00 25.00
30 Tim Horton 25.00 60.00

2006-07 ITG Ultimate Memorabilia Blades of Steel Gold

STATED PRINT RUN 1 SER.#'d SET
NOT PRICED DUE TO SCARCITY

2006-07 ITG Ultimate Memorabilia Bleu Blanc et Rouge Autos

1 Babe Siebert
2 Georges Mantha
3 Bill Durnan
4 Doug Harvey
5 Jacques Plante
6 Armand Mondou
7 Aurel Joliat

2006-07 ITG Ultimate Memorabilia Bloodlines

STATED PRINT RUN 25 SER.#'d SETS
GOLD 1/1s ALSO EXIST
1 Peter Stastny 25.00 60.00
Paul Stastny
Yan Stastny
2 Eric Staal 20.00 50.00
Jordan Staal
Marc Staal
3 Raymond Bourque 20.00 50.00
Chris Bourque
4 Frank Mahovlich 15.00 40.00
Peter Mahovlich
5 Maurice Richard 30.00 80.00
Henri Richard
6 Phil Esposito 20.00 50.00
Tony Esposito
7 Bobby Hull 25.00 60.00
Dennis Hull
Brett Hull

2006-07 ITG Ultimate Memorabilia Bloodlines Gold

STATED PRINT RUN 1 SER.#'d SET
NOT PRICED DUE TO SCARCITY

2006-07 ITG Ultimate Memorabilia Bloodlines Autos

STATED PRINT RUN 9 SER.#'d SETS
NOT PRICED DUE TO SCARCITY
1 Peter Stastny
Paul Stastny
2 Eric Staal
Jordan Staal
3 Raymond Bourque
Chris Bourque
4 Eric Staal
Marc Staal
5 Phil Esposito
Tony Esposito
6 Bobby Hull
Brett Hull
7 Jordan Staal
Marc Staal

2006-07 ITG Ultimate Memorabilia Bloodlines Autos Gold

STATED PRINT RUN 1 SER.#'d SET
NOT PRICED DUE TO SCARCITY

2006-07 ITG Ultimate Memorabilia Bowman Factor

STATED PRINT RUN 25 SER.#'d SETS
GOLD 1/1 VERSION EXISTS
1 Glenn Hall 10.00 25.00
2 Frank Mahovlich 10.00 25.00
3 Yvan Cournoyer 10.00 25.00
4 Guy Lafleur 12.00 30.00
5 Steve Shutt 10.00 25.00
6 Larry Robinson 10.00 25.00
7 Henri Richard 10.00 25.00
8 Serge Savard 10.00 25.00
9 Gilbert Perreault 10.00 25.00
10 Danny Gare 10.00 25.00
11 Ron Francis 10.00 25.00
12 Paul Coffey 10.00 25.00
13 Jaromir Jagr 20.00 50.00
14 Mario Lemieux 25.00 60.00
15 Brett Hull 15.00 40.00
16 Steve Yzerman 20.00 50.00

2006-07 ITG Ultimate Memorabilia Bowman Factor Gold

STATED PRINT RUN 1 SER.#'d SET
NOT PRICED DUE TO SCARCITY

2006-07 ITG Ultimate Memorabilia Bowman Factor Autos

STATED PRINT RUN 20 SER.#'d SETS
GOLD 1/1 VERSION ALSO EXISTS

2006-07 ITG Ultimate Memorabilia Bowman Factor Autos Gold

STATED PRINT RUN 1 SER.#'d SET
NOT PRICED DUE TO SCARCITY

2006-07 ITG Ultimate Memorabilia Boys Will Be Boys

STATED PRINT RUN 25 SER.#'d SETS
GOLD 1/1 VERSION ALSO EXISTS
1 Brett Hull 15.00 40.00
2 Frank Mahovlich 12.00 30.00
3 Guy Lafleur 15.00 40.00
4 Howie Morenz 15.00 40.00
5 Jean Beliveau 15.00 40.00
6 Larry Robinson 10.00 25.00
7 Mario Lemieux 25.00 60.00
8 Glenn Hall 12.00 30.00
9 Norm Ullman 10.00 25.00
10 Dave Keon 15.00 40.00
11 Alex Delvecchio 10.00 25.00
12 Ed Giacomin 15.00 40.00
13 Rod Gilbert 10.00 25.00
14 Steve Shutt 10.00 25.00
15 Guy Lapointe 10.00 25.00
16 Serge Savard 10.00 25.00
17 Billy Smith 12.00 30.00
18 Denis Potvin 12.00 30.00
19 Mike Bossy 15.00 40.00
20 Bryan Trottier 12.00 30.00
21 Peter Stastny 12.00 30.00
22 Red Kelly 12.00 30.00
23 Bobby Hull 15.00 40.00
24 Brad Park 10.00 25.00
25 Bobby Clarke 10.00 25.00
26 Marcel Dionne 12.00 30.00
27 Vladislav Tretiak 25.00 60.00
28 Ed Belfour 12.00 30.00

2006-07 ITG Ultimate Memorabilia Boys Will Be Boys Gold

STATED PRINT RUN 1 SER.#'d SET
NOT PRICED DUE TO SCARCITY

2006-07 ITG Ultimate Memorabilia Broadway Blue Shirts Autos

STATED PRINT RUN 1 SER.#'d SET
NOT PRICED DUE TO SCARCITY
1 Lester Patrick
2 Lynn Patrick
3 Frank Boucher
4 Cecil Dillon
5 Alex Shibicky
6 Bun Cook
7 Ott Heller
8 Mac Colville
9 Neil Colville
10 Ching Johnson
11 Bill Cook

2006-07 ITG Ultimate Memorabilia Builders Autos

STATED PRINT RUN 1 SER.#'d SET
NOT PRICED DUE TO SCARCITY
1 Cecil Hart
2 Conn Smythe
3 Red Dutton
4 Foster Hewitt
5 Hap Day
6 Clarence Campbell
7 Dick Irvin

2006-07 ITG Ultimate Memorabilia Captain-C

STATED PRINT RUN 5 SER.#'d SETS
NOT PRICED DUE TO SCARCITY
1 Steve Yzerman
2 Mario Lemieux
3 Dave Keon
4 Luc Robitaille
5 Phil Esposito
6 Raymond Bourque
7 Lanny McDonald
8 Stan Mikita
9 Darryl Sittler
10 Brian Leetch
11 Mike Modano
12 Joe Sakic

2006-07 ITG Ultimate Memorabilia Captain-C Gold

STATED PRINT RUN 1 SER.#'d SET
NOT PRICED DUE TO SCARCITY

2006-07 ITG Ultimate Memorabilia Chi-Town Immortals Autos

STATED PRINT RUN 1 SER.#'d SET
NOT PRICED DUE TO SCARCITY
1 Charlie Gardiner
2 Bill Mosienko
3 Cy Wentworth
4 Alex Levinsky
5 Roy Conacher
6 Gaye Stewart
7 Charlie Conacher
8 Doug Bentley
9 Mush March

2006-07 ITG Ultimate Memorabilia Complete Jersey

STATED PRINT RUN 9 SER.#'d SETS
NOT PRICED DUE TO SCARCITY
1 Evgeni Malkin
2 Joe Thornton
3 Steve Yzerman
4 Martin Brodeur
5 Patrick Roy Colorado
6 Jaromir Jagr
7 Mark Messier
8 John Tavares
9 Alexander Ovechkin
10 Jean Beliveau
11 Ron Francis
12 Dave Keon
13 Luc Robitaille
14 Milt Schmidt
15 Nicklas Lidstrom
16 Dominik Hasek
17 Borje Salming
18 Joe Sakic
19 Mario Lemieux
20 Mike Modano
21 Vincent Lecavalier
22 Ed Belfour
23 Raymond Bourque
24 Phil Kessel
25 Ilya Kovalchuk
26 Marty Turco
27 Patrick Roy Montreal
28 Jason Spezza
29 Eric Staal
30 Jordan Staal

2006-07 ITG Ultimate Memorabilia Complete Jersey Gold

STATED PRINT RUN 1 SER.#'d SET
NOT PRICED DUE TO SCARCITY

2006-07 ITG Ultimate Memorabilia Complete Package

STATED PRINT RUN 9 SER.#'d SETS
NOT PRICED DUE TO SCARCITY
1 Dominik Hasek
2 Raymond Bourque
3 Bobby Hull
4 Stan Mikita
5 Paul Coffey
6 Eddie Shore
7 Terry Sawchuk
8 Mario Lemieux
9 Alexander Ovechkin
10 Cam Neely
11 Maurice Richard
12 Joe Thornton
13 Tim Horton
14 Guy Lafleur
15 Steve Yzerman
16 Patrick Roy
17 Bernie Parent
18 Martin Brodeur

2006-07 ITG Ultimate Memorabilia Complete Package Gold

STATED PRINT RUN 1 SER.#'d SET
NOT PRICED DUE TO SCARCITY

2006-07 ITG Ultimate Memorabilia Cornerstones

1 Valeri Kharlamov
Vladislav Tretiak
Alexander Ovechkin
Evgeni Malkin
2 Aurel Joliat
Maurice Richard
Jean Beliveau
Guy Lafleur
3 Ted Kennedy
Dave Keon
Darryl Sittler
Wendel Clark
4 Bill Mosienko
Bobby Hull
Stan Mikita
Tony Esposito
5 Sid Abel
Ted Lindsay
Steve Yzerman
Nicklas Lidstrom
6 Jean Ratelle
Rod Gilbert
Brian Leetch
Mark Messier
7 Eddie Shore
Milt Schmidt
Phil Esposito
Joe Thornton
8 Mark Messier
Paul Coffey
Jari Kurri
Grant Fuhr
9 Turk Broda
Johnny Bower
Felix Potvin
Ed Belfour
10 Bill Durnan
Jacques Plante
Patrick Roy
Cristobal Huet

2006-07 ITG Ultimate Memorabilia Cornerstones Gold

STATED PRINT RUN 1 SER.#'d SET
NOT PRICED DUE TO SCARCITY

2006-07 ITG Ultimate Memorabilia Decades

1 Howie Morenz
Ted Lindsay
Maurice Richard
Bobby Hull
Guy Lafleur
Mark Messier
Jaromir Jagr
Evgeni Malkin
2 Charlie Conacher
Ted Kennedy
Tim Horton
Dave Keon
Darryl Sittler
Wendel Clark
Doug Gilmour
Ed Belfour
3 Toe Blake
Maurice Richard
Jean Beliveau
Jacques Plante
Guy Lafleur
Larry Robinson
Patrick Roy
Cristobal Huet
4 Howie Morenz
Chuck Rayner
Bill Gadsby
Ed Giacomin
Rod Gilbert
Brian Leetch
Mark Messier
Jaromir Jagr
5 Sid Abel
Ted Lindsay
Norm Ullman
Roger Crozier
Alex Delvecchio
Steve Yzerman
Nicklas Lidstrom
Henrik Zetterberg
6 George Hainsworth
Bill Durnan
Jacques Plante
Glenn Hall
Bernie Parent
Patrick Roy
Dominik Hasek
Martin Brodeur
7 Eddie Shore
Frank Brimsek
Johnny Bucyk
Phil Esposito
Brad Park
Raymond Bourque
Cam Neely
Joe Thornton
8 Tiny Thompson
Frank Brimsek
Terry Sawchuk
Johnny Bower
Tony Esposito
Grant Fuhr
Martin Brodeur
Henrik Lundqvist

2006-07 ITG Ultimate Memorabilia Double Memorabilia

STATED PRINT RUN 25 SER.#'d SETS
GOLD 1/1 VERSION ALSO EXISTS
1 Mark Messier 15.00 40.00
2 Patrick Roy 30.00 80.00
3 Martin Brodeur 15.00 40.00
4 Mike Modano 12.00 30.00
5 Steve Yzerman 25.00 60.00
6 John Tavares 40.00 80.00
7 Joe Thornton 15.00 40.00
8 Bobby Hull 20.00 50.00
9 Alexander Ovechkin 25.00 60.00
10 Jean Beliveau 15.00 40.00
11 Tim Horton 25.00 60.00
12 Dave Keon 15.00 40.00
13 Aurel Joliat 20.00 50.00
14 Brett Hull 15.00 40.00
15 Chris Chelios 10.00 25.00
16 Dominik Hasek 20.00 50.00
17 Borje Salming 12.00 30.00
18 Cam Neely 12.00 30.00
19 Joe Sakic 25.00 60.00
20 Ed Belfour 15.00 40.00
21 Raymond Bourque 15.00 40.00
22 Vladislav Tretiak
23 Guy Lafleur 15.00 40.00
24 Mario Lemieux 30.00 80.00
25 Henrik Zetterberg 20.00 50.00
26 Jacques Plante 20.00 50.00
27 Doug Harvey 15.00 40.00
28 Jordan Staal 25.00 60.00
29 Eddie Shore 15.00 40.00
30 Stan Mikita 12.00 30.00

2006-07 ITG Ultimate Memorabilia Double Memorabilia Autos

STATED PRINT RUN 50 SER.#'d SETS
GOLD 1/1 VERSION ALSO EXISTS
1 Eric Staal 30.00 60.00
Jordan Staal
2 Ray Emery 20.00 50.00
Dany Heatley
3 Guy Lafleur 25.00 60.00
Marcel Dionne
4 Jaromir Jagr 100.00 175.00
Mario Lemieux
5 Martin Brodeur 100.00 200.00
Patrick Roy
6 Steve Yzerman 40.00 80.00
Doug Gilmour
7 Joe Thornton 25.00 60.00
Phil Esposito
8 Alexander Ovechkin 40.00 80.00
Ilya Kovalchuk
9 John Tavares 100.00 200.00
Mark Messier
10 Dion Phaneuf 20.00 50.00
Nicklas Lidstrom
11 Brett Hull 25.00 60.00
Mike Modano
12 Roberto Luongo 75.00 150.00
Carey Price

2006-07 ITG Ultimate Memorabilia Emblem Attic

STATED PRINT RUN 5 SER.#'d SETS
GOLD 1/1 VERSION ALSO EXISTS
NOT PRICED DUE TO SCARCITY
1 Milt Schmidt
2 Frank Brimsek
3 Doug Harvey
4 Sid Abel
5 Jean Beliveau
6 Harry Lumley
7 Roy Worters
8 Aurel Joliat
9 George Hainsworth
10 Frank Mahovlich
11 Johnny Bower
12 Jacques Plante

2006-07 ITG Ultimate Memorabilia Emblems

1 Evgeni Malkin
2 Alexander Ovechkin
3 Mark Messier
4 Luc Robitaille
5 Patrick Roy
6 Eric Staal
7 Martin Brodeur
8 Mario Lemieux
9 Ray Emery
10 Mike Modano
11 Marty Turco
12 Brett Hull
13 Pat LaFontaine
14 Lanny McDonald
15 Cam Neely
16 Joe Sakic
17 Jason Spezza
18 John Tavares
19 Steve Yzerman
20 Felix Potvin
21 Carey Price
22 Stan Mikita
23 Dion Phaneuf
24 Paul Coffey
25 Manny Fernandez
26 Roberto Luongo

2006-07 ITG Ultimate Memorabilia Fire In His Eyes Autos

STATED PRINT RUN 9 SER.#'d SETS
GOLD 1/1 VERSION ALSO EXISTS
NOT PRICED DUE TO SCARCITY
1 Maurice Richard
2 Maurice Richard
3 Maurice Richard
4 Maurice Richard
5 Maurice Richard

2006-07 ITG Ultimate Memorabilia First Round Picks

STATED PRINT RUN 25 SER.#'d SETS
GOLD 1/1 VERSION ALSO EXISTS
1 Evgeni Malkin 20.00 50.00
2 Alexander Ovechkin 20.00 50.00
3 Ilya Kovalchuk 10.00 25.00
4 Jaromir Jagr 15.00 40.00
5 Joe Thornton 12.00 30.00
6 Carey Price 20.00 50.00
7 Marc-Andre Fleury 12.00 30.00
8 Eric Staal 10.00 25.00
9 Kari Lehtonen 10.00 25.00
10 Anze Kopitar 10.00 25.00
11 Guy Lafleur 12.00 30.00
12 Marcel Dionne 10.00 25.00
13 Mike Bossy 10.00 25.00
14 Paul Coffey 12.00 30.00
15 Ron Francis 12.00 30.00
16 Pat LaFontaine 12.00 30.00
17 Steve Yzerman 20.00 50.00
18 Wendel Clark 12.00 30.00
19 Martin Brodeur 15.00 40.00
20 Joe Sakic 15.00 40.00
21 Mike Modano 12.00 30.00
22 Marc Staal 10.00 25.00
23 Vincent Lecavalier 12.00 30.00
24 Gilbert Perreault 12.00 30.00
25 Jordan Staal 12.00 30.00
26 Jason Spezza 10.00 25.00
27 Roberto Luongo 12.00 30.00
28 Brian Leetch 10.00 25.00
29 Mario Lemieux 20.00 60.00
30 Raymond Bourque 15.00 40.00

2006-07 ITG Ultimate Memorabilia Future Star

STATED PRINT RUN 25 SER.#'d SETS
GOLD 1/1 VERSION ALSO EXISTS
1 Angelo Esposito 20.00 50.00
2 John Tavares 30.00 80.00
3 Evgeni Malkin 20.00 50.00
4 Wojtek Wolski
5 Marek Schwarz
6 Carey Price 30.00 80.00
7 Anze Kopitar 10.00 25.00
8 Jordan Staal 15.00 40.00
9 Gilbert Brule 10.00 25.00
10 Phil Kessel 10.00 25.00
11 Peter Mueller 10.00 25.00
12 Bobby Ryan 12.00 30.00
13 Rob Schremp 12.00 30.00
14 Paul Stastny 12.00 30.00
15 Dustin Penner 8.00 20.00
16 Bryan Little 8.00 20.00
17 Derick Brassard 8.00 20.00
18 Justin Pogge 10.00 25.00
19 Alexander Radulov 15.00 40.00
20 Al Montoya 8.00 20.00
21 Ryan Getzlaf 10.00 25.00
22 Marc Staal 10.00 25.00
23 Alexei Cherepanov 12.00 30.00
24 Ryan Callahan 8.00 20.00
25 Jack Skille 8.00 20.00

2006-07 ITG Ultimate Memorabilia Future Star Autos

PRINT RUN 40 #'d SETS UNLESS NOTED
GOLD VERSION #'d TO 10 ALSO EXISTS
1 Phil Kessel 12.00 30.00
2 Peter Mueller 10.00 25.00
3 Bobby Ryan 10.00 25.00
4 Rob Schremp 8.00 20.00
5 Paul Stastny 15.00 30.00
6 Dustin Penner 8.00 20.00
7 Bryan Little 10.00 25.00
8 Derick Brassard 15.00 30.00
9 Justin Pogge 20.00 40.00
10 Jeff Glass 8.00 20.00
11 Ryan Getzlaf 15.00 30.00
12 Jack Skille 8.00 20.00
13 Ryan Callahan 8.00 20.00
14 Alexei Cherepanov 40.00 80.00
15 Angelo Esposito/30 40.00 80.00
16 John Tavares/30 60.00 125.00
17 Alexander Radulov/30 12.00 30.00
18 Wojtek Wolski/30 10.00 25.00
19 Marek Schwarz/30 8.00 20.00
20 Carey Price/30 60.00 120.00
21 Anze Kopitar/30 20.00 40.00
22 Jordan Staal/30 30.00 60.00
23 Gilbert Brule/30 15.00 30.00
24 Michael Frolik/30 8.00 20.00
25 Jonathan Toews 50.00 100.00

2006-07 ITG Ultimate Memorabilia Future Star Patches Autos

STATED PRINT RUN 40 SER.#'d SETS
GOLD VERSION #'d TO 10 ALSO EXISTS
1 Phil Kessel 30.00 60.00
2 Peter Mueller 25.00 60.00
3 Bobby Ryan 15.00 40.00
4 Rob Schremp 20.00 50.00
5 Paul Stastny 40.00 80.00
6 Dustin Penner 15.00 40.00
7 Bryan Little 15.00 40.00
8 Derick Brassard 20.00 50.00
9 Justin Pogge 20.00 50.00
10 Jeff Glass 15.00 40.00
11 Al Montoya 15.00 40.00
12 Jack Skille 15.00 40.00
13 Ryan Callahan 15.00 40.00
14 Alexei Cherepanov 50.00 100.00
15 Angelo Esposito 30.00 80.00
16 John Tavares 75.00 150.00
17 Hannu Toivonen 15.00 40.00
18 Wojtek Wolski 20.00 50.00
19 Marek Schwarz 20.00 50.00
20 Carey Price 60.00 120.00
21 Anze Kopitar 40.00 80.00
22 Jordan Staal 50.00 100.00
23 Gilbert Brule 15.00 40.00
24 Michael Frolik 15.00 40.00
25 Benoit Pouliot 15.00 40.00
26 Jonathan Toews 60.00 120.00

2006-07 ITG Ultimate Memorabilia Gloves Are Off

STATED PRINT RUN 25 SER.#'d SETS
1 Alexander Ovechkin 30.00 60.00
2 Bobby Clarke 20.00 40.00
3 Brett Hull 15.00 40.00
4 Bryan Trottier 12.00 30.00
5 Cam Neely 15.00 40.00
6 Charlie Conacher 20.00 50.00
7 Dale Hawerchuk 12.00 30.00
8 Dominik Hasek 20.00 40.00
9 Eddie Shore 20.00 50.00
10 Eric Lindros 15.00 40.00
11 Jacques Plante 20.00 50.00
12 Joe Sakic 25.00 50.00
13 Joe Thornton 15.00 40.00
14 Mario Lemieux 30.00 80.00
15 Martin Brodeur 20.00 50.00
16 Pat LaFontaine 10.00 25.00
17 Patrick Roy 30.00 80.00
18 Raymond Bourque 15.00 40.00
19 Stan Mikita 10.00 25.00
20 Steve Yzerman 25.00 60.00

2006-07 ITG Ultimate Memorabilia Going For Gold

STATED PRINT RUN 25 SER.#'d SETS
GOLD 1/1 VERSION ALSO EXISTS
1 Alexander Ovechkin 20.00 50.00
2 Mike Modano 12.00 30.00
3 Bobby Clarke 10.00 25.00
4 Brett Hull 12.00 30.00
5 Brian Leetch 8.00 20.00
6 Cristobal Huet 15.00 30.00
7 Eric Staal 10.00 25.00
8 Evgeni Malkin 25.00 50.00
9 Henrik Lundqvist 15.00 30.00
10 Henrik Zetterberg 15.00 30.00
11 Ilya Kovalchuk 15.00 30.00
12 Jari Kurri 20.00 40.00
13 Jaromir Jagr 20.00 40.00
14 Jason Spezza 10.00 25.00
15 Joe Thornton 15.00 30.00
16 Alexei Cherepanov 15.00 30.00
17 Mario Lemieux 30.00 60.00
18 Mark Messier 20.00 40.00
19 Martin Brodeur 20.00 40.00
20 Nicklas Lidstrom
21 Phil Esposito 12.00 30.00
22 Raymond Bourque
23 Steve Yzerman 20.00 50.00
24 Valeri Kharlamov 12.00 30.00
25 Vladislav Tretiak
26 Dominik Hasek 12.00 30.00
27 Keith Tkachuk 8.00 20.00
28 Vincent Lecavalier 12.00 30.00
29 Joe Sakic 20.00 40.00
30 John Tavares 40.00 80.00

2006-07 ITG Ultimate Memorabilia In The Numbers

STATED PRINT RUN 9 SER.#'d SETS
GOLD 1/1 VERSION ALSO EXISTS
NOT PRICED DUE TO SCARCITY
GOLD NOT PRICED DUE TO SCARCITY
1 Evgeni Malkin
2 Patrick Roy
3 Martin Brodeur
4 Mario Lemieux
5 Angelo Esposito
6 John Tavares
7 Mark Messier
8 Joe Sakic
9 Steve Yzerman
10 Alexander Ovechkin
11 Dominik Hasek
12 Dave Keon
13 Jaromir Jagr
14 Mike Modano
15 Jason Spezza
16 Eric Staal
17 Marty Turco
18 Ray Emery
19 Henrik Zetterberg
20 Milt Schmidt

2006-07 ITG Ultimate Memorabilia Jerseys

STATED PRINT RUN 25 SER.#'d SETS
GOLD 1/1 VERSION ALSO EXISTS
GOLD NOT PRICED DUE TO SCARCITY

1 Evgeni Malkin 20.00 50.00
2 Joe Thornton 12.00 30.00
3 Brett Hull 15.00 40.00
4 Chris Chelios 15.00 40.00
5 Patrick Roy 20.00 50.00
6 Alexander Ovechkin 15.00 40.00
7 Dominik Hasek 12.00 30.00
8 Joe Sakic 15.00 40.00
9 Mark Messier 15.00 40.00
10 Steve Yzerman 15.00 40.00
11 Jean Beliveau 12.00 30.00
12 Milt Schmidt 10.00 25.00
13 Martin Brodeur 15.00 40.00
14 Jaromir Jagr 15.00 40.00
15 Ed Belfour 10.00 25.00
16 Mario Lemieux 20.00 50.00
17 Borje Salming 12.00 30.00
18 Bobby Hull 12.00 30.00
19 Doug Gilmour 12.00 30.00
20 Guy Lafleur 12.00 30.00
21 Dave Keon 12.00 30.00
22 Jason Spezza 10.00 25.00
23 Nicklas Lidstrom 10.00 25.00
24 Eric Staal 10.00 25.00
25 Luc Robitaille 12.00 30.00
26 John Tavares 25.00 60.00
27 Vincent Lecavalier 12.00 30.00

2006-07 ITG Ultimate Memorabilia Jerseys and Emblems

STATED PRINT RUN 25 SER.#'d SETS
GOLD 1/1 VERSIONS ALSO EXISTS
GOLD NOT PRICED DUE TO SCARCITY

1 Evgeni Malkin 40.00 80.00
2 Joe Thornton 30.00 60.00
3 Patrick Roy 50.00 100.00
5 Martin Brodeur 30.00 60.00
6 Alexander Ovechkin 30.00 60.00
7 Mark Messier 30.00 60.00
8 Joe Sakic 30.00 60.00
9 Brian Leetch 30.00 60.00
10 Jean Beliveau 30.00 60.00
11 Mario Lemieux 50.00 100.00
12 Dominik Hasek 25.00 50.00
13 Dave Keon 25.00 50.00
14 Ilya Kovalchuk 25.00 50.00
15 Bobby Hull 30.00 60.00
16 Steve Yzerman 40.00 80.00
17 Jaromir Jagr 30.00 60.00
18 Nicklas Lidstrom 25.00 50.00
19 John Tavares 75.00 125.00
20 Jordan Staal 30.00 60.00
21 Vincent Lecavalier 30.00 60.00

2006-07 ITG Ultimate Memorabilia Jerseys Autos

STATED PRINT RUN 50 SER.#'d SETS
GOLD VERSION /10 ALSO EXISTS
GOLD NOT PRICED DUE TO SCARCITY

1 Tom Barrasso 12.00 30.00
2 Glenn Hall 15.00 40.00
3 Chris Chelios 15.00 40.00
4 Martin Brodeur 40.00 80.00
5 Gerry Cheevers 15.00 40.00
6 Dominik Hasek 25.00 60.00
7 Bobby Clarke 15.00 40.00
8 Paul Coffey 15.00 40.00
9 Yvan Cournoyer 12.00 30.00
10 Ron Hextall 12.00 30.00
11 Marcel Dionne 12.00 30.00
12 Ray Emery 12.00 30.00
13 Angelo Esposito 30.00 60.00
14 Phil Esposito 15.00 40.00
15 Cristobal Huet 12.00 30.00
16 Manny Fernandez 8.00 20.00
17 Ron Francis 12.00 30.00
18 Grant Fuhr 12.00 30.00
19 Ed Giacomin 12.00 30.00
20 Doug Gilmour 12.00 30.00
21 Jean Beliveau 20.00 50.00
22 Wendel Clark 15.00 40.00
23 Alex Delvecchio 10.00 30.00
24 Brett Hull 12.00 30.00
25 Jaromir Jagr 25.00 60.00
26 Dave Keon 15.00 40.00
27 Ilya Kovalchuk 15.00 40.00
28 Jari Kurri 15.00 40.00
29 Guy Lafleur 25.00 60.00
30 Pat LaFontaine 12.00 30.00
31 Brian Leetch 12.00 30.00
32 Kari Lehtonen 12.00 30.00
33 Nicklas Lidstrom 15.00 40.00
34 Henrik Lundqvist 15.00 40.00
35 Roberto Luongo 15.00 40.00
36 Frank Mahovlich 12.00 30.00
37 Lanny McDonald 8.00 20.00
38 Mark Messier 50.00 100.00
39 Stan Mikita 15.00 40.00
40 Mike Modano 15.00 40.00
41 Cam Neely 15.00 40.00
42 Alexander Ovechkin 30.00 80.00
43 Brad Park 12.00 30.00
44 Gilbert Perreault 12.00 30.00
45 Dion Phaneuf 15.00 40.00
46 Denis Potvin 12.00 30.00
47 Petr Prucha 8.00 20.00
48 Jean Ratelle 15.00 40.00
49 Larry Robinson 12.00 30.00
50 Luc Robitaille 25.00 60.00
51 Patrick Roy 50.00 100.00
52 Joe Sakic 30.00 80.00
53 Darryl Sittler 12.00 30.00
54 Jason Spezza 12.00 30.00
55 Eric Staal 12.00 30.00
56 Marek Svatos 8.00 20.00
57 John Tavares 75.00 125.00
58 Joe Thornton 20.00 50.00
59 Vladislav Tretiak 25.00 60.00
60 Bryan Trottier 12.00 30.00
61 Marty Turco 12.00 30.00
62 Rogie Vachon 12.00 30.00
63 Cam Ward 15.00 40.00
64 Steve Yzerman 40.00 80.00
65 Henrik Zetterberg 15.00 40.00
66 Felix Potvin 20.00 50.00
67 Vincent Lecavalier 15.00 40.00
68 Keith Tkachuk 12.00 30.00
69 Thomas Vanek 15.00 40.00

2006-07 ITG Ultimate Memorabilia Journey Emblem

STATED PRINT RUN 10 SER.#'d SETS
GOLD 1/1 VERSION ALSO EXISTS
GOLD NOT PRICED DUE TO SCARCITY
NOT PRICED DUE TO SCARCITY

1 Raymond Bourque
2 Patrick Roy
3 Dave Keon
4 Dany Heatley
5 Joe Sakic
6 Ed Giacomin
7 Eric Lindros
8 Brian Leetch
9 Jaromir Jagr
10 Ron Francis
11 Ed Belfour
12 Doug Gilmour
13 Mark Messier
14 Brett Hull
15 Luc Robitaille
16 Dominik Hasek
17 Paul Coffey
18 Felix Potvin

2006-07 ITG Ultimate Memorabilia Journey Jersey

STATED PRINT RUN 25 SER.#'d SETS
GOLD 1/1 VERSION ALSO EXISTS
GOLD NOT PRICED DUE TO SCARCITY

1 Raymond Bourque 15.00 40.00
2 Patrick Roy 25.00 60.00
3 Dave Keon 12.00 30.00
4 Dany Heatley 12.00 30.00
5 Joe Sakic 15.00 40.00
6 Ed Giacomin 12.00 30.00
7 Eric Lindros 12.00 30.00
8 Brian Leetch 12.00 30.00
9 Jaromir Jagr 15.00 40.00
10 Ron Francis 12.00 30.00
11 Ed Belfour 12.00 30.00
12 Doug Gilmour 12.00 30.00
13 Mark Messier 15.00 40.00
14 Brett Hull 12.00 30.00
15 Luc Robitaille 12.00 30.00
16 Dominik Hasek 15.00 40.00
17 Paul Coffey 12.00 30.00
18 Felix Potvin 12.00 30.00

2006-07 ITG Ultimate Memorabilia Legendary Captains

STATED PRINT RUN 25 SER.#'d SETS
GOLD 1/1 VERSION ALSO EXISTS
GOLD NOT PRICED DUE TO SCARCITY

1 Maurice Richard/10
2 Dave Keon 12.00 30.00
3 Jean Beliveau 15.00 40.00
4 Steve Yzerman 15.00 40.00
5 Mario Lemieux 25.00 60.00
6 Mark Messier 15.00 40.00
7 Bobby Clarke 12.00 30.00
8 Raymond Bourque 12.00 30.00
9 Darryl Sittler 12.00 30.00
10 Phil Esposito 12.00 30.00
11 Henri Richard 12.00 30.00
12 Gilbert Perreault 12.00 30.00
13 Joe Sakic 15.00 40.00
14 Mike Modano 12.00 30.00
15 Bill Durnan/10
16 Milt Schmidt 12.00 30.00

2006-07 ITG Ultimate Memorabilia Lumbergraphs

STATED PRINT RUN 1 SER.#'d SET
NOT PRICED DUE TO SCARCITY

1 Terry Sawchuk
2 Sid Abel
3 Tim Horton
4 Nels Stewart
5 Howie Morenz
6 Sprague Cleghorn
7 Gordie Drillon
8 Aurel Joliat
9 George Hainsworth
10 Ace Bailey
11 Conn Smythe
12 Earl Seibert
13 Red Horner
14 Charlie Conacher
15 Red Dutton

2006-07 ITG Ultimate Memorabilia Maple Leafs Forever Autos

STATED PRINT RUN 1 SER.#'d SET
NOT PRICED DUE TO SCARCITY

1 Ace Bailey
2 Charlie Conacher
3 Baldy Cotton
4 Joe Primeau
5 Bill Barilko
6 Turk Broda
7 Busher Jackson
8 Lorne Chabot

2006-07 ITG Ultimate Memorabilia Marvelous Maroons Autos

STATED PRINT RUN 1 SER.#'d SET
NOT PRICED DUE TO SCARCITY

1 Baldy Northcott
2 Nels Stewart
3 Dave Kerr
4 Lionel Conacher
5 Lorne Chabot
6 Hooley Smith
7 Red Dutton
8 Dave Trottier

2006-07 ITG Ultimate Memorabilia Motown Heroes Autos

STATED PRINT RUN 1 SER.#'d SET
NOT PRICED DUE TO SCARCITY

1 Terry Sawchuk
2 Sid Abel
3 Jack Stewart
4 Normie Smith
5 Roger Crozier

2006-07 ITG Ultimate Memorabilia Paper Cuts Autos

STATED PRINT RUN 1 SER.#'d SET
NOT PRICED DUE TO SCARCITY

1 Howie Morenz
2 Nels Stewart
3 Lionel Conacher
4 George Hainsworth
5 Cecil Hart
6 Earl Seibert
7 Frank Nighbor
8 Cy Wentworth
9 Sprague Cleghorn
10 Frank McCool
11 Hooley Smith
12 Joe Simpson
13 Pelle Lindbergh

2006-07 ITG Ultimate Memorabilia Passing The Torch

STATED PRINT RUN 25 SER.#'d SETS
GOLD 1/1 VERSION ALSO EXISTS
GOLD NOT PRICED DUE TO SCARCITY

1 Jean Beliveau 20.00 50.00
Guy Lafleur
2 Dave Keon 20.00 50.00
Darryl Sittler
3 Marcel Dionne 20.00 50.00
Luc Robitaille
4 Jacques Plante 20.00 50.00
Patrick Roy
5 Steve Yzerman 20.00 50.00
Nicklas Lidstrom
6 Eddie Shore 12.00 30.00
Raymond Bourque
7 Tim Horton 25.00 60.00
Borje Salming
8 Bernie Parent 15.00 40.00
Ron Hextall
9 Bobby Clarke 12.00 30.00
Mark Messier
10 Milt Schmidt 12.00 30.00
Joe Thornton
11 Terry Sawchuk
Martin Brodeur
12 Bobby Hull 15.00 40.00
Brett Hull
13 Ed Belfour 12.00 30.00
Marty Turco
14 Mario Lemieux 30.00 60.00
Jaromir Jagr
15 Dominik Hasek 20.00 50.00
Ryan Miller
16 Glenn Hall 15.00 40.00
Tony Esposito
17 Valeri Kharlamov 12.00 30.00
Alexander Ovechkin
18 Ilya Kovalchuk 20.00 50.00
Evgeni Malkin
19 Eric Lindros 20.00 50.00
John Tavares
20 Ed Giacomin 12.00 30.00
Mike Richter

2006-07 ITG Ultimate Memorabilia Portrait in Courage

STATED PRINT RUN 9 SER.#'d SETS
GOLD 1/1 VERSION ALSO EXISTS
GOLD NOT PRICED DUE TO SCARCITY
NOT PRICED DUE TO SCARCITY

1 Mario Lemieux
2 Mario Lemieux
3 Mario Lemieux
4 Mario Lemieux
5 Mario Lemieux
6 Mario Lemieux
7 Mario Lemieux
8 Mario Lemieux
9 Mario Lemieux
10 Mario Lemieux
11 Mario Lemieux
12 Mario Lemieux
13 Mario Lemieux
14 Mario Lemieux
15 Mario Lemieux
16 Mario Lemieux
17 Mario Lemieux
18 Mario Lemieux
19 Mario Lemieux
20 Mario Lemieux

2006-07 ITG Ultimate Memorabilia R.O.Y. Autos

STATED PRINT RUN 19 SER.#'d SETS
GOLD 1/1 VERSION ALSO EXISTS
GOLD NOT PRICED DUE TO SCARCITY

1 Anze Kopitar 30.00 60.00
2 Gilbert Brule 20.00 40.00
3 Phil Kessel 25.00 50.00
4 Alexander Radulov 25.00 50.00
5 Wojtek Wolski 20.00 40.00
6 Jordan Staal
7 Dustin Penner 10.00 25.00
8 Paul Stastny 30.00 60.00
9 Evgeni Malkin 60.00 100.00
10 Alexander Ovechkin 40.00 80.00
11 Dany Heatley 12.00 30.00
12 Martin Brodeur
13 Ed Belfour
14 Brian Leetch
15 Luc Robitaille 20.00 40.00
16 Mario Lemieux
17 Tony Esposito 20.00 40.00
18 Dave Keon 20.00 40.00
19 Glenn Hall 20.00 40.00
20 Gump Worsley 25.00 50.00

2006-07 ITG Ultimate Memorabilia R.O.Y. Emblems

STATED PRINT RUN 9 SER.#'d SETS
GOLD 1/1 VERSION ALSO EXISTS
GOLD NOT PRICED DUE TO SCARCITY
NOT PRICED DUE TO SCARCITY

1 Anze Kopitar
2 Gilbert Brule
3 Phil Kessel
4 Alexander Radulov
5 Wojtek Wolski
6 Jordan Staal
7 Dustin Penner
8 Paul Stastny
9 Evgeni Malkin
10 Alexander Ovechkin
11 Dany Heatley
12 Martin Brodeur
13 Ed Belfour
14 Brian Leetch
15 Luc Robitaille
16 Mario Lemieux
17 Tony Esposito
18 Dave Keon
19 Glenn Hall
20 Gump Worsley

2006-07 ITG Ultimate Memorabilia R.O.Y. Jerseys

STATED PRINT RUN 25 SER.#'d SETS
GOLD 1/1 VERSION ALSO EXISTS
GOLD NOT PRICED DUE TO SCARCITY

1 Anze Kopitar 20.00 40.00
2 Gilbert Brule 10.00 25.00
3 Phil Kessel 12.00 30.00
4 Alexander Radulov 12.00 30.00
5 Wojtek Wolski 12.00 30.00
6 Jordan Staal
7 Dustin Penner 10.00 25.00
8 Paul Stastny 15.00 40.00
9 Evgeni Malkin 25.00 60.00
10 Alexander Ovechkin 20.00 50.00
11 Dany Heatley 10.00 25.00
12 Martin Brodeur 20.00 50.00
13 Ed Belfour 10.00 25.00
14 Brian Leetch 10.00 25.00
15 Luc Robitaille 10.00 25.00
16 Mario Lemieux 25.00 60.00
17 Tony Esposito 15.00 40.00
18 Dave Keon 15.00 40.00
19 Glenn Hall 12.00 30.00
20 Gump Worsley 15.00 40.00

2006-07 ITG Ultimate Memorabilia R.O.Y. Numbers

STATED PRINT RUN 9 SER.#'d SETS
GOLD 1/1 VERSION ALSO EXISTS
NOT PRICED DUE TO SCARCITY
GOLD NOT PRICED DUE TO SCARCITY

1 Anze Kopitar
2 Gilbert Brule
3 Phil Kessel
4 Alexander Radulov
5 Wojtek Wolski
6 Jordan Staal
7 Dustin Penner
8 Paul Stastny
9 Evgeni Malkin
10 Alexander Ovechkin
11 Dany Heatley
12 Martin Brodeur
13 Ed Belfour
14 Brian Leetch
15 Luc Robitaille
16 Mario Lemieux
17 Tony Esposito
18 Dave Keon
19 Glenn Hall
20 Gump Worsley

2006-07 ITG Ultimate Memorabilia Raised to the Rafters

STATED PRINT RUN 25 SER.#'d SETS
GOLD 1/1 VERSION ALSO EXISTS
GOLD NOT PRICED DUE TO SCARCITY

1 Pat LaFontaine 20.00 40.00
2 Mark Messier 30.00 60.00
3 Yvan Cournoyer 20.00 40.00
4 Bernie Geoffrion 25.00 50.00
5 Paul Coffey 20.00 40.00
6 Luc Robitaille 15.00 40.00
7 Ron Francis 20.00 40.00
8 Milt Schmidt 25.00 50.00
9 Brett Hull 20.00 50.00
10 Steve Yzerman 30.00 60.00
11 Mario Lemieux 30.00 80.00
12 Bobby Hull

2006-07 ITG Ultimate Memorabilia Retro Teammates

STATED PRINT RUN 25 SER.#'d SETS
GOLD 1/1 VERSION ALSO EXISTS
GOLD NOT PRICED DUE TO SCARCITY

1 Howie Morenz 50.00 100.00
Aurel Joliat
George Hainsworth
2 Tiny Thompson 30.00 60.00
Milt Schmidt
Eddie Shore
3 Terry Sawchuk
Sid Abel
Ted Lindsay
4 Jacques Plante 50.00 100.00
Maurice Richard
Doug Harvey
5 Johnny Bower 50.00 100.00
Dave Keon
Tim Horton
6 Jean Beliveau 40.00 80.00
Gump Worsley
Henri Richard
7 Stan Mikita 20.00 50.00
Glenn Hall
Bobby Hull
8 Alex Delvecchio 15.00 40.00
Roger Crozier
Norm Ullman
9 Rod Gilbert 30.00 60.00
Jean Ratelle
Ed Giacomin
10 Gerry Cheevers 25.00 60.00
Johnny Bucyk
Phil Esposito
11 Valeri Kharlamov 50.00 100.00
Vladislav Tretiak
Alexander Yakushev
12 Guy Lafleur 20.00 50.00
Yvan Cournoyer
Steve Shutt
13 Bobby Clarke 50.00 100.00
Bernie Parent
Bill Barber
14 Darryl Sittler
Borje Salming
Lanny McDonald
15 Mike Bossy 30.00 60.00
Bryan Trottier
Denis Potvin
16 Mark Messier 50.00 100.00
Paul Coffey
Jari Kurri
17 Maurice Richard 75.00 150.00
Elmer Lach
Toe Blake
18 Patrick Roy 40.00 80.00
Chris Chelios
Larry Robinson
19 Raymond Bourque 30.00 60.00
Andy Moog
Cam Neely
20 Mark Messier 40.00 80.00
Grant Fuhr
Glenn Anderson
21 Mario Lemieux 50.00 100.00
Ron Francis
Jaromir Jagr
22 Doug Gilmour
Wendel Clark
Felix Potvin
23 Mark Messier 40.00 80.00
Brian Leetch
Mike Richter
24 Steve Yzerman 40.00 80.00
Dominik Hasek
Igor Larionov
25 Brett Hull 40.00 80.00
Steve Yzerman
Nicklas Lidstrom

2006-07 ITG Ultimate Memorabilia Retrospective

STATED PRINT RUN 10 SER.#'d SETS
GOLD 1/1 VERSION ALSO EXISTS
NOT PRICED DUE TO SCARCITY
GOLD NOT PRICED DUE TO SCARCITY

2006-07 ITG Ultimate Memorabilia Ring Leaders

STATED PRINT RUN 25 SER.#'d SETS
GOLD 1/1 VERSION ALSO EXISTS
GOLD NOT PRICED DUE TO SCARCITY

1 Henri Richard 15.00 40.00
2 Jean Beliveau 12.00 30.00
3 Steve Yzerman 20.00 50.00
4 Jaromir Jagr 15.00 40.00
5 Mario Lemieux 20.00 50.00
6 Mark Messier 12.00 30.00
7 Martin Brodeur 15.00 40.00
8 Larry Robinson 10.00 25.00
9 Dave Keon 12.00 30.00
10 Guy Lafleur 12.00 30.00
11 Jari Kurri 10.00 25.00
12 Red Kelly 12.00 30.00
13 Frank Mahovlich 10.00 25.00
14 Johnny Bower 12.00 30.00
15 Serge Savard 10.00 25.00
16 Patrick Roy 20.00 50.00
17 Paul Coffey 10.00 25.00
18 Yvan Cournoyer 12.00 30.00

2006-07 ITG Ultimate Memorabilia Road to the Cup

STATED PRINT RUN 9 SER.#'d SETS
GOLD 1/1 VERSION ALSO EXISTS
GOLD NOT PRICED DUE TO SCARCITY
NOT PRICED DUE TO SCARCITY

1 Terry Sawchuk
Red Kelly
Ted Lindsay
Sid Abel
Alex Delvecchio
2 Maurice Richard
Jacques Plante
Doug Harvey
Jean Beliveau
Henri Richard
3 Tim Horton
Terry Sawchuk
Johnny Bower
Dave Keon
Frank Mahovlich
4 Gerry Cheevers
Wayne Cashman
Ken Hodge
Phil Esposito
Johnny Bucyk
5 Larry Robinson
Serge Savard
Guy Lafleur
Steve Shutt
Yvan Cournoyer
6 Mike Bossy
Denis Potvin
Bryan Trottier
Billy Smith
Bob Nystrom
7 Mark Messier
Grant Fuhr
Jari Kurri
Paul Coffey
Glenn Anderson
8 Mario Lemieux
Ron Francis
Tom Barrasso
Jaromir Jagr
Paul Coffey
9 Bobby Clarke
Bill Barber
Bernie Parent
Dave Schultz
Reggie Leach
10 Steve Yzerman
Chris Chelios
Nicklas Lidstrom
Brett Hull
Dominik Hasek

2006-07 ITG Ultimate Memorabilia Seams Unbelievable

STATED PRINT RUN 9 SER.#'d SETS
GOLD 1/1 VERSION ALSO EXISTS
GOLD NOT PRICED DUE TO SCARCITY

1 Evgeni Malkin
2 John Tavares
3 Terry Sawchuk
4 Dave Keon
5 Milt Schmidt
6 Patrick Roy
7 Mark Messier
8 Ron Francis
9 Jaromir Jagr
10 Joe Thornton

2006-07 ITG Ultimate Memorabilia Sensational Season

STATED PRINT RUN 25 SER.#'d SETS
GOLD 1/1 VERSION ALSO EXISTS
GOLD NOT PRICED DUE TO SCARCITY

1 Phil Esposito 12.00 30.00
2 Mario Lemieux 20.00 50.00
3 Stan Mikita 12.00 30.00
4 George Hainsworth 15.00 40.00
5 Maurice Richard 30.00 80.00
6 Paul Coffey 10.00 25.00
7 John Tavares 30.00 80.00
8 Tony Esposito 10.00 25.00
9 Martin Brodeur 15.00 40.00
10 Mike Bossy
11 Brett Hull 15.00 40.00

2006-07 ITG Ultimate Memorabilia Sensational Sens Autos

STATED PRINT RUN 1 SER.#'d SET
NOT PRICED DUE TO SCARCITY

1 Frank Finnigan
2 Cooney Weiland
3 King Clancy
4 Syd Howe
5 Bill Beveridge
6 Hooley Smith
Tommy Gorman

2006-07 ITG Ultimate Memorabilia Stick Rack

STATED PRINT RUN 25 SER.#'d SETS
GOLD 1/1 VERSION ALSO EXISTS
GOLD NOT PRICED DUE TO SCARCITY

1 Guy Lafleur 60.00 125.00
Jean Beliveau
Yvan Cournoyer
2 Doug Harvey 60.00 125.00
Maurice Richard
Jacques Plante
3 Frank Mahovlich 50.00 100.00
Dave Keon
Johnny Bower
4 Patrick Roy 50.00 100.00
Jacques Plante
Cristobal Huet
5 Brett Hull 40.00 80.00
Steve Yzerman
Dino Ciccarelli
6 Johnny Bucyk 40.00 80.00
Phil Esposito
Gerry Cheevers
7 Doug Harvey 40.00 80.00
Red Kelly
Tim Horton
8 Mario Lemieux 75.00 150.00
Ron Francis
Bryan Trottier
9 Dave Keon 60.00 125.00
Darryl Sittler
Doug Gilmour
10 Larry Robinson 40.00 80.00
Serge Savard
Guy Lapointe
11 Terry Sawchuk 40.00 80.00
Red Kelly
Alex Delvecchio
12 Bobby Hull
Stan Mikita
Glenn Hall
13 Patrick Roy 40.00 80.00
Raymond Bourque
Marek Svatos
14 Gump Worsley 60.00 125.00
Ed Giacomin
Henrik Lundqvist
15 Bobby Clarke 40.00 80.00
Bill Barber
Reggie Leach
16 Mario Lemieux 90.00 150.00
Jean Beliveau
Maurice Richard
17 Eric Staal 50.00 100.00
Alexander Ovechkin
Dion Phaneuf
18 Marian Stastny 25.00 60.00
Anton Stastny
Peter Stastny
19 Bill Durnan 40.00 80.00
Turk Broda
Harry Lumley
20 Georges Vezina
Jacques Plante
Patrick Roy/9
21 Howie Morenz
Maurice Richard
Jean Beliveau/9
22 Darryl Sittler 30.00 80.00
Lanny McDonald
Tiger Williams
23 Bernie Parent 30.00 80.00
Ron Hextall
Antero Niittymaki
24 Mike Bossy 60.00 100.00
Bryan Trottier
Denis Potvin
25 Gump Worsley 40.00 80.00
Ed Giacomin
Mike Richter
26 Jari Kurri 75.00 125.00
Glenn Anderson
Grant Fuhr
27 Raymond Bourque 40.00 80.00
Brian Leetch
Paul Coffey
28 King Clancy 75.00 125.00
Joe Primeau
Bill Barilko

2006-07 ITG Ultimate Memorabilia Sticks and Jerseys

STATED PRINT RUN 25 SER.#'d SETS
GOLD 1/1 VERSION ALSO EXISTS
GOLD NOT PRICED DUE TO SCARCITY

1 Patrick Roy 30.00 60.00
2 Dave Keon 15.00 30.00
3 Steve Yzerman 25.00 50.00
4 Martin Brodeur
5 Ray Emery 10.00 25.00
6 Ron Francis 15.00 30.00
7 Dominik Hasek
8 Eric Staal 10.00 25.00
9 Peter Stastny
10 Roberto Luongo 25.00 50.00
11 Bernie Parent
12 Vincent Lecavalier 15.00 30.00
13 Rogie Vachon 15.00 30.00
14 Gilbert Perreault 15.00 30.00
15 Mario Lemieux 30.00 60.00

2006-07 ITG Ultimate Memorabilia Sticks Autos

STATED PRINT RUN 50 SER.#'d SETS
GOLD VERSION /10 ALSO EXISTS
GOLD NOT PRICED DUE TO SCARCITY

1 Marcel Dionne 15.00 40.00
2 Manny Fernandez 8.00 20.00
3 Bobby Clarke 12.00 30.00
4 Ed Belfour 10.00 25.00
5 Guy Lafleur 20.00 50.00
6 Jari Kurri 15.00 40.00
7 Cam Neely 15.00 40.00
8 Mark Messier 40.00 80.00
9 Roberto Luongo 20.00 50.00
10 Henrik Lundqvist 15.00 40.00
11 Nicklas Lidstrom 15.00 40.00
12 Pat LaFontaine 12.00 30.00
13 Dave Keon 12.00 30.00
14 Paul Coffey 12.00 30.00
15 Petr Prucha 8.00 20.00
16 Luc Robitaille 25.00 60.00
17 Phil Esposito 12.00 30.00
18 Doug Gilmour 12.00 30.00
19 Glenn Hall 12.00 30.00
20 Brett Hull 15.00 40.00
21 Mike Modano 12.00 30.00
22 Alexander Ovechkin 75.00 150.00
23 Brad Park 8.00 20.00
24 Dion Phaneuf 15.00 40.00
25 Patrick Roy 60.00 125.00
26 Joe Sakic 30.00 60.00
27 Darryl Sittler 10.00 25.00
28 Eric Staal 10.00 25.00
29 John Tavares 75.00 150.00

30 Steve Yzerman 40.00 100.00
31 Felix Potvin
32 Vincent Lecavalier 15.00 40.00

2006-07 ITG Ultimate Memorabilia Trifecta Autos

STATED PRINT RUN 10 SER.#'d SETS
GOLD 1/1 VERSION ALSO EXISTS
NOT PRICED DUE TO SCARCITY
GOLD NOT PRICED DUE TO SCARCITY
1 Nicklas Lidstrom
2 Mario Lemieux
3 Jaromir Jagr
4 Alexander Ovechkin
5 Patrick Roy
6 Steve Yzerman

2006-07 ITG Ultimate Memorabilia Triple Thread Jerseys

STATED PRINT RUN 25 SER.#'d SETS
GOLD 1/1 VERSION ALSO EXISTS
GOLD NOT PRICED DUE TO SCARCITY
1 Evgeni Malkin 50.00 100.00
Ilya Kovalchuk
Alexander Ovechkin
2 Gilbert Perreault 25.00 50.00
Bobby Clarke
Guy Lafleur
3 Steve Yzerman
Mario Lemieux
Mark Messier
4 Roberto Luongo 30.00 80.00
Martin Brodeur
Dominik Hasek
5 Patrick Roy 40.00 100.00
Felix Potvin
Ed Belfour
6 Chris Chelios 25.00 60.00
Brian Leetch
Nicklas Lidstrom
7 Dave Keon 20.00 50.00
Jean Beliveau
Bobby Hull
8 Ted Lindsay 40.00 100.00
Maurice Richard
Milt Schmidt
9 Doug Gilmour 20.00 50.00
Cam Neely
Keith Tkachuk
10 Terry Sawchuk 40.00 80.00
Jacques Plante
Johnny Bower
11 Ed Giacomin 40.00 80.00
Gerry Cheevers
Bernie Parent
12 John Tavares 50.00 125.00
Angelo Esposito
Peter Mueller
13 Eric Staal
Jason Spezza
Dion Phaneuf
14 Alexander Radulov 50.00 100.00
Anze Kopitar
Jordan Staal
15 Luc Robitaille
Brett Hull
Eric Lindros
16 Joe Sakic 30.00 80.00
Joe Thornton
Jaromir Jagr

2006-07 ITG Ultimate Memorabilia Ultimate Hero Single Jerseys

STATED PRINT RUN 25 SER.#'d SETS
GOLD 1/1 VERSION ALSO EXISTS
GOLD NOT PRICED DUE TO SCARCITY
1 Maurice Richard 30.00 80.00
2 Terry Sawchuk 15.00 40.00
3 Patrick Roy 25.00 60.00
4 Steve Yzerman 20.00 50.00
5 Mark Messier 15.00 40.00
6 Mario Lemieux 20.00 50.00

2006-07 ITG Ultimate Memorabilia Ultimate Hero Double Jerseys

STATED PRINT RUN 25 SER.#'d SETS
GOLD 1/1 VERSION ALSO EXISTS
GOLD NOT PRICED DUE TO SCARCITY
1 Maurice Richard 30.00 80.00
2 Terry Sawchuk 15.00 40.00
3 Patrick Roy 25.00 60.00
4 Steve Yzerman 20.00 50.00
5 Mark Messier 15.00 40.00
6 Mario Lemieux 25.00 60.00

2006-07 ITG Ultimate Memorabilia Hero Triple Jerseys

STATED PRINT RUN 25 SER.#'d SETS
GOLD 1/1 VERSION ALSO EXISTS
GOLD NOT PRICED DUE TO SCARCITY
1 Maurice Richard 40.00 100.00
2 Terry Sawchuk 25.00 50.00
3 Patrick Roy 40.00 80.00
4 Steve Yzerman 30.00 60.00
5 Mark Messier 25.00 50.00
6 Mario Lemieux 40.00 80.00

2006-07 ITG Ultimate Memorabilia Vintage Lumber

STATED PRINT RUN 9 SER.#'d SETS
GOLD 1/1 VERSION ALSO EXISTS
NOT PRICED DUE TO SCARCITY
GOLD NOT PRICED DUE TO SCARCITY
1 Howie Morenz
2 Maurice Richard
3 Joe Primeau
4 Terry Sawchuk
5 King Clancy
6 Bill Durnan
7 Bob Davidson
8 Doug Harvey
9 Georges Vezina
10 Bill Barilko

2007-08 ITG Ultimate Memorabilia

This set was released on November 12, 2008. The base set consists of 100 cards.

STATED PRINT RUN 90 SERIAL #'d SETS
1 Alexander Ovechkin 15.00 40.00
2 Gilbert Perreault 4.00 10.00
3 Martin Brodeur 12.00 30.00
4 Dave Keon 4.00 10.00
5 Joe Sakic 10.00 25.00
6 Patrick Roy 15.00 40.00
7 Eddie Shore 5.00 12.00
8 Ilya Kovalchuk 6.00 15.00
9 Luc Robitaille 4.00 10.00
10 Bernie Parent 6.00 15.00
11 Glenn Hall 6.00 15.00
12 Maurice Richard 8.00 20.00
13 Cyclone Taylor 5.00 12.00
14 Bobby Hull 8.00 20.00
15 Dany Heatley 6.00 15.00
16 Georges Vezina 5.00 12.00
17 Dominik Hasek 6.00 15.00
18 Brett Hull 8.00 20.00
19 Phil Esposito 8.00 20.00
20 Guy Lafleur 12.00 30.00
21 Brian Leetch 5.00 12.00
22 Ted Lindsay 4.00 10.00
23 Frank Mahovlich 8.00 20.00
24 Johnny Bower 5.00 12.00
25 Larry Robinson 6.00 15.00
26 Jaromir Jagr 8.00 20.00
27 Jean Beliveau 8.00 20.00
28 Turk Broda 4.00 10.00
29 Tony Esposito 8.00 20.00
30 Markus Naslund 5.00 12.00
31 Henri Richard 8.00 20.00
32 Terry Sawchuk 6.00 15.00
33 Howie Morenz 4.00 10.00
34 Patrick Roy 15.00 40.00
35 Marian Gaborik 6.00 15.00
36 Chris Osgood 4.00 10.00
37 Jacques Plante 8.00 20.00
38 Pelle Lindbergh 5.00 12.00
39 Red Kelly 3.00 8.00
40 Peter Forsberg 6.00 15.00
41 Mike Modano 6.00 15.00
42 Pat LaFontaine 3.00 8.00
43 Syl Apps 4.00 10.00
44 Ron Hextall 8.00 20.00
45 Stan Mikita 4.00 10.00
46 Tim Horton 4.00 10.00
47 Roberto Luongo 8.00 20.00
48 Pavel Datsyuk 5.00 12.00
49 Mats Sundin 5.00 12.00
50 Nicklas Lidstrom 5.00 12.00
51 Alex Delvecchio 3.00 8.00
52 Bill Durnan 3.00 8.00
53 Bobby Clarke 5.00 12.00
54 Borje Salming 4.00 10.00
55 Brad Park 3.00 8.00
56 Cam Neely 5.00 12.00
57 Chris Chelios 3.00 8.00
58 Darryl Sittler 4.00 10.00
59 Denis Potvin 4.00 10.00
60 Doug Gilmour 4.00 10.00
61 Drew Doughty 8.00 20.00
62 Ed Belfour 5.00 12.00
63 Ed Giacomin 5.00 12.00
64 George Hainsworth 3.00 8.00
65 Gerry Cheevers 8.00 20.00
66 Grant Fuhr 8.00 20.00
67 Gump Worsley 6.00 15.00
68 Guy Lapointe 4.00 10.00
69 Jari Kurri 5.00 12.00
70 Jean Ratelle 4.00 10.00
71 Joe Thornton 6.00 15.00
72 John Tavares 20.00 50.00
73 Lanny McDonald 4.00 10.00
74 Lord Stanley 5.00 12.00
75 Mario Lemieux 15.00 40.00
76 Marcel Dionne 3.00 8.00
77 Marty Turco 5.00 12.00
78 Michel Goulet 4.00 10.00
79 Mike Bossy 4.00 10.00
80 Milt Schmidt 3.00 8.00
81 Paul Coffey 5.00 12.00
82 Paul Stastny 5.00 12.00
83 Peter Stastny 4.00 10.00
84 Raymond Bourque 5.00 12.00
85 Elmer Lach 5.00 12.00
86 Rogie Vachon 5.00 12.00
87 Ron Francis 3.00 8.00
88 Sam Gagner 6.00 15.00
89 Scott Niedermayer 3.00 8.00
90 Sid Abel 3.00 8.00
91 Steven Stamkos 10.00 25.00
92 Ted Kennedy 3.00 8.00
93 Roy Worters 3.00 8.00
94 Toe Blake 3.00 8.00
95 Valeri Kharlamov 4.00 10.00
96 Victor Hedman 4.00 10.00
97 Vincent Lecavalier 5.00 12.00
98 Vladislav Tretiak 5.00 12.00
99 Wendel Clark 4.00 10.00
100 Yvan Cournoyer 6.00 15.00

2007-08 ITG Ultimate Memorabilia Autos

STATED PRINT RUN 30 SERIAL #'d SETS
1 Alexander Ovechkin 25.00 60.00
2 Bobby Clarke 8.00 20.00
3 Bobby Hull 12.00 30.00
4 Brett Hull
5 Cam Neely 8.00 20.00
6 Chris Chelios 5.00 12.00
7 Chris Osgood 6.00 15.00
8 Dominik Hasek 10.00 25.00
9 Glenn Hall 10.00 25.00
10 Gump Worsley 10.00 25.00
11 Guy Lafleur 20.00 50.00
12 Henri Richard
13 Ilya Kovalchuk 10.00 25.00
14 Jaromir Jagr 12.00 30.00
15 Jean Beliveau 12.00 30.00
16 Joe Sakic 15.00 40.00
17 Joe Thornton 10.00 25.00
18 John Tavares 30.00 80.00
19 Johnny Bower 8.00 20.00
20 Jean-Sebastien Giguere
21 Luc Robitaille 6.00 15.00
22 Marian Gaborik 10.00 25.00
23 Marcel Dionne
24 Mario Lemieux 25.00 60.00
25 Martin Brodeur
26 Martin St. Louis 6.00 15.00
27 Marty Turco 8.00 20.00
28 Mats Sundin 8.00 20.00
29 Mike Modano 8.00 20.00
30 Nicklas Lidstrom 8.00 20.00
31 Patrick Roy 25.00 60.00
32 Pavel Datsyuk 8.00 20.00
33 Peter Forsberg 10.00 25.00
34 Phil Esposito 12.00 30.00
35 Roberto Luongo 12.00 30.00
36 Ron Francis 5.00 12.00
37 Scott Niedermayer 5.00 12.00
38 Stan Mikita 6.00 15.00
39 Steven Stamkos
40 Ted Lindsay 6.00 15.00
41 Tony Esposito 12.00 30.00
42 Vincent Lecavalier 8.00 20.00
43 Vladislav Tretiak
44 Elmer Lach 8.00 20.00
45 Dave Keon 6.00 15.00
46 Milt Schmidt 5.00 12.00
47 Ted Kennedy 5.00 12.00
48 Joe Nieuwendyk/11
49 Red Kelly/11
50 Paul Coffey/11

2007-08 ITG Ultimate Memorabilia Autos Gold

STATED PRINT RUN 10 SERIAL #'d SETS
NOT PRICED DUE TO SCARCITY

2007-08 ITG Ultimate Memorabilia Autos Dual

STATED PRINT RUN 24 SERIAL #'d SETS
1 Alexander Ovechkin
Ilya Kovalchuk
2 Dave Keon 12.00 30.00
Darryl Sittler
3 Bobby Hull
Brett Hull
4 Scott Niedermayer 15.00 40.00
Chris Pronger
5 Tony Esposito 25.00 60.00
Phil Esposito
6 Mario Lemieux
Jaromir Jagr
7 John Tavares
Steven Stamkos
8 Joe Thornton 20.00 50.00
Milt Schmidt
9 Martin Brodeur 50.00 120.00
Patrick Roy
10 Vincent Lecavalier 15.00 40.00
Martin St. Louis
11 Roberto Luongo 25.00 60.00
Jean-Sebastien Giguere
12 Dominik Hasek 20.00 50.00
Chris Osgood
13 Jean Beliveau 40.00 100.00
Guy Lafleur
14 Brian Leetch 20.00 50.00
Raymond Bourque
15 Mats Sundin 15.00 40.00
Markus Naslund
16 Ed Giacomin
Gerry Cheevers
17 Peter Forsberg 30.00 80.00
Joe Sakic
18 Chris Chelios
Nicklas Lidstrom
19 Bobby Clarke 20.00 50.00
Bernie Parent
20 Marian Gaborik 20.00 50.00
Pavel Datsyuk
21 Ron Francis 12.00 30.00
Luc Robitaille
22 Frank Mahovlich 25.00 60.00
Johnny Bower
23 Peter Stastny 15.00 40.00
Paul Stastny

2007-08 ITG Ultimate Memorabilia Autos Dual Gold

STATED PRINT RUN 1 SERIAL #'d SET
NOT PRICED DUE TO SCARCITY

2007-08 ITG Ultimate Memorabilia Autos Triple

STATED PRINT RUN 9 SERIAL #'d SETS
NOT PRICED DUE TO SCARCITY

2007-08 ITG Ultimate Memorabilia Autos Triple Gold

STATED PRINT RUN 1 SERIAL #'d SET
NOT PRICED DUE TO SCARCITY

2007-08 ITG Ultimate Memorabilia Battle of Alberta

STATED PRINT RUN 24 SERIAL #'d SETS
1 Lanny McDonald 15.00 40.00
Jari Kurri
2 Brett Hull 12.00 30.00
Glenn Anderson
3 Mike Vernon 25.00 60.00
Grant Fuhr
4 Joe Nieuwendyk 12.00 30.00
Paul Coffey
5 Phil Housley 12.00 30.00
Bill Ranford

2007-08 ITG Ultimate Memorabilia Battle of Alberta Gold

STATED PRINT RUN 1 SERIAL #'d SET
NOT PRICED DUE TO SCARCITY

2007-08 ITG Ultimate Memorabilia Battle of Quebec

1 Mats Sundin 50.00 120.00
Patrick Roy
2 Dan Bouchard 12.00 30.00
Guy Lafleur
3 Michel Goulet 20.00 50.00
Larry Robinson
4 Peter Stastny 12.00 30.00
Steve Shutt
5 Joe Sakic 50.00 120.00
Patrick Roy

2007-08 ITG Ultimate Memorabilia Battle of Quebec Gold

STATED PRINT RUN 1 SERIAL #'d SET
NOT PRICED DUE TO SCARCITY

2007-08 ITG Ultimate Memorabilia Blades of Steel

STATED PRINT RUN 24 SERIAL #'d SETS
1 Dave Keon 10.00 25.00
2 Jaromir Jagr 20.00 50.00
3 Dany Heatley 15.00 40.00
4 Gerry Cheevers 20.00 50.00
5 Doug Gilmour 10.00 25.00
6 Phil Esposito 20.00 50.00
7 Pavel Datsyuk 12.00 30.00
8 Gilbert Perreault 10.00 25.00
9 Luc Robitaille 10.00 25.00
10 Mario Lemieux 40.00 100.00
11 Paul Coffey 12.00 30.00
12 Alexander Ovechkin 40.00 100.00
13 Darryl Sittler 10.00 25.00
14 Marcel Dionne 8.00 20.00
15 Joe Thornton 15.00 40.00
16 Jacques Plante 20.00 50.00
17 Jean Beliveau 20.00 50.00
18 Maurice Richard 20.00 50.00
19 Tim Horton 10.00 25.00
20 Stan Mikita 10.00 25.00

2007-08 ITG Ultimate Memorabilia Cityscapes

STATED PRINT RUN 24 SERIAL #'d SETS
1 Bobby Hull 15.00 40.00
Ernie Banks
2 Ilya Kovalchuk 12.00 30.00
Dominique Wilkins
3 Dominik Hasek 12.00 30.00
Doug Flutie
4 Marty Turco 10.00 25.00
Deion Sanders
5 Phil Esposito 15.00 40.00
Pele
6 Tony Esposito 15.00 40.00
Andre Dawson
7 Glenn Hall 12.00 30.00
Bob Gibson
8 Patrick Roy 30.00 80.00
Gary Carter
9 Patrick Roy 30.00 80.00
John Elway
10 Pavel Datsyuk 10.00 25.00
Barry Sanders
11 Brian Leetch 10.00 25.00
Reggie Jackson
12 Marian Gaborik 12.00 30.00
Justin Morneau
13 Mario Lemieux 30.00 80.00
Jason Bay
14 Jean Beliveau 15.00 40.00
Tony Perez
15 Mike Modano 10.00 25.00
Michael Irvin
16 Brett Hull 15.00 40.00
Lou Brock
17 Jaromir Jagr 15.00 40.00
Roberto Clemente

2007-08 ITG Ultimate Memorabilia Complete Jersey

1 Alexander Ovechkin
2 Brett Hull
3 Cam Neely
4 Dave Keon
5 Dominik Hasek
6 Guy Lafleur
7 Ilya Kovalchuk
8 Jacques Plante
9 Jaromir Jagr
10 Jean Beliveau
11 Joe Sakic
12 John Tavares
13 Marcel Dionne
14 Mario Lemieux
15 Martin Brodeur
16 Mats Sundin
17 Mike Modano
18 Milt Schmidt
19 Patrick Roy
20 Pavel Datsyuk
21 Peter Forsberg
22 Raymond Bourque
23 Roberto Luongo
24 Sam Gagner
25 Scott Niedermayer
26 Steven Stamkos
27 Vincent Lecavalier
28 Vladislav Tretiak
29 Joe Nieuwendyk
30 Nicklas Lidstrom

2007-08 ITG Ultimate Memorabilia Complete Package

1 Joe Thornton
2 Gerry Cheevers
3 Eddie Shore
4 Alexander Ovechkin
5 Martin Brodeur
6 Patrick Roy
7 Dominik Hasek
8 Mario Lemieux
9 Marcel Dionne
10 Guy Lafleur
11 Raymond Bourque
12 Bernie Parent
13 Cam Neely
14 Bobby Hull
15 Tim Horton
16 Maurice Richard
17 Stan Mikita
18 Paul Coffey
19 Terry Sawchuk
20 Jacques Plante

2007-08 ITG Ultimate Memorabilia Cornerstones

1 Charlie Conacher
Joe Primeau
Busher Jackson
Hap Day
2 Dave Keon
Frank Mahovlich
Nathan Horton
Johnny Bower
3 Howie Morenz
Auriel Joliat
George Hainsworth
Newsy Lalonde
4 Sid Abel
Ted Lindsay
Alex Delvecchio
Terry Sawchuk
5 Eddie Shore
Tiny Thompson
Nels Stewart
Milt Schmidt
6 Bobby Clarke
Bernie Parent
Bill Barber
Reggie Leach
7 Eddie Giacomin
Rod Gilbert
Jean Ratelle
Brad Park
8 Dominik Hasek
Chris Chelios
Brett Hull
Nicklas Lidstrom

2007-08 ITG Ultimate Memorabilia Country Wide

1 Jaromir Jagr 12.00 30.00
2 Jari Kurri 8.00 20.00
3 Roberto Luongo 12.00 30.00
4 Vincent Lecavalier 8.00 20.00
5 Brett Hull 12.00 30.00
6 Michel Goulet 6.00 15.00
7 Marcel Dionne 5.00 12.00
8 Bobby Clarke 8.00 20.00
9 Chris Chelios 5.00 12.00
10 Gilbert Perreault 6.00 15.00
11 Chris Pronger 8.00 20.00
12 Mats Naslund 6.00 15.00
13 Mike Richter
14 Joe Sakic
15 Borje Salming 6.00 15.00
16 Mats Sundin 8.00 20.00
17 Joe Thornton 10.00 25.00
18 Brian Leetch 8.00 20.00
19 Mike Modano 8.00 20.00
20 Nicklas Lidstrom
21 Mario Lemieux
22 Alexander Ovechkin
23 Patrick Roy 25.00 60.00
24 Kyle Okposo 5.00 12.00
25 John Tavares 30.00 80.00
26 Steven Stamkos
27 Sam Gagner 10.00 25.00
28 Martin Brodeur 20.00 50.00
29 Dany Heatley 10.00 25.00
30 Peter Forsberg 10.00 25.00
31 Pelle Lindbergh 8.00 20.00

2007-08 ITG Ultimate Memorabilia Decade Dominance

1 Ted Lindsay
Maurice Richard
Jean Beliveau
Terry Sawchuk
Doug Harvey
Sid Abel 1950's
2 Bobby Hull
Frank Mahovlich
Dave Keon
Alex Delvecchio
Tim Horton
Stan Mikita 1960's
3 Phil Esposito
Borje Salming
Tony Esposito
Marcel Dionne
Bobby Clarke
Guy Lafleur 1970's
4 Patrick Roy
Cam Neely
Jari Kurri
Ray Bourque
Grant Fuhr
Wendell Clark 1980's
5 Mats Sundin
Mario Lemieux
Joe Sakic
Dominik Hasek
Brett Hull
Martin Brodeur 1990's
6 Marian Gaborik
Joe Thornton
Pavel Datsyuk
Ilya Kovalchuk
Roberto Luongo
Alexander Ovechkin 2000's

2007-08 ITG Ultimate Memorabilia Double Memorabilia Autos

STATED PRINT RUN 24 SERIAL #'d SETS
1 Alexander Ovechkin 25.00 60.00
Ilya Kovalchuk
2 Dave Keon 25.00 60.00
Darryl Sittler
3 Bobby Hull 40.00 80.00
Brett Hull
4 Scott Niedermayer 10.00 25.00
Chris Pronger
5 Tony Esposito
Phil Esposito
6 Mario Lemieux 60.00 120.00
Jaromir Jagr
7 John Tavares 40.00 80.00
Steven Stamkos
8 Joe Thornton 15.00 40.00
Milt Schmidt
9 Martin Brodeur 75.00 150.00
Patrick Roy
10 Vincent Lecavalier 20.00 50.00
Martin St. Louis
11 Roberto Luongo 30.00 60.00
Jean-Sebastien Giguere
12 Dominik Hasek 15.00 40.00
Chris Osgood
13 Jean Beliveau 25.00 60.00
Guy Lafleur
14 Brian Leetch 25.00 60.00
Raymond Bourque
15 Mats Sundin 25.00 60.00
Markus Naslund
16 Ed Giacomin
Gerry Cheevers
17 Peter Forsberg 20.00 50.00
Joe Sakic
18 Chris Chelios 25.00 60.00
Nicklas Lidstrom
19 Bobby Clarke 25.00 60.00
Bernie Parent
20 Marian Gaborik
Pavel Datsyuk
21 Ron Francis
Luc Robitaille
22 Frank Mahovlich
Johnny Bower
23 Peter Stastny
Paul Stastny

2007-08 ITG Ultimate Memorabilia Emblem Attic

1 Maurice Richard
2 Terry Sawchuk
3 Sid Abel
4 Frank Brimsek
5 Milt Schmidt
6 Aurel Joliat
7 George Hainsworth
8 Jacques Plante
9 Doug Harvey
10 Stan Mikita
11 Dave Keon
12 Jean Beliveau
13 Frank Mahovlich
14 Roy Worters

2007-08 ITG Ultimate Memorabilia Emblems

1 Mario Lemieux
2 Lanny McDonald
3 Cam Neely
4 Alexander Ovechkin
5 Patrick Roy
6 Mats Sundin
7 Joe Thornton
8 Raymond Bourque
9 Pavel Datsyuk
10 Grant Fuhr
11 Marian Gaborik
12 Scott Niedermayer
13 Jaromir Jagr
14 Steven Stamkos
15 Joe Sakic
16 Gilbert Perreault
17 Joe Nieuwendyk
18 Mike Modano
19 Brian Leetch
20 Vincent Lecavalier
21 Dominik Hasek
22 Brett Hull
23 Ron Francis
24 Peter Forsberg
25 Martin Brodeur

2007-08 ITG Ultimate Memorabilia First Rounders

1 John Tavares 25.00 60.00
2 Victor Hedman 12.00 30.00
3 Steven Stamkos 15.00 40.00
4 Drew Doughty
5 Alex Pietrangelo
6 Luke Schenn 25.00 60.00
7 Karl Alzner 10.00 25.00
8 Sam Gagner 15.00 40.00
9 Peter Mueller 15.00 40.00
10 Kyle Okposo
11 Bryan Little 12.00 30.00
12 Carey Price 30.00 60.00
13 Alexander Ovechkin 15.00 40.00
14 Alexander Semin 15.00 40.00
15 Ilya Kovalchuk 8.00 20.00
16 Dany Heatley 8.00 20.00
17 Marian Gaborik 12.00 30.00
18 Vincent Lecavalier 12.00 30.00
19 Joe Thornton
20 Roberto Luongo 12.00 30.00
21 Scott Niedermayer 10.00 25.00
22 Peter Forsberg 15.00 40.00
23 Jaromir Jagr 20.00 50.00
24 Martin Brodeur
25 Mats Sundin 12.00 30.00
26 Mike Modano 12.00 30.00
27 Joe Sakic
28 Brian Leetch 8.00 20.00
29 Wendel Clark 15.00 40.00
30 Mario Lemieux
31 Raymond Bourque 15.00 40.00
32 Denis Potvin 8.00 20.00
33 Guy Lafleur
34 Gilbert Perreault 10.00 25.00
35 Darryl Sittler

2007-08 ITG Ultimate Memorabilia Franchises

STATED PRINT RUN 24 SERIAL #'d SETS
1 Mats Sundin 15.00 40.00
Doug Gilmour
Felix Potvin
2 Dave Keon 20.00 50.00
Frank Mahovlich
Tim Horton
3 Jean Beliveau 20.00 50.00
Doug Harvey
Jacques Plante
4 Guy Lafleur 30.00 80.00
Lanny Robinson
Serge Savard
5 Alex Delvecchio 10.00 25.00
Sid Abel
Ted Lindsay
6 Pavel Datsyuk 12.00 30.00
Nicklas Lidstrom
Chris Osgood
7 Harry Lumley 12.00 30.00
Bill Mosienko
Bill Gadsby
8 Chris Chelios 12.00 30.00
Ed Belfour
Michel Goulet
9 Eddie Giacomin 12.00 30.00
Brad Park
Jean Ratelle
10 Mike Richter 12.00 30.00
Brian Leetch
John Vanbiesbrouck
11 Eddie Shore 10.00 25.00
Tiny Thompson
Frank Brimsek
12 Cam Neely 15.00 40.00
Andy Moog
Ray Bourque
13 Peter Forsberg 40.00 100.00
Patrick Roy
Joe Sakic
14 Grant Fuhr 20.00 50.00
Jari Kurri
Glenn Anderson
15 Mike Modano 12.00 30.00
Brett Hull
Marty Turco
16 Denis Potvin 12.00 30.00
Billy Smith
Mike Bossy
17 Bernie Parent 15.00 40.00
Bill Barber
Bobby Clarke
18 Mario Lemieux 40.00 100.00
Jaromir Jagr
Ron Francis
19 Jean-Sebastien Giguere 12.00 30.00
Dany Heatley
20 Vincent Lecavalier 25.00 60.00
Martin St. Louis
Steven Stamkos
21 Darryl Sittler 10.00 25.00
Lanny McDonald
Borje Salming

2007-08 ITG Ultimate Memorabilia Future Star Autos

STATED PRINT RUN 40 SERIAL #'d SETS
1 John Tavares 40.00 100.00
2 Ryan Parent 15.00 40.00
3 Ryan O'Marra 6.00 15.00
4 Logan Couture
5 Jonas Hiller
6 Alex Pietrangelo 6.00 15.00
7 Steve Mason 30.00 80.00
8 Andrew Cogliano 15.00 40.00
9 Leland Irving 15.00 40.00
10 Tuukka Rask 15.00 40.00
11 Kyle Okposo
12 Karl Alzner 8.00 20.00
13 Steven Stamkos 20.00 50.00
14 Steve Downie 8.00 20.00
15 Sam Gagner 12.00 30.00
16 Peter Mueller 20.00 50.00
17 Paul Stastny 10.00 25.00
18 Michael Frolik 8.00 20.00
19 Michael Del Zotto 10.00 25.00
20 Marc Staal 15.00 40.00
21 Jordan Staal 12.00 30.00
22 Jiri Tlusty 15.00 40.00
23 Jack Skille 10.00 25.00
24 Drew Doughty 15.00 40.00
25 Devin Setoguchi 12.00 30.00
26 Carey Price 60.00 120.00
27 Bryan Little 8.00 20.00
28 Angelo Esposito
29 Alexei Cherepanov 10.00 25.00
30 Brandon Sutter 8.00 20.00
31 Victor Hedman 15.00 40.00

2007-08 ITG Ultimate Memorabilia Future Star Patches Autos

STATED PRINT RUN 19 SERIAL #'d SETS
NOT PRICED DUE TO SCARCITY

2007-08 ITG Ultimate Memorabilia Gloves Are Off

1 Joe Sakic 25.00 60.00
2 Joe Thornton 15.00 40.00
3 Alexander Ovechkin 40.00 100.00
4 Stan Mikita 10.00 25.00
5 Raymond Bourque 15.00 40.00
6 Pat LaFontaine 8.00 20.00
7 Martin Brodeur 30.00 80.00
8 Mario Lemieux 40.00 100.00
9 Eddie Shore 12.00 30.00
10 Dominik Hasek 15.00 40.00
11 Cam Neely 12.00 30.00
12 Brett Hull 20.00 50.00
13 Bobby Clarke 12.00 30.00
14 Patrick Roy 40.00 100.00
15 Sam Gagner 15.00 40.00
16 Bill Durnan 8.00 20.00
17 Paul Coffey
18 Mats Sundin
19 Drew Doughty 20.00 50.00
20 Charlie Conacher 10.00 25.00

2007-08 ITG Ultimate Memorabilia Jerseys

1 Alexander Ovechkin 40.00 100.00
2 Bobby Hull 20.00 50.00
3 Borje Salming 10.00 25.00
4 Brett Hull 20.00 50.00
5 Carey Price
6 Chris Osgood 10.00 25.00
7 Dave Keon
8 Dominik Hasek 15.00 40.00
9 Glenn Hall
10 Guy Lafleur 30.00 80.00

11 Ilya Kovalchuk 15.00 40.00
12 Jean Beliveau 20.00 50.00
13 Joe Sakic 25.00 60.00
14 Joe Thornton 15.00 40.00
15 John Tavares 50.00 120.00
16 Marian Gaborik
17 Mario Lemieux 40.00 100.00
18 Martin Brodeur 30.00 80.00
19 Marty Turco 12.00 30.00
20 Mats Sundin 12.00 30.00
21 Maurice Richard 20.00 50.00
22 Mike Modano 12.00 30.00
23 Patrick Roy 40.00 100.00
24 Pavel Datsyuk 12.00 30.00
25 Peter Forsberg 15.00 40.00
26 Roberto Luongo 20.00 50.00
27 Scott Niedermayer
28 Steven Stamkos 25.00 60.00
29 Vincent Lecavalier 12.00 30.00
30 Vladislav Tretiak
31 Victor Hedman 10.00 25.00
32 Joe Nieuwendyk 10.00 25.00

2007-08 ITG Ultimate Memorabilia Jerseys Autos

1 Alexander Ovechkin 50.00 120.00
2 Bobby Clarke 15.00 40.00
3 Bobby Hull 25.00 60.00
4 Brett Hull 25.00 60.00
5 Cam Neely 15.00 40.00
6 Chris Chelios 10.00 25.00
7 Chris Osgood 12.00 30.00
8 Dominik Hasek 20.00 50.00
9 Ed Giacomin 15.00 40.00
10 Glenn Hall 20.00 50.00
11 Guy Lafleur 40.00 100.00
12 Ilya Kovalchuk
13 Jaromir Jagr
14 Jean Beliveau 25.00 60.00
15 Joe Sakic 30.00 80.00
16 Joe Thornton 20.00 50.00
17 John Tavares 60.00 150.00
18 Jean-Sebastien Giguere 15.00 40.00
19 Luc Robitaille 12.00 30.00
20 Marian Gaborik 20.00 50.00
21 Marcel Dionne 10.00 25.00
22 Mario Lemieux
23 Martin Brodeur
24 Martin St. Louis
25 Marty Turco 15.00 40.00
26 Mats Sundin 15.00 40.00
27 Mike Modano 15.00 40.00
28 Nicklas Lidstrom 15.00 40.00
29 Patrick Roy 50.00 120.00
30 Paul Stastny 15.00 40.00
31 Pavel Datsyuk 15.00 40.00
32 Peter Forsberg
33 Phil Esposito
34 Roberto Luongo 25.00 60.00
35 Ron Francis 10.00 25.00
36 Scott Niedermayer 10.00 25.00
37 Stan Mikita 12.00 30.00
38 Steven Stamkos 30.00 80.00
39 Tony Esposito 25.00 60.00
40 Vincent Lecavalier 15.00 40.00
41 Vladislav Tretiak 12.00 30.00
42 Joe Nieuwendyk 12.00 30.00
43 Victor Hedman 12.00 30.00
44 Brian Leetch 15.00 40.00
45 Bernie Parent 20.00 50.00
46 Frank Mahovlich
47 Pat LaFontaine 10.00 25.00
48 Red Kelly 10.00 25.00
49 Doug Gilmour 12.00 30.00
50 Alex Delvecchio

2007-08 ITG Ultimate Memorabilia Journey Emblem

1 Mats Sundin
2 Ed Belfour
3 Raymond Bourque
4 Martin Brodeur
5 Chris Chelios
6 Paul Coffey
7 Peter Forsberg
8 Dominik Hasek
9 Brett Hull
10 Jaromir Jagr
11 Brian Leetch
12 Mario Lemieux
13 Nicklas Lidstrom
14 Felix Potvin
15 Luc Robitaille
16 Patrick Roy
17 Dany Heatley
18 Joe Thornton
19 Mike Modano
20 Joe Sakic

2007-08 ITG Ultimate Memorabilia Journey Jersey

1 Mats Sundin 25.00 60.00
2 Ed Belfour 25.00 60.00
3 Raymond Bourque
4 Martin Brodeur
5 Chris Chelios
6 Paul Coffey 25.00 60.00
7 Peter Forsberg 30.00 80.00
8 Dominik Hasek
9 Brett Hull 40.00 100.00
10 Jaromir Jagr 40.00 100.00
11 Brian Leetch 25.00 60.00
12 Mario Lemieux 80.00 200.00
13 Nicklas Lidstrom 25.00 60.00
14 Felix Potvin 30.00 80.00
15 Luc Robitaille
16 Patrick Roy 80.00 200.00
17 Dany Heatley 30.00 80.00
18 Joe Thornton 30.00 80.00
19 Mike Modano 25.00 60.00
20 Joe Sakic 50.00 125.00

2007-08 ITG Ultimate Memorabilia Net Average

1 Roy Worters 15.00 40.00
Tiny Thompson
2 Ed Belfour
Martin Brodeur
3 Marty Turco 10.00 25.00
4 Patrick Roy 30.00 80.00
5 Dominik Hasek 12.00 30.00
6 Bernie Parent 12.00 30.00
7 Tony Esposito 15.00 40.00
8 Frank Brimsek 10.00 25.00

2007-08 ITG Ultimate Memorabilia Net Wins

1 Patrick Roy 50.00 120.00
Martin Brodeur
2 Mike Richter 15.00 40.00
John Vanbiesbrouck
3 Bernie Parent 25.00 60.00
Ron Hextall
4 Ed Belfour 10.00 25.00
6 Jacques Plante 15.00 40.00
7 Tony Esposito 15.00 40.00
8 Glenn Hall 12.00 30.00
9 Grant Fuhr 15.00 40.00
10 Dominik Hasek 12.00 30.00
12 Billy Smith 10.00 25.00

2007-08 ITG Ultimate Memorabilia Net Zero

1 Terry Sawchuk
Martin Brodeur
2 Glenn Hall 15.00 40.00
Tony Esposito
3 Jacques Plante 40.00 100.00
Patrick Roy
4 George Hainsworth 8.00 20.00
5 Tiny Thompson 10.00 25.00
6 Dominik Hasek 15.00 40.00
7 Ed Belfour
8 Harry Lumley
9 Roy Worters 8.00 20.00
10 Bernie Parent 15.00 40.00
11 Ed Giacomin 12.00 30.00
12 Rogie Vachon 12.00 30.00

2007-08 ITG Ultimate Memorabilia New Millennium First Rounders Autos

1 Alexei Cherepanov
2 Angelo Esposito 20.00 50.00
3 Bryan Little 10.00 25.00
4 Carey Price 75.00 150.00
5 Devin Setoguchi 15.00 40.00
6 Jack Skille 12.00 30.00
7 Jiri Tlusty 20.00 50.00
8 Jordan Staal 15.00 40.00
9 Marc Staal 20.00 50.00
10 Michael Del Zotto 12.00 30.00
11 Michael Frolik 10.00 25.00
12 Peter Mueller 25.00 60.00
13 Sam Gagner 15.00 40.00
14 Steve Downie 10.00 25.00
15 Karl Alzner 10.00 25.00
16 Kyle Okposo 8.00 20.00
17 Tuukka Rask 20.00 50.00
18 Leland Irving 12.00 30.00
19 Andrew Cogliano 20.00 50.00
20 Logan Couture 12.00 30.00
21 Ryan O'Marra 8.00 20.00
22 Ryan Parent 10.00 25.00
23 Brandon Sutter 10.00 25.00
24 Thomas Hickey 15.00 40.00
25 Benoit Pouliot
26 Jonathan Blum 8.00 20.00
27 Alex Pietrangelo 8.00 20.00
28 Steven Stamkos 25.00 60.00
29 Drew Doughty 20.00 50.00
30 John Tavares 50.00 120.00
31 Victor Hedman 10.00 25.00

2007-08 ITG Ultimate Memorabilia Past Present and Future

1 Dave Keon 25.00 60.00
Mats Sundin
Luke Schenn
2 Doug Harvey 30.00 80.00
Scott Niedermayer
Drew Doughty
3 Jean Beliveau 30.00 80.00
Vincent Lecavalier
Claude Giroux
4 Glenn Hall 60.00 150.00
Roberto Luongo
Steve Mason
5 Guy Lafleur 80.00 200.00
Marian Gaborik
John Tavares
6 Mario Lemieux
Joe Thornton
Sam Gagner
7 Maurice Richard 30.00 80.00
Martin St. Louis
Gilbert Brule
8 Grant Fuhr 30.00 80.00
Martin Brodeur
Leland Irving
9 Bobby Clarke 30.00 80.00
Dany Heatley
Andrew Cogliano
10 Igor Larionov 60.00 150.00
Alexander Ovechkin
Alexei Cherepanov
11 Patrick Roy
Joe Sakic
Peter Budaj
12 Denis Potvin 20.00 50.00
Chris Pronger
Michael Del Zotto
13 Borje Salming 25.00 60.00
Chris Chelios
Thomas Hickey
14 Mike Richter 50.00 120.00
Mike Modano
Kyle Okposo
15 Ted Lindsay
Pavel Datsyuk
Thomas McCollum
16 Terry Sawchuk 25.00 60.00
Marty Turco
Jonas Hiller
17 Pelle Lindbergh
Jean-Sebastien Giguere
Tuukka Rask
18 Peter Stastny 30.00 80.00
Jaromir Jagr
Jiri Tlusty
19 Tim Horton 20.00 50.00
Nicklas Lidstrom
Alex Pietrangelo
20 Markus Naslund
Peter Forsberg
Victor Hedman
21 Vladislav Tretiak 75.00 150.00
Chris Osgood
Carey Price

2007-08 ITG Ultimate Memorabilia Raised to the Rafters

STATED PRINT RUN 24 SERIAL #'d SETS
1 Glenn Hall 12.00 30.00
2 Brian Leetch 10.00 25.00
3 Tony Esposito 15.00 40.00
4 Guy Lafleur 25.00 60.00
5 Larry Robinson 12.00 30.00
6 Johnny Bucyk 6.00 15.00

2007-08 ITG Ultimate Memorabilia Retro Teammates

1 Tiny Thompson 10.00 25.00
Eddie Shore
2 Sid Abel 6.00 15.00
Alex Delvecchio
3 Raymond Bourque 12.00 30.00
Cam Neely
4 Paul Coffey 10.00 25.00
Ron Francis
5 Joe Sakic 20.00 50.00
Mats Sundin
6 Dominik Hasek 12.00 30.00
Pat LaFontaine
7 Glenn Anderson 15.00 40.00
Grant Fuhr
8 Ed Belfour 10.00 25.00
Chris Chelios
9 Jean Beliveau 15.00 40.00
Jacques Plante
10 Mike Bossy 8.00 20.00
Denis Potvin
11 Bobby Clarke 10.00 25.00
Pelle Lindbergh
12 Bill Barber 12.00 30.00
Bernie Parent
13 Dave Keon 15.00 40.00
Frank Mahovlich
14 Guy Lafleur 25.00 60.00
Yvan Cournoyer
15 Rod Gilbert 10.00 25.00
Ed Giacomin
16 Tony Esposito 15.00 40.00
Stan Mikita
17 Glenn Hall 12.00 30.00
Bobby Hull
18 George Hainsworth 6.00 15.00
Aurel Joliat
19 Tim Horton 10.00 25.00
Johnny Bower
20 Brett Hull 15.00 40.00
Lanny McDonald
21 Mario Lemieux 30.00 80.00
Jaromir Jagr
22 Mike Richter 10.00 25.00
John Vanbiesbrouck
23 Bill Mosienko 10.00 25.00
Harry Lumley
24 Brad Park 8.00 20.00
Jean Ratelle
25 Patrick Roy 30.00 80.00
Peter Forsberg
26 Guy Lapointe 12.00 30.00
Larry Robinson
27 Brian Leetch 10.00 25.00
Luc Robitaille
28 Doug Gilmour 12.00 30.00
Felix Potvin
29 Borje Salming 8.00 20.00
Darryl Sittler
30 Vladislav Tretiak 8.00 20.00
Valeri Kharlamov

2007-08 ITG Ultimate Memorabilia St. Patrick's Legacy

1 Patrick Roy Montreal Jersey 12.00 30.00
2 Patrick Roy Colorado Jersey 12.00 30.00
3 Patrick Roy Dual Jersey 15.00 40.00
4 Patrick Roy Montreal Pad 20.00 50.00
5 Patrick Roy Colorado Pad 20.00 50.00
6 Patrick Roy Dual Pad 25.00 60.00
7 Patrick Roy Montreal Glove 20.00 50.00
8 Patrick Roy Colorado Glove 20.00 50.00
9 Patrick Roy Dual Glove 25.00 60.00

2007-08 ITG Ultimate Memorabilia Stick Rack

1 Martin Brodeur 50.00 120.00
2 Felix Potvin 25.00 60.00
3 Pat LaFontaine 12.00 30.00
4 Mike Richter 50.00 120.00
5 Cam Neely 20.00 50.00
6 Joe Sakic 40.00 100.00
7 Jaromir Jagr 30.00 80.00
8 Vincent Lecavalier 20.00 50.00
9 Rogie Vachon
10 Grant Fuhr 30.00 80.00
11 Mario Lemieux 60.00 150.00
12 Alexander Ovechkin
13 Peter Stastny 15.00 40.00
14 Peter Forsberg 25.00 60.00
15 Martin St. Louis 15.00 40.00
16 Joe Thornton 25.00 60.00
17 Tony Esposito 30.00 80.00
18 Dominik Hasek
19 Chris Osgood 15.00 40.00
20 Luc Robitaille 15.00 40.00
21 Guy Lafleur 50.00 120.00
22 Phil Housley
23 Dale Hawerchuk 15.00 40.00
24 Michel Goulet 15.00 40.00
25 Ron Francis 12.00 30.00

2007-08 ITG Ultimate Memorabilia Sticks Autos

1 Alexander Ovechkin 60.00 150.00
2 Marcel Dionne
3 Cam Neely 20.00 50.00
4 Chris Chelios 12.00 30.00
5 Dominik Hasek 25.00 60.00
6 Guy Lafleur 50.00 120.00
7 Jaromir Jagr 30.00 80.00
8 Joe Sakic 40.00 100.00
9 Joe Thornton 25.00 60.00
10 Jean-Sebastien Giguere 20.00 50.00
11 Luc Robitaille 15.00 40.00
12 Mario Lemieux 60.00 150.00
13 Martin Brodeur 50.00 120.00
14 Martin St. Louis 15.00 40.00
15 Marty Turco 20.00 50.00
16 Mike Modano 20.00 50.00
17 Tony Esposito
18 Mats Sundin 20.00 50.00
19 Pavel Datsyuk 20.00 50.00
20 Peter Forsberg 25.00 60.00
21 Roberto Luongo 30.00 80.00
22 Ron Francis 12.00 30.00
23 Scott Niedermayer 12.00 30.00
24 Stan Mikita 15.00 40.00
25 Vincent Lecavalier 20.00 50.00

2007-08 ITG Ultimate Memorabilia Toronto Fall Expo Memorabilia

1 Jean Beliveau
2 Turk Broda
3 Henri Richard
4 Terry Sawchuk
5 Howie Morenz
6 Jacques Plante
7 Eddie Shore
8 Ted Kennedy
9 Roy Worters
10 Bobby Hull
11 Glenn Hall
12 Maurice Richard
13 Alex Devecchio
14 Stan Mikita
15 Sid Abel
16 Bill Durnan
17 Red Kelly
18 Dave Keon
19 Phil Esposito
20 Tim Horton
21 Frank Mahovlich
22 Ted Lindsay
23 Milt Schmidt
24 Johnny Bower
25 Rogie Vachon

2007-08 ITG Ultimate Memorabilia Toronto Fall Expo Memorabilia Redemptions

1 Alexander Ovechkin
2 Bernie Parent
3 Bobby Clarke
4 Borje Salming
5 Brad Park
6 Brett Hull
7 Brian Leetch
8 Cam Neely
9 Chris Chelios
10 Chris Osgood
11 Dany Heatley
12 Darryl Sittler
13 Denis Potvin
14 Dominik Hasek
15 Doug Gilmour
16 Drew Doughty
17 Ed Belfour
18 Ed Giacomin
19 Gerry Cheevers
20 Gilbert Perreault
21 Grant Fuhr
22 Guy Lafleur
23 Guy Lapointe
24 Jaromir Jagr
25 Jean Ratelle
26 Joe Sakic
27 Joe Thornton
28 John Tavares
29 Lanny McDonald
30 Larry Robinson
31 Ilya Kovalchuk
32 Luc Robitaille
33 Marcel Dionne
34 Marian Gaborik
35 Mario Lemieux
36 Markus Naslund
37 Martin Brodeur
38 Marty Turco
39 Mats Sundin
40 Michel Goulet
41 Mike Bossy
42 Mike Modano
43 Nicklas Lidstrom
44 Pat LaFontaine
45 Patrick Roy-Colorado
46 Patrick Roy-Montreal
47 Paul Stastny
48 Pavel Datsyuk
49 Pelle Lindbergh
50 Peter Forsberg
51 Peter Stastny
52 Raymond Bourque
53 Roberto Luongo
54 Ron Francis
55 Ron Hextall
56 Sam Gagner
57 Scott Niedermayer
58 Steven Stamkos
59 Tony Esposito
60 Valeri Kharlamov
61 Victor Hedman
62 Vincent Lecavalier
63 Vladislav Tretiak
64 Wendel Clark

2007-08 ITG Ultimate Memorabilia Trifecta Autos

1 Alexander Ovechkin
2 Mats Sundin
3 Martin Brodeur
4 Marcel Dionne
5 Patrick Roy
6 Guy Lafleur

2007-08 ITG Ultimate Memorabilia Triple Logo

1 Raymond Bourque
2 Marty Turco
3 Mats Sundin
4 Joe Sakic
5 Dany Heatley
6 Brett Hull
7 Dominik Hasek
8 Brett Hull
9 Ron Francis
10 Peter Forsberg
11 Paul Coffey
12 Grant Fuhr
13 Chris Chelios
14 Mats Sundin
15 Steven Stamkos
16 Alexander Ovechkin
17 Scott Niedermayer
18 Mike Modano
19 Roberto Luongo
20 Vincent Lecavalier
21 Jaromir Jagr
22 Dany Heatley
23 Patrick Roy
24 Joe Thornton
25 Mario Lemieux
26 Jaromir Jagr
27 Mats Sundin
28 Jean-Sebastien Giguere
29 Martin St. Louis
30 Martin Brodeur

2007-08 ITG Ultimate Memorabilia Vintage Lumber

STATED PRINT RUN 24 SERIAL #'d SETS
SOME NOT PRICED DUE TO SCARCITY
1 Doug Harvey/9
2 Red Kelly/9
3 Dave Keon/9
4 Tim Horton/9
5 King Clancy/9
6 Bill Durnan/9
7 Henri Richard/9
8 Howie Morenz/9
9 Jacques Plante/9
10 Gump Worsley/9
11 Johnny Bower/9
12 Bernie Geffrion/9
13 Chuck Rayner 12.00 30.00
14 Ed Giacomin
15 Stan Mikita 12.00 30.00
16 Joe Primeau/19
17 Johnny Bucyk 12.00 30.00
18 Roger Crozier 12.00 30.00
19 Norm Ullman 12.00 30.00
20 Harry Lumley 12.00 30.00

2008-09 ITG Ultimate Memorabilia

(1-15) PRINT RUN 30 SER.#'d SETS
(16-30) PRINT RUN 50 SER.#'d SETS
(31-90) PRINT RUN 90 SER.#'d SETS
1 Alex Delvecchio/30 10.00 25.00
2 Alexander Ovechkin/30 30.00 80.00
3 Denis Potvin/30 6.00 15.00
4 Dominik Hasek/30 12.00 30.00
5 Georges Vezina/30 15.00 40.00
6 Gump Worsley/30 6.00 15.00
7 Howie Morenz/30 5.00 12.00
8 Joe Thornton/30 12.00 30.00
9 Mario Lemieux/30 20.00 50.00
10 Mario Lemieux/30 20.00 50.00
11 Marty Turco/30 6.00 15.00
12 Mike Modano/30 8.00 20.00
13 Raymond Bourque/30 15.00 40.00
14 Ted Lindsay/30 8.00 20.00
15 Terry Sawchuk/30 12.00 30.00
16 Brett Hull/50 15.00 40.00
17 Chris Osgood/50 6.00 15.00
18 Henri Richard/50 8.00 20.00
19 Martin Brodeur/50 12.00 30.00
20 Maurice Richard/50 12.00 30.00
21 Maurice Richard/50 12.00 30.00
22 Maurice Richard/50 12.00 30.00
23 Maurice Richard/50 12.00 30.00
24 Maurice Richard/50 12.00 30.00
25 Maurice Richard/50 12.00 30.00
26 Maurice Richard/50 12.00 30.00
27 Maurice Richard/50 12.00 30.00
28 Maurice Richard/50 12.00 30.00
29 Maurice Richard/50 12.00 30.00
30 Mikko Koivu/50 6.00 15.00
31 Alexander Ovechkin 25.00 60.00
32 Bill Barilko 4.00 10.00
33 Borje Salming 8.00 20.00
34 Cam Neely 8.00 20.00
35 Carey Price 20.00 50.00
36 Chris Chelios 8.00 20.00
37 Chris Chelios 8.00 20.00
38 Chris Osgood 6.00 15.00
39 Darryl Sittler 8.00 20.00
40 Dave Keon 10.00 25.00
41 Dominik Hasek 10.00 25.00
42 Doug Gilmour 8.00 20.00
43 Ed Belfour 8.00 20.00
44 Elmer Lach 10.00 25.00
45 Evgeni Nabokov 6.00 15.00
46 Frank Mahovlich 6.00 15.00
47 Grant Fuhr 6.00 15.00
48 Grant Fuhr 6.00 15.00
49 Guy Lafleur 12.00 30.00
50 Jacques Plante 10.00 25.00
51 Jari Kurri 6.00 15.00
52 Jaromir Jagr 8.00 20.00
53 Jaromir Jagr 8.00 20.00
54 Jean Beliveau 10.00 25.00
55 Joe Sakic 10.00 25.00
56 Joe Sakic 10.00 25.00
57 Joe Sakic 10.00 25.00
58 Joe Thornton 10.00 25.00
59 Johnny Bower 8.00 20.00
60 John Tavares 20.00 50.00
61 Lanny McDonald 6.00 15.00
62 Larry Robinson 6.00 15.00
63 Mario Lemieux 15.00 40.00
64 Martin Brodeur 12.00 30.00
65 Martin Brodeur 12.00 30.00
66 Martin St. Louis 6.00 15.00
67 Mats Sundin 6.00 15.00
68 Mike Modano 6.00 15.00
69 Nicklas Lidstrom 6.00 15.00
70 Nicklas Lidstrom 6.00 15.00
71 Pat LaFontaine 6.00 15.00
72 Pat LaFontaine 6.00 15.00
73 Patrick Roy 20.00 50.00
74 Patrick Roy 20.00 50.00
75 Patrick Roy 20.00 50.00
76 Patrick Roy 20.00 50.00
77 Phil Esposito 10.00 25.00
78 Red Kelly 8.00 20.00
79 Rob Blake 6.00 15.00
80 Roberto Luongo 10.00 25.00
81 Saku Koivu 6.00 15.00
82 Scott Niedermayer 4.00 10.00
83 Sergei Fedorov 10.00 25.00
84 Syl Apps 10.00 25.00
85 Ted Kennedy 6.00 15.00
86 Tim Horton 12.00 30.00
87 Tim Horton 12.00 30.00
88 Tim Thomas 6.00 15.00
89 Tony Esposito 6.00 15.00
90 Turk Broda 6.00 15.00

2008-09 ITG Ultimate Memorabilia Gold

STATED PRINT RUN 9 SER.#'d SETS
NOT PRICED DUE TO SCARCITY

2008-09 ITG Ultimate Memorabilia Onyx

STATED PRINT RUN 1 SER.#'d SET
NOT PRICED DUE TO SCARCITY

2008-09 ITG Ultimate Memorabilia Amazing Amerks

STATED PRINT RUN 1 SER.#'d SETS
NOT PRICED DUE TO SCARCITY
1 Lorne Carr
2 Red Dutton
3 Nels Stewart

2008-09 ITG Ultimate Memorabilia Autographs

STATED PRINT RUN 24 SER.#'d SETS
NOT PRICED DUE TO SCARCITY
1 Alexander Ovechkin
2 Alexander Semin
3 Anze Kopitar
4 Carey Price
5 Chris Chelios
6 Miikka Kiprusoff
7 Evgeni Nabokov
8 Joe Thornton
9 Martin St. Louis
10 Marty Turco
11 Mike Green
12 Mike Modano
13 Mikko Koivu
14 Niklas Backstrom
15 Nicklas Lidstrom
16 Pavel Datsyuk
17 Roberto Luongo
18 Ryan Getzlaf
19 Scott Niedermayer
20 Sergei Fedorov
21 Teemu Selanne
22 Rob Blake
23 Saku Koivu
24 Jaromir Jagr
25 Marian Gaborik
26 Martin Brodeur
27 Daniel Briere
28 Ilya Kovalchuk
29 Patrick Marleau
30 Mats Sundin

2008-09 ITG Ultimate Memorabilia Autographs Duals

STATED PRINT RUN 9 SER.#'d SETS
NOT PRICED DUE TO SCARCITY
1 Alexander Ovechkin
Alexander Yakushev
2 Joe Thornton
Mike Modano
3 Roberto Luongo
Tim Thomas
4 Carey Price
Gump Worsley
5 John Tavares
Victor Hedman
6 Chris Chelios
Raymond Bourque
7 Jaromir Jagr
Marian Gaborik
8 Mikko Koivu
Saku Koivu
9 Niklas Backstrom
Miikka Kiprusoff
10 Nicklas Lidstrom
Borje Salming
11 Dave Keon
Darryl Sittler
12 Johnny Bower
Glenn Hall
13 Charlie Hodge
Rogie Vachon
14 Phil Esposito
Tony Esposito
15 Paul Henderson
Vladislav Tretiak
16 Bobby Hull
Stan Mikita
17 Simeon Varlamov
Vladislav Tretiak
18 Boris Mikhailov
Pavel Datsyuk
19 Scott Niedermayer
Mike Green
20 Marty Turco
J-S Giguere
21 Ted Kennedy
Elmer Lach
22 Guy Lafleur
Henri Richard
23 Mats Sundin
Doug Gilmour
24 Matt Duchene
Evander Kane
25 Darren Helm
Brett Hull
26 Daniel Briere
Bobby Clarke
27 Martin Brodeur
Evgeni Nabokov
28 Ryan Getzlaf
Teemu Selanne
29 Dominik Hasek
Sergei Fedorov
30 Jean Beliveau
Yvan Cournoyer

2008-09 ITG Ultimate Memorabilia Autographs Duals Gold

STATED PRINT RUN 9 SER.#'d SETS
NOT PRICED DUE TO SCARCITY

2008-09 ITG Ultimate Memorabilia Autographs Gold

STATED PRINT RUN 1 SER.#'d SETS
NOT PRICED DUE TO SCARCITY

2008-09 ITG Ultimate Memorabilia Autographs Triple

STATED PRINT RUN 9 SER.#'d SETS
NOT PRICED DUE TO SCARCITY
1 Ovechkin
Datsyuk
Kovalchuk
2 Tavares
Hedman
Duchene
3 Price
Roy
Worsley
4 Henderson
Cournoyer
Esposito
5 Lafleur
Beliveau
Richard
6 Lach
Schmidt
Kennedy
7 Nabokov
Marleau
Thornton
8 Turco
Backstrom
Kiprusoff
9 Yakushev
Mikhailov
Tretiak
10 Brodeur
Giguere
Luongo

2008-09 ITG Ultimate Memorabilia Autographs Triple Gold

STATED PRINT RUN 1 SER.#'d SETS
NOT PRICED DUE TO SCARCITY

2008-09 ITG Ultimate Memorabilia AutoMates

STATED PRINT RUN 24 SER.#'d SETS
NOT PRICED DUE TO SCARCITY
1 Alexander Ovechkin
Alexander Semin
2 Scott Niedermayer
Teemu Selanne
3 Alexander Ovechkin
Mike Green
4 John Tavares
Nazem Kadri
5 Evgeni Nabokov
Patrick Marleau
6 Pavel Datsyuk
Darren Helm
7 Karl Alzner
Simeon Varlamov
8 Mikko Koivu
Niklas Backstrom
9 Rob Blake
Joe Thornton
10 Carey Price
Saku Koivu
11 Marty Turco
Mike Modano
12 Chris Chelios
Nicklas Lidstrom
13 Paul Stastny
Joe Sakic
14 Roberto Luongo
Mats Sundin
15 J-S Giguere
Ryan Getzlaf
16 Tim Thomas
Manny Fernandez
17 Sergei Fedorov
Nicklas Lidstrom
18 Paul Henderson
Phil Esposito
19 Alexander Yakushev
Boris Mikhailov
20 Bernie Parent
Derek Sanderson
21 Evander Kane
Zach Boychuk
22 Thomas Hickey
Jordan Eberle
23 Jaromir Jagr
Mario Lemieux
24 Matt Duchene
Cody Hodgson
25 Martin Brodeur

Roberto Luongo
26 Phil Esposito
Gerry Cheevers
27 Dominik Hasek
Brett Hull
28 Henri Richard
Guy Lafleur
29 Bobby Hull
Stan Mikita
30 Darryl Sittler
Borje Salming

2008-09 ITG Ultimate Memorabilia AutoMates Gold

STATED PRINT RUN 1 SER.#'d SETS
NOT PRICED DUE TO SCARCITY

2008-09 ITG Ultimate Memorabilia Beantown's Best

STATED PRINT RUN 1 SER.#'d SETS
NOT PRICED DUE TO SCARCITY
1 Dit Clapper
2 Frank Brimsek
3 Harry Oliver
4 Bill Cowley
5 Cooney Weiland
6 Tiny Thompson

2008-09 ITG Ultimate Memorabilia Blades of Steel

STATED PRINT RUN 19 SER.#'d SETS
NOT PRICED DUE TO SCARCITY
1 Alexander Ovechkin
2 Ryan Getzlaf
3 Gilbert Perreault
4 Phil Esposito
5 Marcel Dionne
6 Joe Thornton
7 Jacques Plante
8 Stan Mikita
9 Johnny Bucyk
10 Mario Lemieux
11 Pavel Datsyuk
12 Jaromir Jagr

2008-09 ITG Ultimate Memorabilia Blades of Steel Gold

STATED PRINT RUN 1 SER.#'d SETS
NOT PRICED DUE TO SCARCITY

2008-09 ITG Ultimate Memorabilia Bleu Blanc et Rouge

STATED PRINT RUN 1 SER.#'d SETS
NOT PRICED DUE TO SCARCITY
1 Bill Durnan
2 Toe Blake
3 Gerry McNeil
4 Tom Johnson
5 Howie Morenz

2008-09 ITG Ultimate Memorabilia Broadway Blueshirts

STATED PRINT RUN 1 SER.#'d SETS
NOT PRICED DUE TO SCARCITY
1 Neil Colville
2 Lynn Patrick
3 Babe Pratt
4 Dutch Hiller
5 Art Coulter
6 Bryan Hextall Sr.
7 Chuck Rayner

2008-09 ITG Ultimate Memorabilia Builders

STATED PRINT RUN 1 SER.#'d SETS
NOT PRICED DUE TO SCARCITY
1 Punch Imlach
2 Harold Ballard
3 James D. Norris
4 Conn Smythe
5 Foster Hewitt
6 William Wirtz

2008-09 ITG Ultimate Memorabilia Chitown Immortals

STATED PRINT RUN 1 SER.#'d SETS
NOT PRICED DUE TO SCARCITY
1 Mush March
2 Bill Mosienko
3 George Hay

2008-09 ITG Ultimate Memorabilia Cityscapes

STATED PRINT RUN 24 SER.#'d SETS
NOT PRICED DUE TO SCARCITY
1 Bobby Clarke
Mike Schmidt
2 Rod Gilbert
Joe Namath
3 Brett Hull
Kurt Warner
4 Joe Sakic
Patrick Roy
5 Mario Lemieux
Jaromir Jagr
6 Phil Esposito
Reggie Jackson
7 Bobby Hull
Dennis Rodman
8 Brad Park
Pele
9 Jean Beliveau
Gary Carter
10 Martin St. Louis
Warren Sapp

2008-09 ITG Ultimate Memorabilia Cityscapes Gold

STATED PRINT RUN 1 SER.#'d SETS
NOT PRICED DUE TO SCARCITY

2008-09 ITG Ultimate Memorabilia Complete Jersey

STATED PRINT RUN 9 SER.#'d SETS
NOT PRICED DUE TO SCARCITY
1 Alexander Ovechkin
2 John Tavares
3 Mario Lemieux
4 Dominik Hasek
5 Joe Sakic
6 Martin Brodeur
7 Mike Modano
8 Patrick Roy
9 Roberto Luongo
10 Pavel Datsyuk
11 Raymond Bourque
12 Mats Sundin
13 Nicklas Lidstrom
14 Tim Thomas
15 Evgeni Nabokov
16 Matt Duchene
17 Victor Hedman
18 Miikka Kiprusoff

2008-09 ITG Ultimate Memorabilia Complete Jersey Gold

STATED PRINT RUN 1 SER.#'d SETS
NOT PRICED DUE TO SCARCITY

2008-09 ITG Ultimate Memorabilia Complete Package

STATED PRINT RUN 9 SER.#'d SETS
NOT PRICED DUE TO SCARCITY
1 Alexander Ovechkin
2 Eddie Shore
3 Maurice Richard
4 Terry Sawchuk
5 Jacques Plante
6 Joe Thornton
7 Stan Mikita
8 Vladislav Tretiak
9 Mario Lemieux
10 Ryan Getzlaf
11 Patrick Roy
12 Martin Brodeur
13 Guy Lafleur
14 Bobby Hull
15 Raymond Bourque
16 Marcel Dionne
17 Pelle Lindbergh
18 Jaromir Jagr

2008-09 ITG Ultimate Memorabilia Complete Package Gold

STATED PRINT RUN 1 SER.#'d SETS
NOT PRICED DUE TO SCARCITY
1 Alexander Ovechkin
2 Eddie Shore
3 Maurice Richard
4 Terry Sawchuk
5 Jacques Plante
6 Joe Thornton
7 Stan Mikita
8 Vladislav Tretiak
9 Mario Lemieux
10 Ryan Getzlaf
11 Patrick Roy
12 Martin Brodeur
13 Guy Lafleur
14 Bobby Hull
15 Raymond Bourque
16 Marcel Dionne
17 Pelle Lindbergh
18 Jaromir Jagr

2008-09 ITG Ultimate Memorabilia Cornerstones

STATED PRINT RUN 24 SER.#'d SETS
NOT PRICED DUE TO SCARCITY
1 Valeri Kharlamov
Vladislav TretiakPavel Datsyuk
Alexander Ovechkin
2 Tiny Thompson
Frank BrimsekGerry Cheevers
Tim Thomas
3 George Hainsworth
Jacques PlantePatrick Roy
Carey Price
4 Turk Broda
Johnny BowerFelix Potvin
Vesa Toskala
5 Bobby Clarke
Bernie ParentPelle Lindbergh
Daniel Briere
6 Howie Morenz
Maurice RichardGuy Lafleur
Saku Koivu
7 Phil Esposito
Darryl SittlerMario Lemieux
Joe Sakic
8 Borje Salming
Mats NaslundNicklas Lidstrom
Victor Hedman
9 Tony Esposito
Rogie VachonGrant Fuhr
Martin Brodeur
10 Ted Lindsay
Alex DelvecchioMarcel Dionne
Pavel Datsyuk
11 Roberto Luongo
Joe ThorntonCarey Price
John Tavares
12 Terry Sawchuk
Marcel DionneRob Blake
Anze Kopitar

2008-09 ITG Ultimate Memorabilia Cornerstones Gold

STATED PRINT RUN 1 SER.#'d SETS
NOT PRICED DUE TO SCARCITY

2008-09 ITG Ultimate Memorabilia Decade Dominance

STATED PRINT RUN 19 SER.#'d SETS
NOT PRICED DUE TO SCARCITY
1 Marian Gaborik
Joe ThorntonPavel Datsyuk
Nicklas Lidstrom
Roberto Luongo
Alexander Ovechkin
2 Martin Brodeur
Mario LemieuxJaromir Jagr
Patrick Roy
Mats Sundin
Joe Sakic
3 Patrick Roy
Billy SmithCam Neely
Wendel Clark
Raymond Bourque
Mario Lemieux
4 Guy Lafleur
Darryl SittlerPhil Esposito
Bobby Clarke
Vladislav Tretiak
Borje Salming
5 Henri Richard
Dave KeonRod Gilbert
Johnny Bower
Bobby Hull
Stan Mikita
6 Maurice Richard
Ted LindsayJean Beliveau
Jacques Plante
Terry Sawchuk
Sid Abel

2008-09 ITG Ultimate Memorabilia Decade Dominance Gold

STATED PRINT RUN 1 SER.#'d SETS
NOT PRICED DUE TO SCARCITY

2008-09 ITG Ultimate Memorabilia Emblems

STATED PRINT RUN 1 SER.#'d SETS
NOT PRICED DUE TO SCARCITY
1 Alexei Kovalev
2 Alex Ovechkin
3 Bob Probert
4 Brian Leetch
5 Cam Neely
6 Chris Chelios Blackhawks
7 Chris Chelios AS
8 Chris Pronger
9 Denis Savard
10 Dion Phaneuf
11 Dominik Hasek AS
12 Dominik Hasek Sabres
13 Drew Doughty
14 Eric Lindros
15 Eric Staal
16 Gilbert Perreault
17 Gordie Howe Whalers
18 Gordie Howe Aeros
19 Ilya Kovalchuk
20 Jaromir Jagr Rangers
21 Jaromir Jagr AS
22 Jason Spezza
23 Jeremy Roenick AS
24 Jeremy Roenick Blackhawks
25 Joe Sakic
26 Joe Thornton AS
27 Joe Thornton Bruins
28 John Davidson
29 John Tavares
30 John Vanbiesbrouck
31 Marian Gaborik
32 Mario Lemieux Penguins
33 Mario Lemieux Canada
34 Mario Lemieux AS
35 Mark Messier Oilers
36 Mark Messier Rangers
37 Mats Sundin
38 Miikka Kiprusoff
39 Mike Modano
40 Milan Lucic
41 Nicklas Lidstrom
42 Patrick Roy
43 Paul Coffey
44 Paul Kariya
45 Pavel Bure
46 Peter Forsberg
47 Ray Bourque
48 Rob Blake '02 AS
49 Rob Blake '03 AS
50 Saku Koivu
51 Scott Gomez
52 Simon Gagne
53 Teemu Selanne Ducks
54 Teemu Selanne Avs
55 Tony Amonte
56 Victor Hedman
57 Vincent Lecavalier
58 Wayne Gretzky Rangers
59 Wayne Gretzky Kings
60 Pelle Lindbergh
61 Patric Roy
62 Steve Yzerman
63 Mike Modano
64 Mark Messier Canucks
65 Jaromir Jagr Penguins

2008-09 ITG Ultimate Memorabilia Franchises

STATED PRINT RUN 1 SER.#'d SETS
NOT PRICED DUE TO SCARCITY
1 Alexander Ovechkin
Alexander Semin
Simeon Varlamov
2 Bobby Clarke
Rick MacLeish
Bernie Parent
3 Bobby Hull
Stan Mikita
Bill White
4 Brad Park
Vic Hadfield
Walt Tkaczuk
5 Brett Hull
Joe Nieuwendyk
Lanny McDonald
6 Darryl Sittler
Lanny McDonald
Borje Salming
7 Frank Mahovlich
Red Kelly
Terry Sawchuk
8 Joe Thornton
Patrick Marleau
Evgeni Nabokov
9 Johnny Bucyk
Gerry Cheevers
Phil Esposito
10 Larry Robinson
Serge Savard
Guy Lapointe
11 Martin Brodeur
Joe Nieuwendyk
Scott Niedermayer
12 Mats Sundin
Wendel Clark
Doug Gilmour
13 Maurice Richard
Jean Beliveau
Henri Richard
14 Mike Modano
Marty Turco
Fabian Brunnstrom
15 Patrick Roy
Chris Chelios
Mats Naslund
16 Pavel Datsyuk
Nicklas Lidstrom
Chris Osgood
17 Teemu Selanne
Scott Niedermayer
Jonas Hiller
18 Tim Thomas
Milan Lucic
Manny Fernandez

2008-09 ITG Ultimate Memorabilia Franchises Gold

STATED PRINT RUN 1 SER.#'d SETS
NOT PRICED DUE TO SCARCITY

2008-09 ITG Ultimate Memorabilia From Russia with Love

STATED PRINT RUN 24 SER.#'d SETS
NOT PRICED DUE TO SCARCITY
1 Alexander Ovechkin
2 Vladislav Tretiak
3 Pavel Datsyuk
4 Evgeni Nabokov
5 Valeri Kharlamov
6 Alexander Semin
7 Alexander Yakushev
8 Boris Mikhailov
9 Sergei Fedorov
10 Nikolai Kulemin
11 Simeon Varlamov
12 Ilya Kovalchuk

2008-09 ITG Ultimate Memorabilia From Russia with Love Gold

STATED PRINT RUN 1 SER.#'d SETS
NOT PRICED DUE TO SCARCITY

2008-09 ITG Ultimate Memorabilia Future Stars Autographs

STATED PRINT RUN 30 SER.#'d SETS
1 Simeon Varlamov 25.00 50.00
2 Nikolai Kulemin
3 Chet Pickard
4 Zach Boychuk
5 Dana Tyrell
6 Darren Helm
7 Scott Glennie 12.00 30.00
8 Evander Kane 20.00 50.00
9 Fabian Brunnstrom
10 Thomas Hickey
11 John Tavares 50.00 100.00
12 Taylor Hall 40.00 100.00
13 Jordan Eberle 8.00 20.00
14 Guillaume Latendresse
15 Jacob Josefson
16 Matt Duchene
17 Mikkel Boedker
18 Milan Lucic 15.00 40.00
19 Nazem Kadri 20.00 40.00
20 Oliver Ekman-Larsson
21 Ryan Ellis 15.00 40.00
22 Dustin Tokarski
23 Jonas Hiller 10.00 25.00
24 Jared Cowen
25 Victor Hedman 12.00 30.00
26 Carter Ashton
27 Mikhail Grabovski 15.00 40.00
28 Brayden Schenn 12.00 30.00
29 Paul Stastny
30 Cody Hodgson 15.00 40.00

2008-09 ITG Ultimate Memorabilia Future Stars Autographs Gold

STATED PRINT RUN 10 SER.#'d SETS
NOT PRICED DUE TO SCARCITY

2008-09 ITG Ultimate Memorabilia Future Stars Jerseys Autographs

STATED PRINT RUN 19 SER.#'d SETS
NOT PRICED DUE TO SCARCITY
1 Simeon Varlamov
2 Nikolai Kulemin
3 Chet Pickard
4 Zach Boychuk
5 Dana Tyrell
6 Darren Helm
7 Scott Glennie
8 Evander Kane
9 Fabian Brunnstrom
10 Thomas Hickey
11 John Tavares
12 Taylor Hall
13 Jordan Eberle
14 Anze Kopitar
15 Guillaume Latendresse
16 Matt Duchene
17 Mikkel Boedker
18 Milan Lucic
19 Nazem Kadri
20 Ryan Ellis
21 Dustin Tokarski
22 Jonas Hiller
23 Jared Cowen
24 Victor Hedman
25 Carter Ashton
26 Mikhail Grabovski
27 Brayden Schenn
28 Paul Stastny
29 Cody Hodgson
30 Karl Alzner/15

2008-09 ITG Ultimate Memorabilia Future Stars Jerseys Autographs Gold

STATED PRINT RUN 1 SER.#'d SETS
NOT PRICED DUE TO SCARCITY

2008-09 ITG Ultimate Memorabilia Future Stars Patches Autographs

STATED PRINT RUN 19 SER.#'d SETS
NOT PRICED DUE TO SCARCITY
1 Oliver Ekman-Larsson
2 Simeon Varlamov
3 Nikolai Kulemin
4 Chet Pickard
5 Zach Boychuk
6 Dana Tyrell
7 Darren Helm
8 Scott Glennie
9 Evander Kane
10 Fabian Brunnstrom
11 Thomas Hickey
12 John Tavares
13 Taylor Hall
14 Jordan Eberle
15 Karl Alzner
16 Guillaume Latendresse
17 Matt Duchene
18 Mikkel Boedker
19 Milan Lucic
20 Nazem Kadri
21 Ryan Ellis
22 Dustin Tokarski
23 Jonas Hiller
24 Jared Cowen
25 Victor Hedman
26 Carter Ashton
27 Mikhail Grabovski
28 Brayden Schenn
29 Paul Stastny
30 Cody Hodgson
31 Anze Kopitar

2008-09 ITG Ultimate Memorabilia Future Stars Patches Autographs Gold

STATED PRINT RUN 1 SER.#'d SETS
NOT PRICED DUE TO SCARCITY

2008-09 ITG Ultimate Memorabilia Glove

STATED PRINT RUN 1 SER.#'d SETS
NOT PRICED DUE TO SCARCITY
1 Al MacInnis
2 Alexander Ovechkin
3 Bobby Clarke
4 Cam Neely
5 Chris Chelios
6 Dale Hawerchuk
7 Dave Andreychuk
8 Dominik Hasek
9 Doug Weight
10 Ed Belfour
11 Gordie Howe
12 Jack Johnson
13 Jarome Iginla
14 Joe Sakic
15 Joe Thornton
16 John Tavares
17 Keith Tkachuk
18 Marian Gaborik
19 Mats Sundin
20 Pat LaFontaine
21 Patrick Roy
22 Paul Coffey
23 Raymond Bourque
24 Rob Blake
25 Roberto Luongo
26 Ryan Getzlaf
27 Scott Niedermayer
28 Sergei Fedorov
29 Simon Gagne
30 Stan Mikita
31 Thomas Kaberle
32 Vincent Lecavalier
33 Wayne Gretzky
34 Wendel Clark
35 Bryan Trottier

2008-09 ITG Ultimate Memorabilia Gloves are Off

STATED PRINT RUN 24 SER.#'d SETS
NOT PRICED DUE TO SCARCITY
1 Alexander Ovechkin
2 Bobby Clarke
3 Ryan Getzlaf
4 Dominik Hasek
5 Ed Belfour
6 Evgeni Nabokov
7 Joe Sakic
8 Joe Thornton
9 John Tavares
10 Marian Gaborik
11 Mario Lemieux
12 Martin Brodeur
13 Patrick Roy Canadiens
14 Patrick Roy Avs
15 Raymond Bourque
16 Rob Blake
17 Chris Chelios
18 Scott Niedermayer
19 Sergei Fedorov
20 Stan Mikita

2008-09 ITG Ultimate Memorabilia Gloves are Off Gold

STATED PRINT RUN 1 SER.#'d SETS
NOT PRICED DUE TO SCARCITY

2008-09 ITG Ultimate Memorabilia Hometown Heroes

STATED PRINT RUN 24 SER.#'d SETS
NOT PRICED DUE TO SCARCITY
1 Alexander Ovechkin
2 Joe Sakic
3 Joe Thornton
4 John Tavares
5 Martin Brodeur
6 Patrick Roy
7 Bobby Clarke
8 Borje Salming
9 Mario Lemieux
10 Guy Lafleur
11 Teemu Selanne
12 Jaromir Jagr
13 Miikka Kiprusoff
14 Raymond Bourque
15 Roberto Luongo
16 Dominik Hasek
17 Ryan Getzlaf
18 Mike Modano

2008-09 ITG Ultimate Memorabilia Jerseys-Emblems Gold

STATED PRINT RUN 1 SER.#'d SETS
NOT PRICED DUE TO SCARCITY

2008-09 ITG Ultimate Memorabilia Jerseys Gold

STATED PRINT RUN 1 SER.#'d SETS
NOT PRICED DUE TO SCARCITY

2008-09 ITG Ultimate Memorabilia Journey Jersey

STATED PRINT RUN 24 SER.#'d SETS
NOT PRICED DUE TO SCARCITY
1 Mats Sundin
2 Joe Sakic
3 Raymond Bourque
4 Patrick Roy
5 Joe Thornton
6 Roberto Luongo

2008-09 ITG Ultimate Memorabilia Journey Jersey Gold

STATED PRINT RUN 1 SER.#'d SETS
NOT PRICED DUE TO SCARCITY

2008-09 ITG Ultimate Memorabilia Legends Autographs

STATED PRINT RUN 24 SER.#'d SETS
NOT PRICED DUE TO SCARCITY
1 Jean Beliveau
2 Raymond Bourque
3 Johnny Bower
4 Gerry Cheevers
5 Wendel Clark
6 Bobby Clarke
7 Yvan Cournoyer
8 Marcel Dionne
9 Phil Esposito
10 Tony Esposito
11 Grant Fuhr
12 Glenn Hall
13 Dominik Hasek
14 Bobby Hull
15 Doug Gilmour
16 Brett Hull
17 Dave Keon
18 Derek Sanderson
19 Elmer Lach
20 Guy Lafleur
21 Ted Lindsay
22 Lanny McDonald
23 Stan Mikita
24 Boris Mikhailov
25 Alexander Yakushev
26 Joe Sakic
27 Henri Richard
28 Vladislav Tretiak
29 Mario Lemieux
30 Joe Nieuwendyk

2008-09 ITG Ultimate Memorabilia Legends Autographs Gold

STATED PRINT RUN 1 SER.#'d SETS
NOT PRICED DUE TO SCARCITY

2008-09 ITG Ultimate Memorabilia Lumbergraphs

STATED PRINT RUN 1 SER.#'d SETS
NOT PRICED DUE TO SCARCITY
1 Terry Sawchuk
2 Syd Howe
3 Herbie Lewis
4 Hec Kilrea
5 Ted Kennedy
6 Tom Johnson
7 Tim Horton
8 Harold Cotton
9 Normie Smith
10 Herb Cain

2008-09 ITG Ultimate Memorabilia Maple Leafs Forever

STATED PRINT RUN 1 SER.#'d SETS
NOT PRICED DUE TO SCARCITY
1 Hap Day
2 Syl Apps
3 Bob Davidson
4 Ace Bailey
5 Frank King Clancey
6 Joe Primeau
7 Dave Schriner
8 Gordie Drillon
9 Bill Barilko

2008-09 ITG Ultimate Memorabilia Marvellous Maroons

STATED PRINT RUN 1 SER.#'d SETS
NOT PRICED DUE TO SCARCITY
1 Mickey Blake
Vern Ayres
2 George Boucher
3 Baldy Northcott
4 Teddy Graham

2008-09 ITG Ultimate Memorabilia Memorabilia Autographs Duals

STATED PRINT RUN 9 SER.#'d SETS
NOT PRICED DUE TO SCARCITY
1 Alexander Ovechkin
Alexander Yakushev
2 Roberto Luongo
Tim Thomas
3 John Tavares
Victor Hedman
4 Joe Thornton
Mike Modano
5 Mikko Koivu
Saku Koivu
6 Nicklas Lidstrom
Borje Salming
7 Johnny Bower
Glenn Hall
8 Phil Esposito
Tony Esposito
9 Dave Keon
Darryl Sittler
10 Bobby Hull
Stan Mikita
11 Scott Niedermayer
Mike Green
12 Guy Lafleur
Henri Richard
13 Mats Sundin
Doug Gilmour
14 Matt Duchene
Evander Kane
15 Darren Helm
Brett Hull
16 Carey Price
Gump Worsley
17 Simeon Varlamov
Vladislav Tretiak
18 Ilya Kovalchuk
Pavel Datsyuk
19 Nicklas Lidstrom
Borje Salming
20 Ted Lindsay
Milt Schmidt

2008-09 ITG Ultimate Memorabilia Memorabilia Autographs Duals Gold

STATED PRINT RUN 1 SER.#'d SETS
NOT PRICED DUE TO SCARCITY

2008-09 ITG Ultimate Memorabilia Motown Heroes

STATED PRINT RUN 1 SER.#'d SETS
NOT PRICED DUE TO SCARCITY
1 Jack Adams
2 Syd Howe
3 Jack Stewart
4 Ebbie Goodfellow
5 Sid Abel
6 Harry Lumley

2008-09 ITG Ultimate Memorabilia Numbers

STATED PRINT RUN 1 SER.#'d SETS
NOT PRICED DUE TO SCARCITY
1 Alexander Ovechkin
2 Alexei Kovalev
3 Anze Kopitar
4 Bob Probert
5 Brett Hull
6 Brian Leetch
7 Cam Neely
8 Carey Price
9 Chris Pronger
10 Dominik Hasek Sabres
11 Dominik Hasek Red Wings
12 Drew Doughty
13 Eric Lindros Flyers
14 Eric Lindros AS
15 Eric Staal
16 Gilbert Perreault
17 Gordie Howe
18 Ilya Kovalchuk
19 Jaromir Jagr
20 Jeremy Roenick AS
21 Jeremy Roenick Blackhawks
22 Joe Sakic
23 Joe Thornton AS
24 Joe Thornton Bruins
25 John Vanbiesbrouck
26 Kevin Lowe
27 Marian Gaborik
28 Mario Lemieux Penguins
29 Mario Lemieux AS
30 Mark Messier
31 Mats Sundin Nordiques
32 Mats Sundin Leafs
33 Miikka Kiprusoff
34 Milan Lucic
35 Nicklas Lidstrom '03 AS
36 Nicklas Lidstrom '01 AS
37 Patrick Roy '02 AS
38 Patrick Roy Canadiens
39 Patrick Roy '03 AS
40 Paul Coffey Penguins
41 Paul Coffey Oilers
42 Paul Kariya
43 Pavel Bure Canucks
44 Pavel Bure Panthers
45 Pavel Datsyuk
46 Peter Forsberg
47 Phil Kessel
48 Raymond Bourque
49 Richard Brodeur
50 Rob Blake '03 AS
51 Rob Blake '02 AS
52 Ron Hextall
53 Saku Koivu
54 Scott Gomez
55 Scott Stevens
56 Simon Gagne
57 Teemu Selanne Avs
58 Teemu Selanne Jets
59 Tony Amonte
60 Tony Esposito

61 Wayne Gretzky Kings
62 Wayne Gretzky Rangers
63 Wendel Clark
64 Pelle Lindbergh
65 Bernie Parent
66 Marcel Dionne
67 Vladislav Tretiak

2008-09 ITG Ultimate Memorabilia Numerology

STATED PRINT RUN 24 SER.#'d SETS
NOT PRICED DUE TO SCARCITY
1 Alexander Ovechkin
2 Mario Lemieux
3 Joe Sakic
4 Martin Brodeur
5 Patrick Roy
6 Pavel Datsyuk
7 Nicklas Lidstrom
8 John Tavares
9 Mats Sundin
10 Raymond Bourque
11 Jaromir Jagr
12 Frank Brimsek
13 Mike Modano
14 Carey Price
15 Vladislav Tretiak
16 Bobby Hull
17 Stan Mikita
18 Dominik Hasek
19 Ed Belfour
20 Brett Hull
21 Doug Harvey
22 Miikka Kiprusoff
23 Ilya Kovalchuk
24 Ryan Getzlaf

2008-09 ITG Ultimate Memorabilia Numerology Gold

STATED PRINT RUN 1 SER.#'d SETS
NOT PRICED DUE TO SCARCITY

2008-09 ITG Ultimate Memorabilia Paper Cuts

STATED PRINT RUN 1 SER.#'d SETS
NOT PRICED DUE TO SCARCITY
1 Tim Horton
2 Ching Johnson
3 Frank Fredrickson
4 Eddie Shore
5 Art Ross
6 Terry Sawchuk
7 Turk Broda
8 Sugar Jim Henry

2008-09 ITG Ultimate Memorabilia Past, Present and Future

STATED PRINT RUN 24 SER.#'d SETS
NOT PRICED DUE TO SCARCITY
1 Borje Salming
Nicklas Lidstrom
Victor Hedman
2 Brett Hull
Marty Turco
Scott Glennie
3 Cam Neely
Tim Thomas
Milan Lucic
4 Darryl Sittler
Mikhail Grabovski
Nazem Kadri
5 Doug Gilmour
Vesa Toskala
Nikolai Kulemin
6 Grant Fuhr
Roberto Luongo
Carey Price
7 Joe Nieuwendyk
Mike Modano
Fabian Brunnstrom
8 Joe Sakic
Paul Stastny
Matt Duchene
9 Marcel Dionne
Anze Kopitar
Brayden Schenn
10 Marcel Dionne
Pavel Datsyuk
Darren Helm
11 Mario Lemieux
Joe Thornton
John Tavares
12 Olaf Kolzig
Alexander Ovechkin
Simeon Varlamov
13 Patrick Roy
Martin Brodeur
Chet Pickard
14 Raymond Bourque
Scott Niedermayer
Jared Cowen
15 Rob Blake
Anze Kopitar
Thomas Hickey
16 Rogie Vachon
Martin Brodeur
Dustin Tokarski
17 Sergei Fedorov
Ryan Getzlaf
Jonas Hiller
18 Vladislav Tretiak
Evgeni Nabokov
Simeon Varlamov

2008-09 ITG Ultimate Memorabilia Past, Present and Future Gold

STATED PRINT RUN 1 SER.#'d SETS
NOT PRICED DUE TO SCARCITY

2008-09 ITG Ultimate Memorabilia Patch Autographs

STATED PRINT RUN 9 SER.#'d SETS
NOT PRICED DUE TO SCARCITY
1 Alexander Ovechkin
2 Alexander Semin
3 Jaromir Jagr
4 Joe Sakic
5 Evgeni Nabokov
6 Stan Mikita
7 Marty Turco
8 Mike Modano
9 Miikka Kiprusoff
10 Joe Nieuwendyk
11 Nicklas Lidstrom
12 Brett Hull
13 Pavel Datsyuk
14 Mats Sundin
15 Ryan Getzlaf
16 Saku Koivu
17 Scott Niedermayer
18 Sergei Fedorov
19 Bobby Hull
20 Teemu Selanne
21 Tim Thomas
22 Marcel Dionne
23 Tony Esposito
24 Dominik Hasek
25 Mike Green
26 Martin Brodeur
27 Daniel Briere
28 Martin St. Louis
29 Patrick Marleau
30 Jean-Sebastien Giguere

2008-09 ITG Ultimate Memorabilia Patch Autographs Gold

STATED PRINT RUN 1 SER.#'d SETS
NOT PRICED DUE TO SCARCITY

2008-09 ITG Ultimate Memorabilia Retro Teammates

STATED PRINT RUN 24 SER.#'d SETS
NOT PRICED DUE TO SCARCITY
1 Bernie Parent
Bobby Clarke
2 Bobby Hull
Glenn Hall
3 Brad Park
Rod Gilbert
4 Darryl Sittler
Lanny McDonald
5 Dave Keon
Frank Mahovlich
6 Felix Potvin
Wendel Clark
7 Gilbert Perreault
Rick Martin
8 Guy Lafleur
Steve Shutt
9 Jacques Plante
Henri Richard
10 Jean Beliveau
Maurice Richard
11 Joe Sakic
Patrick Roy
12 Mario Lemieux
Jaromir Jagr
13 Phil Esposito
Johnny Bucyk
14 Stan Mikita
Tony Esposito
15 Ted Lindsay
Alex Delvecchio
16 Terry Sawchuk
Johnny Bower
17 Tim Horton
Red Kelly
18 Valeri Kharlamov
Vladislav Tretiak

2008-09 ITG Ultimate Memorabilia Retro Teammates Gold

STATED PRINT RUN 1 SER.#'d SETS
NOT PRICED DUE TO SCARCITY

2008-09 ITG Ultimate Memorabilia Sensational Sens

STATED PRINT RUN 1 SER.#'d SETS
NOT PRICED DUE TO SCARCITY
1 Jack Adams
2 Alex Smith
3 King Clancy

2008-09 ITG Ultimate Memorabilia Stick Autographs

STATED PRINT RUN 24 SER.#'d SETS
NOT PRICED DUE TO SCARCITY
1 Mike Modano
2 Pavel Datsyuk
3 Jean-Sebastien Giguere
4 Alexander Ovechkin
5 John Tavares
6 Ryan Getzlaf
7 Doug Gilmour
8 Brett Hull
9 Jaromir Jagr
10 Guy Lafleur
11 Chris Chelios
12 Nicklas Lidstrom
13 Joe Nieuwendyk
14 Joe Sakic
15 Borje Salming
16 Derek Sanderson
17 Teemu Selanne
18 Alexander Semin
19 Darryl Sittler
20 Mats Sundin
21 Marian Gaborik
22 Joe Thornton
23 Dominik Hasek
24 Evgeni Nabokov
25 Sergei Fedorov
26 Patrick Roy
27 Martin Brodeur
28 Daniel Briere
29 Roberto Luongo
30 Carey Price

2008-09 ITG Ultimate Memorabilia Stick Autographs Gold

STATED PRINT RUN 1 SER.#'d SETS
NOT PRICED DUE TO SCARCITY

2008-09 ITG Ultimate Memorabilia Stick Rack

STATED PRINT RUN 24 SER.#'d SETS
NOT PRICED DUE TO SCARCITY
1 Alexander Ovechkin
2 Chris Chelios
3 Marian Gaborik
4 Nicklas Lidstrom
5 Joe Thornton
6 Pavel Datsyuk
7 Dominik Hasek
8 Ryan Getzlaf
9 John Tavares
10 Evgeni Nabokov
11 Joe Sakic
12 Teemu Selanne
13 Jaromir Jagr
14 Martin Brodeur
15 Patrick Roy
16 Roberto Luongo
17 Mike Modano
18 Milan Lucic

2008-09 ITG Ultimate Memorabilia Stick Rack Gold

STATED PRINT RUN 1 SER.#'d SETS
NOT PRICED DUE TO SCARCITY

2008-09 ITG Ultimate Memorabilia Tag

STATED PRINT RUN 1 SER.#'d SETS
NOT PRICED DUE TO SCARCITY
1 Al MacInnis
2 Alexander Ovechkin
3 Alexei Kovalev
4 Bob Probert
5 Brett Hull
6 Brian Leetch
7 Cam Neely
8 Carey Price
9 Chris Chelios
10 Dominik Hasek
11 Eric Lindros Flyers
12 Eric Lindros AS
13 Eric Staal
14 Gilbert Perreault
15 Ilya Kovalchuk
16 Jaromir Jagr
17 Jeremy Roenick
18 Joe Thornton AS
19 Joe Thornton Bruins
20 John Vanbiesbrouck
21 Kevin Lowe
22 Marian Gaborik
23 Mario Lemieux
24 Mark Messier
25 Martin Brodeur
26 Martin Brodeur
27 Mats Sundin Nordiques
28 Mats Sundin Maple Leafs
29 Nicklas Lidstrom '03 AS
30 Nicklas Lidstrom '01 AS
31 Owen Nolan
32 Patrick Roy AS
33 Patrick Roy Canadiens
34 Paul Coffey
35 Paul Kariya
36 Pavel Bure Canucks
37 Pavel Bure Panthers
38 Pavel Datsyuk
39 Peter Forsberg
40 Phil Esposito
41 Raymond Bourque
42 Rob Blake '02 AS
43 Rob Blake '03 AS
44 Ron Hextall
45 Scott Stevens
46 Teemu Selanne Avs
47 Teemu Selanne Jets
48 Tony Amonte
49 Wayne Gretzky Kings
50 Wayne Gretzky Rangers

2008-09 ITG Ultimate Memorabilia Tribute Autographs

STATED PRINT RUN 9 SER.#'d SETS
NOT PRICED DUE TO SCARCITY
1 Alexei Cherepanov
2 Luc Bourdon
3 Lorne Worsley
4 Bernie Geoffrion
5 Ted Kennedy

2008-09 ITG Ultimate Memorabilia Tribute Autographs Gold

STATED PRINT RUN 1 SER.#'d SETS
NOT PRICED DUE TO SCARCITY

2008-09 ITG Ultimate Memorabilia Triple Memorabilia Autographs

STATED PRINT RUN 9 SER.#'d SETS
NOT PRICED DUE TO SCARCITY
1 Alexander Ovechkin
2 Chris Chelios
3 Evgeni Nabokov
4 John Tavares
5 Brett Hull
6 Joe Thornton
7 Jean-Sebastien Giguere
8 Vladislav Tretiak
9 Marty Turco
10 Mats Sundin
11 Nicklas Lidstrom
12 Roberto Luongo
13 Ryan Getzlaf
14 Teemu Selanne
15 Jean Beliveau
16 Raymond Bourque
17 Marcel Dionne
18 Phil Esposito
19 Tony Esposito
20 Grant Fuhr
21 Johnny Bower
22 Glenn Hall
23 Dominik Hasek
24 Bobby Hull
25 Joe Sakic
26 Patrick Roy
27 Mario Lemieux
28 Jaromir Jagr
29 Martin Brodeur
30 Doug Gilmour

2008-09 ITG Ultimate Memorabilia Triple Memorabilia Autographs Gold

STATED PRINT RUN 1 SER.#'d SETS
NOT PRICED DUE TO SCARCITY

2008-09 ITG Ultimate Memorabilia Trophy Winners

STATED PRINT RUN 24 SER.#'d SETS
NOT PRICED DUE TO SCARCITY
1 Alexander Ovechkin
2 Alexander Ovechkin
3 Mario Lemieux
4 Sergei Fedorov
5 Alexander Ovechkin
6 Pavel Datsyuk
7 Nicklas Lidstrom
8 Alexander Ovechkin
9 Alexander Ovechkin
10 Martin Brodeur
11 Jaromir Jagr
12 Martin Brodeur
13 Patrick Roy
14 Doug Gilmour
15 Joe Sakic
16 Joe Sakic
17 Raymond Bourque
18 Mario Lemieux
19 Ilya Kovalchuk
20 Patrick Roy

2008-09 ITG Ultimate Memorabilia Trophy Winners Gold

STATED PRINT RUN 9 SER.#'d SETS
NOT PRICED DUE TO SCARCITY

2008-09 ITG Ultimate Memorabilia Trophy Winners Onyx

STATED PRINT RUN 1 SER.#'d SETS
NOT PRICED DUE TO SCARCITY

2008-09 ITG Ultimate Memorabilia Ultimate Defensemen

STATED PRINT RUN 24 SER.#'d SETS
NOT PRICED DUE TO SCARCITY
1 Scott Niedermayer
Nicklas LidstromChris Chelios
Borje SalmingLarry Robinson
Doug Harvey

2008-09 ITG Ultimate Memorabilia Ultimate Defensemen Gold

STATED PRINT RUN 1 SER.#'d SETS
NOT PRICED DUE TO SCARCITY

2008-09 ITG Ultimate Memorabilia Ultimate Draft Pick Autographs

STATED PRINT RUN 19 SER.#'d SETS
NOT PRICED DUE TO SCARCITY
1 John Tavares
Alexander Ovechkin
2 John Tavares
Alexander Ovechkin
3 John Tavares
4 John Tavares
5 John Tavares
6 John Tavares
7 John Tavares
8 John Tavares
9 John Tavares

2008-09 ITG Ultimate Memorabilia Ultimate Draft Pick Autographs Gold

STATED PRINT RUN 1 SER.#'d SETS
NOT PRICED DUE TO SCARCITY

2008-09 ITG Ultimate Memorabilia Ultimate Forwards

STATED PRINT RUN 24 SER.#'d SETS
NOT PRICED DUE TO SCARCITY
1 Alexander Ovechkin
Joe ThorntonJoe Sakic
Bobby HullSid Abel
Aurel Joliat
2 John Tavares
Mats SundinMarcel Dionne
Dave KeonMaurice Richard
Milt Schmidt
3 Pavel Datsyuk
Mario LemieuxPhil Esposito
Guy LafleurJean Beliveau
Howie Morenz

2008-09 ITG Ultimate Memorabilia Ultimate Forwards Gold

STATED PRINT RUN 1 SER.#'d SETS
NOT PRICED DUE TO SCARCITY

2008-09 ITG Ultimate Memorabilia Ultimate Goalies

STATED PRINT RUN 24 SER.#'d SETS
NOT PRICED DUE TO SCARCITY
1 Jacques Plante
Carey PricePatrick Roy
Roberto LuongoTim Thomas
Martin Brodeur
2 Evgeni Nabokov
Dominikk HasekPatrick Roy
Bernie ParentTony Esposito
Terry Sawchuk

2008-09 ITG Ultimate Memorabilia Ultimate Goalies Gold

STATED PRINT RUN 1 SER.#'d SETS
NOT PRICED DUE TO SCARCITY

2008-09 ITG Ultimate Memorabilia Ultimate Players Dual Swatch

STATED PRINT RUN 19 SER.#'d SETS
NOT PRICED DUE TO SCARCITY
1 Alexander Ovechkin
2 John Tavares
3 Roberto Luongo
4 Nicklas Lidstrom
5 Mario Lemieux
6 Martin Brodeur
7 Patrick Roy
8 Joe Sakic
9 Jaromir Jagr

2008-09 ITG Ultimate Memorabilia Ultimate Players Dual Swatch Gold

STATED PRINT RUN 9 SER.#'d SETS
NOT PRICED DUE TO SCARCITY

2008-09 ITG Ultimate Memorabilia Ultimate Players Five Swatch

STATED PRINT RUN 19 SER.#'d SETS
NOT PRICED DUE TO SCARCITY
1 Alexander Ovechkin
2 John Tavares
3 Roberto Luongo
4 Nicklas Lidstrom
5 Mario Lemieux
6 Martin Brodeur
7 Patrick Roy
8 Joe Sakic
9 Jaromir Jagr

2008-09 ITG Ultimate Memorabilia Ultimate Players Five Swatch Gold

STATED PRINT RUN 9 SER.#'d SETS
NOT PRICED DUE TO SCARCITY

2008-09 ITG Ultimate Memorabilia Ultimate Players Quad Swatch

STATED PRINT RUN 19 SER.#'d SETS
NOT PRICED DUE TO SCARCITY
1 Alexander Ovechkin
2 John Tavares
3 Roberto Luongo
4 Nicklas Lidstrom
5 Mario Lemieux
6 Martin Brodeur
7 Patrick Roy
8 Joe Sakic
9 Jaromir Jagr

2008-09 ITG Ultimate Memorabilia Ultimate Players Quad Swatch Gold

STATED PRINT RUN 9 SER.#'d SETS
NOT PRICED DUE TO SCARCITY

2008-09 ITG Ultimate Memorabilia Ultimate Players Six Swatch

STATED PRINT RUN 19 SER.#'d SETS
NOT PRICED DUE TO SCARCITY
1 Alexander Ovechkin
2 John Tavares
3 Roberto Luongo
4 Nicklas Lidstrom
5 Mario Lemieux
6 Martin Brodeur
7 Patrick Roy
8 Joe Sakic
9 Jaromir Jagr

2008-09 ITG Ultimate Memorabilia Ultimate Players Six Swatch Gold

STATED PRINT RUN 9 SER.#'d SETS
NOT PRICED DUE TO SCARCITY

2008-09 ITG Ultimate Memorabilia Ultimate Players Triple Swatch

STATED PRINT RUN 19 SER.#'d SETS
NOT PRICED DUE TO SCARCITY
1 Alexander Ovechkin
2 John Tavares
3 Roberto Luongo
4 Nicklas Lidstrom
5 Mario Lemieux
6 Martin Brodeur
7 Patrick Roy
8 Joe Sakic
9 Jaromir Jagr

2008-09 ITG Ultimate Memorabilia Ultimate Players Triple Swatch Gold

STATED PRINT RUN 9 SER.#'d SETS
NOT PRICED DUE TO SCARCITY

2008-09 ITG Ultimate Memorabilia Vintage Lumber

STATED PRINT RUN 9 SER.#'d SETS
NOT PRICED DUE TO SCARCITY
1 King Clancy
2 Jean Beliveau
3 Henri Richard
4 Joe Primeau
5 Bob Davidson
6 Bill Durnan
7 Maurice Richard
8 Bernie Geoffrion
9 Bobby Hull
10 Harry Lumley
11 Tim Horton
12 Chuck Rayner

2008-09 ITG Ultimate Memorabilia Vintage Lumber Gold

STATED PRINT RUN 1 SER.#'d SETS
NOT PRICED DUE TO SCARCITY

2008-09 ITG Ultimate Memorabilia Hometown Heroes Gold

STATED PRINT RUN 1 SER.#'d SETS
NOT PRICED DUE TO SCARCITY

2008-09 ITG Ultimate Memorabilia Jerseys

STATED PRINT RUN 24 SER.#'d SETS
NOT PRICED DUE TO SCARCITY
1 Alexander Ovechkin
2 Joe Sakic
3 John Tavares
4 Ryan Getzlaf
5 Martin Brodeur
6 Patrick Roy
7 Mario Lemieux
8 Raymond Bourque
9 Mike Modano
10 Miikka Kiprusoff
11 Milan Lucic
12 Pavel Datsyuk

2008-09 ITG Ultimate Memorabilia Jerseys-Emblems

STATED PRINT RUN 9 SER.#'d SETS
NOT PRICED DUE TO SCARCITY
1 Alexander Ovechkin
2 Joe Sakic
3 John Tavares
4 Ryan Getzlaf
5 Martin Brodeur
6 Patrick Roy
7 Mario Lemieux
8 Raymond Bourque
9 Mike Modano
10 Miikka Kiprusoff
11 Milan Lucic
12 Pavel Datsyuk

2002-03 ITG Used

This 200-card set was printed on two types of card stock. Card 1-100 were printed on a shimmerboard stock and pictured players in their away jerseys. Cards 101-200 were printed on dufex card stock and pictured players in the road jerseys. Cards 81-100 and 181-200 were shortprinted rookies and were serial-numbered to just 100 copies each.

COMP.SET w/o SP's (160)	300.00	600.00
1 Adam Oates	1.00	2.50
2 Paul Kariya	2.00	5.00
3 Petr Sykora	1.00	2.50
4 Dany Heatley	2.50	6.00
5 Ilya Kovalchuk	2.50	6.00
6 Jeff O'Neill	1.00	2.50
7 Joe Thornton	3.00	8.00
8 Sergei Samsonov	1.00	2.50
9 Jarome Iginla	2.50	6.00
10 Ron Francis	1.50	4.00
11 Jocelyn Thibault	1.50	4.00
12 Alex Tanguay	1.50	4.00
13 Joe Sakic	3.00	8.00
14 Milan Hejduk	2.00	5.00
15 Patrick Roy	8.00	20.00
16 Peter Forsberg	4.00	10.00
17 Rob Blake	1.50	4.00
18 Rostislav Klesla	1.00	2.50
19 Brett Hull	2.50	6.00
20 Marty Turco	1.50	4.00
21 Mike Modano	3.00	8.00
22 Bill Guerin	1.00	2.50
23 Brendan Shanahan	2.00	5.00
24 Chris Chelios	1.50	4.00
25 Curtis Joseph	2.00	5.00
26 Luc Robitaille	1.50	4.00
27 Nicklas Lidstrom	2.00	5.00
28 Pavel Datsyuk	2.00	5.00
29 Sergei Fedorov	2.50	6.00
30 Steve Yzerman	8.00	20.00
31 Mike Comrie	1.00	2.50
32 Erik Cole	1.00	2.50
33 Kristian Huselius	1.00	2.50
34 Roberto Luongo	2.50	6.00
35 Felix Potvin	2.00	5.00
36 Jason Allison	1.00	2.50
37 Zigmund Palffy	1.50	4.00
38 Marian Gaborik	4.00	10.00
39 Jose Theodore	2.50	6.00
40 Saku Koivu	2.00	5.00
41 Martin Brodeur	4.00	10.00
42 Patrik Elias	1.00	2.50
43 Scott Gomez	1.00	2.50
44 Alexei Yashin	1.00	2.50
45 Chris Osgood	1.50	4.00
46 Rick DiPietro	1.50	4.00
47 Brian Leetch	1.50	4.00
48 Eric Lindros	2.00	5.00
49 Mark Messier	2.00	5.00
50 Mike Richter	2.00	5.00
51 Pavel Bure	2.00	5.00
52 Daniel Alfredsson	1.50	4.00
53 Marian Hossa	2.00	5.00
54 Martin Havlat	1.50	4.00
55 Jeremy Roenick	2.50	6.00
56 John LeClair	1.50	4.00
57 Mark Recchi	1.50	4.00
58 Simon Gagne	2.00	5.00
59 Nikolai Khabibulin	2.00	5.00
60 Sean Burke	1.00	2.50
61 Johan Hedberg	1.00	2.50
62 Mario Lemieux	8.00	20.00
63 Evgeni Nabokov	1.50	4.00
64 Owen Nolan	1.00	2.50
65 Teemu Selanne	2.00	5.00
66 Al MacInnis	1.00	2.50
67 Chris Pronger	1.50	4.00
68 Doug Weight	1.50	4.00
69 Keith Tkachuk	2.00	5.00
70 Vincent Lecavalier	1.50	4.00
71 Ed Belfour	2.00	5.00
72 Mats Sundin	2.00	5.00
73 Daniel Sedin	1.00	2.50
74 Henrik Sedin	1.00	2.50
75 Markus Naslund	2.00	5.00
76 Todd Bertuzzi	2.00	5.00
77 Jaromir Jagr	2.50	6.00
78 Olaf Kolzig	1.50	4.00
79 Peter Bondra	1.50	4.00
80 Tony Amonte	1.00	2.50
81 P-M Bouchard RC	15.00	30.00
82 Rick Nash RC	75.00	200.00
83 Dennis Seidenberg RC	8.00	20.00
84 Jay Bouwmeester RC	15.00	40.00
85 Stanislav Chistov RC	8.00	20.00
86 Tom Koivisto RC	8.00	20.00
87 Ivan Majesky RC	8.00	20.00
88 Chuck Kobasew RC	10.00	25.00
89 Ales Hemsky RC	30.00	80.00
90 Radovan Somik RC	8.00	20.00
91 Dmitri Bykov RC	8.00	20.00
92 Ryan Miller RC	40.00	80.00
93 Ron Hainsey RC	8.00	20.00
94 Anton Volchenkov RC	8.00	20.00
95 Dick Tarnstrom RC	8.00	20.00
96 Scottie Upshall RC	10.00	25.00
97 Jordan Leopold RC	8.00	20.00
98 Carlo Colaiacovo RC	8.00	20.00
99 Levente Szuper RC	8.00	20.00
100 Lynn Loyns RC	8.00	20.00
101 Adam Oates	1.00	2.50
102 Paul Kariya	2.00	5.00
103 Petr Sykora	1.00	2.50
104 Dany Heatley	2.50	6.00
105 Ilya Kovalchuk	2.50	6.00
106 Jeff O'Neill	1.00	2.50
107 Joe Thornton	3.00	8.00
108 Sergei Samsonov	1.00	2.50
109 Jarome Iginla	2.50	6.00
110 Ron Francis	1.00	2.50
111 Jocelyn Thibault	1.00	2.50
112 Alex Tanguay	1.50	4.00
113 Joe Sakic	4.00	10.00
114 Milan Hejduk	2.00	5.00
115 Patrick Roy	10.00	25.00
116 Peter Forsberg	3.00	8.00
117 Rob Blake	1.50	4.00
118 Rostislav Klesla	1.00	2.50
119 Brett Hull	2.50	6.00
120 Marty Turco	1.50	4.00
121 Mike Modano	3.00	8.00
122 Bill Guerin	1.00	2.50
123 Brendan Shanahan	3.00	8.00
124 Chris Chelios	1.50	4.00
125 Curtis Joseph	2.00	5.00
126 Luc Robitaille	1.50	4.00
127 Nicklas Lidstrom	2.00	5.00
128 Pavel Datsyuk	2.00	5.00
129 Sergei Fedorov	4.00	10.00
130 Steve Yzerman	10.00	25.00
131 Mike Comrie	1.00	2.50
132 Erik Cole	1.00	2.50
133 Kristian Huselius	1.00	2.50
134 Roberto Luongo	2.50	6.00
135 Felix Potvin	2.00	5.00
136 Jason Allison	1.00	2.50
137 Zigmund Palffy	2.00	5.00
138 Marian Gaborik	4.00	10.00
139 Jose Theodore	2.50	6.00
140 Saku Koivu	2.00	5.00
141 Martin Brodeur	5.00	12.00
142 Patrik Elias	1.00	2.50
143 Scott Gomez	1.00	2.50
144 Alexei Yashin	1.00	2.50
145 Chris Osgood	1.50	4.00
146 Rick DiPietro	1.50	4.00
147 Brian Leetch	1.50	4.00
148 Eric Lindros	3.00	8.00
149 Mark Messier	2.50	6.00
150 Mike Richter	2.00	5.00
151 Pavel Bure	2.50	6.00
152 Daniel Alfredsson	1.50	4.00
153 Marian Hossa	2.00	5.00
154 Martin Havlat	1.00	2.50
155 Jeremy Roenick	2.50	6.00
156 John LeClair	2.00	4.00
157 Mark Recchi	1.00	2.50
158 Simon Gagne	2.00	5.00
159 Nikolai Khabibulin	2.00	5.00
160 Sean Burke	1.50	4.00
161 Johan Hedberg	1.00	2.50
162 Mario Lemieux	12.50	30.00
163 Evgeni Nabokov	1.50	4.00
164 Owen Nolan	1.00	2.50
165 Teemu Selanne	2.00	5.00
166 Al MacInnis	1.50	4.00
167 Chris Pronger	1.50	4.00
168 Doug Weight	1.50	4.00
169 Keith Tkachuk	2.00	5.00
170 Vincent Lecavalier	1.50	4.00
171 Ed Belfour	2.00	5.00
172 Mats Sundin	2.00	5.00
173 Daniel Sedin	1.00	2.50
174 Henrik Sedin	1.00	2.50
175 Markus Naslund	2.00	5.00
176 Todd Bertuzzi	2.00	5.00
177 Jaromir Jagr	3.00	8.00
178 Olaf Kolzig	1.50	4.00
179 Peter Bondra	1.00	2.50
180 Tony Amonte	1.00	2.50
181 Shaone Morrisonn RC	8.00	20.00
182 Kari Haakana RC	8.00	20.00
183 Ray Emery RC	20.00	50.00
184 Mike Cammalleri RC	12.00	30.00
185 Ari Ahonen RC	8.00	20.00
186 Martin Gerber RC	12.00	30.00
187 Adam Hall RC	8.00	20.00
188 Lasse Pirjeta RC	8.00	20.00
189 Stephane Veilleux RC	8.00	20.00
190 Jeff Taffe RC	8.00	20.00
191 Mikael Tellqvist RC	12.00	30.00
192 Alexander Frolov RC	20.00	50.00
193 Steve Eminger RC	8.00	20.00
194 Shawn Thornton RC	8.00	20.00
195 Alexander Svitov RC	8.00	20.00
196 Alexei Smirnov RC	8.00	20.00
197 Curtis Sanford RC	10.00	25.00

198 Henrik Zetterberg RC 75.00 125.00
199 Eric Godard RC 8.00 20.00
200 Jason Spezza RC 100.00 250.00

2002-03 ITG Used Calder Jerseys

STATED PRINT RUN 50 SETS
C1 Jason Spezza 20.00 50.00
C2 Rick Nash 20.00 50.00
C3 Jay Bouwmeester 10.00 20.00
C4 Stephen Weiss 8.00 20.00
C5 Chuck Kobasew 6.00 15.00
C6 Ales Hemsky 10.00 25.00
C7 Alexander Svitov 6.00 15.00
C8 Ron Hainsey 6.00 15.00
C9 Jordan Leopold 6.00 15.00
C10 Stanislav Chistov 6.00 15.00
C11 Alexei Smirnov 6.00 15.00
C12 Ryan Miller 12.00 30.00
C13 Dennis Seidenberg 6.00 15.00
C14 Adam Hall 6.00 15.00
C15 Niko Kapanen 6.00 15.00
C16 Alexander Frolov 12.00 30.00
C17 Anton Volchenkov 6.00 15.00
C18 Radovan Somik 6.00 15.00
C19 Ivan Huml 6.00 15.00
C20 Mike Cammalleri 8.00 20.00

2002-03 ITG Used Calder Jerseys Gold

STATED PRINT RUN 10 SETS
NOT PRICED DUE TO SCARCITY

2002-03 ITG Used Franchise Players

Limited to 65 copies each, this 30-card set carried swatches of game-worn jerseys.

F1 Paul Kariya 8.00 20.00
F2 Ilya Kovalchuk 12.50 30.00
F3 Joe Thornton 15.00 40.00
F4 Miroslav Satan 8.00 20.00
F5 Jarome Iginla 10.00 25.00
F6 Jeff O'Neill 8.00 20.00
F7 Eric Daze 8.00 20.00
F8 Patrick Roy 25.00 60.00
F9 Rostislav Klesla 8.00 20.00
F10 Mike Modano 12.50 30.00
F11 Steve Yzerman 20.00 50.00
F12 Mike Comrie 8.00 20.00
F13 Roberto Luongo 12.50 30.00
F14 Zigmund Palffy 8.00 20.00
F15 Marian Gaborik 12.00 30.00
F16 Jose Theodore 8.00 20.00
F17 Scott Hartnell 8.00 20.00
F18 Martin Brodeur 20.00 50.00
F19 Alexei Yashin 8.00 20.00
F20 Pavel Bure 8.00 20.00
F21 Marian Hossa 8.00 20.00
F22 Simon Gagne 8.00 20.00
F23 Daniel Briere 8.00 20.00
F24 Mario Lemieux 25.00 60.00
F25 Chris Pronger 8.00 20.00
F26 Owen Nolan 8.00 20.00
F27 Nikolai Khabibulin 8.00 20.00
F28 Mats Sundin 8.00 20.00
F29 Markus Naslund 8.00 20.00
F30 Jaromir Jagr 12.50 30.00

2002-03 ITG Used Franchise Players Autographs

This 30-card set paralleled the basic insert set but also carried certified autographs. Cards were limited to just 10 copies each and are not priced due to scarcity.

NOT PRICED DUE TO SCARCITY

2002-03 ITG Used Franchise Players Gold

STATED PRINT RUN 10 SETS
NOT PRICED DUE TO SCARCITY

2002-03 ITG Used Goalie Pad and Jersey

This 20-card set featured jersey and goalie pad swatches. Cards were limited to 50 copies each.

GP1 Jose Theodore 20.00 50.00
GP2 Patrick Roy 40.00 100.00
GP3 Martin Brodeur 40.00 100.00
GP4 Jocelyn Thibault 12.50 30.00
GP5 Mike Dunham 12.50 30.00
GP6 Ed Belfour 15.00 40.00
GP7 J-S Aubin 12.50 30.00

GP8 Dan Cloutier 12.50 30.00
GP9 Roman Turek 12.50 30.00
GP10 Chris Osgood 12.50 30.00
GP11 Marty Turco 12.50 30.00
GP12 Roman Cechmanek 12.50 30.00
GP13 Sean Burke 12.50 30.00
GP14 Tomas Vokoun 12.50 30.00
GP15 Gerry Cheevers 15.00 40.00
GP16 Bernie Parent 12.50 30.00
GP17 Brian Boucher 12.50 30.00
GP18 Jeff Hackett 12.50 30.00
GP19 Ron Hextall 15.00 40.00
GP20 Terry Sawchuk 50.00 125.00

2002-03 ITG Used Goalie Pad and Jersey Gold

STATED PRINT RUN 10 SETS
NOT PRICED DUE TO SCARCITY

2002-03 ITG Used International Experience

This 28-card set featured swatches of jersey used in world championship competition. Cards were limited to 60 copies each.

IE1 Mario Lemieux 30.00 80.00
IE2 Jaromir Jagr 15.00 40.00
IE3 Mats Sundin 12.50 30.00
IE4 Steve Yzerman 25.00 60.00
IE5 Nicklas Lidstrom 12.50 30.00
IE6 Mike Modano 15.00 40.00
IE7 Peter Forsberg 20.00 50.00
IE8 Zigmund Palffy 12.50 30.00
IE9 Olaf Kolzig 12.50 30.00
IE10 Teemu Selanne 12.50 30.00
IE11 Bill Guerin 12.50 30.00
IE12 Alexander Mogilny 12.50 30.00
IE13 Alexei Yashin 12.50 30.00
IE14 Saku Koivu 12.50 30.00
IE15 Bobby Holik 12.50 30.00
IE16 Tony Amonte 12.50 30.00
IE17 Joe Sakic 15.00 40.00
IE18 Chris Chelios 12.50 30.00
IE19 Curtis Joseph 12.50 30.00
IE20 Martin Brodeur 20.00 50.00
IE21 Radek Bonk 12.50 30.00
IE22 Brian Leetch 15.00 40.00
IE23 Darius Kasparaitis 12.50 30.00
IE24 Tommy Salo 12.50 30.00
IE25 Roman Turek 12.50 30.00
IE26 Johan Hedberg 12.50 30.00
IE27 Roman Cechmanek 12.50 30.00
IE28 Nikolai Khabibulin 12.50 30.00

2002-03 ITG Used International Experience Gold

STATED PRINT RUN 10 SETS
NOT PRICED DUE TO SCARCITY

2002-03 ITG Used Jerseys

STATED PRINT RUN 75 SETS
GUJ1 Mario Lemieux 20.00 50.00
GUJ2 Steve Yzerman 15.00 40.00
GUJ3 Peter Forsberg 12.50 30.00
GUJ4 Patrick Roy 15.00 40.00
GUJ5 Jarome Iginla 8.00 20.00
GUJ6 Pavel Bure 8.00 20.00
GUJ7 Jaromir Jagr 10.00 25.00
GUJ8 Eric Lindros 8.00 20.00
GUJ9 Paul Kariya 8.00 20.00
GUJ10 Ilya Kovalchuk 10.00 25.00
GUJ11 Mike Modano 10.00 25.00
GUJ12 Joe Thornton 10.00 25.00
GUJ13 Jose Theodore 10.00 25.00
GUJ14 Jeremy Roenick 10.00 25.00
GUJ15 Martin Brodeur 15.00 40.00
GUJ16 Mats Sundin 8.00 20.00
GUJ17 Mark Messier 8.00 20.00
GUJ18 Alexei Yashin 8.00 20.00
GUJ19 Marian Gaborik 12.50 30.00
GUJ20 Brendan Shanahan 8.00 20.00
GUJ21 Owen Nolan 8.00 20.00
GUJ22 Joe Sakic 12.50 30.00
GUJ23 Daniel Alfredsson 8.00 20.00
GUJ24 Teemu Selanne 8.00 20.00
GUJ25 Nicklas Lidstrom 8.00 20.00
GUJ26 John LeClair 8.00 20.00
GUJ27 Keith Tkachuk 8.00 20.00
GUJ28 Brian Leetch 8.00 20.00
GUJ29 Milan Hejduk 8.00 20.00
GUJ30 Dany Heatley 10.00 25.00
GUJ31 Sergei Samsonov 8.00 20.00
GUJ32 Todd Bertuzzi 8.00 20.00
GUJ33 Markus Naslund 8.00 20.00
GUJ34 Chris Chelios 8.00 20.00
GUJ35 Rob Blake 8.00 20.00
GUJ36 Sergei Fedorov 10.00 25.00
GUJ37 Al MacInnis 8.00 20.00
GUJ38 Luc Robitaille 8.00 20.00
GUJ39 Eric Daze 8.00 20.00
GUJ40 Ron Francis 8.00 20.00
GUJ41 Alexander Mogilny 8.00 20.00
GUJ42 Chris Pronger 8.00 20.00
GUJ43 Doug Weight 8.00 20.00
GUJ44 Zigmund Palffy 8.00 20.00
GUJ45 Peter Bondra 8.00 20.00
GUJ46 Mike Comrie 8.00 20.00
GUJ47 Mark Recchi 8.00 20.00
GUJ48 Marian Hossa 8.00 20.00
GUJ49 Saku Koivu 8.00 20.00
GUJ50 Pierre Turgeon 8.00 20.00

2002-03 ITG Used Jersey Autographs

STATED PRINT RUN 10 SETS
NOT PRICED DUE TO SCARCITY

2002-03 ITG Used Jerseys Gold

STATED PRINT RUN 10 SETS
NOT PRICED DUE TO SCARCITY

2002-03 ITG Used Emblems

This 40-card set partially paralleled the basic jersey set but with emblem pieces. Cards were limited to 9 copies each and are not priced due to scarcity. Gold one of one's were also created.

NOT PRICED DUE TO SCARCITY

2002-03 ITG Used Jersey and Stick

This 50-card set combined swatches of game jerseys with game-used sticks. Cards were limited to 75 copies each.

*STK/JSY: .5X TO 1.25X BASIC JERSEY

2002-03 ITG Used Jersey and Stick Gold

STATED PRINT RUN 10 SETS
NOT PRICED DUE TO SCARCITY

2002-03 ITG Used Magnificent Inserts

This 10-card set featured game-used equipment from the career of Mario Lemieux. Cards MI1-MI5 had a print run of 40 copies each and cards MI6-MI10 were limited to just 10 copies each. Cards MI6-MI10 are not priced due to scarcity.

MI6-MI10 NOT PRICED DUE TO SCARCITY
MI1 2000-01 Jersey 30.00 80.00
MI2 1985-86 Jersey 30.00 80.00
MI3 2002 All-Star Jersey 30.00 80.00
MI4 1987 Canada Cup Jersey 30.00 80.00
MI5 Dual Jersey 50.00 125.00
MI6 Number
MI7 Emblem
MI8 Triple Jersey
MI9 Quad Jersey
MI10 Complete Package

2002-03 ITG Used Magnificent Inserts Autographs

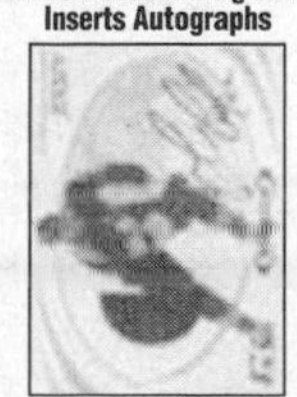

This 10-card set paralleled the base Magnificent Inserts but carried certified autographs and each card was hand numbered. Cards MI1-MI5 were serial-numbered to 15 each and cards MI6-MI10 were serial numbered out of 5.

NOT PRICED DUE TO SCARCITY

2002-03 ITG Used Teammates

Limited to 70 copies each, this 20-card set featured swatches of game jerseys from players on the same club.

T1 Mario Lemieux / Alexei Kovalev 30.00 80.00
T2 Peter Forsberg / Patrick Roy 40.00 100.00
T3 Joe Thornton / Sergei Samsonov 15.00 40.00
T4 Pavel Bure / Eric Lindros 10.00 25.00
T5 Steve Yzerman / Chris Chelios 30.00 80.00
T6 Saku Koivu / Jose Theodore 12.50 30.00
T7 Ilya Kovalchuk / Dany Heatley 15.00 40.00
T8 Chris Pronger / Keith Tkachuk 10.00 25.00
T9 Nicklas Lidstrom / Brendan Shanahan 12.50 30.00
T10 Rob Blake / Joe Sakic 15.00 40.00
T11 Brian Leetch / Mark Messier 12.50 30.00
T12 Mats Sundin / Alexander Mogilny 12.50 30.00
T13 M.Modano/M.Turco 15.00 40.00
T14 M.Brodeur/S.Niedermayer 12.50 30.00
T15 Simon Gagne / John LeClair 10.00 25.00
T16 Owen Nolan / Teemu Selanne 12.50 30.00
T17 Zigmund Palffy / Felix Potvin 10.00 25.00
T18 Jaromir Jagr / Olaf Kolzig 12.50 30.00
T19 Markus Naslund / Todd Bertuzzi 10.00 25.00
T20 Sergei Fedorov / Brett Hull 15.00 40.00

2002-03 ITG Used Teammates Gold

STATED PRINT RUN 10 SETS
NOT PRICED DUE TO SCARCITY

2002-03 ITG Used Triple Memorabilia

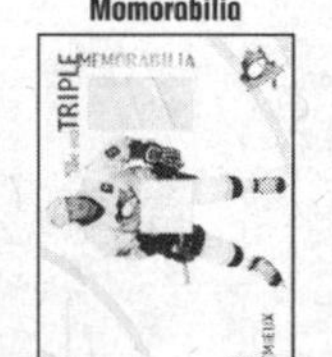

This 20-card set featured three different pieces of game-used equipment. Each card was limited to just 35 copies.

TM1 Joe Thornton 25.00 60.00
TM2 Mario Lemieux 75.00 200.00
TM3 Mats Sundin 15.00 40.00
TM4 Jarome Iginla 20.00 50.00
TM5 Nicklas Lidstrom 15.00 40.00
TM6 John LeClair 15.00 40.00
TM7 Chris Chelios 15.00 40.00
TM8 Joe Sakic 40.00 100.00
TM9 Eric Lindros 15.00 40.00
TM10 Al MacInnis 15.00 40.00
TM11 Sergei Fedorov 25.00 60.00
TM12 Sergei Samsonov 15.00 40.00
TM13 Simon Gagne 15.00 40.00
TM14 Doug Weight 15.00 40.00
TM15 Alexei Yashin 15.00 40.00
TM16 Scott Niedermayer 15.00 40.00
TM17 Steve Yzerman 50.00 125.00
TM18 Rob Blake 15.00 40.00
TM19 Brett Hull 40.00 100.00
TM20 Adam Deadmarsh 15.00 40.00

2002-03 ITG Used Triple Memorabilia Gold

STATED PRINT RUN 10 SETS
NOT PRICED DUE TO SCARCITY

2002-03 ITG Used Vintage Memorabilia

Limited to just 38 sets, this 20-card set featured swatches of game-used equipment or jersey from great players of the past.

VM1 Newsy Lalonde 30.00 80.00
VM2 Jacques Plante 30.00 80.00
VM3 Roy Worters 30.00 80.00
VM4 Tiny Thompson 12.50 30.00
VM5 Ace Bailey 40.00 100.00
VM6 Jean Beliveau 25.00 60.00
VM7 Maurice Richard 40.00 100.00
VM8 Red Kelly 20.00 50.00
VM9 Harry Lumley 20.00 50.00
VM10 Eddie Shore 40.00 100.00
VM11 Alex Delvecchio 12.50 30.00
VM12 Bill Mosienko 12.50 30.00
VM13 Tim Horton 30.00 80.00
VM14 Doug Harvey 12.50 30.00
VM15 Johnny Bower 12.50 30.00
VM16 George Hainsworth 20.00 50.00
VM17 Bill Durnan 12.50 30.00
VM18 Terry Sawchuk 30.00 80.00
VM19 Frank Brimsek 12.50 30.00
VM20 King Clancy 50.00 125.00

2002-03 ITG Used Vintage Memorabilia Gold

STATED PRINT RUN 10 SETS
NOT PRICED DUE TO SCARCITY

2003-04 ITG Used Signature Series

This 200-card set consisted of 110 veteran cards limited to 300 copies each, 10 legends cards (111-120) limited to 100 sets each; 30 rookie autograph cards (121-150) serial-numbered out of 135 and 50 rookie cards (151-200) serial-numbered to 390 copies each. Please note that cards 151 and 152 both had autographed parallels serial-numbered to just 25 copies each, those cards can be found in the autograph set checklist. Also note that cards 112B (Hull) and 114B (Bower) were supposedly pulled and destroyed prior to distribution. However, copies have been confirmed to be in circulation. Unfortunately, we have no confirmed sales at this point, and thus no pricing information.

1-100 PRINT RUN 300 SETS
101-120 PRINT RUN 100 SETS
COMMON RC (151-200) 4.00 10.00
RC PRINT RUN 390 SER.#'d SETS
1 Rick Nash 2.00 5.00
2 Tomas Vokoun 1.25 3.00
3 Alexander Frolov 1.00 2.50
4 Eric Brewer 1.00 2.50
5 Pavel Datsyuk 1.50 4.00
6 Bill Guerin 1.25 3.00
7 Rob Blake 1.25 3.00
8 Rostislav Klesla 1.00 2.50
9 Ron Francis 1.25 3.00
10 Glen Murray 1.00 2.50
11 Chris Drury 1.25 3.00
12 Alexei Yashin 1.00 2.50
13 Teemu Selanne 1.50 4.00
14 Henrik Zetterberg 1.50 4.00
15 Olli Jokinen 1.25 3.00
16 Marian Gaborik 3.00 8.00
17 Patrik Elias 1.25 3.00
18 Alex Kovalev 1.25 3.00
19 Simon Gagne 1.50 4.00
20 Martin St. Louis 1.25 3.00
21 Chris Pronger 1.25 3.00
22 Jeremy Roenick 2.00 5.00
23 Manny Fernandez 1.25 3.00
24 Zigmund Palffy 1.25 3.00
25 Erik Cole 1.00 2.50
26 Sergei Samsonov 1.25 3.00
27 Niko Kapanen 1.00 2.50
28 Ales Hemsky 1.25 3.00
29 Eric Daze 1.25 3.00
30 Vincent Lecavalier 1.50 4.00
31 Shane Doan 1.00 2.50
32 Marian Hossa 1.50 4.00
33 Scott Stevens 1.25 3.00
34 Roberto Luongo 2.00 5.00
35 Joe Thornton 2.50 6.00
36 Marc Denis 1.25 3.00
37 Marty Turco 1.25 3.00
38 Daniel Alfredsson 1.25 3.00
39 Ryan Smyth 1.00 2.50
40 Miroslav Satan 1.25 3.00
41 Nicklas Lidstrom 1.50 4.00
42 Chuck Kobasew 1.00 2.50
43 Mark Recchi 1.25 3.00
44 Rick DiPietro 1.25 3.00
45 Nikolai Khabibulin 1.50 4.00
46 Keith Tkachuk 1.50 4.00
47 Jason Spezza 1.50 4.00
48 Felix Potvin 1.50 4.00
49 Patrick Lalime 1.25 3.00
50 Milan Hejduk 1.50 4.00
51 Sergei Fedorov 2.00 5.00
52 Ed Jovanovski 1.25 3.00
53 Jarome Iginla 2.00 5.00
54 Jocelyn Thibault 1.25 3.00
55 Brian Leetch 1.25 3.00
56 Michael Ryder 1.25 3.00
57 Jay Bouwmeester 1.00 2.50
58 Saku Koivu 1.50 4.00
59 Jose Theodore 2.00 5.00
60 Anson Carter 1.25 3.00
61 John LeClair 1.50 4.00
62 Sean Burke 1.25 3.00
63 Markus Naslund 1.50 4.00
64 Olaf Kolzig 1.50 4.00
65 Peter Bondra 1.25 3.00
66 Doug Weight 1.25 3.00
67 Sergei Gonchar 1.00 2.50
68 Dwayne Roloson 1.25 3.00
69 Roman Cechmanek 1.25 3.00
70 David Legwand 1.25 3.00
71 Mike Peca 1.00 2.50
72 Mike Dunham 1.25 3.00
73 Dany Heatley 2.00 5.00
74 Chris Osgood 1.25 3.00
75 Tommy Salo 1.25 3.00
76 David Aebischer 1.25 3.00
77 Jeff O'Neill 1.00 2.50
78 Tyler Arnason 1.00 2.50
79 Roman Turek 1.25 3.00
80 Ryan Miller 1.25 3.00
81 Pasi Nurminen 1.25 3.00
82 Kevin Weekes 1.25 3.00
83 Byron Dafoe 1.25 3.00
84 Ray Whitney 1.00 2.50
85 Al MacInnis 1.25 3.00
86 Adam Oates 1.25 3.00
87 Vincent Damphousse 1.00 2.50
88 Evgeni Nabokov 1.25 3.00
89 Daymond Langkow 1.00 2.50
90 Todd Bertuzzi 1.50 4.00
91 Dan Cloutier 1.25 3.00
92 Aleksey Morozov 1.00 2.50
93 Tony Amonte 1.25 3.00
94 Brett Hull 2.00 5.00
95 Martin Biron 1.25 3.00
96 Ilya Kovalchuk 2.00 5.00
97 Andrew Raycroft 1.25 3.00
98 Curtis Joseph 1.50 4.00
99 Peter Forsberg 4.00 10.00
100 Joe Sakic 3.00 8.00
101 Steve Yzerman 10.00 25.00
102 Brendan Shanahan 2.00 5.00
103 Owen Nolan 2.00 5.00
104 Mike Modano 3.00 8.00
105 Dominik Hasek 4.00 10.00
106 Martin Brodeur 5.00 12.00
107 Eric Lindros 2.00 5.00
108 Jaromir Jagr 3.00 8.00
109 Mats Sundin 2.00 5.00
110 Mario Lemieux 12.50 30.00
111 Jean Beliveau 6.00 15.00
112 Frank Mahovlich 5.00 12.00
112B Bobby Hull
113 Ted Lindsay 6.00 15.00
114 Red Kelly 4.00 10.00
114B Johnny Bower
115 Bobby Orr 12.50 30.00
116 Ray Bourque 4.00 10.00
117 Patrick Roy 10.00 25.00
118 Guy Lafleur 5.00 12.00
119 Ted Kennedy 4.00 10.00
120 Phil Esposito 4.00 10.00
121 Tuomo Ruutu AU RC 20.00 50.00
122 Chris Higgins AU RC 25.00 60.00
123 Antoine Vermette AU RC 12.50 30.00
124 David Hale AU RC 10.00 25.00
125 Pavel Vorobiev AU RC 10.00 25.00
126 Antti Miettinen AU RC 10.00 25.00
127 Patrice Bergeron AU RC 30.00 80.00
128 Nathan Horton AU RC 25.00 60.00
129 Tim Gleason AU RC 12.50 30.00
130 Matthew Lombardi AU RC 12.50 30.00
131 Paul Martin AU RC 10.00 25.00
132 Marek Zidlicky AU RC 12.50 30.00
133 Joni Pitkanen AU RC 12.50 30.00
134 Marc-Andre Fleury AU RC 75.00 125.00
135 Jordin Tootoo AU RC 25.00 60.00
136 Eric Staal AU RC 40.00 100.00
137 Fredrik Sjostrom AU RC 12.50 30.00
138 Dustin Brown AU RC 15.00 40.00
139 Jiri Hudler AU RC 15.00 40.00
140 Derek Roy AU RC 15.00 40.00
141 Ryan Malone AU RC 12.00 30.00
142 Chris Kunitz AU RC 12.50 30.00
143 Jozef Balej AU RC 12.50 30.00
144 Boyd Gordon AU RC 12.50 30.00
145 Alexander Semin AU RC 30.00 80.00
146 Dan Fritsche AU RC 12.00 30.00
147 Brent Burns AU RC 12.50 30.00
148 Milan Michalek AU RC 20.00 50.00
149 Matt Stajan AU RC 15.00 40.00
150 Nikolai Zherdev AU RC 15.00 40.00
151 Darryl Bootland RC 4.00 10.00
152 Kari Lehtonen RC 25.00 50.00
153 Noah Clarke RC 4.00 10.00
154 Sean Bergenheim RC 4.00 10.00
155 Niklas Kronwall RC 6.00 15.00
156 Matt Murley RC 4.00 10.00
157 Mark Popovic RC 4.00 10.00
158 John-Michael Liles RC 4.00 10.00
159 Brent Krahn RC 4.00 10.00
160 Sergei Zinovjev RC 4.00 10.00
161 Trevor Daley RC 4.00 10.00
162 Matt Ellison RC 4.00 10.00
163 Timofei Shishkanov RC 4.00 10.00
164 John Pohl RC 4.00 10.00
165 Adam Munro RC 4.00 10.00
166 Rastislav Stana RC 4.00 10.00
167 Peter Sejna RC 4.00 10.00
168 Jed Ortmeyer RC 4.00 10.00
169 Aleksander Suglobov RC 4.00 10.00
170 Seamus Kotyk RC 4.00 10.00
171 Andy Chiodo RC 4.00 10.00
172 Ryan Kesler RC 4.00 10.00
173 Mikhail Yakubov RC 4.00 10.00
174 Nathan Robinson RC 4.00 10.00
175 Tom Preissing RC 4.00 10.00
176 Jeff Hamilton RC 4.00 10.00
177 Dan Hamhuis RC 4.00 10.00
178 Antero Niittymaki RC 8.00 20.00
179 Joffrey Lupul RC 6.00 15.00
180 Garth Murray RC 4.00 10.00
181 Denis Grebeshkov RC 4.00 10.00
182 Dan Ellis RC 4.00 10.00
183 Tomas Plekanec RC 8.00 20.00
184 Tuomas Pihlman RC 4.00 10.00
185 Nolan Schaefer RC 4.00 10.00
186 Joey MacDonald RC 4.00 10.00
187 Carl Corazzini RC 4.00 10.00
188 Mike Smith RC 5.00 12.00
189 Anton Babchuk RC 4.00 10.00
190 Kyle Wellwood RC 8.00 20.00
191 Marek Svatos RC 8.00 20.00
192 Ryan Barnes RC 4.00 10.00
193 Fedor Tyutin RC 4.00 10.00
194 Dominic Moore RC 4.00 10.00
195 Colton Orr RC 4.00 10.00
196 Andrew Peters RC 4.00 10.00
197 Wade Brookbank RC 4.00 10.00
198 Cody McCormick RC 4.00 10.00
199 Michal Barinka RC 4.00 10.00
200 Mikhail Kuleshov RC 4.00 10.00

2003-04 ITG Used Signature Series Gold

*1-100 STARS: 2X TO 5X
1-100 PRINT RUN 50 SETS
*101-120 STARS: .75X TO 2X
*151-200 ROOKIES: .5X TO 1.25X
101-120 PRINT RUN 50 SETS

2003-04 ITG Used Signature Series Autographs

This 123-card set paralleled the veteran and legend subsets of the base set with certified player autographs. Print runs for basic veteran cards were 170 copies each unless otherwise noted. Cards listed as SP's were limited to 70 copies each. Please note that several players had two different versions of their cards, one with their former team and one with their most recent team. Those different versions are noted below with "1" and "2" designations after the card number. Also note that cards 151A and 152A are the only cards in this set featuring rookie players and carrying the same numbering as the base set; the "A" designation was added for checklisting purposes.

151A Darryl Bootland/25 40.00 100.00
152A Kari Lehtonen/25 150.00 300.00
AC1 Anson Carter NYR 6.00 15.00
AC2 Anson Carter LA/20
AF Alexander Frolov 6.00 15.00
AH Ales Hemsky 6.00 15.00
AK1 Alex Kovalev NYR 6.00 15.00
AK2 Alexei Kovalev MON/20
AM Alexei Morozov 6.00 15.00
AO Adam Oates 6.00 15.00
AR Andrew Raycroft 8.00 20.00
AY Alexei Yashin 6.00 15.00
BD Byron Dafoe 6.00 15.00
BG Bill Guerin 6.00 15.00
BJ Barret Jackman 6.00 15.00
BL Brian Leetch/100 12.50 30.00
CD Chris Drury 6.00 15.00
CJ Curtis Joseph 8.00 20.00
CK Chuck Kobasew 6.00 15.00
CO Chris Osgood 6.00 15.00
CP Chris Pronger 6.00 15.00
DA Daniel Alfredsson 6.00 15.00
DC Dan Cloutier 6.00 15.00
DL David Legwand 6.00 15.00
DR Dwayne Roloson 6.00 15.00
DW Doug Weight 6.00 15.00
EB Eric Brewer 6.00 15.00
EC Erik Cole 6.00 15.00
ED Eric Daze 6.00 15.00
EJ Ed Jovanovski 6.00 15.00
EN Evgeni Nabokov 6.00 15.00
FP Felix Potvin 8.00 20.00
GM Glen Murray 6.00 15.00
HZ Henrik Zetterberg 10.00 25.00
IK Ilya Kovalchuk 10.00 25.00
JH Jeff Hackett 6.00 15.00
JI Jarome Iginla 10.00 25.00
JL John LeClair 8.00 20.00
JO Jeff O'Neill 6.00 15.00
JR Jeremy Roenick 10.00 25.00
JS Jason Spezza 8.00 20.00
JT Joe Thornton 12.50 30.00
KT Keith Tkachuk 8.00 20.00
KW Kevin Weekes 6.00 15.00
MD Marc Denis 6.00 15.00
MF Manny Fernandez 6.00 15.00
MG Marian Gaborik 15.00 40.00
MH Marian Hossa 8.00 20.00
MN Markus Naslund 8.00 20.00
MP Mike Peca 6.00 15.00
MR Mark Recchi 6.00 15.00
MS Martin St. Louis 6.00 15.00
MT Marty Turco 6.00 15.00
NK Niko Kapanen 6.00 15.00
NL Nicklas Lidstrom 8.00 20.00
OJ Olli Jokinen 6.00 15.00
OK Olaf Kolzig 6.00 15.00
PB1 Peter Bondra WAS 6.00 15.00
PB2 Peter Bondra OTT/20
PD Pavel Datsyuk 12.50 30.00
PE Patrik Elias 6.00 15.00
PF Peter Forsberg 20.00 50.00
PL Patrick Lalime 6.00 15.00
PN Pasi Nurminen 6.00 15.00
PS Petr Sykora 6.00 15.00
RB Rob Blake 6.00 15.00
RC Roman Cechmanek 6.00 15.00
RD Rick DiPietro 6.00 15.00
RF1 Ron Francis CAR 6.00 15.00
RF2 Ron Francis TOR/20
RK1 Rostislav Klesla 6.00 15.00
RL Roberto Luongo 10.00 25.00
RM Ryan Miller 8.00 20.00
RN Rick Nash/195 10.00 25.00
RS Ryan Smyth 8.00 20.00
RT Roman Turek 6.00 15.00
RW Ray Whitney 6.00 15.00
SB1 Sean Burke PHX 6.00 15.00
SB2 Sean Burke PHI/20
SD Shane Doan 6.00 15.00
SF Sergei Fedorov 8.00 20.00
SG Simon Gagne 8.00 20.00

SK Saku Koivu 8.00 20.00
SS Sergei Samsonov 6.00 15.00
TA Tyler Arnason 6.00 15.00
TB Todd Bertuzzi 8.00 20.00
TS Teemu Selanne 8.00 20.00
TV Tomas Vokoun 6.00 15.00
VD Vincent Damphousse 6.00 15.00
VL Vincent Lecavalier 8.00 20.00
ZP Zigmund Palffy 6.00 15.00
AMA Al MacInnis 6.00 15.00
BHU Brett Hull 10.00 25.00
DAE David Aebischer 6.00 15.00
DHE Dany Heatley 10.00 25.00
DLA Daymond Langkow 6.00 15.00
JBO Jay Bouwmeester 6.00 15.00
JHE Johan Hedberg 6.00 15.00
JSA Joe Sakic 20.00 50.00
JTH Jocelyn Thibault 6.00 15.00
MBI Martin Biron 6.00 15.00
MDU Mike Dunham 6.00 15.00
MHE Milan Hejduk 8.00 20.00
MRY Michael Ryder 10.00 25.00
MSA Miroslav Satan 6.00 15.00
NKH Nikolai Khabibulin 8.00 20.00
SGO1 Sergei Gonchar WAS 6.00 15.00
SGO2 Sergei Gonchar BOS/20
SST Scott Stevens 6.00 15.00
TAM Tony Amonte 6.00 15.00
TSA1 Tommy Salo EDM 6.00 15.00
TSA2 Tommy Salo COL/20
JTHE Jose Theodore 10.00 25.00
BS Brendan Shanahan SP 75.00 200.00
DH Dominik Hasek SP 30.00 80.00
EL Eric Lindros SP 20.00 40.00
JJ Jaromir Jagr SP 40.00 100.00
MB Martin Brodeur SP 75.00 200.00
ML Mario Lemieux SP 75.00 200.00
MM Mike Modano SP 20.00 40.00
ON Owen Nolan SP 12.50 30.00
SY Steve Yzerman SP 60.00 125.00
MSU Mats Sundin SP 30.00 80.00
BO Bobby Orr/50 150.00 250.00
FM Frank Mahovlich/50 20.00 50.00
GL Guy Lafleur/50 20.00 50.00
JB Jean Beliveau/50 20.00 50.00
PE Phil Esposito/50 20.00 50.00
PR Patrick Roy/50 75.00 150.00
RK Red Kelly/50 15.00 40.00
TK Ted Kennedy/50 20.00 50.00
TL Ted Lindsay/50 15.00 40.00
RBO Ray Bourque/50 25.00 60.00

2003-04 ITG Used Signature Series Autographs Gold

*STARS: .6X TO 1.5X
PRINT RUN 70 SETS
*ROOKIES: .75X TO 2X
ROOKIE PRINT RUN 25 SETS
SP/VINT.AU PRINT RUN 10 SETS
PRINT RUNS UNDER 25 NOT PRICED
DUE TO SCARCITY
134 Marc-Andre Fleury 75.00 200.00
136 Eric Staal 75.00 150.00

2003-04 ITG Used Signature Series Franchise

*MULT.COLOR SWATCH: .6X TO 1.5X
PRINT RUN 70 SETS
1 Sergei Fedorov 10.00 25.00
2 Ilya Kovalchuk 10.00 25.00
3 Joe Thornton 10.00 25.00
4 Miroslav Satan 6.00 15.00
5 Jarome Iginla 10.00 25.00
6 Jeff O'Neill 6.00 15.00
7 Tyler Arnason 6.00 15.00
8 Peter Forsberg 10.00 25.00
9 Rick Nash 8.00 20.00
10 Mike Modano 10.00 25.00
11 Steve Yzerman 15.00 40.00
12 Ryan Smyth 6.00 15.00
13 Roberto Luongo 10.00 25.00
14 Zigmund Palffy 8.00 20.00
15 Marian Gaborik 12.50 30.00
16 Jose Theodore 10.00 25.00
17 Tomas Vokoun 8.00 20.00
18 Martin Brodeur 20.00 50.00
19 Eric Lindros 8.00 20.00
20 Rick DiPietro 8.00 20.00
21 Marian Hossa 8.00 20.00
22 Jeremy Roenick 10.00 25.00
23 Shane Doan 6.00 15.00
24 Mario Lemieux 20.00 50.00
25 Evgeni Nabokov 8.00 20.00
26 Chris Pronger 8.00 20.00
27 Vincent Lecavalier 8.00 20.00
28 Mats Sundin 8.00 20.00
29 Markus Naslund 8.00 20.00
30 Olaf Kolzig 8.00 20.00

2003-04 ITG Used Signature Series Franchise Autographs

PRINT RUN 10 SETS
NOT PRICED DUE TO SCARCITY

2003-04 ITG Used Signature Series Franchise Gold

PRINT RUN 10 SETS
NOT PRICED DUE TO SCARCITY

2003-04 ITG Used Signature Series Game-Day Jerseys

*MULT.COLOR SWATCH: .6X TO 1.5X
PRINT RUN 50 SETS
1 Mats Sundin 10.00 25.00
2 Mike Modano 12.50 30.00
3 Steve Yzerman 25.00 60.00
4 Mario Lemieux 30.00 80.00

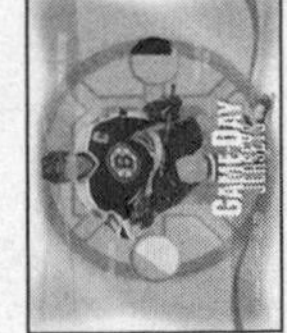

5 Ray Bourque 20.00 50.00
6 Patrick Roy 25.00 60.00
7 Martin Brodeur 25.00 60.00
8 Peter Forsberg 12.00 30.00
9 John LeClair 10.00 25.00
10 Brendan Shanahan 10.00 25.00
11 Joe Sakic 25.00 60.00

2003-04 ITG Used Signature Series Game-Day Jerseys Gold

PRINT RUN 10 SETS
NOT PRICED DUE TO SCARCITY

2003-04 ITG Used Signature Series Goalie Gear

*MULT.COLOR SWATCH: .6X TO 1.5X
PRINT RUNS LISTED BELOW
PRINT RUNS UNDER 25
NOT PRICED DUE TO SCARCITY
1 Martin Brodeur/60 25.00 60.00
2 Roberto Luongo/50 10.00 25.00
3 Sean Burke/50 8.00 20.00
4 Rick DiPietro/50 8.00 20.00
5 Nikolai Khabibulin/60 10.00 25.00
6 Marty Turco/60 10.00 25.00
7 Jose Theodore/50 12.50 30.00
8 Patrick Roy/15
9 Jocelyn Thibault/60 10.00 25.00
10 Tomas Vokoun/60 8.00 20.00
11 Olaf Kolzig/60 8.00 20.00
12 Felix Potvin/60 10.00 25.00
13 Roman Cechmanek/60 8.00 20.00
14 Roman Turek/60 8.00 20.00
15 Evgeni Nabokov/60 8.00 20.00
16 Tommy Salo/60 8.00 20.00
17 Mike Dunham/60 8.00 20.00
18 Jeff Hackett/60 8.00 20.00
19 Chris Osgood/60 8.00 20.00
20 Byron Dafoe/60 8.00 20.00
21 David Aebischer/60 12.50 30.00
22 Dominik Hasek/15
23 Gerry Cheevers/15
24 Tony Esposito/15
25 Bernie Parent/60 20.00 50.00
26 Patrick Lalime/60 8.00 20.00
27 Dan Cloutier/60 8.00 20.00
28 Jean-Sebastien Giguere/60 8.00 20.00
29 Gump Worsley/15
30 Glenn Hall/15
31 Vladislav Tretiak/60 50.00 125.00
32 Frank Brimsek/20
33 Andrew Raycroft/60 12.50 30.00
34 Ed Belfour/60 10.00 25.00
35 Harry Lumley/30 12.50 30.00
36 Roger Crozier/40 12.50 30.00

2003-04 ITG Used Signature Series Goalie Gear Autographs

PRINT RUN 10 SETS
NOT PRICED DUE TO SCARCITY

2003-04 ITG Used Signature Series Goalie Gear Gold

PRINT RUN 10 SETS
NOT PRICED DUE TO SCARCITY

2003-04 ITG Used Signature Series International Experience

*MULT.COLOR SWATCH: .6X TO 1.5X
PRINT RUN 70 SETS
1 Martin Brodeur 15.00 40.00
2 Mario Lemieux 20.00 50.00
3 Steve Yzerman 15.00 40.00
4 Joe Sakic 12.50 30.00
5 Curtis Joseph 8.00 20.00
6 Jarome Iginla 10.00 25.00
7 Jason Spezza 8.00 20.00
8 Barret Jackman 6.00 15.00
9 Joe Nieuwendyk 6.00 15.00
10 Rob Blake 6.00 15.00
11 Paul Kariya 8.00 20.00
12 Ed Jovanovski 6.00 15.00
13 Chris Pronger 6.00 15.00
14 Dany Heatley 10.00 25.00
15 Jaromir Jagr 10.00 25.00
16 Teemu Selanne 8.00 20.00
17 Saku Koivu 8.00 20.00
18 Vladislav Tretiak 25.00 60.00
19 Alexander Mogilny 6.00 15.00
20 Alexei Yashin 6.00 15.00
21 Nikolai Khabibulin 8.00 20.00
22 Zigmund Palffy 6.00 15.00
23 Nicklas Lidstrom 8.00 20.00
24 Peter Forsberg 15.00 40.00
25 Mats Sundin 8.00 20.00
26 Mike Modano 10.00 25.00
27 Bill Guerin 6.00 15.00
28 Brian Leetch 8.00 20.00
29 Chris Chelios 8.00 20.00
30 Tony Amonte 6.00 15.00

2003-04 ITG Used Signature Series International Experience Autographs

PRINT RUN 10 SETS
NOT PRICED DUE TO SCARCITY

2003-04 ITG Used Signature Series International Experience Emblems

PRINT RUN 9 SETS
NOT PRICED DUE TO SCARCITY
UNPRICED GOLD 1/1 EXIST

2003-04 ITG Used Signature Series International Experience Gold

PRINT RUN 10 SETS
NOT PRICED DUE TO SCARCITY

2003-04 ITG Used Signature Series Jerseys

*MULT.COLOR SWATCH: .6X TO 1.5X
PRINT RUN 80 SETS
GOLD PRINT RUN 10 SETS
GOLD NOT PRICED DUE TO SCARCITY
1 Alex Kovalev 4.00 10.00
2 Alexei Yashin 4.00 10.00
3 Bill Guerin 4.00 10.00
4 Bobby Orr 60.00 150.00
5 Brett Hull 10.00 25.00
6 Chris Pronger 4.00 10.00
7 Dominik Hasek 10.00 25.00
8 Eric Lindros 8.00 20.00
9 Felix Potvin 8.00 20.00
10 Henrik Zetterberg 8.00 20.00
11 Ilya Kovalchuk 10.00 25.00
12 Jarome Iginla 10.00 25.00
13 Jaromir Jagr 10.00 25.00
14 Jason Spezza 8.00 15.00
15 Jeremy Roenick 10.00 25.00
16 Joe Sakic 12.00 30.00
17 Joe Thornton 10.00 25.00
18 John LeClair 4.00 10.00
19 Jose Theodore 10.00 25.00
20 Keith Tkachuk 8.00 20.00
21 Marc-Andre Fleury 10.00 25.00
22 Marian Gaborik 10.00 25.00
23 Marian Hossa 8.00 20.00
24 Mario Lemieux 15.00 40.00
25 Martin Brodeur 15.00 40.00
26 Marty Turco 6.00 15.00
27 Mats Sundin 8.00 20.00
28 Mike Modano 10.00 25.00
29 Milan Hejduk 8.00 20.00
30 Nicklas Lidstrom 8.00 20.00
31 Nikolai Khabibulin 8.00 20.00
32 Olaf Kolzig 6.00 15.00
33 Patrick Roy 20.00 50.00
34 Pavel Datsyuk 8.00 20.00
35 Peter Forsberg 10.00 25.00
36 Ray Bourque 10.00 25.00
37 Rick Dipietro 6.00 15.00
38 Rick Nash 10.00 25.00
39 Rob Blake 4.00 10.00
40 Roberto Luongo 10.00 25.00
41 Roman Cechmanek 4.00 10.00
42 Ron Francis 4.00 10.00
43 Steve Yzerman 15.00 40.00
44 Teemu Selanne 8.00 20.00
45 Vincent Lecavalier 8.00 20.00
46 Zigmund Palffy 6.00 15.00
47 Markus Naslund 8.00 20.00
48 Todd Bertuzzi 8.00 20.00
49 Jean-Sebastien Giguere 6.00 15.00
50 Sergei Fedorov 10.00 25.00
51 Kari Lehtonen 12.00 30.00

2003-04 ITG Used Signature Series Jersey Autos

PRINT RUN 10 SER.#'d SETS
NOT PRICED DUE TO SCARCITY

2003-04 ITG Used Signature Series Emblems

PRINT RUN 9 SETS
NOT PRICED DUE TO SCARCITY
UNPRICED GOLD 1/1's EXIST
1 Henrik Zetterberg
2 Rick Nash
3 Paul Kariya
4 Steve Yzerman
5 Peter Forsberg
6 Mario Lemieux
7 Teemu Selanne
8 Martin Brodeur

9 Sergei Fedorov
10 Ray Bourque
11 Bobby Orr
12 Ron Francis
13 Joe Sakic
14 Jean-Sebastien Giguere
15 Joe Thornton
16 Jarome Iginla
17 Patrick Roy
18 Milan Hejduk
19 Marty Turco
20 Mike Modano
21 Marian Gaborik
22 Ilya Kovalchuk
23 Jason Spezza
24 Marc-Andre Fleury
25 Mats Sundin
26 Nikolai Khabibulin
27 Pavel Datsyuk
28 Rick DiPietro
29 Rob Blake
30 Roberto Luongo
31 Roman Cechmanek
32 Vincent Lecavalier
33 Zigmund Palffy
34 Markus Naslund
35 Todd Bertuzzi
36 John LeClair
37 Jeremy Roenick
38 Bill Guerin
39 Dominik Hasek
40 Sergei Samsonov
41 Kari Lehtonen

2003-04 ITG Used Signature Series Jersey and Stick

PRINT RUN 80 SETS
GOLD PRINT RUN 10 SETS
GOLD NOT PRICED DUE TO SCARCITY
1 Alex Kovalev 10.00 25.00
2 Alexei Yashin 10.00 25.00
3 Bill Guerin 10.00 25.00
4 Bobby Orr 125.00 250.00
5 Sergei Samsonov 10.00 25.00
6 Chris Pronger 10.00 25.00
7 Dominik Hasek 15.00 40.00
8 Eric Lindros 12.50 30.00
9 Felix Potvin 12.50 30.00
10 Henrik Zetterberg 12.50 30.00
11 Ilya Kovalchuk 15.00 40.00
12 Jarome Iginla 15.00 40.00
13 Brendan Shanahan 12.50 30.00
14 Jason Spezza 10.00 25.00
15 Jeremy Roenick 15.00 40.00
16 Joe Sakic 20.00 50.00
17 Saku Koivu 12.50 30.00
18 Paul Kariya
19 Jose Theodore 15.00 40.00
20 Keith Tkachuk 12.50 30.00
21 Mark Messier 15.00 40.00
22 Marian Gaborik 20.00 50.00
23 Marian Hossa 12.50 30.00
24 Mario Lemieux 25.00 60.00
25 Martin Brodeur 25.00 60.00
26 Marty Turco 10.00 25.00
27 Mats Sundin 12.50 30.00
28 Mike Modano 15.00 40.00
29 Milan Hejduk 12.50 30.00
30 Brian Leetch 10.00 25.00
31 Nikolai Khabibulin 12.50 30.00
32 Olaf Kolzig 10.00 25.00
33 Patrick Roy 25.00 60.00
34 Pavel Datsyuk 12.50 30.00
35 Peter Forsberg 25.00 60.00
36 Ray Bourque 20.00 50.00
37 Rick Dipietro 10.00 25.00
38 Rick Nash 20.00 50.00
39 Rob Blake 10.00 25.00
40 Roberto Luongo 15.00 40.00
41 Roman Cechmanek 10.00 25.00
42 Ron Francis 10.00 25.00
43 Steve Yzerman 25.00 60.00
44 Teemu Selanne 12.50 30.00
45 Vincent Lecavalier 12.50 30.00
46 Zigmund Palffy 10.00 25.00
47 Markus Naslund 12.50 30.00
48 Todd Bertuzzi 12.50 30.00
49 Jean-Sebastien Giguere 10.00 25.00
50 Sergei Fedorov 15.00 40.00

2003-04 ITG Used Signature Series Norris Trophy

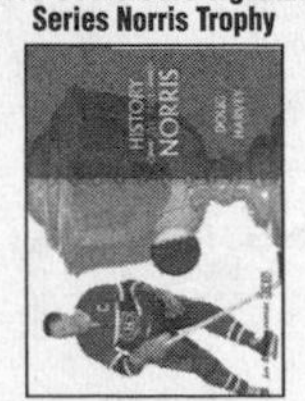

*MULT.COLOR SWATCH: .6X TO 1.5X
PRINT RUN 50 SETS
GOLD PRINT RUN 10 SETS
GOLD NOT PRICED DUE TO SCARCITY
1 Nicklas Lidstrom 8.00 20.00
2 Chris Pronger 8.00 20.00
3 Al MacInnis 8.00 20.00
4 Rob Blake 8.00 20.00
5 Chris Chelios 8.00 20.00
6 Chris Chelios 8.00 20.00
7 Bobby Orr 40.00 100.00
8 Doug Harvey 12.50 30.00
9 Ray Bourque 15.00 40.00
10 Brian Leetch 8.00 20.00
11 Larry Robinson 8.00 20.00
12 Denis Potvin 8.00 20.00
13 Jacques Laperriere 8.00 20.00

2003-04 ITG Used Signature Series Oh Canada

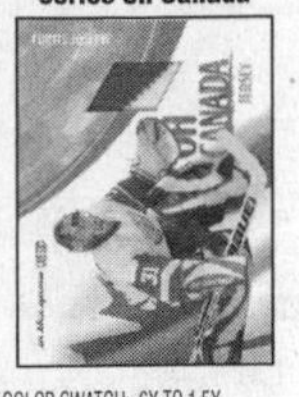

*MULT.COLOR SWATCH: .6X TO 1.5X
PRINT RUN 50 SETS
GOLD PRINT RUN 10 SETS
GOLD NOT PRICED DUE TO SCARCITY
1 Curtis Joseph 10.00 25.00
2 Martin Brodeur 25.00 60.00
3 Ed Jovanovski 8.00 20.00
4 Scott Niedermayer 8.00 20.00
5 Al MacInnis 8.00 20.00
6 Rob Blake 8.00 20.00
7 Eric Brewer 8.00 20.00
8 Owen Nolan 8.00 20.00
9 Eric Lindros 10.00 25.00
10 Paul Kariya 10.00 25.00
11 Steve Yzerman 20.00 50.00
12 Mike Peca 8.00 20.00
13 Brendan Shanahan 15.00 40.00
14 Ryan Smyth 8.00 20.00
15 Joe Nieuwendyk 8.00 20.00
16 Jarome Iginla 12.50 30.00

2003-04 ITG Used Signature Series Oh Canada Emblems

PRINT RUN 19 SETS
NOT PRICED DUE TO SCARCITY
UNPRICED GOLD 1/1 EXIST

2003-04 ITG Used Signature Series Retrospectives

*MULT.COLOR SWATCH: .6X TO 1.5X
PRINT RUN 50 SETS
GOLD PRINT RUN 10 SETS
GOLD NOT PRICED DUE TO SCARCITY
1A Patrick Roy 20.00 50.00
1B Patrick Roy 20.00 50.00
1C Patrick Roy 20.00 50.00
1D Patrick Roy 20.00 50.00
1E Patrick Roy 20.00 50.00
1F Patrick Roy 20.00 50.00
2A Jaromir Jagr 12.50 30.00
2B Jaromir Jagr 12.50 30.00
2C Jaromir Jagr 12.50 30.00
2D Jaromir Jagr 12.50 30.00
2E Jaromir Jagr 12.50 30.00
2F Jaromir Jagr 12.50 30.00
3A Brett Hull 12.50 30.00
3B Brett Hull 12.50 30.00
3C Brett Hull 12.50 30.00
3D Brett Hull 12.50 30.00
3E Brett Hull 12.50 30.00
3F Brett Hull 12.50 30.00
4A Mario Lemieux 15.00 40.00
4B Mario Lemieux 15.00 40.00
4C Mario Lemieux 15.00 40.00
4D Mario Lemieux 15.00 40.00
4E Mario Lemieux 15.00 40.00
4F Mario Lemieux 15.00 40.00
5A Mats Sundin 10.00 25.00
5B Mats Sundin 10.00 25.00
5C Mats Sundin 10.00 25.00
5D Mats Sundin 10.00 25.00
5E Mats Sundin 10.00 25.00
5F Mats Sundin 10.00 25.00
6A Curtis Joseph 10.00 25.00
6B Curtis Joseph PAD 10.00 25.00
6C Curtis Joseph 10.00 25.00
6D Curtis Joseph 10.00 25.00
6E Curtis Joseph 10.00 25.00
6F Curtis Joseph 10.00 25.00
7A Paul Kariya 10.00 25.00
7B Paul Kariya 10.00 25.00
7C Paul Kariya 10.00 25.00
7D Paul Kariya 10.00 25.00
7E Paul Kariya 10.00 25.00
7F Paul Kariya 10.00 25.00
8A Pavel Bure 10.00 25.00
8B Pavel Bure 10.00 25.00
8C Pavel Bure 10.00 25.00
8D Pavel Bure 10.00 25.00
8E Pavel Bure 10.00 25.00
8F Pavel Bure 10.00 25.00
9A Ed Belfour 10.00 25.00
9B Ed Belfour 10.00 25.00
9C Ed Belfour 10.00 25.00
9D Ed Belfour 10.00 25.00
9E Ed Belfour 10.00 25.00
9F Ed Belfour 10.00 25.00
10A Mark Messier 12.50 30.00
10B Mark Messier 12.50 30.00
10C Mark Messier 12.50 30.00
10D Mark Messier 12.50 30.00
10E Mark Messier 12.50 30.00
10F Mark Messier 12.50 30.00
11A Martin Brodeur 15.00 40.00
11B Martin Brodeur 15.00 40.00
11C Martin Brodeur 15.00 40.00
11D Martin Brodeur 15.00 40.00
11E Martin Brodeur 15.00 40.00
11F Martin Brodeur 15.00 40.00
12A Dominik Hasek 12.50 30.00
12B Dominik Hasek 12.50 30.00
12C Dominik Hasek STK 12.50 30.00
12D Dominik Hasek 12.50 30.00
12E Dominik Hasek 12.50 30.00
12F Dominik Hasek 12.50 30.00
13A Steve Yzerman 15.00 40.00
13B Steve Yzerman 15.00 40.00
13C Steve Yzerman 15.00 40.00
13D Steve Yzerman 15.00 40.00
13E Steve Yzerman 15.00 40.00
13F Steve Yzerman 15.00 40.00
14A Brian Leetch 10.00 25.00
14B Brian Leetch 10.00 25.00
14C Brian Leetch 10.00 25.00
14D Brian Leetch 10.00 25.00
14E Brian Leetch 10.00 25.00
14F Brian Leetch 10.00 25.00

2003-04 ITG Used Signature Series Teammates

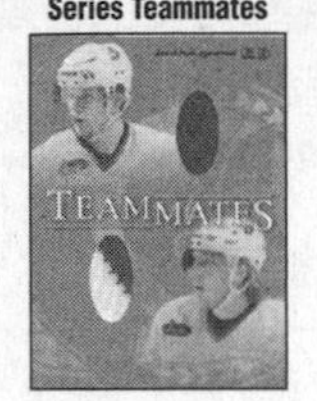

*MULT.COLOR SWATCH: .6X TO 1.5X
PRINT RUN 50 SETS
GOLD PRINT RUN 10 SETS
GOLD NOT PRICED DUE TO SCARCITY
1 Paul Kariya 12.50 30.00
Teemu Selanne
2 Mark Recchi 12.50 30.00
John LeClair
3 Jason Spezza 12.50 30.00
Marian Hossa
4 Brett Hull 20.00 50.00
Henrik Zetterberg
5 Todd Bertuzzi 12.50 30.00
Markus Naslund
6 Tony Amonte 12.50 30.00
Jeremy Roenick
7 Joe Sakic 20.00 50.00
Peter Forsberg
8 Doug Weight 12.50 30.00
Keith Tkachuk
9 Mario Lemieux 25.00 60.00
Marc-Andre Fleury
10 Eric Lindros 12.50 30.00
Alex Kovalev
11 Roberto Luongo 12.50 30.00
Jay Bouwmeester
12 Mark Messier 12.50 30.00
Brian Leetch
13 Steve Yzerman 20.00 50.00
Dominik Hasek
14 Jean-Sebastien Giguere 12.50 30.00
Sergei Fedorov
15 Mats Sundin 12.50 30.00
Ed Belfour
16 M.Brodeur/S.Stevens 20.00 50.00
17 Joe Thornton 12.50 30.00
Glen Murray
18 Ray Bourque 25.00 60.00
Cam Neely
19 M.Modano/M.Turco 12.50 30.00
20 Patrick Roy 15.00 40.00
Rob Blake

2003-04 ITG Used Signature Series Triple Memorabilia

PRINT RUNS LISTED BELOW
PRINT RUNS UNDER 25
NOT PRICED DUE TO SCARCITY
GOLD PRINT RUN 10 SETS
GOLD NOT PRICED DUE TO SCARCITY
1 Henrik Zetterberg/30 30.00 80.00
2 Mats Sundin/15
3 Ray Bourque/20
4 Bobby Orr/20
5 Eddie Shore/15
6 Stan Mikita/25 15.00 40.00
7 Pavel Datsyuk/35 30.00 80.00
8 Aurel Joliat/20
9 Marty Turco/50 12.50 30.00
10 Martin Brodeur/40 50.00 125.00
11 Jocelyn Thibault/50 12.50 30.00
12 Sean Burke/50 12.50 30.00
13 Gerry Cheevers/45 25.00 60.00
14 Jean-Sebastien Giguere/30 12.50 30.00
15 Milan Hejduk/40 12.50 30.00
16 Jarome Iginla/40 25.00 60.00
17 Olaf Kolzig/45 12.50 30.00
18 Eric Lindros/35 20.00 50.00
19 Evgeni Nabokov/35 12.50 30.00
20 Mario Lemieux/45 40.00 100.00
21 Cam Neely/40 20.00 50.00
22 Bernie Parent/45 30.00 80.00
23 Jacques Plante/35 50.00 125.00
24 Patrick Roy/20
25 Joe Sakic/35 30.00 80.00
26 Joe Thornton/35 25.00 60.00
27 Keith Tkachuk/35 20.00 50.00
28 Alexei Yashin/40 12.50 30.00
29 Andrew Raycroft/45 20.00 50.00
30 David Aebischer/50 12.50 30.00

2003-04 ITG Used Signature Series Vintage Memorabilia

*MULT.COLOR SWATCH: .75X TO 2X
PRINT RUNS LISTED BELOW
GOLD PRINT RUN 10 SETS
GOLD NOT PRICED DUE TO SCARCITY
1 Bobby Orr/25 75.00 200.00
2 Ray Bourque/25 30.00 80.00
3 Phil Esposito/25 15.00 40.00
4 Tony Esposito/25 15.00 40.00
5 Ted Lindsay/25 15.00 40.00
6 Bobby Hull/25 25.00 60.00
7 Jean Beliveau/25 25.00 60.00
8 Ted Kennedy/25 15.00 40.00
9 Ed Giacomin/25 30.00 80.00
10 Red Kelly/40 20.00 50.00
11 Borje Salming/45 20.00 50.00
12 Bernie Parent/45 15.00 40.00
13 Gerry Cheevers/45 15.00 40.00
14 Guy Lafleur/25 20.00 50.00
15 Henri Richard/25 15.00 40.00
16 Bill Gadsby/45 15.00 40.00
17 Gump Worsley/25 25.00 60.00
18 Stan Mikita/45 15.00 40.00
19 Mike Bossy/45 15.00 40.00
20 Marcel Dionne/45 15.00 40.00
21 Aurel Joliat/50 25.00 60.00
22 Tiny Thompson/50 15.00 40.00
23 George Hainsworth/45 25.00 60.00
24 Eddie Shore/45 25.00 60.00
25 Tim Horton/45 30.00 80.00
26 Bill Mosienko/45 15.00 40.00
27 Chuck Gardiner/45 20.00 50.00
28 Doug Harvey/45 15.00 40.00
29 Rocket Richard/25 40.00 100.00
30 Jacques Plante/45 25.00 60.00

2003-04 ITG Used Signature Series Vintage Memorabilia Autographs

*AUTO: .75X TO 2X BASIC INSERTS
PRINT RUN 25 SETS

2003-04 ITG VIP Brightest Stars

All cards carried a "BS" prefix on the card back.

STATED PRINT RUN 30 SETS
1 Mario Lemieux 25.00 60.00
2 Marian Gaborik 20.00 50.00
3 Dany Heatley 15.00 40.00
4 Ilya Kovalchuk 15.00 40.00
5 Jason Spezza 20.00 50.00
6 Dominik Hasek 20.00 50.00
7 Peter Forsberg 25.00 60.00
8 Steve Yzerman 30.00 80.00
9 Martin Brodeur 25.00 60.00
10 Patrick Roy 25.00 60.00

2003-04 ITG VIP Collages

This set consisted of 35 sepia-toned, oversized (approx. 4"x 5") collage cards serial-numbered consecutively to a total of 6000 total cards. Cards were placed in tin "packs" and a memorabilia card was attached to the larger collage card with removable glue. Approximately 50 each of several of the collages were also autographed.

1 Mario Lemieux 10.00 25.00
2 Martin Brodeur 8.00 20.00
3 Steve Yzerman 8.00 20.00
4 Patrick Roy 8.00 20.00
5 Paul Kariya 3.00 8.00
6 Peter Forsberg 6.00 15.00
7 Joe Sakic 6.00 15.00

8 Marian Gaborik 6.00 15.00
9 Mark Messier 5.00 12.00
10 Ilya Kovalchuk 5.00 12.00
11 Mike Modano 5.00 12.00
12 Brett Hull 5.00 12.00
13 Jean-Sebastien Giguere 2.00 5.00
14 Joe Thornton 5.00 12.00
15 Pavel Bure 2.00 5.00
16 Dany Heatley 5.00 12.00
17 Rick Nash 4.00 10.00
18 Henrik Zetterberg 4.00 10.00
19 Dominik Hasek 6.00 15.00
20 Jose Theodore 4.00 10.00
21 Jason Spezza 5.00 12.00
22 Ed Belfour 3.00 8.00
23 Nicklas Lidstrom 3.00 8.00
24 Roberto Luongo 4.00 10.00
25 Tony Esposito 4.00 10.00
26 Ted Lindsay 3.00 8.00
27 Bobby Hull 6.00 15.00
28 Jacques Plante 4.00 10.00
29 Phil Esposito 2.00 5.00
30 Turk Broda 2.00 5.00
31 Georges Vezina 4.00 12.00
32 Terry Sawchuk 4.00 10.00
33 Rocket Richard 5.00 12.00
34 Jean Beliveau 3.00 8.00
35 Doug Harvey 2.00 5.00

2003-04 ITG VIP Collage Autographs

PRINT RUN 50 SETS
UNLESS OTHERWISE NOTED
1 Mario Lemieux 50.00 125.00
2 Martin Brodeur/20 50.00 125.00
3 Steve Yzerman/20 50.00 125.00
6 Peter Forsberg 30.00 80.00
7 Joe Sakic 25.00 60.00
10 Ilya Kovalchuk 20.00 50.00
12 Brett Hull 20.00 50.00
14 Joe Thornton 20.00 50.00
17 Rick Nash 20.00 50.00
18 Henrik Zetterberg 25.00 60.00
19 Dominik Hasek/20 25.00 60.00
23 Nicklas Lidstrom 15.00 40.00
24 Roberto Luongo 15.00 40.00
25 Tony Esposito 20.00 50.00
26 Ted Lindsay 12.50 30.00
27 Bobby Hull 15.00 40.00
29 Phil Esposito 12.50 30.00
34 Jean Beliveau 20.00 50.00

2003-04 ITG VIP International Experience

All cards carried an "IE" prefix on the card back.
STATED PRINT RUN 50 SETS
1 Mario Lemieux 30.00 80.00
2 Jay Bouwmeester 12.50 30.00
3 Jason Spezza 20.00 50.00
4 Mike Modano 12.50 30.00
5 Joe Sakic 25.00 60.00
6 Nicklas Lidstrom 12.50 30.00
7 Peter Forsberg 15.00 40.00
8 Mats Sundin 12.50 30.00
9 Jaromir Jagr 20.00 50.00
10 Steve Yzerman 25.00 60.00
11 Dany Heatley 12.50 30.00
12 Martin Brodeur 30.00 80.00

2003-04 ITG VIP Jerseys

All cards carried a "GUJ" prefix on the card back.
STATED PRINT RUN 50 SETS
1 Joe Thornton 12.50 30.00
2 Mario Lemieux 25.00 60.00
3 Mats Sundin 8.00 20.00
4 Pavel Bure 8.00 20.00
5 Dany Heatley 15.00 40.00
6 Joe Sakic 25.00 60.00
7 Rick Nash 15.00 40.00
8 Nicklas Lidstrom 8.00 20.00
9 Markus Naslund 8.00 20.00
10 Patrick Roy 25.00 60.00
11 Peter Forsberg 20.00 50.00
12 Dominik Hasek 15.00 40.00
13 Henrik Zetterberg 15.00 40.00
14 Mike Modano 12.50 30.00
15 Jay Bouwmeester 12.50 30.00
16 Ilya Kovalchuk 12.50 30.00
17 Marian Gaborik 15.00 40.00
18 Brett Hull 12.50 30.00
19 Martin Brodeur 25.00 60.00
20 Milan Hejduk 8.00 20.00
21 Steve Yzerman 25.00 60.00
22 Jeremy Roenick 12.50 30.00
23 Jean-Sebastien Giguere 6.00 15.00
24 Brendan Shanahan 8.00 20.00
25 Todd Bertuzzi 8.00 20.00
26 Jarome Iginla 12.50 30.00
27 Al MacInnis 6.00 15.00
28 Saku Koivu 8.00 20.00
29 Jason Spezza 20.00 50.00
30 Ed Belfour 8.00 20.00

2003-04 ITG VIP Jersey Autographs

STATED PRINT RUN 20 SETS
UNLESS OTHERWISE NOTED BELOW
NOT PRICED DUE TO SCARCITY
1 Joe Thornton
2 Mario Lemieux
3 Mats Sundin
6 Joe Sakic
7 Rick Nash
8 Nicklas Lidstrom
11 Peter Forsberg
12 Dominik Hasek/10
13 Henrik Zetterberg
16 Ilya Kovalchuk
18 Brett Hull
19 Martin Brodeur/10
20 Milan Hejduk
21 Steve Yzerman
24 Brendan Shanahan
26 Jarome Iginla

2003-04 ITG VIP Jersey and Emblems

All cards carried a "JE" prefix on the card back.
STATED PRINT RUN 10 SETS
NOT PRICED DUE TO SCACITY
1 Joe Thornton
2 Mario Lemieux
3 Dany Heatley
4 Joe Sakic
5 Rick Nash
6 Jean-Sebastien Giguere
7 Jason Spezza
8 Patrick Roy
9 Peter Forsberg
10 Mike Modano
11 Ilya Kovalchuk
12 Marian Gaborik
13 Martin Brodeur
14 Dominik Hasek
15 Steve Yzerman

2003-04 ITG VIP Jersey and Numbers

All cards carried a "JN" prefix on the card back.
STATED PRINT RUN 10 SETS
NOT PRICED DUE TO SCARCITY
1 Joe Thornton
2 Mario Lemieux
3 Dany Heatley
4 Joe Sakic
5 Rick Nash
6 Jean-Sebastien Giguere
7 Jason Spezza
8 Patrick Roy
9 Peter Forsberg
10 Mike Modano
11 Ilya Kovalchuk
12 Marian Gaborik
13 Martin Brodeur
14 Dominik Hasek
15 Steve Yzerman

2003-04 ITG VIP Making the Bigs

All cards carried a "MTB" prefix on the card back.
STATED PRINT RUN 50 SETS
1 Jay Bouwmeester 15.00 40.00
2 Rick Nash 25.00 60.00
3 Scottie Upshall 12.50 30.00
4 Jason Spezza 20.00 50.00
5 Ron Hainsey 12.50 30.00
6 Barret Jackman 12.50 30.00
7 Dany Heatley 15.00 40.00
8 Dan Blackburn 12.50 30.00

2003-04 ITG VIP Mighty Mario

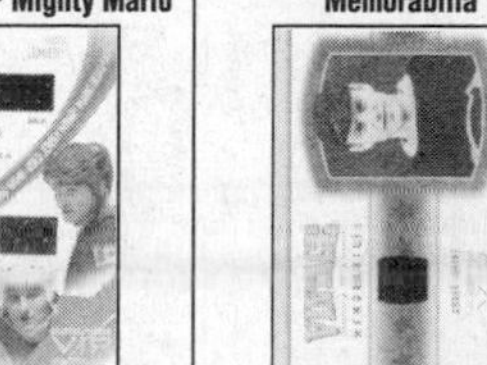

All cards carried a "MM" prefix on the card back.
STATED PRINT RUN 10 SETS
NOT PRICED DUE TO SCARCITY
1 M.Lemieux/2000-01 Jersey
2 M.Lemieux/1985-86 Jersey
3 M.Lemieux/2002All-Star Jersey
4 M.Lemieux/1987 Canada Cup Jersey
5 M.Lemieux/Dual Jersey
6 M.Lemieux/Number
7 M.Lemieux/Emblem
8 M.Lemieux/Triple Jersey
9 M.Lemieux/Quad Jersey
10 M.Lemieux/Complete Package

2003-04 ITG VIP MVP

All cards carried a "MVP" prefix on the card back.
STATED PRINT RUNS LISTED BELOW
PRINT RUNS OF LESS THAN 25 NOT
PRICED DUE TO SCARCITY
1 Howie Morenz/10
2 Roy Worters/10
3 Eddie Shore/10
4 Aurel Joliat/10
5 Maurice Richard/10
6 Ted Kennedy/10
7 Jacques Plante/10
8 Bobby Hull/50 20.00 50.00
9 Stan Mikita/50 15.00 40.00
10 Phil Esposito/50 15.00 40.00
11 Bobby Clarke/50 12.50 30.00
12 Dominik Hasek/50 15.00 40.00
13 Roger Crozier/50 15.00 40.00
14 Glenn Hall/40 20.00 50.00
15 Bernie Parent/50 20.00 50.00
16 Mike Bossy/50 12.50 30.00
17 Patrick Roy/50 30.00 80.00
18 Patrick Roy/50 30.00 80.00
19 Steve Yzerman/50 25.00 60.00
20 Jean-Sebastien Giguere/50 12.50 30.00
21 Bryan Trottier/50 12.50 30.00
22 Jean Beliveau/50 25.00 60.00
23 Guy Lafleur/50 15.00 40.00
24 Mark Messier/50 15.00 40.00
25 Mario Lemieux/50 30.00 80.00
26 Joe Sakic/50 20.00 50.00

2003-04 ITG VIP Netminders

All cards carried a "N" prefix on the card back.
STATED PRINT RUN 50 SETS
1 Martin Brodeur 25.00 60.00
2 Roberto Luongo 12.50 30.00
3 Ed Belfour 10.00 25.00
4 Patrick Roy 25.00 60.00
5 Marty Turco 10.00 25.00
6 Jean-Sebastien Giguere 10.00 25.00
7 Olaf Kolzig 10.00 25.00
8 Patrick Lalime 10.00 25.00
9 Dan Blackburn 15.00 40.00
10 Rick DiPietro 10.00 25.00
11 Ryan Miller 12.50 30.00
12 Jose Theodore 12.50 30.00

2003-04 ITG VIP Sophomores

All cards carried a "S" prefix on the card back.
STATED PRINT RUN 50 SETS
1 Rick Nash 15.00 40.00
2 Jay Bouwmeester 6.00 15.00
3 Barret Jackman 15.00 40.00
4 Henrik Zetterberg 15.00 40.00
5 Ryan Miller 12.50 30.00
6 Stanislav Chistov 6.00 15.00
7 Jason Spezza 15.00 40.00
8 Alexander Frolov 6.00 15.00

2003-04 ITG VIP Vintage Memorabilia

All cards carried a "VM" prefix on the card back.
STATED PRINT RUNS LISTED BELOW
PRINT RUNS LESS THAN 25 NOT
PRICED DUE TO SCARCITY
1 Cyclone Taylor/10
2 Georges Vezina/10
3 George Hainsworth/20
4 Aurel Joliat/20
5 Charlie Conacher/10
6 Howie Morenz/10
7 Sid Abel/20
8 Frank Brimsek/20
9 Ted Lindsay/30 20.00 50.00
10 Bill Barilko/10
11 Tim Horton/30 20.00 50.00
12 Jacques Plante/30 30.00 80.00
13 Terry Sawchuk/10
14 Doug Harvey/30 12.50 30.00
15 Maurice Richard/10
16 Harry Lumley/30 15.00 40.00
17 Tony Esposito/30 12.50 30.00
18 Jean Beliveau/30 30.00 80.00
19 Frank Mahovlich/30 20.00 50.00
20 Glenn Hall/30 20.00 50.00
21 Bobby Hull/30 30.00 80.00
22 Stan Mikita/30 15.00 40.00

2003-04 ITG VIP Rookie Debut

Cards in this 149-card set were made available for online orders after the players made their NHL debut. Collectors could order as many cards as they wanted for a period of 90 days after the debut at which time ordering was ceased. Print runs listed below were provided by BAP, the cards are not serial numbered.

1 Tuomo Ruutu/114 4.00 10.00
2 Joffrey Lupul/101 5.00 12.00
3 Brent Burns/71 5.00 12.00
4 David Hale/65 4.00 10.00
5 Paul Martin/52 4.00 10.00
6 Patrice Bergeron/166 8.00 20.00
7 Travis Moen/64 5.00 12.00
8 Lasse Kukkonen/58 4.00 10.00
9 Christoph Brandner/62 5.00 12.00
10 Garrett Burnett/48 4.00 10.00
11 Antti Miettinen/59 5.00 12.00
12 Antoine Vermette/50 4.00 10.00
13 Andrew Peters/63 4.00 10.00
14 Joni Pitkanen/81 5.00 12.00
15 Sean Bergenheim/54 5.00 12.00
16 Boyd Gordon/53 4.00 10.00
17 Dan Fritsche/54 6.00 15.00
18 Eric Staal/165 12.50 30.00
19 Nathan Horton/102 6.00 15.00
20 Dustin Brown/65 6.00 15.00
21 Tim Gleason/58 4.00 10.00
22 Esa Pirnes/51 4.00 10.00
23 Wade Brookbank/51 4.00 10.00
24 Dan Hamhuis/56 5.00 12.00
25 Jordin Tootoo/156 8.00 20.00
26 Marek Zidlicky/61 5.00 12.00
27 Christian Ehrhoff/54 4.00 10.00
28 Milan Michalek/58 12.00 30.00
29 Matthew Lombardi/70 4.00 10.00
30 John-Michael Liles/56 4.00 10.00
31 Marek Svatos/53 4.00 10.00
32 Marc-Andre Fleury/580 10.00 25.00
33 Martin Strbak/66 4.00 10.00
34 Ryan Malone/84 8.00 20.00
35 Matt Murley/74 4.00 10.00
36 Matthew Spiller/62 4.00 10.00
37 Chris Higgins/67 10.00 25.00
38 Maxim Kondratiev/62 4.00 10.00
39 Tom Preissing/58 4.00 10.00
40 Cody McCormick/37 4.00 10.00
41 Pavel Vorobiev/30 4.00 10.00
42 Alexander Semin/47 10.00 25.00
43 Brent Krahn/32 4.00 10.00
44 Jiri Hudler/122 5.00 12.00
45 Boyd Kane/38 4.00 10.00
46 Gregory Campbell/36 4.00 10.00
47 Andrew Hutchinson/36 4.00 10.00
48 Mike Stuart/24 4.00 10.00
49 Sergei Zinovjev/45 4.00 10.00
50 Trevor Daley/34 4.00 10.00
51 Julien Vauclair/32 4.00 10.00
52 Alan Rourke/33 4.00 10.00
53 Tony Salmelainen/34 4.00 10.00
54 John Pohl/36 4.00 10.00
55 Dominic Moore/42 4.00 10.00
56 Peter Sarno/34 4.00 10.00
57 Rastislav Stana/66 4.00 10.00
58 Karl Stewart/58 4.00 10.00
59 Darryl Bootland/43 4.00 10.00
60 Pat Rissmiller/35 4.00 10.00
61 Jed Ortmeyer/42 4.00 10.00
62 Nathan Smith/31 4.00 10.00
63 Grant McNeill/31 4.00 10.00
64 Seamus Kotyk/39 4.00 10.00
65 Phil Osaer/35 4.00 10.00
66 Ryan Kesler/62 4.00 10.00
67 Libor Pivko/39 4.00 10.00
68 Mikhail Yakubov/33 4.00 10.00
69 Nathan Robinson/35 4.00 10.00
70 Fredrik Sjostrom/37 4.00 10.00
71 Tony Martensson/43 4.00 10.00
72 Aaron Johnson/48 4.00 10.00
73 Jeff Hamilton/47 4.00 10.00
74 Nikolai Zherdev/255 15.00 40.00
75 Gavin Morgan/53 4.00 10.00
76 Patrick Leahy/30 4.00 10.00
77 Jeff MacMillan/47 4.00 10.00
78 Antero Niittymaki/90 8.00 20.00
79 Niklas Kronwall/77 12.50 30.00
80 Joey MacDonald/56 4.00 10.00
81 Doug Doull/59 12.50 30.00
82 Dwayne Zinger/50 4.00 10.00
83 Jason MacDonald/47 4.00 10.00
84 Rob Skrlac/39 4.00 10.00
85 Derek Roy/88 12.50 30.00
86 Ryan Barnes/39 4.00 10.00
87 Noah Clarke/48 12.50 30.00
88 Steve McLaren/54 4.00 10.00
89 Tim Jackman/32 6.00 15.00
90 Timofei Shishkanov/39 8.00 20.00
91 Jason Pominville/40 4.00 10.00
92 Mikko Luoma/36 4.00 10.00
93 Jeremy Yablonski/39 4.00 10.00
94 Tomas Plekanec/37 4.00 10.00
95 Tuomas Pihlman/36 4.00 10.00
96 Darcy Verot/55 4.00 10.00
97 Mark Popovic/38 4.00 10.00
98 Doug Lynch/36 4.00 10.00
99 Aleksander Suglobov/31 4.00 10.00
100 Nolan Schaefer/35 4.00 10.00
101 Colton Orr/54 4.00 10.00
102 Mike Smith/64 4.00 10.00
103 Anton Babchuk/37 4.00 10.00
104 Kyle Wellwood/41 4.00 10.00
105 Jame Pollock/36 4.00 10.00
106 Carl Corazzini/49 4.00 10.00
107 Zbynek Michalek/31 4.00 10.00
108 Chris Kunitz/27 4.00 10.00
109 Lawrence Nycholat/37 6.00 15.00
110 Jozef Balej/56 8.00 20.00
111 Mike Bishai/33 4.00 10.00
112 Garth Murray/39 4.00 10.00
113 Matt Ellison/29 4.00 10.00
114 Joe Motzko/36 4.00 10.00
115 Graham Mink/54 4.00 10.00
116 Brooks Laich/46 4.00 10.00
117 Mike Green/27 4.00 10.00
118 Dan Ellis/37 4.00 10.00
119 Robert Scuderi/37 4.00 10.00
120 Fedor Tyutin/50 4.00 10.00
121 Michael Morrison/37 4.00 10.00
122 Cory Larose/38 4.00 10.00
123 Andy Chiodo/62 4.00 10.00
124 Adam Munro/43 4.00 10.00
125 Mikhail Kuleshov/76 4.00 10.00
126 Matt Keith/31 4.00 10.00
127 Denis Grebeshkov/32 4.00 10.00
128 Quintin Laing/16 4.00 10.00
129 Benoit Dusablon/23 4.00 10.00
130 Matt Underhill/27 4.00 10.00
131 Fred Meyer/20 4.00 10.00
132 Randy Jones/23 4.00 10.00
133 Brad Boyes/67 12.50 30.00
134 Erik Westrum/16 4.00 10.00
135 Bryce Lampman/23 4.00 10.00
136 Goran Bezina/32 4.00 10.00
137 Owen Fussey/48 4.00 10.00
138 Josh Olson/14 4.00 10.00
139 Michal Barinka/21 4.00 10.00
140 Kari Lehtonen/526 15.00 40.00
141 Matt Hussey/28 4.00 10.00
142 Mike Stutzel/18 4.00 10.00
143 Roman Tvrdon/34 4.00 10.00
144 Matthew Yeats/50 4.00 10.00
145 Thomas Pock/40 4.00 10.00
146 Wade Dubielewicz/59 4.00 10.00
147 Greg Mauldin/34 4.00 10.00
148 Mike Pandolfo/32 4.00 10.00
149 Eric Perrin/48 4.00 10.00

2009-10 ITG 1972 The Year In Hockey

COMPLETE SET (200) 30.00 60.00
1 Phil Esposito .75 2.00
2 Johnny Bucyk .60 1.50
3 Ken Hodge .40 1.00
4 Wayne Cashman .75 2.00
5 Terry O'Reilly .30 .75
6 Don Awrey .40 1.00
7 Dallas Smith .50 1.25
8 Jacques Plante .60 1.50
9 Eddie Johnston .50 1.25
10 Jacques Lemaire .40 1.00
11 Frank Mahovlich .50 1.25
12 Yvan Cournoyer .50 1.25
13 Guy Lafleur .60 1.50
14 Guy Lapointe .30 .75
15 Rejean Houle .25 .60
16 Serge Savard .50 1.25
17 Larry Robinson .50 1.25
18 Michel Plasse .25 .60
19 Steve Shutt .40 1.00
20 Darryl Sittler .50 1.25
21 Rick Kehoe .30 .75
22 Dave Keon .30 .75
23 Norm Ullman .30 .75
24 Ron Ellis .25 .60
25 Paul Henderson .30 .75
26 Brian Glennie .75 2.00
27 Gerry Desjardins .30 .75
28 Ed Westfall .30 .75
29 Bob Nystrom .30 .75
30 Billy Smith .60 1.50
31 Gilles Villemure .50 1.25
32 Rod Gilbert .50 1.25
33 Walt Tkaczuk .30 .75
34 Vic Hadfield .40 1.00
35 Brad Park .40 1.00
36 Rod Seiling .30 .75
37 Ed Giacomin .50 1.25
38 Red Berenson .75 2.00
39 Marcel Dionne .50 1.25
40 Alex Delvecchio .50 1.25
41 Nick Libett .30 .75
42 Roy Edwards .25 .60
43 Rene Robert .40 1.00
44 Gilbert Perreault .40 1.00
45 Rick Martin .40 1.00
46 Jim Lorentz .30 .75
47 Tim Horton .40 1.00
48 Roger Crozier .25 .60
49 Jim Schoenfeld .25 .60
50 Bobby Schmautz .25 .60
51 Andre Boudrias .30 .75
52 Don Lever .60 1.50
53 Dunc Wilson .40 1.00
54 Doug Jarrett .25 .60
55 Bill White .25 .60
56 Dennis Hull .50 1.25
57 Pit Martin .25 .60
58 Stan Mikita .60 1.50
59 Pat Stapleton .30 .75
60 Tony Esposito .60 1.50
61 Keith Magnuson .30 .75
62 Garry Unger .25 .60
63 Jack Egers .25 .60
64 Noel Picard .25 .60
65 Gary Sabourin .30 .75
66 Phil Myre .25 .60
67 Dan Bouchard .60 1.50
68 Pat Quinn .50 1.25
69 Bob Leiter .25 .60
70 Curt Bennett .25 .60
71 Bobby Clarke .60 1.50
72 Rick MacLeish .30 .75
73 Gary Dornhoefer .40 1.00
74 Bill Flett .25 .60
75 Bill Barber .30 .75
76 Joe Watson .30 .75
77 Dave Schultz .40 1.00
78 Doug Favell .40 1.00
79 Serge Bernier .25 .60
80 Rogie Vachon .60 1.50
81 Gary Edwards .25 .60
82 Butch Goring .40 1.00
83 Harry Howell .30 .75
84 Bill Goldsworthy .25 .60
85 Dennis Hextall .25 .60
86 J.P. Parise .40 1.00
87 Gump Worsley .60 1.50
88 Danny Grant .50 1.25
89 Cesare Maniago .30 .75
90 Eddie Shack .40 1.00
91 Bryan Hextall .30 .75
92 Syl Apps Jr. .40 1.00
93 Lowell MacDonald .25 .60
94 Al McDonough .25 .60
95 Denis Herron .30 .75
96 Walt McKechnie .30 .75
97 Stan Weir .25 .60
98 Joey Johnston .25 .60
99 Gilles Meloche .50 1.25
100 Checklist .25 .60
101 Rick Smith .30 .75
102 Wayne Rutledge .30 .75
103 Poul Popiel .30 .75
104 Larry Lund .25 .60
105 Ted Taylor .25 .60
106 Gord Labossiere .25 .60
107 Andre Lacroix .30 .75
108 Bernie Parent .40 1.00
109 Derek Sanderson .25 .60
110 John McKenzie .60 1.50
111 Rosaire Paiement .25 .60
112 Bob Sicinski .25 .60
113 Jim McLeod .25 .60
114 Larry Mavety .25 .60
115 Gary Jarrett .30 .75
116 Gerry Pinder .25 .60
117 Gerry Cheevers .75 2.00
118 Paul Shmyr .25 .60
119 Wayne Connelly .25 .60
120 Ted Hampson .30 .75
121 Mike Antonovich .30 .75
122 Mike Curran .30 .75
123 Bob MacMillan .25 .60
124 Bobby Hull 1.00 2.50
125 Joe Daley .25 .60
126 Ernie Wakely .30 .75
127 Chris Bordeleau .40 1.00
128 Ab McDonald .30 .75
129 Wayne Carleton .25 .60
130 Gilles Gratton .30 .75
131 Les Binkley .40 1.00
132 J.C. Tremblay .25 .60
133 Richard Brodeur .40 1.00
134 Jean-Guy Gendron .30 .75
135 Ken Brown .25 .60
136 Val Fonteyne .30 .75
137 Al Hamilton .25 .60
138 Jack Norris .30 .75
139 Bill Hicke .25 .60
140 Ron Ward .25 .60
141 Norm Ferguson .25 .60
142 Kent Douglas .25 .60
143 Alton White .25 .60
144 Gary Veneruzzo .30 .75
145 Bart Crashley .25 .60
146 Gerry Odrowski .25 .60
147 Tom Webster .25 .60
148 Larry Pleau .25 .60
149 Jim Dorey .25 .60
150 Al Smith .25 .60
151 Rick Ley .25 .60
152 Don Awrey .40 1.00
153 Red Berenson .75 2.00
154 Gary Bergman .25 .60
155 Wayne Cashman .75 2.00
156 Bobby Clarke .60 1.50
157 Yvan Cournoyer .50 1.25
158 Ron Ellis .25 .60
159 Phil Esposito .75 2.00
160 Tony Esposito .60 1.50
161 Rod Gilbert .50 1.25
162 Vic Hadfield .40 1.00
163 Paul Henderson .30 .75
164 Dennis Hull .50 1.25
165 Valeri Kharlamov .25 .60
166 Guy Lapointe .30 .75
167 Frank Mahovlich .50 1.25
168 Pete Mahovlich .60 1.50
169 Alexander Maltsev .25 .60
170 Bill Goldsworthy .25 .60
171 Boris Mikhailov .60 1.50
172 Stan Mikita .60 1.50
173 J.P. Parise .40 1.00
174 Brad Park .40 1.00
175 Gilbert Perreault .40 1.00
176 Vladimir Petrov .75 2.00
177 Alexander Ragulin .25 .60
178 Eddie Johnston .50 1.25
179 Serge Savard .50 1.25
180 Rod Seiling .30 .75
181 Pat Stapleton .30 .75
182 Dale Tallon .75 2.00
183 Vladislav Tretiak .40 1.00
184 Valeri Vasiliev .60 1.50
185 Vladimir Shadrin .60 1.50
186 Bill White .25 .60
187 Alexander Yakushev .50 1.25
188 Harry Sinden .25 .60
189 Vsevolod Bobrov .25 .60
190 Valeri Kharlamov .60 1.50
Bobby Clarke
191 Tony Esposito .60 1.50
Vladislav Tretiak
192 Paul Henderson .40 1.00
Vladislav Tretiak
193 Boris Mikhailov .75 2.00
Phil Esposito
194 Vladimir Petrov .75 2.00
Tony Esposito
195 Gary Bergman .50 1.25
Alexander Yakushev
196 Bill White .60 1.50
Boris Mikhailov
197 Paul Henderson .50 1.25
Alexander Yakushev
198 Paul Henderson .30 .75
199 Vladislav Tretiak .40 1.00
200 Checklist .25 .60

2009-10 ITG 1972 The Year In Hockey Autographs

AAB Andre Boudrias 5.00 12.00
AAD Alex Delvecchio SP 8.00 20.00
AAG Alexander Gusev 8.00 20.00
AAH Al Hamilton 4.00 10.00
AAL Andre Lacroix 5.00 12.00
AAM Al McDonough 4.00 10.00
AAW Alton White 4.00 10.00
AAY Alexander Yakushev 8.00 20.00
ABB Bill Barber SP
ABC Bobby Clarke SP
ABG Butch Goring 6.00 15.00
ABH Bryan Hextall 5.00 12.00
ABL Bob Leiter 4.00 10.00
ABM Bob MacMillan 4.00 10.00
ABN Bob Nystrom 5.00 12.00
ABP Brad Park SP 30.00 60.00
ABS Bobby Schmautz 4.00 10.00
ABW Bill White 4.00 10.00
ACB Curt Bennett 4.00 10.00
ACM Cesare Maniago 5.00 12.00
ADA Don Awrey 6.00 15.00
ADB Dan Bouchard 10.00 25.00
ADF Doug Favell 6.00 15.00
ADG Danny Grant 8.00 20.00
ADH Denis Herron 5.00 12.00
ADJ Doug Jarrett 4.00 10.00
ADK Dave Keon SP 50.00 100.00
ADL Don Lever 10.00 25.00
ADS Dallas Smith 8.00 20.00
ADT Dale Tallon 12.00 30.00
Summit Series
ADW Dunc Wilson 6.00 15.00
AEG Ed Giacomin SP
AEJ Eddie Johnston 8.00 20.00
AES Eddie Shack 6.00 15.00
AEW Ernie Wakely 5.00 12.00
AFM Frank Mahovlich SP 60.00 100.00
AGC Gerry Cheevers 12.00 30.00
AGD Gerry Desjardins 5.00 12.00
AGE Gary Edwards 4.00 10.00
AGG Gilles Gratton 5.00 12.00
AGJ Gary Jarrett 5.00 12.00
AGL Guy Lafleur SP
AGM Gilles Meloche 8.00 20.00
AGO Gerry Odrowski 4.00 10.00
AGP Gilbert Perreault SP 6.00 15.00
AGS Gary Sabourin 5.00 12.00
AGU Garry Unger 4.00 10.00
AGV Gilles Villemure 8.00 20.00
AHH Harry Howell 5.00 12.00
AHS Harry Sinden
Summit Series
AJB Johnny Bucyk 10.00 25.00
AJD Joe Daley 4.00 10.00
AJE Jack Egers 4.00 10.00
AJJ Joey Johnston 4.00 10.00
AJL Jacques Lemaire 6.00 15.00
AJN Jack Norris 4.00 10.00
AJS Jim Schoenfeld 4.00 10.00
AJW Joe Watson 5.00 12.00
AKB Ken Brown 6.00 15.00
AKH Ken Hodge 6.00 15.00
ALB Les Binkley 6.00 15.00
ALL Larry Lund 4.00 10.00
ALM Lowell MacDonald 4.00 10.00
ALP Larry Pleau 4.00 10.00
ALR Larry Robinson 8.00 20.00
AMA Mike Antonovich 5.00 12.00
AMC Mike Curran 5.00 12.00
AMD Marcel Dionne SP
ANF Norm Ferguson 4.00 10.00
ANL Nick Libett 5.00 12.00
ANP Noel Picard 4.00 10.00
ANU Norm Ullman 5.00 12.00
APE Phil Esposito 12.00 30.00
APH Paul Henderson 5.00 12.00
APM Phil Myre 4.00 10.00
APP Poul Popiel 5.00 12.00
APQ Pat Quinn 8.00 20.00
APS Pat Stapleton 5.00 12.00
ARB Richard Brodeur 6.00 15.00
ARE Ron Ellis SP
ARG Rod Gilbert SP 8.00 20.00
ARH Rejean Houle SP
ARK Rick Kehoe 5.00 12.00
ARL Rick Ley 4.00 10.00
ARM Rick Martin 6.00 15.00
ARP Rosaire Paiement 4.00 10.00
ARR Rene Robert 6.00 15.00
ARS Rod Seiling 5.00 12.00
ARV Rogie Vachon 10.00 25.00
ARW Ron Ward 4.00 10.00
ASA Syl Apps 6.00 15.00
ASB Serge Bernier 4.00 10.00
ASM Stan Mikita SP 20.00 40.00

ASS Serge Savard SP 8.00 20.00
ASW Stan Weir 4.00 10.00
ATE Tony Esposito SP
ATH Ted Hampson 5.00 12.00
ATO Terry O'Reilly
ATT Ted Taylor 4.00 10.00
ATW Tom Webster 4.00 10.00
AVF Val Fonteyne 5.00 12.00
AVH Vic Hadfield 6.00 15.00
AVP Vladimir Petrov 12.00 30.00
AVS Vladimir Shadrin 10.00 25.00
AVT Vladislav Tretiak
AVV Valeri Vasiliev 10.00 25.00
AWC Wayne Cashman 12.00 30.00
AWM Walt McKechnie 5.00 12.00
AWT Walt Tkaczuk 5.00 12.00
AYC Yvan Cournoyer SP
AAMC Ab McDonald 5.00 12.00
ABC2 Bobby Clarke SP
Summit Series
ABCR Bart Crashley 4.00 10.00
ABGL Brian Glennie 12.00 30.00
ABHU Bobby Hull SP 15.00 40.00
ABMI Boris Mikhailov 10.00 25.00
ABP2 Brad Park SP
Summit Series
ABPA Bernie Parent SP
ABSC Bob Sicinski 4.00 10.00
ABSM Billy Smith 10.00 25.00
ABW2 Bill White 4.00 10.00
Summit Series
ACBO Chris Bordeleau 6.00 15.00
ADA2 Don Awrey 6.00 15.00
Summit Series
ADHE Dennis Hextall 4.00 10.00
ADHU Dennis Hull 8.00 20.00
ADSA Derek Sanderson SP 4.00 10.00
Philadelphia
ADSC Dave Schultz 6.00 15.00
ADSI Darryl Sittler SP 40.00 80.00
AEWE Ed Westfall 5.00 12.00
AFM2 Frank Mahovlich SP
Summit Series
AGDO Gary Dornhoefer 6.00 15.00
AGLA Guy Lapointe SP 40.00 80.00
AGP2 Gilbert Perreault SP 10.00 25.00
Summit Series
AGPI Gerry Pinder
AGVE Gary Veneruzzo 5.00 12.00
AJDO Jim Dorey 4.00 10.00
AJGG Jean-Guy Gendron 5.00 12.00
AJLO Jim Lorentz 5.00 12.00
AJMC Jim McKenny 4.00 10.00
AJPP J.P. Parise 6.00 15.00
ALMA Larry Mavety 4.00 10.00
AMD2 Marcel Dionne SP
Summit Series
APE2 Phil Esposito 12.00 30.00
Summit Series
APH2 Paul Henderson
Summit Series
APMA Pete Mahovlich 10.00 25.00
APS2 Pat Stapleton
Summit Series
ARBE Red Berenson 12.00 30.00
ARE2 Ron Ellis SP 25.00 50.00
Summit Series
ARG2 Rod Gilbert SP 8.00 20.00
Summit Series
ARMA Rick MacLeish 5.00 12.00
ARSM Rick Smith 5.00 12.00
ASM2 Stan Mikita SP
Summit Series
ASS2 Serge Savard SP 20.00 40.00
Summit Series
ASSH Steve Shutt 6.00 15.00
ATE2 Tony Esposito SP 10.00 25.00
Summit Series
AVH2 Vic Hadfield 6.00 15.00
Summit Series
AWC2 Wayne Cashman
Summit Series
AWCA Wayne Carleton 4.00 10.00
AWCO Wayne Connelly 4.00 10.00
AYC2 Yvan Cournoyer SP
Summit Series
ABGL2 Brian Glennie
Summit Series
ADHU2 Dennis Hull 8.00 20.00
Summit Series
ADSAN Derek Sanderson SP
Boston
AGLA2 Guy Lapointe SP 5.00 12.00
Summit Series
AGLAB Gord Labossiere 4.00 10.00
AJMCK John McKenzie 10.00 25.00
AJMCL Jimmy McLeod 4.00 10.00
AJPP2 J.P. Parise 6.00 15.00
Summit Series
APMA2 Pete Mahovlich
Summit Series
ARBE2 Red Berenson 12.00 30.00
Summit Series

2009-10 ITG 1972 The Year In Hockey Coaches

COMPLETE SET (10) 10.00 25.00
C01 Scotty Bowman 1.50 4.00
C02 Tom Johnson 1.00 2.50
C03 Emile Francis 1.00 2.50
C04 Phil Goyette 1.00 2.50
C05 Billy Reay 1.00 2.50
C06 Fred Shero 1.00 2.50
C07 Al Arbour 1.00 2.50
C08 Bob Pulford 1.00 2.50
C09 Red Kelly 1.50 4.00
C10 Bernie Geoffrion 1.50 4.00

2009-10 ITG 1972 The Year In Hockey Forever Linked

FL01 Paul Henderson 2.50 6.00
Vladislav Tretiak
FL02 Bobby Hull 6.00 15.00
Gerry Cheevers
FL03 Bobby Clarke 4.00 10.00
Valeri Kharlamov
FL04 Jean Beliveau 4.00 10.00
Guy Lafleur

2009-10 ITG 1972 The Year In Hockey Great Moments

COMPLETE SET (8) 10.00 25.00
COMMON CARD .75 2.00
SEMISTARS/GOALIES 1.00 2.50
UNLISTED STARS 1.25 3.00
GM01 Gerry Cheevers 2.50 6.00
The Streak
GM02 Johnny Bucyk 2.00 5.00
Bruins Win The Cup
GM03 Bobby Hull 3.00 8.00
Signs with Jets
GM04 Vladislav Tretiak 1.25 3.00
Russian Surprise
GM05 Phil Esposito 2.50 6.00
The Speech
GM06 Paul Henderson 1.00 2.50
The Goal
GM07 Billy Smith 2.00 5.00
NHL Expansion
GM08 Les Binkley 1.25 3.00
First WHA Game

2009-10 ITG 1972 The Year In Hockey Masked Men

COMPLETE SET (10) 15.00 40.00
MM01 Doug Favell 2.50 6.00
MM02 Gerry Cheevers 5.00 12.00
MM03 Rogie Vachon 4.00 10.00
MM04 Ed Giacomin 3.00 8.00
MM05 Gilles Villemure 3.00 8.00
MM06 Tony Esposito 4.00 10.00
MM07 Jacques Plante 4.00 10.00
MM08 Cesare Maniago 2.00 5.00
MM09 Bernie Parent 2.50 6.00
MM10 Ken Brown 1.50 4.00

2009-10 ITG 1972 The Year In Hockey Past and Present

COMPLETE SET (10) 12.00 30.00
PP01 Guy Lafleur 3.00 8.00
Carey Price
PP02 Tony Esposito 3.00 8.00
Martin Brodeur
PP03 Marcel Dionne 1.50 4.00
Pavel Datsyuk
PP04 Bobby Clarke 2.00 5.00
Daniel Briere
PP05 Alex Delvecchio 1.50 4.00
Nicklas Lidstrom
PP06 Bill Goldsworthy 1.25 3.00
Mike Modano
PP07 Dunc Wilson 3.00 8.00
Roberto Luongo
PP08 Jacques Plante 2.00 5.00
Vesa Toskala
PP09 Gerry Cheevers 2.50 6.00
Tim Thomas
PP10 Ed Westfall 6.00 15.00
John Tavares

2009-10 ITG 1972 The Year In Hockey Rookies

COMPLETE SET (8) 8.00 20.00
R01 Dan Bouchard 2.00 5.00
Jim Schoenfeld
R02 Denis Herron 2.00 5.00
Billy Smith
R03 Bill Barber 1.25 3.00
Dave Schultz
R04 Steve Shutt 1.25 3.00
Terry O'Reilly
R05 Bob Nystrom 1.25 3.00
Richard Brodeur
R06 Larry Robinson 1.50 4.00
Gilles Gratton
R07 Bob MacMillan .75 2.00
Bob Sicinski
R08 Don Lever 2.00 5.00
Mike Antonovich

2009-10 ITG 1972 The Year In Hockey '71-'72 Cup Winners Jerseys

STATED PRINT RUN 10 SER.#'d SETS
NOT PRICED DUE TO SCARCITY
CWA01 Phil Esposito
John Bucyk
Derek Sanderson
Bobby Orr
Gerry Cheevers
Dallas Smith

2009-10 ITG 1972 The Year In Hockey '71-'72 First Team All Star Jerseys

STATED PRINT RUN 10 SER.#'d SETS
NOT PRICED DUE TO SCARCITY
FATA01 Tony Esposito
Bobby Orr
Brad Park
Phil Esposito
Rod Gilbert
Bobby Hull
FATA02 Tony Esposito
FATA03 Bobby Orr
FATA04 Brad Park
FATA05 Phil Esposito
FATA06 Rod Gilbert
FATA07 Bobby Hull

2009-10 ITG 1972 The Year In Hockey '71-'72 Quest For The Cup Jerseys

STATED PRINT RUN 10 SER.#'d SETS
NOT PRICED DUE TO SCARCITY
QCA01 Phil Esposito
Dave Keon
QCA02 Gump Worsley
Noel Picard
QCA03 Bill White
Tim Horton
QCA04 Jean Ratelle
Pete Mahovlich
QCA05 Gerry Cheevers
Gary Unger
QCA06 Bobby Hull
Rod Gilbert
QCA07 Bobby Orr
Giacomin

2009-10 ITG 1972 The Year In Hockey '71-'72 Scoring Leaders Jerseys

STATED PRINT RUN 10 SER.#'d SETS
NOT PRICED DUE TO SCARCITY
SLA01 Phil Esposito
Bobby Orr
Jean Ratelle
Vic Hadfield
Rod Gilbert
Frank Mahovlich
SLA02 Phil Esposito
SLA03 Bobby Orr
SLA04 Jean Ratelle
SLA05 Vic Hadfield
SLA06 Rod Gilbert
SLA07 Frank Mahovlich
SLA08 Bobby Hull
SLA09 Yvan Cournoyer
SLA10 Johnny Bucyk
SLA11 Bobby Clarke

2009-10 ITG 1972 The Year In Hockey '71-'72 Second Team All Star Jerseys

STATED PRINT RUN 10 SER.#'d SETS
NOT PRICED DUE TO SCRCITY
SATA01 Ken Dryden
Bill White
Pat Stapleton
Jean Ratelle
Yvan Cournoyer
Vic Hadfield
SATA02 Ken Dryden
SATA03 Bill White
SATA04 Pat Stapleton
SATA05 Jean Ratelle
SATA06 Yvan Cournoyer
SATA07 Vic Hadfield

2009-10 ITG 1972 The Year In Hockey '71-'72 Trophy Winners Jerseys

STATED PRINT RUN 10 SER.#'d SETS
NOT PRICED DUE TO SCARCITY
TWA01 Phil Esposito
Art Ross Trophy
TWA02 Bobby Orr
Conn Smythe
TWA03 Bobby Orr
Hart Memorial Trophy
TWA04 Bobby Orr
Norris Trophy
TWA05 Jean Ratelle
Lady Byng Trophy
TWA06 Tony Esposito
Vezina Trophy

2009-10 ITG 1972 The Year In Hockey '72-'73 Cup Winners Jerseys

STATED PRINT RUN 10 SER.#'d SETS
NOT PRICED DUE TO SCARCITY
CWB01 Guy Lafleur
Frank Mahovlich
Jacques Lemaire
Guy Lapointe
Ken Dryden
Serge Savard

2009-10 ITG 1972 The Year In Hockey '72-'73 First Team All Star Jerseys

STATED PRINT RUN 10 SER.#'d SETS
NOT PRICED DUE TO SCARCITY
FATB01 Ken Dryden
Bobby Orr
Guy Lapointe
Phil Esposito
Mickey Redmond
Frank Mahovlich
FATB02 Ken Dryden
FATB03 Bobby Orr
FATB04 Guy Lapointe
FATB05 Phil Esposito
FATB06 Mickey Redmond
FATB07 Frank Mahovlich

2009-10 ITG 1972 The Year In Hockey '72-'73 Quest For The Cup Jerseys

STATED PRINT RUN 10 SER.#'d SETS
NOT PRICED DUE TO SCARCITY
QCB01 Henri Richard
Gilbert Perreault
QCB02 Bobby Clarke
Drouin
QCB03 Dennis Hull
Unger
QCB04 Bobby Orr
Park
QCB05 Guy Lafleur
Barber
QCB06 Stan Mikita
Hadfield
QCB07 Ken Dryden
Tony Esposito

2009-10 ITG 1972 The Year In Hockey '72-'73 Scoring Leaders Jerseys

STATED PRINT RUN 10 SER.#'d SETS
NOT PRICED DUE TO SCARCITY
SLB01 Phil Esposito
Bobby Clarke
Bobby Orr
Rick MacLeish
Jaques Lemaire
Jean Ratelle
SLB02 Phil Esposito
SLB03 Bobby Clarke
SLB04 Bobby Orr
SLB05 Rick MacLeish
SLB06 Jacques Lemaire
SLB07 Jean Ratelle

2009-10 ITG 1972 The Year In Hockey '72-'73 Second Team All Star Jerseys

STATED PRINT RUN 10 SER.#'d SETS
NOT PRICED DUE TO SCARCITY
SATB01 Tony Esposito
Brad Park
Bill White
Bobby Clarke
Yvan Cournoyer
Dennis Hull
SATB02 Tony Esposito
SATB03 Brad Park
SATB04 Bill White
SATB05 Bobby Clarke
SATB06 Yvan Cournoyer
SATB07 Dennis Hull

2009-10 ITG 1972 The Year In Hockey '72-'73 Trophy Winners Jerseys

STATED PRINT RUN 10 SER.#'d SETS
NOT PRICED DUE TO SCARCITY
TWB01 Phil Esposito
Art Ross Trophy
TWB02 Yvan Cournoyer
Conn Smythe
TWB03 Bobby Clarke
Hart Memorial Trophy
TWB04 Bobby Orr
Norris Trophy
TWB05 Gilbert Perreault
Lady Byng Trophy
TWB06 Ken Dryden
Vezina Trophy

1979-80 Islanders Transparencies

These standard postcard size cards featured black and white posed photos on a thin, transparent paper stock. Cards were unnumbered and checklisted below alphabetically.

COMPLETE SET (22) 20.00 40.00
1 Mike Bossy 7.50 15.00
2 Bob Bourne .38 .75
3 Clark Gillies .38 .75
4 Billy Harris .38 .75
5 Lerne Henning .38 .75
6 Anders Kallur .38 .75
7 Mike Kaszycki .38 .75
8 Dave Langevin .38 .75
9 Dave Lewis .38 .75
10 Bob Lorimer .38 .75
11 Wayne Merrick .38 .75
12 Bob Nystrom 1.00 2.00
13 Stefan Persson .38 .75
14 Denis Potvin 1.00 2.00
15 Jean Potvin .38 .75
16 Garry Howatt .38 .75
17 Glenn Resch 2.50 5.00
18 Bill Smith 2.50 5.00
19 Steven Tambellini .38 .75
20 John Tonelli .75 1.50
21 Bryan Trottier 2.00 4.00
22 Header Card .30 .60

1983-84 Islanders Team Issue

This 19-card set measured approximately 4" by 5 1/2" and featured the 1983-84 New York Islanders. The cards were printed on thin paper stock. The fronts had black-and-white action player photos with white borders. The player's name and the team logo appeared below the photo. The cards were unnumbered and checklisted below in alphabetical order. The set featured an early card of Kelly Hrudey pre-dating his O-Pee-Chee and Topps Rookie Cards by two years.

COMPLETE SET (19) 12.00 30.00
1 Mike Bossy 2.00 5.00
2 Bob Bourne .40 1.00
3 Billy Carroll .40 1.00
4 Clark Gillies .75 2.00
5 Mats Hallin .40 1.00
6 Kelly Hrudey 1.50 4.00
7 Tomas Jonsson .40 1.00
8 Dave Langevin .40 1.00
9 Roland Melanson .60 1.50
10 Wayne Merrick .40 1.00
11 Ken Morrow .60 1.50
12 Bob Nystrom .60 1.50
13 Denis Potvin 1.50 4.00
14 Billy Smith 1.50 4.00
15 Brent Sutter .75 2.00
16 Duane Sutter .60 1.50
17 John Tonelli .75 2.00
18 Bryan Trottier 1.50 4.00
19 Team Photo .75 2.00

1984 Islanders News

This 38-card standard-size set of New York Islanders was sponsored by Islander News and issued during the summer of 1984 to commemorate the Islanders' fourth consecutive Stanley Cup victory. The color photo on the front was framed by a thin black border. Another thin black border (with rounded corners) outlined the card front, and the space in between was pale blue. The player's name was given below the picture and sandwiched between a trophy cup icon and the New York Islanders' logo. The back had biographical information and a career summary on the player.

COMPLETE SET (38) 10.00 25.00
1 Checklist Card .20 .50
2 Mike Bossy 1.50 4.00
3 Bob Bourne .20 .50
4 Billy Carroll .20 .50
5 Greg Gilbert .20 .50
6 Clark Gillies .50 1.25
7 Butch Goring .40 1.00
8 Mats Hallin .20 .50
9 Anders Kallur .20 .50
10 Wayne Merrick .20 .50
11 Bob Nystrom .30 .75
12 Brent Sutter .50 1.25
13 Duane Sutter .40 1.00
14 John Tonelli .50 1.25
15 Bryan Trottier 1.25 3.00
16 Tomas Jonsson .20 .50
17 Gordie Lane .20 .50
18 Dave Langevin .20 .50
19 Ken Morrow .40 1.00
20 Stefan Persson .20 .50
21 Denis Potvin 1.00 2.50
22 Roland Melanson .30 .75
23 Billy Smith .75 2.00
24 Cup Number 1 .20 .50
25 Cup Number 2 .20 .50
26 Cup Number 4 .20 .50
27 Lorne Henning CO .20 .50
28 Bill Torrey GM .20 .50
29 Al Arbour CO .40 1.00
30 Waske-Pickard .08 .25
Two Trainers
31 1979-80 Team Photo .40 1.00
32 1980-81 Team Photo .40 1.00
33 1981-82 Team Photo .40 1.00
34 1982-83 Team Photo .40 1.00
35 Mike Bossy .75 2.00
'82 Conn Smythe Winner
36 Billy Smith .50 1.25
'83 Conn Smythe Winner
37 Bryan Trottier .60 1.50
'80 Conn Smythe Winner
38 Butch Goring .30 .75
'81 Conn Smythe Winner

1985 Islanders News

This 37-card standard-size set of New York Islanders was sponsored by Islander News and issued during the summer of 1985. The color photo on the front was enframed by a thin black border. A red and blue hockey stick formed the border on the left side of the picture, with the end of the stick below the picture. The words "Islander News" appeared on the end of the stick, and the player's name was given to the right. The back had biographical information including a career summary on the player as well as the notation "Second Series". The key card in the set was the Pat LaFontaine card as it was issued concurrently with his O-Pee-Chee and Topps Rookie Cards.

COMPLETE SET (37) 12.00 30.00
1 Checklist Card .20 .50
2 Mike Bossy 1.50 4.00
3 Bob Bourne .20 .50
4 Pat Flatley .30 .75
5 Greg Gilbert .20 .50
6 Clark Gillies .40 1.00
7 Mats Hallin .20 .50
8 Anders Kallur .20 .50
9 Alan Kerr .20 .50
10 Roger Kortko .20 .50
11 Pat LaFontaine 3.00 8.00
12 Bob Nystrom .30 .75
13 Brent Sutter .40 1.00
14 Duane Sutter .30 .75
15 John Tonelli .40 1.00
16 Bryan Trottier 1.25 3.00
17 Paul Boutilier .20 .50
18 Gerald Diduck .20 .50
19 Gord Dineen .20 .50
20 Tomas Jonsson .20 .50
21 Gordie Lane .20 .50
22 Dave Langevin .20 .50
23 Ken Morrow .30 .75
24 Stefan Persson .20 .50
25 Denis Potvin 1.00 2.50
26 Kelly Hrudey 1.25 3.00
27 Billy Smith .75 2.00
28 Bill Torrey GM/P .30 .75
29 Al Arbour CO .40 1.00
30 Brian Kilrea CO .08 .25
31 Pickard/Smith .08 .25
Two Trainers
32 Mike Bossy .75 2.00
Milestone-400 Goals
33 Denis Potvin .60 1.50
Milestone-600 Assists
34 Billy Smith .40 1.00
Milestone-500 Games
35 Bryan Trottier .60 1.50
Milestone-1000 Points
36 1984-85 Team .40 1.00
37 Wales Champs .30 .75

1985 Islanders News Trottier

This 33-card standard-size set was sponsored by the New York Islander News and issued during the summer of 1985 supposedly by the Port Washington Police Department. It highlighted the early career of then-Islander, Bryan Trottier, who is credited with writing the drug and alcohol prevention tips on the back of the cards. The cards featured color or black and white photos of Trottier on the front. They were framed by a red border on two sides, and white border; the white border is in the shape of a hockey stick, with Trottier's signature across the bottom of the stick. The cards were numbered on both sides. In addition to the anti-drug or alcohol message, the back also had Trottier's own comments about each photo.

COMPLETE SET (33) 10.00 25.00
1 Penalty box .40 1.00
2 Swift Current Broncos .40 1.00
3 Three goals in first .20 .50
game at Nassau Coliseum
4 All-Star game .30 .75
5 Four goals vs. Atlanta .20 .50
6 Ross and Hart Trophies .30 .75
7 Street hockey equipment .20 .50
8 Bearing down on the .30 .75
draw against Maruk
9 Pleading with referee .20 .50
10 Trottier/Rangers action .20 .50
11 Trottier/Holmgren action .30 .75
12 Trottier/Canadiens action .30 .75
13 1980 Boston playoff .30 .75
14 1980 Final Game .30 .75
vs. Flyers
15 NHL Awards Luncheon .20 .50
16 Trottier/Rangers action .30 .75
17 Watching action in .20 .50
resting area
18 Warm-up time .20 .50
19 Debating with referee .20 .50
20 1981 Playoff with Oilers .30 .75
21 Trottier/Gretzky action 4.00 10.00
22 Trottier/North Stars .30 .75
action
23 Congratulating Don .30 .75
Beaupre
24 Second Stanley Cup .20 .50
Championship
25 Trottier/Sutter celebrate .30 .75
26 Trottier psyching himself .20 .50
27 Trottier/Devils action .30 .75
28 1983 All-Star .30 .75
29 Trottier defending goal 3.00 8.00
(Gretzky behind net)
30 Fourth Stanley Cup .20 .50
Championship
31 Trottier and Denis .60 1.50
Potvin celebrate
32 Trottier and Mike .75 2.00
Bossy celebrate
33 1984 Canada Cup Series .40 1.00

1986-87 Islanders Team Issue

This 30-card set was issued by the team and used at promotional events.

COMPLETE SET (30) 10.00 25.00
1 Alan Kerr .20 .50
2 Ari Haanpaa .20 .50
3 Bill Smith 1.25 3.00
4 Bob Nystrom .30 .75
5 Bob Bassen .20 .50
6 Brad Lauer .20 .50
7 Brent Sutter .60 1.50
8 Brian Curran .20 .50
9 Bryan Trottier .60 1.50
10 Trainers .08 .25
11 Dale Henry .20 .50
12 Denis Potvin 1.25 3.00
13 Duane Sutter .30 .75
14 Gerald Diduck .20 .50
15 Gord Dineen .20 .50
16 Greg Gilbert .20 .50
17 Islander Emblem .02 .10
18 Kelly Hrudey .75 2.00
19 Ken Leiter .20 .50
20 Ken Morrow .30 .75
21 Mike Bossy 1.25 3.00
22 Mikko Makela .20 .50
23 Pat Lafontaine .75 2.00
24 Patrick Flatley .20 .50
25 Randy Boyd .20 .50
26 Richard Kromm .20 .50
27 Roger Kortko .20 .50
28 Steve Konroyd .20 .50
29 Terry Simpson CO .08 .25
30 Tomas Jonsson .20 .50

1989-90 Islanders Team Issue

This 22-card set measured approximately 3 7/8" by 7 1/8". The fronts featured autographed color action photos. The player's name, jersey number, position, team logo and team name were printed in the wider bottom border. The cards were unnumbered and checklisted below in alphabetical order.

COMPLETE SET (22) 4.80 12.00
1 Al Arbour CO .30 .75
2 Dean Chynoweth .20 .50
3 Dave Chyzowski .20 .50
4 Doug Crossman .20 .50
5 Gerald Diduck .20 .50
6 Tom Fitzgerald .20 .50
7 Mark Fitzpatrick .60 1.50
8 Patrick Flatley .30 .75
9 Glenn Healy .40 1.00
10 Alan Kerr .20 .50
11 Pat LaFontaine 1.00 2.50
12 Mikko Makela .20 .50
13 Don Maloney .20 .50
14 Jeff Norton .20 .50
15 Gary Nylund .20 .50
16 Rich Pilon .20 .50
17 Brent Sutter .30 .75
18 Gilles Thibaudeau .20 .50
19 Bryan Trottier .75 2.00
20 David Volek .20 .50
21 Mick Vukota .20 .50
22 Randy Wood .20 .50

1993-94 Islanders Chemical Bank Alumni

This ten-card set was issued as a promotional give-away to honor prestigious members of the Islanders alumni on January 28, 1994. The cards were standard size and featured color action photos surrounded by an orange border. The logos of Chemical Bank and the Isles adorned the corners, and the player name appeared along the bottom. The two-color backs included career highlights. As the cards were unnumbered, they are listed in alphabetical order.

COMPLETE SET (10) 3.00 8.00
1 Title Card .08 .25
2 Mike Bossy .75 2.00
3 Clark Gillies .30 .75
4 Gerry Hart .20 .50
5 Wayne Merrick .20 .50
6 Bob Nystrom .30 .75
7 Denis Potvin .60 1.50
8 Bill Smith .60 1.50
9 John Tonelli .30 .75
10 Eddie Westfall .20 .50

1996-97 Islander Postcards

This 23-postcard set was produced by the Islanders for promotional giveaways and autograph signings. They featured black and white action photos on the front, with a white border along the bottom containing the player's name and the club's special 25th anniversary logo. The backs were blank and unnumbered, hence the alphabetical listing below.

COMPLETE SET (23) 6.00 15.00
1 Niclas Andersson .20 .50
2 Derek Armstrong .20 .50
3 Todd Bertuzzi .30 .75
4 Eric Fichaud .75 2.00
5 Travis Green .30 .75
6 Doug Houda .20 .50
7 Brent Hughes .20 .50
8 Kenny Jonsson .30 .75
9 Derek King .30 .75
10 Paul Kruse .20 .50
11 Claude Lapointe .20 .50
12 Scott Lachance .20 .50
13 Bryan McCabe .20 .50
14 Marty McInnis .20 .50
15 Mike Milbury CO .20 .50
16 Zigmund Palffy 1.25 3.00
17 Dan Plante .20 .50
18 Rich Pilon .20 .50
19 Tommy Salo .60 1.50
20 Bryan Smolinski .30 .75
21 Dennis Vaske .20 .50
22 Mick Vukota .20 .50
23 Randy Wood .20 .50

1998-99 Islanders Power Play

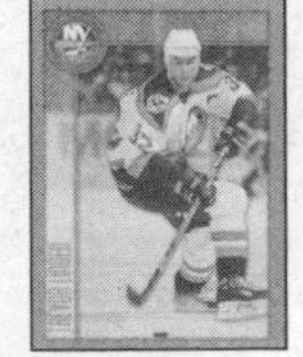

Cards were distributed in a sealed pack and were made available through give-always at various arenas, in conjunction with Power Play magazine. Each packet contained 4-cards, similar in design to the base set from each manufacturer, but featured a different card number on the back.

COMPLETE SET (4) 2.50 6.00
NYI1 Trevor Linden .75 2.00
NYI2 Bryan Smolinski .40 1.00
NYI3 Mike Watt .20 .50
NYI4 Zigmund Palffy 2.00 5.00

1997-98 Jell-O Juniors To Pros

This 12-card set featured two photos of each superstar player: one from his participation in the World Junior Championships, and the other with his NHL team. The cards were found on the back of specially marked boxes of Jell-O Pudding in Canada.

COMPLETE SET (12)
1 Wayne Gretzky 2.00 5.00
2 Paul Kariya 1.00 2.50
3 Eric Lindros .40 1.00
4 Mark Messier .40 1.00
5 Patrick Roy 1.50 4.00
6 Joe Sakic .75 2.00
7 Chris Chelios .40 1.00
8 Sergei Fedorov .75 2.00
9 Jaromir Jagr .75 2.00
10 Saku Koivu .40 1.00
11 Zigmund Palffy .40 1.00
12 Mats Sundin .40 1.00

1998 Jell-O Spoons

Available one per pack in select boxes of Jell-O Pudding mix. These small stickers featured a head shot of the selected player.

COMPLETE SET (8) 6.00 15.00
1 Rod Brind'Amour .25 .60
2 Theo Fleury .30 .75
3 Wayne Gretzky 1.50 4.00
4 Curtis Joseph .30 .75
5 Paul Kariya 1.00 2.50
6 Eric Lindros .75 2.00
7 Patrick Roy 1.25 3.00
8 Joe Sakic .60 1.50

1999-00 Jell-O Goalie Collection

1 Ron Tugnutt
2 Martin Brodeur
3 Curtis Joseph
4 Dominik Hasek
5 Patrick Roy
6 Byron Dafoe

1999-00 Jell-O Partners of Power

This 12-card set was issued by Kraft to promote their Jell-O Stanley Cup 2000 sweepstakes. Cards 1-6 were available in Jell-O pudding snacks, cards 7-12 were available in Jell-O powder. Each card featured color photos of the goalie and captain of that team and opened up to reveal individual stats and contest rules.

COMPLETE SET (6) 6.00 15.00
1 Scott Stevens .75 2.00
Martin Brodeur
2 Jaromir Jagr .40 1.00
Tom Barrasso
3 Eric Lindros .60 1.50
John Vanbiesbrouck
4 Mike Peca .40 1.00
Dominik Hasek
5 Ray Bourque .75 2.00
Byron Dafoe
6 Mats Sundin .40 1.00
Curtis Joseph
7 Derian Hatcher .30 .75
Ed Belfour
8 Doug Weight .20 .50
Tommy Salo
9 Joe Sakic 2.00 5.00
Patrick Roy
10 Steve Yzerman 1.25 3.00
Chris Osgood
11 Paul Kariya .75 2.00
Guy Hebert
12 Owen Nolan .20 .50
Mike Vernon

1999-00 Jell-O Pudding Super Skills

These oversized issues came in packs of Jell-O Pudding Snacks. The cards featured an action photo on the front, along with a set checklist. The card back offered instructions on how to use the pudding paddles, which were found "inside" this card.

COMPLETE SET (6) 1.50 4.00
1 Peter Bondra .30 .75
2 Ray Bourque .60 1.50
3 John LeClair .40 1.00
4 Al MacInnis .30 .75
5 Mike Modano .40 1.00
6 Jeremy Roenick .30 .75

2000-01 Jell-O NHL Tattoos

Issued in sets of two per pack of Jell-O Pudding 4 Pack Snacks, this set included one sticker of each team in the NHL and two stickers of the NHL logo. This issue was exclusive to Canada.

COMPLETE SET (32) 8.00 20.00
COMMON DUAL TEAM (1-30) .80 2.00
COMMON NHL LOGO (31-32) .20 .50

1978-79 Jets Postcards

This 23-postcard set measured approximately 3 1/2" by 5 1/2". The fronts featured posed-on-ice borderless color player photos with a facsimile player autograph near the bottom. The backs had a postcard format and carried the player's name and a brief biography. The postcards were unnumbered and checklisted below in alphabetical order.

COMPLETE SET (23) 12.50 25.00
1 Mike Amodeo .38 .75
2 Scott Campbell .38 .75
3 Kim Clackson .50 1.00
4 Joe Daley 1.00 2.00
5 John Gray .38 .75
6 Ted Green 1.00 2.00
7 Robert Guindon .38 .75
8 Glenn Hicks .38 .75
9 Larry Hillman .38 .75
10 Bill Lesuk .50 1.00
11 Willy Lindstrom .75 1.50
12 Barry Long .38 .75
13 Morris Lukowich .75 1.50
14 Paul MacKinnon .38 .75
15 Markus Mattsson .75 1.50
16 Lyle Moffat .38 .75
17 Kent Nilsson 2.50 5.00
18 Rich Preston .50 1.00
19 Terry Ruskowski 1.25 2.50
20 Lars-Erik Sjoberg 1.25 2.50
21 Peter Sullivan .38 .75
22 Paul Terbenche .38 .75
23 Steve West .38 .75

1979-80 Jets Postcards

These 28 postcards measured approximately 3 1/2" by 5 1/2" and featured posed-on-ice color player photos on their borderless fronts. A facsimile player autograph rested near the bottom. The backs had a postcard format and carried the player's name and brief biography. The postcards were unnumbered and checklisted below in alphabetical order.

COMPLETE SET (28) 12.50 25.00
1 Mike Amodeo .38 .75
2 Al Cameron .38 .75
3 Scott Campbell .38 .75
4 Wayne Dillon .38 .75
5 Jude Drouin .38 .75
6 John Ferguson GM .50 1.00
7 Hilliard Graves .38 .75
8 Pierre Hamel .38 .75
9 Dave Hoyda .38 .75
10 Bobby Hull 4.00 8.00
11 Bill Lesuk .38 .75
12 Willy Lindstrom .75 1.50
13 Morris Lukowich .75 1.50
14 Jimmy Mann .75 1.50
15 Peter Marsh .50 1.00
16 Gord McTavish .38 .75
17 Tom McVie CO .38 .75
18 Barry Melrose 1.50 3.00
19 Lyle Moffat .38 .75
20 Craig Norwich .38 .75
21 Lars-Erik Sjoberg 1.25 2.50
22 Gary Smith .50 1.00
23 Gordon Smith .38 .75
24 Lorne Stamler .38 .75
25 Peter Sullivan .38 .75
26 Bill Sutherland ACO .25 .50
27 Ron Wilson .50 1.00
28 Title Card .25 .50

1980-81 Jets Postcards

This 23-card set of the Winnipeg Jets measured approximately 3 1/2" by 5 1/2". The fronts featured borderless black-and-white action player photos. A facsimile autograph rounded out the front. The backs were blank. The cards were unnumbered and checklisted below in alphabetical order.

COMPLETE SET (24) 10.00 20.00
1 David Babych 1.00 2.50
2 Al Cameron .40 1.00
3 Scott Campbell .40 1.00
4 Dave Chartier .40 1.00
5 Dave Christian .40 1.00
6 Jude Drouin .40 1.00
7 Norm Dupont .40 1.00
8 Dan Geoffrion .40 1.00
9 Pierre Hamel .40 1.00
10 Barry Legge .40 1.00
11 Willy Lindstrom .60 1.50
12 Barry Long .60 1.50
13 Morris Lukowich .40 1.00
14 Kris Manery .40 1.00
15 Jimmy Mann .60 1.50
16 Moe Mantha .60 1.50
17 Markus Mattsson .60 1.50
18 Richard Mulhern .40 1.00
19 Doug Smail .60 1.50
20 Don Spring .40 1.00
21 Anders Steen .40 1.00
22 Pete Sullivan .40 1.00
23 Tim Trimper .40 1.00
24 Ron Wilson .60 1.50

1981-82 Jets Postcards

This 24-card set of the Winnipeg Jets measured approximately 3 1/2" by 5 1/2". The fronts featured black-and-white action player photos with a white border and a facsimile autograph near the bottom. The backs were blank. The cards were unnumbered and checklisted below in alphabetical order. This set featured a postcard of Dale Hawerchuk that predated his RC by one year.

COMPLETE SET (24) 12.00 30.00
1 Scott Arniel .40 1.00
2 Dave Babych .60 1.50
3 Dave Christian .60 1.50
4 Lucien Deblois .40 1.00
5 Normand Dupont .30 .75
6 Dale Hawerchuk 4.00 10.00
7 Larry Hopkins .30 .75
8 Craig Levie .30 .75
9 Willy Lindstrom .40 1.00
10 Morris Lukowich .40 1.00
11 Bengt Lundholm .30 .75
12 Paul MacLean .60 1.50
13 Jimmy Mann .40 1.00
14 Bryan Maxwell .30 .75
15 Serge Savard .50 1.25
16 Doug Smail .60 1.50
17 Doug Soetaert .60 1.50
18 Don Spring .30 .75
19 Ed Staniowski .30 .75
20 Thomas Steen .75 2.00
21 Bill Sutherland CO .30 .75
22 Tim Trimper .30 .75
23 Tom Watt CO .30 .75
24 Tim Watters .30 .75

1982-83 Jets Postcards

This 28-card set measured approximately 3 1/2" by 5 1/2". The fronts featured white-bordered posed color player photos with the player's name and jersey number printed in blue inside a white bar at the bottom. The backs were blank. The cards were unnumbered and checklisted below in alphabetical order.

COMPLETE SET (28) 10.00 25.00
1 Scott Arniel .30 .75
2 Dave Babych .40 1.00
3 Jerry Butler .20 .50
4 Wade Campbell .20 .50
5 Dave Christian .40 1.00
6 Lucien DeBlois .20 .50
7 Norm Dupont .20 .50
8 Dale Hawerchuk 3.00 8.00
(Sitting holding trophy)
9 Dale Hawerchuk 3.00 8.00
10 Jim Kyte .20 .50
11 Craig Levie .20 .50
12 Willy Lindstrom .30 .75
13 Morris Lukowich .20 .50
14 Bengt Lundholm .30 .75
15 Paul MacLean .30 .75
16 Jimmy Mann .20 .50
17 Bryan Maxwell .20 .50
18 Brian Mullen .20 .50
19 Serge Savard .40 1.00
20 Doug Smail .40 1.00
21 Doug Soetaert .30 .75
22 Don Spring .20 .50
23 Ed Staniowski .20 .50
24 Thomas Steen .60 1.50
25 Bill Sutherland ACO .20 .50
26 Tom Watt CO .20 .50
27 Tim Watters .20 .50
28 Team Photo .20 .50

1983-84 Jets Postcards

This 25-card set measured 3 1/4" by 5 1/4". The fronts featured full-bleed color action photos with the player's name and jersey number at the lower right corner. The backs were blank. The cards were unnumbered and checklisted below in alphabetical order.

COMPLETE SET (25) 6.00 15.00
1 Scott Arniel .20 .50
2 Dave Babych .30 .75
3 Laurie Boschman .20 .50
4 Wade Campbell .20 .50
5 Lucien DeBlois .30 .75
6 John Ferguson VP/GM .30 .75
7 John Gibson .20 .50
8 Dale Hawerchuk 1.50 4.00
9 Brian Hayward .40 1.00
10 Jim Kyte .30 .75
11 Barry Long CO .20 .50
12 Morris Lukowich .20 .50
13 Bengt Lundholm .20 .50
14 Paul MacLean .30 .75
15 Jimmy Mann .20 .50
16 Moe Mantha .20 .50
17 Andrew McBain .20 .50
18 Brian Mullen .20 .50
19 Robert Picard .20 .50
20 Doug Smail .30 .75
21 Doug Soetaert .30 .75
22 Thomas Steen .30 .75
23 Tim Watters .20 .50
24 Ron Wilson .20 .50
25 Tim Young .20 .50

1993-94 Jets Readers Club

This set features the Winnipeg Jets of the NHL. These are actually collectible bookmarks that were handed out to Winnipeg-area school children as a reward for reading books. The cards are unnumbered and so are listed below in alphabetical order.

COMPLETE SET (23) 6.00 15.00
1 Stu Barnes .20 .50
2 Sergei Bautin .08 .25
3 Stephane Beauregard .20 .50
4 Arto Blomsten .20 .50
5 Luciano Borsato .08 .25
6 Tie Domi .60 1.50
7 Mike Eagles .08 .25
8 Nelson Emerson .20 .50
9 Bryan Erickson .08 .25
10 Bob Essensa .20 .50
11 Yan Kaminsky .08 .25
12 Dean Kennedy .08 .25
13 Boris Mironov .08 .25
14 Teppo Numminen .40 1.00
15 Fredrik Olausson .40 1.00
16 Stephane Quintal .08 .25
17 Teemu Selanne 2.00 5.00
18 Darrin Shannon .08 .25
19 Thomas Steen .08 .25
20 Keith Tkachuk .20 .50
21 Igor Ulanov .08 .25
22 Paul Ysebaert .08 .25
23 Alexei Zhamnov .20 .50

1984-85 Jets Police

This 24-card set of Winnipeg Jets was sponsored by The Kinsmen Club of Winnipeg and all police forces in Manitoba. The cards measured approximately 2 5/8" by 3 11/16" and were issued in panels of two cards each. The front featured a color posed photo of the player shot against a blue background. The borders were white, and the player information beneath the picture was sandwiched between the Jets' and the Kinsmen logos. The back had "Jets Tips" in the form of a hockey tip paralleled by an anti-crime or safety tip. We have checklisted the cards below in alphabetical order, with the uniform number to the right of the player's name.

COMPLETE SET (24) 3.00 8.00
1 Scott Arniel 11 .08 .25
2 Dave Babych 44 .30 .75
3 Marc Behrend 29 .20 .50
4 Laurie Boschman 16 .20 .50
5 Randy Carlyle 8 .30 .75
6 Dave Ellett 2 .40 1.00
7 John Ferguson VP/GM .30 .75
8 Dale Hawerchuk 10 .75 2.00
9 Brian Hayward 1 .40 1.00
10 Jim Kyte 6 .08 .25
11 Morris Lukowich 12 .20 .50
12 Bengt Lundholm 22 .08 .25
13 Paul MacLean 15 .30 .75
14 Andrew McBain 20 .08 .25
15 Brian Mullen 19 .20 .50
16 Robert Picard 3 .08 .25
17 Paul Pooley 23 .08 .25
18 Doug Smail 9 .30 .75
19 Thomas Steen 25 .50 1.25
20 Perry Turnbull 27 .08 .25
21 Tim Watters 7 .08 .25
22 Ron Wilson 24 .08 .25
23 Assistant Coaches .08 .25
Bill Sutherland
Barry Long
Rick Bowness
24 Team Photo .30 .75

1985-86 Jets Police

This 24-card set of Winnipeg Jets was sponsored by The Kinsmen Club of Winnipeg and all police forces in Manitoba. The cards measured approximately 2 5/8" by 3 3/4" and were issued in panels of two cards each. The front featured a color action shot of the player. The borders were white, and the player information beneath the picture was sandwiched between the Jets' and the Kinsmen logos. The back had "Jets Tips" in the form of a hockey tip paralleled by an anti-crime or safety tip. We have checklisted the cards below in alphabetical order, with the uniform number to the right of the player's name.

COMPLETE SET (24) 3.00 8.00
1 Scott Arniel 11 .08 .25
2 Laurie Boschman 16 .20 .50
3 Dan Bouchard 35 .20 .50
4 Randy Carlyle 8 .30 .75
5 Dave Ellett 2 .40 1.00
6 John Ferguson VP/GM .20 .50
7 Dale Hawerchuk 10 .75 2.00
8 Brian Hayward 1 .40 1.00
9 Jim Kyte 6 .08 .25
10 Paul MacLean 15 .30 .75
11 Mario Marois 22 .08 .25
12 Andrew McBain 20 .08 .25
13 Anssi Melametsa 14 .08 .25
14 Brian Mullen 19 .08 .25
15 Ray Neufeld 28 .08 .25
16 Jim Nill 17 .08 .25
17 Dave Silk 34 .08 .25
18 Doug Smail 9 .30 .75
19 Thomas Steen 25 .50 1.25
20 Perry Turnbull 27 .08 .25
21 Tim Watters 7 .20 .50
22 Ron Wilson 24 .20 .50
23 Assistant Coaches .08 .25
Bill Sutherland
Barry Long
Rick Bowness
24 Team Photo .20 .50

1985-86 Jets Silverwood Dairy

This six-panel set of Winnipeg Jets was issued by Silverwood Dairy on the side of half-gallon milk cartons. The picture and text were printed in blue. The top of the panel featured an oval-shaped head and shoulders shot of the player, with his name immediately below the picture. The bottom of the panel presented the instructions for the Silverwood Game of the Month contest, in which ten lucky winners would win a pair of tickets to see the featured game of the month. The panels were unnumbered and checklisted below in alphabetical order.

COMPLETE SET (6) 24.00 60.00
1 Laurie Boschman 4.00 10.00
2 Randy Carlyle 5.00 12.00
3 Dave Ellett 5.00 12.00
4 Dale Hawerchuk 10.00 25.00
5 Paul MacLean 4.00 10.00
6 Brian Mullen 5.00 12.00

1986-87 Jets Postcards

This blank-backed 26-card set measured approximately 3 1/4" by 5 1/4". The fronts had borderless color action player photos. The player's name and uniform number appeared on the bottom. The cards were unnumbered and checklisted below in alphabetical order.

COMPLETE SET (26) 8.00 20.00
1 Brad Berry .30 .75
2 Laurie Boschman .40 1.00
3 Rick Bowness ACO .20 .50
Dan Maloney CO
Bill Sutherland ACO
4 Randy Carlyle .75 2.00
5 Bill Derlago .40 1.00
6 Dave Ellett .60 1.50
7 John Ferguson GM .40 1.00
8 Gilles Hamel .30 .75
9 Dale Hawerchuk 1.50 4.00
10 Hannu Jarvenpaa .30 .75
11 Jim Kyte .30 .75
12 Paul MacLean .40 1.00
13 Mario Marois .30 .75
14 Andrew McBain .30 .75
15 Brian Mullen .40 1.00
16 Ray Neufeld .30 .75
17 Jim Nill .30 .75
18 Fredrik Olausson .60 1.50
19 Steve Penney .40 1.00
20 Eldon Reddick .40 1.00
21 Doug Smail .40 1.00
22 Thomas Steen .60 1.50
23 Perry Turnbull .30 .75
24 Tim Watters .30 .75
25 Ron Wilson .30 .75
26 Team Photo .75 2.00

1987-88 Jets Postcards

This 24-card set measured approximately 3 1/4" by 5 1/4". The fronts featured autographed color action player photos with the player's jersey number and name in the lower right. The backs were blank. The cards were unnumbered and checklisted below in alphabetical order.

COMPLETE SET (24) 4.80 12.00
1 Brad Berry .20 .50
2 Daniel Berthiaume .40 1.00
3 Laurie Boschman .20 .50
4 Randy Carlyle .30 .75
5 Iain Duncan .20 .50
6 Dave Ellett .30 .75
7 Pat Elynuik .20 .50
8 Gilles Hamel .20 .50
9 Dale Hawerchuk .60 1.50
10 Hannu Jarvenpaa .20 .50
11 Jim Kyte .20 .50
12 Paul MacLean .30 .75
13 Mario Marois .20 .50
14 Andrew McBain .20 .50
15 Ray Neufeld .20 .50
16 Fredrik Olausson .40 1.00
17 Eldon Reddick .40 1.00
18 Steve Rooney .30 .75
19 Doug Smail .30 .75
20 Thomas Steen .40 1.00
21 Peter Taglianetti .20 .50
22 Tim Watters .20 .50
23 Ron Wilson .20 .50
24 Team Photo .40 1.00

1988-89 Jets Police

This 24-card set of Winnipeg Jets was sponsored by The Kinsmen Club of Winnipeg and all police forces in Manitoba. The cards measured approximately 2 5/8" by 3 3/4" and were issued as 12 panels of two cards each. By uniform numbers, the panel pairs were CO/TEAM, 39/ACO, 23/4, 6/10, 16/20, 25/32, 19/22, 8/7, 27/28, 2/34, 9/12, and 31/33. The front featured a color action shot of the player. The borders were white, and the player information beneath the picture was sandwiched between the Jets' and the Kinsmen logos. The back had "Jets Tips" in the form of a hockey tip paralleled by an anti-crime or safety tip. We have checklisted the cards below in alphabetical order, with the uniform number to the right of the player's name.

COMPLETE SET (24) 3.00 8.00
1 Brent Ashton 7 .08 .25
2 Laurie Boschman 16 .08 .25
3 Randy Carlyle 8 .30 .75
4 Alain Chevrier 31 .20 .50
5 Iain Duncan 19 .08 .25
6 Dave Ellett 2 .30 .75
7 Pat Elynuik 34 .08 .25
8 Randy Gilhen 00 .08 .25
9 Dale Hawerchuk 10 .60 1.50
10 Dave Hunter 12 .08 .25
11 Hannu Jarvenpaa 23 .08 .25
12 Jim Kyte 6 .08 .25
13 Dan Maloney CO .08 .25
14 Mario Marois 22 .08 .25
15 Andrew McBain 20 .08 .25
16 Ray Neufeld 28 .08 .25
17 Teppo Numminen 27 .30 .75
18 Fredrik Olausson 4 .20 .50
19 Eldon Reddick 33 .20 .50
20 Doug Smail 9 .20 .50
21 Thomas Steen 25 .30 .75
22 Peter Taglianetti 32 .08 .25
23 Assistant Coaches .08 .25
Bill Sutherland
Bruce Southern
Rick St.Croix
24 Team Photo .30 .75

1988-89 Jets Postcards

These postcards were issued by the team at promotional events. They are unnumbered and are listed below in alphabetical order.

COMPLETE SET (24) 8.00 15.00
1 Brent Ashton .20 .50
2 Mascot .02 .10
3 Daniel Berthiaume .40 1.00
4 Laurie Boschman .20 .50
5 Randy Carlyle .30 .75
6 Iain Duncan .20 .50
7 Dave Ellett .30 .75
8 Pat Elynuik .20 .50
9 Paul Fenton .20 .50
10 Randy Gilhen .20 .50
11 Dale Hawerchuk .75 2.00
12 Hannu Jarvenpaa .20 .50
13 Brad Jones .20 .50
14 Jim Kyte .20 .50
15 Dan Maloney CO .08 .25
16 Andrew McBain .20 .50
17 Teppo Numminen .75 2.00
18 Fredrik Olausson .30 .75
19 Eldon Reddick .40 1.00
20 Doug Smail .30 .75
21 Thomas Steen .40 1.00
22 Coaches .08 .25
23 Peter Taglianetti .20 .50
24 Team Photo .40 1.00

1989-90 Jets Safeway

This 30-card set was sponsored by Safeway Limited of Canada and featured players from the Winnipeg Jets. The cards measured approximately 3 3/4" by 6 7/8". The front had a color action photo of the player, with his number and name above the picture between the Jets' and Safeway logos. The back was outlined in black boxes and included player information as well as a oversized Safeway logo and advertisement. Since the cards were unnumbered, they are listed below in alphabetical order with the player's sweater number after the name.

COMPLETE SET (30) 4.80 12.00
1 Brent Ashton 7 .20 .50
2 Stu Barnes 14 .30 .75
3 Brad Berry 29 .20 .50
4 Daniel Berthiaume 30 .30 .75
5 Laurie Boschman 16 .20 .50
6 Randy Carlyle 8 .30 .75
7 Shawn Cronin 44 .20 .50
8 Randy Cunneyworth 18 .20 .50
9 Gord Donnelly 34 .20 .50
10 Tom Draper 37 .30 .75
11 Iain Duncan 19 .20 .50
12 Dave Ellett 2 .30 .75
13 Pat Elynuik 15 .20 .50
14 Bob Essensa 35 .30 .75
15 Paul Fenton 11 .20 .50
16 Dale Hawerchuk 10 .60 1.50
17 Brent Hughes 46 .20 .50
18 Mark Kumpel 21 .20 .50
19 Moe Mantha 22 .20 .50
20 Dave McLlwain 20 .20 .50
21 Brian McReynolds 26 .20 .50
22 Teppo Numminen 27 .30 .75
23 Fredrik Olausson 4 .30 .75
24 Greg Paslawski 28 .20 .50
25 Doug Smail 12 .30 .75
26 Thomas Steen 25 .30 .75
27 Peter Taglianetti 32 .20 .50
28 Benny 00 (Mascot) .08 .25
29 Coaches Card .08 .25
Alpo Suhonen
Bob Murdoch
Clare Drake
30 Team Photo .40 1.00

1990-91 Jets IGA

This 35-card set measured approximately 3 1/2" by 6 1/2" and featured color action player photos with white borders. The team logo, sweater number, player's name, and sponsor logo appeared at the card top between two thin purple stripes. The back was divided into two sections; in the upper appeared player information, while in the lower appeared a GreenCare advertisement (environmentally safe and carried in IGA stores). The cards were unnumbered and checklisted below in alphabetical order.

COMPLETE SET (35) 4.00 10.00
1 Scott Arniel .15 .40
2 Brent Ashton .15 .40
3 Don Barber .15 .40
4 Stephane Beauregard .20 .50
5 Randy Carlyle .30 .75
6 Danton Cole .15 .40
7 Shawn Cronin .15 .40
8 Gord Donnelly .15 .40
9 Clare Drake CO .08 .25
10 Kris Draper .40 1.00
11 Iain Duncan .15 .40
12 Pat Elynuik .15 .40
13 Bob Essensa .20 .50
14 Doug Evans .15 .40
15 Phil Housley .40 1.00
16 Sergei Kharin .15 .40
17 Mark Kumpel .15 .40
18 Guy Larose .15 .40
19 Paul MacDermid .15 .40
20 Moe Mantha .15 .40
21 Brian Marchment .20 .50
22 Dave McLlwain .15 .40
23 Bob Murdoch CO .08 .25
24 Teppo Numminen .30 .75
25 Fredrik Olausson .20 .50
26 Ed Olczyk .20 .50
27 Mark Osborne .15 .40
28 Greg Paslawski .15 .40
29 Terry Simpson CO .08 .25
30 Thomas Steen .30 .75
31 Phil Sykes .15 .40
32 Rick Tabaracci .25 .60
33 Simon Wheeldon .15 .40
34 Benny (Mascot) .08 .25
35 Team Photo .40 1.00

1991 Jets Panini Team Stickers

This 32-sticker set was issued in a plastic bag that contained two 16-sticker sheets (approximately 9" by 12") and a foldout poster, "Super Poster - Hockey 91", on which the stickers could be affixed. The players' names appeared only on the poster, not on the stickers. Each sticker measured about 2 1/8" by 2 7/8" and featured a color player action shot on its white-bordered front. The back of the white sticker sheet was lined off into 16 panels, each carrying the logos for Panini, the NHL, and the NHLPA, as well as the same number that appeared on the front of the sticker. Every Canadian NHL team was featured in this promotion. Each team set was available by mail-order from Panini Canada Ltd. for 2.99 plus 50 cents for shipping and handling.

COMPLETE SET (32) 1.00 2.50
1 Scott Arniel .02 .10
2 Brent Ashton .02 .10
3 Stephane Beauregard .02 .10
4 Randy Carlyle .02 .10
5 Danton Cole .01 .05
6 Shawn Cronin .02 .10
7 Gord Donnelly .01 .05
8 Kris Draper .05 .15
9 Dave Ellett .02 .10
10 Pat Elynuik .01 .05
11 Doug Evans .01 .05
12 Paul Fenton .01 .05
13 Phil Housley .08 .25
14 Mark Kumpel .01 .05
15 Paul MacDermid .01 .05
16 Moe Mantha .01 .05
17 Dave McLlwain .01 .05
18 Teppo Numminen .05 .15
19 Fredrik Olausson .02 .10
20 Greg Paslawski .01 .05
21 Doug Smail .01 .05
22 Thomas Steen .02 .10
23 Phil Sykes .01 .05
24 Rick Tabaracci .05 .15
A Team Logo .01 .05
Left Side
B Team Logo .01 .05
Right Side
C Jets in Action .01 .05
Upper Left Corner
D Jets in Action .01 .05
Lower Left Corner
E Jets in Action .01 .05
Upper Right Corner
F Jets in Action .01 .05
Lower Right Corner
G Paul Fenton .01 .05
H Phil Housley .08 .25

1991-92 Jets IGA

This 35-card set measured approximately 3 1/2" by 6 1/2" and featured color action player photos with white borders. The IGA logo, sweater number, player's name, and a picture of Cadbury's Caramilk candy appeared at the card bottom between two thin purple stripes. The back was divided into three sections; in the top appeared player information; in the middle and bottom appeared ads for Caramilk and GreenCare, respectively. The front of the Thomas Steen card showed (in lower right corner) another Cadbury candy bar/product, "Crunchie". The cards were unnumbered and checklisted below in alphabetical order.

COMPLETE SET (35) 4.00 10.00
1 Stu Barnes .20 .50
2 Stephane Beauregard .20 .50
3 Luciano Borsato .15 .40
4 Randy Carlyle .20 .50
5 Danton Cole .15 .40
6 Shawn Cronin .15 .40
7 Burton Cummings .20 .50
8 Mike Eagles .15 .40
9 Pat Elynuik .15 .40
10 Bryan Erickson .15 .40
11 Bob Essensa .20 .50
12 Doug Evans .15 .40
13 Mike Hartman .15 .40
14 Phil Housley .30 .75
15 Dean Kennedy .15 .40
16 Paul MacDermid .15 .40
17 Moe Mantha .15 .40
18 Rob Murray .15 .40
19 Troy Murray .15 .40
20 Teppo Numminen .20 .50
21 Fredrik Olausson .20 .50
22 Ed Olczyk .15 .40
23 Mark Osborne .15 .40
24 John Paddock CO .08 .25
25 Kent Paynter .15 .40
26 Dave Prior .15 .40
27 Russ Romaniuk .15 .40
28 Darrin Shannon .20 .50
29 Terry Simpson CO .08 .25
30 Thomas Steen .20 .50
31 Phil Sykes .15 .40
32 Rick Tabaracci .20 .50
33 Glen Williamson CO .08 .25
34 Benny (Mascot) .08 .25
35 Team Photo UER .30 .75
(Incorrectly
marked 1990-91)

1993-94 Jets Ruffles

This 29-postcard set measured approximately 3 1/2" by 6 1/2" and featured color action player photos with a thin black border on a white background. The player's name was printed in white in a black bar across the bottom in the wide white border with the team logo, jersey number and sponsor logo printed in red and blue above the bar. The backs carried the player's name, jersey number, position, and biographical information in black print on a white background above a Ruffles Challenge logo and checklist for an all-star potato chip. The cards were unnumbered and checklisted below in alphabetical order.

COMPLETE SET (29) 6.00 15.00
1 Stu Barnes .30 .75
2 Sergei Bautin .15 .40
3 Stephane Beauregard .20 .50
4 Benny (Mascot) .08 .25
5 Zinetula Bilyaletdinov ACO .08 .25
6 Arto Blomsten .15 .40
7 Luciano Borsato .15 .40
8 Tie Domi .40 1.00
9 Mike Eagles .15 .40
10 Nelson Emerson .30 .75
11 Bryan Erickson .15 .40
12 Bob Essensa .20 .50
13 Yan Kaminsky .15 .40
14 Dean Kennedy .15 .40
15 Kris King .15 .40
16 Boris Mironov .25 .60
17 Andy Murray ACO .08 .25
18 Teppo Numminen .25 .60
19 Fredrik Olausson .15 .40
20 John Paddock CO .08 .25
21 Stephane Quintal .15 .40
22 Teemu Selanne 2.00 5.00
23 Darrin Shannon .15 .40
24 Thomas Steen .30 .75
25 Keith Tkachuk 1.00 2.50
26 Igor Ulanov .15 .40
27 Paul Ysebaert .15 .40
28 Alexei Zhamnov .40 1.00
29 Team Picture .20 .50

1995-96 Jets Readers Club

This set of 12 bookmarks featured the Winnipeg Jets. The top of the front featured a player photo, his name and jersey number along with a quote on the importance of reading and a pre-printed autograph. The backs displayed the logos of the various corporate sponsors of this program. The bookmarks were distributed to children who successfully read a number of books.

COMPLETE SET (12) 3.00 8.00
1 Tim Cheveldae .20 .50
2 Dallas Drake .08 .25
3 Mike Eastwood .08 .25
4 Nikolai Khabibulin .40 1.00
5 Kris King .20 .50
6 Igor Korolev .08 .25
7 Dave Manson .08 .25
8 Teppo Numminen .20 .50
9 Teemu Selanne 1.25 3.00
10 Darrin Shannon .08 .25
11 Keith Tkachuk .60 1.50
12 Alexei Zhamnov .40 1.00

1995-96 Jets Team Issue

This 26-card set measured approximately 3 1/2" by 6 1/2" and featured color action player photos in a white border. The player's name, position, and jersey number were printed in the wide bottom margin. The backs carried player information. The cards were unnumbered and checklisted below in alphabetical order.

COMPLETE SET (26) 6.00 15.00
1 Title Card .08 .25
2 Benny (Mascot) .02 .10
3 Tim Cheveldae .30 .75
4 Coaches Card .08 .25
Terry Simpson CO
Perry Pearn ACO
Randy Carlyle ACO
5 Shane Doan .30 .75
6 Jason Doig .20 .50
7 Dallas Drake .20 .50
8 Mike Eastwood .20 .50
9 Randy Gilhen .20 .50
10 Nikolai Khabibulin .40 1.00
11 Kris King .20 .50
12 Igor Korolev .20 .50
13 Stewart Malgunas .20 .50
14 Dave Manson .20 .50
15 Jim McKenzie .20 .50
16 Teppo Numminen .30 .75
17 Eddie Olczyk .20 .50
18 Deron Quint .20 .50
19 Ed Ronan .20 .50
20 Teemu Selanne 1.50 4.00
21 Darrin Shannon .20 .50
22 Darryl Shannon .20 .50
23 Mike Stapleton .20 .50
24 Keith Tkachuk .75 2.00
25 Darren Turcotte .20 .50
26 Alexei Zhamnov .30 .75

1992 Jofa/Koho

This six-card standard-size set was apparently sponsored by four major brands of hockey equipment: Jofa, Koho, Titan, and Canadien. The set was also known as "The Endorsers" and features six famous current players who endorsed their respective products. The cards were printed on thin card stock. The fronts featured color close-up player photos. The borders shade from one color to another and were studded with miniature stars. On various pastel-colored backs, biographical information was presented inside black border stripes. The cards were unnumbered and checklisted below in alphabetical order. The manufacturer's name that appears at the bottom of the card front was listed below beneath the player's name.

COMPLETE SET (6) 4.80 12.00
1 Theo Fleury .75 2.00
Jofa
2 Jari Kurri .40 1.00
Koho
3 Mario Lemieux 2.00 5.00
Koho
4 Eric Lindros 1.50 4.00
Titan
5 Denis Savard .40 1.00
Canadien

6 Mats Sundin .60 1.50
Jofa

2003 Jose Theodore Mike's Postcards

This three-card set was available by purchasing a special meal at Mike's Restaurants in Montreal. They are the size of typical postcards and have perforated edges, along with a Trio Theo logo in the upper left corner and Mike's logo in the bottom right.

COMPLETE SET (3)
1 Jose Theodore
2 Jose Theodore
3 Jose Theodore

1997-98 Katch

The 1997-98 Katch set was issued in one series totaling 168 cards. Gold and silver parallels were also created. Gold were randomly inserted at 1:48 and silver at 1:16.

COMPLETE SET (168) 100.00 100.00
COMP.GOLD SET (168) 2500.00 4000.00
*GOLD: 7.5X TO 15X HI COLUMN
COMP.SILVER SET (168) 1000.00 600.00
*SILVER: 3X TO 6X HI COLUMN
1 Guy Hebert .40 1.00
2 Paul Kariya 2.50 5.00
3 Espen Knutsen .10 .30
4 Tomas Sandstrom .10 .30
5 Teemu Selanne 1.00 2.50
6 Scott Young .10 .30
7 Per Johan Axelsson .10 .30
8 Ray Bourque .60 1.50
9 Jim Carey .40 1.00
10 Ted Donato .10 .30
11 Dimitri Khristich .40 1.00
12 Sergei Samsonov .50 1.25
13 Matthew Barnaby .40 1.00
14 Jason Dawe .10 .30
15 Dominik Hasek 1.00 2.50
16 Mike Peca .40 1.00
17 Rob Ray .40 1.00
18 Alexei Zhitnik .10 .30
19 Andrew Cassels .10 .30
20 Theo Fleury .50 1.25
21 Jarome Iginla .40 1.00
22 Sandy McCarthy .10 .30
23 Tyler Moss .10 .30
24 Cory Stillman .10 .30
25 Sean Burke .40 1.00
26 Kevin Dineen .10 .30
27 Stu Grimson .40 1.00
28 Steven Rice .10 .30
29 Keith Primeau .40 1.00
30 Geoff Sanderson .40 1.00
31 Tony Amonte .40 1.00
32 Chris Chelios .50 1.25
33 Daniel Cleary .10 .30
34 Jeff Hackett .40 1.00
35 Ethan Moreau .10 .30
36 Bob Probert .10 .30
37 Adam Deadmarsh .40 1.00
38 Peter Forsberg 1.25 3.00
39 Claude Lemieux .40 1.00
40 Sandis Ozolinsh .40 1.00
41 Patrick Roy 3.00 6.00
42 Joe Sakic 1.00 2.50
43 Ed Belfour .50 1.25
44 Derian Hatcher .10 .30
45 Jere Lehtinen .40 1.00
46 Mike Modano .60 1.50
47 Joe Nieuwendyk .40 1.00
48 Darryl Sydor .40 1.00
49 Sergei Fedorov 1.00 2.50
50 Vyacheslav Kozlov .40 1.00
51 Darren McCarty .40 1.00
52 Chris Osgood .50 1.25
53 Brendan Shanahan .75 2.00
54 Steve Yzerman 1.50 4.00
55 Jason Arnott .40 1.00
56 Boyd Devereaux .10 .30
57 Curtis Joseph .60 1.50
58 Andrei Kovalenko .10 .30
59 Ryan Smyth .40 1.00
60 Doug Weight .40 1.00
61 Ed Jovanovski .10 .30
62 Scott Mellanby .10 .30
63 David Nemirovsky .10 .30
64 Rob Niedermayer .10 .30
65 Ray Sheppard .40 1.00
66 John Vanbiesbrouck .50 1.25
67 Aki Berg .10 .30
68 Rob Blake .10 .30
69 Stephane Fiset .40 1.00
70 Donald MacLean .10 .30
71 Yanic Perreault .10 .30
72 Luc Robitaille .40 1.00
73 Valeri Bure .40 1.00
74 Vincent Damphousse .40 1.00
75 Saku Koivu .50 1.25
76 Vladimir Malakhov .10 .30
77 Mark Recchi .40 1.00
78 Jocelyn Thibault .40 1.00
79 Martin Brodeur .75 2.00
80 Patrik Elias .40 1.00
81 Doug Gilmour .50 1.25
82 Bill Guerin .40 1.00
83 Scott Niedermayer .10 .30
84 Scott Stevens .40 1.00
85 Bryan Berard .10 .30
86 Eric Fichaud .40 1.00
87 Travis Green .10 .30
88 Kenny Jonsson .10 .30
89 Bryan McCabe .10 .30
90 Zigmund Palffy .50 1.25
91 Adam Graves .40 1.00
92 Wayne Gretzky 4.00 8.00
93 Pat LaFontaine .40 1.00
94 Brian Leetch .50 1.25
95 Mike Richter .50 1.25
96 Kevin Stevens .10 .30
97 Daniel Alfredsson .10 .30
98 Alexandre Daigle .10 .30
99 Chris Phillips .10 .30
100 Wade Redden .10 .30
101 Damian Rhodes .10 .30
102 Alexei Yashin .40 1.00
103 Paul Coffey .50 1.25
104 Chris Gratton .10 .30
105 Ron Hextall .40 1.00
106 John LeClair .75 2.00
107 Eric Lindros 1.25 3.00
108 Dainius Zubrus .10 .30
109 Mike Gartner .40 1.00
110 Brad Isbister .10 .30
111 Nikolai Khabibulin .40 1.00
112 Jeremy Roenick .50 1.25
113 Keith Tkachuk .50 1.25
114 Oleg Tverdovsky .10 .30
115 Tom Barrasso .40 1.00
116 Ron Francis .40 1.00
117 Kevin Hatcher .40 1.00
118 Jaromir Jagr 1.50 4.00
119 Alexei Morozov .10 .30
120 Petr Nedved .40 1.00
121 Patrick Marleau .40 1.00
122 Marty McSorley .10 .30
123 Bernie Nicholls .10 .30
124 Owen Nolan .40 1.00
125 Marco Sturm .40 1.00
126 Mike Vernon .40 1.00
127 Jim Campbell .40 1.00
128 Grant Fuhr .40 1.00
129 Brett Hull .60 1.50
130 Al MacInnis .40 1.00
131 Pierre Turgeon .40 1.00
132 Tony Twist .40 1.00
133 Brian Bradley .10 .30
134 Dino Ciccarelli .10 .30
135 Roman Hamrlik .10 .30
136 Daymond Langkow .10 .30
137 Darren Puppa .10 .30
138 Mikael Renberg .10 .30
139 Wendel Clark .10 .30
140 Tie Domi .40 1.00
141 Alyn McCauley .10 .30
142 Felix Potvin .40 1.00
143 Mathieu Schneider .10 .30
144 Mats Sundin .50 1.25
145 Pavel Bure 1.25 3.00
146 Trevor Linden .40 1.00
147 Kirk McLean .40 1.00
148 Mark Messier .60 1.50
149 Alexander Mogilny .40 1.00
150 Mattias Ohlund .40 1.00
151 Peter Bondra .50 1.25
152 Joe Juneau .10 .30
153 Adam Oates .40 1.00
154 Bill Ranford .40 1.00
155 Jaroslav Svejkovsky .10 .30
156 Richard Zednik .10 .30
157 Wayne Gretzky TL 1.50 4.00
158 Eric Lindros TL .60 1.50
159 Paul Kariya TL 1.00 2.50
160 Patrick Roy TL 1.25 3.00
161 Steve Yzerman TL .75 2.00
162 Jaromir Jagr TL .75 2.00
163 Brett Hull TL .30 .75
164 Joe Thornton .50 1.25
165 Vaclav Prospal .40 1.00
166 Mike Johnson .40 1.00
167 Eric Messier .40 1.00
168 Jan Bulis .40 1.00

1972 Kellogg's Iron-On Transfers

These six iron-on transfers each measured approximately 6 1/2" by 10". Each transfer consisted of a cartoon drawing of the player's body with an oversized head. The puck was comically portrayed with human characteristics (face, arms, and legs). A facsimile player autograph appeared below the drawing. At the bottom were instructions in English and French for applying the iron-on to clothing; these were to be cut off before application. These iron-on transfers were unnumbered and checklisted below in alphabetical order.

COMPLETE SET (6) 150.00 300.00
1 Ron Ellis 12.50 25.00
2 Phil Esposito 37.50 75.00
3 Rod Gilbert 20.00 40.00
4 Bobby Hull 62.50 125.00
5 Frank Mahovlich 20.00 40.00
6 Stan Mikita 25.00 50.00

1984-85 Kellogg's Accordion Discs

The entire set consisted of eight picture pucks: six different pro hockey pucks each containing action shots and personal records for six NHL players, and two different sports pucks each featuring achievements of six famous female athletes. Each puck came with a sticker on NHL Team Emblem or Sports Crest. The pucks were inserted in specially marked packages of Kellogg's Cereals in Canada. By finding instant prize messages inside the picture pucks, one could win sports equipment, such as hockey jerseys, skates, sport bags, or hockey sticks. The promotion also included a mail-in offer for a plastic collector's shield that would hold all the picture pucks and be mounted on a wall. This set of thin cardboard discs measured approximately 2" in diameter. Six discs were joined together at their sides (like the bellows of an accordion) and were issued in a thin black plastic case. The front featured a round-shaped color action photo with white border. The back provided biographical and statistical information in French and English, with the team logo at the top and a facsimile autograph at the bottom. The complete set price below includes only one of the variation pairs.

COMPLETE SET (8) 12.00 30.00
1 Dino Ciccarelli 2.50 6.00
Mike Bossy
Richard Brodeur
Michel Goulet
Jari Kurri
Paul Reinhart
2 Reed Larson 1.50 4.00
Marcel Dionne
Peter Statsny
Paul MacLean
Doug Risebrough
Larry Robinson
3A Stanley Cup 2.00 5.00
Gilbert Perreault
Rick Middleton
Bob Gainey
Kevin Lowe
Borje Salming
3B Stanley Cup 2.00 5.00
Gilbert Perreault
Rick Middleton
Guy Lafleur
Kevin Lowe
Borje Salming
4 Bernie Federko 2.00 5.00
Ron Francis
Stan Smyl
Mike Gartner
Dave Babych
Lanny McDonald
5A Barry Beck 1.50 4.00
Rick Kehoe
Dale Hawerchuk
John Anderson
Mario Tremblay
Paul Coffey
5B Barry Beck 1.50 4.00
Denis Herron
Dale Hawerchuk
Dan Daoust
Mario Tremblay
Paul Coffey
6 Thomas Gradin 1.50 4.00
Dale Hunter
Doug Wilson
Darryl Sittler
Glenn Resch
Rick Vaive
7 Tracy Austin 1.25 3.00
Tennis
Olga Korbut
Gymnastics
Kathy Kreiner
Alpine Skiing
Angela Taylor
Track and Field
Anne Ottenbrite
Swimming
Paul Martini
Skating
Barbara Underhill
Skating
8 Tatiana Kolpakova 1.25 3.00
Long Jump
Kay Thompson
Skating
Kornelia Ender
Swimming
Melanie Smith
Equestrian
Nadia Comaneci
Gymnastics
Carling Bassett
Tennis

1992 Kellogg's All-Star Posters

Posters measured approximately 14" x 10" and were full color. One posted could be found in each specially marked box of Kellogg's cereal in Canada, for a limited time.

COMPLETE SET (3) 2.00 5.00
1 Campbell Conf. All-Stars .75 2.00
2 Wales Conf. All-Stars .75 2.00
3 Snap, Crackle, Pop .40 1.00

1992 Kellogg's Trophies

Protected by a clear plastic cello pack, these 11 cards were inserted into Kellogg's Rice Krispies cereal boxes in Canada. The cards measured approximately 2 3/8" by 3 1/4" and were printed on thin card stock. The fronts featured a color photo of the trophy inside a gold border on a turquoise card face. The name of the trophy appeared in a red circle at the center of the top. The backs were red and carried text in white print about the trophy. All text on both sides is in English and French. The cards were numbered on the front at the bottom center. This set is condition sensitive.

COMPLETE SET (11) 8.00 20.00
1 Stanley Cup 1.25 3.00
2 Presidents' Trophy .75 2.00
3 Hart Memorial Trophy .75 2.00
4 Conn Smythe Trophy .75 2.00
5 Vezina Trophy .75 2.00
6 James Norris Memorial .75 2.00
Trophy
7 Calder Memorial Trophy .75 2.00
8 Frank J. Selke Trophy .75 2.00
9 Lady Byng Memorial .75 2.00
Trophy
10 Art Ross Trophy .75 2.00
11 Jack Adams Trophy .75 2.00

1992-93 Kellogg's Posters

These 9 1/4" by 14" posters were inserted inside specially marked Kellogg's products. The two-sided posters each bore the same photo, with the descriptive legend at the top written in French on one side and English on the other. The bottom of the poster featured the player's name, along with the logos of the NHL and Kellogg's. The posters were folded into card-sized squares and then placed into a protective cellophane seal. All posters, therefore, were subject to extreme creasing, and are considered in top condition in this form. The checklist below may be incomplete. Collectors with additional information are encouraged to forward it to the publisher.

COMPLETE SET 16.00 40.00
1 Mario Lemieux 8.00 20.00
2 Mark Messier 2.00 5.00
3 Luc Robitaille 1.25 3.00
4 Patrick Roy 6.00 15.00
5 Cornelius Rooster 1.25 3.00
Mascot

1995-96 Kellogg's Donruss

This six-card set was distributed in specially-marked boxes of Kellogg's Cereal in Canada and featured color photos of hockey stars Mario Lemieux and Brett Hull. The backs carried another color player photo with the card title and explanation of the title. The cards are unnumbered and listed below as Mario Lemieux (1-4) and Brett Hull (5-6).

COMPLETE SET (6) 12.00 30.00
1 Mario Lemieux 3.00 8.00
The Fiver
2 Mario Lemieux 3.00 8.00
The Cup
3 Mario Lemieux 3.00 8.00
The 500th
4 Mario Lemieux 3.00 8.00
The Comeback
5 Brett Hull 1.25 3.00
50 in 49
6 Brett Hull 1.25 3.00
The MVP

1993 Kenner Starting Lineup Cards

These cards were packaged with their corresponding individual Starting Lineup figures produced by Kenner.

COMPLETE SET (12) 40.00 100.00
1 Ed Belfour 8.00 20.00
2 Ray Bourque 1.00 2.50
3 Grant Fuhr 10.00 25.00
4 Brett Hull .75 2.00
5 Jaromir Jagr 1.25 3.00
6 Pat LaFontaine 1.00 2.50
7 Mario Lemieux 1.50 4.00
8 Eric Lindros 1.00 2.50
9 Mark Messier 1.00 2.50
10 Jeremy Roenick .75 2.00
11 Patrick Roy 2.00 5.00
12 Steve Yzerman 2.00 5.00

1994 Kenner Starting Lineup Cards

These cards were included in the packaging for Kenner Starting Lineups. Because few SLUs are broken from their packaging, these cards made for unique collectibles. This year's cards were made by Pinnacle, and featured an SLU logo on the front.

COMPLETE SET (21) 32.00 80.00
1 Tom Barrasso .75 2.00
2 Ray Bourque .75 2.00
3 Pavel Bure 1.00 2.50
4 Sergei Fedorov 1.00 2.50
5 Grant Fuhr 1.25 3.00
6 Doug Gilmour .60 1.50
7 Brett Hull .60 1.50
8 Arturs Irbe .60 1.50
9 Jaromir Jagr .60 1.50
10 Pat Lafontaine .60 1.50
11 Brian Leetch .60 1.50
12 Mario Lemieux 1.00 2.50
13 Eric Lindros .75 2.00
14 Mark Messier .60 1.50
15 Alexander Mogilny .60 1.50
16 Adam Oates .60 1.50
17 Mike Richter .75 2.00
18 Luc Robitaille .75 2.00
19 Jeremy Roenick .50 1.25
20 Teemu Selanne 1.00 2.50
21 Steve Yzerman 1.50 4.00

1995 Kenner Starting Lineup Cards

These cards were included in the packaging for Kenner Starting Lineups. Because few SLUs were broken from their packaging, these cards made for unique collectibles. This year's cards were made by Fleer, and featured an SLU logo on the front.

COMPLETE SET (21) 24.00 60.00
1 Tom Barrasso .60 1.50
2 Rob Blake .60 1.50
3 Martin Brodeur 1.50 4.00
4 Pavel Bure .60 1.50
5 Chris Chelios .75 2.00
6 Bob Corkum .30 .75
7 Sergei Fedorov .60 1.50
8 Theo Fleury .60 1.50
9 Adam Graves .30 .75
10 Dominik Hasek 1.25 3.00
11 Brett Hull .60 1.50
12 Arturs Irbe .40 1.00
13 Mike Modano .75 2.00
14 Kirk Muller .40 1.00
15 Cam Neely .60 1.50
16 Sandis Ozolinsh .60 1.50
17 Felix Potvin .75 2.00
18 Luc Robitaille .60 1.50
19 Brendan Shanahan 1.00 2.50
20 Scott Stevens .30 .75
21 Pierre Turgeon .75 2.00

1996 Kenner Starting Lineup Cards

These cards were included in the packaging for Kenner Starting Lineups. Because few SLUs are broken from their packaging, these cards make for unique collectibles. This year's cards were made by Skybox, and featured an SLU logo on the front.

COMPLETE SET (24) 24.00 60.00
1 Tom Barrasso .60 1.50
2 Brian Bradley .30 .75
3 Jim Carey .75 2.00
4 Paul Coffey .75 2.00
5 Sergei Fedorov .60 1.50
6 Ron Francis .75 2.00
7 Dominik Hasek .60 1.50
8 Paul Kariya 1.00 2.50
9 Pat Lafontaine .60 1.50
10 John LeClair .75 2.00
11 Brian Leetch .40 1.00
12 Eric Lindros .60 1.50
13 Al MacInnis .60 1.50
14 Scott Mellanby .30 .75
15 Mark Messier .60 1.50
16 Mike Modano .40 1.00
17 Adam Oates .40 1.00
18 Mikael Renberg .30 .75
19 Stephane Richer .30 .75
20 Jeremy Roenick .50 1.25
21 Patrick Roy 1.25 3.00
22 Joe Sakic 1.50 4.00
23 Brendan Shanahan .75 2.00
24 Mats Sundin .75 2.00

1997 Kenner Starting Lineup Cards

These cards were included in the packaging for Kenner Starting Lineups. Because few SLUs are broken from their packaging, these cards made for unique collectibles. This year's cards were made by Fleer, and featured an SLU logo on the front.

COMPLETE SET (20) 16.00 40.00
1 Daniel Alfredsson .30 .75
2 Jason Arnott .40 1.00
3 Peter Bondra .60 1.50
4 Martin Brodeur 1.00 2.50
5 Paul Coffey .50 1.25
6 Chris Chelios .60 1.50
7 Peter Forsberg 1.00 2.50
8 Wayne Gretzky 2.50 6.00
9 Ron Hextall .75 2.00
10 Jaromir Jagr .60 1.50
11 Patrick Lalime .60 1.50
12 Eric Lindros .60 1.50
13 Mark Messier .60 1.50
14 Chris Osgood .75 2.00
15 Sandis Ozolinsh .40 1.00
16 Zigmund Palffy .50 1.25
17 Daren Puppa .50 1.25
18 Mark Recchi .60 1.50
19 Teemu Selanne .60 1.50
20 Keith Tkachuk .60 1.50
21 John Vanbiesbrouck .60 1.50

1998 Kenner Starting Lineup Cards

These cards were included in the packaging for Kenner Starting Lineups. Because few SLUs are broken from their packaging, these cards made for unique collectibles. This year's cards were made by Upper Deck, and featured a SLU logo on the front.

COMPLETE SET (34) 20.00 50.00
1 Tony Amonte .40 1.00
2 Bryan Berard .30 .75
3 Ed Belfour .75 2.00
4 Peter Bondra .30 .75
5 Martin Brodeur 1.00 2.50
6 Jim Campbell .30 .75
7 Vincent Damphousse FP .30 .75
8 Theo Fleury .40 1.00
9 Grant Fuhr .60 1.50
10 Doug Gilmour .40 1.00
11 Wayne Gretzky 2.00 5.00
12 Wayne Gretzky Cup 2.00 5.00
13 Dominik Hasek .75 2.00
14 Jaromir Jagr .60 1.50
15 Paul Kariya .60 1.50
16 Trevor Kidd .40 1.00
17 Nikolai Khabibulin .40 1.00
18 Olaf Kolzig .40 1.00
19 Brian Leetch .40 1.00
20 Eric Lindros .60 1.50
21 Kirk McLean .40 1.00
22 Mark Messier .60 1.50
23 Rob Neidermayer .30 .75
24 Chris Osgood .60 1.50
25 Felix Potvin .60 1.50
26 Daren Puppa .30 .75
27 Jeremy Roenick .60 1.50
28 Patrick Roy 1.25 3.00
29 Joe Sakic Cup .75 2.00
30 Brendan Shanahan .60 1.50
31 Joe Thornton .75 2.00
32 John Vanbiesbrouck .40 1.00
33 Alexei Yashin .40 1.00
34 Steve Yzerman Cup 1.25 3.00

1980-81 Kings Card Night

The cards in this 14-card set were in color and are standard size. The set was produced during the 1980-81 season by All-Star Cards Ltd. for the Los Angeles Kings at the request of owner Jerry Buss. Reportedly 5000 sets were produced, virtually all of which were given away at the Kings' "Card Night." The fronts featured color "mug shots" of the players; the backs provided career highlights and brief biographical information.

COMPLETE SET (14) 10.00 20.00
1 Marcel Dionne 4.00 8.00
2 Glenn Goldup .30 .75
3 Doug Halward .30 .75
4 Billy Harris .40 1.00
5 Steve Jensen .40 1.00
6 Jerry Korab .30 .75
7 Mario Lessard .60 1.50
8 Dave Lewis .40 1.00
9 Mike Murphy .30 .75
10 Rob Palmer .30 .75
11 Charlie Simmer .75 2.00
12 Dave Taylor 1.25 3.00
13 Garry Unger .60 1.50
14 Jay Wells .40 1.00

1984-85 Kings Smokey

This fire safety set contained 23 cards which were numbered on the back. Players in the set were members of the Los Angeles Kings hockey team. The cards measured approximately 2 15/16" by 4 3/8" and were numbered on the back in the upper right corner. Card backs contained a fire safety cartoon and minimal information about the player. The set was sponsored by the California Department of Forestry.

COMPLETE SET (23) 8.00 20.00
1 Russ Anderson .20 .50
2 Marcel Dionne 2.00 5.00
3 Brian Engblom .30 .75
4 Daryl Evans .20 .50
5 Jim Fox .30 .75
6 Garry Galley .60 1.50
7 Anders Hakansson .20 .50
8 Mark Hardy .20 .50
9 Bob Janecyk .30 .75
10 John Paul Kelly .20 .50
11 Brian MacLellan .20 .50
12 Bernie Nicholls 1.00 2.50
13 Craig Redmond .20 .50
14 Terry Ruskowski .30 .75
15 Doug Smith .20 .50
16 Dave Taylor .75 2.00
17 Jay Wells .20 .50
18 Darren Eliot .30 .75
19 Rick Lapointe .20 .50
20 Bob Miller .20 .50
21 Steve Seguin .20 .50
22 Phil Sykes .20 .50
23 Pat Quinn CO .20 .50

1986-87 Kings 20th Anniversary Team Issue

Cards measured 4" x 6 1/4" and featured black and white photos on the front along with player name and 20th anniversary logo. Backs were blank.

COMPLETE SET (23) 10.00 25.00
1 Bob Bourne .08 .25
2 Jimmy Carson .75 2.00
3 Steve Duchesne .75 2.00
4 Darren Eliot .08 .25
5 Bryan Erickson .08 .25
6 Jim Fox .08 .25
7 Garry Galley .40 1.00
8 Paul Guay .08 .25
9 Mark Hardy .08 .25
10 Bob Janecyk .30 .75
11 Dean Kennedy .08 .25
12 Grant Ledyard .20 .50
13 Morris Lukowich .08 .25
14 Sean McKenna .08 .25
15 Roland Melanson .30 .75
16 Bernie Nicholls .75 2.00
17 Joe Paterson .08 .25
18 Larry Playfair .08 .25
19 Luc Robitaille 5.00 12.00
20 Phil Sykes .08 .25
21 Dave Taylor .30 .75
22 Jay Wells .08 .25
23 Dave Williams .30 .75

1988-89 Kings Smokey

This fire safety set contained 25 cards and featured members of the Los Angeles Kings hockey team in their then-new silver and black colors. The cards were unnumbered; not even the player's uniform number was given on the card. The players are listed below alphabetically by name. The cards measured approximately 2 1/2" by 3 1/2". Card backs contained a fire safety cartoon and minimal information about the player. The set was sponsored by the California Department of Forestry and Fire Protection.

COMPLETE SET (25) 12.00 30.00
1 Mike Allison .20 .50
2 Ken Baumgartner .30 .75
3 Bob Carpenter .20 .50
4 Doug Crossman .20 .50
5 Dale DeGray .20 .50
6 Steve Duchesne .60 1.50
7 Ron Duguay .30 .75
8 Mark Fitzpatrick .40 1.00
9 Jim Fox .20 .50
10 Robbie Ftorek CO .20 .50
11 Wayne Gretzky 6.00 15.00
12 Gilles Hamel .20 .50
13 Glenn Healy .40 1.00
14 Mike Krushelnyski .20 .50
15 Tom Laidlaw .20 .50
16 Bryan Maxwell CO .08 .25
17 Wayne McBean .20 .50
18 Marty McSorley 1.25 3.00
19 Bernie Nicholls .60 1.50
20 Cap Raeder CO .08 .25
21 Luc Robitaille 1.50 4.00
22 Dave Taylor .60 1.50
23 John Tonelli .30 .75
24 Tim Watters .20 .50
25 Title Card .20 .50
(Checklist on back)

1989-90 Kings Smokey

This 24-card standard-size set of Los Angeles Kings was sponsored by the USDA Forest Service in cooperation with other agencies. The front featured a color action photo, banded above and below with gray stripes. The Smokey the Bear logo appeared in the upper left-hand corner, and the Los Angeles Kings logo in the lower right-hand corner. A black border below and on the right of the picture created the impression of a shadow. The back provided player information, card number, and a fire prevention cartoon. The cards were numbered in the upper right corner of the reverse.

COMPLETE SET (24) 10.00 25.00
1 Wayne Gretzky 5.00 12.00
2 Tim Watters .20 .50
3 Mikael Lindholm .20 .50
4 Mike Allison .20 .50
5 Steve Kasper .20 .50
6 Dave Taylor .40 1.00
7 Larry Robinson .75 2.00
8 Luc Robitaille 1.25 3.00
9 Barry Beck .30 .75
10 Keith Crowder .20 .50
11 Petr Prajsler .20 .50
12 Mike Krushelnyski .20 .50
13 John Tonelli .30 .75
14 Steve Duchesne .40 1.00
15 Jay Miller .20 .50
16 Kelly Hrudey .60 1.50
17 Marty McSorley .75 2.00
18 Mario Gosselin .30 .75
19 Craig Duncanson .20 .50
20 Bob Kudelski .20 .50
21 Brian Benning .20 .50
22 Mikko Makela .20 .50
23 Tom Laidlaw .20 .50
24 Checklist Card .20 .50

1989-90 Kings Smokey Gretzky 8x10

This 8" by 10" blowup of Wayne Gretzky's regular Smokey issue featured a white-bordered color action shot of him on the front. The team name appeared at the top, and his name and position, along with the Kings and Smokey logos, were shown at the bottom. The black-and-white back had his name and biography in the upper left corner and featured a cartoon of bears on skates scoring a goal against a wildfire goalie while Smokey looked on. The card was unnumbered.

NNO Wayne Gretzky 6.00 15.00

1990-91 Kings Smokey

This 25-card set of Los Angeles Kings was sponsored by Royal Crown Cola in cooperation with the USDA Forest Service and other agencies and features members of the Los Angeles Kings. The cards measured the standard size (2 1/2" by 3 1/2"). The fronts featured color action player photos with white borders. The player's name appeared in a silver-gray stripe above the picture, while his position and several logos appearedin a white rectangle below the picture. The backs had biographical information and a fire prevention cartoon starring Smokey, enframed by thin black borders. The cards were numbered on the back in the upper left corner. The mascot card had a checklist on its reverse.

COMPLETE SET (25) 6.00 15.00
1 Wayne Gretzky 3.00 8.00
2 Brian Benning .08 .25
3 Rob Blake .40 1.00
4 Tim Watters .08 .25
5 Todd Elik .08 .25
6 Tomas Sandstrom .20 .50
7 Steve Kasper .08 .25
8 Dave Taylor .40 1.00
9 Larry Robinson .40 1.00
10 Luc Robitaille .60 1.50
11 Tony Granato .20 .50
12 Tom Laidlaw .08 .25
13 Francois Breault .08 .25
14 John Tonelli .20 .50
15 Steve Duchesne .20 .50
16 Jay Miller .08 .25
17 Kelly Hrudey .60 1.50
18 Marty McSorley .40 1.00
19 Daniel Berthiaume .20 .50
20 Bob Kudelski .08 .25
21 Brad Jones .08 .25
22 John McIntyre .08 .25
23 Rod Buskas .08 .25
24 Kingston (Mascot) .02 .10
(Checklist on back)
NNO RC Cola Challenge .02 .10

1991-92 Kings Upper Deck Season Ticket

This approximately 5" by 3 1/2" horizontally oriented card was sent out to 7,000 Los Angeles Kings season ticket holders along with a Christmas card from Upper Deck in December 1991 celebrating the Kings' 25th anniversary. The front featured a borderless color action shot of several Kings players and opponent(s) in a pileup in front of the Kings' net with Kings' goalie Kelly Hrudey. The limited edition seal with production number was placed in the upper left. The Upper Deck Hockey logo was in the upper right. The horizontal back carrieda drawing of Wayne Gretzky, Rogie Vachon, Bruce McNall, Marcel Dionne, and Luc Robitaille.

NNO Los Angeles Kings 40.00 100.00
Season Ticket Holders
25th Anniversary
Kelly Hrudey

1992-93 Kings Upper Deck Season Ticket

This approximately 5" by 3 1/2" horizontally oriented card was sent out to Los Angeles Kings season ticket holders along with a Christmas card from Upper Deck in December 1992. The card was numbered out of 10,000.

NNO Los Angeles Kings 30.00 75.00
Season Ticket Holders

1993 Kings Forum

This set commemorated various athletes who appeared at the Great Western Forum. Cards were standard size and full color. Only three hockey playerrs appeared in the set, and they are the ones listed below.

8 Rogie Vachon .40 1.00
9 Marcel Dionne .40 1.00
10 Wayne Gretzky 4.00 10.00

1993-94 Kings Upper Deck Season Ticket

This approximately 5" by 3 1/2" horizontally oriented card was sent out to 10,000 Los Angeles Kings season ticket holders along with a Christmas card from Upper Deck in December 1993.

NNO Los Angeles Kings Season Ticket Holders 20.00 50.00

1994-95 Kings Upper Deck Season Ticket

This approximately 5" by 3 1/2" horizontally oriented card was sent out to Los Angeles Kings season ticket holders as a seasonal greeting from the Kings and Upper Deck in December 1994. The front of the card carried a yuletide message over a ghosted image of Wayne Gretzky. The back had another message, a color photo of Gretzky, and the individual serial number out of 45,000.

NNO Los Angeles Kings Season Ticket Holders Wayne Gretzky 10.00 25.00

1998-99 Kings LA Times Coins

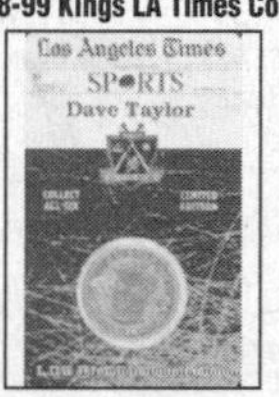

Coins were given out at one coin per game for six games.

COMPLETE SET (6) 12.00 30.00
1 Rob Blake .75 2.00
2 Marcel Dionne 4.00 10.00
3 Larry Robinson 2.50 6.00
4 Luc Robitaille 4.00 10.00
5 Dave Taylor .75 2.00
6 Rogie Vachon 1.50 4.00

1999 Kings AAA Magnets

These magnets were issued as promotional giveaways and were sponsored by AAA.

COMPLETE SET (2) 1.50 4.00
1 Luc Robitaille 1.25 3.00
2 Ziggy Palffy .75 2.00

2002-03 Kings Game Sheets

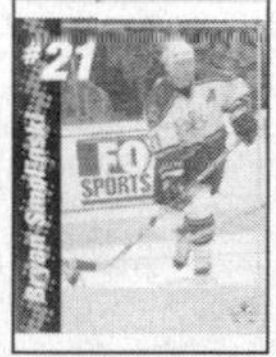

These 8 X 10 player sheets were apparently given away at home games during the 02-03 season. The fronts carried a player image, name and jersey number. The back of the sheets carried lineups for the Kings and their opponents for that particular game along with the sponsor's logo. Please note that several players have more than one card with differing backs.

COMPLETE SET (40) 30.00 75.00
1 Bryan Smolinski Wetzel's Pretzels 1.00 2.50
2 Bryan Smolinski Wilshire Grand 1.00 2.50
3 Dmitry Yushkevich Wetzel's Pretzels 1.00 2.50
4 Dmitry Yushkevich Wilshire Grand 1.00 2.50
5 Craig Johnson Wetzel's Pretzels 1.00 2.50
6 Craig Johnson Wilshire Grand 1.00 2.50
7 Jaroslav Modry Wetzel's Pretzels 1.00 2.50
8 Jaroslav Modry Wilshire Grand 1.00 2.50
9 Eric Belanger Wetzel's Pretzels 1.00 2.50
10 Eric Belanger Wilshire Grand 1.00 2.50
11 Erik Rasmussen Wetzel's Pretzels 1.00 2.50
12 Erik Rasmussen Wilshire Grand 1.00 2.50
13 Ian Laperriere Wetzel's Pretzels 1.00 2.50
14 Ian Laperriere Wilshire Grand 1.00 2.50
15 Felix Potvin Wetzel's Pretzels 2.00 5.00
16 Felix Potvin Wilshire Grand 2.00 5.00
17 Brad Chartrand Wetzel's Pretzels 1.00 2.50
18 Brad Chartrand Wilshire Grand 1.00 2.50
19 Mathieu Schneider Wetzel's Pretzels 1.00 2.50
20 Mathieu Schneider Wilshire Grand 1.00 2.50
21 Mikko Eloranta Wetzel's Pretzels 1.00 2.50
22 Mikko Eloranta Wilshire Grand 1.00 2.50
23 Jason Allison Wetzel's Pretzels 1.25 3.00
24 Jason Allison Wilshire Grand 1.25 3.00
25 Mattias Norstrom Wetzel's Pretzels 1.00 2.50
26 Mattias Norstrom Wilshire Grand 1.00 2.50
27 Jamie Storr Wetzel's Pretzels 1.00 2.50
28 Jamie Storr Wilshire Grand 1.00 2.50
29 Lubomir Visnovsky Wetzel's Pretzels 1.00 2.50
30 Lubomir Visnovsky Wilshire Grand 1.00 2.50
31 Aaron Miller Wetzel's Pretzels 1.00 2.50
32 Aaron Miller Wilshire Grand 1.00 2.50
33 Alexander Frolov Wetzel's Pretzels 1.50 4.00
34 Alexander Frolov Wilshire Grand 1.50 4.00
35 Zigmund Palffy Wetzel's Pretzels 1.50 4.00
36 Zigmund Palffy Wilshire Grand 1.50 4.00
37 Adam Deadmarsh Wetzel's Pretzels 1.00 2.50
38 Adam Deadmarsh Wilshire Grand 1.00 2.50
39 Derek Armstrong Wetzel's Pretzels 1.00 2.50
40 Derek Armstrong Wilshire Grand 1.00 2.50

2005-06 Kings Team Issue

COMPLETE SET (15) 5.00 10.00
1 Header Card .02 .10
2 Luc Robitaille .75 2.00
3 Jeremy Roenick .75 2.00
4 Derek Armstrong .20 .50
5 Craig Conroy .20 .50
6 Alexander Frolov .40 1.00
7 Mathieu Garon .40 1.00
8 Joe Corvo .20 .50
9 Lubomir Visnovsky .20 .50
10 Aaron Miller .20 .50
11 Mattias Norstrom .20 .50
12 Eric Belanger .20 .50
13 Dustin Brown .40 1.00
14 Michael Cammalleri .40 1.00
15 Pavol Demitra .20 .50

1994 Kollectorfest

This five-card standard-size set was issued in conjunction with a collectibles show on October 9, 1994 in Kitchener, Ontario. The three players in this set were all Kitchener natives and donated their time for this show. Reportedly only 3,000 sets were produced, and each set had its own serial number on a title card. The fronts featured black-and-white posed player photos with team color-coded borders and the player's name on the bottom. The players' uniforms had been colorized. The backs carried player profiles. The cards were unnumbered and checklisted below in alphabetical order.

COMPLETE SET (5) 4.00 10.00
1 Woody Dumart 1.25 3.00
2 Dutch Hiller .75 2.00
3 Milt Schmidt 2.00 5.00
4 Title Card Kollectorfest '94 .20 .50
5 Title Card Oktoberfest 1994 .20 .50

1986-87 Kraft Drawings

The 1986-87 Kraft Hockey Drawings set contained 81 standard-size unnumbered cards featuring players from Canadian-based NHL teams. The fronts featured black and white drawings of the players in action, along with each player's team logo. Each back showed the entire checklist for the set. Noted sports artists Jerry Hersh and Carlton McDiarmid drew 42 and 30, respectively, of the 81 cards in the set. The cards were unnumbered and so they are presented below in alphabetical order. Prints of these cards were available through an offer detailed on the card backs. These tended to sell in the two to five times the values listed below. Dealers have reported the existence of a John Kordic print, which apparently was not released to the public. This print sells for $5-$10. An album for the cards was also offered. The set featured early cards of Wendel Clark, Stephane Richer, Patrick Roy, and Mike Vernon.

COMPLETE SET (81) 36.00 90.00
COMPLETE FACT.SET (81) 50.00 125.00
1 Glenn Anderson .40 1.00
2 Brent Ashton .20 .50
3 Laurie Boschman .20 .50
4 Richard Brodeur .30 .75
5 Guy Carbonneau .30 .75
6 Randy Carlyle .30 .75
7 Chris Chelios 1.25 3.00
8 Wendel Clark 3.00 8.00
9 Glen Cochrane .20 .50
10 Paul Coffey 1.25 3.00
11 Alain Cote .20 .50
12 Russ Courtnall .40 1.00
13 Kjell Dahlin .20 .50
14 Dan Daoust .20 .50
15 Bill Derlago .20 .50
16 Tom Fergus .20 .50
17 Grant Fuhr .75 2.00
18 Bob Gainey .40 1.00
19 Gaston Gingras .20 .50
20 Mario Gosselin .30 .75
21 Michel Goulet .40 1.00
22 Rick Green .20 .50
23 Wayne Gretzky 15.00 40.00
24 Doug Halward .20 .50
25 Dale Hawerchuk .60 1.50
26 Brian Hayward .30 .75
27 Dale Hunter .40 1.00
28 Mike Krushelnyski .20 .50
29 Jari Kurri 1.00 2.50
30 Mike Lalor .20 .50
31 Gary Leeman .20 .50
32 Rejean Lemelin .40 1.00
33 Claude Lemieux 2.00 5.00
34 Doug Lidster .20 .50
35 Hakan Loob .30 .75
36 Kevin Lowe .30 .75
37 Craig Ludwig .20 .50
38 Paul MacLean .20 .50
39 Clint Malarchuk .30 .75
40 Mario Marois .20 .50
41 Lanny McDonald .40 1.00
42 Mike McPhee .30 .75
43 Mark Messier 3.00 8.00
44 Randy Moller .20 .50
45 Sergio Momesso .20 .50
46 Andy Moog .75 2.00
47 Brian Mullen .20 .50
48 Joe Mullen .40 1.00
49 Mark Napier .20 .50
50 Mats Naslund .40 1.00
51 Chris Nilan .30 .75
52 Barry Pederson .30 .75
53 Steve Penney .30 .75
54 Jim Peplinski .20 .50
55 Brent Peterson .20 .50
56 Pat Price .20 .50
57 Paul Reinhart .20 .50
58 Stephane Richer .60 1.50
59 Doug Risebrough .20 .50
60 Larry Robinson .40 1.00
61 Patrick Roy 15.00 40.00
62 Borje Salming .40 1.00
63 Petri Skriko .20 .50
64 Brian Skrudland .30 .75
65 Bobby Smith .30 .75
66 Stan Smyl UER (Misspelled Syml on card front) .30 .75
67 Anton Stastny .20 .50
68 Peter Stastny .40 1.00
69 Thomas Steen .30 .75
70 Patrik Sundstrom .20 .50
71 Gary Suter .40 1.00
72 Petr Svoboda .30 .75
73 Tony Tanti .20 .50
74 Greg Terrion .20 .50
75 Steve Thomas .40 1.00
76 Perry Turnbull .20 .50
77 Rick Vaive .30 .75
78 Mike Vernon 1.25 3.00
79 Ryan Walter .20 .50
80 Carey Wilson .20 .50
81 Ken Wregget .60 1.50
x Album 10.00 25.00

1989-90 Kraft

This set of 64 standard-size cards featuring players from Canadian-based NHL teams was available on the package backs of specially marked boxes of Kraft Dinner, Spirals, and Egg Noodles. Also specially marked boxes of Jell-O Puddings and Pie Fillings and Kraft Singles featured additional NHL hockey cards. Each card featured a color action photo of the player, with his name, number and team logo in different color strips running across the bottom of the picture. Kraft also issued a special album to house the cards. The cards were distributed in a variety of ways. There were 26 different Kraft boxes each with two cards on the package back. A sheet of six All-Star cards was packed in each unopened case of Kraft Dinners. Sticker sheets were found in specially marked 500g packages of Kraft Singles. Cards could also be obtained in exchange for UPCs and a small handling fee. The set numbering is listed below according to the company's checklist.

COMPLETE SET (64) 36.00 90.00
COMPLETE FACT.SET (64) 50.00 125.00
1 Doug Gilmour .75 2.00
2 Theo Fleury 2.00 5.00
3 Al MacInnis .40 1.00
4 Sergei Makarov .30 .75
5 Joe Nieuwendyk .40 1.00
6 Joel Otto .20 .50
7 Colin Patterson .20 .50
8 Sergei Priakin .20 .50
9 Paul Ranheim .20 .50
10 Glenn Anderson .40 1.00
11 Grant Fuhr .40 1.00
12 Charlie Huddy .20 .50
13 Jari Kurri .75 2.00
14 Kevin Lowe .30 .75
15 Mark Messier 1.25 3.00
16 Craig Simpson .20 .50
17 Steve Smith .20 .50
18 Esa Tikkanen .40 1.00
19 Guy Carbonneau .30 .75
20 Chris Chelios .75 2.00
21 Shayne Corson .30 .75
22 Russ Courtnall .40 1.00
23 Mats Naslund .30 .75
24 Stephane Richer .30 .75
25 Patrick Roy 3.00 8.00
26 Bobby Smith .30 .75
27 Petr Svoboda .20 .50
28 Jeff Brown .20 .50
29 Paul Gillis .20 .50
30 Michel Goulet .30 .75
31 Guy Lafleur .75 2.00
32 Joe Sakic 2.00 5.00
33 Peter Stastny .30 .75
34 Wendel Clark .40 1.00
35 Vincent Damphousse .40 1.00
36 Gary Leeman .20 .50
37 Daniel Marois .20 .50
38 Ed Olczyk .20 .50
39 Rob Ramage .20 .50
40 Vladimir Krutov .20 .50
41 Igor Larionov .40 1.00
42 Trevor Linden .40 1.00
43 Kirk McLean .40 1.00
44 Paul Reinhart .20 .50
45 Tony Tanti .20 .50
46 Brent Ashton .20 .50
47 Randy Carlyle .20 .50
48 Randy Cunneyworth .20 .50
49 Dave Ellett .20 .50
50 Dale Hawerchuk .40 1.00
51 Fredrik Olausson .20 .50
52 Ray Bourque AS .75 2.00
53 Sean Burke AS .40 1.00
54 Paul Coffey AS .75 2.00
55 Mario Lemieux AS 3.00 8.00
56 Cam Neely AS .75 2.00
57 Rick Tocchet AS .40 1.00
58 Steve Duchesne AS .20 .50
59 Wayne Gretzky AS 4.00 10.00
60 Joe Mullen AS .40 1.00
61 Gary Suter AS .20 .50
62 Mike Vernon AS .40 1.00
63 Steve Yzerman AS 2.00 5.00
64 Checklist Card .20 .50
xx Album 10.00 25.00

1989-90 Kraft All-Stars Stickers

Distributed by Kraft General Foods Canada in packages of Kraft Singles, these six bilingual sticker-sheets measured approximately 4 1/2" by 2 3/4" and each featured stickers of two players in their NHL All-Star uniforms and four NHL team logo stickers. The sheets were white, with color player action shots and color team logos on the peel-away stickers. The white back of each sticker-sheet carried a bilingual order form for the Kraft NHL Hockey sticker/card album. The stickers were numbered on the front.

COMPLETE SET (6) 8.00 20.00
1 Mike McPhee and Paul Reinhart .40 1.00
2 Wayne Gretzky and Rick Tocchet 5.00 12.00
3 Paul Coffey and Steve Yzerman 2.50 6.00
4 Mike Vernon and Ray Bourque 1.25 3.00
5 Jari Kurri and Mario Lemieux 3.00 8.00
6 Kevin Lowe and Sean Burke .40 1.00

1990-91 Kraft

This 115-card standard-size set was issued by Kraft to honor some of the stars of the NHL. There was also a special album, which included advertisements for various Kraft products, issued to store all the cards. The set was divided into three parts: Cards 1-64 were NHL star players listed alphabetically while 65-91 were the Conference All-Stars (Campbell 65-78 and Wales 79-91). Card numbers 92-115 were team photos along with three unnumbered team checklist cards. To complete the set, the consumer had to purchase items from eight different Kraft product groups. Only card number 66 (Wayne Gretzky) was available in two different product groups: Jell-O Instant Pudding (four servings) and Jell-O Lemon Pie Filling (tri-portion).

COMPLETE SET (115) 50.00 125.00
COMPLETE FACT.SET (115) 56.00 140.00
1 Dave Babych .20 .50
2 Brian Bellows .30 .75
3 Ray Bourque .60 1.50
4 Sean Burke .40 1.00
5 Jimmy Carson .20 .50
6 Chris Chelios .60 1.50
7 Dino Ciccarelli .30 .75
8 Paul Coffey .60 1.50
9 Geoff Courtnall .30 .75
10 Doug Crossman .20 .50
11 Kevin Dineen .20 .50
12 Pat Elynuik .20 .50
13 Ron Francis .40 1.00
14 Gerard Gallant .20 .50
15 Wayne Gretzky 4.00 10.00
16 Dale Hawerchuk .40 1.00
17 Ron Hextall .40 1.00
18 Phil Housley .30 .75
19 Mark Howe .30 .75
20 Brett Hull .75 2.00
21 Al Iafrate .25 .60
22 Guy Lafleur .60 1.50
23 Pat LaFontaine .40 1.00
24 Rod Langway .20 .50
25 Igor Larionov .40 1.00
26 Steve Larmer .30 .75
27 Gary Leeman .20 .50
28 Brian Leetch .60 1.50
29 Mario Lemieux 3.00 8.00
30 Trevor Linden .40 1.00
31 Mike Liut .25 .60
32 Mark Messier .75 2.00
33 Al MacInnis .30 .75
34 Mike Modano .75 2.00
35 Andy Moog .40 1.00
36 Joe Mullen .30 .75
37 Kirk Muller .30 .75
38 Petr Nedved .50 1.25
39 Cam Neely .60 1.50
40 Bernie Nicholls .30 .75
41 Joe Nieuwendyk .30 .75
42 Mats Sundin .60 1.50
43 Daren Puppa .20 .50
44 Rob Ramage .20 .50
45 Bill Ranford .40 1.00
46 Stephane Richer .30 .75
47 Larry Robinson .30 .75
48 Luc Robitaille .40 1.00
49 Patrick Roy 3.00 8.00
50 Joe Sakic 1.25 3.00
51 Denis Savard .40 1.00
52 Craig Simpson .20 .50
53 Bobby Smith .25 .60
54 Peter Stastny .40 1.00
55 Thomas Steen .20 .50
56 Scott Stevens .30 .75
57 Brent Sutter .20 .50
58 Rick Tocchet .40 1.00
59 Pierre Turgeon .40 1.00
60 John Vanbiesbrouck .60 1.50
61 Mike Vernon .40 1.00
62 Doug Wilson .20 .50
63 Steve Yzerman 2.00 5.00
64 Checklist Card .20 .50
65 Steve Duchesne AS .20 .50
66 Wayne Gretzky AS 2.50 6.00
67 Brett Hull AS .50 1.25
68 Jari Kurri AS .40 1.00
69 Mike Gartner AS .30 .75
70 Kirk McLean AS .30 .75
71 Mark Messier AS .50 1.25
72 Joe Mullen AS .25 .60
73 Bernie Nicholls AS .25 .60
74 Joe Nieuwendyk AS .30 .75
75 Luc Robitaille AS .30 .75
76 Mike Vernon AS .30 .75
77 Doug Wilson AS .20 .50
78 Steve Yzerman AS 1.25 3.00
79 Joe Sakic AS .75 2.00
80 Ray Bourque AS .50 1.25
81 Chris Chelios AS .50 1.25
82 Paul Coffey AS .50 1.25
83 Ron Francis AS .40 1.00
84 Cam Neely AS .40 1.00
85 Phil Housley AS .25 .60
86 Pat LaFontaine AS .40 1.00
87 Mario Lemieux AS 2.00 5.00
88 Kirk Muller AS .25 .60
89 Stephane Richer AS .25 .60
90 Patrick Roy AS 2.00 5.00
91 Pierre Turgeon AS .40 1.00
92 Boston Bruins .25 .60
93 Buffalo Sabres .20 .50
94 Calgary Flames .20 .50
95 Chicago Blackhawks .25 .60
96 Detroit Red Wings .25 .60
97 Edmonton Oilers .20 .50
98 Hartford Whalers .20 .50
99 Los Angeles Kings .25 .60
100 Minnesota North Stars .20 .50
101 Montreal Canadiens .25 .60
102 New Jersey Devils .20 .50
103 New York Islanders .20 .50
104 New York Rangers .25 .60
105 Philadelphia Flyers .20 .50
106 Pittsburgh Penguins .20 .50
107 Quebec Nordiques .20 .50
108 St. Louis Blues .25 .60
109 Toronto Maple Leafs .25 .60
110 Vancouver Canucks .20 .50
111 Washington Capitals .20 .50
112 Winnipeg Jets .20 .50
113 Unnumbered Checklist .08 .25
114 Unnumbered Checklist .08 .25
115 Unnumbered Checklist .08 .25
xx Album 10.00 25.00

1991-92 Kraft

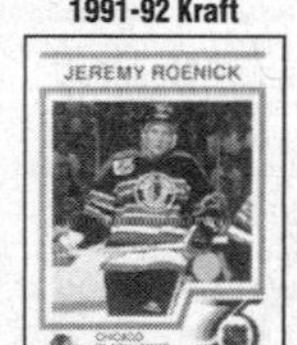

This set of 92 collectibles was sponsored by Kraft-General Foods Canada to commemorate the 75th anniversary of the NHL. It consisted of 68 standard-size cards and 24 discs. To store the set, a 75th Anniversary NHL hockey card album could be purchased. Kraft also provided the opportunity for the collector to purchase any combination of ten cards or discs through the mail to complete the set. Cards 1-40 were issued in Kraft Dinners, cards 41-56 in Kraft Spirals, and cards 57-64 in Kraft Noodles. An eight-card subset highlights "Great Moments" in NHL history. The fronts featured action player photos framed inside a team color border. The player's name was printed in black lettering across the top while the team name, team logo, and 75th NHL Anniversary logo appeared below the picture. The horizontally oriented backs were light gray with red print and carry biography, career statistics, and logos. Measuring 2 3/4" in diameter, the discs (65-88) were available under the caps of Kraft Peanut Butter. They featured action cut-out photos of two players (superimposed on a blue background), pairing today's All-Stars with legends of the past. Players' names and their teams appeared in a white semi-circular margin. The bilingual disc backs were bright yellow with black print and carried biographical and statistical information. Both discs and cards were numbered on the back.

COMPLETE SET (92) 40.00 100.00
COMPLETE FACT.SET (92) 50.00 125.00
1 Mario Lemieux 3.00 8.00
2 Mark Recchi .40 1.00
3 Jaromir Jagr 3.00 8.00
4 Mats Sundin .75 2.00
5 Adam Oates .60 1.50
6 Great Moments Canadien Dynasty Maurice Richard Jacques Plante .60 1.50
7 Brendan Shanahan 1.50 4.00
8 Pat Falloon .20 .50
9 Grant Fuhr .40 1.00
10 Gary Leeman .20 .50
11 Petr Nedved .50 1.25
12 Kirk Muller .30 .75
13 Theo Fleury .75 2.00
14 Dino Ciccarelli .25 .60
15 Geoff Courtnall .20 .50
16 Mark Messier 1.00 2.50
17 Ken Hodge Jr. .20 .50
18 Chris Chelios .75 2.00
19 Mike Vernon .30 .75
20 Kevin Hatcher .25 .60
21 Stephane Richer .20 .50
22 Mark Tinordi .20 .50
23 Pat Verbeek .25 .60
24 John Cullen .20 .50
25 Pat LaFontaine .40 1.00
26 Stephan Lebeau .20 .50
27 Mike Gartner .30 .75
28 Great Moments Last Leaf Dynasty Bobby Baun .30 .75
29 Shayne Corson .25 .60
30 Trevor Linden .40 1.00
31 Craig Janney .25 .60
32 Al MacInnis .30 .75
33 Phil Housley .25 .60
34 Doug Wilson .20 .50
35 Tony Granato .20 .50
36 Dale Hawerchuk .30 .75
37 Bill Durnan Turk Broda .75 2.00
38 Brian Bellows .20 .50
39 Great Moments Number 23 with number 23 Bob Gainey .30 .75
40 Great Moments A Night to Remember Darryl Sittler .30 .75
41 Joe Sakic 1.50 4.00
42 Wendel Clark .40 1.00
43 Brent Sutter .20 .50
44 Bill Ranford .30 .75
45 Rick Tocchet .25 .60
46 Paul Ysebaert .20 .50
47 Adam Creighton .20 .50
48 Mike Modano .75 2.00
49 Russ Courtnall .20 .50
50 Great Moments Evolution of Stanley Cup Syl Apps .20 .50
51 Sergei Fedorov 1.25 3.00
52 Mike Ricci .25 .60
53 Scott Stevens .25 .60
54 Great Moments The Ultimate Expansion Bobby Clarke .40 1.00
55 Owen Nolan .30 .75
56 Jeremy Roenick .60 1.50
57 Ray Bourque .75 2.00
58 Gerard Gallant .20 .50
59 Andy Moog .40 1.00
60 Alexander Mogilny .50 1.25
61 Great Moments Islander Tradition Denis Potvin .20 .50
62 Ed Olczyk .20 .50
63 Tomas Sandstrom .20 .50
64 Checklist .20 .50
65 Wayne Gretzky Maurice Richard 4.00 10.00
66 Brett Hull Guy Lafleur .75 2.00
67 Jari Kurri Bobby Clarke .40 1.00
68 Steve Yzerman Jean Beliveau 2.00 5.00
69 Steve Larmer Pat Stapleton .30 .75
70 Luc Robitaille Ted Lindsay .60 1.50
71 Larry Murphy Doug Harvey .40 1.00
72 Denis Potvin Gary Suter .30 .75
73 Brian Leetch Harry Howell .75 2.00
74 Paul Coffey Bill Gadsby .75 2.00
75 Jon Casey Terry Sawchuk .60 1.50
76 Patrick Roy Jacques Plante 3.00 8.00
77 Denis Savard Serge Savard .40 1.00
78 Doug Gilmour Bob Baun .60 1.50
79 Guy Carbonneau Yvan Cournoyer .30 .75
80 Gilbert Perreault Larry Robinson .40 1.00
81 Red Kelly Craig Simpson .30 .75
82 Bobby Smith Rod Gilbert .30 .75
83 Syl Apps Peter Stastny .30 .75
84 BoomBoom Geoffrion Vincent Damphousse .60 1.50
85 Marcel Dionne Steve Smith .30 .75
86 Tim Horton Kevin Dineen .75 2.00
87 Michel Goulet Frank Mahovlich .40 1.00
88 Mike Richter Henri Richard .60 1.50
89 Boston Bruins logo New York Rangers logo Original Six (Unnumbered) .20 .50
90 Montreal Canadiens logo Toronto Maple Leafs logo Original Six (Unnumbered) .20 .50
91 Chicago Blackhawks logo Detroit Red Wings logo Original Six (Unnumbered) .20 .50
92 Stanley Cup (Unnumbered) .40 1.00
xx Album 10.00 25.00

1992-93 Kraft

This set of 48 collectibles was sponsored by Kraft General Foods Canada to commemorate the 100th anniversary of the Stanley Cup. It consisted of 24 team cards, 12 discs, and 12 All-Star cards. To store the set, a Stanley Cup 100th anniversary album could be purchased by sending in three UPC symbols from Kraft Dinner, one UPC symbol from both Kraft Peanut Butter and Kraft Singles, and 12.99 along with sales tax and shipping and handling charges. The album included special storage sheets for the cards, the history of the Stanley Cup, and team autographs. The team cards, which measured approximately 5 3/16" by 3 7/16" and were distributed on the back of Kraft Dinner boxes, showed players in their centennial uniforms. The team name and logo appeared in a team color-coded stripe at the bottom. The backs were plain cardboard with the team history in red print. The discs, which measure approximately 2 3/4" in diameter and were distributed under the lids of Kraft Peanut Butter jars, are double-sided and feature 24 NHL goaltenders. The goalies are shown in action in a three-quarter-moon shaped picture against a team color-coded background. Statistics are included on the disc. The 12 All-Star cards, which measured approximately 1 3/4" by 2 1/2" and were distributed in groups of four in packages of Kraft Singles, carry color action player photos with white borders. A facsimile autograph was near the bottom of the picture. The player's name was printed in the wider bottom border between sponsor logos. The backs were white and included biographical information, statistics, and career highlights. Collectors who did not complete the series by purchasing the products could obtain any combination of eight cards or discs by sending the same UPC symbols, 3.00, plus shipping and handling charges. The cards were unnumbered and checklisted below in alphabetical order within each subset. The factory set price includes the album.

COMPLETE SET (48) 28.00 70.00
COMPLETE FACT.SET (48) 34.00 85.00
1 Boston Bruins .60 1.50
2 Buffalo Sabres .40 1.00
3 Calgary Flames .40 1.00
4 Chicago Blackhawks .60 1.50
5 Detroit Red Wings .60 1.50
6 Edmonton Oilers .40 1.00
7 Hartford Whalers .40 1.00
8 Los Angeles Kings .60 1.50
9 Minnesota North Stars .40 1.00
10 Montreal Canadiens .60 1.50
11 New Jersey Devils .40 1.00
12 New York Islanders .40 1.00
13 New York Rangers .60 1.50
14 Ottawa Senators .40 1.00
15 Philadelphia Flyers .40 1.00
16 Pittsburgh Penguins .60 1.50
17 Quebec Nordiques .40 1.00
18 San Jose Sharks .40 1.00
19 St. Louis Blues .40 1.00
20 Tampa Bay Lightning .40 1.00
21 Toronto Maple Leafs .60 1.50
22 Vancouver Canucks .40 1.00
23 Washington Capitals .40 1.00
24 Winnipeg Jets .40 1.00
25 Tom Barrasso Wendell Young .40 1.00
26 Don Beaupre Bob Essensa .40 1.00
27 Jon Casey Dominic Roussel .40 1.00
28 Tim Cheveldae Sean Burke .40 1.00
29 Jeff Hackett Kirk McLean .60 1.50
30 Dominik Hasek Chris Terreri 1.25 3.00
31 Ron Hextall Curtis Joseph .75 2.00
32 Andy Moog Mark Fitzpatrick .60 1.50
33 Bill Ranford Kelly Hrudey .60 1.50
34 Patrick Roy John Vanbiesbrouck 4.00 10.00
35 Peter Sidorkiewicz Grant Fuhr .60 1.50
36 Mike Vernon Ed Belfour .75 2.00
37 Ray Bourque AS .60 1.50
38 Chris Chelios AS .60 1.50
39 Paul Coffey AS .60 1.50
40 Wayne Gretzky AS 3.00 8.00
41 Brett Hull AS .75 2.00
42 Jaromir Jagr AS 1.50 4.00
43 Mario Lemieux AS 2.00 5.00
44 Trevor Linden AS .30 .75
45 Mark Messier AS .75 2.00
46 Jeremy Roenick AS .60 1.50
47 Patrick Roy AS 2.00 5.00
48 Steve Yzerman AS 1.25 3.00
xx Album 6.00 15.00

1993-94 Kraft

This set of 72 collectibles was sponsored by Kraft General Foods Canada. It consisted of 26 team cards (1-26), 23 discs (27-49), 17 cut-outs (50-66), three Rookie cards (67-69), and three Trophy Winner cards (70-72). The album was available for purchase and contained special storage sheets for all the collectibles. It was organized by team and also included information (both in French and English) and a picture of the teams' stadiums. The team cards measured approximately 3 1/2" by 5 1/8" and were distributed on the back of Kraft Dinner boxes. The fronts showed a color action player photo with the player's name and number, and the team logo printed in a team color-coded stripe at the bottom. The backs had a ghosted light red team logo with biography (both in French and English) and statistics printed over the team logo. The discs, which measured approximately 3 3/4" in diameter and were distributed under the lids of Kraft Peanut Butter Jars, featured NHL captains and coaches. The captains' cards are double-sided and featured a blue border, while the double-sided coaches' cards had a gray border around the photo. The cut-outs, which were distributed in Jell-O boxes, featured color action poses. Also distributed in Kraft dinner boxes, the Rookie and Trophy Winner cards measured the same size as the team cards. The Trophy Winner cards showed the players with their respective trophies. The cards were unnumbered and checklisted below in alphabetical order within each subset. The factory set price includes the album.

COMPLETE SET (72) 40.00 100.00
COMPLETE FACT.SET (72) 50.00 125.00
1 Ed Belfour .60 1.50
2 Brian Bradley .20 .50
3 Pavel Bure .75 2.00
4 Paul Coffey .40 1.00
5 Russ Courtnall .20 .50
6 Alexandre Daigle .30 .75
7 Pat Falloon .20 .50
8 Theo Fleury .40 1.00
9 Doug Gilmour .40 1.00
10 Adam Graves .30 .75
11 Stu Grimson .20 .50
12 Al Iafrate .20 .50
13 Jaromir Jagr 1.25 3.00
14 Joe Juneau .30 .75
15 Eric Lindros 1.25 3.00
16 Alexander Mogilny .60 1.50
17 Kirk Muller .20 .50
18 Bill Ranford .30 .75
19 Mike Ricci .20 .50
20 Luc Robitaille .40 1.00
21 Geoff Sanderson .25 .60
22 Teemu Selanne 1.00 2.50
23 Brendan Shanahan 1.00 2.50
24 Pierre Turgeon .40 1.00
25 John Vanbiesbrouck .75 2.00
26 Valeri Zelepukin .20 .50
27 Al Arbour CO .75 2.00
28 Bob Berry CO .75 2.00
29 Ray Bourque 1.25 3.00
Patrick Flatley
30 Scott Bowman CO 1.25 3.00
31 Pat Burns CO .75 2.00
32 Jacques Demers CO .75 2.00
33 Kevin Dineen .75 2.00
Kevin Hatcher
34 Wayne Gretzky 3.00 8.00
Wendel Clark
35 Brett Hull 1.25 3.00
Brad Shaw
36 Eddie Johnston CO .75 2.00
37 Dean Kennedy .75 2.00
Denis Savard
38 Dave King CO .75 2.00
39 Pat LaFontaine 1.00 2.50
Pat Verbeek
40 Mike Lalor .75 2.00
Mark Tinordi
41 Trevor Linden .50 1.25
Troy Loney
42 Barry Melrose CO .75 2.00
43 Mark Messier 3.00 8.00
Mario Lemieux
44 John Muckler CO .75 2.00
45 Joe Nieuwendyk 1.00 2.50
Joe Sakic
46 Pierre Page CO .75 2.00
47 Jeremy Roenick 1.25 3.00
Guy Carbonneau
48 Brian Skrudland .75 2.00
Craig MacTavish
49 Scott Stevens 1.50 4.00
Steve Yzerman
50 Tom Barrasso .20 .50
51 Pavel Bure .75 2.00
52 Stephane Fiset .30 .75
53 Doug Gilmour .40 1.00
54 Wayne Gretzky 2.50 6.00
55 Kelly Hrudey .20 .50
56 Mario Lemieux 1.50 4.00
57 Eric Lindros 1.25 3.00
58 Kirk McLean .20 .50
59 Kirk Muller .20 .50
60 Joe Nieuwendyk .20 .50
61 Felix Potvin .40 1.00
63 Dominic Roussel .20 .50
64 Patrick Roy 1.50 4.00
65 Joe Sakic 1.00 2.50
66 Mike Vernon .20 .50
67 Jason Arnott .40 1.00
68 Rob Niedermayer .60 1.50
69 Chris Pronger .30 .75
70 Chris Chelios .30 .75
71 Mario Lemieux 1.50 4.00
72 Patrick Roy 1.50 4.00
xx Album 10.00 25.00

1993-94 Kraft Recipes

Packaged in a folding cardboard cover, this set of recipe cards featured one card for each of the Canadian NHL teams. Each card featured a favorite recipe of a Canadian hockey star. The cards measured approximately 4 3/4" by 4 3/4" and consised of two pages bound by a perforated hinge. The front page displayed a color picture of the prepared food item, while its inside presented the recipe. On the page opposite the recipe appeared a color action player photo with a white-and-red inner border and a ice-blue outer border. The back page carried in its center a color panel displaying biography, statistics, and career summary; the wide surrounding border was a bright color (blue, green, orange, or red) and carried a player cutout as well as team and league logos. The recipe cards were unnumbered and checklisted below in alphabetical order. A Manufacturer's Rebate Coupon was also included in the package but is not considered part of the card set.

COMPLETE SET (8) 2.00 5.00
1 Vincent Damphousse .30 .75
2 Bob Essensa .20 .50
3 Doug Gilmour .50 1.25
4 Trevor Linden .30 .75
5 Al MacInnis .30 .75
6 Bill Ranford .30 .75
7 Mike Ricci .20 .50
8 Brad Shaw .20 .50

1994-95 Kraft

This set of 72 collectibles was sponsored by Kraft General Foods of Canada. Available from January to March 1995, it consisted of five distinct series: 14 Hockey Heroes cards (1-14), 16 Sharp Shooter cards (15-30), 26 Masked Defender cards (31-56), ten Award Winner discs (57-66), and six All-Star discs (67-72). Back panels of the seven different Jell-O Instant Pudding flavors showcased 14 Hockey Hero Action cards measuring 4 5/8" by 1 1/8". The horizontal fronts featured borderless color action player photos with the player's name, uniform number and team logo in a team color-coded bar alongside the left or right. The horizontal backs carried player biography, stats and sponsor logos, both in English and French. Measuring approximately 2 1/2" by 3 3/4", a pair of Sharp Shooter action cards together with an NHL team logo were inserted in Jell-O Pudding Snacks. The fronts featured borderless color action player photos on computerized backgrounds. The player's name and uniform number appeared in a team color-coded bar alongside the left or right. The backs carried player biography, stats and sponsor logos, both in English and French. Kraft Dinner boxes featured 26 oversized Masked Defenders goalie cards, measuring 3 1/2" by 5", on back panels of boxes. The fronts showed color action player photos on team color-coded backgrounds, with the player's name and uniform number in a team color-coded bar alongside the left or right, along with his nickname in stylized script. The backs carried player biography and stats, both in English and French, along with sponsor logos. Finally, two discs of 1994 Award Winners and the All-Star team were placed under each lid of Kraft Peanut Butter jars. The discs measured 2 3/4" in diameter. The Award Winner fronts had color action player photos with the player's name and uniform number, while the backs showed the trophy on a blue background. The All-Star fronts had color action player photos on a ghosted player background, the backs carried player biography, season and NHL career totals. A collectible album to house all the cards was offered for 21.99. The cards were unnumbered and checklisted below in alphabetical order within each subset.

COMPLETE SET (72) 40.00 100.00
1 Dave Andreychuk .20 .50
2 Chris Chelios .60 1.50
3 Wendel Clark .25 .60
4 Theo Fleury .60 1.50
5 Wayne Gretzky 2.00 5.00
6 Brett Hull .75 2.00
7 Al Iafrate .20 .50
8 Jaromir Jagr 2.00 5.00
9 Kirk Muller .20 .50
10 Pat LaFontaine .30 .75
11 Mark Recchi .30 .75
12 Gary Roberts .20 .50
13 Mats Sundin .60 1.50
14 Steve Yzerman 2.00 5.00
15 Jason Arnott .30 .75
16 Vincent Damphousse .20 .50
17 Doug Gilmour .60 1.50
18 Craig Janney .20 .50
19 Joe Juneau .20 .50
20 Trevor Linden .20 .50
21 Eric Lindros 2.00 5.00
22 Mark Messier .75 2.00
23 Mike Modano .75 2.00
Dallas Star
24 Alexander Mogilny .40 1.00
25 Adam Oates .25 .60
26 Robert Reichel .20 .50
27 Jeremy Roenick .40 1.00
28 Joe Sakic 1.25 3.00
29 Keith Tkachuk .60 1.50
30 Alexei Yashin .50 1.25
31 Tom Barrasso .20 .50
32 Don Beaupre .20 .50
33 Ed Belfour .60 1.50
34 Craig Billington .20 .50
35 Martin Brodeur 1.50 4.00
New Jers
36 Sean Burke .20 .50
37 Tim Cheveldae .20 .50
38 Stephane Fiset .30 .75
39 Dominik Hasek 1.25 3.00
40 Guy Hebert .20 .50
41 Ron Hextall .20 .50
42 Kelly Hrudey .20 .50
43 Arturs Irbe .20 .50
44 Curtis Joseph .75 2.00
45 Trevor Kidd .30 .75
46 Kirk McLean .30 .75
47 Jamie McLennan .20 .50
48 Andy Moog .40 1.00
49 Felix Potvin .60 1.50
50 Daren Puppa .30 .75
51 Bill Ranford .30 .75
52 Mike Richter .60 1.50
53 Vincent Riendeau .20 .50
54 Patrick Roy 3.00 8.00
55 John Vanbiesbrouck .60 1.50
56 Mike Vernon .30 .75
57 Ray Bourque .75 2.00
58 Martin Brodeur 1.50 4.00
New Jers
59 Sergei Fedorov 1.25 3.00
60 Dominik Hasek 1.25 3.00
61 Jacques Lemaire .40 1.00
62 Adam Graves .40 1.00
63 Wayne Gretzky 4.00 10.00
64 Brian Leetch .60 1.50
65 Cam Neely .60 1.50
66 New York Rangers 1.25 3.00
Stanley Cup Winners
67 Ray Bourque .75 2.00
68 Pavel Bure 1.50 4.00
69 Sergei Fedorov 1.25 3.00
70 Dominik Hasek 1.25 3.00
71 Brendan Shanahan 1.25 3.00
72 Scott Stevens .40 1.00
NNO Collector's Album 10.00 25.00

1994-95 Kraft Goalie Masks

Inserted as a chiptopper at a rate of one per Kraft Dinner case, this set featured perforated cardboard masks of eight NHL goalies. Unassembled, the masks measured approximately 14" by 13 1/4". The fronts carried the goalie's mask with a photo of his face, along with his name, team name, and instructions on how to assemble the mask. All text was in French and English. The backs were blank. Additional masks could be ordered by mailing in three UPC's from Kraft dinner cartons plus 3.00 for shipping and handling. The masks were unnumbered and checklisted below in alphabetical order.

COMPLETE SET (8) 8.00 20.00
1 Ed Belfour 1.25 3.00
2 Guy Hebert .60 1.50
3 Curtis Joseph 1.25 3.00
4 Andy Moog .75 2.00
5 Felix Potvin .75 2.00
6 Vincent Riendeau .60 1.50
7 Patrick Roy 3.00 8.00
8 John Vanbiesbrouck .75 2.00

1995-96 Kraft

This 79-card set continued the fine tradition of Kraft hockey series. The cards were issued in several sizes and over several Kraft products. The Hottest Ticket were issued with Jell-O Pudding, while Crease Keepers were issued with Jell-O gelatin. The first group were standard card size, while the second group of eight were about half-standard size. 12 All-Stars discs were issued with Kraft Peanut Butter, while 26 Star cards were found on the back of Kraft Dinner boxes. The 79th card was a disc picturing Conn Smythe winner Claude Lemieux and honoring the Cup champ NJ Devils. The cards were unnumbered, and so are listed below in the order in which they appeared in the factory version of the set.

COMPLETE SET (79) 40.00 100.00
1 Sergei Fedorov .75 2.00
2 Jason Arnott .20 .50
3 Teemu Selanne .75 2.00
4 Pierre Turgeon .25 .60
5 Joe Juneau .15 .40
6 Scott Stevens .25 .60
7 Cam Neely .20 .50
8 Mario Lemieux 1.50 4.00
9 Wendel Clark .20 .50
10 Alexandre Daigle .15 .40
11 Peter Forsberg 1.00 2.50
12 Trevor Linden .20 .50
13 Phil Housley .15 .40
14 Doug Gilmour .30 .75
15 Sean Burke .25 .60
16 Dominik Hasek .75 2.00
17 Patrick Roy 1.50 4.00
18 Kirk McLean .20 .50
19 Blaine Lacher .15 .40
20 Jim Carey .20 .50
21 Martin Brodeur 1.00 2.50
22 Mike Richter .30 .75
23 Felix Potvin .30 .75
24 Trevor Kidd .20 .50
25 Ed Belfour .30 .75
26 Stephane Fiset .20 .50
27 Ron Hextall .20 .50
28 Grant Fuhr .20 .50
29 Daren Puppa .20 .50
30 Andy Moog .20 .50
31 Mike Vernon .20 .50
32 John Vanbiesbrouck .40 1.00
33 Bill Ranford .25 .60
34 Tommy Soderstrom .20 .50
35 Tom Barrasso .20 .50
36 Kelly Hrudey .20 .50
37 Guy Hebert .25 .60
38 Arturs Irbe .20 .50
39 Tim Cheveldae .20 .50
40 Don Beaupre .20 .50
41 Eric Lindros 1.25 3.00
42 Jaromir Jagr 1.25 3.00
43 Paul Coffey .30 .75
44 Chris Chelios .30 .75
45 Dominik Hasek .75 2.00
46 John LeClair .60 1.50
47 Alexei Zhamnov .15 .40
48 Keith Tkachuk .40 1.00
49 Theo Fleury .30 .75
50 Larry Murphy .15 .40
51 Ray Bourque .75 2.00
52 Ed Belfour .40 1.00
53 Wayne Gretzky 2.00 5.00
54 Adam Oates .25 .60
55 Paul Kariya 1.25 3.00
56 Alexander Mogilny .25 .60
57 Dave Gagner .15 .40
58 Theo Fleury .30 .75
59 Jesse Belanger .15 .40
60 Joe Sakic .75 2.00
61 Peter Bondra .30 .75
62 Andrew Cassels .15 .40
63 Alexandre Daigle .15 .40
64 Paul Coffey .30 .75
65 Ulf Dahlen .15 .40
66 Brett Hull .40 1.00
67 Bernie Nicholls .15 .40
68 Doug Weight .25 .60
69 Brian Bradley .15 .40
70 Mark Messier .50 1.25
71 Stephane Richer .15 .40
72 Eric Lindros 1.25 3.00
73 Mark Recchi .25 .60
74 Ray Ferraro .15 .40
75 Mats Sundin .30 .75
76 Alexei Zhamnov .20 .50
77 Pavel Bure 1.00 2.50
78 Jaromir Jagr 1.25 3.00
79 Claude Lemieux 10.00 25.00
NNO Binder 4.00 10.00

1996-97 Kraft Upper Deck

MVP (1-26) were found on the backs of specially marked boxes of Kraft Dinner regular or specialty flavours. All-Stars (27-32) were found on the backs of Jell-O instant pudding. Team Rivals (33-39) were available through a redemption offer found on specially marked jars of Kraft Peanut Butter. Award Winners (40-59) were found on specially marked 4 cup packs of Jell-O pudding snacks. Mascots (60-64) were found in 85g boxes of Jell-O jelly powder packs. Magnets (65-72) were found one per unopened case of Kraft Dinner. The existence of a Wayne Gretzky magnet has been reported, but not confirmed.

COMPLETE SET (72) 40.00 100.00
1 Brian Leetch .40 1.00
2 Keith Tkachuk .60 1.50
3 Geoff Sanderson .30 .75
4 Owen Nolan .30 .75
5 Saku Koivu .60 1.50
6 Adam Oates .30 .75
7 Mats Sundin .40 1.00
8 Theo Fleury .30 .75
9 Zigmund Palffy .40 1.00
10 Alexei Yashin .30 .75
11 Brett Hull .40 1.00
12 Michal Pivonka .20 .50
13 Joe Nieuwendyk .30 .75
14 Martin Brodeur .75 2.00
15 Ed Belfour .40 1.00
16 Guy Hebert .30 .75
17 Patrick Roy 1.50 4.00
18 Dominik Hasek .75 2.00
19 John Vanbiesbrouck .60 1.50
20 Yanic Perreault .20 .50
21 Doug Weight .30 .75
22 Mario Lemieux 1.50 4.00
23 Eric Lindros 1.00 2.50
24 Alexander Mogilny .40 1.00
25 Sergei Fedorov .75 2.00
26 Daren Puppa .30 .75
27 Chris Chelios .40 1.00
28 Mario Lemieux 1.50 4.00
29 Paul Kariya 1.25 3.00
30 Ray Bourque .60 1.50
31 Chris Osgood .40 1.00
32 Jaromir Jagr 1.25 3.00
33 Rob Blake 1.50 4.00
Paul Kariya
Kevin Dineen
Peter Bondra
34 Ray Bourque 1.00 2.50
Adam Graves
Randy Cunneyworth
Pat LaFontaine
35 Al MacInnis 1.00 2.50
Trevor Linden
Kris King
Mike Modano
36 Paul Ysebaert 1.00 2.50
Owen Nolan
Theo Fleury
Kelly Buchberger
37 Vince Damphousse 2.00 5.00
Doug Gilmour
Mario Lemieux
Eric Lindros
38 Ziggy Palffy 1.50 4.00
Scott Stevens
Steve Yzerman
Chris
39 Brian Skrudland 1.50 4.00
Joe Sakic
40 Scott Bowman .40 1.00
41 Marc Crawford CO .30 .75
42 Chris Chelios .30 .75
43 Paul Kariya 1.25 3.00
44 Ron Francis .30 .75
45 Daniel Alfredsson .30 .75
46 Adam Oates .30 .75
47 Joe Sakic .75 2.00
48 Peter Forsberg 1.00 2.50
49 Jarome Iginla .30 .75
50 Jim Carey .30 .75
51 C.Osgood/M.Vernon .40 1.00
52 Mike Richter .40 1.00
53 Jocelyn Thibault .30 .75
54 Mario Lemieux 1.50 4.00
55 Ed Jovanovski .30 .75
56 Mario Lemieux 1.50 4.00
57 J.LeClair/B.Shanahan/J.Jagr 1.25 3.00
58 Eric Lindros 1.00 2.50
59 Sergei Fedorov .75 2.00
60 Teemu Selanne 1.25 3.00
Wild Wing
61 Felix Potvin .40 1.00
Carlton the Bear
62 Marty McSorley .30 .75
S.J. Sharkie
63 Rob Niedermayer .30 .75
Stanley C. Panther
64 Dave Gagner .20 .50
Harvey the Hound
65 Theo Fleury .75 2.00
66 Saku Koivu 1.25 3.00
67 Mario Lemieux 4.00 10.00
68 Eric Lindros 2.00 5.00
69 Alexander Mogilny .60 1.50
70 Mats Sundin 1.00 2.50
71 Doug Weight .60 1.50
72 Alexei Yashin .60 1.50

1997-98 Kraft 3-D World's Best

This eight card set was put out by Pinnacle in conjunction with Kraft. Each card measured 3. 1/4" X4 1/2" and is enhanced with a 3-D background.

COMPLETE SET (8) 2.50 6.00
1 Doug Weight .25 .60
2 Mats Sundin .30 .75
3 Alexei Yashin .25 .60
4 Saku Koivu .30 .75
5 Theo Fleury .30 .75
6 Mark Messier .40 1.00
7 Vincent Damphousse .20 .50
8 Paul Kariya 1.25 3.00

1997-98 Kraft Team Canada

COMPLETE SET (12) 8.00 20.00
1 Ray Bourque .75 2.00
Shayne Corson
2 Martin Brodeur 1.25 3.00
Joe Sakic
3 Marc Crawford .40 1.00
Eric Lindros
4 Eric Desjardins .40 1.00
Adam Foote
5 Theoren Fleury .40 1.00
Al MacInnis
6 Curtis Joseph 2.00 5.00
Patrick Roy
7 Paul Kariya .75 2.00
Rod Brind'Amour
8 Trevor Linden .75 2.00
Keith Primeau
9 Joe Nieuwendyk .40 1.00
Rob Blake
10 Scott Stevens .40 1.00
Rob Zamuner
11 Brendan Shanahan 2.50 6.00
Wayne Gretzky
12 Steve Yzerman 1.25 3.00
Chris Pronger

1998-99 Kraft Dinners Zoomer Stickers

Available only in Kraft Dinner 12-packs, this 5-card set made by Pinnacle featured holographic 'magic motion' technology on smaller 3" X 3" cards.

COMPLETE SET 8.00 20.00
1 Atlanta Thrashers 1.50 4.00
2 Columbus Blue Jackets 1.50 4.00
3 Los Angeles Kings 1.50 4.00
4 Minnesota Wild 1.50 4.00
5 Nashville Predators 1.50 4.00

1998-99 Kraft Fearless Forwards

COMPLETE SET (13) 6.00 15.00
1 Peter Bondra .40 1.00
2 Pavel Bure .75 2.00
3 Vincent Damphousse .40 1.00
4 Jaromir Jagr 1.25 3.00
5 Paul Kariya .75 2.00
6 John Leclair .40 1.00
7 Claude Lemieux .40 1.00
8 Mike Modano .75 2.00
9 Brendan Shanahan .75 2.00
10 Cory Stillman .40 1.00
11 Mats Sundin .75 2.00
12 Doug Weight .40 1.00
13 Alexei Yashin .40 1.00

1998-99 Kraft Peanut Butter

COMPLETE SET (8) 4.00 10.00
1 Rob Blake .75 2.00
Larry Murphy
2 Brian Leetch .75 2.00
Robert Svehla
3 Patrice Brisebois .75 2.00
Scott Niedermayer
4 Vladimir Malakhov .40 1.00
Darryl Sydor
5 Al MacInnis .40 1.00
Alexei Zhitnik
6 Ray Bourque 1.25 3.00
Boris Mironov
7 Mathieu Schneider 1.25 3.00
Nicklas Lidstrom
8 Teppo Numminen .75 2.00
Chris Chelios

1999-00 Kraft Dinner

These oversized cards were issued on the backs of boxes of Kraft Dinner in Canada. Factory versions can also be found which were not cut from boxes. Because they tended to be in better condition, these cards earned a premium of up to 2X.

COMPLETE SET (15) 4.80 12.00
1 Shayne Corson .20 .50
2 Jaromir Jagr .60 1.50
3 Curtis Joseph .40 1.00
4 Paul Kariya .75 2.00
5 Saku Koivu .30 .75
6 Mike Modano .40 1.00
7 Eric Lindros .60 1.50
8 Mattias Ohlund .20 .50
9 Chris Pronger .20 .50
10 Joe Sakic .60 1.50
11 Brendan Shanahan .40 1.00
12 Scott Stevens .20 .50
13 Mats Sundin .30 .75
14 Alexei Yashin .20 .50
15 Steve Yzerman 1.25 3.00

1999-00 Kraft Face Off Rivals

COMPLETE SET (6) 4.00 10.00
1 Mats Sundin .75 2.00
Stu Barnes
2 Theoren Fleury .75 2.00
Joe Nieuwendyk
3 Pierre Turgeon .75 2.00
Guy Carbonneau
4 Yanic Perreault .40 1.00
Curtis Brown
5 Steve Yzerman 1.25 3.00
Claude Lemieux
6 Mike Modano .75 2.00
Mike Eastwood

1999-00 Kraft Peanut Butter

These discs were found under the lids of specially marked jars of Kraft Peanut Butter in Canada.

COMPLETE SET (11) 6.00 15.00
1 Ray Bourque .75 2.00
2 Martin Brodeur .75 2.00
3 Peter Forsberg .75 2.00
4 Dominik Hasek .60 1.50
5 Jaromir Jagr .75 2.00
6 Paul Kariya 1.25 3.00
7 Nicklas Lidstrom .40 1.00
8 Al MacInnis .20 .50
9 Teppo Numminen .20 .50
10 Teemu Selanne .60 1.50
11 Brendan Shanahan .60 1.50

1999-00 Kraft Overtime Winners

COMPLETE SET (6) 2.50 6.00
1 Brett Hull .75 2.00
2 Garry Valk .08 .25
3 Mike Modano .75 2.00
4 Pierre Turgeon .40 1.00
5 Jaromir Jagr 1.25 3.00
6 Milan Hejduk .40 1.00

1999-00 Kraft Stanley Cup Moments

COMPLETE SET (15) 2.00 5.00
1 Mark Messier 1.25 3.00
2 Eric Desjardins .20 .50
3 Brett Hull 1.25 3.00
4 Claude Lemieux .20 .50
5 Michael Peca .20 .50
6 Bill Ranford .40 1.00

1999-00 Kraft Whiz Kid

COMPLETE SET (8) 1.50 4.00
1 Milan Hejduk .40 1.00
2 Marian Hossa .40 1.00
3 Jan Hrdina .08 .25
4 Tomas Kaberle .08 .25
5 Chris Drury .40 1.00
6 Daniil Markov .08 .25
7 Erik Rasmussen .08 .25
8 Brendan Morrison .40 1.00

2000-01 Kraft

This set of 30 standard-size cards had an unusual story: they were not supposed to be issued. Despite Kraft's long history of hockey premiums, the company decided to skip a year to work on another promotion. However, it did contract In The Game to produce this set as a sales incentive for grocery store managers. While these cards were not widely distributed, a small quantity did make its way into the secondary market. The cards featured gray borders surrounding an action photo on the front, with another photo and bio info on the back. Kraft logos appeared on both sides. Each of the cards mimicked the base cards that appeared in 2000-01 Be A Player Memorabilia, except for the cards of Scott Pellerin, which pictured him in his new Minnesota Wild sweater, and Ron Tugnutt, who was pictured with the Columbus Blue Jackets.

COMPLETE SET (30) 40.00 100.00
1 Jaromir Jagr 4.80 12.00
2 Markus Naslund 1.20 3.00
3 Luc Robitaille 1.20 3.00
4 Scott Stevens .40 1.00
5 Mike Modano 2.40 6.00
6 Doug Weight 1.20 3.00
7 Peter Bondra 1.20 3.00
8 Paul Kariya 6.00 15.00
9 Radek Bonk .40 1.00
10 John LeClair 2.40 6.00
11 Sandis Ozolinsh .40 1.00
12 Steve Yzerman 10.00 25.00
13 Joe Thornton 2.40 6.00
14 Valeri Bure .40 1.00
15 Pavel Bure
16 Cliff Ronning .40 1.00
17 Dominik Hasek 2.40 6.00
18 Vincent Lecavalier 1.20 3.00
19 Andrew Brunette .40 1.00
20 Chris Pronger 1.20 3.00
21 Owen Nolan 1.20 3.00
22 Joe Sakic 4.00 10.00
23 Jeremy Roenick 2.40 6.00
24 Tony Amonte 2.00 5.00
25 Mariusz Czerkawski .40 1.00
26 Trevor Linden .40 1.00
27 Mats Sundin 1.20 3.00
28 Mark Messier
29 Ron Tugnutt 2.00 5.00
30 Scott Pellerin 2.00 5.00

2003-04 Kraft

These cards were issued on the backs of Kraft Dinner boxes in Canada in mid-winter, 2003/04. They are condition-sensitive as they had to be cut from the box backs.

COMPLETE SET (10) 8.00 15.00
1 Ed Belfour 1.25 3.00
2 Anson Carter .40 1.00
3 Paul Kariya .75 2.00
4 Trevor Linden .40 1.00
5 Vincent Lecavalier .75 2.00
6 Al MacInnis .40 1.00
7 Mike Ribeiro .40 1.00
8 Ryan Smyth .40 1.00
9 Joe Thornton 1.25 3.00
10 Jordin Tootoo .75 2.00

1927-28 La Patrie

The 1927-28 La Patrie set contained 21 notebook paper-sized (approximately 8 1/2" by 11") photos. The front had a sepia-toned posed photo of the player, enframed by a thin black border. The words "La Patrie" appeared above the picture, with the player's name below it. The photo number and year appeared at the lower right corner of the picture. A patterned border completed the front. The back was blank. Reports indicate a folder may have been issued to hold the photos.

COMPLETE SET (21) 1250.00 2500.00
1 Sylvio Mantha 50.00 100.00
2 Art Gagne 30.00 60.00
3 Leo Lafrance 30.00 60.00
4 Aurel Joliat 150.00 300.00
5 Pit Lepine 40.00 80.00
6 Gizzy Hart 30.00 60.00
7 Wildor Larochelle 40.00 80.00
8 Georges Hainsworth 100.00 200.00
9 Herb Gardiner 40.00 80.00
10 Albert Leduc 40.00 80.00
11 Marty (Martin) Burke 40.00 80.00
12 Charlie Langlois 30.00 60.00
13 Leonard Gaudreault 30.00 60.00
14 Howie Morenz 350.00 700.00
15 Cecil M. Hart 40.00 80.00
16 Leo Dandurand 30.00 60.00
17 Newsy Lalonde 150.00 300.00
18 Didier Pitre 30.00 60.00
19 Jack Laviolette 50.00 100.00
20 Georges Patterson 30.00 60.00
21 Georges Vezina 250.00 500.00

1927-28 La Presse Photos

1 Howie Morenz 200.00 300.00
2 Aurel Joliat 125.00 200.00
3 Sylvio Mantha 50.00 100.00
4 Pit Lepine 50.00 100.00
5 George Hainsworth 125.00 200.00
6 Art Gagne 50.00 100.00
7 Herb Gardiner 50.00 100.00
8 Art Gagne 50.00 100.00
9 Herb Gardiner 50.00 100.00
10 Albert Leduc 50.00 100.00
11 Wildor Larochelle 50.00 100.00
12 Leonard Gaudreault 50.00 100.00
13 Gizzy Hart 50.00 100.00
14 Charles Langlois 50.00 100.00
15 Georges Vezina 200.00 300.00
16 Joseph Cattarinich 60.00 150.00
Cecil Hart
Leo Dandurand
Letourneau
17 Eddie Shore 150.00 250.00
18 Lionel Conacher 125.00 200.00
19 Red Porter 50.00 100.00
20 George Patterson 50.00 100.00

1928-29 La Presse Photos

These oversized (10 X16) photos were issued over the course of the 1928-29 season as a premium with the Montreal newspaper, La Presse. They featured color posed images on the front. Because they had standard newspaper coverage on the back, some hobbyists do not consider them true collectibles. However, recent sales information suggests there is significant interest in these pieces. Because of their age and the natural deterioration of newsprint, it is rare to find these in high grade. As they are unnumbered, they are listed below in alphabetical order.

COMPLETE SET (14) 400.00 800.00
1 Clint Benedict 50.00 100.00
2 Frank Boucher 37.50 75.00
3 George Boucher 37.50 75.00
4 Lucien Brunet 10.00 20.00
5 Marty Burke 37.50 75.00
6 Bun Cook 50.00 100.00
7 Hap Day 37.50 75.00
8 Red Dutton 37.50 75.00
9 Georges Mantha 50.00 100.00
10 Armand Mondou 37.50 75.00
11 Bill Phillips 37.50 75.00
12 Babe Siebert 50.00 100.00
13 Nels Stewart 62.50 125.00
14 Jimmy Ward 37.50 75.00

1964 Lamberts Sports and Games

Card measures approximately 1 1/2" x 3 1/2" and featured full color fronts. Came from a series of 25 cards given as a premium for Lambert tea of Norwich, England.

20 Ice Hockey 10.00 20.00

1993 Leaf Chicago National

This huge card (approximately 8 X 11) was given to dealers at the Donruss dinner during the 1993 Chicago National. It heralded the union between Donruss and their new spokesman, Mario Lemieux.

1 Mario Lemieux 5.00 12.00

1993-94 Leaf

The 1993-94 Leaf hockey set consisted of 440 standard-size cards that were issued in two series of 220. The fronts displayed color action player photos that were full-bleed except at the bottom, where a red diagonal edges the picture. Below the diagonal was a black stripe carrying the player's name in gold foil lettering, and a team color-coded triangle displaying the team logo. Against the background of the home team's skyline or another prominent architectural landmark, the backs carried a color action player cut-out overprinted at the bottom with biographical and statistical information. A holographic team logo appeared in the lower right corner. Rookie Cards included Jason Arnott, Damian Rhodes and Jocelyn Thibault. An oversized (8" by 11 3/4") blowup of Mario Lemieux's card #1 was distributed as a promotional item in advance of the release of the set. The card was primarily handed out at the National Convention in Chicago.

COMPLETE SET (440) 12.00 30.00
COMP.SERIES 1 (220) 6.00 15.00
COMP.SERIES 2 (220) 6.00 15.00
1 Mario Lemieux .60 1.50
2 Curtis Joseph .10 .30
3 Steve Leach .02 .10
4 Vincent Damphousse .02 .10
5 Murray Craven .02 .10
6 Pat Elynuik .02 .10
7 Bill Guerin .02 .10
8 Zarley Zalapski .02 .10
9 Rob Gaudreau RC .02 .10
10 Pavel Bure .10 .30
11 Brad Shaw .02 .10
12 Pat LaFontaine .10 .30
13 Teemu Selanne .10 .30
14 Trent Klatt .02 .10
15 Kevin Todd .02 .10
16 Larry Murphy .05 .15
17 Tony Amonte .05 .15
18 Dino Ciccarelli .05 .15
19 Doug Bodger .02 .10
20 Luc Robitaille .05 .15
21 John Tucker .02 .10
22 Todd Gill .02 .10
23 Mike Ricci .02 .10
24 Evgeny Davydov .02 .10
25 Pierre Turgeon .05 .15
26 Rod Brind'Amour .05 .15
27 Jeremy Roenick .15 .40
28 Joel Otto .02 .10
29 Jeff Brown .02 .10
30 Brendan Shanahan .10 .30
31 Jiri Slegr .02 .10
32 Vladimir Malakhov .02 .10
33 Patrick Roy .60 1.50
34 Kevin Hatcher .02 .10
35 Alexander Semak .02 .10
36 Gary Roberts .02 .10
37 Tommy Soderstrom .05 .15
38 Bob Essensa .05 .15
39 Kelly Hrudey .05 .15
40 Shawn Chambers .02 .10
41 Glenn Anderson .05 .15
42 Owen Nolan .05 .15
43 Patrick Flatley .02 .10
44 Ray Sheppard .05 .15
45 Darren Turcotte .02 .10
46 Shayne Corson .02 .10
47 Brad May .05 .15
48 Bob Kudelski .02 .10
49 Pat Falloon .02 .10
50 Andrew Cassels .02 .10
51 Chris Chelios .10 .30
52 Sylvain Cote .02 .10
53 Mathieu Schneider .02 .10
54 Ted Donato .02 .10
55 Kirk McLean .05 .15
56 Bruce Driver .02 .10
57 Uwe Krupp .02 .10
58 Brent Fedyk .02 .10
59 Robert Reichel .02 .10
60 Scott Stevens .05 .15
61 Phil Housley .05 .15
62 Ed Belfour .10 .30
63 Dave Andreychuk .05 .15
64 Claude Lapointe .02 .10
65 Russ Courtnall .02 .10
66 Grant Fuhr .05 .15
67 Paul Coffey .10 .30
68 Bill Ranford .05 .15
69 Kevin Stevens .02 .10
70 Brian Leetch .10 .30
71 Dale Hawerchuk .05 .15
72 Geoff Courtnall .02 .10
73 Sandis Ozolinsh .02 .10
74 Sylvain Turgeon .02 .10
75 Nelson Emerson .02 .10
76 Brian Bellows .02 .10
77 Geoff Sanderson .05 .15
78 Petr Nedved .05 .15
79 Peter Bondra .05 .15
80 Scott Niedermayer .02 .10
81 Steve Thomas .02 .10
82 Dimitri Yushkevich .02 .10
83 Mike Vernon .05 .15
84 Alexei Zhamnov .05 .15
85 Adam Creighton .02 .10
86 Dave Ellett .02 .10
87 Joe Sakic .25 .60
88 Mike Craig .02 .10
89 Nicklas Lidstrom .10 .30
90 Ed Olczyk .02 .10
91 Alexander Mogilny .05 .15
92 Ulf Samuelsson .02 .10
93 Doug Gilmour .05 .15
94 Michael Nylander .02 .10
95 Steve Smith .02 .10
96 Igor Korolev .02 .10
97 Dixon Ward .02 .10
98 John LeClair .10 .30
99 Cam Neely .10 .30
100 Patrick Roy/Cup Champs .60 1.50
101 Darius Kasparaitis .02 .10
102 Mike Ridley .02 .10
103 Josef Beranek .02 .10
104 Valeri Zelepukin .02 .10
105 Keith Tkachuk .10 .30
106 Tomas Sandstrom .02 .10
107 Peter Zezel .02 .10
108 Scott Young .02 .10
109 Rick Tocchet .05 .15
110 Teemu Selanne CL .10 .30
111 Steve Chiasson .02 .10
112 Doug Zmolek .02 .10
113 Patrick Poulin .02 .10
114 Stephane Matteau .02 .10
115 Yves Racine .02 .10
116 Steve Heinze .02 .10
117 Gilbert Dionne .02 .10
118 Dale Hunter .02 .10
119 Derek King .02 .10
120 Garry Galley .02 .10
121 Ray Ferraro .02 .10
122 Andrei Kovalenko .02 .10
123 Alexei Zhitnik .02 .10
124 Fredrik Olausson .02 .10
125 Claude Lemieux .02 .10
126 Joe Nieuwendyk .05 .15
127 Travis Green .05 .15
128 Dave Gagner .05 .15
129 Sergei Fedorov .20 .50
130 Adam Graves .02 .10
131 Petr Svoboda .02 .10
132 Sean Burke .05 .15
133 Johan Garpenlov .02 .10
134 Jamie Baker .02 .10
135 Teppo Numminen .02 .10
136 Mats Sundin .10 .30
137 Nikolai Borschevsky .02 .10
138 Stephane Richer .05 .15
139 Scott Lachance .02 .10
140 Gary Suter .02 .10
141 Al Iafrate .02 .10
142 Brent Sutter .02 .10
143 Dimitri Kvartalnov .02 .10
144 Pat Verbeek .02 .10
145 Ed Courtenay .02 .10
146 Mark Tinordi .02 .10
147 Alexei Kovalev .05 .15
148 Dallas Drake RC .02 .10
149 Jimmy Carson .02 .10
150 Florida Panthers Logo .20 .50
151 Roman Hamrlik .05 .15
152 Martin Rucinsky .02 .10
153 Calle Johansson .02 .10
154 Theo Fleury .02 .10
155 Benoit Hogue .02 .10
156 Kevin Dineen .02 .10
157 Jody Hull .02 .10
158 Mark Messier .10 .30
159 Dave Manson .02 .10
160 Chris Kontos .02 .10
161 Ron Francis .05 .15
162 Steve Yzerman .60 1.50
163 Igor Kravchuk .02 .10
164 Sergei Zubov .02 .10
165 Thomas Steen .02 .10
166 Wendel Clark .05 .15
167 Scott Pellerin RC .02 .10
168 Dimitri Khristich .02 .10
169 Bernie Nicholls .02 .10
170 Paul Ranheim .02 .10
171 Robert Kron .02 .10
172 Rob Blake .05 .15
173 Rob Zamuner .02 .10
174 Rob Pearson .02 .10
175 Ed Belfour CL .10 .30
176 Steve Duchesne .02 .10
177 Pelle Eklund .02 .10
178 Michal Pivonka .02 .10
179 Joe Murphy .02 .10
180 Al MacInnis .05 .15
181 Craig Janney .05 .15
182 Kirk Muller .02 .10
183 Cliff Ronning .02 .10
184 Doug Weight .05 .15
185 Mike Richter .10 .30
186 Bob Probert .05 .15
187 Robert Petrovicky .02 .10
188 Richard Smehlik .02 .10
189 Norm Maciver .02 .10
190 Stephan Lebeau .02 .10
191 Patrice Brisebois .02 .10
192 Kevin Miller .02 .10
193 Trevor Linden .05 .15
194 Darrin Shannon .02 .10
195 Tim Cheveldae .05 .15
196 Tom Barrasso .05 .15
197 Zdeno Ciger .02 .10
198 Ulf Dahlen .02 .10
199 Arturs Irbe .05 .15
200 Anaheim Mighty Ducks Logo .20 .50
201 Tony Granato .02 .10
202 Mike Modano .20 .50
203 Eric Desjardins .05 .15
204 Bryan Smolinski .02 .10
205 Mark Recchi .05 .15
206 Darryl Sydor .02 .10
207 Valeri Kamensky .05 .15
208 Kelly Kisio .02 .10
209 Brian Bradley .02 .10
210 Mario Lemieux CL .20 .50
211 Yuri Khmylev .02 .10
212 Dorian Hatcher .02 .10
213 Mike Gartner .05 .15
214 Mike Needham UER .02 .10
(Grant Jennings on back)
215 Ray Bourque .20 .50
216 Tie Domi .05 .15
217 Shawn McEachern .02 .10
218 Joe Juneau .05 .15
219 Greg Adams .02 .10
220 Martin Straka .02 .10
221 Tom Fitzgerald .02 .10
222 Gary Shuchuk .02 .10
223 Kevin Haller .02 .10
224 Bryan Marchment .02 .10
225 Louie DeBrusk .02 .10
226 Randy Wood .02 .10
227 Bobby Holik .02 .10
228 Troy Mallette .02 .10
229 Adam Foote .02 .10
230 Bob Rouse .02 .10
231 Jyrki Lumme .02 .10
232 James Patrick .02 .10
233 Eric Lindros .10 .30
234 Joe Reekie .02 .10
235 Adam Oates .05 .15
236 Frank Musil .02 .10
237 Vladimir Konstantinov .05 .15
238 Dave Lowry .02 .10
239 Garth Butcher .02 .10
240 Jari Kurri .10 .30
241 Rick Tabaracci .05 .15
242 Sergei Bautin .02 .10
243 Scott Scissons .02 .10
244 Dominic Roussel .05 .15
245 John Cullen .02 .10
246 Sheldon Kennedy .02 .10
247 Mike Hough .02 .10
248 Paul DiPietro .02 .10
249 David Shaw .02 .10
250 Sergio Momesso .02 .10
251 Jeff Daniels .02 .10
252 Sergei Nemchinov .02 .10
253 Kris King .02 .10
254 Kelly Miller .02 .10
255 Brett Hull .15 .40
256 Dominik Hasek .40 1.00
257 Chris Pronger .15 .40
258 Derek Plante RC .02 .10
259 Mark Howe .02 .10
260 Oleg Petrov .02 .10
261 Ronnie Stern .02 .10
262 Scott Mellanby .05 .15
263 Warren Rychel .02 .10
264 John MacLean .05 .15
265 Radek Hamr RC .02 .10
266 Greg Hawgood .02 .10
267 Sylvain Lefebvre .02 .10
268 Glen Wesley .02 .10
269 Joe Cirella .02 .10
270 Dirk Graham .02 .10
271 Eric Weinrich .02 .10
272 Donald Audette .02 .10
273 Jason Woolley .02 .10
274 Kjell Samuelsson .02 .10
275 Ron Sutter .02 .10
276 Keith Primeau .02 .10
277 Ron Tugnutt .05 .15
278 Jesse Belanger .02 .10
279 Mike Keane .02 .10
280 Adam Burt .02 .10
281 Don Sweeney .02 .10
282 Mike Donnelly .02 .10
283 Lyle Odelein .02 .10
284 Gord Murphy .02 .10
285 Mikael Andersson .02 .10
286 Bret Hedican .02 .10
287 Bill Berg .02 .10
288 Esa Tikkanen .02 .10
289 Markus Naslund .10 .30
290 Checklist .02 .10
291 Kerry Huffman .02 .10
292 Dana Murzyn .02 .10
293 Rob Niedermayer .05 .15
294 Andre Racicot .05 .15
295 Ken Sutton .02 .10
296 Shawn Burr .02 .10
297 Scott Pearson .02 .10
298 Joby Messier RC .02 .10
299 Darrin Madeley RC .02 .10
300 Joe Mullen .05 .15
301 Stephane Fiset .05 .15
302 Geoff Smith .02 .10
303 Vyacheslav Kozlov .05 .15
304 Wayne Gretzky .75 2.00
305 Curtis Leschyshyn .02 .10
306 Mike Sillinger .02 .10
307 Vyacheslav Butsayev .02 .10
308 Mark Lamb .02 .10
309 German Titov RC .02 .10
310 Gerard Gallant .02 .10
311 Alexandre Daigle .02 .10
312 Jim Hrivnak .05 .15
313 Corey Hirsch .05 .15
314 Craig Berube .02 .10
315 Bill Houlder .02 .10
316 Ron Wilson .02 .10
317 Glen Murray .02 .10
318 Bryan Trottier .05 .15
319 Jeff Hackett .05 .15
320 Brad Dalgarno .02 .10
321 Petr Klima .02 .10
322 Jon Casey .05 .15
323 Mikael Renberg .10 .30
324 Jimmy Waite .05 .15
325 Brian Skrudland .02 .10
326 Vitali Prokhorov .02 .10
327 Glenn Healy .05 .15
328 Brian Benning .02 .10
329 Tony Hrkac .02 .10
330 Stu Grimson .02 .10
331 Chris Gratton .05 .15
332 Dave Poulin .02 .10
333 Jarrod Skalde .02 .10
334 Christian Ruuttu .02 .10
335 Mark Fitzpatrick .05 .15
336 Martin Lapointe .02 .10
337 Cam Stewart RC .02 .10
338 Anatoli Semenov .02 .10
339 Gaetan Duchesne .02 .10
340 Checklist .02 .10
341 Ron Hextall .05 .15
342 Mikhail Tatarinov .02 .10
343 Danny Lorenz .02 .10
344 Craig Simpson .02 .10
345 Martin Brodeur .40 1.00
346 Jaromir Jagr .20 .50
347 Tyler Wright .02 .10
348 Greg Gilbert .02 .10
349 Dave Tippett .02 .10
350 Stu Barnes .02 .10
351 Daniel Lacroix RC .02 .10
352 Marty McSorley .02 .10
353 Sean Hill .02 .10
354 Craig Billington .05 .15
355 Donald Dufresne .02 .10
356 Guy Hebert .05 .15
357 Neil Wilkinson .02 .10
358 Sandy McCarthy .02 .10
359 Aaron Ward RC .02 .10
360 Scott Thomas RC .02 .10
361 Corey Millen .02 .10
362 Matthew Barnaby .05 .15
363 Benoit Brunet .02 .10
364 Boris Mironov .02 .10
365 Doug Lidster .02 .10
366 Pavol Demitra .05 .15
367 Damian Rhodes RC .05 .15
368 Shawn Antoski .02 .10
369 Andy Moog .05 .15
370 Greg Johnson .02 .10
371 John Vanbiesbrouck .05 .15
372 Denis Savard .05 .15
373 Michel Goulet .05 .15
374 Dave Taylor .05 .15
375 Enrico Ciccone .02 .10
376 Sergei Zholtok .02 .10
377 Bob Errey .02 .10
378 Doug Brown .02 .10
379 Bill McDougall RC .02 .10
380 Pat Conacher .02 .10
381 Alexei Kasatonov .02 .10
382 Jason Arnott RC .60 1.50
383 Jarkko Varvio .02 .10
384 Sergei Makarov .02 .10
385 Trevor Kidd .05 .15
386 Alexei Yashin .02 .10
387 Gerald Diduck .02 .10
388 Paul Ysebaert .02 .10
389 Jason Smith RC .02 .10
390 Jeff Norton .02 .10
391 Igor Larionov .02 .10
392 Pierre Sevigny .02 .10
393 Wes Walz .02 .10
394 Grant Ledyard .02 .10
395 Brad McCrimmon .02 .10
396 Martin Gelinas .02 .10
397 Paul Cavallini .02 .10
398 Brian Noonan .02 .10
399 Mike Lalor .02 .10
400 Dimitri Filimonov .02 .10
401 Andrei Lomakin .02 .10
402 Steve Junker RC .02 .10
403 Daren Puppa .05 .15
404 Jozef Stumpel .02 .10
405 Jeff Shantz RC .02 .10
406 Terry Yake .02 .10
407 Mike Peluso .02 .10
408 Vitali Karamnov .02 .10
409 Felix Potvin .10 .30
410 Steven King .02 .10
411 Roman Oksiuta RC .02 .10
412 Mark Greig .02 .10
413 Wayne McBean .02 .10
414 Nick Kypreos .02 .10
415 Dominic Lavoie .02 .10
416 Chris Simon RC .30 .75
417 Peter Popovic RC .02 .10
418 Gino Odjick .02 .10
419 Mike Rathje .02 .10
420 Keith Acton .02 .10
421 Bob Carpenter .02 .10
422 Steven Finn .02 .10
423 Ian Herbers RC .02 .10
424 Ted Drury .02 .10
425 Sergei Petrenko .02 .10
426 Mattias Norstrom RC .02 .10
427 Todd Ewen .02 .10
428 Jocelyn Thibault RC .40 1.00
429 Robert Burakovsky RC .02 .10
430 Chris Terreri .05 .15
431 Michal Sykora RC .02 .10
432 Craig Ludwig .02 .10
433 Vesa Vitakoski RC .02 .10
434 Sergei Krivokrasov .02 .10
435 Darren McCarty RC .25 .60
436 Dean McAmmond .02 .10
437 J.J. Daigneault .02 .10
438 Vladimir Ruzicka .02 .10
439 Vlastimil Kroupa RC .02 .10
440 Checklist .02 .10

1993-94 Leaf Freshman Phenoms

Randomly inserted in Series II packs, these ten standard-size cards featured borderless color player action shots on their fronts. The player's name appeared in white lettering beneath the set's title in the darkened area at the bottom of the player photo. The horizontal back carried a color player action shot on one side, and player information within a black rectangle on the other.

COMPLETE SET (10) 4.00 10.00
1 Alexandre Daigle .20 .50
2 Chris Pronger 1.00 2.50
3 Chris Gratton .20 .50
4 Markus Naslund 1.00 2.50
5 Mikael Renberg .20 .50
6 Rob Niedermayer .20 .50
7 Jason Arnott .60 1.50
8 Jarkko Varvio .20 .50
9 Alexei Yashin .20 .50
10 Jocelyn Thibault .60 1.50

1993-94 Leaf Gold All-Stars

This 10-card set was randomly inserted in first (1-5) and second (6-10) series foil packs. These standard-size cards featured the NHL's top players at each position, with one player portrayed on each card side.

COMPLETE SET (10) 20.00 50.00
COMP.SERIES 1 (5) 10.00 25.00
COMP.SERIES 2 (5) 10.00 25.00
1 Mario Lemieux 4.00 10.00
Pat LaFontaine
2 Chris Chelios 1.25 3.00
Larry Murphy
3 Brett Hull 2.00 5.00
Teemu Selanne
4 Kevin Stevens 1.25 3.00
Dave Andreychuk
5 Patrick Roy 4.00 10.00
Tom Barrasso
6 Wayne Gretzky 6.00 15.00
Doug Gilmour
7 Ray Bourque 2.50 6.00
Paul Coffey
8 Alexander Mogilny 1.25 3.00
Pavel Bure
9 Luc Robitaille 1.25 3.00
Brendan Shanahan
10 Ed Belfour 1.25 3.00
Felix Potvin

1993-94 Leaf Gold Rookies

Randomly inserted in first series foil packs, this 15-card standard-size set showcased top rookies from the 1992-93 season. Borderless horizontal fronts had a photo of the player along with "Gold Leaf Rookie 1992-93" prominent on the front. Red backs carried a player photo and rookie year highlights. The cards were numbered on back as "X of 15".

COMPLETE SET (15) 4.00 10.00
1 Teemu Selanne .60 1.50
2 Joe Juneau .20 .50
3 Eric Lindros .60 1.50
4 Felix Potvin .60 1.50
5 Alexei Zhamnov .20 .50
6 Andrei Kovalenko .20 .50
7 Shawn McEachern .20 .50
8 Alexei Zhitnik .20 .50
9 Vladimir Malakhov .20 .50
10 Patrick Poulin .20 .50
11 Keith Tkachuk .40 1.00
12 Tommy Soderstrom .20 .50
13 Darius Kasparaitis .20 .50
14 Scott Niedermayer .20 .50
15 Darryl Sydor .20 .50

1993-94 Leaf Hat Trick Artists

This 10-card set was randomly inserted in first (1-5) and second (6-10) series U.S. foil and magazine distribution packs. These standard-size cards honored players who scored three or more hat tricks in the 1992-93 season.

COMPLETE SET (10) 8.00 20.00
COMP.SERIES 1 (5) 5.00 12.00
COMP.SERIES 2 (5) 3.00 8.00
1 M.Lemieux Title Card 2.00 5.00
2 Alexander Mogilny .40 1.00
3 Teemu Selanne .75 2.00
4 Mario Lemieux 2.00 5.00
5 Pierre Turgeon .40 1.00
6 Kevin Dineen .20 .50
7 Eric Lindros .75 2.00
8 Adam Oates .40 1.00
9 Kevin Stevens .20 .50
10 Steve Yzerman 2.00 5.00

1993-94 Leaf Mario Lemieux

As part of a 10-card subset randomly inserted in first (1-5) and second (6-10) series foil packs, these standard-size cards traced Lemieux's illustrious career. Mario Lemieux personally autographed 2,000 of his cards.

COMPLETE SET (10) 8.00 20.00
COMP.SERIES 1 (5) 4.00 10.00
COMP.SERIES 2 (5) 4.00 10.00
COMMON LEMIEUX (1-10) 1.00 2.50
NNO Mario Lemieux AU/2000 75.00 150.00

1993-94 Leaf Painted Warriors

As part of a 10-card subset randomly inserted in first (1-5) and second (6-10) series foil packs, these standard-size cards featured up-close shots of NHL goalies with emphasis on mask design. The back had a small color photo, biography and career highlights.

COMPLETE SET (10) 6.00 15.00
COMP.SERIES 1 (5) 4.00 10.00
COMP.SERIES 2 (5) 2.00 5.00
1 Felix Potvin .60 1.50
2 Curtis Joseph .60 1.50
3 Kirk McLean .30 .75
4 Patrick Roy 3.00 8.00
5 Grant Fuhr .40 1.00
6 Ed Belfour .60 1.50
7 Mike Vernon .30 .75
8 John Vanbiesbrouck .30 .75
9 Tom Barrasso UER .30 .75
(Notes he was traded to Pittsburgh in 1968 instead of '88)
10 Bill Ranford .30 .75

1993-94 Leaf Studio Signature

As part of a 10-card subset randomly inserted in first (1-5) and second (6-10) series Canadian and magazine distribution foil packs, these standard-size cards spotlighted the NHL's top players. Against a colorful background of the team's uniform, the fronts displayed a cut out player photo with his gold foil signature stamped across the bottom. The backs carried a full-bleed color close-up photo and text that defines the player's personal style.

COMPLETE SET (10) 15.00 35.00
COMP.SERIES 1 (5) 10.00 20.00
COMP.SERIES 2 (5) 6.00 15.00
1 Doug Gilmour .40 1.00
2 Pat Falloon .25 .60
3 Pat LaFontaine .75 2.00
4 Wayne Gretzky 6.00 12.00
5 Steve Yzerman 5.00 10.00
6 Patrick Roy 5.00 10.00
7 Jeremy Roenick 1.00 2.50
8 Brett Hull 1.00 2.50
9 Alexandre Daigle .25 .60
10 Eric Lindros .75 2.00

1994-95 Leaf

This 550-card standard-size set was released in two series. Series 1 was 330 cards while series 2 contained 220 cards. Each came in 12-card hobby and 18-card retail packs. These full-bleed cards carried a small Leaf logo above the player's name in gold foil along the bottom. The team name was stamped across the top, also in gold foil. Card backs featured four photos with brief personal and statistical information. The set contained no subsets. Rookie Cards included Mariusz Czerkawski, Byron Dafoe, Eric Fichaud, Ian Laperriere and Jason Wiemer.

COMPLETE SET (550) 17.50 35.00
COMPLETE SERIES 1 (330) 10.00 20.00
COMPLETE SERIES 2 (220) 7.50 15.00
1 Mario Lemieux .60 1.50
2 Tony Amonte .05 .15
3 Steve Duchesne .02 .10
4 Glen Murray .02 .10
5 John LeClair .10 .30
6 Glen Wesley .02 .10
7 Chris Chelios .10 .30
8 Alexei Zhitnik .02 .10
9 Mike Modano .20 .50
10 Pavel Bure .10 .30
11 Mark Messier .10 .30
12 Rob Blake .05 .15
13 Tony Twist .02 .10
14 Glenn Anderson .05 .15
15 Keith Redmond .02 .10
16 Brett Hull .15 .40
17 Valeri Zelepukin .02 .10
18 Mike Richter .10 .30
19 Alexei Yashin .02 .10
20 Luc Robitaille .05 .15
21 Tim Sweeney .02 .10
22 Ted Drury .02 .10
23 Guy Carbonneau .02 .10
24 Stephane Richer .05 .15
25 Ulf Dahlen .02 .10
26 Fred Brathwaite .05 .15
27 Darius Kasparaitis .02 .10
28 Kris Draper .02 .10
29 Alexander Godynyuk .02 .10
30 Brent Sutter .02 .10
31 Josef Beranek .02 .10
32 Stephane Matteau .02 .10
33 Derek Plante .02 .10
34 Vesa Viitakoski .02 .10
35 Dave Ellett .02 .10
36 Martin Straka .02 .10
37 Dimitri Yushkevich .02 .10
38 John Tucker .02 .10
39 Rob Gaudreau .02 .10
40 Doug Weight .05 .15
41 Patrick Roy .60 1.50
42 Brian Bradley .02 .10
43 Bob Beers .02 .10
44 Dino Ciccarelli .05 .15
45 Dean Evason .02 .10
46 Ron Tugnutt .05 .15
47 Andy Moog .10 .30
48 Jason Dawe .02 .10
49 Ted Donato .02 .10
50 Ron Hextall .05 .15
51 Derek Armstrong RC .02 .10
52 Craig Janney .05 .15
53 Geoff Courtnall .02 .10
54 Mikael Renberg .05 .15
55 Theo Fleury .02 .10
56 Martin Brodeur .30 .75
57 Mattias Norstrom .02 .10
58 David Sacco .02 .10
59 Jeff Reese .02 .10
60 Bill Ranford .05 .15
61 Dan Quinn .02 .10
62 Joe Juneau .05 .15
63 Jeremy Roenick .15 .40
64 Donald Audette .02 .10
65 Zdeno Ciger .02 .10
66 Cliff Ronning .02 .10
67 Steve Thomas .02 .10
68 Norm Maciver .02 .10
69 Vincent Damphousse .02 .10
70 John Vanbiesbrouck .05 .15
71 Andrei Kovalenko .02 .10
72 Dave Andreychuk .05 .15
73 Stu Barnes .02 .10
74 Jamie McLennan .05 .15
75 Rudy Poeschek .02 .10
76 Ken Wregget .05 .15
77 Ray Bourque .20 .50
78 Grant Fuhr .05 .15
79 Paul Cavallini .02 .10
80 Nelson Emerson .02 .10
81 Tim Cheveldae .05 .15
82 Mariusz Czerkawski RC .15 .40
83 Pat Peake .02 .10
84 Craig Billington .05 .15
85 Sean Burke .05 .15
86 Chris Gratton .02 .10
87 Andrei Trefilov .02 .10
88 Terry Yake .02 .10
89 Mark Recchi .05 .15
90 Igor Korolev .02 .10
91 Mark Tinordi .02 .10
92 Alexei Kovalev .05 .15
93 Bob Essensa .05 .15
94 Keith Tkachuk .10 .30
95 Pat Falloon .02 .10
96 John Slaney .02 .10
97 Alexei Zhamnov .05 .15
98 Jeff Norton .02 .10
99 Doug Gilmour .05 .15
100 Rick Tocchet .05 .15
101 Robert Kron .02 .10
102 Patrik Carnback .02 .10
103 Tom Barrasso .05 .15
104 Jari Kurri .05 .15
105 Iain Fraser .02 .10
106 Mike Donnelly .02 .10
107 Ray Sheppard .05 .15
108 Scott Young .02 .10
109 Kirk McLean .05 .15
110 Checklist .02 .10
111 Sergei Zubov .02 .10
112 Ivan Droppa .02 .10
113 Brendan Shanahan .10 .30
114 Michal Pivonka .02 .10
115 Pavol Demitra .05 .15
116 Doug Brown .02 .10
117 Valeri Kamensky .05 .15
118 Alexander Karpovtsev .02 .10
119 Alexandre Daigle .02 .10
120 Dominik Hasek .25 .60
121 Murray Craven .02 .10
122 Michal Sykora .02 .10
123 Aris Brimanis RC .02 .10
124 Benoit Hogue .02 .10
125 Arto Blomsten .02 .10
126 Russ Courtnall .02 .10
127 Bryan Marchment .02 .10
128 Jeff Hackett .05 .15
129 Kevin Miller .02 .10
130 Bryan Smolinski .02 .10
131 John Druce .02 .10
132 Roman Hamrlik .05 .15
133 Jason Arnott .02 .10
134 Chris Terreri .05 .15
135 Mike Gartner .05 .15
136 Darryl Sydor .02 .10
137 Lyle Odelein .02 .10
138 Martin Gelinas .02 .10
139 Mike Rathje .02 .10
140 Sylvain Cote .02 .10
141 Nicklas Lidstrom .10 .30
142 Guy Hebert .05 .15
143 Jozef Stumpel .02 .10
144 Owen Nolan .05 .15
145 Jesse Belanger .02 .10
146 Bill Guerin .05 .15
147 Mike Stapleton .02 .10
148 Steve Yzerman .60 1.50
149 Michael Nylander .02 .10
150 Rod Brind'Amour .05 .15
151 Jaromir Jagr .20 .50
152 Darcy Wakaluk .05 .15
153 Sergei Nemchinov .02 .10
154 Wes Walz .02 .10
155 Sergei Fedorov .20 .50

1994-95 Leaf

156 Dan Laperriere .02 .10
157 Marty McInnis .02 .10
158 Chris Joseph .02 .10
159 Matt Martin .02 .10
160 Checklist .02 .10
161 Denis Tsygurov RC .02 .10
162 Stephan Lebeau .02 .10
163 Kirk Muller .02 .10
164 Shayne Corson .02 .10
165 Joe Sakic .25 .60
166 Denis Savard .05 .15
167 Kevin Dineen .02 .10
168 Paul Coffey .10 .30
169 Sandis Ozolinsh .02 .10
170 Stewart Malgunas .02 .10
171 Petr Klima .02 .10
172 Pat Verbeek .02 .10
173 Yan Kaminsky .02 .10
174 Marty McSorley .02 .10
175 Arturs Irbe .05 .15
176 Peter Popovic .02 .10
177 Brian Skrudland .02 .10
178 John Lilley .02 .10
179 Boris Mironov .02 .10
180 Garth Snow .05 .15
181 Alexei Kudashov .02 .10
182 Scott Mellanby .05 .15
183 Dale Hunter .02 .10
184 Tommy Soderstrom .05 .15
185 Claude Lemieux .02 .10
186 Felix Potvin .10 .30
187 Corey Millen .02 .10
188 Derek King .02 .10
189 Kelly Hrudey .05 .15
190 Dimitri Khristich .02 .10
191 Sylvain Turgeon .02 .10
192 John Gruden RC .02 .10
193 Mike Peca .02 .10
194 Vladimir Malakhov .02 .10
195 Mathieu Schneider .02 .10
196 Jeff Shantz .02 .10
197 Darren McCarty .02 .10
198 Craig Simpson .02 .10
199 Jarkko Varvio .02 .10
200 Gino Odjick .02 .10
201 Martin Lapointe .02 .10
202 Paul Ysebaert .02 .10
203 Mike McPhee .02 .10
204 John MacLean .05 .15
205 Ulf Samuelsson .02 .10
206 Garry Valk .02 .10
207 Tomas Sandstrom .02 .10
208 Curtis Joseph .10 .30
209 Mikhail Shtalenkov RC .02 .10
210 Darren Turcotte .02 .10
211 Markus Naslund .10 .30
212 Al Iafrate .02 .10
213 Jim Storm .02 .10
214 Dan Plante RC .02 .10
215 Brad May .02 .10
216 Nathan Lafayette .02 .10
217 Brian Noonan .02 .10
218 Brent Hughes .02 .10
219 Geoff Sanderson .05 .15
220 Checklist .02 .10
221 Eric Weinrich .02 .10
222 Greg Adams .02 .10
223 Dominic Roussel .05 .15
224 Daren Puppa .05 .15
225 Rob Niedermayer .05 .15
226 Todd Elik .02 .10
227 Donald Brashear RC .02 .10
228 Joe Nieuwendyk .05 .15
229 Tony Granato .02 .10
230 Kirk Maltby .02 .10
231 Jocelyn Thibault .10 .30
232 Shawn McEachern .02 .10
233 Teppo Numminen .02 .10
234 Johan Garpenlov .02 .10
235 Ron Francis .05 .15
236 Slava Kozlov .05 .15
237 Scott Niedermayer .02 .10
238 Sergei Krivokrasov .02 .10
239 Dave Manson .02 .10
240 Mike Ricci .02 .10
241 Chad Penney .02 .10
242 Calle Johansson .02 .10
243 Robert Reichel .02 .10
244 Igor Kravchuk .02 .10
245 Jason Smith .02 .10
246 Neal Broten .05 .15
247 Jeff Brown .02 .10
248 Jason Bowen .02 .10
249 Larry Murphy .05 .15
250 Gord Murphy .02 .10
251 Darrin Shannon .02 .10
252 Bobby Holik .02 .10
253 Zigmund Palffy .05 .15
254 Dmitri Mironov .02 .10
255 Adam Graves .02 .10
256 Alexander Mogilny .05 .15
257 Steve Smith .02 .10
258 Jim Montgomery .02 .10
259 Danton Cole .02 .10
260 Dave McLlwain .02 .10
261 German Titov .02 .10
262 Tom Chorske .02 .10
263 Grant Ledyard .02 .10
264 Garry Galley .02 .10
265 Vlastimil Kroupa .02 .10
266 Keith Primeau .02 .10
267 Cam Neely .10 .30
268 Chris Pronger .10 .30
269 Richard Matvichuk .02 .10
270 Steve Larmer .05 .15
271 James Patrick .02 .10
272 Joel Otto .02 .10
273 Todd Nelson .02 .10
274 Joe Sacco .02 .10
275 Jason York RC .02 .10
276 Andrew Cassels .02 .10
277 Peter Bondra .05 .15
278 Pat LaFontaine .10 .30
279 Nikolai Borschevsky .02 .10
280 Dave Mackey .02 .10
281 Cam Stewart .02 .10
282 Sergei Makarov .02 .10
283 Byron Dafoe RC .40 1.00
284 Joe Murphy .02 .10
285 Matthew Barnaby .05 .15
286 Derian Hatcher .02 .10
287 Jyrki Lumme .02 .10
288 Travis Green .05 .15
289 Milos Holan .02 .10
290 Ed Patterson .02 .10
291 Randy Burridge .02 .10
292 Brian Savage .02 .10
293 Stephane Quintal .02 .10
294 Zarley Zalapski .02 .10
295 Vitali Prokhorov .02 .10
296 Ed Belfour .10 .30
297 Yuri Khmylev .02 .10
298 Dean McAmmond .02 .10
299 Bob Corkum .02 .10
300 Darrin Madeley .02 .10
301 Brian Bellows .02 .10
302 Andrei Lomakin .02 .10
303 Anatoli Semenov .02 .10
304 Claude Lapointe .02 .10
305 Adam Oates .05 .15
306 Richard Smehlik .02 .10
307 Jim Dowd .02 .10
308 Mark Fitzpatrick .05 .15
309 Pierre Sevigny .02 .10
310 Glenn Healy .05 .15
311 Igor Larionov .02 .10
312 Aaron Ward .02 .10
313 Dale Hawerchuk .05 .15
314 Bob Kudelski .02 .10
315 Chris Osgood .20 .50
316 Trent Klatt .02 .10
317 Gary Suter .02 .10
318 Tie Domi .05 .15
319 Dave Gagner .05 .15
320 Kevin Smyth .02 .10
321 Philippe Bozon .02 .10
322 Trevor Kidd .05 .15
323 Warren Rychel .02 .10
324 Steven Rice .02 .10
325 Patrice Brisebois .02 .10
326 Gary Roberts .02 .10
327 Fredrik Olausson .02 .10
328 Andrei Nazarov .02 .10
329 Stephane Fiset .05 .15
330 Checklist .02 .10
331 Fred Knipscheer .02 .10
332 Shawn Chambers .02 .10
333 Kelly Buchberger .02 .10
334 Ray Ferraro .02 .10
335 Dirk Graham .02 .10
336 Ken Daneyko .02 .10
337 Mark Lamb .02 .10
338 Shaun Van Allen .02 .10
339 Chris Simon .02 .10
340 Brent Gilchrist .02 .10
341 Greg Gilbert .02 .10
342 Brent Severyn .02 .10
343 Craig Berube .02 .10
344 Randy Moller .02 .10
345 Wayne Gretzky .75 2.00
346 Shawn Anderson .02 .10
347 Mikael Andersson .02 .10
348 Jim Montgomery .02 .10
349 Scott Pearson .02 .10
350 Kevin Todd .02 .10
351 Ron Sutter .02 .10
352 Paul Kruse RC .02 .10
353 Doug Lidster .02 .10
354 Oleg Petrov .02 .10
355 Greg Johnson .02 .10
356 Kevin Stevens .02 .10
357 Doug Bodger .02 .10
358 Troy Mallette .02 .10
359 Keith Carney .02 .10
360 Petr Nedved .05 .15
361 Mark Janssens .02 .10
362 Teemu Selanne .10 .30
363 Scott Stevens .05 .15
364 Shane Churla .02 .10
365 John McIntyre .02 .10
366 Geoff Smith .02 .10
367 Pierre Turgeon .05 .15
368 Shawn Burr .02 .10
369 Kevin Hatcher .02 .10
370 Paul Ranheim .02 .10
371 Kevin Haller .02 .10
372 Scott Lachance .02 .10
373 Craig Muni .02 .10
374 Mike Ridley .02 .10
375 Joby Messier .02 .10
376 Thomas Steen .02 .10
377 Bruce Driver .02 .10
378 Mike Eastwood .02 .10
379 Brian Benning .02 .10
380 Dallas Drake .02 .10
381 Patrick Flatley .02 .10
382 Cam Russell .02 .10
383 Bobby Dollas .02 .10
384 Marc Bergevin .02 .10
385 Joe Mullen .05 .15
386 Chris Dahlquist .02 .10
387 Robert Petrovicky .02 .10
388 Yves Racine .02 .10
389 Adam Bennett .02 .10
390 Patrick Poulin .02 .10
391 Vladimir Konstantinov .05 .15
392 Frank Kucera .02 .10
393 Petr Svoboda .02 .10
394 Mike Sillinger .02 .10
395 Kris King .02 .10
396 Kelly Chase .05 .15
397 Peter Douris .02 .10
398 Bob Errey .02 .10
399 Ronnie Stern .02 .10
400 Randy McKay .02 .10
401 Benoit Brunet .02 .10
402 Gerald Diduck .02 .10
403 Brian Leetch .10 .30
404 Steve Heinze .02 .10
405 Jimmy Waite .05 .15
406 Nick Kypreos .02 .10
407 J.J. Daigneault .02 .10
408 Alexei Gusarov .02 .10
409 Paul Broten .02 .10
410 Drake Berehowsky .02 .10
411 Sandy McCarthy .02 .10
412 John Cullen .02 .10
413 Dan Quinn .02 .10
414 Dave Lowry .02 .10
415 Eric Lindros .10 .30
416 Igor Ulanov .02 .10
417 Bob Sweeney .02 .10
418 Jamie Macoun .02 .10
419 Brian Mullen .02 .10
420 Steve Leach .02 .10
421 Jamie Baker .02 .10
422 Uwe Krupp .02 .10
423 Steve Konowalchuk .02 .10
424 Craig Ludwig .02 .10
425 Bret Hedican .02 .10
426 Steve Dubinsky .02 .10
427 Rob Zamuner .02 .10
428 Dave Brown .02 .10
429 Robert Lang .02 .10
430 Dave Babych .02 .10
431 Scott Thornton .02 .10
432 Dave Archibald .02 .10
433 Eric Desjardins .05 .15
434 Jim Cummins .02 .10
435 Troy Loney .02 .10
436 Bob Carpenter .02 .10
437 Joe Reekie .02 .10
438 Mike Krushelnyski .02 .10
439 Jeff Odgers .02 .10
440 Checklist .02 .10
441 Brian Rolston .02 .10
442 Adam Deadmarsh .02 .10
443 Eric Fichaud RC .05 .15
444 Michel Petit .02 .10
445 Brett Lindros .02 .10
446 Pat Jablonski .05 .15
447 Janne Laukkanen .02 .10
448 Ray Whitney .02 .10
449 Tom Kurvers .02 .10
450 Phil Housley .05 .15
451 Viktor Kozlov .02 .10
452 Aaron Gavey .02 .10
453 Doug Zmolek .02 .10
454 Tony Twist .02 .10
455 Paul Kariya .10 .30
456 Vladislav Boulin RC .02 .10
457 Kevin Brown RC .02 .10
458 David Wilkie .02 .10
459 Jamie Pushor .02 .10
460 Glen Wesley .02 .10
461 Al MacInnis .05 .15
462 Bernie Nicholls .05 .15
463 Luc Robitaille .05 .15
464 Mike Vernon .05 .15
465 Alex Cherbayev .02 .10
466 Garth Butcher .02 .10
467 Todd Harvey .02 .10
468 Viktor Gordiouk .02 .10
469 Pat Neaton .02 .10
470 Jason Muzzatti .05 .15
471 Valeri Bure .02 .10
472 Kenny Jonsson .02 .10
473 Alexei Kasatonov .02 .10
474 Rick Tocchet .05 .15
475 Peter Forsberg .50 1.25
476 Sean Hill .02 .10
477 Steven Rice .02 .10
478 David Roberts .02 .10
479 Justin Hocking RC .02 .10
480 Chris Therien .02 .10
481 Cale Hulse RC .02 .10
482 Jeff Friesen .02 .10
483 Brandon Convery .02 .10
484 Ian Laperriere RC .02 .10
485 Brent Grieve RC .02 .10
486 Valeri Karpov RC .02 .10
487 Steve Chiasson .02 .10
488 Jassen Cullimore .02 .10
489 Jason Wiemer RC .02 .10
490 Checklist .02 .10
491 Len Barrie .02 .10
492 Turner Stevenson .02 .10
493 Kelly Kisio .02 .10
494 Dwayne Norris .02 .10
495 Ron Hextall .05 .15
496 Jaroslav Modry .02 .10
497 Todd Gill .02 .10
498 Ken Sutton .02 .10
499 Sergio Momesso .02 .10
500 Dean Kennedy .02 .10
501 David Reid .02 .10
502 Jocelyn Lemieux .02 .10
503 Mark Osborne .02 .10
504 Mike Hough .02 .10
505 Todd Marchant .02 .10
506 Keith Jones .02 .10
507 Sylvain Lefebvre .02 .10
508 Sergei Zholtok .02 .10
509 Jay More .02 .10
510 Mike Craig .02 .10
511 Jason Allison .02 .10
512 Jim Paek .02 .10
513 Chris Tamer RC .02 .10
514 Craig MacTavish .02 .10
515 Mikko Makela .02 .10
516 Tom Fitzgerald .02 .10
517 Brent Fedyk .02 .10
518 Don Sweeney .02 .10
519 Kelly Miller .02 .10
520 Jiri Slegr .02 .10
521 Wayne Presley .02 .10
522 Mark Greig .02 .10
523 Doug Houda .02 .10
524 Kay Whitmore .05 .15
525 Craig Ferguson RC .02 .10
526 Kent Manderville .02 .10
527 Trevor Linden .05 .15
528 Jeff Beukeboom .02 .10
529 Adam Foote .05 .15
530 Mats Sundin .10 .30
531 Shjon Podein .02 .10
532 Louie DeBrusk .02 .10
533 Peter Zezel .02 .10
534 Greg Hawgood .02 .10
535 Pat Elynuik .02 .10
536 Mike Ramsey .02 .10
537 Bob Beers .02 .10
538 David Williams .02 .10
539 Philippe Boucher .02 .10
540 Rob Brown .02 .10
541 Marc Potvin .02 .10
542 Wendel Clark .05 .15
543 Alexander Semak .02 .10
544 Randy Wood .02 .10
545 Frank Musil .02 .10
546 Mike Peluso .02 .10
547 Gaetan Duchesne .02 .10
548 Curtis Leschyshyn .02 .10
549 Rob DiMaio .02 .10
550 Checklist .02 .10

1994-95 Leaf Crease Patrol

The ten cards in this set were randomly inserted in Leaf series 2 product at the rate of 1:9 packs. Complete sets also were available in randomly inserted Super-Packs. Cards featured a full bleed, horizontally-oriented front, with the set name, player name and logo along the bottom. Backs had a standard card look, with full stats, text, and small player photo. Cards were numbered "X of ten".

COMPLETE SET (10) 3.00 6.00
1 Patrick Roy 1.25 3.00
2 Ed Belfour .25 .60
3 Curtis Joseph .25 .60
4 Felix Potvin .25 .60
5 John Vanbiesbrouck .10 .30
6 Dominik Hasek .50 1.25
7 Kirk McLean .10 .30
8 Mike Richter .25 .60
9 Martin Brodeur .60 1.50
10 Bill Ranford .10 .30

1994-95 Leaf Fire on Ice

This 12-card set was inserted in Leaf series one packs at the rate of 1:18. Cards featured a cutout player image over the words "Fire On Ice", which embellished the silver foil background. The player name was at the bottom of the card next to the Leaf logo. Card backs featured another photo, another Fire On Ice logo and stats. Cards were numbered "X" of 12.

COMPLETE SET (12) 10.00 25.00
1 Sergei Fedorov 1.00 2.50
2 Jeremy Roenick .75 2.00
3 Pavel Bure .60 1.50
4 Wayne Gretzky 4.00 10.00
5 Doug Gilmour .30 .75
6 Eric Lindros .60 1.50
7 Joe Juneau .30 .75
8 Paul Coffey .60 1.50
9 Mario Lemieux 3.00 8.00
10 Alexander Mogilny .30 .75
11 Mike Gartner .30 .75
12 Teemu Selanne .60 1.50

1994-95 Leaf Gold Rookies

The 15 cards in this set were randomly inserted in Leaf series 1 product at the rate of 1:18 packs. Card fronts were very crowded, featuring one large color photo and three black-and-white photos. The set title was written in speckled gold foil over the large color shot. The team logo, team name and player name appear on the right-hand side with the black and white shots. Card backs featured another photo, along with personal info and stats as well as a short blurb. The cards were numbered "X of 15".

COMPLETE SET (15) 10.00 25.00
1 Martin Brodeur 3.00 8.00
2 Jason Arnott .75 2.00
3 Alexei Yashin .75 2.00
4 Chris Gratton .75 2.00
5 Alexandre Daigle .75 2.00
6 Mikael Renberg .75 2.00
7 Rob Niedermayer .75 2.00
8 Boris Mironov .75 2.00
9 Chris Pronger 1.25 3.00
10 Chris Osgood 1.25 3.00
11 Derek Plante .75 2.00
12 Pat Peake .75 2.00
13 Jason Allison .75 2.00
14 Bryan Smolinski .75 2.00
15 Jocelyn Thibault .75 2.00

1994-95 Leaf Gold Stars

The 15 double-front cards in this set were randomly inserted in Leaf series 1 and 2 product at the rate of 1:72 packs. Cards 1-10 appeared in series 1, 11-15 in series 2. Cards featured a gold prismatic border. The player photo was in a diamond shaped gold prismatic border, surrounded by the set title. A gold foil facsimile autograph appeared under the gold diamond, just over the player name and team affiliation. One side of each card bore a serial number out of 10,000. Cards were numbered "X of 15".

COMPLETE SET (15) 60.00 150.00
1 Sergei Fedorov 12.00 30.00
Wayne Gretzky
2 Doug Gilmour 5.00 12.00
Jeremy Roenick
3 Patrick Roy 8.00 20.00
Mike Richter
4 Brett Hull 4.00 10.00
Pavel Bure
5 Mark Messier 4.00 10.00
Alexei Yashin
6 Ray Bourque 5.00 12.00
Brian Leetch
7 Chris Joseph 5.00 12.00
Ed Belfour
8 Martin Brodeur 6.00 15.00
Dominik Hasek
9 Cam Neely 4.00 10.00
Mikael Renberg
10 Mike Modano 4.00 10.00
Jason Arnott
11 Mario Lemieux 8.00 20.00
Eric Lindros
12 Scott Stevens 4.00 10.00
Rob Blake
13 John Vanbiesbrouck 5.00 12.00
Felix Potvin
14 Adam Oates 4.00 10.00
Pat LaFontaine
15 Jaromir Jagr 4.00 10.00
Mark Recchi

1994-95 Leaf Leaf Limited Inserts

This 28-card insert set was issued in two series of 18 and 10 cards, in first and second series Leaf packs, respectively. Cards were randomly inserted at the rate of 1:18 packs, while series two could also be found randomly inserted into Super Packs. The cards were notable for the reflective silver border with rainbow lines coming out of the centered player photo. Player name was written in black at the base of the card below the team name printed in silver foil. The card backs had a ghosted photo covered by text and a small color portrait. These cards were identical in design to the Leaf Limited set issued in packs later in the season. Although the photos were different, the easiest way to determine which set your card belonged to is the numbering system. The inserts were numbered out of 28, while the regular issue cards simply bore a number. This set was condition sensitive.

COMPLETE SET (28) 20.00 50.00
1 Guy Hebert .20 .50
2 Adam Oates .40 1.00
3 Dominik Hasek 1.00 2.50
4 Robert Reichel .20 .50
5 Jeremy Roenick .75 2.00
6 Mike Modano 1.00 2.50
7 Sergei Fedorov .75 2.00
8 Jason Arnott .20 .50
9 John Vanbiesbrouck .40 1.00
10 Chris Pronger .40 1.00
11 Wayne Gretzky 5.00 12.00
12 Patrick Roy 3.00 8.00
13 Martin Brodeur 2.00 5.00
14 Pierre Turgeon .20 .50
15 Mark Messier 1.00 2.50
16 Alexei Yashin .20 .50
17 Eric Lindros .75 2.00
18 Mario Lemieux 4.00 10.00
19 Joe Sakic 1.25 3.00
20 Brendan Shanahan .75 2.00
21 Arturs Irbe .20 .50
22 Chris Gratton .20 .50
23 Doug Gilmour .40 1.00
24 Pavel Bure .75 2.00
25 Joe Juneau .20 .50
26 Teemu Selanne .75 2.00
27 Paul Kariya .75 2.00
28 Peter Forsberg 2.00 5.00

1994-95 Leaf Phenoms

The ten cards in this set were randomly inserted in Leaf series 2 product at the rate of 1:18 packs. Complete sets were also available in random Super Packs. The card fronts came out of packs with a translucent protective film as well as a white sticker which read "Remove Protective Film". The cards were made of a thick Mylar-type stock, and featured a player action photo superimposed over a black background. Set logo and player name appeared at the bottom. The back carried a brief paragraph of information over a cut-out action photo. Cards were numbered "X of 10".

COMPLETE SET (10) 12.00 25.00
1 Jamie Storr .60 1.50
2 Brett Lindros .40 1.00
3 Peter Forsberg 5.00 12.00
4 Jason Wiemer .40 1.00
5 Paul Kariya 1.25 3.00
6 Oleg Tverdovsky .60 1.50
7 Eric Fichaud .60 1.50
8 Viktor Kozlov .40 1.00
9 Jeff Friesen .40 1.00
10 Valeri Karpov .40 1.00

1994-95 Leaf Limited

This 120-card super-premium set was issued in five-card packs, in 20 pack boxes, which were individually numbered out of 60,000. The card designs were identical to the Limited Inserts which were randomly inserted in Leaf product earlier in the season. The cards had a large reflective silver border with rainbow lines coming out of the centered player photo. The player name was in black at the base of the card below the team name, which was printed in silver foil. The card backs had a ghosted photo covered by text and a small color portrait. Cards were numbered in silver foil. Rookie cards in the set included Mariusz Czerkawski, Eric Fichaud and Jason Wiemer. Although different photos were used, it is often difficult to distinguish a Leaf Limited card from a Leaf Limited Insert. The best way to differentiate between these cards and the Leaf Limited Inserts was the numbering system. These cards were numbered 1-120, while the inserts are numbered out of 28.

COMPLETE SET (120) 15.00 40.00
1 Mario Lemieux 3.00 6.00
2 Brett Hull .60 1.50
3 Ed Belfour .50 1.25
4 Brian Rolston .08 .25
5 Garry Galley .08 .25
6 Steve Thomas .08 .25
7 Kevin Brown RC .08 .25
8 Doug Gilmour .20 .50
9 Bill Ranford .20 .50
10 Wayne Gretzky 4.00 8.00
11 Rob Niedermayer .20 .50
12 Larry Murphy .20 .50
13 Glen Wesley .08 .25
14 Pat Falloon .08 .25
15 Jocelyn Thibault .50 1.25
16 Felix Potvin .50 1.25
17 Mike Richter .50 1.25
18 Jeff Brown .08 .25
19 Jesse Belanger .08 .25
20 Benoit Hogue .08 .25
21 Viktor Kozlov .08 .25
22 Chris Pronger .50 1.25
23 Kirk McLean .20 .50
24 Oleg Tverdovsky .20 .50
25 Derian Hatcher .08 .25
26 Ray Sheppard .20 .50
27 Pat Verbeek .08 .25
28 Patrick Roy 2.50 5.00
29 Mariusz Czerkawski RC .50 1.25
30 Ron Francis .20 .50
31 Wendel Clark .20 .50
32 Rob Blake .20 .50
33 Brian Leetch .50 1.25
34 Dave Andreychuk .20 .50
35 Russ Courtnall .08 .25
36 Alexander Mogilny .20 .50
37 Kirk Muller .08 .25
38 Joe Juneau .20 .50
39 Robert Reichel .08 .25
40 Scott Niedermayer .08 .25
41 Owen Nolan .20 .50
42 Mats Sundin .50 1.25
43 Sandis Ozolinsh .08 .25
44 Derek Plante .08 .25
45 Eric Fichaud RC .20 .50
46 Kevin Stevens .08 .25
47 Igor Larionov .08 .25
48 Mikael Renberg .20 .50
49 Cam Neely .50 1.25
50 Brett Lindros .08 .25
51 Valeri Karpov RC .08 .25
52 Pierre Turgeon .20 .50
53 Doug Weight .20 .50
54 Geoff Sanderson .20 .50
55 Slava Kozlov .20 .50
56 Chris Gratton .08 .25
57 Bryan Smolinski .08 .25
58 Eric Lindros .50 1.25
59 Alexei Kovalev .20 .50
60 Mike Modano .75 2.00
61 Jeremy Roenick .60 1.50
62 Martin Straka .08 .25
63 Pat LaFontaine .50 1.25
64 Vlastimil Kroupa .08 .25
65 Sergei Zubov .08 .25
66 Jason Arnott .08 .25
67 Petr Nedved .20 .50
68 Teemu Selanne .50 1.25
69 Geoff Courtnall .08 .25
70 Martin Brodeur 1.25 3.00
71 Mark Recchi .20 .50
72 John Vanbiesbrouck .20 .50
73 Adam Graves .08 .25
74 Arturs Irbe .20 .50
75 Paul Coffey .50 1.25
76 Ulf Dahlen .08 .25
77 Phil Housley .20 .50
78 Rod Brind'Amour .20 .50
79 Al MacInnis .20 .50
80 Alexei Yashin .08 .25
81 Sergei Fedorov .75 2.00
82 Joe Nieuwendyk .20 .50
83 Chris Chelios .50 1.25
84 Ray Bourque .75 2.00
85 Scott Stevens .20 .50
86 Jaromir Jagr .75 2.00
87 Alexandre Daigle .08 .25
88 Luc Robitaille .20 .50
89 Mark Messier .50 1.25
90 Vincent Damphousse .08 .25
91 Craig Janney .20 .50
92 John MacLean .20 .50
93 Steve Duchesne .08 .25
94 Dale Hawerchuk .20 .50
95 Curtis Joseph .50 1.25
96 Chris Osgood .75 2.00
97 Brendan Shanahan .50 1.25
98 Jason Allison .08 .25
99 Theo Fleury .08 .25
100 Pavel Bure .50 1.25
101 Mathieu Schneider .08 .25
102 Dominik Hasek 1.00 2.50
103 Scott Mellanby .20 .50
104 Adam Oates .20 .50
105 Jari Kurri .20 .50
106 Joe Sakic 1.00 2.50
107 Paul Kariya .50 1.25
108 Keith Tkachuk .50 1.25
109 Daren Puppa .20 .50
110 Keith Primeau .08 .25
111 Alexei Zhitnik .08 .25
112 Trevor Linden .20 .50
113 Alexei Zhamnov .20 .50
114 Gary Roberts .08 .25
115 Kenny Jonsson .08 .25
116 Peter Forsberg 1.50 4.00
117 Rick Tocchet .20 .50
118 Aaron Gavey .08 .25
119 Jason Wiemer RC .08 .25
120 Steve Yzerman 2.50 6.00

1994-95 Leaf Limited Gold

The ten cards in this set were randomly inserted into Limited packs at the rate of 1:48 packs. The cards were designed identically to Limited except for being gold in color rather than silver and featured some of the league's most exciting players. The card backs had a ghosted photo background and featured a player profile and a small color portrait. The cards were individually numbered on the back out of 2,500.

COMPLETE SET (10) 40.00 100.00
1 Mario Lemieux 10.00 25.00
2 Brett Hull 5.00 12.00
3 Doug Gilmour 2.50 6.00
4 Eric Lindros 5.00 12.00
5 Paul Kariya 5.00 12.00
6 Jaromir Jagr 5.00 12.00
7 Wayne Gretzky 15.00 40.00
8 Jeremy Roenick 5.00 12.00
9 Sergei Fedorov 5.00 12.00
10 Pavel Bure 4.00 10.00

1994-95 Leaf Limited World Juniors Canada

The ten cards in this set were randomly inserted into Limited packs; cards from either the Canadian or U.S. World Juniors could be found at the rate of 1:12 packs. The card fronts were designed identically to Limited except for being bronze in color rather than silver. The cards featured top Canadian players who competed in the 1995 World Junior Championships. The cards were individually numbered on the back out of 5,000. Card backs also contained a small up-close photo and a brief scouting report.

COMPLETE SET (10) 30.00 60.00
1 Nolan Baumgartner 2.00 5.00
2 Eric Daze 2.00 5.00
3 Jeff Friesen 4.00 10.00
4 Todd Harvey 2.00 5.00
5 Ed Jovanovski 4.00 10.00
6 Jeff O'Neill 2.00 5.00
7 Wade Redden 4.00 10.00
8 Jamie Rivers 2.00 5.00
9 Ryan Smyth 6.00 15.00
10 Jamie Storr 2.00 5.00

1994-95 Leaf Limited World Juniors USA

The 10 cards in this set were randomly inserted into Limited packs; cards from either the U.S. or Canadian World Juniors could be found at the rate of 1:12 packs. The card fronts were designed identically to Limited save for being bronze in color rather than silver. The cards featured top American players who competed in the 1995 World Junior Championships. The cards were individually numbered on the back out of 5,000. Card backs also contained a small headshot and a brief scouting report.

COMPLETE SET (10) 20.00 40.00
1 Bryan Berard 2.00 5.00
2 Doug Bonner 2.00 5.00
3 Jason Bonsignore 2.00 5.00
4 Adam Deadmarsh 2.00 5.00
5 Rory Fitzpatrick 2.00 5.00
6 Sean Haggerty 2.00 5.00
7 Jamie Langenbrunner 4.00 8.00
8 Jeff Mitchell 2.00 5.00
9 Richard Park 2.00 5.00
10 Deron Quint 2.00 5.00

1995-96 Leaf

The 1995-96 Leaf set was released in one series of 330-cards. The 12-card packs had an SRP of $1.99. The cards boasted a simple design featuring an action photo with the team name in reflective foil along the right border. A wrapper offer on the packs gave collectors the chance to redeem two wrappers and $9.95 for a special Mario Lemieux Tribute card limited to 15,000 sequentially numbered copies.

COMPLETE SET (330) 12.50 25.00
1 Mario Lemieux .60 1.50
2 Todd Harvey .05 .15
3 Blaine Lacher .05 .15
4 Alexei Zhitnik .02 .10
5 Cory Stillman .02 .10
6 Murray Craven .02 .10
7 Mike Kennedy RC .02 .10
8 Mike Vernon .05 .15
9 David Oliver .02 .10
10 Magnus Svensson RC .02 .10
11 Andrei Nikolishin .02 .10
12 Jamie Storr .05 .15
13 David Roberts .02 .10
14 Chris McAlpine RC .02 .10
15 Brett Lindros .02 .10
16 Pat Verbeek .02 .10
17 Tony Amonte .05 .15

18 Chris Therien .02 .10
19 Ken Wregget .05 .15
20 Peter Forsberg .30 .75
21 Jeff Friesen .02 .10
22 Patrice Tardif .02 .10
23 Jason Wiemer .02 .10
24 Kenny Jonsson .02 .10
25 Jassen Cullimore .02 .10
26 Sergei Gonchar .02 .10
27 Nikolai Khabibulin .05 .15
28 Oleg Tverdovsky .02 .10
29 Rick Tocchet .05 .15
30 Garry Galley .02 .10
31 German Titov .02 .10
32 Sergei Krivokrasov .02 .10
33 Sylvain Turgeon .02 .10
34 Sergei Fedorov .15 .40
35 Ralph Intranuovo RC .02 .10
36 Stu Barnes .02 .10
37 Mike Gartner .05 .15
38 Kevin Brown .02 .10
39 Valeri Bure .02 .10
40 Sergei Brylin .02 .10
41 Kirk Muller .02 .10
42 Mike Richter .10 .30
43 Stanislav Neckar .02 .10
44 Patrik Juhlin .02 .10
45 Ron Francis .05 .15
46 Janne Laukkanen .02 .10
47 Shean Donovan .02 .10
48 Igor Korolev .02 .10
49 Alexander Selivanov .02 .10
50 Frantisek Kucera .02 .10
51 Russ Courtnall .02 .10
52 Don Beaupre .05 .15
53 Michal Grosek .02 .10
54 Steve Rucchin .05 .15
55 Mariusz Czerkawski .02 .10
56 Dominik Hasek .25 .60
57 Trent Klatt .02 .10
58 Sergio Momesso .02 .10
59 Mark Lawrence .02 .10
60 Steve Yzerman .60 1.50
61 Todd Marchant .02 .10
62 Jesse Belanger .02 .10
63 Sean Burke .05 .15
64 Matt Johnson .02 .10
65 Mark Recchi .05 .15
66 Martin Brodeur .30 .75
67 Mathieu Schneider .02 .10
68 Mark Messier .10 .30
69 Radim Bicanek .02 .10
70 Eric Desjardins .05 .15
71 Jaromir Jagr .20 .50
72 Adam Deadmarsh .02 .10
73 Viktor Kozlov .05 .15
74 Jeff Norton .02 .10
75 Brantt Myhres RC .02 .10
76 Darby Hendrickson .02 .10
77 Roman Oksiuta .02 .10
78 Jim Carey .05 .15
79 Keith Tkachuk .10 .30
80 Valeri Karpov .02 .10
81 Adam Oates .05 .15
82 Eric Lindros .10 .30
83 Trevor Kidd .05 .15
84 Bernie Nicholls .02 .10
85 Craig Conroy RC .02 .10
86 Bill Ranford .05 .15
87 Scott Mellanby .02 .10
88 Geoff Sanderson .02 .10
89 Wayne Gretzky .75 2.00
90 Pierre Turgeon .05 .15
91 Stephane Richer .05 .15
92 Chris Marinucci RC .02 .10
93 Brian Leetch .05 .15
94 Steve Larouche .02 .10
95 John LeClair .10 .30
96 Dmitri Mironov .02 .10
97 Jocelyn Thibault .10 .30
98 Craig Janney .02 .10
99 Ian Laperriere .02 .10
100 Dino Ciccarelli .05 .15
101 Todd Warriner RC .02 .10
102 Kirk McLean .05 .15
103 Jason Allison .02 .10
104 Alexei Zhamnov .05 .15
105 Keith Jones .05 .15
106 Ray Bourque .20 .50
107 John Druce .02 .10
108 Scott Walker RC .02 .10
109 Joe Murphy .02 .10
110 Checklist (1-110) .02 .10
111 Philippe DeRouville .05 .15
112 Greg Adams .02 .10
113 Cam Neely .10 .30
114 Mike Peca .05 .15
115 Theo Fleury .02 .10
116 Jeremy Roenick .15 .40
117 Kevin Hatcher .02 .10
118 Ray Sheppard .02 .10
119 Jason Arnott .02 .10
120 Mark Fitzpatrick .05 .15
121 Brendan Shanahan .10 .30
122 Jari Kurri .10 .30
123 Shayne Corson .02 .10
124 Scott Stevens .05 .15
125 Steve Thomas .05 .15
126 Sergei Zubov .02 .10
127 Denis Savard .05 .15
128 Mikael Renberg .05 .15
129 Luc Robitaille .05 .15
130 Andrei Kovalenko .02 .10
131 Andrei Nazarov .02 .10
132 Denis Chasse .02 .10
133 Chris Gratton .02 .10
134 Benoit Hogue .02 .10
135 Pavel Bure .10 .30
136 Peter Bondra .10 .30
137 Teemu Selanne .10 .30
138 Darren Van Impe RC .02 .10
139 Dimitri Khristich .02 .10
140 Pat LaFontaine .10 .30
141 Phil Housley .05 .15
142 Chris Chelios .10 .30
143 Steve Duchesne .02 .10
144 Paul Coffey .10 .30
145 Doug Weight .05 .15
146 Gord Murphy .02 .10
147 Andrew Cassels .02 .10
148 Rob Blake .05 .15
149 Vladimir Malakhov .02 .10
150 Scott Niedermayer .02 .10
151 Patrick Flatley .02 .10
152 Adam Graves .05 .15
153 Alexei Yashin .02 .10
154 Rod Brind'Amour .05 .15
155 Joe Mullen .05 .15
156 Mike Ricci .05 .15
157 Ulf Dahlen .02 .10
158 Dave Manson .02 .10
159 Brian Bradley .02 .10
160 Felix Potvin .10 .30
161 Trevor Linden .05 .15
162 Michal Pivonka .02 .10
163 Nelson Emerson .05 .15
164 Joe Sacco .02 .10
165 Todd Elik .02 .10
166 Derek Plante .02 .10
167 Mike Sullivan .02 .10
168 Randy Wood .02 .10
169 Manny Fernandez .10 .30
170 Keith Primeau .02 .10
171 Marko Tuomainen .02 .10
172 John Vanbiesbrouck .05 .15
173 Darren Turcotte .02 .10
174 Tony Granato .02 .10
175 Brian Savage .02 .10
176 John MacLean .05 .15
177 Tommy Salo RC .40 1.00
178 Steve Larmer .05 .15
179 Alexandre Daigle .02 .10
180 Petr Svoboda .02 .10
181 John Cullen .02 .10
182 Joe Sakic .25 .60
183 Sandis Ozolinsh .02 .10
184 Dale Hawerchuk .10 .30
185 Paul Ysebaert .02 .10
186 Larry Murphy .05 .15
187 Alexander Mogilny .05 .15
188 Joe Juneau .02 .10
189 Craig Martin RC .02 .10
190 Jason Marshall .02 .10
191 Don Sweeney .02 .10
192 Ron Hextall .05 .15
193 Steve Chiasson .02 .10
194 Steve Smith .02 .10
195 Lyle Odelein .02 .10
196 Ryan Smyth .05 .15
197 Rob Niedermayer .05 .15
198 Steven Rice .02 .10
199 Darryl Sydor .05 .15
200 Patrick Roy .60 1.50
201 Bill Guerin .05 .15
202 Scott Lachance .02 .10
203 Alexei Kovalev .02 .10
204 Ronnie Stern .02 .10
205 Kevin Dineen .02 .10
206 Ulf Samuelsson .02 .10
207 Wendel Clark .05 .15
208 Ray Whitney .05 .15
209 Brett Hull .15 .40
210 Slava Kozlov .05 .15
211 Doug Gilmour .05 .15
212 Mike Ridley .02 .10
213 Mike Torchia .05 .15
214 Tavis Hansen RC .02 .10
215 Dale Hunter .05 .15
216 Kevin Stevens .02 .10
217 Mike Donnelly .02 .10
218 Sylvain Cote .02 .10
219 Gary Suter .02 .10
220 Checklist (111-120) .02 .10
221 Richard Park .02 .10
222 Dave Gagner .02 .10
223 Jozef Stumpel .02 .10
224 Brad May .02 .10
225 Zarley Zalapski .02 .10
226 Eric Daze .05 .15
227 Mike Modano .20 .50
228 Nicklas Lidstrom .10 .30
229 Jason Bonsignore .02 .10
230 Robert Svehla RC .02 .10
231 Glen Wesley .02 .10
232 Josef Beranek .02 .10
233 Geoff Courtnall .02 .10
234 Shawn Chambers .02 .10
235 Darius Kasparaitis .02 .10
236 Sergei Nemchinov .02 .10
237 Patrick Poulin .02 .10
238 Anatoli Semenov .02 .10
239 Bryan Smolinski .02 .10
240 Owen Nolan .05 .15
241 Pat Falloon .02 .10
242 Chris Pronger .10 .30
243 Daren Puppa .05 .15
244 Mats Sundin .10 .30
245 Jeff Brown .02 .10
246 Jeff Nelson .02 .10
247 Teppo Numminen .02 .10
248 Shaun Van Allen .02 .10
249 Yanic Perreault .02 .10
250 Brian Holzinger RC .10 .30
251 Paul Kruse .02 .10
252 Jeff Shantz .02 .10
253 Martin Straka .02 .10
254 Chris Osgood .05 .15
255 Joaquin Gage RC .05 .15
256 Dave Lowry .02 .10
257 Robert Kron .02 .10
258 Dan Quinn .02 .10
259 David Wilkie .02 .10
260 Valeri Zelepukin .02 .10
261 Derek King .02 .10
262 Darren Langdon RC .02 .10
263 Radek Bonk .02 .10
264 Karl Dykhuis .02 .10
265 Tomas Sandstrom .02 .10
266 Uwe Krupp .02 .10
267 Arturs Irbe .05 .15
268 Dallas Drake .02 .10
269 John Tucker .02 .10
270 Dave Andreychuk .05 .15
271 Guy Hebert .05 .15
272 Sandy Moger RC .02 .10
273 Craig Johnson .02 .10
274 Donald Audette .02 .10
275 Cory Cross RC .02 .10
276 Richard Smehlik .02 .10
277 Gary Roberts .02 .10
278 Todd Gill .02 .10
279 Derian Hatcher .02 .10
280 Slava Fetisov .02 .10
281 Curtis Joseph .10 .30
282 Johan Garpenlov .02 .10
283 Vladimir Konstantinov .05 .15
284 Ray Ferraro .02 .10
285 Turner Stevenson .02 .10
286 Neal Broten .05 .15
287 Jason Wiemer RC .02 .10
288 Mattias Norstrom .02 .10
289 Michel Picard .02 .10
290 Brent Fedyk .02 .10
291 Dimitri Yushkevich .02 .10
292 Sylvain Lefebvre .02 .10
293 Sergei Makarov .02 .10
294 Brian Rolston .02 .10
295 Roman Hamrlik .05 .15
296 Mark Wotton RC .02 .10
297 Alek Stojanov RC .02 .10
298 Calle Johansson .02 .10
299 Mike Eastwood .02 .10
300 Bob Corkum .02 .10
301 Petr Nedved .05 .15
302 Vincent Damphousse .02 .10
303 Brett Harkins RC .02 .10
304 Paul Kariya .10 .30
305 Joe Nieuwendyk .05 .15
306 Dennis Bonvie RC .02 .10
307 Jason Woolley .02 .10
308 Jimmy Carson .02 .10
309 Marty McSorley .02 .10
310 Craig Rivet RC .02 .10
311 Claude Lemieux .02 .10
312 Al MacInnis .05 .15
313 Gerald Diduck .02 .10
314 Randy McKay .02 .10
315 Bob Errey .02 .10
316 Rusty Fitzgerald RC .02 .10
317 Scott Young .02 .10
318 Igor Larionov .02 .10
319 Esa Tikkanen .02 .10
320 Darren McCarty .02 .10
321 Petr Klima .02 .10
322 Jon Rohloff .02 .10
323 Steve Konowalchuk .02 .10
324 Milos Holan .02 .10
325 Checklist (221-330) .02 .10
326 Ted Donato .02 .10
327 Grant Marshall .02 .10
328 Jyrki Lumme .02 .10
329 Ed Belfour .10 .30
330 Checklist (inserts) .02 .10
NNO Mario Lemieux wrapper redemption 4.00 10.00

1995-96 Leaf Fire On Ice

This 12-card set featured some of the NHL's most dangerous snipers. The cards were sequentially numbered out of 10,000 and were randomly inserted at a rate of about 1:48 packs.

COMPLETE SET (12) 10.00 20.00
1 Pavel Bure .60 1.50
2 Eric Lindros .60 1.50
3 Alexei Zhamnov .30 .75
4 Paul Coffey .60 1.50
5 Theo Fleury .20 .50
6 Peter Forsberg 1.50 4.00
7 Sergei Fedorov .75 2.00
8 Mats Sundin .60 1.50
9 Brett Hull .75 2.00
10 Wayne Gretzky 4.00 10.00
11 Paul Kariya .60 1.50
12 Mikael Renberg .30 .75

1995-96 Leaf Freeze Frame

These eight cards, which focused on special moments for a team or player form the 1994-95 season, were randomly inserted at indeterminate odds (estimated at around 1:72). The cards were serially numbered out of 10,000.

COMPLETE SET (8) 10.00 25.00
1 Jim Carey 1.00 2.50
2 Pierre Turgeon 1.00 2.50
3 Mikael Renberg 1.00 2.50
4 Jaromir Jagr 1.50 4.00
5 Alexei Zhamnov 1.00 2.50
6 New Jersey Devils 1.00 2.50
7 Mario Lemieux 4.00 10.00
8 A.Mogilny/P.Bure 2.00 5.00

1995-96 Leaf Gold Stars

The twelve players featured in this six-card set were the tops at their position in 1994-95. The cards were individually numbered out of 5,000 and were randomly inserted in retail packs at indeterminate odds (estimated at around 1:90).

COMPLETE SET (6) 10.00 20.00
1 Dominik Hasek 2.50 6.00
Jim Carey
2 Paul Coffey 1.50 4.00
Chris Chelios
3 Ray Bourque 1.50 4.00
Brian Leetch
4 Eric Lindros 2.00 5.00
Alexei Zhamnov
5 Jaromir Jagr 2.50 6.00
Theo Fleury
6 Brett Hull 1.50 4.00
Mikael Renberg

1995-96 Leaf Lemieux's Best

This set captured ten of the greatest moments in the career of one of the greatest players ever, Mario Lemieux. The cards were randomly inserted at indeterminate odds (estimated at around 1:18).

COMPLETE SET (10) 20.00 40.00
COMMON CARD (1-10) 3.00 6.00

1995-96 Leaf Road To The Cup

This ten-card set recognized several key moments from the 1994-95 Stanley Cup playoffs. The cards were serially numbered out of 5,000, and were randomly inserted into hobby packs only at indeterminate odds (estimated at around 1:90).

COMPLETE SET (10) 5.00 10.00
1 Ray Whitney .30 .75
2 Martin Brodeur 1.50 4.00
3 Jaromir Jagr 1.00 2.50
4 Eric Lindros .60 1.50
5 Paul Coffey .60 1.50
6 Chris Chelios .60 1.50
7 Neal Broten .30 .75
8 Slava Kozlov .30 .75
9 Scott Niedermayer .30 .75
10 Claude Lemieux .30 .75

1995-96 Leaf Studio Rookies

This 20-card set resembled credit cards, down to the shape, the embossed membership data on the front and the signature and metallic data strips on the back. The cards were randomly inserted into packs at indeterminate odds, estimated to be around 1:12.

COMPLETE SET (20) 15.00 30.00
1 Jim Carey 1.00 2.50
2 Peter Forsberg 2.50 6.00
3 Paul Kariya 1.50 4.00
4 David Oliver .75 2.00
5 Blaine Lacher 1.00 2.50
6 Oleg Tverdovsky .75 2.00
7 Jeff Friesen .75 2.00
8 Todd Marchant 1.00 2.50
9 Todd Harvey 1.00 2.50
10 Ian Laperriere .75 2.00
11 Eric Daze 1.00 2.50
12 Jason Bonsignore .75 2.00
13 Jamie Storr 1.00 2.50
14 Brian Holzinger 1.50 4.00
15 Brian Savage .75 2.00
16 Roman Oksiuta .75 2.00
17 Mariusz Czerkawski .75 2.00
18 Sergei Krivokrasov .75 2.00
19 Jason Wiemer .75 2.00
20 Radek Bonk .75 2.00

1996-97 Leaf

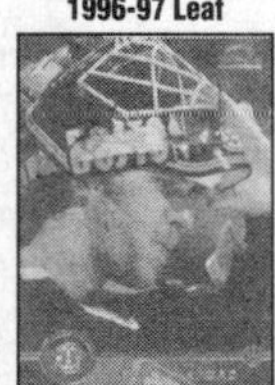

The 1996-97 Leaf set, consisting of 240 cards, was distributed in 10-card packs with a suggested retail price of $2.99. The fronts featured a color action player photo printed on common card stock with silver foil. The backs carried another player photo with season and career statistics. Marin Biron was the only rookie of note.

COMPLETE SET (240) 12.50 30.00
1 Sergei Fedorov .20 .50
2 Bill Ranford .07 .20
3 Oleg Tverdovsky .07 .20
4 Brad May .07 .20
5 Chris Pronger .07 .20
6 Martin Brodeur .40 1.00
7 Yanic Perreault .02 .10
8 Garry Galley .02 .10
9 Shawn McEachern .02 .10
10 Brian Bellows .02 .10
11 Ron Francis .07 .20
12 Mike Modano .25 .60
13 Steve Yzerman .75 2.00
14 Joe Mullen .07 .20
15 Pavel Bure .15 .40
16 Dino Ciccarelli .07 .20
17 Claude Lemieux .02 .10
18 Stephane Richer .07 .20
19 Dominik Hasek .30 .75
20 Adam Graves .07 .20
21 Joe Juneau .02 .10
22 Rob Niedermayer .07 .20
23 Zigmund Palffy .07 .20
24 Dave Andreychuk .07 .20
25 Steve Thomas .07 .20
26 Tom Barrasso .07 .20
27 Eric Desjardins .07 .20
28 Curtis Joseph .15 .40
29 Russ Courtnall .02 .10
30 Stu Barnes .02 .10
31 Mark Tinordi .02 .10
32 Gary Suter .02 .10
33 Greg Johnson .02 .10
34 Joe Nieuwendyk .07 .20
35 Norm Maciver .02 .10
36 Craig Janney .07 .20
37 Mark Recchi .07 .20
38 Patrick Roy .75 2.00
39 Petr Klima .02 .10
40 Ken Wregget .07 .20
41 Rod Brind'Amour .07 .20
42 Slava Fetisov .02 .10
43 Kirk McLean .07 .20
44 Pat LaFontaine .15 .40
45 Brett Hull .20 .50
46 Chris Chelios .15 .40
47 Damian Rhodes .07 .20
48 Kevin Hatcher .02 .10
49 Uwe Krupp .02 .10
50 Bernie Nicholls .02 .10
51 Tommy Soderstrom .07 .20
52 Teemu Selanne .15 .40
53 Mats Sundin .15 .40
54 Jeff Hackett .07 .20
55 Ulf Dahlen .02 .10
56 Dale Hunter .02 .10
57 Robert Kron .02 .10
58 Brian Bradley .02 .10
59 Pat Verbeek .02 .10
60 Kenny Jonsson .02 .10
61 Theo Fleury .02 .10
62 Alexander Selivanov .02 .10
63 Nikolai Khabibulin .07 .20
64 Grant Fuhr .07 .20
65 Phil Housley .07 .20
66 Bill Lindsay .02 .10
67 Trevor Kidd .07 .20
68 Jim Carey .15 .40
69 Brian Skrudland .02 .10
70 Todd Krygier .02 .10
71 Petr Nedved .07 .20
72 Kirk Muller .02 .10
73 Daren Puppa .07 .20
74 Doug Gilmour .07 .20
75 Nicklas Lidstrom .15 .40
76 Zdeno Ciger .02 .10
77 Robert Svehla .02 .10
78 Andrew Cassels .02 .10
79 Vincent Damphousse .02 .10
80 Alexandre Daigle .02 .10
81 Tomas Sandstrom .02 .10
82 Brent Fedyk .02 .10
83 John LeClair .15 .40
84 Mario Lemieux .75 2.00
85 Sean Burke .07 .20
86 Cam Neely .15 .40
87 Jeff Friesen .02 .10
88 Guy Hebert .07 .20
89 Jon Casey .07 .20
90 Rick Tocchet .07 .20
91 Mike Gartner .07 .20
92 Tony Amonte .07 .20
93 Jason Dawe .02 .10
94 Chris Terreri .07 .20
95 Zarley Zalapski .02 .10
96 Martin Rucinsky .02 .10
97 Garth Snow .07 .20
98 Sylvain Lefebvre .02 .10
99 Andy Moog .07 .20
100 Larry Murphy .07 .20
101 Alexei Yashin .07 .20
102 Pat Falloon .02 .10
103 Greg Adams .02 .10
104 Igor Larionov .02 .10
105 Geoff Sanderson .07 .20
106 Jaromir Jagr .25 .60
107 Alexei Zhamnov .07 .20
108 Mikael Renberg .07 .20
109 Kelly Hrudey .07 .20
110 Vladimir Konstantinov .07 .20
111 Brian Savage .02 .10
112 Adam Oates .07 .20
113 Teppo Numminen .02 .10
114 Ray Sheppard .07 .20
115 Michael Nylander .02 .10
116 Jozef Stumpel .02 .10
117 Ed Olczyk .02 .10
118 Roman Hamrlik .07 .20
119 Kris Draper .02 .10
120 Chris Gratton .07 .20
121 Randy Burridge .02 .10
122 Ray Bourque .25 .60
123 Jyrki Lumme .02 .10
124 Dale Hawerchuk .07 .20
125 Dave Lowry .02 .10
126 Curtis Leschyshyn .02 .10
127 Martin Gelinas .02 .10
128 Owen Nolan .07 .20
129 Radek Bonk .02 .10
130 Sergei Zubov .02 .10
131 Travis Green .02 .10
132 Scott Mellanby .07 .20
133 Keith Tkachuk .15 .40
134 Luc Robitaille .07 .20
135 Alexei Kovalev .02 .10
136 Doug Weight .07 .20
137 Benoit Hogue .02 .10
138 Cory Stillman .02 .10
139 Joe Sakic .30 .75
140 Wayne Gretzky 1.00 2.50
141 Mike Ricci .02 .10
142 Kyle McLaren .02 .10
143 Deron Quint .02 .10
144 Ville Peltonen .02 .10
145 Todd Harvey .02 .10
146 Brendan Shanahan .15 .40
147 Mike Vernon .07 .20
148 Eric Lindros .15 .40
149 Rick Tabaracci .02 .10
150 Stephane Yelle .02 .10
151 Chris Osgood .07 .20
152 Corey Hirsch .07 .20
153 Todd Marchant .07 .20
154 Keith Primeau .02 .10
155 Alexei Zhitnik .02 .10
156 Felix Potvin .15 .40
157 Vitali Yachmenev .02 .10
158 Geoff Courtnall .02 .10
159 Peter Forsberg .40 1.00
160 Radek Dvorak .02 .10
161 Bryan McCabe .02 .10
162 Alexander Mogilny .07 .20
163 Shayne Corson .02 .10
164 Paul Coffey .15 .40
165 Brian Leetch .15 .40
166 Wendel Clark .07 .20
167 Aaron Gavey .02 .10
168 Dimitri Khristich .02 .10
169 Grant Marshall .02 .10
170 Valeri Kamensky .07 .20
171 Ryan Smyth .15 .40
172 Niklas Sundstrom .02 .10
173 Cliff Ronning .02 .10
174 Al MacInnis .07 .20
175 Scott Stevens .07 .20
176 Paul Kariya .15 .40
177 Rob Blake .07 .20
178 Mike Richter .15 .40
179 Jason Arnott .02 .10
180 Mark Messier .15 .40
181 Scott Young .02 .10
182 Jocelyn Thibault .15 .40
183 Marcus Ragnarsson .02 .10
184 Darren Turcotte .02 .10
185 Joe Murphy .02 .10
186 Pierre Turgeon .07 .20
187 Trevor Linden .07 .20
188 Stephane Fiset .07 .20
189 Miroslav Satan .02 .10
190 Mathieu Schneider .02 .10
191 Jeremy Roenick .20 .50
192 Craig MacTavish .02 .10
193 John Vanbiesbrouck .07 .20
194 Ron Hextall .07 .20
195 John MacLean .07 .20
196 Vyacheslav Kozlov .02 .10
197 Sandis Ozolinsh .02 .10
198 Scott Niedermayer .02 .10
199 Ed Belfour .15 .40
200 Peter Bondra .07 .20
201 Jere Lehtinen .02 .10
202 Eric Daze .07 .20
203 Chad Kilger .02 .10
204 Saku Koivu .15 .40
205 Todd Bertuzzi .15 .40
206 Petr Sykora .02 .10
207 Valeri Bure .02 .10
208 Ed Jovanovski .07 .20
209 Jeff O'Neill .02 .10
210 Daniel Alfredsson .07 .20
211 Byron Dafoe .07 .20
212 Brian Holzinger .07 .20
213 Martin Biron RC .75 2.00
214 Anders Eriksson .02 .10
215 Landon Wilson .02 .10
216 Alexei Yegorov RC .02 .10
217 Jan Caloun RC .02 .10
218 David Sacco .02 .10
219 David Nemirovsky .02 .10
220 Anders Myrvold .02 .10
221 Tommy Salo .07 .20
222 Jan Vopat .02 .10
223 Steve Staios RC .02 .10
224 Patrick Labrecque .02 .10
225 Jamie Langenbrunner .02 .10
226 Denis Pederson .02 .10
227 Marek Malik .02 .10
228 Geoff Sarjeant .02 .10
229 Chris Ferraro .02 .10
230 Zdenek Nedved .02 .10
231 Wayne Primeau .02 .10
232 Daymond Langkow .07 .20
233 Marko Kiprusoff .02 .10
234 Niklas Sundblad .02 .10
235 Jamie Ram RC .02 .10
236 Jamie Rivers .02 .10
237 Steve Washburn RC .02 .10
238 Teemu Selanne CL .15 .40
239 Steve Yzerman CL .15 .40
240 Eric Lindros CL .15 .40

1996-97 Leaf Press Proofs

This 240-card set was a die-cut parallel rendition of the regular Leaf set. Only 1,500 sets were produced, with each card sequentially numbered. The words "Press Proof" appeared on the card front in gold foil.

*VETS: 8X TO 20X BASIC CARDS
*ROOKIES: 4X TO 10X

1996-97 Leaf Fire On Ice

This 15-card insert set, found only in retail packs, featured megastar players who heated up the ice with their play. Color player photos were printed on foil-laminated, micro-etched card stock. Only 2,500 sets were produced, with each card sequentially numbered.

COMPLETE SET (15) 20.00 50.00
1 Mario Lemieux 5.00 12.00
2 Alexander Mogilny .75 2.00
3 Joe Sakic 2.50 6.00
4 Paul Kariya 1.25 3.00
5 Wayne Gretzky 6.00 15.00
6 Doug Weight .75 2.00
7 Zigmund Palffy .75 2.00
8 Eric Lindros 1.25 3.00
9 Teemu Selanne 1.25 3.00
10 Doug Gilmour .75 2.00
11 Jeremy Roenick 1.50 4.00
12 Steve Yzerman 4.00 10.00
13 Ed Jovanovski .75 2.00
14 Mike Modano 1.50 4.00
15 Mark Messier 1.50 4.00

1996-97 Leaf Gold Rookies

COMPLETE SET (10) 10.00 25.00
1 Ethan Moreau .75 2.00
2 Kevin Hodson .75 2.00
3 Jose Theodore 2.50 6.00
4 Peter Ferraro .75 2.00
5 Ralph Intranuovo .75 2.00
6 Nolan Baumgartner .75 2.00
7 Brandon Convery .75 2.00
8 Darcy Tucker 1.50 4.00
9 Eric Fichaud .75 2.00
10 Steve Sullivan 1.50 4.00

1996-97 Leaf Leather And Laces Promos

This 20 card set was intended to promote the upcoming Leather and Lace insert set. Unlike the regular set in which 5,000 serial numbered sets were issued, these cards were issued as Promo/5000 in the serial numbered box. Forsberg and Modano were the two most commonly found cards in this set

COMPLETE SET (20) 30.00 80.00
*PROMOS: .3X TO .8X BASIC INSERTS

1996-97 Leaf Leather And Laces

This 20-card set featured color action player photos of the NHL's top skaters printed on embossed leather cards with skate laces in the background and gold foil stamping. The backs carried another player photo and player statistics on a black background. Only 5,000 of these sets were produced and were sequentially numbered.

COMPLETE SET (20) 50.00 100.00
1 Joe Sakic 5.00 12.00
2 Keith Tkachuk 2.00 5.00
3 Brett Hull 3.00 8.00
4 Paul Coffey 2.00 5.00
5 Jaromir Jagr 4.00 10.00
6 Peter Forsberg 4.00 10.00
7 Zigmund Palffy 1.25 3.00
8 Wayne Gretzky 12.00 30.00
9 Pavel Bure 3.00 8.00
10 Eric Lindros 2.00 5.00
11 Alexander Mogilny 1.25 3.00
12 Trevor Linden 1.25 3.00
13 Jeremy Roenick 3.00 8.00
14 Doug Gilmour 1.25 3.00
15 Mike Modano 3.00 8.00
16 Sergei Fedorov 3.00 8.00
17 Brendan Shanahan 2.00 5.00
18 Pierre Turgeon 1.25 3.00
19 Ed Jovanovski 1.25 3.00
20 Saku Koivu 2.00 5.00

1996-97 Leaf Shut Down

The dominant goaltenders of the NHL (as a group averaging 27 wins in 95-96), were the focus of this 15-card hobby-only chase set. The fronts featured color player photos printed on sailcloth canvas card stock while the backs carried player information. Only 2,500 of this set were produced, with each card sequentially numbered.

COMPLETE SET (15) 75.00 150.00
1 Patrick Roy 12.00 30.00
2 John Vanbiesbrouck 4.00 10.00
3 Jocelyn Thibault 2.00 5.00
4 Ed Belfour 4.00 10.00
5 Curtis Joseph 4.00 10.00
6 Martin Brodeur 7.50 15.00
7 Damian Rhodes 2.00 5.00
8 Felix Potvin 4.00 10.00
9 Nikolai Khabibulin 4.00 10.00
10 Jim Carey 2.00 5.00
11 Mike Richter 4.00 10.00
12 Corey Hirsch 2.00 5.00
13 Chris Osgood 4.00 10.00
14 Ron Hextall 4.00 10.00
15 Daren Puppa 2.00 5.00

1996-97 Leaf Sweaters Away

This 15-card insert set was printed on embossed, nylon jersey-style card stock in colors simulating the road uniforms of the league's superstars. The fronts displayed color player photos while the backs carried player information. Just 5,000 of these sets were produced and each card was sequentially numbered.

COMPLETE SET (15) 40.00 100.00
*HOME: .8X TO 2X AWAY
HOME PRINT RUN 1000 SER.#'d SETS
1 Mario Lemieux 10.00 25.00
2 Patrick Roy 10.00 25.00
3 Eric Lindros 2.50 6.00
4 John Vanbiesbrouck 2.50 6.00
5 Paul Kariya 2.50 6.00
6 Martin Brodeur 6.00 15.00
7 Eric Daze 1.25 3.00
8 Mark Messier 3.00 8.00
9 Jim Carey 1.25 3.00
10 Brendan Shanahan 2.50 6.00
11 Sergei Fedorov 2.50 6.00

12 Brett Hull	2.50	6.00
13 Pavel Bure	2.50	6.00
14 Daniel Alfredsson	2.50	6.00
15 Saku Koivu	2.50	6.00

1996-97 Leaf The Best Of

This nine-card insert set featured NHL record breakers and was found exclusively in pre-priced retail packs. Printed on clear plastic with holographic foil, just 1,500 of this die-cut insert set were produced, with each card sequentially numbered.

COMPLETE SET (9)	20.00	50.00
1 Jaromir Jagr	6.00	15.00
2 Eric Daze	2.00	5.00
3 Eric Lindros	3.00	8.00
4 Chris Osgood	3.00	8.00
5 Keith Tkachuk	3.00	8.00
6 Nikolai Khabibulin	3.00	8.00
7 Doug Weight	2.00	5.00
8 Peter Forsberg	6.00	15.00
9 Jocelyn Thibault	2.00	5.00

1997-98 Leaf

The 1997-98 Leaf set was issued in one series totaling 200 cards and was distributed in 10-card packs with a suggested retail price of $2.99. The fronts featured borderless color action player photos. The backs carried player information. The set contained the topical subsets: Gold Leaf Rookies (148-167), Gamers (168-187), and Day in the Life (188-197).

COMPLETE SET (200)	60.00	120.00
1 Eric Lindros	.20	.50
2 Dominik Hasek	.40	1.00
3 Peter Forsberg	.50	1.25
4 Steve Yzerman	1.00	2.50
5 John Vanbiesbrouck	.15	.40
6 Paul Kariya	.20	.50
7 Martin Brodeur	.50	1.25
8 Wayne Gretzky	1.25	3.00
9 Mark Messier	.20	.50
10 Jaromir Jagr	.30	.75
11 Brett Hull	.25	.60
12 Brendan Shanahan	.20	.50
13 Ray Bourque	.30	.75
14 Jarome Iginla	.25	.60
15 Mike Modano	.30	.75
16 Curtis Joseph	.20	.50
17 Ed Jovanovski	.15	.40
18 Teemu Selanne	.20	.50
19 Saku Koivu	.20	.50
20 Eric Fichaud	.15	.40
21 Paul Coffey	.20	.50
22 Jeremy Roenick	.25	.60
23 Owen Nolan	.15	.40
24 Felix Potvin	.20	.50
25 Alexander Mogilny	.15	.40
26 Alexandre Daigle	.05	.15
27 Chris Gratton	.15	.40
28 Geoff Sanderson	.15	.40
29 Dimitri Khristich	.05	.15
30 Bryan Berard	.05	.15
31 Vyacheslav Kozlov	.05	.15
32 Jeff Hackett	.15	.40
33 Bill Ranford	.15	.40
34 Pat LaFontaine	.20	.50
35 Joe Sakic	.40	1.00
36 Niklas Sundstrom	.05	.15
37 Martin Gelinas	.05	.15
38 Mikael Renberg	.15	.40
39 Trevor Linden	.15	.40
40 Jozef Stumpel	.15	.40
41 Joe Thornton CL	.20	.50
42 Jocelyn Thibault	.15	.40
43 Pierre Turgeon	.15	.40
44 Ron Francis	.15	.40
45 Damian Rhodes	.15	.40
46 Jamie Langenbrunner	.05	.15
47 Chris Osgood	.15	.40
48 Vaclav Varada	.05	.15
49 Ryan Smyth	.15	.40
50 Daren Puppa	.15	.40
51 Petr Nedved	.15	.40
52 Ron Hextall	.15	.40
53 Joe Juneau	.15	.40
54 Jim Campbell	.05	.15
55 Zigmund Palffy	.15	.40
56 Roman Turek	.15	.40
57 Adam Deadmarsh	.05	.15
58 Rob Niedermayer	.15	.40
59 Alexei Yashin	.15	.40
60 Pavel Bure	.20	.50
61 Jason Arnott	.05	.15
62 Nikolai Khabibulin	.15	.40
63 Sean Burke	.15	.40
64 Chris Chelios	.20	.50
65 Mike Ricci	.05	.15
66 Sergei Berezin	.05	.15
67 Jaroslav Svejkovsky CL	.15	.40
68 Brian Savage	.05	.15
69 Roman Vopat	.05	.15
70 Mike Richter	.20	.50
71 Jim Carey	.15	.40
72 Guy Hebert	.15	.40
73 Keith Tkachuk	.20	.50
74 Kirk McLean	.15	.40
75 Janne Niinimaa	.05	.15
76 Roman Hamrlik	.05	.15
77 Darcy Tucker	.05	.15
78 Pat Verbeek	.05	.15
79 Hnat Domenichelli	.05	.15
80 Doug Gilmour	.15	.40
81 Mike Grier	.05	.15
82 Ken Wregget	.15	.40
83 Dino Ciccarelli	.05	.15
84 Steve Sullivan	.05	.15
85 Anson Carter	.15	.40
86 Steve Shields RC	.30	.75
87 Ed Belfour	.20	.50
88 Darren McCarty	.05	.15
89 Adam Graves	.05	.15
90 Chris Pronger	.15	.40
91 Peter Bondra	.15	.40
92 Oleg Tverdovsky	.05	.15
93 Stephane Fiset	.15	.40
94 Mike Vernon	.15	.40
95 Scott Lachance	.05	.15
96 Corey Schwab	.15	.40
97 Eric Daze	.15	.40
98 Jere Lehtinen	.05	.15
99 Donald Audette	.05	.15
100 John LeClair	.20	.50
101 Steve Rucchin	.05	.15
102 Jeff Friesen	.05	.15
103 Daymond Langkow	.15	.40
104 Mike Dunham	.15	.40
105 Marc Denis CL	.05	.15
106 Andrew Cassels	.05	.15
107 Mike Peca	.05	.15
108 Joe Nieuwendyk	.15	.40
109 Vincent Damphousse	.05	.15
110 Scott Mellanby	.05	.15
111 Patrick Lalime	.15	.40
112 Derek Plante	.05	.15
113 Wade Redden	.05	.15
114 Marcel Cousineau	.15	.40
115 Ray Sheppard	.15	.40
116 Dave Andreychuk	.15	.40
117 Brian Leetch	.20	.50
118 Sandis Ozolinsh	.05	.15
119 Keith Primeau	.05	.15
120 Brian Holzinger	.05	.15
121 Luc Robitaille	.15	.40
122 Jose Theodore	.25	.60
123 Grant Fuhr	.15	.40
124 Dainius Zubrus	.20	.50
125 Rod Brind'Amour	.15	.40
126 Trevor Kidd	.15	.40
127 Mark Recchi	.15	.40
128 Patrick Roy	1.00	2.50
129 Kevin Hatcher	.05	.15
130 Adam Oates	.15	.40
131 Doug Weight	.15	.40
132 Vaclav Prospal RC UER front & back Vinny	.20	.50
133 Harry York	.05	.15
134 Todd Bertuzzi	.20	.50
135 Sergei Fedorov	.30	.75
136 Theo Fleury	.05	.15
137 Chad Kilger	.05	.15
138 Jamie Storr	.15	.40
139 Tony Amonte	.15	.40
140 Rem Murray	.05	.15
141 Chris O'Sullivan	.05	.15
142 Mats Sundin	.20	.50
143 Ethan Moreau	.05	.15
144 Derian Hatcher	.05	.15
145 Daniel Alfredsson	.15	.40
146 Corey Hirsch	.05	.15
147 Landon Wilson	.05	.15
148 Marc Denis GLR	.30	.75
149 Boyd Devereaux GLR	.30	.75
150 Joe Thornton GLR	1.50	4.00
151 Sergei Samsonov GLR	1.00	2.50
152 Alyn McCauley GLR	.30	.75
153 Erik Rasmussen GLR	.30	.75
154 Patrick Marleau GLR	1.00	2.50
155 Olli Jokinen GLR RC	1.00	2.50
156 Chris Phillips GLR	.30	.75
157 Tomas Vokoun GLR RC	.75	2.00
158 Chris Dingman GLR RC	.30	.75
159 Daniel Cleary GLR	.30	.75
160 Juha Lind GLR RC	.30	.75
161 Jean-Yves Leroux RC GLR	.30	.75
162 Brad Isbister GLR	.30	.75
163 Vadim Sharifijanov GLR	.30	.75
164 Alexei Morozov GLR	.30	.75
165 Vaclav Prospal GLR UER front & back Vinny	.30	.75
166 Vaclav Varada GLR	.30	.75
167 Jaroslav Svejkovsky GLR	.30	.75
168 Eric Lindros GM	.50	1.25
169 Dominik Hasek GM	2.00	5.00
170 Peter Forsberg GM	2.50	6.00
171 Steve Yzerman GM	5.00	12.00
172 John Vanbiesbrouck GM	1.00	2.50
173 Paul Kariya GM	.50	1.25
174 Martin Brodeur GM	2.50	6.00
175 Wayne Gretzky GM	6.00	15.00
176 Mark Messier GM	.50	1.25
177 Jaromir Jagr GM	1.50	4.00
178 Brett Hull GM	1.25	3.00
179 Brendan Shanahan GM	.60	1.50
180 Jarome Iginla GM	.60	1.50
181 Mike Modano GM	.50	1.25
182 Teemu Selanne GM	.50	1.25
183 Bryan Berard GM	.40	1.00
184 Ryan Smyth GM	.40	1.00
185 Keith Tkachuk GM	.50	1.25
186 Dainius Zubrus GM	.40	1.00
187 Patrick Roy GM	5.00	12.00
188 Trevor Linden DIL	.40	1.00
189 Trevor Linden DIL	.40	1.00
190 Trevor Linden DIL	.40	1.00
191 Trevor Linden DIL	.40	1.00
192 Trevor Linden DIL	.40	1.00
193 Trevor Linden DIL	.40	1.00
194 Trevor Linden DIL	.40	1.00
195 Trevor Linden DIL	.40	1.00
196 Trevor Linden DIL	.40	1.00
197 Trevor Linden DIL	.40	1.00
198 Chris Phillips CL	.20	.50
199 Sergei Samsonov CL	.40	1.00
200 Daniel Cleary CL	.40	1.00
P5 Felix Potvin PROMO	.60	1.50
P6 Martin Brodeur PROMO	3.00	8.00
P10 Jim Carey PROMO	.50	1.25
NNO Trevor Linden AU/500	10.00	25.00

1997-98 Leaf Fractal Matrix

This 200-card set is parallel to the base set and featured color player photos with either a bronze, silver or gold finish. Only 100 cards were bronze, 60 cards were silver, and 40 cards were gold. No card was available in more than one of the color. Bronze-X cards had a stated print run 1400 sets. Bronze-Y cards had a stated print run 1600 sets. Bronze-Z cards had a stated print run 1700 sets. Silver-X cards had a stated print run of 500 sets. Silver-Y cards had a stated print run of 700 sets. Silver-Z cards had a stated print run of 800 cards. Gold-X cards had a stated print run of 50 sets. Gold-Y cards had a stated print run of 250 sets. Gold-Z cards had a stated print run of 350 sets. These cards were randomly inserted in leaf and Leaf International packs.

COMMON BRONZE/1400-1700	.40	1.00
BRONZE SEMISTARS	1.00	2.50
BRONZE UNL.STARS	1.25	3.00
COMMON SILVER/500-800	1.25	3.00
SILVER SEMISTARS	3.00	8.00
SILVER UNL.STARS	4.00	10.00
COMMON GOLD/250-350	2.00	5.00
GOLD SEMISTARS/250-350	5.00	12.00
GOLD UNL.STARS/250-350	6.00	15.00
1 Eric Lindros GX	6.00	15.00
2 Dominik Hasek GZ	12.50	30.00
3 Peter Forsberg GZ	15.00	40.00
4 Steve Yzerman GZ	30.00	80.00
6 Paul Kariya GX	40.00	100.00
7 Martin Brodeur GZ	15.00	40.00
8 Wayne Gretzky GX	125.00	300.00
11 Brett Hull GY	10.00	25.00
13 Ray Bourque GY	12.50	30.00
15 Mike Modano GY	12.50	30.00
35 Joe Sakic GY	15.00	40.00
41 Joe Thornton CL SZ	5.00	12.00
128 Patrick Roy GY	40.00	100.00
135 Sergei Fedorov GY	12.50	30.00
150 Joe Thornton GLR GX	20.00	50.00
154 Patrick Marleau GLR SX	8.00	20.00
155 Olli Jokinen GLR BX	2.50	6.00
169 Dominik Hasek GM BY	2.50	6.00
170 Peter Forsberg GM BY	3.00	8.00
171 Steve Yzerman GM SY	15.00	40.00
172 J.Vanbiesbrouck GM BX	1.50	4.00
173 Paul Kariya GM SY	6.00	15.00
174 Martin Brodeur GM BZ	3.00	8.00
175 Wayne Gretzky GM SY	20.00	50.00
177 Jaromir Jagr GM BZ	2.00	5.00
178 Brett Hull GM BX	2.00	5.00
180 Jarome Iginla GM BX	1.50	4.00
181 Mike Modano GM BY	2.00	5.00
187 Patrick Roy GM BX	8.00	20.00

1997-98 Leaf Fractal Matrix Die Cuts

Randomly inserted in packs, this 200-card set was a parallel to the base set and featured three different die-cut versions in three different finishes. Only 100 cards of the set were produced in the X-Axis cut with 75 of those bronze, 20 silver, and five gold. Only 60 were produced in the Y-Axis cut with 20 of those bronze, 30 silver and 10 gold. Only 40 were produced in the Z-Axis cut with five bronze, 10 silver, and 25 gold. X-Axis cards had a stated print run of 400 sets. Y-Axis cards had a stated print run of 200 sets. Z-Axis cards had a stated print run of 100 sets. No card was available in more than one color nor in more than one die-cut version.

COMMON X-AXIS/400	1.50	4.00
X-AXIS SEMISTARS	4.00	10.00
X-AXIS UNL.STARS	5.00	12.00
COMMON Y-AXIS/200	2.50	6.00
Y-AXIS SEMISTARS	6.00	15.00
Y-AXIS UNL.STARS	8.00	20.00
COMMON Z-AXIS/100	4.00	10.00
Z-AXIS SEMISTARS	10.00	25.00
Z-AXIS UNL.STARS	12.50	30.00
2 Dominik Hasek GZ	25.00	60.00
3 Peter Forsberg GZ	30.00	80.00
4 Steve Yzerman GZ	60.00	150.00
7 Martin Brodeur GZ	30.00	80.00
8 Wayne Gretzky GX	30.00	80.00
10 Jaromir Jagr GZ	20.00	50.00
11 Brett Hull GY	12.50	30.00
13 Ray Bourque GY	12.50	30.00
14 Jarome Iginla GY	10.00	25.00
15 Mike Modano GY	12.50	30.00
16 Curtis Joseph GY	12.50	30.00
21 Paul Coffey SX	12.50	30.00
22 Jeremy Roenick SX	6.00	15.00
35 Joe Sakic GY	15.00	40.00
41 Joe Thornton CL SZ	15.00	40.00
122 Jose Theodore SX	6.00	15.00
128 Patrick Roy GY	40.00	100.00
134 Todd Bertuzzi BX	5.00	12.00
135 Sergei Fedorov GY	12.50	30.00
157 Tomas Vokoun GLR BX	5.00	12.00
169 Dominik Hasek GM BY	15.00	40.00
170 Peter Forsberg GM BY	20.00	50.00
171 Steve Yzerman GM SY	40.00	100.00
174 Martin Brodeur GM BZ	30.00	80.00
175 Wayne Gretzky GM SY	50.00	125.00
177 Jaromir Jagr GM BZ	20.00	50.00
178 Brett Hull GM BX	6.00	15.00
180 Jarome Iginla GM BX	6.00	15.00
181 Mike Modano GM BY	12.50	30.00
187 Patrick Roy GM BX	25.00	60.00

1997-98 Leaf Banner Season

Randomly inserted in packs, this 24-card set featured color player photos of top players printed on die-cut banner-shaped canvas card stock. Each card was individually numbered to 3,500.

COMPLETE SET (24)	40.00	80.00
1 Paul Kariya	1.50	4.00
2 Eric Lindros	1.50	4.00
3 Wayne Gretzky	10.00	25.00
4 Jaromir Jagr	2.50	6.00
5 Steve Yzerman	8.00	20.00
6 Brendan Shanahan	1.50	4.00
7 John LeClair	1.50	4.00
8 Teemu Selanne	1.50	4.00
9 Mike Modano	2.50	6.00
10 Ryan Smyth	1.25	3.00
11 Brett Hull	2.00	5.00
12 Zigmund Palffy	1.25	3.00
13 Peter Forsberg	4.00	10.00
14 Keith Tkachuk	1.50	4.00
15 Saku Koivu	1.50	4.00
16 Sergei Fedorov	2.50	6.00
17 Brian Leetch	1.50	4.00
18 Bryan Berard	.50	1.25
19 Mats Sundin	1.50	4.00
20 Jarome Iginla	2.00	5.00
21 Sergei Berezin	.50	1.25
22 Dainius Zubrus	1.50	4.00
23 Mike Grier	.50	1.25
24 Joe Sakic	3.00	8.00

1997-98 Leaf Fire On Ice

Randomly inserted in packs, this 16-card set featured color photos of top players on a background of fire and ice printed using dot matrix hologram technology. Each card was individually numbered to 1,000.

COMPLETE SET (16)	75.00	150.00
1 Wayne Gretzky	15.00	40.00
2 Eric Lindros	2.50	6.00
3 Jaromir Jagr	4.00	10.00
4 Steve Yzerman	12.50	30.00
5 Brendan Shanahan	2.50	6.00
6 Mike Modano	4.00	10.00
7 Joe Sakic	5.00	12.00
8 Pavel Bure	2.50	6.00
9 Ryan Smyth	2.00	5.00
10 Teemu Selanne	2.50	6.00
11 Mark Messier	2.50	6.00
12 Peter Forsberg	6.00	15.00
13 Dainius Zubrus	2.50	6.00
14 Joe Thornton	20.00	50.00
15 Sergei Samsonov	12.50	30.00
16 Paul Kariya	2.50	6.00

1997-98 Leaf Lindros Collection

Randomly inserted in packs, this five-card set featured color photos of Eric Lindros with actual pieces of game used equipment inserted into the cards. Pieces of his game-used jerseys, sticks, stirrups, and gloves were used. Each card was individually numbered to 100.

1 E.Lindros Home Jersey	25.00	60.00
2 E.Lindros Away Jersey	25.00	60.00
3 E.Lindros Stick	25.00	60.00
4 E.Lindros Glove	25.00	60.00
5 E.Lindros Stirrups	25.00	60.00

1997-98 Leaf Pipe Dreams

Randomly inserted in packs, this 16-card set featured color photos of top goalies printed on silver foil board and micro-etched. Each card was individually numbered to 2,500.

COMPLETE SET (16)	50.00	100.00
*PROMOS: .3X TO .8X BASIC INSERTS		
1 Dominik Hasek	6.00	15.00
2 John Vanbiesbrouck	3.00	8.00
3 Patrick Roy	12.00	30.00
4 Curtis Joseph	3.00	8.00
5 Felix Potvin	3.00	8.00
6 Martin Brodeur	8.00	20.00
7 Guy Hebert	1.50	4.00
8 Mike Richter	3.00	8.00
9 Jose Theodore	5.00	12.00
10 Jim Carey	1.50	4.00
11 Damian Rhodes	1.50	4.00
12 Jocelyn Thibault	1.50	4.00
13 Nikolai Khabibulin	3.00	8.00
14 Chris Osgood	3.00	8.00
15 Eric Fichaud	1.50	4.00
16 Mike Dunham	1.50	4.00

1995-96 Leaf Limited

This 120-card super-premium set was released in five-card packs with a suggested retail price of $4.99 per pack. The product was produced to order; hence 25,722 individually numbered boxes were produced, much less than the initially announced figure of 60,000. This reduction wreaked havoc with insertion

ratios on the chase cards, which initially hampered interest in the product. It has since recovered nicely. Rookie Cards in this set included Daniel Alfredsson, Todd Bertuzzi, Radek Dvorak, Daymond Langkow and Marcus Ragnarsson.

COMPLETE SET (120)	25.00	50.00
1 Mario Lemieux	2.50	6.00
2 Peter Forsberg	1.25	3.00
3 Geoff Courtnall	.08	.25
4 Vincent Damphousse	.08	.25
5 Jason Allison	.08	.25
6 Theo Fleury	.08	.25
7 Shane Doan RC	1.25	3.00
8 Chris Gratton	.08	.25
9 Paul Kariya	.30	.75
10 Radek Dvorak RC	.50	1.25
11 Adam Graves	.08	.25
12 Donald Audette	.08	.25
13 Craig Janney	.08	.25
14 Sean Burke	.15	.40
15 Ed Belfour	.30	.75
16 Ray Bourque	.75	2.00
17 Pavel Bure	.30	.75
18 Martin Brodeur	1.25	3.00
19 Todd Bertuzzi RC	2.00	5.00
20 Aki Berg RC	.15	.40
21 Dave Andreychuk	.15	.40
22 Jason Arnott	.08	.25
23 Ron Francis	.15	.40
24 Paul Coffey	.30	.75
25 Daniel Alfredsson RC	1.25	3.00
26 Todd Harvey	.15	.40
27 Claude Lemieux	.08	.25
28 Brett Hull	.60	1.50
29 Felix Potvin	.30	.75
30 Peter Bondra	.15	.40
31 Trevor Kidd	.15	.40
32 Igor Korolev	.08	.25
33 Roman Hamrlik	.15	.40
34 Chad Kilger RC	.08	.25
35 Rob Niedermayer	.15	.40
36 Richard Park	.08	.25
37 Mathieu Dandenault	.08	.25
38 Alexandre Daigle	.08	.25
39 Jere Lehtinen	.15	.40
40 Chris Chelios	.30	.75
41 Blaine Lacher	.15	.40
42 Trevor Linden	.15	.40
43 Scott Niedermayer	.08	.25
44 Teemu Selanne	.30	.75
45 Daymond Langkow RC	.50	1.25
46 Oleg Tverdovsky	.08	.25
47 John Vanbiesbrouck	.15	.40
48 Alexei Kovalev	.08	.25
49 Sergei Fedorov	.60	1.50
50 Alexei Yashin	.15	.40
51 Mike Modano	.75	2.00
52 Sandis Ozolinsh	.08	.25
53 Ian Laperriere	.08	.25
54 Mark Recchi	.15	.40
55 Jim Carey	.15	.40
56 Joe Nieuwendyk	.15	.40
57 Keith Tkachuk	.30	.75
58 Daren Puppa	.15	.40
59 Jason Bonsignore	.08	.25
60 Tomas Sandstrom	.08	.25
61 Chris Osgood	.15	.40
62 Jeff Friesen	.08	.25
63 Jeff O'Neill	.08	.25
64 Joe Sakic	1.00	2.50
65 Eric Daze	.15	.40
66 Patrick Roy	2.50	6.00
67 Kirk McLean	.15	.40
68 Stephane Richer	.15	.40
69 Rod Brind'Amour	.15	.40
70 Wendel Clark	.15	.40
71 Rob Blake	.15	.40
72 Doug Gilmour	.15	.40
73 Jaromir Jagr	.75	2.00
74 Sergei Zubov	.08	.25
75 Mark Messier	.30	.75
76 Dominik Hasek	1.00	2.50
77 Viktor Kozlov	.15	.40
78 Marcus Ragnarsson RC	.15	.40
79 Jocelyn Thibault	.30	.75
80 Jeremy Roenick	.40	1.00
81 Cam Neely	.30	.75
82 Brian Savage	.08	.25
83 Alexander Mogilny	.15	.40
84 Steve Thomas	.15	.40
85 John LeClair	.30	.75
86 Brett Lindros	.08	.25
87 Wayne Gretzky	3.00	8.00
88 Kenny Jonsson	.08	.25
89 David Oliver	.08	.25
90 Brian Leetch	.15	.40
91 Luc Robitaille	.15	.40
92 Keith Primeau	.08	.25
93 Owen Nolan	.15	.40
94 Brendan Shanahan	.30	.75
95 Al MacInnis	.15	.40
96 Kevin Stevens	.08	.25
97 Larry Murphy	.15	.40
98 Joe Juneau	.08	.25
99 Eric Lindros	.30	.75
100 Travis Green	.15	.40
101 Jamie Storr	.15	.40
102 Pierre Turgeon	.15	.40
103 Bill Ranford	.15	.40
104 Niklas Sundstrom	.15	.40
105 Steve Yzerman	2.50	6.00
106 Ray Sheppard	.08	.25
107 Chris Pronger	.30	.75
108 Adam Oates	.15	.40
109 Mike Gartner	.15	.40
110 Doug Weight	.15	.40
111 Jason Dawe	.08	.25
112 Rick Tocchet	.15	.40
113 Pat LaFontaine	.30	.75
114 Scott Mellanby	.08	.25
115 Vitali Yachmenev	.08	.25
116 Alexei Zhamnov	.15	.40
117 Brendan Witt	.08	.25
118 Saku Koivu	.30	.75
119 Mikael Renberg	.15	.40
120 Mats Sundin	.30	.75

1995-96 Leaf Limited Rookie Phenoms

This ten-card set saluted some of the league's top first year players. Each card was printed on gold patterned holographic foil and was individually numbered out of 5,000. The odds were announced at 1:24, but the reduction in production altered those somewhat; the actual odds were closer to 1:12.

COMPLETE SET (10)	5.00	12.00
1 Marcus Ragnarsson	.20	.50
2 Daniel Alfredsson	2.00	5.00
3 Chad Kilger	.20	.50
4 Niklas Sundstrom	.20	.50
5 Vitali Yachmenev	.20	.50
6 Eric Daze	.40	1.00
7 Radek Dvorak	.20	.50
8 Jeff O'Neill	.20	.50
9 Saku Koivu	2.00	5.00
10 Todd Bertuzzi	1.00	2.50

1995-96 Leaf Limited Stars of the Game

This twelve-card set celebrated some of the biggest stars playing the game. Every card featured a photo on micro-etched silver holographic foil. Each card was sequentially numbered of 5,000. The announced odds were 1:20 packs, but the reduced production totals made the real odds closer to 1:10.

COMPLETE SET (12)	20.00	40.00
1 Mario Lemieux	5.00	12.00
2 Eric Lindros	.60	1.50
3 Wayne Gretzky	6.00	15.00
4 Peter Forsberg	2.50	6.00
5 Paul Kariya	.60	1.50
6 Alexander Mogilny	.30	.75
7 Teemu Selanne	.60	1.50
8 Jaromir Jagr	1.50	4.00
9 Mats Sundin	.60	1.50
10 Brett Hull	1.25	3.00
11 Sergei Fedorov	1.25	3.00
12 Jeremy Roenick	.75	2.00

1995-96 Leaf Limited Stick Side

This eight-card set was printed on an unusual wood veneer stock and featured some of the NHL's top goalies. Each card was sequentially numbered out of 2,500. The announced odds were 1:60, but the reduced production run meant the actual odds were closer to 1:30.

COMPLETE SET (8)	30.00	60.00
1 Jim Carey	5.00	12.00
2 Martin Brodeur	6.00	15.00
3 Felix Potvin	2.00	5.00
4 Patrick Roy	5.00	12.00
5 Dominik Hasek	3.00	8.00
6 John Vanbiesbrouck	5.00	12.00
7 Ron Hextall	5.00	12.00
8 Ed Belfour	2.00	5.00
P2 Martin Brodeur PROMO	1.50	4.00

1996-97 Leaf Limited

Leaf Limited was a 90-card set featuring the best players in the NHL. The product was hobby-only, with production limited to 27,000 boxes. The cards featured a silver foil effect. Each sealed box also contained an Eric Lindros card measuring 3 3/4" by 3 3/4". This card featured Lindros on the front, along with a serial number out of 27,000, while the reverse held a series checklist.

COMPLETE SET (90)	15.00	40.00
1 Chris Chelios	.40	1.00
2 Brendan Shanahan	.40	1.00
3 Keith Tkachuk	.20	.50
4 Roman Hamrlik	.20	.50
5 Adam Oates	.20	.50
6 Chris Osgood	.20	.50
7 Wayne Gretzky	2.00	5.00
8 Alexander Mogilny	.20	.50
9 Patrick Roy	1.50	4.00
10 Saku Koivu	.40	1.00
11 Jaromir Jagr	.75	2.00
12 Wendel Clark	.20	.50
13 Mike Modano	.40	1.00
14 Ed Jovanovski	.20	.50
15 John LeClair	.20	.50
16 Jim Carey	.20	.50
17 Paul Kariya	.40	1.00
18 Paul Coffey	.40	1.00
19 Todd Bertuzzi	.40	1.00
20 Owen Nolan	.20	.50
21 Dominik Hasek	.75	2.00
22 Bill Ranford	.20	.50
23 Scott Stevens	.20	.50
24 Brett Hull	.40	1.00
25 Trevor Kidd	.20	.50
26 Slava Fetisov	.08	.25
27 Luc Robitaille	.20	.50
28 Mats Sundin	.40	1.00
29 Peter Forsberg	.60	1.50
30 John Vanbiesbrouck	.20	.50
31 Alexei Yashin	.08	.25
32 Pavel Bure	.40	1.00
33 Pat Verbeek	.08	.25
34 Vitali Yachmenev	.08	.25
35 Ron Hextall	.20	.50
36 Michal Pivonka	.08	.25
37 Eric Daze	.20	.50
38 Pierre Turgeon	.20	.50
39 Petr Nedved	.20	.50
40 Steve Yzerman	1.25	3.00
41 Mike Richter	.40	1.00
42 Marcus Ragnarsson	.08	.25
43 Jason Arnott	.08	.25
44 Jocelyn Thibault	.20	.50
45 Alexander Selivanov	.08	.25
46 Claude Lemieux	.08	.25
47 Eric Lindros	.40	1.00
48 Grant Fuhr	.20	.50
49 Ray Bourque	.75	2.00
50 Scott Mellanby	.20	.50
51 Craig Janney	.20	.50
52 Ron Francis	.20	.50
53 Ed Belfour	.40	1.00
54 Petr Sykora	.08	.25
55 Damian Rhodes	.20	.50
56 Joe Sakic	.75	2.00
57 Zigmund Palffy	.20	.50
58 Daren Puppa	.20	.50
59 Pat LaFontaine	.40	1.00
60 Nikolai Khabibulin	.20	.50
61 Sergei Fedorov	.40	1.00
62 Valeri Bure	.08	.25
63 Peter Bondra	.20	.50
64 Teemu Selanne	.40	1.00
65 Mark Messier	.40	1.00
66 Shayne Corson	.08	.25
67 Theo Fleury	.08	.25
68 Jeff O'Neill	.08	.25
69 Eric Fichaud	.20	.50
70 Doug Gilmour	.20	.50
71 Doug Weight	.20	.50
72 Stephane Fiset	.20	.50
73 Daniel Alfredsson	.20	.50
74 Trevor Linden	.20	.50
75 Joe Nieuwendyk	.20	.50
76 Brian Bradley	.08	.25
77 Jere Lehtinen	.08	.25
78 Rob Niedermayer	.20	.50
79 Mikael Renberg	.20	.50
80 Felix Potvin	.40	1.00
81 Valeri Kamensky	.20	.50
82 Brian Leetch	.40	1.00
83 Jeff Friesen	.08	.25
84 Vincent Damphousse	.08	.25
85 Mario Lemieux	1.50	4.00
86 Jeremy Roenick	.40	1.00
87 Martin Brodeur	.75	2.00
88 Vyacheslav Kozlov	.08	.25
89 Corey Hirsch	.20	.50
90 Curtis Joseph	.40	1.00
NNO Eric Lindros CL Jumbo	.75	2.00

1996-97 Leaf Limited Gold

A 90-card parallel of the regular Leaf Limited set, this gold version was randomly inserted in packs at an in-determinate rate. Only the values for the most heavily traded cards are listed below. Values for the remaining cards may be determined by using the multipliers below on the values of the regular counterparts.

*SINGLES: 2.5X TO 6X BASIC CARDS
RANDOM INSERTS IN PACKS

1996-97 Leaf Limited Bash The Boards Promos

This 10-card set was intended to promote the Leaf Limited Bash the Boards insert set. Unlike the regular set which is serial numbered to 3500, these cards were numbered as Promo/2500. Doug Gilmour was the most readily found of these cards.

COMPLETE SET (10)	40.00	100.00
*PROMOS: .6X TO 1.5X BASIC INSERTS	4.00	10.00

1996-97 Leaf Limited Bash The Boards

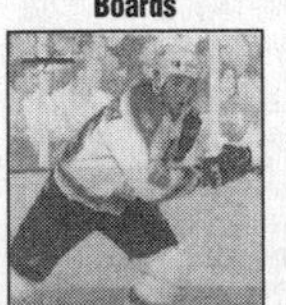

Sequentially numbered to 3500, this insert featured ten players on a rigid plastic stock simulating Plexiglas. Cards were randomly inserted in packs. A limited parallel was also created. These cards were alike the base cards in everyway except that they were serial numbered out of 350.

COMPLETE SET (10)	25.00	60.00
STATED PRINT RUN 3500 SER.#'d SETS		
*LIMITED EDIT: 1.5X TO 4X BASIC INSERTS		
1 Eric Lindros	4.00	10.00
2 Mark Messier	4.00	10.00
3 Owen Nolan	2.00	5.00
4 Doug Gilmour	4.00	10.00
5 Keith Tkachuk	4.00	10.00
6 Claude Lemieux	2.00	5.00
7 Ed Jovanovski	2.00	5.00
8 Peter Forsberg	6.00	15.00
9 Brendan Shanahan	4.00	10.00
10 Eric Daze	2.00	5.00

1996-97 Leaf Limited Rookies

A ten-card random insert, this set consisted of top rookie prospects. Fronts featured a team logo with rays of holographic foil shooting from behind a player photo, while the backs added another photo and a brief player biography. A gold parallel version of this set was known to exist, though quantity produced and distribution source was not entirely clear. Gold parallels are not priced due to scarcity.

COMPLETE SET (10) 25.00 50.00
1 Ethan Moreau .75 2.00
2 Jarome Iginla 4.00 10.00
3 Bryan Berard .75 2.00
4 Hnat Domenichelli .75 2.00
5 Wade Redden 1.25 3.00
6 Dainius Zubrus 1.25 3.00
7 Sergei Berezin .75 2.00
8 Jamie Langenbrunner 1.25 3.00
9 Tomas Holmstrom 2.00 5.00
10 Jonas Hoglund .75 2.00

1996-97 Leaf Limited Stubble

Based upon the old NHL superstition of not shaving while winning during the playoffs, Stubble was a randomly-inserted set highlighted by a felt-like treatment in the beard area. The 20 cards in the set were sequentially numbered to 1500. A promo version of the set was also produced. Those cards resembled the base set in everyway except that they were numbered Promo/1500.

COMPLETE SET (20) 75.00 150.00
1 Patrick Roy 12.00 30.00
2 Eric Lindros 2.50 6.00
3 Wayne Gretzky 15.00 40.00
4 Paul Coffey 1.50 4.00
5 Jim Carey 1.50 4.00
6 Ed Belfour 2.50 6.00
7 Mario Lemieux 12.00 30.00
8 Mike Modano 2.50 6.00
9 Todd Bertuzzi 1.50 4.00
10 Pavel Bure 2.50 6.00
11 Martin Brodeur 6.00 15.00
12 Petr Nedved 1.50 4.00
13 Alexander Mogilny 1.50 4.00
14 Steve Yzerman 10.00 25.00
15 Brett Hull 2.50 6.00
16 Joe Sakic 4.00 10.00
17 Scott Mellanby 1.50 4.00
18 Trevor Linden 1.50 4.00
19 Rob Niedermayer 1.50 4.00
20 Wendel Clark 2.50 6.00

1996-97 Leaf Preferred

The 1996-97 Leaf Preferred set was issued in one series totaling 150 cards. Suggested retail on packs was $3.49, which included five standard cards and one metal card. Card fronts featured color action photos, a small team logo, and the player's name in team colors. One edge was also enhanced with etched silver foil with the Leaf Preferred logo. Key RCs included Dainiuis Zubrus and Sergei Berezin.

COMPLETE SET (150) 12.00 30.00
1 Patrick Roy .75 2.00
2 Alexander Mogilny .08 .25
3 Bill Ranford .08 .25
4 Jeremy Roenick .20 .50
5 Travis Green .08 .25
6 Owen Nolan .08 .25
7 Paul Kariya .15 .40
8 Pat Verbeek .02 .10
9 Jeff O'Neill .02 .10
10 Nikolai Khabibulin .08 .25
11 Pat LaFontaine .15 .40
12 Rob Niedermayer .08 .25
13 Luc Robitaille .08 .25
14 Mats Sundin .15 .40
15 Cory Stillman .02 .10
16 Ray Ferraro .02 .10
17 Alexei Yashin .02 .10
18 Brian Bradley .02 .10
19 Chris Chelios .15 .40
20 Jason Arnott .02 .10
21 Petr Sykora .02 .10
22 Jaromir Jagr .25 .60
23 Jim Carey .15 .40
24 Claude Lemieux .02 .10
25 Vincent Damphousse .02 .10
26 Shayne Corson .02 .10
27 Joe Nieuwendyk .08 .25
28 Kenny Jonsson .02 .10
29 Peter Bondra .08 .25
30 Ed Belfour .15 .40
31 Brendan Shanahan .15 .40
32 Eric Desjardins .08 .25
33 Corey Hirsch .08 .25
34 Slava Fetisov .02 .10
35 Craig Janney .08 .25
36 Felix Potvin .15 .40
37 Joe Sakic .30 .75
38 Scott Stevens .08 .25
39 Kelly Hrudey .08 .25
40 Adam Oates .08 .25
41 John Vanbiesbrouck .08 .25
42 Brian Leetch .15 .40
43 Alexander Selivanov .02 .10
44 Mike Modano .25 .60
45 Saku Koivu .15 .40
46 Tom Barrasso .08 .25
47 Jere Lehtinen .02 .10
48 Daniel Alfredsson .08 .25
49 Joe Juneau .02 .10
50 Chris Osgood .08 .25
51 Dave Andreychuk .08 .25
52 Marcus Ragnarsson .02 .10
53 Valeri Kamensky .08 .25
54 Doug Weight .08 .25
55 Mike Richter .15 .40
56 Teemu Selanne .15 .40
57 Stephane Fiset .08 .25
58 Mikael Renberg .08 .25
59 Trevor Linden .08 .25
60 Bernie Nicholls .02 .10
61 Eric Daze .08 .25
62 Ron Francis .08 .25
63 Sergei Zubov .02 .10
64 Rod Brind'Amour .08 .25
65 Sergei Fedorov .25 .60
66 Mark Messier .15 .40
67 Theo Fleury .02 .10
68 Ed Jovanovski .08 .25
69 Daren Puppa .08 .25
70 Pierre Turgeon .08 .25
71 Oleg Tverdovsky .08 .25
72 Ryan Smyth .15 .40
73 Jocelyn Thibault .15 .40
74 Brendan Witt .02 .10
75 Igor Larionov .02 .10
76 Stephane Richer .08 .25
77 Ron Hextall .08 .25
78 Mike Ricci .02 .10
79 Dimitri Khristich .02 .10
80 Derian Hatcher .02 .10
81 Martin Brodeur .40 1.00
82 Petr Nedved .08 .25
83 Ray Bourque .25 .60
84 Keith Primeau .02 .10
85 Sean Burke .08 .25
86 Geoff Sanderson .08 .25
87 Wendel Clark .08 .25
88 Valeri Bure .02 .10
89 Keith Tkachuk .15 .40
90 Roman Hamrlik .08 .25
91 Dominik Hasek .30 .75
92 Ray Sheppard .08 .25
93 Todd Bertuzzi .15 .40
94 Pavel Bure .15 .40
95 Alexei Zhamnov .08 .25
96 Alexei Kovalev .02 .10
97 Jeff Friesen .02 .10
98 Scott Young .02 .10
99 Vitali Yachmenev .02 .10
100 Michal Pivonka .02 .10
101 Paul Coffey .15 .40
102 Steve Yzerman .75 2.00
103 Zigmund Palffy .08 .25
104 Doug Gilmour .08 .25
105 John LeClair .15 .40
106 Brett Hull .20 .50
107 Yanic Perreault .02 .10
108 Bill Guerin .02 .10
109 Damian Rhodes .08 .25
110 Peter Forsberg .40 1.00
111 Scott Mellanby .08 .25
112 Wayne Gretzky 1.00 2.50
113 Mario Lemieux .75 2.00
114 Todd Harvey .02 .10
115 Mark Recchi .08 .25
116 Trevor Kidd .08 .25
117 Eric Lindros .15 .40
118 Jarome Iginla .20 .50
119 Eric Fichaud .08 .25
120 Mattias Timander RC .02 .10
121 Hnat Domenichelli .02 .10
122 Chris O'Sullivan .02 .10
123 Sergei Berezin RC .40 1.00
124 Jonas Hoglund .02 .10
125 Anders Eriksson .02 .10
126 Corey Schwab .08 .25
127 Janne Niinimaa .15 .40
128 Dainius Zubrus RC .30 .75
129 Bryan Berard .15 .40
130 Wade Redden .02 .10
131 Wayne Primeau .02 .10
132 Brandon Convery .02 .10
133 Richard Zednik RC .20 .50
134 Darcy Tucker .02 .10
135 Christian Dube .02 .10
136 Rem Murray RC .02 .10
137 Kevin Hodson RC .15 .40
138 Steve Washburn RC .02 .10
139 Ethan Moreau RC .15 .40
140 Daymond Langkow .08 .25
141 Terry Ryan RC .02 .10
142 Curtis Brown .02 .10
143 Steve Sullivan RC .20 .50
144 Jamie Langenbrunner .02 .10
145 Daniel Goneau RC .02 .10
146 Anson Carter .08 .25
147 Jim Campbell .02 .10
148 Keith Tkachuk CL (1-76) .15 .40
149 Eric Daze CL (77-150) .08 .25
150 Mike Modano CL (inserts) .08 .25

1996-97 Leaf Preferred Press Proofs

Paralleling the standard 150-card Leaf Preferred set, the randomly inserted Press Proofs were limited to a production run of 250. A gold strip on the left-hand side of the card distinguished this version from its regular counterpart.

*VETS: 15X TO 40X BASIC CARDS
*ROOKIES: 6X TO 15X

1996-97 Leaf Preferred Steel

Inserted one per pack, this 63-card set was the first standard-sized, all-metal hockey set. Cards are silver-colored and come with a protective covering. A gold parallel version also existed; values for these cards can be determined by using the multipliers below. Furthermore, an Eric Lindros promo card was created. It was easy to differentiate from the regular version as it is numbered 77 of 77, and included the word SAMPLE on the back.

*GOLDS: 2X TO 5X SILVER
1 Sergei Fedorov 1.50 4.00
2 Martin Brodeur 2.50 6.00
3 Corey Hirsch .60 1.50
4 Ray Bourque 1.50 4.00
5 Saku Koivu 1.00 2.50
6 Ron Francis .60 1.50
7 Chris Chelios 1.00 2.50
8 Scott Mellanby .60 1.50
9 Ron Hextall .60 1.50
10 Doug Gilmour .60 1.50
11 Joe Sakic 2.00 5.00
12 Petr Sykora .40 1.00
13 Marcus Ragnarsson .40 1.00
14 Pat Verbeek .40 1.00
15 Stephane Fiset .60 1.50
16 Alexei Yashin .40 1.00
17 Daren Puppa .60 1.50
18 Eric Lindros 1.00 2.50
19 Jason Arnott .40 1.00
20 Todd Bertuzzi 1.00 2.50
21 Jim Carey 1.00 2.50
22 Pat LaFontaine 1.00 2.50
23 Brian Leetch 1.00 2.50
24 Trevor Linden .60 1.50
25 Eric Daze .60 1.50
26 Pierre Turgeon .60 1.50
27 Tom Barrasso .60 1.50
28 Mike Modano 1.50 4.00
29 Brendan Shanahan 1.00 2.50
30 Nikolai Khabibulin .60 1.50
31 Claude Lemieux .40 1.00
32 Zigmund Palffy .60 1.50
33 Mats Sundin 1.00 2.50
34 Paul Kariya 1.00 2.50
35 Daniel Alfredsson .60 1.50
36 Patrick Roy 5.00 12.00
37 Jaromir Jagr 1.50 4.00
38 Vyacheslav Kozlov .40 1.00
39 John LeClair 1.00 2.50
40 Bill Ranford .60 1.50
41 Vitali Yachmenev .40 1.00
42 Mark Messier 1.00 2.50
43 Valeri Bure .40 1.00
44 Roman Hamrlik .60 1.50
45 Joe Nieuwendyk .40 1.00
46 Mike Richter 1.00 2.50
47 Theo Fleury .40 1.00
48 Wendel Clark .60 1.50
49 Doug Weight .60 1.50
50 Damian Rhodes .60 1.50
51 Alexander Mogilny .60 1.50
52 Dominik Hasek 2.00 5.00
53 Eric Fichaud .60 1.50
54 Adam Oates .60 1.50
55 Jocelyn Thibault 1.00 2.50
56 Petr Nedved .40 1.00
57 Mike Vernon .40 1.00
58 Mikael Renberg .60 1.50
59 Valeri Kamensky .40 1.00
60 Peter Forsberg 2.50 6.00
61 Rob Niedermayer .40 1.00
62 Owen Nolan .60 1.50
63 Jere Lehtinen .40 1.00
77 Eric Lindros promo .40 1.00

1996-97 Leaf Preferred Masked Marauders

Featuring twelve of the game's top goaltenders, the Masked Marauders were randomly inserted in Leaf Preferred packs and were sequentially numbered to 2500.

COMPLETE SET (12) 30.00 80.00
1 Jim Carey 2.00 5.00
2 Martin Brodeur 6.00 15.00
3 John Vanbiesbrouck 3.00 8.00
4 Patrick Roy 12.00 30.00
5 Felix Potvin 3.00 8.00
6 Chris Osgood 3.00 8.00
7 Dominik Hasek 5.00 12.00
8 Jocelyn Thibault 2.00 5.00
9 Nikolai Khabibulin 3.00 8.00
10 Curtis Joseph 3.00 8.00
11 Mike Richter 3.00 8.00
12 Ed Belfour 4.00 10.00

1996-97 Leaf Preferred Steel Power

With a stated print run of 2500 serial-numbered sets, the Steel Power set consisted of a dozen of the top offensive players. Card fronts featured a color action photo with silver foil at the bottom, and two lightning bolt die-cuts.

COMPLETE SET (12) 40.00 80.00
1 Joe Sakic 4.00 8.00
2 Mario Lemieux 10.00 20.00
3 Pavel Bure 1.50 4.00
4 Mark Messier 1.50 4.00
5 Wayne Gretzky 12.50 25.00
6 Peter Forsberg 5.00 10.00
7 Sergei Fedorov 3.00 6.00
8 Jaromir Jagr 3.00 6.00
9 Brett Hull 2.50 5.00
10 Teemu Selanne 1.50 4.00
11 Paul Kariya 1.50 4.00
12 Eric Lindros 1.50 4.00

1996-97 Leaf Preferred Vanity Plates

Patterned after the theme of vanity license plates, these 14 cards sported the player's nickname, team, and facsimile signature along with a photo on the front. Card backs included a brief player biography and photo. A protective coating covered the silver-colored metal cards, which were inserted randomly into packs. A tougher gold parallel version also was available.

COMPLETE SET (14) 25.00 60.00
*GOLD: 1X TO 2.5X SILVER
1 Wayne Gretzky 8.00 20.00
2 John Vanbiesbrouck 1.50 4.00
3 Chris Osgood .75 2.00
4 Steve Yzerman 4.00 10.00
5 Brett Hull 2.00 5.00
6 Mario Lemieux 5.00 12.00
7 Eric Lindros 1.50 4.00
8 Ed Jovanovski .75 2.00
9 Pavel Bure 1.50 4.00
10 Felix Potvin 1.50 4.00
11 Teemu Selanne 1.50 4.00
12 Keith Tkachuk .75 2.00
13 Curtis Joseph 1.50 4.00
14 Ed Belfour 1.50 4.00

1997-98 Leaf International

This 150-card set featured color player images with a map of their home country in the background and printed on full foil board with heliogram technology and puff ink treatment. The cards were divided into Canadian or U.S./Euro packs, with only Canadian players being found in Canadian packs and the rest of the set in the U.S./Euro version.

COMPLETE SET (150) 30.00 60.00
1 Eric Lindros .25 .60
2 Dominik Hasek .50 1.25
3 Peter Forsberg .60 1.50
4 Steve Yzerman 1.25 3.00
5 John Vanbiesbrouck .20 .50
6 Paul Kariya .25 .60
7 Martin Brodeur .60 1.50
8 Wayne Gretzky 1.50 4.00
9 Mark Messier .25 .60
10 Jaromir Jagr .40 1.00
11 Brett Hull .30 .75
12 Brendan Shanahan .25 .60
13 Ray Bourque .40 1.00
14 Jarome Iginla .30 .75
15 Mike Modano .40 1.00
16 Curtis Joseph .25 .60
17 Ed Jovanovski .20 .50
18 Teemu Selanne .25 .60
19 Saku Koivu .25 .60
20 Eric Fichaud .20 .50
21 Paul Coffey .25 .60
22 Jeremy Roenick .30 .75
23 Owen Nolan .20 .50
24 Felix Potvin .25 .60
25 Alexander Mogilny .20 .50
26 Alexandre Daigle .10 .30
27 Chris Gratton .20 .50
28 Geoff Sanderson .20 .50
29 Dimitri Khristich .10 .30
30 Bryan Berard .10 .30
31 Vyacheslav Kozlov .10 .30
32 Jeff Hackett .20 .50
33 Bill Ranford .20 .50
34 Pat LaFontaine .25 .60
35 Joe Sakic .50 1.25
36 Niklas Sundstrom .10 .30
37 Martin Gelinas .10 .30
38 Mikael Renberg .20 .50
39 Trevor Linden .20 .50
40 Jozef Stumpel .20 .50
41 Joe Thornton CL .10 .30
42 Jocelyn Thibault .20 .50
43 Pierre Turgeon .20 .50
44 Ron Francis .20 .50
45 Damian Rhodes .20 .50
46 Jamie Langenbrunner .10 .30
47 Chris Osgood .20 .50
48 Vaclav Varada .20 .50
49 Ryan Smyth .20 .50
50 Daren Puppa .20 .50
51 Petr Nedved .20 .50
52 Ron Hextall .20 .50
53 Joe Juneau .20 .50
54 Jim Campbell .10 .30
55 Zigmund Palffy .20 .50
56 Roman Turek .20 .50
57 Adam Deadmarsh .20 .50
58 Rob Niedermayer .20 .50
59 Alexei Yashin .10 .30
60 Pavel Bure .25 .60
61 Jason Arnott .10 .30
62 Nikolai Khabibulin .20 .50
63 Sean Burke .20 .50
64 Chris Chelios .25 .60
65 Mike Ricci .20 .50
66 Sergei Berezin .10 .30
67 Jaroslav Svejkovsky CL .10 .30
68 Brian Savage .10 .30
69 Roman Vopat .10 .30
70 Mike Richter .25 .60
71 Jim Carey .20 .50
72 Guy Hebert .20 .50
73 Keith Tkachuk .25 .60
74 Kirk McLean .20 .50
75 Janne Niinimaa .20 .50
76 Roman Hamrlik .10 .30
77 Darcy Tucker .10 .30
78 Pat Verbeek .10 .30
79 Hnat Domenichelli .10 .30
80 Doug Gilmour .20 .50
81 Mike Grier .10 .30
82 Ken Wregget .10 .30
83 Dino Ciccarelli .10 .30
84 Steve Sullivan .10 .30
85 Anson Carter .20 .50
86 Steve Shields RC .40 1.00
87 Ed Belfour .25 .60
88 Darren McCarty .10 .30
89 Adam Graves .10 .30
90 Chris Pronger .20 .50
91 Peter Bondra .10 .30
92 Oleg Tverdovsky .10 .30
93 Stephane Fiset .20 .50
94 Mike Vernon .20 .50
95 Scott Lachance .10 .30
96 Corey Schwab .10 .30
97 Eric Daze .20 .50
98 Jere Lehtinen .10 .30
99 Donald Audette .10 .30
100 John LeClair .25 .60
101 Steve Rucchin .10 .30
102 Jeff Friesen .10 .30
103 Daymond Langkow .20 .50
104 Mike Dunham .20 .50
105 Marc Denis CL .10 .30
106 Andrew Cassels .10 .30
107 Mike Peca .10 .30
108 Joe Nieuwendyk .20 .50
109 Vincent Damphousse .10 .30
110 Scott Mellanby .10 .30
111 Patrick Lalime .20 .50
112 Derek Plante .10 .30
113 Wade Redden .10 .30
114 Marcel Cousineau .10 .30
115 Ray Sheppard .10 .30
116 Dave Andreychuk .10 .30
117 Brian Leetch .25 .60
118 Sandis Ozolinsh .10 .30
119 Keith Primeau .10 .30
120 Brian Holzinger .10 .30
121 Luc Robitaille .20 .50
122 Jose Theodore .30 .75
123 Grant Fuhr .20 .50
124 Dainius Zubrus .25 .60
125 Rod Brind'Amour .20 .50
126 Trevor Kidd .20 .50
127 Mark Recchi .20 .50
128 Patrick Roy 1.25 3.00
129 Kevin Hatcher .10 .30
130 Adam Oates .20 .50
131 Doug Weight .20 .50
132 Vaclav Prospal RC .25 .60
133 Harry York .10 .30
134 Todd Bertuzzi .25 .60
135 Sergei Fedorov .40 1.00
136 Theo Fleury .10 .30
137 Chad Kilger .10 .30
138 Jamie Storr .20 .50
139 Tony Amonte .20 .50
140 Rem Murray .10 .30
141 Chris O'Sullivan .10 .30
142 Mats Sundin .25 .60
143 Ethan Moreau .10 .30
144 Derian Hatcher .10 .30
145 Daniel Alfredsson .20 .50
146 Corey Hirsch .10 .30
147 Landon Wilson .10 .30
148 Chris Phillips CL .10 .30
149 Sergei Samsonov CL .10 .30
150 Daniel Cleary CL .10 .30

1997-98 Leaf International Universal Ice

This 150-card set was parallel to the base set and was printed on holofoil board. Only 250 of each card was produced and numbered. All cards of this parallel set appeared in both Canadian packs and U.S./Euro packs.

*VETS: 4X TO 10X BASIC CARDS
*ROOKIES: 2X TO 5X BASIC CARDS

1971-72 Letraset Action Replays

This set of 24 Hockey Action Replays was issued in Canada by Letraset. Printed on thin paper stock, each replay measured approximately 5 1/4" by 6 1/4" and was folded in the center. All replays had a common front consisting of a color photo of a face-off between Danny O'Shea of the Hawks and Jean Ratelle of the Rangers. On the reverse side, a "Know Your Signals" series illustrated arm signals used by hockey referees. The inside unfolded to display a 5" by 4 1/2" color drawings of NHL action scenes. Immediately above was a description of the play plus slots for photos of the players involved in the action. The center photos and some of the players needed to complete the play were missing and supplied on a separate run-on transfer sheet. The action scene could be completed by rubbing the players on the transfer sheet onto the action scene. The replays were numbered in the white panel that presents the referee arm signals, and checklisted below accordingly.

COMPLETE SET (24) 100.00 200.00
1 Rogatien Vachon 5.00 10.00
Dave Keon
Gilles Marotte
2 Ken Dryden 10.00 20.00
Chico Maki
Jacques Laperriere
3 Gary Dornhoefer 4.00 8.00
Roger Crozier
Tracy Pratt
4 Walt Tkaczuk 4.00 8.00
Gump Worsley
Vic Hadfield
5 Dallas Smith 17.50 35.00
Bobby Orr
Walt McKechnie
6 Ab McDonald 4.00 8.00
Gary Sabourin
Garry Unger
7 Jim Rutherford 4.00 8.00
Orland Kurtenbach
Bob Woytovich
8 Gerry Cheevers 6.00 12.00
Frank Mahovlich
Don Awrey
9 Tim Ecclestone 5.00 10.00
Bob Baun
Jacques Plante
10 Stan Mikita 6.00 12.00
Ed Giacomin
Jim Pappin
11 Doug Favell 4.00 8.00
Danny Grant
Ed Van Impe
12 Ernie Wakely 4.00 8.00
Barclay Plager
Gary Croteau
13 Bryan Hextall 5.00 10.00
Tony Esposito
Pat Stapleton
14 Jean Ratelle 5.00 10.00
Rod Gilbert
Jim Roberts
15 Jacques Lemaire 6.00 12.00
Henri Richard
Yvan Cournoyer
16 George Gardiner 4.00 8.00
Dennis Hull
Lou Angotti
17 Ed Johnston 17.50 35.00
Norm Ullman
Bobby Orr
18 Gilles Meloche 4.00 8.00
Wayne Carleton
Dick Redmond
19 Al Smith 4.00 8.00
Gary Bergman
Stan Gilbertson
20 Dunc Wilson 4.00 8.00
Brad Park
Dale Tallon
21 Jude Drouin 4.00 8.00
Doug Favell
Barry Ashbee
22 Ron Ellis 10.00 20.00
Ken Dryden
Paul Henderson
23 Gary Edwards 4.00 8.00
Jean Pronovost
Ron Shock
24 Cesare Maniago 4.00 8.00
Chris Bordeleau
Ted Harris

1980 Liberty Matchbooks

This yellow matchbook was part of a multi-sport set, featuring athletes from all the major leagues and Olympics.

NNO Ray Bourque 10.00 20.00

1992-93 Lightning Sheraton

Sponsored by the Sheraton Inn Tampa Conference Center, this album and its 28 perforated cards commemorated the Tampa Bay Lightning's inaugural season. Folded closed, the album measured 10" by 13". The 28 standard-size cards folded out and feature color player action shots on their fronts. These photos were borderless on their top and right sides, and white-bordered on the left and bottom edges. The player's name appeared vertically in blue lettering in the margin on the left side, his position appeared in blue in the bottom margin, and his uniform number was shown in silver, just above the Lightning logo in the lower left. The white backs displayed the player's name, uniform number, and biography in the upper left. Below were stats from the player's previous seasons. In the upper right, the Sheraton logo rounded out the card. The cards were unnumbered and checklisted below in alphabetical order.

COMPLETE SET (28) 8.00 20.00
1 Mikael Andersson .20 .50
2 Bob Beers .20 .50
3 J.C. Bergeron .30 .75
4 Marc Bergevin .20 .50
5 Tim Bergland .20 .50
6 Brian Bradley .60 1.50
7 Marc Bureau .20 .50
8 Wayne Cashman CO .20 .50
9 Shawn Chambers .20 .50
10 Danton Cole .20 .50
11 Adam Creighton .30 .75
12 Terry Crisp CO .20 .50
13 Rob DiMaio .30 .75
14 Phil Esposito GM .75 2.00
15 Tony Esposito DIR .60 1.50
16 Roman Hamrlik .75 2.00
17 Pat Jablonski .30 .75
18 Steve Kasper .20 .50
19 Chris Kontos .20 .50
20 Steve Maltais .20 .50
21 Joe Reekie .20 .50
22 Thunderbug (Mascot) .08 .25
23 John Tucker .30 .75
24 Wendell Young .30 .75
25 Rob Zamuner .30 .75
26 Title card .20 .50
27 Inaugural season card .08 .25
28 Sheraton logo card .08 .25

1993-94 Lightning Kash n'Karry

Sponsored by Kash n'Karry, this six-card set measured approximately 5" by 7". Inside gray borders, the fronts featured color action player photos. A blue bar on the left side carried the player's name and number. The sponsor's logo appeared in the bottom gray border. The horizontal backs had a postcard design, with the player's name, position, a short biography, and career highlights on the left side. The cards were unnumbered and checklisted below in alphabetical order. The checklist below is incomplete.

COMPLETE SET (6) 3.00 8.00
1 Brian Bradley .75 2.00
2 Shawn Chambers .40 1.00
3 Chris Gratton .75 2.00
4 Adam Creighton .40 1.00
5 Rob DiMaio .40 1.00
6 Wendell Young .60 1.50

1993-94 Lightning Season in Review

Subtitled "1993-94 Season in Review," the 28 cards comprising this set of the Tampa Bay Lightning were issued in a perforated sheet, which also included a 10" by 13" title page. Each card measured approximately 2 1/2" by 3 1/4" and featured on its front a color player action shot, which was borderless at the top and right. The player's name appeared vertically within the white margin to the left of the photo; his position appeared within the white margin below. His uniform number and the team logo appeared at the lower left. The white back carried the player's name and uniform number at the top, followed below by biography and statistics. Logos for the NHL and The Sky Box Sports Cafe at the upper right roundedout the card. The cards were unnumbered and checklisted below in alphabetical order.

COMPLETE SET (28) 6.00 15.00
1 Mikael Andersson .20 .50
2 Marc Bergevin .20 .50
3 Brian Bradley .30 .75
4 Marc Bureau .20 .50
5 Wayne Cashman ACO .20 .50
6 Shawn Chambers .20 .50
7 Enrico Ciccone .20 .50
8 Danton Cole .20 .50
9 Adam Creighton .20 .50
10 Terry Crisp CO .20 .50
11 Jim Cummins .20 .50
12 Pat Elynuik .20 .50
13 Phil Esposito GM .60 1.50
14 Tony Esposito DIR .40 1.00
15 Gerard Gallant .20 .50
16 Danny Gare ACO .08 .25
17 Chris Gratton .60 1.50
18 Roman Hamrlik .60 1.50
19 Chris Joseph .20 .50
20 Petr Klima .20 .50
21 Chris LiPuma .20 .50
22 Rudy Poeschek .30 .75
23 Daren Puppa .60 1.50
24 Denis Savard .40 1.00
25 Thunderbug MASCOT .08 .25
26 John Tucker .20 .50
27 Wendell Young .25 .60
28 Rob Zamuner .20 .50

1994-95 Lightning Health Plan

This two-card set was sponsored by Health Plan of Florida and the Tampa Tribune. Twenty thousand sets were produced. The front and back panels were connected at their tops and each measure 4" by 5". The front displayed blue-tinted action photo edged by black stripes, while the back carried a color head shot, biography, and sponsor logos. When unfolded, the inside panel measured 4" by 10" and featured a pop-up color player photo and statistics. The cards were numbered on the back at the bottom.

COMPLETE SET (2) 2.50 6.00
1 Daren Puppa 1.50 4.00
2 Chris Gratton 1.25 3.00

1994-95 Lightning Photo Album

The 1994-95 Tampa Bay Lightning Commemorative Photo Album was sponsored by the Sky Box Sports Cafe at the Sheraton Inn in Tampa. It consists of three perforated sheets, each measuring 12 1/2" by 9 3/4" and joined together to form one continuous sheet. The first panel had an array different size color shots, capturing the Lightning off and on the ice. The second and third panels each displayed three rows of player cards; if perforated, the cards would measure the standard size. The fronts featured color action photos with team color-coded borders. The team logo, player's name, position, and number were printed in the borders. On a team color-coded background, the backs carried a color head shot, biography, statistics, and career highlights. The cards were unnumbered and checklisted below in alphabetical order.

COMPLETE SET (29) 4.80 12.00
1 Mikael Andersson .15 .40
2 J.C. Bergeron .20 .50
3 Marc Bergevin .15 .40
4 Brian Bradley .30 .75
5 Marc Bureau .15 .40
6 Wayne Cashman ACO .15 .40
7 Eric Charron .15 .40
8 Enrico Ciccone .15 .40
9 Terry Crisp CO .15 .40
10 Cory Cross .15 .40
11 Phil Esposito PRES/GM .40 1.00
12 Tony Esposito DIR .15 .40
13 Danny Gare ACO .15 .40
14 Chris Gratton .30 .75
15 Bob Halkidis .15 .40
16 Roman Hamrlik .40 1.00
17 Ben Hankinson .15 .40
18 Petr Klima .15 .40
19 Brantt Myhres .15 .40
20 Adrien Plavsic .15 .40
21 Rudy Poeschek .20 .50
22 Daren Puppa .50 1.25
23 Alexander Selivanov .40 1.00

24 Alexander Semak .15 .40
25 John Tucker .20 .50
26 Jason Wiemer .30 .75
27 Paul Ysebaert .15 .40
28 Rob Zamuner .15 .40
29 Team Photo .40 1.00

1994-95 Lightning Postcards

These oversized postcards were issued by the Lightning as promotional giveaways at team events. The postcards were unnumbered, and thus are listed below in alphabetical order.

COMPLETE SET (20) 8.00 20.00
1 Mikael Andersson .30 .75
2 Brian Bradley .40 1.00
3 Shawn Burr .30 .75
4 Terry Crisp CO .20 .50
5 Cory Cross .30 .75
6 John Cullen .30 .75
7 Phil Esposito PRES/GM .75 2.00
8 Tony Esposito DIR .75 2.00
9 Chris Gratton .40 1.00
10 Roman Hamrlik .40 1.00
11 Bill Houlder .30 .75
12 Daymond Langkow .75 2.00
13 Brantt Myhres .30 .75
14 Daren Puppa .40 1.00
15 Chris Reichart .30 .75
16 Alexander Selivanov .30 .75
17 David Shaw .30 .75
18 Jason Wiemer .30 .75
19 Paul Ysebaert .30 .75
20 Rob Zamuner .30 .75

1995-96 Lightning Team Issue

This 21-card set of the Tampa Bay Lightning measured approximately 3 3/4" by 9" and featured color action player photos with player information printed below. The cards were unnumbered and checklisted below in alphabetical order.

COMPLETE SET (21) 8.00 20.00
1 Mikael Andersson .40 1.00
2 Brian Bellows .40 1.00
3 J.C. Bergeron .50 1.25
4 Brian Bradley .50 1.25
5 Shawn Burr .40 1.00
6 Enrico Ciccone .40 1.00
7 Cory Cross .40 1.00
8 John Cullen .40 1.00
9 Aaron Gavey .40 1.00
10 Chris Gratton .60 1.50
11 Roman Hamrlik .50 1.25
12 Bill Houlder .40 1.00
13 Petr Klima .40 1.00
14 Rudy Poeschek .40 1.00
15 Daren Puppa .50 1.25
16 Alexander Selivanov .40 1.00
17 David Shaw .40 1.00
18 John Tucker .40 1.00
19 Jason Wiemer .40 1.00
20 Paul Ysebaert .40 1.00
21 Rob Zamuner .40 1.00

2002-03 Lightning Team Issue

These oversized (4X8) blank-backed cards were issued by the Lightning. The checklist below is incomplete. If you have information on distribution or additional cards, please contact hockeymag@beckett.com.

COMPLETE SET (?)
1 Nikita Alexeev .40 1.00
2 Dave Andreychuk .75 2.00
3 Dan Boyle .75 2.00
4 Chris Dingman .40 1.00
5 Nikolai Khabibulin .75 2.00
6 Pavel Kubina .40 1.00
7 Vincent Lecavalier 2.00 5.00
8 Brad Lukowich .40 1.00
9 Fredrik Modin .40 1.00
10 Brad Richards 1.25 3.00
11 Andre Roy .40 1.00
12 Martin St-Louis .75 2.00

2003-04 Lightning Team Issue

COMPLETE SET (36) 15.00 30.00
1 Cover Card .02 .10
2 Team Card .02 .10
3 John Tortorella CO .20 .50
4 Craig Ramsay ACO .20 .50
5 Jeff Reese ACO .20 .50
6 Nigel Kirwan ACO .20 .50
7 Paul Kennedy ANN .20 .50
8 Rick Peckham ANN .20 .50
9 Phil Esposito ANN .75 2.00
10 Vincent Lecavalier 2.00 5.00
11 Jassen Cullimore .40 1.00
12 Ben Clymer .40 1.00
13 Martin Cibak .40 1.00
14 Eric Perrin .75 2.00
15 Brian Bradley Alumni .40 1.00
16 Chris Dingman .40 1.00
17 Pavel Kubina .40 1.00
18 John Tucker Alumni .40 1.00
19 Alexander Svitov .40 1.00
20 Ruslan Fedotenko .40 1.00
21 Brad Richards 1.50 4.00
22 Cory Sarich .40 1.00
23 Dan Boyle .40 1.00
24 Shane Willis .40 1.00
25 Dave Andreychuk .40 1.00
26 Martin St. Louis 1.25 3.00
27 Tim Taylor .40 1.00
28 Sheldon Keefe .40 1.00
29 Dmitry Afanasenkov .40 1.00
30 Fredrik Modin .40 1.00
31 Nikolai Khabibulin .75 2.00
32 Andre Roy .75 2.00
33 Brad Lukowich .40 1.00
34 Nolan Pratt .40 1.00
35 Cory Stillman .40 1.00
36 Daren Puppa Alumni .40 1.00

2005-06 Lightning Team Issue

These cards were issued by the Lightning at team events and by mail. The checklist is known to be incomplete. If you have additional information, please forward it to hockeymag@beckett.com. Thanks to Andy Hatzos for this partial list.

COMPLETE SET (?)
1 John Tortorella CO .40 1.00
2 Craig Ramsay ACO .40 1.00
3 Jeff Reese ACO .40 1.00
4 Vincent Lecavalier 2.00 5.00
5 Darryl Sydor .75 2.00
6 Chris Dingman .75 2.00
7 Vaclav Prospal .75 2.00
8 Dan Boyle .75 2.00
9 Martin St. Louis 1.25 3.00
10 Tim Taylor .75 2.00
11 Nolan Pratt .75 2.00

2006-07 Lightning Postcards

COMPLETE SET (23) 15.00 30.00
1 Logo Card .10 .25
2 Dmitry Afanasenkov .40 1.00
3 Nikita Alexeev .40 1.00
4 Dan Boyle .40 1.00
5 Ryan Craig .40 1.00
6 Marc Denis .60 1.50
7 Ruslan Fedotenko .40 1.00
8 Doug Janik .40 1.00
9 Johan Holmqvist .75 2.00
10 Andreas Karlsson .40 1.00
11 Filip Kuba .40 1.00
12 Vincent Lecavalier 2.00 5.00
13 Eric Perrin .40 1.00
14 Nolan Pratt .40 1.00
15 Vaclav Prospal .40 1.00
16 Paul Ranger .40 1.00
17 Brad Richards 1.25 3.00
18 Luke Richardson .40 1.00
19 Andre Roy .40 1.00
20 Cory Sarich .40 1.00
21 Martin St. Louis 1.25 3.00
22 Nick Tarnasky .40 1.00
23 Tim Taylor .40 1.00

1974-75 Lipton Soup

The 1974-75 Lipton Soup NHL set contained 50 color cards measuring approximately 2 1/4" by 3 1/4". The set was issued in two-card panels on the back of Lipton Soup packages. The backs featured statistics in French and English. Both varieties of Salming were included in the complete set below.

COMPLETE SET (51) 175.00 350.00
1 Norm Ullman 4.00 8.00
2 Gilbert Perreault 4.00 8.00
3 Darryl Sittler 6.00 12.00
4 Jean-Paul Parise 2.00 4.00
5 Garry Unger 2.00 4.00
6 Ron Ellis 2.50 5.00
7 Rogatien Vachon 5.00 10.00
8 Bobby Orr 50.00 100.00
9 Wayne Cashman 2.50 5.00
10 Brad Park 3.00 6.00
11 Serge Savard 2.50 5.00
12 Walt Tkaczuk 2.00 4.00
13 Yvan Cournoyer 4.00 8.00
14 Andre Boudrias 1.50 3.00
15 Gary Smith 2.50 5.00
16 Guy Lapointe 2.00 4.00
17 Dennis Hull 2.50 5.00
18 Bernie Parent 5.00 10.00
19 Ken Dryden 25.00 50.00
20 Rick MacLeish 2.50 5.00
21 Bobby Clarke 7.50 15.00
22 Dale Tallon 2.00 4.00
23 Jim McKenny 1.50 3.00
24 Rene Robert 2.50 5.00
25 Red Berenson 2.00 4.00
26 Ed Giacomin 5.00 10.00
27 Cesare Maniago 3.00 6.00
28 Ken Hodge 2.50 5.00
29 Gregg Sheppard 1.50 3.00
30 Dave Schultz 5.00 10.00
31 Bill Barber 4.00 8.00
32 Henry Boucha 2.00 4.00
33 Richard Martin 2.50 5.00
34 Steve Vickers 2.00 4.00
35 Billy Harris 1.50 3.00
36 Jim Pappin 1.50 3.00
37 Pit Martin 1.50 3.00
38 Jacques Lemaire 4.00 8.00
39 Peter Mahovlich 2.50 5.00
40 Rod Gilbert 4.00 8.00
41A Borje Salming 6.00 12.00
(Horizontal pose)
41B Borje Salming 6.00 12.00
(Vertical pose)
42 Pete Stemkowski 1.50 3.00
43 Ron Schock 1.50 3.00
44 Dan Bouchard 3.00 6.00
45 Tony Esposito 6.00 12.00
46 Craig Patrick 2.00 4.00
47 Ed Westfall 1.50 3.00
48 Jocelyn Guevremont 1.50 3.00
49 Syl Apps 2.00 4.00
50 Dave Keon 4.00 8.00

1972-73 Los Angeles Sharks WHA

This 19-card standard-size set featured on the front black and white posed player photos, surrounded by a white border. The player's name was given in black lettering below the picture. The backs read "The Original Los Angeles Sharks, 1972-73" and had the Sharks' logo in the center.

COMPLETE SET (19) 20.00 40.00
1 Mike Byers 1.25 2.50
2 Bart Crashley 2.00 4.00
3 George Gardner 1.25 2.50
4 Russ Gillow 1.25 2.50
5 Tom Gilmore 1.25 2.50
6 Earl Heiskala 1.25 2.50
7 J.P. LeBlanc 1.50 3.00
8 Ralph McSweyn 1.25 2.50
9 Ted McCaskill 1.25 2.50
10 Jim Niekamp 1.25 2.50
11 Gerry Odrowski 1.50 3.00
12 Tom Serviss 1.25 2.50
13 Peter Slater 1.25 2.50
14 Steve Sutherland 1.25 2.50
15 Joe Szura 1.50 3.00
16 Gary Veneruzzo 1.25 2.50
17 Jim Watson 1.25 2.50
18 Alton White 1.25 2.50
19 Bill Young 1.25 2.50

1998 Lunchables Goalie Greats Rounds

Available only as a premium found in select packs of Lunchables lunch products, these cards featured color action photos on the front while backs were blank. As the title suggests, these were round, and about the size of a peanut butter lid.

COMPLETE SET (8) 4.00 10.00
1 Ed Belfour .30 .75
2 Martin Brodeur .75 2.00
3 Dominik Hasek .60 1.50
4 Olaf Kolzig .25 .60
5 Chris Osgood .30 .75
6 Damian Rhodes .25 .60
7 Mike Richter .30 .75
8 Patrick Roy 1.50 4.00

1998 Lunchables Goalie Greats Squares

Available only as a premium found in select packs of Lunchables lunch products. Color action photos were featured on the front while backs were blank. As the name suggests, these were square, while the other set was rounded.

COMPLETE SET (8) 4.00 10.00
1 Ed Belfour .30 .75
2 Martin Brodeur .75 2.00
3 Dominik Hasek .60 1.50
4 Olaf Kolzig .25 .60
5 Chris Osgood .30 .75
6 Damian Rhodes .25 .60
7 Mike Richter .30 .75
8 Patrick Roy 1.50 4.00

1973-74 Mac's Milk

The 1973-74 Mac's Milk set contained 30 unnumbered discs measuring approximately 3" in diameter. These round discs were actually cloth stickers with a peel-off back. They were unnumbered and featured popular players in the National Hockey League. There was no identifying mark anywhere on the discs identifying the sponsor as Mac's Milk. They are checklisted below in alphabetical order by player's name.

COMPLETE SET (30) 75.00 150.00
1 Gary Bergman 1.50 3.00
2 Johnny Bucyk 2.50 5.00
3 Wayne Cashman 2.00 4.00
4 Bobby Clarke 7.50 15.00
5 Yvan Cournoyer 3.00 6.00
6 Ron Ellis 1.50 3.00
7 Rod Gilbert 2.50 5.00
8 Brian Glennie 1.50 3.00
9 Paul Henderson 2.50 5.00
10 Ed Johnston 2.50 5.00
11 Rick Kehoe 1.50 3.00
12 Orland Kurtenbach 1.50 3.00
13 Guy Lapointe 2.50 5.00
14 Jacques Lemaire 2.50 5.00
15 Frank Mahovlich 5.00 10.00
16 Pete Mahovlich 2.50 5.00
17 Richard Martin 2.00 4.00
18 Jim McKenny 1.50 3.00
19 Bobby Orr 20.00 40.00
20 Jean-Paul Parise 1.50 3.00
21 Brad Park 4.00 8.00
22 Jacques Plante 7.50 15.00
23 Jean Ratelle 2.50 5.00
24 Mickey Redmond 2.50 5.00
25 Serge Savard 2.50 5.00
26 Darryl Sittler 5.00 10.00
27 Pat Stapleton 1.50 3.00
28 Dale Tallon 1.50 3.00
29 Norm Ullman 2.50 5.00
30 Bill White 2.00 4.00

1996 Maggers

This 108 laser die-cut magnet premier edition set measured approximately 6" by 7 1/2" and was distributed one to a package with a suggested retail price of $1.99. Produced by Corporate Magnates of Ontario, the player's image could be separated from the magnet background and used alone. The magnets were checklisted below in alphabetical order.

COMPLETE SET (108) 90.00 180.00
1 Jason Arnott .50 1.25
2 Tom Barrasso .50 1.25
3 Ed Belfour .60 1.50
4 Peter Bondra .50 1.25
5 Ray Bourque 1.25 3.00
6 Martin Brodeur 1.50 4.00
7 Benoit Brunet .40 1.00
8 Pavel Bure 1.50 4.00
9 Sean Burke .50 1.25
10 Jim Carey .50 1.25
11 Chris Chelios .60 1.50
12 Steve Chiasson .40 1.00
13 Dino Ciccarelli .40 1.00
14 Zdeno Ciger .40 1.00
15 Wendel Clark .40 1.00
16 Paul Coffey .50 1.25
17 Shayne Corson .40 1.00
18 Alexandre Daigle .40 1.00
19 Vincent Damphousse .50 1.25
20 Eric Daze .40 1.00
21 Tie Domi .50 1.25
22 Sergei Fedorov 1.25 3.00
23 Eric Fichaud .40 1.00
24 Theo Fleury .60 1.50
25 Peter Forsberg 1.50 4.00
26 Ron Francis .50 1.25
27 Grant Fuhr .50 1.25
28 Doug Gilmour .60 1.50
29 Sergei Gonchar .40 1.00
30 Tony Granato .40 1.00
31 Adam Graves .50 1.25
32 Wayne Gretzky 4.00 10.00
33 Alexei Gusarov .40 1.00
34 Derian Hatcher .40 1.00
35 Dale Hawerchuk .40 1.00
36 Guy Hebert .50 1.25
37 Ron Hextall .40 1.00
38 Corey Hirsch .40 1.00
39 Phil Housley .40 1.00
40 Kelly Hrudey .40 1.00
41 Brett Hull .75 2.00
42 Jaromir Jagr 1.50 4.00
43 Ed Jovanovski .50 1.25
44 Joe Juneau .40 1.00
45 Valeri Kamensky .50 1.25
46 Paul Kariya 2.00 5.00
47 Trevor Kidd .50 1.25
48 Petr Klima .40 1.00
49 Saku Koivu .50 1.25
50 Andrei Kovalenko .40 1.00
51 Vyacheslav Kozlov .40 1.00
52 Igor Larionov .40 1.00
53 John LeClair .75 2.00
54 Brian Leetch .50 1.25
55 Claude Lemieux .50 1.25
56 Mario Lemieux 4.00 10.00
57 Trevor Linden .50 1.25
58 Eric Lindros 1.00 2.50
59 Al MacInnis .50 1.25
60 Mark Messier .75 2.00
61 Mike Modano 1.00 2.50
62 Alexander Mogilny .50 1.25
63 Andy Moog .50 1.25
64 Joe Murphy .40 1.00
65 Petr Nedved .40 1.00
66 Cam Neely .50 1.25
67 Bernie Nicholls .40 1.00
68 Joe Nieuwendyk .50 1.25
69 Owen Nolan .50 1.25
70 Adam Oates .50 1.25
71 Jeff Odgers .40 1.00
72 Chris Osgood .75 2.00
73 Sandis Ozolinsh .50 1.25
74 Zigmund Palffy .60 1.50
75 Yanic Perreault .40 1.00
76 Michal Pivonka .40 1.00
77 Felix Potvin .60 1.50
78 Keith Primeau .50 1.25
79 Chris Pronger .40 1.00
80 Daren Puppa .40 1.00
81 Bill Ranford .40 1.00
82 Mikael Renberg .40 1.00
83 Mike Ricci .40 1.00
84 Mike Richter .60 1.50
85 Gary Roberts .40 1.00
86 Luc Robitaille .60 1.50
87 Jeremy Roenick .60 1.50
88 Patrick Roy 3.00 8.00
89 Joe Sakic 1.25 3.00
90 Tomas Sandstrom .40 1.00
91 Denis Savard .40 1.00
92 Teemu Selanne 1.25 3.00
93 Brendan Shanahan 1.00 2.50
94 Kevin Stevens .40 1.00
95 Scott Stevens .40 1.00
96 Mats Sundin .60 1.50
97 Gary Suter .40 1.00
98 Chris Terreri .50 1.25
99 Jocelyn Thibault .50 1.25
100 Esa Tikkanen .40 1.00
101 German Titov .40 1.00
102 Rick Tocchet .40 1.00
103 Pierre Turgeon .50 1.25
104 John Vanbiesbrouck .60 1.50
105 Pat Verbeek .50 1.25
106 Mike Vernon .50 1.25
107 Alexei Yashin .50 1.25
108 Steve Yzerman 2.50 6.00

1963-64 Maple Leafs Team Issue

This 22-card set of postcards measured approximately 3 1/2" by 5 1/2" and featured black and white action and posed player photos with white borders. The old Toronto Maple Leafs logo was in the bottom right corner. The player's name and position appeared at the bottom. The backs were blank. The cards were unnumbered and checklisted below in alphabetical order.

COMPLETE SET (22) 62.50 125.00
1 Bob Baun 2.50 5.00
(Posed)
2 Bob Baun 2.50 5.00
(Posed in white uniform& position not listed)
3 Carl Brewer 2.50 5.00
(White uniform)
4 Carl Brewer 2.50 5.00
(Dark uniform)
5 Kent Douglas 1.50 3.00
6 Dick Duff 2.00 4.00
7 Ron Ellis 2.00 4.00
8 Billy Harris 1.50 3.00
(Portrait)
9 Billy Harris 1.50 3.00
(Action)
10 Larry Hillman 1.50 3.00
11 Red Kelly 4.00 8.00
12 Dave Keon 7.50 15.00
(No number)
13 Dave Keon 7.50 15.00
(Number 14)
14 Frank Mahovlich 7.50 15.00
(Dark uniform)
15 Frank Mahovlich 7.50 15.00
(Dark uniform with added line NHL All-Star)
16 Don McKenney 1.50 3.00
17 Dickie Moore 4.00 8.00
18 Bob Nevin 2.00 4.00
19 Bert Olmstead 2.50 5.00
20 Eddie Shack 5.00 10.00
21 Don Simmons 2.00 4.00
22 Allan Stanley 3.00 6.00

1965-66 Maple Leafs White Border

This 17-card set of postcards measured approximately 3 1/2" by 5 1/2" and featured black and white portrait and full length photos with white borders. The Toronto Maple Leafs logo was printed in both bottom corners. A facsimile autograph appeared at the bottom between the logos. The backs were blank. The cards were unnumbered and checklisted below in alphabetical order.

COMPLETE SET (17) 30.00 60.00
1 George Armstrong 4.00 8.00
2 Bob Baun 2.00 4.00
3 Johnny Bower 4.00 8.00
4 John Brenneman 1.50 3.00
5 Brian Conacher 1.50 3.00
6 Ron Ellis 2.00 4.00
(Portrait)
7 Ron Ellis 2.00 4.00
(Full length; name in print)
8 Larry Hillman 1.50 3.00
9 Larry Jeffrey 1.50 3.00
10 Bruce Gamble 2.00 4.00
11 Red Kelly 4.00 8.00
12 Dave Keon 5.00 10.00
13 Orland Kurtenbach 2.00 4.00
14 Jim Pappin 1.50 3.00
15 Marcel Pronovost 3.00 6.00
16 Eddie Shack 4.00 8.00
17 Allan Stanley 3.00 6.00

1966-67 Maple Leafs Hockey Talks

Distributed by Esso, this set of 10 albums was a popular premium among Maple Leafs fans. Set consisted of ten records inside colorful paper sleeves. Each set was also housed in a large blue Esso Hockey Talks envelope.

COMPLETE SET (10) 300.00 600.00
1 George Armstrong 30.00 60.00
2 Johnny Bower 40.00 80.00
3 Dave Keon 30.00 60.00
4 Frank Mahovlich 30.00 60.00
5 Tim Horton 30.00 60.00
6 Bob Pulford 40.00 80.00
7 Brit Selby 25.00 50.00
8 Eddie Shack 30.00 60.00
9 Ron Ellis 30.00 60.00
10 Punch Imlach 30.00 60.00
NNO Hockey Caravan Envelope 15.00 30.00

1968-69 Maple Leafs White Border

This 11-card set of postcards measured approximately 3 1/2" by 5 1/2" and featured black and white player photos with white borders. The Pelyk and Smith cards were portraits while the other cards have posed action shots. The Maple Leafs logo was at the bottom left corner. A facsimile autograph appeared at the bottom. The backs were blank. The cards were unnumbered and checklisted below in alphabetical order.

COMPLETE SET (11) 20.00 40.00
1 Johnny Bower 4.00 8.00
2 Jim Dorey 1.50 3.00
3 Paul Henderson 2.00 4.00
4 Tim Horton 5.00 10.00
5 Rick Ley 1.50 3.00
6 Murray Oliver 1.50 3.00
7 Mike Pelyk 1.50 3.00
8 Pierre Pilote 3.00 6.00
9 Darryl Sly 1.50 3.00
10 Floyd Smith 1.50 3.00
11 Bill Sutherland 1.50 3.00

1969-70 Maple Leafs White Border Glossy

This 40-card set of postcards measured approximately 3 1/2" by 5 1/2" and features glossy black and white player photos (posed action or portraits) with white borders. The Maple Leafs logo is printed in black in the bottom left corner. The player's name appears at the bottom in block letters. The backs are blank. The cards are unnumbered and checklisted below in alphabetical order.

COMPLETE SET (40) 75.00 150.00
1 George Armstrong 3.00 6.00
2 Johnny Bower 4.00 8.00
3 Wayne Carleton 1.00 2.00
4 King Clancy 3.00 6.00
5 Terry Clancy 1.00 2.00
6 Brian Conacher 1.00 2.00
7 Marv Edwards 1.50 3.00
8 Ron Ellis 1.50 3.00
(Number 6)
9 Ron Ellis 1.50 3.00
(Number 8)
10 Ron Ellis 1.50 3.00
(No number)
11 Bruce Gamble 1.50 3.00
(Front view)
12 Bruce Gamble 1.50 3.00
(Side view)
13 Brian Glennie 1.50 3.00
(Portrait)
14 Brian Glennie 1.50 3.00
(Full length)
15 Jim Harrison 1.00 2.00
16 Larry Hillman 1.00 2.00
17 Tim Horton 5.00 10.00
18 Dave Keon 3.00 6.00
(A on sweater)
19 Dave Keon 3.00 6.00
(C on sweater)
20 Rick Ley 1.50 3.00
21 Frank Mahovlich 5.00 10.00
22 Jim McKenny 1.00 2.00
23 Larry Mickey 1.00 2.00
24 Murray Oliver 1.00 2.00
25 Jim Pappin 1.00 2.00
26 Mike Pelyk 1.00 2.00
27 Marcel Pronovost 2.00 4.00
28 Bob Pulford 2.50 5.00
(Number on gloves)
29 Bob Pulford 2.50 5.00
(No number on gloves)
30 Pat Quinn 2.00 4.00
31 Brit Selby 1.00 2.00
32 Al Smith 1.00 2.00
33 Floyd Smith 1.00 2.00
34 Allan Stanley 2.50 5.00
35 Norm Ullman 2.50 5.00
36 Mike Walton 1.50 3.00
(Stick touching border)
37 Mike Walton 1.50 3.00
(Stick away from border)
38 Ron Ward 1.00 2.00
39 Team Photo 1966-67 3.00 6.00
40 Punch Imlach and King Clancy 3.00 6.00

1969-70 Maple Leafs White Border Matte

This six-card set of postcards measured approximately 3 1/2" by 5 1/2" and featured matte black and white player photos with white borders. The Toronto Maple Leafs logo was printed in black in the bottom left corner. The player's name appeared at the bottom in block letters. The backs were blank. The cards were unnumbered and checklisted below in alphabetical order.

COMPLETE SET (6) 10.00 20.00
1 Brian Glennie 1.50 3.00
2 Dave Keon 4.00 8.00
3 Bill MacMillan 1.25 2.50
4 Larry McIntyre 1.25 2.50
5 Brian Spencer 2.50 5.00
6 Norm Ullman 3.00 6.00

1970-71 Maple Leafs Postcards

This 15-card set measured approximately 3 1/2" by 5 1/2" and featured matte black and white player photos with white borders. The Maple Leafs logo was printed in the bottom left corner. The player's name appeared in block letters, and a facsimile autograph was printed in black. The backs were blank. The cards were unnumbered and checklisted below in alphabetical order. Key card in the set was Darryl Sittler appearing in his Rookie Card year.

COMPLETE SET (15) 25.00 50.00
1 Jim Dorey 1.00 2.00
2 Ron Ellis 1.50 3.00
3 Bruce Gamble 1.50 3.00
4 Jim Harrison 1.00 2.00
5 Paul Henderson 1.50 3.00
6 Rick Ley 1.25 2.50
7 Bob Liddington 1.00 2.00
8 Jim McKenny 1.00 2.00
9 Garry Monahan 1.00 2.00
10 Mike Pelyk 1.00 2.00
11 Jacques Plante 6.00 12.00
12 Brad Selwood 1.00 2.00
13 Darryl Sittler 12.50 25.00
14 Guy Trottier 1.00 2.00
15 Mike Walton 1.50 3.00

1971-72 Maple Leafs Postcards

This 21-card set measured approximately 3 1/2" by 5 1/2" and featured posed color player photos with black backgrounds. (The sweaters had lace-style neck.) The cards featured a facsimile autograph. The backs are blank. The cards were unnumbered and checklisted below in alphabetical order.

COMPLETE SET (21) 25.00 50.00
1 Bob Baun 1.50 3.00
2 Jim Dorey 1.00 2.00
3 Denis Dupere 1.00 2.00
4 Ron Ellis 1.50 3.00
5 Brian Glennie 1.00 2.00
6 Jim Harrison 1.00 2.00
7 Paul Henderson 1.50 3.00
8 Dave Keon 2.50 5.00
9 Rick Ley 1.00 2.00
10 Billy MacMillan 1.00 2.00
11 Don Marshall 1.00 2.00
12 Jim McKenny 1.00 2.00
13 Garry Monahan 1.00 2.00
14 Bernie Parent 4.00 8.00
15 Mike Pelyk 1.00 2.00
16 Jacques Plante 4.00 8.00
17 Brad Selwood 1.00 2.00
18 Darryl Sittler 5.00 10.00
19 Brian Spencer 1.50 3.00
20 Guy Trottier 1.00 2.00
21 Norm Ullman 2.00 4.00

1972-73 Maple Leafs Postcards

This 30-card set measured approximately 3 1/2" by 5 1/2" and featured posed color player photos with a black background. The players were pictured wearing "V-neck" sweaters. The cards featured a facsimile autograph. The backs were blank. The cards were unnumbered and checklisted below in alphabetical order.

COMPLETE SET (30) 40.00 80.00
1 Bob Baun 1.25 2.50
2 Terry Clancy .75 1.50
3 Denis Dupere .75 1.50
4 Ron Ellis 1.25 2.50
(Dark print)
5 Ron Ellis 1.25 2.50
(Light print)
6 George Ferguson .75 1.50
7 Brian Glennie .75 1.50
(Autograph touches stick)
8 Brian Glennie .75 1.50
(Autograph away from stick)
9 John Grisdale .75 1.50
10 Paul Henderson 1.25 2.50
(Light print)
11 Paul Henderson 1.25 2.50
(Dark print)
12 Pierre Jarry .75 1.50
13 Rick Kehoe 1.25 2.50
14 Dave Keon 2.50 5.00
(Autograph touches skate)
15 Dave Keon 2.50 5.00
(Autograph away from skate)
16 Ron Low 1.25 2.50
17 Joe Lundrigan .75 1.50
18 Larry McIntyre .75 1.50
19 Jim McKenny .75 1.50
(Blue tinge)
20 Jim McKenny .75 1.50
(Red tinge)
21 Garry Monahan .75 1.50
22 Randy Osburn .75 1.50
23 Mike Pelyk .75 1.50
24 Jacques Plante 5.00 10.00
(Autograph through tape)
25 Jacques Plante 5.00 10.00
(Autograph under tape)
26 Darryl Sittler 5.00 10.00
(Autograph over stick)
27 Darryl Sittler 5.00 10.00
(Autograph away from stick)
28 Errol Thompson .75 1.50
29 Norm Ullman 2.00 4.00
(Best Wishes above blueline)
30 Norm Ullman 2.00 4.00
(Best Wishes across blueline)

1973-74 Maple Leafs Postcards

This 29-card set measured approximately 3 1/2" by 5 1/2" and featured posed color player photos with a blue-green background. The cards featured a facsimile autograph. The backs were blank. The cards were unnumbered and checklisted below in alphabetical order. The key card in the set was Lanny McDonald, whose card predated his Rookie Card.

COMPLETE SET (29) 45.00 90.00
1 Johnny Bower 2.50 5.00
2 Willie Brossart .75 1.50
3 Denis Dupere .75 1.50
4 Ron Ellis 1.25 2.50
5 Doug Favell 1.50 3.00
(Standing)
6 Doug Favell 1.50 3.00
(Bending)
7 Brian Glennie .75 1.50
8 Jim Gregory .75 1.50
9 Inge Hammarstrom .75 1.50
10 Paul Henderson 1.25 2.50
11 Eddie Johnston 1.50 3.00
12 Rick Kehoe 1.50 3.00
(Same as 1972-73 set)
13 Rick Kehoe 1.50 3.00
(Bending)
14 Rick Kehoe 1.50 3.00
(Standing)
15 Red Kelly 3.00 6.00
16 Dave Keon 3.00 6.00
17 Lanny McDonald 6.00 12.00
18 Jim McKenny .75 1.50
19 Garry Monahan .75 1.50
20 Bob Neely .75 1.50
21 Mike Pelyk .75 1.50
22 Borje Salming 4.00 8.00
23 Eddie Shack 3.00 6.00
24 Darryl Sittler 3.00 6.00
(Bending)
25 Darryl Sittler 3.00 6.00
(Standing)
26 Errol Thompson .75 1.50
27 Ian Turnbull .75 1.50
28 Norm Ullman 1.75 3.50
29 Dunc Wilson 1.25 2.50

1974-75 Maple Leafs Postcards

This 27-card set measured approximately 3 1/2" by 5 1/2" and featured posed color player photos with a pale-blue background and a "Venetian blind" effect. The cards featured facsimile autographs. The backs were blank. The cards were unnumbered and are checklisted below in alphabetical order.

COMPLETE SET (27) 25.00 50.00
1 Claire Alexander .75 1.50
2 Dave Dunn .75 1.50
3 Ron Ellis 1.00 2.00
4 George Ferguson .75 1.50
(Bending)
5 George Ferguson .75 1.50
(Standing)
6 Bill Flett .75 1.50
(Front view)
7 Bill Flett .75 1.50
(Side view)
8 Brian Glennie .75 1.50
9 Inge Hammarstrom .75 1.50
10 Dave Keon 2.00 4.00
(Bending)
11 Dave Keon 2.00 4.00
(Standing)
12 Lanny McDonald 3.00 6.00
13 Jim McKenny .75 1.50
14 Gord McRae .75 1.50
15 Lyle Moffat .75 1.50
16 Bob Neely .75 1.50
17 Gary Sabourin .75 1.50
18 Borje Salming 2.00 4.00
19 Rod Seiling .75 1.50
20 Eddie Shack 2.00 4.00
21 Darryl Sittler 2.00 4.00
22 Blaine Stoughton 1.00 2.00
23 Errol Thompson .75 1.50
24 Ian Turnbull 1.00 2.00
25 Norm Ullman 1.50 3.00
26 Dave(Tiger) Williams 2.00 4.00
27 Dunc Wilson 1.00 2.00

1975-76 Maple Leafs Postcards

This 30-card set of postcards measured approximately 3 1/2" by 5 1/2" and featured posed color photos of players in blue uniforms. The Maple Leafs logo, the player's name, and number appeared in a white panel at the bottom. A facsimile autograph was inscribed across the picture. The backs had player information. The cards were unnumbered and are checklisted below in alphabetical order.

COMPLETE SET (30) 25.00 50.00
1 Claire Alexander .75 1.50
2 Don Ashby .75 1.50
(Bending)
3 Don Ashby .75 1.50
(Standing)
4 Pat Boutette .75 1.50
5 Dave Dunn .75 1.50
6 Doug Favell 1.00 2.00
7 George Ferguson .75 1.50
8 Brian Glennie .75 1.50
9 Inge Hammarstrom .75 1.50
(Bending)
10 Inge Hammarstrom .75 1.50
(Standing)
11 Greg Hubick .75 1.50
12 Lanny McDonald 2.50 5.00
13 Jim McKenny .75 1.50
14 Gord McRae .75 1.50
15 Bob Neely .75 1.50
16 Borje Salming 2.00 4.00
(Side view)
17 Borje Salming 2.00 4.00
(Front view)
18 Rod Seiling .75 1.50
19 Darryl Sittler 2.00 4.00
(Bending)
20 Darryl Sittler 2.50 5.00
(Standing)
21 Blaine Stoughton 1.00 2.00
22 Wayne Thomas 1.25 2.50
(Crouching)
23 Wayne Thomas 1.25 2.50
(Standing)
24 Errol Thompson .75 1.50
25 Ian Turnbull 1.00 2.00
(Bending)
26 Ian Turnbull 1.00 2.00
(Standing)
27 Stan Weir .75 1.50
28 Dave(Tiger) Williams 1.25 2.50
(Bending)
29 Dave(Tiger) Williams 1.25 2.50
(Standing)
30 Maple Leaf Gardens 1.00 2.00
(Painting)

1976-77 Maple Leafs Postcards

This 24-card set in the postcard format measured approximately 3 1/2" by 5 1/2" and featured posed color photos of players in blue uniforms. A white panel at the bottom contained the Maple Leafs logo in each corner, the player's name, and uniform number. A facsimile autograph was inscribed across the picture. The cards were unnumbered and checklisted below in alphabetical order. Key card in the set was Randy Carlyle appearing prior to his Rookie Card year.

COMPLETE SET (24) 20.00 40.00
1 Claire Alexander .63 1.25
2 Don Ashby .63 1.25
3 Pat Boutette .63 1.25
4 Randy Carlyle 1.50 3.00
5 George Ferguson .63 1.25
6 Scott Garland .63 1.25
7 Brian Glennie .63 1.25
8 Inge Hammarstrom .63 1.25
9 Lanny McDonald 2.00 4.00
10 Jim McKenny .63 1.25
11 Gord McRae .63 1.25
12 Bob Neely .63 1.25
13 Mike Palmateer 2.00 4.00
14 Mike Pelyk .63 1.25
15 Borje Salming 1.50 3.00
16 Darryl Sittler 2.00 4.00
17 Wayne Thomas 1.00 2.00
18 Errol Thompson .63 1.25
19 Ian Turnbull .75 1.50
(Dark printing)
20 Ian Turnbull .75 1.50
(Light printing)
21 Jack Valiquette .63 1.25
22 Kurt Walker .63 1.25
23 Stan Weir .63 1.25
24 Dave(Tiger) Williams 2.00 4.00

1977-78 Maple Leafs Postcards

This 19-card set measures approximately 3 1/2" by 5 1/2" and featured posed color photos of players in white uniforms. At the bottom were the Toronto Maple Leafs logo in each corner, the player's uniform number, and the player's name in blue print. The backs were blank. The cards were unnumbered and checklisted below in alphabetical order.

COMPLETE SET (19) 12.50 25.00
1 Pat Boutette .50 1.00
2 Randy Carlyle 1.00 2.00
3 Ron Ellis .75 1.50
4 George Ferguson .50 1.00
5 Brian Glennie .50 1.00
6 Inge Hammarstrom .50 1.00
7 Trevor Johansen .50 1.00
8 Jim Jones .50 1.00
9 Lanny McDonald 2.00 4.00
10 Jim McKenny .50 1.00
11 Gord McRae .50 1.00
12 Mike Palmateer 1.50 3.00
13 Borje Salming 1.50 3.00
14 Darryl Sittler 2.00 4.00
15 Errol Thompson .50 1.00
16 Ian Turnbull .50 1.00
17 Jack Valiquette .50 1.00
18 Kurt Walker .50 1.00
19 Dave(Tiger) Williams 1.50 3.00

1978-79 Maple Leafs Postcards

This 25-card set in the postcard format measured approximately 3 1/2" by 5 1/2" and featured posed color player photos. At the bottom were the Toronto Maple Leafs logo in each corner, the player's uniform number in the logo at the bottom right, and the player's name in blue print. The cards were unnumbered and checklisted below in alphabetical order.

COMPLETE SET (25) 15.00 30.00
1 John Anderson .75 1.50
2 Bruce Boudreau .50 1.00
(Black and white)
3 Pat Boutette .50 1.00
4 Pat Boutette .50 1.00
5 Dave Burrows .50 1.00
6 Jerry Butler .50 1.00
7 Ron Ellis .75 1.50
8 Paul Harrison .50 1.00
9 Dave Hutchison .50 1.00
10 Trevor Johansen .50 1.00
11 Jimmy Jones .50 1.00
12 Dan Maloney .75 1.50
13 Lanny McDonald 2.00 4.00
14 Walt McKechnie .50 1.00
15 Garry Monahan .50 1.00
16 Roger Neilson 1.00 2.00
17 Mike Palmateer 1.25 2.50
18 Borje Salming 1.25 2.50
19 Darryl Sittler 2.00 4.00
20 Lorne Stamler .50 1.00
21 Ian Turnbull .50 1.00
22 Dave(Tiger) Williams 1.25 2.50
23 Ron Wilson .50 1.00
24 Harold Ballard and 1.00 2.00
King Clancy
25 Team Photo 1.25 2.50

1979-80 Maple Leafs Postcards

This 34-card set in the postcard format measured approximately 3 1/2" by 5 1/2" and featured posed color photos of players in blue uniforms. The Toronto Maple Leafs logo was in each bottom corner. A blue panel across the bottom contained the player's name in white print. The player's uniform number was printed in the logo at the bottom right. Most of the pictures had a light blue tint and are taken against a studio background. These cards also featured facsimile autographs on the lower portion of the picture. The backs were printed with a light blue postcard design and carry the player's name and position. The cards were unnumbered and checklisted below in alphabetical order.

COMPLETE SET (34) 20.00 40.00
1 John Anderson .50 1.00
2 Harold Ballard .75 1.50
3 Laurie Boschman .50 1.00
4 Pat Boutette .38 .75
5 Carl Brewer .75 1.50
(Action shot taken at rink; borderless; no facsimile autograph; black print on back)
6 Dave Burrows .38 .75
7 Jerry Butler .38 .75
8 Jiri Crha .75 1.50
9 Ron Ellis .50 1.00
10 Paul Gardner .38 .75
11 Paul Harrison .38 .75
12 Greg Hotham .38 .75
13 Dave Hutchison .38 .75
14 Punch Imlach CO 1.00 2.00
15 Jimmy Jones .38 .75
16 Mark Kirton .38 .75
17 Dan Maloney .38 .75
18 Terry Martin .50 1.00
(Action shot taken at rink; borderless; no facsimile autograph; black print on back)
19 Lanny McDonald 2.00 4.00
20 Walt McKechnie .38 .75
21 Mike Palmateer 1.00 2.00
22 Mike Palmateer 1.00 2.00
(Autograph at different angle)
23 Joel Quenneville .50 1.00
24 Rocky Saganiuk .38 .75
25 Borje Salming 1.25 2.50
(Autograph touches blue panel)
26 Borje Salming 1.25 2.50
(Autograph away from blue panel)
27 Darryl Sittler 2.00 4.00
(Autograph closer to blue panel)
28 Darryl Sittler 2.00 4.00
29 Floyd Smith .38 .75
30 Bob Stephenson .50 1.00
(Action shot taken at rink; borderless; no facsimile autograph; black print on back)
31 Ian Turnbull .38 .75
32 Dave(Tiger) Williams 1.00 2.00
33 Ron Wilson .38 .75
34 Faceoff with Cardinal .63 1.25

1980-81 Maple Leafs Postcards

This 28-card set measured approximately 3 1/2" by 5 1/2" and featured horizontally oriented color player photos on the left half of the card. The right half displayed player information, blue logos, and a facsimile autograph printed in sky blue along with the team logo and a maple leaf carrying the player's jersey number. The backs were blank. The cards were unnumbered and checklisted below in alphabetical order.

COMPLETE SET (28) 12.50 25.00
1 John Anderson .40 1.00
2 Harold Ballard .60 1.50
3 Laurie Boschman .40 1.00
(Portrait)
4 Laurie Boschman .40 1.00
(Action)
5 Johnny Bower 1.25 3.00
6 King Clancy .75 2.00
7 Jiri Crha .60 1.50
8 Joe Crozier CO .30 .75
9 Bill Derlago .40 1.00
10 Dick Duff .40 1.00
11 Vitezslav Duris .30 .75
12 Dave Farrish .30 .75
13 Stewart Gavin .40 1.00
14 Paul Harrison .30 .75
15 Pat Hickey .30 .75
16 Mark Kirton .30 .75
17 Terry Martin .30 .75
18 Gerry McNamara .30 .75
19 Wilf Paiement .40 1.00
20 Robert Picard .30 .75
21 Curt Ridley .30 .75
22 Rocky Saganiuk .30 .75
23 Borje Salming .75 2.00
24 Dave Shand .30 .75
25 Darryl Sittler 1.50 4.00
(Portrait)
26 Darryl Sittler 1.50 4.00
(Action)
27 Ian Turnbull .30 .75
28 Rick Vaive .60 1.50

1981-82 Maple Leafs Postcards

This 26-card set in the postcard format measured approximately 3 1/2" by 5 1/2" and featured full-bleed color photos of players posed on the ice against a dark background. A white Maple Leafs logo appeared in each top corner and the player's name in white between the logos. The player's number was printed in the right top logo. These cards also featured facsimile autographs. The backs were white and have a basic postcard design printed in light blue. The cards were unnumbered and checklisted below in alphabetical order.

COMPLETE SET (26) 10.00 25.00
1 John Anderson .40 1.00
2 Harold Ballard .75 2.00
(Painting)
3 Jim Benning .30 .75
4 Fred Boimistruck .30 .75
5 Laurie Boschman .30 .75
6 Bill Derlago .40 1.00
7 Stewart Gavin .40 1.00
8 Bunny Larocque .60 1.50
9 Don Luce .30 .75
10 Dan Maloney .30 .75
11 Bob Manno .30 .75
12 Paul Marshall .30 .75
13 Terry Martin .30 .75
14 Bob McGill .30 .75
15 Barry Melrose .60 1.50
16 Mike Nykoluk CO .30 .75
17 Wilf Paiement .40 1.00
18 Rene Robert .40 1.00
19 Rocky Saganiuk .30 .75
20 Borje Salming .75 2.00
21 Darryl Sittler 1.50 4.00
22 Vincent Tremblay .30 .75
23 Rick Vaive .60 1.50
24 Gary Yaremchuk .30 .75
25 Ron Zanussi .30 .75
26 Frank J. Selke and .60 1.50
Harold Ballard

1982-83 Maple Leafs Postcards

This 37-card set in the postcard format measured approximately 3 1/2" by 5 1/2" and featured color photos of players on the ice against a dark background. A white Maple Leafs logo, the sweater number, and the player's name appeared in a blue panel at the bottom. A facsimile autograph appeared near the bottom of the picture. A blue Maple Leafs logo was printed in one of the top corners. The postcard backs were printed in light blue, in contrast to the 1984-85 issue, which featured black print on the back. The cards were unnumbered and checklisted below in alphabetical order.

COMPLETE SET (37) 10.00 25.00
1 Russ Adam .30 .75
2 John Anderson .40 1.00
3 Normand Aubin .30 .75
4 Jim Benning .30 .75
5 Fred Boimistruck .30 .75
6 Serge Boisvert .30 .75
7 Dan Daoust .30 .75
8 Bill Derlago .40 1.00
(Autograph 1/8 from border)
9 Bill Derlago .40 1.00
(Autograph 1/4 from border)
10 Vitezslav Duris .30 .75
11 Miroslav Frycer .30 .75
(Autograph touching skate blade)
12 Miroslav Frycer .30 .75
(Autograph away from skate blade)
13 Stewart Gavin .40 1.00
14 Gaston Gingras .30 .75
(Dark background)
15 Gaston Gingras .30 .75
(Light background)
16 Billy Harris .30 .75
17 Paul Higgins .30 .75
18 Peter Inhacak .30 .75
19 Jim Korn .30 .75
20 Bunny Larocque .40 1.00
(Bunny touching stick)
21 Bunny Larocque .40 1.00
(Bunny touching goalie pad)
22 Dan Maloney .40 1.00
23 Terry Martin .30 .75
24 Bob McGill .30 .75
25 Frank Nigro .30 .75
26 Mike Nykoluk CO .30 .75
27 Gary Nylund .30 .75
28 Mike Palmateer .75 2.00
29 Walt Poddubny .40 1.00
30 Borje Salming .75 2.00
(Autograph 1/8 from skate)
31 Borje Salming .75 2.00
(Autograph 1/4 from skate)
32 Rick St. Croix .40 1.00
33 Greg Terrion .30 .75
(Dark background)
34 Greg Terrion .30 .75
(Light background)
35 Vincent Tremblay .30 .75
36 Rick Vaive .50 1.25
(Autograph touching blade)
37 Rick Vaive .50 1.25
(Autograph touching toe of skate)

1983-84 Maple Leafs Postcards

This 26-card set in the postcard format measured approximately 3 1/2" by 5 1/2" and featured posed color photos of players on the ice. A pale blue border contained a blue Maple Leafs logo in the bottom right corner. The player's name and number was printed running up the left side and across the top in the left corner. A facsimile autograph was printed in black on the front near the bottom of the photo. The backs were white and carry a basic postcard design in light blue. The cards were unnumbered and checklisted below in alphabetical order.

COMPLETE SET (26) 8.00 20.00
1 John Anderson .40 1.00
2 Jim Benning .30 .75
3 Dan Daoust .30 .75
4 Bill Derlago .40 1.00
5 Dave Farrish .30 .75
6 Miroslav Frycer .30 .75
7 Stewart Gavin .40 1.00
8 Gaston Gingras .30 .75
9 Pat Graham .30 .75
10 Billy Harris .30 .75
11 Peter Inhacak .30 .75
12 Jim Korn .30 .75
13 Gary Leeman .40 1.00
14 Dan Maloney .30 .75
15 Terry Martin .30 .75
16 Basil McRae .40 1.00
17 Frank Nigro .30 .75
18 Mike Nykoluk CO .30 .75
19 Gary Nylund .30 .75
20 Mike Palmateer .60 1.50
21 Walt Poddubny .40 1.00
22 Borje Salming .75 2.00
23 Bill Stewart .30 .75
24 Rick St. Croix .40 1.00
25 Greg Terrion .30 .75
26 Rick Vaive .50 1.25

1984-85 Maple Leafs Postcards

This 25-card set in the postcard format measured approximately 3 1/2" by 5 1/2" and featured posed color photos of players on the ice with facsimile autographs. A blue panel at the bottom contained the player's name, sweater number, and a white Maple Leafs logo. A blue Toronto Maple Leafs logo appeared in one of the top corners. The backs had a basic postcard design printed in black. The cards were unnumbered and checklisted below in alphabetical order. Both Russ Courtnall and Al Iafrate appeared in this set prior to their Rookie Card year. This set could be distinguished from the similarly designed 1982-83 postcard set by the black jersey number and black outline around the team logo in the bottom border stripe.

COMPLETE SET (25) 10.00 25.00
1 John Anderson .40 1.00
2 Jim Benning .30 .75
3 Allan Bester .50 1.25
4 John Brophy CO .40 1.00
5 Jeff Brubaker .30 .75
6 Russ Courtnall 1.25 3.00
7 Dan Daoust .30 .75
8 Bill Derlago .30 .75
9 Miroslav Frycer .30 .75
10 Stewart Gavin .40 1.00
11 Al Iafrate 1.50 4.00
12 Peter Inhacak .30 .75
13 Jeff Jackson .30 .75
14 Jim Korn .30 .75
15 Gary Leeman .40 1.00
16 Dan Maloney CO .30 .75
17 Bob McGill .30 .75
18 Gary Nylund .30 .75
19 Walt Poddubny .40 1.00
20 Bill Root .30 .75
21 Borje Salming .75 2.00
22 Bill Stewart .30 .75
23 Greg Terrion .30 .75
24 Rick Vaive .50 1.25
25 Ken Wregget 1.00 2.50

1905-06 Maple Leafs Postcards

This 34-card set in the postcard format measured approximately 3 1/2" by 5 1/2" and featured color action photos of players on the ice. A blue panel at the bottom contained the player's name, number, and a white Maple Leafs logo. The cards were unnumbered and checklisted below in alphabetical order. Wendel Clark appeared in this set the year before his Rookie Card. In addition to the regular set, a special John Bower card was also available.

COMPLETE SET (35) 12.00 30.00
1 Harold Ballard PRES .40 1.00
2 Jim Benning .30 .75
3 Tim Bernhardt .40 1.00
4 Johnny Bower ACO .60 1.50
5 Jeff Brubaker .30 .75
6 Wendel Clark 4.00 10.00
7 Russ Courtnall .75 2.00
(Dark uniform)
8 Russ Courtnall .75 2.00
(Light uniform)
9 Dan Daoust .30 .75
10 Don Edwards .60 1.50
11 Tom Fergus .30 .75
12 Miroslav Frycer .30 .75
13 Dan Hodgson .30 .75
14 Al Iafrate 1.25 3.00
15 Miroslav Inhacak .30 .75
16 Peter Inhacak .30 .75
17 Jim Korn .30 .75
18 Chris Kotsopoulos .30 .75
19 Gary Leeman .40 1.00
20 Brad Maxwell .40 1.00
(Dark uniform)
21 Brad Maxwell .40 1.00
(Light uniform)
22 Bob McGill .30 .75
23 Gary Nylund .30 .75
24 Walt Poddubny .40 1.00
25 Bill Root .30 .75
26 Borje Salming .75 2.00
27 Marian Stastny .30 .75
28 Greg Terrion .30 .75
29 Steve Thomas 1.00 2.50
30 Rick Vaive .40 1.00
(Taking slapshot& visor on helmet)
31 Rick Vaive .40 1.00
(Light uniform)
32 Blake Wesley .30 .75
33 Ken Wregget .60 1.50
34 Team Photo 1.25 3.00
(5 1/2- by 8 1/2-)
35 John Bower SPECIAL .30 .75

1986-87 Maple Leafs Postcards

This 22-card set measured approximately 3 1/2" by 5 1/2". The fronts featured full-bleed color action player photos; the player's name, number and team logo were printed in a blue-and-white bar at the top or bottom. The backs were white and show a postcard design. The cards were unnumbered and checklisted below in alphabetical order.

COMPLETE SET (22) 10.00 25.00
1 Mike Allison .30 .75
2 Harold Ballard PR .60 1.50
3 Tim Bernhardt .40 1.00
4 Wendel Clark 2.00 5.00
5 Russ Courtnall .75 2.00
6 Vincent Damphousse 2.00 5.00
7 Jerome Dupont .30 .75
8 Tom Fergus .30 .75
9 Miroslav Frycer .30 .75
10 Todd Gill .30 .75
11 Al Iafrate 1.25 3.00
12 Peter Ihnacak .30 .75
13 Jeff Jackson .30 .75
14 Terry Johnson .30 .75
15 Chris Kotsopoulos .30 .75
16 Gary Leeman .30 .75
17 Borje Salming .75 2.00
18 Brad Smith .40 1.00
19 Greg Terrion .30 .75
20 Steve Thomas .60 1.50
21 Rick Vaive .40 1.00
22 Ken Wregget 1.00 2.50

1987-88 Maple Leafs PLAY

This set contained 30 P.L.A.Y. (Police, Law and Youth) cards, and it was sponsored by Kellogg Salada Canada Inc. in conjunction with the Toronto Maple Leafs and various police agencies. The cards could be collected from members of the London City Police and the Ontario Provincial Police, at a rate of three new cards per week. Three special "make-up weeks" were held to acquire any cards that were missed. The cards measured approximately 2 3/4" by 3 1/4".

COMPLETE SET (30) 8.00 20.00
1 N.Laverne Shipley .02 .10
(Police Chief)
2 Tom Gosnell (Mayor) .02 .10
3 Sponsor's Card .02 .10
Kellogg Salada Canada& Inc.
4 Harold E. Ballard PR .20 .50
5 D. Almond .02 .10
(Police Superintendent)
6 Wendel Clark 17 2.00 5.00
7 Tom Fergus 19 .30 .75
8 Borje Salming 21 .60 1.50
9 Ed Olczyk 16 .30 .75
10 Gary Leeman 11 .30 .75
11 Rick Lanz 4 .20 .50
12 Allan Bester 30 .30 .75
13 Todd Gill 23 .30 .75
14 Al Secord 20 .30 .75
15 Miroslav Frycer 14 .20 .50
16 Chris Kotsopoulos 26 .20 .50
17 Vincent Damphousse 10 1.50 4.00
18 Mike Allison 8 .20 .50
19 Al Iafrate 33 .75 2.00
20 Dan Daoust 24 .20 .50
21 Greg Terrion 7 .20 .50
22 Brad Smith 29 .30 .75
23 Mark Osborne 12 .20 .50
24 Peter Ihnacak 18 .20 .50
25 Dale Degray 3 .20 .50
26 Dave Semenko 27 .30 .75
27 Luke Richardson 2 .30 .75
28 John Brophy CO .20 .50
29 Ken Wregget 31 .60 1.50
30 Russ Courtnall 9 .40 1.00

1987-88 Maple Leafs Postcards

Measuring approximately 5" by 8", this set of oversized postcards featured the Toronto Maple Leafs. The fronts had full-bleed color action player photos; the player's name, number, and team logo were printed in a blue-and-white bar at the bottom. The backs were white and show a postcard design. The cards were unnumbered and checklisted below in alphabetical order.

COMPLETE SET (21) 8.00 20.00
1 Allan Bester .30 .75
2 Wendel Clark 2.00 5.00
3 Russ Courtnall .40 1.00
4 Vincent Damphousse 1.50 4.00
5 Dan Daoust .20 .50
6 Tom Fergus .30 .75
7 Miroslav Frycer .20 .50
8 Todd Gill .30 .75
9 Al Iafrate .75 2.00
10 Peter Ihnacak .20 .50
11 Chris Kotsopoulos .20 .50
12 Rick Lanz .20 .50
13 Gary Leeman .30 .75
14 Ed Olczyk .30 .75
15 Mark Osborne .20 .50
16 Luke Richardson .30 .75
17 Borje Salming .60 1.50
18 Al Secord .30 .75
19 Dave Semenko .30 .75
20 Ken Wregget .60 1.50
21 Team Photo .75 2.00

1987-88 Maple Leafs Postcards Oversized

This set was similar in design and checklist to the regular size set, yet measures 6" x 10".

COMPLETE SET (21) 8.00 20.00
1 Allan Bester .30 .75
2 Wendel Clark 2.00 5.00
3 Russ Courtnall .40 1.00
4 Vincent Damphousse 1.50 4.00
5 Dan Daoust .20 .50
6 Tom Fergus .30 .75
7 Miroslav Frycer .20 .50
8 Todd Gill .30 .75
9 Al Iafrate .75 2.00
10 Peter Ihnacak .20 .50
11 Chris Kotsopoulos .20 .50
12 Rick Lanz .20 .50
13 Gary Leeman .30 .75
14 Ed Olczyk .30 .75
15 Mark Osborne .20 .50
16 Luke Richardson .20 .50
17 Borje Salming .60 1.50
18 Al Secord .30 .75
19 Dave Semenko .30 .75
20 Ken Wregget .60 1.50
21 Team Photo .75 2.00

1988-89 Maple Leafs PLAY

This set contained 30 P.L.A.Y. (Police, Law and Youth) cards, and it was sponsored by Kellogg's in conjunction with Toronto Maple Leafs and various police agencies. The cards could be collected from members of the London City Police and the Ontario Provincial Police, at a rate of three new cards per week. Three special "make-up weeks" were held to acquire any cards that were missed. After collecting the first 12 cards, they were to be brought to police stations in order to obtain the collector album, which measured approximately 7" by 10". The P.L.A.Y. cards measured 2 3/4" by 3 1/2" and the album had three slots per page in a horizontal format. Below each picture the album had the player's name, number, and a hockey tip paralleled by an anti-crime message.

COMPLETE SET (30) 4.80 12.00
1 Rules and Tips .08 .25
2 Wendel Clark 17 .75 2.00
3 Tom Fergus 19 .20 .50
4 D. Almond .08 .25
(Superintendent)
5 Borje Salming 21 .60 1.50
6 Ed Olczyk 16 .20 .50
7 Sponsor's Card .08 .25
Kellogg Canada& Inc.
8 Gary Leeman 11 .20 .50
9 Rick Lanz 4 .20 .50
10 N.LaVerne Shipley .08 .25
(Chief of Police)
11 Allan Bester 30 .30 .75
12 Todd Gill 23 .30 .75
13 Harold E. Ballard PR .40 1.00
14 Al Secord 20 .30 .75
15 Daniel Marois 32 .20 .50
16 Chris Kotsopoulos 26 .20 .50
17 Vincent Damphousse 10 .75 2.00
18 Craig Laughlin 14 .20 .50
19 Al Iafrate 33 .40 1.00
20 Dan Daoust 24 .20 .50
21 Derek Laxdal 35 .20 .50
22 Darren Veitch 25 .20 .50
23 Mark Osborne 12 .20 .50
24 David Reid 34 .30 .75
25 Brad Marsh 3 .30 .75
26 Brian Curran 28 .20 .50
27 Sean McKenna 8 .20 .50
28 John Brophy CO .20 .50
29 Ken Wregget 31 .40 1.00
30 Russ Courtnall 9 .40 1.00

1990-91 Maple Leafs Postcards

This postcard-like issue featured color action photos on the front, with an unusual design element of Leafs logos surrounding the action. It was believed that the cards were distributed by local police officers to children. The cards were unnumbered, so are listed in alphabetical order.

COMPLETE SET (21) 4.80 12.00
1 Aaron Broten .20 .50
2 Vincent Damphousse .60 1.50
3 Dave Ellett .20 .50
4 Paul Fenton .20 .50
5 Tom Fergus .20 .50
6 Lou Franceschetti .30 .75
7 Al Iafrate .30 .75
8 Peter Ing .30 .75
9 Mike Krushelnyski .30 .75
10 Tom Kurvers .20 .50
11 Gary Leeman .20 .50
12 Kevin Maguire .30 .75
13 Brad Marsh .30 .75
14 Scott Pearson .20 .50
15 Michel Petit .20 .50
16 Rob Ramage .20 .50
17 Dave Reid .20 .50
18 Luke Richardson .20 .50
19 Joe Sacco .20 .50
20 Doug Shedden .20 .50
21 Scott Thornton .20 .50

1991 Maple Leafs Panini Team Stickers

This 32-sticker set was issued in a plastic bag that contained two 16-sticker sheets (approximately 9" by 12") and a foldout poster, "Super Poster - Hockey 91", on which the stickers could be affixed. The players' names appeared only on the poster, not on the stickers. Each sticker measured about 2 1/8" by 2 7/8" and featured a color player action shot on its white-bordered front. The back of the white sticker sheet was lined off into 16 panels, each carrying the logos for Panini, the NHL, and the NHLPA, as well as the same number that appeared on the front of the sticker. Every Canadian NHL team was featured in this promotion. Each team set was available by mail-order from Panini Canada Ltd. for 2.99 plus 50 cents for shipping and handling.

COMPLETE SET (32) 1.25 3.00
1 Drake Berehowsky .01 .05
2 Allan Bester .02 .10
3 Wendel Clark .20 .50
4 Brian Curran .01 .05
5 Vincent Damphousse .20 .50
6 Lou Franceschetti .01 .05
7 Todd Gill .01 .05
8 Dave Hannan .01 .05
9 Al Iafrate .02 .10
10 Peter Ing .02 .10
11 Tom Kurvers .01 .05
12 Gary Leeman .01 .05
13 Kevin Maguire .01 .05
14 Daniel Marois .01 .05
15 Brad Marsh .02 .10
16 John McIntyre .01 .05
17 Ed Olczyk .01 .05
18 Mark Osborne .01 .05
19 Scott Pearson .01 .05
20 Rob Ramage .02 .10
21 Jeff Reese .02 .10
22 Dave Reid .02 .10
23 Luke Richardson .01 .05
24 Maple Leafs in Action .01 .05
A Team Logo .01 .05
Left Side
B Team Logo .01 .05
Right Side
C Maple Leafs in Action .01 .05
Upper Left Corner
Al Iafrate
Dave Reid
D Maple Leafs in Action .01 .05
Lower Left Corner
Al Iafrate
Dave Reid
E Maple Leafs in Action .01 .05
Upper Right Corner
Al Iafrate
Dave Reid
F Maple Leafs in Action .01 .05
Lower Right Corner
Al Iafrate
Dave Reid
G Al Iafrate .05 .15
Ken Wregget
H Gary Leeman .08 .25
John Kordic

1991-92 Maple Leafs PLAY

This postcard-like set featured action photos on the front, along with player information. The cards were handed out by local police officers to children.

COMPLETE SET (30) 6.00 15.00
1 Glenn Anderson .40 1.00
2 Craig Berube .20 .50
3 Brian Bradley .20 .50
4 Mike Bullard .20 .50
5 Rob Cimetta .20 .50
6 Wendel Clark .75 2.00
7 Bryan Cousineau .20 .50
8 Lucien Deblois .20 .50
9 Dave Ellett .20 .50
10 Tom Fergus .20 .50
11 Cliff Fletcher .08 .25
12 Mike Foligno .20 .50
13 Grant Fuhr .75 2.00
14 Todd Gill .20 .50
15 Alexander Godynyuk .20 .50
16 Bob Halkidis .20 .50
17 Dave Hannan .20 .50
19 Mike Krushelnyski .20 .50
20 Lanny the Police Dog .02 .10
21 Gary Leeman .30 .75
22 Claude Loiselle .20 .50
23 Daniel Marois .20 .50
24 Rob Pearson .20 .50
25 Michel Petit .20 .50
26 Jeff Reese .25 .60
27 Bob Rouse .20 .50
28 Darryl Shannon .20 .50
29 Tom Watt .08 .25
30 Peter Zezel .20 .50

1992-93 Maple Leafs Kodak

This oversized set (4" X 6 1/8") featured full color photos on luscious Kodak paper. The backs were blank. The cards were believed to have been issued as a game-night promotion, although that has not been confirmed.

COMPLETE SET (22) 8.00 20.00
1 Glenn Anderson .30 .75
2 Dave Andreychuk .30 .75
3 Dave Andreychuk .30 .75
(In front of the net
4 Ken Baumgartner .20 .50
5 Drake Berehowsky .20 .50
6 Bill Berg .20 .50
7 Nikolai Borschevsky .20 .50
8 Wendel Clark .75 2.00
9 John Cullen .20 .50
10 Mike Eastwood .20 .50
11 Dave Ellett .20 .50
12 Doug Gilmour .75 2.00
13 Sylvain Lefebvre .20 .50
14 Jamie Macoun .20 .50
15 Kent Manderville .20 .50
16 Dave McIlwain .20 .50
17 Dmitri Mironov .20 .50
18 Mark Osborne .20 .50
19 Rob Pearson .20 .50
20 Felix Potvin 1.25 3.00
21 Bob Rouse .20 .50
22 Peter Zezel .20 .50
23 Mike Foligno .20 .50
24 Grant Fuhr .60 1.50
25 Todd Gill .20 .50
26 Mike Krushelnyski .20 .50
27 Guy Larose .20 .50
28 Bob McGill .20 .50
29 Dave McLLwain .20 .50
30 Daren Puppa .30 .75
31 Joe Sacco .20 .50
32 Darryl Shannon .20 .50
33 Rick Wamsley .30 .75

1993-94 Maple Leafs Score Black's

This 24-card, standard-size Toronto Maple Leafs team set was produced by Score and sponsored by Black's Photography. The cards were distributed free in four-card packs, when a customer brought in film for developing, or with a second order of prints, or when purchasing two rolls of Black's P.I. film. The fronts featured a pop-up photo cut-out. The pop-up was accomplished by gently bending the card to pop up the player's head and then pulling a tab at the top to stand the player up. The fronts had an white outer border with a wider purple inner border overlaid with a thin red and purple line. The words "Collector's Edition" were printed in white at the top of the picture. The logo for Black's Photography was printed on the upper left vertical side. Player identification appeared under the action photo. The purple backs had a white border with a second player portrait and biography. The Black's Photography logo was printed in the upper left corner. The cards were numbered on the front. There was also an album available for this set; it is not included in the complete set price below.

COMPLETE SET (24)	12.00	30.00
1 Wendel Clark	1.50	4.00
2 Doug Gilmour	2.00	5.00
3 Glenn Anderson	.60	1.50
4 Peter Zezel	.30	.75
5 Bob Rouse	.20	.50
6 Rob Pearson	.20	.50
7 Mark Osborne	.20	.50
8 Dmitri Mironov	.40	1.00
9 Dave McLlwain	.20	.50
10 Kent Manderville	.20	.50
11 Jamie Macoun	.20	.50
12 Sylvain Lefebvre	.30	.75
13 Dave Andreychuk	.75	2.00
14 Drake Berehowsky	.20	.50
15 Bill Berg	.20	.50
16 John Cullen	.30	.75
17 Ken Baumgartner	.30	.75
18 Nikolai Borschevsky	.20	.50
19 Mike Eastwood	.20	.50
20 Dave Ellett	.30	.75
21 Mike Foligno	.30	.75
22 Todd Gill	.20	.50
23 Mike Krushelnyski	.20	.50
24 Felix Potvin	3.00	8.00
xx Album	2.00	5.00

1994-95 Maple Leafs Gangsters

This 17-card set measured approximately 4 3/4" by 7". The fronts had borderless color action player photos. The backs carried black-and-white player portraits with a 1920's style gangster motif.

COMPLETE SET (17)	4.80	12.00
1 Dave Andreychuk	.40	1.00
2 Ken Baumgartner	.20	.50
3 Bill Berg	.20	.50
4 Nikolai Borschevsky	.20	.50
5 Mike Eastwood	.20	.50
6 Dave Ellett	.30	.75
7 Mike Gartner	.40	1.00
8 Todd Gill	.30	.75
9 Doug Gilmour	.75	2.00
10 Alexei Kudashov	.20	.50
11 Jamie Macoun	.20	.50
12 Kent Manderville	.20	.50
13 Dmitri Mironov	.20	.50
14 Mark Osborne	.20	.50
15 Felix Potvin	.75	2.00
16 Damian Rhodes	.40	1.00
17 Title Card	.08	.25

1994-95 Maple Leafs Kodak

This set measured approximately 4" x 6" and featured full color action photos on the front. Cards featured blank backs and are checklisted below in alphabetical order.

COMPLETE SET (30)	6.00	15.00
1 Dave Andreychuk	.40	1.00
2 Ken Baumgartner	.20	.50
3 Drake Berehowsky	.20	.50
4 Bill Berg	.20	.50
5 Nikolai Borschevsky	.20	.50
6 Pat Burns	.08	.25
7 Garth Butcher	.20	.50
8 Mike Craig	.20	.50
9 Paul Dipietro	.08	.25
10 Tie Domi	.30	.75
11 Mike Gartner	.40	1.00
12 Todd Gill	.30	.75
13 Doug Gilmour	.75	2.00
14 David Harlock	.30	.75
15 Benoit Hogue	.20	.50
16 Grant Jennings	.08	.25
17 Kenny Jonsson	.30	.75
18 Jamie Macoun	.20	.50
19 Terry Martin	.08	.25
20 Dmitri Mironov	.20	.50
21 Felix Potvin	1.25	3.00
22 Damian Rhodes	.40	1.00
23 Mike Ridley	.20	.50
24 Warren Rychel	.08	.25
25 Mats Sundin	.75	2.00
26 Rich Sutter	.08	.25
27 Dixon Ward	.20	.50
28 Todd Warriner	.20	.50
29 Randy Wood	.08	.25
30 Terry Yake	.08	.25

1994-95 Maple Leafs Pin-up Posters

Cards measure 11 1/2" x 15" and were issued in Saturday and Sunday Toronto Sun newspapers. 1995 MAPLE LEAFS appeared in red at the bottom of the pin-up.

COMPLETE SET (30)	6.00	15.00
1 Mats Sundin	.75	2.00
2 Doug Gilmour	.75	2.00
3 Dave Ellett	.20	.50
4 Mike Eastland	.20	.50
5 Garth Butcher	.20	.50
6 Nikolai Borschevsky	.20	.50
7 Kenny Jonsson	.30	.75
8 Todd Gill	.20	.50
9 Bill Berg	.20	.50
10 Jamie Macoun	.20	.50
11 Damian Rhodes	.30	.75
12 Mike Ridley	.20	.50
13 Terry Yake	.08	.25
14 Felix Potvin	1.25	3.00
15 Warren Rychel	.08	.25
16 Randy Wood	.08	.25
17 Kent Manderville	.20	.50
18 Dave Andreychuk	.30	.75
19 Ken Baumgartner	.20	.50
20 Dmitri Mironov	.20	.50
21 Mike Craig	.20	.50
21A Mike Gartner	.30	.75
23 Matt Martin	.20	.50
24 Tie Domi	.40	1.00
25 Paul DiPietro	.08	.25
26 Rich Sutter	.08	.25
27 Grant Jennings	.08	.25
28 Benoit Hogue	.20	.50
29 Darby Hendrickson	.20	.50
30 Pat Burns CL	.08	.25

1994-95 Maple Leafs Postcards

Sponsored by Coca-Cola, this four-card set measured approximately 5 3/4" by 4". The horizontal and vertical fronts featured borderless color action player photos. The words "1995 Collector Postcard" and Coca-Cola's logo appeared on the bottom. The backs had a postcard format and carried a short description of the scene depicted on the front. The cards were distributed to fans at Maple Leaf Gardens before a game in March, 1995, and came attached to a series of coupons for Beckers convenience stores. The cards were unnumbered and checklisted below in alphabetical order.

COMPLETE SET (4)	3.00	8.00
1 Dave Andreychuk	1.00	2.50
Todd Gill		
Doug Gilmour		
Jamie Macoun		
Mats Sundin		
2 Garth Butcher	1.25	3.00
Doug Gilmour		
Felix Potvin		
Mats Sundin		
3 Dmitri Mironov	.60	1.50
Mike Ridley		
Mats Sundin		
4 Felix Potvin	1.00	2.50

1996-97 Maple Leafs Postcards

These four postcard-sized singles were available for sale at Maple Leaf Gardens souvenir stands throughout this season. They featured the Leafs' most popular players in action.

COMPLETE SET (4)	2.50	6.00
1 Mats Sundin	.75	2.00
Wendel Clark		
Doug Gilmour		
2 Felix Potvin	1.25	3.00
Mario Lemieux		
3 Wendel Clark	.75	2.00
4 Tie Domi	.40	1.00
Sergei Berezin		

1998 Maple Leafs Postcards

A limited edition of postcards, with just 10,000 sets made, these collectibles were distributed by Beckers to commemorate the 65th Anniversary of Maple Leaf Gardens.

COMPLETE SET	4.00	10.00
1 Mats Sundin	1.00	2.50
2 Felix Potvin	1.00	2.50
3 Wendel Clark	1.00	2.50
4 Tie Domi/Sergei Berezin	1.00	2.50

1999-00 Maple Leafs Pizza Pizza

Released by Pizza Pizza, this 20-card set featured the 1999-2000 Toronto Maple Leafs. The set was divided up into four sheets of five cards each. One sheet was available each week from March 27 to April 23 with the purchase of a Big Bacon 16-inch pizza.

COMPLETE SET (20)	4.80	12.00
1 Dimitri Khristich	.20	.50
2 Jonas Hoglund	.20	.50
3 Tomas Kaberle	.20	.50
4 Garry Valk	.20	.50
5 Curtis Joseph AS	1.25	3.00
6 Danny Markov	.20	.50
7 Bryan Berard	.20	.50
8 Kevyn Adams	.20	.50
9 Alexander Karpovtsev	.20	.50
10 Steve Thomas	.20	.50
11 Alyn McCauley	.20	.50
12 Tie Domi	.60	1.50
13 Nikolai Antropov	.20	.50
14 Sergei Berezin	.20	.50
15 Alexander Karpovtsev AS	.20	.50
16 Igor Korolev	.20	.50
17 Darcy Tucker	.30	.75
18 Glenn Healy	.30	.75
19 Yanic Perreault	.20	.50
20 Mats Sundin AS	.60	1.50

2002-03 Maple Leafs Platinum Collection

Produced by Topps and available through MLG, this 120-card set featured current players and former Maple

Leaf greats. Each box set also contained a Maple Leafs pin and one autographed card. Cards were also available at the ACC in five different 22-card packs.

COMPLETE SET (120)	30.00	80.00
1 Wade Belak	.20	.50
2 Ed Belfour	1.25	3.00
3 Aki Berg	.20	.50
4 Shayne Corson	.30	.75
5 Tie Domi	.75	2.00
6 Tom Fitzgerald	.20	.50
7 Travis Green	.20	.50
8 Jonas Hoglund	.20	.50
9 Tomas Kaberle	.20	.50
10 Trevor Kidd	.30	.75
11 Jyrki Lumme	.20	.50
12 Bryan McCabe	.20	.50
13 Alyn McCauley	.20	.50
14 Alexander Mogilny	.30	.75
15 Robert Reichel	.20	.50
16 Mikael Renberg	.30	.75
17 Gary Roberts	.30	.75
18 Mats Sundin	.75	2.00
19 Robert Svehla	.20	.50
20 Darcy Tucker	.30	.75
21 Nik Antropov	.30	.75
22 Karel Pilar	.20	.50
23 Richard Jackman	.20	.50
24 Carlo Colaiacovo	.30	.75
25 Dave Andreychuk	.30	.75
26 Andy Bathgate	.30	.75
27 Wendel Clark	.75	2.00
28 Bill Derlago	.20	.50
29 Todd Gill	.20	.50
30 Doug Gilmour	.75	2.00
31 Billy Harris	.20	.50
32 Curtis Joseph	1.25	3.00
33 Bob Nevin	.20	.50
34 Felix Potvin	1.25	3.00
35 Eddie Shack	.40	1.00
36 Sid Smith	.20	.50
37 Ron Stewart	.20	.50
38 Ian Turnbull	.30	.75
39 Dave Williams	.75	2.00
40 Syl Apps	.40	1.00
41 George Armstrong	.40	1.00
42 Ace Bailey	.75	2.00
43 Max Bentley	.30	.75
44 Johnny Bower	.75	2.00
45 Turk Broda	.75	2.00
46 King Clancy	.75	2.00
47 Charlie Conacher	.40	1.00
48 Hap Day	.30	.75
49 Gordie Drillon	.30	.75
50 Babe Dye	.30	.75
51 Mike Gartner	.30	.75
52 Red Horner	.30	.75
53 Tim Horton	1.25	3.00
54 Busher Jackson	.30	.75
55 Red Kelly	.30	.75
56 Ted Kennedy	.40	1.00
57 Harry Lumley	.40	1.00
58 Frank Mahovlich	.40	1.00
59 Lanny McDonald	.40	1.00
60 Babe Pratt	.30	.75
61 Joe Primeau	.30	.75
62 Marcel Pronovost	.30	.75
63 Bob Pulford	.40	1.00
64 Borje Salming	.40	1.00
65 Terry Sawchuk	1.25	3.00
66 Sweeney Schriner	.30	.75
67 Darryl Sittler	.40	1.00
68 Allan Stanley	.30	.75
69 Norm Ullman	.30	.75
70 Harry Watson	.30	.75
71 Bobby Baun	.30	.75
72 Ron Ellis	.30	.75
73 Pat Quinn	.30	.75
74 Rick Vaive	.30	.75
75 Paul Henderson	.30	.75
76 Red Kelly	.30	.75
77 Frank Mahovlich	.40	1.00
78 Lanny McDonald	.30	.75
79 Jim McKenny	.30	.75
80 Mike Palmateer	.40	1.00
81 John Anderson	.20	.50
82 Laurie Boschman	.20	.50
83 Randy Carlyle	.20	.50
84 Wendel Clark	.75	2.00
85 Ron Ellis	.30	.75
86 Jim McKenny	.20	.50
87 Gary Nylund	.20	.50
88 Mike Palmateer	.40	1.00
89 Joel Quenneville	.20	.50
90 Borje Salming	.40	1.00
91 Brit Selby	.20	.50
92 Darryl Sittler	.40	1.00
93 MLG Opening Night	.20	.50
94 MLG Closing Night	.20	.50
95 AAC Opening Night	.20	.50
96 Bill Barilko	.40	1.00
The Goal		
97 1991-92 St. Pats	.20	.50
98 1st NHL All-Star Game	.20	.50
99 50th NHL All-Star Game	.20	.50
100 Tim Horton	1.25	3.00
101 Darryl Sittler	.40	1.00
10 Point Night		
102 Gordie Drillon	.30	.75
Art Ross Trophy		
103 Ted Kennedy	.40	1.00
Hart Memorial Trophy		
104 Sid Smith	.20	.50
Lady Byng Trophy		
105 Terry Sawchuk	1.25	3.00
Johnny Bower		
Vezina Trophy		
106 Harry Lumley	.40	1.00
Bickell Memorial Trophy		
107 Curtis Joseph	1.25	3.00
King Clancy Memorial Trophy		
108 Borje Salming	.40	1.00
Molson Cup		
109 Doug Gilmour	.75	2.00
Selke Trophy		
110 Pat Burns	.30	.75
Jack Adams Trophy		
111 Gus Bodnar	.30	.75
Calder Trophy		
112 1931-92 Stanley Cup Winners	.30	.75
113 1941-42 Stanley Cup Winners	.30	.75
114 1946-47 Stanley Cup Winners	.30	.75
115 1948-49 Stanley Cup Winners	.30	.75
116 1961-62 Stanley Cup Winners	.30	.75
117 1962-63 Stanley Cup Winners	.30	.75
118 1963-64 Stanley Cup Winners	.30	.75
119 1966-67 Stanley Cup Winners	.30	.75
120 Checklist	.01	.01

2002-03 Maple Leafs Platinum Collection Autographs

Due to a lack of market activity, we are unable to price this set.

ONE PER BOX SET
71 Bobby Baun
72 Ron Ellis
73 Pat Quinn
74 Rick Vaive
75 Paul Henderson
76 Red Kelly
77 Frank Mahovlich
78 Lanny McDonald
79 Jim McKenny
80 Mike Palmateer

2002-03 Maple Leafs Team Issue

This postcard-size team issue features glossy prints on actual Kodak photo paper. The fronts include player and sponsor names and the backs are blank. If you have information about additional singles in this set, please forward to hockeymag@beckett.com.

COMPLETE SET (?)	8.00	20.00
1 Nik Antropov	.40	1.00
2 Ed Belfour	1.25	3.00
3 Tie Domi	.75	2.00
4 Tom Fitzgerald	.40	1.00
5 Travis Green	.40	1.00
6 Tomas Kaberle	.40	1.00
7 Trevor Kidd	.60	1.50
8 Alexander Mogilny	.60	1.50
9 Robert Reichel	.40	1.00
10 Mikael Renberg	.40	1.00
11 Mats Sundin	1.25	3.00
12 Robert Svehla	.40	1.00
13 Mikael Tellqvist	.75	2.00
14 Darcy Tucker	.60	1.50

2003-04 Maple Leafs Team Issue

COMPLETE SET (?)
1 Owen Nolan
2 Mikael Tellqvist

2007 Maple Leafs 1967 Commemorative

COMPLETE SET (30)	10.00	25.00
1 Bob Baun	.20	.50
2 Johnny Bower	.40	1.00
3 John Brennemman	.10	.25
4 Wayne Carleton	.20	.50
5 Brian Conacher	.20	.50
6 Kent Douglas	.20	.50
7 Ron Ellis	.20	.50
8 Aut Erickson	.20	.50
9 Bob Haggert	.20	.50
10 Larry Hillman	.20	.50
11 Tim Horton	.75	2.00
12 Larry Jeffrey	.20	.50
13 Red Kelly	.20	.50
14 Dave Keon	.75	2.00
15 Frank Mahovlich	.40	1.00
16 Frank Mahovlich/Red Kelly	.40	1.00
17 Milan Marcetta	.20	.50
18 Jim McKenny	.20	.50
19 Jim Pappin	.20	.50
20 Marcel Pronovost	.20	.50
21 Bob Pulford	.20	.50
22 Terry Sawchuk	.75	2.00
23 Brit Selby	.20	.50
24 Eddie Shack	.40	1.00
25 Allan Stanley	.20	.50
26 Pete Stemkowski	.20	.50
27 Mike Walton	.20	.50
28 Group Photo	.10	.25
29 Victory Parade	.10	.25
30 Johnny Bower CL	.20	.50

2007 Maple Leafs 1967 Commemorative Autographs

RANDOM INSERTS IN SEALED SETS		
ABB1 Bob Baun	12.00	30.00
ABB2 Bob Baun	12.00	30.00
ABC1 Brian Conacher	6.00	15.00
ABC2 Brian Conacher	6.00	15.00
ABP1 Bob Pulford	12.00	30.00
ABP2 Bob Pulford	12.00	30.00
AES1 Eddie Shack	15.00	40.00
AES2 Eddie Shack	15.00	40.00
AJB1 Johnny Bower	15.00	40.00
AJB2 Johnny Bower	15.00	40.00
ALJ1 Larry Jeffrey	6.00	15.00
ALJ2 Larry Jeffrey	6.00	15.00
ARE1 Ron Ellis	12.00	30.00
ARE2 Ron Ellis	12.00	30.00
ARK1 Red Kelly	12.00	30.00
ARK2 Red Kelly	12.00	30.00

2007 Maple Leafs 1967 Commemorative Box Topper

ML67 Group Photo	.40	1.00

2007 Maple Leafs 1967 Commemorative Jerseys

RANDOM INSERTS IN SEALED SETS		
JES Eddie Shack	6.00	15.00
JJB Johnny Bower	8.00	20.00

2007 Maple Leafs 1967 Commemorative Sticks

RANDOM INSERTS IN SEALED SETS		
SDK Dave Keon	30.00	80.00
SFM Frank Mahovlich	30.00	80.00

2003 Marc-Andre Fleury Stadium Giveaways

This 4-card set of Penguins' goalie Marc-Andre Fleury was given away during a game in October 2003.

COMPLETE SET (4)	15.00	35.00

2004 MasterCard Priceless Moments

This 10-card set was produced by MasterCard and highlighted Stanley Cup winners of the past 5 decades. The cards were available at participating restaurants in Canada during the 2004 playoffs. Due to lack of market activity, this set is not priced.

COMPLETE SET (10)	20.00
1 Bobby Baun	1.00
1964 Stanley Cup	
2 Bobby Orr	5.00
1970 Stanley Cup	
3 Bob Nystrom	1.00
1980 Stanley Cup	
4 Jari Kurri	2.00
1984 Stanley Cup	
5 Lanny McDonald	1.00
1989 Stanley Cup	
6 Mario Lemieux	5.00
1991 Stanley Cup	
7 Mark Messier	2.00
1994 Stanley Cup	
8 Ray Bourque	2.00
2001 Stanley Cup	
9 Scotty Bowman	1.00
2002 Stanley Cup	
10 Martin Brodeur	3.00
2003 Stanley Cup	

1971 Mattel Mini-Records *

This eight-disc set was designed to be played on a special Mattel mini-record player, which was not included in the complete set price. Measuring roughly 2 1/2" in diameter, the discs were packaged in sets of four. In contrast to basketball and football, hockey only double-sided discs are unknown. The discs were unnumbered and checklisted below in alphabetical order.

COMPLETE SET (8)	100.00	200.00
1 Yvan Cournoyer	5.00	10.00
2 Tony Esposito	6.00	12.00
3 Phil Esposito	7.50	15.00
4 Ed Giacomin	5.00	10.00
5 Gordie Howe	20.00	40.00
6 Frank Mahovlich	6.00	12.00
7 Bobby Orr	25.00	50.00
8 Jacques Plante	12.50	25.00
NNO Record Player	50.00	100.00

1982-83 McDonald's Stickers

This set consisted of 36 full-color stickers measuring 2" by 2 1/2". A 12-page album was also available. The stickers were only issued in the province of Quebec. The stickers were numbered on the front and on the back. The sticker numbering was by position, i.e., goalies (1-5), right wings (6-10), left wings (11-15), all-stars (16-21), centers (22-26), and defensemen (27-36). The all-star stickers were gold foils; the other stickers all had a distinctive red border and showed the McDonald's logo in the lower right corner.

COMPLETE SET (36)	14.00	35.00
1 Dan Bouchard	.20	.50
2 Richard Brodeur	.25	.60
3 Gilles Meloche	.20	.50
4 Billy Smith	.40	1.00
5 Rick Wamsley	.20	.50
6 Mike Bossy	.75	2.00
7 Dino Ciccarelli	.30	.75
8 Guy Lafleur	.75	2.00
9 Rick Middleton	.30	.75
10 Marian Stastny	.15	.40
11 Bill Barber	.25	.60
12 Bob Gainey	.40	1.00
13 Clark Gillies	.20	.50
14 Michel Goulet	.30	.75
15 Mark Messier	1.50	4.00
16 Billy Smith AS	.25	.60
17 Larry Robinson AS	.25	.60
18 Denis Potvin AS	.25	.60
19 Michel Goulet AS	.25	.60
20 Wayne Gretzky AS	3.00	8.00
21 Mike Bossy AS	.30	.75
22 Wayne Gretzky	4.00	10.00
23 Denis Savard	.30	.75
24 Peter Stastny	.30	.75
25 Bryan Trottier	.40	1.00
26 Doug Wickenheiser	.15	.40
27 Barry Beck	.15	.40
28 Ray Bourque	1.00	2.50
29 Brian Engblom	.15	.40
30 Craig Hartsburg	.20	.50
31 Mark Howe	.25	.60
32 Rod Langway	.20	.50
33 Denis Potvin	.30	.75
34 Larry Robinson	.40	1.00
35 Normand Rochefort	.15	.40
36 Doug Wilson	.25	.60
NNO Album	2.00	5.00

1991-92 McDonald's Upper Deck

This 31-card standard-size set, which featured 25 regular cards and six hologram cards and was produced by Upper Deck for McDonald's Restaurants across Canada to honor NHL All-Stars. For 29 cents plus tax, with the purchase of any soft drink, customers could receive a pack with three regular cards and one hologram sticker card. The fronts featured a mix of posed and action pictures enclosed in red and white borders. The Upper Deck logo appeared in the upper right corner while the McDonald's All-Stars logo appeared in a red circle in the lower right corner. The player's name and position appeared in the bottom white border. The backs carried a second color photo and career summary was presented in English and French. Upper Deck's unique anti-counterfeiting device appeared in the upper right corner in the shape of McDonald's golden arches. Six players wearing their 1991 All-Star uniforms on the regular cards appeared on the hologram cards in their regular team uniforms. The holograms had blank backs and were numbered on the front. The card numbers showed a "Mc" prefix.

COMPLETE SET (31)	6.00	15.00
1 Cam Neely	.15	.40
2 Rick Tocchet	.15	.40
3 Kevin Stevens	.08	.25
4 Mark Recchi	.15	.40
5 Joe Sakic	.40	1.00
6 Pat LaFontaine	.15	.40
7 Darren Turcotte	.08	.25
8 Patrick Roy	1.00	2.50
9 Andy Moog	.15	.40
10 Ray Bourque	.25	.60
11 Paul Coffey	.20	.50
12 Brian Leetch	.20	.50
13 Brett Hull	.25	.60
14 Luc Robitaille	.15	.40
15 Steve Larmer	.08	.25
16 Vincent Damphousse	.15	.40
17 Wayne Gretzky	1.25	3.00
18 Theo Fleury	.20	.50
19 Steve Yzerman	.60	1.50
20 Mike Vernon	.15	.40
21 Bill Ranford	.15	.40
22 Chris Chelios	.20	.50
23 Al MacInnis	.15	.40
24 Scott Stevens	.08	.25
25 Checklist	.08	.25
H1 Wayne Gretzky	1.50	4.00
H2 Chris Chelios	.20	.50
H3 Ray Bourque	.25	.60
H4 Brett Hull	.30	.75
H5 Cam Neely	.20	.50
H6 Patrick Roy	1.25	3.00

1992-93 McDonald's Upper Deck Iron-Ons

Printed in Canada, these 26 iron-on transfers measured approximately 3" by 3". They featured the NHL team logos and commemorated the 44th All-Star Game in Montreal. The backs carried ironing instructions. These iron-ons were a test issue to be distributed along with the McDonald's All-Star cards, and surfaced just in parts of Quebec. The iron-ons were unnumbered and checklisted below in alphabetical order.

COMPLETE SET (26)	16.00	40.00
1 Boston Bruins	.75	2.00
2 Buffalo Sabres	.75	2.00
3 Calgary Flames	.75	2.00
4 Chicago Blackhawks	.75	2.00
5 Minnesota North Stars	.75	2.00
6 Detroit Red Wings	.75	2.00
7 Edmonton Oilers	.75	2.00
8 Hartford Whalers	.75	2.00
9 Los Angeles Kings	.75	2.00
10 Montreal Canadiens	.75	2.00
11 New Jersey Devils	.75	2.00
12 New York Islanders	.75	2.00
13 New York Rangers	.75	2.00
14 Ottawa Senators	.75	2.00
15 Philadelphia Flyers	.75	2.00
16 Pittsburgh Penguins	.75	2.00
17 Quebec Nordiques	.75	2.00
18 St. Louis Blues	.75	2.00
19 San Jose Sharks	.75	2.00
20 Tampa Bay Lightning	.75	2.00
21 Toronto Maple Leafs	.75	2.00
22 Vancouver Canucks	.75	2.00
23 Washington Capitals	.75	2.00
24 Winnipeg Jets	.75	2.00
25 All-Stars Logo	.75	2.00
26 44th NHL All-Star	2.00	5.00
Game Logo		

1992-93 McDonald's Upper Deck

Produced by Upper Deck for McDonald's of Canada, this set consisted of 27 regular cards and six hologram cards in honor of 33 of hockey's most exciting players. Four-card packs were available for 39 cents plus tax with a purchase at participating McDonald's restaurants. All cards measured the standard size. The regular cards featured color action photos of the players in their 1992 All-Star uniforms. A black border, which edged the photo on three sides, contained the player's name and position. Featuring six NHL post-season First Team All-Stars, the six hologram cards were randomly inserted in a limited number of card packs. The full-bleed cards featured a small, cut-out action player photos against a facial shot. The player's name appeared in a stripe across the bottom. The backs of the regular cards and holograms were identical, each showing a narrow, vertical player photo against a white background with a bilingual (English and French) player profile to the right. The regular cards were arranged according to conference: Campbell (1-14) and Wales (15-27). The cards were numbered on the back with an "McD" prefix.

COMPLETE SET (34)	8.00	20.00
1 Ed Belfour	.25	.60
2 Brian Bellows	.08	.25
3 Chris Chelios	.25	.60
4 Vincent Damphousse	.10	.30
5 Dave Ellett	.08	.25
6 Sergei Fedorov	.50	1.25
7 Theo Fleury	.25	.60
8 Phil Housley	.08	.25
9 Trevor Linden	.10	.30
10 Al MacInnis	.10	.30
11 Adam Oates	.20	.50
12 Luc Robitaille	.20	.50
13 Jeremy Roenick	.25	.60
14 Steve Yzerman	.75	2.00
15 Don Beaupre	.10	.30
16 Rod Brind'Amour	.10	.30
17 Paul Coffey	.25	.60
18 John Cullen	.08	.25
19 Kevin Hatcher	.08	.25
20 Jaromir Jagr	.75	2.00
21 Mario Lemieux	1.00	2.50
22 Alexander Mogilny	.20	.50
23 Kirk Muller	.08	.25
24 Owen Nolan	.10	.30
25 Mike Richter	.25	.60
26 Joe Sakic	.50	1.25
27 Scott Stevens	.10	.30
H1 Mark Messier HOLO	.50	1.25
H2 Brett Hull HOLO	.60	1.50
H3 Kevin Stevens HOLO	.20	.50
H4 Brian Leetch HOLO	.30	.75
H5 Ray Bourque HOLO	.50	1.25
H6 Patrick Roy HOLO	1.50	4.00
NNO Checklist UER SP	.75	2.00
(Bourque listed as 4 and Leetch as 5)		

1993-94 McDonald's Upper Deck

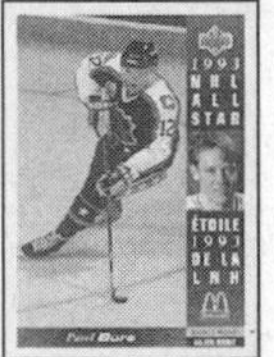

Produced by Upper Deck for McDonald's of Canada, this set was similar in concept to the previous year's Upper Deck McDonald's set. The 27 regular cards and six hologram-type cards honored 33 of the NHL's most exciting players. The holograms were random inserts in the four-card packs. An oversized (4" by 5 1/2") Patrick Roy card (23) was also available via a redemption card randomly inserted in packs. The redemption card could be redeemed at McDonald's or through the mail. A number of redemption cards for other prizes, such as trips to games, autographed pucks and sticks, etc, also were included. These cards obviously were extremely difficult to locate, but also experience limited demand from collectors at this point. Most would be valued in the $10-$20 range. Also, Upper Deck had confirmed that the unnumbered checklist card was short-printed. All cards measured the standard size. The regular cards featured on their fronts white-bordered color action shots of players in their 1993 All-Star uniforms. The hologram cards were horizontal on their fronts and backs. The front of each card featured a hologram-type action photo of a first team All-Star on the right and a posed close-up on the left. The player's name and position appeared within blue, black, and gray stripes near the bottom. The back carried the player's All-Star highlights in both English and French. Variations of the cards with incorrect backs were known to exist. The regular cards were arranged according to conference: Campbell (1-13) and Wales (14-27). The regular cards were numbered on the back with an "McD" prefix; the hologram-types are numbered with an "McH" prefix.

COMPLETE SET (34)	6.00	15.00

1 Brian Bradley	.08	.25
2 Pavel Bure	.50	1.25
3 Jon Casey	.08	.25
4 Paul Coffey	.25	.60
5 Doug Gilmour	.25	.60
6 Phil Housley	.08	.25
7 Brett Hull	.40	1.00
8 Jari Kurri	.08	.25
9 Dave Manson	.08	.25
10 Mike Modano	.40	1.00
11 Gary Roberts	.08	.25
12 Jeremy Roenick	.25	.60
13 Steve Yzerman	.60	1.50
14 Steve Duchesne	.08	.25
15 Mike Gartner	.08	.25
16 Al Iafrate	.08	.25
17 Jaromir Jagr	.60	1.50
18 Pat LaFontaine	.15	.40
19 Alexander Mogilny	.15	.40
20A Kirk Muller (Full stick blade showing)	.08	.25
20B Kirk Muller (Stick blade partly cut off by cropping)	.08	.25
21 Adam Oates	.15	.40
22 Mark Recchi	.15	.40
23 Patrick Roy	1.00	2.50
23L Patrick Roy Large (4- by 5 1/2-; only available from redemption card)	4.00	10.00
24 Joe Sakic	.50	1.25
25 Kevin Stevens	.08	.25
26 Scott Stevens	.08	.25
27 Pierre Turgeon	.15	.40
H1 Mario Lemieux	1.25	3.00
H2 Teemu Selanne	.75	2.00
H3 Luc Robitaille	.25	.60
H4 Ray Bourque	.25	.60
H5 Chris Chelios	.25	.60
H6 Ed Belfour	.40	1.00
NNO Checklist SP	1.00	2.50

1994-95 McDonald's Upper Deck

Produced by Upper Deck for McDonald's of Canada, this set consisted of 40 standard-size cards and honored some of hockey's most exciting players. Three-card packs were available for 39 cents plus tax with a purchase of a soft drink at participating McDonald's restaurants across Canada. The offer began March 24 and ran as long as supplies lasted. The horizontal fronts featured color action player cutouts on holographic backgrounds. The player's name appeared in a team color-coded bar alongside the left, while a small color player portrait in his 1994 All-Star uniform was on the right. The bilingual backs carried another small color player portrait, with profile and statistics. The cards were arranged as follows: 1994 NHL All-Stars Eastern Conference (1-10), 1994 NHL All-Stars Western Conference (11-20), Hat Tricks Eastern Conference (21-25), Hat Tricks Western Conference (26-30), Future NHL All-Stars Eastern Conference (31-35), and Future NHL All-Stars Western Conference (36-39). An unnumbered checklist card featuring All-Star Game MVP Mike Richter completed the set. This card was thought by some to be short printed. Since we cannot confirm this, we have not applied this designation.

COMPLETE SET (40)	10.00	25.00
McD1 Joe Sakic	.60	1.50
McD2 Adam Graves	.08	.25
McD3 Alexei Yashin	.08	.25
McD4 Patrick Roy	1.50	4.00
McD5 Ray Bourque	.40	1.00
McD6 Brian Leetch	.25	.60
McD7 Scott Stevens	.08	.25
McD8 Alexander Mogilny	.15	.40
McD9 Eric Lindros	.75	2.00
McD10 Jaromir Jagr	1.00	2.50
McD11 Sandis Ozolinsh	.08	.25
McD12 Sergei Fedorov	.60	1.50
McD13 Brett Hull	.40	1.00
McD14 Felix Potvin	.08	.25
McD15 Al MacInnis	.08	.25
McD16 Chris Chelios	.25	.60
McD17 Rob Blake	.08	.25
McD18 Dave Andreychuk	.08	.25
McD19 Paul Coffey	.25	.60
McD20 Jeremy Roenick	.25	.60
McD21 Joe Nieuwendyk	.15	.40
McD22 Cam Neely	.15	.40
McD23 Pavel Bure	.75	2.00
McD24 Wendel Clark	.15	.40
McD25 Teemu Selanne	.60	1.50
McD26 Pierre Turgeon	.15	.40
McD27 Alexei Zhamnov	.08	.25
McD28 Doug Gilmour	.25	.60
McD29 Vincent Damphousse	.08	.25
McD30 Brendan Shanahan	.50	1.25
McD31 Peter Forsberg	1.00	2.50
McD32 Paul Kariya	1.25	3.00
McD33 Viktor Kozlov	.08	.25
McD34 Brett Lindros	.08	.25
McD35 Martin Brodeur	.75	2.00
McD36 Alexandre Daigle	.08	.25
McD37 Jason Arnott	.15	.40
McD38 Alexei Kovalev	.08	.25
McD39 Mikael Renberg	.25	.60
NNO Mike Richter CL	.25	.60

1995-96 McDonald's Pinnacle

This 41-card set featured borderless color player cut-out photos on a 3-D, lenticular background. The backs carried information about the player in both English and French. The cards were divided into three categories as follows: Game Winners (McD-1-McD-24), Game Savers (McD-25-McD-30), and Future Game Winners (McD-31-McD-40). They were available in 3-card packs for 79 cents (with purchase) at participating McDonald's restaurants in Canada.

COMPLETE SET (41)	10.00	25.00
MCD1 Jaromir Jagr	.75	2.00
MCD2 Eric Lindros	.60	1.50
MCD3 Alexei Zhamnov	.08	.25
MCD4 Paul Coffey	.25	.60
MCD5 Mark Messier	.30	.75
MCD6 Brett Hull	.30	.75
MCD7 Peter Forsberg	.60	1.50
MCD8 Pavel Bure	.60	1.50
MCD9 Doug Gilmour	.25	.60
MCD10 Owen Nolan	.25	.60
MCD11 Paul Kariya	1.00	2.50
MCD12 Joe Nieuwendyk	.15	.40
MCD13 Pierre Turgeon	.15	.40
MCD14 Jason Arnott	.15	.40
MCD15 Mario Lemieux	1.25	3.00
MCD16 Jeremy Roenick	.25	.60
MCD17 Sergei Fedorov	.40	1.00
MCD18 Mats Sundin	.25	.60
MCD19 Teemu Selanne	.40	1.00
MCD20 John LeClair	.40	1.00
MCD21 Alexander Mogilny	.25	.60
MCD22 Mikael Renberg	.08	.25
MCD23 Chris Chelios	.25	.60
MCD24 Mark Recchi	.15	.40
MCD25 Patrick Roy	1.25	3.00
MCD26 Felix Potvin	.08	.25
MCD27 Martin Brodeur	.60	1.50
MCD28 Dominik Hasek	.40	1.00
MCD29 Ed Belfour	.25	.60
MCD30 Kirk McLean	.15	.40
MCD31 Jeff Friesen	.15	.40
MCD32 Todd Harvey	.08	.25
MCD33 Brett Lindros	.08	.25
MCD34 Valeri Bure	.15	.40
MCD35 Oleg Tverdovsky	.08	.25
MCD36 Kenny Jonsson	.08	.25
MCD37 Mariusz Czerkawski	.08	.25
MCD38 Alexandre Daigle	.08	.25
MCD39 Saku Koivu	.25	.60
MCD40 Jim Carey	.15	.40
NNO Joe Sakic CL	.25	.60

1996-97 McDonald's Pinnacle

This 40-card set was available through McDonald's Restaurants of Canada and featured advanced 3D and Full-Motion Video technology. The set contained three subsets: IceBreakers (3D Cards #1-20 which consisted of 20 of the top NHL players), Premier IceBreakers (Full-Motion Video Cards #21-31 which showcased approximately three seconds of live footage of 11 outstanding NHL players), and Caged IceBreakers (3D Cards #32-40 which featured nine of the league's best goaltenders).

COMPLETE SET (40)	15.00	30.00
1 Paul Coffey	.10	.30
2 Teemu Selanne	.40	1.00
3 Eric Daze	.08	.25
4 John LeClair	.40	1.00
5 Saku Koivu	.30	.75
6 Ed Jovanovski	.25	.60
7 Chris Osgood	.30	.75
8 Chris Chelios	.10	.30
9 Daniel Alfredsson	.08	.25
10 Joe Sakic	.50	1.25
11 Alexander Mogilny	.08	.25
12 Jeremy Roenick	.10	.30
13 Keith Tkachuk	.30	.75
14 Doug Gilmour	.10	.30
15 Theo Fleury	.25	.60
16 Doug Weight	.08	.25
17 Steve Yzerman	.60	1.50
18 Zigmund Palffy	.25	.60
19 Pierre Turgeon	.08	.25
20 Brian Leetch	.10	.30
21 Mario Lemieux SP	2.00	5.00
22 Mark Messier SP	.60	1.50
23 Jaromir Jagr SP	1.25	3.00
24 Brett Hull SP	.60	1.50
25 Eric Lindros SP	1.25	3.00
26 Sergei Fedorov SP	.75	2.00
27 Pavel Bure SP	1.00	2.50
28 Peter Forsberg SP	1.00	2.50
29 Paul Kariya SP	1.50	4.00
30 Patrick Roy SP	2.00	5.00
31 Ray Bourque SP	.50	1.25
32 Jim Carey	.08	.25
33 Martin Brodeur	.60	1.50
34 Trevor Kidd	.15	.40
35 John Vanbiesbrouck	.50	1.25
36 Jocelyn Thibault	.20	.50
37 Ed Belfour	.25	.60
38 Felix Potvin	.25	.60
39 Damian Rhodes	.15	.40
40 Curtis Joseph	.30	.75
NNO Checklist	.01	.05

1997 McDonald's Team Canada Coins

COMPLETE SET (10)	10.00	25.00
1 Rod Brind'Amour Trevor Linden	.75	2.00
2 Rob Blake Al MacInnis	.75	2.00
3 Martin Brodeur Curtis Joseph	1.25	3.00
4 Ray Bourque Chris Pronger	1.25	3.00
5 Shayne Corson Brendan Shanahan	.75	2.00
6 Eric DesJardins Adam Foote	.75	2.00
7 Theoren Fleury Paul Kariya	.75	2.00
8 Wayne Gretzky Joe Sakic	1.50	4.00
9 Eric Lindros Joe Nieuwendyk	.75	2.00
10 Keith Primeau Steve Yzerman	1.25	3.00
11 Patrick Roy Olympic Games Logo	1.25	3.00
12 Scott Stevens Rob Zamuner	.75	2.00

1997-98 McDonald's Upper Deck

This 40-card set was available through McDonald's Restaurants of Canada and featured a design similar to that of the 1996-97 Upper Deck Ice set. Redemption cards for various Wayne Gretzky prizes were also inserted randomly into packs. These prizes included autographed sticks, photos and jerseys, these items are not priced due to scarcity.

COMPLETE SET (40)	12.50	25.00
1 Wayne Gretzky	1.50	4.00
2 Theo Fleury	.25	.60
3 Pavel Bure	.60	1.50
4 Saku Koivu	.25	.60
5 Joe Sakic	.50	1.25
6 Wade Redden	.08	.25
7 Keith Tkachuk	.30	.75
8 Eric Lindros	.75	2.00
9 Paul Kariya	1.00	2.50
10 Bryan Berard	.15	.40
11 Teemu Selanne	.50	1.25
12 Jarome Iginla	.15	.40
13 Mats Sundin	.25	.60
14 Brendan Shanahan	.50	1.25
15 Peter Forsberg	.60	1.50
16 Brett Hull	.30	.75
17 Ray Bourque	.25	.60
18 Doug Weight	.15	.40
19 Steve Yzerman	.75	2.00
20 Jaromir Jagr	.75	2.00
21 Vincent Damphousse	.15	.40
22 Trevor Linden	.15	.40
23 Patrick Roy	1.25	3.00
24 John Vanbiesbrouck	.25	.60
25 Martin Brodeur	.60	1.50
26 Dominik Hasek	.50	1.25
27 Curtis Joseph	.30	.75
28 Andy Moog	.15	.40
29 Mike Richter	.25	.60
30 Damian Rhodes	.15	.40
31 Felix Potvin		
32 Chris Osgood	.25	.60
33 Joe Thornton	.40	1.00
34 Patrick Marleau	.40	1.00
35 Jaroslav Svejkovsky	.15	.40
36 Daniel Cleary	.15	.40
37 Chris Phillips	.08	.25
38 Alexei Morozov	.15	.40
39 Vaclav Prospal	.25	.60
40 Sergei Samsonov	.40	1.00

1997-98 McDonald's Upper Deck Game Film

This 10-card set was randomly inserted into packs of McDonalds hockey cards. Each set featured a design similar to a strip of film.

COMPLETE SET (10)	60.00	120.00
1 Wayne Gretzky	15.00	30.00
2 Alexander Mogilny	1.50	4.00
3 Steve Yzerman	7.50	15.00
4 Eric Lindros	2.00	5.00
5 Patrick Roy	12.50	25.00
6 Paul Kariya	10.00	20.00
7 Ray Bourque	2.50	6.00
8 Saku Koivu	2.00	5.00
9 Theo Fleury	1.50	4.00
10 Mats Sundin	2.50	5.00

1998-99 McDonald's Upper Deck

Issued by McDonalds of Canada, these cards were available with any french fry purchase for 79 cents. Cards featured color action photos and statistical information.

COMPLETE SET (28)	7.50	15.00
1 Wayne Gretzky	1.50	4.00
2 Theo Fleury	.20	.50
3 Joe Sakic	.60	1.50
4 Saku Koivu	.20	.50
5 Brendan Shanahan	.40	1.00
6 Steve Yzerman	1.25	3.00
7 Peter Forsberg	.60	1.50
8 Paul Kariya	.75	2.00
9 Alexei Yashin	.15	.40
10 Eric Lindros	.60	1.50
11 Jaromir Jagr	.60	1.50
12 Mats Sundin	.20	.50
13 Sergei Samsonov	.20	.50
14 Pavel Bure	.60	1.50
15 Patrick Roy	1.25	3.00
16 Dominik Hasek	.40	1.00
17 Martin Brodeur	.60	1.50
18 Curtis Joseph	.40	1.00
19 Jocelyn Thibault	.20	.50
20 Chris Osgood	.20	.50
21 Ed Belfour	.20	.50
22 Mattias Ohlund	.15	.40
23 Marian Hossa	.20	.50
24 Brendan Morrison	.15	.40
25 Jason Botterill	.15	.40
26 Cameron Mann	.15	.40
27 Daniel Briere	.20	.50
28 Terry Ryan	.15	.40

1998-99 McDonald's Upper Deck Gretzky's Moments

Random inserts in packs of McDonalds cards. Entire set featured some of Gretzky's greatest accomplishments.

COMPLETE SET (10)	25.00	30.00
COMMON CARD (1-10)	1.50	4.00

1998-99 McDonald's Upper Deck Gretzky's Teammates

Random inserts in packs of McDonalds cards. Each card featured Gretzky along with a past or present teammate.

COMPLETE SET (13)	2.00	5.00
T1 Walter Gretzky	.10	.30
T2 Gordie Howe	.75	2.00
T3 Marty McSorley	.10	.30
T4 Brian Leetch	.20	.50
T5 Brett Hull	.30	.75
T6 Esa Tikkanen	.10	.30
T7 Grant Fuhr	.20	.50
T8 Mike Richter	.20	.50
T9 Jari Kurri	.20	.50
T10 Paul Coffey	.20	.50
T11 Rob Blake	.20	.50
T12 Mario Lemieux	.75	2.00
T13 Luc Robitaille	.20	.50

1999-00 McDonald's Upper Deck Gretzky Performance for the Record

COMPLETE SET (24)	15.00	30.00
COMMON RECORD (1-15)	.75	2.00
COMMON CHECKLIST (C1-C9)	.60	1.50

1999-00 McDonald's Upper Deck

Produced by Upper Deck in conjunction with McDonalds of Canada at the cost of an order of french fries and 89 cents, this 35-card set utilized set designs from Upper Deck and Upper Deck Retro.

COMPLETE SET (35)	8.00	20.00
MCD1 Paul Kariya	.50	1.25
MCD1R Paul Kariya	.50	1.25
MCD2 Eric Lindros	.20	.50
MCD2R Eric Lindros	.20	.50
MCD3 Dominik Hasek	.40	1.00
MCD3R Dominik Hasek	.40	1.00
MCD4 Steve Yzerman	1.00	2.50
MCD4R Steve Yzerman	1.00	2.50
MCD5 Jarome Iginla	.20	.50
MCD5R Jarome Iginla	.20	.50
MCD6 Jaromir Jagr	.30	.75
MCD6R Jaromir Jagr	.30	.75
MCD7 Brett Hull	.25	.60
MCD7R Brett Hull	.25	.60
MCD8 Ed Belfour	.20	.50
MCD8R Ed Belfour	.20	.50
MCD9 Mats Sundin	.20	.50
MCD9R Mats Sundin	.20	.50
MCD10 Peter Forsberg	.50	1.25
MCD10R Peter Forsberg	.50	1.25
MCD11 Doug Weight	.20	.50
MCD11R Doug Weight	.20	.50
MCD12 Curtis Joseph	.20	.50
MCD12R Curtis Joseph	.20	.50
MCD13 Michael Peca	.20	.50
MCD13R Michael Peca	.20	.50
MCD14 Saku Koivu	.20	.50
MCD14R Saku Koivu	.20	.50
MCD15 Patrick Roy	.75	2.00
MCD15R Patrick Roy	.75	2.00
MCD16 Jose Theodore	.20	.50
MCD17 David Legwand	.20	.50
MCD18 Chris Drury	.20	.50
MCD19 Milan Hejduk	.20	.50
MCD20 Marian Hossa	.20	.50
NNO Wayne Gretzky 5 x 7	4.00	10.00

1999-00 McDonald's Upper Deck Game Jerseys

Randomly inserted in McDonald's Upper Deck Packs, this 11-card set featured players coupled with a swatch of game jersey. Stated print run for the set was 300, with Wayne Gretzky limited to 99, and a special autographed version of the Gretzky card.

GJCP Chris Pronger	40.00	100.00
GJDS Darryl Sydor	40.00	100.00
GJEL Eric Lindros	60.00	150.00
GJGF Grant Fuhr	80.00	120.00
GJJJ Jaromir Jagr	75.00	200.00
GJMM Mike Modano	50.00	125.00
GJPB Peter Bondra	40.00	100.00
GJPF Peter Forsberg	100.00	250.00
GJSS Scott Stevens	75.00	200.00
GJTA Tony Amonte	40.00	100.00
GJWG Wayne Gretzky/99	600.00	1000.00
GJWG Wayne Gretzky AU	750.00	1500.00

1999-00 McDonald's Upper Deck Signatures

Randomly inserted in McDonald's packs, this 16-card set featured player action photography coupled with an authentic player autograph. Each card was sequentially numbered to 500. The Gretzky card was known to exist, but it is not priced due to scarcity.

AY Alexei Yashin	25.00	50.00
BH Brett Hull	40.00	80.00
CJ Curtis Joseph	40.00	80.00
CO Chris Osgood	30.00	60.00
EB Ed Belfour	25.00	50.00
GF Grant Fuhr	40.00	80.00
JL John LeClair	20.00	40.00
JT Jose Theodore	25.00	50.00
LR Luc Robitaille	25.00	50.00
RB Ray Bourque	75.00	150.00
SK Saku Koivu	40.00	80.00
ST Steve Thomas	20.00	40.00
SY Steve Yzerman	75.00	150.00
TA Tony Amonte	25.00	50.00
TD Tie Domi	25.00	50.00
WG Wayne Gretzky/25		

1999-00 McDonald's Upper Deck The Great Career

Randomly inserted in McDonald's Upper Deck packs at the rate of one in six, this five card set payed tribute to the great career of Wayne Gretzky.

COMPLETE SET (5)	4.00	10.00
COMMON (GR81-1 to GR81-5)	.75	2.00

2000-01 McDonald's Pacific

Released by Pacific in conjunction with McDonald's, this 36-card set was available through McDonald's of Canada with the purchase of a large french fry or hash brown and 89 cents from December 18, 2000 through January 11, 2001. Cards utilized the 00-01 Pacific Prism card stock and carried both English and French on the card backs.

COMPLETE SET (36)	6.00	15.00
1 Paul Kariya	.50	1.25
2 Teemu Selanne	.50	1.25
3 Patrik Stefan	.05	.15
4 Joe Thornton	.30	.75
5 Dominik Hasek	.40	1.00
6 Valeri Bure	.05	.15
7 Ray Bourque	.40	1.00
8 Peter Forsberg	.50	1.25
9 Patrick Roy	1.00	2.50
10 Joe Sakic	.40	1.00
11 Brett Hull	.25	.60
12 Mike Modano	.30	.75
13 Chris Osgood	.15	.40
14 Brendan Shanahan	.20	.50
15 Steve Yzerman	1.00	2.50
16 Doug Weight	.15	.40
17 Pavel Bure	.20	.50
18 Jeff Hackett	.15	.40
19 Saku Koivu	.20	.50
20 Martin Brodeur	.50	1.25
21 Scott Gomez	.05	.15
22 Scott Stevens	.15	.40
23 Marian Hossa	.20	.50
24 Brian Boucher	.20	.50
25 John LeClair	.20	.50
26 Eric Lindros	.20	.50
27 Jaromir Jagr	.30	.75
28 Chris Pronger	.15	.40
29 Roman Turek	.15	.40
30 Vincent Lecavalier	.15	.40
31 Nikolai Antropov	.05	.15
32 Curtis Joseph	.20	.50
33 Mats Sundin	.20	.50
34 Mattias Ohlund	.05	.15
35 Felix Potvin	.20	.50
36 Olaf Kolzig	.20	.50

2000-01 McDonald's Pacific Blue

Randomly inserted in packs at the rate of one in four, this 36-card set paralleled the base McDonald's Pacific set enhanced with a blue foil background.

COMPLETE SET (36)	25.00	50.00

*BLUE STARS: 2X TO 5X BASIC CARDS

2000-01 McDonald's Pacific Checklists

Randomly inserted in packs at the rate of one in one, this nine card set featured full color player action photography set on a card with white borders, and contained a checklist of the McDonald's Pacific set on the back.

COMPLETE SET (9)	1.50	3.00
1 Valeri Bure	.10	.25
2 Doug Weight	.15	.40
3 Jeff Hackett	.15	.40
4 Saku Koivu	.20	.50
5 Marian Hossa	.20	.50
6 Curtis Joseph	.20	.50
7 Mats Sundin	.20	.50
8 Mattias Ohlund	.10	.25
9 Felix Potvin	.20	.50

2000-01 McDonald's Pacific Dial-A-Stats

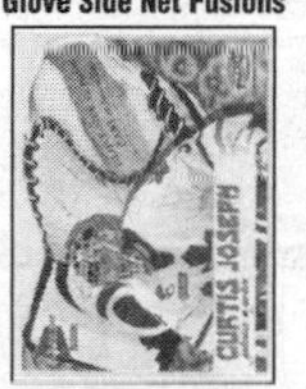

Randomly inserted in McDonald's Pacific packs at the rate of one in 16, this six card set featured a framed player action shot on the top half of the card and a rotating wheel and display window that when turned displays the featured player's career statistics versus selected NHL teams. Cards contained gold foil highlights.

COMPLETE SET (6)	7.50	15.00
1 Paul Kariya	2.50	6.00
2 Steve Yzerman	5.00	12.00
3 Pavel Bure	1.00	2.50
4 Eric Lindros	1.00	2.50
5 Jaromir Jagr	1.50	4.00
6 Mats Sundin	1.00	2.50

2000-01 McDonald's Pacific Glove Side Net Fusions

Randomly inserted in packs at the rate of one in 16, this six card set featured a die cut card around a white goalie glove with actual "netting" in the die cut holes for the glove netting. Goalie action photography was set in front of the backdrop and names were highlighted in gold foil.

COMPLETE SET (6)	10.00	20.00
1 Dominik Hasek	2.00	5.00
2 Patrick Roy	5.00	12.00
3 Chris Osgood	1.00	2.50
4 Martin Brodeur	2.50	6.00
5 Brian Boucher	1.00	2.50
6 Curtis Joseph	1.00	2.50

2000-01 McDonald's Pacific Gold Crown Die Cuts

Randomly inserted in McDonald's Pacific packs at the rate of one in eight, this six card set featured player action shots set against a green background and a maroon die-cut crown along the top of the card. Both the crown and the name box along the bottom of the card were highlighted in gold foil.

COMPLETE SET (6)	4.00	8.00
1 Patrik Stefan	.60	1.50
2 Alex Tanguay	.60	1.50
3 David Legwand	.60	1.50
4 Scott Gomez	.60	1.50
5 Tim Connolly	.60	1.50
6 Vincent Lecavalier	.60	1.50

2000-01 McDonald's Pacific Game Jerseys

Randomly inserted in McDonald's Pacific packs at the rate of one in 11,915, this 10-card set featured player

action photography coupled with a circular game jersey swatch. Cards were accented with gold foil highlights.

*MULT.COLOR SWATCH: 1X TO 2X

1 Teemu Selanne	40.00	100.00
2 Peter Forsberg	75.00	150.00
3 Patrick Roy	60.00	150.00
4 Mike Modano	50.00	100.00
5 Steve Yzerman	100.00	175.00
6 Pavel Bure	50.00	100.00
7 Martin Brodeur	75.00	150.00
8 Eric Lindros	50.00	125.00
9 Jaromir Jagr	40.00	100.00
10 Mats Sundin	30.00	80.00

2001-02 McDonald's Pacific

Produced by Pacific in conjunction with McDonalds of Canada at the cost of an order of french fries or hash browns and 89 cents, this 42-card set utilized set designs from Pacific Prism Gold. Card backs carried stats and player bios in both English and French.

COMPLETE SET (42)	12.50	25.00
1 Paul Kariya	.20	.50
2 Joe Thornton	.30	.75
3 Jarome Iginla	.25	.60
4 Ray Bourque	.40	1.00
5 Peter Forsberg	.50	1.25
6 Patrick Roy SP	1.50	4.00
7 Joe Sakic	.40	1.00
8 Ed Belfour SP	.50	1.25
9 Brett Hull	.25	.60
10 Mike Modano	.30	.75
11 Sergei Fedorov	.30	.75
12 Dominik Hasek SP	.60	1.50
13 Chris Osgood SP	.40	1.00
14 Brendan Shanahan	.20	.50
15 Steve Yzerman	1.00	2.50
16 Tommy Salo SP	.40	1.00
17 Ryan Smyth	.15	.40
18 Pavel Bure	.20	.50
19 Felix Potvin SP	.50	1.25
20 Marian Gaborik	.40	1.00
21 Saku Koivu	.20	.50
22 Jose Theodore SP	.60	1.50
23 Jason Arnott	.15	.40
24 Martin Brodeur SP	.75	2.00
25 Rick DiPietro SP	.40	1.00
26 Marian Hossa	.20	.50
27 Patrick Lalime SP	.40	1.00
28 Roman Cechmanek SP	.40	1.00
29 John LeClair	.20	.50
30 Johan Hedberg SP	.40	1.00
31 Mario Lemieux SP	2.00	5.00
32 Fred Brathwaite SP	.40	1.00
33 Chris Pronger	.15	.40
34 Doug Weight	.15	.40
35 Evgeni Nabokov SP	.40	1.00
36 Teemu Selanne	.20	.50
37 Vincent Lecavalier	.20	.50
38 Curtis Joseph SP	.50	1.25
39 Mats Sundin	.20	.50
40 Dan Cloutier SP	.40	1.00
41 Markus Naslund	.20	.50
42 Jaromir Jagr SP	.50	1.25

2001-02 McDonald's Pacific Cosmic Force

Inserted at odds of 1:16, this 6-card set featured a "starlight" sparkle effect which revealed a player silhouette when tilted in the light.

COMPLETE SET (6)	15.00	30.00
1 Pavel Bure	2.00	5.00
2 Mario Lemieux	5.00	12.00
3 Doug Weight	1.50	4.00
4 Teemu Selanne	2.00	5.00
5 Mats Sundin	2.00	5.00
6 Jaromir Jagr	2.00	5.00

2001-02 McDonald's Pacific Future Legends

Inserted at 1:16, this 6-card die-cut set featured both large profile photos in black-and-white and smaller color action photos.

COMPLETE SET (6)	15.00	30.00
1 Mike Comrie	2.00	5.00
2 Rick DiPietro	2.00	5.00
3 Martin Havlat	2.00	5.00
4 Evgeni Nabokov	2.00	5.00

5 Daniel Sedin 2.00 5.00
6 Henrik Sedin 2.00 5.00

2001-02 McDonald's Pacific Glove-Side Net-Fusion

Inserted at 1:16, this 6-card die-cut set featured color goalie photos over a goalie trapper background. Realistic "netting" was used in the die-cut pocket of the glove.

COMPLETE SET (6) 20.00 40.00
1 Patrick Roy 5.00 12.00
2 Tommy Salo 2.50 6.00
3 Jose Theodore 3.00 8.00
4 Martin Brodeur 4.00 10.00
5 Johan Hedberg 3.00 8.00
6 Curtis Joseph 2.50 6.00

2001-02 McDonald's Pacific Hockey Greats

Inserted at 1:16, this 6-card set featured bronzed player profiles on sepia toned card fronts.

COMPLETE SET (6) 15.00 30.00
1 Ray Bourque 3.00 8.00
2 Joe Sakic 3.00 8.00
3 Brett Hull 2.50 6.00
4 Dominik Hasek 3.00 8.00
5 Steve Yzerman 5.00 12.00
6 Mark Messier 2.00 5.00

2001-02 McDonald's Pacific Hometown Pride

This 10-card set was inserted one per pack and featured dual player photos on the card fronts and set checklists on the card backs.

COMPLETE SET (10) 5.00 10.00
1 J.Friesen/W.Redden .40 1.00
2 P.Kariya/B.Morrison .40 1.00
3 S.Pellerin/D.Sweeney .40 1.00
4 M.Comrie/J.Iginla .40 1.00
5 B.Richards/G.Sanderson .40 1.00
6 E.Belfour/T.Fleury .40 1.00
7 L.Robitaille/V.Lecavalier .40 1.00
8 D.Cleary/H.Druken .40 1.00
9 A.MacInnis/C.White .40 1.00
10 G.Roberts/S.Thomas .40 1.00

2001-02 McDonald's Pacific Jersey Patches Silver

This 20-card set featured game-worn swatches of jersey patches. Each card was serial-numbered to a number equal to 250 minus their jersey numbers. Actual redeemed numbers are listed below.

1 Jarome Iginla/238 50.00 125.00
150 actually redeemed
2 Peter Forsberg/229 75.00 200.00
160 actually redeemed
3 Patrick Roy/217 125.00 250.00
136 actually redeemed
4 Joe Sakic/231 60.00 150.00
140 actually redeemed
5 Ed Belfour/230 50.00 125.00
144 actually redeemed
6 Brett Hull/234 60.00 150.00
147 actually redeemed
7 Mike Modano/241 60.00 150.00
149 actually redeemed
8 Joe Nieuwendyk/225 40.00 100.00
139 actually redeemed
9 Dominik Hasek/211 75.00 200.00
121 actually redeemed
10 Brendan Shanahan/236 40.00 100.00
149 actually redeemed
11 Steve Yzerman/231 75.00 200.00
150 actually redeemed
12 Saku Koivu/239 60.00 150.00
161 actually redeemed
13 Theo Fleury/236 40.00 100.00
149 actually redeemed
14 Daniel Alfredsson/239 50.00 125.00
143 actually redeemed
15 Mario Lemieux/184 75.00 200.00
16 Teemu Selanne/242 40.00 100.00
139 actually redeemed
17 Vincent Lecavalier/246 75.00 200.00
163 actually redeemed
18 Curtis Joseph/219 50.00 125.00
145 actually redeemed
19 Mats Sundin/237 40.00 100.00
146 actually redeemed
20 Jaromir Jagr/182 60.00 150.00
117 actually redeemed

2001-02 McDonald's Pacific Jersey Patches Gold

This 20-card set paralleled the base jersey set but was on gold card stock. Each card was serial-numbered to the player's jersey number. Print runs less than 25 were not priced due to scarcity. Actual redeemed numbers are listed below.

1 Jarome Iginla/12
8 actually redeemed
2 Peter Forsberg/21
14 actually redeemed
3 Patrick Roy/33 250.00 600.00
21 actually redeemed
4 Joe Sakic/19
10 actually redeemed
5 Ed Belfour/20
8 actually redeemed
6 Brett Hull/16
10 actually redeemed
7 Mike Modano/9
4 actually redeemed
8 Joe Nieuwendyk/25 150.00 300.00
15 actually redeemed
9 Dominik Hasek/39 200.00 400.00
26 actually redeemed
10 Brendan Shanahan/14
8 actually redeemed
11 Steve Yzerman/19
17 actually redeemed
12 Saku Koivu/11
6 actually redeemed
13 Theo Fleury/14
9 actually redeemed
14 Daniel Alfredsson/11
8 actually redeemed
15 Mario Lemieux/66 350.00 700.00
16 Teemu Selanne/8
7 actually redeemed
17 Vincent Lecavalier/4
2 actually redeemed
18 Curtis Joseph/31
19 actually redeemed
19 Mats Sundin/13
9 actually redeemed
20 Jaromir Jagr/68 150.00 300.00
45 actually redeemed

2002-03 McDonald's Pacific

Produced by Pacific in conjunction with McDonalds of Canada at the cost of an order of french fries or hash browns and 89 cents, this 42-card set utilized set designs from Pacific Prism Platinum. Card backs carried stats and player bios in both English and French.

COMPLETE SET (42) 15.00 30.00
COMP.SET w/CL's (52) 20.00 40.00
COMP.MASTER SET (76) 60.00 125.00
1 Paul Kariya .30 .75
2 Dany Heatley .40 1.00
3 Ilya Kovalchuk .50 1.25
4 Joe Thornton .50 1.25
5 Jarome Iginla .40 1.00
6 Derek Morris .12 .30
7 Roman Turek .25 .60
8 Peter Forsberg .75 2.00
9 Patrick Roy 1.50 4.00
10 Joe Sakic .60 1.50
11 Dominik Hasek .60 1.50
12 Brendan Shanahan .30 .75
13 Steve Yzerman 1.50 4.00
14 Anson Carter .25 .60
15 Mike Comrie .25 .60
16 Ryan Smyth .12 .30
17 Roberto Luongo .40 1.00
18 Jason Allison .12 .30
19 Marian Gaborik .60 1.50
20 Doug Gilmour .25 .60
21 Saku Koivu .30 .75
22 Jose Theodore .75 2.00
23 Martin Brodeur .75 2.00
24 Michael Peca .12 .30
25 Alexei Yashin .12 .30
26 Pavel Bure .30 .75
27 Eric Lindros .30 .75
28 Daniel Alfredsson .25 .60
29 Marian Hossa .30 .75
30 Patrick Lalime .25 .60
31 Simon Gagne .25 .60
32 Mario Lemieux 2.00 5.00
33 Chris Pronger .25 .60
34 Evgeni Nabokov .25 .60
35 Teemu Selanne .30 .75
36 Curtis Joseph .30 .75
37 Gary Roberts .12 .30
38 Mats Sundin .30 .75
39 Todd Bertuzzi .30 .75
40 Brendan Morrison .25 .60
41 Markus Naslund .30 .75
42 Jaromir Jagr .50 1.25

2002-03 McDonald's Pacific Atomic

Randomly inserted into packs at 1:16, this 6-card set borrowed from the Pacific Atomic diecut design.

COMPLETE SET (6)
1 Paul Kariya 1.50 4.00
2 Ron Francis 1.50 4.00
3 Brett Hull 2.00 5.00
4 Steve Yzerman 5.00 12.00
5 Mats Sundin 1.50 4.00
6 Jaromir Jagr 1.50 4.00

2002-03 McDonald's Pacific Clear Advantage

Inserted at 1:16, this 6-card set featured color photos of up and coming stars on sparkle effect backgrounds.

COMPLETE SET (6) 12.50 30.00
1 Dany Heatley 2.50 6.00
2 Ilya Kovalchuk 4.00 10.00
3 Jarome Iginla 3.00 8.00
4 Mike Comrie 3.00 8.00
5 Martin Havlat 2.00 5.00
6 Todd Bertuzzi 2.00 5.00

2002-03 McDonald's Pacific Cup Contenders Die-Cuts

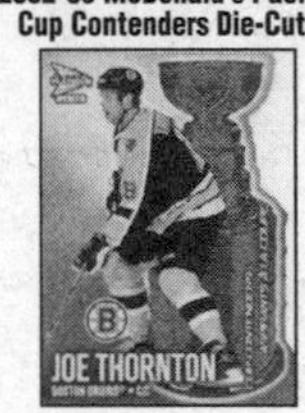

Inserted at 1:16, this 6-card set featured full color action player photos skating over an image of the Stanley Cup. All cards were die-cut.

COMPLETE SET (6) 15.00 30.00
1 Joe Thornton 2.50 6.00
2 Patrick Roy 5.00 12.00
3 Sergei Fedorov 2.50 6.00
4 Saku Koivu 2.00 5.00
5 Daniel Alfredsson 1.50 4.00
6 Mats Sundin 1.50 4.00

2002-03 McDonald's Pacific Glove Side Net-Fusions

Inserted at 1:16, this 6-card die-cut set featured color goalie photos over a goalie trapper background. Realistic "netting" was used in the die-cut pocket of the glove.

COMPLETE SET (6) 15.00 30.00
1 Patrick Roy 4.00 10.00
2 Dominik Hasek 2.50 6.00
3 Tommy Salo 2.00 5.00
4 Jose Theodore 2.50 6.00
5 Patrick Lalime 2.50 6.00
6 Evgeni Nabokov 2.00 5.00

2002-03 McDonald's Pacific Jersey Patches Silver

Randomly inserted into packs as redemption cards, this 20-card set featured authentic game-worn jersey patches of the featured players. Both silver and gold variations were produced for a total of 250 cards of each player. Gold versions were serial-numbered to the player's jersey and silver versions were numbered to the remainder.

1 Dany Heatley/235 100.00 200.00
2 Ilya Kovalchuk/233 75.00 150.00
3 Ron Francis/240 50.00 100.00
4 Joe Sakic/231 75.00 150.00
5 Dominik Hasek/211 125.00 250.00
6 Mike Comrie/161 50.00 100.00
7 Yanic Perreault/156 40.00 80.00
8 Jose Theodore/190 125.00 250.00
9 Martin Brodeur/220 125.00 250.00
10 Pavel Bure/241 40.00 80.00
11 Eric Lindros/162 75.00 150.00
12 Daniel Alfredsson/239 40.00 80.00
13 Adam Oates/173 50.00 100.00
14 Mario Lemieux/184 200.00 400.00
15 Chris Pronger/206 50.00 100.00
16 Curtis Joseph/219 50.00 100.00
17 Alexander Mogilny/161 40.00 80.00
18 Gary Roberts/243 50.00 100.00
19 Markus Naslund/231 50.00 100.00
20 Jaromir Jagr/182 75.00 150.00

2002-03 McDonald's Pacific Jersey Patches Gold

This 20-card set paralleled the base jersey set but was on gold card stock. Each card was serial-numbered to the player's jersey number. Print runs less than 25 were not priced due to scarcity.

1 Dany Heatley/15
2 Ilya Kovalchuk/17
3 Ron Francis/10
4 Joe Sakic/19
5 Dominik Hasek/39 250.00 500.00
6 Mike Comrie/89 200.00 400.00
7 Yanic Perreault/94
8 Jose Theodore/60
9 Martin Brodeur/30 200.00 400.00
10 Pavel Bure/9
11 Eric Lindros/88 75.00 200.00
12 Daniel Alfredsson/11
13 Adam Oates/77 75.00 200.00
14 Mario Lemieux/66 300.00 800.00
15 Chris Pronger/44 75.00 200.00
16 Curtis Joseph/31 125.00 250.00
17 Alexander Mogilny/89 60.00 150.00
18 Gary Roberts/7
19 Markus Naslund/19
20 Jaromir Jagr/68 150.00 300.00

2002-03 McDonald's Pacific Salt Lake Gold

Randomly inserted in packs, this 10-card set features players who were members of the 2002 gold medal Canadian Olympic team. Card backs carry checklists for the rest of the product.

COMPLETE SET (10) 5.00 10.00
1 M.Brodeur/C.Joseph/E.Belfour .40 1.00
2 Adam Foote .25 .60
Rob Blake
Scott Niedermayer
3 Ed Jovanovski .25 .60
Chris Pronger
Al MacInnis
4 Ryan Smyth .25 .60
Eric Brewer
5 B.Shanahan/S.Yzerman 1.25 3.00
6 Eric Lindros .30 .75
Theoren Fleury
7 Paul Kariya .25 .60
Joe Nieuwendyk
8 Jarome Iginla .25 .60
Owen Nolan
9 Joe Sakic .25 .60
Michael Peca
10 M.Lemieux/S.Gagne 1.25 3.00

2003-04 McDonald's Pacific

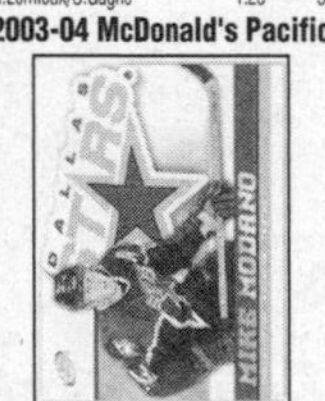

In 2003-04, Pacific Trading Cards utilized their Atomic brand for the McDonald's promotion. This set consisted of 55 veteran cards and 6 rookie autograph cards originally found in packs as redemption cards. The redeemed cards were serial-numbered out of 100.

COMP.SET w/o SP's (55) 12.00 25.00
COMP.SET w/CL's (65) 15.00 30.00
COMP.MASTER SET (89) 50.00 100.00
1 Jean-Sebastien Giguere .25 .60
2 Dany Heatley .40 1.00
3 Ilya Kovalchuk .40 1.00
4 Joe Thornton .50 1.25
5 Martin Biron .25 .60
6 Chris Drury .25 .60
7 Jarome Iginla .40 1.00
8 Chuck Kobasew .12 .30
9 Jocelyn Thibault .25 .60
10 Peter Forsberg .75 2.00
11 Milan Hejduk .30 .75
12 Paul Kariya .30 .75
13 Joe Sakic .60 1.50
14 Rick Nash .40 1.00
15 Mike Modano .50 1.25
16 Marty Turco .25 .60
17 Sergei Fedorov .40 1.00
18 Curtis Joseph .30 .75
19 Steve Yzerman 1.50 4.00
20 Henrik Zetterberg .30 .75
21 Mike Comrie .25 .60
22 Georges Laraque .12 .30
23 Ryan Smyth .12 .30
24 Jay Bouwmeester .12 .30
25 Roberto Luongo .40 1.00
26 Marian Gaborik .60 1.50
27 Marcel Hossa .30 .75
28 Saku Koivu .30 .75
29 Jose Theodore .40 1.00
30 Martin Brodeur .75 2.00
31 Scott Stevens .25 .60
32 Michael Peca .12 .30
33 Eric Lindros .30 .75
34 Mark Messier .30 .75
35 Daniel Alfredsson .25 .60
36 Marian Hossa .30 .75
37 Patrick Lalime .25 .60
38 Simon Gagne .30 .75
39 Jeremy Roenick .40 1.00
40 Sean Burke .25 .60
41 Mario Lemieux 2.00 5.00
42 Barret Jackman .25 .60
43 Peter Sejna .50 1.25
44 Vincent Lecavalier .30 .75
45 Martin St. Louis .25 .60
46 Ed Belfour .30 .75
47 Tie Domi .25 .60
48 Owen Nolan .25 .60
49 Matt Stajan .40 1.00
50 Mats Sundin .30 .75
51 Todd Bertuzzi .30 .75
52 Ed Jovanovski .25 .60
53 Brendan Morrison .25 .60
54 Markus Naslund .30 .75
55 Jaromir Jagr .50 1.25
56 Eric Staal AU 200.00 350.00
57 Tuomo Ruutu AU 100.00 200.00
58 Nathan Horton AU 100.00 250.00
59 Chris Higgins AU 150.00 300.00
60 Jordin Tootoo AU 150.00 300.00
61 Marc-Andre Fleury AU 200.00 400.00

2003-04 McDonald's Pacific Canadian Pride

COMPLETE SET (6) 12.00 25.00
STATED ODDS 1:16
1 Dany Heatley 2.00 5.00
2 Joe Thornton 2.50 6.00
3 Rick Nash 2.00 5.00
4 Jay Bouwmeester 1.25 3.00
5 Jason Spezza 2.00 5.00
6 Vincent Lecavalier 1.25 3.00

2003-04 McDonald's Pacific Etched in Time

COMPLETE SET (6) 12.00 25.00
STATED ODDS 1:16
1 Mark Messier 1.50 4.00
2 Joe Sakic 3.00 8.00
3 Brett Hull 2.00 5.00
4 Steve Yzerman 5.00 12.00
5 Mario Lemieux 6.00 15.00
6 Jaromir Jagr 2.50 6.00

2003-04 McDonald's Pacific Hockey Roots Checklists

COMPLETE SET (10) 3.00 6.00
STATED ODDS 1:1
1 Dany Heatley .25 .60
2 Joe Thornton .25 .60
3 Jarome Iginla .30 .75
4 Rob Blake .30 .75
5 Paul Kariya .25 .60
6 Rick Nash .25 .60
7 Jeff Friesen .25 .60
8 Vincent Lecavalier .30 .75
9 Brad Richards .40 1.00
10 Gary Roberts .25 .60

2003-04 McDonald's Pacific Patches Silver

Randomly inserted into packs as redemption cards, this 25-card set featured authentic game-worn jersey patches of the featured players. Each card was serial-numbered out of 150, though there is no information currently as to how many cards were actually redeemed.

STATED PRINT RUN 150 SER.#'d SETS
1 Paul Kariya 60.00 150.00
2 Dany Heatley 60.00 150.00
3 Joe Thornton 75.00 200.00
4 Jarome Iginla 60.00 150.00
5 Peter Forsberg 60.00 150.00
6 Ilya Kovalchuk 50.00 125.00
7 Joe Sakic 75.00 200.00
8 Mike Modano 50.00 125.00
9 Marty Turco 50.00 125.00
10 Brendan Shanahan 50.00 125.00
11 Steve Yzerman 75.00 200.00
12 Mike Comrie 30.00 80.00
13 Ryan Smyth 60.00 150.00
14 Saku Koivu 60.00 125.00
15 Jose Theodore 60.00 150.00
16 Martin Brodeur 150.00 250.00
17 Marian Hossa 60.00 150.00
18 Patrick Lalime 50.00 125.00
19 Jason Spezza 75.00 200.00
20 Mario Lemieux 125.00 300.00
21 Vincent Lecavalier 60.00 150.00
22 Ed Belfour 75.00 200.00
23 Mats Sundin 50.00 125.00
24 Todd Bertuzzi 60.00 150.00
25 Markus Naslund 60.00 150.00

2003-04 McDonald's Pacific Patches Gold

*STARS: .6X TO 1.5X BASIC INSERTS
STATED PRINT RUN 100 SER.#'d SETS

2003-04 McDonald's Pacific Patches and Sticks

*STARS: .75X TO 2X BASIC INSERT
STATED PRINT RUN 50 SETS
1 Paul Kariya 125.00 250.00
2 Dany Heatley 125.00 250.00
3 Joe Thornton 150.00 400.00
4 Jarome Iginla 150.00 400.00
5 Peter Forsberg 125.00 250.00
6 Ilya Kovalchuk 125.00 250.00
7 Joe Sakic 150.00 400.00
8 Mike Modano 100.00 200.00
9 Marty Turco 100.00 200.00
10 Brendan Shanahan 100.00 200.00
11 Steve Yzerman 150.00 400.00
12 Mike Comrie 60.00 150.00
13 Ryan Smyth 125.00 250.00
14 Saku Koivu 100.00 200.00
15 Jose Theodore 125.00 250.00
16 Martin Brodeur 200.00 400.00
17 Marian Hossa 125.00 250.00
18 Patrick Lalime 100.00 200.00
19 Jason Spezza 150.00 400.00
20 Mario Lemieux 250.00 500.00
21 Vincent Lecavalier 125.00 250.00
22 Ed Belfour 150.00 300.00
23 Mats Sundin 100.00 200.00
24 Todd Bertuzzi 125.00 250.00
25 Markus Naslund 125.00 250.00

2003-04 McDonald's Pacific Net Fusions

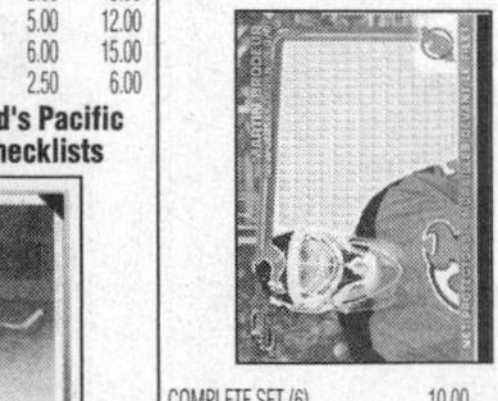

COMPLETE SET (6) 10.00 20.00
STATED ODDS 1:16
1 Jean-Sebastien Giguere 1.25 3.00
2 Curtis Joseph 1.50 4.00
3 Roberto Luongo 2.00 5.00
4 Jose Theodore 2.00 5.00
5 Martin Brodeur 2.50 6.00
6 Ed Belfour 1.50 4.00

2003-04 McDonald's Pacific Saturday Night Rivals

COMPLETE SET (1-6) 8.00 15.00
STATED ODDS 1:16
1 Jarome Iginla 1.25 3.00
Mike Comrie
2 Todd Bertuzzi 1.50 4.00
Ryan Smyth
3 Brendan Morrison 1.25 3.00

Craig Conroy
4 Mats Sundin 2.00 5.00
Saku Koivu
5 Patrick Lalime 2.00 5.00
Ed Belfour
6 Marian Hossa 2.00 5.00
Marcel Hossa

2005-06 McDonald's Upper Deck

COMPLETE SET (51) 15.00 40.00
1 Jay Bouwmeester .12 .30
2 Eric Lindros .30 .75
3 Sergei Fedorov .40 1.00
4 Vincent Lecavalier .30 .75
5 Miikka Kiprusoff .40 1.00
6 Scott Niedermayer .12 .30
7 Chris Pronger .25 .60
8 Joe Thornton .40 1.00
9 Rick Nash .40 1.00
10 Saku Koivu .30 .75
11 Wade Redden .12 .30
12 Mats Sundin .30 .75
13 Jason Smith .12 .30
14 Tuomo Ruutu .25 .60
15 Olaf Kolzig .25 .60
16 Simon Gagne .30 .75
17 Brendan Shanahan .30 .75
18 Jean-Sebastien Giguere .25 .60
19 Roberto Luongo .40 1.00
20 Michael Ryder .40 1.00
21 Ed Jovanovski .25 .60
22 Daniel Briere .12 .30
23 Jarome Iginla .40 1.00
24 Joe Sakic .60 1.50
25 Dany Heatley .40 1.00
26 Steve Yzerman 1.25 3.00
27 Mike Ribeiro .12 .30
28 Mario Lemieux 1.50 4.00
29 Brendan Morrison .25 .60
30 Brad Richards .25 .60
31 Luc Robitaille .25 .60
32 Daniel Alfredsson .25 .60
33 Andrew Raycroft .25 .60
34 Eric Staal .40 1.00
35 Jose Theodore .40 1.00
36 Jaromir Jagr .50 1.25
37 Jeremy Roenick .40 1.00
38 Martin St. Louis .25 .60
39 Ed Belfour .30 .75
40 Mike Modano .40 1.00
41 Marian Hossa .30 .75
42 Ilya Kovalchuk .40 1.00
43 Jonathan Cheechoo .30 .75
44 Ryan Smyth .12 .30
45 Peter Forsberg .60 1.50
46 Shean Donovan .12 .30
47 Marian Gaborik .40 1.00
48 Martin Brodeur .75 2.00
49 Bryan McCabe .12 .30
50 Markus Naslund .30 .75
51 Sidney Crosby RC 10.00 25.00

2005-06 McDonald's Upper Deck Autographs

COMMON CARD
PRINT RUN 50 SER.#'d SETS
MA1 Wayne Gretzky 400.00 750.00
MA2 Markus Naslund 50.00 125.00
MA3 Joe Thornton 200.00 400.00
MA4 Dominik Hasek 100.00 200.00
MA5 Jarome Iginla 125.00 250.00
MA6 Martin Brodeur 250.00 400.00
MA7 Rick Nash 125.00 250.00
MA8 Jose Theodore 150.00 300.00
MA9 Mats Sundin 150.00 300.00

2005-06 McDonald's Upper Deck Chasing the Cup

PRINT RUN 100 SER.#'d SETS
CC1 Simon Gagne 40.00 80.00
CC2 Jose Theodore 50.00 100.00
CC3 Jarome Iginla 50.00 100.00
CC4 Markus Naslund 50.00 100.00
CC5 Jason Spezza 60.00 125.00
CC6 Mats Sundin 60.00 125.00
CC7 Joe Thornton 75.00 150.00
CC8 Ilya Kovalchuk 60.00 125.00

2005-06 McDonald's Upper Deck CHL Graduates

COMPLETE SET (6) 2.00 4.00
STATED ODDS 1:1
CG1 Joe Sakic .50 1.25
CG2 Jarome Iginla .30 .75
CG3 Wade Redden .25 .60
CG4 Vincent Lecavalier .25 .60
CG5 Joe Thornton .40 1.00
CG6 Rick Nash .30 .75

2005-06 McDonald's Upper Deck Goalie Factory

COMPLETE SET (15) 25.00 60.00
STATED ODDS 1:14
GF1 Dominik Hasek 4.00 10.00

GF2 Roberto Luongo 3.00 8.00
GF3 Martin Brodeur 5.00 12.00
GF4 Marty Turco 2.50 6.00
GF5 Miikka Kiprusoff 2.50 6.00
GF6 Jean-Sebastien Giguere 2.50 6.00
GF7 Tomas Vokoun 2.50 6.00
GF8 Dan Cloutier 2.50 6.00
GF9 Jose Theodore 3.00 8.00
GF10 Nikolai Khabibulin 2.50 6.00
GF11 Marc-Andre Fleury 2.50 6.00
GF12 Kari Lehtonen 2.50 6.00
GF13 Ed Belfour 1.50 4.00
GF14 Curtis Joseph 1.50 4.00
GF15 Andrew Raycroft 2.50 6.00

2005-06 McDonald's Upper Deck Goalie Gear

PRINT RUN 50 SER.#'d SETS
MG1 Marc-Andre Fleury 125.00 250.00
MG2 Jocelyn Thibault 60.00 150.00
MG3 Roberto Luongo 75.00 200.00
MG4 Rick DiPietro 60.00 150.00
MG5 Olaf Kolzig 100.00 200.00
MG6 Jose Theodore 75.00 150.00
MG7 Andrew Raycroft 60.00 150.00
MG8 Marty Turco 60.00 150.00
MG9 Dominik Hasek 125.00 250.00
MG10 Ed Belfour 125.00 250.00
MG11 Chris Osgood 60.00 150.00
MG12 Curtis Joseph 60.00 125.00

2005-06 McDonald's Upper Deck Jerseys

PRINT RUN 120 SER.#'d SETS
MJ1 Mario Lemieux 125.00 250.00
MJ2 Joe Thornton 75.00 200.00
MJ3 Mats Sundin 60.00 150.00
MJ4 Markus Naslund 60.00 150.00
MJ5 Dany Heatley 60.00 150.00
MJ6 Martin Brodeur 150.00 300.00
MJ7 Steve Yzerman 150.00 300.00
MJ8 Saku Koivu 75.00 150.00
MJ9 Jose Theodore 75.00 150.00
MJ10 Ed Belfour 100.00 200.00
MJ11 Jarome Iginla 150.00 250.00
MJ12 Jason Spezza 75.00 150.00
MJ13 Martin Havlat 75.00 150.00
MJ14 Sergei Fedorov 75.00 150.00
MJ15 Jeremy Roenick 75.00 150.00

2005-06 McDonald's Upper Deck Patches

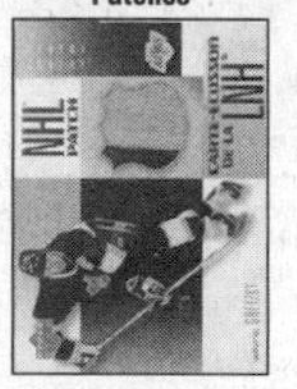

*PATCHES: .75X TO 1.5X JSY HI
PRINT RUN 25 SER.#'d SETS
MP1 Mario Lemieux 150.00 400.00
MP2 Joe Thornton 175.00 300.00
MP3 Mats Sundin 100.00 225.00
MP4 Markus Naslund 100.00 225.00
MP5 Dany Heatley 125.00 300.00
MP6 Martin Brodeur 200.00 450.00
MP7 Wayne Gretzky
MP8 Saku Koivu 100.00 225.00
MP9 Jose Theodore 125.00 300.00
MP10 Ed Belfour 125.00 300.00
MP11 Jarome Iginla 125.00 300.00
MP12 Jeremy Roenick 125.00 300.00
MP13 Martin Havlat 100.00 225.00
MP14 Sergei Fedorov 100.00 225.00

2005-06 McDonald's Upper Deck Next Generation

COMPLETE SET (15) 30.00 60.00
STATED ODDS 1:18
NG1 Andrew Raycroft 2.50 6.00
NG2 Rick Nash 4.00 10.00
NG3 Marc-Andre Fleury 3.00 8.00
NG4 Nikolai Zherdev 2.00 5.00
NG5 Tuomo Ruutu 2.00 5.00
NG6 Jonathan Cheechoo 2.50 6.00
NG7 Kari Lehtonen 3.00 8.00
NG8 Jason Spezza 4.00 10.00
NG9 Alexander Frolov 2.00 5.00
NG10 Stephen Weiss 2.00 5.00
NG11 Patrice Bergeron 2.50 6.00
NG12 Derek Roy 2.00 5.00
NG13 Eric Staal 5.00 12.00
NG14 Michael Ryder 2.50 6.00
NG15 Matthew Lombardi 2.00 5.00

2005-06 McDonald's Upper Deck Superstar Spotlight

COMPLETE SET (10) 30.00 60.00
COMMON CARD (SS1-SS10) 1.50 4.00
STATED ODDS 1:16
SS1 Mario Lemieux 6.00 15.00
SS2 Joe Thornton 2.50 6.00
SS3 Mats Sundin 1.50 4.00
SS4 Jarome Iginla 2.00 5.00
SS5 Martin Brodeur 5.00 12.00
SS6 Jose Theodore 2.00 5.00
SS7 Martin St. Louis 1.50 4.00
SS8 Joe Sakic 3.00 8.00
SS9 Steve Yzerman 5.00 12.00
SS10 Vincent Lecavalier 1.50 4.00

2005-06 McDonald's Upper Deck Top Scorers

COMPLETE SET (15) 100.00 175.00
STATED ODDS 1:18
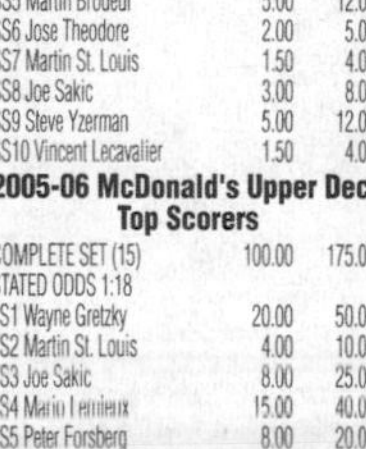
TS1 Wayne Gretzky 20.00 50.00
TS2 Martin St. Louis 4.00 10.00
TS3 Joe Sakic 8.00 25.00
TS4 Mario Lemieux 15.00 40.00
TS5 Peter Forsberg 8.00 20.00
TS6 Steve Yzerman 12.00 30.00
TS7 Mike Modano 8.00 20.00
TS8 Mike Ribeiro 4.00 10.00

TS9 Mats Sundin 6.00 15.00
TS10 Markus Naslund 6.00 15.00
TS11 Jarome Iginla 8.00 20.00
TS12 Daniel Alfredsson 6.00 15.00
TS13 Ilya Kovalchuk 8.00 20.00
TS14 Rick Nash 8.00 20.00
TS15 Joe Thornton 8.00 20.00

2006-07 McDonald's Upper Deck

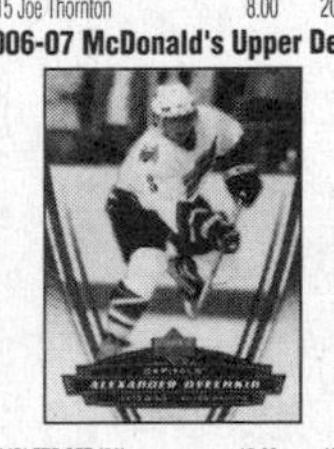

COMPLETE SET (56) 15.00 40.00
1 Teemu Selanne .50 1.25
2 Ilya Kovalchuk .60 1.50
3 Patrice Bergeron .40 1.00
4 Ryan Miller .50 1.25
5 Jarome Iginla .75 2.00
6 Miikka Kiprusoff .50 1.25
7 Dion Phaneuf .60 1.50
8 Eric Staal .40 1.00
9 Nikolai Khabibulin .50 1.25
10 Joe Sakic 1.00 2.50
11 Milan Hejduk .40 1.00
12 Rick Nash .50 1.25
13 Mike Modano .50 1.25
14 Marty Turco .40 1.00
15 Steve Yzerman 1.50 4.00
16 Brendan Shanahan .50 1.25
17 Jarret Stoll .30 .75
18 Ales Hemsky .30 .75
19 Ryan Smyth .40 1.00
20 Jay Bouwmeester .30 .75
21 Alexander Frolov .30 .75
22 Marian Gaborik .75 2.00
23 Saku Koivu .50 1.25
24 Michael Ryder .40 1.00
25 Mike Ribeiro .30 .75
26 Paul Kariya .50 1.25
27 Martin Brodeur 1.50 4.00
28 Miroslav Satan .30 .75
29 Jaromir Jagr .75 2.00
30 Henrik Lundqvist .75 2.00
31 Jason Spezza .50 1.25
32 Dany Heatley .50 1.25
33 Daniel Alfredsson .40 1.00
34 Peter Forsberg .75 2.00
35 Simon Gagne .50 1.25
36 Shane Doan .40 1.00
37 Marc-Andre Fleury .50 1.25
38 Joe Thornton .75 2.00
39 Jonathan Cheechoo .50 1.25
40 Keith Tkachuk .40 1.00
41 Brad Richards .50 1.25
42 Martin St. Louis .50 1.25
43 Vincent Lecavalier .50 1.25
44 Darcy Tucker .30 .75
45 Mats Sundin .50 1.25
46 Alexander Steen .40 1.00
47 Markus Naslund .50 1.25
48 Ed Jovanovski .30 .75
49 Brendan Morrison .30 .75
50 Alexander Ovechkin 2.00 5.00
51 Saku Koivu CL 1.00 2.50
52 Mats Sundin CL 1.00 2.50
53 Jarome Iginla CL 1.50 4.00
54 Markus Naslund CL 1.00 2.50
55 Daniel Alfredsson CL .75 2.00
56 Jason Smith CL .60 1.50

2006-07 McDonald's Upper Deck Autographs

STATED ODDS 1:4,000
PRINT RUN 25 SER. #'d SETS
AAH Ales Hemsky 125.00 250.00
AAO Alexander Ovechkin
AAT Alex Tanguay 75.00 150.00
ABM Bryan McCabe 75.00 150.00
ADP Dion Phaneuf 100.00 175.00
AES Eric Staal 100.00 200.00
AHL Henrik Lundqvist 125.00 250.00
AHZ Henrik Zetterberg 125.00 250.00
AIK Ilya Kovalchuk 125.00 300.00
AJC Jonathan Cheechoo 100.00 200.00
AJI Jarome Iginla 125.00 250.00
AJT Joe Thornton
AKD Kris Draper 100.00 175.00
ALR Luc Robitaille 100.00 200.00
AMB Martin Brodeur
AMF Marc-Andre Fleury 125.00 250.00
AMK Miikka Kiprusoff 100.00 200.00
AMN Markus Naslund 100.00 200.00
AMP Michael Peca 75.00 150.00
AMR Michael Ryder 75.00 150.00
AMT Marty Turco 75.00 150.00
APB Patrice Bergeron 75.00 150.00
APM Patrick Marleau 75.00 150.00
ARL Roberto Luongo 150.00 250.00
ARM Ryan Miller 125.00 225.00
ARN Rick Nash 125.00 225.00
ARS Ryan Smyth 75.00 150.00
ASH Shawn Horcoff 75.00 150.00
ASK Saku Koivu
AVL Vincent Lecavalier

2006-07 McDonald's Upper Deck Clear Cut Winners

COMPLETE SET (10) 300.00 400.00
STATED ODDS 1:100
CC1 Joe Sakic 25.00 60.00
CC2 Jarome Iginla 20.00 50.00
CC3 Rick Nash 20.00 50.00
CC4 Eric Staal 20.00 50.00
CC5 Saku Koivu 20.00 50.00
CC6 Martin Brodeur 25.00 60.00
CC7 Dany Heatley 20.00 50.00
CC8 Joe Thornton 20.00 50.00
CC9 Mats Sundin 20.00 50.00
CC10 Ryan Smyth 20.00 50.00

2006-07 McDonald's Upper Deck Hardware Heroes

COMPLETE SET (10) 30.00 60.00
STATED ODDS 1:6
HH1 Joe Thornton 5.00 12.00
HH2 Alexander Ovechkin 6.00 15.00
HH3 Nicklas Lidstrom 3.00 8.00
HH4 Joe Thornton 5.00 12.00
HH5 Cam Ward 4.00 10.00
HH6 Miikka Kiprusoff 4.00 10.00
HH7 Jonathan Cheechoo 3.00 8.00
HH8 Eric Staal 4.00 10.00
HH9 Ryan Smyth 3.00 8.00
HH10 Rod Brind'Amour 3.00 8.00

2006-07 McDonald's Upper Deck Hot Gloves

COMPLETE SET (10) 30.00 80.00
STATED ODDS 1:20
HG1 Martin Brodeur 6.00 15.00
HG2 Dominik Hasek 6.00 15.00
HG3 Dwayne Roloson 4.00 10.00
HG4 Miikka Kiprusoff 6.00 15.00
HG5 Cristobal Huet 6.00 15.00
HG6 Jean-Sebastien Giguere 6.00 15.00
HG7 Roberto Luongo 4.00 10.00
HG8 Marty Turco 4.00 10.00
HG9 Marc-Andre Fleury 4.00 10.00
HG10 Henrik Lundqvist 4.00 10.00

2006-07 McDonald's Upper Deck Jerseys

STATED PRINT RUN 100 #'d SETS
JAH Ales Hemsky 75.00 150.00
JAO Alexander Ovechkin 150.00 250.00
JAT Alex Tanguay 75.00 150.00
JBS Brendan Shanahan 75.00 150.00
JCP Chris Pronger 50.00 125.00
JDH Dany Heatley 75.00 150.00
JDT Darcy Tucker 50.00 125.00
JES Eric Staal 75.00 150.00
JHZ Henrik Zetterberg 75.00 150.00
JIK Ilya Kovalchuk 100.00 200.00
JJG Jean-Sebastien Giguere 100.00 200.00
JJI Jarome Iginla 75.00 200.00
JJJ Jaromir Jagr 100.00 200.00
JJS Joe Sakic 125.00 250.00
JJT Joe Thornton 100.00 200.00
JMB Martin Brodeur 100.00 200.00
JMK Miikka Kiprusoff 100.00 200.00
JMN Markus Naslund 75.00 150.00
JMR Michael Ryder 50.00 125.00
JMS Mats Sundin 75.00 150.00
JMT Marty Turco 60.00 125.00
JPB Patrice Bergeron 60.00 125.00
JPF Peter Forsberg 75.00 150.00
JPK Paul Kariya 75.00 150.00
JRL Roberto Luongo 75.00 150.00
JRN Rick Nash 75.00 150.00
JSC Brad Richards 75.00 150.00
JSK Saku Koivu 75.00 150.00
JSP Jason Spezza 75.00 150.00
JVL Vincent Lecavalier 100.00 200.00

2006-07 McDonald's Upper Deck Patches

STATED PRINT RUN 10 #'d SETS
NOT PRICED DUE TO SCARCITY

2006-07 McDonald's Upper Deck Rookie Review

COMPLETE SET (15) 15.00 40.00
STATED ODDS 1:20
RR1 Kyle Wellwood 1.50 4.00
RR2 Alexander Ovechkin 6.00 15.00
RR3 Henrik Lundqvist 2.50 6.00
RR4 Dion Phaneuf 2.50 6.00
RR5 Alexander Steen 1.50 4.00
RR6 Thomas Vanek 2.00 5.00
RR7 Corey Perry 2.00 5.00
RR8 Andrej Meszaros 1.50 4.00
RR9 Jeff Carter 2.00 5.00
RR10 Patrick Eaves 1.50 4.00
RR11 Ryan Miller 2.00 5.00
RR12 Marek Svatos 1.50 4.00
RR13 Brad Boyes 1.50 4.00
RR14 Chris Higgins 2.00 5.00
RR15 Cam Ward 2.00 5.00

2007-08 McDonald's Upper Deck

COMPLETE SET (50) 10.00 25.00
1 Alexander Ovechkin 1.50 4.00
2 Markus Naslund .50 1.25
3 Roberto Luongo .75 2.00
4 Daniel Sedin .30 .75
5 Mats Sundin .50 1.25
6 Bryan McCabe .30 .75
7 Darcy Tucker .40 1.00
8 Vincent Lecavalier .50 1.25
9 Martin St. Louis .40 1.00
10 Doug Weight .30 .75
11 Joe Thornton .60 1.50
12 Jonathan Cheechoo .40 1.00
13 Marc-Andre Fleury .50 1.25
14 Jordan Staal .60 1.50
15 Evgeni Malkin 1.25 3.00
16 Shane Doan .30 .75
17 Simon Gagne .50 1.25
18 Dany Heatley .40 1.00
19 Ray Emery .40 1.00
20 Jason Spezza .50 1.25
21 Jaromir Jagr .75 2.00
22 Henrik Lundqvist .60 1.50
23 Rick DiPietro .40 1.00
24 Martin Brodeur 1.25 3.00
25 Alexander Radulov .50 1.25
26 Saku Koivu .40 1.00
27 Guillaume Latendresse .40 1.00
28 Cristobal Huet .40 1.00
29 Marian Gaborik .60 1.50
30 Anze Kopitar .50 1.25
31 Nathan Horton .30 .75
32 Ales Hemsky .30 .75
33 Dwayne Roloson .40 1.00
34 Rob Schremp .40 1.00
35 Nicklas Lidstrom .50 1.25
36 Henrik Zetterberg .50 1.25
37 Pavel Datsyuk .50 1.25
38 Marty Turco .50 1.25
39 Rick Nash .50 1.25
40 Joe Sakic 1.00 2.50
41 Martin Havlat .40 1.00
42 Eric Staal .50 1.25
43 Jarome Iginla .75 2.00
44 Miikka Kiprusoff .60 1.50
45 Dion Phaneuf .50 1.25
46 Thomas Vanek .40 1.00
47 Ryan Miller .50 1.25
48 Patrice Bergeron .50 1.25
49 Marian Hossa .50 1.25
50 Scott Niedermayer .30 .75

2007-08 McDonald's Upper Deck Autographs

STATED PRINT RUN 30 #'d SETS
MAAH Ales Hemsky 60.00 150.00
MAAR Andrew Raycroft 80.00 200.00
MAAS Alexander Steen 60.00 150.00
MAAT Alex Tanguay 80.00 200.00
MABM Brendan Morrison 60.00 150.00
MACH Chris Higgins 80.00 200.00
MACW Cam Ward 100.00 250.00
MADB Daniel Briere 100.00 250.00
MADH Dany Heatley 150.00 300.00
MADR Dwayne Roloson 80.00 200.00
MAEC Erik Cole 60.00 150.00
MAEM Evgeni Malkin 150.00 300.00
MAES Eric Staal 100.00 250.00
MAGL Guillaume Latendresse 80.00 200.00
MAHU Cristobal Huet 80.00 200.00
MAJC Jonathan Cheechoo 80.00 200.00
MAJI Jarome Iginla 150.00 400.00
MAJS Jarret Stoll 60.00 150.00
MAKL Kari Lehtonen 100.00 250.00
MAMF Marc-Andre Fleury 100.00 250.00
MAMR Michael Ryder 60.00 150.00
MAMT Marty Turco 100.00 250.00
MAPM Patrick Marleau 80.00 200.00
MAPS Paul Stastny 100.00 250.00
MARL Roberto Luongo 150.00 300.00
MARN Rick Nash 100.00 250.00
MASK Saku Koivu 80.00 200.00
MAST Jordan Staal 150.00 300.00
MATV Thomas Vanek 80.00 200.00
MAWR Wade Redden 60.00 150.00

2007-08 McDonald's Upper Deck In the Crease

COMPLETE SET (6) 10.00 25.00
STATED ODDS 1:15
ICDH Dominik Hasek 2.50 6.00
ICMB Martin Brodeur 5.00 12.00
ICMF Marc-Andre Fleury 2.00 5.00
ICMK Miikka Kiprusoff 2.50 6.00
ICRL Roberto Luongo 3.00 8.00
ICRM Ryan Miller 2.00 5.00

2007-08 McDonald's Upper Deck Jerseys

STATED PRINT RUN 100 SER.#'d SETS
MJAH Ales Hemsky 40.00 100.00
MJAO Alexander Ovechkin 125.00
MJAR Andrew Raycroft 50.00 120.00
MJAT Alex Tanguay 50.00 120.00
MJBS Brendan Shanahan 60.00 150.00
MJCH Cristobal Huet 50.00 120.00
MJDH Dany Heatley 100.00
MJDR Dwayne Roloson 50.00 120.00
MJEM Evgeni Malkin 100.00 200.00
MJES Eric Staal 60.00 150.00
MJIK Ilya Kovalchuk 100.00
MJJC Jonathan Cheechoo 50.00 120.00
MJJI Jarome Iginla 100.00 250.00
MJJS Joe Sakic 100.00
MJJT Joe Thornton 100.00
MJMB Martin Brodeur 100.00
MJMK Miikka Kiprusoff 100.00
MJMN Markus Naslund 60.00 150.00
MJMR Michael Ryder 40.00 100.00
MJMS Martin St. Louis 50.00 120.00
MJMT Marty Turco 60.00 150.00
MJPB Patrice Bergeron 60.00 150.00
MJPK Paul Kariya 60.00 150.00
MJRL Roberto Luongo 100.00
MJRN Rick Nash 60.00 150.00
MJSG Simon Gagne 60.00 150.00
MJSK Saku Koivu 50.00 120.00
MJSP Jason Spezza 60.00 150.00
MJSU Mats Sundin 60.00 150.00
MJVL Vincent Lecavalier 60.00 150.00

2007-08 McDonald's Upper Deck Pride of Canada

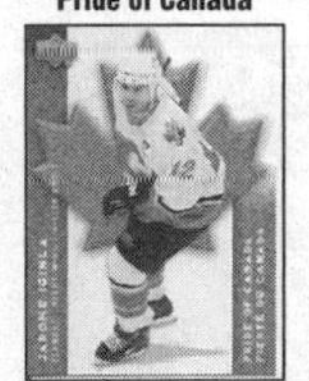

COMPLETE SET (6) 8.00 20.00
STATED ODDS 1:15
PC1 Joe Sakic 3.00 8.00
PC2 Rick Nash 1.50 4.00
PC3 Joe Thornton 2.00 5.00
PC4 Vincent Lecavalier 1.50 4.00
PC5 Eric Staal 1.50 4.00
PC6 Jarome Iginla 2.50 6.00

2007-08 McDonald's Upper Deck Season in Review

COMPLETE SET (6) 10.00 25.00
STATED ODDS 1:15
SR1 Evgeni Malkin 4.00 10.00
SR2 Mats Sundin 1.50 4.00
SR3 Mike Modano 1.50 4.00
SR4 Martin Brodeur 4.00 10.00
SR5 Roberto Luongo 2.50 6.00
SR6 Joe Sakic 3.00 8.00

2007-08 McDonald's Upper Deck Superstar Spotlight

COMPLETE SET (10) 15.00 40.00
STATED ODDS 1:15
SS1 Ray Emery 1.25 3.00
SS2 Joe Sakic 3.00 8.00
SS3 Alexander Ovechkin 5.00 12.00
SS4 Dany Heatley 2.00 5.00
SS5 Martin St. Louis 1.25 3.00
SS6 Jaromir Jagr 2.50 6.00
SS7 Jarome Iginla 2.50 6.00
SS8 Joe Thornton 2.00 5.00
SS9 Vincent Lecavalier 1.50 4.00
SS10 Teemu Selanne 1.50 4.00

2007-08 McDonald's Upper Deck Three Stars Checklists

COMPLETE SET (6) 1.00 2.50
ONE PER PACK
CL1 Saku Koivu .15 .40
Michael Ryder
Cristobal Huet
CL2 Mats Sundin .20 .50
Darcy Tucker
Bryan McCabe
CL3 Jason Spezza .25 .60
Dany Heatley
Ray Emery
CL4 Shawn Horcoff .15 .40
Dwayne Roloson
Ales Hemsky
CL5 Jarome Iginla .30 .75
Miikka Kiprusoff
Dion Phaneuf
CL6 Markus Naslund .30 .75
Roberto Luongo
Daniel Sedin

2008-09 McDonald's Upper Deck

COMPLETE SET (50) 8.00 20.00
1 Ryan Getzlaf .60 1.50
2 Teemu Selanne .50 1.25
3 Ilya Kovalchuk .60 1.50
4 Patrice Bergeron .50 1.25
5 Ryan Miller .50 1.25
6 Jarome Iginla 1.00 2.50
7 Miikka Kiprusoff .50 1.25
8 Dion Phaneuf .50 1.25
9 Eric Staal .75 2.00
10 Patrick Kane 1.25 3.00
11 Jonathan Toews 1.50 4.00
12 Paul Stastny .50 1.25
13 Peter Forsberg .75 2.00
14 Joe Sakic .75 2.00
15 Rick Nash .50 1.25
16 Marty Turco .40 1.00
17 Mike Modano .50 1.25
18 Henrik Zetterberg 1.00 2.50
19 Chris Osgood .50 1.25
20 Nicklas Lidstrom .50 1.25
21 Sam Gagner .75 2.00
22 Ales Hemsky .30 .75
23 Andrew Cogliano .75 2.00
24 Anze Kopitar .50 1.25
25 Marian Gaborik .75 2.00
26 Carey Price 1.50 4.00
27 Saku Koivu .50 1.25
28 Alex Kovalev .50 1.25
29 Martin Brodeur 1.00 2.50
30 Rick DiPietro .50 1.25
31 Marc Staal .60 1.50
32 Henrik Lundqvist 1.00 2.50
33 Dany Heatley .60 1.50
34 Daniel Alfredsson .40 1.00
35 Jason Spezza .60 1.50
36 Simon Gagne .40 1.00
37 Shane Doan .30 .75
38 Jordan Staal .75 2.00
39 Evgeni Malkin 1.25 3.00
40 Marc-Andre Fleury .50 1.25
41 Joe Thornton .75 2.00
42 Paul Kariya .50 1.25
43 Vincent Lecavalier .50 1.25
44 Martin St. Louis .50 1.25
45 Mats Sundin .50 1.25
46 Vesa Toskala .50 1.25
47 Tomas Kaberle .30 .75
48 Roberto Luongo .75 2.00
49 Markus Naslund .50 1.25
50 Alexander Ovechkin 2.00 5.00

2008-09 McDonald's Upper Deck Gold

*GOLD: 10X TO 25X BASE

2008-09 McDonald's Upper Deck Autographs

STATED PRINT RUN 25 SERIAL #'d SETS
AAC Andrew Cogliano 175.00 300.00
AAH Ales Hemsky
AAK Anze Kopitar 175.00 300.00
AAO Alexander Ovechkin
ACP Carey Price
ADH Dany Heatley
AEJ Erik Johnson
AEM Evgeni Malkin
AES Eric Staal
AHZ Henrik Zetterberg 250.00 400.00
AIK Ilya Kovalchuk
AJI Jarome Iginla
AJJ Jack Johnson
AJT Jonathan Toews 200.00 350.00
AKP Phil Kessel 75.00 150.00
AMG Marian Gaborik
AMM Mike Modano
AMS Martin St. Louis 175.00 300.00
AMT Marty Turco
ANF Nick Foligno
ANL Nicklas Lidstrom
APK Patrick Kane
APM Peter Mueller
APS Paul Stastny 175.00 300.00
ARG Ryan Getzlaf
ARM Ryan Miller
ASG Sam Gagner 100.00 200.00
ASK Saku Koivu 200.00 350.00
ATH Joe Thornton
ATK Tomas Kaberle

2008-09 McDonald's Upper Deck Canadian Goalie Checklist

COMPLETE SET (6) 5.00 12.00
CLCGY Miikka Kiprusoff 1.00 2.50
CLEDM Mathieu Garon 1.00 2.50
CLMTL Carey Price 3.00 8.00
CLOTT Martin Gerber .75 2.00
CLTOR Vesa Toskala 1.00 2.50
CLVAN Roberto Luongo 1.50 4.00

2008-09 McDonald's Upper Deck Clear Path to Greatness

COMPLETE SET (14) 250.00 500.00
CP1 Joe Sakic 20.00 50.00
CP2 Alexander Ovechkin 50.00 120.00
CP3 Vincent Lecavalier 12.00 30.00
CP4 Dany Heatley 15.00 40.00
CP5 Ilya Kovalchuk 15.00 40.00
CP6 Joe Thornton 20.00 50.00
CP7 Jaromir Jagr 15.00 40.00
CP8 Martin Brodeur 25.00 60.00
CP9 Henrik Zetterberg 25.00 60.00
CP10 Markus Naslund 12.00 30.00
CP11 Mats Sundin 12.00 30.00
CP12 Jarome Iginla 25.00 60.00
CP13 Mike Modano 12.00 30.00
CP14 Evgeni Malkin 30.00 80.00

2008-09 McDonald's Upper Deck Jerseys

STATED PRINT RUN 100 SERIAL #'d SETS
JAO Alexander Ovechkin 150.00 250.00
JBS Brendan Shanahan 60.00 150.00
JDA Daniel Alfredsson 50.00 120.00
JDH Dany Heatley
JDS Daniel Sedin 60.00 150.00
JEM Evgeni Malkin
JES Eric Staal 100.00 250.00
JGA Simon Gagne 50.00 120.00
JHZ Henrik Zetterberg 125.00
JIK Ilya Kovalchuk
JJI Jarome Iginla 100.00 200.00
JJJ Jaromir Jagr 100.00 200.00
JJS Joe Sakic 125.00
JJT Joe Thornton 100.00
JKA Patrick Kane 100.00 200.00
JMB Martin Brodeur 150.00 250.00
JMG Marian Gaborik 125.00
JMK Miikka Kiprusoff 60.00 150.00
JMM Mike Modano 60.00 150.00
JMS Mats Sundin 60.00 150.00
JNL Nicklas Lidstrom 60.00 150.00
JPF Peter Forsberg
JPK Paul Kariya 60.00 150.00
JRG Ryan Getzlaf 80.00 200.00
JRL Roberto Luongo 100.00 200.00
JRM Ryan Miller
JRN Rick Nash 60.00 150.00
JSG Sam Gagner 125.00
JSK Saku Koivu 60.00 150.00
JVL Vincent Lecavalier

2008-09 McDonald's Upper Deck Patches

STATED PRINT RUN 5 SERIAL #'d SETS
NOT PRICED DUE TO SCARCITY

2008-09 McDonald's Upper Deck Profiles

COMPLETE SET (10) 20.00 50.00
PRO1 Roberto Luongo 5.00 12.00
PRO2 Mats Sundin 3.00 8.00
PRO3 Jarome Iginla 6.00 15.00
PRO4 Dany Heatley 4.00 10.00
PRO5 Saku Koivu 3.00 8.00
PRO6 Vincent Lecavalier 3.00 8.00
PRO7 Martin Brodeur 6.00 15.00
PRO8 Alexander Ovechkin 12.00 30.00
PRO9 Nicklas Lidstrom 3.00 8.00
PRO10 Joe Thornton 5.00 12.00

2008-09 McDonald's Upper Deck Speed Skaters

COMPLETE SET (10) 30.00 60.00
SS1 Martin St. Louis 4.00 10.00
SS2 Paul Kariya 4.00 10.00
SS3 Teemu Selanne 4.00 10.00
SS4 Marian Hossa 6.00 15.00
SS5 Jaromir Jagr 5.00 12.00
SS6 Marian Gaborik 6.00 15.00
SS7 Simon Gagne 3.00 8.00
SS8 Ilya Kovalchuk 5.00 12.00
SS9 Alexander Ovechkin 15.00 40.00
SS10 Scott Niedermayer 2.50 6.00

2008-09 McDonald's Upper Deck Superstar Spotlight

COMPLETE SET (14) 20.00 50.00
IS1 Carey Price 6.00 15.00
IS2 Vincent Lecavalier 2.00 5.00
IS3 Jonathan Toews 6.00 15.00
IS4 Vesa Toskala 2.00 5.00
IS5 Miikka Kiprusoff 2.00 5.00
IS6 Joe Thornton 3.00 8.00
IS7 Pavel Datsyuk 2.00 5.00
IS8 Evgeni Malkin 5.00 12.00
IS9 Roberto Luongo 3.00 8.00

IS10 Jarome Iginla 4.00 10.00
IS11 Daniel Alfredsson 1.50 4.00
IS12 Jaromir Jagr 2.50 6.00
IS13 Alexander Ovechkin 8.00 20.00
IS14 Martin Brodeur 4.00 10.00

2009-10 McDonald's Upper Deck

COMPLETE SET (50) 8.00 20.00
1 Ryan Getzlaf .75 2.00
2 Ilya Kovalchuk .60 1.50
3 Tim Thomas .50 1.25
4 Marc Savard .30 .75
5 Thomas Vanek .50 1.25
6 Ryan Miller .50 1.25
7 Jarome Iginla 1.00 2.50
8 Miikka Kiprusoff .50 1.25
9 Dion Phaneuf .75 2.00
10 Eric Staal .60 1.50
11 Jonathan Toews 1.25 3.00
12 Patrick Kane 1.00 2.50
13 Paul Stastny .50 1.25
14 Rick Nash .50 1.25
15 Steve Mason .75 2.00
16 Marty Turco .40 1.00
17 Henrik Zetterberg 1.00 2.50
18 Pavel Datsyuk .50 1.25
19 Andrew Cogliano .60 1.50
20 Sheldon Souray .30 .75
21 Ales Hemsky .40 1.00
22 Drew Doughty 1.00 2.50
23 Niklas Backstrom .50 1.25
24 Carey Price 1.25 3.00
25 Andrei Markov .40 1.00
26 Saku Koivu .50 1.25
27 Shea Weber .40 1.00
28 Martin Brodeur 1.25 3.00
29 Zach Parise .50 1.25
30 Rick DiPietro .50 1.25
31 Henrik Lundqvist 1.00 2.50
32 Dany Heatley 1.00 2.50
33 Jason Spezza .60 1.50
34 Daniel Alfredsson .50 1.25
35 Jeff Carter .50 1.25
36 Mike Richards 1.00 2.50
37 Shane Doan .40 1.00
38 Evgeni Malkin 1.25 3.00
39 Marc-Andre Fleury .50 1.25
40 Joe Thornton 1.00 2.50
41 Patrick Marleau .50 1.25
42 Paul Kariya .50 1.25
43 Steven Stamkos 1.25 3.00
44 Vincent Lecavalier .60 1.50
45 Matt Stajan .40 1.00
46 Luke Schenn .75 2.00
47 Ryan Kesler .40 1.00
48 Roberto Luongo 1.25 3.00
49 Alexander Ovechkin 2.00 5.00
50 Mike Green 1.00 2.50

2009-10 McDonald's Upper Deck Checklists

COMPLETE SET (6) 2.50 6.00
STATED ODDS 1:4
CL1 Patrick Roy 1.25 3.00
CL2 Jarome Iginla .75 2.00
CL3 Roberto Luongo 1.00 2.50
CL4 Grant Fuhr .50 1.25
CL5 Jason Spezza .50 1.25
CL6 Doug Gilmour .40 1.00

2009-10 McDonald's Upper Deck Goaltending Greats

COMPLETE SET (6) 8.00 20.00
STATED ODDS 1:10
GG1 Carey Price 2.50 6.00
GG2 Roberto Luongo 2.50 6.00
GG3 Miikka Kiprusoff 1.00 2.50
GG4 Steve Mason 1.50 4.00
GG5 Marc-Andre Fleury 1.00 2.50
GG6 Martin Brodeur 2.50 6.00

2009-10 McDonald's Upper Deck Horizons

COMPLETE SET (14) 40.00 80.00
STATED ODDS 1:20
H1 Tim Thomas 2.00 5.00
H2 Jarome Iginla 4.00 10.00
H3 Jonathan Toews 5.00 12.00
H4 Henrik Zetterberg 4.00 10.00
H5 Andrew Cogliano 2.50 6.00
H6 Carey Price 5.00 12.00
H7 Henrik Lundqvist 4.00 10.00
H8 Dany Heatley 4.00 10.00
H9 Luke Schenn 3.00 8.00
H10 Roberto Luongo 5.00 12.00
H11 Drew Doughty 4.00 10.00
H12 Marty Turco 1.50 4.00
H13 Evgeni Malkin 5.00 12.00
H14 Alexander Ovechkin 8.00 20.00

2009-10 McDonald's Upper Deck In the Spotlight

COMPLETE SET (10) 175.00 350.00
STATED ODDS 1:60
IS1 Alexander Ovechkin 30.00 80.00
IS2 Evgeni Malkin 20.00 50.00
IS3 Joe Thornton 15.00 40.00
IS4 Jarome Iginla 15.00 40.00
IS5 Ilya Kovalchuk 10.00 25.00
IS6 Carey Price 20.00 50.00
IS7 Martin Brodeur 20.00 50.00
IS8 Steven Stamkos 20.00 50.00
IS9 Jonathan Toews 20.00 50.00
IS10 Vincent Lecavalier 10.00 25.00

2009-10 McDonald's Upper Deck Pride of Canada

COMPLETE SET (14) 75.00 150.00
STATED ODDS 1:40
PC1 Dany Heatley 12.00 30.00
PC2 Vincent Lecavalier 8.00 20.00
PC3 Jarome Iginla 12.00 30.00
PC4 Rick Nash 6.00 15.00
PC5 Mike Richards 12.00 30.00
PC6 Joe Thornton 12.00 30.00
PC7 Ryan Getzlaf 10.00 25.00
PC8 Mike Green 12.00 30.00
PC9 Jeff Carter 6.00 15.00
PC10 Jonathan Toews 15.00 40.00
PC11 Dion Phaneuf 10.00 25.00
PC12 Chris Pronger 5.00 12.00
PC13 Martin Brodeur 15.00 40.00
PC14 Roberto Luongo 15.00 40.00

1906 McGill Men at Hockey Postcard

Standard sized postcard featured a photo of unknown men playing ice hockey. Back featured U.P.S. Montreal Series No 402.

NNO McGill Men at Hockey Montreal 60.00 120.00

1995-96 Metal

The 1995-96 Fleer Metal set was issued in one series totaling 200 cards. The 8-card packs had a suggested retail of $2.49 each. The hand-engraved etched cards each featured a colorful action photo with the player cutting through a unique metallic foil background. The cards were grouped alphabetically within teams. The Joe Sakic SkyMint Exchange card was randomly inserted 1:360 packs. When exchanged collectors received a unique card with a dime-sized coin featuring the Avalanche star embedded in the corner. The exchange offer expired January 1, 1997. Rookie Cards in this set included Daniel Alfredsson, Radek Dvorak, Chad Kilger, Daymond Langkow, and Kyle McLaren.

COMPLETE SET (200) 12.00 30.00
1 Guy Hebert .10 .30
2 Paul Kariya .20 .50
3 Todd Krygier .05 .15
4 Steve Rucchin .10 .30
5 Oleg Tverdovsky .05 .15
6 Ray Bourque .30 .75
7 Blaine Lacher .05 .15
8 Shawn McEachern .05 .15
9 Cam Neely .20 .50
10 Adam Oates .10 .30
11 Kevin Stevens .05 .15
12 Donald Audette .05 .15
13 Randy Burridge .05 .15
14 Jason Dawe .05 .15
15 Dominik Hasek .40 1.00
16 Pat LaFontaine .20 .50
17 Alexei Zhitnik .05 .15
18 Theo Fleury .05 .15
19 Phil Housley .10 .30
20 Trevor Kidd .10 .30
21 Joe Nieuwendyk .10 .30
22 Michael Nylander .05 .15
23 Ed Belfour .20 .50
24 Chris Chelios .20 .50
25 Joe Murphy .05 .15
26 Bernie Nicholls .05 .15
27 Patrick Poulin .05 .15
28 Jeremy Roenick .25 .60
29 Gary Suter .05 .15
30 Adam Deadmarsh .05 .15
31 Stephane Fiset .10 .30
32 Peter Forsberg .50 1.25
33 Valeri Kamensky .10 .30
34 Claude Lemieux .05 .15
35 Sandis Ozolinsh .05 .15
36 Joe Sakic .40 1.00
37 Greg Adams .05 .15
38 Dave Gagner .05 .15
39 Todd Harvey .10 .30
40 Derian Hatcher .05 .15
41 Kevin Hatcher .05 .15
42 Mike Modano .30 .75
43 Andy Moog .20 .50
44 Paul Coffey .20 .50
45 Sergei Fedorov .30 .75
46 Vladimir Konstantinov .10 .30
47 Slava Kozlov .10 .30
48 Nicklas Lidstrom .20 .50
49 Chris Osgood .10 .30
50 Keith Primeau .05 .15
51 Steve Yzerman .75 2.00
52 Jason Arnott .05 .15
53 Zdeno Ciger .05 .15
54 Todd Marchant .05 .15
55 David Oliver .05 .15
56 Bill Ranford .10 .30
57 Doug Weight .10 .30
58 Stu Barnes .05 .15
59 Jody Hull .05 .15
60 Scott Mellanby .05 .15
61 Rob Niedermayer .10 .30
62 John Vanbiesbrouck .10 .30
63 Sean Burke .10 .30
64 Andrew Cassels .05 .15
65 Nelson Emerson .05 .15
66 Geoff Sanderson .10 .30
67 Brendan Shanahan .20 .50
68 Glen Wesley .05 .15
69 Rob Blake .10 .30
70 Tony Granato .05 .15
71 Wayne Gretzky 1.25 3.00
72 Dimitri Khristich .05 .15
73 Yanic Perreault .05 .15
74 Rick Tocchet .10 .30
75 Benoit Brunet .05 .15
76 Vincent Damphousse .05 .15
77 Mark Recchi .10 .30
78 Patrick Roy 1.00 2.50
79 Brian Savage .05 .15
80 Pierre Turgeon .10 .30
81 Martin Brodeur .50 1.25
82 Neal Broten .10 .30
83 John MacLean .10 .30
84 Scott Niedermayer .05 .15
85 Scott Stevens .10 .30
86 Stephane Richer .10 .30
87 Esa Tikkanen .05 .15
88 Steve Thomas .10 .30
89 Wendel Clark .10 .30
90 Travis Green .10 .30
91 Kirk Muller .05 .15
92 Zigmund Palffy .10 .30
93 Mathieu Schneider .05 .15
94 Ray Ferraro .05 .15
95 Alexei Kovalev .05 .15
96 Brian Leetch .10 .30
97 Mark Messier .20 .50
98 Mike Richter .20 .50
99 Luc Robitaille .10 .30
100 Ulf Samuelsson .05 .15
101 Pat Verbeek .05 .15
102 Radek Bonk .05 .15
103 Don Beaupre .05 .15
104 Alexandre Daigle .05 .15
105 Steve Duchesne .05 .15
106 Dan Quinn .05 .15
107 Martin Straka .05 .15
108 Rod Brind'Amour .10 .30
109 Eric Desjardins .10 .30
110 Ron Hextall .10 .30
111 John LeClair .20 .50
112 Eric Lindros .20 .50
113 Mikael Renberg .10 .30
114 Chris Therien .05 .15
115 Tom Barrasso .10 .30
116 Ron Francis .10 .30
117 Jaromir Jagr .30 .75
118 Mario Lemieux 1.00 2.50
119 Tomas Sandstrom .05 .15
120 Bryan Smolinski .05 .15
121 Sergei Zubov .05 .15
122 Shayne Corson .05 .15
123 Grant Fuhr .20 .50
124 Dale Hawerchuk .20 .50
125 Brett Hull .25 .60
126 Al MacInnis .10 .30
127 Chris Pronger .20 .50
128 Ulf Dahlen .05 .15
129 Jeff Friesen .05 .15
130 Arturs Irbe .10 .30
131 Craig Janney .05 .15
132 Andrei Nazarov .05 .15
133 Owen Nolan .10 .30
134 Ray Sheppard .05 .15
135 Brian Bradley .05 .15
136 Chris Gratton .05 .15
137 Roman Hamrlik .10 .30
138 Petr Klima .05 .15
139 Daren Puppa .10 .30
140 Alexander Selivanov .05 .15
141 Dave Andreychuk .10 .30
142 Mike Gartner .10 .30
143 Doug Gilmour .10 .30
144 Kenny Jonsson .05 .15
145 Larry Murphy .10 .30
146 Felix Potvin .20 .50
147 Mats Sundin .20 .50
148 Jeff Brown .05 .15
149 Pavel Bure .20 .50
150 Russ Courtnall .05 .15
151 Trevor Linden .10 .30
152 Kirk McLean .10 .30
153 Alexander Mogilny .10 .30
154 Roman Oksiuta .05 .15
155 Mike Ridley .05 .15
156 Peter Bondra .10 .30
157 Jim Carey .10 .30
158 Sylvain Cote .05 .15
159 Sergei Gonchar .05 .15
160 Keith Jones .10 .30
161 Joe Juneau .05 .15
162 Nikolai Khabibulin .10 .30
163 Igor Korolev .05 .15
164 Teppo Numminen .05 .15
165 Teemu Selanne .20 .50
166 Keith Tkachuk .20 .50
167 Darren Turcotte .05 .15
168 Alexei Zhamnov .10 .30
169 Daniel Alfredsson RC .60 1.50
170 Aki Berg RC .10 .30
171 Todd Bertuzzi RC .60 1.50
172 Jason Bonsignore .05 .15
173 Byron Dafoe .10 .30
174 Eric Daze .10 .30
175 Shane Doan RC .60 1.50
176 Radek Dvorak RC .30 .75
177 Brian Holzinger RC .10 .30
178 Ed Jovanovski .20 .50
179 Chad Kilger RC .10 .30
180 Saku Koivu .20 .50
181 Darren Langdon RC .05 .15
182 Daymond Langkow RC .30 .75
183 Jere Lehtinen .10 .30
184 Kyle McLaren RC .10 .30
185 Marty Murray .05 .15
186 Jeff O'Neill .10 .30
187 Richard Park .05 .15
188 Deron Quint .05 .15
189 Marcus Ragnarsson RC .10 .30
190 Miroslav Satan RC .40 1.00
191 Tommy Salo RC .40 1.00
192 Jamie Storr .10 .30
193 Niklas Sundstrom .05 .15
194 Robert Svehla RC .05 .15
195 Denis Pederson .05 .15
196 Antti Tormanen RC .05 .15
197 Brendan Witt .05 .15
198 Vitali Yachmenev .05 .15
199 Checklist (1 114) .05 .15
200 Checklist (115-200/inserts) .05 .15
UER Bure is Number 1 in International Steel, not Berg
NNO Joe Sakic Coin/Card 8.00 20.00
NNO Joe Sakic EXCH .75 2.00

1995-96 Metal Heavy Metal

Randomly inserted in packs at a rate of 1:30 packs, this 12-card set highlighted some of the league's top players. The fronts featured an isolated player photo over a dynamic starburst metallic background. The backs included another photo, and the card number out of 12.

COMPLETE SET (12) 30.00 60.00
1 Pavel Bure 1.25 3.00
2 Sergei Fedorov 1.25 3.00
3 Theo Fleury .60 1.50
4 Wayne Gretzky 8.00 20.00
5 Brett Hull 1.25 3.00
6 Jaromir Jagr 2.00 5.00
7 Paul Kariya 1.25 3.00
8 Brian Leetch .60 1.50
9 Mario Lemieux 6.00 15.00
10 Mike Modano 2.00 5.00
11 Adam Oates .60 1.50
12 Joe Sakic 3.00 8.00

1995-96 Metal International Steel

Randomly inserted in packs at a rate of 1:3 packs, this 24-card set featured the top skaters from around the globe. The checklist card for this set found in the regular Fleer Metal series suggested that card number one is Aki-Petteri Berg. This was incorrect as this card did not exist. The remaining cards existed as checklisted, save for their number being one less than listed.

COMPLETE SET (24) 15.00 30.00
1 Pavel Bure .60 1.50
2 Chris Chelios .40 1.00
3 Sergei Fedorov .75 2.00
4 Peter Forsberg 1.25 3.00
5 Wayne Gretzky 2.50 6.00
6 Roman Hamrlik .20 .50
7 Dominik Hasek 1.25 3.00
8 Brett Hull .75 2.00
9 Jaromir Jagr 1.00 2.50
10 Saku Koivu .60 1.50
11 Pat LaFontaine .40 1.00
12 Brian Leetch .40 1.00
13 Jere Lehtinen .40 1.00
14 Mario Lemieux 2.00 5.00
15 Alexander Mogilny .40 1.00
16 Mikael Renberg .20 .50
17 Jeremy Roenick .60 1.50
18 Joe Sakic 1.25 3.00
19 Teemu Selanne .60 1.50
20 Mats Sundin .60 1.50
21 Niklas Sundstrom .20 .50
22 Vitali Yachmenev .20 .50
23 Alexei Zhamnov .20 .50
24 Sergei Zubov .20 .50

1995-96 Metal Iron Warriors

Randomly inserted in packs at a rate of 1:12 packs, this 15-card set had a razor-sharp design and featured the NHL's toughest competitors.

COMPLETE SET (15) 20.00 40.00
1 Jason Arnott .60 1.50
2 Ed Belfour 1.25 3.00
3 Theo Fleury .60 1.50
4 Ron Francis .75 2.00
5 John LeClair .75 2.00
6 Claude Lemieux .60 1.50
7 Eric Lindros 2.00 5.00
8 Mark Messier 2.00 5.00
9 Cam Neely 2.00 5.00
10 Keith Primeau .60 1.50
11 Kevin Stevens .60 1.50
12 Scott Stevens .60 1.50
13 Brendan Shanahan 2.00 5.00
14 Keith Tkachuk 1.25 3.00
15 Rick Tocchet .75 2.00

1995-96 Metal Promo Panel

Measuring 7" by 7", this promo panel was issued to preview the 1995-96 Fleer Metal series. Its left side consisted of a 2" by 7" strip with ad copy; to the right were four standard-size perforated cards. The fronts displayed color action cutouts on a silver metallic background. On a background consisting of a close-up photo and a jagged ice design, the backs carried biography and a bar graph presenting statistics. The cards were numbered "SAMPLE X" in the upper left corner.

COMPLETE SHEET .75 2.00
1 Felix Potvin .40 1.00
2 Jeremy Roenick .30 .75
3 Theo Fleury .20 .50
4 Richard Park .08 .25

1995-96 Metal Winners

Randomly inserted in packs at a rate of 1:60 packs, this 9-card set emblazoned on a high-tech design, showed players who have won medals in international competitions such as the Olympics or World Championships.

COMPLETE SET (9) 8.00 20.00
1 Peter Forsberg 4.00 10.00
2 Saku Koivu 2.00 5.00
3 Alexei Kovalev .40 1.00
4 Eric Lindros 2.00 5.00
5 Alexander Mogilny .75 2.00
6 Tommy Salo .75 2.00
7 Brian Savage .40 1.00
8 Sergei Zubov .40 1.00
9 Alexei Zhamnov .40 1.00

1996-97 Metal Universe

Issued in eight-card packs with a SRP of $2.49, this single-series set consisted of 200 cards. The design is comprised of a cutout player photo placed atop a surrealistic, etched-metal background. Key rookies include Dainius Zubrus, Mike Grier, and Sergei Berezin.

COMPLETE SET (200) 20.00 40.00
1 Guy Hebert .08 .25
2 Paul Kariya .20 .50
3 Jari Kurri .08 .25
4 Roman Oksiuta .05 .15
5 Steve Rucchin .05 .15
6 Teemu Selanne .20 .50
7 Ray Bourque .30 .75
8 Kyle McLaren .05 .15
9 Adam Oates .08 .25
10 Bill Ranford .08 .25
11 Rick Tocchet .08 .25
12 Donald Audette .05 .15
13 Jason Dawe .05 .15
14 Dominik Hasek .40 1.00
15 Pat LaFontaine .20 .50
16 Derek Plante .05 .15
17 Wayne Primeau .05 .15
18 Theo Fleury .05 .15
19 Dave Gagner .08 .25
20 Trevor Kidd .08 .25
21 James Patrick .05 .15
22 Robert Reichel .05 .15
23 German Titov .05 .15
24 Tony Amonte .08 .25
25 Ed Belfour .20 .50
26 Chris Chelios .20 .50
27 Eric Daze .08 .25
28 Gary Suter .05 .15
29 Alexei Zhamnov .05 .15
30 Adam Deadmarsh .05 .15
31 Adam Foote .05 .15
32 Peter Forsberg .50 1.25
33 Valeri Kamensky .08 .25
34 Uwe Krupp .05 .15
35 Claude Lemieux .05 .15
36 Sandis Ozolinsh .05 .15
37 Patrick Roy 1.00 2.50
38 Joe Sakic .40 1.00
39 Derian Hatcher .05 .15
40 Mike Modano .30 .75
41 Andy Moog .08 .25
42 Joe Nieuwendyk .08 .25
43 Pat Verbeek .05 .15
44 Sergei Zubov .05 .15
45 Sergei Fedorov .30 .75
46 Vladimir Konstantinov .08 .25
47 Slava Kozlov .08 .25
48 Nicklas Lidstrom .20 .50
49 Chris Osgood .08 .25
50 Brendan Shanahan .20 .50
51 Steve Yzerman 1.00 2.50
52 Jason Arnott .05 .15
53 Curtis Joseph .20 .50
54 Andrei Kovalenko .05 .15
55 Miroslav Satan .05 .15
56 Doug Weight .08 .25
57 Radek Dvorak .05 .15
58 Per Gustafsson RC .05 .15
59 Ed Jovanovski .08 .25
60 Scott Mellanby .08 .25
61 Rob Niedermayer .08 .25
62 Ray Sheppard .08 .25
63 Robert Svehla .08 .25
64 John Vanbiesbrouck .08 .25
65 Jeff Brown .05 .15
66 Sean Burke .08 .25
67 Paul Coffey .20 .50
68 Nelson Emerson .05 .15
69 Jeff O'Neill .05 .15
70 Keith Primeau .05 .15
71 Geoff Sanderson .08 .25
72 Aki Berg .05 .15
73 Rob Blake .08 .25
74 Stephane Fiset .08 .25
75 Dimitri Khristich .05 .15
76 Petr Klima .05 .15
77 Ed Olczyk .05 .15
78 Vitali Yachmenev .05 .15
79 Vincent Damphousse .05 .15
80 Saku Koivu .20 .50
81 Mark Recchi .08 .25
82 Stephane Richer .08 .25
83 Jocelyn Thibault .20 .50
84 Pierre Turgeon .08 .25
85 Dave Andreychuk .08 .25
86 Martin Brodeur .50 1.25
87 Scott Niedermayer .05 .15
88 Scott Stevens .08 .25
89 Petr Sykora .05 .15
90 Steve Thomas .05 .15
91 Todd Bertuzzi .20 .50
92 Travis Green .08 .25
93 Kenny Jonsson .05 .15
94 Bryan McCabe .05 .15
95 Zigmund Palffy .08 .25
96 Wayne Gretzky 1.50 4.00
97 Alexei Kovalev .05 .15
98 Brian Leetch .20 .50
99 Mark Messier .20 .50
100 Mike Richter .20 .50
101 Luc Robitaille .08 .25
102 Niklas Sundstrom .05 .15
103 Daniel Alfredsson .08 .25
104 Radek Bonk .05 .15
105 Alexandre Daigle .05 .15
106 Steve Duchesne .05 .15
107 Damian Rhodes .08 .25
108 Alexei Yashin .05 .15
109 Rod Brind'Amour .08 .25
110 Eric Desjardins .08 .25
111 Dale Hawerchuk .08 .25
112 Ron Hextall .08 .25
113 John LeClair .20 .50
114 Eric Lindros .20 .50
115 Mikael Renberg .08 .25
116 Mike Gartner .08 .25
117 Craig Janney .08 .25
118 Nikolai Khabibulin .08 .25
119 Dave Manson .05 .15
120 Teppo Numminen .05 .15
121 Jeremy Roenick .25 .60
122 Keith Tkachuk .20 .50
123 Oleg Tverdovsky .08 .25
124 Tom Barrasso .08 .25
125 Ron Francis .08 .25
126 Kevin Hatcher .05 .15
127 Jaromir Jagr .30 .75
128 Mario Lemieux 1.00 2.50
129 Petr Nedved .08 .25
130 Shayne Corson .05 .15
131 Grant Fuhr .08 .25
132 Brett Hull .25 .60
133 Al MacInnis .08 .25
134 Joe Murphy .05 .15
135 Chris Pronger .08 .25
136 Kelly Hrudey .08 .25
137 Al Iafrate .05 .15
138 Bernie Nicholls .05 .15
139 Owen Nolan .08 .25
140 Marcus Ragnarsson .05 .15
141 Darren Turcotte .05 .15
142 Brian Bradley .05 .15
143 Dino Ciccarelli .08 .25
144 Chris Gratton .08 .25
145 Roman Hamrlik .08 .25
146 Daren Puppa .08 .25
147 Alexander Selivanov .05 .15
148 Wendel Clark .08 .25
149 Doug Gilmour .08 .25
150 Kirk Muller .05 .15
151 Larry Murphy .08 .25
152 Felix Potvin .20 .50
153 Mathieu Schneider .05 .15
154 Mats Sundin .20 .50
155 Pavel Bure .20 .50
156 Russ Courtnall .05 .15
157 Trevor Linden .08 .25
158 Kirk McLean .08 .25
159 Alexander Mogilny .08 .25
160 Esa Tikkanen .05 .15
161 Peter Bondra .08 .25
162 Jim Carey .20 .50
163 Sergei Gonchar .08 .25
164 Phil Housley .08 .25
165 Calle Johansson .05 .15
166 Joe Juneau .05 .15
167 Michal Pivonka .05 .15
168 Brendan Witt .05 .15
169 Nolan Baumgartner .05 .15
170 Bryan Berard .20 .50
171 Sergei Berezin RC .50 1.25
172 Curtis Brown .05 .15
173 Jan Caloun RC .05 .15
174 Andreas Dackell RC .05 .15
175 Hnat Domenichelli .05 .15
176 Christian Dube .05 .15
177 Anders Eriksson .05 .15
178 Peter Ferraro .05 .15
179 Eric Fichaud .08 .25
180 Daniel Goneau RC .05 .15
181 Mike Grier RC .50 1.25
182 Jarome Iginla .25 .60
183 Steve Kelly RC .05 .15
184 Jamie Langenbrunner .05 .15
185 Daymond Langkow .05 .15
186 Jay McKee RC .05 .15
187 Ethan Moreau RC .20 .50
188 Rem Murray RC .05 .15
189 Janne Niinimaa .20 .50
190 Wade Redden .05 .15
191 Rustan Salei RC .08 .25
192 Jamie Storr .08 .25
193 Darren Van Impe .05 .15
194 Roman Vopat .05 .15
195 David Wilkie .05 .15
196 Landon Wilson .05 .15
197 Richard Zednik RC .25 .60
198 Dainius Zubrus RC .40 1.00
199 Checklist (1-118) .05 .15
200 Checklist (119-200/inserts) .05 .15

1996-97 Metal Universe Armor Plate

Randomly inserted in packs at a rate of 1:72, this 12-card set was comprised of hockey's top netminders. Cutout player photos were placed over a bubbled metallic surface, with a short write-up and photo on the reverse. A Super Power parallel with enhanced holographic foil backgrounds was inserted one per 720 packs. There was no distinction other than the special holofoil treatment.

COMPLETE SET (12) 30.00 60.00
*SUPER POWER: 1.5X TO 4X BASIC INSERTS
1 Ed Belfour 3.00 8.00
2 Martin Brodeur 8.00 20.00
3 Jim Carey 2.00 5.00
4 Dominik Hasek 6.00 15.00
5 Ron Hextall 2.00 5.00
6 Chris Osgood 3.00 8.00
7 Felix Potvin 3.00 8.00
8 Daren Puppa 2.00 5.00
9 Damian Rhodes 2.00 5.00
10 Mike Richter 3.00 8.00
11 Patrick Roy 15.00 40.00
12 John Vanbiesbrouck 3.00 8.00

1996-97 Metal Universe Cool Steel

Randomly inserted in packs at a rate of 1:48, this 12-card set featured cutout player photos on a brushed metal background. Two photos graced the reverse, including an extreme face close-up, as well as a description of each player's strengths. A Super Power parallel with an enhanced holographic foil background was inserted one per 480 packs. There was no distinction between the two versions other than the special holofoil treatment.

COMPLETE SET (12) 20.00 40.00
*SUPER POWER: 1.5X TO 4X BASIC INSERTS
1 Chris Chelios 2.00 5.00
2 Peter Forsberg 5.00 12.00
3 Ron Francis 1.50 4.00
4 Dominik Hasek 4.00 10.00
5 Ed Jovanovski 1.50 4.00
6 Vladimir Konstantinov 1.50 4.00
7 Eric Lindros 2.00 5.00
8 Mark Messier 2.00 5.00
9 Patrick Roy 10.00 25.00
10 Brendan Shanahan 2.00 5.00
11 Keith Tkachuk 2.00 5.00
12 John Vanbiesbrouck 1.50 4.00

1996-97 Metal Universe Ice Carvings

This 12-card set was randomly inserted in retail packs at a rate of 1:24. An etched, blue-foil player image accompanied a cutout photo on the front, while the flip side added a close-up photo and interesting text on each player. A Super Power parallel with an enhanced holographic foil background was inserted one per 240 packs. There was no distinction between the two versions other than the special holofoil treatment.

COMPLETE SET (12) 30.00 60.00
*SUPER POWER: 1.5X TO 4X BASIC INSERTS
1 Martin Brodeur 5.00 12.00
2 Pavel Bure 4.00 10.00
3 Jim Carey 2.00 5.00
4 Paul Coffey 4.00 10.00
5 Sergei Fedorov 3.00 8.00
6 Jaromir Jagr 3.00 8.00
7 Paul Kariya 4.00 10.00
8 Pat LaFontaine 2.00 5.00
9 Brian Leetch 4.00 10.00
10 Mario Lemieux 10.00 25.00
11 Alexander Mogilny 2.00 5.00
12 Joe Sakic 4.00 10.00

1996-97 Metal Universe Lethal Weapons

The most common of the Metal inserts, this 20-card set was randomly inserted 1:12 packs and featured the top scorers in the NHL. Cutout player photos leaped off of bronze metallic backgrounds with a second photo on the card back as well as a description of each player's scoring prowess. Super Power parallels were inserted every 120 packs and differed only by an enhanced holographic foil background.

COMPLETE SET (20) 20.00 40.00
*SUPER POWER: 1.5X TO 4X BASIC INSERTS

1 Peter Bondra 1.00 2.50
2 Pavel Bure 1.50 4.00
3 Sergei Fedorov 1.50 4.00
4 Peter Forsberg 2.50 6.00
5 Ron Francis 1.50 4.00
6 Wayne Gretzky 6.00 15.00
7 Brett Hull 1.25 3.00
8 Jaromir Jagr 1.50 4.00
9 Paul Kariya 1.50 4.00
10 John LeClair 1.50 4.00
11 Mario Lemieux 5.00 12.00
12 Eric Lindros 1.50 4.00
13 Mark Messier 1.50 4.00
14 Alexander Mogilny 1.00 2.50
15 Adam Oates 1.00 2.50
16 Joe Sakic 2.00 5.00
17 Teemu Selanne 1.50 4.00
18 Brendan Shanahan 1.50 4.00
19 Keith Tkachuk 1.50 4.00
20 Doug Weight 1.50 4.00

1996 Metallic Ice Series

Produced by Cityscope Digital Imaging, this standard size card was given out at a Dallas Stars game in 1996. It was made of metal and weighed significantly more than a standard card. Card is serial numbered out of 1000.

NNO Mike Modano 4.00 10.00

1995-96 Metallic Impressions Team Metal Mario Lemieux

1 Mario Lemieux
2 Mario Lemieux
3 Mario Lemieux
4 Mario Lemieux
NNO Mario Lemieux Tin

1972-73 Minnesota Fighting Saints Postcards WHA

These borderless postcards featured action photos on the front, along with player name and biographical information. They were issued as promotional giveaways at autograph signings and to by-mail requesters.

COMPLETE SET (25) 35.00 70.00
1 Mike Antonovich 2.00 4.00
2 John Arbour 1.50 3.00
3 Terry Ball 1.50 3.00
4 Keith Christiansen 1.50 3.00
5 Wayne Connelly 2.50 5.00
6 Mike Curran 1.50 3.00
7 Craig Falkman 1.50 3.00
8 Ted Hampson 2.00 4.00
9 Jimmy Johnson 1.50 3.00
10 Bill Klatt 1.50 3.00
11 George Konik 1.50 3.00
12 Leonard Lilyholm 1.50 3.00
13 Bob MacMillan 1.50 3.00
14 Jack McCartan 2.50 5.00
15 Mike McMahon 1.50 3.00
16 George Morrison 1.50 3.00
17 Dick Paradise 1.50 3.00
18 Mel Pearson 1.50 3.00
19 Terry Ryan 1.50 3.00
20 Blaine Rydman 1.50 3.00
21 Frank Sanders 1.50 3.00
22 Glen Sonmor CO 1.50 3.00
23 Fred Speck 1.50 3.00
24 Bill Young 1.50 3.00
25 Carl Wetzel 1.50 3.00

1974-75 Minnesota Fighting Saints WHA

These cards set measure 3 1/2" x 5 1/2" and featured borderless color action photos on the front. Backs featured a head shot and statistics, along with the players position. The Saints logo could be found in black along the top of card back. Several cards are as yet unconfirmed.

1 Mike Antonovich 2.00 4.00
2 John Arbour 1.50 3.00
3 Terry Ball (unconfirmed)
4 Bob Boyd (unconfirmed)
5 Ron Busniuk 1.50 3.00
6 Wayne Connelly 2.00 4.00
7 Mike Curran 1.50 3.00
8 Gord Gallant 2.00 4.00
9 Gary Gambucci 1.50 3.00
10 John Garrett 5.00 10.00
11 Ted Hampson 2.00 4.00
12 Murray Heatley 1.50 3.00
13 Fran Huck 1.50 3.00
14 Jim Johnson 1.50 3.00
15 Jack McCartan (unconfirmed)
16 Mike McMahon 1.50 3.00
17 George Morrison (unconfirmed)
18 Harry Neale (unconfirmed)
19 Danny O'Shea (unconfirmed)
20 Rich Smith 1.50 3.00
21 Glen Sonmor (unconfirmed)
22 Don Tannahill (unconfirmed)
23 Mike Walton 2.50 5.00

1911 Murad College Series T51 *

Produced in 1910, these cards measured approximately 2 x 2 3/4 and featured full color fronts. Backs featured a list of colleges in the set along with 2nd Edition. Also noted was S.Anargyros New York.

NNO Swarthmore Field Hockey 20.00 40.00
NNO Rochester Ice Hockey 25.00 50.00

1974 Nabisco Sugar Daddy *

COMPLETE SET ()
11 Phil Esposito 4.00 10.00
12 Dennis Hull 2.00 5.00
13 Reg Fleming 2.00 5.00
14 Garry Unger 2.00 5.00
15 Derek Sanderson 4.00 10.00
16 Jerry Korab 2.00 5.00
22 Mickey Redmond 4.00 10.00

1975 Nabisco Sugar Daddy *

COMPLETE SET ()
11 Phil Esposito 4.00 10.00
12 Dennis Hull 2.00 5.00
13 Brad Park 2.00 5.00
14 Tom Lysiak 2.00 5.00
15 Bernie Parent 4.00 10.00
16 Mickey Redmond 4.00 10.00
22 Don Awrey 2.00 5.00

2004 National Trading Card Day

This 53-card set (49 basic cards plus four cover cards) was given out in five separate sealed packs (one from each of the following manufacturers: Donruss, Fleer, Press Pass, Topps and Upper Deck). One of the five packs was distributed at no cost to each patron that visited a participating sports card shop on April 3rd, 2004 as part of the National Trading Card Day promotion in an effort to increase awareness of collecting sports cards. The 50-card set is composed of 16 baseball, 9 basketball, 10 football, 4 golf, 5 hockey and 4 NASCAR cards. Of note, first year cards of NBA rookie stars LeBron James and Carmelo Anthony were included respectively within the UD and Fleer packs. An early Alex Rodriguez Yankees card was also highlighted within the Fleer pack.

F1-F9 ISSUED IN FLEER PACK
T1-T12 ISSUED IN TOPPS PACK
DP1-DP6 ISSUED IN DONRUSS PACK
PP1-PP7 ISSUED IN PRESS PASS PACK
UD1-UD15 ISSUED IN UPPER DECK PACK
T7 Rick Nash .20 .50
T8 Jean-Sebastian Giguere .30 .75
T12 Jaromir Jagr .40 1.00
UD10 Patrick Roy .40 1.00
UD15 Wayne Gretzky .50 1.25

1982-83 Neilson's Gretzky

This 50-card set was issued to honor one of hockey's all-time great players, Wayne Gretzky. The cards measured 2 1/2" by 3 1/2". The first nine cards featured vintage black and white photos from Gretzky's childhood up to age 17. The rest of the cards featured color action photos highlighting Gretzky's pro career. All the pictures on the cards are framed by white and orange borders on a dark blue background. The card number appeared in a star at the upper left hand corner of the card face. A facsimile autograph was inscribed across the bottom of each picture. The card backs had captions to the pictures and include a discussion of some aspect of the game. The card backs were bilingual, i.e., French and English. Many of these discussions were accompanied by illustrations. The cards were issued as inserts with Neilson's candy bars.

COMPLETE SET (50) 60.00 150.00
1 Discard Broken Stick 4.00 10.00
2 Handling the Puck 2.00 6.00
3 Offsides 2.00 5.00
4 Penalty Shot 2.00 5.00
5 Icing the Puck 2.00 5.00
6 Taping your Stick 2.00 5.00
7 Skates 2.00 5.00
8 The Helmet 2.00 5.00
9 Selecting Skates 2.00 5.00
10 Choosing a Stick (with Gordie Howe) 10.00 25.00
11 General Equipment Care 2.00 5.00
12 The Hook Check (with Marcel Dionne) 3.00 8.00
13 The Hip Check 2.00 5.00
14 Forward Skating (With Mike Gartner) 4.00 10.00
15 Stopping 2.00 5.00
16 Sharp Turning 2.00 5.00
17 Fast Starts 2.00 5.00
18 Backward Skating 2.00 5.00
19 The Grip 2.00 5.00
20 The Wrist Shot 2.00 5.00
21 The Back Hand Shot 2.00 5.00
22 The Slap Shot 2.00 5.00
23 The Flip Shot 2.00 5.00
24 Pass Receiving 2.00 5.00
25 Faking 2.00 5.00
26 Puck Handling 2.00 5.00
27 Deflecting Shots 2.00 5.00
28 One On One 2.00 5.00
29 Keep Your Head Up 2.00 5.00
30 Passing to the Slot 2.00 5.00
31 Winning Face-Offs (with Guy Lafleur and Mike Bossy) 5.00 12.00
32 Forechecking 2.00 5.00
33 Body Checking 2.00 5.00
34 Breaking Out 2.00 5.00
35 The Drop Pass 2.00 5.00
36 Backchecking (with Phil Esposito) 4.00 10.00
37 Using the Boards 2.00 5.00
38 The Power Play 3.00 8.00
39 Passing the Puck 2.00 5.00
40 Clear the Slot 2.00 5.00
41 Leg Lifts 2.00 5.00
42 Balance Exercise 2.00 5.00
43 Leg Stretches 2.00 5.00
44 Hip and Groin Stretch 2.00 5.00
45 Toe Touches (With Mark Messier) 4.00 10.00
46 Goalie Warm Up Drill 2.00 5.00
47 Leg Exercises 2.00 5.00
48 Arm Exercises 2.00 5.00
49 Wrist Exercises 2.00 5.00
50 Flip Pass 2.00 5.00

2002 Nextel NHL All-Star Game

Handed out exclusively at the Nextel booth at the All-Star Fantasy, this 4-card set featured three players per card of either the World or North American team. Collectors had to answer trivia questions to receive the cards. Each card was approximately 7 1/2" x 3 1/2". The cards were unnumbered.

COMPLETE SET (4) 4.00 10.00
1 Rob Blake Patrick Roy Chris Pronger 1.60 4.00
2 Brendan Shanahan Vincent Damphousse Owen Nolan .80 2.00
3 Jaromir Jagr Sergei Fedorov Teemu Selanne 1.20 3.00
4 Nicklas Lidstrom Dominik Hasek Sandis Ozolinsh .80 2.00

1974-75 NHL Action Stamps

This set of NHL Action Stamps was distributed throughout North America in large grocery chains such as Loblaw's, IGA, A and P, and Acme. Some of these small stickers (or stamps) mentioned the particular grocery store on back; others had blank backs. A strip of eight player stamps was given out with a grocery purchase. The stamps measured approximately 1 5/8" by 2 1/8". These unnumbered stamps were ordered below alphabetically by teams as follows, Atlanta Flames (1-18), Boston Bruins (19-36), Buffalo Sabres (37-54), California Golden Seals (55-72), Chicago Blackhawks (73-90), Detroit Red Wings (91-108), Kansas City Scouts (109-126), Los Angeles Kings (127-144), Minnesota North Stars (145-162), Montreal Canadiens (163-180), New York Islanders (181-198), New York Rangers (199-216), Philadelphia Flyers (217-234), Pittsburgh Penguins (235-252), St. Louis Blues (253-270), Toronto Maple Leafs (271-288), Vancouver Canucks (289-306), and Washington Capitals (307-324). An album was available for this set which included 20 stamps in the back. Some of the stamps (29, 57, 94, and 164) were only available in the album. Intact strips would be valued at 50 to 75 percent more than the sum of the respective player prices listed below.

COMPLETE SET (324) 100.00 200.00
1 Eric Vail .25 .50
2 Jerry Byers .18 .35
3 Rey Comeau .18 .35
4 Curt Bennett .18 .35
5 Bob Murray .18 .35
6 Dan Bouchard .50 1.00
7 Pat Quinn .50 1.00
8 Larry Romanchych .18 .35
9 Randy Manery .10 .35
10 Phil Myre .50 1.00
11 Buster Harvey .18 .35
12 Keith McCreary .18 .35
13 Jean Lemieux .18 .35
14 Arnie Brown .18 .35
15 Bob Leiter .18 .35
16 Jacques Richard .25 .50
17 Noel Price .18 .35
18 Tom Lysiak .38 .75
19 Bobby Orr 10.00 20.00
20 Al Sims .25 .50
21 Don Marcotte .18 .35
22 Terry O'Reilly .50 1.00
23 Carol Vadnais .18 .35
24 Gilles Gilbert .75 1.50
25 Bobby Schmautz .25 .50
26 Phil Esposito 2.50 5.00
27 Walt McKechnie .25 .50
28 Ken Hodge .38 .75
29 Dave Forbes .18 .35
30 Wayne Cashman .38 .75
31 Johnny Bucyk .75 1.50
32 Ross Brooks .25 .50
33 Dallas Smith .18 .35
34 Darryl Edestrand .18 .35
35 Gregg Sheppard .18 .35
36 Andre Savard .25 .50
37 Jim Schoenfeld .38 .75
38 Brian Spencer .38 .75
39 Rick Dudley .25 .50
40 Craig Ramsay .18 .35
41 Gary Bromley .38 .75
42 Lee Fogolin .18 .35
43 Jerry Korab .18 .35
44 Larry Mickey .18 .35
45 Roger Crozier .50 1.00
46 Larry Carriere .18 .35
47 Norm Gratton .18 .35
48 Jim Lorentz .18 .35
49 Rene Robert .38 .75
50 Gilbert Perreault (74/75 season on back) 2.00 4.00
51 Mike Robitaille .18 .35
52 Don Luce .18 .35
53 Richard Martin .38 .75
54 Gerry Meehan .25 .50
55 Bruce Affleck .18 .35
56 Wayne King .18 .35
57 Joseph Johnston .18 .35
58 Ron Huston .18 .35
59 Dave Hrechkosy .18 .35
60 Stan Gilbertson .18 .35
61 Mike Christie .18 .35
62 Larry Wright .18 .35
63 Stan Weir .18 .35
64 Larry Patey .18 .35
65 Al MacAdam .25 .50
66 Ted McAneeley .18 .35
67 Jim Neilson .18 .35
68 Rick Hampton .18 .35
69 Len Frig .18 .35
70 Gilles Meloche .38 .75
71 Robert Stewart .18 .35
72 Craig Patrick .38 .75
73 Dennis Hull .38 .75
74 Dale Tallon .25 .50
75 Bill White .25 .50
76 Jim Pappin .18 .35
77 Cliff Koroll .18 .35
78 Tony Esposito 2.50 5.00
79 Doug Jarrett .18 .35
80 John Marks .18 .35
81 Stan Mikita 2.00 4.00
82 Darcy Rota .18 .35
83 J.P. Bordeleau .18 .35
84 Ivan Boldirev .18 .35
85 Germaine Gagnon UER .18 .35
86 Dick Redmond .18 .35
87 Pit Martin .18 .35
88 Keith Magnuson .25 .50
89 Phil Russell .18 .35
90 Chico Maki .25 .50
91 Jean Hamel .18 .35
92 Nick Libett .25 .50
93 Hank Nowak .18 .35
94 Guy Charron .25 .50
95 Bryan Watson .18 .35
96 Nelson Pyatt .18 .35
97 Billy Lochead .18 .35
98 Danny Grant .25 .50
99 Bill Hogaboam .18 .35
100 Jim Rutherford .50 1.00
101 Doug Grant .18 .35
102 Pierre Jarry .18 .35
103 Doug Roberts .18 .35
104 Red Berenson .38 .75
105 Marcel Dionne 1.75 3.50
106 Mickey Redmond .75 1.50
107 Jack Lynch .18 .35
108 Thommie Bergman .18 .35
109 Mike Corrigan .18 .35
110 Frank St.Marseille .18 .35
111 Gene Carr .18 .35
112 Neil Komadoski .18 .35
113 Gary Edwards .38 .75
114 Sheldon Kannegiesser .18 .35
115 Bob Murdoch .18 .35
116 Rogatien Vachon 1.25 2.50
117 Dave Hutchinson .18 .35
118 Tom Williams .18 .35
119 Butch Goring .38 .75
120 Bob Berry .25 .50
121 Dan Maloney .25 .50
122 Mike Murphy .18 .35
123 Juha Widing .25 .50
124 Don Kozak .18 .35
125 Bob Nevin .18 .35
126 Terry Harper .25 .50
127 Bill Goldsworthy .38 .75
128 Dennis O'Brien .18 .35
129 Dennis Hextall .25 .50
130 Murray Oliver .18 .35
131 Lou Nanne .25 .50
132 Fred Stanfield .18 .35
133 Jean-Paul Parise .25 .50
134 Tom Reid .18 .35
135 Fred Barrett .18 .35
136 Gary Bergman .18 .35
137 Barry Gibbs .18 .35
138 Cesare Maniago .50 1.00
139 Jude Drouin .18 .35
140 Blake Dunlop .18 .35
141 Henry Boucha .25 .50
142 Fern Rivard .18 .35
143 Chris Ahrens .18 .35
144 Don Martineau .18 .35
145 Jacques Lemaire .75 1.50
146 Peter Mahovlich .38 .75
147 Yvon Lambert .18 .35
148 Yvan Cournoyer 1.25 2.50
149 Michel Larocque .38 .75
150 Guy Lapointe .50 1.00
151 Steve Shutt 1.50 3.00
152 Guy Lafleur 3.50 7.00
153 Larry Robinson 1.00 2.00
154 Jacques Laperriere .38 .75
155 Chuck Lefley .18 .35
156 Henri Richard 1.25 2.50
157 Claude Larose .18 .35
158 Ken Dryden 6.00 12.00
159 Pierre Bouchard .18 .35
160 Murray Wilson .18 .35
161 Jim Roberts .25 .50
162 Serge Savard .50 1.00
163 Clark Gillies 1.25 2.50
164 Garry Howatt .18 .35
165 Ernie Hicke .18 .35
166 Craig Cameron .18 .35
167 Ralph Stewart .18 .35
168 Lorne Henning .18 .35
169 Glenn Resch .50 1.00
170 Bill MacMillan .18 .35
171 Doug Rombough .18 .35
172 Jean Potvin .18 .35
173 Gerry Hart .18 .35
174 Bert Marshall .18 .35
175 Billy Harris .18 .35
176 Bob Nystrom .38 .75
177 Dave Lewis .18 .35
178 Billy Smith 1.00 2.00
179 Denis Potvin 4.00 8.00
180 Ed Westfall .25 .50
181 Jerry Butler .18 .35
182 Bobby Rousseau .25 .50
183 Ron Harris .18 .35
184 Bill Fairbairn .18 .35
185 Derek Sanderson 1.50 3.00
186 Jean Ratelle 1.00 2.00
187 Greg Polis .18 .35
188 Rod Gilbert 1.00 2.00
189 Ed Giacomin 1.00 2.00
190 Rod Seiling .18 .35
191 Dale Rolfe .18 .35
192 Walt Tkaczuk .25 .50
193 Pete Stemkowski .25 .50
194 Gilles Villemure .38 .75
195 Ted Irvine .18 .35
196 Brad Park 1.00 2.00
197 Gilles Marotte .25 .50
198 Steve Vickers .25 .50
199 Ross Lonsberry .18 .35
200 Bob Kelly .25 .50
201 Reggie Leach .38 .75
202 Bernie Parent 1.75 3.50
203 Terry Crisp .38 .75
204 Bill Clement .50 1.00
205 Bill Barber .50 1.00
206 Dave Schultz .50 1.00
207 Ed Van Impe .18 .35
208 Jimmy Watson .25 .50
209 Tom Bladon .18 .35
210 Rick MacLeish .38 .75
211 Andre Dupont .25 .50
212 Orest Kindrachuk .25 .50
213 Gary Dornhoefer .38 .75
214 Joe Watson .25 .50
215 Don Saleski .18 .35
216 Bobby Clarke 3.00 6.00
217 Jean Pronovost .38 .75
218 Ab DeMarco .18 .35
219 Wayne Bianchin .18 .35
220 Dave Burrows .18 .35
221 Ron Lalonde .18 .35
222 Syl Apps .38 .75
223 Bob Kelly .18 .35
224 Chuck Arnason .18 .35
225 Steve Durbano .18 .35
226 Ron Schock .18 .35
227 Bob Paradise .18 .35
228 Ron Stackhouse .18 .35
229 Lowell MacDonald .25 .50
230 Bob Johnson .18 .35
231 Rick Kehoe .38 .75
232 Nelson Debenedet .18 .35
233 Vic Hadfield .25 .50
234 Denis Herron .50 1.00
235 Phil Roberto .18 .35
236 Floyd Thomson .18 .35
237 Don Awrey .18 .35
238 Rick Wilson .18 .35
239 John Davidson 1.50 3.00
240 Pierre Plante .18 .35
241 Barclay Plager .38 .75
242 Larry Giroux .18 .35
243 Bob Gassoff .38 .75
244 Dave Gardner .18 .35
245 Brian Ogilvie .18 .35
246 Ed Johnston .50 1.00
247 Bob Plager .25 .50
248 Wayne Merrick .18 .35
249 Larry Sacharuk .18 .35
250 Bill Collins .18 .35
251 Garnet Bailey .18 .35
252 Garry Unger .38 .75
253 Gary Sabourin .18 .35
254 Willie Brossart .18 .35
255 Tim Ecclestone .18 .35
256 Dave Keon .75 1.50
257 Darryl Sittler 1.50 3.00
258 Inge Hammarstrom .18 .35
259 Ian Turnbull .25 .50
260 Jim McKenny .18 .35
261 Norm Ullman .75 1.50
262 Doug Favell .50 1.00
263 Bob Neely .18 .35
264 Lanny McDonald 1.50 3.00
265 Dunc Wilson .38 .75
266 Errol Thompson .18 .35
267 Brian Glennie .18 .35
268 Bill Flett .18 .35
269 Borje Salming .75 1.50
270 Ron Ellis .25 .50
271 Dave Dunn .18 .35
272 Chris Oddleifson .18 .35
273 Barry Wilkins .18 .35
274 Gary Smith .38 .75
275 Dennis Ververgaert .18 .35
276 Jocelyn Guevremont .18 .35
277 Andre Boudrias .25 .50
278 John Gould .18 .35
279 Jim Wiley .18 .35
280 Bob Dailey .18 .35
281 Tracy Pratt .18 .35
282 Ken Lockett .18 .35
283 Paulin Bordeleau .18 .35
284 Gerry O'Flaherty .18 .35
285 Bryan McSheffrey .18 .35
286 Gregg Boddy .18 .35
287 Don Lever .25 .50
288 Dennis Kearns .18 .35
289 Robin Burns .18 .35
290 Gary Coalter .18 .35
291 John Wright .18 .35
292 Peter McDuffe .38 .75
293 Simon Nolet .18 .35
294 Ted Snell .18 .35
295 Gary Croteau .18 .35
296 Lynn Powis .18 .35
297 Dave Hudson .18 .35
298 Richard Lemieux .18 .35
299 Bryan Lefley .18 .35
300 Doug Horbul .18 .35
301 Brent Hughes .18 .35
302 Ed Gilbert .18 .35
303 Michel Plasse .38 .75
304 Dennis Patterson .18 .35
305 Randy Rota .18 .35
306 Chris Evans .18 .35
307 Bill Mikkelson .18 .35
308 Ron Low .50 1.00
309 Doug Mohns .25 .50
310 Joe Lundrigan .18 .35
311 Steve Atkinson .18 .35
312 Ron Anderson .18 .35
313 Mike Marson .38 .75
314 Lew Morrison .18 .35
315 Jack Egers .18 .35
316 Gordy Brooks .18 .35
317 Pete Laframboise .18 .35
318 Mike Bloom .18 .35
319 Bob Collyard .18 .35
320 Dave Kryskow .18 .35
321 Greg Joly .18 .35
322 Jim Hrycuik .18 .35
323 Bob Gryp .18 .35
324 Larry Fullan .18 .35
NNO Album 10.00 20.00

1974-75 NHL Action Stamps Update

A group of 43 previously uncatalogued NHL Action (Loblaw's) stamps had been reported. Thirty-six of these stamps are recropped or airbrushed versions of original stamps listing the player's new team. The remaining seven were completely new stamps to replace nine originals dropped from the set. The discrepancy between the seven added and the nine dropped stamps had led some to speculate that there were at least two other stamps in the set, all the more so since two teams (Islanders and Vancouver) have one less player than all the other teams. These stamps were grouped alphabetically within teams and checklisted below alphabetically according to teams as follows: Atlanta Flames (1), Boston Bruins (2), Buffalo Sabres (3-5), California Golden Seals (6-8), Detroit Red Wings (9-13), Kansas City Scouts (14-16), Minnesota North Stars (17-21), Montreal Canadiens (22-23), New York Islanders (24-25), New York Rangers (26), Pittsburgh Penguins (27-29), St. Louis Blues (30-34), Toronto Maple Leafs (35-37), Vancouver Canucks (38-40), and Washington Capitals (41-43).

COMPLETE SET (43) 25.00 50.00
1 Barry Gibbs .50 1.00
2 Henry Nowak .50 1.00
3 Jocelyn Guevremont .50 1.00
4 Bryan McSheffrey .50 1.00
5 Fred Stanfield .50 1.00
6 Dave Gardner .50 1.00
7 Morris Mott NEW .50 1.00
8 Gary Simmons NEW 2.00 4.00
9 Gary Bergman .75 1.50
10 Dave Kryskow .50 1.00
11 Walt McKechnie .50 1.00
12 Phil Roberto .50 1.00
13 Ted Snell .50 1.00
14 Guy Charron .75 1.50
15 Jean-Guy Lagace NEW .50 1.00
16 Denis Herron 2.00 4.00
17 Craig Cameron .50 1.00
18 John Flesch NEW .50 1.00
19 Norm Gratton .50 1.00
20 Ernie Hicke .50 1.00
21 Doug Rombough .50 1.00
22 Don Awrey .50 1.00
23 Wayne Thomas NEW 2.00 4.00
24 Jude Drouin .50 1.00
25 Jean Paul Parise .50 1.00
26 Rick Middleton NEW 2.50 5.00
27 Lew Morrison .50 1.00
28 Michel Plasse 2.00 4.00
29 Barry Wilkins .50 1.00
30 Red Berenson .75 1.50
31 Chris Evans .50 1.00
32 Claude Larose .50 1.00
33 Chuck Lefley .50 1.00
34 Craig Patrick .75 1.50
35 Dave Dunn .50 1.00
36 George Ferguson NEW .50 1.00
37 Rod Seiling .50 1.00
38 Ab Demarco .50 1.00
39 Gerry Meehan .50 1.00
40 Mike Robitaille .50 1.00
41 Willie Brossart .50 1.00
42 Ron Lalonde .50 1.00
43 Jack Lynch .50 1.00

1995-96 NHL Aces Playing Cards

This 55 standard-size playing card set featured National Hockey League players. The fronts of these rounded-corner cards featured full-color action player shots. The team logo appeared in the upper right of each picture. The player's name and position appeared in either a blue or aqua stripe at the bottom. The backs had the NHL Aces design and sponsor logos on a black background. Since this set was similar to a playing card set, the set was checklisted below as if it were a playing card deck. In the checklist C meant Clubs, D meant Diamonds, H meant Hearts and S meant Spades. The cards were checklisted in playing order by suits and numbers are assigned to Aces (1), Jacks (11), Queens (12) and Kings (13).

COMPLETE SET (55) 6.00 15.00
1C Paul Coffey .25 .60
1D Wayne Gretzky 1.25 3.00
1H Eric Lindros .60 1.50
1S Patrick Roy 1.00 2.50
2C Scott Stevens .01 .05
2D Al MacInnis .01 .05
2H Craig Janney .01 .05
2S Kirk Muller .01 .05
3C Bill Ranford .05 .15
3D Mike Modano .25 .60
3H Doug Gilmour .25 .60
3S Steve Yzerman .60 1.50
4C Brian Bradley .01 .05
4D Alexandre Daigle .01 .05
4H Claude Lemieux .05 .15
4S Felix Potvin .15 .40
5C Ed Belfour .25 .60
5D Jeremy Roenick .25 .60
5H Trevor Linden .02 .10
5S Pat Lafontaine .05 .15
6C Brian Leetch .25 .60
6D Jason Arnott .02 .10
6H Geoff Sanderson .01 .05
6S Jim Carey .15 .40
7C Ron Francis .05 .15
7D Peter Bondra .25 .60
7H Paul Kariya .75 2.00
7S John Vanbiesbrouck .20 .50
8C Teemu Selanne .40 1.00
8D Ray Bourque .25 .60
8H Pierre Turgeon .05 .15
8S Alexei Yashin .15 .40
9C Martin Brodeur .50 1.25
9D Pavel Bure .50 1.25
9H Peter Forsberg .50 1.25
9S Chris Chelios .25 .60
10C Joe Nieuwendyk .07 .20
10D Mats Sundin .25 .60
10H Adam Oates .05 .15
10S Cam Neely .07 .20
11C Mark Messier .25 .60
11D Brett Hull .25 .60
11H Sergei Fedorov .40 1.00
11S Keith Tkachuk .25 .60
12C Mikael Renberg .05 .15
12D Jaromir Jagr .60 1.50
12H Mario Lemieux 1.00 2.50
12S John LeClair .30 .75
13C Joe Sakic .40 1.00
13D Dominik Hasek .40 1.00
13H Alexei Zhamnov .02 .10
13S Theo Fleury .25 .60
NNO Eastern Conference Logo .01 .05
NNO Checklist of Players in Deck .01 .05
NNO Western Conference Logo .01 .05

1996-97 NHL Aces Playing Cards

This 55-card set was standard playing card size and featured NHL players in action. A color action photo took up the bulk of the front, with the team logo in the upper right corner. The suits and numbers were located in the upper left and lower right hand corners. Player name and position could be found along the bottom. If the player was a finalist for or winner of any major NHL award, that achievement was noted with a golden icon in the lower left corner. The backs carried a uniformly indistinguishable NHL Hockey Aces logo.

COMPLETE SET (55) 4.80 12.00
1 Daniel Alfredsson .10 .30
2 Jason Arnott .10 .30
3 Ray Bourque .30 .75
4 Rod Brind'Amour .10 .30
5 Martin Brodeur .30 .75
6 Pavel Bure .30 .75
7 Jim Carey .08 .25
8 Chris Chelios .10 .30
9 Vincent Damphousse .05 .15
10 Eric Daze .08 .25
11 Sergei Fedorov .30 .75
12 Ray Ferraro .02 .10
13 Theo Fleury .10 .30
14 Peter Forsberg .30 .75
15 Ron Francis .10 .30
16 Grant Fuhr .07 .20
17 Mike Gartner .05 .15
18 Doug Gilmour .10 .30
19 Travis Green .02 .10
20 Wayne Gretzky .75 2.00
21 Roman Hamrlik .05 .15
22 Brett Hull .15 .40
23 Jaromir Jagr .40 1.00
24 Ed Jovanovski .07 .20
25 Joe Juneau .07 .20
26 Paul Kariya .40 1.00
27 Pat LaFontaine .08 .25
28 Brian Leetch .10 .30
29 Mario Lemieux .60 1.50
30 Trevor Linden .10 .30
31 Eric Lindros .30 .75
32 Mark Messier .15 .40
33 Mike Modano .15 .40
34 Alexander Mogilny .08 .25
35 Owen Nolan .10 .30
36 Adam Oates .10 .30
37 Chris Osgood .10 .30
38 Daren Puppa .05 .15
39 Gary Roberts .05 .15
40 Jeremy Roenick .10 .30
41 Patrick Roy .60 1.50
42 Joe Sakic .30 .75
43 Teemu Selanne .30 .75
44 Brendan Shanahan .30 .75
45 Mats Sundin .10 .30
46 Jocelyn Thibault .08 .25
47 Keith Tkachuk .10 .30
48 Pierre Turgeon .08 .25
49 John Vanbiesbrouck .10 .30
50 Doug Weight .10 .30
51 Alexei Yashin .08 .25
52 Steve Yzerman .60 1.50
NNO Western Conference .02 .10
NNO Checklist .02 .10
NNO Eastern Conference .02 .10

1997-98 NHL Aces Playing Cards

COMPLETE SET (55) 8.00 20.00
1 Dominik Hasek .40 1.00
2 Mike Vernon .08 .25
3 Doug Gilmour .20 .50
4 Dimitri Kristich .02 .10
5 Mark Recchi .08 .25
6 Daniel Alfredsson .08 .25
7 Eric Lindros .08 .25
8 Keith Tkachuk .08 .25
9 Pavel Bure .30 .75
10 Brendan Shanahan .30 .75
11 Sandis Ozolinsh .02 .10
12 Mark Messier .30 .75
13 Patrick Roy .75 2.00
14 Paul Kariya .30 .75
15 Ray Bourque .40 1.00
16 Ryan Smyth .20 .50
17 Jarome Iginla .40 1.00
18 Chris Gratton .02 .10
19 Jeremy Roenick .40 1.00
20 Mike Modano .40 1.00

21 Doug Weight .08 .25
22 Jim Campbell .02 .10
23 Sheldon Kennedy .02 .10
24 Jason Arnott .02 .10
25 Peter Forsberg .40 1.00
26 Brian Leetch .40 1.00
27 Mike Peca .02 .10
28 Jere Lehtinen .08 .25
29 Trevor Linden .40 1.00
30 John LeClair .08 .25
31 Owen Nolan .08 .25
32 Pierre Turgeon .02 .10
33 Tony Amonte .02 .10
34 Alexei Yashin .02 .10
35 Mats Sundin .40 1.00
36 Jaromir Jagr .60 1.50
37 Wayne Gretzky 1.25 3.00
38 Martin Brodeur .60 1.50
39 Tony Granato .02 .10
40 Bryan Berard .02 .10
41 Geoff Sanderson .02 .10
42 Chris Chelios .20 .50
43 Felix Potvin .30 .75
44 Adam Oates .08 .25
45 Roman Hamrlik .02 .10
46 Theoren Fleury .08 .25
47 Vincent Damphousse .02 .10
48 Zigmund Palffy .08 .25
49 Saku Koivu .40 1.00
50 Teemu Selanne .40 1.00
51 John Vanbiesbrouck .20 .50
52 Vladimir Konstantinov .40 1.00
NNO Checklist .01 .01
NNO Eastern Conference .01 .01
NNO Western Conference .01 .01

1998-99 NHL Aces Playing Cards

COMPLETE SET (55) 6.00 15.00
1 Olaf Kolzig .20 .50
2 Marcel Cousineau .08 .25
3 Corey Schwab .08 .25
4 Dwayne Roloson .08 .25
5 Mark Fitzpatrick .08 .25
6 Guy Hebert .08 .25
7 Jamie McLennan .08 .25
8 Rick Tabaracci .08 .25
9 Jose Theodore .40 1.00
10 Grant Fuhr .40 1.00
11 Ed Belfour .40 1.00
12 Felix Potvin .40 1.00
13 Damian Rhodes .08 .25
14 Patrick Roy 1.00 2.50
15 Ken Wregget .08 .25
16 Bill Ranford .08 .25
17 Jamie Storr .08 .25
18 Chris Terreri .08 .25
19 Kelly Hrudey .08 .25
20 Ron Tugnutt .08 .25
21 Mike Vernon .08 .25
22 Mikhail Shtalenkov .08 .25
23 Darren Puppa .08 .25
24 Bryon Dafoe .08 .25
25 Arthurs Irbe .20 .50
26 Chris Osgood .20 .50
27 Dominik Hasek .60 1.50
28 Robbie Tallas .08 .25
29 Kirk McLean .08 .25
30 Peter Skudra .08 .25
31 Eric Fichaud .08 .25
32 Bob Essensa .08 .25
33 Sean Burke .08 .25
34 Jocelyn Thibault .08 .25
35 Ron Hextall .40 1.00
36 Nikolai Khabibulin .40 1.00
37 Mike Richter .40 1.00
38 Tommy Salo .08 .25
39 John Vanbiesbrouck .40 1.00
40 Curtis Joseph .40 1.00
41 Glenn Healy .08 .25
42 Mike Dunham .08 .25
43 Roman Turek .08 .25
44 Steve Shields .08 .25
45 Garth Snow .08 .25
46 Kevin Hodson .08 .25
47 Craig Billington .08 .25
48 Trevor Kidd .08 .25
49 Jeff Hackett .08 .25
50 Stephane Fiset .08 .25
51 Tom Barrasso .20 .50
52 Martin Brodeur .75 2.00
NNO Western Conference .01 .01
NNO Eastern Conference .01 .01
NNO Checklist .01 .01

1960s NHL Ceramic Tiles

These unique collectibles featured artistic renditions of top NHL players on smallish ceramic tiles. As they were unnumbered, the tiles were checklisted below by the number that appears on their original box. The checklist below is believed to be incomplete -- any updates can be forwarded to hockeymag@beckett.com. Although these are being seen more often lately, the tiles are not priced due to lack of secondary market sales evidence.

1 Charlie Burns
2 Red Berenson
3 Ralph Backstrom
4 Larry Cahan
5 Bernie Geoffrion
6 Phil Goyette
7 Doug Harvey
8 Bronco Horvath
9 Harry Howell
10 Andy Hebenton
11 Jim Langlois
12 Bert Marshall
13 Marcel Pronovost
14 Henri Richard
15 Bobby Rousseau
16 Gilles Tremblay
17 Jerry Toppazzini
18 Gump Worsley
19 Dave Balon
20 Jean Beliveau
21 Claude Provost
22 Vic Hadfield
23 Jean-Guy Talbot
24 Dickie Moore
25 Jean Ratelle
26 Tom Johnson
27 Earl Ingarfield
28 Lou Fontinato
29 Cesare Maniago
30 Ted Hampson
31 Muzz Patrick
32 Andy Bathgate
33 Bill Hicke
34 J.C. Tremblay

1995-96 NHL Cool Trade

This 20-card standard-size set was the result of a unique collaboration between the NHL, the NHLPA and the five card manufacturers. Each of the latter created four cards for inclusion in the set, which was available to collectors who sent in 20 wrappers plus postage and handling to a mailing address. The set also was available at the NHLPA booth at the 1996 National Convention for between five and ten wrappers, depending upon when you went to the booth. The set included five different designs, one unique to each contributing manufacturer. There also was the possibility of acquiring limited-edition upgrade versions of the cards. Cool Trade exchange cards were randomly inserted in packs of Bowman, Donruss Elite, Summit, Ultra series 2, and Upper Deck series 2. These could be mailed in to the participating licensee for redemption. The Emotion exchange card inserted in '95-96 Ultra series two was by far the most difficult to acquire. The redemption cards are priced individually below, and have an RP prefix amended to them for cataloguing purposes only, the RP prefix is not on the actual cards.

COMPLETE SET (20) 3.00 10.00
1 Cam Neely .20 .50
2 Wayne Gretzky 1.50 4.00
3 Jeremy Roenick .20 .50
4 Mario Lemieux 1.00 2.50
5 Mark Messier .30 .75
6 Ray Bourque .20 .50
7 Sergei Fedorov .40 1.00
8 Paul Kariya .40 1.00
9 Eric Lindros .40 1.00
10 Pavel Bure .30 .75
11 Chris Chelios .20 .50
12 Peter Forsberg .50 1.25
13 Saku Koivu .20 .50
14 Ed Belfour .20 .50
15 Brett Hull .30 .75
16 Patrick Roy 1.00 2.50
17 Doug Gilmour .20 .50
18 Martin Brodeur .40 1.00
19 Alexander Mogilny .20 .50
20 Jaromir Jagr .30 .75
RP1 Cam Neely .75 2.00
RP2 Wayne Gretzky 6.00 15.00
RP3 Jeremy Roenick 4.00 10.00
RP4 Mario Lemieux 2.00 5.00
RP5 Mark Messier 2.00 5.00
RP6 Ray Bourque 1.00 2.50
RP7 Sergei Fedorov 1.50 4.00
RP8 Paul Kariya 10.00 25.00
RP9 Eric Lindros 1.00 2.50
RP10 Pavel Bure 3.00 8.00
RP11 Chris Chelios .75 2.00
RP12 Peter Forsberg 1.25 3.00
RP13 Saku Koivu 4.00 10.00
RP14 Ed Belfour 1.00 2.50
RP15 Brett Hull 3.00 6.00
RP16 Patrick Roy 5.00 10.00
RP17 Doug Gilmour .75 2.00
RP18 Martin Brodeur 8.00 20.00
RP19 Alexander Mogilny 1.00 2.50
RP20 Jaromir Jagr 2.50 6.00

1996-97 NHL Pro Stamps

This set of 130 postage stamp-style collectibles was released by Chris Martin Enterprises. The series was issued in 12 numbered sheets of 12 stamps each. There were several double prints-they are noted below with a DP suffix.

COMPLETE SET (130) 7.20 18.00
1 Stephane Fiset .05 .15
2 Peter Forsberg .20 .50
3 Claude Lemieux DP .05 .15
4 Mike Ricci .02 .10
5 Joe Sakic .15 .40
6 Ed Belfour .08 .25
7 Chris Chelios .08 .25
8 Joe Murphy .02 .10
9 Bernie Nicholls .02 .10
10 Jeremy Roenick DP .08 .25
11 Geoff Courtnall .02 .10
12 Brett Hull .15 .40
13 Al MacInnis .05 .15
14 Chris Pronger .05 .15
15 Esa Tikkanen .05 .15
16 Ray Bourque .08 .25
17 Blaine Lacher .05 .15
18 Cam Neely .07 .20
19 Adam Oates DP .07 .20
20 Kevin Stevens .02 .10
21 Valeri Bure .02 .10
22 Vincent Damphousse .05 .15
23 Mark Recchi .05 .15
24 Patrick Roy .30 .75
25 Pierre Turgeon .07 .20
26 Pavel Bure .15 .40
27 Trevor Linden .05 .15
28 Kirk McLean .05 .15
29 Alexander Mogilny .08 .25
30 Cliff Ronning .02 .10
31 Jason Allison .02 .10
32 Jim Carey .10 .30
33 Dale Hunter .02 .10
34 Joe Juneau DP .07 .20
35 Brendan Witt .02 .10
36 Martin Brodeur DP .15 .40
37 John MacLean .05 .15
38 Scott Niedermayer .05 .15
39 Stephane Richer .02 .10
40 Scott Stevens .05 .15
41 Patrik Carnback .02 .10
42 Guy Hebert .07 .20
43 Paul Kariya .25 .60
44 Oleg Tverdovsky .05 .15
45 Garry Valk .02 .10
46 Theo Fleury .07 .20
47 Trevor Kidd .05 .15
48 Joe Nieuwendyk .05 .15
49 Gary Roberts .02 .10
50 German Titov .02 .10
51 Rod Brind'Amour .05 .15
52 Ron Hextall .05 .15
53 John LeClair .10 .30
54 Eric Lindros .20 .50
55 Mikael Renberg .07 .20
56 Brett Lindros .02 .10
57 Wendel Clark .05 .15
58 Patrick Flatley .02 .10
59 Kirk Muller .02 .10
60 Mathieu Schneider .02 .10
61 Tim Cheveldae .05 .15
62 Dallas Drake .02 .10
63 Teemu Selanne .15 .40
64 Keith Tkachuk .10 .30
65 Alexei Zhamnov .05 .15
66 Rob Blake .05 .15
67 Wayne Gretzky DP .40 1.00
68 Jari Kurri .05 .15
69 Jamie Storr .05 .15
70 Rick Tocchet .05 .15
71 Brian Bradley .02 .10
72 Chris Gratton .05 .15
73 Roman Hamrlik .05 .15
74 Paul Ysebaert .02 .10
75 Rob Zamuner .02 .10
76 Dave Andreychuk .05 .15
77 Doug Gilmour .08 .25
78 Kenny Jonsson .05 .15
79 Felix Potvin .10 .30
80 Mats Sundin .07 .20
81 Jason Arnott .07 .20
82 Jason Bonsignore .02 .10
83 Todd Marchant .02 .10
84 Bill Ranford .07 .20
85 Doug Weight .07 .20
86 Jody Hull .02 .10
87 Bob Kudelski .02 .10
88 Scott Mellanby .05 .15
89 Rob Niedermayer .05 .15
90 John Vanbiesbrouck .08 .25
91 Ron Francis .07 .20
92 Jaromir Jagr .20 .50
93 Mario Lemieux DP .30 .75
94 Bryan Smolinski .02 .10
95 Sergei Zubov .02 .10
96 Adam Graves .05 .15
97 Brian Leetch .07 .20
98 Mark Messier DP .15 .40
99 Mike Richter .08 .25
100 Luc Robitaille .07 .20
101 Paul Coffey .07 .20
102 Sergei Fedorov DP .15 .40
103 Nicklas Lidstrom .05 .15
104 Ray Sheppard .02 .10
105 Steve Yzerman .20 .50
106 Donald Audette .02 .10
107 Dominik Hasek DP .15 .40
108 Yuri Khmylev .02 .10
109 Pat LaFontaine .05 .15
110 Alexei Zhitnik .02 .10
111 Radek Bonk .02 .10
112 Randy Cunneyworth .02 .10
113 Alexandre Daigle .05 .15
114 Steve Larouche .02 .10
115 Martin Straka .02 .10
116 Ulf Dahlen .02 .10
117 Pat Falloon .02 .10
118 Jeff Friesen .05 .15
119 Arturs Irbe DP .05 .15
120 Craig Janney .02 .10
121 Shane Churla .02 .10
122 Todd Harvey .02 .10
123 Derian Hatcher .02 .10
124 Mike Modano .07 .20
125 Andy Moog .07 .20
126 Sean Burke .05 .15
127 Andrew Cassels .02 .10
128 Geoff Sanderson .05 .15
129 Brendan Shanahan .15 .40
130 Darren Turcotte .02 .10

1994 NHLPA Phone Cards

This set was issued by the Player's Association in 1994. The photos are from the 4 on 4 tournament held in Canada during the NHL lockout. Each card carried the player's name and the denomination of the card on front.

COMPLETE SET (9) 16.00 40.00
1 Doug Gilmour 1.50 4.00
2 Brett Hull 2.00 5.00
3 Paul Kariya 3.00 8.00
4 Eric Lindros 2.50 6.00
5 Luc Robitaille 1.50 4.00
6 Jeremy Roenick 1.50 4.00
7 Patrick Roy 4.00 10.00
8 John Vanbiesbrouck 1.50 4.00
9 Team Ontario 1.25 3.00

2003 NHL Sticker Collection

This 300-card sticker set was sold in packs of 10 stickers. The stickers measured approximately 2" X 1 1/2". A collector album was also available with pages separated by team.

COMPLETE SET (300) 25.00 50.00
1 Atlanta Thrashers .10 .25
Home Logo
2 Atlanta Thrashers .10 .25
Away Logo
3 Dany Heatley .20 .50
4 Ilya Kovalchuk .20 .50
5 Patrik Stefan .10 .25
6 Frantisek Kaberle .10 .25
7 Yannick Tremblay .10 .25
8 Tony Hrkac .10 .25
9 Shawn Mceachern .10 .25
10 Byron Dafoe .10 .25
11 Boston Bruins .10 .25
Home Logo
12 Boston Bruins .10 .25
Away Logo
13 Martin Lapointe .10 .25
14 Glen Murray .20 .50
15 Brian Rolston .10 .25
16 Sergei Samsonov .20 .50
17 Joe Thornton .40 1.00
18 Jozef Stumpel .10 .25
19 Nick Boynton .10 .25
20 Steve Shields .10 .25
21 Buffalo Sabres .10 .25
Home Logo
22 Buffalo Sabres .10 .25
Away Logo
23 Stu Barnes .10 .25
24 Curtis Brown .10 .25
25 Miroslav Satan .20 .50
26 Jochen Hecht .10 .25
27 Tim Connolly .10 .25
28 Jay McKee .10 .25
29 Chris Gratton .10 .25
30 Martin Biron .20 .50
31 Carolina Hurricanes .10 .25
Home Logo
32 Carolina Hurricanes .10 .25
Away Logo
33 Rod Brind'Amour .20 .50
34 Erik Cole .10 .25
35 Ron Francis .20 .50
36 Sami Kapanen .10 .25
37 Jeff O'Neill .10 .25
38 Bret Hedican .10 .25
39 Sean Hill .10 .25
40 Kevin Weekes .10 .25
41 Florida Panthers .10 .25
Home Logo
42 Florida Panthers .10 .25
Away Logo
43 Valeri Bure .10 .25
44 Olli Jokinen .10 .25
45 Marcus Nilsson .10 .25
46 Stephen Weiss .10 .25
47 Kristian Huselius .10 .25
48 Sandis Ozolinsh .10 .25
49 Jay Bouwmeester .20 .50
50 Roberto Luongo .60 1.50
51 Montreal Canadians .10 .25
Home Logo
52 Montreal Canadians .10 .25
Away Logo
53 Randy McKay .10 .25
54 Richard Zednik .10 .25
55 Doug Gilmour .40 1.00
56 Saku Koivu .40 1.00
57 Yanic Perreault .10 .25
58 Craig Rivet .10 .25
59 Patrice Brisebois .10 .25
60 Jose Theodore .30 .75
61 New Jersey Devils .10 .25
Home Logo
62 New Jersey Devils .10 .25
Away Logo
63 Patrik Elias .10 .25
64 Jeff Friesen .10 .25
65 Joe Nieuwendyk .20 .50
66 Sergei Brylin .10 .25
67 Jamie Langenbrunner .10 .25
68 Scott Stevens .10 .25
69 Scott Niedermayer .20 .50
70 Martin Brodeur .40 1.00
71 New York Islanders .10 .25
Home Logo
72 New York Islanders .10 .25
Away Logo
73 Shawn Bates .10 .25
74 Brad Isbister .10 .25
75 Mark Parrish .10 .25
76 Michael Peca .10 .25
77 Alexei Yashin .10 .25
78 Kenny Jonsson .10 .25
79 Roman Hamrlik .10 .25
80 Chris Osgood .20 .50
81 New York Rangers .10 .25
Home Logo
82 New York Rangers .10 .25
Away Logo
83 Pavel Bure .40 1.00
84 Bobby Holik .10 .25
85 Eric Lindros .40 1.00
86 Mark Messier .40 1.00
87 Petr Nedved .10 .25
88 Brian Leetch .20 .50
89 Darius Kasparitis .10 .25
90 Mike Richter .20 .50
91 Ottawa Senators .10 .25
Home Logo
92 Ottawa Senators .10 .25
93 Daniel Alfredsson .20 .50
94 Jason Spezza .20 .50
95 Marian Hossa .30 .75
96 Magnus Arvedson .10 .25
97 Martin Havlat .20 .50
98 Wade Redden .10 .25
99 Chris Phillips .10 .25
100 Patrick Lalime .10 .25
101 Philadelphia Flyers .10 .25
Home Logo
102 Philadelphia Flyers .10 .25
Away Logo
103 Simon Gagne .20 .50
104 John LeClair .10 .25
105 Keith Primeau .10 .25
106 Mark Recchi .20 .50
107 Jeremy Roenick .40 1.00
108 Eric Desjardins .10 .25
109 Kim Johnsson .10 .25
110 Roman Cechmanek .10 .25
111 Pittsburgh Penguins .10 .25
Home Logo
112 Pittsburgh Penguins .10 .25
Away Logo
113 Jan Hrdina .10 .25
114 Alexei Kovalev .10 .25
115 Mario Lemieux .75 2.00
116 Alexei Morozov .10 .25
117 Wayne Primeau .10 .25
118 Michal Rozsival .10 .25
119 Dick Tarnstrom .10 .25
120 Johan Hedberg .10 .25
121 Tampa Bay Lightning .10 .25
Home Logo
122 Tampa Bay Lightning .10 .25
Away Logo
123 Dave Andreychuk .10 .25
124 Vincent Lecavalier .40 1.00
125 Vaclav Prospal .10 .25
126 Brad Richards .20 .50
127 Martin St. Louis .20 .50
128 Pavel Kubina .10 .25
129 Dan Boyle .10 .25
130 Nikolai Khabibulin .40 1.00
131 Toronto Maple Leafs .10 .25
Home Logo
132 Toronto Maple Leafs .10 .25
Away Logo
133 Mats Sundin .40 1.00
134 Tie Domi .10 .25
135 Darcy Tucker .10 .25
136 Alexander Mogilny .10 .25
137 Gary Roberts .10 .25
138 Tomas Kaberle .10 .25
139 Bryan McCabe .10 .25
140 Ed Belfour .40 1.00
141 Washington Capitals .10 .25
Home Logo
142 Washington Capitals .10 .25
Away Logo
143 Peter Bondra .10 .25
144 Jaromir Jagr .30 .75
145 Robert Lang .10 .25
146 Jeff Halpern .10 .25
147 Sergei Gonchar .10 .25
148 Dainius Zubrus .10 .25
149 Steve Konowalchuk .10 .25
150 Olaf Kolzig .20 .50
151 Anaheim Mighty Ducks .10 .25
Home Logo
152 Anaheim Mighty Ducks .10 .25
Away Logo
153 Paul Kariya .40 1.00
154 Matt Cullen .10 .25
155 Steve Rucchin .10 .25
156 Mike Leclerc .10 .25
157 Petr Sykora .10 .25
158 Stanislav Chistov .10 .25
159 Keith Carney .10 .25
160 Jean-Sebastien Giguere .20 .50
161 Calgary Flames .10 .25
Home Logo
162 Calgary Flames .10 .25
Away Logo
163 Craig Conroy .10 .25
164 Jarome Iginla .40 1.00
165 Chris Drury .20 .50
166 Martin Gelinas .10 .25
167 Stephane Yelle .10 .25
168 Denis Gauthier .10 .25
169 Bob Boughner .10 .25
170 Roman Turek .10 .25
171 Chicago Blackhawks .10 .25
Home Logo
172 Chicago Blackhawks .10 .25
Away Logo
173 Eric Daze .10 .25
174 Steve Sullivan .10 .25
175 Alexei Zhamnov .10 .25
176 Kyle Calder .10 .25
177 Phil Housley .10 .25
178 Tyler Arnason .10 .25
179 Lyle Odelein .10 .25
180 Jocelyn Thibault .20 .50
181 Colorado Avalanche .10 .25
Home Logo
182 Colorado Avalanche .10 .25
Away Logo
183 Peter Forsberg .40 1.00
184 Milan Hejduk .20 .50
185 Joe Sakic .40 1.00
186 Alex Tanguay .20 .50
187 Rob Blake .10 .25
188 Adam Foote .10 .25
189 Derek Morris .10 .25
190 Patrick Roy .75 2.00
191 Columbus Blue Jackets .10 .25
Home Logo
192 Columbus Blue Jackets .10 .25
Away Logo
193 Rick Nash .40 1.00
194 Geoff Sanderson .10 .25
195 Andrew Cassels .10 .25
196 Ray Whitney .10 .25
197 Luke Richardson .10 .25
198 Scott Lachance .10 .25
199 Mike Sillinger .10 .25
200 Marc Denis .20 .50
201 Dallas Stars .10 .25
Home Logo
202 Dallas Stars .10 .25
Away Logo
203 Ulf Dahlen .10 .25
204 Bill Guerin .10 .25
205 Mike Modano .30 .75
206 Pierre Turgeon .10 .25
207 Scott Young .10 .25
208 Sergei Zubov .10 .25
209 Darryl Sydor .10 .25
210 Marty Turco .20 .50
211 Detroit Red Wings .10 .25
Home Logo
212 Detroit Red Wings .10 .25
Away Logo
213 Sergei Fedorov .20 .50
214 Brett Hull .30 .75
215 Brendan Shanahan .20 .50
216 Steve Yzerman .75 2.00
217 Chris Chelios .20 .50
218 Nicklas Lidstrom .20 .50
219 Kris Draper .10 .25
220 Curtis Joseph .20 .50
221 Edmonton Oilers .10 .25
Home Logo
222 Edmonton Oilers .10 .25
Away Logo
223 Anson Carter .10 .25
224 Mike Comrie .10 .25
225 Ryan Smyth .20 .50
226 Mike York .10 .25
227 Eric Brewer .10 .25
228 Jason Smith .10 .25
229 Janne Niinimaa .10 .25
230 Tommy Salo .10 .25
231 Los Angeles Kings .10 .25
Home Logo
232 Los Angeles Kings .10 .25
Away Logo
233 Jason Allison .10 .25
234 Adam Deadmarsh .10 .25
235 Bryan Smolinski .10 .25
236 Mathieu Schneider .10 .25
237 Jaroslav Modry .10 .25
238 Zigmund Palffy .20 .50
239 Lubomir Visnovsky .10 .25
240 Felix Potvin .20 .50
241 Minnesota Wild .10 .25
Home Logo
242 Minnesota Wild .10 .25
Away Logo
243 Andrew Brunette .10 .25
244 Marian Gaborik .40 1.00
245 Cliff Ronning .10 .25
246 Sergei Zholtok .10 .25
247 Jim Dowd .10 .25
248 Antti Laaksonen .10 .25
249 Willie Mitchell .10 .25
250 Manny Fernandez .20 .50
251 Nashville Predators .10 .25
Home Logo
252 Nashville Predators .10 .25
Away Logo
253 Andreas Johansson .10 .25
254 Greg Johnson .10 .25
255 Denis Arkhipov .10 .25
256 David Legwand .10 .25
257 Vladimir Orszagh .10 .25
258 Andy Delmore .10 .25
259 Kimmo Timonen .10 .25
260 Tomas Vokoun .20 .50
261 Phoenix Coyotes .10 .25
Home Logo
262 Phoenix Coyotes .10 .25
Away Logo
263 Tony Amonte .10 .25
264 Daniel Briere .10 .25
265 Shane Doan .10 .25
266 Daymond Langkow .10 .25
267 Ladislav Nagy .10 .25
268 Teppo Numminen .10 .25
269 Danny Markov .10 .25
270 Sean Burke .20 .50
271 St. Louis Blues .10 .25
Home Logo
272 St. Louis Blues .10 .25
Away Logo
273 Pavol Demitra .10 .25
274 Cory Stillman .10 .25
275 Keith Tkachuk .20 .50
276 Doug Weight .10 .25
277 Al MacInnis .20 .50
278 Chris Pronger .20 .50
279 Eric Boguniecki .10 .25
280 Brent Johnson .10 .25
281 San Jose Sharks .10 .25
Home Logo
282 San Jose Sharks .10 .25
Away Logo
283 Vincent Damphousse .10 .25
284 Adam Graves .10 .25
285 Patrick Marleau .20 .50
286 Owen Nolan .10 .25
287 Teemu Selanne .30 .75
288 Marco Sturm .10 .25
289 Mike Ricci .10 .25
290 Evgeni Nabokov .20 .50
291 Vancouver Canucks .10 .25
Home Logo
292 Vancouver Canucks .10 .25
Away Logo
293 Todd Bertuzzi .20 .50
294 Trevor Linden .40 1.00
295 Brendan Morrison .10 .25
296 Markus Naslund .20 .50
297 Henrik Sedin .10 .25
298 Ed Jovanovski .10 .25
299 Mattias Ohlund .10 .25
300 Dan Cloutier .10 .25

1995-96 No Fear Ad Cards

These large (6X9") photocards featured close-up color photos of Fuhr and Fleury, two spokesman for the No Fear company. It was not known whether these were the only cards issued, nor how exactly they were distributed. Any additional information would be appreciated.

COMPLETE SET (2) 3.00 8.00
1 Grant Fuhr 2.00 5.00
2 Theo Fleury 2.00 5.00

1972-73 Nordiques Postcards

This standard size postcard featured color photos surrounded by a white border. Card fronts featured a facsimile autograph and were issued by Pro Star Promotions. Backs were blank. The postcards were unnumbered and checklisted below in alphabetical order.

COMPLETE SET (22) 20.00 40.00
1 Michel Archambeault 1.00 2.00
2 Serge Aubry 1.00 2.00
3 Yves Bergeron 1.00 2.00
4 Jacques Blain 1.00 2.00
5 Alain Caron 1.00 2.00
6 Ken Desjardine 1.00 2.00
7 Maurice Filion 1.00 2.00
8 Andre Gaudette 1.00 2.00
9 Jean-Guy Gendron 1.00 2.00
10 Rejean Giroux 1.00 2.00
11 Frank Golembrosky 1.00 2.00
12 Robert Guindon 1.00 2.00
13 Pierre Guite 1.00 2.00
14 Francois Lacombe 1.00 2.00
15 Paul Larose 1.00 2.00
16 Jacques Lemelin 1.00 2.00
17 Michel Parizeau 1.00 2.00
18 Jean Payette 1.00 2.00
19 Michel Rouleau 1.00 2.00
20 Pierre Roy 1.00 2.00
21 J.C. Tremblay 1.50 3.00
NNO Header Card .50 1.00

1973-74 Nordiques Team Issue

This 21-card team issue set featured the 1973-74 Quebec Nordiques of the World Hockey Association. The oversized cards measured approximately 3 1/2" by 5 1/2". The fronts featured glossy color posed photos with white borders. The team and WHA logos were superimposed in the upper corners of the picture. A facsimile autograph was inscribed across the bottom of the picture. The backs were blank. The cards were unnumbered and checklisted below in alphabetical order.

COMPLETE SET (21) 25.00 50.00
1 Mike Archambault 1.25 2.50
2 Serge Aubry 1.25 2.50
3 Yves Bergeron 1.25 2.50
4 Jacques Blain 1.25 2.50
5 Richard Brodeur 4.00 8.00
6 Alain Caron 1.25 2.50
7 Ken Desjardins 1.25 2.50
8 Maurice Filion 1.25 2.50
9 Andre Gaudette 1.25 2.50
10 Jean-Guy Gendron 1.50 3.00
11 Rejean Giroux 1.25 2.50
12 Frank Golembrosky 1.25 2.50
13 Bob Guindon 1.25 2.50
14 Pierre Guite 1.25 2.50
15 Frank Lacombe 1.25 2.50
16 Paul Larose 1.25 2.50
17 Michel Parizeau 1.25 2.50
18 Jean Payette 1.25 2.50
19 Michel Rouleau 1.25 2.50
20 Pierre Roy 1.25 2.50
21 J.C. Tremblay 2.50 5.00

1976 Nordiques Marie Antoinette

This 14-card set measured approximately 8" by 10 1/2" and featured on the fronts color player portraits of the Quebec Nordiques by the artist Claude Laroche. The player's name was printed in black in the lower right with the card logo on the left. The backs were blank. The cards were unnumbered and checklisted below in alphabetical order.

COMPLETE SET (14) 30.00 60.00
1 Paul Baxter 2.00 4.00
2 Serge Bernier 2.00 4.00
3 Paulin Bordeleau 2.00 4.00
4 Andre Boudrias 2.50 5.00
5 Curt Brackenbury 2.00 4.00
6 Richard Brodeur 4.00 8.00
7 Real Cloutier 3.00 6.00
8 Charles Constantin 2.00 4.00
9 Bob Fitchner 2.00 4.00
10 Richard Grenier 2.00 4.00
11 Marc Tardif 3.00 6.00
12 Jean-Claude Tremblay 3.00 6.00
13 Steve Sutherland 2.00 4.00
14 Wally Weir 2.00 4.00

1976-77 Nordiques Postcards

These 20 postcards measured approximately 3 1/2" by 5 1/2" and featured posed-on-ice color player photos on their borderless fronts. A facsimile player autograph rested near the bottom. The backs carried the player's name, uniform number, brief biography, and Nordiques team logo at the upper left. Places for stamp and address appeared on the right. All text is in French. The postcards are unnumbered and checklisted below in alphabetical order.

COMPLETE SET (20) 15.00 30.00
1 Serge Aubry .75 1.50
2 Paul Baxter 1.00 2.00
3 Jean Bernier .75 1.50
4 Serge Bernier 1.50 3.00
5 Christian Bordeleau .75 1.50
6 Paulin Bordeleau 1.00 2.00
7 Andre Boudrias 1.00 2.00
8 Curt Brackenbury .75 1.50
9 Richard Brodeur 2.00 4.00
10 Real Cloutier 1.50 3.00
11 Charles Constantin .75 1.50
12 Jim Dorey 1.00 2.00
13 Robert Fitchner .75 1.50
14 Richard Grenier .75 1.50
15 Francois Lacombe .75 1.50
16 Pierre Roy .75 1.50
17 Steve Sutherland .75 1.50
18 Marc Tardif 1.50 3.00
19 J.C. Tremblay 1.50 3.00
20 Wally Weir .75 1.50

1980-81 Nordiques Postcards

Printed in Canada, this 24-card set measured approximately 3" by 5 1/2" and featured members of the 1980-81 Quebec Nordiques. The fronts had borderless, posed color player photos. The backs were in postcard format with a short player biography both in French and in English. The text on some cards was printed in royal blue and on other cards in turquoise. The cards were unnumbered and checklisted below in alphabetical order.

COMPLETE SET (29) 20.00 40.00
1 Michel Bergeron .40 1.00
2 Serge Bernier .75 2.00
3 Daniel Bouchard .40 1.00
4 Ron Chipperfield .40 1.00
5 Kim Clackson .60 1.50
6 Real Cloutier .75 2.00
7 Alain Cote .60 1.50

8 Michel Dion .60 1.50
9 Andre Dupont .60 1.50
10 Robbie Florek .75 2.00
11 Michel Goulet 2.50 5.00
12 Ron Grahame .40 1.00
13 Jamie Hislop .40 1.00
14 Dale Hoganson .40 1.00
15 Dale Hunter 2.50 5.00
16 Pierre Lacroix .40 1.00
17 Garry Lariviere .40 1.00
18 Richard Leduc .40 1.00
19 Lee Norwood .60 1.50
20 John Paddock .60 1.50
21 Dave Pichette .40 1.00
22 Michel Plasse .75 2.00
23 Jacques Richard .60 1.50
24 Normand Rochefort .40 1.00
25 Anton Stastny .75 2.00
26 Peter Stastny 4.00 8.00
27 Marc Tardif .75 2.00
28 Wally Weir .40 1.00
29 John Wensink .60 1.50

1981-82 Nordiques Postcards

Printed in Canada, this 21-card set measured approximately 3" by 5 1/2" and featured members of the 1981-82 Quebec Nordiques. The fronts had borderless, posed color player portraits. The backs were in postcard format with a short player biography both in French and in English. The cards were unnumbered and checklisted below in alphabetical order.

COMPLETE SET (21) 10.00 25.00
1 Pierre Aubry .40 1.00
2 Michel Bergeron CO .60 1.50
3 Daniel Bouchard .75 2.00
4 Real Cloutier .75 2.00
5 Alain Cote .40 1.00
6 Andre Dupont .40 1.00
7 Miroslav Frycer UER .40 1.00
(Last and first names are reversed)
8 Michel Goulet 1.50 4.00
9 Dale Hunter 1.25 3.00
10 Pierre Lacroix .40 1.00
11 Mario Marois .40 1.00
12 Dave Pichette .40 1.00
13 Michel Plasse .60 1.50
14 Jacques Richard .60 1.50
15 Normand Rochefort .40 1.00
16 Anton Stastny .60 1.50
17 Peter Stastny 2.00 5.00
18 Marian Stastny 1.00 2.50
19 Marc Tardif .60 1.50
20 Charles Thiffault CO .30 .75
21 Wally Weir .40 1.00

1982-83 Nordiques Postcards

This 24-card set measured approximately 3" by 5 1/2" and featured members of the 1982-83 Quebec Nordiques. The fronts had borderless color action player photos. The backs were in postcard format with a short player biography both in French and in English and a facsimile player autograph on the bottom. The cards were unnumbered and checklisted below in alphabetical order.

COMPLETE SET (25) 10.00 25.00
1 Pierre Aubry .30 .75
2 Michel Bergeron CO .60 1.50
3 Daniel Bouchard .20 .50
4 Real Cloutier .75 2.00
5 Alain Cote .30 .75
6 Andre Dupont .30 .75
7 John Garrett .60 1.50
8 Michel Goulet 1.25 3.00
9 Jean Hamel .30 .75
10 Dale Hunter 1.00 2.50
11 Rick Lapointe .40 1.00
12 Clint Malarchuk .75 2.00
13 Mario Marois .30 .75
14 Randy Moller .30 .75
15 Wilf Paiement .40 1.00
16 Dave Pichette .30 .75
17 Jacques Richard .60 1.50
18 Normand Rochefort .30 .75
19 Louis Sleigher .30 .75
20 Anton Stastny .60 1.50
21 Marian Stastny .60 1.50
22 Peter Stastny 1.25 3.00
23 Marc Tardif .60 1.50
24 Charles Thiffault ACO .20 .50
25 Wally Weir .30 .75

1983-84 Nordiques Postcards

This 32-card set measured approximately 3 1/2" by 5 1/2" and featured members of the 1983-84 Quebec Nordiques. This set featured borderless full-color action shots on the front. The back was in postcard format with a brief identification of the player written in blue ink. This unnumbered set had been checklisted in alphabetical order.

COMPLETE SET (32) 10.00 25.00
1 Pierre Aubry .30 .75
2 Michel Bergeron CO .40 1.00
3 Dan Bouchard .50 1.25
4 Real Cloutier .60 1.50
5 Alain Cote .30 .75
6 Andre Dore .30 .75
7 Andre Dupont .30 .75
8 John Garrett .50 1.25
9 Paul Gillis .30 .75
10 Mario Gosselin .50 1.25
11 Michel Goulet 1.00 2.50
12 Jean Hamel .30 .75
13 Dale Hunter .60 1.50
14 Rick Lapointe .30 .75
15 Clint Malarchuk .60 1.50
16 Jimmy Mann .30 .75
17 Mario Marois .40 1.00
18 Randy Moller .40 1.00
19 Wilf Paiement .40 1.00
20 Dave Pichette .30 .75
21 Pat Price .30 .75
22 Jacques Richard .40 1.00
23 Normand Rochefort .30 .75
24 Jean-Francois Sauve .30 .75
25 Andre Savard .30 .75
26 Louis Sleigher .30 .75
27 Anton Stastny .40 1.00
28 Marian Stastny .40 1.00
29 Peter Stastny 1.00 2.50
30 Marc Tardif .50 1.25
31 Wally Weir .30 .75
32 Blake Wesley .30 .75

1984-85 Nordiques Postcards

This 27-card set measured approximately 3" by 5 1/2" and featured members of the 1984-85 Quebec Nordiques. The fronts had borderless color action player photos. The backs were in postcard format with a short player biography both in French and in English. The years "84-85" appeared in the spot where the stamp is supposed to go. The cards were unnumbered and checklisted below in alphabetical order.

COMPLETE SET (27) 8.00 20.00
1 Brent Ashton .30 .75
2 Bruce Bell .30 .75
3 Michel Bergeron CO .40 1.00
4 Daniel Bouchard .40 1.00
5 Alain Cote .30 .75
6 Gord Donnelly .30 .75
7 Luc Dufour .30 .75
8 Jean-Marc Gaulin .30 .75
9 Paul Gillis .30 .75
10 Mario Gosselin .40 1.00
11 Michel Goulet 1.00 2.50
12 Dale Hunter .60 1.50
13 Guy Lapointe ACO .40 1.00
14 Jimmy Mann .30 .75
15 Mario Marois .30 .75
16 Brad Maxwell .30 .75
17 Randy Moller .30 .75
18 Simon Nolet ACO .30 .75
19 Wilf Paiement .40 1.00
20 Pat Price .30 .75
21 Normand Rochefort .40 1.00
22 Jean-Francois Sauve .40 1.00
23 Andre Savard .30 .75
24 Richard Sevigny .40 1.00
25 Anton Stastny .40 1.00
26 Marian Stastny .40 1.00
27 Peter Stastny 1.00 2.50

1985-86 Nordiques General Foods

These 27 cards measured approximately 3 1/2" by 5 1/2". The fronts featured color close-ups of the players against a light background. The pictures were full-bleed, except at the bottom where the player's number, name and the sponsor's logo appeared in a white bar. The backs were blank. The cards were unnumbered and checklisted below in alphabetical order.

COMPLETE SET (27) 12.00 30.00
1 John Anderson .40 1.00
2 Brent Ashton .40 1.00
3 Michel Bergeron CO .40 1.00
4 Alain Cote .40 1.00
5 Gilbert Delorme .40 1.00
6 Mike Eagles .40 1.00
7 Steven Finn .40 1.00
8 Jean-Marc Gaulin .40 1.00
9 Paul Gillis .40 1.00
10 Mario Gosselin .60 1.50
11 Michel Goulet 1.00 2.50
12 Ron Harris CO .20 .50
13 Dale Hunter 1.00 2.50
14 Mark Kumpel .40 1.00
15 Clint Malarchuk .60 1.50
16 Jimmy Mann .40 1.00
17 Mario Marois .40 1.00
18 Randy Moller .40 1.00
19 Simon Nolet CO .20 .50
20 Pat Price .40 1.00
21 Normand Rochefort .40 1.00
22 Jean-Francois Sauve .40 1.00
23 Richard Sevigny .60 1.50
24 David Shaw .40 1.00
25 Anton Stastny .60 1.50
26 Peter Stastny 1.50 4.00
27 Trevor Stienburg .40 1.00

1985-86 Nordiques McDonald's

This 22-card set measured approximately 3 1/2" by 5 1/2" and featured members of the 1985-86 Quebec Nordiques. The fronts featured borderless color action player photos. The sponsors' logos (McDonald's, Le Soleil and CHRC 80) appeared across the bottom; there were no player names on the fronts. The backs were blank. The cards were unnumbered and checklisted below in alphabetical order.

COMPLETE SET (22) 10.00 25.00
1 Brent Ashton .40 1.00
2 Jeff Brown 1.00 2.50
3 Alain Cote .40 1.00
4 Gilbert Delorme .40 1.00
5 Gord Donnelly .40 1.00
6 Mike Eagles .40 1.00
7 Paul Gillis .40 1.00
8 Mario Gosselin .60 1.50
9 Michel Goulet 1.00 2.50
10 Dale Hunter 1.00 2.50
11 Mark Kumpel .40 1.00
12 Jason Lafreniere .40 1.00
13 Clint Malarchuk .60 1.50
14 Randy Moller .40 1.00
15 Robert Picard .40 1.00
16 Pat Price .40 1.00
17 Normand Rochefort .40 1.00
18 Richard Sevigny .60 1.50
19 David Shaw .40 1.00
20 Risto Siltanen .40 1.00
21 Anton Stastny .60 1.50
22 Peter Stastny 1.50 4.00

1985-86 Nordiques Placemats

This 6-card placemat set of the Quebec Nordiques was sponsored by Pepsi-Cola and Seven-up and measured approximately 11" by 17". The fronts featured a painted portrait, action shot, and facsimile autograph on a yellow background with white border. The player's name, position, jersey number, date and place of birth, and career statistics in French were also found on the front. The sponsors' logos appeared in the upper right corner. The backs carried the sponsors' and team logos on a white background with thin blue, white, and purple borders. The mats were unnumbered, and one placemat showed portraits of all twelve players with their facsimile autographs.

COMPLETE SET (6) 8.00 20.00
1 Brent Ashton 1.25 3.00
Randy Moller
2 Mario Gosselin 1.50 4.00
Clint Malarchuk
3 Dale Hunter 2.00 5.00
Michel Goulet
4 Pat Price 1.25 3.00
Robert Picard
5 Peter Stastny 2.00 5.00
Anton Stastny
6 Player Portraits 2.00 5.00
Dale Hunter
Michel Goulet
Peter Stastny
Anton Stastny
Brent Ashton
Randy Moller
Pat Price
Robert Picard
Mario Gosselin
Clint Malarchuk
Alain Cote
John Anderson

1985-86 Nordiques Provigo

This 25-sticker set of Quebec Nordiques was released through Provigo. The puffy stickers measured approximately 1 1/8" by 2 1/4" and featured a color head and shoulders photo of the player, with the player's number and name bordered by star-studded banners across the bottom of the picture. The player's signature was inscribed just above the banner. The Nordiques' logo was superimposed over the banner at its right end. The backs were blank. We have checklisted them below in alphabetical order, with the uniform number to the right of the player's name. The 25 Styrofoam stickers were to be attached to a cardboard poster. The poster measured approximately 20" by 11" and had 25 white spaces (designated for the stickers) on blue background. At the center was a picture of a goalie mask, with the Nordiques' logo above and slightly to the right. The back of the poster had a checklist, stripes in the team's colors, and two team logos.

COMPLETE SET (25) 8.00 20.00
1 John Anderson 14 .40 1.00
2 Brent Ashton 9 .30 .75
3 Wayne Babych 18 .40 1.00
4 Michel Bergeron CO .40 1.00
5 Alain Cote 19 .30 .75
6 Gilbert Delorme 6 .30 .75
7 Mike Eagles 11 .30 .75
8 Steven Finn 25 .30 .75
9 Paul Gillis 23 .30 .75
10 Mario Gosselin 33 .40 1.00
11 Michel Goulet 16 .75 2.00
12 Dale Hunter 32 .75 2.00
13 Mark Kumpel 17 .30 .75
14 Clint Malarchuk 30 .40 1.00
15 Jimmy Mann 10 .30 .75
16 Mario Marois 22 .40 1.00
17 Randy Moller 21 .30 .75
18 Wilf Paiement 27 .40 1.00
19 Pat Price 7 .30 .75
20 Normand Rochefort 5 .30 .75
21 J.F. Sauve 15 .30 .75
22 Richard Sevigny 1 .40 1.00
23 David Shaw 4 .30 .75
24 Anton Stastny 20 .40 1.00
25 Peter Stastny 26 1.25 3.00
NNO Poster 2.00 5.00

1985-86 Nordiques Team Issue

This 27-card set measured approximately 3 1/2" by 5 1/2" and featured members of the 1985-86 Quebec Nordiques. The fronts featured posed color close-up shots of the players against a light background. The pictures were borderless except at the bottom, where the player's name, uniform number and the team logo appeared in a white bar. The backs were blank. The cards were unnumbered and checklisted below in alphabetical order.

COMPLETE SET (27) 10.00 25.00
1 Brent Ashton .40 1.00
2 Michel Bergeron CO .40 1.00
3 Jeff Brown 1.00 2.50
4 Alain Cote .40 1.00
5 Gilbert Delorme .40 1.00
6 Gord Donnelly .40 1.00
7 Mike Eagles .40 1.00
8 Paul Gillis .40 1.00
9 Mario Gosselin .60 1.50
10 Michel Goulet 1.00 2.50
11 Dale Hunter 1.00 2.50
12 Mark Kumpel .40 1.00
13 Jason Lafreniere .40 1.00
14 Clint Malarchuk .60 1.50
15 Randy Moller .40 1.00
16 Simon Nolet CO .20 .50
17 Robert Picard .40 1.00
18 Pat Price .40 1.00
19 Ken Quinney .40 1.00
20 Normand Rochefort .40 1.00
21 Richard Sevigny .60 1.50
22 David Shaw .40 1.00
23 Risto Siltanen .40 1.00
24 Anton Stastny .60 1.50
25 Peter Stastny 1.50 4.00
26 Charles Thiffault CO .20 .50
27 Richard Zemlak .40 1.00

1986-87 Nordiques General Foods

This 28-card set measured approximately 3 1/2" by 5 1/2" and featured members of the 1986-87 Quebec Nordiques. The fronts featured posed color close-up shots of the players against a light background. The pictures were borderless except at the bottom, where the player's name, uniform number and the sponsor's logo appeared in a white bar. The backs were blank. The cards were unnumbered and checklisted below in alphabetical order.

COMPLETE SET (28) 10.00 25.00
1 Brent Ashton .30 .75
2 Michel Bergeron CO .60 1.50
3 Jeff Brown .60 1.50
4 Alain Cote .30 .75
5 Gilbert Delorme .30 .75
6 Gord Donnelly .30 .75
7 Mike Eagles .30 .75
8 Paul Gillis .30 .75
9 Mario Gosselin .60 1.50
10 Michel Goulet .75 2.00
11 Mike Hough .30 .75
12 Dale Hunter .60 1.50
13 Mark Kumpel .30 .75
14 Jason Lafreniere .30 .75
15 Clint Malarchuk .50 1.25
16 Randy Moller .30 .75
17 Simon Nolet CO .20 .50
18 Robert Picard .30 .75
19 Pat Price .30 .75
20 Ken Quinney .30 .75
21 Normand Rochefort .30 .75
22 Richard Sevigny .50 1.25
23 David Shaw .30 .75
24 Risto Siltanen .30 .75
25 Anton Stastny .40 1.00
26 Peter Stastny 1.25 3.00
27 Charles Thiffault CO .20 .50
28 Richard Zemlak .40 1.00

1986-87 Nordiques McDonald's

This 25-card set measured approximately 3 1/2" by 5 1/2" and featured members of the 1986-87 Quebec Nordiques. The fronts featured borderless color action player photos. The sponsors' logos (McDonald's and Le Soleil) appeared across the bottom; there were no player names on the fronts. The backs were blank. The cards were unnumbered and checklisted below in alphabetical order.

COMPLETE SET (25) 12.00 30.00
1 John Anderson .60 1.50
2 Brent Ashton .40 1.00
3 Jeff Brown .75 2.00
4 Alain Cote .40 1.00
5 Gilbert Delorme .40 1.00
6 Mike Eagles .40 1.00
7 Steven Finn .40 1.00
8 Paul Gillis .40 1.00
9 Mario Gosselin .60 1.50
10 Michel Goulet 1.00 2.50
11 Mike Hough .40 1.00
12 Dale Hunter .75 2.00
13 Mark Kumpel .40 1.00
14 Alain Lemieux .40 1.00
15 Clint Malarchuk .60 1.50
16 Jimmy Mann .60 1.50
17 Randy Moller .40 1.00
18 Wilf Paiement .60 1.50
19 Pat Price .40 1.00
20 Normand Rochefort .40 1.00
21 Jean-Francois Sauve .40 1.00
22 Richard Sevigny .60 1.50
23 David Shaw .40 1.00
24 Anton Stastny .60 1.50
25 Peter Stastny 1.50 4.00

1986-87 Nordiques Team Issue

This 29-card set measured approximately 3 1/2" by 5 1/2" and featured members of the 1986-87 Quebec Nordiques. The fronts featured borderless color action photos. The player's name and number appeared in white or black lettering at the lower right corner. The backs were blank. The cards were unnumbered and checklisted below in alphabetical order.

COMPLETE SET (29) 8.00 20.00
1 Jeff Brown .75 2.00
2 Alain Cote .30 .75
3 Bill Derlago .30 .75
4 Gord Donnelly .30 .75
5 Mike Eagles .30 .75
6 Steven Finn .30 .75
7 Paul Gillis .30 .75
8 Mario Gosselin .40 1.00
9 Michel Goulet .75 2.00
10 Mike Hough .30 .75
11 Dale Hunter .60 1.50
12 Jason Lafreniere .30 .75
13 Clint Malarchuk .50 1.25
14 Basil McRae .40 1.00
15 Randy Moller .30 .75
16 John Ogrodnick .40 1.00
17 Robert Picard .30 .75
18 Pat Price .30 .75
19 Normand Rochefort .30 .75
20 Richard Sevigny .50 1.25
21 David Shaw .30 .75
22 Doug Shedden .30 .75
23 Risto Siltanen .30 .75
24 Anton Stastny .40 1.00
25 Peter Stastny 1.25 3.00

1986-87 Nordiques Yum-Yum

Each card in this ten-card set measured approximately 2" by 2 1/2". The fronts featured color action player photos with blue, white, and red borders. The player's name and number, along with sponsor and team logos, appearedon the front. The backs carried a team checklist. The cards were unnumbered and checklisted below in alphabetical order.

COMPLETE SET (10) 10.00 25.00
1 Alain Cote .75 2.00
2 Gilbert Delorme .75 2.00
3 Paul Gillis .75 2.00
4 Michel Goulet 2.00 5.00
5 Dale Hunter 1.50 4.00
6 Clint Malarchuk 1.25 3.00
7 Robert Picard .75 2.00
8 Normand Rochefort .75 2.00
9 Anton Stastny 1.00 2.50
10 Peter Stastny 2.50 6.00

1987-88 Nordiques General Foods

Each card in this 32-card set measured approximately 3 3/4" by 5 5/8". The fronts featured a full color action photo of the player, with the Quebec Nordiques' logo superimposed at the upper left-hand corner of the picture. At the bottom the player's number and name were given in the white triangle. The backs were blank. The set was issued in two versions, one with and one without the General Foods logo at the lower right corner. Both versions are valued equally. The set featured an early card of Ron Tugnutt pre-dating his O-Pee-Chee rookie card by two years.

COMPLETE SET (32) 8.00 20.00
1 Tommy Albelin 28 .20 .50
2 Jeff Brown 22 .50 1.25
3 Mario Brunetta 30 .30 .75
4 Terry Carkner 4 .30 .75
5 Alain Cote 19 .20 .50
6 Gord Donnelly 34 .20 .50
7 Gaetan Duchesne 14 .30 .75
8 Mike Eagles 11 .20 .50
9 Steven Finn 29 .20 .50
10 Paul Gillis 23 .20 .50
11 Mario Gosselin 33 .40 1.00
12 Michel Goulet 16 .75 2.00
13 Stephane Guerard 46 .20 .50
14 Alan Haworth 15 .20 .50
15 Mike Hough 18 .20 .50
16 Jeff Jackson 25 .20 .50
17 Stu Kulak 17 .20 .50
18 Jason Lafreniere 10 .20 .50
19 Lane Lambert 7 .20 .50
20 David Latta 27 .20 .50
21 Max Middendorf 12 .20 .50
22 Randy Moller 21 .20 .50
23 Robert Picard 24 .20 .50
24 Daniel Poudrier 2 .20 .50
25 Ken Quinney 54 .20 .50
26 Normand Rochefort 5 .20 .50
27 Richard Sevigny 1 .30 .75
28 Anton Stastny 20 .30 .75
29 Peter Stastny 26 1.25 3.00
30 Ron Tugnutt 50 1.50 4.00
31 Alain Chainey .08 .25
Andre Savard
Guy Lapointe
32 Badaboum (Mascot) .08 .25

1987-88 Nordiques Team Issue

COMPLETE SET (32) 15.00 30.00
1 Richard Sevigny .75 2.00
2 Daniel Poudrier .40 1.00
3 Terry Carkner .40 1.00
4 Normand Rochefort .40 1.00
5 Lane Lambert .40 1.00
6 Jason Lafreniere .40 1.00
7 Mike Eagles .40 1.00
8 Max Middendorf .40 1.00
9 Gaetan Duchesne .40 1.00
10 Alan Haworth .40 1.00
11 Michel Goulet .75 2.00
12 Stu Kulak .40 1.00
13 Mike Hough .40 1.00
14 Alain Cote .40 1.00
15 Anton Stastny .75 2.00
16 Randy Moller .40 1.00
17 Jeff Brown .40 1.00
18 Paul Gillis .40 1.00
19 Robert Picard .40 1.00
20 Jeff Jackson .40 1.00
21 Peter Stastny 1.50 4.00
22 David Latta .40 1.00
23 Tommy Albelin .40 1.00
24 Steven Finn .40 1.00
25 Mario Brunetta .40 1.00
26 Mario Gosselin .75 2.00
27 Gord Donnelly .40 1.00
28 Stephane Guerard .40 1.00
29 Ron Tugnutt .75 2.00
30 Ken Quinney .40 1.00
31 Badaboum on sled .08 .25
32 Alain Chainey .20 .50
Andre Savard
Guy Lapointe

1987-88 Nordiques Yum-Yum

Each card in this ten-card set measured approximately 2" by 2 1/2". The front had a color action photo of the player, enframed by red, white, and blue borders. At the bottom the player's number and name was sandwiched between the Nordiques' logo and the Yum-Yum potato chips logo. The back was printed in red, white, and blue, and presented in two columns a checklist of the ten players. We have checklisted the cards below in alphabetical order, with the uniform number to the right of the player's name.

COMPLETE SET (10) 8.00 20.00
1 Alain Cote 19 .60 1.50
2 Paul Gillis 23 .60 1.50
3A Mario Gosselin 33 ERR 1.25 3.00
(Reverse has 83 for sweater number; three numbers messed up)
3B Mario Gosselin 33 COR 1.25 3.00
4 Michel Goulet 16 1.50 4.00
5 Alan Haworth 15 UER .60 1.50
(Reverse has 38 for sweater number)
6 Jason Lafreniere 10 UER .60 1.50
(Reverse has 30 for sweater number)
7 Robert Picard 24 .60 1.50
8 Normand Rochefort 5 .60 1.50
9 Anton Stastny 20 .75 2.00
10 Peter Stastny 26 2.00 5.00

1988-89 Nordiques General Foods

The 31 blank-backed cards comprising this set measured approximately 3 3/4" by 5 5/8" and feature white-bordered color player action shots. The Nordiques logo is displayed at the upper right. The player's first name appears at the lower left of the photo. His last name appears in cursive lettering in the wide white margin below. The player's uniform number and the logos for General Foods, Le Journal de Quebec, and CHRC Sport Radio appear at the bottom right. The cards are unnumbered and checklisted below in alphabetical order. Joe Sakic's card predates his Rookie Card by one year.

COMPLETE SET (31) 14.00 35.00
1 Tommy Albelin .20 .50
2 Badaboum MASCOT .20 .50
3 Joel Baillargeon .20 .50
4 Jeff Brown .30 .75
5 Mario Brunetta .30 .75
6 Coaches .20 .50
Serge Aubry
Ron Lapointe
Guy Lapointe
Alain Chainey
7 Alain Cote .20 .50
8 Gord Donnelly .30 .75
9 Daniel Dore .20 .50
10 Gaetan Duchesne .30 .75
11 Steven Finn .20 .50
12 Marc Fortier .20 .50
13 Paul Gillis .20 .50
14 Mario Gosselin .30 .75
15 Michel Goulet .60 1.50
16 Jari Gronstrand .20 .50
17 Stephane Guerard .20 .50
18 Mike Hough .20 .50
19 Jeff Jackson .20 .50
20 Iiro Jarvi .20 .50
21 Darin Kimble .40 1.00
22 Lane Lambert .20 .50
23 David Latta .20 .50
24 Curtis Leschyshyn .40 1.00
25 Bob Mason .30 .75
26 Mario Marois .20 .50
27 Ken McRae .20 .50
28 Randy Moller .20 .50
29 Robert Picard .20 .50
30 Walt Poddubny .30 .75
31 Joe Sakic 6.00 15.00
32 Greg Smyth .20 .50
33 Anton Stastny .40 1.00
34 Peter Stastny 1.00 2.50
35 Trevor Steinberg .20 .50
36 Ron Tugnutt .75 2.00
37 Mark Vermette .20 .50
38 Team Picture .40 1.00

1988-89 Nordiques Team Issue

The 41 blank-backed cards comprising this set measure approximately 3 3/4" by 5 5/8" and featured white-bordered player action shots. The team logo was displayed at the upper right. The player's first name in all capital letters appeared at the lower left of the photo. His last name was a facsimile autograph in the wide white margin right below, with his uniform number next to it. The cards were unnumbered and checklisted below in alphabetical order. The Joe Sakic issue predated his RC by one year.

COMPLETE SET (33) 15.00 30.00
1 Tommy Albelin .20 .50
2 Serge Aubry CO .30 .75
Ron Lapointe CO
Guy Lapointe CO
Alain Chainey CO
3 Badaboum (Mascot) .08 .25
4 Joel Baillargeon .20 .50
5 Jeff Brown .60 1.50
6 Mario Brunetta .30 .75
7 Alain Cote .20 .50
8 Gord Donnelly .30 .75
9 Daniel Dore .20 .50
10 Gaetan Duchesne .30 .75
11 Steven Finn .20 .50
12 Marc Fortier .20 .50
13 Paul Gillis .20 .50
14 Mario Gosselin .30 .75
15 Michel Goulet .75 2.00
16 Jari Gronstrand .20 .50
17 Stephane Guerard .20 .50
18 Jeff Jackson .20 .50
19 Iiro Jarvi .20 .50
20 Lane Lambert .20 .50
21 David Latta .20 .50
22 Curtis Leschyshyn .40 1.00
23 Bob Mason .30 .75
24 Randy Moller .20 .50
25 Robert Picard .20 .50
26 Walt Poddubny .30 .75
27 Joe Sakic 6.00 15.00
28 Greg Smyth .20 .50
29 Anton Stastny .30 .75
30 Peter Stastny 1.00 2.50
31 Trevor Steinburg .20 .50
32 Mark Vermette .20 .50
33 Team Photo .75 2.00
34 Bobby Dollas .20 .50
35 Mike Hough .20 .50
36 Darin Kimble .20 .50
37 Ken McRae .20 .50
38 Martin Madded .20 .50
39 Ron Tugnutt .40 1.00
40 Mario Marois .20 .50
41 Jean Perron .20 .50

1989-90 Nordiques Team Issue

This 39-card set of the Quebec Nordiques printed on white card stock measured approximately 5 5/8" by 3 3/4" and featured a borderless posed head shot of the player against a blue background. The team logo and the player's name and jersey number appeared to the left of each picture. The backs were blank. The cards were unnumbered and checklisted below in alphabetical order.

COMPLETE SET (39) 10.00 25.00
1 Serge Aubry .20 .50
2 Michel Bergeron CO .20 .50
3 Jeff Brown .30 .75
4 Alain Chainey .20 .50
5 Joe Cirella .20 .50
6 Lucien DeBlois .20 .50
7 Daniel Dore .20 .50
8 Steven Finn .20 .50
9 Stephane Fiset .60 1.50
10 Bryan Fogarty .20 .50
11 Marc Fortier .20 .50
12 Paul Gillis .20 .50
13 Michel Goulet .40 1.00
14 Jari Gronstrand .20 .50
15 Stephane Guerard .20 .50
16 Mike Hough .20 .50
17 Tony Hrkac .20 .50
18 Jeff Jackson .20 .50
19 Iiro Jarvi .20 .50
20 Kevin Kaminski .20 .50
21 Darin Kimble .20 .50
22 Guy Lafleur 1.00 2.50
23 Guy Lapointe .20 .50
24 David Latta .20 .50
25 Brian Lawton .20 .50
26 Curtis Leschyshyn .30 .75
27 Claude Loiselle .20 .50
28 Mario Marois .20 .50
29 Tony McKegney .20 .50
30 Ken McRae .20 .50
31 Greg Millen .30 .75
32 Randy Moller .20 .50
33 Sergei Mylnikov .30 .75
34 Michel Petit .20 .50
35 Robert Picard .20 .50
36 Joe Sakic 6.00 15.00
37 Peter Stastny .60 1.50
38 Ron Tugnutt .60 1.50
39 Team Picture .20 .50

1989-90 Nordiques General Foods

This 30-card set of Quebec Nordiques printed on white card stock measured approximately 5 5/8" by 3 3/4" and featured a borderless posed head shot of the player against a blue background. It was essentially the same as the 1989-90 Quebec Nordiques set save for the smaller set size and the appearance of a General Foods logo in the lower left corner. Card backs were blank and unnumbered; thus the cards are listed below alphabetically. Joe Sakic's card appeared during his Rookie Card year.

COMPLETE SET (30) 10.00 25.00
1 Michel Bergeron CO .20 .50
2 Jeff Brown .30 .75
3 Joe Cirella .20 .50
4 Lucien DeBlois .20 .50
5 Daniel Dore .20 .50
6 Steven Finn .20 .50
7 Stephane Fiset .60 1.50
8 Marc Fortier .20 .50
9 Paul Gillis .20 .50
10 Michel Goulet .40 1.00
11 Jari Gronstrand .20 .50
12 Stephane Guerard .20 .50
13 Mike Hough .20 .50
14 Jeff Jackson .20 .50
15 Iiro Jarvi .20 .50
16 Kevin Kaminski .20 .50
17 Darin Kimble .20 .50
18 Guy Lafleur 1.00 2.50
19 David Latta .20 .50
20 Curtis Leschyshyn .30 .75
21 Claude Loiselle .20 .50
22 Mario Marois .20 .50
23 Ken McRae .20 .50
24 Sergei Mylnikov .30 .75
25 Michel Petit .20 .50
26 Robert Picard .20 .50
27 Joe Sakic 6.00 15.00
28 Peter Stastny .60 1.50
29 Ron Tugnutt .60 1.50
30 Team Photo .60 1.50

1989-90 Nordiques Police

This 27-card police set of Quebec Nordiques was sponsored by the city of Vanier. The cards measured approximately 4" by 2 3/4" and featured a borderless posed head and shoulders photo against a blue background. The team logo appeared to the left of each player picture. The backs, which read "Un Project Stupefiant..Sss" across the top, were printed in French and present biography and an anti-drug or alcohol message on the left side. The right side had a local police number and slot for a police officer's signature. The cards were unnumbered and checklisted below in alphabetical order. Joe Sakic's card appears during his Rookie Card year.

COMPLETE SET (27) 8.00 20.00
1 Jeff Brown .30 .75
2 Joe Cirella .20 .50
3 Lucien DeBlois .20 .50
4 Daniel Dore .20 .50
5 Steven Finn .20 .50
6 Stephane Fiset .60 1.50
7 Marc Fortier .20 .50
8 Paul Gillis .20 .50
9 Michel Goulet .40 1.00
10 Stephane Guerard .20 .50
11 Mike Hough .20 .50
12 Jeff Jackson .20 .50
13 Iiro Jarvi .20 .50
14 Darin Kimble .20 .50
15 Guy Lafleur 1.00 2.50
16 David Latta .20 .50
17 Curtis Leschyshyn .30 .75
18 Claude Loiselle .20 .50
19 Mario Marois .20 .50
20 Ken McRae .20 .50
21 Sergei Mylnikov .30 .75
22 Michel Petit .20 .50
23 Robert Picard .20 .50
24 Jean-Marc Routhier .20 .50
25 Joe Sakic 6.00 15.00
26 Peter Stastny .60 1.50
27 Ron Tugnutt .60 1.50

1990-91 Nordiques Petro-Canada

These blank-backed cards measured approximately 3 3/4" by 5 5/8" and featured white-bordered color player action shots. The player's name, uniform number, Nordiques logo, and Petro-Canada logo appeared on the bottom. The words "Les Nordiques" in blue letters was printed in the upper right corner. The cards were unnumbered and checklisted below in alphabetical order.

COMPLETE SET (28) 15.00 30.00
1 Aaron Broten .20 .50
2 Dave Chambers CO .20 .50
3 Joe Cirella .30 .75
4 Lucien DeBlois .20 .50
5 Steven Finn .20 .50

6 Bryan Fogarty .20 .50
7 Marc Fortier .20 .50
8 Robbie Ftorek ACO .20 .50
9 Paul Gillis .20 .50
10 Scott Gordon .30 .75
11 Mike Hough .20 .50
12 Tony Hrkac .30 .75
13 Darin Kimble .30 .75
14 Guy Lafleur .75 2.00
15 Curtis Leschyshyn .20 .50
16 Claude Loiselle .20 .50
17 Jacques Martin ACO .20 .50
18 Tony McKegney .20 .50
19 Owen Nolan 1.00 2.50
20 Michel Petit .20 .50
21 Joe Sakic 2.00 5.00
22 Everett Sanipass .20 .50
23 Mats Sundin 1.25 3.00
24 John Tanner .30 .75
25 Ron Tugnutt .40 1.00
26 Daniel Vincelette .20 .50
27 Craig Wolanin .20 .50
28 Team Photo .30 .75
29 Shawn Anderson .20 .50
30 Jacques Cloutier .30 .75
31 Alexei Gusarov .20 .50
32 Jeff Jackson .20 .50
33 Claude Lapointe .20 .50
34 Stephane Morin .20 .50
35 Scott Pearson .20 .50
36 Ken Quinney .20 .50
37 Serge Roberge .20 .50
38 Tony Twist .40 1.00
39 Randy Velischek .20 .50
40 Wayne Van Dorp .40 1.00
41 Mark Vermette .20 .50
42 Badaboum MASCOT .08 .25

1990-91 Nordiques Team Issue

The 25 blank-backed cards comprising this set measured approximately 5 5/8" by 3 3/4" and featured white-bordered posed color player head shots against blue backgrounds. The Quebec Nordiques logo was prominently displayed to the left of the player. The player's name and uniform number appeared in white lettering below the logo. The cards were unnumbered and checklisted below in alphabetical order.

COMPLETE SET (25) 6.00 15.00
1 Joe Cirella .20 .50
2 Lucien DeBlois .20 .50
3 Daniel Dore .20 .50
4 Steven Finn .20 .50
5 Stephane Fiset .60 1.50
6 Bryan Fogarty .20 .50
7 Marc Fortier .20 .50
8 Paul Gillis .20 .50
9 Michel Goulet .50 1.25
10 Stephane Guerard .20 .50
11 Mike Hough .20 .50
12 Tony Hrkac .25 .60
13 Jeff Jackson .20 .50
14 Iiro Jarvi .20 .50
15 Kevin Kaminski .20 .50
16 Darin Kimble .25 .60
17 David Latta .20 .50
18 Curtis Leschyshyn .20 .50
19 Claude Loiselle .20 .50
20 Mario Marois .20 .50
21 Tony McKegney .20 .50
22 Ken McRae .20 .50
23 Michel Petit .20 .50
24 Peter Stastny .60 1.50
25 Ron Tugnutt .40 1.00

1991 Nordiques Panini Team Stickers

This 32-sticker set was issued in a plastic bag that contained two 16-sticker sheets (approximately 9" by 12") and a foldout poster, "Super Poster - Hockey 91", on which the stickers could be affixed. The players' names appeared only on the poster, not on the stickers. Each sticker measured about 2 1/8" by 2 7/8" and featured a color player action shot on its white-bordered front. The back of the white sticker sheet was lined off into 16 panels, each carried the logos for Panini, the NHL, and the NHLPA, as well as the same number that appears on the front of the sticker. Every Canadian NHL team was featured in this promotion. Each team set was available by mail-order from Panini Canada Ltd. for 2.99 plus 50 cents for shipping and handling.

COMPLETE SET (32) 2.00 5.00
1 Joe Cirella .01 .05
2 Daniel Dore .01 .05
3 Steven Finn .01 .05
4 Bryan Fogarty .01 .05
5 Marc Fortier .01 .05
6 Paul Gillis .01 .05
7 Scott Gordon .02 .10
8 Stephane Guerard .01 .05
9 Mike Hough .01 .05
10 Tony Hrkac .01 .05
11 Darin Kimble .01 .05
12 Guy Lafleur .20 .50
13 Curtis Leschyshyn .02 .10
14 Claude Loiselle .01 .05
15 Tony McKegney .01 .05
16 Ken McRae .01 .05
17 Owen Nolan .20 .50
18 Joe Sakic .50 1.25
19 Everett Sanipass .01 .05
20 Mats Sundin .30 .75
21 John Tanner .02 .10
22 Ron Tugnutt .05 .15
23 Randy Velischek .01 .05
24 Craig Wolanin .01 .05
A Team Logo Left Side .01 .05
B Team Logo Right Side .01 .05
C Guy Lafleur Upper Left Corner .08 .25
D Guy Lafleur Lower Left Corner .08 .25
E Benoit Hogue Upper Right Corner .02 .10
F Benoit Hogue Lower Right Corner .02 .10
G Guy Lafleur .20 .50
H Mats Sundin .30 .75

1991-92 Nordiques Petro-Canada

These blank-backed cards measured approximately 3 1/2" by 5 5/8" and featured white-bordered color player action shots. The player's name, uniform number, Nordiques logo, and Petro-Canada logo appeared within the purplish margin on the left and below the photo. The cards were unnumbered and checklisted below in alphabetical order.

COMPLETE SET (35) 8.00 20.00
1 Badaboum (Mascot) .08 .25
2 Don Barber .20 .50
3 Jacques Cloutier .30 .75
4 Steven Finn .20 .50
5 Stephane Fiset .50 1.25
6 Bryan Fogarty .20 .50
7 Adam Foote .40 1.00
8 Marc Fortier .20 .50
9 Alexei Gusarov .20 .50
10 Mike Hough .20 .50
11 Don Jackson ACO .08 .25
12 Valeri Kamensky .60 1.50
13 John Kordic .30 .75
14 Claude Lapointe .20 .50
15 Curtis Leschyshyn .25 .60
16 Jacques Martin ACO .20 .50
17 Mike McNeill .20 .50
18 Ken McRae .20 .50
19 Kip Miller .20 .50
20 Stephane Morin .20 .50
21 Owen Nolan .60 1.50
22 Pierre Page GM/CO .20 .50
23 Greg Paslawski .20 .50
24 Herb Raglan .20 .50
25 Joe Sakic 1.50 4.00
26 Doug Smail .20 .50
27 Greg Smyth .20 .50
28 Mats Sundin .75 2.00
29 Mikhail Tatarinov .20 .50
30 Ron Tugnutt .30 .75
31 Tony Twist .50 1.25
32 Wayne Van Dorp .20 .50
33 Randy Velischek .20 .50
34 Mark Vermette .20 .50
35 Craig Wolanin .20 .50

1992-93 Nordiques Petro-Canada

These blank-backed cards measured approximately 3 1/2" by 5 5/8" and featured white-bordered color player action shots. The player's name, uniform number, Nordiques logo, and Petro-Canada logo appeared within the purplish margin on the left and below the photo. The cards were unnumbered and checklisted below in alphabetical order.

COMPLETE SET (39) 8.00 20.00
1 Badaboum (Mascot) .08 .25
2 Daniel Bouchard CO .20 .50
3 Gino Cavallini .20 .50
4 Jacques Cloutier .30 .75
5 Steve Duchesne .20 .50
6 Steven Finn .20 .50
7 Stephane Fiset .40 1.00
8 Adam Foote .40 1.00
9 Alexei Gusarov .20 .50
10 Ron Hextall .40 1.00
11 Mike Hough .20 .50
12 Kerry Huffman .20 .50
13 Tim Hunter .20 .50
14 Don Jackson ACO .08 .25
15 Valeri Kamensky .20 .50
16 David Karpa .20 .50
17 Andrei Kovalenko .20 .50
18 Claude Lapointe .20 .50
19 Curtis Leschyshyn .20 .50
20 Bill Lindsay .20 .50
21 Jacques Martin ACO .08 .25
22 Owen Nolan .40 1.00
23 Pierre Page GM/CO .08 .25
24 Scott Pearson .20 .50
25 Herb Raglan .20 .50
26 Mike Ricci .30 .75
27 Martin Rucinsky .20 .50
28 Joe Sakic 1.50 4.00
29 Andre Savard ACO .08 .25
30 Chris Simon .40 1.00
31 Mats Sundin .75 2.00
32 John Tanner .25 .60
33 Mikhail Tatarinov .20 .50
34 Tony Twist .30 .75
35 Wayne Van Dorp .20 .50
36 Mark Vermette .20 .50
37 Craig Wolanin .20 .50
38 Scott Young .30 .75
39 Team Photo .08 .25

1994-95 Nordiques Burger King

Sponsored by Burger King, this 24-card set measured approximately 3 1/2" by 6" and featured members of the 1994-95 Quebec Nordiques. The fronts had white-bordered color action player shots, with the player's name and uniform number was a team color-coded bar alongside the left or right. A small color player portrait with red borders appeared on the bottom. The backs carried another small blue-toned action shot, along with biography, career statistics and highlights (both in English and French) and the sponsor logo. The cards were unnumbered and checklisted below in alphabetical order.

COMPLETE SET (28) 8.00 20.00
1 Badaboum .20 .50
2 Bob Bassen .20 .50
3 Wendel Clark .40 1.00
4 Adam Deadmarsh .40 1.00
5 Steven Finn .20 .50
6 Stephane Fiset .40 1.00
7 Adam Foote .30 .75
8 Peter Forsberg 2.00 5.00
9 Alexei Gusarov .20 .50
10 Valeri Kamensky .20 .50
11 Jon Klemm .20 .50
12 Andrei Kovalenko .20 .50
13 Uwe Krupp .20 .50
14 Claude Lapointe .20 .50
15 Janne Laukkanen .20 .50
16 Sylvain Lefebvre .20 .50
17 Curtis Leschyshyn .20 .50
18 Paul MacDermid .20 .50
19 Owen Nolan .60 1.50
20 Mike Ricci .30 .75
21 Martin Rucinsky .30 .75
22 Joe Sakic 1.25 3.00
23 Reggie Savage .20 .50
24 Chris Simon .20 .50
25 Jocelyn Thibault .60 1.50
26 Craig Wolanin .20 .50
27 Scott Young .30 .75
28 Team Card .20 .50

2001 Nortel All-Star Game Sheets

Sponsored by Nortel Networks, this 10-card set featured two sheets containing six perforated cards each of the NHL's Top All-Stars. The sheets were given to participants in a shooting contest at the All-Star Fan Fest, and so are extremely difficult to acquire. Each card featured a full color action photo set against the colored All-Star Game logo for 2001. The cards were bound together by a gray sheet that displayed the Nortel Networks logo and the North America vs. The World logo.

COMPLETE SET (12) 24.00 60.00
1 Jaromir Jagr 3.00 7.50
2 Peter Forsberg 3.00 7.50
3 Pavel Bure 1.00 2.50
4 Nicklas Lidstrom 1.00 2.50
5 Dominik Hasek 2.00 5.00
6 Sandis Ozolinsh .40 1.00
7 Paul Kariya 4.00 10.00
8 Joe Sakic 3.00 7.50
9 Theo Fleury 1.00 2.50
10 Ray Bourque 3.00 7.50
11 Patrick Roy 6.00 15.00
12 Chris Pronger 1.00 2.50

1970-71 North Stars Postcards

This 10-card set measured 3 1/2" by 5 1/2" and was stapled together in a booklet with the team name and logo above two hockey sticks on a pale green background. The fronts featured posed, color player photos. The backs carried the player's name, biographical information and career highlights printed in blue on a white background. The cards were unnumbered and checklisted below in alphabetical order.

COMPLETE SET (10) 17.50 35.00
1 Barry Gibbs 1.00 2.00
2 Bill Goldsworthy 2.50 5.00
3 Danny Grant 2.00 4.00
4 Ted Harris 1.00 2.00
5 Cesare Maniago 3.00 6.00
6 Jean Paul Parise 1.50 3.00
7 Tom Reid 1.00 2.00
8 Bobby Rousseau 1.00 2.00
9 Tom Williams 1.00 2.00
10 Lorne Worsley 5.00 10.00

1972-73 North Stars Glossy Photos

These 20 blank-backed approximately 8" by 10" glossy white-bordered black-and-white photo sheets featured a suited-up posed player photo on the right and, on the left, a posed player head shot. Below the head shot appeared the player's name and the Minnesota North Stars name and logo. The photos were unnumbered and checklisted below in alphabetical order.

COMPLETE SET (20) 10.00 20.00
1 Fred Barrett .50 1.00
2 Charlie Burns .50 1.00
3 Jude Drouin .50 1.00
4 Barry Gibbs .50 1.00
5 Bill Goldsworthy 1.25 2.50
6 Danny Grant .75 1.50
7 Ted Harris .50 1.00
8 Fred(Buster) Harvey .50 1.00
9 Dennis Hextall .75 1.50
10 Cesare Maniago 1.00 2.00
11 Doug Mohns .75 1.50
12 Lou Nanne .75 1.50
13 Bob Nevin .50 1.00
14 Dennis O'Brien .50 1.00
15 Murray Oliver .50 1.00
16 J.P. Parise .50 1.00
17 Dean Prentice .75 1.50
18 Tom Reid .50 1.00
19 Gump Worsley 2.50 5.00
20 Wren Blair GM Jack Gordon CO .50 1.00

1973-74 North Stars Action Posters

These 14 x 20 color action posters were distributed by Mr. Steak restaurants in the Minneapolis area. They were distributed one every two weeks for twenty weeks.

COMPLETE SET (10) 10.00 20.00
1 Henry Boucha 1.00 2.00
2 Jude Drouin 1.00 2.00
3 Barry Gibbs 1.00 2.00
4 Bill Goldsworthy 1.50 3.00
5 Dennis Hextall 1.00 2.00
6 Cesare Maniago 1.50 3.00
7 Lou Nanne 1.50 3.00
8 Dennis O'Brien 1.00 2.00
9 J.P. Parise 1.50 3.00
10 Tom Reid 1.00 2.00

1973-74 North Stars Postcards

These postcard sized cards featured black and white posed photos on the front, and were blank backed. Cards were unnumbered and checklisted below alphabetically.

COMPLETE SET (20) 10.00 20.00
1 Fred Barrett .38 .75
2 Gary Bergman .38 .75
3 Jude Drouin .38 .75
4 Tony Featherstone .38 .75
5 Barry Gibbs .38 .75
6 Bill Goldsworthy .63 1.25
7 Danny Grant .38 .75
8 Buster Harvey .38 .75
9 Dennis Hextall .50 1.00
10 Parker MacDonald .38 .75
11 Cesare Maniago .50 1.00
12 Lou Nanne .50 1.00
13 Rod Norrish .38 .75
14 Dennis O'Brien .38 .75
15 Murray Oliver .38 .75
16 Jean-Paul Parise .38 .75
17 Dean Prentice .50 1.00
18 Tom Reid .38 .75
19 Fred Stanfield .63 1.25
20 Lorne Worsley 1.50 3.00

1978-79 North Stars Cloverleaf Dairy

This ten-panel set of Minnesota North Stars was issued on the side of half gallon milk cartons as part of a sweepstakes. The picture and text were printed in either red or purple. The panels measured approximately 3 3/4" by 7 5/8", with two players per panel. The North Stars' logo, the team name, year, and panel number appeared at the top of each panel. Each panel featured a "mug shot" and brief biographical information on two players. A North Stars question was included at the bottom of each panel. There were ten questions in all: one per panel, and a tenth question on the final entry panel, which also included a list of all ten questions and gave complete entry information. The unnumbered panel described the sweepstakes promotion and lists the prizes.

COMPLETE SET (11) 62.50 125.00
1 Gilles Meloche and Gary Sargent 7.50 15.00
2 Fred Barrett and Per-Olov Brasar 6.00 12.00
3 Jean-Paul Parise and Greg Smith 6.00 12.00
4 Al MacAdam and Kent-Erik Andersson 6.00 12.00
5 Gary Edwards and Bobby Smith 12.50 25.00
6 Mike Polich and Brad Maxwell 6.00 12.00
7 Steve Payne and Glen Sharpley 6.00 12.00
8 Tim Young and Kris Manery 6.00 12.00
9 Ron Zanussi and Tom Younghans 6.00 12.00
10 Final Entry Panel 6.00 12.00
NNO Sweepstakes Promotion 2.50 5.00

1979-80 North Stars Postcards

This 21-card set measured approximately 3 1/2" by 5 1/2" and featured the 1979-80 Minnesota North Stars. The fronts had borderless black-and-white player action photos. The backs had a postcard format and carry the player's name, position, short biography, and the team logo. The cards were unnumbered and checklisted below in alphabetical order.

COMPLETE SET (21) 10.00 20.00
1 Kent-Erik Andersson .38 .75
2 Fred Barrett .38 .75
3 Gary Edwards .75 1.50
4 Mike Fidler .38 .75
5 Craig Hartsburg 1.00 2.00
6 Al MacAdam .50 1.00
7 Kris Manery .38 .75
8 Brad Maxwell .38 .75
9 Tom McCarthy .50 1.00
10 Gilles Meloche 1.00 2.00
11 Steve Payne .50 1.00
12 Mike Polich .38 .75
13 Gary Sargent .50 1.00
14 Glen Sharpley .38 .75
15 Paul Shmyr .38 .75
16 Bobby Smith 1.50 3.00
17 Greg Smith .38 .75
18 Glen Sonmor CO .38 .75
19 Tim Young .50 1.00
20 Tom Younghans .38 .75
21 Ron Zanussi .38 .75

1980-81 North Stars Postcards

This 24-card set measured approximately 3 1/2" by 5 1/2" and featured the 1980-81 Minnesota North Stars. The fronts had borderless color posed player photos with facsimile autographs across the bottom. The backs had a postcard format and carry a short player biography and the team logo in green print. The cards were unnumbered and checklisted below in alphabetical order.

COMPLETE SET (24) 9.00 18.00
1 Kent-Erik Andersson .30 .75
2 Fred Barrett .30 .75
3 Don Beaupre 1.00 2.50
4 Jack Carlson 1.00 2.50
5 Steve Christoff .40 1.00
6 Mike Eaves .30 .75
7 Gary Edwards .60 1.50
8 Curt Giles .40 1.00
9 Craig Hartsburg .75 2.00
10 Al MacAdam .30 .75
11 Brad Maxwell .30 .75
12 Tom McCarthy .30 .75
13 Gilles Meloche .60 1.50
14 Murray Oliver ACO J.P. Parise ACO Glen Sonmor CO .30 .75
15 Steve Payne .30 .75
16 Mike Polich .30 .75
17 Gary Sargent .40 1.00
18 Glen Sharpley .30 .75
19 Paul Shmyr .30 .75
20 Bobby Smith 1.00 2.50
21 Greg Smith .30 .75
22 Tim Young .30 .75
23 Tom Younghans .30 .75
24 Ron Zanussi .30 .75

1981-82 North Stars Postcards

This 24-card set measured approximately 3 1/2" by 5 1/2" and featured color player photos on the fronts. The backs had a green postcard design with the North Stars' logo printed in pale green on the left side. The player's name, position, and biographical information appeared in the upper left corner. The season and team name appeared vertically in the middle, bisecting the cards. The cards were unnumbered and checklisted below in alphabetical order.

COMPLETE SET (24) 10.00 25.00
1 Kent-Erik Andersson .30 .75
2 Fred Barrett .30 .75
3 Don Beaupre 1.00 2.50
4 Neal Broten 1.50 4.00
5 Jack Carlson .75 2.00
6 Steve Christoff .30 .75
7 Dino Ciccarelli 2.50 6.00
8 Mike Eaves .30 .75
9 Curt Giles .40 1.00
10 Anders Hakansson .30 .75
11 Craig Hartsburg .60 1.50
12 Al Macadam .30 .75
13 Brad Maxwell .30 .75
14 Kevin Maxwell .30 .75
15 Tom McCarthy .30 .75
16 Gilles Meloche .60 1.50
17 Bill Nyrop .30 .75
18 Steve Payne .30 .75
19 Brad Palmer .30 .75
20 Gordie Roberts .30 .75
21 Gary Sargent .30 .75
22 Bobby Smith .75 2.00
23 Glen Sonmor CO J.P. Parise ACO Murray Oliver ACO .30 .75
24 Tim Young .30 .75

1982-83 North Stars Postcards

This 25-card set measured approximately 3 1/2" by 5 1/2" and featured color player photos on the fronts. The backs had a green postcard design with the North Stars' logo printed in pale green on the left side. The player's name, position, and biographical information appeared in the upper left corner. The season and team name appeared vertically in the middle, bisecting the cards. The cards were unnumbered and checklisted below in alphabetical order.

COMPLETE SET (24) 10.00 25.00
1 Fred Barrett .30 .75
2 Don Beaupre .60 1.50
3 Brian Bellows 1.25 3.00
4 Neal Broten 1.00 2.50
5 Dino Ciccarelli 1.50 4.00
6 Dino Ciccarelli Neal Broten 1.00 2.50
7 Jordy Douglas .30 .75
8 Mike Eaves .30 .75
9 George Ferguson .30 .75
10 Ron Friest .30 .75
11 Curt Giles .40 1.00
12 Craig Hartsburg .60 1.50
13 Al MacAdam .30 .75
14 Dan Mandich .30 .75
15 Brad Maxwell .30 .75
16 Tom McCarthy .30 .75
17 Gilles Meloche .60 1.50
18 Steve Payne .30 .75
19 Willi Plett .40 1.00
20 Gordie Roberts .30 .75
21 Gary Sargent .30 .75
22 Bobby Smith .75 2.00
23 Ken Solheim .30 .75
24 Tim Young .30 .75
25 Team Photo .60 1.50

1983-84 North Stars Postcards

This 27-card set measured approximately 3 1/2" by 5 1/2" and featured color player photos on the fronts. The backs had a green postcard design with the North Stars' logo printed in pale green on the left side. The player's name, position, and biographical information appeared in the upper left corner. The season and team name appeared vertically in the middle, bisecting the cards. The cards wereunnumbered and checklisted below in alphabetical order.

COMPLETE SET (27) 8.00 20.00
1 Keith Acton .30 .75
2 Brent Ashton .30 .75
3 Don Beaupre .60 1.50
4 Brian Bellows .75 2.00
5 Neal Broten .75 2.00
6 Dino Ciccarelli 1.00 2.50
7 Jordy Douglas .30 .75
8 George Ferguson .30 .75
9 Curt Giles .40 1.00
10 Craig Hartsburg .40 1.00
11 Brian Lawton .30 .75
12 Craig Levie .30 .75
13 Lars Lindgren .30 .75
14 Al MacAdam .30 .75
15 Bill Mahoney CO .20 .50
16 Dan Mandich .30 .75
17 Dennis Maruk .50 1.25
18 Brad Maxwell .30 .75
19 Tom McCarthy .30 .75
20 Gilles Meloche .40 1.00
21 Mark Napier .30 .75
22 Steve Payne .30 .75
23 Willi Plett .40 1.00
24 Dave Richter .30 .75
25 Gordie Roberts .30 .75
26 Randy Velischek .30 .75
27 Team Photo .60 1.50

1984-85 North Stars 7-Eleven

This 12-card safety set was sponsored by the Southland Corporation in cooperation with the Fire Marshalls Assn. of Minnesota and the Minnesota North Stars. The cards measured 2 5/8" by 4 1/8". The front had a color action photo enframed by a thin green border on white card stock. The green box below the picture gave the uniform number, player's name, player's position, the team name, and team logo. The card number on the back was sandwiched between the North Stars' and 7-Eleven logos. The back also had basic biographical information, career scoring statistics, and a fire prevention tip in a yellow box on the lower portion of the card back.

COMPLETE SET (12) 3.00 8.00
1 Neal Broten .50 1.25
2 Willi Plett .30 .75
3 Craig Hartsburg .50 1.25
4 Brian Bellows .75 2.00
5 Gordie Roberts .20 .50
6 Keith Acton .30 .75
7 Paul Holmgren .30 .75
8 Gilles Meloche .30 .75
9 Dennis Maruk .50 1.25
10 Tom McCarthy .20 .50
11 Steve Payne .30 .75
12 Dino Ciccarelli .75 2.00

1984-85 North Stars Postcards

This 25-card set measured approximately 3 1/2" by 5 1/2" and featured full-bleed, posed, color player photos. The backs had a green postcard design. The North Stars' logo was printed in pale green on the left side. The player's name, position, and biographical information appeared in the upper left corner. The season and team name appeared vertically in the middle, bisecting the cards. The cards were unnumbered and checklisted below in alphabetical order.

COMPLETE SET (29) 6.00 15.00
1 Keith Acton .30 .75
2 Don Beaupre .60 1.50
3 Brian Bellows .75 2.00
4 Scott Bjugstad .20 .50
5 Neal Broten .60 1.50
6 Dino Ciccarelli .75 2.00
7 Curt Giles .30 .75
8 Curt Giles w/captains C .20 .50
9 Craig Hartsburg .60 1.50
10 Tom Hirsch .20 .50
11 Paul Holmgren .40 1.00
12 Brian Lawton .20 .50
13 Dan Mandich .20 .50
14 Dennis Maruk .60 1.50
15 Brad Maxwell .20 .50
16 Tom McCarthy .20 .50
17 Tony McKegney .20 .50
18 Roland Melanson .30 .75
19 Gilles Meloche .30 .75
20 Mark Napier .20 .50
21 Steve Payne .30 .75
22 Willi Plett .30 .75
23 Dave Richter .20 .50
24 Gordie Roberts .20 .50
25 Bob Rouse .20 .50
26 Gord Sherven .20 .50
27 Harold Snepsts .40 1.00
28 Ken Solheim .20 .50
29 Randy Velischek .20 .50

1985-86 North Stars 7-Eleven

This 12-card safety set was sponsored by the Southland Corporation in cooperation with the Fire Marshalls Assn. of Minnesota and the Minnesota North Stars. The cards measured the standard size, 2 1/2" by 3 1/2". The front had a color action photo enframed by a thin green border on white card stock. The green box below the picture gave the uniform number, player's name, position, the team name, and team logo. The card number on the back was sandwiched between the North Stars' and 7-Eleven logos. The back also had basic biographical information, career scoring statistics, and a fire prevention tip in a yellow box on the lower portion of the card back.

COMPLETE SET (12) 3.00 8.00
1 Dino Ciccarelli .75 2.00
2 Scott Bjugstad .20 .50
3 Curt Giles .30 .75
4 Don Beaupre .40 1.00
5 Tony McKegney .20 .50
6 Neal Broten .60 1.50
7 Willi Plett .30 .75
8 Craig Hartsburg .40 1.00
9 Brian Bellows .40 1.00
10 Keith Acton .30 .75
11 Dave Langevin .20 .50
12 Dirk Graham .60 1.50

1985-86 North Stars Postcards

This 27-card set measured 3 1/2" by 5 1/2" and featured full-bleed, posed, color player photos on thin card stock. The backs had a green postcard design. The North Stars' logo was printed in pale green outline lettering on the left side. The player's name and biographical information appeared in the upper left corner. The cards were unnumbered and checklisted below in alphabetical order. The year of the set is established by the Dave Langevin card; he played with the North Stars only during the 1985-86 season.

COMPLETE SET (27) 6.00 15.00
1 Keith Acton .30 .75
2 Don Beaupre .40 1.00
3 Brian Bellows .40 1.00
4 Bo Berglund .20 .50
5 Scott Bjugstad .20 .50
6 Neal Broten .60 1.50
7 Jon Casey .60 1.50
8 Dino Ciccarelli .75 2.00
9 Tim Coulis .20 .50
10 Curt Giles .30 .75
11 Dirk Graham .60 1.50
12 Mats Hallin .20 .50
13 Craig Hartsburg .40 1.00
14 Tom Hirsch .20 .50
15 Dave Langevin .20 .50
16 Brian Lawton .20 .50
17 Craig Levie .20 .50
18 Dan Mandich .20 .50
19 Dennis Maruk .40 1.00
20 Tom McCarthy .20 .50
21 Tony McKegney .20 .50
22 Roland Melanson .30 .75
23 Steve Payne .20 .50
24 Willi Plett .30 .75
25 Gordie Roberts .20 .50
26 Bob Rouse .30 .75
27 Gord Sherven .20 .50

1986-87 North Stars 7-Eleven

This 12-card safety set was sponsored by the Southland Corporation in cooperation with the Fire Marshalls Assn. of Minnesota and the Minnesota North Stars. The cards measured the standard size, 2 1/2" by 3 1/2". The front had a color action photo enframed by a thin green border on white card stock. The green box below the picture gave the uniform number, player's name, position, the team name, and team logo. The card number on the back was sandwiched between the North Stars' and 7-Eleven logos. The back also had basic biographical information, career scoring statistics, and a fire prevention tip in a yellow box on the lower portion of the card back. The copyright notice on the back said 1987.

COMPLETE SET (12) 3.00 8.00
1 Neal Broten .40 1.00
2 Brian MacLellan .20 .50
3 Willi Plett .30 .75
4 Scott Bjugstad .20 .50
5 Don Beaupre .40 1.00
6 Dino Ciccarelli .75 2.00
7 Craig Hartsburg .40 1.00
8 Dennis Maruk .60 1.50
9 Bob Rouse .20 .50
10 Gordie Roberts .20 .50
11 Bob Brooke .20 .50
12 Brian Bellows .60 1.50

1987-88 North Stars Postcards

This 31-card set of Minnesota North Stars featured color action photos without borders. The cards measured approximately 3 1/2" by 5 3/8" and are of the postcard type format. The backs were printed in green, provided brief biographical information, and had the North Stars' logo on the left-hand portion. These cards were unnumbered and we have checklisted them below in alphabetical order.

COMPLETE SET (31) 8.00 20.00
1 Keith Acton .25 .60
2 Dave Archibald .20 .50
3 Warren Babe .20 .50
4 Don Beaupre .40 1.00
5 Brian Bellows .40 1.00
6 Mike Berger .20 .50
7 Scott Bjugstad .20 .50
8 Bob Brooke .20 .50
9 Herb Brooks CO .30 .75
10 Neal Broten .40 1.00
11 Dino Ciccarelli .60 1.50
12 Larry DePalma .20 .50
13 Dave Gagner 1.00 2.50
14 Curt Giles .30 .75
15 Dirk Graham .40 1.00
16 Craig Hartsburg .40 1.00
17 Tom Hirsch .20 .50
18 Brian Lawton .20 .50
19 Brian MacLellan .20 .50
20 Dennis Maruk .30 .75
21 Basil McRae .30 .75
22 Frantisek Musil .20 .50
23 Steve Payne .25 .60
24 Pat Price .20 .50
25 Chris Pryor .20 .50
26 Gordie Roberts .20 .50
27 Bob Rouse .25 .60
28 Terry Ruskowski .25 .60
29 Kari Takko .30 .75
30 Ron Wilson .20 .50
31 Richard Zemlak .20 .50

1988-89 North Stars ADA

This 23-card set measured 3 1/2" by 7 1/8" and was sponsored by the American Dairy Association and Pro Ex Photo Systems. The fronts featured color action player photos with the team logo, player's name, and sponsors' logos at the bottom in the wide white margin. On the horizontal backs, the left box carried the team logo and player information. The right box displayed a nutrition tip from the American Dairy Association of Minnesota. The cards were unnumbered and checklisted below in alphabetical order.

COMPLETE SET (23) 4.80 12.00
1 Brian Bellows .40 1.00
2 Bob Brooke .20 .50
3 Neal Broten .40 1.00
4 Jon Casey .60 1.50
5 Shawn Chambers .20 .50
6 Dino Ciccarelli .75 2.00
7 Larry DePalma .20 .50
8 Curt Fraser .20 .50
9 Link Gaetz .30 .75
10 Dave Gagner .75 2.00
11 Stewart Gavin .20 .50
12 Curt Giles .20 .50
13 Marc Habscheid .20 .50
14 Mark Hardy .20 .50
15 Craig Hartsburg .40 1.00
16 Brian MacLellan .20 .50
17 Moe Mantha .20 .50
18 Basil McRae .30 .75
19 Frantisek Musil .20 .50
20 Dusan Pasek .20 .50
21 Bob Rouse .20 .50
22 Terry Ruskowski .20 .50
23 Kari Takko .30 .75

1989-90 North Stars ADA

This postcard-sized set featured the old Minnesota North Stars. The cards were issued as a promotional giveaway, likely at one home game. The set was noteworthy for the inclusion of a card on Mike Modano, a full year before his RC appearance.

COMPLETE SET (23) 8.00 20.00
1 Brian Bellows .20 .50
2 Perry Berezan .08 .25
3 Bob Brooke .08 .25
4 Neal Broten .40 1.00
5 Jon Casey .30 .75
6 Shawn Chambers .08 .25
7 Shane Churla .40 1.00

Clark Donatelli .08 .25
Gaetan Duchesne .08 .25
0 Curt Fraser .08 .25
1 Dave Gagner .20 .50
12 Mike Gartner .30 .75
13 Stewart Gavin .08 .25
14 Curt Giles .20 .50
15 Ken Leiter .08 .25
16 Basil McRae .30 .75
17 Mike Modano 4.00 10.00
18 Larry Murphy .30 .75
19 Frantisek Musil .08 .25
20 Pierre Page .08 .25
21 Ville Siren .08 .25
22 Kari Takko .30 .75
23 Mark Tinordi .08 .25

1990 Oakville Horton

Card was produced to promote a show in Oakville, Ontario.

1 Tim Horton 1.50 4.00

1979-80 Oilers Postcards

Measuring approximately 3 1/2" by 5 1/4", this 24-card set featured borderless posed-on-ice photos of the Edmonton Oilers on the fronts. The postcard format had each of the horizontal backs bisected by a vertical line, with the player's name, position, and biography on the left side, and the team logo on the right. The cards were unnumbered and checklisted below in alphabetical order. Early cards of Wayne Gretzky, Kevin Lowe, and Mark Messier were featured in this set. The complete set price includes both Mio variations.

COMPLETE SET (24) 50.00 100.00
1 Brett Callighen .50 1.00
2 Colin Campbell 1.00 2.00
3 Ron Chipperfield .50 1.00
4 Cam Connor .50 1.00
5 Peter Driscoll .50 1.00
6 Dave Dryden 1.00 2.00
7 Bill Flett .50 1.00
8 Lee Fogolin .50 1.00
9 Wayne Gretzky 30.00 60.00
10 Al Hamilton .50 1.00
11 Doug Hicks .50 1.00
12 Dave Hunter .50 1.00
13 Kevin Lowe 2.00 4.00
14 Dave Lumley .50 1.00
15 Blair MacDonald .50 1.00
16 Kari Makkonen .50 1.00
17 Mark Messier 12.50 25.00
18A Ed Mio ERR 1.00 2.00
(Back says DOB Jan. 31, 1979)
18B Ed Mio ERR 1.00 2.00
(Back says DOB Jan. 31, 1979)
19 Pat Price .50 1.00
20 Dave Semenko 1.00 2.00
21 Bobby Schmautz .50 1.00
22 Risto Siltanen .75 1.50
23 Stan Weir .50 1.00

1981-82 Oilers Red Rooster

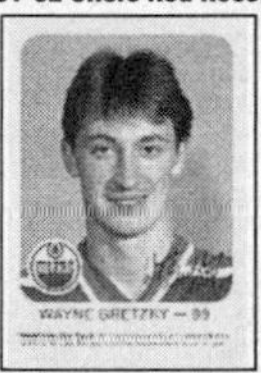

This 30-card set of Edmonton Oilers was sponsored by Red Rooster Food Stores in conjunction with Sun-Rype, Jell-O, Maxwell House, and Post. The player cards could be collected from any police officer or Red Rooster store. The cards measured approximately 2 3/4" by 3 9/16". The front had a color photo (with rounded corners) of the player, with the Oilers' logo and player's signature across the bottom of the picture. The player's name, uniform number, and a hockey tip were given below the photo. The back had the Red Rooster logo at the upper left-hand corner as well as biographical and statistical information on the player. The bottom included logos of the sponsors and an anti-crime message. The original printing included four "long-hair" Gretzky cards as well as coaches' cards of Billy Harris and Ted Green. Reportedly those involved didn't approve of the photos and thus most of the offending pictures were destroyed. Consequently, the new poses were much more common and the old ones more scarce. The mass-produced second printing produced six variations so that the total possible cards is 36. These (original) other six cards were very hard to find as they were apparently not released to the general collecting public. The set is checklisted below using sweater numbers for reference.

COMPLETE SET (30) 24.00 60.00
1 Grant Fuhr 1.50 4.00
2 Lee Fogolin .20 .50
4 Kevin Lowe .60 1.50
5 Doug Hicks .20 .50
6 Garry Lariviere .20 .50
7 Paul Coffey 3.00 8.00
8 Risto Siltanen .20 .50
9 Glenn Anderson 1.25 3.00
10 Matti Hagman .20 .50
11 Mark Messier 3.00 8.00
12 Dave Hunter .20 .50
15 Curt Brackenbury .20 .50
16 Pat Hughes .20 .50
17 Jari Kurri 2.00 5.00
18 Brett Callighen .20 .50
20 Dave Lumley .20 .50
21 Stan Weir .20 .50
26 Mike Forbes .20 .50
27 Dave Semenko .40 1.00
30 Ron Low .40 1.00
35 Andy Moog 1.50 4.00
77 Garry Unger .30 .75
99 Wayne Gretzky 5.00 12.00
99A Wayne Gretzky-long hair 30.00 80.00
99B Wayne Gretzky 5.00 12.00
99C Wayne Gretzky 5.00 12.00
99D Wayne Gretzky 5.00 12.00
xx Team Autographs .40 1.00
xx Glen Sather CO .30 .75
xx Billy Harris CO .20 .50
xx Ted Green CO .20 .50

1981-82 Oilers West Edmonton Mall

These nine blank-backed photos measured approximately 5" by 7" and featured white-bordered black-and-white player head shots. The player's name and uniform number, along with the name and logo of the West Edmonton Mall, appeared in the wide bottom white margin. The photos were unnumbered and checklisted below in alphabetical order.

COMPLETE SET (9) 50.00 125.00
1 Lee Fogolin 1.50 4.00
2 Grant Fuhr 6.00 15.00
3 Wayne Gretzky 40.00 100.00
4 Billy Harris ACO 1.50 4.00
5 Charlie Huddy 2.00 5.00
6 Gary Lariviere 1.50 4.00
7 Dave Lumley 1.50 4.00
8 Risto Siltanen 1.50 4.00
9 Stan Weir 1.50 4.00

1982-83 Oilers Red Rooster

This 30-card set of Edmonton Oilers was sponsored by Red Rooster Food Stores, and the player cards could be collected at any of these stores. The cards measured approximately 2 3/4" by 3 9/16" and the set included four different cards of Wayne Gretzky. The front had a color photo (with rounded corners) of the player, with the Edmonton Oilers' logo and player's signature across the bottom of the picture. The player's name, uniform number, and a hockey tip were given below the photo. The back had the Red Rooster logo at the upper left-hand corner as well as biographical and statistical information on the player. The bottom had an anti-crime message. The set is checklisted below using sweater numbers for reference.

COMPLETE SET (30) 16.00 40.00
2 Lee Fogolin .20 .50
4 Kevin Lowe .40 1.00
6 Garry Lariviere .20 .50
7 Paul Coffey 1.50 4.00
9 Glenn Anderson .50 1.25
10 Jaroslav Pouzar .20 .50
11 Mark Messier 2.00 5.00
12 Dave Hunter .20 .50
13 Ken Linseman .20 .50
14 Laurie Boschman .20 .50
16 Pat Hughes .20 .50
17 Jari Kurri 1.25 3.00
20 Dave Lumley .20 .50
21 Randy Gregg .20 .50
22 Charlie Huddy .30 .75
23 Marc Habscheid .20 .50
24 Tom Roulston .20 .50
27 Dave Semenko .30 .75
29 Don Jackson .20 .50
30 Ron Low .30 .75
31 Grant Fuhr 1.00 2.50
35 Andy Moog 1.00 2.50
77 Garry Unger .30 .75
99A Wayne Gretzky 4.00 10.00
99B Wayne Gretzky 4.00 10.00
99C Wayne Gretzky 4.00 10.00
99D Wayne Gretzky 4.00 10.00
NNO Glen Sather CO .30 .75
NNO John Muckler ACO .20 .50
NNO Ted Green ACO .20 .50

1983-84 Oilers Dollars

These seven cards, measuring approximately 3" by 5" and perforated on each end, were issued with Hockey Dollars or what may be better described as silver-colored coins. Each coin displayed an engraving of the player's face on the obverse and the team logo on the reverse. The card fronts were gray with tan lettering. They hadthe player's name, number, year, team logo, and a picture of the coin. In a horizontal format, the backs carried biography, career highlights, and career statistics. The cards were numbered on the back in the upper right corner. The prices below refer to the coin-card combination intact.

COMPLETE SET (7) 30.00 75.00
H14 Wayne Gretzky 4.00 10.00
H15 Andy Moog 2.00 5.00
H16 Dave Hunter 1.25 3.00
H17 Ken Linseman SP 12.00 30.00
H18 Lee Fogolin SP 12.00 30.00
H19 Dave Semenko 2.00 5.00
H20 Mark Messier 3.00 8.00

1983-84 Oilers McDonald's

This 25-card set of Edmonton Oilers (entitled McDonald's Playoff Action Album) was issued in seven panels. After perforation, the standard issue cards measured 1 1/2" by 2 1/2" and number 22; three cards (3, 19, and 20) are oversized and measure 3" by 2 1/2". The card fronts featured color action photos with dark blue borders. The card backs gave the player's name and number and often included a bit of trivia about player's career or preferences. Cards could be collected from participating McDonald's restaurants and pasted in a playoff album. An adhesive strip on the back could be used to stick the card in a special album. We have checklisted the names below according to the order of the album.

COMPLETE SET (25) 10.00 25.00
1 Ken Linseman 13 .20 .50
2 Dave Semenko 27 .20 .50
3 Andy Moog 35 .75 2.00
4 Raimo Summanen 25 .15 .40
5 Jari Kurri 17 .75 2.00
6 Rick Chartraw 6 .15 .40
7 Don Jackson 29 .15 .40
8 Dave Hunter 12 .15 .40
9 Charlie Huddy 22 .20 .50
10 Emery Award .15 .40
11 Pat Conacher 15 .15 .40
12 Lee Fogolin 2 .15 .40
13 Kevin Lowe 4 .30 .75
14 Randy Gregg 21 .20 .50
15 Pat Hughes 16 .15 .40
16 Kevin McClelland 24 .15 .40
17 Willy Lindstrom 19 .15 .40
18 Mark Messier 11 1.50 4.00
19 Grant Fuhr 31 .75 2.00
20 Coaches .30 .75
Ted Green
Glen Sather
John Muckler
21 Wayne Gretzky 99 4.00 10.00
22 Dave Lumley 20 .15 .40
23 Jaroslav Pouzar 10 .15 .40
24 Glenn Anderson 9 .40 1.00
25 Paul Coffey 7 1.00 2.50
xx Playoff Album 1.25 3.00

1984-85 Oilers Red Rooster

This 30-card set of Edmonton Oilers was sponsored by Red Rooster Food Stores in conjunction with Old Dutch Potato Chips and Post. The player cards could be collected at Red Rooster stores. The cards measured approximately 2 3/4" by 3 9/16" and the set included four different cards of Wayne Gretzky. The front had a color photo of the player, with the Oilers' logo and player's signature across the bottom of the picture. The player's name, uniform number, and a hockey tip were given below the photo. The top half of the back had biographical and statistical information on the player, while the bottom half had company logos and an anti-crime message. There was a second print version of Glen Sather, which color corrected his first print card to reduce the redness in his face. The set is checklisted below using sweater numbers for reference.

COMPLETE SET (30) 12.00 30.00
2 Lee Fogolin .15 .40
4 Kevin Lowe .20 .50
7 Paul Coffey 1.00 2.50
8 Dave Lumley .15 .40
9 Glenn Anderson .40 1.00
10 Jaroslav Pouzar .15 .40
11 Mark Messier 1.50 4.00
12 Dave Hunter .15 .40
16 Pat Hughes .15 .40
17 Jari Kurri .75 2.00
18 Mark Napier .15 .40
19 Willy Lindstrom .15 .40
20 Billy Carroll .15 .40
21 Randy Gregg .15 .40
22 Charlie Huddy .15 .40
23 Marc Habscheid .15 .40
24 Kevin McClelland .15 .40
26 Mike Krushelnyski .15 .40
27 Dave Semenko .20 .50
28 Larry Melnyk .15 .40
29 Don Jackson .15 .40
31 Grant Fuhr .75 2.00
35 Andy Moog .75 2.00
99A Wayne Gretzky 3.00 8.00
99B Wayne Gretzky 3.00 8.00
99C Wayne Gretzky 3.00 8.00
99D Wayne Gretzky 3.00 8.00
NNO Ted Green ACO .15 .40
NNO John Muckler ACO .15 .40
NNO Glen Sather CO P1 .20 .50
(Facsimile autograph on front& redness in face)
NNO Glen Sather CO P2 2.00 5.00
(No facsimile autograph on front& softer colors)

1984-85 Oilers Team Issue

Each of these collectibles measured approximately 4 1/2" by 6 1/2" and was printed on thin glossy paper. The set was packaged in a plastic bag that included three small stickers. Two of the stickers ("Go 2 It Oilers" and "do it again Oilers") determined the date of the set as 1984-85, the season following the Oilers' 1983-84 championship. On the top half, the front featured player information on the left and a color portrait with a light blue studio background on the right. On the bottom half, a white-bordered 4" by 3" color action player photo appeared. The backs were blank. The cards were unnumbered and checklisted below in alphabetical order.

COMPLETE SET (23) 12.00 30.00
1 Glenn Anderson .50 1.25
2 Billy Carroll .20 .50
3 Paul Coffey 1.25 3.00
4 Lee Fogolin .20 .50
5 Grant Fuhr .75 2.00
6 Randy Gregg .20 .50
7 Wayne Gretzky 4.00 10.00
8 Charlie Huddy .20 .50
9 Pat Hughes .20 .50
10 Dave Hunter .20 .50
11 Don Jackson .20 .50
12 Mike Krushelnyski .30 .75
13 Jari Kurri .75 2.00
14 Willy Lindstrom .20 .50
15 Kevin Lowe .40 1.00
16 Dave Lumley .20 .50
17 Kevin McClelland .20 .50
18 Larry Melnyk .20 .50
19 Mark Messier 2.00 5.00
20 Andy Moog .75 2.00
21 Mark Napier .20 .50
22 Jaroslav Pouzar .20 .50
23 Dave Semenko .30 .75

1985-86 Oilers Red Rooster

This 30-card set of Edmonton Oilers was sponsored by Red Rooster Food Stores in conjunction with Old Dutch Potato Chips and Post. The player cards could be collected from any Red Rooster stores. The cards measured approximately 2 3/4" by 3 9/16" and the set included three different cards of Wayne Gretzky. The front had a color photo (with rounded corners) of the player, with the player's signature across the bottom of the picture. The player's name, uniform number, and a hockey tip were given below the photo. In contrast to earlier issues, the team logo appeared beneath the picture. The top half of the back had biographical and statistical information on the player, while the bottom half had company logos and an anti-crime message. The cards of Marty McSorley, Steve Smith, and Esa Tikkanen predated their O-Pee-Chee Rookie Cards by at least a year. The set is checklisted below using sweater numbers for reference.

COMPLETE SET (30) 14.00 35.00
2 Lee Fogolin .15 .40
4 Kevin Lowe .20 .50
5 Steve Smith .60 1.50
7 Paul Coffey 1.00 2.50
8 Gord Sherven .15 .40
9 Glenn Anderson .30 .75
10 Esa Tikkanen 1.25 3.00
11 Mark Messier 1.50 4.00
12 Dave Hunter .15 .40
14 Craig MacTavish .30 .75
17 Jari Kurri .75 2.00
18 Mark Napier .20 .50
19 Mike Rogers .15 .40
20 Dave Lumley .15 .40
21 Randy Gregg .15 .40
22 Charlie Huddy .15 .40
24 Kevin McClelland .15 .40
25 Raimo Summanen .15 .40
26 Mike Krushelnyski .15 .40
27 Dave Semenko .20 .50
29 Don Jackson .15 .40
31 Grant Fuhr .75 2.00
33 Marty McSorley 1.00 2.50
35 Andy Moog .75 2.00
99A Wayne Gretzky 3.00 8.00
99B Wayne Gretzky 3.00 8.00
99C Wayne Gretzky 3.00 8.00
NNO Bob McCammon ACO .15 .40
NNO John Muckler ACO .15 .40
NNO Glen Sather CO .20 .50

1986-87 Oilers Red Rooster

This 30-card set of Edmonton Oilers was sponsored by Red Rooster Food Stores in conjunction with Old Dutch Potato Chips. The player cards could be collected from any Red Rooster stores. The cards measured approximately 2 3/4" by 3 9/16" and the set included two different cards of Wayne Gretzky and of Andy Moog. The front had a color photo (with rounded corners) of the player, with the player's signature across the bottom of the picture. The player's name, uniform number, the team logo, and a safety tip were given below the photo. The top half of the back had biographical and statistical information on the player, while the bottom half had the sponsor's advertisements and the anti-crime slogan "Support Crime Stoppers." The set is checklisted below using sweater numbers for reference.

COMPLETE SET (30) 10.00 25.00
2 Lee Fogolin .15 .40
4 Kevin Lowe .20 .50
5 Steve Smith .30 .75
6 Jeff Beukeboom .20 .50
7 Paul Coffey .75 2.00
8 Stu Kulak .15 .40
9 Glenn Anderson .30 .75
10 Esa Tikkanen .75 2.00
11 Mark Messier 1.25 3.00
12 Dave Hunter .15 .40
14 Craig MacTavish .40 1.00
15 Steve Graves .15 .40
17 Jari Kurri .60 1.50
18 Danny Gare .20 .50
21 Randy Gregg .15 .40
22 Charlie Huddy .20 .50
24 Kevin McClelland .15 .40
25 Raimo Summanen .15 .40
26 Mike Krushelnyski .15 .40
28 Craig Muni .15 .40
31 Grant Fuhr .60 1.50
33 Marty McSorley .75 2.00
35A Andy Moog .60 1.50
35B Andy Moog .60 1.50
65 Mark Napier .20 .50
99A Wayne Gretzky 3.00 8.00
99B Wayne Gretzky 3.00 8.00
NNO Ted Green ACO .20 .50
NNO John Muckler ACO .08 .25
NNO Glen Sather CO .20 .50

1986-87 Oilers Team Issue

This set of Edmonton Oilers consisted of 24 cards, each measuring approximately 3 11/16" by 6 13/16". The front featured a full color action shot of the player on white card stock, with a color "mug shot" superimposed for the most part at one of the lower corners of the picture. The player's uniform number, name, Oilers' logo, and brief biographical information were given above the photo. The back of each card was blank. The set is checklisted below using sweater numbers for reference.

COMPLETE SET (24) 14.00 35.00
2 Lee Fogolin .20 .50
4 Kevin Lowe .30 .75
5 Steve Smith .30 .75
6 Jeff Beukeboom .30 .75
7 Paul Coffey 1.25 3.00
8 Stu Kulak .20 .50
9 Glenn Anderson .50 1.25
10 Esa Tikkanen 1.25 3.00
11 Mark Messier 2.00 5.00
12 Dave Hunter .20 .50
14 Craig MacTavish .40 1.00
17 Jari Kurri 1.00 2.50
20 Jaroslav Pouzar .20 .50
21 Randy Gregg .20 .50
22 Charlie Huddy .20 .50
24 Kevin McClelland .20 .50
25 Raimo Summanen .20 .50
26 Mike Krushelnyski .20 .50
28 Craig Muni .20 .50
31 Grant Fuhr 1.00 2.50
33 Marty McSorley 1.25 3.00
35 Andy Moog 1.00 2.50
65 Mark Napier .30 .75
99 Wayne Gretzky 6.00 15.00

1987-88 Oilers Team Issue

This set of Edmonton Oilers consisted of 22 cards, each measuring approximately 3 11/16" by 6 13/16". The front featured a full color action shot of the player on white card stock, with a color "mug shot" superimposed for the most part at one of the lower corners of the picture. The player's uniform number, name, Oilers' logo, and brief biographical information were given above the photo. The back of each card was blank. The set is checklisted below using sweater numbers for reference.

COMPLETE SET (22) 12.00 30.00
4 Kevin Lowe .30 .75
5 Steve Smith .40 1.00
6 Jeff Beukeboom .40 1.00
9 Glenn Anderson .40 1.00
10 Esa Tikkanen .60 1.50
11 Mark Messier 1.50 4.00
12 Dave Hannan .20 .50
14 Craig MacTavish .30 .75
17 Jari Kurri .75 2.00
18 Craig Simpson .40 1.00
19 Normand Lacombe .20 .50
22 Charlie Huddy .20 .50
23 Keith Acton .30 .75
24 Kevin McClelland .20 .50
26 Mike Krushelnyski .20 .50
28 Craig Muni .20 .50
29 Daryl Reaugh .30 .75
30 Warren Skorodenski .30 .75
31 Grant Fuhr .75 2.00
33 Marty McSorley .60 1.50
36 Selmar Odelein .20 .50
99 Wayne Gretzky 6.00 15.00

1988-89 Oilers Tenth Anniversary

This set contained 164 cards and commemoraleed the tenth anniversary of the Edmonton Oilers. The cards were issued in four card panels, and each regular season edition of Action Magazine (Edmonton Oilers game program) contained one panel. The panels measured approximately 9 1/4 by 7 7/16", and the horizontally oriented cards were in between a gray stripe at the top and card information at the bottom. The cards were not perforated, but after cutting they measure approximately 2 9/16" by 4 5/16". The front featured a color action photo of the player, with a thin black border on white card stock. The box below the picture had player identification and three logos. The back had biographical and statistical information in a horizontal format concerning the player's history with the Oilers.

COMPLETE SET (164) 50.00 125.00
1 Garry Unger .40 1.00
2 Chris Joseph .20 .50
3 Raimo Summanen .20 .50
4 Mike Zanier .30 .75
5 Kevin Lowe .60 1.50
6 Dave Semenko .40 1.00
7 Peter Driscoll .20 .50
8 Ken Solheim .20 .50
9 Glenn Anderson 1.00 2.50
10 Curt Brackenbury .20 .50
11 Ron Shudra .20 .50
12 Gord Sherven .20 .50
13 Randy Gregg .30 .75
14 Larry Melnyk .20 .50
15 Tom Roulston .20 .50
16 Billy Carroll .20 .50
17 Jeff Beukeboom .30 .75
18 Jaroslav Pouzar .20 .50
19 Jeff Brubaker .20 .50
20 Danny Gare .30 .75
21 Craig MacTavish .30 .75
22 Reijo Ruotsalainen .30 .75
23 Willy Lindstrom .20 .50
24 Pat Hughes .20 .50
25 Jim Wiemer .20 .50
26 Selmar Odelein .20 .50
27 Kent Nilsson .40 1.00
28 Mark Napier .20 .50
29 Esa Tikkanen 1.00 2.50
30 John Miner .20 .50
31 Tom McMurchy .20 .50
32 Steve Graves .20 .50
33 Craig Muni .20 .50
34 Moe Mantha .20 .50
35 Dave Lumley .20 .50
36 Ron Low .20 .50
37 Marty McSorley 1.00 2.50
38 Steve Dykstra .20 .50
39 Risto Jalo .20 .50
40 Dave Hunter .20 .50
41 Jari Kurri 2.00 5.00
42 Lee Fogolin .20 .50
43 Moe Lemay .20 .50
44 Stu Kulak .20 .50
45 Charlie Huddy .20 .50
46 Wayne Gretzky 15.00 40.00
47 Ken Linseman .30 .75
48 Risto Siltanen .30 .75
49 Glen Sather .40 1.00
50 Brett Callighen .20 .50
51 Eddie Mio .30 .75
52 Ken Hammond .20 .50
53 Jimmy Carson .30 .75
54 Paul Coffey 2.00 5.00
55 Wayne Gretzky 1050th 10.00 25.00
56 Reed Larson .20 .50
57 Ted Green .30 .75
58 Matti Hagman .20 .50
59 Marc Habscheid .20 .50
60 Bill Ranford 2.00 5.00
61 Mark Lamb .20 .50
62 Daryl Reaugh .40 1.00
63 Al Hamilton .20 .50
64 Paul Coffey's 47th 1.25 3.00
65 Grant Fuhr 2.00 5.00
66 Stan Weir .20 .50
67 Ken Berry .20 .50
68 John Muckler CO .30 .75
69 Doug Smith .20 .50
70 Lance Nethery .20 .50
71 Bill Flett .20 .50
72 Mike Forbes .20 .50
73 Martin Gelinas .40 1.00
74 Ron Chipperfield .20 .50
75 Reg Kerr .20 .50
76 Don Jackson .20 .50
77 Keith Acton .30 .75
78 Gary Edwards .30 .75
79 Mike Krushelnyski .30 .75
80 Trainers .20 .50
Lyle Kulchisky
Peter Millar
Barrie Stafford
81 Normand Lacombe .20 .50
82 Pat Price .20 .50
83 Dave Hannan .20 .50
84 Garry Lariviere .20 .50
85 Greg Adams .20 .50
86 Poul Popiel .20 .50
87 Tom Gorence .20 .50
88 Geoff Courtnall .75 2.00
89 Mark Messier 3.00 8.00
90 Dave Dryden .30 .75
91 Andy Moog 2.00 5.00
92 Jim Ennis .20 .50
93 Craig Simpson .40 1.00
94 Laurie Boschman .20 .50
95 Doug Hicks .20 .50
96 Rick Chartraw .20 .50
97 1984 Stanley Cup .40 1.00
Champs
98 Ron Carter .20 .50
99 Blair MacDonald .20 .50
100 Dean Clark .20 .50
101 Glen Cochrane .20 .50
102 Lindsay Middlebrook .20 .50
103 Ron Areshenkoff .20 .50
104 Billy Harris CO .20 .50
105 Conn Smythe Trophy .30 .75
106 John Blum .20 .50
107 Wayne Bianchin .20 .50
108 Tom Bladon .20 .50
109 Kevin McClelland .20 .50
110 Roy Sommer .20 .50
111 Mike Toal .20 .50
112 Don Ashby .20 .50
113 Don Nachbaur .20 .50
114 1985 Stanley Cup .40 1.00
Champions
115 Jim Corsi .20 .50
116 John Hughes .20 .50
117 Coach of the Year .40 1.00
Glen Sather
118 Bob Dupuis .20 .50
119 Jim Harrison .20 .50
120 Don Murdoch .20 .50
121 Steve Smith .40 1.00
122 Pete Lopresti .20 .50
123 Colin Campbell .40 1.00
124 Bryan Watson .20 .50
125 John Bednarski .20 .50
126 1987 Stanley Cup .40 1.00
Champions
127 Scott Metcalfe .20 .50
128 Mike Rogers .20 .50
129 Dan Newman .20 .50
130 Fuhr's 75th .75 2.00
131 Warren Skorodenski .30 .75
132 Todd Strueby .20 .50
133 Kelly Buchberger .40 1.00
134 Cam Connor .20 .50
135 Dean Hopkins .20 .50
136 Mike Moller .20 .50
137 1988 Stanley Cup 3.00 8.00
Champions
(Wayne Gretzky)
138 Bryon Baltimore .20 .50
139 Pat Conacher .20 .50
140 Ray Cote .20 .50
141 Walt Poddubny .20 .50
142 Jim Playfair .20 .50
143 Nick Fotiu .20 .50
144 Kari Makkonen .20 .50
145 Dave Brown .20 .50
146 Terry Martin .20 .50
147 Francois Leroux .20 .50
148 Kari Jalonen .20 .50
149 Tomas Jonsson .30 .75
150 Dave Donnelly .20 .50
151 Mike Ware .20 .50
152 Don Cutts .20 .50
153 Miroslav Fryer .20 .50
154 Bruce MacGregor GM .20 .50
155 Kim Issel .20 .50
156 Marco Baron .30 .75
157 Doug Halward .20 .50
158 Barry Fraser DIR .20 .50
159 Alan May .20 .50
160 Bobby Schmautz .20 .50
161 Craig Redmond .20 .50
162 Oilers Host '89 .30 .75
All-Star Game
163 Alex Tidey .20 .50
164 Wayne Van Dorp .20 .50

1988-89 Oilers Team Issue

This 27-card set measured approximately 3 3/4" by 6 7/8". On a white background, the fronts featured a color action player photo with a color player portrait superimposed in one of the corners. The player's name, uniform number, a short biography, and the team logo appeared above the picture. The backs were blank. The cards are unnumbered and checklisted below in alphabetical order.

COMPLETE SET (27) 8.00 20.00
1 Glenn Anderson .40 1.00
2 Jeff Beukeboom .40 1.00
3 Dave Brown .30 .75
4 Kelly Buchberger .40 1.00
5 Jimmy Carson .30 .75
6 Miroslav Frycer .20 .50
7 Grant Fuhr .75 2.00
8 Randy Gregg .30 .75
9 Doug Halward .20 .50
10 Charlie Huddy .30 .75
11 Dave Hunter .20 .50
12 Tomas Jonsson .30 .75
13 Chris Joseph .20 .50
14 Jari Kurri .60 1.50
15 Normand Lacombe .20 .50
16 Mark Lamb .20 .50
17 John LoBlanc .20 .50
18 Kevin Lowe .30 .75
19 Craig MacTavish .30 .75
20 Kevin McClelland .20 .50
21 Mark Messier 1.50 4.00
22 Craig Muni .20 .50
23 Bill Ranford 1.25 3.00
24 Craig Redmond .20 .50
25 Craig Simpson .30 .75
26 Steve Smith .40 1.00
27 Esa Tikkanen .60 1.50

1989-90 Oilers Team Issue

This standard size set featured color action photos on a white background. Players name, number, and a short bio appeared at the top of the card. Cards featured blank backs and are checklisted below alphabetically.

COMPLETE SET (24) 10.00 25.00
1 Glenn Anderson .30 .75
2 Jeff Beukeboom .25 .60
3 Dave Brown .25 .60
4 Kelly Buchberger .25 .60
5 Peter Eriksson .15 .40
6 Grant Fuhr .60 1.50
7 Martin Gelinas .75 2.00
8 Adam Graves 1.50 4.00
9 Randy Gregg .25 .60
10 Charlie Huddy .25 .60
11 Petr Klima .30 .75
12 Jari Kurri .60 1.50
13 Normand Lacombe .15 .40
14 Mark Lamb .15 .40
15 Kevin Lowe .25 .60
16 Craig Mactavish .25 .60
17 Mark Messier 1.25 3.00
18 Craig Muni .15 .40
19 Joe Murphy .75 2.00
20 Bill Ranford .75 2.00
21 Craig Simpson .25 .60
22 Geoff Smith .25 .60
23 Steve Smith .30 .75
24 Esa Tikkanen .30 .75

1990-91 Oilers IGA

This 30-card standard-size set was sponsored by IGA food stores in conjunction with McGavin's, a distributor of bread and other products in Alberta. Protected by a cello pack, one card was inserted in bread loaves distributed by McGavin's to IGA stores in Calgary and Edmonton. Calgary consumers received a Flames' card, while Edmonton consumers received an Oilers' card. Checklist and coaches cards were not inserted in the loaves but were included on five hundred individually numbered and uncut sheets not offered to the general public. The cards were printed on thin card stock. The fronts had posed color player photos, with a border that shades from blue to orange and back to blue. Most of the photos were shot against the background of the equipment room or dressing room. The player's name was printed in the bottom border, and his uniform number was printed in a circle in the upper left corner of each picture. The horizontally oriented backs featured biographical information, with year-by-year statistics presented in a pink rectangle. Sponsor logos at the bottom rounded out the back. The cards were unnumbered and checklisted below in alphabetical order. Adam Graves appears during his Rookie Card year.

COMPLETE SET (30) 14.00 35.00
1 Glenn Anderson .60 1.50
2 Jeff Beukeboom .30 .75
3 Dave Brown .40 1.00
4 Kelly Buchberger .40 1.00
5 Martin Gelinas .40 1.00
6 Adam Graves 1.50 4.00
7 Ted Green CO SP 1.25 3.00
8 Charlie Huddy .30 .75
9 Chris Joseph .30 .75
10 Petr Klima .20 .50
11 Mark Lamb .20 .50
12 Ken Linseman .30 .75
13 Ron Low CO SP 1.25 3.00
14 Kevin Lowe .50 1.25
15 Craig MacTavish .30 .75
16 Mark Messier 2.50 6.00
17 Joey Moss .20 .50
18 John Muckler CO SP 1.25 3.00
19 Craig Muni .20 .50
20 Joe Murphy .30 .75
21 Bill Ranford 1.25 3.00
22 Anatoli Semenov .20 .50
23 Craig Simpson .20 .50
24 Geoff Smith .20 .50
25 Steve Smith .40 1.00
26 Kari Takko .30 .75
27 Esa Tikkanen .60 1.50
28 Training Staff SP .60 1.50
Ken Low TR/THER
Lyle Kulchisky TR
Barrie Stafford TR
Stewart Poirier THER
29 Edmonton Oilers .20 .50
Year-by-Year Record
30 Checklist Card SP 1.25 3.00

1991 Oilers Panini Team Stickers

This 32-sticker set was issued in a plastic bag that contained two 16-sticker sheets (approximately 9" by 12") and a foldout poster, "Super Poster - Hockey 91", on which the stickers could be affixed. The players' names appeared only on the poster, not on the stickers. Each sticker measured about 2 1/8" by 2 7/8" and featured a color player action shot on its white-bordered front. The back of the white sticker sheet was lined off into 16 panels, each carried the logos for Panini, the NHL, and the NHLPA, as well as the same number that appeared on the front of the sticker. Every Canadian NHL team was featured in this promotion. Each team set was available by mail-order from Panini Canada Ltd. for 2.99 plus 50 cents for shipping and handling.

COMPLETE SET (32) 1.50 4.00
1 Glenn Anderson .07 .20
2 Jeff Beukeboom .01 .05
3 Dave Brown .01 .05
4 Kelly Buchberger .02 .10
5 Martin Gelinas .02 .10
6 Adam Graves .15 .40
7 Charlie Huddy .01 .05
8 Chris Joseph .01 .05
9 Petr Klima .02 .10
10 Mark Lamb .01 .05

11 Ken Linesman	.01	.05
12 Kevin Lowe	.05	.15
13 Craig MacTavish	.02	.10
14 Mark Messier	.20	.50
15 Craig Muni	.01	.05
16 Joe Murphy	.02	.10
17 Bill Ranford	.15	.40
18 Eldon Reddick	.02	.10
19 Anatoli Semenov	.01	.05
20 Craig Simpson	.02	.10
21 Geoff Smith	.01	.05
22 Steve Smith	.02	.10
23 Esa Tikkanen	.07	.20
24 Oilers In Action	.05	.15
A Team Logo Left Side	.01	.05
B Team Logo Right Side	.01	.05
C Oilers in Action Upper Left Corner	.01	.05
D Oilers in Action Lower Left Corner	.01	.05
E Bill Ranford Upper Right Corner	.08	.25
F Bill Ranford Lower Right Corner	.08	.25
G Mark Messier	.20	.50
H Action in the Crease	.05	.15

1991-92 Oilers IGA

This 30-card standard-size set of Edmonton Oilers was sponsored by IGA food stores and included manufacturers' discount coupons. One pack of cards was distributed in Calgary and Edmonton IGA stores with any grocery purchase of 10.00 or more. The cards were printed on thin card stock. The fronts have posed color action photos bordered in dark blue. The player's name was printed vertically in the wider left border, and his uniform number and the team name appeared at the bottom of the picture. In black print on a white background, the backs presented biography and statistics (regular season and playoff). Packs were kept under the cash till drawer, and therefore many of the cards were creased. Each pack contained three Oilers and two Flame cards. The checklist and coaches cards for both teams were not included in the packs but were available on a very limited basis through an uncut team sheet offer. The cards were unnumbered and checklisted below in alphabetical order, with the coaches cards listed after the players.

COMPLETE SET (30)	8.00	20.00
1 Josef Beranek	.20	.50
2 Kelly Buchberger	.30	.75
3 Vincent Damphousse	.60	1.50
4 Louie DeBrusk	.20	.50
5 Martin Gelinas	.30	.75
6 Peter Ing	.25	.60
7 Petr Klima	.20	.50
8 Mark Lamb	.20	.50
9 Kevin Lowe	.30	.75
10 Norm Maciver	.20	.50
11 Craig MacTavish	.30	.75
12 Troy Mallette	.20	.50
13 Dave Manson	.40	1.00
14 Scott Mellanby	.40	1.00
15 Craig Muni	.20	.50
16 Joe Murphy	.30	.75
17 Bill Ranford	.75	2.00
18 Steven Rice	.20	.50
19 Luke Richardson	.20	.50
20 Anatoli Semenov	.20	.50
21 David Shaw	.20	.50
22 Craig Simpson	.30	.75
23 Geoff Smith	.20	.50
24 Scott Thornton	.20	.50
25 Esa Tikkanen	.40	1.00
26 Training Staff SP	.60	1.50
27 Ted Green CO SP	1.00	2.50
28 Ron Low CO SP	1.00	2.50
29 Kevin Primeau CO SP	1.00	2.50
30 Checklist Card SP	1.00	2.50

1991-92 Oilers Team Issue

Printed on thin card stock, this 28-card set measured approximately 3 3/4" by 6 7/8". On the fronts, the white-bordered color action shots had player information and team logo in the top white border. The backs were blank. The cards were unnumbered and checklisted below in alphabetical order.

COMPLETE SET (28)	6.00	15.00
1 Josef Beranek	.20	.50
2 Jeff Beukeboom	.20	.50
3 Kelly Buchberger	.30	.75
4 Vincent Damphousse	.60	1.50
5 Louie DeBrusk	.20	.50
6 Martin Gelinas	.20	.50
7 Peter Ing	.25	.60
8 Chris Joseph	.20	.50
9 Petr Klima	.20	.50
10 Mark Lamb	.20	.50
11 Kevin Lowe	.30	.75
12 Norm Maciver	.20	.50
13 Craig MacTavish	.20	.50
14 Troy Mallette	.20	.50
15 Dave Manson	.40	1.00
16 Scott Mellanby	.40	1.00
17 Craig Muni	.20	.50
18 Joe Murphy	.30	.75
19 Bill Ranford	.75	2.00
20 Eldon(Pokey) Reddick	.30	.75
21 Steve Rice	.20	.50
22 Luke Richardson	.20	.50
23 Martin Rucinsky	.60	1.50
24 Anatoli Semenov	.20	.50
25 Craig Simpson	.20	.50
26 Geoff Smith	.20	.50
27 Scott Thornton	.20	.50
28 Esa Tikkanen	.40	1.00

1992-93 Oilers IGA

Sponsored by IGA food stores, the 30 standard-size cards comprising this Special Edition Collector Series set featured color player action shots on their fronts. Each photo was trimmed with a black line and offset flush with the thin white border on the right, which surrounds the card. On the remaining three sides, the picture was edged with a gray and white netlike pattern. The player's name appeared in the upper right and the Oilers logo rests in the lower left. The back carried the player's name at the top, with his position, uniform number, biography, and stat table set within a bluish-gray screened background. The Oilers logo in the upper right rounded out the card.

COMPLETE SET (30)	6.00	15.00
1 Checklist	.08	.25
2 Joseph Beranek	.20	.50
3 Kelly Buchberger	.30	.75
4 Shayne Corson	.40	1.00
5 Louie DeBrusk	.20	.50
6 Martin Gelinas	.30	.75
7 Brent Gilchrist	.20	.50
8 Brian Glynn	.20	.50
9 Greg Hawgood	.20	.50
10 Petr Klima	.20	.50
11 Chris Joseph	.20	.50
12 Craig MacTavish	.20	.50
13 Dan Currie	.20	.50
14 Dave Manson	.20	.50
15 Scott Mellanby	.20	.50
16 Craig Muni	.20	.50
17 Bernie Nicholls	.30	.75
18 Bill Ranford	.40	1.00
19 Luke Richardson	.20	.50
20 Craig Simpson	.25	.60
21 Geoff Smith	.20	.50
22 Vladimir Vujtek	.20	.50
23 Esa Tikkanen	.40	1.00
24 Ron Tugnutt	.60	1.50
25 Shaun Van Allen	.20	.50
26 Glen Sather GM	.20	.50
27 Ted Green CO	.20	.50
28 Ron Low CO	.20	.50
29 Kevin Primeau CO	.08	.25
30 Oilers Yearly Record	.08	.25

1992-93 Oilers Team Issue

The 22 blank-backed cards comprising this set were printed on thin white card stock and measured approximately 3 3/4" by 6 7/8". They featured white-bordered color player action photos and displayed the Oilers logo, the player's name, jersey number, and brief biography within the broad white border at the top. The cards were unnumbered and checklisted below in alphabetical order.

COMPLETE SET (22)	4.80	12.00
1 Kelly Buchberger	.25	.60
2 Zdeno Ciger	.20	.50
3 Shayne Corson	.30	.75
4 Louie DeBrusk	.20	.50
5 Todd Elik	.20	.50
6 Brian Glynn	.20	.50
7 Mike Hudson	.20	.50
8 Chris Joseph	.20	.50
9 Igor Kravchuk	.20	.50
10 Francois Leroux	.20	.50
11 Craig MacTavish	.20	.50
12 Dave Manson	.20	.50
13 Shjon Podein	.20	.50
14 Bill Ranford	.40	1.00
15 Steve Rice	.20	.50
16 Luke Richardson	.20	.50
17 Craig Simpson	.25	.60
18 Geoff Smith	.20	.50
19 Kevin Todd	.20	.50
20 Vladimir Vujtek	.20	.50
21 Doug Weight	.75	2.00
22 Brad Werenka	.20	.50

1996-97 Oilers Postcards

This 27-card set of Oilers postcards was the first to picture the team in their new sweaters. These odd size postcards (3 3/4" by 6 7/8") featured sharp action photography on the front, along with team logo, player name and biographical data. The backs were blank. As the players' jersey numbers were displayed prominently on the upper left corner, they are listed below accordingly.

COMPLETE SET (27)	6.00	15.00
2 Boris Mironov	.20	.50
4 Kevin Lowe	.20	.50
5 Greg de Vries	.20	.50
6 Jeff Norton	.15	.40
7 Jason Arnott	.40	1.00
8 Sean Brown	.15	.40
10 Steve Kelly	.20	.50
14 Mats Lindgren	.20	.50
16 Kelly Buchberger	.20	.50
17 Rem Murray	.20	.50
18 Miroslav Satan	.60	1.50
19 Boyd Devereaux	.40	1.00
21 Mariusz Czerkawski	.20	.50
22 Luke Richardson	.20	.50
23 Dan McGillis	.20	.50
24 Bryan Marchment	.20	.50
25 Mike Grier	.60	1.50
26 Todd Marchant	.20	.50
29 Louie DeBrusk	.15	.40
30 Bob Essensa	.30	.75
31 Curtis Joseph	.75	2.00
34 Donald Dufresne	.15	.40
37 Dean McAmmond	.15	.40
39 Doug Weight	.40	1.00
51 Andrei Kovalenko	.20	.50
85 Petr Klima	.15	.40
94 Ryan Smyth	.75	2.00

2002-03 Oilers Postcards

This 22-card set was issued by the team. Cards measure approximately 4" x 7" and are unnumbered. The checklist below is in order by jersey number.

COMPLETE SET (22)	10.00	20.00
1 Eric Brewer	.20	.50
2 Daniel Cleary	.20	.50
3 Ales Pisa	.20	.50
4 Shawn Horcoff	.40	1.00
5 Mike York	.20	.50
6 Ethan Moreau	.20	.50
7 Marty Reasoner	.20	.50
8 Jason Smith	.20	.50
9 Anson Carter	.40	1.00
10 Steve Staios	.20	.50
11 Todd Marchant	.40	1.00
12 Georges Laraque	.75	2.00
14 Jussi Markkanen	.40	1.00
15 Scott Ferguson	.20	.50
16 Jiri Dopita	.20	.50
17 Tommy Salo	.40	1.00
18 Brian Swanson	.20	.50
19 Janne Niinimaa	.20	.50
20 Ales Hemsky	1.25	3.00
21 Mike Comrie	.75	2.00
22 Ryan Smyth	1.00	2.50
113 Jason Chimera	.20	.50

2003-04 Oilers Postcards

These postcards were offered by the team in singles form at club events and in response to fan requests. It is believed that this list is complete.

COMPLETE SET (22)	8.00	20.00
1 Marc-Andre Bergeron	.30	.75
2 Eric Brewer	.30	.75
3 Jason Chimera	.30	.75
4 Ty Conklin	.40	1.00
5 Cory Cross	.30	.75
6 Radek Dvorak	.30	.75
7 Scott Ferguson	.30	.75
8 Ales Hemsky	.60	1.50
9 Shawn Horcoff	.40	1.00
10 Brad Isbister	.30	.75
11 Georges Laraque	.60	1.50
12 Ethan Moreau	.40	1.00
13 Fernando Pisani	.40	1.00
14 Marty Reasoner	.30	.75
15 Tommy Salo	.40	1.00
16 Alexei Semenov	.30	.75
17 Jason Smith	.30	.75
18 Ryan Smyth	.75	2.00
19 Steve Staios	.30	.75
20 Jarret Stoll	.40	1.00
21 Raffi Torres	.40	1.00
22 Mike York	.40	1.00

1932-33 O'Keefe Maple Leafs

This 20-card set was issued by O'Keefe's Beverages and featured the Toronto Maple Leafs, 1931-32 Stanley Cup Champions. Each was designed for use as a coaster. The shape of each card is an eight-pointed star, which measures approximately 5" from one point across to its opposite. Inside a blue border, the front had a black and blue ink portrait or drawing of the player, which was surrounded by cartoons and captions presenting player information. The backs read "O'-Keefe's Big 4" and "Each a Leader in its Class." The coasters were numbered on the front near the top and are checklisted below accordingly. Card numbers 13 and 15 are unknown, although many collectors believe it likely that the Ken Doraty and Thoms cards were slated to fill those slots.

COMPLETE SET (20)	6000.00	12000.00
1 Lorne Chabot	250.00	600.00
2 Red Horner	250.00	600.00
3 Alex Levinsky	200.00	500.00
4 Hap Day	200.00	500.00
5 Andy Blair	200.00	500.00
6 Ace Bailey	500.00	1200.00
7 King Clancy	500.00	1200.00
8 Harold Cotton	250.00	600.00
9 Charlie Conacher	400.00	1000.00
10 Joe Primeau	400.00	1000.00
11 Harvey Jackson	400.00	1000.00
12 Frank Finnigan	200.00	500.00
14 Bob Gracie	200.00	500.00
16 Harold Darragh	200.00	500.00
17 Benny Grant	200.00	500.00
18 Fred Robertson	200.00	500.00
19 Conn Smythe	400.00	1000.00
20 Dick Irvin	300.00	800.00
NNO Ken Doraty	250.00	600.00
NNO Bill Thoms	250.00	600.00

1933-34 O-Pee-Chee V304A

This first of five O-Pee-Chee 1930's hockey card issues featured a black and white photo of the player portrayed on a colored field of stars. The cards in the set were approximately 2 5/16" by 3 9/16". The player's name appeared in a rectangle at the bottom of the front of the card. Four possible color background fields existed, red, blue, orange and green. The cards were numbered on the back, and a short biography in both English and French is also contained on the back. The catalog designation for this set is V304A. The existence of an album designed to store the cards has been confirmed. It is valued at approximately $250.

COMPLETE SET (48)	9000.00	15000.00
WRAPPER (1-CENT)	175.00	350.00
1 Danny Cox RC	150.00	250.00
2 Joe Lamb RC	60.00	100.00
3 Eddie Shore RC	900.00	1500.00
4 Ken Doraty RC	60.00	100.00
5 Fred Hitchman	60.00	100.00
6 Nels Stewart RC	500.00	800.00
7 Walter Galbraith RC	60.00	100.00
8 Dit Clapper RC	400.00	600.00
9 Harry Oliver RC	200.00	400.00
10 Red Horner RC	175.00	300.00
11 Alex Levinsky RC	60.00	100.00
12 Joe Primeau RC	400.00	600.00
13 Ace Bailey RC	300.00	500.00
14 George Patterson RC	60.00	100.00
15 George Hainsworth RC	250.00	400.00
16 Ott Heller RC	60.00	100.00
17 Art Somers RC	60.00	100.00
18 Lorne Chabot RC	175.00	300.00
19 Johnny Gagnon RC	60.00	100.00
20 Pit Lepine RC	60.00	100.00
21 Wildor Larochelle RC	90.00	150.00
22 Georges Mantha RC	90.00	150.00
23 Howie Morenz	1200.00	2500.00
24 Syd Howe RC	200.00	350.00
25 Frank Finnigan	90.00	150.00
26 Bill Touhey RC	60.00	100.00
27 Cooney Weiland RC	200.00	400.00
28 Leo Bourgeault RC	60.00	100.00
29 Normie Himes RC	90.00	150.00
30 Johnny Sheppard RC	60.00	100.00
31 King Clancy	600.00	1000.00
32 Clarence Day	150.00	250.00
33 Harvey Jackson RC	300.00	500.00
34 Charlie Conacher RC	600.00	1000.00
35 Harold Cotton RC	125.00	200.00
36 Butch Keeling RC	60.00	100.00
37 Murray Murdoch RC	60.00	100.00
38 Bill Cook	150.00	250.00
39 Ivan Johnson RC	300.00	600.00
40 Happy Emms RC	90.00	150.00
41 Bert McInenly RC	60.00	100.00
42 John Sorrell RC	90.00	150.00
43 Bill Phillips RC	60.00	100.00
44 Charley McVeigh RC	60.00	100.00
45 Roy Worters RC	250.00	400.00
46 Albert Leduc RC	100.00	200.00
47 Nick Wasnie RC	60.00	100.00
48 Armand Mondou RC	125.00	200.00

1933-34 O-Pee-Chee V304B

The second O-Pee-Chee hockey series of the 1930's contained 24 cards and continues the numbering sequence of the Series A cards. The format was exactly the same as the cards of Series A. The cards in the set measured approximately 2 5/16" by 3 9/16". The catalog designation for this set is V304B.

COMPLETE SET (24)	3000.00	5000.00
WRAPPER (1-CENT)	175.00	350.00
49 Babe Siebert RC	250.00	400.00
50 Aurel Joliat	500.00	800.00
51 Larry Aurie RC	175.00	300.00
52 Ebbie Goodfellow RC	150.00	300.00
53 John Roach	125.00	200.00
54 Bill Beveridge RC	125.00	200.00
55 Earl Robinson RC	90.00	150.00
56 Jimmy Ward RC	90.00	150.00
57 Archie Wilcox RC	90.00	150.00
58 Lorne Duguid RC	90.00	150.00
59 Dave Kerr RC	125.00	200.00
60 Baldy Northcott RC	100.00	200.00
61 Marvin Wentworth RC	125.00	200.00
62 Dave Trottier RC	100.00	200.00
63 Wally Kilrea RC	90.00	150.00
64 Glen Brydson RC	125.00	200.00
65 Vernon Ayres RC	90.00	150.00
66 Bob Gracie RC	90.00	150.00
67 Vic Ripley RC	90.00	150.00
68 Tiny Thompson RC	300.00	500.00
69 Alex Smith RC	90.00	150.00
70 Andy Blair RC	90.00	150.00
71 Cecil Dillon RC	90.00	150.00
72 Bun Cook RC	250.00	400.00

1935-36 O-Pee-Chee V304C

While Series C in the O-Pee-Chee 1930's hockey card set continued the numbering sequence of the previous two years, this 24-card set differed significantly in both format and size. The cards in this set measured approximately 2 3/8" by 2 7/8". Each black and white photo portraying the player on the front could be found on four possible color fields, green, orange, maroon, or yellow. The field consisted of a star in the center and cartooned hockey players flanking the center of the card. The backs contained the player's name, the card number, and biographical data in both English and French. The catalog designation for this set is V304C.

COMPLETE SET (24)	2500.00	4000.00
WRAPPER (1-CENT)	175.00	350.00
73 Wilfred Cude RC	175.00	300.00
74 Jack McGill RC	75.00	125.00
75 Russ Blinco RC	75.00	125.00
76 Hooley Smith	150.00	250.00
77 Herb Cain RC	90.00	150.00
78 Gus Marker RC	75.00	125.00
79 Lynn Patrick RC	175.00	300.00
80 Johnny Gottselig RC	75.00	125.00
81 Marty Barry	125.00	200.00
82 Sylvio Mantha	150.00	250.00
83 Flash Hollett RC	75.00	125.00
84 Nick Metz RC	75.00	125.00
85 Bill Thoms	75.00	125.00
86 Hec Kilrea	75.00	125.00
87 Pep Kelly RC	75.00	125.00
88 Art Jackson RC	75.00	125.00
89 Allan Shields RC	75.00	125.00
90 Buzz Boll	75.00	125.00
91 Jean Pusie RC	75.00	125.00
92 Roger Jenkins RC	75.00	125.00
93 Arthur Coulter RC	90.00	150.00
94 Art Chapman	75.00	125.00
95 Paul Haynes	75.00	125.00
96 Leroy Goldsworthy RC	150.00	250.00

1936-37 O-Pee-Chee V304D

The most significant difference between Series D cards and cards from the previous three O-Pee-Chee sets was the fact that these cards are die-cut and could be folded to give a stand-up figure, like the 1934-36 Batter-Up baseball cards. The cards were in black and white with no colored background field. The cards in the set measured approximately 2 3/8" by 2 15/16". As these cards are difficult to find without the backs missing, this set was the most valuable of the 1930's O-Pee-Chee sets. The backs contained the card number and biographical data in English and French. The player's name was given on the front of the card only. The catalog designation for this set is V304D.

COMPLETE SET (36)	9000.00	15000.00
WRAPPER (1-CENT)	175.00	350.00
97 Turk Broda RC	700.00	1200.00
98 Sweeney Schriner RC	250.00	400.00
99 Jack Shill RC	100.00	150.00
100 Bob Davidson RC	100.00	150.00
101 Syl Apps RC	500.00	800.00
102 Lionel Conacher	400.00	600.00
103 Jimmy Fowler RC	100.00	150.00
104 Al Murray RC	100.00	150.00
105 Neil Colville RC	175.00	300.00
106 Paul Runge RC	100.00	150.00
107 Mike Karakas RC	125.00	200.00
108 John Gallagher RC	100.00	150.00
109 Alex Shibicky RC	150.00	250.00
110 Herb Cain	150.00	250.00
111 Bill McKenzie	100.00	150.00
112 Harold Jackson	100.00	150.00
113 Art Wiebe RC	100.00	150.00
114 Joffre Desilets RC	100.00	150.00
115 Earl Robinson	100.00	150.00
116 Cy Wentworth	150.00	250.00
117 Ebbie Goodfellow	125.00	200.00
118 Eddie Shore	1200.00	1800.00
119 Buzz Boll	100.00	150.00
120 Wilfred Cude	125.00	200.00
121 Howie Morenz	1400.00	2200.00
122 Red Horner	250.00	400.00
123 Charlie Conacher	500.00	800.00
124 Harvey(Busher)Jackson	300.00	500.00
125 King Clancy	600.00	1000.00
126 Dave Trottier	100.00	150.00
127 Russ Blinco	100.00	150.00
128 Lynn Patrick	300.00	500.00
129 Aurel Joliat	500.00	800.00
130 Baldy Northcott	100.00	150.00
131 Larry Aurie	100.00	150.00
132 Hooley Smith	250.00	400.00

1937-38 O-Pee-Chee V304E

Series E cards continued the numerical series of the 1930's O-Pee-Chee sets and featured a black and white photo of the player within a serrated, colored (blue or purple) frame. A facsimile autograph and a cartooned hockey player appeared on the front in the same color as the frame. The cards in the set measured approximately 2 3/8" by 2 7/8". The backs contained the card number, the player's name, and biographical data in both English and French. The catalog designation for this set is V304E.

COMPLETE SET (48)	4000.00	7500.00
WRAPPER (1-CENT)	150.00	300.00
133 Turk Broda	400.00	600.00
134 Red Horner	125.00	200.00
135 Jimmy Fowler	60.00	100.00
136 Bob Davidson	60.00	100.00
137 Reg. Hamilton RC	60.00	100.00
138 Charlie Conacher	300.00	500.00
139 Busher Jackson	175.00	300.00
140 Buzz Boll	60.00	100.00
141 Syl Apps	250.00	400.00
142 Gordie Drillon RC	175.00	300.00
143 Bill Thoms	60.00	100.00
144 Nick Metz	60.00	100.00
145 Pep Kelly	60.00	100.00
146 Murray Armstrong RC	60.00	100.00
147 Murph Chamberlain RC	60.00	100.00
148 Des Smith RC	60.00	100.00
149 Wilfred Cude	90.00	150.00
150 Babe Siebert	125.00	200.00
151 Bill MacKenzie	60.00	100.00
152 Aurel Joliat	300.00	500.00
153 Georges Mantha	60.00	100.00
154 Johnny Gagnon	60.00	100.00
155 Paul Haynes	60.00	100.00
156 Joffre Desilets	60.00	100.00
157 George Allen Brown RC	60.00	100.00
158 Paul Drouin RC	60.00	100.00
159 Pit Lepine	60.00	100.00
160 Toe Blake RC	500.00	800.00
161 Bill Beveridge	90.00	150.00
162 Allan Shields	60.00	100.00
163 Cy Wentworth	125.00	200.00
164 Stew Evans RC	60.00	100.00
165 Earl Robinson	60.00	100.00
166 Baldy Northcott	90.00	150.00
167 Paul Runge	60.00	100.00
168 Dave Trottier	60.00	100.00
169 Russ Blinco	60.00	100.00
170 Jimmy Ward	60.00	100.00
171 Bob Gracie	60.00	100.00
172 Herb Cain	125.00	200.00
173 Gus Marker	60.00	100.00
174 Walter Buswell RC	60.00	100.00
175 Carl Voss RC	125.00	200.00
176 Rod Lorraine RC	60.00	100.00
177 Armand Mondou	60.00	100.00
178 Cliff Goupille RC	60.00	100.00
179 Jerry Shannon RC	60.00	100.00
180 Tom Cook RC	125.00	200.00

1939-40 O-Pee-Chee V301-1

This O-Pee-Chee set of 100 large cards was apparently issued during the 1939-40 season. The catalog designation for this set is V301-1. The cards are black and white and measured approximately 5" by 7". The card backs were blank. The cards were numbered on the front in the lower right corner. Cards in the set were identified on the front by name, team, and position. These cards were premiums and were issued one per cello pack.

COMPLETE SET (100)	4000.00	7000.00
1 Reg Hamilton	35.00	60.00
2 Turk Broda	175.00	300.00
3 Bingo Kampman RC	25.00	50.00
4 Gordie Drillon	50.00	80.00
5 Bob Davidson	25.00	50.00
6 Syl Apps	125.00	200.00
7 Pete Langelle RC	25.00	50.00
8 Don Metz RC	25.00	50.00
9 Pep Kelly	25.00	50.00
10 Red Horner	60.00	100.00
11 Wally Stanowsky RC	25.00	50.00
12 Murph Chamberlain	25.00	50.00
13 Bucko MacDonald	25.00	50.00
14 Sweeney Schriner	60.00	100.00
15 Billy Taylor RC	25.00	50.00
16 Gus Marker	25.00	50.00
17 Hooley Smith	60.00	100.00
18 Art Chapman	25.00	50.00
19 Murray Armstrong	25.00	50.00
20 Harvey(Busher) Jackson	90.00	150.00
21 Buzz Boll	25.00	50.00
22 Cliff(Red) Goupille	25.00	50.00
23 Rod Lorraine	25.00	50.00
24 Paul Drouin	25.00	50.00
25 Johnny Gagnon	25.00	50.00
26 Georges Mantha	25.00	50.00
27 Armand Mondou	25.00	50.00
28 Claude Bourque RC	25.00	50.00
29 Ray Getliffe RC	25.00	50.00
30 Cy Wentworth	50.00	80.00
31 Paul Haynes	25.00	50.00
32 Walter Buswell	25.00	50.00
33 Ott Heller	25.00	50.00
34 Arthur Coulter	35.00	60.00
35 Clint Smith RC	60.00	100.00
36 Lynn Patrick	60.00	100.00
37 Dave Kerr	50.00	80.00
38 Murray Patrick RC	25.00	50.00
39 Neil Colville	60.00	100.00
40 Jack Portland RC	25.00	50.00
41 Flash Hollett	25.00	50.00
42 Herb Cain	50.00	80.00
43 Mud Bruneteau	25.00	50.00
44 Joffre DeSilets	25.00	50.00
45 Harold(Mush) March	25.00	50.00
46 Cully Dahlstrom RC	25.00	50.00
47 Mike Karakas	35.00	60.00
48 Bill Thoms	25.00	50.00
49 Art Wiebe	25.00	50.00
50 Johnny Gottselig	25.00	50.00
51 Nick Metz	25.00	50.00
52 Jack Church RC	25.00	50.00
53 Bob Heron RC	25.00	50.00
54 Hank Goldup RC	25.00	50.00
55 Jimmy Fowler	25.00	50.00
56 Charlie Sands	25.00	50.00
57 Marty Barry	35.00	60.00
58 Doug Young	25.00	50.00
59 Charlie Conacher	150.00	250.00
60 John Sorrell	25.00	50.00
61 Tommy Anderson RC	25.00	50.00
62 Lorne Carr	25.00	50.00
63 Earl Robertson RC	35.00	60.00
64 Wilfy Field RC	25.00	50.00
65 Jimmy Orlando RC	25.00	50.00
66 Ebbie Goodfellow	35.00	60.00
67 Jack Keating RC	25.00	50.00
68 Sid Abel RC	250.00	400.00
69 Gus Giesebrecht RC	25.00	50.00
70 Don Deacon RC	25.00	50.00
71 Hec Kilrea	25.00	50.00
72 Syd Howe	60.00	100.00
73 Eddie Wares RC	25.00	50.00
74 Carl Liscombe RC	25.00	50.00
75 Tiny Thompson	90.00	150.00
76 Earl Seibert RC	25.00	50.00
77 Des Smith RC	25.00	50.00
78 Les Cunningham RC	25.00	50.00
79 George Allen RC	25.00	50.00
80 Bill Carse RC	25.00	50.00
81 Bill McKenzie	25.00	50.00
82 Ab DeMarco RC	25.00	50.00
83 Phil Watson	30.00	50.00
84 Alf Pike RC	25.00	50.00
85 Babe Pratt RC	50.00	80.00
86 Bryan Hextall Sr. RC	50.00	80.00
87 Kilby MacDonald RC	25.00	50.00
88 Alex Shibicky	25.00	50.00
89 Dutch Hiller RC	25.00	50.00
90 Mac Colville	25.00	50.00
91 Roy Conacher RC	60.00	100.00
92 Cooney Weiland	60.00	100.00
93 Art Jackson	25.00	50.00
94 Woody Dumart RC	75.00	150.00
95 Dit Clapper	125.00	200.00
96 Mel Hill RC	25.00	50.00
97 Frank Brimsek RC	150.00	300.00
98 Bill Cowley RC	75.00	150.00
99 Bobby Bauer RC	50.00	80.00
100 Eddie Shore	400.00	600.00

1940-41 O-Pee-Chee V301-2

This O-Pee-Chee set was continuously numbered from the 1939-40 O-Pee-Chee set. These large cards were apparently issued during the 1940-41 season. The catalog designation for this set is V301-2. The cards were sepia and measure approximately 5" by 7". The second series numbers were somewhat larger than the numbers used for the first series. The card backs were blank. The cards were numbered on the front in the lower right corner. Cards in the set were identified on the front by name, team, and position. These cards were premiums and were issued one per cello pack.

COMPLETE SET (50)	3000.00	5000.00
101 Toe Blake	175.00	300.00
102 Charlie Sands	30.00	50.00
103 Wally Stanowski	30.00	50.00
104 Jack Adams	30.00	50.00
105 Johnny Mowers RC	50.00	80.00
106 Johnny Quilty RC	30.00	50.00
107 Billy Taylor	30.00	50.00
108 Turk Broda	175.00	300.00
109 Bingo Kampman	30.00	50.00
110 Gordie Drillon	75.00	125.00
111 Don Metz	30.00	50.00
112 Paul Haynes	30.00	50.00
113 Gus Marker	30.00	50.00
114 Alex Singbush RC	30.00	50.00
115 Alex Motter RC	30.00	50.00
116 Ken Reardon RC	90.00	150.00
117 Pete Langelle	30.00	50.00
118 Syl Apps	125.00	200.00
119 Reg. Hamilton	30.00	50.00
120 Cliff(Red) Goupille	30.00	50.00
121 Joe Benoit RC	30.00	50.00
122 Sweeney Schriner	75.00	125.00
123 Joe Carveth RC	30.00	50.00
124 Jack Stewart RC	75.00	125.00
125 Elmer Lach RC	125.00	200.00
126 Jack Schewchuk RC	50.00	80.00
127 Norman Larson RC	50.00	80.00
128 Don Grosso RC	50.00	80.00
129 Lester Douglas RC	50.00	80.00
130 Turk Broda	250.00	400.00
131 Max Bentley RC	175.00	300.00
132 Milt Schmidt RC	250.00	400.00
133 Nick Metz	50.00	80.00
134 Jack Crawford RC	50.00	80.00
135 Bill Benson RC	50.00	80.00
136 Lynn Patrick	90.00	150.00
137 Cully Dahlstrom	50.00	80.00
138 Mud Bruneteau	50.00	80.00
139 Dave Kerr	90.00	150.00
140 Bob(Red) Heron	50.00	80.00
141 Nick Metz	50.00	80.00
142 Ott Heller	50.00	80.00
143 Phil Hergesheimer RC	50.00	80.00
144 Tony Demers RC	50.00	80.00
145 Archie Wilder RC	50.00	80.00
146 Syl Apps	150.00	250.00
147 Ray Getliffe	50.00	80.00
148 Lex Chisholm RC	50.00	80.00
149 Eddie Wiseman RC	50.00	80.00
150 Paul Goodman RC	60.00	120.00

1968-69 O-Pee-Chee

The 1968-69 O-Pee-Chee set contained 216 standard-size color cards. Included are players from the six expansion teams: Philadelphia, Pittsburgh, St. Louis, Minnesota, Los Angeles and Oakland. The cards were originally sold in five-cent wax packs. The horizontally oriented fronts featured the player in the foreground with an artistically rendered hockey scene in the background. The bilingual backs were printed in red and black ink. The player's 1967-68 and career statistics, a short biography, and a cartoon-illustrated fact about the player were included on the back. The cards were printed in Canada and were issued by O-Pee-Chee, even though the Topps Gum copyright is found on the reverse. For the most part, the cards were grouped by teams. However, numerous cards are updated to reflect off-season transactions. The O-Pee-Chee set featured many different poses from the corresponding Topps cards. Card No. 193 can be found either numbered or unnumbered. Rookie Cards in this set included Bernie Parent, Mickey Redmond, Gary Smith and Garry Unger.

COMPLETE SET (216)	1500.00	2500.00
1 Doug Harvey	25.00	60.00
2 Bobby Orr	200.00	350.00
3 Don Awrey UER	5.00	8.00

(Photo actually
Skip Krake)
4 Ted Green 6.00 10.00
5 Johnny Bucyk 9.00 15.00
6 Derek Sanderson 25.00 50.00
7 Phil Esposito 25.00 40.00
8 Ken Hodge 6.00 10.00
9 John McKenzie 6.00 10.00
10 Fred Stanfield 5.00 8.00
11 Tom Williams 5.00 8.00
12 Denis DeJordy 6.00 10.00
13 Doug Jarrett 5.00 8.00
14 Gilles Marotte 5.00 8.00
15 Pat Stapleton 6.00 10.00
16 Bobby Hull 50.00 75.00
17 Chico Maki 5.00 8.00
18 Pit Martin 6.00 10.00
19 Doug Mohns 5.00 8.00
20 John Ferguson 6.00 10.00
21 Jim Pappin 5.00 8.00
22 Ken Wharram 5.00 8.00
23 Roger Crozier 6.00 10.00
24 Bob Baun 6.00 10.00
25 Gary Bergman 5.00 8.00
26 Kent Douglas 5.00 8.00
27 Ron Harris RC 5.00 8.00
28 Alex Delvecchio 9.00 15.00
29 Gordie Howe 60.00 100.00
30 Bruce MacGregor 5.00 8.00
31 Frank Mahovlich 12.00 20.00
32 Dean Prentice 5.00 8.00
33 Pete Stemkowski 5.00 8.00
34 Terry Sawchuk 30.00 50.00
35 Larry Cahan 5.00 8.00
36 Real Lemieux RC 5.00 8.00
37 Bill White RC 7.00 12.00
38 Gord Labossiere RC 5.00 8.00
39 Ted Irvine RC 5.00 8.00
40 Eddie Joyal 5.00 8.00
41 Dale Rolfe RC 5.00 8.00
42 Lowell MacDonald RC 7.00 12.00
43 Skip Krake UER 5.00 8.00
(Photo actually
Don Awrey)
44 Terry Gray 5.00 8.00
45 Cesare Maniago 6.00 10.00
46 Mike McMahon 5.00 8.00
47 Wayne Hillman 5.00 8.00
48 Larry Hillman 5.00 8.00
49 Bob Woytowich 5.00 8.00
50 Wayne Connelly 5.00 8.00
51 Claude Larose 5.00 8.00
52 Danny Grant RC 10.00 20.00
53 Andre Boudrias RC 5.00 8.00
54 Ray Cullen RC 6.00 10.00
55 Parker MacDonald 5.00 8.00
56 Gump Worsley 9.00 15.00
57 Terry Harper 5.00 8.00
58 Jacques Laperriere 6.00 10.00
59 J.C. Tremblay 6.00 10.00
60 Ralph Backstrom 6.00 10.00
61 Checklist 1 125.00 200.00
62 Yvan Cournoyer 12.00 20.00
63 Jacques Lemaire 15.00 25.00
64 Mickey Redmond RC 40.00 70.00
65 Bobby Rousseau 5.00 8.00
66 Gilles Tremblay 5.00 8.00
67 Ed Giacomin 12.00 20.00
68 Arnie Brown 5.00 8.00
69 Harry Howell 6.00 10.00
70 Al Hamilton RC 5.00 8.00
71 Rod Seiling 5.00 8.00
72 Rod Gilbert 7.00 12.00
73 Phil Goyette 5.00 8.00
74 Larry Jeffrey 5.00 8.00
75 Don Marshall 5.00 8.00
76 Bob Nevin 6.00 10.00
77 Jean Ratelle 7.00 12.00
78 Charlie Hodge 6.00 10.00
79 Bert Marshall 5.00 8.00
80 Billy Harris 5.00 8.00
81 Carol Vadnais 6.00 10.00
82 Howie Young 5.00 8.00
83 John Brenneman RC 5.00 8.00
84 Gerry Ehman 5.00 8.00
85 Ted Hampson 5.00 8.00
86 Bill Hicke 5.00 8.00
87 Gary Jarrett 5.00 8.00
88 Doug Roberts 5.00 8.00
89 Bernie Parent RC 100.00 250.00
90 Joe Watson 5.00 8.00
91 Ed Van Impe 5.00 8.00
92 Larry Zeidel 5.00 8.00
93 John Miszuk RC 5.00 8.00
94 Gary Dornhoefer 6.00 10.00
95 Leon Rochefort RC 5.00 8.00
96 Brit Selby 5.00 8.00
97 Forbes Kennedy 5.00 8.00
98 Ed Hoekstra RC 5.00 8.00
99 Garry Peters 5.00 8.00
100 Les Binkley RC 10.00 20.00
101 Leo Boivin 6.00 10.00
102 Earl Ingarfield 5.00 8.00
103 Lou Angotti 5.00 8.00
104 Andy Bathgate 7.00 12.00
105 Wally Boyer 5.00 8.00
106 Ken Schinkel 5.00 8.00
107 Ab McDonald 5.00 8.00
108 Charlie Burns 5.00 8.00
109 Val Fonteyne 5.00 8.00
110 Noel Price 5.00 8.00
111 Glenn Hall 12.00 20.00
112 Bob Plager RC 12.50 25.00
113 Jim Roberts 5.00 8.00
114 Red Berenson 6.00 10.00
115 Larry Keenan 5.00 8.00
116 Camille Henry 5.00 8.00
117 Gary Sabourin RC 5.00 8.00
118 Ron Schock 5.00 8.00
119 Gary Veneruzzo RC 5.00 8.00
120 Gerry Melnyk 5.00 8.00
121 Checklist 2 150.00 250.00
122 Johnny Bower 9.00 15.00
123 Tim Horton 15.00 25.00
124 Pierre Pilote 7.00 12.00
125 Marcel Pronovost 6.00 10.00
126 Ron Ellis 6.00 10.00
127 Paul Henderson 6.00 10.00
128 Al Arbour 6.00 10.00
129 Bob Pulford 6.00 10.00
130 Floyd Smith 5.00 8.00
131 Norm Ullman 7.00 12.00
132 Mike Walton 6.00 10.00
133 Ed Johnston 6.00 10.00
134 Glen Sather 9.00 15.00
135 Ed Westfall 6.00 10.00
136 Dallas Smith 5.00 8.00
137 Eddie Shack 7.00 12.00
138 Gary Doak 5.00 8.00
139 Ron Murphy 5.00 8.00
140 Gerry Cheevers 12.00 20.00
141 Bob Falkenberg RC 5.00 8.00
142 Garry Unger RC 18.00 30.00
143 Peter Mahovlich 6.00 10.00
144 Roy Edwards 6.00 10.00
145 Gary Bauman RC 5.00 8.00
146 Bob McCord 5.00 8.00
147 Elmer Vasko 5.00 8.00
148 Bill Goldsworthy RC 7.00 12.00
149 Jean-Paul Parise RC 7.00 12.00
150 Dave Dryden 6.00 10.00
151 Howie Young 5.00 8.00
152 Matt Ravlich 5.00 8.00
153 Dennis Hull 6.00 10.00
154 Eric Nesterenko 5.00 8.00
155 Stan Mikita 18.00 30.00
156 Bob Wall 5.00 8.00
157 Dave Amadio RC 5.00 8.00
158 Howie Hughes RC 5.00 8.00
159 Bill Flett RC 7.00 12.00
160 Doug Robinson 5.00 8.00
161 Dick Duff 6.00 10.00
162 Ted Harris 5.00 8.00
163 Claude Provost 5.00 8.00
164 Rogatien Vachon 25.00 40.00
165 Henri Richard 12.00 20.00
166 Jean Beliveau 20.00 40.00
167 Reg Fleming 5.00 8.00
168 Ron Stewart 5.00 8.00
169 Dave Balon 5.00 8.00
170 Orland Kurtenbach 5.00 8.00
171 Vic Hadfield 6.00 10.00
172 Jim Neilson 5.00 8.00
173 Bryan Watson 5.00 8.00
174 George Swarbrick RC 5.00 8.00
175 Joe Szura RC 5.00 8.00
176 Gary Smith RC 10.00 20.00
177 Barclay Plager UER RC 9.00 15.00
178 Tim Ecclestone RC 5.00 8.00
179 Jean-Guy Talbot 6.00 10.00
180 Ab McDonald 5.00 8.00
181 Jacques Plante 30.00 60.00
182 Bill McCreary RC 5.00 8.00
183 Allan Stanley 7.00 12.00
184 Andre Lacroix RC 7.00 12.00
185 Jean-Guy Gendron 5.00 8.00
186 Jim Johnson RC 5.00 8.00
187 Simon Nolet RC 7.00 12.00
188 Joe Daley RC 7.00 12.00
189 John Arbour RC 5.00 8.00
190 Billy Dea 5.00 8.00
191 Bob Dillabaugh 5.00 8.00
192 Bob Woytowich 5.00 8.00
193A Keith McCreary ERR RC 20.00 40.00
193B Keith McCreary COR RC 5.00 8.00
194 Murray Oliver 5.00 8.00
195 Larry Mickey RC 5.00 8.00
196 Bill Sutherland RC 5.00 8.00
197 Bruce Gamble 6.00 10.00
198 Dave Keon 9.00 15.00
199 Gump Worsley AS1 7.00 12.00
200 Bobby Orr AS1 90.00 150.00
201 Tim Horton AS1 8.00 15.00
202 Stan Mikita AS1 9.00 15.00
203 Gordie Howe AS1 40.00 60.00
204 Bobby Hull AS1 30.00 50.00
205 Ed Giacomin AS2 9.00 15.00
206 J.C. Tremblay AS2 6.00 10.00
207 Jim Neilson AS2 5.00 8.00
208 Phil Esposito AS2 15.00 25.00
209 Rod Gilbert AS2 6.00 10.00
210 Johnny Bucyk AS2 6.00 10.00
211 Stan Mikita 9.00 15.00
Hart Trophy
Ross Trophy
Lady Byng Trophy
212 Worsley/Vachon 18.00 30.00
Vezina Trophy
213 Derek Sanderson 25.00 50.00
Calder Trophy
214 Bobby Orr 90.00 150.00
Norris Trophy
215 Glenn Hall 7.00 12.00
Conn Smythe Trophy
216 Claude Provost 7.50 15.00
Masterson Trophy

1968-69 O-Pee-Chee Puck Stickers

This set consisted of 22 numbered (on the front), full-color stickers measuring 2 1/2" by 3 1/2". The card backs were blank and contained an adhesive. These stickers were printed in Canada and were inserted one per pack in 1968-69 O-Pee-Chee regular issue hockey packs. The pucks were perforated so that they could be punched out. This was obviously not recommended. Sticker card 22 is a special card honoring Gordie Howe's 700th goal.

COMPLETE SET (22) 250.00 500.00
1 Stan Mikita 10.00 25.00
2 Frank Mahovlich 10.00 25.00
3 Bobby Hull 25.00 50.00
4 Bobby Orr 125.00 250.00
5 Phil Esposito 15.00 30.00
6 Gump Worsley 10.00 20.00
7 Jean Beliveau 15.00 30.00
8 Elmer Vasko 7.50 15.00
9 Rod Gilbert 10.00 20.00
10 Roger Crozier 10.00 20.00
11 Lou Angotti 7.50 15.00
12 Charlie Hodge 7.50 15.00
13 Glenn Hall 10.00 25.00
14 Doug Harvey 10.00 25.00
15 Jacques Plante 25.00 50.00
16 Allan Stanley 7.50 15.00
17 Johnny Bower 15.00 30.00
18 Tim Horton 15.00 30.00
19 Dave Keon 15.00 40.00
20 Terry Sawchuk 25.00 50.00
21 Henri Richard 10.00 25.00
22 Gordie Howe Special 30.00 60.00
(700th Goal)

1969-70 O-Pee-Chee

The 1969-70 O-Pee-Chee set contained 231 standard-size cards issued in two series of 132 and 99. The cards were issued in ten-cent wax packs. Bilingual backs contain 1968-69 and career statistics, a short biography and a cartoon-illustrated fact about the player. The cards were printed in Canada with the Topps Gum Company copyright appearing on the reverse. Many player poses in this set were different from the corresponding player poses of the Topps set of this year. Card 193, Gordie Howe "Mr. Hockey" existed with or without the card number. Stamps inserted in wax packs could be placed on the back of the corresponding player's regular-issue cards in a space provided. A card with a stamp on the back was considered to be of less value than one without the stamp. Rookie Cards include Tony Esposito and Serge Savard.

COMPLETE SET (231) 1200.00 2000.00
1 Gump Worsley 18.00 30.00
2 Ted Harris 4.00 6.00
3 Jacques Laperriere 4.00 6.00
4 Serge Savard RC 20.00 50.00
5 J.C. Tremblay 5.00 8.00
6 Yvan Cournoyer 6.00 10.00
7 John Ferguson 5.00 8.00
8 Jacques Lemaire 6.00 10.00
9 Bobby Rousseau 4.00 6.00
10 Jean Beliveau 12.00 20.00
11 Dick Duff 5.00 8.00
12 Glenn Hall 7.00 12.00
13 Bob Plager 4.00 6.00
14 Ron Anderson RC 4.00 6.00
15 Jean-Guy Talbot 5.00 8.00
16 Andre Boudrias 4.00 6.00
17 Camille Henry 4.00 6.00
18 Ab McDonald 4.00 6.00
19 Gary Sabourin 4.00 6.00
20 Red Berenson 4.00 6.00
21 Phil Goyette 4.00 6.00
22 Gerry Cheevers 9.00 15.00
23 Ted Green 4.00 6.00
24 Bobby Orr 100.00 250.00
25 Dallas Smith 4.00 6.00
26 Johnny Bucyk 8.00 12.00
27 Ken Hodge 5.00 8.00
28 John McKenzie 5.00 8.00
29 Ed Westfall 5.00 8.00
30 Phil Esposito 18.00 30.00
31 Checklist 1 100.00 150.00
32 Fred Stanfield 4.00 6.00
33 Ed Giacomin 9.00 15.00
34 Arnie Brown 4.00 6.00
35 Jim Neilson 4.00 6.00
36 Rod Seiling 4.00 6.00
37 Rod Gilbert 6.00 10.00
38 Vic Hadfield 5.00 8.00
39 Don Marshall 4.00 6.00
40 Bob Nevin 4.00 6.00
41 Ron Stewart 4.00 6.00
42 Jean Ratelle 6.00 10.00
43 Walt Tkaczuk RC 6.00 10.00
44 Bruce Gamble 6.00 10.00
45 Jim Dorey RC 4.00 6.00
46 Ron Ellis 4.00 6.00
47 Paul Henderson 5.00 8.00
48 Brit Selby 4.00 6.00
49 Floyd Smith 4.00 6.00
50 Mike Walton 5.00 8.00
51 Dave Keon 6.00 10.00
52 Murray Oliver 4.00 6.00
53 Bob Pulford 5.00 8.00
54 Norm Ullman 6.00 10.00
55 Roger Crozier 5.00 8.00
56 Roy Edwards 5.00 8.00
57 Bob Baun 5.00 8.00
58 Gary Bergman 4.00 6.00
59 Carl Brewer 5.00 8.00
60 Wayne Connelly 4.00 6.00
61 Gordie Howe 50.00 80.00
62 Frank Mahovlich 7.00 12.00
63 Bruce MacGregor 4.00 6.00
64 Ron Harris 4.00 6.00
65 Pete Stemkowski 4.00 6.00
66 Denis DeJordy 5.00 8.00
67 Doug Jarrett 4.00 6.00
68 Gilles Marotte 4.00 6.00
69 Pat Stapleton 5.00 8.00
70 Bobby Hull 40.00 80.00
71 Dennis Hull 5.00 8.00
72 Doug Mohns 4.00 6.00
73 Howie Menard RC 4.00 6.00
74 Ken Wharram 4.00 6.00
75 Pit Martin 5.00 8.00
76 Stan Mikita 12.00 20.00
77 Charlie Hodge 5.00 8.00
78 Gary Smith 5.00 8.00
79 Harry Howell 5.00 8.00
80 Bert Marshall 4.00 6.00
81 Doug Roberts 4.00 6.00
82 Carol Vadnais 5.00 8.00
83 Gerry Ehman 4.00 6.00
84 Brian Perry RC 4.00 6.00
85 Gary Jarrett 4.00 6.00
86 Ted Hampson 4.00 6.00
87 Earl Ingarfield 4.00 6.00
88 Doug Favell RC 9.00 15.00
89 Bernie Parent 25.00 40.00
90 Larry Hillman 4.00 6.00
91 Wayne Hillman 4.00 6.00
92 Ed Van Impe 4.00 6.00
93 Joe Watson 4.00 6.00
94 Gary Dornhoefer 5.00 8.00
95 Reg Fleming 4.00 6.00
96 Ralph McSweyn RC 4.00 6.00
97 Jim Johnson 4.00 6.00
98 Andre Lacroix 5.00 8.00
99 Gerry Desjardins RC 7.00 12.00
100 Dale Rolfe 4.00 6.00
101 Bill White 4.00 6.00
102 Bill Flett 4.00 6.00
103 Ted Irvine 4.00 6.00
104 Ross Lonsberry 4.00 6.00
105 Leon Rochefort 4.00 6.00
106 Bryan Campbell RC 4.00 6.00
107 Dennis Hextall RC 6.00 10.00
108 Eddie Joyal 4.00 6.00
109 Gord Labossiere 4.00 6.00
110 Les Binkley 5.00 8.00
111 Tracy Pratt RC 4.00 6.00
112 Bryan Watson 4.00 6.00
113 Bob Blackburn RC 4.00 6.00
114 Keith McCreary 4.00 6.00
115 Dean Prentice 4.00 6.00
116 Glen Sather 5.00 8.00
117 Ken Schinkel 4.00 6.00
118 Wally Boyer 4.00 6.00
119 Val Fonteyne 4.00 6.00
120 Ron Schock 4.00 6.00
121 Cesare Maniago 5.00 8.00
122 Leo Boivin 4.00 6.00
123 Bob McCord 4.00 6.00
124 John Miszuk 4.00 6.00
125 Danny Grant 5.00 8.00
126 Bill Collins RC 4.00 6.00
127 Jean-Paul Parise 5.00 8.00
128 Tom Williams 4.00 6.00
129 Charlie Burns 4.00 6.00
130 Ray Cullen 4.00 6.00
131 Danny O'Shea RC 4.00 6.00
132 Checklist 2 150.00 250.00
133 Jim Pappin 4.00 6.00
134 Lou Angotti 4.00 6.00
135 Terry Cafery RC 5.00 8.00
136 Eric Nesterenko 5.00 8.00
137 Chico Maki 5.00 8.00
138 Tony Esposito RC 75.00 150.00
139 Eddie Shack 6.00 10.00
140 Bob Wall 4.00 6.00
141 Skip Krake RC 5.00 8.00
142 Howie Hughes 4.00 6.00
143 Jimmy Peters RC 5.00 8.00
144 Brent Hughes RC 5.00 8.00
145 Bill Hicke 4.00 6.00
146 Norm Ferguson RC 5.00 8.00
147 Dick Mattiussi RC 5.00 8.00
148 Mike Laughton RC 5.00 8.00
149 Gene Ubriaco RC 5.00 8.00
150 Bob Dillabaugh 4.00 6.00
151 Bob Woytowich 4.00 6.00
152 Joe Daley 5.00 8.00
153 Duane Rupp 4.00 6.00
154 Bryan Hextall RC 6.00 10.00
155 Jean Pronovost RC 6.00 10.00
156 Jim Morrison 4.00 6.00
157 Alex Delvecchio 8.00 12.00
158 Paul Popiel 4.00 6.00
159 Garry Unger 6.00 10.00
160 Garry Monahan 4.00 6.00
161 Matt Ravlich 4.00 6.00
162 Nick Libett RC 6.00 10.00
163 Henri Richard 7.00 12.00
164 Terry Harper 5.00 8.00
165 Rogatien Vachon 10.00 18.00
166 Ralph Backstrom 5.00 8.00
167 Claude Provost 5.00 8.00
168 Gilles Tremblay 5.00 8.00
169 Jean-Guy Gendron 5.00 8.00
170 Earl Heiskala RC 5.00 8.00
171 Garry Peters 4.00 6.00
172 Bill Sutherland 4.00 6.00
173 Dick Cherry RC 5.00 8.00
174 Jim Roberts 5.00 8.00
175 Noel Picard RC 5.00 8.00
176 Barclay Plager RC 5.00 8.00
177 Frank St. Marseille RC 5.00 8.00
178 Al Arbour 5.00 8.00
179 Tim Ecclestone 4.00 6.00
180 Jacques Plante 25.00 40.00
181 Bill McCreary 4.00 6.00
182 Tim Horton 12.00 20.00
183 Rick Ley RC 6.00 10.00
184 Wayne Carleton 4.00 6.00
185 Marv Edwards RC 6.00 10.00
186 Pat Quinn RC 9.00 15.00
187 Johnny Bower 7.00 12.00
188 Orland Kurtenbach 5.00 8.00
189 Terry Sawchuk 25.00 40.00
190 Real Lemieux 4.00 6.00
191 Dave Balon 4.00 6.00
192 Al Hamilton 4.00 6.00
193A Gordie Howe ERR 90.00 150.00
Mr. Hockey
(No number)
193B Gordie Howe COR 100.00 175.00
Mr. Hockey
194 Claude Larose 4.00 6.00
195 Bill Goldsworthy 5.00 8.00
196 Bob Barlow RC 4.00 6.00
197 Ken Broderick RC 5.00 8.00
198 Lou Nanne RC 6.00 10.00
199 Tom Polonic RC 5.00 8.00
200 Ed Johnston 5.00 8.00
201 Derek Sanderson 15.00 25.00
202 Gary Doak 4.00 6.00
203 Don Awrey 4.00 6.00
204 Ron Murphy 4.00 6.00
205A Phil Esposito 15.00 25.00
Art Ross Trophy
Hart Trophy
(214 on back and
no number on front)
205B Phil Esposito 12.00 20.00
Art Ross Trophy
Hart Trophy
(214 on back and
205 on front)
206 Alex Delvecchio 4.00 6.00
Lady Byng
207 Jacques Plante 30.00 50.00
Glenn Hall
Vezina Trophy
208 Danny Grant 4.00 6.00
Calder Trophy
209 Bobby Orr 50.00 100.00
Norris Trophy
210 Serge Savard 4.00 6.00
Conn Smythe Trophy
211 Glenn Hall AS 9.00 15.00
212 Bobby Orr AS 50.00 100.00
213 Tim Horton AS 12.00 20.00
214 Phil Esposito AS 12.00 20.00
215 Gordie Howe AS 30.00 50.00
216 Bobby Hull AS 20.00 35.00
217 Ed Giacomin AS 7.00 12.00
218 Ted Green AS 4.00 6.00
219 Ted Harris AS 4.00 6.00
220 Jean Beliveau AS 12.00 20.00
221 Yvan Cournoyer AS 4.00 6.00
222 Frank Mahovlich AS 6.00 10.00
223 Art Ross Trophy 5.00 8.00
224 Hart Trophy 5.00 8.00
225 Lady Byng Trophy 5.00 8.00
226 Vezina Trophy 6.00 10.00
227 Calder Trophy 5.00 8.00
228 James Norris Trophy 5.00 8.00
229 Conn Smythe Trophy 5.00 8.00
230 Prince of Wales 5.00 8.00
Trophy
231 The Stanley Cup 25.00 60.00

1969-70 O-Pee-Chee Four-in-One

The 1969-70 O-Pee-Chee Four-in-One set contained 18 four-player adhesive-backed color cards. The cards were standard size, 2 1/2" by 3 1/2", whereas the individual mini-cards were approximately 1" by 1 1/2". These small cards could be separated and then stuck in a small team album/booklet that was also available that year from O-Pee-Chee. This set was distributed as an insert with the second series of regular 1969-70 O-Pee-Chee cards. Cards that had been separated into the mini-cards have very little value. The cards were unnumbered and so they are checklisted below alphabetically by the (upper left corner) player's name.

COMPLETE SET (18) 600.00 1000.00
1 Bob Baun 30.00 60.00
Ken Schinkel
Tim Horton
Bernie Parent
2 Les Binkley 30.00 60.00
Ken Hodge
Reg Fleming
Jacques Laperriere
3 Yvan Cournoyer 30.00 60.00
Jim Neilson
Gary Sabourin
John Miszuk
4 Bruce Gamble 30.00 60.00
Carol Vadnais
Frank Mahovlich
Larry Hillman
5 Ed Giacomin 30.00 60.00
Jean Beliveau
Eddie Joyal
Leo Boivin
6 Phil Goyette 30.00 60.00
Doug Jarrett
Ted Green
Bill Hicke
7 Ted Hampson 30.00 60.00
Carl Brewer
Denis DeJordy
Leon Rochefort
8 Charlie Hodge 30.00 60.00
Pat Quinn
Derek Sanderson
Duane Rupp
9 Earl Ingarfield 50.00 100.00
Jim Roberts
Gump Worsley
Bobby Hull
10 Andre Lacroix 30.00 60.00
Bob Wall
Serge Savard
Roger Crozier
11 Cesare Maniago 150.00 300.00
Bobby Orr
Dave Keon
Jean-Guy Gendron
12 Keith McCreary 30.00 60.00
Claude Larose
Rod Gilbert
Gerry Cheevers
13 Stan Mikita 30.00 60.00
Al Arbour
Rod Seiling
Ron Schock
14 Doug Mohns 75.00 150.00
Bob Woytowich
Gordie Howe
Gerry Desjardins
15 Bob Nevin 30.00 60.00
Jacques Plante
Mike Walton
Ray Cullen
16 Bob Pulford 40.00 80.00
Henri Richard
Red Berenson
Eddie Shack
17 Pat Stapleton 30.00 60.00
Danny Grant
Bert Marshall
Jean Ratelle
18 Ed Van Impe 30.00 60.00
Dale Rolfe
Alex Delvecchio
Phil Esposito

1969-70 O-Pee-Chee Stamps

The 1969-70 O-Pee-Chee Stamps set contained 26 black and white stamps measuring approximately 1 1/2" by 1 1/4". The stamps were distributed with the first series of regular 1969-70 O-Pee-Chee hockey cards and may also have been available in some of the Topps wax packs of that year as well. The stamps were unnumbered and hence are checklisted below alphabetically for convenience. OPC intended for the stamps to be stuck on the blank space provided on the backs of the corresponding regular card; collectors are strongly encouraged NOT to follow that procedure. The stamps were produced as pairs; intact pairs are now valued at 1.5 to 2 times the sum of the individual player prices listed below.

COMPLETE SET (26) 125.00 250.00
1 Jean Beliveau 7.50 15.00
2 Red Berenson 4.00 8.00
3 Les Binkley 5.00 10.00
4 Yvan Cournoyer 6.00 12.00
5 Ray Cullen 4.00 8.00
6 Gerry Desjardins 5.00 10.00
7 Phil Esposito 7.50 15.00
8 Ed Giacomin 6.00 12.00
9 Rod Gilbert 6.00 12.00
10 Danny Grant 4.00 8.00
11 Glenn Hall 7.50 15.00
12 Ted Hampson 4.00 8.00
13 Ken Hodge 4.00 8.00
14 Gordie Howe 20.00 40.00
15 Bobby Hull 15.00 30.00
16 Eddie Joyal 4.00 8.00
17 Dave Keon 7.50 15.00
18 Andre Lacroix 4.00 8.00
19 Frank Mahovlich 6.00 12.00
20 Keith McCreary 4.00 8.00
21 Stan Mikita 7.50 15.00
22 Bobby Orr 25.00 60.00
23 Bernie Parent 7.50 15.00
24 Jean Ratelle 5.00 10.00
25 Norm Ullman 5.00 10.00
26 Carol Vadnais 4.00 8.00

1970-71 O-Pee-Chee

The 1970-71 O-Pee-Chee set contained 264 standard-size cards. Players from expansion Buffalo and Vancouver are included. Bilingual backs featured a short biography as well as the player's 1969-70 and career statistics. The cards were printed in Canada, and the O-Pee-Chee copyright, and not the Topps, appeared on the back for the first time. Many player poses were different from the Topps set of this year. Cards were grouped by teams. However, there are a number of cards that had updated team names reflecting off-season trades. Card no. 231 is a special memorial to Terry Sawchuk, who passed away in 1970. Card nos. 111, Brit Selby, and 175 Mickey Redmond, could be found with or without a line of text acknowledging trades. Rookie Cards included Wayne Cashman, Bobby Clarke, Brad Park, Guy Lapointe, Gilbert Perreault, and Darryl Sittler.

COMPLETE SET (264) 900.00 1500.00
1 Gerry Cheevers 15.00 25.00
2 Johnny Bucyk 3.50 7.00
3 Bobby Orr 75.00 200.00
4 Don Awrey 2.00 4.00
5 Fred Stanfield 2.00 4.00
6 John McKenzie 2.50 5.00
7 Wayne Cashman RC 9.00 15.00
8 Ken Hodge 2.50 5.00
9 Wayne Carleton 2.00 4.00
10 Garnet Bailey RC 2.50 5.00
11 Phil Esposito 15.00 25.00
12 Lou Angotti 2.00 4.00
13 Jim Pappin 2.00 4.00
14 Dennis Hull 2.50 5.00
15 Bobby Hull 35.00 50.00
16 Doug Mohns 2.00 4.00
17 Pat Stapleton 2.50 5.00
18 Pit Martin 2.50 5.00
19 Eric Nesterenko 2.50 5.00
20 Stan Mikita 10.00 20.00
21 Roy Edwards 2.50 5.00
22 Frank Mahovlich 6.00 12.00
23 Ron Harris 2.00 4.00
24 Checklist 1 100.00 200.00
25 Pete Stemkowski 2.00 4.00
26 Garry Unger 2.00 4.00
27 Bruce MacGregor 2.00 4.00
28 Larry Jeffrey 2.00 4.00
29 Gordie Howe 50.00 80.00
30 Billy Dea 2.00 4.00
31 Denis DeJordy 2.50 5.00
32 Matt Ravlich 2.00 4.00
33 Dave Amadio 2.00 4.00
34 Gilles Marotte 2.00 4.00
35 Eddie Shack 6.00 12.00
36 Bob Pulford 2.50 5.00
37 Ross Lonsberry 2.00 4.00
38 Gord Labossiere 2.00 4.00
39 Eddie Joyal 2.00 4.00
40 Gump Worsley 6.00 12.00
41 Bob McCord 2.00 4.00
42 Leo Boivin 2.50 5.00
43 Tom Reid RC 2.00 4.00
44 Charlie Burns 2.00 4.00
45 Bob Barlow 2.00 4.00
46 Bill Goldsworthy 2.50 5.00
47 Danny Grant 2.50 5.00
48 Norm Beaudin RC 2.00 4.00
49 Rogatien Vachon 6.00 12.00
50 Yvan Cournoyer 6.00 12.00
51 Serge Savard 6.00 12.00
52 Jacques Laperriere 2.50 5.00
53 Terry Harper 2.00 4.00
54 Ralph Backstrom 2.50 5.00
55 Jean Beliveau 6.00 12.00
56 Claude Larose 2.00 4.00
57 Jacques Lemaire 6.00 12.00
58 Peter Mahovlich 2.50 5.00
59 Tim Horton 9.00 15.00
60 Bob Nevin 2.00 4.00
61 Dave Balon 2.00 4.00
62 Vic Hadfield 2.50 5.00
63 Rod Gilbert 6.00 12.00
64 Ron Stewart 2.00 4.00
65 Ted Irvine 2.00 4.00
66 Arnie Brown 2.00 4.00
67 Brad Park RC 25.00 40.00
68 Ed Giacomin 6.00 12.00
69 Gary Smith 2.50 5.00
70 Carol Vadnais 2.50 5.00
71 Doug Roberts 2.00 4.00
72 Harry Howell 2.50 5.00
73 Joe Szura 2.00 4.00
74 Mike Laughton 2.00 4.00
75 Gary Jarrett 2.00 4.00
76 Bill Hicke 2.00 4.00
77 Paul Andrea RC 2.00 4.00
78 Bernie Parent 15.00 25.00
79 Joe Watson 2.00 4.00
80 Ed Van Impe 2.00 4.00
81 Larry Hillman 2.00 4.00
82 George Swarbrick 2.00 4.00
83 Bill Sutherland 2.00 4.00
84 Andre Lacroix 2.50 5.00
85 Gary Dornhoefer 2.50 5.00
86 Jean-Guy Gendron 2.00 4.00
87 Al Smith RC 2.50 5.00
88 Bob Woytowich 2.00 4.00
89 Duane Rupp 2.00 4.00
90 Jim Morrison 2.00 4.00
91 Ron Schock 2.00 4.00
92 Ken Schinkel 2.00 4.00
93 Keith McCreary 2.00 4.00
94 Bryan Hextall 2.50 5.00
95 Wayne Hicks RC 2.00 4.00
96 Gary Sabourin 2.00 4.00
97 Ernie Wakely RC 2.50 5.00
98 Bob Wall 2.00 4.00
99 Barclay Plager 2.50 5.00
100 Jean-Guy Talbot 2.00 4.00
101 Gary Veneruzzo 2.00 4.00
102 Tim Ecclestone 2.00 4.00
103 Red Berenson 2.50 5.00
104 Larry Keenan 2.00 4.00
105 Bruce Gamble 2.50 5.00
106 Jim Dorey 2.00 4.00
107 Mike Pelyk RC 2.00 4.00
108 Rick Ley 2.00 4.00
109 Mike Walton 2.00 4.00
110 Norm Ullman 6.00 12.00
111A Brit Selby 2.00 4.00
(No mention of trade)
111B Brit Selby 10.00 20.00
(Trade noted)
112 Garry Monahan 2.00 4.00
113 George Armstrong 6.00 12.00
114 Gary Doak 2.00 4.00
115 Darryl Sly RC 2.00 4.00
116 Wayne Maki 2.00 4.00
117 Orland Kurtenbach 2.00 4.00
118 Murray Hall 2.00 4.00
119 Marc Reaume 2.00 4.00
120 Pat Quinn 6.00 12.00
121 Andre Boudrias 2.00 4.00
122 Paul Popiel 2.00 4.00
123 Paul Terbenche 2.00 4.00
124 Howie Menard 2.00 4.00
125 Gerry Meehan RC 2.50 5.00
126 Skip Krake 2.00 4.00
127 Phil Goyette 2.00 4.00
128 Reg Fleming 2.00 4.00
129 Don Marshall 2.50 5.00
130 Bill Inglis RC 2.00 4.00
131 Gilbert Perreault RC 60.00 100.00
132 Checklist 2 100.00 200.00
133 Ed Johnston 2.50 5.00
134 Ted Green 2.50 5.00
135 Rick Smith RC 2.00 4.00
136 Derek Sanderson 12.00 20.00
137 Dallas Smith 2.00 4.00
138 Don Marcotte RC 2.50 5.00
139 Ed Westfall 2.50 5.00
140 Floyd Smith 2.00 4.00
141 Randy Wyrozub RC 2.00 4.00
142 Cliff Schmautz RC 2.00 4.00
143 Mike McMahon 2.00 4.00
144 Jim Watson 2.00 4.00
145 Roger Crozier 2.50 5.00
146 Tracy Pratt 2.00 4.00
147 Cliff Koroll RC 2.50 5.00
148 Gerry Pinder RC 2.50 5.00
149 Chico Maki 2.00 4.00
150 Doug Jarrett 2.00 4.00
151 Keith Magnuson RC 5.00 10.00
152 Gerry Desjardins 2.50 5.00
153 Tony Esposito 30.00 50.00
154 Gary Bergman 2.00 4.00
155 Tom Webster RC 2.50 5.00
156 Dale Rolfe 2.00 4.00
157 Alex Delvecchio 6.00 12.00
158 Nick Libett 2.00 4.00
159 Wayne Connelly 2.00 4.00
160 Mike Byers RC 2.00 4.00

Card		
161 Bill Flett	2.00	4.00
162 Larry Mickey	2.00	4.00
163 Noel Price	2.00	4.00
164 Larry Cahan	2.00	4.00
165 Jack Norris	2.50	5.00
166 Ted Harris	2.00	4.00
167 Murray Oliver	2.00	4.00
168 Jean-Paul Parise	2.50	5.00
169 Tom Williams	2.00	4.00
170 Bobby Rousseau	2.00	4.00
171 Jude Drouin RC	2.50	5.00
172 Walt McKechnie RC	2.50	5.00
173 Cesare Maniago	2.50	5.00
174 Rejean Houle RC	6.00	12.00
175A Mickey Redmond TR	5.00	8.00
175B Mickey Redmond NoTR	9.00	15.00
176 Henri Richard	6.00	10.00
177 Guy Lapointe RC	12.00	20.00
178 J.C. Tremblay	2.50	5.00
179 Marc Tardif RC	6.00	12.00
180 Walt Tkaczuk	2.50	5.00
181 Jean Ratelle	6.00	12.00
182 Pete Stemkowski	2.00	4.00
183 Gilles Villemure	2.50	5.00
184 Rod Seiling	2.00	4.00
185 Jim Neilson	2.00	4.00
186 Dennis Hextall	2.50	5.00
187 Gerry Ehman	2.00	4.00
188 Bert Marshall	2.00	4.00
189 Gary Croteau RC	2.00	4.00
190 Ted Hampson	2.00	4.00
191 Earl Ingarfield	2.00	4.00
192 Dick Mattiussi	2.00	4.00
193 Earl Heiskala	2.00	4.00
194 Simon Nolet	2.00	4.00
195 Bobby Clarke RC	60.00	125.00
196 Garry Peters	2.00	4.00
197 Lew Morrison RC	2.00	4.00
198 Wayne Hillman	2.00	4.00
199 Doug Favell	6.00	12.00
200 Les Binkley	2.50	5.00
201 Dean Prentice	2.00	4.00
202 Jean Pronovost	2.50	5.00
203 Wally Boyer	2.00	4.00
204 Bryan Watson	2.00	4.00
205 Glen Sather	2.50	5.00
206 Lowell MacDonald	2.00	4.00
207 Andy Bathgate	2.50	5.00
208 Val Fonteyne	2.00	4.00
209 Jim Lorentz RC	2.00	4.00
210 Glenn Hall	6.00	12.00
211 Bob Plager	2.50	5.00
212 Noel Picard	2.00	4.00
213 Jim Roberts	2.50	5.00
214 Frank St.Marseille	2.00	4.00
215 Ab McDonald	2.00	4.00
216 Brian Glennie RC	2.00	4.00
217 Paul Henderson	2.50	5.00
218 Darryl Sittler RC	75.00	100.00
219 Dave Keon	6.00	12.00
220 Jim Harrison RC	2.00	4.00
221 Ron Ellis	2.50	5.00
222 Jacques Plante	15.00	25.00
223 Bob Baun	2.50	5.00
224 George Gardner RC	2.00	4.00
225 Dale Tallon RC	2.50	5.00
226 Rosaire Paiement RC	2.00	4.00
227 Mike Corrigan RC	2.00	4.00
228 Ray Cullen	2.00	4.00
229 Charlie Hodge	2.50	5.00
230 Len Lunde	2.00	4.00
231 Terry Sawchuk Memorial	35.00	60.00
232 Boston Bruins Team Stanley Cup Champs	7.00	12.00
233 Esposito line: Cashman/Hodge	12.00	20.00
234 Tony Esposito AS1	15.00	25.00
235 Bobby Hull AS1	15.00	25.00
236 Bobby Orr AS1	30.00	60.00
237 Phil Esposito AS1	9.00	15.00
238 Gordie Howe AS1	25.00	40.00
239 Brad Park AS1	9.00	15.00
240 Stan Mikita AS2	5.00	10.00
241 John McKenzie AS2	2.00	4.00
242 Frank Mahovlich AS2	2.00	4.00
243 Carl Brewer AS2	2.00	4.00
244 Ed Giacomin AS2	5.00	8.00
245 Jacques Laperriere AS2	2.00	4.00
246 Bobby Orr Hart Trophy	30.00	60.00
247 Tony Esposito Calder Trophy	15.00	25.00
248A Bobby Orr Norris	30.00	60.00
248B Bobby Orr Norris	30.00	60.00
249 Bobby Orr Ross	30.00	60.00
250 Tony Esposito Vezina Trophy	15.00	25.00
251 Phil Goyette Lady Byng Trophy	2.00	4.00
252 Bobby Orr Conn Smythe	30.00	60.00
253 Pit Martin Bill Masterton Trophy	2.00	4.00
254 The Stanley Cup	9.00	15.00
255 Prince of Wales Trophy	2.50	5.00
256 Conn Smythe Trophy	2.50	5.00
257 James Norris Trophy	2.50	5.00
258 Calder Trophy	2.50	5.00
259 Vezina Trophy	2.50	5.00
260 Lady Byng Trophy	2.50	5.00
261 Hart Trophy	2.50	5.00
262 Art Ross Trophy	2.50	5.00
263 Clarence S. Campbell Bowl	2.50	5.00
264 John Ferguson	5.00	10.00

1970-71 O-Pee-Chee Deckle

This set consisted of 48 numbered black and white deckle edge cards measuring approximately 2 1/8" by 3 1/8". The set was issued as an insert with the second series regular issue of the same year. The set was printed in Canada.

Card		
COMPLETE SET (48)	200.00	400.00
1 Pat Quinn	2.00	5.00
2 Eddie Shack	3.00	6.00
3 Eddie Joyal	2.00	5.00
4 Bobby Orr	40.00	80.00
5 Derek Sanderson	6.00	12.00
6 Phil Esposito	7.50	15.00
7 Fred Stanfield	2.00	5.00
8 Bob Woytowich	2.00	5.00
9 Ron Schock	2.00	5.00
10 Les Binkley	3.00	6.00
11 Roger Crozier	3.00	6.00
12 Reg Fleming	2.00	5.00
13 Charlie Burns	2.00	5.00
14 Bobby Rousseau	2.00	5.00
15 Leo Boivin	3.00	6.00
16 Garry Unger	2.00	5.00
17 Frank Mahovlich	5.00	10.00
18 Gordie Howe	25.00	50.00
19 Jacques Lemaire	3.00	8.00
20 Jacques Laperriere	2.00	5.00
21 Jean Beliveau	10.00	20.00
22 Rogatien Vachon	4.00	8.00
23 Yvan Cournoyer	3.00	8.00
24 Henri Richard	6.00	12.00
25 Red Berenson	2.00	5.00
26 Frank St Marseille	2.00	5.00
27 Glenn Hall	5.00	10.00
28 Gary Sabourin	2.00	5.00
29 Doug Mohns	2.00	5.00
30 Bobby Hull	20.00	40.00
31 Ray Cullen	2.00	5.00
32 Tony Esposito	10.00	20.00
33 Gary Dornhoefer	2.00	5.00
34 Ed Van Impe	2.00	5.00
35 Doug Favell	3.00	6.00
36 Carol Vadnais	2.00	5.00
37 Harry Howell	2.00	5.00
38 Bill Hicke	2.00	5.00
39 Rod Gilbert	3.00	6.00
40 Jean Ratelle	3.00	6.00
41 Walt Tkaczuk	3.00	6.00
42 Ed Giacomin	4.00	8.00
43 Brad Park	5.00	10.00
44 Bruce Gamble	3.00	6.00
45 Orland Kurtenbach	2.00	5.00
46 Ron Ellis	2.00	5.00
47 Dave Keon	5.00	10.00
48 Norm Ullman	3.00	6.00

1971-72 O-Pee-Chee

The 1971-72 O-Pee-Chee set contained 264 standard-size cards. The unopened wax packs consisted of eight cards plus a piece of bubble gum. Player photos were framed in an oval. Bilingual backs featured a short biography, year-by-year statistics and a cartoon-illustrated fact about the player. Rookie Cards in this set included Marcel Dionne, Ken Dryden, Butch Goring, Guy Lafleur, Reggie Leach, Richard Martin, and Rick MacLeish.

Card		
COMPLETE SET (264)	900.00	1500.00
1 Paul Popiel	5.00	8.00
2 Pierre Bouchard RC	2.50	5.00
3 Don Awrey	2.00	4.00
4 Paul Curtis RC	2.00	4.00
5 Guy Trottier RC	2.00	4.00
6 Paul Shmyr RC	2.00	4.00
7 Fred Stanfield	2.00	4.00
8 Mike Robitaille RC	2.00	4.00
9 Vic Hadfield	2.50	5.00
10 Jim Harrison	2.00	4.00
11 Bill White	2.00	4.00
12 Andre Boudrias	2.00	4.00
13 Gary Sabourin	2.00	4.00
14 Arnie Brown	2.00	4.00
15 Yvan Cournoyer	4.00	8.00
16 Bryan Hextall	2.50	5.00
17 Gary Croteau	2.00	4.00
18 Gilles Villemure	2.50	5.00
19 Serge Bernier RC	2.50	5.00
20 Phil Esposito	12.00	20.00
21 Tom Reid	2.00	4.00
22 Doug Barrie RC	2.00	4.00
23 Eddie Joyal	2.00	4.00
24 Dunc Wilson RC	4.00	8.00
25 Pat Stapleton	2.50	5.00
26 Garry Unger	2.50	5.00
27 Al Smith	2.50	5.00
28 Bob Woytowich	2.00	4.00
29 Marc Tardif	2.50	5.00
30 Norm Ullman	4.00	8.00
31 Tom Williams	2.00	4.00
32 Ted Harris	2.00	4.00
33 Andre Lacroix	2.50	5.00
34 Mike Byers	2.00	4.00
35 Johnny Bucyk	4.00	8.00
36 Roger Crozier	2.50	5.00
37 Alex Delvecchio	6.00	10.00
38 Frank St.Marseille	2.00	4.00
39 Pit Martin	2.50	5.00
40 Brad Park	9.00	15.00
41 Greg Polis RC	2.00	4.00
42 Orland Kurtenbach	2.00	4.00
43 Jim McKenny RC	2.00	4.00
44 Bob Nevin	2.00	4.00
45 Ken Dryden RC	125.00	300.00
46 Carol Vadnais	2.50	5.00
47 Bill Flett	2.00	4.00
48 Jim Johnson	2.00	4.00
49 Al Hamilton	2.00	4.00
50 Bobby Hull	25.00	40.00
51 Chris Bordeleau RC	2.00	4.00
52 Tim Ecclestone	2.00	4.00
53 Rod Seiling	2.00	4.00
54 Gerry Cheevers	6.00	10.00
55 Bill Goldsworthy	2.50	5.00
56 Ron Schock	2.00	4.00
57 Jim Dorey	2.00	4.00
58 Wayne Maki	2.00	4.00
59 Terry Harper	2.00	4.00
60 Gilbert Perreault	15.00	25.00
61 Ernie Hicke RC	2.00	4.00
62 Wayne Hillman	2.00	4.00
63 Denis DeJordy	2.50	5.00
64 Ken Schinkel	2.00	4.00
65 Derek Sanderson	7.00	12.00
66 Barclay Plager	2.50	5.00
67 Paul Henderson	2.50	5.00
68 Jude Drouin	2.00	4.00
69 Keith Magnuson	2.50	5.00
70 Ron Harris	2.00	4.00
71 Jacques Lemaire	4.00	8.00
72 Doug Favell	2.50	5.00
73 Bert Marshall	2.00	4.00
74 Ted Irvine	2.00	4.00
75 Walt Tkaczuk	2.50	5.00
76 Bob Berry RC	4.00	8.00
77 Syl Apps RC	4.00	8.00
78 Tom Webster	2.50	5.00
79 Danny Grant	2.50	5.00
80 Dave Keon	4.00	8.00
81 Ernie Wakely	2.50	5.00
82 John McKenzie	2.50	5.00
83 Ron Stackhouse RC	2.00	4.00
84 Peter Mahovlich	2.50	5.00
85 Dennis Hull	2.50	5.00
86 Juha Widing RC	2.00	4.00
87 Gary Doak	2.00	4.00
88 Phil Goyette	2.00	4.00
89 Lew Morrison	2.00	4.00
90 Ab DeMarco RC	2.00	4.00
91 Red Berenson	2.50	5.00
92 Mike Pelyk	2.00	4.00
93 Gary Jarrett	2.00	4.00
94 Bob Pulford	2.50	5.00
95 Dan Johnson RC	2.00	4.00
96 Eddie Shack	4.00	8.00
97 Jean Ratelle	4.00	8.00
98 Jim Pappin	2.00	4.00
99 Roy Edwards	2.50	5.00
100 Bobby Orr	60.00	100.00
101 Ted Hampson	2.00	4.00
102 Mickey Redmond	4.00	8.00
103 Bob Plager	4.00	8.00
104 Barry Ashbee RC	2.50	5.00
105 Frank Mahovlich	6.00	10.00
106 Dick Redmond RC	2.00	4.00
107 Tracy Pratt	2.00	4.00
108 Ralph Backstrom	2.50	5.00
109 Murray Hall	2.00	4.00
110 Tony Esposito	20.00	35.00
111 Checklist Card	350.00	500.00
112 Jim Neilson	2.00	4.00
113 Ron Ellis	2.50	5.00
114 Bobby Clarke	40.00	60.00
115 Ken Hodge	2.50	5.00
116 Jim Roberts	2.50	5.00
117 Cesare Maniago	2.50	5.00
118 Jean Pronovost	2.50	5.00
119 Gary Bergman	2.00	4.00
120 Henri Richard	6.00	10.00
121 Ross Lonsberry	2.00	4.00
122 Pat Quinn	2.50	5.00
123 Rod Gilbert	4.00	8.00
124 Walt McKechnie	2.50	5.00
125 Stan Mikita	9.00	15.00
126 Ed Van Impe	2.00	4.00
127 Terry Crisp RC	6.00	10.00
128 Fred Barrett RC	2.00	4.00
129 Wayne Cashman	4.00	8.00
130 J.C. Tremblay	2.50	5.00
131 Bernie Parent	12.00	20.00
132 Bryan Watson	2.50	5.00
133 Marcel Dionne RC	75.00	150.00
134 Ab McDonald	2.50	5.00
135 Leon Rochefort	2.50	5.00
136 Serge Lajeunesse RC	2.50	5.00
137 Joe Daley	3.00	6.00
138 Brian Conacher	2.50	5.00
139 Bill Collins	2.50	5.00
140 Nick Libett	2.50	5.00
141 Bill Sutherland	2.50	5.00
142 Bill Hicke	2.50	5.00
143 Serge Savard	5.00	10.00
144 Jacques Laperriere	3.00	6.00
145 Guy Lapointe	3.00	6.00
146 Claude Larose UER	2.50	5.00
147 Rejean Houle	3.00	6.00
148 Guy Lafleur UER RC !	75.00	200.00
149 Dale Hoganson RC	2.50	5.00
150 Al McDonough RC	2.50	5.00
151 Gilles Marotte	2.50	5.00
152 Butch Goring RC	6.00	10.00
153 Harry Howell	3.00	6.00
154 Real Lemieux	2.50	5.00
155 Gary Edwards RC	3.00	6.00
156 Rogatien Vachon	5.00	10.00
157 Mike Corrigan	2.50	5.00
158 Floyd Smith	2.50	5.00
159 Dave Dryden	3.00	6.00
160 Gerry Meehan	3.00	6.00
161 Richard Martin RC	10.00	20.00
162 Steve Atkinson RC	2.50	5.00
163 Ron Anderson	2.50	5.00
164 Dick Duff	3.00	6.00
165 Jim Watson	2.50	5.00
166 Don Luce RC	2.50	5.00
167 Larry Mickey	2.50	5.00
168 Larry Hillman	2.50	5.00
169 Ed Westfall	3.00	6.00
170 Dallas Smith	2.50	5.00
171 Mike Walton	2.50	5.00
172 Ed Johnston	3.00	6.00
173 Ted Green	3.00	6.00
174 Rick Smith	2.50	5.00
175 Reggie Leach RC	10.00	20.00
176 Don Marcotte	2.50	5.00
177 Bobby Sheehan RC	2.50	5.00
178 Wayne Carleton	2.50	5.00
179 Norm Ferguson	2.50	5.00
180 Don O'Donoghue RC	2.50	5.00
181 Gary Kurt RC	3.00	6.00
182 Joey Johnston RC	2.50	5.00
183 Stan Gilbertson RC	2.50	5.00
184 Craig Patrick RC	6.00	10.00
185 Gerry Pinder	2.50	5.00
186 Tim Horton	7.00	12.00
187 Darryl Edestrand RC	2.50	5.00
188 Keith McCreary	2.50	5.00
189 Val Fonteyne	2.50	5.00
190 Sheldon Kannegiesser RC	2.50	5.00
191 Nick Harbaruk RC	2.50	5.00
192 Les Binkley	3.00	6.00
193 Darryl Sittler	25.00	40.00
194 Rick Ley	2.50	5.00
195 Jacques Plante	15.00	30.00
196 Bob Baun	3.00	6.00
197 Brian Glennie	2.50	5.00
198 Brian Spencer RC	6.00	10.00
199 Don Marshall	3.00	6.00
200 Denis Dupere RC	2.50	5.00
201 Bruce Gamble	3.00	6.00
202 Gary Dornhoefer	2.50	5.00
203 Bob Kelly RC	3.00	6.00
204 Jean-Guy Gendron	2.50	5.00
205 Brent Hughes	2.50	5.00
206 Simon Nolet	2.50	5.00
207 Rick MacLeish RC	10.00	20.00
208 Doug Jarrett	2.50	5.00
209 Cliff Koroll	2.50	5.00
210 Chico Maki	2.50	5.00
211 Danny O'Shea	2.50	5.00
212 Lou Angotti	2.50	5.00
213 Eric Nesterenko	3.00	6.00
214 Bryan Campbell	2.50	5.00
215 Bill Fairbairn RC	2.50	5.00
216 Bruce MacGregor	2.50	5.00
217 Pete Stemkowski	2.50	5.00
218 Bobby Rousseau	2.50	5.00
219 Dale Rolfe	2.50	5.00
220 Ed Giacomin	5.00	10.00
221 Glen Sather	3.00	6.00
222 Carl Brewer	3.00	6.00
223 George Morrison RC	2.50	5.00
224 Noel Picard	2.50	5.00
225 Peter McDuffe RC	3.00	6.00
226 Brit Selby	2.50	5.00
227 Jim Lorentz	2.50	5.00
228 Phil Roberto RC	2.50	5.00
229 Dave Balon	2.50	5.00
230 Barry Wilkins RC	2.50	5.00
231 Dennis Kearns RC	2.50	5.00
232 Jocelyn Guevremont RC	3.00	6.00
233 Rosaire Paiement	2.50	5.00
234 Dale Tallon	2.50	5.00
235 George Gardner	2.50	5.00
236 Ron Stewart	2.50	5.00
237 Wayne Connelly	2.50	5.00
238 Charlie Burns	2.50	5.00
239 Murray Oliver	2.50	5.00
240 Lou Nanne	3.00	6.00
241 Gump Worsley	5.00	10.00
242 Doug Mohns	2.50	5.00
243 Jean-Paul Parise	2.50	5.00
244 Dennis Hextall	3.00	6.00
245 Bobby Orr Double	30.00	50.00
246 Gilbert Perreault Calder	9.00	15.00
247 Phil Esposito Ross	6.00	10.00
248 Ed Giacomin and Gilles Villemure Vezina Trophy	3.00	6.00
249 Johnny Bucyk Byng	3.00	6.00
250 Ed Giacomin AS1	3.00	6.00
251 Bobby Orr AS1	30.00	50.00
252 J.C. Tremblay AS1	3.00	6.00
253 Phil Esposito AS1 UER	7.00	12.00
254 Ken Hodge AS1	3.00	6.00
255 Johnny Bucyk AS1	3.00	6.00
256 Jacques Plante AS2 UER	9.00	15.00
257 Brad Park AS2	3.00	6.00
258 Pat Stapleton AS2	3.00	6.00
259 Dave Keon AS2	3.00	6.00
260 Yvan Cournoyer AS2	3.00	6.00
261 Bobby Hull AS2	15.00	25.00
262 Gordie Howe Retires	50.00	100.00
263 Jean Beliveau Retires	40.00	80.00
264 Checklist Card	100.00	175.00

1971-72 O-Pee-Chee/Topps Booklets

This set consisted of 24 colorful comic booklets (eight pages in format) each measuring 2 1/2" by 3 1/2". The booklets were included as an insert with the regular issue of the same year and gave a mini-biography of the player. These booklets were also put out by Topps and were printed in the United States. They could be found in either French or English language versions. The booklets were numbered on the fronts with a complete set checklist on the backs. The prices below are valid as well for the 1971-72 Topps version of these booklets although the English version is probably a little easier to find.

Card		
COMPLETE SET (24)	50.00	125.00
1 Bobby Hull	6.00	15.00
2 Phil Esposito	3.00	6.00
3 Dale Tallon	1.25	3.00
4 Jacques Plante	4.00	8.00
5 Roger Crozier	1.25	3.00
6 Henri Richard	1.25	3.00
7 Ed Giacomin	2.50	5.00
8 Gilbert Perreault	3.00	6.00
9 Greg Polis	1.25	3.00
10 Bobby Clarke	5.00	10.00
11 Danny Grant	1.25	3.00
12 Alex Delvecchio	1.25	3.00
13 Tony Esposito	3.00	6.00
14 Garry Unger	1.25	3.00
15 Frank St.Marseille	1.25	3.00
16 Dave Keon	2.50	5.00
17 Ken Dryden	8.00	20.00
18 Rod Gilbert	1.25	3.00
19 Juha Widing	1.25	3.00
20 Orland Kurtenbach	1.25	3.00
21 Jude Drouin	1.25	3.00
22 Gary Smith	1.25	3.00
23 Gordie Howe	8.00	20.00
24 Bobby Orr	10.00	25.00

1971-72 O-Pee-Chee Posters

The 1971-72 O-Pee-Chee Posters set contained 24 color pictures measuring approximately 10" by 18". They were originally issued (as a separate issue) in folded form, two to a wax pack. Attached pairs are still sometimes found; these pairs are valued at 25 percent greater than the sum of the individual players included in the pair. The current scarcity of these posters suggests that they may have been a test issue. These posters are numbered and blank backed.

Card		
COMPLETE SET (24)	600.00	1000.00
1 Bobby Orr	125.00	250.00
2 Bob Pulford	10.00	20.00
3 Dave Keon	15.00	30.00
4 Yvan Cournoyer	15.00	30.00
5 Dale Tallon	10.00	20.00
6 Richard Martin	7.50	15.00
7 Rod Gilbert	15.00	30.00
8 Tony Esposito	20.00	40.00
9 Bobby Hull	25.00	50.00
10 Red Berenson	7.50	15.00
11 Norm Ullman	8.00	20.00
12 Orland Kurtenbach	7.50	15.00
13 Guy Lafleur	50.00	100.00
14 Gilbert Perreault	20.00	40.00
15 Jacques Plante	25.00	50.00
16 Bruce Gamble	10.00	25.00
17 Walt McKechnie	7.50	15.00
18 Tim Horton	25.00	50.00
19 Jean Ratelle	15.00	30.00
20 Garry Unger	7.50	15.00
21 Phil Esposito	25.00	50.00
22 Ken Dryden	75.00	150.00
23 Gump Worsley	15.00	30.00
24 Montreal Canadiens	20.00	40.00

1972-73 O-Pee-Chee

The 1972-73 O-Pee-Chee set featured 340 standard-size cards that were printed in Canada. The set featured players from the expansion New York Islanders and Atlanta Flames. Unopened packs consisted of eight cards plus a bubble-gum piece. Tan borders on the front included the team name on the left-hand side. Bilingual backs featured a year-by-year record of the player's career, a short biography and a cartoon-illustrated fact about the player. There were a number of In-Action (IA) cards of popular players distributed throughout the set. Card number 208 was never issued. The last series (290-341), which was printed in lesser quantities, featured players from the newly formed World Hockey Association. There were apparently 22 double-printed cards in the first series (1-110), but the identity of these 22 is not known at this time except for card no.1 Johnny Bucyk, and no.102, Frank Mahovlich. There were also 22 known double-printed cards in the second series (111-209). These cards were identified by DP in the checklist below.

Card		
COMPLETE SET (340)	900.00	1500.00
1 Johnny Bucyk DP	5.00	8.00
2 Rene Robert RC	3.00	5.00
3 Gary Croteau	1.25	2.50
4 Pat Stapleton	1.25	2.50
5 Ron Harris	1.25	2.50
6 Checklist 1	30.00	45.00
7 Playoff Game 1 Bruins 6 Rangers 5	1.25	2.50
8 Marcel Dionne	15.00	25.00
9 Bob Berry	1.25	2.50
10 Lou Nanne	1.25	2.50
11 Marc Tardif	1.25	2.50
12 Jean Ratelle	2.00	4.00
13 Craig Cameron RC	1.25	2.50
14 Bobby Clarke	18.00	30.00
15 Jim Rutherford RC	6.00	10.00
16 Andre Dupont RC	2.00	4.00
17 Mike Pelyk	1.25	2.50
18 Dunc Wilson	1.25	2.50
19 Checklist 2 (See also card 190; 160 is Bill Harris)	30.00	50.00
20 Playoff Game 2 Bruins 2 Rangers 1	1.25	2.50
21 Dallas Smith	1.25	2.50
22 Gerry Meehan	1.25	2.50
23 Rick Smith UER (Wrong total games should be 262	1.25	2.50
24 Pit Martin	1.25	2.50
25 Keith McCreary	1.25	2.50
26 Alex Delvecchio	2.00	4.00
27 Gilles Marotte	1.25	2.50
28 Gump Worsley	2.00	4.00
29 Yvan Cournoyer	2.00	4.00
30 Playoff Game 3 Rangers 5 Bruins 2	1.25	2.50
31 Vic Hadfield	1.25	2.50
32 Tom Miller RC	1.25	2.50
33 Ed Van Impe	1.25	2.50
34 Greg Polis	1.25	2.50
35 Barclay Plager	1.25	2.50
36 Ron Ellis	1.25	2.50
37 Jocelyn Guevremont	1.25	2.50
38 Playoff Game 4 Bruins 3 Rangers 2	1.25	2.50
39 Carol Vadnais	1.25	2.50
40 Steve Atkinson	1.25	2.50
41 Ivan Boldirev RC	2.00	4.00
42 Jim Pappin	1.25	2.50
43 Phil Myre RC	5.00	8.00
44 Yvan Cournoyer IA	1.50	3.00
45 Nick Libett	1.25	2.50
46 Juha Widing	1.25	2.50
47 Jude Drouin	1.25	2.50
48A Jean Ratelle IA ERR (Defense on back)	2.00	4.00
48B Jean Ratelle IA COR (Center on back)	1.50	3.00
49 Ken Hodge	1.25	2.50
50 Roger Crozier	1.25	2.50
51 Reggie Leach	2.00	4.00
52 Dennis Hull	1.25	2.50
53 Larry Hale RC	1.25	2.50
54 Playoff Game 5 Rangers 3 Bruins 2	1.25	2.50
55 Tim Ecclestone	1.25	2.50
56 Butch Goring	1.50	3.00
57 Danny Grant	1.25	2.50
58 Bobby Orr IA	20.00	40.00
59 Guy Lafleur	30.00	60.00
60 Jim Neilson	1.25	2.50
61 Brian Spencer	1.25	2.50
62 Joe Watson	1.25	2.50
63 Playoff Game 6 Bruins 3 Rangers 0	1.25	2.50
64 Jean Pronovost	1.25	2.50
65 Frank St.Marseille	1.25	2.50
66 Bob Baun	1.25	2.50
67 Paul Popiel	1.25	2.50
68 Wayne Cashman	1.25	2.50
69 Tracy Pratt	1.25	2.50
70 Stan Gilbertson	1.25	2.50
71 Keith Magnuson	1.25	2.50
72 Ernie Hicke	1.25	2.50
73 Gary Doak	1.25	2.50
74 Mike Corrigan	1.25	2.50
75 Doug Mohns	1.25	2.50
76 Phil Esposito IA	5.00	8.00
77 Jacques Lemaire	2.00	4.00
78 Pete Stemkowski	1.25	2.50
79 Bill Mikkelson RC	1.25	2.50
80 Rick Foley RC	1.25	2.50
81 Ron Schock	1.25	2.50
82 Phil Roberto	1.25	2.50
83 Jim McKenny	1.25	2.50
84 Wayne Maki	1.25	2.50
85A Brad Park IA Centre	5.00	8.00
85B Brad Park IA Defense	2.50	5.00
86 Guy Lapointe	1.50	3.00
87 Bill Fairbairn	1.25	2.50
88 Terry Crisp	1.25	2.50
89 Doug Favell	1.25	2.50
90 Bryan Watson	1.25	2.50
91 Gary Sabourin	1.25	2.50
92 Jacques Plante	12.00	20.00
93 Andre Boudrias	1.25	2.50
94 Mike Walton	1.25	2.50
95 Don Luce	1.25	2.50
96 Joey Johnston	1.25	2.50
97 Doug Jarrett	1.25	2.50
98 Bill MacMillan RC	1.25	2.50
99 Mickey Redmond	1.50	3.00
100 Rogatien Vachon UER	2.00	4.00
101 Barry Gibbs RC	1.25	2.50
102 Frank Mahovlich DP	2.00	4.00
103 Bruce MacGregor	1.25	2.50
104 Ed Westfall	1.25	2.50
105 Rick MacLeish	3.00	5.00
106 Nick Harbaruk	1.25	2.50
107 Jack Egers RC	1.25	2.50
108 Dave Keon	2.00	4.00
109 Barry Wilkins	1.25	2.50
110 Walt Tkaczuk	1.25	2.50
111 Phil Esposito	9.00	15.00
112 Gilles Meloche RC	5.00	8.00
113 Gary Edwards	1.50	3.00
114 Brad Park	6.00	10.00
115 Syl Apps DP	1.50	3.00
116 Jim Lorentz	1.50	3.00
117 Gary Smith	1.50	3.00
118 Ted Harris	1.50	3.00
119 Gerry Desjardins DP	.50	1.00
120 Garry Unger	1.50	3.00
121 Dale Tallon	1.50	3.00
122 Bill Plager RC	2.00	4.00
123 Red Berenson DP	.50	1.00
124 Peter Mahovlich DP	1.50	3.00
125 Simon Nolet	1.50	3.00
126 Paul Henderson	1.50	3.00
127 Hart Trophy Winners	1.50	3.00
128 Frank Mahovlich IA	1.50	3.00
129 Bobby Orr	40.00	80.00
130 Bert Marshall	1.50	3.00
131 Ralph Backstrom	1.50	3.00
132 Gilles Villemure	1.50	3.00
133 Dave Burrows RC	1.50	3.00
134 Calder Trophy Winners	1.50	3.00
135 Dallas Smith IA	1.50	3.00
136 Gilbert Perreault DP	7.00	12.00
137 Tony Esposito DP	12.00	20.00
138 Cesare Maniago DP	.50	1.00
139 Gerry Hart RC	1.50	3.00
140 Jacques Caron RC	1.50	3.00
141 Orland Kurtenbach	1.50	3.00
142 Norris Trophy Winners	1.50	3.00
143 Lew Morrison	1.50	3.00
144 Arnie Brown	1.50	3.00
145 Ken Dryden DP	25.00	50.00
146 Gary Dornhoefer	1.50	3.00
147 Norm Ullman	2.50	5.00
148 Art Ross Trophy	1.50	3.00
149 Orland Kurtenbach IA	1.50	3.00
150 Fred Stanfield	1.50	3.00
151 Dick Redmond DP	.50	1.00
152 Serge Bernier	1.50	3.00
153 Rod Gilbert	2.50	5.00
154 Duane Rupp	1.50	3.00
155 Vezina Trophy Winners	1.50	3.00
156 Stan Mikita IA	3.00	5.00
157 Richard Martin DP	3.00	5.00
158 Bill White DP	.50	1.00
159 Bill Goldsworthy DP	.50	1.00
160 Jack Lynch RC	1.50	3.00
161 Bob Plager DP	.50	1.00
162 Dave Balon UER	1.50	3.00
163 Noel Price	1.50	3.00
164 Gary Bergman DP	.50	1.00
165 Pierre Bouchard	1.50	3.00
166 Ross Lonsberry	1.50	3.00
167 Denis Dupere	1.50	3.00
168 Byng Trophy Winners DP	.50	1.00
169 Ken Hodge	1.50	3.00
170 Don Awrey DP	.50	1.00
171 Marshall Johnston DP RC	.50	1.00
172 Terry Harper	1.50	3.00
173 Ed Giacomin	2.50	5.00
174 Bryan Hextall DP	.50	1.00
175 Conn Smythe Trophy Winners	1.50	3.00
176 Larry Hillman	1.50	3.00
177 Stan Mikita DP	4.00	8.00
178 Charlie Burns	1.50	3.00
179 Brian Marchinko	1.50	3.00
180 Noel Picard DP	.50	1.00
181 Bobby Schmautz RC	2.00	4.00
182 Richard Martin IA UER	2.00	4.00
183 Pat Quinn	1.50	3.00
184 Denis DeJordy UER	1.50	3.00
185 Serge Savard	2.50	5.00
186 Eddie Shack	2.00	4.00
187 Bill Flett	1.50	3.00
188 Darryl Sittler	12.00	20.00
189 Gump Worsley IA	2.00	4.00
190 Checklist	35.00	60.00
191 Garnet Bailey DP	.50	1.00
192 Walt McKechnie	1.50	3.00
193 Harry Howell	1.50	3.00
194 Rod Seiling	1.50	3.00
195 Darryl Edestrand	1.50	3.00
196 Tony Esposito IA	5.00	8.00
197 Tim Horton	5.00	8.00
198 Chico Maki DP	.50	1.00
199 Jean-Paul Parise	1.50	3.00
200 Germaine Gagnon UER RC	1.50	3.00
201 Danny O'Shea	1.50	3.00
202 Richard Lemieux RC	1.50	3.00
203 Dan Bouchard RC	6.00	10.00
204 Leon Rochefort	1.50	3.00
205 Jacques Laperriere	2.00	4.00
206 Barry Ashbee	1.50	3.00
207 Garry Monahan	1.50	3.00
208 Never Issued		
209 Dave Keon IA	2.50	5.00
210 Rejean Houle	2.00	4.00
211 Dave Hudson RC	2.00	4.00
212 Ted Irvine	2.00	4.00
213 Don Saleski RC	3.00	5.00
214 Lowell MacDonald	2.00	4.00
215 Mike Murphy RC	2.00	4.00
216 Brian Glennie	2.00	4.00
217 Bobby Lalonde RC	2.00	4.00
218 Bob Leiter	2.00	4.00
219 Don Marcotte	2.00	4.00
220 Jim Schoenfeld RC	7.00	12.00
221 Craig Patrick	2.00	4.00
222 Cliff Koroll	2.00	4.00
223 Guy Charron RC	2.00	4.00
224 Jim Peters	2.00	4.00
225 Dennis Hextall	2.00	4.00
226 Tony Esposito AS1	9.00	15.00
227 Orr/Park AS1	20.00	40.00
228 Bobby Hull AS1	15.00	30.00
229 Rod Gilbert AS1	2.00	4.00
230 Phil Esposito AS1 (Brother Tony pictured in background)	6.00	10.00
231 Claude Larose UER (Misspelled La Rose on both sides)	2.00	4.00
232 Jim Mair RC	2.00	4.00
233 Bobby Rousseau	2.00	4.00
234 Brent Hughes	2.00	4.00
235 Al McDonough	2.00	4.00
236 Chris Evans RC	2.00	4.00
237 Pierre Jarry RC	2.00	4.00
238 Don Tannahill RC	2.00	4.00
239 Rey Comeau RC	2.00	4.00
240 Gregg Sheppard RC	2.00	4.00
241 Dave Dryden	2.00	4.00
242 Ted McAneeley RC	2.00	4.00
243 Lou Angotti	2.00	4.00
244 Len Fontaine RC	2.00	4.00
245 Bill Lesuk RC	2.00	4.00
246 Fred Harvey RC	2.00	4.00
247 Ken Dryden AS2	18.00	30.00
248 Bill White AS2	2.00	4.00
249 Pat Stapleton AS2	2.00	4.00
250 Ratelle/Cournoyer/ Hadfield AS2	3.50	6.00
251 Henri Richard	2.00	4.00
252 Bryan Lefley RC	2.00	4.00
253 Stanley Cup Trophy	9.00	15.00
254 Steve Vickers RC	4.00	8.00
255 Wayne Hillman	2.00	4.00
256 Ken Schinkel UER (Misspelled Shinkel on card front)	2.00	4.00
257 Kevin O'Shea RC	2.00	4.00
258 Ron Low RC	9.00	15.00
259 Don Lever RC	2.50	5.00
260 Randy Manery RC	2.00	4.00
261 Ed Johnston	2.00	4.00
262 Craig Ramsay RC	3.50	6.00
263 Pete Laframboise RC	2.00	4.00
264 Dan Maloney RC	2.50	5.00
265 Bill Collins	2.00	4.00
266 Paul Curtis	2.00	4.00
267 Bob Nevin	2.00	4.00
268 Penalty Min. Leaders Bryan Watson Keith Magnuson	2.00	4.00
269 Jim Roberts	2.00	4.00
270 Brian Lavender RC	2.00	4.00
271 Dale Rolfe	2.00	4.00
272 Goals Leaders	10.00	20.00
273 Michel Belhumeur RC	4.00	8.00
274 Eddie Shack	2.00	4.00
275 Wayne Stephenson RC UER	6.00	10.00
276 Stanley Cup Winner Boston Bruins Team	4.00	8.00

277 Rick Kehoe RC 5.00 8.00
278 Gerry O'Flaherty RC 2.00 4.00
279 Jacques Richard RC 2.00 4.00
280 Scoring Leaders 15.00 25.00
Phil Esposito
Bobby Orr
Jean Ratelle
281 Nick Beverley RC 3.50 6.00
282 Larry Carriere RC 2.00 4.00
283 Assists Leaders 15.00 25.00
Bobby Orr
Phil Esposito
Jean Ratelle
284 Rick Smith IA 2.00 4.00
285 Jerry Korab RC 2.50 5.00
286 Goals Against 7.00 12.00
Average Leaders
Tony Esposito
Gilles Villemure
Gump Worsley
287 Ron Stackhouse 2.00 4.00
288 Barry Long RC 2.00 4.00
289 Dean Prentice 2.00 4.00
290 Norm Beaudin 5.00 8.00
291 Mike Amodeo RC 5.00 8.00
292 Jim Harrison 5.00 8.00
293 J.C. Tremblay 5.00 8.00
294 Murray Hall 5.00 8.00
295 Bart Crashley 5.00 8.00
296 Wayne Connelly 5.00 8.00
297 Bobby Sheehan 5.00 8.00
298 Ron Anderson 5.00 8.00
299 Chris Bordeleau 5.00 8.00
300 Les Binkley 5.00 8.00
301 Ron Walters 5.00 8.00
302 Jean-Guy Gendron 5.00 8.00
303 Gord Labossiere 5.00 8.00
304 Gerry Odrowski 5.00 8.00
305 Mike McMahon 5.00 8.00
306 Gary Kurt 5.00 8.00
307 Larry Cahan 5.00 8.00
308 Wally Boyer 5.00 8.00
309 Bob Charlebois RC 5.00 8.00
310 Bob Falkenberg 5.00 8.00
311 Jean Payette RC 5.00 8.00
312 Ted Taylor 5.00 8.00
313 Joe Szura 5.00 8.00
314 George Morrison 5.00 8.00
315 Wayne Rivers 5.00 8.00
316 Reg Fleming 5.00 8.00
317 Larry Hornung RC 5.00 8.00
318 Ron Climie RC 5.00 8.00
319 Val Fonteyne 5.00 8.00
320 Michel Archambault RC 5.00 8.00
321 Al McDonald 5.00 8.00
322 Bob Leduc RC 5.00 8.00
323 Bob Wall 5.00 8.00
324 Alain Caron RC 5.00 8.00
325 Bob Woytowich 5.00 8.00
326 Guy Trottier 5.00 8.00
327 Bill Hicke 5.00 8.00
328 Guy Dufour RC 5.00 8.00
329 Wayne Rutledge RC 5.00 8.00
330 Gary Veneruzzo 5.00 8.00
331 Fred Speck RC 5.00 8.00
332 Ron Ward RC 5.00 8.00
333 Rosaire Paiement 5.00 8.00
334A Checklist 3 50.00 80.00
(Numbers 335-341
listed as More
WHA Stars)
334B Checklist 3 40.00 70.00
(Numbers 335-341
listed correctly)
335 Michel Parizeau RC 5.00 8.00
336 Bobby Hull 30.00 60.00
337 Wayne Carleton 5.00 8.00
338 John McKenzie 5.00 8.00
339 Jim Dorey 5.00 8.00
340 Gerry Cheevers 18.00 30.00
341 Gerry Pinder 12.00 20.00

1972-73 O-Pee-Chee Player Crests

This set consisted of 22 full-color cardboard stickers measuring 2 1/2" by 3 1/2". The set was issued as an insert with the regular issue of the same year in with the first series wax packs. These cards were numbered on the front and have a blank adhesive back. Although the cards were designed so that the crest could be popped out, this is strongly discouraged. These stickers were printed in Canada.

COMPLETE SET (22) 100.00 200.00
1 Pat Quinn 3.00 10.00
2 Phil Esposito 8.00 20.00
3 Bobby Orr 30.00 80.00
4 Richard Martin 2.50 6.00
5 Stan Mikita 4.00 10.00
6 Bill White 2.50 6.00
7 Red Berenson 2.50 6.00
8 Gary Bergman 2.50 6.00
9 Gary Edwards 2.50 6.00
10 Bill Goldsworthy 2.50 6.00
11 Jacques Laperriere 2.50 6.00
12 Ken Dryden 20.00 40.00
13 Ed Westfall 2.50 6.00
14 Walt Tkaczuk 2.50 6.00
15 Brad Park 5.00 12.00
16 Doug Favell 5.00 12.00
17 Eddie Shack 5.00 10.00
18 Jacques Caron 2.50 6.00
19 Paul Henderson 4.00 10.00
20 Jim Harrison 2.50 6.00
21 Dale Tallon 2.50 6.00
22 Orland Kurtenbach 2.50 6.00

1972-73 O-Pee-Chee Team Canada

This attractive set consisted of 28 unnumbered color cards measuring 2 1/2" by 3 1/2". The 28 players are those who represented Team Canada against Russia in the 1972 Summit Series. Only the players' heads were shown surrounded by a border of maple leaves with a Canadian and Russian flag in each corner. The card back provided a summary of that player's performance in the eight-game series. The set was issued as an insert with the second series of the 1972-73 O-Pee-Chee regular issue. Backs were written in both French and English. The cards were printed in Canada.

COMPLETE SET (28) 150.00 300.00
1 Don Awrey 3.00 8.00
2 Red Berenson 3.00 8.00
3 Gary Bergman 3.00 8.00
4 Wayne Cashman 3.00 8.00
5 Bobby Clarke 12.50 25.00
6 Yvan Cournoyer 7.50 15.00
7 Ken Dryden 25.00 50.00
8 Ron Ellis 3.00 8.00
9 Phil Esposito 12.50 25.00
10 Tony Esposito 15.00 30.00
11 Rod Gilbert 4.00 10.00
12 Bill Goldsworthy 3.00 8.00
13 Vic Hadfield 3.00 8.00
14 Paul Henderson 15.00 30.00
15 Dennis Hull 3.00 8.00
16 Guy Lapointe 3.00 8.00
17 Frank Mahovlich 7.50 15.00
18 Pete Mahovlich 3.00 8.00
19 Stan Mikita 10.00 20.00
20 Jean-Paul Parise 3.00 8.00
21 Brad Park 6.00 12.00
22 Gilbert Perreault 3.00 8.00
23 Jean Ratelle 4.00 10.00
24 Mickey Redmond 4.00 10.00
25 Serge Savard 3.00 8.00
26 Rod Seiling 3.00 8.00
27 Pat Stapleton 3.00 8.00
28 Bill White 3.00 8.00

1972-73 O-Pee-Chee Team Logos

This set of 30 team logo pushouts included logos for the 15 NHL established teams as well as the two new NHL teams, the 12 WHA teams, and the WHA League emblem. The cards were die-cut and adhesive backed. They were inserted in with the third series of the 1972-73 O-Pee-Chee wax packs. The expansion and WHA emblems were more difficult to find and are listed as SP in the checklist below. These inserts were standard size, 2 1/2" by 3 1/2". These team logos cards were distinguished by their lack of instructions on the front.

COMPLETE SET (30) 500.00 900.00
1 NHL Logo 4.00 10.00
2 Atlanta Flames SP 150.00 250.00
3 Boston Bruins 4.00 10.00
4 Buffalo Sabres 4.00 10.00
5 California Seals 5.00 12.00
6 Chicago Blackhawks 4.00 10.00
7 Detroit Red Wings 4.00 10.00
8 Los Angeles Kings 4.00 10.00
9 Minnesota North Stars 5.00 12.00
10 Montreal Canadiens 4.00 10.00
11 New York Islanders SP 60.00 150.00
12 New York Rangers 4.00 10.00
13 Philadelphia Flyers 4.00 10.00
14 Pittsburgh Penguins 5.00 12.00
15 St. Louis Blues 4.00 10.00
16 Toronto Maple Leafs 4.00 10.00
17 Vancouver Canucks 5.00 12.00
18 WHA Logo SP 25.00 60.00
19 Chicago Cougars SP 25.00 60.00
20 Cleveland Crusaders SP 40.00 80.00
21 Edmonton Oilers SP 40.00 80.00
22 Houston Aeros SP 25.00 60.00
23 Los Angeles Sharks SP 20.00 50.00
24 Minnesota Fighting Saints SP 50.00 100.00
25 New England Whalers SP 30.00 80.00
26 New York Raiders SP 30.00 80.00
27 Ottawa Nationals SP 25.00 60.00
28 Phila. Blazers SP 40.00 80.00
29 Quebec Nordiques SP 30.00 60.00
30 Winnipeg Jets SP 40.00 80.00

1973-74 O-Pee-Chee

The 1973-74 O-Pee-Chee NHL set featured 264 standard-size cards. The cards measured 2 1/2" by 3 1/2". The border color on the fronts differed from the Topps set. Cards 1-198 had a red border and cards 199-264 had a green border. Topps cards were a mix of blue and green. Bilingual backs contained 1972-73 and career statistics, a short biography and a cartoon-illustrated fact about the player. Team cards (92-107) contained team and player records on the back. The cards were printed in Canada on cream or gray card stock. Rookie Cards in this set included Bill Barber, Terry O'Reilly, Larry Robinson, Dave Schultz, and Billy Smith.

COMPLETE SET (264) 300.00 500.00
1 Alex Delvecchio 2.50 5.00
2 Gilles Meloche 1.25 3.00
3 Phil Roberto 1.25 3.00
4 Orland Kurtenbach 1.00 2.50
5 Gilles Marotte 1.00 2.50
6 Stan Mikita 5.00 8.00
7 Paul Henderson 1.25 3.00
8 Gregg Sheppard 1.00 2.50
9 Rod Seiling 1.00 2.50
10 Red Berenson 1.25 3.00
11 Jean Pronovost 1.25 3.00
12 Dick Redmond 1.00 2.50
13 Keith McCreary 1.00 2.50
14 Bryan Watson 1.00 2.50
15 Garry Unger 1.25 3.00
16 Neil Komadoski RC 1.00 2.50
17 Marcel Dionne 9.00 15.00
18 Ernie Hicke 1.00 2.50
19 Andre Boudrias 1.00 2.50
20 Bill Flett 1.00 2.50
21 Marshall Johnston 1.00 2.50
22 Gerry Meehan 1.00 2.50
23 Ed Johnston 1.25 3.00
24 Serge Savard 2.50 5.00
25 Walt Tkaczuk 1.25 3.00
26 Ken Hodge 1.25 3.00
27 Norm Ullman 2.50 5.00
28 Cliff Koroll 1.00 2.50
29 Rey Comeau 1.00 2.50
30 Bobby Orr 30.00 50.00
31 Jocelyn Guevremont 1.25 3.00
32 Dan Maloney 1.25 3.00
33 Henry Boucha RC 1.00 2.50
34 Gerry Hart 1.00 2.50
35 Bobby Schmautz 1.00 2.50
36 Ross Lonsberry 1.00 2.50
37 Ted McAneeley 1.00 2.50
38 Don Luce 1.00 2.50
39 Jim McKenny 1.00 2.50
40 Jacques Laperriere 1.25 3.00
41 Bill Fairbairn 1.00 2.50
42 Craig Cameron 1.00 2.50
43 Bryan Hextall 1.00 2.50
44 Chuck Lefley RC 1.00 2.50
45 Dan Bouchard 1.25 3.00
46 Jean-Paul Parise 1.00 2.50
47 Barclay Plager 1.25 3.00
48 Mike Corrigan 1.00 2.50
49 Nick Libett 1.00 2.50
50 Bobby Clarke 12.00 20.00
51 Bert Marshall 1.00 2.50
52 Craig Patrick 1.25 3.00
53 Richard Lemieux 1.00 2.50
54 Tracy Pratt 1.00 2.50
55 Ron Ellis 1.25 3.00
56 Jacques Lemaire 2.50 5.00
57 Steve Vickers 1.25 3.00
58 Carol Vadnais 1.00 2.50
59 Jim Rutherford 1.25 3.00
60 Rick Kehoe 1.25 3.00
61 Pat Quinn 1.25 3.00
62 Bill Goldsworthy 1.25 3.00
63 Dave Dryden 1.25 3.00
64 Rogatien Vachon 2.50 5.00
65 Gary Bergman 1.00 2.50
66 Bernie Parent 6.00 10.00
67 Ed Westfall 1.25 3.00
68 Ivan Boldirev 1.25 3.00
69 Don Tannahill 1.00 2.50
70 Gilbert Perreault 7.00 12.00
71 Mike Pelyk 1.00 2.50
72 Guy Lafleur 15.00 25.00
73 Pit Martin 1.25 3.00
74 Gilles Gilbert RC 5.00 8.00
75 Jim Lorentz 1.00 2.50
76 Syl Apps 1.25 3.00
77 Phil Myre 1.25 3.00
78 Bill White 1.00 2.50
79 Jack Egers 1.00 2.50
80 Terry Harper 1.00 2.50
81 Bill Barber RC 12.00 20.00
82 Roy Edwards 1.25 3.00
83 Brian Spencer 1.25 3.00
84 Reggie Leach 1.25 2.50
85 Wayne Cashman 1.25 3.00
86 Jim Schoenfeld 2.50 5.00
87 Henri Richard 2.50 5.00
88 Dennis O'Brien RC 1.00 2.50
89 Al McDonough 1.00 2.50
90 Tony Esposito 7.00 12.00
91 Joe Watson 1.00 2.50
92 Flames Team 2.50 5.00
93 Bruins Team 2.50 5.00
94 Sabres Team 2.50 5.00
95 Golden Seals Team 2.50 5.00
96 Blackhawks Team 2.50 5.00
97 Red Wings Team 2.50 5.00
98 Kings Team 2.50 5.00
99 North Stars Team 2.50 5.00
100 Canadiens Team 2.50 5.00
101 Islanders Team 2.50 5.00
102 Rangers Team 2.50 5.00
103 Flyers Team 2.50 5.00
104 Penguins Team 2.50 5.00
105 Blues Team 2.50 5.00
106 Maple Leafs Team 2.50 5.00
107 Canucks Team 2.50 5.00
108 Vic Hadfield 1.25 3.00
109 Tom Reid 1.00 2.50
110 Hilliard Graves RC 1.00 2.50
111 Don Lever 1.25 3.00
112 Jim Pappin 1.00 2.50
113 Andre Dupont 1.00 2.50
114 Guy Lapointe 1.25 3.00
115 Dennis Hextall 1.00 2.50
116 Checklist 1 20.00 40.00
117 Bob Leiter 1.00 2.50
118 Ab DeMarco 1.00 2.50
119 Gilles Villemure 1.25 3.00
120 Phil Esposito 6.00 10.00
121 Mike Robitaille 1.00 2.50
122 Real Lemieux 1.00 2.50
123 Jim Neilson 1.00 2.50
124 Steve Durbano RC 1.00 2.50
125 Jude Drouin 1.00 2.50
126 Gary Smith 1.25 3.00
127 Cesare Maniago 1.25 3.00
128 Lowell MacDonald 1.00 2.50
129 Checklist 2 20.00 40.00
130 Billy Harris RC 1.00 2.50
131 Randy Manery 1.00 2.50
132 Darryl Sittler 7.50 15.00
133 Goals Leaders 2.50 5.00
Phil Esposito
Rick MacLeish
134 Assists Leaders 2.50 5.00
Phil Esposito
Bobby Clarke
135 Scoring Leaders 2.50 5.00
Phil Esposito
Bobby Clarke
136 Goals Against 6.00 10.00
Average Leaders
Ken Dryden
Tony Esposito
137 Penalty Min. Leaders 2.50 5.00
Jim Schoenfeld
Dave Schultz
138 Power Play Goal 2.50 5.00
Leaders
Phil Esposito
Rick MacLeish
139 Rene Robert 1.25 3.00
140 Dave Burrows 1.00 2.50
141 Jean Ratelle 2.50 5.00
142 Billy Smith RC 30.00 50.00
143 Jocelyn Guevremont 1.00 2.50
144 Tim Ecclestone 1.00 2.50
145 Frank Mahovlich 2.50 5.00
146 Rick MacLeish 2.50 5.00
147 Johnny Bucyk 2.50 5.00
148 Bob Plager 1.25 3.00
149 Curt Bennett RC 1.00 2.50
150 Dave Keon 2.50 5.00
151 Keith Magnuson 1.25 3.00
152 Walt McKechnie 1.00 2.50
153 Roger Crozier 1.25 3.00
154 Ted Harris 1.00 2.50
155 Butch Goring 1.25 3.00
156 Rod Gilbert 2.50 5.00
157 Yvan Cournoyer 2.50 5.00
158 Doug Favell 1.25 3.00
159 Juha Widing 1.00 2.50
160 Ed Giacomin 2.50 5.00
161 Germaine Gagnon UER 1.00 2.50
162 Dennis Kearns 1.00 2.50
163 Bill Collins 1.00 2.50
164 Peter Mahovlich 1.25 3.00
165 Brad Park 3.00 6.00
166 Dave Schultz RC 7.50 15.00
167 Dallas Smith 1.00 2.50
168 Gary Sabourin 1.00 2.50
169 Jacques Richard 1.00 2.50
170 Brian Glennie 1.00 2.50
171 Dennis Hull 1.25 3.00
172 Joey Johnston 1.00 2.50
173 Richard Martin 2.50 5.00
174 Barry Gibbs 1.00 2.50
175 Bob Berry 1.00 2.50
176 Greg Polis 1.00 2.50
177 Dale Rolfe 1.00 2.50
178 Gerry Desjardins 1.25 3.00
179 Bobby Lalonde 1.00 2.50
180 Mickey Redmond 1.25 3.00
181 Jim Roberts 1.00 2.50
182 Gary Dornhoefer 1.25 3.00
183 Derek Sanderson 2.50 5.00
184 Brent Hughes 1.00 2.50
185 Larry Romanchych RC 1.00 2.50
186 Pierre Jarry 1.00 2.50
187 Doug Jarrett 1.00 2.50
188 Bob Stewart RC 1.00 2.50
189 Tim Horton 3.00 6.00
190 Fred Harvey 1.00 2.50
191 Series A .75 1.50
Canadiens 4
Sabres 2
192 Series B .75 1.50
Flyers 4
North Stars 2
193 Series C .75 1.50
Blackhawks 4
Blues 1
194 Series D .75 1.50
Rangers 4
Bruins
195 Series E .75 1.50
Canadiens 4
Flyers 1
196 Series F .75 1.50
Blackhawks 4
Rangers 1
197 Series G .75 1.50
Canadiens 4
Blackhawks 2
198 Stanley Cup Champs 2.50 5.00
199 Gary Edwards 1.25 3.00
200 Ron Schock 1.00 2.50
201 Bruce MacGregor 1.00 2.50
202 Bob Nystrom RC 3.00 5.00
203 Jerry Korab 1.00 2.50
204 Thommie Bergman RC 1.00 2.50
205 Bill Lesuk 1.00 2.50
206 Ed Van Impe 1.00 2.50
207 Doug Roberts 1.00 2.50
208 Chris Evans 1.00 2.50
209 Lynn Powis RC 1.00 2.50
210 Denis Dupere 1.00 2.50
211 Dale Tallon 1.00 2.50
212 Stan Gilbertson 1.00 2.50
213 Craig Ramsay 1.25 3.00
214 Danny Grant 1.25 3.00
215 Doug Volmar RC 1.00 2.50
216 Darryl Edestrand 1.00 2.50
217 Pete Stemkowski 1.00 2.50
218 Lorne Henning RC 1.00 2.50
219 Bryan McSheffrey RC 1.00 2.50
220 Guy Charron 1.25 3.00
221 Wayne Thomas RC 2.50 5.00
222 Simon Nolet 1.00 2.50
223 Fred O'Donnell RC 1.00 2.50
224 Lou Angotti 1.00 2.50
225 Arnie Brown 1.00 2.50
226 Garry Monahan 1.00 2.50
227 Chico Maki 1.00 2.50
228 Gary Croteau 1.00 2.50
229 Paul Terbenche 1.00 2.50
230 Gump Worsley 2.50 5.00
231 Jim Peters 1.00 2.50
232 Jack Lynch 1.00 2.50
233 Bobby Rousseau 1.00 2.50
234 Dave Hudson 1.00 2.50
235 Gregg Boddy RC 1.00 2.50
236 Ron Stackhouse 1.00 2.50
237 Larry Robinson RC 40.00 80.00
238 Bobby Taylor RC 2.50 5.00
239 Nick Beverley 1.00 2.50
240 Don Awrey 1.00 2.50
241 Doug Mohns 1.00 2.50
242 Eddie Shack 2.50 5.00
243 Phil Russell RC 1.25 3.00
244 Pete Laframboise 1.00 2.50
245 Steve Atkinson 1.00 2.50
246 Lou Nanne 1.25 3.00
247 Yvon Labre RC 1.00 2.50
248 Ted Irvine 1.00 2.50
249 Tom Miller 1.00 2.50
250 Gerry O'Flaherty 1.00 2.50
251 Larry Johnston RC 1.00 2.50
252 Michel Plasse RC 2.50 5.00
253 Bob Kelly 1.00 2.50
254 Terry O'Reilly RC 10.00 25.00
255 Pierre Plante RC 1.00 2.50
256 Noel Price 1.00 2.50
257 Dunc Wilson 1.25 3.00
258 J.P. Bordeleau RC 1.00 2.50
259 Terry Murray RC 1.25 2.50
260 Larry Carriere 1.00 2.50
261 Pierre Bouchard 1.25 3.00
262 Frank St.Marseille 1.00 2.50
263 Checklist 3 20.00 40.00
264 Fred Barrett 1.00 2.50

1973-74 O-Pee-Chee Rings

The 1973-74 O-Pee-Chee Rings set contained 17 standard-size cards, featuring the NHL league and team logos. The fronts have a push-out cardboard ring and instructions in English and French. The rings are yellow-colored and feature a NHL team logo in the team's colors. The cards are numbered on the front and the backs are blank.

COMPLETE SET (17) 75.00 175.00
1 Vancouver Canucks 3.00 8.00
2 Montreal Canadiens 5.00 12.00
3 Toronto Maple Leafs 3.00 8.00
4 NHL Logo 3.00 8.00
5 Minnesota North Stars 3.00 8.00
6 New York Rangers 3.00 8.00
7 California Seals 8.00 20.00
8 Pittsburgh Penguins 5.00 12.00
9 Philadelphia Flyers 3.00 8.00
10 Chicago Blackhawks 3.00 8.00
11 Boston Bruins 3.00 8.00
12 Los Angeles Kings 3.00 8.00
13 Detroit Red Wings 3.00 8.00
14 St. Louis Blues 3.00 8.00
15 Buffalo Sabres 3.00 8.00
16 Atlanta Flames 8.00 20.00
17 New York Islanders 3.00 8.00

1973-74 O-Pee-Chee Team Logos

The 1973-74 O-Pee-Chee Team Logos set contains 17 unnumbered, standard-size color stickers, featuring the NHL league and team logos. The cards were die-cut and adhesive backed. After the NHL logo, they were ordered below alphabetically by team city/location. This set was distinguished from the similar set of the previous year by the presence of written instructions on the fronts.

COMPLETE SET (17) 25.00 60.00
1 NHL Logo 2.00 5.00
2 Atlanta Flames 6.00 15.00
3 Boston Bruins 3.00 6.00
4 Buffalo Sabres 2.00 5.00
5 California Seals 5.00 10.00
6 Chicago Blackhawks 2.00 5.00
7 Detroit Red Wings 3.00 6.00
8 Los Angeles Kings 2.00 5.00
9 Minnesota North Stars 3.00 6.00
10 Montreal Canadiens 3.00 6.00
11 New York Islanders 5.00 10.00
12 New York Rangers 2.00 5.00
13 Philadelphia Flyers 2.00 5.00
14 Pittsburgh Penguins 3.00 6.00
15 St. Louis Blues 2.00 5.00
16 Toronto Maple Leafs 3.00 6.00
17 Vancouver Canucks 2.00 5.00

1973-74 O-Pee-Chee WHA Posters

Players featured in this set are from the World Hockey Association (WHA). The set consisted of 20 large posters each measuring approximately 7 1/2" by 13 3/4" and was a separate issue in wax packs. The packs contained two posters and gum; gum stains are frequently seen. Posters were numbered on the front and were issued folded. As a result, folded copies are accepted as being in near mint condition. The posters are blank backed.

COMPLETE SET (20) 50.00 100.00
1 Al Smith 2.50 5.00
2 J.C. Tremblay 2.50 5.00
3 Guy Dufour 1.50 3.00
4 Pat Stapleton 2.50 5.00
5 Rosaire Paiement 1.50 3.00
6 Gerry Cheevers 5.00 10.00
7 Gerry Pinder 2.00 4.00
8 Wayne Carleton 1.50 3.00
9 Bob Leduc 1.50 3.00
10 Andre Lacroix 2.50 5.00
11 Jim Harrison 1.50 3.00
12 Ron Climie 1.50 3.00
13 Gordie Howe 12.50 25.00
14 The Howe Family 12.50 25.00
Gordie/Mark/Marty
15 Mike Walton 2.00 4.00
16 Bobby Hull 10.00 20.00
17 Chris Bordeleau 1.50 3.00
18 Claude St.Sauveur 1.50 3.00
19 Bryan Campbell 1.50 3.00
20 Marc Tardif 2.50 5.00

1974-75 O-Pee-Chee NHL

The 1974-75 O-Pee-Chee NHL set contained 396 standard-size cards. The first 264 cards are identical to those of Topps in terms of numbering and photos. Wax packs consisted of eight cards plus a piece of bubble gum. Bilingual backs featured the player's 1973-74 and career statistics, a short biography and a cartoon-illustrated fact about the player. The first six cards in the set (1-6) featured league leaders of the previous season. The set included players from the expansion Washington Capitals and Kansas City Scouts (presently New Jersey Devils). The set marked the return of coach cards, including Rookie Cards of Don Cherry and Scotty Bowman.

COMPLETE SET (396) 300.00 500.00
1 Goal Leaders 2.50 5.00
Phil Esposito
Bill Goldsworthy
2 Assists Leaders 9.00 15.00
Bobby Orr
Dennis Hextall
3 Scoring Leaders 3.00 6.00
Phil Esposito
Bobby Clarke
4 Goals Against Leaders .50 1.25
Doug Favell
Bernie Parent
5 Penalty Min. Leaders .50 1.25
Bryan Watson
Dave Schultz
6 Power Play Goal .50 1.25
Leaders
Mickey Redmond
Rick MacLeish
7 Gary Bromley RC 1.00 2.50
8 Bill Barber 3.00 6.00
9 Emile Francis CO .75 2.00
10 Gilles Gilbert 1.00 2.50
11 John Davidson RC 10.00 15.00
12 Ron Ellis 1.00 2.50
13 Syl Apps .75 2.00
14 Flames Leaders .50 1.25
Jacques Richard
Tom Lysiak
Tom Lysiak
Keith McCreary
15 Dan Bouchard 1.00 2.50
16 Ivan Boldirev 1.00 2.50
17 Gary Coalter RC .75 2.00
18 Bob Berry .75 2.00
19 Red Berenson 1.00 2.50
20 Stan Mikita 3.00 6.00
21 Fred Shero CO RC 2.50 5.00
22 Gary Smith 1.00 2.50
23 Bill Mikkelson .75 2.00
24 Jacques Lemaire UER 1.50 3.00
25 Gilbert Perreault 4.00 8.00
26 Cesare Maniago 1.00 2.50
27 Bobby Schmautz .75 2.00
28 Bruins Leaders 9.00 15.00
Phil Esposito
Bobby Orr
Phil Esposito
Johnny Bucyk
29 Steve Vickers 1.00 2.50
30 Lowell MacDonald UER .75 2.00
31 Fred Stanfield .75 2.00
32 Ed Westfall 1.00 2.50
33 Curt Bennett .75 2.00
34 Bep Guidolin CO .75 2.00
35 Cliff Koroll .75 2.00
36 Gary Croteau .75 2.00
37 Mike Corrigan .75 2.00
38 Henry Boucha .75 2.00
39 Ron Low 1.00 2.50
40 Darryl Sittler 6.00 10.00
41 Tracy Pratt .75 2.00
42 Sabres Leaders .50 1.25
Richard Martin
Rene Robert
Richard Martin
Richard Martin
43 Larry Carriere .75 2.00
44 Gary Dornhoefer .75 2.00
45 Denis Herron RC 2.50 5.00
46 Doug Favell 1.00 2.50
47 Dave Gardner RC .75 2.00
48 Morris Mott RC .75 2.00
49 Marc Boileau CO .75 2.00
50 Brad Park 2.50 5.00
51 Bob Leiter .75 2.00
52 Tom Reid .75 2.00
53 Serge Savard 1.50 3.00
54 Checklist 1-132 UER 18.00 30.00
55 Terry Harper .75 2.00
56 Golden Seals .50 1.25
Leaders
Joey Johnston
Joey Johnston
Joey Johnston
Walt McKechnie
57 Guy Charron 1.00 2.50
58 Pit Martin .75 2.00
59 Chris Evans .75 2.00
60 Bernie Parent 3.00 6.00
61 Jim Lorentz .75 2.00
62 Dave Kryskow RC .75 2.00
63 Lou Angotti CO .75 2.00
64 Bill Flett .75 2.00
65 Vic Hadfield 1.00 2.50
66 Wayne Merrick RC .75 2.00
67 Andre Dupont .75 2.00
68 Tom Lysiak RC 1.50 3.00
69 Blackhawks Leaders 1.00 2.50
Jim Pappin
Stan Mikita
J.P. Bordeleau
70 Guy Lapointe 1.00 2.50
71 Gerry O'Flaherty .75 2.00
72 Marcel Dionne 6.00 10.00
73 Butch Deadmarsh RC .75 2.00
74 Butch Goring 1.00 2.50
75 Keith Magnuson .75 2.00
76 Red Kelly CO .75 2.00
77 Pete Stemkowski .75 2.00
78 Jim Roberts .75 2.00
79 Don Luce .75 2.00
80 Don Awrey .75 2.00
81 Rick Kehoe 1.00 2.50
82 Billy Smith 6.00 10.00
83 Jean-Paul Parise .75 2.00
84 Red Wings Leaders 1.00 2.50
Mickey Redmond
Marcel Dionne
Marcel Dionne
Bill Hogaboam
85 Ed Van Impe .75 2.00
86 Randy Manery .75 2.00
87 Barclay Plager 1.00 2.50
88 Inge Hammarstrom RC .75 2.00
89 Ab DeMarco .75 2.00
90 Bill White .75 2.00
91 Al Arbour CO 1.50 3.00
92 Bob Stewart .75 2.00
93 Jack Egers .75 2.00
94 Don Lever 1.00 2.50
95 Reggie Leach 1.00 2.50
96 Dennis O'Brien .75 2.00
97 Peter Mahovlich 1.00 2.50
98 Kings Leaders .50 1.25
Butch Goring
Frank St.Marseille
Butch Goring
Don Kozak
99 Gerry Meehan .75 2.00
100 Bobby Orr 25.00 50.00
101 Jean Potvin RC .75 2.00
102 Rod Seiling .75 2.00
103 Keith McCreary .75 2.00
104 Phil Maloney CO RC .75 2.00
105 Denis Dupere .75 2.00
106 Steve Durbano .75 2.00
107 Bob Plager UER 1.00 2.50
(Photo actually
Barclay Plager)
108 Chris Oddleifson RC .75 2.00
109 Jim Neilson .75 2.00
110 Jean Pronovost 1.00 2.50
111 Don Kozak RC .75 2.00
112 North Stars Leaders .50 1.25
Bill Goldsworthy
Dennis Hextall
Dennis Hextall
Danny Grant
113 Jim Pappin .75 2.00
114 Richard Lemieux .75 2.00
115 Dennis Hextall .75 2.00
116 Bill Hogaboam RC .75 2.00
117 Canucks Leaders .50 1.25
Dennis Ververgaert
Bobby Schmautz
Andre Boudrias
Andre Boudrias
Don Tannahill
118 Jimmy Anderson CO .75 2.00
119 Walt Tkaczuk 1.00 2.50
120 Mickey Redmond 1.00 2.50
121 Jim Schoenfeld 1.00 2.50
122 Jocelyn Guevremont .75 2.00
123 Bob Nystrom 1.00 2.50
124 Canadiens Leaders 1.50 3.00
Yvan Cournoyer
Frank Mahovlich
Frank Mahovlich
Claude Larose
125 Lew Morrison .75 2.00
126 Terry Murray 1.00 2.50
127 Richard Martin AS .50 1.25
128 Ken Hodge AS .50 1.25
129 Phil Esposito AS 2.00 4.00
130 Bobby Orr AS 12.00 20.00
131 Brad Park AS .50 1.25
132 Gilles Gilbert AS .50 1.25
133 Lowell MacDonald AS .50 1.25
134 Bill Goldsworthy AS .50 1.25
135 Bobby Clarke AS 3.00 6.00
136 Bill White AS .50 1.25
137 Dave Burrows AS .50 1.25
138 Bernie Parent AS 1.50 3.00
139 Jacques Richard .75 2.00
140 Yvan Cournoyer 1.50 3.00
141 Rangers Leaders 1.50 3.00
Rod Gilbert
Brad Park
Brad Park
Rod Gilbert
142 Rene Robert 1.00 2.50
143 J. Bob Kelly RC .75 2.00
144 Ross Lonsberry .75 2.00
145 Jean Ratelle 1.50 3.00
146 Dallas Smith .75 2.00
147 Bernie Geoffrion CO 2.00 4.00
148 Ted McAneeley .75 2.00
149 Pierre Plante .75 2.00
150 Dennis Hull 1.00 2.50
151 Dave Keon 1.50 3.00
152 Dave Dunn RC .75 2.00
153 Michel Belhumeur 1.00 2.50
154 Flyers Leaders 2.00 4.00
Bobby Clarke
Bobby Clarke
Bobby Clarke
Dave Schultz
155 Ken Dryden 15.00 25.00
156 John Wright RC .75 2.00
157 Larry Romanchych .75 2.00
158 Ralph Stewart RC .75 2.00
159 Mike Robitaille .75 2.00
160 Ed Giacomin 2.00 4.00

161 Don Cherry CO RC 40.00 60.00
162 Checklist 133-264 18.00 30.00
163 Rick MacLeish 1.00 2.50
164 Greg Polis .75 2.00
165 Carol Vadnais .75 2.00
166 Pete Laframboise .75 2.00
167 Ron Schock .75 2.00
168 Lanny McDonald RC 15.00 25.00
169 Scouts Emblem 1.00 2.50
(Draft Selections
on back)
170 Tony Esposito 4.00 8.00
171 Pierre Jarry .75 2.00
172 Dan Maloney 1.00 2.50
173 Peter McDuffe 1.00 2.50
174 Danny Grant 1.00 2.50
175 John Stewart RC .75 2.00
176 Floyd Smith CO .75 2.00
177 Bert Marshall .75 2.00
178 Chuck Lefley UER .75 2.00
(Photo actually
Pierre Bouchard)
179 Gilles Villemure 1.00 2.50
180 Borje Salming RC 15.00 25.00
181 Doug Mohns .75 2.00
182 Barry Wilkins .75 2.00
183 Penguins Leaders .50 1.25
Lowell MacDonald
Syl Apps
Syl Apps
Lowell MacDonald
184 Gregg Sheppard .75 2.00
185 Joey Johnston .75 2.00
186 Dick Redmond .75 2.00
187 Simon Nolet .75 2.00
188 Ron Stackhouse .75 2.00
189 Marshall Johnston .75 2.00
190 Richard Martin 1.00 2.50
191 Andre Boudrias .75 2.00
192 Steve Atkinson .75 2.00
193 Nick Libett .75 2.00
194 Bob Murdoch RC .75 2.00
195 Denis Potvin RC 25.00 40.00
196 Dave Schultz 2.00 4.00
197 Blues Leaders .50 1.25
Garry Unger
Garry Unger
Garry Unger
Pierre Plante
198 Jim McKenny .75 2.00
199 Gerry Hart .75 2.00
200 Phil Esposito 3.00 6.00
201 Rod Gilbert 1.50 3.00
202 Jacques Laperriere 1.00 2.50
203 Barry Gibbs .75 2.00
204 Billy Reay CO 1.00 2.50
205 Gilles Meloche 1.00 2.50
206 Wayne Cashman 1.00 2.50
207 Dennis Ververgaert RC .75 2.00
208 Phil Roberto .75 2.00
209 Quarter Finals .50 1.25
Flyers sweep
Flames
210 Quarter Finals .50 1.25
Rangers over
Canadiens
211 Quarter Finals .50 1.25
Bruins sweep
Maple Leafs
212 Quarter Finals .50 1.25
Blackhawks over
L.A. Kings
213 Semi-Finals .50 1.25
Flyers over Rangers
214 Semi-Finals .50 1.25
Bruins over
Blackhawks
215 '73-'74 Finals .50 1.25
Flyers over Bruins
216 Cup Championship 1.00 2.50
217 Joe Watson .75 2.00
218 Wayne Stephenson 1.00 2.50
219 Maple Leaf Leaders 1.00 2.50
Darryl Sittler
Norm Ullman
Darryl Sittler
Paul Henderson
Denis Dupere
220 Bill Goldsworthy 1.00 2.50
221 Don Marcotte .75 2.00
222 Alex Delvecchio CO .75 2.00
223 Stan Gilbertson .75 2.00
224 Mike Murphy .75 2.00
225 Jim Rutherford 1.00 2.50
226 Phil Russell .75 2.00
227 Lynn Powis .75 2.00
228 Billy Harris .75 2.00
229 Bob Pulford CO 1.00 2.50
230 Ken Hodge 1.00 2.50
231 Bill Fairbairn .75 2.00
232 Guy Lafleur 7.50 15.00
233 Islanders Leaders UER 2.00 4.00
Billy Harris
Ralph Stewart
Denis Potvin
Denis Potvin
Ralph Stewart
(Steward on front)
234 Fred Barrett .75 2.00
235 Rogatien Vachon 2.00 4.00
236 Norm Ullman 1.50 3.00
237 Garry Unger 1.00 2.50
238 Jack Gordon CO RC .75 2.00
239 Johnny Bucyk 1.50 3.00
240 Bob Dailey RC .75 2.00
241 Dave Burrows .75 2.00
242 Len Frig RC .75 2.00
243 Masterson Trophy 1.00 2.50
Henri Richard
244 Hart Trophy 2.00 4.00
Phil Esposito
245 Byng Trophy .50 1.25
Johnny Bucyk
246 Ross Trophy 2.00 4.00
Phil Esposito
247 Prince of Wales .50 1.25
Trophy
248 Norris Trophy 12.00 20.00
Bobby Orr
249 Vezina Trophy .50 1.25
Bernie Parent
250 Stanley Cup 1.00 2.50
251 Smythe Trophy .50 1.25
Bernie Parent
252 Calder Trophy 6.00 10.00
Denis Potvin
253 Campbell Trophy .50 1.25
254 Pierre Bouchard .50 1.25
255 Jude Drouin .75 2.00
256 Capitals Emblem 1.00 2.50
(Draft Selections
on back)
257 Michel Plasse 1.00 2.50
258 Juha Widing .75 2.00
259 Bryan Watson .75 2.00
260 Bobby Clarke UER 7.00 12.00
Back mentions Art Ross
Trophy. Should be Hart
Trophy
261 Scotty Bowman CO RC 40.00 60.00
262 Craig Patrick 1.00 2.50
263 Craig Cameron .75 2.00
264 Ted Irvine .75 2.00
265 Ed Johnston 1.00 2.50
266 Dave Forbes RC .75 2.00
267 Detroit Red Wings 2.00 4.00
Team Card
268 Rick Dudley RC 1.00 2.50
269 Darcy Rota RC 1.00 2.50
270 Phil Myre 1.00 2.50
271 Larry Brown RC .75 2.00
272 Bob Neely RC .75 2.00
273 Jerry Byers RC .75 2.00
274 Pittsburgh Penguins 2.00 4.00
Team Card
275 Glenn Goldup RC .75 2.00
276 Ron Harris .75 2.00
277 Joe Lundrigan RC .75 2.00
278 Mike Christie RC .75 2.00
279 Doug Rombough RC .75 2.00
280 Larry Robinson RC 12.00 20.00
281 St. Louis Blues 2.00 4.00
Team Card
282 John Marks RC .75 2.00
283 Don Saleski 1.00 2.50
284 Rick Wilson RC .75 2.00
285 Andre Savard RC .75 2.00
286 Pat Quinn 1.00 2.50
287 Los Angeles Kings 2.00 4.00
Team Card
288 Norm Gratton .75 2.00
289 Ian Turnbull RC 1.00 2.50
290 Derek Sanderson 2.00 4.00
291 Murray Oliver .75 2.00
292 Wilf Paiement RC 1.50 3.00
293 Nelson Debenedet RC .75 2.00
294 Greg Joly RC .75 2.00
295 Terry O'Reilly 2.00 4.00
296 Rey Comeau .75 2.00
297 Michel Larocque RC 2.50 5.00
298 Floyd Thomson RC .75 2.00
299 Jean-Guy Lagace RC .75 2.00
300 Philadelphia Flyers 2.00 4.00
Team Card
301 Al MacAdam RC 1.50 3.00
302 George Ferguson RC .75 2.00
303 Jimmy Watson RC 1.50 3.00
304 Rick Middleton RC 12.00 20.00
305 Craig Ramsay UER .75 2.00
(Name on front is Graig)
306 Hilliard Graves .75 2.00
307 New York Islanders 2.00 4.00
Team Card
308 Blake Dunlop RC .75 2.00
309 J.P. Bordeleau .75 2.00
310 Brian Glennie .75 2.00
311 Checklist 265-396 UER 18.00 30.00
312 Doug Roberts .75 2.00
313 Darryl Edestrand .75 2.00
314 Ron Anderson .75 2.00
315 Chicago Blackhawks 2.00 4.00
Team Card
316 Steve Shutt RC 15.00 25.00
317 Doug Horbul RC .75 2.00
318 Billy Lochead RC .75 2.00
319 Fred Harvey .75 2.00
320 Gene Carr RC .75 2.00
321 Henri Richard 1.50 3.00
322 Vancouver Canucks 2.00 4.00
Team Card
323 Tim Ecclestone .75 2.00
324 Dave Lewis RC .75 2.00
325 Lou Nanne 1.00 2.50
326 Bobby Rousseau .75 2.00
327 Dunc Wilson 1.00 2.50
328 Brian Spencer .75 2.00
329 Rick Hampton RC .75 2.00
330 Montreal Canadiens 2.00 4.00
Team Card UER
331 Jack Lynch .75 2.00
332 Garnet Bailey .75 2.00
333 Al Sims RC .75 2.00
334 Orest Kindrachuk RC 1.00 2.50
335 Dave Hudson .75 2.00
336 Bob Murray RC 1.00 2.50
337 Buffalo Sabres 2.00 4.00
Team Card
338 Sheldon Kannegiesser .75 2.00
339 Bill MacMillan .75 2.00
340 Paulin Bordeleau RC .75 2.00
341 Dale Rolfe .75 2.00
342 Yvon Lambert RC 1.00 2.50
343 Bob Paradise RC .75 2.00
344 Germaine Gagnon UER .75 2.00
345 Yvon Labre .75 2.00
346 Chris Ahrens RC .75 2.00
347 Doug Grant RC .75 2.00
348 Blaine Stoughton RC 2.00 4.00
349 Gregg Boddy .75 2.00
350 Boston Bruins 2.00 4.00
Team Card
351 Doug Jarrett .75 2.00
352 Terry Crisp 1.00 2.50
353 Glenn Resch RC 12.00 20.00
354 Jerry Korab .75 2.00
355 Stan Weir RC .75 2.00
356 Noel Price .75 2.00
357 Bill Clement RC 9.00 15.00
358 Neil Komadoski .75 2.00
359 Murray Wilson RC .75 2.00
360 Dale Tallon UER .75 2.00
(Misspelled Talon
on card front)
361 Gary Doak .75 2.00
362 Randy Rota RC .75 2.00
363 Minnesota North Stars 2.00 4.00
Team Card
364 Bill Collins .75 2.00
365 Thommie Bergman UER .75 2.00
(Misspelled Tommie
on card front)
366 Dennis Kearns .75 2.00
367 Lorne Henning .75 2.00
368 Gary Sabourin .75 2.00
369 Mike Bloom RC .75 2.00
370 New York Rangers 2.00 4.00
Team Card
371 Gary Simmons RC 2.50 5.00
372 Dwight Bialowas RC .75 2.00
373 Gilles Marotte .75 2.00
374 Frank St.Marseille .75 2.00
375 Garry Howatt RC .75 2.00
376 Ross Brooks RC 1.00 2.50
377 Atlanta Flames 2.00 4.00
Team Card
378 Bob Nevin .75 2.00
379 Lyle Moffat RC .75 2.00
380 Bob Kelly .75 2.00
381 John Gould RC .75 2.00
382 Dave Fortier RC .75 2.00
383 Jean Hamel RC .75 2.00
384 Bert Wilson RC .75 2.00
385 Chuck Arnason RC .75 2.00
386 Bruce Cowick RC .75 2.00
387 Ernie Hicke .75 2.00
388 Bob Gainey RC 18.00 30.00
389 Vic Venasky RC .75 2.00
390 Toronto Maple Leafs 2.00 4.00
Team Card
391 Eric Vail RC 1.00 2.50
392 Bobby Lalonde .75 2.00
393 Jerry Butler RC .75 2.00
394 Tom Williams .75 2.00
395 Chico Maki .75 2.00
396 Tom Bladon RC 2.00 4.00

1974-75 O-Pee-Chee WHA

The 1974-75 O-Pee-Chee WHA set consisted of 66 color standard-size cards. The cards were originally sold in eight-card ten-cent wax packs. Bilingual backs featured a short biography, the player's 1973-74 and career WHA statistics as well as a cartoon-illustrated hockey fact or interpretation of a referee's signal. Rookie Cards in this set included Anders Hedberg and Ulf Nilsson, although some collectors and dealers considered the Howe Family card to be the Rookie Card for Mark and Marty Howe.

COMPLETE SET (66) 75.00 200.00
1 The Howes 50.00 80.00
Gordie Howe
Mark Howe
Marty Howe
2 Bruce MacGregor 1.50 3.00
3 Wayne Dillon RC 1.50 3.00
4 Ulf Nilsson RC 7.00 12.00
5 Serge Bernier 2.00 4.00
6 Bryan Campbell 1.50 3.00
7 Rosaire Paiement 1.50 3.00
8 Tom Webster 2.00 4.00
9 Gerry Pinder 1.50 3.00
10 Mike Walton 1.50 3.00
11 Norm Beaudin 1.50 3.00
12 Bob Whitlock RC 1.50 3.00
13 Wayne Rivers 1.50 3.00
14 Gerry Odrowski 1.50 3.00
15 Ron Climie 1.50 3.00
16 Tom Simpson RC 1.50 3.00
17 Anders Hedberg RC 7.00 12.00
18 J.C. Tremblay 1.50 3.00
19 Mike Pelyk 1.50 3.00
20 Dave Dryden 2.00 4.00
21 Ron Ward 1.50 3.00
22 Larry Lund RC 1.50 3.00
23 Ron Buchanan RC 1.50 3.00
24 Pat Hickey RC 2.00 4.00
25 Danny Lawson RC 2.00 4.00
26 Bob Guindon RC 1.50 3.00
27 Gene Peacosh RC 1.50 3.00
28 Fran Huck 1.50 3.00
29 Al Hamilton 1.50 3.00
30 Gerry Cheevers 7.50 15.00
31 Heikki Riihiranta RC 2.00 4.00
32 Don Burgess RC 1.50 3.00
33 John French RC 1.50 3.00
34 Jim Wiste RC 1.50 3.00
35 Pat Stapleton 4.00 8.00
36 J.P. LeBlanc RC 1.50 3.00
37 Mike Antonovich RC 1.50 3.00
38 Joe Daley 2.00 4.00
39 Ross Perkins RC 1.50 3.00
40 Frank Mahovlich 7.00 12.00
41 Rejean Houle 1.50 3.00
42 Ron Chipperfield RC 3.00 5.00
43 Marc Tardif 1.50 3.00
44 Murray Keogan RC 1.50 3.00
45 Wayne Carleton 1.50 3.00
46 Andre Gaudette RC 1.50 3.00
47 Ralph Backstrom 2.00 4.00
48 Don McLeod RC 2.00 4.00
49 Vaclav Nedomansky RC 3.00 5.00
50 Bobby Hull 25.00 40.00
51 Rusty Patenaude RC 1.50 3.00
52 Michel Parizeau 1.50 3.00
53 Checklist 20.00 40.00
54 Wayne Connelly 2.00 4.00
55 Gary Veneruzzo 1.50 3.00
56 Dennis Sobchuk RC 2.00 4.00
57 Paul Henderson 2.00 4.00
58 Andy Brown RC 2.00 4.00
59 Paul Popiel 1.50 3.00
60 Andre Lacroix 2.00 4.00
61 Gary Jarrett 1.50 3.00
62 Claude St.Sauveur RC 1.50 3.00
63 Real Cloutier RC 3.00 5.00
64 Jacques Plante 25.00 40.00
65 Gilles Gratton RC 4.00 8.00
66 Lars-Erik Sjoberg RC 4.00 8.00

1975-76 O-Pee-Chee NHL

The 1975-76 O-Pee-Chee NHL set consisted of 396 color standard-size cards. The cards were originally sold in ten-cent wax packs. The first 330 cards had identical fronts (except perhaps for a short traded line) to the Topps set of this year. Number 395 was not issued; however, the set contained two of number 267, which are checklist cards. Team cards (81-98) had a team checklist on the back. Bilingual backs contained year-by-year and career statistics, a short biography and a cartoon-illustrated NHL fact or interpretation of a referee's signal.

COMPLETE SET (396) 200.00 400.00
1 Stanley Cup Finals 1.50 3.00
Philadelphia 4
Buffalo 2
2 Semi-Finals .40 1.00
Philadelphia 4
N.Y. Islanders 3
3 Semi-Finals .40 1.00
Buffalo 4
Montreal
4 Quarter Finals .40 1.00
N.Y. Islanders 4
Pittsburgh 2
5 Quarter Finals .40 1.00
Montreal 4
Vancouver 1
6 Quarter Finals .40 1.00
Buffalo 4
Chicago 1
7 Quarter Finals .40 1.00
Philadelphia 4
Toronto 0
8 Curt Bennett .40 1.00
9 Johnny Bucyk 1.00 2.50
10 Gilbert Perreault 3.00 6.00
11 Darryl Edestrand .40 1.00
12 Ivan Boldirev .40 1.00
13 Nick Libett .40 1.00
14 Jim McElmury RC .40 1.00
15 Frank St.Marseille .40 1.00
16 Blake Dunlop .40 1.00
17 Yvon Lambert .60 1.50
18 Gerry Hart .40 1.00
19 Steve Vickers .40 1.00
20 Rick MacLeish .60 1.50
21A Bob Paradise .40 1.00
21B Bob Paradise .60 1.50
Traded to Washington notation
22 Red Berenson .60 1.50
23 Lanny McDonald 4.00 7.00
24 Mike Robitaille .40 1.00
25 Ron Low .60 1.50
26A Bryan Hextall .35 .75
(No mention of trade)
26B Bryan Hextall .35 .75
(Trade noted)
27A Carol Vadnais .35 .75
(No mention of trade)
27B Carol Vadnais .35 .75
(Trade noted)
28 Jim Lorentz .40 1.00
29 Gary Simmons .60 1.50
30 Stan Mikita 2.50 5.00
31 Bryan Watson .40 1.00
32 Guy Charron .40 1.00
33 Bob Murdoch .40 1.00
34 Norm Gratton .40 1.00
35 Ken Dryden 12.00 20.00
36 Jean Potvin .40 1.00
37 Rick Middleton 2.50 5.00
38 Ed Van Impe .40 1.00
39 Rick Kehoe .60 1.50
40 Garry Unger .60 1.50
41 Ian Turnbull .60 1.50
42 Dennis Ververgaert .40 1.00
43 Mike Marson RC .60 1.50
44 Randy Manery .40 1.00
45 Gilles Gilbert .60 1.50
46 Rene Robert .60 1.50
47 Bob Stewart .40 1.00
48 Pit Martin .40 1.00
49 Danny Grant .60 1.50
50 Peter Mahovlich .60 1.50
51 Dennis Patterson RC .40 1.00
52 Mike Murphy .40 1.00
53 Dennis O'Brien .40 1.00
54 Garry Howatt .40 1.00
55 Ed Giacomin 1.25 2.50
56 Andre Dupont .40 1.00
57 Chuck Arnason .40 1.00
58 Bob Gassoff RC .40 1.00
59 Ron Ellis .60 1.50
60 Andre Boudrias .40 1.00
61 Yvon Labre .40 1.00
62 Hilliard Graves .40 1.00
63 Wayne Cashman .60 1.50
64 Danny Gare RC 1.50 3.00
65 Rick Hampton .40 1.00
66 Darcy Rota .40 1.00
67 Bill Hogaboam .40 1.00
68 Denis Herron .60 1.50
69 Sheldon Kannegiesser .40 1.00
70 Yvan Cournoyer 1.00 2.50
71 Ernie Hicke .40 1.00
72 Bert Marshall .40 1.00
73 Derek Sanderson 2.00 4.00
74 Tom Bladon .40 1.00
75 Ron Schock .40 1.00
76 Larry Sacharuk RC .40 1.00
77 George Ferguson .40 1.00
78 Ab DeMarco .40 1.00
79 Tom Williams .40 1.00
80 Phil Roberto .40 1.00
81 Bruins Team 2.00 4.00
82 Seals Team 2.00 4.00
83 Sabres Team 2.00 4.00
84 Blackhawks Team 2.00 4.00
85 Flames Team 2.00 4.00
86 Kings Team 2.00 4.00
87 Red Wings Team 2.00 4.00
88 Scouts Team 2.00 4.00
89 North Stars Team 2.00 4.00
90 Canadiens Team 2.00 4.00
91 Maple Leafs Team 2.00 4.00
92 Islanders Team 2.00 4.00
93 Penguins Team 2.00 4.00
94 Rangers Team 2.00 4.00
95 Flyers Team 2.00 4.00
96 Blues Team 2.00 4.00
97 Canucks Team 2.00 4.00
98 Capitals Team 2.00 4.00
99 Checklist 1-110 8.00 15.00
100 Bobby Orr 20.00 30.00
101 Germain Gagnon UER .40 1.00
(First name spelled Germaine)
102 Phil Russell .40 1.00
103 Billy Lochead .40 1.00
104 Robin Burns RC .40 1.00
105 Gary Edwards .60 1.50
106 Dwight Bialowas .40 1.00
107 Doug Risebrough UER RC 1.50 3.00
108 Dave Lewis .40 1.00
109 Bill Fairbairn .40 1.00
110 Ross Lonsberry .40 1.00
111 Ron Stackhouse .40 1.00
112 Claude Larose .40 1.00
113 Don Luce .40 1.00
114 Errol Thompson RC .40 1.00
115 Gary Smith .60 1.50
116 Jack Lynch .40 1.00
117 Jacques Richard .40 1.00
118 Dallas Smith .40 1.00
119 Dave Gardner .40 1.00
120 Mickey Redmond .60 1.50
121 John Marks .40 1.00
122 Dave Hudson .40 1.00
123 Bob Nevin .40 1.00
124 Fred Barrett .40 1.00
125 Gerry Desjardins .60 1.50
126 Guy Lafleur UER 9.00 15.00
127 Jean-Paul Parise .40 1.00
128 Walt Tkaczuk .60 1.50
129 Gary Dornhoefer .60 1.50
130 Syl Apps .40 1.00
131 Bob Plager .60 1.50
132 Stan Weir .40 1.00
133 Tracy Pratt .40 1.00
134 Jack Egers .40 1.00
135 Eric Vail .40 1.00
136 Al Sims .40 1.00
137 Larry Patey RC .40 1.00
138 Jim Schoenfeld .60 1.50
139 Cliff Koroll .40 1.00
140 Marcel Dionne 4.00 7.00
141 Jean-Guy Lagace .40 1.00
142 Juha Widing .40 1.00
143 Lou Nanne .60 1.50
144 Serge Savard 1.00 2.50
145 Glenn Resch 2.50 5.00
146 Ron Greschner RC 1.50 3.00
147 Dave Schultz 1.00 2.50
148 Barry Wilkins .40 1.00
149 Floyd Thomson .40 1.00
150 Darryl Sittler 4.00 8.00
151 Paulin Bordeleau .40 1.00
152 Ron Lalonde RC .40 1.00
153 Larry Romanchych .40 1.00
154 Larry Carriere .40 1.00
155 Andre Savard .40 1.00
156 Dave Hrechkosy RC .40 1.00
157 Bill White .40 1.00
158 Dave Kryskow .40 1.00
159 Denis Dupere .40 1.00
160 Rogatien Vachon 1.50 3.00
161 Doug Rombough .40 1.00
162 Murray Wilson .40 1.00
163 Bob Bourne RC 1.50 3.00
164 Gilles Marotte .40 1.00
165 Vic Hadfield .60 1.50
166 Reggie Leach .60 1.50
167 Jerry Butler .40 1.00
168 Inge Hammarstrom .40 1.00
169 Chris Oddleifson .40 1.00
170 Greg Joly RC .40 1.00
171 Checklist 111-220 8.00 15.00
172 Pat Quinn .60 1.50
173 Dave Forbes .40 1.00
174 Len Frig .40 1.00
175 Richard Martin .60 1.50
176 Keith Magnuson .40 1.00
177 Dan Maloney .40 1.00
178 Craig Patrick .60 1.50
179 Tom Williams .40 1.00
180 Bill Goldsworthy .60 1.50
181 Steve Shutt 2.50 5.00
182 Ralph Stewart .40 1.00
183 John Davidson 2.50 5.00
184 Bob Kelly .40 1.00
185 Ed Johnston .60 1.50
186 Dave Burrows .40 1.00
187 Dave Dunn .40 1.00
188 Dennis Kearns .40 1.00
189 Bill Clement 2.50 5.00
190 Gilles Meloche .60 1.50
191 Bob Leiter .40 1.00
192 Jerry Korab .40 1.00
193 Joey Johnston .40 1.00
194 Walt McKechnie .40 1.00
195 Wilf Paiement .60 1.50
196 Bob Berry .40 1.00
197 Dean Talafous RC .40 1.00
198 Guy Lapointe .60 1.50
199 Clark Gillies RC 4.00 8.00
200A Phil Esposito 4.00 8.00
(No mention of trade)
200B Phil Esposito 2.50 5.00
(Trade noted)
201 Greg Polis .40 1.00
202 Jimmy Watson .60 1.50
203 Gord McRae RC .60 1.50
204 Lowell MacDonald .40 1.00
205 Barclay Plager .60 1.50
206 Don Lever .40 1.00
207 Bill Mikkelson .40 1.00
208 Goals Leaders 2.50 5.00
Phil Esposito
Guy Lafleur
Richard Martin
209 Assists Leaders 4.00 8.00
Bobby Clarke
Bobby Orr
Pete Mahovlich
210 Scoring Leaders 4.00 8.00
Bobby Orr
Phil Esposito
Marcel Dionne
211 Penalty Min. Leaders 2.00 4.00
Dave Schultz
Andre Dupont
Phil Russell
212 Power Play 1.50 3.00
Goal Leaders
Phil Esposito
Richard Martin
Danny Grant
213 Goals Against 4.00 8.00
Average Leaders
Bernie Parent
Rogatien Vachon
Ken Dryden
214 Barry Gibbs .40 1.00
215 Ken Hodge .60 1.50
216 Jocelyn Guevremont .40 1.00
217 Warren Williams RC .40 1.00
218 Dick Redmond .40 1.00
219 Jim Rutherford .60 1.50
220 Simon Nolet .40 1.00
221 Butch Goring .60 1.50
222 Glen Sather .60 1.50
223 Mario Tremblay UER RC 2.50 5.00
224 Jude Drouin .40 1.00
225 Rod Gilbert 1.00 2.50
226 Bill Barber 2.00 4.00
227 Gary Inness RC .60 1.50
228 Wayne Merrick .40 1.00
229 Rod Seiling .40 1.00
230 Tom Lysiak .60 1.50
231 Bob Dailey .40 1.00
232 Michel Belhumeur .60 1.50
233 Bill Hajt RC .40 1.00
234 Jim Pappin .40 1.00
235 Gregg Sheppard .40 1.00
236A Gary Bergman .35 .75
(No mention of trade)
236B Gary Bergman .35 .75
(Trade noted)
237 Randy Rota .40 1.00
238 Neil Komadoski .40 1.00
239 Craig Cameron .40 1.00
240 Tony Esposito 3.00 6.00
241 Larry Robinson 7.00 12.00
242 Billy Harris .40 1.00
243A Jean Ratelle 1.50 3.00
(No mention of trade)
243B Jean Ratelle 1.00 2.50
(Trade noted)
244 Ted Irvine UER .40 1.00
(Photo actually
Ted Harris)
245 Bob Neely .40 1.00
246 Bobby Lalonde .40 1.00
247 Ron Jones RC .40 1.00
248 Rey Comeau .40 1.00
249 Michel Plasse .60 1.50
250 Bobby Clarke 5.00 10.00
251 Bobby Schmautz .40 1.00
252 Peter McNab RC 2.00 4.00
253 Al MacAdam .40 1.00
254 Dennis Hull .60 1.50
255 Terry Harper .40 1.00
256 Peter McDuffe .60 1.50
257 Jean Hamel .40 1.00
258 Jacques Lemaire 1.00 2.50
259 Bob Nystrom .60 1.50
260A Brad Park 2.00 4.00
(No mention of trade)
260B Brad Park 1.50 3.00
(Trade noted)
261 Cesare Maniago .60 1.50
262 Don Saleski .40 1.00
263 J. Bob Kelly .40 1.00
264 Bob Hess RC .40 1.00
265 Blaine Stoughton .60 1.50
266 John Gould .40 1.00
267A Checklist 221-330 8.00 15.00
267B Checklist 331-396 8.00 15.00
268 Dan Bouchard .60 1.50
269 Don Marcotte .40 1.00
270 Jim Neilson .40 1.00
271 Craig Ramsay .40 1.00
272 Grant Mulvey RC .60 1.50
273 Larry Giroux RC .40 1.00
274 Real Lemieux .40 1.00
275 Denis Potvin 7.00 12.00
276 Don Kozak .40 1.00
277 Tom Reid .40 1.00
278 Bob Gainey 4.00 7.00
279 Nick Beverley .40 1.00
280 Jean Pronovost .60 1.50
281 Joe Watson .40 1.00
282 Chuck Lefley .40 1.00
283 Borje Salming 4.00 8.00
284 Garnet Bailey .40 1.00
285 Gregg Boddy .40 1.00
286 Bobby Clarke AS1 2.50 5.00
287 Denis Potvin AS1 2.50 5.00
288 Bobby Orr AS1 9.00 15.00
289 Richard Martin AS1 .60 1.50
290 Guy Lafleur AS1 3.00 6.00
291 Bernie Parent AS1 1.00 2.50
292 Phil Esposito AS2 2.00 4.00
293 Guy Lapointe AS2
294 Borje Salming AS2 2.00 4.00
295 Steve Vickers AS2
296 Rene Robert AS2
297 Rogatien Vachon AS2 1.00 2.50
298 Buster Harvey RC .40 1.00
299 Gary Sabourin .40 1.00
300 Bernie Parent 2.00 4.00
301 Terry O'Reilly 1.00 2.50
302 Ed Westfall .60 1.50
303 Pete Stemkowski .40 1.00
304 Pierre Bouchard .40 1.00
305 Pierre Larouche RC 4.00 8.00
306 Lee Fogolin RC .40 1.00
307 Gerry O'Flaherty .40 1.00
308 Phil Myre .60 1.50
309 Pierre Plante .40 1.00
310 Dennis Hextall .40 1.00
311 Jim McKenny .40 1.00
312 Vic Venasky .40 1.00
313 Flames Leaders .40 1.00
Eric Vail
Tom Lysiak
314 Bruins Leaders 9.00 15.00
Phil Esposito
Bobby Orr
Johnny Bucyk
315 Sabres Leaders .60 1.50
Richard Martin
Rene Robert
316 Seals Leaders .35 .75
Dave Hrechkosy
Larry Patey
Stan Weir
317 Blackhawks Leaders 1.00 2.50
Stan Mikita
Jim Pappin
318 Red Wings Leaders 1.00 2.50
Danny Grant
Marcel Dionne
319 Scouts Leaders .35 .75
Simon Nolet
Wilf Paiement
Guy Charron
320 Kings Leaders .35 .75
Bob Nevin
Juha Widing
Bob Berry
321 North Stars Leaders .35 .75
Bill Goldsworthy
Dennis Hextall
322 Canadiens Leaders 1.50 3.00
Guy Lafleur
Pete Mahovlich
323 Islanders Leaders 1.25 2.50
Bob Nystrom
Denis Potvin
Denis Potvin
Clark Gillies
324 Rangers Leaders 1.00 2.50
Steve Vickers
Rod Gilbert
Jean Ratelle
325 Flyers Leaders 1.00 2.00
Reggie Leach
Bobby Clarke
326 Penguins Leaders .35 .75
Jean Pronovost
Ron Schock
327 Blues Leaders .60 1.50
Garry Unger
Larry Sacharuk
328 Maple Leafs Leaders 1.25 2.50
Darryl Sittler
329 Canucks Leaders .35 .75
Don Lever
Andre Boudrias
330 Capitals Leaders .35 .75
Tommy Williams
Garnet Bailey
331 Noel Price .40 1.00
332 Fred Stanfield .40 1.00
333 Doug Jarrett .40 1.00
334 Gary Coalter .40 1.00
335 Murray Oliver .40 1.00
336 Dave Fortier .40 1.00
337 Terry Crisp UER .40 1.00
338 Bert Wilson .40 1.00
339 John Grisdale RC .40 1.00
340 Ken Broderick .60 1.50
341 Frank Spring RC .40 1.00
342 Mike Korney RC .40 1.00
343 Gene Carr .40 1.00
344 Don Awrey .40 1.00
345 Pat Hickey .40 1.00
346 Colin Campbell RC 1.00 2.50
347 Wayne Thomas .60 1.50
348 Bob Gryp RC .40 1.00
349 Bill Flett .40 1.00
350 Roger Crozier .60 1.50
351 Dale Tallon .40 1.00
352 Larry Johnston .40 1.00
353 John Flesch RC .40 1.00
354 Lorne Henning .40 1.00
355 Wayne Stephenson .60 1.50
356 Rick Wilson .40 1.00
357 Garry Monahan .40 1.00

358 Gary Doak .40 1.00
359A Pierre Jarry .35 .75
(No mention of trade)
359B Pierre Jarry .35 .75
(Trade noted)
360 George Pesut RC .40 1.00
361 Mike Corrigan .40 1.00
362 Michel Larocque 1.00 2.50
363 Wayne Dillon .40 1.00
364 Pete Laframboise .40 1.00
365 Brian Glennie .40 1.00
366 Mike Christie .40 1.00
367 Jean Lemieux RC .40 1.00
368 Gary Bromley .60 1.50
369 J.P. Bordeleau .40 1.00
370 Ed Gilbert RC .40 1.00
371 Chris Ahrens .40 1.00
372 Billy Smith 4.00 7.00
373 Larry Goodenough RC .40 1.00
374 Leon Rochefort .40 1.00
375 Doug Gibson RC .40 1.00
376 Mike Bloom .40 1.00
377 Larry Brown .40 1.00
378 Jim Roberts .40 1.00
379 Gilles Villemure .60 1.50
380 Dennis Owchar RC .40 1.00
381 Doug Favell .60 1.50
382 Stan Gilbertson UER .40 1.00
(Photo actually
Denis Dupere)
383 Ed Kea RC .40 1.00
384 Brian Spencer .40 1.00
385 Mike Veisor RC .60 1.50
386 Bob Murray .40 1.00
387 Andre St.Laurent RC .40 1.00
388 Rick Chartraw RC .40 1.00
389 Orest Kindrachuk .40 1.00
390 Dave Hutchinson RC .40 1.00
391 Glenn Goldup .40 1.00
392 Jerry Holland RC .40 1.00
393 Peter Sturgeon RC .40 1.00
394 Alain Daigle RC .40 1.00
395 Never Issued
(Checklist 330-396&
numbered as 267
and listed as 267B)
396 Harold Snepsts RC 12.00 20.00

1975-76 O-Pee-Chee WHA

The 1975-76 O-Pee-Chee WHA set consisted of 132 color cards. Printed in Canada, the cards measured 2 1/2" by 3 1/2". Bilingual backs featured 1974-75 and career WHA statistics as well as a short biography.

COMPLETE SET (132) 250.00 400.00
1 Bobby Hull 25.00 50.00
2 Dale Hoganson 2.50 5.00
3 Serge Aubry 3.00 6.00
4 Ron Chipperfield 2.00 4.00
5 Paul Shmyr 2.00 4.00
6 Perry Miller RC 2.00 4.00
7 Mark Howe RC 20.00 50.00
8 Mike Rogers RC 3.00 6.00
9 Bryon Baltimore 2.00 4.00
10 Andre Lacroix 2.50 5.00
11 Nick Harbaruk 2.00 4.00
12 John Garrett RC 7.00 12.00
13 Lou Nistico RC 2.00 4.00
14 Rick Ley 2.00 4.00
15 Veli-Pekka Ketola RC 4.00 8.00
16 Real Cloutier 2.50 5.00
17 Pierre Guite RC 2.00 4.00
18 Duane Rupp 2.00 4.00
19 Robbie Ftorek RC 7.50 15.00
20 Gerry Cheevers 9.00 15.00
21 John Schella RC 2.00 4.00
22 Bruce MacGregor 2.00 4.00
23 Ralph Backstrom 2.50 5.00
24 Gene Peacosh 2.00 4.00
25 Pierre Roy 2.00 4.00
26 Mike Walton 3.00 6.00
27 Vaclav Nedomansky 2.50 5.00
28 Christer Abrahamsson RC 6.00 10.00
29 Thommie Bergman 2.00 4.00
30 Marc Tardif 2.00 4.00
31 Bryan Campbell 2.00 4.00
32 Don McLeod 2.50 5.00
33 Al McDonough 2.00 4.00
34 Jacques Plante 25.00 40.00
35 Andre Hinse RC 2.00 4.00
36 Eddie Joyal 2.00 4.00
37 Ken Baird RC 2.00 4.00
38 Wayne Rivers 2.00 4.00
39 Ron Buchanan 2.00 4.00
40 Anders Hedberg 3.00 6.00
41 Rick Smith 2.00 4.00
42 Paul Henderson 2.50 5.00
43 Wayne Carleton 2.50 5.00
44 Richard Brodeur RC 7.00 12.00
45 John Hughes RC 2.00 4.00
46 Larry Israelson RC 2.00 4.00
47 Jim Harrison 2.00 4.00
48 Cam Connor RC 2.00 4.00
49 Al Hamilton 2.00 4.00
50 Ron Grahame 3.00 6.00
51 Frank Rochon RC 2.00 4.00
52 Ron Climie 2.00 4.00
53 Murray Heatley RC 2.00 4.00
54 John Arbour 2.00 4.00
55 Jim Shaw RC 2.50 5.00
56 Larry Pleau RC 3.00 6.00
57 Ted Green 3.00 6.00
58 Rick Dudley 2.00 4.00
59 Butch Deadmarsh 2.00 4.00
60 Serge Bernier 2.50 5.00
61 Ron Grahame AS 2.00 4.00
62 J.C. Tremblay AS 2.00 4.00
63 Kevin Morrison AS 2.00 4.00
64 Andre Lacroix AS 2.00 4.00
65 Bobby Hull AS 12.00 20.00
66 Gordie Howe AS 18.00 30.00
67 Gerry Cheevers AS 4.00 8.00
68 Poul Popiel AS 2.00 4.00
69 Barry Long AS 2.00 4.00
70 Serge Bernier AS 2.00 4.00
71 Marc Tardif AS 2.00 4.00
72 Anders Hedberg AS 2.00 4.00
73 Ron Ward 2.00 4.00
74 Michel Cormier RC 2.00 4.00
75 Marty Howe RC 3.00 6.00
76 Rusty Patenaude 2.00 4.00
77 John McKenzie 2.50 5.00
78 Mark Napier RC 3.00 6.00
79 Henry Boucha 2.00 4.00
80 Kevin Morrison RC 2.00 4.00
81 Tom Simpson 2.00 4.00
82 Brad Selwood RC 3.00 6.00
83 Ulf Nilsson 3.00 6.00
84 Rejean Houle 2.50 5.00
85 Normand Lapointe RC 2.00 4.00
86 Danny Lawson 2.50 5.00
87 Gary Jarrett 2.00 4.00
88 Al McLeod RC 2.00 4.00
89 Gord Labossiere 2.00 4.00
90 Barry Long 2.50 5.00
91 Rick Morris RC 2.00 4.00
92 Norm Ferguson 2.00 4.00
93 Bob Whitlock 2.00 4.00
94 Jim Dorey 2.00 4.00
95 Tom Webster 2.50 5.00
96 Gordie Gallant 2.00 4.00
97 Dave Keon 3.00 6.00
98 Ron Plumb RC 2.50 5.00
99 Rick Jodzio RC 2.00 4.00
100 Gordie Howe 35.00 50.00
101 Joe Daley 3.00 6.00
102 Wayne Muloin RC 2.00 4.00
103 Gavin Kirk RC 2.00 4.00
104 Dave Dryden 2.50 5.00
105 Bob Liddington RC 2.00 4.00
106 Rosaire Paiement 2.00 4.00
107 John Sheridan 4.00 8.00
108 Nick Fotiu RC 6.00 10.00
109 Lars-Erik Sjoberg 2.00 4.00
110 Frank Mahovlich 3.00 6.00
111 Mike Antonovich 2.00 4.00
112 Paul Terbenche 2.00 4.00
113 Rich Leduc RC 2.00 4.00
114 Jack Norris 2.50 5.00
115 Dennis Sobchuk 2.00 4.00
116 Chris Bordeleau 2.00 4.00
117 Doug Barrie 2.00 4.00
118 Hugh Harris RC 2.00 4.00
119 Cam Newton RC 2.00 4.00
120 Poul Popiel 2.00 4.00
121 Fran Huck 2.00 4.00
122 Tony Featherstone 2.00 4.00
123 Bob Woytowich 2.00 4.00
124 Claude St.Sauveur 2.00 4.00
125 Heikki Riihiranta 2.50 5.00
126 Gary Kurt 2.50 5.00
127 Thommy Abrahamsson RC 3.00 5.00
128 Danny Gruen RC 2.00 4.00
129 Jacques Locas RC 2.00 4.00
130 J.C. Tremblay 2.00 4.00
131 Checklist Card 25.00 50.00
132 Ernie Wakely 4.00 8.00

1976-77 O-Pee-Chee NHL

The 1976-77 O-Pee-Chee NHL set consisted of 396 color standard-size cards. Printed in Canada, the cards contained both the O-Pee-Chee and the NHL Players Association copyright. The wax packs issued contained eight cards in ten-cent packs along with a bubble-gum slab. Several Record Breaker (RB) cards featured achievements from the previous season. Team cards (132-149) had a team checklist on the back. Bilingual backs contained the player's statistics from the 1975-76 season, career numbers, a short biography and a cartoon-illustrated fact about the player. Cards that featured California players in the 1976-77 Topps set had been updated in this set to show them with the Cleveland Barons. One of those was card 176 Gary Simmons. There are reportedly three variations of the Simmons card. In addition to the basic card, one version had "Team transferred to Colorado" on front. This is an error in itself because the Barons disbanded with players going to Minnesota. The other version had the text shaded or airbrushed out. Information on values and scarcities is not known at this time. Rookie Cards included Bryan Trottier and Dave "Tiger" Williams.

COMPLETE SET (396) 150.00 300.00
1 Goals Leaders 1.50 3.00
Reggie Leach
Guy Lafleur
Pierre Larouche
2 Assists Leaders 1.50 3.00
Bobby Clarke
Peter Mahovlich
Guy Lafleur
Gilbert Perrault
Jean Ratelle
3 Scoring Leaders 1.50 3.00
Guy Lafleur
Bobby Clarke
Gilbert Perreault
4 Penalty Min. Leaders .20 .50
Steve Durbano
Bryan Watson
Dave Schultz
5 Power Play Goals 1.50 3.00
Leaders
Phil Esposito
Guy Lafleur
Richard Martin
Pierre Larouche
Denis Potvin
6 Goals Against 2.50 5.00
Average Leaders
Ken Dryden
Glenn Resch
Michel Larocque
7 Gary Doak .40 1.00
8 Jacques Richard .40 1.00
9 Wayne Dillon .40 1.00
10 Bernie Parent .75 2.00
11 Ed Westfall .60 1.50
12 Dick Redmond .40 1.00
13 Bryan Hextall .40 1.00
14 Jean Pronovost .40 1.00
15 Peter Mahovlich .60 1.50
16 Danny Grant .40 1.00
17 Phil Myre .40 1.00
18 Wayne Merrick .40 1.00
19 Steve Durbano .40 1.00
20 Derek Sanderson .75 2.00
21 Mike Murphy .40 1.00
22 Borje Salming 2.50 5.00
23 Mike Walton .40 1.00
24 Randy Manery .40 1.00
25 Ken Hodge .40 1.00
26 Mel Bridgman RC 1.25 2.50
27 Jerry Korab .40 1.00
28 Gilles Gratton .40 1.00
29 Andre St.Laurent .40 1.00
30 Yvan Cournoyer .75 2.00
31 Phil Russell .40 1.00
32 Dennis Hextall .40 1.00
33 Lowell MacDonald .40 1.00
34 Dennis O'Brien .40 1.00
35 Gerry Meehan .40 1.00
36 Gilles Meloche .60 1.50
37 Wilf Paiement .40 1.00
38 Bob MacMillan RC .75 2.00
39 Ian Turnbull .40 1.00
40 Rogatien Vachon .75 2.00
41 Nick Beverley .40 1.00
42 Rene Robert .60 1.50
43 Andre Savard .40 1.00
44 Bob Gainey 2.00 4.00
45 Joe Watson .40 1.00
46 Billy Smith 2.50 5.00
47 Darcy Rota .40 1.00
48 Rick Lapointe RC .40 1.00
49 Pierre Jarry .40 1.00
50 Syl Apps .40 1.00
51 Eric Vail .40 1.00
52 Greg Joly .40 1.00
53 Don Lever .40 1.00
54 Bob Murdoch .40 1.00
55 Denis Herron .40 1.00
56 Mike Bloom .40 1.00
57 Bill Fairbairn .40 1.00
58 Fred Stanfield .40 1.00
59 Steve Shutt .75 2.00
60 Brad Park .75 2.00
61 Gilles Villemure .40 1.00
62 Bert Marshall .40 1.00
63 Chuck Lefley .40 1.00
64 Simon Nolet .40 1.00
65 Reggie Leach RB .20 .50
66 Darryl Sittler RB .75 2.00
67 Bryan Trottier RB 5.00 10.00
68 Garry Unger RB .20 .50
69 Ron Low .40 1.00
70 Bobby Clarke 3.00 6.00
71 Michel Bergeron RC .40 1.00
72 Ron Stackhouse .40 1.00
73 Bill Hogaboam .40 1.00
74 Bob Murdoch .40 1.00
75 Steve Vickers .40 1.00
76 Pit Martin .40 1.00
77 Gerry Hart .40 1.00
78 Craig Ramsay .40 1.00
79 Michel Larocque .40 1.00
80 Jean Ratelle .75 2.00
81 Don Saleski .40 1.00
82 Bill Clement .75 2.00
83 Dave Burrows .40 1.00
84 Wayne Thomas .40 1.00
85 John Gould .40 1.00
86 Dennis Maruk RC 1.50 3.00
87 Ernie Hicke .40 1.00
88 Jim Rutherford .40 1.00
89 Dale Tallon .40 1.00
90 Rod Gilbert .75 2.00
91 Marcel Dionne 3.00 6.00
92 Chuck Arnason .40 1.00
93 Jean Potvin .40 1.00
94 Don Luce .40 1.00
95 Johnny Bucyk .75 2.00
96 Larry Goodenough .40 1.00
97 Mario Tremblay .60 1.50
98 Nelson Pyatt RC .40 1.00
99 Brian Glennie .40 1.00
100 Tony Esposito 2.00 4.00
101 Dan Maloney .40 1.00
102 Dunc Wilson .40 1.00
103 Dean Talafous .40 1.00
104 Ed Staniowski RC .40 1.00
105 Dallas Smith .40 1.00
106 Jude Drouin .40 1.00
107 Pat Hickey .40 1.00
108 Jocelyn Guevremont .40 1.00
109 Doug Risebrough .75 2.00
110 Reggie Leach .60 1.50
111 Dan Bouchard .60 1.50
112 Chris Oddleifson .40 1.00
113 Rick Hampton .40 1.00
114 John Marks .40 1.00
115 Bryan Trottier RC 30.00 60.00
116 Checklist 1-132 6.00 10.00
117 Greg Polis .40 1.00
118 Peter McNab .75 2.00
119 Jim Roberts .40 1.00
120 Gerry Cheevers 1.50 3.00
121 Rick MacLeish .60 1.50
122 Billy Lochead .40 1.00
123 Tom Reid .40 1.00
124 Rick Kehoe .40 1.00
125 Keith Magnuson .40 1.00
126 Clark Gillies .75 2.00
127 Rick Middleton .75 2.00
128 Bill Hajt .40 1.00
129 Jacques Lemaire .75 2.00
130 Terry O'Reilly .75 2.00
131 Andre Dupont .40 1.00
132 Flames Team 1.50 3.00
133 Bruins Team 1.50 3.00
134 Sabres Team 1.50 3.00
135 Seals Team 1.50 3.00
136 Blackhawks Team 1.50 3.00
137 Red Wings Team 1.50 3.00
138 Scouts Team 1.50 3.00
139 Kings Team 1.50 3.00
140 North Stars Team 1.50 3.00
141 Canadiens Team 1.50 3.00
142 Islanders Team 1.50 3.00
143 Rangers Team 1.50 3.00
144 Flyers Team 1.50 3.00
145 Penguins Team 1.50 3.00
146 Blues Team 1.50 3.00
147 Maple Leafs Team 1.50 3.00
148 Canucks Team 1.50 3.00
149 Capitals Team 1.50 3.00
150 Dave Schultz .75 2.00
151 Larry Robinson 3.00 6.00
152 Al Smith .60 1.50
153 Bob Nystrom .60 1.50
154 Ron Greschner .60 1.50
155 Gregg Sheppard .40 1.00
156 Alain Daigle .40 1.00
157 Ed Van Impe .40 1.00
158 Tim Young RC .60 1.50
159 Bryan Lefley .40 1.00
160 Ed Giacomin .75 2.00
161 Yvon Labre .40 1.00
162 Jim Lorentz .40 1.00
163 Guy Lafleur 7.00 12.00
164 Tom Bladon .40 1.00
165 Wayne Cashman .60 1.50
166 Pete Stemkowski .40 1.00
167 Grant Mulvey .40 1.00
168 Yves Belanger RC .40 1.00
169 Bill Goldsworthy .60 1.50
170 Denis Potvin 3.00 6.00
171 Nick Libett .40 1.00
172 Michel Plasse .40 1.00
173 Lou Nanne .40 1.00
174 Tom Lysiak .40 1.00
175 Dennis Ververgaert .40 1.00
176 Gary Simmons .60 1.50
177 Pierre Bouchard .40 1.00
178 Bill Barber .75 2.00
179 Darryl Edestrand .40 1.00
180 Gilbert Perreault 1.50 3.00
181 Dave Maloney RC .75 2.00
182 Jean-Paul Parise .40 1.00
183 Jim Harrison .40 1.00
184 Pete Lopresti RC .40 1.00
185 Don Kozak .40 1.00
186 Guy Charron .40 1.00
187 Stan Gilbertson .40 1.00
188 Bill Nyrop RC .40 1.00
189 Bobby Schmautz .40 1.00
190 Wayne Stephenson .40 1.00
191 Brian Spencer .40 1.00
192 Gilles Marotte .40 1.00
193 Lorne Henning .40 1.00
194 Bob Neely .40 1.00
195 Dennis Hull .40 1.00
196 Walt McKechnie .40 1.00
197 Curt Ridley RC .40 1.00
198 Dwight Bialowas .40 1.00
199 Pierre Larouche .75 2.00
200 Ken Dryden 10.00 20.00
201 Ross Lonsberry .40 1.00
202 Curt Bennett .40 1.00
203 Hartland Monahan RC .40 1.00
204 John Davidson 1.50 3.00
205 Serge Savard .75 2.00
206 Garry Howatt .40 1.00
207 Darryl Sittler 2.50 5.00
208 J.P. Bordeleau .40 1.00
209 Henry Boucha .40 1.00
210 Richard Martin .60 1.50
211 Vic Venasky .40 1.00
212 Buster Harvey .40 1.00
213 Bobby Orr 20.00 50.00
214 French Connection 1.50 3.00
Richard Martin
Gilbert Perreault
Rene Robert
215 LCB Line 2.00 4.00
Reggie Leach
Bobby Clarke
Bill Barber
216 Long Island Lightning 2.50 5.00
Clark Gillies
Bryan Trottier
Billy Harris
217 Checking Line .75 2.00
Bob Gainey
Doug Jarvis
Jim Roberts
218 Bicentennial Line .40 1.00
Lowell MacDonald
Syl Apps
Jean Pronovost
219 Bob Kelly .40 1.00
220 Walt Tkaczuk .40 1.00
221 Dave Lewis .40 1.00
222 Danny Gare .75 2.00
223 Guy Lapointe .60 1.50
224 Hank Nowak RC .40 1.00
225 Stan Mikita 2.00 4.00
226 Vic Hadfield .40 1.00
227 Bernie Wolfe RC .60 1.50
228 Bryan Watson .40 1.00
229 Ralph Stewart .40 1.00
230 Gerry Desjardins .60 1.50
231 John Bednarski RC .40 1.00
232 Yvon Lambert .40 1.00
233 Orest Kindrachuk .40 1.00
234 Don Marcotte .40 1.00
235 Bill White .40 1.00
236 Red Berenson .40 1.00
237 Al MacAdam .40 1.00
238 Rick Blight RC .40 1.00
239 Butch Goring .60 1.50
240 Cesare Maniago .60 1.50
241 Jim Schoenfeld .60 1.50
242 Cliff Koroll .40 1.00
243 Scott Garland RC .40 1.00
244 Rick Chartraw .40 1.00
245 Phil Esposito 2.00 4.00
246 Dave Forbes .40 1.00
247 Joe Watson .40 1.00
248 Ron Schock .40 1.00
249 Fred Barrett .40 1.00
250 Glenn Resch 1.50 3.00
251 Ivan Boldirev .40 1.00
252 Billy Harris .40 1.00
253 Lee Fogolin .40 1.00
254 Murray Wilson .40 1.00
255 Gilles Gilbert .60 1.50
256 Gary Dornhoefer .60 1.50
257 Carol Vadnais .40 1.00
258 Checklist 133-264 6.00 10.00
259 Errol Thompson .40 1.00
260 Garry Unger .60 1.50
261 J. Bob Kelly .40 1.00
262 Terry Harper .40 1.00
263 Blake Dunlop .40 1.00
264 Stanley Cup Champs 1.25 2.50
265 Richard Mulhern RC .40 1.00
266 Gary Sabourin .40 1.00
267 Bill McKenzie UER RC .40 1.00
268 Mike Corrigan .40 1.00
269 Rick Smith .40 1.00
270 Stan Weir .40 1.00
271 Ron Sedlbauer RC .40 1.00
272 Jean Lemieux .40 1.00
273 Hilliard Graves .40 1.00
274 Dave Gardner .40 1.00
275 Tracy Pratt .40 1.00
276 Frank St.Marseille .40 1.00
277 Bob Hess .40 1.00
278 Bobby Lalonde .40 1.00
279 Tony White RC .40 1.00
280 Rod Seiling .40 1.00
281 Larry Romanchych .40 1.00
282 Ralph Klassen RC .40 1.00
283 Gary Croteau .40 1.00
284 Neil Komadoski .40 1.00
285 Ed Johnston .40 1.00
286 George Ferguson .40 1.00
287 Gerry O'Flaherty .40 1.00
288 Jack Lynch .40 1.00
289 Pat Quinn .60 1.50
290 Gene Carr .40 1.00
291 Bob Stewart .40 1.00
292 Doug Favell .60 1.50
293 Rick Wilson .40 1.00
294 Jack Valiquette RC .40 1.00
295 Garry Monahan .40 1.00
296 Michel Belhumeur .40 1.00
297 Larry Carriere .40 1.00
298 Fred Ahern RC .40 1.00
299 Dave Hudson .40 1.00
300 Bob Berry .40 1.00
301 Bob Gassoff .40 1.00
302 Jim McKenny .40 1.00
303 Gord Smith RC .40 1.00
304 Garnet Bailey .40 1.00
305 Bruce Affleck RC .40 1.00
306 Doug Halward RC .40 1.00
307 Lew Morrison .40 1.00
308 Bob Sauve RC 1.50 3.00
309 Bob Murray RC .40 1.00
310 Claude Larose .40 1.00
311 Don Awrey .40 1.00
312 Bill MacMillan .40 1.00
313 Doug Jarvis RC 1.25 2.50
314 Dennis Owchar .40 1.00
315 Jerry Holland .40 1.00
316 Guy Chouinard RC .75 2.00
317 Gary Smith .60 1.50
318 Pat Price RC .40 1.00
319 Tom Williams .40 1.00
320 Larry Patey .40 1.00
321 Claire Alexander .40 1.00
322 Larry Bolonchuk RC .40 1.00
323 Bob Sirois RC .40 1.00
324 Joe Zanussi RC .40 1.00
325 Joey Johnston .40 1.00
326 J.P. LeBlanc .40 1.00
327 Craig Cameron .40 1.00
328 Dave Fortier .40 1.00
329 Ed Gilbert .40 1.00
330 John Van Boxmeer RC .40 1.00
331 Gary Inness .60 1.50
332 Bill Flett .40 1.00
333 Mike Christie .40 1.00
334 Denis Dupere .40 1.00
335 Sheldon Kannegiesser .40 1.00
336 Jerry Butler .40 1.00
337 Gord McRae .40 1.00
338 Dennis Kearns .40 1.00
339 Ron Lalonde .40 1.00
340 Jean Hamel .40 1.00
341 Barry Gibbs .40 1.00
342 Mike Pelyk .40 1.00
343 Rey Comeau .40 1.00
344 Jim Neilson .40 1.00
345 Phil Roberto .40 1.00
346 Dave Hutchinson RC .40 1.00
347 Ted Irvine .40 1.00
348 Lanny McDonald 2.00 4.00
349 Jim Moxey RC .40 1.00
350 Bob Dailey .40 1.00
351 Tim Ecclestone .40 1.00
352 Len Frig .40 1.00
353 Randy Rota .40 1.00
354 Juha Widing .40 1.00
355 Larry Brown .40 1.00
356 Floyd Thomson .40 1.00
357 Richard Nantais RC .40 1.00
358 Inge Hammarstrom .40 1.00
359 Mike Robitaille .40 1.00
360 Rejean Houle .40 1.00
361 Ed Kea .40 1.00
362 Bob Girard RC .40 1.00
363 Bob Murray .40 1.00
364 Dave Hrechkosy .40 1.00
365 Gary Edwards .40 1.00
366 Harold Snepsts 2.00 4.00
367 Pat Boutette RC .75 2.00
368 Bob Paradise .40 1.00
369 Bob Plager .60 1.50
370 Tim Jacobs RC .40 1.00
371 Pierre Plante .40 1.00
372 Colin Campbell .60 1.50
373 Dave Williams RC 12.50 25.00
374 Ab DeMarco .40 1.00
375 Mike Lampman RC .40 1.00
376 Mark Heaslip RC .40 1.00
377 Checklist Card 6.00 10.00
378 Bert Wilson .40 1.00
379 Flames Leaders .20 .50
Curt Bennett
Tom Lysiak
Pat Quinn
Claude St.Sauveur
380 Sabres Leaders .20 .50
Danny Gare
Gilbert Perreault
Richard Martin
381 Bruins Leaders 1.25 2.50
Johnny Bucyk
Jean Ratelle
Terry O'Reilly
382 Blackhawks Leaders .20 .50
Pit Martin
Dale Tallon
Phil Russell
Cliff Koroll
383 Seals Leaders .20 .50
Wayne Merrick
Al MacAdam
Rick Hampton
Mike Christie
Bob Murdoch
384 Scouts Leaders .20 .50
Guy Charron
Steve Durbano
385 Red Wings Leaders .20 .50
Michel Bergeron
Walt McKechnie
Bryan Watson
386 Kings Leaders .20 .50
Marcel Dionne
Dave Hutchison
Mike Corrigan
387 North Stars Leaders .20 .50
Bill Hogaboam
Tim Young
Dennis O'Brien
388 Canadiens Leaders 1.50 3.00
Guy Lafleur
Pete Mahovlich
Doug Risebrough
389 Islanders Leaders 1.25 2.50
Clark Gillies
Denis Potvin
Garry Howatt
390 Rangers Leaders 1.25 2.50
Rod Gilbert
Steve Vickers
Carol Vadnais
Phil Esposito
391 Flyers Leaders 1.25 2.50
Reggie Leach
Bobby Clarke
Dave Schultz
Bill Barber
392 Penguins Leaders .20 .50
Pierre Larouche
Syl Apps
Ron Schock
393 Blues Leaders .20 .50
Chuck Lefley
Garry Unger
Bob Gassoff
394 Maple Leafs Leaders .20 .50
Errol Thompson
Darryl Sittler
Dave(Tiger) Williams
395 Canucks Leaders .20 .50
Dennis Ververgaert
Chris Oddleifson
Dennis Kearns
Harold Snepsts
396 Capitals Leaders .20 .50
Nelson Pyatt
Gerry Meehan
Yvon Labre
Tony White

1976-77 O-Pee-Chee WHA

The 1976-77 O-Pee-Chee WHA set consisted of 132 color cards featuring WHA players. Cards were 2 1/2" by 3 1/2". The cards were originally sold in ten-cent wax packs. The backs, in both French and English, told a short biography of the player and career statistics. The cards were printed in Canada. Cards 1-6 featured the league leaders from the previous season in various statistical categories. The backs of cards 62-65, 67, and 71 formed a puzzle of Gordie Howe. A puzzle of Bobby Hull was derived from the backs of cards 61, 66, 68-70 and 72. These cards (61-72) comprised the All-Star subset.

COMPLETE SET (132) 100.00 200.00
1 Goals Leaders 2.00 4.00
Marc Tardif
Real Cloutier
Vaclav Nedomansky
2 Assists Leaders 1.50 3.00
J.C. Tremblay
Marc Tardif
Ulf Nilsson
3 Scoring Leaders 4.00 8.00
Marc Tardif
Bobby Hull
Real Cloutier
Ulf Nilsson
4 Penalties Leaders 1.00 2.00
Curt Brackenbury
Gord Gallant
5 Points Leaders 4.00 8.00
Marc Tardif
Bobby Hull
Ulf Nilsson
6 Goals Against 1.00 2.00
Average Leaders
Michel Dion
Joe Daley
Wayne Rutledge
7 Barry Long .60 1.50
8 Danny Lawson .60 1.50
9 Ulf Nilsson 1.25 3.00
10 Kevin Morrison .60 1.50
11 Gerry Pinder .60 1.50
12 Richard Brodeur 3.00 5.00
13 Robbie Ftorek 4.00 8.00
14 Tom Webster .75 2.00
15 Marty Howe 1.25 3.00
16 Bryan Campbell .60 1.50
17 Rick Dudley .60 1.50
18 Jim Turkiewicz RC .60 1.50
19 Rusty Patenaude .60 1.50
20 Joe Daley .75 2.00
21 Gary Veneruzzo .60 1.50
22 Chris Evans .60 1.50
23 Mike Antonovich .60 1.50
24 Jim Dorey .60 1.50
25 John Gray RC .60 1.50
26 Larry Pleau .60 1.50
27 Poul Popiel .60 1.50
28 Renald Leclerc RC .60 1.50
29 Dennis Sobchuk .60 1.50
30 Lars-Erik Sjoberg .60 1.50
31 Wayne Wood RC .75 2.00
32 Ron Chipperfield .60 1.50
33 Tim Sheehy RC .60 1.50
34 Brent Hughes .60 1.50
35 Ron Ward .60 1.50
36 Ron Huston RC .60 1.50
37 Rosaire Paiement .60 1.50
38 Terry Ruskowski RC 3.00 5.00
39 Hugh Harris .60 1.50
40 J.C. Tremblay .60 1.50
41 Rich Leduc .60 1.50
42 Peter Sullivan RC .60 1.50
43 Jerry Rollins RC .60 1.50
44 Ken Broderick .75 2.00
45 Peter Driscoll RC .60 1.50
46 Joe Noris RC .60 1.50
47 Al McLeod .00 1.50
48 Bruce Landon RC .75 2.00
49 Chris Bordeleau .60 1.50
50 Gordie Howe 20.00 40.00
51 Thommie Bergman .60 1.50
52 Dave Keon 1.25 3.00
53 Butch Deadmarsh .60 1.50
54 Bryan Maxwell .60 1.50
55 John Garrett .75 2.00
56 Glen Sather .75 2.00
57 John Miszuk .60 1.50
58 Heikki Riihiranta .75 2.00
59 Richard Grenier RC .60 1.50
60 Gene Peacosh .60 1.50
61 Joe Daley AS 1.00 2.00
62 J.C. Tremblay AS 1.00 2.00
63 Lars-Erik Sjoberg AS 1.00 2.00
64 Vaclav Nedomansky AS 1.00 2.00
65 Bobby Hull AS 10.00 20.00
66 Anders Hedberg AS 1.00 2.00
67 Chris Abrahamsson AS 1.00 2.00
68 Kevin Morrison AS 1.00 2.00
69 Paul Shmyr AS 1.00 2.00
70 Andre Lacroix AS 1.00 2.00
71 Gene Peacosh AS 1.00 2.00
72 Gordie Howe AS 15.00 25.00
73 Bob Nevin .60 1.50
74 Richard Lemieux .60 1.50
75 Mike Ford RC .60 1.50
76 Real Cloutier .75 2.00
77 Al McDonough .60 1.50
78 Del Hall RC .60 1.50
79 Thommy Abrahamsson .60 1.50
80 Andre Lacroix .75 2.00
81 Frank Hughes RC .60 1.50
82 Reg Thomas RC .60 1.50
83 Dave Inkpen RC .60 1.50
84 Paul Henderson .75 2.00
85 Dave Dryden .75 2.00
86 Lynn Powis .60 1.50
87 Andre Boudrias .60 1.50
88 Veli-Pekka Ketola .75 2.00
89 Cam Connor .60 1.50
90 Claude St.Sauveur .60 1.50
91 Garry Swain RC .60 1.50
92 Ernie Wakely .75 2.00
93 Blair MacDonald RC .60 1.50
94 Ron Plumb .60 1.50
95 Mark Howe 7.00 12.00
96 Peter Marrin RC 1.25 3.00
97 Al Hamilton .75 2.00
98 Paulin Bordeleau .60 1.50
99 Gavin Kirk .60 1.50
100 Bobby Hull 15.00 30.00
101 Rick Ley .60 1.50
102 Gary Kurt .75 2.00
103 John McKenzie .75 2.00
104 Al Karlander RC .60 1.50
105 John French .60 1.50

106 John Hughes .60 1.50
107 Ron Grahame .75 2.00
108 Mark Napier .75 2.00
109 Serge Bernier .75 2.00
110 Christer Abrahamsson .75 2.00
111 Frank Mahovlich 3.50 6.00
112 Ted Green .75 2.00
113 Rick Jodzio .60 1.50
114 Michel Dion RC 3.00 6.00
115 Rich Preston RC .60 1.50
116 Pekka Rautakallio RC 3.00 6.00
117 Checklist Card 12.00 30.00
118 Marc Tardif .75 2.00
119 Doug Barrie .60 1.50
120 Vaclav Nedomansky .75 2.00
121 Bill Lesuk .60 1.50
122 Wayne Connelly .60 1.50
123 Pierre Guite .60 1.50
124 Ralph Backstrom .75 2.00
125 Anders Hedberg 1.25 3.00
126 Norm Ullman 1.25 3.00
127 Steve Sutherland RC .60 1.50
128 John Schella .60 1.50
129 Don McLeod .75 2.00
130 Canadian Finals 1.50 4.00
131 U.S. Finals 1.50 4.00
132 World Trophy Final 6.00 15.00

1977-78 O-Pee-Chee NHL

The 1977-78 O-Pee-Chee NHL set consisted of 396 color standard-size cards. Unopened packs consisted of 12 cards plus a bubble-gum stick. Cards 203 and 255 featured different players than corresponding Topps cards. Bilingual backs contained yearly statistics and a cartoon-illustrated fact about the player. Cards 322-339 had a team logo on the front with team records on the back. Rookie Cards included Mike Milbury, Mike Palmateer and Paul Holmgren. The Rick Bourbonnais card (312) actually depicted Bernie Federko, predating his Rookie Card by one year.

COMPLETE SET (396) 75.00 150.00
1 Goals Leaders 1.50 3.00
Steve Shutt
Guy Lafleur
Marcel Dionne
2 Assists Leaders 1.00 2.00
Guy Lafleur
Marcel Dionne
Larry Robinson
Borje Salming
Tim Young
3 Scoring Leaders 1.25 2.50
Guy Lafleur
Marcel Dionne
Steve Shutt
4 Penalty Min. Leaders .30 .75
Dave(Tiger) Williams
Dennis Polonich
Bob Gassoff
5 Power Play Goals .40 1.00
Leaders
Lanny McDonald
Phil Esposito
Tom Williams
6 Goals Against 2.00 4.00
Average Leaders
Michel Larocque
Ken Dryden
Glenn Resch
7 Game Winning 1.25 2.50
Goals Leaders
Gilbert Perreault
Steve Shutt
Guy Lafleur
Rick MacLeish
Peter McNab
8 Shutouts Leaders 2.50 5.00
Ken Dryden
Rogatien Vachon
Bernie Parent
Dunc Wilson
9 Brian Spencer .20 .50
10 Denis Potvin AS2 2.00 4.00
11 Nick Fotiu .40 1.00
12 Bob Murray .20 .50
13 Pete Lopresti .30 .75
14 J. Bob Kelly .30 .75
15 Rick MacLeish .30 .75
16 Terry Harper .20 .50
17 Willi Plett RC 1.50 3.00
18 Peter McNab .30 .75
19 Wayne Thomas .30 .75
20 Pierre Bouchard .20 .50
21 Dennis Maruk .40 1.00
22 Mike Murphy .20 .50
23 Cesare Maniago .30 .75
24 Paul Gardner RC .30 .75
25 Rod Gilbert .40 1.00
26 Orest Kindrachuk .20 .50
27 Bill Hajt .20 .50
28 John Davidson .75 1.50
29 Jean-Paul Parise .20 .50
30 Larry Robinson AS1 2.50 5.00
31 Yvon Labre .20 .50
32 Walt McKechnie .20 .50
33 Rick Kehoe .30 .75
34 Randy Holt RC .20 .50
35 Garry Unger .30 .75
36 Lou Nanne .20 .50
37 Dan Bouchard .30 .75
38 Darryl Sittler 1.50 3.00
39 Bob Murdoch .20 .50
40 Jean Ratelle .40 1.00
41 Dave Maloney .20 .50
42 Danny Gare .30 .75
43 Jimmy Watson .20 .50
44 Tom Williams .20 .50
45 Serge Savard .40 1.00
46 Derek Sanderson 1.00 2.00
47 John Marks .20 .50
48 Al Cameron RC .20 .50
49 Dean Talafous .20 .50
50 Glenn Resch 1.00 2.00
51 Ron Schock .20 .50
52 Gary Croteau .20 .50
53 Gerry Meehan .20 .50
54 Ed Staniowski .20 .50
55 Phil Esposito UER 1.50 3.00
(Goal total reads 78(should be 55)
56 Dennis Ververgaert .20 .50
57 Rick Wilson .20 .50
58 Jim Lorentz .20 .50
59 Bobby Schmautz .20 .50
60 Guy Lapointe AS2 .30 .75
61 Ivan Boldirev .20 .50
62 Bob Nystrom .20 .50
63 Rick Hampton .20 .50
64 Jack Valiquette .20 .50
65 Bernie Parent 1.25 2.50
66 Dave Burrows .20 .50
67 Butch Goring .30 .75
68 Checklist 1-132 4.00 8.00
69 Murray Wilson .20 .50
70 Ed Giacomin .75 1.50
71 Flames Team .75 2.00
72 Bruins Team .75 2.00
73 Sabres Team .75 2.00
74 Blackhawks Team .75 2.00
75 Barons Team .75 2.00
76 Rockies Team .75 2.00
77 Red Wings Team .75 2.00
78 Kings Team .75 2.00
79 North Stars Team .75 2.00
80 Canadiens Team .75 2.00
81 Islanders Team .75 2.00
82 Rangers Team .75 2.00
83 Flyers Team .75 2.00
84 Penguins Team .75 2.00
85 Blues Team .75 2.00
86 Maple Leafs Team .75 2.00
87 Canucks Team .75 2.00
88 Capitals Team .75 2.00
89 Keith Magnuson .20 .50
90 Walt Tkaczuk .30 .75
91 Bill Nyrop .20 .50
92 Michel Plasse .30 .75
93 Bob Bourne .30 .75
94 Lee Fogolin .20 .50
95 Gregg Sheppard .20 .50
96 Hartland Monahan .20 .50
97 Curt Bennett .20 .50
98 Bob Dailey .20 .50
99 Bill Goldsworthy .30 .75
100 Ken Dryden AS1 7.50 15.00
101 Grant Mulvey .20 .50
102 Pierre Larouche .40 1.00
103 Nick Libett .20 .50
104 Rick Smith .20 .50
105 Bryan Trottier 10.00 20.00
106 Pierre Jarry .20 .50
107 Red Berenson .30 .75
108 Jim Schoenfeld .30 .75
109 Gilles Meloche .30 .75
110 Lanny McDonald AS2 1.25 2.50
111 Don Lever .20 .50
112 Greg Polis .20 .50
113 Gary Sargent RC .20 .50
114 Earl Anderson RC .20 .50
115 Bobby Clarke 2.50 5.00
116 Dave Lewis .20 .50
117 Darcy Rota .20 .50
118 Andre Savard .20 .50
119 Denis Herron .30 .75
120 Steve Shutt AS1 1.00 2.00
121 Mel Bridgman .20 .50
122 Buster Harvey .20 .50
123 Roland Eriksson RC .20 .50
124 Dale Tallon .20 .50
125 Gilles Gilbert .30 .75
126 Billy Harris .20 .50
127 Tom Lysiak .30 .75
128 Jerry Korab .20 .50
129 Bob Gainey 1.25 2.50
130 Wilf Paiement .30 .75
131 Tom Bladon .20 .50
132 Ernie Hicke .20 .50
133 J.P. LeBlanc .20 .50
134 Mike Milbury RC 4.00 8.00
135 Pit Martin .20 .50
136 Steve Vickers .20 .50
137 Don Awrey .20 .50
138 Bernie Wolfe .30 .75
139 Doug Jarvis .30 .75
140 Borje Salming AS1 1.50 3.00
141 Bob MacMillan .20 .50
142 Wayne Stephenson .30 .75
143 Dave Forbes .20 .50
144 Jean Potvin .20 .50
145 Guy Charron .20 .50
146 Cliff Koroll .20 .50
147 Danny Grant .30 .75
148 Bill Hogaboam .20 .50
149 Al MacAdam .20 .50
150 Gerry Desjardins .30 .75
151 Yvon Lambert .20 .50
152 Rick Lapointe .20 .50
153 Ed Westfall .30 .75
154 Carol Vadnais .20 .50
155 Johnny Bucyk .40 1.00
156 J.P. Bordeleau .20 .50
157 Ron Stackhouse .20 .50
158 Glen Sharpley RC .20 .50
159 Michel Bergeron .20 .50
160 Rogatien Vachon AS2 .75 1.50
161 Fred Stanfield .20 .50
162 Gerry Hart .20 .50
163 Mario Tremblay .30 .75
164 Andre Dupont .20 .50
165 Don Marcotte .20 .50
166 Wayne Dillon .20 .50
167 Claude Larose .20 .50
168 Eric Vail .20 .50
169 Tom Edur RC .20 .50
170 Tony Esposito 1.50 3.00
171 Andre St.Laurent .20 .50
172 Dan Maloney .20 .50
173 Dennis O'Brien .20 .50
174 Blair Chapman RC .20 .50
175 Dennis Kearns .20 .50
176 Wayne Merrick .20 .50
177 Michel Larocque .30 .75
178 Bob Kelly .20 .50
179 Dave Farrish RC .20 .50
180 Richard Martin AS2 .30 .75
181 Gary Doak .20 .50
182 Jude Drouin .20 .50
183 Barry Dean RC .20 .50
184 Gary Smith .30 .75
185 Reggie Leach .30 .75
186 Ian Turnbull .30 .75
187 Vic Venasky .20 .50
188 Wayne Bianchin RC .20 .50
189 Doug Risebrough .30 .75
190 Brad Park 1.00 2.00
191 Craig Ramsay .20 .50
192 Ken Hodge .30 .75
193 Phil Myre .30 .75
194 Garry Howatt .20 .50
195 Stan Mikita 1.50 3.00
196 Garnet Bailey .20 .50
197 Dennis Hextall .20 .50
198 Nick Beverley .20 .50
199 Larry Patey .20 .50
200 Guy Lafleur AS1 6.00 10.00
201 Don Edwards RC 2.00 4.00
202 Gary Dornhoefer .30 .75
203 Bob Paradise .20 .50
204 Alex Pirus RC .20 .50
205 Peter Mahovlich .30 .75
206 Bert Marshall .20 .50
207 Gilles Gratton .30 .75
208 Alain Daigle .20 .50
209 Chris Oddleifson .20 .50
210 Gilbert Perreault AS2 1.25 2.50
211 Mike Palmateer RC 4.00 8.00
212 Billy Lochead .20 .50
213 Dick Redmond .20 .50
214 Guy Lafleur RB 1.25 2.50
215 Ian Turnbull RB .20 .50
216 Guy Lafleur RB 1.25 2.50
217 Steve Shutt RB .30 .75
218 Guy Lafleur RB 1.25 2.50
219 Lorne Henning .20 .50
220 Terry O'Reilly .30 .75
221 Pat Hickey .20 .50
222 Rene Robert .30 .75
223 Tim Young .20 .50
224 Dunc Wilson .30 .75
225 Dennis Hull .30 .75
226 Rod Seiling .20 .50
227 Bill Barber .40 1.00
228 Dennis Polonich RC .20 .50
229 Billy Smith 1.25 2.50
230 Yvan Cournoyer .40 1.00
231 Don Luce .20 .50
232 Mike McEwen RC .20 .50
233 Don Saleski .20 .50
234 Wayne Cashman .30 .75
235 Phil Russell .20 .50
236 Mike Corrigan .20 .50
237 Guy Chouinard .30 .75
238 Steve Jensen RC .20 .50
239 Jim Rutherford .30 .75
240 Marcel Dionne AS1 2.00 4.00
241 Rejean Houle .20 .50
242 Jocelyn Guevremont .20 .50
243 Jim Harrison .20 .50
244 Don Murdoch RC .20 .50
245 Rick Green RC .40 1.00
246 Rick Middleton 1.00 2.00
247 Joe Watson .20 .50
248 Syl Apps .20 .50
249 Checklist 133-264 4.00 8.00
250 Clark Gillies .30 .75
251 Bobby Orr 15.00 25.00
252 Nelson Pyatt .20 .50
253 Gary McAdam RC .20 .50
254 Jacques Lemaire .40 1.00
255 Bob Girard .20 .50
256 Ron Greschner .30 .75
257 Ross Lonsberry .20 .50
258 Dave Gardner .20 .50
259 Rick Blight .20 .50
260 Gerry Cheevers 1.00 2.00
261 Jean Pronovost .30 .75
262 Cup Semi-Finals .20 .50
263 Cup Semi-Finals .20 .50
264 Canadiens Champs .40 1.00
265 Rick Bowness RC .30 .75
266 George Ferguson .20 .50
267 Mike Kitchen RC .20 .50
268 Bob Berry .20 .50
269 Greg Smith RC .20 .50
270 Stan Jonathan RC 1.00 3.00
271 Dwight Bialowas .20 .50
272 Pete Stemkowski .20 .50
273 Greg Joly .20 .50
274 Ken Houston RC .20 .50
275 Brian Glennie .20 .50
276 Ed Johnston .30 .75
277 John Grisdale .20 .50
278 Craig Patrick .30 .75
279 Ken Breitenbach RC .20 .50
280 Fred Ahern .20 .50
281 Jim Roberts .20 .50
282 Harvey Bennett RC .20 .50
283 Ab DeMarco .20 .50
284 Pat Boutette .20 .50
285 Bob Plager .30 .75
286 Hilliard Graves .20 .50
287 Gordie Lane RC .20 .50
288 Ron Andruff RC .20 .50
289 Larry Brown .20 .50
290 Mike Fidler RC .20 .50
291 Fred Barrett .20 .50
292 Bill Clement .30 .75
293 Errol Thompson .20 .50
294 Doug Grant .30 .75
295 Harold Snepsts 1.00 2.00
296 Rick Bragnalo RC .20 .50
297 Bryan Lefley .20 .50
298 Gene Carr .20 .50
299 Bob Stewart .20 .50
300 Lew Morrison .20 .50
301 Ed Kea .20 .50
302 Scott Garland .20 .50
303 Bill Fairbairn .20 .50
304 Larry Carriere .20 .50
305 Ron Low .30 .75
306 Tom Reid .20 .50
307 Paul Holmgren RC 2.50 5.00
308 Pat Price .20 .50
309 Kirk Bowman RC .20 .50
310 Bobby Simpson RC .20 .50
311 Ron Ellis .30 .75
312 Rick Bourbonnais UER .40 1.00
(Photo actually
Bernie Federko)
313 Bobby Lalonde .20 .50
314 Tony White .20 .50
315 John Van Boxmeer .30 .75
316 Don Kozak .20 .50
317 Jim Neilson .20 .50
318 Terry Martin RC .20 .50
319 Barry Gibbs .20 .50
320 Inge Hammarstrom .20 .50
321 Darryl Edestrand .20 .50
322 Flames Logo .75 2.00
323 Bruins Logo .75 2.00
324 Sabres Logo .75 2.00
325 Blackhawks Logo .75 2.00
326 Barons Logo .75 2.00
327 Rockies Logo .75 2.00
328 Red Wings Logo .75 2.00
329 Kings Logo .75 2.00
330 North Stars Logo .75 2.00
331 Canadiens Logo .75 2.00
332 Islanders Logo .75 2.00
333 Rangers Logo .75 2.00
334 Flyers Logo .75 2.00
335 Penguins Logo .75 2.00
336 Blues Logo .75 2.00
337 Maple Leafs Logo .75 2.00
338 Canucks Logo .75 2.00
339 Capitals Logo .75 2.00
340 Chuck Lefley .20 .50
341 Garry Monahan .20 .50
342 Dryan Watson .20 .50
343 Dave Hudson .20 .50
344 Neil Komadoski .20 .50
345 Gary Edwards .30 .75
346 Rey Comeau .20 .50
347 Bob Neely .20 .50
348 Jean Hamel .20 .50
349 Jerry Butler .20 .50
350 Mike Walton .20 .50
351 Bob Sirois .20 .50
352 Jim McElmury .20 .50
353 Dave Schultz .30 .75
354 Doug Palazzari RC .20 .50
355 David Shand RC .20 .50
356 Stan Weir .20 .50
357 Mike Christie .20 .50
358 Floyd Thomson .20 .50
359 Larry Goodenough .20 .50
360 Bill Riley RC .20 .50
361 Doug Hicks RC .20 .50
362 Dan Newman RC .20 .50
363 Rick Chartraw .20 .50
364 Tim Ecclestone .20 .50
365 Don Ashby RC .20 .50
366 Jacques Richard .20 .50
367 Yves Belanger .20 .50
368 Ron Sedlbauer .20 .50
369 Jack Lynch UER .20 .50
(Photo actually
Bill Collins)
370 Doug Favell .30 .75
371 Bob Murdoch .20 .50
372 Ralph Klassen .20 .50
373 Richard Mulhern .20 .50
374 Jim McKenny .20 .50
375 Mike Bloom .20 .50
376 Bruce Affleck .20 .50
377 Gerry O'Flaherty .20 .50
378 Ron Lalonde .20 .50
379 Chuck Arnason .20 .50
380 Dave Hutchinson .20 .50
381A Checklist ERR 4.00 8.00
(Topps heading)
381B Checklist COR 4.00 8.00
(No Topps heading)
382 John Gould .20 .50
383 Dave(Tiger) Williams 2.00 4.00
384 Len Frig .20 .50
385 Pierre Plante .20 .50
386 Ralph Stewart .20 .50
387 Gord Smith .20 .50
388 Denis Dupere .20 .50
389 Randy Manery .20 .50
390 Lowell MacDonald .20 .50
391 Dennis Owchar .20 .50
392 Jim Roberts RC .20 .50
393 Mike Veisor .30 .75
394 Bob Hess .20 .50
395 Curt Ridley .20 .50
396 Mike Lampman .40 1.00

1977-78 O-Pee-Chee WHA

The 1977-78 O-Pee-Chee WHA set consistedof 66 color standard-size cards. Printed in Canada, the cards were originally sold in 15-cent wax packs containing 12 cards and gum. Bilingual backs featured player statistics and a short biography. Card number 1 featured Gordie Howe's 1000th career goal. There were no key Rookie Cards in this set. This was the final WHA set. The league disbanded following the 1978-79 season with the four surviving teams (Edmonton, New England/Hartford, Quebec and Winnipeg) merging with the NHL.

COMPLETE SET (66) 35.00 70.00
1 Gordie Howe 15.00 30.00
2 Jean Bernier RC .30 .75
3 Anders Hedberg .75 2.00
4 Ken Broderick .60 1.50
5 Joe Noris .30 .75
6 Blaine Stoughton .60 1.50
7 Claude St.Sauveur .30 .75
8 Real Cloutier .60 1.50
9 Joe Daley .60 1.50
10 Ron Chipperfield .30 .75
11 Wayne Rutledge .60 1.50
12 Mark Napier .60 1.50
13 Rich Leduc .30 .75
14 Don McLeod .60 1.50
15 Ulf Nilsson .75 2.00
16 Blair MacDonald .30 .75
17 Mike Rogers .60 1.50
18 Gary Inness .60 1.50
19 Larry Lund .30 .75
20 Marc Tardif .60 1.50
21 Lars-Erik Sjoberg .60 1.50
22 Bryan Campbell .30 .75
23 John Garrett .60 1.50
24 Ron Plumb .30 .75
25 Mark Howe 3.00 6.00
26 Garry Lariviere RC .30 .75
27 Peter Sullivan .30 .75
28 Dave Dryden .60 1.50
29 Reg Thomas .30 .75
30 Andre Lacroix .60 1.50
31 Paul Henderson .60 1.50
32 Paulin Bordeleau .30 .75
33 Juha Widing .60 1.50
34 Mike Antonovich .30 .75
35 Robbie Ftorek .60 1.50
36 Rosaire Paiement .30 .75
37 Terry Ruskowski .60 1.50
38 Richard Brodeur 1.75 3.00
39 Willy Lindstrom RC 1.00 2.50
40 Al Hamilton .30 .75
41 John McKenzie .60 1.50
42 Wayne Wood .60 1.50
43 Claude Larose .30 .75
44 J.C. Tremblay .30 .75
45 Gary Bromley .60 1.50
46 Ken Baird .30 .75
47 Bobby Sheehan .30 .75
48 Don Larway RC .30 .75
49 Al Smith .60 1.50
50 Bobby Hull 10.00 20.00
51 Peter Marrin .30 .75
52 Norm Ferguson .30 .75
53 Dennis Sobchuk .30 .75
54 Norm Dube RC .30 .75
55 Tom Webster .30 .75
56 Jim Park RC .60 1.50
57 Dan Labraaten RC .75 2.00
58 Checklist Card 6.00 10.00
59 Paul Shmyr .30 .75
60 Serge Bernier .60 1.50
61 Frank Mahovlich 2.00 4.00
62 Michel Dion .60 1.50
63 Poul Popiel .30 .75
64 Lyle Moffat .30 .75
65 Marty Howe .60 1.50
66 Don Burgess .75 2.00

1978-79 O-Pee-Chee

The 1978-79 O-Pee-Chee set consisted of 396 standard-size cards. Bilingual backs featured the card number (pictured in a hockey skate), year-by-year player statistics, a short biography and a facsimile autograph. Unlike Topps, All-Star designations did not appear on the front of cards of those players named to the All-Star team. An All-Star subset (325-336) served to recognize these players. Card number 300 honored Bobby Orr's retirement early in the season.

COMPLETE SET (396) 100.00 200.00
1 Mike Bossy HL 6.00 12.00
Goals by Rookie
2 Phil Esposito HL .75 1.50
29th Hat Trick
3 Guy Lafleur HL .75 1.50
Scores against Every Team
4 Darryl Sittler HL .30 .75
Goals In Nine
Straight Games
5 Garry Unger HL .15 .40
803 Consec. Games
6 Gary Edwards .15 .40
7 Rick Blight .10 .25
8 Larry Patey .10 .25
9 Craig Ramsay .10 .25
10 Bryan Trottier 5.00 10.00
11 Don Murdoch .10 .25
12 Phil Russell .10 .25
13 Doug Jarvis .15 .40
14 Gene Carr .10 .25
15 Bernie Parent 1.00 2.00
16 Perry Miller .10 .25
17 Kent-Erik Andersson RC .10 .25
18 Gregg Sheppard .10 .25
19 Dennis Owchar .10 .25
20 Rogatien Vachon .30 .75
21 Dan Maloney .10 .25
22 Guy Charron .10 .25
23 Dick Redmond .10 .25
24 Checklist 1-132 2.50 5.00
25 Anders Hedberg .15 .40
26 Mel Bridgman .10 .25
27 Lee Fogolin .10 .25
28 Gilles Meloche .15 .40
29 Garry Howatt .10 .25
30 Darryl Sittler 1.25 2.50
31 Curt Bennett .10 .25
32 Andre St.Laurent .10 .25
33 Blair Chapman .10 .25
34 Keith Magnuson .10 .25
35 Pierre Larouche .15 .40
36 Michel Plasse .15 .40
37 Gary Sargent .10 .25
38 Mike Walton .10 .25
39 Robert Picard RC .10 .25
40 Terry O'Reilly .15 .40
41 Dave Farrish .10 .25
42 Gary McAdam .10 .25
43 Joe Watson .10 .25
44 Yves Belanger .15 .40
45 Steve Jensen .10 .25
46 Bob Stewart .10 .25
47 Darcy Rota .10 .25
48 Dennis Hextall .10 .25
49 Bert Marshall .10 .25
50 Ken Dryden 6.00 12.00
51 Peter Mahovlich .15 .40
52 Dennis Ververgaert .10 .25
53 Inge Hammarstrom .10 .25
54 Doug Favell .15 .40
55 Steve Vickers .10 .25
56 Syl Apps .10 .25
57 Errol Thompson .10 .25
58 Don Luce .10 .25
59 Mike Milbury .30 .75
60 Yvan Cournoyer .30 .75
61 Kirk Bowman .10 .25
62 Billy Smith .75 1.50
63 Goal Leaders 2.50 5.00
Guy Lafleur
Mike Bossy
Steve Shutt
64 Assist Leaders 1.25 2.50
Bryan Trottier
Guy Lafleur
Darryl Sittler
65 Scoring Leaders 1.25 2.50
Guy Lafleur
Bryan Trottier
Darryl Sittler
66 Penalty Minutes .20 .50
Leaders
Dave Schultz
Dave(Tiger) Williams
Dennis Polonich
67 Power Play Goal 2.00 4.00
Leaders
Mike Bossy
Phil Esposito
Steve Shutt
68 Goals Against 2.00 4.00
Average Leaders
Ken Dryden
Bernie Parent
Gilles Gilbert
69 Game Winning 1.00 2.00
Goal Leaders
Guy Lafleur
Bill Barber
Darryl Sittler
Bob Bourne
70 Shutout Leaders 2.50 5.00
Bernie Parent
Ken Dryden
Don Edwards
Tony Esposito
Mike Palmateer
71 Bob Kelly .10 .25
72 Ron Stackhouse .10 .25
73 Wayne Dillon .10 .25
74 Jim Rutherford .15 .40
75 Stan Mikita 1.25 2.50
76 Bob Gainey .75 1.50
77 Gerry Hart .10 .25
78 Lanny McDonald .75 1.50
79 Brad Park .75 1.50
80 Richard Martin .15 .40
81 Bernie Wolfe .15 .40
82 Bob MacMillan .10 .25
83 Brad Maxwell RC .10 .25
84 Mike Fidler .10 .25
85 Carol Vadnais .10 .25
86 Don Lever .10 .25
87 Phil Myre .15 .40
88 Paul Gardner .10 .25
89 Bob Murray .10 .25
90 Guy Lafleur 4.00 7.00
91 Bob Murdoch .10 .25
92 Ron Ellis .15 .40
93 Jude Drouin .10 .25
94 Jocelyn Guevremont .10 .25
95 Gilles Gilbert .15 .40
96 Bob Sirois .10 .25
97 Tom Lysiak .15 .40
98 Andre Dupont .10 .25
99 Per-Olov Brasar RC .10 .25
100 Phil Esposito 1.50 3.00
101 J.P. Bordeleau .10 .25
102 Pierre Mondou RC .30 .75
103 Wayne Bianchin .10 .25
104 Dennis O'Brien .10 .25
105 Glenn Resch .30 .75
106 Dennis Polonich .10 .25
107 Kris Manery RC .10 .25
108 Bill Hajt .10 .25
109 Jere Gillis RC .10 .25
110 Garry Unger .15 .40
111 Nick Beverley .10 .25
112 Pat Hickey .10 .25
113 Rick Middleton .30 .75
114 Orest Kindrachuk .10 .25
115 Mike Bossy RC 50.00 100.00
116 Pierre Bouchard .10 .25
117 Alain Daigle .10 .25
118 Terry Martin .10 .25
119 Tom Edur .10 .25
120 Marcel Dionne 1.50 3.00
121 Barry Beck RC 1.00 2.00
122 Billy Lochead .10 .25
123 Paul Harrison RC .15 .40
124 Wayne Cashman .15 .40
125 Rick MacLeish .15 .40
126 Bob Bourne .15 .40
127 Ian Turnbull .10 .25
128 Gerry Meehan .10 .25
129 Eric Vail .10 .25
130 Gilbert Perreault .30 .75
131 Bob Dailey .10 .25
132 Dale McCourt RC .15 .40
133 John Wensink RC .30 .75
134 Bill Nyrop .10 .25
135 Ivan Boldirev .10 .25
136 Lucien DeBlois RC .10 .25
137 Brian Spencer .10 .25
138 Tim Young .10 .25
139 Ron Sedlbauer .10 .25
140 Gerry Cheevers .75 1.50
141 Dennis Maruk .15 .40
142 Barry Dean .10 .25
143 Bernie Federko RC 5.00 10.00
144 Stefan Persson RC .10 .25
145 Wilf Paiement .15 .40
146 Dale Tallon .10 .25
147 Yvon Lambert .10 .25
148 Greg Joly .10 .25
149 Dean Talafous .10 .25
150 Don Edwards .15 .40
151 Butch Goring .15 .40
152 Tom Bladon .10 .25
153 Bob Nystrom .10 .25
154 Ron Greschner .15 .40
155 Jean Ratelle .30 .75
156 Russ Anderson RC .10 .25
157 John Marks .10 .25
158 Michel Larocque .15 .40
159 Paul Woods RC .10 .25
160 Mike Palmateer .15 .40
161 Jim Lorentz .10 .25
162 Dave Lewis .10 .25
163 Harvey Bennett .10 .25
164 Rick Smith .10 .25
165 Reggie Leach .15 .40
166 Wayne Thomas .15 .40
167 Dave Forbes .10 .25
168 Doug Wilson RC 5.00 10.00
169 Dan Bouchard .15 .40
170 Steve Shutt .30 .75
171 Mike Kaszycki RC .10 .25
172 Denis Herron .15 .40
173 Rick Bowness .15 .40
174 Rick Hampton .10 .25
175 Glen Sharpley .10 .25
176 Bill Barber .30 .75
177 Ron Duguay RC 2.50 5.00
178 Jim Schoenfeld .15 .40
179 Pierre Plante .10 .25
180 Jacques Lemaire .30 .75
181 Stan Jonathan .10 .25
182 Billy Harris .10 .25
183 Chris Oddleifson .10 .25
184 Jean Pronovost .15 .40
185 Fred Barrett .10 .25
186 Ross Lonsberry .10 .25
187 Mike McEwen .10 .25
188 Rene Robert .15 .40
189 J. Bob Kelly .10 .25
190 Serge Savard .30 .75
191 Dennis Kearns .10 .25
192 Flames Team .40 1.00
193 Bruins Team .40 1.00
194 Sabres Team .40 1.00
195 Blackhawks Team .40 1.00
196 Rockies Team .40 1.00
197 Red Wings Team .40 1.00
198 Kings Team .40 1.00
199 North Stars Team .40 1.00
200 Canadiens Team .40 1.00
201 Islanders Tedm .40 1.00
202 Rangers Team .40 1.00
203 Flyers Team .40 1.00
204 Penguins Team .40 1.00
205 Blues Team .40 1.00
206 Maple Leafs Team .40 1.00
207 Canucks Team .40 1.00
208 Capitals Team .40 1.00
209 Danny Gare .15 .40
210 Larry Robinson 1.25 2.50
211 John Davidson .30 .75
212 Peter McNab .15 .40
213 Rick Kehoe .15 .40
214 Terry Harper .10 .25
215 Bobby Clarke 1.50 3.00
216 Bryan Maxwell UER .10 .25
(Photo actually
Brad Maxwell)
217 Ted Bulley RC .10 .25
218 Red Berenson .15 .40
219 Ron Grahame .15 .40
220 Clark Gillies .15 .40
221 Dave Maloney .10 .25
222 Derek Smith RC .10 .25
223 Wayne Stephenson .15 .40
224 John Van Boxmeer .10 .25
225 Dave Schultz .15 .40
226 Reed Larson RC .30 .75
227 Rejean Houle .10 .25
228 Doug Hicks .10 .25
229 Mike Murphy .10 .25
230 Pete Lopresti .15 .40
231 Jerry Korab .10 .25
232 Ed Westfall .15 .40
233 Greg Malone RC .10 .25
234 Paul Holmgren .15 .40
235 Walt Tkaczuk .15 .40
236 Don Marcotte .10 .25

237 Ron Low .15 .40
238 Rick Chartraw .10 .25
239 Cliff Koroll .10 .25
240 Borje Salming 1.00 2.00
241 Roland Eriksson .10 .25
242 Ric Seiling RC .10 .25
243 Jim Bedard RC .15 .40
244 Peter Lee RC .15 .40
245 Denis Potvin 1.25 2.50
246 Greg Polis .10 .25
247 Jimmy Watson .10 .25
248 Bobby Schmautz .10 .25
249 Doug Risebrough .15 .40
250 Tony Esposito 1.25 2.50
251 Nick Libett .10 .25
252 Ron Zanussi RC .10 .25
253 Andre Savard .10 .25
254 Dave Burrows .10 .25
255 Ulf Nilsson .30 .75
256 Richard Mulhern .10 .25
257 Don Saleski .10 .25
258 Wayne Merrick .10 .25
259 Checklist 133-264 2.50 5.00
260 Guy Lapointe .15 .40
261 Grant Mulvey .10 .25
262 Stanley Cup Semifinals .20 .50
Canadiens Sweep
Maple Leafs
263 Stanley Cup Semifinals .20 .50
Bruins Skate
Past Flyers
264 Stanley Cup Finals .30 .75
Canadiens Win Third
Straight Cup
265 Bob Sauve .15 .40
266 Randy Manery .10 .25
267 Bill Fairbairn .10 .25
268 Garry Monahan .10 .25
269 Colin Campbell .15 .40
270 Dan Newman .10 .25
271 Dwight Foster RC .10 .25
272 Larry Carriere .10 .25
273 Michel Bergeron .10 .25
274 Scott Garland .10 .25
275 Bill McKenzie .15 .40
276 Garnet Bailey .10 .25
277 Ed Kea .10 .25
278 Dave Gardner .10 .25
279 Bruce Affleck .10 .25
280 Bruce Boudreau RC .10 .25
281 Jean Hamel .10 .25
282 Kurt Walker RC .10 .25
283 Denis Dupere .10 .25
284 Gordie Lane .10 .25
285 Bobby Lalonde .10 .25
286 Pit Martin .10 .25
287 Jean Potvin .10 .25
288 Jimmy Jones RC .10 .25
289 Dave Hutchinson .10 .25
290 Pete Stemkowski .10 .25
291 Mike Christie .10 .25
292 Bill Riley .10 .25
293 Rey Comeau .10 .25
294 Jack McIlhargey RC .10 .25
295 Tom Younghans RC .10 .25
296 Mario Faubert RC .10 .25
297 Checklist 265-396 2.50 5.00
298 Rob Palmer RC .10 .25
299 Dave Hudson .10 .25
300 Bobby Orr 25.00 40.00
301 Lorne Stamler RC .10 .25
302 Curt Ridley .10 .25
303 Greg Smith .10 .25
304 Jerry Butler .10 .25
305 Gary Doak .10 .25
306 Danny Grant .15 .40
307 Mark Suzor RC .10 .25
308 Rick Bragnalo .10 .25
309 John Gould .10 .25
310 Sheldon Kannegiesser .10 .25
311 Bobby Sheehan .10 .25
312 Randy Carlyle RC 2.50 5.00
313 Lorne Henning .10 .25
314 Tom Williams .10 .25
315 Ron Andruff .10 .25
316 Bryan Watson .10 .25
317 Willi Plett .10 .25
318 John Grisdale .10 .25
319 Brian Sutter RC 4.00 8.00
320 Trevor Johansen RC .10 .25
321 Vic Venasky .10 .25
322 Rick Lapointe .10 .25
323 Ron Delorme RC .10 .25
324 Yvon Labre .10 .25
325 Bryan Trottier AS UER 2.00 4.00
326 Guy Lafleur AS 1.25 2.50
327 Clark Gillies AS .15 .40
328 Borje Salming AS .15 .40
329 Larry Robinson AS .30 .75
330 Ken Dryden AS 2.50 5.00
331 Darryl Sittler AS .30 .75
332 Terry O'Reilly AS .20 .50
333 Steve Shutt AS .15 .40
334 Denis Potvin AS .30 .75
335 Serge Savard AS .15 .40
336 Don Edwards AS .20 .50
337 Glenn Goldup .10 .25
338 Mike Kitchen .10 .25
339 Bob Girard .10 .25
340 Guy Chouinard .10 .25
341 Randy Holt .10 .25
342 Jim Roberts .10 .25
343 Dave Logan RC .10 .25
344 Walt McKechnie .10 .25
345 Brian Glennie .10 .25
346 Ralph Klassen .10 .25
347 Gord Smith .10 .25
348 Ken Houston .10 .25
349 Bob Manno RC .10 .25
350 Jean-Paul Parise .10 .25
351 Don Ashby .10 .25
352 Fred Stanfield .10 .25
353 Dave Taylor RC ! 18.00 30.00
354 Nelson Pyatt .10 .25
355 Blair Stewart RC .10 .25
356 David Shand .10 .25
357 Hilliard Graves .10 .25
358 Bob Hess .10 .25
359 Dave(Tiger) Williams .75 1.50
360 Larry Wright RC .10 .25
361 Larry Brown .10 .25
362 Gary Croteau .10 .25
363 Rick Green .15 .40
364 Bill Clement .15 .40
365 Gerry O'Flaherty .15 .40
366 John Baby RC .10 .25
367 Nick Fotiu .15 .40
368 Pat Price .10 .25
369 Bert Wilson .10 .25
370 Bryan Lefley .10 .25
371 Ron Lalonde .10 .25
372 Bobby Simpson .10 .25
373 Doug Grant .15 .40
374 Pat Boutette .10 .25
375 Bob Paradise .10 .25
376 Mario Tremblay .15 .40
377 Darryl Edestrand .10 .25
378 Andy Spruce RC .10 .25
379 Jack Brownschidle RC .10 .25
380 Harold Snepsts .30 .75
381 Al MacAdam .10 .25
382 Neil Komadoski .10 .25
383 Don Awrey .10 .25
384 Ron Schock .10 .25
385 Gary Simmons .15 .40
386 Fred Ahern .10 .25
387 Larry Bolonchuk .10 .25
388 Brad Gassoff RC .10 .25
389 Chuck Arnason .10 .25
390 Barry Gibbs .10 .25
391 Jack Valiquette .10 .25
392 Doug Halward .10 .25
393 Hartland Monahan .10 .25
394 Rod Seiling .10 .25
395 George Ferguson .10 .25
396 Al Cameron .30 .75

1979-80 O-Pee-Chee

The 1979-80 O-Pee-Chee set consisted of 396 standard-size cards. Cards 81, 82, 141, 163, and 263 differed from that of the corresponding Topps issue. Wax packs had 14 cards plus a bubble-gum piece. The fronts featured distinctive blue borders (that are prone to chipping), while bilingual backs featured 1978-79 and career stats, a short biography and a cartoon-illustrated fact about the player. Team cards (#244-261) had checklist backs. The Rookie Card of Wayne Gretzky (No. 18) had been illegally reprinted. Most of the reprints were discovered and then destroyed or clearly marked as reprints. However some still exist in the market. The reprint is difficult to distinguish from the real card, hence, collectors and dealers should be careful.

COMPLETE SET (396) 750.00 1400.00
1 Goal Leaders 2.50 5.00
Mike Bossy
Marcel Dionne
Guy Lafleur
2 Assist Leaders 1.50 3.00
Bryan Trottier
Guy Lafleur
Marcel Dionne
Bob MacMillan
3 Scoring Leaders 1.50 3.00
Bryan Trottier
Marcel Dionne
Guy Lafleur
4 Penalty Minute .30 .75
Leaders
Dave(Tiger) Williams
Randy Holt
Dave Schultz
5 Power Play 1.25 3.00
Goal Leaders
Mike Bossy
Marcel Dionne
Paul Gardner
Lanny McDonald
6 Goals Against 2.00 4.00
Average Leaders
Ken Dryden
Glenn Resch
Bernie Parent
7 Game Winning 2.00 4.00
Goals Leaders
Guy Lafleur
Mike Bossy
Bryan Trottier
Jean Pronovost
Ted Bulley
8 Shutout Leaders 2.50 5.00
Ken Dryden
Tony Esposito
Mario Lessard
Mike Palmateer
Bernie Parent
9 Greg Malone .25 .60
10 Rick Middleton .60 1.50
11 Greg Smith .25 .60
12 Rene Robert .40 1.00
13 Doug Risebrough .40 1.00
14 Bob Kelly .25 .60
15 Walt Tkaczuk .40 1.00
16 John Marks .25 .60
17 Willie Huber RC .25 .60
18 Wayne Gretzky RC ! 500.00 800.00
19 Ron Sedlbauer .25 .60
20 Glenn Resch AS2 .60 1.50
21 Blair Chapman .25 .60
22 Ron Zanussi .25 .60
23 Brad Park .60 1.50
24 Yvon Lambert .25 .60
25 Andre Savard .25 .60
26 Jimmy Watson .25 .60
27 Hal Philipoff RC .25 .60
28 Dan Bouchard .40 1.00
29 Bob Sirois .25 .60
30 Ulf Nilsson .40 1.00
31 Mike Murphy .25 .60
32 Stefan Persson .25 .60
33 Garry Unger .40 1.00
34 Rejean Houle .25 .60
35 Barry Beck .40 1.00
36 Tim Young .25 .60
37 Rick Dudley .25 .60
38 Wayne Stephenson .40 1.00
39 Peter McNab .40 1.00
40 Borje Salming AS2 .60 1.50
41 Tom Lysiak .25 .60
42 Don Maloney RC .60 1.50
43 Mike Rogers .40 1.00
44 Dave Lewis .25 .60
45 Peter Lee .25 .60
46 Marty Howe .60 1.50
47 Serge Bernier .25 .60
48 Paul Woods .25 .60
49 Bob Sauve .40 1.00
50 Larry Robinson AS1 1.00 2.50
51 Tom Gorence RC .25 .60
52 Gary Sargent .25 .60
53 Thomas Gradin RC .60 1.50
54 Dean Talafous .25 .60
55 Bob Murray .25 .60
56 Bob Bourne .40 1.00
57 Larry Patey .25 .60
58 Ross Lonsberry .25 .60
59 Rick Smith UER .25 .60
(Born Kinston
should be Kingston)
60 Guy Chouinard .40 1.00
61 Danny Gare .40 1.00
62 Jim Bedard .40 1.00
63 Dale McCourt UER .25 .60
(Pictured in Kings'
sweater but he never
played for the Kings)
64 Steve Payne RC .25 .60
65 Pat Hughes RC .25 .60
66 Mike McEwen .25 .60
67 Reg Kerr RC .25 .60
68 Walt McKechnie .25 .60
69 Michel Plasse .40 1.00
70 Denis Potvin AS1 .75 2.00
71 Dave Dryden .60 1.50
72 Gary McAdam .25 .60
73 Andre St.Laurent .25 .60
74 Jerry Korab .25 .60
75 Rick MacLeish .60 1.50
76 Dennis Kearns .25 .60
77 Jean Pronovost .40 1.00
78 Ron Greschner .40 1.00
79 Wayne Cashman .60 1.50
80 Tony Esposito .75 2.00
81 Jets Emblem 5.00 10.00
82 Oilers Emblem 6.00 12.00
83 Stanley Cup Finals .60 1.50
84 Brian Sutter 1.00 2.50
85 Gerry Cheevers .60 1.50
86 Pat Hickey .25 .60
87 Mike Kaszycki .25 .60
88 Grant Mulvey .25 .60
89 Derek Smith .25 .60
90 Steve Shutt .60 1.50
91 Robert Picard .25 .60
92 Dan Labraaten .25 .60
93 Glen Sharpley .25 .60
94 Denis Herron .40 1.00
95 Reggie Leach .60 1.50
96 John Van Boxmeer .25 .60
97 Dave(Tiger) Williams .60 1.50
98 Butch Goring .40 1.00
99 Don Marcotte .25 .60
100 Bryan Trottier AS1 2.00 4.00
101 Serge Savard AS2 .60 1.50
102 Cliff Koroll .25 .60
103 Gary Smith .40 1.00
104 Al MacAdam .25 .60
105 Don Edwards .40 1.00
106 Errol Thompson .25 .60
107 Andre Lacroix .40 1.00
108 Marc Tardif .40 1.00
109 Rick Kehoe .40 1.00
110 John Davidson .60 1.50
111 Behn Wilson RC .25 .60
112 Doug Jarvis .40 1.00
113 Tom Rowe RC .25 .60
114 Mike Milbury .60 1.50
115 Billy Harris .25 .60
116 Greg Fox RC .25 .60
117 Curt Fraser RC .25 .60
118 Jean-Paul Parise .25 .60
119 Ric Seiling .25 .60
120 Darryl Sittler .60 1.50
121 Rick Lapointe .25 .60
122 Jim Rutherford .40 1.00
123 Mario Tremblay .60 1.50
124 Randy Carlyle .60 1.50
125 Bobby Clarke 1.25 2.50
126 Wayne Thomas .40 1.00
127 Ivan Boldirev .25 .60
128 Ted Bulley .25 .60
129 Dick Redmond .25 .60
130 Clark Gillies AS1 .60 1.50
131 Checklist 1-132 5.00 10.00
132 Vaclav Nedomansky .25 .60
133 Richard Mulhern .25 .60
134 Dave Schultz .60 1.50
135 Guy Lapointe .40 1.00
136 Gilles Meloche .60 1.50
137 Randy Pierce RC .25 .60
138 Cam Connor .25 .60
139 George Ferguson .25 .60
140 Bill Barber .60 1.50
141 Terry Ruskowski UER .40 1.00
142 Wayne Babych RC .40 1.00
143 Phil Russell .25 .60
144 Bobby Schmautz .25 .60
145 Carol Vadnais .25 .60
146 John Tonelli RC 3.00 6.00
147 Peter Marsh RC .25 .60
148 Thommie Bergman .25 .60
149 Richard Martin .60 1.50
150 Ken Dryden AS1 6.00 10.00
151 Kris Manery .25 .60
152 Guy Charron .25 .60
153 Lanny McDonald .60 1.50
154 Ron Stackhouse .25 .60
155 Stan Mikita 1.25 2.50
156 Paul Holmgren .25 .60
157 Perry Miller .25 .60
158 Gary Croteau .25 .60
159 Dave Maloney .25 .60
160 Marcel Dionne AS2 1.50 3.00
161 Mike Bossy RB 2.00 4.00
162 Don Maloney RB .30 .75
163 Whalers Emblem 5.00 10.00
(checklist back)
164 Brad Park RB .30 .75
165 Bryan Trottier RB .60 1.50
166 Al Hill RC .25 .60
167 Gary Bromley UER .40 1.00
168 Don Murdoch .25 .60
169 Wayne Merrick .25 .60
170 Bob Gainey .60 1.50
171 Jim Schoenfeld .60 1.50
172 Gregg Sheppard .25 .60
173 Dan Bolduc RC .25 .60
174 Blake Dunlop .25 .60
175 Gordie Howe 18.00 30.00
176 Richard Brodeur .60 1.50
177 Tom Younghans .25 .60
178 Andre Dupont .25 .60
179 Ed Johnstone RC .25 .60
180 Gilbert Perreault .60 1.50
181 Bob Lorimer RC .25 .60
182 John Wensink .25 .60
183 Lee Fogolin .25 .60
184 Greg Carroll RC .25 .60
185 Bobby Hull 15.00 25.00
186 Harold Snepsts .25 .60
187 Peter Mahovlich .40 1.00
188 Eric Vail .25 .60
189 Phil Myre .40 1.00
190 Wilf Paiement .40 1.00
191 Charlie Simmer RC 3.00 6.00
192 Per-Olov Brasar .25 .60
193 Lorne Henning .25 .60
194 Don Luce .25 .60
195 Steve Vickers .25 .60
196 Bob Miller RC .25 .60
197 Mike Palmateer .40 1.00
198 Nick Libett .25 .60
199 Pat Ribble RC .25 .60
200 Guy Lafleur AS1 3.00 6.00
201 Mel Bridgman .40 1.00
202 Morris Lukowich RC .25 .60
203 Don Lever .25 .60
204 Tom Bladon .25 .60
205 Garry Howatt .25 .60
206 Bobby Smith RC 3.00 6.00
207 Craig Ramsay .40 1.00
208 Ron Duguay .60 1.50
209 Gilles Gilbert .40 1.00
210 Bob MacMillan .25 .60
211 Pierre Mondou .25 .60
212 J.P. Bordeleau .25 .60
213 Reed Larson .40 1.00
214 Dennis Ververgaert .25 .60
215 Bernie Federko 2.50 5.00
216 Mark Howe 1.50 3.00
217 Bob Nystrom .25 .60
218 Orest Kindrachuk .25 .60
219 Mike Fidler .25 .60
220 Phil Esposito .60 1.50
221 Bill Hajt .25 .60
222 Mark Napier .40 1.00
223 Dennis Maruk .40 1.00
224 Dennis Polonich .25 .60
225 Jean Ratelle .60 1.50
226 Bob Dailey .25 .60
227 Alain Daigle .25 .60
228 Ian Turnbull .25 .60
229 Jack Valiquette .25 .60
230 Mike Bossy AS2 10.00 20.00
231 Brad Maxwell .25 .60
232 Dave Taylor 2.50 5.00
233 Pierre Larouche .60 1.50
234 Rod Schutt RC .25 .60
235 Rogatien Vachon .60 1.50
236 Ryan Walter RC .60 1.50
237 Checklist 133-264 UER 5.00 10.00
238 Terry O'Reilly .60 1.50
239 Real Cloutier .40 1.00
240 Anders Hedberg .40 1.00
241 Ken Linseman RC 2.00 4.00
242 Billy Smith .60 1.50
243 Rick Chartraw .25 .60
244 Flames Team 1.00 2.50
245 Bruins Team 1.00 2.50
246 Sabres Team 1.00 2.50
247 Blackhawks Team 1.00 2.50
248 Rockies Team 1.00 2.50
249 Red Wings Team 1.00 2.50
250 Kings Team 1.00 2.50
251 North Stars Team 1.00 2.50
252 Canadiens Team 1.00 2.50
253 Islanders Team 1.00 2.50
254 Rangers Team 1.00 2.50
255 Flyers Team 1.00 2.50
256 Penguins Team 1.00 2.50
257 Blues Team 1.00 2.50
258 Maple Leafs Team 1.00 2.50
259 Canucks Team 1.00 2.50
260 Capitals Team 1.00 2.50
261 Nordiques Team 5.00 10.00
262 Jean Hamel .25 .60
263 Stan Jonathan .25 .60
264 Russ Anderson .25 .60
265 Gordie Roberts RC .25 .60
266 Bill Flett .25 .60
267 Robbie Florek .40 1.00
268 Mike Amodeo .25 .60
269 Vic Venasky .25 .60
270 Bob Manno .25 .60
271 Dan Maloney .25 .60
272 Al Sims .25 .60
273 Greg Polis .25 .60
274 Doug Favell .60 1.50
275 Pierre Plante .25 .60
276 Bob Murdoch .25 .60
277 Lyle Moffat .25 .60
278 Jack Brownschidle .25 .60
279 Dave Keon .60 1.50
280 Darryl Edestrand .25 .60
281 Greg Millen RC 2.00 4.00
282 John Gould .25 .60
283 Rich Leduc .25 .60
284 Ron Delorme .25 .60
285 Gord Smith .25 .60
286 Nick Fotiu .40 1.00
287 Kevin McCarthy RC .25 .60
288 Jimmy Jones .25 .60
289 Pierre Bouchard .25 .60
290 Wayne Bianchin .25 .60
291 Garry Lariviere .25 .60
292 Steve Jensen .25 .60
293 John Garrett .40 1.00
294 Hilliard Graves .25 .60
295 Bill Clement .40 1.00
296 Michel Larocque .60 1.50
297 Bob Stewart .25 .60
298 Doug Patey RC .25 .60
299 Dave Farrish .25 .60
300 Al Smith .40 1.00
301 Billy Lochead .25 .60
302 Dave Hutchinson .25 .60
303 Bill Riley .25 .60
304 Barry Gibbs .25 .60
305 Chris Oddleifson .25 .60
306 J. Bob Kelly UER .25 .60
307 Al Hangsleben RC .25 .60
308 Curt Brackenbury RC .25 .60
309 Rick Green .40 1.00
310 Ken Houston .25 .60
311 Greg Joly .25 .60
312 Bill Lesuk .25 .60
313 Bill Stewart RC .25 .60
314 Rick Ley .25 .60
315 Brett Callighen RC .25 .60
316 Michel Dion .40 1.00
317 Randy Manery .25 .60
318 Barry Dean .25 .60
319 Pat Boutette .25 .60
320 Mark Heaslip .25 .60
321 Dave Inkpen .25 .60
322 Jere Gillis .25 .60
323 Larry Brown .25 .60
324 Alain Cote RC .25 .60
325 Gordie Lane .25 .60
326 Bobby Lalonde .25 .60
327 Ed Staniowski .25 .60
328 Ron Plumb .25 .60
329 Jude Drouin .25 .60
330 Rick Hampton .25 .60
331 Stan Weir .25 .60
332 Blair Stewart .25 .60
333 Mike Polich RC .25 .60
334 Jean Potvin .25 .60
335 Jordy Douglas RC .25 .60
336 Joel Quenneville RC .25 .60
337 Glen Hanlon RC 1.00 2.50
338 Dave Hoyda RC .25 .60
339 Colin Campbell .40 1.00
340 John Smrke .25 .60
341 Brian Glennie .25 .60
342 Don Kozak .25 .60
343 Yvon Labre .25 .60
344 Curt Bennett .25 .60
345 Mike Christie .25 .60
346 Checklist 265-396 5.00 10.00
347 Pat Price .25 .60
348 Ron Low .40 1.00
349 Mike Antonovich .25 .60
350 Roland Eriksson .25 .60
351 Bob Murdoch .25 .60
352 Rob Palmer .25 .60
353 Brad Gassoff .25 .60
354 Bruce Boudreau .25 .60
355 Al Hamilton .25 .60
356 Blaine Stoughton .40 1.00
357 John Baby .25 .60
358 Gary Inness .40 1.00
359 Wayne Dillon .25 .60
360 Darcy Rota .25 .60
361 Brian Engblom RC .40 1.00
362 Bill Hogaboam .25 .60
363 Dave Debol RC .25 .60
364 Pete Lopresti .40 1.00
365 Gerry Hart .25 .60
366 Syl Apps .25 .60
367 Jack McIlhargey .25 .60
368 Willy Lindstrom .25 .60
369 Don Laurence RC .25 .60
370 Chuck Luksa RC .25 .60
371 Dave Semenko RC 2.00 4.00
372 Paul Baxter RC .25 .60
373 Ron Ellis .40 1.00
374 Leif Svensson RC .25 .60
375 Dennis O'Brien .25 .60
376 Glenn Goldup .25 .60
377 Terry Richardson .25 .60
378 Peter Sullivan .25 .60
379 Doug Hicks .25 .60
380 Jamie Hislop RC .25 .60
381 Jocelyn Guevremont .25 .60
382 Willi Plett .40 1.00
383 Larry Goodenough .25 .60
384 Jim Warner RC .25 .60
385 Rey Comeau .25 .60
386 Barry Melrose RC 5.00 10.00
387 Dave Hunter RC .25 .60
388 Wally Weir RC .25 .60
389 Mario Lessard RC .40 1.00
390 Ed Kea .25 .60
391 Bob Stephenson RC .25 .60
392 Dennis Hextall .25 .60
393 Jerry Butler .25 .60
394 David Shand .25 .60
395 Rick Blight .25 .60
396 Lars-Erik Sjoberg 1.00 3.00

1980-81 O-Pee-Chee

Card fronts of this 396-card standard-size set contained the player's name and position (bilingual text) in a hockey puck on the lower right of the front. Unlike the Topps set of this year, the puck was not issued with a black scratch-off covering. The team name was listed to the left of the puck. The cards were originally sold in 10-card 20-cent wax packs. Bilingual backs featured a short list of career milestones, 1979-80 season and career statistics along with short trivia comments. Members of the U.S. Olympic hockey team (USA in checklist below) were honored with the USA hockey emblem on the card front. Beware when purchasing the cards of Ray Bourque and Mark Messier as they have been counterfeited.

COMPLETE SET (396) 200.00 400.00
1 Flyers Streak to 35 RB .50 1.25
Longest in
Sports History
2 Ray Bourque RB 10.00 20.00
65 Pts.& Record for
Rookie Defenseman
3 Wayne Gretzky RB 15.00 30.00
Youngest Ever
50-goal Scorer
4 Charlie Simmer RB .30 .75
Scores 13th Straight
Game& NHL Record
5 Billy Smith RB .30 .75
First Goalie to
Score a Goal
6 Jean Ratelle .40 1.00
7 Dave Maloney .20 .50
8 Phil Myre .40 1.00
9 Ken Morrow OLY RC .60 1.50
10 Guy Lafleur 1.25 3.00
11 Bill Derlago RC .20 .50
12 Doug Wilson .50 1.25
13 Craig Ramsay .20 .50
14 Pat Boutette .20 .50
15 Eric Vail .20 .50
16 Mike Foligno .30 .75
Red Wings Scoring Leaders
(checklist back)
17 Bobby Smith .75 2.00
18 Rick Kehoe .40 1.00
19 Joel Quenneville .20 .50
20 Marcel Dionne .60 1.50
21 Kevin McCarthy .20 .50
22 Jim Craig OLY RC 2.00 5.00
23 Steve Vickers .20 .50
24 Ken Linseman .50 1.25
25 Mike Bossy 3.00 8.00
26 Serge Savard .50 1.25
27 Grant Mulvey .30 .75
Blackhawks Scoring Leaders
(checklist back)
28 Pat Hickey .20 .50
29 Peter Sullivan .20 .50
30 Blaine Stoughton .40 1.00
31 Mike Liut RC 5.00 10.00
32 Blair MacDonald .20 .50
33 Rick Green .20 .50
34 Al MacAdam .20 .50
35 Robbie Ftorek .20 .50
36 Dick Redmond .20 .50
37 Ron Duguay .20 .50
38 Danny Gare .30 .75
Sabres Scoring Leaders
(checklist back)
39 Brian Propp RC 2.00 5.00
40 Bryan Trottier 1.00 2.50
41 Rich Preston .20 .50
42 Pierre Mondou .20 .50
43 Reed Larson .20 .50
44 George Ferguson .20 .50
45 Guy Chouinard .40 1.00
46 Billy Harris .20 .50
47 Gilles Meloche .40 1.00
48 Blair Chapman .20 .50
49 Mike Gartner 3.00 6.00
Capitals Scoring Leaders
(checklist back)
50 Darryl Sittler .50 1.25
51 Richard Martin .40 1.00
52 Ivan Boldirev .20 .50
53 Craig Norwich RC .20 .50
54 Dennis Polonich .20 .50
55 Bobby Clarke .60 1.50
56 Terry O'Reilly .40 1.00
57 Carol Vadnais .20 .50
58 Bob Gainey .50 1.25
59 Blaine Stoughton .30 .75
Whalers Scoring Leaders
(checklist back)
60 Billy Smith .40 1.00
61 Mike O'Connell RC .40 1.00
62 Lanny McDonald .50 1.25
63 Lee Fogolin .20 .50
64 Rocky Saganiuk RC .20 .50
65 Rolf Edberg RC .20 .50
66 Paul Shmyr .20 .50
67 Michel Goulet RC 7.50 15.00
68 Dan Bouchard .40 1.00
69 Mark Johnson OLY RC .40 1.00
70 Reggie Leach .40 1.00
71 Bernie Federko .30 .75
Blues Scoring Leaders
(checklist back)
72 Peter Mahovlich .40 1.00
73 Anders Hedberg .40 1.00
74 Brad Park .40 1.00
75 Clark Gillies .40 1.00
76 Doug Jarvis .20 .50
77 John Garrett .40 1.00
78 Dave Hutchinson .20 .50
79 John Anderson RC .20 .50
80 Gilbert Perreault .50 1.25
81 Marcel Dionne ASI .50 1.25
82 Guy Lafleur AS1 .60 1.50
83 Charlie Simmer AS1 .30 .75
84 Larry Robinson AS1 .30 .75
85 Borje Salming AS1 .30 .75
86 Tony Esposito AS1 .50 1.25
87 Wayne Gretzky AS2 25.00 50.00
88 Danny Gare AS2 .30 .75
89 Steve Shutt AS2 .30 .75
90 Barry Beck AS2 .30 .75
91 Mark Howe AS2 .30 .75
92 Don Edwards AS2 .30 .75
93 Tom McCarthy RC .20 .50
94 Peter McNab/Rick Middleton .30 .75
Bruins Scoring Leaders
(checklist back)
95 Mike Palmateer .40 1.00
96 Jim Schoenfeld .40 1.00
97 Jordy Douglas .20 .50
98 Keith Brown RC .20 .50
99 Dennis Ververgaert .20 .50
100 Phil Esposito .50 1.25
101 Jack Brownschidle .20 .50
102 Bob Nystrom .20 .50
103 Steve Christoff OLY RC .30 .75
104 Rob Palmer .20 .50
105 Dave(Tiger) Williams .40 1.00
106 Kent Nilsson .30 .75
Flames Scoring Leaders
(checklist back)
107 Morris Lukowich .40 1.00
108 Jack Valiquette .20 .50
109 Richie Dunn RC .20 .50
110 Rogatien Vachon .40 1.00
111 Mark Napier .20 .50
112 Gordie Roberts .20 .50
113 Stan Jonathan .20 .50
114 Brett Callighen .20 .50
115 Rick MacLeish .40 1.00
116 Ulf Nilsson .40 1.00
117 Rick Kehoe .30 .75
Penguins Scoring Leaders
(checklist back)
118 Dan Maloney .20 .50
119 Terry Ruskowski .20 .50
120 Denis Potvin .60 1.50
121 Wayne Stephenson .40 1.00
122 Rich Leduc .20 .50
123 Checklist 1-132 3.00 6.00
124 Don Lever .20 .50
125 Jim Rutherford .40 1.00
126 Ray Allison RC .20 .50
127 Mike Ramsey OLY RC 1.25 3.00
128 Stan Smyl .30 .75
Canucks Scoring Leaders
(checklist back)
129 Al Secord RC 1.50 4.00
130 Denis Herron .40 1.00
131 Bob Dailey .20 .50
132 Dean Talafous .20 .50
133 Ian Turnbull .20 .60
134 Ron Sedlbauer .20 .50
135 Tom Bladon .20 .50
136 Bernie Federko 1.00 2.50
137 Dave Taylor 1.25 3.00
138 Bob Lorimer .20 .50
139 Al MacAdam/Steve Payne .30 .75
North Stars Scoring Leaders
(checkist back)
140 Ray Bourque RC 40.00 100.00
141 Glen Hanlon .40 1.00
142 Willy Lindstrom .20 .50
143 Mike Rogers .20 .50
144 Tony McKegney RC .20 .50
145 Behn Wilson .20 .50
146 Lucien DeBlois .20 .50
147 Dave Burrows .20 .50
148 Paul Woods .20 .50
149 Phil Esposito .50 1.25
Rangers Scoring Leaders
(checklist back)
150 Tony Esposito .60 1.50
151 Pierre Larouche .40 1.00
152 Brad Maxwell .20 .50
153 Stan Weir .20 .50
154 Ryan Walter .20 .50
155 Dale Hoganson .20 .50
156 Anders Kallur RC .20 .50
157 Paul Reinhart RC .50 1.25
158 Greg Millen .40 1.00
159 Ric Seiling .20 .50
160 Mark Howe .60 1.50
161 Goals Leaders .30 .75
Danny Gare (1)
Charlie Simmer (1)
B. Stoughton (1)
162 Assists Leaders 10.00 25.00
Wayne Gretzky (1)
Marcel Dionne (2)
Guy Lafleur (3)
163 Scoring Leaders 10.00 25.00
Marcel Dionne (1)
Wayne Gretzky (1)
Guy Lafleur (3)
164 Penalty Minutes .30 .75
Leaders
Jimmy Mann (1)
Dave(Tiger) Williams (2)
Paul Holmgren (3)
165 Power Play Goals .50 1.25
Leaders
Charlie Simmer (1)
Marcel Dionne (2)
Danny Gare (2)
Steve Shutt (2)
Darryl Sittler (2)
166 Goals Against Avg. .30 .75
Leaders
Bob Sauve (1)

Denis Herron (2)
Don Edwards (3)
167 Game-Winning Goals .30 .75
Leaders
Danny Gare (1)
Peter McNab (2)
Blaine Stoughton (2)
168 Shutout Leaders .60 1.50
Tony Esposito (1)
Gerry Cheevers (2)
Bob Sauve (2)
Rogatien Vachon (2)
169 Perry Turnbull RC .20 .50
170 Barry Beck .40 1.00
171 Charlie Simmer .30 .75
Kings Scoring Leaders
(checklist back)
172 Paul Holmgren .40 1.00
173 Willie Huber .20 .50
174 Tim Young .20 .50
175 Gilles Gilbert .40 1.00
176 Dave Christian OLY RC 1.25 3.00
177 Lars Lindgren RC .20 .50
178 Real Cloutier .20 .50
179 Laurie Boschman RC .20 .50
180 Steve Shutt .20 .50
181 Bob Murray .20 .50
182 Wayne Gretzky 10.00 20.00
Oilers Scoring Leaders
(checklist back)
183 John Van Boxmeer .20 .50
184 Nick Fotiu .40 1.00
185 Mike McEwen .20 .50
186 Greg Malone .20 .50
187 Mike Foligno RC 1.50 4.00
188 Dave Langevin RC .20 .50
189 Mel Bridgman .20 .50
190 John Davidson .40 1.00
191 Mike Milbury .40 1.00
192 Ron Zanussi .20 .50
193 Darryl Sittler .40 1.00
Maple Leafs Scoring Leaders
(checklist back)
194 John Marks .20 .50
195 Mike Gartner RC 20.00 40.00
196 Dave Lewis .20 .50
197 Kent Nilsson RC 2.00 5.00
198 Rick Ley .20 .50
199 Derek Smith .20 .50
200 Bill Barber .40 1.00
201 Guy Lapointe .40 1.00
202 Vaclav Nedomansky .20 .50
203 Don Murdoch .20 .50
204 Mike Bossy .60 1.50
Islanders Scoring Leaders
(checklist back)
205 Pierre Hamel RC .40 1.00
206 Mike Eaves RC .20 .50
207 Doug Halward .20 .50
208 Stan Smyl RC .50 1.25
209 Mike Zuke RC .20 .50
210 Borje Salming .40 1.00
211 Walt Tkaczuk .40 1.00
212 Grant Mulvey .20 .50
213 Rob Ramage RC 1.25 3.00
214 Tom Rowe .20 .50
215 Don Edwards .20 .50
216 Guy Lafleur .50 1.25
Pierre Larouche
Canadiens Scoring Leaders
(checklist back)
217 Dan Labraaten .20 .50
218 Glen Sharpley .20 .50
219 Stefan Persson .20 .50
220 Peter McNab .20 .50
221 Doug Hicks .20 .50
222 Bengt Gustafsson RC .20 .50
223 Michel Dion .40 1.00
224 Jimmy Watson .20 .50
225 Wilf Paiement .20 .50
226 Phil Russell .20 .50
227 Morris Lukowich .40 1.00
Jets Scoring Leaders
(checklist back)
228 Ron Stackhouse .20 .50
229 Ted Bulley .20 .50
230 Larry Robinson .50 1.25
231 Don Maloney .20 .50
232 Rob McClanahan OLY RC .30 .75
233 Al Sims .20 .50
234 Errol Thompson .20 .50
235 Glenn Resch .40 1.00
236 Bob Miller .20 .50
237 Gary Sargent .20 .50
238 Real Cloutier .30 .75
Nordiques Scoring Leaders
(checklist back)
239 Rene Robert .50 1.25
240 Charlie Simmer .75 2.00
241 Thomas Gradin .20 .50
242 Rick Vaive RC 1.25 3.00
243 Ron Wilson RC .20 .50
244 Brian Sutter .50 1.25
245 Dale McCourt .20 .50
246 Yvon Lambert .20 .50
247 Tom Lysiak .20 .50
248 Ron Greschner .20 .50
249 Reggie Leach .30 .75
Flyers Scoring Leaders
(checklist back)
250 Wayne Gretzky 40.00 100.00
251 Rick Middleton .40 1.00
252 Al Smith .40 1.00
253 Fred Barrett .20 .50
254 Butch Goring .40 1.00
255 Robert Picard .20 .50
256 Marc Tardif .20 .50
257 Checklist 133-264 3.00 6.00
258 Barry Long .20 .50
259 Rene Robert .30 .75
Rockies Scoring Leaders
(checklist back)
260 Danny Gare .40 1.00
261 Rejean Houle .20 .50
262 Stanley Cup Semifinals .30 .75
Islanders-Sabres
263 Stanley Cup Semifinals .30 .75
Flyers-North Stars
264 Stanley Cup Finals .50 1.25
Islanders win 1st
265 Bobby Lalonde .20 .50
266 Bob Sauve .40 1.00
267 Bob MacMillan .20 .50
268 Greg Fox .20 .50
269 Hardy Astrom RC .40 1.00
270 Greg Joly .20 .50
271 Dave Lumley RC .20 .50
272 Dave Keon .50 1.25
273 Garry Unger .40 1.00
274 Steve Payne .20 .50
275 Doug Risebrough UER .20 .50
(Photo actually
Serge Savard)
276 Bob Bourne .20 .50
277 Ed Johnstone .20 .50
278 Peter Lee .20 .50
279 Pete Peeters RC 3.00 6.00
280 Ron Chipperfield .20 .50
281 Wayne Babych .40 1.00
282 David Shand .20 .50
283 Jere Gillis .20 .50
284 Dennis Maruk .40 1.00
285 Jude Drouin .20 .50
286 Mike Murphy .20 .50
287 Curt Fraser .20 .50
288 Gary McAdam .20 .50
289 Mark Messier UER RC ! 50.00 100.00
290 Vic Venasky .20 .50
291 Per-Olov Brasar .20 .50
292 Orest Kindrachuk .20 .50
293 Dave Hunter .20 .50
294 Steve Jensen .20 .50
295 Chris Oddleifson .20 .50
296 Larry Playfair RC .40 1.00
297 Mario Tremblay .20 .50
298 Gilles Lupien RC .20 .50
299 Pat Price .20 .50
300 Jerry Korab .20 .50
301 Darcy Rota .20 .50
302 Don Luce .20 .50
303 Ken Houston .20 .50
304 Brian Engblom .20 .50
305 John Tonelli .75 2.00
306 Doug Sulliman RC .20 .50
307 Rod Schutt .20 .50
308 Norm Barnes RC .20 .50
309 Serge Bernier .20 .50
310 Larry Patey .20 .50
311 Dave Farrish .20 .50
312 Harold Snepsts .40 1.00
313 Bob Sirois .20 .50
314 Peter Marsh .20 .50
315 Risto Siltanen RC .20 .50
316 Andre St.Laurent .20 .50
317 Craig Hartsburg RC 1.25 3.00
318 Wayne Cashman .40 1.00
319 Lindy Ruff RC .40 1.00
320 Willi Plett .40 1.00
321 Ron Delorme .20 .50
322 Gaston Gingras RC .20 .50
323 Gordie Lane .20 .50
324 Doug Soetaert RC .20 .50
325 Gregg Sheppard .20 .50
326 Mike Busniuk RC .20 .50
327 Jamie Hislop .20 .50
328 Ed Staniowski .20 .50
329 Ron Ellis .40 1.00
330 Gary Bromley UER .40 1.00
(Photo actually
Curt Ridley)
331 Mark Lofthouse RC .20 .50
332 Dave Hoyda .20 .50
333 Ron Low .20 .50
334 Barry Gibbs .20 .50
335 Gary Edwards .60 1.50
336 Don Marcotte .20 .50
337 Bill Hajt .20 .50
338 Brad Marsh RC 1.50 4.00
339 J.P. Bordeleau .20 .50
340 Randy Pierce .20 .50
341 Eddie Mio RC .40 1.00
342 Randy Manery .20 .50
343 Tom Younghans .20 .50
344 Rod Langway RC 3.00 6.00
345 Wayne Merrick .20 .50
346 Steve Baker RC .40 1.00
347 Pat Hughes .20 .50
348 Al Hill .20 .50
349 Gerry Hart .20 .50
350 Richard Mulhern .20 .50
351 Jerry Butler .20 .50
352 Guy Charron .20 .50
353 Jimmy Mann RC .40 1.00
354 Brad McCrimmon RC .75 2.00
355 Rick Dudley .20 .50
356 Pekka Rautakallio .20 .50
357 Tim Trimper RC .20 .50
358 Mike Christie .20 .50
359 John Ogrodnick RC 1.25 3.00
360 Dave Semenko .40 1.00
361 Mike Veisor .40 1.00
362 Syl Apps .20 .50
363 Mike Polich .20 .50
364 Rick Chartraw .20 .50
365 Steve Tambellini RC .20 .50
366 Ed Hospodar RC .20 .50
367 Randy Carlyle .40 1.00
368 Tom Gorence .20 .50
369 Pierre Plante .20 .50
370 Blake Dunlop .20 .50
371 Mike Kaszycki .20 .50
372 Rick Blight .20 .50
373 Pierre Bouchard .20 .50
374 Gary Doak .20 .50
375 Andre Savard .20 .50
376 Bill Clement .40 1.00
377 Reg Kerr .20 .50
378 Walt McKechnie .20 .50
379 George Lyle RC .20 .50
380 Colin Campbell .20 .50
381 Dave Debol .20 .50
382 Glenn Goldup .20 .50
383 Kent-Erik Andersson .20 .50
384 Tony Currie RC .20 .50
385 Richard Sevigny RC .60 1.50
386 Gary Howatt .20 .50
387 Cam Connor .20 .50
388 Ross Lonsberry .20 .50
389 Frank Bathe RC .20 .50
390 John Wensink .20 .50
391 Paul Harrison .40 1.00
392 Dennis Kearns .20 .50
393 Pat Ribble .20 .50
394 Markus Mattsson RC .40 1.00
395 Chuck Lefley .20 .50
396 Checklist 265-396 4.00 8.00

1980-81 O-Pee-Chee Super

These large (approximately 5" by 7") full-color photos were numbered on the back. They were made of thicker cardboard stock. They were a separate issue rather than an insert. Player information on the card back was sparse.

COMPLETE SET (24) 20.00 40.00
1 Brad Park .75 2.00
2 Gilbert Perreault .60 1.50
3 Kent Nilsson .30 .75
4 Tony Esposito .75 2.00
5 Lanny McDonald .60 1.50
6 Pete Mahovlich .30 .75
7 Wayne Gretzky 10.00 20.00
8 Marcel Dionne 1.00 2.50
9 Bob Gainey .60 1.50
10 Guy Lafleur 1.50 4.00
11 Larry Robinson .75 2.00
12 Mike Bossy 3.00 6.00
13 Denis Potvin .60 1.50
14 Phil Esposito 1.25 3.00
15 Anders Hedberg .25 .60
16 Bobby Clarke 1.00 2.50
17 Marc Tardif .20 .50
18 Bernie Federko .30 .75
19 Borje Salming .40 1.00
20 Darryl Sittler .75 2.00
21 Ian Turnbull .20 .50
22 Glen Hanlon .25 .60
23 Mike Palmateer .40 1.00
24 Morris Lukowich .20 .50

1981-82 O-Pee-Chee

The 396 standard-size cards in this set featured the player's name, position and team logo along the front bottom border. The team name appeared in bold letters across the lower portion of the photo. Bilingual backs featured yearly and career statistics and biographical data. Super Action (SA) cards were designated in the list below. The set was essentially numbered in team order with the team leader (TL) card typically portrayed the team's leading scorer. However, team names were updated to reflect off-season trades. Beware when purchasing the Rookie Card of Paul Coffey as it has been counterfeited.

COMPLETE SET (396) 200.00 400.00
1 Ray Bourque 30.00 50.00
2 Rick Middleton .25 .60
3 Dwight Foster .15 .40
4 Steve Kasper RC .60 1.50
5 Peter McNab .15 .40
6 Mike O'Connell .25 .60
7 Terry O'Reilly .25 .60
8 Brad Park .25 .60
9 Dick Redmond .15 .40
10 Rogatien Vachon .25 .60
11 Wayne Cashman .25 .60
12 Mike Gillis RC .15 .40
13 Stan Jonathan .15 .40
14 Don Marcotte .15 .40
15 Brad McCrimmon .25 .60
16 Mike Milbury .25 .60
17 Ray Bourque SA 5.00 10.00
18 Rick Middleton SA .25 .60
19 Rick Middleton .15 .40
Bruins Leaders
20 Danny Gare .25 .60
21 Don Edwards .15 .40
22 Tony McKegney .15 .40
23 Bob Sauve .25 .60
24 Andre Savard .15 .40
25 Derek Smith .15 .40
26 John Van Boxmeer .15 .40
27 Danny Gare SA .25 .60
28 Danny Gare .15 .40
Sabres Leaders
29 Richie Dunn .15 .40
30 Gilbert Perreault .30 .75
31 Craig Ramsay .15 .40
32 Ric Seiling .15 .40
33 Guy Chouinard .25 .60
34 Kent Nilsson .25 .60
35 Willi Plett .15 .40
36 Paul Reinhart .15 .40
37 Pat Riggin RC .25 .60
38 Eric Vail .15 .40
39 Bill Clement .25 .60
40 Jamie Hislop .15 .40
41 Randy Holt .15 .40
42 Dan Labraaten .15 .40
43 Kevin Lavallee RC .15 .40
44 Rejean Lemelin RC 2.50 5.00
45 Don Lever .15 .40
46 Bob MacMillan .15 .40
47 Brad Marsh .30 .75
48 Bob Murdoch .15 .40
49 Jim Peplinski RC .75 2.00
50 Pekka Rautakallio .15 .40
51 Phil Russell .15 .40
52 Kent Nilsson SA .25 .60
53 Kent Nilsson .15 .40
Flames Leaders
54 Tony Esposito .30 .75
55 Keith Brown .15 .40
56 Ted Bulley .15 .40
57 Tim Higgins RC .15 .40
58 Reg Kerr .15 .40
59 Tom Lysiak .15 .40
60 Grant Mulvey .15 .40
61 Bob Murray .15 .40
62 Terry Ruskowski .15 .40
63 Denis Savard RC 15.00 30.00
64 Glen Sharpley .15 .40
65 Darryl Sutter RC .60 1.50
66 Doug Wilson .30 .75
67 Tony Esposito SA .25 .60
68 Murray Bannerman RC .25 .60
69 Greg Fox .15 .40
70 John Marks .15 .40
71 Peter Marsh .15 .40
72 Al Secord .30 .75
73 Tom Lysiak .15 .40
Blackhawks Leaders
74 Lucien DeBlois .15 .40
75 Paul Gagne RC .15 .40
76 Merlin Malinowski RC .15 .40
77 Lanny McDonald .25 .60
78 Joel Quenneville .15 .40
79 Rob Ramage .25 .60
80 Glenn Resch .25 .60
81 Steve Tambellini .15 .40
82 Ron Delorme .15 .40
83 Mike Kitchen .15 .40
84 Yvon Vautour RC .15 .40
85 Lanny McDonald .15 .40
Rockies Leaders
86 Dale McCourt .15 .40
87 Mike Foligno .25 .60
88 Gilles Gilbert .25 .60
89 Willie Huber .15 .40
90 Mark Kirton RC .15 .40
91 Jim Korn RC .15 .40
92 Reed Larson .15 .40
93 Gary McAdam .15 .40
94 Vaclav Nedomansky .15 .40
95 John Ogrodnick .15 .40
96 Dale McCourt SA .15 .40
97 Jean Hamel .15 .40
98 Glen Hicks RC .15 .40
99 Larry Lozinski RC .25 .60
100 George Lyle .15 .40
101 Perry Miller .15 .40
102 Brad Maxwell .15 .40
103 Brad Smith RC .15 .40
104 Paul Woods .15 .40
105 Dale McCourt .15 .40
Red Wings Leaders
106 Wayne Gretzky 40.00 80.00
107 Jari Kurri RC 15.00 40.00
108 Glenn Anderson RC ! 7.50 15.00
109 Curt Brackenbury .15 .40
110 Brett Callighen .15 .40
111 Paul Coffey RC ! 30.00 80.00
112 Lee Fogolin .15 .40
113 Matti Hagman RC .15 .40
114 Doug Hicks .15 .40
115 Dave Hunter .15 .40
116 Garry Lariviere .15 .40
117 Kevin Lowe RC 3.00 6.00
118 Mark Messier 8.00 20.00
119 Eddie Mio .25 .60
120 Andy Moog RC 12.50 25.00
121 Dave Semenko .25 .60
122 Risto Siltanen .15 .40
123 Garry Unger .25 .60
124 Stan Weir .15 .40
125 Wayne Gretzky SA 12.50 25.00
126 Wayne Gretzky 5.00 10.00
Oilers Leaders
127 Mike Rogers .15 .40
128 Mark Howe .30 .75
129 Dave Keon .30 .75
130 Warren Miller RC .15 .40
131 Al Sims .15 .40
132 Blaine Stoughton .25 .60
133 Rick MacLeish .25 .60
134 Greg Millen .25 .60
135 Mike Rogers SA .15 .40
136 Mike Fidler .15 .40
137 John Garrett .15 .40
138 Don Nachbaur RC .15 .40
139 Tom Rowe .15 .40
140 Mike Rogers .15 .40
Whalers Leaders
141 Marcel Dionne .30 .75
142 Charlie Simmer .30 .75
143 Dave Taylor .60 1.50
144 Billy Harris .15 .40
145 Jerry Korab .15 .40
146 Mario Lessard .25 .60
147 Don Luce .15 .40
148 Larry Murphy RC 6.00 15.00
149 Mike Murphy .15 .40
150 Marcel Dionne SA .30 .75
151 Charlie Simmer SA .25 .60
152 Dave Taylor SA .25 .60
153 Jim Fox RC .15 .40
154 Steve Jensen .15 .40
155 Greg Terrion RC .15 .40
156 Marcel Dionne .25 .60
Kings Leaders
157 Bobby Smith .25 .60
158 Kent-Erik Andersson .15 .40
159 Don Beaupre RC 2.50 5.00
160 Steve Christoff .15 .40
161 Dino Ciccarelli RC 10.00 20.00
162 Craig Hartsburg .15 .40
163 Al MacAdam .15 .40
164 Tom McCarthy .15 .40
165 Gilles Meloche .25 .60
166 Steve Payne .15 .40
167 Gordie Roberts .15 .40
168 Greg Smith .15 .40
169 Tim Young .15 .40
170 Bobby Smith SA .25 .60
171 Mike Eaves .15 .40
172 Mike Polich .15 .40
173 Tom Younghans .15 .40
174 Bobby Smith .15 .40
North Stars Leaders
175 Brian Engblom .15 .40
176 Bob Gainey .30 .75
177 Guy Lafleur 1.00 2.50
178 Mark Napier .15 .40
179 Larry Robinson .30 .75
180 Steve Shutt .15 .40
181 Keith Acton RC .30 .75
182 Gaston Gingras .15 .40
183 Rejean Houle .15 .40
184 Doug Jarvis .15 .40
185 Yvon Lambert .15 .40
186 Rod Langway .60 1.50
187 Pierre Larouche .25 .60
188 Pierre Mondou .15 .40
189 Robert Picard .15 .40
190 Doug Risebrough .15 .40
191 Richard Sevigny .25 .60
192 Mario Tremblay .15 .40
193 Doug Wickenheiser RC .40 1.00
194 Bob Gainey SA .25 .60
195 Guy Lafleur SA .30 .75
196 Larry Robinson SA .15 .40
197 Steve Shutt .15 .40
Canadiens Leaders
198 Mike Bossy 1.50 4.00
199 Denis Potvin .40 1.00
200 Bryan Trottier .60 1.50
201 Bob Bourne .15 .40
202 Clark Gillies .25 .60
203 Butch Goring .25 .60
204 Anders Kallur .15 .40
205 Ken Morrow .25 .60
206 Stefan Persson .15 .40
207 Billy Smith .25 .60
208 Mike Bossy SA .60 1.50
209 Denis Potvin SA .25 .60
210 Bryan Trottier SA .30 .75
211 Duane Sutter RC .40 1.00
212 Gordie Lane .15 .40
213 Dave Langevin RC .15 .40
214 Bob Lorimer .15 .40
215 Mike McEwen .15 .40
216 Wayne Merrick .15 .40
217 Bob Nystrom .15 .40
218 John Tonelli .30 .75
219 Mike Bossy .30 .75
Islanders Leaders
220 Barry Beck .25 .60
221 Mike Allison RC .15 .40
222 John Davidson .25 .60
223 Ron Duguay .15 .40
224 Ron Greschner .15 .40
225 Anders Hedberg .25 .60
226 Ed Johnstone .15 .40
227 Dave Maloney .15 .40
228 Don Maloney .15 .40
229 Ulf Nilsson .25 .60
230 Barry Beck SA .25 .60
231 Steve Baker .25 .60
232 Jere Gillis .15 .40
233 Ed Hospodar .15 .40
234 Tom Laidlaw RC .15 .40
235 Dean Talafous .15 .40
236 Carol Vadnais .15 .40
237 Anders Hedberg .15 .40
Rangers Leaders
238 Bill Barber .25 .60
239 Behn Wilson .15 .40
240 Bobby Clarke .30 .75
241 Bob Dailey .15 .40
242 Paul Holmgren .25 .60
243 Reggie Leach .25 .60
244 Ken Linseman .25 .60
245 Pete Peeters .60 1.50
246 Brian Propp .75 2.00
247 Bill Barber SA .25 .60
248 Mel Bridgman .15 .40
249 Mike Busniuk .15 .40
250 Tom Gorence .15 .40
251 Tim Kerr RC 1.50 4.00
252 Rick St.Croix RC .25 .60
253 Bill Barber .15 .40
Flyers Leaders
254 Rick Kehoe .25 .60
255 Pat Boutette .15 .40
256 Randy Carlyle .25 .60
257 Paul Gardner .15 .40
258 Peter Lee .15 .40
259 Rod Schutt .15 .40
260 Rick Kehoe SA .25 .60
261 Mario Faubert .15 .40
262 George Ferguson .15 .40
263 Ross Lonsberry .15 .40
264 Greg Malone .15 .40
265 Pat Price .15 .40
266 Ron Stackhouse .15 .40
267 Rick Kehoe .15 .40
Penguins Leaders
268 Jacques Richard .15 .40
269 Peter Stastny RC 7.50 15.00
270 Dan Bouchard .25 .60
271 Kim Clackson RC .15 .40
272 Alain Cote .15 .40
273 Andre Dupont .15 .40
274 Robbie Ftorek .15 .40
275 Michel Goulet 1.25 3.00
276 Dale Hoganson .15 .40
277 Dale Hunter RC ! 4.00 8.00
278 Pierre Lacroix .15 .40
279 Mario Marois RC .15 .40
280 Dave Pichette RC .15 .40
281 Michel Plasse .25 .60
282 Anton Stastny RC .30 .75
283 Marc Tardif .15 .40
284 Wally Weir .15 .40
285 Jacques Richard SA .15 .40
286 Peter Stastny SA 2.50 5.00
287 Peter Stastny 1.25 3.00
Nordiques Leaders
288 Bernie Federko .60 1.50
289 Mike Liut .60 1.50
290 Wayne Babych .15 .40
291 Blair Chapman .15 .40
292 Tony Currie .15 .40
293 Blake Dunlop .15 .40
294 Ed Kea .15 .40
295 Rick Lapointe .15 .40
296 Jorgen Pettersson RC .15 .40
297 Brian Sutter .25 .60
298 Perry Turnbull .15 .40
299 Mike Zuke .15 .40
300 Bernie Federko SA .25 .60
301 Mike Liut SA .25 .60
302 Jack Brownschidle .15 .40
303 Larry Patey .15 .40
304 Bernie Federko .15 .40
Blues Leaders
305 Bill Derlago .15 .40
306 Wilf Paiement .15 .40
307 Borje Salming .25 .60
308 Darryl Sittler .30 .75
309 Ian Turnbull .15 .40
310 Rick Vaive .25 .60
311 Wilf Paiement SA .15 .40
312 Darryl Sittler SA .25 .60
313 John Anderson .15 .40
314 Laurie Boschman .25 .60
315 Jiri Crha RC .25 .60
316 Vitezslav Duris RC .15 .40
317 Dave Farrish .15 .40
318 Pat Hickey .15 .40
319 Michel Larocque .25 .60
320 Dan Maloney .15 .40
321 Terry Martin .15 .40
322 Rene Robert .25 .60
323 Rocky Saganiuk .15 .40
324 Ron Sedlbauer .15 .40
325 Ron Zanussi .15 .40
326 Wilf Paiement .15 .40
Maple Leafs Leaders
327 Thomas Gradin .25 .60
328 Stan Smyl .25 .60
329 Ivan Boldirev .15 .40
330 Per-Olov Brasar UER .15 .40
(Photo actually
Brent Ashton)
331 Richard Brodeur .25 .60
332 Jerry Butler .15 .40
333 Colin Campbell .15 .40
334 Curt Fraser .15 .40
335 Doug Halward .15 .40
336 Glen Hanlon .25 .60
337 Dennis Kearns .15 .40
338 Rick Lanz RC .15 .40
339 Pat Ribble .15 .40
340 Blair MacDonald .15 .40
341 Kevin McCarthy .15 .40
342 Gerry Minor RC .15 .40
343 Darcy Rota .15 .40
344 Harold Snepsts .15 .40
345 Dave(Tiger) Williams .25 .60
346 Thomas Gradin .15 .40
Canucks Leaders
347 Mike Gartner 6.00 12.00
348 Rick Green .15 .40
349 Bob Kelly .15 .40
350 Dennis Maruk .25 .60
351 Mike Palmateer .25 .60
352 Ryan Walter .15 .40
353 Bengt Gustafsson .15 .40
354 Al Hangsleben .15 .40
355 Jean Pronovost .25 .60
356 Dennis Ververgaert .15 .40
357 Dennis Maruk .15 .40
Capitals Leaders
358 Dave Babych RC .60 1.50
359 Dave Christian .25 .60
360 Dave Christian SA .25 .60
361 Rick Bowness .25 .60
362 Rick Dudley .15 .40
363 Norm Dupont RC .15 .40
364 Dan Geoffrion RC .15 .40
365 Pierre Hamel .25 .60
366 Dave Hoyda UER .15 .40
(Photo actually
Doug Lecuyer)
367 Doug Lecuyer RC .15 .40
368 Willy Lindstrom .15 .40
369 Barry Long .15 .40
370 Morris Lukowich .15 .40
371 Kris Manery .15 .40
372 Jimmy Mann .25 .60
373 Moe Mantha RC .30 .75
374 Markus Mattsson .25 .60
375 Don Spring RC .15 .40
376 Tim Trimper .15 .40
377 Ron Wilson .15 .40
378 Dave Christian .15 .40
Jets Leaders
379 Checklist 1-132 2.50 5.00
380 Checklist 133-264 2.50 5.00
381 Checklist 265-396 2.50 5.00
382 Mike Bossy .30 .75
Goals Leader
383 Wayne Gretzky 5.00 10.00
Assists Leader
384 Wayne Gretzky 5.00 10.00
Scoring Leader
385 Dave(Tiger) Williams .15 .40
Penalty Minutes Leader
386 Mike Bossy .30 .75
Power-play Goals Leader
387 Richard Sevigny .15 .40
Goals Against Ave. Leader
388 Mike Bossy .30 .75
Game Winning Goals Ldr.
389 Don Edward .15 .40
Glenn Resch
Shutout Leaders
390 Mike Bossy RB .30 .75
Eight hat tricks
in one season
391 Marcel Dionne 1.00 2.50
Charlie Simmer
Dave Taylor RB
100 points each
392 Wayne Gretzky RB 5.00 10.00
Season scoring record
393 Larry Murphy RB 1.25 3.00
Highest scoring
rookie defenseman
394 Mike Palmateer RB .15 .40
Seventh assist&
new goalie record
395 Peter Stastny RB 1.25 3.00
Rookie scoring record
396 Bob Manno .30 .75

1981-82 O-Pee-Chee Stickers

Similar in size and format to the baseball and football stickers of recent years, this 269-sticker set featured foil cards of significant events and star players. Stickers measured approximately 1 15/16" by 2 9/16". The backs printed in both English and French contained the card number, the player's name and team, an advertisement for an O-Pee-Chee hockey sticker album, and a 1981 O-Pee-Chee copyright date. The sticker number also appeared within the border at the lower left corner on the front. On the inside back cover of the sticker album the company offered (via direct mail-order) any ten different stickers (but no more than two foil) of your choice for one dollar; this is one reason why the values of the most popular players in these sticker sets are somewhat depressed compared to traditional card set prices.

COMPLETE SET (269) 18.00 45.00
1 The Stanley Cup .08 .25
FOIL
2 The Stanley Cup .08 .25
FOIL
3 The Stanley Cup .08 .25
FOIL
4 The Stanley Cup .08 .25
FOIL
5 The Stanley Cup .08 .25
FOIL
6 The Stanley Cup .08 .25
FOIL
7 Oilers vs. Islanders .08 .25
8 Oilers vs. Islanders .08 .25
9 Oilers vs. Islanders .08 .25
10 Oilers vs. Islanders .08 .25
11 Jari Kurri 1.50 4.00
12 Pat Riggin .08 .25
13 Flames vs. Flyers .01 .05
14 Flames vs. Flyers .01 .05
15 Flames vs. Flyers .01 .05
16 Flames vs. Flyers .01 .05
17 Stanley Cup Winner .01 .05
1980-81
18 Stanley Cup Winner .01 .05
1980-81
19 Conn Smythe Trophy .08 .25
FOIL
20 Butch Goring .01 .05
21 North Stars vs. .01 .05
Islanders
22 Steve Payne .01 .05
23 North Stars vs. .01 .05
Islanders
24 North Stars vs. .01 .05
Islanders
25 North Stars vs. .01 .05
Islanders
26 North Stars vs. .01 .05
Islanders
27 Prince of Wales .08 .25
Trophy FOIL
28 Prince of Wales .08 .25
Trophy FOIL
29 Guy Lafleur .30 .75
30 Bob Gainey .08 .25
31 Larry Robinson .08 .25
32 Steve Shutt .08 .25
33 Brian Engblom .01 .05
34 Doug Jarvis .01 .05
35 Yvon Lambert .01 .05
36 Mark Napier .01 .05
37 Rejean Houle .01 .05
38 Pierre Larouche .08 .25
39 Rod Langway .08 .25
40 Richard Sevigny .08 .25
41 Guy Lafleur .30 .75
42 Larry Robinson .08 .25
43 Bob Gainey .08 .25
44 Steve Shutt .08 .25
45 Rick Middleton .08 .25
46 Peter McNab .01 .05
47 Rogatien Vachon .08 .25
48 Brad Park .08 .25
49 Ray Bourque 1.25 3.00
50 Terry O'Reilly .08 .25
51 Steve Kasper .01 .05
52 Dwight Foster .01 .05
53 Danny Gare .08 .25
54 Andre Savard .01 .05
55 Don Edwards .01 .05
56 Bob Sauve .08 .25
57 Tony McKegney .01 .05
58 John Van Boxmeer .01 .05
59 Derek Smith .01 .05
60 Gilbert Perreault .08 .25
61 Mike Rogers .01 .05
62 Mark Howe .08 .25
63 Blaine Stoughton .08 .25
64 Rick Ley .01 .05
65 Jordy Douglas .01 .05
66 Al Sims .01 .05
67 Norm Barnes .01 .05
68 John Garrett .08 .25
69 Peter Stastny .60 1.50
70 Anton Stastny .08 .25
71 Jacques Richard .01 .05
72 Robbie Ftorek .01 .05
73 Dan Bouchard .08 .25
74 Real Cloutier .01 .05
75 Michel Goulet .30 .75
76 Marc Tardif .01 .05
77 Capitals vs. Maple .01 .05
Leafs
78 Capitals vs. Maple .01 .05
Leafs
79 Capitals vs. Maple .01 .05

Leafs
80 Capitals vs. Maple .01 .05
Leafs
81 Whalers vs. Capitals .01 .05
82 Whalers vs. Capitals .01 .05
83 Canadiens vs. Capitals .01 .05
84 Dan Bouchard .08 .25
85 North Stars vs. .01 .05
Capitals
86 North Stars vs. .01 .05
Capitals
87 Bruins vs. Capitals .01 .05
88 Bobby Smith .08 .25
89 Don Beaupre .08 .25
90 Al MacAdam .01 .05
91 Craig Hartsburg .08 .25
92 Steve Payne .01 .05
93 Gilles Meloche .08 .25
94 Tim Young .01 .05
95 Tom McCarthy .01 .05
96 Wilf Paiement .01 .05
97 Darryl Sittler .08 .25
98 Borje Salming .08 .25
99 Bill Derlago .01 .05
100 Ian Turnbull .01 .05
101 Rick Vaive .08 .25
102 Dan Maloney .01 .05
103 Laurie Boschman .01 .05
104 Pat Hickey .01 .05
105 Michel Larocque .08 .25
106 Jiri Crha .01 .05
107 John Anderson .01 .05
108 Bill Derlago .01 .05
109 Darryl Sittler .08 .25
110 Wilf Paiement .01 .05
111 Borje Salming .08 .25
112 Denis Savard .75 2.00
113 Tony Esposito .08 .25
114 Tom Lysiak .08 .25
115 Keith Brown .01 .05
116 Glen Sharpley .01 .05
117 Terry Ruskowski .01 .05
118 Reg Kerr .01 .05
119 Bob Murray .01 .05
120 Dale McCourt .01 .05
121 John Ogrodnick .08 .25
122 Mike Foligno .08 .25
123 Gilles Gilbert .08 .25
124 Reed Larson .01 .05
125 Vaclav Nedomansky .01 .05
126 Willie Huber .01 .05
127 Jim Korn .01 .05
128 Bernie Federko .08 .25
129 Mike Liut .08 .25
130 Wayne Babych .01 .05
131 Blake Dunlop .01 .05
132 Mike Zuke .01 .05
133 Brian Sutter .08 .25
134 Rick Lapointe .01 .05
135 Jorgen Pettersson .01 .05
136 Dave Christian .08 .25
137 Dave Babych .01 .05
138 Morris Lukowich .01 .05
139 Norm Dupont .01 .05
140 Ron Wilson .01 .05
141 Dan Geoffrion .01 .05
142 Barry Long .01 .05
143 Pierre Hamel .01 .05
144 Charlie Simmer AS .08 .25
FOIL
145 Mark Howe AS FOIL .08 .25
146 Don Beaupre AS FOIL .08 .25
147 Marcel Dionne AS .30 .75
FOIL
148 Larry Robinson AS .30 .75
FOIL
149 Dave Taylor AS FOIL .08 .25
150 Mike Bossy AS FOIL .40 1.00
151 Denis Potvin AS FOIL .30 .75
152 Bryan Trottier AS .30 .75
FOIL
153 Mike Liut AS FOIL .08 .25
154 Rob Ramage AS FOIL .08 .25
155 Bill Barber AS FOIL .08 .25
156 Campbell Bowl FOIL .08 .25
157 Campbell Bowl FOIL .08 .25
158 Mike Bossy .30 .75
159 Denis Potvin .08 .25
160 Bryan Trottier .08 .25
161 Billy Smith .08 .25
162 Anders Kallur .01 .05
163 Bob Bourne .01 .05
164 Clark Gillies .01 .05
165 Ken Morrow .08 .25
166 Anders Hedberg .08 .25
167 Ron Greschner .08 .25
168 Barry Beck .01 .05
169 Ed Johnstone .01 .05
170 Don Maloney .08 .25
171 Ron Duguay .08 .25
172 Ulf Nilsson .01 .05
173 Dave Maloney .01 .05
174 Bill Barber .08 .25
175 Behn Wilson .01 .05
176 Ken Linseman .08 .25
177 Pete Peeters .08 .25
178 Bobby Clarke
179 Paul Holmgren .08 .25
180 Brian Propp
181 Reggie Leach .08 .25
182 Rick Kehoe .01 .05
183 Randy Carlyle .01 .05
184 George Ferguson .01 .05
185 Peter Lee .01 .05
186 Rod Schutt .01 .05
187 Paul Gardner .01 .05
188 Ron Stackhouse .01 .05
189 Mario Faubert .01 .05
190 Mike Gartner .50 1.25
191 Dennis Maruk .01 .05
192 Ryan Walter .08 .25
193 Rick Green .01 .05
194 Mike Palmateer .08 .25
195 Bob Kelly .01 .05
196 Jean Pronovost .01 .05
197 Al Hangsleben .01 .05
198 Flames vs. Capitals .01 .05
199 Oilers vs. Islanders .08 .25
200 Oilers vs. Islanders .08 .25
201 Oilers vs. Islanders .08 .25
202 Oilers vs. Islanders .08 .25
203 Rangers vs. Islanders .01 .05
204 Rangers vs. Islanders .01 .05
205 Flyers vs. Capitals .01 .05
206 Flyers vs. Capitals .01 .05
207 Rangers vs. Capitals .01 .05
208 Canadiens vs. Capitals .01 .05
209 Wayne Gretzky 4.00 10.00
210 Mark Messier 2.00 5.00
211 Jari Kurri 1.25 3.00
212 Brett Callighen .01 .05
213 Matti Hagman .01 .05
214 Risto Siltanen .08 .25
215 Lee Fogolin .01 .05
216 Eddie Mio .01 .05
217 Glenn Anderson .50 1.25
218 Kent Nilsson .08 .25
219 Guy Chouinard .01 .05
220 Eric Vail .01 .05
221 Pat Riggin .08 .25
222 Willi Plett .01 .05
223 Pekka Rautakallio .01 .05
224 Paul Reinhart .01 .05
225 Brad Marsh .08 .25
226 Phil Russell .01 .05
227 Lanny McDonald .08 .25
228 Merlin Malinowski .01 .05
229 Rob Ramage .08 .25
230 Glenn Resch .08 .25
231 Ron Delorme .01 .05
232 Lucien DeBlois .01 .05
233 Paul Gagne .01 .05
234 Joel Quenneville .01 .05
235 Marcel Dionne .08 .25
236 Charlie Simmer .08 .25
237 Dave Taylor .08 .25
238 Mario Lessard .01 .05
239 Larry Murphy .50 1.25
240 Jerry Korab .01 .05
241 Mike Murphy .01 .05
242 Billy Harris .01 .05
243 Thomas Gradin .08 .25
244 Per-Olov Brasar .01 .05
245 Glen Hanlon .08 .25
246 Chris Oddleifson .01 .05
247 Dave(Tiger) Williams .08 .25
248 Kevin McCarthy .01 .05
249 Dennis Kearns .01 .05
250 Harold Snepsts .08 .25
251 Art Ross Trophy FOIL .08 .25
252 Wayne Gretzky 4.00 10.00
253 Mike Bossy .30 .75
254 Norris Trophy FOIL .08 .25
255 Randy Carlyle .01 .05
256 Richard Sevigny .08 .25
257 Vezina Trophy FOIL .08 .25
258 Denis Herron .01 .05
259 Michel Larocque .08 .25
260 Lady Byng Trophy FOIL .08 .25
261 Rick Kehoe .01 .05
262 Calder Trophy FOIL .08 .25
263 Peter Stastny .60 1.50
264 Wayne Gretzky 4.00 10.00
265 Hart Trophy FOIL .08 .25
266 Charlie Simmer .08 .25
267 Marcel Dionne .08 .25
268 Dave Taylor .08 .25
269 Bob Gainey .08 .25
xx Sticker Album 2.00 5.00

1982-83 O-Pee-Chee

Because Topps did not issue a set for a two-year period, this 396-card set marks the first time since the pre-war era that O-Pee-Chee manufactured hockey cards without competition. Card fronts displayed the player's name, team and position at the top. The backs had yearly statistics, highlights and a section devoted to team records. A team logo appeared at the bottom. Highlight cards, team scoring leaders cards, league leaders cards and In-Action cards were contained within the set. The cards were essentially in team order. However, text on front was updated to reflect off-season trades.

COMPLETE SET (396) 60.00 100.00
COMMON CARD (1-396) .07 .20
1 Wayne Gretzky HL 4.00 10.00
2 Mike Bossy HL .30 .75
Record 147 Points
3 Dale Hawerchuk HL 2.00 5.00
4 Mikko Leinonen HL .07 .20
Six Assists One Game
5 Bryan Trottier HL .30 .75
Sets Assist Mark
6 Rick Middleton .15 .40
7 Ray Bourque 6.00 15.00
8 Wayne Cashman .15 .40
9 Bruce Crowder RC .07 .20
10 Keith Crowder RC .07 .20
11 Tom Fergus RC .15 .40
12 Steve Kasper .07 .20
13 Normand Leveille RC .30 .75
14 Don Marcotte .07 .20
15 Rick Middleton .15 .40
16 Peter McNab .07 .20
17 Mike O'Connell .07 .20
18 Terry O'Reilly .15 .40
19 Brad Park .15 .40
20 Barry Pederson RC .40 1.00
21 Brad Palmer RC .07 .20
22 Pete Peeters .30 .75
23 Rogatien Vachon .15 .40
24 Ray Bourque IA 2.00 5.00
25 Gilbert Perreault .15 .40
26 Mike Foligno .15 .40
27 Yvon Lambert .07 .20
28 Dale McCourt .07 .20
29 Tony McKegney .07 .20
30 Gilbert Perreault .30 .75
31 Lindy Ruff .07 .20
32 Mike Ramsey .07 .20
33 J.F. Sauve RC .07 .20
34 Bob Sauve .15 .40
35 Ric Seiling .07 .20
36 John Van Boxmeer .07 .20
37 John Van Boxmeer IA .07 .20
38 Lanny McDonald .15 .40
39 Mel Bridgman .07 .20
40 Mel Bridgman IA .07 .20
41 Guy Chouinard .07 .20
42 Steve Christoff .07 .20
43 Denis Cyr RC .07 .20
44 Bill Clement .15 .40
45 Richie Dunn .07 .20
46 Don Edwards .07 .20
47 Jamie Hislop .07 .20
48 Steve Konroyd RC .07 .20
49 Kevin Lavallee .07 .20
50 Rejean Lemelin .40 1.00
51 Lanny McDonald .15 .40
52 Lanny McDonald IA .15 .40
53 Bob Murdoch .07 .20
54 Kent Nilsson .15 .40
55 Jim Peplinski .07 .20
56 Paul Reinhart .07 .20
57 Doug Risebrough .07 .20
58 Phil Russell .07 .20
59 Howard Walker RC .07 .20
60 Al Secord .15 .40
61 Murray Bannerman .15 .40
62 Keith Brown .07 .20
63 Doug Crossman RC .30 .75
64 Tony Esposito .30 .75
65 Greg Fox .07 .20
66 Tim Higgins .07 .20
67 Reg Kerr .07 .20
68 Tom Lysiak .07 .20
69 Grant Mulvey .07 .20
70 Bob Murray .07 .20
71 Rich Preston .07 .20
72 Terry Ruskowski .07 .20
73 Denis Savard 1.50 4.00
74 Al Secord .15 .40
75 Glen Sharpley .07 .20
76 Darryl Sutter .15 .40
77 Doug Wilson .30 .75
78 Doug Wilson IA .15 .40
79 John Ogrodnick .07 .20
80 John Barrett RC .07 .20
81 Mike Blaisdell RC .07 .20
82 Colin Campbell .07 .20
83 Danny Gare .15 .40
84 Gilles Gilbert .15 .40
85 Willie Huber .07 .20
86 Greg Joly .07 .20
87 Mark Kirton .07 .20
88 Reed Larson .07 .20
89 Reed Larson IA .07 .20
90 Reggie Leach .15 .40
91 Walt McKechnie .07 .20
92 John Ogrodnick .07 .20
93 Mark Osborne RC .15 .40
94 Jim Schoenfeld .15 .40
95 Derek Smith .07 .20
96 Greg Smith .07 .20
97 Eric Vail .07 .20
98 Paul Woods .07 .20
99 Wayne Gretzky TL 2.50 5.00
100 Glenn Anderson 1.25 3.00
101 Paul Coffey 5.00 12.00
102 Paul Coffey IA 2.50 5.00
103 Brett Callighen .07 .20
104 Lee Fogolin .07 .20
105 Grant Fuhr RC 15.00 40.00
106 Wayne Gretzky 20.00 40.00
107 Wayne Gretzky IA 6.00 15.00
108 Matti Hagman .07 .20
109 Pat Hughes .07 .20
110 Dave Hunter .07 .20
111 Jari Kurri 3.00 8.00
112 Ron Low .07 .20
113 Kevin Lowe UER .60 1.50
114 Dave Lumley .07 .20
115 Ken Linseman .15 .40
116 Garry Lariviere .07 .20
117 Mark Messier ! 4.00 10.00
118 Tom Roulston RC .07 .20
119 Dave Semenko .15 .40
120 Garry Unger .15 .40
121 Checklist 1-132 1.00 2.50
122 Blaine Stoughton .15 .40
123 Ron Francis RC 8.00 20.00
124 Chris Kotsopoulos RC .07 .20
125 Pierre Larouche .15 .40
126 Greg Millen .15 .40
127 Warren Miller .07 .20
128 Merlin Malinowski .07 .20
129 Risto Siltanen .07 .20
130 Blaine Stoughton .15 .40
131 Blaine Stoughton IA .15 .40
132 Doug Sulliman .07 .20
133 Blake Wesley RC .07 .20
134 Steve Tambellini .07 .20
135 Brent Ashton RC .20 .50
136 Aaron Broten RC .07 .20
137 Joe Cirella RC .20 .50
138 Dwight Foster .07 .20
139 Paul Gagne .07 .20
140 Garry Howatt .07 .20
141 Don Lever .07 .20
142 Bob Lorimer .07 .20
143 Bob MacMillan .07 .20
144 Rick Meagher RC .20 .50
145 Glenn Resch .15 .40
146 Glenn Resch IA .15 .40
147 Steve Tambellini .07 .20
148 Carol Vadnais .07 .20
149 Marcel Dionne .15 .40
150 Dan Bonar RC .07 .20
151 Steve Bozek RC .20 .50
152 Marcel Dionne .30 .75
153 Marcel Dionne IA .15 .40
154 Jim Fox .07 .20
155 Mark Hardy RC .07 .20
156 Mario Lessard .07 .20
157 Dave Lewis .07 .20
158 Larry Murphy 1.25 3.00
159 Charlie Simmer .30 .75
160 Doug Smith RC .07 .20
161 Dave Taylor .30 .75
162 Dino Ciccarelli .30 .75
163 Don Beaupre .40 1.00
164 Neal Broten RC 4.00 10.00
165 Dino Ciccarelli 1.50 4.00
166 Curt Giles RC .40 1.00
167 Craig Hartsburg .07 .20
168 Brad Maxwell .07 .20
169 Tom McCarthy .07 .20
170 Gilles Meloche .15 .40
171 Al MacAdam .07 .20
172 Steve Payne .07 .20
173 Willi Plett .07 .20
174 Gordie Roberts .07 .20
175 Bobby Smith .15 .40
176 Bobby Smith IA .15 .40
177 Tim Young .07 .20
178 Mark Napier .15 .40
179 Keith Acton .07 .20
180 Keith Acton IA .15 .40
181 Bob Gainey .30 .75
182 Gaston Gingras .07 .20
183 Rick Green .07 .20
184 Rejean Houle .07 .20
185 Mark Hunter RC .15 .40
186 Guy Lafleur .30 .75
187 Guy Lafleur IA .30 .75
188 Pierre Mondou .07 .20
189 Mark Napier .07 .20
190 Robert Picard .07 .20
191 Larry Robinson .15 .40
192 Steve Shutt .07 .20
193 Mario Tremblay .07 .20
194 Ryan Walter .07 .20
195 Rick Wamsley RC .60 1.50
196 Doug Wickenheiser .07 .20
197 Mike Bossy .30 .75
198 Bob Bourne .07 .20
199 Mike Bossy .40 1.00
200 Butch Goring .15 .40
201 Clark Gillies .15 .40
202 Tomas Jonsson RC .15 .40
203 Anders Kallur .07 .20
204 Dave Langevin .07 .20
205 Wayne Merrick .07 .20
206 Ken Morrow .15 .40
207 Mike McEwen .07 .20
208 Bob Nystrom .07 .20
209 Stefan Persson .07 .20
210 Denis Potvin .30 .75
211 Billy Smith .15 .40
212 Duane Sutter .07 .20
213 John Tonelli .30 .75
214 Bryan Trottier .30 .75
215 Bryan Trottier IA .30 .75
216 Brent Sutter RC 1.25 3.00
217 Ron Duguay .07 .20
218 Kent-Erik Andersson .07 .20
219 Barry Beck .07 .20
220 Barry Beck IA .07 .20
221 Ron Duguay .07 .20
222 Nick Fotiu .15 .40
223 Robbie Ftorek .07 .20
224 Ron Greschner .07 .20
225 Anders Hedberg .15 .40
226 Ed Johnstone .07 .20
227 Tom Laidlaw .07 .20
228 Dave Maloney .07 .20
229 Don Maloney .07 .20
230 Eddie Mio .15 .40
231 Mark Pavelich RC .20 .50
232 Mike Rogers .15 .40
233 Reijo Ruotsalainen RC .30 .75
234 Steve Weeks RC .30 .75
235 Wayne Gretzky LL 2.50 5.00
236 Paul Gardner .07 .20
(Power Play Goals Leader)
237 W.Gretzky/M.Goulet LL 2.50 5.00
238 Paul Baxter .07 .20
(Penalty Minutes Leader)
239 Denis Herron .15 .40
(Goals Against Average Leader)
240 Wayne Gretzky LL 2.50 5.00
241 Denis Herron .15 .40
(Shutouts Leader)
242 Wayne Gretzky LL 2.50 5.00
243 Wayne Gretzky LL 2.50 5.00
244 Bill Barber .15 .40
(Flyers Scoring Leaders)
245 Fred Arthur RC .07 .20
246 Bill Barber .15 .40
247 Bill Barber IA .15 .40
248 Bobby Clarke .30 .75
249 Ron Flockhart RC .07 .20
250 Tom Gorence .07 .20
251 Paul Holmgren .15 .40
252 Mark Howe .30 .75
253 Tim Kerr .40 1.00
254 Brad Marsh .07 .20
255 Brad McCrimmon .15 .40
256 Brian Propp .40 1.00
257 Darryl Sittler .30 .75
258 Rick St.Croix .07 .20
259 Jimmy Watson .07 .20
260 Behn Wilson .07 .20
261 Checklist 133-264 1.00 2.50
262 Mike Bullard .07 .20
263 Pat Boutette .07 .20
264 Mike Bullard RC .40 1.00
265 Randy Carlyle .15 .40
266 Randy Carlyle IA .07 .20
267 Michel Dion .15 .40
268 George Ferguson .07 .20
269 Paul Gardner .07 .20
270 Denis Herron .15 .40
271 Rick Kehoe .15 .40
272 Greg Malone .07 .20
273 Rick MacLeish .15 .40
274 Pat Price .07 .20
275 Ron Stackhouse .07 .20
276 Peter Stastny .30 .75
277 Pierre Aubry RC .07 .20
278 Dan Bouchard .15 .40
279 Real Cloutier .07 .20
280 Real Cloutier IA .07 .20
281 Alain Cote .07 .20
282 Andre Dupont .07 .20
283 John Garrett .07 .20
284 Michel Goulet .75 2.00
285 Dale Hunter .75 2.00
286 Pierre Lacroix .07 .20
287 Mario Marois .07 .20
288 Wilf Paiement .07 .20
289 Dave Pichette .07 .20
290 Jacques Richard .07 .20
291 Normand Rochefort RC .07 .20
292 Peter Stastny 1.25 3.00
293 Peter Stastny IA .60 1.50
294 Anton Stastny .15 .40
295 Marian Stastny RC .15 .40
296 Marc Tardif .07 .20
297 Wally Weir .07 .20
298 Brian Sutter .15 .40
299 Wayne Babych .07 .20
300 Jack Brownschidle .07 .20
301 Blake Dunlop .07 .20
302 Bernie Federko .30 .75
303 Bernie Federko IA .15 .40
304 Pat Hickey .07 .20
305 Guy Lapointe .15 .40
306 Mike Liut .30 .75
307 Joe Mullen RC 3.00 8.00
308 Larry Patey .07 .20
309 Jorgen Pettersson .07 .20
310 Rob Ramage .07 .20
311 Brian Sutter .15 .40
312 Perry Turnbull .07 .20
313 Mike Zuke .07 .20
314 Rick Vaive .07 .20
315 John Anderson .07 .20
316 Normand Aubin RC .07 .20
317 Jim Benning RC .07 .20
318 Fred Boimistruck RC .07 .20
319 Bill Derlago .07 .20
320 Bill Derlago IA .07 .20
321 Miroslav Frycer RC .07 .20
322 Billy Harris .07 .20
323 Jim Korn .07 .20
324 Michel Larocque .15 .40
325 Bob Manno .07 .20
326 Dan Maloney .07 .20
327 Bob McGill RC .07 .20
328 Barry Melrose .15 .40
329 Terry Martin .07 .20
330 Rene Robert .15 .40
331 Rocky Saganiuk .07 .20
332 Borje Salming .15 .40
333 Greg Terrion .07 .20
334 Vincent Tremblay RC .07 .20
335 Rick Vaive .07 .20
336 Rick Vaive IA .07 .20
337 Thomas Gradin .07 .20
338 Ivan Boldirev .07 .20
339 Richard Brodeur .15 .40
340 Richard Brodeur IA .15 .40
341 Tony Currie .07 .20
342 Marc Crawford RC .75 2.00
343 Curt Fraser .07 .20
344 Thomas Gradin .07 .20
345 Thomas Gradin IA .07 .20
346 Ivan Hlinka UER RC .07 .20
347 Ron Delorme .07 .20
348 Rick Lanz .07 .20
349 Lars Lindgren .07 .20
350 Blair MacDonald .07 .20
351 Kevin McCarthy .07 .20
352 Gerry Minor .07 .20
353 Lars Molin RC .07 .20
354 Gary Lupul RC .07 .20
355 Darcy Rota .07 .20
356 Stan Smyl .07 .20
357 Harold Snepsts .07 .20
358 Dave(Tiger) Williams .15 .40
359 Dennis Maruk .15 .40
360 Ted Bulley .07 .20
361 Bob Carpenter RC .40 1.00
362 Brian Engblom .07 .20
363 Mike Gartner 2.50 5.00
364 Bengt Gustafsson .07 .20
365 Doug Hicks .07 .20
366 Ken Houston .07 .20
367 Doug Jarvis .07 .20
368 Rod Langway .30 .75
369 Dennis Maruk .15 .40
370 Dennis Maruk IA .15 .40
371 Dave Parro RC .15 .40
372 Pat Riggin .15 .40
373 Chris Valentine RC .07 .20
374 Dale Hawerchuk TL 1.50 4.00
375 Dave Babych .07 .20
376 Dave Babych IA .07 .20
377 Dave Christian .15 .40
378 Norm Dupont .07 .20
379 Lucien DeBlois .07 .20
380 Dale Hawerchuk RC ! 10.00 20.00
381 Dale Hawerchuk IA 2.00 5.00
382 Craig Levie RC .07 .20
383 Morris Lukowich .07 .20
384 Willy Lindstrom .07 .20
385 Bengt Lundholm RC .07 .20
386 Paul MacLean UER RC .30 .75
387 Bryan Maxwell .07 .20
388 Doug Smail RC .20 .50
389 Doug Soetaert .15 .40
390 Serge Savard .30 .75
391 Thomas Steen RC 1.25 3.00
392 Don Spring .07 .20
393 Ed Staniowski .07 .20
394 Tim Trimper .07 .20
395 Tim Watters RC .07 .20
396 Checklist 265-396 1.00 2.50

1982-83 O-Pee-Chee Stickers

This set of 263 stickers was exactly the same as the Topps stickers issued this year except for minor back differences. Foil cards of players and trophies were contained within this set. The stickers in the set were 1 15/16" by 2 9/16". The card numbers appeared at the lower right within the border on the fronts of the cards as well as appearing on the back. The backs of the stickers contained an ad for an O-Pee-Chee hockey sticker album (in both English and French), the player's name and team, a 1982 Topps copyright date, and a statement to the fact that these cards were made in Italy. The checklist and prices below apply to both O-Pee-Chee and Topps stickers for this year. On the inside back cover of the sticker album the company offered (via direct mail-order) any ten different stickers (but no more than two foil) of your choice for one dollar; this is one reason why the values of the most popular players in these sticker sets are somewhat depressed compared to traditional card set prices.

COMPLETE SET (263) 18.00 45.00
1 Mike Bossy .20 .50
2 Conn Smythe Trophy .08 .25
FOIL
3 1981-82 Stanley Cup .01 .05
Winners
4 1981-82 Stanley Cup .01 .05
Winners
5 Stanley Cup Finals .08 .25
6 Stanley Cup Finals .08 .25
7 Richard Brodeur .08 .25
8 Victory/Victoire .01 .05
9 Stanley Cup Finals .08 .25
10 Stanley Cup Finals .08 .25
11 Canucks vs. Chicago .01 .05
12 Canucks vs. Chicago .01 .05
13 Canucks vs. Chicago .01 .05
14 Tom Lysiak .08 .25
15 Peter Stastny .30 .75
16 Islanders vs. Quebec .01 .05
17 Islanders vs. Quebec .01 .05
18 Islanders vs. Quebec .01 .05
19 Peter Stastny .30 .75
20 Marian Stastny .01 .05
21 Marc Tardif .08 .25
22 Wilf Paiement .01 .05
23 Real Cloutier .01 .05
24 Anton Stastny .08 .25
25 Michel Goulet .20 .50
26 Dale Hunter .08 .25
27 Dan Bouchard .08 .25
28 Guy Lafleur .20 .50
29 Guy Lafleur .20 .50
30 Mario Tremblay .08 .25
31 Larry Robinson .08 .25
32 Steve Shutt .08 .25
33 Steve Shutt .08 .25
34 Rod Langway .08 .25
35 Pierre Mondou .01 .05
36 Bob Gainey .08 .25
37 Rick Wamsley .08 .25
38 Mark Napier .08 .25
39 Mark Napier .08 .25
40 Doug Jarvis .08 .25
41 Denis Herron .08 .25
42 Keith Acton .01 .05
43 Keith Acton .01 .05
44 Prince of Wales .08 .25
Trophy FOIL
45 Prince of Wales .08 .25
Trophy FOIL
46 Denis Potvin .08 .25
47 Bryan Trottier .08 .25
48 Bryan Trottier .08 .25
49 John Tonelli .08 .25
50 Mike Bossy .20 .50
51 Mike Bossy .20 .50
52 Duane Sutter .08 .25
53 Bob Bourne .01 .05
54 Clark Gillies .08 .25
55 Clark Gillies .08 .25
56 Brent Sutter .08 .25
57 Anders Kallur .01 .05
58 Ken Morrow .08 .25
59 Bob Nystrom .08 .25
60 Billy Smith .08 .25
61 Billy Smith .08 .25
62 Rick Vaive .08 .25
63 Rick Vaive .08 .25
64 Jim Benning .01 .05
65 Miroslav Frycer .01 .05
66 Terry Martin .01 .05
67 Bill Derlago .01 .05
68 Bill Derlago .01 .05
69 Rocky Saganiuk .01 .05
70 Vincent Tremblay .01 .05
71 Bob Manno .01 .05
72 Dan Maloney .08 .25
73 John Anderson .01 .05
74 John Anderson .01 .05
75 Borje Salming .08 .25
76 Borje Salming .08 .25
77 Michel Larocque .08 .25
78 Rick Middleton .08 .25
79 Rick Middleton .08 .25
80 Keith Crowder .01 .05
81 Steve Kasper .08 .25
82 Brad Park .08 .25
83 Peter McNab .08 .25
84 Peter McNab .08 .25
85 Terry O'Reilly .08 .25
86 Ray Bourque .60 1.50
87 Ray Bourque .60 1.50
88 Tom Fergus .01 .05
89 Mike O'Connell .01 .05
90 Brad McCrimmon .08 .25
91 Don Marcotte .01 .05
92 Barry Pederson .08 .25
93 Barry Pederson .08 .25
94 Mark Messier 1.50 4.00
95 Grant Fuhr .75 2.00
96 Kevin Lowe .20 .50
97 Wayne Gretzky 2.50 6.00
98 Wayne Gretzky 2.50 6.00
99 Glenn Anderson .20 .50
100 Glenn Anderson .20 .50
101 Dave Lumley .01 .05
102 Dave Hunter .01 .05
103 Matti Hagman .01 .05
104 Paul Coffey .75 2.00
105 Paul Coffey .75 2.00
106 Lee Fogolin .01 .05
107 Ron Low .08 .25
108 Jari Kurri .40 1.00
109 Jari Kurri .40 1.00
110 Bill Barber .08 .25
111 Brian Propp .08 .25
112 Ken Linseman .08 .25
113 Ron Flockhart .08 .25
114 Darryl Sittler .08 .25
115 Bobby Clarke .20 .50
116 Paul Holmgren .08 .25
117 Pete Peeters .08 .25
118 Gilbert Perreault .08 .25
119 Dale McCourt .01 .05
120 Mike Foligno .08 .25
121 John Van Boxmeer .01 .05
122 Tony McKegney .08 .25
123 Ric Seiling .01 .05
124 Don Edwards .08 .25
125 Yvon Lambert .01 .05
126 Blaine Stoughton .08 .25
127 Pierre Larouche .08 .25
128 Doug Sulliman .01 .05
129 Ron Francis 1.25 3.00
130 Greg Millen .08 .25
131 Mark Howe .08 .25
132 Chris Kotsopoulos .01 .05
133 Garry Howatt .01 .05
134 Ron Duguay .08 .25
135 Barry Beck .08 .25
136 Mike Rogers .01 .05
137 Don Maloney .08 .25
138 Mark Pavelich .08 .25
139 Ed Johnstone .01 .05
140 Dave Maloney .01 .05
141 Steve Weeks .08 .25
142 Eddie Mio .08 .25
143 Rick Kehoe .08 .25
144 Randy Carlyle .08 .25
145 Paul Gardner .01 .05
146 Michel Dion .08 .25
147 Rick MacLeish .08 .25
148 Pat Boutette .08 .25
149 Mike Bullard .08 .25
150 George Ferguson .01 .05
151 Dennis Maruk .08 .25
152 Ryan Walter .08 .25
153 Mike Gartner .20 .50
154 Bob Carpenter .20 .50
155 Chris Valentine .01 .05
156 Rick Green .08 .25
157 Bengt Gustafsson .01 .05
158 Dave Parro .01 .05
159 Mark Messier AS FOIL 1.50 4.00
160 Paul Coffey AS FOIL 1.25 3.00
161 Grant Fuhr AS FOIL 1.25 3.00
162 Wayne Gretzky AS 4.00 10.00
FOIL
163 Doug Wilson AS FOIL .20 .50
164 Dave Taylor AS FOIL .20 .50
165 Mike Bossy AS FOIL .40 1.00
166 Ray Bourque AS FOIL 1.00 2.50
167 Peter Stastny AS .40 1.00
FOIL
168 Michel Dion AS FOIL .08 .25
169 Larry Robinson AS .20 .50
FOIL
170 Bill Barber AS FOIL .20 .50
171 Denis Savard .20 .50
172 Doug Wilson .08 .25
173 Grant Mulvey .08 .25
174 Tom Lysiak .08 .25
175 Al Secord .08 .25
176 Reg Kerr .01 .05
177 Tim Higgins .01 .05
178 Terry Ruskowski .08 .25
179 John Ogrodnick .08 .25
180 Reed Larson .01 .05
181 Bob Sauve .08 .25
182 Mark Osborne .01 .05
183 Jim Schoenfeld .08 .25
184 Danny Gare .08 .25
185 Willie Huber .01 .05
186 Walt McKechnie .01 .05
187 Paul Woods .08 .25
188 Bobby Smith .08 .25
189 Dino Ciccarelli .30 .75
190 Neal Broten .20 .50
191 Steve Payne .08 .25
192 Craig Hartsburg .08 .25
193 Don Beaupre .08 .25
194 Steve Christoff .08 .25
195 Gilles Meloche .08 .25
196 Mike Liut .08 .25
197 Bernie Federko .08 .25
198 Brian Sutter .08 .25
199 Blake Dunlop .01 .05
200 Joe Mullen .40 1.00
201 Wayne Babych .01 .05
202 Jorgen Pettersson .01 .05
203 Perry Turnbull .01 .05
204 Dale Hawerchuk 1.00 2.50
205 Morris Lukowich .01 .05
206 Dave Christian .08 .25
207 Dave Babych .08 .25
208 Paul MacLean .08 .25
209 Willy Lindstrom .01 .05
210 Ed Staniowski .01 .05
211 Doug Soetaert .08 .25
212 Lucien DeBlois .01 .05
213 Mel Bridgman .08 .25
214 Lanny McDonald .08 .25
215 Guy Chouinard .08 .25
216 Jim Peplinski .08 .25
217 Kent Nilsson .08 .25
218 Pekka Rautakallio .08 .25
219 Paul Reinhart .08 .25
220 Kevin Lavallee .01 .05

221 Ken Houston .01 .05
222 Glenn Resch .08 .25
223 Rob Ramage .08 .25
224 Don Lever .01 .05
225 Bob MacMillan .01 .05
226 Steve Tambellini .01 .05
227 Brent Ashton .01 .05
228 Bob Lorimer .01 .05
229 Merlin Malinowski .01 .05
230 Marcel Dionne .08 .25
231 Dave Taylor .08 .25
232 Larry Murphy .20 .50
233 Steve Bozek .01 .05
234 Greg Terrion .01 .05
235 Jim Fox .01 .05
236 Mario Lessard .08 .25
237 Charlie Simmer .08 .25
238 Campbell Bowl FOIL .08 .25
239 Campbell Bowl FOIL .08 .25
240 Thomas Gradin .08 .25
241 Ivan Boldirev .01 .05
242 Stan Smyl .08 .25
243 Harold Snepsts .08 .25
244 Curt Fraser .01 .05
245 Lars Molin .01 .05
246 Kevin McCarthy .01 .05
247 Richard Brodeur .08 .25
248 Calder Trophy FOIL .08 .25
249 Dale Hawerchuk 1.00 2.50
250 Vezina Trophy FOIL .08 .25
251 Billy Smith .08 .25
252 Denis Herron and .10 .25
Rick Wamsley
253 Steve Kasper .08 .25
254 Doug Wilson .08 .25
255 Norris Trophy FOIL .08 .25
256 Wayne Gretzky 2.50 6.00
257 Wayne Gretzky 2.50 6.00
258 Wayne Gretzky 2.50 6.00
259 Wayne Gretzky 2.50 6.00
260 Hart Trophy FOIL .08 .25
261 Art Ross Trophy FOIL .08 .25
262 Rick Middleton .08 .25
263 Lady Byng Trophy FOIL .08 .25
xx Sticker Album 2.00 5.00

1983-84 O-Pee-Chee

This 396-card standard-size set featured card fronts that contain player name, position, team name and team logo at the top. The player's position appeared within an area that resembles a hockey stick blade with the team logo fronting the blade as if to be a puck. Bilingual backs contained yearly, career statistics and a section devoted to team records. Each team had a Highlight (HL) and scoring leaders (SL) card. However, updated text on front reflected off-season trades. For the second straight year, Topps did not produce a set.

COMPLETE SET (396) 60.00 120.00
1 Mike Bossy SL .30 .75
2 Denis Potvin HL .15 .40
3 Mike Bossy .40 1.00
4 Bob Bourne .07 .20
5 Billy Carroll RC .07 .20
6 Clark Gillies .15 .40
7 Butch Goring .15 .40
8 Mats Hallin RC .07 .20
9 Tomas Jonsson .07 .20
10 Gordie Lane .07 .20
11 Dave Langevin .07 .20
12 Rollie Melanson RC .30 .75
13 Ken Morrow .07 .20
14 Bob Nystrom .07 .20
15 Stefan Persson .07 .20
16 Denis Potvin .30 .75
17 Billy Smith .15 .40
18 Brent Sutter .30 .75
19 Duane Sutter .07 .20
20 John Tonelli .15 .40
21 Bryan Trottier .30 .75
22 Wayne Gretzky SL 2.50 5.00
23 Mark Messier 15.00 30.00
Wayne Gretzky
(Oilers Highlights)
24 Glenn Anderson .60 1.50
25 Paul Coffey 5.00 10.00
26 Lee Fogolin .07 .20
27 Grant Fuhr 3.00 8.00
28 Randy Gregg RC .30 .75
29 Wayne Gretzky 15.00 30.00
30 Charlie Huddy RC .40 1.00
31 Pat Hughes .07 .20
32 Dave Hunter .07 .20
33 Don Jackson RC .07 .20
34 Jari Kurri 3.00 6.00
35 Willy Lindstrom .07 .20
36 Ken Linseman .15 .40
37 Kevin Lowe .30 .75
38 Dave Lumley .07 .20
39 Mark Messier 2.50 6.00
40 Andy Moog 3.00 6.00
41 Jaroslav Pouzar RC .07 .20
42 Tom Roulston .07 .20
43 Rick Middleton SL .15 .40
44 Pete Peeters HL .15 .40
45 Ray Bourque UER 5.00 10.00
(Text on back indicates Ray
won the Calder in 1978-79; he
won it in 1979-80)
46 Bruce Crowder .07 .20
47 Keith Crowder .07 .20
48 Luc Dufour RC .15 .40
49 Tom Fergus .07 .20
50 Steve Kasper .07 .20
51 Gord Kluzak RC .30 .75
52 Mike Krushelnyski RC .15 .40
53 Peter McNab .07 .20
54 Rick Middleton .15 .40
55 Mike Milbury .15 .40
56 Mike O'Connell .07 .20
57 Barry Pederson .07 .20
58 Pete Peeters .15 .40
59 Jim Schoenfeld .15 .40
60 Tony McKegney SL .07 .20
61 Bob Sauve HL .15 .40
62 Real Cloutier .07 .20
63 Mike Foligno .15 .40
64 Bill Hajt .07 .20
65 Phil Housley RC 2.00 5.00
66 Dale McCourt .07 .20
67 Gilbert Perreault .30 .75
68 Brent Peterson RC .07 .20
69 Craig Ramsay .07 .20
70 Mike Ramsey .07 .20
71 Bob Sauve .15 .40
72 Ric Seiling .07 .20
73 John Van Boxmeer .07 .20
74 Lanny McDonald SL .15 .40
75 Lanny McDonald HL .15 .40
76 Ed Beers RC .07 .20
77 Steve Bozek .07 .20
78 Guy Chouinard .07 .20
79 Mike Eaves .07 .20
80 Don Edwards .07 .20
81 Kari Eloranta RC .07 .20
82 Dave Hindmarch RC .07 .20
83 Jamie Hislop .07 .20
84 Jim Jackson RC .07 .20
85 Steve Konroyd .07 .20
86 Rejean Lemelin .30 .75
87 Lanny McDonald .15 .40
88 Greg Meredith RC .07 .20
89 Kent Nilsson .15 .40
90 Jim Peplinski .07 .20
91 Paul Reinhart .07 .20
92 Doug Risebrough .07 .20
93 Steve Tambellini .07 .20
94 Mickey Volcan RC .07 .20
95 Al Secord SL .15 .40
96 Denis Savard HL .15 .40
97 Murray Bannerman .15 .40
98 Keith Brown .07 .20
99 Tony Esposito .30 .75
100 Dave Feamster RC .07 .20
101 Greg Fox .07 .20
102 Curt Fraser .07 .20
103 Bill Gardner RC .07 .20
104 Tim Higgins .07 .20
105 Steve Larmer UER RC 3.00 8.00
106 Steve Ludzik UER RC .75 2.00
107 Tom Lysiak .07 .20
108 Bob Murray .07 .20
109 Rick Paterson RC .07 .20
110 Rick Preston .07 .20
111 Denis Savard 1.00 2.50
112 Al Secord .15 .40
113 Darryl Sutter .07 .20
114 Doug Wilson .30 .75
115 John Ogrodnick SL .07 .20
116 Corrado Micalef HL .07 .20
117 John Barrett .07 .20
118 Ivan Boldirev .07 .20
119 Colin Campbell .07 .20
120 Murray Craven RC .30 .75
121 Ron Duguay .07 .20
122 Dwight Foster .07 .20
123 Danny Gare .15 .40
124 Ed Johnstone .07 .20
125 Reed Larson .07 .20
126 Corrado Micalef RC .07 .20
127 Eddie Mio .15 .40
128 John Ogrodnick .07 .20
129 Brad Park .15 .40
130 Greg Smith .07 .20
131 Ken Solheim RC .07 .20
132 Bob Manno .07 .20
133 Paul Woods .07 .20
134 Checklist 1-132 1.00 2.50
135 Blaine Stoughton SL .15 .40
136 Blaine Stoughton HL .15 .40
137 Richie Dunn .07 .20
138 Ron Francis 3.00 6.00
139 Marty Howe .15 .40
140 Mark Johnson .07 .20
141 Paul Lawless RC .07 .20
142 Merlin Malinowski .07 .20
143 Greg Millen .15 .40
144 Ray Neufeld RC .07 .20
145 Joel Quenneville .07 .20
146 Risto Siltanen .07 .20
147 Blaine Stoughton .15 .40
148 Doug Sulliman .07 .20
149 Bob Sullivan RC .07 .20
150 Marcel Dionne SL .15 .40
151 Marcel Dionne HL .15 .40
152 Marcel Dionne .30 .75
153 Daryl Evans RC .07 .20
154 Jim Fox .07 .20
155 Mark Hardy .07 .20
156 Gary Laskoski RC .07 .20
157 Kevin Lavallee .07 .20
158 Dave Lewis .07 .20
159 Larry Murphy .60 1.50
160 Bernie Nicholls RC 2.50 6.00
161 Terry Ruskowski .07 .20
162 Charlie Simmer .15 .40
163 Dave Taylor .30 .75
164 Dino Ciccarelli SL .15 .40
165 Brian Bellows HL .30 .75
166 Don Beaupre .30 .75
167 Brian Bellows RC 1.50 4.00
168 Neal Broten .30 .75
169 Steve Christoff .07 .20
170 Dino Ciccarelli 1.00 2.50
171 George Ferguson .07 .20
172 Craig Hartsburg .07 .20
173 Al MacAdam .07 .20
174 Dennis Maruk .15 .40
175 Brad Maxwell .07 .20
176 Tom McCarthy .07 .20
177 Gilles Meloche .15 .40
178 Steve Payne .07 .20
179 Willi Plett .07 .20
180 Gordie Roberts .07 .20
181 Bobby Smith .15 .40
182 Mark Napier SL .07 .20
183 Guy Lafleur HL .30 .75
184 Keith Acton .07 .20
185 Guy Carbonneau RC 3.00 6.00
186 Gilbert Delorme RC .07 .20
187 Bob Gainey .30 .75
188 Rick Green .07 .20
189 Guy Lafleur .30 .75
190 Craig Ludwig RC .40 1.00
191 Pierre Mondou .07 .20
192 Mark Napier .07 .20
193 Mats Naslund UER RC 1.25 3.00
194 Chris Nilan RC .60 1.50
195 Larry Robinson .15 .40
196 Bill Root RC .07 .20
197 Richard Sevigny .15 .40
198 Steve Shutt .07 .20
199 Mario Tremblay .07 .20
200 Ryan Walter .07 .20
201 Rick Wamsley .15 .40
202 Doug Wickenheiser .07 .20
203 Wayne Gretzky 2.50 5.00
(Hart Trophy)
204 Wayne Gretzky 2.50 5.00
(Ross Trophy)
205 Mike Bossy .30 .75
(Lady Byng Trophy)
206 Steve Larmer 1.25 3.00
(Calder Trophy)
207 Rod Langway .08 .25
(Norris Trophy)
208 Lanny McDonald .08 .25
(Masterton Trophy)
209 Pete Peeters .08 .25
(Vezina Trophy)
210 Mike Bossy RB .30 .75
Scores 50 goals&
first six seasons
211 Marcel Dionne RB .15 .40
Scores 100 points
in seven seasons
212 Wayne Gretzky RB 2.50 5.00
Scores in 30
consecutive games
213 Pat Hughes RB .07 .20
Two short-handed goals
within 25 seconds
214 Rick Middleton RB .15 .40
19 points in one
playoff series
215 Wayne Gretzky 2.50 5.00
(Goals Leaders)
216 Wayne Gretzky 2.50 5.00
(Assists Leaders)
217 Wayne Gretzky 2.50 5.00
(Scoring Leaders)
218 Brian Propp .07 .20
(Game Winning Goal Leaders)
219 Paul Gardner/Al Secord .07 .20
(Power Play Goal Leaders)
220 Randy Holt .07 .20
(Penalty Minute Leaders)
221 Pete Peeters .15 .40
(Goals Against Average Leaders)
222 Pete Peeters .15 .40
(Shutout Leaders)
223 Steve Tambellini .07 .20
(Devils Scoring Leaders)
224 Don Lever .07 .20
(Devils Highlights)
225 Brent Ashton .07 .20
226 Mel Bridgman .07 .20
227 Aaron Broten .07 .20
228 Murray Brumwell RC .07 .20
229 Garry Howatt .07 .20
230 Jeff Larmer RC .07 .20
231 Don Lever .07 .20
232 Bob Lorimer .07 .20
233 Ron Low .07 .20
234 Bob MacMillan .07 .20
235 Hector Marini RC .07 .20
236 Glenn Resch .15 .40
237 Phil Russell .07 .20
238 Mark Pavelich SL .07 .20
239 Mark Pavelich HL .07 .20
240 Bill Baker RC .15 .40
241 Barry Beck .07 .20
242 Mike Blaisdell .07 .20
243 Nick Fotiu .15 .40
244 Robbie Ftorek .07 .20
245 Anders Hedberg .15 .40
246 Willie Huber .07 .20
247 Tom Laidlaw .07 .20
248 Mikko Leinonen RC .07 .20
249 Dave Maloney .07 .20
250 Don Maloney .15 .40
251 Rob McClanahan .07 .20
252 Mark Osborne .07 .20
253 Mark Pavelich .07 .20
254 Mike Rogers .07 .20
255 Reijo Ruotsalainen .07 .20
256 Checklist 133-264 1.00 2.50
257 Darryl SittlerSL .15 .40
258 Darryl Sittler HL .15 .40
259 Ray Allison .07 .20
260 Bill Barber .07 .20
261 Lindsay Carson RC .07 .20
262 Bobby Clarke .30 .75
263 Doug Crossman .07 .20
264 Ron Flockhart .07 .20
265 Bob Froese RC .30 .75
266 Paul Holmgren .15 .40
267 Mark Howe .30 .75
268 Pelle Lindbergh RC 6.00 15.00
269 Brad Marsh .07 .20
270 Brad McCrimmon .15 .40
271 Brian Propp .30 .75
272 Darryl Sittler .30 .75
273 Mark Taylor RC .07 .20
274 Rick Kehoe SL .15 .40
275 Paul Gardner HL .07 .20
276 Pat Boutette .07 .20
277 Mike Bullard .07 .20
278 Randy Carlyle .07 .20
279 Michel Dion .07 .20
280 Paul Gardner .07 .20
281 Dave Hannan RC .15 .40
282 Rick Kehoe .15 .40
283 Randy Boyd RC .07 .20
284 Greg Malone .07 .20
285 Doug Shedden RC .20 .50
286 Andre St.Laurent .07 .20
287 Michel Goulet SL .30 .75
288 Michel Goulet HL .30 .75
289 Pierre Aubry .07 .20
290 Dan Bouchard .15 .40
291 Alain Cote .07 .20
292 Michel Goulet .30 .75
293 Dale Hunter .30 .75
294 Rick Lapointe .07 .20
295 Mario Marois .07 .20
296 Tony McKegney .07 .20
297 Randy Moller RC .07 .20
298 Wilf Paiement .07 .20
299 Dave Pichette .07 .20
300 Normand Rochefort .07 .20
301 Louis Sleigher RC .07 .20
302 Anton Stastny .15 .40
303 Marian Stastny .15 .40
304 Peter Stastny .60 1.50
305 Marc Tardif .07 .20
306 Wally Weir .07 .20
307 Blake Wesley .07 .20
(Stat line on back has '82-38
instead of '83-84)
308 Brian Sutter SL .15 .40
309 Mike Liut HL .15 .40
310 Wayne Babych .07 .20
311 Jack Brownschidle .07 .20
312 Mike Crombeen RC .07 .20
313 Andre Dore RC .07 .20
314 Blake Dunlop .07 .20
315 Bernie Federko .30 .75
316 Mike Liut .30 .75
317 Joe Mullen 1.00 2.50
318 Jorgen Pettersson .07 .20
319 Rob Ramage .07 .20
320 Brian Sutter .15 .40
321 Perry Turnbull .07 .20
322 Mike Zuke .07 .20
323 Rick Vaive SL .07 .20
324 Rick Vaive HL .07 .20
325 John Anderson .07 .20
326 Jim Benning .07 .20
327 Bill Derlago .07 .20
328 Dan Daoust RC .07 .20
329 Dave Farrish .07 .20
330 Miroslav Frycer .07 .20
331 Stewart Gavin RC .07 .20
332 Gaston Gingras .07 .20
333 Billy Harris .07 .20
334 Peter Ihnacak RC .07 .20
335 Jim Korn .07 .20
336 Terry Martin .07 .20
337 Frank Nigro RC .07 .20
338 Mike Palmateer .15 .40
339 Walt Poddubny RC .20 .50
340 Rick St.Croix .07 .20
341 Borje Salming .15 .40
342 Greg Terrion .07 .20
343 Rick Vaive .07 .20
344 Darcy Rota SL .07 .20
345 Darcy Rota HL .07 .20
346 Richard Brodeur .15 .40
347 Jiri Bubla RC .07 .20
348 Ron Delorme .07 .20
349 John Garrett .07 .20
350 Thomas Gradin .07 .20
351 Doug Halward .07 .20
352 Mark Kirton .07 .20
353 Rick Lanz .07 .20
354 Lars Lindgren .07 .20
355 Gary Lupul .07 .20
356 Kevin McCarthy .07 .20
357 Jim Nill RC .07 .20
358 Darcy Rota .07 .20
359 Stan Smyl .07 .20
360 Harold Snepsts .07 .20
361 Patrik Sundstrom RC .20 .50
362 Tony Tanti RC .30 .75
363 Dave(Tiger) Williams .15 .40
364 Mike Gartner SL .30 .75
365 Rod Langway HL .15 .40
366 Bob Carpenter .07 .20
367 Dave Christian .07 .20
368 Brian Engblom .07 .20
369 Mike Gartner 1.50 4.00
370 Bengt Gustafsson .07 .20
371 Ken Houston .07 .20
372 Doug Jarvis .07 .20
373 Al Jensen RC .30 .75
374 Rod Langway .15 .40
375 Craig Laughlin RC .07 .20
376 Scott Stevens RC 5.00 10.00
377 Dale Hawerchuk SL .30 .75
378 Lucien DeBlois HL .07 .20
379 Scott Arniel RC .07 .20
380 Dave Babych .07 .20
381 Laurie Boschman .07 .20
382 Wade Campbell RC .07 .20
383 Lucien DeBlois .07 .20
384 Murray Eaves RC .07 .20
385 Dale Hawerchuk 1.50 4.00
386 Morris Lukowich .07 .20
387 Bengt Lundholm .07 .20
388 Paul MacLean .07 .20
389 Brian Mullen RC .20 .50
390 Doug Smail .07 .20
391 Doug Soetaert .15 .40
392 Don Spring .07 .20
393 Thomas Steen .30 .75
394 Tim Watters .07 .20
395 Tim Young .07 .20
396 Checklist 265-396 1.00 2.50

1983-84 O-Pee-Chee Stickers

This sticker set consisted of 330 stickers in full color and was put out by both O-Pee-Chee and Topps. The foil stickers were numbers 1-4, 15, 22-24, 299-300, 304-305, 308-311, 314-315, 319-330. Stickers measured 1 15/16" by 2 9/16". An album was available for these stickers. The Topps set was distinguishable only by minor back differences. The checklist and prices below apply to both O-Pee-Chee and Topps stickers for this year. On the inside back cover of the sticker album the company offered (via direct mail-order) any ten different stickers of your choice for one dollar; this is one reason why the values of the most popular players in these sticker sets are somewhat depressed compared to traditional card set prices.

COMPLETE SET (330) 16.00 40.00
1 Marcel Dionne FOIL .20 .50
2 Guy Lafleur FOIL .40 1.00
3 Darryl Sittler FOIL .20 .50
4 Gilbert Perreault FOIL .20 .50
5 Bill Barber .08 .25
6 Steve Shutt .08 .25
7 Wayne Gretzky 2.50 6.00
8 Lanny McDonald .08 .25
9 Reggie Leach .08 .25
10 Mike Bossy .20 .50
11 Rick Kehoe .08 .25
12 Bobby Clarke .08 .25
13 Butch Goring .08 .25
14 Rick Middleton .08 .25
15 Conn Smythe .05 .15
Trophy FOIL
16 Billy Smith .08 .25
17 Lee Fogolin .01 .05
18 Stanley Cup Finals .08 .25
19 Stanley Cup Finals .08 .25
20 Stanley Cup Finals .08 .25
21 Stanley Cup Finals .08 .25
22 Stanley Cup FOIL .08 .25
23 Stanley Cup FOIL .08 .25
24 Stanley Cup FOIL .08 .25
25 Rick Vaive .08 .25
26 Rick Vaive .08 .25
27 Billy Harris .01 .05
28 Dan Daoust .01 .05
29 Dan Daoust .01 .05
30 John Anderson .01 .05
31 John Anderson .01 .05
32 Peter Ihnacak .01 .05
33 Borje Salming .08 .25
34 Borje Salming .08 .25
35 Bill Derlago .01 .05
36 Rick St.Croix .01 .05
37 Greg Terrion .01 .05
38 Miroslav Frycer .01 .05
39 Mike Palmateer .08 .25
40 Gaston Gingras .01 .05
41 Pete Peeters .08 .25
42 Pete Peeters .08 .25
43 Mike Krushelnyski .08 .25
44 Rick Middleton .08 .25
45 Rick Middleton .08 .25
46 Ray Bourque .40 1.00
47 Ray Bourque .40 1.00
48 Brad Park .08 .25
49 Barry Pederson .08 .25
50 Barry Pederson .08 .25
51 Peter McNab .08 .25
52 Mike O'Connell .01 .05
53 Steve Kasper .08 .25
54 Marty Howe .08 .25
55 Tom Fergus .01 .05
56 Keith Crowder .01 .05
57 Steve Shutt .08 .25
58 Guy Lafleur .20 .50
59 Guy Lafleur .20 .50
60 Larry Robinson .08 .25
61 Larry Robinson .08 .25
62 Ryan Walter .08 .25
63 Ryan Walter .08 .25
64 Mark Napier .01 .05
65 Mark Napier .01 .05
66 Bob Gainey .08 .25
67 Doug Wickenheiser .01 .05
68 Pierre Mondou .01 .05
69 Mario Tremblay .01 .05
70 Gilbert Delorme .01 .05
71 Mats Naslund .08 .25
72 Rick Wamsley .08 .25
73 Ken Morrow .01 .05
74 John Tonelli .08 .25
75 John Tonelli .08 .25
76 Bryan Trottier .08 .25
77 Bryan Trottier .08 .25
78 Mike Bossy .20 .50
79 Mike Bossy .20 .50
80 Bob Bourne .01 .05
81 Denis Potvin .08 .25
82 Denis Potvin .08 .25
83 Dave Langevin .01 .05
84 Clark Gillies .08 .25
85 Bob Nystrom .08 .25
86 Billy Smith .08 .25
87 Tomas Jonsson .01 .05
88 Rollie Melanson .08 .25
89 Wayne Gretzky 2.50 6.00
90 Wayne Gretzky 2.50 6.00
91 Willy Lindstrom .01 .05
92 Glenn Anderson .20 .50
93 Glenn Anderson .20 .50
94 Paul Coffey .40 1.00
95 Paul Coffey .40 1.00
96 Charlie Huddy .08 .25
97 Mark Messier .75 2.00
98 Mark Messier .75 2.00
99 Andy Moog .40 1.00
100 Lee Fogolin .01 .05
101 Kevin Lowe .08 .25
102 Ken Linseman .08 .25
103 Tom Roulston .01 .05
104 Jari Kurri .40 1.00
105 Darryl Sutter .08 .25
106 Denis Savard .08 .25
107 Denis Savard .08 .25
108 Steve Larmer .75 2.00
109 Bob Murray .01 .05
110 Tom Lysiak .08 .25
111 Al Secord .08 .25
112 Doug Wilson .08 .25
113 Murray Bannerman .08 .25
114 Gordie Roberts .01 .05
115 Tom McCarthy .01 .05
116 Bobby Smith .08 .25
117 Craig Hartsburg .08 .25
118 Dino Ciccarelli .20 .50
119 Dino Ciccarelli .20 .50
120 Neal Broten .08 .25
121 Steve Payne .01 .05
122 Don Beaupre .08 .25
123 Jorgen Pettersson .01 .05
124 Perry Turnbull .01 .05
125 Bernie Federko .08 .25
126 Mike Crombeen .01 .05
127 Brian Sutter .08 .25
128 Brian Sutter .08 .25
129 Mike Liut .08 .25
130 Rob Ramage .08 .25
131 Blake Dunlop .01 .05
132 Ivan Boldirev .01 .05
133 Dwight Foster .01 .05
134 Reed Larson .01 .05
135 Danny Gare .08 .25
136 Jim Schoenfeld .08 .25
137 John Ogrodnick .08 .25
138 John Ogrodnick .08 .25
139 Willie Huber .01 .05
140 Greg Smith .01 .05
141 Ed Beers .01 .05
142 Brian Bellows .20 .50
143 Jiri Bubla .01 .05
144 Daryl Evans .01 .05
145 Randy Gregg .01 .05
146 Jim Jackson .01 .05
147 Corrado Micalef .01 .05
148 Brian Mullen .08 .25
149 Frank Nigro .01 .05
150 Walt Poddubny .01 .05
151 Jaroslav Pouzar .01 .05
152 Patrik Sundstrom .08 .25
153 Denis Savard .20 .50
154 Dave Hunter .01 .05
155 Andy Moog .40 1.00
156 Al Secord .08 .25
157 Mark Messier .75 2.00
158 Glenn Anderson .20 .50
159 Jaroslav Pouzar .01 .05
160 Al Secord AS .08 .25
161 Wayne Gretzky AS 2.50 6.00
162 Lanny McDonald AS .08 .25
163 Dave Babych AS .01 .05
164 Murray Bannerman AS .08 .25
165 Doug Wilson AS .08 .25
166 Michel Goulet AS .08 .25
167 Peter Stastny AS .20 .50
168 Marian Stastny AS .08 .25
169 Denis Potvin AS .08 .25
170 Pete Peeters AS .08 .25
171 Mark Howe AS .08 .25
172 Luc Dufour .01 .05
173 Ray Bourque .40 1.00
174 Bob Bourne .01 .05
175 Denis Potvin .08 .25
176 Mike Bossy .20 .50
177 Butch Goring .08 .25
178 Brad Park .08 .25
179 Murray Brumwell .01 .05
180 Guy Carbonneau .40 1.00
181 Lindsay Carson .01 .05
182 Luc Dufour .01 .05
183 Bob Froese .08 .25
184 Mats Hallin .01 .05
185 Gord Kluzak .08 .25
186 Jeff Larmer .01 .05
187 Milan Novy .01 .05
188 Scott Stevens .75 2.00
189 Bob Sullivan .01 .05
190 Mark Taylor .01 .05
191 Darryl Sittler .08 .25
192 Ron Flockhart .01 .05
193 Brad McCrimmon .08 .25
194 Bill Barber .08 .25
195 Mark Howe .08 .25
196 Mark Howe .08 .25
197 Pelle Lindbergh 1.50 4.00
198 Bobby Clarke .08 .25
199 Brian Propp .08 .25
200 Ken Houston .01 .05
201 Rod Langway .08 .25
202 Al Jensen .08 .25
203 Brian Engblom .01 .05
204 Dennis Maruk .08 .25
205 Dennis Maruk .08 .25
206 Bob Carpenter .08 .25
207 Mike Gartner .20 .50
208 Doug Jarvis .08 .25
209 Eddie Mio .08 .25
210 Barry Beck .08 .25
211 Dave Maloney .08 .25
212 Don Maloney .08 .25
213 Mark Pavelich .08 .25
214 Mark Pavelich .01 .05
215 Anders Hedberg .08 .25
216 Reijo Ruotsalainen .01 .05
217 Mike Rogers .01 .05
218 Don Lever .01 .05
219 Steve Tambellini .01 .05
220 Bob MacMillan .01 .05
221 Hector Marini .01 .05
222 Glenn Resch .08 .25
223 Glenn Resch .08 .25
224 Carol Vadnais .01 .05
225 Joel Quenneville .01 .05
226 Aaron Broten .01 .05
227 Randy Carlyle .08 .25
228 Doug Shedden .01 .05
229 Greg Malone .01 .05
230 Paul Gardner .01 .05
231 Rick Kehoe .08 .25
232 Rick Kehoe .08 .25
233 Pat Boutette .01 .05
234 Michel Dion .08 .25
235 Mike Bullard .08 .25
236 Dale McCourt .01 .05
237 Mike Foligno .08 .25
238 Phil Housley .40 1.00
239 Tony McKegney .08 .25
240 Gilbert Perreault .08 .25
241 Gilbert Perreault .08 .25
242 Bob Sauve .08 .25
243 Mike Ramsey .08 .25
244 John Van Boxmeer .01 .05
245 Dan Bouchard .08 .25
246 Real Cloutier .01 .05
247 Marc Tardif .08 .25
248 Randy Moller .01 .05
249 Michel Goulet .08 .25
250 Michel Goulet .08 .25
251 Marian Stastny .08 .25
252 Anton Stastny .08 .25
253 Peter Stastny .20 .50
254 Mark Johnson .08 .25
255 Ron Francis .60 1.50
256 Doug Sulliman .01 .05
257 Risto Siltanen .01 .05
258 Blaine Stoughton .08 .25
259 Blaine Stoughton .08 .25
260 Ray Neufeld .01 .05
261 Pierre Lacroix .01 .05
262 Greg Millen .08 .25
263 Lanny McDonald .08 .25
264 Paul Reinhart .08 .25
265 Mel Bridgman .08 .25
266 Rejean Lemelin .08 .25
267 Kent Nilsson .08 .25
268 Kent Nilsson .08 .25
269 Doug Risebrough .08 .25
270 Kari Eloranta .01 .05
271 Phil Russell .01 .05
272 Darcy Rota .01 .05
273 Thomas Gradin .08 .25
274 Stan Smyl .08 .25
275 John Garrett .08 .25
276 Richard Brodeur .08 .25
277 Richard Brodeur .08 .25
278 Doug Halward .01 .05
279 Kevin McCarthy .01 .05
280 Rick Lanz .01 .05
281 Morris Lukowich .01 .05
282 Dale Hawerchuk .40 1.00
283 Paul MacLean .08 .25
284 Lucien DeBlois .01 .05
285 Dave Babych .08 .25
286 Dave Babych .01 .05
287 Doug Smail .01 .05
288 Doug Soetaert .01 .05
289 Thomas Steen .08 .25
290 Charlie Simmer .08 .25
291 Terry Ruskowski .08 .25
292 Bernie Nicholls .75 2.00
293 Jim Fox .01 .05
294 Marcel Dionne .08 .25
295 Marcel Dionne .08 .25
296 Gary Laskoski .01 .05
297 Jerry Korab .01 .05
298 Larry Murphy .20 .50
299 Hart Trophy FOIL .05 .15
300 Hart Trophy FOIL .05 .15
301 Wayne Gretzky 2.50 6.00
302 Bobby Clarke .08 .25
303 Lanny McDonald .08 .25
304 Lady Byng .05 .15
Trophy FOIL
305 Lady Byng .05 .15
Trophy FOIL
306 Mike Bossy .20 .50
307 Wayne Gretzky 2.50 6.00
308 Art Ross .05 .15
Trophy FOIL
309 Art Ross .05 .15
Trophy FOIL
310 Calder Trophy FOIL .05 .15
311 Calder Trophy FOIL .05 .15
312 Steve Larmer .60 1.50
313 Rod Langway .08 .25
314 Norris Trophy FOIL .05 .15
315 Norris Trophy FOIL .05 .15
316 Billy Smith .08 .25
317 Roland Melanson .08 .25
318 Pete Peeters .08 .25
319 Vezina Trophy FOIL .05 .15
320 Vezina Trophy FOIL .05 .15
321 Mike Bossy FOIL .20 .50
322 Mike Bossy FOIL .20 .50
323 Marcel Dionne FOIL .20 .50
324 Marcel Dionne FOIL .20 .50
325 Wayne Gretzky FOIL 3.00 8.00
326 Wayne Gretzky FOIL 3.00 8.00
327 Pat Hughes FOIL .05 .15
328 Pat Hughes FOIL .05 .15
329 Rick Middleton FOIL .05 .15
330 Rick Middleton FOIL .05 .15
xx Sticker Album 1.50 4.00

1984-85 O-Pee-Chee

This 396-card standard-size set featured two player photos on the front. A small head shot appeared in a circle toward the bottom of the card. Bilingual backs contained yearly and career statistics and career highlights. All-Stars were featured on cards 207-218. Cards 352-372 featured each team's leading goal scorer on the front and team individual scoring statistics on the back. The cards were essentially in team order. However, updated text on some card fronts reflected off-season trades. The Instant Winner card (one in 662 packs) could be redeemed for prizes including Stanley Cup Finals tickets, hockey equipment and sets of uncut card sheets from this year.

COMPLETE SET (396) 150.00 250.00
1 Ray Bourque 4.00 8.00
2 Keith Crowder .07 .20

3 Luc Dufour	.15	.40
4 Tom Fergus	.07	.20
5 Doug Keans RC	.15	.40
6 Gord Kluzak	.07	.20
7 Ken Linseman	.15	.40
8 Nevin Markwart RC	.07	.20
9 Rick Middleton	.15	.40
10 Mike Milbury	.07	.20
11 Jim Nill	.07	.20
12 Mike O'Connell	.07	.20
13 Terry O'Reilly	.15	.40
14 Barry Pederson	.07	.20
15 Pete Peeters	.15	.40
16 Dave Silk RC	.15	.40
17 Dave Andreychuk RC !	3.00	6.00
18 Tom Barrasso RC !	2.00	5.00
19 Real Cloutier	.07	.20
20 Mike Foligno	.15	.40
21 Bill Hajt	.07	.20
22 Gilles Hamel RC	.07	.20
23 Phil Housley	.30	.75
24 Gilbert Perreault	.15	.40
25 Brent Peterson	.07	.20
26 Larry Playfair	.07	.20
27 Craig Ramsay	.07	.20
28 Mike Ramsey	.07	.20
29 Lindy Ruff	.07	.20
30 Bob Sauve	.15	.40
31 Ric Seiling	.07	.20
32 Murray Bannerman	.15	.40
33 Keith Brown	.07	.20
34 Curt Fraser	.07	.20
35 Bill Gardner	.07	.20
36 Jeff Larmer	.07	.20
37 Steve Larmer	1.00	2.50
38 Steve Ludzik	.07	.20
39 Tom Lysiak	.07	.20
40 Bob MacMillan	.07	.20
41 Bob Murray	.07	.20
42 Troy Murray RC	.30	.75
43 Jack O'Callahan RC	.07	.20
44 Rick Paterson	.07	.20
45 Denis Savard	.30	.75
46 Al Secord	.15	.40
47 Darryl Sutter	.07	.20
48 Doug Wilson	.15	.40
49 John Barrett	.07	.20
50 Ivan Boldirev	.07	.20
51 Colin Campbell	.07	.20
52 Ron Duguay	.15	.40
53 Dwight Foster	.07	.20
54 Danny Gare	.07	.20
55 Ed Johnstone	.07	.20
56 Kelly Kisio RC	.15	.40
57 Lane Lambert	.07	.20
58 Reed Larson	.07	.20
59 Bob Manno	.07	.20
60 Randy Ladouceur RC	.07	.20
61 Eddie Mio	.15	.40
62 John Ogrodnick	.07	.20
63 Brad Park	.15	.40
64 Greg Smith	.07	.20
65 Greg Stefan RC	.15	.40
66 Paul Woods	.15	.40
67 Steve Yzerman RC	50.00	100.00
68 Bob Crawford RC	.07	.20
69 Richie Dunn	.07	.20
70 Ron Francis	1.50	4.00
71 Marty Howe	.07	.20
72 Mark Johnson	.07	.20
73 Chris Kotsopoulos	.07	.20
74 Greg Malone	.07	.20
75 Greg Millen	.15	.40
76 Ray Neufeld	.07	.20
77 Joel Quenneville	.07	.20
78 Risto Siltanen	.07	.20
79 Sylvain Turgeon RC	.15	.40
80 Mike Zuke	.07	.20
81 Steve Christoff	.07	.20
82 Marcel Dionne	.30	.75
83 Brian Engblom	.07	.20
84 Jim Fox	.07	.20
85 Anders Hakansson RC	.07	.20
86 Mark Hardy	.07	.20
87 Brian MacLellan RC	.07	.20
88 Bernie Nicholls	.75	2.00
89 Terry Ruskowski	.07	.20
90 Charlie Simmer	.15	.40
91 Doug Smith	.07	.20
92 Dave Taylor	.15	.40
93 Keith Acton	.07	.20
94 Don Beaupre	.15	.40
95 Brian Bellows	.30	.75
96 Neal Broten	.30	.75
97 Dino Ciccarelli	.30	.75
98 Craig Hartsburg	.07	.20
99 Tom Hirsch RC	.07	.20
100 Paul Holmgren	.15	.40
101 Dennis Maruk	.15	.40
102 Brad Maxwell	.07	.20
103 Tom McCarthy	.07	.20
104 Gilles Meloche	.15	.40
105 Mark Napier	.07	.20
106 Steve Payne	.07	.20
107 Gordie Roberts	.07	.20
108 Harold Snepsts	.07	.20
109 Mel Bridgman	.07	.20
110 Joe Cirella	.07	.20
111 Tim Higgins	.07	.20
112 Don Lever	.07	.20
113 Dave Lewis	.07	.20
114 Bob Lorimer	.07	.20
115 Ron Low	.07	.20
116 Jan Ludvig RC	.07	.20
117 Gary McAdam	.07	.20
118 Rich Preston	.07	.20
119 Glenn Resch	.15	.40
120 Phil Russell	.07	.20
121 Pat Verbeek RC	3.00	6.00
122 Mike Bossy	.40	1.00
123 Bob Bourne	.07	.20
124 Pat Flatley RC	.30	.75
125 Greg Gilbert RC	.15	.40
126 Clark Gillies	.15	.40
127 Butch Goring	.15	.40
128 Tomas Jonsson	.07	.20
129 Pat LaFontaine RC	7.50	15.00
130 Rollie Melanson	.15	.40
131 Ken Morrow	.07	.20
132 Bob Nystrom	.07	.20
133 Stefan Persson	.07	.20
134 Denis Potvin	.30	.75
135 Billy Smith	.15	.40
136 Brent Sutter	.07	.20
137 Duane Sutter	.07	.20
138 John Tonelli	.15	.40
139 Bryan Trottier	.30	.75
140 Barry Beck	.07	.20
141 Ron Greschner	.07	.20
142 Glen Hanlon	.15	.40
143 Anders Hedberg	.15	.40
144 Tom Laidlaw	.07	.20
145 Pierre Larouche	.15	.40
146 Dave Maloney	.07	.20
147 Don Maloney	.07	.20
148 Mark Osborne	.07	.20
149 Larry Patey	.07	.20
150 James Patrick RC	.30	.75
151 Mark Pavelich	.07	.20
152 Mike Rogers	.07	.20
153 Reijo Ruotsalainen	.07	.20
154 Blaine Stoughton	.15	.40
155 Peter Sundstrom RC	.15	.40
156 Bill Barber	.15	.40
157 Doug Crossman	.07	.20
158 Thomas Eriksson RC	.07	.20
159 Bob Froese	.15	.40
160 Paul Guay RC	.07	.20
161 Mark Howe	.15	.40
162 Tim Kerr	.15	.40
163 Brad Marsh	.07	.20
164 Brad McCrimmon	.15	.40
165 Dave Poulin RC	.75	2.00
166 Brian Propp	.15	.40
167 Ilkka Sinisalo RC	.15	.40
168 Darryl Sittler	.30	.75
169 Rich Sutter RC	.15	.40
170 Ron Sutter RC	.30	.75
171 Pat Boutette	.07	.20
172 Mike Bullard	.07	.20
173 Michel Dion	.15	.40
174 Ron Flockhart	.07	.20
175 Greg Fox	.07	.20
176 Denis Herron	.15	.40
177 Rick Kehoe	.15	.40
178 Kevin McCarthy	.07	.20
179 Tom Roulston	.07	.20
180 Mark Taylor	.07	.20
181 Wayne Babych	.07	.20
182 Tim Bothwell RC	.07	.20
183 Kevin Lavallee	.07	.20
184 Bernie Federko	.15	.40
185 Doug Gilmour RC	12.50	30.00
186 Terry Johnson RC	.07	.20
187 Mike Liut	.15	.40
188 Joe Mullen	.60	1.50
189 Jorgen Pettersson	.07	.20
190 Rob Ramage	.07	.20
191 Dwight Schofield RC	.07	.20
192 Brian Sutter	.15	.40
193 Doug Wickenheiser	.07	.20
194 Bob Carpenter	.07	.20
195 Dave Christian	.07	.20
196 Bob Gould RC	.07	.20
197 Mike Gartner	1.25	3.00
198 Bengt Gustafsson	.07	.20
199 Alan Haworth RC	.07	.20
200 Doug Jarvis	.07	.20
201 Al Jensen	.15	.40
202 Rod Langway	.15	.40
203 Craig Laughlin	.07	.20
204 Larry Murphy	.30	.75
205 Pat Riggin	.15	.40
206 Scott Stevens	1.25	3.00
207 Michel Goulet AS	.15	.40
208 Wayne Gretzky AS	2.50	5.00
209 Mike Bossy AS	.30	.75
210 Rod Langway AS	.15	.40
211 Ray Bourque AS	.75	2.00
212 Tom Barrasso AS	.30	.75
213 Mark Messier AS	2.00	5.00
214 Bryan Trottier AS	.30	.75
215 Jari Kurri AS	.30	.75
216 Denis Potvin AS	.15	.40
217 Paul Coffey AS	.60	1.50
218 Pat Riggin AS	.07	.20
219 Ed Beers	.07	.20
220 Steve Bozek	.07	.20
221 Mike Eaves	.07	.20
222 Don Edwards	.07	.20
223 Kari Eloranta	.07	.20
224 Dave Hindmarch	.07	.20
225 Jim Jackson	.07	.20
226 Steve Konroyd	.07	.20
227 Richard Kromm RC	.07	.20
228 Rejean Lemelin	.15	.40
229 Hakan Loob RC	1.00	2.50
230 Jamie Macoun RC	.15	.40
231 Lanny McDonald	.15	.40
232 Kent Nilsson	.15	.40
233 Jim Peplinski	.07	.20
234 Dan Quinn RC	.30	.75
235 Paul Reinhart	.07	.20
236 Doug Risebrough	.07	.20
237 Steve Tambellini	.07	.20
238 Glenn Anderson	.30	.75
239 Paul Coffey	3.00	6.00
240 Lee Fogolin	.07	.20
241 Grant Fuhr	2.50	5.00
242 Randy Gregg	.07	.20
243 Wayne Gretzky	10.00	20.00
244 Charlie Huddy	.07	.20
245 Pat Hughes	.07	.20
246 Dave Hunter	.07	.20
247 Don Jackson	.07	.20
248 Mike Krushelnyski	.07	.20
249 Jari Kurri	1.50	4.00
250 Willy Lindstrom	.07	.20
251 Kevin Lowe	.30	.75
252 Dave Lumley	.07	.20
253 Kevin McClelland RC	.07	.20
254 Mark Messier	2.00	5.00
255 Andy Moog	1.50	4.00
256 Jaroslav Pouzar	.07	.20
257 Guy Carbonneau	.30	.75
258 John Chabot RC	.07	.20
259 Chris Chelios RC !	10.00	25.00
260 Lucien DeBlois	.07	.20
261 Bob Gainey	.30	.75
262 Rick Green	.07	.20
263 Jean Hamel	.07	.20
264 Guy Lafleur	.30	.75
265 Craig Ludwig	.07	.20
266 Pierre Mondou	.07	.20
267 Mats Naslund	.30	.75
268 Chris Nilan	.07	.20
269 Steve Penney RC	.15	.40
270 Larry Robinson	.15	.40
271 Bill Root	.07	.20
272 Steve Shutt	.07	.20
273 Bobby Smith	.15	.40
274 Mario Tremblay	.07	.20
275 Ryan Walter	.07	.20
276 Bo Berglund RC	.07	.20
277 Dan Bouchard	.15	.40
278 Alain Cote	.07	.20
279 Andre Dore	.07	.20
280 Michel Goulet	.30	.75
281 Dale Hunter	.15	.40
282 Mario Marois	.07	.20
283 Tony McKegney	.07	.20
284 Randy Moller	.07	.20
285 Wilf Paiement	.07	.20
286 Pat Price	.07	.20
287 Normand Rochefort	.07	.20
288 Andre Savard	.07	.20
289 Richard Sevigny	.07	.20
290 Louis Sleigher	.07	.20
291 Anton Stastny	.15	.40
292 Marian Stastny	.15	.40
293 Peter Stastny	.30	.75
294 Blake Wesley	.07	.20
295 John Anderson	.07	.20
296 Jim Benning	.07	.20
297 Allan Bester UER RC	.15	.40
298 Rich Costello RC	.07	.20
299 Dan Daoust	.07	.20
300 Bill Derlago	.07	.20
301 Dave Farrish	.07	.20
302 Stewart Gavin	.07	.20
303 Gaston Gingras	.07	.20
304 Jim Korn	.07	.20
305 Gary Leeman RC	.30	.75
306 Terry Martin	.07	.20
307 Gary Nylund RC	.07	.20
308 Mike Palmateer	.15	.40
309 Walt Poddubny	.07	.20
310 Rick St.Croix	.07	.20
311 Borje Salming	.15	.40
312 Greg Terrion	.07	.20
313 Rick Vaive	.07	.20
314 Richard Brodeur	.07	.20
315 Jiri Bubla	.07	.20
316 Ron Delorme	.07	.20
317 John Garrett	.15	.40
318 Jere Gillis	.07	.20
319 Thomas Gradin	.07	.20
320 Doug Halward	.07	.20
321 Rick Lanz	.07	.20
322 Moe Lemay RC	.07	.20
323 Gary Lupul	.07	.20
324 Al MacAdam	.07	.20
325 Rob McClanahan	.07	.20
326 Peter McNab	.07	.20
327 Cam Neely RC	15.00	40.00
328 Darcy Rota	.07	.20
329 Andy Schliebener RC	.07	.20
330 Stan Smyl	.07	.20
331 Patrik Sundstrom	.07	.20
332 Tony Tanti	.07	.20
333 Scott Arniel	.07	.20
334 Dave Babych	.07	.20
335 Laurie Boschman	.07	.20
336 Wade Campbell	.07	.20
337 Randy Carlyle	.07	.20
338 Jordy Douglas	.07	.20
339 Dale Hawerchuk	1.25	3.00
340 Morris Lukowich	.07	.20
341 Bengt Lundholm	.07	.20
342 Paul MacLean	.07	.20
343 Andrew McBain RC	.07	.20
344 Brian Mullen	.07	.20
345 Robert Picard	.07	.20
346 Doug Smail	.07	.20
347 Doug Soetaert	.15	.40
348 Thomas Steen	.07	.20
349 Perry Turnbull	.07	.20
350 Tim Watters	.07	.20
351 Tim Young	.07	.20
352 Rick Middleton SL	.15	.40
353 Dave Andreychuk SL	.60	1.50
354 Ed Beers SL	.07	.20
355 Denis Savard SL	.15	.40
356 John Ogrodnick SL	.07	.20
357 Wayne Gretzky SL	2.50	5.00
358 Charlie Simmer SL	.15	.40
359 Brian Bellows SL	.15	.40
360 Guy Lafleur SL	.30	.75
361 Mel Bridgman SL	.07	.20
362 Mike Bossy SL	.30	.75
363 Pierre Larouche SL	.15	.40
364 Tim Kerr SL	.15	.40
365 Mike Bullard SL	.07	.20
366 Michel Goulet SL	.15	.40
367 Bernie Federko	.30	.75
Joe Mullen UER SL		
368 Rick Vaive	.07	.20
369 Tony Tanti	.07	.20
370 Mike Gartner	.30	.75
371 Paul MacLean SL	.07	.20
372 Sylvain Turgeon SL	.15	.40
373 Wayne Gretzky	2.50	5.00
(Art Ross Trophy)		
374 Wayne Gretzky	2.50	5.00
(Hart Trophy)		
375 Tom Barrasso	.30	.75
(Calder Trophy)		
376 Mike Bossy	.30	.75
(Lady Byng Trophy)		
377 Rod Langway	.07	.20
(Norris Trophy)		
378 Brad Park	.15	.40
(Masterton Trophy)		
379 Tom Barrasso	.30	.75
(Vezina Trophy)		
380 Wayne Gretzky	2.50	5.00
(Scoring Leaders)		
381 Wayne Gretzky	2.50	5.00
(Goals Leaders)		
382 Wayne Gretzky	2.50	5.00
(Assists Leaders)		
383 Wayne Gretzky	2.50	5.00
(Power Play Goal Leaders)		
384 Michel Goulet	.15	.40
(Game Winning Goal Leaders)		
385 Steve Yzerman UER	10.00	20.00
(Rookie Scoring Leaders)		
(Gilmour misspelled as		
Gilmore on reverse)		
386 Pat Riggin	.15	.40
(Goals Against Average Leaders)		
387 Rollie Melanson	.15	.40
(Save Percentage Leaders)		
388 Wayne Gretzky RB	2.50	5.00
Scores in 51		
Straight Games		
389 Denis Potvin RB	.15	.40
20 Goals, Eight		
Seasons, Defenseman		
390 Brad Park RB	.15	.40
Most Career Assists,		
Defenseman		
391 Michel Goulet RB	.15	.40
Most Points, Season,		
Left Wing		
392 Pat LaFontaine RB	1.50	4.00
Rookie Scoring Mark		
393 Dale Hawerchuk RB	.30	.75
Five Assists& Period		
394 Checklist 1-132	.75	2.00
395 Checklist 133-264 UER	.75	2.00
(185 Gilmore)		
396 Checklist 265-396	.75	2.00
NNO Instant Winner Card	60.00	100.00

1984-85 O-Pee-Chee Stickers

This sticker set consisted of 292 stickers in full color and was put out by O-Pee-Chee. The foil stickers are listed in the checklist below explicitly. The stickers measured approximately 1 15/16" by 2 9/16". An album was available for these stickers. Those stickers which are pairs are indicated in the checklist below by noting parenthetically the other member of the pair. On the inside back cover of the sticker album the company offered (via direct mail-order) any ten different stickers of your choice for one dollar; this is one reason why the values of the most popular players in these sticker sets are somewhat depressed compared to traditional card set prices.

COMPLETE SET (292)	16.00	40.00
1 Stanley Cup	.08	.25
2 Stanley Cup	.08	.25
3 Stanley Cup	.08	.25
4 Stanley Cup	.08	.25
5 Mark Messier	.50	1.25
6 Maple Leafs Logo (23)	.05	.15
FOIL		
7 Borje Salming	.01	.05
8 Borje Salming	.01	.05
9 Dan Daoust	.01	.05
10 Dan Daoust	.01	.05
11 Rick Vaive	.01	.05
12 Rick Vaive	.01	.05
13 Dale McCourt	.01	.05
14 Bill Derlago	.01	.05
15 Gary Nylund	.01	.05
16 Gary Nylund	.01	.05
17 Jim Korn	.01	.05
18 John Anderson	.01	.05
19 Greg Terrion	.01	.05
20 Allan Bester	.01	.05
21 Jim Benning	.01	.05
22 Mike Palmateer	.08	.25
23 Blackhawks Logo (6)	.05	.15
FOIL		
24 Denis Savard	.20	.50
25 Denis Savard	.20	.50
26 Bob Murray	.01	.05
27 Doug Wilson	.01	.05
28 Keith Brown	.01	.05
29 Steve Larmer	.20	.50
30 Darryl Sutter	.01	.05
31 Tom Lysiak	.01	.05
32 Murray Bannerman	.08	.25
33 Red Wings Logo (43)	.05	.15
FOIL		
34 John Ogrodnick	.01	.05
35 John Ogrodnick	.01	.05
36 Reed Larson	.01	.05
37 Steve Yzerman	5.00	12.00
38 Brad Park	.08	.25
39 Ivan Boldirev	.01	.05
40 Kelly Kisio	.01	.05
41 Greg Stefan	.08	.25
42 Ron Duguay	.01	.05
43 North Stars Logo (33)	.05	.15
FOIL		
44 Brian Bellows	.08	.25
45 Brian Bellows	.08	.25
46 Neal Broten	.08	.25
47 Dino Ciccarelli	.20	.50
48 Dennis Maruk	.01	.05
49 Steve Payne	.01	.05
50 Brad Maxwell	.01	.05
51 Gilles Meloche	.08	.25
52 Tom McCarthy	.01	.05
53 Blues Logo (67)	.05	.15
FOIL		
54 Bernie Federko	.01	.05
55 Bernie Federko	.01	.05
56 Brian Sutter	.01	.05
57 Mike Liut	.08	.25
58 Doug Wickenheiser	.01	.05
59 Jorgen Pettersson	.01	.05
60 Doug Gilmour	1.50	4.00
61 Joe Mullen	.08	.25
62 Rob Ramage	.01	.05
63 Wayne Gretzky (64)	2.50	6.00
FOIL		
64 Michel Goulet (63)	2.50	6.00
FOIL		
65 Pat Riggin (66)	.05	.15
FOIL		
66 Denis Potvin (65)	.05	.15
FOIL		
67 Devils Logo (53)	.05	.15
FOIL		
68 Glenn Resch	.08	.25
69 Glenn Resch	.08	.25
70 Don Lever	.01	.05
71 Mel Bridgman	.01	.05
72 Bob MacMillan	.01	.05
73 Pat Verbeek	.20	.50
74 Joe Cirella	.01	.05
75 Phil Russell	.01	.05
76 Jan Ludvig	.01	.05
77 Islanders Logo (94)	.05	.15
FOIL		
78 Denis Potvin	.08	.25
79 Denis Potvin	.08	.25
80 John Tonelli	.01	.05
81 John Tonelli	.01	.05
82 Mike Bossy	.20	.50
83 Mike Bossy	.20	.50
84 Butch Goring	.01	.05
85 Bob Nystrom	.01	.05
86 Bryan Trottier	.08	.25
87 Bryan Trottier	.08	.25
88 Brent Sutter	.01	.05
89 Bob Bourne	.01	.05
90 Greg Gilbert	.01	.05
91 Billy Smith	.01	.05
92 Rollie Melanson	.08	.25
93 Ken Morrow	.01	.05
94 Rangers Logo (77)	.05	.15
FOIL		
95 Don Maloney	.01	.05
96 Don Maloney	.01	.05
97 Mark Pavelich	.01	.05
98 Glen Hanlon	.08	.25
99 Mike Rogers	.01	.05
100 Barry Beck	.01	.05
101 Reijo Ruotsalainen	.01	.05
102 Anders Hedberg	.01	.05
103 Pierre Larouche	.08	.25
104 Flyers Logo (114)	.05	.15
FOIL		
105 Tim Kerr	.01	.05
106 Tim Kerr	.01	.05
107 Ron Sutter	.08	.25
108 Darryl Sittler	.08	.25
109 Mark Howe	.08	.25
110 Dave Poulin	.01	.05
111 Rich Sutter	.08	.25
112 Brian Propp	.01	.05
113 Bob Froese	.08	.25
114 Penguins Logo (104)	.05	.15
FOIL		
115 Ron Flockhart	.01	.05
116 Ron Flockhart	.01	.05
117 Rick Kehoe	.01	.05
118 Mike Bullard	.01	.05
119 Kevin McCarthy	.01	.05
120 Doug Shedden	.01	.05
121 Mark Taylor	.01	.05
122 Denis Herron	.01	.05
123 Tom Roulston	.01	.05
124 Capitals Logo (146)	.05	.15
FOIL		
125 Rod Langway	.01	.05
126 Rod Langway	.01	.05
127 Larry Murphy	.08	.25
128 Al Jensen	.01	.05
129 Doug Jarvis	.01	.05
130 Bengt Gustafsson	.01	.05
131 Mike Gartner	.20	.50
132 Bob Carpenter	.01	.05
133 Dave Christian	.01	.05
134 Paul Coffey FOIL	.40	1.00
135 Murray Bannerman	.08	.25
FOIL		
136 Rob Ramage FOIL	.08	.25
137 John Ogrodnick	.08	.25
FOIL		
138 Wayne Gretzky	2.50	6.00
FOIL		
139 Rick Vaive FOIL	.08	.25
140 Michel Goulet	.20	.50
FOIL		
141 Peter Stastny FOIL	.20	.50
142 Rick Middleton	.08	.25
FOIL		
143 Ray Bourque FOIL	.40	1.00
144 Pete Peeters FOIL	.08	.25
145 Denis Potvin FOIL	.20	.50
146 Canadiens Logo (124)	.05	.15
FOIL		
147 Larry Robinson	.08	.25
148 Larry Robinson	.08	.25
149 Guy Lafleur	.20	.50
150 Guy Lafleur	.20	.50
151 Bobby Smith	.01	.05
152 Bobby Smith	.01	.05
153 Bob Gainey	.08	.25
154 Craig Ludwig	.01	.05
155 Mats Naslund	.08	.25
156 Mats Naslund	.08	.25
157 Rick Wamsley	.08	.25
158 Jean Hamel	.01	.05
159 Ryan Walter	.01	.05
160 Guy Carbonneau	.08	.25
161 Mario Tremblay	.01	.05
162 Pierre Mondou	.01	.05
163 Nordiques Logo (180)	.05	.15
FOIL		
164 Peter Stastny	.20	.50
165 Peter Stastny	.20	.50
166 Mario Marois	.01	.05
167 Mario Marois	.01	.05
168 Michel Goulet	.08	.25
169 Michel Goulet	.08	.25
170 Andre Savard	.01	.05
171 Tony McKegney	.01	.05
172 Dan Bouchard	.08	.25
173 Dan Bouchard	.08	.25
174 Randy Moller	.01	.05
175 Wilf Paiement	.01	.05
176 Normand Rochefort	.01	.05
177 Marian Stastny	.01	.05
178 Anton Stastny	.01	.05
179 Dale Hunter	.08	.25
180 Bruins Logo (163)	.05	.15
FOIL		
181 Rick Middleton	.08	.25
182 Rick Middleton	.08	.25
183 Ray Bourque	.30	.75
184 Pete Peeters	.08	.25
185 Mike O'Connell	.01	.05
186 Gord Kluzak	.01	.05
187 Barry Pederson	.01	.05
188 Mike Krushelnyski	.01	.05
189 Tom Fergus	.01	.05
190 Whalers Logo (200)	.05	.15
FOIL		
191 Sylvain Turgeon	.01	.05
192 Sylvain Turgeon	.01	.05
193 Mark Johnson	.01	.05
194 Greg Malone	.01	.05
195 Mike Zuke	.01	.05
196 Ron Francis	.40	1.00
197 Bob Crawford	.01	.05
198 Greg Millen	.08	.25
199 Ray Neufeld	.01	.05
200 Sabres Logo (190)	.05	.15
FOIL		
201 Gilbert Perreault	.08	.25
202 Gilbert Perreault	.08	.25
203 Phil Housley	.20	.50
204 Phil Housley	.20	.50
205 Tom Barrasso	.30	.75
206 Tom Barrasso	.30	.75
207 Larry Playfair	.01	.05
208 Bob Sauve	.08	.25
209 Dave Andreychuk	.40	1.00
210 Dave Andreychuk	.40	1.00
211 Mike Ramsey	.01	.05
212 Mike Foligno	.01	.05
213 Lindy Ruff	.01	.05
214 Bill Hajt	.01	.05
215 Craig Ramsay	.01	.05
216 Ric Seiling	.01	.05
217 Hart Trophy (224)	.05	.15
FOIL		
218 Vezina Trophy (223)	.05	.15
FOIL		
219 Jennings Trophy (221)	.05	.15
FOIL		
220 Calder Trophy (225)	.05	.15
FOIL		
221 Art Ross Trophy (219)	.05	.15
FOIL		
222 Norris Trophy (283)	.05	.15
FOIL		
223 Masterton Trophy	.05	.15
(218) FOIL		
224 Selke Trophy (217)	.05	.15
FOIL		
225 Lady Byng Trophy(220)	.05	.15
FOIL		
226 Wayne Gretzky (227)	1.50	4.00
227 Tom Barrasso (226)	1.50	4.00
228 Tom Barrasso (229)	1.50	4.00
229 Wayne Gretzky (228)	1.50	4.00
230 Rod Langway (231)	.08	.25
231 Brad Park (230)	.08	.25
232 Al Jensen (233)	.08	.25
233 Pat Riggin (232)	.08	.25
234 Doug Jarvis (235)	.08	.25
235 Mike Bossy (234)	.08	.25
236 Flames Logo (246)	.05	.15
FOIL		
237 Lanny McDonald	.08	.25
238 Lanny McDonald	.08	.25
239 Steve Tambellini	.01	.05
240 Rejean Lemelin	.08	.25
241 Doug Risebrough	.01	.05
242 Hakan Loob	.08	.25
243 Ed Beers	.01	.05
244 Mike Eaves	.01	.05
245 Kent Nilsson	.01	.05
246 Oilers Logo (236)	.05	.15
FOIL		
247 Glenn Anderson	.08	.25
248 Glenn Anderson	.08	.25
249 Jari Kurri	.20	.50
250 Jari Kurri	.20	.50
251 Paul Coffey	.30	.75
252 Paul Coffey	.30	.75
253 Kevin Lowe	.08	.25
254 Lee Fogolin	.01	.05
255 Wayne Gretzky	1.50	4.00
256 Wayne Gretzky	1.50	4.00
257 Randy Gregg	.01	.05
258 Charlie Huddy	.01	.05
259 Grant Fuhr	.20	.50
260 Willy Lindstrom	.01	.05
261 Mark Messier	.50	1.25
262 Andy Moog	.20	.50
263 Kings Logo (273)	.05	.15
FOIL		
264 Marcel Dionne	.08	.25
265 Marcel Dionne	.08	.25
266 Charlie Simmer	.01	.05
267 Dave Taylor	.01	.05
268 Jim Fox	.01	.05
269 Bernie Nicholls	.20	.50
270 Terry Ruskowski	.01	.05
271 Brian Engblom	.01	.05
272 Mark Hardy	.01	.05
273 Canucks Logo (263)	.05	.15
FOIL		
274 Tony Tanti	.01	.05
275 Tony Tanti	.01	.05
276 Rick Lanz	.01	.05
277 Richard Brodeur	.08	.25
278 Doug Halward	.01	.05
279 Patrik Sundstrom	.08	.25
280 Darcy Rota	.01	.05
281 Stan Smyl	.01	.05
282 Thomas Gradin	.01	.05
283 Jets Logo (222)	.05	.15
FOIL		
284 Dale Hawerchuk	.20	.50
285 Dale Hawerchuk	.20	.50
286 Scott Arniel	.01	.05
287 Dave Babych	.01	.05
288 Laurie Boschman	.01	.05
289 Paul MacLean	.01	.05
290 Lucien DeBlois	.01	.05
291 Randy Carlyle	.01	.05
292 Thomas Steen	.01	.05
xx Sticker Album	2.00	5.00

1985-86 O-Pee-Chee

The 1985-86 O-Pee-Chee set contained 264 standard-size cards. The fronts had player name and position at the bottom with team logo at the top right or left. Bilingual backs contained yearly and career stats and highlights. The key Rookie Card in this set was Mario Lemieux. Printed later than Topps, O-Pee-Chee was able to issue a Memorial card of the late Pelle Lindbergh. Beware when purchasing the Rookie Card of Mario Lemieux as it has been counterfeited.

COMPLETE SET (264)	250.00	500.00
1 Lanny McDonald	.75	2.00
2 Mike O'Connell	.15	.40
3 Curt Fraser	.15	.40
4 Steve Penney	.15	.40
5 Brian Engblom	.15	.40
6 Ron Sutter	.15	.40
7 Joe Mullen	.60	1.50
8 Rod Langway	.30	.75
9 Mario Lemieux RC !	75.00	200.00
10 Dave Babych	.15	.40
11 Bob Nystrom	.15	.40
12 Andy Moog	1.50	4.00
13 Dino Ciccarelli	.60	1.50
14 Dwight Foster	.15	.40
15 James Patrick	.15	.40
16 Thomas Gradin	.15	.40
17 Mike Foligno	.30	.75
18 Mario Gosselin RC	.15	.40
19 Mike Zuke	.15	.40
20 John Anderson	.15	.40
21 Dave Pichette	.15	.40
22 Nick Fotiu	.30	.75
23 Tom Lysiak	.15	.40
24 Peter Zezel RC	.60	1.50
25 Denis Potvin	.30	.75
26 Bob Carpenter	.15	.40
27 Murray Bannerman	.30	.75
28 Gordie Roberts	.15	.40
29 Steve Yzerman !	25.00	50.00
30 Phil Russell	.15	.40
31 Peter Stastny	.60	1.50
32 Craig Ramsay	.15	.40
33 Terry Ruskowski	.15	.40
34 Kevin Dineen RC	1.50	4.00
35 Mark Howe	.30	.75
36 Glenn Resch	.30	.75
37 Danny Gare	.30	.75
38 Doug Bodger RC	.30	.75
39 Mike Rogers	.15	.40
40 Ray Bourque	4.00	8.00
41 John Tonelli	.30	.75
42 Mel Bridgman	.15	.40
43 Sylvain Turgeon	.30	.75
44 Mark Johnson	.15	.40
45 Doug Wilson	.30	.75
46 Mike Gartner	1.25	3.00
47 Brent Peterson	.15	.40
48 Paul Reinhart	.15	.40
49 Mike Krushelnyski	.30	.75
50 Brian Bellows	.60	1.50
51 Chris Chelios	4.00	8.00
52 Barry Pederson	.15	.40
53 Murray Craven	.15	.40
54 Pierre Larouche	.30	.75
55 Reed Larson	.15	.40
56 Pat Verbeek	.15	.40
57 Randy Carlyle	.15	.40
58 Ray Neufeld	.15	.40
59 Keith Brown	.15	.40
60 Bryan Trottier	.60	1.50
61 Jim Fox	.15	.40
62 Scott Stevens	1.25	3.00
63 Phil Housley	.60	1.50
64 Rick Middleton	.30	.75
65 Steve Payne	.15	.40
66 Dave Lewis	.15	.40
67 Mike Bullard	.15	.40
68 Stan Smyl	.15	.40
69 Mark Pavelich	.15	.40
70 John Ogrodnick	.15	.40
71 Bill Derlago	.15	.40
72 Brad Marsh	.15	.40
73 Denis Savard	.60	1.50
74 Mark Fusco RC	.15	.40
75 Pete Peeters	.30	.75
76 Doug Gilmour	5.00	10.00
77 Mike Ramsey	.15	.40
78 Anton Stastny	.30	.75
79 Steve Kasper	.15	.40
80 Bryan Erickson RC	.15	.40
81 Clark Gillies	.30	.75
82 Keith Acton	.15	.40
83 Pat Flatley	.15	.40
84 Kirk Muller RC	1.50	4.00
85 Paul Coffey	3.00	6.00
86 Ed Olczyk RC	.40	1.00

87 Charlie Simmer .30 .75
88 Mike Liut .30 .75
89 Dave Maloney .15 .40
90 Marcel Dionne .30 .75
91 Tim Kerr .30 .75
92 Ivan Boldirev .15 .40
93 Ken Morrow .15 .40
94 Don Maloney .15 .40
95 Rejean Lemelin .30 .75
96 Curt Giles .15 .40
97 Bob Bourne .15 .40
98 Joe Cirella .15 .40
99 Dave Christian .15 .40
100 Darryl Sutter .15 .40
101 Kelly Kisio .30 .75
102 Mats Naslund .30 .75
103 Joel Quenneville .15 .40
104 Bernie Federko .30 .75
105 Tom Barrasso .60 1.50
106 Rick Vaive .15 .40
107 Brent Sutter .15 .40
108 Wayne Babych .15 .40
109 Dale Hawerchuk 1.25 3.00
110 Pelle Lindbergh 6.00 12.00
(Memorial)
111 Dennis Maruk .30 .75
112 Reijo Ruotsalainen .15 .40
113 Tom Fergus .15 .40
114 Bob Murray .15 .40
115 Patrik Sundstrom .15 .40
116 Ron Duguay .15 .40
117 Alan Haworth .15 .40
118 Greg Malone .15 .40
119 Bill Hajt .15 .40
120 Wayne Gretzky 15.00 40.00
121 Craig Redmond RC .15 .40
122 Kelly Hrudey RC 2.50 5.00
123 Tomas Sandstrom RC 2.50 5.00
124 Neal Broten .30 .75
125 Moe Mantha .15 .40
126 Greg Gilbert .15 .40
127 Bruce Driver RC .60 1.50
128 Dave Poulin .15 .40
129 Morris Lukowich .15 .40
130 Mike Bossy .75 2.00
131 Larry Playfair .15 .40
132 Steve Larmer .60 1.50
133 Doug Keans .15 .40
134 Bob Manno .15 .40
135 Brian Sutter .30 .75
136 Pat Riggin .30 .75
137 Pat LaFontaine 2.50 5.00
138 Barry Beck .15 .40
139 Rich Preston .15 .40
140 Ron Francis 1.50 4.00
141 Brian Propp .30 .75
142 Don Beaupre .30 .75
143 Dave Andreychuk .60 1.50
144 Ed Beers .15 .40
145 Paul MacLean .15 .40
146 Troy Murray .15 .40
147 Larry Robinson .30 .75
148 Bernie Nicholls .60 1.50
149 Glen Hanlon .30 .75
150 Michel Goulet .60 1.50
151 Doug Jarvis .15 .40
152 Warren Young RC .15 .40
153 Tony Tanti .15 .40
154 Tomas Jonsson .15 .40
155 Jari Kurri 1.50 4.00
156 Tony McKegney .15 .40
157 Greg Stefan .30 .75
158 Brad McCrimmon .30 .75
159 Keith Crowder .15 .40
160 Gilbert Perreault .30 .75
161 Tim Bothwell .15 .40
162 Bob Crawford .15 .40
163 Paul Gagne .15 .40
164 Dan Daoust .15 .40
165 Checklist 1-132 1.50 4.00
166 Tim Bernhardt RC .15 .40
167 Gord Kluzak .15 .40
168 Glenn Anderson .60 1.50
169 Bob Gainey .60 1.50
170 Brent Ashton .15 .40
171 Ron Flockhart .15 .40
172 Gary Nylund .15 .40
173 Moe Lemay .15 .40
174 Bob Sauve .30 .75
175 Doug Smail .15 .40
176 Dan Quinn .15 .40
177 Mark Messier 2.00 5.00
178 Jay Wells RC .30 .75
179 Dale Hunter .30 .75
180 Richard Brodeur .30 .75
181 Bobby Smith .30 .75
182 Ron Greschner .15 .40
183 Don Edwards .15 .40
184 Hakan Loob .30 .75
185 Dave Ellett RC .30 .75
186 Denis Herron .15 .40
187 Charlie Huddy .30 .75
188 Ilkka Sinisalo .15 .40
189 Doug Halward .15 .40
190 Craig Laughlin .15 .40
191 Carey Wilson RC .15 .40
192 Craig Ludwig .15 .40
193 Bob MacMillan .15 .40
194 Mario Marois .15 .40
195 Brian Mullen .15 .40
196 Rob Ramage .15 .40
197 Rick Lanz .15 .40
198 Miroslav Frycer .15 .40
199 Randy Gregg .15 .40
200 Corrado Micalef .15 .40
201 Jamie Macoun .15 .40
202 Bob Brooke RC .15 .40
203 Billy Carroll .15 .40
204 Brian MacLellan .15 .40
205 Alain Cote .15 .40
206 Thomas Steen .15 .40
207 Grant Fuhr 1.50 4.00
208 Rich Sutter .15 .40
209 Al MacAdam .15 .40
210 Al Iafrate RC 2.50 5.00
211 Pierre Mondou .15 .40
212 Randy Hillier RC .15 .40
213 Mike Eaves .15 .40
214 Dave Taylor .30 .75
215 Robert Picard .15 .40
216 Randy Ladouceur .15 .40
217 Willy Lindstrom .15 .40
218 Torrie Robertson RC .15 .40
219 Tom Kurvers RC .30 .75
220 John Garrett .15 .40
221 Greg Millen .30 .75
222 Richard Kromm .15 .40
223 Bob Janecyk RC .30 .75
224 Brad Maxwell .15 .40
225 Mike McPhee RC .60 1.50
226 Brian Hayward RC .60 1.50
227 Duane Sutter .15 .40
228 Cam Neely 5.00 10.00
229 Doug Wickenheiser .15 .40
230 Rollie Melanson .30 .75
231 Bruce Bell RC .15 .40
232 Harold Snepsts .15 .40
233 Guy Carbonneau .60 1.50
234 Doug Sulliman .15 .40
235 Lee Fogolin .15 .40
236 Larry Murphy .60 1.50
237 Al MacInnis RC 18.00 30.00
238 Don Lever .15 .40
239 Kevin Lowe .30 .75
240 Randy Moller .15 .40
241 Doug Lidster RC .30 .75
242 Craig Hartsburg .15 .40
243 Doug Risebrough .15 .40
244 John Chabot .15 .40
245 Mario Tremblay .15 .40
246 Dan Bouchard .30 .75
247 Doug Shedden .15 .40
248 Borje Salming .30 .75
249 Aaron Broten .15 .40
250 Jim Benning .15 .40
251 Laurie Boschman .15 .40
252 George McPhee RC .15 .40
253 Mark Napier .15 .40
254 Perry Turnbull .15 .40
255 Warren Skorodenski RC .30 .75
256 Checklist 133-264 1.50 4.00
257 Wayne Gretzky 1.50 4.00
(Goals Leaders)
258 Wayne Gretzky 1.50 4.00
(Assists Leaders)
259 Wayne Gretzky 1.50 4.00
(Scoring Leaders)
260 Tim Kerr .30 .75
(Power Play Goals Leaders)
261 Jari Kurri .60 1.50
(Game Winning Goals Leaders)
262 Mario Lemieux LL 25.00 40.00
263 Tom Barrasso .30 .75
(Goals Against Average Leaders)
264 Warren Skorodenski .30 .75
(Save Percentage Leaders)

1985-86 O-Pee-Chee Box Bottoms

This sixteen-card standard-size set was issued in sets of four on the bottom of the 1985-86 O-Pee-Chee wax pack boxes. Complete box bottom panels are valued at a 25 percent premium above the prices listed below. The card back included statistical information,and was written in English and French. The cards were lettered rather than numbered. The key card in the set was obviously Mario Lemieux, pictured in his rookie year for cards.

COMPLETE SET (16) 40.00 100.00
A Brian Bellows .30 .75
B Ray Bourque 2.00 5.00
C Bob Carpenter .20 .50
D Chris Chelios 2.00 5.00
E Marcel Dionne .75 2.00
F Ron Francis 1.25 3.00
G Wayne Gretzky 12.00 30.00
H Tim Kerr .20 .50
I Mario Lemieux 40.00 100.00
J John Ogrodnick .20 .50
K Gilbert Perreault .40 1.00
L Glenn Resch .40 1.00
M Reijo Ruotsalainen .20 .50
N Brian Sutter .30 .75
O John Tonelli .20 .50
P Doug Wilson .30 .75

1985-86 O-Pee-Chee Stickers

This sticker set consisted of 255 stickers in full color and was put out by O-Pee-Chee. The foil stickers are listed in the checklist below explicitly. The stickers measured approximately 2 1/8" by 3". An album was available for these stickers. Those stickers which are pairs are indicated in the checklist below by noting parenthetically the other member of the pair. On the inside back cover of the sticker album the company offered (via direct mail-order) any ten different stickers of your choice for one dollar; this is one reason why the values of the most popular players in these sticker sets are somewhat depressed compared to traditional card set prices. For example, anyone wanting Mario Lemieux, Wayne Gretzky, and eight others could get them for one dollar directly through this offer.

COMPLETE SET (255) 16.00 40.00
1 Stanley Cup Finals .08 .25
2 Stanley Cup Finals .02 .10
3 Stanley Cup Finals .02 .10
4 Stanley Cup Finals .02 .10
5 Wayne Gretzky 2.00 5.00
6 Rick Vaive .02 .10
7 Bill Derlago .02 .10
8 Rick St. Croix (136) .01 .05
9 Tim Bernhardt (137) .01 .05
10 John Anderson (138) .01 .05
11 Dan Daoust (139) .01 .05
12 Borje Salming .02 .10
13 Al Iafrate (143) .20 .50
14 Gary Nylund (144) .01 .05
15 Bob McGill (145) .01 .05
16 Jim Benning (146) .08 .25
17 Stewart Gavin (148) .01 .05
18 Greg Terrion (149) .01 .05
19 Peter Ihnacak (150) .01 .05
20 Russ Courtnall (151) .20 .50
21 Miroslav Frycer .02 .10
22 Denis Savard .08 .25
23 Steve Yzerman (152) .75 2.00
24 Curt Fraser (153) .01 .05
25 Doug Wilson .02 .10
26 Ed Olczyk (154) .08 .25
27 Murray Bannerman .01 .05
(155)
28 Steve Larmer (158) .08 .25
29 Troy Murray (159) .02 .10
30 Steve Yzerman 1.25 3.00
31 Greg Stefan (161) .01 .05
32 Ron Duguay (162) .02 .10
33 Reed Larson (163) .01 .05
34 Ivan Boldirev (164) .01 .05
35 Danny Gare (166) .01 .05
36 Darryl Sittler (167) .01 .05
37 John Ogrodnick .02 .10
38 Keith Acton .02 .10
39 Dino Ciccarelli (168) .08 .25
40 Neal Broten (169) .08 .25
41 Brian Bellows .08 .25
42 Steve Payne (170) .01 .05
43 Gordie Roberts (171) .01 .05
44 Harold Snepsts (175) .02 .10
45 Tony McKegney (176) .01 .05
46 Brian Sutter .02 .10
47 Joe Mullen (177) .08 .25
48 Doug Gilmour (178) .40 1.00
49 Tim Bothwell (180) .01 .05
50 Mark Johnson (181) .01 .05
51 Greg Millen (182) .01 .05
52 Doug Wickenheiser .01 .05
(183)
53 Bernie Federko .02 .10
54 Wayne Gretzky (197) 1.50 4.00
FOIL
55 Tom Barrasso (203) .08 .25
FOIL
56 Paul Coffey (204) .20 .50
FOIL
57 Mel Bridgman .02 .10
58 Phil Russell (184) .01 .05
59 Dave Lewis (185) .01 .05
60 Paul Gagne (186) .01 .05
61 Glenn Resch (187) .08 .25
62 Aaron Broten (189) .08 .25
63 Dave Pichette (190) .01 .05
64 Kirk Muller .40 1.00
65 Bryan Trottier .08 .25
66 Mike Bossy .08 .25
67 Bob Bourne (191) .08 .25
68 Clark Gillies (192) .02 .10
69 Bob Nystrom (193) .01 .05
70 Denis Potvin (198) .08 .25
71 Brent Sutter .02 .10
72 Duane Sutter (199) .02 .10
73 Pat Flatley (200) .02 .10
74 Pat LaFontaine (201) .40 1.00
75 Greg Gilbert (202) .01 .05
76 Billy Smith (209) .08 .25
77 Gordie Lane (210) .01 .05
78 Tomas Jonsson (211) .01 .05
79 Kelly Hrudey (212) .30 .75
80 John Tonelli .02 .10
81 Reijo Ruotsalainen .02 .10
82 Barry Beck (213) .02 .10
83 James Patrick (214) .08 .25
84 Mark Pavelich .02 .10
85 Pierre Larouche .01 .05
86 Mike Rogers (219) .08 .25
87 Glen Hanlon (220) .08 .25
88 John Vanbiesbrouck 1.25 3.00
(221)
89 Dave Poulin .02 .10
90 Brian Propp (223) .02 .10
91 Pelle Lindbergh (224) .75 2.00
92 Brad McCrimmon (225) .02 .10
93 Mark Howe (226) .08 .25
94 Peter Zezel (227) .08 .25
95 Murray Craven (228) .20 .50
96 Tim Kerr .02 .10
97 Mario Lemieux 6.00 15.00
98 Moe Mantha (229) .01 .05
99 Doug Bodger (230) .01 .05
100 Warren Young .02 .10
101 John Chabot (233) .01 .05
102 Doug Shedden (234) .01 .05
103 Wayne Babych (236) .01 .05
104 Mike Bullard (237) .01 .05
105 Rod Langway .02 .10
106 Pat Riggin (238) .02 .10
107 Scott Stevens (239) .08 .25
108 Alan Haworth (241) .01 .05
109 Doug Jarvis (242) .01 .05
110 Dave Christian (243) .01 .05
111 Mike Gartner (244) .08 .25
112 Bob Carpenter .02 .10
113 Rod Langway FOIL .05 .15
114 Tom Barrasso FOIL .08 .25
115 Ray Bourque FOIL .40 1.00
116 John Tonelli FOIL .05 .15
117 Brent Sutter FOIL .05 .15
118 Mike Bossy FOIL .20 .50
119 John Ogrodnick FOIL .05 .15
120 Wayne Gretzky FOIL 2.00 5.00
121 Jari Kurri FOIL .30 .75
122 Doug Wilson FOIL .05 .15
123 Andy Moog FOIL .20 .50
124 Paul Coffey FOIL .40 1.00
125 Chris Chelios .40 1.00
126 Steve Penney .02 .10
127 Chris Nilan (245) .02 .10
128 Ron Flockhart (246) .01 .05
129 Tom Kurvers (249) .01 .05
130 Craig Ludwig (250) .01 .05
131 Mats Naslund .01 .05
132 Bobby Smith (252) .02 .10
133 Pierre Mondou (253) .01 .05
134 Mario Tremblay (254) .01 .05
135 Guy Carbonneau (255) .08 .25
136 Doug Soetaert (8) .01 .05
137 Mark Hunter (9) .01 .05
138 Bob Gainey (10) .01 .05
139 Petr Svoboda (11) .01 .05
140 Larry Robinson .08 .25
141 Michel Goulet .08 .25
142 Bruce Bell .02 .10
143 Dan Bouchard (13) .20 .50
144 Mario Marois (14) .01 .05
145 Randy Moller (15) .01 .05
146 Mario Gosselin (16) .08 .25
147 Anton Stastny .02 .10
148 Normand Rochefort(17) .01 .05
149 Alain Cote (18) .01 .05
150 Paul Gillis (19) .01 .05
151 Dale Hunter (20) .20 .50
152 Wilf Paiement (23) .01 .05
153 Brent Ashton (24) .01 .05
154 Brad Maxwell (26) .08 .25
155 J.F. Sauve (27) .01 .05
156 Peter Stastny .08 .25
157 Ray Bourque .20 .50
158 Charlie Simmer (28) .08 .25
159 Rick Middleton (29) .02 .10
160 Pete Peeters .02 .10
161 Mike O'Connell (31) .01 .05
162 Terry O'Reilly (32) .02 .10
163 Keith Crowder (33) .01 .05
164 Tom Fergus (34) .01 .05
165 Sylvain Turgeon .02 .10
166 Greg Malone (35) .01 .05
167 Bob Crawford (36) .01 .05
168 Kevin Dineen (39) .08 .25
169 Mike Liut (40) .08 .25
170 Joel Quenneville (42) .01 .05
171 Ray Neufeld (43) .01 .05
172 Ron Francis .20 .50
173 Phil Housley .08 .25
174 Mike Foligno .02 .10
175 Craig Ramsay (44) .01 .05
176 Bill Hajt (45) .01 .05
177 Dave Maloney (47) .08 .25
178 Brent Peterson (48) .01 .05
179 Tom Barrasso .08 .25
180 Mike Ramsey (49) .01 .05
181 Bob Sauve (50) .01 .05
182 Ric Seiling (51) .01 .05
183 Paul Cyr (52) .01 .05
184 John Tucker (58) .01 .05
185 Gilles Hamel (59) .01 .05
186 Malcolm Davis (60) .01 .05
187 Dave Andreychuk (61) .08 .25
188 Gilbert Perreault .08 .25
189 Tom Barrasso (62) .08 .25
190 Bob Sauve (63) .01 .05
191 Paul Coffey (67) .08 .25
192 Craig Ramsay (68) .01 .05
193 Pelle Lindbergh (69) .75 2.00
194 Jennings Trophy (205) .02 .10
FOIL
195 Norris Trophy (206) .02 .10
FOIL
196 Selke Trophy (207) .02 .10
FOIL
197 Vezina Trophy (54) .02 .10
FOIL
198 Wayne Gretzky (70) 1.50 4.00
199 Mario Lemieux (72) 3.00 8.00
200 Anders Hedberg (73) .02 .10
201 Jari Kurri (74) .08 .25
202 Wayne Gretzky (75) 1.50 4.00
203 Hart Trophy (55) .08 .25
FOIL
204 Calder Trophy (56) .20 .50
FOIL
205 Masterton Trophy(194) .02 .10
FOIL
206 Lady Byng Trophy(195) .02 .10
FOIL
207 Art Ross Trophy (207) .02 .10
FOIL
208 Kent Nilsson .02 .10
209 Paul Reinhart (76) .08 .25
210 Rejean Lemelin (77) .02 .10
211 Al MacInnis (78) .75 2.00
212 Jamie Macoun (79) .02 .10
213 Carey Wilson (82) .08 .25
214 Ed Beers (83) .08 .25
215 Lanny McDonald .08 .25
216 Charlie Huddy .02 .10
217 Paul Coffey .20 .50
218 Lee Fogolin (85) .01 .05
219 Kevin Lowe (86) .08 .25
220 Andy Moog (87) .08 .25
221 Grant Fuhr (88) .08 .25
222 Wayne Gretzky 2.00 5.00
223 Mike Krushelnyski(90) .02 .10
224 Billy Carroll (91) .01 .05
225 Randy Gregg (92) .02 .10
226 Willy Lindstrom (93) .08 .25
227 Glenn Anderson (94) .08 .25
228 Mark Messier (95) .20 .50
229 Pat Hughes (98) .01 .05
230 Kevin McClelland (99) .01 .05
231 Jari Kurri .20 .50
232 Bernie Nicholls .08 .25
233 Brian Engblom (101) .01 .05
234 Mark Hardy (102) .01 .05
235 Marcel Dionne .08 .25
236 Jim Fox (103) .01 .05
237 Terry Ruskowski (104) .01 .05
238 Dave Taylor (106) .02 .10
239 Bob Janecyk (107) .08 .25
240 Thomas Gradin .02 .10
241 Patrik Sundstrom(108) .01 .05
242 Al MacAdam (109) .01 .05
243 Doug Halward (110) .01 .05
244 Peter McNab (111) .01 .05
245 Tony Tanti (127) .02 .10
246 Moe Lemay (128) .01 .05
247 Stan Smyl .02 .10
248 Dale Hawerchuk .20 .50
249 Dave Babych (129) .01 .05
250 Paul MacLean (130) .01 .05
251 Randy Carlyle .02 .10
252 Robert Picard (132) .01 .05
253 Thomas Steen (133) .01 .05
254 Laurie Boschman (134) .01 .05
255 Doug Smail (135) .08 .25
xx Sticker Album 2.00 5.00

1986-87 O-Pee-Chee

This 1986-87 O-Pee-Chee set consisted of 264 standard-size cards. Card fronts featured player name, team, team logo and position at the bottom. Bilingual backs featured yearly and career statistics as well as the number of game-winning goals scored in 1985-86. The key Rookie Card in this set was Patrick Roy. Beware when purchasing the Patrick Roy card from this set as it has been counterfeited.

COMPLETE SET (264) 200.00 350.00
1 Ray Bourque 2.50 5.00
2 Pat LaFontaine 1.25 3.00
3 Wayne Gretzky 15.00 25.00
4 Lindy Ruff .08 .25
5 Brad McCrimmon .08 .25
6 Dave(Tiger) Williams .20 .50
7 Denis Savard .50 1.25
8 Lanny McDonald .20 .50
9 John Vanbiesbrouck RC 10.00 25.00
10 Greg Adams RC .60 1.50
11 Steve Yzerman 15.00 30.00
12 Craig Hartsburg .08 .25
13 John Anderson .08 .25
14 Bob Bourne .08 .25
15 Kjell Dahlin RC .08 .25
16 Dave Andreychuk .50 1.25
17 Rob Ramage .08 .25
18 Ron Greschner .08 .25
19 Bruce Driver .20 .50
20 Peter Stastny .20 .50
21 Dave Christian .08 .25
22 Doug Keans .08 .25
23 Scott Bjugstad RC .08 .25
24 Doug Bodger .08 .25
25 Troy Murray .08 .25
26 Al Iafrate .40 1.00
27 Kelly Hrudey .50 1.25
28 Doug Jarvis .08 .25
29 Rich Sutter .08 .25
30 Marcel Dionne .20 .50
31 Curt Fraser .08 .25
32 Doug Lidster .08 .25
33 Brian MacLellan .08 .25
34 Barry Pederson .08 .25
35 Craig Laughlin .08 .25
36 Ilkka Sinisalo .08 .25
37 John MacLean RC 1.50 4.00
38 Brian Mullen .08 .25
39 Duane Sutter .08 .25
40 Brian Engblom .08 .25
41 Chris Cichocki RC .08 .25
42 Gordie Roberts .08 .25
43 Ron Francis 1.00 2.50
44 Joe Mullen .50 1.25
45 Moe Mantha .08 .25
46 Pat Verbeek .08 .25
47 Clint Malarchuk RC .50 1.25
48 Bob Brooke .08 .25
49 Darryl Sutter .08 .25
50 Stan Smyl .08 .25
51 Greg Stefan .20 .50
52 Bill Hajt .08 .25
53 Patrick Roy RC 75.00 150.00
54 Gord Kluzak .08 .25
55 Bob Froese .20 .50
56 Grant Fuhr 1.00 2.50
57 Mark Hunter .08 .25
58 Dana Murzyn RC .50 1.25
59 Mike Gartner .50 1.25
60 Dennis Maruk .08 .25
61 Rich Preston .08 .25
62 Larry Robinson .20 .50
63 Dave Taylor .20 .50
64 Bob Murray .08 .25
65 Ken Morrow .08 .25
66 Mike Ridley RC .50 1.25
67 John Tucker RC .20 .50
68 Miroslav Frycer .08 .25
69 Danny Gare .20 .50
70 Randy Burridge RC .40 1.00
71 Dave Poulin .08 .25
72 Brian Sutter .20 .50
73 Dave Babych .08 .25
74 Dale Hawerchuk .50 1.25
75 Brian Bellows .50 1.25
76 Dave Pasin RC .08 .25
77 Pete Peeters .20 .50
78 Tomas Jonsson .08 .25
79 Gilbert Perreault .20 .50
80 Glenn Anderson .50 1.25
81 Don Maloney .08 .25
82 Ed Olczyk .08 .25
83 Mike Bullard .08 .25
84 Tom Fergus .08 .25
85 Dave Lewis .08 .25
86 Brian Propp .20 .50
87 John Ogrodnick .08 .25
88 Kevin Dineen .40 1.00
89 Don Beaupre .20 .50
90 Mike Bossy .60 1.50
91 Tom Barrasso .40 1.00
92 Michel Goulet .20 .50
93 Doug Gilmour 2.50 5.00
94 Kirk Muller .40 1.00
95 Larry Melnyk RC .08 .25
96 Bob Gainey .50 1.25
97 Steve Kasper .08 .25
98 Petr Klima RC .40 1.00
99 Neal Broten .20 .50
100 Al Secord .08 .25
101 Bryan Erickson .08 .25
102 Rejean Lemelin .20 .50
103 Sylvain Turgeon .08 .25
104 Bob Nystrom .08 .25
105 Bernie Federko .20 .50
106 Doug Wilson .20 .50
107 Alan Haworth .08 .25
108 Jari Kurri 1.00 2.50
109 Ron Sutter .08 .25
110 Reed Larson .08 .25
111 Terry Ruskowski .08 .25
112 Mark Johnson .08 .25
113 James Patrick .08 .25
114 Paul MacLean .08 .25
115 Mike Ramsey .08 .25
116 Kelly Kisio .08 .25
117 Brent Sutter .08 .25
118 Joel Quenneville .08 .25
119 Curt Giles .08 .25
120 Tony Tanti .08 .25
121 Doug Sulliman .08 .25
122 Mario Lemieux ! 40.00 60.00
123 Mark Howe .20 .50
124 Bob Sauve .20 .50
125 Anton Stastny .08 .25
126 Scott Stevens .40 1.00
127 Mike Foligno .08 .25
128 Reijo Ruotsalainen .08 .25
129 Denis Potvin .20 .50
130 Keith Crowder .08 .25
131 Bob Janecyk .20 .50
132 John Tonelli .08 .25
133 Mike Liut .20 .50
134 Tim Kerr .20 .50
135 Al Jensen .08 .25
136 Mel Bridgman .08 .25
137 Paul Coffey 1.50 4.00
138 Dino Ciccarelli .50 1.25
139 Steve Larmer .50 1.25
140 Mike O'Connell .08 .25
141 Clark Gillies .20 .50
142 Phil Russell .08 .25
143 Dirk Graham RC .75 2.00
144 Randy Carlyle .08 .25
145 Charlie Simmer .20 .50
146 Ron Flockhart .08 .25
147 Tom Laidlaw .08 .25
148 Dave Tippett RC .20 .50
149 Wendel Clark RC 7.50 15.00
150 Bob Carpenter .08 .25
151 Bill Watson RC .08 .25
152 Roberto Romano RC .20 .50
153 Doug Shedden .08 .25
154 Phil Housley .40 1.00
155 Bryan Trottier .50 1.25
156 Patrik Sundstrom .08 .25
157 Rick Middleton .20 .50
158 Glenn Resch .20 .50
159 Bernie Nicholls .20 .50
160 Ray Ferraro RC 2.00 5.00
161 Mats Naslund .20 .50
162 Pat Flatley .08 .25
163 Joe Cirella .08 .25
164 Rod Langway .20 .50
165 Checklist 1-132 1.25 3.00
166 Carey Wilson .08 .25
167 Murray Craven .20 .50
168 Paul Gillis RC .08 .25
169 Borje Salming .08 .25
170 Perry Turnbull .08 .25
171 Chris Chelios 2.00 5.00
172 Keith Acton .08 .25
173 Al MacInnis 3.00 6.00
174 Russ Courtnall RC 1.50 4.00
175 Brad Marsh .20 .50
176 Guy Carbonneau .20 .50
177 Ray Neufeld .08 .25
178 Craig MacTavish RC .75 2.00
179 Rick Lanz .08 .25
180 Murray Bannerman .08 .25
181 Brent Ashton .08 .25
182 Jim Peplinski .08 .25
183 Mark Napier .08 .25
184 Laurie Boschman .08 .25
185 Larry Murphy .40 1.00
186 Mark Messier .75 2.00
187 Risto Siltanen .08 .25
188 Bobby Smith .20 .50
189 Gary Suter RC 1.25 3.00
190 Peter Zezel .08 .25
191 Rick Vaive .08 .25
192 Dale Hunter .20 .50
193 Mike Krushelnyski .08 .25
194 Scott Arniel .08 .25
195 Larry Playfair .08 .25
196 Doug Risebrough .08 .25
197 Kevin Lowe .20 .50
198 Checklist 133-264 1.25 3.00
199 Chris Nilan .08 .25
200 Paul Cyr RC .08 .25
201 Ric Seiling .08 .25
202 Doug Smith .08 .25
203 Jamie Macoun .08 .25
204 Dan Quinn .08 .25
205 Paul Reinhart .08 .25
206 Keith Brown .08 .25
207 Jack O'Callahan .08 .25
208 Steve Richmond RC .08 .25
209 Warren Young .08 .25
210 Lee Fogolin .08 .25
211 Charlie Huddy .08 .25
212 Andy Moog 1.00 2.50
213 Wayne Babych .08 .25
214 Torrie Robertson .08 .25
215 Jim Fox .08 .25
216 Phil Sykes RC .08 .25
217 Jay Wells .08 .25
218 Dave Langevin .08 .25
219 Steve Payne .08 .25
220 Craig Ludwig .08 .25
221 Mike McPhee .08 .25
222 Steve Penney .08 .25
223 Mario Tremblay .08 .25
224 Ryan Walter .08 .25
225 Alain Chevrier RC .20 .50
226 Uli Hiemer RC .08 .25
227 Tim Higgins .08 .25
228 Billy Smith .20 .50
229 Richard Kromm .08 .25
230 Tomas Sandstrom .50 1.25
231 Jim Johnson RC .20 .50
232 Willy Lindstrom .08 .25
233 Alain Cote .08 .25
234 Gilbert Delorme .08 .25
235 Mario Gosselin .20 .50
236 David Shaw RC .40 1.00
237 Dave Barr RC .40 1.00
238 Ed Beers .08 .25
239 Charlie Bourgeois RC .08 .25
240 Rick Wamsley .08 .25
241 Dan Daoust .08 .25
242 Brad Maxwell .08 .25
243 Gary Nylund .08 .25
244 Greg Terrion .08 .25
245 Steve Thomas RC 2.50 5.00
246 Richard Brodeur .08 .25
247 Joel Otto UER RC .40 1.00
248 Doug Halward .08 .25
249 Moe Lemay UER .08 .25
(Photo actually
Joel Otto)
250 Cam Neely 2.50 5.00
251 Brent Peterson .08 .25
252 Petri Skriko RC .40 1.00
253 Greg C. Adams RC .20 .50
254 Bill Derlago .08 .25
255 Brian Hayward .20 .50
256 Doug Smail .08 .25
257 Thomas Steen .08 .25
258 Jari Kurri .50 1.25
(Goals Leaders)
259 Wayne Gretzky 3.00 6.00
(Assists Leaders)
260 Wayne Gretzky 3.00 6.00
(Points Leaders)
261 Tim Kerr .10 .30
(Power Play Goal Leaders)
262 Kjell Dahlin .10 .30
(Rookie Scoring Leaders)
263 Bob Froese .10 .30
(Goals Against Average Leaders)
264 Bob Froese .10 .30
(Save Percentage Leaders)

1986-87 O-Pee-Chee Box Bottoms

This sixteen-card standard-size set was issued in sets of four on the bottom of the 1986-87 O-Pee-Chee wax pack boxes. Complete box bottom panels are valued at a 25 percent premium above the prices listed below. This set featured some of the leading NHL players including Mike Bossy, Wayne Gretzky, Mario Lemieux, and Bryan Trottier. The front presented a color action photo with various color borders, with the team's logo in the lower right hand corner. The back included statistical information, was written in English and French, and was printed in blue with black ink. The cards were lettered rather than numbered.

COMPLETE SET (16) 16.00 40.00
A Greg Adams .20 .50
B Mike Bossy .60 1.50
C Dave Christian .08 .25
D Mike Foligno .20 .50
E Michel Goulet .30 .75
F Wayne Gretzky 8.00 20.00
G Tim Kerr .08 .25
H Jari Kurri 1.00 2.50
I Mario Lemieux 10.00 25.00
J Lanny McDonald .30 .75
K Bernie Nicholls .30 .75
L Mike Ridley .30 .75
M Larry Robinson .30 .75
N Denis Savard .30 .75
O Brian Sutter .08 .25
P Bryan Trottier .40 1.00

1986-87 O-Pee-Chee Stickers

This sticker set consisted of 255 stickers in full color and was put out by O-Pee-Chee. The foil stickers are listed in the checklist below explicitly. The stickers measured approximately 2 1/8" by 3". An album was available for these stickers. Those stickers which are pairs are indicated in the checklist below by noting parenthetically the other member of the pair. On the inside back cover of the sticker album the company offered (via direct mail-order) any ten different stickers of your choice for one dollar; this is one reason why the values of the most popular players in these sticker sets are somewhat depressed compared to traditional card set prices.

COMPLETE SET (255) 16.00 40.00
1 Stanley Cup Action .20 .50
2 Stanley Cup Action .08 .25
3 Stanley Cup Action .08 .25
4 Stanley Cup Action .08 .25
5 Patrick Roy FOIL 6.00 15.00
6 Chris Chelios (151) .08 .25
7 Guy Carbonneau (152) .01 .05
8 Larry Robinson .02 .10
9 Mario Tremblay (154) .01 .05
10 Tom Kurvers (155) .01 .05
11 Mats Naslund .02 .10
12 Bob Gainey .30 .75
13 Bobby Smith .02 .10
14 Craig Ludwig (156) .01 .05
15 Mike McPhee (157) .01 .05
16 Doug Soetaert (159) .01 .05
17 Petr Svoboda (160) .01 .05
18 Kjell Dahlin .02 .10
19 Patrick Roy 4.00 10.00
20 Alain Cote (161) .01 .05
21 Mario Gosselin (162) .01 .05
22 Michel Goulet .08 .25
23 J.F. Sauve (163) .01 .05
24 Paul Gillis (164) .01 .05
25 Brent Ashton .02 .10
26 Peter Stastny .08 .25
27 Anton Stastny .02 .10
28 Gilbert Delorme (167) .01 .05
29 Risto Siltanen (168) .01 .05
30 Robert Picard (170) .01 .05
31 David Shaw (171) .01 .05
32 Dale Hunter .02 .10
33 Clint Malarchuk .08 .25
34 Ray Bourque .20 .50

35 Rick Middleton (172) .01 .05
36 Charlie Simmer (173) .01 .05
37 Keith Crowder .02 .10
38 Barry Pederson (175) .01 .05
39 Reed Larson (176) .01 .05
40 Steve Kasper (177) .01 .05
41 Pat Riggin (178) .01 .05
42 Mike Foligno .02 .10
43 Gilbert Perreault .01 .05
(179)
44 Mike Ramsey (180) .01 .05
45 Tom Barrasso (186) .08 .25
46 Brian Engblom (187) .01 .05
47 Phil Housley (188) .08 .25
48 John Tucker (189) .01 .05
49 Dave Andreychuk .08 .25
50 Dave Babych .02 .10
51 Ron Francis (190) .08 .25
52 Mike Liut (191) .08 .25
53 Sylvain Turgeon .02 .10
54 John Anderson (192) .01 .05
55 Joel Quenneville (193) .01 .05
56 Kevin Dineen (194) .08 .25
57 Ray Ferraro (195) .01 .05
58 Action Sticker .02 .10
59 Action Sticker .02 .10
60 Action Sticker .02 .10
61 Action Sticker .02 .10
62 Action Sticker .02 .10
63 Action Sticker .02 .10
64 Action Sticker .02 .10
65 Action Sticker .02 .10
66 Andy Moog (197) .08 .25
67 Grant Fuhr (198) .08 .25
68 Paul Coffey .20 .50
69 Charlie Huddy (199) .01 .05
70 Kevin Lowe (200) .08 .25
71 Lee Fogolin .02 .10
72 Wayne Gretzky 1.50 4.00
73 Jari Kurri .08 .25
74 Mike Krushelnyski .01 .05
(201)
75 Mark Napier (202) .01 .05
76 Craig MacTavish (204) .01 .05
77 Kevin McClelland .01 .05
(205)
78 Glenn Anderson .08 .25
79 Mark Messier .30 .75
80 Lanny McDonald .08 .25
81 John Tonelli (207) .01 .05
82 Joe Mullen (208) .08 .25
83 Reggie Lemelin .08 .25
84 Jim Peplinski (212) .01 .05
85 Jamie Macoun (213) .01 .05
86 Al MacInnis (214) .20 .50
87 Dan Quinn (215) .01 .05
88 Marcel Dionne .08 .25
89 Jim Fox (219) .01 .05
90 Dave Taylor (220) .01 .05
91 Bob Janecyk (222) .01 .05
92 Jay Wells (223) .01 .05
93 Bryan Erickson (224) .01 .05
94 Dave(Tiger) Williams .01 .05
(225)
95 Bernie Nicholls .08 .25
96 Stan Smyl .02 .10
97 Doug Halward (227) .01 .05
98 Richard Brodeur (228) .01 .05
99 Tony Tanti .02 .10
100 Brent Peterson (229) .01 .05
101 Patrik Sundstrom .01 .05
(230)
102 Doug Lidster (231) .01 .05
103 Petri Skriko (232) .01 .05
104 Dale Hawerchuk .08 .25
105 Bill Derlago (234) .01 .05
106 Ray Neufeld (235) .01 .05
107 Randy Carlyle (237) .01 .05
108 Paul MacLean (238) .01 .05
109 Brian Mullen (242) .01 .05
110 Thomas Steen (243) .01 .05
111 Laurie Boschman .02 .10
112 Paul Coffey (126) .20 .50
FOIL
113 Michel Goulet (127) .05 .15
FOIL
114 John Vanbiesbrouck 1.00 2.50
(128) FOIL
115 Wayne Gretzky (129) 1.25 3.00
FOIL
116 Mark Howe (130) .05 .15
FOIL
117 Mike Bossy (131) .20 .50
FOIL
118 Jari Kurri (132) .20 .50
FOIL
119 Ray Bourque (133) .20 .50
FOIL
120 Mario Lemieux (134) 1.25 3.00
FOIL
121 Grant Fuhr (135) .05 .15
FOIL
122 Mats Naslund (182) .05 .15
FOIL
123 Larry Robinson (183) .05 .15
FOIL
124 Chris Cichocki (184) .05 .15
FOIL
125 Wendel Clark (185) .75 2.00
FOIL
126 Kjell Dahlin (112) .05 .15
FOIL
127 Pelle Eklund (113) .05 .15
FOIL
128 Jim Johnson (114) .05 .15
FOIL
129 Petr Klima (115) .05 .15
FOIL
130 Joel Otto (116) .05 .15
FOIL
131 Mike Ridley (117) .20 .50
FOIL
132 Patrick Roy (118) 3.00 8.00
FOIL
133 David Shaw (119) .05 .15
FOIL
134 Gary Suter (120) .05 .15
FOIL
135 Steve Thomas (121) .05 .15
FOIL
136 Borje Salming (244) .01 .05
137 Gary Nylund (245) .01 .05
138 Rick Vaive .02 .10
139 Don Edwards (249) .01 .05
140 Steve Thomas (250) .08 .25
141 Wendel Clark .40 1.00
142 Miroslav Frycer .02 .10
143 Tom Fergus .02 .10
144 Marian Stastny (252) .01 .05
145 Brad Maxwell (253) .01 .05
146 Dan Daoust (254) .01 .05
147 Greg Terrion (255) .01 .05
148 Al Iafrate .08 .25
149 Russ Courtnall .08 .25
150 Dennis Savard .08 .25
151 Darryl Sutter (6) .01 .05
152 Bob Sauve (7) .01 .05
153 Doug Wilson .02 .10
154 Troy Murray (9) .01 .05
155 Al Secord (10) .01 .05
156 Ed Olczyk (14) .01 .05
157 Steve Larmer (15) .08 .25
158 John Ogrodnick .02 .10
159 Danny Gare (16) .01 .05
160 Petr Svoboda (160) .01 .05
161 Steve Yzerman (20) .75 2.00
162 Petr Klima (21) .01 .05
163 Kelly Kisio (23) .01 .05
164 Doug Shedden (24) .01 .05
165 Greg Stefan .02 .10
166 Neal Broten .08 .25
167 Brian Bellows (28) .01 .05
168 Scott Bjugstad (29) .01 .05
169 Dino Ciccarelli .08 .25
170 Dennis Maruk (30) .01 .05
171 Dirk Graham (31) .08 .25
172 Curt Giles (35) .01 .05
173 Craig Hartsburg (36) .01 .05
174 Bernie Federko .02 .10
175 Brian Sutter (38) .01 .05
176 Ron Flockhart (39) .01 .05
177 Doug Gilmour (40) .20 .50
178 Charlie Bourgeois .01 .05
(41)
179 Rick Wamsley (43) .01 .05
180 Rob Ramage (44) .01 .05
181 Mark Hunter .02 .10
182 Bob Froese (122) .05 .15
FOIL
183 Wayne Gretzky (123) 1.25 3.00
FOIL
184 Mark Howe (124) .05 .15
FOIL
185 Jari Kurri (125) .20 .50
FOIL
186 Bob Froese (45) .01 .05
187 Darren Jensen (46) .01 .05
188 Paul Coffey (47) .08 .25
189 Troy Murray (48) .01 .05
190 John Vanbiesbrouck .40 1.00
191 Wayne Gretzky (52) 1.25 3.00
192 Gary Suter (54) .01 .05
193 Bob Froese (55) .08 .25
194 Mike Bossy (56) .01 .05
195 Wayne Gretzky (57) 1.25 3.00
196 Greg Adams .02 .10
197 Dave Lewis (66) .01 .05
198 Joe Cirella (67) .01 .05
199 Rich Preston (69) .01 .05
200 Mark Johnson (70) .01 .05
201 Kirk Muller (74) .08 .25
202 Pat Verbeek (75) .08 .25
203 Mel Bridgman .02 .10
204 Bob Nystrom (76) .01 .05
205 Clark Gillies (77) .01 .05
206 Pat LaFontaine .30 .75
207 Pat Flatley (81) .01 .05
208 Bob Bourne (82) .01 .05
209 Denis Potvin .08 .25
210 Duane Sutter .02 .10
211 Brent Sutter .02 .10
212 Kelly Hrudey (84) .20 .50
213 Billy Smith (85) .08 .25
214 Tomas Jonsson (86) .01 .05
215 Ken Morrow (87) .01 .05
216 Bryan Trottier .08 .25
217 Mike Bossy .08 .25
218 John Vanbiesbrouck .75 2.00
219 Bob Brooke (89) .01 .05
220 James Patrick (90) .01 .05
221 Mike Ridley .08 .25
222 Ron Greschner (91) .01 .05
223 Tom Laidlaw (92) .01 .05
224 Larry Melnyk (93) .01 .05
225 Reijo Ruotsalainen .01 .05
(94)
226 Terry Ruskowski .02 .10
227 Willy Lindstrom (97) .01 .05
228 Mike Bullard (98) .01 .05
229 Roberto Romano (100) .01 .05
230 John Chabot (101) .01 .05
231 Moe Mantha (102) .01 .05
232 Doug Bodger (103) .01 .05
233 Mario Lemieux 3.00 8.00
234 Glenn Resch (105) .08 .25
235 Brad Marsh (106) .01 .05
236 Bob Froese .02 .10
237 Doug Crossman (107) .01 .05
238 Ilkka Sinisalo (108) .01 .05
239 Brian Propp .02 .10
240 Tim Kerr .02 .10
241 Dave Poulin .40 1.00
242 Rich Sutter (109) .01 .05
243 Ron Sutter (110) .01 .05
244 Murray Craven (136) .01 .05
245 Peter Zezel (137) .01 .05
246 Mark Howe .02 .10
247 Brad McCrimmon .02 .10
248 Dave Christian .02 .10
249 Rod Langway (139) .01 .05
250 Bob Carpenter (140) .01 .05
251 Mike Gartner .08 .25
252 Al Jensen (144) .01 .05
253 Craig Laughlin (145) .01 .05
254 Scott Stevens (146) .08 .25
255 Alan Haworth (147) .01 .05
xx Sticker Album 1.50 4.00

1987-88 O-Pee-Chee

Card fronts in this 264-card standard-size set featured a bottom border that contains the design of a hockey stick with which the player's name appears. Also, the team name appeared within a puck. Bilingual backs contain yearly and career statistics along with highlights. Beware when purchasing the cards of Wayne Gretzky, Adam Oates and Luc Robitaille from this set as they have been counterfeited.

COMPLETE SET (264) 75.00 150.00
COMPLETE FACT.SET (264) 75.00 150.00
1 Denis Potvin .15 .40
2 Rick Tocchet RC 3.00 8.00
3 Dave Andreychuk .30 .75
4 Stan Smyl .05 .15
5 Dave Babych .05 .15
6 Pat Verbeek .05 .15
7 Esa Tikkanen RC 2.50 6.00
8 Mike Ridley .15 .40
9 Randy Carlyle UER .05 .15
(Misspelled Calryle on card front)
10 Greg Paslawski RC .15 .40
11 Neal Broten .15 .40
12 Wendel Clark 2.50 5.00
13 Bill Ranford RC 3.00 8.00
14 Doug Wilson .15 .40
15 Mario Lemieux 15.00 30.00
16 Mats Naslund .15 .40
17 Mel Bridgman .05 .15
18 James Patrick .05 .15
19 Rollie Melanson .15 .40
20 Lanny McDonald .15 .40
21 Peter Stastny .15 .40
22 Murray Craven .05 .15
23 Ulf Samuelsson RC 1.50 4.00
24 Michael Thelven RC .05 .15
25 Scott Stevens .30 .75
26 Petr Klima .05 .15
27 Brent Sutter .05 .15
28 Tomas Sandstrom .30 .75
29 Tim Bothwell .05 .15
30 Bob Carpenter .05 .15
31 Brian MacLellan .05 .15
32 John Chabot .05 .15
33 Phil Housley .15 .40
34 Patrik Sundstrom .05 .15
35 Dave Ellett .15 .40
36 John Vanbiesbrouck 4.00 10.00
37 Dave Lewis .05 .15
38 Tom McCarthy .05 .15
39 Dave Poulin .05 .15
40 Mike Foligno .05 .15
41 Gordie Roberts .05 .15
42 Luc Robitaille RC 15.00 30.00
43 Duane Sutter .05 .15
44 Pete Peeters .15 .40
45 John Anderson .05 .15
46 Aaron Broten .05 .15
47 Keith Brown .05 .15
48 Bobby Smith .15 .40
49 Don Maloney .05 .15
50 Mark Hunter .05 .15
51 Moe Mantha .05 .15
52 Charlie Simmer .15 .40
53 Wayne Gretzky 10.00 25.00
54 Mark Howe .15 .40
55 Bob Gould .05 .15
56 Steve Yzerman 6.00 12.00
57 Larry Playfair .05 .15
58 Alain Chevrier .05 .15
59 Steve Larmer .30 .75
60 Bryan Trottier .30 .75
61 Stewart Gavin .05 .15
62 Russ Courtnall .30 .75
63 Mike Ramsey .05 .15
64 Bob Brooke .05 .15
65 Rick Wamsley .05 .15
66 Ken Morrow .05 .15
67 Gerard Gallant UER RC .15 .40
68 Kevin Hatcher RC .75 2.00
69 Cam Neely 1.25 3.00
70 Sylvain Turgeon .05 .15
71 Peter Zezel .05 .15
72 Al MacInnis 1.50 4.00
73 Terry Ruskowski .05 .15
74 Troy Murray .05 .15
75 Jim Fox .05 .15
76 Kelly Kisio .05 .15
77 Michel Goulet .15 .40
78 Tom Barrasso .30 .75
79 Bruce Driver .05 .15
80 Craig Simpson RC .40 1.00
81 Dino Ciccarelli .15 .40
82 Gary Nylund .05 .15
83 Bernie Federko .15 .40
84 John Tonelli .05 .15
85 Brad McCrimmon .05 .15
86 Dave Tippett .05 .15
87 Ray Bourque 1.50 4.00
88 Dave Christian .05 .15
89 Glen Hanlon .15 .40
90 Brian Curran RC .05 .15
91 Paul MacLean .05 .15
92 Jimmy Carson RC .30 .75
93 Willie Huber .05 .15
94 Brian Bellows .15 .40
95 Doug Jarvis .05 .15
96 Clark Gillies .15 .40
97 Tony Tanti .05 .15
98 Pelle Eklund RC .30 .75
99 Paul Coffey 1.25 3.00
100 Brent Ashton .05 .15
101 Mark Johnson .05 .15
102 Greg Johnston RC .05 .15
103 Ron Flockhart .05 .15
104 Ed Olczyk .05 .15
105 Mike Bossy .40 1.00
106 Chris Chelios 1.25 3.00
107 Gilles Meloche .15 .40
108 Rod Langway .15 .40
109 Ray Ferraro .30 .75
110 Ron Duguay .05 .15
111 Al Secord .05 .15
112 Mark Messier .30 .75
113 Ron Sutter .05 .15
114 Darren Veitch RC .05 .15
115 Rick Middleton .15 .40
116 Doug Sulliman .05 .15
117 Dennis Maruk .05 .15
118 Dave Taylor .15 .40
119 Kelly Hrudey .30 .75
120 Tom Fergus .05 .15
121 Christian Ruuttu RC .30 .75
122 Brian Benning RC .15 .40
123 Adam Oates RC 6.00 15.00
124 Kevin Dineen .15 .40
125 Doug Bodger .05 .15
126 Joe Mullen .15 .40
127 Denis Savard .15 .40
128 Brad Marsh .15 .40
129 Marcel Dionne .15 .40
130 Bryan Erickson .05 .15
131 Reed Larson .05 .15
132 Don Beaupre .15 .40
133 Larry Murphy .15 .40
134 John Ogrodnick .15 .40
135 Greg Adams .05 .15
136 Pat Flatley .05 .15
137 Scott Arniel .05 .15
138 Dana Murzyn .05 .15
139 Greg C. Adams .05 .15
140 Bob Sauve .05 .15
141 Mike O'Connell .05 .15
142 Walt Poddubny .05 .15
143 Paul Reinhart .05 .15
144 Tim Kerr .15 .40
145 Brian Lawton RC .05 .15
146 Gino Cavallini RC .15 .40
147 Doug Keans .05 .15
148 Jari Kurri .30 .75
149 Dale Hawerchuk .30 .75
150 Randy Cunneyworth RC .05 .15
151 Jay Wells .05 .15
152 Mike Liut .15 .40
153 Steve Konroyd .05 .15
154 John Tucker .05 .15
155 Rick Vaive .15 .40
156 Bob Murray .05 .15
157 Kirk Muller .30 .75
158 Brian Propp .05 .15
159 Ron Greschner .05 .15
160 Rob Ramage .05 .15
161 Craig Laughlin .05 .15
162 Steve Kasper .05 .15
163 Patrick Roy 15.00 40.00
164 Shawn Burr RC .30 .75
165 Craig Hartsburg .05 .15
166 Dean Evason RC .15 .40
167 Bob Bourne .05 .15
168 Mike Gartner .30 .75
169 Ron Hextall RC 5.00 10.00
170 Joe Cirella .05 .15
171 Dan Quinn .05 .15
172 Tony McKegney .05 .15
173 Pat LaFontaine .30 .75
174 Allen Pedersen RC .05 .15
175 Doug Gilmour .15 .40
176 Gary Suter .30 .75
177 Barry Pederson .05 .15
178 Grant Fuhr .30 .75
179 Wayne Presley RC .15 .40
180 Wilf Paiement .05 .15
181 Doug Smail .05 .15
182 Doug Crossman .05 .15
183 Bernie Nicholls UER .15 .40
(Misspelled Nichols on both sides)
184 Dirk Graham UER .15 .40
(Misspelled Dick)
185 Anton Stastny .05 .15
186 Greg Stefan .15 .40
187 Ron Francis .30 .75
188 Steve Thomas .15 .40
189 Kelly Miller RC .15 .40
190 Tomas Jonsson .05 .15
191 John MacLean .30 .75
192 Larry Robinson .15 .40
193 Doug Wickenheiser .05 .15
194 Keith Crowder .05 .15
195 Bob Froese .15 .40
196 Jim Johnson .05 .15
197 Checklist 1-132 .60 1.50
198 Checklist 133-264 .60 1.50
199 Glenn Anderson .05 .15
200 Kevin Lowe .15 .40
201 Kevin McClelland .05 .15
202 Mike Krushelnyski .05 .15
203 Craig MacTavish .15 .40
204 Andy Moog .60 1.50
205 Marty McSorley RC 2.00 5.00
206 Craig Muni RC .15 .40
207 Charlie Huddy .05 .15
208 Hakan Loob .15 .40
209 Jim Peplinski .05 .15
210 Mike Bullard .05 .15
211 Carey Wilson .05 .15
212 Joel Otto .05 .15
213 Neil Sheehy RC .05 .15
214 Jamie Macoun .05 .15
215 Mike Vernon RC 3.00 10.00
216 Steve Bozek .05 .15
217 Daniel Berthiaume RC .30 .75
218 Gilles Hamel .05 .15
219 Tim Watters .05 .15
220 Mario Marois .05 .15
221 Thomas Steen .05 .15
222 Laurie Boschman .05 .15
223 Steve Rooney RC .05 .15
224 Ron Wilson .05 .15
225 Fredrik Olausson RC .30 .75
226 Jim Kyte RC .05 .15
227 Claude Lemieux RC 2.50 6.00
228 Bob Gainey .30 .75
229 Gaston Gingras .05 .15
230 Brian Hayward .15 .40
231 Ryan Walter .05 .15
232 Guy Carbonneau .15 .40
233 Stephane Richer RC 2.50 5.00
234 Rick Green .05 .15
235 Brian Skrudland RC .60 1.50
236 Allan Bester .15 .40
237 Borje Salming .15 .40
238 Al Iafrate .30 .75
239 Rick Lanz .05 .15
240 Gary Leeman .05 .15
241 Greg Terrion .05 .15
242 Ken Wregget RC 1.25 3.00
243 Vincent Damphousse RC 3.00 8.00
244 Chris Kotsopoulos .05 .15
245 Dale Hunter .15 .40
246 Clint Malarchuk .15 .40
247 Paul Gillis .05 .15
248 Robert Picard .05 .15
249 Doug Shedden .05 .15
250 Mario Gosselin .15 .40
251 Randy Moller .05 .15
252 David Shaw .05 .15
253 Mike Eagles RC .15 .40
254 Alain Cote .05 .15
255 Petri Skriko .05 .15
256 Doug Lidster .05 .15
257 Richard Brodeur UER .15 .40
(Photo actually Frank Caprice)
258 Rich Sutter .05 .15
259 Steve Tambellini .05 .15
260 Jim Benning .05 .15
261 Dave Richter RC .15 .40
262 Michel Petit RC .15 .40
263 Brent Peterson .05 .15
264 Jim Sandlak RC .15 .40

1987-88 O-Pee-Chee Box Bottoms

This sixteen-card set was issued in sets of four on the bottom of the 1987-88 O-Pee-Chee wax pack boxes. Complete box bottom panels are valued at a 25 percent premium above the prices listed below. The cards were in the same design as the 1987-88 O-Pee-Chee regular issues except they were bordered in yellow. The backs were printed in red and black ink and give statistical information. The cards were lettered rather than numbered.

COMPLETE SET (16) 14.00 35.00
A Wayne Gretzky 6.00 15.00
B Tim Kerr .15 .40
C Steve Yzerman 3.00 8.00
D Luc Robitaille 3.00 8.00
E Doug Gilmour .75 2.00
F Ray Bourque .75 2.00
G Joe Mullen .30 .75
H Larry Murphy .30 .75
I Dale Hawerchuk .40 1.00
J Ron Francis .75 2.00
K Walt Poddubny .08 .25
L Mats Naslund .20 .50
M Michel Goulet .30 .75
N Denis Savard .30 .75
O Bryan Trottier .40 1.00
P Russ Courtnall .30 .75

1987-88 O-Pee-Chee Minis

The 1987-88 O-Pee-Chee Minis set contained 42 cards measuring approximately 2 1/8" by 3". The fronts were white with vignette-style color photos and player names in navy blue. The backs were pale pink and blue, and show 1986-87 stats. The cards were distributed five per cello pack at a suggested retail price of 25 cents.

COMPLETE SET (42) 8.00 20.00
1 Glenn Anderson .08 .25
2 Brian Benning .02 .10
3 Daniel Berthiaume .02 .10
4 Ray Bourque .40 1.00
5 Shawn Burr .02 .10
6 Jimmy Carson .05 .15
7 Dino Ciccarelli .08 .25
8 Paul Coffey .40 1.00
9 Pelle Eklund .02 .10
10 Ron Francis .40 1.00
11 Doug Gilmour .40 1.00
12 Michel Goulet .08 .25
13 Wayne Gretzky 2.50 6.00
14 Glen Hanlon .05 .15
15 Brian Hayward .05 .15
16 Ron Hextall .75 2.00
17 Phil Housley .08 .25
18 Mark Howe .05 .15
19 Doug Jarvis .02 .10
20 Tim Kerr .05 .15
21 Jari Kurri .20 .50
22 Pat LaFontaine .20 .50
23 Mario Lemieux 2.50 6.00
24 Mike Liut .07 .20
25 Kevin Lowe .05 .15
26 Al MacInnis .15 .40
27 Brad McCrimmon .02 .10
28 Mark Messier .60 1.50
29 Joe Mullen .08 .25
30 Craig Muni .02 .10
31 Larry Murphy .08 .25
32 Dave Poulin .05 .15
33 Brian Propp .05 .15
34 Paul Reinhart .05 .15
35 Luc Robitaille 1.50 4.00
36 Patrick Roy 4.00 10.00
37 Christian Ruuttu .02 .10
38 Tomas Sandstrom .08 .25
39 Denis Savard .08 .25
40 Petri Skriko .02 .10
41 Bryan Trottier .20 .50
42 Checklist 1-42 .02 .10

1987-88 O-Pee-Chee Stickers

This sticker set consisted of 255 stickers in full color and was put out by O-Pee-Chee. There were no foil stickers in this set. The stickers measured approximately 2 1/8" by 3". An album was available for these stickers. Those stickers which are pairs are indicated in the checklist below by noting parenthetically the other member of the pair. On the inside back cover of the sticker album the company offered (via direct mail-order) up to 25 different stickers of your choice for ten cents each; this is one reason why the values of the most popular players in these sticker sets are somewhat depressed compared to traditional card set prices.

COMPLETE SET (255) 12.00 30.00
1 Ron Hextall MVP .08 .25
2 Stanley Cup Action .08 .25
3 Stanley Cup Action .08 .25
4 Stanley Cup Action .08 .25
5 Stanley Cup Action .08 .25
6 Mats Naslund .08 .25
7 Guy Carbonneau (146) .08 .25
8 Gaston Gingras (147) .01 .05
9 Chris Chelios .20 .50
10 Bobby Smith .08 .25
11 Rick Green (149) .01 .05
12 Bob Gainey (150) .08 .25
13 Patrick Roy 3.00 8.00
14 Kjell Dahlin (153) .01 .05
15 Chris Nilan (154) .01 .05
16 Larry Robinson .08 .25
17 Ryan Walter (157) .01 .05
18 Petr Svoboda (158) .01 .05
19 Claude Lemieux .60 1.50
20 Rob Ramage (160) .01 .05
21 Mark Hunter (161) .01 .05
22 Rick Wamsley (162) .01 .05
23 Greg Paslawski (164) .01 .05
24 Bernie Federko .08 .25
25 Ron Flockhart (166) .01 .05
26 Tim Bothwell (167) .01 .05
27 Doug Gilmour .20 .50
28 Kelly Kisio (168) .01 .05
29 Don Maloney (169) .01 .05
30 James Patrick (171) .01 .05
31 Willie Huber (172) .01 .05
32 Walt Poddubny .02 .10
33 John Vanbiesbrouck .20 .50
(178)
34 Marcel Dionne (179) .08 .25
35 Tomas Sandstrom .08 .25
36 Joe Mullen .08 .25
37 Mike Bullard (180) .01 .05
38 Neil Sheehy (181) .01 .05
39 Paul Reinhart .02 .10
40 Al MacInnis .08 .25
41 Mike Vernon (182) .20 .50
42 Joel Otto (183) .01 .05
43 Lanny McDonald .08 .25
44 Hakan Loob (184) .08 .25
45 Carey Wilson (185) .01 .05
46 Jim Peplinski .02 .10
47 John Tonelli (186) .01 .05
48 Jamie Macoun (187) .01 .05
49 Gary Suter .08 .25
50 Dennis Maruk (189) .01 .05
51 Don Beaupre (190) .08 .25
52 Neal Broten (193) .08 .25
53 Brian Bellows (194) .08 .25
54 Craig Hartsburg .01 .05
55 Gordie Roberts (196) .01 .05
56 Steve Payne (197) .01 .05
57 Dino Ciccarelli .08 .25
58 Pat Verbeek (199) .01 .05
59 Doug Sulliman (200) .01 .05
60 Bruce Driver (202) .01 .05
61 Joe Cirella (203) .01 .05
62 Aaron Broten .02 .10
63 Alain Chevrier (204) .01 .05
64 Mark Johnson (205) .01 .05
65 Kirk Muller .08 .25
66A Face-Off Action .02 .10
(Sandlak)
66B Face-Off Action .02 .10
(Kasper)
67 Action Sticker .02 .10
68 Action Sticker .02 .10
69 Murray Craven IA .02 .10
70 Bruins Action .02 .10
71 Islanders Action .02 .10
72 Action Sticker .02 .10
73 Action Sticker .02 .10
74 Al Secord (207) .01 .05
75 Bob Sauve (208) .01 .05
76 Ed Olczyk (210) .01 .05
77 Doug Wilson (211) .01 .05
78 Denis Savard .08 .25
79 Troy Murray (212) .01 .05
80 Gary Nylund (213) .01 .05
81 Steve Larmer .08 .25
82 Jari Kurri .08 .25
83 Esa Tikkanen (215) .20 .50
84 Kevin Lowe (216) .01 .05
85 Grant Fuhr .08 .25
86 Wayne Gretzky 1.50 4.00
87 Charlie Huddy (219) .01 .05
88 Kent Nilsson (220) .01 .05
89 Paul Coffey .20 .50
90 Mike Krushelnyski .01 .05
(223)
91 Craig MacTavish (224) .01 .05
92 Mark Messier .40 1.00
93 Andy Moog (226) .08 .25
94 Randy Gregg (227) .01 .05
95 Glenn Anderson .08 .25
96 Peter Zezel (229) .08 .25
97 Brian Propp (230) .08 .25
98 Dave Poulin (232) .01 .05
99 Brad McCrimmon (233) .01 .05
100 Mark Howe .08 .25
101 Ron Hextall (234) .20 .50
102 Ron Sutter (235) .01 .05
103 Tim Kerr .02 .10
104 Petr Klima (237) .08 .25
105 Adam Oates (238) .60 1.50
106 Gerard Gallant (240) .01 .05
107 Mike O'Connell (241) .01 .05
108 Brent Ashton .02 .10
109 Glen Hanlon (242) .01 .05
110 Harold Snepsts (243) .01 .05
111 Steve Yzerman .40 1.00
112 Mark Howe (124) .08 .25
113 Michel Goulet (125) .08 .25
114 Ron Hextall (126) .20 .50
115 Wayne Gretzky (127) 1.25 3.00
116 Ray Bourque (128) .08 .25
117 Jari Kurri (129) .08 .25
118 Dino Ciccarelli (130) .08 .25
119 Larry Murphy (131) .08 .25
120 Mario Lemieux (132) .75 2.00
121 Mike Liut (133) .08 .25
122 Luc Robitaille (134) .40 1.00
123 Al MacInnis (135) .08 .25
124 Brian Benning (112) .01 .05
125 Shawn Burr (113) .01 .05
126 Jimmy Carson (114) .08 .25
127 Shayne Corson (115) .08 .25
128 Vincent Damphousse .20 .50
(116)
129 Ron Hextall (117) .20 .50
130 Jason Lafreniere .01 .05
(118)
131 Ken Leiter (119) .01 .05
132 Allen Pedersen (120) .01 .05
133 Luc Robitaille (121) .40 1.00
134 Christian Ruuttu .08 .25
(122)
135 Jim Sandlak (123) .01 .05
136 Keith Crowder (245) .01 .05
137 Charlie Simmer (246) .01 .05
138 Rick Middleton (248) .01 .05
139 Doug Keans (249) .01 .05
140 Ray Bourque .08 .25
141 Tom McCarthy (250) .01 .05
142 Reed Larson (251) .01 .05
143 Cam Neely .20 .50
144 Christian Ruuttu .01 .05
(253)
145 John Tucker (254) .01 .05
146 Steve Dykstra (7) .01 .05
147 Dave Andreychuk (8) .01 .05
148 Tom Barrasso .08 .25
149 Mike Ramsey (11) .01 .05
150 Mike Foligno (12) .01 .05
151 Phil Housley .08 .25
152 Wendel Clark .20 .50
153 Greg Terrion (14) .01 .05
154 Steve Thomas (15) .08 .25
155 Rick Vaive .02 .10
156 Russ Courtnall .08 .25
157 Rick Lanz (17) .01 .05
158 Miroslav Frycer (18) .01 .05
159 Tom Fergus .02 .10
160 Al Iafrate .08 .25
161 Gary Leeman (21) .01 .05
162 Allan Bester .08 .25
163 Todd Gill (22) .01 .05
164 Ken Wregget (23) .20 .50
165 Borje Salming .08 .25
166 Craig Simpson (25) .08 .25
167 Terry Ruskowski (26) .01 .05
168 Gilles Meloche (28) .01 .05
169 John Chabot (29) .01 .05
170 Mario Lemieux 1.25 3.00
171 Moe Mantha (30) .01 .05
172 Jim Johnson (31) .01 .05
173 Dan Quinn .01 .05
174 Wayne Gretzky (176) 1.25 3.00
175 Brian Hayward (177) .08 .25
176 Mark Howe (174) .08 .25
177 Luc Robitaille (175) .40 1.00
178 Ray Bourque (33) .08 .25
179 Dave Poulin (34) .01 .05
180 Wayne Gretzky (37) 1.25 3.00
Hart Trophy Winner
181 Wayne Gretzky (38) 1.25 3.00
Ross Trophy Winner
182 Ron Hextall (41) .20 .50
183 Doug Jarvis (42) .01 .05
184 Brian Hayward (44) .08 .25
185 Patrick Roy (45) 1.50 4.00
186 Joe Mullen (47) .08 .25
187 Luc Robitaille (48) .40 1.00
188 Barry Pederson .02 .10
189 Richard Brodeur (50) .01 .05
190 Dave Richter (51) .01 .05
191 Doug Lidster .02 .10
192 Petri Skriko .02 .10
193 Rich Sutter (52) .01 .05
194 Jim Sandlak (53) .01 .05
195 Tony Tanti .02 .10
196 Michel Petit (55) .01 .05
197 Jim Benning (56) .01 .05
198 Stan Smyl .02 .10
199 Brent Peterson (58) .01 .05
200 Garth Butcher (59) .08 .25
201 Patrik Sundstrom .02 .10
202 Kevin Dineen (60) .01 .05
203 Sylvain Turgeon (61) .01 .05
204 John Anderson (63) .01 .05
205 Ulf Samuelsson (64) .08 .25
206 Ron Francis .20 .50
207 Doug Jarvis (74) .01 .05
208 Dave Babych (75) .01 .05
209 Mike Liut .08 .25
210 Jimmy Carson (76) .08 .25

211 Larry Playfair (77) .01 .05
212 Jay Wells (79) .01 .05
213 Rollie Melanson (80) .01 .05
214 Bernie Nicholls .08 .25
215 Dave Taylor (83) .01 .05
216 Jim Fox (84) .01 .05
217 Luc Robitaille 1.25 3.00
218 John Ogrodnick .02 .10
219 Jason Lafreniere (87) .01 .05
220 Mike Hough (88) .01 .05
221 Paul Gillis .02 .10
222 Peter Stastny .08 .25
223 David Shaw (90) .01 .05
224 Bill Derlago (91) .01 .05
225 Michel Goulet .08 .25
226 Doug Shedden (93) .01 .05
227 Basil McRae (94) .01 .05
228 Anton Stastny .02 .10
229 Randy Moller (96) .01 .05
230 Robert Picard (97) .01 .05
231 Mario Gosselin .08 .25
232 Larry Murphy (98) .08 .25
233 Scott Stevens (99) .08 .25
234 Mike Ridley (101) .08 .25
235 Dave Christian (102) .01 .05
236 Rod Langway .08 .25
237 Bob Gould (104) .01 .05
238 Bob Mason (105) .01 .05
239 Mike Gartner .08 .25
240 Bryan Trottier (106) .08 .25
241 Brent Sutter (107) .01 .05
242 Kelly Hrudey (109) .08 .25
243 Pat LaFontaine (110) .20 .50
244 Mike Bossy .08 .25
245 Pat Flatley (136) .01 .05
246 Ken Morrow (137) .01 .05
247 Denis Potvin .08 .25
248 Randy Carlyle (138) .01 .05
249 Daniel Berthiaume .08 .25
(139)
250 Mario Marois (141) .01 .05
251 Dave Ellett (142) .01 .05
252 Paul MacLean .02 .10
253 Gilles Hamel (144) .01 .05
254 Doug Smail (145) .01 .05
255 Dale Hawerchuk .08 .25
xx Sticker Album 1.50 4.00

1988-89 O-Pee-Chee

The 1988-89 O-Pee-Chee set consisted of 264 cards. The card fronts contain the player's name within a team-colored banner, position and team logo at the top. Bilingual backs had yearly and career statistics, number of game winning goals from previous season, playoff scoring records and highlights. Printed later than Topps, O-Pee-Chee was able to get Wayne Gretzky (120) in a Kings uniform in an arena setting. In the Topps set, Gretzky was holding a Kings jersey during a press conference. Beware when purchasing the cards of Gretzky, Hull, Lemieux, Nieuwendyk, and Turgeon as they have been counterfeited.

COMPLETE SET (264) 60.00 125.00
COMPLETE FACT.SET (264) 75.00 150.00
1 Mario Lemieux 6.00 12.00
2 Bob Joyce RC .05 .15
3 Joel Quenneville .05 .15
4 Tony McKegney .05 .15
5 Stephane Richer .30 .75
6 Mark Howe .05 .15
7 Brent Sutter .05 .15
8 Gilles Meloche .15 .40
9 Jimmy Carson .05 .15
10 John MacLean .15 .40
11 Gary Leeman .05 .15
12 Gerard Gallant .05 .15
13 Marcel Dionne .15 .40
14 Dave Christian .05 .15
15 Gary Nylund .05 .15
16 Joe Nieuwendyk RC 4.00 10.00
17 Billy Smith .15 .40
18 Christian Ruuttu .05 .15
19 Randy Cunneyworth .05 .15
20 Brian Lawton .05 .15
21 Scott Mellanby RC 1.00 2.50
22 Peter Stastny .15 .40
23 Gord Kluzak .05 .15
24 Sylvain Turgeon .05 .15
25 Clint Malarchuk .15 .40
26 Denis Savard .15 .40
27 Craig Simpson .05 .15
28 Petr Klima .05 .15
29 Pat Verbeek .05 .15
30 Moe Mantha .05 .15
31 Chris Nilan .05 .15
32 Barry Pederson .05 .15
33 Randy Burridge .05 .15
34 Ron Hextall .75 2.00
35 Gaston Gingras .05 .15
36 Kevin Dineen .05 .15
37 Tom Laidlaw .05 .15
38 Paul MacLean .05 .15
39 John Chabot .05 .15
40 Lindy Ruff .05 .15
41 Dan Quinn .05 .15
42 Don Beaupre .15 .40
43 Gary Suter .15 .40
44 Mikko Makela RC .15 .40
45 Mark Johnson .05 .15
46 Dave Taylor .15 .40
47 Ulf Dahlen RC .30 .75
48 Jeff Sharples RC .05 .15
49 Chris Chelios .75 2.00
50 Mike Gartner .15 .40
51 Darren Pang RC .75 2.00
52 Ron Francis .30 .75
53 Ken Morrow .05 .15
54 Michel Goulet .15 .40
55 Ray Sheppard RC 1.00 2.50
56 Doug Gilmour .30 .75
57 David Shaw .05 .15
58 Cam Neely .40 1.00
59 Grant Fuhr .40 1.00
60 Scott Stevens .15 .40
61 Bob Brooke .05 .15
62 Dave Hunter .05 .15
63 Alan Kerr RC .05 .15
64 Brad Marsh .05 .15
65 Dale Hawerchuk .15 .40
66 Brett Hull RC ! 20.00 50.00
67 Patrik Sundstrom .05 .15
68 Greg Stefan .15 .40
69 James Patrick .05 .15
70 Dale Hunter .15 .40
71 Al Iafrate .15 .40
72 Bob Carpenter .05 .15
73 Ray Bourque 1.00 2.50
74 John Tucker .05 .15
75 Carey Wilson .05 .15
76 Joe Mullen .15 .40
77 Rick Vaive .05 .15
78 Shawn Burr .05 .15
79 Murray Craven .05 .15
80 Clark Gillies .15 .40
81 Bernie Federko .15 .40
82 Tony Tanti .05 .15
83 Greg Gilbert .05 .15
84 Kirk Muller .15 .40
85 Dave Tippett .05 .15
86 Kevin Hatcher .15 .40
87 Rick Middleton .15 .40
88 Bobby Smith .15 .40
89 Doug Wilson .15 .40
90 Scott Arniel .05 .15
91 Brian Mullen .05 .15
92 Mike O'Connell .05 .15
93 Mark Messier .40 1.00
94 Sean Burke RC 1.50 4.00
95 Brian Bellows .05 .15
96 Doug Bodger .05 .15
97 Bryan Trottier .30 .75
98 Anton Stastny .05 .15
99A Checklist 1-99 .30 .75
(found in vending cases)
99B Checklist 1-132 .30 .75
(found in wax cases)
100 Dave Poulin .05 .15
101 Bob Bourne .05 .15
102 John Vanbiesbrouck .15 .40
103 Allen Pedersen .05 .15
104 Mike Ridley .05 .15
105 Andrew McBain .05 .15
106 Troy Murray .05 .15
107 Tom Barrasso .15 .40
108 Tomas Jonsson .05 .15
109 Rob Brown RC .30 .75
110 Hakan Loob .05 .15
111 Ilkka Sinisalo .05 .15
112 Dave Archibald RC .05 .15
113 Doug Halward .05 .15
114 Ray Ferraro .05 .15
115 Doug Brown RC .30 .75
116 Patrick Roy 7.50 15.00
117 Greg Millen .15 .40
118 Ken Linseman .05 .15
119 Phil Housley .15 .40
120 Wayne Gretzky UER 7.50 15.00
(No position on front)
121 Tomas Sandstrom .15 .40
122 Brendan Shanahan RC 15.00 30.00
123 Pat LaFontaine .30 .75
124 Luc Robitaille 2.00 5.00
125 Ed Olczyk .05 .15
126 Ron Sutter .05 .15
127 Mike Liut .15 .40
128 Brent Ashton .05 .15
129 Tony Hrkac RC .30 .75
130 Kelly Miller .05 .15
131 Alan Haworth .05 .15
132 Dave McLlwain RC .15 .40
133 Mike Ramsey .15 .40
134 Bob Sweeney RC .15 .40
135 Dirk Graham .05 .15
136 Ulf Samuelsson .30 .75
137 Petri Skriko .05 .15
138 Aaron Broten .05 .15
139 Jim Fox .05 .15
140 Randy Wood RC .15 .40
141 Larry Murphy .15 .40
142 Daniel Berthiaume .05 .15
143 Kelly Kisio .05 .15
144 Neal Broten .15 .40
145 Reed Larson .05 .15
146 Peter Zezel .05 .15
147 Jari Kurri .30 .75
148 Jim Johnson .05 .15
149 Gino Cavallini .05 .15
150 Glen Hanlon .15 .40
151 Bengt Gustafsson .05 .15
152 Mike Bullard .05 .15
153 John Ogrodnick .05 .15
154 Steve Larmer .15 .40
155 Kelly Hrudey .15 .40
156 Mats Naslund .05 .15
157 Bruce Driver .05 .15
158 Randy Hillier .05 .15
159 Craig Hartsburg .05 .15
160 Rollie Melanson .15 .40
161 Adam Oates 1.50 4.00
162 Greg Adams .05 .15
163 Dave Andreychuk .15 .40
164 Dave Babych .05 .15
165 Brian Noonan RC .15 .40
166 Glen Wesley RC .30 .75
167 Dave Ellett .05 .15
168 Brian Propp .05 .15
169 Bernie Nicholls .15 .40
170 Walt Poddubny .05 .15
171 Steve Konroyd .05 .15
172 Doug Sulliman .05 .15
173 Mario Gosselin .15 .40
174 Brian Benning .05 .15
175 Dino Ciccarelli .15 .40
176 Steve Kasper .05 .15
177 Rick Tocchet .75 2.00
178 Brad McCrimmon .05 .15
179 Paul Coffey .75 2.00
180 Pete Peeters .15 .40
181 Bob Probert RC 2.00 5.00
182 Steve Duchesne RC .75 2.00
183 Russ Courtnall .15 .40
184 Mike Foligno .05 .15
185 Wayne Presley .05 .15
186 Rejean Lemelin .15 .40
187 Mark Hunter .05 .15
188 Joe Cirella .05 .15
189 Glenn Anderson .15 .40
190 John Anderson .05 .15
191 Pat Flatley .05 .15
192 Rod Langway .05 .15
193 Brian MacLellan .05 .15
194 Pierre Turgeon RC 5.00 12.00
195 Brian Hayward .05 .15
196 Steve Yzerman 3.00 8.00
197 Doug Crossman .05 .15
198A Checklist 100-198 .30 .75
(Found in vending cases)
198B Checklist 133-264 UER .30 .75
(Found in wax cases;
233 Mario Marios)
199 Greg C. Adams .05 .15
200 Laurie Boschman .05 .15
201 Jeff Brown RC .30 .75
202 Garth Butcher RC .15 .40
203 Guy Carbonneau .15 .40
204 Randy Carlyle .05 .15
205 Alain Cote .05 .15
206 Keith Crowder .05 .15
207 Vincent Damphousse .75 2.00
208 Gaetan Duchesne RC .15 .40
209 Iain Duncan RC .05 .15
210 Tommy Albelin RC .05 .15
211 Pelle Eklund .05 .15
212 Jan Erixon RC .15 .40
213 Paul Fenton RC .05 .15
214 Tom Fergus .05 .15
215 Dave Gagner RC .40 1.00
216 Bob Gainey .30 .75
217 Stewart Gavin .05 .15
218 Charlie Huddy .05 .15
219 Jeff Jackson RC .05 .15
220 Uwe Krupp RC .40 1.00
221 Mike Krushelnyski .05 .15
222 Tom Kurvers .05 .15
223 Jason Lafreniere RC .05 .15
224 Lane Lambert .05 .15
225 Rick Lanz .05 .15
226 Brad Lauer RC .05 .15
227 Claude Lemieux 1.25 3.00
228 Doug Lidster .05 .15
229 Kevin Lowe UER .15 .40
(Has Gretzky's stats)
230 Craig Ludwig .05 .15
231 Al MacInnis .60 1.50
232 Craig MacTavish .15 .40
233 Mario Marois .05 .15
(misspelled Marios
on checklist 198b)
234 Lanny McDonald .15 .40
235 Rick Meagher .05 .15
236 Craig Muni .05 .15
237 Mike McPhee .05 .15
238 Ric Nattress RC .15 .40
239 Ray Neufeld .05 .15
240 Lee Norwood RC .15 .40
241 Mark Osborne UER .05 .15
(Misspelled Osbourne
on both sides)
242 Joel Otto .05 .15
243 Jim Peplinski .05 .15
244 Rob Ramage .05 .15
245 Luke Richardson RC .30 .75
246 Larry Robinson .15 .40
247 Borje Salming .05 .15
248 David Saunders RC .05 .15
249 Al Secord .05 .15
250 Charlie Simmer .05 .15
251 Doug Smail .05 .15
252 Steve Smith UER RC .30 .75
253 Stan Smyl .05 .15
254 Thomas Steen .05 .15
255 Rich Sutter .05 .15
256 Petr Svoboda RC .30 .75
257 Peter Taglianetti RC .05 .15
258 Steve Tambellini .05 .15
259 Steve Thomas .05 .15
260 Esa Tikkanen .60 1.50
261 Mike Vernon 1.25 3.00
262 Ryan Walter .05 .15
263 Doug Wickenheiser .05 .15
264 Ken Wregget .30 .75

1988-89 O-Pee-Chee Box Bottoms

This sixteen-card set was issued in sets of four on the bottom of the 1988-89 O-Pee-Chee wax pack boxes. Complete box bottom panels are valued at a 25 percent premium above the prices listed below. The cards were in the same design as the 1988-89 O-Pee-Chee regular issues. The backs were printed in purple on orange background and give statistical information. The cards were lettered rather than numbered.

COMPLETE SET (16) 6.00 15.00
A Ron Francis .40 1.00
B Wayne Gretzky 3.00 8.00
C Pat LaFontaine .40 1.00
D Bobby Smith .15 .40
E Bernie Federko .15 .40
F Kirk Muller .30 .75
G Ed Olczyk .08 .25
H Denis Savard .30 .75
I Ray Bourque .75 2.00
J Murray Craven and .08 .25
Brian Propp
K Dale Hawerchuk .30 .75
L Steve Yzerman 2.00 5.00
M Dave Andreychuk .20 .50
N Mike Gartner .30 .75
O Hakan Loob .15 .40
P Luc Robitaille .60 1.50

1988-89 O-Pee-Chee Minis

The 1988-89 O-Pee-Chee Minis set contained 46 numbered cards measuring approximately 2 1/8" by 3". The fronts were white with vignette-style color photos and player names in navy blue. The backs were pale pink and blue, and show 1987-88 stats. The key card in the set was Brett Hull, appearing in his Rookie Card year. The set numbering was alphabetical by player's name.

COMPLETE SET (46) 8.00 20.00
1 Tom Barrasso .08 .25
2 Bob Bourne .01 .05
3 Ray Bourque .30 .75
4 Guy Carbonneau .05 .15
5 Jimmy Carson .02 .10
6 Paul Coffey .30 .75
7 Ulf Dahlen .05 .15
8 Marcel Dionne .15 .40
9 Grant Fuhr .20 .50
10 Michel Goulet .08 .25
11 Wayne Gretzky 2.50 6.00
12 Dale Hawerchuk .15 .40
13 Brian Hayward .01 .05
14 Ron Hextall .20 .50
15 Tony Hrkac .01 .05
16 Brett Hull 2.00 5.00
17 Steve Larmer .08 .25
18 Rejean Lemelin .05 .15
19 Mario Lemieux 2.00 5.00
20 Mike Liut .05 .15
21 Hakan Loob .08 .25
22 Al MacInnis .08 .25
23 Paul MacLean .02 .10
24 Brad McCrimmon .01 .05
25 Mark Messier .60 1.50
26 Mats Naslund .08 .25
27 Cam Neely .30 .75
28 Bernie Nicholls .08 .25
29 Joe Nieuwendyk .75 2.00
30 Pete Peeters .08 .25
31 Stephane Richer .15 .40
32 Luc Robitaille .30 .75
33 Patrick Roy 2.00 5.00
34 Denis Savard .15 .40
35 Ray Sheppard .20 .50
36 Craig Simpson .02 .10
37 Peter Stastny .15 .40
38 Greg Stefan .02 .10
39 Scott Stevens .08 .25
40 Gary Suter .05 .15
41 Petr Svoboda .02 .10
42 John Vanbiesbrouck 1.25 3.00
43 Pat Verbeek .15 .40
44 Mike Vernon .20 .50
45 Carey Wilson .01 .05
46 Checklist Card .01 .05

1988-89 O-Pee-Chee Stickers

This set consisted of 270 stickers in full color and was put out by O-Pee-Chee. There were no foil stickers in this set. The stickers measured approximately 2 1/8" by 3". An album was available for these stickers. Those stickers which are pairs are indicated in the checklist below by noting parenthetically the other member of the pair. The backs of the stickers were three types: trivia questions and answers (42 different red Level I and blue Level II), various souvenir offers, and the colorful Future Stars (which are considered a separate set in their own right). On the inside back cover of the sticker album the company offered (via direct mail-order) up to 20 different stickers of your choice for ten cents each; this is one reason why the values of the most popular players in these sticker sets are somewhat depressed compared to traditional card set prices.

COMPLETE SET (270) 8.00 20.00
1 Wayne Gretzky MVP 1.50 4.00
2 Oilers/Bruins Action .02 .10
3 Oilers/Bruins Action .08 .25
4 Oilers/Bruins Action .08 .25
5 Oilers/Bruins Action .02 .10
6 Doug Wilson (135) .01 .05
7 Dirk Graham (136) .01 .05
8 Darren Pang (137) .01 .05
9 Rick Vaive (138) .01 .05
10 Troy Murray (139) .01 .05
11 Brian Noonan (140) .01 .05
Kirk McLean-Future Star
12 Steve Larmer .08 .25
13 Denis Savard .08 .25
14 Mark Hunter (141) .01 .05
15 Brian Sutter (142) .01 .05
16 Brett Hull (145) .75 2.00
17 Tony McKegney (146) .01 .05
18 Brian Benning (151) .01 .05
Darren Pang-Future Star
19 Tony Hrkac (152) .01 .05
20 Doug Gilmour .20 .50
21 Bernie Federko .02 .10
22 Cam Neely .20 .50
23 Ray Bourque .20 .50
Doug Brown-Future Star
24 Rejean Lemelin (153) .01 .05
25 Gord Kluzak (154) .01 .05
26 Rick Middleton (155) .08 .25
27 Steve Kasper (156) .01 .05
28 Bob Sweeney (168) .01 .05
29 Randy Burridge (169) .01 .05
30 Bruins/Whalers Action .02 .10
31 Canadiens/Bruins .02 .10
Action
32 Canadiens/Bruins .02 .10
Action
33 Blues/Red Wings .02 .10
Action
34 Canadiens/Bruins .02 .10
Action
35 Canadiens/Bruins .02 .10
Action
36 Canadiens/Bruins .02 .10
Action, Tony Hrkac-Future Star
37 Canadiens/Bruins .02 .10
Action
38 Canadiens/Bruins .02 .10
Action
39 Larry Robinson (170) .08 .25
40 Ryan Walter (171) .01 .05
41 Guy Carbonneau (172) .01 .05
42 Bob Gainey (173) .08 .25
43 Claude Lemieux (176) .20 .50
44 Petr Svoboda (177) .01 .05
45 Patrick Roy 1.25 3.00
46 Bobby Smith .08 .25
47 Mike McPhee (182) .01 .05
48 Craig Ludwig (183) .01 .05
49 Stephane Richer .08 .25
50 Mats Naslund .02 .10
51 Chris Chelios .20 .50
52 Brian Hayward .08 .25
53 Larry Melnyk (184) .01 .05
David Archibald-Future Star
54 Garth Butcher (185) .01 .05
55 Kirk McLean (186) .08 .25
56 Doug Wickenheiser .01 .05
(187)
57 Rich Sutter (190) .01 .05
58 Jim Benning (191) .01 .05
59 Tony Tanti .02 .10
60 Stan Smyl .02 .10
61 David Saunders (196) .01 .05
62 Steve Tambellini .01 .05
(197)
63 Doug Lidster .02 .10
Rob Brown-Future Star
64 Petri Skriko .02 .10
65 Barry Pederson .02 .10
66 Greg Adams .02 .10
67 Mike Gartner .08 .25
68 Scott Stevens .08 .25
Bob Sweeney-Future Star
69 Rod Langway (198) .01 .05
Pierre Turgeon-Future Star
70 Dave Christian (199) .01 .05
71 Larry Murphy (200) .01 .05
72 Clint Malarchuk (201) .08 .25
73 Dale Hunter (204) .08 .25
74 Mike Ridley (205) .02 .10
Jeff Sharples-Future Star
75 Kirk Muller .08 .25
76 Aaron Broten .02 .10
77 Bruce Driver (206) .01 .05
78 John MacLean (207) .08 .25
79 Joe Cirella (208) .01 .05
80 Doug Brown (209) .01 .05
81 Pat Verbeek (210) 1.25 3.00
Brett Hull-Future Star
82 Sean Burke (211) .08 .25
83 Joel Otto (212) .01 .05
84 Rob Ramage (213) .01 .05
85 Lanny McDonald (215) .08 .25
Glen Wesley-Future Star
86 Mike Vernon (216) .08 .25
87 John Tonelli (217) .01 .05
88 Jim Peplinski (218) .01 .05
89 Gary Suter .08 .25
90 Joe Nieuwendyk .40 1.00
Craig Janney-Future Star
91 Ric Nattress (219) .01 .05
92 Al MacInnis (220) .08 .25
93 Mike Bullard .02 .10
94 Hakan Loob .02 .10
95 Joe Mullen .08 .25
96 Brad McCrimmon .02 .10
97 Brian Propp (221) .01 .05
98 Murray Craven (222) .01 .05
99 Rick Tocchet (225) .20 .50
100 Doug Crossman (226) .01 .05
101 Brad Marsh (233) .01 .05
102 Peter Zezel (234) .01 .05
103 Ron Hextall .08 .25
104 Mark Howe .08 .25
105 Brent Sutter (235) .01 .05
106 Alan Kerr (236) .01 .05
107 Randy Wood (237) .01 .05
108 Mikko Makela (238) .01 .05
Iain Duncan-Future Star
109 Kelly Hrudey (241) .08 .25
110 Steve Konroyd (242) .01 .05
111 Pat LaFontaine .20 .50
112 Bryan Trottier .08 .25
113 Gary Suter (243) .01 .05
114 Luc Robitaille (244) .20 .50
115 Patrick Roy (245) .60 1.50
116 Mario Lemieux (246) .60 1.50
117 Ray Bourque (247) .08 .25
118 Hakan Loob (248) .01 .05
119 Mike Bullard (249) .01 .05
120 Brad McCrimmon (250) .01 .05
121 Wayne Gretzky (251) .75 2.00
122 Grant Fuhr (252) .08 .25
123 Craig Simpson (255) .08 .25
Glenn Healy-Future Star
124 Mark Howe (256) .01 .05
125 Joe Nieuwendyk (257) .08 .25
126 Ray Sheppard (258) .08 .25
Ulf Dahlen-Future Star
127 Brett Hull (259) .75 2.00
128 Ulf Dahlen (260) .08 .25
129 Tony Hrkac (261) .01 .05
130 Bob Sweeney (266) .01 .05
131 Rob Brown (267) .08 .25
132 Iain Duncan (268) .01 .05
133 Pierre Turgeon (269) .40 1.00
134 Calle Johansson (270) .01 .05
Joe Nieuwendyk-Future Star
135 Darren Pang (6) .08 .25
136 Kirk McLean (7) .08 .25
137 Doug Smail (8) .01 .05
138 Thomas Steen (9) .01 .05
139 Laurie Boschman (10) .01 .05
140 Iain Duncan (11) .01 .05
Kirk McLean-Future Star
141 Ray Neufeld (14) .01 .05
142 Mario Marois (15) .01 .05
143 Dale Hawerchuk .08 .25
144 Paul MacLean .02 .10
145 Jim Kyte (16) .01 .05
146 Pokey Reddick (17) .01 .05
147 Andrew McBain .02 .10
Brian Noonan-Future Star
148 Randy Carlyle .02 .10
149 Daniel Berthiaume .08 .25
150 Dave Ellett .02 .10
151 Roland Melanson (18) .01 .05
Darren Pang-Future Star
152 Steve Duchesne (19) .08 .25
153 Bob Carpenter (24) .01 .05
154 Jim Fox (25) .01 .05
155 Dave Taylor (26) .01 .05
156 Bernie Nicholls (27) .08 .25
157 Luc Robitaille .30 .75
158 Jimmy Carson .20 .50
Sean Burke-Future Star
159 Canadiens/Bruins .02 .10
Action
160 Devils/Nordiques .02 .10
Action
161 Devils/Nordiques .02 .10
Action, Ray Sheppard-Future Star
162 Devils/North Stars .02 .10
Action
163 Oilers/Flames Action .02 .10
164 Oilers/Flames Action .02 .10
165 Oilers/Flames Action .02 .10
166 Oilers/Flames Action .02 .10
167 Canadiens/Bruins .02 .10
Action
168 Mark Osborne (28) .01 .05
169 Dan Daoust (29) .01 .05
170 Tom Fergus (39) .01 .05
171 Vincent Damphousse .08 .25
(40)
172 Wendel Clark (41) .08 .25
173 Luke Richardson (42) .01 .05
174 Borje Salming .08 .25
175 Russ Courtnall .08 .25
176 Rick Lanz (43) .01 .05
177 Ken Wregget (44) .08 .25
178 Gary Leeman .02 .10
179 Al Secord .02 .10
180 Al Iafrate .08 .25
181 Ed Olczyk .02 .10
182 Normand Rochefort .01 .05
(47)
183 Lane Lambert (48) .01 .05
184 Tommy Albelin (53) .01 .05
David Archibald-Future Star
185 Jason Lafreniere (54) .01 .05
186 Alain Cote (55) .01 .05
187 Gaetan Duchesne (56) .01 .05
188 Michel Goulet .08 .25
189 Peter Stastny .08 .25
Brian Leetch-Future Star
190 Jeff Jackson (57) .01 .05
191 Mike Eagles (58) .01 .05
192 Jeff Brown .20 .50
193 Mario Gosselin .08 .25
194 Anton Stastny .02 .10
195 Alan Haworth .02 .10
196 Don Beaupre (61) .08 .25
197 Brian MacLellan (62) .01 .05
198 Brian Lawton (69) .01 .05
Pierre Turgeon-Future Star
199 Craig Hartsburg (70) .01 .05
200 Moe Mantha (71) .01 .05
201 Neal Broten (72) .01 .05
202 Dino Ciccarelli .08 .25
Randy Wood-Future Star
203 Brian Bellows .02 .10
204 Mario Lemieux (73) .60 1.50
205 Joe Nieuwendyk (74) .08 .25
Jeff Sharples-Future Star
206 Brad McCrimmon (77) .01 .05
207 Pete Peeters (78) .08 .25
208 Norris Trophy Winner .08 .25
Ray Bourque (79)
209 Frank J. Selke .02 .10
Trophy Winner
Guy Carbonneau (80)
210 Hart Trophy Winner 1.50 4.00
Mario Lemieux (81),
Brett Hull-Future Star
211 Art Ross .40 1.00
Trophy Winner#
212 Vezina Trophy Winner .08 .25
Grant Fuhr (83)
213 Bill Masterton .02 .10
Trophy Winner
Bob Bourne (84)
214 William Jennings .40 1.00
Trophy Winners
Brian Hayward and
Patrick Roy
215 Lady Byng .08 .25
Trophy Winner
Mats Naslund (85),
Glen Wesley-Future Star
216 Calder Trophy Winner .20 .50
Joe Nieuwendyk (86)
217 Craig MacTavish (87) .01 .05
218 Chris Joseph (88) .01 .05
219 Kevin Lowe (91) .01 .05
220 Esa Tikkanen (92) .20 .50
221 Charlie Huddy (97) .01 .05
222 Geoff Courtnall (98) .08 .25
223 Grant Fuhr .08 .25
224 Wayne Gretzky 1.50 4.00
225 Steve Smith (99) .08 .25
226 Mike Krushelnyski .01 .05
(100)
227 Jari Kurri .08 .25
228 Craig Simpson .02 .10
229 Glenn Anderson .08 .25
230 Mark Messier .20 .50
231 Randy Cunneyworth .02 .10
232 Mario Lemieux 1.25 3.00
233 Paul Coffey (101) .08 .25
234 Doug Bodger (102) .01 .05
235 Dave Hunter (105) .01 .05
236 Dan Quinn (106) .01 .05
237 Rob Brown (107) .01 .05
238 Gilles Meloche (108) .01 .05
Iain Duncan-Future Star
239 Kelly Kisio .02 .10
240 Walt Poddubny .02 .10
241 John Vanbiesbrouck .20 .50
(109)
242 Tomas Sandstrom (110) .01 .05
243 David Shaw (113) .01 .05
244 Marcel Dionne (114) .08 .25
245 Chris Nilan (115) .01 .05
246 James Patrick (116) .01 .05
247 Bob Probert (117) .20 .50
248 Mike O'Connell (118) .01 .05
249 Jeff Sharples (119) .01 .05
250 Brent Ashton (120) .01 .05
251 Petr Klima (121) .01 .05
252 Greg Stefan (122) .01 .05
253 Steve Yzerman .40 1.00
254 Gerard Gallant .08 .25
Calle Johansson-Future Star
255 Phil Housley (123) .08 .25
Glenn Healy-Future Star
256 Christian Ruuttu .01 .05
(124)
257 Mike Foligno (125) .01 .05
258 Scott Arniel (126) .08 .25
Ulf Dahlen-Future Star
259 Tom Barrasso (127) .08 .25
260 Mike Ramsey (128) .01 .05
261 Dave Andreychuk .08 .25
262 Ray Sheppard .08 .25
263 Mike Liut .08 .25
264 Ron Francis .20 .50
265 Ulf Samuelsson (129) .01 .05
266 Carey Wilson (130) .01 .05
267 Dave Babych (131) .01 .05
268 Ray Ferraro (132) .01 .05
269 Kevin Dineen (133) .01 .05
270 John Anderson (134) .01 .05
Joe Nieuwendyk-Future Star
xx Sticker Album 1.25 3.00

1989-90 O-Pee-Chee

This 330-card standard-size set was O-Pee-Chee's largest issue since 1984-85. The fronts featured color action photos with "blue ice" borders and player name and team logo at the lower right-hand corner. Solid blue borders appeared at the top and bottom on the card face. Bilingual backs were tinted red with black lettering and provided career and playoff statistics as well as highlights. The team cards in the set (298-318) were actually action scenes with no players explicitly identified. This set was produced in mass quantity as O-Pee-Chee gave dealers the option to order vending cases following the initial printing. A second printing allowed for these orders to be filled, saturating the market. Most dealers believe that this O-Pee-Chee set was produced in an amount much greater than the Topps production of this year.

COMPLETE SET (330) 10.00 20.00
COMP.FACT.SET (330) 10.00 20.00
1 Mario Lemieux .75 2.00
2 Ulf Dahlen .01 .05
3 Terry Carkner RC .05 .15
4 Tony McKegney .01 .05
5 Denis Savard .05 .15
6 Derek King RC .10 .30
7 Lanny McDonald .05 .15
8 John Tonelli .01 .05
9 Tom Kurvers .01 .05
10 Dave Archibald .01 .05
11 Peter Sidorkiewicz RC .10 .30
12 Esa Tikkanen .05 .15
13 Dave Barr .01 .05
14 Brent Sutter .01 .05
15 Cam Neely .10 .30
16 Calle Johansson RC .10 .30
17 Patrick Roy .60 1.50
18 Dale DeGray RC .01 .05
19 Phil Bourque RC .05 .15
20 Kevin Dineen .01 .05
21 Mike Bullard .01 .05
22 Gary Leeman .01 .05
23 Greg Stefan .05 .15
24 Brian Mullen .01 .05
25 Pierre Turgeon .20 .50
26 Bob Rouse RC .01 .05
27 Peter Zezel .01 .05
28 Jeff Brown .05 .15
29 Andy Brickley RC .10 .30
30 Mike Gartner .05 .15
31 Darren Pang .05 .15
32 Pat Verbeek .05 .15
33 Petri Skriko .01 .05
34 Tom Laidlaw .01 .05
35 Randy Wood .01 .05
36 Tom Barrasso .05 .15
37 John Tucker .01 .05
38 Andrew McBain .01 .05
39 David Shaw .01 .05
40 Rejean Lemelin .05 .15
41 Dino Ciccarelli .05 .15
42 Jeff Sharples .01 .05
43 Jari Kurri .05 .15
44 Murray Craven .01 .05
45 Cliff Ronning RC .40 1.00
46 Dave Babych .01 .05
47 Bernie Nicholls .05 .15
48 Jon Casey RC .10 .30
49 Al MacInnis .05 .15
50 Bob Errey RC .05 .15
51 Glen Wesley .01 .05
52 Dirk Graham .01 .05
53 Guy Carbonneau .05 .15
54 Tomas Sandstrom .05 .15
55 Rod Langway .01 .05
56 Patrik Sundstrom .01 .05
57 Michel Goulet .05 .15
58 Dave Taylor .05 .15

59 Phil Housley .01 .05
60 Pat LaFontaine .05 .15
61 Kirk McLean RC .25 .60
62 Ken Linseman .01 .05
63 Randy Cunneyworth .01 .05
64 Tony Hrkac .01 .05
65 Mark Messier .10 .30
66 Carey Wilson .01 .05
67 Stephen Leach RC .05 .15
68 Christian Ruuttu .01 .05
69 Dave Ellett .01 .05
70 Ray Ferraro .01 .05
71 Colin Patterson RC .01 .05
72 Tim Kerr .01 .05
73 Bob Joyce .01 .05
74 Doug Gilmour .05 .15
75 Lee Norwood .01 .05
76 Dale Hunter .05 .15
77 Jim Johnson .01 .05
78 Mike Foligno .01 .05
79 Al Iafrate .05 .15
80 Rick Tocchet .10 .30
81 Greg Hawgood RC .05 .15
82 Steve Thomas .01 .05
83 Steve Yzerman .60 1.50
84 Mike McPhee .01 .05
85 David Volek RC .05 .15
86 Brian Benning .01 .05
87 Neal Broten .01 .05
88 Luc Robitaille .05 .15
89 Trevor Linden RC .40 1.00
90 James Patrick .01 .05
91 Brian Lawton .01 .05
92 Sean Burke .05 .15
93 Scott Stevens .05 .15
94 Pat Elynuik RC .05 .15
95 Paul Coffey .10 .30
96 Jan Erixon .01 .05
97 Mike Liut .05 .15
98 Wayne Presley .01 .05
99 Craig Simpson .01 .05
100 Kjell Samuelsson RC .05 .15
101 Shawn Burr .01 .05
102 John MacLean .05 .15
103 Tom Fergus .01 .05
104 Mike Krushelnyski .01 .05
105 Gary Nylund .01 .05
106 Dave Andreychuk .05 .15
107 Bernie Federko .05 .15
108 Gary Suter .01 .05
109 Dave Gagner .01 .05
110 Ray Bourque .20 .50
111 Geoff Courtnall RC .20 .50
112 Doug Wilson .05 .15
113 Joe Sakic RC 5.00 12.00
114 John Vanbiesbrouck .05 .15
115 Dave Poulin .01 .05
116 Rick Meagher .01 .05
117 Kirk Muller .05 .15
118 Mats Naslund .01 .05
119 Ray Sheppard .05 .15
120 Jeff Norton RC .05 .15
121 Randy Burridge .01 .05
122 Dale Hawerchuk .05 .15
123 Steve Duchesne .05 .15
124 John Anderson .01 .05
125 Rick Vaive .01 .05
126 Randy Hillier .01 .05
127 Jimmy Carson .01 .05
128 Larry Murphy .05 .15
129 Paul MacLean .01 .05
130 Joe Cirella .01 .05
131 Kelly Miller .01 .05
132 Alain Chevrier .05 .15
133 Ed Olczyk .01 .05
134 Dave Tippett .01 .05
135 Bob Sweeney .01 .05
136 Brian Leetch RC 1.25 3.00
137 Greg Millen .05 .15
138 Joe Nieuwendyk .05 .15
139 Brian Propp .01 .05
140 Mike Ramsey .01 .05
141 Mike Allison .01 .05
142 Shawn Chambers RC .05 .15
143 Peter Stastny .05 .15
144 Glen Hanlon .05 .15
145 John Cullen RC .10 .30
146 Kevin Hatcher .05 .15
147 Brendan Shanahan .10 .30
148 Paul Reinhart .01 .05
149 Bryan Trottier .10 .30
150 Dave Manson RC .05 .15
151 Marc Habscheid RC .01 .05
152 Dan Quinn .01 .05
153 Stephane Richer .05 .15
154 Doug Bodger .01 .05
155 Ron Hextall .10 .30
156 Wayne Gretzky .75 2.00
157 Steve Tuttle RC .01 .05
158 Charlie Huddy .01 .05
159 Dave Christian .01 .05
160 Andy Moog .10 .30
161 Tony Granato RC .10 .30
162 Sylvain Cote RC .05 .15
163 Mike Vernon .05 .15
164 Steve Chiasson RC .10 .30
165 Mike Ridley .01 .05
166 Kelly Hrudey .05 .15
167 Bob Carpenter .01 .05
168 Zarley Zalapski RC .10 .30
169 Derek Laxdal RC .01 .05
170 Clint Malarchuk .05 .15
171 Kelly Kisio .01 .05
172 Gerard Gallant .01 .05
173 Ron Sutter .01 .05
174 Chris Chelios .10 .30
175 Ron Francis .05 .15
176 Gino Cavallini .01 .05
177 Brian Bellows .01 .05
178 Greg C. Adams .01 .05
179 Steve Larmer .05 .15
180 Aaron Broten .01 .05
181 Brent Ashton .01 .05
182 Gerald Diduck RC .01 .05
183 Paul MacDermid RC .01 .05
184 Walt Poddubny .01 .05
185 Adam Oates .10 .30
186 Brett Hull .60 1.50
187 Scott Arniel .01 .05
188 Bobby Smith .05 .15
189 Guy Lafleur .05 .15
190 Craig Janney RC .20 .50
191 Mark Howe .01 .05
192 Grant Fuhr .10 .30
193 Rob Brown .01 .05
194 Steve Kasper .01 .05
195 Pete Peeters .05 .15
196 Joe Mullen .05 .15
197 Checklist 1-110 .02 .10
198 Checklist 111-220 .02 .10
199 Keith Crowder .01 .05
200 Daren Puppa RC .30 .75
201 Benoit Hogue RC .10 .30
202 Gary Roberts RC .20 .50
203 Brad McCrimmon .01 .05
204 Rick Wamsley .01 .05
205 Joel Otto .01 .05
206 Jim Peplinski .01 .05
207 Jamie Macoun .01 .05
208 Brian MacLellan .01 .05
209 Scott Young RC .50 1.25
210 Ulf Samuelsson .01 .05
211 Joel Quenneville UER .01 .05
(Misspelled Quennville
on card back)
212 Tim Watters .01 .05
213 Curt Giles .01 .05
214 Stewart Gavin .01 .05
215 Bob Brooke .01 .05
216 Basil McRae RC .10 .30
217 Frank Musil RC .05 .15
218 Adam Creighton RC .05 .15
219 Troy Murray .01 .05
220 Steve Konroyd .01 .05
221 Duane Sutter .01 .05
222 Trent Yawney RC .05 .15
223 Mike O'Connell .01 .05
224 Jim Nill .01 .05
225 John Chabot .01 .05
226 Glenn Anderson .05 .15
227 Kevin Lowe .05 .15
228 Steve Smith .01 .05
229 Randy Gregg .01 .05
230 Craig MacTavish .05 .15
231 Craig Muni .01 .05
232 Theo Fleury RC 2.00 5.00
233 Bill Ranford .10 .30
234 Claude Lemieux .05 .15
235 Larry Robinson .05 .15
236 Craig Ludwig .01 .05
237 Brian Hayward .05 .15
238 Petr Svoboda .05 .15
239 Russ Courtnall .05 .15
240 Ryan Walter .01 .05
241 Tommy Albelin .01 .05
242 Doug Brown RC .01 .05
243 Ken Daneyko RC .05 .15
244 Mark Johnson .01 .05
245 Randy Velischek RC .05 .15
246 Brad Dalgarno RC .05 .15
247 Mikko Makela .01 .05
248 Shayne Corson RC .50 1.25
249 Marc Bergevin RC .01 .05
250 Pat Flatley .01 .05
251 Michel Petit .01 .05
252 Mark Hardy .01 .05
253 Scott Mellanby .05 .15
254 Keith Acton .01 .05
255 Ken Wregget .01 .05
256 Gord Dineen RC .05 .15
257 Dave Hannan .01 .05
258 Mario Gosselin .05 .15
259 Randy Moller .01 .05
260 Mario Marois .01 .05
261 Robert Picard .01 .05
262 Marc Fortier RC .01 .05
263 Ron Tugnutt RC .75 2.00
264 Iiro Jarvi RC .01 .05
265 Paul Gillis .01 .05
266 Mike Hough RC .01 .05
267 Jim Sandlak .01 .05
268 Greg Paslawski .01 .05
269 Paul Cavallini RC .05 .15
270 Gaston Gingras .01 .05
271 Allan Bester .05 .15
272 Vincent Damphousse .05 .15
273 Daniel Marois RC .05 .15
274 Mark Osborne UER .01 .05
(Misspelled Osbourne
on card front)
275 Craig Laughlin .01 .05
276 Brad Marsh .01 .05
277 Dan Daoust .01 .05
278 Borje Salming .01 .05
279 Chris Kotsopoulos .01 .05
280 Tony Tanti .01 .05
281 Barry Pederson .01 .05
282 Rich Sutter .01 .05
283 Stan Smyl .01 .05
284 Doug Lidster .01 .05
285 Steve Weeks .01 .05
286 Harold Snepsts .01 .05
287 Brian Bradley RC .10 .30
288 Larry Melnyk .01 .05
289 Bob Gould .01 .05
290 Thomas Steen .01 .05
291 Randy Carlyle .01 .05
292 Hannu Jarvenpaa RC .01 .05
293 Iain Duncan .01 .05
294 Doug Smail .01 .05
295 Jim Kyte .01 .05
296 Daniel Berthiaume .05 .15
297 Peter Taglianetti .05 .15
298 Boston Bruins .01 .05
Action Scene
(Craig Janney)
299 Buffalo Sabres .01 .05
300 Calgary Flames .01 .05
301 Chicago Blackhawks .01 .05
302 Detroit Red Wings .01 .05
303 Edmonton Oilers .01 .05
304 Hartford Whalers .01 .05
305 Los Angeles Kings .01 .05
306 Minnesota North Stars .01 .05
307 Montreal Canadiens .05 .15
308 New Jersey Devils .01 .05
309 New York Islanders .01 .05
310 New York Rangers .01 .05
311 Philadelphia Flyers .01 .05
312 Penguins/Lemieux .15 .40
313 Quebec Nordiques .25 .60
Gerard Gallant AS
Action Scene
(Joe Sakic)
314 St. Louis Blues .01 .05
315 Toronto Maple Leafs .01 .05
316 Vancouver Canucks .01 .05
Action Scene
(Jim Sandlak,
Ray Bourque defending)
317 Washington Capitals .01 .05
318 Winnipeg Jets .01 .05
319 Mario Lemieux Ross .40 1.00
320 Hart Trophy .30 .75
Wayne Gretzky
321 Calder Trophy .10 .30
Brian Leetch
322 Vezina Trophy .30 .75
Patrick Roy
323 Norris Trophy .05 .15
324 Lady Byng Trophy .01 .05
325 1988-89 Highlight .30 .75
Wayne Gretzky
326 1988-89 Highlight .10 .30
Brian Leetch UER
(Photo actually
David Shaw)
327 Mario Lemieux HL .40 1.00
328 1988-89 Highlight .01 .05
329 Coupe Stanley Cup .01 .05
330 Checklist 221-330 .02 .10

1989-90 O-Pee-Chee Box Bottoms

This sixteen-card set was issued in sets of four on the bottom of the 1989-90 O-Pee-Chee wax pack boxes. Complete box bottom panels are valued at a 25 percent premium above the prices listed below. The cards featured sixteen NHL star players who were scoring leaders on their teams. A color action photo appeared on the front and the player's name, team, and team logo at the bottom of the picture. The back was printed in red and black ink and gave the player's position and statistical information. The cards were lettered rather than numbered.

COMPLETE SET (16) 4.00 10.00
A Mario Lemieux 1.50 4.00
B Mike Ridley .08 .25
C Tomas Sandstrom .08 .25
D Petri Skriko .08 .25
E Wayne Gretzky 1.50 4.00
F Brett Hull .75 2.00
G Tim Kerr .08 .25
H Mats Naslund .08 .25
I Jari Kurri .20 .50
J Steve Larmer .20 .50
K Cam Neely .30 .75
L Steve Yzerman .75 2.00
M Kevin Dineen .08 .25
N Dave Gagner .15 .40
O Joe Mullen .15 .40
P Pierre Turgeon .30 .75

1989-90 O-Pee-Chee Stickers

The 1989-90 O-Pee-Chee set contained 270 stickers. The standard size stickers measured 2 1/8" by 3"; some stickers consisted of two half-size stickers. The fronts featured color action photos of players, teams, and trophies. The sticker backs were of four types: trivia questions and answers (green Level III), souvenir offers, Future Stars, and All-Stars. A full-color glossy album was issued with the set for holding the stickers. Some team action shots were a composite of two or four stickers; in the checklist below these stickers are denoted by L (left half) and R (right half), with the additional prefixes U (upper) and L (lower) for the four sticker pictures. The stickers were numbered on the front and are checklisted below accordingly. For those stickers that consist of two half-size stickers, we have noted the other number of the pair parenthetically after the player's name.

COMPLETE SET (270) 8.00 20.00
1 Flames/Canadiens .02 .10
action UL
2 Flames/Canadiens .08 .25
action UR, Zarley Zalapski FS
3 Flames/Canadiens .02 .10
action LL
4 Flames/Canadiens .02 .10
action LR, Bob Joyce FS
5 Al MacInnis .08 .25
Conn Smythe
Trophy Winner
6 Flames/Canadiens .02 .10
action UL
7 Flames/Canadiens .02 .10
action UR, Iiro Jarvi FS
8 Flames/Canadiens .02 .10
action LL
9 Flames/Canadiens .02 .10
action LR
10 Darren Pang (150) .08 .25
Tony Granato FS
11 Troy Murray (151) .01 .05
12 Dirk Graham (152) .01 .05
13 Dave Manson (153) .01 .05
14 Doug Wilson (156) .01 .05
Patrick Roy AS
15 Steve Thomas (157) .01 .05
16 Denis Savard .08 .25
17 Steve Larmer .08 .25
18 Paul MacLean (158) .01 .05
19 Paul Cavallini (159) .01 .05
20 Cliff Ronning (160) .08 .25
21 Gaston Gingras (161) .08 .25
Al MacInnis AS
22 Brett Hull .40 1.00
23 Peter Zezel .02 .10
24 Brian Benning (162) .01 .05
25 Tony Hrkac (163) .01 .05
26 Ken Linseman (164) .01 .05
27 Glen Wesley (165) .01 .05
28 Randy Burridge (166) .01 .05
29 Craig Janney (167) .08 .25
30 Andy Moog (170) .08 .25
31 Bob Joyce (171) .01 .05
32 Ray Bourque .20 .50
Gerard Gallant AS
33 Cam Neely .20 .50
34 Sean Burke (174) .01 .05
35 Pat Elynuik (175) .20 .50
Craig Janney FS
36 Tony Granato (176) .01 .05
37 Benoit Hogue (177) .08 .25
38 Craig Janney (180) .08 .25
39 Brian Leetch (181) .20 .50
40 Trevor Linden (184) .20 .50
41 Joe Sakic (185) 1.25 3.00
Joe Sakic FS
42 Peter Sidorkiewicz .01 .05
(188)
43 Dave Volek (189) .01 .05
44 Scott Young (190) .01 .05
45 Zarley Zalapski (191) .01 .05
46 Mats Naslund .02 .10
47 Bobby Smith .02 .10
Wayne Gretzky AS
48 Guy Carbonneau (194) .01 .05
49 Shayne Corson (195) .01 .05
50 Brian Hayward .02 .10
51 Stephane Richer .02 .10
52 Claude Lemieux (196) .20 .50
53 Russ Courtnall (197) .01 .05
54 Petr Svoboda (198) .20 .50
Chris Chelios AS
55 Larry Robinson (199) .08 .25
Mario Lemieux AS
56 Chris Chelios .20 .50
57 Patrick Roy .60 1.50
58 Bob Gainey (200) .01 .05
59 Mike McPhee (201) .01 .05
60 Barry Pederson .02 .10
Jiri Hrdina AS
61 Trevor Linden .30 .75
Joe Mullen AS
62 Rich Sutter (204) .01 .05
63 Brian Bradley (205) .08 .25
Bob Essensa FS
64 Kirk McLean .08 .25
John Cullen FS
65 Paul Reinhart .08 .25
Steve Duchesne AS
66 Robert Nordmark (206) .01 .05
Pat Elynuik FS
67 Steve Bozek (207) .01 .05
Greg Hawgood FS
68 Stan Smyl (208) .01 .05
69 Doug Lidster (209) .01 .05
70 Petri Skriko .02 .10
71 Tony Tanti .02 .10
72 Garth Butcher (210) .20 .50
Ray Bourque AS
73 Larry Melnyk (212) .01 .05
74 Kelly Miller (213) .01 .05
75 Dino Ciccarelli (214) .01 .05
76 Scott Stevens (215) .08 .25
Mike Vernon AS
77 Rod Langway (216) .08 .25
Benoit Hogue FS
78 Dave Christian (219) .01 .05
79 Stephen Leach (220) .01 .05
80 Geoff Courtnall .08 .25
81 Mike Ridley .08 .25
82 Patrik Sundstrom .01 .05
(223)
83 Kirk Muller (224) .01 .05
84 Tom Kurvers (225) .01 .05
85 Walt Poddubny (226) .01 .05
86 Sean Burke .08 .25
87 John MacLean .08 .25
88 Aaron Broten (229) .01 .05
Gordon Murphy FS
89 Brendan Shanahan .40 1.00
(230)
90 Joe Mullen .08 .25
91 Brad McCrimmon .02 .10
Brian Leetch FS
92 Lanny McDonald (231) .01 .05
93 Rick Wamsley (232) .01 .05
94 Mike Vernon .08 .25
95 Al MacInnis .08 .25
96 Joel Otto (233) .01 .05
Scott Young FS
97 Jiri Hrdina (234) .01 .05
98 Gary Roberts (235) .08 .25
99 Jim Peplinski (236) .01 .05
100 Gary Suter .02 .10
101 Joe Nieuwendyk .08 .25
102 Colin Patterson (239) .01 .05
Dan Marois FS
103 Doug Gilmour (240) .08 .25
104 Mike Bullard (241) .01 .05
105 Pelle Eklund (242) .01 .05
106 Brian Propp (245) .01 .05
107 Ron Sutter (246) .08 .25
Geoff Courtnall AS
108 Rick Tocchet (247) .08 .25
109 Mark Howe (248) .01 .05
110 Tim Kerr .02 .10
111 Ron Hextall .08 .25
112 Mikko Makela (249) .01 .05
Trevor Linden AS
113 Dave Volek (250) .01 .05
114 Gary Nylund (251) .01 .05
115 Brent Sutter (252) .01 .05
116 Derek King (255) .08 .25
117 Gerald Diduck (256) .01 .05
118 Bryan Trottier .08 .25
Peter Sidorkiewicz FS
119 Pat LaFontaine .20 .50
120 Blues/Bruins action L .02 .10
121 Blues/Bruins action R .02 .10
122 Bruins/Rangers .02 .10
action L
123 Bruins/Rangers .02 .10
action R
124 Blackhawks action .02 .10
125 Bruins/Canadiens .08 .25
action (Ray Bourque)
126 Devils/Bruins action .02 .10
127 Flames/Devils action .02 .10
128 Canadiens/Flyers .02 .10
action
129 Flyers/Oilers action .02 .10
130 Canucks/Bruins .02 .10
action L
131 Canucks/Bruins .02 .10
action R
132 North Stars/Bruins .02 .10
action L
133 North Stars/Bruins .02 .10
action R
134 Dale Hawerchuk .08 .25
135 Andrew McBain .08 .25
136 Iain Duncan (257) .01 .05
137 Eldon Reddick (258) .01 .05
138 Brent Ashton .02 .10
139 Dave Ellett .02 .10
140 Jim Kyte (259) .01 .05
141 Doug Smail (260) .01 .05
142 Pat Elynuik (263) .01 .05
143 Randy Carlyle (264) .01 .05
144 Thomas Steen .02 .10
145 Hannu Jarvenpaa .02 .10
146 Peter Taglianetti .01 .05
(265)Vincent Riendeau FS
147 Laurie Boschman (266) .01 .05
148 Luc Robitaille (267) .20 .50
149 Kelly Hrudey (268) .01 .05
150 Steve Duchesne (10) .01 .05
Tony Granato FS
151 Dave Taylor (11) .01 .05
152 Steve Kasper (12) .01 .05
153 Mike Krushelnyski .01 .05
(13)
154 Wayne Gretzky .75 2.00
155 Bernie Nicholls .02 .10
156 Chris Chelios (14) .08 .25
Patrick Roy AS
157 Gerard Gallant (15) .01 .05
158 Mario Lemieux (18) .40 1.00
159 Al MacInnis (19) .01 .05
160 Joe Mullen (20) .01 .05
161 Patrick Roy (21) .40 1.00
Al MacInnis AS
162 Ray Bourque (24) .08 .25
163 Rob Brown (25) .01 .05
164 Geoff Courtnall (26) .01 .05
165 Steve Duchesne (27) .01 .05
166 Wayne Gretzky (28) .60 1.50
167 Mike Vernon (29) .08 .25
168 Gary Leeman .02 .10
169 Allan Bester .02 .10
170 David Reid (30) .01 .05
171 Craig Laughlin (31) .01 .05
172 Ed Olczyk .02 .10
173 Tom Fergus .02 .10
174 Mark Osborne (34) .01 .05
175 Brad Marsh (35) .20 .50
Craig Janney FS
176 Daniel Marois (36) .01 .05
177 Dan Daoust (37) .01 .05
178 Al Iafrate .08 .25
179 Vincent Damphousse .08 .25
180 Chris Kotsopoulos .01 .05
(38)
181 Derek Laxdal (39) .01 .05
182 Peter Stastny .08 .25
183 Paul Gillis .02 .10
184 Jeff Jackson (40) .01 .05
185 Mario Marois (41) .01 .05
Joe Sakic FS
186 Michel Goulet .08 .25
187 Joe Sakic 1.50 4.00
Dave Volek FS
188 Bob Mason (42) .01 .05
189 Marc Fortier (43) .01 .05
190 Robert Picard (44) .01 .05
191 Steve Finn (45) .01 .05
192 Iiro Jarvi .02 .10
193 Jeff Brown .08 .25
194 Gaetan Duchesne (48) .01 .05
195 Randy Moller (49) .01 .05
196 Mike Gartner (52) .08 .25
197 Jon Casey (53) .08 .25
198 Marc Habscheid (54) .20 .50
Chris Chelios AS
199 Larry Murphy (55) .01 .05
200 Brian Bellows (58) .01 .05
201 Dave Archibald (59) .01 .05
202 Neal Broten .02 .10
203 Dave Gagner .20 .50
Sean Burke FS
204 Vezina Trophy (62) .01 .05
205 Jennings Trophy (63) .08 .25
Bob Essensa FS
206 Selke Trophy (66) .01 .05
Pat Elynuik FS
207 Masterton Trophy (67) .01 .05
Greg Hawgood FS
208 Mario Lemieux (68) .40 1.00
Ross
209 Wayne Gretzky (69) .60 1.50
Hart Winner
210 Patrick Roy (72) .40 1.00
Vezina Winner,
Ray Bourque AS
211 Patrick Roy and .30 .75
Brian Hayward
Jennings Trophy Winners
212 Chris Chelios (73) .08 .25
Norris Winner
213 Guy Carbonneau (74) .01 .05
Selke Winner
214 Joe Mullen (75) .01 .05
Lady Byng Winner
215 Brian Leetch (76) .20 .50
CalderWinner, Mike Vernon AS
216 Tim Kerr (77) .08 .25
Masterton Winner,
Benoit Hogue FS
217 Craig Simpson .02 .10
218 Glenn Anderson .02 .10
219 Esa Tikkanen (78) .08 .25
220 Charlie Huddy (79) .01 .05
221 Jari Kurri .08 .25
222 Jimmy Carson .02 .10
223 Steve Smith (82) .01 .05
224 Kevin Lowe (83) .01 .05
225 Chris Joseph (84) .01 .05
226 Craig MacTavish (85) .01 .05
227 Mark Messier .20 .50
228 Grant Fuhr .08 .25
229 Craig Muni (88) .01 .05
Gordon Murphy FS
230 Bill Ranford (89) .20 .50
231 John Cullen (92) .08 .25
232 Zarley Zalapski (93) .01 .05
233 Bob Errey (96) .01 .05
Scott Young FS
234 Dan Quinn (97) .01 .05
235 Tom Barrasso (98) .01 .05
236 Rob Brown (99) .01 .05
237 Paul Coffey .20 .50
238 Mario Lemieux .60 1.50
239 Carey Wilson (102) .01 .05
Dan Marois FS
240 Brian Leetch (103) .20 .50
241 Tony Granato (104) .01 .05
242 James Patrick (105) .01 .05
243 Brian Mullen .02 .10
244 Tomas Sandstrom .02 .10
245 Guy Lafleur (106) .08 .25
246 John Vanbiesbrouck .20 .50
(107)Geoff Courtnall AS
247 Bernie Federko (108) .01 .05
248 Greg Stefan (109) .01 .05
249 Mike O'Connell (112) .01 .05
Trevor Linden AS
250 Dave Barr (113) .08 .25
251 Lee Norwood (114) .01 .05
252 Shawn Burr (115) .01 .05
253 Gerard Gallant .02 .10
254 Steve Yzerman .30 .75
255 Christian Ruuttu .01 .05
(116)
256 Rick Vaive (117) .01 .05
Rob Brown AS
257 Doug Bodger (136) .01 .05
258 Dave Andreychuk (137) .01 .05
259 Ray Sheppard (140) .01 .05
260 Mike Foligno (141) .01 .05
261 Phil Housley .08 .25
262 Pierre Turgeon .20 .50
263 Ray Ferraro (142) .01 .05
264 Scott Young (143) .01 .05
265 Dave Babych (146) .01 .05
Vincent Riendeau FS
266 Paul MacDermid (147) .01 .05
267 Mike Liut (148) .01 .05
268 Dave Tippett (149) .01 .05
269 Ron Francis .20 .50
270 Kevin Dineen .02 .10
xx Sticker Album .75 2.00

1990-91 O-Pee-Chee

At 528 cards, this was the largest set ever issued by O-Pee-Chee. Cards measured the standard 2 1/2" by 3 1/2". The fronts featured color photos bordered by team colors. A hockey stick is superimposed over the picture at the top border. Bilingual backs had blue lettering on a pale green background and had biographical information and career statistics.

COMPLETE SET (528) 6.00 15.00
COMP.FACT.SET (528) 10.00 20.00
1 Gretzky Tribute .50 1.25
Indianapolis Racers
2 Gretzky Tribute .30 .75
3 Gretzky Tribute .30 .75
4 Brett Hull HL .08 .25
5 Jari Kurri HL .02 .10
6 Bryan Trottier HL .02 .10
7 Jeremy Roenick RC .50 1.25
8 Brian Propp .01 .05
9 Jim Hrivnak RC .02 .10
10 Mick Vukota RC .01 .05
11 Tom Kurvers .01 .05
12 Ulf Dahlen .01 .05
13 Bernie Nicholls .02 .10
14 Peter Sidorkiewicz .01 .05
15 Peter Zezel .01 .05
16 Mike Hartman RC .01 .05
17 Kings Team .01 .05
18 Jim Sandlak .01 .05
19 Rob Brown .01 .05
20 Paul Ranheim RC .01 .05
21 Rick Zombo RC .01 .05
22 Paul Gillis .01 .05
23 Brian Hayward .02 .10
24 Brent Ashton .01 .05
25 Mark Lamb .01 .05
26 Rick Tocchet .02 .10
27 Slava Fetisov RC .01 .05
28 Denis Savard .02 .10
29 Chris Chelios .08 .25
30 Janne Ojanen RC .01 .05
31 Don Maloney .01 .05
32 Allan Bester .02 .10
33 Geoff Smith RC .01 .05
34 Daniel Shank RC .01 .05
35 Mikael Andersson RC .01 .05
36 Gino Cavallini .01 .05
37 Rob Murphy RC .01 .05
38 Flames Team .01 .05
39 Laurie Boschman .01 .05
40 Craig Wolanin RC .01 .05
41 Phil Bourque .01 .05
42 Alexander Mogilny RC .50 1.25
43 Ray Bourque .15 .40
44 Mike Liut .02 .10
45 Ron Sutter .01 .05
46 Bob Kudelski RC .01 .05
47 Larry Murphy .02 .10
48 Darren Turcotte RC .01 .05
49 Paul Ysebaert RC .01 .05
50 Alan Kerr .01 .05
51 Randy Carlyle .01 .05
52 Iiro Jarvi .01 .05
53 Don Barber RC .01 .05
54 Carey Wilson .01 .05
55 Joey Kocur RC .15 .40
56 Steve Larmer .02 .10
57 Paul Cavallini .01 .05
58 Shayne Corson .01 .05
59 Canucks Team .01 .05
60 Sergei Makarov RC .01 .05
61 Kjell Samuelsson .01 .05
62 Tony Granato .01 .05
63 Tom Fergus .01 .05
64 Mario Gelinas RC .10 .30
65 Tom Barrasso .02 .10
66 Pierre Turgeon .02 .10
67 Randy Cunneyworth .01 .05
68 Michal Pivonka RC .01 .05
69 Cam Neely .08 .25
70 Brian Bellows .01 .05
71 Pat Elynuik .01 .05
72 Doug Crossman .01 .05
73 Sylvain Turgeon .01 .05
74 Shawn Burr .01 .05
75 John Vanbiesbrouck .02 .10
76 Steve Bozek .01 .05
77 Brett Hull .25 .60
78 Zarley Zalapski .01 .05
79 Wendel Clark .02 .10
80 Flyers Team .01 .05
81 Kelly Miller .01 .05
82 Mark Pederson RC .01 .05
83 Adam Creighton .01 .05
84 Scott Young .01 .05
85 Petr Klima .01 .05
86 Steve Duchesne .01 .05
87 Joe Nieuwendyk .02 .10
88 Andy Brickley .01 .05
89 Phil Housley .02 .10
90 Neal Broten .02 .10
91 Al Iafrate .02 .10
92 Steve Thomas .01 .05
93 Guy Carbonneau .02 .10
94 Steve Chiasson .01 .05
95 Mike Tomlak RC .01 .05
96 Roger Johansson RC .01 .05
97 Randy Wood .01 .05
98 Jim Johnson .01 .05
99 Bob Sweeney .01 .05
100 Dino Ciccarelli .02 .10
101 Rangers Team .01 .05
102 Mike Ramsey .01 .05
103 Kelly Hrudey .02 .10
104 Dave Ellett .01 .05
105 Bob Brooke .01 .05
106 Greg Adams .01 .05
107 Joe Cirella .01 .05
108 Jari Kurri .02 .10
109 Pete Peeters .02 .10
110 Paul MacLean .01 .05
111 Doug Wilson .02 .10
112 Pat Verbeek .01 .05
113 Bob Beers RC .01 .05
114 Mike O'Connell .01 .05
115 Brian Bradley .01 .05
116 Paul Coffey .08 .25
117 Doug Brown .01 .05
118 Aaron Broten .01 .05
119 Bob Essensa RC .02 .10
120 Wayne Gretzky UER .60 1.50
(1302 career assists&
not 13102)
121 Vincent Damphousse .01 .05
122 Nordiques Team .01 .05
123 Mike Foligno .01 .05
124 Russ Courtnall .01 .05
125 Rick Meagher .01 .05
126 Craig Fisher RC .01 .05
127 Al MacInnis .02 .10
128 Derek King .01 .05
129 Dale Hunter .01 .05
130 Mark Messier UER .08 .25
(Position LW&
should be C)
131 James Patrick UER .01 .05
(Blue border&
should be orange)
132 Checklist 1-132 UER .01 .05
(132 Cary Wilson&
should be Carey)
133 Red Wings Team .08 .25
134 Barry Pederson .01 .05
135 Gary Leeman .01 .05
136 Doug Gilmour .02 .10
137 Mike McPhee .01 .05
138 Bob Murphy .01 .05
139 Bob Carpenter .01 .05
140 Sean Burke .01 .05
141 Dale Hawerchuk .02 .10
142 Guy Lafleur .08 .25
143 Lindy Ruff .01 .05
144 Whalers Team .01 .05
145 Glenn Anderson .02 .10
146 Dave Chyzowski RC .01 .05
147 Kevin Hatcher .01 .05
148 Rick Vaive .01 .05
149 Adam Oates .02 .10
150 Garth Butcher .01 .05
151 Basil McRae .01 .05
152 Ilkka Sinisalo .01 .05
153 Steve Kasper .01 .05
154 Greg Paslawski .01 .05
155 Brad Marsh .01 .05
156 Esa Tikkanen .01 .05

157 Tony Tanti .01 .05
158 Mario Marois UER .01 .05
(On front, oi in
Marois is out of line)
159 Sylvain Lefebvre RC .01 .05
160 Troy Murray .01 .05
161 Gary Roberts .01 .05
162 Randy Ladouceur .01 .05
163 John Chabot .01 .05
164 Calle Johansson .01 .05
165 Bruins Team .01 .05
166 Jeff Norton .01 .05
167 Mike Krushelnyski .01 .05
168 Dave Gagner .02 .10
169 Dave Andreychuk .02 .10
170 Dave Capuano RC .01 .05
171 Curtis Joseph RC .60 1.50
172 Bruce Driver .01 .05
173 Scott Mellanby .02 .10
174 John Ogrodnick .01 .05
175 Mario Lemieux .60 1.50
176 Marc Fortier .01 .05
177 Vincent Riendeau RC .02 .10
178 Mark Johnson .01 .05
179 Dirk Graham .01 .05
180 Jets Team .01 .05
(Keith Acton breaking in on
Daniel Berthiaume)
181 Robb Stauber RC .02 .10
182 Christian Ruuttu .01 .05
183 Dave Tippett .01 .05
184 Pat LaFontaine .08 .25
185 Mark Howe .01 .05
186 Stephane Richer .02 .10
187 Jan Erixon .01 .05
188 Neil Sheehy .01 .05
189 Craig MacTavish .01 .05
190 Randy Burridge .01 .05
191 Bernie Federko .02 .10
192 Shawn Chambers .01 .05
193 Mark Messier AS1 .08 .25
194 Luc Robitaille AS1 .02 .10
195 Brett Hull AS1 .08 .25
196 Ray Bourque AS1 .08 .25
197 Al MacInnis AS1 .02 .10
198 Patrick Roy AS1 .20 .50
199 Wayne Gretzky AS2 .30 .75
200 Brian Bellows AS2 .01 .05
201 Cam Neely AS2 .02 .10
202 Paul Coffey AS2 .08 .25
203 Doug Wilson AS2 .02 .10
204 Daren Puppa AS2 .02 .10
205 Gary Suter .01 .05
206 Ed Olczyk .01 .05
207 Doug Lidster .01 .05
208 John Cullen .01 .05
209 Luc Robitaille .02 .10
210 Tim Kerr .01 .05
211 Scott Stevens .02 .10
212 Craig Janney .02 .10
213 Kevin Dineen .01 .05
214 Jimmy Waite RC .02 .10
215 Benoit Hogue .01 .05
216 Curtis Leschyshyn RC .01 .05
217 Brad Lauer .01 .05
218 Joe Mullen .02 .10
219 Patrick Roy .50 1.25
220 Blues Team .01 .05
221 Brian Leetch .10 .30
222 Steve Yzerman .50 1.25
223 Stephane Beauregard RC .02 .10
224 John MacLean .02 .10
225 Trevor Linden .02 .10
226 Bill Ranford .02 .10
227 Mark Osborne .01 .05
228 Curt Giles .01 .05
229 Mikko Makela .01 .05
230 Bob Errey .01 .05
231 Jimmy Carson .01 .05
232 Kay Whitmore RC .02 .10
233 Gary Nylund .01 .05
234 Jiri Hrdina RC .01 .05
235 Stephen Leach RC .01 .05
236 Greg Hawgood .01 .05
237 Jocelyn Lemieux RC .01 .05
238 Daren Puppa .02 .10
239 Kelly Kisio .01 .05
240 Craig Simpson .01 .05
241 Maple Leafs Team .01 .05
242 Fredrik Olausson .01 .05
243 Ron Hextall .02 .10
244 Sergio Momesso RC .01 .05
245 Kirk Muller .01 .05
246 Petr Svoboda .01 .05
247 Daniel Berthiaume .02 .10
248 Andrew McBain .01 .05
249 Jeff Jackson UER .01 .05
('89-90 stats should
be 65& not 0)
250 Randy Gilhen RC .01 .05
251 Oilers Team .01 .05
(Adam Graves)
252 Rick Bennett RC .01 .05
253 Don Beaupre .02 .10
254 Pelle Eklund .01 .05
255 Greg Gilbert .01 .05
256 Gordie Roberts .01 .05
257 Kirk McLean .02 .10
258 Brent Sutter .01 .05
259 Brendan Shanahan .08 .25
260 Todd Krygier RC .01 .05
261 Larry Robinson UER .02 .10
('80-81 season stats
missing making career
totals wrong)
262 Sabres Team .01 .05
263 Dave Christian .01 .05
264 Checklist 133-264 .01 .05
265 Jamie Macoun .01 .05
266 Glen Hanlon .02 .10
267 Daniel Marois .01 .05
268 Doug Smail .01 .05
269 Jon Casey .02 .10
270 Brian Skrudland .01 .05
271 Michel Petit .01 .05
272 Dan Quinn .01 .05
273 Geoff Courtnall .01 .05
274 Mike Bullard .01 .05
275 Randy Gregg .01 .05
276 Keith Brown .01 .05
277 Troy Mallette RC .01 .05
278 Steve Tuttle .01 .05
279 Brad Shaw RC .01 .05
280 Mark Recchi RC .60 1.50
281 John Tonelli .01 .05
282 Doug Bodger .01 .05
283 Thomas Steen .01 .05
284 Devils Team .01 .05
285 Lee Norwood .01 .05
286 Brian MacLellan .01 .05
287 Bobby Smith .02 .10
288 Rob Cimetta RC .01 .05
289 Rob Zettler RC .01 .05
290 David Reid RC .01 .05
291 Bryan Trottier .02 .10
292 Brian Mullen .01 .05
293 Paul Reinhart .01 .05
294 Andy Moog .02 .10
295 Jeff Brown .01 .05
296 Ryan Walter .01 .05
297 Trent Yawney .01 .05
298 John Druce RC .01 .05
299 Dave McLlwain .01 .05
300 David Volek .01 .05
301 Tomas Sandstrom .01 .05
302 Gord Murphy RC .01 .05
303 Lou Franceschetti RC .01 .05
304 Dana Murzyn .01 .05
305 North Stars Team .01 .05
306 Patrik Sundstrom .01 .05
307 Kevin Lowe .01 .05
308 Dave Barr .01 .05
309 Wendell Young .02 .10
310 Darrin Shannon RC .01 .05
311 Ron Francis .02 .10
312 Stephane Fiset RC .20 .50
313 Paul Fenton .01 .05
314 Dave Taylor .02 .10
315 Islanders Team .01 .05
316 Petri Skriko .01 .05
317 Rob Ramage .01 .05
318 Murray Craven .01 .05
319 Gaetan Duchesne .01 .05
320 Brad McCrimmon .01 .05
321 Grant Fuhr .02 .10
322 Gerard Gallant .01 .05
323 Tommy Albelin .01 .05
324 Scott Arniel .01 .05
325 Mike Keane RC .01 .05
326 Penguins Team .01 .05
327 Mike Ridley .01 .05
328 Dave Babych .01 .05
329 Michel Goulet .02 .10
330 Mike Richter RC .40 1.00
331 Garry Galley RC .01 .05
332 Rod Brind'Amour RC .40 1.00
333 Tony McKegney .01 .05
334 Peter Stastny .02 .10
335 Greg Millen .02 .10
336 Ray Ferraro .01 .05
337 Miloslav Horava RC .01 .05
338 Paul MacDermid .01 .05
339 Craig Coxe RC .01 .05
340 Dave Snuggerud .01 .05
341 Mike Lalor RC .01 .05
342 Marc Habscheid .01 .05
343 Rejean Lemelin .02 .10
344 Charlie Huddy .01 .05
345 Ken Linseman .01 .05
346 Canadiens Team .01 .05
347 Troy Loney RC .01 .05
348 Mike Modano RC .60 1.50
349 Jeff Reese RC .01 .05
350 Pat Flatley .01 .05
351 Mike Vernon .02 .10
352 Todd Elik RC .01 .05
353 Rod Langway .01 .05
354 Moe Mantha .01 .05
355 Keith Acton .01 .05
356 Scott Pearson RC .01 .05
357 Perry Berezan RC .01 .05
358 Alexei Kasatonov RC .01 .05
359 Igor Larionov RC .20 .50
360 Kevin Stevens RC .01 .05
361 Yves Racine RC .01 .05
362 Dave Poulin .01 .05
363 Blackhawks Team .01 .05
364 Yvon Corriveau RC .01 .05
365 Brian Benning .01 .05
366 Hubie McDonough RC .01 .05
367 Ron Tugnutt .02 .10
368 Steve Smith .01 .05
369 Joel Otto .01 .05
370 Dave Lowry RC .01 .05
371 Clint Malarchuk .02 .10
372 Mathieu Schneider RC .01 .05
373 Mike Gartner .02 .10
374 John Tucker .01 .05
375 Chris Terreri RC .02 .10
376 Dean Evason .01 .05
377 Jamie Leach RC .01 .05
378 Jacques Cloutier RC .02 .10
379 Glen Wesley .01 .05
380 Vladimir Krutov RC .02 .10
381 Terry Carkner .01 .05
382 John McIntyre RC .01 .05
383 Ville Siren RC .01 .05
384 Joe Sakic .30 .75
385 Teppo Numminen RC .01 .05
386 Theo Fleury .01 .05
387 Glen Featherstone RC .01 .05
388 Stephan Lebeau RC .01 .05
389 Kevin McClelland .01 .05
390 Uwe Krupp .01 .05
391 Mark Janssens RC .01 .05
392 Marty McSorley .01 .05
393 Vladimir Ruzicka RC .01 .05
394 Capitals Team .01 .05
395 Mark Fitzpatrick RC .02 .10
396 Checklist 265-396 .01 .05
397 Dave Manson .01 .05
398 Bob Gould .01 .05
399 Bill Houlder RC .01 .05
400 Glenn Healy RC .02 .10
401 John Kordic RC .01 .05
402 Stewart Gavin .01 .05
403 David Shaw .01 .05
404 Ed Kastelic RC .01 .05
405 Rich Sutter .01 .05
406 Grant Ledyard RC .01 .05
407 Steve Weeks .02 .10
408 Randy Hillier .01 .05
409 Rick Wamsley .02 .10
410 Doug Houda RC .01 .05
411 Ken McRae RC .01 .05
412 Craig Ludwig .01 .05
413 Doug Evans RC .01 .05
414 Ken Baumgartner RC .01 .05
415 Ken Wregget .02 .10
416 Eric Weinrich RC .01 .05
417 Mike Allison .01 .05
418 Joel Quenneville .01 .05
419 Larry Melnyk .01 .05
420 Colin Patterson .01 .05
421 Gerald Diduck .01 .05
422 Brent Gilchrist RC .01 .05
423 Craig Muni .01 .05
424 Mike Hudson RC .01 .05
425 Eric Desjardins RC .20 .50
426 Walt Poddubny .01 .05
427 Mike Hough .01 .05
428 Luke Richardson .01 .05
429 Joe Murphy RC .01 .05
430 Tim Cheveldae RC .02 .10
431 Adam Burt RC .01 .05
432 Kelly Chase RC .01 .05
433 Robert Nordmark RC .01 .05
434 Tim Hunter RC .01 .05
435 Peter Taglianetti .01 .05
436 Alain Chevrier .02 .10
437 Darin Kimble RC .01 .05
438 David Maley RC .01 .05
439 Jim Wiemer RC .01 .05
440 Nick Kypreos RC .01 .05
441 Lucien DeBlois .01 .05
442 Mario Gosselin .02 .10
443 Neil Wilkinson RC .01 .05
444 Mark Kumpel RC .01 .05
445 Sergei Mylnikov RC .01 .05
446 Ray Sheppard .02 .10
447 Ron Greschner .01 .05
448 Craig Berube RC .01 .05
449 Dave Hannan .01 .05
450 Jim Korn .01 .05
451 Claude Lemieux .01 .05
452 Eldon Reddick RC .02 .10
453 Randy Velischek .01 .05
454 Chris Nilan .01 .05
455 Jim Benning .01 .05
456 Wayne Presley .01 .05
457 Jon Morris RC .01 .05
458 Clark Donatelli RC .01 .05
459 Ric Nattress .01 .05
460 Rob Murray RC .01 .05
461 Tim Watters .01 .05
462 Checklist 397-528 .01 .05
463 Derrick Smith RC .01 .05
464 Lyndon Byers RC .01 .05
465 Jeff Chychrun RC .01 .05
466 Duane Sutter .01 .05
467 Conn Smythe Trophy .02 .10
468 Anatoli Semenov RC .01 .05
469 Konstantin Kurashov RC .01 .05
470 Gord Dineen .01 .05
471 Jeff Beukeboom RC .01 .05
472 Andrei Lomakin RC .01 .05
473 Doug Sulliman .01 .05
474 Alexander Kerch RC .01 .05
475 Norris Trophy .02 .10
476 Keith Crowder .01 .05
477 Oleg Znarok RC .01 .05
478 Dimitri Zinovyev RC .01 .05
479 Igor Esmantovich .01 .05
480 Adam Graves RC .20 .50
481 Petr Prajsler RC .01 .05
482 Sergei Yashin RC .01 .05
483 Jeff Bloemberg RC .01 .05
484 Yuri Strakhov RC .01 .05
485 Sergei B. Makarov RC .01 .05
486 Jennings Trophy .02 .10
487 Sergei Zaltsev RC .01 .05
488 Selke Trophy .01 .05
489 Yuri Kusnetsov RC .01 .05
490 Tom Chorske RC .01 .05
491 Igor Akulinin .01 .05
492 Mikhail Panin RC .01 .05
493 Sergei Nemchinov RC .01 .05
494 Vladimir Yurzinov RC .01 .05
495 Gord Kluzak .01 .05
496 Sergei Skosyrev RC .01 .05
497 Jeff Parker RC .01 .05
498 Tom Tilley RC .01 .05
499 Alexander Smirnov RC .01 .05
500 Alexander Lysenko RC .01 .05
501 Arturs Irbe RC UER 1.00 2.50
(Misspelled Artur;
played in 7 games of
Dynamo Riga's tour)
502 Alexei Frolikov RC .01 .05
503 Calder Trophy .01 .05
Sergei Makarov
504 Nikolai Varjanov RC .01 .05
505 Allen Pedersen .01 .05
506 Vladimir Shashov RC .01 .05
507 Tim Bergland RC .01 .05
508 Gennady Lebedev RC .01 .05
509 Rod Buskas RC .01 .05
510 Grant Jennings RC .01 .05
511 Ulf Samuelsson .01 .05
512 Vezina Trophy .20 .50
Patrick Roy
513 Lady Byng Trophy .08 .25
Brett Hull
514 Dimitri Mironov RC .01 .05
515 Randy Moller .01 .05
516 Kerry Huffman RC .01 .05
517 Gilbert Delorme .01 .05
518 Greg C. Adams .01 .05
519 Hart Trophy .08 .25
520 Sheldon Kennedy RC .01 .05
521 Harijs Vitolins RC .01 .05
522 Art Ross Trophy .30 .75
Wayne Gretzky
523 Dmitri Frolov RC .01 .05
524 Tom Laidlaw .01 .05
525 Oleg Bratash RC .02 .10
526 Kris King RC .01 .05
527 Wayne Van Dorp RC .01 .05
528 Chris Dahlquist .01 .05

1990-91 O-Pee-Chee Box Bottoms

This sixteen-card set was issued in sets of four on the bottom of the 1990-91 O-Pee-Chee wax pack boxes. Complete box bottom panels are valued at a 25 percent premium above the prices listed below. The cards are lettered rather than numbered.

COMPLETE SET (16) 4.00 10.00
A Alexander Mogilny .30 .75
B Jon Casey .15 .40
C Paul Coffey .30 .75
D Wayne Gretzky 1.25 3.00
E Patrick Roy .75 2.00
F Mike Modano .40 1.00
G Mario Lemieux .75 2.00
H Al MacInnis .20 .50
I Ray Bourque .30 .75
J Steve Yzerman .60 1.50
K Darren Turcotte .08 .25
L Mike Vernon .20 .50
M Pierre Turgeon .20 .50
N Doug Wilson .08 .25
O Don Beaupre .15 .40
P Sergei Makarov .20 .50

1990-91 O-Pee-Chee Red Army

This 22-card standard-size set was distributed one card per 1990-91 O-Pee-Chee wax pack. The fronts featured color action photos surrounded by red borders. The words "Central Red Army" appeared above the photos in the red border. The horizontally designed backs contained the player's statistics compiled from the Super Series tour against the NHL. The statistical information on the back was superimposed over a white Soviet star and a "hammer and sickle" insignia. The card number was followed by an R suffix. Parts of the first print run suffered from pin punctures and other quality control flaws. First cards of Sergei Fedorov, Arturs Irbe, and Valeri Kamensky were a part of this set. Because this was an insert set, these cards are not considered Rookie Cards.

COMPLETE SET (22) 3.00 8.00
1R Ilya Byalsin .08 .25
2R Vladimir Malakhov .08 .25
3R Andrei Khomutov .08 .25
4R Valeri Kamensky .08 .25
5R Dimitri Motkov .08 .25
6R Evgeny Shastin .08 .25
7R Arturs Irbe UER .60 1.50
(Misspelled Artur;
played in 3 games in
Red Army's NHL tour)
8R Igor Chibirev .08 .25
9R Maxim Mikhailovsky UER .08 .25
(Played one game not one
minute on 1990 NHL tour)
10R Viacheslav Bykov .08 .25
11R Central Red Army Team .08 .25
12R Central Red Army Team .08 .25
13R Valeri Shirjaev .08 .25
14R Igor Maslennikov .08 .25
15R Igor Malykhin .08 .25
16R Dimitri Khristich .08 .25
17R Viktor Tikhonov CO .08 .25
18R Eugeny Davydov .08 .25
19R Sergei Fedorov 1.25 3.00
20R Pavel Kostichkin .08 .25
21R Vladimir Konstantinov .60 1.50
22R Checklist Card .08 .25

1991-92 O-Pee-Chee

This 528-card set parallels the Topps set of the same season. See the Topps listing for complete prices and checklist.

COMPLETE SET (528) 5.00 12.00
COMP.FACT.SET (528) 5.00 12.00
*O-PEE-CHEE: .4X TO 1X TOPPS

1991-92 O-Pee-Chee Inserts

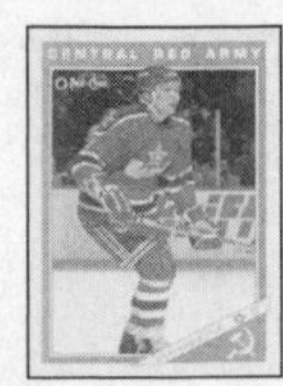

Inserted one per 1991-92 O-Pee-Chee nine-card wax pack, this 66-card standard-size set features ten cards of San Jose Sharks (1S-10S) and 56 Russian hockey players (11R-66R). Among the 56 Russian player cards are those from Central Red Army (11R 30R), Dynamo Moscow (31R-48R), and Khimik (49R-66R). The Sharks' cards have either posed or action player photos with gray and teal border stripes. Card backs present biography and statistics. The Russian player cards have color action player photos enclosed by yellow and red borders. On a red and white background, the backs carry a blue hammer and sickle emblem, a blue Russian star, biography, and statistics versus NHL clubs while touring.

COMPLETE SET (66) 2.50 6.00
1S Link Gaetz .08 .25
2S Bengt Gustafsson .02 .10
3S Dan Keczmer .02 .10
4S Dean Kolstad .02 .10
5S Peter Lappin .02 .10
6S Jeff Madill .02 .10
7S Mike McHugh .02 .10
8S Jarmo Myllys UER .08 .25
(Stat line is for
Offense/Defense)
9S Doug Zmolek .02 .10
10S Sharks Checklist .02 .10
11R Vadim Brezgunov .02 .10
12R Vyacheslav Butsayev .02 .10
13R Ilya Byakin .02 .10
14R Igor Chibirev .02 .10
15R Victor Gordiouk .02 .10
16R Yuri Khmylev .02 .10
17R Pavel Kostichkin .02 .10
18R Andrei Kovalenko .08 .25
19R Igor Kravchuk .02 .10
20R Igor Malykhin .02 .10
21R Igor Maslennikov .02 .10
22R Maxim Mikhailovsky .02 .10
23R Dimitri Mironov .02 .10
24R Sergei Nemchinov .02 .10
25R Alexander Prokopjev .02 .10
26R Igor Stelnov .02 .10
27R Sergei Vostrikov .02 .10
28R Sergei Zubov .20 .50
29R Central Red Army Team .02 .10
30R Central Red Army Team .08 .25
31R Alexander Andreivsky .02 .10
32R Igor Dorofeyev .02 .10
33R Alexander Galchenyuk .02 .10
34R Roman Ilyin .02 .10
35R Alexander Karpovtsev .02 .10
36R Ravil Khaidarov .02 .10
37R Igor Korolytov .02 .10
38R Andrei Kovalyov .02 .10
39R Yuri Leonov .02 .10
40R Andrei Lomakin UER .02 .10
(Misspelled Adrei
on card front)
41R Evgeny Popikhin .02 .10
42R Alexander Semak .08 .25
43R Mikhail Shtalenkov .08 .25
44R Sergei Sorokin .02 .10
45R Andrei Trefilov .08 .25
46R Ravil Yakubov .02 .10
47R Alexander Yudin .02 .10
48R Alexei Zhamnov .08 .25
49R Andrei Basalgin .02 .10
50R Lev Berdichevsky .02 .10
51R Konstantin Kapkaikin .02 .10
52R Konstantin Kurashov .02 .10
53R Andrei Kvartalnov UER .02 .10
54R Albert Malgin .02 .10
55R Nikolai Maslov .02 .10
56R Anatoli Naida .02 .10
57R Roman Oksiuta .08 .25
58R Sergei Selyanin .02 .10
59R Valeri Shiryev .02 .10
60R Alexander Smirnov .02 .10
61R Leonid Trukhno .02 .10
62R Igor Ulanov UER .08 .25
(Misspelled Vlanov
on card front)
63R Andrei Yakovenko .02 .10
64R Oleg Yashin .02 .10
65R Valeri Zelepukin .08 .25
66R Russian Checklist .02 .10

1992-93 O-Pee-Chee

The 1992-93 set marks O-Pee-Chee's 25th consecutive year of manufacturing hockey cards. The set contains 396 standard-size cards. The set includes 25 special 25th Anniversary Tribute cards. The same 25 players are featured in a 25th Anniversary wax pack insert set. O-Pee-Chee produced 12,000 Special Anniversary Collector sets which included the complete 396-card set and the 26-card (including checklist) anniversary insert set. Also, 750 additional factory sets were allocated across Canada for confectionary customers and O-Pee-Chee employees to purchase. Card fronts feature color player photos bordered by a metallic blue stripe on the left and full-bleed on the other three sides. The player's name, team name, and position appear in a gray stripe toward the bottom of the card. The bilingual backs carry the team logo, biography, complete statistics, and player profile. Guy Hebert is the only Rookie Card of note.

COMPLETE SET (396) 8.00 20.00
COMP.FACT.SET (396) 12.50 25.00
COMP.ANN.FACT.SET (422) 45.00 70.00
1 Kevin Todd .01 .05
2 Robert Kron .01 .05
3 David Volek .01 .05
4 Teppo Numminen .01 .05
5 Paul Coffey .02 .10
6 Luc Robitaille .02 .10
7 Steven Finn .01 .05
8 Gord Hynes .01 .05
9 Dave Ellett .01 .05
10 Alexander Godynyuk .01 .05
11 Darryl Sydor .01 .05
12 Randy Carlyle .01 .05
13 Chris Chelios .08 .25
14 Kent Manderville .01 .05
15 Wayne Gretzky .60 1.50
16 Jon Casey .02 .10
17 Mark Tinordi .01 .05
18 Dale Hunter .02 .10
19 Martin Gelinas UER .01 .05
(Trade was 8-9-88,
not 8-9-89)
20 Todd Elik .01 .05
21 Bob Sweeney .01 .05
22 Chris Dahlquist .01 .05
23 Joe Mullen .02 .10
24 Shawn Burr .01 .05
25 Pavel Bure .08 .25
26 Randy Gilhen .01 .05
27 Brian Bradley .01 .05
28 Don Beaupre .02 .10
29 Kevin Stevens .01 .05
30 Michal Pivonka .01 .05
31 Grant Fuhr .02 .10
32 Steve Larmer .02 .10
33 Gary Leeman .01 .05
34 Tony Tanti .01 .05
35 Denis Savard .02 .10
36 Paul Ranheim .01 .05
37 Andrei Lomakin .01 .05
38 Perry Anderson .01 .05
39 Stu Barnes .01 .05
40 Don Sweeney .01 .05
41 Jamie Baker .01 .05
42 Ray Ferraro .01 .05
43 Bobby Clarke 70-71 .08 .25
44 Kelly Hrudey .02 .10
45 Brian Skrudland .01 .05
46 Paul Ysebaert .01 .05
47 Pierre Turgeon .02 .10
48 Keith Brown .01 .05
49 Rod Brind'Amour .02 .10
50 Wayne McBean .01 .05
51 Doug Lidster .01 .05
52 Bernie Nicholls .02 .10
53 Daren Puppa .02 .10
54 Joe Sakic .15 .40
55 Joe Sakic 89-90 .30 .75
56 Dave Manson .01 .05
57 Denis Potvin 74-75 .02 .10
58 Daniel Marois .01 .05
59 Martin Brodeur .30 .75
60 Brent Sutter .01 .05
61 Steve Yzerman .40 1.00
62 Neal Broten .02 .10
63 Darcy Wakaluk .02 .10
64 Troy Murray .01 .05
65 Tony Granato .01 .05
66 Frank Musil .01 .05
67 Claude Lemieux .01 .05
68 Brian Benning .01 .05
69 Stephane Matteau .01 .05
70 Tomas Forslund .01 .05
71 Dmitri Mironov .01 .05
72 Gary Roberts .01 .05
73 Felix Potvin .08 .25
74 Glen Murray UER .01 .05
(Misspelled Glenn
on both sides)
75 Stephane Fiset .02 .10
76 Stephane Richer .02 .10
77 Jeff Reese .01 .05
78 Marc Bureau .01 .05
79 Derek King .01 .05
80 Dave Gagner .01 .05
81 Ed Belfour .08 .25
82 Joel Otto .01 .05
83 Anatoli Semenov .01 .05
84 Ron Hextall .02 .10
85 Adam Creighton .01 .05
86 Kris King .01 .05
87 Brett Hull .10 .30
88 Zdeno Ciger .01 .05
89 Petr Nedved .02 .10
90 Sergei Makarov .01 .05
91 Tomas Sandstrom .02 .10
92 Steve Heinze .01 .05
93 Robert Reichel .01 .05
94 Cliff Ronning .01 .05
95 Eric Weinrich .01 .05
96 Wendel Clark .02 .10
97 Rick Zombo .01 .05
98 Ric Nattress .01 .05
99 Theo Fleury .01 .05
100 Joe Murphy .01 .05
101 Gord Murphy .01 .05
102 Jaromir Jagr .10 .30
103 Mike Craig .01 .05
104 John Cullen .01 .05
105 John Druce .01 .05
106 Peter Bondra .02 .10
107 Bryan Trottier 76-77 .08 .25
108 Steve Smith .01 .05
109 Petr Svoboda .01 .05
110 Mats Sundin .08 .25
111 Patrick Roy 86-87 .75 2.00
112 Steve Leach .01 .05
113 Jacques Cloutier .02 .10
114 Doug Weight .08 .25
115 Frank Pietrangelo .02 .10
116 Guy Hebert RC .25 .60
117 Donald Audette .01 .05
118 Craig MacTavish .01 .05
119 Grant Fuhr 82-83 .08 .25
120 Trevor Linden .02 .10
121 Fredrik Olausson .01 .05
122 Geoff Sanderson .02 .10
123 Derian Hatcher .01 .05
124 Brett Hull 88-89 .25 .60
125 Kelly Buchberger .01 .05
126 Ray Bourque .15 .40
127 Murray Craven .01 .05
128 Tim Cheveldae .02 .10
129 Ulf Dahlen .01 .05
130 Bryan Trottier .02 .10
131 Bob Carpenter .01 .05
132 Benoit Hogue .01 .05
133 Claude Vilgrain .01 .05
134 Glenn Anderson .02 .10
135 Marty McInnis .01 .05
136 Rob Pearson .01 .05
137 Bill Ranford .02 .10
138 Mario Lemieux .40 1.00
139 Bob Bassen .01 .05
140 Scott Mellanby .01 .05
141 Dave Andreychuk .02 .10
142 Kelly Miller .01 .05
143 Gaetan Duchesne .01 .05
144 Mike Sullivan .01 .05
145 Kevin Hatcher .01 .05
146 Doug Bodger .01 .05
147 Craig Berube .01 .05
148 Rick Tocchet .02 .10
149 Luciano Borsato .01 .05
150 Glen Wesley .01 .05
151 Mike Donnelly .01 .05
152 Jimmy Carson .01 .05
153 Jocelyn Lemieux .01 .05
154 Ray Sheppard .01 .05
155 Tony Amonte .02 .10
156 Adrien Plavsic .01 .05
157 Mark Pederson .01 .05
158 Adam Graves .01 .05
159 Igor Larionov .01 .05
160 Steve Chiasson .01 .05
161 Igor Kravchuk .01 .05
162 Slava Fetisov .01 .05
163 Gerard Gallant .01 .05
164 Patrick Roy .40 1.00
165 Ken Sutton .01 .05
166 Mathieu Schneider .01 .05
167 Larry Robinson 73-74 .08 .25
168 Jim Sandlak .01 .05
169 Joey Kocur .02 .10
170 Rob Brown .01 .05
171 Luke Richardson .01 .05
172 Adam Oates 87-88 .08 .25
173 Uwe Krupp .01 .05
174 Cam Neely .08 .25
175 Peter Sidorkiewicz .02 .10
176 Geoff Courtnall .01 .05
177 Doug Gilmour .02 .10
178 Josef Beranek .01 .05
179 Michel Picard .01 .05
180 Terry Carkner .01 .05
181 Nelson Emerson .01 .05
182 Perry Berezan .01 .05
183 Checklist C .01 .05
184 Andy Moog .08 .25
185 Michel Petit .01 .05
186 Mark Greig .01 .05
187 Paul Coffey 81-82 .08 .25
188 Ron Francis .02 .10
189 Joe Juneau .02 .10
190 Jeff Odgers .01 .05
191 Darryl Sittler 75-76 .02 .10
192 Vincent Damphousse .01 .05
193 Greg Paslawski .01 .05
194 Tony Esposito 69-70 .08 .25
195 Sergei Fedorov .10 .30
196 Doug Smail .01 .05
197 Pat Verbeek .01 .05
198 Dominic Roussel .02 .10
199 Mike McPhee .01 .05
200 Kevin Dineen .01 .05
201 Pat Elynuik .01 .05
202 Tom Kurvers .01 .05
203 Chris Joseph .01 .05
204 Mark Fitzpatrick .02 .10
205 Jari Kurri .08 .25
206 Guy Carbonneau .02 .10
207 Jan Erixon .01 .05
208 Mark Messier .08 .25
209 Larry Murphy .02 .10
210 Dirk Graham .01 .05
211 Ron Tugnutt .02 .10
212 Dale Hawerchuk .02 .10
213 Dave Babych .01 .05
214 Mikael Andersson .01 .05
215 James Patrick .01 .05
216 Peter Stastny .02 .10
217 Bernie Parent 68-69 .08 .25
218 Jeff Hackett .02 .10
219 Dave Lowry .01 .05
220 Wayne Gretzky 79-80 1.25 3.00
221 Brent Gilchrist .01 .05
222 Andrew Cassels .01 .05
223 Calle Johansson .01 .05
224 Joe Reekie .01 .05
225 Craig Simpson .01 .05
226 Bob Essensa .02 .10
227 Pat Falloon .01 .05
228 Vladimir Ruzicka .01 .05
229 Igor Ulanov .01 .05
230 Kjell Samuelsson .01 .05
231 Shayne Corson .01 .05
232 Kelly Kisio .01 .05
233 Gordie Roberts .01 .05
234 Brian Noonan .01 .05
235 Slava Kozlov UER .02 .10
236 Checklist B .01 .05
237 Jeff Beukeboom .01 .05
238 Steve Konroyd .01 .05
239 Patrice Brisebois .01 .05
240 Mario Lemieux Smythe .20 .50
241 Dana Murzyn .01 .05
242 Pelle Eklund .01 .05
243 Rob Blake .02 .10
244 Brendan Shanahan .08 .25
245 Mike Gartner HL .01 .05
246 David Bruce .01 .05
247 Mike Vernon .02 .10
248 Zarley Zalapski .01 .05
249 Dino Ciccarelli .02 .10
250 David Williams RC .01 .05

251 Scott Stevens 83-84 .08 .25
252 Bob Probert .02 .10
253 Mikhail Tatarinov .01 .05
254 Bobby Holik .02 .10
255 Tony Amonte 91-92 .02 .10
256 Brad May .01 .05
257 Philippe Bozon .01 .05
258 Mark Messier 80-81 .08 .25
259 Mike Richter .08 .25
260 Brian Mullen .01 .05
261 Marty McSorley .01 .05
262 Glenn Healy .02 .10
263 Russ Romaniuk .01 .05
264 Dan Quinn .01 .05
265 Jyrki Lumme .01 .05
266 Valeri Kamensky .01 .05
267 Vladimir Konstantinov .08 .25
268 Peter Ahola .01 .05
269 Guy Larose .01 .05
270 Ulf Samuelsson .01 .05
271 Dale Craigwell .01 .05
272 Adam Oates .02 .10
273 Pat MacLeod .01 .05
274 Mike Keane .01 .05
275 John Vanbiesbrouck .02 .10
276 Brian Lawton .01 .05
277 Sylvain Cote .01 .05
278 Gary Suter .01 .05
279 Alexander Mogilny .02 .10
280 Garth Butcher .01 .05
281 Doug Wilson .02 .10
282 Chris Terreri .02 .10
283 Phil Esposito 77-78 .08 .25
284 Russ Courtnall .01 .05
285 Pat LaFontaine .08 .25
286 Dimitri Khristich .01 .05
287 John LeBlanc RC .01 .05
288 Randy Velischek .01 .05
289 Dave Christian .01 .05
290 Kevin Haller .01 .05
291 Kevin Miller .01 .05
292 Mario Lemieux 85 .75 2.00
293 Stephan Lebeau .01 .05
294 Marcel Dionne 71-72 .08 .25
295 Barry Pederson .01 .05
296 Steve Duchesne .01 .05
297 Yves Racine .01 .05
298 Phil Housley .02 .10
299 Randy Ladouceur .01 .05
300 Mike Gartner .02 .10
301 Dominik Hasek .30 .75
302 Kevin Lowe .02 .10
303 Sylvain Lefebvre .01 .05
304 J.J. Daigneault .01 .05
305 Mike Ridley .01 .05
306 Curtis Leschyshyn .01 .05
307 Gilbert Dionne .01 .05
308 Bill Guerin RC .30 .75
309 Gerald Diduck .01 .05
310 Rick Wamsley .02 .10
311 Pat Jablonski UER .02 .10
(Listed as Ottawa Senator on both sides, should be Tampa Bay Lightning)
312 Jay More .01 .05
313 Mike Modano .20 .50
314 Checklist A .01 .05
315 Sylvain Turgeon .01 .05
316 Sergei Nemchinov .01 .05
317 Garry Galley .01 .05
318 Paul Coffey HL .05 .15
319 Esa Tikkanen .01 .05
320 Claude LaPointe .01 .05
321 Steve Yzerman 84-85 .75 2.00
322 Mark Lamb .01 .05
323 Bob Errey .01 .05
324 Pavel Bure 92-93 .08 .25
325 Craig Janney .02 .10
326 Bob Kudelski .01 .05
327 Kirk Muller .01 .05
328 Jim Paek .01 .05
329 Mike Ricci .02 .10
330 Al MacInnis .02 .10
331 Mike Hudson .01 .05
332 Darrin Shannon .01 .05
333 Doug Brown .01 .05
334 Corey Millen .01 .05
335 Mike Krushelnyski .01 .05
336 Scott Stevens .02 .10
337 Peter Zezel .01 .05
338 Geoff Smith .01 .05
339 Curtis Joseph .08 .25
340 Tom Barrasso .02 .10
341 Al Iafrate .02 .10
342 Patrick Flatley .02 .10
343 Gerry Cheevers 72-73 .02 .10
Cleveland Crusaders
344 Norm Maciver .01 .05
345 Jeremy Roenick .10 .30
346 Keith Tkachuk UER .08 .25
(Photo actually Petri Skriko)
347 Rod Langway .01 .05
348 Ray Bourque HL .07 .20
349 Kirk McLean .02 .10
350 Brian Propp .01 .05
351 John Ogrodnick .01 .05
352 Benoit Brunet .01 .05
353 Alexei Kasatonov .01 .05
354 Joe Nieuwendyk .02 .10
355 Joe Sacco .01 .05
356 Tom Fergus .01 .05
357 Dan Lambert .01 .05
358 Michel Goulet .02 .10
359 Shawn McEachern .01 .05
360 Eric Desjardins .02 .10
361 Paul Stanton .01 .05
362 Ron Sutter .01 .05
363 Derrick Smith .01 .05
364 Paul Broten .01 .05
365 Greg Adams .01 .05
366 Rob Zettler .01 .05
367 Dave Poulin .01 .05
368 Keith Acton .01 .05
369 Nicklas Lidstrom .08 .25
370 Randy Burridge .01 .05
371 Jamie Macoun .01 .05
372 Craig Billington .02 .10
373 Mark Recchi .02 .10
374 Kris Draper .01 .05
375 Ed Olczyk .01 .05
376 Tom Draper .01 .05
377 Sergio Momesso .01 .05
378 Brian Leetch .08 .25
379 Paul Cavallini .01 .05
380 Paul Fenton .01 .05
381 Dean Evason .01 .05
382 Owen Nolan .02 .10
383 Jeremy Roenick 90-91 .10 .30
384 Brian Bellows .01 .05
385 Thomas Steen .01 .05
386 John LeClair .15 .40
387 Darren Turcotte .01 .05
388 James Black .01 .05
389 Alexei Gusarov .01 .05
390 Scott Lachance .01 .05
391 Mike Bossy 78-79 .10 .30
392 Mike Hough .01 .05
393 Grant Ledyard .01 .05
394 Tim Fitzgerald .01 .05
395 Steve Thomas .02 .10
396 Bobby Smith .02 .10

1992-93 O-Pee-Chee 25th Anniversary

This insert was included in 1992-93 O-Pee-Chee wax packs. The first 25 cards commemorate each of the past 25 years, beginning with the 1968-69 series. The cards measure the standard size and each one is a reproduction of the actual card design from each of the past 25 years; the front is bordered in silver metallic ink with a "watermark" mat varnish logo to commemorate the 25th Anniversary. The cards are numbered on the back as originally issued; however, the set has been renumbered on the front at the lower left and are checklisted below accordingly. Cards can be found with and without the 25th Anniversary emblem embossed on the front.

COMPLETE SET (26) 6.00 15.00
1 Bernie Parent .20 .50
2 Tony Esposito .20 .50
3 Bobby Clarke .07 .20
4 Marcel Dionne .07 .20
5 Gerry Cheevers .20 .50
6 Larry Robinson .07 .20
7 Denis Potvin .07 .20
8 Darryl Sittler .07 .20
9 Bryan Trottier .07 .20
10 Phil Esposito .20 .50
11 Mike Bossy .20 .50
12 Wayne Gretzky 1.50 4.00
13 Mark Messier .30 .75
14 Paul Coffey .30 .75
15 Grant Fuhr .20 .50
16 Scott Stevens .07 .20
17 Steve Yzerman 1.25 3.00
18 Mario Lemieux 1.25 3.00
19 Patrick Roy 1.25 3.00
20 Adam Oates .20 .50
21 Brett Hull .30 .75
22 Joe Sakic .50 1.25
23 Jeremy Roenick .30 .75
24 Tony Amonte .07 .20
25 Pavel Bure .60 1.50
NNO Checklist .07 .20

1992-93 O-Pee-Chee Trophy Winners

These four oversized cards measure approximately 4 7/8" by 6 3/4" and were bottoms from 1992-93 O-Pee-Chee pack boxes. Each features on its front a white-bordered color shot of the player in a tuxedo, holding his trophy and standing in front of an NHL backdrop. The player's name, team, and the trophy name appear in a dark gray stripe near the bottom. O-Pee-Chee appears vertically in a blue stripe along the left edge of the photo. In both French and English, the back has the trophy name, player name and team, and stats in blue lettering. The cards are unnumbered and checklisted below in alphabetical order.

COMPLETE SET (4) 2.00 5.00
1 Pavel Bure .60 1.50
2 Brian Leetch .20 .50
3 Mark Messier .25 .60
4 Patrick Roy 1.00 2.50

1993 O-Pee-Chee Canadiens Hockey Fest

Sold initially only at Hockey Fest '93 (February 4-7, 1993) and the Montreal Forum, this 66-card standard-size set features tribute cards to the Stanley Cup, the Montreal Forum, and past and present stars of the Montreal Canadiens. The production run was 5,000 sets, and each set came in a puck-shaped display box that bore the set serial number. A portion of the proceeds went to the Montreal Canadiens Old Timers Association. Current players are shown in color action photos with white borders and a red stripe at the top. Cards showing former players and people associated with the team have either color or sepia-tone photos framed by red borders on a white card face. The backs of all cards display a variegated pale blue panel containing text or statistics. The current player cards also carry a close-up player photo on the back. Former player cards have a red border around the panel. All the cards have a royal blue outer border.

COMPLETE SET (66) 28.00 70.00
1 Montreal Forum 1924 .40 1.00
2 Emile Bouchard .08 .25
3 Henri Richard .75 2.00
4 Serge Savard .20 .50
5 Toe Blake CO HL .75 2.00
6 Maurice Richard HL 2.00 5.00
7 Stephan Lebeau .08 .25
8 Kevin Haller .08 .25
9 Guy Carbonneau .20 .50
10 Jacques Demers CO .15 .40
11 Serge Savard .20 .50
12 Montreal Forum 1968 .40 1.00
13 Howie Morenz 2.00 5.00
14 Jean Beliveau 1.25 3.00
15 Jacques Laperriere .20 .50
16 Bob Gainey .30 .75
17 Guy Lafleur HL .75 2.00
18 Jacques Raymond .08 .25
19 Sean Hill .08 .25
20 Eric Desjardins .15 .40
21 Aurel Joliat .75 2.00
22 Doug Harvey .75 2.00
23 Yvan Cournoyer .30 .75
24 Frank Mahovlich HL .40 1.00
25 J.J. Daigneault .08 .25
26 Kirk Muller .15 .40
27 Jean Beliveau 1.50 4.00
28 Georges Vezina 2.00 5.00
29 Maurice Richard 3.00 8.00
30 Patrick Roy 5.00 12.00
31 Benoit Brunet .08 .25
32 Jacques Plante HL 1.25 3.00
33 Ralph Backstrom .08 .25
34 Elmer Lach .40 1.00
35 Stanley Cup Champions .20 .50
36 Jacques Laperriere .20 .50
37 Montreal Individual Records--Playoffs .08 .25
38 Vincent Damphousse .30 .75
39 Frank Mahovlich .75 2.00
40 Jacques Plante 2.00 5.00
41 Stanley Cup Champions .20 .50
42 Kenny Reardon .30 .75
43 Claude Provost .08 .25
44 Jean Beliveau HL 1.00 2.50
45 Edward Ronan .08 .25
46 Canadiens NHL Individual Records .08 .25
47 Bill Durnan .75 2.00
48 Stanley Cup .20 .50
49 Patrice Brisebois .08 .25
50 Denis Savard .30 .75
51 Ken Dryden 2.00 5.00
52 Lou Fontinato .15 .40
53 Jean-Guy Talbot .20 .50
54 BoomBoom Geoffrion .75 2.00
55 Joe Malone .40 1.00
56 Oleg Petrov .08 .25
57 Guy Lafleur 1.00 2.50
58 Bert Olmstead .20 .50
59 The Dream Team 2.00 5.00
Jacques Plante
Larry Robinson
Toe Blake CO
Jean Beliveau
Dickie Moore
Doug Harvey
Maurice Richard
Aurel Joliat
Bob Gainey
60 Brian Bellows .15 .40
61 Henri Richard HL .40 1.00
62 Jacques Lemaire .30 .75
63 Dickie Moore .60 1.50
64 Lorne Worsley .60 1.50
65 Toe Blake .75 2.00
66 Checklist Card .02 .10
NNO Advertisement Card .01

1993 O-Pee-Chee Canadiens Panel

This approximately 5" by 7" panel displays samples of the O-Pee-Chee Canadiens Hockey Fest cards. If the cards were cut, they would measure the standard size. The front features three cards with posed color player photos with red borders, and one sepia-tone action player photo with red borders. The cards are printed on a white card face. The back show variegated pale blue panels containing statistics. The panels are bordered in dark blue and set on a red background.

1 Canadiens Panel 6.00 15.00
Henri Richard
Jean Beliveau
Yvan Cournoyer
Maurice Richard

1998-99 OPC Chrome

The 1998-99 OPC Chrome set was issue in one series by Topps totaling 242 cards and was distributed in four card packs with a suggested retail price of $3. The fronts feature color action photos of veteran players, 1998 NHL Draft Picks, and CHL All-Stars. The backs carry player information and career statistics.

COMPLETE SET (242) 40.00 100.00
1 Peter Forsberg 1.00 2.50
2 Petr Sykora .20 .50
3 Byron Dafoe .30 .75
4 Ron Francis .30 .75
5 Alexei Yashin .20 .50
6 Dave Ellett .20 .50
7 Jamie Langenbrunner .20 .50
8 Doug Weight .30 .75
9 Jason Woolley .20 .50
10 Paul Coffey .40 1.00
11 Uwe Krupp .20 .50
12 Tomas Sandstrom .20 .50
13 Scott Mellanby .20 .50
14 Vladimir Tsyplakov .20 .50
15 Martin Rucinsky .20 .50
16 Mikael Renberg .30 .75
17 Marco Sturm .20 .50
18 Eric Lindros .40 1.00
19 Sean Burke .20 .50
20 Martin Brodeur 1.25 3.00
21 Boyd Devereaux .20 .50
22 Kelly Buchberger .20 .50
23 Scott Stevens .30 .75
24 Jamie Storr .30 .75
25 Anders Eriksson .20 .50
26 Gary Suter .20 .50
27 Theo Fleury .20 .50
28 Steve Leach .20 .50
29 Felix Potvin .40 1.00
30 Brett Hull .60 1.50
31 Mike Grier .20 .50
32 Cale Hulse .20 .50
33 Larry Murphy .30 .75
34 Rick Tocchet .30 .75
35 Eric Desjardins .30 .75
36 Igor Kravchuk .20 .50
37 Rob Niedermayer .20 .50
38 Bryan Smolinski .20 .50
39 Valeri Kamensky .20 .50
40 Ryan Smyth .30 .75
41 Bruce Driver .20 .50
42 Mike Johnson .20 .50
43 Rob Zamuner .20 .50
44 Steve Duchesne .20 .50
45 Martin Straka .20 .50
46 Bill Houlder .20 .50
47 Craig Conroy .20 .50
48 Guy Hebert .20 .50
49 Colin Forbes .20 .50
50 Mike Modano .60 1.50
51 Jamie Pushor .20 .50
52 Jarome Iginla .75 2.00
53 Paul Kariya .40 1.00
54 Mattias Ohlund .20 .50
55 Sergei Berezin .30 .75
56 Peter Zezel .20 .50
57 Teppo Numminen .20 .50
58 Dale Hunter .20 .50
59 Sandy Moger .20 .50
60 John LeClair .40 1.00
61 Wade Redden .20 .50
62 Patrik Elias .30 .75
63 Rob Blake .30 .75
64 Todd Marchant .20 .50
65 Claude Lemieux .20 .50
66 Trevor Kidd .20 .50
67 Sergei Fedorov .60 1.50
68 Joe Sakic 1.00 2.50
69 Derek Morris .20 .50
70 Alexei Morozov .20 .50
71 Mats Sundin .40 1.00
72 Daymond Langkow .20 .50
73 Kevin Hatcher .20 .50
74 Damian Rhodes .30 .75
75 Brian Leetch .40 1.00
76 Saku Koivu .40 1.00
77 Rick Tabaracci .20 .50
78 Bernie Nicholls .30 .75
79 Alyn McCauley .30 .75
80 Patrice Brisebois .20 .50
81 Bret Hedican .20 .50
82 Sandy McCarthy .20 .50
83 Viktor Kozlov .20 .50
84 Derek King .20 .50
85 Alexander Selivanov .20 .50
86 Mike Vernon .30 .75
87 Jeff Beukeboom .20 .50
88 Tommy Salo .30 .75
89 Adam Graves .30 .75
90 Randy McKay .20 .50
91 Rich Pilon .20 .50
92 Richard Zednik .20 .50
93 Jeff Hackett .30 .75
94 Michael Peca .20 .50
95 Brent Gilchrist .20 .50
96 Stu Grimson .20 .50
97 Bob Probert .20 .50
98 Stu Barnes .20 .50
99 Ruslan Salei .20 .50
100 Al MacInnis .30 .75
101 Ken Daneyko .20 .50
102 Paul Ranheim .20 .50
103 Marty McInnis .20 .50
104 Marian Hossa .40 1.00
105 Darren McCarty .20 .50
106 Guy Carbonneau .20 .50
107 Dallas Drake .20 .50
108 Sergei Samsonov .30 .75
109 Teemu Selanne .40 1.00
110 Checklist .20 .50
111 Jaromir Jagr 1.00 2.50
112 Joe Thornton 1.00 2.50
113 Jon Klemm .20 .50
114 Grant Fuhr .30 .75
115 Nikolai Khabibulin .30 .75
116 Rod Brind'Amour .30 .75
117 Trevor Linden .30 .75
118 Vincent Damphousse .30 .75
119 Dino Ciccarelli .30 .75
120 Pat Verbeek .20 .50
121 Sandis Ozolinsh .20 .50
122 Garth Snow .30 .75
123 Ed Belfour .40 1.00
124 Keith Primeau .20 .50
125 Jason Allison .20 .50
126 Peter Bondra .30 .75
127 Ulf Samuelsson .20 .50
128 Jeff Friesen .20 .50
129 Jason Bonsignore .20 .50
130 Daniel Alfredsson .30 .75
131 Bobby Holik .20 .50
132 Jozef Stumpel .20 .50
133 Brian Bellows .20 .50
134 Chris Osgood .30 .75
135 Alexei Zhamnov .20 .50
136 Mattias Norstrom .20 .50
137 Drake Berehowsky .20 .50
138 Mark Messier .40 1.00
139 Geoff Courtnall .20 .50
140 Marc Bureau .20 .50
141 Don Sweeney .20 .50
142 Wendel Clark .30 .75
143 Scott Niedermayer .20 .50
144 Chris Therien .20 .50
145 Kirk Muller .20 .50
146 Wayne Primeau .20 .50
147 Tony Granato .20 .50
148 Derian Hatcher .20 .50
149 Daniel Briere .20 .50
150 Fredrik Olausson .20 .50
151 Joe Juneau .30 .75
152 Michal Grosek .20 .50
153 Janne Laukkanen .20 .50
154 Keith Tkachuk .40 1.00
155 Marty McSorley .20 .50
156 Owen Nolan .30 .75
157 Mark Tinordi .20 .50
158 Steve Washburn .20 .50
159 Luke Richardson .20 .50
160 Kris King .20 .50
161 Joe Nieuwendyk .30 .75
162 Travis Green .20 .50
163 Dominik Hasek 1.00 2.50
164 Dimitri Khristich .20 .50
165 Dave Manson .20 .50
166 Chris Chelios .40 1.00
167 Claude LaPointe .20 .50
168 Kris Draper .20 .50
169 Brad Isbister .20 .50
170 Patrick Marleau .20 .50
171 Jeremy Roenick .60 1.50
172 Darren Langdon .20 .50
173 Kevin Dineen .20 .50
174 Luc Robitaille .30 .75
175 Steve Yzerman 1.50 4.00
176 Sergei Zubov .20 .50
177 Ed Jovanovski .20 .50
178 Sami Kapanen .20 .50
179 Adam Oates .30 .75
180 Pavel Bure .40 1.00
181 Chris Pronger .30 .75
182 Pat Falloon .20 .50
183 Darcy Tucker .20 .50
184 Zigmund Palffy .30 .75
185 Curtis Brown .20 .50
186 Curtis Joseph .40 1.00
187 Valeri Zelepukin .20 .50
188 Russ Courtnall .20 .50
189 Adam Foote .20 .50
190 Patrick Roy 1.50 4.00
191 Cory Stillman .20 .50
192 Alexei Zhitnik .20 .50
193 Olaf Kolzig .30 .75
194 Mark Fitzpatrick .20 .50
195 Eric Daze .30 .75
196 Zarley Zalapski .20 .50
197 Niklas Sundstrom .20 .50
198 Bryan Berard .30 .75
199 Jason Arnott .20 .50
200 Mike Richter .40 1.00
201 Ken Baumgartner .20 .50
202 Jason Dawe .20 .50
203 Nicklas Lidstrom .40 1.00
204 Tony Amonte .30 .75
205 Kjell Samuelsson .20 .50
206 Ray Bourque .60 1.50
207 Alexander Mogilny .30 .75
208 Pierre Turgeon .30 .75
209 Tom Barrasso .30 .75
210 Richard Matvichuk .20 .50
211 Sergei Krivokrasov .20 .50
212 Ted Drury .20 .50
213 Matthew Barnaby .20 .50
214 Denis Pederson .20 .50
215 John Vanbiesbrouck .30 .75
216 Brendan Shanahan .40 1.00
217 Jocelyn Thibault .30 .75
218 Nelson Emerson .20 .50
219 Wayne Gretzky 2.00 5.00
220 Checklist .20 .50
221 Ramzi Abid RC .40 1.00
222 Mark Bell RC .75 2.00
223 Michael Henrich RC .40 1.00
224 Vincent Lecavalier .75 2.00
225 Rico Fata .40 1.00
226 Bryan Allen .40 1.00
227 Daniel Tkaczuk .40 1.00
228 Brad Stuart RC .75 2.00
229 Derrick Walser RC .40 1.00
230 Jonathan Cheechoo RC 3.00 8.00
231 Sergei Varlamov .40 1.00
232 Scott Gomez RC 1.50 4.00
233 Jeff Heerema RC .40 1.00
234 David Legwand .40 1.00
235 Manny Malhotra .40 1.00
236 Michael Rupp RC .40 1.00
237 Alex Tanguay .40 1.00
238 Mathieu Biron RC .40 1.00
239 Bujar Amidovski RC .40 1.00
240 Brian Finley RC .40 1.00
241 Philippe Sauve RC .40 1.00
242 Jiri Fischer RC .40 1.00
*232 S.Gomez Refractor 40.00 100.00

1998-99 OPC Chrome Refractors

Randomly inserted in packs at the rate of 1:12, this 242-card set is a refractive parallel version of the base set.

*VETERANS: 4X TO 10X BASIC CARDS
*ROOKIES: .8X TO 2X BASIC CARDS

1998-99 OPC Chrome Blast From the Past

Randomly inserted into packs at the rate of 1:28, this 10-card set features reprints of the rookie cards of selected great retirees as well as current stars. A refractor parallel version of this set was also produced with an insertion rate of 1:112.

COMPLETE SET (10) 40.00 80.00
*REFRACTORS: 1.2X TO 3X BASIC INSERTS
1 Wayne Gretzky 8.00 20.00
2 Mark Messier 3.00 8.00
3 Ray Bourque 5.00 12.00
4 Patrick Roy 6.00 15.00
5 Grant Fuhr 3.00 8.00
6 Brett Hull 3.00 8.00
7 Gordie Howe 8.00 20.00
8 Stan Mikita 4.00 10.00
9 Bobby Hull 5.00 12.00
10 Phil Esposito 4.00 10.00

1998-99 OPC Chrome Board Members

Randomly inserted into packs at the rate of 1:12, this 15-card set features color action photos of some of the great defensive superstars of the NHL. A refractor parallel version of this set was also produced with an insertion rate of 1:36.

COMPLETE SET (15) 30.00 60.00
*REFRACTORS: .8X TO 2X BASIC INSERTS
B1 Chris Pronger 2.00 5.00
B2 Chris Chelios 3.00 8.00
B3 Brian Leetch 2.00 5.00
B4 Ray Bourque 5.00 12.00
B5 Mattias Ohlund 2.00 5.00
B6 Nicklas Lidstrom 3.00 8.00
B7 Sergei Zubov 2.00 5.00
B8 Scott Niedermayer 1.25 3.00
B9 Larry Murphy 2.00 5.00
B10 Sandis Ozolinsh 1.25 3.00
B11 Rob Blake 2.00 5.00
B12 Scott Stevens 2.00 5.00
B13 Derian Hatcher 1.25 3.00
B14 Kevin Hatcher 1.25 3.00
B15 Wade Redden 1.25 3.00

1998-99 OPC Chrome Season's Best

Randomly inserted into packs at the rate of 1:8, this 30-card set features color action photos of top players in five distinct categories: Net Minders, the league's top goalies; Sharpshooters, the top scoring leaders; Puck Providers, assist leaders; Performers Plus, leaders in ice time by plus/minus ratio; and Ice Hot, powerful rookies. A refractor parallel version of this set was also produced with an insertion rate of 1:24.

COMPLETE SET (30) 30.00 60.00
*REFRACTORS: 1X TO 2.5X BASIC INSERTS
SB1 Dominik Hasek 2.00 5.00
SB2 Martin Brodeur 2.50 6.00
SB3 Ed Belfour 1.00 2.50
SB4 Curtis Joseph 1.00 2.50
SB5 Jeff Hackett .75 2.00
SB6 Tom Barrasso .75 2.00
SB7 Mike Johnson .40 1.00
SB8 Sergei Samsonov .75 2.00
SB9 Patrik Elias .75 2.00
SB10 Patrick Marleau .75 2.00
SB11 Mattias Ohlund .75 2.00
SB12 Marco Sturm .75 2.00
SB13 Teemu Selanne 1.00 2.50
SB14 Peter Bondra .75 2.00
SB15 Pavel Bure 1.00 2.50
SB16 John LeClair 1.00 2.50
SB17 Zigmund Palffy .75 2.00
SB18 Keith Tkachuk 1.00 2.50
SB19 Jaromir Jagr 1.50 4.00
SB20 Wayne Gretzky 6.00 15.00
SB21 Peter Forsberg 2.50 6.00
SB22 Ron Francis .40 1.00
SB23 Adam Oates .40 1.00
SB24 Jozef Stumpel .40 1.00
SB25 Chris Pronger .75 2.00
SB26 Larry Murphy .40 1.00
SB27 Jason Allison .40 1.00
SB28 John LeClair 1.00 2.50
SB29 Randy McKay .40 1.00
SB30 Dainius Zubrus .40 1.00

1999-00 O-Pee-Chee

This 286-card set parallels the Topps set of the same season. See the Topps listings for complete prices and checklists.

COMPLETE SET (286) 20.00 50.00
*O-PEE-CHEE: .5X TO 1.2X TOPPS

1999-00 O-Pee-Chee All-Topps

COMPLETE SET (15) 20.00 40.00
*O-PEE-CHEE: .4X TO 1X TOPPS
STATED ODDS 1:16 OPC
AT1 Dominik Hasek 1.50 4.00
AT2 Martin Brodeur 2.00 5.00
AT3 Ray Bourque 1.25 3.00
AT4 Al MacInnis .60 1.50
AT5 Nicklas Lidstrom .75 2.00
AT6 Brian Leetch .75 2.00
AT7 John LeClair 1.00 2.50
AT8 Paul Kariya 2.00 5.00
AT9 Keith Tkachuk .75 2.00
AT10 Eric Lindros 1.25 3.00
AT11 Peter Forsberg 2.00 5.00
AT12 Steve Yzerman 4.00 10.00
AT13 Jaromir Jagr 1.25 3.00
AT14 Teemu Selanne 1.50 4.00
AT15 Pavel Bure 1.00 2.50

1999-00 O-Pee-Chee Autographs

Randomly inserted in Topps packs at the rate of 1:517, this 10-card set features authentic player autographs

STATED ODDS 1:517 OPC
TA1 John LeClair 20.00 50.00
TA2 Dominik Hasek 30.00 80.00
TA3 Curtis Joseph 15.00 40.00
TA4 Alexei Yashin 12.00 30.00
TA5 Mats Sundin 15.00 40.00
TA6 Chris Drury 12.00 30.00
TA7 Milan Hejduk 15.00 40.00
TA8 Marian Hossa 15.00 40.00
TA9 Vincent Lecavalier 12.00 30.00
TA10 Joe Thornton 20.00 50.00

1999-00 O-Pee-Chee Chrome

COMPLETE SET (297) 200.00 400.00
*OPC CHROME: .6X TO 1.5X TOPPS CHROME

1999-00 O-Pee-Chee Chrome All Topps

COMPLETE SET (15) 15.00 40.00
*O-PEE-CHEE: .4X TO 1X TOPPS CHROME
STATED ODDS 1:24 OPC
*REFRACTORS: 1.2X TO 3X OPC INSERTS
REFRACTOR ODDS 1:120 OPC

1999-00 O-Pee-Chee Chrome Ice Masters

COMPLETE SET (20) 25.00 50.00
*O-PEE-CHEE: .4X TO 1X TOPPS CHROME
STATED ODDS 1:18 OPC
*REFRACTORS: 1.2X TO 3X OPC INSERTS
REFRACTOR ODDS 1:90 OPC

1999-00 O-Pee-Chee Chrome A-Men

COMPLETE SET (6) 10.00 20.00
*O-PEE-CHEE: .4X TO 1X TOPPS CHROME
STATED ODDS 1:24 OPC
*REFRACTORS: 1.2X TO 3X OPC INSERTS
REFRACTOR ODDS 1:120 OPC

1999-00 O-Pee-Chee Chrome Fantastic Finishers

COMPLETE SET (6) 6.00 15.00
*O-PEE-CHEE: .4X TO 1X TOPPS CHROME
STATED ODDS 1:24 OPC
*REFRACTORS: 1.2X TO 3X OPC INSERTS
REFRACTOR ODDS 1:120 OPC

1999-00 O-Pee-Chee Chrome Ice Futures

COMPLETE SET (6) 5.00 12.00
*O-PEE-CHEE: .4X TO 1X TOPPS CHROME
STATED ODDS 1:24 OPC
*REFRACTORS: 1.2X TO 3X OPC INSERTS
REFRACTOR ODDS 1:120 OPC

1999-00 O-Pee-Chee Chrome Positive Performers

COMPLETE SET (6) 3.00 8.00
*O-PEE-CHEE: .4X TO 1X TOPPS CHROME
STATED ODDS 1:24 OPC
*REFRACTORS: 1.2X TO 3X OPC INSERTS
REFRACTOR ODDS 1:120 OPC

1999-00 O-Pee-Chee Chrome Postmasters

COMPLETE SET (6)
*O-PEE-CHEE: .4X TO 1X TOPPS CHROME
STATED ODDS 1:24
*REFRACTORS: 1.2X TO 3X OPC INSERTS

1999-00 O-Pee-Chee Ice Masters

COMPLETE SET (20) 40.00 80.00
*O-PEE-CHEE: .4X TO 1X TOPPS
STATED ODDS 1:25 OPC

1999-00 O-Pee-Chee Now Starring

COMPLETE SET (15) 10.00 20.00
*O-PEE-CHEE: .4X TO 1X TOPPS
STATED ODDS 1:16 OPC

1999-00 O-Pee-Chee A-Men

COMPLETE SET (6) 5.00 12.00
*O-PEE-CHEE: .4X TO 1X TOPPS
STATED ODDS 1:8 OPC

1999-00 O-Pee-Chee Fantastic Finishers

COMPLETE SET (6) 3.00 8.00
*O-PEE-CHEE: .4X TO 1X TOPPS
STATED ODDS 1:10 TOPPS/1:8 OPC

1999-00 O-Pee-Chee Ice Futures

COMPLETE SET (6) 1.25 3.00
*O-PEE-CHEE: .4X TO 1X TOPPS
STATED ODDS 1:8 OPC

1999-00 O-Pee-Chee Positive Performers

COMPLETE SET (6) 2.50 6.00
*O-PEE-CHEE: .4X TO 1X TOPPS
STATED ODDS 1:8 OPC

1999-00 O-Pee-Chee Postmasters

COMPLETE SET (6) 5.00 12.00
*O-PEE-CHEE: .4X TO 1X TOPPS
STATED ODDS 1:8 OPC

1999-00 O-Pee-Chee Top of the World

COMPLETE SET (20) 30.00 60.00
*O-PEE-CHEE: .4X TO 1X TOPPS

2000-01 O-Pee-Chee

This 330-card set parallels the Topps set of the same season. See the Topps listing for complete prices and checklist.

COMPLETE SET (300)
*O-PEE-CHEE: .4X TO 1X TOPPS

2000-01 O-Pee-Chee Combos

Card	Lo	Hi
TC1 Pavel Bure Valeri Bure	1.50	4.00
TC2 Teemu Selanne Paul Kariya	1.25	3.00
TC3 John LeClair Tony Amonte	1.00	2.50
TC4 Curtis Joseph Dominik Hasek	2.00	5.00
TC5 Mike Modano Peter Forsberg	2.00	5.00
TC6 Ray Bourque Chris Pronger	2.00	5.00
TC7 Vincent Lecavalier Joe Thornton	2.00	5.00
TC8 Patrick Roy Martin Brodeur	4.00	10.00
TC9 Steve Yzerman Brett Hull	3.00	8.00
TC10 Jaromir Jagr Mario Lemieux	3.00	8.00

2001-02 O-Pee-Chee

This 360-card set parallels the Topps set of the same season. See the Topps listing for complete prices and checklist. Pack SRP was $1.49 for a 10-card pack and there were 36 packs per box.

*BASE CARDS SAME VALUE AS TOPPS
*ROOKIES: .75X TO 2X

2001-02 O-Pee-Chee Heritage Parallel

Inserted at a rate of 1:1, this 110-card set parallels the first 110 cards of the O-Pee-Chee base set. The card fronts carry the same photo as the base cards, but use the 1971-72 O-Pee-Chee design. Card backs are the same as the base set. A limited parallel to these inserts were also created, these parallels look the same but carry different colored foil and serial numbering out of 50.

*STARS: 1.25X TO 2.5X BASIC CARDS
*LIMITED: 40X TO 80X BASIC CARD

2001-02 O-Pee-Chee Premier Parallel

This parallel to the base set was inserted at 1:4 packs. Cards from this set were stamped with a OPC Premier silver foil stamp on the card fronts.

*STARS: 1.5X TO 4X BASIC CARDS

2001-02 O-Pee-Chee Jumbos

Inserted in retail value boxes only as box toppers, very little is known about these eight oversized cards other than that they were numbered "X of 8".

Card	Lo	Hi
1 Mario Lemieux	2.00	5.00
2 Steve Yzerman	2.00	5.00
3 Martin Brodeur	.75	2.00
4 Paul Kariya	1.00	2.50
5 Patrick Roy	2.00	5.00
6 Curtis Joseph	.75	2.00
7 Martin Havlat	.75	2.00
8 Mike Comrie	.40	1.00

2002-03 O-Pee-Chee

Available in Canada only, this 341-card set minors the Topps issue. Values for singles can be found by using the multipliers below. Cards 331-340 were available via mail-in redemption.

*BASE CARDS SAME VALUE AS TOPPS
*ROOKIES: .6X TO 1.5X

2002-03 O-Pee-Chee Jumbos

Inserted as boxtoppers in OPC boxes, this 25-card set consists of jumbo-sized reprints of 25 base cards.

Card	Price
COMPLETE SET (25)	60.00
1 Joe Thornton	5.00
2 Jarome Iginla	3.00
3 Roman Turek	2.00
4 Ron Francis	2.00
5 Patrick Roy	10.00
6 Joe Sakic	7.00
7 Steve Yzerman	10.00
8 Brendan Shanahan	5.00
9 Mike Comrie	3.00
10 Ryan Smyth	2.00
11 Paul Kariya	5.00
12 Jose Theodore	3.00
13 Saku Koivu	3.00
14 Martin Brodeur	5.00
15 Mike Peca	1.00
16 Daniel Alfredsson	1.00
17 Martin Havlat	3.00
18 Sean Burke	2.00
19 Mario Lemieux	10.00
20 Owen Nolan	2.00
21 Chris Pronger	2.00
22 Mats Sundin	3.00
23 Curtis Joseph	3.00
24 Markus Naslund	2.00
25 Todd Bertuzzi	2.00

2002-03 O-Pee-Chee Premier Blue Parallel

This set paralleled the base set but carried blue borders and blue foil accents. The OPC Premier logo was stamped on the card fronts in blue foil and each card was serial-numbered out of 500.

*STARS: 3X TO 8X BASIC CARDS
*ROOKIES: 1.25X TO 3X

2002-03 O-Pee-Chee Premier Red Parallel

Issued as a redemption, this parallel set carried red borders and red foil accents. The OPC Premier logo was stamped on the card fronts in red foil and each card was serial-numbered out of 100.

*STARS: 8X TO 20X BASIC CARDS
*ROOKIES: 4X TO 10X HI

2002-03 O-Pee-Chee Factory Set

	Lo	Hi
COMPLETE FACTORY SET	30.00	60.00

*STARS: .6X TO 1.5X REG.TOPPS
*ROOKIES: 1X TO 2.5X REG.TOPPS

2002-03 O-Pee-Chee Factory Set Hometown Heroes

*SAME VALUE AS REGULAR INSERTS

2003-04 O-Pee-Chee

Released in late-August, this 340-card set consisted of 330-base cards and a special 10-card rookie redemption subset. Rookie redemption cards were seeded at 1:36.

*OPC: .6X TO 1.5X TOPPS

2003-04 O-Pee-Chee Blue

This 330-card set paralleled the base set but carried blue glitter borders and the Topps logo. These parallels were inserted at 1:5 and each card was serial numbered out of 500. The Rookie Redemption parallel card was inserted at 1:1562.

*STARS: 5X TO 12X TOPPS BASE
*ROOKIES: 1X TO 2.5X TOPPS

2003-04 O-Pee-Chee Gold

This 330-card set paralleled the base set but carried gold glitter borders and the Topps logo. These parallels were inserted at 1:23 and each card was serial numbered out of 50. The Rookie Redemption parallel card was inserted at 1:7485.

*STARS: 10X TO 25X TOPPS BASE
*ROOKIES: 3X TO 8X TOPPS

2003-04 O-Pee-Chee Red

This 330-card set paralleled the base set but carried blue glitter borders and the Topps logo. These parallels were inserted at 2:36 and each card was serial numbered out of 100. The Rookie Redemption parallel card was inserted at 1:5852.

*STARS: 8X TO 20X TOPPS BASE
*ROOKIES: 2.5X TO 6X TOPPS

2006-07 O-Pee-Chee

This 700-card set was released in March, 2007. The set was issued into the hobby in six-card packs, with a $1.59 SRP, which came 36 packs to a box and 12 boxes to a case. Cards numbered 1-500 feature veterans and the rest of the set is broken down into subsets. Cards numbered 501-600 are Rookie Cards, while cards 601-615 are Stat Leaders, Cards numbered 616-645 are Rookie/Sophmore Showdowns, Cards numbered 646-670 is an Hall Worthy subset and the set concludes with Team Checklists from cards 671-700.

Card	Lo	Hi
COMPLETE SET (700)	100.00	250.00
COMP. SET w/o SP's (500)	30.00	80.00
1 Chris Pronger	.30	.75
2 Samuel Pahlsson	.12	.30
3 Andy McDonald	.25	.60
4 Todd Fedoruk	.12	.30
5 Teemu Selanne	.40	1.00
6 Chris Kunitz	.25	.60
7 Scott Niedermayer	.25	.60
8 Corey Perry	.30	.75
9 Sean O'Donnell	.12	.30
10 Ryan Getzlaf	.30	.75
11 Francois Beauchemin	.12	.30
12 Dustin Penner	.25	.60
13 Rob Niedermayer	.12	.30
14 Todd Marchant	.12	.30
15 Ilya Bryzgalov	.40	1.00
16 Stanislav Chistov	.12	.30
17 Jean-Sebastien Giguere	.40	1.00
18 Andy Sutton	.12	.30
19 Steve Rucchin	.25	.60
20 Greg de Vries	.12	.30
21 Vitaly Vishnevski	.12	.30
22 Ilya Kovalchuk	.50	1.25
23 Scott Mellanby	.12	.30
24 Jim Slater	.12	.30
25 Kari Lehtonen	.40	1.00
26 Johan Hedberg	.20	.50
27 Niclas Havelid	.12	.30
28 Marian Hossa	.30	.75
29 Bobby Holik	.25	.60
30 Garnet Exelby	.25	.60
31 Steve McCarthy	.12	.30
32 Niko Kapanen	.12	.30
33 Slava Kozlov	.25	.60
34 P.J. Axelsson	.12	.30
35 Hannu Toivonen	.40	1.00
36 Patrice Bergeron	.30	.75
37 Tim Thomas	.40	1.00
38 Marc Savard	.25	.60
39 Nathan Dempsey	.12	.30
40 Glen Murray	.25	.60
41 Brad Stuart	.25	.60
42 Shean Donovan	.12	.30
43 Marco Sturm	.25	.60
44 Mark Mowers	.12	.30
45 Paul Mara	.12	.30
46 Andrew Alberts	.12	.30
47 Brad Boyes	.25	.60
48 Wayne Primeau	.25	.60
49 Milan Jurcina	.25	.60
50 Jason York	.12	.30
51 Zdeno Chara	.25	.60
52 Jiri Novotny	.12	.30
53 Derek Roy	.25	.60
54 Teppo Numminen	.12	.30
55 Jason Pominville	.12	.30
56 Henrik Tallinder	.12	.30
57 Adam Mair	.12	.30
58 Daniel Briere	.30	.75
59 Chris Drury	.30	.75
60 Ryan Miller	.40	1.00
61 Ales Kotalik	.25	.60
62 Tomas Vanek	.30	.75
63 Brian Campbell	.25	.60
64 Paul Gaustad	.12	.30
65 Jaroslav Spacek	.12	.30
66 Jochen Hecht	.12	.30
67 Maxim Afinogenov	.25	.60
68 Martin Biron	.30	.75
69 Robyn Regehr	.25	.60
70 Dion Phaneuf	.50	1.25
71 Miikka Kiprusoff	.40	1.00
72 Jamie Lundmark	.12	.30
73 Roman Hamrlik	.12	.30
74 Kristian Huselius	.25	.60
75 Darren McCarty	.12	.30
76 Stephane Yelle	.12	.30
77 Marcus Nilson	.12	.30
78 Daymond Langkow	.25	.60
79 Jamie McLennan	.20	.50
80 Tony Amonte	.12	.30
81 Chuck Kobasew	.25	.60
82 Jarome Iginla	.60	1.50
83 Alex Tanguay	.30	.75
84 Andrew Ference	.12	.30
85 Matthew Lombardi	.12	.30
86 Jeff Friesen	.12	.30
87 Glen Wesley	.12	.30
88 Cory Stillman	.25	.60
89 John Grahame	.20	.50
90 Erik Cole	.25	.60
91 Chad Larose	.12	.30
92 Andrew Ladd	.25	.60
93 Craig Adams	.12	.30
94 Eric Staal	.30	.75
95 Rod Brind'Amour	.30	.75
96 Mike Commodore	.25	.60
97 Ray Whitney	.12	.30
98 Justin Williams	.25	.60
99 Kevyn Adams	.25	.60
100 Cam Ward	.60	1.50
101 Eric Belanger	.12	.30
102 Scott Walker	.25	.60
103 Bret Hedican	.12	.30
104 Tim Gleason	.12	.30
105 Adrian Aucoin	.25	.60
106 Nikolai Khabibulin	.40	1.00
107 Michal Handzus	.12	.30
108 Tuomo Ruutu	.25	.60
109 Martin Lapointe	.12	.30
110 Jim Vandermeer	.12	.30
111 Martin Havlat	.30	.75
112 Bryan Smolinski	.12	.30
113 Michael Holmqvist	.12	.30
114 Rene Bourque	.25	.60
115 Brandon Bochenski	.25	.60
116 Patrick Sharp	.12	.30
117 Brent Seabrook	.25	.60
118 Duncan Keith	.50	1.25
119 Jeffrey Hamilton	.12	.30
120 Radim Vrbata	.25	.60
121 Joe Sakic	.75	2.00
122 Peter Budaj	.30	.75
123 Tyler Arnason	.12	.30
124 Mark Rycroft	.12	.30
125 John-Michael Liles	.25	.60
126 Milan Hejduk	.30	.75
127 Andrew Brunette	.25	.60
128 Ian Laperriere	.12	.30
129 Antti Laaksonen	.12	.30
130 Marek Svatos	.25	.60
131 Wojtek Wolski	.25	.60
132 Patrice Brisebois	.12	.30
133 Pierre Turgeon	.25	.60
134 Brett McLean	.12	.30
135 Karlis Skrastins	.12	.30
136 Brad Richardson	.12	.30
137 Brett Clark	.12	.30
138 Jose Theodore	.40	1.00
139 Rick Nash	.40	1.00
140 Nikolai Zherdev	.25	.60
141 Rostislav Klesla	.25	.60
142 David Vyborny	.25	.60
143 Anders Eriksson	.12	.30
144 Adam Foote	.12	.30
145 Jody Shelley	.25	.60
146 Duvie Westcott	.12	.30
147 Gilbert Brule	.25	.60
148 Jason Chimera	.12	.30
149 Pascal LeClaire	.40	1.00
150 Manny Malhotra	.25	.60
151 Ron Hainsey	.12	.30
152 Anson Carter	.25	.60
153 Fredrik Modin	.25	.60
154 Dan Fritsche	.12	.30
155 Sergei Fedorov	.40	1.00
156 Marty Turco	.30	.75
157 Jussi Jokinen	.25	.60
158 Steve Ott	.25	.60
159 Jaroslav Modry	.12	.30
160 Patrik Stefan	.12	.30
161 Matthew Barnaby	.12	.30
162 Jeff Halpern	.25	.60
163 Eric Lindros	.40	1.00
164 Sergei Zubov	.25	.60
165 Darryl Sydor	.12	.30
166 Brenden Morrow	.30	.75
167 Antti Miettinen	.12	.30
168 Jere Lehtinen	.25	.60
169 Philippe Boucher	.12	.30
170 Mike Ribeiro	.25	.60
171 Stu Barnes	.12	.30
172 Mike Modano	.40	1.00
173 Dominik Hasek	.50	1.25
174 Tomas Holmstrom	.25	.60
175 Johan Franzen	.25	.60
176 Robert Lang	.12	.30
177 Mathieu Schneider	.12	.30
178 Nicklas Lidstrom	.40	1.00
179 Chris Osgood	.40	1.00
180 Jason Williams	.12	.30
181 Mikael Samuelsson	.12	.30
182 Chris Chelios	.20	.50
183 Pavel Datsyuk	.40	1.00
184 Dan Cleary	.12	.30
185 Kirk Maltby	.12	.30
186 Kris Draper	.25	.60
187 Andreas Lilja	.12	.30
188 Brett Lebda	.12	.30
189 Jiri Hudler	.20	.50
190 Henrik Zetterberg	.40	1.00
191 Ales Hemsky	.25	.60
192 Fernando Pisani	.25	.60
193 Joffrey Lupul	.25	.60
194 Dwayne Roloson	.30	.75
195 Matt Greene	.12	.30
196 Jason Smith	.25	.60
197 Ethan Moreau	.12	.30
198 Jarret Stoll	.25	.60
199 Jussi Markkanen	.20	.50
200 Brad Winchester	.25	.60
201 Marc-Andre Bergeron	.12	.30
202 Raffi Torres	.12	.30
203 Petr Sykora	.12	.30
204 Shawn Horcoff	.25	.60
205 Steve Staios	.12	.30
206 Ryan Smyth	.30	.75
207 Jay Bouwmeester	.25	.60
208 Ed Belfour	1.00	2.50
209 Ruslan Salei	.12	.30
210 Stephen Weiss	.12	.30
211 Rostislav Olesz	.25	.60
212 Mike Van Ryn	.25	.60
213 Jozef Stumpel	.12	.30
214 Nathan Horton	.25	.60
215 Alexander Auld	.30	.75
216 Juraj Kolnik	.12	.30
217 Martin Gelinas	.12	.30
218 Joe Nieuwendyk	.30	.75
219 Gary Roberts	.12	.30
220 Todd Bertuzzi	.30	.75
221 Chris Gratton	.12	.30
222 Bryan Allen	.12	.30
223 Olli Jokinen	.25	.60
224 Alexander Frolov	.25	.60
225 Mathieu Garon	.30	.75
226 Dustin Brown	.25	.60
227 Lubomir Visnovsky	.25	.60
228 Sean Avery	.25	.60
229 Brent Sopel	.12	.30
230 Craig Conroy	.25	.60
231 Aaron Miller	.12	.30
232 Scott Thornton	.12	.30
233 Mattias Norstrom	.25	.60
234 Dan Cloutier	.20	.50
235 Mike Cammalleri	.25	.60
236 Oleg Tverdovsky	.12	.30
237 Derek Armstrong	.12	.30
238 Tom Kostopoulos	.12	.30
239 Rob Blake	.30	.75
240 Marian Gaborik	.60	1.50
241 Derek Boogaard	.25	.60
242 Brian Rolston	.25	.60
243 Keith Carney	.12	.30
244 Mark Parrish	.25	.60
245 Wes Walz	.12	.30
246 Todd White	.25	.60
247 Pierre-Marc Bouchard	.25	.60
248 Nick Schultz	.25	.60
249 Kurtis Foster	.25	.60
250 Pascal Dupuis	.12	.30
251 Mikko Koivu	.25	.60
252 Manny Fernandez	.40	1.00
253 Wyatt Smith	.12	.30
254 Brent Burns	.25	.60
255 Kim Johnsson	.12	.30
256 Pavol Demitra	.25	.60
257 Michael Ryder	.30	.75
258 David Aebischer	.30	.75
259 Andrei Markov	.25	.60
260 Alexander Perezhogin	.25	.60
261 Sheldon Souray	.25	.60
262 Cristobal Huet	.40	1.00
263 Chris Higgins	.25	.60
264 Steve Begin	.12	.30
265 Radek Bonk	.12	.30
266 Janne Niinimaa	.12	.30
267 Mike Komisarek	.12	.30
268 Tomas Plekanec	.12	.30
269 Sergei Samsonov	.30	.75
270 Alexei Kovalev	.25	.60
271 Craig Rivet	.12	.30
272 Mathieu Dandenault	.12	.30
273 Mike Johnson	.12	.30
274 Saku Koivu	.40	1.00
275 Tomas Vokoun	.30	.75
276 Scott Hartnell	.12	.30
277 Marek Zidlicky	.12	.30
278 Josef Vasicek	.12	.30
279 Jordin Tootoo	.20	.50
280 Ryan Suter	.25	.60
281 Martin Erat	.12	.30
282 David Legwand	.25	.60
283 Kimmo Timonen	.25	.60
284 Chris Mason	.20	.50
285 Steve Sullivan	.25	.60
286 Jason Arnott	.25	.60
287 Dan Hamhuis	.25	.60
288 J.P. Dumont	.25	.60
289 Darcy Hordichuk	.12	.30
290 Paul Kariya	.40	1.00
291 Martin Brodeur	1.25	3.00
292 Brian Gionta	.25	.60
293 Paul Martin	.12	.30
294 John Madden	.12	.30
295 Brian Rafalski	.25	.60
296 Colin White	.12	.30
297 Zach Parise	.30	.75
298 Jay Pandolfo	.12	.30
299 Jamie Langenbrunner	.12	.30
300 Scott Gomez	.25	.60
301 Sergei Brylin	.12	.30
302 Scott Clemmensen	.20	.50
303 Jim Fahey	.12	.30
304 Erik Rasmussen	.12	.30
305 Brad Lukowich	.12	.30
306 Patrik Elias	.25	.60
307 Rick DiPietro	.40	1.00
308 Jason Blake	.25	.60
309 Tom Poti	.25	.60
310 Trent Hunter	.25	.60
311 Brendan Witt	.12	.30
312 Chris Simon	.25	.60
313 Arron Asham	.12	.30
314 Alexei Yashin	.25	.60
315 Mike Sillinger	.25	.60
316 Alexei Zhitnik	.12	.30
317 Jeff Tambellini	.25	.60
318 Mike Dunham	.20	.50
319 Mike York	.12	.30
320 Shawn Bates	.25	.60
321 Viktor Kozlov	.12	.30
322 Miroslav Satan	.25	.60
323 Henrik Lundqvist	.60	1.50
324 Fedor Tyutin	.12	.30
325 Michal Rozsival	.12	.30
326 Michael Nylander	.25	.60
327 Sandis Ozolinsh	.12	.30
328 Matt Cullen	.25	.60
329 Brendan Shanahan	.40	1.00
330 Darius Kasparaitis	.12	.30
331 Kevin Weekes	.20	.50
332 Petr Prucha	.25	.60
333 Martin Straka	.25	.60
334 Aaron Ward	.25	.60
335 Marek Malik	.12	.30
336 Blair Betts	.12	.30
337 Jason Ward	.12	.30
338 Jaromir Jagr	.60	1.50
339 Dany Heatley	.40	1.00
340 Wade Redden	.25	.60
341 Peter Schaefer	.12	.30
342 Mike Fisher	.12	.30
343 Ray Emery	.40	1.00
344 Tom Preissing	.12	.30
345 Patrick Eaves	.25	.60
346 Daniel Alfredsson	.30	.75
347 Chris Phillips	.25	.60
348 Andrej Meszaros	.25	.60
349 Martin Gerber	.40	1.00
350 Joe Corvo	.12	.30
351 Antoine Vermette	.25	.60
352 Chris Neil	.12	.30
353 Anton Volchenkov	.12	.30
354 Chris Kelly	.12	.30
355 Jason Spezza	.40	1.00
356 Simon Gagne	.40	1.00
357 Antero Niittymaki	.40	1.00
358 Joni Pitkanen	.25	.60
359 Jeff Carter	.40	1.00
360 Randy Jones	.12	.30
361 R.J. Umberger	.25	.60
362 Mike Knuble	.25	.60
363 Derian Hatcher	.12	.30
364 Sami Kapanen	.12	.30
365 Fredrick Meyer	.12	.30
366 Mike Richards	.40	1.00
367 Robert Esche	.30	.75
368 Randy Robitaille	.12	.30
369 Stefan Ruzicka	.12	.30
370 Geoff Sanderson	.12	.30
371 Kyle Calder	.25	.60
372 Peter Forsberg	.60	1.50
373 Curtis Joseph	.40	1.00
374 Ladislav Nagy	.25	.60
375 Nick Boynton	.12	.30
376 Dave Scatchard	.12	.30
377 Derek Morris	.12	.30
378 Mike Comrie	.25	.60
379 Ed Jovanovski	.25	.60
380 Georges Laraque	.25	.60
381 Oleg Saprykin	.12	.30
382 Keith Ballard	.25	.60
383 Steven Reinprecht	.12	.30
384 Jeremy Roenick	.40	1.00
385 Zbynek Michalek	.12	.30
386 Owen Nolan	.30	.75
387 Fredrik Sjostrom	.12	.30
388 David Leneveu	.30	.75
389 Shane Doan	.30	.75
390 Marc-Andre Fleury	.40	1.00
391 Sergei Gonchar	.12	.30
392 Dominic Moore	.12	.30
393 Ryan Whitney	.25	.60
394 Nils Ekman	.12	.30
395 Brooks Orpik	.12	.30
396 Mark Eaton	.12	.30
397 Jocelyn Thibault	.20	.50
398 Andre Roy	.12	.30
399 Colby Armstrong	.25	.60
400 Ryan Malone	.25	.60
401 Jarkko Ruutu	.12	.30
402 Mark Recchi	.25	.60
403 John LeClair	.30	.75
404 Josef Melichar	.12	.30
405 Sidney Crosby	2.00	5.00
406 Jonathan Cheechoo	.40	1.00
407 Steve Bernier	.25	.60
408 Evgeni Nabokov	.30	.75
409 Marcel Goc	.12	.30
410 Christian Ehrhoff	.12	.30
411 Mark Bell	.25	.60
412 Mike Grier	.12	.30
413 Patrick Marleau	.30	.75
414 Scott Hannan	.12	.30
415 Mark Smith	.12	.30
416 Milan Michalek	.25	.60
417 Ville Nieminen	.12	.30
418 Kyle McLaren	.12	.30
419 Vesa Toskala	.30	.75
420 Josh Gorges	.25	.60
421 Joe Thornton	.60	1.50
422 Keith Tkachuk	.30	.75
423 Barret Jackman	.12	.30
424 Lee Stempniak	.25	.60
425 Jay McClement	.12	.30
426 Dallas Drake	.12	.30
427 Curtis Sanford	.30	.75
428 Petr Cajanek	.25	.60
429 Eric Brewer	.25	.60
430 Bill Guerin	.25	.60
431 Jamal Mayers	.25	.60
432 Manny Legace	.30	.75
433 Christian Backman	.12	.30
434 Martin Rucinsky	.12	.30
435 Dennis Wideman	.12	.30
436 Jay McKee	.12	.30
437 Doug Weight	.25	.60
438 Brad Richards	.40	1.00
439 Ruslan Fedotenko	.25	.60
440 Johan Holmqvist	.40	1.00
441 Filip Kuba	.12	.30
442 Dimitry Afanasenkov	.12	.30
443 Ryan Craig	.12	.30
444 Dan Boyle	.25	.60
445 Paul Ranger	.12	.30
446 Marc Denis	.30	.75
447 Vaclav Prospal	.25	.60
448 Tim Taylor	.25	.60
449 Martin St. Louis	.40	1.00
450 Cory Sarich	.12	.30
451 Nikita Alexeev	.12	.30
452 Nolan Pratt	.12	.30
453 Vincent Lecavalier	.40	1.00
454 Mats Sundin	.40	1.00
455 Darcy Tucker	.25	.60
456 Kyle Wellwood	.25	.60
457 Nik Antropov	.12	.30
458 Tomas Kaberle	.25	.60
459 Hal Gill	.25	.60
460 Jean-Sebastien Aubin	.20	.50
461 Matt Stajan	.25	.60
462 Alexander Steen	.30	.75
463 Bryan McCabe	.25	.60
464 Jeff O'Neill	.12	.30
465 Wade Belak	.12	.30
466 Michael Peca	.25	.60
467 Carlo Colaiacovo	.12	.30
468 Chad Kilger	.12	.30
469 Alexei Ponikarovsky	.12	.30
470 Andrew Raycroft	.30	.75
471 Roberto Luongo	.75	2.00
472 Ryan Kesler	.25	.60
473 Jan Bulis	.12	.30
474 Matt Cooke	.12	.30
475 Sami Salo	.25	.60
476 Brendan Morrison	.25	.60
477 Henrik Sedin	.25	.60
478 Daniel Sedin	.25	.60
479 Mattias Ohlund	.25	.60
480 Willie Mitchell	.12	.30
481 Dany Sabourin	.20	.50
482 Lukas Krajicek	.12	.30
483 Marc Chouinard	.12	.30
484 Trevor Linden	.12	.30
485 Taylor Pyatt	.12	.30
486 Markus Naslund	.40	1.00
487 Olaf Kolzig	.50	1.25
488 Donald Brashear	.12	.30
489 Chris Clark	.25	.60
490 Dainius Zubrus	.25	.60
491 Matt Pettinger	.30	.75
492 Jamie Heward	.12	.30
493 Bryan Muir	.25	.60
494 Steve Eminger	.25	.60
495 Brian Pothier	.25	.60
496 Brian Sutherby	.12	.30
497 Richard Zednik	.12	.30
498 Brent Johnson	.20	.50
499 Matt Bradley	.12	.30
500 Alexander Ovechkin	1.50	4.00
501 Dustin Byfuglien RC	3.00	8.00
502 Yan Stastny RC	1.50	4.00
503 Mark Stuart RC	1.50	4.00
504 Eric Fehr RC	2.00	5.00
505 Bill Thomas RC	1.50	4.00
506 Joel Perrault RC	1.50	4.00
507 Frank Doyle RC	2.00	5.00
508 Carsen Germyn RC	1.50	4.00
509 Ryan Potulny RC	2.00	5.00
510 David Printz RC	1.50	4.00
511 Rob Collins RC	1.50	4.00
512 Steve Regier RC	1.50	4.00
513 Matt Koalska RC	1.50	4.00
514 Ryan Caldwell RC	1.50	4.00
515 Masi Marjamaki RC	1.50	4.00
516 Cole Jarrett RC	.75	2.00
517 Konstantin Pushkaryov RC	1.50	4.00
518 Ben Ondrus RC	1.50	4.00
519 Brendan Bell RC	1.50	4.00
520 Ian White RC	1.50	4.00
521 Jeremy Williams RC	1.50	4.00
522 Marc-Antoine Pouliot RC	2.00	5.00
523 Noah Welch RC	1.50	4.00
524 Michel Ouellet RC	2.00	5.00
525 Shea Weber RC	1.50	4.00
526 Jarkko Immonen RC	1.50	4.00
527 David Liffiton RC	1.50	4.00
528 Tomas Kopecky RC	1.50	4.00
529 Billy Thompson RC	1.50	4.00
530 Filip Novak RC	1.50	4.00
531 Matt Carle RC	1.50	4.00
532 Dan Jancevski RC	1.50	4.00
533 Erik Reitz RC	1.50	4.00
534 Miroslav Kopriva RC	1.50	4.00
535 Jonas Johansson RC	.75	2.00
536 Shane O'Brien RC	1.50	4.00
537 Ryan Shannon RC	1.50	4.00
538 Patrick O'Sullivan RC	1.50	4.00
539 Anze Kopitar RC	3.00	8.00
540 John Oduya RC	1.50	4.00
541 Travis Zajac RC	2.50	6.00
542 Fredrik Norrena RC	1.50	4.00
543 Phil Kessel RC	4.00	10.00
544 Guillaume Latendresse RC	3.00	8.00
545 Nigel Dawes RC	1.50	4.00
546 Jordan Staal RC	3.00	8.00
547 Kristopher Letang RC	2.50	6.00
548 Paul Stastny RC	3.00	8.00
549 Niklas Backstrom RC	1.50	4.00
550 D.J. King RC	.75	2.00
551 Marc-Edouard Vlasic RC	1.50	4.00
552 Patrick Thoresen RC	1.50	4.00
553 Ladislav Smid RC	1.50	4.00
554 Loui Eriksson RC	1.50	4.00
555 Patrick Fischer RC	.75	2.00
556 Mikko Lehtonen RC	.75	2.00
557 Roman Polak RC	.75	2.00
558 Luc Bourdon RC	2.00	5.00
559 Keith Yandle RC	1.50	4.00
560 Enver Lisin RC	1.50	4.00
561 Adam Burish RC	.75	2.00
562 Alexei Kaigorodov RC	1.50	4.00
563 Alex Brooks RC	.75	2.00
564 Evgeni Malkin RC	6.00	15.00
565 Nate Thompson RC	.75	2.00
566 Janis Sprukts RC	1.50	4.00
567 Alexander Radulov RC	3.00	8.00
568 Alexei Mikhnov RC	1.50	4.00
569 Dave Bolland RC	3.00	8.00
570 Michael Blunden RC	1.50	4.00
571 Lars Jonsson RC	.75	2.00
572 Triston Grant RC	.75	2.00
573 Matt Lashoff RC	1.50	4.00
574 Dustin Boyd RC	2.00	5.00
575 Brandon Prust RC	1.50	4.00
576 Alexander Edler RC	1.50	4.00
577 Jan Hejda RC	.75	2.00
578 Drew Stafford RC	1.50	4.00
579 Kelly Guard RC	2.00	5.00
580 Patrick Coulombe RC	.75	2.00
581 Nathan McIver RC	.75	2.00
582 Mike Brown RC	1.25	3.00
583 Jean-Francois Racine RC	2.00	5.00
584 Adam Dennis RC	.75	2.00
585 Drew Larman RC	.75	2.00
586 Mike Card RC	.75	2.00
587 Michael Funk RC	.75	2.00
588 Stefan Liv RC	2.00	5.00
589 David Booth RC	1.50	4.00
590 Blair Jones RC	1.50	4.00
591 Jussi Timonen RC	.75	2.00
592 David McKee RC	2.00	5.00
593 Michael Ryan RC	.75	2.00
594 Peter Harrold RC	.75	2.00
595 Joe Pavelski RC	5.00	12.00
596 Karl Goehring RC	1.25	3.00
597 Benoit Pouliot RC	2.00	5.00
598 Jesse Schultz RC	1.50	4.00
599 Jeff Drouin-Deslauriers RC	2.00	5.00
600 Martin Houle RC	2.00	5.00
601 Joe Thornton	.60	1.50
602 Jonathan Cheechoo	.40	1.00
603 Wade Redden	.25	.60
604 Michal Rozsival	.12	.30
605 Ilya Kovalchuk	.50	1.25
606 Marian Hossa	.30	.75
607 Sean Avery	.25	.60
608 Martin Brodeur	1.25	3.00
609 Miikka Kiprusoff	.40	1.00
610 Cristobal Huet	.40	1.00
611 Eric Staal	.30	.75
612 Fernando Pisani	.25	.60
613 Dwayne Roloson	.30	.75
614 Ilya Bryzgalov	.40	1.00
615 Alexander Ovechkin	1.50	4.00
616 Patrick Eaves Alexei Kaigorodov	.75	2.00
617 Keith Ballard Keith Yandle	.75	2.00
618 Dion Phaneuf Luc Bourdon	.75	2.00
619 Jussi Jokinen Loui Eriksson	.75	2.00
620 Marek Svatos Paul Stastny	.75	2.00
621 Sidney Crosby Evgeni Malkin	2.00	5.00
622 Chris Higgins Guillaume Latendresse	.75	2.00
623 Brad Boyes Phil Kessel	.75	2.00
624 Alexander Ovechkin Evgeni Malkin	1.25	3.00
625 Petr Prucha Nigel Dawes	.75	2.00
626 Andrej Meszaros Ladislav Smid	.75	2.00
627 Jeff Carter Patrick O'Sullivan	.75	2.00
628 Zach Parise Travis Zajac	.75	2.00
629 Ryan Whitney Noah Welch	.75	2.00
630 Ryan Suter Shea Weber	.75	2.00
631 Josh Gorges Matt Carle	.75	2.00
632 Ryan Getzlaf Ryan Shannon	.75	2.00
633 Mike Richards Ryan Potulny	.75	2.00
634 Pascal LeClaire Fredrik Norrena	.75	2.00
635 Brad Winchester Marc-Antoine Pouliot	.75	2.00
636 Mikko Koivu Anze Kopitar	.75	2.00
637 Andrew Alberts	.75	2.00

Mark Stuart
638 Thomas Vanek 1.00 2.50
Drew Stafford
639 Johan Franzen .75 2.00
Tomas Kopecky
640 Carlo Colaiacovo .75 2.00
Ian White
641 Francois Beauchemin .75 2.00
Shane O'Brien
642 Steve Bernier .75 2.00
Eric Fehr
643 Corey Perry 1.25 3.00
Jordan Staal
644 Alexander Steen .75 2.00
Patrick Thoresen
645 Brent Seabrook .75 2.00
Kristopher Letang
646 Teemu Selanne .40 1.00
647 Joe Sakic .75 2.00
648 Mike Modano .40 1.00
649 Eric Lindros .40 1.00
650 Dominik Hasek .50 1.25
651 Nicklas Lidstrom .40 1.00
652 Chris Chelios .20 .50
653 Joe Nieuwendyk .30 .75
654 Ed Belfour 1.00 2.50
655 Rob Blake .30 .75
656 Saku Koivu .40 1.00
657 Paul Kariya .40 1.00
658 Martin Brodeur 1.25 3.00
659 Jaromir Jagr .60 1.50
660 Brendan Shanahan .40 1.00
661 Daniel Alfredsson .30 .75
662 Peter Forsberg .60 1.50
663 Jeremy Roenick .40 1.00
664 Curtis Joseph .40 1.00
665 Sidney Crosby 2.00 5.00
666 Mark Recchi .25 .60
667 Doug Weight .25 .60
668 Keith Tkachuk .30 .75
669 Mats Sundin .40 1.00
670 Markus Naslund .40 1.00
671 Teemu Selanne .40 1.00
672 Ilya Kovalchuk .50 1.25
673 Patrice Bergeron .30 .75
674 Ryan Miller .40 1.00
675 Miikka Kiprusoff .40 1.00
676 Eric Staal .30 .75
677 Nikolai Khabibulin .40 1.00
678 Rick Nash .40 1.00
679 Joe Sakic .75 2.00
680 Mike Modano .40 1.00
681 Nicklas Lidstrom .40 1.00
682 Ryan Smyth .30 .75
683 Olli Jokinen .25 .60
684 Rob Blake .30 .75
685 Marian Gaborik .60 1.50
686 Saku Koivu .40 1.00
687 Martin Brodeur 1.25 3.00
688 Paul Kariya .40 1.00
689 Miroslav Satan .25 .60
690 Jaromir Jagr .60 1.50
691 Daniel Alfredsson .30 .75
692 Peter Forsberg .60 1.50
693 Shane Doan .30 .75
694 Sidney Crosby 2.00 5.00
695 Patrick Marleau .30 .75
696 Keith Tkachuk .30 .75
697 Vincent Lecavalier .40 1.00
698 Mats Sundin .40 1.00
699 Markus Naslund .40 1.00
700 Alexander Ovechkin 1.50 4.00

2006-07 O-Pee-Chee Rainbow

RAINBOW: 6X to 15X BASE HI
PRINT RUN 100 #'d SETS
5 Teemu Selanne 12.00 30.00
121 Joe Sakic 25.00 60.00
173 Dominik Hasek 12.00 30.00
291 Martin Brodeur 30.00 80.00
405 Sidney Crosby 30.00 80.00
500 Alexander Ovechkin 30.00 80.00
539 Anze Kopitar 20.00 50.00
544 Guillaume Latendresse 20.00 50.00
546 Jordan Staal 20.00 50.00
548 Paul Stastny 25.00 60.00
564 Evgeni Malkin 30.00 80.00
567 Alexander Radulov 15.00 40.00
608 Martin Brodeur 30.00 80.00
615 Alexander Ovechkin 40.00 100.00
621 Sidney Crosby 50.00 100.00
Evgeni Malkin
624 Alexander Ovechkin 15.00 40.00
Evgeni Malkin
643 Corey Perry 10.00 25.00
Jordan Staal
647 Joe Sakic 15.00 40.00
650 Dominik Hasek 8.00 20.00
658 Martin Brodeur 15.00 40.00
665 Sidney Crosby 30.00 80.00
679 Joe Sakic 15.00 40.00
687 Martin Brodeur 15.00 40.00
694 Sidney Crosby 30.00 80.00
700 Alexander Ovechkin 20.00 50.00

2006-07 O-Pee-Chee Autographs

ODDS 1:360
AAH Ales Hemsky 6.00 15.00
AAM Andy McDonald 10.00 25.00
AAN Antero Niittymaki SP 20.00 50.00
AAR Andrew Raycroft SP 20.00 50.00
ABB Brad Boyes SP 20.00 50.00
ABG Brian Gionta 6.00 15.00
ABM Brendan Morrison 6.00 15.00
ABO Bobby Orr SP 400.00 700.00
ACC Chris Campoli 6.00 15.00
ACH Cristobal Huet 12.00 30.00
ACK Chris Kunitz 6.00 15.00
ACS Cory Stillman 8.00 20.00
ACW Cam Ward SP 40.00 100.00
ADB Daniel Briere 15.00 30.00
ADH Dany Heatley SP 30.00 60.00
ADR Dwayne Roloson 12.00 30.00
AEM Evgeni Malkin 125.00 200.00
AGB Gilbert Brule SP 30.00 60.00
AHA Dominik Hasek SP 40.00 80.00
AHT Hannu Toivonen 10.00 25.00
AIK Ilya Kovalchuk SP 30.00 80.00
AJA Jason Arnott 6.00 15.00
AJC Jeff Carter 15.00 30.00
AJI Jarome Iginla SP 40.00 80.00
AJL John-Michael Liles 6.00 15.00
AJS Jordan Staal 30.00 80.00
AJT Joe Thornton SP
AKB Keith Ballard 6.00 15.00
AKC Kyle Calder 8.00 30.00
AKD Kris Draper SP
AKO Mikko Koivu 6.00 15.00
AMC Mike Cammalleri 10.00 25.00
AMG Marian Gaborik SP 50.00 100.00
AMP Marc-Antoine Pouliot 10.00 25.00
AMR Mike Richards 15.00 40.00
AMS Marek Svatos 6.00 15.00
ANA Rick Nash 20.00 50.00
ANH Nathan Horton 10.00 25.00
ANL Nicklas Lidstrom SP 40.00 100.00
AOJ Olli Jokinen SP
APB Pierre-Marc Bouchard 6.00 15.00
APK Phil Kessel SP 60.00 125.00
APP Petr Prucha 10.00 25.00
APS Paul Stastny 40.00 100.00
ARB Rob Blake 15.00 40.00
ARL Roberto Luongo SP 75.00 150.00
ARM Ryan Malone 8.00 20.00
ARN Robert Nilsson 6.00 15.00
ARS Ryan Smyth 10.00 25.00
ASB Steve Bernier 10.00 25.00
ASW Stephen Weiss 6.00 15.00
AWR Wade Redden 6.00 15.00
AWW Wojtek Wolski 12.00 30.00

2006-07 O-Pee-Chee Swatches

STATED ODDS 1:24
SAA Arron Asham 3.00 8.00
SAE David Aebischer 8.00 20.00
SAF Alexander Frolov 6.00 15.00
SAH Ales Hemsky 6.00 15.00
SAM Andrej Meszaros 6.00 15.00
SAO Alexander Ovechkin 30.00 80.00
SAS Alexander Steen 12.00 30.00
SAT Alex Tanguay 8.00 20.00
SAY Alexei Yashin 8.00 20.00
SBB Brandon Bochenski 6.00 15.00
SBM Brendan Morrison 6.00 15.00
SBS Brad Stuart 6.00 15.00
SCC Chris Chelios 5.00 12.00
SCD Chris Drury 8.00 20.00
SCH Jonathan Cheechoo 15.00 40.00
SCK Chuck Kobasew 6.00 15.00
SCP Chris Pronger 8.00 20.00
SDA Daniel Alfredsson 8.00 20.00
SDE Pavol Demitra 6.00 15.00
SDH Dominik Hasek 12.00 30.00
SDK Duncan Keith 12.00 30.00
SDT Darcy Tucker 6.00 15.00
SDW Doug Weight 6.00 15.00
SEN Evgeni Nabokov 6.00 15.00
SES Eric Staal 8.00 20.00
SFP Fernando Pisani 6.00 15.00
SGA Mathieu Garon 8.00 20.00
SGL Guy Lafleur SP 75.00 125.00
SGM Glen Murray 6.00 15.00
SGR Gary Roberts 3.00 8.00
SHA Martin Havlat 8.00 20.00
SHE Milan Hejduk 8.00 20.00
SHO Shawn Horcoff 6.00 15.00
SHS Henrik Sedin 6.00 15.00
SHT Hannu Toivonen 10.00 25.00
SJA Jason Arnott 6.00 15.00
SJB Jay Bouwmeester 6.00 15.00
SJC Jeff Carter 10.00 25.00
SJG Jean-Sebastien Giguere 10.00 25.00
SJI Jarome Iginla 15.00 40.00
SJJ Jaromir Jagr 15.00 40.00
SJL Jere Lehtinen 6.00 15.00
SJP Joni Pitkanen 6.00 15.00
SJR Jeremy Roenick 10.00 25.00
SJS Jason Spezza 10.00 25.00
SKL Kari Lehtonen 10.00 25.00
SLE Jordan Leopold 6.00 15.00
SLX Mario Lemieux SP 50.00 100.00
SMA Maxim Afinogenov 6.00 15.00
SMB Martin Brodeur 30.00 80.00
SMC Mike Cammalleri 6.00 15.00
SMD Marc Denis 8.00 20.00
SMF Manny Fernandez 10.00 25.00
SMG Marian Gaborik 15.00 40.00
SMH Marian Hossa 8.00 20.00
SMI Miroslav Satan 6.00 15.00
SML Manny Legace 8.00 20.00
SMM Mike Modano 10.00 25.00
SMN Markus Naslund 10.00 25.00
SMR Mark Recchi 6.00 15.00
SMS Martin St. Louis SP 10.00 25.00
SMT Marty Turco 8.00 20.00
SNL Nicklas Lidstrom 10.00 25.00
SOJ Olli Jokinen 6.00 15.00
SOT Steve Ott 10.00 25.00
SPB Patrice Bergeron 8.00 20.00
SPD Pavel Datsyuk 15.00 40.00
SPF Peter Forsberg 12.00 30.00
SPK Paul Kariya 15.00 40.00
SPL Pascal LeClaire 10.00 25.00
SPM Patrick Marleau 8.00 20.00
SPR Patrick Roy 25.00 60.00
SPS Peter Stastny 6.00 15.00
SRB Rod Brind'Amour 8.00 20.00
SRD Rick DiPietro 10.00 25.00
SRE Robert Esche 8.00 20.00
SRF Ruslan Fedotenko 6.00 15.00
SRI Mike Ribeiro 6.00 15.00
SRK Rostislav Klesla 6.00 15.00
SRL Robert Lang 3.00 8.00
SRM Ryan Miller 10.00 25.00
SRN Rick Nash 12.00 30.00
SRS Ryan Smyth 8.00 20.00
SRY Michael Ryder 8.00 20.00
SSA Joe Sakic 30.00 80.00
SSB Steve Bernier 6.00 15.00
SSC Sidney Crosby SP 90.00 150.00
SSD Shane Doan 8.00 20.00
SSF Sergei Fedorov 10.00 25.00
SSG Scott Gomez 6.00 15.00
SSH Brendan Shanahan 10.00 25.00
SSO Sandis Ozolinsh 3.00 8.00
SSS Sergei Samsonov 8.00 20.00
SST Martin Straka 6.00 15.00
SSU Mats Sundin 10.00 25.00
STR Tuomo Ruutu 6.00 15.00
STS Teemu Selanne 12.00 30.00
STV Tomas Vokoun 8.00 20.00
SVL Vincent Lecavalier 10.00 25.00
SZC Zdeno Chara 6.00 15.00

2007-08 O-Pee-Chee

This 600-card set was released in December, 2007. The set was issued into the hobby in six-card packs, with a $1.59 SRP, which came 36 packs to a box and 12 boxes to a case. Cards numbered 1-500 feature veterans while cards numbered 501-600 are Rookie Cards. Those Rookie Cards were inserted into packs at a stated rate of one in two.

COMPLETE SET (600) 100.00 200.00
COMP.SET w/o SP's (500) 60.00 100.00
MARQUEE RCs STATED ODDS 1:2
1 Jean-Sebastien Giguere .40 1.00
2 Andy McDonald .25 .60
3 Teemu Selanne .40 1.00
4 Travis Moen .25 .60
5 George Parros .25 .60
6 Samuel Pahlsson .25 .60
7 Rob Niedermayer .25 .60
8 Scott Niedermayer .25 .60
9 Francois Beauchemin .25 .60
10 Dustin Penner .25 .60
11 Ryan Getzlaf .30 .75
12 Corey Perry .30 .75
13 Chris Kunitz .25 .60
14 Chris Pronger .40 1.00
15 Ilya Bryzgalov .40 1.00
16 Mathieu Schneider .25 .60
17 Todd Bertuzzi .30 .75
18 Marian Hossa .40 1.00
19 Bobby Holik .25 .60
20 Eric Belanger .25 .60
21 Ken Klee .25 .60
22 Alexei Zhitnik .25 .60
23 Johan Hedberg .25 .60
24 Steve Rucchin .25 .60
25 Ilya Kovalchuk .50 1.25
26 Niclas Havelid .25 .60
27 Jim Slater .25 .60
28 Kari Lehtonen .40 1.00
29 Garnet Exelby .25 .60
30 Slava Kozlov .25 .60
31 Chris Thorburn .25 .60
32 Pascal Dupuis .25 .60
33 Andy Sutton .25 .60
34 Patrice Bergeron .40 1.00
35 Phil Kessel .40 1.00
36 Manny Fernandez .30 .75
37 Aaron Ward .25 .60
38 Zdeno Chara .25 .60
39 Glen Murray .25 .60
40 Marco Sturm .25 .60
41 Chuck Kobasew .25 .60
42 P.J. Axelsson .25 .60
43 Dennis Wideman .25 .60
44 Tim Thomas .50 1.25
45 Andrew Ference .25 .60
46 Mark Mowers .25 .60
47 Marc Savard .25 .60
48 Brandon Bochenski .25 .60
49 Andrew Alberts .25 .60
50 Shean Donovan .25 .60
51 Ryan Miller .40 1.00
52 Thomas Vanek .30 .75
53 Derek Roy .25 .60
54 Jochen Hecht .25 .60
55 Dmitri Kalinin .25 .60
56 Jason Pominville .25 .60
57 Daniel Paille .25 .60
58 Drew Stafford .30 .75
59 Brian Campbell .25 .60
60 Nathan Paetsch .25 .60
61 Jocelyn Thibault .30 .75
62 Andrew Peters .25 .60
63 Teppo Numminen .25 .60
64 Tim Connolly .25 .60
65 Ales Kotalik .25 .60
66 Maxim Afinogenov .25 .60
67 Jarome Iginla .60 1.50
68 Matthew Lombardi .25 .60
69 Rhett Warrener .25 .60
70 Robyn Regehr .25 .60
71 Daymond Langkow .25 .60
72 David Hale .25 .60
73 Miikka Kiprusoff .50 1.25
74 Stephane Yelle .25 .60
75 Adrian Aucoin .25 .60
76 Mark Giordano .25 .60
77 Alex Tanguay .30 .75
78 Kristian Huselius .25 .60
79 Owen Nolan .30 .75
80 Dion Phaneuf .40 1.00
81 Craig Conroy .25 .60
82 Cory Sarich .25 .60
83 Cam Ward .40 1.00
84 Ray Whitney .25 .60
85 Erik Cole .25 .60
86 Mike Commodore .25 .60
87 Eric Staal .40 1.00
88 Chad Larose .25 .60
89 Justin Williams .25 .60
90 Tim Gleason .25 .60
91 Andrew Ladd .25 .60
92 David Tanabe .25 .60
93 John Grahame .30 .75
94 Cory Stillman .25 .60
95 Craig Adams .25 .60
96 Rod Brind'Amour .30 .75
97 Scott Walker .25 .60
98 Jeffrey Hamilton .25 .60
99 Glen Wesley .25 .60
100 Martin Havlat .30 .75
101 Rene Bourque .25 .60
102 Andrei Zyuzin .25 .60
103 Duncan Keith .40 1.00
104 Jim Vandermeer .25 .60
105 Patrick Sharp .25 .60
106 Martin Lapointe .25 .60
107 Tuomo Ruutu .25 .60
108 Patrick Lalime .30 .75
109 Jason Williams .25 .60
110 Radim Vrbata .25 .60
111 Brent Seabrook .25 .60
112 Robert Lang .25 .60
113 Cam Barker .25 .60
114 Sergei Samsonov .25 .60
115 Nikolai Khabibulin .40 1.00
116 Nikita Alexeev .25 .60
117 Joe Sakic .75 2.00
118 Peter Budaj .30 .75
119 Andrew Brunette .25 .60
120 John-Michael Liles .25 .60
121 Ian Laperriere .25 .60
122 Scott Hannan .25 .60
123 Marek Svatos .25 .60
124 Brett Clark .25 .60
125 Jose Theodore .40 1.00
126 Jordan Leopold .25 .60
127 Tyler Arnason .25 .60
128 Wojtek Wolski .25 .60
129 Kurt Sauer .25 .60
130 Paul Stastny .40 1.00
131 Brad Richardson .25 .60
132 Ryan Smyth .30 .75
133 Milan Hejduk .30 .75
134 Rick Nash .40 1.00
135 Nikolai Zherdev .25 .60
136 Jody Shelley .25 .60
137 Adam Foote .25 .60
138 Ole-Kristian Tollefsen .25 .60
139 Jason Chimera .25 .60
140 Fredrik Norrena .30 .75
141 Sergei Fedorov .40 1.00
142 Rostislav Klesla .25 .60
143 Dan Fritsche .25 .60
144 Fredrik Modin .25 .60
145 Manny Malhotra .25 .60
146 Jiri Novotny .25 .60
147 David Vyborny .25 .60
148 Alexander Svitov .25 .60
149 Gilbert Brule .25 .60
150 Pascal LeClaire .30 .75
151 Mike Modano .40 1.00
152 Sergei Zubov .25 .60
153 Mike Smith .30 .75
154 Jussi Jokinen .25 .60
155 Philippe Boucher .25 .60
156 Trevor Daley .25 .60
157 Antti Miettinen .25 .60
158 Steve Ott .25 .60
159 Brenden Morrow .30 .75
160 Loui Eriksson .25 .60
161 Todd Fedoruk .25 .60
162 Mike Ribeiro .25 .60
163 Jere Lehtinen .25 .60
164 Stu Barnes .25 .60
165 Jeff Halpern .25 .60
166 Mattias Norstrom .25 .60
167 Marty Turco .40 1.00
168 Nicklas Lidstrom .40 1.00
169 Dan Cleary .30 .75
170 Kris Draper .30 .75
171 Chris Osgood .30 .75
172 Andreas Lilja .25 .60
173 Henrik Zetterberg .40 1.00
174 Brett Lebda .25 .60
175 Chris Chelios .25 .60
176 Tomas Holmstrom .30 .75
177 Pavel Datsyuk .40 1.00
178 Jiri Hudler .25 .60
179 Kyle Quincey .25 .60
180 Valtteri Filppula .25 .60
181 Brian Rafalski .25 .60
182 Johan Franzen .25 .60
183 Mikael Samuelsson .25 .60
184 Dominik Hasek .50 1.25
185 Ales Hemsky .25 .60
186 Mathieu Garon .30 .75
187 Jarret Stoll .25 .60
188 Ladislav Smid .25 .60
189 Marc-Antoine Pouliot .25 .60
190 Matt Greene .25 .60
191 Joni Pitkanen .25 .60
192 Marty Reasoner .25 .60
193 Shawn Horcoff .25 .60
194 Steve Staios .25 .60
195 Ethan Moreau .25 .60
196 Patrick Thoresen .25 .60
197 Dwayne Roloson .30 .75
198 Fernando Pisani .25 .60
199 Geoff Sanderson .25 .60
200 Jean-Francois Jacques .25 .60
201 Raffi Torres .25 .60
202 Olli Jokinen .25 .60
203 Mike Van Ryn .25 .60
204 Stephen Weiss .25 .60
205 Bryan Allen .25 .60
206 Richard Zednik .25 .60
207 Steve Montador .25 .60
208 Alexander Auld .30 .75
209 Nathan Horton .25 .60
210 Ruslan Salei .25 .60
211 Rostislav Olesz .25 .60
212 David Booth .25 .60
213 Gregory Campbell .25 .60
214 Noah Welch .25 .60
215 Brett McLean .25 .60
216 Tomas Vokoun .40 1.00
217 Jay Bouwmeester .25 .60
218 Radek Dvorak .25 .60
219 Rob Blake .30 .75
220 Patrick O'Sullivan .30 .75
221 Derek Armstrong .25 .60
222 Dan Cloutier .30 .75
223 Scott Thornton .25 .60
224 Michal Handzus .25 .60
225 Anze Kopitar .40 1.00
226 Dustin Brown .25 .60
227 Raitis Ivanans .25 .60
228 Kyle Calder .25 .60
229 Brad Stuart .25 .60
230 Mike Cammalleri .30 .75
231 Ladislav Nagy .25 .60
232 Jason LaBarbera .30 .75
233 Lubomir Visnovsky .25 .60
234 Alexander Frolov .25 .60
235 Marian Gaborik .50 1.25
236 Kim Johnsson .25 .60
237 Niklas Backstrom .30 .75
238 Branko Radivojevic .25 .60
239 Dominic Moore .25 .60
240 Pavol Demitra .25 .60
241 Nick Schultz .25 .60
242 Brian Rolston .25 .60
243 Josh Harding .30 .75
244 Derek Boogaard .25 .60
245 Kurtis Foster .25 .60
246 Stephane Veilleux .25 .60
247 Keith Carney .25 .60
248 Mikko Koivu .25 .60
249 Mark Parrish .25 .60
250 Brent Burns .25 .60
251 Pierre-Marc Bouchard .25 .60
252 Saku Koivu .30 .75
253 Chris Higgins .30 .75
254 Mike Komisarek .25 .60
255 Maxim Lapierre .25 .60
256 Guillaume Latendresse .30 .75
257 Bryan Smolinski .25 .60
258 Sheldon Souray .25 .60
259 Andrei Kostitsyn .25 .60
260 Cristobal Huet .30 .75
261 Michael Ryder .25 .60
262 Andrei Markov .30 .75
263 Josh Gorges .25 .60
264 Alexander Perezhogin .25 .60
265 Tomas Plekanec .25 .60
266 Roman Hamrlik .25 .60
267 Mark Streit .25 .60
268 Alexei Kovalev .25 .60
269 Jerred Smithson .25 .60
270 Jason Arnott .25 .60
271 Dan Hamhuis .25 .60
272 Jordin Tootoo .30 .75
273 Darcy Hordichuk .25 .60
274 Vernon Fiddler .25 .60
275 Steve Sullivan .25 .60
276 Shea Weber .25 .60
277 Alexander Radulov .40 1.00
278 Marek Zidlicky .25 .60
279 David Legwand .25 .60
280 Radek Bonk .25 .60
281 Ryan Suter .25 .60
282 Chris Mason .30 .75
283 Greg de Vries .25 .60
284 J.P. Dumont .25 .60
285 Martin Erat .25 .60
286 Brian Gionta .25 .60
287 Travis Zajac .25 .60
288 Johnny Oduya .25 .60
289 Jamie Langenbrunner .25 .60
290 Colin White .25 .60
291 Sergei Brylin .25 .60
292 Dainius Zubrus .25 .60
293 Jay Pandolfo .25 .60
294 Cam Janssen .25 .60
295 Martin Brodeur 1.00 2.50
296 Zach Parise .30 .75
297 Paul Martin .25 .60
298 John Madden .25 .60
299 Michael Rupp .25 .60
300 Kevin Weekes .30 .75
301 Patrik Elias .25 .60
302 Rick DiPietro .30 .75
303 Mike Sillinger .25 .60
304 Marc-Andre Bergeron .25 .60
305 Mike Comrie .25 .60
306 Jon Sim .25 .60
307 Chris Campoli .25 .60
308 Ruslan Fedotenko .25 .60
309 Bill Guerin .25 .60
310 Trent Hunter .25 .60
311 Radek Martinek .25 .60
312 Frederick Meyer .25 .60
313 Richard Park .25 .60
314 Jeff Tambellini .25 .60
315 Wade Dubielewicz .30 .75
316 Brendan Witt .25 .60
317 Andy Hilbert .25 .60
318 Miroslav Satan .25 .60
319 Jaromir Jagr .60 1.50
320 Sean Avery .25 .60
321 Michal Rozsival .25 .60
322 Petr Prucha .25 .60
323 Matt Cullen .25 .60
324 Marcel Hossa .25 .60
325 Paul Mara .25 .60
326 Scott Gomez .25 .60
327 Blair Betts .25 .60
328 Colton Orr .25 .60
329 Marek Malik .25 .60
330 Chris Drury .30 .75
331 Martin Straka .25 .60
332 Nigel Dawes .25 .60
333 Ryan Hollweg .25 .60
334 Fedor Tyutin .25 .60
335 Henrik Lundqvist .50 1.25
336 Dany Heatley .50 1.25
337 Wade Redden .25 .60
338 Joe Corvo .25 .60
339 Jason Spezza .40 1.00
340 Patrick Eaves .25 .60
341 Chris Kelly .25 .60
342 Mike Fisher .30 .75
343 Ray Emery .30 .75
344 Andrej Meszaros .25 .60
345 Peter Schaefer .25 .60
346 Anton Volchenkov .25 .60
347 Chris Neil .25 .60
348 Chris Phillips .25 .60
349 Christoph Schubert .25 .60
350 Antoine Vermette .25 .60
351 Martin Gerber .30 .75
352 Daniel Alfredsson .30 .75
353 Jason Smith .25 .60
354 Simon Gagne .40 1.00
355 Antero Niittymaki .30 .75
356 Joffrey Lupul .25 .60
357 Jeff Carter .25 .60
358 Ben Eager .25 .60
359 Scott Hartnell .25 .60
360 Martin Biron .30 .75
361 Mike Richards .50 1.25
362 Kimmo Timonen .25 .60
363 R.J. Umberger .25 .60
364 Daniel Briere .40 1.00
365 Scottie Upshall .25 .60
366 Mike Knuble .25 .60
367 Shane Doan .25 .60
368 Niko Kapanen .25 .60
369 Mathias Tjarnqvist .25 .60
370 Zbynek Michalek .25 .60
371 Fredrik Sjostrom .25 .60
372 Bill Thomas .25 .60
373 Josh Gratton .25 .60
374 Mikael Tellqvist .30 .75
375 Derek Morris .25 .60
376 Kevyn Adams .25 .60
377 Michael Zigomanis .25 .60
378 Ed Jovanovski .25 .60
379 David Leneveu .30 .75
380 Steven Reinprecht .25 .60
381 Nick Boynton .25 .60
382 Keith Ballard .25 .60
383 Marc-Andre Fleury .40 1.00
384 Jordan Staal .50 1.25
385 Gary Roberts .25 .60
386 Georges Laraque .25 .60
387 Ryan Whitney .30 .75
388 Petr Sykora .25 .60
389 Jarkko Ruutu .25 .60
390 Evgeni Malkin 1.00 2.50
391 Brooks Orpik .25 .60
392 Maxime Talbot .25 .60
393 Mark Recchi .25 .60
394 Ryan Malone .25 .60
395 Colby Armstrong .25 .60
396 Sergei Gonchar .25 .60
397 Erik Christensen .25 .60
398 Darryl Sydor .25 .60
399 Sidney Crosby 2.00 5.00
400 Evgeni Nabokov .30 .75
401 Milan Michalek .25 .60
402 Marc-Edouard Vlasic .25 .60
403 Patrick Marleau .30 .75
404 Christian Ehrhoff .25 .60
405 Pat Rissmiller .25 .60
406 Craig Rivet .25 .60
407 Jonathan Cheechoo .30 .75
408 Joe Pavelski .25 .60
409 Curtis Brown .25 .60
410 Mike Grier .25 .60
411 Kyle McLaren .25 .60
412 Steve Bernier .25 .60
413 Matt Carle .25 .60
414 Marcel Goc .25 .60
415 Ryan Clowe .25 .60
416 Joe Thornton .50 1.25
417 Manny Legace .30 .75
418 Brad Boyes .30 .75
419 Eric Brewer .25 .60
420 Jay McClement .25 .60
421 Martin Rucinsky .25 .60
422 Jay McKee .25 .60
423 Petr Cajanek .25 .60
424 Doug Weight .25 .60
425 Christian Backman .25 .60
426 Jamal Mayers .25 .60
427 Jeff Woywitka .25 .60
428 Lee Stempniak .25 .60
429 David Backes .25 .60
430 Barret Jackman .25 .60
431 Paul Kariya .40 1.00
432 Keith Tkachuk .30 .75
433 Bryce Salvador .25 .60
434 Vincent Lecavalier .40 1.00
435 Paul Ranger .25 .60
436 Vaclav Prospal .25 .60
437 Shane O'Brien .25 .60
438 Michel Ouellet .25 .60
439 Marc Denis .30 .75
440 Jason Ward .25 .60
441 Martin St. Louis .30 .75
442 Blair Jones .25 .60
443 Filip Kuba .25 .60
444 Ryan Craig .25 .60
445 Tim Taylor .25 .60
446 Dan Boyle .25 .60
447 Nick Tarnasky .25 .60
448 Johan Holmqvist .30 .75
449 Brad Richards .30 .75
450 Andre Roy .25 .60
451 Mats Sundin .40 1.00
452 Kyle Wellwood .25 .60
453 Bryan McCabe .25 .60
454 Jason Blake .25 .60
455 Ian White .25 .60
456 Alexei Ponikarovsky .25 .60
457 Hal Gill .25 .60
458 Pavel Kubina .25 .60
459 Andrew Raycroft .30 .75
460 Alexander Steen .25 .60
461 Nik Antropov .25 .60
462 Mark Bell .25 .60
463 Carlo Colaiacovo .25 .60
464 Matt Stajan .25 .60
465 Tomas Kaberle .25 .60
466 Vesa Toskala .30 .75
467 Darcy Tucker .30 .75
468 Roberto Luongo .60 1.50
469 Sami Salo .25 .60
470 Ryan Kesler .25 .60
471 Trevor Linden .30 .75
472 Kevin Bieksa .25 .60
473 Matt Cooke .25 .60
474 Aaron Miller .25 .60
475 Henrik Sedin .25 .60
476 Mattias Ohlund .25 .60
477 Brendan Morrison .25 .60
478 Willie Mitchell .25 .60
479 Curtis Sanford .30 .75
480 Markus Naslund .40 1.00
481 Taylor Pyatt .25 .60
482 Alexandre Burrows .25 .60
483 Lukas Krajicek .25 .60
484 Daniel Sedin .25 .60
485 Alexander Ovechkin 1.25 3.00
486 Chris Clark .25 .60
487 Milan Jurcina .25 .60
488 Boyd Gordon .25 .60
489 Michael Nylander .25 .60
490 Donald Brashear .25 .60
491 Shaone Morrisonn .25 .60
492 Steve Eminger .25 .60
493 Olaf Kolzig .40 1.00
494 Matt Pettinger .25 .60
495 Viktor Kozlov .25 .60
496 Brooks Laich .25 .60
497 Mike Green .25 .60
498 Jakub Klepis .25 .60
499 Brent Johnson .30 .75
500 Alexander Semin .40 1.00
501 Bobby Ryan RC 4.00 10.00
502 Drew Miller RC 1.00 2.50
503 Aaron Rome RC 1.00 2.50
504 Ryan Carter RC 1.25 3.00
505 Jonas Hiller RC 2.50 6.00
506 Kent Huskins RC 1.00 2.50
507 Bjorn Melin RC 1.00 2.50
508 Bryan Little RC 1.50 4.00
509 Brett Sterling RC 1.00 2.50
510 Tobias Enstrom RC 1.50 4.00
511 David Krejci RC 2.00 5.00
512 Jonathan Sigalet RC 1.00 2.50
513 Milan Lucic RC 2.50 6.00
514 Curtis McElhinney RC 1.25 3.00
515 David Moss RC 1.50 4.00
516 Tomi Maki RC 1.00 2.50
517 Jonathan Toews RC 6.00 15.00
518 Patrick Kane RC 6.00 15.00
519 Colin Fraser RC 1.00 2.50
520 Bryan Bickell RC 1.00 2.50
521 Magnus Johansson RC 1.00 2.50
522 Pierre Parenteau RC 1.00 2.50
523 Jonas Nordqvist RC 1.00 2.50
524 David Koci RC 1.00 2.50
525 Tyler Weiman RC 1.25 3.00
526 Jaroslav Hlinka RC 1.25 3.00
527 Jeff Finger RC 1.00 2.50
528 Kris Russell RC 1.50 4.00
529 Danny Bois RC 1.00 2.50
530 Tomas Popperle RC 1.25 3.00
531 Marc Methot RC 1.00 2.50
532 Jared Boll RC 1.00 2.50
533 Curtis Glencross RC 1.00 2.50
534 Matt Niskanen RC 1.00 2.50
535 Tobias Stephan RC 1.25 3.00
536 Joel Lundqvist RC 1.00 2.50
537 Krys Barch RC 1.00 2.50
538 Chris Conner RC 1.00 2.50
539 Matt Ellis RC 1.00 2.50
540 Sam Gagner RC 2.00 5.00
541 Andrew Cogliano RC 2.50 6.00
542 Rob Schremp RC 1.25 3.00
543 Tom Gilbert RC 1.25 3.00
544 Bryan Young RC 1.00 2.50
545 Zack Stortini RC 1.00 2.50
546 Sebastien Bisaillon RC 1.00 2.50
547 Martin Lojek RC 1.00 2.50
548 Cory Murphy RC 1.00 2.50
549 Jack Johnson RC 1.50 4.00
550 Jonathan Bernier RC 2.50 6.00

551 Lauri Tukonen RC 1.00 2.50
552 Brady Murray RC 1.00 2.50
553 John Zeiler RC 1.00 2.50
554 Gabe Gauthier RC 1.00 2.50
555 Shay Stephenson RC 1.00 2.50
556 Joe Piskula RC 1.00 2.50
557 Petr Kalus RC 1.00 2.50
558 James Sheppard RC 1.00 2.50
559 Joel Ward RC 1.00 2.50
560 Carey Price RC 5.00 12.00
561 Kyle Chipchura RC 1.50 4.00
562 Jaroslav Halak RC 3.00 8.00
563 Duncan Milroy RC 1.00 2.50
564 Ville Koistinen RC 1.00 2.50
565 Rich Peverley RC 1.00 2.50
566 Nicklas Bergfors RC 1.25 3.00
567 Andy Greene RC 1.00 2.50
568 Mark Fraser RC 1.00 2.50
569 David Clarkson RC 1.00 2.50
570 Rod Pelley RC 1.00 2.50
571 Frans Nielsen RC 1.00 2.50
572 Marc Staal RC 2.50 6.00
573 Brandon Dubinsky RC 1.50 4.00
574 Ryan Callahan RC 1.50 4.00
575 Daniel Girardi RC 1.00 2.50
576 Nick Foligno RC 1.50 4.00
577 Brian Elliott RC 1.25 3.00
578 Ryan Parent RC 1.25 3.00
579 Scott Munroe RC 1.00 2.50
580 Denis Tolpeko RC 1.00 2.50
581 Riley Cote RC 1.25 3.00
582 Nathan Guenin RC 1.00 2.50
583 Peter Mueller RC 3.00 8.00
584 Martin Hanzal RC 1.25 3.00
585 Craig Weller RC 1.00 2.50
586 Daniel Winnik RC 1.00 2.50
587 Daniel Carcillo RC 1.25 3.00
588 Mark Mancari RC 1.25 3.00
589 Torrey Mitchell RC 1.25 3.00
590 Thomas Pilhal RC 1.25 3.00
591 Erik Johnson RC 2.00 5.00
592 Darcy Campbell RC 1.00 2.50
593 Steve Wagner RC 1.00 2.50
594 Matt Smaby RC 1.00 2.50
595 Mike Lundin RC 1.00 2.50
596 Mason Raymond RC 2.50 6.00
597 Jannik Hansen RC 1.00 2.50
598 Nicklas Backstrom RC 4.00 10.00
599 Jeff Schultz RC 1.00 2.50
600 Jamie Hunt RC 1.00 2.50

2007-08 O-Pee-Chee Micromotion

*MICRO: 4X TO 10X
STATED ODDS 1:6

2007-08 O-Pee-Chee Micromotion Black

*MICRO BLACK: 8X TO 20X
*MICRO BLACK ROOKIES: 1.5X TO 4X
STATED PRINT RUN 100 SER.#'d SETS

2007-08 O-Pee-Chee Silver

*SILVER: 1.2X TO 3X

2007-08 O-Pee-Chee 3x5 Toys R' Us

INSERTS IN TOYS R US PACKS
TRU1 Saku Koivu 3.00 8.00
TRU2 Michael Ryder 2.50 6.00
TRU3 Guillaume Latendresse 3.00 8.00
TRU4 Cristobal Huet 3.00 8.00
TRU5 Alexei Kovalev 2.50 6.00
TRU6 Chris Higgins 3.00 8.00
TRU7 Miikka Kiprusoff 5.00 12.00
TRU8 Jarome Iginla 6.00 15.00
TRU9 Dion Phaneuf 4.00 10.00
TRU10 Alex Tanguay 3.00 8.00
TRU11 Daymond Langkow 2.50 6.00
TRU12 Kristian Huselius 2.50 6.00
TRU13 Ray Emery 3.00 8.00
TRU14 Dany Heatley 5.00 12.00
TRU15 Daniel Alfredsson 3.00 8.00
TRU16 Jason Spezza 4.00 10.00
TRU17 Wade Redden 2.50 6.00
TRU18 Mike Fisher 3.00 8.00
TRU19 Roberto Luongo 6.00 15.00
TRU20 Markus Naslund 4.00 10.00
TRU21 Daniel Sedin 2.50 6.00
TRU22 Henrik Sedin 2.50 6.00
TRU23 Brendan Morrison 2.50 6.00
TRU24 Ryan Kesler 2.50 6.00
TRU25 Mats Sundin 4.00 10.00
TRU26 Jason Blake 2.50 6.00
TRU27 Darcy Tucker 3.00 8.00
TRU28 Alexander Steen 2.50 6.00
TRU29 Tomas Kaberle 2.50 6.00
TRU30 Vesa Toskala 3.00 8.00
TRU31 Ales Hemsky 2.50 6.00
TRU32 Dwayne Roloson 3.00 8.00
TRU33 Joni Pitkanen 2.50 6.00
TRU34 Geoff Sanderson 2.50 6.00
TRU35 Jarret Stoll 2.50 6.00
TRU36 Shawn Horcoff 2.50 6.00
TRU37 Sidney Crosby 20.00 50.00
TRU38 Martin Brodeur 10.00 25.00
TRU39 Nicklas Lidstrom 4.00 10.00
TRU40 Evgeni Malkin 10.00 25.00
TRU41 Scott Niedermayer 2.50 6.00
TRU42 Sidney Crosby 20.00 50.00

2007-08 O-Pee-Chee Autographed Buybacks

NOT PRICED DUE TO SCARCITY

2007-08 O-Pee-Chee Bobby Orr Panoramic Cards

COMPLETE SET (6) 30.00 60.00
COMMON ORR 6.00 15.00
ORR1 Bobby Orr 6.00 15.00
ORR2 Bobby Orr 6.00 15.00
ORR3 Bobby Orr 6.00 15.00
ORR4 Bobby Orr 6.00 15.00
ORR5 Bobby Orr 6.00 15.00
ORR6 Bobby Orr 6.00 15.00

2007-08 O-Pee-Chee In Action

COMPLETE SET (20) 12.00 30.00
IA1 Sidney Crosby 2.50 6.00
IA2 Alexander Ovechkin 1.50 4.00
IA3 Evgeni Malkin 1.25 3.00
IA4 Dany Heatley .60 1.50
IA5 Rick Nash .50 1.25
IA6 Ilya Kovalchuk .60 1.50
IA7 Vincent Lecavalier .50 1.25
IA8 Jaromir Jagr .75 2.00
IA9 Thomas Vanek .40 1.00
IA10 Jarome Iginla .75 2.00
IA11 Henrik Zetterberg .50 1.25
IA12 Michael Ryder .30 .75
IA13 Mats Sundin .50 1.25
IA14 Joe Sakic 1.00 2.50
IA15 Martin Brodeur 1.25 3.00
IA16 Roberto Luongo .75 2.00
IA17 Ray Emery .40 1.00
IA18 Ryan Miller .50 1.25
IA19 Joe Thornton .60 1.50
IA20 Ryan Getzlaf .40 1.00

2007-08 O-Pee-Chee Materials Quad

STATED ODDS 1:144
QMANGE Daniel Alfredsson 10.00 25.00
Scott Niedermayer
Jean-Sebastien Giguere
Ray Emery
QMASHE Daniel Alfredsson 12.00 30.00
Jason Spezza
Dany Heatley
Ray Emery
QMASOW Nik Antropov 6.00 15.00
Matt Stajan
Ben Ondrus
Ian White
QMBEGP Martin Brodeur 25.00 60.00
Patrik Elias
Brian Gionta
Zach Parise
QMBFCK Rob Blake 10.00 25.00
Alexander Frolov
Mike Cammalleri
Anze Kopitar
QMBJBH Ed Belfour 25.00 60.00
Curtis Joseph
Martin Brodeur
Dominik Hasek
QMCBMA Tim Connolly 10.00 25.00
Maxim Afinogenov
Ryan Miller
Thomas Vanek
QMCBTK Zdeno Chara 12.00 30.00
Patrice Bergeron
Tim Thomas
Phil Kessel
QMCHOD Chris Chelios 12.00 30.00
Dominik Hasek
Chris Osgood
Kris Draper
QMDGHB Pavol Demitra 12.00 30.00
Marian Gaborik
Adam Hall
Pierre-Marc Bouchard
QMDLAF David Legwand 12.00 30.00
Jason Arnott
Peter Forsberg
J.P. Dumont
QMDNLW Shane Doan 10.00 25.00
Rick Nash
Matthew Lombardi
Cam Ward
QMGBRC Simon Gagne 12.00 30.00
Daniel Briere
Mike Richards
Jeff Carter
QMGFCM Sergei Gonchar 50.00 120.00
Marc-Andre Fleury
Sidney Crosby
Evgeni Malkin
QMITKP Jarome Iginla 15.00 40.00
Alex Tanguay
Miikka Kiprusoff
Dion Phaneuf
QMJBWH Olli Jokinen 6.00 15.00
Jay Bouwmeester
Stephen Weiss
Nathan Horton
QMJDSB Ed Jovanovski 6.00 15.00
Shane Doan
Fredrik Sjostrom
Brendan Bell
QMJHEH Jaromir Jagr 15.00 40.00
Milan Hejduk
Patrik Elias
Martin Havlat
QMJHSH Jaromir Jagr 15.00 40.00
Marian Hossa
Martin St. Louis
Dany Heatley
QMJROM Barret Jackman
Andrew Raycroft
Alexander Ovechkin
Evgeni Malkin
QMJSLP Jaromir Jagr 15.00 40.00
Martin Straka
Henrik Lundqvist
Petr Prucha
QMKHHK Saku Koivu 8.00 20.00
Cristobal Huet
Chris Higgins
Alexei Kovalev
QMKMOJ Olaf Kolzig
Shaone Morrisonn
Alexander Ovechkin
Milan Jurcina
QMKOMR Ilya Kovalchuk 30.00 80.00
Alexander Ovechkin
Evgeni Malkin
Alexander Radulov
QMLHDZ Nicklas Lidstrom 10.00 25.00
Tomas Holmstrom
Pavel Datsyuk
Henrik Zetterberg
QMLLMK Roberto Luongo 15.00 40.00
Trevor Linden
Brendan Morrison
Ryan Kesler
QMLNFB Pascal LeClaire 10.00 25.00
Rick Nash
Sergei Fedorov
Gilbert Brule
QMLNMG Nicklas Lidstrom 10.00 25.00
Scott Niedermayer
Bryan McCabe
Sergei Gonchar
QMLREK Roberto Luongo 15.00 40.00
Andrew Raycroft
Ray Emery
Miikka Kiprusoff
QMLRSC Vincent Lecavalier 10.00 25.00
Brad Richards
Martin St. Louis
Ryan Craig
QMMLRT Mike Modano 10.00 25.00
Jere Lehtinen
Mike Ribeiro
Marty Turco
QMMTNC Patrick Marleau 12.00 30.00
Joe Thornton
Evgeni Nabokov
Jonathan Cheechoo
QMNSOS Markus Naslund 10.00 25.00
Henrik Sedin
Mattias Ohlund
Daniel Sedin
QMRNGW Brad Richards 10.00 25.00
Scott Niedermayer
Jean-Sebastien Giguere
Cam Ward
QMSBTI Joe Sakic 25.00 60.00
Martin Brodeur
Joe Thornton
Jarome Iginla
QMSCCL Cory Stillman 6.00 15.00
Mike Commodore
Erik Cole
Andrew Ladd
QMSDRD Joe Sakic 20.00 50.00
Pavol Demitra
Brad Richards
Pavel Datsyuk
QMSGDH Bill Guerin 8.00 20.00
Miroslav Satan
Rick DiPietro
Trent Hunter
QMSHRH Jarret Stoll 8.00 20.00
Shawn Horcoff
Dwayne Roloson
Ales Hemsky
QMSHRK Sergei Samsonov 10.00 25.00
Martin Havlat
Tuomo Ruutu
Nikolai Khabibulin
QMSHSB Joe Sakic 20.00 50.00
Milan Hejduk
Marek Svatos
Peter Budaj
QMSJSS Joe Sakic 20.00 50.00
Brendan Shanahan
Jaromir Jagr
Mats Sundin
QMSKAI Mats Sundin 15.00 40.00
Saku Koivu
Daniel Alfredsson
Jarome Iginla
QMSLHO Teemu Selanne 30.00 80.00
Vincent Lecavalier
Dany Heatley
Alexander Ovechkin
QMSLKJ Teemu Selanne 10.00 25.00
Jere Lehtinen
Saku Koivu
Olli Jokinen
QMSLTC Joe Sakic 50.00 120.00
Vincent Lecavalier
Joe Thornton
Sidney Crosby
QMSMKB Marc Savard 6.00 15.00
Glen Murray
Chuck Kobasew
Brandon Bochenski
QMSMSR Teemu Selanne 10.00 25.00
Mike Modano
Mats Sundin
Mark Recchi
QMSNGG Teemu Selanne 10.00 25.00
Scott Niedermayer
Jean-Sebastien Giguere
Ryan Getzlaf
QMSNLF Mats Sundin 12.00 30.00
Markus Naslund
Nicklas Lidstrom
Peter Forsberg
QMSOVM Daniel Sedin 30.00 80.00
Alexander Ovechkin
Thomas Vanek
Evgeni Malkin
QMSSKW Patrick Sharp 10.00 25.00
Brent Seabrook
Duncan Keith
Jason Williams
QMSTMS Mats Sundin 10.00 25.00
Darcy Tucker
Bryan McCabe
Alexander Steen
QMTFSC Joe Thornton 50.00 120.00
Peter Forsberg
Martin St. Louis
Sidney Crosby
QMTLLW Jose Theodore 10.00 25.00
Jordan Leopold
John-Michael Liles
Wojtek Wolski
QMTPPP Raffi Torres 6.00 15.00
Fernando Pisani
Joni Pitkanen
Marc-Antoine Pouliot
QMVSZP David Vyborny 6.00 15.00
Jody Shelley
Nikolai Zherdev
Alexandre Picard
QMWBSW Justin Williams 10.00 25.00
Rod Brind' Amour
Eric Staal
Cam Ward
QMWJLB Doug Weight 8.00 20.00
Barret Jackman
Manny Legace
Brad Boyes
QMZMOJ Sergei Zubov 8.00 20.00
Brenden Morrow
Steve Ott
Jussi Jokinen

2007-08 O-Pee-Chee Record Breakers

COMPLETE SET (10) 8.00 20.00
RB1 Mike Modano .50 1.25
RB2 Martin Brodeur 1.25 3.00
RB3 Paul Stastny .50 1.25
RB4 Vincent Lecavalier .50 1.25
RB5 Sidney Crosby 2.50 6.00
RB6 Sheldon Souray .30 .75
RB7 Evgeni Malkin 1.25 3.00
RB8 Jaromir Jagr .75 2.00
RB9 Alexander Ovechkin 1.50 4.00
RB10 Roberto Luongo .75 2.00

2007-08 O-Pee-Chee Season Highlights

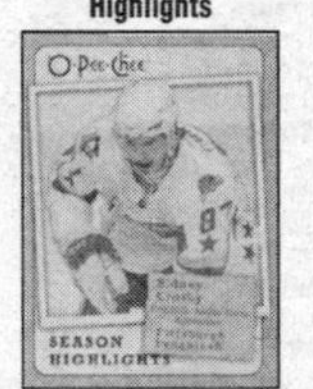

COMPLETE SET (19) 10.00 25.00
SH1 Scott Niedermayer .30 .75
SH2 Daniel Alfredsson .40 1.00
SH3 Ryan Miller .50 1.25
SH4 Evgeni Malkin 1.25 3.00
SH5 Joe Sakic 1.00 2.50
SH6 Daniel Briere .50 1.25
SH7 Sidney Crosby 2.50 6.00
SH8 Brendan Shanahan .50 1.25
SH9 Jaromir Jagr .75 2.00
SH10 Mats Sundin .50 1.25
SH11 Teemu Selanne .50 1.25
SH12 Dean McAmmond .30 .75
SH13 Jean-Sebastien Giguere .50 1.25
SH14 Wade Dubielewicz .40 1.00
SH15 Sidney Crosby 2.50 6.00
SH16 Roberto Luongo .75 2.00
SH17 Dominik Hasek .60 1.50
SH18 Joe Thornton .60 1.50
SH19 Nicklas Lidstrom .50 1.25
SH20 Jordan Staal .60 1.50

2007-08 O-Pee-Chee Signatures

STATED ODDS 1:432
SAB Adam Burish 8.00 20.00
SAD Adam Dennis 8.00 20.00
SAE Alexander Edler 6.00 15.00
SAF Alexander Frolov 6.00 15.00
SAO Alexander Ovechkin SP 250.00 350.00
SAT Alex Tanguay SP
SBA Christian Backman 6.00 15.00
SBJ Blair Jones 6.00 15.00
SBM Brenden Morrow
SBO Ben Ondrus 6.00 15.00
SBP Benoit Pouliot 6.00 15.00
SBR Alex Brooks 6.00 15.00
SBW Ben Walter 6.00 15.00
SCK Chuck Kobasew 6.00 15.00
SCP Chris Phillips 6.00 15.00
SCT Chris Thorburn 6.00 15.00
SCW Cam Ward 10.00 25.00
SDB Dave Bolland 6.00 15.00
SDH Dany Heatley SP
SDL Drew Larman 6.00 15.00
SDS Drew Stafford 8.00 20.00
SDW Doug Weight 6.00 15.00
SEC Erik Christensen
SEL Patrik Elias
SEM Evgeni Malkin 25.00 60.00
SES Eric Staal SP
SFN Filip Novak 6.00 15.00
SFP Fernando Pisani 6.00 15.00
SGA Simon Gagne SP
SGH Gordie Howe SP 75.00 150.00
SHL Henrik Lundqvist SP
SIW Ian White 6.00 15.00
SJC Jeff Carter 6.00 15.00
SJG Jean-Sebastien Giguere SP 25.00 60.00
SJI Jarome Iginla SP
SJM Jay McClement 6.00 15.00
SJP Joe Pavelski 6.00 15.00
SJS Jordan Staal 12.00 30.00
SJT Joe Thornton SP 150.00 250.00
SMC Mike Cammalleri
SMG Marian Gaborik SP
SMH Marian Hossa SP
SMJ Milan Jurcina 6.00 15.00
SML Mario Lemieux SP
SMM Mark Messier SP
SMO Michel Ouellet 6.00 15.00
SMP Marc-Antoine Pouliot 6.00 15.00
SMR Michael Ryder
SMV Marc-Edouard Vlasic 6.00 15.00
SNG Niklas Grossman 6.00 15.00
SNZ Nikolai Zherdev 6.00 15.00
SOR Bobby Orr SP
SPE Corey Perry 8.00 20.00
SPM Paul Mara 6.00 15.00
SPR Brandon Prust 6.00 15.00
SPS Paul Stastny 10.00 25.00
SRA Paul Ranger 6.00 15.00
SRC Ryan Clowe SP
SRG Ryan Getzlaf 8.00 20.00
SRI Mike Richards 12.00 30.00
SRM Ryan Malone 6.00 15.00
SRN Rick Nash SP 40.00 80.00
SRY Ryan Miller 10.00 25.00
SSB Steve Bernier 6.00 15.00
SSC Sidney Crosby SP 400.00 600.00
SSG Scott Gomez 6.00 15.00
SSO Shane O'Brien 6.00 15.00
SST Martin St. Louis SP 50.00 100.00
SSW Shea Weber 6.00 15.00
STV Tomas Vokoun
SVL Vincent Lecavalier SP 75.00 150.00
SWW Wojtek Wolski 6.00 15.00

2007-08 O-Pee-Chee Stat Leaders

COMPLETE SET (20) 12.00 30.00
SL1 Teemu Selanne .60 1.50
Vincent Lecavalier
Dany Heatley
SL2 Joe Thornton 2.50 6.00
Marc Savard
Sidney Crosby
SL3 Vincent Lecavalier 2.50 6.00
Joe Thornton
Sidney Crosby
SL4 Nicklas Lidstrom .50 1.25
Daniel Alfredsson
Thomas Vanek
SL5 Teemu Selanne .60 1.50
Ilya Kovalchuk
Sheldon Souray
SL6 Vincent Lecavalier .60 1.50
Kris Draper
Jordan Staal
SL7 Teemu Selanne .60 1.50
Henrik Zetterberg
Dany Heatley
SL8 Chris Neil .30 .75
Josh Gratton
Ben Eager
SL9 Martin Brodeur 1.25 3.00
Dominik Hasek
Niklas Backstrom
SL10 Martin Brodeur 1.25 3.00
Roberto Luongo
Miikka Kiprusoff
SL11 Martin Brodeur 1.25 3.00
Chris Mason
Niklas Backstrom
SL12 Martin Brodeur 1.25 3.00
Dominik Hasek
Miikka Kiprusoff
SL13 Daniel Alfredsson .50 1.25
Andy McDonald
Pavel Datsyuk
SL14 Nicklas Lidstrom .60 1.50
Jason Spezza
Dany Heatley
SL15 Daniel Alfredsson .60 1.50
Jason Spezza
Dany Heatley
SL16 Chris Pronger .50 1.25
Teppo Numminen
Samuel Pahlsson
SL17 Chris Drury .40 1.00
Daniel Alfredsson
Ryan Getzlaf
SL18 Dominik Hasek .60 1.50
Jean-Sebastien Giguere
Ray Emery
SL19 Dominik Hasek .75 2.00
Roberto Luongo
Marty Turco
SL20 Scott Niedermayer .30 .75
Sergei Gonchar
Sheldon Souray

2007-08 O-Pee-Chee Team Checklists

COMPLETE SET (30) 20.00 50.00
STATED ODDS 1:14
CL1 Anaheim Ducks 1.00 2.50
CL2 Atlanta Thrashers 1.00 2.50
CL3 Boston Bruins 1.00 2.50
CL4 Buffalo Sabres 1.00 2.50
CL5 Calgary Flames 1.00 2.50
CL6 Carolina Hurricanes 1.00 2.50
CL7 Chicago Blackhawks 1.00 2.50
CL8 Colorado Avalanche 1.00 2.50
CL9 Columbus Blue Jackets 1.00 2.50
CL10 Dallas Stars 1.00 2.50
CL11 Detroit Red Wings 1.00 2.50
CL12 Edmonton Oilers 1.00 2.50
CL13 Florida Panthers 1.00 2.50
CL14 Los Angeles Kings 1.00 2.50
CL15 Minnesota Wild 1.00 2.50
CL16 Montreal Canadiens 1.00 2.50
CL17 Nashville Predators 1.00 2.50
CL18 New Jersey Devils 1.00 2.50
CL19 New York Islanders 1.00 2.50
CL20 New York Rangers 1.00 2.50
CL21 Ottawa Senators 1.00 2.50
CL22 Philadelphia Flyers 1.00 2.50
CL23 Phoenix Coyotes 1.00 2.50
CL24 Pittsburgh Penguins 1.00 2.50
CL25 San Jose Sharks 1.00 2.50
CL26 St. Louis Blues 1.00 2.50
CL27 Tampa Bay Lightning 1.00 2.50
CL28 Toronto Maple Leafs 1.00 2.50
CL29 Vancouver Canucks 1.00 2.50
CL30 Washington Capitals 1.00 2.50

2008-09 O-Pee-Chee

This set was released on October 7, 2008. The base set consists of 600 cards, including rookies as cards 501-560.

COMPLETE SET (800) 250.00 400.00
COMP.SET SET (600) 175.00 300.00
COMP.SET w/o SPs (500) 60.00 120.00
COMP.UPD.SET (200) 75.00 150.00
1 Markus Naslund .25 .60
2 Dan Hinote .15 .40
3 Pascal Dupuis .15 .40
4 Frantisek Kaberle .15 .40
5 Derek Morris .15 .40
6 Scottie Upshall .15 .40
7 Richard Park .15 .40
8 Josh Gorges .15 .40
9 Rob Blake .25 .60
10 Cory Murphy .15 .40
11 Sheldon Souray .15 .40
12 Mike Modano .25 .60
13 Wojtek Wolski .15 .40
14 Hal Gill .15 .40
15 Dustin Boyd .15 .40
16 Jason Pominville .20 .50
17 Slava Kozlov .15 .40
18 Sidney Crosby 1.25 3.00
19 Kamil Kreps .15 .40
20 Bryan McCabe .20 .50
21 Karri Ramo .20 .50
22 Joe Pavelski .15 .40
23 Mikael Tellqvist .25 .60
24 Braydon Coburn .15 .40
25 Nigel Dawes .15 .40
26 Jay Pandolfo .15 .40
27 Niklas Backstrom .25 .60
28 Shaone Morrisonn .15 .40
29 Bryan Allen .15 .40
30 Jiri Hudler .15 .40
31 Marc-Andre Bergeron .15 .40
32 Pascal Leclaire .20 .50
33 Tim Gleason .15 .40
34 Patrice Bergeron .25 .60
35 Eric Perrin .15 .40
36 Francois Beauchemin .15 .40
37 Fredrik Norrena .25 .60
38 Mats Sundin .25 .60
39 Jay McClement .15 .40
40 Jarkko Ruutu .15 .40
41 Ladislav Smid .15 .40
42 Daniel Carcillo .15 .40
43 Ryan Parent .15 .40
44 Antoine Vermette .15 .40
45 Brendan Shanahan .25 .60
46 Josef Vasicek .30 .75
47 Roman Hamrlik .15 .40
48 Michal Handzus .15 .40
49 Ales Hemsky .15 .40
50 Brooks Orpik .15 .40
51 Scott Parker .15 .40
52 Chad LaRose .15 .40
53 Ryan Miller .25 .60
54 Tobias Enstrom .25 .60
55 George Parros .15 .40
56 Viktor Kozlov .15 .40
57 Kyle Wellwood .15 .40
58 Evgeni Nabokov .25 .60
59 Corey Perry .25 .60
60 Boyd Gordon .15 .40
61 Dan Cleary .25 .60
62 Mike Fisher .15 .40
63 John Madden .15 .40
64 Tomas Plekanec .15 .40
65 Nathan Horton .15 .40
66 Dwayne Roloson .20 .50
67 Niklas Kronwall .20 .50
68 Radim Vrbata .15 .40
69 Manny Malhotra .15 .40
70 Martin Havlat .20 .50
71 Curtis Joseph .25 .60
72 Saku Koivu .25 .60
73 Bryan Little .15 .40
74 Marc-Edouard Vlasic .20 .40
75 Jonas Hiller .25 .60
76 Brendan Morrison .15 .40
77 Nikolai Antropov .20 .50
78 Ryan Johnson .15 .40
79 Craig Rivet .15 .40
80 Marian Hossa .40 1.00
81 Simon Gagne .20 .50
82 Cory Stillman .20 .50
83 Chris Campoli .20 .50
84 Zach Parise .25 .60
85 David Legwand .20 .50
86 Andrei Kostitsyn .20 .50
87 Maxim Afinogenov .15 .40
88 Kyle Calder .15 .40
89 Henrik Zetterberg .50 1.25
90 Rostislav Klesla .25 .60
91 Travis Zajac .15 .40
92 Brent Seabrook .20 .50
93 Toni Lydman .15 .40
94 Todd White .15 .40
95 Tomas Fleischmann .15 .40
96 Devin Setoguchi .25 .60
97 Henrik Sedin .25 .60
98 Boyd Devereaux .15 .40
99 Michel Ouellet .15 .40
100 Matt Carle .15 .40
101 Zbynek Michalek .15 .40
102 Scott Gomez .20 .50
103 Dainius Zubrus .15 .40
104 Nikolai Khabibulin .25 .60
105 James Sheppard .25 .60
106 Richard Zednik .15 .40
107 Chris Osgood .25 .60
108 Alexander Semin .25 .60
109 Paul Stastny .25 .60
110 Justin Williams .15 .40
111 Eric Nystrom .15 .40
112 Tuukka Rask .25 .60
113 Mathieu Schneider .15 .40
114 Mikael Samuelsson .15 .40
115 Vincent Lecavalier .25 .60
116 Eric Brewer .15 .40
117 Pat Rissmiller .15 .40
118 Niko Kapanen .15 .40
119 Jaromir Jagr .30 .75
120 Paul Martin .15 .40
121 Guillaume Latendresse .20 .50
122 Pierre-Marc Bouchard .15 .40
123 Olli Jokinen .15 .40
124 Brian Rafalski .15 .40
125 Rob Niedermayer .15 .40
126 Jiri Novotny .15 .40
127 Matt Cullen .15 .40
128 Tim Thomas .25 .60
129 Dennis Wideman .15 .40
130 Garnet Exelby .15 .40
131 Nicklas Lidstrom .25 .60
132 Sami Salo .15 .40
133 Alexei Ponikarovsky .15 .40
134 Paul Ranger .15 .40
135 Andy McDonald .15 .40
136 Chris Kunitz .15 .40
137 Mike Richards .40 1.00
138 Andrej Meszaros .15 .40
139 Michal Rozsival .15 .40
140 Brendan Witt .15 .40
141 Marek Zidlicky .15 .40
142 Mark Parrish .15 .40
143 Craig Anderson .15 .40
144 Mathieu Garon .25 .60
145 Brett Lebda .15 .40
146 Loui Eriksson .15 .40
147 Marek Svatos .15 .40
148 Scott Walker .15 .40
149 Anders Eriksson .15 .40
150 Aaron Ward .15 .40
151 Nicklas Backstrom .50 1.25
152 Anton Stralman .20 .50
153 Dmitri Kalinin .15 .40
154 Mike Grier .15 .40
155 Keith Yandle .15 .40
156 Ray Emery .20 .50
157 Chris Drury .25 .60
158 Blake Comeau .15 .40
159 Kevin Weekes .25 .60
160 Marian Gaborik .40 1.00
161 Rostislav Olesz .15 .40
162 Tomas Kopecky .20 .50
163 Jason Chimera .15 .40
164 Tuomo Ruutu .25 .60
165 Henrik Tallinder .15 .40
166 Matt Stajan .20 .50
167 Marc Savard .15 .40
168 Alexei Zhitnik .15 .40
169 Scott Niedermayer .15 .40
170 Mike Green .15 .40
171 Pavel Kubina .15 .40
172 David Perron .20 .50
173 Jaroslav Halak .25 .60
174 Torrey Mitchell .25 .60
175 Shane Doan .15 .40
176 Johnny Oduya .15 .40
177 Carey Price .75 2.00
178 David Backes .15 .40
179 Martin Skoula .20 .50
180 David Booth .15 .40
181 Kris Draper .15 .40
182 Paul Gaustad .20 .50
183 Donald Brashear .15 .40
184 Roberto Luongo .40 1.00
185 Brooks Laich .20 .50
186 Craig MacDonald .15 .40
187 Patrick Marleau .20 .50
188 Steven Reinprecht .25 .60
189 Chris Kelly .15 .40
190 Ryan Hollweg .15 .40
191 Andy Hilbert .15 .40
192 Andy Greene .20 .50
193 Jason Arnott .15 .40
194 Nick Schultz .15 .40
195 Jozef Stumpel .15 .40
196 Matt Niskanen .15 .40
197 John-Michael Liles .15 .40
198 Dave Bolland .20 .50
199 Patrick Eaves .15 .40
200 Cory Sarich .15 .40
201 Marco Sturm .15 .40
202 Martin St. Louis .25 .60
203 Jeff Schultz .15 .40
204 Alexander Steen .25 .60
205 Shane O'Brien .15 .40
206 Thomas Greiss .20 .50
207 Nick Boynton .15 .40
208 Daniel Girardi .15 .40
209 Alex Kovalev .25 .60
210 Henrik Lundqvist .50 1.25
211 Shea Weber .15 .40

212 Mikko Koivu .25 .60
213 Karlis Skrastins .15 .40
214 Jere Lehtinen .15 .40
215 Fredrik Modin .15 .40
216 Petr Budaj .20 .50
217 Andrew Ladd .15 .40
218 Joe Corvo .15 .40
219 Zdeno Chara .15 .40
220 Sean O'Donnell .15 .40
221 Ian White .15 .40
222 Andre Roy .15 .40
223 Steve Wagner .20 .50
224 Ty Conklin .20 .50
225 Daniel Winnik .15 .40
226 Jason Spezza .30 .75
227 Martin Brodeur .50 1.25
228 Ryan Callahan .15 .40
229 Ryan O'Byrne .15 .40
230 Brian Rolston .15 .40
231 Ladislav Nagy .15 .40
232 Tomas Holmstrom .20 .50
233 Kris Russell .25 .60
234 Jason LaBarbera .20 .50
235 Ben Guite .15 .40
236 Rene Bourque .25 .60
237 David Moss .20 .50
238 Jaroslav Spacek .15 .40
239 Jean-Sebastien Giguere .25 .60
240 Jason Blake .15 .40
241 Dan Boyle .20 .50
242 Joe Thornton .40 1.00
243 Ilya Bryzgalov .15 .40
244 Martin Gerber .20 .50
245 Andy Sutton .15 .40
246 Patrik Elias .15 .40
247 Mike Komisarek .20 .50
248 Eric Belanger .15 .40
249 Andrew Raycroft .25 .60
250 David Vyborny .15 .40
251 Pavel Datsyuk .25 .60
252 Ron Hainsey .15 .40
253 Patrick Sharp .15 .40
254 Mike Sillinger .15 .40
255 Adrian Aucoin .15 .40
256 Thomas Vanek .25 .60
257 Derek Armstrong .15 .40
258 Teemu Selanne .25 .60
259 Ryan Kesler .15 .40
260 Darcy Tucker .20 .50
261 Alexander Frolov .15 .40
262 Erik Johnson .30 .75
263 Willie Mitchell .15 .40
264 Ryan Whitney .15 .40
265 Jeff Carter .25 .60
266 Bruno Gervais .15 .40
267 Brent Sopel .15 .40
268 Martin Erat .25 .60
269 Raitis Ivanans .15 .40
270 Drew Stafford .25 .60
271 Robert Nilsson .15 .40
272 Lee Stempniak .15 .40
273 Dan Fritsche .15 .40
274 Ryan Smyth .20 .50
275 Owen Nolan .25 .60
276 David Krejci .20 .50
277 Jim Slater .15 .40
278 Alexander Ovechkin 1.00 2.50
279 Drew MacIntyre .25 .60
280 Stephane Robidas .15 .40
281 Manny Legace .20 .50
282 Jordan Staal .40 1.00
283 Scott Hartnell .20 .50
284 Brandon Dubinsky .20 .50
285 Bill Guerin .15 .40
286 R.J. Umberger .15 .40
287 Ryan Suter .15 .40
288 Lubomir Visnovsky .15 .40
289 Joni Pitkanen .15 .40
290 Dominik Hasek .40 1.00
291 Niklas Hagman .15 .40
292 Jordan Leopold .15 .40
293 Miroslav Satan .15 .40
294 Erik Cole .15 .40
295 Kristian Huselius .15 .40
296 Kari Lehtonen .15 .40
297 Mason Raymond .15 .40
298 Marc Denis .25 .60
299 Dan Ellis .15 .40
300 Randy Jones .15 .40
301 Cam Ward .25 .60
302 Tom Gilbert .15 .40
303 Daniel Alfredsson .20 .50
304 Radek Martinek .15 .40
305 Vernon Fiddler .15 .40
306 Tyler Kennedy .20 .50
307 Patrick O'Sullivan .20 .50
308 Chris Thorburn .15 .40
309 Dany Heatley .30 .75
310 Denis Grebeshkov .15 .40
311 Steve Ott .20 .50
312 Ian Laperriere .15 .40
313 Adam Burish .20 .50
314 Stephane Yelle .15 .40
315 Ilya Kovalchuk .30 .75
316 Brian Willsie .15 .40
317 Olaf Kolzig .25 .60
318 Daniel Sedin .25 .60
319 Filip Kuba .15 .40
320 Chris Neil .15 .40
321 Hannu Toivonen .20 .50
322 Milan Michalek .15 .40
323 Martin Hanzal .20 .50
324 Dean McAmmond .15 .40
325 Marc Staal .30 .75
326 Michael Rupp .15 .40
327 Kim Johnsson .15 .40
328 Stephen Weiss .15 .40
329 Chris Chelios .30 .75
330 Mike Ribeiro .15 .40
331 Tyler Arnason .15 .40
332 Duncan Keith .20 .50
333 Rod Brind'Amour .20 .50
334 Peter Schaefer .15 .40
335 Colby Armstrong .15 .40
336 Ryan Carter .15 .40
337 Lukas Krajicek .15 .40
338 Mike Smith .20 .50
339 Maxime Talbot .20 .50
340 Steve Downie .25 .60
341 Christoph Schubert .15 .40
342 Jeff Halpern .15 .40
343 Jeff Tambellini .15 .40
344 Jordin Tootoo .25 .60
345 Anze Kopitar .25 .60
346 Evgeni Malkin .60 1.50
347 Zach Stortini .15 .40
348 Dustin Penner .15 .40
349 Trevor Daley .15 .40
350 Milan Hejduk .20 .50
351 Corey Crawford .20 .50
352 Robyn Regehr .15 .40
353 Daniel Paille .20 .50
354 Milan Lucic .50 1.25
355 Chris Pronger .20 .50
356 Taylor Pyatt .15 .40
357 Jussi Jokinen .15 .40
358 Petr Sykora .15 .40
359 Jack Johnson .20 .50
360 Daymond Langkow .15 .40
361 Antero Niittymaki .25 .60
362 Trent Hunter .15 .40
363 Aaron Voros .15 .40
364 Craig Conroy .15 .40
365 Brett McLean .15 .40
366 Jarret Stoll .20 .50
367 Marty Turco .20 .50
368 Gilbert Brule .25 .60
369 Joe Sakic .40 1.00
370 Mike Knuble .25 .60
371 Jarome Iginla .50 1.25
372 Stephane Veilleux .15 .40
373 Mark Stuart .15 .40
374 Mattias Ohlund .15 .40
375 Mike Lundin .15 .40
376 Sergei Gonchar .25 .60
377 Ed Jovanovski .15 .40
378 Kimmo Timonen .15 .40
379 Rick DiPietro .25 .60
380 J.P. Dumont .15 .40
381 Mattias Norstrom .15 .40
382 Andrei Markov .20 .50
383 Josh Harding .20 .50
384 Steve Staios .15 .40
385 Francis Bouillon .15 .40
386 Brenden Morrow .20 .50
387 Scott Hannan .15 .40
388 Dustin Byfuglien .20 .50
389 Bret Hedican .15 .40
390 Matthew Lombardi .15 .40
391 Derek Roy .15 .40
392 Phil Kessel .25 .60
393 Milan Jurcina .15 .40
394 Nick Foligno .25 .60
395 Jiri Tlusty .25 .60
396 Jonathan Cheechoo .25 .60
397 Peter Mueller .30 .75
398 Daniel Briere .25 .60
399 Anton Volchenkov .15 .40
400 Brian Pothier .15 .40
401 Sergei Brylin .15 .40
402 Sergei Kostitsyn .25 .60
403 Tomas Vokoun .25 .60
404 Valtteri Filppula .15 .40
405 Bobby Ryan .40 1.00
406 Antti Miettinen .15 .40
407 Nikolai Zherdev .15 .40
408 Jack Skille .20 .50
409 Jochen Hecht .15 .40
410 Chuck Kobasew .15 .40
411 Brad Richards .20 .50
412 Todd Bertuzzi .25 .60
413 Trevor Linden .25 .60
414 Nick Tarnasky .15 .40
415 Brian Campbell .40 1.00
416 Marc-Andre Fleury .25 .60
417 Martin Biron .20 .50
418 Dan Hamhuis .15 .40
419 Petr Prucha .15 .40
420 David Clarkson .15 .40
421 Scott Nichol .15 .40
422 Christian Backman .15 .40
423 Brent Burns .15 .40
424 Pavol Demitra .15 .40
425 Sam Gagner .40 1.00
426 Fernando Pisani .15 .40
427 Philippe Boucher .15 .40
428 Peter Forsberg .40 1.00
429 Cam Barker .15 .40
430 Miikka Kiprusoff .25 .60
431 Clarke MacArthur .15 .40
432 Glen Murray .15 .40
433 Ruslan Fedotenko .15 .40
434 Ales Kotalik .15 .40
435 Vesa Toskala .25 .60
436 Keith Tkachuk .25 .60
437 Ryan Malone .15 .40
438 Joffrey Lupul .15 .40
439 Chris Phillips .15 .40
440 Frederick Meyer .15 .40
441 P.J. Axelsson .15 .40
442 Colin White .15 .40
443 Chris Mason .20 .50
444 Mark Streit .15 .40
445 Andrew Cogliano .40 1.00
446 Michael Ryder .20 .50
447 Rick Nash .25 .60
448 Patrick Kane .60 1.50
449 Steve Bernier .15 .40
450 Alexandre Burrows .20 .50
451 Ondrej Pavelec .20 .50
452 Alexander Edler .20 .50
453 Tomas Kaberle .15 .40
454 Jay McKee .15 .40
455 Christian Ehrhoff .15 .40
456 Kristopher Letang .15 .40
457 Vaclav Prospal .15 .40
458 Fedor Tyutin .15 .40
459 Jamie Langenbrunner .15 .40
460 Barret Jackman .15 .40
461 Chris Higgins .15 .40
462 Kyle Brodziak .15 .40
463 Mike Cammalleri .25 .60
464 Johan Franzen .15 .40
465 Jared Boll .20 .50
466 Andrew Brunette .15 .40
467 Robert Lang .15 .40
468 Glen Wesley .15 .40
469 Tim Connolly .15 .40
470 Nicklas Havelid .15 .40
471 Cristobal Huet .25 .60
472 Kevin Bieksa .15 .40
473 Jason Ward .15 .40
474 Brad Boyes .20 .50
475 Trevor Gionta .25 .60
476 Kyle McLaren .15 .40
477 Keith Ballard .15 .40
478 Wade Redden .15 .40
479 Martin Straka .15 .40
480 Radek Bonk .15 .40
481 Ray Whitney .15 .40
482 Kurtis Foster .15 .40
483 Dustin Brown .15 .40
484 Mike Van Ryn .15 .40
485 Sergei Zubov .15 .40
486 T.J. Hensick .20 .50
487 Eric Staal .40 1.00
488 Alexander Radulov .25 .60
489 Alex Tanguay .20 .50
490 Manny Fernandez .25 .60
491 Jamal Mayers .15 .40
492 Colton Orr .15 .40
493 Jay Bouwmeester .20 .50
494 Jonathan Toews .75 2.00
495 Ryan Getzlaf .30 .75
496 Checklist .15 .40
497 Checklist .15 .40
498 Checklist .15 .40
499 Checklist .15 .40
500 Checklist .15 .40
501 Sami Lepisto RC 1.25 3.00
502 Mike Brown RC 1.50 4.00
503 Zach Fitzgerald RC 1.25 3.00
504 Robbie Earl RC 1.00 2.50
505 Darryl Boyce RC 1.00 2.50
506 Alex Foster RC 1.00 2.50
507 Mike Iggulden RC 1.00 2.50
508 Tom Cavanagh RC 1.00 2.50
509 Alex Goligoski RC 2.50 6.00
510 Jon Filewich RC 1.00 2.50
511 Ryan Stone RC 1.25 3.00
512 Chris Minard RC 1.25 3.00
513 Kyle Turris RC 2.50 6.00
514 Claude Giroux RC 2.50 6.00
515 Kyle Greentree RC 1.50 4.00
516 Brian Lee RC 1.25 3.00
517 Ilya Zubov RC 1.25 3.00
518 Jesse Winchester RC 1.25 3.00
519 Kyle Okposo RC 2.50 6.00
520 Mike Mole RC 1.00 2.50
521 Jack Hillen RC 1.00 2.50
522 Jordan LaVallee RC 1.25 3.00
523 Matt D'Agostini RC 2.00 5.00
524 Corey Locke RC 1.25 3.00
525 Brian Boyle RC 1.25 3.00
526 Teddy Purcell RC 1.25 3.00
527 Danny Taylor RC 1.25 3.00
528 Erik Ersberg RC 1.25 3.00
529 Shawn Matthias RC 1.25 3.00
530 David Brine RC 1.00 2.50
531 Tyler Plante RC 1.25 3.00
532 Theo Peckham RC 1.25 3.00
533 Tom Sestito RC 1.00 2.50
534 Justin Abdelkader RC 2.50 6.00
535 Jonathan Ericsson RC 2.00 5.00
536 Darren Helm RC 2.00 5.00
537 Mattias Ritola RC 1.50 4.00
538 Garrett Stafford RC 1.50 4.00
539 Mark Fistric RC 1.00 2.50
540 B.J. Crombeen RC 1.00 2.50
541 Derick Brassard RC 2.50 6.00
542 Steve Mason RC 3.00 8.00
543 Adam Pineault RC 1.25 3.00
544 Dan LaCosta RC 1.50 4.00
545 Andrew Murray RC 1.00 2.50
546 Clay Wilson RC .75 2.00
547 Cody McLeod RC 1.00 2.50
548 Jordan Hendry RC 1.00 2.50
549 Niklas Hjalmarsson RC 2.00 5.00
550 Brandon Nolan RC 1.50 4.00
551 Tim Conboy RC 1.00 2.50
552 Joey Mormina RC 1.00 2.50
553 Joe Jensen RC 1.25 3.00
554 Tim Ramholt RC 1.00 2.50
555 Marc-Andre Gragnani RC 1.00 2.50
556 Pascal Pelletier RC 1.00 2.50
557 Boris Valabik RC 1.50 4.00
558 Colin Stuart RC 1.00 2.50
559 Kevin Doell RC .75 2.00
560 Andrew Ebbett RC 1.25 3.00
561 Checklist .15 .40
562 Dale Hawerchuk .75 2.00
563 Bobby Hull 1.50 4.00
564 Richard Brodeur .60 1.50
565 Borje Salming .75 2.00
566 Johnny Bower .75 2.00
567 Eddie Shack .75 2.00
568 Doug Wilson .50 1.25
569 Peter Stastny .75 2.00
570 Mario Lemieux 2.00 5.00
571 Joe Mullen .75 2.00
572 Ron Hextall .75 2.00
573 Rick MacLeish .60 1.50
574 Bernie Parent .75 2.00
575 Mark Messier 1.50 4.00
576 Brian Leetch 1.00 2.50
577 Mike Bossy .75 2.00
578 Pat LaFontaine .75 2.00
579 Guy Lafleur 1.50 4.00
580 Jean Beliveau 1.25 3.00
581 Frank Mahovlich .75 2.00
582 Dino Ciccarelli .50 1.25
583 Rogie Vachon .75 2.00
584 Wayne Gretzky 4.00 10.00
585 Glenn Anderson .60 1.50
586 Grant Fuhr .75 2.00
587 Luc Robitaille .60 1.50
588 Scotty Bowman .75 2.00
589 Alex Delvecchio 1.00 2.50
590 Patrick Roy 2.50 6.00
591 Jari Kurri .75 2.00
592 Denis Savard .75 2.00
593 Tony Esposito .75 2.00
594 Stan Mikita .75 2.00
595 Lanny McDonald .75 2.00
596 Gilbert Perreault .75 2.00
597 Ray Bourque 1.50 4.00
598 Cam Neely 1.00 2.50
599 Phil Esposito 1.25 3.00
600 Bobby Orr 2.50 6.00
601 Steve Montador .15 .40
602 Brendan Morrison .15 .40
603 Mathieu Schneider .15 .40
604 Ron Hainsey .15 .40
605 Michael Ryder .20 .50
606 Patrick Lalime .15 .40
607 Craig Rivet .15 .40
608 Teppo Numminen .20 .50
609 Todd Bertuzzi .25 .60
610 Mike Cammalleri .25 .60
611 Curtis Glencross .15 .40
612 Rene Bourque .25 .60
613 Jarome Iginla .50 1.25
614 Joni Pitkanen .15 .40
615 Brian Campbell .40 1.00
616 Cristobal Huet .25 .60
617 Adam Foote .15 .40
618 Darcy Tucker .20 .50
619 Andrew Raycroft .25 .60
620 Joe Sakic .40 1.00
621 Kristian Huselius .15 .40
622 R.J. Umberger .15 .40
623 Mike Commodore .15 .40
624 Sean Avery .20 .50
625 Mark Parrish .15 .40
626 Marian Hossa .40 1.00
627 Ty Conklin .20 .50
628 Lubomir Visnovsky .15 .40
629 Erik Cole .15 .40
630 Jeff Drouin-Deslauriers .15 .40
631 Keith Ballard .15 .40
632 Cory Stillman .15 .40
633 Bryan McCabe .20 .50
634 Jarret Stoll .20 .50
635 Andrew Brunette .15 .40
636 Owen Nolan .25 .60
637 Marek Zidlicky .15 .40
638 Marc-Andre Bergeron .15 .40
639 Craig Weller .15 .40
640 Antti Miettinen .15 .40
641 Alex Tanguay .20 .50
642 Marc Denis .25 .60
643 Georges Laraque .20 .50
644 Robert Lang .15 .40
645 Joel Ward .15 .40
646 Brian Rolston .15 .40
647 Doug Weight .15 .40
648 Mark Streit .15 .40
649 Nikolai Zherdev .15 .40
650 Wade Redden .15 .40
651 Markus Naslund .25 .60
652 Filip Kuba .15 .40
653 Alex Auld .15 .40
654 Alexandre Picard .15 .40
655 Ryan Shannon .15 .40
656 Jason Smith .15 .40
657 Brendan Bell .15 .40
658 Samuel Pahlsson .15 .40
659 Matt Carle .15 .40
660 Arron Asham .20 .50
661 Ossi Vaananen .15 .40
662 Olli Jokinen .15 .40
663 Joakim Lindstrom .15 .40
664 Todd Fedoruk .15 .40
665 Ken Klee .15 .40
666 Eric Godard .15 .40
667 Miroslav Satan .15 .40
668 Ruslan Fedotenko .15 .40
669 Matt Cooke .15 .40
670 Sidney Crosby 1.25 3.00
671 Evgeni Malkin .60 1.50
672 Rob Blake .25 .60
673 Dan Boyle .20 .50
674 Jody Shelley .15 .40
675 Chris Mason .20 .50
676 Andy McDonald .15 .40
677 David Koci .15 .40
678 Andy Wozniewski .25 .60
679 Matt Foy .15 .40
680 Brad Winchester .15 .40
681 Mark Recchi .20 .50
682 Radim Vrbata .15 .40
683 Ryan Malone .15 .40
684 Vaclav Prospal .15 .40
685 Andrej Meszaros .15 .40
686 Gary Roberts .15 .40
687 Olaf Kolzig .25 .60
688 Steve Eminger .15 .40
689 Vincent Lecavalier .25 .60
690 Curtis Joseph .25 .60
691 Jeff Finger .15 .40
692 Ryan Hollweg .15 .40
693 Niklas Hagman .15 .40
694 Pavol Demitra .15 .40
695 Steve Bernier .15 .40
696 Shane O'Brien .15 .40
697 Darcy Hordichuk .15 .40
698 Rob Davison .15 .40
699 Jose Theodore .25 .60
702 Bret Hedican .15 .40
703 Cory Schneider RC 2.50 6.00
704 Jason Williams .15 .40
705 Karl Alzner RC 2.00 5.00
706 Johan Hedberg .20 .50
707 Erik Christensen .15 .40
708 Stephane Yelle .15 .40
709 Andrew Ference .15 .40
710 Andrej Sekera .15 .40
711 Andrew Peters .15 .40
712 Wayne Primeau .15 .40
713 Brandon Prust .15 .40
714 Sergei Samsonov .15 .40
715 Michael Leighton .15 .40
716 Nathan Gerbe RC 2.50 6.00
717 Kris Versteeg .40 1.00
718 Aaron Johnson .15 .40
719 Ben Eager .15 .40
720 David Jones .15 .40
721 Brett Clark .15 .40
722 Raffi Torres .15 .40
723 Michael Peca .20 .50
724 Kenndal McArdle RC 1.25 3.00
725 Kirk Maltby .15 .40
726 Ethan Moreau .15 .40
727 Marc-Antoine Pouliot .25 .60
728 Wade Belak .15 .40
729 Kyle Quincey .15 .40
730 Matt Greene .15 .40
731 Derek Boogaard .15 .40
732 Cal Clutterbuck .15 .40
733 Maxim Lapierre .15 .40
734 Pekka Rinne .25 .60
735 Scott Clemmensen .15 .40
736 Mike Comrie .15 .40
737 Joey MacDonald .15 .40
738 Michal Repik RC 1.50 4.00
739 Jesse Winchester .25 .60
740 Riley Cote .15 .40
741 Dany Sabourin .15 .40
742 Brad Lukowich .15 .40
743 Brian Boucher .15 .40
744 Doug Murray .15 .40
745 Adam Hall .15 .40
746 Mikhail Grabovski .40 1.00
747 Mike Van Ryn .15 .40
748 Chris Stewart RC 1.50 4.00
749 Zach Bogosian RC 2.50 6.00
750 Nathan Oystrick RC 1.25 3.00
751 Blake Wheeler RC 3.00 8.00
752 Adam Pardy RC 1.25 3.00
753 Zach Boychuk RC 2.00 5.00
754 Brandon Sutter RC 1.50 4.00
755 Dwight Helminen RC 1.25 3.00
756 Patrick Dwyer RC 1.25 3.00
757 Nikita Filatov RC 5.00 12.00
758 Jakub Voracek RC 2.50 6.00
759 Derek Dorsett RC 1.50 4.00
760 James Neal RC 2.00 5.00
761 Fabian Brunnstrom RC 2.00 5.00
762 Steve MacIntyre RC 1.25 3.00
763 Michael Frolik RC 2.50 6.00
764 Wayne Simmonds RC 1.25 3.00
765 Oscar Moller RC 1.25 3.00
766 Drew Doughty RC 4.00 10.00
767 Colton Gillies RC 1.25 3.00
768 Patric Hornqvist RC 1.25 3.00
769 Ryan Jones RC 1.50 4.00
770 Pierre-Luc Letourneau-Leblond RC .75 2.00
771 Patrick Davis RC 1.00 2.50
772 Anssi Salmela RC 1.50 4.00
773 Matthew Halischuk RC 1.50 4.00
774 Petr Vrana RC 1.50 4.00
775 Josh Bailey RC 2.00 5.00
776 Brett Skinner RC 1.00 2.50
777 Mitch Fritz RC 1.00 2.50
778 Jared Ross RC 1.50 4.00
779 Andreas Nodl RC 1.25 3.00
780 Luca Sbisa RC 2.00 5.00
781 Darrel Powe RC 1.25 3.00
782 Ben Maxwell RC 2.00 5.00
783 Kevin Porter RC 1.00 2.50
784 Viktor Tikhonov RC 1.25 3.00
785 Mikkel Boedker RC 2.00 5.00
786 Janne Pesonen RC 1.00 2.50
787 Brad Staubitz RC 1.00 2.50
788 Jamie McGinn RC 1.25 3.00
789 Ben Bishop RC 2.00 5.00
790 T.J. Oshie RC 3.00 8.00
791 Patrik Berglund RC 3.00 8.00
792 Chris Porter RC 1.25 3.00
793 Alex Pietrangelo RC 2.00 5.00
794 Vladimir Mihalik RC 1.25 3.00
795 Steven Stamkos RC 10.00 25.00
796 John Mitchell RC 1.25 3.00
797 Jonas Frogren RC 1.50 4.00
798 Luke Schenn RC 4.00 10.00
799 Nikolai Kulemin RC 1.25 3.00
800 Simeon Varlamov RC 6.00 15.00

2008-09 O-Pee-Chee 1979-80 Retro

COMPLETE SET (800) 500.00 750.00
COMP.SET (600) 300.00 500.00
COMP.UPD.SET (200) 125.00 300.00
*RETRO (1-500,601-747): 2.5X TO 6X
*RETRO RCS (501-560,748-800): .8X TO 2X
*RETRO (561-600): 1X TO 2.5X
COMMON CL .75 2.00

2008-09 O-Pee-Chee 1979-80 Retro Blank Backs

*BLANK (1-500,601-747): 25X TO 60X BASE
*BLANK RCs (501-560, 748-800): 4X TO 10X BASE
*BLANK SPs (561-600): 5X TO 12X BASE
COMMON CL 4.00 10.00

2008-09 O-Pee-Chee 1979-80 Retro Rainbow

RAINBOW (1-500,601-747): 6X TO 15X BASE
RAINBOW RCs (501-560,748-800): 2X TO 5X BASE
RAINBOW SPs (561-600): 2.5X TO 6X BASE
COMMON CL 2.00 5.00

2008-09 O-Pee-Chee Gold

*GOLD (1-500,601-747): 2.5X TO 6X BASE
*GOLD RCs (501-560,748-800): .6X TO 1.5X BASE
*GOLD SPs (561-600): .8X TO 2X BASE
COMMON CL .60 1.50
18 Sidney Crosby 12.00 30.00

2008-09 O-Pee-Chee Metal

*METAL: 1.5X TO 4X BASE
*METAL RC: .5X TO 1.2X BASE RC
STATED ODDS 2 PER UPD.PACKS

2008-09 O-Pee-Chee Metal X

*METAL X: 3X TO 8 X BASE
METAL X RC: 1X TO 2.5X BASE RC
STATED ODDS 1:4 UPD.PACKS

2008-09 O-Pee-Chee All-Rookie Team

COMPLETE SET (6) 8.00 20.00
STATED ODDS 1:4
ARTCP Carey Price 2.50 6.00
ARTJT Jonathan Toews 2.50 6.00
ARTNB Nicklas Backstrom 1.50 4.00
ARTPK Patrick Kane 2.00 5.00
ARTTE Tobias Enstrom .75 2.00
ARTTG Tom Gilbert .50 1.25

2008-09 O-Pee-Chee Autographed Buybacks

STATED ODDS 1:432
BBAC Andrew Cogliano
BBAG Andy Greene 10.00 25.00
BBAM Al MacInnis
BBAO Adam Oates
BBBA Nicklas Backstrom
BBBC Bobby Clarke
BBBD Brandon Dubinsky
BBBE Brian Elliott 12.00 30.00
BBBF Bernie Federko
BBBL Brian Leetch
BBBN Bernie Nicholls
BBBR Bobby Ryan 12.00 30.00
BBBS Billy Smith
BBBU Martin Brodeur
BBCG Clark Gillies 15.00 40.00
BBCI Dino Ciccarelli
BBCM Cory Murphy 8.00 20.00
BBCN Cam Neely
BBCP Carey Price
BBDC Daniel Carcillo 10.00 25.00
BBDG Daniel Girardi 12.00 30.00
BBDH Dale Hawerchuk 20.00 50.00
BBDN Marcel Dionne
BBDP Denis Potvin
BBDS Denis Savard 25.00 60.00
BBDW Doug Wilson 8.00 20.00
BBDY Ron Duguay 15.00 40.00
BBEG Ed Giacomin
BBEJ Erik Johnson
BBEM Evgeni Malkin
BBES Tony Esposito
BBFN Frans Nielsen
BBGA Glenn Anderson
BBGF Grant Fuhr 25.00 60.00
BBGH Gordie Howe
BBGL Tom Gilbert
BBGP Gilbert Perreault 15.00 40.00
BBHA Jaroslav Halak 12.00 30.00
BBHI Jonas Hiller
BBHZ Henrik Zetterberg
BBJB Jared Boll
BBJH Jannik Hansen
BBJI Jarome Iginla
BBJJ Jack Johnson 20.00 50.00
BBJK Jari Kurri
BBJO Jonathan Bernier
BBJS James Sheppard 10.00 25.00
BBJT Jonathan Toews
BBKA Petr Kalus
BBKC Kyle Chipchura
BBLI Bryan Little 12.00 30.00
BBLM Mario Lemieux
BBLR Larry Robinson
BBLT Lauri Tukonen 12.00 30.00
BBLU Mike Lundin
BBMB Mike Bossy 25.00 60.00
BBMC Curtis McElhinney 10.00 25.00
BBMD Lanny McDonald 15.00 40.00
BBME Matt Ellis
BBMF Mark Fraser 8.00 20.00
BBMH Martin Hanzal
BBMI Drew Miller
BBMK Mark Mancari 8.00 20.00
BBMM Mark Messier
BBMN Matt Niskanen
BBMR Mason Raymond 20.00 50.00
BBMS Marc Staal 20.00 50.00
BBNB Neal Broten 25.00 60.00
BBNF Nick Foligno
BBOV Alexander Ovechkin
BBPE Phil Esposito 20.00 50.00
BBPK Patrick Kane
BBPM Peter Mueller
BBPO Tomas Popperle
BBPP Pete Peeters 12.00 30.00
BBPR Patrick Roy
BBPS Peter Stastny 15.00 40.00
BBPT Ryan Parent
BBPV Rich Peverley 10.00 25.00
BBRC Ryan Carter 8.00 20.00
BBRH Ron Hextall
BBRL Rod Langway
BBRM Rick MacLeish
BBRO Luc Robitaille 20.00 50.00
BBRP Rod Pelley 8.00 20.00
BBRS Rob Schremp 15.00 40.00
BBRY Ryan Callahan 12.00 30.00
BBSC Sidney Crosby
BBSG Sam Gagner 25.00 60.00
BBSM Matt Smaby 8.00 20.00
BBST Brett Sterling 8.00 20.00
BBSW Steve Wagner 10.00 25.00
BBTE Tobias Enstrom 20.00 50.00
BBTF Theoren Fleury
BBTH Joe Thornton
BBTM Torrey Mitchell
BBTO Terry O'Reilly 25.00 60.00
BBTP Tomas Plihal
BBTW Tyler Weiman 12.00 30.00
BBVK Ville Koistinen 8.00 20.00

2008-09 O-Pee-Chee Box Bottoms

COMP.PANEL IGINLA/LUONGO /KOVALCHUK/GABORIK 2.50 6.00
COMP.PANEL LECAVALIER/NASH/STAAL /LUNDQVIST 1.50 4.00
COMP.PANEL BRODEUR/THORNTON/ZETTERBERG /TOEWS 1.50 4.00
COMP.PANEL OVECHKIN/ALFREDSSON/PRICE /SUNDIN 2.50 6.00
COMP.PANEL STAMKOS/SUTTER/FILATOV /OKPOSO 2.50 6.00
COMP.PANEL VORACEK/BOEDKER/GILLIES /SCHENN 1.50 4.00
COMP.PANEL BRUNNCTROM/DNACCARD /OSHIE/BOGOSIAN U 2.00 5.00
COMP.PANEL TURRIS/WHEELER/BOYCHUK /DOUGHTY U 2.00 5.00
NNO Kyle Turris U .30 .75
NNO Rick Nash .15 .40
NNO Zach Boychuk U .25 .60
NNO Joe Thornton .25 .60
NNO Henrik Zetterberg .30 .75
NNO Kyle Okposo U .30 .75
NNO Henrik Lundqvist .30 .75
NNO Derick Brassard U .30 .75
NNO Marian Gaborik .25 .60
NNO Nikita Filatov U .60 1.50
NNO Steven Stamkos U 1.25 3.00
NNO Fabian Brunnstrom U .25 .60
NNO Martin Brodeur .30 .75
NNO Zach Bogosian U .30 .75
NNO Ilya Kovalchuk .20 .50
NNO Brandon Sutter U .20 .50
NNO T.J. Oshie U .40 1.00
NNO Daniel Alfredsson .12 .30
NNO Jarome Iginla .30 .75
NNO Jonathan Toews .50 1.25
NNO Drew Doughty U .50 1.25
NNO Vincent LeCavalier .15 .40
NNO Roberto Luongo .25 .60
NNO Jakub Voracek U .30 .75
NNO Blake Wheeler U .40 1.00
NNO Colton Gillies U .15 .40
NNO Eric Staal .25 .60
NNO Mats Sundin .15 .40
NNO Carey Price .50 1.25
NNO Mikkel Boedker U .25 .60
NNO Luke Schenn U .50 1.25
NNO Alexander Ovechkin .60 1.50

2008-09 O-Pee-Chee First Team All-Stars

COMPLETE SET (6) 8.00 20.00
STATED ODDS 1:4
1STAO Alexander Ovechkin 5.00 12.00
1STDP Dion Phaneuf 1.25 3.00
1STEM Evgeni Malkin 3.00 8.00
1STEN Evgeni Nabokov 1.25 3.00

1STJI Jarome Iginla 2.50 6.00
1STNL Nicklas Lidstrom 1.25 3.00

2008-09 O-Pee-Chee Materials Triple

STATED ODDS 1:108
3MADR Alexander Radulov 10.00 25.00
Jason Arnott
J.P. Dumont
3MASH Dany Heatley 12.00 30.00
Daniel Alfredsson
Jason Spezza
3MASZ Daniel Alfredsson 20.00 50.00
Henrik Zetterberg
Henrik Sedin
3MBBJ Dustin Brown 10.00 25.00
Rob Blake
Jack Johnson
3MBBK Anze Kopitar 10.00 25.00
Dustin Brown
Rob Blake
3MBBP Carey Price 25.00 60.00
Francis Bouillon
Patrice Brisebois
3MBCP Dion Phaneuf 10.00 25.00
Mike Cammalleri
Todd Bertuzzi
3MBDL Martin Brodeur 20.00 50.00
Henrik Lundqvist
Rick DiPietro
3MBEP Martin Brodeur 20.00 50.00
Zach Parise
Patrik Elias
3MBHH Chris Higgins 8.00 20.00
Francis Bouillon
Roman Hamrlik
3MBLG Martin Brodeur 20.00 50.00
Roberto Luongo
Jean-Sebastien Giguere
3MBLR Daniel Briere 15.00 40.00
Mike Richards
Joffrey Lupul
3MBMR Ray Bourque
Larry Robinson
Al MacInnis SP
3MBOT Kyle Turris 20.00 50.00
Kyle Okposo
Derick Brassard
3MBPM Borje Salming 15.00 40.00
Peter Forsberg
Mats Sundin
3MBRE Rod Brind'Amour 10.00 25.00
Tuomo Ruutu
Patrick Eaves
3MBSP Brad Boyes 10.00 25.00
David Perron
Lee Stempniak
3MBSW Eric Staal 15.00 40.00
Cam Ward
Rod Brind'Amour
3MCBP Tim Connolly 8.00 20.00
Daniel Paille
Steve Bernier
3MCFH Trent Hunter 6.00 15.00
Mike Comrie
Ruslan Fedotenko
3MCHO Dominik Hasek 15.00 40.00
Chris Osgood
Chris Chelios
3MCOK Sidney Crosby 50.00 120.00
Alexander Ovechkin
Patrick Kane
3MCPC Zach Parise 10.00 25.00
Erik Cole
Matt Carle
3MCRL Nicklas Lidstrom 12.00 30.00
Chris Chelios
Brian Rafalski
3MCSK Anze Kopitar 10.00 25.00
Jarret Stoll
Kyle Calder
3MDGK Marian Gaborik 15.00 40.00
Mikko Koivu
Pavol Demitra
3MDMJ Shane Doan 12.00 30.00
Peter Mueller
Olli Jokinen
3MDSG Rick DiPietro 10.00 25.00
Miroslav Satan
Bill Guerin
3MFCM Sidney Crosby 40.00 100.00
Evgeni Malkin
Marc-Andre Fleury
3MFCT Tim Thomas 10.00 25.00
Manny Fernandez
Zdeno Chara
3MFIN Teemu Selanne 10.00 25.00
Saku Koivu
Mikko Koivu
3MFTW Peter Forsberg 15.00 40.00
Wojtek Wolski
Darcy Tucker
3MGAC Brian Gionta 10.00 25.00
David Clarkson
Arron Asham
3MGCM Sidney Crosby 25.00 60.00
Evgeni Malkin
Sergei Gonchar
3MGKM Ryan Getzlaf 12.00 30.00
Peter Mueller
Anze Kopitar
3MGLN Simon Gagne 15.00 40.00
Joffrey Lupul
Antero Niittymaki
3MGNL Henrik Lundqvist 20.00 50.00
Markus Naslund
Scott Gomez
3MGRC Simon Gagne 15.00 40.00
Mike Richards
Jeff Carter
3MGRP Scott Gomez 8.00 20.00
Wade Redden
Petr Prucha
3MGSD Chris Drury 10.00 25.00
Scott Gomez
Martin Straka
3MGWL Sergei Gonchar 10.00 25.00
Ryan Whitney
Kristopher Letang
3MHGS Marian Gaborik 15.00 40.00
Marian Hossa
Marek Svatos
3MHHG Sam Gagner 15.00 40.00
Ales Hemsky
Shawn Horcoff
3MHLH Nicklas Lidstrom 15.00 40.00
Marian Hossa
Tomas Holmstrom
3MHMS Marian Hossa 15.00 40.00
Jordan Staal
Ryan Malone
3MHSD Tomas Holmstrom 8.00 20.00
Kris Draper
Brad Stuart
3MHSG Marian Gaborik 15.00 40.00
Marian Hossa
Miroslav Satan
3MHSV Dany Heatley 12.00 30.00
Thomas Vanek
Alexander Steen
3MHTK Patrick Kane 30.00 80.00
Jonathan Toews
Martin Havlat
3MHTS Paul Stastny 10.00 25.00
Milan Hejduk
Darcy Tucker
3MICP Jarome Iginla
Mike Cammalleri
Dion Phaneuf
3MIGS Jarome Iginla 20.00 50.00
Simon Gagne
Eric Staal
3MISH Jarome Iginla 20.00 50.00
Martin St. Louis
Dany Heatley
3MITP Jarome Iginla 20.00 50.00
Alex Tanguay
Dion Phaneuf
3MJBH Martin Brodeur 20.00 50.00
Dominik Hasek
Curtis Joseph
3MJDM Peter Mueller 12.00 30.00
Shane Doan
Olli Jokinen
3MJEM Jaromir Jagr 12.00 30.00
Patrik Elias
Milan Michalek
3MJLJ Manny Legace 12.00 30.00
Erik Johnson
Barret Jackman
3MJNJ Jack Johnson 12.00 30.00
Erik Johnson
Matt Niskanen
3MJTS Vesa Toskala 10.00 25.00
Curtis Joseph
Matt Stajan
3MKGH Olaf Kolzig 10.00 25.00
Cristobal Huet
Mike Green
3MKKP Saku Koivu 40.00 80.00
Carey Price
Alex Kovalev
3MKLE Ilya Kovalchuk 12.00 30.00
Kari Lehtonen
Tobias Enstrom
3MKLH Gordie Howe
Guy Lafleur
Jari Kurri SP
3MKMC Ryan Malone 10.00 25.00
Olaf Kolzig
Matt Carle
3MKOR Ilya Kovalchuk 40.00 100.00
Alexander Ovechkin
Alexander Radulov
3MKPK Saku Koivu 10.00 25.00
Mike Komisarek
Tomas Plekanec
3MKSF Sergei Fedorov 15.00 40.00
Alexander Semin
Viktor Kozlov
3MKSS Patrick Kane 12.00 30.00
Duncan Keith
Brent Seabrook
3MKTB Paul Kariya 10.00 25.00
Keith Tkachuk
Brad Boyes
3MKWP Paul Kariya 10.00 25.00
David Perron
Andy Wozniewski
3MKZO Alexander Ovechkin
Ilya Kovalchuk
Nikolai Zherdev
3MLCT Vincent Lecavalier 15.00 40.00
Jonathan Cheechoo
Jonathan Toews
3MLDZ Henrik Zetterberg 20.00 50.00
Nicklas Lidstrom
Pavel Datsyuk
3MLEZ David Legwand 10.00 25.00
Martin Erat
Marek Zidlicky
3MLGM Wayne Gretzky
Mario Lemieux
Mark Messier SP
3MLMK Ryan Kesler 10.00 25.00
Trevor Linden
Brendan Morrison
3MLMO Brenden Morrow 8.00 20.00
Jere Lehtinen
Steve Ott
3MLNP Nicklas Lidstrom 10.00 25.00
Dion Phaneuf
Scott Niedermayer
3MLNZ Rick Nash 10.00 25.00
Nikolai Zherdev
Pascal Leclaire
3MLOB Roberto Luongo 15.00 40.00
Mattias Ohlund
Steve Bernier
3MLOE Roberto Luongo 15.00 40.00
Mattias Ohlund
Alexander Edler
3MLRV Roberto Luongo 15.00 40.00
Vesa Toskala
Dwayne Roloson
3MLSJ Vincent Lecavalier 10.00 25.00
Martin St. Louis
Jussi Jokinen
3MLSW Robert Lang 6.00 15.00
Patrick Sharp
Jason Williams
3MLTT Vincent Lecavalier 25.00 60.00
Joe Thornton
Jonathan Toews
3MMCM Jonathan Cheechoo 10.00 25.00
Patrick Marleau
Milan Michalek
3MMCW Bryan McCabe 8.00 20.00
Ian White
Carlo Colaiacovo
3MMFG Steve Mason 15.00 40.00
Mark Fistric
Alex Goligoski
3MMHK Alex Kovalev 10.00 25.00
Chris Higgins
Andrei Markov
3MMKG Glen Murray 20.00 50.00
Chuck Kobasew
Milan Lucic
3MMKP Mike Modano 10.00 25.00
Paul Kariya
Zach Parise
3MMRR Mike Modano 10.00 25.00
Mike Ribeiro
Brad Richards
3MMRT Mike Modano 10.00 25.00
Jeremy Roenick
Keith Tkachuk
3MMSS Jason Spezza 12.00 30.00
Matt Stajan
Shawn Matthias
3MMVS Ryan Miller 10.00 25.00
Thomas Vanek
Drew Stafford
3MNJL Jarome Iginla 20.00 50.00
Matthew Lombardi
Owen Nolan
3MNLR Kari Lehtonen 10.00 25.00
Antero Niittymaki
Tuukka Rask
3MNSS Markus Naslund 10.00 25.00
Henrik Sedin
Daniel Sedin
3MPRB Brian Rolston 6.00 15.00
Pierre-Marc Bouchard
Mark Parrish
3MPRM Wade Redden 6.00 15.00
Chris Phillips
Andrej Meszaros
3MRCL Ryan Craig 8.00 20.00
Mike Lundin
Mark Recchi
3MRDS Jason Spezza 12.00 30.00
Shane Doan
Brad Richards
3MRFH Patrick Roy
Grant Fuhr
Ron Hextall SP
3MRGH Dany Heatley 12.00 30.00
Martin Gerber
Wade Redden
3MRHA Mark Recchi 8.00 20.00
Bobby Holik
Colby Armstrong
3MRHL Michael Ryder 30.00 60.00
Guillaume Latendresse
Chris Higgins
3MRHS Luc Robitaille
Bobby Hull
Steve Shutt SP
3MRK1 Steven Stamkos
Drew Doughty
Zach Bogosian
3MRK2 Derick Brassard 20.00 50.00
Kyle Turris
Kyle Okposo
3MRTL Michael Ryder 20.00 50.00
Tim Thomas
Milan Lucic
3MSAS Alexander Steen 10.00 25.00
Nikolai Antropov
Matt Stajan
3MSBK Patrice Bergeron 10.00 25.00
Marc Savard
Phil Kessel
3MSBR Rod Brind'Amour 10.00 25.00
Sergei Samsonov
Tuomo Ruutu
3MSBS Eric Staal 15.00 40.00
Daniel Briere
Joe Sakic
3MSBT Mats Sundin 10.00 25.00
Darcy Tucker
Jason Blake
3MSCW Erik Cole 6.00 15.00
Justin Williams
Sergei Samsonov
3MSDL Shane Doan 8.00 20.00
Ryan Smyth
Joffrey Lupul
3MSFB Peter Forsberg 20.00 50.00
Mats Sundin
Nicklas Backstrom
3MSFS Joe Sakic 15.00 40.00
Peter Forsberg
Ryan Smyth
3MSGN Teemu Selanne 12.00 30.00
Ryan Getzlaf
Rob Niedermayer
3MSJL Jaromir Jagr 20.00 50.00
Brendan Shanahan
Henrik Lundqvist
3MSKA Mats Sundin 10.00 25.00
Saku Koivu
Daniel Alfredsson
3MSKK Nikolai Khabibulin 10.00 25.00
Patrick Sharp
Duncan Keith
3MSKT Paul Kariya 10.00 25.00
Brendan Shanahan
Teemu Selanne
3MSLB Joe Sakic 15.00 40.00
Peter Budaj
John-Michael Liles
3MSLJ Teemu Selanne 10.00 25.00
Jere Lehtinen
Jussi Jokinen
3MSNG Jean-Sebastien Giguere 10.00 25.00
Teemu Selanne
Scott Niedermayer
3MSOB Alexander Ovechkin 30.00 60.00
Nicklas Backstrom
Alexander Semin
3MSSS Eric Staal 15.00 40.00
Jordan Staal
Marc Staal
3MSWS Paul Stastny 10.00 25.00
Marek Svatos
Wojtek Wolski
3MTLU Pascal Leclaire 8.00 20.00
R.J. Umberger
Rafi Torres
3MTRM Joe Thornton 15.00 40.00
Jeremy Roenick
Patrick Marleau
3MTTL Hannu Toivonen 10.00 25.00
Kari Lehtonen
Vesa Toskala
3MVKB David Vyborny 10.00 25.00
Gilbert Brule
Rostislav Klesla
3MVWH Tomas Vokoun 10.00 25.00
Stephen Weiss
Nathan Horton
3MWPG Ryan Getzlaf 12.00 30.00
Corey Perry
Doug Weight
3MWPG Doug Weight 10.00 25.00
Zach Parise
Scott Gomez
3MZBW Stephen Weiss 8.00 20.00
Jay Bouwmeester
Richard Zednik
3MZEG Claude Giroux 15.00 40.00
Ilya Zubov
Robbie Earl
3MZKA Nikolai Khabibulin 10.00 25.00
Nikolai Zherdev
Nik Antropov
3MZRT Marty Turco 8.00 20.00
Mike Ribeiro
Sergei Zubov
3MZTN Marty Turco 8.00 20.00
Sergei Zubov
Matt Niskanen

2008-09 O-Pee-Chee Season Highlights

COMPLETE SET (19) 25.00 60.00
STATED ODDS 1:4
SH1 Alexander Ovechkin 4.00 10.00
SH2 Alexander Ovechkin 4.00 10.00
SH3 Andrew Cogliano 1.50 4.00
SH4 Chris Chelios 1.25 3.00
SH5 Evgeni Nabokov 1.00 2.50
SH6 Jarome Iginla 2.00 5.00
SH7 Jarome Iginla 2.00 5.00
SH8 Jeremy Roenick 1.00 2.50
SH9 Joe Sakic 1.50 4.00
SH10 Marian Gaborik 1.50 4.00
SH11 Martin Brodeur 2.00 5.00
SH12 Mats Sundin 1.00 2.50
SH13 Mike Modano 1.00 2.50
SH14 Paul Kariya 1.00 2.50
SH15 Robert Nilsson .60 1.50
SH16 Sidney Crosby 5.00 12.00
SH17 Carey Price 3.00 8.00
SH18 Johan Franzen .60 1.50
SH19 Jonathan Toews 3.00 8.00

2008-09 O-Pee-Chee Second Team All-Stars

COMPLETE SET (6) 5.00 12.00
STATED ODDS 1:4
2NDAK Alex Kovalev 1.50 4.00
2NDBC Brian Campbell 2.50 6.00
2NDHZ Henrik Zetterberg 3.00 8.00
2NDJT Joe Thornton 2.50 6.00
2NDMB Martin Brodeur 3.00 8.00
2NDZC Zdeno Chara 1.00 2.50

2008-09 O-Pee-Chee Signatures

COMMON CARD 8.00 20.00
SEMISTARS/GOALIES 10.00 25.00
UNLISTED STARS 12.00 30.00
STATED ODDS 1:432
SAK Anze Kopitar 15.00 40.00
SAO Alexander Ovechkin
SBC Blake Comeau
SBD Brandon Dubinsky 15.00 40.00
SBE Jonathan Bernier
SBL Michael Blunden
SBO Bobby Orr
SBR Bobby Ryan 20.00 50.00
SBY Dustin Byfuglien 20.00 50.00
SCA Casey Borer 12.00 30.00
SCB Cam Barker
SCD Chris Drury 12.00 30.00
SCH Chris Higgins 15.00 40.00
SCK Chris Kunitz 12.00 30.00
SCM Cory Murphy 8.00 20.00
SDA Daniel Carcillo
SDB Dan Boyle 10.00 25.00
SDC Dan Cleary 15.00 40.00
SDG Daniel Girardi 15.00 40.00
SDJ David Jones 8.00 20.00
SDP Daniel Paille 10.00 25.00
SDS Daniel Sedin 15.00 40.00
SDU Dustin Penner
SEJ Erik Johnson
SEN Eric Nystrom
SFN Frans Nielsen 8.00 20.00
SGL Guillaume Latendresse 30.00 60.00
SGM Greg Moore
SHA Josh Harding 10.00 25.00
SHE T.J. Hensick 10.00 25.00
SHI Jonas Hiller 10.00 25.00
SHL Jaroslav Hlinka 8.00 20.00
SHS Henrik Sedin 12.00 30.00
SHZ Henrik Zetterberg
SJB Jared Boll 10.00 25.00
SJC Jeff Carter 25.00 60.00
SJH Jaroslav Halak
SJJ Jack Johnson 15.00 40.00
SJO Johnny Boychuk 8.00 20.00
SJP Jason Pominville 12.00 30.00
SJS Jack Skille 15.00 40.00
SJT Jiri Tlusty 15.00 40.00
SKA Petr Kalus 10.00 25.00
SKC Kyle Chipchura 12.00 30.00
SKE Phil Kessel 15.00 40.00
SKY Keith Yandle
SLK Lukas Kaspar 8.00 20.00
SMA Mark Mancari
SMB Martin Brodeur 60.00 120.00
SME Matt Ellis 8.00 20.00
SMF Mark Fraser 10.00 25.00
SMI Milan Michalek 8.00 20.00
SML Matt Lashoff
SMM Marc Methot 10.00 25.00
SMN Matt Niskanen 12.00 30.00
SMR Mike Ribeiro 8.00 20.00
SMS Matt Smaby 10.00 25.00
SMT Marty Turco
SNA Evgeni Nabokov 12.00 30.00
SNB Nicklas Backstrom 25.00 60.00
SNG Niklas Grossman
SNH Nathan Horton
SNI Nicklas Bergfors 10.00 25.00
SNK Niklas Kronwall
SOP Ondrej Pavelec 10.00 25.00
SPA Ryan Parent 15.00 40.00
SPB Peter Budaj 10.00 25.00
SPE David Perron 12.00 30.00
SPI Pierre-Marc Bouchard 10.00 25.00
SPK Patrick Kane 50.00 100.00
SPM Peter Mueller 20.00 50.00
SPS Paul Stastny
SRC Ryan Callahan 12.00 30.00
SRG Ryan Getzlaf
SRI Mike Richards 20.00 50.00
SRO Rostislav Olesz
SRP Rod Pelley 8.00 20.00
SRS Ryan Smyth
SRY Ryan Carter 8.00 20.00
SSC Sidney Crosby 125.00 200.00
SSD Steve Downie 15.00 40.00
SSE Devin Setoguchi 12.00 30.00
SSG Sam Gagner 20.00 50.00
SSH James Sheppard 10.00 25.00
SSJ Jordan Staal 25.00 60.00
SSK Sergei Kostitsyn
SSM Matt Stajan 12.00 30.00
SST Drew Stafford 12.00 30.00
STA Maxime Talbot
STE Tobias Enstrom 15.00 40.00
STG Tom Gilbert 15.00 40.00
STH Joe Thornton 25.00 60.00
STK Tomas Kaberle
STO Jonathan Toews 50.00 100.00
STP Tomas Plihal 10.00 25.00
STR Tuukka Rask 20.00 50.00
STS Tobias Stephan 10.00 25.00
STV Tomas Vokoun
STW Tyler Weiman 12.00 30.00
STY Tyler Kennedy 12.00 30.00
OPSAB Adam Burish
OPSAE Andrew Ebbett
OPSBB Brian Boyle
OPSBE Brendan Bell 8.00 20.00
OPSBG Brian Gionta 12.00 30.00
OPSBJ Jonathan Bernier
OPSBL Brian Lee 12.00 30.00
OPSBM Brenden Morrow
OPSBO Brad Boyes
OPSBW Blake Wheeler
OPSCG Colton Gillies
OPSCP Chris Phillips 8.00 20.00
OPSCR Sidney Crosby 125.00
OPSDC David Clarkson 8.00 20.00
OPSDG Daniel Girardi 8.00 20.00
OPSDL Dan LaCosta 15.00 40.00
OPSDP Daniel Paille 10.00 25.00
OPSDU Dustin Boyd
OPSEF Eric Fehr
OPSEL Patrik Elias 8.00 20.00
OPSFB Fabian Brunnstrom 20.00 50.00
OPSFR Michael Frolik 25.00 60.00
OPSHA Michal Handzus
OPSHE Josh Hennessy 8.00 20.00
OPSJA Jarret Stoll
OPSJD Jeff Drouin-Deslauriers
OPSJH Jannik Hansen
OPSJI Jarome Iginla
OPSJJ Jack Johnson 10.00 25.00
OPSJL John-Michael Liles
OPSJM Jamie McGinn 12.00 30.00
OPSJO Joel Perrault
OPSJP Jason Pominville 10.00 25.00
OPSJS James Sheppard 12.00 30.00
OPSJT Jiri Tlusty
OPSKD Kris Draper
OPSKN Kevin Nastiuk 8.00 20.00
OPSKQ Kyle Quincey 8.00 20.00
OPSKT Kyle Turris 15.00 40.00
OPSKV Kris Versteeg 40.00 80.00
OPSLA Drew Larman 8.00 20.00
OPSLI Bryan Little
OPSLS Luke Schenn
OPSMA Mark Fraser
OPSMB Mikkel Boedker
OPSMC Bryan McCabe 10.00 25.00
OPSME Matt Ellis
OPSMF Mark Fistric 10.00 25.00
OPSMG Martin Gerber 10.00 25.00
OPSMH Martin Havlat 10.00 25.00
OPSMI Mike Iggulden
OPSMK Mike Knuble 12.00 30.00
OPSMM Mark Mancari 10.00 25.00
OPSMP Marc-Antoine Pouliot
OPSMR Mattias Ritola 15.00 40.00
OPSMS Marco Sturm 8.00 20.00
OPSNB Nicklas Backstrom 25.00 60.00
OPSND Nigel Dawes 8.00 20.00
OPSNF Nikita Filatov
OPSNK Nikolai Kulemin
OPSNW Noah Welch 8.00 20.00
OPSOP Ondrej Pavelec 10.00 25.00
OPSPA Dimitri Patzold
OPSPD Dustin Penner 8.00 20.00
OPSPO Ryan Potulny 8.00 20.00
OPSRA Mason Raymond
OPSRC Ryane Clowe 8.00 20.00
OPSRP Rich Peverley 8.00 20.00
OPSSA Miroslav Satan
OPSSC Marek Schwarz
OPSSM Stefan Meyer
OPSSS Steven Stamkos 75.00 150.00
OPSSW Steve Wagner
OPSTG Tom Gilbert
OPSTO T.J. Oshie
OPSTS Tom Sestito
OPSTW Tyler Weiman 8.00 20.00
OPSVF Valtteri Filppula 8.00 20.00
OPSVT Viktor Tikhonov
OPSZB Zach Bogosian 25.00 60.00

2008-09 O-Pee-Chee Stat Leaders

COMPLETE SET (14) 12.00 30.00
STATED ODDS 1:4
SL1 Alexander Ovechkin 3.00 8.00
Evgeni Malkin
Jarome Iginla
SL2 Alexander Ovechkin 3.00 8.00
Ilya Kovalchuk
Jarome Iginla
SL3 Joe Thornton 1.25 3.00
Pavel Datsyuk
Marc Savard
SL4 Pavel Datsyuk 1.00 2.50
Nicklas Lidstrom
Dany Heatley
SL5 Daniel Carcillo .60 1.50
Jared Boll
Adam Burish
SL6 Nicklas Lidstrom .75 2.00
Sergei Gonchar
Mark Streit
SL7 Evgeni Nabokov 1.50 4.00
Martin Brodeur
Miikka Kiprusoff
SL8 Chris Osgood 1.25 3.00
Jean-Sebastien Giguere
Dominik Hasek
SL9 Henrik Lundqvist 1.50 4.00
Pascal Leclaire
Evgeni Nabokov
SL10 Dan Ellis .75 2.00
Ty Conklin
Jean-Sebastien Giguere
SL11 Patrick Kane 2.50 6.00
Nicklas Backstrom
Jonathan Toews
SL12 Sidney Crosby 4.00 10.00
Henrik Zetterberg
Marian Hossa
SL13 Johan Franzen 1.50 4.00
Henrik Zetterberg
Marian Hossa
SL14 Chris Osgood .75 2.00
Marc-Andre Fleury
Marty Turco

2008-09 O-Pee-Chee Team Checklists

COMPLETE SET (30) 20.00 50.00
STATED ODDS 1:4
CL1 Anaheim Ducks 1.25 3.00
CL2 Atlanta Thrashers 1.25 3.00
CL3 Boston Bruins 1.25 3.00
CL4 Buffalo Sabres 1.25 3.00
CL5 Calgary Flames 1.25 3.00
CL6 Carolina Hurricanes 1.25 3.00
CL7 Chicago Blackhawks 1.25 3.00
CL8 Colorado Avalanche 1.25 3.00
CL9 Columbus Blue Jackets 1.25 3.00
CL10 Dallas Stars 1.25 3.00
CL11 Detroit Red Wings 1.25 3.00
CL12 Edmonton Oilers 1.25 3.00
CL13 Florida Panthers 1.25 3.00
CL14 Los Angeles Kings 1.25 3.00
CL15 Minnesota Wild 1.25 3.00
CL16 Montreal Canadiens 1.25 3.00
CL17 Nashville Predators 1.25 3.00
CL18 New Jersey Devils 1.25 3.00
CL19 New York Islanders 1.25 3.00
CL20 New York Rangers 1.25 3.00
CL21 Ottawa Senators 1.25 3.00
CL22 Philadelphia Flyers 1.25 3.00
CL23 Phoenix Coyotes 1.25 3.00
CL24 Pittsburgh Penguins 1.25 3.00
CL25 San Jose Sharks 1.25 3.00
CL26 St. Louis Blues 1.25 3.00
CL27 Tampa Bay Lightning 1.25 3.00
CL28 Toronto Maple Leafs 1.25 3.00
CL29 Vancouver Canucks 1.25 3.00
CL30 Washington Capitals 1.25 3.00

2008-09 O-Pee-Chee Trophy Cards

COMPLETE SET (19) 15.00 40.00
STATED ODDS 1:4
AWDAL Art Ross 1.00 2.50
AWDAO Hart Memorial 1.00 2.50
AWDDA Lady Byng 1.00 2.50
AWDDE Roger Crozier 1.00 2.50
AWDDR Clarence Campbell 1.00 2.50
AWDDW Stanley Cup 1.00 2.50
AWDHO William Jennings 1.00 2.50
AWDHZ Conn Smythe 1.00 2.50
AWDJB Bill Masterton 1.00 2.50
AWDMB Vezina 1.00 2.50
AWDNL James Norris 1.00 2.50
AWDOA Maurice Richard 1.00 2.50
AWDOV Lester B Pearson 1.00 2.50
AWDPD Frank J Selke 1.00 2.50
AWDPK Calder 1.00 2.50
AWDPP Prince of Whales 1.00 2.50
AWDPV Plus/Minus Award 1.00 2.50
AWDRE Presidents' Trophy 1.00 2.50
AWDVL King Clancy Memorial Trophy 1.00 2.50

2008-09 O-Pee-Chee Wayne Gretzky Retro Cards

COMPLETE SET (4) 150.00 300.00
COMMON GRETZKY 40.00 80.00
STATED ODDS 1:
18 Wayne Gretzky Team Canada 40.00 80.00
18 Wayne Gretzky Oilers 40.00 80.00
18 Wayne Gretzky Kings 40.00 80.00
18 Wayne Gretzky Rangers 40.00 80.00

2008-09 O-Pee-Chee Winter Classic Highlights

STATED ODDS 1:36
SP SEMISTARS/GOALIES 10.00 25.00
WC1 Buffalo Sabres 4.00 10.00
WC2 Brian Campbell 8.00 20.00
WC3 Brian Campbell 8.00 20.00
WC4 Erik Christensen 3.00 8.00
WC5 Ty Conklin 4.00 10.00
WC6 Ty Conklin 4.00 10.00
WC7 Ty Conklin 4.00 10.00
WC8 Daniel Paille 4.00 10.00
WC9 Sidney Crosby 8.00 20.00
WC10 Sidney Crosby 8.00 20.00
WC11 Pittsburgh Penguins 4.00 10.00
WC12 Paul Gaustad 4.00 10.00
WC13 Sergei Gonchar 5.00 12.00
WC14 Sergei Gonchar 5.00 12.00
WC15 Tyler Kennedy 4.00 10.00
WC16 Ales Kotalik 3.00 8.00
WC17 Buffalo Sabres 4.00 10.00
WC18 Georges Laraque 4.00 10.00
WC19 Evgeni Malkin 12.00 30.00
WC20 Ryan Malone 3.00 8.00
WC21 Ryan Miller 5.00 12.00
WC22 Derek Roy 3.00 8.00
WC23 Michael Ryan 3.00 8.00
WC24 Colby Armstrong 3.00 8.00
WC25 Jaroslav Spacek 3.00 8.00
WC26 Jordan Staal 8.00 20.00
WC27 Ralph Wilson Stadium 3.00 8.00
WC28 Thomas Vanek 5.00 12.00
WC29 Jason Pominville 4.00 10.00
WC30 Maxim Afinogenov 3.00 8.00
WC31 Jordan Staal SP 20.00 50.00
WC32 Ryan Miller SP 12.00 30.00
WC33 Evgeni Malkin SP 30.00 80.00
WC34 Thomas Vanek SP 12.00 30.00
WC35 Thomas Vanek SP 12.00 30.00
WC36 Evgeni Malkin SP 30.00 80.00

WC37 Sidney Crosby SP 25.00 60.00
WC38 Sidney Crosby SP 25.00 60.00
WC39 Sidney Crosby SP 25.00 60.00
WC40 Sidney Crosby SP 25.00 60.00

2009-10 O-Pee-Chee

COMPLETE SET (800) 150.00 250.00
COMP.SET w/SPs (600) 125.00 225.00
COMP.SET w/o SPs (500) 40.00 80.00
COMP.FACT.UPDATE (205) 20.00 40.00
STATED ROOKIE ODDS 1:2
STATED LEGEND ODDS 1:2
1 Roberto Luongo .60 1.50
2 Zdeno Chara .15 .40
3 Patrick Lalime .20 .50
4 Sergei Samsonov .15 .40
5 Troy Brouwer .15 .40
6 Mike Commodore .15 .40
7 Marian Hossa .40 1.00
8 Alexander Ovechkin 1.00 2.50
9 Alexander Frolov .20 .50
10 Colton Gillies .30 .75
11 Jamie Langenbrunner .15 .40
12 Paul Mara .15 .40
13 Scottie Upshall .15 .40
14 Jordan Staal .30 .75
15 Anton Stralman .20 .50
16 Andrej Meszaros .15 .40
17 Henrik Sedin .40 1.00
18 Karl Alzner .25 .60
19 Jonathan Toews .60 1.50
20 Jim Slater .15 .40
21 Andrew Ference .15 .40
22 David Moss .20 .50
23 Bruno Gervais .15 .40
24 David Jones .15 .40
25 James Neal .25 .60
26 Ty Conklin .20 .50
27 Gregory Campbell .15 .40
28 Jonathan Quick .40 1.00
29 Roman Hamrlik .15 .40
30 Martin Brodeur .60 1.50
31 Carey Price .60 1.50
32 Alex Auld .20 .50
33 Martin Hanzal .20 .50
34 Eric Godard .15 .40
35 Chris Mason .20 .50
36 Tomas Kaberle .15 .40
37 Erik Cole .15 .40
38 Joel Ward .15 .40
39 Colby Armstrong .15 .40
40 Stephane Yelle .15 .40
41 Craig Conroy .15 .40
42 Mike Comrie .15 .40
43 Cody McLeod .15 .40
44 Loui Eriksson .15 .40
45 Jiri Tlusty .20 .50
46 Cory Stillman .15 .40
47 Erik Ersberg .20 .50
48 Sergei Kostitsyn .25 .60
49 Brendan Shanahan .25 .60
50 Scott Gomez .25 .60
51 Chris Phillips .15 .40
52 Steven Reinprecht .15 .40
53 Ryan Whitney .15 .40
54 T.J. Oshie .40 1.00
55 Alexei Ponikarovsky .15 .40
56 Willie Mitchell .15 .40
57 David Legwand .20 .50
58 Brendan Mikkelson .15 .40
59 Milan Lucic .25 .60
60 Adam Mair .15 .40
61 Joni Pitkanen .20 .50
62 Ryan Smyth .25 .60
63 Michael Peca .20 .50
64 Jiri Hudler .15 .40
65 Sam Gagner .30 .75
66 Patrick O'Sullivan .20 .50
67 Josh Harding .20 .50
68 Dainius Zubrus .15 .40
69 Daniel Alfredsson .25 .60
70 Daniel Briere .25 .60
71 Alex Goligoski .25 .60
72 Brian Boucher .25 .60
73 Paul Ranger .15 .40
74 Mats Sundin .25 .60
75 Rick Rypien .15 .40
76 Zbynek Michalek .15 .40
77 Corey Perry .25 .60
78 Zach Bogosian .30 .75
79 Ales Kotalik .15 .40
80 Cory Sarich .15 .40
81 Andrew Ladd .25 .60
82 Andrew Raycroft .25 .60
83 Fabian Brunnstrom .25 .60
84 Ales Hemsky .20 .50
85 Keith Ballard .15 .40
86 Marek Zidlicky .15 .40
87 Sidney Crosby 1.25 3.00
88 Patrick Kane .50 1.25
89 Daniel Girardi .15 .40
90 Jeff Carter .25 .60
91 Viktor Tikhonov .25 .60
92 Dan Boyle .15 .40
93 Barret Jackman .15 .40
94 Nikolai Kulemin .20 .50
95 Alexander Semin .25 .60
96 Wade Belak .15 .40
97 Jonas Hiller .30 .75
98 Chuck Kobasew .15 .40
99 Craig Rivet .15 .40
100 Adam Pardy .20 .50
101 Milan Hejduk .25 .60
102 Kris Russell .25 .60
103 Brian Rafalski .15 .40
104 Dwayne Roloson .20 .50
105 Kyle Quincey .15 .40
106 Niklas Backstrom .25 .60
107 Johnny Oduya .15 .40
108 Jason Spezza .30 .75
109 Luca Sbisa .30 .75
110 Kristopher Letang .25 .60
111 Evgeni Nabokov .25 .60
112 Evgeni Artyukhin .15 .40
113 Kevin Bieksa .15 .40
114 Donald Brashear .15 .40
115 Jonas Frogren .20 .50
116 Rob Niedermayer .15 .40
117 Patrice Bergeron .25 .60
118 Jochen Hecht .15 .40
119 Chad LaRose .15 .40
120 Paul Stastny .25 .60
121 Jared Boll .20 .50
122 Nicklas Lidstrom .30 .75
123 Jeff Drouin-Deslauriers .15 .40
124 Michal Handzus .15 .40
125 Andrei Markov .20 .50
126 David Clarkson .15 .40
127 Filip Kuba .15 .40
128 Martin Biron .20 .50
129 Pascal Dupuis .15 .40
130 Brad Boyes .20 .50
131 Ty Wishart .25 .60
132 Pavol Demitra .20 .50
133 Matt Bradley .15 .40
134 Steve Montador .15 .40
135 Matt Hunwick .15 .40
136 Jarome Iginla .50 1.25
137 Justin Williams .15 .40
138 Wojtek Wolski .15 .40
139 Rostislav Klesla .25 .60
140 Johan Franzen .25 .60
141 Robert Nilsson .15 .40
142 Drew Doughty .50 1.25
143 Robert Lang .15 .40
144 John Madden .15 .40
145 Antoine Vermette .15 .40
146 Antero Niittymaki .25 .60
147 Marc-Andre Fleury .25 .60
148 Keith Tkachuk .20 .50
149 Mike Smith .20 .50
150 Alexandre Burrows .20 .50
151 Boyd Gordon .15 .40
152 Teemu Selanne .20 .50
153 Phil Kessel .25 .60
154 Teppo Numminen .25 .60
155 Eric Staal .30 .75
156 Ben Eager .15 .40
157 Jakub Voracek .25 .60
158 Marty Turco .20 .50
159 Tom Gilbert .15 .40
160 Craig Anderson .20 .50
161 James Sheppard .25 .60
162 Zach Parise .25 .60
163 Trevor Smith .15 .40
164 Colton Orr .15 .40
165 Joffrey Lupul .25 .60
166 Chris Drury .20 .50
167 Christian Ehrhoff .15 .40
168 Ryan Malone .15 .40
169 Justin Pogge .50 1.25
170 Tomas Fleischmann .15 .40
171 Kyle Brodziak .15 .40
172 Ilya Kovalchuk .30 .75
173 Tim Thomas .25 .60
174 Mike Cammalleri .25 .60
175 Brandon Sutter .20 .50
176 John-Michael Liles .20 .50
177 Nikita Filatov .50 1.25
178 Mikael Samuelsson .15 .40
179 Steve Staios .15 .40
180 Oscar Moller .20 .50
181 Alex Kovalev .25 .60
182 Paul Martin .15 .40
183 Mike Fisher .15 .40
184 Arron Asham .20 .50
185 Mathieu Garon .25 .60
186 David Perron .25 .60
187 Ryan Bayda .15 .40
188 Steve Bernier .15 .40
189 Jean-Pierre Dumont .15 .40
190 Todd White .15 .40
191 Manny Fernandez .20 .50
192 Daymond Langkow .15 .40
193 Zach Boychuk .30 .75
194 Marek Svatos .15 .40
195 Steve Mason .40 1.00
196 Tomas Holmstrom .20 .50
197 Marc-Antoine Pouliot .20 .50
198 Wayne Simmonds .25 .60
199 Andrei Kostitsyn .20 .50
200 Brian Rolston .15 .40
201 Chris Kelly .15 .40
202 Riley Cote .15 .40
203 Tyler Kennedy .25 .60
204 Patrik Berglund .50 1.25
205 Vladimir Mihalik .25 .60
206 Alexander Edler .15 .40
207 Martin Erat .25 .60
208 Slava Kozlov .15 .40
209 P.J. Axelsson .25 .60
210 Todd Bertuzzi .25 .60
211 Dennis Seidenberg .15 .40
212 Jordan Leopold .15 .40
213 Pascal Leclaire .25 .60
214 Niklas Kronwall .20 .50
215 Stephen Weiss .15 .40
216 Trevor Lewis .15 .40
217 Saku Koivu .25 .60
218 Colin White .15 .40
219 Alexandre Picard .20 .50
220 Shane Doan .20 .50
221 Matt Cooke .15 .40
222 David Backes .20 .50
223 Nik Antropov .20 .50
224 Jannik Hansen .15 .40
225 Shea Weber .20 .50
226 Brad Winchester .15 .40
227 Boris Valabik .25 .60
228 Derek Roy .25 .60
229 Mark Giordano .15 .40
230 Patrick Sharp .20 .50
231 Adam Foote .15 .40
232 Steve Ott .15 .40
233 Brad Stuart .15 .40
234 Radek Dvorak .15 .40
235 Antti Miettinen .15 .40
236 Patrice Brisebois .15 .40
237 Bill Guerin .15 .40
238 Michal Rozsival .15 .40
239 Brian Lee .25 .60
240 Mikkel Boedker .20 .50
241 Patrick Marleau .25 .60
242 Carlo Colaiacovo .15 .40
243 Lee Stempniak .15 .40
244 Shane O'Brien .15 .40
245 Vernon Fiddler .15 .40
246 Tobias Enstrom .25 .60
247 Thomas Vanek .25 .60
248 Matthew Lombardi .15 .40
249 Kris Versteeg .30 .75
250 Darcy Tucker .20 .50
251 Trevor Daley .15 .40
252 Chris Osgood .30 .75
253 Michael Frolik .20 .50
254 Mikko Koivu .25 .60
255 Maxim Lapierre .15 .40
256 Doug Weight .15 .40
257 Brandon Dubinsky .20 .50
258 Brian Elliott .20 .50
259 Keith Yandle .15 .40
260 Joe Thornton .50 1.25
261 Manny Legace .20 .50
262 Niklas Hagman .15 .40
263 Cory Schneider .40 1.00
264 Dan Hamhuis .15 .40
265 Sami Salo .25 .60
266 Dennis Wideman .15 .40
267 Maxim Afinogenov .15 .40
268 Rod Brind'Amour .20 .50
269 Nikolai Khabibulin .25 .60
270 Fredrik Modin .15 .40
271 Tobias Stephan .15 .40
272 Denis Grebeshkov .15 .40
273 Dustin Brown .20 .50
274 Benoit Pouliot .15 .40
275 Patrik Elias .20 .50
276 Rick DiPietro .25 .60
277 Henrik Lundqvist .50 1.25
278 Kimmo Timonen .20 .50
279 Petr Sykora .15 .40
280 Jonathan Cheechoo .25 .60
281 Steve Eminger .15 .40
282 John Mitchell .20 .50
283 Sergei Fedorov .50 1.25
284 Fernando Pisani .15 .40
285 Travis Moen .15 .40
286 Michael Ryder .20 .50
287 Ryan Miller .25 .60
288 Tuomo Ruutu .15 .40
289 Cristobal Huet .25 .60
290 Jason Arnott .15 .40
291 Pavel Datsyuk .25 .60
292 Dustin Penner .15 .40
293 Anze Kopitar .25 .60
294 Marian Gaborik .40 1.00
295 Travis Zajac .15 .40
296 Joey MacDonald .15 .40
297 Stephen Valiquette .15 .40
298 Braydon Coburn .15 .40
299 Miroslav Satan .15 .40
300 Mike Grier .15 .40
301 Steven Stamkos .60 1.50
302 Daniel Sedin .30 .75
303 Milan Jurcina .15 .40
304 Cal Clutterbuck .20 .50
305 Ryan Getzlaf .40 1.00
306 Kari Lehtonen .25 .60
307 Jason Pominville .25 .60
308 Dustin Boyd .15 .40
309 Brian Campbell .20 .50
310 Brett Clark .15 .40
311 Stephane Robidas .15 .40
312 Brett Lebda .15 .40
313 Bryan McCabe .20 .50
314 Pierre-Marc Bouchard .20 .50
315 Max Pacioretty .25 .60
316 Trent Hunter .15 .40
317 Ryan Callahan .15 .40
318 Ilya Zubov .20 .50
319 Kyle Turris .30 .75
320 Devin Setoguchi .15 .40
321 Jay McClement .15 .40
322 Mikhail Grabovski .20 .50
323 George Parros .15 .40
324 Jordin Tootoo .25 .60
325 Scott Niedermayer .15 .40
326 Mathieu Schneider .15 .40
327 Clarke MacArthur .15 .40
328 Curtis Glencross .15 .40
329 Duncan Keith .20 .50
330 Rick Nash .25 .60
331 Jere Lehtinen .20 .50
332 Shawn Horcoff .15 .40
333 Anthony Stewart .15 .40
334 Eric Belanger .15 .40
335 Jaroslav Halak .25 .60
336 Kyle Okposo .25 .60
337 Nigel Dawes .15 .40
338 Mike Richards .50 1.25
339 Daniel Carcillo .25 .60
340 Joe Pavelski .20 .50
341 Martin St. Louis .25 .60
342 Ian White .15 .40
343 Mike Green .50 1.25
344 Dan Ellis .20 .50
345 Francois Beauchemin .15 .40
346 Blake Wheeler .30 .75
347 Daniel Paille .20 .50
348 Joe Corvo .20 .50
349 Jack Skille .15 .40
350 Manny Malhotra .15 .40
351 Henrik Zetterberg .50 1.25
352 Ethan Moreau .15 .40
353 Jarret Stoll .20 .50
354 Derek Boogaard .20 .50
355 Brian Gionta .25 .60
356 Dany Heatley .50 1.25
357 Matt Carle .15 .40
358 Ruslan Fedotenko .15 .40
359 Jeremy Roenick .20 .50
360 Jussi Jokinen .25 .60
361 Ryan Kesler .20 .50
362 Jose Theodore .25 .60
363 Derek Morris .15 .40
364 Bobby Ryan .30 .75
365 Eric Perrin .15 .40
366 Jaroslav Spacek .15 .40
367 Miikka Kiprusoff .25 .60
368 Cam Barker .15 .40
369 Kristian Huselius .15 .40
370 Matt Niskanen .15 .40
371 Sheldon Souray .15 .40
372 Shawn Matthias .25 .60
373 Owen Nolan .25 .60
374 Chris Higgins .15 .40
375 Andy Hilbert .15 .40
376 Aaron Voros .15 .40
377 Simon Gagne .25 .60
378 Mike Weaver .15 .40
379 Milan Michalek .15 .40
380 Vincent Lecavalier .30 .75
381 Jeff Finger .15 .40
382 Viktor Kozlov .15 .40
383 Pekka Rinne .20 .50
384 Chris Kunitz .25 .60
385 David Krejci .20 .50
386 Paul Gaustad .20 .50
387 Ray Whitney .15 .40
388 Brent Seabrook .20 .50
389 Derick Brassard .25 .60
390 Darryl Sydor .15 .40
391 Andrew Cogliano .30 .75
392 Tomas Vokoun .25 .60
393 Brent Burns .15 .40
394 Matt D'Agostini .30 .75
395 Josh Bailey .20 .50
396 Lauri Korpikoski .15 .40
397 Mike Knuble .25 .60
398 Evgeni Malkin .60 1.50
399 Marc-Edouard Vlasic .15 .40
400 Vaclav Prospal .15 .40
401 Vesa Toskala .25 .60
402 Michael Nylander .15 .40
403 Anton Babchuk .20 .50
404 Rich Peverley .20 .50
405 Marco Sturm .15 .40
406 Adrian Aucoin .15 .40
407 Martin Havlat .20 .50
408 Chris Stewart .25 .60
409 Mike Modano .25 .60
410 Chris Chelios .30 .75
411 Jay Bouwmeester .25 .60
412 Jack Johnson .20 .50
413 Guillaume Latendresse .20 .50
414 Mark Streit .15 .40
415 Jamal Mayers .15 .40
416 Chris Neil .15 .40
417 Ed Jovanovski .15 .40
418 Philippe Boucher .15 .40
419 Paul Kariya .25 .60
420 Dominic Moore .25 .60
421 Mathias Ohlund .15 .40
422 Radek Bonk .15 .40
423 Jean-Sebastien Giguere .25 .60
424 Johan Hedberg .20 .50
425 Drew Stafford .25 .60
426 Robyn Regehr .20 .50
427 Dave Bolland .20 .50
428 Peter Budaj .25 .60
429 Brenden Morrow .20 .50
430 Kirk Maltby .15 .40
431 Michal Repik .20 .50
432 Andrew Brunette .15 .40
433 Mike Komisarek .15 .40
434 Richard Park .15 .40
435 Wade Redden .15 .40
436 Jesse Winchester .20 .50
437 Enver Lisin .15 .40
438 Ryane Clowe .15 .40
439 Mason Raymond .15 .40
440 Pavel Kubina .15 .40
441 Nicklas Backstrom .50 1.25
442 Patric Hornqvist .20 .50
443 Ron Hainsey .15 .40
444 Mark Stuart .15 .40
445 Dion Phaneuf .40 1.00
446 Brooks Orpik .15 .40
447 Tyler Arnason .15 .40
448 Brad Richards .20 .50
449 Valtteri Filppula .25 .60
450 Nathan Horton .15 .40
451 Raitis Ivanans .15 .40
452 Tomas Plekanec .20 .50
453 Bobby Holik .15 .40
454 Nikolai Zherdev .15 .40
455 Jarkko Ruutu .15 .40
456 Peter Mueller .30 .75
457 Maxime Talbot .25 .60
458 Andy McDonald .15 .40
459 Matt Stajan .20 .50
460 Kyle Wellwood .15 .40
461 Ryan Suter .15 .40
462 Chris Pronger .20 .50
463 Marc Savard .20 .50
464 Tim Connolly .15 .40
465 Curtis McElhinney .15 .40
466 Dustin Byfuglien .20 .50
467 R.J. Umberger .20 .50
468 Sergei Zubov .15 .40
469 Lubomir Visnovsky .15 .40
470 Kenndal McArdle .20 .50
471 Marc-Andre Bergeron .15 .40
472 Alexander Steen .15 .40
473 Chris Campoli .20 .50
474 Marc Staal .30 .75
475 Scott Hartnell .15 .40
476 Ilya Bryzgalov .20 .50
477 Rob Blake .25 .60
478 Mark Recchi .15 .40
479 Luke Schenn .40 1.00
480 Brooks Laich .20 .50
481 Steve Sullivan .15 .40
482 Bryan Little .20 .50
483 Jason Blake .15 .40
484 Rene Bourque .15 .40
485 Cam Ward .25 .60
486 T.J. Hensick .15 .40
487 Mike Ribeiro .15 .40
488 Dan Cleary .25 .60
489 Mike Weber .15 .40
490 David Booth .15 .40
491 Alex Tanguay .20 .50
492 Scott Clemmensen .15 .40
493 Brendan Witt .15 .40
494 Nick Foligno .25 .60
495 Olli Jokinen .15 .40
496 Checklist .15 .40
497 Checklist .15 .40
498 Checklist .15 .40
499 Checklist .15 .40
500 Checklist .15 .40
501 Yannick Weber RC 1.50 4.00
502 Ville Leino RC 1.50 4.00
503 Troy Bodie RC 1.00 2.50
504 Tom Wandell RC 4.00 10.00
505 Tim Wallace RC .75 2.00
506 Tim Stapleton RC 1.25 3.00
507 T.J. Galiardi RC 1.50 4.00
508 Spencer Machacek RC 1.00 2.50
509 Sean Collins RC 1.00 2.50
510 Scott Lehman RC .75 2.00
511 Christian Hanson RC 1.50 4.00
512 Riley Armstrong RC 1.00 2.50
513 Riku Helenius RC 1.25 3.00
514 Phil Oreskovic RC 1.25 3.00
515 Peter Regin RC 1.50 4.00
516 Mike Santorelli RC .75 2.00
517 Mike McKenna RC 1.00 2.50
518 Mikael Backlund RC 2.00 5.00
519 Michal Neuvirth RC 3.00 8.00
520 Michael Vernace RC 1.00 2.50
521 Matt Hendricks RC 1.00 2.50
522 Matt Beleskey RC 1.25 3.00
523 Luca Caputi RC 1.50 4.00
524 Kurtis McLean RC 1.00 2.50
525 Kris Chucko RC 1.00 2.50
526 Kevin Westgarth RC 1.00 2.50
527 Kevin Quick RC .75 2.00
528 John Scott RC 1.25 3.00
529 Joel Rechlicz RC 1.25 3.00
530 Jhonas Enroth RC 1.50 4.00
531 Jesse Joensuu RC 1.50 4.00
532 Jay Beagle RC 1.25 3.00
533 Jaime Sifers RC 1.00 2.50
534 Taylor Chorney RC 1.25 3.00
535 Grant Lewis RC 1.00 2.50
536 Derek Peltier RC .75 2.00
537 Davis Drewiske RC 1.25 3.00
538 David Van Der Gulik RC 1.00 2.50
539 David Schlemko RC 1.00 2.50
540 John Negrin RC 1.00 2.50
541 Cal O'Reilly RC 1.25 3.00
542 Byron Bitz RC 1.00 2.50
543 Ivan Vishnevskiy RC 1.50 4.00
544 Brian Salcido RC 1.00 2.50
545 Brandon Segal RC 1.00 2.50
546 Ben Lovejoy RC 2.00 5.00
547 Artem Anisimov RC 1.50 4.00
548 Antti Niemi RC 4.00 10.00
549 Andrew MacDonald RC 1.00 2.50
550 Alexander Sulzer RC .75 2.00
551 Wayne Gretzky L 4.00 10.00
552 Denis Potvin L .60 1.50
553 Steve Shutt L .75 2.00
554 Dale Hawerchuk L .75 2.00
555 Don Cherry L .75 2.00
556 Stan Mikita L 1.25 3.00
557 Al MacInnis L .75 2.00
558 Denis Savard L .75 2.00
559 Bernie Federko L .60 1.50
560 Darryl Sutter L .60 1.50
561 Alex Delvecchio L 1.00 2.50
562 Rod Langway L .60 1.50
563 Johnny Bucyk L 1.25 3.00
564 Mark Messier L 1.50 4.00
565 Ted Lindsay L .75 2.00
566 Bobby Hull L 2.00 5.00
567 Scotty Bowman L .75 2.00
568 Clark Gillies L .75 2.00
569 Red Kelly L .75 2.00
570 Gilbert Perreault L .75 2.00
571 Terry O'Reilly L .60 1.50
572 Jean Beliveau L 1.25 3.00
573 Ron Ellis L .50 1.25
574 Harry Howell L .60 1.50
575 Guy Carbonneau L 1.25 3.00
576 Butch Bouchard L .60 1.50
577 Frank Mahovlich L 1.00 2.50
578 Lanny McDonald L .75 2.00
579 Peter Stastny L .75 2.00
580 Dick Duff L .60 1.50
581 Grant Fuhr L 1.00 2.50
582 Cam Neely L 1.25 3.00
583 Rogie Vachon L 1.25 3.00
584 Phil Esposito L 1.50 4.00
585 Theoren Fleury L 1.25 3.00
586 Bobby Orr L 3.00 8.00
587 Johnny Bower L 1.00 2.50
588 Luc Robitaille L .75 2.00
589 Jari Kurri L .75 2.00
590 Doug Wilson L .50 1.25
591 Borje Salming L .75 2.00
592 Marty McSorley L .60 1.50
593 Bob Bourne L .60 1.50
594 Doug Gilmour L .75 2.00
595 Mike Bossy L .75 2.00
596 Bobby Clarke L 1.25 3.00
597 Mario Lemieux L 2.00 5.00
598 Patrick Roy L 2.50 6.00
599 Tony Esposito L 1.25 3.00
600 Gordie Howe L 3.00 8.00
601 Scott Hartnell .15 .40
602 Jason Williams .15 .40
603 Rob Scuderi .15 .40
604 Aaron Ward .15 .40
605 Rickard Wallin .15 .40
606 Niclas Wallin .15 .40
607 Stephane Veilleux .15 .40
608 Ole-Kristian Tollefsen .15 .40
609 Alex Tanguay .20 .50
610 Petr Sykora .15 .40
611 Darryl Sydor .15 .40
612 Jaroslav Spacek .15 .40
613 Ryan Smyth .25 .60
614 Dennis Seidenberg .15 .40
615 Jeff Schultz .15 .40
616 Rob Schremp .15 .40
617 Luca Sbisa .30 .75
618 Mikael Samuelsson .15 .40
619 Dwayne Roloson .20 .50
620 Andrew Raycroft .25 .60
621 Kyle Quincey .15 .40
622 Vaclav Prospal .15 .40
623 Chris Pronger .20 .50
624 Wayne Primeau .15 .40
625 Roman Polak .15 .40
626 Patrick O'Sullivan .20 .50
627 Colton Orr .15 .40
628 Mattias Ohlund .15 .40
629 Antero Niittymaki .25 .60
630 Rob Niedermayer .15 .40
631 Scott Nichol .15 .40
632 Cory Murphy .15 .40
633 Matt Moulson .15 .40
634 Brendan Morrison .20 .50
635 Steve Montador .15 .40
636 Travis Moen .15 .40
637 Drew Miller .15 .40
638 Milan Michalek .15 .40
639 Steve McCarthy .15 .40
640 Paul Mara .15 .40
641 Manny Malhotra .15 .40
642 John Madden .15 .40
643 Joey MacDonald .15 .40
644 Joffrey Lupul .25 .60
645 Pascal Leclaire .25 .60
646 Ian Laperriere .15 .40
647 Robert Lang .15 .40
648 Quintin Laing .15 .40
649 Jason LaBarbera .20 .50
650 Pavel Kubina .15 .40
651 Alex Kovalev .25 .60
652 Ales Kotalik .15 .40
653 Lauri Korpikoski .15 .40
654 Mike Komisarek .20 .50
655 Saku Koivu .25 .60
656 Chuck Kobasew .15 .40
657 Mike Knuble .25 .60
658 Nikolai Khabibulin .25 .60
659 Phil Kessel .25 .60
660 Boyd Kane .15 .40
661 Ryan Johnson .15 .40
662 Brent Johnson .15 .40
663 Cam Janssen .15 .40
664 Marian Hossa .40 1.00
665 Darcy Hordichuk .15 .40
666 Chris Higgins .15 .40
667 Dany Heatley .50 1.25
668 Martin Havlat .20 .50
669 Jeff Halpern .15 .40
670 Scott Gomez .25 .60
671 Brian Gionta .25 .60
672 Hal Gill .15 .40
673 Mathieu Garon .25 .60
674 Marian Gaborik .40 1.00
675 Maxim Afinogenov .15 .40
676 Todd Fedoruk .15 .40
677 Garnet Exelby .15 .40
678 Ray Emery .20 .50
679 Christian Ehrhoff .15 .40
680 Andrew Ebbett .20 .50
681 Steve Downie .15 .40
682 Nigel Dawes .15 .40
683 Ty Conklin .20 .50
684 Mike Comrie .15 .40
685 Scott Clemmensen .15 .40
686 Jonathan Cheechoo .25 .60
687 Mike Cammalleri .25 .60
688 Jay Bouwmeester .25 .60
689 Chris Bourque .25 .60
690 Paul Bissonnette .15 .40
691 Martin Biron .20 .50
692 Todd Bertuzzi .25 .60
693 Marc-Andre Bergeron .15 .40
694 Francois Beauchemin .15 .40
695 Alex Auld .20 .50
696 Keith Aucoin .30 .75
697 Evgeni Artyukhin .15 .40
698 Nik Antropov .20 .50
699 Craig Anderson .20 .50
700 Checklist .15 .40
701 Checklist .15 .40
702 Toni Lydman .15 .40
703 Brian McGrattan .15 .40
704 Matt Ellis .15 .40
705 Fredrik Sjostrom .15 .40
706 Tomas Kopecky .20 .50
707 Brent Sopel .15 .40
708 Bryan Bickell .15 .40
709 Niklas Hjalmarsson .20 .50
710 Henrik Tallinder .15 .40
711 Nathan Paetsch .15 .40
712 Mike Grier .15 .40
713 Jordan Hendry .20 .50
714 Aaron Johnson .15 .40
715 Johnny Boychuk .20 .50
716 Derek Morris .15 .40
717 Daniel Paille .20 .50
718 Steve Begin .15 .40
719 Ondrej Pavelec .20 .50
720 Christoph Schubert .15 .40
721 Eric Boulton .15 .40
722 Chris Thorburn .15 .40
723 Ryan Carter .15 .40
724 Erik Christensen .15 .40
725 Sheldon Brookbank .15 .40
726 Petteri Nokelainen .15 .40
727 Nick Boynton .15 .40
728 Ruslan Salei .15 .40
729 Scott Hannan .15 .40
730 David Koci .15 .40
731 Stephane Yelle .15 .40
732 Tom Kostopoulos .15 .40
733 Georges Laraque .15 .40
734 Ryan Shannon .20 .50
735 Anton Volchenkov .15 .40
736 Steve MacIntyre .15 .40
737 Gilbert Brule .30 .75
738 Jean-Francois Jacques .15 .40
739 Derek Meech .15 .40
740 Jim Howard .30 .75
741 Kyle Chipchura .15 .40
742 Matt Carkner .15 .40
743 Ryan Stone .15 .40
744 Anton Stralman .20 .50
745 Derek Dorsett .20 .50
746 Patrick Eaves .15 .40
747 Brad May .15 .40
748 Mathieu Roy .15 .40
749 Tanner Glass .15 .40
750 Shean Donovan .15 .40
751 Craig Adams .15 .40
752 Martin Skoula .15 .40
753 Steven Zalewski RC .40 1.00
754 Matthew Corrente RC .50 1.25
755 Bryan Rodney RC .40 1.00
756 Ryan Vesce RC .40 1.00
757 David Sloane RC .60 1.50
758 Lars Eller RC .75 2.00
759 Tyson Strachan RC .30 .75
760 Wes O'Neill RC .50 1.25
761 Matt Climie RC .40 1.00
762 Daniel Larsson RC .60 1.50
763 James Wright RC .60 1.50
764 Teemu Laakso RC .30 .75
765 Devan Dubnyk RC .60 1.50
766 Jason Demers RC .40 1.00
767 Benn Ferriero RC .50 1.25
768 Frazer McLaren RC .30 .75
769 Johan Backlund RC .50 1.25
770 Mika Pyorala RC .50 1.25
771 Tyler Myers RC 2.00 5.00
772 Ryan O'Reilly RC 1.00 2.50
773 Jamie Benn RC .75 2.00
774 Dmitry Kulikov RC .50 1.25
775 Alec Martinez RC .30 .75
776 Matt Gilroy RC .60 1.50
777 Michael Del Zotto RC 1.00 2.50
778 Jay Rosehill RC .30 .75
779 Sergei Shirokov RC .75 2.00
780 Tyler Ennis RC 1.25 3.00
781 Chris Butler RC .50 1.25
782 James Reimer RC .50 1.25
783 Perttu Lindgren RC .50 1.25
784 Bobby Sanguinetti RC .40 1.00
785 Braden Holtby RC .60 1.50
786 Ryan Wilson RC .50 1.25
787 Aaron Gagnon RC .30 .75
788 Viktor Stalberg RC .75 2.00
789 Erik Karlsson RC 1.50 4.00
790 Brad Marchand RC .60 1.50
791 Colin Wilson RC 1.00 2.50
792 Michael Grabner RC .60 1.50
793 Tyler Bozak RC 1.25 3.00
794 Logan Couture RC 1.00 2.50
795 Evander Kane RC 1.25 3.00
796 Jonas Gustavsson RC 1.25 3.00
797 Victor Hedman RC 1.00 2.50
798 James Van Riemsdyk RC 1.25 3.00
799 Matt Duchene RC 2.00 5.00
800 John Tavares RC 4.00 10.00

2009-10 O-Pee-Chee Rainbow

*SINGLES: 2.5X TO 6X BASIC CARDS
*ROOKIES: .6X TO 1.5X BASIC
*LEGENDS: 1X TO 2.5X BASIC
STATED ODDS 1:4
*UPD (601-752): 3X TO 8X BASIC CARDS
*UPD ROOKIES (753-800): 2X TO 5X BASIC CARDS
UPDATE STATED ODDS 2-5 PER FACT.SET
800 John Tavares 15.00 40.00

2009-10 O-Pee-Chee Retro

*SINGLES: 2X TO 5X BASIC CARDS
*ROOKIES: .5 X TO 1.2X BASIC CARDS
*LEGENDS: .8X TO 2X BASIC CARDS
STATED ODDS 1 PER PACK

2009-10 O-Pee-Chee Retro Blank Backs

*BLANK: 25X TO 60X BASIC CARDS
*BLANK RCs: 4X TO 10X BASIC CARDS
*BLANK SPs: 5X TO 12X BASIC CARDS
COMMON CLs 4.00 10.00

2009-10 O-Pee-Chee Retro Rainbow

*SINGLES: 8X TO 20X BASIC CARDS
*ROOKIES: 1X TO 2.5X BASIC
*LEGENDS: 2.5X TO 6X BASIC
STATED PRINT RUN 100 SER. #'d SETS

2009-10 O-Pee-Chee All Rookie Team

COMPLETE SET (6) 6.00 15.00
STATED ODDS 1:4
ART1 Steve Mason 1.25 3.00
ART2 Drew Doughty 1.50 4.00
ART3 Luke Schenn 1.25 3.00
ART4 Patrik Berglund 1.50 4.00
ART5 Bobby Ryan 1.00 2.50
ART6 Kris Versteeg 1.00 2.50

2009-10 O-Pee-Chee All Star Team

COMPLETE SET (12) 10.00 25.00
STATED ODDS 1:4
AST1 Tim Thomas .75 2.00
AST2 Mike Green 1.50 4.00
AST3 Zdeno Chara .50 1.25
AST4 Evgeni Malkin 2.00 5.00
AST5 Jarome Iginla 1.50 4.00
AST6 Alexander Ovechkin 3.00 8.00
AST7 Steve Mason 1.25 3.00
AST8 Nicklas Lidstrom 1.00 2.50
AST9 Dan Boyle .50 1.25
AST10 Pavel Datsyuk .75 2.00
AST11 Marian Hossa 1.25 3.00
AST12 Zach Parise .75 2.00

2009-10 O-Pee-Chee Box Bottoms

NNO Rod Brind'Amour .20 .50
NNO Henrik Zetterberg .50 1.25
NNO Rick Nash .25 .60
NNO Evgeni Malkin .60 1.50
NNO Ilya Kovalchuk .30 .75
NNO Jonathan Toews .60 1.50
NNO Vincent Lecavalier .30 .75
NNO Nicklas Lidstrom .30 .75
NNO Alexander Ovechkin 1.00 2.50
NNO Roberto Luongo .60 1.50
NNO Jarome Iginla .50 1.25
NNO Steven Stamkos .60 1.50
NNO Sidney Crosby 1.25 3.00
NNO Joe Thornton .50 1.25

NNO Carey Price .60 1.50
NNO Luke Schenn .40 1.00

2009-10 O-Pee-Chee Buyback Autographs

BBCG Claude Giroux 15.00 40.00
BBHW Dale Hawerchuk 8.00 20.00

2009-10 O-Pee-Chee Canadian Heroes

COMPLETE SET (42) 15.00 40.00
STATED ODDS 1:4
CBBC Braydon Coburn .50 1.25
CBBK Becky Kellar .50 1.25
CBCH Chris Mason .60 1.50
CBCL Charline Labonte .50 1.25
CBCM Carla MacLeod .50 1.25
CBCO Caroline Ouellette .50 1.25
CBCP Chris Phillips .50 1.25
CBCS Colleen Sostorics .50 1.25
CBCW Catherine Ward .50 1.25
CBDD Drew Doughty 1.50 4.00
CBDH Dan Hamhuis .50 1.25
CBDR Dwayne Roloson .60 1.50
CBGA Gillian Apps .50 1.25
CBGF Gillian Ferrari .50 1.25
CBGK Gina Kingsbury .50 1.25
CBHA Josh Harding .60 1.50
CBHE Dany Heatley 1.50 4.00
CBHI Haley Irwin .50 1.25
CBHW Hayley Wickenheiser .50 1.25
CBIW Ian White .50 1.25
CBJB Jennifer Botterill .50 1.25
CBJH Jayna Hefford .50 1.25
CBJS Jason Spezza 1.00 2.50
CBKS Kim St-Pierre .50 1.25
CBLS Luke Schenn 1.25 3.00
CBMA Meghan Agosta .50 1.25
CBML Matthew Lombardi .50 1.25
CBMM Meaghan Mikkelson .50 1.25
CBMP Marie-Philip Poulin .50 1.25
CBMS Martin St. Louis .75 2.00
CBMV Marc-Edouard Vlasic .50 1.25
CBRJ Rebecca Johnston .50 1.25
CBRO Derek Roy .75 2.00
CBSD Shane Doan .60 1.50
CBSH Shawn Horcoff .50 1.25
CBSS Shannon Szabados .50 1.25
CBST Steven Stamkos 2.00 5.00
CBSU Scottie Upshall .50 1.25
CBSV Sarah Vaillancourt .50 1.25
CBSW Shea Weber .60 1.50
CBTB Tessa Bonhomme .50 1.25
CBTZ Travis Zajac .50 1.25

2009-10 O-Pee-Chee Canadian Heroes Autographs

CBABO Bobby Orr
CBACP Carey Price 150.00 300.00
CBADD Drew Doughty 40.00 80.00
CBADH Dany Heatley 40.00 80.00
CBADP Dion Phaneuf
CBADR Dwayne Roloson
CBAGH Gordie Howe 125.00 250.00
CBAHA Josh Harding 30.00 60.00
CBAJI Jarome Iginla 125.00 250.00
CBAJT Jonathan Toews 125.00 250.00
CBALS Luke Schenn 50.00 100.00
CBAML Mario Lemieux 125.00 250.00
CBAMM Mark Messier
CBAMR Mike Richards 75.00 150.00
CBAMS Martin St. Louis
CBAPR Patrick Roy 275.00 400.00
CBARB Ray Bourque 150.00 250.00
CBARN Rick Nash 125.00 250.00
CBASC Sidney Crosby 125.00 250.00
CBAST Steven Stamkos 100.00 200.00
CBAWG Wayne Gretzky 450.00 600.00

2009-10 O-Pee-Chee Canadian Heroes Foil

STATED ODDS 1:36
CBH1 Wayne Gretzky 15.00 40.00
CBH2 Gordie Howe 12.00 30.00
CBH3 Bobby Orr 12.00 30.00
CBH4 Steven Stamkos 8.00 20.00
CBH5 Mark Messier 6.00 15.00
CBH6 Sidney Crosby 15.00 40.00
CBH7 Phil Esposito 6.00 15.00
CBH8 Tony Esposito 5.00 12.00
CBH9 Gilbert Perreault 3.00 8.00
CBH10 Lanny McDonald 3.00 8.00
CBH11 Ray Bourque 5.00 12.00
CBH12 Theoren Fleury 5.00 12.00
CBH13 Luc Robitaille 3.00 8.00
CBH14 Manon Rheaume 5.00 12.00
CBH15 Mike Bossy 3.00 8.00
CBH16 Bobby Clarke 5.00 12.00
CBH17 Patrick Roy 10.00 25.00
CBH18 Mario Lemieux 8.00 20.00
CBH19 Joe Thornton 6.00 15.00
CBH20 Jarome Iginla 6.00 15.00
CBH21 Vincent Lecavalier 4.00 10.00
CBH22 Ryan Getzlaf 5.00 12.00
CBH23 Patrick Marleau 3.00 8.00
CBH24 Martin St. Louis 3.00 8.00
CBH25 Mike Richards 6.00 15.00
CBH26 Shane Doan 2.50 6.00
CBH27 Jonathan Toews 8.00 20.00
CBH28 Steve Mason 5.00 12.00
CBH29 Martin Brodeur 8.00 20.00
CBH30 Marc-Andre Fleury 3.00 8.00
CBH31 Roberto Luongo 8.00 20.00
CBH32 Mike Green 6.00 15.00
CBH33 Brian Campbell 2.50 6.00
CBH34 Scott Niedermayer 2.00 5.00
CBH35 Dion Phaneuf 5.00 12.00
CBH36 Joe Sakic 6.00 15.00
CBH37 Marty Turco 2.50 6.00
CBH38 Carey Price 8.00 20.00
CBH39 Jason Spezza 4.00 10.00
CBH40 Rick Nash 3.00 8.00

2009-10 O-Pee-Chee In Action

COMPLETE SET (12) 12.00 30.00
STATED ODDS 1:4
ACT1 Sidney Crosby 4.00 10.00
ACT2 Evgeni Malkin 2.00 5.00
ACT3 Alexander Ovechkin 3.00 8.00
ACT4 Jarome Iginla 1.50 4.00
ACT5 Bobby Ryan 1.00 2.50
ACT6 Jonathan Toews 2.00 5.00
ACT7 Ilya Kovalchuk 1.00 2.50
ACT8 Henrik Zetterberg 1.50 4.00
ACT9 Ales Hemsky .60 1.50
ACT10 Zach Parise .75 2.00
ACT11 Dany Heatley 1.50 4.00
ACT12 Mikko Koivu .75 2.00

2009-10 O-Pee-Chee Materials

STATED ODDS 1:144
JBEES Blake Wheeler 10.00 25.00
Marc Savard
Patrice Bergeron
Phil Kessel
JBLUE David Perron 15.00 40.00
Keith Tkachuk
Patrik Berglund
Paul Kariya
JBOLT Martin St. Louis 20.00 50.00
Steven Stamkos
Vaclav Prospal
Vincent Lecavalier
JBOST Manny Fernandez 10.00 25.00
Michael Ryder
Milan Lucic
Tuukka Rask
JCANE Cam Ward 10.00 25.00
Eric Staal
Erik Cole
Rod Brind'Amour
JCAPS Alexander Ovechkin 30.00 80.00
Mike Green
Nicklas Backstrom
Tomas Fleischmann
JCATS David Booth 8.00 20.00
Nathan Horton
Stephen Weiss
Tomas Vokoun
JCNDS Alex Kovalev 8.00 20.00
Andrei Kostitsyn
Andrei Markov
Mike Komisarek
JCNKS Alexander Edler 20.00 50.00
Daniel Sedin
Kevin Bieksa
Roberto Luongo
JCOLO Joe Sakic 15.00 40.00
Marek Svatos
Paul Stastny
Wojtek Wolski
JCYTE Matthew Lombardi 10.00 25.00
Mikkel Boedker
Peter Mueller
Shane Doan
JDEVL David Clarkson 20.00 50.00
Martin Brodeur
Patrik Elias
Zach Parise
JDRFT Drew Doughty 20.00 50.00
Luke Schenn
Mikkel Boedker
Steven Stamkos
JDUCK Chris Pronger 12.00 30.00
Corey Perry
Jean-Sebastien Giguere
Ryan Getzlaf
JEURO Mats Sundin 15.00 40.00
Olaf Kolzig
Sergei Fedorov
Teemu Selanne
JFLAM Dion Phaneuf 12.00 30.00
Jarome Iginla
Miikka Kiprusoff
Olli Jokinen
JFLYR Antero Niittymaki 15.00 40.00
Jeff Carter
Mike Richards
Simon Gagne
JGCML Mario Lemieux 100.00 200.00
Mark Messier
Sidney Crosby
Wayne Gretzky
JHABS Alex Tanguay 6.00 15.00
Carey Price
Saku Koivu
Tomas Plekanec
JHAWK Brent Seabrook 20.00 50.00
Jonathan Toews
Patrick Kane
Patrick Sharp
JISLE Doug Weight
Jeff Tambellini
Rick DiPietro
Trent Hunter SP
JJACK Jakub Voracek 8.00 20.00
R.J. Umberger
Rick Nash
Rostislav Klesla
JKING Alexander Frolov 15.00 40.00
Anze Kopitar
Drew Doughty
Dustin Brown
JKMLP Darcy Tucker 15.00 40.00
Jarome Iginla
Scott Niedermayer
Shane Doan
JLEAF Jason Blake 12.00 30.00
Luke Schenn
Matt Stajan
Vesa Toskala
JLGND Gordie Howe 75.00 150.00
Mark Messier
Patrick Roy
Wayne Gretzky
JOILR Andrew Cogliano 10.00 25.00
Marc-Antoine Pouliot
Sam Gagner
Shawn Horcoff
JPENS Evgeni Malkin 40.00 100.00
Jordan Staal
Marc-Andre Fleury
Sidney Crosby
JRBLF Marc-Andre Fleury 25.00 60.00
Martin Brodeur
Patrick Roy
Roberto Luongo
JRNGR Brandon Dubinsky 15.00 40.00
Henrik Lundqvist
Marc Staal
Markus Naslund
JSABR Derek Roy 8.00 20.00
Jason Pominville
Ryan Miller
Thomas Vanek
JSBBS Brendan Shanahan 20.00 50.00
Joe Sakic
Martin Brodeur
Rob Blake
JSENS Chris Campoli 15.00 40.00
Chris Phillips
Dany Heatley
Jason Spezza
JSHRK Devin Setoguchi 15.00 40.00
Evgeni Nabokov
Joe Thornton
Patrick Marleau
JSTAR Marty Turco 8.00 20.00
Matt Niskanen
Mike Modano
Sergei Zubov
JTHRS Bryan Little 10.00 25.00
Ilya Kovalchuk
Kari Lehtonen
Tobias Enstrom
JVANC Mats Sundin 20.00 50.00
Mattias Ohlund
Roberto Luongo
Steve Bernier
JWILD Marian Gaborik 12.00 30.00
Mikko Koivu
Owen Nolan
Pierre-Marc Bouchard
JWING Henrik Zetterberg 15.00 40.00
Marian Hossa
Nicklas Lidstrom
Pavel Datsyuk
JWNGS Brian Rafalski 10.00 25.00
Chris Chelios
Chris Osgood
Kris Draper
JPREDS David Legwand 6.00 15.00
Pekka Rinne
Shea Weber
Steve Sullivan

2009-10 O-Pee-Chee Record Breakers

COMPLETE SET (10) 10.00 25.00
STATED ODDS 1:4
RB1 Zdeno Chara .50 1.25
RB2 Alexander Ovechkin 3.00 8.00
RB3 Steve Mason 1.25 3.00
RB4 Patrik Elias .60 1.50
RB5 Jarome Iginla 1.50 4.00
RB6 Miikka Kiprusoff .75 2.00
RB7 Mike Green 1.50 4.00
RB8 Martin Brodeur 2.00 5.00
RB9 Brendan Shanahan .75 2.00
RB10 Mike Richards 1.50 4.00

2009-10 O-Pee-Chee Signatures

STATED ODDS 1:216
SAP Adam Pineault 8.00 20.00
SBB Ben Bishop 10.00 25.00
SBL Brian Lee 10.00 25.00
SBM Brendan Mikkelson 6.00 15.00
SBO Bobby Orr 150.00 250.00
SBR Brian Boyle 8.00 20.00
SBS Brandon Sutter 10.00 25.00
SBU Peter Budaj 10.00 25.00
SBW Blake Wheeler 12.00 30.00
SCB Cam Barker 6.00 15.00
SCG Colton Gillies 12.00 30.00
SCK Chris Kunitz 10.00 25.00
SCL David Clarkson 6.00 15.00
SCO Cory Schneider 15.00 40.00
SCP Carey Price 25.00 60.00
SCS Chris Stewart 10.00 25.00
SDC Daniel Carcillo 10.00 25.00
SDD Drew Doughty 20.00 50.00
SDJ David Jones 6.00 15.00
SDP Dion Phaneuf 15.00 40.00
SDR Dwayne Roloson
SDS Daniel Sedin 12.00 30.00
SEN Evgeni Nabokov 10.00 25.00
SFB Fabian Brunnstrom 10.00 25.00
SGA Marian Gaborik 15.00 40.00
SGH Gordie Howe
SGI Claude Giroux 20.00 50.00
SGL Guillaume Latendresse 8.00 20.00
SHL Henrik Lundqvist 40.00 80.00
SHS Henrik Sedin 12.00 30.00
SHU Matt Hunwick 6.00 15.00
SJB Josh Bailey 8.00 20.00
SJD Jean-Pierre Dumont 6.00 15.00
SJH Jonas Hiller 12.00 30.00
SJI Jarome Iginla 20.00 50.00
SJM Jamie McGinn 8.00 20.00
SJN James Neal 10.00 25.00
SJP Justin Pogge 20.00 50.00
SJS Jack Skille 6.00 15.00
SJT Joe Thornton 20.00 50.00
SJV Jakub Voracek
SKA Karl Alzner 10.00 25.00
SKE Tyler Kennedy 10.00 25.00
SKM Kenndal McArdle 8.00 20.00
SKO Kyle Okposo 10.00 25.00
SKV Kris Versteeg 15.00 40.00
SLS Luke Schenn 15.00 40.00
SMA Steve Mason 15.00 40.00
SMB Mikkel Boedker 8.00 20.00
SMD Matt D'Agostini 12.00 30.00
SMG Mike Green 20.00 50.00
SMH Matthew Halischuk
SMI Michael Peca 8.00 20.00
SMK Mike Knuble 10.00 25.00
SMM Milan Michalek 6.00 15.00
SMN Markus Naslund 10.00 25.00
SMO Brendan Morrison 8.00 20.00
SMP Max Pacioretty 10.00 25.00
SMR Michal Repik 8.00 20.00
SMS Marc Staal 12.00 30.00
SMX Ben Maxwell 15.00 40.00
SNB Nicklas Backstrom 20.00 50.00
SNF Nikita Filatov 20.00 50.00
SNG Nathan Gerbe 12.00 30.00
SNI Matt Niskanen 6.00 15.00
SNK Nikolai Kulemin 8.00 20.00
SPB Patrik Berglund 20.00 50.00
SPD Pavel Datsyuk
SPE Patrik Elias 8.00 20.00
SPH Chris Phillips 6.00 15.00
SPI Alex Pietrangelo 8.00 20.00
SPO Jason Pominville 10.00 25.00
SRI Mike Ribeiro 6.00 15.00
SRS Ryan Smyth 10.00 25.00
SRY Bobby Ryan 12.00 30.00
SSC Sidney Crosby 125.00 200.00
SSD Steve Downie 6.00 15.00
SSG Simon Gagne 10.00 25.00
SSM Matt Smaby 8.00 20.00
SSS Steven Stamkos
SST Marco Sturm
SSV Simeon Varlamov 40.00 80.00
SSW Stephen Weiss 6.00 15.00
STE Tobias Enstrom
STG Tom Gilbert 6.00 15.00
STH Tomas Holmstrom 8.00 20.00
STK Tim Kennedy 10.00 25.00
STL Trevor Lewis 6.00 15.00
STO T.J. Oshie 15.00 40.00
STV Tomas Vokoun 10.00 25.00
STW Ty Wishart 10.00 25.00
SVT Viktor Tikhonov 10.00 25.00
SWG Wayne Gretzky 250.00 400.00
SZA Zach Boychuk 12.00 30.00
SZB Zach Bogosian 12.00 30.00

2009-10 O-Pee-Chee Stat Leaders

COMPLETE SET (17) 15.00 40.00
STATED ODDS 1:4
SL1 Evgeni Malkin 2.00 5.00
SL2 Alexander Ovechkin 3.00 8.00
SL3 Evgeni Malkin 2.00 5.00
SL4 Mike Richards 1.50 4.00
SL5 David Krejci .60 1.50
SL6 Daniel Carcillo .75 2.00
SL7 Thomas Vanek .75 2.00
SL8 Alexander Ovechkin 3.00 8.00
SL9 Jeff Carter .75 2.00
SL10 Alexander Ovechkin 3.00 8.00
SL11 Cal Clutterbuck .60 1.50
SL12 Evgeni Malkin 2.00 5.00
SL13 Steve Mason 1.25 3.00
SL14 Miikka Kiprusoff .75 2.00
SL15 Tim Thomas .75 2.00
SL16 Tim Thomas .75 2.00
SL17 Henrik Lundqvist 1.50 4.00

2009-10 O-Pee-Chee Top Draws Triple Jerseys

RANDOM INSERTS IN UPDATE SETS
TJATL Evander Kane 15.00 40.00
Nik Antropov
Ilya Kovalchuk
TJBOS Michael Ryder 15.00 40.00
Milan Lucic
Tuukka Rask
TJCGY Matt Pelech 12.00 30.00
Mikael Backlund
Kris Chucko
TJGR8 Mario Lemieux 50.00 100.00
Steve Yzerman
Wayne Gretzky
TJHOF Steve Shutt 12.00 30.00
Peter Stastny
Lanny McDonald
TJBEES Cam Neely 20.00 50.00
Adam Oates
Ray Bourque
TJBUFF Thomas Vanek 15.00 40.00
Jason Pominville
Derek Roy
TJCALG Al MacInnis 12.00 30.00
Theoren Fleury
Lanny McDonald
TJCAPS Mike Green 25.00 60.00
Alexander Ovechkin
Nicklas Backstrom
TJCOUV Steve Bernier 15.00 40.00
Michael Grabner
Sergei Shirokov
TJDALL Jamie Benn 12.00 30.00
Mike Modano
Marty Turco
TJNEXT James van Riemsdyk 20.00 50.00
John Tavares
Matt Duchene
TJPHIL James van Riemsdyk 15.00 40.00
Oskars Bartulis
Claude Giroux
TJRANG Matt Gilroy 20.00 50.00
Artem Anisimov
Michael Del Zotto
TJSANJ Benn Ferriero 15.00 40.00
Logan Couture
Jason Demers
TJCANES Eric Staal 15.00 40.00
Rod Brind'Amour
Cam Ward
TJFLAME Jarome Iginla 12.00 30.00
Miikka Kiprusoff
Dion Phaneuf
TJFLYER Mike Richards 15.00 40.00
Jeff Carter
Ray Emery
TJHTOWN Tomas Holmstrom 15.00 40.00
Chris Osgood
Johan Franzen
TJKINGS Alec Martinez 15.00 40.00
Alexander Frolov
Ryan Smyth
TJROOKD Victor Hedman 15.00 40.00
Tyler Myers
Erik Karlsson
TJROOKF Matt Duchene 20.00 50.00
James van Riemsdyk
Evander Kane
TJROOKG Antti Niemi 20.00 50.00
Jonas Gustavsson
Jhonas Enroth
TJTHRSH Evander Kane 15.00 40.00
Spencer Machacek
Ilya Kovalchuk
TJPHILLY James van Riemsdyk 20.00 50.00
Jeff Carter
Mike Richards

2009-10 O-Pee-Chee Trophy Winners

COMPLETE SET (13)
STATED ODDS 1:4
TW1 Alexander Ovechkin 3.00 8.00
TW2 Alexander Ovechkin 3.00 8.00
TW3 Alexander Ovechkin 3.00 8.00
TW4 Steve Sullivan .50 1.25
TW5 Tim Thomas .75 2.00
TW6 Pavel Datsyuk .75 2.00
TW7 Pavel Datsyuk .75 2.00
TW8 Zdeno Chara .50 1.25
TW9 Steve Mason 1.25 3.00
TW10 Evgeni Malkin 2.00 5.00
TW11 Ethan Moreau .50 1.25
TW12 Evgeni Malkin 2.00 5.00
TW13 Pittsburgh Penguins 2.00 5.00

1990-91 OPC Premier

The 1990-91 O-Pee-Chee Premier hockey set contained 132 standard-size cards. The fronts featured color action photos of the players and have the words "O-Pee-Chee Premier" in a gold border above the picture. Border colors according to team framed the photo. Horizontal backs contained 1989-90 and career statistics. A player photo appeared in the upper left hand corner. The checklist was numbered alphabetically.

COMPLETE SET (132) 25.00 50.00
COMP.FACT.SET (132) 40.00 80.00
1 Scott Arniel .05 .15
2 Jergus Baca RC .05 .15
3 Brian Bellows .05 .15
4 Jean-Claude Bergeron RC .05 .15
5 Daniel Berthiaume .15 .40
6 Rob Blake RC 1.00 2.50
7 Peter Bondra RC 1.00 2.50
8 Laurie Boschman .05 .15
9 Ray Bourque .40 1.00
10 Aaron Broten .05 .15
11 Greg Brown RC .05 .15
12 Jimmy Carson .05 .15
13 Chris Chelios .30 .75
14 Dino Ciccarelli .15 .40
15 Zdeno Ciger RC .05 .15
16 Paul Coffey .30 .75
17 Danton Cole RC .05 .15
18 Geoff Courtnall .05 .15
19 Mike Craig RC UER .05 .15
(Played Juniors at Oshawa, not Minors)
20 John Cullen .05 .15
21 Vincent Damphousse .05 .15
22 Gerald Diduck .05 .15
23 Kevin Dineen .05 .15
24 Per Djoos RC .05 .15
25 Tie Domi RC 1.00 2.50
26 Peter Douris RC .05 .15
27 Rob DiMaio RC .05 .15
28 Pat Elynuik .05 .15
29 Bob Essensa RC .40 1.00
30 Sergei Fedorov RC 2.50 6.00
31 Brent Fedyk RC .05 .15
32 Ron Francis .15 .40
33 Link Gaetz RC .05 .15
34 Troy Gamble RC .15 .40
35 Johan Garpenlov RC .05 .15
36 Mike Gartner .15 .40
37 Rick Green .05 .15
38 Wayne Gretzky 2.00 5.00
39 Jeff Hackett RC .60 1.50
40 Dale Hawerchuk .15 .40
41 Ron Hextall .15 .40
42 Bruce Hoffort RC .05 .15
43 Bobby Holik RC .40 1.00
44 Martin Hostak RC .05 .15
45 Phil Housley .15 .40
46 Jody Hull RC .05 .15
47 Brett Hull .75 2.00
48 Al Iafrate .15 .40
49 Peter Ing RC .15 .40
50 Jaromir Jagr RC 5.00 12.00
51 Curtis Joseph RC 2.00 5.00
52 Robert Kron RC .05 .15
53 Frantisek Kucera RC .05 .15
54 Dale Kushner RC .05 .15
55 Guy Lafleur .30 .75
56 Pat LaFontaine .30 .75
57 Mike Lalor RC .05 .15
58 Steve Larmer .15 .40
59 Jiri Latal RC .05 .15
60 Jamie Leach RC .05 .15
61 Brian Leetch .40 1.00
62 Claude Lemieux .05 .15
63 Mario Lemieux 1.50 4.00
64 Craig Ludwig .05 .15
65 Al MacInnis .15 .40
66 Mikko Makela .05 .15
67 David Marcinyshyn RC .05 .15
68 Stephane Matteau RC .05 .15
69 Brad McCrimmon .05 .15
70 Kirk McLean .15 .40
71 Mark Messier .30 .75
72 Kelly Miller .05 .15
73 Kevin Miller RC .05 .15
74 Mike Modano RC 2.50 6.00
75 Alexander Mogilny RC 1.00 2.50
76 Andy Moog .30 .75
77 Joe Mullen .15 .40
78 Kirk Muller .05 .15
79 Pat Murray RC .05 .15
80 Jarmo Myllys RC .05 .15
81 Petr Nedved RC .40 1.00
82 Cam Neely .30 .75
83 Bernie Nicholls .15 .40
84 Joe Nieuwendyk .15 .40
85 Chris Nilan .05 .15
86 Owen Nolan RC 1.00 2.50
87 Brian Noonan RC .05 .15
88 Adam Oates .15 .40
89 Greg Parks RC .05 .15
90 Adrien Plavsic RC .05 .15
91 Keith Primeau RC .60 1.50
92 Brian Propp .05 .15
93 Dan Quinn .05 .15
94 Bill Ranford .15 .40
95 Robert Reichel RC .40 1.00
96 Mike Ricci RC .40 1.00
97 Steven Rice RC .05 .15
98 Stephane Richer .15 .40
99 Luc Robitaille .15 .40
100 Jeremy Roenick RC 2.00 5.00
101 Patrick Roy 1.50 4.00
102 Joe Sakic 1.00 2.50
103 Denis Savard .15 .40
104 Anatoli Semenov RC .05 .15
105 Brendan Shanahan .30 .75
106 Ray Sheppard .15 .40
107 Mike Sillinger RC UER .05 .15
(Played Juniors at Regina, not Minors)
108 Ilkka Sinisalo .05 .15
109 Bobby Smith .15 .40
110 Paul Stanton RC .05 .15
111 Kevin Stevens RC .30 .75
112 Scott Stevens .15 .40
113 Alan Stewart RC .05 .15
114 Mats Sundin RC 2.00 5.00
115 Brent Sutter .05 .15
116 Tim Sweeney RC .05 .15
117 Peter Taglianetti .05 .15
118 John Tanner RC .05 .15
119 Dave Tippett .05 .15
120 Rick Tocchet .15 .40
121 Bryan Trottier .15 .40
122 John Tucker .05 .15
123 Darren Turcotte RC .20 .50
124 Pierre Turgeon .15 .40
125 Randy Velischek .05 .15
126 Mike Vernon .15 .40
127 Wes Walz RC .05 .15
128 Carey Wilson .05 .15
129 Doug Wilson .15 .40
130 Steve Yzerman 1.25 3.00
131 Peter Zezel .05 .15
132 Checklist 1-132 .05 .15

1991-92 OPC Premier

The 1991-92 O-Pee-Chee Premier hockey set contains 198 standard-size cards. Color player photos are bordered above and below in gold. Player name, team and position appear at the bottom. The backs have a small color player photo, biography, team logo and statistics. A Konstantinov variation can be found with Lidstrom's photo on the back. Very few of these variations have been located. To commemorate the 75th Anniversary of the NHL, throwback sweaters were worn several times during the 1991-92 campaign by the original six teams. Cards portraying players in those sweaters are indicated by ORIG6.

COMPLETE SET (198) 4.00 10.00
COMP.FACT.SET (198) 5.00 12.00
1 Dale Hawerchuk .05 .15
2 Ray Sheppard .01 .05
3 Wayne Gretzky UER .60 1.50
(Canada Cup stats incorrect)
4 John MacLean .05 .15
5 Pat Verbeek .01 .05
6 Doug Wilson .05 .15
7 Adam Oates .05 .15
8 Bob McGill .01 .05
9 Mike Vernon .05 .15
10 Glenn Anderson .05 .15
11 Tony Amonte RC .60 1.50
12 Stephen Leach .01 .05
13 Steve Duchesne .01 .05
14 Patrick Roy .50 1.25
15 Jarmo Myllys .01 .05
16 Yanic Dupre RC .01 .05
17 Chris Chelios .08 .25
18 Bill Ranford .05 .15
19 Ed Belfour .08 .25
20 Michel Picard RC .01 .05
21 Rob Zettler .01 .05
22 Kevin Todd RC .01 .05
23 Mike Ricci .08 .25
24 Jaromir Jagr .15 .40
25 Sergei Nemchinov .01 .05
26 Kevin Stevens .01 .05
27 Dan Quinn .01 .05
28 Adam Graves .05 .15
29 Pat Jablonski RC .05 .15
30 Scott Mellanby .01 .05
31 Tomas Forslund RC .01 .05
32 Doug Weight RC .50 1.25
33 Peter Ing .05 .15
34 Luc Robitaille .05 .15
35 Scott Niedermayer .01 .05
36 Dean Evason .01 .05
37 John Tonelli .01 .05
38 Ron Hextall .05 .15
39 Troy Mallette .01 .05
40 Tony Hrkac .01 .05
41 Ken Hodge Jr. .01 .05
42 Kip Miller .01 .05
43 Randy Burridge .01 .05
44 Rob Blake .05 .15
45 Sergei Makarov .01 .05
46 Luke Richardson .01 .05
47 Craig Berube .01 .05
48 Joe Nieuwendyk .05 .15
49 Brett Hull .10 .30
50 Phil Housley .05 .15
51 Mark Messier .08 .25
52 Jeremy Roenick .08 .25
53 Dave Christian .01 .05
54 Dave Barr .01 .05
55 Sergio Momesso .01 .05
56 Pat Falloon .01 .05
57 Brian Leetch .08 .25
58 Russ Courtnall .01 .05
59 Pierre Turgeon .05 .15
60 Steve Larmer .05 .15
61 Petr Klima .01 .05
62 Mikhail Tatarinov .01 .05
63 Rick Tocchet .05 .15
64 Pat LaFontaine .08 .25
65 Rob Pearson RC .01 .05
66 Glen Featherstone .01 .05
67 Pavel Bure .08 .25
68 Sergei Fedorov .15 .40
69 Kelly Kisio .01 .05
70 Joe Sakic .20 .50
71 Denis Savard .05 .15
72 Andrew Cassels .01 .05
73 Steve Yzerman .50 1.25
74 Todd Elik .01 .05
75 Troy Murray .01 .05
76 Rob Ramage .01 .05
77 Trevor Linden .05 .15
78 Mike Richter .08 .25
79 Paul Coffey .08 .25
80 Craig Ludwig .01 .05
81 Al MacInnis .05 .15
82 Tomas Sandstrom .01 .05
83 Tim Kerr .01 .05
84 Scott Stevens .05 .15
85 Steve Kasper .01 .05
86 Kirk Muller .01 .05
87 Pat MacLeod RC .01 .05
88 Kevin Hatcher .01 .05
89 Wayne Presley .01 .05
90 Darryl Sydor .05 .15
91 Tom Chorske .01 .05
92 Theo Fleury .05 .15
93 Craig Janney .05 .15
94 Rod Brind'Amour .08 .25
95 Ron Sutter .01 .05
96 Matt DelGuidice RC .01 .05
97 Rollie Melanson .01 .05
98 Tom Kurvers .01 .05
99 Bryan Marchment RC .05 .15
100 Grant Fuhr .08 .25
101 Geoff Courtnall .05 .15
102 Joel Otto .01 .05
103 Tom Barrasso .05 .15
104 Vincent Damphousse .01 .05
105 John LeClair RC .60 1.50
106 Gary Leeman .01 .05
107 Cam Neely .08 .25
108 Jeff Hackett .05 .15
109 Stu Barnes .01 .05
110 Neil Wilkinson .01 .05
111 Jari Kurri .08 .25
112 Jon Casey .05 .15
113 Stephane Richer .05 .15
114 Mario Lemieux .60 1.50
115 Brad Jones .01 .05
116 Wendel Clark .05 .15
117 Nicklas Lidstrom RC .60 1.50
118A Vladimir Konstantinov RC 15.00 30.00
ERR
(Lidstrom photo on back)
118B Vladimir Konstantinov RC .30 .75
COR
119 Ray Bourque .15 .40
120 Ron Francis .05 .15
121 Esa Tikkanen .01 .05
122 Randy Hillier .01 .05
123 Randy Gilhen .01 .05
124 Barry Pederson .01 .05
125 Charlie Huddy .01 .05
(Bruce McNall in background)
126 Gary Roberts .05 .15
127 John Cullen .01 .05
128 Dave Gagner .01 .05
129 Bob Kudelski .01 .05
130 Brendan Shanahan .08 .25
131 Dirk Graham .01 .05
132 Checklist 1-99 .01 .05
133 Andy Moog .08 .25
134 Gary Leeman ORIG6 .01 .05
135 Steve Larmer ORIG6 .05 .15
136 Steve Smith .01 .05
137 Dave Manson .01 .05
138 Nelson Emerson .01 .05
139 Doug Weight ORIG6 .08 .25
140 Uwe Krupp .01 .05
141 Peter Douris ORIG6 .01 .05
142 Steve Yzerman ORIG6 .30 .75
143 Derian Hatcher .05 .15
144 Vladimir Ruzicka ORIG6 .01 .05
145 Kirk Muller ORIG6 .01 .05
146 Darrin Shannon .01 .05
147 Mike Gartner ORIG6 .05 .15
148 Bob Carpenter ORIG6 .01 .05
149 Josef Beranek RC .01 .05
150 Chris Chelios ORIG6 .08 .25
151 Bob Rouse ORIG6 .01 .05
152 Guy Carbonneau ORIG6 .05 .15
153 Joe Mullen .05 .15
154 Ken Hodge Jr. ORIG6 .01 .05
155 Vladimir Konstantinov ORIG6 .08 .25

2009-10 O-Pee-Chee Buyback Autographs

156 Brent Sutter .01 .05
157 Eric Desjardins ORIG6 .05 .15
158 Kirk McLean UER .05 .15
(Photo on back actually Frank Caprice)
159 John Tonelli ORIG6 .01 .05
160 Rob Cimetta ORIG6 .01 .05
161 Shayne Corson .01 .05
162 Russ Romaniuk RC .01 .05
163 Nicklas Lidstrom ORIG6 .08 .25
164 Mike Gartner .05 .15
165 Curtis Joseph .08 .25
166 Brian Mullen .01 .05
167 Jimmy Carson .01 .05
168 Petr Svoboda ORIG6 .01 .05
169 Troy Crowder .01 .05
170 Patrick Roy ORIG6 .30 .75
171 Adam Creighton .01 .05
172 James Patrick ORIG6 .01 .05
173 Sergei Fedorov ORIG6 .15 .40
174 Jeremy Roenick ORIG6 .08 .25
175 Tim Cheveldae ORIG6 .05 .15
176 Dimitri Khristich .01 .05
177 Wendel Clark ORIG6 .05 .15
178 Andrei Lomakin .01 .05
179 Benoit Hogue .01 .05
180 Dave Ellett ORIG6 .01 .05
181 Mathieu Schneider ORIG6 .01 .05
182 Kay Whitmore .05 .15
183 Brian Leetch ORIG6 .08 .25
184 Sylvain Turgeon ORIG6 .01 .05
185 Brian Bradley ORIG6 .01 .05
186 John LeClair ORIG6 .20 .50
187 Paul Fenton .01 .05
188 Alain Cote ORIG6 .01 .05
189 Mike Krushelnyski .01 .05
(ORIG6 UER
(Misspelled on back as Krushelnynski)
190 Brian Bradley .01 .05
191 Grant Fuhr ORIG6 .08 .25
192 Ray Bourque ORIG6 .08 .25
193 Owen Nolan .08 .25
194 Russ Courtnall ORIG6 .01 .05
195 Steve Thomas .01 .05
196 Ed Olczyk .01 .05
197 Chris Terreri .05 .15
198 Checklist 100-198 .01 .05

1992-93 OPC Premier

The 1992-93 O-Pee-Chee Premier hockey set consists of 132 standard-sized cards. The fronts feature action color player photos with white borders. A team color-coded stripe accents the top edge of each picture. The O-Pee-Chee logo overlaps the picture at the lower right corner. The player's name and position appear in the bottom border. The backs show a slightly offset, pale, team color-coded panel which carries a close-up photo and biographical data. A darker team color-coded bar with a speckled effect presents statistics and appears at the bottom. The team logo overlaps the picture panel at the lower left corner of the photo. Each pack contained an insert from either the Top Rookie set or the 22-card Star Performers set. According to O-Pee-Chee, every ninth pack contained a Top Rookie card as its insert with the other packs containing a Star Performers card. The production quantity reportedly was 7,500 20-box wax cases.

COMPLETE SET (132) 4.00 10.00
1 Dave Christian .01 .05
2 Christian Ruuttu .01 .05
3 Vincent Damphousse .01 .05
4 Chris Lindberg .01 .05
5 Bill Lindsay RC .01 .05
6 Dmitri Kvartalnov RC .01 .05
7 Darcy Loewen .01 .05
8 Ed Courtenay .01 .05
9 Sergei Krivokrasov .01 .05
10 Shawn Antoski .01 .05
11 Andre Racicot .02 .10
12 Marty McInnis .01 .05
13 Alexei Zhamnov .02 .10
14 Keith Jones RC .08 .25
15 Steve Konowalchuk RC .02 .10
16 Darryl Sydor .01 .05
17 Janne Ojanen .01 .05
18 Doug Zmolek RC .01 .05
19 Michael Nylander RC .02 .10
20 Russ Courtnall .01 .05
21 Martin Straka RC .40 1.00
22 Kevin Dahl RC .01 .05
23 Kent Manderville .01 .05
24 Steve Heinze .01 .05
25 Philippe Bozon .01 .05
26 Brent Fedyk .01 .05
27 Kris Draper .02 .10
28 Brad Schlegel .01 .05
29 Patric Kjellberg RC .08 .25
30 Ted Donato .01 .05
31 Vyatcheslav Butsayev RC .01 .05
32 Tyler Wright .01 .05
33 Tom Pederson RC .01 .05
34 Jim Hiller RC .01 .05
35 Chris Luongo RC .01 .05
36 Robert Petrovicky RC .01 .05
37 Jean-Francois Quintin .01 .05
38 Chris Dahlquist .01 .05
39 Daniel Laperriere RC .01 .05
40 Guy Hebert RC .30 .75
41 Ed Ronan RC .01 .05
42 Shawn Cronin .01 .05
43 Keith Tkachuk .08 .25
44 Dino Ciccarelli .02 .10
45 Doug Evans .01 .05
46 Roman Hamrlik RC .15 .40
47 Robert Lang RC .01 .05
48 Kerry Huffman .01 .05
49 Pat Conacher .01 .05
50 Dominik Hasek .40 1.00
51 Dominic Roussel .02 .10
52 Glen Murray .01 .05
53 Igor Korolev RC .02 .10
54 Jiri Slegr .01 .05
55 Mikael Andersson .01 .05
56 Bob Babcock RC .01 .05
57 Ron Hextall .02 .10
58 Jeff Daniels .01 .05
59 Doug Crossman .01 .05
60 Viktor Gordiouk RC .01 .05
61 Adam Creighton .01 .05
62 Rob DiMaio .01 .05
63 Eric Weinrich .01 .05
64 Vitali Prokhorov RC .01 .05
65 Dimitri Yushkevich RC .02 .10
66 Evgeny Davydov .01 .05
67 Dixon Ward RC .02 .10
68 Teemu Selanne .50 1.25
69 Rob Zamuner RC .02 .10
70 Joe Reekie .01 .05
71 Slava Kozlov .02 .10
72 Philippe Boucher .01 .05
73 Phil Bourque .01 .05
74 Yvon Corriveau .01 .05
75 Brian Bellows .01 .05
76 Wendell Young .02 .10
77 Bobby Holik .02 .10
78 Bob Carpenter .01 .05
79 Scott Lachance .01 .05
80 John Druce .01 .05
81 Keith Carney RC .30 .75
82 Neil Brady .01 .05
83 Richard Matvichuk RC .02 .10
84 Sergei Bautin RC .01 .05
85 Patrick Poulin .01 .05
86 Gordie Roberts .01 .05
87 Kay Whitmore .02 .10
88 Steph Beauregard .02 .10
89 Vladimir Malakhov .01 .05
90 Richard Smehlik RC .01 .05
91 Mike Ricci .02 .10
92 Sean Burke .02 .10
93 Andrei Kovalenko RC .02 .10
94 Shawn McEachern .01 .05
95 Pat Jablonski .02 .10
96 Oleg Petrov RC .01 .05
97 Glenn Mulvenna RC .01 .05
98 Jason Woolley RC .01 .05
99 Mark Greig .01 .05
100 Nikolai Borschevsky RC .01 .05
101 Joe Juneau .02 .10
102 Eric Lindros .08 .25
103 Darius Kasparaitis .01 .05
104 Sandis Ozolinsh .01 .05
105 Stan Drulia RC .01 .05
106 Mike Needham RC .01 .05
107 Norm Maciver .01 .05
108 Sylvain Lefebvre .01 .05
109 Tommy Sjodin RC .01 .05
110 Bob Sweeney .01 .05
111 Brian Mullen .01 .05
112 Peter Sidorkiewicz .02 .10
113 Scott Niedermayer .01 .05
114 Felix Potvin .08 .25
115 Robb Stauber .02 .10
116 Sylvain Turgeon .01 .05
117 Mark Janssens .01 .05
118 Darren Banks RC .01 .05
119 Pat Elynuik .01 .05
120 Bill Guerin RC .60 1.50
121 Reggie Savage .01 .05
122 Enrico Ciccone .01 .05
123 Chris Kontos RC .01 .05
124 Martin Rucinsky .01 .05
125 Alexei Zhitnik .01 .05
126 Alexei Kovalev .01 .05
127 Tim Kerr .01 .05
128 Guy Larose .01 .05
129 Brent Gilchrist .01 .05
130 Steve Duchesne .01 .05
131 Drake Berehowsky .01 .05
132 Checklist 1-132 .01 .05

1992-93 OPC Premier Star Performers

This 22-card standard-size set was randomly inserted in 1992-93 O-Pee-Chee Premier foil packs. According to O-Pee-Chee, the insertion rate was eight out of every nine packs. The other packs contained Top Rookie inserts.

COMPLETE SET (22) 4.00 10.00
1 Ray Ferraro .05 .15
2 Dale Hunter .15 .40
3 Murray Craven .05 .15
4 Paul Coffey .20 .50
5 Jeremy Roenick .25 .60
6 Denis Savard .15 .40
7 Jon Casey .15 .40
8 Doug Gilmour .15 .40
9 Rod Brind'Amour .15 .40
10 Pavel Bure .20 .50
11 Joe Sakic .40 1.00
12 Pat Falloon .05 .15
13 Adam Oates .15 .40
14 Gary Roberts .05 .15
15 Mark Messier .20 .50
16 Phil Housley .05 .15
17 Pat LaFontaine .20 .50
18 Stephane Richer .15 .40
19 Bill Ranford .15 .40
20 Sergei Fedorov .30 .75
21 Brett Hull .30 .75
22 Mario Lemieux 1.00 2.50

1992-93 OPC Premier Top Rookies

This four-card standard-size set was randomly inserted in 1992-93 O-Pee-Chee Premier foil packs. According to O-Pee-Chee, eight out of nine packs contained a Star Performer insert card, while the ninth pack contained a Top Rookie card as its insert.

COMPLETE SET (4) .60 1.50
1 Eric Lindros .20 .50
2 Roman Hamrlik .30 .75
3 Dominic Roussel .08 .25
4 Felix Potvin .20 .50

1993-94 OPC Premier

COMPLETE SET (528) 8.00 20.00
COMPLETE SERIES 1 (264) 4.00 10.00
COMPLETE SERIES 2 (264) 4.00 10.00
*OPC PREMIER: .4X TO 1X TOPPS PREMIER

1993-94 OPC Premier Gold

COMPLETE SET (528) 100.00 200.00
COMP.SERIES 1 (264) 50.00 100.00
COMP.SERIES 2 (264) 50.00 100.00
*GOLD VETS: 2.5X TO 6X BASIC CARDS
*GOLD ROOKIES: 1.5X TO 4X BASIC CARDS
ONE PER OPC PACK/FOUR PER OPC JUMBO

1993-94 OPC Premier Black Gold

These 24 standard-size Black Gold cards were randomly inserted in O-Pee-Chee packs. The white-bordered fronts feature color player action shots with darkened backgrounds. Gold-foil stripes above and below the photo carry multiple-set logos. The player's name appears in white lettering within a black stripe through the lower gold-foil stripe. The white-bordered and horizontal back carries a color player cutout on one side, and career highlights in French and English within a purple rectangle on the other.

1 Wayne Gretzky 8.00 20.00
2 Vincent Damphousse .60 1.50
3 Adam Oates 1.00 2.50
4 Phil Housley .60 1.50
5 Mike Vernon .60 1.50
6 Mats Sundin 1.50 4.00
7 Pavel Bure 6.00 15.00
8 Patrick Roy 4.00 10.00
9 Tom Barrasso .60 1.50
10 Alexander Mogilny 1.50 4.00
11 Doug Gilmour 1.00 2.50
12 Eric Lindros 10.00 25.00
13 Theo Fleury .60 1.50
14 Pat LaFontaine 1.00 2.50
15 Joe Sakic 1.50 4.00
16 Ed Belfour 1.00 2.50
17 Felix Potvin 4.00 10.00
18 Mario Lemieux 5.00 12.00
19 Jaromir Jagr 3.00 8.00
20 Teemu Selanne 3.00 8.00
21 Ray Bourque 1.00 2.50
22 Brett Hull 2.50 6.00
23 Steve Yzerman 2.00 5.00
24 Kirk Muller .60 1.50

1993-94 OPC Premier Team Canada

Randomly inserted in second-series OPC Premier packs, these 19 standard-size cards feature borderless color player action shots on their fronts. The player's name and the Hockey Canada logo appear at the bottom. The red back carries the player's name and position at the top, followed below by biography, player photo, career highlights in English and French, and statistics. The cards are numbered on the back as "X of 19."

COMPLETE SET (19) 10.00 25.00
1 Brett Lindros .75 2.00
2 Manny Legace .75 2.00
3 Adrian Aucoin .60 1.50
4 Ken Lovsin .60 1.50
5 Craig Woodcroft .60 1.50
6 Derek Mayer .60 1.50
7 Fabian Joseph .60 1.50
8 Todd Brost .60 1.50
9 Chris Therien .75 2.00
10 Brad Turner .60 1.50
11 Trevor Sim .60 1.50
12 Todd Hlushko .60 1.50
13 Dwayne Norris .60 1.50
14 Chris Kontos .60 1.50
15 Petr Nedved .75 2.00
16 Brian Savage .75 2.00
17 Paul Kariya 1.50 4.00
18 Corey Hirsch .75 2.00
19 Todd Warriner .75 2.00

1994-95 OPC Premier

COMPLETE SET (550) 15.00 40.00
COMP.SERIES 1 (275) 6.00 15.00
COMP.SERIES 2 (275) 10.00 25.00
*OPC PREMIER: .6X TO 1.5X TOPPS PREMIER

1994-95 OPC Premier Finest Inserts

The 23 cards in this set were randomly inserted at a rate of 1:36 OPC Premier series 1 packs. The set includes top rookies of 1993-94. Cards feature an isolated player photo over a textured rainbow background. A reflective rainbow border is broken up by the player name. Premier Finest is written across the top of the card. Backs have a small player photo with brief personal information, and statistical breakdown. Cards are numbered "X of 23".

COMPLETE SET (23) 20.00 50.00
1 Patrik Carnback .60 1.50
2 Bryan Smolinski .60 1.50
3 Derek Plante .60 1.50
4 Alexander Karpovtsev .60 1.50
5 Trevor Kidd 1.25 3.00
6 Iain Fraser .60 1.50
7 Alexandre Daigle .60 1.50
8 Chris Osgood 2.00 5.00
9 Rob Niedermayer .60 1.50
10 Jason Arnott .60 1.50
11 Chris Pronger 2.00 5.00
12 Jesse Belanger .60 1.50
13 Oleg Petrov .60 1.50
14 Martin Brodeur 8.00 20.00
15 Alexei Yashin .60 1.50
16 Mikael Renberg 1.25 3.00
17 Boris Mironov .60 1.50
18 Damian Rhodes 1.25 3.00
19 Darren McCarty .60 1.50
20 Chris Gratton 1.25 3.00
21 Jamie McLennan .60 1.50
22 Nathan Lafayette .60 1.50
23 Jeff Shantz .60 1.50

1994-95 OPC Premier Special Effects

*OPC SE: .6X TO 1.5X TOPPS SPEC.EFFECT
STATED ODDS 1:2 HOB/RET, 2:1 JUMBO

2007-08 OPC Premier

STATED PRINT RUN 299 SERIAL #'d SETS
STATED PRINT RUN 299 SERIAL #'d SETS
1 Bernie Parent 3.00 8.00
2 Al MacInnis 2.00 5.00
3 Rob Blake 2.00 5.00
4 Bobby Orr 10.00 25.00
5 Denis Potvin 2.00 5.00
6 Nicklas Lidstrom 2.50 6.00
7 Phil Esposito 4.00 10.00
8 Cam Neely 2.50 6.00
9 Gordie Howe 6.00 15.00
10 Guy Lafleur 6.00 15.00
11 Mark Messier 5.00 12.00
12 Jarome Iginla 4.00 10.00
13 Mats Sundin 2.50 6.00
14 Brendan Shanahan 2.50 6.00
15 Dany Heatley 3.00 8.00
16 Bobby Clarke 2.50 6.00
17 Jari Kurri 2.50 6.00
18 Larry Robinson 3.00 8.00
19 Joe Sakic 5.00 12.00
20 Dino Ciccarelli 2.00 5.00
21 Borje Salming 2.00 5.00
22 Mike Bossy 2.50 6.00
23 Milan Hejduk 2.00 5.00
24 Bernie Federko 1.50 4.00
25 Stan Mikita 2.00 5.00
26 Peter Stastny 2.00 5.00
27 Frank Mahovlich 4.00 10.00
28 Alexander Semin 2.50 6.00
29 Marc-Andre Fleury 2.50 6.00
30 Martin Brodeur 6.00 15.00
31 Grant Fuhr 4.00 10.00
32 Billy Smith 2.50 6.00
33 Patrick Roy 8.00 20.00
34 Miikka Kiprusoff 3.00 8.00
35 Tony Esposito 4.00 10.00
36 Jean-Sebastien Giguere 2.00 5.00
37 Patrice Bergeron 2.50 6.00
38 Dominik Hasek 3.00 8.00
39 Henrik Zetterberg 2.50 6.00
40 Lee Stempniak 1.50 4.00
41 Keith Tkachuk 2.00 5.00
42 Alexander Ovechkin 8.00 20.00
43 Zach Parise 2.00 5.00
44 Andy Bathgate 2.00 5.00
45 Rick DiPietro 2.00 5.00
46 Alexander Radulov 2.50 6.00
47 Daniel Briere 2.50 6.00
48 Jason Spezza 2.50 6.00
49 Ray Emery 2.00 5.00
50 Marian Gaborik 3.00 8.00
51 Simon Gagne 2.50 6.00
52 Roberto Luongo 4.00 10.00
53 Saku Koivu 2.50 6.00
54 Paul Kariya 2.50 6.00
55 Lanny McDonald 2.50 6.00
56 Darryl Sittler 2.00 5.00
57 Scott Stevens 2.00 5.00
58 Joe Thornton 3.00 8.00
59 Mike Modano 2.50 6.00
60 Clark Gillies 2.00 5.00
61 Rick Nash 2.50 6.00
62 Dale Hawerchuk 2.00 5.00
63 Anze Kopitar 2.50 6.00
64 Gilbert Perreault 2.00 5.00
65 Daniel Alfredsson 2.00 5.00
66 Mario Lemieux 8.00 20.00
67 Brad Richards 2.00 5.00
68 Jaromir Jagr 4.00 10.00
69 Bobby Hull 4.00 10.00
70 Mark Recchi 1.50 4.00
71 Evgeni Malkin 6.00 15.00
72 Jordan Staal 3.00 8.00
73 Michael Ryder 1.50 4.00
74 Eric Staal 2.50 6.00
75 Olli Jokinen 1.50 4.00
76 Pavel Datsyuk 2.50 6.00
77 Ray Bourque 3.00 8.00
78 Vincent Lecavalier 2.50 6.00
79 Dwayne Roloson 2.00 5.00
80 Henrik Lundqvist 3.00 8.00
81 Phil Kessel 2.50 6.00
82 Tomas Vokoun 2.50 6.00
83 Steve Shutt 2.00 5.00
84 Thomas Vanek 2.00 5.00
85 Patrik Elias 1.50 4.00
86 Martin St. Louis 2.00 5.00
87 Sidney Crosby 12.00 30.00
88 Paul Stastny 2.50 6.00
89 Cam Ward 2.50 6.00
90 Marty Turco 2.50 6.00
91 Sergei Fedorov 2.50 6.00
92 Patrick Marleau 2.00 5.00
93 Jason Arnott 1.50 4.00
94 Jonathan Cheechoo 2.00 5.00
95 Ryan Getzlaf 2.00 5.00
96 Shane Doan 1.50 4.00
97 Ryan Miller 2.50 6.00
98 Markus Naslund 2.50 6.00
99 Wayne Gretzky 12.00 30.00
100 Alexander Frolov 1.50 4.00
101 Andrew Cogliano JSY AU RC 15.00 40.00
102 Andy Greene JSY AU RC 6.00 15.00
103 Anton Stralman JSY AU RC 8.00 20.00
104 Bobby Ryan JSY AU RC 25.00 60.00
105 Brandon Dubinsky JSY AU RC 10.00 25.00
106 Brian Elliott JSY AU RC 8.00 20.00
107 Bryan Little JSY AU RC 10.00 25.00
108 Carey Price JSY AU RC 75.00 150.00
109 Cory Murphy JSY AU RC 6.00 15.00
110 Curtis McElhinney JSY AU RC 8.00 20.00
111 Casey Borer JSY AU RC 6.00 15.00
112 David Krejci JSY AU RC 12.00 30.00
113 David Perron JSY AU RC 10.00 25.00
114 Drew Miller JSY AU RC 6.00 15.00
115 Erik Johnson JSY AU RC 12.00 30.00
116 Frans Nielsen JSY AU RC 6.00 15.00
117 Devin Setoguchi JSY AU RC 12.00 30.00
118 Jack Johnson JSY AU RC 10.00 25.00
119 James Sheppard JSY AU RC 6.00 15.00
120 Jannik Hansen JSY AU RC 6.00 15.00
121 Jared Boll JSY AU RC 6.00 15.00
122 Jaroslav Halak JSY AU RC 20.00 50.00
123 Jaroslav Hlinka JSY AU RC 8.00 20.00
124 Jiri Tlusty JSY AU RC 15.00 40.00
125 Jack Skille JSY AU RC 10.00 25.00
126 Jonathan Bernier JSY AU RC 15.00 40.00
127 Jonathan Sigalet JSY AU RC 6.00 15.00
128 Jonathan Toews JSY AU RC 60.00 120.00
129 Tuukka Rask JSY AU RC 15.00 40.00
130 Kyle Chipchura JSY AU RC 10.00 25.00
131 Lauri Tukonen JSY AU RC 6.00 15.00
132 Sergei Kostitsyn JSY AU RC 20.00 50.00
133 Marc Staal JSY AU RC 15.00 40.00
134 Martin Hanzal JSY AU RC 8.00 20.00
135 Mason Raymond JSY AU RC 15.00 40.00
136 T.J. Hensick JSY AU RC 8.00 20.00
137 Matt Niskanen JSY AU RC 6.00 15.00
138 Matt Smaby JSY AU RC 6.00 15.00
139 Milan Lucic JSY AU RC 15.00 40.00
140 Nick Foligno JSY AU RC 10.00 25.00
141 Nicklas Backstrom JSY AU RC 25.00 60.00
142 Nicklas Bergfors JSY AU RC 8.00 20.00
143 Ondrej Pavelec JSY AU RC 10.00 25.00
144 Patrick Kane JSY AU RC 50.00 100.00
145 Peter Mueller JSY AU RC 20.00 50.00
146 Petr Kalus JSY AU RC 6.00 15.00
147 Rob Schremp JSY AU RC 8.00 20.00
148 Rod Pelley JSY AU RC 6.00 15.00
149 Ryan Callahan JSY AU RC 10.00 25.00
150 Ryan Carter JSY AU RC 8.00 20.00
151 Steve Downie JSY AU RC 8.00 20.00
152 Sam Gagner JSY AU RC 12.00 30.00
153 Stefan Meyer JSY AU RC 6.00 15.00
154 Steve Wagner JSY AU RC 6.00 15.00
155 Tobias Enstrom JSY AU RC 10.00 25.00
156 Tobias Stephan JSY AU RC 8.00 20.00
157 David Jones JSY AU RC 8.00 20.00
158 Torrey Mitchell JSY AU RC 8.00 20.00
159 Tyler Weiman JSY AU RC 8.00 20.00
160 Ville Koistinen JSY AU RC 6.00 15.00

2007-08 OPC Premier Black

STATED PRINT RUN 1 SER.#'d SET
NOT PRICED DUE TO SCARCITY

2007-08 OPC Premier Gold

*GOLD: .3X TO .8X BASE
STATED PRINT RUN 75 SER.#'d SETS
*GOLD JSY AU: .5X TO 1.2X BASE
GOLD JSY AU PRINT RUN 50 SER.#'d SETS
108 Carey Price JSY AU 75.00 150.00
128 Jonathan Toews JSY AU 100.00 200.00

2007-08 OPC Premier Gold Spectrum

(1-100) STATED PRINT RUN 5 SER.#'d SETS
(101-160) STATED PRINT RUN 15 SER.#'d SETS
NOT PRICED DUE TO SCARCITY

2007-08 OPC Premier Silver Spectrum

*SILVER SPECTRUM: .8X TO 2X
STATED PRINT RUN 25 SER.#'d SETS
*SILVER SPECTRUM JSY AU: .6X TO 1.5X
JSY AU PRINT RUN 35 SER.#'d SETS
108 Carey Price JSY AU 100.00 200.00
128 Jonathan Toews JSY AU 100.00 200.00

2007-08 OPC Premier Autographed Premier Stitchings

STATED PRINT RUN 50 SERIAL #'d SETS
APSAB Andy Bathgate 15.00 40.00
APSAK Anze Kopitar 40.00 80.00
APSBC Bobby Clarke 20.00 50.00
APSBY Mike Bossy 40.00 80.00
APSCN Cam Neely 20.00 50.00
APSCW Cam Ward 20.00 50.00
APSDS Darryl Sittler 15.00 40.00
APSES Eric Staal 30.00 60.00
APSJB Johnny Bucyk 20.00 50.00
APSJC Jonathan Cheechoo 20.00 50.00
APSJG Jean-Sebastien Giguere 15.00 40.00
APSJI Jarome Iginla 30.00 60.00
APSLR Larry Robinson 15.00 40.00
APSMF Marc-Andre Fleury 20.00 50.00
APSMM Mike Modano 20.00 50.00
APSMN Markus Naslund 20.00 50.00
APSMR Michael Ryder 12.00 30.00
APSMS Martin St. Louis 15.00 40.00
APSMT Marty Turco 20.00 50.00
APSNL Nicklas Lidstrom 25.00 50.00
APSPS Peter Stastny 15.00 40.00
APSRN Rick Nash 20.00 50.00
APSSA Borje Salming 15.00 40.00
APSSD Shane Doan 12.00 30.00
APSSG Simon Gagne 20.00 50.00
APSSK Saku Koivu 25.00 50.00
APSSM Stan Mikita 15.00 40.00
APSST Paul Stastny 25.00 50.00
APSTV Thomas Vanek 15.00 40.00
APSVL Vincent Lecavalier 20.00 50.00
APSVO Tomas Vokoun 20.00 50.00

2007-08 OPC Premier Autographed Premier Stitchings 15

STATED PRINT RUN 15 SERIAL #'d SETS
NOT PRICED DUE TO SCARCITY

2007-08 OPC Premier Autographs Duos

STATED PRINT RUN 75 SERIAL #'d SETS
PP2BC Johnny Bucyk 12.00 30.00
Bobby Clarke
PP2BF Martin Brodeur 50.00 100.00
Marc-Andre Fleury
PP2BK Patrice Bergeron 12.00 30.00
Phil Kessel
PP2CH Bobby Clarke 20.00 50.00
Ron Hextall
PP2DF Nicklas Lidstrom 15.00 40.00
Borje Salming
PP2EM Tony Esposito 20.00 50.00
Stan Mikita
PP2FM Bernie Federko 8.00 20.00
Joe Mullen
PP2FR Grant Fuhr 15.00 40.00
Bill Ranford
PP2FS Marc-Andre Fleury 20.00 50.00
Jordan Staal
PP2GK Marian Gaborik 15.00 40.00
Petr Kalus
PP2GO Bobby Orr 150.00 300.00
Gordie Howe
PP2GS Simon Gagne 12.00 30.00
Martin St. Louis
PP2GT Jean-Sebastien Giguere 12.00 30.00
Marty Turco
PP2HK Marian Hossa 15.00 40.00
Ilya Kovalchuk
PP2IC Jarome Iginla 15.00 40.00
Jonathan Cheechoo
PP2IN Jarome Iginla 20.00 50.00
Rick Nash
PP2IT Jarome Iginla 15.00 40.00
Alex Tanguay
PP2KR Ilya Kovalchuk 15.00 40.00
Alexander Radulov
PP2LB Vincent Lecavalier 12.00 30.00
Dan Boyle
PP2LK Ted Lindsay 12.00 30.00
Red Kelly
PP2LS Guy Lafleur 20.00 50.00
Steve Shutt
PP2MB Mike Modano 12.00 30.00
Brenden Morrow
PP2NB Cam Neely 20.00 50.00
Ray Bourque
PP2NK Markus Naslund 12.00 30.00
Ryan Kesler
PP2OM Alexander Ovechkin 75.00 150.00
Evgeni Malkin
PP2RG Rick Nash 12.00 30.00
Gilbert Brule
PP2SJ Rob Schremp 12.00 30.00
Jack Johnson
PP2SS Marek Svatos 12.00 30.00
Paul Stastny
PP2VH Tomas Vokoun 15.00 40.00
Dominik Hasek
PP2VM Vincent Lecavalier 12.00 30.00
Martin St. Louis

2007-08 OPC Premier Autographs Trios

Originally five cards were released in packs as exchange cards: Gagne/Lupul/Carter, Hull/Steen/Hawerchuk, Iginla/Gagne/Cheechoo, Lindsay/Howe/Kelly and St. Louis/Heatley/Nash.

STATED PRINT RUN 35 SERIAL #'d SETS
PP3CKJ Mike Cammalleri 15.00 40.00
Anze Kopitar
Jack Johnson
PP3EHM Tony Esposito 75.00 150.00
Bobby Hull
Stan Mikita
PP3FKM Grant Fuhr 100.00 200.00
Jari Kurri
Mark Messier
PP3GLC Simon Gagne 15.00 40.00
Joffrey Lupul
Jeff Carter
PP3HSH Bobby Hull 50.00 100.00
Tomas Steen
Dale Hawerchuk
PP3IGC Jarome Iginla 25.00 60.00
Simon Gagne
Jonathan Cheechoo
PP3LHK Ted Lindsay 75.00 150.00
Gordie Howe
Red Kelly
PP3LSR Guy Lafleur 50.00 100.00
Steve Shutt
Larry Robinson
PP3MRM Mike Modano 15.00 40.00
Mike Ribeiro
Brenden Morrow
PP3NMK Markus Naslund 15.00 40.00
Brendan Morrison
Ryan Kesler
PP3OGH Bobby Orr 600.00 900.00
Wayne Gretzky
Gordie Howe
PP3RLO Mario Lemieux 200.00 300.00
Patrick Roy
Bobby Orr
PP3SBK Marc Savard 50.00 100.00
Patrice Bergeron
Phil Kessel
PP3SHN Martin St. Louis 50.00 100.00
Dany Heatley
Rick Nash

2007-08 OPC Premier Autographs Foursomes

STATED PRINT RUN 15 SERIAL #'d SETS
NOT PRICED DUE TO SCARCITY

2007-08 OPC Premier Black Autographs

STATED PRINT RUN 1 SER.#'d SET
NOT PRICED DUE TO SCARCITY

2007-08 OPC Premier Original Six Signatures

STATED PRINT RUN 100 SERIAL #'d SETS
O6AB Andy Bathgate 5.00 12.00
O6BD Bill Dineen 6.00 15.00
O6BH Bobby Hull 20.00 50.00
O6BO Bobby Orr 125.00 200.00
O6BS Borje Salming 8.00 20.00
O6DS Darryl Sittler 5.00 12.00
O6DW Doug Wilson 8.00 20.00
O6EG Ed Giacomin 6.00 15.00
O6FM Frank Mahovlich 10.00 25.00
O6GC Gerry Cheevers 10.00 25.00
O6GL Guy Lafleur 20.00 50.00
O6JB Jean Beliveau 15.00 40.00
O6LR Larry Robinson 8.00 20.00
O6MS Milt Schmidt 12.00 30.00
O6RD Ron Duguay 8.00 20.00
O6RE Ron Ellis 6.00 15.00
O6RK Red Kelly 6.00 15.00
O6SS Steve Shutt 6.00 15.00
O6TE Tony Esposito 12.00 30.00
O6TL Ted Lindsay 10.00 25.00
O6WT Walt Tkaczuk 6.00 15.00

2007-08 OPC Premier Original Six Signatures Gold

*GOLD: .8X TO 2X BASE
STATED PRINT RUN 25 SERIAL #'d SETS
O6BD Bill Dineen 12.00 30.00
O6BO Bobby Orr 125.00 250.00
O6GH Gordie Howe 50.00 120.00
O6RK Red Kelly 12.00 30.00
O6TL Ted Lindsay 12.00 30.00
O6TO Terry O'Reilly 8.00 20.00

2007-08 OPC Premier Original Six Signatures Silver

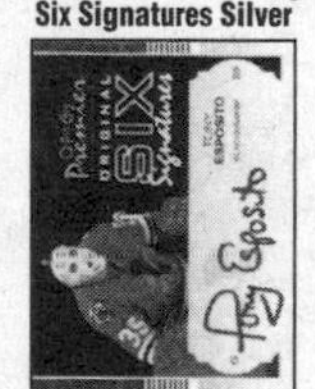

*SILVER: .6X TO 1.5X BASE
STATED PRINT RUN 50 SERIAL #'d SETS
O6BH Bobby Hull 25.00 60.00
O6BO Bobby Orr 125.00 200.00
O6BS Borje Salming 12.00 30.00
O6DS Darryl Sittler 12.00 30.00
O6DW Doug Wilson 10.00 25.00
O6GH Gordie Howe 125.00 200.00

2007-08 OPC Premier Pairings Autographs

STATED PRINT RUN 50 SERIAL #'d SETS
PCAS Colby Armstrong 15.00 40.00
Jordan Staal
PCBP Johnny Bucyk 12.00 30.00
Gilbert Perreault
PCBS Mike Bossy 12.00 30.00
Steve Shutt
PCCK Mike Cammalleri 16.00 40.00
Anze Kopitar
PCCP Cam Neely 15.00 40.00
Phil Kessel
PCDH Marcel Dionne 30.00 60.00
Dale Hawerchuk
PCDN Marcel Dionne 15.00 40.00

Bernie Nicholls
PCEJ Evgeni Malkin 40.00 80.00
Jordan Staal
PCFR Grant Fuhr 30.00 60.00
Bill Ranford
PCHK Marian Hossa 15.00 40.00
Ilya Kovalchuk
PCIM Jarome Iginla 30.00 60.00
Lanny McDonald
PCIT Jarome Iginla 12.00 30.00
Alex Tanguay
PCLG Mario Lemieux 200.00 400.00
Wayne Gretzky
PCLM Brian Leetch 75.00 150.00
Mark Messier
PCLN Pascal Leclaire 12.00 30.00
Rick Nash
PCLS Vincent Lecavalier 15.00 40.00
Martin St. Louis
PCLT Vincent Lecavalier 12.00 30.00
Joe Thornton
PCMH Al MacInnis 12.00 30.00
Dale Hawerchuk
PCMK Brendan Morrison 12.00 30.00
Ryan Kesler
PCMM Mike Modano 12.00 30.00
Joe Mullen
PCMR Mike Modano 12.00 30.00
Mike Ribeiro
PCMS Stan Mikita 15.00 40.00
Denis Savard
PCNB Rick Nash 15.00 40.00
Gilbert Brule
PCNM Markus Naslund 15.00 40.00
Brendan Morrison
PCNO Cam Neely 15.00 40.00
Adam Oates
PCNS Alex Tanguay 15.00 40.00
Henrik Zetterberg
PCPE Patrice Bergeron 15.00 40.00
Eric Staal
PCRB Patrick Roy 60.00 120.00
Ray Bourque
PCRT Mike Ribeiro 12.00 30.00
Marty Turco
PCSH Martin St. Louis 12.00 30.00
Nathan Horton
PCSM Simon Gagne 12.00 30.00
Alex Tanguay
PCSW Marek Svatos 10.00 25.00
Wojtek Wolski
PCWH Tomas Vokoun 12.00 30.00
Nathan Horton
PCWS Justin Williams 12.00 30.00
Eric Staal

2007-08 OPC Premier Pairings Patches Autographs

STATED PRINT RUN 25 SERIAL #'d SETS
PCBP Johnny Bucyk 15.00 40.00
Gilbert Perreault
PCGD Simon Gagne 15.00 40.00
Shane Doan
PCIM Jarome Iginla 60.00 120.00
Lanny McDonald
PCIT Jarome Iginla 20.00 50.00
Alex Tanguay
PCLN Pascal Leclaire 20.00 50.00
Rick Nash
PCMM Mike Modano 12.00 30.00
Joe Mullen
PCNM Markus Naslund 15.00 40.00
Brendan Morrison
PCNO Cam Neely 30.00 60.00
Adam Oates
PCPE Patrice Bergeron 12.00 30.00
Eric Staal
PCRB Patrick Roy 100.00 175.00
Ray Bourque
PCRT Mike Ribeiro 15.00 40.00
Marty Turco
PCSM Simon Gagne 15.00 40.00
Alex Tanguay
PCWH Tomas Vokoun 20.00 50.00
Nathan Horton
PCWS Justin Williams 10.00 25.00
Eric Staal

2007-08 OPC Premier Penmanship

STATED PRINT RUN 100 SER.#'d SETS
PPAK Anze Kopitar 8.00 20.00
PPBF Bernie Federko 5.00 12.00
PPCG Clark Gillies 6.00 15.00
PPDH Dany Heatley 10.00 25.00
PPDR Dwayne Roloson 6.00 15.00
PPEM Evgeni Malkin 50.00 100.00
PPHJ Milan Hejduk 8.00 20.00
PPHX Ron Hextall 12.00 30.00
PPIK Ilya Kovalchuk 10.00 25.00
PPJG Jean-Sebastien Giguere 8.00 20.00
PPJK Jari Kurri 8.00 20.00
PPJS Jordan Staal 10.00 25.00
PPMG Marian Gaborik 10.00 25.00
PPMN Markus Naslund 8.00 20.00
PPMR Michael Ryder
PPMT Marty Turco 8.00 20.00
PPNL Nicklas Lidstrom 8.00 20.00
PPPB Patrice Bergeron 8.00 20.00
PPPS Paul Stastny 8.00 20.00
PPRG Ryan Getzlaf 6.00 15.00
PPSC Sidney Crosby 100.00 175.00
PPSD Shane Doan 5.00 12.00
PPSG Simon Gagne 8.00 20.00
PPSK Saku Koivu 8.00 20.00
PPVL Vincent Lecavalier
PPVO Tomas Vokoun 6.00 15.00

2007-08 OPC Premier Penmanship Gold

*GOLD: 8X TO 2X BASE
STATED PRINT RUN 25 SERIAL #'d SETS
PPEM Evgeni Malkin 50.00 100.00

2007-08 OPC Premier Penmanship Silver

*SILVER: .6X TO 1.5X BASE
STATED PRINT RUN 50 SERIAL #'d SETS
PPEM Evgeni Malkin 40.00 80.00
PPSC Sidney Crosby 125.00 200.00

2007-08 OPC Premier Rare Remnants Triples

STATED PRINT RUN 50 SERIAL #'d SETS
PTAJD David Aebischer 15.00 40.00
Ed Jovanovski
Shane Doan
PTAMV Maxim Afinogenov 15.00 40.00
Ryan Miller
Thomas Vanek
PTAVS Maxim Afinogenov 12.00 30.00
Thomas Vanek
Drew Stafford
PTBES Martin Brodeur 20.00 50.00
Patrik Elias
Scott Stevens
PTBGP Martin Brodeur 15.00 40.00
Brian Gionta
Zach Parise
PTBLB Rob Blake 15.00 40.00
Vincent Lecavalier
Luc Bourdon
PTBLK Martin Brodeur 20.00 50.00
Roberto Luongo
Miikka Kiprusoff
PTBLM Jean Beliveau 20.00 50.00
Guy Lafleur
Frank Mahovlich
PTBPS Mike Bossy 15.00 40.00
Denis Potvin
Billy Smith
PTBRS Ray Bourque 15.00 40.00
Larry Robinson
Scott Stevens
PTBSW Rod Brind'Amour 12.00 30.00
Eric Staal
Cam Ward
PTCFM Marc-Andre Fleury 50.00 100.00
Sidney Crosby
Evgeni Malkin
PTCGH Bobby Clarke 20.00 50.00
Simon Gagne
Ron Hextall
PTCMS Sidney Crosby 50.00 100.00
Evgeni Malkin
Jordan Staal
PTDFM Pavel Datsyuk 15.00 40.00
Sergei Fedorov
Evgeni Malkin
PTDGK Pavol Demitra 15.00 40.00
Marian Gaborik
Mikko Koivu
PTFBK Manny Fernandez 12.00 30.00
Patrice Bergeron
Phil Kessel
PTFCK Alexander Frolov 12.00 30.00
Mike Cammalleri
Anze Kopitar
PTFCT Manny Fernandez 10.00 25.00
Zdeno Chara
Tim Thomas
PTGBL Simon Gagne 15.00 40.00
Daniel Briere
Joffrey Lupul
PTGDP Scott Gomez 12.00 30.00
Chris Drury
Petr Prucha
PTGRC Simon Gagne 15.00 40.00
Mike Richards
Jeff Carter
PTGSD Bill Guerin 15.00 40.00
Miroslav Satan
Rick DiPietro
PTHDG Marian Hossa 12.00 30.00
Pavol Demitra
Marian Gaborik
PTHHK Cristobal Huet 12.00 30.00
Chris Higgins
Alex Kovalev
PTHKL Marian Hossa 15.00 40.00
Ilya Kovalchuk
Kari Lehtonen
PTHLD Dominik Hasek 15.00 40.00
Nicklas Lidstrom
Pavel Datsyuk
PTJHE Jaromir Jagr 20.00 50.00
Dominik Hasek
Patrik Elias
PTKOF Olaf Kolzig 15.00 40.00
Alexander Ovechkin
Eric Fehr
PTKOR Ilya Kovalchuk 20.00 50.00
Alexander Ovechkin
Alexander Radulov
PTKRK Saku Koivu 12.00 30.00
Michael Ryder
Alex Kovalev
PTKSK Saku Koivu 15.00 40.00
Jordan Staal
Anze Kopitar
PTKST Paul Kariya 12.00 30.00
Keith Tkachuk
Lee Stempniak
PTLEK Roberto Luongo 12.00 30.00
Ray Emery
Miikka Kiprusoff
PTLHZ Nicklas Lidstrom 15.00 40.00
Tomas Holmstrom
Henrik Zetterberg
PTMGM Lanny McDonald 12.00 30.00
Doug Gilmour
Al MacInnis
PTMSR Mike Modano 12.00 30.00
Mats Sundin
Mark Recchi
PTMTK Mike Modano 15.00 40.00
Keith Tkachuk
Phil Kessel
PTNBO Cam Neely 15.00 40.00
Ray Bourque
Adam Oates
PTNSS Markus Naslund 10.00 25.00
Henrik Sedin
Daniel Sedin
PTNZF Rick Nash 10.00 25.00
Nikolai Zherdev
Sergei Fedorov
PTPGB Mark Parrish 10.00 25.00
Marian Gaborik
Pierre-Marc Bouchard
PTRLG Patrick Roy 75.00 150.00
Mario Lemieux
Wayne Gretzky
PTROV Brad Richards 10.00 25.00
Steve Ott
Rick Vaive
PTSBS Jason Spezza 10.00 25.00
Patrice Bergeron
Eric Staal
PTSHP Jarret Stoll 12.00 30.00
Ales Hemsky
Marc-Antoine Pouliot
PTSNG Teemu Selanne 15.00 40.00
Scott Niedermayer
Jean-Sebastien Giguere
PTSRT Joe Sakic 12.00 30.00
Brad Richards
Joe Thornton
PTSSN Owen Nolan 15.00 40.00
Joe Sakic
Mats Sundin
PTSTS Joe Sakic 12.00 30.00
Jose Theodore
Ryan Smyth
PTTSC Joe Thornton 20.00 50.00
Martin St. Louis
Sidney Crosby
PTVNB David Vyborny 10.00 25.00
Rick Nash
Gilbert Brule

2007-08 OPC Premier Rare Remnants Triples Patches Gold

STATED PRINT RUN 3 SERIAL #'d SETS
NOT PRICED DUE TO SCARCITY

2007-08 OPC Premier Rare Remnants Triples Patches Silver

STATED PRINT RUN 10 SERIAL #'d SETS
NOT PRICED DUE TO SCARCITY
PTAJD David Aebischer
Ed Jovanovski
Shane Doan
PTAMV Maxim Afinogenov
Ryan Miller
Thomas Vanek
PTASH Daniel Alfredsson
Jason Spezza
Dany Heatley
PTASR Jason Arnott
Steve Sullivan
Alexander Radulov
PTAVS Maxim Afinogenov
Thomas Vanek
Drew Stafford
PTBES Martin Brodeur
Patrik Elias
Scott Stevens
PTBGP Martin Brodeur
Brian Gionta
Zach Parise
PTBLB Rob Blake
Vincent Lecavalier
Luc Bourdon
PTBLK Martin Brodeur
Roberto Luongo
Miikka Kiprusoff
PTBPG Todd Bertuzzi
Corey Perry
Ryan Getzlaf
PTBPW Jay Bouwmeester
Dion Phaneuf
Shea Weber
PTBRS Ray Bourque
Larry Robinson
Scott Stevens
PTBSW Rod Brind'Amour
Eric Staal
Cam Ward
PTCFM Marc-Andre Fleury
Sidney Crosby
Evgeni Malkin
PTCMS Sidney Crosby
Evgeni Malkin
Jordan Staal
PTDFM Pavel Datsyuk
Sergei Fedorov
Evgeni Malkin
PTDGK Pavol Demitra
Marian Gaborik
Mikko Koivu
PTFBK Manny Fernandez
Patrice Bergeron
Phil Kessel
PTFCK Alexander Frolov
Mike Cammalleri
Anze Kopitar
PTFCT Manny Fernandez
Zdeno Chara
Tim Thomas
PTGBL Simon Gagne
Daniel Briere
Joffrey Lupul
PTGDP Scott Gomez
Chris Drury
Petr Prucha
PTGRC Simon Gagne
Mike Richards
Jeff Carter
PTGSD Bill Guerin
Miroslav Satan
Rick DiPietro
PTHDG Marian Hossa
Pavol Demitra
Marian Gaborik
PTHHK Cristobal Huet
Chris Higgins
Alex Kovalev
PTHKL Marian Hossa
Ilya Kovalchuk
Kari Lehtonen
PTHLD Dominik Hasek
Nicklas Lidstrom
Pavel Datsyuk
PTHRK Martin Havlat
Tuomo Ruutu
Nikolai Khabibulin
PTHSW Milan Hejduk
Marek Svatos
Wojtek Wolski
PTIKP Jarome Iginla
Miikka Kiprusoff
Dion Phaneuf
PTJHE Jaromir Jagr
Dominik Hasek
Patrik Elias
PTKIH Paul Kariya
Jarome Iginla
Dany Heatley
PTKOF Olaf Kolzig
Alexander Ovechkin
Eric Fehr
PTKOR Ilya Kovalchuk
Alexander Ovechkin
Alexander Radulov
PTKSK Saku Koivu
Jordan Staal
Anze Kopitar
PTKST Paul Kariya
Keith Tkachuk
Lee Stempniak
PTLAR David Legwand
Jason Arnott
Alexander Radulov
PTLEK Roberto Luongo
Ray Emery
Miikka Kiprusoff
PTLHZ Nicklas Lidstrom
Tomas Holmstrom
Henrik Zetterberg
PTLRS Vincent Lecavalier
Brad Richards
Martin St. Louis
PTMGM Lanny McDonald
Doug Gilmour
Al MacInnis
PTMSR Mike Modano
Mats Sundin
Mark Recchi
PTMTK Mike Modano
Keith Tkachuk
Phil Kessel
PTNBO Cam Neely
Ray Bourque
Adam Oates
PTNLM Markus Naslund
Roberto Luongo
Brendan Morrison
PTNSS Markus Naslund
Henrik Sedin
Daniel Sedin
PTNZF Rick Nash
Nikolai Zherdev
Sergei Fedorov
PTPGB Mark Parrish
Marian Gaborik
Pierre-Marc Bouchard
PTRLG Patrick Roy
Mario Lemieux
Wayne Gretzky
PTROV Brad Richards
Steve Ott
Rick Vaive
PTRRM Gary Roberts
Mark Recchi
Ryan Malone
PTSBS Jason Spezza
Patrice Bergeron
Eric Staal
PTSFA Mats Sundin
Peter Forsberg
Daniel Alfredsson
PTSHP Jarret Stoll
Ales Hemsky
Marc-Antoine Pouliot
PTSKT Brent Seabrook
Duncan Keith
Jonathan Toews
PTSLJ Teemu Selanne
Jere Lehtinen
Olli Jokinen
PTSNG Teemu Selanne
Scott Niedermayer
Jean-Sebastien Giguere
PTSOH Peter Stastny
Adam Oates
Dale Hawerchuk
PTSRT Joe Sakic
Brad Richards
Joe Thornton
PTSSB Mats Sundin
Mark Bell
Alexander Steen
PTSSN Owen Nolan
Joe Sakic
Mats Sundin
PTSSW Darryl Sittler
Borje Salming
Tiger Williams
PTSTS Joe Sakic
Jose Theodore
Ryan Smyth
PTSWS Cory Stillman
Justin Williams
Eric Staal
PTTKN Vesa Toskala
Miikka Kiprusoff
Antero Niittymaki
PTTNC Joe Thornton
Evgeni Nabokov
Jonathan Cheechoo
PTTSC Joe Thornton
Martin St. Louis
Sidney Crosby
PTVJH Tomas Vokoun
Olli Jokinen
Nathan Horton
PTVNB David Vyborny
Rick Nash
Gilbert Brule

2007-08 OPC Premier Rare Remnants Quads

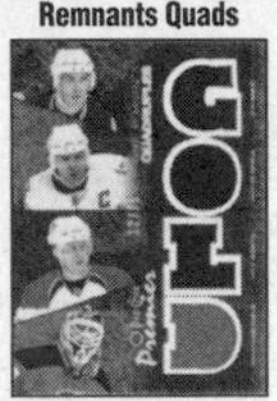

STATED PRINT RUN 25 SERIAL #'d SETS
NOT PRICED DUE TO LACK OF MARKET ACTIVITY
PQASHE Daniel Alfredsson 25.00 60.00
Jason Spezza
Dany Heatley
Ray Emery
PQCFMS Marc-Andre Fleury 60.00 120.00
Sidney Crosby
Evgeni Malkin
Jordan Staal
PQCWPS Chris Chelios 25.00 60.00
Tiger Williams
Bob Probert
Scott Stevens
PQITKP Jarome Iginla 20.00 50.00
Alex Tanguay
Miikka Kiprusoff
Dion Phaneuf
PQJFIC Jaromir Jagr 60.00 120.00
Peter Forsberg
Jarome Iginla
Sidney Crosby
PQLNFB Pascal Leclaire 20.00 50.00
Rick Nash
Sergei Fedorov
Gilbert Brule
PQMTCC Patrick Marleau 25.00 60.00
Joe Thornton
Jonathan Cheechoo
Matt Carle
PQRNWS Brad Richards 25.00 60.00
Scott Niedermayer
Cam Ward
Scott Stevens
PQSJDL Brendan Shanahan 50.00 100.00
Jaromir Jagr
Chris Drury
Henrik Lundqvist
PQSKRD Joe Sakic 50.00 100.00
Paul Kariya
Brad Richards
Pavel Datsyuk
PQSOMA Teemu Selanne 60.00 120.00
Daniel Alfredsson
Alexander Ovechkin
Evgeni Malkin
PQTNCO Joe Thornton 60.00 120.00
Rick Nash
Sidney Crosby
Alexander Ovechkin

2007-08 OPC Premier Rare Remnants Quads Gold

STATED PRINT RUN 10 SERIAL #'d SETS
NOT PRICED DUE TO SCARCITY

2007-08 OPC Premier Rare Remnants Quads Patches Gold

STATED PRINT RUN 1 SERIAL #'d SET
NOT PRICED DUE TO SCARCITY

2007-08 OPC Premier Rare Remnants Quads Patches Silver

STATED PRINT RUN 5 SERIAL #'d SETS
NOT PRICED DUE TO SCARCITY

2007-08 OPC Premier Remnants Triples

STATED PRINT RUN 100 SER.#'d SETS
PRAF Alexander Frolov 5.00 12.00
PRAK Alex Kovalev 5.00 12.00
PRAO Alexander Ovechkin 15.00 40.00
PRAS Alexander Steen 5.00 12.00
PRBL Rob Blake 6.00 15.00
PRBM Brendan Morrison 5.00 12.00
PRBO Mike Bossy 10.00 25.00
PRBR Rod Brind'Amour 6.00 15.00
PRBS Billy Smith 8.00 20.00
PRCH Jonathan Cheechoo 6.00 15.00
PRCW Cam Ward 8.00 20.00
PRDA Daniel Alfredsson 6.00 15.00
PRDE Pavol Demitra 5.00 12.00
PRDH Dale Hawerchuk 6.00 15.00
PRDL David Legwand 5.00 12.00
PRDR Dwayne Roloson 6.00 15.00
PRDS Darryl Sittler 6.00 15.00
PREB Ed Belfour 8.00 20.00
PREJ Ed Jovanovski 5.00 12.00
PREL Eric Lindros 8.00 20.00
PREM Evgeni Malkin 20.00 50.00
PRES Eric Staal 8.00 20.00
PRGA Simon Gagne 8.00 20.00
PRGP Gilbert Perreault 6.00 15.00
PRHA Dominik Hasek 10.00 25.00
PRHL Henrik Lundqvist 10.00 25.00
PRHM Milan Hejduk 6.00 15.00
PRHZ Henrik Zetterberg 8.00 20.00
PRIK Ilya Kovalchuk 10.00 25.00
PRJA Jason Arnott 5.00 12.00
PRJB Jay Bouwmeester 5.00 12.00
PRJC Jeff Carter/75 5.00 12.00
PRJG Jean-Sebastien Giguere 8.00 20.00
PRJI Jarome Iginla 12.00 30.00
PRJO Joe Sakic 15.00 40.00
PRJP Joni Pitkanen 5.00 12.00
PRJS Jason Spezza 8.00 20.00
PRJT Joe Thornton 10.00 25.00
PRJW Justin Williams 5.00 12.00
PRKL Kari Lehtonen 8.00 20.00
PRKO Mikko Koivu 5.00 12.00
PRLM Lanny McDonald 6.00 15.00
PRLR Larry Robinson 10.00 25.00
PRMA Martin Havlat 6.00 15.00
PRMB Martin Brodeur 20.00 50.00
PRMC Mike Cammalleri 6.00 15.00
PRMG Marian Gaborik 10.00 25.00
PRMH Marian Hossa 8.00 20.00
PRMI Mike Richards 10.00 25.00
PRML Mario Lemieux 20.00 50.00
PRMN Markus Naslund 8.00 20.00
PRMR Mark Recchi 5.00 12.00
PRMS Marc Savard 5.00 12.00
PRMT Marty Turco 8.00 20.00
PRNH Nathan Horton 5.00 12.00
PRNL Nicklas Lidstrom 8.00 20.00
PROJ Olli Jokinen 5.00 12.00
PROK Olaf Kolzig 8.00 20.00
PRPB Patrice Bergeron 8.00 20.00
PRPD Pavel Datsyuk 8.00 20.00
PRPE Patrik Elias 5.00 12.00
PRPF Peter Forsberg 10.00 25.00
PRPI Pierre-Marc Bouchard 5.00 12.00
PRPK Paul Kariya 8.00 20.00
PRPM Patrick Marleau 6.00 15.00
PRPR Patrick Roy 25.00 60.00
PRPS Peter Stastny 6.00 15.00
PRRB Ray Bourque 10.00 25.00
PRRD Rick DiPietro 10.00 25.00
PRRI Mike Ribeiro 5.00 12.00
PRRL Roberto Luongo 12.00 30.00
PRRM Ryan Miller 8.00 20.00
PRRN Rick Nash 8.00 20.00
PRRS Ryan Smyth 6.00 15.00
PRRY Michael Ryder 5.00 12.00
PRSA Borje Salming 6.00 15.00
PRSC Sidney Crosby 40.00 80.00
PRSD Shane Doan 5.00 12.00
PRSF Sergei Fedorov 8.00 20.00
PRSG Scott Gomez 5.00 12.00
PRSH Brendan Shanahan 8.00 20.00
PRSK Saku Koivu 6.00 15.00
PRSM Miroslav Satan 10.00 25.00
PRSS Steve Shutt 6.00 15.00
PRST Martin St. Louis 6.00 15.00
PRSU Mats Sundin 8.00 20.00
PRSV Marek Svatos 5.00 12.00
PRTB Todd Bertuzzi 6.00 15.00
PRTH Tomas Holmstrom 6.00 15.00
PRTR Tuomo Ruutu 5.00 12.00
PRTS Teemu Selanne 8.00 20.00
PRTV Tomas Vokoun 8.00 20.00
PRVL Vincent Lecavalier 8.00 20.00
PRZC Zdeno Chara

2007-08 OPC Premier Remnants Triples Patches

*PATCHES: 1.5X TO 4X BASE
STATED PRINT RUN 35 SERIAL #'d SETS

2007-08 OPC Premier Remnants Quads

STATED PRINT RUN 25 SERIAL #'d SETS
PRAF Alexander Frolov 12.00 30.00
PRAK Alex Kovalev 12.00 30.00
PRAO Alexander Ovechkin 40.00 100.00
PRAS Alexander Steen 12.00 30.00
PRBO Mike Bossy 15.00 40.00
PRBR Rod Brind'Amour 20.00 50.00
PRBS Billy Smith 12.00 30.00
PRCH Jonathan Cheechoo 15.00 40.00
PRCW Cam Ward 20.00 50.00
PRDE Pavol Demitra 12.00 30.00
PRDH Dale Hawerchuk 15.00 40.00
PRDS Darryl Sittler 15.00 40.00
PREB Ed Belfour 20.00 50.00
PREJ Ed Jovanovski 12.00 30.00
PREM Evgeni Malkin 20.00 50.00
PRES Eric Staal 20.00 50.00
PRGA Simon Gagne 20.00 50.00
PRHE Dany Heatley 20.00 50.00
PRHL Henrik Lundqvist 25.00 60.00
PRHM Milan Hejduk 15.00 40.00
PRHZ Henrik Zetterberg 20.00 50.00
PRIK Ilya Kovalchuk 12.00 30.00
PRJA Jason Arnott 12.00 30.00
PRJB Jay Bouwmeester 12.00 30.00
PRJC Jeff Carter 12.00 30.00
PRJG Jean-Sebastien Giguere 20.00 50.00
PRJI Jarome Iginla 20.00 50.00
PRJJ Jaromir Jagr 25.00 60.00
PRJO Joe Sakic 20.00 50.00
PRJP Joni Pitkanen 12.00 30.00
PRJS Jason Spezza 20.00 50.00
PRJT Joe Thornton 15.00 40.00
PRKL Kari Lehtonen 15.00 40.00
PRLM Lanny McDonald 12.00 30.00
PRLR Larry Robinson 25.00 60.00
PRMA Martin Havlat 12.00 25.00
PRMB Martin Brodeur 30.00 60.00
PRMC Mike Cammalleri 12.00 12.00
PRMG Marian Gaborik 25.00 60.00
PRMH Marian Hossa 20.00 50.00
PRMI Mike Richards 25.00 60.00
PRML Mario Lemieux 40.00 80.00
PRMM Mike Modano 12.00 25.00
PRMN Markus Naslund 20.00 50.00
PRMR Mark Recchi 12.00 30.00
PRMS Marc Savard 12.00 30.00
PRMT Marty Turco 20.00 50.00
PRNH Nathan Horton 12.00 20.00
PRNL Nicklas Lidstrom 20.00 50.00
PROJ Olli Jokinen 12.00 30.00
PROK Olaf Kolzig 20.00 50.00
PRPB Patrice Bergeron 20.00 50.00
PRPF Peter Forsberg 12.00 20.00
PRPI Pierre-Marc Bouchard 12.00 30.00
PRPK Paul Kariya 15.00 40.00
PRPM Patrick Marleau 15.00 40.00
PRPR Patrick Roy 50.00 100.00
PRPS Peter Stastny 15.00 40.00
PRRB Ray Bourque 25.00 60.00
PRRD Rick DiPietro 15.00 40.00
PRRI Mike Ribeiro 12.00 30.00
PRRM Ryan Miller 20.00 50.00
PRRN Rick Nash 20.00 50.00
PRRS Ryan Smyth 15.00 40.00
PRSA Borje Salming 15.00 40.00
PRSC Sidney Crosby 60.00 120.00
PRSD Shane Doan 12.00 30.00
PRSE Sergei Samsonov 12.00 30.00
PRSF Sergei Fedorov 20.00 50.00
PRSG Scott Gomez 12.00 30.00
PRSH Brendan Shanahan 12.00 30.00
PRSK Saku Koivu 20.00 50.00
PRSM Miroslav Satan/15 15.00 40.00
PRSS Steve Shutt 15.00 40.00
PRST Martin St. Louis 15.00 40.00
PRSU Mats Sundin 12.00 30.00
PRTH Tomas Holmstrom 12.00 30.00
PRTS Teemu Selanne 20.00 50.00
PRTV Tomas Vokoun 20.00 50.00

2007-08 OPC Premier Remnants Quads Patches

STATED PRINT RUN 20 SERIAL #'d SETS
NOT PRICED DUE TO SCARCITY

2007-08 OPC Premier Remnants Quads Autographs

STATED PRINT RUN 10 SERIAL #'d SETS
NOT PRICED DUE TO SCARCITY

2007-08 OPC Premier Remnants Quads Patches Autographs

STATED PRINT RUN 5 SERIAL #'d SETS
NOT PRICED DUE TO SCARCITY

2007-08 OPC Premier Stitchings

STATED PRINT RUN 199 SERIAL #'d SETS
PSAB Andy Bathgate 5.00 12.00
PSAO Alexander Ovechkin 20.00 50.00
PSBC Bobby Clarke 6.00 15.00
PSBH Bobby Hull 10.00 25.00
PSBL Rob Blake 5.00 12.00
PSBO Bobby Orr 25.00 60.00
PSBP Bernie Parent 8.00 20.00
PSBS Brendan Shanahan 6.00 15.00
PSCD Chris Drury 5.00 12.00
PSCN Cam Neely 6.00 15.00
PSCT Cyclone Taylor 6.00 15.00
PSDA Daniel Alfredsson 5.00 12.00
PSDH Dany Heatley 8.00 20.00
PSDS Darryl Sittler 5.00 12.00
PSEG Ed Giacomin 6.00 15.00
PSEJ Ed Jovanovski 4.00 10.00
PSEM Evgeni Malkin 15.00 40.00
PSES Eddie Shack 6.00 15.00
PSFN Frank Nighbor 6.00 15.00
PSGC Gerry Cheevers 10.00 25.00
PSGH Gordie Howe 15.00 40.00
PSGR Wayne Gretzky 20.00 50.00
PSIK Ilya Kovalchuk 8.00 20.00
PSJB Jean Beliveau 10.00 25.00
PSJI Jarome Iginla 8.00 20.00
PSJJ Jaromir Jagr 10.00 25.00
PSJL Jacques Lemaire 5.00 12.00
PSJS Jason Spezza 6.00 15.00
PSJT Joe Thornton 8.00 20.00
PSKL Kari Lehtonen 6.00 15.00
PSLR Larry Robinson 8.00 20.00
PSMA Martin Brodeur 15.00 40.00
PSMH Martin Havlat 5.00 12.00
PSMK Miikka Kiprusoff 8.00 20.00
PSML Mario Lemieux 15.00 40.00
PSMM Mark Messier 12.00 30.00
PSMS Mats Sundin 6.00 15.00
PSOK Olaf Kolzig 6.00 15.00
PSPD Pavel Datsyuk 6.00 15.00
PSPE Phil Esposito 10.00 25.00
PSPK Paul Kariya 6.00 15.00
PSPL Pat LaFontaine 4.00 10.00
PSPR Patrick Roy 20.00 50.00
PSRA Ray Bourque 8.00 20.00
PSRB Richard Brodeur 5.00 12.00
PSRK Red Kelly 4.00 10.00
PSRL Roberto Luongo 10.00 25.00
PSRO Patrick Roy 20.00 50.00
PSSA Joe Sakic 12.00 30.00

PSSF Sergei Fedorov 6.00 15.00
PSSM Billy Smith 6.00 15.00
PSST Jordan Staal 8.00 20.00
PSTE Tony Esposito 10.00 25.00
PSTS Teemu Selanne 6.00 15.00
PSVL Vincent Lecavalier 6.00 15.00
PSWA Wayne Gretzky 15.00 40.00
PSWG Wayne Gretzky/100 20.00 50.00

2007-08 OPC Premier Stitchings 25

*25: .6X TO 1.5X BASE
STATED PRINT RUN 25 SERIAL #'d SETS

2007-08 OPC Premier Stitchings 50

*50: .5X TO 1.2X BASE
STATED PRINT RUN 50 SERIAL #'d SETS
PSBR Brad Richards 6.00 15.00

2007-08 OPC Premier Stitchings Variation

STATED PRINT RUN 99 SERIAL #'d SETS
PSAB Andy Bathgate 5.00 12.00
PSAO Alexander Ovechkin 20.00 50.00
PSBC Bobby Clarke 6.00 15.00
PSBH Bobby Hull 10.00 25.00
PSBL Rob Blake 5.00 12.00
PSBO Bobby Orr 25.00 60.00
PSBP Bernie Parent 8.00 20.00
PSBR Brad Richards 5.00 12.00
PSBS Brendan Shanahan 6.00 15.00
PSCD Chris Drury 5.00 12.00
PSCN Cam Neely 10.00 25.00
PSCT Cyclone Taylor 6.00 15.00
PSDA Daniel Alfredsson 6.00 15.00
PSDH Dany Heatley 8.00 20.00
PSDS Darryl Sittler 5.00 12.00
PSEG Ed Giacomin/50 6.00 15.00
PSEJ Ed Jovanovski 4.00 10.00
PSEM Evgeni Malkin 12.00 30.00
PSES Eddie Shack 6.00 15.00
PSFN Frank Nighbor 6.00 15.00
PSGC Gerry Cheevers 10.00 25.00
PSGR Wayne Gretzky 30.00 80.00
PSIK Ilya Kovalchuk 8.00 20.00
PSJB Jean Beliveau 10.00 25.00
PSJI Jarome Iginla 15.00 40.00
PSJJ Jaromir Jagr 10.00 25.00
PSJL Jacques Lemaire 5.00 12.00
PSJS Jason Spezza 6.00 15.00
PSJT Joe Thornton 8.00 20.00
PSKL Kari Lehtonen 6.00 15.00
PSLR Larry Robinson 8.00 20.00
PSMA Martin Brodeur 15.00 40.00
PSMH Martin Havlat 5.00 12.00
PSMK Miikka Kiprusoff 8.00 20.00
PSML Mario Lemieux 20.00 50.00
PSMM Mark Messier 12.00 30.00
PSMS Mats Sundin 6.00 15.00
PSOK Olaf Kolzig 6.00 15.00
PSPD Pavel Datsyuk 6.00 15.00
PSPE Phil Esposito 10.00 25.00
PSPK Paul Kariya 6.00 15.00
PSPR Patrick Roy 20.00 50.00
PSRA Ray Bourque 8.00 20.00
PSRB Richard Brodeur 5.00 12.00
PSRK Red Kelly 4.00 10.00
PSRL Roberto Luongo 10.00 25.00
PSRO Patrick Roy 20.00 50.00
PSSF Sergei Fedorov 6.00 15.00
PSSM Billy Smith 6.00 15.00
PSST Jordan Staal 8.00 20.00
PSTE Tony Esposito 10.00 25.00
PSTS Teemu Selanne 6.00 15.00
PSVL Vincent Lecavalier 6.00 15.00
PSWA Wayne Gretzky 30.00 80.00
PSWG Wayne Gretzky 30.00 80.00

2007-08 OPC Premier Stitchings Variation 10

STATED PRINT RUN 10 SERIAL #'d SETS
NOT PRICED DUE TO SCARCITY

2007-08 OPC Premier Stitchings Variation 25

*25: .6X TO 1.5X BASE
STATED PRINT RUN 25 SERIAL #'d SETS

2008-09 OPC Premier

The T.J. Oshie AU RC was issued in packs as an exchange card. The live cards were not available at the time of the pack out process.

COMP.SET w/o SPs (42) 175.00 300.00
STATED PRINT RUN 299 SER.#'d SETS
1 Wayne Gretzky 10.00 25.00
2 Vincent Lecavalier 2.00 5.00
3 Tony Esposito 2.00 5.00
4 Sidney Crosby 10.00 25.00
5 Saku Koivu 2.00 5.00
6 Rick Nash 2.00 5.00
7 Ray Bourque 4.00 10.00
8 Phil Esposito 3.00 8.00
9 Peter Mueller 2.50 6.00
10 Pavel Datsyuk 2.00 5.00
11 Paul Stastny 2.00 5.00
12 Patrick Roy 6.00 15.00
13 Patrick Kane 5.00 12.00
14 Nicklas Lidstrom 2.00 5.00
15 Mike Bossy 2.00 5.00
16 Martin St. Louis 2.00 5.00
17 Martin Brodeur 4.00 10.00
18 Mark Messier 4.00 10.00
19 Mario Lemieux 5.00 12.00
20 Marian Gaborik 3.00 8.00
21 Jonathan Toews 6.00 15.00
22 Jonathan Cheechoo 2.00 5.00
23 Joe Thornton 3.00 8.00
24 Joe Sakic 3.00 8.00
25 Jarome Iginla 4.00 10.00
26 Jari Kurri 2.00 5.00
27 Ilya Kovalchuk 2.50 6.00
28 Henrik Zetterberg 4.00 10.00
29 Guy Lafleur 4.00 10.00
30 Grant Fuhr 2.00 5.00
31 Gordie Howe 8.00 20.00
32 Gilbert Perreault 2.00 5.00
33 Evgeni Malkin 5.00 12.00
34 Eric Staal 3.00 8.00
35 Dany Heatley 2.50 6.00
36 Dale Hawerchuk 2.00 5.00
37 Carey Price 6.00 15.00
38 Cam Neely 2.50 6.00
39 Bobby Orr 6.00 15.00
40 Bobby Hull 4.00 10.00
41 Bobby Clarke 2.00 5.00
42 Alexander Ovechkin 8.00 20.00
43 Zach Bogosian JSY AU RC 12.00 30.00
44 Blake Wheeler JSY AU RC 15.00 40.00
45 Zach Boychuk JSY AU RC 10.00 25.00
46 Brandon Sutter JSY AU RC 8.00 20.00
47 Nikita Filatov JSY AU RC 25.00 60.00
48 Jakub Voracek JSY AU RC 12.00 30.00
49 Derick Brassard JSY AU RC 12.00 30.00
50 Steve Mason JSY AU RC 25.00 50.00
51 Justin Pogge JSY AU RC 12.00 30.00
52 Fabian Brunnstrom JSY AU RC 10.00 25.00
53 James Neal JSY AU RC 10.00 25.00
54 Justin Abdelkader JSY AU RC 12.00 30.00
55 Darren Helm JSY AU RC 10.00 25.00
56 Mattias Ritola JSY AU RC 8.00 20.00
57 Michael Frolik JSY AU RC 12.00 30.00
58 Shawn Matthias JSY AU RC 6.00 15.00
59 Drew Doughty JSY AU RC 20.00 50.00
60 Oscar Moller JSY AU RC 6.00 15.00
61 Erik Ersberg JSY AU RC 6.00 15.00
62 Brian Boyle JSY AU RC 6.00 15.00
63 Colton Gillies JSY AU RC 6.00 15.00
64 Patric Hornqvist JSY AU RC 6.00 15.00
65 Ben Maxwell JSY AU RC 10.00 25.00
66 Josh Bailey JSY AU RC 10.00 25.00
67 Kyle Okposo JSY AU RC 12.00 30.00
68 Lauri Korpikoski JSY AU RC 6.00 15.00
69 Ilya Zubov JSY AU RC 6.00 15.00
70 Claude Giroux JSY AU RC 12.00 30.00
71 Luca Sbisa JSY AU RC 10.00 25.00
72 Viktor Tikhonov JSY AU RC 6.00 15.00
73 Mikkel Boedker JSY AU RC 10.00 25.00
74 Kyle Turris JSY AU RC 12.00 30.00
75 Alex Goligoski JSY AU RC 12.00 30.00
76 Jamie McGinn JSY AU RC 6.00 15.00
77 Alex Pietrangelo JSY AU RC 10.00 25.00
78 Patrik Berglund JSY AU RC 15.00 40.00
79 T.J. Oshie JSY AU RC EXCH
80 Ben Bishop JSY AU RC 10.00 25.00
81 Steven Stamkos JSY AU RC 60.00 120.00
82 Luke Schenn JSY AU RC 20.00 50.00
83 Nikolai Kulemin JSY AU RC 6.00 15.00
84 Cory Schneider JSY AU RC 12.00 30.00

2008-09 OPC Premier Black Spectrum

STATED PRINT RUN 1 SERIAL #'d SET
NOT PRICED DUE TO SCARCITY

2008-09 OPC Premier Gold Spectrum

STATED PRINT RUN 5 SERIAL #'d SETS
ROOKIE PRINT RUN 15 SERIAL #'d SETS
NOT PRICED DUE TO SCARCITY

2008-09 OPC Premier Silver

*SINGLES: .6X TO 1.5X BASIC CARDS
STATED PRINT RUN 75 SER.#'d SETS

2008-09 OPC Premier Duos

STATED PRINT RUN 75 SER.#'d SETS
PP2-BF Derick Brassard 25.00 60.00
Nikita Filatov
PP2-BN Fabian Brunnstrom 20.00 50.00
James Neal
PP2-DH Pavel Datsyuk 20.00 50.00
Marian Hossa
PP2-DK Alex Delvecchio 15.00 40.00
Red Kelly
PP2-DZ Nikolai Zherdev
Chris Drury
PP2-EN Phil Esposito 50.00 100.00
Cam Neely
PP2-FA Grant Fuhr 15.00 40.00
Glenn Anderson
PP2-FH Tomas Holmstrom
Johan Franzen
PP2-GG Colton Gillies 12.00 30.00
Clark Gillies
PP2-GM Wayne Gretzky 150.00 250.00
Mark Messier
PP2-HE Bobby Hull 50.00 100.00
Tony Esposito
PP2-HO Bobby Orr 150.00 250.00
Gordie Howe
PP2-KR Jari Kurri 15.00 40.00
Luc Robitaille
PP2-KT Jonathan Toews 125.00 200.00
Patrick Kane
PP2-LN Markus Naslund 40.00 100.00
Henrik Lundqvist
PP2-LS Vincent Lecavalier 12.00 30.00
Martin St. Louis
PP2-MF Evgeni Malkin 50.00 100.00
Marc-Andre Fleury
PP2-MK Evgeni Malkin 40.00 80.00
Ilya Kovalchuk
PP2-ML Brian Leetch 50.00 100.00
Mark Messier
PP2-OB Bobby Orr 100.00 200.00
Ray Bourque
PP2-PV Thomas Vanek 12.00 30.00
Gilbert Perreault
PP2-RP Carey Price 50.00 100.00
Patrick Roy
PP2-SB Zach Boychuk 20.00 50.00
Brandon Sutter
PP2-TC Jonathan Cheechoo 20.00 50.00
Joe Thornton
PP2-TM Kyle Turris 15.00 40.00
Peter Mueller
PP2-ZL Nicklas Lidstrom 25.00 60.00
Henrik Zetterberg

2008-09 OPC Premier Dynasty Duos

STATED PRINT RUN 100 SER.#'d SETS
DD-AF Grant Fuhr 12.00 30.00
Glenn Anderson
DD-BP Mike Bossy 12.00 30.00
Denis Potvin
DD-DH Tomas Holmstrom 12.00 30.00
Pavel Datsyuk
DD-GM Mark Messier 125.00 250.00
Wayne Gretzky
DD-LK Ted Lindsay 15.00 40.00
Red Kelly
DD-LS Steve Shutt
Guy Lafleur
DD-MB Frank Mahovlich 15.00 40.00
Johnny Bower
DD-OE Bobby Orr 100.00 200.00
Phil Esposito

2008-09 OPC Premier Dynasty Duos Gold Spectrum

*SINGLES: .6X TO 1.5X BASIC INSERTS
STATED PRINT RUN 25 SER.#'d SETS

2008-09 OPC Premier Inductions Ink

STATED PRINT RUN 100 SER.#'d SETS
PI-AM Al MacInnis 10.00 25.00
PI-BS Borje Salming 8.00 20.00
PI-DS Denis Savard 8.00 20.00
PI-JM Joe Mullen 8.00 20.00
PI-LM Lanny McDonald 8.00 20.00
PI-MD Marcel Dionne 8.00 20.00
PI-PS Peter Stastny 8.00 20.00
PI-RB Ray Bourque 15.00 40.00
PI-SS Steve Shutt 8.00 20.00

2008-09 OPC Premier Inductions Ink Dual

STATED PRINT RUN 50 SER.#'d SETS
2PI-BP Denis Potvin 15.00 40.00
Mike Bossy
2PI-DM Marcel Dionne 15.00 40.00
Lanny McDonald
2PI-EL Guy Lafleur 30.00 80.00
Tony Esposito
2PI-GL Rod Langway 20.00 50.00
Clark Gillies
2PI-HB Jean Beliveau 75.00 150.00
Gordie Howe
2PI-KH Jari Kurri 15.00 40.00
Dale Hawerchuk
2PI-MM Mark Messier 50.00 100.00
Al MacInnis
2PI-MS Joe Mullen 15.00 40.00
Denis Savard
2PI-OH Harry Howell 75.00 150.00
Bobby Orr

2008-09 OPC Premier Inductions Ink Dual Gold

STATED PRINT RUN 10 SERIAL #'d SETS
NOT PRICED DUE TO SCARCITY

2008-09 OPC Premier Inductions Ink Gold Spectrum

*SINGLES: .5X TO 1.2X BASIC INSERTS
STATED PRINT RUN 25 SER.#'d SETS

2008-09 OPC Premier Penmanship

STATED PRINT RUN 100 SER.#'d SETS
PP-AK Anze Kopitar 8.00 20.00
PP-AO Alexander Ovechkin 40.00 80.00
PP-CP Carey Price 25.00 60.00
PP-DH Dany Heatley 10.00 25.00
PP-EM Evgeni Malkin 40.00 80.00
PP-HZ Henrik Zetterberg
PP-JG Jean-Sebastien Giguere 8.00 20.00
PP-JS Jordan Staal 12.00 30.00
PP-MH Milan Hejduk 6.00 15.00
PP-MR Mike Richards 12.00 30.00
PP-MT Marty Turco 6.00 15.00
PP-PK Patrick Kane 20.00 50.00
PP-PS Paul Stastny 8.00 20.00
PP-RG Ryan Getzlaf 10.00 25.00
PP-RH Ron Hextall 10.00 25.00
PP-SC Sidney Crosby 75.00 150.00
PP-SG Simon Gagne 6.00 15.00
PP-TH Joe Thornton 12.00 30.00
PP-TV Thomas Vanek 8.00 20.00
PP-VL Vincent Lecavalier 8.00 20.00

2008-09 OPC Premier Penmanship Gold Spectrum

*SINGLES: .6X TO 1.5X BASIC INSERTS
STATED PRINT RUN 25 SER.#'d SETS

2008-09 OPC Premier Rare Remnants Quads

STATED PRINT RUN 10 SERIAL #'d SETS
NOT PRICED DUE TO SCARCITY
RR4-PTML Kari Lehtonen
Carey Price
Ryan Miller
Marty Turco
RR4-RBLF Roberto Luongo
Martin Brodeur
Marc-Andre Fleury
Patrick Roy

2008-09 OPC Premier Rare Remnants Quads Gold

STATED PRINT RUN 3 SERIAL #'d SETS
NOT PRICED DUE TO SCARCITY

2008-09 OPC Premier Rare Remnants Quads Patches

STATED PRINT RUN 5 SERIAL #'d SETS
NOT PRICED DUE TO SCARCITY
RR4-ILSS Vincent Lecavalier
Joe Sakic
Jarome Iginla
Jason Spezza
RR4-LCMS Evgeni Malkin
Sidney Crosby
Jordan Staal
Mario Lemieux
RR4-OMKF Evgeni Malkin
Nikita Filatov
Ilya Kovalchuk
Alexander Ovechkin
RR4-PTML Kari Lehtonen
Carey Price
Ryan Miller
Marty Turco
RR4-RBLF Roberto Luongo
Martin Brodeur
Marc-Andre Fleury
Patrick Roy

2008-09 OPC Premier Rare Remnants Quads Patches Gold

STATED PRINT RUN 1 SERIAL #'d SET
NOT PRICED DUE TO SCARCITY

2008-09 OPC Premier Rare Remnants Triples

STATED PRINT RUN 20 SERIAL #'d SETS
NOT PRICED DUE TO SCARCITY
RR3-BON Adam Oates
Ray Bourque
Cam Neely
RR3-GML Mark Messier
Wayne Gretzky
Mario Lemieux
RR3-HSW Milan Hejduk
Marek Svatos
Wojtek Wolski
RR3-LNG Ryan Getzlaf
Rick Nash
Vincent Lecavalier
RR3-PMK Phil Kessel
Peter Mueller
Zach Parise
RR3-RBH Martin Brodeur
Dominik Hasek
Patrick Roy
RR3-RLB Patrick Roy
Martin Brodeur
Roberto Luongo
RR3-SBV Fabian Brunnstrom
Jakub Voracek
Steven Stamkos
RR3-SDB Zach Bogosian
Drew Doughty
Luke Schenn
RR3-SRL Steve Shutt
Rod Langway
Larry Robinson
RR3-SSB Patrice Bergeron
Eric Staal
Jason Spezza
RR3-ZLH Henrik Zetterberg
Nicklas Lidstrom
Tomas Holmstrom

2008-09 OPC Premier Rare Remnants Triples Gold

The checklist parallels that of the Rare Remnants Triples with the addition of one card, Carey Price/Saku Koivu/Alex Kovalev. These are serial numbered to 5.

STATED PRINT RUN 5 SERIAL #'d SETS
NOT PRICED DUE TO SCARCITY

2008-09 OPC Premier Rare Remnants Triples Patches

STATED PRINT RUN 10 SERIAL #'d SETS
NOT PRICED DUE TO SCARCITY
RR3-GML Mark Messier
Wayne Gretzky
Mario Lemieux
RR3-HSW Milan Hejduk
Marek Svatos
Wojtek Wolski
RR3-IPB Todd Bertuzzi
Mike Cammalleri
Jarome Iginla
RR3-PKK Carey Price
Alex Kovalev
Saku Koivu
RR3-RBH Martin Brodeur
Dominik Hasek
Patrick Roy
RR3-RLB Patrick Roy
Martin Brodeur
Roberto Luongo
RR3-SDB Zach Bogosian
Drew Doughty
Luke Schenn
RR3-SSB Patrice Bergeron
Eric Staal
Jason Spezza
RR3-VMA Ryan Miller
Thomas Vanek
Maxim Afinogenov

2008-09 OPC Premier Rare Remnants Triples Patches Gold

STATED PRINT RUN 3 SERIAL #'d SETS
NOT PRICED DUE TO SCARCITY

2008-09 OPC Premier Remnants Quads

STATED PRINT RUN 25 SER.#'d SETS
PR-AO Adam Oates 8.00 20.00
PR-BS Borje Salming 8.00 20.00
PR-CP Carey Price 25.00 60.00
PR-DH Dale Hawerchuk 8.00 20.00
PR-DS Darryl Sittler 8.00 20.00
PR-EM Evgeni Malkin 20.00 50.00
PR-ES Eric Staal 12.00 30.00
PR-HA Dominik Hasek 12.00 30.00
PR-HL Henrik Lundqvist 15.00 40.00
PR-HZ Henrik Zetterberg 15.00 40.00
PR-IK Ilya Kovalchuk 10.00 25.00
PR-JC Jonathan Cheechoo 8.00 20.00
PR-JI Jarome Iginla 15.00 40.00
PR-KB Nicklas Backstrom 15.00 40.00
PR-LM Lanny McDonald 8.00 20.00
PR-LR Larry Robinson 8.00 20.00
PR-MB Martin Brodeur 15.00 40.00
PR-MG Marian Gaborik 12.00 30.00
PR-MK Mikko Koivu 8.00 20.00
PR-ML Mario Lemieux 20.00 50.00
PR-MM Mike Modano 8.00 20.00
PR-MR Mike Richards 12.00 30.00
PR-NL Nicklas Lidstrom 8.00 20.00
PR-OV Alexander Ovechkin 30.00 80.00
PR-PB Patrice Bergeron 8.00 20.00
PR-PM Peter Mueller 10.00 25.00
PR-PR Patrick Roy 25.00 60.00
PR-RB Ray Bourque 15.00 40.00
PR-RL Roberto Luongo 12.00 30.00
PR-RN Rick Nash 8.00 20.00
PR-SC Sidney Crosby 40.00 100.00
PR-SD Shane Doan 5.00 12.00
PR-SG Simon Gagne 6.00 15.00
PR-SK Saku Koivu 8.00 20.00
PR-SS Steve Shutt 8.00 20.00
PR-TR Tuomo Ruutu 8.00 20.00
PR-VL Vincent Lecavalier 8.00 20.00
PR-ZP Marian Hossa 12.00 30.00

2008-09 OPC Premier Remnants Quads Autographs

STATED PRINT RUN 10 SERIAL #'d SETS
NOT PRICED DUE TO SCARCITY

2008-09 OPC Premier Remnants Quads Autographs Gold

STATED PRINT RUN 5 SERIAL #'d SETS
NOT PRICED DUE TO SCARCITY

2008-09 OPC Premier Remnants Quads Gold

*GOLD: .5X TO 1.2X BASIC
STATED PRINT RUN 20 SERIAL #'d SETS

2008-09 OPC Premier Remnants Triples

STATED PRINT RUN 100 SER.#'d SETS
PR-AO Adam Oates 5.00 12.00
PR-BS Borje Salming 5.00 12.00
PR-CP Carey Price 15.00 40.00
PR-DH Dale Hawerchuk 5.00 12.00
PR-DS Darryl Sittler 5.00 12.00
PR-EM Evgeni Malkin 12.00 30.00
PR-ES Eric Staal 8.00 20.00
PR-HA Dominik Hasek 8.00 20.00
PR-HL Henrik Lundqvist 10.00 25.00
PR-HZ Henrik Zetterberg 10.00 25.00
PR-IK Ilya Kovalchuk 6.00 15.00
PR-JC Jonathan Cheechoo 5.00 12.00
PR-JI Jarome Iginla 10.00 25.00
PR-KB Nicklas Backstrom 10.00 25.00
PR-LM Lanny McDonald 5.00 12.00
PR-LR Larry Robinson 5.00 12.00
PR-MB Martin Brodeur 10.00 25.00
PR-MG Marian Gaborik 8.00 20.00
PR-MK Mikko Koivu 5.00 12.00
PR-ML Mario Lemieux 12.00 30.00
PR-MM Mike Modano 5.00 12.00
PR-MR Mike Richards 8.00 20.00
PR-NL Nicklas Lidstrom 5.00 12.00
PR-OV Alexander Ovechkin 20.00 50.00
PR-PB Patrice Bergeron 5.00 12.00
PR-PM Peter Mueller 6.00 15.00
PR-PR Patrick Roy 15.00 40.00
PR-RB Ray Bourque 10.00 25.00
PR-RN Rick Nash 5.00 12.00
PR-SC Sidney Crosby 25.00 60.00
PR-SD Shane Doan 3.00 8.00
PR-SG Simon Gagne 4.00 10.00
PR-SK Saku Koivu 5.00 12.00
PR-SS Steve Shutt 5.00 12.00
PR-TR Tuomo Ruutu 5.00 12.00
PR-VL Vincent Lecavalier 5.00 12.00
PR-ZP Marian Hossa 8.00 20.00

2008-09 OPC Premier Remnants Triples Gold

*SINGLES: .6X TO 1.5X BASIC INSERTS
STATED PRINT RUN 35 SER.#'d SETS

2008-09 OPC Premier Stitchings

STATED PRINT RUN 99 SER.#'d SETS
PS-BH Bobby Hull 6.00 15.00
PS-BO Bobby Orr 10.00 25.00
PS-CN Cam Neely 4.00 10.00
PS-CP Carey Price 10.00 25.00
PS-DH Dany Heatley 4.00 10.00
PS-EM Evgeni Malkin 8.00 20.00
PS-GH Gordie Howe 12.00 30.00
PS-HL Henrik Lundqvist 6.00 15.00
PS-HZ Henrik Zetterberg 6.00 15.00
PS-IK Ilya Kovalchuk 4.00 10.00
PS-JI Jarome Iginla 6.00 15.00
PS-JS Joe Sakic 5.00 12.00
PS-JT Joe Thornton 5.00 12.00
PS-MB Martin Brodeur 6.00 15.00
PS-ME Mark Messier 6.00 15.00
PS-MG Marian Gaborik 5.00 12.00
PS-ML Mario Lemieux 8.00 20.00
PS-MM Mike Modano 3.00 8.00
PS-OV Alexander Ovechkin 12.00 30.00
PS-PD Pavel Datsyuk 3.00 8.00
PS-PE Phil Esposito 4.00 10.00
PS-PK Patrick Kane 8.00 20.00
PS-PR Patrick Roy 10.00 25.00
PS-RB Ray Bourque 6.00 15.00
PS-RL Roberto Luongo 5.00 12.00
PS-RN Rick Nash 3.00 8.00
PS-SS Steven Stamkos 10.00 25.00
PS-TO Jonathan Toews 10.00 25.00
PS-VL Vincent Lecavalier 3.00 8.00
PS-WG Wayne Gretzky 15.00 40.00

2008-09 OPC Premier Stitchings Autographs

STATED PRINT RUN 50 SER.#'d SETS
CARDS #'d TO 15 NOT PRICED DUE TO SCARCITY
APS-BH Bobby Hull 20.00 50.00
APS-BO Bobby Orr/15
APS-CN Cam Neely 20.00 50.00
APS-CP Carey Price 30.00 80.00
APS-EM Evgeni Malkin/15
APS-GH Gordie Howe/15
APS-HE Dany Heatley
APS-HZ Henrik Zetterberg 25.00 60.00
APS-JI Jarome Iginla 15.00 40.00
APS-JT Joe Thornton 12.00 30.00
APS-MB Martin Brodeur 50.00 100.00
APS-ML Mario Lemieux/15
APS-MM Mark Messier/15
APS-PE Phil Esposito 12.00 30.00
APS-PK Patrick Kane 20.00 50.00
APS-PR Patrick Roy/15
APS-TO Jonathan Toews 25.00 60.00
APS-WG Wayne Gretzky/15

2008-09 OPC Premier Stitchings Blue

*BLUE: .6X TO 1.5X STITCHINGS
STATED PRINT RUN 25 SER.#'d SETS

2008-09 OPC Premier Stitchings Variation

*VARIATION: .5X TO 1.2X STITCHINGS
STATED PRINT RUN 75 SER.#'d SETS

2008-09 OPC Premier Stitchings Variation Black

STATED PRINT RUN 1 SERIAL #'d SET
NOT PRICED DUE TO SCARCITY

2008-09 OPC Premier Trios

STATED PRINT RUN 35 SER.#'d SETS
PP3-BPF Carey Price 40.00 100.00
Marc-Andre Fleury
Martin Brodeur
PP3-BPG Clark Gillies 50.00 100.00
Denis Potvin
Mike Bossy
PP3-BVF Nikita Filatov
Jakub Voracek
Derick Brassard
PP3-GOH Gordie Howe 250.00 400.00
Wayne Gretzky
Bobby Orr
PP3-HTK Patrick Kane
Bobby Hull
Jonathan Toews
PP3-MLS Mark Messier
Steven Stamkos
Mario Lemieux
PP3-RFH Ron Hextall 125.00 200.00
Patrick Roy
Grant Fuhr
PP3-TBW Blake Wheeler
Fabian Brunnstrom
Kyle Turris

2009-10 OPC Premier

STATED PRINT RUN 299 SER.#'d SETS
1 Al MacInnis 2.00 5.00
2 Alexander Ovechkin 8.00 20.00
3 Anze Kopitar 2.00 5.00
4 Bobby Hull 5.00 12.00
5 Bobby Orr 8.00 20.00
6 Brian Leetch 2.00 5.00
7 Cam Neely 3.00 8.00
8 Carey Price 5.00 12.00
9 Dale Hawerchuk 2.00 5.00
10 Daniel Sedin 2.50 6.00
11 Dany Heatley 4.00 10.00
12 Dion Phaneuf 3.00 8.00
13 Eric Staal 2.50 6.00
14 Evgeni Malkin 5.00 12.00
15 Gordie Howe 8.00 20.00
16 Grant Fuhr 2.50 6.00
17 Guy Lafleur 3.00 8.00
18 Henrik Sedin 3.00 8.00
19 Henrik Zetterberg 4.00 10.00
20 Ilya Kovalchuk 2.50 6.00
21 Jari Kurri 2.00 5.00
22 Jarome Iginla 4.00 10.00
23 Jason Spezza 2.50 6.00
24 Jean Beliveau 3.00 8.00
25 Joe Thornton 4.00 10.00
26 Jonathan Toews 5.00 12.00
27 Luc Robitaille 2.00 5.00
28 Marc-Andre Fleury 2.00 5.00
29 Marian Gaborik 3.00 8.00
30 Mario Lemieux 5.00 12.00
31 Mark Messier 4.00 10.00
32 Martin Brodeur 5.00 12.00
33 Martin St. Louis 2.00 5.00
34 Marty Turco 1.50 4.00
35 Mike Richards 4.00 10.00
36 Nicklas Backstrom 4.00 10.00
37 Nicklas Lidstrom 2.50 6.00
38 Patrick Kane 4.00 10.00
39 Patrick Roy 6.00 15.00
40 Paul Stastny 2.00 5.00
41 Pavel Datsyuk 2.00 5.00
42 Phil Esposito 4.00 10.00
43 Ray Bourque 3.00 8.00
44 Rick Nash 3.00 8.00
45 Roberto Luongo 5.00 12.00
46 Ron Hextall 5.00 12.00
47 Ryan Getzlaf 3.00 8.00
48 Ryan Miller 2.00 5.00
49 Saku Koivu 2.00 5.00
50 Sam Gagner 2.50 6.00
51 Sidney Crosby 10.00 25.00
52 Steve Mason 3.00 8.00
53 Steve Yzerman 6.00 15.00
54 Steven Stamkos 5.00 12.00
55 Teemu Selanne 2.00 5.00
56 Thomas Vanek 2.00 5.00
57 Tony Esposito 3.00 8.00
58 Vincent Lecavalier 2.50 6.00
59 Walt Tkaczuk 1.50 4.00
60 Wayne Gretzky 10.00 25.00
61 John Tavares JSY AU RC 75.00 150.00
62 James van Riemsdyk JSY AU RC 25.00 50.00
63 Evander Kane JSY AU RC 15.00 40.00
64 Victor Hedman JSY AU RC 15.00 40.00
65 Jonas Gustavsson JSY AU RC 10.00 25.00
66 Matt Duchene JSY AU RC 40.00 80.00
67 Colin Wilson JSY AU RC 10.00 25.00
68 T.J. Galiardi JSY AU RC 8.00 20.00
69 Yannick Weber JSY AU RC 8.00 20.00
70 Spencer Machacek JSY AU RC 8.00 20.00
71 Antti Niemi JSY AU RC 15.00 40.00
72 Viktor Stalberg JSY AU RC 10.00 25.00
73 Michael Del Zotto JSY AU RC 12.00 30.00
74 Dmitry Kulikov JSY AU RC 6.00 15.00
75 Jamie Benn JSY AU RC 10.00 25.00
76 Ryan O'Reilly JSY AU RC 12.00 30.00
77 Tyler Myers JSY AU RC 25.00 60.00
78 Erik Karlsson JSY AU RC 15.00 40.00
79 Matt Gilroy JSY AU RC 8.00 20.00
80 Sergei Shirokov JSY AU RC 10.00 25.00
81 Ville Leino JSY AU RC 8.00 20.00
82 Riku Helenius JSY AU RC 6.00 15.00
83 Mikael Backlund JSY AU RC 10.00 25.00
84 Michal Neuvirth JSY AU RC 15.00 40.00
85 Cody Franson JSY AU RC 6.00 15.00
86 Luca Caputi JSY AU RC 8.00 20.00
87 Kris Chucko JSY AU RC 5.00 12.00
88 Jhonas Enroth JSY AU RC 8.00 20.00
89 Ivan Vishnevskiy JSY AU RC 8.00 20.00
90 Jakub Kindl JSY AU RC 8.00 20.00
91 Artem Anisimov JSY AU RC 8.00 20.00
92 Taylor Chorney JSY AU RC 6.00 15.00
93 Benn Ferriero JSY AU RC 6.00 15.00
94 Cal O'Reilly JSY AU RC 6.00 15.00
95 Matthew Corrente JSY AU RC 6.00 15.00
96 Jason Demers JSY AU RC 5.00 12.00
97 Ryan Stoa JSY AU RC 6.00 15.00
98 Lars Eller JSY AU RC 10.00 25.00
99 Ryan O'Marra JSY AU RC 5.00 12.00
100 Logan Couture JSY AU RC 12.00 30.00
101 Brad Marchand JSY AU RC 8.00 20.00
102 Michael Grabner JSY AU RC 8.00 20.00

2009-10 OPC Premier Black

(1-60) PRINT RUN 1 SER.#'d SET
(61-102) PRINT RUN 10 SER.#'d SETS
NOT PRICED DUE TO SCARCITY

2009-10 OPC Premier Gold

*SINGLES: .8X TO 2X BASIC CARDS
STATED PRINT RUN 25 SER.#'d SETS
51 Sidney Crosby 20.00 50.00
60 Wayne Gretzky 20.00 50.00

2009-10 OPC Premier Gold Spectrum

(1-60) PRINT RUN 10 SER.#'d SETS
(1-60) NOT PRICED DUE TO SCARCITY
(61-102) PRINT RUN 35 SER.#'d SETS
1 Al MacInnis
2 Alexander Ovechkin
3 Anze Kopitar
4 Bobby Hull
5 Bobby Orr
6 Brian Leetch
7 Cam Neely
8 Carey Price
9 Dale Hawerchuk
10 Daniel Sedin
11 Dany Heatley
12 Dion Phaneuf
13 Eric Staal
14 Evgeni Malkin
15 Gordie Howe
16 Grant Fuhr
17 Guy Lafleur
18 Henrik Sedin
19 Henrik Zetterberg
20 Ilya Kovalchuk
21 Jari Kurri
22 Jarome Iginla
23 Jason Spezza
24 Jean Beliveau
25 Joe Thornton
26 Jonathan Toews
27 Luc Robitaille
28 Marc-Andre Fleury
29 Marian Gaborik
30 Mario Lemieux
31 Mark Messier
32 Martin Brodeur
33 Martin St. Louis
34 Marty Turco
35 Mike Richards
36 Nicklas Backstrom
37 Nicklas Lidstrom
38 Patrick Kane
39 Patrick Roy
40 Paul Stastny
41 Pavel Datsyuk
42 Phil Esposito
43 Ray Bourque
44 Rick Nash
45 Roberto Luongo
46 Ron Hextall
47 Ryan Getzlaf
48 Ryan Miller
49 Saku Koivu
50 Sam Gagner
51 Sidney Crosby
52 Steve Mason
53 Steve Yzerman
54 Steven Stamkos
55 Teemu Selanne
56 Thomas Vanek
57 Tony Esposito
58 Vincent Lecavalier
59 Walt Tkaczuk
60 Wayne Gretzky
61 John Tavares JSY/PATCH 125.00 250.00
62 James van Riemsdyk JSY/PATCH 50.00 100.00
63 Evander Kane JSY/PATCH 30.00 60.00
64 Victor Hedman JSY/PATCH 30.00 60.00
65 Jonas Gustavsson JSY/PATCH 60.00 120.00
66 Matt Duchene JSY/PATCH 75.00 150.00
67 Colin Wilson JSY/PATCH
68 T.J. Galiardi JSY/PATCH 15.00 40.00
69 Yannick Weber JSY/PATCH 15.00 40.00
70 Spencer Machacek JSY/PATCH 12.00 30.00
71 Antti Niemi JSY/PATCH 40.00 80.00
72 Viktor Stalberg JSY/PATCH 25.00 60.00
73 Michael Del Zotto JSY/PATCH 25.00 60.00
74 Dmitry Kulikov JSY/PATCH 20.00 50.00
75 Jamie Benn JSY/PATCH 25.00 60.00
76 Ryan O'Reilly JSY/PATCH 25.00 60.00
77 Tyler Myers JSY/PATCH 50.00 100.00
78 Erik Karlsson JSY/PATCH 60.00 120.00
79 Matt Gilroy JSY/PATCH 12.00 30.00
80 Sergei Shirokov JSY/PATCH
81 Ville Leino JSY/PATCH 15.00 40.00
82 Riku Helenius JSY/PATCH 15.00 40.00
83 Mikael Backlund JSY/PATCH 25.00 60.00
84 Michal Neuvirth JSY/PATCH 40.00 80.00
85 Cody Franson JSY/PATCH 15.00 40.00
86 Luca Caputi JSY/PATCH 15.00 40.00
87 Kris Chucko JSY/PATCH 10.00 25.00
88 Jhonas Enroth JSY/PATCH 15.00 40.00
89 Ivan Vishnevskiy JSY/PATCH
90 Jakub Kindl JSY/PATCH 12.00 30.00
91 Artem Anisimov JSY/PATCH 15.00 40.00

92 Taylor Chorney JSY/PATCH 25.00 60.00
93 Benn Ferriero JSY/PATCH
94 Cal O'Reilly JSY/PATCH 15.00 40.00
95 Matthew Corrente JSY/PATCH 12.00 30.00
96 Jason Demers JSY/PATCH 25.00 60.00
97 Ryan Stoa JSY/PATCH 12.00 30.00
98 Lars Eller JSY/PATCH 25.00 60.00
99 Ryan O'Marra JSY/PATCH 12.00 30.00
100 Logan Couture JSY/PATCH 25.00 60.00
101 Brad Marchand JSY/PATCH 15.00 40.00
102 Michael Grabner JSY/PATCH 20.00 50.00

2009-10 OPC Premier Gold Spectrum Autographs

STATED PRINT RUN 1 SER.#'d SETS
NOT PRICED DUE TO SCARCITY
1 Al MacInnis
2 Alexander Ovechkin
4 Bobby Hull
5 Bobby Orr
6 Brian Leetch
7 Cam Neely
8 Carey Price
9 Dale Hawerchuk
10 Daniel Sedin
12 Dion Phaneuf
13 Eric Staal
15 Gordie Howe
16 Grant Fuhr
17 Guy Lafleur
19 Henrik Zetterberg
21 Jari Kurri
22 Jarome Iginla
24 Jean Beliveau
25 Joe Thornton
26 Jonathan Toews
27 Luc Robitaille
28 Marc-Andre Fleury
29 Marian Gaborik
31 Mark Messier
32 Martin Brodeur
33 Martin St. Louis
34 Marty Turco
36 Nicklas Backstrom
37 Nicklas Lidstrom
39 Patrick Roy
40 Paul Stastny
41 Pavel Datsyuk
42 Phil Esposito
43 Ray Bourque
44 Rick Nash
48 Ryan Miller
51 Sidney Crosby
52 Steve Mason
53 Steve Yzerman
54 Steven Stamkos
56 Thomas Vanek
57 Tony Esposito

2009-10 OPC Premier Foursomes

STATED PRINT RUN 25 SER.#'d SETS
4JAVKS Artem Anisimov 12.00 30.00
Sergei Shirokov
Dmitry Kulikov
Ivan Vishnevskiy
4JCKWM Logan Couture 12.00 30.00
Evander Kane
Colin Wilson
Brad Marchand
4JCTDM Matthew Corrente 30.00 60.00
John Tavares
Michael Del Zotto
Tyler Myers
4JDENG Jonas Gustavsson 25.00 60.00
Antti Niemi
Jhonas Enroth
Devan Dubnyk
4JDKOM Alexander Ovechkin 20.00 50.00
Evgeni Malkin
Ilya Kovalchuk
Pavel Datsyuk
4JDMKH Victor Hedman 30.00 80.00
Michael Del Zotto
Erik Karlsson
Tyler Myers
4JEBHH Phil Esposito
Jean Beliveau
Bobby Hull
Gordie Howe
4JEMEB Jhonas Enroth 25.00 60.00
Tyler Myers
Tyler Ennis
Chris Butler
4JFCMS Marc-Andre Fleury 40.00 100.00
Sidney Crosby
Evgeni Malkin
Jordan Staal
4JGMCP Carey Price
Scott Gomez
Mike Cammalleri
Andrei Markov
4JHGBS Jonas Gustavsson 30.00 80.00
Tyler Bozak
Viktor Stalberg
Christian Hanson
4JISHN Jarome Iginla 15.00 40.00
Dany Heatley
Rick Nash
Martin St. Louis
4JJIKP Jarome Iginla
Miikka Kiprusoff
Dion Phaneuf
Olli Jokinen
4JKCOT Ilya Kovalchuk 50.00 120.00
Sidney Crosby
Alexander Ovechkin
John Tavares
4JLDZF Nicklas Lidstrom
Pavel Datsyuk
Henrik Zetterberg
Johan Franzen
4JLSSK Henrik Sedin
Daniel Sedin
Ryan Kesler
Roberto Luongo
4JLTSS Jason Spezza
Eric Staal
Vincent Lecavalier
Joe Thornton
4JLYCO Mario Lemieux 100.00 175.00
Steve Yzerman
Sidney Crosby
Alexander Ovechkin
4JLYGM Mark Messier 75.00 150.00
Wayne Gretzky
Mario Lemieux
Steve Yzerman
4JMPOV James van Riemsdyk 12.00 30.00
Mike Modano
Zach Parise
Kyle Okposo
4JMTNS Joe Thornton 12.00 30.00
Patrick Marleau
Devin Setoguchi
Evgeni Nabokov
4JNCTS Sidney Crosby 40.00 100.00
Rick Nash
Steven Stamkos
John Tavares
4JRBLF Patrick Roy 25.00 60.00
Martin Brodeur
Roberto Luongo
Marc-Andre Fleury
4JRBTL Tim Thomas 15.00 40.00
Milan Lucic
Patrice Bergeron
Michael Ryder
4JRCGV James van Riemsdyk 30.00 80.00
Mike Richards
Jeff Carter
Claude Giroux
4JSDSG Michael Del Zotto 10.00 25.00
Matt Gilroy
Bobby Sanguinetti
Michael Sauer
4JSGDO Paul Stastny 30.00 80.00
T.J. Galiardi
Matt Duchene
Ryan O'Reilly
4JSSGS Daniel Sedin
Henrik Sedin
Sergei Shirokov
Michael Grabner
4JTKDH John Tavares
Evander Kane
Matt Duchene
Victor Hedman
4JTWPM Steve Mason 20.00 50.00
Carey Price
Cam Ward
Marty Turco

2009-10 OPC Premier Foursomes Patches

STATED PRINT RUN 10 SER.#'d SETS
NOT PRICED DUE TO SCARCITY
4JAVKS Artem Anisimov
Sergei Shirokov
Dmitry Kulikov
Ivan Vishnevskiy
4JCKWM Logan Couture
Evander Kane
Colin Wilson
Brad Marchand
4JCTDM Matthew Corrente
John Tavares
Michael Del Zotto
Tyler Myers
4JDENG Jonas Gustavsson
Antti Niemi
Jhonas Enroth
Devan Dubnyk
4JDKOM Alexander Ovechkin
Evgeni Malkin
Ilya Kovalchuk
Pavel Datsyuk
4JDMKH Victor Hedman
Michael Del Zotto
Erik Karlsson
Tyler Myers
4JEBHH Phil Esposito
Jean Beliveau
Bobby Hull
Gordie Howe
4JEMEB Jhonas Enroth
Tyler Myers
Tyler Ennis
Chris Butler
4JFCMS Marc-Andre Fleury
Sidney Crosby
Evgeni Malkin
Jordan Staal
4JGMCP Carey Price
Scott Gomez
Mike Cammalleri
Andrei Markov
4JHGBS Jonas Gustavsson
Tyler Bozak
Viktor Stalberg
Christian Hanson
4JISHN Jarome Iginla
Dany Heatley
Rick Nash
Martin St. Louis
4JJIKP Jarome Iginla
Miikka Kiprusoff
Dion Phaneuf
Olli Jokinen
4JKCOT Ilya Kovalchuk
Sidney Crosby
Alexander Ovechkin
John Tavares
4JLDZF Nicklas Lidstrom
Pavel Datsyuk
Henrik Zetterberg
Johan Franzen
4JLSSK Henrik Sedin
Daniel Sedin
Ryan Kesler
Roberto Luongo
4JLTSS Jason Spezza
Eric Staal
Vincent Lecavalier
Joe Thornton
4JLYCO Mario Lemieux
Steve Yzerman
Sidney Crosby
Alexander Ovechkin
4JLYGM Mark Messier
Wayne Gretzky
Mario Lemieux
Steve Yzerman
4JMPOV James van Riemsdyk
Mike Modano
Zach Parise
Kyle Okposo
4JMTNS Joe Thornton
Patrick Marleau
Devin Setoguchi
Evgeni Nabokov
4JNCTS Sidney Crosby
Rick Nash
Steven Stamkos
John Tavares
4JRBLF Patrick Roy
Martin Brodeur
Roberto Luongo
Marc-Andre Fleury
4JRBTL Tim Thomas
Milan Lucic
Patrice Bergeron
Michael Ryder
4JRCGV James van Riemsdyk
Mike Richards
Jeff Carter
Claude Giroux
4JSDSG Michael Del Zotto
Matt Gilroy
Bobby Sanguinetti
Michael Sauer
4JSGDO Paul Stastny
T.J. Galiardi
Matt Duchene
Ryan O'Reilly
4JSSGS Daniel Sedin
Henrik Sedin
Sergei Shirokov
Michael Grabner
4JTKDH John Tavares
Evander Kane
Matt Duchene
Victor Hedman
4JTWPM Steve Mason
Carey Price
Cam Ward
Marty Turco

2009-10 OPC Premier Rare Remnants Quads Patches Autographs

STATED PRINT RUN 5 SER.#'d SETS
NOT PRICED DUE TO SCARCITY

2009-10 OPC Premier Rare Remnants Triples

STATED PRINT RUN 35 SER.#'d SETS
PRTAN Antti Niemi 15.00 40.00
PRTAO Alexander Ovechkin 15.00 40.00
PRTBA Mikael Backlund 12.00 30.00
PRTBH Bobby Hull 12.00 30.00
PRTBL Brian Leetch 5.00 12.00
PRTBM Brad Marchand 6.00 15.00
PRTCN Cam Neely 8.00 20.00
PRTCP Carey Price 15.00 40.00
PRTCW Colin Wilson 10.00 25.00
PRTDB Derick Brassard 5.00 12.00
PRTDE Michael Del Zotto 10.00 25.00
PRTDH Dany Heatley 10.00 25.00
PRTDP Dion Phaneuf 8.00 20.00
PRTEK Evander Kane 8.00 20.00
PRTEM Evgeni Malkin 12.00 30.00
PRTES Eric Staal 8.00 20.00
PRTGH Gordie Howe 20.00 50.00
PRTGR Michael Grabner 5.00 12.00
PRTHL Henrik Lundqvist 10.00 25.00
PRTHZ Henrik Zetterberg 10.00 25.00
PRTIK Ilya Kovalchuk 6.00 15.00
PRTJB Jamie Benn 8.00 20.00
PRTJC Jeff Carter 8.00 20.00
PRTJG Jonas Gustavsson 12.00 30.00
PRTJI Jarome Iginla 10.00 25.00
PRTJS Jordan Staal 6.00 15.00
PRTJT Joe Thornton 10.00 25.00
PRTJV James van Riemsdyk 12.00 30.00
PRTKE Phil Kessel 5.00 12.00
PRTLC Logan Couture 10.00 25.00
PRTLE Lars Eller 15.00 40.00
PRTMB Martin Brodeur 15.00 40.00
PRTMD Matt Duchene 15.00 40.00
PRTMF Marc-Andre Fleury 10.00 25.00
PRTMG Marian Gaborik 8.00 20.00
PRTMK Miikka Kiprusoff 8.00 20.00
PRTML Mario Lemieux 15.00 40.00
PRTMM Mark Messier 12.00 30.00
PRTMO Mike Modano 5.00 12.00
PRTMR Mike Richards 10.00 25.00
PRTMS Martin St. Louis 5.00 12.00
PRTMT Marty Turco 4.00 10.00
PRTNB Nicklas Backstrom 10.00 25.00
PRTNL Nicklas Lidstrom 6.00 15.00
PRTPD Pavel Datsyuk 10.00 25.00
PRTPK Patrick Kane 12.00 30.00
PRTPM Patrick Marleau 12.00 30.00
PRTPR Patrick Roy 15.00 40.00
PRTPS Paul Stastny 5.00 12.00
PRTRB Ray Bourque 8.00 20.00
PRTRL Roberto Luongo 10.00 25.00
PRTRN Rick Nash 8.00 20.00
PRTRO Ryan O'Reilly 10.00 25.00
PRTSC Sidney Crosby 25.00 60.00
PRTSM Steve Mason 8.00 20.00
PRTSP Jason Spezza 6.00 15.00
PRTSS Steven Stamkos 10.00 25.00
PRTSY Steve Yzerman 25.00 60.00
PRTTA John Tavares 20.00 50.00
PRTTB Tyler Bozak 12.00 30.00
PRTTM Tyler Myers 15.00 40.00
PRTTO Jonathan Toews 12.00 30.00
PRTTT Tim Thomas 12.00 30.00
PRTTV Tomas Vokoun 5.00 12.00
PRTVH Victor Hedman 10.00 25.00
PRTVI Ville Leino 6.00 15.00
PRTVL Vincent Lecavalier 6.00 15.00
PRTWA Cam Ward 8.00 20.00
PRTWG Wayne Gretzky 25.00 60.00
PRTZP Zach Parise 6.00 15.00

2009-10 OPC Premier Rare Remnants Triples Patches

STATED PRINT RUN 25 SER.#'d SETS
PRTAN Antti Niemi 30.00 80.00
PRTAO Alexander Ovechkin 75.00 150.00
PRTBA Mikael Backlund 15.00 40.00
PRTBH Bobby Hull
PRTBL Brian Leetch
PRTBM Brad Marchand 12.00 30.00
PRTCN Cam Neely
PRTCP Carey Price
PRTCW Colin Wilson 15.00 40.00
PRTDB Derick Brassard
PRTDE Michael Del Zotto 15.00 40.00
PRTDH Dany Heatley
PRTDP Dion Phaneuf 12.00 30.00
PRTEK Evander Kane 12.00 30.00
PRTEM Evgeni Malkin 50.00 100.00
PRTES Eric Staal
PRTGH Gordie Howe
PRTGR Michael Grabner 15.00 40.00
PRTHL Henrik Lundqvist 20.00 50.00
PRTHZ Henrik Zetterberg 15.00 40.00
PRTIK Ilya Kovalchuk 15.00 40.00
PRTJB Jamie Benn 15.00 40.00
PRTJC Jeff Carter
PRTJG Jonas Gustavsson 25.00 60.00
PRTJI Jarome Iginla 20.00 50.00
PRTJS Jordan Staal 12.00 30.00
PRTJT Joe Thornton 15.00 40.00
PRTJV James van Riemsdyk 20.00 50.00
PRTKE Phil Kessel
PRTLC Logan Couture 20.00 50.00
PRTLE Lars Eller 15.00 40.00
PRTMB Martin Brodeur 25.00 60.00
PRTMD Matt Duchene 40.00 80.00
PRTMF Marc-Andre Fleury 25.00 60.00
PRTMG Marian Gaborik 25.00 60.00
PRTMK Miikka Kiprusoff 20.00 50.00
PRTML Mario Lemieux
PRTMM Mark Messier 20.00 50.00
PRTMO Mike Modano 12.00 30.00
PRTMR Mike Richards 40.00 80.00
PRTMS Martin St. Louis 10.00 25.00
PRTMT Marty Turco 12.00 30.00
PRTNB Nicklas Backstrom 20.00 50.00
PRTNL Nicklas Lidstrom
PRTPD Pavel Datsyuk 12.00 30.00
PRTPK Patrick Kane 25.00 60.00
PRTPM Patrick Marleau 8.00 20.00
PRTPR Patrick Roy
PRTPS Paul Stastny 10.00 25.00
PRTRB Ray Bourque 12.00 30.00
PRTRL Roberto Luongo 20.00 50.00
PRTRN Rick Nash 15.00 40.00
PRTRO Ryan O'Reilly 20.00 50.00
PRTSC Sidney Crosby 100.00 175.00
PRTSM Steve Mason 15.00 40.00
PRTSP Jason Spezza 15.00 40.00
PRTSS Steven Stamkos 25.00 60.00
PRTSY Steve Yzerman 30.00 80.00
PRTTA John Tavares
PRTTB Tyler Bozak 20.00 50.00
PRTTM Tyler Myers 25.00 60.00
PRTTO Jonathan Toews 25.00 60.00
PRTTT Tim Thomas 10.00 25.00
PRTTV Tomas Vokoun 12.00 30.00
PRTVH Victor Hedman 20.00 50.00
PRTVI Ville Leino 12.00 30.00
PRTVL Vincent Lecavalier
PRTWA Cam Ward 15.00 40.00
PRTWG Wayne Gretzky
PRTZP Zach Parise 20.00 50.00

2009-10 OPC Premier Rare Remnants Triples Patches Autographs

STATED PRINT RUN 10 SER.#'d SETS
NOT PRICED DUE TO SCARCITY

2009-10 OPC Premier Remnants Quad Jerseys

STATED PRINT RUN 25 SER.#'d SETS
PRQAO Alexander Ovechkin 25.00 60.00
PRQDP Dion Phaneuf 10.00 25.00
PRQEK Evander Kane 15.00 40.00
PRQEM Evgeni Malkin 15.00 40.00
PRQGH Gordie Howe 25.00 60.00
PRQHL Henrik Lundqvist 25.00 60.00
PRQHZ Henrik Zetterberg 12.00 30.00
PRQIK Ilya Kovalchuk 6.00 15.00
PRQJB Jamie Benn 10.00 25.00
PRQJC Jeff Carter 10.00 25.00
PRQJG Jonas Gustavsson 15.00 40.00
PRQJI Jarome Iginla 12.00 30.00
PRQJT John Tavares 25.00 60.00
PRQJV James van Riemsdyk 25.00 60.00
PRQMB Martin Brodeur 15.00 40.00
PRQMD Matt Duchene 20.00 50.00
PRQMF Marc-Andre Fleury 6.00 15.00
PRQMG Michael Grabner 8.00 20.00
PRQMK Miikka Kiprusoff 10.00 25.00
PRQML Mario Lemieux 20.00 50.00
PRQMM Mark Messier 12.00 30.00
PRQMR Mike Richards 25.00 60.00
PRQNB Nicklas Backstrom 12.00 30.00
PRQNL Nicklas Lidstrom 12.00 30.00
PRQPR Patrick Roy 20.00 50.00
PRQRL Roberto Luongo 20.00 50.00
PRQSC Sidney Crosby 30.00 80.00
PRQSS Steven Stamkos 15.00 40.00
PRQSY Steve Yzerman 25.00 60.00
PRQWG Wayne Gretzky 50.00 100.00

2009-10 OPC Premier Remnants Quad Patches

STATED PRINT RUN 10 SER.#'d SETS
NOT PRICED DUE TO SCARCITY

2009-10 OPC Premier Remnants Quad Jerseys Autographs

STATED PRINT RUN 25 SER.#'d SETS
NOT PRICED DUE TO SCARCITY

2009-10 OPC Premier Remnants Triple Autographs

STATED PRINT RUN 25 SER.#'d SETS
AR3AO Alexander Ovechkin
AR3BH Bobby Hull 25.00 60.00
AR3BL Brian Leetch 12.00 30.00
AR3BW Blake Wheeler 12.00 30.00
AR3CN Cam Neely 15.00 40.00
AR3CP Carey Price
AR3CW Cam Ward 12.00 30.00
AR3DP Dion Phaneuf 15.00 40.00
AR3EM Evgeni Malkin 25.00 60.00
AR3ES Eric Staal 12.00 30.00
AR3GA Glenn Anderson 15.00 40.00
AR3GH Gordie Howe 60.00 120.00
AR3HL Henrik Lundqvist 20.00 50.00
AR3HZ Henrik Zetterberg 20.00 50.00
AR3IK Ilya Kovalchuk
AR3JC Jeff Carter
AR3JI Jarome Iginla 20.00 50.00
AR3JK Jari Kurri 20.00 50.00
AR3JT Joe Thornton 20.00 50.00
AR3LR Luc Robitaille 20.00 50.00
AR3MB Martin Brodeur 50.00 100.00
AR3MF Marc-Andre Fleury 15.00 40.00
AR3MG Marian Gaborik 15.00 40.00
AR3ML Mario Lemieux 50.00 100.00
AR3MM Mark Messier 20.00 50.00
AR3MR Mike Richards
AR3NB Nicklas Backstrom 20.00 50.00
AR3NL Nicklas Lidstrom 15.00 40.00
AR3PD Pavel Datsyuk
AR3PR Patrick Roy
AR3RB Ray Bourque 25.00 60.00
AR3RM Ryan Miller 20.00 50.00
AR3RN Rick Nash 15.00 40.00
AR3SC Sidney Crosby 100.00 175.00
AR3SM Steve Mason 15.00 40.00
AR3SS Steven Stamkos 25.00 60.00
AR3SY Steve Yzerman 50.00 100.00
AR3TO Jonathan Toews 25.00 60.00
AR3VL Vincent Lecavalier
AR3WG Wayne Gretzky 125.00 200.00

2009-10 OPC Premier Signings

STATED PRINT RUN 50 SER.#'d SETS
PSAA Artem Anisimov
PSAK Anze Kopitar 10.00 25.00
PSAN Antti Niemi 15.00 40.00
PSAT Alex Tanguay 8.00 20.00
PSBA David Backes 8.00 20.00
PSBH Bobby Hull 15.00 40.00
PSBL Brian Leetch 10.00 25.00
PSBO Bobby Orr 60.00 120.00
PSBR Martin Brodeur 30.00 60.00
PSBW Blake Wheeler 8.00 20.00
PSCP Carey Price 25.00 60.00
PSCR Sidney Crosby 75.00 150.00
PSCS Sidney Crosby 75.00 150.00
PSCW Cam Ward 10.00 25.00
PSDB Derick Brassard 10.00 25.00
PSDD Drew Doughty 15.00 40.00
PSDE Michael Del Zotto 8.00 20.00
PSDG Doug Gilmour 15.00 40.00
PSDH Dany Heatley
PSDP Dion Phaneuf 8.00 20.00
PSDS Daniel Sedin 12.00 30.00
PSEK Evander Kane 12.00 30.00
PSEM Evgeni Malkin 20.00 50.00
PSEP Phil Esposito 12.00 30.00
PSES Eric Staal 12.00 30.00
PSGA Glenn Anderson
PSGH Gordie Howe 40.00 100.00
PSGI Matt Gilroy
PSGO Scott Gomez
PSGP Gilbert Perreault 10.00 25.00
PSGR Mike Green
PSHL Henrik Lundqvist 12.00 30.00
PSHS Henrik Sedin
PSHZ Henrik Zetterberg 12.00 30.00
PSIK Ilya Kovalchuk
PSJA Jason Arnott 6.00 15.00
PSJB Jean Beliveau 15.00 40.00
PSJC Jeff Carter 10.00 25.00
PSJE Jhonas Enroth 8.00 20.00
PSJG Jonas Gustavsson 15.00 40.00
PSJI Jarome Iginla 15.00 40.00
PSJS Jordan Staal 12.00 30.00
PSJT Jonathan Toews 25.00 60.00
PSJV Jakub Voracek 10.00 25.00
PSKA Erik Karlsson 25.00 50.00
PSKE Phil Kessel 10.00 25.00
PSLE Vincent Lecavalier 12.00 30.00
PSLR Luc Robitaille 12.00 30.00
PSLS Luke Schenn 10.00 25.00
PSMB Mikael Backlund 10.00 25.00
PSMD Matt Duchene 20.00 50.00
PSME Mark Messier 25.00 60.00
PSMF Marc-Andre Fleury 15.00 40.00
PSMG Marian Gaborik 12.00 30.00
PSMH Milan Hejduk 10.00 25.00
PSML Mario Lemieux 25.00 60.00
PSMM Mike Modano 10.00 25.00
PSMN Markus Naslund
PSMR Mike Ribeiro 6.00 15.00
PSMS Martin St. Louis 10.00 25.00
PSMT Marty Turco 8.00 20.00
PSNB Nicklas Backstrom 15.00 40.00
PSNF Tony Esposito 15.00 40.00
PSNL Nicklas Lidstrom 12.00 30.00
PSOV Alexander Ovechkin 60.00 120.00
PSPB Patrice Bergeron
PSPD Pavel Datsyuk 15.00 40.00
PSPE Patrik Elias 8.00 20.00
PSPK Patrick Kane 20.00 50.00
PSPR Patrick Roy 50.00 100.00
PSPS Paul Stastny 10.00 25.00
PSRB Ray Bourque 15.00 40.00
PSRG Ryan Getzlaf
PSRI Mike Richards
PSRM Ryan Miller 10.00 25.00
PSRN Rick Nash 10.00 25.00
PSRO Ryan O'Reilly 10.00 25.00
PSRS Ryan Stoa 10.00 25.00
PSSC Sidney Crosby 75.00 150.00
PSSD Shane Doan 8.00 20.00
PSSG Sam Gagner 12.00 30.00
PSSH Sergei Shirokov
PSSI Simon Gagne 10.00 25.00
PSSK Saku Koivu
PSSM Steve Mason 10.00 25.00
PSSS Steven Stamkos 25.00 60.00
PSST Peter Stastny
PSSV Steve Shutt 10.00 25.00
PSSW Shea Weber 8.00 20.00
PSSY Steve Yzerman 30.00 80.00
PSTA John Tavares 40.00 80.00
PSTH Joe Thornton 12.00 30.00
PSTM Tyler Myers 20.00 50.00
PSTV Thomas Vanek 10.00 25.00
PSVA James van Riemsdyk 15.00 40.00
PSVH Victor Hedman 12.00 30.00
PSVL Ville Leino 10.00 25.00
PSVO Tomas Vokoun 10.00 25.00
PSWG Wayne Gretzky 100.00 175.00
PSZB Zach Bogosian 8.00 20.00

2009-10 OPC Premier Signings Duals

STATED PRINT RUN 25 SER.#'d SETS
PS2AO Jason Arnott
Cal O'Reilly
PS2BO David Backes
T.J. Oshie
PS2BT John Tavares 50.00 100.00
Mike Bossy
PS2BV Ivan Vishnevskiy 10.00 25.00
Jamie Benn
PS2BW Patrice Bergeron
Blake Wheeler
PS2CV Bobby Clarke 30.00 60.00
James van Riemsdyk
PS2DM Shane Doan
Peter Mueller
PS2DW J.P. Dumont 10.00 25.00
Shea Weber
PS2EO Phil Esposito 75.00 150.00
Bobby Orr
PS2FA Grant Fuhr
Glenn Anderson
PS2FF Mike Foligno 12.00 30.00
Nick Foligno
PS2FK Grant Fuhr 15.00 40.00
Jari Kurri
PS2FL Valtteri Filppula 15.00 40.00
Ville Leino
PS2GB Nicklas Backstrom
Mike Green
PS2GC Jeff Carter 12.00 30.00
Simon Gagne
PS2GG Clark Gillies 10.00 25.00
Colton Gillies
PS2GL Marian Gaborik 25.00 60.00
Henrik Lundqvist
PS2GM Wayne Gretzky 125.00 200.00
Mark Messier
PS2GZ Marian Gaborik 15.00 40.00
Michael Del Zotto
PS2HD Gordie Howe 50.00 120.00
Alex Delvecchio
PS2HG Jonas Gustavsson 20.00 50.00
Christian Hanson
PS2HM Bobby Hull 25.00 60.00
Stan Mikita
PS2HS Dany Heatley
Devin Setoguchi
PS2HT Bobby Hull
Jonathan Toews
PS2IB Jarome Iginla 25.00 60.00
Mikael Backlund
PS2IO Ilya Kovalchuk
Alexander Ovechkin
PS2JD Jack Johnson
Drew Doughty
PS2JV John Tavares 50.00 100.00
Victor Hedman
PS2KB Josh Bailey
Kyle Okposo
PS2KM Evgeni Malkin
Ilya Kovalchuk
PS2KS Patrick Kane 30.00 80.00
Steven Stamkos
PS2KV Patrick Kane
James van Riemsdyk
PS2LB Brian Leetch 12.00 30.00
Andy Bathgate
PS2LE Nicklas Lidstrom 15.00 40.00
Jonathan Ericsson
PS2LG Jonas Gustavsson 30.00 80.00
Henrik Lundqvist
PS2LI Vincent Lecavalier 20.00 50.00
Jarome Iginla
PS2LK Ted Lindsay
Red Kelly
PS2LS Guy Lafleur
Steve Shutt
PS2ME Ryan Miller 15.00 40.00
Jhonas Enroth
PS2MH Dale Hawerchuk 12.00 30.00
Joe Mullen
PS2NV Semyon Varlamov
Michal Neuvirth
PS2NW Cam Neely 20.00 50.00
Blake Wheeler
PS2OB Bobby Orr 75.00 150.00
Ray Bourque
PS2OC Terry O'Reilly
Daniel Carcillo
PS2OM Alexander Ovechkin 75.00 150.00
Evgeni Malkin
PS2PM Dion Phaneuf
Al MacInnis
PS2PP Peter Stastny 12.00 30.00
Paul Stastny
PS2RB Patrick Roy 40.00 100.00
Martin Brodeur
PS2RC Mike Richards 30.00 80.00
Jeff Carter
PS2RO Alexander Ovechkin 50.00 120.00
Luc Robitaille
PS2SD Henrik Sedin
Daniel Sedin
PS2SG Sergei Shirokov
Michael Grabner
PS2SH Victor Hedman 30.00 80.00
Steven Stamkos
PS2SS Martin St. Louis
Steven Stamkos
PS2SW Denis Savard
Doug Wilson
PS2TD John Tavares 50.00 100.00
Matt Duchene
PS2TH Joe Thornton
Dany Heatley
PS2TV Jonathan Toews
Kris Versteeg
PS2VG Thomas Vanek 15.00 40.00
Michael Grabner
PS2YL Steve Yzerman 60.00 120.00
Nicklas Lidstrom

2009-10 OPC Premier Signings Duals Gold

STATED PRINT RUN 10 SER.#'d SETS
NOT PRICED DUE TO SCARCITY

2009-10 OPC Premier Signings Gold

STATED PRINT RUN 15 SER.#'d SETS
NOT PRICED DUE TO SCARCITY

2009-10 OPC Premier Signings Quads

STATED PRINT RUN 10 SER.#'d SETS
NOT PRICED DUE TO SCARCITY
PS4GR8 Wayne Gretzky
Steve Yzerman
Mario Lemieux
Mark Messier
PS4NYI John Tavares
Mike Bossy
Denis Potvin
Clark Gillies
PS4NYR Henrik Lundqvist
Marian Gaborik
Brandon Dubinsky
Chris Drury
PS4CAPT Gordie Howe
Alex Delvecchio
Steve Yzerman
Nicklas Lidstrom
PS4GOAL Patrick Roy
Martin Brodeur
Carey Price
Steve Mason
PS4OMKD Alexander Ovechkin
Evgeni Malkin
Ilya Kovalchuk
Pavel Datsyuk
PS4HAWKS Bobby Hull
Tony Esposito
Jonathan Toews
Patrick Kane
PS4HTOWN Gordie Howe
Red Kelly
Ted Lindsay
Alex Delvecchio
PS4OILER Wayne Gretzky
Mark Messier
Jari Kurri
Glenn Anderson
PS4ROOKS John Tavares
Victor Hedman
Matt Duchene
James van Riemsdyk

2009-10 OPC Premier Signings Quads Gold

STATED PRINT RUN 1 SER.#'d SET
NOT PRICED DUE TO SCARCITY

2009-10 OPC Premier Signings Triples

STATED PRINT RUN 15 SER.#'d SETS
NOT PRICED DUE TO SCARCITY
PS3BEM Steve Mason
Martin Brodeur
Tony Esposito
PS3BUF Thomas Vanek
Drew Stafford
Tim Kennedy
PS3CRC Bobby Clarke
Mike Richards
Jeff Carter
PS3DSG Michael Del Zotto
Matt Gilroy
Michael Sauer
PS3EGM Phil Esposito
Mark Messier
Marian Gaborik
PS3ENO Bobby Orr
Phil Esposito
Cam Neely
PS3FME Grant Fuhr
Ryan Miller
Jhonas Enroth
PS3GDA Marian Gaborik
Brandon Dubinsky
Artem Anisimov
PS3HGT Jonathan Toews
Ryan Getzlaf
Dany Heatley
PS3HTK Bobby Hull
Jonathan Toews
Patrick Kane
PS3HYL Gordie Howe
Steve Yzerman
Nicklas Lidstrom
PS3IMB Mikael Backlund
Lanny McDonald
Jarome Iginla
PS3KVD Matt Duchene
James van Riemsdyk
Evander Kane
PS3LEG Henrik Lundqvist
Jhonas Enroth
Jonas Gustavsson
PS3LHD Alex Delvecchio
Gordie Howe
Ted Lindsay
PS3LSS Vincent Lecavalier
Steven Stamkos

Martin St. Louis
PS3LYG Wayne Gretzky
Mario Lemieux
Steve Yzerman
PS3LZD Nicklas Lidstrom
Henrik Zetterberg
Pavel Datsyuk
PS3MOD Evgeni Malkin
Alexander Ovechkin
Pavel Datsyuk
PS3NVM Rick Nash
Jakub Voracek
Steve Mason
PS3OBG Alexander Ovechkin
Nicklas Backstrom
Mike Green
PS3OGB Mike Green
Ray Bourque
Bobby Orr
PS3ORS Alexander Ovechkin
Luc Robitaille
Steve Shutt
PS3RBM Patrick Roy
Martin Brodeur
Steve Mason
PS3RCV Mike Richards
Jeff Carter
James van Riemsdyk
PS3TKD John Tavares
Matt Duchene
Evander Kane
PS3TOR Luke Schenn
Matt Stajan
Nikolai Kulemin
PS3TSK John Tavares
Steven Stamkos
Patrick Kane
PS3TVD John Tavares
Matt Duchene
James van Riemsdyk
PS3BEST Wayne Gretzky
Bobby Orr
Patrick Roy

2009-10 OPC Premier Signings Triples Gold

STATED PRINT RUN 5 SER.#'d SETS
NOT PRICED DUE TO SCARCITY

2009-10 OPC Premier Stichings

STATED PRINT RUN 199 SER.#'d SETS
PSAC Andrew Cogliano 4.00 10.00
PSAO Alexander Ovechkin 8.00 20.00
PSBA Mikael Backlund 4.00 10.00
PSBF Benn Ferriero 10.00 25.00
PSBH Bobby Hull 4.00 10.00
PSBL Brian Leetch 4.00 10.00
PSBO Bobby Orr 10.00 25.00
PSBR Bobby Ryan 3.00 8.00
PSBW Blake Wheeler 3.00 8.00
PSCG Clark Gillies 2.50 6.00
PSCN Cam Neely 4.00 10.00
PSCP Carey Price 6.00 15.00
PSCW Cam Ward 3.00 8.00
PSDC Don Cherry 8.00 20.00
PSDH Dany Heatley 5.00 12.00
PSDP Dion Phaneuf 4.00 10.00
PSDP Denis Potvin 4.00 10.00
PSEM Evgeni Malkin 6.00 15.00
PSES Eric Staal 4.00 10.00
PSGH Gordie Howe 6.00 15.00
PSGP Gilbert Perreault 4.00 10.00
PSHL Henrik Lundqvist 5.00 12.00
PSHZ Henrik Zetterberg 5.00 12.00
PSIK Ilya Kovalchuk 3.00 8.00
PSJF Johan Franzen 1.50 4.00
PSJI Jarome Iginla 5.00 12.00
PSJK Jari Kurri 6.00 15.00
PSJN John Tavares 8.00 20.00
PSJS Jason Spezza 3.00 8.00
PSJT Joe Thornton 5.00 12.00
PSKA Paul Kariya 2.50 6.00
PSLR Luc Robitaille 4.00 10.00
PSLS Luke Schenn 4.00 10.00
PSMB Martin Brodeur 8.00 20.00
PSMD Matt Duchene 8.00 20.00
PSMF Marc-Andre Fleury 5.00 12.00
PSMG Marian Gaborik 4.00 10.00
PSMI Mike Bossy 2.50 6.00
PSMK Miikka Kiprusoff 2.50 6.00
PSML Mario Lemieux 8.00 20.00
PSMM Mark Messier 5.00 12.00
PSMN Markus Naslund 2.50 6.00
PSMO Mike Modano 2.50 6.00
PSMR Mike Richards 5.00 12.00
PSMS Martin St. Louis 4.00 10.00
PSNB Nicklas Backstrom 5.00 12.00
PSNL Nicklas Lidstrom 4.00 10.00
PSPD Pavel Datsyuk 6.00 15.00
PSPE Phil Esposito 5.00 12.00
PSPK Patrick Kane 5.00 12.00
PSPR Patrick Roy 8.00 20.00
PSRB Ray Bourque 4.00 10.00
PSRL Roberto Luongo 6.00 15.00
PSRM Ryan Miller 5.00 12.00
PSRN Rick Nash 3.00 8.00
PSSC Sidney Crosby 15.00 40.00
PSSG Sam Gagner 4.00 10.00
PSSM Steve Mason 4.00 10.00
PSSS Steven Stamkos 6.00 15.00
PSSY Steve Yzerman 8.00 20.00
PSTO Jonathan Toews 6.00 15.00
PSTS Teemu Selanne 2.50 6.00
PSTV Thomas Vanek 2.50 6.00
PSVL Vincent Lecavalier 4.00 10.00
PSWG Wayne Gretzky 15.00 40.00

2009-10 OPC Premier Stitchings Autographs

STATED PRINT RUN 25 SER.#'d SETS
APSAC Andrew Cogliano 8.00 20.00
APSAO Alexander Ovechkin 60.00 120.00
APSBH Bobby Hull 20.00 50.00
APSBL Brian Leetch 12.00 30.00
APSBO Bobby Orr 100.00 150.00
APSBR Martin Brodeur 40.00 80.00
APSCG Clark Gillies 10.00 25.00
APSCN Cam Neely 15.00 40.00
APSCP Carey Price 20.00 50.00
APSCW Cam Ward 10.00 25.00
APSDC Don Cherry 60.00 120.00
APSDH Dany Heatley 15.00 40.00
APSDP Denis Potvin
APSEM Evgeni Malkin 40.00 100.00
APSES Eric Staal 12.00 30.00
APSGH Gordie Howe 60.00 120.00
APSGP Gilbert Perreault 12.00 30.00
APSGR Wayne Gretzky
APSHL Henrik Lundqvist
APSHZ Henrik Zetterberg 30.00 60.00
APSJI Jarome Iginla 20.00 50.00
APSJK Jari Kurri 15.00 40.00
APSJN John Tavares 50.00 100.00
APSKA Patrick Kane 25.00 60.00
APSLR Luc Robitaille
APSLS Luke Schenn 10.00 25.00
APSMA Mark Messier 25.00 60.00
APSMD Matt Duchene 40.00 80.00
APSMG Marian Gaborik 12.00 30.00
APSML Mario Lemieux 50.00 100.00
APSMM Mike Modano 20.00 50.00
APSMS Martin St. Louis 8.00 20.00
APSNB Nicklas Backstrom 12.00 30.00
APSNL Nicklas Lidstrom 15.00 40.00
APSPD Pavel Datsyuk 15.00 40.00
APSPE Phil Esposito 12.00 30.00
APSPH Dion Phaneuf 10.00 25.00
APSPK Phil Kessel
APSPS Paul Stastny
APSRB Ray Bourque/24 25.00 60.00
APSRM Ryan Miller 15.00 40.00
APSRN Rick Nash 15.00 40.00
APSRO Patrick Roy 40.00 80.00
APSRY Bobby Ryan 12.00 30.00
APSSC Sidney Crosby 175.00 300.00
APSSG Sam Gagner 10.00 25.00
APSSM Steve Mason 10.00 25.00
APSSS Steven Stamkos 20.00 50.00
APSSY Steve Yzerman 50.00 100.00
APSTE Tony Esposito
APSTH Joe Thornton 15.00 40.00
APSTV Thomas Vanek 8.00 20.00
APSTW Jonathan Toews 25.00 60.00
APSVL Vincent Lecavalier 12.00 30.00

2009-10 OPC Premier Trios

STATED PRINT RUN 50 SER.#'d SETS
3JAKA Maxim Afinogenov 6.00 15.00
Ilya Kovalchuk
Nik Antropov
3JASK Daniel Alfredsson 8.00 20.00
Jason Spezza
Alex Kovalev
3JBGB Mike Bossy
Clark Gillies
Bob Bourne
3JBMR Larry Robinson 8.00 20.00
Al MacInnis
Ray Bourque
3JBSW Cam Ward 8.00 20.00
Eric Staal
Rod Brind'Amour
3JCBP Matt Pelech 8.00 20.00
Mikael Backlund
Kris Chucko
3JCDF Logan Couture 10.00 25.00
Jason Demers
Benn Ferriero
3JCTS Sidney Crosby 40.00 80.00
Steven Stamkos
John Tavares
3JCWM Brad Marchand 10.00 25.00
Colin Wilson
Logan Couture
3JDGL Henrik Lundqvist 10.00 25.00
Marian Gaborik
Chris Drury
3JDMO Devan Dubnyk 6.00 15.00
Colin McDonald
Ryan O'Marra
3JDSG Michael Del Zotto 10.00 25.00
Matt Gilroy
Michael Sauer
3JEHH Gordie Howe
Bobby Hull
Phil Esposito
3JEME Jhonas Enroth 20.00 50.00
Tyler Myers
Tyler Ennis
3JENW Phil Esposito
Cam Neely
Blake Wheeler
3JFCS Marc-Andre Fleury
Sidney Crosby
Jordan Staal
3JFOW Colin Wilson 10.00 25.00
Cal O'Reilly
Cody Franson
3JGBS Jonas Gustavsson 12.00 30.00
Viktor Stalberg
Tyler Bozak
3JGDO Matt Duchene 15.00 40.00
Ryan O'Reilly
T.J. Galiardi
3JGKH Jonas Gustavsson 15.00 40.00
Victor Hedman
Erik Karlsson
3JHGV Jakub Voracek
Marian Gaborik
Marian Hossa
3JHTK Jonathan Toews 15.00 40.00
Patrick Kane
Marian Hossa
3JIKP Dion Phaneuf
Miikka Kiprusoff
Jarome Iginla
3JKAM Mark Messier 12.00 30.00
Jari Kurri
Glenn Anderson
3JKBS Phil Kessel 8.00 20.00
Tyler Bozak
Viktor Stalberg
3JKLN Miikka Kiprusoff 15.00 40.00
Kari Lehtonen
Antti Niemi
3JKOM Alexander Ovechkin 20.00 50.00
Evgeni Malkin
Ilya Kovalchuk
3JKSS Jari Kurri 15.00 40.00
Teemu Selanne
Saku Koivu
3JLAM Brian Leetch 15.00 40.00
Glenn Anderson
Mark Messier
3JLCM Mario Lemieux 25.00 60.00
Sidney Crosby
Evgeni Malkin
3JLEG Henrik Lundqvist 12.00 30.00
Jhonas Enroth
Jonas Gustavsson
3JLIN Vincent Lecavalier 10.00 25.00
Jarome Iginla
Rick Nash
3JLMP Brian Leetch 10.00 25.00
Mike Modano
Zach Parise
3JLPM Roberto Luongo 12.00 30.00
Carey Price
Steve Mason
3JLSH Victor Hedman 12.00 30.00
Borje Salming
Nicklas Lidstrom
3JLSS Vincent Lecavalier 10.00 25.00
Martin St. Louis
Steven Stamkos
3JLVB Jamie Benn 8.00 20.00
Ivan Vishnevskiy
Perttu Lindgren
3JLYM Mario Lemieux 25.00 60.00
Steve Yzerman
Mark Messier
3JLYT Steve Yzerman 25.00 60.00
Mario Lemieux
John Tavares
3JLZF Nicklas Lidstrom
Henrik Zetterberg
Johan Franzen
3JMGK Lanny McDonald 12.00 30.00
Doug Gilmour
Phil Kessel
3JMMG Lanny McDonald 6.00 15.00
Joe Mullen
Doug Gilmour
3JMTS Joe Thornton 10.00 25.00
Patrick Marleau
Devin Setoguchi
3JMVM Ryan Miller 12.00 30.00
Thomas Vanek
Tyler Myers
3JNBM Steve Mason 8.00 20.00
Rick Nash
Derick Brassard
3JOCM Alexander Ovechkin 40.00 100.00
Sidney Crosby
Evgeni Malkin
3JPGW Dion Phaneuf
Mike Green
Shea Weber
3JPKW Zach Parise 10.00 25.00
Patrick Kane
Colin Wilson
3JRBF Patrick Roy 25.00 60.00
Martin Brodeur
Marc-Andre Fleury
3JRBL Patrick Roy 25.00 60.00
Martin Brodeur
Roberto Luongo
3JRCG Mike Richards 15.00 40.00
Jeff Carter
Claude Giroux
3JRCR Patrick Roy
Guy Carbonneau
Larry Robinson
3JRCV Mike Richards 20.00 50.00
Jeff Carter
James van Riemsdyk
3JRDG Wayne Gretzky 25.00 60.00
Luc Robitaille
Marcel Dionne
3JRNG Wayne Gretzky 25.00 60.00
Luc Robitaille
Bernie Nicholls
3JSDG Michael Del Zotto 10.00 25.00
Matt Gilroy
Bobby Sanguinetti
3JSDO Paul Stastny 20.00 50.00
Matt Duchene
Ryan O'Reilly
3JSGH Miroslav Satan 12.00 30.00
Marian Gaborik
Marian Hossa
3JSGR Ryan Getzlaf 8.00 20.00
Bobby Ryan
Teemu Selanne
3JSHN Martin St. Louis 10.00 25.00
Dany Heatley
Rick Nash
3JSKK Jason Spezza 15.00 40.00
Alex Kovalev
Erik Karlsson
3JSOG Alexander Semin 15.00 40.00
Alexander Ovechkin
Mike Green
3JSRL Steve Shutt
Larry Robinson
Jacques Lemaire
3JSSL Roberto Luongo 12.00 30.00
Daniel Sedin
Henrik Sedin
3JTDH John Tavares 20.00 50.00
Victor Hedman
Matt Duchene
3JTKD John Tavares 20.00 50.00
Evander Kane
Matt Duchene
3JTVD Matt Duchene 20.00 50.00
John Tavares
James van Riemsdyk
3JVWG James van Riemsdyk 12.00 30.00
Colin Wilson
Matt Gilroy
3JYGM Steve Yzerman 25.00 60.00
Wayne Gretzky
Mark Messier
3JYLH Nicklas Lidstrom 20.00 50.00
Gordie Howe
Steve Yzerman
3JYZH Gordie Howe 40.00 80.00
Steve Yzerman
Henrik Zetterberg

2009-10 OPC Premier Trios Patches

STATED PRINT RUN 15 SER.#'d SETS
NOT PRICED DUE TO SCARCITY

1976 Old Timers

This 18-card set of indeterminate origin measures approximately 2 1/2" by 3 5/8" and features black-and-white player photos in a white border. Members of the Red Wings, Maple Leafs and Blackhawks are pictured. The backs are blank. The cards are unnumbered and checklisted below in alphabetical order.

COMPLETE SET (18) 30.00 60.00
1 Gerry Abel 1.25 2.50
2 Sid Abel 4.00 8.00
3 Doug Barkley 1.25 2.50
4 Joe Carveth 1.25 2.50
5 Billy Dea 1.25 2.50
6 Alex Delvecchio 7.50 15.00
7 Bill Gadsby 1.25 2.50
8 Hal Jackson 1.25 2.50
9 Joe Klukay 1.25 2.50
10 Ted Lindsay 7.50 15.00
11 Jim Orlando 1.25 2.50
12 Marty Pavlich 1.25 2.50
13 Jim Peters 1.25 2.50
14 Marcel Pronovost 1.25 2.50
15 Marc Reaume 1.25 2.50
16 Leo Reise 1.25 2.50
17 Glen Skov 1.25 2.50
18 Jack Stewart 1.25 2.50

1999-00 Oscar Mayer Lunchables

These cards were featured on the backs of Oscar Mayer Lunchables packages. Each package contained both a 3 x 5 player card and a postcard size artist rendition of the player as a comic book superhero. The inside of each package contained a checklist of the set, player stats, and one part of the twelve part comic series.

COMPLETE SET (12) 6.00 15.00
1 Ray Bourque .60 1.50
2 Pavel Bure .75 2.00
3 Dominik Hasek .60 1.50
4 Jaromir Jagr 1.00 2.50
5 Curtis Joseph .40 1.00
6 Paul Kariya 1.25 3.00
7 Saku Koivu .30 .75
8 Eric Lindros 1.00 2.50
9 Al MacInnis .20 .50
10 Mark Messier .40 1.00
11 Mats Sundin .40 1.00
12 Alexei Yashin .25 .60

1997-98 Pacific

The 1997-98 inaugural issue of the Pacific Crown Collection NHL Hockey cards was issued in one series totaling 350 cards and was distributed in eight-card packs. The fronts feature color action player photos with gold foil highlights. The backs carry player information. Pacific chose not to print a card #66, as a tribute to Mario Lemieux

COMPLETE SET (350) 20.00 40.00
1 Ray Bourque .30 .75
2 Brian Leetch .20 .50
3 Claude Lemieux .05 .15
4 Mike Modano .30 .75
5 Zigmund Palffy .15 .40
6 Nikolai Khabibulin .15 .40
7 Chris Chelios .20 .50
8 Teemu Selanne .20 .50
9 Paul Kariya .20 .50
10 John LeClair .20 .50
11 Mark Messier .20 .50
12 Jarome Iginla .25 .60
13 Petr Nedved .05 .15
14 Brendan Shanahan .20 .50
15 Dino Ciccarelli .05 .15
16 Brett Hull .25 .60
17 Wendel Clark .05 .15
18 Peter Bondra .15 .40
19 Steve Yzerman 1.00 2.50
20 Ed Belfour .20 .50
21 Peter Forsberg .50 1.25
22 Mike Gartner .05 .15
23 Jim Carey .15 .40
24 Mike Vernon .15 .40
25 Vincent Damphousse .05 .15
26 Adam Graves .05 .15
27 Ron Hextall .15 .40
28 Keith Tkachuk .20 .50
29 Felix Potvin .20 .50
30 Martin Brodeur .50 1.25
31 Rod Brind'Amour .15 .40
32 Pierre Turgeon .15 .40
33 Patrick Roy 1.00 2.50
34 John Vanbiesbrouck .15 .40
35 Andy Moog .15 .40
36 Sergei Berezin .05 .15
37 Adam Oates .15 .40
38 Joe Sakic .40 1.00
39 Dominik Hasek .40 1.00
40 Patrick Lalime .15 .40
41 Bobby Dollas .05 .15
42 Kyle McLaren .05 .15
43 Wayne Primeau .05 .15
44 Stephane Richer .05 .15
45 Theo Fleury .05 .15
46 Kevin Miller .05 .15
47 Adam Deadmarsh .05 .15
48 Darryl Sydor .05 .15
49 Igor Larionov .05 .15
50 Radek Dvorak .05 .15
51 Andrei Kovalenko .05 .15
52 Keith Primeau .05 .15
53 Ray Ferraro .05 .15
54 David Wilkie .05 .15
55 Bobby Holik .05 .15
56 Tommy Salo .15 .40
57 Jeff Beukeboom .05 .15
58 Daniel Alfredsson .15 .40
59 Mikael Renberg .05 .15
60 Norm Maciver .05 .15
61 Darius Kasparaitis .05 .15
62 Geoff Courtnall .05 .15
63 Jeff Friesen .05 .15
64 Brian Bradley .05 .15
65 Tie Domi .15 .40
67 Martin Gelinas .05 .15
68 Jaromir Jagr .30 .75
69 Steve Konowalchuk .05 .15
70 Brian Bellows .05 .15
71 Jozef Stumpel .05 .15
72 Darryl Shannon .05 .15
73 Todd Simpson .05 .15
74 Ulf Dahlen .05 .15
75 Sandis Ozolinsh .05 .15
76 Sergei Zubov .05 .15
77 Paul Coffey .20 .50
78 Nicklas Lidstrom .20 .50
79 Jason Arnott .05 .15
80 Ray Sheppard .05 .15
81 Sean Burke .15 .40
82 Vladimir Tsyplakov .05 .15
83 Darcy Tucker .05 .15
84 Dave Andreychuk .05 .15
85 Scott Lachance .05 .15
86 Niklas Sundstrom .05 .15
87 Ron Tugnutt .15 .40
88 Eric Lindros .20 .50
89 Alexander Mogilny .15 .40
90 Kris King .05 .15
91 Sergei Fedorov .30 .75
92 Ed Olczyk .05 .15
93 Doug Gilmour .15 .40
94 Ryan Smyth .05 .15
95 Scott Pellerin .05 .15
96 Pavel Bure .20 .50
97 Jeremy Roenick .25 .60
98 Todd Gill .05 .15
99 Wayne Gretzky 1.25 3.00
100 Roman Hamrlik .05 .15
101 Rob Zettler .05 .15
102 Sergei Nemchinov .05 .15
103 Sergei Gonchar .05 .15
104 Steve Rucchin .05 .15
105 Landon Wilson .05 .15
106 Anatoli Semenov .05 .15
107 Corey Millen .05 .15
108 Eric Daze .15 .40
109 Mike Ricci .05 .15
110 Jamie Langenbrunner .05 .15
111 Slava Fetisov .05 .15
112 Rem Murray .05 .15
113 Tom Fitzgerald .05 .15
114 Robert Kron .05 .15
115 Kevin Stevens .05 .15
116 Valeri Bure .05 .15
117 Bill Guerin .15 .40
118 Bryan McCabe .05 .15
119 Alexei Kovalev .05 .15
120 Alexei Yashin .15 .40
121 Eric Desjardins .05 .15
122 Teppo Numminen .05 .15
123 Ron Francis .15 .40
124 Chris Pronger .15 .40
125 Viktor Kozlov .05 .15
126 Corey Schwab .15 .40
127 Fredrik Modin .05 .15
128 Markus Naslund .20 .50
129 Dale Hunter .05 .15
130 Warren Rychel .05 .15
131 Anson Carter .15 .40
132 Miroslav Satan .05 .15
133 Trevor Kidd .15 .40
134 Sergei Krivokrasov .05 .15
135 Adam Foote .05 .15
136 Brent Gilchrist .05 .15
137 Chris Osgood .15 .40
138 Doug Weight .15 .40
139 Martin Straka .05 .15
140 Jeff O'Neill .05 .15
141 Byron Dafoe .15 .40
142 Brian Savage .05 .15
143 Lyle Odelein .05 .15
144 Niklas Andersson .05 .15
145 Luc Robitaille .15 .40
146 Damian Rhodes .05 .15
147 Garth Snow .15 .40
148 Craig Janney .05 .15
149 Fredrik Olausson .05 .15
150 Joe Murphy .05 .15
151 Owen Nolan .15 .40
152 Shawn Burr .05 .15
153 Dimitri Yushkevich .05 .15
154 Trevor Linden .05 .15
155 Joe Juneau .05 .15
156 Sean Pronger .05 .15
157 Jeff Odgers .05 .15
158 Brian Holzinger .05 .15
159 Dave Gagner .05 .15
160 Jeff Hackett .15 .40
161 Eric Lacroix .05 .15
162 Pat Verbeek .05 .15
163 Darren McCarty .05 .15
164 Mike Grier .05 .15
165 Per Gustafsson .05 .15
166 Andrew Cassels .05 .15
167 Vitali Yachmenev .05 .15
168 Jocelyn Thibault .15 .40
169 John MacLean .05 .15
170 Travis Green .05 .15
171 Ulf Samuelsson .05 .15
172 Bruce Gardiner RC .05 .15
173 Janne Niinimaa .05 .15
174 Jim Johnson .05 .15
175 Stu Barnes .05 .15
176 Harry York .05 .15
177 Al Iafrate .05 .15
178 Paul Ysebaert .05 .15
179 Mathieu Schneider .05 .15
180 Corey Hirsch .15 .40
181 Mark Tinordi .05 .15
182 Kevin Todd .05 .15
183 Tim Sweeney .05 .15
184 Donald Audette .05 .15
185 Jonas Hoglund .05 .15
186 Brent Sutter .05 .15
187 Scott Young .05 .15
188 Arturs Irbe .15 .40
189 Vladimir Konstantinov .05 .15
190 Mats Lindgren .05 .15
191 David Nemirovsky .05 .15
192 Sami Kapanen .05 .15
193 Rob Blake .15 .40
194 Sebastien Bordeleau .05 .15
195 Steve Thomas .05 .15
196 Bryan Smolinski .05 .15
197 Mike Richter .20 .50
198 Randy Cunneyworth .05 .15
199 Pat Falloon .05 .15
200 Cliff Ronning .05 .15
201 Ken Wregget .05 .15
202 Al MacInnis .15 .40
203 Tony Granato .05 .15
204 Rob Zamuner .05 .15
205 Mats Sundin .20 .50
206 Mike Ridley .05 .15
207 Sylvain Cote .05 .15
208 Joe Sacco .05 .15
209 Ted Donato .05 .15
210 Matthew Barnaby .05 .15
211 Cory Stillman .05 .15
212 Gary Suter .05 .15
213 Valeri Kamensky .05 .15
214 Derian Hatcher .05 .15
215 Jamie Pushor .05 .15
216 Mariusz Czerkawski .05 .15
217 Kirk Muller .05 .15
218 Kevin Dineen .05 .15
219 Dimitri Khristich .05 .15
220 Martin Rucinsky .05 .15
221 Denis Pederson .05 .15
222 Bryan Berard .05 .15
223 Alexander Karpovtsev .05 .15
224 Shawn McEachern .05 .15
225 Dale Hawerchuk .05 .15
226 Bob Corkum .05 .15
227 Kevin Hatcher .05 .15
228 Grant Fuhr .15 .40
229 Darren Turcotte .05 .15
230 Patrick Poulin .05 .15
231 Jamie Macoun .05 .15
232 Jyrki Lumme .05 .15
233 Bill Ranford .15 .40
234 Dmitri Mironov .05 .15
235 Mattias Timander .05 .15
236 Alexei Zhitnik .05 .15
237 Hnat Domenichelli .05 .15
238 Murray Craven .05 .15
239 Mike Keane .05 .15
240 Benoit Hogue .05 .15
241 Martin Lapointe .05 .15
242 Curtis Joseph .20 .50
243 Robert Svehla .05 .15
244 Glen Wesley .05 .15
245 Stephane Fiset .15 .40
246 Shayne Corson .05 .15
247 Scott Niedermayer .05 .15
248 Steve Webb RC .05 .15
249 Esa Tikkanen .05 .15
250 Alexandre Daigle .05 .15
251 Trent Klatt .05 .15
252 Oleg Tverdovsky .05 .15
253 Dave Roche .05 .15
254 Tony Twist .05 .15
255 Bernie Nicholls .05 .15
256 Rick Tabaracci .15 .40
257 Todd Warriner .05 .15
258 Kirk McLean .15 .40
259 Phil Housley .05 .15
260 Guy Hebert .15 .40
261 Steve Heinze .05 .15
262 Derek Plante .05 .15
263 German Titov .05 .15
264 Tony Amonte .15 .40
265 Uwe Krupp .05 .15
266 Joe Nieuwendyk .15 .40
267 Vyacheslav Kozlov .05 .15
268 Kelly Buchberger .05 .15
269 Rob Niedermayer .05 .15
270 Geoff Sanderson .05 .15
271 Jan Vopat .05 .15
272 Saku Koivu .20 .50
273 Scott Stevens .15 .40
274 Eric Fichaud .05 .15
275 Russ Courtnall .05 .15
276 Wade Redden .05 .15
277 Petr Svoboda .05 .15
278 Andreas Dackell .05 .15
279 Jason Woolley .05 .15
280 Stephane Matteau .05 .15
281 Stephen Guolla RC .05 .15
282 John Cullen .05 .15
283 Steve Sullivan .05 .15
284 Bret Hedican .05 .15
285 Michal Pivonka .05 .15
286 Darren Van Impe .05 .15
287 Rob DiMaio .05 .15
288 Garry Galley .05 .15
289 Kent Manderville .05 .15
290 Bob Probert .05 .15
291 Keith Jones .05 .15
292 Guy Carbonneau .05 .15
293 Tomas Sandstrom .05 .15
294 Daniel McGillis RC .05 .15
295 Brian Skrudland .05 .15
296 Stu Grimson .05 .15
297 Doug Zmolek .05 .15
298 Mark Recchi .15 .40
299 Valeri Zelepukin .05 .15
300 Derek Armstrong .05 .15
301 Eric Cairns RC .05 .15
302 Steve Duchesne .05 .15
303 Dainius Zubrus .05 .15
304 Deron Quint .05 .15
305 Joe Dziedzic .05 .15
306 Mike Peluso .05 .15
307 Andrei Nazarov .05 .15
308 Chris Gratton .05 .15
309 Mike Craig .05 .15
310 Lonny Bohonos .05 .15
311 Rick Tocchet .05 .15
312 Ted Drury .05 .15
313 Jean-Yves Roy .05 .15
314 Jason Dawe .05 .15
315 Jamie Allison .05 .15
316 Alexei Zhamnov .05 .15
317 Aaron Miller .05 .15
318 Todd Krygier .05 .15
319 Tomas Holmstrom .05 .15
320 Todd Marchant .05 .15
321 Scott Mellanby .05 .15
322 Marek Malik .05 .15
323 Dan Bylsma RC .05 .15
324 Stephane Quintal .05 .15
325 Ken Daneyko .05 .15
326 Robert Reichel .05 .15
327 Daniel Goneau .05 .15
328 Sergei Zholtok .05 .15
329 Kjell Samuelsson .05 .15
330 Shane Doan .05 .15
331 Radek Bonk .05 .15
332 Jim Campbell .05 .15
333 Marty McSorley .05 .15
334 Brantt Myhres .05 .15
335 Mike Johnson RC .20 .50
336 Mike Sillinger .05 .15
337 Kelly Hrudey .05 .15
338 Joel Bouchard .05 .15
339 Brian Noonan .05 .15
340 Dean Chynoweth .05 .15
341 Michael Peca .05 .15
342 Jeff Toms RC .05 .15
343 Denis Savard .05 .15
344 Stephane Yelle .05 .15
345 Grant Ledyard .05 .15
346 Ronnie Stern .05 .15
347 Petr Klima .05 .15
348 Johan Garpenlov .05 .15
349 Nelson Emerson .05 .15
350 Matt Johnson .05 .15
351 Ken Belanger RC .05 .15
CM1 Mark Messier .20 .50

1997-98 Pacific Copper

*COPPER: 2.5X TO 6X BASIC CARDS
COPPER STATED ODDS 1:1 HOBBY

1997-98 Pacific Emerald Green

*GREEN: 3X TO 8X BASIC CARDS
GREEN ODDS 1:1 CANADIAN ONLY

1997-98 Pacific Ice Blue

*ICE BLUE: 20X TO 50X BASIC CARDS
ICE BLUE/67 STATED ODDS 1:73

1997-98 Pacific Red

*RED: 5X TO 12X BASIC CARDS
STATED ODDS 1:1 TREAT PACKS

1997-98 Pacific Silver

*SILVER: 2.5X TO 6X BASIC CARDS
SILVER ODDS 1:1 RETAIL PACKS

1997-98 Pacific Card-Supials

Randomly inserted at a rate of 1:37 packs, this 20-card set features color action player photos of some of the great players in Hockey. A smaller card is made to pair with the regular size card of the same player. The backs carry a slot for insertion of the small card.

COMPLETE SET (40) 40.00 80.00
*MINIS: .25X TO .6X LARGE
1 Paul Kariya 1.50 4.00
2 Teemu Selanne 1.50 4.00
3 Jarome Iginla 2.00 5.00
4 Peter Forsberg 2.50 6.00
5 Mike Modano 2.00 5.00
6 Sergei Fedorov 2.00 5.00
7 Vladimir Konstantinov 1.00 2.50
8 Steve Yzerman 4.00 10.00
9 John Vanbiesbrouck 1.00 2.50
10 Martin Brodeur 3.00 8.00
11 Doug Gilmour 1.00 2.50
12 Wayne Gretzky 6.00 15.00
13 Mark Messier 1.50 4.00
14 John LeClair 1.00 2.50
15 Eric Lindros 1.50 4.00
16 Jeremy Roenick 1.50 4.00
17 Keith Tkachuk 1.00 2.50
18 Brett Hull 1.50 4.00
19 Felix Potvin 1.50 4.00
20 Pavel Bure 1.50 4.00

1997-98 Pacific Cramer's Choice

Randomly inserted in packs at the rate of 1:721, this 10-card set features top NHL Hockey players as chosen by Pacific President and CEO, Michael Cramer. The fronts display a color action player cut-out on a pyramid die-cut shaped background.

COMPLETE SET (10) 100.00 200.00
1 Paul Kariya 4.00 10.00

2 Dominik Hasek 8.00 20.00
3 Jarome Iginla 5.00 12.00
4 Peter Forsberg 10.00 25.00
5 Patrick Roy 20.00 50.00
6 Steve Yzerman 20.00 50.00
7 Wayne Gretzky 25.00 60.00
8 Mark Messier 4.00 10.00
9 Eric Lindros 4.00 10.00
10 Jaromir Jagr 6.00 15.00

1997-98 Pacific Gold Crown Die-Cuts

COMPLETE SET (20) 30.00 80.00
STATED ODDS 1:37
1 Paul Kariya 1.50 4.00
2 Teemu Selanne 1.25 3.00
3 Dominik Hasek 3.00 8.00
4 Michael Peca .75 2.00
5 Jarome Iginla 1.50 4.00
6 Chris Chelios .75 2.00
7 Peter Forsberg 2.00 5.00
8 Patrick Roy 8.00 20.00
9 Joe Sakic 3.00 8.00
10 Brendan Shanahan 1.50 4.00
11 Steve Yzerman 6.00 15.00
12 Ryan Smyth .75 2.00
13 John Vanbiesbrouck 1.25 3.00
14 Martin Brodeur 4.00 10.00
15 Wayne Gretzky 10.00 25.00
16 Mark Messier 1.50 4.00
17 Eric Lindros 1.25 3.00
18 Jaromir Jagr 2.00 5.00
19 Brett Hull 1.25 3.00
20 Pavel Bure 1.50 4.00

1997-98 Pacific In The Cage Laser Cuts

Randomly inserted in packs at the rate of 1:145, this 20-card set honors top goalies of the NHL. The laser-cut fronts feature color player photos with the net as the background. The backs carry player information.

COMPLETE SET (20) 40.00 100.00
1 Guy Hebert 2.00 5.00
2 Dominik Hasek 5.00 12.00
3 Trevor Kidd 2.00 5.00
4 Jeff Hackett 2.00 5.00
5 Patrick Roy 10.00 25.00
6 Andy Moog 2.00 5.00
7 Chris Osgood 2.00 5.00
8 Mike Vernon 2.00 5.00
9 Curtis Joseph 4.00 10.00
10 John Vanbiesbrouck 4.00 10.00
11 Jocelyn Thibault 2.00 5.00
12 Martin Brodeur 6.00 15.00
13 Mike Richter 4.00 10.00
14 Ron Hextall 4.00 10.00
15 Garth Snow 2.00 5.00
16 Nikolai Khabibulin 4.00 10.00
17 Patrick Lalime 2.00 5.00
18 Grant Fuhr 4.00 10.00
19 Ed Belfour 4.00 10.00
20 Felix Potvin 4.00 10.00

1997-98 Pacific Slap Shots Die-Cuts

Randomly inserted in packs at the rate of 1:73, this 36-card set features color player photos of top NHL players. Three cards of players from the same team were made to fit on top of each other to form a hockey stick on the cards' right sides with the words, "Pacific Trading Cards," printed on the middle section of the stick. The cards that go together have the same number with the letters, "A, B, or C" after the number to indicate where the cards should be placed to form the giant hockey stick.

COMPLETE SET (36) 50.00 125.00
1A Paul Kariya 2.00 5.00
1B Jari Kurri 1.50 4.00
1C Teemu Selanne 1.50 4.00
2A Peter Forsberg 3.00 8.00
2B Joe Sakic 4.00 10.00
2C Claude Lemieux 1.00 2.50
3A Brendan Shanahan 2.00 5.00
3B Sergei Fedorov 2.00 5.00
3C Steve Yzerman 6.00 15.00
4A Mark Recchi 1.00 2.50
4B Vincent Damphousse 1.00 2.50
4C Stephane Richer 1.00 2.50
5A Wayne Gretzky 10.00 25.00
5B Mark Messier 2.00 5.00
5C Brian Leetch 1.50 4.00
6A Rod Brind'Amour 1.00 2.50
6B Eric Lindros 2.00 5.00
6C John LeClair 1.00 2.50
7A Keith Tkachuk 1.00 2.50
7B Jeremy Roenick 2.00 5.00
7C Mike Gartner 1.00 2.50
8A Petr Nedved 1.00 2.50
8B Ron Francis 1.00 2.50
8C Jaromir Jagr 3.00 8.00
9A Geoff Courtnall 1.00 2.50
9B Pierre Turgeon 1.00 2.50
9C Brett Hull 2.00 5.00
10A Wendel Clark 1.50 4.00
10B Mats Sundin 1.50 4.00
10C Sergei Berezin 1.00 2.50
11A Pavel Bure 2.00 5.00
11B Trevor Linden 1.50 4.00
11C Alexander Mogilny 1.00 2.50
12A Joe Juneau 1.00 2.50
12B Adam Oates 1.00 2.50
12C Peter Bondra 1.00 2.50

1997-98 Pacific Team Checklists

Randomly inserted in packs at the rate of 1:73, this 26-card set features color player photos with the player's team logo in a circle next to the player's image. The backs carry the checklist of the team the player plays on.

COMPLETE SET (26) 40.00 100.00
1 Teemu Selanne 2.00 5.00
2 Ray Bourque 2.00 5.00
3 Dominik Hasek 4.00 8.00
4 Jarome Iginla 2.50 6.00
5 Keith Primeau .75 2.00
6 Chris Chelios 1.25 3.00
7 Patrick Roy 6.00 15.00
8 Mike Modano 2.00 5.00
9 Steve Yzerman 5.00 12.00
10 Curtis Joseph 1.25 3.00
11 John Vanbiesbrouck 1.25 3.00
12 Rob Blake .75 2.00
13 Stephane Richer .75 2.00
14 Martin Brodeur 4.00 10.00
15 Zigmund Palffy 1.25 3.00
16 Wayne Gretzky 10.00 25.00
17 Alexandre Daigle .75 2.00
18 Eric Lindros 1.25 3.00
19 Jeremy Roenick 2.00 5.00
20 Jaromir Jagr 3.00 8.00
21 Brett Hull 2.00 5.00
22 Owen Nolan .75 2.00
23 Dino Ciccarelli .75 2.00
24 Felix Potvin 1.25 3.00
25 Pavel Bure 2.00 5.00
26 Peter Bondra .75 2.00

1998-99 Pacific

The 1998-99 Pacific set was issued in one series totaling 450 cards and was distributed in 10-card packs. The fronts features borderless action color player photos. The backs carry player information and career statistics.

COMPLETE SET (450) 25.00 40.00
1 Damian Rhodes .05 .15
2 Mattias Ohlund .05 .15
3 Craig Ludwig .05 .15
4 Rob Blake .15 .40
5 Nicklas Lidstrom .20 .50
6 Calle Johansson .05 .15
7 Chris Chelios .20 .50
8 Teemu Selanne .20 .50
9 Paul Kariya .20 .50
10 Pavel Bure .20 .50
11 Mark Messier .20 .50
12 Peter Bondra .15 .40
13 Mats Sundin .20 .50
14 Brendan Shanahan .20 .50
15 Jamie Langenbrunner .05 .15
16 Brett Hull .25 .60
17 Rod Brind'Amour .15 .40
18 Adam Deadmarsh .05 .15
19 Steve Yzerman 1.00 2.50
20 Ed Belfour .20 .50
21 Peter Forsberg .50 1.25
22 Dino Ciccarelli .05 .15
23 Brian Bellows .05 .15
24 Janne Niinimaa .05 .15
25 Joe Nieuwendyk .15 .40
26 Patrik Elias .15 .40
27 Michael Peca .05 .15
28 Tie Domi .15 .40
29 Felix Potvin .20 .50
30 Martin Brodeur .50 1.25
31 Grant Fuhr .15 .40
32 Trevor Linden .05 .15
33 Patrick Roy 1.00 2.50
34 John Vanbiesbrouck .15 .40
35 Tom Barrasso .15 .40
36 Matthew Barnaby .05 .15
37 Olaf Kolzig .15 .40
38 Pavol Demitra .15 .40
39 Dominik Hasek .40 1.00
40 Chris Terreri .15 .40
41 Jason Allison .05 .15
42 Richard Smehlik .05 .15
43 Frank Banham .05 .15
44 Chris Pronger .15 .40
45 Matt Cullen .05 .15
46 Mike Rucinski RC .05 .15
47 Mike Crowley RC .15 .40
48 Scott Young .05 .15
49 Brian Savage .05 .15
50 Travis Green .05 .15
51 John LeClair .20 .50
52 Adam Foote .05 .15
53 Derek Morris .05 .15
54 Guy Hebert .15 .40
55 Chris Gratton .15 .40
56 Sergei Zubov .05 .15
57 Dave Karpa .05 .15
58 Sergei Varlamov .05 .15
59 Josef Marha .05 .15
60 Jason Marshall .05 .15
61 Jeff Nielsen RC .05 .15
62 Steve Rucchin .05 .15
63 Tomas Sandstrom .05 .15
64 Jason Bonsignore .05 .15
65 Mikhail Shtalenkov .05 .15
67 Tom Askey RC .05 .15
68 Jaromir Jagr .30 .75
69 Per Axelsson .05 .15
70 Ken Baumgartner .05 .15
71 Jiri Slegr .05 .15
72 Mathieu Schneider .05 .15
73 Anson Carter .15 .40
74 Byron Dafoe .15 .40
75 Rob DiMaio .05 .15
76 Ted Donato .05 .15
77 Ray Bourque .30 .75
78 Dave Ellett .05 .15
79 Steve Heinze .05 .15
80 Geoff Sanderson .15 .40
81 Miroslav Satan .15 .40
82 Martin Straka .05 .15
83 Dimitri Khristich .05 .15
84 Grant Ledyard .05 .15
85 Cameron Mann .05 .15
86 Kyle McLaren .05 .15
87 Sergei Samsonov .15 .40
88 Eric Lindros .20 .50
89 Alexander Mogilny .15 .40
90 Joe Juneau .05 .15
91 Sergei Fedorov .30 .75
92 Rick Tocchet .05 .15
93 Doug Gilmour .15 .40
94 Ryan Smyth .05 .15
95 Alexei Morozov .05 .15
96 Phil Housley .05 .15
97 Jeremy Roenick .25 .60
98 Jay More .05 .15
99 Wayne Gretzky 1.25 3.00
100 Robbie Tallas .05 .15
101 Tim Taylor .05 .15
102 Joe Thornton .30 .75
103 Donald Audette .05 .15
104 Curtis Brown .05 .15
105 Michal Grosek .05 .15
106 Brian Holzinger .05 .15
107 Derek Plante .05 .15
108 Rob Ray .05 .15
109 Darryl Shannon .05 .15
110 Steve Shields .15 .40
111 Vaclav Varada .05 .15
112 Dixon Ward .05 .15
113 Jason Woolley .05 .15
114 Alexei Zhitnik .05 .15
115 Andrew Cassels .05 .15
116 Hnat Domenichelli .05 .15
117 Theo Fleury .05 .15
118 Denis Gauthier .05 .15
119 Cale Hulse .05 .15
120 Jarome Iginla .25 .60
121 Marty McInnis .05 .15
122 Tyler Moss .05 .15
123 Michael Nylander .05 .15
124 Dwayne Roloson .05 .15
125 Cory Stillman .05 .15
126 Rick Tabaracci .05 .15
127 German Titov .05 .15
128 Jason Wiemer .05 .15
129 Steve Chiasson .05 .15
130 Kevin Dineen .05 .15
131 Nelson Emerson .05 .15
132 Martin Gelinas .05 .15
133 Stu Grimson .05 .15
134 Sami Kapanen .05 .15
135 Trevor Kidd .15 .40
136 Robert Kron .05 .15
137 Jeff O'Neill .05 .15
138 Keith Primeau .05 .15
139 Paul Ranheim .05 .15
140 Gary Roberts .05 .15
141 Glen Wesley .05 .15
142 Tony Amonte .15 .40
143 Eric Daze .15 .40
144 Jeff Hackett .15 .40
145 Greg Johnson .05 .15
146 Chad Kilger .05 .15
147 Sergei Krivokrasov .05 .15
148 Christian LaFlamme .05 .15
149 Jean-Yves Leroux .05 .15
150 Dmitri Nabokov .05 .15
151 Jeff Shantz .05 .15
152 Gary Suter .05 .15
153 Eric Weinrich .05 .15
154 Todd White RC .05 .15
155 Alexei Zhamnov .05 .15
156 Wade Belak .05 .15
157 Craig Billington .05 .15
158 Rene Corbet .05 .15
159 Shean Donovan .05 .15
160 Valeri Kamensky .05 .15
161 Uwe Krupp .05 .15
162 Jari Kurri .15 .40
163 Eric Lacroix .05 .15
164 Claude Lemieux .05 .15
165 Eric Messier .05 .15
166 Jeff Odgers .05 .15
167 Sandis Ozolinsh .05 .15
168 Warren Rychel .05 .15
169 Joe Sakic .40 1.00
170 Stephane Yelle .05 .15
171 Greg Adams .05 .15
172 Jason Botterill .05 .15
173 Guy Carbonneau .05 .15
174 Shawn Chambers .05 .15
175 Manny Fernandez .05 .15
176 Derian Hatcher .05 .15
177 Benoit Hogue .05 .15
178 Mike Keane .05 .15
179 Jere Lehtinen .05 .15
180 Juha Lind .05 .15
181 Mike Modano .30 .75
182 Brian Skrudland .05 .15
183 Darryl Sydor .05 .15
184 Roman Turek .15 .40
185 Pat Verbeek .05 .15
186 Jamie Wright .05 .15
187 Doug Brown .05 .15
188 Kris Draper .05 .15
189 Anders Eriksson .05 .15
190 Slava Fetisov .05 .15
191 Brent Gilchrist .05 .15
192 Kevin Hodson .05 .15
193 Tomas Holmstrom .05 .15
194 Michael Knuble .15 .40
195 Joey Kocur .05 .15
196 Vyacheslav Kozlov .15 .40
197 Martin Lapointe .05 .15
198 Igor Larionov .05 .15
199 Kirk Maltby .05 .15
200 Norm Maracle RC .30 .75
201 Darren McCarty .05 .15
202 Dmitri Mironov .05 .15
203 Larry Murphy .15 .40
204 Chris Osgood .15 .40
205 Kelly Buchberger .05 .15
206 Bob Essensa .15 .40
207 Scott Fraser .05 .15
208 Mike Grier .05 .15
209 Bill Guerin .15 .40
210 Tony Hrkac .05 .15
211 Curtis Joseph .20 .50
212 Mats Lindgren .05 .15
213 Todd Marchant .05 .15
214 Dean McAmmond .05 .15
215 Craig Millar .05 .15
216 Boris Mironov .05 .15
217 Doug Weight .15 .40
218 Valeri Zelepukin .05 .15
219 Roman Hamrlik .05 .15
220 Radek Dvorak .05 .15
221 Dave Gagner .05 .15
222 Ed Jovanovski .05 .15
223 Viktor Kozlov .05 .15
224 Paul Laus .05 .15
225 Kirk McLean .05 .15
226 Scott Mellanby .05 .15
227 Kirk Muller .05 .15
228 Robert Svehla .05 .15
229 Steve Washburn .05 .15
230 Kevin Weekes .15 .40
231 Ray Whitney .05 .15
232 Peter Worrell RC .25 .60
233 Russ Courtnall .05 .15
234 Stephane Fiset .15 .40
235 Garry Galley .05 .15
236 Craig Johnson .05 .15
237 Ian Laperriere .05 .15
238 Donald MacLean .05 .15
239 Steve McKenna .05 .15
240 Sandy Moger .05 .15
241 Glen Murray .05 .15
242 Sean O'Donnell .05 .15
243 Yanic Perreault .05 .15
244 Luc Robitaille .15 .40
245 Jamie Storr .15 .40
246 Jozef Stumpel .05 .15
247 Vladimir Tsyplakov .05 .15
248 Benoit Brunet .05 .15
249 Shayne Corson .05 .15
250 Vincent Damphousse .05 .15
251 Eric Houde RC .05 .15
252 Saku Koivu .20 .50
253 Vladimir Malakhov .05 .15
254 Dave Manson .05 .15
255 Andy Moog .15 .40
256 Mark Recchi .15 .40
257 Martin Rucinsky .05 .15
258 Jocelyn Thibault .15 .40
259 Mick Vukota .05 .15
260 Dave Andreychuk .15 .40
261 Jason Arnott .05 .15
262 Mike Dunham .15 .40
263 Bobby Holik .05 .15
264 Randy McKay .05 .15
265 Brendan Morrison .15 .40
266 Scott Niedermayer .05 .15
267 Lyle Odelein .05 .15
268 Krzysztof Oliwa .05 .15
269 Denis Pederson .05 .15
270 Brian Rolston .05 .15
271 Sheldon Souray RC .30 .75
272 Scott Stevens .15 .40
273 Petr Sykora .05 .15
274 Steve Thomas .05 .15
275 Bryan Berard .15 .40
276 Zdeno Chara .05 .15
277 Vladimir Chebaturkin RC .05 .15
278 Tom Chorske .05 .15
279 Mariusz Czerkawski .05 .15
280 Jason Dawe .05 .15
281 Wade Flaherty .15 .40
282 Kenny Jonsson .05 .15
283 Sergei Nemchinov .05 .15
284 Zigmund Palffy .15 .40
285 Rich Pilon .05 .15
286 Robert Reichel .05 .15
287 Joe Sacco .05 .15
288 Tommy Salo .15 .40
289 Bryan Smolinski .05 .15
290 Jeff Beukeboom .05 .15
291 Dan Cloutier .15 .40
292 Bruce Driver .05 .15
293 Adam Graves .05 .15
294 Alexei Kovalev .15 .40
295 Pat LaFontaine .20 .50
296 Darren Langdon .05 .15
297 Brian Leetch .20 .50
298 Mike Richter .20 .50
299 Ulf Samuelsson .05 .15
300 Marc Savard .05 .15
301 Kevin Stevens .05 .15
302 Niklas Sundstrom .05 .15
303 Tim Sweeney .05 .15
304 Vladimir Vorobiev .15 .40
305 Daniel Alfredsson .05 .15
306 Magnus Arvedson .05 .15
307 Radek Bonk .05 .15
308 Andreas Dackell .05 .15
309 Bruce Gardiner .05 .15
310 Igor Kravchuk .05 .15
311 Denny Lambert .05 .15
312 Janne Laukkanen .05 .15
313 Shawn McEachern .05 .15
314 Chris Phillips .05 .15
315 Wade Redden .05 .15
316 Ron Tugnutt .15 .40
317 Shaun Van Allen .05 .15
318 Alexei Yashin .05 .15
319 Jason York .05 .15
320 Sergei Zholtok .05 .15
321 Sean Burke .15 .40
322 Paul Coffey .20 .50
323 Alexandre Daigle .05 .15
324 Eric Desjardins .15 .40
325 Colin Forbes .05 .15
326 Ron Hextall .15 .40
327 Trent Klatt .05 .15
328 Dan McGillis .05 .15
329 Joel Otto .05 .15
330 Shjon Podein .05 .15
331 Mike Sillinger .05 .15
332 Chris Therien .05 .15
333 Dainius Zubrus .05 .15
334 Bob Corkum .05 .15
335 Jim Cummins .05 .15
336 Jason Doig .05 .15
337 Dallas Drake .05 .15
338 Mike Gartner .15 .40
339 Brad Isbister .05 .15
340 Craig Janney .05 .15
341 Nikolai Khabibulin .15 .40
342 Teppo Numminen .05 .15
343 Cliff Ronning .05 .15
344 Keith Tkachuk .20 .50
345 Oleg Tverdovsky .05 .15
346 Jim Waite .15 .40
347 Juha Ylonen .05 .15
348 Stu Barnes .05 .15
349 Rob Brown .05 .15
350 Robert Dome .05 .15
351 Ron Francis .15 .40
352 Kevin Hatcher .05 .15
353 Alex Hicks .05 .15
354 Darius Kasparaitis .05 .15
355 Robert Lang .05 .15
356 Fredrik Olausson .05 .15
357 Ed Olczyk .05 .15
358 Peter Skudra .05 .15
359 Chris Tamer .05 .15
360 Ken Wregget .05 .15
361 Blair Atcheynum .05 .15
362 Jim Campbell .05 .15
363 Kelly Chase .05 .15
364 Craig Conroy .05 .15
365 Geoff Courtnall .05 .15
366 Steve Duchesne .15 .40
367 Todd Gill .05 .15
368 Al MacInnis .15 .40
369 Jamie McLennan .05 .15
370 Scott Pellerin .05 .15
371 Pascal Rheaume .05 .15
372 Jamie Rivers .15 .40
373 Darren Turcotte .05 .15
374 Pierre Turgeon .15 .40
375 Tony Twist .05 .15
376 Terry Yake .05 .15
377 Richard Brennan .05 .15
378 Murray Craven .05 .15
379 Jeff Friesen .05 .15
380 Tony Granato .05 .15
381 Bill Houlder .05 .15
382 Kelly Hrudey .15 .40
383 Alexander Korolyuk .15 .40
384 John MacLean .05 .15
385 Bryan Marchment .05 .15
386 Patrick Marleau .05 .15
387 Stephane Matteau .05 .15
388 Marty McSorley .05 .15
389 Bernie Nicholls .05 .15
390 Owen Nolan .15 .40
391 Mike Ricci .15 .40
392 Marco Sturm .05 .15
393 Mike Vernon .15 .40
394 Andrei Zyuzin .05 .15
395 Mikael Andersson .05 .15
396 Zac Bierk RC .05 .15
397 Enrico Ciccone .05 .15
398 Louie DeBrusk .05 .15
399 Karl Dykhuis .05 .15
400 Daymond Langkow .05 .15
401 Mike McBain .05 .15
402 Sandy McCarthy .05 .15
403 Daren Puppa .15 .40
404 Mikael Renberg .15 .40
405 Stephane Richer .15 .40
406 Alexander Selivanov .05 .15
407 Darcy Tucker .05 .15
408 Paul Ysebaert .05 .15
409 Rob Zamuner .05 .15
410 Sergei Berezin .05 .15
411 Wendel Clark .05 .15
412 Sylvain Cote .05 .15
413 Mike Johnson .05 .15
414 Derek King .05 .15
415 Kris King .05 .15
416 Igor Korolev .05 .15
417 Daniil Markov RC .15 .40
418 Alyn McCauley .05 .15
419 Fredrik Modin .05 .15
420 Martin Prochazka .05 .15
421 Jason Smith .05 .15
422 Steve Sullivan .05 .15
423 Yannick Tremblay .05 .15
424 Todd Bertuzzi .20 .50
425 Donald Brashear .05 .15
426 Bret Hedican .05 .15
427 Arturs Irbe .15 .40
428 Jyrki Lumme .05 .15
429 Brad May .05 .15
430 Bryan McCabe .05 .15
431 Markus Naslund .20 .50
432 Brian Noonan .05 .15
433 Dave Scatchard .05 .15
434 Garth Snow .15 .40
435 Scott Walker RC .05 .15
436 Peter Zezel .05 .15
437 Craig Berube .05 .15
438 Jeff Brown .05 .15
439 Andrew Brunette .15 .40
440 Jan Bulis .05 .15
441 Sergei Gonchar .05 .15
442 Dale Hunter .15 .40
443 Steve Konowalchuk .05 .15
444 Kelly Miller .05 .15
445 Adam Oates .15 .40
446 Bill Ranford .15 .40
447 Jaroslav Svejkovsky .05 .15
448 Esa Tikkanen .05 .15
449 Mark Tinordi .05 .15
450 Brendan Witt .05 .15
451 Richard Zednik .05 .15
S181 Mike Modano SAMPLE .60 1.50

1998-99 Pacific Ice Blue

*VETERANS: 6X TO 15X BASIC CARDS
*ROOKIES: 1.2X TO 3X BASIC CARDS
STATED ODDS 1:73

1998-99 Pacific Red

*VETERANS: 3X TO 8X BASIC CARDS
*ROOKIES: 1.5X TO 4X BASIC CARDS
STATED ODDS 1:1 TREAT PACKS

1998-99 Pacific Cramer's Choice

Randomly inserted in packs at the rate of 1:721, this 10-card set features action color photos of players picked by President/CEO Michael Cramer and printed on die-cut trophy cards.

COMPLETE SET (10) 100.00 200.00
1 Sergei Samsonov 4.00 10.00
2 Dominik Hasek 10.00 25.00
3 Peter Forsberg 12.50 30.00
4 Patrick Roy 25.00 60.00
5 Mike Modano 8.00 20.00
6 Martin Brodeur 12.50 30.00
7 Wayne Gretzky 30.00 80.00
8 Eric Lindros 5.00 12.00
9 Jaromir Jagr 8.00 20.00
10 Pavel Bure 5.00 12.00

1998-99 Pacific Dynagon Ice Inserts

Randomly inserted in packs at the rate of 4:37, this 20-card set features color photos of some of the NHL's most exciting players printed on mirror-patterned full-foil cards. A titanium parallel was also created and randomly inserted in packs. Titanium Ice parallels were numbered to just 99.

COMPLETE SET (20) 30.00 60.00
1 Paul Kariya .75 2.00
2 Teemu Selanne .75 2.00
3 Sergei Samsonov .60 1.50
4 Dominik Hasek 1.50 4.00
5 Peter Forsberg 2.00 5.00
6 Patrick Roy 4.00 10.00
7 Joe Sakic 1.50 4.00
8 Mike Modano 1.25 3.00
9 Sergei Fedorov .75 2.00
10 Steve Yzerman 4.00 10.00
11 Saku Koivu .75 2.00
12 Martin Brodeur 2.00 5.00
13 Wayne Gretzky 5.00 12.00
14 John LeClair .75 2.00
15 Eric Lindros .75 2.00
16 Jaromir Jagr 1.25 3.00
17 Pavel Bure .75 2.00
18 Mark Messier .75 2.00
19 Peter Bondra .60 1.50
20 Olaf Kolzig .60 1.50

1998-99 Pacific Titanium Ice

Randomly inserted into packs, this 20-card set is an insert to the Pacific base set. Only 99 serially numbered sets were made.

STATED PRINT RUN 99 SER.#'d SETS
1 Paul Kariya 10.00 25.00
2 Teemu Selanne 10.00 25.00
3 Sergei Samsonov 8.00 20.00
4 Dominik Hasek 20.00 50.00
5 Peter Forsberg 25.00 60.00
6 Patrick Roy 50.00 120.00
7 Joe Sakic 20.00 50.00
8 Mike Modano 15.00 40.00
9 Sergei Fedorov 15.00 40.00
10 Steve Yzerman 50.00 120.00
11 Saku Koivu 10.00 25.00
12 Martin Brodeur 25.00 60.00
13 Wayne Gretzky 60.00 150.00
14 John LeClair 10.00 25.00
15 Eric Lindros 10.00 25.00
16 Jaromir Jagr 15.00 40.00
17 Pavel Bure 10.00 25.00
18 Mark Messier 10.00 25.00
19 Peter Bondra 8.00 20.00
20 Olaf Kolzig 8.00 20.00

1998-99 Pacific Gold Crown Die-Cuts

Randomly inserted in packs at the rate of 1:37, this 36-card set features color photos of top NHL stars printed on die-cut crown design 24-point card stock with laser cutting and dual foil.

COMPLETE SET (36) 75.00 150.00
1 Paul Kariya 2.00 5.00
2 Teemu Selanne 2.00 5.00
3 Sergei Samsonov 1.50 4.00
4 Dominik Hasek 4.00 10.00
5 Michael Peca .75 2.00
6 Theo Fleury .75 2.00
7 Chris Chelios .75 2.00
8 Peter Forsberg 5.00 12.00
9 Patrick Roy 10.00 25.00
10 Joe Sakic 4.00 10.00
11 Ed Belfour 2.00 5.00
12 Mike Modano 3.00 8.00
13 Sergei Fedorov 2.50 6.00
14 Chris Osgood 1.50 4.00
15 Brendan Shanahan 2.00 5.00
16 Steve Yzerman 10.00 25.00
17 Saku Koivu 2.00 5.00
18 Martin Brodeur 6.00 15.00
19 Patrik Elias .75 2.00
20 Doug Gilmour 1.50 4.00
21 Trevor Linden .75 2.00
22 Zigmund Palffy .75 2.00
23 Wayne Gretzky 12.00 30.00
24 John LeClair .75 2.00
25 Eric Lindros 2.00 5.00
26 Dainius Zubrus .75 2.00
27 Keith Tkachuk .75 2.00
28 Tom Barrasso 1.50 4.00
29 Jaromir Jagr 3.00 8.00
30 Brett Hull 2.50 6.00
31 Felix Potvin 2.00 5.00
32 Mats Sundin 2.00 5.00
33 Pavel Bure 2.00 5.00
34 Mark Messier 2.00 5.00
35 Peter Bondra .75 2.00
36 Olaf Kolzig 1.50 4.00

1998-99 Pacific Martin Brodeur Show Promo

This card was created by Pacific to honor its relationship with new spokesman Martin Brodeur. It was given away free at three shows in early 1999 to those who opened complete boxes of Pacific product at the company's booth. It was reported that 5,000 copies were produced, but few ever make their way onto market.

COMPLETE SET (1) 10.00
1 Martin Brodeur 4.00 10.00

1998-99 Pacific Team Checklists

COMPLETE SET (30) 15.00 30.00
STATED ODDS 2:37
1 Paul Kariya .40 1.00
2 Sergei Samsonov .30 .75
3 Dominik Hasek .75 2.00
4 Theo Fleury .10 .30
5 Keith Primeau .10 .30
6 Chris Chelios .40 1.00
7 Patrick Roy 2.00 5.00
8 Mike Modano .60 1.50
9 Steve Yzerman 2.00 5.00
10 Ryan Smyth .10 .30
11 John Vanbiesbrouck .30 .75
12 Jozef Stumpel .10 .30
13 Saku Koivu .40 1.00
14 Mike Dunham .30 .75
15 Martin Brodeur 1.00 2.50
16 Zigmund Palffy .30 .75
17 Wayne Gretzky 2.50 6.00
18 Alexei Yashin .10 .30
19 Eric Lindros .40 1.00
20 Keith Tkachuk .40 1.00
21 Jaromir Jagr .60 1.50
22 Brett Hull .50 1.25
23 Patrick Marleau .10 .30

24 Rob Zamuner .10 .30
25 Mats Sundin .40 1.00
26 Pavel Bure .40 1.00
27 Olaf Kolzig .30 .75
28 Atlanta Thrashers .40 1.00
29 Minnesota Wild .40 1.00
30 Columbus Blue Jackets .40 1.00

1998-99 Pacific Timelines

COMPLETE SET (20) 60.00 150.00
STATED ODDS 1:181
1 Teemu Selanne 3.00 8.00
2 Dominik Hasek 6.00 15.00
3 Peter Forsberg 6.00 15.00
4 Patrick Roy 12.00 30.00
5 Joe Sakic 6.00 15.00
6 Ed Belfour 3.00 8.00
7 Brendan Shanahan 3.00 8.00
8 Steve Yzerman 10.00 25.00
9 Mike Modano 4.00 10.00
10 Doug Gilmour 2.50 6.00
11 Wayne Gretzky 15.00 40.00
12 Pat LaFontaine 3.00 8.00
13 John LeClair 3.00 8.00
14 Eric Lindros 3.00 8.00
15 Keith Tkachuk 3.00 8.00
16 Jaromir Jagr 4.00 10.00
17 Brett Hull 4.00 10.00
18 Mats Sundin 3.00 8.00
19 Pavel Bure 3.00 8.00
20 Mark Messier 3.00 8.00

1998-99 Pacific Trophy Winners

COMPLETE SET (10) 10.00 20.00
STATED ODDS 1:37 CANADIAN PACKS
1 Martin Brodeur 2.50 6.00
2 Dominik Hasek 1.50 4.00
3 Jaromir Jagr 1.25 3.00
4 Sergei Samsonov .25 .60
5 Sergei Fedorov 1.00 2.50
6 Nicklas Lidstrom .75 2.00
7 Darren McCarty .25 .60
8 Chris Osgood .25 .60
9 Brendan Shanahan .75 2.00
10 Steve Yzerman 3.00 8.00

1999-00 Pacific

Among the first sets released during the 1999-00 hockey season, these cards featured near full bleed photography on the front, along with stars and biographical information on the back. Cards #451-466 were not found in packs. They were available only as part of an arena giveaway program. As such, they are not considered part of the base set. #461 does not exist.

COMPLETE SET (450) 40.00 80.00
1 Matt Cullen .05 .15
2 Johan Davidsson .05 .15
3 Scott Ferguson RC .05 .15
4 Travis Green .05 .15
5 Stu Grimson .05 .15
6 Kevin Haller .05 .15
7 Guy Hebert .15 .40
8 Paul Kariya .20 .50
9 Marty McInnis .05 .15
10 Jim McKenzie .05 .15
11 Fredrik Olausson .05 .15
12 Dominic Roussel .15 .40
13 Steve Rucchin .05 .15
14 Ruslan Salei .05 .15
15 Tomas Sandstrom .05 .15
16 Teemu Selanne .20 .50
17 Jason Allison .05 .15
18 P.J. Axelsson .05 .15
19 Shawn Bates .05 .15
20 Ray Bourque .30 .75
21 Anson Carter .15 .40
22 Byron Dafoe .15 .40
23 Hal Gill .05 .15
24 Steve Heinze .05 .15
25 Dimitri Khristich .05 .15
26 Cameron Mann .05 .15
27 Kyle McLaren .05 .15
28 Sergei Samsonov .15 .40
29 Robbie Tallas .15 .40
30 Joe Thornton .30 .75
31 Landon Wilson .05 .15
32 J.Girard/A.Savage RC .20 .50
33 Stu Barnes .05 .15
34 Martin Biron .05 .15
35 Curtis Brown .05 .15
36 Michal Grosek .05 .15
37 Dominik Hasek .40 1.00
38 Brian Holzinger .15 .40
39 Joe Juneau .15 .40
40 Jay McKee .05 .15
41 Michael Peca .15 .40
42 Erik Rasmussen .05 .15
43 Rob Ray .05 .15
44 Geoff Sanderson .15 .40
45 Miroslav Satan .15 .40
46 Darryl Shannon .05 .15
47 Vaclav Varada .05 .15
48 Dixon Ward .05 .15
49 Jason Woolley .05 .15
50 Alexei Zhitnik .05 .15
51 Fred Brathwaite .15 .40
52 Valeri Bure .05 .15
53 Andrew Cassels .05 .15
54 Rene Corbet .05 .15
55 Jean-Sebastien Giguere .15 .40
56 Phil Housley .05 .15
57 Jarome Iginla .25 .60
58 Derek Morris .05 .15
59 Andrei Nazarov .05 .15
60 Jeff Shantz .05 .15
61 Todd Simpson .05 .15
62 Cory Stillman .05 .15
63 Jason Wiemer .05 .15
64 Clarke Wilm .05 .15
65 Ken Wregget .15 .40
66 Rico Fata RC .05 .15
Tyrone Garner
67 Bates Battaglia .05 .15
68 Paul Coffey .20 .50
69 Kevin Dineen .05 .15
70 Ron Francis .15 .40
71 Martin Gelinas .05 .15
72 Arturs Irbe .15 .40
73 Sami Kapanen .05 .15
74 Trevor Kidd .15 .40
75 Andrei Kovalenko .05 .15
76 Robert Kron .05 .15
77 Kent Manderville .05 .15
78 Jeff O'Neill .05 .15
79 Keith Primeau .05 .15
80 Gary Roberts .05 .15
81 Ray Sheppard .15 .40
82 Glen Wesley .05 .15
83 Byron Ritchie RC .15 .40
Craig MacDonald
84 Tony Amonte .15 .40
85 Eric Daze .15 .40
86 J-P Dumont .15 .40
87 Anders Eriksson .05 .15
88 Mark Fitzpatrick .15 .40
89 Doug Gilmour .15 .40
90 J.Y. Leroux .05 .15
91 Dave Manson .05 .15
92 Josef Marha .05 .15
93 Dean McAmmond .05 .15
94 Boris Mironov .05 .15
95 Ed Olczyk .05 .15
96 Bob Probert .05 .15
97 Jocelyn Thibault .15 .40
98 Alexei Zhamnov .05 .15
99 Remi Royer .05 .15
Ty Jones
100 Craig Billington .15 .40
101 Adam Deadmarsh .05 .15
102 Chris Drury .15 .40
103 Theo Fleury .05 .15
104 Adam Foote .15 .40
105 Peter Forsberg .50 1.25
106 Milan Hejduk .20 .50
107 Dale Hunter .05 .15
108 Valeri Kamensky .15 .40
109 Sylvain Lefebvre .05 .15
110 Claude Lemieux .05 .15
111 Aaron Miller .05 .15
112 Jeff Odgers .05 .15
113 Sandis Ozolinsh .05 .15
114 Patrick Roy 1.00 2.50
115 Joe Sakic .40 1.00
116 Stephane Yelle .05 .15
117 Ed Belfour .20 .50
118 Derian Hatcher .05 .15
119 Benoit Hogue .05 .15
120 Brett Hull .25 .60
121 Mike Keane .05 .15
122 Jamie Langenbrunner .05 .15
123 Jere Lehtinen .15 .40
124 Brad Lukowich RC .05 .15
125 Grant Marshall .05 .15
126 Mike Modano .30 .75
127 Joe Nieuwendyk .15 .40
128 Derek Plante .05 .15
129 Darryl Sydor .05 .15
130 Roman Turek .15 .40
131 Pat Verbeek .05 .15
132 Sergei Zubov .15 .40
133 Jonathan Sim RC .20 .50
Blake Sloan
134 Doug Brown .05 .15
135 Chris Chelios .20 .50
136 Wendel Clark .15 .40
137 Kris Draper .05 .15
138 Sergei Fedorov .30 .75
139 Tomas Holmstrom .05 .15
140 Vyacheslav Kozlov .15 .40
141 Martin Lapointe .05 .15
142 Igor Larionov .05 .15
143 Nicklas Lidstrom .20 .50
144 Darren McCarty .05 .15
145 Larry Murphy .15 .40
146 Chris Osgood .15 .40
147 Bill Ranford .15 .40
148 Ulf Samuelsson .05 .15
149 Brendan Shanahan .20 .50
150 Aaron Ward .05 .15
151 Steve Yzerman 1.00 2.50
152 Josef Beranek .05 .15
153 Pat Falloon .05 .15
154 Mike Grier .05 .15
155 Bill Guerin .15 .40
156 Roman Hamrlik .05 .15
157 Chad Kilger .05 .15
158 Georges Laraque RC .25 .60
159 Todd Marchant .05 .15
160 Ethan Moreau .05 .15
161 Rem Murray .05 .15
162 Janne Niinimaa .05 .15
163 Tom Poti .05 .15
164 Tommy Salo .15 .40
165 Alexander Selivanov .05 .15
166 Ryan Smyth .15 .40
167 Doug Weight .15 .40
168 Steve Passmore RC .20 .50
169 Pavel Bure .20 .50
170 Sean Burke .15 .40
171 Dino Ciccarelli .15 .40
172 Radek Dvorak .05 .15
173 Viktor Kozlov .05 .15
174 Oleg Kvasha .05 .15
175 Paul Laus .05 .15
176 Bill Lindsay .05 .15
177 Kirk McLean .15 .40
178 Scott Mellanby .05 .15
179 Rob Niedermayer .05 .15
180 Mark Parrish .05 .15
181 Jaroslav Spacek .05 .15
182 Robert Svehla .05 .15
183 Ray Whitney .05 .15
184 Peter Worrell .05 .15
185 Dan Boyle RC .15 .40
Marcus Nilson
186 Donald Audette .05 .15
187 Rob Blake .15 .40
188 Russ Courtnall .05 .15
189 Ray Ferraro .05 .15
190 Stephane Fiset .15 .40
191 Craig Johnson .05 .15
192 Olli Jokinen .15 .40
193 Glen Murray .05 .15
194 Mattias Norstrom .05 .15
195 Sean O'Donnell .05 .15
196 Luc Robitaille .15 .40
197 Pavel Rosa .15 .40
198 Jamie Storr .15 .40
199 Jozef Stumpel .15 .40
200 Vladimir Tsyplakov .05 .15
201 Benoit Brunet .05 .15
202 Shayne Corson .05 .15
203 Jeff Hackett .15 .40
204 Matt Higgins .05 .15
205 Saku Koivu .20 .50
206 Vladimir Malakhov .05 .15
207 Patrick Poulin .05 .15
208 Stephane Quintal .05 .15
209 Martin Rucinsky .05 .15
210 Brian Savage .05 .15
211 Turner Stevenson .05 .15
212 Jose Theodore .25 .60
213 Eric Weinrich .05 .15
214 Sergei Zholtok .05 .15
215 Dainius Zubrus .15 .40
216 Terry Ryan .05 .15
Miloslav Guren
217 Drake Berehowsky .05 .15
218 Sebastien Bordeleau .05 .15
219 Bob Boughner .05 .15
220 Andrew Brunette .15 .40
221 Patrick Cote .05 .15
222 Mike Dunham .15 .40
223 Tom Fitzgerald .05 .15
224 Jamie Heward .05 .15
225 Greg Johnson .05 .15
226 Patric Kjellberg .05 .15
227 Sergei Krivokrasov .05 .15
228 Denny Lambert .05 .15
229 David Legwand .20 .50
230 Mark Mowers RC .05 .15
231 Cliff Ronning .05 .15
232 Tomas Vokoun .05 .15
233 Scott Walker .05 .15
234 Jason Arnott .05 .15
235 Martin Brodeur .50 1.25
236 Ken Daneyko .05 .15
237 Patrik Elias .15 .40
238 Bobby Holik .15 .40
239 John Madden RC .30 .75
240 Randy McKay .05 .15
241 Brendan Morrison .15 .40
242 Scott Niedermayer .05 .15
243 Lyle Odelein .05 .15
244 Krzysztof Oliwa .05 .15
245 Jay Pandolfo .05 .15
246 Brian Rolston .05 .15
247 Vadim Sharifijanov .05 .15
248 Petr Sykora .05 .15
249 Chris Terreri .15 .40
250 Scott Stevens .15 .40
251 Eric Brewer .15 .40
252 Zdeno Chara .05 .15
253 Mariusz Czerkawski .15 .40
254 Wade Flaherty .05 .15
255 Kenny Jonsson .05 .15
256 Claude Lapointe .05 .15
257 Mark Lawrence .05 .15
258 Trevor Linden .05 .15
259 Mats Lindgren .05 .15
260 Warren Luhning .05 .15
261 Zigmund Palffy .15 .40
262 Rich Pilon .05 .15
263 Felix Potvin .20 .50
264 Barry Richter .05 .15
265 Bryan Smolinski .05 .15
266 Mike Watt .05 .15
267 Dan Cloutier .05 .15
268 Brent Fedyk .05 .15
269 Adam Graves .05 .15
270 Todd Harvey .05 .15
271 Mike Knuble .05 .15
272 Brian Leetch .20 .50
273 John MacLean .05 .15
274 Manny Malhotra .15 .40
275 Rumun Ndur .05 .15
276 Petr Nedved .05 .15
277 Peter Popovic .05 .15
278 Mike Richter .20 .50
279 Marc Savard .05 .15
280 Mathieu Schneider .05 .15
281 Kevin Stevens .15 .40
282 Niklas Sundstrom .15 .40
283 Daniel Alfredsson .15 .40
284 Magnus Arvedson .05 .15
285 Radek Bonk .05 .15
286 Andreas Dackell .05 .15
287 Bruce Gardiner .05 .15
288 Marian Hossa .20 .50
289 Andreas Johansson .05 .15
290 Igor Kravchuk .05 .15
291 Shawn McEachern .05 .15
292 Vaclav Prospal .05 .15
293 Wade Redden .05 .15
294 Damian Rhodes .15 .40
295 Sami Salo .05 .15
296 Ron Tugnutt .15 .40
297 Alexei Yashin .05 .15
298 Jason York .05 .15
299 Rod Brind'Amour .15 .40
300 Adam Burt .05 .15
301 Eric Desjardins .15 .40
302 Ron Hextall .15 .40
303 Jody Hull .05 .15
304 Keith Jones .05 .15
305 Daymond Langkow .15 .40
306 John LeClair .20 .50
307 Eric Lindros .20 .50
308 Sandy McCarthy .05 .15
309 Dan McGillis .05 .15
310 Mark Recchi .15 .40
311 Mikael Renberg .15 .40
312 Chris Therien .05 .15
313 John Vanbiesbrouck .15 .40
314 Valeri Zelepukin .05 .15
315 Greg Adams .05 .15
316 Keith Carney .05 .15
317 Bob Corkum .05 .15
318 Jim Cummins .05 .15
319 Shane Doan .05 .15
320 Dallas Drake .05 .15
321 Nikolai Khabibulin .15 .40
322 Jyrki Lumme .05 .15
323 Teppo Numminen .05 .15
324 Robert Reichel .05 .15
325 Jeremy Roenick .25 .60
326 Mikhail Shtalenkov .05 .15
327 Mike Stapleton .05 .15
328 Keith Tkachuk .20 .50
329 Rick Tocchet .15 .40
330 Oleg Tverdovsky .05 .15
331 Juha Ylonen .05 .15
332 Robert Esche RC .05 .15
Scott Langkow
333 Matthew Barnaby .15 .40
334 Tom Barrasso .15 .40
335 Rob Brown .05 .15
336 Kevin Hatcher .05 .15
337 Jan Hrdina .05 .15
338 Jaromir Jagr .30 .75
339 Darius Kasparaitis .05 .15
340 Dan Kesa .05 .15
341 Alexei Kovalev .05 .15
342 Robert Lang .05 .15
343 Kip Miller .05 .15
344 Alexei Morozov .15 .40
345 Peter Skudra .15 .40
346 Jiri Slegr .05 .15
347 Martin Straka .05 .15
348 German Titov .05 .15
349 Brad Werenka .05 .15
350 J.S. Aubin RC .15 .40
Brian Bonin
351 Blair Atcheynum .05 .15
352 Lubos Bartecko .05 .15
353 Craig Conroy .05 .15
354 Geoff Courtnall .15 .40
355 Pavol Demitra .15 .40
356 Grant Fuhr .15 .40
357 Michal Handzus .15 .40
358 Al MacInnis .15 .40
359 Jamal Mayers .05 .15
360 Jamie McLennan .15 .40
361 Scott Pellerin .05 .15
362 Chris Pronger .15 .40
363 Pascal Rheaume .05 .15
364 Pierre Turgeon .15 .40
365 Tony Twist .15 .40
366 Scott Young .05 .15
367 Jochen Hecht RC .50 1.25
Brent Johnson
368 Tyson Nash RC .15 .40
Marty Reasoner
369 Vincent Damphousse .05 .15
370 Jeff Friesen .05 .15
371 Tony Granato .05 .15
372 Bill Houlder .05 .15
373 Alexander Korolyuk .05 .15
374 Bryan Marchment .05 .15
375 Patrick Marleau .15 .40
376 Stephane Matteau .05 .15
377 Joe Murphy .05 .15
378 Owen Nolan .15 .40
379 Mike Rathje .05 .15
380 Mike Ricci .05 .15
381 Steve Shields .15 .40
382 Ronnie Stern .05 .15
383 Marco Sturm .05 .15
384 Mike Vernon .15 .40
385 Scott Hannan RC .15 .40
Shawn Heins
386 Cory Cross .05 .15
387 Alexandre Daigle .05 .15
388 Colin Forbes .05 .15
389 Chris Gratton .05 .15
390 Kevin Hodson .15 .40
391 Pavel Kubina .05 .15
392 Vincent Lecavalier .20 .50
393 Michael Nylander .15 .40
394 Stephane Richer .15 .40
395 Corey Schwab .15 .40
396 Mike Sillinger .05 .15
397 Petr Svoboda .05 .15
398 Darcy Tucker .05 .15
399 Rob Zamuner .05 .15
400 Paul Mara RC .20 .50
Mario Larocque
401 Bryan Berard .15 .40
402 Sergei Berezin .15 .40
403 Lonny Bohonos .05 .15
404 Sylvain Cote .05 .15
405 Tie Domi .15 .40
406 Mike Johnson .05 .15
407 Curtis Joseph .20 .50
408 Tomas Kaberle .05 .15
409 Alexander Karpovtsev .05 .15
410 Derek King .05 .15
411 Igor Korolev .05 .15
412 Adam Mair RC .15 .40
413 Alyn McCauley .15 .40
414 Yanic Perreault .15 .40
415 Steve Sullivan .05 .15
416 Mats Sundin .20 .50
417 Steve Thomas .05 .15
418 Garry Valk .05 .15
419 Adrian Aucoin .05 .15
420 Todd Bertuzzi .20 .50
421 Donald Brashear .05 .15
422 Dave Gagner .05 .15
423 Josh Holden .05 .15
424 Ed Jovanovski .05 .15
425 Bryan McCabe .15 .40
426 Mark Messier .20 .50
427 Alexander Mogilny .15 .40
428 Bill Muckalt .15 .40
429 Markus Naslund .20 .50
430 Mattias Ohlund .15 .40
431 Dave Scatchard .05 .15
432 Peter Schaefer .05 .15
433 Garth Snow .15 .40
434 Kevin Weekes .05 .15
435 Brian Bellows .05 .15
436 James Black .05 .15
437 Peter Bondra .15 .40
438 Jan Bulis .05 .15
439 Sergei Gonchar .05 .15
440 Benoit Gratton RC .05 .15
441 Calle Johansson .05 .15
442 Ken Klee .05 .15
443 Olaf Kolzig .15 .40
444 Steve Konowalchuk .05 .15
445 Andrei Nikolishin .05 .15
446 Adam Oates .15 .40
447 Jaroslav Svejkovsky .05 .15
448 Rick Tabaracci .15 .40
449 Richard Zednik .05 .15
450 Nolan Baumgartner RC .20 .50
Alexei Tezikov
451 Ladislav Kohn AG
452 Petr Buzek AG
453 Robyn Regehr AG
454 David Tanabe AG
455 Jiri Fischer AG
456 Paul Comrie AG
457 Brad Chartrand AG
458 Scott Gomez AG
459 Roberto Luongo AG
460 Mike York AG
462 Trevor Letowski AG
463 Brad Stuart AG
464 Ben Clymer AG
465 Nikolai Antropov AG
466 Jeff Halpern AG

1999-00 Pacific Copper

*VETERANS: 10X TO 25X BASIC CARDS
*ROOKIES: 6X TO 15X BASIC CARDS
STATED PRINT RUN 99 SER.#'d SETS

1999-00 Pacific Emerald Green

*VETERANS: 6X TO 15X BASIC CARDS
*ROOKIES: 4X TO 10X BASIC CARDS
STATED PRINT RUN 199 SER.#'d SETS

1999-00 Pacific Gold

*VETERANS: 8X TO 20X BASIC CARDS
*ROOKIES: 5X TO 12X BASIC CARDS
STATED PRINT RUN 199 SER.#'d SETS

1999-00 Pacific Ice Blue

*VETERANS: 15X TO 40X BASIC CARDS
*ROOKIES: 10X TO 25X BASIC CARDS
STATED PRINT RUN 75 SER.#'d SETS

1999-00 Pacific Premiere Date

*VETERANS: 20X TO 50X BASIC CARDS
ROOKIES: 12X TO 30X BASIC CARDS
STATED PRINT RUN 46 SER.#'d SETS

1999-00 Pacific Red

*VETERANS: .6X TO 1.5X BASIC CARDS
*ROOKIES: .4X TO 1X BASIC CARDS

1999-00 Pacific Center Ice

Randomly inserted in the 7-eleven pack release, this set identifies some of the NHL's top stars. A parallel proof version of this set was released also where cards are sequentially numbered to 10. Proofs are not priced due to scarcity.

COMPLETE SET (20) 20.00 40.00
UNPRICED PROOFS SER.#'d OF 10
1 Paul Kariya .75 2.00
2 Teemu Selanne .75 2.00
3 Dominik Hasek 1.50 4.00
4 Jarome Iginla 1.00 2.50
5 Theo Fleury .60 1.50
6 Peter Forsberg 2.00 5.00
7 Patrick Roy 4.00 10.00
8 Joe Sakic 1.50 4.00
9 Mike Modano 1.25 3.00
10 Brendan Shanahan .75 2.00
11 Steve Yzerman 4.00 10.00
12 Doug Weight .60 1.50
13 Trevor Linden .30 .75
14 Martin Brodeur 2.00 5.00
15 Alexei Yashin .30 .75
16 Eric Lindros .75 2.00
17 Jaromir Jagr 1.25 3.00
18 Curtis Joseph .75 2.00
19 Mats Sundin .75 2.00
20 Mark Messier .75 2.00

1999-00 Pacific Cramer's Choice

Randomly inserted into packs, this set continues the tradition of the Cramer's Choice Awards. For the first time, these cards are serial numbered out of 299.

COMPLETE SET (10) 175.00 350.00
1 Paul Kariya 8.00 20.00
2 Dominik Hasek 15.00 40.00
3 Peter Forsberg 20.00 50.00
4 Patrick Roy 40.00 100.00
5 Joe Sakic 15.00 40.00
6 Mike Modano 12.50 30.00
7 Steve Yzerman 40.00 100.00
8 Eric Lindros 8.00 20.00
9 Jaromir Jagr 12.50 30.00
10 Curtis Joseph 8.00 20.00

1999-00 Pacific Gold Crown Die-Cuts

COMPLETE SET (36) 100.00 200.00
COMMON CARD (1-36) 1.25 3.00
SEMISTARS/GOALIES 2.00 5.00
UNLISTED STARS 2.50 6.00
STATED ODDS 1:25
1 Paul Kariya 2.00 5.00
2 Teemu Selanne 2.00 5.00
3 Ray Bourque 3.00 8.00
4 Byron Dafoe 1.25 3.00
5 Dominik Hasek 4.00 10.00
6 Michael Peca 1.25 3.00
7 Chris Drury 1.25 3.00
8 Theo Fleury 1.25 3.00
9 Peter Forsberg 5.00 12.00
10 Milan Hejduk 1.25 3.00
11 Patrick Roy 10.00 25.00
12 Joe Sakic 4.00 10.00
13 Ed Belfour 2.00 5.00
14 Brett Hull 2.50 6.00
15 Mike Modano 2.50 6.00
16 Chris Chelios 1.25 3.00
17 Brendan Shanahan 2.00 5.00
18 Steve Yzerman 10.00 25.00
19 Pavel Bure 2.00 5.00
20 David Legwand 1.25 3.00
21 Martin Brodeur 6.00 15.00
22 Felix Potvin 2.00 5.00
23 Mike Richter 2.00 5.00
24 Alexei Yashin 1.25 3.00
25 John LeClair 1.25 3.00
26 Eric Lindros 1.25 3.00
27 Mark Recchi 1.25 3.00
28 John Vanbiesbrouck 1.25 3.00
29 Jeremy Roenick 2.50 6.00
30 Keith Tkachuk 1.25 3.00
31 Jaromir Jagr 3.00 8.00
32 Vincent Lecavalier 2.00 5.00
33 Sergei Berezin 1.25 3.00
34 Curtis Joseph 2.00 5.00
35 Mats Sundin 2.00 5.00
36 Mark Messier 2.00 5.00

1999-00 Pacific Home and Away

Inserted 2:25 packs, these cards feature players in both their Home and Away jerseys. Cards 1-10 can be found in retail packs, while cards 11-20 can be found in hobby packs.

COMPLETE SET (20) 50.00 100.00
1 Paul Kariya 1.25 3.00
2 Teemu Selanne 1.25 3.00
3 Dominik Hasek 2.50 6.00
4 Peter Forsberg 3.00 8.00
5 Patrick Roy 6.00 15.00
6 Mike Modano 2.00 5.00
7 Steve Yzerman 6.00 15.00
8 John LeClair 1.25 3.00
9 Eric Lindros 1.25 3.00
10 Jaromir Jagr 2.00 5.00
11 Paul Kariya 1.25 3.00
12 Teemu Selanne 1.25 3.00
13 Dominik Hasek 2.50 6.00
14 Peter Forsberg 3.00 8.00
15 Patrick Roy 6.00 15.00
16 Mike Modano 2.00 5.00
17 Steve Yzerman 6.00 15.00
18 John LeClair 1.25 3.00
19 Eric Lindros 1.25 3.00
20 Jaromir Jagr 2.00 5.00

1999-00 Pacific In the Cage Net-Fusions

Inserted 1:97 packs, these cards are die-cut and feature actual netting as the background. Cards are full color and feature goalie action shots.

COMPLETE SET (20) 50.00 100.00
1 Guy Hebert 2.00 5.00
2 Byron Dafoe 2.00 5.00
3 Dominik Hasek 5.00 12.00
4 Arturs Irbe 2.00 5.00
5 Patrick Roy 12.50 30.00
6 Ed Belfour 2.50 6.00
7 Chris Osgood 2.00 5.00
8 Tommy Salo 2.00 5.00
9 Jeff Hackett 2.00 5.00
10 Martin Brodeur 6.00 15.00
11 Felix Potvin 2.50 6.00
12 Mike Richter 2.50 6.00
13 Ron Tugnutt 2.00 5.00
14 John Vanbiesbrouck 2.00 5.00
15 Nikolai Khabibulin 2.00 5.00
16 Tom Barrasso 2.00 5.00
17 Grant Fuhr 2.00 5.00
18 Mike Vernon 2.00 5.00
19 Curtis Joseph 2.50 6.00
20 Olaf Kolzig 2.00 5.00

1999-00 Pacific Past and Present

A hobby only insert seeded 1:49 that features 20 of the NHL's top stars in both their old and current uniforms.

COMPLETE SET (20) 100.00 200.00
1 Paul Kariya 2.00 5.00
2 Teemu Selanne 2.00 5.00
3 Ray Bourque 3.00 8.00
4 Dominik Hasek 6.00 15.00
5 Theo Fleury 1.50 4.00
6 Peter Forsberg 8.00 20.00
7 Patrick Roy 12.00 30.00
8 Joe Sakic 6.00 15.00
9 Ed Belfour 2.00 5.00
10 Brett Hull 3.00 8.00
11 Mike Modano 3.00 8.00
12 Brendan Shanahan 2.00 5.00
13 Steve Yzerman 12.00 30.00
14 Pavel Bure 2.00 5.00
15 Martin Brodeur 8.00 20.00
16 John LeClair 1.50 4.00
17 Eric Lindros 2.00 5.00
18 John Vanbiesbrouck 1.50 4.00
19 Jaromir Jagr 4.00 10.00
20 Curtis Joseph 2.00 5.00

1999-00 Pacific Team Leaders

Randomly inserted in packs at the rate of 2:25, this set features 27 of the NHL's premier team leaders. Each card features holographic foil with a complete team checklist on the back.

COMPLETE SET (28) 30.00 60.00
1 Paul Kariya 1.00 2.50
2 Atlanta Thrashers .40 1.00
3 Ray Bourque 1.50 4.00
4 Dominik Hasek 2.00 5.00
5 Jarome Iginla 1.25 3.00
6 Arturs Irbe .75 2.00
7 Doug Gilmour .75 2.00
8 Patrick Roy 5.00 12.00
9 Mike Modano 1.50 4.00
10 Steve Yzerman 5.00 12.00
11 Bill Guerin .75 2.00
12 Pavel Bure 1.00 2.50
13 Luc Robitaille .75 2.00

14 Saku Koivu 1.00 2.50
15 Mike Dunham .75 2.00
16 Martin Brodeur 2.50 6.00
17 Zigmund Palffy .75 2.00
18 Mike Richter 1.00 2.50
19 Alexei Yashin .40 1.00
20 Eric Lindros 1.00 2.50
21 Keith Tkachuk 1.00 2.50
22 Jaromir Jagr 1.50 4.00
23 Grant Fuhr .75 2.00
24 Mike Vernon .75 2.00
25 Vincent Lecavalier 1.00 2.50
26 Curtis Joseph 1.00 2.50
27 Mark Messier 1.00 2.50
28 Peter Bondra .75 2.00

2000-01 Pacific

Released as a 450-card set, Pacific features full color action shots and cards enhanced with silver foil highlights. Pacific was packaged in 36-pack boxes with packs containing 12 cards each and carried a suggested retail price of $2.99.

COMPLETE SET (450) 30.00 60.00
1 Maxim Balmochnyk .15 .40
2 Matt Cullen .05 .15
3 Ted Donato .05 .15
4 Guy Hebert .15 .40
5 Paul Kariya .20 .50
6 Ladislav Kohn .05 .15
7 Marty McInnis .05 .15
8 Kip Miller .05 .15
9 Dominic Roussel .15 .40
10 Steve Rucchin .05 .15
11 Teemu Selanne .20 .50
12 Oleg Tverdovsky .05 .15
13 Vitali Vishnevski .05 .15
14 Donald Audette .05 .15
15 Andrew Brunette .15 .40
16 Petr Buzek .05 .15
17 Hnat Domenichelli .05 .15
18 Ray Ferraro .05 .15
19 Steve Guolla .05 .15
20 Denny Lambert .05 .15
21 Damian Rhodes .15 .40
22 Mike Stapleton .05 .15
23 Patrik Stefan .05 .15
24 Per Svartvadet .05 .15
25 Dean Sylvester .05 .15
26 Yannick Tremblay .05 .15
27 Bryan Adams .15 .40
Scott Fankhouser
28 Herbert Vasiljevs RC .20 .50
Sergei Vyshedkevich RC
29 Jason Allison .05 .15
30 Per Johan Axelsson .05 .15
31 Anson Carter .15 .40
32 Byron Dafoe .15 .40
33 Hal Gill .05 .15
34 John Grahame .15 .40
35 Steve Heinze .05 .15
36 Joe Hulbig .05 .15
37 Mike Knuble .05 .15
38 Kyle McLaren .05 .15
39 Eric Nickulas RC .05 .15
40 Brian Rolston .05 .15
41 Sergei Samsonov .15 .40
42 Andre Savage .05 .15
43 Joe Thornton .30 .75
44 Darren Van Impe .05 .15
45 Nick Boynton .15 .40
Johnathan Aitken
46 Maxim Afinogenov .05 .15
47 Stu Barnes .05 .15
48 Martin Biron .15 .40
49 Curtis Brown .05 .15
50 Doug Gilmour .15 .40
51 Chris Gratton .05 .15
52 Dominik Hasek .40 1.00
53 Michael Peca .15 .40
54 Erik Rasmussen .05 .15
55 Rob Ray .15 .40
56 Geoff Sanderson .05 .15
57 Miroslav Satan .15 .40
58 Vladimir Tsyplakov .05 .15
59 Vaclav Varada .05 .15
60 Jason Woolley .05 .15
61 Fred Brathwaite .15 .40
62 Valeri Bure .05 .15
63 Bobby Dollas .05 .15
64 Jean-Sebastien Giguere .05 .15
65 Phil Housley .05 .15
66 Jarome Iginla .25 .60
67 Andreas Johansson .05 .15
68 Sergei Krivokrasov .05 .15
69 Bill Lindsay .05 .15
70 Derek Morris .05 .15
71 Andrei Nazarov .05 .15
72 Oleg Saprykin .05 .15
73 Marc Savard .15 .40
74 Jeff Shantz .05 .15
75 Cory Stillman .05 .15
76 Jason Wiemer .05 .15
77 Chris Clark .05 .15
Sergei Varlamov
78 Bates Battaglia .05 .15
79 Rod Brind'Amour .15 .40
80 Paul Coffey .20 .50
81 Ron Francis .15 .40
82 Sean Hill .05 .15
83 Arturs Irbe .15 .40
84 Sami Kapanen .05 .15
85 Dave Karpa .05 .15
86 Andrei Kovalenko .05 .15
87 Robert Kron .05 .15
88 Jeff O'Neill .05 .15
89 Gary Roberts .05 .15
90 Dave Tanabe .15 .40
91 Tommy Westlund .05 .15
92 Tony Amonte .15 .40
93 Eric Daze .15 .40
94 Kevin Dean .05 .15
95 Michal Grosek .05 .15
96 Dean McAmmond .05 .15
97 Bryan McCabe .05 .15
98 Steven McCarthy .05 .15
99 Boris Mironov .05 .15
100 Michael Nylander .05 .15
101 Bob Probert .15 .40
102 Steve Sullivan .05 .15
103 Jocelyn Thibault .15 .40
104 Ryan Vandenbussche .05 .15
105 Alexei Zhamnov .15 .40
106 Dave Andreychuk .15 .40
107 Ray Bourque .40 1.00
108 Adam Deadmarsh .05 .15
109 Marc Denis .15 .40
110 Greg DeVries .05 .15
111 Chris Drury .15 .40
112 Adam Foote .05 .15
113 Peter Forsberg .50 1.25
114 Alexei Gusarov .05 .15
115 Milan Hejduk .20 .50
116 Eric Messier .05 .15
117 Sandis Ozolinsh .05 .15
118 Shjon Podein .05 .15
119 Dave Reid .05 .15
120 Patrick Roy 1.00 2.50
121 Joe Sakic .40 1.00
122 Martin Skoula .15 .40
123 Alex Tanguay .15 .40
124 Stephane Yelle .05 .15
125 Serge Aubin RC .75 2.00
Ville Nieminen RC
126 Ed Belfour .20 .50
127 Guy Carbonneau .05 .15
128 Sylvain Cote .05 .15
129 Manny Fernandez .15 .40
130 Derian Hatcher .05 .15
131 Brett Hull .25 .60
132 Mike Keane .05 .15
133 Jamie Langenbrunner .05 .15
134 Jere Lehtinen .15 .40
135 Dave Manson .05 .15
136 Richard Matvichuk .05 .15
137 Mike Modano .30 .75
138 Brenden Morrow .15 .40
139 Joe Nieuwendyk .15 .40
140 Blake Sloan .05 .15
141 Darryl Sydor .05 .15
142 Scott Thornton .05 .15
143 Sergei Zubov ERR .05 .15
Misnumbered 142
144 Doug Brown .05 .15
145 Chris Chelios .20 .50
146 Kris Draper .05 .15
147 Sergei Fedorov .30 .75
148 Tomas Holmstrom .05 .15
149 Vyacheslav Kozlov .05 .15
150 Darryl Laplante .05 .15
151 Martin Lapointe .05 .15
152 Igor Larionov .05 .15
153 Nicklas Lidstrom .20 .50
154 Kirk Maltby .05 .15
155 Darren McCarty .05 .15
156 Larry Murphy .15 .40
157 Chris Osgood .15 .40
158 Brendan Shanahan .20 .50
159 Pat Verbeek .05 .15
160 Jesse Wallin .05 .15
161 Ken Wregget .15 .40
162 Steve Yzerman 1.00 2.50
163 Boyd Devereaux .05 .15
164 Jim Dowd .05 .15
165 Mike Grier .05 .15
166 Bill Guerin .15 .40
167 Roman Hamrlik .15 .40
168 Georges Laraque .05 .15
169 Todd Marchant .05 .15
170 Ethan Moreau .05 .15
171 Tom Poti .05 .15
172 Tommy Salo .15 .40
173 Alexander Selivanov .05 .15
174 Ryan Smyth .05 .15
175 German Titov .05 .15
176 Doug Weight .15 .40
177 Pavel Bure .20 .50
178 Trevor Kidd .15 .40
179 Viktor Kozlov .05 .15
180 Oleg Kvasha .05 .15
181 Paul Laus .05 .15
182 Scott Mellanby .05 .15
183 Rob Niedermayer .05 .15
184 Ivan Novoseltsev .15 .40
185 Mark Parrish .05 .15
186 Mikhail Shtalenkov .05 .15
187 Robert Svehla .05 .15
188 Mike Vernon .15 .40
189 Ray Whitney .05 .15
190 Peter Worrell .05 .15
191 Erix Boguniecki .05 .15
Brad Ference
192 Aki Berg .05 .15
193 Rob Blake .15 .40
194 Kelly Buchberger .05 .15
195 Nelson Emerson .05 .15
196 Stephane Fiset .15 .40
197 Garry Galley .05 .15
198 Glen Murray .05 .15
199 Jan Nemecek .05 .15
200 Zigmund Palffy .15 .40
201 Luc Robitaille .15 .40
202 Bryan Smolinski .05 .15
203 Jamie Storr .15 .40
204 Jozef Stumpel .15 .40
205 Patrice Brisebois .05 .15
206 Benoit Brunet .05 .15
207 Shayne Corson .05 .15
208 Jeff Hackett .15 .40
209 Saku Koivu .20 .50
210 Trevor Linden .05 .15
211 Oleg Petrov .05 .15
212 Martin Rucinsky .05 .15
213 Brian Savage .05 .15
214 Sheldon Souray .05 .15
215 Jose Theodore .25 .60
216 Eric Weinrich .05 .15
217 Sergei Zholtok .05 .15
218 Dainius Zubrus .05 .15
219 Sebastien Bordeleau .05 .15
220 Mike Dunham .15 .40
221 Tom Fitzgerald .05 .15
222 Greg Johnson .05 .15
223 David Legwand .15 .40
224 Craig Millar .05 .15
225 Cliff Ronning .05 .15
226 Kimmo Timonen .05 .15
227 Tomas Vokoun .05 .15
228 Scott Walker .05 .15
229 Alexandre Boikov RC .15 .40
Marc Moro RC
230 David Gosselin .20 .50
Chris Mason
231 Jason Arnott .05 .15
232 Martin Brodeur .50 1.25
233 Patrik Elias .15 .40
234 Scott Gomez .05 .15
235 Bobby Holik .05 .15
236 Claude Lemieux .05 .15
237 John Madden .15 .40
238 Vladimir Malakhov .05 .15
239 Randy McKay .05 .15
240 Alexander Mogilny .15 .40
241 Scott Niedermayer .05 .15
242 Brian Rafalski .05 .15
243 Scott Stevens .15 .40
244 Petr Sykora .05 .15
245 Chris Terreri .15 .40
246 Willie Mitchell RC .15 .40
Colin White RC
247 Tim Connolly .05 .15
248 Mariusz Czerkawski .05 .15
249 Josh Green .05 .15
250 Brad Isbister .05 .15
251 Jason Krog .05 .15
252 Claude Lapointe .05 .15
253 Roberto Luongo .25 .60
254 Petr Mika RC .05 .15
255 Dave Scatchard .05 .15
256 Steve Valiquette RC .20 .50
257 Kevin Weekes .05 .15
258 Alexandre Daigle .05 .15
259 Radek Dvorak .05 .15
260 Theo Fleury .05 .15
261 Adam Graves .05 .15
262 Jan Hlavac .15 .40
263 Kim Johnsson .05 .15
264 Valeri Kamensky .15 .40
265 Brian Leetch .15 .40
266 John MacLean .05 .15
267 Kirk McLean .05 .15
268 Petr Nedved .15 .40
269 Mike Richter .20 .50
270 Mathieu Schneider .05 .15
271 Johan Witehall RC .05 .15
272 Mike York .05 .15
273 Daniel Alfredsson .15 .40
274 Magnus Arvedson .05 .15
275 Tom Barrasso .15 .40
276 Radek Bonk .05 .15
277 Mike Fisher .15 .40
278 Marian Hossa .20 .50
279 Jani Hurme RC .40 1.00
280 Joe Juneau .15 .40
281 Patrick Lalime .15 .40
282 Grant Ledyard .05 .15
283 Shawn McEachern .05 .15
284 Chris Phillips .05 .15
285 Vaclav Prospal .05 .15
286 Wade Redden .05 .15
287 Sami Salo .05 .15
288 Alexei Yashin .05 .15
289 Jason York .05 .15
290 Rob Zamuner .05 .15
291 Erich Goldmann RC .05 .15
Petr Schastlivy
292 Craig Berube .05 .15
293 Brian Boucher .20 .50
294 Andy Delmore .15 .40
295 Eric Desjardins .15 .40
296 Simon Gagne .20 .50
297 Jody Hull .05 .15
298 Keith Jones .05 .15
299 Daymond Langkow .15 .40
300 John LeClair .20 .50
301 Eric Lindros .20 .50
302 Kent Manderville .05 .15
303 Dan McGillis .05 .15
304 Gino Odjick .05 .15
305 Keith Primeau .05 .15
306 Mark Recchi .15 .40
307 Chris Therien .05 .15
308 Rick Tocchet .15 .40
309 John Vanbiesbrouck .15 .40
310 Valeri Zelepukin .05 .15
311 Sean Burke .05 .15
312 Keith Carney .05 .15
313 Louie DeBrusk .05 .15
314 Shane Doan .05 .15
315 Dallas Drake .05 .15
316 Travis Green .05 .15
317 Nikolai Khabibulin .20 .50
318 Trevor Letowski .05 .15
319 Jyrki Lumme .05 .15
320 Mikael Renberg .05 .15
321 Jeremy Roenick .25 .60
322 Keith Tkachuk .20 .50
323 Robert Esche .05 .15
Wyatt Smith
324 Jean-Sebastien Aubin .15 .40
325 Matthew Barnaby .05 .15
326 Pat Falloon .05 .15
327 Jan Hrdina .05 .15
328 Jaromir Jagr .30 .75
329 Darius Kasparaitis .05 .15
330 Alexei Kovalev .05 .15
331 Robert Lang .05 .15
332 Janne Laukkanen .05 .15
333 Stephen Leach .05 .15
334 Alexei Morozov .05 .15
335 Michal Rozsival .05 .15
336 Jiri Slegr .05 .15
337 Martin Straka .05 .15
338 Ron Tugnutt .15 .40
339 Lubos Bartecko .05 .15
340 Marc Bergevin .05 .15
341 Pavol Demitra .15 .40
342 Mike Eastwood .05 .15
343 Dave Ellett .05 .15
344 Michal Handzus .15 .40
345 Jochen Hecht .05 .15
346 Al MacInnis .15 .40
347 Jamie McLennan .15 .40
348 Tyson Nash .15 .40
349 Chris Pronger .15 .40
350 Marty Reasoner .15 .40
351 Stephane Richer .05 .15
352 Roman Turek .15 .40
353 Pierre Turgeon .15 .40
354 Scott Young .05 .15
355 Derek Bekar RC .15 .40
Ladislav Nagy
356 Vincent Damphousse .05 .15
357 Jeff Friesen .05 .15
358 Todd Harvey .05 .15
359 Alexander Korolyuk .05 .15
360 Patrick Marleau .15 .40
361 Stephane Matteau .05 .15
362 Evgeni Nabokov .15 .40
363 Owen Nolan .15 .40
364 Mike Ricci .15 .40
365 Steve Shields .15 .40
366 Brad Stuart .15 .40
367 Marco Sturm .05 .15
368 Gary Suter .05 .15
369 Dan Cloutier .15 .40
370 Stan Drulia .05 .15
371 Matt Elich RC .05 .15
372 Brian Holzinger .05 .15
373 Mike Johnson .05 .15
374 Ryan Johnson .05 .15
375 Dieter Kochan RC .20 .50
376 Pavel Kubina .05 .15
377 Vincent Lecavalier .20 .50
378 Fredrik Modin .05 .15
379 Wayne Primeau .05 .15
380 Cory Sarich .05 .15
381 Petr Svoboda .05 .15
382 Kaspars Astashenko RC .05 .15
Kyle Freadrich RC
383 Gordie Dwyer .05 .15
Marek Posmyk
384 Nikolai Antropov .05 .15
385 Sergei Berezin .05 .15
386 Wendel Clark .15 .40
387 Tie Domi .15 .40
388 Gerald Diduck .05 .15
389 Jeff Farkas .15 .40
390 Glenn Healy .05 .15
391 Jonas Hoglund .05 .15
392 Curtis Joseph .20 .50
393 Tomas Kaberle .05 .15
394 Alexander Karpovtsev .05 .15
395 Dimitri Khristich .05 .15
396 Igor Korolev .05 .15
397 Yanic Perreault .05 .15
398 DJ Smith .05 .15
399 Mats Sundin .20 .50
400 Steve Thomas .05 .15
401 Darcy Tucker .05 .15
402 Dimitri Yushkevich .05 .15
403 Adrian Aucoin .05 .15
404 Todd Bertuzzi .20 .50
405 Donald Brashear .05 .15
406 Andrew Cassels .05 .15
407 Harold Druken .05 .15
408 Ed Jovanovski .05 .15
409 Steve Kariya .05 .15
410 Trent Klatt .05 .15
411 Mark Messier .20 .50
412 Markus Naslund .20 .50
413 Mattias Ohlund .05 .15
414 Felix Potvin .20 .50
415 Peter Schaefer .05 .15
416 Garth Snow .15 .40
417 Alfie Michaud .05 .15
Jarkko Ruutu
418 Peter Bondra .20 .50
419 Martin Brochu RC .05 .15
420 Jan Bulis .05 .15
421 Sergei Gonchar .05 .15
422 Jeff Halpern .05 .15
423 Calle Johansson .05 .15
424 Ken Klee .05 .15
425 Olaf Kolzig .15 .40
426 Steve Konowalchuk .05 .15
427 Glen Metropolit .05 .15
428 Adam Oates .15 .40
429 Chris Simon .05 .15
430 Richard Zednik .05 .15
431 Jorgen Jonsson SF .05 .15
432 Teemu Selanne SF .15 .40
433 Sami Kapanen SF .05 .15
434 Peter Forsberg SF .20 .50
435 Jere Lehtinen SF .05 .15
436 Nicklas Lidstrom SF .05 .15
437 Janne Niinimaa SF .05 .15
438 Tommy Salo SF .05 .15
439 Saku Koivu SF .05 .15
440 Patric Kjellberg SF .05 .15
441 Olli Jokinen SF .15 .40
442 Kenny Jonsson SF .05 .15
443 Daniel Alfredsson SF .15 .40
444 Andreas Dackell SF .05 .15
445 Teppo Numminen SF .05 .15
446 Marcus Ragnarsson SF .05 .15
447 Niklas Sundstrom SF .05 .15
448 Mats Sundin SF .05 .15
449 Markus Naslund SF .20 .50
450 Ulf Dahlen SF .05 .15

2000-01 Pacific Copper

*STARS: 20X TO 50X BASIC CARDS
*ROOKIES: 8X TO 20X BASIC CARDS
STATED PRINT RUN 40 SERIAL #'d SETS
STATED ODDS 1:37 HOBBY

2000-01 Pacific Gold

*STARS: 20X TO 50X BASIC CARDS
*ROOKIES: 8X TO 20X BASIC CARDS
STATED ODDS 1:37 RETAIL
STATED PRINT RUN 50 SERIAL #'d SETS

2000-01 Pacific Ice Blue

*STARS: 20X TO 50X BASIC CARDS
*ROOKIES: 8X TO 20X BASIC CARDS
STATED ODDS 1:73
STATED PRINT RUN 45 SERIAL #'d SETS

2000-01 Pacific Premiere Date

*STARS: 12X TO 30X BASIC CARDS
*ROOKIES: 8X TO 20X BASIC CARDS
STATED ODDS 1:37 HOBBY
STATED PRINT RUN 40 SERIAL #'d SETS

2000-01 Pacific 2001: Ice Odyssey

COMPLETE SET (20) 30.00 80.00
STATED ODDS 1:37
1 Paul Kariya 2.00 5.00
2 Teemu Selanne 2.00 5.00
3 Martin Biron 1.25 3.00
4 Jarome Iginla 2.50 6.00
5 Chris Drury .75 2.00
6 Peter Forsberg 3.00 8.00
7 Milan Hejduk 1.25 3.00
8 Patrick Roy 6.00 15.00
9 Steve Yzerman 6.00 15.00
10 Pavel Bure 2.00 5.00
11 Jose Theodore 2.00 5.00
12 Martin Brodeur 4.00 10.00
13 Patrik Elias .75 2.00
14 Scott Gomez .75 2.00
15 Roberto Luongo 2.50 6.00
16 Marian Hossa 1.25 3.00
17 Brian Boucher 1.25 3.00
18 Jaromir Jagr 3.00 8.00
19 Vincent Lecavalier 2.00 5.00
20 Mats Sundin 2.00 5.00

2000-01 Pacific Autographs

Randomly inserted in packs, this 20-card set utilizes the base card design and number. Each card is autographed by the featured player and contains a Pacific stamp of authenticity. This set is skip numbered. Card number 262 has recently been confirmed. It appears that they arrived to late to be inserted into packs and were held back at the Pacific offices. When the company folded, the cards were sold to Fairfield, a repackager, and only recently have begun to appear.Each card is serial numbered, and the totals are listed beside the player's name below.

57 Miroslav Satan/500 5.00 12.00
123 Alex Tanguay/250 15.00 30.00
126 Ed Belfour/250 6.00 15.00
137 Mike Modano/250 15.00 30.00
138 Brenden Morrow/500 5.00 12.00
169 Todd Marchant/250 5.00 12.00
172 Tommy Salo/500 5.00 12.00
215 Jose Theodore/250 10.00 25.00
223 David Legwand/250 5.00 12.00
233 Patrik Elias/500 5.00 12.00
234 Scott Gomez/500 5.00 12.00
251 Jason Krog/500 5.00 12.00
262 Jan Hlavac/500 6.00 15.00
272 Mike York/500 5.00 12.00
296 Simon Gagne/1000 6.00 15.00
300 John LeClair/250 12.50 30.00
352 Roman Turek/500 5.00 12.00
377 Vincent Lecavalier/1000 6.00 15.00
384 Nikolai Antropov/250 5.00 12.00

2000-01 Pacific Cramer's Choice

Randomly inserted in packs at the rate of 1:721, this 10-card set features a die-cut holographic foil card stock showcasing Michael Cramer's top player choices.

COMPLETE SET (10) 100.00 200.00
1 Paul Kariya 5.00 12.00
2 Teemu Selanne 5.00 12.00
3 Peter Forsberg 12.50 30.00
4 Patrick Roy 25.00 60.00
5 Steve Yzerman 25.00 60.00
6 Pavel Bure 5.00 12.00
7 Martin Brodeur 12.50 30.00
8 Scott Gomez 1.50 4.00
9 Jaromir Jagr 8.00 20.00
10 Mats Sundin 5.00 12.00

2000-01 Pacific Euro-Stars

COMPLETE SET (10) 30.00 60.00
STATED ODDS 1:37
1 Teemu Selanne 2.50 6.00
2 Dominik Hasek 5.00 12.00
3 Peter Forsberg 6.00 15.00
4 Sergei Fedorov 5.00 12.00
5 Pavel Bure 3.00 8.00
6 Jaromir Jagr 4.00 10.00
7 Pavol Demitra 2.00 5.00
8 Roman Turek 2.00 5.00
9 Mats Sundin 2.50 6.00
10 Olaf Kolzig 2.00 5.00

2000-01 Pacific Jerseys

RANDOM INSERTS IN PACKS
1 Ray Bourque 10.00 25.00
2 Eric Messier 4.00 10.00
3 Patrick Roy 12.50 30.00
4 Joe Sakic 10.00 25.00
5 Mike Modano 6.00 15.00
6 Darryl Sydor 4.00 10.00
7 Brendan Shanahan 4.00 10.00
8 Steve Yzerman 12.50 30.00
9 Pavel Bure 4.00 10.00
10 Eric Desjardins 4.00 10.00
11 Daymond Langkow 4.00 10.00
12 Shane Doan 4.00 10.00
13 Jaromir Jagr 10.00 25.00
14 Mark Messier 4.00 10.00
15 Olaf Kolzig 4.00 10.00

2000-01 Pacific Jersey Patches

Randomly inserted in packs, this 10-card set parallels the base Game-Worn Jersey insert set with cards containing premium jersey swatches of patches and numbers. Each card is sequentially numbered to 10.

NOT PRICED DUE TO SCARCITY

2000-01 Pacific Gold Crown Die Cuts

Randomly seeded in packs at the rate of 1:37, this 36-card set features top NHL players on a crown die-cut card with enhanced holofoil and gold foil stamping. Card number 12 was not released.

COMPLETE SET (36) 60.00 150.00
1 Paul Kariya 2.00 5.00
2 Teemu Selanne 2.00 5.00
3 Joe Thornton 3.00 8.00
4 Dominik Hasek 4.00 10.00
5 Valeri Bure 1.25 3.00
6 Tony Amonte 1.25 3.00
7 Ray Bourque 3.00 8.00
8A Peter Forsberg 3.00 8.00
8B Milan Hejduk 1.25 3.00
9 Joe Sakic 4.00 10.00
10 Patrick Roy 8.00 20.00
11 Brett Hull 2.50 5.00
13 Mike Modano 3.00 5.00
14 Brendan Shanahan 3.00 5.00
15 Steve Yzerman 6.00 15.00
16 Pavel Bure 2.50 6.00
17 Luc Robitaille 1.50 4.00
18 Martin Brodeur 5.00 12.00
19 Scott Gomez 1.25 3.00
20 Roberto Luongo 2.50 6.00
21 Marian Hossa 1.25 3.00
22 Brian Boucher 1.25 3.00
23 John LeClair 1.25 3.00
24 Eric Lindros 2.00 5.00
25 Mark Recchi 1.25 3.00
26 Keith Tkachuk 1.25 3.00
27 Jeremy Roenick 2.50 5.00
28 Jaromir Jagr 3.00 8.00
29 Chris Pronger 1.25 3.00
30 Roman Turek 1.25 3.00
31 Owen Nolan 1.25 3.00
32 Vincent Lecavalier 2.00 5.00
33 Mats Sundin 2.00 5.00
34 Curtis Joseph 2.00 4.00
35 Mark Messier 2.50 5.00
36 Olaf Kolzig 1.50 4.00

2000-01 Pacific In the Cage Net-Fusions

Inserted at 1:73 packs, these cards are die-cut and feature a goalie game action photograph where the goal itself has been die cut out and replaced with "netting."

COMPLETE SET (10) 30.00 60.00
1 Dominik Hasek 5.00 12.00
2 Fred Brathwaite 2.00 5.00
3 Patrick Roy 12.50 30.00
4 Mike Vernon 2.00 5.00
5 Stephane Fiset 2.00 5.00
6 Jeff Hackett 2.00 5.00
7 Martin Brodeur 6.00 15.00
8 Mike Richter 2.50 6.00
9 Brian Boucher 2.50 6.00
10 Curtis Joseph 2.50 6.00

2000-01 Pacific North American Stars

COMPLETE SET (10) 50.00 100.00
STATED ODDS 1:37
1 Paul Kariya 2.50 6.00
2 Joe Sakic 5.00 12.00
3 Patrick Roy 12.50 30.00
4 Mike Modano 4.00 10.00
5 Brendan Shanahan 4.00 10.00
6 Steve Yzerman 12.50 30.00
7 Martin Brodeur 6.00 15.00
8 Scott Gomez 2.50 6.00
9 John LeClair 3.00 8.00
10 Curtis Joseph 2.50 6.00

2000-01 Pacific Reflections

Randomly inserted in packs at the rate of 1:145, this 20-card set features a die cut base card in the shape of a helmet. Each helmet has an iridescent visor that shows the reflection of the featured player.

COMPLETE SET (20) 60.00 150.00
1 Paul Kariya 2.50 6.00
2 Teemu Selanne 2.50 6.00
3 Doug Gilmour 2.00 5.00
4 Ray Bourque 4.00 10.00
5 Peter Forsberg 8.00 20.00
6 Joe Sakic 6.00 15.00
7 Brett Hull 3.00 8.00
8 Mike Modano 4.00 10.00
9 Brendan Shanahan 3.00 8.00
10 Steve Yzerman 12.00 30.00
11 Pavel Bure 3.00 8.00
12 Zigmund Palffy 2.00 5.00
13 Scott Gomez 2.00 5.00
14 Marian Hossa 2.00 5.00
15 John LeClair 2.00 5.00
16 Eric Lindros 3.00 8.00
17 Jaromir Jagr 4.00 10.00
18 Vincent Lecavalier 2.50 6.00
19 Mats Sundin 2.50 6.00
20 Mark Messier 3.00 8.00

2000-01 Pacific 2001: Ice Odyssey Anaheim National

Given away by Pacific at the 21st National card convention in Anaheim, this 20-card set parallels the official base insert release of Pacific 2001: Ice Odyssey. Each card is enhanced with a special gold foil 21st National Anaheim stamp and is hand numbered out of 10.

COMPLETE SET (20)

1 Paul Kariya
2 Teemu Selanne
3 Martin Biron
4 Jarome Iginla
5 Chris Drury
6 Peter Forsberg
7 Milan Hejduk
8 Patrick Roy
9 Steve Yzerman
10 Pavel Bure
11 Jose Theodore
12 Martin Brodeur
13 Patrik Elias
14 Scott Gomez
15 Roberto Luongo
16 Marian Hossa
17 Brian Boucher
18 Jaromir Jagr
19 Vincent Lecavalier
20 Mats Sundin

2001-02 Pacific

Pacific was released as a 452-card set with the last 10 cards of the set available only by mail-in redemption. Cards 444-451 were issued as autographed cards numbered to 500 and card 452 had stated odds of 1 per case. The card front design had only 1 border, with the featured player's name and team, and it was highlighted with silver-foil. The 'Pacific 2002' logo was also done with silver-foil to let it stand out. The card backs had player stats by season and there was a brief synopsis of the career highlights.

COMPLETE SET w/o AU's (444) 40.00 80.00
COMP.UPDATE SET (10) 25.00 50.00
1 Matt Cullen .08 .20
2 Jim Cummins .08 .20
3 Jeff Friesen .08 .20
4 Jean-Sebastien Giguere .20 .50
5 Tony Hrkac .08 .20
6 Paul Kariya .25 .60
7 Mike Leclerc .08 .20
8 Marty McInnis .08 .20
9 Steve Rucchin .08 .20
10 Ruslan Salei .08 .20
11 Steve Shields .20 .50
12 Oleg Tverdovsky .08 .20
13 Bob Wren RC .20 .50
14 Andrew Brunette .08 .20
15 Hnat Domenichelli .08 .20
16 Ray Ferraro .08 .20
17 Stephen Guolla .08 .20
18 Milan Hnilicka .20 .50
19 Tomi Kallio .08 .20
20 Norm Maracle .20 .50
21 Rumun Ndur .08 .20
22 Jeff Odgers .08 .20
23 Damian Rhodes .20 .50
24 Jiri Slegr .08 .20
25 Patrik Stefan .08 .20
26 J.P. Vigier .08 .20
27 Jason Allison .08 .20
28 P.J. Axelsson .08 .20
29 Byron Dafoe .20 .50
30 John Grahame .20 .50
31 Bill Guerin .20 .50
32 Mike Knuble .08 .20
33 Andrei Kovalenko .08 .20
34 Eric Manlow .08 .20
35 Andrei Nazarov .08 .20
36 Brian Rolston .08 .20
37 Sergei Samsonov .20 .50
38 Peter Skudra .08 .20
39 Don Sweeney .08 .20
40 Joe Thornton .40 1.00
41 Eric Weinrich .08 .20
42 Maxim Afinogenov .08 .20
43 Dave Andreychuk .20 .50
44 Donald Audette .08 .20
45 Stu Barnes .08 .20
46 Martin Biron .20 .50
47 J-P Dumont .08 .20
48 Doug Gilmour .20 .50
49 Chris Gratton .08 .20
50 Dominik Hasek .50 1.25
51 Steve Heinze .08 .20
52 Erik Rasmussen .08 .20
53 Rob Ray .08 .20
54 Miroslav Satan .20 .50
55 Alexei Zhitnik .08 .20
56 Tommy Albelin .08 .20
57 Fred Brathwaite .20 .50
58 Valeri Bure .08 .20
59 Craig Conroy .08 .20
60 Phil Housley .08 .20
61 Jarome Iginla .30 .75
62 Dave Lowry .08 .20
63 Derek Morris .08 .20
64 Oleg Saprykin .08 .20
65 Marc Savard .08 .20
66 Daniel Tkaczuk .08 .20
67 Mike Vernon .20 .50
68 Jason Wiemer .08 .20
69 Bates Battaglia .08 .20
70 Rod Brind'Amour .20 .50
71 Ron Francis .20 .50
72 Martin Gelinas .08 .20
73 Kevin Hatcher .08 .20
74 Arturs Irbe .20 .50
75 Sami Kapanen .08 .20
76 Dave Karpa .08 .20
77 Tyler Moss .08 .20
78 Jeff O'Neill .08 .20
79 Sandis Ozolinsh .08 .20
80 Scott Pellerin .08 .20
81 Shane Willis .08 .20
82 Tony Amonte .20 .50
83 Mark Bell .08 .20
84 Eric Daze .20 .50
85 Steve Dubinsky .08 .20
86 Chris Herperger .08 .20
87 Michel Larocque .08 .20
88 Michael Nylander .08 .20
89 Steve Passmore .20 .50
90 Bob Probert .08 .20
91 Stephane Quintal .08 .20
92 Steve Sullivan .08 .20
93 Jocelyn Thibault .20 .50
94 Alexei Zhamnov .08 .20
95 David Aebischer .20 .50
96 Rick Berry .08 .20
97 Rob Blake .20 .50
98 Ray Bourque .50 1.25
99 Chris Drury .20 .50
100 Adam Foote .08 .20
101 Peter Forsberg .60 1.50
102 Milan Hejduk .25 .60
103 Ville Nieminen .20 .50
104 Shjon Podein .08 .20
105 Steven Reinprecht .20 .50
106 Patrick Roy 1.25 3.00
107 Joe Sakic .50 1.25
108 Alex Tanguay .20 .50
109 Serge Aubin .20 .50
110 Mathieu Darche RC .08 .20
111 Matt Davidson RC .08 .20
112 Marc Denis .20 .50
113 Rostislav Klesla .20 .50
114 Espen Knutsen .08 .20
115 Chris Nielsen .08 .20
116 Geoff Sanderson .08 .20
117 Martin Spanhel RC .08 .20
118 Ron Tugnutt .20 .50
119 David Vyborny .08 .20
120 Ray Whitney .08 .20
121 Tyler Wright .08 .20
122 Ed Belfour .25 .60
123 Steve Gainey .20 .50
124 Derian Hatcher .08 .20
125 Sami Helenius .08 .20
126 Brett Hull .30 .75
127 Jamie Langenbrunner .08 .20
128 Jere Lehtinen .08 .20
129 Brad Lukowich .08 .20
130 Grant Marshall .08 .20
131 Mike Modano .40 1.00
132 Brenden Morrow .20 .50
133 Kirk Muller .08 .20
134 Joe Nieuwendyk .20 .50
135 Darryl Sydor .08 .20
136 Marty Turco .20 .50
137 Sergei Zubov .08 .20
138 Chris Chelios .25 .60
139 Sergei Fedorov .40 1.00
140 Todd Gill .08 .20
141 Tomas Holmstrom .08 .20
142 Slava Kozlov .08 .20
143 Martin Lapointe .08 .20
144 Igor Larionov .08 .20
145 Manny Legace .20 .50
146 Nicklas Lidstrom .25 .60
147 Darren McCarty .08 .20
148 Chris Osgood .20 .50
149 Brendan Shanahan .25 .60
150 Pat Verbeek .08 .20
151 Aaron Ward .08 .20
152 Steve Yzerman 1.25 3.00
153 Anson Carter .20 .50
154 Jason Chimera RC .20 .50
155 Daniel Cleary .08 .20
156 Mike Comrie .20 .50
157 Mike Grier .08 .20
158 Shawn Horcoff .08 .20
159 Georges Laraque .08 .20
160 Todd Marchant .08 .20
161 Rem Murray .08 .20
162 Janne Niinimaa .08 .20
163 Dominic Roussel .08 .20
164 Tommy Salo .20 .50
165 Jason Smith .08 .20
166 Ryan Smyth .08 .20
167 Doug Weight .20 .50
168 Kevyn Adams .08 .20
169 Pavel Bure .25 .60
170 Anders Eriksson .08 .20
171 Trevor Kidd .20 .50
172 Viktor Kozlov .08 .20
173 Roberto Luongo .30 .75
174 Rob Niedermayer .08 .20
175 Marcus Nilsson .08 .20
176 Andrej Podkonicky RC .08 .20
177 Robert Svehla .08 .20
178 Peter Worrell .08 .20
179 Eric Belanger .08 .20
180 Adam Deadmarsh .08 .20
181 Stu Grimson .08 .20
182 Andreas Lilja .08 .20
183 Glen Murray .08 .20
184 Zigmund Palffy .20 .50
185 Felix Potvin .25 .60
186 Luc Robitaille .20 .50
187 Mathieu Schneider .08 .20
188 Bryan Smolinski .08 .20
189 Jamie Storr .20 .50
190 Jozef Stumpel .08 .20
191 Lubomir Visnovsky .08 .20
192 Jim Dowd .08 .20
193 Manny Fernandez .20 .50
194 Marian Gaborik .50 1.25
195 Derek Gustafson .08 .20
196 Matt Johnson .08 .20
197 Filip Kuba .08 .20
198 Antti Laaksonen .08 .20
199 Jamie McLennan .08 .20
200 Lubomir Sekeras .08 .20
201 Wes Walz .08 .20
202 Francis Belanger RC .20 .50
203 Patrice Brisebois .08 .20
204 Jan Bulis .08 .20
205 Karl Dykhuis .08 .20
206 Mathieu Garon .20 .50
207 Jeff Hackett .20 .50
208 Chad Kilger .08 .20
209 Saku Koivu .25 .60
210 Oleg Petrov .08 .20
211 Martin Rucinsky .08 .20
212 Brian Savage .08 .20
213 Jose Theodore .30 .75
214 Richard Zednik .08 .20
215 Marian Cisar .08 .20
216 Mike Dunham .20 .50
217 Scott Hartnell .08 .20
218 Greg Johnson .08 .20
219 Patric Kjellberg .08 .20
220 David Legwand .20 .50
221 Cliff Ronning .08 .20
222 Tomas Vokoun .20 .50
223 Scott Walker .08 .20
224 Vitali Yachmenev .08 .20
225 Jason Arnott .08 .20
226 Jiri Bicek .08 .20
227 Martin Brodeur .60 1.50
228 Sergei Brylin .08 .20
229 Patrik Elias .20 .50
230 Scott Gomez .08 .20
231 Bobby Holik .08 .20
232 John Madden .08 .20
233 Randy McKay .08 .20
234 Jim McKenzie .08 .20
235 Alexander Mogilny .20 .50
236 Sergei Nemchinov .08 .20
237 Scott Niedermayer .08 .20
238 Scott Stevens .20 .50
239 Petr Sykora .08 .20
240 John Vanbiesbrouck .20 .50
241 Ed Ward .08 .20
242 Zdeno Chara .08 .20
243 Tim Connolly .08 .20
244 Mariusz Czerkawski .08 .20
245 Rick DiPietro .20 .50
246 Garry Galley .08 .20
247 Kevin Haller .08 .20
248 Roman Hamrlik .08 .20
249 Brad Isbister .08 .20
250 Kenny Jonsson .08 .20
251 Claude Lapointe .08 .20
252 Mark Parrish .08 .20
253 Dave Scatchard .08 .20
254 Chris Terreri .20 .50
255 Radek Dvorak .08 .20
256 Theo Fleury .08 .20
257 Adam Graves .08 .20
258 Guy Hebert .20 .50
259 Jan Hlavac .08 .20
260 Valeri Kamensky .08 .20
261 Brian Leetch .20 .50
262 Sylvain Lefebvre .08 .20
263 Sandy McCarthy .08 .20
264 Mark Messier .25 .60
265 Petr Nedved .08 .20
266 Rich Pilon .08 .20
267 Mike Richter .25 .60
268 Mike York .08 .20
269 Daniel Alfredsson .20 .50
270 Magnus Arvedson .08 .20
271 Radek Bonk .08 .20
272 Martin Havlat .20 .50
273 Marian Hossa .25 .60
274 Jani Hurme .20 .50
275 Patrick Lalime .20 .50
276 Shawn McEachern .08 .20
277 Chris Phillips .08 .20
278 Wade Redden .08 .20
279 Andre Roy .08 .20
280 Mike Sillinger .08 .20
281 Alexei Yashin .08 .20
282 Rob Zamuner .08 .20
283 Brian Boucher .20 .50
284 Roman Cechmanek .20 .50
285 Eric Desjardins .08 .20
286 Ruslan Fedotenko .20 .50
287 Simon Gagne .25 .60
288 Daymond Langkow .08 .20
289 John LeClair .25 .60
290 Eric Lindros .25 .60
291 Dan McGillis .08 .20
292 Keith Primeau .08 .20
293 Paul Ranheim .08 .20
294 Mark Recchi .20 .50
295 Rick Tocchet .08 .20
296 Justin Williams .20 .50
297 Joel Bouchard .08 .20
298 Daniel Briere .08 .20
299 Sean Burke .20 .50
300 Keith Carney .08 .20
301 Shane Doan .08 .20
302 Robert Esche .08 .20
303 Michal Handzus .08 .20
304 Mike Johnson .08 .20
305 Joe Juneau .08 .20
306 Claude Lemieux .08 .20
307 Teppo Numminen .08 .20
308 Jeremy Roenick .30 .75
309 Landon Wilson .08 .20
310 Jean-Sebastien Aubin .20 .50
311 Jan Hrdina .08 .20
312 Jaromir Jagr .40 1.00
313 Darius Kasparaitis .08 .20
314 Alexei Kovalev .20 .50
315 Robert Lang .08 .20
316 Mario Lemieux 1.50 4.00
317 Garth Snow .20 .50
318 Kevin Stevens .08 .20
319 Martin Straka .08 .20
320 Sebastien Bordeleau .08 .20
321 Pavol Demitra .20 .50
322 Dallas Drake .08 .20
323 Jochen Hecht .08 .20
324 Brent Johnson .20 .50
325 Reed Low .08 .20
326 Al MacInnis .20 .50
327 Scott Mellanby .08 .20
328 Jaroslav Obsut RC .20 .50
329 Chris Pronger .20 .50
330 Darren Rumble .08 .20
331 Cory Stillman .08 .20
332 Keith Tkachuk .25 .60
333 Roman Turek .20 .50
334 Pierre Turgeon .20 .50
335 Scott Young .08 .20
336 Vincent Damphousse .08 .20
337 Miikka Kiprusoff .20 .50
338 Bryan Marchment .08 .20
339 Patrick Marleau .20 .50
340 Evgeni Nabokov .20 .50
341 Owen Nolan .20 .50
342 Jeff Norton .08 .20
343 Mike Ricci .08 .20
344 Teemu Selanne .25 .60
345 Brad Stuart .08 .20
346 Marco Sturm .08 .20
347 Niklas Sundstrom .08 .20
348 Scott Thornton .08 .20
349 Matthew Barnaby .08 .20
350 Brian Holzinger .08 .20
351 Nikolai Khabibulin .25 .60
352 Alexander Kharitonov .20 .50
353 Pavel Kubina .08 .20
354 Kristian Kudroc .08 .20
355 Vincent Lecavalier .25 .60
356 Fredrik Modin .08 .20
357 Brad Richards .20 .50
358 Martin St. Louis .20 .50
359 Kevin Weekes .20 .50
360 Thomas Ziegler RC .20 .50
361 Sergei Berezin .08 .20
362 Shayne Corson .08 .20
363 Cory Cross .08 .20
364 Tie Domi .20 .50
365 Glenn Healy .08 .20
366 Jonas Hoglund .08 .20
367 Curtis Joseph .25 .60
368 Don MacLean .08 .20
369 Dave Manson .08 .20
370 Yanic Perreault .08 .20
371 Alexei Ponikarovsky .08 .20
372 Gary Roberts .08 .20
373 Mats Sundin .25 .60
374 Steve Thomas .08 .20
375 Darcy Tucker .08 .20
376 Murray Baron .08 .20
377 Todd Bertuzzi .25 .60
378 Donald Brashear .08 .20
379 Andrew Cassels .08 .20
380 Dan Cloutier .20 .50
381 Bob Essensa .08 .20
382 Ed Jovanovski .20 .50
383 Brendan Morrison .20 .50
384 Markus Naslund .25 .60
385 Mattias Ohlund .08 .20
386 Peter Schaefer .08 .20
387 Daniel Sedin .08 .20
388 Henrik Sedin .08 .20
389 Craig Billington .08 .20
390 Peter Bondra .25 .60
391 Ulf Dahlen .08 .20
392 Sergei Gonchar .08 .20
393 Jeff Halpern .08 .20
394 Dmitri Khristich .08 .20
395 Olaf Kolzig .20 .50
396 Steve Konowalchuk .08 .20
397 Trevor Linden .20 .50
398 Adam Oates .20 .50
399 Chris Simon .08 .20
400 Dainius Zubrus .08 .20
401 Paul Kariya .20 .50
Jim Cummins
402 Ray Ferraro .20 .50
Jeff Odgers
403 Jason Allison .20 .50
Ken Belanger
404 Jean-Pierre Dumont .20 .50
Rob Ray
405 Jarome Iginla .20 .50
Jason Wiemer
406 Ron Francis .20 .50
Darren Langdon
407 Steve Sullivan .20 .50
Bob Probert
408 Joe Sakic .20 .50
Scott Parker
409 Mike Modano .20 .50
Grant Marshall
410 Steve Yzerman .20 .50
Darren McCarty
411 Ryan Smyth .20 .50
Georges Laraque
412 Pavel Bure .20 .50
Peter Worrell
413 Ziggy Palffy .20 .50
Stu Grimson
414 Patrick Elias .20 .50
Colin White
415 Mariusz Czerkawski .20 .50
Zdeno Chara
416 Theoren Fleury .20 .50
Sandy McCarthy
417 Marian Hossa .20 .50
Andre Roy
418 Jeremy Roenick .20 .50
Louie DeBrusk
419 Mario Lemieux .20 .50
Krzysztof Oliwa
420 Pierre Turgeon .20 .50
Reed Low
421 Teemu Selanne .20 .50
Bryan Marchment
422 Vincent Lecavalier .20 .50
Matthew Barnaby
423 Mats Sundin .20 .50
Tie Domi
424 Markus Naslund .20 .50
Donald Brashear
425 Peter Bondra .20 .50
Chris Simon
426 Jason Allison .20 .50
Joe Thornton
427 Joe Sakic 1.25 3.00
Patrick Roy
428 M.Modano/B.Hull .20 .50
429 Sergei Fedorov .20 .50
Nicklas Lidstrom
430 Doug Weight .20 .50
Ryan Smyth
431 Pavel Bure .20 .50
Roberto Luongo
432 Luc Robitaille .20 .50
Ziggy Palffy
433 Patrik Elias .20 .50
Alexander Mogilny
434 Mariusz Czerkawski .20 .50
Rick DiPietro
435 Theoren Fleury .20 .50
Brian Leetch
436 Alexei Yashin .20 .50
Marian Hossa
437 Keith Primeau .20 .50
Roman Cechmanek
438 JeremyRoenick .20 .50
Sean Burke
439 Jaromir Jagr 1.50 4.00
Mario Lemieux
440 Pierre Turgeon .20 .50
Brent Johnson
441 Teemu Selanne .20 .50
Evgeni Nabokov
442 Mats Sundin .20 .50
Curtis Joseph
443 Adam Oates .20 .50
Peter Bondra
444 David Aebischer AU/500 10.00 25.00
445 Steven Reinprecht AU/500 10.00 25.00
446 Marty Turco AU/500 10.00 25.00
447 Marian Gaborik AU/500 15.00 40.00
448 Martin Havlat AU/500 10.00 25.00
449 Brent Johnson AU/500 10.00 25.00
450 Evgeni Nabokov AU/500 10.00 25.00
451 Brad Richards AU/500 10.00 25.00
452 Johan Hedberg SP .20 .50
453 Timo Parssinen RC 2.00 5.00
454 Ilya Kovalchuk RC 10.00 25.00
455 Vaclav Nedorost RC 2.00 5.00
456 Kristian Huselius RC 2.50 6.00
457 Jaroslav Bednar RC 2.00 5.00
458 Dan Blackburn RC 2.00 5.00
459 Jiri Dopita RC 2.00 5.00
460 Krystofer Kolanos RC 2.00 5.00
461 Jeff Jillson RC 2.00 5.00
462 Nikita Alexeev RC 2.00 5.00

2001-02 Pacific Extreme LTD

Randomly inserted at 1 per hobby box or 1:2 retail boxes, this set parallels the base set except that the words "Extreme LTD" are embossed across the front of the card diagonally. These cards were limited to 49 serial-numbered sets.

*EXTREME: 12X TO 30X BASIC CARDS

2001-02 Pacific Gold

Randomly inserted in packs of 2001-02 Pacific, this 43-card set featured a gold version of the base set cards 401-443. Each card was serial numbered to 100, and featured 2 player on the cards.

*GOLD: 8X TO 20X BASIC CARDS

2001-02 Pacific Hobby LTD

Randomly inserted, this set parallels the base set except that the words "Hobby LTD" are embossed across the front of the card diagonally. These cards were limited to 99 serial-numbered sets.

*HOBBY LTD: 5X TO 12X BASIC CARDS

2001-02 Pacific Premiere Date

Randomly inserted in packs of 2001-02 Pacific, this 400-card set was a parallel to the base set along with the 'Premiere Date' stamp on these and each card was serial numbered to 45.

*PREM.DATE: 12X TO 30X BASIC CARDS

2001-02 Pacific Retail LTD

Randomly inserted, this set parallels the base set except that the words "Retail LTD" are embossed across the front of the card diagonally. These cards were limited to 149 serial-numbered sets.

*RETAIL LTD: 8X TO 20X BASIC CARDS

2001-02 Pacific All-Stars

Randomly inserted in packs of 2001-02 Pacific at a rate of 1:37, this 20-card set featured 10 World All Stars and 10 North America All Stars. The cards were die-cut and featured silver-foil lettering and highlights.

COMPLETE SET (20) 60.00 125.00

W1 Dominik Hasek 3.00 8.00
W2 Peter Forsberg 4.00 10.00
W3 Sergei Fedorov 3.00 8.00
W4 Pavel Bure 2.00 5.00
W5 Zigmund Palffy 1.25 3.00
W6 Marian Hossa 1.50 4.00
W7 Roman Cechmanek 3.00 8.00
W8 Alexei Kovalev 1.50 4.00
W9 Evgeni Nabokov 3.00 8.00
W10 Mats Sundin 1.50 4.00
NA1 Paul Kariya 1.50 4.00
NA2 Bill Guerin 1.25 3.00
NA3 Ray Bourque 6.00 15.00
NA4 Patrick Roy 8.00 20.00
NA5 Joe Sakic 3.00 8.00
NA6 Brett Hull 2.00 5.00
NA7 Doug Weight 1.25 3.00
NA8 Luc Robitaille 1.25 3.00
NA9 Martin Brodeur 4.00 10.00
NA10 Mario Lemieux 10.00 25.00

2001-02 Pacific Cramer's Choice

Randomly inserted in packs of 2001-02 Pacific, this 10-card set was serial numbered to 49.

1 Paul Kariya 8.00 20.00
2 Ray Bourque 20.00 50.00
3 Patrick Roy 40.00 100.00
4 Joe Sakic 20.00 50.00
5 Steve Yzerman 30.00 80.00
6 Pavel Bure 15.00 40.00
7 Martin Brodeur 25.00 60.00
8 Jaromir Jagr 12.50 30.00
9 Mario Lemieux 40.00 100.00
10 Curtis Joseph 15.00 40.00

2001-02 Pacific Jerseys

*MULT.COLOR: 1X TO 1.5X
STATED ODDS 2:37 HOBBY/1:145 RETAIL
STATED PRINT RUNS LISTED BELOW
1 Andre Savage/510 2.50 6.00
2 Eric Weinrich/510 2.50 6.00
3 Jay McKee/1135 2.50 6.00
4 Fred Brathwaite/1135 3.00 0.00
5 Marc Savard/760 2.50 6.00
6 Tony Amonte/1135 3.00 8.00
7 Alexei Zhamnov/1135 2.50 6.00
8 Chris Dingman/510 2.50 6.00
9 Joe Sakic/510 6.00 15.00
10 Derian Hatcher/1135 2.50 6.00
11 Jamie Langenbrunner/1135 2.50 6.00
12 Sergei Zubov/760 3.00 8.00
13 Mathieu Dandenault/1135 2.50 6.00
14 Chris Osgood/760 3.00 8.00
15 Doug Weight/260 2.50 6.00
16 Aaron Miller/510 2.50 6.00
17 Cliff Ronning/510 2.50 6.00
18 Bobby Holik/760 2.50 6.00
19 Mariusz Czerkawski/510 2.50 6.00
20 Chris Terreri/1135 2.50 6.00
21 Guy Hebert/760 3.00 8.00
22 Mike Richter/760 3.00 8.00
23 Mika Alatalo/510 2.50 6.00
24 Shane Doan/310 2.50 6.00
25 Jyrki Lumme/1135 2.50 6.00
26 Jan Hrdina/510 2.50 6.00
27 Jaromir Jagr/210 6.00 15.00
28 Mario Lemieux/110 20.00 50.00
29 Kip Miller/1135 2.50 6.00
30 Ian Moran/1135 2.50 6.00
31 Martin Straka/110 2.50 6.00
32 Cory Stillman/1135 2.50 6.00
33 Vincent Damphousse/1010 2.50 6.00
34 Teemu Selanne/1135 3.00 8.00
35 Mats Sundin/760 3.00 8.00
36 Dainius Zubrus/760 2.50 6.00

2001-02 Pacific Gold Crown Die-Cuts

COMPLETE SET (20) 60.00 125.00
STATED ODDS 1:73
1 Paul Kariya 1.50 4.00
2 Joe Thornton 2.50 6.00
3 Dominik Hasek 4.00 10.00
4 Ray Bourque 3.00 8.00
5 Peter Forsberg 5.00 12.00
6 Patrick Roy 8.00 20.00
7 Joe Sakic 4.00 10.00
8 Mike Modano 2.50 6.00
9 Sergei Fedorov 2.50 6.00
10 Steve Yzerman 8.00 20.00
11 Pavel Bure 1.50 4.00
12 Martin Brodeur 6.00 15.00
13 Rick DiPietro 1.50 4.00
14 Mark Messier 2.50 6.00
15 Marian Hossa 1.50 4.00
16 Jaromir Jagr 3.00 8.00
17 Mario Lemieux 12.00 30.00
18 Keith Tkachuk 1.50 4.00
19 Evgeni Nabokov 2.50 6.00
20 Curtis Joseph 1.50 4.00

2001-02 Pacific Impact Zone

COMPLETE SET (20) 15.00 40.00
STATED ODDS 1:37
1 Paul Kariya 1.50 4.00
2 Byron Dafoe .75 2.00
3 Doug Gilmour .75 2.00
4 Dominik Hasek 3.00 8.00
5 Ron Francis .75 2.00
6 Ray Bourque 3.00 8.00
7 Patrick Roy 6.00 15.00
8 Ed Belfour 1.50 4.00
9 Derian Hatcher .40 1.00
10 Mike Modano 2.50 6.00
11 Chris Osgood .75 2.00
12 Martin Brodeur 4.00 10.00
13 Marian Hossa .75 2.00
14 Patrick Lalime .75 2.00
15 Roman Cechmanek .40 1.00
16 Chris Pronger .75 2.00
17 Tie Domi .40 1.00
18 Curtis Joseph 1.50 4.00
19 Mats Sundin 1.50 4.00
20 Andrew Cassels .40 1.00

2001-02 Pacific 97-98 Subset

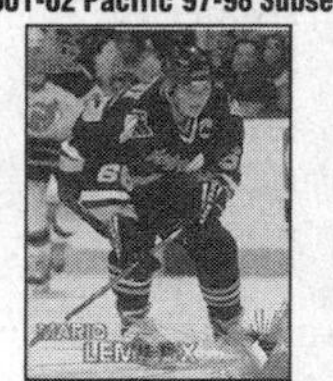

Randomly inserted in packs of 2001-02 Pacific, this 7-card set was issued as an update to the 1997-98 set. The cards featured a similar design as that of the original set and added 7 players who were not originally included in the set. There was also a gold version available in random retail packs. Gold cards were serial-numbered to 100.

COMPLETE SET (7) 10.00 20.00
*GOLD: 10X TO 20X BASIC CARDS
66 Mario Lemieux 2.50 6.00
352 Mike LeClerc 1.25 3.00
353 Sergei Samsonov 1.50 4.00
354 Joe Thornton 2.50 6.00
355 Steve Shields 1.25 3.00
356 Patrik Elias 1.25 3.00
357 Marian Hossa 1.50 4.00

2001-02 Pacific Steel Curtain

COMPLETE SET (20) 30.00 60.00
STATED ODDS 2:37
1 Steve Shields 1.00 2.50
2 Byron Dafoe 1.00 2.50
3 Dominik Hasek 2.50 6.00
4 Jocelyn Thibault 1.00 2.50
5 Patrick Roy 6.00 15.00
6 Ed Belfour 1.25 3.00
7 Manny Legace 1.00 2.50
8 Tommy Salo 1.00 2.50
9 Roberto Luongo 1.50 4.00
10 Jose Theodore 1.50 4.00
11 Martin Brodeur 3.00 8.00
12 Rick DiPietro 1.00 2.50
13 Mike Richter 1.25 3.00
14 Patrick Lalime 1.00 2.50
15 Roman Cechmanek 1.00 2.50
16 Sean Burke 1.00 2.50
17 Roman Turek 1.00 2.50
18 Evgeni Nabokov 1.00 2.50
19 Curtis Joseph 1.25 3.00
20 Olaf Kolzig 1.00 2.50

2001-02 Pacific Top Draft Picks

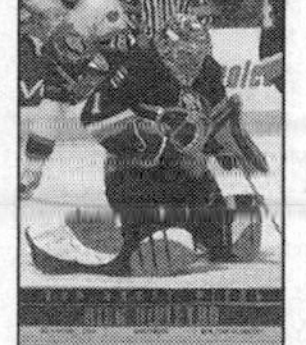

Randomly inserted in packs of 2001-02 Pacific at a rate of 1:37, this 10-card set featured some of the top draft picks from the last 20 years. These cards were identical to the Promos with the exception of gold-foil instead of silver, and these were not serial numbered.

COMPLETE SET (10) 10.00 25.00
1 Rick DiPietro .75 2.00
2 Patrik Stefan .40 1.00
3 Vincent Lecavalier 1.25 3.00
4 Joe Thornton 2.00 5.00
5 Eric Lindros 1.25 3.00
6 Owen Nolan .75 2.00
7 Mats Sundin 1.25 3.00
8 Mike Modano 2.00 5.00
9 Pierre Turgeon .75 2.00
10 Mario Lemieux 4.00 10.00

2001 Pacific Top Draft Picks Draft Day Promos

This 10-card set was given away at the 2001 NHL Draft. Collectors could obtain one card in exchange for a Titanium Draft Day wrapper, or combination of other Pacific wrappers. Although the cards mirror the inserts found in 2001-02 Pacific, these cards differ in that they are serial numbered to 499, and are highlighted by silver foil lettering. It is believed that far fewer than 499 sets were actually distributed.

COMPLETE SET (10) 40.00 100.00
1 Rick DiPietro 6.00 15.00
2 Patrik Stefan 2.00 5.00
3 Vincent LeCavalier 4.80 12.00
4 Joe Thornton 6.00 15.00
5 Eric Lindros 4.80 12.00
6 Owen Nolan 4.00 10.00
7 Mats Sundin 4.80 12.00
8 Mike Modano 6.00 15.00
9 Pierre Turgeon 4.00 10.00
10 Mario Lemieux 12.00 30.00

2002-03 Pacific

This 400-card set was released in late-July 2002 and carried an SRP of $2.99 for a 10-card pack. A red parallel of this set was also created and inserted 1:2 packs. Cards 401-410 were available as a mail-in redemption only and were serial-numbered out of 999.

COMPLETE SET (400) 50.00 100.00
*RED: .5X TO 1.25X BASIC CARD
1 Matt Cullen .08 .20
2 Jeff Friesen .08 .20
3 Jean-Sebastien Giguere .20 .50
4 Paul Kariya .25 .60
5 Mike Leclerc .08 .20
6 Andy McDonald .08 .20
7 Steve Rucchin .08 .20
8 Steve Shields .20 .50
9 German Titov .08 .20
10 Oleg Tverdovsky .08 .20
11 Jason York .08 .20
12 Lubos Bartecko .08 .20
13 Dany Heatley .30 .75
14 Milan Hnilicka .20 .50
15 Tony Hrkac .08 .20
16 Frantisek Kaberle .08 .20
17 Tomi Kallio .08 .20
18 Ilya Kovalchuk .30 .75
19 Jeff Odgers .08 .20
20 Damian Rhodes .20 .50
21 Patrik Stefan .08 .20
22 Daniel Tjarnqvist .08 .20
23 Nicholas Boynton .08 .20
24 Sean Brown .08 .20
25 Byron Dafoe .20 .50
26 Hal Gill .08 .20
27 John Grahame .20 .50
28 Bill Guerin .20 .50
29 Martin Lapointe .08 .20
30 Glen Murray .08 .20
31 Brian Rolston .08 .20
32 Sergei Samsonov .20 .50
33 P.J. Stock .08 .20
34 Jozef Stumpel .08 .20
35 Joe Thornton .40 1.00
36 Maxim Afinogenov .08 .20
37 Stu Barnes .08 .20
38 Martin Biron .20 .50
39 Curtis Brown .08 .20
40 Tim Connolly .08 .20
41 J-P Dumont .08 .20
42 Chris Gratton .08 .20
43 Ales Kotalik .08 .20
44 Slava Kozlov .08 .20
45 Jay McKee .08 .20
46 Mika Noronen .20 .50
47 Rob Ray .08 .20
48 Miroslav Satan .20 .50
49 Alexei Zhitnik .08 .20
50 Bob Boughner .08 .20
51 Chris Clark .08 .20
52 Craig Conroy .08 .20
53 Denis Gauthier .08 .20
54 Jarome Iginla .30 .75
55 Toni Lydman .08 .20
56 Dean McAmmond .08 .20
57 Derek Morris .08 .20
58 Rob Niedermayer .08 .20
59 Marc Savard .08 .20
60 Roman Turek .20 .50
61 Mike Vernon .20 .50
62 Bates Battaglia .08 .20
63 Rod Brind'Amour .20 .50
64 Erik Cole .08 .20
65 Ron Francis .20 .50
66 Bret Hedican .08 .20
67 Arturs Irbe .20 .50
68 Sami Kapanen .08 .20
69 Jeff O'Neill .08 .20
70 Dave Tanabe .08 .20
71 Josef Vasicek .08 .20
72 Kevin Weekes .20 .50
73 Tony Amonte .20 .50
74 Mark Bell .08 .20
75 Kyle Calder .08 .20
76 Eric Daze .20 .50
77 Phil Housley .08 .20
78 Jon Klemm .08 .20
79 Boris Mironov .08 .20
80 Steve Passmore .08 .20
81 Bob Probert .08 .20
82 Steve Sullivan .08 .20
83 Jocelyn Thibault .20 .50
84 Steve Thomas .08 .20
85 Alexei Zhamnov .08 .20
86 David Aebischer .20 .50
87 Rob Blake .20 .50
88 Chris Drury .20 .50
89 Adam Foote .08 .20
90 Peter Forsberg .60 1.50
91 Milan Hejduk .25 .60
92 Darius Kasparaitis .08 .20
93 Scott Parker .08 .20
94 Steven Reinprecht .08 .20
95 Patrick Roy 1.25 3.00
96 Joe Sakic .50 1.25
97 Alex Tanguay .20 .50
98 Radim Vrbata .08 .20
99 Marc Denis .20 .50
100 Rostislav Klesla .08 .20
101 Espen Knutsen .08 .20
102 Grant Marshall .08 .20
103 Deron Quint .08 .20
104 Geoff Sanderson .08 .20
105 Jody Shelley .08 .20
106 Mike Sillinger .08 .20
107 Ron Tugnutt .20 .50
108 David Vyborny .08 .20
109 Ray Whitney .08 .20
110 Jason Arnott .08 .20
111 Ed Belfour .25 .60
112 Derian Hatcher .08 .20
113 Jere Lehtinen .20 .50
114 Mike Modano .40 1.00
115 Brenden Morrow .20 .50
116 Kirk Muller .08 .20
117 Scott Pellerin .08 .20
118 Darryl Sydor .08 .20
119 Marty Turco .20 .50
120 Pierre Turgeon .20 .50
121 Pat Verbeek .08 .20
122 Sergei Zubov .08 .20
123 Chris Chelios .25 .60
124 Pavel Datsyuk .25 .60
125 Boyd Devereaux .08 .20
126 Kris Draper .08 .20
127 Sergei Fedorov .40 1.00
128 Dominik Hasek .50 1.25
129 Brett Hull .30 .75
130 Igor Larionov .08 .20
131 Manny Legace .20 .50
132 Nicklas Lidstrom .25 .60
133 Luc Robitaille .20 .50
134 Brendan Shanahan .25 .60
135 Jiri Slegr .08 .20
136 Jason Williams .08 .20
137 Steve Yzerman 1.25 3.00
138 Eric Brewer .08 .20
139 Anson Carter .20 .50
140 Daniel Cleary .08 .20
141 Mike Comrie .20 .50
142 Mike Grier .08 .20
143 Jochen Hecht .08 .20
144 Georges Laraque .08 .20
145 Todd Marchant .08 .20
146 Jussi Markkanen .08 .20
147 Janne Niinimaa .08 .20
148 Tommy Salo .20 .50
149 Ryan Smyth .08 .20
150 Mike York .08 .20
151 Eric Beaudoin .08 .20
152 Valeri Bure .08 .20
153 Niklas Hagman .08 .20
154 Kristian Huselius .08 .20
155 Trevor Kidd .20 .50
156 Roberto Luongo .30 .75
157 Marcus Nilsson .08 .20
158 Sandis Ozolinsh .08 .20
159 Nick Smith .08 .20
160 Robert Svehla .08 .20
161 Stephen Weiss .08 .20
162 Jason Wiemer .08 .20
163 Peter Worrell .08 .20
164 Jason Allison .08 .20
165 Adam Deadmarsh .08 .20
166 Steve Heinze .08 .20
167 Craig Johnson .08 .20
168 Ian Laperriere .08 .20
169 Aaron Miller .08 .20
170 Jaroslav Modry .08 .20
171 Zigmund Palffy .20 .50
172 Felix Potvin .25 .60
173 Cliff Ronning .08 .20
174 Mathieu Schneider .08 .20
175 Bryan Smolinski .08 .20
176 Jamie Storr .20 .50
177 Andrew Brunette .08 .20
178 Hnat Domenichelli .08 .20
179 Jim Dowd .08 .20
180 Pascal Dupuis .08 .20
181 Manny Fernandez .20 .50
182 Marian Gaborik .50 1.25
183 Darby Hendrickson .08 .20
184 Filip Kuba .08 .20
185 Antti Laaksonen .08 .20
186 Stacy Roest .08 .20
187 Dwayne Roloson .20 .50
188 Wes Walz .08 .20
189 Sergei Zholtok .08 .20
190 Donald Audette .08 .20
191 Sergei Berezin .08 .20
192 Patrice Brisebois .08 .20
193 Andreas Dackell .08 .20
194 Stephane Fiset .08 .20
195 Mathieu Garon .20 .50
196 Doug Gilmour .20 .50
197 Joe Juneau .08 .20
198 Saku Koivu .25 .60
199 Andrei Markov .08 .20
200 Yanic Perreault .08 .20
201 Oleg Petrov .08 .20
202 Mike Ribeiro .08 .20
203 Jose Theodore .30 .75
204 Richard Zednik .08 .20
205 Denis Arkhipov .08 .20
206 Andy Delmore .08 .20
207 Mike Dunham .20 .50
208 Martin Erat .08 .20
209 Stu Grimson .08 .20
210 Scott Hartnell .08 .20
211 Greg Johnson .08 .20
212 David Legwand .20 .50
213 Vladimir Orszagh .08 .20
214 Kimmo Timonen .08 .20
215 Tomas Vokoun .20 .50
216 Scott Walker .08 .20
217 Vitali Yachmenev .08 .20
218 Martin Brodeur .60 1.50
219 Sergei Brylin .08 .20
220 Patrik Elias .20 .50
221 Brian Gionta .08 .20
222 Scott Gomez .08 .20
223 Bobby Holik .08 .20
224 Jamie Langenbrunner .08 .20
225 John Madden .08 .20
226 Scott Niedermayer .08 .20
227 Joe Nieuwendyk .20 .50
228 Brian Rafalski .08 .20
229 Scott Stevens .20 .50
230 Petr Sykora .08 .20
231 John Vanbiesbrouck .20 .50
232 Adrian Aucoin .08 .20
233 Shawn Bates .08 .20
234 Mariusz Czerkawski .08 .20
235 Rick DiPietro .20 .50
236 Roman Hamrlik .08 .20
237 Brad Isbister .08 .20
238 Kenny Jonsson .08 .20
239 Kip Miller .08 .20
240 Chris Osgood .20 .50
241 Mark Parrish .08 .20
242 Michael Peca .08 .20
243 Garth Snow .08 .20
244 Raffi Torres .08 .20
245 Alexei Yashin .08 .20
246 Matthew Barnaby .08 .20
247 Bryan Berard .08 .20
248 Dan Blackburn .20 .50
249 Pavel Bure .25 .60
250 Radek Dvorak .08 .20
251 Theo Fleury .08 .20
252 Brian Leetch .20 .50
253 Eric Lindros .25 .60
254 Vladimir Malakhov .08 .20
255 Sandy McCarthy .08 .20
256 Mark Messier .25 .60
257 Petr Nedved .08 .20
258 Mike Richter .25 .60
259 Martin Rucinsky .08 .20
260 Daniel Alfredsson .20 .50
261 Magnus Arvedson .08 .20
262 Chris Bala .08 .20
263 Radek Bonk .08 .20
264 Zdeno Chara .08 .20
265 Mike Fisher .08 .20
266 Martin Havlat .20 .50
267 Marian Hossa .25 .60
268 Jani Hurme .20 .50
269 Patrick Lalime .20 .50
270 Shawn McEachern .08 .20
271 Chris Phillips .08 .20
272 Wade Redden .08 .20
273 Sami Salo .08 .20
274 Todd White .08 .20
275 Brian Boucher .20 .50
276 Donald Brashear .08 .20
277 Roman Cechmanek .20 .50
278 Eric Desjardins .08 .20
279 Jiri Dopita .08 .20
280 Simon Gagne .25 .60
281 Kim Johnsson .08 .20
282 John LeClair .25 .60
283 Neil Little .08 .20
284 Adam Oates .20 .50
285 Keith Primeau .08 .20
286 Mark Recchi .20 .50
287 Jeremy Roenick .30 .75
288 Bill Tibbetts .08 .20
289 Eric Weinrich .08 .20
290 Justin Williams .08 .20
291 Daniel Briere .08 .20
292 Sean Burke .20 .50
293 Shane Doan .08 .20
294 Robert Esche .08 .20
295 Michal Handzus .08 .20
296 Mike Johnson .08 .20
297 Krystofer Kolanos .08 .20
298 Daymond Langkow .08 .20
299 Claude Lemieux .08 .20
300 Daniil Markov .08 .20
301 Ladislav Nagy .08 .20
302 Andrei Nazarov .08 .20
303 Teppo Numminen .08 .20
304 Brian Savage .08 .20
305 J-S Aubin .08 .20
306 Kris Beech .08 .20
307 Johan Hedberg .20 .50
308 Jan Hrdina .08 .20
309 Alexei Kovalev .20 .50
310 Milan Kraft .08 .20
311 Robert Lang .08 .20
312 Mario Lemieux 1.50 4.00
313 Alexei Morozov .08 .20
314 Toby Petersen .08 .20
315 Wayne Primeau .08 .20
316 Randy Robitaille .08 .20
317 Michal Rozsival .08 .20
318 Martin Straka .08 .20
319 Fred Brathwaite .20 .50
320 Pavol Demitra .20 .50
321 Dallas Drake .08 .20
322 Ray Ferraro .08 .20
323 Brent Johnson .20 .50
324 Reed Low .08 .20
325 Al MacInnis .20 .50
326 Scott Mellanby .08 .20
327 Chris Pronger .20 .50
328 Cory Stillman .08 .20
329 Keith Tkachuk .25 .60
330 Doug Weight .20 .50
331 Scott Young .08 .20
332 Vincent Damphousse .08 .20
333 Adam Graves .08 .20
334 Jeff Jillson .08 .20
335 Bryan Marchment .08 .20
336 Patrick Marleau .20 .50
337 Evgeni Nabokov .20 .50
338 Owen Nolan .20 .50
339 Mike Ricci .08 .20
340 Teemu Selanne .25 .60
341 Brad Stuart .08 .20
342 Marco Sturm .08 .20
343 Gary Suter .08 .20
344 Scott Thornton .08 .20
345 Nikita Alexeev .08 .20
346 Dave Andreychuk .20 .50
347 Ben Clymer .08 .20
348 Nikolai Khabibulin .25 .60
349 Dieter Kochan .20 .50
350 Pavel Kubina .08 .20
351 Vincent Lecavalier .25 .60
352 Fredrik Modin .08 .20
353 Vaclav Prospal .20 .50
354 Brad Richards .20 .50
355 Martin St.Louis .20 .50
356 Shane Willis .08 .20
357 Tom Barrasso .20 .50
358 Shayne Corson .08 .20
359 Tie Domi .20 .50
360 Travis Green .08 .20
361 Curtis Joseph .25 .60
362 Tomas Kaberle .08 .20
363 Bryan McCabe .08 .20
364 Alyn McCauley .08 .20
365 Alexander Mogilny .20 .50
366 Robert Reichel .08 .20
367 Mikael Renberg .08 .20
368 Gary Roberts .08 .20
369 Corey Schwab .20 .50
370 Mats Sundin .25 .60
371 Darcy Tucker .08 .20
372 Dmitri Yushkevich .08 .20
373 Todd Bertuzzi .25 .60
374 Andrew Cassels .08 .20
375 Dan Cloutier .20 .50
376 Matt Cooke .08 .20
377 Jan Hlavac .08 .20
378 Ed Jovanovski .20 .50
379 Trevor Linden .20 .50
380 Brendan Morrison .20 .50
381 Markus Naslund .25 .60
382 Mattias Ohlund .08 .20
383 Daniel Sedin .08 .20
384 Henrik Sedin .08 .20
385 Peter Skudra .08 .20
386 Brent Sopel .08 .20
387 Craig Billington .08 .20
388 Peter Bondra .20 .50
389 Ulf Dahlen .08 .20
390 Sergei Gonchar .08 .20
391 Jeff Halpern .08 .20
392 Jaromir Jagr .40 1.00
393 Calle Johansson .08 .20
394 Dimitri Khristich .08 .20
395 Olaf Kolzig .20 .50
396 Steve Konowalchuk .08 .20
397 Andrei Nikolishin .08 .20
398 Stephen Peat .08 .20
399 Chris Simon .08 .20
400 Dainius Zubrus .08 .20
401 Stanislav Chistov RC 2.00 5.00
402 Alexei Smirnov RC 2.50 6.00
403 Chuck Kobasew RC 2.00 5.00
404 Rick Nash RC 8.00 20.00
405 Henrik Zetterberg RC 8.00 20.00
406 Ales Hemsky RC 5.00 12.00
407 Jay Bouwmeester RC 2.50 6.00
408 Alexander Frolov RC 3.00 8.00
409 P-M Bouchard RC 3.00 8.00
410 Alexander Svitov RC 2.50 6.00

2002-03 Pacific Blue

This 400-card set paralleled the base set but carried blue foil highlights in place of the silver foil on the base set. Cards in this set were serial-numbered out of 45.

*BLUE: 12X TO 30X BASIC CARD

2002-03 Pacific Cramer's Choice

This 10-card set was inserted at 1:732 packs. Each card was serial-numbered to just 95 copies.

1 Dany Heatley 6.00 15.00
2 Ilya Kovalchuk 6.00 15.00
3 Joe Thornton 6.00 15.00
4 Peter Forsberg 10.00 25.00
5 Patrick Roy 25.00 60.00
6 Dominik Hasek 8.00 20.00
7 Steve Yzerman 25.00 60.00
8 Martin Brodeur 15.00 40.00
9 Mario Lemieux 30.00 75.00
10 Mats Sundin 4.00 10.00

2002-03 Pacific Impact Zone

This 10-card set was inserted at 1:9 packs.

COMPLETE SET (10) 8.00 15.00
1 Paul Kariya .40 1.00
2 Ilya Kovalchuk .50 1.25
3 Joe Thornton .60 1.50
4 Jarome Iginla .50 1.25
5 Joe Sakic .75 2.00
6 Brendan Shanahan .60 1.50
7 Saku Koivu .40 1.00
8 Eric Lindros .40 1.00
9 Mario Lemieux 2.50 6.00
10 Teemu Selanne .40 1.00

2002-03 Pacific Jerseys

Inserted at 2:37, this 50-card set featured swatches of game-worn jerseys. The NNO card at the end of this set was inserted at a stated rate of 1:732 and each card was serial-numbered out of 500. A holo-silver hobby only parallel was also created and serial-numbered to 40 sets. The parallel had a silver foil border around the jersey swatch.

*HOLO-SILVER: 1X TO 2.5X BASIC JERSEY
1 Dany Heatley 5.00 12.00
2 Milan Hnilicka 3.00 8.00
3 Joe Thornton 6.00 15.00
4 Miroslav Satan 3.00 8.00
5 Roman Turek 3.00 8.00
6 Arturs Irbe 3.00 8.00
7 Tony Amonte 3.00 8.00
8 Steve Sullivan 3.00 8.00
9 Rob Blake 3.00 8.00
10 Chris Drury 3.00 8.00
11 Joe Sakic 8.00 20.00
12 Marc Denis 3.00 8.00
13 Ron Tugnutt 3.00 8.00
14 Jason Arnott 3.00 8.00
15 Mike Modano 6.00 15.00
16 Sergei Fedorov 5.00 12.00
17 Dominik Hasek 12.50 30.00
18 Jason Williams 3.00 8.00
19 Tommy Salo 3.00 8.00
20 Wade Flaherty 3.00 8.00
21 Jason Allison 3.00 8.00
22 Aaron Miller 3.00 8.00
23 Cliff Ronning 3.00 8.00
24 Manny Fernandez 3.00 8.00
25 Sergei Berezin 3.00 8.00
26 Yanic Perreault 3.00 8.00
27 Jose Theodore 5.00 12.00
28 Martin Erat 3.00 8.00
29 Jukka Hentunen 3.00 8.00
30 Jamie Langenbrunner SP 3.00 8.00
31 Joe Nieuwendyk SP 3.00 8.00
32 Michael Peca 3.00 8.00
33 Alexei Yashin 3.00 8.00
34 Pavel Bure 4.00 10.00
35 Theo Fleury 3.00 8.00
36 Mark Messier 4.00 10.00
37 Martin Havlat 3.00 8.00
38 Jiri Dopita 3.00 8.00
39 Simon Gagne 4.00 10.00
40 Adam Oates 3.00 8.00
41 Daymond Langkow 3.00 8.00
42 Mario Lemieux 12.50 30.00
43 Pavol Demitra 3.00 8.00
44 Ray Ferraro 3.00 8.00
45 Evgeni Nabokov 3.00 8.00
46 Fredrik Modin 3.00 8.00
47 Alexander Mogilny 3.00 8.00
48 Darcy Tucker 3.00 8.00
49 Dan Cloutier 3.00 8.00
50 Jaromir Jagr 6.00 15.00
NNO Ilya Kovalchuk JSY/STK AU 30.00 80.00

2002-03 Pacific Lamplighters

This 14-card set was inserted at 1:20 packs.

COMPLETE SET (14) 25.00 50.00
1 Dany Heatley 1.00 2.50
2 Ilya Kovalchuk 1.00 2.50
3 Joe Thornton 1.25 3.00
4 Jarome Iginla 1.00 2.50
5 Peter Forsberg 2.00 5.00
6 Joe Sakic 1.50 4.00
7 Steve Yzerman 4.00 10.00
8 Alexei Yashin .75 2.00
9 Pavel Bure 1.25 3.00
10 Eric Lindros .75 2.00
11 Mario Lemieux 5.00 12.00
12 Mats Sundin .75 2.00
13 Todd Bertuzzi .75 2.00
14 Jaromir Jagr 1.25 3.00

2002-03 Pacific Main Attractions

This 20-card set was inserted at 1:12 packs.

COMPLETE SET (20) 15.00 30.00
1 Paul Kariya .40 1.00
2 Ilya Kovalchuk 1.50 4.00
3 Joe Thornton .60 1.50
4 Jarome Iginla .50 1.25
5 Patrick Roy 2.00 5.00
6 Mike Modano .60 1.50
7 Steve Yzerman 2.00 5.00
8 Mike Comrie .30 .75
9 Jason Allison .30 .75
10 Jose Theodore .50 1.25
11 Martin Brodeur 1.00 2.50
12 Alexei Yashin .30 .75
13 Pavel Bure .60 1.50
14 Daniel Alfredsson .30 .75
15 Jeremy Roenick .50 1.25
16 Mario Lemieux 2.50 6.00
17 Keith Tkachuk .40 1.00
18 Mats Sundin .40 1.00
19 Markus Naslund .40 1.00
20 Jaromir Jagr .60 1.50

2002-03 Pacific Maximum Impact

This 16-card set was inserted at 1:12 packs.

COMPLETE SET (16) 12.50 25.00
1 Roman Turek .30 .75
2 Patrick Roy 2.00 5.00
3 Dominik Hasek .75 2.00
4 Jose Theodore .50 1.25
5 Martin Brodeur 1.00 2.50
6 Sean Burke .30 .75
7 Evgeni Nabokov .30 .75
8 Curtis Joseph .40 1.00
9 Ilya Kovalchuk 1.50 4.00
10 Joe Thornton .60 1.50
11 Jarome Iginla .50 1.25
12 Joe Sakic .75 2.00
13 Steve Yzerman 2.00 5.00
14 Eric Lindros .40 1.00
15 Mario Lemieux 2.50 6.00
16 Mats Sundin .40 1.00

2002-03 Pacific Shining Moments

This 10-card set was inserted at 1:20 packs.

COMPLETE SET (10) 20.00 40.00
1 Dany Heatley 3.00 8.00
2 Ilya Kovalchuk 3.00 8.00
3 Erik Cole 1.50 4.00
4 Radim Vrbata 1.50 4.00
5 Pavel Datsyuk 2.50 6.00
6 Kristian Huselius 1.50 4.00
7 Stephen Weiss 1.50 4.00
8 Mike Ribeiro 1.50 4.00
9 Dan Blackburn 2.00 5.00
10 Krystofer Kolanos 1.50 4.00

2003-04 Pacific

Released in late July 2003, this 350-card set was the first of the 2003-04 season. Cards 351-360 were available only by a mail-in/internet redemption offer and cards 361-368 were available in packs of Pacific Calder.

351-360 PRINT RUN 999 SER.#'d SETS
361-368 PRINT RUN 1225 SER.#'d SETS
1 Stanislav Chistov .08 .20
2 Martin Gerber .20 .50
3 Jean-Sebastien Giguere .20 .50
4 Niclas Havelid .08 .20
5 Paul Kariya .25 .60
6 Mike Leclerc .08 .20
7 Adam Oates .20 .50
8 Sandis Ozolinsh .08 .20
9 Steve Rucchin .08 .20
10 Petr Sykora .08 .20
11 Steve Thomas .08 .20
12 Byron Dafoe .20 .50
13 Joe DiPenta RC .75 2.00
14 Dany Heatley .30 .75
15 Milan Hnilicka .20 .50
16 Ilya Kovalchuk .30 .75
17 Slava Kozlov .08 .20
18 Shawn McEachern .08 .20
19 Pasi Nurminen .20 .50
20 Jeff Odgers .08 .20
21 Marc Savard .08 .20
22 Patrik Stefan .08 .20
23 P.J. Axelsson .08 .20
24 Bryan Berard .08 .20
25 Nick Boynton .08 .20
26 Jeff Hackett .20 .50
27 Mike Knuble .08 .20
28 Glen Murray .08 .20
29 Brian Rolston .08 .20
30 Sergei Samsonov .20 .50
31 Steve Shields .20 .50
32 P.J. Stock .08 .20
33 Jozef Stumpel .08 .20
34 Joe Thornton .40 1.00
35 Milan Bartovic RC .75 2.00
36 Martin Biron .20 .50
37 Daniel Briere .08 .20
38 Curtis Brown .08 .20
39 Tim Connolly .08 .20
40 J-P Dumont .08 .20
41 Ales Kotalik .08 .20
42 Ryan Miller .20 .50
43 Mika Noronen .20 .50
44 Taylor Pyatt .08 .20
45 Miroslav Satan .20 .50
46 Alexei Zhitnik .08 .20
47 Craig Conroy .08 .20
48 Chris Drury .20 .50
49 Martin Gelinas .08 .20
50 Jarome Iginla .30 .75
51 Chuck Kobasew .08 .20
52 Jordan Leopold .08 .20
53 Toni Lydman .08 .20
54 Dean McAmmond .08 .20
55 Jamie McLennan .08 .20
56 Roman Turek .20 .50
57 Stephane Yelle .08 .20
58 Ryan Bayda .08 .20
59 Rod Brind'Amour .20 .50
60 Erik Cole .08 .20
61 Ron Francis .20 .50
62 Jeff Heerema .08 .20
63 Sean Hill .08 .20
64 Arturs Irbe .20 .50
65 Jeff O'Neill .08 .20
66 Radim Vrbata .08 .20
67 Kevin Weekes .20 .50
68 Craig Andersson .08 .20
69 Tyler Arnason .20 .50
70 Mark Bell .08 .20
71 Kyle Calder .08 .20
72 Eric Daze .20 .50
73 Theoren Fleury .08 .20
74 Steve Passmore .08 .20
75 Chris Simon .08 .20
76 Steve Sullivan .08 .20
77 Jocelyn Thibault .20 .50
78 Alexei Zhamnov .08 .20
79 David Aebischer .20 .50
80 Bates Battaglia .08 .20
81 Rob Blake .20 .50
82 Adam Foote .08 .20
83 Peter Forsberg .50 1.25
84 Milan Hejduk .25 .60
85 Derek Morris .08 .20
86 Vaclav Nedorost .08 .20
87 Steven Reinprecht .08 .20
88 Patrick Roy 1.25 3.00
89 Joe Sakic .50 1.25
90 Alex Tanguay .20 .50
91 Andrew Cassels .08 .20
92 Marc Denis .20 .50
93 Rostislav Klesla .08 .20
94 Pascal Leclaire .20 .50
95 Kent McDonell RC .75 2.00
96 Rick Nash .30 .75
97 Geoff Sanderson .08 .20
98 Mike Sillinger .08 .20
99 David Vyborny .08 .20
100 Ray Whitney .08 .20
101 Tyler Wright .08 .20
102 Jason Arnott .08 .20
103 Ulf Dahlen .08 .20
104 Bill Guerin .20 .50
105 Derian Hatcher .08 .20
106 Jere Lehtinen .20 .50
107 Mike Modano .40 1.00
108 Brenden Morrow .20 .50
109 Steve Ott .08 .20
110 Ron Tugnutt .20 .50
111 Marty Turco .20 .50
112 Pierre Turgeon .20 .50
113 Scott Young .08 .20
114 Sergei Zubov .08 .20
115 Chris Chelios .25 .60
116 Pavel Datsyuk .25 .60
117 Sergei Fedorov .40 1.00
118 Tomas Holmstrom .08 .20
119 Brett Hull .30 .75
120 Curtis Joseph .25 .60
121 Igor Larionov .08 .20
122 Manny Legace .20 .50
123 Nicklas Lidstrom .25 .60
124 Luc Robitaille .20 .50
125 Mathieu Schneider .08 .20
126 Brendan Shanahan .25 .60
127 Steve Yzerman 1.25 3.00
128 Henrik Zetterberg .25 .60
129 Eric Brewer .08 .20
130 Jason Chimera .08 .20
131 Mike Comrie .20 .50
132 Ales Hemsky .20 .50
133 Brad Isbister .08 .20
134 Georges Laraque .08 .20
135 Todd Marchant .08 .20
136 Jussi Markkanen .08 .20
137 Tommy Salo .20 .50
138 Ryan Smyth .08 .20
139 Mike York .08 .20
140 Jaroslav Bednar .08 .20
141 Jay Bouwmeester .08 .20
142 Matt Cullen .08 .20
143 Jani Hurme .20 .50
144 Kristian Huselius .08 .20
145 Olli Jokinen .20 .50
146 Viktor Kozlov .08 .20
147 Roberto Luongo .30 .75
148 Marcus Nilsson .08 .20
149 Stephen Weiss .08 .20
150 Peter Worrell .08 .20
151 Jason Allison .08 .20
152 Jared Aulin .08 .20

153 Michael Cammalleri .08 .20
154 Adam Deadmarsh .08 .20
155 Alexander Frolov .08 .20
156 Cristobal Huet .20 .50
157 Jaroslav Modry .08 .20
158 Zigmund Palffy .20 .50
159 Felix Potvin .25 .60
160 Jamie Storr .20 .50
161 Pierre-Marc Bouchard .08 .20
162 Andrew Brunette .08 .20
163 Pascal Dupuis .08 .20
164 Manny Fernandez .20 .50
165 Marian Gaborik .40 1.00
166 Filip Kuba .08 .20
167 Antti Laaksonen .08 .20
168 Richard Park .08 .20
169 Dwayne Roloson .20 .50
170 Cliff Ronning .08 .20
171 Wes Walz .08 .20
172 Sergei Zholtok .08 .20
173 Donald Audette .08 .20
174 Patrice Brisebois .08 .20
175 Jan Bulis .08 .20
176 Mathieu Garon .08 .20
177 Marcel Hossa .08 .20
178 Saku Koivu .25 .60
179 Andrei Markov .08 .20
180 Yanic Perreault .08 .20
181 Mike Ribeiro .08 .20
182 Niklas Sundstrom .08 .20
183 Jose Theodore .30 .75
184 Richard Zednik .08 .20
185 Denis Arkhipov .08 .20
186 Andy Delmore .08 .20
187 Adam Hall .08 .20
188 Scott Hartnell .08 .20
189 Andreas Johansson .08 .20
190 David Legwand .20 .50
191 Oleg Petrov .08 .20
192 Kimmo Timonen .08 .20
193 Scottie Upshall .08 .20
194 Tomas Vokoun .20 .50
195 Scott Walker .08 .20
196 Martin Brodeur .60 1.50
197 Patrik Elias .20 .50
198 Jeff Friesen .08 .20
199 Brian Gionta .08 .20
200 Scott Gomez .08 .20
201 Jamie Langenbrunner .08 .20
202 John Madden .08 .20
203 Scott Niedermayer .08 .20
204 Joe Nieuwendyk .20 .50
205 Brian Rafalski .08 .20
206 Scott Stevens .20 .50
207 Oleg Tverdovsky .08 .20
208 Arron Asham .08 .20
209 Shawn Bates .08 .20
210 Jason Blake .08 .20
211 Rick DiPietro .20 .50
212 Roman Hamrlik .08 .20
213 Mark Parrish .08 .20
214 Michael Peca .08 .20
215 Dave Scatchard .08 .20
216 Garth Snow .20 .50
217 Mattias Weinhandl .08 .20
218 Alexei Yashin .08 .20
219 Matthew Barnaby .08 .20
220 Dan Blackburn .20 .50
221 Pavel Bure .25 .60
222 Anson Carter .20 .50
223 Mike Dunham .20 .50
224 Bobby Holik .08 .20
225 Alex Kovalev .20 .50
226 Brian Leetch .20 .50
227 Eric Lindros .25 .60
228 Mark Messier .25 .60
229 Petr Nedved .08 .20
230 Tom Poti .08 .20
231 Mike Richter .25 .60
232 Daniel Alfredsson .20 .50
233 Magnus Arvedson .08 .20
234 Radek Bonk .08 .20
235 Zdeno Chara .08 .20
236 Mike Fisher .08 .20
237 Martin Havlat .20 .50
238 Marian Hossa .25 .60
239 Patrick Lalime .20 .50
240 Martin Prusek .20 .50
241 Wade Redden .08 .20
242 Bryan Smolinski .08 .20
243 Jason Spezza .25 .60
244 Vaclav Varada .08 .20
245 Todd White .08 .20
246 Tony Amonte .20 .50
247 Donald Brashear .08 .20
248 Roman Cechmanek .20 .50
249 Eric Desjardins .08 .20
250 Robert Esche .08 .20
251 Simon Gagne .25 .60
252 Michal Handzus .08 .20
253 Kim Johnsson .08 .20
254 John LeClair .25 .60
255 Keith Primeau .20 .50
256 Mark Recchi .20 .50
257 Jeremy Roenick .30 .75
258 Zac Bierk .20 .50
259 Brian Boucher .20 .50
260 Sean Burke .20 .50
261 Shane Doan .08 .20
262 Chris Gratton .08 .20
263 Jan Hrdina .08 .20
264 Mike Johnson .08 .20
265 Daymond Langkow .08 .20
266 Ladislav Nagy .08 .20
267 Teppo Numminen .08 .20
268 Jeff Taffe .08 .20
269 Ramzi Abid .08 .20
270 Rico Fata .08 .20
271 Johan Hedberg .20 .50
272 Brian Holzinger .08 .20
273 Mathias Johansson .08 .20
274 Mario Lemieux 1.50 4.00
275 Alexei Morozov .08 .20
276 Martin Straka .08 .20
277 Tomas Surovy .08 .20
278 Dick Tarnstrom .08 .20
279 Eric Boguniecki .08 .20
280 Pavol Demitra .20 .50
281 Dallas Drake .08 .20
282 Barret Jackman .20 .50
283 Brent Johnson .20 .50
284 Al MacInnis .20 .50
285 Scott Mellanby .08 .20
286 Chris Osgood .20 .50
287 Chris Pronger .20 .50
288 Peter Sejna RC .75 2.00
289 Cory Stillman .08 .20
290 Keith Tkachuk .25 .60
291 Doug Weight .20 .50
292 Jonathan Cheechoo .10 .25
293 Vincent Damphousse .08 .20
294 Niko Dimitrakos .08 .20
295 Miikka Kiprusoff .20 .50
296 Patrick Marleau .20 .50
297 Alyn McCauley .08 .20
298 Evgeni Nabokov .20 .50
299 Mike Ricci .08 .20
300 Teemu Selanne .25 .60
301 Marco Sturm .08 .20
302 Vesa Toskala .08 .20
303 Dave Andreychuk .08 .20
304 Dan Boyle .08 .20
305 Ruslan Fedotenko .08 .20
306 John Grahame .20 .50
307 Nikolai Khabibulin .25 .60
308 Vincent Lecavalier .25 .60
309 Fredrik Modin .08 .20
310 Vaclav Prospal .08 .20
311 Brad Richards .20 .50
312 Martin St. Louis .20 .50
313 Alexander Svitov .08 .20
314 Nik Antropov .08 .20
315 Ed Belfour .25 .60
316 Tie Domi .20 .50
317 Doug Gilmour .20 .50
318 Tomas Kaberle .08 .20
319 Trevor Kidd .20 .50
320 Alexander Mogilny .20 .50
321 Owen Nolan .20 .50
322 Gary Roberts .08 .20
323 Matt Stajan RC 1.50 4.00
324 Mats Sundin .25 .60
325 Robert Svehla .08 .20
326 Darcy Tucker .08 .20
327 Todd Bertuzzi .25 .60
328 Dan Cloutier .20 .50
329 Matt Cooke .08 .20
330 Ed Jovanovski .20 .50
331 Trent Klatt .08 .20
332 Trevor Linden .08 .20
333 Brendan Morrison .20 .50
334 Markus Naslund .25 .60
335 Daniel Sedin .08 .20
336 Henrik Sedin .08 .20
337 Peter Skudra .08 .20
338 Brent Sopel .08 .20
339 Sergei Berezin .08 .20
340 Peter Bondra .20 .50
341 Sebastien Charpentier .20 .50
342 Sergei Gonchar .08 .20
343 Mike Grier .08 .20
344 Jeff Halpern .08 .20
345 Jaromir Jagr .40 1.00
346 Olaf Kolzig .20 .50
347 Robert Lang .08 .20
348 Kip Miller .08 .20
349 Michael Nylander .08 .20
350 Dainius Zubrus .08 .20
351 Joffrey Lupul RC 1.25 3.00
352 Eric Staal RC 4.00 10.00
353 Tuomo Ruutu RC 2.00 5.00
354 Pavel Vorobiev RC .75 2.00
355 Nathan Horton RC 2.00 5.00
356 Dustin Brown RC .75 2.00
357 Jordin Tootoo RC 1.50 4.00
358 Marc-Andre Fleury RC 4.00 10.00
359 Milan Michalek RC 1.25 3.00
360 Boyd Gordon RC .75 2.00
361 Derek Roy RC 1.00 2.50
362 Matthew Lombardi RC .75 2.00
363 Nikolai Zherdev RC 2.00 5.00
364 Jiri Hudler RC 1.25 3.00
365 Niklas Kronwall RC .75 2.00
366 Fredrik Sjostrom RC .75 2.00
367 Ryan Malone RC 1.25 3.00
368 Ryan Kesler RC .75 2.00

2003-04 Pacific Blue

*STARS: 1.25X TO 3X BASIC CARDS
PRINT RUN 250 SER.#'d SETS

2003-04 Pacific Red

*STARS: .5X TO 1.25X BASIC CARDS
STATED ODDS: 1:3

2003-04 Pacific Cramer's Choice

STATED PRINT RUN 99 SER.#'d SETS
1 Peter Forsberg 12.00 30.00
2 Patrick Roy 25.00 60.00
3 Rick Nash 12.00 30.00
4 Mike Modano 8.00 20.00
5 Steve Yzerman 20.00 50.00
6 Henrik Zetterberg 10.00 25.00
7 Martin Brodeur 15.00 40.00
8 Mario Lemieux 30.00 80.00
9 Markus Naslund 4.00 10.00
10 Jaromir Jagr 10.00 25.00

2003-04 Pacific In the Crease

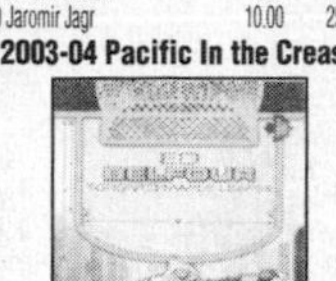

COMPLETE SET (12) 10.00 20.00
STATED ODDS 1:10
1 Jean-Sebastien Giguere .60 1.50
2 Jocelyn Thibault .60 1.50
3 Patrick Roy 1.50 4.00
4 Marty Turco .60 1.50
5 Curtis Joseph .75 2.00
6 Jose Theodore 1.00 2.50
7 Martin Brodeur 1.25 3.00
8 Patrick Lalime .60 1.50
9 Roman Cechmanek .60 1.50
10 Sean Burke .60 1.50
11 Ed Belfour .75 2.00
12 Dan Cloutier .60 1.50

2003-04 Pacific Jerseys

STATED ODDS 1:19
1 Paul Kariya 3.00 8.00
2 Dany Heatley 4.00 10.00
3 Milan Hnilicka 2.50 6.00
4 Ilya Kovalchuk 4.00 10.00
5 Joe Thornton 6.00 15.00
6 J-P Dumont 2.50 6.00
7 Chris Drury 2.50 6.00
8 Peter Forsberg 8.00 20.00
9 Patrick Roy 10.00 25.00
10 Joe Sakic 6.00 15.00
11 Alex Tanguay 2.50 6.00
12 Geoff Sanderson 2.50 6.00
13 Mike Modano 4.00 10.00
14 Marty Turco 2.50 6.00
15 Brendan Shanahan 3.00 8.00
16 Steve Yzerman 8.00 20.00
17 Ryan Smyth 2.50 6.00
18 Ziggy Palffy 2.50 6.00
19 Filip Kuba 2.50 6.00
20 Saku Koivu 3.00 8.00
21 Jose Theodore 4.00 10.00
22 Scott Walker 2.50 6.00
23 Martin Brodeur 10.00 25.00
24 Alexei Yashin 2.50 6.00
25 Pavel Bure 3.00 8.00
26 Eric Lindros 3.00 8.00
27 Daniel Alfredsson 2.50 6.00
28 Jason Spezza 6.00 15.00
29 Roman Cechmanek 2.50 6.00
30 Jeremy Roenick 4.00 10.00
31 Mario Lemieux 10.00 25.00
32 Brent Johnson 2.50 6.00
33 Keith Tkachuk 3.00 8.00
34 Miikka Kiprusoff 2.50 6.00
35 Vincent Lecavalier 2.50 6.00
36 Fredrik Modin 2.50 6.00
37 Ed Belfour 3.00 8.00
38 Todd Bertuzzi 3.00 8.00
39 Dan Cloutier 2.50 6.00
40 Jaromir Jagr 5.00 12.00

2003-04 Pacific Jerseys Gold

*GOLD: 1X TO 2.5X BASIC JERSEY
PRINT RUN 50 SER.#'d SETS

2003-04 Pacific Main Attractions

STATED ODDS 1:10
1 Paul Kariya .60 1.50
2 Ilya Kovalchuk .75 2.00
3 Joe Thornton .75 2.00
4 Peter Forsberg 1.25 3.00
5 Mike Modano .75 2.00
6 Steve Yzerman 1.50 4.00
7 Marian Gaborik 1.00 2.50
8 Saku Koivu .60 1.50
9 Pavel Bure .60 1.50
10 Marian Hossa .60 1.50
11 John LeClair .60 1.50
12 Mario Lemieux 2.00 5.00
13 Teemu Selanne .60 1.50
14 Mats Sundin .60 1.50
15 Markus Naslund .60 1.50
16 Jaromir Jagr .75 2.00

2003-04 Pacific Marty Turco

This 6-card set highlighted the young career of Marty Turco and was inserted at 1:37.

COMPLETE SET (6) 8.00 15.00
COMMON CARD (1-6) 1.25 3.00

2003-04 Pacific Marty Turco Autographs

This 6-card set paralleled the regular insert set but carried certified autographs. Cards #1-5 were serial-numbered to 99 and card #6 was serial-numbered to 35 copies.

COMMON AUTO/99 (1-5) 15.00 40.00
COMMON AUTO/35 (6) 40.00 100.00

2003-04 Pacific Maximum Impact

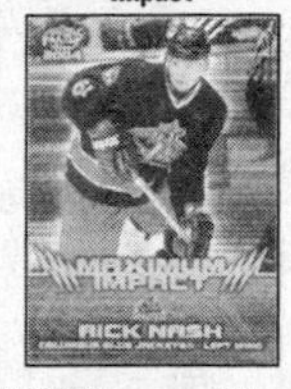

COMPLETE SET (10) 10.00 20.00
STATED ODDS 1:19
1 Joe Thornton 1.25 3.00
2 Jarome Iginla 1.00 2.50
3 Rick Nash 1.00 2.50
4 Brendan Shanahan .75 2.00
5 Michael Peca .60 1.50
6 Eric Lindros .75 2.00
7 Mark Messier .75 2.00
8 Jeremy Roenick 1.00 2.50
9 Owen Nolan .60 1.50
10 Todd Bertuzzi .75 2.00

2003-04 Pacific Milestones

COMPLETE SET (8) 10.00 20.00
STATED ODDS 1:19
1 Patrick Roy 2.50 6.00
2 Joe Sakic 1.50 4.00
3 Mike Modano 1.25 3.00
4 Marty Turco .60 1.50
5 Brett Hull 1.00 2.50
6 Joe Nieuwendyk .60 1.50
7 Mats Sundin .75 2.00
8 Jaromir Jagr 1.25 3.00

2003-04 Pacific View from the Crease

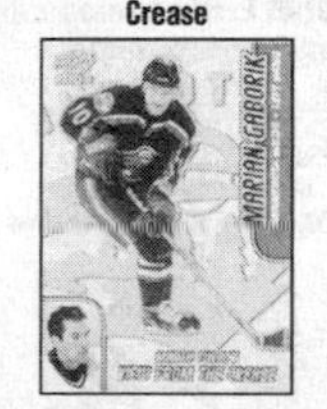

COMPLETE SET (8) 15.00 30.00
STATED ODDS 1:37
1 Paul Kariya 1.25 3.00
2 Joe Thornton 2.00 5.00
3 Joe Sakic 2.50 6.00
4 Mike Modano 2.00 5.00
5 Sergei Fedorov 1.50 4.00
6 Brett Hull 1.50 4.00
7 Marian Gaborik 2.50 6.00
8 Todd Bertuzzi 1.25 3.00

2004-05 Pacific

This 300-card set was issued in the summer of 2004 before the eventual NHL lockout. It was the last set produced by Pacific Trading Cards.

COMPLETE SET (300) 40.00 80.00

1 Stanislav Chistov .08 .20
2 Sergei Fedorov .40 1.00
3 Martin Gerber .20 .50
4 Jean-Sebastien Giguere .20 .50
5 Joffrey Lupul .08 .20
6 Vaclav Prospal .08 .20
7 Steve Rucchin .08 .20
8 Martin Skoula .08 .20
9 Petr Sykora .08 .20
10 Dany Heatley .30 .75
11 Ilya Kovalchuk .30 .75
12 Slava Kozlov .08 .20
13 Shawn McEachern .08 .20
14 Pasi Nurminen .20 .50
15 Ronald Petrovicky .08 .20
16 Randy Robitaille .08 .20
17 Marc Savard .08 .20
18 Patrik Stefan .08 .20
19 Patrice Bergeron .20 .50
20 Sergei Gonchar .08 .20
21 Mike Knuble .08 .20
22 Glen Murray .08 .20
23 Felix Potvin .25 .60
24 Andrew Raycroft .08 .20
25 Brian Rolston .08 .20
26 Sergei Samsonov .20 .50
27 Joe Thornton .40 1.00
28 Maxim Afinogenov .08 .20
29 Martin Biron .20 .50
30 Daniel Briere .08 .20
31 Chris Drury .20 .50
32 J-P Dumont .08 .20
33 Jochen Hecht .08 .20
34 Mika Noronen .20 .50
35 Derek Roy .08 .20
36 Miroslav Satan .20 .50
37 Craig Conroy .08 .20
38 Shean Donovan .08 .20
39 Martin Gelinas .08 .20
40 Jarome Iginla .30 .75
41 Miikka Kiprusoff .20 .50
42 Jordan Leopold .08 .20
43 Matthew Lombardi .08 .20
44 Steven Reinprecht .08 .20
45 Chris Simon .08 .20
46 Rod Brind'Amour .20 .50
47 Erik Cole .08 .20
48 Sean Hill .08 .20
49 Jeff O'Neill .08 .20
50 Eric Staal .08 .20
51 Josef Vasicek .08 .20
52 Radim Vrbata .08 .20
53 Kevin Weekes .20 .50
54 Justin Williams .08 .20
55 Craig Andersson .08 .20
56 Tyler Arnason .20 .50
57 Mark Bell .08 .20
58 Bryan Berard .08 .20
59 Kyle Calder .08 .20
60 Eric Daze .20 .50
61 Brett McLean .08 .20
62 Tuomo Ruutu .20 .50
63 Jocelyn Thibault .20 .50
64 David Aebischer .20 .50
65 Rob Blake .20 .50
66 Peter Forsberg .60 1.50
67 Milan Hejduk .25 .60
68 Paul Kariya .20 .50
69 Joe Sakic .50 1.25
70 Tommy Salo .20 .50
71 Teemu Selanne .25 .60
72 Alex Tanguay .20 .50
73 Andrew Cassels .08 .20
74 Marc Denis .20 .50
75 Anders Eriksson .08 .20
76 Trevor Letowski .08 .20
77 Manny Malhotra .08 .20
78 Todd Marchant .08 .20
79 Rick Nash .30 .75
80 David Vyborny .08 .20
81 Nikolai Zherdev .08 .20
82 Jason Arnott .08 .20
83 Valeri Bure .08 .20
84 Bill Guerin .20 .50
85 Jere Lehtinen .20 .50
86 Mike Modano .40 1.00
87 Brenden Morrow .20 .50
88 Marty Turco .20 .50
89 Pierre Turgeon .20 .50
90 Sergei Zubov .08 .20
91 Pavel Datsyuk .25 .60
92 Kris Draper .08 .20
93 Brett Hull .30 .75
94 Curtis Joseph .25 .60
95 Robert Lang .08 .20
96 Manny Legace .20 .50
97 Nicklas Lidstrom .25 .60
98 Brendan Shanahan .25 .60
99 Steve Yzerman 1.25 3.00
100 Ty Conklin .20 .50
101 Radek Dvorak .08 .20
102 Ales Hemsky .08 .20
103 Shawn Horcoff .08 .20
104 Ethan Moreau .08 .20
105 Petr Nedved .08 .20
106 Ryan Smyth .08 .20
107 Raffi Torres .08 .20
108 Mike York .08 .20
109 Jay Bouwmeester .08 .20
110 Niklas Hagman .08 .20
111 Nathan Horton .08 .20
112 Kristian Huselius .08 .20
113 Olli Jokinen .08 .20
114 Juraj Kolnik .08 .20
115 Roberto Luongo .30 .75
116 Mike Van Ryn .08 .20
117 Stephen Weiss .08 .20
118 Derek Armstrong .08 .20
119 Dustin Brown .08 .20
120 Roman Cechmanek .20 .50
121 Alexander Frolov .08 .20
122 Cristobal Huet .20 .50
123 Trent Klatt .08 .20
124 Ziggy Palffy .20 .50
125 Luc Robitaille .08 .20
126 Jozef Stumpel .08 .20
127 Andrew Brunette .08 .20
128 Brent Burns .08 .20
129 Alexandre Daigle .08 .20
130 Pascal Dupuis .08 .20
131 Manny Fernandez .20 .50
132 Marian Gaborik .50 1.25
133 Filip Kuba .08 .20
134 Antti Laaksonen .08 .20
135 Dwayne Roloson .20 .50
136 Patrice Brisebois .08 .20
137 Saku Koivu .25 .60
138 Alex Kovalev .20 .50
139 Yanic Perreault .08 .20
140 Mike Ribeiro .08 .20
141 Michael Ryder .08 .20
142 Sheldon Souray .08 .20
143 Jose Theodore .30 .75
144 Richard Zednik .08 .20
145 Martin Erat .08 .20
146 Adam Hall .08 .20
147 Scott Hartnell .08 .20
148 David Legwand .20 .50
149 Steve Sullivan .08 .20
150 Jordin Tootoo .08 .20
151 Tomas Vokoun .20 .50
152 Scott Walker .08 .20
153 Marek Zidlicky .08 .20
154 Martin Brodeur .60 1.50
155 Patrik Elias .20 .50
156 Jeff Friesen .08 .20
157 Brian Gionta .08 .20
158 Scott Gomez .08 .20
159 Jamie Langenbrunner .08 .20
160 John Madden .08 .20
161 Scott Niedermayer .08 .20
162 Scott Stevens .20 .50
163 Adrian Aucoin .08 .20
164 Jason Blake .08 .20
165 Mariusz Czerkawski .08 .20
166 Rick DiPietro .20 .50
167 Trent Hunter .08 .20
168 Oleg Kvasha .08 .20
169 Mark Parrish .08 .20
170 Michael Peca .08 .20
171 Alexei Yashin .08 .20
172 Mike Dunham .20 .50
173 Jan Hlavac .08 .20
174 Bobby Holik .08 .20
175 Jaromir Jagr .40 1.00
176 Eric Lindros .25 .60
177 Mark Messier .25 .60
178 Boris Mironov .08 .20
179 Tom Poti .08 .20
180 Fedor Tyutin .08 .20
181 Daniel Alfredsson .20 .50
182 Peter Bondra .20 .50
183 Zdeno Chara .08 .20
184 Martin Havlat .20 .50
185 Marian Hossa .25 .60
186 Patrick Lalime .20 .50
187 Wade Redden .08 .20
188 Bryan Smolinski .08 .20
189 Jason Spezza .25 .60
190 Tony Amonte .20 .50
191 Sean Burke .20 .50
192 Robert Esche .08 .20
193 Simon Gagne .25 .60
194 Michal Handzus .08 .20
195 John LeClair .25 .60
196 Joni Pitkanen .08 .20
197 Mark Recchi .20 .50
198 Jeremy Roenick .30 .75
199 Brian Boucher .20 .50
200 Mike Comrie .20 .50
201 Shane Doan .08 .20
202 Daymond Langkow .08 .20
203 Paul Mara .08 .20
204 Derek Morris .08 .20
205 Ladislav Nagy .08 .20
206 Fredrik Sjostrom .08 .20
207 Jeff Taffe .08 .20
208 Jean-Sebastien Aubin .08 .20
209 Rico Fata .08 .20
210 Marc-Andre Fleury .20 .50
211 Ric Jackman .08 .20
212 Milan Kraft .08 .20
213 Mario Lemieux 1.50 4.00
214 Ryan Malone .08 .20
215 Aleksey Morozov .08 .20
216 Dick Tarnstrom .08 .20
217 Pavol Demitra .08 .20
218 Dallas Drake .08 .20
219 Barret Jackman .08 .20
220 Al MacInnis .20 .50
221 Chris Osgood .20 .50
222 Chris Pronger .20 .50
223 Mark Rycroft .08 .20
224 Keith Tkachuk .25 .60
225 Doug Weight .20 .50
226 Jonathan Cheechoo .10 .25
227 Vincent Damphousse .08 .20
228 Nils Ekman .08 .20
229 Alex Korolyuk .08 .20
230 Patrick Marleau .20 .50
231 Alyn McCauley .08 .20
232 Evgeni Nabokov .20 .50
233 Marco Sturm .08 .20
234 Vesa Toskala .08 .20
235 Dave Andreychuk .08 .20
236 John Grahame .20 .50
237 Nikolai Khabibulin .25 .60
238 Pavel Kubina .08 .20
239 Vincent Lecavalier .25 .60
240 Fredrik Modin .08 .20
241 Brad Richards .20 .50
242 Martin St. Louis .20 .50
243 Cory Stillman .08 .20
244 Ed Belfour .25 .60
245 Brian Leetch .25 .60
246 Bryan McCabe .08 .20
247 Alexander Mogilny .20 .50
248 Joe Nieuwendyk .20 .50
249 Owen Nolan .20 .50
250 Gary Roberts .08 .20
251 Mats Sundin .25 .60
252 Darcy Tucker .08 .20
253 Todd Bertuzzi .25 .60
254 Dan Cloutier .20 .50
255 Ed Jovanovski .20 .50
256 Trevor Linden .08 .20
257 Brendan Morrison .20 .50
258 Markus Naslund .25 .60
259 Mattias Ohlund .08 .20
260 Daniel Sedin .08 .20
261 Henrik Sedin .08 .20
262 Sebastien Charpentier .20 .50
263 Jeff Halpern .08 .20
264 Olaf Kolzig .20 .50
265 Kip Miller .08 .20
266 Maxime Ouellet .20 .50
267 Matt Pettinger .08 .20
268 Brian Willsie .08 .20
269 Brendan Witt .08 .20
270 Dainius Zubrus .08 .20
271 Chris Kunitz .08 .20
272 Kari Lehtonen .20 .50
273 Brett Lysak .08 .20
274 Matt Keith .08 .20
275 Adam Munro .20 .50
276 Mikhail Kuleshov .08 .20
277 John-Michael Liles .08 .20
278 Marek Svatos .08 .20
279 Dan Fritsche .08 .20
280 Greg Mauldin .08 .20
281 Mike Pandolfo .08 .20
282 Dan Ellis .20 .50
283 Mike Bishai .08 .20
284 Lukas Krajicek .08 .20
285 Denis Grebeshkov .08 .20
286 Tomas Plekanec .08 .20
287 Timofei Shishkanov .08 .20
288 Scottie Upshall .08 .20
289 Thomas Pihlman .08 .20
290 Aleksander Suglobov .08 .20
291 Jozef Balej .08 .20
292 Bryce Lampman .08 .20
293 Randy Jones .08 .20
294 Antero Niittymaki .20 .50
295 Mike Stutzel .08 .20
296 Niko Dimitrakos .08 .20
297 Marcel Goc RC .25 .60
298 Matt Stajan .08 .20
299 Alexander Semin .08 .20
300 Roman Tvrdon .08 .20

2004-05 Pacific Blue

*STARS: 1.25X TO 3X BASIC CARDS
STATED PRINT RUN 250 SER.#'d SETS

2004-05 Pacific Red

*STARS: .5X TO 1.25X BASIC CARDS
STATED ODDS 1:3

2004-05 Pacific All-Stars

COMPLETE SET (12) 8.00 15.00
STATED ODDS 1:10
1 Ilya Kovalchuk .75 2.00
2 Joe Thornton .75 2.00
3 Joe Sakic 1.25 3.00
4 Rick Nash .75 2.00
5 Mike Modano 1.00 2.50
6 Marty Turco .50 1.25
7 Robert Lang .50 1.25
8 Nicklas Lidstrom .60 1.50
9 Jose Theodore .75 2.00
10 Martin Brodeur 1.50 4.00
11 Patrick Marleau .50 1.25
12 Martin St. Louis .50 1.25

2004-05 Pacific Cramer's Choice

STATED ODDS 1:721
PRINT RUN 99 SER.#'d SETS
1 Ilya Kovalchuk 12.00 30.00
2 Joe Thornton 12.00 30.00
3 Jarome Iginla 12.00 30.00
4 Joe Sakic 15.00 40.00
5 Rick Nash 12.00 30.00
6 Steve Yzerman 20.00 50.00
7 Martin Brodeur 15.00 40.00
8 Mario Lemieux 20.00 50.00
9 Martin St. Louis 8.00 20.00
10 Ed Belfour 8.00 20.00

2004-05 Pacific Global Connection

COMPLETE SET (8) 8.00 15.00
STATED ODDS 1:19
1 Dany Heatley 1.25 3.00
Ilya Kovalchuk
2 Sergei Samsonov 1.00 2.50
Joe Thornton
3 Peter Forsberg 1.50 4.00
Joe Sakic
4 Paul Kariya 1.00 2.50
Teemu Selanne
5 Pavel Datsyuk 1.25 3.00
Henrik Zetterberg
6 Brett Hull 1.00 2.50
Nicklas Lidstrom
7 Martin Havlat 1.00 2.50
Marian Hossa
8 Alexander Mogilny 1.00 2.50
Mats Sundin

2004-05 Pacific Gold Crown Die-Cuts
COMPLETE SET (8) 10.00 20.00
STATED ODDS 1:37
1 Ilya Kovalchuk 2.00 5.00
2 Andrew Raycroft 1.00 2.50
3 Eric Staal 1.25 3.00
4 Henrik Zetterberg 1.25 3.00
5 Michael Ryder 1.00 2.50
6 Jordin Tootoo 1.25 3.00
7 Jason Spezza 2.00 5.00
8 Jonathan Cheechoo 1.25 3.00

2004-05 Pacific In The Crease
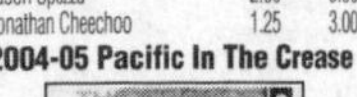

COMPLETE SET (10) 8.00 15.00
STATED ODDS 1:19
1 Andrew Raycroft .75 2.00
2 Miikka Kiprusoff .75 2.00
3 David Aebischer .75 2.00
4 Marty Turco .75 2.00
5 Dominik Hasek 1.25 3.00
6 Roberto Luongo 1.25 3.00
7 Jose Theodore 1.25 3.00
8 Martin Brodeur 1.50 4.00
9 Nikolai Khabibulin 1.00 2.50
10 Ed Belfour 1.00 2.50

2004-05 Pacific Jerseys
Card #45 in this 45-card set featured the Richard Trophy winners for 2003-04. The card carried jersey swatches of both Ilya Kovlachuk and Jarome Iginla on front and a certified Rick Nash autograph on the back.

STAT.ODDS 2:36 HOBBY/1:36 RETAIL
CARD#45 PRINT RUN 100 SER.#'d SETS
*GOLD: 1X TO 2X BASIC JERSEYS
1 Sergei Fedorov 4.00 10.00
2 Patrice Bergeron 3.00 8.00
3 Sergei Samsonov 3.00 8.00
4 Joe Thornton 5.00 12.00
5 Ales Kotalik 2.00 5.00
6 Mark Bell 2.00 5.00
7 Jocelyn Thibault 2.00 5.00
8 Peter Forsberg 8.00 20.00
9 Paul Kariya 4.00 10.00
10 Joe Sakic 6.00 15.00
11 Mike Modano 5.00 12.00
12 Derian Hatcher 2.00 5.00
13 Jason Williams 2.00 5.00
14 Steve Yzerman 10.00 25.00
15 Ryan Smyth 2.00 5.00
16 Roberto Luongo 3.00 8.00
17 Vaclav Nedorost 2.00 5.00
18 Jason Allison 2.00 5.00
19 Alex Kovalev 2.00 5.00
20 Martin Brodeur 10.00 25.00
21 Alexei Yashin 2.00 5.00
22 Pavel Bure 3.00 8.00
23 Eric Lindros 3.00 8.00
24 Daniel Alfredsson 3.00 8.00
25 Martin Havlat 3.00 8.00
26 Jeff Hackett 2.00 5.00
27 Joni Pitkanen 2.00 5.00
28 Jeremy Roenick 3.00 8.00
29 Brent Johnson 2.00 5.00
30 Krystofer Kolanos 2.00 5.00
31 Kris Beech 2.00 5.00
32 Mike Eastwood 2.00 5.00
33 Rico Fata 2.00 5.00
34 Mario Lemieux 12.00 30.00
35 Chris Osgood 2.00 5.00
36 Peter Sejna 2.00 5.00
37 Vincent Lecavalier 3.00 8.00
38 Ed Belfour 3.00 8.00
39 Matt Stajan 2.00 5.00
40 Mats Sundin 3.00 8.00
41 Todd Bertuzzi 3.00 8.00
42 Dan Cloutier 2.00 5.00
43 Brendan Morrison 2.00 5.00
44 Olaf Kolzig 3.00 8.00
45 Ilya Kovalchuk JSY/Jarome Iginla JSY/Rick Nash AU 75.00 200.00

2004-05 Pacific Milestones

COMPLETE SET (6) 10.00 20.00
STATED ODDS 1:37
1 Steve Yzerman 3.00 8.00
2 Martin Brodeur 3.00 8.00
3 Jaromir Jagr 1.50 4.00
4 Mark Messier 1.00 2.50
5 Mario Lemieux 4.00 10.00
6 Ed Belfour 1.00 2.50

2004-05 Pacific Philadelphia
COMPLETE SET (16) 12.50 25.00
STATED ODDS 1:10
1 Sergei Fedorov .75 2.00
2 Joe Sakic 1.25 3.00
3 Chris Chelios .60 1.50
4 Dominik Hasek 1.25 3.00
5 Brett Hull .75 2.00
6 Steve Yzerman 1.50 4.00
7 Luc Robitaille .50 1.25
8 Jaromir Jagr 1.00 2.50

9 Eric Lindros .60 1.50
10 Mark Messier .60 1.50
11 John LeClair .60 1.50
12 Jeremy Roenick .75 2.00
13 Mario Lemieux 2.00 5.00
14 Keith Tkachuk .60 1.50
15 Ron Francis .50 1.25
16 Brian Leetch .60 1.50

2001-02 Pacific Adrenaline

Released in December 2001, this 225-card set carried an SRP of $3.50 for a 5-card pack. Base cards carried full color action photos on white card fronts. Short printed rookies were serial-numbered out of 984, and the Kovalchuk autographed card was inserted at a rate of 1:721 hobby packs/1:1921 retail packs and serial-numbered to 500. The 500 Kovalchuk cards were inserted in both hobby and retail packs.

COMP.SET w/o SP's (200) 15.00 40.00
1 Jeff Friesen .10 .25
2 Jean-Sebastien Giguere .20 .50
3 Paul Kariya .30 .75
4 Marty McInnis .10 .25
5 Steve Shields .20 .50
6 Oleg Tverdovsky .10 .25
7 Ray Ferraro .10 .25
8 Milan Hnilicka .10 .25
9 Tomi Kallio .10 .25
10 Damian Rhodes .10 .25
11 Patrik Stefan .10 .25
12 Byron Dafoe .20 .50
13 Bill Guerin .20 .50
14 Martin Lapointe .10 .25
15 Sergei Samsonov .20 .50
16 Jozef Stumpel .10 .25
17 Joe Thornton .60 1.50
18 Stu Barnes .10 .25
19 Martin Biron .20 .50
20 Tim Connolly .10 .25
21 J-P Dumont .10 .25
22 Chris Gratton .10 .25
23 Slava Kozlov .10 .25
24 Miroslav Satan .20 .50
25 Jarome Iginla .60 1.50
26 Derek Morris .10 .25
27 Rob Niedermayer .10 .25
28 Marc Savard .10 .25
29 Roman Turek .20 .50
30 Mike Vernon .20 .50
31 Rod Brind'Amour .20 .50
32 Ron Francis .20 .50
33 Martin Gelinas .10 .25
34 Arturs Irbe .20 .50
35 Sami Kapanen .10 .25
36 Jeff O'Neill .10 .25
37 Shane Willis .10 .25
38 Tony Amonte .20 .50
39 Eric Daze .20 .50
40 Michael Nylander .10 .25
41 Steve Sullivan .10 .25
42 Jocelyn Thibault .20 .50
43 Alexei Zhamnov .10 .25
44 David Aebischer .20 .50
45 Rob Blake .20 .50
46 Chris Drury .20 .50
47 Peter Forsberg .60 1.50
48 Milan Hejduk .30 .75
49 Patrick Roy 1.50 4.00
50 Joe Sakic .75 2.00
51 Alex Tanguay .20 .50
52 Marc Denis .20 .50
53 Rostislav Klesla .10 .25
54 Espen Knutsen .10 .25
55 Geoff Sanderson .10 .25
56 Ron Tugnutt .20 .50
57 Donald Audette .10 .25
58 Ed Belfour .30 .75
59 Mike Modano .60 1.50
60 Joe Nieuwendyk .20 .50
61 Marty Turco .20 .50
62 Pierre Turgeon .20 .50
63 Chris Chelios .30 .75
64 Sergei Fedorov .40 1.00
65 Dominik Hasek .75 2.00
66 Brett Hull .40 1.00
67 Nicklas Lidstrom .30 .75
68 Luc Robitaille .20 .50
69 Brendan Shanahan .30 .75
70 Steve Yzerman 1.25 3.00
71 Eric Brewer .10 .25
72 Anson Carter .10 .25
73 Daniel Cleary .10 .25
74 Mike Comrie .20 .50
75 Mike Grier .10 .25
76 Jochen Hecht .10 .25
77 Tommy Salo .20 .50
78 Ryan Smyth .20 .50
79 Pavel Bure .30 .75
80 Valeri Bure .10 .25
81 Trevor Kidd .20 .50
82 Viktor Kozlov .10 .25
83 Roberto Luongo .60 1.50
84 Marcus Nilsson .10 .25
85 Jason Allison .10 .25
86 Adam Deadmarsh .10 .25
87 Zigmund Palffy .20 .50
88 Felix Potvin .30 .75
89 Mathieu Schneider .10 .25
90 Bryan Smolinski .10 .25
91 Manny Fernandez .20 .50
92 Marian Gaborik .60 1.50
93 Darby Hendrickson .10 .25
94 Lubomir Sekeras .10 .25
95 Wes Walz .10 .25
96 Joe Juneau .10 .25
97 Yanic Perreault .10 .25
98 Oleg Petrov .10 .25
99 Martin Rucinsky .10 .25
100 Brian Savage .10 .25
101 Jose Theodore .40 1.00
102 Richard Zednik .10 .25
103 Mike Dunham .20 .50
104 Scott Hartnell .10 .25
105 Patric Kjellberg .10 .25
106 David Legwand .20 .50
107 Cliff Ronning .10 .25
108 Tomas Vokoun .20 .50
109 Scott Walker .10 .25
110 Jason Arnott .10 .25
111 Martin Brodeur 1.00 2.50
112 Sergei Brylin .10 .25
113 Patrik Elias .20 .50
114 Scott Gomez .10 .25
115 John Madden .10 .25
116 Randy McKay .10 .25
117 Scott Stevens .20 .50
118 Mariusz Czerkawski .10 .25
119 Rick DiPietro .20 .50
120 Brad Isbister .10 .25
121 Chris Osgood .20 .50
122 Michael Peca .10 .25
123 Alexei Yashin .10 .25
124 Radek Dvorak .10 .25
125 Theo Fleury .10 .25
126 Brian Leetch .20 .50
127 Eric Lindros .30 .75
128 Mark Messier .30 .75
129 Petr Nedved .10 .25
130 Mike Richter .30 .75
131 Daniel Alfredsson .20 .50
132 Radek Bonk .10 .25
133 Martin Havlat .20 .50
134 Marian Hossa .30 .75
135 Patrick Lalime .20 .50
136 Shawn McEachern .10 .25
137 Wade Redden .10 .25
138 Roman Cechmanek .20 .50
139 Simon Gagne .30 .75
140 John LeClair .30 .75
141 Keith Primeau .10 .25
142 Mark Recchi .20 .50
143 Jeremy Roenick .40 1.00
144 Justin Williams .10 .25
145 Sergei Berezin .10 .25
146 Sean Burke .20 .50
147 Shane Doan .10 .25
148 Michal Handzus .10 .25
149 Daymond Langkow .10 .25
150 Claude Lemieux .10 .25
151 Johan Hedberg .20 .50
152 Jan Hrdina .10 .25
153 Alexei Kovalev .20 .50
154 Robert Lang .10 .25
155 Mario Lemieux 2.50 5.00
156 Martin Straka .10 .25
157 Fred Brathwaite .20 .50
158 Pavol Demitra .20 .50
159 Brent Johnson .20 .50
160 Al MacInnis .20 .50
161 Chris Pronger .20 .50
162 Cory Stillman .10 .25
163 Keith Tkachuk .30 .75
164 Doug Weight .20 .50
165 Miikka Kiprusoff .20 .50
166 Patrick Marleau .10 .25
167 Evgeni Nabokov .20 .50
168 Owen Nolan .20 .50
169 Mike Ricci .10 .25
170 Teemu Selanne .30 .75
171 Marco Sturm .10 .25
172 Brian Holzinger .10 .25
173 Nikolai Khabibulin .30 .75
174 Vincent Lecavalier .30 .75
175 Fredrik Modin .10 .25
176 Brad Richards .20 .50
177 Martin St. Louis .20 .50
178 Kevin Weekes .10 .25
179 Tie Domi .20 .50
180 Jonas Hoglund .10 .25
181 Curtis Joseph .30 .75
182 Tomas Kaberle .10 .25
183 Alexander Mogilny .20 .50
184 Gary Roberts .20 .50
185 Mats Sundin .30 .75
186 Darcy Tucker .10 .25
187 Todd Bertuzzi .30 .75
188 Andrew Cassels .10 .25
189 Dan Cloutier .20 .50
190 Brendan Morrison .20 .50
191 Markus Naslund .30 .75
192 Daniel Sedin .10 .25
193 Henrik Sedin .10 .25
194 Peter Bondra .30 .75
195 Sergei Gonchar .10 .25
196 Jeff Halpern .10 .25
197 Jaromir Jagr .60 1.50
198 Olaf Kolzig .20 .50
199 Steve Konowalchuk .10 .25
200 Adam Oates .20 .50
201 Ilja Bryzgalov RC 2.50 5.00
202 Timo Parssinen RC 2.50 5.00
203 Ilya Kovalchuk AU RC 30.00 80.00
204 Kamil Piros RC 2.50 5.00
205 Erik Cole RC 2.50 6.00
206 Vaclav Nedorost RC 2.50 5.00
207 Pavel Datsyuk RC 8.00 20.00
208 Ty Conklin RC 2.00 5.00
209 Niklas Hagman RC 2.00 5.00
210 Kristian Huselius RC 3.00 8.00
211 Jaroslav Bednar RC 2.00 5.00
212 Nick Schultz RC 2.00 5.00
213 Martin Erat RC 2.00 5.00
214 Scott Clemmensen RC 2.00 5.00
215 Andreas Salomonsson RC 2.00 5.00
216 Radek Martinek RC 2.00 5.00
217 Dan Blackburn RC 2.00 5.00
218 Chris Neil RC 2.50 6.00
219 Pavel Brendl SP 2.00 5.00
220 Jiri Dopita RC 2.00 5.00
221 Krystofer Kolanos RC 2.00 5.00
222 Mark Rycroft RC 2.00 5.00
223 Jeff Jillson RC 2.00 5.00
224 Nikita Alexeev RC 2.00 5.00
225 Brian Sutherby RC 2.00 5.00

2001-02 Pacific Adrenaline Blue
This 225-card set directly parallels the base set, with the only difference being a blue foil stamp rather than gold and serial numbering out of 62 on the card front. The cards were inserted randomly in hobby packs at a rate of 1:25.

*STARS: 6X TO 15X BASIC CARD
*SP's: .5X TO 1.25X BASIC CARD

2001-02 Pacific Adrenaline Premiere Date

This 225-card set directly parallels the base set, with the only difference being a gold premiere date stamp and serial numbering out of 62 on the card front. The cards were inserted randomly in hobby packs at a rate of 1:25.

*STARS: 6X TO 15X BASIC CARD
*SP's: .5X TO 1.25X BASIC CARD

2001-02 Pacific Adrenaline Red
Randomly inserted into retail packs at a rate of one per box, this 225 card set paralleled the base set but carried red foil and was serial-numbered to 54 sets.

*STARS: 8X TO 20X BASIC CARD
*SP's: .6X TO 1.5X BASIC CARDS

2001-02 Pacific Adrenaline Retail
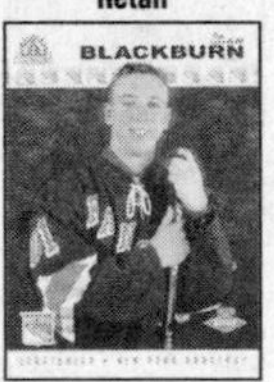
Though similar to the hobby version, the retail set had silver foil highlights and short prints were non-serial numbered. SP's were inserted at a rate of 4:25. There were two versions of the Kovalchuk card, a nonserial-numbered regular card and a serial-numbered out of 500 autographed card. Odds for the Kovalchuk auto card were 1:1921 for retail packs and the cards were inserted in both retail and hobby packs.

*RETAIL BASE SAME VALUE AS HOBBY
*RETAIL SPs: .15X TO .4X HOBBY CARDS
203 Ilya Kovalchuk RC 8.00 20.00
207 Pavel Datsyuk RC 6.00 15.00

2001-02 Pacific Adrenaline Blade Runners
Inserted into hobby packs at a rate of 1:481, this 10-card set featured a color action photo of the featured player on a blue and gold micro-chip design background. Borders were white with the same micro-chip design, and each card was serial-numbered out of 63.

1 Paul Kariya 15.00 40.00
2 Patrick Roy 30.00 80.00
3 Joe Sakic 12.50 30.00
4 Dominik Hasek 12.50 30.00
5 Steve Yzerman 30.00 80.00
6 Pavel Bure 8.00 20.00
7 Martin Brodeur 15.00 40.00
8 Eric Lindros 10.00 25.00
9 Mario Lemieux 40.00 100.00
10 Jaromir Jagr 10.00 25.00

2001-02 Pacific Adrenaline Creased Lightning
COMPLETE SET (20) 20.00 40.00
STATED ODDS 1:25
1 Martin Biron .60 1.50
2 Arturs Irbe .60 1.50
3 Jocelyn Thibault .60 1.50
4 Patrick Roy 4.00 10.00
5 Ed Belfour .75 2.00
6 Dominik Hasek 2.00 5.00
7 Tommy Salo .60 1.50
8 Roberto Luongo 1.00 2.50
9 Felix Potvin .60 1.50
10 Jose Theodore 1.00 2.50
11 Martin Brodeur 2.50 6.00
12 Rick DiPietro .60 1.50
13 Mike Richter .75 2.00
14 Patrick Lalime .60 1.50
15 Roman Cechmanek .60 1.50
16 Sean Burke .60 1.50
17 Johan Hedberg .60 1.50
18 Brent Johnson .60 1.50
19 Evgeni Nabokov .60 1.50
20 Curtis Joseph .75 2.00

2001-02 Pacific Adrenaline Jerseys

*MULT.COLOR SWATCH: 1X TO 1.5X
STATED ODDS 2:25 HOBBY/1:73 RETAIL
1 Oleg Tverdovsky 2.00 5.00
2 Sergei Samsonov 4.00 10.00
3 J-P Dumont 2.00 5.00
4 Jay McKee 2.00 5.00
5 Jarome Iginla 6.00 15.00
6 Roman Turek 2.00 5.00
7 Tony Amonte 4.00 10.00
8 Alexei Zhamnov 2.00 5.00
9 Patrick Roy 15.00 40.00
10 Joe Sakic 8.00 20.00
11 Ed Belfour 4.00 10.00
12 Derian Hatcher 2.00 5.00
13 Joe Nieuwendyk 4.00 10.00
14 Pierre Turgeon 4.00 10.00
15 Brett Hull 6.00 15.00
16 Steve Yzerman 12.00 30.00
17 Jochen Hecht 2.00 5.00
18 Valeri Bure 2.00 5.00
19 Robert Svehla 2.00 5.00
20 Felix Potvin 4.00 10.00
21 Jamie McLennan 2.00 5.00
22 Saku Koivu 4.00 10.00
23 Patric Kjellberg 2.00 5.00
24 Kimmo Timonen 2.00 5.00
25 Martin Brodeur 10.00 25.00
26 Petr Sykora 2.00 5.00
27 Chris Osgood 4.00 10.00
28 Eric Lindros 5.00 12.00
29 Petr Nedved 2.00 5.00
30 Mike Richter 4.00 10.00
31 Zdeno Chara 2.00 5.00
32 John LeClair 2.00 5.00
33 Shane Doan 2.00 5.00
34 Daymond Langkow 2.00 5.00
35 Alexei Kovalev 2.00 5.00
36 Milan Kraft 2.00 5.00
37 Robert Lang 2.00 5.00
38 Mario Lemieux 15.00 40.00
39 Fred Brathwaite 2.00 5.00
40 Cory Stillman 2.00 5.00
41 Doug Weight 4.00 10.00
42 Scott Young 2.00 5.00
43 Teemu Selanne 4.00 10.00
44 Nikolai Khabibulin 4.00 10.00
45 Vincent Lecavalier 5.00 12.00
46 Shayne Corson 2.00 5.00
47 Mats Sundin 5.00 12.00
48 Dimitri Yushkevich 2.00 5.00
49 Andrew Cassels 2.00 5.00
50 Jaromir Jagr 8.00 20.00

2001-02 Pacific Adrenaline Playmakers

COMPLETE SET (10) 10.00 25.00
STATED ODDS 1:49
1 Joe Thornton 2.50 6.00
2 Milan Hejduk .75 2.00
3 Mike Modano 2.50 6.00
4 Brett Hull 1.50 4.00
5 Mike Comrie .75 2.00
6 Marian Gaborik 2.50 6.00
7 Martin Havlat 1.25 3.00
8 Teemu Selanne 1.50 4.00
9 Daniel Sedin 1.25 3.00
10 Henrik Sedin 1.25 3.00

2001-02 Pacific Adrenaline Power Play
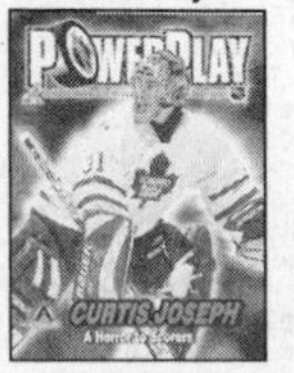
This DC card was inserted at a rate of 1:1. The cards were sponsored by Power Play magazine and the NHLPA. This set featured the top goalies of the league.

COMPLETE SET (36) 8.00 20.00
1 Jean-Sebastien Giguere .20 .50
2 Steve Shields .20 .50
3 Milan Hnilicka .20 .50
4 Byron DaFoe .20 .50
5 Martin Biron .20 .50
6 Roman Turek .20 .50
7 Arturs Irbe .20 .50
8 Jocelyn Thibault .20 .50
9 Patrick Roy 1.50 4.00
10 Marc Denis .20 .50
11 Ron Tugnutt .20 .50
12 Ed Belfour .30 .75
13 Marty Turco .30 .75
14 Dominik Hasek .60 1.50
15 Tommy Salo .20 .50
16 Trevor Kidd .20 .50
17 Roberto Luongo .40 1.00
18 Felix Potvin .30 .75
19 Manny Fernandez .20 .50
20 Jose Theodore .40 1.00
21 Mike Dunham .20 .50
22 Martin Brodeur .75 2.00
23 Rick DiPietro .30 .75
24 Mike Richter .30 .75
25 Patrick Lalime .20 .50
26 Roman Cechmanek .20 .50
27 Sean Burke .20 .50
28 Johan Hedberg .20 .50
29 Fred Brathwaite .20 .50
30 Brent Johnson .20 .50
31 Miikka Kiprusoff .40 1.00
32 Evgeni Nabokov .20 .50
33 Nikolai Khabibulin .30 .75
34 Curtis Joseph .30 .75
35 Dan Cloutier .20 .50
36 Olaf Kolzig .40 1.00

2001-02 Pacific Adrenaline Rookie Report

COMPLETE SET (20) 15.00 40.00
STATED ODDS 2:25
1 Ilja Bryzgalov 1.25 3.00
2 Dany Heatley 3.00 8.00
3 Ilya Kovalchuk 8.00 20.00
4 Erik Cole 1.25 3.00
5 Mark Bell .40 1.00
6 Vaclav Nedorost .40 1.00
7 Rostislav Klesla .40 1.00
8 Pavel Datsyuk 5.00 12.00
9 Kristian Huselius .40 1.00
10 Jaroslav Bednar .40 1.00
11 Rick DiPietro 2.00 5.00
12 Dan Blackburn .40 1.00
13 Pavel Brendl .40 1.00
14 Krystofer Kolanos .40 1.00
15 Kris Beech .40 1.00
16 Johan Hedberg .40 1.00
17 Jeff Jillson .40 1.00
18 Miikka Kiprusoff 2.00 5.00
19 Nikita Alexeev .40 1.00
20 Brian Sutherby .40 1.00

2001-02 Pacific Adrenaline World Beaters

COMPLETE SET (20) 25.00 50.00
STATED ODDS 3:25
1 Paul Kariya .75 2.00
2 Chris Drury .60 1.50
3 Joe Sakic 1.25 3.00
4 Mike Modano 1.00 2.50
5 Brett Hull .75 2.00
6 Steve Yzerman 3.00 8.00
7 Pavel Bure .75 2.00
8 Zigmund Palffy .60 1.50
9 Marian Gaborik 1.50 4.00
10 Patrik Elias .60 1.50
11 Alexei Yashin .60 1.50
12 Eric Lindros 1.00 2.50
13 Martin Havlat .60 1.50
14 John LeClair .75 2.00
15 Alexei Kovalev .60 1.50
16 Mario Lemieux 4.00 10.00
17 Keith Tkachuk .75 2.00
18 Teemu Selanne .75 2.00
19 Mats Sundin .75 2.00
20 Jaromir Jagr 1.00 2.50

2003 Pacific All-Star Game-Used Goal Net Cards
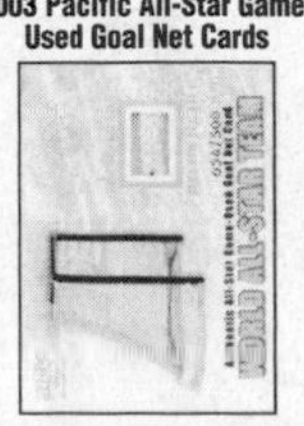
Given away exclusivley at the 2003 NHL All-Star block party as a wrapper redemption, this 2-card set featured swatches of the actual goal netting used during the 2002 NHL All-Star game. Each card was serial-numbered out of 500.

COMPLETE SET (2) 20.00 40.00
1 North American All-Star Team 20.00 25.00
2 World All-Star Team 20.00 25.00

2003 Pacific Atlantic City National Convention
Available via wrapper redemption at the Pacific booth during the 2003 Atlantic City National Sports Collectors Convention, this 6-card dual player set was numbered to just 500 copies.

COMPLETE SET (6) 12.50 30.00
1 Rick Nash / John LeClair 3.00 8.00
2 Henrik Zetterberg / Ilya Kovalchuk 4.00 10.00
3 Ryan Miller / Martin Brodeur 2.50 6.00
4 Jay Bouwmeester / Scott Stevens 2.00 5.00
5 Jason Spezza / Jeremy Roenick 3.00 8.00
6 Stanislav Chistov / Paul Kariya 2.00 5.00

2002 Pacific Calder Collection All-Star Fantasy
Available via wrapper redemption from the Pacific booth at the NHL All-Star Fantasy show, this 10-card set featured top rookies from the 2001-02 season. Each card was serial numbered out of 2000.

COMPLETE SET (10) 20.00 50.00
1 Dany Heatley 3.20 8.00
2 Ilya Kovalchuk 8.00 20.00
3 Erik Cole 2.40 6.00
4 Vaclav Nedorost 2.40 6.00
5 Kristian Huselius 2.40 6.00
6 Jaroslav Bednar 1.20 3.00
7 Martin Erat 1.20 3.00
8 Dan Blackburn 3.20 8.00
9 Krys Kolanos 2.40 6.00
10 Jeff Jillson 1.60 4.00

2003 Pacific Calder Collection NHL All-Star Block Party
Given away as wrapper redemptions exclusively at the Pacific booth during the 2003 NHL All-Star block party, this 10-card set featured players eligible for Calder consideration. Each card was serial-numbered out of 500.

COMPLETE SET 10.00 25.00
1 Stanislav Chistov .75 2.00
2 Chuck Kobasew .75 2.00
3 Jordan Leopold .75 2.00
4 Rick Nash 4.00 10.00
5 Henrik Zetterberg 4.00 10.00
6 Jay Bouwmeester 2.50 6.00
7 Alexander Frolov 2.00 5.00
8 P-M Bouchard 2.00 5.00
9 Jason Spezza 3.00 8.00
10 Alexander Svitov .75 2.00

2003 Pacific Calder Contenders NHL Entry Draft

Distributed exclusively at the 2003 NHL Entry Draft, this 10-card set paralleled the regular Calder Contenders set in Pacific Quest for the Cup, but carried a foil Draft stamp and gold background. Each card was serial-numbered to just 500 copies.

COMPLETE SET 15.00 40.00
1 Stanislav Chistov .75 2.00
2 Ales Kotalik .75 2.00
3 Ryan Miller 2.00 5.00
4 Tyler Arnason .75 2.00
5 Pascal Leclaire 1.25 3.00
6 Rick Nash 4.00 10.00
7 Henrik Zetterberg 3.00 8.00
8 Ales Hemsky .75 2.00
9 Jay Bouwmeester 1.50 4.00
10 Jason Spezza 3.00 8.00

2002-03 Pacific Calder
Released in June, this 150-card set featured veteran players who were nominated for the Calder trophy and rookies. Rookie cards were serial-numbered to 825.

COMP.SET w/o SP'S (100) 10.00 25.00
1 Dany Heatley .40 1.00
2 Ilya Kovalchuk .40 1.00

3 Evgeni Nabokov .25 .60
4 Brad Richards .25 .60
5 Scott Gomez .10 .25
6 Brad Stuart .25 .60
7 Chris Drury .25 .60
8 Marian Hossa .30 .75
9 Sergei Samsonov .25 .60
10 Mattias Ohlund .10 .25
11 Bryan Berard .10 .25
12 Jarome Iginla .40 1.00
13 Daniel Alfredsson .25 .60
14 Eric Daze .25 .60
15 Peter Forsberg .75 2.00
16 Martin Brodeur .75 2.00
17 Jason Arnott .10 .25
18 Teemu Selanne .30 .75
19 Pavel Bure .30 .75
20 Nicklas Lidstrom .30 .75
21 Ed Belfour .30 .75
22 Sergei Fedorov .50 1.25
23 Mike Modano .50 1.25
24 Brian Leetch .25 .60
25 Joe Nieuwendyk .25 .60
26 Luc Robitaille .25 .60
27 Mario Lemieux 2.50 6.00
28 Chris Chelios .30 .75
29 Steve Yzerman 1.50 4.00
30 Paul Kariya .30 .75
31 Joe Thornton .50 1.25
32 Theoren Fleury .10 .25
33 Milan Hejduk .30 .75
34 Patrick Roy 1.50 4.00
35 Joe Sakic .60 1.50
36 Marty Turco .25 .60
37 Brett Hull .40 1.00
38 Curtis Joseph .30 .75
39 Brendan Shanahan .30 .75
40 Mike Comrie .25 .60
41 Marian Gaborik .60 1.50
42 Saku Koivu .30 .75
43 Jose Theodore .40 1.00
44 Alexei Yashin .10 .25
45 Alex Kovalev .25 .60
46 Eric Lindros .30 .75
47 Mark Messier .30 .75
48 Tony Amonte .25 .60
49 Vincent Lecavalier .30 .75
50 Mats Sundin .30 .75
51 Markus Naslund .30 .75
52 Jaromir Jagr .50 1.25
53 Dan Snyder .10 .25
54 Lee Goren .10 .25
55 Ivan Huml .10 .25
56 Andrew Raycroft .25 .60
57 Ales Kotalik .10 .25
58 Mika Noronen .10 .25
59 Henrik Tallinder .10 .25
60 Pavel Brendl .10 .25
61 Jeff Heerema .10 .25
62 Jaroslav Svoboda .10 .25
63 Tyler Arnason .25 .60
64 Riku Hahl .10 .25
65 Vaclav Nedorost .10 .25
66 Niko Kapanen .10 .25
67 Jesse Wallin .10 .25
68 Jason Chimera .10 .25
69 Jani Rita .10 .25
70 Raffi Torres .10 .25
71 Jaroslav Bednar .10 .25
72 Stephen Weiss .10 .25
73 Joe Corvo .10 .25
74 Kyle Wanvig .10 .25
75 Mathieu Garon .25 .60
76 Marcel Hossa .10 .25
77 Jan Lasak .10 .25
78 Christian Berglund .10 .25
79 Jiri Bicek .10 .25
80 Michael Rupp .10 .25
81 Rick DiPietro .25 .60
82 Justin Mapletoft .10 .25
83 Mattias Weinhandl .10 .25
84 Jamie Lundmark .10 .25
85 Ales Pisa .10 .25
86 Toni Dahlman .10 .25
87 Eric Chouinard .10 .25
88 Ramzi Abid .10 .25
89 Sebastien Caron .10 .25
90 Dan Focht .10 .25
91 Barret Jackman .25 .60
92 Justin Papineau .10 .25
93 Jonathan Cheechoo .12 .30
94 Miikka Kiprusoff .25 .60
95 Vesa Toskala .10 .25
96 Karel Pilar .10 .25
97 Fedor Fedorov .10 .25
98 Sebastien Charpentier .25 .60
99 Joel Kwiatkowski .10 .25
100 Brian Sutherby .10 .25
101 Stanislav Chistov RC 2.00 5.00
102 Kurt Sauer RC 2.00 5.00
103 Alexei Smirnov RC 2.00 5.00
104 Shaone Morrisonn RC 2.00 5.00
105 Kris Vernarsky RC 2.00 5.00
106 Ryan Miller RC 2.00 5.00
107 Chuck Kobasew RC 2.00 5.00
108 Jordan Leopold RC 2.00 5.00
109 Ryan Bayda RC 2.00 5.00
110 Igor Radulov RC 2.00 5.00
111 Pascal Leclaire RC 2.00 5.00
112 Rick Nash RC 6.00 15.00
112A Rick Nash AU/100 60.00 125.00
113 Jason Bacashihua RC 2.00 5.00
114 Steve Ott RC 2.00 5.00
115 Dmitri Bykov RC 2.00 5.00
116 Henrik Zetterberg RC 4.00 10.00
117 Ales Hemsky RC 3.00 8.00
118 Fernando Pisani RC 2.00 5.00
119 Jay Bouwmeester RC 2.00 5.00
120 Jared Aulin RC 2.00 5.00
121 Michael Cammalleri RC 2.50 6.00
122 Alexander Frolov RC 2.50 6.00
123 Cristobal Huet RC 4.00 10.00
124 P-M Bouchard RC 2.00 5.00
125 Stephane Veilleux RC 2.00 5.00
126 Ron Hainsey RC 2.00 5.00
127 Mike Komisarek RC 2.00 5.00
128 Vernon Fiddler RC 2.00 5.00
129 Adam Hall RC 2.00 5.00
130 Scottie Upshall RC 2.00 5.00
131 Eric Godard RC 2.00 5.00
132 Ray Emery RC 2.00 5.00
133 Jason Spezza RC 6.00 15.00
134 Anton Volchenkov RC 2.00 5.00
135 Dennis Seidenberg RC 2.00 5.00
136 Radovan Somik RC 2.00 5.00
137 Jim Vandermeer RC 2.00 5.00
138 Jeff Taffe RC 2.00 5.00
139 Brooks Orpik RC 2.00 5.00
140 Tomas Surovy RC 2.00 5.00
141 Curtis Sanford RC 2.00 5.00
142 Matt Walker RC 2.00 5.00
143 Niko Dimitrakos RC 2.00 5.00
144 Jim Fahey RC 2.00 5.00
145 Lynn Loyns RC 2.00 5.00
146 Alexander Svitov RC 2.00 5.00
147 Carlo Colaiacovo RC 2.00 5.00
148 Mikael Tellqvist RC 2.00 5.00
149 Steve Eminger RC 2.00 5.00
150 Alex Henry RC 2.00 5.00

2002-03 Pacific Calder Silver

*STARS: 1.25X TO 3X BASIC CARD
*SP's: .25X TO .75X
PRINT RUN 299 SER.#'d SETS

2002-03 Pacific Calder Chasing Glory

COMPLETE SET (10) 10.00 20.00
STATED ODDS 1:13
1 Joe Thornton 1.00 2.50
2 Peter Forsberg 1.50 4.00
3 Patrick Roy 2.50 6.00
4 Mike Modano 1.00 2.50
5 Marty Turco .60 1.50
6 Martin Brodeur 1.50 4.00
7 Marian Hossa .60 1.50
8 Mario Lemieux 3.00 8.00
9 Ed Belfour .60 1.50
10 Markus Naslund .60 1.50

2002-03 Pacific Calder Hardware Heroes

COMPLETE SET (12) 10.00 20.00
STATED ODDS 1:9
1 Dany Heatley .60 1.50
2 Patrick Roy 2.00 5.00
3 Joe Sakic 1.00 2.50
4 Brett Hull .60 1.50
5 Nicklas Lidstrom .50 1.25
6 Steve Yzerman 2.00 5.00
7 Jose Theodore .60 1.50
8 Eric Lindros .50 1.25
9 Mark Messier .50 1.25
10 Mario Lemieux 2.50 6.00
11 Ed Belfour .50 1.25
12 Jaromir Jagr .75 2.00

2002-03 Pacific Calder Hart Stoppers

COMPLETE SET (8) 10.00 20.00
STATED ODDS 1:13
1 Joe Thornton 1.00 2.50
2 Peter Forsberg 1.50 4.00
3 Patrick Roy 2.50 6.00
4 Mike Modano 1.00 2.50
5 Marty Turco .60 1.50
6 Martin Brodeur 1.50 4.00
7 Marian Hossa .60 1.50
8 Markus Naslund .60 1.50

2002-03 Pacific Calder Jerseys

STATED ODDS 1:13
1 Dany Heatley 5.00 12.00
2 Patrik Stefan 3.00 8.00
3 Glen Murray 3.00 8.00
4 Joe Thornton 5.00 12.00
5 Miroslav Satan 3.00 8.00
6 Alexei Zhamnov 3.00 8.00
7 Peter Forsberg 8.00 20.00
8 Patrick Roy 10.00 25.00
9 Marty Turco 5.00 12.00
10 Luc Robitaille 3.00 8.00
11 Olli Jokinen 3.00 8.00
12 Yanic Perreault 3.00 8.00
13 Tomas Vokoun 3.00 8.00
14 Rick DiPietro 3.00 8.00
15 Daniel Alfredsson 3.00 8.00
16 Jason Spezza 6.00 15.00
17 Roman Cechmanek 3.00 8.00
18 Mario Lemieux 12.50 30.00
19 Valeri Bure 3.00 8.00
20 Doug Weight 3.00 8.00
21 Ed Belfour 4.00 10.00
22 Mats Sundin 4.00 10.00
23 Brendan Morrison 3.00 8.00
24 Markus Naslund 4.00 10.00
25 Jaromir Jagr 6.00 15.00

2002-03 Pacific Calder Reflections

COMPLETE SET (20) 12.00 30.00
STATED ODDS 1:5
1 Stanislav Chistov .60 1.50
2 Ivan Huml .60 1.50
3 Ales Kotalik .60 1.50
4 Ryan Miller 1.50 4.00
5 Jordan Leopold .60 1.50
6 Tyler Arnason .60 1.50
7 Pascal Leclaire 1.00 2.50
8 Rick Nash 2.00 5.00
9 Henrik Zetterberg 1.50 4.00
10 Ales Hemsky 1.25 3.00
11 Jay Bouwmeester .75 2.00
12 Stephen Weiss .75 2.00
13 Michael Cammalleri .75 2.00
14 Alexander Frolov 1.00 2.50
15 P-M Bouchard .75 2.00
16 Marcel Hossa .75 2.00
17 Rick DiPietro 1.00 2.50
18 Jason Spezza 1.50 4.00
19 Barret Jackman .60 1.50
20 Jonathan Cheechoo 1.25 3.00

2003-04 Pacific Calder

The last Pacific brand of the season, Calder focused on rookies and prospects. Cards 101-140 were serial-numbered to 775 copies each. Cards 141 through 175 were jersey cards.

JSY RC PRINT RUN 500 SER.#'d SETS
1 Sergei Fedorov .40 1.00
2 Jean-Sebastien Giguere .25 .60
3 Dany Heatley .40 1.00
4 Ilya Kovalchuk .40 1.00
5 Marc Savard .15 .40
6 Sergei Gonchar .15 .40
7 Glen Murray .15 .40
8 Andrew Raycroft .25 .60
9 Joe Thornton .50 1.25
10 Martin Biron .25 .60
11 Daniel Briere .15 .40
12 Mika Noronen .25 .60
13 Jarome Iginla .40 1.00
14 Miikka Kiprusoff .25 .60
15 Chuck Kobasew .15 .40
16 Erik Cole .15 .40
17 Josef Vasicek .15 .40
18 Justin Williams .15 .40
19 Tyler Arnason .25 .60
20 Mark Bell .15 .40
21 Kyle Calder .15 .40
22 Peter Forsberg .75 2.00
23 Milan Hejduk .30 .75
24 Paul Kariya .30 .75
25 Joe Sakic .60 1.50
26 Philippe Sauve .25 .60
27 Alex Tanguay .25 .60
28 Marc Denis .25 .60
29 Rick Nash .40 1.00
30 Valeri Bure .15 .40
31 Bill Guerin .25 .60
32 Mike Modano .50 1.25
33 Marty Turco .25 .60
34 Pavel Datsyuk .30 .75
35 Kris Draper .15 .40
36 Dominik Hasek .60 1.50
37 Brett Hull .40 1.00
38 Curtis Joseph .30 .75
39 Robert Lang .25 .60
40 Brendan Shanahan .25 .60
41 Steve Yzerman .75 2.00
42 Ryan Smyth .15 .40
43 Raffi Torres .15 .40
44 Mike York .15 .40
45 Jay Bouwmeester .15 .40
46 Olli Jokinen .25 .60
47 Roberto Luongo .40 1.00
48 Roman Cechmanek .25 .60
49 Alexander Frolov .15 .40
50 Ziggy Palffy .25 .60
51 Alexandre Daigle .15 .40
52 Marian Gaborik .60 1.50
53 Dwayne Roloson .25 .60
54 Saku Koivu .30 .75
55 Alex Kovalev .25 .60
56 Mike Ribeiro .15 .40
57 Michael Ryder .15 .40
58 Jose Theodore .40 1.00
59 Scott Hartnell .15 .40
60 Scottie Upshall .15 .40
61 Tomas Vokoun .25 .60
62 Martin Brodeur .75 2.00
63 Patrik Elias .25 .60
64 Jeff Friesen .15 .40
65 Rick DiPietro .25 .60
66 Trent Hunter .15 .40
67 Jaromir Jagr .50 1.25
68 Eric Lindros .30 .75
69 Mark Messier .30 .75
70 Daniel Alfredsson .25 .60
71 Martin Havlat .25 .60
72 Marian Hossa .30 .75
73 Jason Spezza .30 .75
74 Mark Recchi .25 .60
75 Jeremy Roenick .40 1.00
76 Brian Boucher .25 .60
77 Mike Comrie .25 .60
78 Shane Doan .15 .40
79 Ladislav Nagy .15 .40
80 Rico Fata .15 .40
81 Mario Lemieux 1.50 4.00
82 Pavol Demitra .15 .40
83 Chris Osgood .25 .60
84 Keith Tkachuk .30 .75
85 Doug Weight .25 .60
86 Jonathan Cheechoo .20 .50
87 Patrick Marleau .25 .60
88 Evgeni Nabokov .25 .60
89 Nikolai Khabibulin .30 .75
90 Vincent Lecavalier .30 .75
91 Martin St. Louis .25 .60
92 Ed Belfour .30 .75
93 Owen Nolan .25 .60
94 Gary Roberts .15 .40
95 Mats Sundin .30 .75
96 Todd Bertuzzi .30 .75
97 Dan Cloutier .25 .60
98 Jason King .15 .40
99 Brendan Morrison .25 .60
100 Markus Naslund .30 .75
101 Chris Kunitz RC 1.50 4.00
102 Kari Lehtonen RC 8.00 20.00
103 Jason Pominville RC 2.00 5.00
104 Derek Roy RC 1.50 4.00
105 Brent Krahn RC 1.50 4.00
106 Eric Staal RC 6.00 15.00
107 Adam Munro RC 1.50 4.00
108 Tuomo Ruutu RC 2.00 5.00
109 Pavel Vorobiev RC 1.50 4.00
110 Cody McCormick RC 1.50 4.00
111 Dan Fritsche RC 1.50 4.00
112 Tim Jackman RC 1.50 4.00
113 Nikolai Zherdev RC 3.00 8.00
114 Dan Ellis RC 1.50 4.00
115 Jiri Hudler RC 2.50 6.00
116 Niklas Kronwall RC 2.00 5.00
117 Nathan Robinson RC 1.50 4.00
118 Doug Lynch RC 1.50 4.00
119 Scott Barney 1.50 4.00
120 Noah Clarke RC 1.50 4.00
121 Brent Burns RC 1.50 4.00
122 Dan Hamhuis RC 2.00 5.00
123 Timofei Shishkanov RC 1.50 4.00
124 Marek Zidlicky RC 1.50 4.00
125 Tuomas Pihlman RC 1.50 4.00
126 Jozef Balej RC 2.00 5.00
127 Dominic Moore RC 1.50 4.00
128 Chad Wiseman 1.50 4.00
129 Fredrik Sjostrom RC 1.50 4.00
130 Marc-Andre Fleury RC 8.00 20.00
131 Ryan Malone RC 2.50 6.00
132 Matt Murley RC 1.50 4.00
133 John Pohl RC 1.50 4.00
134 Milan Michalek RC 2.00 5.00
135 Kyle Wellwood RC 4.00 10.00
136 Wade Brookbank RC 1.50 4.00
137 Ryan Kesler RC 1.50 4.00
138 Peter Sarno RC 1.50 4.00
139 Alexander Semin RC 4.00 10.00
140 Rastislav Stana RC 1.50 4.00
141 Jean-Sebastien Giguere 2.50 6.00
142 Ilya Kovalchuk 8.00 20.00
143 Joe Thornton 6.00 15.00
144 Jarome Iginla 6.00 15.00
145 Peter Forsberg 8.00 20.00
146 Milan Hejduk 3.00 8.00
147 Rick Nash 4.00 10.00
148 Marty Turco 6.00 15.00
149 Roman Cechmanek 2.50 6.00
150 Martin Brodeur 12.00 30.00
151 Jaromir Jagr 6.00 15.00
152 Daniel Alfredsson 2.50 6.00
153 Marian Hossa 3.00 8.00
154 Jeff Hackett 2.50 6.00
155 Mario Lemieux/66 15.00 40.00
156 Chris Osgood 2.50 6.00
157 Vincent Lecavalier .30 .75
158 Ed Belfour 3.00 8.00
159 Todd Bertuzzi 3.00 8.00
160 Brendan Morrison 2.50 6.00
161 Olaf Kolzig 2.50 6.00
162 Joffrey Lupul RC 4.00 10.00
163 Patrice Bergeron RC 8.00 20.00
164 Matthew Lombardi RC 3.00 8.00
165 Antti Miettinen RC 3.00 8.00
166 Nathan Horton RC 5.00 12.00
167 Dustin Brown RC 3.00 8.00
168 Chris Higgins RC 4.00 10.00
169 Jordin Tootoo RC 5.00 12.00
170 Sean Bergenheim RC 3.00 8.00
171 Antoine Vermette RC 3.00 8.00
172 Joni Pitkanen RC 4.00 10.00
173 Peter Sejna RC 3.00 8.00
174 Matt Stajan RC 4.00 10.00
175 Boyd Gordon RC 3.00 8.00
176 Andrew Raycroft AU/250 12.00 30.00

2003-04 Pacific Calder Silver

*STARS: 2X TO 5X BASIC CARDS
*ROOKIES: .25X TO .6X
PRINT RUN 575 SER.#'d SETS

2003-04 Pacific Calder Reflections

COMPLETE SET 15.00 30.00
STATED ODDS 1:13
1 Joffrey Lupul 2.00 5.00
2 Patrice Bergeron 3.00 8.00
3 Andrew Raycroft 3.00 8.00
4 Eric Staal 2.50 6.00
5 Michael Ryder 2.00 5.00
6 Trent Hunter 2.00 5.00
7 Marc-Andre Fleury 4.00 10.00
8 Ryan Malone 2.00 5.00

2002 Pacific Chicago National *

Available via a wrapper redemption at the Pacific booth during the 2002 Chicago National Convention, this 8-card set was serial-numbered to just 500 copies. Collectors had to open a box of 2002 Pacific football or 2001-02 Pacific hockey product to receive the set. Each card featured an NHL player and an NFL player on either side.

COMPLETE SET (8) 20.00 40.00
1 Ilya Kovalchuk 4.00 10.00
Michael Vick
2 Joe Thornton 2.50 6.00
Tom Brady
3 Eric Daze 2.00 5.00
Anthony Thomas
4 Peter Forsberg 2.50 6.00
Brian Griese
5 Mike Modano 2.50 6.00
Emmitt Smith
6 Steve Yzerman 4.00 10.00
Joey Harrington
7 Eric Lindros 2.50 6.00
Ron Dayne
8 Chris Pronger 2.00 5.00
Kurt Warner

2002-03 Pacific Complete

This 600-card super set was inserted into various Pacific products throughout the season. A red parallel set was also created and sold via an online offer.

*RED: 6X TO 15X BASIC CARDS
*RED ROOKIES: 3X TO 8X
RED PRINT RUN 100 SER.#'d SETS
1 Nicklas Lidstrom .15 .40
2 Mika Noronen .05 .15
3 Alexei Kovalev .12 .30
4 Jason Allison .05 .15
5 Erik Cole .05 .15
6 Sami Kapanen .05 .15
7 Marty Turco .12 .30
8 Brad Isbister .05 .15
9 Saku Koivu .15 .40
10 Jarome Iginla .20 .50
11 Jean-Sebastien Giguere .12 .30
12 Roman Turek .12 .30
13 Joe Sakic .30 .75
14 Peter Bondra .12 .30
15 Dany Heatley .20 .50
16 Vincent Lecavalier .15 .40
17 Manny Fernandez .12 .30
18 Simon Gagne .15 .40
19 Rick DiPietro .12 .30
20 Mark Recchi .12 .30
21 Mike Richter .15 .40
22 Daymond Langkow .05 .15
23 Pavel Datsyuk .15 .40
24 Mark Messier .15 .40
25 Ed Belfour .15 .40
26 Michael Peca .05 .15
27 Krystofer Kolanos .05 .15
28 Alexander Mogilny .12 .30
29 Martin Straka .05 .15
30 Shane Willis .05 .15
31 Alyn McCauley .05 .15
32 Ryan Smyth .05 .15
33 Tomi Kallio .05 .15
34 Doug Weight .12 .30
35 Nicholas Boynton .05 .15
36 Pascal Dupuis .05 .15
37 Jaroslav Svoboda .05 .15
38 Al MacInnis .12 .30
39 Peter Forsberg .40 1.00
40 Rostislav Klesla .05 .15
41 Kimmo Timonen .05 .15
42 Darren McCarty .05 .15
43 Brian Savage .05 .15
44 Ethan Moreau .05 .15
45 Peter Worrell .05 .15
46 Doug Gilmour .12 .30
47 David Aebischer .12 .30
48 Aaron Miller .05 .15
49 Nick Schultz .05 .15
50 Magnus Arvedson .05 .15
51 Cale Hulse .05 .15
52 Brian Gionta .05 .15
53 Trevor Linden .05 .15
54 Raffi Torres .05 .15
55 Jean-Sebastien Aubin .12 .30
56 Zdeno Chara .05 .15
57 Mattias Ohlund .05 .15
58 Travis Green .05 .15
59 Michael Nylander .05 .15
60 Andreas Dackell .05 .15
61 Craig Billington .05 .15
62 Chris Therien .05 .15
63 Eric Brewer .05 .15
64 Shayne Corson .05 .15
65 Patrice Brisebois .05 .15
66 Sean O'Donnell .05 .15
67 Sergei Varlamov .05 .15
68 Donald Brashear .05 .15
69 Vaclav Prospal .05 .15
70 Mike Ricci .05 .15
71 Fredrik Modin .05 .15
72 Stu Grimson .05 .15
73 Jeff Jillson .05 .15
74 Andre Roy .05 .15
75 Filip Kuba .05 .15
76 Martin Skoula .05 .15
77 Sandis Ozolinsh .05 .15
78 Robert Reichel .05 .15
79 Wes Walz .05 .15
80 Keith Carney .05 .15
81 Steve Kariya .05 .15
82 Dave Tanabe .05 .15
83 Robert Svehla .05 .15
84 Rob Ray .05 .15
85 Niklas Hagman .05 .15
86 Stu Barnes .05 .15
87 Scott Gomez .05 .15
88 Rob Niedermayer .05 .15
89 Dave Scatchard .05 .15
90 Petr Nedved .05 .15
91 Bob Probert .05 .15
92 Dallas Drake .05 .15
93 Mike Leclerc .05 .15
94 Janne Niinimaa .05 .15
95 Rob Zamuner .05 .15
96 Jim Dowd .05 .15
97 Richard Matvichuk .05 .15
98 Boyd Devereaux .05 .15
99 Jamie Storr .12 .30
100 Rem Murray .05 .15
101 Jaromir Jagr .25 .60
102 Todd Bertuzzi .15 .40
103 Mike Modano .25 .60
104 Sergei Fedorov .25 .60
105 Ilya Kovalchuk .20 .50
106 Patrik Elias .12 .30
107 Marian Hossa .15 .40
108 Paul Kariya .15 .40
109 Manny Legace .12 .30
110 Milan Hejduk .15 .40
111 Adam Deadmarsh .05 .15
112 Owen Nolan .12 .30
113 Patrick Marleau .12 .30
114 Adam Oates .12 .30
115 Donald Audette .05 .15
116 Steven Reinprecht .05 .15
117 Jere Lehtinen .12 .30
118 Joe Nieuwendyk .12 .30
119 Roman Cechmanek .12 .30
120 Brian Rolston .05 .15
121 Chris Drury .12 .30
122 J-P Dumont .05 .15
123 Denis Arkhipov .05 .15
124 Sergei Zubov .05 .15
125 Scott Hartnell .05 .15
126 Espen Knutsen .05 .15
127 Slava Kozlov .12 .30
128 Roberto Luongo .20 .50
129 John LeClair .15 .40
130 Daniel Sedin .05 .15
131 Justin Williams .05 .15
132 Kyle Calder .05 .15
133 Bryan Smolinski .05 .15
134 Scott Mellanby .05 .15
135 Martin Lapointe .05 .15
136 Dwayne Roloson .12 .30
137 Niklas Sundstrom .05 .15
138 Ladislav Nagy .05 .15
139 Mathieu Schneider .05 .15
140 Scott Walker .05 .15
141 Marcus Nilsson .05 .15
142 Steve Thomas .05 .15
143 Kevin Weekes .12 .30
144 Vladimir Orszagh .05 .15
145 Brad Stuart .05 .15
146 Shawn Bates .05 .15
147 Oleg Tverdovsky .05 .15
148 Andy Delmore .05 .15
149 Stanislav Neckar .05 .15
150 Phil Housley .05 .15
151 Matt Cooke .05 .15
152 Scott Niedermayer .05 .15
153 Jeff Hackett .12 .30
154 Ruslan Fedotenko .05 .15
155 Daniel Cleary .12 .30
156 Martin Prusek .05 .15
157 Matt Cullen .05 .15
158 Jason Woolley .05 .15
159 Fred Brathwaite .12 .30
160 Adam Graves .05 .15
161 Kenny Jonsson .05 .15
162 Todd Marchant .05 .15
163 Jason Williams .05 .15
164 Joe Juneau .05 .15
165 Patrick Roy .75 2.00
166 Tie Domi .12 .30
167 Adrian Aucoin .05 .15
168 Dan Blackburn .12 .30
169 Vitali Yachmenev .05 .15
170 Derian Hatcher .05 .15
171 Mike Ribeiro .05 .15
172 Mike Van Ryn .05 .15
173 Brian Willsie .05 .15
174 Chris Phillips .05 .15
175 Jason York .05 .15
176 Kris Draper .05 .15
177 Sean Burke .12 .30
178 Kevin Dineen .05 .15
179 Toni Lydman .05 .15
180 Artem Chubarov .05 .15
181 Trevor Letowski .05 .15
182 P.J. Axelsson .05 .15
183 Lubos Bartecko .05 .15
184 Mike Knuble .05 .15
185 Ossi Vaananen .05 .15
186 David Vyborny .05 .15
187 Kevyn Adams .05 .15
188 Johan Hedberg .12 .30
189 Brent Gilchrist .05 .15
190 Eric Boguniecki .05 .15
191 Marcus Ragnarsson .05 .15
192 Eric Weinrich .05 .15
193 Yannick Tremblay .05 .15
194 Mike Keane .05 .15
195 Chad Kilger .05 .15
196 Glen Metropolit .05 .15
197 Stephane Quintal .05 .15
198 Tyler Arnason .12 .30
199 Jan Bulis .05 .15
200 Patric Kjellberg .05 .15
201 Eric Lindros .15 .40
202 Markus Naslund .12 .30
203 Ziggy Palffy .15 .40
204 Brian Rafalski .05 .15
205 Miroslav Satan .12 .30
206 Marian Gaborik .30 .75
207 Tony Amonte .12 .30
208 Tomas Kaberle .05 .15
209 Ray Whitney .05 .15
210 Ron Francis .12 .30
211 Steve Sullivan .05 .15
212 Bryan Berard .05 .15
213 Mark Recchi .12 .30
214 Vincent Damphousse .05 .15
215 Richard Zednik .05 .15
216 Ed Jovanovski .12 .30
217 Valeri Bure .05 .15
218 Jozef Stumpel .05 .15
219 Alexei Zhamnov .05 .15
220 Mariusz Czerkawski .05 .15
221 John Grahame .12 .30
222 Mark Parrish .05 .15
223 Mike York .05 .15
224 Chris Osgood .12 .30
225 Scott Young .05 .15
226 Derek Morris .05 .15
227 Brendan Morrison .12 .30
228 Mike Sillinger .05 .15
229 Todd White .05 .15
230 Tom Poti .05 .15
231 Sergei Zholtok .05 .15
232 Kip Miller .05 .15
233 Pasi Nurminen .05 .15
234 Michal Handzus .05 .15
235 Henrik Sedin .05 .15
236 Phil Housley .05 .15
237 Jeff Halpern .05 .15
238 Stephen Weiss .05 .15
239 Pavel Kubina .05 .15
240 Luc Robitaille .12 .30
241 Michal Rozsival .05 .15
242 Martin Gelinas .05 .15
243 Curtis Brown .05 .15
244 Steve Passmore .05 .15
245 Tony Hrkac .05 .15
246 Alexei Yashin .05 .15
247 Richard Park .05 .15
248 Viktor Kozlov .05 .15
249 Andrei Markov .05 .15
250 Dan Boyle .05 .15
251 Paul Mara .05 .15
252 Jeremy Roenick .20 .50
253 Randy McKay .05 .15
254 Tommy Salo .12 .30
255 Jaroslav Spacek .05 .15
256 Adam Foote .12 .30
257 Martin Erat .05 .15
258 Jamal Mayers .05 .15
259 Chris Neil .05 .15
260 Mark Bell .05 .15
261 Matt Bradley .05 .15
262 Boris Mironov .05 .15
263 Trevor Kidd .12 .30
264 Dave Andreychuk .05 .15
265 Jaroslav Modry .05 .15
266 Vaclav Varada .05 .15
267 Marty Murray .05 .15
268 Ben Clymer .05 .15
269 Mikael Renberg .05 .15
270 Sean Hill .05 .15
271 Eric Belanger .05 .15
272 Andy McDonald .05 .15
273 Miikka Kiprusoff .12 .30
274 Brad May .05 .15
275 Dan LaCouture .05 .15
276 Andy Sutton .05 .15
277 Kirk Maltby .05 .15
278 Kirk Muller .05 .15
279 Alex Tanguay .12 .30
280 Bryan Marchment .05 .15
281 Jason Smith .05 .15
282 Dan Bylsma .05 .15
283 Jyrki Lumme .05 .15
284 Chris Gratton .05 .15
285 Chris Clark .05 .15
286 Scott Walker .05 .15
287 Alexander Khavanov .05 .15
288 Marc Chouinard .05 .15
289 Rob DiMaio .05 .15
290 Sean Avery .05 .15
291 Tommy Albelin .05 .15
292 Jean-Francois Fortin .05 .15
293 Matthew Barnaby .05 .15
294 Jan Hrdina .05 .15
295 Harold Druken .05 .15

296 Jody Hull .05 .15
297 Shjon Podein .05 .15
298 Jochen Hecht .05 .15
299 Glen Murray .05 .15
300 Sergei Brylin .05 .15
301 Pavel Bure .15 .40
302 Mike Comrie .12 .30
303 Mario Lemieux 1.00 2.50
304 Mats Sundin .15 .40
305 Jason Blake .05 .15
306 Robert Lang .05 .15
307 Bill Guerin .12 .30
308 Brad Richards .12 .30
309 Radek Bonk .05 .15
310 Craig Conroy .05 .15
311 Brett Hull .20 .50
312 Dainius Zubrus .05 .15
313 Petr Sykora .05 .15
314 Craig Rivet .05 .15
315 Andrew Brunette .05 .15
316 Kristian Huselius .05 .15
317 Rod Brind'Amour .12 .30
318 Tim Connolly .05 .15
319 Anson Carter .12 .30
320 Cory Stillman .05 .15
321 Teppo Numminen .05 .15
322 Jason Arnott .05 .15
323 Oleg Petrov .05 .15
324 Shawn McEachern .05 .15
325 Scott Thornton .05 .15
326 Oleg Kvasha .05 .15
327 Byron Dafoe .12 .30
328 Glen Wesley .05 .15
329 Eric Messier .05 .15
330 Brad Lukowich .05 .15
331 Jon Klemm .05 .15
332 Tomas Vokoun .12 .30
333 Scott Hannan .05 .15
334 Mike Eastwood .05 .15
335 Peter Skudra .05 .15
336 Roman Hamrlik .05 .15
337 Josef Vasicek .05 .15
338 Bryan McCabe .05 .15
339 Igor Larionov .05 .15
340 Darryl Sydor .05 .15
341 Mike Fisher .05 .15
342 Greg Johnson .05 .15
343 Danny Markov .05 .15
344 Frantisek Kaberle .05 .15
345 Michal Grosek .05 .15
346 Ivan Novoseltsev .05 .15
347 Marty McInnis .05 .15
348 Eric Desjardins .05 .15
349 Jason Wiemer .05 .15
350 Fredrik Olausson .05 .15
351 Bill Muckalt .05 .15
352 Ville Nieminen .05 .15
353 Taylor Pyatt .05 .15
354 Mike Rathje .05 .15
355 Trent Klatt .05 .15
356 Bret Hedican .05 .15
357 Tyler Wright .05 .15
358 Greg deVries .05 .15
359 Lubomir Sekeras .05 .15
360 Jonas Hoglund .05 .15
361 Mike Grier .05 .15
362 Wade Redden .05 .15
363 Nik Antropov .05 .15
364 Philippe Boucher .05 .15
365 Clarke Wilm .05 .15
366 Erik Rasmussen .05 .15
367 Per Svartvadet .05 .15
368 Felix Potvin .15 .40
369 Igor Korolev .05 .15
370 Vladimir Malakhov .05 .15
371 Mathieu Dandenault .05 .15
372 Brent Johnson .12 .30
373 Shaun Van Allen .05 .15
374 Scott Pellerin .05 .15
375 Radim Vrbata .05 .15
376 Mike Johnson .05 .15
377 Mikael Samuelsson .05 .15
378 Radek Martinek .05 .15
379 Curtis Joseph .15 .40
380 Craig Johnson .05 .15
381 Kelly Buchberger .05 .15
382 Todd Harvey .05 .15
383 Jason Chimera .05 .15
384 Claude Lapointe .05 .15
385 Marc Denis .12 .30
386 Lyle Odelein .05 .15
387 Dimitri Kalinin .05 .15
388 Scott Nichol .05 .15
389 Tom Fitzgerald .05 .15
390 Darius Kasparaitis .12 .30
391 Bryan Allen .05 .15
392 Jamie McLennan .05 .15
393 Martin St. Louis .12 .30
394 Landon Wilson .05 .15
395 Kim Johnsson .05 .15
396 Pavel Trnka .05 .15
397 P.J. Stock .05 .15
398 Alexandre Daigle .05 .15
399 Andrew Cassels .05 .15
400 Wayne Primeau .05 .15
401 Theo Fleury .05 .15
402 Cliff Ronning .05 .15
403 Sergei Samsonov .12 .30
404 Jean-Francois Labbe .12 .30
405 Darcy Tucker .05 .15
406 Daniel Briere .05 .15
407 Marc Savard .05 .15
408 Blake Sloan .05 .15
409 Sergei Berezin .05 .15
410 Ron Tugnutt .12 .30
411 Jocelyn Thibault .12 .30
412 Jose Theodore .20 .50
413 Sheldon Keefe .05 .15
414 Yanic Perreault .05 .15
415 Jason Krog .05 .15
416 John Madden .05 .15
417 Jonathan Girard .05 .15
418 Niclas Havelid .05 .15
419 Daniel Alfredsson .15 .40
420 Dean McAmmond .05 .15
421 Brenden Morrow .12 .30
422 Dimitri Yushkevich .05 .15
423 Alexei Zhitnik .05 .15
424 Jani Hurme .12 .30
425 Antti Laaksonen .05 .15
426 Corey Schwab .12 .30
427 Geoff Sanderson .05 .15
428 Brian Leetch .12 .30
429 Brad Tapper .05 .15
430 Derek Armstrong .05 .15
431 Evgeni Nabokov .12 .30
432 Jan Hlavac .05 .15
433 Bob Boughner .05 .15
434 Andreas Johansson .05 .15
435 Jeff Odgers .05 .15
436 Teemu Selanne .15 .40
437 Pavol Demitra .05 .15
438 Tomas Holmstrom .05 .15
439 Jeff Friesen .05 .15
440 Eric Boulton .05 .15
441 Oleg Saprykin .05 .15
442 Chris Chelios .15 .40
443 Stephane Yelle .05 .15
444 Martin Havlat .12 .30
445 Jeff O'Neill .05 .15
446 Dan Cloutier .12 .30
447 Nikolai Khabibulin .15 .40
448 Grant Marshall .05 .15
449 Pierre Turgeon .12 .30
450 Jamie Langenbrunner .12 .30
451 Steve Staios .05 .15
452 Alexei Morozov .05 .15
453 Shawn Horcoff .05 .15
454 Adam Mair .05 .15
455 Ruslan Salei .05 .15
456 Robert Esche .05 .15
457 Brent Sopel .05 .15
458 Aaron Ward .05 .15
459 Martin Biron .12 .30
460 Brian Boucher .12 .30
461 Richard Jackman .05 .15
462 Jarkko Ruutu .05 .15
463 Bates Battaglia .05 .15
464 Sergei Gonchar .05 .15
465 Martin Brodeur .40 1.00
466 Patrik Stefan .05 .15
467 Scott Stevens .12 .30
468 Gary Roberts .05 .15
469 Shane Doan .05 .15
470 Keith Tkachuk .15 .40
471 Brendan Witt .05 .15
472 Todd Fedoruk .05 .15
473 Patrick Lalime .12 .30
474 Mike Dunham .12 .30
475 Ulf Dahlen .05 .15
476 Olli Jokinen .12 .30
477 Garth Snow .05 .15
478 Sean Pronger .05 .15
479 Milan Kraft .05 .15
480 Aki Berg .05 .15
481 Steve Shields .12 .30
482 Sami Salo .05 .15
483 Brendan Shanahan .15 .40
484 Niclas Wallin .05 .15
485 Sandy McCarthy .05 .15
486 Olaf Kolzig .12 .30
487 Cory Sarich .05 .15
488 Zac Bierk .12 .30
489 Luke Richardson .05 .15
490 Colin White .05 .15
491 Reed Low .05 .15
492 Joe Thornton .25 .60
493 Rob Blake .12 .30
494 Bobby Holik .05 .15
495 Chris Simon .05 .15
496 Wade Belak .05 .15
497 Eric Daze .05 .15
498 Hal Gill .05 .15
499 Chris Pronger .12 .30
500 Steve Yzerman .75 2.00
501 Justin Papineau .05 .15
502 Alex Auld .05 .15
503 Niko Kapanen .05 .15
504 Michael Cammalleri .05 .15
505 Sebastien Charpentier .05 .15
506 Stanislav Chistov .50 1.25
507 Jiri Bicek .05 .15
508 Ryan Flinn .05 .15
509 Christian Berglund .05 .15
510 Vernon Fiddler .05 .15
511 Andrej Nedorost .05 .15
512 Lynn Loyns .05 .15
513 Niko Dimitrakos .05 .15
514 Ryan Bayda .05 .15
515 Curtis Sanford .05 .15
516 Pierre-Marc Bouchard .50 1.25
517 Sebastien Caron .12 .30
518 Steve Ott .30 .75
519 Dan Snyder .05 .15
520 Mattias Weinhandl .05 .15
521 Henrik Zetterberg .75 2.00
522 Tomas Surovy .05 .15
523 Ales Hemsky .75 2.00
524 Jamie Lundmark .05 .15
525 Barret Jackman .12 .30
526 Toni Dahlman .05 .15
527 Jaroslav Bednar .05 .15
528 Ales Pisa .05 .15
529 Joel Kwiatkowski .05 .15
530 Jan Lasak .05 .15
531 Jim Fahey .05 .15
532 Pavel Brendl .05 .15
533 Stephane Veilleux .05 .15
534 Vaclav Nedorost .05 .15
535 Tomas Malec .05 .15
536 Jeff Heerema .05 .15
537 Dmitri Bykov .05 .15
538 Dennis Seidenberg .05 .15
539 Jonathan Cheechoo .08 .20
540 Fernando Pisani .05 .15
541 Riku Hahl .05 .15
542 Jani Rita .05 .15
543 Jim Vandermeer .05 .15
544 Jordan Leopold .05 .15
545 Joe Corvo .05 .15
546 Ales Kotalik .05 .15
547 Ryan Miller .50 1.25
548 Tomas Kurka .05 .15
549 Arturs Irbe .12 .30
550 Radovan Somik .12 .30
551 Mathieu Garon .12 .30
552 Jesse Wallin .05 .15
553 Steve Eminger .05 .15
554 Jason Bacashihua .40 1.00
555 Ramzi Abid .05 .15
556 Marcel Hossa .05 .15
557 Rick Nash .75 2.00
558 Kris Vernarsky .05 .15
559 Brian Sutherby .05 .15
560 Adam Hall .05 .15
561 Eric Chouinard .05 .15
562 Henrik Tallinder .05 .15
563 Alexander Svitov .05 .15
564 Kurt Sauer .05 .15
565 Matt Walker .05 .15
566 Ray Emery .60 1.50
567 Eric Godard .05 .15
568 Jay Bouwmeester .60 1.50
569 Kip Brennan .05 .15
570 Mike Komisarek .05 .15
571 Alex Henry .05 .15
572 Scottie Upshall .30 .75
573 Chuck Kobasew .30 .75
574 Anton Volchenkov .05 .15
575 Carlo Colaiacovo .05 .15
576 Pascal Leclaire .50 1.25
577 Jason Spezza 1.00 2.50
578 Jeff Taffe .05 .15
579 Alexander Frolov .50 1.25
580 Shaone Morrisonn .05 .15
581 Ron Hainsey .05 .15
582 Alexei Smirnov .05 .15
583 Andrew Raycroft .05 .15
584 Brooks Orpik .05 .15
585 Dan Focht .05 .15
586 Fedor Fedorov .05 .15
587 Ivan Huml .05 .15
588 Jared Aulin .05 .15
589 Justin Mapletoft .05 .15
590 Karel Pilar .05 .15
591 Kyle Wanvig .05 .15
592 Lee Goren .05 .15
593 Cristobal Huet 1.00 2.50
594 Mikael Tellqvist .12 .30
595 Igor Radulov .05 .15
596 Kirill Safronov .05 .15
597 Jerred Smithson .05 .15
598 Vesa Toskala .05 .15
599 Dick Tarnstrom .05 .15
600 Martin Gerber .12 .30

2003-04 Pacific Complete

This 600-card super set was inserted into various Pacific products throughout the season. A red parallel set was also created and available randomly.

*RED: 6X TO 15X BASE HI
*RED ROOKIES: 3X TO 8X
RED PRINT RUN 99 SER.#'d SETS

1 Donald Brashear .05 .15
2 Chris Gratton .05 .15
3 Alyn McCauley .05 .15
4 Mats Sundin .15 .40
5 Brenden Morrow .12 .30
6 Jaroslav Modry .05 .15
7 Brian Rafalski .05 .15
8 Mike Grier .05 .15
9 Marco Sturm .05 .15
10 Mike Comrie .12 .30
11 Derek Morris .05 .15
12 Scott Niedermayer .05 .15
13 Dainius Zubrus .05 .15
14 Jason Krog .05 .15
15 Brian Rolston .05 .15
16 Dany Heatley .20 .50
17 Dean McAmmond .05 .15
18 Glen Murray .05 .15
19 Adam Mair .05 .15
20 Tony Amonte .12 .30
21 David Vyborny .05 .15
22 Tyler Wright .05 .15
23 Doug Gilmour .12 .30
24 Andy Sutton .05 .15
25 Ivan Huml .05 .15
26 Olli Jokinen .12 .30
27 Kimmo Timonen .05 .15
28 Donald Audette .05 .15
29 Martin St. Louis .12 .30
30 Martin Skoula .05 .15
31 Wade Redden .05 .15
32 Kyle Calder .05 .15
33 Shawn Bates .05 .15
34 Brendan Shanahan .05 .15
35 Martin Havlat .12 .30
36 Radim Vrbata .05 .15
37 Eric Daze .12 .30
38 J-P Dumont .05 .15
39 Scott Mellanby .05 .15
40 Brad Richards .12 .30
41 Jason Allison .05 .15
42 Rostislav Klesla .05 .15
43 Tyler Arnason .12 .30
44 Henrik Sedin .05 .15
45 Markus Naslund .15 .40
46 Daniel Sedin .05 .15
47 Niklas Sundstrom .05 .15
48 Rod Brind'Amour .12 .30
49 Martin Straka .05 .15
50 Craig Conroy .05 .15
51 Tomas Kaberle .05 .15
52 Robyn Regehr .05 .15
53 Scott Hartnell .05 .15
54 Sergei Zholtok .05 .15
55 Pierre Turgeon .12 .30
56 Mike Ricci .05 .15
57 Brad Tapper .05 .15
58 Martin Gelinas .05 .15
59 Philippe Boucher .05 .15
60 Alex Tanguay .12 .30
61 Niclas Havelid .05 .15
62 Kristian Huselius .05 .15
63 Dave Lowry .05 .15
64 Tim Connolly .12 .30
65 Robert Lang .05 .15
66 Taylor Pyatt .05 .15
67 Bryan Smolinski .05 .15
68 Keith Primeau .12 .30
69 Anson Carter .12 .30
70 Dallas Drake .05 .15
71 Curtis Brown .05 .15
72 Nik Antropov .05 .15
73 Aaron Ward .05 .15
74 Tie Domi .12 .30
75 Mike Leclerc .05 .15
76 Tom Poti .05 .15
77 Kris Draper .05 .15
78 Joe Juneau .05 .15
79 Milan Kraft .05 .15
80 Marty Reasoner .05 .15
81 Shaun Van Allen .05 .15
82 Kenny Jonsson .05 .15
83 Alexander Khavanov .05 .15
84 Pavel Kubina .05 .15
85 Vladimir Malakhov .05 .15
86 Willie Mitchell .05 .15
87 Jason Smith .05 .15
88 Radoslav Suchy .05 .15
89 Mattias Timander .05 .15
90 Eric Weinrich .05 .15
91 Andrei Zyuzin .05 .15
92 Christian Berglund .05 .15
93 Jamie Lundmark .05 .15
94 Kirk Maltby .05 .15
95 Brian Savage .05 .15
96 Petr Schastlivy .05 .15
97 Ian Laperriere .05 .15
98 Alexei Morozov .05 .15
99 Justin Williams .05 .15
100 Jason Chimera .05 .15
101 Patrick Marleau .12 .30
102 Ryan Smyth .05 .15
103 Michal Handzus .05 .15
104 Brett Hull .20 .50
105 Tom Fitzgerald .05 .15
106 Ben Clymer .05 .15
107 Rick Nash .20 .50
108 Scott Walker .05 .15
109 Rob Niedermayer .05 .15
110 Sergei Gonchar .05 .15
111 Chris Chelios .15 .40
112 Brian Leetch .12 .30
113 David Legwand .12 .30
114 Sean Hill .05 .15
115 Brad Isbister .05 .15
116 Pavel Datsyuk .15 .40
117 Alexei Yashin .05 .15
118 Jere Lehtinen .12 .30
119 Jason Spezza .15 .40
120 Daniel Briere .05 .15
121 Andreas Dackell .05 .15
122 Shane Doan .05 .15
123 Josef Vasicek .05 .15
124 Dan McGillis .05 .15
125 Geoff Sanderson .05 .15
126 Teemu Selanne .15 .40
127 Andreas Johansson .05 .15
128 Al MacInnis .12 .30
129 Ruslan Fedotenko .05 .15
130 Scott Stevens .12 .30
131 Frantisek Kaberle .05 .15
132 Toni Lydman .05 .15
133 Kip Miller .05 .15
134 Dan Hinote .05 .15
135 Mike Modano .25 .60
136 Scott Thornton .05 .15
137 Eric Lindros .15 .40
138 Grant Marshall .05 .15
139 Vincent Damphousse .05 .15
140 Mario Lemieux 1.00 2.50
141 Patrice Brisebois .05 .15
142 Sergei Samsonov .12 .30
143 Sergei Zubov .05 .15
144 Alexei Zhamnov .05 .15
145 Oleg Kvasha .05 .15
146 Brendan Morrison .12 .30
147 Jason York .05 .15
148 Eric Boguniecki .05 .15
149 Henrik Zetterberg .15 .40
150 Nick Boynton .05 .15
151 Trevor Linden .05 .15
152 Joe Nieuwendyk .12 .30
153 Filip Kuba .05 .15
154 Matthew Barnaby .05 .15
155 Ales Hemsky .12 .30
156 Jan Bulis .05 .15
157 Yannick Tremblay .05 .15
158 Andre Roy .05 .15
159 Jaroslav Bednar .05 .15
160 Stephane Yelle .05 .15
161 Paul Mara .05 .15
162 Sandis Ozolinsh .05 .15
163 Trent Klatt .05 .15
164 Brian Gionta .05 .15
165 Jaroslav Spacek .05 .15
166 Rob Blake .12 .30
167 Ziggy Palffy .12 .30
168 Chris Clark .05 .15
169 John LeClair .15 .40
170 Landon Wilson .05 .15
171 Mark Bell .05 .15
172 Simon Gagne .15 .40
173 Michael Nylander .05 .15
174 Andy McDonald .05 .15
175 Todd Bertuzzi .15 .40
176 Dick Tarnstrom .05 .15
177 Radek Dvorak .05 .15
178 Antti Laaksonen .05 .15
179 Steve Rucchin .05 .15
180 Steve Sullivan .05 .15
181 Viktor Kozlov .05 .15
182 Miroslav Satan .12 .30
183 Lubomir Visnovsky .05 .15
184 Stephen Weiss .05 .15
185 John Madden .05 .15
186 Mike Knuble .05 .15
187 Michael Peca .05 .15
188 Adam Foote .05 .15
189 Steve McKenna .05 .15
190 Adam Deadmarsh .05 .15
191 Barret Jackman .12 .30
192 Marian Gaborik .30 .75
193 Zdeno Chara .05 .15
194 Chris Drury .12 .30
195 Sami Salo .05 .15
196 Daniel Tjarnqvist .05 .15
197 Vaclav Varada .05 .15
198 Shawn McEachern .05 .15
199 Kevyn Adams .05 .15
200 Roman Hamrlik .05 .15
201 Keith Carney .05 .15
202 Scott Gomez .05 .15
203 Marcus Nilsson .05 .15
204 Tomas Surovy .05 .15
205 Vladimir Orszagh .05 .15
206 Owen Nolan .12 .30
207 Matt Cooke .05 .15
208 Jeremy Roenick .20 .50
209 Andrew Cassels .05 .15
210 Jim Dowd .05 .15
211 Todd Marchant .05 .15
212 Joe Sakic .30 .75
213 Krystofer Kolanos .05 .15
214 Chris Phillips .05 .15
215 Stanislav Chistov .05 .15
216 Steve Yzerman .75 2.00
217 Jamie Langenbrunner .05 .15
218 Daymond Langkow .12 .30
219 Jarome Iginla .20 .50
220 Darryl Sydor .05 .15
221 Mark Messier .15 .40
222 Richard Matvichuk .05 .15
223 Jay Bouwmeester .05 .15
224 Sheldon Souray .05 .15
225 Niklas Hagman .05 .15
226 Bill Lindsay .05 .15
227 Ray Whitney .05 .15
228 Jordan Leopold .05 .15
229 Daniel Alfredsson .12 .30
230 Kyle McLaren .05 .15
231 Vincent Lecavalier .15 .40
232 Bobby Holik .05 .15
233 Adam Hall .05 .15
234 Mark Recchi .05 .15
235 Alexander Mogilny .12 .30
236 Alexei Zhitnik .05 .15
237 Jay McKee .05 .15
238 Jaromir Jagr .25 .60
239 Ladislav Nagy .05 .15
240 Radek Bonk .12 .30
241 Mike Van Ryn .05 .15
242 Joe Thornton .20 .50
243 Peter Bondra .12 .30
244 Keith Tkachuk .15 .40
245 Luc Robitaille .12 .30
246 Alexandre Daigle .05 .15
247 Jason Blake .05 .15
248 Jonathan Cheechoo .08 .20
249 Alexander Frolov .05 .15
250 Danny Markov .05 .15
251 Oleg Saprykin .05 .15
252 Maxim Afinogenov .05 .15
253 Alexander Karpovtsev .05 .15
254 Peter Forsberg .60 1.50
255 Espen Knutsen .05 .15
256 Erik Cole .05 .15
257 Dan Boyle .05 .15
258 Marc Savard .05 .15
259 Adrian Aucoin .05 .15
260 Brian Holzinger .05 .15
261 Cory Stillman .05 .15
262 Mattias Ohlund .05 .15
263 Petr Sykora .12 .30
264 Jeff Halpern .05 .15
265 Patrik Stefan .05 .15
266 Jeff Jillson .05 .15
267 Mariusz Czerkawski .05 .15
268 Jeff O'Neill .05 .15
269 Brad Stuart .05 .15
270 Ron Francis .12 .30
271 Mike Johnson .05 .15
272 Richard Park .05 .15
273 Yanic Perreault .05 .15
274 Eric Belanger .05 .15
275 Stu Barnes .05 .15
276 Nathan Dempsey .05 .15
277 Bryan McCabe .05 .15
278 Andrew Brunette .05 .15
279 Ville Nieminen .05 .15
280 Greg Johnson .05 .15
281 Alex Kovalev .12 .30
282 Raffi Torres .05 .15
283 Drake Berehowsky .05 .15
284 Steve McCarthy .05 .15
285 Martin Erat .05 .15
286 Pavol Demitra .12 .30
287 Saku Koivu .15 .40
288 Milan Hejduk .15 .40
289 Sami Kapanen .12 .30
290 Nicklas Lidstrom .15 .40
291 Eric Brewer .05 .15
292 Martin Lapointe .05 .15
293 Andrei Markov .05 .15
294 Doug Weight .12 .30
295 Jason Arnott .12 .30
296 Mike York .05 .15
297 Jay Pandolfo .05 .15
298 Ed Jovanovski .12 .30
299 Bill Guerin .12 .30
300 Petr Cajanek .05 .15
301 Shawn Horcoff .05 .15
302 Ales Kotalik .05 .15
303 Chris Dingman .05 .15
304 Arron Asham .05 .15
305 Steve Staios .05 .15
306 Artem Chubarov .05 .15
307 Karlis Skrastins .05 .15
308 Nick Schultz .05 .15
309 Rico Fata .05 .15
310 Jan Hrdina .05 .15
311 Brendan Witt .05 .15
312 Lyle Odelein .05 .15
313 Pascal Dupuis .05 .15
314 Paul Kariya .15 .40
315 Petr Nedved .05 .15
316 Tim Taylor .05 .15
317 Ethan Moreau .05 .15
318 Shean Donovan .05 .15
319 Ruslan Salei .05 .15
320 Rem Murray .05 .15
321 Eric Nickulas .05 .15
322 Rob DiMaio .05 .15
323 Steven Reinprecht .05 .15
324 Cory Cross .05 .15
325 Kim Johnsson .05 .15
326 Chris Simon .05 .15
327 Gary Roberts .05 .15
328 Ken Klee .05 .15
329 Krzysztof Oliwa .05 .15
330 Marian Hossa .15 .40
331 Valeri Bure .05 .15
332 Bret Hedican .05 .15
333 Pavel Trnka .05 .15
334 Darcy Tucker .05 .15
335 Peter Schaefer .05 .15
336 Sergei Brylin .05 .15
337 Hal Gill .05 .15
338 Jason Woolley .05 .15
339 Mike Rathje .05 .15
340 Marty Murray .05 .15
341 Todd White .05 .15
342 Brent Sopel .05 .15
343 Glen Wesley .05 .15
344 Jozef Stumpel .05 .15
345 Scott Nichol .05 .15
346 Derrick Walser .05 .15
347 Marc Bergevin .05 .15
348 Richard Zednik .05 .15
349 Mike Ribeiro .05 .15
350 Mike Eastwood .05 .15
351 Trevor Letowski .05 .15
352 Fredrik Modin .05 .15
353 Mark Parrish .05 .15
354 Sandy McCarthy .05 .15
355 Tomas Holmstrom .05 .15
356 Dmitri Kalinin .05 .15
357 Janne Niinimaa .05 .15
358 Dave Andreychuk .12 .30
359 Boyd Devereaux .05 .15
360 Sergei Fedorov .20 .50
361 Josef Melichar .05 .15
362 Stephane Quintal .05 .15
363 Lasse Pirjeta .05 .15
364 Denis Arkhipov .05 .15
365 Matt Cullen .05 .15
366 Teppo Numminen .05 .15
367 Ilya Kovalchuk .20 .50
368 Reed Low .05 .15
369 Jochen Hecht .05 .15
370 Martin Rucinsky .05 .15
371 Mark Eaton .05 .15
372 Nils Ekman .05 .15
373 Slava Kozlov .05 .15
374 Scott Young .05 .15
375 Mathieu Schneider .05 .15
376 Scott Hannan .05 .15
377 Brad May .05 .15
378 Jeff Friesen .05 .15
379 P.J. Axelsson .05 .15
380 Brian Sutherby .05 .15
381 David Tanabe .05 .15
382 Pierre-Marc Bouchard .05 .15
383 Steve Konowalchuk .05 .15
384 Chris Pronger .12 .30
385 Craig Rivet .05 .15
386 Eric Desjardins .05 .15
387 Jody Shelley .05 .15
388 Vaclav Prospal .05 .15
389 Aaron Miller .05 .15
390 Deron Quint .05 .15
391 Joel Kwiatkowski .05 .15
392 Branko Radivojevic .05 .15
393 Niko Kapanen .05 .15
394 Wayne Primeau .05 .15
395 Patrik Elias .12 .30
396 Ronald Petrovicky .05 .15
397 Mike Cammalleri .05 .15
398 Bryan Berard .05 .15
399 Jason Doig .05 .15
400 Marcus Ragnarsson .05 .15
401 Aaron Downey .05 .15
402 Byron Dafoe .12 .30
403 Jean-Sebastien Giguere .12 .30
404 Dwayne Roloson .12 .30
405 Marc-Andre Fleury 2.50 6.00
406 Ray Emery .12 .30
407 Derek Armstrong .05 .15
408 Randy Robitaille .05 .15
409 Manny Fernandez .12 .30
410 Jeff Hackett .12 .30
411 Nikolai Khabibulin .15 .40
412 Tomas Vokoun .12 .30
413 Chris Neil .05 .15
414 Andrei Nikolishin .05 .15
415 Garth Snow .12 .30
416 Marty Turco .15 .40
417 Roberto Luongo .20 .50
418 Mikael Tellqvist .12 .30
419 Chris Osgood .12 .30
420 Jocelyn Thibault .12 .30
421 Olaf Kolzig .12 .30
422 Tommy Salo .12 .30
423 Corey Schwab .12 .30
424 Johan Hedberg .12 .30
425 Travis Green .05 .15
426 Pascal Leclaire .12 .30
427 Craig Andersson .12 .30
428 John Grahame .12 .30
429 Pasi Nurminen .12 .30
430 Trevor Kidd .12 .30
431 Scott Lachance .12 .30
432 Brent Johnson .12 .30
433 Jamie Storr .12 .30
434 Miikka Kiprusoff .12 .30
435 Cristobal Huet .12 .30
436 Jose Theodore .20 .50
437 Ty Conklin .12 .30
438 Curtis Joseph .15 .40
439 Jussi Markkanen .12 .30
440 Patrick Lalime .12 .30
441 Vesa Toskala .12 .30
442 Dan Cloutier .12 .30
443 Kevin Weekes .12 .30
444 Peter Worrell .05 .15
445 Zac Bierk .12 .30
446 Evgeni Nabokov .12 .30
447 Martin Biron .12 .30
448 Rick DiPietro .12 .30
449 Ed Belfour .15 .40
450 Martin Gerber .12 .30
451 Reinhard Divis .12 .30
452 Brian Finley .12 .30
453 Jason Bacashihua .12 .30
454 Mika Noronen .12 .30
455 Scott Clemmensen .12 .30
456 Brian Boucher .12 .30
457 Jason LaBarbera .12 .30
458 Mike Dunham .12 .30
459 Sean Burke .12 .30
460 Felix Potvin .15 .40
461 Martin Brodeur .75 2.00
462 Sebastien Caron .12 .30
463 Rob Zamuner .05 .15
464 Igor Larionov .05 .15
465 Andrew Raycroft .12 .30
466 Mathieu Garon .05 .15
467 Roman Turek .12 .30
468 Steve Passmore .12 .30
469 Chris Mason .05 .15
470 Jean-Sebastien Aubin .12 .30
471 Milan Hnilicka .12 .30
472 Steve Shields .12 .30
473 Arturs Irbe .12 .30
474 Ilja Bryzgalov .12 .30
475 Roman Cechmanek .12 .30
476 Steve Ott .05 .15
477 Mattias Weinhandl .05 .15
478 Brent Krahn .05 .15
479 Jamie McLennan .12 .30
480 Michael Leighton .12 .30
481 Ryan Miller .12 .30
482 Dominik Hasek .30 .75
483 Marc Denis .12 .30
484 Rastislav Stana .12 .30
485 Alex Auld .12 .30
486 Fred Brathwaite .12 .30
487 Martin Prusek .12 .30
488 Robert Esche .12 .30
489 Sebastien Charpentier .12 .30
490 David Aebischer .12 .30
491 Manny Legace .12 .30
492 Philippe Sauve .12 .30
493 Bob Boughner .05 .15
494 Maxime Ouellet .12 .30
495 Ron Tugnutt .12 .30
496 J.P. Vigier .05 .15
497 Steve Thomas .12 .30
498 Manny Malhotra .05 .15
499 Dany Sabourin .05 .15
500 Pavel Brendl .05 .15
501 Derek Roy .40 1.00
502 Lawrence Nycholat .20 .50
503 Simon Gamache .20 .50
504 Dan Fritsche .20 .50
505 Chris Higgins 1.25 3.00
506 Pierre Hedin .20 .50
507 Marc-Andre Fleury 2.50 6.00
508 Tony Salmelainen .20 .50
509 Ryan Kesler .40 1.00
510 John-Michael Liles .40 1.00
511 Zbynek Michalek .20 .50
512 Trent Hunter .20 .50
513 Matthew Lombardi .20 .50
514 Matt Stajan 1.00 2.50
515 Gregory Campbell .20 .50
516 Chad Wiseman .20 .50
517 Konstantin Koltsov .20 .50
518 Joffrey Lupul .60 1.50
519 Jeff MacMillan .20 .50
520 Wade Brookbank .20 .50
521 Timofei Shishkanov .20 .50
522 Eric Staal 2.00 5.00
523 Nathan Horton 1.00 2.50
524 Julien Vauclair .20 .50
525 Tom Preissing .20 .50
526 Kent McDonell .20 .50
527 Antoine Vermette .20 .50
528 Anton Babchuk .20 .50
529 Grant McNeill .20 .50
530 Chris Hajt .20 .50
531 Burke Henry .20 .50
532 Kyle Rossiter .20 .50
533 Joni Pitkanen .40 1.00
534 Maxim Kondratiev .20 .50
535 Peter Sejna .20 .50
536 Sergei Zinovjev .20 .50
537 Nathan Robinson .20 .50
538 Tuomas Pihlman .20 .50
539 Lasse Kukkonen .20 .50
540 Tomas Plekanec .20 .50
541 Alexander Semin 1.25 3.00
542 Fredrik Sjostrom .20 .50
543 Kari Lehtonen 3.00 8.00
544 Matt Murley .20 .50
545 Dustin Brown .30 .75
546 Tuomo Ruutu 1.25 3.00
547 Dominic Moore .20 .50
548 Garnet Exelby .20 .50
549 Dan Hamhuis .30 .75
550 Ryan Malone 1.00 2.50
551 Milan Michalek 1.00 2.50
552 Aaron Johnson .20 .50
553 Matthew Spiller .20 .50
554 Christian Ehrhoff .20 .50
555 Doug Lynch .20 .50
556 Andrew Peters .20 .50
557 Aleksander Suglobov .20 .50

558 Chuck Kobasew .20 .50
559 Sean Bergenheim .20 .50
560 Jason Pominville .60 1.50
561 Andrew Hutchinson .20 .50
562 Garrett Burnett .20 .50
563 Nikolai Zherdev 1.25 3.00
564 Tony Martensson .20 .50
565 Antti Miettinen .20 .50
566 Scott Barney .20 .50
567 Jordin Tootoo 1.25 3.00
568 Brad Leeb .20 .50
569 Peter Sarno .20 .50
570 Jed Ortmeyer .40 1.00
571 Kyle Wellwood 1.00 2.50
572 Brent Krahn .40 1.00
573 Dmitri Afanasenkov .20 .50
574 Jarret Stoll .20 .50
575 Marek Zidlicky .20 .50
576 Karl Stewart .20 .50
577 Darryl Bootland .20 .50
578 Niklas Kronwall .20 .50
579 Paul Martin .20 .50
580 Adam Munro .20 .50
581 Pat Leahy .20 .50
582 Cody McCormick .20 .50
583 Jozef Balej .20 .50
584 Boyd Gordon .20 .50
585 Jason King .20 .50
586 Trevor Daley .40 1.00
587 Robert Schnabel .20 .50
588 Chris Kunitz .40 1.00
589 Mike Danton .05 .15
590 Mikhail Yakubov .20 .50
591 John Pohl .40 1.00
592 Brent Burns .40 1.00
593 Patrice Bergeron 1.50 4.00
594 Jiri Hudler .75 2.00
595 David Hale .20 .50
596 Travis Moen .40 1.00
597 Michael Ryder .40 1.00
598 Tim Gleason .20 .50
599 Christian Backman .40 1.00
600 Pavel Vorobiev .20 .50

1997-98 Pacific Dynagon

The 1997-98 Pacific Dynagon set was issued in one series totalling 156 cards and was distributed in three-card packs with a suggested retail price of $2.49. The fronts feature color action player photos printed on fully foiled and double etched cards. The backs carry a small circular player head photo and player information.

COMPLETE SET (156) 25.00 60.00
1 Brian Bellows .20 .50
2 Guy Hebert .30 .75
3 Paul Kariya .40 1.00
4 Steve Rucchin .20 .50
5 Teemu Selanne .40 1.00
6 Jason Allison .20 .50
7 Ray Bourque .60 1.50
8 Jim Carey .20 .50
9 Jozef Stumpel .20 .50
10 Dominik Hasek 1.00 2.50
11 Brian Holzinger .20 .50
12 Michael Peca .20 .50
13 Derek Plante .20 .50
14 Miroslav Satan .20 .50
15 Theo Fleury .20 .50
16 Jonas Hoglund .20 .50
17 Jarome Iginla .60 1.50
18 Trevor Kidd .30 .75
19 German Titov .20 .50
20 Sean Burke .30 .75
21 Andrew Cassels .20 .50
22 Keith Primeau .20 .50
23 Geoff Sanderson .20 .50
24 Tony Amonte .30 .75
25 Chris Chelios .40 1.00
26 Eric Daze .20 .50
27 Jeff Hackett .30 .75
28 Ethan Moreau .20 .50
29 Peter Forsberg .75 2.00
30 Valeri Kamensky .20 .50
31 Claude Lemieux .20 .50
32 Sandis Ozolinsh .20 .50
33 Patrick Roy 1.50 4.00
34 Joe Sakic 1.00 2.50
35 Derian Hatcher .20 .50
36 Jamie Langenbrunner .20 .50
37 Mike Modano .60 1.50
38 Joe Nieuwendyk .30 .75
39 Darryl Sydor .20 .50
40 Sergei Zubov .20 .50
41 Sergei Fedorov .60 1.50
42 Vladimir Konstantinov .30 .75
43 Chris Osgood .30 .75
44 Brendan Shanahan .40 1.00
45 Mike Vernon .20 .50
46 Steve Yzerman 1.25 3.00
47 Kelly Buchberger .20 .50
48 Mike Grier .20 .50
49 Curtis Joseph .40 1.00
50 Rem Murray .20 .50
51 Ryan Smyth .30 .75
52 Doug Weight .30 .75
53 Ed Jovanovski .20 .50
54 Scott Mellanby .20 .50
55 Ray Sheppard .20 .50
56 Robert Svehla .20 .50
57 John Vanbiesbrouck .30 .75
58 Rob Blake .30 .75
59 Ray Ferraro .20 .50
60 Dimitri Khristich .20 .50
61 Vladimir Tsyplakov .20 .50
62 Vincent Damphousse .20 .50
63 Saku Koivu .40 1.00
64 Mark Recchi .30 .75
65 Stephane Richer .20 .50
66 Jocelyn Thibault .30 .75
67 Dave Andreychuk .20 .50
68 Martin Brodeur 1.25 3.00
69 Doug Gilmour .30 .75
70 Bobby Holik .20 .50
71 John MacLean .20 .50
72 Bryan Berard .20 .50
73 Travis Green .20 .50
74 Zigmund Palffy .30 .75
75 Tommy Salo .30 .75
76 Bryan Smolinski .20 .50
77 Adam Graves .20 .50
78 Wayne Gretzky 2.00 5.00
79 Alexei Kovalev .20 .50
80 Brian Leetch .40 1.00
81 Mark Messier .40 1.00
82 Mike Richter .40 1.00
83 Daniel Alfredsson .30 .75
84 Alexandre Daigle .20 .50
85 Wade Redden .20 .50
86 Damian Rhodes .20 .50
87 Alexei Yashin .20 .50
88 Rod Brind'Amour .30 .75
89 Ron Hextall .30 .75
90 John LeClair .30 .75
91 Eric Lindros .40 1.00
92 Janne Niinimaa .20 .50
93 Garth Snow .30 .75
94 Dainius Zubrus .20 .50
95 Mike Gartner .30 .75
96 Nikolai Khabibulin .30 .75
97 Jeremy Roenick .60 1.50
98 Keith Tkachuk .30 .75
99 Oleg Tverdovsky .20 .50
100 Ron Francis .30 .75
101 Kevin Hatcher .20 .50
102 Jaromir Jagr .75 2.00
103 Patrick Lalime .20 .50
104 Petr Nedved .20 .50
105 Jim Campbell .20 .50
106 Grant Fuhr .30 .75
107 Brett Hull .60 1.50
108 Pierre Turgeon .30 .75
109 Harry York .20 .50
110 Jeff Friesen .20 .50
111 Tony Granato .20 .50
112 Stephen Guolla RC .30 .75
113 Viktor Kozlov .20 .50
114 Owen Nolan .20 .50
115 Dino Ciccarelli .20 .50
116 John Cullen .20 .50
117 Chris Gratton .20 .50
118 Roman Hamrlik .20 .50
119 Daymond Langkow .20 .50
120 Sergei Berezin .20 .50
121 Wendel Clark .30 .75
122 Felix Potvin .40 1.00
123 Steve Sullivan .20 .50
124 Mats Sundin .40 1.00
125 Pavel Bure .40 1.00
126 Martin Gelinas .20 .50
127 Trevor Linden .30 .75
128 Kirk McLean .30 .75
129 Alexander Mogilny .30 .75
130 Peter Bondra .30 .75
131 Joe Juneau .20 .50
132 Steve Konowalchuk .20 .50
133 Adam Oates .30 .75
134 Bill Ranford .30 .75
135 P.Kariya/T.Selanne .40 1.00
136 D.Hasek/M.Peca .30 .75
137 Theo Fleury .60 1.50
Jarome Iginla
138 P.Forsberg/P.Roy 1.00 2.50
139 B.Shanahan/S.Yzerman 1.00 2.50
140 W.Gretzky/M.Messier 1.25 3.00
141 J.LeClair/E.Lindros .40 1.00
142 J.Jagr/P.Lalime .30 .75
143 J.Campbell/B.Hull .30 .75
144 S.Berezin/M.Sundin .30 .75
NNO Shawn Bates RC .30 .75
NNO Daniel Cleary .20 .50
NNO Marian Hossa RC 4.00 10.00
NNO Olli Jokinen RC 1.25 3.00
NNO Espen Knutsen RC .40 1.00
NNO Patrick Marleau .60 1.50
NNO Alyn McCauley .20 .50
NNO Mattias Ohlund .20 .50
NNO Chris Phillips .20 .50
NNO Erik Rasmussen .20 .50
NNO Sergei Samsonov .40 1.00
NNO Joe Thornton .75 2.00

1997-98 Pacific Dynagon Copper

Randomly inserted in hobby packs only at the rate of 2:37, this 156-card set is a parallel version of the base set and is distinguished by the copper foil enhancements.

*VETS: 3X TO 8X BASIC CARDS
*ROOKIES: 1.2X TO 3X BASIC CARDS

1997-98 Pacific Dynagon Dark Gray

Randomly inserted in hobby packs only at the rate of 2:37, this 156-card set is a parallel version of the base set and is distinguished by the gray foil enhancements.

*VETS: 3X TO 8X BASIC CARDS
*ROOKIES: 1.2X TO 3X BASIC CARDS

1997-98 Pacific Dynagon Emerald Green

Randomly inserted in Canadian packs only at the rate of 2:37, this 156-card set is a parallel version of the base set and is distinguished by the green foil enhancements.

*VETS: 3X TO 8X BASIC CARDS
*ROOKIES: 1.2X TO 3X BASIC CARDS

1997-98 Pacific Dynagon Ice Blue

Randomly inserted in packs at the rate of 1:73, this 156-card set is a parallel version of the base set and is distinguished by the blue foil enhancements.

*STARS: 12.5X TO 25X BASIC CARDS
*ROOKIES: 2.5X TO 6X BASIC CARDS

1997-98 Pacific Dynagon Red

Randomly inserted in packs at the rate of 2:37 Treat packs, this 156-card set is a parallel version of the base set and is distinguished by the red foil enhancements.

*VETS: 2.5X TO 6X BASIC CARDS
*ROOKIES: 1.5X TO 4X BASIC CARDS

1997-98 Pacific Dynagon Silver

Randomly inserted in retail packs only at the rate of 2:37, this 156-card set is a parallel version of the base set and is distinguished by the silver foil enhancements.

*VETS: 3X TO 8X BASIC CARDS
*ROOKIES: 1.2X TO 3X BASIC CARDS

1997-98 Pacific Dynagon Best Kept Secrets

Randomly inserted one per pack, this 110-card set features color action player photos of the top NHL players made to resemble a picture paper clipped to a file. A small slide-look version of the player's picture appears at the top. The backs carry player information and career statistics.

COMPLETE SET (110) 12.50 25.00
1 J.J. Daigneault .02 .10
2 Paul Kariya .15 .40
3 Dave Karpa .02 .10
4 Teemu Selanne .15 .40
5 Ray Bourque .25 .60
6 Jim Carey .08 .25
7 Davis Payne .02 .10
8 Paxton Schafer .02 .10
9 Bob Boughner .02 .10
10 Dominik Hasek .30 .75
11 Brad May .02 .10
12 Cale Hulse .02 .10
13 Jarome Iginla .20 .50
14 James Patrick .02 .10
15 Zarley Zalapski .02 .10
16 Jeff Brown .02 .10
17 Keith Primeau .08 .25
18 Steven Rice .02 .10
19 James Black .02 .10
20 Chris Chelios .15 .40
21 Steve Dubinsky .02 .10
22 Steve Smith .02 .10
23 Craig Billington .08 .25
24 Peter Forsberg .40 1.00
25 Jon Klemm .02 .10
26 Patrick Roy .75 2.00
27 Joe Sakic .30 .75
28 Neal Broten .02 .10
29 Richard Matvichuk .02 .10
30 Mike Modano .25 .60
31 Andy Moog .08 .25
32 Sergei Fedorov .30 .75
33 Kirk Maltby .02 .10
34 Brendan Shanahan .25 .60
35 Tim Taylor .02 .10
36 Steve Yzerman .75 2.00
37 Louie DeBrusk .02 .10
38 Joe Hulbig .02 .10
39 Ryan Smyth .08 .25
40 Mike Hough .02 .10
41 Jody Hull .02 .10
42 Paul Laus .08 .25
43 John Vanbiesbrouck .15 .40
44 Aki Berg .02 .10
45 Ray Ferraro .02 .10
46 Craig Johnson .02 .10
47 Ian Laperriere .02 .10
48 Vincent Damphousse .08 .25
49 Dave Manson .02 .10
50 Stephane Richer .08 .25
51 Craig Rivet .02 .10
52 Martin Brodeur .40 1.00
53 Jay Pandolfo .02 .10
54 Brian Rolston .02 .10
55 Doug Houda .02 .10
56 Brent Hughes .02 .10
57 Zigmund Palffy .15 .40
58 Adam Graves .08 .25
59 Wayne Gretzky 1.00 2.50
60 Chris Ferraro .02 .10
61 Glenn Healy .08 .25
62 Brian Leetch .15 .40
63 Mark Messier .15 .40
64 Radim Bicanek .02 .10
65 Philip Crowe .02 .10
66 Christer Olsson .02 .10
67 Jason York .02 .10
68 Rod Brind'Amour .08 .25
69 John Druce .02 .10
70 Daniel Lacroix .02 .10
71 John LeClair .20 .50
72 Eric Lindros .30 .75
73 Murray Baron .02 .10
74 Mike Gartner .08 .25
75 Brad McCrimmon .02 .10
76 Keith Tkachuk .15 .40
77 Jaromir Jagr .25 .60
78 Patrick Lalime .08 .25
79 Ian Moran .02 .10
80 Petr Nedved .08 .25
81 Brett Hull .20 .50
82 Robert Petrovicky .02 .10
83 Pierre Turgeon .08 .25
84 Trent Yawney .02 .10
85 Tim Hunter .02 .10
86 Marcus Ragnarsson .02 .10
87 Dody Wood .02 .10
88 Dino Ciccarelli .02 .10
89 Alexander Selivanov .02 .10
90 Jason Wiemer .02 .10
91 Sergei Berezin .08 .25
92 Felix Potvin .15 .40
93 Mats Sundin .15 .40
94 Craig Wolanin .02 .10
95 Pavel Bure .25 .60
96 Troy Crowder .02 .10
97 Dana Murzyn .02 .10
98 Gino Odjick .08 .25
99 Craig Berube .02 .10
100 Peter Bondra .15 .40
101 Mike Eagles .02 .10
102 Andrei Nikolishin .02 .10
103 Paul Kariya .15 .40
104 Dominik Hasek .30 .75
105 Michael Peca .02 .10
106 M.Brodeur/M.Dunham .20 .50
107 Bryan Berard .08 .25
108 Brian Leetch .15 .40
109 Tony Granato .02 .10
110 Trevor Linden .08 .25

1997-98 Pacific Dynagon Dynamic Duos

Randomly inserted in packs at the rate of 1:37, this 30-card set features color action images of the NHL's top teammates printed on a die-cut gold foil card and framed with a textured hockey puck border. When placed side by side, the matching cards are joined together by their team logo.

COMPLETE SET (30) 30.00 80.00
1A Paul Kariya 1.50 4.00
1B Teemu Selanne 1.50 4.00
2A Ray Bourque 2.00 5.00
2B Jim Carey .75 2.00
3A Dominik Hasek 3.00 8.00
3B Michael Peca .40 1.00
4A Theo Fleury .75 2.00
4B Jarome Iginla 2.00 5.00
5A Peter Forsberg 2.50 6.00
5B Claude Lemieux .40 1.00
6A Patrick Roy 8.00 20.00
6B Joe Sakic 3.00 8.00
7A Sergei Fedorov 1.50 4.00
7B Vladimir Konstantinov .75 2.00
8A Brendan Shanahan 1.50 4.00
8B Steve Yzerman 6.00 15.00
9A Bryan Berard .40 1.00
9B Zigmund Palffy .75 2.00
10A Wayne Gretzky 10.00 25.00
10B Mark Messier 1.50 4.00
11A Eric Lindros 1.50 4.00
11B Dainius Zubrus .40 1.00
12A Jeremy Roenick 2.00 5.00
12B Keith Tkachuk 1.25 3.00
13A Jaromir Jagr 2.50 6.00
13B Patrick Lalime .75 2.00
14A Jim Campbell .40 1.00
14B Brett Hull 1.50 4.00
15A Pavel Bure 1.50 4.00
15B Alexander Mogilny .75 2.00

1997-98 Pacific Dynagon Kings of the NHL

COMPLETE SET (10) 60.00 125.00
STATED ODDS 1:361
1 Paul Kariya 3.00 8.00
2 Peter Forsberg 6.00 15.00
3 Patrick Roy 12.00 30.00
4 Joe Sakic 6.00 15.00
5 John Vanbiesbrouck 2.50 6.00
6 Wayne Gretzky 20.00 50.00
7 Mark Messier 3.00 8.00
8 Eric Lindros 3.00 8.00
9 Jaromir Jagr 5.00 12.00
10 Pavel Bure 3.00 8.00

1997-98 Pacific Dynagon Stonewallers

COMPLETE SET (20) 25.00 60.00
STATED ODDS 1:73
1 Guy Hebert 1.25 3.00
2 Jim Carey 1.25 3.00
3 Dominik Hasek 4.00 10.00
4 Trevor Kidd 1.25 3.00
5 Jeff Hackett 1.25 3.00
6 Patrick Roy 10.00 25.00
7 Chris Osgood 1.25 3.00
8 Mike Vernon 1.50 4.00
9 Curtis Joseph 1.50 4.00
10 John Vanbiesbrouck 1.50 4.00
11 Jocelyn Thibault 1.25 3.00
12 Martin Brodeur 6.00 15.00
13 Tommy Salo 1.25 3.00
14 Mike Richter 1.50 4.00
15 Ron Hextall 1.50 4.00
16 Garth Snow 1.25 3.00
17 Nikolai Khabibulin 1.50 4.00
18 Patrick Lalime 1.25 3.00
19 Grant Fuhr 1.50 4.00
20 Felix Potvin 2.00 5.00

1997-98 Pacific Dynagon Tandems

Randomly inserted in packs at the rate of 1:37, this 72-card set features color player images printed on double front, holographic fully foiled, double etched cards.

COMPLETE SET (72) 60.00 150.00
1 Wayne Gretzky 10.00 25.00
Eric Lindros

2 Joe Sakic 4.00 10.00
Paul Kariya
3 Jarome Iginla 4.00 10.00
Mark Messier
4 Patrick Roy 8.00 20.00
Dominik Hasek
5 Peter Forsberg 4.00 10.00
Jaromir Jagr
6 Brendan Shanahan 1.25 3.00
Keith Tkachuk
7 Steve Yzerman 4.00 10.00
Teemu Selanne
8 Sergei Fedorov 4.00 10.00
Brett Hull
9 Dainius Zubrus .40 1.00
Patrick Lalime
10 Sergei Berezin .40 1.00
Mike Grier
11 Zigmund Palffy .75 2.00
Curtis Joseph
12 Chris Osgood 4.00 10.00
Martin Brodeur
13 John Vanbiesbrouck .75 2.00
Jocelyn Thibault
14 Saku Koivu 2.00 5.00
Pavel Bure
15 John LeClair .75 2.00
Peter Bondra
16 Mats Sundin .75 2.00
Janne Niinimaa
17 Felix Potvin 1.25 3.00
Jim Carey
18 Grant Fuhr 2.00 5.00
Brett Hull
Jim Campbell
19 Wayne Gretzky 8.00 20.00
Mark Messier
Brian Leetch
20 Eric Lindros 2.00 5.00
John LeClair
Rod Brind'Amour
21 Dominik Hasek 2.00 5.00
Michael Peca
Miroslav Satan
22 Jaromir Jagr 2.00 5.00
Patrick Lalime
Petr Nedved
23 Jarome Iginla 2.00 5.00
Theo Fleury
Trevor Kidd
24 Paul Kariya 2.00 5.00
Teemu Selanne
Guy Hebert
25 Peter Forsberg 8.00 20.00
Patrick Roy
Claude Lemieux
26 Steve Yzerman 8.00 20.00
Brendand Shanahan
Vladimir Konstantinov
27 Mats Sundin 2.00 5.00
Sergei Berezin
Wendel Clark
28 Ray Bourque 2.00 5.00
Derek Plante
29 Brian Bellows .40 1.00
Jason Allison
30 Steve Rucchin .40 1.00
Keith Primeau
31 Jozef Stumpel .40 1.00
Eric Daze
32 Brian Holzinger .40 1.00
Jamie Langenbrunner
33 Michael Peca .40 1.00
Tony Amonte
34 German Titov .40 1.00
Darryl Sydor
35 Theo Fleury .75 2.00
Chris Chelios
36 Jonas Hoglund .40 1.00
Dimitri Khristich
37 Sean Burke .40 1.00
Dave Andreychuk
38 Geoff Sanderson .40 1.00
Derian Hatcher
39 Andrew Cassels .40 1.00
Jeff Hackett
40 Ethan Moreau .40 1.00
Ray Ferraro
41 Sandis Ozolinsh .75 2.00
Doug Gilmour
42 Valeri Kamensky 1.25 3.00
Mike Modano
43 Joe Nieuwendyk .40 1.00
Vladimir Tsyplakov
44 Sergei Zubov .40 1.00
Mike Vernon
45 Rob Blake .40 1.00
Bobby Holik
46 Vincent Damphousse .40 1.00
Doug Weight
47 Mark Recchi .75 2.00
Ryan Smyth
48 Stephane Richer .40 1.00
John MacLean
49 Kelly Buchberger .40 1.00
Ed Jovanovski
50 Rem Murray .40 1.00
Owen Nolan
51 Robert Svehla .40 1.00
Bill Ranford
52 Ray Sheppard .40 1.00
Steve Sullivan
53 Scott Mellanby .40 1.00
John Cullen
54 Garth Snow .40 1.00
Alexandre Daigle
55 Ron Hextall .75 2.00
Alexander Mogilny
56 Kirk McLean .75 2.00
Adam Oates
57 Joe Juneau .40 1.00
Dino Ciccarelli
58 Steve Konowalchuk .40 1.00
Jim Campbell
59 Trevor Linden .40 1.00
Pierre Turgeon
60 Martin Gelinas .40 1.00
Jeff Friesen
61 Roman Hamrlik .40 1.00
Harry York
62 Kevin Hatcher .40 1.00
Chris Gratton
63 Ron Francis 1.25 3.00
Jeremy Roenick
64 Nikolai Khabibulin .75 2.00
Viktor Kozlov
65 Daymond Langkow .40 1.00
Mike Gartner
66 Oleg Tverdovsky .40 1.00
Steve Guolla
67 Tony Granato .40 1.00
Tommy Salo
68 Bryan Smolinski .40 1.00
Wade Redden
69 Adam Graves .40 1.00
Damian Rhodes
70 Mike Richter .75 2.00
Alexei Yashin
71 Daniel Alfredsson .40 1.00
Bryan Berard
72 Travis Green .40 1.00
Alexei Kovalev

1998-99 Pacific Dynagon Ice

The 1998-99 Pacific Dynagon Ice set was issued in one series totaling 200 cards and was distributed in five-card packs with a suggested retail price of $2.49. The set features color action player photos printed on gold foil cards with player highlights and statistics displayed on the backs.

COMPLETE SET (200) 25.00 50.00
1 Travis Green .08 .25
2 Guy Hebert .25 .60
3 Paul Kariya .30 .75
4 Steve Rucchin .08 .25
5 Tomas Sandstrom .08 .25
6 Teemu Selanne .30 .75
7 Jason Allison .08 .25
8 Ray Bourque .50 1.25
9 Byron Dafoe .25 .60
10 Anson Carter .25 .60
11 Dimitri Khristich .08 .25
12 Antti Laaksonen RC .08 .25
13 Peter Nordstrom RC .08 .25
14 Sergei Samsonov .25 .60
15 Joe Thornton .50 1.25
16 Matthew Barnaby .08 .25
17 Michal Grosek .08 .25
18 Dominik Hasek .60 1.50
19 Brian Holzinger .08 .25
20 Michael Peca .25 .60
21 Miroslav Satan .25 .60
22 Vaclav Varada .08 .25
23 Andrew Cassels .08 .25
24 Rico Fata .08 .25
25 Theo Fleury .08 .25
26 Phil Housley .08 .25
27 Jarome Iginla .40 1.00
28 Martin St. Louis RC 2.00 5.00
29 Ken Wregget .25 .60
30 Kevin Dineen .08 .25
31 Ron Francis .25 .60
32 Martin Gelinas .08 .25
33 Arturs Irbe .25 .60
34 Sami Kapanen .25 .60
35 Trevor Kidd .25 .60
36 Robert Kron .08 .25
37 Keith Primeau .08 .25
38 Tony Amonte .25 .60
39 Chris Chelios .30 .75
40 Eric Daze .25 .60
41 Doug Gilmour .25 .60
42 Jeff Hackett .25 .60
43 Ty Jones .25 .60
44 Bob Probert .08 .25
45 Adam Deadmarsh .08 .25
46 Chris Drury .25 .60
47 Peter Forsberg .75 2.00
48 Milan Hejduk RC 1.25 3.00
49 Valeri Kamensky .08 .25
50 Claude Lemieux .08 .25
51 Patrick Roy 1.50 4.00
52 Joe Sakic .60 1.50
53 Ed Belfour .30 .75
54 Sergey Gusev RC .08 .25
55 Derian Hatcher .08 .25
56 Brett Hull .40 1.00
57 Jamie Langenbrunner .08 .25
58 Jere Lehtinen .08 .25
59 Mike Modano .50 1.25
60 Joe Nieuwendyk .25 .60
61 Sergei Zubov .08 .25
62 Sergei Fedorov .50 1.25
63 Vyacheslav Kozlov .25 .60
64 Uwe Krupp .08 .25
65 Nicklas Lidstrom .30 .75
66 Darren McCarty .08 .25
67 Chris Osgood .25 .60
68 Brendan Shanahan .30 .75
69 Steve Yzerman 1.50 4.00
70 Bob Essensa .25 .60
71 Mike Grier .08 .25
72 Bill Guerin .25 .60
73 Roman Hamrlik .08 .25
74 Janne Niinimaa .08 .25
75 Tom Poti .08 .25
76 Ryan Smyth .25 .60
77 Doug Weight .25 .60
78 Sean Burke .08 .25
79 Dino Ciccarelli .25 .60
80 Dave Gagner .08 .25
81 Ed Jovanovski .08 .25
82 Viktor Kozlov .08 .25
83 Oleg Kvasha RC .30 .75
84 Paul Laus .08 .25
85 Mark Parrish RC .40 1.00
86 Rob Blake .25 .60
87 Stephane Fiset .25 .60
88 Josh Green RC .08 .25
89 Yanic Perreault .08 .25
90 Luc Robitaille .25 .60
91 Jozef Stumpel .25 .60
92 Vladimir Tsyplakov .08 .25
93 Brad Brown .08 .25
94 Shayne Corson .25 .60
95 Vincent Damphousse .08 .25
96 Saku Koivu .30 .75
97 Mark Recchi .25 .60
98 Jocelyn Thibault .25 .60
99 Sergei Zholtok .08 .25
100 Andrew Brunette .25 .60
101 Mike Dunham .25 .60
102 Tom Fitzgerald .08 .25
103 Patrik Kjellberg .08 .25
104 Sergei Krivokrasov .08 .25
105 Darren Turcotte .08 .25
106 Dave Andreychuk .25 .60
107 Jason Arnott .08 .25
108 Martin Brodeur .75 2.00
109 Patrik Elias .25 .60
110 Bobby Holik .08 .25
111 Brendan Morrison .25 .60
112 Scott Stevens .25 .60
113 Bryan Berard .25 .60
114 Eric Brewer .08 .25
115 Trevor Linden .25 .60
116 Zigmund Palffy .25 .60
117 Robert Reichel .08 .25
118 Tommy Salo .25 .60
119 Bryan Smolinski .08 .25
120 Adam Graves .25 .60
121 Wayne Gretzky 2.00 5.00
122 Alexei Kovalev .08 .25
123 Brian Leetch .30 .75
124 Manny Malhotra .25 .60
125 Mike Richter .30 .75
126 Daniel Alfredsson .25 .60
127 Igor Kravchuk .08 .25
128 Shawn McEachern .08 .25
129 Vaclav Prospal .25 .60
130 Damian Rhodes .25 .60
131 Sami Salo RC .25 .60
132 Alexei Yashin .08 .25
133 Rod Brind'Amour .25 .60
134 Alexandre Daigle .08 .25
135 Chris Gratton .25 .60
136 Ron Hextall .25 .60
137 John LeClair .30 .75
138 Eric Lindros .30 .75
139 Mike Maneluk RC .08 .25
140 John Vanbiesbrouck .25 .60
141 Dainius Zubrus .08 .25
142 Brad Isbister .08 .25
143 Nikolai Khabibulin .25 .60
144 Jeremy Roenick .40 1.00
145 Keith Tkachuk .30 .75
146 Rick Tocchet .25 .60
147 Oleg Tverdovsky .08 .25
148 Tom Barrasso .25 .60
149 Kevin Hatcher .25 .60
150 Jan Hrdina RC .50 1.25
151 Jaromir Jagr .50 1.25
152 Alexei Morozov .25 .60
153 Jiri Slegr .08 .25
154 Martin Straka .08 .25
155 Jim Campbell .08 .25
156 Geoff Courtnall .08 .25
157 Grant Fuhr .08 .25
158 Michal Handzus RC .40 1.00
159 Al MacInnis .25 .60
160 Jamie McLennan .25 .60
161 Chris Pronger .25 .60
162 Marty Reasoner .25 .60
163 Pierre Turgeon .25 .60
164 Jeff Friesen .08 .25
165 Tony Granato .25 .60
166 Scott Hannan RC .25 .60
167 Patrick Marleau .08 .25
168 Owen Nolan .25 .60
169 Marco Sturm .08 .25
170 Mike Vernon .25 .60
171 Wendel Clark .25 .60
172 John Cullen .25 .60
173 Vincent Lecavalier 1.00 2.50
174 Stephane Richer .25 .60
175 Paul Ysebaert .08 .25
176 Rob Zamuner .08 .25
177 Sergei Berezin .25 .60
178 Tie Domi .25 .60
179 Mike Johnson .08 .25
180 Curtis Joseph .30 .75
181 Tomas Kaberle RC .40 1.00
182 Igor Korolev .08 .25
183 Alyn McCauley .08 .25
184 Mats Sundin .30 .75
185 Todd Bertuzzi .30 .75
186 Donald Brashear .08 .25
187 Pavel Bure .30 .75
188 Matt Cooke RC .08 .25
189 Mark Messier .30 .75
190 Alexander Mogilny .25 .60
191 Mattias Ohlund .08 .25
192 Garth Snow .25 .60
193 Peter Bondra .25 .60

194 Matthew Herr RC .08 .25
195 Calle Johansson .08 .25
196 Joe Juneau .25 .60
197 Olaf Kolzig .25 .60
198 Adam Oates .25 .60
199 Jaroslav Svejkovsky .08 .25
200 Richard Zednik .08 .25

1998-99 Pacific Dynagon Ice Blue

Randomly inserted into packs, this 200-card set is a blue foil parallel version of the base set. Only 67 serially numbered sets were made.

*VETERANS: 10X TO 25X BASIC CARDS
*ROOKIES: 4X TO 10X BASIC CARDS

1998-99 Pacific Dynagon Ice Red

Randomly inserted into Treat retail packs only at the rate of 4:37, this 200-card set is a red foil parallel version of the base set made especially for Treat Entertainment.

*VETERANS: 1.5X TO 4X BASIC CARDS
*ROOKIES: 1.5X TO 4X BASIC CARDS

1998-99 Pacific Dynagon Ice Adrenaline Rush Bronze

Randomly inserted into Canadian retail packs only at the rate of 1:37, this 10-card set is a Canadian insert to the Pacific Dynagon Ice base set. Four limited edition parallel sets were also made and inserted into packs: Bronze with only 160 sets made, Ice Blue with 10 sets made, Red with 79 sets made, and Silver with 120 sets made.

COMPLETE SET (10) 60.00 120.00
UNPRICED ICE BLUE PRINT RUN 10
*RED/79: .8X TO 2X BRONZE/180
*SILVER/120: .5X TO 1.2X BRONZE/180
1 Paul Kariya 2.00 5.00
2 Teemu Selanne 3.00 8.00
3 Dominik Hasek 5.00 12.00
4 Peter Forsberg 6.00 15.00
5 Patrick Roy 12.50 30.00
6 Joe Sakic 5.00 12.00
7 Steve Yzerman 12.50 30.00
8 Wayne Gretzky 20.00 50.00
9 Eric Lindros 3.00 8.00
10 Jaromir Jagr 4.00 10.00

1998-99 Pacific Dynagon Ice Forward Thinking

COMPLETE SET (20) 15.00 40.00
STATED ODDS 1:37
1 Paul Kariya 1.25 3.00
2 Teemu Selanne 1.25 3.00
3 Michael Peca .40 1.00
4 Doug Gilmour .75 2.00
5 Peter Forsberg 2.00 5.00
6 Joe Sakic 2.00 5.00
7 Brett Hull 1.50 4.00
8 Mike Modano 1.50 4.00
9 Sergei Fedorov 1.50 4.00
10 Brendan Shanahan 1.25 3.00
11 Steve Yzerman 3.00 8.00
12 Saku Koivu 1.25 3.00
13 Wayne Gretzky 4.00 10.00
14 John LeClair .40 1.00
15 Eric Lindros 1.25 3.00
16 Jaromir Jagr 2.00 5.00
17 Vincent Lecavalier 1.50 4.00
18 Mats Sundin 1.25 3.00
19 Mark Messier 1.25 3.00
20 Peter Bondra .75 2.00

1998-99 Pacific Dynagon Ice Watchmen

COMPLETE SET (10) 30.00 80.00
STATED ODDS 1:73
1 Dominik Hasek 6.00 15.00
2 Patrick Roy 12.00 30.00
3 Ed Belfour 2.00 5.00
4 Chris Osgood 2.00 5.00
5 Martin Brodeur 8.00 20.00
6 Mike Richter 2.00 5.00
7 John Vanbiesbrouck 2.00 5.00
8 Grant Fuhr 2.00 5.00
9 Curtis Joseph 3.00 8.00
10 Olaf Kolzig 2.00 5.00

1998-99 Pacific Dynagon Ice Preeminent Players

COMPLETE SET (10) 60.00 150.00
STATED ODDS 1:181
1 Paul Kariya 4.00 10.00
2 Dominik Hasek 8.00 20.00
3 Peter Forsberg 6.00 15.00
4 Patrick Roy 12.00 30.00
5 Mike Modano 5.00 12.00
6 Steve Yzerman 12.00 30.00
7 Martin Brodeur 10.00 25.00
8 Wayne Gretzky 15.00 40.00
9 Eric Lindros 4.00 10.00
10 Jaromir Jagr 6.00 15.00

1998-99 Pacific Dynagon Ice Rookies

COMPLETE SET (10) 15.00 40.00
STATED ODDS 1:73 HOBBY
1 Chris Drury 2.00 5.00
2 Milan Hejduk 2.00 5.00
3 Mark Parrish .75 2.00
4 Brendan Morrison 2.00 5.00
5 Mike Maneluk .75 2.00
6 Jan Hrdina .75 2.00
7 Marty Reasoner .75 2.00
8 Vincent Lecavalier 10.00 25.00
9 Tomas Kaberle .75 2.00
10 Bill Muckalt .75 2.00

1998-99 Pacific Dynagon Ice Team Checklists

COMPLETE SET (27) 25.00 60.00
STATED ODDS 2:37
1 Paul Kariya 1.25 3.00
2 Ray Bourque 1.25 3.00
3 Dominik Hasek 2.50 6.00
4 Theo Fleury .40 1.00
5 Keith Primeau .40 1.00
6 Chris Chelios .75 2.00
7 Patrick Roy 6.00 15.00
8 Mike Modano 1.50 4.00
9 Steve Yzerman 4.00 10.00
10 Ryan Smyth .75 2.00
11 Dino Ciccarelli .40 1.00
12 Rob Blake .75 2.00
13 Saku Koivu 1.25 3.00
14 Mike Dunham .75 2.00
15 Martin Brodeur 3.00 8.00
16 Trevor Linden .75 2.00
17 Wayne Gretzky 8.00 20.00
18 Alexei Yashin .40 1.00
19 Eric Lindros 1.25 3.00
20 Keith Tkachuk .75 2.00
21 Jaromir Jagr 2.00 5.00
22 Grant Fuhr .75 2.00
23 Mike Vernon .75 2.00
24 Vincent Lecavalier 2.00 5.00
25 Mats Sundin 1.25 3.00
26 Mark Messier 1.25 3.00
27 Peter Bondra .75 2.00

1999-00 Pacific Dynagon Ice

Released as a 206-card set, Dynagon Ice features base cards with full color action photography set against each respective player's team logo and feature silver foil highlights. Dynagon Ice was packaged in 36-pack boxes with packs containing five cards and carried a suggested retail price of $2.49.

COMPLETE SET (206) 50.00 100.00
COMP.SET w/o SP's (200) 35.00 70.00
1 Steve Kariya SP RC 1.50 4.00
2 Simon Gagne SP 2.50 6.00
3 Mike Fisher SP RC 2.50 6.00
4 Mike Ribeiro SP 1.50 4.00
5 Oleg Saprykin SP RC 4.00 10.00
6 Patrik Stefan SP RC 4.00 10.00
7 Ted Donato .08 .25
8 Niclas Havelid RC .30 .75
9 Guy Hebert .25 .60
10 Paul Kariya .30 .75
11 Steve Rucchin .08 .25
12 Teemu Selanne .30 .75
13 Oleg Tverdovsky .08 .25
14 Kelly Buchberger .08 .25
15 Nelson Emerson .08 .25
16 Ray Ferraro .08 .25
17 Norm Maracle .25 .60
18 Damian Rhodes .25 .60
19 Per Svartvadet RC .08 .25
20 Jason Allison .08 .25
21 Ray Bourque .50 1.25
22 Anson Carter .25 .60
23 Byron Dafoe .25 .60
24 John Grahame RC .60 1.50
25 Sergei Samsonov .25 .60
26 Joe Thornton .50 1.25
27 Stu Barnes .08 .25
28 Martin Biron .25 .60
29 Curtis Brown .08 .25
30 Michal Grosek .08 .25
31 Dominik Hasek .60 1.50
32 Michael Peca .25 .60
33 Miroslav Satan .25 .60
34 Valeri Bure .08 .25
35 Grant Fuhr .25 .60
36 Jarome Iginla .40 1.00
37 Derek Morris .08 .25
38 Marc Savard .08 .25
39 Cory Stillman .08 .25
40 Ron Francis .25 .60
41 Arturs Irbe .25 .60
42 Sami Kapanen .08 .25
43 Keith Primeau .08 .25
44 Dave Tanabe .08 .25
45 Tommy Westlund RC .25 .60
46 Tony Amonte .25 .60
47 Wendel Clark .08 .25
48 Eric Daze .25 .60
49 J-P Dumont .25 .60
50 Doug Gilmour .25 .60
51 Steve McCarthy .08 .25
52 Jocelyn Thibault .25 .60
53 Alexei Zhamnov .08 .25
54 Adam Deadmarsh .08 .25
55 Chris Drury .25 .60
56 Peter Forsberg .75 2.00
57 Milan Hejduk .30 .75
58 Dan Hinote RC .25 .60
59 Patrick Roy 1.50 4.00
60 Joe Sakic .60 1.50
61 Martin Skoula RC .75 2.00
62 Alex Tanguay .25 .60
63 Ed Belfour .30 .75
64 Derian Hatcher .08 .25
65 Brett Hull .40 1.00
66 Jamie Langenbrunner .08 .25
67 Jere Lehtinen .25 .60
68 Mike Modano .50 1.25
69 Joe Nieuwendyk .25 .60
70 Pavel Patera RC .08 .25
71 Yuri Butsayev RC .08 .25
72 Chris Chelios .30 .75
73 Sergei Fedorov .50 1.25
74 Vyacheslav Kozlov .08 .25
75 Nicklas Lidstrom .30 .75
76 Darren McCarty .08 .25
77 Chris Osgood .25 .60
78 Brendan Shanahan .30 .75
79 Steve Yzerman 1.50 4.00
80 Paul Comrie RC .25 .60
81 Mike Grier .08 .25
82 Tom Poti .08 .25
83 Bill Ranford .25 .60
84 Tommy Salo .25 .60
85 Ryan Smyth .08 .25
86 Doug Weight .25 .60
87 Pavel Bure .30 .75
88 Sean Burke .25 .60
89 Trevor Kidd .25 .60
90 Viktor Kozlov .08 .25
91 Ivan Novoseltsev RC .60 1.50
92 Mark Parrish .08 .25
93 Ray Whitney .08 .25
94 Jason Blake RC .25 .60
95 Rob Blake .08 .25
96 Stephane Fiset .25 .60
97 Zigmund Palffy .25 .60
98 Luc Robitaille .25 .60
99 Jozef Stumpel .25 .60
100 Shayne Corson .08 .25
101 Jeff Hackett .25 .60
102 Saku Koivu .30 .75
103 Trevor Linden .25 .60
104 Martin Rucinsky .08 .25
105 Brian Savage .08 .25
106 Mike Dunham .25 .60
107 Greg Johnson .08 .25
108 Sergei Krivokrasov .08 .25
109 David Legwand .25 .60
110 Ville Peltonen .08 .25
111 Cliff Ronning .08 .25
112 Scott Walker .08 .25
113 Jason Arnott .08 .25
114 Martin Brodeur .75 2.00
115 Patrik Elias .25 .60
116 Scott Gomez .08 .25
117 Bobby Holik .08 .25
118 Scott Niedermayer .08 .25
119 Brian Rafalski RC .60 1.50
120 Petr Sykora .25 .60
121 Mathieu Biron .25 .60
122 Tim Connolly .08 .25
123 Mariusz Czerkawski .08 .25
124 Olli Jokinen .25 .60
125 Jorgen Jonsson RC .08 .25
126 Kenny Jonsson .08 .25
127 Felix Potvin .30 .75
128 Theo Fleury .08 .25
129 Adam Graves .08 .25
130 Kim Johnsson RC .25 .60
131 Valeri Kamensky .25 .60
132 Brian Leetch .30 .75
133 Petr Nedved .25 .60
134 Mike Richter .30 .75
135 Mike York .08 .25
136 Daniel Alfredsson .25 .60
137 Magnus Arvedson .08 .25
138 Radek Bonk .08 .25
139 Marian Hossa .30 .75
140 Patrick Lalime .25 .60
141 Ron Tugnutt .25 .60
142 Alexei Yashin .08 .25
143 Rob Zamuner .08 .25
144 Brian Boucher .30 .75
145 Rod Brind'Amour .25 .60
146 Mark Eaton RC .30 .75
147 John LeClair .30 .75
148 Eric Lindros .30 .75
149 Mark Recchi .25 .60
150 John Vanbiesbrouck .25 .60
151 Travis Green .08 .25
152 Nikolai Khabibulin .25 .60
153 Jeremy Roenick .40 1.00
154 Mikhail Shtalenkov .25 .60
155 Keith Tkachuk .30 .75
156 Rick Tocchet .25 .60
157 Matthew Barnaby .08 .25
158 Tom Barrasso .25 .60
159 Jaromir Jagr .50 1.25
160 Alexei Kovalev .08 .25
161 Alexei Morozov .08 .25
162 Michal Rozsival RC .08 .25
163 Martin Straka .08 .25
164 German Titov .08 .25
165 Pavol Demitra .25 .60
166 Al MacInnis .25 .60
167 Chris Pronger .25 .60
168 Roman Turek .25 .60
169 Pierre Turgeon .25 .60
170 Scott Young .08 .25
171 Vincent Damphousse .08 .25
172 Jeff Friesen .08 .25
173 Patrick Marleau .30 .75
174 Owen Nolan .25 .60
175 Steve Shields .25 .60
176 Brad Stuart .25 .60
177 Niklas Sundstrom .08 .25
178 Mike Vernon .25 .60
179 Dan Cloutier .25 .60
180 Chris Gratton .08 .25
181 Vincent Lecavalier .30 .75
182 Fredrik Modin .08 .25
183 Darcy Tucker .08 .25
184 Nikolai Antropov RC .75 2.00
185 Sergei Berezin .08 .25
186 Tie Domi .25 .60
187 Jonas Hoglund .08 .25
188 Mike Johnson .08 .25
189 Curtis Joseph .30 .75
190 Mats Sundin .30 .75
191 Steve Thomas .08 .25
192 Andrew Cassels .08 .25
193 Artem Chubarov .08 .25
194 Mark Messier .30 .75
195 Alexander Mogilny .25 .60
196 Bill Muckalt .08 .25
197 Markus Naslund .30 .75
198 Kevin Weekes .25 .60
199 Peter Bondra .25 .60
200 Jan Bulis .08 .25
201 Jeff Halpern RC .75 2.00
202 Olaf Kolzig .25 .60
203 Adam Oates .25 .60
204 Chris Simon .08 .25
205 Alexander Volchkov RC .25 .60
206 Richard Zednik .08 .25
NNO Martin Brodeur SAMPLE 1.50 4.00

1999-00 Pacific Dynagon Ice Blue

Randomly inserted in packs, this 206-card set parallels the base Dynagon Ice set and is enhanced with blue foil highlights. Each card set sequentially numbered to 67.

*ICE BLUE 1-6: 2.5X TO 6X BASIC CARDS
*ICE BLUE 7-200: 15X TO 40X BASIC CARDS

1999-00 Pacific Dynagon Ice Copper

Randomly inserted in Retail packs, this 206-card set parallels the base Dynagon Ice set and is enhanced with copper foil highlights. Each card set sequentially numbered to 99.

*COPPER 1-6: 1.5X TO 4X BASIC CARDS
*COPPER 7-200: 10X TO 25X BASIC CARDS
STATED PRINT RUN 99 SER.#'d SETS

1999-00 Pacific Dynagon Ice Gold

Randomly inserted in Retail packs, this 206-card set parallels the base Dynagon Ice set and is enhanced with gold foil highlights. Each card set sequentially numbered to 199.

*GOLD 1-6: .8X TO 2X BASIC SP
*GOLD 7-200: 4X TO 10X BASIC CARDS
GOLD PRINT RUN 199 SER.#'d SETS

1999-00 Pacific Dynagon Ice Premiere Date

Randomly inserted in packs, this 206-card set parallels the base Dynagon Ice set and is enhanced with a Premier Date stamp. Each card set sequentially numbered to 63.

*1-6 PREM.DATE: 2.5X TO 6X BASIC SP
*7-200 PREM.DATE: 15X TO 40X BASIC CARDS
STATED PRINT RUN 63 SER.#'d SETS

1999-00 Pacific Dynagon Ice 2000 All-Star Preview

Randomly inserted in Hobby packs at the rate of 2:37, this 20-card set features color player photos set against a circular panoramic shot of a live hockey game and the 1999-2000 All-Star game logo in the lower left corner.

COMPLETE SET (20) 50.00 100.00
1 Paul Kariya 1.25 3.00
2 Teemu Selanne 1.25 3.00
3 Ray Bourque 2.00 5.00
4 Dominik Hasek 2.50 6.00
5 Patrick Roy 6.00 15.00
6 Joe Sakic 2.50 6.00
7 Nicklas Lidstrom 1.25 3.00
8 Steve Yzerman 6.00 15.00
9 Ed Belfour 1.25 3.00
10 Jere Lehtinen 1.00 2.50
11 Mike Modano 2.00 5.00
12 Pavel Bure 1.50 4.00
13 Martin Brodeur 3.00 8.00
14 John LeClair 1.50 4.00
15 Eric Lindros 2.00 5.00
16 Jaromir Jagr 2.00 5.00
17 Keith Tkachuk 1.25 3.00
18 Curtis Joseph 1.25 3.00
19 Mats Sundin 1.25 3.00
20 Peter Bondra 1.00 2.50

1999-00 Pacific Dynagon Ice Checkmates American

Randomly inserted in American packs at the rate of two in 37, this 30-card set pairs a top goal scorer on the card front and an enforcer on the card back for numbers 1-15, then switches to enforcer on the front and scorer on the back for card numbers 16-30.

COMPLETE SET (30) 40.00 100.00
1 Paul Kariya .60 1.50
Steve Kariya
2 Teemu Selanne .60 1.50
Brendan Shanahan
3 Patrik Stefan .60 1.50
Eric Lindros
4 Tony Amonte .60 1.50
Chris Pronger
5 Chris Drury 3.00 8.00
Peter Forsberg
6 Joe Sakic 2.50 6.00
Theo Fleury
7 S.Yzerman/C.Chelios 5.00 12.00
8 Brett Hull 1.50 4.00
Michael Peca
9 M.Modano/D.Hatcher 2.00 5.00
10 Pavel Bure 1.50 4.00
Raymond Bourque
11 Zigmund Palffy 1.00 2.50
Keith Tkachuk
12 Marian Hossa 1.25 3.00
John LeClair
13 Jaromir Jagr 2.00 5.00
Matthew Barnaby
14 Patrick Marleau .60 1.50
Owen Nolan
15 Mats Sundin 1.00 2.50
Tie Domi
16 Steve Kariya .60 1.50
Paul Kariya
17 Brendan Shanahan .60 1.50
Teemu Selanne
18 Eric Lindros 1.25 3.00
Patrik Stefan
19 Chris Pronger 1.00 2.50
Tony Amonte
20 Peter Forsberg 3.00 8.00
Chris Drury
21 Theo Fleury 2.50 6.00
Joe Sakic
22 C.Chelios/S.Yzerman 5.00 12.00
23 Michael Peca 1.50 4.00
Brett Hull
24 D.Hatcher/M.Modano 2.00 5.00
25 Raymond Bourque 1.50 4.00
Pavel Bure
26 Keith Tkachuk 1.00 2.50
Zigmund Palffy
27 John LeClair 1.25 3.00
Marian Hossa
28 Matthew Barnaby 2.00 5.00
Jaromir Jagr
29 Owen Nolan 1.25 3.00
Patrick Marleau
30 Tie Domi 1.25 3.00
Mats Sundin

1999-00 Pacific Dynagon Ice Checkmates Canadian

Randomly inserted in Canadian packs at a rate of 2:37, this 30-cards set features top NHL players in both their home and away jerseys.

COMPLETE SET (30) 40.00 80.00
1 Steve Kariya .60 1.50
2 Brendan Shanahan 2.00 5.00
3 Eric Lindros 2.00 5.00
4 Chris Pronger 1.00 2.50
5 Peter Forsberg 3.00 8.00
6 Theo Fleury .60 1.50
7 Chris Chelios 1.25 3.00
8 Michael Peca 1.00 2.50
9 Derian Hatcher .60 1.50
10 Ray Bourque 2.00 5.00
11 Keith Tkachuk 1.25 3.00
12 John LeClair 1.25 3.00
13 Matthew Barnaby .60 1.50
14 Owen Nolan 1.00 2.50
15 Tie Domi .60 1.50
16 Paul Kariya 1.25 3.00
17 Teemu Selanne 1.25 3.00
18 Patrik Stefan 1.00 2.50
19 Tony Amonte 1.00 2.50
20 Chris Drury 1.00 2.50
21 Joe Sakic 2.50 6.00
22 Steve Yzerman 5.00 12.00
23 Brett Hull 1.50 4.00
24 Mike Modano 2.00 5.00
25 Pavel Bure 1.50 4.00
26 Zigmund Palffy 1.00 2.50
27 Marian Hossa 1.25 3.00
28 Jaromir Jagr 2.00 5.00
29 Patrick Marleau 1.25 3.00
30 Mats Sundin 1.25 3.00

1999-00 Pacific Dynagon Ice Lamplighter Net-Fusions

Randomly inserted in packs at the rate of 1:73, this 10-card set features a laser cut background that has been filled in with actual "netting."

COMPLETE SET (10) 40.00 80.00
1 Paul Kariya 2.50 6.00
2 Teemu Selanne 2.50 6.00
3 Patrik Stefan 2.00 5.00
4 Joe Sakic 5.00 12.00
5 Steve Yzerman 12.50 30.00
6 Pavel Bure 3.00 8.00
7 Theo Fleury 2.50 6.00
8 John LeClair 3.00 8.00
9 Eric Lindros 4.00 10.00
10 Jaromir Jagr 4.00 10.00

1999-00 Pacific Dynagon Ice Lords of the Rink

COMPLETE SET (10) 100.00 200.00
STATED ODDS 1:181
1 Paul Kariya 15.00 40.00
2 Teemu Selanne 15.00 40.00
3 Dominik Hasek 8.00 20.00
4 Peter Forsberg 10.00 25.00
5 Patrick Roy 20.00 50.00
6 Joe Sakic 8.00 20.00
7 Steve Yzerman 20.00 50.00
8 Martin Brodeur 10.00 25.00
9 Eric Lindros 6.00 15.00
10 Jaromir Jagr 6.00 15.00

1999-00 Pacific Dynagon Ice Masks

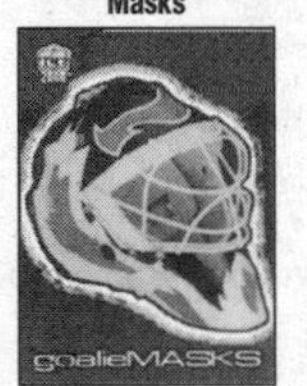

Randomly inserted in packs at the rate of 1:37, this 10-card set showcases some of the NHL's to goalies' masks. Each card is enhanced with holographic foil stamping. Card numbers 1-5 are found only in hobby packs, and card numbers 6-10 are only found in retail packs.

COMPLETE SET (10) 20.00 40.00
UNPRICED HOLO.PURPLE PRINT RUN 1
1 Patrick Roy 6.00 15.00
2 Martin Brodeur 5.00 12.00
3 Mike Richter 1.00 2.50
4 John Vanbiesbrouck 1.00 2.50
5 Curtis Joseph 1.00 2.50
6 Patrick Roy 6.00 15.00
7 Martin Brodeur 3.00 8.00
8 Mike Richter 1.00 2.50
9 John Vanbiesbrouck 1.00 2.50
10 Curtis Joseph 1.00 2.50

2002 Pacific Entry Draft

Available as a wrapper redemption at the 2002 NHL Entry Draft, held in Toronto. Each card was serial-numbered on the back out of 500.

COMPLETE SET (10) 24.00 40.00
1 Ilya Kovalchuk 10.00 20.00

2 Erik Cole 3.20 5.00
3 Mark Bell 1.20 2.00
4 Marcel Hossa 2.00 3.00
5 Mike Ribeiro 1.20 2.00
6 Rick DiPietro 4.00 5.00
7 Raffi Torres 2.00 2.00
8 Dan Blackburn 4.00 5.00
9 Krys Kolanos 3.20 5.00
10 Jeff Jillson 2.00 3.00

2002-03 Pacific Exclusive

This 200-card set consisted of 175 veteran cards, 17 prospect cards and 8 autographed rookie cards short-printed to 1000 copies each. A glitch during production caused two different versions of card #179 to be inserted into packs. Both Alex Henry and Jason Spezza cards were created and have been verified, they are labeled below with "A" and "B" suffixes for checklisting only.

COMP.SET w/o SP's (192) 40.00 100.00
1 Jean-Sebastien Giguere .40 1.00
2 Paul Kariya .40 1.00
3 Adam Oates .20 .50
4 Petr Sykora .20 .50
5 Dany Heatley .60 1.50
6 Milan Hnilicka .10 .25
7 Tomi Kallio .10 .25
8 Ilya Kovalchuk .60 1.50
9 Patrik Stefan .10 .25
10 Nick Boynton .10 .25
11 Glen Murray .20 .50
12 Brian Rolston .20 .50
13 Sergei Samsonov .40 1.00
14 Steve Shields .20 .50
15 Joe Thornton .75 2.00
16 Martin Biron .20 .50
17 Tim Connolly .10 .25
18 J-P Dumont .10 .25
19 Mika Noronen .20 .50
20 Miroslav Satan .20 .50
21 Craig Conroy .10 .25
22 Chris Drury .20 .50
23 Jarome Iginla .60 1.50
24 Roman Turek .20 .50
25 Bates Battaglia .10 .25
26 Rod Brind'Amour .20 .50
27 Erik Cole .20 .50
28 Ron Francis .40 1.00
29 Arturs Irbe .20 .50
30 Sami Kapanen .10 .25
31 Jeff O'Neill .10 .25
32 Jaroslav Svoboda .10 .25
33 Josef Vasicek .10 .25
34 Mark Bell .10 .25
35 Eric Daze .20 .50
36 Theo Fleury .20 .50
37 Jocelyn Thibault .20 .50
38 Alexei Zhamnov .10 .25
39 Rob Blake .40 1.00
40 Peter Forsberg 1.25 3.00
41 Milan Hejduk .40 1.00
42 Dean McAmmond .10 .25
43 Derek Morris .10 .25
44 Steven Reinprecht .10 .25
45 Patrick Roy 2.50 6.00
46 Joe Sakic 1.00 2.50
47 Alex Tanguay .40 1.00
48 Radim Vrbata .10 .25
49 Andrew Cassels .10 .25
50 Marc Denis .20 .50
51 Rostislav Klesla .10 .25
52 Espen Knutsen .10 .25
53 Ray Whitney .10 .25
54 Jason Arnott .10 .25
55 Bill Guerin .20 .50
56 Jere Lehtinen .20 .50
57 Mike Modano .75 2.00
58 Marty Turco .40 1.00
59 Pierre Turgeon .20 .50
60 Chris Chelios .20 .50
61 Pavel Datsyuk .40 1.00
62 Sergei Fedorov .75 2.00
63 Brett Hull .60 1.50
64 Curtis Joseph .40 1.00
65 Nicklas Lidstrom .40 1.00
66 Luc Robitaille .40 1.00
67 Brendan Shanahan .40 1.00
68 Steve Yzerman 2.00 5.00
69 Anson Carter .20 .50
70 Mike Comrie .20 .50
71 Tommy Salo .20 .50
72 Jason Smith .10 .25
73 Ryan Smyth .20 .50
74 Mike York .10 .25
75 Valeri Bure .10 .25
76 Kristian Huselius .10 .25
77 Roberto Luongo .60 1.50
78 Stephen Weiss .10 .25
79 Jason Allison .10 .25
80 Adam Deadmarsh .10 .25
81 Zigmund Palffy .20 .50

82 Felix Potvin .40 1.00
83 Bryan Smolinski .10 .25
84 Andrew Brunette .10 .25
85 Pascal Dupuis .10 .25
86 Manny Fernandez .20 .50
87 Marian Gaborik 1.00 2.50
88 Cliff Ronning .10 .25
89 Mariusz Czerkawski .10 .25
90 Marcel Hossa .10 .25
91 Saku Koivu .40 1.00
92 Yanic Perreault .10 .25
93 Oleg Petrov .10 .25
94 Jose Theodore .60 1.50
95 Richard Zednik .10 .25
96 Denis Arkhipov .10 .25
97 Mike Dunham .20 .50
98 Scott Hartnell .10 .25
99 Greg Johnson .10 .25
100 David Legwand .20 .50
101 Christian Berglund .10 .25
102 Martin Brodeur 1.25 3.00
103 Patrik Elias .20 .50
104 Jeff Friesen .10 .25
105 Joe Nieuwendyk .20 .50
106 Rick DiPietro .20 .50
107 Brad Isbister .10 .25
108 Chris Osgood .20 .50
109 Mark Parrish .10 .25
110 Michael Peca .10 .25
111 Alexei Yashin .10 .25
112 Dan Blackburn .20 .50
113 Pavel Bure .40 1.00
114 Bobby Holik .10 .25
115 Brian Leetch .40 1.00
116 Eric Lindros .40 1.00
117 Mark Messier .40 1.00
118 Mike Richter .20 .50
119 Daniel Alfredsson .20 .50
120 Radek Bonk .10 .25
121 Martin Havlat .20 .50
122 Marian Hossa .40 1.00
123 Patrick Lalime .20 .50
124 Pavel Brendl .10 .25
125 Roman Cechmanek .20 .50
126 Simon Gagne .40 1.00
127 John LeClair .20 .50
128 Mark Recchi .20 .50
129 Jeremy Roenick .60 1.50
130 Tony Amonte .20 .50
131 Brian Boucher .20 .50
132 Daniel Briere .10 .25
133 Sean Burke .20 .50
134 Krystofer Kolanos .10 .25
135 Daymond Langkow .10 .25
136 Johan Hedberg .20 .50
137 Alexei Kovalev .20 .50
138 Mario Lemieux 3.00 8.00
139 Alexei Morozov .10 .25
140 Martin Straka .10 .25
141 Pavol Demitra .20 .50
142 Barret Jackman .20 .50
143 Brent Johnson .20 .50
144 Al MacInnis .20 .50
145 Chris Pronger .20 .50
146 Keith Tkachuk .40 1.00
147 Doug Weight .20 .50
148 Vincent Damphousse .10 .25
149 Patrick Marleau .20 .50
150 Evgeni Nabokov .20 .50
151 Owen Nolan .20 .50
152 Teemu Selanne .40 1.00
153 Scott Thornton .10 .25
154 Dave Andreychuk .20 .50
155 Nikolai Khabibulin .40 1.00
156 Vincent Lecavalier .40 1.00
157 Brad Richards .40 1.00
158 Shane Willis .10 .25
159 Ed Belfour .40 1.00
160 Alyn McCauley .10 .25
161 Alexander Mogilny .20 .50
162 Gary Roberts .10 .25
163 Mats Sundin .40 1.00
164 Darcy Tucker .10 .25
165 Todd Bertuzzi .20 .50
166 Dan Cloutier .20 .50
167 Ed Jovanovski .20 .50
168 Brendan Morrison .20 .50
169 Markus Naslund .40 1.00
170 Peter Bondra .20 .50
171 Sergei Gonchar .10 .25
172 Jaromir Jagr .75 2.00
173 Olaf Kolzig .40 1.00
174 Robert Lang .10 .25
175 Dainius Zubrus .10 .25
176 Martin Gerber RC 1.50 4.00
177 Dmitri Bykov RC 1.50 4.00
178 Ales Hemsky RC 4.00 10.00
179A Alex Henry RC 1.50 4.00
179B Jason Spezza SP RC 6.00 15.00
180 P-M Bouchard RC 4.00 10.00
181 Ron Hainsey RC 1.50 4.00
182 Adam Hall RC 1.50 4.00
183 Scottie Upshall RC 2.00 5.00
184 Mike Danton .10 .25
185 Jamie Lundmark .10 .25
186 Anton Volchenkov RC 1.50 4.00
187 Dennis Seidenberg RC 1.50 4.00
188 Patrick Sharp RC 1.50 4.00
189 Petr Cajanek .10 .25
190 Jonathan Cheechoo .20 .50
191 Fedor Fedorov .10 .25
192 Steve Eminger RC 1.50 4.00
193 Stanislav Chistov AU RC 6.00 15.00
194 Alexei Smirnov AU RC 5.00 12.00
195 Chuck Kobasew AU RC 6.00 15.00
196 Rick Nash AU RC 25.00 60.00
197 Henrik Zetterberg AU RC 25.00 50.00
198 Jay Bouwmeester AU RC 8.00 20.00
199 Alexander Frolov AU RC 10.00 25.00
200 Alexander Svitov AU RC 6.00 15.00

2002-03 Pacific Exclusive Blue

Inserted into hobby packs at a stated rate of 1:11, this 25-card set paralleled the last 25 cards of the base set but carried blue foil backgrounds on the card fronts. No cards in this parallel set were autographed. Each card was serial-numbered out of 699.

*NON-SP's: .3X TO .75X BASE HI
*SP's: .10X TO .25X BASE HI
179B Jason Spezza 6.00 15.00

2002-03 Pacific Exclusive Gold

This 200-card set was inserted at 1:1 hobby and 1:2 retail packs and directly paralleled the base set but card fronts carried a gold foil background. Cards 193-200 were not autographed as in the base set.

*STARS: .5X TO 1.25X BASE HI
*ROOKIE SP's: X TO X BASE HI

2002-03 Pacific Exclusive Retail

The only cards that were different in retail packs than hobby packs of 2002-03 Pacific Exclusive were cards 193-200. Those retail cards were unsigned and carried the same dot matrix pattern as the other players. All other players had the same card in both hobby and retail.

*STARS: SAME VALUE AS HOBBY
193 Stanislav Chistov RC 4.00 10.00
194 Alexei Smirnov RC 2.50 6.00
195 Chuck Kobasew RC 3.00 8.00
196 Rick Nash RC 8.00 20.00
197 Henrik Zetterberg RC 8.00 20.00
198 Jay Bouwmeester RC 5.00 12.00
199 Alexander Frolov RC 4.00 10.00
200 Alexander Svitov RC 2.00 5.00

2002-03 Pacific Exclusive Advantage

COMPLETE SET (15) 10.00 20.00
STATED ODDS 1:6 HOBBY/1:13 RETAIL
1 Jean-Sebastien Giguere .50 1.25
2 Roman Turek .50 1.25
3 Arturs Irbe .50 1.25
4 Patrick Roy 2.00 5.00
5 Marc Denis .50 1.25
6 Marty Turco .50 1.25
7 Curtis Joseph .60 1.50
8 Roberto Luongo .75 2.00
9 Felix Potvin .60 1.50
10 Jose Theodore .75 2.00
11 Martin Brodeur 1.00 2.50
12 Mike Richter .60 1.50
13 Brent Johnson .50 1.25
14 Evgeni Nabokov .50 1.25
15 Ed Belfour .60 1.50

2002-03 Pacific Exclusive Destined

COMPLETE SET (10) 6.00 15.00
STATED ODDS 1:11 HOBBY/1:25 RETAIL
1 Stanislav Chistov .60 1.50
2 Dany Heatley 1.25 3.00
3 Ilya Kovalchuk 1.50 4.00
4 Ivan Huml .60 1.50
5 Rick Nash 2.00 5.00
6 Pavel Datsyuk 1.25 3.00
7 Kristian Huselius .60 1.50
8 Stephen Weiss .60 1.50
9 Jamie Lundmark .60 1.50
10 Jonathan Cheechoo 1.25 3.00

2002-03 Pacific Exclusive Etched in Stone

COMPLETE SET (10) 30.00 60.00
STATED ODDS 1:21 HOBBY/1:25 RETAIL
1 Paul Kariya .75 2.00
2 Ron Francis .75 2.00
3 Patrick Roy 5.00 12.00
4 Joe Sakic 2.00 5.00
5 Brett Hull 1.25 3.00
6 Steve Yzerman 5.00 12.00
7 Martin Brodeur 2.50 6.00
8 Eric Lindros .75 2.00
9 Mario Lemieux 6.00 15.00
10 Jaromir Jagr 1.50 4.00

2002-03 Pacific Exclusive Great Expectations

COMPLETE SET (15) 12.50 25.00
STATED ODDS 1:6 HOBBY/1:13 RETAIL
1 Dany Heatley 1.25 3.00
2 Ilya Kovalchuk 1.25 3.00
3 Ivan Huml .75 2.00
4 Erik Cole .75 2.00
5 Radim Vrbata .75 2.00
6 Pavel Datsyuk 1.00 2.50
7 Mike Comrie .75 2.00
8 Kristian Huselius .75 2.00
9 Stephen Weiss .75 2.00
10 Marian Gaborik 2.00 5.00
11 Marcel Hossa .75 2.00
12 Rick DiPietro .75 2.00
13 Dan Blackburn .75 2.00
14 Krystofer Kolanos .75 2.00
15 Barret Jackman .75 2.00

2002-03 Pacific Exclusive Jerseys

COMMON CARD (1-25) 3.00 8.00
*MULT.COLOR SWATCH: .5X TO 1.25X HI
STATED ODDS 2:21 HOBBY/1:49 RETAIL
1 Tomi Kallio 3.00 8.00
2 Joe Thornton 10.00 25.00
3 Miroslav Satan 5.00 12.00
4 Theo Fleury 3.00 8.00
5 Milan Hejduk 6.00 15.00
6 Pierre Turgeon 5.00 12.00
7 Sergei Fedorov 12.50 30.00
8 Nicklas Lidstrom 6.00 15.00
9 Tommy Salo 5.00 12.00
10 Kristian Huselius 3.00 8.00
11 Roberto Luongo 8.00 20.00
12 Bryan Smolinski 3.00 8.00
13 Manny Fernandez 5.00 12.00
14 Mariusz Czerkawski 3.00 8.00
15 David Legwand 5.00 12.00
16 Bobby Holik 3.00 8.00
17 Eric Lindros 6.00 15.00
18 Marian Hossa 6.00 15.00
19 Michal Handzus 3.00 8.00
20 Alexei Kovalev 5.00 12.00
21 Keith Tkachuk 6.00 15.00
22 Patrick Marleau 5.00 12.00
23 Brad Richards 5.00 12.00
24 Mats Sundin 6.00 15.00
25 Olaf Kolzig 5.00 12.00

2002-03 Pacific Exclusive Jerseys Gold

STATED PRINT RUN 25 SER.#'d SETS
NOT PRICED DUE TO SCARCITY

2002-03 Pacific Exclusive Maximum Overdrive

COMPLETE SET (20) 15.00 30.00
STATED ODDS 1:6 HOBBY/1:13 RETAIL
1 Paul Kariya .40 1.00
2 Dany Heatley .50 1.25
3 Ilya Kovalchuk .50 1.25
4 Joe Thornton .60 1.50
5 Jarome Iginla .50 1.25
6 Peter Forsberg 1.00 2.50
7 Joe Sakic .75 2.00
8 Mike Modano .60 1.50
9 Sergei Fedorov .75 2.00
10 Steve Yzerman 2.00 5.00
11 Saku Koivu .40 1.00
12 Patrik Elias .40 1.00
13 Alexei Yashin .40 1.00
14 Pavel Bure .50 1.25
15 Simon Gagne .40 1.00
16 Mario Lemieux 2.50 6.00
17 Teemu Selanne .40 1.00
18 Mats Sundin .40 1.00
19 Markus Naslund .40 1.00
20 Jaromir Jagr .60 1.50

2003-04 Pacific Exhibit

This 225-card set was released in eraly-October and consisted of four distinct subsets. Cards 1-150 were regular base cards, cards 151-200 were over-sized cards measuring approximatley 3.5" X 5" and cards 201-215 were over-sized jersey cards. Cards 216-225 made up the "Time Warp" subset, the cards were over-sized and contained a jersey swatch of a current player and an authentic autograph of a retired great, each serial-numbered out of 565. Cards 226-235 were available in packs of Pacific Calder.

COMP.SET w/o SP's (150) 30.00 60.00
COMP.SET w/o JSYS (200) 50.00 100.00
1 Stanislav Chistov .10 .25
2 Mike Leclerc .10 .25
3 Adam Oates .20 .50
4 Sandis Ozolinsh .10 .25
5 Vaclav Prospal .10 .25
6 Steve Rucchin .10 .25
7 Steve Thomas .10 .25
8 Byron Dafoe .20 .50
9 Joe DiPenta RC .20 .50
10 Slava Kozlov .10 .25
11 Patrik Stefan .10 .25
12 Bryan Berard .10 .25
13 Mike Knuble .10 .25
14 Glen Murray .10 .25
15 Brian Rolston .20 .50
16 Milan Bartovic RC .20 .50
17 Daniel Briere .10 .25
18 Chris Drury .20 .50
19 J-P Dumont .10 .25
20 Ales Kotalik .10 .25
21 Ryan Miller .20 .50
22 Miroslav Satan .20 .50
23 Craig Conroy .10 .25
24 Martin Gelinas .10 .25
25 Roman Turek .20 .50
26 Rod Brind'Amour .20 .50
27 Erik Cole .10 .25
28 Arturs Irbe .20 .50
29 Jeff O'Neill .10 .25
30 Tyler Arnason .20 .50
31 Kyle Calder .10 .25
32 Eric Daze .10 .25
33 Theoren Fleury .10 .25
34 Alexei Zhamnov .10 .25
35 David Aebischer .20 .50
36 Rob Blake .20 .50
37 Milan Hejduk .25 .60
38 Derek Morris .10 .25
39 Teemu Selanne .25 .60
40 Alex Tanguay .20 .50
41 Andrew Cassels .10 .25
42 Marc Denis .20 .50
43 Kent McDonell RC .20 .50
44 Geoff Sanderson .10 .25
45 Ray Whitney .10 .25
46 Jason Arnott .10 .25
47 Bill Guerin .20 .50
48 Jere Lehtinen .20 .50
49 Brenden Morrow .20 .50
50 Teppo Numminen .10 .25
51 Chris Chelios .25 .60
52 Pavel Datsyuk .25 .60
53 Derian Hatcher .10 .25
54 Nicklas Lidstrom .25 .60
55 Brendan Shanahan .25 .60
56 Henrik Zetterberg .25 .60
57 Mike Comrie .20 .50
58 Ales Hemsky .20 .50
59 Georges Laraque .10 .25
60 Tommy Salo .20 .50
61 Mike York .10 .25
62 Jay Bouwmeester .10 .25
63 Kristian Huselius .10 .25
64 Olli Jokinen .10 .25
65 Stephen Weiss .20 .50
66 Jason Allison .20 .50
67 Roman Cechmanek .20 .50
68 Adam Deadmarsh .10 .25
69 Alexander Frolov .10 .25
70 Felix Potvin .20 .50
71 Andrew Brunette .10 .25
72 Manny Fernandez .20 .50
73 Filip Kuba .10 .25
74 Dwayne Roloson .20 .50
75 Cliff Ronning .10 .25
76 Mathieu Garon .20 .50
77 Marcel Hossa .10 .25
78 Yanic Perreault .10 .25
79 Richard Zednik .10 .25
80 Scott Hartnell .10 .25
81 Andreas Johansson .10 .25
82 Tomas Vokoun .20 .50
83 Scott Walker .10 .25
84 Patrik Elias .20 .50
85 Jeff Friesen .10 .25
86 Scott Gomez .10 .25
87 Jamie Langenbrunner .10 .25
88 John Madden .10 .25
89 Joe Nieuwendyk .20 .50
90 Scott Stevens .20 .50
91 Jason Blake .10 .25
92 Rick DiPietro .20 .50
93 Roman Hamrlik .10 .25
94 Mark Parrish .10 .25
95 Dan Blackburn .20 .50
96 Anson Carter .25 .60
97 Mike Dunham .20 .50
98 Bobby Holik .10 .25
99 Alex Kovalev .20 .50
100 Tom Poti .10 .25
101 Daniel Alfredsson .20 .50
102 Zdeno Chara .10 .25
103 Mike Fisher .10 .25
104 Martin Havlat .20 .50
105 Bryan Smolinski .10 .25
106 Jason Spezza .25 .60
107 Todd White .10 .25
108 Tony Amonte .20 .50
109 Simon Gagne .25 .60
110 Jeff Hackett .20 .50
111 Keith Primeau .20 .50
112 Mark Recchi .20 .50
113 Shane Doan .10 .25
114 Chris Gratton .10 .25
115 Mike Johnson .10 .25
116 Daymond Langkow .10 .25
117 Johan Hedberg .20 .50
118 Aleksey Morozov .10 .25
119 Martin Straka .10 .25
120 Dick Tarnstrom .10 .25
121 Pavol Demitra .20 .50
122 Al MacInnis .20 .50
123 Chris Pronger .20 .50
124 Peter Sejna RC .20 .50
125 Keith Tkachuk .25 .60
126 Doug Weight .20 .50
127 Jonathan Cheechoo .12 .30
128 Vincent Damphousse .10 .25
129 Patrick Marleau .20 .50
130 Dave Andreychuk .10 .25
131 John Grahame .20 .50
132 Brad Richards .20 .50
133 Martin St. Louis .20 .50
134 Nik Antropov .10 .25
135 Tie Domi .20 .50
136 Doug Gilmour .20 .50
137 Alexander Mogilny .20 .50
138 Matt Stajan RC 1.00 2.50
139 Darcy Tucker .10 .25
140 Dan Cloutier .20 .50
141 Ed Jovanovski .20 .50
142 Trevor Linden .10 .25
143 Brendan Morrison .20 .50
144 Daniel Sedin .10 .25
145 Henrik Sedin .10 .25
146 Sergei Berezin .10 .25
147 Peter Bondra .20 .50
148 Sebastien Charpentier .20 .50
149 Sergei Gonchar .10 .25
150 Michael Nylander .10 .25
151 Sergei Fedorov .75 2.00
152 Jean-Sebastien Giguere .60 1.50
153 Dany Heatley .75 2.00
154 Ilya Kovalchuk .75 2.00
155 Joe Thornton .75 2.00
156 Martin Biron .60 1.50
157 Jarome Iginla .75 2.00
158 Ron Francis .60 1.50
159 Jocelyn Thibault .60 1.50
160 Peter Forsberg 1.50 4.00
161 Paul Kariya .10 .25
162 Patrick Roy 2.00 5.00
163 Joe Sakic 1.25 3.00
164 Rick Nash .75 2.00
165 Mike Modano 1.00 2.50
166 Marty Turco .60 1.50
167 Dominik Hasek 1.25 3.00
168 Brett Hull .75 2.00
169 Steve Yzerman 2.00 5.00
170 Ryan Smyth .60 1.50
171 Roberto Luongo .75 2.00
172 Ziggy Palffy .60 1.50
173 Marian Gaborik 1.25 3.00
174 Saku Koivu .60 1.50
175 Jose Theodore .75 2.00
176 David Legwand .60 1.50
177 Martin Brodeur 1.50 4.00
178 Michael Peca .60 1.50
179 Alexei Yashin .60 1.50
180 Pavel Bure .60 1.50
181 Eric Lindros .60 1.50
182 Mark Messier .60 1.50
183 Marian Hossa .60 1.50
184 Patrick Lalime .60 1.50
185 John LeClair .60 1.50
186 Jeremy Roenick .75 2.00
187 Sean Burke .60 1.50
188 Mario Lemieux 2.50 6.00
189 Barret Jackman .60 1.50
190 Chris Osgood .60 1.50
191 Evgeni Nabokov .60 1.50
192 Nikolai Khabibulin .60 1.50
193 Vincent Lecavalier .60 1.50
194 Ed Belfour .60 1.50
195 Owen Nolan .60 1.50
196 Mats Sundin .60 1.50
197 Todd Bertuzzi .60 1.50
198 Markus Naslund .60 1.50
199 Jaromir Jagr 1.00 2.50
200 Olaf Kolzig .60 1.50
201 Stanislav Chistov 6.00 15.00
202 Martin Biron 6.00 15.00
203 Eric Daze 6.00 15.00
204 Milan Hejduk 8.00 20.00
205 Bill Guerin 6.00 15.00
206 Marty Turco 6.00 15.00
207 Jason Allison 6.00 15.00
208 Roman Cechmanek 6.00 15.00
209 David Legwand 6.00 15.00
210 Patrick Lalime 6.00 15.00
211 Tony Amonte 6.00 15.00
212 Jeff Hackett 6.00 15.00
213 Sean Burke 6.00 15.00
214 Chris Osgood 6.00 15.00
215 Nikolai Khabibulin 8.00 20.00
216 B.Hull/B.Hull 20.00 50.00
217 S.Yzerman/T.Esposito 15.00 40.00
218 P.Roy/J.Beliveau 30.00 80.00
219 I.Kovalchuk/G.Lafleur 15.00 40.00
220 D.Heatley/G.Hall 15.00 40.00
221 M.Lemieux/J.Bower 30.00 80.00
222 J.Theodore/D.Sittler 16.00 40.00
223 P.Kariya/M.Dionne 15.00 40.00
224 M.Brodeur/F.Mahovlich 25.00 60.00
225 J.Sakic/B.Park 15.00 40.00
226 Joffrey Lupul RC 1.50 4.00
227 Patrice Bergeron RC 4.00 10.00
228 Matthew Lombardi RC 1.00 2.50
229 Eric Staal RC 3.00 8.00
230 Nikolai Zherdev RC 4.00 10.00
231 Nathan Horton RC 2.50 6.00
232 Brent Burns RC 1.00 2.50
233 Joni Pitkanen RC 1.50 4.00
234 Marc-Andre Fleury RC 6.00 15.00
235 Ryan Malone RC 2.00 5.00

2003-04 Pacific Exhibit Blue Backs

*CARDS 1-150: .75X TO 2X BASE HI
1-150 ODDS 1:10 HOBBY/1:13 RETAIL
1-150 PRINT RUN 275 SER.#'d SETS
*CARDS 151-200: 1X TO 2.5X
151-200 ODDS 1:15 HOBBY/1:25 RETAIL
151-200 PRINT RUN 425 SER.#'d SETS

2003-04 Pacific Exhibit Yellow Backs

*STARS: .5X TO 1.25X BASE HI
ONE PER HOBBY PACK

2003-04 Pacific Exhibit History Makers

COMPLETE SET (8) 12.50 25.00
STATED ODDS 1:29 HOBBY/1:25 RETAIL
1 Paul Kariya .60 1.50
2 Peter Forsberg 1.50 4.00
3 Joe Sakic 1.25 3.00
4 Brett Hull .75 2.00
5 Steve Yzerman 2.50 6.00
6 Mario Lemieux 3.00 8.00
7 Todd Bertuzzi .60 1.50
8 Markus Naslund .60 1.50

2003-04 Pacific Exhibit Pursuing Prominence

COMPLETE SET (12) 8.00 15.00
STATED ODDS 1:15 HOBBY/1:13 RETAIL
1 Dany Heatley 1.00 2.50
2 Ilya Kovalchuk 1.00 2.50
3 Joe Thornton 1.00 2.50
4 Rick Nash 1.00 2.50
5 Henrik Zetterberg 1.00 2.50
6 Ales Hemsky .50 1.25
7 Jay Bouwmeester .50 1.25
8 Marian Gaborik 2.00 5.00
9 Marian Hossa .50 1.25
10 Jason Spezza 1.00 2.50
11 Barret Jackman .50 1.25
12 Vincent Lecavalier .50 1.25

2003-04 Pacific Exhibit Standing on Tradition

COMPLETE SET (10) 10.00 20.00
STATED ODDS 1:29 HOBBY/1:25 RETAIL
1 Jean-Sebastien Giguere .60 1.50
2 Jocelyn Thibault .60 1.50
3 Patrick Roy 2.50 6.00
4 Marty Turco .60 1.50
5 Dominik Hasek 1.50 4.00
6 Roberto Luongo 1.00 2.50
7 Jose Theodore 1.00 2.50
8 Martin Brodeur 2.00 5.00
9 Patrick Lalime .60 1.50
10 Ed Belfour .75 2.00

2001-02 Pacific Heads Up

Released in mid-November 2001, this 120-card set carried an SRP of $3.99 for a five-card hobby pack with 18 packs per box. The set consisted of 100 veteran cards and 20 shortprinted Rookie Cards available in hobby packs only. Rookies (Cards 101-120) were serial-numbered to 999 sets.

COM.SET w/o SP's (100) 20.00 50.00
1 Paul Kariya .30 .75
2 Steve Shields .10 .25
3 Ray Ferraro .10 .25
4 Milan Hnilicka .20 .50
5 Patrik Stefan .10 .25
6 Jason Allison .10 .25
7 Byron Dafoe .20 .50
8 Bill Guerin .20 .50
9 Sergei Samsonov .20 .50
10 Joe Thornton .60 1.50
11 J-P Dumont .10 .25
12 Jarome Iginla .60 1.50
13 Marc Savard .10 .25
14 Roman Turek .20 .50
15 Ron Francis .20 .50
16 Arturs Irbe .20 .50
17 Jeff O'Neill .10 .25
18 Tony Amonte .20 .50
19 Steve Sullivan .10 .25
20 Jocelyn Thibault .20 .50
21 Rob Blake .20 .50
22 Chris Drury .20 .50
23 Peter Forsberg .75 2.00
24 Milan Hejduk .20 .50
25 Patrick Roy 2.00 5.00
26 Joe Sakic .75 2.00
27 Marc Denis .20 .50
28 Geoff Sanderson .10 .25
29 Ed Belfour .30 .75
30 Brett Hull .40 1.00
31 Mike Modano .60 1.50
32 Joe Nieuwendyk .20 .50
33 Pierre Turgeon .20 .50
34 Sergei Fedorov .60 1.50
35 Dominik Hasek .75 2.00
36 Chris Osgood .20 .50
37 Luc Robitaille .20 .50
38 Brendan Shanahan .30 .75
39 Steve Yzerman 1.50 4.00
40 Mike Comrie .20 .50
41 Tommy Salo .20 .50
42 Ryan Smyth .10 .25
43 Pavel Bure .30 .75
44 Roberto Luongo .60 1.50
45 Steve Heinze .10 .25
46 Zigmund Palffy .20 .50
47 Felix Potvin .30 .75
48 Manny Fernandez .20 .50
49 Marian Gaborik .60 1.50
50 Saku Koivu .30 .75
51 Brian Savage .10 .25
52 Jose Theodore .40 1.00
53 Mike Dunham .20 .50
54 David Legwand .20 .50
55 Jason Arnott .10 .25
56 Martin Brodeur 1.00 2.50
57 Patrik Elias .20 .50
58 Scott Stevens .20 .50
59 Mariusz Czerkawski .10 .25
60 Rick DiPietro .20 .50
61 Mike Peca .10 .25
62 Alexei Yashin .10 .25
63 Theo Fleury .20 .50
64 Brian Leetch .20 .50
65 Mark Messier .30 .75
66 Mike Richter .30 .75
67 Daniel Alfredsson .20 .50
68 Martin Havlat .20 .50
69 Marian Hossa .30 .75
70 Patrick Lalime .20 .50
71 Roman Cechmanek .20 .50
72 John LeClair .20 .50
73 Mark Recchi .20 .50
74 Jeremy Roenick .40 1.00
75 Sean Burke .20 .50
76 Johan Hedberg .20 .50
77 Alexei Kovalev .20 .50
78 Mario Lemieux 2.00 5.00
79 Fred Brathwaite .20 .50
80 Chris Pronger .20 .50
81 Keith Tkachuk .20 .50
82 Doug Weight .20 .50
83 Patrick Marleau .20 .50
84 Evgeni Nabokov .20 .50
85 Teemu Selanne .30 .75
86 Nikolai Khabibulin .30 .75
87 Vincent Lecavalier .30 .75
88 Brad Richards .20 .50
89 Curtis Joseph .30 .75
90 Alexander Mogilny .20 .50
91 Gary Roberts .10 .25
92 Mats Sundin .30 .75
93 Dan Cloutier .20 .50
94 Markus Naslund .20 .50
95 Daniel Sedin .10 .25
96 Henrik Sedin .10 .25
97 Peter Bondra .20 .50
98 Jaromir Jagr .60 1.50
99 Olaf Kolzig .20 .50
100 Adam Oates .20 .50
101 Ilja Bryzgalov RC 3.00 8.00
102 Timo Parssinen RC 1.25 3.00
103 Ilya Kovalchuk RC 10.00 25.00
104 Erik Cole RC 3.00 8.00
105 Vaclav Nedorost RC 1.25 3.00
106 Pavel Datsyuk RC 8.00 20.00
107 Kristian Huselius RC 3.00 8.00
108 Jaroslav Bednar RC 1.25 3.00
109 Pascal Dupuis RC 1.25 3.00
110 Martin Erat RC 1.25 3.00
111 Scott Clemmensen RC 1.25 3.00
112 Dan Blackburn RC 1.25 3.00
113 Chris Neil RC 3.00 8.00
114 Pavel Brendl SP 1.25 3.00
115 Jiri Dopita RC 1.25 3.00
116 Krystofer Kolanos RC 1.25 3.00
117 Mark Rycroft RC 1.25 3.00
118 Jeff Jillson RC 1.25 3.00
119 Nikita Alexeev RC 1.25 3.00
120 Brian Sutherby RC 1.25 3.00

2001-02 Pacific Heads Up Blue

Randomly inserted in packs at a rate of 1:37 hobby packs, This 100-card set paralleled the base set but featured full color action card fronts with a blue holographic background. Each card was serial-numbered to 55 on the card fronts.

*BLUE: 10X TO 25X BASIC CARD

2001-02 Pacific Heads Up Premiere Date

Randomly inserted into hobby packs at the rate of one per box, this 100-card set paralleled the base set but was enhanced with a foil premiere date box on the card front. Each card was serial-numbered out of 105.

*STARS: 6X TO 15X BASIC CARD

2001-02 Pacific Heads Up Red

Randomly inserted in retail packs at a rate of 2:25 , this 100 card set paralleled the base set but carried a red holographic background. Each card was serial-numbered to 165.

*RED: 5X TO 12X BASIC CARDS

2001-02 Pacific Heads Up Silver

Randomly inserted into packs at 1:145 hobby and 1:241 retail, this 100-card set paralleled the base set but featured a silver holographic card front. Each card was serial-numbered to 27.

NOT PRICED DUE TO SCARCITY

2001-02 Pacific Heads Up All-Star Net

Randomly inserted in packs at a rate of 1:1153 hobby and 1:2401 retail. This set featured 2 player action color photos on the card front along with a swatch of game-used NHL All-Star goal net located in a gold box at the bottom center of card. Cards were serial-numbered to 65.

1 Evgeni Nabokov 25.00 60.00
Roman Cechmanek
2 Martin Brodeur 50.00 125.00
Rob Blake
3 Bill Guerin 25.00 60.00
Doug Weight
4 Pavel Bure 25.00 60.00
Zigmund Palffy
5 Paul Kariya 25.00 60.00
Mats Sundin
6 Chris Pronger 25.00 60.00
Nicklas Lidstrom

2001-02 Pacific Heads Up Bobble Heads

Randomly inserted in hobby boxes at a rate of 1 per box and in retail packs as redemption cards at 1:121, this 12-player ceramic bobble head doll set featured the Pacific logo on the base along with the Pacific Heads-Up logo with the last name of each player. Please note that the Comrie bobble head was not produced and was redeemable for another randomly chosen bobble head as a replacement. Collectors receiving a bobble head of Pacific president Mike Cramer also received a redemption card good for the entire set. Approximately 12 of these dolls were randomly inserted into boxes.

1 Paul Kariya 12.50 30.00
2 Patrick Roy 15.00 40.00
3 Joe Sakic 12.50 30.00
4 Dominik Hasek 12.50 30.00
5 Steve Yzerman 15.00 40.00
6 Exchange Card 12.50 30.00
7 Martin Brodeur 15.00 40.00
8 Mark Messier 12.50 30.00
9 Johan Hedberg 12.50 30.00
10 Mario Lemieux 20.00 50.00
11 Curtis Joseph 12.50 30.00
12 Jaromir Jagr 12.50 30.00

2001-02 Pacific Heads Up Breaking the Glass

COMPLETE SET (20) 30.00 60.00
STAT.ODDS 1:19 HOBBY/1:25 RETAIL
1 Milan Hnilicka 1.25 3.00
2 Patrik Stefan 1.25 3.00
3 J-P Dumont 1.25 3.00
4 Shane Willis 1.25 3.00
5 David Aebischer 1.25 3.00
6 Chris Drury 1.25 3.00
7 Alex Tanguay 2.00 5.00

8 Marc Denis 1.25 3.00
9 Marty Turco 1.25 3.00
10 Mike Comrie 1.25 3.00
11 Roberto Luongo 1.50 4.00
12 Marian Gaborik 3.00 8.00
13 David Legwand 1.25 3.00
14 Rick DiPietro 1.25 3.00
15 Martin Havlat 1.25 3.00
16 Johan Hedberg 1.25 3.00
17 Evgeni Nabokov 1.25 3.00
18 Brad Richards 1.25 3.00
19 Daniel Sedin 1.25 3.00
20 Henrik Sedin 1.25 3.00

2001-02 Pacific Heads Up HD NHL

Cards 1-10 in this 20-card set were only available in hobby packs at rate of 1:19. Cards 11-20 were only available in retail packs at an insertion rate of 1:25. Cards featured color player photos on silver metallic card stock.

COMPLETE SET (20) 25.00 50.00
1 Paul Kariya .75 2.00
2 Peter Forsberg 2.00 5.00
3 Joe Sakic 1.50 4.00
4 Mike Modano 1.25 3.00
5 Steve Yzerman 4.00 10.00
6 Pavel Bure 1.00 2.50
7 Mario Lemieux 5.00 12.00
8 Teemu Selanne .75 2.00
9 Mats Sundin .75 2.00
10 Jaromir Jagr 1.25 3.00
11 Roman Turek .60 1.50
12 Ed Belfour .75 2.00
13 Chris Osgood .60 1.50
14 Tommy Salo .60 1.50
15 Felix Potvin .75 2.00
16 Jose Theodore 1.00 2.50
17 Martin Brodeur 2.00 5.00
18 Mike Richter .75 2.00
19 Roman Cechmanek .60 1.50
20 Curtis Joseph .75 2.00

2001-02 Pacific Heads Up Prime Picks

COMPLETE SET (10) 15.00 40.00
STAT.ODDS 1:73 HOBBY/1:121 RETAIL
1 Mike Comrie 1.50 4.00
2 Roberto Luongo 4.00 10.00
3 Marian Gaborik 4.00 10.00
4 Rick DiPietro 1.50 4.00
5 Martin Havlat 1.50 4.00
6 Johan Hedberg 1.50 4.00
7 Evgeni Nabokov 1.50 4.00
8 Brad Richards 1.50 4.00
9 Daniel Sedin 1.50 4.00
10 Henrik Sedin 1.50 4.00

2001-02 Pacific Heads Up Quad Jerseys

Randomly inserted in packs at a rate of 2:19 hobby and 1:97 retail, this 29-card set featured color action photo's along with game-used jersey swatches on both card front and back for a total of 4 per card.

1 Jean-Sebastien Giguere 6.00 15.00
Mike Leclerc
Teemu Selanne
Guy Hebert
2 Joe Thornton 8.00 20.00
Sergei Samsonov
Kyle McLaren
Byron Dafoe
3 Scott Niedermeyer 8.00 20.00
Bobby Holik
P.J. Axelsson
Don Sweeney
4 Dominik Hasek 6.00 15.00
Stu Barnes
Mariusz Czerkawski
Kenny Jonsson
5 Jarome Iginla 6.00 15.00
Valeri Bure
Marc Savard
Rico Fata
6 Tony Amonte 6.00 15.00
Eric Daze
Jocelyn Thibault
Kyle Calder
7 Steve Sullivan 6.00 15.00
Alexei Zhamnov
Michael Nylander
Boris Mironov
8 Peter Forsberg 10.00 25.00
Joe Sakic
Aaron Miller
Dave Reid
9 Patrick Roy 8.00 20.00
Chris Dingman
Greg deVries
Jon Klemm
10 Mike Modano 6.00 15.00
Joe Nieuwendyk
Darryl Sydor
Derian Hatcher
11 Brendan Shanahan 8.00 20.00
Chris Chelios
Mathieu Dandenault
Chris Osgood
12 Benoit Brunet 6.00 15.00
Sergei Zholtok
Dainius Zubrus
Ulf Dahlen
13 Mike Dunham 6.00 15.00
David Legwnd
Tom Fitzgerald
Scott Walker
14 Theo Fleury 6.00 15.00
Brian Leetch
Mike Richter
Petr Nedved
15 John LeClair 6.00 15.00
Eric Desjardins
Kevin Stevens
Kip Miller
16 Jeremy Roenick 6.00 15.00
Sean Burke
Mika Alatalo
Shane Doan
17 Mario Lemieux 15.00 40.00
Jaromir Jagr
Jan Hrdina
Darius Kasparaitis
18 Martin Straka 6.00 15.00
Alexei Kovalev
Jean-Sebastien Aubin
Rich Parent
19 Tie Domi 6.00 15.00
Glenn Healy
Daniel Alfredsson
Dan Cloutier
20 Patrick Roy 20.00 50.00
Curtis Joseph
Dominik Hasek
Mike Richter
21 Lemieux/Sakic/Moda./Bure 30.00 80.00
22 Doug Weight 10.00 25.00
Chris Chelios
Derian Hatcher
Brian Leetch
23 Alexei Zhitnik 6.00 15.00
Eric Rasmussen
Rob Ray
Richard Smehlik
24 Jere Lehtinen 6.00 15.00
Mike Keane
Benoit Hogue
Blake Sloan
25 Mike York 6.00 15.00
Adam Graves
Sylvain Lefebvre
Manny Malhotra
26 Sean Burke 6.00 15.00
Teppo Numminen
Radoslav Suchy
Jyrki Lumme
27 Vincent Lecavalier 6.00 15.00
Keith Primeau
Matthew Barnaby
Milan Kraft
28 Martin Straka 6.00 15.00
Alexei Morozov
Josef Beranek
Bob Boughner
29 Alexei Kovalev 6.00 15.00
Michal Rozsival
Rich Parent
Darius Kasparaitis

2001-02 Pacific Heads Up Rink Immortals

Randomly inserted in packs at a rate of 1:289 packs, this 10-card set featured full color action shots with a grey silhouette background. Cards were serial numbered to 99 of each on the front of the card in lower right hand corner.

1 Paul Kariya 8.00 20.00
2 Patrick Roy 20.00 50.00
3 Joe Sakic 10.00 25.00
4 Brett Hull 8.00 20.00
5 Dominik Hasek 10.00 25.00
6 Steve Yzerman 15.00 40.00
7 Pavel Bure 6.00 15.00
8 Martin Brodeur 12.00 30.00
9 Mario Lemieux 25.00 60.00
10 Jaromir Jagr 10.00 25.00

2001-02 Pacific Heads Up Showstoppers

COMPLETE SET (20) 20.00 40.00
STATED ODDS 2:19 HOBBY/2:25 RETAIL
1 Steve Shields .60 1.50
2 Byron Dafoe .60 1.50
3 Roman Turek .60 1.50
4 Patrick Roy 4.00 10.00
5 Ed Belfour .75 2.00
6 Dominik Hasek 1.50 4.00
7 Chris Osgood .60 1.50
8 Tommy Salo .60 1.50
9 Roberto Luongo 1.00 2.50
10 Felix Potvin .75 2.00
11 Jose Theodore 1.00 2.50
12 Martin Brodeur 2.00 5.00
13 Rick DiPietro .60 1.50
14 Mike Richter .60 1.50
15 Patrick Lalime .60 1.50
16 Roman Cechmanek .60 1.50
17 Johan Hedberg .60 1.50
18 Evgeni Nabokov .60 1.50
19 Curtis Joseph .75 2.00
20 Olaf Kolzig .60 1.50

2001-02 Pacific Heads Up Stat Masters

COMPLETE SET (20) 25.00 50.00
STATED ODDS 2:19 HOBBY/2:25 RETAIL
1 Paul Kariya .60 1.50
2 Joe Thornton 1.00 2.50
3 Peter Forsberg 1.50 4.00
4 Joe Sakic 1.25 3.00
5 Brett Hull .75 2.00
6 Mike Modano 1.00 2.50
7 Steve Yzerman 3.00 8.00
8 Pavel Bure .75 2.00
9 Zigmund Palffy .50 1.25
10 Jason Arnott .50 1.25
11 Theo Fleury .50 1.25
12 Marian Hossa .60 1.50
13 Jeremy Roenick .60 1.50
14 Mario Lemieux 4.00 10.00
15 Keith Tkachuk .60 1.50
16 Teemu Selanne .60 1.50
17 Vincent Lecavalier .60 1.50
18 Brad Richards .50 1.25
19 Mats Sundin .60 1.50
20 Jaromir Jagr 1.00 2.50

2002-03 Pacific Heads Up

This 125-card set contained 125 veteran cards and 20 shortprinted rookie cards. Rookies were serial-numbered to 1000 each and were only available via a mail in redemption card found in packs.

COMPLETE SET (145) 100.00 200.00
COMP.SET w/o SP's (125) 30.00 60.00
1 Jean-Sebastien Giguere .30 .75
2 Paul Kariya .40 1.00
3 Adam Oates .30 .75
4 Dany Heatley .50 1.25
5 Milan Hnilicka .30 .75
6 Ilya Kovalchuk .50 1.25
7 Byron Dafoe .30 .75
8 Glen Murray .12 .30
9 Brian Rolston .12 .30
10 Sergei Samsonov .30 .75
11 Joe Thornton .60 1.50
12 Martin Biron .30 .75
13 J-P Dumont .12 .30
14 Miroslav Satan .30 .75
15 Craig Conroy .12 .30
16 Jarome Iginla .50 1.25
17 Dean McAmmond .12 .30
18 Roman Turek .30 .75
19 Erik Cole .12 .30
20 Ron Francis .30 .75
21 Arturs Irbe .30 .75
22 Sami Kapanen .12 .30
23 Jeff O'Neill .12 .30
24 Tony Amonte .30 .75
25 Eric Daze .30 .75
26 Jocelyn Thibault .30 .75
27 Alexei Zhamnov .12 .30
28 Rob Blake .30 .75
29 Chris Drury .30 .75
30 Peter Forsberg 1.00 2.50
31 Milan Hejduk .40 1.00
32 Patrick Roy 2.00 5.00
33 Joe Sakic .75 2.00
34 Marc Denis .30 .75
35 Rostislav Klesla .12 .30
36 Ray Whitney .12 .30
37 Jason Arnott .12 .30
38 Bill Guerin .30 .75
39 Mike Modano .60 1.50
40 Marty Turco .30 .75
41 Sergei Fedorov .60 1.50
42 Dominik Hasek .75 2.00
43 Brett Hull .50 1.25
44 Curtis Joseph .40 1.00
45 Nicklas Lidstrom .40 1.00
46 Luc Robitaille .30 .75
47 Brendan Shanahan .40 1.00
48 Steve Yzerman 2.00 5.00
49 Mike Comrie .30 .75
50 Tommy Salo .30 .75
51 Ryan Smyth .12 .30
52 Kristian Huselius .12 .30
53 Roberto Luongo .50 1.25
54 Stephen Weiss .12 .30
55 Jason Allison .12 .30
56 Adam Deadmarsh .12 .30
57 Zigmund Palffy .30 .75
58 Felix Potvin .40 1.00
59 Andrew Brunette .12 .30
60 Manny Fernandez .30 .75
61 Marian Gaborik .75 2.00
62 Donald Audette .12 .30
63 Doug Gilmour .30 .75
64 Saku Koivu .40 1.00
65 Yanic Perreault .12 .30
66 Jose Theodore .50 1.25
67 Denis Arkhipov .12 .30
68 Scott Hartnell .12 .30
69 David Legwand .30 .75
70 Martin Brodeur 1.00 2.50
71 Patrik Elias .30 .75
72 Joe Nieuwendyk .30 .75
73 Chris Osgood .30 .75
74 Mark Parrish .12 .30
75 Michael Peca .12 .30
76 Alexei Yashin .12 .30
77 Daniel Blackburn .30 .75
78 Pavel Bure .40 1.00
79 Theo Fleury .12 .30
80 Bobby Holik .12 .30
81 Brian Leetch .30 .75
82 Eric Lindros .40 1.00
83 Mike Richter .40 1.00
84 Daniel Alfredsson .30 .75
85 Radek Bonk .12 .30
86 Martin Havlat .30 .75
87 Marian Hossa .40 1.00
88 Patrick Lalime .30 .75
89 Roman Cechmanek .30 .75
90 Simon Gagne .40 1.00
91 John LeClair .40 1.00
92 Mark Recchi .30 .75
93 Jeremy Roenick .50 1.25
94 Daniel Briere .12 .30
95 Sean Burke .30 .75
96 Krystofer Kolanos .12 .30
97 Daymond Langkow .12 .30
98 Johan Hedberg .30 .75
99 Alexei Kovalev .30 .75
100 Mario Lemieux 2.50 6.00
101 Alexei Morozov .12 .30
102 Pavol Demitra .30 .75
103 Brent Johnson .30 .75
104 Chris Pronger .30 .75
105 Keith Tkachuk .40 1.00
106 Doug Weight .30 .75
107 Patrick Marleau .30 .75
108 Evgeni Nabokov .30 .75
109 Owen Nolan .30 .75
110 Teemu Selanne .40 1.00
111 Nikolai Khabibulin .40 1.00
112 Vincent Lecavalier .40 1.00
113 Brad Richards .30 .75
114 Ed Belfour .40 1.00
115 Alyn McCauley .12 .30
116 Alexander Mogilny .30 .75
117 Gary Roberts .12 .30
118 Mats Sundin .40 1.00
119 Todd Bertuzzi .40 1.00
120 Dan Cloutier .30 .75
121 Brendan Morrison .30 .75
122 Markus Naslund .40 1.00
123 Peter Bondra .30 .75
124 Jaromir Jagr .60 1.50
125 Olaf Kolzig .30 .75
126 Stanislav Chistov RC 1.50 4.00
127 Martin Gerber RC 2.50 6.00
128 Alexei Smirnov RC 1.50 4.00
129 Chuck Kobasew RC 2.50 6.00
130 Rick Nash RC 8.00 20.00
131 Dmitri Bykov RC 1.50 4.00
132 Henrik Zetterberg RC 6.00 15.00
133 Ales Hemsky RC 5.00 12.00
134 Jay Bouwmeester RC 3.00 8.00
135 Alexander Frolov RC 3.00 8.00
136 Sylvain Blouin RC 1.50 4.00
137 P-M Bouchard RC 3.00 8.00
138 Ron Hainsey RC 1.50 4.00
139 Scottie Upshall RC 1.50 4.00
140 Mike Danton SP 1.50 4.00
141 Ray Schultz RC 1.50 4.00
142 Anton Volchenkov RC 1.50 4.00
143 Dennis Seidenberg RC 1.50 4.00
144 Alexander Svitov RC 1.50 4.00
145 Steve Eminger RC 1.50 4.00

2002-03 Pacific Heads Up Blue

*BLUE: 1.25X TO 3X BASIC CARDS
STATED PRINT RUN 240 SER.#'d SETS

2002-03 Pacific Heads Up Purple

*PURPLE: 12X TO 30X BASIC CARDS
STATED ODDS 1:73
STATED PRINT RUN 30 SER.#'d SETS

2002-03 Pacific Heads Up Red

*RED: 8X TO 20X BASIC CARDS
STATED ODDS 1:19 HOBBY PACKS
STATED PRINT RUN 80 SER.#'d SETS

2002-03 Pacific Heads Up Bobble Heads

Randomly inserted on per hobby box, this 14-player ceramic bobble head doll set featured the Pacific logo on the base along with the Pacific Heads-Up logo with the last name of each player.

1 Jason Allison 10.00 25.00
2 Pavel Bure 10.00 25.00
3 Mike Comrie 10.00 25.00
4 Peter Forsberg 15.00 50.00
5 Jarome Iginla 15.00 40.00
6 Saku Koivu 10.00 25.00
7 Ilya Kovalchuk 15.00 40.00
8 Eric Lindros 10.00 25.00
9 Evgeni Nabokov 10.00 25.00
10 Brendan Shanahan 10.00 25.00
11 Mats Sundin 10.00 25.00
12 Jose Theodore 15.00 40.00
13 Joe Thornton 15.00 40.00
14 Alexei Yashin 10.00 25.00

2002-03 Pacific Heads Up Etched in Time

This 15-card set was inserted at a rate of 1:289 and each card was serial-numbered to just 85 copies.

1 Paul Kariya 6.00 15.00
2 Ilya Kovalchuk 8.00 20.00
3 Joe Thornton 8.00 20.00
4 Jarome Iginla 8.00 20.00
5 Ron Francis 6.00 15.00
6 Peter Forsberg 15.00 40.00
7 Patrick Roy 20.00 50.00
8 Joe Sakic 12.50 30.00
9 Dominik Hasek 15.00 40.00
10 Steve Yzerman 20.00 50.00
11 Martin Brodeur 15.00 40.00
12 Eric Lindros 6.00 15.00
13 Mario Lemieux 25.00 60.00
14 Mats Sundin 6.00 15.00
15 Jaromir Jagr 10.00 25.00

2002-03 Pacific Heads Up Head First

This 16-card set was inserted at a rate of 1:19.

COMPLETE SET (16) 20.00 40.00
1 Dany Heatley 1.50 4.00
2 Ilya Kovalchuk 2.00 5.00
3 Sergei Samsonov 1.00 2.50
4 Joe Thornton 2.00 5.00
5 Stephen Weiss 1.00 2.50
6 Marian Gaborik 2.50 6.00
7 Scott Hartnell 1.00 2.50
8 Rick DiPietro 1.00 2.50
9 Raffi Torres 1.00 2.50
10 Dan Blackburn 1.00 2.50
11 Martin Havlat 1.00 2.50
12 Simon Gagne 1.25 3.00
13 Krystofer Kolanos 1.00 2.50
14 Vincent Lecavalier 1.25 3.00
15 Daniel Sedin 1.00 2.50
16 Henrik Sedin 1.00 2.50

2002-03 Pacific Heads Up Inside the Numbers

This 24-card set was inserted at a rate of 1:10.

COMPLETE SET (24) 30.00 60.00
1 Adam Oates .60 1.50
2 Dany Heatley 1.00 2.50
3 Ilya Kovalchuk 1.00 2.50
4 Joe Thornton 1.25 3.00
5 Jarome Iginla 1.00 2.50
6 Ron Francis .60 1.50
7 Patrick Roy 3.00 8.00
8 Joe Sakic 1.50 4.00
9 Mike Modano 1.25 3.00
10 Dominik Hasek 2.00 5.00
11 Brendan Shanahan 1.25 3.00
12 Jose Theodore 1.00 2.50
13 Martin Brodeur 2.50 6.00
14 Alexei Yashin .60 1.50
15 Eric Lindros .75 2.00
16 Daniel Alfredsson .60 1.50
17 Mario Lemieux 4.00 10.00
18 Pavol Demitra .60 1.50
19 Evgeni Nabokov .60 1.50
20 Nikolai Khabibulin .75 2.00
21 Mats Sundin .75 2.00
22 Todd Bertuzzi .75 2.00
23 Markus Naslund .75 2.00
24 Jaromir Jagr 1.25 3.00

2002-03 Pacific Heads Up Postseason Picks

This 10-card set was inserted at a rate of 1:37.

COMPLETE SET (10) 20.00 40.00
1 Erik Cole .75 2.00
2 Ron Francis .75 2.00
3 Peter Forsberg 2.00 5.00
4 Patrick Roy 4.00 10.00
5 Joe Sakic 1.50 4.00
6 Dominik Hasek 1.50 4.00
7 Brendan Shanahan 1.25 3.00
8 Steve Yzerman 4.00 10.00
9 Jose Theodore 1.00 2.50
10 Mats Sundin .75 2.00

2002-03 Pacific Heads Up Quad Jerseys

Inserted at 2:19, this 36-card set featured four swatches of game-used jerseys. Two swatches appeared on the card front and two on the card back.

1 Jeff Friesen 5.00 12.00
Oleg Tverdovsky
Jason Allison
Adam Deadmarsh
2 Ilya Kovalchuk 5.00 12.00
Patrik Stefan
Milan Hnilicka
Tomi Kallio
3 Sergei Samsonov 5.00 12.00
Joe Thornton
Kyle McLaren
Don Sweeney
4 J.P. Dumont 5.00 12.00
Martin Biron
Jay McKee
Miroslav Satan
5 Roman Turek 5.00 12.00
Marc Savard
Mike Comrie
Ryan Smyth
6 Franc/Irbe/Brdmour/O'Neill 12.50 30.00
7 Amonte/Daze/Bell/Sulli 5.00 12.00
8 Chris Drury 5.00 12.00
Milan Hejduk
Alex Tanguay
Vaclav Nedorost
9 Rob Blake 15.00 40.00
Joe Sakic
Luc Robitaille
Sergei Fedorov
10 Marc Denis 5.00 12.00
Ron Tugnutt
Rostislav Klesla
Geoff Sanderson
11 Belfour/Turco/Trgeon/Mdno 6.00 15.00
12 Dominik Hasek 10.00 25.00
Brett Hull
Nicklas Lidstrom
Jason Williams
13 Jason Allison 5.00 12.00
Ziggy Palffy
Felix Potvin
Bryan Smolinski
14 Gbrik/Kuba/McLnn/Ferndz 6.00 15.00
15 Jose Theodore 10.00 25.00
Yanic Perreault
Sergei Berezin
Saku Koivu
16 Martin Erat 5.00 12.00
David Legwand
Scott Walker
Jukka Hentunen
17 Martin Brodeur 12.50 30.00
Patrik Elias
Scott Gomez
Scott Stevens
18 Michael Peca 5.00 12.00
Alexei Yashin
Eric Lindros
Theoren Fleury
19 Daniel Alfredsson 10.00 25.00
Patrick Lalime
Martin Havlat
Marian Hossa
20 Adam Oates 5.00 12.00
Jeremy Roenick
Roman Cechmanek
Jiri Dopita
21 Krystofer Kolanos 5.00 12.00
Michal Handzus
Daymond Langkow
Shane Doan
22 Johan Hedberg 5.00 12.00
Robert Lang
Toby Petersen
Kris Beech
23 Chris Pronger 5.00 12.00
Keith Tkachuk
Pavol Demitra
Sergei Varlamov

24 Evgeni Nabokov 8.00 20.00
Owen Nolan
Miikka Kiprusoff
Patrick Marleau
25 Nikolai Khabibulin 10.00 25.00
Brad Richards
Valeri Bure
Roberto Luongo
26 Curtis Joseph 12.50 30.00
Gary Roberts
Alexander Mogilny
Darcy Tucker
27 Dan Cloutier 8.00 20.00
Todd Bertuzzi
Daniel Sedin
Henrik Sedin
28 Lemx/Prnger/Brodeur/Cujo 20.00 50.00
29 Guerin/Mdno/Hull/Leetch 12.50 30.00
30 Pavel Bure 15.00 40.00
Nikolai Khabibulin
Sergei Fedorov
Alexei Yashin
31 Mats Sundin 5.00 12.00
Daniel Alfredsson
Tommy Salo
Johan Hedberg
32 Jaromir Jagr 10.00 25.00
Dominik Hasek
Milan Hejduk
Patrik Elias
33 Teemu Selanne 5.00 12.00
Jere Lehtinen
Jyrki Lumme
Tomi Kallio
34 Bndra/Gbrlk/Demitra/Plfy 8.00 20.00
35 Ilya Kovalchuk 15.00 40.00
Dany Heatley
Krystofer Kolanos
Erik Cole
36 Kristian Huselius 5.00 12.00
Jiri Dopita
Martin Erat
Jukka Hentunen

2002-03 Pacific Heads Up Quad Jerseys Gold

*GOLD: 1X TO 2.5X BASIC JERSEYS
STATED PRINT RUN 30 SER.#'d SETS

2002-03 Pacific Heads Up Showstoppers

This 20-card set was inserted at a rate of 1:10 and featured goalies only.

COMPLETE SET (20) 25.00 50.00
1 Jean-Sebastien Giguere .40 1.00
2 Byron Dafoe .40 1.00
3 Roman Turek .40 1.00
4 Arturs Irbe .40 1.00
5 Jocelyn Thibault .40 1.00
6 Patrick Roy 3.00 8.00
7 Marty Turco .40 1.00
8 Dominik Hasek 1.25 3.00
9 Curtis Joseph .60 1.50
10 Roberto Luongo .75 2.00
11 Felix Potvin .60 1.50
12 Jose Theodore .75 2.00
13 Martin Brodeur 1.50 4.00
14 Chris Osgood .40 1.00
15 Patrick Lalime .40 1.00
16 Sean Burke .40 1.00
17 Brent Johnson .40 1.00
18 Evgeni Nabokov .40 1.00
19 Nikolai Khabibulin .60 1.50
20 Dan Cloutier .40 1.00

2002-03 Pacific Heads Up Stat Masters

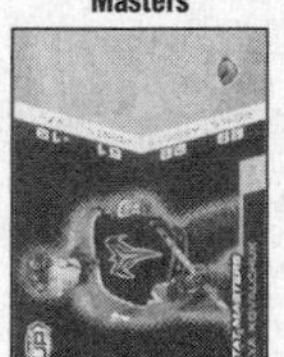

This 15-card set was inserted at a rate of 1:73.

COMPLETE SET (15) 40.00 80.00
1 Paul Kariya 1.25 3.00
2 Dany Heatley 1.50 4.00
3 Ilya Kovalchuk 1.50 4.00
4 Joe Thornton 2.00 5.00
5 Jarome Iginla 1.50 4.00
6 Ron Francis 1.25 3.00
7 Joe Sakic 2.50 6.00
8 Brett Hull 1.50 4.00
9 Steve Yzerman 6.00 15.00
10 Pavel Bure 1.50 4.00
11 Eric Lindros 1.25 3.00
12 Mario Lemieux 8.00 20.00
13 Mats Sundin 1.25 3.00
14 Todd Bertuzzi 1.25 3.00
15 Jaromir Jagr 2.00 5.00

2003-04 Pacific Heads Up

This 136-card set consisted of 100 veteran cards and 36 short-printed rookie cards (101-136). Rookie cards were serial-numbered to just 899 copies each.

COMPLETE SET (136) 75.00 150.00
COMP.SET w/o SP's (100) 15.00 30.00
1 Sergei Fedorov .50 1.25
2 Jean-Sebastien Giguere .30 .75
3 Steve Rucchin .12 .30
4 Ilya Kovalchuk .50 1.25
5 Shawn McEachern .12 .30
6 Pasi Nurminen .30 .75
7 Mike Knuble .12 .30
8 Andrew Raycroft .30 .75
9 Brian Rolston .12 .30
10 Joe Thornton .60 1.50
11 Martin Biron .30 .75
12 Daniel Briere .12 .30
13 J-P Dumont .12 .30
14 Jarome Iginla .50 1.25
15 Jamie McLennan .12 .30
16 Steven Reinprecht .12 .30
17 Ron Francis .30 .75
18 Josef Vasicek .12 .30
19 Kevin Weekes .30 .75
20 Mark Bell .12 .30
21 Michael Leighton .30 .75
22 Jocelyn Thibault UER .30 .75
Michael Leighton
pictured on front
23 David Aebischer .30 .75
24 Peter Forsberg 1.00 2.50
25 Paul Kariya .40 1.00
26 Joe Sakic .75 2.00
27 Alex Tanguay .30 .75
28 Marc Denis .30 .75
29 Rick Nash .50 1.25
30 David Vyborny .12 .30
31 Bill Guerin .30 .75
32 Mike Modano .60 1.50
33 Marty Turco .30 .75
34 Pavel Datsyuk .40 1.00
35 Dominik Hasek .75 2.00
36 Brett Hull .50 1.25
37 Brendan Shanahan .40 1.00
38 Steve Yzerman 2.00 5.00
39 Henrik Zetterberg .40 1.00
40 Ty Conklin .30 .75
41 Ales Hemsky .12 .30
42 Ryan Smyth .12 .30
43 Jay Bouwmeester .12 .30
44 Olli Jokinen .30 .75
45 Roberto Luongo .50 1.25
46 Roman Cechmanek .30 .75
47 Cristobal Huet .30 .75
48 Ziggy Palffy .30 .75
49 Pierre-Marc Bouchard .12 .30
50 Marian Gaborik .75 2.00
51 Dwayne Roloson .30 .75
52 Saku Koivu .40 1.00
53 Mike Ribeiro .12 .30
54 Michael Ryder UER .12 .30
Front pictures Andrei Markov
55 Jose Theodore .50 1.25
56 Scott Hartnell .12 .30
57 David Legwand .30 .75
58 Martin Brodeur 1.00 2.50
59 Patrik Elias .30 .75
60 Jamie Langenbrunner .12 .30
61 Mariusz Czerkawski .12 .30
62 Rick DiPietro .30 .75
63 Trent Hunter .12 .30
64 Alexei Yashin .12 .30
65 Alex Kovalev .30 .75
66 Eric Lindros .40 1.00
67 Mark Messier .40 1.00
68 Daniel Alfredsson .30 .75
69 Marian Hossa .40 1.00
70 Patrick Lalime .30 .75
71 Jason Spezza .40 1.00
72 Tony Amonte .30 .75
73 Robert Esche .30 .75
74 Jeremy Roenick .50 1.25
75 Justin Williams .12 .30
76 Sean Burke .30 .75
77 Ladislav Nagy .12 .30
78 Rico Fata .12 .30
79 Mario Lemieux 2.50 6.00
80 Barret Jackman .12 .30
81 Chris Osgood .30 .75
82 Chris Pronger .30 .75
83 Patrick Marleau .30 .75
84 Alyn McCauley .12 .30
85 Marco Sturm .12 .30
86 Nikolai Khabibulin .40 1.00
87 Vincent Lecavalier .40 1.00
88 Martin St. Louis .30 .75
89 Cory Stillman .12 .30
90 Ed Belfour .40 1.00
91 Alexander Mogilny .30 .75
92 Owen Nolan .30 .75
93 Mats Sundin .40 1.00
94 Todd Bertuzzi .40 1.00
95 Dan Cloutier .30 .75
96 Jason King .12 .30
97 Brendan Morrison .12 .30
98 Markus Naslund .40 1.00
99 Jaromir Jagr .60 1.50
100 Robert Lang .12 .30
101 Jeffrey Lupul RC 2.00 5.00
102 Patrice Bergeron RC 4.00 10.00
103 Pat Leahy RC 1.50 4.00
104 Brent Krahn RC 1.50 4.00
105 Matthew Lombardi RC 1.50 4.00
106 Eric Staal RC 6.00 15.00
107 Tuomo Ruutu RC 3.00 8.00
108 Mikhail Yakubov RC 1.50 4.00
109 Cody McCormick RC 1.50 4.00
110 Dan Fritsche RC 1.50 4.00
111 Nikolai Zherdev RC 2.50 6.00
112 Antti Miettinen RC 1.50 4.00
113 Darryl Bootland RC 1.50 4.00
114 Jiri Hudler RC 2.00 5.00
115 Nathan Robinson RC 1.50 4.00
116 Tony Salmelainen RC 1.50 4.00
117 Peter Sarno RC 1.50 4.00
118 Nathan Horton RC 3.00 8.00
119 Dustin Brown RC 1.50 4.00
120 Brent Burns RC 1.50 4.00
121 Christopher Higgins RC 4.00 10.00
122 Dan Hamhuis RC 1.50 4.00
123 Jordin Tootoo RC 3.00 8.00
124 Marek Zidlicky RC 1.50 4.00
125 Paul Martin RC 1.50 4.00
126 Dominic Moore RC 1.50 4.00
127 Antoine Vermette RC 1.50 4.00
128 Joni Pitkanen RC 1.50 4.00
129 Fredrik Sjostrom RC 1.50 4.00
130 Marc-Andre Fleury RC 6.00 15.00
131 John Pohl RC 1.50 4.00
132 Peter Sejna RC 1.50 4.00
133 Milan Michalek RC 1.50 4.00
134 Matt Stajan RC 3.00 8.00
135 Boyd Gordon RC 1.50 4.00
136 Alexander Semin RC 4.00 10.00

2003-04 Pacific Heads Up Hobby LTD

*STARS: 2X TO 5X BASIC CARDS
1-100 PRINT RUN
*ROOKIES: .5X TO 1.25X
101-136 PRINT RUN 250 SER.#'d SETS

2003-04 Pacific Heads Up Retail LTD

*STARS: .5X TO 1.25X
*ROOKIES: .25X TO .5X
STATED ODDS 1:2 RETAIL PACKS

2003-04 Pacific Heads Up Fast Forwards

STATED ODDS 1:9
*LTD: .75X TO 2X
LTD PRINT RUN 175 SER.#'d SETS
1 Sergei Fedorov 1.00 2.50
2 Ilya Kovalchuk 1.00 2.50
3 Rick Nash 1.00 2.50
4 Mike Modano 1.25 3.00
5 Marian Gaborik 1.50 4.00
6 Marian Hossa .75 2.00
7 Jeremy Roenick 1.00 2.50
8 Alexander Mogilny .75 2.00
9 Markus Naslund .75 2.00

2003-04 Pacific Heads Up In Focus

STATED ODDS 1:13
*LTD: .75X TO 2X
LTD PRINT RUN 175 SER.#'d SETS
1 Sergei Fedorov 1.00 2.50
2 Ilya Kovalchuk 1.00 2.50
3 Eric Staal 1.00 2.50
4 Joe Sakic 1.50 4.00
5 Alex Tanguay .75 2.00
6 Rick Nash 1.00 2.50
7 Henrik Zetterberg .75 2.00
8 Jay Bouwmeester .75 2.00
9 Jason Spezza .75 2.00
10 Todd Bertuzzi .75 2.00

2003-04 Pacific Heads Up Jerseys

This 25-card memorabilia set was inserted at 2 per 24-pack box. Known SP's are noted below.

1 Jeffrey Lupul 2.00 5.00
2 Ilya Kovalchuk SP 8.00 20.00
3 Joe Thornton SP 10.00 25.00
4 Ales Kotalik 2.00 5.00
5 Ryan Miller 3.00 8.00
6 Matthew Lombardi 2.00 5.00
7 David Aebischer 3.00 8.00
8 Peter Forsberg SP 10.00 25.00
9 Antti Miettinen 2.00 5.00
10 Steve Yzerman SP 12.50 30.00
11 Ales Hemsky 2.00 5.00
12 Jay Bouwmeester 2.00 5.00
13 Nathan Horton 3.00 8.00
14 Dustin Brown 2.00 5.00
15 Ziggy Palffy 3.00 8.00
16 Chris Higgins 4.00 10.00
17 Jordin Tootoo 6.00 15.00
18 Martin Brodeur 8.00 20.00
19 Rick DiPietro 3.00 8.00
20 Jason Spezza 6.00 15.00
21 Antoine Vermette 2.00 5.00
22 Mario Lemieux SP 15.00 40.00
23 Barret Jackman 2.00 5.00
24 Owen Nolan 2.00 5.00
25 Boyd Gordon 2.00 5.00

2003-04 Pacific Heads Up Mini Sweaters

Inserted at one per hobby box, these small replica sweaters measured about 6" high.

1 Marc-Andre Fleury 12.00 30.00
2 Ilya Kovalchuk 12.00 30.00
3 Joe Thornton 12.00 30.00
4 Peter Forsberg 12.00 30.00
5 Steve Yzerman 15.00 40.00
6 Martin Brodeur 15.00 40.00
7 Marian Gaborik 12.00 30.00
8 Ed Belfour 8.00 20.00
9 Todd Bertuzzi 8.00 20.00

2003-04 Pacific Heads Up Prime Prospects

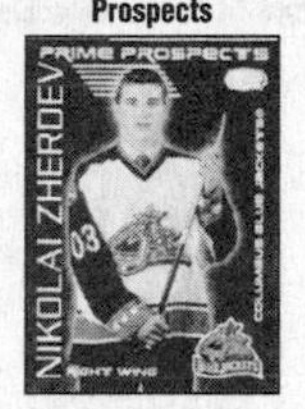

COMPLETE SET (10) 10.00 20.00
STATED ODDS 1:7
*LTD: .6X TO 1.5X
LTD PRINT RUN 175 SER.#'d SETS
1 Joffrey Lupul .75 2.00
2 Patrice Bergeron 1.50 4.00
3 Ryan Miller 1.25 3.00
4 Matthew Lombardi .40 1.00
5 Eric Staal 2.00 5.00
6 Philippe Sauve .40 1.00
7 Nikolai Zherdev 1.25 3.00
8 Jiri Hudler .75 2.00
9 Nathan Horton .75 2.00
10 Dustin Brown .40 1.00
11 Brent Burns .40 1.00
12 Christopher Higgins 1.25 3.00
13 Michael Ryder 1.25 3.00
14 Jordin Tootoo 1.25 3.00
15 Antoine Vermette .40 1.00
16 Joni Pitkanen .75 2.00
17 Marc-Andre Fleury 2.00 5.00
18 Milan Michalek .75 2.00
19 Matt Stajan .75 2.00
20 Jason King .40 1.00

2003-04 Pacific Heads Up Rink Immortals

STATED ODDS 1:13
*LTD: .75X TO 2X
LTD PRINT RUN 175 SER.#'d SETS
1 Joe Thornton 1.00 2.50
2 Peter Forsberg 2.00 5.00
3 Joe Sakic 1.50 4.00
4 Dominik Hasek 1.50 4.00
5 Brett Hull 1.00 2.50
6 Steve Yzerman 2.50 6.00
7 Martin Brodeur 2.50 6.00
8 Mark Messier 1.00 2.50
9 Mario Lemieux 3.00 8.00
10 Ed Belfour 1.00 2.50

2003-04 Pacific Heads Up Stonewallers

STATED ODDS 1:9
*LTD: .75X TO 2X
LTD.PRINT RUN 175 SER.#'d SETS
1 Jean-Sebastien Giguere .60 1.50
2 Pasi Nurminen .60 1.50
3 David Aebischer .60 1.50
4 Marty Turco .60 1.50
5 Dominik Hasek 1.50 4.00
6 Jose Theodore 1.00 2.50
7 Martin Brodeur 2.50 6.00
8 Rick DiPietro .60 1.50
9 Patrick Lalime .60 1.50
10 Nikolai Khabibulin .75 2.00
11 Ed Belfour .75 2.00
12 Dan Cloutier .60 1.50

2001-02 Pacific High Voltage

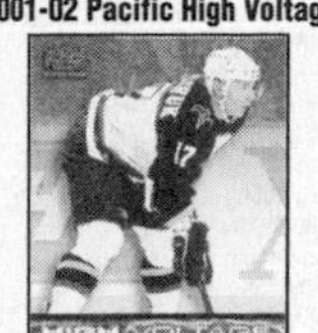

Available via a mail-in offer advertised in Powerplay magazine, this 10-card set featured hot rookies from the 2001-02 season. To receive a set, collectors had to send in wrappers from other Pacific products.

COMPLETE SET (10) 20.00 50.00
1 Dany Heatley 2.40 6.00
2 Ilya Kovalchuk 10.00 25.00
3 Erik Cole 2.40 6.00
4 Vaclav Nedorost 2.40 6.00
5 Kristian Huselius 3.20 8.00
6 Martin Erat .80 2.00
7 Dan Blackburn 1.00 2.50
8 Krystofer Kolanos 2.40 6.00
9 Jeff Jillson 1.60 4.00
10 Nikita Alexeev 1.60 4.00

1997-98 Pacific Invincible

The 1997-98 Pacific Invincible set was issued in one series totaling 150 cards and distributed in three-card packs. The fronts feature color action player images with gold foil background enhancements and a small player head photo in a clear, circular "window" at the bottom. The backs carry player information.

COMPLETE SET (150) 20.00 50.00
1 Brian Bellows .20 .50
2 Guy Hebert .30 .75
3 Paul Kariya .40 1.00
4 Teemu Selanne .40 1.00
5 Darren Van Impe .20 .50
6 Jason Allison .20 .50
7 Ray Bourque .40 1.00
8 Jim Carey .30 .75
9 Ted Donato .20 .50
10 Jozef Stumpel .20 .50
11 Jason Dawe .20 .50
12 Dominik Hasek 1.00 2.50
13 Michael Peca .20 .50
14 Derek Plante .20 .50
15 Miroslav Satan .20 .50
16 Theo Fleury .20 .50
17 Dave Gagner .20 .50
18 Jonas Hoglund .20 .50
19 Jarome Iginla .60 1.50
20 Trevor Kidd .30 .75
21 German Titov .20 .50
22 Sean Burke .30 .75
23 Andrew Cassels .20 .50
24 Derek King .20 .50
25 Keith Primeau .20 .50
26 Geoff Sanderson .20 .50
27 Tony Amonte .30 .75
28 Chris Chelios .30 .75
29 Eric Daze .20 .50
30 Jeff Hackett .30 .75
31 Ethan Moreau .20 .50
32 Alexei Zhamnov .20 .50
33 Adam Deadmarsh .20 .50
34 Peter Forsberg .60 1.50
35 Valeri Kamensky .20 .50
36 Claude Lemieux .20 .50
37 Sandis Ozolinsh .20 .50
38 Patrick Roy 1.50 4.00
39 Joe Sakic 1.00 2.50
40 Jamie Langenbrunner .20 .50
41 Mike Modano .40 1.00
42 Andy Moog .30 .75
43 Joe Nieuwendyk .30 .75
44 Pat Verbeek .20 .50
45 Sergei Zubov .20 .50
46 Sergei Fedorov .40 1.00
47 Vladimir Konstantinov .40 1.00
48 Vyacheslav Kozlov .20 .50
49 Nicklas Lidstrom .40 1.00
50 Chris Osgood .30 .75
51 Brendan Shanahan .40 1.00
52 Mike Vernon .30 .75
53 Steve Yzerman 1.25 3.00
54 Jason Arnott .20 .50
55 Mike Grier .20 .50
56 Curtis Joseph .40 1.00
57 Rem Murray .20 .50
58 Ryan Smyth .30 .75
59 Doug Weight .30 .75
60 Ed Jovanovski .30 .75
61 Scott Mellanby .20 .50
62 Kirk Muller .20 .50
63 Ray Sheppard .20 .50
64 John Vanbiesbrouck .40 1.00
65 Rob Blake .30 .75
66 Ray Ferraro .20 .50
67 Stephane Fiset .30 .75
68 Dimitri Khristich .20 .50
69 Vladimir Tsyplakov .20 .50
70 Vincent Damphousse .20 .50
71 Saku Koivu .40 1.00
72 Mark Recchi .30 .75
73 Stephane Richer .20 .50
74 Jocelyn Thibault .30 .75
75 Dave Andreychuk .20 .50
76 Martin Brodeur 1.25 3.00
77 Doug Gilmour .30 .75
78 Bobby Holik .20 .50
79 Denis Pederson .20 .50
80 Bryan Berard .20 .50
81 Travis Green .20 .50
82 Zigmund Palffy .30 .75
83 Tommy Salo .30 .75
84 Bryan Smolinski .20 .50
85 Adam Graves .20 .50
86 Wayne Gretzky 2.00 5.00
87 Alexei Kovalev .20 .50
88 Brian Leetch .30 .75
89 Mark Messier .40 1.00
90 Mike Richter .30 .75
91 Luc Robitaille .40 1.00
92 Daniel Alfredsson .40 1.00
93 Alexandre Daigle .20 .50
94 Steve Duchesne .20 .50
95 Wade Redden .20 .50
96 Ron Tugnutt .20 .50
97 Alexei Yashin .20 .50
98 Rod Brind'Amour .20 .50
99 Paul Coffey .30 .75
100 Ron Hextall .30 .75
101 John LeClair .30 .75
102 Eric Lindros .40 1.00
103 Janne Niinimaa .20 .50
104 Mikael Renberg .20 .50
105 Dainius Zubrus .20 .50
106 Mike Gartner .30 .75
107 Nikolai Khabibulin .30 .75
108 Jeremy Roenick .40 1.00
109 Keith Tkachuk .20 .50
110 Oleg Tverdovsky .20 .50
111 Ron Francis .30 .75
112 Kevin Hatcher .20 .50
113 Jaromir Jagr .60 1.50
114 Patrick Lalime .20 .50
115 Petr Nedved .20 .50
116 Ed Olczyk .20 .50
117 Jim Campbell .20 .50
118 Geoff Courtnall .20 .50
119 Grant Fuhr .30 .75
120 Brett Hull .40 1.00
121 Sergio Momesso .20 .50
122 Pierre Turgeon .30 .75
123 Ed Belfour .40 1.00
124 Jeff Friesen .20 .50
125 Tony Granato .20 .50
126 Stephen Guolla RC .20 .50
127 Bernie Nicholls .20 .50
128 Owen Nolan .30 .75
129 Dino Ciccarelli .20 .50
130 John Cullen .20 .50
131 Chris Gratton .20 .50
132 Roman Hamrlik .20 .50
133 Daymond Langkow .20 .50
134 Paul Ysebaert .20 .50
135 Sergei Berezin .20 .50
136 Wendel Clark .30 .75
137 Felix Potvin .40 1.00
138 Steve Sullivan .20 .50
139 Mats Sundin .40 1.00
140 Pavel Bure .40 1.00
141 Martin Gelinas .20 .50
142 Trevor Linden .30 .75
143 Kirk McLean .30 .75
144 Alexander Mogilny .30 .75
145 Peter Bondra .30 .75
146 Dale Hunter .20 .50
147 Joe Juneau .20 .50
148 Steve Konowalchuk .20 .50
149 Adam Oates .30 .75
150 Bill Ranford .30 .75

1997-98 Pacific Invincible Copper

Randomly inserted in U.S. hobby packs only at the rate of 2:37, this 150-card set is parallel to the regular gold foil base set only with copper foil enhancements.

*COPPER: 1.5X TO 4X BASIC CARDS

1997-98 Pacific Invincible Emerald Green

Randomly inserted in Canadian packs only at the rate of 2:37, this 150-card set is parallel to the regular gold foil base set only with green foil enhancements.

*GREEN: 1.5X TO 4X BASIC CARDS

1997-98 Pacific Invincible Ice Blue

Randomly inserted in packs at the rate of 1:73, this 150-card set is parallel to the regular gold foil base set only with blue foil enhancements.

*ICE BLUE: 6X TO 15X BASIC CARDS

1997-98 Pacific Invincible Red

Randomly inserted at the rate of 2:37 into special packs found only in Wal-Mart stores, this 150-card set is parallel to the regular gold foil base set only with red foil enhancements.

*RED: 2.5X TO 6X BASIC CARDS

1997-98 Pacific Invincible Silver

Randomly inserted in U.S. retail packs only at the rate of 2:37, this 150-card set is parallel to the regular gold foil base set only with silver foil enhancements.

*SILVER: 1.5X TO 4X BASIC CARDS

1997-98 Pacific Invincible Attack Zone

Randomly inserted in packs at the rate of 1:37, this 24-card set features color action player images on a bright, colorful background. The backs carry player information.

COMPLETE SET (24) 50.00 100.00
1 Paul Kariya 2.50 6.00
2 Teemu Selanne 2.50 6.00
3 Michael Peca 1.00 2.50
4 Jarome Iginla 3.00 8.00
5 Peter Forsberg 6.00 15.00
6 Claude Lemieux 1.00 2.50
7 Joe Sakic 5.00 12.00
8 Mike Modano 4.00 10.00
9 Sergei Fedorov 4.00 10.00
10 Brendan Shanahan 2.50 6.00
11 Steve Yzerman 12.50 30.00
12 Bryan Berard 2.00 5.00
13 Zigmund Palffy 2.00 5.00
14 Wayne Gretzky 15.00 40.00
15 Brian Leetch 2.50 6.00
16 Mark Messier 2.50 6.00
17 John LeClair 2.50 6.00
18 Eric Lindros 2.50 6.00
19 Ron Francis 2.00 5.00
20 Jaromir Jagr 4.00 10.00
21 Brett Hull 3.00 8.00
22 Dino Ciccarelli 1.00 2.50
23 Pavel Bure 2.50 6.00
24 Alexander Mogilny 2.00 5.00

1997-98 Pacific Invincible Feature Performers

Randomly inserted in packs at the rate of 2:37, this 36-card set features color action player made to look as if they are breaking through the ice.

COMPLETE SET (36) 30.00 80.00
1 Paul Kariya 1.25 3.00
2 Teemu Selanne 1.25 3.00
3 Ray Bourque 2.00 5.00
4 Dominik Hasek 3.00 8.00
5 Jarome Iginla 2.00 5.00
6 Chris Chelios 1.25 3.00
7 Peter Forsberg 2.50 6.00
8 Claude Lemieux .40 1.00
9 Patrick Roy 6.00 15.00
10 Joe Sakic 3.00 8.00
11 Mike Modano 1.50 4.00
12 Sergei Fedorov 1.25 3.00
13 Vladimir Konstantinov 1.25 3.00
14 Brendan Shanahan 1.25 3.00
15 Mike Vernon .75 2.00
16 Steve Yzerman 4.00 10.00
17 John Vanbiesbrouck .75 2.00
18 Saku Koivu 1.25 3.00
19 Martin Brodeur 4.00 10.00
20 Zigmund Palffy .75 2.00
21 Wayne Gretzky 8.00 20.00
22 Mark Messier 1.25 3.00
23 Alexandre Daigle .40 1.00
24 John LeClair .75 2.00
25 Eric Lindros 1.25 3.00
26 Janne Niinimaa .40 1.00
27 Jeremy Roenick 2.00 5.00
28 Jaromir Jagr 2.50 6.00
29 Patrick Lalime .75 2.00
30 Jim Campbell .40 1.00
31 Brett Hull 1.25 3.00
32 Sergei Berezin .40 1.00
33 Felix Potvin 1.25 3.00
34 Mats Sundin 1.25 3.00
35 Alexander Mogilny .75 2.00
36 Peter Bondra .75 2.00

1997-98 Pacific Invincible NHL Regime

Randomly inserted one in every pack, this 220-card set features color action player photos with a faint lavender border. The backs carry player information.

COMPLETE SET (220) 8.00 20.00
1 Ken Baumgartner .05 .15
2 Mark Janssens .05 .15
3 Jean-Francois Jomphe .05 .15
4 Paul Kariya .10 .30
5 Jason Marshall .05 .15
6 Richard Park .05 .15
7 Teemu Selanne .10 .30
8 Mikhail Shtalenkov .05 .15
9 Bob Beers .05 .15
10 Ray Bourque .20 .50
11 Jim Carey .05 .15
12 Brett Harkins .05 .15
13 Sheldon Kennedy .05 .15
14 Troy Mallette .05 .15
15 Sandy Moger .05 .15
16 Jon Rohloff .05 .15
17 Don Sweeney .05 .15
18 Randy Burridge .05 .15
19 Michal Grosek .05 .15
20 Dominik Hasek .25 .60
21 Rob Ray .05 .15
22 Steve Shields .08 .25
23 Richard Smehlik .05 .15
24 Dixon Ward .05 .15
25 Mike Wilson .05 .15
26 Tommy Albelin .05 .15

27 Aaron Gavey .05 .15
28 Todd Hlushko .05 .15
29 Jarome Iginla .15 .40
30 Yves Racine .05 .15
31 Dwayne Roloson .08 .25
32 Mike Sullivan .05 .15
33 Ed Ward .05 .15
34 Adam Burt .05 .15
35 Nelson Emerson .05 .15
36 Kevin Haller .05 .15
37 Derek King .05 .15
38 Curtis Leschyshyn .05 .15
39 Chris Murray .05 .15
40 Jason Muzzatti .05 .15
41 Keith Carney .05 .15
42 Chris Chelios .10 .30
43 Enrico Ciccone .05 .15
44 Jim Cummins .05 .15
45 Cam Russell .05 .15
46 Jeff Shantz .05 .15
47 Michal Sykora .05 .15
48 Chris Terreri .08 .25
49 Eric Weinrich .05 .15
50 Rene Corbet .05 .15
51 Peter Forsberg .30 .75
52 Alexei Gusarov .05 .15
53 Uwe Krupp .05 .15
54 Sylvain Lefebvre .05 .15
55 Eric Messier .08 .25
56 Patrick Roy .60 1.50
57 Joe Sakic .25 .60
58 Brent Severyn .05 .15
59 Greg Adams .05 .15
60 Todd Harvey .05 .15
61 Jere Lehtinen .05 .15
62 Craig Ludwig .05 .15
63 Mike Modano .20 .50
64 Andy Moog .08 .25
65 Dave Reid .05 .15
66 Roman Turek .05 .15
67 Doug Brown .05 .15
68 Kris Draper .05 .15
69 Sergei Fedorov .20 .50
70 Joey Kocur .05 .15
71 Kirk Maltby .05 .15
72 Bob Rouse .05 .15
73 Brendan Shanahan .10 .30
74 Aaron Ward .05 .15
75 Steve Yzerman .60 1.50
76 Greg DeVries .05 .15
77 Bob Essensa .08 .25
78 Kevin Lowe .05 .15
79 Bryan Marchment .05 .15
80 Dean McAmmond .05 .15
81 Boris Mironov .05 .15
82 Luke Richardson .05 .15
83 Ryan Smyth .08 .25
84 Terry Carkner .05 .15
85 Ed Jovanovski .05 .15
86 Bill Lindsay .05 .15
87 Dave Lowry .05 .15
88 Gord Murphy .05 .15
89 John Vanbiesbrouck .08 .25
90 Steve Washburn .05 .15
91 Chris Wells .05 .15
92 Philippe Boucher .05 .15
93 Steven Finn .05 .15
94 Mattias Norstrom .05 .15
95 Kai Nurminen .05 .15
96 Sean O'Donnell .05 .15
97 Yanic Perreault .05 .15
98 Jeff Shevalier .05 .15
99 Brad Smyth .05 .15
100 Brad Brown RC .05 .15
101 Jassen Cullimore .05 .15
102 Vincent Damphousse .05 .15
103 Vladimir Malakhov .05 .15
104 Peter Popovic .05 .15
105 Stephane Richer .08 .25
106 Turner Stevenson .05 .15
107 Jose Theodore .15 .40
108 Martin Brodeur .30 .75
109 Bob Carpenter .05 .15
110 Mike Dunham .08 .25
111 Patrik Elias .08 .25
112 Dave Ellett .05 .15
113 Doug Gilmour .08 .25
114 Randy McKay .05 .15
115 Todd Bertuzzi .10 .30
116 Kenny Jonsson .05 .15
117 Paul Kruse .05 .15
118 Claude Lapointe .05 .15
119 Zigmund Palffy .08 .25
120 Rich Pilon .05 .15
121 Dan Plante .05 .15
122 Dennis Vaske .05 .15
123 Shane Churla .05 .15
124 Bruce Driver .05 .15
125 Mike Eastwood .05 .15
126 Patrick Flatley .05 .15
127 Adam Graves .05 .15
128 Wayne Gretzky .75 2.00
129 Brian Leetch .10 .30
130 Doug Lidster .05 .15
131 Mark Messier .10 .30
132 Tom Chorske .05 .15
133 Sean Hill .05 .15
134 Denny Lambert .05 .15
135 Janne Laukkanen .05 .15
136 Frank Musil .05 .15
137 Lance Pitlick .05 .15
138 Shaun Van Allen .05 .15
139 Rod Brind'Amour .08 .25
140 Paul Coffey .10 .30
141 Karl Dykhuis .05 .15
142 Dan Kordic .05 .15
143 Daniel Lacroix .05 .15
144 John LeClair .10 .30
145 Eric Lindros .10 .30
146 Joel Otto .05 .15
147 Shjon Podein .05 .15
148 Chris Therien .05 .15
149 Shane Doan .05 .15
150 Dallas Drake .05 .15
151 Jeff Finley .05 .15
152 Mike Gartner .05 .15
153 Nikolai Khabibulin .08 .25
154 Darrin Shannon .05 .15
155 Mike Stapleton .05 .15
156 Keith Tkachuk .10 .30
157 Tom Barrasso .08 .25
158 Josef Beranek .05 .15
159 Alex Hicks .05 .15
160 Jaromir Jagr .20 .50
161 Patrick Lalime .08 .25
162 Francois Leroux .05 .15
163 Petr Nedved .08 .25
164 Roman Oksiuta .05 .15
165 Chris Tamer .05 .15
166 Marc Bergevin .05 .15
167 Jon Casey .08 .25
168 Craig Conroy .05 .15
169 Brett Hull .15 .40
170 Igor Kravchuk .05 .15
171 Stephen Leach .05 .15
172 Ricard Persson .05 .15
173 Pierre Turgeon .08 .25
174 Ed Belfour .10 .30
175 Doug Bodger .05 .15
176 Shean Donovan .05 .15
177 Bob Errey .05 .15
178 Todd Ewen .05 .15
179 Wade Flaherty .05 .15
180 Mike Rathje .05 .15
181 Ron Sutter .05 .15
182 Mikael Andersson .05 .15
183 Dino Ciccarelli .05 .15
184 Cory Cross .05 .15
185 Jamie Huscroft .05 .15
186 Rudy Poeschek .05 .15
187 Daren Puppa .08 .25
188 David Shaw .05 .15
189 Jay Wells .05 .15
190 Jamie Baker .05 .15
191 Sergei Berezin .08 .25
192 Brandon Convery .05 .15
193 Darby Hendrickson .05 .15
194 Matt Martin .05 .15
195 Felix Potvin .10 .30
196 Jason Smith .05 .15
197 Craig Wolanin .05 .15
198 Adrian Aucoin .05 .15
199 Dave Babych .05 .15
200 Donald Brashear .05 .15
201 Pavel Bure .10 .30
202 Chris Joseph .05 .15
203 Alexander Mogilny .08 .25
204 David Roberts .05 .15
205 Scott Walker .05 .15
206 Peter Bondra .08 .25
207 Andrew Brunette .08 .25
208 Calle Johansson .05 .15
209 Ken Klee .05 .15
210 Olaf Kolzig .08 .25
211 Kelly Miller .05 .15
212 Joe Reekie .05 .15
213 Chris Simon .05 .15
214 Brendan Witt .05 .15
215 Paul Kariya TL .10 .30
216 Peter Forsberg TL .10 .30
217 Patrick Roy TL .10 .30
218 Wayne Gretzky TL .10 .30
219 Eric Lindros TL .10 .30
220 Jaromir Jagr TL .10 .30

1997-98 Pacific Invincible Off The Glass

Randomly inserted in packs at the rate of 1:73, this 20-card set features borderless color action photos of top hockey players with gold foil highlights.

COMPLETE SET (20) 25.00 60.00
1 Paul Kariya 1.25 3.00
2 Teemu Selanne 1.25 3.00
3 Michael Peca .75 2.00
4 Jarome Iginla 2.00 5.00
5 Peter Forsberg 3.00 8.00
6 Joe Sakic 4.00 10.00
7 Sergei Fedorov 1.50 4.00
8 Brendan Shanahan 1.25 3.00
9 Steve Yzerman 6.00 15.00
10 Mike Grier .75 2.00
11 Saku Koivu 1.25 3.00
12 Wayne Gretzky 10.00 25.00
13 Mark Messier 1.50 4.00
14 Eric Lindros 1.25 3.00
15 Dainius Zubrus .75 2.00
16 Keith Tkachuk 1.25 3.00
17 Jaromir Jagr 3.00 8.00
18 Brett Hull 1.50 4.00
19 Sergei Berezin .75 2.00
20 Pavel Bure 1.50 4.00

2003-04 Pacific Invincible

This 125-card set consisted of 100 veteran cards (1-100) and 25 shortprinted rookie cards (101-125). Rookies were serial-numbered to 799.

COMPLETE SET (125)
COMP.SET w/o SP's (100) 20.00 50.00
1 Stanislav Chistov .20 .50
2 Sergei Fedorov .50 1.25
3 Jean-Sebastien Giguere .30 .75
4 Dany Heatley .50 1.25
5 Ilya Kovalchuk .50 1.25
6 Glen Murray .20 .50
7 Sergei Samsonov .30 .75
8 Joe Thornton .60 1.50
9 Martin Biron .30 .75
10 Ryan Miller .30 .75
11 Miroslav Satan .30 .75
12 Craig Conroy .20 .50
13 Jarome Iginla .50 1.25
14 Roman Turek .30 .75
15 Ron Francis .30 .75
16 Jeff O'Neill .20 .50
17 Eric Daze .30 .75
18 Jocelyn Thibault .30 .75
19 Alexei Zhamnov .20 .50
20 David Aebischer .30 .75
21 Peter Forsberg .60 1.50
22 Milan Hejduk .40 1.00
23 Paul Kariya .40 1.00
24 Patrick Roy 2.00 5.00
25 Joe Sakic .75 2.00
26 Teemu Selanne .40 1.00
27 Marc Denis .30 .75
28 Rick Nash .40 1.00
29 Bill Guerin .30 .75
30 Mike Modano .60 1.50
31 Marty Turco .30 .75
32 Dominik Hasek .75 2.00
33 Brett Hull .40 1.00
34 Nicklas Lidstrom .40 1.00
35 Brendan Shanahan .40 1.00
36 Steve Yzerman 1.50 4.00
37 Henrik Zetterberg .40 1.00
38 Mike Comrie .30 .75
39 Ales Hemsky .30 .75
40 Ryan Smyth .20 .50
41 Jay Bouwmeester .20 .50
42 Olli Jokinen .30 .75
43 Roberto Luongo .50 1.25
44 Jason Allison .20 .50
45 Roman Cechmanek .30 .75
46 Zigmund Palffy .30 .75
47 Manny Fernandez .20 .50
48 Marian Gaborik .60 1.50
49 Marcel Hossa .20 .50
50 Saku Koivu .40 1.00
51 Jose Theodore .40 1.00
52 David Legwand .30 .75
53 Scottie Upshall .20 .50
54 Tomas Vokoun .30 .75
55 Martin Brodeur 1.00 2.50
56 Patrik Elias .30 .75
57 Jeff Friesen .20 .50
58 Jamie Langenbrunner .20 .50
59 Scott Stevens .30 .75
60 Rick DiPietro .30 .75
61 Mark Parrish .20 .50
62 Michael Peca .20 .50
63 Alexei Yashin .20 .50
64 Pavel Bure .40 1.00
65 Alex Kovalev .30 .75
66 Eric Lindros .40 1.00
67 Mark Messier .40 1.00
68 Daniel Alfredsson .30 .75
69 Marian Hossa .40 1.00
70 Patrick Lalime .30 .75
71 Jason Spezza .40 1.00
72 Tony Amonte .30 .75
73 Jeff Hackett .30 .75
74 John LeClair .40 1.00
75 Jeremy Roenick .40 1.00
76 Sean Burke .30 .75
77 Daymond Langkow .20 .50
78 Mario Lemieux 2.00 5.00
79 Pavol Demitra .30 .75
80 Barret Jackman .30 .75
81 Chris Osgood .30 .75
82 Doug Weight .30 .75
83 Patrick Marleau .30 .75
84 Evgeni Nabokov .30 .75
85 John Grahame .30 .75
86 Nikolai Khabibulin .40 1.00
87 Vincent Lecavalier .40 1.00
88 Martin St. Louis .30 .75
89 Ed Belfour .40 1.00
90 Alexander Mogilny .30 .75
91 Owen Nolan .30 .75
92 Mats Sundin .40 1.00
93 Todd Bertuzzi .40 1.00
94 Dan Cloutier .30 .75
95 Johan Hedberg .30 .75
96 Brendan Morrison .30 .75
97 Markus Naslund .40 1.00
98 Peter Bondra .30 .75
99 Jaromir Jagr .60 1.50
100 Olaf Kolzig .30 .75
101 Joffrey Lupul RC 2.00 5.00
102 Patrice Bergeron RC 5.00 12.00
103 Milan Bartovic RC 1.50 4.00
104 Matthew Lombardi RC 2.00 5.00
105 Eric Staal RC 6.00 15.00
106 Tuomo Ruutu RC 3.00 8.00
107 Pavel Vorobiev RC 1.50 4.00
108 Dan Fritsche RC 1.50 4.00
109 Kent McDonell RC 1.50 4.00
110 Antti Miettinen RC 1.50 4.00
111 Nathan Horton RC 4.00 10.00
112 Dustin Brown RC 1.50 4.00
113 Tim Gleason RC 1.50 4.00
114 Brent Burns RC 1.50 4.00
115 Christopher Higgins RC 4.00 10.00
116 Dan Hamhuis RC 1.50 4.00
117 Jordin Tootoo RC 4.00 10.00
118 Sean Bergenheim RC 1.50 4.00
119 Antoine Vermette RC 1.50 4.00
120 Joni Pitkanen RC 1.50 4.00
121 Marc-Andre Fleury RC 8.00 20.00
122 Peter Sejna RC 1.50 4.00
123 Milan Michalek RC 2.00 5.00
124 Matt Stajan RC 4.00 10.00
125 Boyd Gordon RC 1.50 4.00

2003-04 Pacific Invincible Blue

*STARS: 2X TO 5X BASIC CARDS
*ROOKIES: .5X TO 1.25X
STATED PRINT RUN 350 SER.#'d SETS

2003-04 Pacific Invincible Red

This retail only parallel carried a red foil logo and was serial-numbered out of 850.

*STARS: 1.25X TO 3X BASIC CARDS
*ROOKIES: .25X TO .75X

2003-04 Pacific Invincible Retail

*STARS: SAME VALUE HOBBY
*ROOKIES: .25X TO .75X

2003-04 Pacific Invincible Afterburners

STAT.ODDS 1:41 HBBY/1:49 RETAIL
1 Ilya Kovalchuk 1.25 3.00
2 Paul Kariya .75 2.00
3 Teemu Selanne .75 2.00
4 Mike Modano 1.50 4.00
5 Henrik Zetterberg .75 2.00
6 Marian Gaborik 2.00 5.00
7 Pavel Bure .75 2.00
8 Marian Hossa .75 2.00
9 Martin St. Louis .75 2.00
10 Markus Naslund .75 2.00

2003-04 Pacific Invincible Featured Performers

COMPLETE SET (30) 20.00 40.00
STAT.ODDS 1:11 HBBY/1:25 RETAIL
1 Jean-Sebastien Giguere .40 1.00
2 Dany Heatley .75 2.00
3 Joe Thornton 1.00 2.50
4 Miroslav Satan .40 1.00
5 Jarome Iginla .50 1.25
6 Ron Francis .40 1.00
7 Jocelyn Thibault .40 1.00
8 Peter Forsberg 1.50 4.00
9 Rick Nash .75 2.00
10 Mike Modano 1.00 2.50
11 Steve Yzerman 2.00 5.00
12 Ales Hemsky .40 1.00
13 Olli Jokinen .40 1.00
14 Ziggy Palffy .40 1.00
15 Marian Gaborik 1.25 3.00
16 Jose Theodore .50 1.25
17 David Legwand .40 1.00
18 Martin Brodeur 1.50 4.00
19 Michael Peca .40 1.00
20 Eric Lindros .40 1.00
21 Jason Spezza .75 2.00
22 Jeremy Roenick .50 1.25
23 Sean Burke .40 1.00
24 Mario Lemieux 2.50 6.00
25 Pavol Demitra .40 1.00
26 Patrick Marleau .40 1.00
27 Vincent Lecavalier .40 1.00
28 Mats Sundin .40 1.00
29 Todd Bertuzzi .40 1.00
30 Jaromir Jagr 1.00 2.50

2003-04 Pacific Invincible Freeze Frame

COMPLETE SET (24) 10.00 20.00
STAT.ODDS 1:11/1:25 RETAIL
1 Jean-Sebastien Giguere .30 .75
2 Ryan Miller .30 .75
3 Jocelyn Thibault .30 .75
4 Patrick Roy 2.50 6.00
5 Marc Denis .30 .75
6 Marty Turco .30 .75
7 Dominik Hasek 1.00 2.50
8 Roberto Luongo .50 1.25
9 Roman Cechmanek .30 .75
10 Jose Theodore .50 1.25
11 Tomas Vokoun .30 .75
12 Martin Brodeur 1.25 3.00
13 Rick DiPietro .30 .75
14 Garth Snow .30 .75
15 Mike Dunham .30 .75
16 Patrick Lalime .30 .75
17 Sean Burke .30 .75
18 Chris Osgood .30 .75
19 Evgeni Nabokov .30 .75
20 John Grahame .30 .75
21 Nikolai Khabibulin .40 1.00
22 Ed Belfour .40 1.00
23 Dan Cloutier .30 .75
24 Olaf Kolzig .30 .75

2003-04 Pacific Invincible Jerseys

Known SP's are noted below.

STAT.ODDS 1:11 HBBY/1:25 RETAIL
1 Byron Dafoe 3.00 8.00
2 Milan Hnilicka 3.00 8.00
3 Martin Biron 3.00 8.00

4 Jamie McLennan 3.00 8.00
5 Roman Turek 3.00 8.00
6 Patrick Roy SP 15.00 40.00
7 Fred Brathwaite SP 5.00 12.00
8 Marc Denis 3.00 8.00
9 Ron Tugnutt 3.00 8.00
10 Marty Turco 5.00 12.00
11 Dominik Hasek SP 10.00 25.00
12 Curtis Joseph 3.00 8.00
13 Roman Cechmanek 3.00 8.00
14 Felix Potvin 3.00 8.00
15 Manny Fernandez 3.00 8.00
16 Jose Theodore 4.00 10.00
17 Tomas Vokoun 5.00 12.00
18 Martin Brodeur 8.00 20.00
19 Rick DiPietro 5.00 12.00
20 Mike Richter 3.00 8.00
21 Patrick Lalime 3.00 8.00
22 Jeff Hackett 3.00 8.00
23 Sean Burke 3.00 8.00
24 Johan Hedberg 3.00 8.00
25 Brent Johnson 3.00 8.00
26 Chris Osgood 3.00 8.00
27 Miikka Kiprusoff 5.00 12.00
28 Evgeni Nabokov 5.00 12.00
29 Nikolai Khabibulin 3.00 8.00
30 Ed Belfour SP 6.00 15.00
31 Dan Cloutier 3.00 8.00
32 Olaf Kolzig 4.00 10.00

2003-04 Pacific Invincible New Sensations

STAT.ODDS 1:21 HBBY/1:49 RETAIL
1 Stanislav Chistov .60 1.50
2 Dany Heatley 1.25 3.00
3 Ilya Kovalchuk 1.25 3.00
4 Ales Kotalik .60 1.50
5 Ryan Miller .60 1.50
6 Chuck Kobasew .60 1.50
7 Jordan Leopold .60 1.50
8 Tyler Arnason .60 1.50
9 Rick Nash 1.00 2.50
10 Pavel Datsyuk .60 1.50
11 Henrik Zetterberg 1.00 2.50
12 Ales Hemsky .60 1.50
13 Jay Bouwmeester .60 1.50
14 Alexander Frolov .60 1.50
15 Marcel Hossa .60 1.50
16 Rick DiPietro .60 1.50
17 Mattias Weinhandl .60 1.50
18 Jason Spezza 1.00 2.50
19 Barret Jackman .60 1.50
20 Jonathan Cheechoo .75 2.00

2003-04 Pacific Invincible Top Line

STATED ODDS 1:41 HOBBY
1 Sergei Fedorov 1.50 3.00
2 Peter Forsberg 2.50 6.00
3 Paul Kariya 1.00 2.50
4 Joe Sakic 2.00 5.00
5 Brett Hull 1.25 3.00
6 Steve Yzerman 4.00 10.00
7 Marian Gaborik 2.00 5.00
8 Mario Lemieux 5.00 12.00
9 Markus Naslund 1.00 2.50
10 Jaromir Jagr 1.50 4.00

2002 Pacific Les Gardiens

This 7-card set was available via a wrapper redemption at the Pacific booth during the Montreal show in October 2002. Each card was serial-numbered to just 199 copies. A gold parallel was also created and available randomly.

COMPLETE SET (7) 30.00
*GOLD: .6X TO 1.5X BASIC CARDS
GOLD PRINT RUN 99 SER.#'d SETS
1 Jean-Sebastien Giguere 2.00 5.00
2 Jocelyn Thibault 2.00 3.00
3 Patrick Roy 4.80 10.00
4 Roberto Luongo 2.00 5.00
5 Jose Theodore 3.20 5.00
6 Martin Brodeur 4.00 8.00
7 Patrick Lalime 2.00 3.00

2003-04 Pacific Luxury Suite

This mostly memorabilia set consisted of 23 veteran cards with up to 4 versions of each player; 25 dual-player cards with as many as 4 versions of each card; 30 short-printed rookie cards and 20 short-printed rookie cards that carried certified autographs and memorabilia swatches. Single player stick/blade cards were serial-numbered out of 20 and single player patch/blade cards were serial-numbered out of 10. Dual-player jerseys were serial-numbered out of 650 (unless otherwise noted below); dual-player patch cards were serial-numbered out of 100 (unless otherwise noted); dual-player blade cards were serial-numbered out of 10 and dual-player patch/blade cards were serial-numbered out of 10. Rookie cards #51-80 were serial-numbered out of 599 and rookie autograph/memorabilia cards #81-100 were serial-numbered out of 299.

PRINT RUNS UNDER 25 NOT PRICED DUE TO SCARCITY
1A Sergei Fedorov J/S-150 12.50 30.00
1B Sergei Fedorov J/P-100 15.00 40.00
1C Sergei Fedorov S/B
1D Sergei Fedorov P/B
2A Ilya Kovalchuk J/S-300 12.50 30.00
2B Ilya Kovalchuk J/P-100 20.00 50.00
2C Ilya Kovalchuk S/B
2D Ilya Kovalchuk P/B
3A Jarome Iginla J/S-150 20.00 50.00
3B Jarome Iginla J/P-100 30.00 80.00
3C Jarome Iginla S/B
3D Jarome Iginla P/B
4A Ron Francis P/S-65 30.00 80.00
4B Ron Francis S/B
4C Ron Francis P/B
5A Peter Forsberg J/S-150 15.00 40.00
5B Peter Forsberg J/P-100 20.00 50.00
5C Peter Forsberg S/B
5D Peter Forsberg P/B
6A Joe Sakic J/S-300 15.00 30.00
6B Joe Sakic J/P-100 20.00 50.00
6C Joe Sakic S/B
6D Joe Sakic P/B
7A Marc Denis P/S-175 12.50 30.00
7B Marc Denis S/B
7C Marc Denis P/B
8A Mike Modano J/S-150 15.00 40.00
8B Mike Modano J/P-100 15.00 40.00
8C Mike Modano S/B
8D Mike Modano P/B
9A Dominik Hasek P/S-30 50.00 100.00
9B Dominik Hasek S/B 50.00 100.00
9C Dominik Hasek P/B
10A Steve Yzerman J/S-150 30.00 80.00
10B Steve Yzerman J/P-100 30.00 80.00
10C Steve Yzerman S/B
10D Steve Yzerman P/B
11A Ziggy Palffy J/S-150 8.00 20.00
11B Ziggy Palffy J/P-100 12.50 30.00
11C Ziggy Palffy S/B
11D Ziggy Palffy P/B
12A Jose Theodore J/S-300 15.00 40.00
12B Jose Theodore J/P-100 20.00 50.00
12C Jose Theodore S/B
12D Jose Theodore P/B
13A Martin Brodeur J/S-300 15.00 40.00
13B Martin Brodeur J/P-100 30.00 60.00
13C Martin Brodeur S/B
13D Martin Brodeur P/B
14A Jason Spezza J/S-300 10.00 25.00
14B Jason Spezza J/P-50 30.00 80.00
14C Jason Spezza S/B
14D Jason Spezza P/B
15A Mike Comrie J/S-300 6.00 15.00
15B Mike Comrie J/P-50 10.00 25.00
15C Mike Comrie S/B
15D Mike Comrie P/B
16A Mario Lemieux J/S-100 40.00 100.00
16B Mario Lemieux S/B
16C Mario Lemieux P/B
17A Nikolai Khabibulin J/S-150 12.50 30.00
17B Nikolai Khabibulin J/P-50 25.00 60.00
17C Nikolai Khabibulin S/B
17D Nikolai Khabibulin P/B
18A Vincent Lecavalier J/S-100 20.00 50.00
18B Vincent Lecavalier J/P-50 25.00 60.00
18C Vincent Lecavalier S/B
18D Vincent Lecavalier P/B
19A Ed Belfour J/S-300 12.50 30.00
19B Ed Belfour J/P-50 15.00 40.00
19C Ed Belfour S/B
19D Ed Belfour P/B
20A Mats Sundin J/S-300 12.00 30.00
20B Mats Sundin J/P-50 15.00 40.00
20C Mats Sundin S/B
20D Mats Sundin P/B
21A Todd Bertuzzi J/S-300 12.50 30.00
21B Todd Bertuzzi J/P-50 20.00 50.00
21C Todd Bertuzzi S/B
21D Todd Bertuzzi P/B
22A Markus Naslund J/S-300 10.00 25.00
22B Markus Naslund J/P-50 15.00 40.00
22C Markus Naslund S/B
22D Markus Naslund P/B
23A Olaf Kolzig J/S-150 6.00 15.00
23B Olaf Kolzig J/P-50 15.00 40.00
23C Olaf Kolzig S/B
23D Olaf Kolzig P/B
24A Sergei Fedorov JSY 8.00 20.00
Jean-Sebastien Giguere JSY
24B Sergei Fedorov JSY 15.00 40.00
Jean-Sebastien Giguere JSY
24C Sergei Fedorov JSY
Jean-Sebastien Giguere JSY
25A Ilya Kovalchuk 10.00 25.00
Dany Heatley
25B Kovalchuk/Heatley P/P-50 30.00 80.00
25C Kovalchuk/Heatley B/B
26A Joe Thornton 8.00 20.00
Sergei Samsonov
26B J.Thornton/S.Samsonov P/P 20.00 50.00
26C J.Thornton/S.Samsonov J/S 12.50 30.00
26D J.Thornton/S.Samsonov P/B
27A Ryan Miller 8.00 20.00
Ales Kotalik
27B R.Miller/A.Kotalik P/P 12.00 30.00
28A Peter Forsberg 12.50 30.00
Joe Sakic
28B P.Forsberg/J.Sakic P/P 40.00 100.00
28C P.Forsberg/J.Sakic B/B
29A Paul Kariya 5.00 12.00
Teemu Selanne
29B P.Kariya/T.Selanne P/P 25.00 60.00
29C P.Kariya/T.Selanne B/B
30A Paul Kariya 10.00 25.00
Milan Hejduk
30B P.Kariya/M.Hejduk P/P 25.00 60.00
30C P.Kariya/M.Hejduk P/B
31A Teemu Selanne 8.00 20.00
David Aebischer
31B T.Selanne/D.Aebischer P/P 15.00 40.00
32A M.Modano/M.Turco J/J 6.00 15.00
32B M.Modano/M.Turco P/P 20.00 50.00
32C M.Modano/M.Turco B/B
33A Brett Hull 8.00 20.00
Brendan Shanahan
33B B.Hull/B. Shanahan P/P 20.00 50.00
33C B.Hull/B. Shanahan P/B
34A Chris Chelios 40.00 100.00
Nicklas Lidstrom
34B C.Chelios/N.Lidstrom B/B
35A Ryan Smyth 6.00 15.00
Ales Hemsky
35B R.Smyth/A.Hemsky P/P 25.00 60.00
35C R.Smyth/A.Hemsky P/B
36A Jay Bouwmeester 6.00 15.00
Roberto Luongo
36B Bouwmeester/Luongo P/P 25.00 60.00
37A Ziggy Palffy 5.00 12.00
Adam Deadmarsh
37B Palffy/Deadmarsh P/P 10.00 25.00
37C Palffy/Deadmarsh B/B 15.00 40.00
38A Saku Koivu 10.00 25.00
Jose Theodore
38B S.Koivu/J.Theodore P/P 25.00 60.00
38C S.Koivu/J.Theodore B/B
39A Tomas Vokoun 5.00 12.00
Scott Walker
39B Vokoun/Walker P/P 20.00 50.00
39C Vokoun/Walker J/S-100 8.00 20.00
39D T.Vokoun/S.Walker P/B
40A Martin Brodeur 8.00 20.00
Patrick Elias
40B M.Brodeur/P.Elias P/P 30.00 80.00
40C M.Brodeur/P.Elias P/B
41A Alexei Yashin 8.00 20.00
Rick DiPietro
41B A.Yashin/R.DiPietro P/P 20.00 50.00
42A Eric Lindros 8.00 20.00
Brian Leetch
42B Lindros/Leetch P/P-75 20.00 50.00
42C Lindros/Leetch B/B
43A Marian Hossa 6.00 15.00
Patrick Lalime
43B M. Hossa/P.Lalime P/P 20.00 50.00
43C M. Hossa/P.Lalime B/B
44A Jeremy Roenick 8.00 20.00
Jeff Hackett
44B J.Roenick/J.Hackett P/P 15.00 40.00
45A Barret Jackman 8.00 20.00
Chris Pronger
45B Jackman/Pronger P/P-50 20.00 50.00
46A Doug Weight 8.00 20.00
Chris Osgood
46B D.Weight/C.Osgood P/P 20.00 50.00
46C D.Weight/C.Osgood B/B
47A Nikolai Khabibulin 10.00 25.00
Vincent Lecavalier
47B N.Khabibulin/V.Lecavalier P/P 20.00 50.00
47C N.Khabibulin/V.Lecavalier B/B
48A Mats Sundin 6.00 15.00
Alexander Mogilny
48B Sundin/Mogilny P/P-25 25.00 60.00
48C Sundin/Mogilny B/B
49A Brendan Morrison 6.00 15.00
Dan Cloutier
49B B.Morrison/D.Cloutier P/P 15.00 40.00
50A Jaromir Jagr 10.00 25.00
Peter Bondra
50B J.Jagr/P.Bondra P/P 25.00 60.00
50C J.Jagr/P.Bondra B/B
51 Garrett Burnett RC 3.00 8.00
52 Tony Martensson RC 3.00 8.00
53 Sergei Zinovjev RC 3.00 8.00
54 Andrew Peters RC 3.00 8.00
55 Matthew Lombardi RC 3.00 8.00
56 Travis Moen RC 3.00 8.00
57 Pavel Vorobiev RC 3.00 8.00
58 Mikhail Yakubov RC 3.00 8.00
59 Cody McCormick RC 3.00 8.00
60 Dan Fritsche RC 3.00 8.00
61 Kent McDonell RC 3.00 8.00
62 Nikolai Zherdev RC 8.00 20.00
63 Darryl Bootland RC 3.00 8.00
64 Nathan Robinson RC 3.00 8.00
65 Tony Salmelainen RC 3.00 8.00
66 Peter Sarno RC 3.00 8.00
67 Gregory Campbell RC 3.00 8.00
68 Dan Hamhuis RC 3.00 8.00
69 Marek Zidlicky RC 3.00 8.00
70 David Hale RC 3.00 8.00
71 Paul Martin RC 3.00 8.00
72 Dominic Moore RC 3.00 8.00

73 Fredrik Sjostrom RC 3.00 8.00
74 Matt Murley RC 3.00 8.00
75 John Pohl RC 3.00 8.00
76 Tom Preissing RC 3.00 8.00
77 Maxim Kondratiev RC 3.00 8.00
78 Ryan Kesler RC 4.00 10.00
79 Alexander Semin RC 10.00 25.00
80 Rastislav Stana RC 4.00 10.00
81 Joffrey Lupul JSY AU RC 12.00 30.00
82 Patrice Bergeron JSY AU RC 25.00 50.00
83 Brent Krahn PCK AU RC 8.00 20.00
84 Eric Staal PCK AU RC 40.00 100.00
85 Tuomo Ruutu PCK AU RC 10.00 25.00
86 Antti Miettinen JSY AU RC 8.00 20.00
87 Jiri Hudler PCK AU RC 12.00 30.00
88 Nathan Horton JSY AU RC 15.00 40.00
89 Dustin Brown JSY AU RC 12.00 30.00
90 Brent Burns PCK AU RC 12.00 30.00
91 Chris Higgins JSY AU RC 15.00 40.00
92 Jordin Tootoo JSY AU RC 20.00 40.00
93 S.Bergenheim PCK AU RC 8.00 20.00
94 Antoine Vermette JSY AU RC 10.00 25.00
95 Joni Pitkanen JSY AU RC 8.00 20.00
96 Marc-Andre Fleury 50.00 100.00
PCK AU RC
97 Peter Sejna PCK AU RC 8.00 20.00
98 Milan Michalek PCK AU RC 15.00 40.00
99 Matt Stajan PCK AU RC 10.00 25.00
100 Boyd Gordon JSY AU RC 8.00 20.00

2003-04 Pacific Luxury Suite Gold

STATED PRINT RUN 10 SER.#'d SETS
NOT PRICED DUE TO SCARCITY

2003 Pacific Montreal International

This set was issued at the Spring 2003 Montreal show as a wrapper redemption by Pacific. The cards feature members of the Montreal Canadiens on one side and Montreal Alouettes on the other.

COMPLETE SET (6) 15.00
1 Saku Koivu 5.00
Anthony Calvillo
2 Jose Theodore 5.00
Jermaine Copeland
3 Yanic Perreault 2.00
Ben Cahoon
4 Richard Zednik 2.00
Eric Lapointe
5 Jan Bulis 2.00
Bruno Heppell
6 Patrice Brisebois 2.00
Kevin Johnson

2003 Pacific Montreal Olympic Stadium Show

Serial-numbered to 299, this 8-card set was available via wrapper redemption at the Pacific booth during the 2003 Spring " Collections Sport et Jouet" in Montreal at the Olympic Stadium. A gold version was also created and numbered to 99. Values for gold parallels can be found by using the multipliers below.

COMPLETE SET (8) 40.00
*GOLD: .75X TO 2X BASIC CARDS
1 Stanislav Chistov 3.20 5.00
2 Pascal Leclaire 3.20 5.00
3 Rick Nash 4.80 15.00
4 Henrik Zetterberg 4.80 15.00
5 Jay Bouwmeester 3.20 8.00
6 Alexander Frolov 2.40 5.00
7 Ron Hainsey 2.40 5.00
8 Jason Spezza 4.00 12.00

2004 Pacific Montreal International

Available via redemption only at the 2004 Montreal International show, this 8-card set featured promising prospects.

COMPLETE SET (8) 15.00
STATED PRINT RUN 499 SER.#'d SETS
*GOLD: 2X TO 4X BASIC CARDS
GOLD PRINT RUN 99 SER.#'d SETS
1 Patrice Bergeron 4.00
2 Eric Staal 2.00
3 Nathan Horton 2.00
4 Chris Higgins 1.00
5 Jordin Tootoo 2.00
6 Antoine Vermette 1.00
7 Joni Pitkanen 2.00
8 Marc-Andre Fleury 4.00

2004 Pacific NHL All-Star FANtasy

This 10-card set was available via wrapper redemption at the Pacific booth during the 2004 NHL All-Star FANtasy. Cards were serial-numbered out of 499.

COMPLETE SET (10)
1 Joffrey Lupul 1.50
2 Patrice Bergeron 4.00
3 Eric Staal 2.00
4 Jiri Hudler 2.00
5 Brent Burns 1.50
6 Jordin Tootoo 2.00
7 Joni Pitkanen 2.00
8 Marc-Andre Fleury 4.00
9 Peter Sejna 1.00
10 Matt Stajan 2.50

2004 Pacific NHL All-Star Nets

These cards were available via redemption at the Pacific booth during the 2004 NHL All-Star FANtasy. Cards were serial-numbered out of 499. A gold parallel was also created and available randomly.

*GOLD: 1X TO 2.5X BASIC CARDS
GOLD PRINT RUN 99 SER.#'d SETS
1 Eastern Team 12.50 30.00
Joe Thornton
Martin Brodeur
Marian
2 Western Team 15.00 25.00
Mike Modano
Marty Turco
Marian Gab

2004 Pacific NHL Draft All-Star Nets

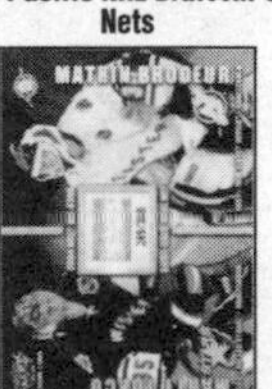

Available via wrapper redemption at the Pacific booth during the 2004 NHL Draft, this 3-card set features pieces of netting from the 2004 All-Star game. Each card was serial numbered out of 250.

COMPLETE SET (3) 60.00 125.00
1 I.Kovalchuk/R.Nash 20.00 50.00
2 Martin St. Louis 15.00 40.00
Joe Sakic
3 M.Turco/M.Brodeur 20.00 50.00

2004 Pacific NHL Draft Show Calder Reflections

COMPLETE SET (8)
1 Joffrey Lupul .75 2.00
2 Patrice Bergeron 1.50 4.00
3 Andrew Raycroft 1.25 3.00
4 Eric Staal .75 2.00
5 Michael Ryder .75 2.00
6 Trent Hunter .40 1.00
7 Marc-Andre Fleury 1.50 4.00
8 Ryan Malone .40 1.00

1997-98 Pacific Omega

The 1997-98 Pacific Omega set was issued in one series totaling 250 cards and was distributed in six-card packs with a suggested retail price of $1.99. The fronts feature color action photos etched in foil of players who are popular with fans. The backs carry another photo and the player's accomplishments.

COMPLETE SET (250) 12.00 30.00
1 Matt Cullen RC .20 .50
2 Guy Hebert .10 .30
3 Paul Kariya .15 .40
4 Dmitri Mironov .05 .15
5 Steve Rucchin .05 .15
6 Tomas Sandstrom .05 .15
7 Teemu Selanne .15 .40
8 Mikhail Shtalenkov .05 .15
9 Pavel Trnka .05 .15
10 Jason Allison .05 .15
11 Per Axelsson .05 .15
12 Ray Bourque .25 .60
13 Anson Carter .10 .30
14 Byron Dafoe .10 .30
15 Ted Donato .05 .15
16 Hal Gill RC .05 .15
17 Dimitri Khristich .05 .15
18 Sergei Samsonov .10 .30
19 Joe Thornton .40 1.00
20 Jason Dawe .05 .15
21 Michal Grosek .05 .15
22 Dominik Hasek .30 .75
23 Brian Holzinger .05 .15
24 Michael Peca .05 .15
25 Derek Plante .05 .15
26 Miroslav Satan .10 .30
27 Steve Shields RC .25 .60
28 Andrew Cassels .05 .15
29 Theo Fleury .05 .15
30 Jarome Iginla .20 .50
31 Derek Morris RC .20 .50
32 Tyler Moss RC .05 .15
33 Michael Nylander .05 .15
34 Dwayne Roloson .10 .30
35 Cory Stillman .05 .15
36 Rick Tabaracci .10 .30
37 German Titov .05 .15
38 Bates Battaglia RC .05 .15
39 Nelson Emerson .05 .15
40 Martin Gelinas .05 .15
41 Sami Kapanen .05 .15
42 Trevor Kidd .10 .30
43 Kevin Dineen .05 .15
44 Keith Primeau .05 .15
45 Gary Roberts .05 .15
46 Tony Amonte .10 .30
47 Keith Carney .05 .15
48 Chris Chelios .15 .40
49 Eric Daze .10 .30
50 Brian Felsner .10 .30
51 Jeff Hackett .10 .30
52 Christian Laflamme RC .05 .15
53 Alexei Zhamnov .05 .15
54 Craig Billington .10 .30
55 Adam Deadmarsh .05 .15
56 Peter Forsberg .30 .75
57 Valeri Kamensky .10 .30
58 Uwe Krupp .05 .15
59 Jari Kurri .10 .30
60 Claude Lemieux .05 .15
61 Eric Messier RC .05 .15
62 Jeff Odgers .05 .15
63 Sandis Ozolinsh .05 .15
64 Patrick Roy .75 2.00
65 Joe Sakic .30 .75
66 Greg Adams .05 .15
67 Ed Belfour .15 .40
68 Manny Fernandez .05 .15
69 Derian Hatcher .05 .15
70 Jamie Langenbrunner .05 .15
71 Jere Lehtinen .05 .15
72 Juha Lind RC .05 .15
73 Mike Modano .20 .50
74 Joe Nieuwendyk .10 .30
75 Darryl Sydor .05 .15
76 Pat Verbeek .05 .15
77 Sergei Zubov .05 .15
78 Slava Fetisov .05 .15
79 Brent Gilchrist .05 .15
80 Kevin Hodson .10 .30
81 Vyacheslav Kozlov .05 .15
82 Igor Larionov .05 .15
83 Nicklas Lidstrom .15 .40
84 Darren McCarty .05 .15
85 Larry Murphy .05 .15
86 Chris Osgood .10 .30
87 Brendan Shanahan .15 .40
88 Steve Yzerman .60 1.50
89 Kelly Buchberger .05 .15
90 Mike Grier .05 .15
91 Bill Guerin .10 .30
92 Roman Hamrlik .05 .15
93 Curtis Joseph .15 .40
94 Boris Mironov .05 .15
95 Ryan Smyth .10 .30
96 Doug Weight .10 .30
97 Dino Ciccarelli .05 .15
98 Dave Gagner .05 .15
99 Ed Jovanovski .10 .30
100 Scott Mellanby .05 .15
101 Robert Svehla .05 .15
102 John Vanbiesbrouck .10 .30
103 Steve Washburn .05 .15
104 Kevin Weekes RC .40 1.00
105 Ray Whitney .05 .15
106 Rob Blake .10 .30
107 Stephane Fiset .10 .30
108 Garry Galley .05 .15
109 Steve McKenna RC .05 .15
110 Glen Murray .05 .15
111 Yanic Perreault .10 .30
112 Luc Robitaille .10 .30
113 Jamie Storr .10 .30
114 Jozef Stumpel .10 .30
115 Vladimir Tsyplakov .05 .15
116 Shayne Corson .05 .15
117 Vincent Damphousse .05 .15
118 Saku Koivu .15 .40
119 Vladimir Malakhov .05 .15
120 Andy Moog .10 .30
121 Mark Recchi .10 .30
122 Martin Rucinsky .05 .15
123 Brian Savage .05 .15
124 Jocelyn Thibault .10 .30
125 Jason Arnott .05 .15
126 Brad Bombardir RC .05 .15
127 Martin Brodeur .40 1.00
128 Patrik Elias RC 1.00 2.50
129 Doug Gilmour .10 .30
130 Bobby Holik .05 .15
131 Randy McKay .05 .15
132 Scott Niedermayer .05 .15
133 Krzysztof Oliwa RC .05 .15
134 Scott Stevens .10 .30
135 Petr Sykora .05 .15
136 Bryan Berard .05 .15
137 Travis Green .05 .15
138 Bryan McCabe .05 .15
139 Sergei Nemchinov .05 .15
140 Zigmund Palffy .10 .30
141 Robert Reichel .05 .15
142 Tommy Salo .10 .30
143 Bryan Smolinski .05 .15
144 Adam Graves .05 .15
145 Wayne Gretzky 1.00 2.50
146 Pat LaFontaine .15 .40
147 Brian Leetch .15 .40
148 Mike Richter .15 .40
149 Kevin Stevens .10 .30
150 Niklas Sundstrom .05 .15
151 Tim Sweeney .05 .15
152 Daniel Alfredsson .10 .30
153 Magnus Arvedson .05 .15
154 Andreas Dackell .05 .15
155 Igor Kravchuk .05 .15
156 Shawn McEachern .05 .15
157 Damian Rhodes .10 .30
158 Ron Tugnutt .10 .30
159 Alexei Yashin .05 .15
160 Rod Brind'Amour .10 .30
161 Paul Coffey .15 .40
162 Eric Desjardins .10 .30
163 Colin Forbes .05 .15
164 Chris Gratton .10 .30
165 Ron Hextall .10 .30
166 Trent Klatt .05 .15
167 John LeClair .15 .40
168 Eric Lindros .15 .40
169 Joel Otto .05 .15
170 Garth Snow .10 .30
171 Dainius Zubrus .15 .40
172 Dallas Drake .05 .15
173 Mike Gartner .10 .30
174 Nikolai Khabibulin .10 .30
175 Teppo Numminen .05 .15
176 Jeremy Roenick .20 .50
177 Keith Tkachuk .15 .40
178 Rick Tocchet .10 .30
179 Oleg Tverdovsky .05 .15
180 Juha Ylonen .05 .15
181 Stu Barnes .05 .15
182 Tom Barrasso .10 .30
183 Rob Brown .05 .15
184 Ron Francis .10 .30
185 Kevin Hatcher .05 .15
186 Jaromir Jagr .25 .60
187 Alexei Morozov .10 .30
188 Ed Olczyk .05 .15
189 Jim Campbell .05 .15
190 Geoff Courtnall .05 .15
191 Pavol Demitra .10 .30
192 Steve Duchesne .05 .15
193 Grant Fuhr .10 .30
194 Brett Hull .20 .50
195 Al MacInnis .10 .30
196 Chris Pronger .10 .30
197 Pascal Rheaume RC .05 .15
198 Jamie Rivers .05 .15
199 Pierre Turgeon .10 .30
200 Jeff Friesen .05 .15
201 Tony Granato .05 .15
202 John MacLean .05 .15
203 Patrick Marleau .25 .60
204 Marty McSorley .05 .15
205 Owen Nolan .10 .30
206 Marco Sturm RC .25 .60
207 Mike Vernon .10 .30
208 Andrei Zyuzin RC .05 .15
209 Karl Dykhuis .05 .15
210 Daymond Langkow .10 .30
211 Louie DeBrusk .05 .15
212 Daren Puppa .10 .30
213 Mikael Renberg .10 .30
214 Alexander Selivanov .05 .15
215 Paul Ysebaert .05 .15
216 Rob Zamuner .05 .15
217 Sergei Berezin .05 .15
218 Wendel Clark .10 .30
219 Marcel Cousineau .10 .30
220 Tie Domi .10 .30
221 Mike Johnson RC .15 .40
222 Igor Korolev .05 .15
223 Felix Potvin .15 .40
224 Mathieu Schneider .05 .15
225 Mats Sundin .15 .40
226 Yannick Tremblay RC .05 .15
227 Donald Brashear .05 .15
228 Pavel Bure .15 .40
229 Sean Burke .10 .30
230 Trevor Linden .10 .30
231 Mark Messier .15 .40
232 Alexander Mogilny .10 .30
233 Markus Naslund .15 .40
234 Mattias Ohlund .10 .30
235 Dave Scatchard RC .05 .15
236 Peter Bondra .10 .30
237 Andrew Brunette .10 .30
238 Phil Housley .05 .15
239 Dale Hunter .05 .15
240 Calle Johansson .05 .15
241 Joe Juneau .10 .30
242 Olaf Kolzig .10 .30
243 Adam Oates .10 .30
244 Richard Zednik .05 .15
245 Chris Chelios .15 .40
Keith Tkachuk
246 M.Modano/E.Belfour .15 .40
247 Teemu Selanne .15 .40
Saku Koivu
248 Eric Lindros .15 .40
Shayne Corson
249 Patrick Roy .40 1.00
Martin Brodeur
250 Wayne Gretzky .60 1.50
Mark Messier
S73 Mike Modano SAMPLE .75 2.00

1997-98 Pacific Omega Copper

Inserted one in every hobby pack, this 250-card set is parallel to the base set with copper foil highlights.

*COPPER: 1.5X TO 4X BASIC CARDS

1997-98 Pacific Omega Dark Gray

Inserted one in every Canadian retail pack, this 250-card set is parallel to the base set with dark gray foil highlights.

*DARK GRAY: 2X TO 5X BASIC CARDS

1997-98 Pacific Omega Emerald Green

Inserted one in every Canadian pack only, this 250-card set is parallel to the base set with green foil highlights.

*GREEN: 2X TO 4X BASIC CARDS

1997-98 Pacific Omega Gold

Inserted one in every U.S. retail pack only, this 250-card set is parallel to the base set with gold foil highlights.

*GOLD: 2X TO 5X BASIC CARDS

1997-98 Pacific Omega Ice Blue

Randomly inserted in both Canadian and U.S. hobby and retail packs at the rate of 1:73, this 250-card set is parallel to the base set with blue foil highlights.

*ICE BLUE: 20X TO 50X BASIC CARDS

1997-98 Pacific Omega Game Face

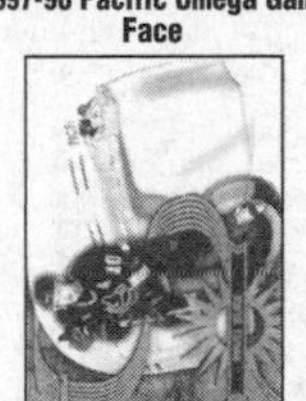

Randomly inserted in hobby and retail packs at the rate of 1:37, this 20-card set features color photos of top goalies printed on die-cut helmet-shaped cards with a cel facemask. The backs carry player information and describe his talents as a goalie.

COMPLETE SET (20) 20.00 40.00
1 Paul Kariya .60 1.50
2 Teemu Selanne .60 1.50
3 Peter Forsberg 1.50 4.00
4 Joe Sakic 1.25 3.00
5 Mike Modano 1.00 2.50
6 Nicklas Lidstrom .60 1.50
7 Brendan Shanahan .60 1.50
8 Steve Yzerman 3.00 8.00
9 Ryan Smyth .50 1.25
10 Saku Koivu .60 1.50
11 Wayne Gretzky 4.00 10.00
12 John LeClair .60 1.50
13 Eric Lindros .60 1.50
14 Dainius Zubrus .60 1.50
15 Keith Tkachuk .60 1.50
16 Jaromir Jagr 1.00 2.50
17 Brett Hull .75 2.00
18 Pavel Bure .60 1.50
19 Mark Messier .60 1.50
20 Peter Bondra .50 1.25

1997-98 Pacific Omega No Scoring Zone

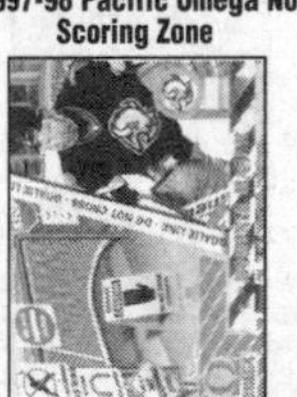

COMPLETE SET (10) 6.00 12.00
STATED ODDS 2:37
1 Dominik Hasek 1.00 2.50
2 Patrick Roy 2.50 6.00
3 Ed Belfour .50 1.25
4 Chris Osgood .40 1.00
5 John Vanbiesbrouck .40 1.00
6 Andy Moog .40 1.00
7 Martin Brodeur 1.25 3.00
8 Mike Richter .50 1.25
9 Ron Hextall .40 1.00
10 Felix Potvin .50 1.25

1997-98 Pacific Omega Silks

Randomly inserted in hobby and retail packs at the rate of 1:73, this 12-card set features color photos of top players printed on a silk-like fabric card stock.

COMPLETE SET (12) 30.00 60.00
1 Paul Kariya 1.25 3.00
2 Teemu Selanne 2.50 6.00
3 Peter Forsberg 3.00 8.00
4 Patrick Roy 6.00 15.00
5 Joe Sakic 2.50 6.00
6 Steve Yzerman 6.00 15.00
7 Martin Brodeur 3.00 8.00
8 Wayne Gretzky 8.00 20.00
9 Eric Lindros 1.25 3.00
10 Jaromir Jagr 2.00 5.00
11 Pavel Bure 1.25 3.00
12 Mark Messier 1.25 3.00

1997-98 Pacific Omega Stick Handle Laser Cuts

Randomly inserted in hobby and retail packs at the rate of 1:145, this 20-card set features color photos of popular players printed on full foil card stock with laser-cut hockey sticks crossing in the background. The backs carry a description of the player's accomplishments on ice.

COMPLETE SET (20) 60.00 120.00
1 Paul Kariya 5.00 12.00
2 Teemu Selanne 6.00 15.00
3 Theo Fleury 2.00 5.00
4 Chris Chelios 2.00 5.00
5 Peter Forsberg 6.00 15.00
6 Joe Sakic 4.00 10.00
7 Mike Modano 3.00 8.00
8 Brendan Shanahan 2.00 5.00
9 Steve Yzerman 12.50 30.00
10 Saku Koivu 2.00 5.00
11 Doug Gilmour 2.00 5.00
12 Zigmund Palffy 2.00 5.00
13 Wayne Gretzky 15.00 40.00
14 Pat LaFontaine 2.00 5.00
15 John LeClair 2.00 5.00
16 Eric Lindros 2.00 5.00
17 Jaromir Jagr 3.00 8.00
18 Mats Sundin 2.00 5.00
19 Pavel Bure 2.00 5.00
20 Mark Messier 2.00 5.00

1997-98 Pacific Omega Team Leaders

COMPLETE SET (20) 15.00 30.00
STATED ODDS 2:48 CANADIAN PACKS
1 Paul Kariya .50 1.25
2 Ray Bourque .75 2.00
3 Theo Fleury .20 .50
4 Patrick Roy 2.50 6.00
5 Joe Sakic 1.00 2.50
6 Ed Belfour .50 1.25
7 Joe Nieuwendyk .40 1.00
8 Brendan Shanahan .50 1.25
9 Steve Yzerman 2.50 6.00
10 Ryan Smyth .40 1.00
11 Shayne Corson .20 .50
12 Mark Recchi .40 1.00
13 Martin Brodeur 1.25 3.00
14 Wayne Gretzky 3.00 8.00
15 Rod Brind'Amour .40 1.00
16 Eric Lindros .50 1.25
17 Chris Pronger .40 1.00
18 Felix Potvin .50 1.25
19 Pavel Bure .50 1.25
20 Mark Messier .50 1.25

1998-99 Pacific Omega

The 1998-99 Pacific Omega set was issued in one series totaling 250 cards and was distributed in six-card packs with a suggested retail price of $1.99. The fronts feature color action photos of the NHL's greatest stars and most exciting rookies printed on etched silver foil cards. The backs carry player information and career statistics.

COMPLETE SET (252) 40.00 80.00
COMP.SET w/o SP's (1-250) 30.00 60.00
1 Travis Green .05 .15
2 Stu Grimson .05 .15
3 Guy Hebert .10 .30
4 Paul Kariya .15 .40
5 Marty McInnis .05 .15
6 Fredrik Olausson .05 .15
7 Steve Rucchin .05 .15
8 Teemu Selanne .15 .40
9 Johan Davidsson .15 .40
Antti Aalto
10 Jason Allison .05 .15
11 Ken Belanger .05 .15
12 Ray Bourque .25 .60
13 Anson Carter .10 .30
14 Byron Dafoe .10 .30
15 Steve Heinze .05 .15
16 Dimitri Khristich .05 .15
17 Sergei Samsonov .10 .30
18 Robbie Tallas .10 .30
19 Joe Thornton .25 .60
20 Matthew Barnaby .10 .30
21 Curtis Brown .05 .15
22 Michal Grosek .05 .15
23 Dominik Hasek .30 .75
24 Brian Holzinger .10 .30
25 Micael Peca .10 .30
26 Rob Ray .05 .15
27 Geoff Sanderson .10 .30
28 Miroslav Satan .10 .30
29 Dixon Ward .05 .15
30 Valeri Bure .05 .15
31 Theo Fleury .05 .15
32 Jean-Sebastien Giguere .10 .30
33 Jarome Iginla .20 .50
34 Tyler Moss .05 .15
35 Cory Stillman .05 .15
36 Jason Wiemer .05 .15
37 Clarke Wilm RC .05 .15
38 Martin St.Louis RC 2.00 5.00
Rico Fata
39 Paul Coffey .15 .40
40 Ron Francis .10 .30
41 Martin Gelinas .05 .15
42 Arturs Irbe .10 .30
43 Sami Kapanen .05 .15
44 Trevor Kidd .10 .30
45 Keith Primeau .05 .15
46 Gary Roberts .05 .15
47 Ray Sheppard .10 .30
48 Tony Amonte .10 .30
49 Chris Chelios .15 .40
50 Eric Daze .10 .30
51 Nelson Emerson .05 .15
52 Doug Gilmour .10 .30
53 Mike Maneluk RC .05 .15
54 Bob Probert .05 .15
55 Jocelyn Thibault .10 .30
56 Alexei Zhamnov .05 .15
57 Todd White RC .05 .15
Brad Brown
58 Adam Deadmarsh .05 .15
59 Marc Denis .10 .30
60 Peter Forsberg .40 1.00
61 Claude Lemieux .05 .15
62 Jeff Odgers .05 .15
63 Sandis Ozolinsh .05 .15
64 Patrick Roy .75 2.00
65 Joe Sakic .30 .75
66 Wade Belak RC .10 .30
Scott Parker
67 Chris Drury RC 2.00 5.00
Milan Hejduk
68 Ed Belfour .15 .40
69 Derian Hatcher .05 .15
70 Brett Hull .20 .50
71 Jamie Langenbrunner .05 .15
72 Jere Lehtinen .10 .30
73 Mike Modano .25 .60
74 Joe Nieuwendyk .10 .30
75 Darryl Sydor .05 .15
76 Roman Turek .10 .30
77 Sergei Zubov .05 .15
78 Sergei Gusev RC .05 .15
Jamie Wright
79 Sergei Fedorov .25 .60
80 Joey Kocur .05 .15
81 Martin LaPointe .05 .15
82 Igor Larionov .05 .15
83 Nicklas Lidstrom .15 .40
84 Darren McCarty .05 .15
85 Larry Murphy .10 .30
86 Chris Osgood .10 .30
87 Brendan Shanahan .15 .40
88 Steve Yzerman .75 2.00
89 Norm Maracle RC .25 .60
Stacy Roest
90 Josef Beranek .05 .15
91 Sean Brown .05 .15
92 Bill Guerin .10 .30
93 Roman Hamrlik .05 .15
94 Janne Niinimaa .05 .15
95 Mikhail Shtalenkov .05 .15
96 Ryan Smyth .10 .30
97 Doug Weight .10 .30
98 Tom Poti .10 .30
Craig Millar
99 Pavel Bure .15 .40
100 Sean Burke .10 .30
101 Dino Ciccarelli .05 .15
102 Bret Hedican .05 .15
103 Viktor Kozlov .05 .15
104 Paul Laus .05 .15
105 Rob Niedermayer .05 .15
106 Mark Parrish RC .10 .30
107 Ray Whitney .05 .15
108 Oleg Kvasha RC .20 .50
Peter Worrell
109 Rob Blake .10 .30
110 Stephane Fiset .10 .30
111 Glen Murray .05 .15
112 Luc Robitaille .10 .30
113 Jamie Storr .10 .30
114 Jozef Stumpel .05 .15
115 Vladimir Tsyplakov .05 .15
116 M.Visheau RC/J.Green RC .10 .30
117 Olli Jokinen RC .10 .30
Pavel Rosa
118 Benoit Brunet .05 .15
119 Shayne Corson .10 .30
120 Vincent Damphousse .05 .15
121 Jeff Hackett .10 .30
122 Matt Higgins RC .05 .15
123 Saku Koivu .15 .40
124 Mark Recchi .10 .30
125 Martin Rucinsky .05 .15
126 Brian Savage .05 .15
127 Andrew Brunette .10 .30
128 Mike Dunham .10 .30
129 Greg Johnson .05 .15

130 Sergei Krivokrasov .05 .15
131 Denny Lambert .05 .15
132 Cliff Ronning .05 .15
133 Tomas Vokoun .05 .15
134 Patrick Cote .10 .30
Kimmo Timonen
135 Jason Arnott .05 .15
136 Martin Brodeur .40 1.00
137 Patrik Elias .10 .30
138 Bobby Holik .05 .15
139 Brendan Morrison .10 .30
140 Krzysztof Oliwa .05 .15
141 Brian Rolston .05 .15
142 Vadim Sharifijanov .05 .15
143 Scott Stevens .10 .30
144 Petr Sykora .05 .15
145 Ted Donato .05 .15
146 Kenny Jonsson .05 .15
147 Trevor Linden .10 .30
148 Gino Odjick .05 .15
149 Zigmund Palffy .10 .30
150 Felix Potvin .15 .40
151 Robert Reichel .05 .15
152 Tommy Salo .10 .30
153 Mike Watt .10 .30
Eric Brewer
154 Dan Cloutier .10 .30
155 Adam Graves .05 .15
156 Wayne Gretzky 1.00 2.50
157 Todd Harvey .05 .15
158 Brian Leetch .15 .40
159 Manny Malhotra .10 .30
160 Petr Nedved .10 .30
161 Mike Richter .15 .40
162 Esa Tikkanen .05 .15
163 Daniel Alfredsson .10 .30
164 Marian Hossa .15 .40
165 Andreas Johansson .05 .15
166 Shawn McEachern .05 .15
167 Wade Redden .05 .15
168 Damian Rhodes .10 .30
169 Ron Tugnutt .10 .30
170 Alexei Yashin .05 .15
171 Patrick Traverse RC .05 .15
Sami Salo
172 Rod Brind'Amour .10 .30
173 Eric Desjardins .10 .30
174 Ron Hextall .10 .30
175 Keith Jones .10 .30
176 John LeClair .15 .40
177 Eric Lindros .15 .40
178 Mikael Renberg .10 .30
179 Dimitri Tertyshny RC .05 .15
180 John Vanbiesbrouck .10 .30
181 Dainius Zubrus .05 .15
182 Daniel Briere .05 .15
183 Dallas Drake .05 .15
184 Nikolai Khabibulin .10 .30
185 Jyrki Lumme .05 .15
186 Teppo Numminen .05 .15
187 Jeremy Roenick .20 .50
188 Keith Tkachuk .15 .40
189 Rick Tocchet .10 .30
190 Oleg Tverdovsky .05 .15
191 Jim Waite .10 .30
192 Jean-Sebastien Aubin RC .30 .75
193 Stu Barnes .05 .15
194 Tom Barrasso .10 .30
195 Jaromir Jagr .25 .60
196 Alexei Kovalev .05 .15
197 Robert Lang .05 .15
198 Alexei Morozov .05 .15
199 Martin Straka .05 .15
200 Jan Hrdina RC .25 .60
Maxim Galanov
201 Pavol Demitra .10 .30
202 Grant Fuhr .10 .30
203 Al MacInnis .10 .30
204 Jamie McLennan .10 .30
205 Chris Pronger .10 .30
206 Pierre Turgeon .10 .30
207 Tony Twist .05 .15
208 Marty Reasoner RC .30 .75
Lubos Bartecko
209 Jeff Friesen .05 .15
210 Bryan Marchment .05 .15
211 Patrick Marleau .10 .30
212 Owen Nolan .10 .30
213 Mike Ricci .10 .30
214 Steve Shields .10 .30
215 Marco Sturm .10 .30
216 Mike Vernon .10 .30
217 Wendel Clark .10 .30
218 Chris Gratton .05 .15
219 Vincent Lecavalier .50 1.25
220 Sandy McCarthy .05 .15
221 Stephane Richer .10 .30
222 Darcy Tucker .05 .15
223 Rob Zamuner .05 .15
224 Pavel Kubina RC .50 1.25
Zac Bierk
225 Bryan Berard .05 .15
226 Tie Domi .10 .30
227 Mike Johnson .10 .30
228 Curtis Joseph .15 .40
229 Igor Korolev .05 .15
230 Alyn McCauley .05 .15
231 Mats Sundin .15 .40
232 Steve Thomas .05 .15
233 Tomas Kaberle RC .20 .50
Daniil Markov
234 Adrian Aucoin .05 .15
235 Corey Hirsch .10 .30
236 Mark Messier .15 .40
237 Alexander Mogilny .10 .30
238 Bill Muckalt RC .10 .30
239 Markus Naslund .15 .40
240 Mattias Ohlund .10 .30
241 Garth Snow .10 .30
242 Matt Cooke RC .05 .15
Peter Schaefer
243 Brian Bellows .05 .15
244 Craig Berube .05 .15
245 Peter Bondra .10 .30
246 Matt Herr RC .05 .15
247 Joe Juneau .10 .30
248 Olaf Kolzig .10 .30
249 Adam Oates .10 .30
250 Richard Zednik .05 .15
251 Last Game at MLG SP 2.00 5.00
252 First Game at ACC SP 2.00 5.00
S136 Martin Brodeur SAMPLE .20 .50

1998-99 Pacific Omega Red

Found at a rate of 4:25 Treat packs, this tough insert features red foil on the front as its distinguishing mark.

*VETERANS: 2X TO 5X BASIC CARDS
*ROOKIES: .8X TO 2X BASIC CARDS

1998-99 Pacific Omega Opening Day Issue

Randomly inserted into packs, this 250-card set is parallel to the base set. Only 56 serially numbered sets were made.

*VETERANS: 30X TO 80X BASIC CARDS
*ROOKIES: 8X TO 20X BASIC CARDS

1998-99 Pacific Omega Championship Spotlight

Randomly inserted in special packs at the rate of 1:49, this 10-card set features color action photos of top NHL players with player information on the backs. Three limited edition parallel sets were also produced to be inserted into Treat packs. Only 50 serially numbered Green parallel versions were made, 10 serially numbered Red parallel versions, and one Gold parallel version. Gold parallels not priced due to scarcity.

COMPLETE SET (10) 75.00 150.00
*GREEN/50: 3X TO 8X BASIC INSERTS
UNPRICED RED PRINT RUN 10
UNPRICED GOLD PRINT RUN 1
1 Paul Kariya 4.00 10.00
2 Dominik Hasek 6.00 15.00
3 Patrick Roy 12.50 30.00
4 Steve Yzerman 12.50 30.00
5 Pavel Bure 4.00 10.00
6 Martin Brodeur 8.00 20.00
7 Wayne Gretzky 15.00 40.00
8 Eric Lindros 4.00 10.00
9 Jaromir Jagr 5.00 12.00
10 Curtis Joseph 4.00 10.00

1998-99 Pacific Omega EO Portraits

Randomly inserted into packs at the rate of 1:73, this 20-card set features color player images of some of hockey's biggest superstars printed using Electro-Optical technology to laser-cut the player image into every card. A special one of a kind Hobby only parallel set was also produced with "1/1" laser-cut into each card, they are not priced due to scarcity.

COMPLETE SET (20) 30.00 60.00
UNPRICED HOBBY 1/1 PARALLEL EXISTS
1 Paul Kariya .75 2.00
2 Teemu Selanne .75 2.00
3 Dominik Hasek 1.50 4.00
4 Peter Forsberg 2.00 5.00
5 Patrick Roy 4.00 10.00
6 Joe Sakic 1.50 4.00
7 Brett Hull 1.25 3.00
8 Mike Modano 1.25 3.00
9 Sergei Fedorov 1.25 3.00
10 Brendan Shanahan .75 2.00
11 Steve Yzerman 4.00 10.00
12 Pavel Bure .75 2.00
13 Martin Brodeur 2.00 5.00
14 Wayne Gretzky 5.00 12.00
15 John LeClair .75 2.00
16 Eric Lindros .75 2.00
17 Keith Tkachuk .75 2.00
18 Jaromir Jagr 1.25 3.00
19 Mats Sundin .75 2.00
20 Mark Messier .75 2.00

1998-99 Pacific Omega Face to Face

Randomly inserted into packs at the rate of 1:145, this 10-card set features color portraits of top NHL players printed on silver-foiled and etched cards. Two players are matched on every card creating an all-star face-off effect.

COMPLETE SET (10) 75.00 150.00
1 P.Roy/M.Brodeur 12.50 30.00
2 Wayne Gretzky 15.00 40.00
Paul Kariya
3 Dominik Hasek 5.00 12.00
Jaromir Jagr
4 Sergei Fedorov 5.00 12.00
Pavel Bure
5 Keith Tkachuk 4.00 10.00
Brendan Shanahan
6 Steve Yzerman 12.50 30.00
Joe Sakic
7 Teemu Selanne 4.00 10.00
Saku Koivu
8 Peter Forsberg 10.00 25.00
Mats Sundin
9 Mike Modano 5.00 12.00
John LeClair
10 Eric Lindros 4.00 10.00
Mark Messier

1998-99 Pacific Omega Online

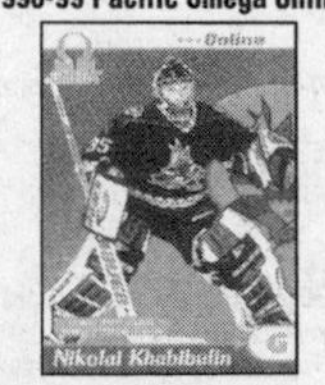

Randomly inserted into packs at the rate of 4:37, this 36-card set features color photos of NHL stars with interesting player facts on the backs. Each card invites fans to learn more about each player and team by logging on to their respective internet sites at www.nhlpa.com and www.nhl.com.

COMPLETE SET (36) 10.00 20.00
1 Paul Kariya .20 .50
2 Teemu Selanne .20 .50
3 Ray Bourque .30 .75
4 Dominik Hasek .20 .50
5 Theo Fleury .07 .20
6 Chris Chelios .20 .50
7 Doug Gilmour .15 .40
8 Peter Forsberg .50 1.25
9 Patrick Roy 1.00 2.50
10 Joe Sakic .40 1.00
11 Ed Belfour .20 .50
12 Brett Hull .25 .60
13 Mike Modano .30 .75
14 Sergei Fedorov .30 .75
15 Brendan Shanahan .20 .50
16 Steve Yzerman 1.00 2.50
17 Pavel Bure .20 .50
18 Saku Koivu .20 .50
19 Martin Brodeur .50 1.25
20 Brendan Morrison .15 .40
21 Zigmund Palffy .15 .40
22 Felix Potvin .20 .50
23 Wayne Gretzky 1.25 3.00
24 Alexei Yashin .07 .20
25 John LeClair .20 .50
26 Eric Lindros .20 .50
27 John Vanbiesbrouck .15 .40
28 Nikolai Khabibulin .15 .40
29 Keith Tkachuk .20 .50
30 Jaromir Jagr .30 .75
31 Vincent Lecavalier .60 1.50
32 Curtis Joseph .20 .50
33 Mats Sundin .20 .50
34 Mark Messier .20 .50
35 Bill Muckalt .07 .20
36 Peter Bondra .15 .40

1998-99 Pacific Omega Planet Ice

Randomly inserted into hobby packs only with an insertion rate of 4:37, this 30-card set features action color photos of top NHL players. The backs carry player information.

COMPLETE SET (30) 8.00 15.00
*1-6 PARALLEL/100: 6X TO 15X BASIC INSERTS
*7-12 PARALLEL/75: 8X TO 20X BASIC INSERTS
*13-18 PARALLEL/50: 12X TO 30X BASIC INSERTS
*19-24 PARALLEL/25: 25X TO 60X BASIC INSERTS
UNPRICED 25-30 PARALLEL PRINT RUN 1
1 Ray Bourque .30 .75
2 Chris Chelios .15 .40
3 Vincent Lecavalier .08 .25
4 Mark Parrish .08 .25
5 Felix Potvin .15 .40
6 Alexei Yashin .08 .25
7 Ed Belfour .15 .40
8 Peter Bondra .08 .25
9 Brett Hull .25 .60
10 Mark Messier .25 .60
11 Mats Sundin .08 .25
12 John Vanbiesbrouck .08 .25
13 Sergei Fedorov .30 .75
14 Curtis Joseph .15 .40
15 John LeClair .15 .40
16 Mike Modano .30 .75
17 Brendan Shanahan .15 .40
18 Keith Tkachuk .15 .40
19 Martin Brodeur 1.00 2.50
20 Pavel Bure .15 .40
21 Dominik Hasek .40 1.00
22 Joe Sakic .40 1.00
23 Teemu Selanne .15 .40
24 Steve Yzerman 1.00 2.50
25 Peter Forsberg .50 1.25
26 Wayne Gretzky 1.25 3.00
27 Jaromir Jagr .30 .75
28 Paul Kariya .15 .40
29 Eric Lindros .15 .40
30 Patrick Roy 1.00 2.50

1998-99 Pacific Omega Prism

COMPLETE SET (20) 20.00 40.00
STATED ODDS 1:37
1 Paul Kariya .60 1.50
2 Teemu Selanne .60 1.50
3 Dominik Hasek .60 1.50
4 Peter Forsberg 1.50 4.00
5 Patrick Roy 3.00 8.00
6 Joe Sakic 1.25 3.00
7 Mike Modano 1.00 2.50
8 Sergei Fedorov 1.00 2.50
9 Brendan Shanahan .60 1.50
10 Steve Yzerman 3.00 8.00
11 Pavel Bure .60 1.50
12 Martin Brodeur 1.50 4.00
13 Wayne Gretzky 4.00 10.00
14 Alexei Yashin .25 .60
15 John LeClair .60 1.50
16 Eric Lindros .60 1.50
17 Keith Tkachuk .60 1.50
18 Jaromir Jagr 1.00 2.50
19 Mats Sundin .60 1.50
20 Mark Messier .60 1.50

1998-99 Pacific Omega Toronto Spring Expo

Available via wrapper redemption at the 1999 Toronto Spring Expo from the Pacific booth, these cards are stamped on the front in silver foil with the Expo logo. Each card was serial numbered to just 20. Although these cards have a secondary market interest, there is not enough data to accurately price them. The list below is partial, please forward any additional information to Beckett.com.

8 Teemu Selanne
31 Theo Fleury
65 Joe Sakic
88 Steve Yzerman
156 Wayne Gretzky
177 Eric Lindros
195 Jaromir Jagr

1999-00 Pacific Omega

The 1999-00 Pacific Omega set was released as a 250-card set. It is available in both hobby and retail version, limiting certain inserts to hobby only or retail only. The base card features full-color photography and a silver foil player portrait in the bottom right corner, while prospect cards contain two players in split screen format. Each pack contains 6 cards, and carries a suggested retail price of $1.99.

COMPLETE SET (250) 30.00 60.00
1 Matt Cullen .05 .15
2 Guy Hebert .10 .30
3 Paul Kariya .15 .40
4 Marty McInnis .05 .15
5 Steve Rucchin .05 .15
6 Teemu Selanne .15 .40
7 Pascal Trepanier .10 .30
8 Ladislav Kohn .10 .30
Vitaly Vishnevski
9 Andrew Brunette .10 .30
10 Nelson Emerson .05 .15
11 Ray Ferraro .05 .15
12 Damian Rhodes .10 .30
13 Patrik Stefan RC .30 .75
14 Dean Sylvester RC .30 .75
15 Petr Buzek RC .30 .75
Scott Fankhouser
16 Jason Allison .05 .15
17 Dave Andreychuk .10 .30
18 Ray Bourque .25 .60
19 Anson Carter .10 .30
20 Byron Dafoe .10 .30
21 Sergei Samsonov .10 .30
22 Joe Thornton .25 .60
23 J.GrahameRC/J.HendersonRC .30 .75
24 Maxim Afinogenov .05 .15
25 Martin Biron .10 .30
26 Curtis Brown .05 .15
27 Brian Campbell RC .30 .75
28 Dominik Hasek .30 .75
29 Dimitri Kalinin RC .30 .75
30 Michael Peca .05 .15
31 Miroslav Satan .10 .30
32 Rhett Warrener .05 .15
33 Jean-Luc Grand-Pierre RC .30 .75
David Moravec
34 Fred Brathwaite .05 .15
35 Valeri Bure .05 .15
36 Grant Fuhr .05 .15
37 Phil Housley .05 .15
38 Jarome Iginla .20 .50
39 Oleg Saprykin RC .60 1.50
40 Marc Savard .05 .15
41 Cory Stillman .05 .15
42 Travis Brigley RC .30 .75
Robyn Regehr
43 Ron Francis .10 .30
44 Sean Hill .05 .15
45 Arturs Irbe .10 .30
46 Sami Kapanen .05 .15
47 Curtis Leschyshyn .05 .15
48 Jeff O'Neill .05 .15
49 Gary Roberts .05 .15
50 D.Tanabe RC/T.Westlund .30 .75
51 Tony Amonte .10 .30
52 Eric Daze .10 .30
53 Doug Gilmour .10 .30
54 Michael Nylander .05 .15
55 Steve Sullivan .05 .15
56 Jocelyn Thibault .10 .30
57 Alexei Zhamnov .05 .15
58 J-P Dumont .30 .75
Marc Lamothe RC
59 Chris Harperger RC .30 .75
Steve McCarthy
60 Adam Deadmarsh .05 .15
61 Chris Drury .10 .30
62 Peter Forsberg .40 1.00
63 Milan Hejduk .15 .40
64 Sandis Ozolinsh .05 .15
65 Patrick Roy .75 2.00
66 Joe Sakic .30 .75
67 Alex Tanguay .10 .30
68 Marc Denis RC .30 .75
Martin Skoula
69 Sami Helenius RC .30 .75
Brian Willsie
70 Ed Belfour .15 .40
71 Manny Fernandez .10 .30
72 Brett Hull .20 .50
73 Jere Lehtinen .10 .30
74 Mike Modano .25 .60
75 Brenden Morrow .15 .40
76 Joe Nieuwendyk .10 .30
77 Sergei Zubov .05 .15
78 Ryan Christie RC .30 .75
Roman Lyashenko
79 R.Jackman/A.Letang RC .30 .75
80 Chris Chelios .15 .40
81 Sergei Fedorov .25 .60
82 Igor Larionov .05 .15
83 Nicklas Lidstrom .15 .40
84 Chris Osgood .10 .30
85 Brendan Shanahan .15 .40
86 Pat Verbeek .05 .15
87 Ken Wregget .10 .30
88 Steve Yzerman .75 2.00
89 Paul Comrie RC .10 .30
90 Bill Guerin .05 .15
91 Tom Poti .05 .15
92 Bert Robertsson RC .30 .75
93 Tommy Salo .10 .30
94 Alexander Selivanov .05 .15
95 Ryan Smyth .05 .15
96 Doug Weight .10 .30
97 Pavel Bure .15 .40
98 Viktor Kozlov .05 .15
99 Mark Parrish .05 .15
100 Mikhail Shtalenkov .05 .15
101 Robert Svehla .05 .15
102 Mike Vernon .10 .30
103 Ray Whitney .10 .30
104 Dave Duerden RC .30 .75
Ivan Novoseltsev
105 John Jakopin RC .30 .75
Filip Kuba
106 Rob Blake .10 .30
107 Stephane Fiset .10 .30
108 Jaroslav Modry .05 .15
109 Glen Murray .05 .15
110 Zigmund Palffy .10 .30
111 Luc Robitaille .10 .30
112 Bryan Smolinski .10 .30
113 Jamie Storr .10 .30
114 Marko Tuomainen .05 .15
115 Brad Chartrand RC .30 .75
Frantisek Kaberle
116 Shayne Corson .05 .15
117 Craig Darby .05 .15
118 Jeff Hackett .10 .30
119 Saku Koivu .15 .40
120 Trevor Linden .05 .15
121 Martin Rucinsky .10 .30
122 Brian Savage .05 .15
123 Jose Theodore .20 .50
124 Francis Bouillon RC .30 .75
Stephane Robidas
125 Mike Ribeiro .10 .30
Jason Ward
126 Mike Dunham .10 .30
127 Patric Kjellberg .05 .15
128 Cliff Ronning .10 .30
129 Tomas Vokoun .05 .15
130 David Legwand .10 .30
Randy Robitaille
131 Richard Lintner RC .30 .75
Karlis Skrastins
132 Jason Arnott .05 .15
133 Martin Brodeur .40 1.00
134 Patrik Elias .10 .30
135 Scott Gomez .05 .15
136 Bobby Holik .05 .15
137 Claude Lemieux .05 .15
138 Petr Sykora .05 .15
139 John Madden RC .30 .75
Brian Rafalski
140 Mariusz Czerkawski .05 .15
141 Brad Isbister .05 .15
142 Jorgen Jonsson RC .30 .75
143 Roberto Luongo .20 .50
144 Bill Muckalt .05 .15
145 Kevin Weekes .10 .30
146 Tim Connolly RC .30 .75
Evgeny Korolev
147 Alexandre Daigle .05 .15
148 Radek Dvorak .05 .15
149 Theo Fleury .05 .15
150 Adam Graves .05 .15
151 Brian Leetch .15 .40
152 Petr Nedved .10 .30
153 Mike Richter .15 .40
154 Michael York .05 .15
155 Jan Hlavac .30 .75
Kim Johnsson RC RC
156 Daniel Alfredsson .10 .30
157 Magnus Arvedson .05 .15
158 Radek Bonk .05 .15
159 Marian Hossa .15 .40
160 Patrick Lalime .10 .30
161 Shawn McEachern .05 .15
162 Petr Schastlivy RC .30 .75
163 Ron Tugnutt .10 .30
164 Shaun Van Allen .05 .15
165 Alexei Yashin .05 .15
166 Mike Fisher RC .30 .75
Andre Roy
167 Brian Boucher .15 .40
168 Eric Desjardins .10 .30
169 Simon Gagne .15 .40
170 Daymond Langkow .10 .30
171 John LeClair .15 .40
172 Eric Lindros .15 .40
173 Keith Primeau .05 .15
174 Mark Recchi .10 .30
175 Mikael Renberg .10 .30
176 John Vanbiesbrouck .10 .30
177 Andy Delmore RC .30 .75
Mark Eaton
178 Shane Doan .05 .15
179 Dallas Drake .05 .15
180 Robert Esche RC .10 .30
181 Travis Green .10 .30
182 Nikolai Khabibulin .10 .30
183 Teppo Numminen .05 .15
184 Jeremy Roenick .20 .50
185 Keith Tkachuk .15 .40
186 Trevor Letowski RC .30 .75
Radoslav Suchy
187 Jan Hrdina .05 .15
188 Jaromir Jagr .25 .60
189 Hans Jonsson RC .30 .75
190 Alexei Kovalev .10 .30
191 Martin Straka .05 .15
192 German Titov .05 .15
193 Tyler Wright .05 .15
194 Jean-Sebastien Aubin RC .30 .75
Michael Rozsival
195 Pavol Demitra .10 .30
196 Al MacInnis .10 .30
197 Jamie McLennan .10 .30
198 Tyson Nash RC .30 .75
199 Chris Pronger .10 .30
200 Todd Reirden RC .30 .75
201 Roman Turek .10 .30
202 Pierre Turgeon .10 .30
203 Jochen Hecht RC .75 2.00
Ladislav Nagy
204 Vincent Damphousse .05 .15
205 Jeff Friesen .05 .15
206 Todd Harvey .05 .15
207 Alexander Korolyuk .05 .15
208 Patrick Marleau .10 .30
209 Owen Nolan .10 .30
210 Steve Shields .10 .30
211 Gary Suter .05 .15
212 Evgeni Nabokov RC 2.00 5.00
Brad Stuart
213 Dan Cloutier .05 .15
214 Stan Drulia .05 .15
215 Chris Gratton .05 .15
216 Vincent Lecavalier .15 .40
217 Steve Martins RC .30 .75
218 Fredrik Modin .05 .15
219 Mike Sillinger .05 .15
220 Ben Clymer RC .30 .75
Nils Ekman
221 Nikolai Antropov RC .60 1.50
222 Sergei Berezin .10 .30
223 Tie Domi .10 .30
224 Jonas Hoglund .05 .15
225 Curtis Joseph .15 .40
226 Tomas Kaberle .05 .15
227 Dimitri Khristich .05 .15
228 Mats Sundin .15 .40
229 Steve Thomas .10 .30
230 Adam Mair RC .30 .75
Dmitri Yakushin
231 Todd Bertuzzi .15 .40
232 Andrew Cassels .05 .15
233 Steve Kariya RC .30 .75
234 Mark Messier .15 .40
235 Alexander Mogilny .10 .30
236 Markus Naslund .15 .40
237 Felix Potvin .15 .40
238 Ryan Bonni RC .30 .75
Zenith Komarniski
239 Harold Druken .05 .15
Peter Schaefer
240 Brad Leeb RC .30 .75
Alfie Michaud
241 Peter Bondra .10 .30
242 Jan Bulis .05 .15
243 Olaf Kolzig .10 .30
244 Steve Konowalchuk .05 .15
245 Adam Oates .10 .30
246 Jeff Halpern RC .30 .75
Glen Metropolit
247 Alexei Tezikov RC .30 .75
Alexandre Volchkov
248 North American All-Stars .10 .30
249 World All-Stars .10 .30
250 Pavel Bure .15 .40
Valeri Bure
NNO Martin Brodeur SAMPLE .40 1.00

1999-00 Pacific Omega Copper

Randomly inserted in packs, this 250-card Hobby Only set parallels the base set and enhances the base card design with copper foil on the text and on the player portrait in the bottom right front corner. Just above the player portrait is a box that contains each card's serial number. Each of the Copper parallel version cards are numbered out of 99.

*VETS: 12X TO 30 BASIC CARDS
*ROOKIES: 6X TO 15X BASIC CARDS

1999-00 Pacific Omega Gold

Randomly inserted in packs, this 250-card Retail Only set parallels the base set and enhances the base card design with gold foil on the text and on the player portrait in the bottom right front corner. Just above the player portrait is a box that contains each card's serial number. Each of the Gold parallel version cards are numbered out of 299.

*VETS: 5X TO 12X BASIC CARDS
*ROOKIES: 2.5X TO 6X BASIC CARDS

1999-00 Pacific Omega Ice Blue

Randomly inserted in packs, this 250-card set parallels the base set and enhances the base card design with blue foil on the text and on the player portrait in the bottom right front corner. Just above the player portrait is a box that contains each card's serial number. Each of the Ice Blue parallel version cards are numbered out of 75. This set was available in both Hobby and Retail packs.

*VETS: 20X TO 50X BASIC CARDS
*ROOKIES: 10X TO 25X BASIC CARDS

1999-00 Pacific Omega Premiere Date

Randomly inserted in packs at a rate of 1:37, this 250 card set paralleled the base set except for a gold foil stamp just above the player's name. The stamps carried a serial number out of 68. The date of the player's 'premiere' in the NHL is under the stamp.

*VETS: 20X TO 50X BASIC CARDS
*ROOKIES: 10X TO 25X BASIC CARDS

1999-00 Pacific Omega Cup Contenders

COMPLETE SET (20) 50.00 100.00
STATED ODDS 1:37
1 Paul Kariya 1.50 4.00
2 Dominik Hasek 3.00 8.00
3 Peter Forsberg 4.00 10.00
4 Patrick Roy 8.00 20.00
5 Joe Sakic 3.00 8.00
6 Brett Hull 2.00 5.00
7 Mike Modano 2.50 6.00
8 Sergi Fedorov 3.00 8.00
9 Brendan Shanahan 2.50 6.00
10 Steve Yzerman 8.00 20.00
11 Pavel Bure 2.00 5.00
12 Martin Broedur 4.00 10.00
13 Theo Fleury 1.50 4.00
14 Mike Richter 1.50 4.00
15 John LeClair 2.00 5.00
16 Jeremy Roenick 2.00 5.00
17 Jaromir Jagr 2.50 6.00
18 Al MacInnis 1.25 3.00
19 Curtis Joseph 1.50 4.00
20 Mark Messier 2.00 5.00

1999-00 Pacific Omega EO Portraits

Randomly inserted in packs at 1:73, this 20-card set features laser-cut player images on one side and a full color photo on the other. Parallels numbered 1/1 also exist; they are not priced due to scarcity.

COMPLETE SET (20) 25.00 50.00
1 Paul Kariya .75 2.00
2 Teemu Selanne .75 2.00

3 Patrik Stefan .75 2.00
4 Dominik Hasek 1.50 4.00
5 Peter Forsberg 2.00 5.00
6 Patrick Roy 4.00 10.00
7 Mike Modano 1.25 3.00
8 Brendan Shanahan .75 2.00
9 Steve Yzerman 4.00 10.00
10 Pavel Bure .75 2.00
11 Martin Brodeur 2.00 5.00
12 Scott Gomez .75 2.00
13 Eric Lindros .75 2.00
14 John Vanbiesbrouck .75 2.00
15 Keith Tkachuk .75 2.00
16 Jaromir Jagr 1.25 3.00
17 Vincent Lecavalier .75 2.00
18 Curtis Joseph .75 2.00
19 Mats Sundin .75 2.00
20 Mark Messier .75 2.00

1999-00 Pacific Omega Game-Used Jerseys

Randomly inserted in packs at 1:180, this 10-card set features a swatch of game used jersey on each card. This set was not announced in the initial release, and was a last minute addition.

1 Teemu Selanne 4.00 10.00
2 Mike Modano 4.00 10.00
3 Steve Yzerman 10.00 25.00
4 Martin Brodeur 8.00 20.00
5 Mike Richter 4.00 10.00
6 John LeClair 4.00 10.00
7 Eric Lindros 4.00 10.00
8 John Vanbiesbrouck 4.00 10.00
9 Jaromir Jagr 6.00 15.00
10 Mats Sundin 4.00 10.00

1999-00 Pacific Omega NHL Generations

Randomly seeded in packs at one in 1:145, this 10-card set features two players on each card. The left side pictures an NHL standout veteran paired with a top rated prospect on the right. The green background on each side contains a silhouette of both respective players.

COMPLETE SET (10) 50.00 120.00
1 Paul Kariya 6.00 15.00
Steve Kariya
2 Teemu Selanne 6.00 15.00
Milan Hejduk
3 Peter Forsberg 8.00 20.00
Chris Drury
4 Patrick Roy 15.00 40.00
Roberto Luongo
5 M.Modano/D.Legwand 6.00 15.00
6 Steve Yzerman 12.00 30.00
Scott Gomez
7 Pavel Bure 6.00 15.00
Marian Hossa
8 John LeClair 4.00 10.00
Simon Gagne
9 Eric Lindros 6.00 15.00
Vincent Lecavalier
10 Jaromir Jagr 8.00 20.00
Patrik Stefan

1999-00 Pacific Omega North American All-Stars

Randomly inserted in packs at 2:37, this 10-card die-cut set pictured some of North America's most dominating All-Stars set against the Toronto All-Star logo.

COMPLETE SET (10) 15.00 30.00
1 Paul Kariya 1.00 2.50
2 Ray Bourque 1.25 3.00
3 Joe Sakic 1.50 4.00
4 Mike Modano 1.25 3.00
5 Brendan Shanahan 1.25 3.00
6 Steve Yzerman 4.00 10.00
7 Martin Brodeur 2.00 5.00
8 Scott Gomez 1.00 2.50
9 Curtis Joseph 1.00 2.50
10 Mark Messier 1.00 2.50

1999-00 Pacific Omega 5 Star Talents

Randomly inserted in Hobby packs at the rate of 4:37, this 30-card set segments NHL players into five different groups of six cards each. Card #'s 1-6 are top prospects (Rookies), card #'s 7-12 are power players (Power Game), card #'s 13-18 are some of the NHL's

quickest (Speed Merchants), card #'s 19-24 are some of the top set-up guys (Playmakers), and card #'s 25-30 are some of the NHL's most dominating goaltenders (Netminders). A five-tier serial #'d parallel of this set was released also.

COMPLETE SET (30) 20.00 40.00
*1-6 PARALLEL/100: 10X TO 25X BASIC INSERT
*7-12 PARALLEL/75: 15X TO 40X BASIC INSERT
*13-18 PARALLEL/50: 25X TO 60X BASIC INSERT
*19-24 PARALLEL/25: 40X TO 100X BASIC INSERT
25-30 UNPRICED PARALLEL PRINT RUN 1
1 Patrik Stefan .75 2.00
2 Alex Tanguay .40 1.00
3 David Legwand .40 1.00
4 Scott Gomez .40 1.00
5 Roberto Luongo .60 1.50
6 Steve Kariya .50 1.25
7 Brendan Shanahan .50 1.25
8 John LeClair .50 1.25
9 Eric Lindros .50 1.25
10 Keith Tkachuk .50 1.25
11 Owen Nolan .40 1.00
12 Mark Messier .50 1.25
13 Paul Kariya .50 1.25
14 Teemu Selanne .50 1.25
15 Pavel Bure .50 1.25
16 Theo Fleury .50 1.25
17 Marian Hossa .40 1.00
18 Jaromir Jagr .75 2.00
19 Peter Forsberg 1.25 3.00
20 Mike Modano .75 2.00
21 Steve Yzerman 2.50 6.00
22 Mark Recchi .40 1.00
23 Vincent Lecavalier .50 1.25
24 Mats Sundin .50 1.25
25 Dominik Hasek 1.00 2.50
26 Patrick Roy 2.50 6.00
27 Ed Belfour .50 1.25
28 Martin Brodeur 1.25 3.00
29 John Vanbiesbrouck .50 1.25
30 Curtis Joseph .50 1.25

1999-00 Pacific Omega World All-Stars

Randomly inserted in packs at 2:37, this 10-card die-cut set pictured some of the World's most dominating All-Stars set against the Toronto All-Star logo.

COMPLETE SET (10) 6.00 12.00
1 Teemu Selanne .60 1.50
2 Valeri Bure .60 1.50
3 Nicklas Lidstrom .60 1.50
4 Pavel Bure .60 1.50
5 Viktor Kozlov .60 1.50
6 Jaromir Jagr 1.25 3.00
7 Pavol Demitra .60 1.50
8 Roman Turek .60 1.50
9 Mats Sundin .75 2.00
10 Olaf Kolzig .60 1.50

1999-00 Pacific Prism

The 1999-00 Pacific Prism set was released in both hobby and retail versions as a 150-card set featuring both veterans and prospects. The base cards are printed on silver holo-foil, and the prospects are denoted by a red diamond in the lower front right corner. Prism was packaged in 20-pack boxes with three cards per pack.

COMPLETE SET (150) 30.00 60.00
1 Guy Hebert .15 .40
2 Paul Kariya .20 .50
3 Mike Leclerc .10 .30
4 Steve Rucchin .10 .30
5 Teemu Selanne .20 .50
6 Andrew Brunette .15 .40
7 Petr Buzek .15 .40
8 Damian Rhodes .10 .30
9 Patrik Stefan RC .75 2.00
10 Jason Allison .10 .30
11 Dave Andreychuk .15 .40
12 Ray Bourque .30 .75
13 Byron Dafoe .15 .40
14 Sergei Samsonov .15 .40
15 Joe Thornton .30 .75
16 Maxim Afinogenov .10 .30
17 Martin Biron .15 .40
18 Curtis Brown .10 .30
19 Dominik Hasek .40 1.00
20 Michael Peca .10 .30
21 Miroslav Satan .15 .40
22 Valeri Bure .10 .30
23 Grant Fuhr .15 .40
24 Jarome Iginla .25 .60
25 Oleg Saprykin RC .60 1.50
26 Cory Stillman .10 .30
27 Bates Battaglia .10 .30
28 Ron Francis .10 .30
29 Arturs Irbe .15 .40
30 Sami Kapanen .10 .30
31 Keith Primeau .10 .30
32 Tony Amonte .15 .40
33 J-P Dumont .15 .40
34 Doug Gilmour .15 .40
35 Jocelyn Thibault .15 .40
36 Alexei Zhamnov .10 .30
37 Chris Drury .15 .40
38 Peter Forsberg .50 1.25
39 Milan Hejduk .20 .50
40 Patrick Roy 1.00 2.50
41 Joe Sakic .40 1.00
42 Alex Tanguay .15 .40
43 Ed Belfour .20 .50
44 Brett Hull .25 .60
45 Roman Lyashenko .10 .30
46 Mike Modano .30 .75
47 Joe Nieuwendyk .15 .40
48 Brendan Shanahan .20 .50
49 Chris Chelios .20 .50
50 Sergei Fedorov .30 .75
51 Jiri Fischer .10 .30
52 Nicklas Lidstrom .20 .50
53 Chris Osgood .15 .40
54 Steve Yzerman 1.00 2.50
55 Bill Guerin .10 .30
56 Tommy Salo .15 .40
57 Alexander Selivanov .10 .30
58 Ryan Smyth .10 .30
59 Doug Weight .15 .40
60 Pavel Bure .20 .50
61 Trevor Kidd .10 .30
62 Viktor Kozlov .15 .40
63 Mark Parrish .10 .30
64 Ray Whitney .15 .40
65 Rob Blake .15 .40
66 Stephane Fiset .15 .40
67 Frantisek Kaberle .15 .40
68 Zigmund Palffy .15 .40
69 Luc Robitaille .15 .40
70 Francis Bouillon RC .20 .50
71 Jeff Hackett .15 .40
72 Saku Koivu .20 .50
73 Trevor Linden .15 .40
74 Brian Savage .10 .30
75 Mike Dunham .15 .40
76 David Legwand .20 .50
77 Cliff Ronning .10 .30
78 Rob Valicevic RC .20 .50
79 Martin Brodeur .50 1.25
80 Patrik Elias .15 .40
81 Scott Gomez .10 .30
82 Bobby Holik .10 .30
83 Claude Lemieux .10 .30
84 Petr Sykora .10 .30
85 Tim Connolly .10 .30
86 Mariusz Czerkawski .10 .30
87 Brad Isbister .10 .30
88 Roberto Luongo .25 .60
89 Theo Fleury .10 .30
90 Jan Hlavac .10 .30
91 Brian Leetch .20 .50
92 Mike Richter .20 .50
93 Mike York .10 .30
94 Daniel Alfredsson .15 .40
95 Radek Bonk .10 .30
96 Marian Hossa .20 .50
97 Shawn McEachern .10 .30
98 Ron Tugnutt .15 .40
99 Alexei Yashin .10 .30
100 Brian Boucher .20 .50
101 Simon Gagne .20 .50
102 John LeClair .20 .50
103 Eric Lindros .20 .50
104 Mark Recchi .15 .40
105 John Vanbiesbrouck .15 .40
106 Mike Alatalo RC .20 .50
107 Travis Green .10 .30
108 Nikolai Khabibulin .15 .40
109 Jeremy Roenick .25 .60
110 Keith Tkachuk .20 .50
111 Rick Tocchet .15 .40
112 Jean-Sebastien Aubin .15 .40
113 Andrew Ference .10 .30
114 Jaromir Jagr .30 .75
115 Alexei Kovalev .10 .30
116 Martin Straka .10 .30
117 Pavol Demitra .15 .40
118 Jochen Hecht RC .75 2.00
119 Al MacInnis .15 .40
120 Chris Pronger .15 .40
121 Roman Turek .15 .40
122 Pierre Turgeon .15 .40
123 Vincent Damphousse .10 .30
124 Jeff Friesen .10 .30
125 Patrick Marleau .15 .40
126 Owen Nolan .15 .40
127 Steve Shields .15 .40
128 Brad Stuart .15 .40
129 Dan Cloutier .10 .30
130 Ben Clymer RC .20 .50
131 Chris Gratton .10 .30
132 Vincent Lecavalier .20 .50
133 Darcy Tucker .10 .30
134 Nikolai Antropov RC 1.25 3.00
135 Sergei Berezin .10 .30
136 Tie Domi .15 .40
137 Curtis Joseph .20 .50
138 Dimitri Khristich .10 .30
139 Mats Sundin .20 .50
140 Steve Kariya RC .60 1.50
141 Mark Messier .20 .50
142 Alfie Michaud RC .40 1.00
143 Alexander Mogilny .15 .40
144 Jarkko Ruutu RC .20 .50
145 Peter Schaefer .15 .40
146 Peter Bondra .15 .40
147 Jan Bulis .10 .30
148 Olaf Kolzig .15 .40
149 Glen Metropolit RC .60 1.50
150 Adam Oates .15 .40
NNO Martin Brodeur SAMPLE .75 2.00

1999-00 Pacific Prism Holographic Blue

Randomly inserted in packs, this 150-card set parallels the base set in a holographic blue foil version. Each card is numbered out of 80 in the top left-hand corner.

*VETS: 6X TO 15X BASIC CARDS
*ROOKIES: 3X TO 8X BASIC CARDS

1999-00 Pacific Prism Holographic Gold

Randomly inserted in packs, this 150-card set parallels the base set in a holographic gold foil version. Each card is numbered out of 480 in the top left-hand corner.

*VETS: 1.2X TO 3X BASIC CARDS
*ROOKIES: .8X TO 2X BASIC CARDS

1999-00 Pacific Prism Holographic Mirror

Randomly inserted in packs, this 150-card set parallels the base set in a holographic silver rainbow foil version. Each card is numbered out of 160 in the top left-hand corner.

*VETS: 4X TO 10X BASIC CARDS
*ROOKIES: 2X TO 5X BASIC CARDS
STATED PRINT RUN 160 SER.#'d SETS

1999-00 Pacific Prism Holographic Purple

Randomly inserted in hobby packs, this 150-card set parallels the base set in a holographic purple foil version. Each card is numbered out of 99 in the top left-hand corner.

*VETS: 5X TO 12X BASIC CARDS
*ROOKIES: 2.5X TO 6X BASIC CARDS

1999-00 Pacific Prism Premiere Date

Randomly inserted in packs, the 150-card set parallels the base set and is serial numbered in the upper-left front corner out of 69. The center of the cards also contains a "premiere date" embossed stamp.

*VETS: 8X TO 20X BASIC CARDS
*ROOKIES: 4X TO 10X BASIC CARDS

1999-00 Pacific Prism Clear Advantage

Randomly seeded in packs at 2:25, this 20-card set features 20 of hockey's most exciting players. Action player photos are set against an icy-looking blue background.

COMPLETE SET (20) 20.00 40.00
1 Paul Kariya .60 1.50
2 Teemu Selanne .60 1.50
3 Dominik Hasek 1.25 3.00
4 Peter Forsberg 1.50 4.00
5 Patrick Roy 3.00 8.00
6 Alex Tanguay .50 1.25
7 Brett Hull .75 2.00
8 Brendan Shanahan 1.00 2.50
9 Steve Yzerman 3.00 8.00
10 Pavel Bure .75 2.00
11 Zigmund Palffy .50 1.25
12 Martin Brodeur 1.50 4.00
13 Theo Fleury .50 1.25
14 Marian Hossa .60 1.50
15 John LeClair .75 2.00
16 Eric Lindros 1.00 2.50
17 Mark Recchi .50 1.25
18 Jaromir Jagr 1.00 2.50
19 Vincent Lecavalier .60 1.50
20 Mats Sundin .60 1.50

1999-00 Pacific Prism Ice Prospects

Randomly inserted in hobby packs at 1:97, this 10-card set features some of hockey's up and coming prospects.

COMPLETE SET (10) 30.00 60.00
1 Patrik Stefan 3.00 8.00
2 Martin Biron 3.00 8.00
3 Alex Tanguay 3.00 8.00
4 David Legwand 3.00 8.00
5 Scott Gomez 3.00 8.00
6 Simon Gagne 3.00 8.00
7 Brad Stuart 3.00 8.00
8 Nikolai Antropov 3.00 8.00
9 Steve Kariya 3.00 8.00
10 Peter Schaefer 3.00 8.00

1999-00 Pacific Prism Dial-a-Stats

Randomly inserted in packs at 1:193, this 20-card set showcases NHL superstars that boast impressive statistics. The card is cut and fitted with a fastener in the middle to allow a wheel with stat numbers on it to be spun to display the player's career statistics versus the various NHL teams faced.

COMPLETE SET (10) 40.00 80.00
1 Paul Kariya 6.00 15.00
2 Teemu Selanne 6.00 15.00
3 Dominik Hasek 4.00 10.00
4 Peter Forsberg 5.00 12.00
5 Patrick Roy 10.00 25.00
6 Mike Modano 3.00 8.00
7 Steve Yzerman 10.00 25.00
8 Eric Lindros 3.00 8.00
9 Jaromir Jagr 3.00 8.00
10 Mark Messier 2.50 6.00

1999-00 Pacific Prism Sno-Globe Die-Cuts

Randomly seeded in packs at one in 1:25, this 20-card set features NHL greats on a full foil die-cut card shaped like a glass sno-globe.

COMPLETE SET (20) 20.00 40.00
1 Paul Kariya .60 1.50
2 Teemu Selanne .60 1.50
3 Ray Bourque 1.00 2.50
4 Dominik Hasek 1.25 3.00
5 Peter Forsberg 1.50 4.00
6 Patrick Roy 3.00 8.00
7 Joe Sakic 1.25 3.00
8 Ed Belfour .60 1.50
9 Mike Modano 1.00 2.50
10 Brendan Shanahan 1.00 2.50
11 Steve Yzerman 3.00 8.00
12 Pavel Bure .75 2.00
13 Martin Brodeur 1.50 4.00
14 Theo Fleury .60 1.50
15 John LeClair .75 2.00
16 Eric Lindros 1.00 2.50
17 John Vanbiesbrouck .60 1.50
18 Keith Tkachuk .60 1.50
19 Jaromir Jagr 1.00 2.50
20 Curtis Joseph .60 1.50

2003-04 Pacific Prism

Released in mid-August, this 150-card set consisted of 100 base cards and 50 jersey cards. Jersey cards were one per pack and were serial-numbered. Numbering for individual cards can be found below. Cards 101-150 were available only in packs of Pacific Calder.

COMPSET w/o JSY's (100) 30.00 60.00
1 Stanislav Chistov .10 .25
2 Jean-Sebastien Giguere .25 .60
3 Adam Oates .25 .60
4 Petr Sykora .10 .25
5 Joe DiPenta RC 1.50 4.00
6 Slava Kozlov .10 .25
7 Marc Savard .10 .25
8 Patrik Stefan .10 .25
9 Jeff Hackett .25 .60
10 Mike Knuble .10 .25
11 Sergei Samsonov .25 .60
12 Steve Shields .25 .60
13 Milan Bartovic RC 1.50 4.00
14 Martin Biron .25 .60
15 Daniel Briere .10 .25
16 Ryan Miller .25 .60
17 Miroslav Satan .25 .60
18 Craig Conroy .10 .25
19 Roman Turek .25 .60
20 Ron Francis .25 .60
21 Arturs Irbe .25 .60
22 Jeff O'Neill .10 .25
23 Tyler Arnason .25 .60
24 Theo Fleury .10 .25
25 Jocelyn Thibault .25 .60
26 Alexei Zhamnov .10 .25
27 Rob Blake .25 .60
28 Alex Tanguay .25 .60
29 Marc Denis .25 .60
30 Kent McDonell RC .30 .75
31 Rick Nash .40 1.00
32 Geoff Sanderson .10 .25
33 Ray Whitney .10 .25
34 Jason Arnott .10 .25
35 Jere Lehtinen .25 .60
36 Pavel Datsyuk .30 .75
37 Brett Hull .40 1.00
38 Curtis Joseph .30 .75
39 Henrik Zetterberg .30 .75
40 Ales Hemsky .25 .60
41 Tommy Salo .25 .60
42 Ryan Smyth .10 .25
43 Jay Bouwmeester .10 .25
44 Olli Jokinen .25 .60
45 Roberto Luongo .40 1.00
46 Stephen Weiss .10 .25
47 Michael Cammalleri .10 .25
48 Adam Deadmarsh .10 .25
49 Alexander Frolov .10 .25
50 Felix Potvin .30 .75
51 Andrew Brunette .10 .25
52 Manny Fernandez .25 .60
53 Marian Gaborik .60 1.50
54 Dwayne Roloson .25 .60
55 Cliff Ronning .25 .60
56 Marcel Hossa .10 .25
57 Yanic Perreault .25 .60
58 Scottie Upshall .10 .25
59 Tomas Vokoun .25 .60
60 Scott Walker .10 .25
61 Patrik Elias .25 .60
62 Jamie Langenbrunner .10 .25
63 John Madden .10 .25
64 Joe Nieuwendyk .25 .60
65 Scott Stevens .25 .60
66 Jason Blake .10 .25
67 Rick DiPietro .25 .60
68 Mark Parrish .10 .25
69 Mike Dunham .25 .60
70 Alex Kovalev .25 .60
71 Brian Leetch .25 .60
72 Mark Messier .30 .75
73 Zdeno Chara .10 .25
74 Martin Havlat .25 .60
75 Todd White .10 .25
76 John LeClair .30 .75
77 Mark Recchi .25 .60
78 Shane Doan .10 .25
79 Mike Johnson .10 .25
80 Johan Hedberg .25 .60
81 Martin Straka .10 .25
82 Pavol Demitra .25 .60
83 Barret Jackman .25 .60
84 Al MacInnis .25 .60
85 Peter Sejna RC 1.50 4.00
86 Keith Tkachuk .30 .75
87 Patrick Marleau .25 .60
88 Evgeni Nabokov .25 .60
89 Teemu Selanne .30 .75
90 Dave Andreychuk .10 .25
91 Brad Richards .25 .60
92 Alexander Mogilny .25 .60
93 Owen Nolan .25 .60
94 Matt Stajan RC 1.50 4.00
95 Ed Jovanovski .25 .60
96 Daniel Sedin .10 .25
97 Henrik Sedin .10 .25
98 Peter Bondra .25 .60
99 Sergei Gonchar .10 .25
100 Olaf Kolzig .25 .60
101 Paul Kariya/935 4.00 10.00
102 Dany Heatley/924 5.00 12.00
103 Ilya Kovalchuk/935 5.00 12.00
104 Glen Murray/1185 3.00 8.00
105 Joe Thornton/674 5.00 12.00
106 Chris Drury/935 3.00 8.00
107 Jarome Iginla/1183 5.00 12.00
108 Eric Daze/1171 3.00 8.00
109 Milan Hejduk/1183 4.00 10.00
110 Peter Forsberg/685 5.00 12.00
111 Patrick Roy/185 12.50 30.00
112 Joe Sakic/935 6.00 15.00
113 Bill Guerin/1136 3.00 8.00
114 Mike Modano/935 4.00 10.00
115 Marty Turco/685 4.00 10.00
116 Sergei Fedorov/685 4.00 10.00
117 Brendan Shanahan/935 4.00 10.00
118 Steve Yzerman/185 15.00 40.00
119 Mike Comrie/935 3.00 8.00
120 Jason Allison/1176 3.00 8.00
121 Roman Cechmanek/1185 3.00 8.00
122 Zigmund Palffy/1060 3.00 8.00
123 Saku Koivu/935 4.00 10.00
124 Jose Theodore/1185 4.00 10.00
125 Richard Zednik/1185 3.00 8.00
126 David Legwand/1185 3.00 8.00
127 Martin Brodeur/685 8.00 20.00
128 Michael Peca/1185 3.00 8.00
129 Alexei Yashin/1185 3.00 8.00
130 Pavel Bure/935 4.00 10.00
131 Eric Lindros/935 4.00 10.00
132 Daniel Alfredsson/185 5.00 12.00
133 Marian Hossa/185 5.00 12.00
134 Jason Spezza/185 8.00 20.00
135 Tony Amonte/1163 3.00 8.00
136 Jeremy Roenick/1185 4.00 10.00
137 Sean Burke/1185 3.00 8.00
138 Mario Lemieux/305 12.50 30.00
139 Chris Osgood/1185 3.00 8.00
140 Doug Weight/1185 3.00 8.00
141 Nikolai Khabibulin/1125 4.00 10.00
142 Vincent Lecavalier/935 3.00 8.00
143 Martin St. Louis/1185 3.00 8.00
144 Ed Belfour/685 4.00 10.00
145 Mats Sundin/685 4.00 10.00
146 Todd Bertuzzi/935 4.00 10.00
147 Dan Cloutier/1185 3.00 8.00
148 Brendan Morrison/685 3.00 8.00
149 Markus Naslund/185 8.00 20.00
150 Jaromir Jagr/185 10.00 25.00
151 Joffrey Lupul RC 2.00 5.00
152 Patrice Bergeron RC 4.00 10.00
153 Matthew Lombardi RC 2.00 5.00
154 Eric Staal RC 5.00 12.00
155 Nikolai Zherdev RC 2.50 6.00
156 Jiri Hudler RC 2.00 5.00
157 Nathan Horton RC 3.00 8.00
158 Jordin Tootoo RC 3.00 8.00
159 Antoine Vermette RC 2.00 5.00
160 Marc-Andre Fleury RC 6.00 15.00

2003-04 Pacific Prism Blue

*STARS 1-100: .6X TO 1.5X BASE CARDS
*ROOKIES 1-100: .3X TO .75X
*CARDS 101-150: .75X TO 2X BASIC JERSEYS
1-100 ODDS: ONE PER U.S. PACK
1-100 PRINT RUN 325 SER.#'d SETS
101-150 PRINT RUN 90 SER.#'d SETS
U.S. PACKS ONLY

2003-04 Pacific Prism Gold

Inserted at a rate of 6 per retail box, this 100-card set paralleled the base cards of the regular set but carried gold foil highlights and serial-numbering out of 425.

*GOLD: .5X TO 1.25X BASIC CARDS
*ROOKIES: .3X TO .75X

2003-04 Pacific Prism Patches

*PATCHES: 1X TO 2.5X BASIC JERSEYS
118 Steve Yzerman SP 50.00 125.00

2003-04 Pacific Prism Red

*CARDS 1-100: .75X TO 2X BASE CARDS
*ROOKIES 1-100: .4X TO 1X
*JSYS 101-150: .75X TO 2X BASIC JERSEYS
CARDS 1-100: ONE PER CANADIAN PACK
1-100 PRINT RUN 260 SER.#'d SETS
101-150 PRINT RUN 75 SER.#'d SETS
CANADIAN PACKS ONLY

2003-04 Pacific Prism Retail

This 150-card set mirrored the hobby set but cards 101-150 carried silver foil highlights and were serial numbered out of 150.

*RETAIL JERSEYS: .6X TO 1.5X HOBBY

2003-04 Pacific Prism Crease Police

COMPLETE SET (8) 10.00 20.00
STATED ODDS 1:9
1 Jean-Sebastien Giguere 1.50 4.00
2 Patrick Roy 3.00 8.00
3 Marty Turco 1.50 4.00
4 Curtis Joseph 1.50 4.00
5 Jose Theodore 2.00 5.00
6 Martin Brodeur 2.50 6.00
7 Patrick Lalime 1.50 4.00
8 Ed Belfour 1.50 4.00

2003-04 Pacific Prism Paramount Prodigies

COMPLETE SET (20) 15.00 30.00
STATED ODDS 1:3
1 Stanislav Chistov .60 1.50
2 Jean-Sebastien Giguere .60 1.50
3 Dany Heatley 1.00 2.50
4 Ilya Kovalchuk 1.00 2.50
5 Tyler Arnason .60 1.50
6 Rick Nash 1.00 2.50
7 Pavel Datsyuk .75 2.00
8 Henrik Zetterberg 1.00 2.50
9 Mike Comrie .60 1.50
10 Ales Hemsky .60 1.50
11 Jay Bouwmeester .60 1.50
12 Stephen Weiss .60 1.50
13 Alexander Frolov .60 1.50
14 Marian Gaborik 1.25 3.00
15 David Legwand .60 1.50
16 Martin Havlat .60 1.50
17 Marian Hossa .75 2.00
18 Jason Spezza 1.00 2.50
19 Barret Jackman .60 1.50
20 Vincent Lecavalier .60 1.50

2003-04 Pacific Prism Rookie Revolution

COMPLETE SET (12) 8.00 15.00
STATED ODDS 1:5
1 Stanislav Chistov .40 1.00
2 Ales Kotalik .40 1.00
3 Ryan Miller 1.00 2.50
4 Tyler Arnason .40 1.00
5 Rick Nash 1.00 2.50
6 Henrik Zetterberg .75 2.00
7 Ales Hemsky .75 2.00
8 Jay Bouwmeester .60 1.50
9 Alexander Frolov .60 1.50
10 Pierre-Marc Bouchard .60 1.50
11 Jason Spezza 1.00 2.50
12 Jonathan Cheechoo .75 2.00

2003-04 Pacific Prism Stat Masters

COMPLETE SET (10) 8.00 15.00
STATED ODDS 1:9
1 Paul Kariya .40 1.00
2 Joe Thornton .50 1.25
3 Peter Forsberg 1.00 2.50
4 Milan Hejduk .40 1.00
5 Mike Modano .60 1.50
6 Steve Yzerman 1.50 4.00
7 Mario Lemieux 2.00 5.00
8 Todd Bertuzzi .40 1.00
9 Markus Naslund .40 1.00
10 Jaromir Jagr .60 1.50

2002-03 Pacific Quest for the Cup

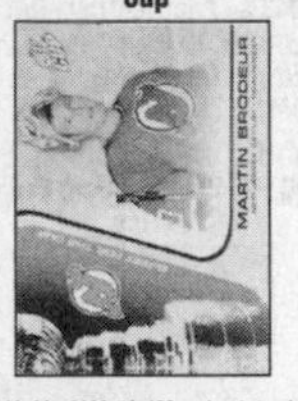

Released in May 2003, this 150-card set featured color player photos on the right side of the card fronts and a silver holographic image of the Stanley Cup on the left. Cards 151-150 were shortprinted to 950 and inserted at 1:5 hobby packs and 1:9 retail packs. Hobby packs contained 6 cards, and retail packs contained 4 cards.

COMP.SET w/o SP's (100) 20.00 40.00
1 Jean-Sebastien Giguere .25 .60
2 Paul Kariya .30 .75
3 Sandis Ozolinsh .10 .25
4 Dany Heatley .40 1.00
5 Ilya Kovalchuk .40 1.00
6 Jeff Hackett .25 .60
7 Glen Murray .10 .25
8 Joe Thornton .50 1.25
9 Martin Biron .25 .60
10 Miroslav Satan .25 .60
11 Chris Drury .25 .60
12 Jarome Iginla .40 1.00
13 Roman Turek .25 .60
14 Ron Francis .25 .60
15 Jeff O'Neill .10 .25
16 Eric Daze .25 .60
17 Theo Fleury .10 .25
18 Jocelyn Thibault .25 .60
19 Alexei Zhamnov .10 .25
20 Rob Blake .25 .60
21 Peter Forsberg .75 2.00
22 Milan Hejduk .30 .75
23 Patrick Roy 1.50 4.00
24 Joe Sakic .60 1.50
25 Marc Denis .25 .60
26 Ray Whitney .10 .25
27 Bill Guerin .25 .60
28 Jere Lehtinen .25 .60
29 Mike Modano .50 1.25
30 Marty Turco .25 .60
30AU Marty Turco AU/500 8.00 20.00
31 Pierre Turgeon .25 .60
32 Sergei Fedorov .50 1.25
33 Brett Hull .40 1.00
34 Curtis Joseph .30 .75
35 Nicklas Lidstrom .30 .75
36 Brendan Shanahan .30 .75
37 Steve Yzerman 1.50 4.00
38 Mike Comrie .25 .60
39 Tommy Salo .25 .60
40 Ryan Smyth .10 .25
41 Olli Jokinen .25 .60
42 Roberto Luongo .40 1.00
43 Jason Allison .10 .25
44 Zigmund Palffy .25 .60
45 Felix Potvin .30 .75
46 Pascal Dupuis .10 .25
47 Manny Fernandez .25 .60
48 Marian Gaborik .60 1.50
49 Cliff Ronning .10 .25
50 Saku Koivu .30 .75
51 Yanic Perreault .10 .25
52 Jose Theodore .40 1.00
53 Richard Zednik .10 .25
54 David Legwand .25 .60
55 Tomas Vokoun .25 .60
56 Martin Brodeur .75 2.00
57 Patrik Elias .25 .60
58 Jeff Friesen .10 .25
59 Jamie Langenbrunner .10 .25
60 Rick DiPietro .25 .60
61 Michael Peca .10 .25
62 Alexei Yashin .10 .25
63 Pavel Bure .30 .75
64 Anson Carter .25 .60
65 Alexei Kovalev .25 .60
66 Eric Lindros .30 .75
67 Mark Messier .30 .75
68 Daniel Alfredsson .25 .60
69 Radek Bonk .10 .25
70 Martin Havlat .25 .60
71 Marian Hossa .30 .75
72 Patrick Lalime .25 .60
73 Tony Amonte .25 .60
74 Roman Cechmanek .25 .60
75 Simon Gagne .30 .75
76 Sami Kapanen .10 .25
77 Jeremy Roenick .40 1.00
78 Sean Burke .25 .60
79 Johan Hedberg .25 .60
80 Mario Lemieux 2.50 6.00
81 Pavol Demitra .25 .60
82 Brent Johnson .25 .60
83 Cory Stillman .10 .25
84 Keith Tkachuk .30 .75
85 Doug Weight .25 .60
86 Evgeni Nabokov .25 .60
87 Teemu Selanne .30 .75
88 Nikolai Khabibulin .30 .75
89 Vincent Lecavalier .30 .75
90 Martin St. Louis .25 .60
91 Ed Belfour .30 .75
92 Alexander Mogilny .25 .60
93 Mats Sundin .30 .75
94 Todd Bertuzzi .30 .75
95 Dan Cloutier .25 .60
96 Brendan Morrison .25 .60
97 Markus Naslund .30 .75
98 Jaromir Jagr .50 1.25
99 Olaf Kolzig .25 .60
100 Michael Nylander .10 .25
101 Stanislav Chistov RC 1.50 4.00
102 Martin Gerber RC 2.00 5.00
103 Kurt Sauer RC 1.50 4.00
104 Alexei Smirnov RC 1.50 4.00
105 Shaone Morrisonn RC 1.50 4.00
106 Tim Thomas RC 2.00 5.00
107 Ryan Miller RC 4.00 10.00
108 Chuck Kobasew RC 2.00 5.00
109 Jordan Leopold RC 1.50 4.00
110 Ryan Bayda RC 1.50 4.00
111 Tomas Malec RC 1.50 4.00
112 Pascal Leclaire RC 2.00 5.00
113 Rick Nash RC 6.00 15.00
114 Jason Bacashihua RC 2.00 5.00
115 Steve Ott RC 2.00 5.00
116 Dmitri Bykov RC 1.50 4.00
117 Henrik Zetterberg RC 5.00 12.00
118 Ales Hemsky RC 5.00 12.00
119 Fernando Pisani RC 2.00 5.00
120 Jay Bouwmeester RC 3.00 8.00
121 Kip Brennan .10 .25
122 Michael Cammalleri RC 2.00 5.00
123 Alexander Frolov RC 3.00 8.00
124 P-M Bouchard RC 3.00 8.00
125 Stephane Veilleux RC 1.50 4.00
126 Ron Hainsey RC 1.50 4.00
127 Mike Komisarek RC 1.50 4.00
128 Vernon Fiddler RC 1.50 4.00
129 Adam Hall RC 1.50 4.00
130 Scottie Upshall RC 1.50 4.00
131 Eric Godard RC 1.50 4.00
132 Ray Emery RC 3.00 8.00
133 Jason Spezza RC 6.00 15.00
134 Anton Volchenkov RC 1.50 4.00
135 Dennis Seidenberg RC 1.50 4.00
136 Radovan Somik RC 1.50 4.00
137 Jim Vandermeer RC 1.50 4.00
138 Jeff Taffe RC 1.50 4.00
139 Brooks Orpik RC 1.50 4.00
140 Tomas Surovy RC 1.50 4.00
141 Dick Tarnstrom RC 1.50 4.00
142 Curtis Sanford RC 2.00 5.00
143 Matt Walker RC 1.50 4.00
144 Niko Dimitrakos RC 1.50 4.00
145 Jim Fahey RC 1.50 4.00
146 Lynn Loyns RC 1.50 4.00
147 Alexander Svitov RC 1.50 4.00
148 Carlo Colaiacovo RC 1.50 4.00
149 Mikael Tellqvist RC 2.00 5.00
150 Steve Eminger RC 1.50 4.00

2002-03 Pacific Quest for the Cup Gold

This 150-card set directly paralleled the base set but carried gold foil highlights on the card fronts. Each card was also serial-numbered out of 325 on the card back.

*STARS: 1.25X TO 3X BASIC CARD
*SP's: .25X TO .75X

2002-03 Pacific Quest For the Cup Calder Contenders

Inserted at 1:13 hobby and 1:25 retail, this 10-card set featured color player photos on gold foil backgrounds on the card fronts.

COMPLETE SET (10) 15.00 30.00
1 Stanislav Chistov 2.00 5.00
2 Ales Kotalik 1.00 2.50
3 Ryan Miller 1.50 4.00
4 Tyler Arnason 1.00 2.50
5 Pascal Leclaire 2.00 5.00
6 Rick Nash 2.50 6.00
7 Henrik Zetterberg 3.00 8.00
8 Ales Hemsky 1.50 4.00
9 Jay Bouwmeester 1.50 4.00
10 Jason Spezza 2.00 5.00

2002-03 Pacific Quest For the Cup Chasing the Cup

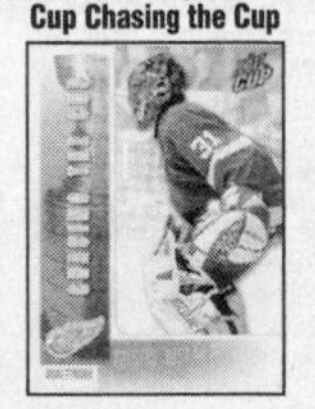

COMPLETE SET (20) 10.00 20.00
STATED ODDS 1:5 HOBBY/1:13 RETAIL
1 Paul Kariya .50 1.25
2 Dany Heatley .60 1.50
3 Ilya Kovalchuk .60 1.50
4 Joe Thornton .75 2.00
5 Marty Turco .40 1.00
6 Curtis Joseph .50 1.25
7 Marian Gaborik 1.00 2.50
8 Jose Theodore .60 1.50
9 Alexei Yashin .40 1.00
10 Pavel Bure .50 1.25
11 Eric Lindros .50 1.25
12 Daniel Alfredsson .40 1.00
13 Marian Hossa .50 1.25
14 Jeremy Roenick .60 1.50
15 Teemu Selanne .50 1.25
16 Owen Nolan .40 1.00
17 Mats Sundin .50 1.25
18 Todd Bertuzzi .50 1.25
19 Brendan Morrison .40 1.00
20 Markus Naslund .60 1.50

2002-03 Pacific Quest for the Cup Itech Masks

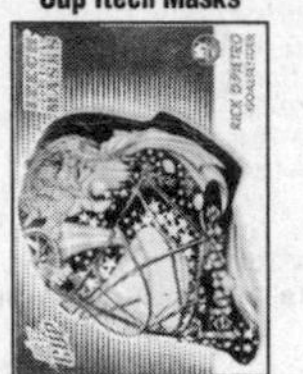

This insert set was pulled from production because of licensing issues, but a few random copies apparently made it into packs The only confirmed single to exist is the DiPietro card. Due to the scarcity of the card, it is not priced. If you know of other singles, please send information to hockeymag@beckett.com.

6 Rick DiPietro

2002-03 Pacific Quest for the Cup Jerseys

*MULT.COLOR SWATCH: .75X TO 1.5X
STATED ODDS 1:9 HOBBY/1:25 RETAIL
1 Dany Heatley 5.00 12.00
2 Glen Murray 3.00 8.00
3 Joe Thornton 6.00 15.00
4 Rob Blake 3.00 8.00
5 Peter Forsberg 8.00 20.00
6 Patrick Roy 12.50 30.00
7 Mike Modano 6.00 15.00
8 Marty Turco 5.00 12.00
9 Nicklas Lidstrom 4.00 10.00
10 Rick DiPietro 3.00 8.00
11 Mark Messier 4.00 10.00
12 Daniel Alfredsson 3.00 8.00
13 Marian Hossa 4.00 10.00
14 Jason Spezza 8.00 20.00
15 Roman Cechmanek 3.00 8.00
16 Jeremy Roenick 5.00 12.00
17 Mario Lemieux 12.50 30.00
18 Brent Johnson 3.00 8.00
19 Doug Weight 3.00 8.00
20 Martin St. Louis 3.00 8.00
21 Ed Belfour 4.00 10.00
22 Gary Roberts 3.00 8.00
23 Markus Naslund 4.00 10.00
24 Jaromir Jagr 6.00 15.00
25 Olaf Kolzig 3.00 8.00

2002-03 Pacific Quest For the Cup Raising the Cup

STATED ODDS 1:9 HOBBY/1:13 RETAIL
1 Peter Forsberg 1.50 4.00
2 Patrick Roy 2.50 6.00
3 Joe Sakic 1.25 3.00
4 Mike Modano 1.00 2.50
5 Sergei Fedorov 1.00 2.50
6 Brett Hull .75 2.00
7 Brendan Shanahan .60 1.50
8 Steve Yzerman 2.50 6.00
9 Martin Brodeur 1.50 4.00
10 Mark Messier .60 1.50
11 Mario Lemieux 3.00 8.00
12 Jaromir Jagr 1.00 2.50

2003-04 Pacific Quest for the Cup

This 140-card set consisted of 100 veteran cards and 40 rookie cards (101-140) that were serial-numbered out of 950.

COMP.SET w/o SP's 20.00 40.00
1 Sergei Fedorov .40 1.00
2 Jean-Sebastien Giguere .25 .60
3 Dany Heatley .40 1.00
4 Ilya Kovalchuk .40 1.00
5 Slava Kozlov .15 .40
6 Pasi Nurminen .25 .60
7 Mike Knuble .15 .40
8 Glen Murray .15 .40
9 Andrew Raycroft .25 .60
10 Joe Thornton .40 1.00
11 Daniel Briere .15 .40
12 Ales Kotalik .15 .40
13 Miroslav Satan .25 .60
14 Shean Donovan .15 .40
15 Jarome Iginla .40 1.00
16 Miikka Kiprusoff .25 .60
17 Erik Cole .15 .40
18 Ron Francis .25 .60
19 Tyler Arnason .25 .60
20 Mark Bell .15 .40
21 Kyle Calder .15 .40
22 David Aebischer .25 .60
23 Peter Forsberg .75 2.00
24 Milan Hejduk .30 .75
25 Paul Kariya .30 .75
26 Joe Sakic .60 1.50
27 Teemu Selanne .30 .75
28 Alex Tanguay .25 .60
29 Marc Denis .25 .60
30 Rick Nash .40 1.00
31 Bill Guerin .25 .60
32 Mike Modano .50 1.25
33 Marty Turco .25 .60
34 Pavel Datsyuk .30 .75
35 Kris Draper .15 .40
36 Dominik Hasek .60 1.50
37 Brett Hull .40 1.00
38 Curtis Joseph .30 .75
39 Robert Lang .25 .60
40 Brendan Shanahan .30 .75
41 Steve Yzerman 1.50 4.00
42 Ales Hemsky .25 .60
43 Ryan Smyth .15 .40
44 Raffi Torres .15 .40
45 Jay Bouwmeester .15 .40
46 Valeri Bure .15 .40
47 Olli Jokinen .25 .60
48 Roberto Luongo .40 1.00
49 Roman Cechmanek .25 .60
50 Alexander Frolov .15 .40
51 Ziggy Palffy .25 .60
52 Andrew Brunette .15 .40
53 Alexandre Daigle .15 .40
54 Marian Gaborik .60 1.50
55 Saku Koivu .30 .75
56 Mike Ribeiro .15 .40
57 Michael Ryder .15 .40
58 Sheldon Souray .15 .40
59 Jose Theodore .40 1.00
60 Martin Erat .15 .40
61 Scott Hartnell .15 .40
62 Tomas Vokoun .25 .60
63 Martin Brodeur .75 2.00
64 Patrik Elias .25 .60
65 Scott Stevens .25 .60
66 Rick DiPietro .25 .60
67 Trent Hunter .15 .40
68 Alexei Yashin .15 .40
69 Jaromir Jagr .50 1.25
70 Alex Kovalev .25 .60
71 Eric Lindros .30 .75
72 Daniel Alfredsson .25 .60
73 Peter Bondra .25 .60
74 Martin Havlat .25 .60
75 Marian Hossa .30 .75
76 Patrick Lalime .25 .60
77 Jason Spezza .30 .75
78 Tony Amonte .25 .60
79 Mark Recchi .25 .60
80 Jeremy Roenick .40 1.00
81 Shane Doan .15 .40
82 Ladislav Nagy .15 .40
83 Rico Fata .15 .40
84 Mario Lemieux 2.00 5.00
85 Pavol Demitra .25 .60
86 Keith Tkachuk .30 .75
87 Doug Weight .25 .60
88 Jonathan Cheechoo .20 .50
89 Patrick Marleau .25 .60
90 Evgeni Nabokov .25 .60
91 Nikolai Khabibulin .30 .75
92 Vincent Lecavalier .30 .75
93 Martin St. Louis .25 .60
94 Ed Belfour .30 .75
95 Owen Nolan .25 .60
96 Mats Sundin .30 .75
97 Todd Bertuzzi .30 .75
98 Jason King .15 .40
99 Brendan Morrison .25 .60
100 Markus Naslund .30 .75
101 Joffrey Lupul RC 1.25 3.00
102 Patrice Bergeron RC 4.00 10.00
103 Derek Roy RC 1.50 4.00
104 Brent Krahn RC 1.25 3.00
105 Matthew Lombardi RC 1.25 3.00
106 Eric Staal RC 5.00 12.00
107 Anton Babchuk RC 1.25 3.00
108 Tuomo Ruutu RC 2.00 5.00
109 Pavel Vorobiev RC 1.25 3.00
110 Mikhail Yakubov RC 1.25 3.00
111 Dan Fritsche RC 1.25 3.00
112 Nikolai Zherdev RC 2.50 6.00
113 Antti Miettinen RC 1.25 3.00
114 Darryl Bootland RC 1.25 3.00
115 Jiri Hudler RC 2.00 5.00
116 Nathan Robinson RC 1.25 3.00
117 Tony Salmelainen RC 1.25 3.00
118 Nathan Horton RC 3.00 8.00
119 Dustin Brown RC 1.25 3.00
120 Brent Burns RC 1.25 3.00
121 Christopher Higgins RC 3.00 8.00
122 Dan Hamhuis RC 1.25 3.00
123 Jordin Tootoo RC 3.00 8.00
124 Marek Zidlicky RC 1.25 3.00
125 David Hale RC 1.25 3.00
126 Paul Martin RC 1.25 3.00
127 Dominic Moore RC 1.25 3.00
128 Antoine Vermette RC 1.25 3.00
129 Joni Pitkanen RC 1.25 3.00
130 Fredrik Sjostrom RC 1.25 3.00
131 Marc-Andre Fleury RC 6.00 15.00
132 Ryan Malone RC 2.00 5.00
133 John Pohl RC 1.25 3.00
134 Peter Sejna RC 1.25 3.00
135 Milan Michalek RC 1.25 3.00
136 Matt Stajan RC 2.00 5.00
137 Ryan Kesler RC 1.25 3.00
138 Boyd Gordon RC 1.25 3.00
139 Alexander Semin RC 4.00 10.00
140 Rastislav Stana RC 1.25 3.00

2003-04 Pacific Quest for the Cup Blue

*STARS: 2X TO 5X BASE HI
STATED ODDS 1:25
STATED PRINT RUN 150 SER.#'d SETS

2003-04 Pacific Quest for the Cup Calder Contenders

COMPLETE SET (20) 15.00 30.00
STATED ODDS 1:7
1 Patrice Bergeron 2.50 6.00
2 Andrew Raycroft 2.50 6.00
3 Matthew Lombardi 1.25 3.00
4 Eric Staal 2.00 5.00
5 Tuomo Ruutu 2.00 5.00
6 Philippe Sauve 1.25 3.00
7 Nikolai Zherdev 2.00 5.00
8 Jiri Hudler 1.25 3.00
9 Nathan Horton 1.50 4.00
10 Dustin Brown 1.25 3.00
11 Brent Burns 1.25 3.00
12 Michael Ryder 1.50 4.00
13 Jordin Tootoo 1.50 4.00
14 Trent Hunter 1.25 3.00
15 Antoine Vermette 1.25 3.00
16 Joni Pitkanen 1.25 3.00
17 Marc-Andre Fleury 3.00 8.00
18 Ryan Malone 1.25 3.00
19 Matt Stajan 1.50 4.00
20 Jason King 1.25 3.00

2003-04 Pacific Quest for the Cup Chasing the Cup

COMPLETE SET (9) 5.00 10.00
STATED ODDS 1:16
1 Dany Heatley 1.00 2.50
2 Ilya Kovalchuk 1.00 2.50
3 Joe Thornton 1.00 2.50
4 Paul Kariya .50 1.25
5 Rick Nash .60 1.50
6 Marty Turco .50 1.25
7 Jason Spezza .50 1.25
8 Mats Sundin .50 1.25
9 Todd Bertuzzi .50 1.25

2003-04 Pacific Quest for the Cup Connquest

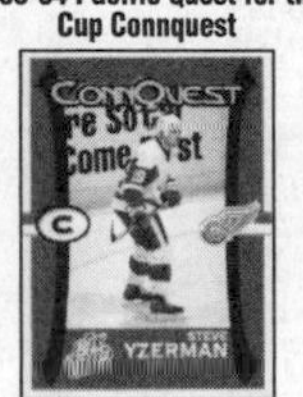

COMPLETE SET (6) 8.00 15.00
STATED ODDS 1:48
1 Jean-Sebastien Giguere .75 2.00
2 Joe Sakic 1.50 4.00
3 Nicklas Lidstrom .75 2.00
4 Steve Yzerman 2.50 6.00
5 Scott Stevens .75 2.00
6 Mario Lemieux 3.00 8.00

2003-04 Pacific Quest for the Cup Eternal Champions

This 2-card set featured certified player autographs from two retired great who participated in the 2003 Heritage Classic game. Due to unknown reasons, it is thought that the cards were pulled from production at the last minute and the mention of the cards was crossed off of packs. Since Pacific went out of business soon afterwards, there is no way to confirm the exact distribution of these cards as a handful have made their way onto the secondary market. The cards are not pirced due to scarcity.

NOT PRICED DUE TO SCARCITY
1 Guy Lafleur
2 Grant Fuhr

2003-04 Pacific Quest for the Cup Jerseys

COMPLETE SET (19)
STATED ODDS 1:25
1 Ilya Kovalchuk SP 5.00 12.00
2 Joe Thornton 4.00 10.00
3 Jarome Iginla 3.00 8.00
4 Jocelyn Thibault 2.50 6.00
5 David Aebischer SP 4.00 10.00
6 Joe Sakic 5.00 12.00
7 Rick Nash 4.00 10.00
8 Marty Turco 2.50 6.00
9 Steve Yzerman SP 8.00 20.00
10 Ryan Smyth 2.50 6.00
11 Scott Walker 2.50 6.00
12 Patrik Elias 2.50 6.00
13 Jaromir Jagr 4.00 10.00
14 Martin Havlat 2.50 6.00
15 Jeff Hackett 2.50 6.00
16 Mario Lemieux SP 10.00 25.00
17 Nikolai Khabibulin 2.50 6.00
18 Ed Belfour SP 5.00 12.00
19 Dan Cloutier 2.50 6.00

2003-04 Pacific Quest for the Cup Raising the Cup

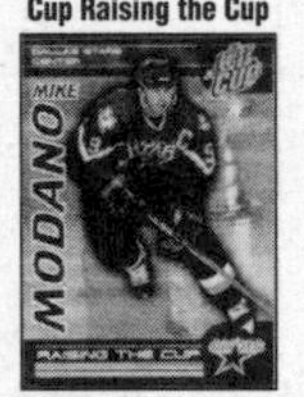

STATED ODDS 1:9
1 Sergei Fedorov .75 2.00
2 Rob Blake .60 1.50
3 Peter Forsberg 1.50 4.00
4 Milan Hejduk .60 1.50
5 Joe Sakic 1.25 3.00
6 Mike Modano 1.00 2.50
7 Dominik Hasek 1.25 3.00
8 Brett Hull .75 2.00
9 Nicklas Lidstrom .60 1.50
10 Brendan Shanahan .60 1.50
11 Steve Yzerman 2.00 5.00
12 Martin Brodeur 2.00 5.00
13 Scott Stevens .60 1.50
14 Mark Messier .60 1.50
15 Mario Lemieux 2.50 6.00

2003-04 Pacific Supreme

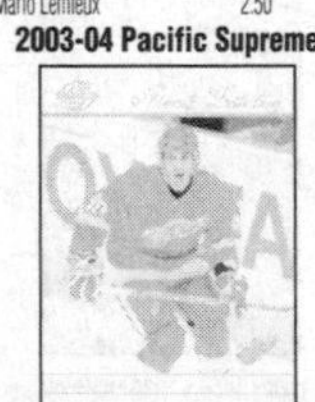

This 140-card set consisted of 100 veteran cards and 40 rookie cards (101-140) serial-numbered to 775 copies each. There were also 14 autographed parallels of rookie players that were seeded randomly and serial-numbered out of 375. These cards are noted below with a "A" suffix which does not appear on the actual cards.

COMP. SET w/o SP's (100) 20.00 40.00
COMMON ROOKIE AUTO 5.00 12.00
ROOK.AUTO PRINT RUN 375 SER.#'d SETS
1 Sergei Fedorov .30 .75
2 Jean-Sebastien Giguere .20 .50
3 Petr Sykora .12 .30
4 Dany Heatley .30 .75
5 Ilya Kovalchuk .30 .75
6 Glen Murray .12 .30
7 Sergei Samsonov .20 .50
8 Joe Thornton .40 1.00
9 Daniel Briere .12 .30
10 Chris Drury .20 .50
11 Ales Kotalik .12 .30
12 Ryan Miller .20 .50
13 Jarome Iginla .30 .75
14 Chuck Kobasew .12 .30
15 Ron Francis .20 .50
16 Jeff O'Neill .12 .30
17 Radim Vrbata .12 .30
18 Tyler Arnason .20 .50
19 Steve Sullivan .12 .30
20 Jocelyn Thibault .20 .50
21 Peter Forsberg .60 1.50
22 Milan Hejduk .25 .60
23 Paul Kariya .25 .60
24 Patrick Roy 1.25 3.00
25 Joe Sakic .40 1.00
26 Marc Denis .20 .50
27 Rick Nash .30 .75
28 Geoff Sanderson .12 .30
29 Jason Arnott .20 .50
30 Mike Modano .50 1.25
31 Marty Turco .20 .50
32 Dominik Hasek .50 1.25
33 Brett Hull .30 .75
34 Ray Whitney .12 .30
35 Steve Yzerman 1.25 3.00
36 Henrik Zetterberg .25 .60
37 Mike Comrie .20 .50
38 Ales Hemsky .20 .50
39 Tommy Salo .20 .50
40 Ryan Smyth .12 .30
41 Jay Bouwmeester .12 .30
42 Olli Jokinen .20 .50
43 Roberto Luongo .30 .75
44 Roman Cechmanek .20 .50
45 Alexander Frolov .12 .30
46 Ziggy Palffy .20 .50
47 Pierre-Marc Bouchard .12 .30
48 Marian Gaborik .50 1.25
49 Dwayne Roloson .20 .50
50 Marcel Hossa .12 .30
51 Saku Koivu .25 .60
52 Jose Theodore .30 .75
53 Richard Zednik .12 .30
54 Andreas Johansson .12 .30
55 David Legwand .20 .50
56 Tomas Vokoun .20 .50
57 Martin Brodeur .60 1.50
58 Patrik Elias .20 .50
59 John Madden .12 .30
60 Jamie Langenbrunner .12 .30
61 Jason Blake .20 .50
62 Rick DiPietro .12 .30
63 Michael Peca .12 .30
64 Alexei Yashin .12 .30
65 Anson Carter .20 .50
66 Alex Kovalev .20 .50
67 Eric Lindros .25 .60
68 Petr Nedved .12 .30
69 Daniel Alfredsson .20 .50
70 Marian Hossa .25 .60
71 Patrick Lalime .20 .50
72 Jason Spezza .25 .60
73 Tony Amonte .20 .50
74 John LeClair .25 .60
75 Jeremy Roenick .30 .75
76 Sean Burke .20 .50
77 Mike Johnson .12 .30
78 Sebastien Caron .20 .50
79 Mario Lemieux 1.50 4.00
80 Pavol Demitra .20 .50
81 Barret Jackman .20 .50
82 Chris Pronger .20 .50
83 Keith Tkachuk .25 .60
84 Patrick Marleau .20 .50
85 Evgeni Nabokov .20 .50
86 Marco Sturm .12 .30
87 Nikolai Khabibulin .25 .60
88 Vincent Lecavalier .25 .60
89 Martin St. Louis .20 .50
90 Ed Belfour .25 .60
91 Alexander Mogilny .20 .50
92 Owen Nolan .20 .50
93 Mats Sundin .25 .60
94 Todd Bertuzzi .25 .60
95 Dan Cloutier .20 .50
96 Brendan Morrison .20 .50
97 Markus Naslund .25 .60
98 Peter Bondra .20 .50
99 Jaromir Jagr .40 1.00
100 Olaf Kolzig .20 .50
101 Garrett Burnett RC 1.50 4.00
102 Joffrey Lupul RC 2.50 6.00
102A Joffrey Lupul AU 6.00 15.00
103 Joe DiPenta RC 1.50 4.00
104 Patrice Bergeron RC 5.00 12.00
105 Milan Bartovic RC 1.50 4.00
106 Andrew Peters RC 1.50 4.00
107 Brent Krahn RC 1.50 4.00
108 Matthew Lombardi RC 1.50 4.00
109 Eric Staal RC 6.00 15.00
109A Eric Staal AU 20.00 50.00
110 Travis Moen RC 1.50 4.00
111 Tuomo Ruutu RC 2.50 6.00
111A Tuomo Ruutu AU 6.00 15.00
112 Pavel Vorobiev RC 1.50 4.00
113 Cody McCormick RC 1.50 4.00
114 Dan Fritsche RC 1.50 4.00
115 Kent McDonell RC 1.50 4.00
116 Antti Miettinen RC 1.50 4.00
117 Jiri Hudler RC 2.50 6.00
117A Jiri Hudler AU 8.00 20.00
118 Nathan Horton RC 3.00 8.00
118A Nathan Horton AU 10.00 25.00
119 Dustin Brown RC 1.50 4.00
119A Dustin Brown AU 5.00 12.00
120 Tim Gleason RC 1.50 4.00
121 Esa Pirnes RC 1.50 4.00
122 Brent Burns RC 1.50 4.00
123 Chris Higgins RC 3.00 8.00
123A Chris Higgins AU 10.00 25.00
124 Dan Hamhuis RC 1.50 4.00
125 Jordin Tootoo RC 3.00 8.00
125A Jordin Tootoo AU 10.00 25.00
126 Marek Zidlicky RC 1.50 4.00
127 David Hale RC 1.50 4.00
128 Paul Martin RC 1.50 4.00
129 Sean Bergenheim RC 1.50 4.00
130 Antoine Vermette RC 1.50 4.00
130A Antoine Vermette AU 5.00 12.00
131 Joni Pitkanen RC 1.50 4.00
131A Joni Pitkanen AU 6.00 15.00
132 Matthew Spiller RC 1.50 4.00
133 Marc-Andre Fleury RC 6.00 15.00

133A Marc-Andre Fleury AU	20.00	50.00
134 Matt Murley RC	1.50	4.00
135 Peter Sejna RC	1.50	4.00
135A Peter Sejna AU	5.00	12.00
136 Milan Michalek RC	2.50	6.00
136A Milan Michalek AU	8.00	20.00
137 Tom Preissing RC	1.50	4.00
138 Maxim Kondratiev RC	1.50	4.00
139 Matt Stajan RC	3.00	8.00
139A Matt Stajan AU	8.00	20.00
140 Boyd Gordon RC	1.50	4.00

2003-04 Pacific Supreme Blue

*STARS: 1.5X TO 4X BASIC CARDS
1-100 ODDS 1:2
*ROOKIES: .75X TO 2X
STATED PRINT RUN 250 SER.#'d SETS

2003-04 Pacific Supreme Red

*STARS: 1.5X TO 4X BASIC CARD
1-100 ODDS 1:3
*ROOKIES: .5X TO 1.25X
ROOKIE PRINT RUN 425 SER.#'d SETS

2003-04 Pacific Supreme Retail

This 140-card set mirrored the hobby version but carried silver foil highlights in place of the gold foil. Rookie cards were not serial-numbered and were inserted at 1:4.

*STARS: SAME VALUE AS HOBBY
*ROOKIES: .25X TO .75X HOBBY

2003-04 Pacific Supreme Generations

COMPLETE SET (24)	25.00	50.00
STATED ODDS 1:7		
1 Ron Francis Radim Vrbata	1.50	4.00
2 Patrick Roy David Aebischer	3.00	8.00
3 Geoff Sanderson Rick Nash	1.50	4.00
4 Steve Yzerman Pavel Datysuk	4.00	10.00
5 Brett Hull Henrik Zetterberg	3.00	8.00
6 Daniel Alfredsson Jason Spezza	2.50	6.00
7 Sean Burke Zac Bierk	1.50	4.00
8 Mario Lemieux Marc-Andre Fleury	5.00	12.00
9 Al MacInnis Barret Jackman	1.50	4.00
10 V.Damphousse/J.Cheechoo	1.50	4.00
11 Mats Sundin Nik Antropov	1.50	4.00
12 Markus Naslund Daniel Sedin	1.50	4.00

2003-04 Pacific Supreme Jerseys

STATED ODDS 2:10		
1 Sergei Fedorov	4.00	10.00
2 Ilya Kovalchuk	4.00	10.00
3 Joe Thornton	5.00	12.00
4 Chris Drury	2.50	6.00
5 Miroslav Satan	2.50	6.00
6 Jarome Iginla	4.00	10.00
7 Eric Daze	2.50	6.00
8 Peter Forsberg SP	8.00	20.00
9 Paul Kariya	3.00	8.00
10 Patrick Roy	10.00	25.00
11 Brett Hull	4.00	10.00
12 Steve Yzerman SP	10.00	25.00
13 Mike Comrie	2.50	6.00
14 Ryan Smyth	2.50	6.00
15 Olli Jokinen	2.50	6.00
16 Jose Theodore	4.00	10.00
17 Pavel Bure	3.00	8.00
18 Eric Lindros	3.00	8.00
19 Tony Amonte	2.50	6.00
20 Jeremy Roenick	4.00	10.00
21 Mario Lemieux	10.00	25.00
22 Vincent Lecavalier	2.50	6.00
23 Mats Sundin	3.00	8.00
24 Markus Naslund	3.00	8.00
25 Jaromir Jagr	5.00	12.00

2003-04 Pacific Supreme Standing Guard

COMPLETE SET (12)	20.00	40.00
STATED ODDS 1:12		
1 Jean-Sebastien Giguere	1.25	3.00
2 Jocelyn Thibault	1.25	3.00
3 Patrick Roy	3.00	8.00
4 Marc Denis	1.25	3.00
5 Marty Turco	1.25	3.00
6 Dominik Hasek	2.00	5.00
7 Roberto Luongo	2.00	5.00
8 Jose Theodore	2.00	5.00
9 Martin Brodeur	2.50	6.00
10 Patrick Lalime	1.25	3.00
11 Sean Burke	1.25	3.00
12 Ed Belfour	1.50	4.00

2003-04 Pacific Supreme Team

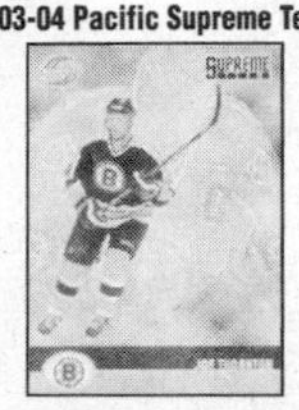

COMPLETE SET (10)	8.00	15.00
STATED ODDS 1:12		
1 Joe Thornton	.50	1.25
2 Peter Forsberg	1.00	2.50
3 Joe Sakic	.60	1.50
4 Brett Hull	.40	1.00
5 Steve Yzerman	2.00	5.00
6 Marian Gaborik	.60	1.50
7 Mario Lemieux	2.50	6.00
8 Todd Bertuzzi	.30	.75
9 Markus Naslund	.30	.75
10 Jaromir Jagr	.50	1.25

2002 Pacific Toronto Fall Expo

Available as a wrapper redemption at the 2002 Toronto Fall Expo, this 10-card set focused on goalies from around the league. One goalie was pictured on each side of the cards and each card was serial-numbered out of 500. A gold parallel was also created and available randomly.

COMPLETE SET (10)		25.00
*GOLD: 1.5X TO 4X		
GOLD PRINT RUN 99 SER.#'d SETS		
1 Ed Belfour Curtis Joseph	1.20	5.00
2 Jose Theodore Patrick Roy	1.60	10.00
3 Roman Turek Tommy Salo		1.00
4 Patrick Lalime Dan Cloutier		1.00
5 Roberto Luongo Nikolai Khabibulin		3.00
6 Martin Brodeur Mike Richter	1.20	5.00
7 Jean-Sebastien Giguere Felix Potvin		5.00
8 Marty Turco Sean Burke		3.00
9 Martin Biron Jocelyn Thibault		1.00
10 Brent Johnson Evgeni Nabokov		1.00

2002 Pacific Toronto Spring Expo Rookie Collection

Available as a wrapper redemption at the Pacific booth during the 2002 Spring Expo in Toronto, this 10-card set featured some of the hottest rookies of the year. Each card was serial-numbered out of 500.

COMPLETE SET (10)	10.00	25.00
1 Dany Heatley	2.00	5.00
2 Ilya Kovalchuk	3.00	8.00
5 Rostislav Klesla	1.25	3.00
6 Pavel Datsyuk	3.00	8.00
9 Dan Blackburn	1.25	3.00

2003 Pacific Toronto Spring Expo

Serial-numbered to 499, this 8-card set was available only via wrapper redemption at the Pacific booth during the Toronto Spring Expo. A gold parallel numbered to 99 was also available for the first 99 visitors to open a Pacific box at the booth. Values for gold parallels can be found by using the multipliers below.

COMPLETE SET (8)	15.00	35.00
*GOLD: 1.5X TO 4X BASIC CARDS		
1 Stanislav Chistov	2.40	3.00
2 Ryan Miller	2.00	5.00
3 Rick Nash	4.00	10.00
4 Henrik Zetterberg	4.00	10.00
5 Jay Bouwmeester	2.40	6.00
6 Mike Cammalleri	2.00	5.00
7 Jason Spezza	3.20	8.00
8 Carlo Colaiacovo	2.00	3.00

2003 Pacific Toronto Fall Expo

This 6-card set was part of a wrapper redemption during the 2003 Fall Expo. Cards were serial-numbered out of 500 and featured a NHL player on the front and a CFL player on the back.

COMPLETE SET (6)	10.00	20.00
1 Todd Bertuzzi Dave Dickenson	1.50	4.00
2 Jarome Iginla Marcus Crandell	2.00	5.00
3 Ryan Smyth Ricky Ray	1.25	3.00
4 Jose Theodore Anthony Calvillo	2.00	5.00
5 Marian Hossa Josh Ranek	1.25	3.00
6 Ed Belfour Damon Allen	1.50	4.00

2004 Pacific National Convention

These cards were intended to be issued as part of a wrapper redemption at the 2004 National Sports Collectors Convention in Cleveland, due to circumstances, Pacific did not attend the show and the entire lot was sold on consignment. The cards are serial numbered out of 499. The full bleed borders make them susceptible to chipping.

COMPLETE SET (6)	8.00	20.00
1 Ilya Kovalchuk	2.00	5.00
2 Joe Thornton	2.00	5.00
3 Rick Nash	2.00	5.00
4 Rick DiPietro	.75	2.00
5 Marc-Andre Fleury	1.50	4.00
6 Vincent Lecavalier	1.25	3.00

2004 Pacific Toronto Spring Expo

Available only via wrapper redemption at the 2004 Toronto Spring Expo, this 8-card set featured rookies from the 2003-04 season. Each card was serial-numbered out of 499. A gold parallel was also randomly available.

COMPLETE SET (8)	
*GOLD: 1.5X TO 3X BASIC CARDS	
GOLD PRINT RUN 99 SER.#'d SETS	
1 Patrice Bergeron	4.00
2 Eric Staal	2.00
3 Nathan Horton	2.00
4 Dustin Brown	1.00
5 Jordin Tootoo	2.00
6 Antoine Vermette	1.00
7 Marc-Andre Fleury	4.00
8 Matt Stajan	2.00

2004 Pacific WHA Autographs

These two autographed cards were the only two WHA cards that Pacific produced before the company shut their doors in 2004. Each card was serial-numbered to 1972 and were available only via the Pacific website and various other online dealers for $25US.

1 Bobby Hull	25.00
2 Andre Lacroix	20.00

1987-88 Panini Stickers

This set of 396 hockey stickers was produced and distributed by Panini. The sticker number is only on the backing of the sticker. The stickers measure approximately 2 1/8" by 2 11/16". The team logos are foil stickers. On the inside back cover of the sticker album the company offered (via direct mail-order) up to 30 different stickers of your choice for either ten cents each or in trade one-for-one for your unwanted extra stickers plus 1.00 for postage and handling; this is one reason why the values of the most popular players in these sticker sets are somewhat depressed compared to traditional card prices.

COMPLETE SET (396)	14.00	35.00
1 Stanley Cup	.02	.10
2 Bruins Action	.01	.05
3 Bruins Emblem	.01	.05
4 Doug Keans	.01	.05
5 Bill Ranford	.60	1.50
6 Ray Bourque	.40	1.00
7 Reed Larson	.01	.05
8 Mike Milbury	.01	.05
9 Michael Thelven	.01	.05
10 Cam Neely	.20	.50
11 Charlie Simmer	.01	.05
12 Rick Middleton	.01	.05
13 Tom McCarthy	.01	.05
14 Keith Crowder	.01	.05
15 Steve Kasper	.01	.05
16 Ken Linseman	.01	.05
17 Dwight Foster	.01	.05
18 Jay Miller	.01	.05
19 Sabres Action	.01	.05
20 Sabres Emblem	.01	.05
21 Jacques Cloutier	.02	.10
22 Tom Barrasso	.02	.10
23 Daren Puppa	.02	.10
24 Phil Housley	.01	.05
25 Mike Ramsey	.01	.05
26 Bill Hajt	.01	.05
27 Dave Andreychuk	.02	.10
28 Christian Ruuttu	.01	.05
29 Mike Foligno	.01	.05
30 John Tucker	.01	.05
31 Adam Creighton	.01	.05
32 Wilf Paiement	.01	.05
33 Paul Cyr	.01	.05
34 Clark Gillies	.01	.05
35 Lindy Ruff	.01	.05
36 Whalers Action	.01	.05
37 Whalers Emblem	.01	.05
38 Mike Liut	.02	.10
39 Steve Weeks	.01	.05
40 Dave Babych	.01	.05
41 Ulf Samuelsson	.20	.50
42 Dana Murzyn	.01	.05
43 Ron Francis	.02	.10
44 Kevin Dineen	.01	.05
45 John Anderson	.01	.05
46 Ray Ferraro	.01	.05
47 Dean Evason	.01	.05
48 Paul Lawless	.01	.05
49 Stewart Gavin	.01	.05
50 Sylvain Turgeon	.01	.05
51 Dave Tippett	.01	.05
52 Doug Jarvis	.01	.05
53 Canadiens Action	.01	.05
54 Canadiens Emblem	.01	.05
55 Brian Hayward	.02	.10
56 Patrick Roy	1.25	3.00
57 Larry Robinson	.02	.10
58 Chris Chelios	.30	.75
59 Craig Ludwig	.01	.05
60 Rick Green	.01	.05
61 Mats Naslund	.01	.05
62 Bobby Smith	.01	.05
63 Claude Lemieux	.60	1.50
64 Guy Carbonneau	.02	.10
65 Stephane Richer	.30	.75
66 Mike McPhee	.02	.10
67 Brian Skrudland	.01	.05
68 Chris Nilan	.01	.05
69 Bob Gainey	.02	.10
70 Devils Action	.01	.05
71 Devils Emblem	.01	.05
72 Craig Billington	.02	.10
73 Alain Chevrier	.01	.05
74 Bruce Driver	.01	.05
75 Joe Cirella	.01	.05
76 Ken Daneyko	.01	.05
77 Craig Wolanin	.01	.05
78 Aaron Broten	.01	.05
79 Kirk Muller	.02	.10
80 John MacLean	.01	.05
81 Pat Verbeek	.01	.05
82 Doug Sulliman	.01	.05
83 Mark Johnson	.01	.05
84 Greg Adams	.01	.05
85 Claude Loiselle	.01	.05
86 Andy Brickley	.01	.05
87 Islanders Action	.01	.05
88 Islanders Emblem	.01	.05
89 Billy Smith	.02	.10
90 Kelly Hrudey	.02	.10
91 Denis Potvin	.01	.05
92 Tomas Jonsson	.01	.05
93 Ken Leiter	.01	.05
94 Ken Morrow	.01	.05
95 Brian Curran	.01	.05
96 Bryan Trottier	.02	.10
97 Mike Bossy	.20	.50
98 Pat LaFontaine	.20	.50
99 Brent Sutter	.01	.05
100 Mikko Makela	.01	.05
101 Pat Flatley	.01	.05
102 Duane Sutter	.01	.05
103 Rich Kromm	.01	.05
104 Rangers Action	.01	.05
105 Rangers Emblem	.01	.05
106 John Vanbiesbrouck	.75	2.00
107 James Patrick	.01	.05
108 Ron Greschner	.01	.05
109 Willie Huber	.01	.05
110 Curt Giles	.01	.05
111 Larry Melnyk	.01	.05
112 Walt Poddubny	.01	.05
113 Marcel Dionne	.20	.50
114 Tomas Sandstrom	.01	.05
115 Kelly Kisio	.01	.05
116 Pierre Larouche	.01	.05
117 Don Maloney	.01	.05
118 Tony McKegney	.01	.05
119 Ron Duguay	.01	.05
120 Jan Erixon	.01	.05
121 Flyers Action	.01	.05
122 Flyers Emblem	.01	.05
123 Ron Hextall	.40	1.00
124 Mark Howe	.01	.05
125 Doug Crossman	.01	.05
126 Brad McCrimmon	.01	.05
127 Brad Marsh	.01	.05
128 Tim Kerr	.01	.05
129 Peter Zezel	.01	.05
130 Dave Poulin	.01	.05
131 Brian Propp	.01	.05
132 Pelle Eklund	.01	.05
133 Murray Craven	.01	.05
134 Rick Tocchet	.40	1.00
135 Derrick Smith	.01	.05
136 Ilkka Sinisalo	.01	.05
137 Ron Sutter	.01	.05
138 Penguins Action	.01	.05
139 Penguins Emblem	.01	.05
140 Gilles Meloche	.02	.10
141 Doug Bodger	.01	.05
142 Moe Mantha	.01	.05
143 Jim Johnson	.01	.05
144 Rod Buskas	.01	.05
145 Randy Hillier	.01	.05
146 Mario Lemieux	1.25	3.00
147 Dan Quinn	.01	.05
148 Randy Cunneyworth	.01	.05
149 Craig Simpson	.01	.05
150 Terry Ruskowski	.01	.05
151 John Chabot	.01	.05
152 Bob Errey	.01	.05
153 Dan Frawley	.01	.05
154 Dave Hannan	.01	.05
155 Nordiques Action	.01	.05
156 Nordiques Emblem	.01	.05
157 Mario Gosselin	.02	.10
158 Clint Malarchuk	.02	.10
159 Risto Siltanen	.01	.05
160 Robert Picard	.01	.05
161 Normand Rochefort	.01	.05
162 Randy Moller	.01	.05
163 Michel Goulet	.02	.10
164 Peter Stastny	.02	.10
165 John Ogrodnick	.01	.05
166 Anton Stastny	.01	.05
167 Paul Gillis	.01	.05
168 Dale Hunter	.01	.05
169 Alain Cote	.01	.05
170 Mike Eagles	.01	.05
171 Jason Lafreniere	.01	.05
172 Capitals Action	.01	.05
173 Capitals Emblem	.01	.05
174 Pete Peeters	.02	.10
175 Bob Mason	.02	.10
176 Larry Murphy	.20	.50
177 Scott Stevens	.02	.10
178 Rod Langway	.01	.05
179 Kevin Hatcher	.20	.50
180 Mike Gartner	.20	.50
181 Mike Ridley	.01	.05
182 Craig Laughlin	.01	.05
183 Gaetan Duchesne	.01	.05
184 Dave Christian	.01	.05
185 Greg Adams	.01	.05
186 Kelly Miller	.01	.05
187 Alan Haworth	.01	.05
188 Lou Franceschetti	.01	.05
189 Stanley Cup (top half)	.02	.10
190 Stanley Cup (bottom half)	.02	.10
191 Ron Hextall	.60	1.50
192 Wayne Gretzky	1.50	4.00
193 Brian Propp	.01	.05
194 Mark Messier	.40	1.00
195 Flyers/Oilers Action	.01	.05
196 Flyers/Oilers Action	.01	.05
197 Gretzky Holding Cup (upper left)	.40	1.00
198 Gretzky Holding Cup (upper right)	.40	1.00
199 Gretzky Holding Cup (lower left)	.40	1.00
200 Gretzky Holding Cup (lower right)	.40	1.00
201 Flames Action	.01	.05
202 Flames Emblem	.01	.05
203 Mike Vernon	.60	1.50
204 Rejean Lemelin	.02	.10
205 Al MacInnis	.20	.50
206 Paul Reinhart	.01	.05
207 Gary Suter	.02	.10
208 Jamie Macoun	.01	.05
209 Neil Sheehy	.01	.05
210 Joe Mullen	.02	.10
211 Carey Wilson	.01	.05
212 Joel Otto	.01	.05
213 Jim Peplinski	.01	.05
214 Hakan Loob	.01	.05
215 Lanny McDonald	.01	.05
216 Tim Hunter	.01	.05
217 Gary Roberts	.02	.10
218 Blackhawks Action	.01	.05
219 Blackhawks Emblem	.01	.05
220 Bob Sauve	.02	.10
221 Murray Bannerman	.01	.05
222 Doug Wilson	.01	.05
223 Bob Murray	.01	.05
224 Gary Nylund	.01	.05
225 Denis Savard	.02	.10
226 Steve Larmer	.02	.10
227 Troy Murray	.01	.05
228 Wayne Presley	.01	.05
229 Al Secord	.01	.05
230 Ed Olczyk	.01	.05
231 Curt Fraser	.01	.05
232 Bill Watson	.01	.05
233 Keith Brown	.01	.05
234 Darryl Sutter	.01	.05
235 Red Wings Action	.01	.05
236 Red Wings Emblem	.01	.05
237 Greg Stefan	.01	.05
238 Glen Hanlon	.02	.10
239 Darren Veitch	.01	.05
240 Mike O'Connell	.01	.05
241 Harold Snepsts	.01	.05
242 Dave Lewis	.01	.05
243 Steve Yzerman	.75	2.00
244 Brent Ashton	.01	.05
245 Gerard Gallant	.01	.05
246 Petr Klima	.01	.05
247 Shawn Burr	.01	.05
248 Adam Oates	.02	.10
249 Mel Bridgman	.01	.05
250 Tim Higgins	.01	.05
251 Joey Kocur	.01	.05
252 Oilers Action	.01	.05
253 Oilers Emblem	.01	.05
254 Grant Fuhr	.20	.50
255 Andy Moog	.02	.10
256 Paul Coffey	.20	.50
257 Kevin Lowe	.02	.10
258 Craig Muni	.01	.05
259 Steve Smith	.01	.05
260 Charlie Huddy	.01	.05
261 Wayne Gretzky	1.50	4.00
262 Jari Kurri	.20	.50
263 Mark Messier	.40	1.00
264 Esa Tikkanen	.01	.05
265 Glenn Anderson	.02	.10
266 Mike Krushelnyski	.01	.05
267 Craig MacTavish	.01	.05
268 Dave Hunter	.01	.05
269 Kings Action	.01	.05
270 Kings Emblem	.01	.05
271 Roland Melanson	.02	.10
272 Darren Eliot	.01	.05
273 Grant Ledyard	.01	.05
274 Jay Wells	.01	.05
275 Mark Hardy	.01	.05
276 Dean Kennedy	.01	.05
277 Luc Robitaille	1.00	2.50
278 Bernie Nicholls	.02	.10
279 Jimmy Carson	.01	.05
280 Dave Taylor	.01	.05
281 Jim Fox	.01	.05
282 Bryan Erickson	.01	.05
283 Dave(Tiger) Williams	.01	.05
284 Sean McKenna	.01	.05
285 Phil Sykes	.01	.05
286 North Stars Action	.01	.05
287 North Stars Emblem	.01	.05
288 Kari Takko	.02	.10
289 Don Beaupre	.02	.10
290 Craig Hartsburg	.01	.05
291 Ron Wilson	.01	.05
292 Frantisek Musil	.01	.05
293 Dino Ciccarelli	.02	.10
294 Brian MacLellan	.01	.05
295 Dirk Graham	.01	.05
296 Brian Bellows	.01	.05
297 Neal Broten	.01	.05
298 Dennis Maruk	.01	.05
299 Keith Acton	.01	.05
300 Brian Lawton	.01	.05
301 Bob Brooke	.01	.05
302 Willi Plett	.01	.05
303 Blues Action	.01	.05
304 Blues Emblem	.01	.05
305 Rick Wamsley	.02	.10
306 Rob Ramage	.01	.05
307 Ric Nattress	.01	.05
308 Bruce Bell	.01	.05
309 Charlie Bourgeois	.01	.05
310 Jim Pavese	.01	.05
311 Doug Gilmour	.20	.50
312 Bernie Federko	.01	.05
313 Mark Hunter	.01	.05
314 Greg Paslawski	.01	.05
315 Gino Cavallini	.01	.05
316 Rick Meagher	.01	.05
317 Ron Flockhart	.01	.05
318 Doug Wickenheiser	.01	.05
319 Jocelyn Lemieux	.01	.05
320 Maple Leafs Action	.01	.05
321 Maple Leafs Emblem	.01	.05
322 Ken Wregget	.02	.10
323 Allan Bester	.02	.10
324 Todd Gill	.01	.05
325 Al Iafrate	.01	.05
326 Borje Salming	.01	.05
327 Russ Courtnall	.01	.05
328 Rick Vaive	.01	.05
329 Steve Thomas	.01	.05
330 Wendel Clark	.30	.75
331 Gary Leeman	.01	.05
332 Tom Fergus	.01	.05
333 Vincent Damphousse	.20	.50
334 Peter Ihnacak	.01	.05
335 Brad Smith	.01	.05
336 Miroslav Ihnacak	.01	.05
337 Canucks Action	.01	.05
338 Canucks Emblem	.01	.05
339 Frank Caprice	.01	.05
340 Richard Brodeur	.01	.05
341 Doug Lidster	.01	.05
342 Michel Petit	.01	.05
343 Garth Butcher	.01	.05
344 Dave Richter	.01	.05
345 Tony Tanti	.01	.05
346 Barry Pederson	.01	.05
347 Petri Skriko	.01	.05
348 Patrik Sundstrom	.01	.05
349 Stan Smyl	.01	.05
350 Rich Sutter	.01	.05
351 Steve Tambellini	.01	.05
352 Jim Sandlak	.01	.05
353 Dave Lowry	.01	.05
354 Jets Action	.01	.05
355 Jets Emblem	.01	.05
356 Daniel Berthiaume	.02	.10
357 Pokey Reddick	.01	.05
358 Dave Ellett	.01	.05
359 Mario Marois	.01	.05
360 Randy Carlyle	.01	.05
361 Fredrick Olausson	.01	.05
362 Jim Kyte	.01	.05
363 Dale Hawerchuk	.02	.10
364 Paul MacLean	.01	.05
365 Thomas Steen	.01	.05
366 Gilles Hamel	.01	.05
367 Doug Smail	.01	.05
368 Laurie Boschman	.01	.05
369 Ray Neufeld	.01	.05
370 Andrew McBain	.01	.05
371 Wayne Gretzky	1.50	4.00
372 Hart Trophy	.01	.05
373 Wayne Gretzky	1.50	4.00
374 Art Ross Trophy	.01	.05
375 Jennings Trophy	.01	.05
376A Brian Hayward	.02	.10
376B Patrick Roy	1.25	3.00
377 Vezina Trophy	.01	.05
378 Ron Hextall	.20	.50
379 Luc Robitaille	1.00	2.50
380 Calder Trophy	.01	.05
381 Ray Bourque	.20	.50
382 Norris Trophy	.01	.05
383 Lady Byng Trophy	.01	.05
384 Joe Mullen	.02	.10
385 Frank Selke Trophy	.01	.05
386 Dave Poulin	.01	.05
387 Doug Jarvis	.01	.05
388 Masterton Trophy	.01	.05
389 Wayne Gretzky	1.50	4.00
390 Emery Edge Award	.01	.05
391 Flyers Team Photo (left half)	.01	.05
392 Flyers Team Photo (right half)	.01	.05
393 Prince of Wales Trophy	.01	.05
394 Clarence S. Campbell Bowl	.01	.05
395 Oilers Team Photo (left half)	.01	.05
396 Oilers Team Photo (right half)	.01	.05
xx Sticker Album	2.00	5.00

1988-89 Panini Stickers

This set of 408 hockey stickers was produced and distributed by Panini. The sticker number is only on the backing of the sticker. The stickers measure approximately 2 1/8" by 2 11/16". The team picture cards are double stickers with each sticker showing half of the photo; in the checklist below these halves are denoted by LH (left half) and RH (right half). There was an album issued with the set for holding the stickers. On the inside back cover of the sticker album the company offered (via direct mail-order) up to 30 different stickers of your choice for either ten cents each or in trade one-for-one for your unwanted extra stickers plus 1.00 for postage and handling; this is one reason why the values of the most popular players in these sticker sets are somewhat depressed compared to traditional card prices.

COMPLETE SET (408)	12.00	30.00
1 Road to the Cup Stanley Cup Draw	.01	.05
2 Flames Emblem	.01	.05
3 Flames Uniform	.01	.05
4 Mike Vernon	.02	.10
5 Al MacInnis	.02	.10
6 Brad McCrimmon	.01	.05
7 Gary Suter	.02	.10
8 Mike Bullard	.01	.05
9 Hakan Loob	.01	.05
10 Lanny McDonald	.01	.05
11 Joe Mullen	.02	.10
12 Joe Nieuwendyk	.20	.50
13 Joel Otto	.01	.05
14 Jim Peplinski	.01	.05
15 Gary Roberts	.02	.10
16 Flames Team LH	.01	.05
17 Flames Team RH	.01	.05
18 Blackhawks Emblem	.01	.05
19 Blackhawks Uniform	.01	.05
20 Bob Mason	.02	.10
21 Darren Pang	.02	.10
22 Bob Murray	.01	.05
23 Gary Nylund	.01	.05
24 Doug Wilson	.01	.05
25 Dirk Graham	.01	.05
26 Steve Larmer	.02	.10
27 Troy Murray	.01	.05
28 Brian Noonan	.01	.05
29 Denis Savard	.02	.10
30 Steve Thomas	.01	.05
31 Rick Vaive	.01	.05
32 Blackhawks Team LH	.01	.05
33 Blackhawks Team RH	.01	.05
34 Red Wings Emblem	.01	.05
35 Red Wings Uniform	.01	.05
36 Glen Hanlon	.02	.10
37 Greg Stefan	.02	.10
38 Jeff Sharples	.01	.05
39 Darren Veitch	.01	.05
40 Brent Ashton	.01	.05
41 Shawn Burr	.01	.05
42 John Chabot	.01	.05
43 Gerard Gallant	.01	.05
44 Petr Klima	.01	.05
45 Adam Oates	.02	.10
46 Bob Probert	.02	.10
47 Steve Yzerman	.60	1.50
48 Red Wings Team LH	.01	.05
49 Red Wings Team RH	.01	.05
50 Oilers Emblem	.01	.05
51 Oilers Uniform	.01	.05
52 Grant Fuhr	.20	.50
53 Charlie Huddy	.01	.05
54 Kevin Lowe	.02	.10
55 Steve Smith	.01	.05
56 Jeff Beukeboom	.01	.05
57 Glenn Anderson	.02	.10
58 Wayne Gretzky	1.00	2.50
59 Jari Kurri	.20	.50
60 Craig MacTavish	.01	.05
61 Mark Messier	.30	.75
62 Craig Simpson	.01	.05
63 Esa Tikkanen	.02	.10
64 Oilers Team LH	.01	.05
65 Oilers Team RH	.01	.05
66 Kings Emblem	.01	.05
67 Kings Uniform	.01	.05
68 Glenn Healy	.20	.50
69 Roland Melanson	.02	.10
70 Steve Duchesne	.20	.50
71 Tom Laidlaw	.01	.05
72 Jay Wells	.01	.05

73 Mike Allison .01 .05
74 Bob Carpenter .01 .05
75 Jimmy Carson .01 .05
76 Jim Fox .01 .05
77 Bernie Nicholls .02 .10
78 Luc Robitaille .20 .50
79 Dave Taylor .01 .05
80 Kings Team LH .01 .05
81 Kings Team RH .01 .05
82 North Stars Emblem .01 .05
83 North Stars Uniform .01 .05
84 Don Beaupre .02 .10
85 Kari Takko .02 .10
86 Craig Hartsburg .01 .05
87 Frantisek Musil .01 .05
88 Dave Archibald .01 .05
89 Brian Bellows .01 .05
90 Scott Bjugstad .01 .05
91 Bob Brooke .01 .05
92 Neal Broten .01 .05
93 Dino Ciccarelli .02 .10
94 Brian Lawton .01 .05
95 Brian MacLellan .01 .05
96 North Stars Team LH .01 .05
97 North Stars Team RH .01 .05
98 Blues Emblem .01 .05
99 Blues Uniform .01 .05
100 Greg Millen .02 .10
101 Brian Benning .01 .05
102 Gordie Roberts .01 .05
103 Gino Cavallini .01 .05
104 Bernie Federko .01 .05
105 Doug Gilmour .20 .50
106 Tony Hrkac .01 .05
107 Brett Hull .20 .50
108 Mark Hunter .01 .05
109 Tony McKegney .01 .05
110 Rick Meagher .01 .05
111 Brian Sutter .01 .05
112 Blues Team LH .01 .05
113 Blues Team RH .01 .05
114 Maple Leafs Emblem .01 .05
115 Maple Leafs Uniform .01 .05
116 Allan Bester .02 .10
117 Ken Wregget .02 .10
118 Al Iafrate .01 .05
119 Luke Richardson .01 .05
120 Borje Salming .01 .05
121 Wendel Clark .02 .10
122 Russ Courtnall .01 .05
123 Vincent Damphousse .02 .10
124 Dan Daoust .01 .05
125 Gary Leeman .01 .05
126 Ed Olczyk .01 .05
127 Mark Osborne .01 .05
128 Maple Leafs Team LH .01 .05
129 Maple Leafs Team RH .01 .05
130 Canucks Emblem .01 .05
131 Canucks Uniform .01 .05
132 Kirk McLean .02 .10
133 Jim Benning .01 .05
134 Garth Butcher .01 .05
135 Doug Lidster .01 .05
136 Greg Adams .01 .05
137 David Bruce .01 .05
138 Barry Pederson .01 .05
139 Jim Sandlak .01 .05
140 Petri Skriko .01 .05
141 Stan Smyl .01 .05
142 Rich Sutter .01 .05
143 Tony Tanti .01 .05
144 Canucks Team LH .01 .05
145 Canucks Team RH .01 .05
146 Jets Emblem .01 .05
147 Jets Uniform .01 .05
148 Daniel Berthiaume .02 .10
149 Randy Carlyle .01 .05
150 Dave Ellett .01 .05
151 Mario Marois .01 .05
152 Peter Taglianetti .01 .05
153 Laurie Boschman .01 .05
154 Iain Duncan .01 .05
155 Dale Hawerchuk .02 .10
156 Paul MacLean .01 .05
157 Andrew McBain .01 .05
158 Doug Smail .01 .05
159 Thomas Steen .01 .05
160 Jets Team LH .01 .05
161 Jets Team RH .01 .05
162 Prince of Wales Trophy .01 .05
163 Caps/Flyers Action .01 .05
164 Bruins/Canadiens Action .01 .05
165 Caps/Devils Action .01 .05
166 Bruins/Devils Action LH .01 .05
167 Bruins/Devils Action RH .01 .05
168 Flames/Kings Action .01 .05
169 Clarence S. Campbell Bowl .01 .05
170 Oilers/Flames Action .01 .05
171 Blues/Red Wings Action .01 .05
172 Oilers/Red Wings Action LH .01 .05
173 Oilers/Red Wings Action RH .01 .05
174 Oilers Celebrate .01 .05
175 Oilers/Bruins Action .01 .05
176 Stanley Cup (top half) .02 .10
177 Stanley Cup (bottom half) .02 .10
178 Wayne Gretzky 1.00 2.50
178 Bruins Action .01 .05
179 Oilers/Bruins Action RH .01 .05
180 Oilers/Bruins Action .01 .05
181 Wayne Gretzky 1.00 2.50
182 Conn Smythe Trophy .01 .05
183 Oilers Celebrate UL .01 .05
184 Oilers Celebrate UR .01 .05
185 Oilers Celebrate LL .01 .05
186 Oilers Celebrate LR .01 .05
187 Flames Action .01 .05
188 Grant Fuhr .20 .50
189 Devils Action .01 .05
190 Marcel Dionne .20 .50
191 Cam Neely .20 .50
192 Capitals Action .01 .05
193 Wayne Gretzky 1.00 2.50
194 Jets/Bruins Action .01 .05
195 Bruins/Canadiens Action .01 .05
196 Blues Action .01 .05
197 Caps/Flyers Action .01 .05
198 Islanders Action .01 .05
199 Flames Action .01 .05
200 Penguins Action .01 .05
201 Bruins Emblem .01 .05
202 Bruins Uniform .01 .05
203 Rejean Lemelin .02 .10
204 Ray Bourque .20 .50
205 Gord Kluzak .01 .05
206 Michael Thelven .01 .05
207 Glen Wesley .01 .05
208 Randy Burridge .01 .05
209 Keith Crowder .01 .05
210 Steve Kasper .01 .05
211 Ken Linseman .01 .05
212 Jay Miller .01 .05
214 Bob Sweeney .01 .05
215 Bruins Team LH .01 .05
216 Bruins Team RH .01 .05
217 Sabres Emblem .01 .05
218 Sabres Uniform .01 .05
219 Tom Barrasso .02 .10
220 Phil Housley .01 .05
221 Calle Johansson .01 .05
222 Mike Ramsey .01 .05
223 Dave Andreychuk .02 .10
224 Scott Arniel .01 .05
225 Adam Creighton .01 .05
226 Mike Foligno .01 .05
227 Christian Ruuttu .01 .05
228 Ray Sheppard .20 .50
229 John Tucker .01 .05
230 Pierre Turgeon .20 .50
231 Sabres Team LH .01 .05
232 Sabres Team RH .01 .05
233 Whalers Emblem .01 .05
234 Whalers Uniform .01 .05
235 Mike Liut .02 .10
236 Dave Babych .01 .05
237 Sylvain Cote .01 .05
238 Ulf Samuelsson .01 .05
239 John Anderson .01 .05
240 Kevin Dineen .01 .05
241 Ray Ferraro .01 .05
242 Ron Francis .02 .10
243 Paul MacDermid .01 .05
244 Dave Tippett .01 .05
245 Sylvain Turgeon .01 .05
246 Carey Wilson .01 .05
247 Whalers Team LH .01 .05
248 Whalers Team RH .01 .05
249 Canadiens Emblem .01 .05
250 Canadiens Uniform .01 .05
251 Brian Hayward .02 .10
252 Patrick Roy .75 2.00
253 Chris Chelios .20 .50
254 Craig Ludwig .01 .05
255 Petr Svoboda .01 .05
256 Guy Carbonneau .02 .10
257 Claude Lemieux .20 .50
258 Mike McPhee .01 .05
259 Mats Naslund .01 .05
260 Stephane Richer .02 .10
261 Bobby Smith .01 .05
262 Ryan Walter .01 .05
263 Canadiens Team LH .01 .05
264 Canadiens Team RH .01 .05
265 Devils Emblem .01 .05
266 Devils Uniform .01 .05
267 Sean Burke .20 .50
268 Joe Cirella .01 .05
269 Bruce Driver .01 .05
270 Craig Wolanin .01 .05
271 Aaron Broten .01 .05
272 Doug Brown .01 .05
273 Claude Loiselle .01 .05
274 John MacLean .01 .05
275 Kirk Muller .02 .10
276 Brendan Shanahan .20 .50
277 Patrik Sundstrom .01 .05
278 Pat Verbeek .01 .05
279 Devils Team LH .01 .05
280 Devils Team RH .01 .05
281 Islanders Emblem .01 .05
282 Islanders Uniform .01 .05
283 Kelly Hrudey .02 .10
284 Steve Konroyd .01 .05
285 Ken Morrow .01 .05
286 Pat Flatley .01 .05
287 Greg Gilbert .01 .05
288 Alan Kerr .01 .05
289 Derek King .01 .05
290 Pat LaFontaine .20 .50
291 Mikko Makela .01 .05
292 Brent Sutter .01 .05
293 Bryan Trottier .02 .10
294 Randy Wood .01 .05
295 Islanders Team .01 .05
296 Islanders Team .01 .05
297 Rangers Emblem .01 .05
298 Rangers Uniform .01 .05
299 Bob Froese .02 .10
300 John Vanbiesbrouck .20 .50
301 Brian Leetch .20 .50
302 Norm Maciver .01 .05
303 James Patrick .01 .05
304 Michel Petit .01 .05
305 Ulf Dahlen .01 .05
306 Jan Erixon .01 .05
307 Kelly Kisio .01 .05
308 Don Maloney .01 .05
309 Walt Poddubny .01 .05
310 Tomas Sandstrom .01 .05
311 Rangers Team LH .01 .05
312 Rangers Team RH .01 .05
313 Flyers Emblem .01 .05
314 Flyers Uniform .01 .05
315 Ron Hextall .02 .10
316 Mark Howe .01 .05
317 Kerry Huffman .01 .05
318 Kjell Samuelsson .01 .05
319 Dave Brown .01 .05
320 Murray Craven .01 .05
321 Tim Kerr .01 .05
322 Scott Mellanby .02 .10
323 Dave Poulin .01 .05
324 Brian Propp .01 .05
325 Ilkka Sinisalo .01 .05
326 Rick Tocchet .02 .10
327 Flyers Team LH .01 .05
328 Flyers Team RH .01 .05
329 Penguins Emblem .01 .05
330 Penguins Uniform .01 .05
331 Frank Pietrangelo .02 .10
332 Doug Bodger .01 .05
333 Paul Coffey .20 .50
334 Jim Johnson .01 .05
335 Ville Siren .01 .05
336 Rob Brown .01 .05
337 Randy Cunneyworth .01 .05
338 Dan Frawley .01 .05
339 Dave Hunter .01 .05
340 Mario Lemieux .75 2.00
341 Troy Loney .01 .05
342 Dan Quinn .01 .05
343 Penguins Team LH .01 .05
344 Penguins Team RH .01 .05
345 Nordiques Emblem .01 .05
346 Nordiques Uniform .01 .05
347 Mario Gosselin .02 .10
348 Tommy Albelin .01 .05
349 Jeff Brown .01 .05
350 Steven Finn .01 .05
351 Randy Moller .01 .05
352 Alain Cote .01 .05
353 Gaetan Duchesne .01 .05
354 Mike Eagles .01 .05
355 Michel Goulet .02 .10
356 Lane Lambert .01 .05
357 Anton Stastny .01 .05
358 Peter Stastny .02 .10
359 Nordiques Team LH .01 .05
360 Nordiques Team RH .01 .05
361 Capitals Emblem .01 .05
362 Capitals Uniform .01 .05
363 Clint Malarchuk .02 .10
364 Pete Peeters .02 .10
365 Kevin Hatcher .02 .10
366 Rod Langway .01 .05
367 Larry Murphy .02 .10
368 Scott Stevens .02 .10
369 Dave Christian .01 .05
370 Mike Gartner .20 .50
371 Bengt Gustafsson .01 .05
372 Dale Hunter .01 .05
373 Kelly Miller .01 .05
374 Mike Ridley .01 .05
375 Capitals Team LH .01 .05
376 Capitals Team RH .01 .05
377 Hockey Rink Schematic .01 .05
378 Hockey Rink Schematic .01 .05
379 Cross-checking .01 .05
380 Elbowing .01 .05
381 High-sticking .01 .05
382 Holding .01 .05
383 Hooking .01 .05
384 Interference .01 .05
385 Spearing .01 .05
386 Tripping .01 .05
387 Boarding .01 .05
388 Charging .01 .05
389 Delayed Calling of Penalty .01 .05
390 Kneeing .01 .05
391 Misconduct .01 .05
392 Roughing .01 .05
393 Slashing .01 .05
394 Unsportsmanlike Conduct .01 .05
395 Wash-out .01 .05
396 Icing .01 .05
397 Off-side .01 .05
398 Wash-out .01 .05
399 Bill Masterton Memorial Trophy Bob Bourne .01 .05
400 Hart Memorial Trophy Mario Lemieux .20 .50
401 Art Ross Trophy Mario Lemeiux .20 .50
402 William M. Jennings Trophy Brian Hayward and Patrick Roy .20 .50
403 Vezina Trophy Grant Fuhr .02 .10
404 Calder Memorial Trophy Joe Nieuwendyk .02 .10
405 James Norris Memorial Trophy Ray Bourque .20 .50
406 Lady Byng Trophy Mats Naslund .02 .10
407 Frank J. Selke Trophy Guy Carbonneau .02 .10
408 Emery Edge Award Brad McCrimmon .02 .10
xx Sticker Album 2.00 5.00

1989-90 Panini Stickers

This set of 384 hockey stickers was produced and distributed by Panini. The stickers are numbered on the back and measure 1 7/8" by 3". The stickers display color action shots of players, teams, arenas, and logos. Some team pictures consist of two stickers, each showing half of the photo, in the checklist below these halves are denoted by LH (left half) and RH (right half), and in the case of a four sticker picture, note the additional prefixes U (upper) and L (lower). A 52-page, full-color glossy album was issued with the set for holding the stickers. The album includes player information and statistics in English and French.

COMPLETE SET (384) 10.00 25.00
1 NHL Logo .01 .05
2 Playoff schedule .01 .05
3 Flames/Blackhawks action .01 .05
4 Flames/Canucks action .01 .05
5 Kings/Oilers action .01 .05
6 Vernon goal LH .01 .05
7 Vernon goal RH .01 .05
8 Bruins/Sabres action .01 .05
9 Canadiens/Bruins action .01 .05
10 Flyers score .01 .05
11 Canadiens/Flyers action LH .01 .05
12 Canadiens/Flyers action RH .01 .05
13 Canadiens/Flames action .01 .05
14 Canadiens celebration .01 .05
15 Canadiens/Flames action .01 .05
16 Canadiens/Flames action .01 .05
17 Flames celebration .01 .05
18 Flames/Canadiens action LH .01 .05
19 Flames/Canadiens action RH .01 .05
20 Al MacInnis Conn Smythe Trophy .02 .10
21 Stanley Cup/Flames UL .02 .10
22 Stanley Cup/Flames UR .02 .10
23 Stanley Cup/Flames LL .02 .10
24 Stanley Cup/Flames LR .02 .10
25 Stanley Cup .02 .10
26 Calgary Flames logo .01 .05
27 Joe Mullen .02 .10
28 Doug Gilmour .20 .50
29 Joe Nieuwendyk .02 .10
30 Gary Suter .02 .10
31 Flames team .01 .05
32 Al MacInnis .02 .10
33 Brad McCrimmon .01 .05
34 Mike Vernon .02 .10
35 Gary Roberts .02 .10
36 Colin Patterson .01 .05
37 Jim Peplinski .01 .05
38 Jamie Macoun .01 .05
39 Lanny McDonald .02 .10
40 Saddledome .01 .05
41 Chicago Blackhawks logo .01 .05
42 Darren Pang .02 .10
43 Steve Larmer .02 .10
44 Dirk Graham .01 .05
45 Doug Wilson .01 .05
46 Blackhawks/Oilers action (Ed Belfour shown) .01 .05
47 Dave Manson .01 .05
48 Troy Murray .01 .05
49 Denis Savard .02 .10
50 Steve Thomas .01 .05
51 Adam Creighton .01 .05
52 Wayne Presley .01 .05
53 Trent Yawney .01 .05
54 Alain Chevrier .01 .05
55 Chicago Stadium .01 .05
56 Detroit Red Wings logo .01 .05
57 Steve Yzerman .50 1.25
58 Gerard Gallant .01 .05
59 Greg Stefan .02 .10
60 Dave Barr .01 .05
61 Red Wings team .01 .05
62 Steve Chiasson .01 .05
63 Shawn Burr .01 .05
64 Rick Zombo .01 .05
65 Glen Hanlon .02 .10
66 Jeff Sharples .01 .05
67 Joey Kocur .01 .05
68 Lee Norwood .01 .05
69 Mike O'Connell .01 .05
70 Joe Louis Arena .01 .05
71 Edmonton Oilers logo .01 .05
72 Jimmy Carson .01 .05
73 Jari Kurri .20 .50
74 Mark Messier .20 .50
75 Craig Simpson .01 .05
76 Oilers/Flyers action .01 .05
77 Glenn Anderson .02 .10
78 Craig MacTavish .01 .05
79 Kevin Lowe .02 .10
80 Craig Muni .01 .05
81 Bill Ranford .02 .10
82 Charlie Huddy .01 .05
83 Steve Smith .01 .05
84 Normand Lacombe .01 .05
85 Northlands Coliseum .01 .05
86 L.A. Kings logo .01 .05
87 Wayne Gretzky 1.00 2.50
88 Bernie Nicholls .02 .10
89 Kelly Hrudey .02 .10
90 John Tonelli .01 .05
91 Oilers/Kings action .01 .05
92 Steve Kasper .01 .05
93 Steve Duchesne .01 .05
94 Mike Krushelnyski .01 .05
95 Luc Robitaille .20 .50
96 Ron Duguay .01 .05
97 Glenn Healy .02 .10
98 Dave Taylor .01 .05
99 Marty McSorley .01 .05
100 The Great Western Forum .01 .05
101 Minnesota North Stars logo .01 .05
102 Kari Takko .02 .10
103 Dave Gagner .01 .05
104 Mike Gartner .20 .50
105 Brian Bellows .01 .05
106 North Stars team .01 .05
107 Neal Broten .01 .05
108 Larry Murphy .02 .10
109 Basil McRae .01 .05
110 Perry Berezan .01 .05
111 Shane Chambers .01 .05
112 Curt Giles .01 .05
113 Stewart Gavin .01 .05
114 Jon Casey .02 .10
115 Metropolitan Sports Center .01 .05
116 St. Louis Blues logo .01 .05
117 Brett Hull .20 .50
118 Peter Zezel .01 .05
119 Tony Hrkac .01 .05
120 Vincent Riendeau .02 .10
121 Blues/Islanders action .01 .05
122 Cliff Ronning .01 .05
123 Gino Cavallini .01 .05
124 Brian Benning .01 .05
125 Rick Meagher .01 .05
126 Steve Tuttle .01 .05
127 Paul Cavallini .01 .05
128 Tom Tilley .01 .05
129 Greg Millen .02 .10
130 St. Louis Arena .01 .05
131 Toronto Maple Leafs logo .01 .05
132 Ed Olczyk .01 .05
133 Gary Leeman .01 .05
134 Vincent Damphousse .02 .10
135 Tom Fergus .01 .05
136 Maple Leafs action .01 .05
137 Daniel Marois .01 .05
138 Mark Osborne .01 .05
139 Allan Bester .02 .10
140 Al Iafrate .01 .05
141 Brad Marsh .01 .05
142 Luke Richardson .01 .05
143 Todd Gill .01 .05
144 Wendel Clark .02 .10
145 Maple Leafs Gardens .01 .05
146 Vancouver Canucks logo .01 .05
147 Petri Skriko .01 .05
148 Trevor Linden .02 .10
149 Tony Tanti .01 .05
150 Steve Weeks .01 .05
151 Canucks/Islanders action .01 .05
152 Brian Bradley .01 .05
153 Barry Pederson .01 .05
154 Greg Adams .01 .05
155 Kirk McLean .02 .10
156 Jim Sandlak .01 .05
157 Rich Sutter .01 .05
158 Garth Butcher .01 .05
159 Stan Smyl .01 .05
160 Pacific Coliseum .01 .05
161 Winnipeg Jets logo .01 .05
162 Dale Hawerchuk .02 .10
163 Thomas Steen .01 .05
164 Brent Ashton .01 .05
165 Pat Elynuik .01 .05
166 Jets/Islanders action .01 .05
167 Dave Ellett .01 .05
168 Randy Carlyle .01 .05
169 Laurie Boschman .01 .05
170 Iain Duncan .01 .05
171 Doug Smail .01 .05
172 Teppo Numminen .01 .05
173 Bob Essensa .02 .10
174 Peter Taglianetti .01 .05
175 Winnipeg Arena .01 .05
176 Steve Duchesne AS .01 .05
177 Luc Robitaille AS .02 .10
178 Mike Vernon AS .02 .10
179 Wayne Gretzky AS .50 1.25
180 Kevin Lowe AS .02 .10
181 Jari Kurri AS .20 .50
182 Cam Neely AS .20 .50
183 Paul Coffey AS .20 .50
184 Mario Lemieux AS .40 1.00
185 Sean Burke AS .02 .10
186 Rob Brown AS .01 .05
187 Ray Bourque AS .20 .50
188 Boston Bruins logo .01 .05
189 Greg Hawgood .01 .05
190 Ken Linseman .01 .05
191 Andy Moog .02 .10
192 Cam Neely .20 .50
193 Bruins/Flyers action .01 .05
194 Andy Brickley .01 .05
195 Rejean Lemelin .02 .10
196 Bob Carpenter .01 .05
197 Randy Burridge .01 .05
198 Craig Janney .01 .05
199 Bob Joyce .01 .05
200 Glen Wesley .01 .05
201 Ray Bourque .20 .50
202 Boston Garden .01 .05
203 Buffalo Sabres logo .01 .05
204 Pierre Turgeon .02 .10
205 Phil Housley .01 .05
206 Rick Vaive .01 .05
207 Christian Ruuttu .01 .05
208 Flyers/Sabres action .01 .05
209 Doug Bodger .01 .05
210 Mike Foligno .01 .05
211 Ray Sheppard .01 .05
212 John Tucker .01 .05
213 Scott Arniel .01 .05
214 Daren Puppa .02 .10
215 Dave Andreychuk .02 .10
216 Uwe Krupp .01 .05
217 Memorial Auditorium .01 .05
218 Hartford Whalers logo .01 .05
219 Kevin Dineen .01 .05
220 Peter Sidorkiewicz .02 .10
221 Ron Francis .02 .10
222 Ray Ferraro .01 .05
223 Islanders/Whalers action .01 .05
224 Scott Young .01 .05
225 Dave Babych .01 .05
226 Dave Tippett .01 .05
227 Paul MacDermid .01 .05
228 Ulf Samuelsson .01 .05
229 Sylvain Cote .01 .05
230 Jody Hull .01 .05
231 Don Maloney .01 .05
232 Hartford Civic Center .01 .05
233 Montreal Canadiens logo .01 .05
234 Mats Naslund .01 .05
235 Patrick Roy .75 2.00
236 Bobby Smith .01 .05
237 Chris Chelios .20 .50
238 Flames/Canadiens action .01 .05
239 Stephane Richer .02 .10
240 Claude Lemieux .02 .10
241 Guy Carbonneau .02 .10
242 Shayne Corson .01 .05
243 Mike McPhee .01 .05
244 Petr Svoboda .01 .05
245 Larry Robinson .01 .05
246 Brian Hayward .01 .05
247 Montreal Forum .01 .05
248 New Jersey Devils logo .01 .05
249 John MacLean .01 .05
250 Patrik Sundstrom .01 .05
251 Kirk Muller .02 .10
252 Tom Kurvers .01 .05
253 Bruins/Devils action .01 .05
254 Aaron Broten .01 .05
255 Brendan Shanahan .20 .50
256 Sean Burke .02 .10
257 Tommy Albelin .01 .05
258 Ken Daneyko .01 .05
259 Randy Velischek .01 .05
260 Mark Johnson .01 .05
261 Jim Korn .01 .05
262 Brendan Byrne Arena .01 .05
263 New York Islanders logo .01 .05
264 Pat LaFontaine .02 .10
265 Mark Fitzpatrick .02 .10
266 Brent Sutter .01 .05
267 David Volek .01 .05
268 Islanders/Rangers action .01 .05
269 Bryan Trottier .02 .10
270 Mikko Makela .01 .05
271 Derek King .01 .05
272 Pat Flatley .01 .05
273 Jeff Norton .01 .05
274 Gerald Diduck .01 .05
275 Alan Kerr .01 .05
276 Jeff Hackett .02 .10
277 Nassau Veterans Memorial Coliseum .01 .05
278 New York Rangers logo .01 .05
279 Brian Leetch .20 .50
280 Carey Wilson .01 .05
281 Tomas Sandstrom .01 .05
282 John Vanbiesbrouck .20 .50
283 Oilers/Rangers action .01 .05
284 Bob Froese .02 .10
285 Tony Granato .01 .05
286 Brian Mullen .01 .05
287 Kelly Kisio .01 .05
288 Ulf Dahlen .01 .05
289 James Patrick .01 .05
290 John Ogrodnick .01 .05
291 Michel Petit .01 .05
292 Madison Square Garden .01 .05
293 Philadelphia Flyers logo .01 .05
294 Tim Kerr .01 .05
295 Rick Tocchet .02 .10
296 Pelle Eklund .01 .05
297 Terry Carkner .01 .05
298 Flyers/Canadiens action .01 .05
299 Ron Sutter .01 .05
300 Mark Howe .01 .05
301 Keith Acton .01 .05
302 Ron Hextall .02 .10
303 Gord Murphy .01 .05
304 Derrick Smith .01 .05
305 Dave Poulin .01 .05
306 Brian Propp .01 .05
307 The Spectrum .01 .05
308 Pittsburgh Penguins logo .01 .05
309 Mario Lemieux .75 2.00
310 Rob Brown .01 .05
311 Paul Coffey .20 .50
312 Tom Barrasso .02 .10
313 Penguins/Flyers action .01 .05
314 Dan Quinn .01 .05
315 Bob Errey .01 .05
316 John Cullen .01 .05
317 Phil Bourque .01 .05
318 Zarley Zalapski .01 .05
319 Troy Loney .01 .05
320 Jim Johnson .01 .05
321 Kevin Stevens .01 .05
322 Civic Arena .01 .05
323 Quebec Nordiques logo .01 .05
324 Peter Stastny .02 .10
325 Jeff Brown .01 .05
326 Michel Goulet .02 .10
327 Joe Sakic .20 .50
328 Flyers/Nordiques action .01 .05
329 Iiro Jarvi .01 .05
330 Paul Gillis .01 .05
331 Randy Moller .01 .05
332 Ron Tugnutt .02 .10
333 Robert Picard .01 .05
334 Curtis Leschyshyn .01 .05
335 Marc Fortier .01 .05
336 Mario Marois .01 .05
337 Le Colisee .01 .05
338 Washington Capitals logo .01 .05
339 Mike Ridley .01 .05
340 Geoff Courtnall .01 .05
341 Scott Stevens .02 .10
342 Dino Ciccarelli .02 .10
343 Capitals/Flames action .01 .05
344 Bob Mason .02 .10
345 Dave Christian .01 .05
346 Dale Hunter .01 .05
347 Kevin Hatcher .02 .10
348 Kelly Miller .01 .05
349 Stephen Leach .01 .05
350 Rod Langway .01 .05
351 Bob Rouse .01 .05
352 Capital Centre .01 .05
353 Calgary Flames logo .01 .05
354 Edmonton Oilers logo .01 .05
355 Winnipeg Jets logo .01 .05
356 Toronto Maple Leafs logo .01 .05
357 Buffalo Sabres logo .01 .05
358 Montreal Canadiens logo .01 .05
359 Quebec Nordiques logo .01 .05
360 New Jersey Devils logo .01 .05
361 Boston Bruins logo .01 .05
362 Hartford Whalers logo .01 .05
363 Vancouver Canucks logo .01 .05
364 Minnesota North Stars logo .01 .05
365 Los Angeles Kings logo .01 .05
366 St. Louis Blues logo .01 .05
367 Chicago Blackhawks logo .01 .05
368 Detroit Red Wings logo .01 .05
369 Pittsburgh Penguins logo .01 .05
370 Washington Capitals logo .01 .05
371 Philadelphia Flyers logo .01 .05
372 New York Rangers logo .01 .05
373 New York Islanders logo .01 .05
374 Wayne Gretzky 1.00 2.50
375 Mario Lemieux .75 2.00
376 Patrick Roy and Brian Hayward .30 .75
377 Tim Kerr .01 .05
378 Brian Leetch .20 .50
379 Chris Chelios .20 .50
380 Joe Mullen .02 .10
381 Guy Carbonneau .02 .10
382 Bryan Trottier .02 .10
383 Patrick Roy .75 2.00
384 Joe Mullen .02 .10
xx Sticker Album 1.00 2.50

1990-91 Panini Stickers

This set of 351 hockey stickers was produced and distributed by Panini. The stickers are numbered on the back and measure approximately 2 1/16" by 2 15/16". The fronts feature full color action photos of the players. Different color triangles (in one of the team's colors) overlay the upper left corner of the pictures, with the team name in white lettering. A variegated stripe appears below the player photos, with the player's name below. The team logo and conference stickers are in foil. The stickers are arranged according to alphabetical team order.

COMPLETE SET (351) 8.00 20.00
1 Prince of Wales Conference .01 .05
2 Clarence Campbell Conference .01 .05
3 Stanley Cup .02 .10
4 Dave Poulin .01 .05
5 Brian Propp .01 .05
6 Glen Wesley .01 .05
7 Bob Carpenter .01 .05
8 John Carter .01 .05
9 Cam Neely .20 .50
10 Greg Hawgood .01 .05
11 Andy Moog .02 .10
12 Boston Bruins logo .01 .05
13 Rejean Lemelin .02 .10
14 Craig Janney .01 .05
15 Bob Sweeney .01 .05
16 Andy Brickley .01 .05
17 Ray Bourque .20 .50
18 Dave Christian .01 .05
19 Dave Snuggerud .01 .05
20 Christian Ruuttu .01 .05
21 Phil Housley .01 .05
22 Uwe Krupp .01 .05
23 Rick Vaive .01 .05
24 Mike Ramsey .01 .05
25 Mike Foligno .01 .05
26 Clint Malarchuk .02 .10
27 Buffalo Sabres logo .01 .05
28 Pierre Turgeon .02 .10
29 Dave Andreychuk .02 .10
30 Scott Arniel .01 .05
31 Daren Puppa .02 .10
32 Mike Hartman .01 .05
33 Doug Bodger .01 .05
34 Scott Young .01 .05
35 Todd Krygier .01 .05
36 Pat Verbeek .01 .05
37 Dave Tippett .01 .05
38 Peter Sidorkiewicz .02 .10
39 Ron Francis .02 .10
40 Dave Babych .01 .05
41 Randy Ladouceur .01 .05
42 Hartford Whalers logo .01 .05
43 Kevin Dineen .01 .05
44 Dean Evason .01 .05
45 Ray Ferraro .01 .05

46 Mike Tomlak .01 .05
47 Mikael Andersson .01 .05
48 Brad Shaw .01 .05
49 Chris Chelios .20 .50
50 Petr Svoboda .01 .05
51 Patrick Roy .60 1.50
52 Bobby Smith .01 .05
53 Stephane Richer .02 .10
54 Shayne Corson .01 .05
55 Brian Skrudland .01 .05
56 Russ Courtnall .01 .05
57 Montreal Canadiens logo .01 .05
58 Guy Carbonneau .02 .10
59 Sylvain Lefebvre .01 .05
60 Mathieu Schneider .01 .05
61 Brian Hayward .02 .10
62 Mats Naslund .01 .05
63 Mike McPhee .01 .05
64 Brendan Shanahan .20 .50
65 Patrik Sundstrom .01 .05
66 Mark Johnson .01 .05
67 Doug Brown .01 .05
68 Chris Terreri .02 .10
69 Bruce Driver .01 .05
70 Peter Stastny .02 .10
71 Sylvain Turgeon .01 .05
72 New Jersey Devils logo .01 .05
73 Kirk Muller .02 .10
74 John MacLean .01 .05
75 Slava Fetisov .01 .05
76 Tommy Albelin .01 .05
77 Sean Burke .02 .10
78 Janne Ojanen .01 .05
79 Randy Wood .01 .05
80 Gary Nylund .01 .05
81 Pat LaFontaine .20 .50
82 Pat Flatley .01 .05
83 Bryan Trottier .02 .10
84 Don Maloney .01 .05
85 Gerald Diduck .01 .05
86 Mark Fitzpatrick .02 .10
87 New York Islanders logo .01 .05
88 Glenn Healy .02 .10
89 Alan Kerr .01 .05
90 Brent Sutter .01 .05
91 Doug Crossman .01 .05
92 Hubie McDonough .01 .05
93 Jeff Norton .01 .05
94 Kelly Kisio .01 .05
95 Brian Leetch .20 .50
96 Brian Mullen .01 .05
97 James Patrick .01 .05
98 Mike Richter .02 .10
99 John Ogrodnick .01 .05
100 Troy Mallette .01 .05
101 Mark Janssens .01 .05
102 New York Rangers logo .01 .05
103 Mike Gartner .20 .50
104 Jan Erixon .01 .05
105 Carey Wilson .01 .05
106 Bernie Nicholls .02 .10
107 Darren Turcotte .02 .10
108 John Vanbiesbrouck .20 .50
109 Ron Sutter .01 .05
110 Kjell Samuelsson .01 .05
111 Ken Linseman .01 .05
112 Ken Wregget .02 .10
113 Pelle Eklund .01 .05
114 Terry Carkner .01 .05
115 Gord Murphy .01 .05
116 Murray Craven .01 .05
117 Philadelphia Flyers logo .01 .05
118 Ron Hextall .02 .10
119 Mike Bullard .01 .05
120 Tim Kerr .01 .05
121 Rick Tocchet .02 .10
122 Mark Howe .01 .05
123 Ilkka Sinisalo .01 .05
124 Tony Tanti .01 .05
125 John Cullen .01 .05
126 Zarley Zalapski .01 .05
127 Wendell Young .02 .10
128 Rob Brown .01 .05
129 Phil Bourque .01 .05
130 Mark Recchi .20 .50
131 Kevin Stevens .01 .05
132 Pittsburgh Penguins logo .01 .05
133 Bob Errey .01 .05
134 Tom Barrasso .02 .10
135 Paul Coffey .20 .50
136 Mario Lemieux .60 1.50
137 Randy Hillier .01 .05
138 Troy Loney .01 .05
139 Joe Sakic .20 .50
140 Lucien DeBlois .01 .05
141 Joe Cirella .01 .05
142 Ron Tugnutt .02 .10
143 Paul Gillis .01 .05
144 Bryan Fogarty .01 .05
145 Guy Lafleur .02 .10
146 Tony Hrkac .01 .05
147 Quebec Nordiques logo .01 .05
148 Michel Petit .01 .05
149 Tony McKegney .01 .05
150 Curtis Leschyshyn .01 .05
151 Claude Loiselle .01 .05
152 Mario Brunetta .01 .05
153 Marc Fortier .01 .05
154 Michal Pivonka .01 .05
155 Scott Stevens .02 .10
156 Kelly Miller .01 .05
157 John Tucker .01 .05
158 Don Beaupre .02 .10
159 Geoff Courtnall .01 .05
160 Alan May .01 .05
161 Dino Ciccarelli .02 .10
162 Washington Capitals logo .01 .05
163 Mike Ridley .01 .05
164 Bob Rouse .01 .05
165 Mike Liut .02 .10
166 Stephen Leach .01 .05
167 Kevin Hatcher .02 .10
168 Dale Hunter .01 .05
169 Prince of Wales Trophy .01 .05
170 Clarence Campbell Trophy .01 .05
171 Stanley Cup Championship .02 .10
172 Doug Gilmour .20 .50
173 Brad McCrimmon .01 .05
174 Joe Nieuwendyk .02 .10
175 Mike Vernon .02 .10
176 Theo Fleury .20 .50
177 Gary Suter .02 .10
178 Jamie Macoun .01 .05
179 Gary Roberts .02 .10
180 Calgary Flames logo .01 .05
181 Paul Ranheim .01 .05
182 Jiri Hrdina .01 .05
183 Joe Mullen .02 .10
184 Sergei Makarov .01 .05
185 Al MacInnis .02 .10
186 Rick Wamsley .02 .10
187 Trent Yawney .01 .05
188 Greg Millen .02 .10
189 Doug Wilson .02 .10
190 Jocelyn Lemieux .01 .05
191 Dirk Graham .01 .05
192 Keith Brown .01 .05
193 Adam Creighton .01 .05
194 Steve Larmer .02 .10
195 Chicago Blackhawks logo .01 .05
196 Greg Gilbert .01 .05
197 Jacques Cloutier .02 .10
198 Denis Savard .02 .10
199 Dave Manson .01 .05
200 Troy Murray .01 .05
201 Jeremy Roenick .20 .50
202 Lee Norwood .01 .05
203 Glen Hanlon .02 .10
204 Marc Habscheid .01 .05
205 Gerard Gallant .01 .05
206 Rick Zombo .01 .05
207 Steve Chiasson .01 .05
208 Steve Yzerman .40 1.00
209 Bernie Federko .01 .05
210 Detroit Red Wings logo .01 .05
211 Joey Kocur .01 .05
212 Tim Cheveldae .02 .10
213 Shawn Burr .01 .05
214 Jimmy Carson .01 .05
215 Mike O'Connell .01 .05
216 John Chabot .01 .05
217 Craig Muni .01 .05
218 Bill Ranford .02 .10
219 Mark Messier .20 .50
220 Craig MacTavish .01 .05
221 Charlie Huddy .01 .05
222 Jari Kurri .20 .50
223 Esa Tikkanen .02 .10
224 Kevin Lowe .02 .10
225 Edmonton Oilers logo .01 .05
226 Steve Smith .01 .05
227 Glenn Anderson .02 .10
228 Petr Klima .01 .05
229 Craig Simpson .01 .05
230 Grant Fuhr .20 .50
231 Randy Gregg .01 .05
232 Bob Kudelski .01 .05
233 Luc Robitaille .02 .10
234 Marty McSorley .01 .05
235 John Tonelli .01 .05
236 Dave Taylor .01 .05
237 Mikko Makela .01 .05
238 Steve Kasper .01 .05
239 Tony Granato .01 .05
240 Los Angeles Kings logo .01 .05
241 Steve Duchesne .01 .05
242 Wayne Gretzky .75 2.00
243 Tomas Sandstrom .01 .05
244 Larry Robinson .02 .10
245 Mike Krushelnyski .01 .05
246 Kelly Hrudey .02 .10
247 Aaron Broten .01 .05
248 Dave Gagner .01 .05
249 Basil McRae .01 .05
250 Curt Giles .01 .05
251 Larry Murphy .02 .10
252 Shawn Chambers .01 .05
253 Mike Modano .20 .50
254 Jon Casey .02 .10
255 Minnesota North Stars logo .01 .05
256 Gaetan Duchesne .01 .05
257 Brian Bellows .01 .05
258 Frantisek Musil .01 .05
259 Don Barber .01 .05
260 Stewart Gavin .01 .05
261 Neal Broten .01 .05
262 Brett Hull .20 .50
263 Sergio Momesso .01 .05
264 Peter Zezel .01 .05
265 Gino Cavallini .01 .05
266 Rod Brind'Amour .20 .50
267 Mike Lalor .01 .05
268 Vincent Riendeau .02 .10
269 Gordie Roberts .01 .05
270 St. Louis Blues logo .01 .05
271 Paul MacLean .01 .05
272 Curtis Joseph .20 .50
273 Rick Meagher .01 .05
274 Jeff Brown .01 .05
275 Adam Oates .02 .10
276 Paul Cavallini .01 .05
277 Brad Marsh .01 .05
278 Mark Osborne .01 .05
279 Gary Leeman .01 .05
280 Rob Ramage .01 .05
281 Jeff Reese .02 .10
282 Tom Fergus .01 .05
283 Ed Olczyk .01 .05
284 Daniel Marois .01 .05
285 Toronto Maple Leafs logo .01 .05
286 Wendel Clark .02 .10
287 Tom Kurvers .01 .05
288 Gilles Thibaudeau .01 .05
289 Lou Franceschetti .01 .05
290 Al Iafrate .01 .05
291 Vincent Damphousse .02 .10
292 Stan Smyl .01 .05
293 Paul Reinhart .01 .05
294 Igor Larionov .01 .05
295 Doug Lidster .01 .05
296 Kirk McLean .02 .10
297 Andrew McBain .01 .05
298 Petri Skriko .01 .05
299 Trevor Linden .02 .10
300 Vancouver Canucks logo .01 .05
301 Steve Bozek .01 .05
302 Brian Bradley .01 .05
303 Greg Adams .01 .05
304 Vladimir Krutov .01 .05
305 Dan Quinn .01 .05
306 Jim Sandlak .01 .05
307 Teppo Numminen .01 .05
308 Doug Smail .01 .05
309 Greg Paslawski .01 .05
310 Dave Ellett .01 .05
311 Bob Essensa .02 .10
312 Pat Elynuik .01 .05
313 Paul Fenton .01 .05
314 Randy Carlyle .01 .05
315 Winnipeg Jets logo .01 .05
316 Thomas Steen .01 .05
317 Dale Hawerchuk .02 .10
318 Fredrik Olausson .01 .05
319 Dave McLlwain .01 .05
320 Laurie Boschman .01 .05
321 Brent Ashton .01 .05
322 Ray Bourque .20 .50
323 Patrick Roy .60 1.50
324 Paul Coffey .20 .50
325 Brian Propp .01 .05
326 Mario Lemieux .60 1.50
327 Cam Neely .20 .50
328 Al MacInnis .02 .10
329 Mike Vernon .02 .10
330 Kevin Lowe .02 .10
331 Luc Robitaille .02 .10
332 Wayne Gretzky .75 2.00
333 Brett Hull .20 .50
334 Sergei Makarov .01 .05
335 Alexei Kasatonov .01 .05
336 Igor Larionov .01 .05
337 Vladimir Krutov .01 .05
338 Alexander Mogilny .02 .10
339 Slava Fetisov .01 .05
340 Mike Modano .20 .50
341 Mark Recchi .20 .50
342 Paul Ranheim .01 .05
343 Rod Brind'Amour .01 .05
344 Brad Shaw .01 .05
345 Mike Richter .02 .10
346 Hart Trophy .01 .05
347 Art Ross Trophy .01 .05
348 Calder Memorial Trophy .01 .05
349 Lady Byng Trophy .01 .05
350 Norris Trophy .01 .05
351 Vezina Trophy .01 .05
xx Sticker Album 1.00 2.50

1991-92 Panini Stickers

This set of 344 stickers was produced by Panini. They measure approximately 1 7/8" by 2 7/8" and were to be pasted in a 8 1/4" by 10 1/2" bilingual sticker album. The fronts feature color action shots of the players. Pages 2-5 of the album picture highlights of the 1991 Stanley Cup playoffs and finals. Team pages have team colors that highlight player stickers. The NHL 75th Anniversary logo (3-4) and the circular-shaped team logos (148-169) are foil. The stickers are numbered on the back and checklisted below alphabetically according to team.

COMPLETE SET (344) 8.00 20.00
1 NHL Logo .01 .05
2 NHLPA Logo .01 .05
3 NHL Logo 75th Anniversary (Left) .01 .05
4 NHL Logo 75th Anniversary (Right) .01 .05
5 Clarence Campbell Conference Logo .01 .05
6 Prince of Wales Conference Logo .01 .05
7 Stanley Cup Championship Logo .02 .10
8 Steve Larmer .02 .10
9 Ed Belfour .20 .50
10 Chris Chelios .20 .50
11 Michel Goulet .01 .05
12 Jeremy Roenick .20 .50
13 Adam Creighton .01 .05
14 Steve Thomas .01 .05
15 Dave Manson .01 .05
16 Dirk Graham .01 .05
17 Troy Murray .01 .05
18 Doug Wilson .01 .05
19 Wayne Presley .01 .05
20 Jocelyn Lemieux .01 .05
21 Keith Brown .01 .05
22 Curtis Joseph .20 .50
23 Jeff Brown .01 .05
24 Gino Cavallini .01 .05
25 Brett Hull .20 .50
26 Scott Stevens .02 .10
27 Dan Quinn .01 .05
28 Garth Butcher .01 .05
29 Bob Bassen .01 .05
30 Rod Brind'Amour .01 .05
31 Adam Oates .02 .10
32 Dave Lowry .01 .05
33 Rich Sutter .01 .05
34 Ron Wilson .01 .05
35 Paul Cavallini .01 .05
36 Trevor Linden .02 .10
37 Troy Gamble .01 .05
38 Geoff Courtnall .01 .05
39 Greg Adams .01 .05
40 Doug Lidster .01 .05
41 Dave Capuano .01 .05
42 Igor Larionov .01 .05
43 Tom Kurvers .01 .05
44 Sergio Momesso .01 .05
45 Kirk McLean .02 .10
46 Cliff Ronning .01 .05
47 Robert Kron .01 .05
48 Steve Bozek .01 .05
49 Petr Nedved .02 .10
50 Al MacInnis .02 .10
51 Theo Fleury .20 .50
52 Gary Roberts .02 .10
53 Joe Nieuwendyk .02 .10
54 Paul Ranheim .01 .05
55 Mike Vernon .02 .10
56 Carey Wilson .01 .05
57 Gary Suter .02 .10
58 Sergei Makarov .01 .05
59 Doug Gilmour .20 .50
60 Joel Otto .01 .05
61 Jamie Macoun .01 .05
62 Stephane Matteau .01 .05
63 Robert Reichel .01 .05
64 Ed Olczyk .01 .05
65 Phil Housley .01 .05
66 Pat Elynuik .01 .05
67 Fredrik Olausson .01 .05
68 Thomas Steen .01 .05
69 Paul MacDermid .01 .05
70 Brent Ashton .01 .05
71 Teppo Numminen .01 .05
72 Danton Cole .01 .05
73 Dave McLlwain .01 .05
74 Scott Arniel .01 .05
75 Bob Essensa .02 .10
76 Randy Carlyle .01 .05
77 Mark Osborne .01 .05
78 Wayne Gretzky 1.25 3.00
79 Tomas Sandstrom .01 .05
80 Steve Duchesne .01 .05
81 Kelly Hrudey .02 .10
82 Larry Robinson .02 .10
83 Tony Granato .01 .05
84 Marty McSorley .01 .05
85 Todd Elik .01 .05
86 Rob Blake .02 .10
87 Bob Kudelski .01 .05
88 Steve Kasper .01 .05
89 Dave Taylor .01 .05
90 John Tonelli .01 .05
91 Luc Robitaille .02 .10
92 Vincent Damphousse .02 .10
93 Brian Bradley .01 .05
94 Dave Ellett .01 .05
95 Daniel Marois .01 .05
96 Rob Ramage .01 .05
97 Mike Krushelnyski .01 .05
98 Michel Petit .01 .05
99 Peter Ing .01 .05
100 Lucien DeBlois .01 .05
101 Bob Rouse .01 .05
102 Wendel Clark .02 .10
103 Peter Zezel .01 .05
104 David Reid .01 .05
105 Aaron Broten .01 .05
106 Brian Hayward .02 .10
107 Neal Broten .02 .10
108 Brian Bellows .01 .05
109 Mark Tinordi .01 .05
110 Ulf Dahlen .01 .05
111 Doug Smail .01 .05
112 Dave Gagner .01 .05
113 Bobby Smith .01 .05
114 Brian Glynn .01 .05
115 Brian Propp .01 .05
116 Mike Modano .02 .10
117 Gaetan Duchesne .01 .05
118 Jon Casey .02 .10
119 Basil McRae .01 .05
120 Glenn Anderson .02 .10
121 Steve Smith .01 .05
122 Adam Graves .02 .10
123 Esa Tikkanen .02 .10
124 Mark Messier .20 .50
125 Bill Ranford .02 .10
126 Petr Klima .01 .05
127 Anatoli Semenov .01 .05
128 Martin Gelinas .01 .05
129 Charlie Huddy .01 .05
130 Craig Simpson .01 .05
131 Kevin Lowe .02 .10
132 Craig MacTavish .01 .05
133 Craig Muni .01 .05
134 Steve Yzerman .60 1.50
135 Shawn Burr .01 .05
136 Tim Cheveldae .02 .10
137 Rick Zombo .01 .05
138 Marc Habscheid .01 .05
139 Jimmy Carson .01 .05
140 Brent Fedyk .01 .05
141 Yves Racine .01 .05
142 Gerard Gallant .01 .05
143 Steve Chiasson .01 .05
144 Johan Garpenlov .01 .05
145 Sergei Fedorov .20 .50
146 Bob Probert .02 .10
147 Rick Green .01 .05
148 Chicago Blackhawks Logo .01 .05
149 Detroit Red Wings Logo .01 .05
150 Minnesota North Stars Logo .01 .05
151 St. Louis Blues Logo .01 .05
152 Toronto Maple Leafs Logo .01 .05
153 Calgary Flames Logo .01 .05
154 Edmonton Oilers Logo .01 .05
155 Los Angeles Kings Logo .01 .05
156 San Jose Sharks Logo .01 .05
157 Vancouver Canucks Logo .01 .05
158 Winnipeg Jets Logo .01 .05
159 Boston Bruins Logo .01 .05
160 Buffalo Sabres Logo .01 .05
161 Hartford Whalers Logo .01 .05
162 Montreal Canadiens Logo .01 .05
163 Quebec Nordiques Logo .01 .05
164 New Jersey Devils Logo .01 .05
165 New York Islanders Logo .01 .05
166 New York Rangers Logo .01 .05
167 Philadelphia Flyers Logo .01 .05
168 Pittsburgh Penguins Logo .01 .05
169 Washington Capitals Logo .01 .05
170 Craig Janney .01 .05
171 Ray Bourque .20 .50
172 Rejean Lemelin .02 .10
173 Dave Christian .01 .05
174 Randy Burridge .01 .05
175 Garry Galley .01 .05
176 Cam Neely .20 .50
177 Bob Sweeney .01 .05
178 Ken Hodge Jr. .01 .05
179 Andy Moog .02 .10
180 Don Sweeney .01 .05
181 Bob Carpenter .01 .05
182 Glen Wesley .01 .05
183 Chris Nilan .01 .05
184 Patrick Roy 1.00 2.50
185 Petr Svoboda .01 .05
186 Russ Courtnall .01 .05
187 Denis Savard .02 .10
188 Mike McPhee .01 .05
189 Eric Desjardins .02 .10
190 Mike Keane .01 .05
191 Stephan Lebeau .01 .05
192 J.J. Daigneault .01 .05
193 Stephane Richer .02 .10
194 Brian Skrudland .01 .05
195 Mathieu Schneider .02 .10
196 Shayne Corson .01 .05
197 Guy Carbonneau .02 .10
198 Kevin Hatcher .02 .10
199 Mike Ridley .01 .05
200 John Druce .01 .05
201 Don Beaupre .02 .10
202 Kelly Miller .01 .05
203 Dale Hunter .01 .05
204 Nick Kypreos .01 .05
205 Calle Johansson .01 .05
206 Michal Pivonka .01 .05
207 Dino Ciccarelli .02 .10
208 Al Iafrate .01 .05
209 Rod Langway .01 .05
210 Mikhail Tatarinov .01 .05
211 Stephen Leach .01 .05
212 Sean Burke .02 .10
213 John MacLean .01 .05
214 Lee Norwood .01 .05
215 Laurie Boschman .01 .05
216 Alexei Kasatonov .01 .05
217 Patrik Sundstrom .01 .05
218 Ken Daneyko .01 .05
219 Kirk Muller .02 .10
220 Peter Stastny .02 .10
221 Chris Terreri .02 .10
222 Brendan Shanahan .20 .50
223 Eric Weinrich .01 .05
224 Claude Lemieux .02 .10
225 Bruce Driver .01 .05
226 Tim Kerr .01 .05
227 Ron Hextall .02 .10
228 Pelle Eklund .01 .05
229 Rick Tocchet .02 .10
230 Gord Murphy .01 .05
231 Mike Ricci .01 .05
232 Derrick Smith .01 .05
233 Ron Sutter .01 .05
234 Murray Craven .01 .05
235 Terry Carkner .01 .05
236 Ken Wregget .02 .10
237 Keith Acton .01 .05
238 Scott Mellanby .01 .05
239 Kjell Samuelsson .01 .05
240 Jeff Hackett .02 .10
241 David Volek .01 .05
242 Craig Ludwig .01 .05
243 Pat LaFontaine .20 .50
244 Randy Wood .01 .05
245 Pat Flatley .01 .05
246 Brent Sutter .01 .05
247 Derek King .01 .05
248 Jeff Norton .01 .05
249 Glenn Healy .02 .10
250 Ray Ferraro .01 .05
251 Gary Nylund .01 .05
252 Joe Reekie .01 .05
253 Dave Chyzowski .01 .05
254 Mike Hough .01 .05
255 Mats Sundin .02 .10
256 Curtis Leschyshyn .01 .05
257 Joe Sakic .20 .50
258 Stephane Fiset .02 .10
259 Bryan Fogarty .01 .05
260 Alexei Gusarov .01 .05
261 Steven Finn .01 .05
262 Everett Sanipass .01 .05
263 Stephane Morin .01 .05
264 Craig Wolanin .01 .05
265 Randy Velischek .01 .05
266 Owen Nolan .02 .10
267 Ron Tugnutt .02 .10
268 Mario Lemieux 1.00 2.50
269 Kevin Stevens .01 .05
270 Larry Murphy .02 .10
271 Tom Barrasso .02 .10
272 Phil Bourque .01 .05
273 Scott Young .01 .05
274 Paul Stanton .01 .05
275 Jaromir Jagr .20 .50
276 Paul Coffey .20 .50
277 Ulf Samuelsson .01 .05
278 Joe Mullen .02 .10
279 Bob Errey .01 .05
280 Mark Recchi .02 .10
281 Ron Francis .02 .10
282 John Vanbiesbrouck .20 .50
283 Jan Erixon .01 .05
284 Brian Leetch .20 .50
285 Darren Turcotte .01 .05
286 Ray Sheppard .01 .05
287 James Patrick .01 .05
288 Bernie Nicholls .02 .10
289 Brian Mullen .01 .05
290 Mike Richter .02 .10
291 Kelly Kisio .01 .05
292 Mike Gartner .20 .50
293 John Ogrodnick .01 .05
294 David Shaw .01 .05
295 Troy Mallette .01 .05
296 Dale Hawerchuk .02 .10
297 Rick Vaive .01 .05
298 Daren Puppa .02 .10
299 Mike Ramsey .01 .05
300 Benoit Hogue .01 .05
301 Clint Malarchuk .02 .10
302 Mikko Makela .01 .05
303 Pierre Turgeon .02 .10
304 Alexander Mogilny .02 .10
305 Uwe Krupp .01 .05
306 Christian Ruuttu .01 .05
307 Doug Bodger .01 .05
308 Dave Snuggerud .01 .05
309 Dave Andreychuk .02 .10
310 Peter Sidorkiewicz .02 .10
311 Brad Shaw .01 .05
312 Dean Evason .01 .05
313 Pat Verbeek .02 .10
314 John Cullen .01 .05
315 Rob Brown .01 .05
316 Bobby Holik .01 .05
317 Todd Krygier .01 .05
318 Adam Burt .01 .05
319 Mike Tomlak .01 .05
320 Randy Cunneyworth .01 .05
321 Paul Cyr .01 .05
322 Zarley Zalapski .01 .05
323 Kevin Dineen .02 .10
324 Luc Robitaille .02 .10
325 Brett Hull .20 .50
326 All-Star Game Logo .01 .05
327 Wayne Gretzky 1.25 3.00
328 Mike Vernon .02 .10
329 Chris Chelios .20 .50
330 Al MacInnis .02 .10
331 Rick Tocchet .02 .10
332 Cam Neely .20 .50
333 Patrick Roy 1.00 2.50
334 Joe Sakic .20 .50
335 Ray Bourque .20 .50
336 Paul Coffey .20 .50
337 Ed Belfour .20 .50
338 Mike Ricci .01 .05
339 Rob Blake .02 .10
340 Sergei Fedorov .50 1.25
341 Ken Hodge Jr. .01 .05
342 Bobby Holik .01 .05
343 Robert Reichel .01 .05
344 Jaromir Jagr .20 .50
xx Sticker Album .60 1.50

1992-93 Panini Stickers

This set of 330 stickers was produced by Panini. They measure approximately 2 3/8" by 3 3/8" and were to be pasted in a 9" by 11" album. The fronts have action color player photos with statistics running down the right side in a colored bar. The player's name appears at the top. The team logo is superimposed on the photo at the lower left corner. The backs feature questions and answers that go with the Slap-shot game that is included in the album. The team logos scattered throughout the set are foil. The stickers are numbered on the front on a puck icon at the lower right corner. They are checklisted below alphabetically according to teams in the Campbell and Wales Conferences. Also included are subsets of the 1992 NHL's Top Rookies (270-275), the 1992 All-Star Game (276-289), the European Invasion (290-302), and The Trophies (303-308). Randomly inserted throughout the packs were 22 lettered "Ice-Breaker" stickers, each featuring a star player from each of the 22 NHL teams (minus the new expansion teams, the Tampa Bay Lightning and the Ottawa Senators.

COMPLETE SET (330) 14.00 35.00
*FRENCH: SAME VALUE
1 Stanley Cup .02 .10
2 Blackhawks logo .01 .05
3 Ed Belfour .20 .50
4 Jeremy Roenick .20 .50
5 Steve Larmer .01 .05
6 Michel Goulet .01 .05
7 Dirk Graham .01 .05
8 Jocelyn Lemieux .01 .05
9 Brian Noonan .01 .05
10 Rob Brown .01 .05
11 Chris Chelios .20 .50
12 Steve Smith .01 .05
13 Keith Brown .01 .05
14 St. Louis Blues .01 .05
15 Curtis Joseph .20 .50
16 Brett Hull .30 .75
17 Brendan Shanahan .50 1.25
18 Ron Wilson .01 .05
19 Rich Sutter .01 .05
20 Ron Sutter .01 .05
21 Dave Lowry .01 .05
22 Craig Janney .01 .05
23 Paul Cavallini .01 .05
24 Garth Butcher .01 .05
25 Jeff Brown .01 .05
26 Canucks Logo .01 .05
27 Kirk McLean .02 .10
28 Trevor Linden .02 .10
29 Geoff Courtnall .01 .05
30 Cliff Ronning .01 .05
31 Petr Nedved .02 .10
32 Igor Larionov .01 .05
33 Robert Kron .01 .05
34 Jim Sandlak .01 .05
35 Dave Babych .01 .05
36 Jyrki Lumme .01 .05
37 Doug Lidster .01 .05
38 Flames Logo .01 .05
39 Mike Vernon .02 .10
40 Joe Nieuwendyk .02 .10
41 Gary Leeman .01 .05
42 Robert Reichel .01 .05
43 Joel Otto .01 .05
44 Paul Ranheim .01 .05
45 Gary Roberts .01 .05
46 Theo Fleury .20 .50
47 Sergei Makarov .01 .05
48 Gary Suter .02 .10
49 Al MacInnis .02 .10
50 Jets Logo .01 .05
51 Bob Essensa .02 .10
52 Teppo Numminen .01 .05
53 Thomas Steen .01 .05
54 Pat Elynuik .01 .05
55 Ed Olczyk .01 .05
56 Danton Cole .01 .05
57 Troy Murray .01 .05
58 Darrin Shannon .01 .05
59 Russ Romaniuk .01 .05
60 Fredrik Olausson .01 .05
61 Phil Housley .01 .05
62 Kings Logo .01 .05
63 Kelly Hrudey .02 .10
64 Wayne Gretzky .75 2.00
65 Luc Robitaille .02 .10
66 Jari Kurri .02 .10
67 Tomas Sandstrom .01 .05
68 Tony Granato .01 .05
69 Bob Kudelski .01 .05
70 Corey Millen .01 .05
71 Rob Blake .02 .10
72 Paul Coffey .20 .50
73 Marty McSorley .01 .05
74 Maple Leafs Logo .01 .05
75 Grant Fuhr .02 .10
76 Glenn Anderson .02 .10
77 Doug Gilmour .20 .50
78 Mike Krushelnyski .01 .05
79 Wendel Clark .02 .10
80 Rob Pearson .01 .05
81 Peter Zezel .01 .05
82 Todd Gill .01 .05
83 Dave Ellett .01 .05
84 Mike Foligno .01 .05
85 Ken Baumgartner .01 .05
86 North Stars Logo .01 .05
87 Jon Casey .02 .10
88 Brian Bellows .01 .05
89 Neal Broten .01 .05
90 Dave Gagner .01 .05
91 Mike Modano .30 .75
92 Ulf Dahlen .01 .05
93 Brian Propp .01 .05
94 Jim Johnson .01 .05
95 Mike Craig .01 .05
96 Bobby Smith .01 .05
97 Mark Tinordi .01 .05
98 Oilers Logo .01 .05
99 Bill Ranford .02 .10
100 Joe Murphy .02 .10
101 Craig MacTavish .01 .05
102 Craig Simpson .01 .05
103 Esa Tikkanen .02 .10
104 Vincent Damphousse .02 .10
105 Petr Klima .01 .05
106 Martin Gelinas .01 .05
107 Kevin Lowe .02 .10
108 Dave Manson .01 .05
109 Bernie Nicholls .01 .05
110 Red Wings Logo .01 .05
111 Tim Cheveldae .02 .10
112 Steve Yzerman .75 2.00
113 Sergei Fedorov .50 1.25
114 Jimmy Carson .01 .05
115 Kevin Miller .01 .05
116 Gerard Gallant .01 .05
117 Keith Primeau .01 .05
118 Paul Ysebaert .01 .05
119 Yves Racine .01 .05
120 Steve Chiasson .01 .05
121 Ray Sheppard .01 .05
122 Sharks Logo .01 .05
123 Jeff Hackett .02 .10
124 Kelly Kisio .01 .05
125 Brian Mullen .01 .05
126 David Bruce .01 .05
127 Rob Zettler .01 .05
128 Neil Wilkinson .01 .05
129 Doug Wilson .01 .05
130 Jeff Odgers .01 .05
131 Dean Evason .01 .05
132 Brian Lawton .01 .05
133 Dale Craigwell .01 .05
134 Bruins Logo .01 .05
135 Andy Moog .02 .10
136 Adam Oates .02 .10
137 Dave Poulin .01 .05
138 Vladimir Ruzicka .01 .05

139 Jeff Lazaro .01 .05
140 Bob Carpenter .01 .05
141 Peter Douris .01 .05
142 Glen Murray .01 .05
143 Cam Neely .20 .50
144 Ray Bourque .30 .75
145 Glen Wesley .01 .05
146 Canadiens Logo .01 .05
147 Patrick Roy .60 1.50
148 Kirk Muller .02 .10
149 Guy Carbonneau .02 .10
150 Shayne Corson .01 .05
151 Stephan Lebeau .01 .05
152 Denis Savard .02 .10
153 Brent Gilchrist .01 .05
154 Russ Courtnall .01 .05
155 Patrice Brisebois .01 .05
156 Eric Desjardins .02 .10
157 Matt Schneider .01 .05
158 Capitals Logo .01 .05
159 Don Beaupre .02 .10
160 Dino Ciccarelli .02 .10
161 Michal Pivonka .01 .05
162 Mike Ridley .01 .05
163 Randy Burridge .01 .05
164 Peter Bondra .20 .50
165 Dale Hunter .01 .05
166 Kelly Miller .01 .05
167 Kevin Hatcher .02 .10
168 Al Iafrate .01 .05
169 Rod Langway .01 .05
170 Devils Logo .01 .05
171 Chris Terreri .02 .10
172 Claude Lemieux .02 .10
173 Stephane Richer .02 .10
174 Peter Stastny .02 .10
175 Zdeno Ciger .01 .05
176 Alexander Semak .01 .05
177 Valeri Zelepukin .01 .05
178 Bruce Driver .01 .05
179 Scott Niedermayer .01 .05
180 Alexei Kasatonov .01 .05
181 Scott Stevens .02 .10
182 Flyers Logo .01 .05
183 Dominic Roussel .02 .10
184 Mike Ricci .01 .05
185 Mark Recchi .02 .10
186 Kevin Dineen .01 .05
187 Rod Brind'Amour .01 .05
188 Mark Pederson .01 .05
189 Pelle Eklund .01 .05
190 Terry Carkner .01 .05
191 Mark Howe .01 .05
192 Steve Duchesne .01 .05
193 Andrei Lomakin .01 .05
194 Islanders Logo .01 .05
195 Mark Fitzpatrick .02 .10
196 Pierre Turgeon .02 .10
197 Benoit Hogue .01 .05
198 Ray Ferraro .01 .05
199 Derek King .01 .05
200 David Volek .01 .05
201 Patrick Flatley .01 .05
202 Uwe Krupp .01 .05
203 Steve Thomas .01 .05
204 Adam Creighton .01 .05
205 Jeff Norton .01 .05
206 Nordiques Logo .01 .05
207 Stephane Fiset .02 .10
208 Mikhail Tatarinov .01 .05
209 Joe Sakic .50 1.25
210 Owen Nolan .02 .10
211 Mike Hough .01 .05
212 Mats Sundin .20 .50
213 Claude Lapointe .01 .05
214 Stephane Morin .01 .05
215 Alexei Gusarov .01 .05
216 Steven Finn .01 .05
217 Curtis Leschyshyn .01 .05
218 Penguins Logo .01 .05
219 Tom Barrasso .02 .10
220 Mario Lemieux .60 1.50
221 Kevin Stevens .01 .05
222 Shawn McEachern .01 .05
223 Joe Mullen .02 .10
224 Ron Francis .02 .10
225 Phil Bourque .01 .05
226 Rick Tocchet .02 .10
227 Bryan Trottier .02 .10
228 Larry Murphy .02 .10
229 Ulf Samuelsson .01 .05
230 Rangers Logo .01 .05
231 Mike Richter .20 .50
232 John Vanbiesbrouck .20 .50
233 Mark Messier .30 .75
234 Sergei Nemchinov .01 .05
235 Darren Turcotte .02 .10
236 Doug Weight .02 .10
237 Mike Gartner .02 .10
238 Adam Graves .02 .10
239 Brian Leetch .20 .50
240 James Patrick .01 .05
241 Jan Erixon .01 .05
242 Sabres Logo .01 .05
243 Tom Draper .01 .05
244 Grant Ledyard .01 .05
245 Doug Bodger .01 .05
246 Pat LaFontaine .20 .50
247 Dale Hawerchuk .02 .10
248 Alexander Mogilny .02 .10
249 Dave Andreychuk .02 .10
250 Christian Ruuttu .01 .05
251 Randy Wood .01 .05
252 Brad May .02 .10
253 Mike Ramsey .01 .05
254 Whalers Logo .01 .05
255 Kay Whitmore .01 .05
256 Pat Verbeek .02 .10
257 John Cullen .01 .05
258 Mikael Andersson .01 .05
259 Yvon Corriveau .01 .05
260 Randy Cunneyworth .01 .05
261 Robert Holik .01 .05
262 Murray Craven .01 .05
263 Zarley Zalapski .01 .05
264 Adam Burt .01 .05
265 Brad Shaw .01 .05
266 Lightning Logo .01 .05
267 Lightning Jersey .01 .05
268 Senators Logo .01 .05
269 Senators Jersey .01 .05
270 Tony Amonte .02 .10
271 Pavel Bure .60 1.50
272 Gilbert Dionne .01 .05
273 Pat Falloon .01 .05
274 Nicklas Lidstrom .20 .50
275 Kevin Todd .01 .05
276 Prince of Wales .01 .05
Conference Logo
277 Patrick Roy AS .60 1.50
278 Paul Coffey AS .20 .50
279 Ray Bourque AS .30 .75
280 Mario Lemieux AS .60 1.50
281 Kevin Stevens AS .01 .05
282 Jaromir Jagr AS .75 2.00
283 Clarence Campbell .01 .05
Conference Logo
284 Ed Belfour AS .20 .50
285 Al MacInnis AS .02 .10
286 Chris Chelios AS .20 .50
287 Wayne Gretzky AS .75 2.00
288 Luc Robitaille AS .02 .10
289 Brett Hull AS .20 .50
290 Pavel Bure .60 1.50
291 Sergei Fedorov .50 1.25
292 Dominik Hasek .50 1.25
293 Robert Holik .01 .05
294 Jaromir Jagr .75 2.00
295 Valeri Kamensky .01 .05
296 Alexander Semak .01 .05
297 Igor Kravchuk .01 .05
298 Nicklas Lidstrom .20 .50
299 Alexander Mogilny .02 .10
300 Petr Nedved .02 .10
301 Robert Reichel .01 .05
302 Mats Sundin .20 .50
303 Calder Trophy .01 .05
304 Hart Trophy .01 .05
305 Lady Byng Trophy .01 .05
306 Norris Trophy .01 .05
307 Selke Trophy .01 .05
308 Vezina Trophy .01 .05
A Igor Kravchuk .15 .40
B Nelson Emerson .15 .40
C Pavel Bure 1.50 4.00
D Tomas Forslund .15 .40
E Luciano Borsato .15 .40
F Darryl Sydor .15 .40
G Felix Potvin .20 .50
H Derian Hatcher .15 .40
I Joseph Beranek .15 .40
J Nicklas Lidstrom .20 .50
K Pat Falloon .15 .40
L Joe Juneau .15 .40
M Gilbert Dionne .15 .40
N Dimitri Khristich .15 .40
O Kevin Todd .15 .40
P Eric Lindros 2.00 5.00
Q Scott Lachance .15 .40
R Valeri Kamensky .15 .40
S Jaromir Jagr 2.00 5.00
T Tony Amonte .15 .40
U Donald Audette .15 .40
V Geoff Sanderson .15 .40
xx Sticker Album .60 1.50

1993-94 Panini Stickers

This set of 300 stickers was produced by Panini. They measure approximately 2 3/8" by 3 3/8" and were to be pasted in a 9" by 11" sticker album. The fronts have action color player photos with the player's name and the team name printed to the left side of the photo. The backs promote collecting Panini stickers. Also included are a subset Best of the Best (133-144), and a subset of 24 glitter stickers of Panini's superstars (A-X), one per team. The stickers are numbered on the back. The album also includes players' statistics and a Stanley Cup final review.

COMPLETE SET (300) 10.00 25.00
1 Bruins Logo .01 .05
2 Adam Oates .02 .10
3 Cam Neely .20 .50
4 Dave Poulin .01 .05
5 Steve Leach .01 .05
6 Glen Wesley .01 .05
7 Dmitri Kvartalnov .01 .05
8 Ted Donato .01 .05
9 Andy Moog .02 .10
10 Ray Bourque .40 1.00
11 Don Sweeney .01 .05
12 Canadiens Logo .01 .05
13 Vincent Damphousse .02 .10
14 Kirk Muller .02 .10
15 Brian Bellows .01 .05
16 Stephan Lebeau .01 .05
17 Denis Savard .02 .10
18 Gilbert Dionne .01 .05
19 Guy Carbonneau .02 .10
20 Benoit Brunet .01 .05
21 Eric Desjardins .02 .10
22 Mathieu Schneider .01 .05
23 Capitals Logo .01 .05
24 Peter Bondra .02 .10
25 Mike Ridley .01 .05
26 Dale Hunter .01 .05
27 Michal Pivonka .01 .05
28 Dimitri Khristich .02 .10
29 Pat Elynuik .01 .05
30 Kelly Miller .01 .05
31 Calle Johansson .01 .05
32 Al Iafrate .01 .05
33 Don Beaupre .02 .10
34 Devils Logo .01 .05
35 Claude Lemieux .02 .10
36 Alexander Semak .01 .05
37 Stephane Richer .02 .10
38 Valeri Zelepukin .01 .05
39 Bernie Nicholls .02 .10
40 John MacLean .01 .05
41 Peter Stastny .02 .10
42 Scott Niedermayer .02 .10
43 Scott Stevens .02 .10
44 Bruce Driver .01 .05
45 Flyers Logo .01 .05
46 Mark Recchi .02 .10
47 Rod Brind'Amour .01 .05
48 Brent Fedyk .01 .05
49 Kevin Dineen .01 .05
50 Keith Acton .01 .05
51 Pelle Eklund .01 .05
52 Andrei Lomakin .01 .05
53 Garry Galley .01 .05
54 Terry Carkner .01 .05
55 Tommy Soderstrom .01 .05
56 Islanders Logo .01 .05
57 Steve Thomas .01 .05
58 Derek King .01 .05
59 Benoit Hogue .01 .05
60 Patrick Flatley .01 .05
61 Brian Mullen .01 .05
62 Marty McInnis .01 .05
63 Scott Lachance .01 .05
64 Jeff Norton .01 .05
65 Glenn Healy .02 .10
66 Mark Fitzpatrick .02 .10
67 Nordiques Logo .01 .05
68 Mats Sundin .02 .10
69 Mike Ricci .02 .10
70 Owen Nolan .02 .10
71 Andrei Kovalenko .01 .05
72 Valeri Kamensky .01 .05
73 Scott Young .01 .05
74 Martin Rucinsky .01 .05
75 Steven Finn .01 .05
76 Steve Duchesne .01 .05
77 Ron Hextall .02 .10
78 Penguins Logo .01 .05
79 Kevin Stevens .01 .05
80 Rick Tocchet .02 .10
81 Ron Francis .02 .10
82 Jaromir Jagr .20 .50
83 Joe Mullen .02 .10
84 Shawn McEachern .01 .05
85 Dave Tippett .01 .05
86 Larry Murphy .02 .10
87 Ulf Samuelsson .01 .05
88 Tom Barrasso .02 .10
89 Rangers Logo .01 .05
90 Tony Amonte .02 .10
91 Mike Gartner .20 .50
92 Adam Graves .01 .05
93 Sergei Nemchinov .01 .05
94 Darren Turcotte .02 .10
95 Esa Tikkanen .02 .10
96 Brian Leetch .20 .50
97 Kevin Lowe .02 .10
98 John Vanbiesbrouck .20 .50
99 Mike Richter .20 .50
100 Sabres Logo .01 .05
101 Pat LaFontaine .20 .50
102 Dale Hawerchuk .02 .10
103 Donald Audette .02 .10
104 Bob Sweeney .01 .05
105 Randy Wood .01 .05
106 Yuri Khmylev .01 .05
107 Wayne Presley .01 .05
108 Grant Fuhr .20 .50
109 Doug Bodger .01 .05
110 Richard Smehlik .01 .05
111 Senators Logo .01 .05
112 Norm Maciver .01 .05
113 Jamie Baker .01 .05
114 Bob Kudelski .01 .05
115 Jody Hull .01 .05
116 Mike Peluso .01 .05
117 Mark Lamb .01 .05
118 Mark Freer .01 .05
119 Neil Brady .01 .05
120 Brad Shaw .01 .05
121 Peter Sidorkiewicz .02 .10
122 Whalers Logo .01 .05
123 Andrew Cassels .01 .05
124 Pat Verbeek .01 .05
125 Terry Yake .01 .05
126 Patrick Poulin .01 .05
127 Mark Janssens .01 .05
128 Michael Nylander .01 .05
129 Zarley Zalapski .01 .05
130 Eric Weinrich .01 .05
131 Sean Burke .02 .10
132 Frank Pietrangelo .01 .05
133 Phil Housley .01 .05
134 Paul Coffey .20 .50
135 Larry Murphy .02 .10
136 Mario Lemieux .60 1.50
137 Pat LaFontaine .20 .50
138 Adam Oates .02 .10
139 Felix Potvin .20 .50
140 Ed Belfour .20 .50
141 Tom Barrasso .02 .10
142 Teemu Selanne .30 .75
143 Joe Juneau .01 .05
144 Eric Lindros .20 .50
145 Blackhawks Logo .01 .05
146 Steve Larmer .01 .05
147 Dirk Graham .01 .05
148 Michel Goulet .01 .05
149 Brian Noonan .01 .05
150 Stephane Matteau .01 .05
151 Brent Sutter .01 .05
152 Jocelyn Lemieux .01 .05
153 Chris Chelios .20 .50
154 Steve Smith .01 .05
155 Ed Belfour .20 .50
156 Blues Logo .01 .05
157 Craig Janney .01 .05
158 Brendan Shanahan .20 .50
159 Nelson Emerson .01 .05
160 Rich Sutter .01 .05
161 Ron Sutter .01 .05
162 Ron Wilson .01 .05
163 Bob Bassen .01 .05
164 Garth Butcher .01 .05
165 Jeff Brown .01 .05
166 Curtis Joseph .02 .10
167 Canucks Logo .01 .05
168 Cliff Ronning .01 .05
169 Murray Craven .01 .05
170 Geoff Courtnall .01 .05
171 Petr Nedved .02 .10
172 Trevor Linden .02 .10
173 Greg Adams .01 .05
174 Anatoli Semenov .01 .05
175 Jyrki Lumme .01 .05
176 Doug Lidster .01 .05
177 Kirk McLean .02 .10
178 Flames Logo .01 .05
179 Theo Fleury .20 .50
180 Robert Reichel .01 .05
181 Gary Roberts .02 .10
182 Joe Nieuwendyk .02 .10
183 Sergei Makarov .01 .05
184 Paul Ranheim .01 .05
185 Joel Otto .01 .05
186 Gary Suter .02 .10
187 Jeff Reese .01 .05
188 Mike Vernon .02 .10
189 Jets Logo .01 .05
190 Alexei Zhamnov .01 .05
191 Thomas Steen .01 .05
192 Darrin Shannon .01 .05
193 Keith Tkachuk .20 .50
194 Evgeny Davydov .01 .05
195 Luciano Borsato .01 .05
196 Phil Housley .01 .05
197 Teppo Numminen .01 .05
198 Fredrik Olausson .01 .05
199 Bob Essensa .02 .10
200 Kings Logo .01 .05
201 Luc Robitaille .02 .10
202 Jari Kurri .20 .50
203 Tony Granato .01 .05
204 Jimmy Carson .01 .05
205 Tomas Sandstrom .01 .05
206 Dave Taylor .01 .05
207 Corey Millen .01 .05
208 Marty McSorley .01 .05
209 Rob Blake .02 .10
210 Kelly Hrudey .02 .10
211 Lightning Logo .01 .05
212 John Tucker .01 .05
213 Chris Kontos .01 .05
214 Rob Zamuner .01 .05
215 Adam Creighton .01 .05
216 Mikael Andersson .01 .05
217 Bob Beers .01 .05
218 Rob DiMaio .01 .05
219 Shawn Chambers .01 .05
220 J.C. Bergeron .01 .05
221 Wendell Young .02 .10
222 Maple Leafs Logo .01 .05
223 Dave Andreychuk .02 .10
224 Nikolai Borschevsky .01 .05
225 Glenn Anderson .02 .10
226 John Cullen .01 .05
227 Wendel Clark .02 .10
228 Mike Foligno .01 .05
229 Mike Krushelnyski .01 .05
230 James Macoun .01 .05
231 Dave Ellett .01 .05
232 Felix Potvin .20 .50
233 Oilers Logo .01 .05
234 Petr Klima .01 .05
235 Doug Weight .02 .10
236 Shayne Corson .01 .05
237 Craig Simpson .01 .05
238 Todd Elik .01 .05
239 Zdeno Ciger .01 .05
240 Craig MacTavish .01 .05
241 Kelly Buchberger .01 .05
242 Dave Manson .01 .05
243 Scott Mellanby .02 .10
244 Red Wings Logo .01 .05
245 Dino Ciccarelli .02 .10
246 Sergei Fedorov .20 .50
247 Ray Sheppard .01 .05
248 Paul Ysebaert .01 .05
249 Bob Probert .02 .10
250 Keith Primeau .01 .05
251 Steve Chiasson .01 .05
252 Paul Coffey .20 .50
253 Nicklas Lidstrom .20 .50
254 Tim Cheveldae .02 .10
255 Sharks Logo .01 .05
256 Kelly Kisio .01 .05
257 Johan Garpenlov .01 .05
258 Robert Gaudreau .01 .05
259 Dean Evason .01 .05
260 Jeff Odgers .01 .05
261 Ed Courtenay .01 .05
262 Mike Sullivan .01 .05
263 Doug Zmolek .01 .05
264 Doug Wilson .01 .05
265 Brian Hayward .02 .10
266 Stars Logo .01 .05
267 Brian Propp .01 .05
268 Russ Courtnall .01 .05
269 Dave Gagner .01 .05
270 Ulf Dahlen .01 .05
271 Mike Craig .01 .05
272 Neal Broten .01 .05
273 Gaetan Duchesne .01 .05
274 Derian Hatcher .01 .05
275 Mark Tinordi .01 .05
276 Jon Casey .02 .10
A Joe Juneau .15 .40
B Patrick Roy 1.25 3.00
C Kevin Hatcher .15 .40
D Chris Terreri .15 .40
E Eric Lindros .20 .50
F Pierre Turgeon .20 .50
G Joe Sakic .75 2.00
H Mario Lemieux 1.25 3.00
I Mark Messier .30 .75
J Alexander Mogilny .20 .50
K Sylvain Turgeon .15 .40
L Geoff Sanderson .15 .40
M Jeremy Roenick .20 .50
N Brett Hull .20 .50
O Pavel Bure .50 1.25
P Al MacInnis .15 .40
Q Teemu Selanne .60 1.50
R Wayne Gretzky 1.50 4.00
S Brian Bradley .15 .40
T Doug Gilmour .20 .50
U Bill Ranford .20 .50
V Steve Yzerman .75 2.00
W Pat Falloon .15 .40
X Mike Modano .20 .50

1995-96 Panini Stickers

This popular set of NHL player stickers was distributed primarily in Europe by Panini. The stickers -- which are about half the size of a regulation trading card -- feature action photos on the front, with the card number and licensing logos on the back.

COMPLETE SET (306) 32.00 80.00
1 Claude Lemieux .15 .40
2 Claude Lemieux .15 .40
3 Adam Oates .15 .40
4 Ted Donato .02 .10
5 Mariusz Czerkawski .02 .10
6 Sandy Moger .02 .10
7 Kevin Stevens .02 .10
8 Cam Neely .20 .50
9 Ray Bourque .40 1.00
10 Bruins Logo .02 .10
11 Don Sweeney .02 .10
12 Al Iafrate .15 .40
13 Blaine Lacher .15 .40
14 Brian Holzinger .15 .40
15 Pat LaFontaine .20 .50
16 Derek Plante .15 .40
17 Yuri Khmylev .02 .10
18 Jason Dawe .02 .10
19 Donald Audette .02 .10
20 Alexei Zhitnik .02 .10
21 Sabres Logo .02 .10
22 Richard Smehlik .02 .10
23 Garry Galley .02 .10
24 Dominik Hasek .40 1.00
25 Andrew Cassels .02 .10
26 Jimmy Carson .02 .10
27 Darren Turcotte .15 .40
28 Geoff Sanderson .15 .40
29 Andrei Nikolishin .02 .10
30 Kevin Smyth .02 .10
31 Brendan Shanahan .40 1.00
32 Whalers Logo .02 .10
33 Steven Rice .02 .10
34 Frantisek Kucera .02 .10
35 Sean Burke .15 .40
36 Brian Savage .02 .10
37 Pierre Turgeon .15 .40
38 Vincent Damphousse .15 .40
39 Benoit Brunet .02 .10
40 Mike Keane .02 .10
41 Mark Recchi .15 .40
42 Vladimir Malakhov .02 .10
43 Canadiens Logo .02 .10
44 Patrice Brisebois .02 .10
45 Stephane Quintal .02 .10
46 Patrick Roy 1.25 3.00
47 Alexandre Daigle .15 .40
48 Alexei Yashin .15 .40
49 Dan Quinn .02 .10
50 Radek Bonk .15 .40
51 Scott Levins .02 .10
52 Sylvain Turgeon .15 .40
53 Pavol Demitra .15 .40
54 Senators Logo .02 .10
55 Steve Larouche .02 .10
56 Sean Hill .02 .10
57 Don Beaupre .15 .40
58 Ron Francis .15 .40
59 Mario Lemieux 1.25 3.00
60 Bryan Smolinski .15 .40
61 Luc Robitaille .15 .40
62 Tomas Sandstrom .15 .40
63 Jaromir Jagr .60 1.50
64 Joe Mullen .15 .40
65 Penguins Logo .02 .10
66 Ulf Samuelsson .02 .10
67 Dmitri Mironov .02 .10
68 Ken Wregget .15 .40
69 Stu Barnes .02 .10
70 Jesse Belanger .02 .10
71 Rob Niedermayer .15 .40
72 Brian Skrudland .02 .10
73 Dave Lowry .02 .10
74 Jody Hull .02 .10
75 Scott Mellanby .02 .10
76 Panthers Logo .02 .10
77 Gord Murphy .02 .10
78 Magnus Svensson .02 .10
79 John Vanbiesbrouck .20 .50
80 Neal Broten .15 .40
81 Bill Guerin .15 .40
82 Claude Lemieux .15 .40
83 John Maclean .15 .40
84 Randy McKay .02 .10
85 Stephane Richer .15 .40
86 Shawn Chambers .02 .10
87 Devils Logo .02 .10
88 Scott Niedermayer .15 .40
89 Scott Stevens .15 .40
90 Martin Brodeur .50 1.25
91 Kirk Muller .02 .10
92 Derek King .02 .10
93 Patrick Flatley .02 .10
94 Brett Lindros .02 .10
95 Steve Thomas .02 .10
96 Darius Kasparaitis .15 .40
97 Scott Lachance .02 .10
98 Islanders Logo .02 .10
99 Mathieu Schneider .02 .10
100 Dennis Vaske .02 .10
101 Tommy Salo .15 .40
102 Mark Messier .25 .60
103 Ray Ferraro .02 .10
104 Petr Nedved .02 .10
105 Adam Graves .15 .40
106 Alexei Kovalev .15 .40
107 Steve Larmer .02 .10
108 Pat Verbeek .15 .40
109 Rangers Logo .02 .10
110 Brian Leetch .20 .50
111 Sergei Zubov .15 .40
112 Mike Richter .20 .50
113 Eric Lindros .60 1.50
114 Rod Brind'Amour .15 .40
115 Joel Otto .02 .10
116 John LeClair .30 .75
117 Mikael Renberg .15 .40
118 Chris Therien .15 .40
119 Eric Desjardins .15 .40
120 Flyers Logo .02 .10
121 Dimitri Yushkevich .02 .10
122 Karl Dykhuis .02 .10
123 Ron Hextall .15 .40
124 Brian Bradley .02 .10
125 John Tucker .02 .10
126 Chris Gratton .15 .40
127 Alexander Semak .02 .10
128 Brian Bellows .02 .10
129 Paul Ysebaert .02 .10
130 Petr Klima .02 .10
131 Lightning Logo .02 .10
132 Alexander Selivanov .02 .10
133 Roman Hamrlik .02 .10
134 Daren Puppa .15 .40
135 Dale Hunter .15 .40
136 Michal Pivonka .02 .10
137 Steve Konowalchuk .02 .10
138 Joe Juneau .15 .40
139 Peter Bondra .20 .50
140 Keith Jones .15 .40
141 Sergei Gonchar .02 .10
142 Capitals Logo .02 .10
143 Calle Johansson .02 .10
144 Mark Tinordi .02 .10
145 Jim Carey .02 .10
146 Eric Lindros AW .30 .75
147 Paul Coffey AW .08 .25
148 Peter Forsberg AW .25 .60
149 Dominik Hasek AW .20 .50
150 Jaromir Jagr AW .30 .75
151 Peter Bondra LL .08 .25
152 Ron francis LL .02 .10
153 Cam Neely LL .05 .15
154 Dominik Hasek LL .20 .50
155 Ian Laperriere LL .02 .10
156 Bernie Nicholls .02 .10
157 Jeremy Roenick .20 .50
158 Patrick Poulin .02 .10
159 Eric Daze .02 .10
160 Tony Amonte .15 .40
161 Sergei Krivokrasov .02 .10
162 Joe Murphy .02 .10
163 Blackhawks Logo .02 .10
164 Chris Chelios .20 .50
165 Gary Suter .02 .10
166 Ed Belfour .20 .50
167 Dave Gagner .02 .10
168 Mike Modano .25 .60
169 Todd Harvey .15 .40
170 Mike Donnelly .02 .10
171 Mike Kennedy .02 .10
172 Trent Klatt .02 .10
173 Derian Hatcher .02 .10
174 Stars Logo .02 .10
175 Kevin Hatcher .02 .10
176 Grant Ledyard .02 .10
177 Andy Moog .15 .40
178 Sergei Fedorov .40 1.00
179 Steve Yzerman .75 2.00
180 Vyacheslav Kozlov .15 .40
181 Keith Primeau .15 .40
182 Dino Ciccarelli .15 .40
183 Ray Sheppard .15 .40
184 Paul Coffey .20 .50
185 Red Wings Logo .02 .10
186 Nicklas Lidstrom .20 .50
187 Chris Osgood .20 .50
188 Mike Vernon .15 .40
189 Dale Hawerchuk .15 .40
190 Ian Laperriere .02 .10
191 David Roberts .02 .10
192 Esa Tikkanen .02 .10
193 Geoff Courtnall .02 .10
194 Brett Hull .25 .60
195 Steve Duchesne .15 .40
196 Blues Logo .02 .10
197 Al MacInnis .15 .40
198 Chris Pronger .15 .40
199 Jon Casey .15 .40
200 Doug Gilmour .20 .50
201 Mats Sundin .20 .50
202 Benoit Hogue .02 .10
203 Dave Andreychuk .15 .40
204 Mike Gartner .15 .40
205 Dave Ellett .02 .10
206 Todd Gill .02 .10
207 Maple Leafs Logo .02 .10
208 Kenny Jonsson .02 .10
209 Larry Murphy .15 .40
210 Felix Potvin .20 .50
211 Dallas Drake .02 .10
212 Alexei Zhamnov .15 .40
213 Mike Eastwood .02 .10
214 Keith Tkachuk .20 .50
215 Igor Korolev .02 .10
216 Nelson Emerson .02 .10
217 Teemu Selanne .40 1.00
218 Jets Logo .02 .10
219 Dave Manson .02 .10
220 Teppo Numminen .02 .10
221 Nikolai Khabibulin .15 .40
222 Steve Rucchin .02 .10
223 Shaun Van Allen .02 .10
224 Patrik Carnback .02 .10
225 Peter Douris .02 .10
226 Todd Krygier .02 .10
227 Paul Kariya .75 2.00
228 Bobby Dollas .02 .10
229 Ducks Logo .02 .10
230 Milos Holan .02 .10
231 Oleg Tverdovsky .15 .40
232 Guy Hebert .15 .40
233 Joe Nieuwendyk .15 .40
234 German Titov .02 .10
235 Paul Kruse .02 .10
236 Gary Roberts .02 .10
237 Theo Fleury .20 .50
238 Ronnie Stern .02 .10
239 Steve Chiasson .15 .40
240 Flames Logo .02 .10
241 Phil Housley .02 .10
242 Zarley Zalapski .02 .10
243 Trevor Kidd .02 .10
244 Peter Forsberg .50 1.25
245 Mike Ricci .15 .40
246 Joe Sakic .40 1.00
247 Wendel Clark .15 .40
248 Valeri Kamensky .15 .40
249 Owen Nolan .15 .40
250 Scott Young .02 .10
251 Avalanche Logo .02 .10
252 Uwe Krupp .02 .10
253 Curtis Leschyshyn .02 .10
254 Jocelyn Thibault .15 .40
255 Jason Arnott .15 .40
256 Jason Bonsignore .02 .10
257 Todd Marchant .02 .10
258 Scott Thornton .02 .10
259 Doug Weight .15 .40
260 Shayne Corson .15 .40
261 Kelly Buchberger .02 .10
262 Oilers Logo .02 .10
263 David Oliver .02 .10
264 Igor Kravchuk .02 .10
265 Curtis Joseph .25 .60
266 Wayne Gretzky 1.50 4.00
267 Tony Granato .15 .40
268 Dimitri Khristich .15 .40
269 John Druce .02 .10
270 Jari Kurri .02 .10
271 Rick Tocchet .15 .40
272 Rob Blake .15 .40
273 Kings Logo .02 .10
274 Marty McSorley .02 .10
275 Darryl Sydor .02 .10
276 Kelly Hrudey .15 .40
277 Craig Janney .15 .40
278 Jeff Friesen .15 .40
279 Viktor Kozlov .15 .40
280 Ray Whitney .02 .10
281 Ulf Dahlen .02 .10
282 Sergei Makarov .02 .10
283 Sandis Ozolinsh .15 .40
284 Sharks Logo .02 .10
285 Mike Rathje .02 .10
286 Michal Sykora .02 .10
287 Arturs Irbe .15 .40
288 Trevor Linden .15 .40
289 Mike Ridley .02 .10
290 Cliff Ronning .15 .40
291 Josef Beranek .15 .40
292 Roman Oksiuta .02 .10
293 Pavel Bure .50 1.25
294 Alexander Mogilny .15 .40
295 Canucks Logo .02 .10
296 Russ Courtnall .15 .40
297 Jeff Brown .02 .10
298 Kirk McLean .15 .40
299 Peter Forsberg .50 1.25
300 Paul Kariya .75 2.00
301 Chris Therien .02 .10
302 Blaine Lacher .02 .10
303 Jim Carey .15 .40
304 Jeff Friesen .15 .40
305 Ian Laperriere .02 .10
306 Kenny Jonsson .02 .10

1998-99 Panini Photocards

These postcard-like collectibles were issued in packs of five by Panini for sale primarily in Europe. The fronts featured a full-bleed action photo, while the backs carried the player's name and team. These issues were printed on very thin paper stock, which makes them somewhat condition sensitive.

COMPLETE SET (108) 20.00 40.00
1 Daniel Alfredsson .20 .50
2 Jason Allison .25 .60
3 Tony Amonte .30 .75
4 Jason Arnott .25 .60
5 Tom Barrasso .25 .60
6 Stu Barnes .20 .50
7 Ed Belfour .30 .75
8 Bryan Berard .20 .50
9 Rob Blake .25 .60
10 Peter Bondra .30 .75
11 Ray Bourque .60 1.50
12 Rod Brind'Amour .25 .60
13 Martin Brodeur .75 2.00
14 Andrew Brunette .20 .50
15 Pavel Bure .30 .75
16 Chris Chelios .30 .75
17 Vincent Damphousse .25 .60
18 Eric Daze .20 .50
19 Detroit Red Wings .20 .50
20 Mike Dunham .25 .60
21 Sergei Fedorov .50 1.25
22 Stephane Fiset .20 .50
23 Theo Fleury .30 .75
24 Peter Forsberg .75 2.00
25 Ron Francis .25 .60
26 Jeff Friesen .25 .60
27 Grant Fuhr .25 .60
28 Doug Gilmour .30 .75
29 Adam Graves .25 .60
30 Wayne Gretzky 2.00 5.00
31 Michal Grosek .20 .50
32 Dominik Hasek .60 1.50
33 Kevin Hatcher .20 .50
34 Brett Hull .40 1.00
35 Jaromir Jagr .75 2.00
36 Mike Johnson .20 .50
37 Curtis Joseph .40 1.00
38 Joe Juneau .20 .50

39 Paul Kariya 1.00 2.50
40 Nikolai Khabibulin .25 .60
41 Saku Koivu .25 .60
42 Olaf Kolzig .25 .60
43 Oleg Kvasha .20 .50
44 Vincent Lecavalier .30 .75
45 John LeClair .40 1.00
46 Brian Leetch .25 .60
47 Claude Lemieux .20 .50
48 Trevor Linden .20 .50
49 Eric Lindros .30 .75
50 Al MacInnis .25 .60
51 Mark Messier .30 .75
52 Mike Modano .50 1.25
53 Alexander Mogilny .25 .60
54 Brendan Morrison .20 .50
55 Scott Niedermayer .25 .60
56 Joe Nieuwendyk .25 .60
57 Adam Oates .25 .60
58 Chris Osgood .30 .75
59 Zigmund Palffy .30 .75
60 Mark Parrish .20 .50
61 Michael Peca .20 .50
62 Yanic Perreault .20 .50
63 Felix Potvin .30 .75
64 Keith Primeau .25 .60
65 Chris Pronger .25 .60
66 Daren Puppa .20 .50
67 Mark Recchi .25 .60
68 Mike Richter .30 .75
69 Luc Robitaille .30 .75
70 Jeremy Roenick .30 .75
71 Patrick Roy 1.50 4.00
72 Joe Sakic .60 1.50
73 Tommy Salo .25 .60
74 Sergei Samsonov .25 .60
75 Geoff Sanderson .20 .50
76 Teemu Selanne .60 1.50
77 Brendan Shanahan .30 .75
78 Ryan Smyth .20 .50
79 Garth Snow .25 .60
80 Cory Stillman .20 .50
81 Mats Sundin .30 .75
82 Jocelyn Thibault .25 .60
83 Joe Thornton .30 .75
84 Keith Tkachuk .30 .75
85 Pierre Turgeon .25 .60
86 Oleg Tverdovsky .20 .50
87 John Vanbiesbrouck .30 .75
88 Mike Vernon .25 .60
89 Doug Weight .25 .60
90 Alexei Yashin .25 .60
91 Steve Yzerman 1.25 3.00
92 Steve Yzerman w/CUP 1.25 3.00
93 Rob Blake AW .25 .60
94 Martin Brodeur AW .75 2.00
95 Ron Francis AW .25 .60
96 Dominik Hasek AW .60 1.50
97 Jaromir Jagr AW .75 2.00
98 Sergei Samsonov AW .25 .60
99 Peter Bondra AS .30 .75
100 Ray Bourque AS .60 1.50
101 Peter Forsberg AS .75 2.00
102 Wayne Gretzky AS 2.00 5.00
103 Saku Koivu AS .25 .60
104 Eric Lindros AS .30 .75
105 Mark Messier AS .30 .75
106 Patrick Roy 1.50 4.00
107 Teemu Selanne AS .60 1.50
108 Mats Sundin AS .30 .75

1998-99 Panini Stickers

This set of undersized stickers were issued in packs of five, primarily in Europe. The fronts feature action photos, while the backs display card number and player name.

COMPLETE SET (248) 10.00 25.00
1 Teemu Selanne .60 1.50
2 Peter Bondra .30 .75
3 Wayne Gretzky 2.00 5.00
4 Jaromir Jagr .75 2.00
5 Chris Pronger .25 .60
6 Ed Belfour .30 .75
7 Bruins logo .20 .50
8 Dmitri Khristich .20 .50
9 P.J Axelsson .20 .50
10 Byron Dafoe .25 .60
11 Ted Donato .20 .50
12 Ray Bourque .60 1.50
13 Sergei Samsonov .25 .60
14 Jason Allison .25 .60
15 Sabres logo .20 .50
16 Miroslav Satan .25 .60
17 Donald Audette .25 .60
18 Michal Grosek .20 .50
19 Dominik Hasek .60 1.50
20 Richard Smehlik .20 .50
21 Mike Peca .20 .50
22 Alexei Zhitnik .20 .50
23 Hurricanes logo .20 .50
24 Trevor Kidd .25 .60
25 Nelson Emerson .20 .50
26 Curtis Leschyshyn .20 .50
27 Robert Kron .20 .50
28 Gary Roberts .20 .50
29 Sami Kapanen .20 .50
30 Keith Primeau .25 .60
31 Canadiens logo .20 .50
32 Saku Koivu .25 .60
33 Vladimir Malakhov .20 .50
34 Mark Recchi .25 .60
35 Jocelyn Thibault .25 .60
36 Peter Popovic .20 .50
37 Martin Rucinsky .20 .50
38 Jonas Hoglund .20 .50
39 Senators logo .20 .50
40 Damian Rhodes .25 .60
41 Radek Bonk .25 .60
42 Daniel Alfredsson .25 .60
43 Alexei Yashin .25 .60
44 Magnus Arvedson .20 .50
45 Janne Laukkanen .20 .50
46 Igor Kravchuk .20 .50
47 Penguins logo .20 .50
48 Jaromir Jagr .75 2.00
49 Ron Francis .25 .60
50 Darius Kasparaitis .20 .50
51 Tom Barrasso .25 .60
52 Martin Straka .25 .60
53 Alexei Morozov .20 .50
54 Fredrik Olausson .20 .50
55 Panthers logo .20 .50
56 Radek Dvorak .20 .50
57 Robert Svehla .20 .50
58 Ray Whitney .20 .50
59 Dave Gagner .20 .50
60 John Vanbiesbrouck .30 .75
61 Ed Jovanovski .25 .60
62 Viktor Kozlov .20 .50
63 Devils logo .20 .50
64 Petr Sykora .25 .60
65 Scott Niedermayer .25 .60
66 Dave Andreychuk .25 .60
67 Martin Brodeur .75 2.00
68 Bobby Holik .20 .50
69 Doug Gilmour .30 .75
70 Patrik Elias .30 .75
71 Islanders logo .20 .50
72 Tommy Salo .25 .60
73 Zigmund Palffy .30 .75
74 Bryan Smolinski .20 .50
75 Robert Reichel .20 .50
76 Sergei Nemchinov .20 .50
77 Kenny Jonsson .20 .50
78 Bryan Berard .20 .50
79 Rangers logo .20 .50
80 Wayne Gretzky 2.00 5.00
81 Adam Graves .25 .60
82 Mike Richter .30 .75
83 Brian Leetch .25 .60
84 Alexei Kovalev .25 .60
85 Ulf Samuelsson .20 .50
86 Niklas Sundstrom .20 .50
87 Flyers logo .20 .50
88 John LeClair .40 1.00
89 Petr Svoboda .20 .50
90 Rod Brind'Amour .25 .60
91 Sean Burke .25 .60
92 Dainius Zubrus .20 .50
93 Alexandre Daigle .20 .50
94 Eric Lindros .50 1.25
95 Lightning logo .20 .50
96 Mark Fitzpatrick .20 .50
97 Alexander Selivanov .20 .50
98 Mikael Renberg .20 .50
99 Rob Zamuner .20 .50
100 Karl Dykhuis .20 .50
101 Paul Ysebaert .20 .50
102 Mikael Andersson .20 .50
103 Capitals logo .20 .50
104 Peter Bondra .30 .75
105 Sergei Gonchar .60 1.50
106 Adam Oates .25 .60
107 Calle Johansson .20 .50
108 Olaf Kolzig .25 .60
109 Esa Tikkanen .20 .50
110 Andrei Nikolishin .20 .50
111 Blackhawks logo .20 .50
112 Alexei Zhamnov .20 .50
113 Eric Daze .20 .50
114 Chris Chelios .30 .75
115 Jeff Hackett .20 .50
116 Gary Suter .20 .50
117 Eric Weinrich .20 .50
118 Tony Amonte .30 .75
119 Stars logo .20 .50
120 Jere Lehtinen .25 .60
121 Joe Nieuwendyk .25 .60
122 Ed Belfour .30 .75
123 Mike Modano .50 1.25
124 Sergei Zubov .20 .50
125 Darryl Sydor .20 .50
126 Pat Verbeek .25 .60
127 Red Wings logo .20 .50
128 Chris Osgood .30 .75
129 Sergei Fedorov .60 1.50
130 Stanley Cup .20 .50
131 Igor Larionov .20 .50
132 Slava Kozlov .20 .50
133 Brendan Shanahan .50 1.25
134 Nicklas Lidstrom .30 .75
135 Steve Yzerman 1.25 3.00
136 Predators logo .20 .50
137 Jan Vopat .20 .50
138 Sergei Krivokrasov .20 .50
139 Darren Turcotte .20 .50
140 Tom Fitzgerald .20 .50
141 Joel Bouchard .20 .50
142 Scott Walker .20 .50
143 Coyotes logo .20 .50
144 Keith Tkachuk .30 .75
145 Craig Janney .20 .50
146 Oleg Tverdovsky .20 .50
147 Nikolai Khabibulin .25 .60
148 Teppo Numminen .20 .50
149 Cliff Ronning .20 .50
150 Jeremy Roenick .30 .75
151 Blues logo .20 .50
152 Brett Hull .40 1.00
153 Chris Pronger .25 .60
154 Pierre Turgeon .25 .60
155 Grant Fuhr .25 .60
156 Geoff Courtnall .20 .50
157 Pavol Demitra .25 .60
158 Steve Duchesne .20 .50
159 Maple Leafs logo .20 .50
160 Fredrik Modin .20 .50
161 Dimitri Yushkevich .20 .50
162 Tie Domi .25 .60
163 Igor Korolev .20 .50
164 Mats Sundin .30 .75
165 Felix Potvin .30 .75
166 Sergei Berezin .20 .50
167 Mighty Ducks logo .20 .50
168 Guy Hebert .25 .60
169 Teemu Selanne .60 1.50
170 Paul Kariya 1.00 2.50
171 Steve Rucchin .20 .50
172 Tomas Sandstrom .20 .50
173 Josef Marha .20 .50
174 Ruslan Salei .20 .50
175 Flames logo .20 .50
176 Theo Fleury .30 .75
177 Michael Nylander .20 .50
178 German Titov .20 .50
179 Rick Tabaracci .20 .50
180 Cory Stillman .20 .50
181 Jarome Iginla .25 .60
182 Tommy Albelin .20 .50
183 Avalanche logo .20 .50
184 Patrick Roy 1.50 4.00
185 Peter Forsberg .75 2.00
186 Alexei Gusarov .20 .50
187 Uwe Krupp .20 .50
188 Valeri Kamensky .25 .60
189 Joe Sakic .60 1.50
190 Sandis Ozolinsh .25 .60
191 Oilers logo .20 .50
192 Boris Mironov .20 .50
193 Mats Lindren .20 .50
194 Andrei Kovalenko .20 .50
195 Curtis Joseph .40 1.00
196 Roman Hamrlik .20 .50
197 Doug Weight .25 .60
198 Janne Niinimaa .20 .50
199 Kings logo .20 .50
200 Stephane Fiset .20 .50
201 Jozef Stumpel .20 .50
202 Aki Berg .20 .50
203 Glenn Murray .20 .50
204 Vladimir Tsyplakov .20 .50
205 Rob Blake .25 .60
206 Mattias Norstrom .20 .50
207 Sharks logo .20 .50
208 Marcus Ragnarsson .20 .50
209 Jeff Friesen .25 .60
210 Owen Nolan .25 .60
211 Mike Vernon .25 .60
212 John MacLean .20 .50
213 Andrei Zyuzin .20 .50
214 Marco Sturm .20 .50
215 Canucks logo .20 .50
216 Pavel Bure .75 2.00
217 Alexander Mogilny .25 .60
218 Arturs Irbe .25 .60
219 Mark Messier .20 .50
220 Markus Naslund .30 .75
221 Mattias Ohlund .20 .50
222 Jyrki Lumme .20 .50
223 Dominik Hasek .60 1.50
224 Rob Blake .25 .60
225 Sergei Samsonov .25 .60
226 Jere Lehtinen .25 .60
227 Ron Francis .25 .60
228 Jamie McLennan .20 .50

2000-01 Panini Stickers

COMPLETE SET (212) 15.00 40.00
1 NHL logo .02 .10
2 NHLPA logo .02 .10
3 Atlanta logo .02 .10
4 Johan Garpenlov .08 .20
5 Patrik Stefan .08 .20
6 Andrew Brunette .08 .20
7 Andreas Karlsson .08 .20
8 Ray Ferraro .08 .20
9 Petr Buzek .08 .20
10 Boston logo .02 .10
11 Sergei Samsonov .20 .50
12 P.J. Axelsson .08 .20
13 Anson Carter .08 .20
14 Eric Nickulas .08 .20
15 Mikko Eloranta .08 .20
16 Joe Thornton .40 1.00
17 Buffalo logo .02 .10
18 Dominik Hasek .40 1.00
19 Curtis Brown .08 .20
20 Michael Peca .08 .20
21 Vaclav Varada .08 .20
22 Alexei Zhitnik .08 .20
23 Miroslav Satan .08 .20
24 Carolina logo .02 .10
25 Sami Kapanen .08 .20
26 Paul Coffey .20 .50
27 Marek Malik .08 .20
28 Andrei Kovalenko .08 .20
29 Arturs Irbe .20 .50
30 Ron Francis .20 .50
31 Florida logo .02 .10
32 Scott Mellanby .08 .20
33 Viktor Kozlov .08 .20
34 Jaroslav Spacek .08 .20
35 Ray Whitney .08 .20
36 Robert Svehla .08 .20
37 Pavel Bure .30 .75
38 Montreal logo .02 .10
39 Saku Koivu .20 .50
40 Trevor Linden .20 .50
41 Karl Dykhuis .08 .20
42 Sergei Zholtok .08 .20
43 Martin Rucinsky .08 .20
44 Dainius Zubrus .08 .20
45 New Jersey logo .02 .10
46 Alexander Mogilny .08 .20
47 Petr Sykora .08 .20
48 Martin Brodeur .75 2.00
49 Bobby Holik .08 .20
50 Scott Gomez .08 .20
51 Patrik Elias .20 .50
52 NY Islanders logo .02 .10
53 Brad Isbister .08 .20
54 Mariusz Czerkawski .08 .20
55 Mats Lindgren .08 .20
56 Tim Connolly .08 .20
57 Kenny Jonsson .08 .20
58 Olli Jokinen .08 .20
59 NY Rangers logo .02 .10
60 Brian Leetch .20 .50
61 Petr Nedved .08 .20
62 Radek Dvorak .08 .20
63 Valeri Kamensky .08 .20
64 Theo Fleury .20 .50
65 Jan Hlavac .08 .20
66 Ottawa logo .02 .10
67 Magnus Arvedson .08 .20
68 Igor Kravchuk .08 .20
69 Vaclav Prospal .08 .20
70 Daniel Alfredsson .20 .50
71 Shawn McEachern .08 .20
72 Radek Bonk .08 .20
73 Philadelphia logo .02 .10
74 John LeClair .08 .20
75 Eric Lindros .20 .50
76 Mark Recchi .20 .50
77 Daymond Langkow .08 .20
78 Ulf Samuelsson .08 .20
79 Valeri Zelepukin .08 .20
80 Pittsburgh logo .02 .10
81 Jaromir Jagr .60 1.50
82 Martin Straka .08 .20
83 Alexei Morozov .08 .20
84 Alexei Kovalev .08 .20
85 Robert Lang .08 .20
86 Darius Kasparaitis .08 .20
87 Tampa Bay logo .02 .10
88 Vincent Lecavalier .40 1.00
89 Fredrik Modin .08 .20
90 Jaroslav Svejkovsky .08 .20
91 Mike Johnson .08 .20
92 Pavel Kubina .08 .20
93 Petr Svoboda .08 .20
94 Toronto logo .02 .10
95 Mats Sundin .40 1.00
96 Darcy Tucker .08 .20
97 Steve Thomas .08 .20
98 Jonas Hoglund .08 .20
99 Igor Korolev .08 .20
100 Yanic Perreault .08 .20
101 Washington logo .02 .10
102 Peter Bondra .20 .50
103 Sergei Gonchar .08 .20
104 Joe Sacco .08 .20
105 Ulf Dahlen .08 .20
106 Adam Oates .08 .20
107 Calle Johansson .08 .20
108 Anaheim logo .02 .10
109 Paul Kariya .40 1.00
110 Guy Hebert .08 .20
111 Teemu Selanne .60 1.50
112 Ruslan Salei .08 .20
113 Vitali Vishnevsky .08 .20
114 Oleg Tverdovsky .08 .20
115 Calgary logo .02 .10
116 Valeri Bure .08 .20
117 Jarome Iginla .60 1.50
118 Marc Savard .08 .20
119 Andrei Nazarov .08 .20
120 Phil Housley .08 .20
121 Derek Morris .08 .20
122 Chicago logo .02 .10
123 Michael Nylander .08 .20
124 Boris Mironov .08 .20
125 Alexei Zhamnov .08 .20
126 Tony Amonte .20 .50
127 Michal Grosek .08 .20
128 Steve Sullivan .08 .20
129 Colorado logo .02 .10
130 Peter Forsberg .60 1.50
131 Patrick Roy 1.00 2.50
132 Joe Sakic .60 1.50
133 Stephane Yelle .08 .20
134 Sandis Ozolinsh .08 .20
135 Milan Hejduk .40 1.00
136 Columbus logo .02 .10
137 Geoff Sanderson .08 .20
138 Ron Tugnutt .08 .20
139 Radim Bicanek .08 .20
140 Mattias Timander .08 .20
141 Krzysztof Oliwa .08 .20
142 Espen Knutsen .08 .20
143 Dallas logo .02 .10
144 Mike Modano .40 1.00
145 Joe Nieuwendyk .40 1.00
146 Sergei Zubov .08 .20
147 Richard Matvichuk .08 .20
148 Brett Hull .40 1.00
149 Jamie Langenbrunner .08 .20
150 Detroit logo .02 .10
151 Sergei Fedorov .40 1.00
152 Brendan Shanahan .40 1.00
153 Nicklas Lidstrom .40 1.00
154 Slava Kozlov .08 .20
155 Igor Larionov .08 .20
156 Steve Yzerman .75 2.00
157 Edmonton logo .02 .10
158 Doug Weight .08 .20
159 German Titov .08 .20
160 Janne Niinimaa .08 .20
161 Roman Hamrlik .08 .20
162 Ryan Smyth .40 1.00
163 Alexander Selivanov .08 .20
164 Los Angeles logo .02 .10
165 Rob Blake .20 .50
166 Luc Robitaille .40 1.00
167 Ziggy Palffy .08 .20
168 Jozef Stumpel .08 .20
169 Glen Murray .20 .50
170 Mattias Norstrom .08 .20
171 Minnesota logo .02 .10
172 Curtis Leschyshyn .08 .20
173 Sergei Krivokrasov .08 .20
174 Antti Laaksonen .08 .20
175 Pavel Patera .08 .20
176 Sean O'Donnell .08 .20
177 Manny Fernandez .20 .50
178 Nashville logo .02 .10
179 Vitali Yachmenev .08 .20
180 Patric Kjellberg .08 .20
181 Ville Peltonen .08 .20
182 Cliff Ronning .08 .20
183 Greg Johnson .08 .20
184 Kimmo Timonen .08 .20
185 Phoenix logo .02 .10
186 Jeremy Roenick .40 1.00
187 Jyrki Lumme .08 .20
188 Travis Green .08 .20
189 Teppo Numminen .08 .20
190 Keith Tkachuk .20 .50
191 Radoslav Suchy .08 .20
192 St. Louis logo .02 .10
193 Chris Pronger .20 .50
194 Pierre Turgeon .08 .20
195 Pavol Demitra .08 .20
196 Roman Turek .08 .20
197 Michal Handzus .08 .20
198 Stephane Richer .08 .20
199 San Jose logo .02 .10
200 Vincent Damphousse .08 .20
201 Niklas Sundstrom .08 .20
202 Stephane Matteau .08 .20
203 Marcus Ragnarsson .08 .20
204 Owen Nolan .08 .20
205 Aleksander Korolyuk .08 .20
206 Vancouver logo .02 .10
207 Andrew Cassels .08 .20
208 Mark Messier .40 1.00
209 Artem Chubarov .08 .20
210 Mattias Ohlund .08 .20
211 Todd Bertuzzi .20 .50
212 Markus Naslund .20 .50

2005-06 Panini Stickers

1 Sidney Crosby 4.00 10.00
2 Alexander Ovechkin 1.50 4.00
3 Mike Richards .40 1.00
4 Dion Phaneuf .75 2.00
5 Corey Perry .40 1.00
6 Henrik Lundqvist .75 2.00
7 Ilya Kovalchuk .60 1.50
8 Marian Hossa .20 .50
9 Bobby Holik .10 .25
10 Kari Lehtonen .20 .50
11 Marc Savard .10 .25
12 Jaroslav Modry .10 .25
13 Thrashers Team Logo .10 .25
14 Thrashers Action Shot A .10 .25
15 Thrashers Action Shot B .10 .25
16 Peter Bondra .10 .25
17 Slava Kozlov .10 .25
18 Patrik Stefan .10 .25
19 Joe Thornton .75 2.00
20 Brian Leetch .20 .50
21 Sergei Samsonov .10 .25
22 Patrice Bergeron .20 .50
23 Glen Murray .20 .50
24 Bruins Team Logo .10 .25
25 Bruins Action Shot A .10 .25
26 Bruins Action Shot B .10 .25
27 Andrew Raycroft .20 .50
28 Jiri Slegr .10 .25
29 Shawn McEachern .10 .25
30 P.J. Axelsson .10 .25
31 Sabres Action Shot A .10 .25
32 Sabres Action Shot B .10 .25
33 Chris Drury .20 .50
34 Daniel Briere .20 .50
35 Ryan Miller .40 1.00
36 Maxim Afinogenov .10 .25
37 J.P. Dumont .10 .25
38 Sabres Team Logo .10 .25
39 Jochen Hecht .10 .25
40 Thomas Vanek .75 2.00
41 Andrew Peters .10 .25
42 Teppo Numminen .10 .25
43 Rod Brind'Amour .10 .25
44 Eric Staal .40 1.00
45 Erik Cole .10 .25
46 Justin Williams .10 .25
47 Oleg Tverdovsky .10 .25
48 Hurricanes Action Shot A .10 .25
49 Hurricanes Action Shot B .10 .25
50 Hurricanes Team Logo .10 .25
51 Cory Stillman .10 .25
52 Ray Whitney .10 .25
53 Glen Wesley .10 .25
54 Martin Gerber .20 .50
55 Roberto Luongo .75 2.00
56 Olli Jokinen .10 .25
57 Gary Roberts .10 .25
58 Joe Nieuwendyk .20 .50
59 Jay Bouwmeester .20 .50
60 Panthers Action Shot A .10 .25
61 Panthers Action Shot B .10 .25
62 Panthers Team Logo .10 .25
63 Nathan Horton .20 .50
64 Stephen Weiss .10 .25
65 Kristian Huselius .10 .25
66 Jozef Stumpel .10 .25
67 Canadiens Action Shot A .10 .25
68 Canadiens Action Shot B .10 .25
69 Jose Theodore .40 1.00
70 Saku Koivu .40 1.00
71 Alex Kovalev .10 .25
72 Michael Ryder .20 .50
73 Canadiens Team Logo .10 .25
74 Mike Ribeiro .10 .25
75 Sheldon Souray .10 .25
76 Richard Zednik .10 .25
77 Mathieu Dandenault .10 .25
78 Radek Bonk .10 .25
79 Martin Brodeur .20 .50
80 Scott Gomez .20 .50
81 Alexander Mogilny .20 .50
82 Vladimir Malakhov .10 .25
83 Brian Rafalski .10 .25
84 Jamie Langenbrunner .10 .25
85 Devils Team Logo .10 .25
86 Devils Action Shot A .10 .25
87 Devils Action Shot B .10 .25
88 Brian Gionta .10 .25
89 John Madden .10 .25
90 Zach Parise .75 2.00
91 Alexei Yashin .10 .25
92 Rick DiPietro .40 1.00
93 Miroslav Satan .10 .25
94 Jason Blake .10 .25
95 Mark Parrish .10 .25
96 Islanders Action Shot A .10 .25
97 Islanders Action Shot B .10 .25
98 Islanders Team Logo .10 .25
99 Trent Hunter .10 .25
100 Mike York .10 .25
101 Alexei Zhitnik .10 .25
102 Garth Snow .20 .50
103 Jaromir Jagr .75 2.00
104 Michael Nylander .10 .25
105 Martin Straka .10 .25
106 Darius Kasparaitis .10 .25
107 Rangers Action Shot A .10 .25
108 Rangers Action Shot B .10 .25
109 Kevin Weekes .20 .50
110 Tom Poti .10 .25
111 Rangers Team Logo .10 .25
112 Martin Rucinsky .10 .25
113 Steve Rucchin .10 .25
114 Marek Malik .10 .25
115 Dany Heatley .60 1.50
116 Jason Spezza .40 1.00
117 Dominik Hasek .75 2.00
118 Daniel Alfredsson .30 .75
119 Senators Action Shot A .10 .25
120 Senators Action Shot B .10 .25
121 Zdeno Chara .10 .25
122 Martin Havlat .20 .50
123 Senators Team Logo .10 .25
124 Mike Fisher .10 .25
125 Wade Redden .10 .25
126 Chris Phillips .10 .25
127 Flyers Action Shot A .10 .25
128 Flyers Action Shot B .10 .25
129 Peter Forsberg .75 2.00
130 Keith Primeau .10 .25
131 Simon Gagne .20 .50
132 Robert Esche .20 .50
133 Joni Pitkanen .10 .25
134 Flyers Team Logo .10 .25
135 Derian Hatcher .10 .25
136 Mike Knuble .10 .25
137 Eric Desjardins .10 .25
138 Jeff Carter 1.00 2.50
139 Sidney Crosby 4.00 10.00
140 Mario Lemieux 1.25 3.00
141 Mark Recchi .10 .25
142 Zigmund Palffy .10 .25
143 Sergei Gonchar .10 .25
144 Penguins Action Shot A .10 .25
145 Penguins Action Shot B .10 .25
146 Penguins Team Logo .10 .25
147 Marc-Andre Fleury .40 1.00
148 John LeClair .10 .25
149 Ryan Malone .10 .25
150 Dick Tarnstrom .10 .25
151 Vincent Lecavalier .40 1.00
152 Brad Richards .20 .50
153 Martin St. Louis .20 .50
154 Lightning Action Shot A .10 .25
155 Lightning Action Shot B .10 .25
156 John Grahame .20 .50
157 Fredrik Modin .10 .25
158 Lightning Team Logo .10 .25
159 Ruslan Fedotenko .10 .25
160 Dan Boyle .10 .25
161 Pavel Kubina .10 .25
162 Dave Andreychuk .10 .25
163 Mats Sundin .40 1.00
164 Ed Belfour .40 1.00
165 Eric Lindros .40 1.00
166 Darcy Tucker .10 .25
167 Jeff O'Neill .10 .25
168 Bryan McCabe .10 .25
169 Maple Leafs Team Logo .10 .25
170 Maple Leafs Action Shot A .10 .25
171 Maple Leafs Action Shot B .10 .25
172 Tie Domi .20 .50
173 Tomas Kaberle .10 .25
174 Matt Stajan .20 .50
175 Alexander Ovechkin 1.50 4.00
176 Olaf Kolzig .40 1.00
177 Brian Sutherby .10 .25
178 Jeff Halpern .10 .25
179 Dainius Zubrus .10 .25
180 Capitals Action Shot A .10 .25
181 Capitals Action Shot B .10 .25
182 Capitals Team Logo .10 .25
183 Brendan Witt .10 .25
184 Andrew Cassels .10 .25
185 Jeff Friesen .10 .25
186 Steve Eminger .10 .25
187 Jean Sebastien Giguere .40 1.00
188 Ruslan Salei .10 .25
189 Scott Niedermayer .20 .50
190 Rob Niedermayer .10 .25
191 Sandis Ozolinsh .10 .25
192 Teemu Selanne .40 1.00
193 Mighty Ducks Team Logo .10 .25
194 Mighty Ducks Action Shot A .10 .25
195 Mighty Ducks Action Shot B .10 .25
196 Joffrey Lupul .20 .50
197 Petr Sykora .10 .25
198 Ryan Getzlaf .75 2.00
199 Jarome Iginla .75 2.00
200 Miikka Kiprusoff .60 1.50
201 Shean Donovan .10 .25
202 Roman Hamrlik .10 .25
203 Daymond Langkow .10 .25
204 Steven Reinprecht .10 .25
205 Flames Team Logo .10 .25
206 Flames Action Shot A .10 .25
207 Flames Action Shot B .10 .25
208 Chuck Kobasew .10 .25
209 Jordan Leopold .10 .25
210 Tony Amonte .10 .25
211 Tuomo Ruutu .20 .50
212 Nikolai Khabibulin .20 .50
213 Jassen Cullimore .10 .25
214 Adrian Aucoin .10 .25
215 Tyler Arnason .10 .25
216 Blackhawks Team Logo .10 .25
217 Matthew Barnaby .10 .25
218 Blackhawks Action Shot A .10 .25
219 Blackhawks Action Shot B .10 .25
220 Mark Bell .10 .25
221 Kyle Calder .10 .25
222 Martin Lapointe .10 .25
223 Joe Sakic 1.25 3.00
224 Milan Hejduk .20 .50
225 Rob Blake .20 .50
226 Alex Tanguay .20 .50
227 David Aebischer .20 .50
228 John-Michael Liles .10 .25
229 Avalanche Team Logo .10 .25
230 Avalanche Action Shot A .10 .25
231 Avalanche Action Shot B .10 .25
232 Pierre Turgeon .10 .25
233 Andrew Brunette .10 .25
234 Steve Konowalchuk .10 .25
235 Rick Nash .60 1.50
236 Adam Foote .10 .25
237 Marc Denis .20 .50
238 Nikolai Zherdev .20 .50
239 Dan Fritsche .10 .25
240 Manny Malhotra .10 .25
241 Blue Jackets Team Logo .10 .25
242 Blue Jackets Action Shot A .10 .25
243 Blue Jackets Action Shot B .10 .25
244 Bryan Berard .10 .25
245 David Vyborny .10 .25
246 Sergei Fedorov .40 1.00
247 Mike Modano .40 1.00
248 Bill Guerin .20 .50
249 Sergei Zubov .10 .25
250 Jere Lehtinen .20 .50
251 Jason Arnott .10 .25
252 Stars Team Logo .10 .25
253 Brenden Morrow .20 .50
254 Stars Action Shot A .10 .25
255 Stars Action Shot B .10 .25
256 Stu Barnes .10 .25
257 Antti Miettinen .10 .25
258 Marty Turco .30 .75
259 Steve Yzerman 1.00 2.50
260 Brendan Shanahan .40 1.00
261 Nicklas Lidstrom .40 1.00
262 Kris Draper .10 .25
263 Robert Lang .10 .25
264 Pavel Datsyuk .40 1.00
265 Red Wings Team Logo .10 .25
266 Red Wings Action Shot A .10 .25
267 Red Wings Action Shot B .10 .25
268 Chris Osgood .20 .50
269 Chris Chelios .20 .50
270 Henrik Zetterberg .40 1.00
271 Ryan Smyth .20 .50
272 Chris Pronger .20 .50
273 Michael Peca .10 .25
274 Ty Conklin .20 .50
275 Georges Laraque .20 .50
276 Oilers Action Shot A .10 .25
277 Oilers Action Shot B .10 .25
278 Oilers Team Logo .10 .25
279 Ales Hemsky .20 .50
280 Jason Smith .10 .25
281 Steve Staios .10 .25
282 Radek Dvorak .10 .25
283 Luc Robitaille .40 1.00
284 Jeremy Roenick .75 2.00
285 Alexander Frolov .20 .50
286 Pavol Demitra .10 .25
287 Mattias Norstrom .10 .25
288 Kings Team Logo .10 .25
289 Kings Action Shot A .10 .25
290 Kings Action Shot B .10 .25
291 Lubomir Visnovsky .10 .25
292 Eric Belanger .10 .25
293 Mathieu Garon .20 .50
294 Mike Cammalleri .20 .50
295 Marian Gaborik .75 2.00
296 Dwayne Roloson .20 .50
297 Marc Chouinard .10 .25
298 Brian Rolston .10 .25
299 Pierre-Marc Bouchard .20 .50
300 Willie Mitchell .10 .25
301 Wild Team Logo .10 .25
302 Wild Action Shot A .10 .25
303 Wild Action Shot B .10 .25
304 Manny Fernandez .20 .50
305 Alexandre Daigle .10 .25
306 Wes Walz .10 .25
307 Paul Kariya .40 1.00
308 Steve Sullivan .10 .25
309 Tomas Vokoun .20 .50
310 Kimmo Timonen .10 .25
311 Marek Zidlicky .10 .25
312 Dan Hamuis .10 .25
313 David Legwand .10 .25
314 Predators Team Logo .10 .25
315 Scott Walker .10 .25
316 Predators Action Shot A .10 .25
317 Predators Action Shot B .10 .25
318 Greg Johnson .10 .25
319 Shane Doan .10 .25
320 Geoff Sanderson .10 .25
321 Mike Comrie .10 .25
322 Curtis Joseph .20 .50
323 Mike Ricci .10 .25
324 Paul Mara .10 .25
325 Coyotes Team Logo .10 .25
326 Coyotes Action Shot A .10 .25
327 Coyotes Action Shot B .10 .25
328 Oleg Saprykin .10 .25
329 Petr Nedved .10 .25
330 Derek Morris .10 .25
331 Blues Action Shot A .10 .25
332 Blues Action Shot B .10 .25
333 Doug Weight .10 .25
334 Keith Tkachuk .20 .50
335 Barret Jackman .10 .25
336 Eric Brewer .10 .25
337 Patrick Lalime .20 .50
338 Blues Team Logo .10 .25
339 Dallas Drake .10 .25
340 Scott Young .10 .25
341 Petr Cajanek .10 .25
342 Bryce Salvador .10 .25
343 Evgeni Nabokov .20 .50
344 Patrick Marleau .20 .50
345 Marco Sturm .10 .25
346 Brad Stuart .10 .25
347 Jonathan Cheechoo .20 .50
348 Scott Hannan .10 .25
349 Sharks Team Logo .10 .25
350 Sharks Action Shot A .10 .25
351 Sharks Action Shot B .10 .25
352 Alyn McCauley .10 .25
353 Niko Dimitrakos .10 .25
354 Wayne Primeau .10 .25
355 Markus Naslund .20 .50
356 Brendan Morrison .10 .25
357 Ed Jovanovski .10 .25
358 Todd Bertuzzi .20 .50
359 Dan Cloutier .20 .50
360 Canucks Action Shot A .10 .25
361 Canucks Action Shot B .10 .25
362 Canucks Team Logo .10 .25

363 Trevor Linden .20 .50
364 Daniel Sedin .20 .50
365 Henrik Sedin .20 .50
366 Mattias Ohlund .10 .25
367 Action Shot 1A .10 .25
368 Action Shot 1B .10 .25
369 Action Shot 2A .10 .25
370 Action Shot 2B .10 .25
371 Action Shot 3A .10 .25
372 Action Shot 3B .10 .25
373 Action Shot 4A .10 .25
374 Action Shot 4B .10 .25
375 Action Shot 5A .10 .25
376 Action Shot 5B .10 .25
377 Action Shot 6A .10 .25
378 Action Shot 6B .10 .25
379 Action Shot 7A .10 .25
380 Action Shot 7B .10 .25
381 Action Shot 8A .10 .25
382 Action Shot 8B .10 .25
383 Action Shot 9A .10 .25
384 Action Shot 9B .10 .25
385 Action Shot 10A .10 .25
386 Action Shot 10B .10 .25
387 Action Shot 11A .10 .25
388 Action Shot 11B .10 .25
389 Action Shot 12A .10 .25
390 Action Shot 12B .10 .25

2006-07 Panini Stickers

COMPLETE SET (360) 25.00 60.00
1 Atlanta Thrashers Puzzle Piece .07 .20
2 Atlanta Thrashers Puzzle Piece .07 .20
3 Atlanta Thrashers Team Logo .07 .20
4 Bobby Holik .15 .40
5 Marian Hossa .25 .60
6 Ilya Kovalchuk .40 1.00
7 Vyacheslav Kozlov .15 .40
8 Scott Mellanby .15 .40
9 Kari Lehtonen .30 .75
10 Niclas Havelid .15 .40
11 Steve Rucchin .15 .40
12 Andy Sutton .15 .40
13 Boston Bruins Puzzle Piece .07 .20
14 Boston Bruins Puzzle Piece .07 .20
15 Boston Bruins Team Logo .07 .20
16 P.J. Axelsson .15 .40
17 Patrice Bergeron .30 .75
18 Brad Boyes .15 .40
19 Glen Murray .15 .40
20 Marc Savard .15 .40
21 Marco Sturm .15 .40
22 Zdeno Chara .15 .40
23 Brad Stuart .15 .40
24 Paul Mara .15 .40
25 Buffalo Sabres Puzzle Piece .07 .20
26 Buffalo Sabres Puzzle Piece .07 .20
27 Buffalo Sabres Team Logo .07 .20
28 Ryan Miller .30 .75
29 Chris Drury .15 .40
30 Maxim Afinogenov .15 .40
31 Ales Kotalik .15 .40
32 Daniel Briere .25 .60
33 Thomas Vanek .25 .60
34 Derek Roy .15 .40
35 Brian Campbell .15 .40
36 Tim Connolly .15 .40
37 Carolina Hurricanes Puzzle Piece .07 .20
38 Carolina Hurricanes Puzzle Piece .07 .20
39 Carolina Hurricanes Team Logo .07 .20
40 Cam Ward .30 .75
41 Rod Brind'Amour .25 .60
42 Erik Cole .15 .40
43 Eric Staal .30 .75
44 Cory Stillman .15 .40
45 Ray Whitney .15 .40
46 Justin Williams .15 .40
47 Frantisek Kaberle .15 .40
48 Bret Hedican .15 .40
49 Florida Panthers Puzzle Piece .07 .20
50 Florida Panthers Puzzle Piece .07 .20
51 Florida Panthers Team Logo .07 .20
52 Todd Bertuzzi .25 .60
53 Nathan Horton .15 .40
54 Olli Jokinen .15 .40
55 Joe Nieuwendyk .25 .60
56 Rostislav Olesz .15 .40
57 Gary Roberts .15 .40
58 Josef Stumpel .15 .40
59 Jay Bouwmeester .15 .40
60 Ed Belfour .30 .75
61 Montreal Canadiens Puzzle Piece .07 .20
62 Montreal Canadiens Puzzle Piece .07 .20
63 Montreal Canadiens Team Logo .07 .20
64 Saku Koivu .30 .75
65 Alexei Kovalev .15 .40
66 Chris Higgins .15 .40
67 Mike Ribeiro .15 .40
68 Michael Ryder .25 .60
69 Sergei Samsonov .25 .60
70 Andrei Markov .15 .40
71 Sheldon Souray .15 .40
72 Cristobal Huet .40 1.00
73 New Jersey Devils Puzzle Piece .07 .20
74 New Jersey Devils Puzzle Piece .07 .20
75 New Jersey Devils Team Logo .07 .20
76 Martin Brodeur 1.00 2.50
77 Brian Gionta .15 .40
78 Patrik Elias .15 .40
79 Scott Gomez .15 .40
80 Brian Rafalski .15 .40
81 Colin White .15 .40
82 Jamie Langenbrunner .15 .40
83 John Madden .15 .40
84 Zach Parise .25 .60
85 New York Islanders Puzzle Piece .07 .20
86 New York Islanders Puzzle Piece .07 .20
87 New York Islanders Team Logo .07 .20
88 Rick DiPietro .25 .60
89 Miroslav Satan .15 .40
90 Alexei Yashin .15 .40
91 Mike York .15 .40
92 Jason Blake .15 .40
93 Brendan Witt .15 .40
94 Alexei Zhitnik .15 .40
95 Mike Sillinger .15 .40
96 Trent Hunter .15 .40
97 New York Rangers Puzzle Piece .07 .20
98 New York Rangers Puzzle Piece .07 .20
99 New York Rangers Team Logo .07 .20
100 Jaromir Jagr .50 1.25
101 Brendan Shanahan .30 .75
102 Henrik Lundqvist .40 1.00
103 Marek Malik .15 .40
104 Michal Rozsival .15 .40
105 Petr Prucha .15 .40
106 Martin Straka .15 .40
107 Michael Nylander .15 .40
108 Darius Kasparaitis .15 .40
109 Ottawa Senators Puzzle Piece .07 .20
110 Ottawa Senators Puzzle Piece .07 .20
111 Ottawa Senators Team Logo .07 .20
112 Daniel Alfredsson .25 .60
113 Jason Spezza .30 .75
114 Dany Heatley .40 1.00
115 Mike Fisher .15 .40
116 Patrick Eaves .15 .40
117 Chris Phillips .15 .40
118 Wade Redden .15 .40
119 Martin Gerber .30 .75
120 Ray Emery .25 .60
121 Philadelphia Flyers Puzzle Piece .07 .20
122 Philadelphia Flyers Puzzle Piece .07 .20
123 Philadelphia Flyers Team Logo .07 .20
124 Peter Forsberg .50 1.25
125 Kyle Calder .15 .40
126 Simon Gagne .30 .75
127 Petr Nedved .15 .40
128 Derian Hatcher .15 .40
129 Joni Pitkanen .15 .40
130 Robert Esche .25 .60
131 Mike Knuble .15 .40
132 Jeff Carter .30 .75
133 Pittsburgh Penguins Puzzle Piece .07 .20
134 Pittsburgh Penguins Puzzle Piece .07 .20
135 Pittsburgh Penguins Team Logo .07 .20
136 Sidney Crosby 2.50 6.00
137 Mark Recchi .15 .40
138 Marc-Andre Fleury .30 .75
139 Sergei Gonchar .15 .40
140 Ronald Petrovicky .15 .40
141 John LeClair .25 .60
142 Ryan Malone .15 .40
143 Ryan Whitney .15 .40
144 Nils Ekman .15 .40
145 Tampa Bay Lightning Puzzle Piece .07 .20
146 Tampa Bay Lightning Puzzle Piece .07 .20
147 Tampa Bay Lightning Team Logo .07 .20
148 Marc Denis .25 .60
149 Vincent Lecavalier .30 .75
150 Brad Richards .25 .60
151 Vaclav Prospal .15 .40
152 Dan Boyle .15 .40
153 Martin St. Louis .25 .60
154 Filip Kuba .15 .40
155 Ruslan Fedotenko .15 .40
156 Cory Sarich .15 .40
157 Toronto Maple Leafs Puzzle Piece .07 .20
158 Toronto Maple Leafs Puzzle Piece .07 .20
159 Toronto Maple Leafs Team Logo .07 .20
160 Andrew Raycroft .25 .60
161 Mats Sundin .30 .75
162 Pavel Kubina .15 .40
163 Michael Peca .15 .40
164 Darcy Tucker .15 .40
165 Tomas Kaberle .15 .40
166 Bryan McCabe .15 .40
167 Jeff O'Neill .15 .40
168 Alexander Steen .25 .60
169 Washington Capitals Puzzle Piece .07 .20
170 Washington Capitals Puzzle Piece .07 .20
171 Washington Capitals Team Logo .07 .20
172 Alexander Ovechkin 1.00 2.50
173 Richard Zednik .15 .40
174 Dainius Zubrus .15 .40
175 Olaf Kolzig .30 .75
176 Chris Clark .15 .40
177 Matt Pettinger .15 .40
178 Ben Clymer .15 .40
179 Brian Sutherby .15 .40
180 Brian Pothier .15 .40
181 Anaheim Ducks Puzzle Piece .07 .20
182 Anaheim Ducks Puzzle Piece .07 .20
183 Anaheim Ducks Team Logo .07 .20
184 Chris Pronger .25 .60
185 Scott Niedermayer .15 .40
186 Jean-Sebastien Giguere .25 .60
187 Teemu Selanne .30 .75
188 Andy McDonald .15 .40
189 Rob Niedermayer .15 .40
190 Ilya Bryzgalov .25 .60
191 Ryan Getzlaf .25 .60
192 Chris Kunitz .15 .40
193 Calgary Flames Puzzle Piece .07 .20
194 Calgary Flames Puzzle Piece .07 .20
195 Calgary Flames Team Logo .07 .20
196 Jarome Iginla .40 1.00
197 Miikka Kiprusoff .30 .75
198 Alex Tanguay .25 .60
199 Dion Phaneuf .40 1.00
200 Tony Amonte .15 .40
201 Robyn Regehr .15 .40
202 Rhett Warrener .15 .40
203 Daymond Langkow .15 .40
204 Kristian Huselius .15 .40
205 Chicago Blackhawks Puzzle Piece .07 .20
206 Chicago Blackhawks Puzzle Piece .07 .20
207 Chicago Blackhawks Team Logo .07 .20
208 Nikolai Khabibulin .30 .75
209 Martin Havlat .25 .60
210 Tuomo Ruutu .25 .60
211 Michal Handzus .15 .40
212 Radim Vrbata .15 .40
213 Bryan Smolinski .15 .40
214 Patrick Sharp .15 .40
215 Adrian Aucoin .15 .40
216 Martin Lapointe .15 .40
217 Colorado Avalanche Puzzle Piece .07 .20
218 Colorado Avalanche Puzzle Piece .07 .20
219 Colorado Avalanche Team Logo .07 .20
220 Jose Theodore .30 .75
221 Joe Sakic .60 1.50
222 Milan Hejduk .15 .40
223 Marek Svatos .15 .40
224 Pierre Turgeon .15 .40
225 Andrew Brunette .15 .40
226 Steve Konowalchuk .15 .40
227 John-Michael Liles .15 .40
228 Ian Laperriere .15 .40
229 Columbus Blue Jackets Puzzle Piece .07 .20
230 Columbus Blue Jackets Puzzle Piece .07 .20
231 Columbus Blue Jackets Team Logo .07 .20
232 Rick Nash .30 .75
233 Sergei Fedorov .30 .75
234 Fredrik Modin .15 .40
235 David Vyborny .15 .40
236 Adam Foote .15 .40
237 Rostislav Klesla .15 .40
238 Pascal Leclaire .25 .60
239 Nikolai Zherdev .15 .40
240 Jason Chimera .15 .40
241 Dallas Stars Puzzle Piece .07 .20
242 Dallas Stars Puzzle Piece .07 .20
243 Dallas Stars Team Logo .07 .20
244 Marty Turco .25 .60
245 Mike Modano .30 .75
246 Eric Lindros .30 .75
247 Sergei Zubov .15 .40
248 Jere Lehtinen .15 .40
249 Brenden Morrow .25 .60
250 Jaroslav Modry .15 .40
251 Stu Barnes .15 .40
252 Phillippe Boucher .15 .40
253 Detroit Red Wings Puzzle Piece .07 .20
254 Detroit Red Wings Puzzle Piece .07 .20
255 Detroit Red Wings Team Logo .07 .20
256 Dominik Hasek .50 1.25
257 Pavel Datsyuk .25 .60
258 Chris Chelios .25 .60
259 Nicklas Lidstrom .30 .75
260 Henrik Zetterberg .30 .75
261 Robert Lang .15 .40
262 Mathieu Schneider .15 .40
263 Kris Draper .15 .40
264 Tomas Holmstrom .15 .40
265 Edmonton Oilers Puzzle Piece .07 .20
266 Edmonton Oilers Puzzle Piece .07 .20
267 Edmonton Oilers Team Logo .07 .20
268 Dwayne Roloson .30 .75
269 Ryan Smyth .25 .60
270 Jason Smith .15 .40
271 Joffrey Lupul .15 .40
272 Ales Hemsky .15 .40
273 Fernando Pisani .15 .40
274 Raffi Torres .15 .40
275 Shawn Horcoff .15 .40
276 Jarret Stoll .15 .40
277 Los Angeles Kings Puzzle Piece .07 .20
278 Los Angeles Kings Puzzle Piece .07 .20
279 Los Angeles Kings Team Logo .07 .20
280 Alexander Frolov .15 .40
281 Rob Blake .25 .60
282 Dan Cloutier .25 .60
283 Mattias Norstrom .15 .40
284 Lubomir Visnovsky .15 .40
285 Craig Conroy .15 .40
286 Sean Avery .15 .40
287 Mike Cammalleri .15 .40
288 Dustin Brown .15 .40
289 Minnesota Wild Puzzle Piece .07 .20
290 Minnesota Wild Puzzle Piece .07 .20
291 Minnesota Wild Team Logo .07 .20
292 Manny Fernandez .25 .60
293 Marian Gaborik .40 1.00
294 Mark Parrish .15 .40
295 Pavol Demitra .15 .40
296 Brian Rolston .15 .40
297 Wes Walz .15 .40
298 Pierre-Marc Bouchard .15 .40
299 Todd White .15 .40
300 Martin Skoula .15 .40
301 Nashville Predators Puzzle Piece .07 .20
302 Nashville Predators Puzzle Piece .07 .20
303 Nashville Predators Team Logo .07 .20
304 Paul Kariya .30 .75
305 Jason Arnott .15 .40
306 Steve Sullivan .15 .40
307 Tomas Vokoun .25 .60
308 Marek Zidlicky .15 .40
309 David Legwand .15 .40
310 Martin Erat .15 .40
311 Kimmo Timonen .15 .40
312 Scott Hartnell .15 .40
313 Phoenix Coyotes Puzzle Piece .07 .20
314 Phoenix Coyotes Puzzle Piece .07 .20
315 Phoenix Coyotes Team Logo .07 .20
316 Ed Jovanovski .15 .40
317 Jeremy Roenick .40 1.00
318 Curtis Joseph .30 .75
319 Shane Doan .15 .40
320 Mike Comrie .15 .40
321 Ladislav Nagy .15 .40
322 Nick Boynton .15 .40
323 Derek Morris .15 .40
324 Steve Reinprecht .15 .40
325 San Jose Sharks Puzzle Piece .07 .20
326 San Jose Sharks Puzzle Piece .07 .20
327 San Jose Sharks Team Logo .07 .20
328 Vesa Toskala .25 .60
329 Evgeni Nabokov .25 .60
330 Joe Thornton .50 1.25
331 Jonathan Cheechoo .30 .75
332 Mark Bell .15 .40
333 Patrick Marleau .25 .60
334 Steve Bernier .15 .40
335 Scott Hannan .15 .40
336 Milan Michalek .15 .40
337 St. Louis Blues Puzzle Piece .07 .20
338 St. Louis Blues Puzzle Piece .07 .20
339 St. Louis Blues Team Logo .07 .20
340 Doug Weight .15 .40
341 Bill Guerin .15 .40
342 Martin Rucinsky .15 .40
343 Jay McKee .15 .40
344 Barret Jackman .15 .40
345 Eric Brewer .15 .40
346 Keith Tkachuk .25 .60
347 Manny Legace .25 .60
348 Petr Cajanek .15 .40
349 Vancouver Canucks Puzzle Piece .07 .20
350 Vancouver Canucks Puzzle Piece .07 .20
351 Vancouver Canucks Team Logo .07 .20
352 Roberto Luongo .60 1.50
353 Jan Bulis .15 .40
354 Markus Naslund .30 .75
355 Brendan Morrison .15 .40
356 Daniel Sedin .15 .40
357 Henrik Sedin .15 .40
358 Mattias Ohlund .15 .40
359 Sami Salo .15 .40
360 Matt Cooke .15 .40

1993-94 Panthers Team Issue

These eight blank-backed cards were printed on thin stock and measure approximately 3 3/4" by 7". They feature on their white-bordered fronts black-and-white action shots framed by a thin red line. The player's uniform number (in large red characters), his name and position, and the Panthers' logo are printed across the top. The cards are unnumbered and checklisted below in alphabetical order.

COMPLETE SET (8) 4.80 12.00
1 Joe Cirella .60 1.50
2 Tom Fitzgerald .60 1.50
3 Mike Foligno .60 1.50
4 Paul Laus .75 2.00
5 Bill Lindsay .60 1.50
6 Andrei Lomakin .60 1.50
7 Scott Mellanby .75 2.00
8 Brent Severyn .60 1.50

1994-95 Panthers Pop-ups

Issued by Health Plan of Florida, these cards measure 4" x 10". They were given away at five different home games throughout the season. Back has biographical information.

COMPLETE SET (5) 4.00 10.00
1 Brian Skrudland .60 1.50
2 John Vanbiesbrouck 1.25 3.00
3 Scott Mellanby .60 1.50
4 Stu Barnes .60 1.50
5 Jesse Belanger .60 1.50

2000-01 Panthers Team Issue

This set features the Panthers of the NHL. The cards were issued as a promotional giveaway. The perforated card sheets were stapled into a booklet with four cards per page.

COMPLETE SET (32) 10.00 25.00
1 Bill Torrey CO .04 .10
2 Chuck Fletcher GM .04 .10
3 Duane Sutter CO .10 .25
4 Panther MASCOT .04 .10
5 Slavomir Lener TR .04 .10
6 Billy Smith CO .40 1.00
7 Roberto Luongo 2.00 5.00
8 Lance Pitlick .20 .50
9 Paul Laus .40 1.00
10 Bret Hedican .20 .50
11 Mike Wilson .20 .50
12 Peter Worrell .60 1.50
13 Len Barrie .20 .50
14 Pavel Bure 2.00 5.00
15 Olli Jokinen .30 .75
16 Vaclav Prospal .20 .50
17 Ray Whitney .20 .50
18 John Jakopin .20 .50
19 Mike Sillinger .20 .50
20 Greg Adams .20 .50
21 Marcus Nilsson .20 .50
22 Serge Payer .20 .50
23 Todd Simpson .20 .50
24 Robert Svehla .20 .50
25 Viktor Kozlov .30 .75
26 Dan Boyle .20 .50
27 Scott Mellanby .20 .50
28 Anders Eriksson .20 .50
29 Trevor Kidd .30 .75
30 Ivan Novoseltsev .30 .75
31 Rob Niedermayer .20 .50
32 Lance Ward .20 .50

2003-04 Panthers Team Issue

These cards are oversized and were distributed by the team at club events. It's likely this checklist is incomplete. Additional information can be forwarded to hockeymag@beckett.com.

COMPLETE SET (18) 8.00 20.00
1 Mathieu Biron .20 .50
2 Jay Bouwmeester .40 1.00
3 Valeri Bure .20 .50
4 Matt Cullen .20 .50
5 Niklas Hagman .20 .50
6 Darcy Hordichuk .40 1.00
7 Nathan Horton 1.50 4.00
8 Kristian Huselius .30 .75
9 Olli Jokinen .40 1.00
10 Viktor Kozlov .20 .50
11 Roberto Luongo 1.25 3.00
12 Eric Messier .20 .50
13 Branislav Mezei .20 .50
14 Lyle Odelein .20 .50
15 Mikael Samuelsson .20 .50
16 Pavel Trnka .20 .50
17 Mike Van Ryn .20 .50
18 Stephen Weiss .40 1.00

1943-48 Parade Sportive *

These blank-backed photo sheets of sports figures from the Montreal area in the mid-1940s measure approximately 5" by 8 1/4". They were issued to promote a couple of Montreal radio stations that used to broadcast interviews with some of the pictured athletes. The sheets feature white-bordered black-and-white player photos, some of them crudely retouched. The player's name appears in the bottom white margin and also as a facsimile autograph across the photo. The sheets are unnumbered and are listed below in alphabetical order. It's possible that other example exist of hockey players, so any additions to this checklist are appreciated. Many players are known to appear on two versions of these cards, and those players with (2) following their name, have been found with additional cards. Photos on these cards are often the same, with only the correspondence address at the top being different. A complete checklist for this set, covering all sports, is found in the Beckett Almanac of Baseball Cards and Collectibles.

COMPLETE SET (97) 500.00 1000.00
1 George Allen 5.00 10.00
2 Aldrege Bastien 5.00 10.00
3 Bobby Bauer 12.50 25.00
Milt Schmidt
Bill Durnan
4 Joe Benoit 5.00 10.00
5 Paul Bibeault 5.00 10.00
6 Butch Bouchard 7.50 15.00
8 Toe Blake 12.50 25.00
9 Butch Bouchard (2) 7.50 15.00
10 Butch Bouchard (3) 7.50 15.00
11 Butch Bouchard 12.50 25.00
Leo Lamoureux
Bill Durnan
12 Lionel Bouvrette 5.00 10.00
13 Lionel Bouvrette (2) 5.00 10.00
14 Frank Brimsek 12.50 25.00
15 Turk Broda 12.50 25.00
16 Turk Broda (2) 12.50 25.00
17 Eddie Bruneteau 5.00 10.00
18 Modere Bruneteau 5.00 10.00
19 Modere (Mud) Bruneteau 5.00 10.00
20 J.C. Campeau 5.00 10.00
21 J.C. Campeau 5.00 10.00
22 Bob Carse 5.00 10.00
23 Joe Carveth 5.00 10.00
24 Denys Casavant 5.00 10.00
25 Denys Casavant (2) 5.00 10.00
26 Murph Chamberlain 5.00 10.00
27 Bill Cowley 10.00 20.00
28 Floyd Curry 5.00 10.00
29 Tony Demers 5.00 10.00
30 Tony Demers (2) 5.00 10.00
31 Connie Dion 5.00 10.00
32 Bill Durnan 12.50 25.00
33 Bill Durnan (2) 12.50 25.00
34 Normand Dussault 5.00 10.00
35 Normand Dussault (2) 5.00 10.00
36 Frank Eddolls 5.00 10.00
37 Bob Fillion 5.00 10.00
38 Bob Fillion (2) 5.00 10.00
39 Johnny Gagnon 5.00 10.00
40 Johnny Gagnon 17.50 35.00
Aurel Joliat
Howie Morenz
41 Armand Gaudreault 5.00 10.00
42 Armand Gaudreault (2) 5.00 10.00
43 Fernand Gauthier 5.00 10.00
44 Fernand Gauthier (2) 5.00 10.00
45 Fernand Gauthier 5.00 10.00
Buddy O'Connor
Dutch Hiller
46 Jean Gladu 5.00 10.00
47 Jean Gladu (2) 5.00 10.00
48 Leo Gravelle 5.00 10.00
49 Glen Harmon 5.00 10.00
50 Glen Harmon (2) 5.00 10.00
51 Glen Harmon (close up) 5.00 10.00
52 Doug Harvey 12.50 25.00
53 Jerry Heffernan 5.00 10.00
Buddy O'Connor
Pete Morin
54 Sugar Jim Henry 10.00 20.00
55 Dutch Hiller 7.50 15.00
56 Dutch Hiller (2) 7.50 15.00
57 Rosario Joanette 5.00 10.00
58 Michael Karakas 10.00 20.00
59 Mike Karakas 10.00 20.00
60 Elmer Lach 10.00 20.00
61 Ernest Laforce 5.00 10.00
62 Leo Lamoureux 5.00 10.00
63 Edgar Laprade 7.50 15.00
64 Jerry Plamondon 5.00 10.00
65 Hal Laycoe 5.00 10.00
66 Paul Raymond 5.00 10.00
67 Billy Reay 7.50 15.00
68 Roger Leger 5.00 10.00
69 John Quilty 5.00 10.00
70 Jacques Locas 5.00 10.00
71 Jacques Locas (2) 5.00 10.00
72 Kenny Reardon 7.50 15.00
73 Maurice Richard 30.00 60.00
74 Harry Lumley 12.50 25.00
75 Maurice Richard (2) 30.00 60.00
76 Fernand Mageau 5.00 10.00
77 Maurice Richard 37.50 75.00
Elmer Lach
Toe Blake
78 Georges Mantha 10.00 20.00
79 Howie(Rip) Riopelle 5.00 10.00
80 Gaye Stewart 5.00 10.00
81 Georges Mantha (2) 5.00 10.00
82 Jean Marois 6.00 12.00
83 Phil Watson 5.00 10.00
84 Mike McMahon 5.00 10.00
85 Montreal Canadiens 10.00 20.00
Team Photo 1943-44
86 Montreal Canadiens
(Team Photo 1944-45
87 Montreal Canadiens
(Team Photo 1945-46
88 Montreal Canadiens
(Team Photo 1946-47
89 Gerry McNeil 12.50 25.00
90 Pierre(Pete) Morin 5.00 10.00
91 Ken Mosdell 5.00 10.00
92 Bill Mosienko 10.00 20.00
Max Bentley
Doug Bentley
93 Buddy O'Connor 5.00 10.00
94 Robert (Bob) Pepin 5.00 10.00
95 Jimmy Peters 5.00 10.00
96 Gerry Plamondon 5.00 10.00
97 Gerry Plamondon UER 5.00 10.00
(misspelled as Jerry

1997-98 Paramount

The 1997-98 Pacific Paramount set was issued in one series totaling 200 cards and distributed in five-card packs. The fronts feature color action player photos with holographic gold foil highlights. The backs carry another action player photo and player information.

COMPLETE SET (200) 10.00 25.00
1 Guy Hebert .08 .25

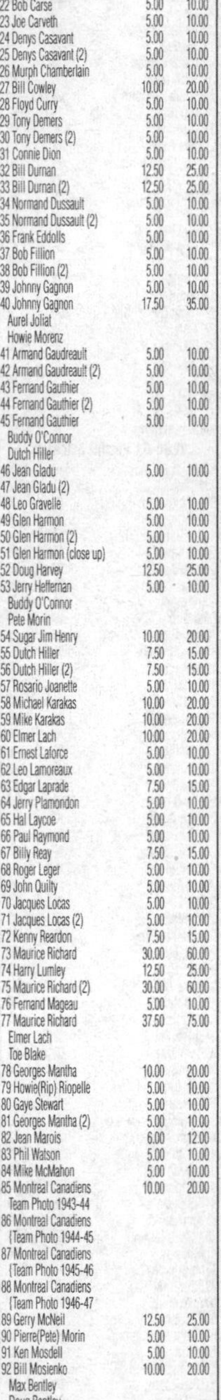

2 Paul Kariya .10 .30
3 Espen Knutsen RC .20 .50
4 Dmitri Mironov .02 .10
5 Steve Rucchin .02 .10
6 Tomas Sandstrom .02 .10
7 Teemu Selanne .10 .30
8 Scott Young .02 .10
9 Ray Bourque .20 .50
10 Jim Carey .08 .25
11 Anson Carter .08 .25
12 Ted Donato .02 .10
13 Dave Ellett .02 .10
14 Dimitri Khristich .02 .10
15 Sergei Samsonov .08 .25
16 Joe Thornton .25 .60
17 Matthew Barnaby .02 .10
18 Jason Dawe .02 .10
19 Dominik Hasek .25 .60
20 Brian Holzinger .02 .10
21 Michael Peca .02 .10
22 Derek Plante .02 .10
23 Erik Rasmussen .02 .10
24 Miroslav Satan .02 .10
25 Steve Begin RC .02 .10
26 Andrew Cassels .02 .10
27 Chris Dingman RC .02 .10
28 Theo Fleury .02 .10
29 Jonas Hoglund .02 .10
30 Jarome Iginla .15 .40
31 Rick Tabaracci .08 .25
32 German Titov .02 .10
33 Kevin Dineen .02 .10
34 Nelson Emerson .02 .10
35 Trevor Kidd .08 .25
36 Stephen Leach .02 .10
37 Keith Primeau .02 .10
38 Steven Rice .02 .10
39 Gary Roberts .02 .10
40 Tony Amonte .08 .25
41 Chris Chelios .10 .30
42 Daniel Cleary .08 .25
43 Eric Daze .08 .25
44 Jeff Hackett .08 .25
45 Sergei Krivokrasov .02 .10
46 Ethan Moreau .02 .10
47 Alexei Zhamnov .02 .10
48 Adam Deadmarsh .02 .10
49 Peter Forsberg .20 .50
50 Valeri Kamensky .08 .25
51 Jari Kurri .08 .25
52 Claude Lemieux .02 .10
53 Sandis Ozolinsh .02 .10
54 Patrick Roy .60 1.50
55 Joe Sakic .25 .60
56 Ed Belfour .10 .30
57 Derian Hatcher .02 .10
58 Jamie Langenbrunner .02 .10
59 Jere Lehtinen .02 .10
60 Mike Modano .20 .50
61 Joe Nieuwendyk .08 .25
62 Darryl Sydor .02 .10
63 Pat Verbeek .02 .10
64 Anders Eriksson .02 .10
65 Sergei Fedorov .15 .40
66 Vyacheslav Kozlov .02 .10
67 Nicklas Lidstrom .10 .30
68 Darren McCarty .02 .10
69 Chris Osgood .08 .25
70 Brendan Shanahan .10 .30
71 Steve Yzerman .40 1.00
72 Jason Arnott .02 .10
73 Boyd Devereaux .02 .10
74 Mike Grier .02 .10
75 Curtis Joseph .10 .30
76 Andrei Kovalenko .02 .10
77 Ryan Smyth .08 .25
78 Doug Weight .08 .25
79 Dave Gagner .02 .10
80 Ed Jovanovski .08 .25
81 Scott Mellanby .02 .10
82 Kirk Muller .02 .10
83 Rob Niedermayer .02 .10
84 Ray Sheppard .02 .10
85 Esa Tikkanen .02 .10
86 John Vanbiesbrouck .08 .25
87 Rob Blake .08 .25
88 Stephane Fiset .08 .25
89 Garry Galley .02 .10
90 Olli Jokinen RC .75 2.00
91 Luc Robitaille .08 .25
92 Jozef Stumpel .02 .10
93 Shayne Corson .02 .10
94 Vincent Damphousse .02 .10
95 Saku Koivu .10 .30
96 Andy Moog .08 .25
97 Mark Recchi .08 .25
98 Stephane Richer .02 .10
99 Brian Savage .02 .10
100 Dave Andreychuk .02 .10
101 Martin Brodeur .30 .75
102 Doug Gilmour .08 .25
103 Bobby Holik .02 .10
104 John MacLean .02 .10
105 Brian Rolston .02 .10
106 Bryan Berard .08 .25
107 Todd Bertuzzi .10 .30
108 Travis Green .02 .10
109 Zigmund Palffy .08 .25
110 Robert Reichel .02 .10
111 Tommy Salo .08 .25
112 Bryan Smolinski .02 .10
113 Christian Dube .02 .10
114 Adam Graves .02 .10
115 Wayne Gretzky .75 2.00
116 Alexei Kovalev .02 .10
117 Pat LaFontaine .10 .30
118 Brian Leetch .10 .30
119 Mike Richter .10 .30
120 Brian Skrudland .02 .10
121 Kevin Stevens .08 .25
122 Daniel Alfredsson .08 .25
123 Radek Bonk .02 .10
124 Alexandre Daigle .02 .10
125 Marian Hossa RC 1.25 3.00
126 Igor Kravchuk .02 .10
127 Chris Phillips .02 .10
128 Damian Rhodes .08 .25
129 Alexei Yashin .02 .10
130 Rod Brind'Amour .08 .25
131 Chris Gratton .08 .25
132 Ron Hextall .08 .25
133 John LeClair .10 .30
134 Eric Lindros .10 .30
135 Janne Niinimaa .08 .25
136 Vaclav Prospal RC .10 .30
137 Garth Snow .08 .25
138 Dainius Zubrus .10 .30
139 Mike Gartner .08 .25
140 Brad Isbister .02 .10
141 Nikolai Khabibulin .08 .25
142 Jeremy Roenick .15 .40
143 Cliff Ronning .02 .10
144 Keith Tkachuk .10 .30
145 Rick Tocchet .08 .25
146 Oleg Tverdovsky .02 .10
147 Tom Barrasso .08 .25
148 Ron Francis .08 .25
149 Kevin Hatcher .02 .10
150 Jaromir Jagr .20 .50
151 Darius Kasparaitis .02 .10
152 Alexei Morozov .08 .25
153 Petr Nedved .08 .25
154 Ed Olczyk .02 .10
155 Jim Campbell .02 .10
156 Kelly Chase .02 .10
157 Geoff Courtnall .02 .10
158 Grant Fuhr .08 .25
159 Brett Hull .15 .40
160 Joe Murphy .02 .10
161 Pierre Turgeon .08 .25
162 Tony Twist .08 .25
163 Shawn Burr .02 .10
164 Jeff Friesen .02 .10
165 Tony Granato .02 .10
166 Viktor Kozlov .02 .10
167 Patrick Marleau .15 .40
168 Stephane Matteau .02 .10
169 Owen Nolan .08 .25
170 Mike Vernon .08 .25
171 Dino Ciccarelli .02 .10
172 Karl Dykhuis .02 .10
173 Roman Hamrlik .02 .10
174 Daymond Langkow .08 .25
175 Mikael Renberg .08 .25
176 Alexander Selivanov .02 .10
177 Paul Ysebaert .02 .10
178 Sergei Berezin .02 .10
179 Wendel Clark .08 .25
180 Glenn Healy .08 .25
181 Derek King .02 .10
182 Alyn McCauley .08 .25
183 Felix Potvin .10 .30
184 Martin Prochazka RC .02 .10
185 Mats Sundin .10 .30
186 Pavel Bure .10 .30
187 Martin Gelinas .02 .10
188 Trevor Linden .08 .25
189 Kirk McLean .08 .25
190 Mark Messier .10 .30
191 Lubomir Vaic .02 .10
192 Mattias Ohlund .08 .25
193 Peter Bondra .08 .25
194 Dale Hunter .02 .10
195 Joe Juneau .08 .25
196 Olaf Kolzig .08 .25
197 Steve Konowalchuk .02 .10
198 Adam Oates .08 .25
199 Bill Ranford .08 .25
200 Jaroslav Svejkovsky .08 .25
P60 Mike Modano PROMO .40 1.00

1997-98 Paramount Copper

*COPPER: .8X TO 2X BASIC CARDS
STATED ODDS 1:1 HOBBY

1997-98 Paramount Dark Gray

*DARK GRAY: .8X TO 2X BASIC CARDS
STATED ODDS 1:1 HOBBY

1997-98 Paramount Emerald Green

*GREEN: .8X TO 2X BASIC CARDS
STATED ODDS 1:1 CANADIAN PACKS

1997-98 Paramount Ice Blue

*ICE BLUE: 15X TO 40X BASIC CARDS
STATED ODDS 1:73

1997-98 Paramount Red

*RED: .8X TO 2X BASIC CARDS
STATED ODDS 1:1 TREAT

1997-98 Paramount Silver

*SILVER: .8X TO 2X BASIC CARDS
STATED ODDS 1:1 RETAIL

1997-98 Paramount Big Numbers Die-Cuts

Randomly inserted in packs at the rate of 1:37, this 20-card set features die-cut textured cards in the shape of the players jersey number. The backs carry a small player head photo and player information in a newspaper story design.

COMPLETE SET (20) 25.00 50.00
1 Paul Kariya .75 2.00
2 Teemu Selanne .75 2.00
3 Joe Thornton 2.00 5.00
4 Dominik Hasek 1.50 4.00
5 Peter Forsberg 2.00 5.00
6 Patrick Roy 4.00 10.00

7 Joe Sakic 1.50 4.00
8 Sergei Fedorov 1.25 3.00
9 Brendan Shanahan .75 2.00
10 Steve Yzerman 4.00 10.00
11 John Vanbiesbrouck .60 1.50
12 Martin Brodeur 2.00 5.00
13 Doug Gilmour .60 1.50
14 Wayne Gretzky 5.00 12.00
15 Eric Lindros .75 2.00
16 Keith Tkachuk .75 2.00
17 Jaromir Jagr 1.25 3.00
18 Brett Hull 1.00 2.50
19 Pavel Bure .75 2.00
20 Mark Messier .75 2.00

1997-98 Paramount Canadian Greats

Randomly inserted at 2:48 Canadian retail packs only, this 12-card set features color photos of star players. The backs carry player information.

COMPLETE SET (12) 15.00 30.00
1 Paul Kariya .60 1.50
2 Joe Thornton 1.50 4.00
3 Jarome Iginla .75 2.00
4 Patrick Roy 3.00 8.00
5 Joe Sakic 1.25 3.00
6 Brendan Shanahan .60 1.50
7 Steve Yzerman 3.00 8.00
8 Ryan Smyth .50 1.25
9 Martin Brodeur 1.50 4.00
10 Wayne Gretzky 4.00 10.00
11 Eric Lindros .60 1.50
12 Mark Messier .60 1.50

1997-98 Paramount Glove Side Laser Cuts

Randomly inserted in packs at the rate of 1:73, this 20-card set features color photos of top goalies printed on a die-cut card in the shape of the goalie's glove.

COMPLETE SET (20) 50.00 100.00
1 Guy Hebert 2.00 5.00
2 Dominik Hasek 5.00 12.00
3 Trevor Kidd 2.00 5.00
4 Jeff Hackett 2.00 6.00
5 Patrick Roy 12.50 30.00
6 Ed Belfour 2.50 6.00
7 Chris Osgood 2.00 5.00
8 Curtis Joseph 2.50 6.00
9 John Vanbiesbrouck 2.00 5.00
10 Andy Moog 2.00 5.00
11 Martin Brodeur 6.00 15.00
12 Tommy Salo 2.00 5.00
13 Mike Richter 2.50 6.00
14 Ron Hextall 2.00 5.00
15 Garth Snow 2.00 5.00
16 Nikolai Khabibulin 2.00 5.00
17 Tom Barrasso 2.00 5.00
18 Grant Fuhr 2.00 5.00
19 Mike Vernon 2.00 5.00
20 Felix Potvin 2.50 6.00

1997-98 Paramount Photoengravings

Randomly inserted in packs at the rate of 2:37, this 20-card set features color images of top stars using photo-engraving technology and printed with a textured paper stock finish.

COMPLETE SET (20) 20.00 40.00
1 Paul Kariya .60 1.50
2 Teemu Selanne .60 1.50
3 Joe Thornton 1.50 4.00
4 Dominik Hasek 1.25 3.00
5 Peter Forsberg 1.50 4.00
6 Patrick Roy 3.00 8.00
7 Joe Sakic 1.25 3.00
8 Mike Modano 1.00 2.50
9 Brendan Shanahan .60 1.50
10 Steve Yzerman 3.00 8.00
11 John Vanbiesbrouck .50 1.25
12 Saku Koivu .60 1.50
13 Wayne Gretzky 4.00 10.00
14 John LeClair .60 1.50
15 Eric Lindros .60 1.50
16 Keith Tkachuk .60 1.50
17 Jaromir Jagr 1.00 2.50
18 Brett Hull .75 2.00
19 Pavel Bure .60 1.50
20 Mark Messier .60 1.50

1998-99 Paramount

The 1998-99 Pacific Paramount set consists of 250 standard-size cards. The fronts feature full bleed action photos with the player's name and team logo on holographic gold foil. The flipside offers the player's statistics. Each pack contains six cards. The cards were released around October, 1998.

COMPLETE SET (250) 15.00 30.00
1 Travis Green .02 .10
2 Guy Hebert .08 .25
3 Paul Kariya .02 .10
4 Josef Marha .02 .10
5 Steve Rucchin .02 .10
6 Tomas Sandstrom .02 .10
7 Teemu Selanne .10 .30
8 Jason Allison .02 .10
9 Per Axelsson .02 .10
10 Ray Bourque .20 .50
11 Anson Carter .08 .25
12 Byron Dafoe .08 .25
13 Ted Donato .02 .10
14 Dave Ellett .02 .10
15 Dimitri Khristich .02 .10
16 Sergei Samsonov .08 .25
17 Matthew Barnaby .02 .10
18 Michal Grosek .02 .10
19 Dominik Hasek .25 .60
20 Brian Holzinger .02 .10
21 Michael Peca .02 .10
22 Miroslav Satan .08 .25
23 Vaclav Varada .02 .10
24 Dixon Ward .02 .10
25 Alexei Zhitnik .02 .10
26 Andrew Cassels .02 .10
27 Theo Fleury .02 .10
28 Jarome Iginla .15 .40
29 Marty McInnis .02 .10
30 Derek Morris .02 .10
31 Michael Nylander .02 .10
32 Cory Stillman .02 .10
33 Rick Tabaracci .02 .10
34 Kevin Dineen .02 .10
35 Nelson Emerson .02 .10
36 Martin Gelinas .02 .10
37 Sami Kapanen .02 .10
38 Trevor Kidd .08 .25
39 Robert Kron .02 .10
40 Jeff O'Neill .02 .10
41 Keith Primeau .02 .10
42 Gary Roberts .02 .10
43 Tony Amonte .08 .25
44 Chris Chelios .10 .30
45 Paul Coffey .10 .30
46 Eric Daze .08 .25
47 Doug Gilmour .08 .25
48 Jeff Hackett .08 .25
49 Jean-Yves Leroux .02 .10
50 Eric Weinrich .02 .10
51 Alexei Zhamnov .02 .10
52 Craig Billington .08 .25
53 Adam Deadmarsh .02 .10
54 Adam Foote .02 .10
55 Peter Forsberg .30 .75
56 Valeri Kamensky .02 .10
57 Claude Lemieux .02 .10
58 Eric Messier .02 .10
59 Sandis Ozolinsh .02 .10
60 Patrick Roy .60 1.50
61 Joe Sakic .25 .60
62 Ed Belfour .10 .30
63 Derian Hatcher .02 .10
64 Brett Hull .15 .40
65 Jamie Langenbrunner .02 .10
66 Jere Lehtinen .02 .10
67 Juha Lind .02 .10
68 Mike Modano .20 .50
69 Joe Nieuwendyk .08 .25
70 Darryl Sydor .02 .10
71 Roman Turek .08 .25
72 Sergei Zubov .02 .10
73 Anders Eriksson .02 .10
74 Sergei Fedorov .20 .50
75 Kevin Hodson .08 .25
76 Vyacheslav Kozlov .08 .25
77 Igor Larionov .02 .10
78 Nicklas Lidstrom .10 .30
79 Darren McCarty .02 .10
80 Larry Murphy .08 .25
81 Chris Osgood .08 .25
82 Brendan Shanahan .10 .30
83 Steve Yzerman .60 1.50
84 Kelly Buchberger .02 .10
85 Mike Grier .02 .10
86 Bill Guerin .08 .25
87 Roman Hamrlik .02 .10
88 Todd Marchant .02 .10
89 Dean McAmmond .02 .10
90 Boris Mironov .02 .10
91 Janne Niinimaa .02 .10
92 Ryan Smyth .08 .25
93 Doug Weight .08 .25
94 Dino Ciccarelli .08 .25
95 Dave Gagner .02 .10
96 Ed Jovanovski .02 .10
97 Viktor Kozlov .02 .10
98 Paul Laus .02 .10
99 Scott Mellanby .02 .10
100 Robert Svehla .02 .10
101 Ray Whitney .02 .10
102 Rob Blake .08 .25
103 Russ Courtnall .02 .10
104 Stephane Fiset .08 .25
105 Glen Murray .02 .10
106 Yanic Perreault .02 .10
107 Luc Robitaille .08 .25
108 Jamie Storr .08 .25
109 Jozef Stumpel .08 .25
110 Vladimir Tsyplakov .02 .10
111 Shayne Corson .02 .10
112 Vincent Damphousse .02 .10
113 Saku Koivu .10 .30
114 Vladimir Malakhov .02 .10
115 Dave Manson .02 .10
116 Mark Recchi .08 .25
117 Martin Rucinsky .02 .10
118 Brian Savage .02 .10
119 Jocelyn Thibault .08 .25
120 Blair Atcheynum .02 .10
121 Andrew Brunette .08 .25
122 Mike Dunham .08 .25
123 Tom Fitzgerald .02 .10
124 Sergei Krivokrasov .02 .10
125 Denny Lambert .02 .10
126 Jay More .02 .10
127 Mikhail Shtalenkov .02 .10
128 Darren Turcotte .02 .10
129 Scott Walker .02 .10
130 Dave Andreychuk .08 .25
131 Jason Arnott .02 .10
132 Martin Brodeur .30 .75
133 Patrik Elias .08 .25
134 Bobby Holik .02 .10
135 Randy McKay .02 .10
136 Scott Niedermayer .02 .10
137 Krzysztof Oliwa .02 .10
138 Sheldon Souray RC .40 1.00
139 Scott Stevens .08 .25
140 Bryan Berard .08 .25
141 Mariusz Czerkawski .02 .10
142 Jason Dawe .02 .10
143 Kenny Jonsson .02 .10
144 Trevor Linden .08 .25
145 Zigmund Palffy .08 .25
146 Rich Pilon .02 .10
147 Robert Reichel .02 .10
148 Tommy Salo .08 .25
149 Bryan Smolinski .02 .10
150 Dan Cloutier .02 .10
151 Adam Graves .02 .10
152 Wayne Gretzky .75 2.00
153 Alexei Kovalev .02 .10
154 Pat LaFontaine .10 .30
155 Brian Leetch .10 .30
156 Mike Richter .10 .30
157 Ulf Samuelsson .02 .10
158 Kevin Stevens .02 .10
159 Niklas Sundstrom .02 .10
160 Daniel Alfredsson .08 .25
161 Magnus Arvedson .02 .10
162 Andreas Dackell .02 .10
163 Igor Kravchuk .02 .10
164 Shawn McEachern .02 .10
165 Chris Phillips .02 .10
166 Damian Rhodes .08 .25
167 Ron Tugnutt .08 .25
168 Alexei Yashin .02 .10
169 Rod Brind'Amour .08 .25
170 Alexandre Daigle .02 .10
171 Eric Desjardins .08 .25
172 Colin Forbes .02 .10
173 Chris Gratton .08 .25
174 Ron Hextall .08 .25
175 Trent Klatt .02 .10
176 John LeClair .10 .30
177 Eric Lindros .10 .30
178 John Vanbiesbrouck .08 .25
179 Dainius Zubrus .02 .10
180 Dallas Drake .02 .10
181 Brad Isbister .02 .10
182 Nikolai Khabibulin .08 .25
183 Teppo Numminen .02 .10
184 Jeremy Roenick .15 .40
185 Cliff Ronning .02 .10
186 Keith Tkachuk .10 .30
187 Rick Tocchet .08 .25
188 Oleg Tverdovsky .02 .10
189 Stu Barnes .02 .10
190 Tom Barrasso .08 .25
191 Kevin Hatcher .02 .10
192 Jaromir Jagr .20 .50
193 Darius Kasparaitis .02 .10
194 Alexei Morozov .02 .10
195 Fredrik Olausson .02 .10
196 Jiri Slegr .02 .10
197 Martin Straka .08 .25
198 Jim Campbell .02 .10
199 Kelly Chase .02 .10
200 Craig Conroy .02 .10
201 Geoff Courtnall .02 .10
202 Pavol Demitra .08 .25
203 Grant Fuhr .08 .25
204 Al MacInnis .08 .25
205 Jamie McLennan .08 .25
206 Chris Pronger .08 .25
207 Pierre Turgeon .08 .25
208 Tony Twist .02 .10
209 Jeff Friesen .02 .10
210 Tony Granato .02 .10
211 Patrick Marleau .02 .10
212 Stephane Matteau .02 .10
213 Marty McSorley .02 .10
214 Owen Nolan .08 .25
215 Marco Sturm .08 .25
216 Mike Vernon .08 .25
217 Karl Dykhuis .02 .10
218 Sandy McCarty .02 .10
219 Mikael Renberg .08 .25
220 Stephane Richer .08 .25
221 Alexander Selivanov .02 .10
222 Paul Ysebaert .02 .10
223 Rob Zamuner .02 .10
224 Sergei Berezin .08 .25
225 Tie Domi .08 .25
226 Mike Johnson .02 .10
227 Curtis Joseph .10 .30
228 Derek King .02 .10
229 Igor Korolev .02 .10
230 Mathieu Schneider .02 .10
231 Mats Sundin .10 .30
232 Todd Bertuzzi .10 .30
233 Donald Brashear .02 .10
234 Pavel Bure .10 .30
235 Arturs Irbe .08 .25
236 Mark Messier .10 .30
237 Alexander Mogilny .08 .25
238 Mattias Ohlund .08 .25
239 Dave Scatchard .02 .10
240 Garth Snow .08 .25
241 Brian Bellows .02 .10
242 Peter Bondra .08 .25
243 Jeff Brown .02 .10
244 Sergei Gonchar .02 .10
245 Calle Johansson .02 .10
246 Joe Juneau .08 .25
247 Olaf Kolzig .08 .25
248 Steve Konowalchuk .02 .10
249 Adam Oates .08 .25
250 Richard Zednik .02 .10
NNO Martin Brodeur SAMPLE .60 1.50

1998-99 Paramount Copper

*COPPER: 2.5X TO 6X BASIC CARDS
STATED ODDS 1:1 US HOBBY

1998-99 Paramount Emerald

*EMERALD: 2.5X TO 6X BASIC CARDS
STATED ODDS 1:1 CANADIAN HOBBY

1998-99 Paramount HoloElectric

This 250-card parallel set carried a holographic silver foil and gold foil impression. Cards were numbered out of 99.

*HOLOELECTRIC: 20X TO 50X BASIC CARDS

1998-99 Paramount Ice Blue

*ICE BLUE: 6X TO 15X BASIC CARDS
ICE BLUE STATED ODDS 1:73

1998-99 Paramount Silver

*SILVER: 3X TO 8X BASIC CARDS
SILVER STATED ODDS 1:1 RETAIL

1998-99 Paramount Glove Side Laser Cuts

The 1998-99 Pacific Paramount Glove Side Laser Cuts set consists of 20 cards and is an insert of the regular Pacific Paramount base set. The cards are randomly inserted in packs at a rate of 1:73. The cards feature 20 superstar goalies delivered on one of the most unique designs.

COMPLETE SET (20) 40.00 80.00
1 Guy Hebert 2.00 5.00
2 Byron Dafoe 2.00 5.00
3 Dominik Hasek 5.00 12.00
4 Trevor Kidd 2.00 5.00
5 Jeff Hackett 2.00 5.00
6 Patrick Roy 12.50 30.00
7 Ed Belfour 2.50 6.00
8 Chris Osgood 2.00 5.00
9 Mike Dunham 2.00 5.00
10 Martin Brodeur 6.00 15.00
11 Tommy Salo 2.00 5.00
12 Mike Richter 2.00 5.00
13 Damian Rhodes 2.00 5.00
14 Ron Hextall 2.00 5.00
15 Nikolai Khabibulin 2.00 5.00
16 Tom Barrasso 2.00 5.00
17 Grant Fuhr 2.00 5.00
18 Mike Vernon 2.00 5.00
19 Curtis Joseph 2.50 6.00
20 Olaf Kolzig 2.00 5.00

1998-99 Paramount Hall of Fame Bound

This 10-card set was inserted in packs at a rate of 1:361. The cards honor 10 NHL superstars on a fully foiled and etched card. A proof parallel was also created and randomly inserted in packs. Each parallel card is limited to only 20 copies.

COMPLETE SET (10) 100.00 200.00
*PACIFIC PROOF/20: 2.5X TO 6X BASIC INSERTS
1 Teemu Selanne 5.00 12.00
2 Dominik Hasek 8.00 20.00
3 Peter Forsberg 10.00 25.00
4 Patrick Roy 15.00 40.00
5 Steve Yzerman 15.00 40.00
6 Martin Brodeur 12.50 30.00
7 Wayne Gretzky 20.00 50.00
8 Eric Lindros 5.00 12.00
9 Jaromir Jagr 6.00 15.00
10 Mark Messier 5.00 12.00

1998-99 Paramount Ice Galaxy

Randomly inserted into Canadian retail packs only at a rate of 1:97, this 10-card set features action color player photos with bronze foil highlights. Only 140 sets were made. A silver foil parallel set was also produced. Only 50 of these sets were made. A very limited gold foil parallel set was produced with a print run of only 10 sets.

COMPLETE SET (10) 100.00 200.00
*SILVER/50: 1X TO 2.5X BRONZE/140
1 Paul Kariya 6.00 15.00

2 Peter Forsberg 8.00 20.00
3 Patrick Roy 15.00 40.00
4 Joe Sakic 6.00 15.00
5 Steve Yzerman 15.00 40.00
6 Martin Brodeur 8.00 20.00
7 Wayne Gretzky 20.00 50.00
8 Alexei Yashin 3.00 8.00
9 Eric Lindros 6.00 15.00
10 Curtis Joseph 6.00 15.00

1998-99 Paramount Special Delivery Die-Cuts

This 20-card set was inserted in packs at a rate of 1:37.

COMPLETE SET (20) 20.00 40.00
1 Paul Kariya .25 .60
2 Teemu Selanne .75 2.00
3 Sergei Samsonov .60 1.50
4 Peter Forsberg 2.00 5.00
5 Joe Sakic 1.50 4.00
6 Mike Modano 1.25 3.00
7 Sergei Fedorov 1.25 3.00
8 Brendan Shanahan .75 2.00
9 Steve Yzerman 4.00 10.00
10 Saku Koivu .75 2.00
11 Zigmund Palffy .60 1.50
12 Wayne Gretzky 5.00 12.00
13 John LeClair .75 2.00
14 Eric Lindros .75 2.00
15 Keith Tkachuk .75 2.00
16 Jaromir Jagr 1.25 3.00
17 Mats Sundin .75 2.00
18 Pavel Bure .75 2.00
19 Mark Messier .75 2.00
20 Peter Bondra .60 1.50

1998-99 Paramount Team Checklists Die-Cuts

This 27-card set was inserted in packs at a rate of 2:37. The set included the league's 1998-99 expansion franchise, the Nashville Predators.

COMPLETE SET (27) 20.00 40.00
1 Teemu Selanne .60 1.50
2 Sergei Samsonov .50 1.25
3 Dominik Hasek 1.25 3.00
4 Theo Fleury .20 .50
5 Keith Primeau .20 .50
6 Chris Chelios .60 1.50
7 Patrick Roy 3.00 8.00
8 Mike Modano 1.00 2.50
9 Steve Yzerman 3.00 8.00
10 Ryan Smyth .50 1.25
11 Dino Ciccarelli .50 1.25
12 Rob Blake .50 1.25
13 Saku Koivu .60 1.50
14 Tom Fitzgerald .20 .50
15 Martin Brodeur 1.50 4.00
16 Zigmund Palffy .50 1.25
17 Wayne Gretzky 4.00 10.00
18 Alexei Yashin .20 .50
19 Eric Lindros .60 1.50
20 Keith Tkachuk .60 1.50
21 Jaromir Jagr 1.00 2.50
22 Grant Fuhr .20 .50
23 Patrick Marleau .20 .50
24 Rob Zamuner .20 .50
25 Mats Sundin .60 1.50
26 Mark Messier .60 1.50
27 Peter Bondra .50 1.25

1999-00 Paramount

Released as a 251-card set, Paramount featured white bordered base cards with color action photography and silver foil highlights. Paramount was packaged in 36-pack boxes with packs containing six cards and carried an SRP of $1.49. Cards #251-269 were not found in packs. They were available only as stadium giveaways as part of an NHL/NHLPA trading card promotion. They are not included in the complete set price and are not found in any of the parallel versions. Reportedly, cards #262 and #265 were not issued.

COMPLETE SET (251) 15.00 30.00
1 Matt Cullen .02 .10
2 Guy Hebert .08 .25
3 Paul Kariya .10 .30
4 Marty McInnis .02 .10
5 Fredrik Olausson .02 .10
6 Steve Rucchin .08 .25
7 Ruslan Salei .02 .10
8 Teemu Selanne .10 .30
9 Jason Botterill .02 .10
10 Andrew Brunette .08 .25
11 Kelly Buchberger .02 .10
12 Matt Johnson .02 .10
13 Norm Maracle .08 .25
14 Damian Rhodes .08 .25
15 Steve Staios .02 .10
16 Jason Allison .02 .10
17 Ray Bourque .20 .50
18 Anson Carter .08 .25
19 Byron Dafoe .08 .25
20 Jonathan Girard .02 .10
21 Steve Heinze .02 .10
22 Dimitri Khristich .02 .10
23 Sergei Samsonov .08 .25
24 Joe Thornton .20 .50
25 Stu Barnes .02 .10
26 Curtis Brown .02 .10
27 Michal Grosek .02 .10
28 Dominik Hasek .25 .60
29 Michael Peca .08 .25
30 Geoff Sanderson .08 .25
31 Miroslav Satan .08 .25
32 Dixon Ward .02 .10
33 Jason Woolley .02 .10
34 Alexei Zhitnik .02 .10
35 Valeri Bure .02 .10
36 Rene Corbet .02 .10
37 Rico Fata .02 .10
38 Jean-Sebastien Giguere .08 .25
39 Phil Housley .08 .25
40 Jarome Iginla .15 .40
41 Derek Morris .02 .10
42 Steve Smith .02 .10
43 Cory Stillman .02 .10
44 Ron Francis .08 .25
45 Martin Gelinas .02 .10
46 Arturs Irbe .08 .25
47 Sami Kapanen .02 .10
48 Jeff O'Neill .02 .10
49 Keith Primeau .02 .10
50 Gary Roberts .02 .10
51 Shane Willis .02 .10
52 Tony Amonte .08 .25
53 Eric Daze .08 .25
54 J-P Dumont .08 .25
55 Doug Gilmour .08 .25
56 Dean McAmmond .02 .10
57 Boris Mironov .02 .10
58 Jocelyn Thibault .08 .25
59 Alexei Zhamnov .02 .10
60 Adam Deadmarsh .02 .10
61 Marc Denis .08 .25
62 Chris Drury .08 .25
63 Peter Forsberg .30 .75
64 Milan Hejduk .10 .30
65 Claude Lemieux .02 .10
66 Sandis Ozolinsh .02 .10
67 Patrick Roy .60 1.50
68 Joe Sakic .25 .60
69 Ed Belfour .10 .30
70 Guy Carbonneau .02 .10
71 Derian Hatcher .02 .10
72 Brett Hull .15 .40
73 Jamie Langenbrunner .02 .10
74 Jere Lehtinen .02 .10
75 Mike Modano .20 .50
76 Joe Nieuwendyk .08 .25
77 Darryl Sydor .02 .10
78 Sergei Zubov .02 .10
79 Chris Chelios .10 .30
80 Sergei Fedorov .20 .50
81 Vyacheslav Kozlov .08 .25
82 Igor Larionov .02 .10
83 Nicklas Lidstrom .10 .30
84 Darren McCarty .02 .10
85 Larry Murphy .08 .25
86 Chris Osgood .08 .25
87 Brendan Shanahan .10 .30
88 Steve Yzerman .60 1.50
89 Josef Beranek .02 .10
90 Pat Falloon .02 .10
91 Mike Grier .02 .10
92 Bill Guerin .02 .10
93 Rem Murray .02 .10
94 Tom Poti .02 .10
95 Tommy Salo .08 .25
96 Ryan Smyth .08 .25
97 Doug Weight .08 .25
98 Pavel Bure .10 .30
99 Sean Burke .08 .25
100 Viktor Kozlov .02 .10
101 Oleg Kvasha .02 .10
102 Scott Mellanby .02 .10
103 Rob Niedermayer .02 .10
104 Marcus Nilsson .02 .10
105 Mark Parrish .08 .25
106 Ray Whitney .02 .10
107 Donald Audette .02 .10
108 Rob Blake .08 .25
109 Stephane Fiset .08 .25
110 Glen Murray .02 .10
111 Zigmund Palffy .08 .25
112 Jamie Storr .08 .25
113 Jozef Stumpel .02 .10
114 Benoit Brunet .02 .10
115 Shayne Corson .02 .10
116 Jeff Hackett .08 .25
117 Saku Koivu .10 .30
118 Trevor Linden .08 .25
119 Vladimir Malakhov .02 .10
120 Martin Rucinsky .02 .10
121 Igor Ulanov .02 .10
122 Dainius Zubrus .08 .25
123 Mike Dunham .08 .25
124 Tom Fitzgerald .02 .10
125 Greg Johnson .02 .10
126 Sergei Krivokrasov .02 .10
127 David Legwand .08 .25
128 Cliff Ronning .08 .25
129 Scott Walker .02 .10
130 Jason Arnott .02 .10
131 Martin Brodeur .30 .75
132 Patrik Elias .08 .25
133 Bobby Holik .02 .10
134 John Madden RC .25 .60
135 Randy McKay .02 .10
136 Brendan Morrison .08 .25
137 Scott Niedermayer .02 .10
138 Brian Rolston .02 .10
139 Petr Sykora .02 .10
140 Eric Brewer .02 .10
141 Mariusz Czerkawski .02 .10
142 Kenny Jonsson .02 .10
143 Claude Lapointe .02 .10
144 Mats Lindgren .02 .10
145 Vladimir Orszagh RC .02 .10
146 Felix Potvin .10 .30
147 Mike Watt .02 .10
148 Theo Fleury .02 .10
149 Adam Graves .02 .10
150 Todd Harvey .08 .25
151 Valeri Kamensky .08 .25
152 Brian Leetch .10 .30
153 John MacLean .02 .10
154 Manny Malhotra .08 .25
155 Petr Nedved .02 .10
156 Mike Richter .10 .30
157 Kevin Stevens .08 .25
158 Daniel Alfredsson .08 .25
159 Magnus Arvedson .02 .10
160 Radek Bonk .02 .10
161 Andreas Dackell .02 .10
162 Marian Hossa .10 .30
163 Shawn McEachern .02 .10
164 Wade Redden .02 .10
165 Sami Salo .08 .25
166 Ron Tugnutt .08 .25
167 Alexei Yashin .02 .10
168 Rod Brind'Amour .08 .25
169 Eric Desjardins .08 .25
170 Keith Jones .02 .10
171 Daymond Langkow .08 .25
172 John LeClair .10 .30
173 Eric Lindros .10 .30
174 Mark Recchi .02 .10
175 Mikael Renberg .02 .10
176 John Vanbiesbrouck .08 .25
177 Greg Adams .02 .10
178 Dallas Drake .02 .10
179 Nikolai Khabibulin .08 .25
180 Jyrki Lumme .02 .10
181 Teppo Numminen .08 .25
182 Jeremy Roenick .15 .40
183 Mike Sullivan .02 .10
184 Keith Tkachuk .10 .30
185 Rick Tocchet .08 .25
186 Matthew Barnaby .02 .10
187 Tom Barrasso .08 .25
188 Jan Hrdina .02 .10
189 Jaromir Jagr .20 .50
190 Alexei Kovalev .02 .10
191 Ian Moran .02 .10
192 Martin Straka .08 .25
193 German Titov .02 .10
194 Craig Conroy .02 .10
195 Pavol Demitra .08 .25
196 Grant Fuhr .08 .25
197 Jochen Hecht RC .50 1.25
198 Al MacInnis .08 .25
199 Ricard Persson .02 .10
200 Chris Pronger .08 .25
201 Pierre Turgeon .08 .25
202 Scott Young .02 .10
203 Vincent Damphousse .02 .10
204 Jeff Friesen .02 .10
205 Alexander Korolyuk .02 .10
206 Patrick Marleau .08 .25
207 Owen Nolan .08 .25
208 Mike Ricci .02 .10
209 Steve Shields .08 .25
210 Marco Sturm .08 .25
211 Ron Sutter .02 .10
212 Mike Vernon .08 .25
213 Karel Betik RC .02 .10
214 Dan Cloutier .08 .25
215 Jassen Cullimore .02 .10
216 Colin Forbes .02 .10
217 Chris Gratton .08 .25
218 Pavel Kubina .02 .10
219 Vincent Lecavalier .10 .30
220 Darcy Tucker .02 .10
221 Bryan Berard .08 .25
222 Sergei Berezin .08 .25
223 Tie Domi .08 .25
224 Mike Johnson .02 .10
225 Curtis Joseph .10 .30
226 Derek King .02 .10
227 Igor Korolev .02 .10
228 Yanic Perreault .02 .10
229 Steve Sullivan .02 .10
230 Mats Sundin .10 .30
231 Steve Thomas .02 .10
232 Adrian Aucoin .02 .10
233 Donald Brashear .02 .10
234 Ed Jovanovski .02 .10
235 Mark Messier .10 .30
236 Alexander Mogilny .08 .25
237 Bill Muckalt .08 .25
238 Markus Naslund .10 .30
239 Mattias Ohlund .08 .25
240 Garth Snow .08 .25
241 Brian Bellows .02 .10
242 Peter Bondra .08 .25
243 Jan Bulis .02 .10
244 Sergei Gonchar .02 .10
245 Olaf Kolzig .08 .25
246 Steve Konowalchuk .02 .10
247 Andrei Nikolishin .02 .10
248 Adam Oates .08 .25

249 Alexei Tezikov RC .02 .10
250 Richard Zednik .02 .10
251 Patrik Stefan RC .60 4.00
252 Jonathan Girard AG
253 Maxim Afinogenov AG
254 Byron Ritchie AG
255 Alex Tanguay AG
256 Brenden Morrow AG
257 Yuri Butsayev AG
258 Ivan Novoseltsev AG
259 Frantisek Kaberle AG
260 Richard Lintner AG
261 Tim Connolly AG
263 Jason Doig AG
264 Mike Fisher AG
266 Stan Neckar AG
267 Andrew Ference AG
268 Paul Mara AG
269 Steve Kariya AG

1999-00 Paramount Copper

*COPPER: 2X TO 5X BASIC CARDS
COPPER STATED ODDS 1:1 HOBBY

1999-00 Paramount Emerald

*EMERALD: 2X TO 5X BASIC CARDS
EMERALD STATED ODDS 1:1 CANADIAN

1999-00 Paramount Gold

*GOLD: 2.5X TO 6X BASIC CARDS
GOLD STATED ODDS 1:1 RETAIL

1999-00 Paramount Holographic Emerald

Randomly inserted in Canadian 7-11 packs, this 251-card set parallels the base Paramount set and is enhanced with green foil highlights. Each card is serial numbered out of 99.

*HOLO.EMERALD: 25X TO 60X BASIC CARDS

1999-00 Paramount Holographic Gold

*HOLO.GOLD: 10X TO 25X BASIC CARDS
RANDOM INSERTS IN RETAIL PACKS
HOLO.GOLD PRINT RUN 199 SER.#'d SETS

1999-00 Paramount Holographic Silver

*HOLO.SILVER: 20X TO 50X BASIC CARDS
RANDOM INSERTS IN HOBBY PACKS
STATED PRINT RUN 99 SER.#'d SETS

1999-00 Paramount Ice Blue

*ICE BLUE: 15X TO 40X BASIC CARDS
ICE BLUE STATED ODDS 1:73

1999-00 Paramount Premiere Date

*PREM.DATE: 30X TO 80X BASIC CARDS
PREM.DATE/50 ODDS 1:37 HOBBY

1999-00 Paramount Red

Randomly inserted in Jewel Boxes, this 251-card set parallels the base Paramount set and is enhanced with red foil highlights.

*RED: .6X TO 1.5X BASIC CARDS

1999-00 Paramount Glove Side Net Fusions

Randomly inserted in packs at the rate of 1:73, this 20-card set features circular goalie portraits on a die cut card in the shape of a goalie's glove with actual netting.

COMPLETE SET (20) 50.00 100.00
1 Guy Hebert 2.00 5.00
2 Byron Dafoe 2.00 5.00
3 Dominik Hasek 5.00 12.00
4 Arturs Irbe 2.00 5.00
5 Jocelyn Thibault 2.00 5.00
6 Patrick Roy 12.50 30.00
7 Ed Belfour 2.50 6.00
8 Chris Osgood 2.00 5.00
9 Tommy Salo 2.00 5.00
10 Jeff Hackett 2.00 5.00
11 Martin Brodeur 6.00 15.00
12 Felix Potvin 2.50 6.00
13 Mike Richter 2.50 6.00
14 Ron Tugnutt 2.00 5.00
15 John Vanbiesbrouck 2.00 5.00
16 Nikolai Khabibulin 2.00 5.00
17 Tom Barrasso 2.00 5.00
18 Grant Fuhr 2.00 5.00
19 Curtis Joseph 2.50 6.00
20 Olaf Kolzig 2.00 5.00

1999-00 Paramount Hall of Fame Bound

Randomly inserted in packs at the rate of 1:361, this 10-card set features future NHL hall of famers. Card fronts contain action player photos and the respective player's team logo on a "mesh jersey" card stock. A proof parallel was also croutod and inserted randomly. Proof were serial numbered to just 35 and their value can be determined by using the multiplier below.

COMPLETE SET (10) 75.00 150.00
*PROOFS/35: 1.2X TO 3X BASIC INSERTS
1 Paul Kariya 5.00 12.00
2 Ray Bourque 8.00 20.00
3 Dominik Hasek 8.00 20.00
4 Peter Forsberg 10.00 25.00
5 Patrick Roy 15.00 40.00
6 Steve Yzerman 15.00 40.00
7 Martin Brodeur 12.50 30.00
8 Eric Lindros 5.00 12.00
9 Jaromir Jagr 6.00 15.00
10 Mark Messier 5.00 12.00

1999-00 Paramount Ice Advantage

Randomly inserted in Canadian packs at the rate of 2:25, this 20-card set featured top NHL players. A proof parallel was also created and randomly inserted Canadian 7-11 retail packs. Proofs were numbered to just 10 and are not priced due to scarcity.

COMPLETE SET (20) 20.00 40.00
1 Paul Kariya .60 1.50
2 Teemu Selanne .60 1.50
3 Dominik Hasek 1.25 3.00
4 Jarome Iginla .75 2.00
5 Peter Forsberg 1.50 4.00
6 Patrick Roy 3.00 8.00
7 Joe Sakic 1.25 3.00
8 Joe Nieuwendyk .50 1.25
9 Brendan Shanahan .60 1.50
10 Steve Yzerman 3.00 8.00
11 Doug Weight .50 1.25
12 Pavel Bure .60 1.50
13 Jeff Hackett .50 1.25
14 Martin Brodeur 1.50 4.00
15 Marian Hossa .60 1.50
16 Eric Lindros .60 1.50
17 Jaromir Jagr 1.00 2.50
18 Curtis Joseph .60 1.50
19 Mats Sundin .60 1.50
20 Mark Messier .60 1.50

1999-00 Paramount Ice Alliance

Randomly inserted in packs at the rate of 2:37, this 28-card set features NHL team leader portraits with their team's logo in gold foil.

COMPLETE SET (28) 20.00 40.00
1 Paul Kariya .60 1.50
2 Damian Rhodes .50 1.25
3 Ray Bourque 1.00 2.50
4 Dominik Hasek 1.50 4.00
5 Jarome Iginla .75 2.00
6 Keith Primeau .50 1.25
7 Tony Amonte .50 1.25
8 Patrick Roy 3.00 8.00
9 Mike Modano 1.00 2.50
10 Steve Yzerman 3.00 8.00
11 Bill Guerin .50 1.25
12 Pavel Bure .60 1.50
13 Luc Robitaille .50 1.25
14 Jeff Hackett .50 1.25
15 Cliff Ronning .50 1.25
16 Martin Brodeur 1.50 4.00
17 Felix Potvin .60 1.50
18 Brian Leetch .50 1.25
19 Alexei Yashin .50 1.25
20 Eric Lindros .60 1.50
21 Keith Tkachuk .60 1.50
22 Jaromir Jagr 1.00 2.50
23 Pierre Turgeon .50 1.25
24 Vincent Damphousse .50 1.25
25 Vincent Lecavalier .60 1.50
26 Curtis Joseph .60 1.50
27 Mark Messier .60 1.50
28 Peter Bondra .50 1.25

1999-00 Paramount Personal Best

Randomly inserted in packs at the rate of 1:37, this 36-card set features color portraits set against a blue background with silver foil highlights of some of the NHL's marquee players.

COMPLETE SET (36) 30.00 60.00
1 Paul Kariya .75 2.00
2 Teemu Selanne .75 2.00
3 Ray Bourque 1.25 3.00
4 Sergei Samsonov .40 1.00
5 Dominik Hasek 1.50 4.00
6 Michael Peca .40 1.00
7 Tony Amonte .40 1.00
8 Chris Drury .40 1.00
9 Peter Forsberg 2.00 5.00
10 Patrick Roy 4.00 10.00
11 Joe Sakic 1.50 4.00
12 Ed Belfour .75 2.00
13 Brett Hull 1.00 2.50
14 Mike Modano 1.25 3.00
15 Joe Nieuwendyk .40 1.00
16 Sergei Fedorov 1.50 4.00
17 Brendan Shanahan .75 2.00
18 Steve Yzerman 4.00 10.00
19 Pavel Bure .75 2.00
20 Saku Koivu .75 2.00
21 Martin Brodeur 2.00 5.00
22 Theo Fleury .40 1.00
23 Mike Richter .75 2.00
24 Alexei Yashin .40 1.00
25 John LeClair .75 2.00
26 Eric Lindros .75 2.00
27 Mark Recchi .40 1.00
28 John Vanbiesbrouck .40 1.00
29 Jeremy Roenick 1.00 2.50
30 Keith Tkachuk .75 2.00
31 Jaromir Jagr 1.25 3.00
32 Pavol Demitra .40 1.00
33 Vincent Lecavalier .75 2.00
34 Curtis Joseph .75 2.00
35 Mats Sundin .75 2.00
36 Mark Messier .75 2.00

2000-01 Paramount

Released as a 252-card set, Paramount features a white bordered card stock with full color player action photography centered on the card. The majority of the background is white, but in the areas directly around the player photo, the real life background can be seen. The featured player's team name is in gold and is overlaid with the player's name in silver foil. Paramount was packaged in 36-pack boxes with each pack containing six cards.

COMPLETE SET (252) 20.00 40.00
1 Antti Aalto .05 .15
2 Maxim Balmochnykh .15 .40
3 Matt Cullen .05 .15
4 Guy Hebert .15 .40
5 Paul Kariya .20 .50
6 Steve Rucchin .05 .15
7 Teemu Selanne .20 .50
8 Oleg Tverdovsky .05 .15
9 Donald Audette .05 .15
10 Andrew Brunette .05 .15
11 Shean Donovan .05 .15
12 Scott Fankhouser .05 .15
13 Ray Ferraro .05 .15
14 Damian Rhodes .05 .15
15 Patrik Stefan .05 .15
16 Jason Allison .05 .15
17 Anson Carter .15 .40
18 Byron Dafoe .15 .40
19 John Grahame .15 .40
20 Brian Rolston .15 .40
21 Sergei Samsonov .15 .40
22 Don Sweeney .05 .15
23 Joe Thornton .30 .75
24 Maxim Afinogenov .05 .15
25 Stu Barnes .05 .15
26 Martin Biron .15 .40
27 Curtis Brown .05 .15
28 Doug Gilmour .15 .40
29 Chris Gratton .05 .15
30 Dominik Hasek .40 1.00
31 Michael Peca .05 .15
32 Miroslav Satan .15 .40
33 Fred Brathwaite .15 .40
34 Valeri Bure .05 .15
35 Phil Housley .05 .15
36 Jarome Iginla .25 .60
37 Oleg Saprykin .05 .15
38 Marc Savard .05 .15
39 Cory Stillman .05 .15
40 Clarke Wilm .05 .15
41 Rod Brind'Amour .15 .40
42 Ron Francis .15 .40
43 Arturs Irbe .15 .40
44 Sami Kapanen .05 .15
45 Jeff O'Neill .05 .15
46 Dave Tanabe .05 .15
47 Glen Wesley .05 .15
48 Tony Amonte .15 .40
49 Michal Grosek .05 .15
50 Dean McAmmond .05 .15
51 Boris Mironov .05 .15
52 Michael Nylander .05 .15
53 Steve Sullivan .05 .15
54 Jocelyn Thibault .15 .40
55 Alexei Zhamnov .15 .40
56 Ray Bourque .40 1.00
57 Adam Deadmarsh .05 .15
58 Chris Drury .15 .40
59 Adam Foote .15 .40
60 Peter Forsberg .50 1.25
61 Milan Hejduk .20 .50
62 Patrick Roy 1.00 2.50
63 Joe Sakic .40 1.00
64 Martin Skoula .05 .15
65 Alex Tanguay .15 .40
66 Kevyn Adams .05 .15
67 Serge Aubin RC .20 .50
68 Marc Denis .15 .40
69 Ted Drury .05 .15
70 Steve Heinze .05 .15
71 Lyle Odelein .05 .15
72 Ron Tugnutt .15 .40
73 Ed Belfour .20 .50
74 Derian Hatcher .05 .15
75 Brett Hull .25 .60
76 Jamie Langenbrunner .05 .15
77 Jere Lehtinen .15 .40
78 Roman Lyashenko .05 .15
79 Mike Modano .30 .75
80 Brenden Morrow .15 .40
81 Joe Nieuwendyk .15 .40
82 Sergei Zubov .05 .15
83 Chris Chelios .20 .50
84 Mathieu Dandenault .05 .15
85 Sergei Fedorov .30 .75
86 Martin Lapointe .05 .15
87 Nicklas Lidstrom .20 .50
88 Chris Osgood .15 .40
89 Brendan Shanahan .20 .50
90 Pat Verbeek .05 .15
91 Jesse Wallin .05 .15
92 Ken Wregget .15 .40
93 Steve Yzerman 1.00 2.50
94 Mike Grier .15 .40
95 Bill Guerin .15 .40
96 Todd Marchant .05 .15
97 Tom Poti .05 .15
98 Tommy Salo .15 .40
99 Alexander Selivanov .15 .40
100 Ryan Smyth .15 .40
101 Doug Weight .15 .40
102 Pavel Bure .20 .50
103 Brad Ference .05 .15
104 Trevor Kidd .15 .40
105 Viktor Kozlov .15 .40
106 Scott Mellanby .05 .15
107 Ivan Novoseltsev .15 .40
108 Robert Svehla .05 .15
109 Ray Whitney .15 .40
110 Rob Blake .15 .40
111 Stephane Fiset .15 .40
112 Glen Murray .05 .15
113 Zigmund Palffy .15 .40
114 Luc Robitaille .15 .40
115 Bryan Smolinski .05 .15
116 Jamie Storr .15 .40
117 Jozef Stumpel .05 .15
118 Manny Fernandez .15 .40
119 Sergei Krivokrasov .05 .15
120 Jamie McLennan .15 .40
121 Jeff Nielsen .05 .15
122 Sean O'Donnell .05 .15
123 Jeff Odgers .05 .15
124 Scott Pellerin .05 .15
125 Jeff Hackett .05 .15
126 Saku Koivu .20 .50
127 Trevor Linden .15 .40
128 Patrick Poulin .05 .15
129 Mike Ribeiro .05 .15
130 Martin Rucinsky .05 .15
131 Brian Savage .05 .15
132 Jose Theodore .25 .60
133 Dainius Zubrus .05 .15
134 Mike Dunham .15 .40
135 Greg Johnson .05 .15
136 David Legwand .15 .40
137 Cliff Ronning .05 .15
138 Rob Valicevic .05 .15
139 Tomas Vokoun .05 .15
140 Vitali Yachmenev .05 .15
141 Jason Arnott .05 .15
142 Martin Brodeur .50 1.25
143 Patrik Elias .15 .40
144 Scott Gomez .05 .15
145 John Madden .05 .15
146 Alexander Mogilny .15 .40
147 Scott Niedermayer .05 .15
148 Brian Rafalski .05 .15
149 Scott Stevens .15 .40
150 Petr Sykora .05 .15
151 Colin White RC .15 .40
152 Tim Connolly .05 .15
153 Mariusz Czerkawski .05 .15
154 Brad Isbister .05 .15
155 Jason Krog .05 .15
156 Claude Lapointe .05 .15
157 Bill Muckalt .05 .15
158 Steve Valiquette RC .20 .50
159 Radek Dvorak .05 .15
160 Theo Fleury .05 .15
161 Adam Graves .05 .15
162 Jan Hlavac .15 .40
163 Brian Leetch .15 .40
164 Sylvain Lefebvre .05 .15
165 Mark Messier .20 .50
166 Petr Nedved .15 .40
167 Mike Richter .20 .50
168 Mike York .05 .15
169 Daniel Alfredsson .15 .40
170 Magnus Arvedson .05 .15
171 Radek Bonk .05 .15
172 Marian Hossa .20 .50
173 Jani Hurme RC 1.25 3.00
174 Patrick Lalime .15 .40
175 Shawn McEachern .05 .15
176 Vaclav Prospal .05 .15
177 Brian Boucher .20 .50
178 Andy Delmore .15 .40
179 Eric Desjardins .05 .15
180 Simon Gagne .20 .50
181 Daymond Langkow .15 .40
182 John LeClair .20 .50
183 Eric Lindros .20 .50
184 Keith Primeau .05 .15
185 Mark Recchi .15 .40
186 Rick Tocchet .15 .40
187 Shane Doan .05 .15
188 Robert Esche .05 .15
189 Travis Green .05 .15
190 Trevor Letowski .05 .15
191 Stanislav Neckar .05 .15
192 Teppo Numminen .05 .15
193 Jeremy Roenick .25 .60
194 Keith Tkachuk .20 .50
195 Jean-Sebastien Aubin .15 .40
196 Matthew Barnaby .05 .15
197 Jan Hrdina .05 .15
198 Jaromir Jagr .30 .75
199 Alexei Kovalev .15 .40
200 Robert Lang .05 .15
201 John Slaney .05 .15
202 Martin Straka .05 .15
203 Lubos Bartecko .05 .15
204 Pavol Demitra .15 .40
205 Michal Handzus .05 .15
206 Al MacInnis .15 .40
207 Jamal Mayers .05 .15
208 Chris Pronger .15 .40
209 Roman Turek .15 .40
210 Pierre Turgeon .15 .40
211 Scott Young .05 .15
212 Vincent Damphousse .05 .15
213 Jeff Friesen .05 .15
214 Patrick Marleau .15 .40
215 Owen Nolan .15 .40
216 Mike Ricci .15 .40
217 Steve Shields .15 .40
218 Brad Stuart .15 .40
219 Dan Cloutier .15 .40
220 Brian Holzinger .05 .15
221 Mike Johnson .05 .15
222 Vincent Lecavalier .20 .50
223 Fredrik Modin .05 .15
224 Petr Svoboda .05 .15
225 Todd Warriner .05 .15
226 Nikolai Antropov .05 .15
227 Sergei Berezin .05 .15
228 Tie Domi .15 .40
229 Jeff Farkas .05 .15
230 Curtis Joseph .20 .50
231 Tomas Kaberle .05 .15
232 Yanic Perreault .05 .15
233 Mats Sundin .20 .50
234 Steve Thomas .05 .15
235 Darcy Tucker .05 .15
236 Todd Bertuzzi .20 .50
237 Andrew Cassels .05 .15
238 Ed Jovanovski .05 .15
239 Steve Kariya .05 .15
240 Markus Naslund .20 .50
241 Mattias Ohlund .05 .15
242 Felix Potvin .20 .50
243 Peter Bondra .20 .50
244 Sergei Gonchar .05 .15
245 Jeff Halpern .05 .15
246 Olaf Kolzig .15 .40
247 Steve Konowalchuk .05 .15
248 Adam Oates .15 .40
249 Chris Simon .05 .15
250 Richard Zednik .05 .15
251 Daniel Sedin .05 .15
252 Henrik Sedin .05 .15

2000-01 Paramount Copper

*STARS: 1.5X TO 4X BASIC CARDS
*ROOKIES: 1X TO 2.5X BASIC CARDS
STATED ODDS 1:1 HOBBY

2000-01 Paramount Gold

*STARS: 2.5X TO 6X BASIC CARDS
*ROOKIES: 1.5X TO 4X BASIC CARDS
STATED ODDS 1:1 RETAIL

2000-01 Paramount Holo-Gold

Randomly inserted in Retail packs at the rate of 2:37, this 252-card set parallels the base set enhanced with a holographic gold foil shift from the base set silver on the player's name. Each card is sequentially numbered to 74.

*STARS: 10X TO 25X BASIC CARDS
*ROOKIES: 5X TO 12X

2000-01 Paramount Holo-Silver

Randomly inserted in Hobby packs, this 252-card set parallels the base set enhanced with a holographic silver foil shift from the base set silver on the player's name. Each card is sequentially numbered to 74.

*STARS: 12.5X TO 30X BASIC CARDS
*ROOKIES: 5X TO 12X BASIC CARDS

2000-01 Paramount Ice Blue

*STARS: 20X TO 50X BASIC CARDS
*ROOKIES: 8X TO 20X BASIC CARDS
STATED PRINT RUN 50 SER.#'d SETS
STATED ODDS 1:73 HOBBY

2000-01 Paramount Premiere Date

*STARS: 20X TO 50X BASIC CARDS
*ROOKIES: 8X TO 20X BASIC CARDS
STATED PRINT RUN 45 SER.#'d SETS
RANDOM INSERTS IN HOBBY PACKS

2000-01 Paramount Epic Scope

This 20-card set was inserted at a rate of 2:37.

COMPLETE SET (20) 30.00 60.00
1 Paul Kariya 1.00 2.50
2 Teemu Selanne 1.00 2.50
3 Dominik Hasek 2.00 5.00
4 Ray Bourque 2.00 5.00
5 Peter Forsberg 2.50 6.00
6 Patrick Roy 5.00 12.00
7 Joe Sakic 2.00 5.00
8 Brett Hull 1.25 3.00
9 Mike Modano 1.50 4.00
10 Brendan Shanahan 1.00 2.50
11 Steve Yzerman 5.00 12.00
12 Pavel Bure 1.00 2.50
13 Martin Brodeur 2.50 6.00
14 Scott Gomez .75 2.00
15 Brian Boucher .75 2.00
16 John LeClair 1.00 2.50
17 Jaromir Jagr 1.50 4.00
18 Vincent Lecavalier 1.00 2.50
19 Curtis Joseph 1.00 2.50
20 Mats Sundin 1.00 2.50

2000-01 Paramount Freeze Frame

Randomly inserted in packs at the rate of 1:37, this 36-card set features full color player action shots and a filmstrip border along the top and bottom of the card. Cards are highlighted with copper foil.

COMPLETE SET (36) 50.00 100.00
1 Paul Kariya 1.25 3.00
2 Teemu Selanne 1.25 3.00
3 Doug Gilmour 1.00 2.50
4 Dominik Hasek 2.50 6.00
5 Valeri Bure .40 1.00
6 Tony Amonte 1.00 2.50
7 Ray Bourque 2.50 6.00
8 Peter Forsberg 3.00 8.00
9 Joe Sakic 2.50 6.00
10 Patrick Roy 6.00 15.00
11 Ed Belfour 1.25 3.00
12 Brett Hull 1.50 4.00
13 Mike Modano 2.00 5.00
14 Sergei Fedorov 2.50 6.00
15 Brendan Shanahan 1.25 3.00
16 Steve Yzerman 6.00 15.00
17 Doug Weight 1.00 2.50
18 Pavel Bure 1.25 3.00
19 Luc Robitaille 1.00 2.50
20 Saku Koivu 1.25 3.00
21 Martin Brodeur 3.00 8.00
22 Scott Gomez .40 1.00
23 Tim Connolly .40 1.00
24 Marian Hossa 1.25 3.00
25 Brian Boucher 1.25 3.00
26 John LeClair 1.25 3.00
27 Mark Recchi 1.00 2.50
28 Jaromir Jagr 2.00 5.00
29 Jeremy Roenick 1.50 4.00
30 Chris Pronger 1.00 2.50
31 Roman Turek 1.00 2.50
32 Owen Nolan 1.00 2.50
33 Vincent Lecavalier 1.25 3.00
34 Mats Sundin 1.25 3.00
35 Curtis Joseph 1.25 3.00
36 Olaf Kolzig 1.00 2.50

2000-01 Paramount Game Used Sticks

Randomly inserted in packs, this 17-card set features player action photography on a horizontal design front coupled with an oval swatch of a game used stick. Each card is individually serial numbered in a gold foil box in the lower right hand corner of the card front.

1 Ron Francis/165 10.00 25.00
2 Ray Bourque/190 20.00 50.00
3 Adam Deadmarsh/200 10.00 25.00
4 Chris Drury/205 10.00 25.00
5 Joe Sakic/190 15.00 40.00
6 Martin Skoula/200 10.00 25.00
7 Alex Tanguay/200 10.00 25.00
8 Ed Belfour/205 15.00 40.00
9 Chris Chelios/165 12.50 30.00
10 Chris Osgood/205 10.00 25.00
11 Doug Weight/165 10.00 25.00
12 Luc Robitaille/185 10.00 25.00
13 Alexander Mogilny/155 10.00 25.00
14 Theo Fleury/190 10.00 25.00
15 Eric Lindros/190 12.50 30.00
16 Al MacInnis/165 10.00 25.00
17 Curtis Joseph/150 12.50 30.00

2000-01 Paramount Jersey and Patches

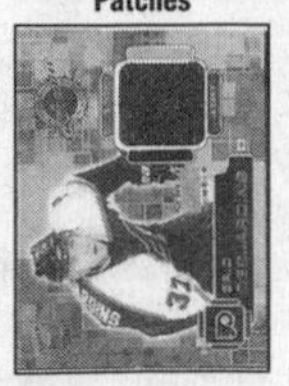

Randomly inserted in Hobby packs, this 10-card set features full color action photography coupled with a swatch of a game worn jersey on the card front and a game worn jersey patch on the back. Each card is sequentially numbered to 30.

1 Jarome Iginla 50.00 125.00
2 Tony Amonte 40.00 100.00
3 Ray Bourque 100.00 200.00
4 Joe Sakic 75.00 200.00
5 Darryl Sydor 40.00 100.00
6 Saku Koivu 40.00 100.00
7 John Vanbiesbrouck 40.00 100.00
8 Eric Desjardins 40.00 100.00
9 Shane Doan 40.00 100.00
10 Olaf Kolzig 40.00 100.00

2000-01 Paramount Glove Side Net Fusions

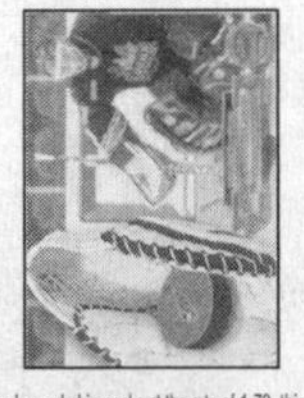

Randomly seeded in packs at the rate of 1:73, this 20-card set features a close-up of a goalie glove on the left side, player action shots on the right, and a die cut goal in the background with goal "netting." A platinum parallel numbered to just 25 was also created and inserted randomly.

COMPLETE SET (20) 50.00 100.00
*PLATINUM: 2.5X TO 6X BASIC CARDS
1 Byron Dafoe 2.00 5.00
2 Martin Biron 2.00 5.00
3 Dominik Hasek 5.00 12.00
4 Fred Brathwaite 2.00 5.00
5 Arturs Irbe 2.00 5.00
6 Jocelyn Thibault 2.00 5.00
7 Patrick Roy 12.50 30.00
8 Ed Belfour 2.50 6.00
9 Chris Osgood 2.00 5.00
10 Tommy Salo 2.00 5.00
11 Jose Theodore 3.00 8.00
12 Martin Brodeur 6.00 15.00
13 Mike Richter 2.50 6.00
14 Brian Boucher 2.00 5.00
15 Jean-Sebastien Aubin 2.00 5.00
16 Roman Turek 2.00 5.00
17 Steve Shields 2.00 5.00
18 Curtis Joseph 2.50 6.00
19 Felix Potvin 2.50 6.00
20 Olaf Kolzig 2.00 5.00

2000-01 Paramount Hall of Fame Bound

Randomly inserted in packs at the rate of 1:361, this 10-card set features embossed oval portraits of top NHL players and a banner bearing the line "Hall of Fame Bound." Two different proof parallels were also created. Regular proofs were randomly inserted and numbered to just 25, canvas proofs were randomly inserted and numbered 1/1. Canvas proofs not priced due to scarcity.

COMPLETE SET (10) 75.00 150.00
*PROOFS: 1.25X TO 3X BASIC CARDS
1 Paul Kariya 5.00 12.00
2 Dominik Hasek 8.00 20.00
3 Ray Bourque 8.00 20.00
4 Patrick Roy 15.00 40.00
5 Brett Hull 10.00 25.00
6 Steve Yzerman 15.00 40.00
7 Pavel Bure 5.00 12.00
8 Martin Brodeur 12.50 30.00
9 John LeClair 5.00 12.00
10 Jaromir Jagr 6.00 15.00

2000-01 Paramount Sub Zero

Randomly inserted in Canadian Retail packs at the rate of 1:49, this 10-card set features top NHL players on a card enhanced with silver foil highlights. Each card is sequentially numbered to 159. A gold parallel was also created and numbered to 99. Red 1/1 parallels also were created, they are not priced due to scarcity.

*GOLD: 1X TO 2X BASIC CARDS
1 Paul Kariya 4.00 10.00
2 Peter Forsberg 6.00 15.00
3 Patrick Roy 20.00 50.00
4 Brendan Shanahan 4.00 10.00

5 Steve Yzerman 12.00 30.00
6 Pavel Bure 4.00 10.00
7 Martin Brodeur 10.00 25.00
8 Jaromir Jagr 6.00 15.00
9 Curtis Joseph 4.00 10.00
10 Mats Sundin 4.00 10.00

1951-52 Parkhurst

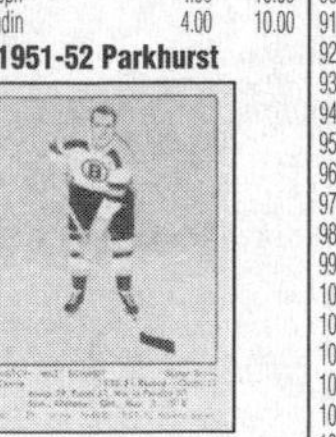

The 1951-52 Parkhurst set contains 105 small cards in crude color. Cards are 1 3/4" by 2 1/2". The player's name, team, card number, and 1950-51 statistics all appear on the front of the card. The backs of the cards are blank. Unopened wax packs, though rarely seen, consist of five cards. The cards feature players from each of the six NHL teams. The set numbering is basically according to teams, i.e., Montreal Canadiens (1-18), Boston Bruins (19-35), Chicago Blackhawks (36-51 and 53), Detroit Red Wings (54-69), Toronto Maple Leafs (70-88), and New York Rangers (89-105). Card #52 features a photo of one of the most famous goals in hockey history as Bill Barilko scored the Stanley Cup winning goal and then went flying into the air. The set features the first cards of hockey greats Gordie Howe and Maurice Richard. Please be alert when purchasing cards of Maurice Richard, Gordie Howe and Terry Sawchuk as counterfeits are known to exist of these players.

COMPLETE SET (105) 6000.00 12000.00
1 Elmer Lach 350.00 500.00
2 Paul Meger RC 40.00 60.00
3 Butch Bouchard RC 75.00 200.00
4 Maurice Richard RC 1200.00 1500.00
5 Bert Olmstead RC 75.00 125.00
6 Bud MacPherson RC 40.00 60.00
7 Tom Johnson RC 60.00 125.00
8 Paul Masnick RC 40.00 60.00
9 Calum Mackay RC 40.00 60.00
10 Doug Harvey RC 400.00 600.00
11 Ken Mosdell RC 50.00 80.00
12 Floyd Curry RC 50.00 80.00
13 Billy Reay RC 50.00 80.00
14 Bernie Geoffrion RC 400.00 600.00
15 Gerry McNeil RC 175.00 300.00
16 Dick Gamble RC 50.00 80.00
17 Gerry Couture RC 40.00 60.00
18 Ross Robert Lowe RC 40.00 60.00
19 Jim Henry RC 90.00 150.00
20 Victor Ivan Lynn RC 40.00 60.00
21 Walter Kyle RC 40.00 60.00
22 Ed Sandford RC 40.00 60.00
23 John Henderson RC 50.00 80.00
24 Dunc Fisher RC 40.00 60.00
25 Hal Laycoe RC 50.00 80.00
26 Bill Quackenbush RC 75.00 125.00
27 George Sullivan RC 50.00 80.00
28 Woody Dumart 50.00 100.00
29 Milt Schmidt 100.00 150.00
30 Adam Brown RC 40.00 60.00
31 Pentti Lund RC 50.00 80.00
32 Ray Barry RC 40.00 60.00
33 Ed Kryznowski UER RC 40.00 60.00
34 Johnny Peirson RC 50.00 80.00
35 Lorne Ferguson RC 40.00 60.00
36 Clare Raglan RC 40.00 60.00
37 Bill Gadsby RC 60.00 125.00
38 Al Dewsbury RC 40.00 60.00
39 George Clare Martin RC 40.00 60.00
40 Gus Bodnar RC 50.00 80.00
41 Jim Peters RC 40.00 60.00
42 Bep Guidolin RC 50.00 80.00
43 George Gee RC 40.00 60.00
44 Jim McFadden RC 40.00 60.00
45 Fred Hucul RC 40.00 60.00
46 Lee Fogolin RC 40.00 60.00
47 Harry Lumley RC 90.00 150.00
48 Doug Bentley RC 60.00 125.00
49 Bill Mosienko RC 60.00 125.00
50 Roy Conacher 50.00 80.00
51 Pete Babando RC 40.00 60.00
52 Bill Barilko 250.00 500.00
Gerry McNeil IA
53 Jack Stewart 50.00 80.00
54 Marty Pavelich RC 40.00 60.00
55 Red Kelly RC 200.00 300.00
56 Ted Lindsay RC 200.00 300.00
57 Glen Skov RC 40.00 60.00
58 Benny Woit RC 40.00 60.00
59 Tony Leswick RC 50.00 80.00
60 Fred Glover RC 40.00 60.00
61 Terry Sawchuk RC 800.00 1200.00
62 Vic Stasiuk RC 50.00 80.00
63 Alex Delvecchio RC 275.00 400.00
64 Sid Abel 60.00 100.00
65 Metro Prystai RC 40.00 60.00
66 Gordie Howe RC 2000.00 3000.00
67 Bob Goldham RC 40.00 60.00
68 Marcel Pronovost RC 60.00 125.00
69 Leo Reise 40.00 60.00
70 Harry Watson RC 50.00 80.00
71 Danny Lewicki RC 40.00 60.00
72 Howie Meeker RC 90.00 150.00
73 Gus Mortson RC 50.00 80.00
74 Joe Klukay RC 40.00 60.00
75 Turk Broda 125.00 200.00
76 Al Rollins RC 75.00 150.00
77 Bill Juzda RC 40.00 60.00
78 Ray Timgren RC 40.00 60.00
79 Hugh Bolton RC 40.00 60.00
80 Fern Flaman RC 60.00 125.00
81 Max Bentley 60.00 100.00
82 Jim Thomson RC 40.00 60.00
83 Fleming Mackell RC 50.00 80.00
84 Sid Smith RC 60.00 125.00
85 Cal Gardner RC 50.00 80.00
86 Teeder Kennedy RC 175.00 275.00
87 Tod Sloan RC 50.00 80.00
88 Bob Solinger RC 40.00 60.00
89 Frank Eddolls RC 40.00 60.00
90 Jack Evans RC 50.00 100.00
91 Hy Buller RC 40.00 60.00
92 Steve Kraftcheck RC 40.00 60.00
93 Don Raleigh RC 40.00 60.00
94 Allan Stanley RC 90.00 150.00
95 Paul Ronty RC 40.00 60.00
96 Edgar Laprade RC 60.00 100.00
97 Nick Mickoski RC 40.00 60.00
98 Jack McLeod RC 40.00 60.00
99 Gaye Stewart RC 40.00 60.00
100 Wally Hergesheimer RC 50.00 80.00
101 Ed Kullman RC 40.00 60.00
102 Ed Slowinski RC 40.00 60.00
103 Reg Sinclair RC 40.00 60.00
104 Chuck Rayner RC 75.00 125.00
105 Jim Conacher RC 100.00 200.00

1952-53 Parkhurst

The 1952-53 Parkhurst set contains 105 color, line-drawing cards. Cards are approximately 1 15/16" by 2 15/16". The obverse contains a facsimile autograph of the player pictured while the backs contain a short biography in English and 1951-52 statistics. The backs also contain the card number and a special album (for holding a set of cards) offer. The cards feature players from each of the Original Six NHL teams. The set numbering is roughly according to teams, i.e., Montreal Canadiens (1-15, 52, 93), Boston Bruins (68-85), Chicago Blackhawks (16-17, 26-27, 29-33, 35-41, 55-56), Detroit Red Wings (53, 60-67, 86-92, 104), Toronto Maple Leafs (28, 34, 42-48, 50-51, 54, 58-59, 94-96, 105), and New York Rangers (18-25, 49, 57, 97-103). The key Rookie Cards in this set are George Armstrong, Tim Horton, and Dickie Moore.

COMPLETE SET (105) 4500.00 7000.00
1 Maurice Richard 800.00 1200.00
2 Billy Reay 25.00 40.00
3 Bernie Geoffrion 150.00 250.00
UER (Misspelled Geoffrion on back)
4 Paul Meger 18.00 30.00
5 Dick Gamble 25.00 40.00
6 Elmer Lach 50.00 80.00
7 Floyd Curry 25.00 40.00
8 Ken Mosdell 25.00 40.00
9 Tom Johnson 25.00 40.00
10 Dickie Moore RC 150.00 250.00
11 Bud MacPherson 18.00 30.00
12 Gerry McNeil 60.00 100.00
13 Butch Bouchard 25.00 40.00
14 Doug Harvey 150.00 250.00
15 John McCormack RC 18.00 30.00
16 Pete Babando 18.00 30.00
17 Al Dewsbury 18.00 30.00
18 Ed Kullman 18.00 30.00
19 Ed Slowinski 18.00 30.00
20 Wally Hergesheimer 25.00 40.00
21 Allan Stanley 50.00 80.00
22 Chuck Rayner 40.00 60.00
23 Steve Kraftcheck 18.00 30.00
24 Paul Ronty 18.00 30.00
25 Gaye Stewart 18.00 30.00
26 Fred Hucul 18.00 30.00
27 Bill Mosienko 30.00 50.00
28 Jim Morrison RC 18.00 30.00
29 Ed Kryznowski 18.00 30.00
30 Cal Gardner 25.00 40.00
31 Al Rollins 40.00 60.00
32 Enio Sclisizzi RC 18.00 30.00
33 Pete Conacher RC 25.00 40.00
34 Leo Boivin RC 40.00 60.00
35 Jim Peters 18.00 30.00
36 George Gee 18.00 30.00
37 Gus Bodnar 25.00 40.00
38 Jim McFadden 18.00 30.00
39 Gus Mortson 25.00 40.00
40 Fred Glover 18.00 30.00
41 Gerry Couture 18.00 30.00
42 Howie Meeker 50.00 80.00
43 Jim Thomson 18.00 30.00
44 Teeder Kennedy 60.00 100.00
45 Sid Smith 25.00 40.00
46 Harry Watson 30.00 50.00
47 Fern Flaman 25.00 40.00
48 Tod Sloan 25.00 40.00
49 Leo Reise 18.00 30.00
50 Bob Solinger 18.00 30.00
51 George Armstrong RC 150.00 250.00
52 Dollard St.Laurent RC 25.00 40.00
53 Alex Delvecchio 90.00 150.00
54 Gord Hannigan RC 18.00 30.00
55 Lee Fogolin 18.00 30.00
56 Bill Gadsby 30.00 50.00
57 Herb Dickenson RC 18.00 30.00
58 Tim Horton RC 500.00 700.00
59 Harry Lumley 60.00 100.00
60 Metro Prystai 18.00 30.00
61 Marcel Pronovost 25.00 40.00
62 Benny Woit 18.00 30.00
63 Glen Skov 18.00 30.00
64 Bob Goldham 18.00 30.00
65 Tony Leswick 18.00 30.00
66 Marty Pavelich 18.00 30.00
67 Red Kelly 90.00 150.00
68 Bill Quackenbush 30.00 50.00
69 Ed Sandford 18.00 30.00
70 Milt Schmidt 40.00 60.00
71 Hal Laycoe 25.00 40.00
72 Woody Dumart 25.00 40.00
73 Zellio Toppazzini RC 18.00 30.00
74 Jim Henry 25.00 40.00
75 Joe Klukay 18.00 30.00
76 Dave Creighton RC 25.00 40.00
77 Jack McIntyre RC 18.00 30.00
78 Johnny Peirson 18.00 30.00
79 George Sullivan 25.00 40.00
80 Real Chevrefils RC 25.00 40.00
81 Leo Labine RC 30.00 50.00
82 Fleming Mackell 25.00 40.00
83 Pentti Lund 18.00 30.00
84 Bob Armstrong RC 18.00 30.00
85 Warren Godfrey RC 18.00 30.00
86 Terry Sawchuk 300.00 500.00
87 Ted Lindsay 90.00 150.00
88 Gordie Howe 600.00 1000.00
89 Johnny Wilson RC 18.00 30.00
90 Vic Stasiuk 25.00 40.00
91 Larry Zeidel RC 18.00 30.00
92 Larry Wilson RC 18.00 30.00
93 Bert Olmstead 25.00 40.00
94 Ron Stewart RC 25.00 40.00
95 Max Bentley 30.00 50.00
96 Rudy Migay RC 18.00 30.00
97 Jack Stoddard RC 18.00 30.00
98 Hy Buller 18.00 30.00
99 Don Raleigh 18.00 30.00
100 Edgar Laprade 25.00 40.00
101 Nick Mickoski 18.00 30.00
102 Jack McLeod UER 18.00 30.00
(Robert on back)
103 Jim Conacher 25.00 40.00
104 Reg Sinclair 18.00 30.00
105 Bob Hassard RC ! 75.00 125.00

1953-54 Parkhurst

The 1953-54 Parkhurst set contains 100 cards in full color. Cards measure approximately 2 1/2" by 3 5/8". The cards were sold in five-cent wax packs each containing four cards and gum. The size of the card increased from the previous year, and the picture and color show marked improvement. A facsimile autograph of the player is found on the front. The backs contain the card number, 1952-53 statistics, a short biography, and an album offer. The back data is presented in both English and French. The cards feature players from each of the six NHL teams. The set numbering is basically according to teams, i.e., Toronto Maple Leafs (1-17), Montreal Canadiens (18-35), Detroit Red Wings (36-52), New York Rangers (53-68), Chicago Blackhawks (69-84), and Boston Bruins (85-100). The key Rookie Cards in this set are Al Arbour, Andy Bathgate, Jean Beliveau, Harry Howell, and Gump Worsley.

COMPLETE SET (100) 3000.00 4500.00
1 Harry Lumley 150.00 250.00
2 Sid Smith 20.00 40.00
3 Gord Hannigan 20.00 40.00
4 Bob Hassard 20.00 40.00
5 Tod Sloan 20.00 40.00
6 Leo Boivin 20.00 40.00
7 Teeder Kennedy 35.00 70.00
8 Jim Thomson 20.00 40.00
9 Ron Stewart 20.00 40.00
10 Eric Nesterenko RC 40.00 80.00
11 George Armstrong 60.00 100.00
12 Harry Watson 30.00 60.00
13 Tim Horton 175.00 300.00
14 Fern Flaman 25.00 50.00
15 Jim Morrison 20.00 40.00
16 Bob Solinger 20.00 40.00
17 Rudy Migay 20.00 40.00
18 Dick Gamble 20.00 40.00
19 Bert Olmstead 25.00 50.00
20 Eddie Mazur RC 20.00 40.00
21 Paul Meger 20.00 40.00
22 Bud MacPherson 20.00 40.00
23 Dollard St.Laurent 20.00 40.00
24 Maurice Richard 300.00 500.00
25 Gerry McNeil 50.00 80.00
26 Doug Harvey 125.00 200.00
27 Jean Beliveau RC 450.00 600.00
28 Dickie Moore UER 75.00 125.00
(Photo actually Jean Beliveau)
29 Bernie Geoffrion 125.00 200.00
30 Lach/Richard 125.00 200.00
Elmer Lach and Maurice Richard
31 Elmer Lach 35.00 70.00
32 Butch Bouchard 25.00 50.00
33 Ken Mosdell 20.00 40.00
34 John McCormack 20.00 40.00
35 Floyd (Busher) Curry 20.00 40.00
36 Earl Reibel RC 20.00 40.00
37 Bill Dineen UER RC 20.00 40.00
38 Al Arbour RC UER 60.00 100.00
39 Vic Stasiuk 20.00 40.00
40 Red Kelly 60.00 100.00
41 Marcel Pronovost 25.00 50.00
42 Metro Prystai 20.00 40.00
43 Tony Leswick 20.00 40.00
44 Marty Pavelich 20.00 40.00
45 Benny Woit 20.00 40.00
46 Terry Sawchuk 200.00 350.00
47 Alex Delvecchio 60.00 100.00
48 Glen Skov 20.00 40.00
49 Bob Goldham 20.00 40.00
50 Gordie Howe 500.00 800.00
51 Johnny Wilson 20.00 40.00
52 Ted Lindsay 60.00 100.00
53 Gump Worsley RC 275.00 400.00
54 Jack Evans 20.00 40.00
55 Max Bentley 30.00 60.00
56 Andy Bathgate RC 90.00 150.00
57 Harry Howell RC 90.00 150.00
58 Hy Buller 20.00 40.00
59 Chuck Rayner 25.00 50.00
60 Jack Stoddard 20.00 40.00
61 Ed Kullman 20.00 40.00
62 Nick Mickoski 20.00 40.00
63 Paul Ronty 20.00 40.00
64 Allan Stanley 30.00 60.00
65 Leo Reise 20.00 40.00
66 Aldo Guidolin RC 20.00 40.00
67 Wally Hergesheimer 20.00 40.00
68 Don Raleigh 20.00 40.00
69 Jim Peters 20.00 40.00
70 Pete Conacher 20.00 40.00
71 Fred Hucul 20.00 40.00
72 Lee Fogolin 20.00 40.00
73 Larry Zeidel 20.00 40.00
74 Larry Wilson 20.00 40.00
75 Gus Bodnar 20.00 40.00
76 Bill Gadsby 30.00 60.00
77 Jim McFadden 20.00 40.00
78 Al Dewsbury 20.00 40.00
79 Clare Raglan 20.00 40.00
80 Bill Mosienko 30.00 60.00
81 Gus Mortson 20.00 40.00
82 Al Rollins 25.00 50.00
83 George Gee 20.00 40.00
84 Gerry Couture 20.00 40.00
85 Dave Creighton 20.00 40.00
86 Jim Henry 25.00 50.00
87 Hal Laycoe 20.00 40.00
88 Johnny Peirson UER 25.00 50.00
(Misspelled Pierson on card back)
89 Real Chevrefils 20.00 40.00
90 Ed Sandford 20.00 40.00
91A Fleming Mackell ERR 25.00 50.00
(No bio)
91B Fleming Mackell COR 25.00 50.00
92 Milt Schmidt 35.00 70.00
93 Leo Labine 20.00 40.00
94 Joe Klukay 20.00 40.00
95 Warren Godfrey 20.00 40.00
96 Woody Dumart 25.00 50.00
97 Frank Martin RC 20.00 40.00
98 Jerry Toppazzini RC 20.00 40.00
99 Cal Gardner 20.00 40.00
100 Bill Quackenbush 75.00 150.00

1954-55 Parkhurst

The 1954-55 Parkhurst set contains 100 cards in full color with both the card number and a facsimile autograph on the fronts. Cards in the set measure approximately 2 1/2" by 3 5/8". Unopened wax packs consisted of four cards. The backs, in both English and French, contain 1953-54 statistics, a short player biography, and an album offer (contained only on cards 1-88). Cards 1-88 feature players from each of the six NHL teams and the remaining cards are action scenes. Cards 1-88 were available with either a stat or a premium back. The cards with the statistics on the back are more desirable but there is currently no price differential. The player/set numbering is basically according to teams, i.e., Montreal Canadiens (1-15), Toronto Maple Leafs (16-32), Detroit Red Wings (33-48), Boston Bruins (49-64), New York Rangers (65-76), and Chicago Blackhawks (77-88), and All-Star selections from the previous season are noted discreetly on the card front by a red star (first team selection) or blue star (second team). The key Rookie Card in this set is Johnny Bower, although there are several Action Scene cards featuring Jacques Plante in the year before his regular Rookie Card.

COMPLETE SET (100) 2500.00 4000.00
*PREM.BACKS 1-88: SAME VALUE
1 Gerry McNeil 75.00 125.00
2 Dickie Moore 50.00 80.00
3 Jean Beliveau 200.00 300.00
4 Eddie Mazur 15.00 25.00
5 Bert Olmstead 18.00 30.00
6 Butch Bouchard 18.00 30.00
7 Maurice Richard 275.00 400.00
8 Bernie Geoffrion 75.00 125.00
9 John McCormack 15.00 25.00
10 Tom Johnson 18.00 30.00
11 Calum Mackay 15.00 25.00
12 Ken Mosdell 15.00 25.00
13 Paul Masnick 15.00 25.00
14 Doug Harvey 75.00 125.00
15 Floyd(Busher) Curry 15.00 25.00
16 Harry Lumley 25.00 40.00
17 Harry Watson 25.00 40.00
18 Jim Morrison 15.00 25.00
19 Eric Nesterenko 15.00 25.00
20 Fern Flaman 18.00 30.00
21 Rudy Migay 15.00 25.00
22 Sid Smith 15.00 25.00
23 Ron Stewart 15.00 25.00
24 George Armstrong 50.00 80.00
25 Earl Balfour RC 15.00 25.00
26 Leo Boivin 15.00 25.00
27 Gord Hannigan 15.00 25.00
28 Bob Bailey RC 15.00 25.00
29 Teeder Kennedy 30.00 50.00
30 Tod Sloan 15.00 25.00
31 Tim Horton 150.00 250.00
32 Jim Thomson 15.00 25.00
33 Terry Sawchuk 150.00 250.00
34 Marcel Pronovost 18.00 30.00
35 Metro Prystai 15.00 25.00
36 Alex Delvecchio 50.00 80.00
37 Earl Reibel 15.00 25.00
38 Benny Woit 15.00 25.00
39 Bob Goldham 15.00 25.00
40 Glen Skov 15.00 25.00
41 Gordie Howe 400.00 600.00
42 Red Kelly 50.00 80.00
43 Marty Pavelich 15.00 25.00
44 Johnny Wilson 15.00 25.00
45 Tony Leswick 15.00 25.00
46 Ted Lindsay 50.00 80.00
47 Keith Allen RC 18.00 30.00
48 Bill Dineen 15.00 25.00
49 Jim Henry 25.00 40.00
50 Fleming Mackell 18.00 30.00
51 Bill Quackenbush 25.00 40.00
52 Hal Laycoe 15.00 25.00
53 Cal Gardner 15.00 25.00
54 Joe Klukay 15.00 25.00
55 Bob Armstrong 15.00 25.00
56 Warren Godfrey 15.00 25.00
57 Doug Mohns RC 25.00 40.00
58 Dave Creighton 15.00 25.00
59 Milt Schmidt 30.00 50.00
60 Johnny Peirson 15.00 25.00
61 Leo Labine 15.00 25.00
62 Gus Bodnar 15.00 25.00
63 Real Chevrefils 15.00 25.00
64 Ed Sandford 15.00 25.00
65 Johnny Bower UER RC 200.00 400.00
66 Paul Ronty 15.00 25.00
67 Leo Reise 15.00 25.00
68 Don Raleigh 15.00 25.00
69 Bob Chrystal RC 15.00 25.00
70 Harry Howell 35.00 60.00
71 Wally Hergesheimer 15.00 25.00
72 Jack Evans 15.00 25.00
73 Camille Henry RC 18.00 30.00
74 Dean Prentice RC 25.00 40.00
75 Nick Mickoski 15.00 25.00
76 Ron Murphy RC 15.00 25.00
77 Al Rollins 25.00 40.00
78 Al Dewsbury 15.00 25.00
79 Lou Jankowski RC 15.00 25.00
80 George Gee 15.00 25.00
81 Gus Mortson 15.00 25.00
82 Fred Saskamoose RC 75.00 125.00
83 Ike Hildebrand RC 15.00 25.00
84 Lee Fogolin 15.00 25.00
85 Larry Wilson 15.00 25.00
86 Pete Conacher 15.00 25.00
87 Bill Gadsby 25.00 40.00
88 Jack McIntyre 15.00 25.00
89 Busher Curry goes up and over 15.00 25.00
90 Delvecchio finds Leaf defense hard to crack (Tim Horton) 18.00 30.00
91 Battle of All-Stars (Red Kelly and Harry Lumley) 25.00 40.00
92 Lum stops Howe With help of Stewart's stick 60.00 100.00
93 Net-minders nightmare (Harry Lumley and others) 15.00 25.00
94 Meger goes down and under (Jim Morrison) 15.00 25.00
95 Harvey takes nosedive (Eric Nesterenko) 30.00 50.00
96 Terry boots out Teeder's blast (Terry Sawchuk and Teeder Kennedy) 60.00 100.00
97 Reibel tests Habs Rookie Mr. Zero (Jacques Plante and Bert Olmstead) 60.00 100.00
98 Plante protects against slippery Sloan (Doug Harvey) 60.00 100.00
99 Placid Plante foils tireless Teeder 60.00 100.00
100 Sawchuk stops Boom Boom 125.00 200.00

1955-56 Parkhurst

The 1955-56 Parkhurst set contains 79 cards in full color with the number and team insignia on the fronts. Cards in the set measure approximately 2 1/2" by 3 9/16". The set features players from Montreal and Toronto as well as Old-Time Greats. The Old-Time Great selections are numbers 21-32 and 55-66. The backs, printed in red ink, in both English and French, contain 1954-55 statistics, a short biography, a "Do You Know" information section, and an album offer. The key Rookie Card in this set is Jacques Plante. The same 79 cards can also be found with Quaker Oats backs, i.e., green printing on back. The Quaker Oats version is much tougher to locate. Using regular Parkhurst card values as a base, multipliers can be found in the header below to determine value for these. Reportedly, cards #1, 33 and 37 are extremely difficult to acquire in the Quaker Oats version, and can sell for much more than the suggested multipliers.

COMPLETE SET (79) 2800.00 5000.00
*QUAKER OATS: 2X TO 3X BASIC CARDS
1 Harry Lumley 200.00 300.00
2 Sid Smith 15.00 30.00
3 Tim Horton 150.00 250.00
4 George Armstrong 50.00 80.00
5 Ron Stewart 15.00 30.00
6 Joe Klukay 12.00 20.00
7 Marc Reaume RC 12.00 20.00
8 Jim Morrison 12.00 20.00
9 Parker MacDonald RC 12.00 20.00
10 Tod Sloan 12.00 20.00
11 Jim Thomson 12.00 20.00
12 Rudy Migay 12.00 20.00
13 Brian Cullen RC 15.00 30.00
14 Hugh Bolton 12.00 20.00
15 Eric Nesterenko 15.00 30.00
16 Larry Cahan RC 12.00 20.00
17 Willie Marshall RC 12.00 20.00
18 Dick Duff RC 50.00 100.00
19 Jack Caffery RC 12.00 20.00
20 Billy Harris RC 15.00 30.00
21 Lorne Chabot OTG 15.00 30.00
22 Busher Jackson OTG 30.00 50.00
23 Turk Broda OTG 60.00 100.00
24 Joe Primeau OTG 25.00 40.00
25 Gordie Drillon OTG 15.00 30.00
26 Chuck Conacher OTG 25.00 40.00
27 Sweeney Schriner OTG 15.00 30.00
28 Syl Apps OTG 25.00 40.00
29 Teeder Kennedy OTG 30.00 50.00
30 Ace Bailey OTG 40.00 60.00
31 Babe Pratt OTG 15.00 30.00
32 Harold Cotton OTG 15.00 30.00
33 King Clancy 60.00 100.00
34 Hap Day 15.00 30.00
35 Don Marshall RC 30.00 50.00
36 Jackie LeClair RC 15.00 30.00
37 Maurice Richard 275.00 400.00
38 Dickie Moore 50.00 80.00
39 Ken Mosdell 15.00 30.00
40 Floyd(Busher) Curry 12.00 20.00
41 Calum Mackay 12.00 20.00
42 Bert Olmstead 12.00 20.00
43 Bernie Geoffrion 75.00 125.00
44 Jean Beliveau 250.00 350.00
45 Doug Harvey 75.00 125.00
46 Butch Bouchard 15.00 30.00
47 Bud MacPherson 12.00 20.00
48 Dollard St.Laurent 12.00 20.00
49 Tom Johnson 15.00 30.00
50 Jacques Plante RC 600.00 800.00
51 Paul Meger 12.00 20.00
52 Gerry McNeil 25.00 40.00
53 Jean-Guy Talbot RC 15.00 30.00
54 Bob Turner 12.00 20.00
55 Newsy Lalonde OTG 40.00 60.00
56 Georges Vezina OTG 75.00 125.00
57 Howie Morenz OTG 60.00 100.00
58 Aurel Joliat OTG 40.00 60.00
59 Geo. Hainsworth OTG 60.00 100.00
60 Sylvio Mantha OTG 15.00 30.00
61 Battleship Leduc OTG 15.00 30.00
62 Babe Siebert OTG UER 18.00 40.00
(Misspelled Seibert on both sides)
63 Bill Durnan OTG RC 40.00 60.00
64 Ken Reardon OTG RC 40.00 60.00
65 Johnny Gagnon OTG 15.00 30.00
66 Billy Reay OTG 15.00 30.00
67 Toe Blake CO 30.00 50.00
68 Frank Selke MG 18.00 30.00
69 Hugh beats Hodge (Hugh Bolton and Charlie Hodge) 18.00 30.00
70 Lum stops Boom Boom (Harry Lumley) 40.00 60.00
71 Plante is protected (Butch Bouchard and Tom Johnson) 50.00 80.00
72 Rocket roars through (Maurice Richard) 50.00 80.00
73 Richard tests Lumley (Maurice Richard) 50.00 80.00
74 Beliveau bats puck (Harry Lumley) 40.00 60.00
75 Leaf speedsters attack (Eric Nesterenko& Sid Smith& and Jacques Plante) 50.00 80.00
76 Curry scores again (Harry Lumley and Jim Morrison) 15.00 30.00
77 Jammed on the boards (Tod Sloan& Parker MacDonald& Doug Harvey& and Jean Beliveau) 50.00 80.00
78 The Montreal Forum 150.00 300.00
79 Maple Leaf Gardens 150.00 300.00

1957-58 Parkhurst

The 1957-58 Parkhurst set contains 50 color cards featuring Montreal and Toronto players. Cards are approximately 2 7/16" by 3 5/8". There are card numbers 1 to 25 for Montreal (M prefix in checklist) and card numbers 1 to 25 for Toronto (T prefix in checklist). The cards are numbered on the fronts and the backs feature resumes in both French and English. The card number, the player's name, and his position appear in a red rectangle on the front. The backs are printed in blue ink. The key Rookie Cards in this set are Frank Mahovlich and Henri Richard. There was no Parkhurst hockey set in 1956-57 reportedly due to market re-evaluation.

COMPLETE SET (50) 2000.00 3500.00
M1 Doug Harvey 150.00 275.00
M2 Bernie Geoffrion 75.00 125.00
M3 Jean Beliveau 200.00 300.00
M4 Henri Richard RC 400.00 600.00
M5 Maurice Richard 300.00 400.00
M6 Tom Johnson 15.00 25.00
M7 Andre Pronovost RC 20.00 40.00
M8 Don Marshall 12.00 20.00
M9 Jean-Guy Talbot 12.00 20.00
M10 Dollard St.Laurent 12.00 20.00
M11 Phil Goyette RC 25.00 40.00
M12 Claude Provost RC 25.00 40.00
M13 Bob Turner 12.00 20.00
M14 Dickie Moore 35.00 60.00
M15 Jacques Plante 250.00 400.00
M16 Toe Blake CO 25.00 40.00
M17 Charlie Hodge RC 50.00 80.00
M18 Marcel Bonin 12.00 20.00
M19 Bert Olmstead 15.00 25.00
M20 Floyd (Busher) Curry 12.00 20.00
M21 Len Broderick IA RC 25.00 40.00
M22 Brian Cullen scores 12.00 20.00
M23 Puck and sticks high (Len Broderick and Doug Harvey) 25.00 40.00
M24 Geoffrion side-steps Chadwick 30.00 50.00
M25 Olmstead beats Chadwick 20.00 40.00
T1 George Armstrong 60.00 100.00
T2 Ed Chadwick RC 75.00 125.00
T3 Dick Duff 15.00 25.00
T4 Bob Pulford RC 90.00 150.00
T5 Tod Sloan 15.00 25.00
T6 Rudy Migay
T7 Ron Stewart
T8 Gerry James RC 15.00 25.00
T9 Brian Cullen
T10 Sid Smith
T11 Jim Morrison
T12 Marc Reaume
T13 Hugh Bolton
T14 Pete Conacher
T15 Billy Harris
T16 Mike Nykoluk RC
T17 Frank Mahovlich RC 300.00 500.00
T18 Ken Girard RC
T19 Al MacNeil RC
T20 Bob Baun RC 60.00 100.00
T21 Barry Cullen RC
T22 Tim Horton 100.00 175.00
T23 Gary Collins RC
T24 Gary Aldcorn RC
T25 Billy Reay CO 20.00 40.00

1958-59 Parkhurst

The 1958-59 Parkhurst set contains 50 color cards of Montreal and Toronto players. Cards are approximately 2 7/16" by 3 5/8". In contrast to the 1957-58 Parkhurst set, the cards, numbered on the fronts, are numbered continuously from 1 to 50. Resumes on the backs of the cards are in both French and English. The player's name and the team logo appears in a yellow rectangle at the bottom on the front. The number, position, and (usually) a hockey stick appear on the front at the upper left. The backs are printed in black ink. The key Rookie Card in this set is Ralph Backstrom.

COMPLETE SET (50) 1200.00 1800.00
1 Pulford Comes Close 30.00 50.00
2 Henri Richard 125.00 200.00
3 Andre Pronovost 10.00 15.00
4 Billy Harris 12.00 20.00
5 Albert Langlois RC 10.00 15.00
6 Noel Price RC 10.00 15.00
7 Armstrong Breaks Through (Tom Johnson) 15.00 25.00
8 Dickie Moore 25.00 40.00
9 Toe Blake CO 15.00 25.00
10 Tom Johnson 12.00 20.00
11 An Object of Interest (Jacques Plante and George Armstrong) 35.00 50.00
12 Ed Chadwick 25.00 40.00
13 Bob Nevin RC 15.00 25.00
14 Ron Stewart 12.00 18.00
15 Bob Baun 25.00 40.00
16 Ralph Backstrom RC 30.00 50.00
17 Charlie Hodge 25.00 40.00
18 Gary Aldcorn 10.00 15.00
19 Willie Marshall 10.00 15.00
20 Marc Reaume 10.00 15.00
21 All Eyes on Puck (Jacques Plante and others) 40.00 60.00
22 Jacques Plante 200.00 300.00
23 Allan Stanley 15.00 25.00
24 Ian Cushenan RC 10.00 15.00
25 Billy Reay CO 12.00 18.00
26 Plante Catches a Shot 40.00 60.00
27 Bert Olmstead 12.00 18.00
28 Bernie Geoffrion 50.00 80.00
29 Dick Duff 12.00 18.00
30 Ab McDonald RC 10.00 15.00
31 Barry Cullen 10.00 15.00
32 Marcel Bonin 10.00 15.00
33 Frank Mahovlich 125.00 200.00
34 Jean Beliveau 125.00 200.00
35 Canadiens on Guard (Jacques Plante and others) 40.00 60.00
36 Brian Cullen Shoots 12.00 18.00
37 Steve Kraftcheck 10.00 15.00
38 Maurice Richard 200.00 300.00
39 Action Around the Net (Jacques Plante and others) 40.00 60.00
40 Bob Turner 10.00 15.00
41 Jean-Guy Talbot 12.00 18.00
42 Tim Horton 75.00 125.00
43 Claude Provost 12.00 18.00
44 Don Marshall 12.00 18.00
45 Bob Pulford 18.00 30.00
46 Johnny Bower UER 90.00 150.00
(Misspelled Bowers on card front)
47 Phil Goyette 12.00 18.00
48 George Armstrong 25.00 40.00
49 Doug Harvey 50.00 80.00
50 Brian Cullen 20.00 40.00

1959-60 Parkhurst

The 1959-60 Parkhurst set contains 50 color cards of Montreal and Toronto players. Cards are approximately 2 7/16" by 3 5/8". The cards are numbered on the fronts. The backs, which contain 1958-59 statistics, a short biography, and a Hockey Gum contest ad, are written in both French and English. The key Rookie Cards in this set are Carl Brewer and Punch Imlach.

COMPLETE SET (50)	700.00	1400.00
1 Canadiens on Guard	75.00	125.00
(Versus Maple Leafs)		
2 Maurice Richard	150.00	250.00
3 Carl Brewer RC	40.00	60.00
4 Phil Goyette	12.50	25.00
5 Ed Chadwick	15.00	30.00
6 Jean Beliveau	75.00	125.00
7 George Armstrong	15.00	30.00
8 Doug Harvey	40.00	60.00
9 Billy Harris	12.50	25.00
10 Tom Johnson	12.50	25.00
11 Marc Reaume	12.50	25.00
12 Marcel Bonin	12.50	25.00
13 Johnny Wilson	12.50	25.00
14 Dickie Moore	20.00	40.00
15 Punch Imlach CO/MG RC	25.00	40.00
16 Charlie Hodge	15.00	30.00
17 Larry Regan	12.50	25.00
18 Claude Provost	12.50	25.00
19 Gerry Ehman RC	12.50	25.00
20 Ab McDonald	12.50	25.00
21 Bob Baun	12.50	25.00
22 Ken Reardon VP	12.50	25.00
23 Tim Horton	65.00	100.00
24 Frank Mahovlich	75.00	125.00
25 Johnny Bower IA	25.00	40.00
26 Ron Stewart	12.50	25.00
27 Toe Blake CO	12.50	25.00
28 Bob Pulford	12.50	25.00
29 Ralph Backstrom	12.50	25.00
30 Action Around the Net	15.00	30.00
31 Bill Hicke RC	15.00	30.00
32 Johnny Bower	65.00	100.00
33 Bernie Geoffrion	40.00	60.00
34 Ted Hampson RC	12.50	25.00
35 Andre Pronovost	12.50	25.00
36 Stafford Smythe CHC	12.50	25.00
37 Don Marshall	12.50	25.00
38 Dick Duff	12.50	25.00
39 Henri Richard	75.00	125.00
40 Bert Olmstead	12.50	25.00
41 Jacques Plante	100.00	200.00
42 Noel Price	12.50	25.00
43 Bob Turner	12.50	25.00
44 Allan Stanley	20.00	40.00
45 Albert Langlois	12.50	25.00
46 Officials Intervene	12.50	25.00
47 Frank Selke MD	12.50	25.00
48 Gary Edmundson RC	12.50	25.00
49 Jean-Guy Talbot	12.50	25.00
50 King Clancy AGM	50.00	80.00

1960-61 Parkhurst

The 1960-61 Parkhurst set of 61 color cards, numbered on the fronts, contains players from Montreal, Toronto, and Detroit. The numbering of the players in the set is basically by teams, i.e., Toronto Maple Leafs (1-19), Detroit Red Wings (20-37), and Montreal Canadiens (38-55). Cards in the set are 2 7/16" by 3 5/8". The backs, in both French and English, are printed in blue ink and contain NHL lifetime records, vital statistics, and biographical data of the player. This set contains the last card of Maurice "Rocket" Richard. The key Rookie Card in this set is John McKenzie.

COMPLETE SET (61)	1100.00	1700.00
1 Tim Horton	90.00	150.00
2 Frank Mahovlich	65.00	100.00
3 Johnny Bower	50.00	80.00
4 Bert Olmstead	10.00	18.00
5 Gary Edmundson	9.00	15.00
6 Ron Stewart	9.00	15.00
7 Gerry James	9.00	15.00
8 Gerry Ehman	9.00	15.00
9 Red Kelly	18.00	30.00
10 Dave Creighton	9.00	15.00
11 Bob Baun	10.00	18.00
12 Dick Duff	10.00	18.00
13 Larry Regan	9.00	15.00
14 Johnny Wilson	9.00	15.00
15 Billy Harris	9.00	15.00
16 Allan Stanley	12.00	20.00
17 George Armstrong	12.00	20.00
18 Carl Brewer	10.00	18.00
19 Bob Pulford	10.00	18.00
20 Gordie Howe	200.00	350.00
21 Val Fonteyne RC	9.00	15.00
22 Murray Oliver RC	12.00	20.00
23 Sid Abel CO	12.00	20.00
24 Jack McIntyre	9.00	15.00
25 Marc Reaume	9.00	15.00
26 Norm Ullman	30.00	50.00
27 Brian Smith RC	9.00	15.00
28 Gerry Melnyk UER RC	9.00	15.00
29 Marcel Pronovost	10.00	18.00
30 Warren Godfrey	9.00	15.00
31 Terry Sawchuk	75.00	150.00
32 Barry Cullen	9.00	15.00
33 Gary Aldcorn	9.00	15.00
34 Pete Goegan	9.00	15.00
35 Len Lunde	9.00	15.00
36 Alex Delvecchio	18.00	30.00
37 John McKenzie RC	15.00	25.00
38 Dickie Moore	15.00	25.00
39 Albert Langlois	9.00	15.00
40 Bill Hicke	9.00	15.00
41 Ralph Backstrom	9.00	15.00
42 Don Marshall	9.00	15.00
43 Bob Turner	9.00	15.00
44 Tom Johnson	10.00	18.00
45 Maurice Richard	100.00	200.00
46 Bernie Geoffrion	30.00	50.00
47 Henri Richard	65.00	100.00
48 Doug Harvey	30.00	50.00
49 Jean Beliveau	60.00	100.00
50 Phil Goyette	9.00	15.00
51 Marcel Bonin	9.00	15.00
52 Jean-Guy Talbot	10.00	18.00
53 Jacques Plante	125.00	200.00
54 Claude Provost	9.00	15.00
55 Andre Pronovost	9.00	15.00
56 Bill Hicke	12.00	20.00
Ab McDonald		
Ralph Backstrom		
57 Don Marshall	30.00	50.00
Dickie Moore		
Henri Richard		
58 Claude Provost	12.00	20.00
Jean Pronovost		
Phil Goyette		
59 Boom Boom Geoffrion	50.00	80.00
Don Marshall		
Jean Beliveau		
60 Ab McDonald	9.00	15.00
61 Jim Morrison	60.00	100.00

1961-62 Parkhurst

The 1961-62 Parkhurst set contains 51 cards in full color, numbered on the fronts. Cards are 2 7/16" by 3 5/8". The backs contain 1960-61 statistics and a cartoon; the punch line for which could be seen by rubbing the card with a coin. The cards contain players from Montreal, Toronto, and Detroit. The numbering of the players in the set is basically by teams, i.e., Toronto Maple Leafs (1-18), Detroit Red Wings (19-34), and Montreal Canadiens (35-51). The backs are in both French and English. The key Rookie Card in this set is Dave Keon.

COMPLETE SET (51)	1000.00	1600.00
1 Tim Horton	100.00	200.00
2 Frank Mahovlich	50.00	80.00
3 Johnny Bower	35.00	60.00
4 Bert Olmstead	10.00	18.00
5 Dave Keon RC	150.00	250.00
6 Ron Stewart	10.00	18.00
7 Eddie Shack	60.00	100.00
8 Bob Pulford	10.00	18.00
9 Red Kelly	15.00	25.00
10 Bob Nevin	10.00	18.00
11 Bob Baun	10.00	18.00
12 Dick Duff	10.00	18.00
13 Larry Keenan RC	9.00	15.00
14 Larry Hillman	10.00	18.00
15 Billy Harris	9.00	15.00
16 Allan Stanley	12.00	20.00
17 George Armstrong	12.00	20.00
18 Carl Brewer	10.00	18.00
19 Howie Glover RC	9.00	15.00
20 Gordie Howe	150.00	250.00
21 Val Fonteyne	9.00	15.00
22 Al Johnson RC	9.00	15.00
23 Pete Goegan	9.00	15.00
24 Len Lunde	9.00	15.00
25 Alex Delvecchio	15.00	25.00
26 Norm Ullman	25.00	40.00
27 Bill Gadsby	9.00	15.00
28 Ed Litzenberger	9.00	15.00
29 Marcel Pronovost	10.00	18.00
30 Warren Godfrey	9.00	15.00
31 Terry Sawchuk	75.00	125.00
32 Vic Stasiuk	9.00	15.00
33 Leo Labine	9.00	15.00
34 John McKenzie	12.00	20.00
35 Bernie Geoffrion	30.00	50.00
36 Dickie Moore	12.00	20.00
37 Albert Langlois	9.00	15.00
38 Bill Hicke	9.00	15.00
39 Ralph Backstrom	10.00	18.00
40 Don Marshall	10.00	18.00
41 Bob Turner	9.00	15.00
42 Tom Johnson	10.00	18.00
43 Henri Richard	50.00	80.00
44 Wayne Connelly RC	12.00	20.00
45 Jean Beliveau	50.00	80.00
46 Phil Goyette	9.00	15.00
47 Marcel Bonin	9.00	15.00
48 Jean-Guy Talbot	10.00	18.00
49 Jacques Plante	100.00	175.00
50 Claude Provost	10.00	18.00
51 Andre Pronovost UER	25.00	40.00
(Shown as Montreal&		
should be Boston)		

1962-63 Parkhurst

The 1962-63 Parkhurst set contains 55 cards in full color, with the card number and, on some cards, a facsimile autograph on the front. There is also one unnumbered checklist which is part of the complete set price. An unnumbered game or tally card, which is also referred to as the "Zip" card, is not part of the set. Both of these are considered rather difficult to obtain. Cards are approximately 2 7/16" by 3 5/8". The backs, in both French and English, contain player lifetime statistics and player vital statistics in paragraph form. There are several different styles or designs within this set depending on card number, e.g., some cards have a giant puck as background for their photo on the front. Other cards have the player's team logo as background. The numbering of the players in the set is basically by teams, i.e., Toronto Maple Leafs (1-18), Detroit Red Wings (19-36), and Montreal Canadiens (37-54). The notable Rookie Cards in this set are Bobby Rousseau, Gilles Tremblay, and J.C.Tremblay.

COMPLETE SET (55)	1200.00	2000.00
1 Billy Harris	25.00	40.00
2 Dick Duff	9.00	15.00
3 Bob Baun	9.00	15.00
4 Frank Mahovlich	50.00	80.00
5 Red Kelly	18.00	30.00
6 Ron Stewart	7.00	12.00
7 Tim Horton	60.00	100.00
8 Carl Brewer	9.00	15.00
9 Allan Stanley	10.00	20.00
10 Bob Nevin	9.00	15.00
11 Bob Pulford	9.00	15.00
12 Ed Litzenberger	7.00	12.00
13 George Armstrong	10.00	20.00
14 Eddie Shack	35.00	60.00
15 Dave Keon	60.00	100.00
16 Johnny Bower	30.00	50.00
17 Larry Hillman	9.00	15.00
18 Frank Mahovlich	40.00	70.00
19 Hank Bassen	9.00	15.00
20 Gerry Odrowski RC	7.00	12.00
21 Norm Ullman	18.00	30.00
22 Vic Stasiuk	7.00	12.00
23 Bruce MacGregor RC	7.00	12.00
24 Claude Laforge	7.00	12.00
25 Bill Gadsby	7.00	12.00
26 Leo Labine	7.00	12.00
27 Val Fonteyne	7.00	12.00
28 Howie Glover	7.00	12.00
29 Marc Boileau RC	7.00	12.00
30 Gordie Howe	150.00	250.00
31 Gordie Howe	150.00	250.00
32 Alex Delvecchio	15.00	25.00
33 Marcel Pronovost	9.00	15.00
34 Sid Abel CO	9.00	15.00
35 Len Lunde	7.00	12.00
36 Warren Godfrey	7.00	12.00
37 Phil Goyette	7.00	12.00
38 Henri Richard	50.00	80.00
39 Jean Beliveau	50.00	80.00
40 Bill Hicke	7.00	12.00
41 Claude Provost	7.00	12.00
42 Dickie Moore	10.00	20.00
43 Don Marshall	9.00	15.00
44 Ralph Backstrom	9.00	15.00
45 Marcel Bonin	7.00	12.00
46 Gilles Tremblay RC	20.00	40.00
47 Bobby Rousseau RC	15.00	25.00
48 Bernie Geoffrion	25.00	40.00
49 Jacques Plante	75.00	125.00
50 Tom Johnson	9.00	15.00
51 Jean-Guy Talbot	9.00	15.00
52 Lou Fontinato	9.00	15.00
53 Bernie Geoffrion	25.00	40.00
54 J.C. Tremblay RC !	40.00	60.00
NNO1 Tally Game Card	125.00	250.00
NNO2 Checklist Card	250.00	400.00

1963-64 Parkhurst

The 1963-64 Parkhurst set contains 99 color cards. Cards measure approximately 2 7/16" by 3 5/8". The fronts of the cards feature the player with a varying background depending upon whether the player is on Detroit (American flag), Toronto (Canadian Red Ensign), or Montreal (multi-color striped background). The numbering of the players in the set is basically by teams, i.e., Toronto Maple Leafs (1-20 and 61-79), Detroit Red Wings (41-60), and Montreal Canadiens (21-40 and 80-99). The backs, in both French and English, contain the card number, player lifetime NHL statistics, player biography, and a Stanley Cup replica offer. The set includes two different cards of each Montreal and Toronto player and only one of each Detroit player (with the following exceptions, numbers 15, 20, and 75 (single card Maple Leafs). Each Toronto player's double is obtained by adding 60, e.g., 1 and 61, 2 and 62, 3 and 63, etc., are the same player. Each Montreal player's double is obtained by adding 59, e.g., 21 and 80, 22 and 81, 23 and 82, etc., are the same player. The key Rookie Cards in the set are Red Berenson, Alex Faulkner, John Ferguson, Jacques Laperriere, and Cesare Maniago. Maniago is the last card in the set and is not often found in top condition.

COMPLETE SET (99)	1500.00	2500.00
1 Allan Stanley	25.00	40.00
2 Don Simmons	9.00	15.00
3 Red Kelly	12.00	25.00
4 Dick Duff	9.00	15.00
5 Johnny Bower	30.00	50.00
6 Ed Litzenberger	7.00	12.00
7 Kent Douglas RC	7.00	12.00
8 Carl Brewer	9.00	15.00
9 Eddie Shack	40.00	80.00
10 Bob Nevin	9.00	15.00
11 Billy Harris	7.00	12.00
12 Bob Pulford	9.00	15.00
13 George Armstrong	10.00	20.00
14 Ron Stewart	7.00	12.00
15 John McMillan RC	7.00	12.00
16 Tim Horton	50.00	100.00
17 Frank Mahovlich	40.00	70.00
18 Bob Baun	9.00	15.00
19 Punch Imlach ACO/GM	12.00	25.00
20 King Clancy ACO	18.00	30.00
21 Gilles Tremblay	9.00	15.00
22 Jean-Guy Talbot	9.00	15.00
23 Henri Richard	40.00	70.00
24 Ralph Backstrom	9.00	15.00
25 Bill Hicke	7.00	12.00
26 Red Berenson RC	25.00	40.00
27 Jacques Laperriere RC	30.00	50.00
28 Jean Gauthier RC	7.00	12.00
29 Bernie Geoffrion	25.00	40.00
30 Jean Beliveau	45.00	75.00
31 J.C. Tremblay	9.00	15.00
32 Terry Harper RC	18.00	30.00
33 John Ferguson RC	50.00	80.00
34 Toe Blake CO	12.00	25.00
35 Bobby Rousseau	9.00	15.00
36 Claude Provost	7.00	12.00
37 Marc Reaume	7.00	12.00
38 Dave Balon	7.00	12.00
39 Gump Worsley	25.00	40.00
40 Cesare Maniago RC	25.00	50.00
41 Bruce MacGregor	7.00	12.00
42 Alex Faulkner RC	60.00	125.00
43 Pete Goegan	7.00	12.00
44 Parker MacDonald	7.00	12.00
45 Andre Pronovost	7.00	12.00
46 Marcel Pronovost	9.00	15.00
47 Bob Dillabough RC	7.00	12.00
48 Larry Jeffrey RC	7.00	12.00
49 Ian Cushenan	7.00	12.00
50 Alex Delvecchio	12.00	25.00
51 Hank Ciesla	7.00	12.00
52 Norm Ullman	18.00	30.00
53 Terry Sawchuk	70.00	110.00
54 Ron Ingram RC	7.00	12.00
55 Gordie Howe	300.00	450.00
56 Billy McNeil	7.00	12.00
57 Floyd Smith RC	7.00	12.00
58 Vic Stasiuk	7.00	12.00
59 Bill Gadsby	7.00	12.00
60 Doug Barkley RC	7.00	12.00
61 Allan Stanley	10.00	20.00
62 Don Simmons	9.00	15.00
63 Red Kelly	12.00	25.00
64 Dick Duff	9.00	15.00
65 Johnny Bower	30.00	50.00
66 Ed Litzenberger	7.00	12.00
67 Kent Douglas	7.00	12.00
68 Carl Brewer	9.00	15.00
69 Eddie Shack	30.00	50.00
70 Bob Nevin	9.00	15.00
71 Billy Harris	7.00	12.00
72 Bob Pulford	9.00	15.00
73 George Armstrong	10.00	20.00
74 Ron Stewart	7.00	12.00
75 Dave Keon	50.00	80.00
76 Tim Horton	50.00	80.00
77 Frank Mahovlich	40.00	70.00
78 Bob Baun	9.00	15.00
79 Punch Imlach ACO/GM	12.00	25.00
80 Gilles Tremblay	9.00	15.00
81 Jean-Guy Talbot	7.00	12.00
82 Henri Richard	40.00	70.00
83 Ralph Backstrom	9.00	15.00
84 Bill Hicke	7.00	12.00
85 Red Berenson RC	25.00	40.00
86 Jacques Laperriere RC	25.00	40.00
87 Jean Gauthier RC	7.00	12.00
88 Bernie Geoffrion	25.00	40.00
89 Jean Beliveau	50.00	80.00
90 J.C. Tremblay	9.00	15.00
91 Terry Harper RC	20.00	30.00
92 John Ferguson RC	50.00	80.00
93 Toe Blake CO	12.00	25.00
94 Bobby Rousseau	9.00	15.00
95 Claude Provost	7.00	12.00
96 Marc Reaume	7.00	12.00
97 Dave Balon	7.00	12.00
98 Gump Worsley	25.00	40.00
99 Cesare Maniago RC	100.00	175.00

1991-92 Parkhurst

The 1991-92 Parkhurst hockey set marks Pro Set's resurrection of this venerable hockey card brand. The set was primarily released in two series. Both series contain 225 standard-size cards and five (four in the second series) special PHC collectible cards randomly inserted into foil packs. First and second series production quantities were each reported to be 15,000 numbered ten-box foil cases, including 2,500 cases that were translated into French and distributed predominantly to Quebec. The fronts feature full-bleed glossy color photos, bordered on the left by a dark brown marbled border stripe. The player's name appears in the stripe; Parkhurst's teal oval-shaped logo in the lower left corner rounds out the card face. The backs carry a color head shot, with biography, career statistics, and player profile all on a bronze background. The NNO Santa Claus card was randomly inserted in first series packs. A special promotion offer for a 25-card Final Update set was included on Parkhurst Series II packs. It is estimated that less than 15,000 of these sets exist.

COMPLETE SET (450)	10.00	20.00
COMP.SERIES 1 (225)	5.00	10.00
COMP.SERIES 2 (225)	5.00	10.00
COMP.FINAL UPDATE (25)	30.00	60.00
1 Matt DelGuidice RC	.05	.15
2 Ken Hodge Jr.	.01	.05
3 Vladimir Ruzicka UER	.01	.05
(Misspelled Vladimar		
Ruzika on card front)		
4 Craig Janney	.05	.15
5 Glen Wesley	.01	.05
6 Stephen Leach	.01	.05
7 Garry Galley	.01	.05
8 Andy Moog	.08	.25
9 Ray Bourque	.15	.40
10 Brad May	.01	.05
11 Donald Audette	.01	.05
12 Alexander Mogilny	.08	.25
13 Randy Wood	.01	.05
14 Daren Puppa	.05	.15
15 Doug Bodger	.01	.05
16 Pat LaFontaine	.08	.25
17 Dave Andreychuk	.05	.15
18 Dale Hawerchuk	.05	.15
19 Mike Ramsey	.01	.05
20 Tomas Forslund RC UER	.01	.05
(Misspelled Thomas		
on card back)		
21 Robert Reichel	.01	.05
22 Theo Fleury	.01	.05
23 Joe Nieuwendyk	.05	.15
24 Gary Roberts	.05	.15
25 Gary Suter	.01	.05
26 Doug Gilmour	.05	.15
27 Mike Vernon	.05	.15
28 Al MacInnis	.05	.15
29 Jeremy Roenick	.08	.25
30 Ed Belfour	.08	.25
31 Steve Smith	.01	.05
32 Chris Chelios	.08	.25
33 Dirk Graham	.01	.05
34 Steve Larmer	.05	.15
35 Brent Sutter	.01	.05
36 Michel Goulet	.05	.15
37 Nicklas Lidstrom RC	.60	1.50
38 Sergei Fedorov	.15	.40
39 Tim Cheveldae	.05	.15
40 Kevin Miller	.01	.05
41 Ray Sheppard	.01	.05
42 Paul Ysebaert	.01	.05
43 Jimmy Carson	.01	.05
44 Steve Yzerman	.50	1.25
45 Shawn Burr	.01	.05
46 Vladimir Konstantinov RC	.30	.75
47 Josef Beranek RC	.01	.05
48 Vincent Damphousse	.01	.05
49 Dave Manson	.01	.05
50 Scott Mellanby	.01	.05
51 Kevin Lowe	.05	.15
52 Joe Murphy	.01	.05
53 Bill Ranford	.05	.15
54 Craig Simpson	.01	.05
55 Esa Tikkanen	.01	.05
56 Michel Picard RC	.01	.05
57 Geoff Sanderson RC	.08	.25
58 Kay Whitmore	.05	.15
59 John Cullen	.01	.05
60 Rob Brown	.01	.05
61 Zarley Zalapski	.01	.05
62 Brad Shaw	.01	.05
63 Mikael Andersson	.01	.05
64 Pat Verbeek	.01	.05
65 Peter Ahola RC	.01	.05
66 Tony Granato	.01	.05
67 Dave Taylor	.05	.15
68 Luc Robitaille	.05	.15
69 Marty McSorley	.01	.05
70 Tomas Sandstrom	.01	.05
71 Kelly Hrudey	.05	.15
72 Jari Kurri	.08	.25
73 Wayne Gretzky	.60	1.50
74 Larry Robinson	.05	.15
75 Derian Hatcher	.05	.15
76 Ulf Dahlen	.01	.05
77 Jon Casey	.05	.15
78 Dave Gagner	.01	.05
79 Brian Bellows	.01	.05
80 Neal Broten	.05	.15
81 Mike Modano	.20	.50
82 Brian Propp	.01	.05
83 Bobby Smith	.05	.15
84 John LeClair RC	.60	1.50
85 Eric Desjardins	.05	.15
86 Shayne Corson	.01	.05
87 Stephan Lebeau	.01	.05
88 Mathieu Schneider	.01	.05
89 Kirk Muller	.01	.05
90 Patrick Roy	.50	1.25
91 Sylvain Turgeon	.01	.05
92 Guy Carbonneau	.05	.15
93 Denis Savard	.05	.15
94 Scott Niedermayer	.01	.05
95 Tom Chorske	.01	.05
96 Slava Fetisov	.01	.05
97 Kevin Todd RC	.01	.05
98 Chris Terreri	.05	.15
99 David Maley	.01	.05
100 Stephane Richer	.05	.15
101 Claude Lemieux	.01	.05
102 Scott Stevens	.05	.15
103 Peter Stastny	.05	.15
104 David Volek	.01	.05
105 Steve Thomas	.01	.05
106 Pierre Turgeon	.05	.15
107 Glenn Healy	.05	.15
108 Derek King	.01	.05
109 Uwe Krupp	.01	.05
110 Ray Ferraro	.01	.05
111 Pat Flatley	.01	.05
112 Tom Kurvers	.01	.05
113 Adam Creighton	.01	.05
114 Tony Amonte RC	.60	1.50
115 John Ogrodnick	.01	.05
116 Doug Weight RC	.50	1.25
117 Mike Richter	.08	.25
118 Darren Turcotte	.01	.05
119 Brian Leetch	.08	.25
120 James Patrick	.01	.05
121 Mark Messier	.08	.25
122 Mike Gartner	.05	.15
123 Mike Ricci	.08	.25
124 Rod Brind'Amour	.08	.25
125 Steve Duchesne	.01	.05
126 Ron Hextall	.05	.15
127 Brad Jones	.01	.05
128 Pelle Eklund	.01	.05
129 Rick Tocchet	.05	.15
130 Mark Howe	.01	.05
131 Andrei Lomakin	.01	.05
132 Jaromir Jagr	.15	.40
133 Jim Paek RC	.01	.05
134 Mark Recchi	.08	.25
135 Kevin Stevens	.01	.05
136 Phil Bourque	.01	.05
137 Mario Lemieux	.60	1.50
138 Bob Errey	.01	.05
139 Tom Barrasso	.05	.15
140 Paul Coffey	.08	.25
141 Joe Mullen	.05	.15
142 Kip Miller	.01	.05
143 Owen Nolan	.08	.25
144 Mats Sundin	.08	.25
145 Mikhail Tatarinov	.01	.05
146 Bryan Fogarty	.01	.05
147 Stephane Morin	.01	.05
148 Joe Sakic	.20	.50
149 Ron Tugnutt	.05	.15
150 Mike Hough	.01	.05
151 Nelson Emerson	.01	.05
152 Curtis Joseph	.08	.25
153 Brendan Shanahan	.08	.25
154 Paul Cavallini	.01	.05
155 Adam Oates	.05	.15
156 Jeff Brown	.01	.05
157 Brett Hull	.10	.30
158 Ron Sutter	.01	.05
159 Dave Christian	.01	.05
160 Pat Falloon	.01	.05
161 Pat MacLeod RC	.01	.05
162 Jarmo Myllys	.01	.05
163 Wayne Presley	.01	.05
164 Perry Anderson	.01	.05
165 Kelly Kisio	.01	.05
166 Brian Mullen	.01	.05
167 Brian Lawton	.01	.05
168 Doug Wilson	.05	.15
169 Rob Pearson RC	.01	.05
170 Wendel Clark	.05	.15
171 Brian Bradley	.01	.05
172 Dave Ellett	.01	.05
173 Gary Leeman	.01	.05
174 Peter Zezel	.01	.05
175 Grant Fuhr	.08	.25
176 Bob Rouse	.01	.05
177 Glenn Anderson	.05	.15
178 Petr Nedved	.05	.15
179 Trevor Linden	.05	.15
180 Jyrki Lumme	.01	.05
181 Kirk McLean	.05	.15
182 Cliff Ronning	.01	.05
183 Greg Adams	.01	.05
184 Doug Lidster	.01	.05
185 Sergio Momesso	.01	.05
186 Geoff Courtnall	.05	.15
187 Dave Babych	.01	.05
188 Peter Bondra	.05	.15
189 Dimitri Khristich	.01	.05
190 Randy Burridge	.01	.05
191 Kevin Hatcher	.05	.15
192 Mike Ridley	.01	.05
193 Dino Ciccarelli	.05	.15
194 Al Iafrate	.05	.15
195 Dale Hunter	.01	.05
196 Mike Liut	.05	.15
197 Rod Langway	.01	.05
198 Russell Romaniuk RC	.01	.05
199 Bob Essensa	.05	.15
200 Teppo Numminen	.01	.05
201 Darrin Shannon	.01	.05
202 Pat Elynuik	.01	.05
203 Fredrik Olausson	.01	.05
204 Ed Olczyk	.01	.05
205 Phil Housley	.05	.15
206 Troy Murray	.01	.05
207 Wayne Gretzky 1000	.40	1.00
208 Bryan Trottier 1000	.05	.15
209 Peter Stastny 1000	.05	.15
210 Jari Kurri 1000	.05	.15
211 Denis Savard 1000	.01	.05
212 Paul Coffey 1000	.05	.15
213 Mark Messier 1000	.08	.25
214 Dave Taylor 1000	.01	.05
215 Michel Goulet 1000	.01	.05
216 Dale Hawerchuk 1000	.01	.05
217 Bobby Smith 1000	.05	.15
218 Ed Belfour LL	.08	.25
219 Brett Hull LL	.08	.25
220 Patrick Roy AS	.30	.75
221 Ray Bourque AS	.08	.25
222 Wayne Gretzky AS	.30	.75
223 Jari Kurri AS	.05	.15
224 Luc Robitaille AS	.05	.15
225 Paul Coffey AS	.05	.15
226 Bob Carpenter	.01	.05
227 Gord Murphy	.01	.05
228 Don Sweeney	.01	.05
229 Glen Murray RC	.20	.50
230 Ted Donato RC	.01	.05
231 Jozef Stumpel RC	.20	.50
232 Stephen Heinze RC	.01	.05
233 Adam Oates	.05	.15
234 Joe Juneau RC	.30	.75
235 Gord Hynes RC	.01	.05
236 Tony Tanti	.01	.05
237 Petr Svoboda	.01	.05
238 Bob Corkum	.01	.05
239 Ken Sutton RC	.01	.05
240 Tom Draper RC	.05	.15
241 Grant Ledyard	.01	.05
242 Christian Ruuttu	.01	.05
243 Brad Miller	.01	.05
244 Clint Malarchuk	.05	.15
245 Trent Yawney	.01	.05
246 Craig Berube	.01	.05
247 Sergei Makarov	.01	.05
248 Alexander Godynyuk RC	.01	.05
249 Paul Ranheim	.01	.05
250 Jeff Reese	.01	.05
251 Chris Lindberg RC	.01	.05
252 Michel Petit	.01	.05
253 Joel Otto	.01	.05
254 Gary Leeman	.01	.05
255 Ray Leblanc RC	.05	.15
256 Jocelyn Lemieux	.01	.05
257 Igor Kravchuk RC	.01	.05
258 Rob Brown	.01	.05
259 Stephane Matteau	.01	.05
260 Mike Hudson	.01	.05
261 Keith Brown	.01	.05
262 Karl Dykhuis	.01	.05
263 Dominik Hasek RC	2.00	5.00
264 Brian Noonan	.01	.05
265 Yves Racine	.01	.05
266 Slava Kozlov RC	.20	.50
267 Martin Lapointe	.05	.15
268 Steve Chiasson	.01	.05
269 Gerard Gallant	.01	.05
270 Brent Fedyk	.01	.05
271 Brad McCrimmon	.01	.05
272 Bob Probert	.05	.15
273 Alan Kerr	.01	.05
274 Luke Richardson	.01	.05
275 Kelly Buchberger	.01	.05
276 Craig MacTavish	.01	.05
277 Ron Tugnutt	.05	.15
278 Bernie Nicholls	.05	.15
279 Anatoli Semenov	.01	.05
280 Petr Klima	.01	.05
281 Louie DeBrusk RC	.01	.05
282 Norm Maciver RC	.01	.05
283 Martin Gelinas	.01	.05
284 Randy Cunneyworth	.01	.05
285 Andrew Cassels	.01	.05
286 Peter Sidorkiewicz	.05	.15
287 Steve Konroyd	.01	.05
288 Murray Craven	.01	.05
289 Randy Ladouceur	.01	.05
290 Bobby Holik	.05	.15
291 Adam Burt	.01	.05
292 Corey Millen RC	.01	.05
293 Rob Blake	.05	.15
294 Mike Donnelly RC	.01	.05
295 Kyosti Karjalainen RC	.05	.15
296 John McIntyre	.01	.05
297 Paul Coffey	.08	.25
298 Charlie Huddy	.01	.05
299 Bob Kudelski	.01	.05
300 Todd Elik	.01	.05
301 Mike Craig	.01	.05
302 Marc Bureau	.01	.05
303 Jim Johnson	.01	.05
304 Mark Tinordi	.01	.05
305 Gaetan Duchesne	.01	.05
306 Darcy Wakaluk RC	.05	.15
307 Sylvain Lefebvre	.01	.05
308 Russ Courtnall	.01	.05
309 Patrice Brisebois	.01	.05
310 Mike McPhee	.01	.05
311 Mike Keane	.01	.05
312 J.J. Daigneault	.01	.05
313 Gilbert Dionne RC	.05	.15
314 Brian Skrudland	.01	.05
315 Brent Gilchrist	.01	.05
316 Laurie Boschman	.01	.05
317 Ken Daneyko	.01	.05
318 Eric Weinrich	.01	.05
319 Alexei Kasatonov	.01	.05
320 Craig Billington RC	.05	.15
321 Claude Vilgrain	.01	.05
322 Bruce Driver	.01	.05
323 Alexander Semak RC	.01	.05
324 Valeri Zelepukin RC	.01	.05
325 Rob DiMaio	.01	.05
326 Scott Lachance RC	.05	.15
327 Marty McInnis RC	.01	.05
328 Joe Reekie	.01	.05
329 Daniel Marois	.01	.05
330 Wayne McBean	.01	.05
331 Jeff Norton	.01	.05
332 Benoit Hogue	.01	.05
333 Tie Domi	.08	.25
334 Sergei Nemchinov	.01	.05
335 Randy Gilhen	.01	.05
336 Paul Broten	.01	.05
337 Kris King	.01	.05
338 John Vanbiesbrouck	.05	.15
339 Adam Graves	.05	.15
340 Joe Cirella	.01	.05
341 Jeff Beukeboom	.01	.05
342 Terry Carkner	.01	.05
343 Mark Freer RC	.01	.05
344 Corey Foster RC	.01	.05
345 Mark Pederson	.01	.05
346 Kimbi Daniels RC	.01	.05
347 Mark Recchi	.08	.25
348 Kevin Dineen	.01	.05
349 Kerry Huffman	.01	.05
350 Garry Galley	.01	.05
351 Dan Quinn	.01	.05
352 Troy Loney	.01	.05
353 Ron Francis	.05	.15
354 Rick Tocchet	.05	.15
355 Shawn McEachern RC	.20	.50
356 Kjell Samuelsson	.01	.05
357 Ken Wreggett	.05	.15
358 Larry Murphy	.05	.15
359 Ken Priestlay	.01	.05
360 Bryan Trottier	.08	.25
361 Ulf Samuelsson	.01	.05
362 Valeri Kamensky RC	.05	.15
363 Stephane Fiset	.05	.15
364 Alexei Gusarov RC	.05	.15
365 Greg Paslawski	.01	.05
366 Martin Rucinsky RC	.08	.25
367 Curtis Leschyshyn	.01	.05
368 Jacques Cloutier	.05	.15
369 Craig Wolanin	.01	.05
370 Claude Lapointe RC	.01	.05
371 Adam Foote RC	.15	.40
372 Rich Sutter	.01	.05
373 Lee Norwood	.01	.05
374 Garth Butcher	.01	.05
375 Philippe Bozon RC	.01	.05
376 Dave Lowry	.01	.05
377 Darin Kimble	.01	.05
378 Craig Janney	.05	.15
379 Bob Bassen	.01	.05
380 Rick Zombo	.01	.05
381 Perry Berezan	.01	.05
382 Neil Wilkinson	.01	.05
383 Mike Sullivan RC	.01	.05
384 David Bruce RC	.01	.05
385 Johan Garpenlov	.01	.05
386 Jeff Odgers RC	.01	.05
387 Jay More RC	.01	.05
388 Dean Evason	.01	.05
389 Dale Craigwell	.01	.05
390 Darryl Shannon RC	.01	.05
391 Dimitri Mironov	.05	.15
392 Kent Manderville	.01	.05

393 Todd Gill .01 .05
394 Rick Wamsley .05 .15
395 Joe Sacco RC .01 .05
396 Doug Gilmour .05 .15
397 Mike Bullard .01 .05
398 Felix Potvin .40 1.00
399 Guy Larose RC .01 .05
400 Tom Fergus .01 .05
401 Ryan Walter .01 .05
402 Troy Gamble .05 .15
403 Robert Dirk .01 .05
404 Pavel Bure .08 .25
405 Jim Sandlak .01 .05
406 Igor Larionov .01 .05
407 Gerald Diduck .01 .05
408 Todd Krygier .01 .05
409 Tim Bergland .01 .05
410 Calle Johansson .01 .05
411 Nick Kypreos .01 .05
412 Michal Pivonka .01 .05
413 Brad Schlegel RC .01 .05
414 Kelly Miller .01 .05
415 John Druce .01 .05
416 Don Beaupre .05 .15
417 Alan May .01 .05
418 Randy Carlyle .01 .05
419 Stu Barnes .01 .05
420 Mike Eagles .01 .05
421 Igor Ulanov RC .05 .15
422 Evgeny Davydov RC .01 .05
423 Shawn Cronin .01 .05
424 Keith Tkachuk RC 1.00 2.50
425 Luciano Borsato RC .01 .05
426 Stephane Beauregard .05 .15
427 Mike Lalor .01 .05
428 Michel Goulet 500 .01 .05
429 Wayne Gretzky 500 .40 1.00
430 Mike Gartner 500 .01 .05
431 Bryan Trottier 500 .05 .15
432 Brett Hull LL .08 .25
433 Wayne Gretzky LL .30 .75
434 Steve Yzerman LL .25 .60
435 Paul Ysebaert LL .01 .05
436 Gary Roberts LL .01 .05
437 Dave Andreychuk LL .01 .05
438 Brian Leetch LL .05 .15
439 Jeremy Roenick LL .08 .25
440 Kirk McLean LL .01 .05
441 Tim Cheveldae LL .01 .05
442 Patrick Roy LL .30 .75
443 Tony Amonte RL .30 .75
444 Kevin Todd RL .01 .05
445 Nicklas Lidstrom RL .30 .75
446 Pavel Bure RL .08 .25
447 Gilbert Dionne RL .01 .05
448 Tom Draper RL .05 .15
449 Dominik Hasek RL .40 1.00
450 Dominic Roussel RL RC .05 .15
451 Header/Checklist .30 .75
452 Trent Klatt XRC .30 .75
453 Bill Guerin XRC 1.50 4.00
454 Ray Whitney XRC 1.00 2.50
455 Boston Bruins .30 .75
Adams Winner
456 Pittsburgh Penguins .30 .75
Patrick Winner
(Larry Murphy et al.)
457 Chicago Blackhawks .30 .75
Norris Winner
(Pile up in front of net)
458 Edmonton Oilers .30 .75
Smythe Winner
(Oiler celebrate win;
Joe Murphy/Petr Klima et al.)
459 Pittsburgh Penguins 1.25 3.00
Wales Winner
(Andy Moog with glove save;
Mario Lemieux in background)
460 Chicago Blackhawks .30 .75
Campbell Winner
(Brent Sutter and Craig Muni
in front of Bill Ranford)
461 Pittsburgh Penguins .30 .75
Stanley Cup Winner
(Igor Kravchuk checking Bryan Trottier)
462 Pavel Bure .08 .25
Calder Winner
463 Patrick Roy 5.00 12.00
Vezina Winner
464 Brian Leetch 1.25 3.00
Norris Winner
465 Wayne Gretzky 6.00 15.00
Lady Byng Winner
466 Guy Carbonneau 1.25 3.00
Selke Winner
467 Mario Lemieux AW 5.00 12.00
468 Mark Messier 2.50 6.00
Pearson Winner
469 Ray Bourque 2.50 6.00
Clancy Winner
470 Patrick Roy AS 5.00 12.00
471 Brian Leetch AS 1.00 2.50
472 Ray Bourque AS 2.50 6.00
473 Kevin Stevens AS 1.00 2.50
474 Brett Hull AS 2.00 5.00
475 Mark Messier AS .08 .25
NNO Santa Claus .40 1.00
NNO Robert Reichel PROMO .40 1.00
NNO Doug Gilmour PROMO 1.00 2.50

1991-92 Parkhurst French

COMPLETE SET (450) 15.00 35.00
COMP.SERIES 1 (225) 7.00 15.00
COMP.SERIES 2 (225) 8.00 20.00
COMP.FINAL UPDATE (25) 30.00 60.00
*FRENCH: .4X TO 1X PARKHURST

1991-92 Parkhurst PHC

This nine card standard-size set was randomly inserted in packs of 1991-92 Parkhurst hockey cards with cards 1-5 being in the first series and 6-9 in the second series, which featured award winners. PHC stands for Parkhurst Collectibles. The cards are numbered with a "PHC" prefix. A French version of these cards exist and are valued the same.

COMPLETE SET (9) 7.50 15.00
PHC1 Gordie Howe 1.25 3.00
PHC2 Alex Delvecchio .40 1.00
PHC3 Ken Hodge Jr. .40 1.00
PHC4 Robert Kron .40 1.00
PHC5 Sergei Fedorov 1.00 2.50
PHC6 Brett Hull .75 2.00
PHC7 Mario Lemieux 2.50 6.00
PHC8 New York Rangers .60 1.50
(Brian Leetch/Mark Messier/
Mike Gartner/John Ziegler)
PHC9 Terry Sawchuk .60 1.50

1992-93 Parkhurst Previews

Randomly inserted in 1992-93 Pro Set foil packs, these five preview standard-size cards were issued to show the design of the 1992-93 Parkhurst issue. The fronts feature color action player photos that are full-bleed except for one edge that is bordered by a dark blue-green marbleized stripe. The player's name is printed vertically in this stripe. The Parkhurst logo overlays the stripe. The backs have a bluish-green background and carry small close-up shots, biography, statistics, and career highlights in French and English. The cards are numbered on the back with a "PV" prefix.

PV1 Paul Ysebaert .60 1.50
PV2 Sean Burke .75 2.00
PV3 Gilbert Dionne .60 1.50
PV4 Ken Hammond .60 1.50
PV5 Grant Fuhr .75 2.00

1992-93 Parkhurst

The 1992-93 Parkhurst set consists of 480 standard-size cards plus a 30-card update set. The set was released in two series of 240. The final 30 cards were issued in set form only and are slightly more difficult to obtain. The fronts feature color action player photos that are full-bleed except for one edge that is bordered by a dark blue-green marbleized stripe. The Parkhurst logo overlays the stripe. The backs have a bluish green background and carry small close-up shots, biographies, statistics, and career highlights in French and English. The second series featured traded players in their new uniforms as well as 35 Calder Candidates. The cards are checklisted alphabetically according to teams.

COMPLETE SET (480) 12.00 30.00
COMP.SERIES 1 (240) 8.00 20.00
COMP.SERIES 2 (240) 5.00 12.00
COMP.FINAL UPDATE (30) 5.00 10.00
1 Ray Bourque .20 .50
2 Joe Juneau .02 .10
3 Andy Moog .08 .25
4 Adam Oates .02 .10
5 Vladimir Ruzicka .01 .05
6 Glen Wesley .01 .05
7 Dmitri Kvartalnov RC .01 .05
8 Ted Donato .01 .05
9 Glen Murray .01 .05
10 Dave Andreychuk .02 .10
11 Dale Hawerchuk .02 .10
12 Pat LaFontaine .08 .25
13 Alexander Mogilny .02 .10
14 Richard Smehlik RC .01 .05
15 Keith Carney RC .30 .75
16 Philippe Boucher .01 .05
17 Viktor Gordiouk RC .01 .05
18 Donald Audette .01 .05
19 Theo Fleury .02 .10
20 Al MacInnis .02 .10
21 Joe Nieuwendyk .02 .10
22 Gary Roberts .01 .05
23 Gary Suter .01 .05
24 Mike Vernon .02 .10
25 Sergei Makarov .01 .05
26 Robert Reichel .01 .05
27 Chris Lindberg .01 .05
28 Ed Belfour .08 .25
29 Chris Chelios .08 .25
30 Steve Larmer .02 .10
31 Jeremy Roenick .08 .25
32 Steve Smith .01 .05
33 Brent Sutter .01 .05
34 Christian Ruuttu .01 .05
35 Igor Kravchuk .01 .05
36 Sergei Krivokrasov .01 .05
37 Tim Cheveldae .02 .10
38 Mike Sillinger .01 .05
39 Sergei Fedorov .15 .40
40 Viacheslav Kozlov .02 .10
41 Bob Probert .02 .10
42 Nicklas Lidstrom .08 .25
43 Paul Ysebaert .01 .05
44 Steve Yzerman .50 1.25
45 Dino Ciccarelli .02 .10
46 Esa Tikkanen .01 .05
47 Dave Manson .01 .05
48 Craig MacTavish .01 .05
49 Bernie Nicholls .02 .10
50 Bill Ranford .02 .10
51 Craig Simpson .01 .05
52 Scott Mellanby .01 .05
53 Shayne Corson .01 .05
54 Petr Klima .01 .05
55 Murray Craven .01 .05
56 Eric Weinrich .01 .05
57 Sean Burke .02 .10
58 Pat Verbeek .01 .05
59 Zarley Zalapski .01 .05
60 Robert Poulin .01 .05
61 Robert Petrovicky RC UER .01 .05
(Assists total for 1990-91
reads 114)
62 Geoff Sanderson .02 .10
63 Paul Coffey .08 .25
64 Robert Lang RC .01 .05
65 Wayne Gretzky .60 1.50
66 Kelly Hrudey .02 .10
67 Jari Kurri .08 .25
68 Luc Robitaille .02 .10
69 Darryl Sydor .01 .05
70 Jim Hiller RC .01 .05
71 Alexei Zhitnik .01 .05
72 Derian Hatcher .01 .05
73 Jon Casey .02 .10
74 Richard Matvichuk RC .02 .10
75 Mike Modano .20 .50
76 Mark Tinordi .01 .05
77 Todd Elik .01 .05
78 Russ Courtnall .01 .05
79 Tommy Sjodin RC .01 .05
80 Eric Desjardins .02 .10
81 Gilbert Dionne .01 .05
82 Stephan Lebeau .01 .05
83 Kirk Muller .01 .05
84 Patrick Roy .50 1.25
85 Denis Savard .02 .10
86 Vincent Damphousse .01 .05
87 Brian Bellows .01 .05
88 Ed Ronan RC .01 .05
89 Claude Lemieux .01 .05
90 John MacLean .02 .10
91 Stephane Richer .02 .10
92 Scott Stevens .02 .10
93 Chris Terreri .01 .05
94 Kevin Todd .01 .05
95 Scott Niedermayer .01 .05
96 Bobby Holik .02 .10
97 Bill Guerin RC .30 .75
98 Ray Ferraro .01 .05
99 Mark Fitzpatrick .02 .10
100 Derek King .01 .05
101 Uwe Krupp .01 .05
102 Darius Kasparaitis .01 .05
103 Pierre Turgeon .02 .10
104 Benoit Hogue .01 .05
105 Scott Lachance .01 .05
106 Marty McInnis .01 .05
107 Tony Amonte .02 .10
108 Mike Gartner .02 .10
109 Alexei Kovalev .02 .10
110 Brian Leetch .08 .25
111 Mark Messier .08 .25
112 Mike Richter .08 .25
113 James Patrick .01 .05
114 Sergei Nemchinov .01 .05
115 Doug Weight .08 .25
116 Mark Lamb .01 .05
117 Norm Maciver .01 .05
118 Mike Peluso .01 .05
119 Jody Hull .01 .05
120 Peter Sidorkiewicz .02 .10
121 Sylvain Turgeon .01 .05
122 Laurie Boschman .01 .05
123 Brad Marsh .01 .05
124 Neil Brady .01 .05
125 Brian Benning .01 .05
126 Rod BrindAmour .02 .10
127 Kevin Dineen .01 .05
128 Eric Lindros .08 .25
129 Dominic Roussel .02 .10
130 Mark Recchi .01 .05
131 Brent Fedyk .01 .05
132 Greg Paslawski .01 .05
133 Dimitri Yushkevich RC .02 .10
134 Tom Barrasso .02 .10
135 Jaromir Jagr .15 .40
136 Mario Lemieux .50 1.25
137 Larry Murphy .02 .10
138 Kevin Stevens .01 .05
139 Rick Tocchet .02 .10
140 Martin Straka RC .40 1.00
141 Ron Francis .02 .10
142 Shawn McEachern .01 .05
143 Steve Duchesne .01 .05
144 Ron Hextall .02 .10
145 Owen Nolan .02 .10
146 Mike Ricci .01 .05
147 Joe Sakic .20 .50
148 Mats Sundin .08 .25
149 Martin Rucinsky .01 .05
150 Andrei Kovalenko RC .02 .10
151 Dave Karpa RC .01 .05
152 Nelson Emerson .01 .05
153 Brett Hull .15 .40
154 Craig Janney .02 .10
155 Curtis Joseph .08 .25
156 Brendan Shanahan .08 .25
157 Vitali Prokhorov RC .01 .05
158 Igor Korolev RC .02 .10
159 Philippe Bozon .01 .05
160 Ray Whitney RC .15 .40
161 Pat Falloon .01 .05
162 Jeff Hackett .02 .10
163 Brian Lawton .01 .05
164 Sandis Ozolinsh .02 .10
165 Neil Wilkinson .01 .05
166 Kelly Kisio .01 .05
167 Doug Wilson .02 .10
168 Dale Craigwell .01 .05
169 Mikael Andersson .01 .05
170 Wendell Young .02 .10
171 Rob Zamuner RC .02 .10
172 Adam Creighton .01 .05
173 Roman Hamrlik RC .15 .40
174 Brian Bradley .01 .05
175 Rob Ramage .01 .05
176 Chris Kontos RC .01 .05
177 Stan Drulia RC .01 .05
178 Glenn Anderson .02 .10
179 Wendel Clark .02 .10
180 John Cullen .01 .05
181 Dave Ellett .01 .05
182 Grant Fuhr .08 .25
183 Doug Gilmour .02 .10
184 Kent Manderville .01 .05
185 Joe Sacco .01 .05
186 Nikolai Borschevsky RC .01 .05
187 Felix Potvin .08 .25
188 Pavel Bure .08 .25
189 Geoff Courtnall .01 .05
190 Trevor Linden .02 .10
191 Jyrki Lumme .01 .05
192 Kirk McLean .02 .10
193 Cliff Ronning .01 .05
194 Dixon Ward RC .02 .10
195 Greg Adams .01 .05
196 Jiri Slegr .01 .05
197 Don Beaupre .02 .10
198 Kevin Hatcher .01 .05
199 Brad Schlegel .01 .05
200 Mike Ridley .01 .05
201 Calle Johansson .01 .05
202 Steve Konowalchuk RC .01 .05
203 Al Iafrate .01 .05
204 Peter Bondra .01 .05
205 Pat Elynuik .01 .05
206 Keith Tkachuk .08 .25
207 Bob Essensa .02 .10
208 Phil Housley .01 .05
209 Teemu Selanne .50 1.25
210 Alexei Zhamnov .02 .10
211 Evgeny Davydov .01 .05
212 Fredrik Olausson .01 .05
213 Ed Olczyk .01 .05
214 Thomas Steen .01 .05
215 Darius Kasparaitis .01 .05
216 Nikolai Borschevsky .02 .10
217 Teemu Selanne .25 .60
218 Alexander Mogilny .02 .10
219 Sergei Fedorov .08 .25
220 Jaromir Jagr .08 .25
221 Mats Sundin .02 .10
222 Dimitri Kvartalnov .01 .05
223 Andrei Kovalenko .01 .05
224 Tommy Sjodin .01 .05
225 Alexei Kovalev .02 .10
226 Evgeny Davydov .01 .05
227 Robert Lang .01 .05
228 Valeri Zelepukin .01 .05
229 Doug Weight .08 .25
230 Valeri Kamensky .01 .05
231 Donald Audette .01 .05
232 Nelson Emerson .01 .05
233 Pat Falloon .01 .05
234 Pavel Bure .07 .20
235 Tony Amonte .05 .15
236 Sergei Nemchinov .01 .05
237 Gilbert Dionne .01 .05
238 Kevin Todd .01 .05
239 Nicklas Lidstrom .01 .05
240 Brad May .01 .05
241 Stephen Leach .01 .05
242 Dave Poulin .01 .05
243 Grigori Panteleyev RC .01 .05
244 Don Sweeney .01 .05
245 John Blue RC .01 .05
246 C.J. Young RC .01 .05
247 Stephen Heinze .01 .05
248 Cam Neely .08 .25
249 David Reid .01 .05
250 Grant Fuhr .08 .25
251 Bob Sweeney .01 .05
252 Rob Ray .02 .10
253 Doug Bodger .01 .05
254 Ken Sutton .01 .05
255 Yuri Khmylev RC .01 .05
256 Mike Ramsey .01 .05
257 Brad May .01 .05
258 Brent Ashton .01 .05
259 Joel Otto .01 .05
260 Paul Ranheim .01 .05
261 Kevin Dahl RC .01 .05
262 Trent Yawney .01 .05
263 Roger Johansson .01 .05
264 Jeff Reese .01 .05
265 Ron Stern .01 .05
266 Brian Skrudland .01 .05
267 Bryan Marchment .01 .05
268 Stephane Matteau .01 .05
269 Frantisek Kucera .01 .05
270 Jim Waite .01 .05
271 Dirk Graham .01 .05
272 Michel Goulet .01 .05
273 Joe Murphy .01 .05
274 Keith Brown .01 .05
275 Jocelyn Lemieux .01 .05
276 Paul Coffey .08 .25
277 Keith Primeau .01 .05
278 Vincent Riendeau .02 .10
279 Mark Howe .01 .05
280 Ray Sheppard .01 .05
281 Jim Hiller .01 .05
282 Steve Chiasson .01 .05
283 Vladimir Konstantinov .08 .25
284 Brian Ronning .01 .05
285 Kevin Todd .01 .05
286 Zdeno Ciger .01 .05
287 Brian Glynn .01 .05
288 Shaun Van Allen .01 .05
289 Brad Werenka RC .01 .05
290 Ron Tugnutt .02 .10
291 Igor Kravchuk .01 .05
292 Todd Elik .01 .05
293 Terry Yake .01 .05
294 Michael Nylander RC .02 .10
295 Yvon Corriveau .01 .05
296 Frank Pietrangelo .02 .10
297 Nick Kypreos .01 .05
298 Andrew Cassels .01 .05
299 Steve Konroyd .01 .05
300 Allen Pedersen .01 .05
301 Tony Granato .01 .05
302 Rob Blake .02 .10
303 Robb Stauber .02 .10
304 Marty McSorley .01 .05
305 Lonnie Loach RC .01 .05
306 Corey Millen .01 .05
307 Dave Taylor .02 .10
308 Jimmy Carson .01 .05
309 Warren Rychel RC .01 .05
310 Ulf Dahlen .01 .05
311 Dave Gagner .02 .10
312 Brad Berry RC .01 .05
313 Neal Broten .02 .10
314 Mike Craig .01 .05
315 Darcy Wakaluk .02 .10
316 Shane Churla .01 .05
317 Trent Klatt RC .02 .10
318 Mike Keane .01 .05
319 Mathieu Schneider .01 .05
320 Patrice Brisebois .01 .05
321 Andre Racicot .02 .10
322 Mario Roberge .01 .05
323 Gary Leeman .01 .05
324 Jean-Jacques Daigneault .01 .05
325 Lyle Odelein .01 .05
326 John LeClair .20 .50
327 Valeri Zelepukin .01 .05
328 Bernie Nicholls .02 .10
329 Alexander Semak .01 .05
330 Craig Billington .02 .10
331 Randy McKay .01 .05
332 Ken Daneyko .01 .05
333 Bruce Driver .01 .05
334 Slava Fetisov .01 .05
335 Dennis Vaske .01 .05
336 Brad Dalgarno .01 .05
337 Jeff Norton .01 .05
338 Steve Thomas .02 .10
339 Vladimir Malakhov .01 .05
340 David Volek .01 .05
341 Glenn Healy .02 .10
342 Patrick Flatley .01 .05
343 Travis Green RC .25 .60
344 Corey Hirsch RC .08 .25
345 Darren Turcotte .01 .05
346 Adam Graves .01 .05
347 Steve King RC .01 .05
348 Kevin Lowe .02 .10
349 John Vanbiesbrouck .02 .10
350 Ed Olczyk .01 .05
351 Sergei Zubov RC .25 .60
352 Brad Shaw .01 .05
353 Jamie Baker .01 .05
354 Mark Freer .01 .05
355 Darcy Loewen .01 .05
356 Darren Rumble RC .01 .05
357 Bob Kudelski .01 .05
358 Ken Hammond .01 .05
359 Daniel Berthiaume .02 .10
360 Josef Beranek .01 .05
361 Greg Hawgood .01 .05
362 Terry Carkner .01 .05
363 Vyatcheslav Butsayev RC .01 .05
364 Garry Galley .01 .05
365 Andre Faust RC .01 .05
366 Ryan McGill RC .01 .05
367 Tommy Soderstrom RC .02 .10
368 Joe Mullen .02 .10
369 Ulf Samuelsson .01 .05
370 Mike Needham RC .05 .15
371 Ken Wregget .02 .10
372 Dave Tippett .01 .05
373 Kjell Samuelsson .01 .05
374 Bob Errey .01 .05
375 Jim Paek .01 .05
376 Bill Lindsay RC .01 .05
377 Valeri Kamensky .01 .05
378 Stephane Fiset .02 .10
379 Steven Finn .01 .05
380 Mike Hough .01 .05
381 Scott Pearson .01 .05
382 Kerry Huffman .01 .05
383 Scott Young .01 .05
384 Stephane Quintal .01 .05
385 Bret Hedican RC .01 .05
386 Guy Hebert RC .30 .75
387 Vitali Karamnov RC .01 .05
388 Doug Crossman .01 .05
389 Ron Sutter .01 .05
390 Garth Butcher .01 .05
391 Basil McRae .01 .05
392 Dean Evason .01 .05
393 Doug Zmolek RC .01 .05
394 Jay More .01 .05
395 Mike Sullivan .01 .05
396 Arturs Irbe .08 .25
397 Johan Garpenlov .01 .05
398 Jeff Odgers .01 .05
399 Jaroslav Otevrel RC .01 .05
400 Marc Bureau .01 .05
401 Bob Beers .01 .05
402 Rob DiMaio .01 .05
403 Steve Kasper .01 .05
404 Pat Jablonski .02 .10
405 John Tucker .01 .05
406 Shawn Chambers .01 .05
407 Mike Hartman .01 .05
408 Danton Cole .01 .05
409 Dave Andreychuk .02 .10
410 Peter Zezel .01 .05
411 Mike Krushelnyski .01 .05
412 Daren Puppa .02 .10
413 Ken Baumgartner .01 .05
414 Rob Pearson .01 .05
415 Mike Foligno .01 .05
416 Sylvain Lefebvre .01 .05
417 Dimitri Mironov .01 .05
418 Petr Nedved .02 .10
419 Gerald Diduck .01 .05
420 Anatoli Semenov .01 .05
421 Sergio Momesso .01 .05
422 Gino Odjick .01 .05
423 Kay Whitmore .02 .10
424 Dave Babych .01 .05
425 Robert Dirk .01 .05
426 Reggie Savage .01 .05
427 Keith Jones RC .08 .25
428 Dimitri Khristich .01 .05
429 Jason Woolley RC .01 .05
430 Jim Hrivnak .02 .10
431 Sylvain Cote .01 .05
432 Michal Pivonka .01 .05
433 Rod Langway .01 .05
434 Tie Domi .08 .25
435 Sergei Bautin RC .01 .05
436 Darrin Shannon .01 .05
437 John Druce .01 .05
438 Teppo Numminen .01 .05
439 Luciano Borsato .01 .05
440 Igor Ulanov .01 .05
441 Mike O'Neill RC .01 .05
442 Kris King .01 .05
443 Roman Hamrlik .02 .10
444 Steve Smith .01 .05
445 Jari Kurri .08 .25
446 Ulf Samuelsson .01 .05
447 Sergei Nemchinov .01 .05
448 Tommy Soderstrom .02 .10
449 Petr Nedved .01 .05
450 Peter Sidorkiewicz .02 .10
451 Nicklas Lidstrom .02 .10
452 Philippe Bozon .01 .05
453 Uwe Krupp .01 .05
454 Steve Thomas .02 .10
455 Owen Nolan .01 .05
456 Steve Yzerman .25 .60
457 Chris Chelios .08 .25
458 Paul Coffey .08 .25
459 Brett Hull .08 .25
460 Pavel Bure .07 .20
461 Ed Belfour .02 .10
462 Mario Lemieux AS .25 .60
463 Patrick Roy .25 .60
464 Ray Bourque .08 .25
465 Jaromir Jagr .08 .25
466 Kevin Stevens .01 .05
467 Brian Leetch .02 .10
468 Bobby Clarke .02 .10
469 Bill Barber .01 .05
470 Bernie Parent .02 .10
471 Reggie Leach .01 .05
472 Rick MacLeish .01 .05
473 Dave Schultz .02 .10
474 Joe Watson .01 .05
475 Bobby Taylor .01 .05
476 Orest Kindrachuk .01 .05
477 Bob Kelly .01 .05
478 Bill Clement .02 .10
479 Ed Van Impe .01 .05
480 Fred Shero .02 .10
481 Bryan Smolinski RC .25 .60
482 Sergei Zholtok .10 .30
483 Matthew Barnaby RC .10 .30
484 Gary Shuchuk .10 .30
485 Guy Carbonneau .10 .30
486 Oleg Petrov RC .10 .30
487 Sean Hill RC .10 .30
488 Jesse Belanger RC .10 .30
489 Paul DiPietro .05 .15
490 Rich Pilon .05 .15
491 Greg Parks .10 .30
492 Jeff Daniels .10 .30
493 Denny Felsner RC .10 .30
494 Mike Eastwood RC .10 .30
495 Murray Craven .10 .30
496 Vincent Damphousse .05 .15
497 Grant Fuhr .25 .60
498 Mario Lemieux SCP 1.25 3.00
499 Ray Ferraro .05 .15
500 Teemu Selanne .75 2.00
501 Luc Robitaille .10 .30
502 Doug Gilmour .10 .30
503 Curtis Joseph .25 .60
504 Kirk Muller .05 .15
505 Glenn Healy .10 .30
506 Pavel Bure .08 .25
507 Felix Potvin .10 .30
508 Guy Carbonneau .10 .30
509 Wayne Gretzky 1.50 4.00
510 Patrick Roy 1.25 3.00

1992-93 Parkhurst Emerald Ice

The 1992-93 Parkhurst Emerald Ice set consists of 480 cards and a 30 card update set. This parallel set version can be differentiated from its basic set counterpart by the company's use of an "emerald green" embossed-foil Parkhurst logo on the lower left of the card. Cards 1-240 were inserted one per foil pack, two per jumbo pack in series one product; likewise for cards 241-480 in series two product. Cards 481-510 were available in Update set form only, and are slightly more difficult to obtain.

COMPLETE SET (480) 80.00 180.00
COMP.SERIES 1 (240) 40.00 100.00
COMP.SERIES 2 (240) 40.00 80.00
COMP.FINAL UPDATE (30) 12.50 25.00
*VETS: 2X TO 5X BASIC CARDS
*ROOKIES: 1.2X TO 3X BASIC CARDS
*UPDATE: 1.2X TO 3X BASIC CARDS

1992-93 Parkhurst Cherry Picks

Randomly inserted in second series Parkhurst foil packs, this 21-card standard-size set features Don Cherry's "Cherry Picks" as selected by the ex-coach and host of "Coach's Corner" on Hockey Night in Canada. The cards feature full-bleed, color action player photos. The player's name is printed in gold foil near the bottom of the card along with the Cherry Picks logo. The backs have a dark blue-gray and black stripe background. Set at an angle on this background is a hockey arena graphic design that carries comments from Don Cherry in French and English. Overlapping the arena design is a small, action player photo. The cards are numbered on the backs with a "CP" prefix. The cover card carries a message from Don Cherry. The Doug Gilmour card (CP 1993) was randomly inserted in Final Update sets.

COMPLETE SET (21) 30.00 60.00
CP1 Doug Gilmour 1.00 2.50
CP2 Jeremy Roenick 2.50 6.00
CP3 Brent Sutter 1.00 2.50
CP4 Mark Messier 2.00 5.00
CP5 Kirk Muller 1.00 2.50
CP6 Eric Lindros 2.00 5.00
CP7 Dale Hunter 1.00 2.50
CP8 Gary Roberts 1.00 2.50
CP9 Bob Probert 1.00 2.50
CP10 Brendan Shanahan 2.00 5.00
CP11 Wendel Clark 1.00 2.50
CP12 Rick Tocchet 1.00 2.50
CP13 Owen Nolan 1.25 3.00
CP14 Cam Neely 2.00 5.00
CP15 Dave Manson 1.00 2.50
CP16 Chris Chelios 2.00 5.00
CP17 Marty McSorley 1.00 2.50
CP18 Scott Stevens 1.00 2.50
CP19 John Blue 1.00 2.50
CP20 Ron Hextall 1.00 2.50
CP1993 Doug Gilmour 6.00 15.00
Cherry Pick of the Year
NNO Don Cherry AU 40.00 100.00
NNO Don Cherry 8.00 20.00
Checklist back
NNO Don Cherry 4.00 10.00
Redemption

1992-93 Parkhurst Cherry Picks Sheet

This approximately 11" by 8 1/2" sheet displays the cards of the 1992-93 Parkhurst Cherry Picks insert set. The sheet could be obtained by collectors in exchange for four Don Cherry redemption cards, which were randomly inserted in 1992-93 Parkhurst series II packs. The sheet pictures the fronts of the cards from the 1992-93 Cherry Picks set with Don Cherry's card in the middle. The words "1993 Cherry Picks Promo" are printed in a pink to purple shaded bar at the top of the sheet. The back is blank and the sheet is unnumbered.

1 D.Hunter 5.00 10.00
D.Manson
D.Gilmour
G.Roberts
C.Chelios
J.Roenick
B.Probert
M.McSorley
B.Sutter
B.Shanahan
D.Cherry
M.Messier
W.Clark
K.Muller
R.Tocchet
S.Stevens
E.Lindros
O.Nolan
J.Blue
R.Hextall

1992-93 Parkhurst Parkie Reprints

This set of 36 cards was issued in four separate series. The cards are reprints of cards from the 1950s. Capturing eight goalies from the 1950's Parkhurst collections, the first set was inserted into first series 12-card foil packs. The second eight cards showcase defensemen; these cards were randomly inserted in series 1 jumbo packs. Forwards (17-24) were inserted in second series foil with the remaining forwards (25-32) inserted in second series jumbo packs. The cover cards, which reproduce Parkhurst wrappers on their fronts (1953-54 and 1955-56), have a checklist on their backs. The fronts vary in design but all carry a color shot of the featured player. The players' names are on the fronts, some in print, some in signature form. The backs carry the information from the original card. The print varies from red to black to a combination. The Turk Broda and Terry Sawchuk cards are blank on the back as the originals are. Only Canadian cases included a newly created 1954-55 Don Cherry Parkie 101 card. The Parkie Reprints set is considered complete without it.

COMPLETE SET (36) 75.00 150.00
PR1 Jacques Plante 3.00 8.00
PR2 Terry Sawchuk 3.00 8.00
PR3 Johnny Bower 2.00 5.00
PR4 Gump Worsley 2.00 5.00
PR5 Harry Lumley 2.00 5.00
PR6 Turk Broda 2.00 5.00
PR7 Jim Henry 2.00 5.00
PR8 Al Rollins 2.00 5.00
PR9 Bill Gadsby 2.00 5.00
PR10 Red Kelly 2.00 5.00
PR11 Allan Stanley 2.00 5.00
PR12 Bob Baun 2.00 5.00
PR13 Carl Brewer 2.00 5.00
PR14 Doug Harvey 2.00 5.00
PR15 Harry Howell 2.00 5.00
PR16 Tim Horton 2.00 5.00
PR17 George Armstrong 2.00 5.00
PR18 Ralph Backstrom 2.00 5.00
PR19 Alex Delvecchio 2.00 5.00
PR20 Bill Mosienko 2.00 5.00
PR21 Dave Keon 2.00 5.00
PR22 Andy Bathgate 2.00 5.00
PR23 Milt Schmidt 2.00 5.00
PR24 Dick Duff 2.00 5.00

PR25 Norm Ullman 2.00 5.00
PR26 Dickie Moore 2.00 5.00
PR27 Jerry Toppazzini 2.00 5.00
PR28 Henri Richard 2.00 5.00
PR29 Frank Mahovlich 2.00 5.00
PR30 Jean Beliveau 2.00 5.00
PR31 Ted Lindsay 2.00 5.00
PR32 Bernie Geoffrion 2.00 5.00
CL1 Parkies Checklist 1 2.00 5.00
(Repro of 1955-56 Parkie Wrapper)
CL2 Parkies Checklist 2 2.00 5.00
(Repro of 1953-54 Parkie Wrapper)
CL3 Parkies Checklist 3 2.00 5.00
(Repro of 1958-59 Parkie Wrapper)
CL4 Parkies Checklist 4 2.00 5.00
(Repro of 1954-55 Parkie Wrapper)
AU Don Cherry Parkie AU 40.00 100.00
NNO Don Cherry Parkie 101 6.00 15.00

1992-93 Parkhurst Arena Tour Sheets

Each sheet in this set of eight measures approximately 11" by 8 1/2" and commemorates a stop on the Canadian Arena Tour. The fronts feature color photos of 1992-93 Parkhurst hockey cards against a blue-green background that shades from dark to light. A thin metallic gold line frames the cards, and the word "Commemorative" is printed in large white letters on this line at the top of the sheet. Near the center are the words "Canadian Arena Tour" and a specific arena name along with the date the sheet was distributed. The team logo is printed above this text. Each sheet carries a serial number and the production run (noted beside the dates below). The backs are blank. The sheets are unnumbered and checklisted below in chronological order. The Montreal sheet was not distributed at the Forum; reportedly because the sheet was not bilingual.

1 Calgary Flames 4.00 10.00
Olympic Saddledome
April 1 1993 (22,000)
Mike Vernon
Theoren Fleury
Trent Yawney
Brian Skrudland
Joel Otto
Al MacInnis
2 Edmonton Oilers 4.00 10.00
Northlands Coliseum
April 3 1993 (22,000)
Zdeno Ciger
Bill Ranford
Todd Elik
Igor Kravchuk
Craig MacTavish
Shayne Corson
3 Quebec Nordiques 4.00 10.00
Colisee de Quebec
April 6 1993 (22,000)
Bill Lindsay
Ron Hextall
Valeri Kamensky
Kerry Huffman
Mats Sundin
Joe Sakic
4 Vancouver Canucks 6.00 15.00
Pacific Coliseum
April 11 1993 (22,000)
Dave Babych
Pavel Bure
Petr Nedved
Anatoli Semenov
Kirk McLean
Trevor Linden
5 Montreal Canadiens 10.00 25.00
The Forum
April 12 1993 (22,000)
Denis Savard
Kirk Muller
J.J. Daigneault
Patrice Brisebois
Mathieu Schneider
Patrick Roy
6 Toronto Maple Leafs 8.00 20.00
Maple Leaf Gardens
April 13 1993 (22,000)
Felix Potvin
Dave Andreychuk
Wendel Clark
Peter Zezel
Doug Gilmour
Sylvain Lefebvre
7 Ottawa Senators 4.00 10.00
Ottawa Civic Centre
April 14 1993 (22,000)
Brad Marsh
Ken Hammond
Bob Kudelski
Peter Sidorkiewicz
Sylvain Turgeon
Mark Freer
8 Winnipeg Jets 4.00 10.00
Winnipeg Arena
April 15 1993 (22,000)
Phil Housley
John Druce
Sergei Bautin
Tie Domi
Evgeny Davydov
Teemu Selanne

1992-93 Parkhurst Parkie Sheets

These five commemorative sheets measure approximately 8 1/2" by 11". The sheets are individually numbered; the production quantities are listed in the checklist below. The sheets were distributed one per case as an insert with the various series of 1992-93 Parkhurst hockey cards. The players pictured are the players in that respective Parkie reprint series. The Stanley Cup Commemorative Update sheet was issued one per case of Final Update. These unnumbered sheets are numbered chronologically below for convenience in reference.

1 Goalies 8.00 20.00
(7000 sheets issued)
2 Defensemen 10.00 25.00
(3000 sheets issued)
3 Forwards/Wingers 8.00 20.00
(7000 sheets issued)
4 Forwards/Centers 12.00 30.00
(3000 sheets issued)
5 Stanley Cup Update 15.00 40.00
(1000 sheets issued)

1992-93 Parkhurst Promo Sheets

These 11" by 8 1/2" sheets were promos of the 1992-93 Parkhurst Limited Edition Commemorative Sheets. The fronts feature color photos of actual Parkhurst Parkies. The cards are set against a dark green marbleized background. A thin metallic gold line frames the cards. The words "Commemorative Sheet" are printed in white over the gold line near the top of the sheet. Above this, are the words "1992-93 Parkhurst Limited Edition" printed in metallic gold. A gold or white oval at the bottom right corner carries the word "Promo." The backs are blank. The sheets are unnumbered.

1 Toronto Maple Leafs 10.00 25.00
vs. Montreal Canadiens
Alumni Game
April 4& 1993
Maple Leaf Gardens
Johnny Bower
Harry Lumley
Jacques Plante
Dave Keon
Doug Harvey
Tim Horton
Ralph Backstrom
Frank Mahovlich
2 Dave Keon 6.00 15.00
Milt Schmidt
Dick Duff
Bill Mosienko
Alex Delvecchio
Ralph Backstrom
George Armstrong
Andy Bathgate

1993-94 Parkhurst

Issued in two series, these 540 standard-size cards feature color player action shots on their fronts. They are borderless, except on the right, where black and green stripes set off by a silver-foil line carry the player's name in white lettering; and at the lower left, where a black and green corner backs up the silver-foil-stamped Parkhurst logo. The player's team name appears near the right edge in vertical silver-foil lettering. The horizontal back carries another color player action shot on the right. On the left are the player's team name, position, biography, career highlights, and statistics. Card numbers 398 and 498 were not issued.

COMPLETE SET (540) 15.00 30.00
COMP.SERIES 1 (270) 7.50 15.00
COMP.SERIES 2 (270) 7.50 15.00
1 Steven King .02 .10
2 Sean Hill .02 .10
3 Anatoli Semenov .02 .10
4 Garry Valk .02 .10
5 Todd Ewen .02 .10
6 Bob Corkum .02 .10
7 Tim Sweeney .02 .10
8 Patrick Carnback RC .20 .50
9 Troy Loney .02 .10
10 Cam Neely .08 .25
11 Adam Oates .05 .15
12 Jon Casey .05 .15
13 Don Sweeney .02 .10
14 Ray Bourque .15 .40
15 Jozef Stumpel .02 .10
16 Glen Murray .02 .10
17 Glen Wesley .02 .10
18 Fred Knipscheer RC .20 .50
19 Craig Simpson .02 .10
20 Richard Smehlik .02 .10
21 Alexander Mogilny .05 .15
22 Grant Fuhr .05 .15
23 Dale Hawerchuk .05 .15
24 Philippe Boucher .02 .10
25 Scott Thomas RC .20 .50
26 Donald Audette .02 .10
27 Brad May .05 .15
28 Theo Fleury .02 .10
29 Andrei Trefilov .02 .10
30 Sandy McCarthy .02 .10
31 Joe Nieuwendyk .05 .15
32 Paul Ranheim .02 .10
33 Kelly Kisio .02 .10
34 Joel Otto .02 .10
35 Ted Drury .02 .10
36 Al MacInnis .05 .15
37 Kevin Todd .02 .10
38 Joe Murphy .02 .10
39 Christian Ruuttu .02 .10
40 Steve Dubinsky RC .20 .50
41 Stephane Matteau .02 .10
42 Ivan Droppa RC .20 .50
43 Jocelyn Lemieux .02 .10
44 Ed Belfour .08 .25
45 Chris Chelios .08 .25
46 Derian Hatcher .02 .10
47 Andy Moog .05 .15
48 Trent Klatt .02 .10
49 Mike Modano .15 .40
50 Paul Cavallini .02 .10
51 Mike McPhee .02 .10
52 Brent Gilchrist .02 .10
53 Russ Courtnall .02 .10
54 Neal Broten .05 .15
55 Steve Chiasson .02 .10
56 Paul Coffey .08 .25
57 Slava Kozlov .05 .15
58 Sergei Fedorov .15 .40
59 Tim Cheveldae .05 .15
60 Dino Ciccarelli .05 .15
61 Dallas Drake RC .20 .50
62 Nicklas Lidstrom .08 .25
63 Martin Lapointe .02 .10
64 Dean McAmmond .02 .10
65 Igor Kravchuk .02 .10
66 Shjon Podein RC .20 .50
67 Bill Ranford .05 .15
68 Brad Werenka .02 .10
69 Doug Weight .05 .15
70 Ian Herbers RC .20 .50
71 Todd Elik .02 .10
72 Steven Rice .02 .10
73 John Vanbiesbrouck .05 .15
74 Alexander Godynyuk .02 .10
75 Brian Skrudland .02 .10
76 Jody Hull .02 .10
77 Brent Severyn RC .20 .50
78 Evgeny Davydov .02 .10
79 Dave Lowry .02 .10
80 Scott Levins RC .20 .50
81 Scott Mellanby .05 .15
82 Dan Keczmer .02 .10
83 Michael Nylander .02 .10
84 Jim Sandlak .02 .10
85 Brian Propp .02 .10
86 Geoff Sanderson .05 .15
87 Mike Lenarduzzi RC .20 .50
88 Zarley Zalapski .02 .10
89 Robert Petrovicky .02 .10
90 Robert Kron .02 .10
91 Luc Robitaille .05 .15
92 Alexei Zhitnik .02 .10
93 Tony Granato .02 .10
94 Rob Blake .05 .15
95 Gary Shuchuk .02 .10
96 Darryl Sydor .02 .10
97 Kelly Hrudey .05 .15
98 Warren Rychel .02 .10
99 Wayne Gretzky .60 1.50
100 Patrick Roy .50 1.25
101 Gilbert Dionne .02 .10
102 Eric Desjardins .05 .15
103 Peter Popovic RC .20 .50
104 Vincent Damphousse .02 .10
105 Patrice Brisebois .02 .10
106 Pierre Sevigny .02 .10
107 John LeClair .08 .25
108 Paul DiPietro .02 .10
109 Alexander Semak .02 .10
110 Claude Lemieux .02 .10
111 Scott Niedermayer .02 .10
112 Chris Terreri .05 .15
113 Stephane Richer .05 .15
114 Scott Stevens .05 .15
115 John MacLean .05 .15
116 Scott Pellerin RC .20 .50
117 Bernie Nicholls .02 .10
118 Ron Hextall .05 .15
119 Derek King .02 .10
120 Scott Lachance .02 .10
121 Scott Scissons .02 .10
122 Darius Kasparaitis .02 .10
123 Ray Ferraro .02 .10
124 Steve Thomas .02 .10
125 Vladimir Malakhov .02 .10
126 Travis Green .05 .15
127 Mark Messier .08 .25
128 Sergei Nemchinov .02 .10
129 Tony Amonte .08 .25
130 Alexei Kovalev .05 .15
131 Brian Leetch .08 .25
132 Mike Richter .08 .25
133 Sergei Zubov .02 .10
134 Adam Graves .02 .10
135 Esa Tikkanen .02 .10
136 Sylvain Turgeon .02 .10
137 Norm Maciver .02 .10
138 Craig Billington .05 .15
139 Dmitri Filimonov .02 .10
140 Pavel Demitra .05 .15
141 Brian Glynn .02 .10
142 Darrin Madeley RC .20 .50
143 Radek Hamr RC .20 .50
144 Robert Burakovsky RC .20 .50
145 Dimitri Yushkevich .02 .10
146 Claude Boivin .02 .10
147 Pelle Eklund .02 .10
148 Brent Fedyk .02 .10
149 Mark Recchi .05 .15
150 Tommy Soderstrom .05 .15
151 Vyacheslav Butsayev .02 .10
152 Rod Brind'Amour .05 .15
153 Josef Beranek .02 .10
154 Jaromir Jagr .15 .40
155 Ulf Samuelsson .02 .10
156 Martin Straka .02 .10
157 Tom Barrasso .05 .15
158 Kevin Stevens .02 .10
159 Joe Mullen .05 .15
160 Ron Francis .05 .15
161 Marty McSorley .02 .10
162 Larry Murphy .05 .15
163 Owen Nolan .05 .15
164 Stephane Fiset .05 .15
165 Dave Karpa .02 .10
166 Martin Gelinas .02 .10
167 Andrei Kovalenko .02 .10
168 Steve Duchesne .02 .10
169 Joe Sakic .20 .50
170 Martin Rucinsky .02 .10
171 Chris Simon RC .20 .50
172 Brendan Shanahan .08 .25
173 Jeff Brown .02 .10
174 Phil Housley .05 .15
175 Curtis Joseph .08 .25
176 Jim Montgomery RC .20 .50
177 Bret Hedican .02 .10
178 Kevin Miller .02 .10
179 Philippe Bozon .02 .10
180 Brett Hull .10 .30
181 Jimmy Waite .05 .15
182 Ray Whitney .02 .10
183 Pat Falloon .02 .10
184 Tom Pederson .02 .10
185 Igor Larionov .02 .10
186 Dody Wood RC .20 .50
187 Sandis Ozolinsh .02 .10
188 Sergei Makarov .02 .10
189 Rob Gaudreau RC .20 .50
190 Roman Hamrlik .05 .15
191 Stan Drulia .02 .10
192 Pat Jablonski .05 .15
193 Denis Savard .05 .15
194 Rob Zamuner .02 .10
195 Petr Klima .02 .10
196 Rob Dimiao .02 .10
197 Chris Kontos .02 .10
198 Mikael Andersson .02 .10
199 Drake Berehowsky .02 .10
200 Dave Andreychuk .05 .15
201 Glenn Anderson .05 .15
202 Felix Potvin .08 .25
203 Nikolai Borschevsky .02 .10
204 Kent Manderville .02 .10
205 Dave Ellett .02 .10
206 Peter Zezel .02 .10
207 Ken Baumgartner .02 .10
208 Murray Craven .02 .10
209 Dixon Ward .02 .10
210 Cliff Ronning .02 .10
211 Pavel Bure .08 .25
212 Sergio Momesso .02 .10
213 Kirk McLean .05 .15
214 Jiri Slegr .02 .10
215 Trevor Linden .05 .15
216 Geoff Courtnall .02 .10
217 Al Iafrate .02 .10
218 Mike Ridley .02 .10
219 Enrico Ciccone .02 .10
220 Dimitri Khristich .02 .10
221 Kevin Hatcher .02 .10
222 Peter Bondra .05 .15
223 Steve Konowalchuk .02 .10
224 Pat Elynuik .02 .10
225 Don Beaupre .05 .15
226 Stu Barnes .02 .10
227 Fredrik Olausson .02 .10
228 Keith Thachuk .08 .25
229 Mike Eagles .02 .10
230 Tie Domi .05 .15
231 Teppo Numminen .02 .10
232 Arto Blomsten .02 .10
233 Teemu Selanne .08 .25
234 Bob Essensa .05 .15
235 Teemu Selanne SPH .08 .25
236 Eric Lindros SPH .08 .25
237 Felix Potvin SPH .05 .15
238 Alexei Kovalev SPH .05 .15
239 Vladimir Malakhov SPH .02 .10
240 Scott Niedermayer SPH .02 .10
241 Joe Juneau SPH .05 .15
242 Shawn McEachern SPH .02 .10
243 Alexei Zhamnov SPH .05 .15
244 Alexandre Daigle PKP .02 .10
245 Markus Naslund PKP .08 .25
246 Rob Niedermayer PKP .05 .15
247 Jocelyn Thibault RC .20 .50
248 Brent Gretzky PKP RC .20 .50
249 Chris Pronger PKP .10 .30
250 Chris Gratton PKP .05 .15
251 Mikael Renberg PKP .08 .25
252 Jarkko Varvio PKP .02 .10
253 Micah Aivazoff PKP RC .20 .50
254 Alexei Yashin PKP .02 .10
255 German Titov PKP RC .20 .50
256 Mattias Norstrom PKP RC .20 .50
257 Michal Sykora PKP RC .20 .50
258 Roman Oksiuta PKP RC .20 .50
259 Bryan Smolinski PKP .02 .10
260 Alexei Kudashov PKP RC .20 .50
261 Jason Arnott PKP RC .50 1.25
262 Aaron Ward PKP RC .20 .50
263 Vesa Vitakoski PKP RC .20 .50
264 Boris Mironov PKP .02 .10
265 Darren McCarty PKP RC .20 .50
266 Vlastimil Kroupa PKP RC .20 .50
267 Denny Felsner PKP .02 .10
268 Milos Holan PKP RC .20 .50
269 Alex. Karpovtsev PKP .02 .10
270 Greg Johnson PKP .02 .10
271 Terry Yake .02 .10
272 Bill Houlder .02 .10
273 Joe Sacco .02 .10
274 Myles O'Connor .02 .10
275 Mark Ferner RC .20 .50
276 Alexei Kasatanov .02 .10
277 Stu Grimson .02 .10
278 Shaun Van Allen .02 .10
279 Guy Hebert .05 .15
280 Joe Juneau .05 .15
281 Sergei Zholtok .02 .10
282 Daniel Marois .02 .10
283 Ted Donato .02 .10
284 Cam Stewart RC .20 .50
285 Stephen Leach .02 .10
286 Darren Banks .02 .10
287 Dmitri Kvartalnov .02 .10
288 Paul Stanton .02 .10
289 Pat LaFontaine .08 .25
290 Bob Sweeney .02 .10
291 Craig Muni .02 .10
292 Sergei Petrenko .02 .10
293 Derek Plante RC .20 .50
294 Wayne Presley .02 .10
295 Mark Astley RC .20 .50
296 Matthew Barnaby .05 .15
297 Randy Wood .02 .10
298 Kevin Dahl .02 .10
299 Gary Suter .02 .10
300 Robert Reichel .02 .10
301 Mike Vernon .05 .15
302 Gary Roberts .02 .10
303 Ronnie Stern .02 .10
304 Michel Petit .02 .10
305 Wes Walz .02 .10
306 Brad Miller RC .20 .50
307 Patrick Poulin .02 .10
308 Brent Sutter .02 .10
309 Jeremy Roenick .10 .30
310 Steve Smith .02 .10
311 Eric Weinrich .02 .10
312 Jeff Hackett .05 .15
313 Michel Goulet .05 .15
314 Jeff Shantz RC .20 .50
315 Neil Wilkinson .02 .10
316 Shane Churla .02 .10
317 Dave Gagner .05 .15
318 Chris Tancill .02 .10
319 Dean Evason .02 .10
320 Mark Tinordi .02 .10
321 Grant Ledyard .02 .10
322 Ulf Dahlen .02 .10
323 Mike Craig .02 .10
324 Paul Broten .02 .10
325 Vladimir Konstantinov .05 .15
326 Steve Yzerman .50 1.25
327 Keith Primeau .02 .10
328 Shawn Burr .02 .10
329 Chris Osgood RC .60 1.50
330 Ray Sheppard .05 .15
331 Mike Sillinger .02 .10
332 Terry Carkner .02 .10
333 Bob Probert .05 .15
334 Adam Bennett .02 .10
335 Dave Manson .02 .10
336 Zdeno Ciger .02 .10
337 Louie DeBrusk .02 .10
338 Shayne Corson .02 .10
339 Vladimir Vujtek .02 .10
340 Tyler Wright .02 .10
341 Ilya Byakin RC .20 .50
342 Craig MacTavish .02 .10
343 Brian Benning .02 .10
344 Mark Fitzpatrick .05 .15
345 Gord Murphy .02 .10
346 Jesse Belanger .02 .10
347 Joe Cirella .02 .10
348 Tom Fitzgerald .02 .10
349 Andrei Lomakin .02 .10
350 Bill Lindsay .02 .10
351 Len Barrie .02 .10
352 Frank Pietrangelo .05 .15
353 Pat Verbeek .02 .10
354 Jim Storm .02 .10
355 Mark Janssens .02 .10
356 Darren Turcotte .02 .10
357 Jim McKenzie .02 .10
358 Brad McCrimmon .02 .10
359 Andrew Cassels .02 .10
360 James Patrick .02 .10
361 Bob Jay RC .20 .50
362 Tomas Sandstrom .02 .10
363 Pat Conacher .02 .10
364 Shawn McEachern .02 .10
365 Jari Kurri .08 .25
366 Dominic Lavoie .02 .10
367 Dave Taylor .05 .15
368 Jimmy Carson .02 .10
369 Mike Donnelly .02 .10
370 Lyle Odelein .02 .10
371 Brian Bellows .02 .10
372 Guy Carbonneau .02 .10
373 Mathieu Schneider .02 .10
374 Stephan Lebeau .02 .10
375 Benoit Brunet .02 .10
376 Kevin Haller .02 .10
377 J.J. Daigneault .02 .10
378 Kirk Muller .02 .10
379 Jason Smith RC .20 .50
380 Martin Brodeur .30 .75
381 Corey Millen .02 .10
382 Bill Guerin .02 .10
383 Valeri Zelepukin .02 .10
384 Tom Chorske .02 .10
385 Bobby Holik .02 .10
386 Jaroslav Modry RC .20 .50
387 Ken Daneyko .02 .10
388 Uwe Krupp .02 .10
389 Pierre Turgeon .05 .15
390 Marty McInnis .02 .10
391 Patrick Flatley .02 .10
392 Tom Kurvers .02 .10
393 Brad Dalgarno .02 .10
394 Steve Junker RC .20 .50
395 David Volek .02 .10
396 Benoit Hogue .02 .10
397 Zigmund Palffy .05 .15
399 Joby Messier RC .20 .50
400 Mike Gartner .05 .15
401 Joey Kocur .02 .10
402 Ed Olczyk .02 .10
403 Doug Lidster .02 .10
404A Greg Gilbert .02 .10
404B Steve Larmer UER .05 .15
(Should be 398)
405 Glenn Healy .05 .15
406 Dennis Vial .02 .10
407 Darcy Loewen .02 .10
408 Bob Kudelski .02 .10
409 Hank Lammens RC .20 .50
410 Jarmo Kekalainen .02 .10
411 Darren Rumble .02 .10
412 Francois Leroux .02 .10
413 Troy Mallette .02 .10
414 Bill Huard RC .20 .50
415 Ryan McGill .02 .10
416 Eric Lindros .08 .25
417 Dominic Roussel .05 .15
418 Jason Bowen RC .20 .50
419 Andre Faust .02 .10
420 Stewart Malgunas RC .20 .50
421 Kevin Dineen .02 .10
422 Yves Racine .02 .10
423 Garry Galley .02 .10
424 Doug Brown .02 .10
425 Mario Lemieux .50 1.25
426 Ladislav Karabin RC .20 .50
427 Grant Jennings .02 .10
428 Rick Tocchet .05 .15
429 Jeff Daniels .02 .10
430 Peter Taglianetti .02 .10
431 Bryan Trottier .05 .15
432 Kjell Samuelsson .02 .10
433 Rene Corbet RC .20 .50
434 Iain Fraser RC .20 .50
435 Mats Sundin .08 .25
436 Curtis Leschyshyn .02 .10
437 Claude LaPointe .02 .10
438 Valeri Kamensky .05 .15
439 Mike Ricci .02 .10
440 Chris Lindberg .02 .10
441 Alexei Gusarov .02 .10
442 Tom Tilley .02 .10
443 Craig Janney .05 .15
444 Vitali Karamnov .02 .10
445 Bob Bassen .02 .10
446 Igor Korolev .02 .10
447 Kevin Miehm .02 .10
448 Tony Hrkac .02 .10
449 Garth Butcher .02 .10
450 Vitali Prokhorov .02 .10
451 Arturs Irbe .05 .15
452 Jay More .02 .10
453 Bob Errey .02 .10
454 Mike Sullivan .02 .10
455 Jeff Norton .02 .10
456 Gaeten Duchesne .02 .10
457 Doug Zmolek .02 .10
458 Mike Rathje .02 .10
459 Jamie Baker .02 .10
460 Joe Reekie .02 .10
461 Mark Bureau .02 .10
462 John Tucker .02 .10
463 Bill McDougall RC .20 .50
464 Danton Cole .02 .10
465 Brian Bradley .02 .10
466 Jason Lafreniere .02 .10
467 Donald Dufresne .02 .10
468 Daren Puppa .05 .15
469 Doug Gilmour .05 .15
470 Damian Rhodes RC .20 .50
471 Matt Martin RC .20 .50
472 Bill Berg .02 .10
473 John Cullen .02 .10
474 Rob Pearson .02 .10
475 Wendel Clark .05 .15
476 Mark Osborne .02 .10
477 Dmitri Mironov .02 .10
478A Kay Whitmore .05 .15
478B Kris King UER .02 .10
(Should be 498)
479 Shawn Antoski .02 .10
480 Greg Adams .02 .10
481 Dave Babych .02 .10
482 John McIntyre .02 .10
483 Jyrki Lumme .02 .10
484 Jose Charbonneau RC .20 .50
485 Gino Odjick .02 .10
486 Dana Murzyn .02 .10
487 Michal Pivonka .02 .10
488 Dave Poulin .02 .10
489 Sylvain Cote .02 .10
490 Jason Woolley .02 .10
491 Kelly Miller .02 .10
492 Randy Burridge .02 .10
493 Kevin Kaminski RC .20 .50
494 John Slaney .02 .10
495 Keith Jones .02 .10
496 Harijs Vitolinsh .02 .10
497 Nelson Emerson .02 .10
499 Darrin Shannon .02 .10
500 Stephane Quintal .02 .10
501 Luciano Borsato .02 .10
502 Thomas Steen .02 .10
503 Alexei Zhamnov .05 .15
504 Paul Ysebaert .02 .10
505 Jeff Friesen RC .60 1.50
506 Niklas Sundstrom .02 .10
507 Nick Stajduhar RC .20 .50
508 Jamie Storr RC .20 .50
509 Valeri Bure RC .20 .50
510 Jason Bonsignore RC .20 .50
511 Mats Lindgren RC .20 .50
512 Yannick Dube RC .20 .50
513 Todd Harvey RC .20 .50
514 Ladislav Prokupek RC .20 .50
515 Tomas Vlasak RC .20 .50
516 Josef Marha RC .20 .50
517 Tomas Blazek RC .20 .50
518 Zdenek Nedved RC .20 .50
519 Jaroslav Miklenda RC .20 .50
520 Janne Niinimaa RC .20 .50
521 Saku Koivu .08 .25
522 Tommi Miettinen RC .20 .50
523 Tuomas Gronman .02 .10
524 Jani Nikko RC .20 .50
525 Jouni Vauhkonen .02 .10
526 Nikolai Tsulygin .02 .10
527 Vadim Sharifjanov .05 .15
528 Valeri Bure RC .20 .50
529 Alexander Kharlamov RC .20 .50
530 Nikolai Zavarukhin RC .20 .50
531 Oleg Tverdovsky RC .20 .50
532 Sergei Kondrashkin RC .20 .50
533 Evgeni Ryabchikov RC .20 .50
534 Mats Lindgren RC .20 .50
535 Kenny Jonsson .02 .10
536 Edvin Frylen RC .20 .50
537 Mathias Johansson RC .20 .50
538 Johan Davidsson RC .20 .50
539 Mikael Hakansson RC .20 .50
540 Anders Eriksson RC .20 .50

1993-94 Parkhurst Emerald Ice

The 540 cards in this parallel set can be found one per foil pack and two per jumbo pack. The Parkhurst logo, team name, and vertical strip near the right edge of the card are adorned with green foil, as opposed to the silver foil used for the basic card set.

*VETS: 2.5X TO 6X BASIC CARDS
*ROOKIES: 1.5X TO 4X BASIC CARDS

1993-94 Parkhurst Calder Candidates

The silver trade card randomly inserted in '93-94 Parkhurst packs was redeemable for this Calder Candidates insert set.This set was also randomly inserted in U.S. Series 2 retail packs. The gold trade card was redeemable for a gold foil-enhanced edition; multipliers can be found below to determine values for these. The expiration date for both trade cards was July 31st, 1994.

*GOLD: .6X TO 1.5X SILVER INSERTS
C1 Alexandre Daigle .40 1.00
C2 Chris Pronger 1.50 4.00
C3 Chris Gratton .40 1.00
C4 Rob Niedermayer .40 1.00
C5 Markus Naslund .40 1.00
C6 Jason Arnott 1.00 2.50
C7 Pierre Sevigny .40 1.00
C8 Jarkko Varvio .40 1.00
C9 Dean McAmmond .40 1.00
C10 Alexei Yashin .40 1.00
C11 Philippe Boucher .40 1.00
C12 Mikael Renberg .40 1.00
C13 Chris Simon .40 1.00
C14 Brent Gretzky .40 1.00
C15 Jesse Belanger .40 1.00
C16 Jocelyn Thibault .75 2.00
C17 Chris Osgood .40 1.00
C18 Derek Plante .40 1.00
C19 Iain Fraser .40 1.00
C20 Vesa Viitakoski .40 1.00

1993-94 Parkhurst Cherry's Playoff Heroes

Randomly inserted in Canadian second-series foil packs, these twenty different cards feature color player action shots on their fronts and a photo of Machiavellian TV personality Don Cherry -- who chose the players to be featured in this set based on his unique set of standards -- on the back. The cards are numbered with a "D" prefix.

COMPLETE SET (20) 20.00 40.00
D1 Wayne Gretzky 3.00 8.00
D2 Mario Lemieux 2.50 6.00
D3 Al MacInnis .40 1.00
D4 Mark Messier .60 1.50
D5 Dino Ciccarelli .40 1.00
D6 Dale Hunter .40 1.00
D7 Grant Fuhr .60 1.50
D8 Paul Coffey .60 1.50
D9 Doug Gilmour .50 1.25
D10 Patrick Roy 2.50 6.00
D11 Alexandre Daigle .40 1.00
D12 Chris Gratton .40 1.00
D13 Chris Pronger .50 1.25
D14 Felix Potvin .60 1.50
D15 Eric Lindros .60 1.50
D16 Maurice Richard 2.50 6.00
D17 Gordie Howe 2.00 5.00
D18 Henri Richard .50 1.25
D19 Reggie Leach .40 1.00
D20 Checklist 1.00 2.50
Don Cherry and Blue

1993-94 Parkhurst East/West Stars

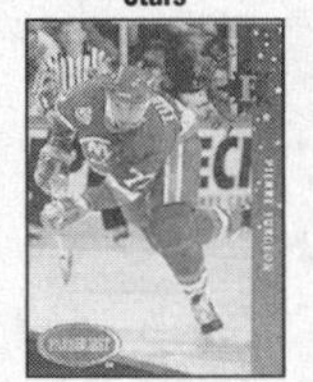

Randomly inserted in U.S. second-series hobby packs, these cards feature color player action shots on their fronts. The first ten cards feature Eastern Conference stars, numbered with an "E" prefix, while the last ten cards present Western Conference stars, numbered with a "W" prefix.

COMPLETE SET (20) 15.00 35.00
COMP.EAST SERIES (10) 6.00 15.00
COMP.WEST SERIES (10) 8.00 20.00
E1 Eric Lindros .60 1.50
E2 Mario Lemieux 2.50 6.00
E3 Alexandre Daigle .20 .50
E4 Patrick Roy 2.50 6.00
E5 Rob Niedermayer .30 .75
E6 Chris Gratton .30 .75
E7 Alexei Yashin .20 .50
E8 Pat LaFontaine .40 1.00
E9 Joe Sakic 1.00 2.50
E10 Pierre Turgeon .30 .75
W1 Wayne Gretzky 3.00 8.00
W2 Pavel Bure .60 1.50
W3 Teemu Selanne .60 1.50
W4 Doug Gilmour .30 .75
W5 Steve Yzerman 2.50 6.00
W6 Jeremy Roenick .60 1.50
W7 Brett Hull .60 1.50
W8 Jason Arnott .60 1.50
W9 Felix Potvin .60 1.50
W10 Sergei Fedorov .75 2.00

1993-94 Parkhurst First Overall

Randomly inserted in Canadian Series I retail foil packs, this ten-card set featured color action shots of players drafted first overall in the annual NHL Entry Draft over the past decade. The cards are numbered on the back with an "F" prefix.

COMPLETE SET (10) 8.00 20.00
F1 Alexandre Daigle .30 .75
F2 Roman Hamrlik .50 1.25
F3 Eric Lindros .75 2.00
F4 Owen Nolan .30 .75
F5 Mats Sundin .75 2.00
F6 Mike Modano 1.25 3.00
F7 Pierre Turgeon .50 1.25
F8 Joe Murphy .30 .75
F9 Wendel Clark .50 1.25
F10 Mario Lemieux 4.00 10.00

1993-94 Parkhurst Parkie Reprints

A continuation of the '92-93 Parkie Reprints set, these 40 (numbered 33-68, plus four checklists) cards measure the standard-size. The first ten cards (33-41, plus checklist (5) were randomly inserted in '93-94 Parkhurst series I foil packs. The second series (42-50, plus checklist (6) were random inserts in Parkhurst series one jumbo packs only. The third series (51-59, plus checklist (7) were random inserts in all series two Parkhurst packs. The fourth Parkie Reprints series (60-68, plus checklist (8) were random inserts in Parkhurst series two jumbo packs. The fronts are that of 1951-64 Parkhurst styles, but all carry a color player photo. The backs carry the information from the original card. The print varies from red to black to a combination. The cards are numbered on the back with a "PR" prefix. A hobby exclusive Parkie Reprints bonus pack was included in every series one and series two case.

COMPLETE SET (40)	25.00	60.00
PR33 Gordie Howe	2.50	6.00
PR34 Tim Horton	1.25	3.00
PR35 Bill Barilko	1.25	3.00
PR36 Elmer Lach Maurice Richard	1.50	4.00
PR37 Terry Sawchuk	1.50	4.00
PR38 George Armstrong	.75	2.00
PR39 William Harris	.75	2.00
PR40 Doug Harvey	.75	2.00
PR41 Gump Worsley	1.25	3.00
PR42 Gordie Howe	2.50	6.00
PR43 Jacques Plante	1.25	3.00
PR44 Frank Mahovlich	1.25	3.00
PR45 Fern Flaman	.75	2.00
PR46 Bernie Geoffrion	1.50	4.00
PR47 Toe Blake CO	.75	2.00
PR48 Maurice Richard	1.50	4.00
PR49 Ted Lindsay	.75	2.00
PR50 Camille Henry	.75	2.00
PR51 Gordie Howe	2.50	6.00
PR52 Jean-Guy Talbot	.75	2.00
PR53 Terry Sawchuk	1.50	4.00
PR54 Warren Godfrey	.75	2.00
PR55 Tom Johnson	.75	2.00
PR56 Bert Olmstead	.75	2.00
PR57 Cal Gardner	.75	2.00
PR58 Red Kelly	.75	2.00
PR59 Phil Goyette	.75	2.00
PR60 Gordie Howe	2.50	6.00
PR61 Lou Fontinato	.75	2.00
PR62 Bill Dineen	.75	2.00
PR63 Maurice Richard	1.25	3.00
PR64 Vic Stasiuk	.75	2.00
PR65 Marcel Pronovost	.75	2.00
PR66 Ed Litzenberger	.75	2.00
PR67 Dave Keon	1.25	3.00
PR68 Dollard St. Laurent	.75	2.00
CL5 Parkies Checklist 5	.40	1.00
CL6 Parkies Checklist 6	.40	1.00
CL7 Parkies Checklist 7	.40	1.00
CL8 Parkies Checklist 8	.40	1.00

1993-94 Parkhurst Parkie Reprints Case Inserts

These sets were inserted one per hobby case. Cards 1-6 were found in series I cases, while 7-12 were inserted in series II cases. Parkhurst selected vintage cards from its past to reprint in this 12-card standard-size set. The cards are coated on both sides and are easily recognizable as reprints. The cards are numbered on the back with the prefix "DPR".

COMPLETE SET (12)	25.00	60.00
COMP.SERIES 1 SET (6)	12.50	30.00
COMP.SERIES 2 SET (6)	12.50	30.00
1 Gordie Howe	6.00	15.00
2 Milt Schmidt	2.50	6.00
3 Tim Horton	3.00	8.00
4 Al Rollins	2.50	6.00
5 Maurice Richard	4.00	10.00
6 Harry Howell	2.50	6.00
7 Gordie Howe	6.00	15.00
8 Johnny Bower	4.00	10.00
9 Dean Prentice	2.50	6.00
10 Leo Labine	2.50	6.00
11 Harry Watson	3.00	8.00
12 Dickie Moore	3.00	8.00

1993-94 Parkhurst USA/Canada Gold

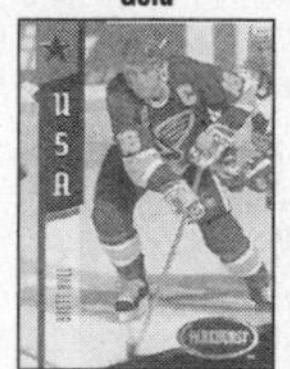

Randomly inserted at the rate of 1:30 U.S. Series I foil packs, this 10-card set depicted the 10 best NHL players form both the U.S. and Canada. Accordingly, cards 1-5 are USA Gold while cards 6-10 are Canadian Gold. The cards are numbered on the back with a "G" prefix.

COMPLETE SET (10)	10.00	25.00
G1 Wayne Gretzky	3.00	8.00
G2 Mario Lemieux	2.50	6.00
G3 Eric Lindros	.50	1.25
G4 Brett Hull	.60	1.50
G5 Rob Niedermayer	.30	.75
G6 Alexandre Daigle	.20	.50
G7 Pavel Bure	.50	1.25
G8 Teemu Selanne	.50	1.25
G9 Patrick Roy	2.50	6.00
G10 Doug Gilmour	.30	.75

1994 Parkhurst Missing Link

This 180-card set attempts to capture what a Parkhurst set might have looked like had one been produced for the 1956-57 NHL campaign. Although the inclusion of all six original teams may seem somewhat anachronistic (keeping in mind that Parkhurst, at that time, issued cards featuring Canadian-based players only) the set does capture the old-time flavor. The simple design includes an isolated player photo (taken during the 1955-56 season) over a cream colored background. A black bar runs along the left side of the card front, and contains the player name and team logo. Card backs include stats for the 1955-56 season and biographical information in both French and English. Subsets include All-Stars (135-146), Trophy Winners (147-152), Action Shots (153-168), Team Leaders (169-174) and Playoffs (175-178). The set was issued in 10-card wax packs and production was limited to 1956 numbered cases for each of the Canadian and American markets.

COMPLETE SET (180)	20.00	35.00
COMMON CARD (1-180)	.02	.10
CL (179/180)	.08	.25
STARS	.15	.40
HOF STARS	.20	.50
1 Jerry Toppazzini	.02	.10
2 Fern Flaman	.15	.40
3 Fleming MacKell	.02	.10
4 Leo Labine	.07	.20
5 John Peirson	.05	.15
6 Don McKenney	.05	.15
7 Bob Armstrong	.02	.10
8 Real Chevrefils	.02	.10
9 Vic Stasiuk	.05	.15
10 Cal Gardner	.02	.10
11 Leo Boivin	.15	.40
12 Jack Caffery	.02	.10
13 Bob Beckett RC	.02	.10
14 Jack Bionda	.02	.10
15 Claude Pronovost RC	.15	.40
16 Larry Regan	.02	.10
17 Terry Sawchuk	1.00	2.50
18 Doug Mohns	.07	.20
19 Marcel Bonin	.05	.15
20 Allan Stanley	.20	.50
21 Milt Schmidt CO	.20	.50
22 Al Dewsbury	.02	.10
23 Glen Skov	.05	.15
24 Ed Litzenberger	.05	.15
25 Nick Mickoski	.02	.10
26 Wally Hergesheimer	.02	.10
27 Jack McIntyre	.02	.10
28 Al Rollins	.20	.50
29 Hank Ciesla	.02	.10
30 Gus Mortson	.02	.10
31 Elmer Vasko	.05	.15
32 Pierre Pilote	.20	.50
33 Ron Ingram	.02	.10
34 Frank Martin	.02	.10
35 Forbes Kennedy	.07	.20
36 Harry Watson	.05	.15
37 Eddie Kachur RC	.05	.15
38 Hec Lalande	.02	.10
39 Eric Nesterenko	.07	.20
40 Ben Woit	.02	.10
41 Ken Mosdell	.05	.15
42 Tommy Ivan CO RC	.15	.40
43 Gordie Howe	1.50	4.00
44 Ted Lindsay	.20	.50
45 Norm Ullman	.20	.50
46 Glenn Hall	.40	1.00
47 Billy Dea	.02	.10
48 Bill McNeill	.02	.10
49 Earl Reibel	.02	.10
50 Bill Dineen	.07	.20
51 Warren Godfrey	.05	.15
52 Red Kelly	.20	.50
53 Marty Pavelich	.02	.10
54 Lorne Ferguson	.02	.10
55 Larry Hillman	.05	.15
56 John Bucyk	.20	.50
57 Metro Prystai	.02	.10
58 Marcel Pronovost	.20	.50
59 Alex Delvecchio	.20	.50
60 Murray Costello RC	.02	.10
61 Al Arbour	.20	.50
62 Bucky Hollingworth	.02	.10
63 Jim Skinner CO RC	.02	.10
64 Jean Beliveau	.75	2.00
65 Maurice Richard	1.00	2.50
66 Henri Richard	.20	.50
67 Doug Harvey	.20	.50
68 Bernie Geoffrion	.30	.75
69 Dollard St. Laurent	.08	.25
70 Dickie Moore	.20	.50
71 Bert Olmstead	.08	.25
72 Jacques Plante	1.00	2.50
73 Claude Provost	.15	.40
74 Phil Goyette	.05	.15
75 Andre Pronovost	.05	.15
76 Don Marshall	.08	.25
77 Ralph Backstrom	.07	.20
78 Floyd Curry	.07	.20
79 Tom Johnson	.20	.50
80 Jean Guy Talbot	.07	.20
81 Bob Turner	.02	.10
82 Connie Broden RC	.02	.10
83 Jackie Leclair	.02	.10
84 Toe Blake CO	.30	.75
85 Frank Selke MD	.20	.50
86 George Sullivan	.02	.10
87 Larry Cahan	.02	.10
88 Jean Guy Gendron	.02	.10
89 Bill Gadsby	.20	.50
90 Andy Bathgate	.20	.50
91 Dean Prentice	.02	.10
92 Gump Worsley	.40	1.00
93 Lou Fontinato	.05	.15
94 Gerry Foley	.02	.10
95 Larry Popein	.05	.15
96 Harry Howell	.20	.50
97 Andy Hebenton	.02	.10
98 Danny Lewicki	.02	.10
99 Dave Creighton	.02	.10
100 Camille Henry	.02	.10
101 Jack Evans	.02	.10
102 Ron Murphy	.02	.10
103 Johnny Bower	.30	.75
104 Parker MacDonald	.02	.10
105 Bronco Horvath	.07	.20
106 Bruce Cline RC	.02	.10
107 Ivan Irwin	.02	.10
108 Phil Watson CO	.02	.10
109 Sid Smith	.02	.10
110 Ron Stewart	.02	.10
111 Rudy Migay	.02	.10
112 Tod Sloan	.05	.15
113 Bob Pulford	.20	.50
114 Marc Reaume	.05	.15
115 Jim Morrison	.05	.15
116 Ted Kennedy	.20	.50
117 Gerry James	.07	.20
118 Brian Cullen	.08	.25
119 Jim Thomson	.02	.10
120 Barry Cullen	.02	.10
121 Al MacNeil	.05	.15
122 Gary Aldcorn	.02	.10
123 Bob Baun	.20	.50
124 Hugh Bolton	.02	.10
125 George Armstrong	.20	.50
126 Dick Duff	.20	.50
127 Tim Horton	.75	2.00
128 Ed Chadwick	.20	.50
129 Billy Harris	.15	.40
130 Mike Nykoluk	.02	.10
131 Noel Price	.02	.10
132 Ken Girard	.02	.10
133 Howie Meeker	.20	.50
134 Hap Day CO	.08	.25
135 Jacques Plante AS	.40	1.00
136 Doug Harvey AS	.20	.50
137 Bill Gadsby AS	.20	.50
138 Jean Beliveau AS	.30	.75
139 Maurice Richard AS	.40	1.00
140 Ted Lindsay AS	.15	.40
141 Glenn Hall AS	.20	.50
142 Red Kelly AS	.20	.50
143 Tom Johnson AS	.20	.50
144 Tod Sloan AS	.05	.15
145 Gordie Howe AS	.60	1.50
146 Bert Olmstead AS	.08	.25
147 Earl Reibel AW Lady Byng	.02	.10
148 Doug Harvey AW Norris	.20	.50
149 Jean Beliveau AW Hart	.30	.75
150 Jean Beliveau AW Art Ross	.30	.75
151 Jacques Plante AW Vezina	.40	1.00
152 Glenn Hall AW Calder	.20	.50
153 Terry Sawchuk IA	.40	1.00
154 Action Shot	.08	.25
155 Action Shot	.08	.25
156 Jean Beliveau IA	.30	.75
157 Jean Beliveau IA	.30	.75
158 Action Shot	.08	.25
159 Action Shot	.08	.25
160 Gordie Howe IA	.60	1.50
161 Jacques Plante IA	.40	1.00
162 Gordie Howe IA	.60	1.50
163 Jacques Plante IA	.40	1.00
164 Action Shot	.08	.25
165 Action Shot	.08	.25
166 Action Shot	.08	.25
167 Terry Sawchuk IA	.40	1.00
168 Terry Sawchuk IA	.40	1.00
169 Vic Stasiuk SL	.05	.15
170 George Sullivan SL	.05	.15
171 Gordie Howe SL	.60	1.50
172 Jean Beliveau SL	.30	.75
173 Andy Bathgate SL	.20	.50
174 Tod Sloan SL	.05	.15
175 Stanley Cup	.08	.25
176 Stanley Cup	.08	.25
177 Stanley Cup	.08	.25
178 Stanley Cup	.08	.25
179 Checklist 1	.02	.10
180 Checklist 2	.02	.10

1994 Parkhurst Missing Link Autographs

The 1994 Parkhurst Missing Link Autograph set is comprised of six Hall of Famers. Randomly inserted in Missing Link packs, the cards are autographed on the front and numbered "X of 956" on the back. The cards are also numbered for set purposes A1-A6. The design is different from those found in the Missing Link issue. Card fronts are color, but do not contain the player's name (except for autograph) or team name. The backs provide a congratulatory note to the collector.

1 Gordie Howe	75.00	150.00
2 Maurice Richard	100.00	200.00
3 Bernie Geoffrion	40.00	80.00
4 Gump Worsley	40.00	100.00
5 Jean Beliveau	75.00	150.00
6 Frank Mahovlich	25.00	60.00

1994 Parkhurst Missing Link Future Stars

The six cards in this set were randomly inserted in both US and Canadian product and featured well-known players who had yet to make their mark in the league by the 1956-57 season, the year which is represented in this set. Cards are numbered with an "FS" prefix.

COMPLETE SET (6)	30.00	70.00
RANDOM INSERTS IN PACKS		
FS1 Carl Brewer	3.00	8.00
FS2 Dave Keon	5.00	12.00
FS3 Stan Mikita	6.00	15.00
FS4 Eddie Shack	5.00	12.00
FS5 Frank Mahovlich	6.00	15.00
FS6 Charlie Hodge	5.00	12.00

1994 Parkhurst Missing Link Pop-Ups

These 12 die-cut cards were randomly inserted over two distribution channels: cards 1-6 in Canadian cases and 7-12 in American product. The cards feature the heroes of hockey's past in a design which approximates the style made famous by the 1936-37 O-Pee-Chee V304D set. The cards are created in such a way that they may be popped open for a 3-D effect; collectors are strongly urged not to follow this course of action unless you're not concerned about the card's value. Card backs contain brief personal information, as well as a wrap-up of career statistics. The cards are numbered with a P prefix in the top left corner. Only 1,000 of each card were circulated.

COMPLETE SET (12)	200.00	350.00
RANDOM INSERTS IN US PACKS		
P1 Howie Morenz	20.00	50.00
P2 George Hainsworth	12.00	30.00
P3 Georges Vezina	20.00	50.00
P4 King Clancy	15.00	40.00
P5 Syl Apps	12.00	30.00
P6 Turk Broda	12.00	30.00
P7 Eddie Shore	25.00	50.00
P8 Bill Cook	10.00	25.00
P9 Woody Dumart	10.00	25.00
P10 Lester Patrick	12.00	30.00
P11 Doug Bentley	10.00	25.00
P12 Earl Seibert	10.00	25.00

1994 Parkhurst Tall Boys

This 180-card set recreates what might have been had the Parkhurst company issued a set of NHL player cards for the 1964-65 season. As the title suggests, the card size matches that of the 1964-65 Topps Tall Boys set (2 1/2" by 4 11/16"). Announced production was 1,964 cases for each of the US and Canadian hobby markets.

COMPLETE SET (180)	10.00	12.00
1 John Bucyk	.15	.40
2 Murray Oliver	.02	.10
3 Ted Green	.05	.15
4 Tom Williams	.02	.10
5 Dean Prentice	.02	.10
6 Ed Westfall	.02	.10
7 Orland Kurtenbach	.02	.10
8 Reg Fleming	.02	.10
9 Leo Boivin	.05	.15
10 Bob McCord	.02	.10
11 Bob Leiter	.02	.10
12 Tom Johnson	.08	.25
13 Bob Woytowich	.02	.10
14 Ab McDonald	.02	.10
15 Ed Johnston	.08	.25
16 Forbes Kennedy	.05	.15
17 Murray Balfour	.02	.10
18 Wayne Cashman	.05	.15
19 Don Awrey	.02	.10
20 Gary Dornhoofer	.05	.15
21 Ron Schock	.02	.10
22 Milt Schmidt	.20	.50
23 Ken Wharram	.05	.15
24 Chico Maki	.02	.10
25 Bobby Hull	.75	2.00
26 Stan Mikita	.30	.75
27 Doug Mohns	.05	.15
28 Denis DeJordy	.07	.20
29 Phil Esposito	.20	.50
30 Elmer Vasko	.02	.10
31 Pierre Pilote	.08	.25
32 Glenn Hall	.30	.75
33 Eric Nesterenko	.02	.10
34 Doug Robinson	.02	.10
35 Matt Ravlich	.02	.10
36 John McKenzie	.05	.15
37 Fred Stanfield	.02	.10
38 Doug Jarrett	.02	.10
39 Dennis Hull	.07	.20
40 Al MacNeil	.02	.10
41 Wayne Hillman	.02	.10
42 Bill Hay	.02	.10
43 Billy Reay	.02	.10
44 Parker MacDonald	.02	.10
45 Floyd Smith	.02	.10
46 Gordie Howe	1.00	2.50
47 Bruce MacGregor	.02	.10
48 Ron Murphy	.02	.10
49 Doug Barkley	.02	.10
50 Paul Henderson	.05	.15
51 Pit Martin	.05	.15
52 Al Langlois	.02	.10
53 Roger Crozier	.08	.25
54 Bill Gadsby	.08	.25
55 Marcel Pronovost	.15	.40
56 Alex Delvecchio	.15	.40
57 Gary Bergman	.02	.10
58 Norm Ullman	.15	.40
59 Larry Jeffrey	.02	.10
60 Lowell MacDonald	.02	.10
61 Pete Goegan	.02	.10
62 Andre Pronovost	.05	.15
63 Warren Godfrey	.02	.10
64 Ted Lindsay	.15	.40
65 Sid Abel	.15	.40
66 John Ferguson	.05	.15
67 Henri Richard	.20	.50
68 Dave Balon	.02	.10
69 Noel Picard	.02	.10
70 Claude Provost	.05	.15
71 Claude Larose	.02	.10
72 Jacques Laperriere	.08	.25
73 Ralph Backstrom	.05	.15
74 J.C. Tremblay	.05	.15
75 Yvan Cournoyer	.15	.40
76 Jean-Guy Talbot	.05	.15
77 Gilles Tremblay	.02	.10
78 Ted Harris	.02	.10
79 Jim Roberts	.02	.10
80 Red Berenson	.05	.15
81 Gump Worsley	.30	.75
82 Charlie Hodge	.08	.25
83 Terry Harper	.02	.10
84 Bobby Rousseau	.02	.10
85 Jean Beliveau	.60	1.50
86 Bill Hicke	.02	.10
87 Toe Blake	.20	.50
88 Don Marshall	.05	.15
89 Jean Ratelle	.15	.40
90 Vic Hadfield	.02	.10
91 Earl Ingarfield	.02	.10
92 Harry Howell	.15	.40
93 Rod Seiling	.02	.10
94 Dave Richardson	.02	.10
95 Val Fonteyne	.02	.10
96 Lou Angotti	.02	.10
97 Arnie Brown	.02	.10
98 Don Johns	.02	.10
99 Jim Mikol	.02	.10
100 Jacques Plante	.75	2.00
101 Marcel Paille	.05	.15
102 Jim Neilson	.02	.10
103 Bob Nevin	.02	.10
104 Rod Gilbert	.15	.40
105 Phil Goyette	.02	.10
106 Dick Duff	.08	.25
107 Camille Henry	.02	.10
108 Red Sullivan	.02	.10
109 Kent Douglas	.02	.10
110 Bob Pulford	.05	.15
111 Dave Keon	.20	.50
112 Don McKenney	.02	.10
113 Pete Stemkowski	.02	.10
114 Carl Brewer	.05	.15
115 Allan Stanley	.08	.25
116 Dickie Moore	.15	.40
117 Ed Shack	.20	.50
118 Larry Hillman	.02	.10
119 Terry Sawchuk	.75	2.00
120 Bob Baun	.08	.25
121 Brit Selby	.02	.10
122 George Armstrong	.20	.50
123 Jim Pappin	.02	.10
124 Andy Bathgate	.15	.40
125 Ron Ellis	.02	.10
126 Billy Harris	.02	.10
127 Red Kelly	.07	.20
128 Ron Stewart	.02	.10
129 Johnny Bower	.20	.50
130 Frank Mahovlich	.20	.50
131 Tim Horton	.60	1.50
132 King Clancy	.15	.40
133 Glenn Hall AS	.20	.50
134 Pierre Pilote AS	.08	.25
135 Tim Horton AS	.30	.75
136 Bobby Hull AS	.40	1.00
137 Ken Wharram AS	.05	.15
138 Stan Mikita AS	.20	.50
139 Charlie Hodge AS	.05	.15
140 Jacques Laperriere AS	.05	.15
141 Elmer Vasko AS	.02	.10
142 Jean Beliveau AS	.30	.75
143 Frank Mahovlich AS	.15	.40
144 Gordie Howe AS	.60	1.50
145 Pierre Pilote	.08	.25
146 Jean Beliveau	.30	.75
147 Stan Mikita	.15	.40
148 Charlie Hodge	.08	.25
149 Jacques Laperriere	.08	.25
150 Ken Wharram	.05	.15
151 1964 All Star Game	.05	.15
152 Ratelle Invades Crease	.08	.25
153 Center Ice Action	.05	.15
154 Old Teammates Duel	.60	1.50
155 All Eyes on the Puck	.05	.15
156 Detroit Defense Stands Tall	.40	1.00
157 Crozier Makes The Stretch	.05	.15
158 Crozier Plays Center Field	.08	.25
159 Hawks Eye Beliveau	.30	.75
160 Montreal's Speedy Rookie	.05	.15
161 Laperriere Wins Race	.05	.15
162 Ellis Robbed by Habs	.05	.15
163 Sawchuk Eyes Bouncing Disc	.40	1.00
164 Shack Entertains	.15	.40
165 ~Mr. Goalie~ In Action	.20	.50
166 Hall Holds His Ground	.15	.40
167 Johnston Freezes Action	.05	.15
168 Ellis Robbed By Johnston	.05	.15
169 Murray Oliver LL	.02	.10
170 Stan Mikita LL	.20	.50
171 Gordie Howe LL	.60	1.50
172 Jean Beliveau LL	.30	.75
173 Phil Goyette LL	.02	.10
174 Andy Bathgate LL	.08	.25
175 Stanley Cup Semi-Finals	.02	.10
176 Stanley Cup Semi-Finals	.02	.10
177 Stanley Cup Finals	.60	1.50
178 Stanley Cup	.08	.25
179 Checklist 1	.02	.10
180 Checklist 2	.02	.10

1994 Parkhurst Tall Boys Autographs

This 6-card set was randomly inserted throughout the production run of 1994 Parkhurst Tall Boys. The player's autograph appears in a white, oblong box along the bottom. A congratulatory note appears on the back. The cards are serially numbered out of 964 on the back.

COMPLETE SET (6)	350.00	500.00
A1 Rod Gilbert	25.00	50.00
A2 Yvan Cournoyer	40.00	60.00
A3 Bobby Hull	40.00	100.00
A4 Phil Esposito	60.00	100.00
A5 Gordie Howe	75.00	150.00
A6 Dave Keon	50.00	80.00

1994 Parkhurst Tall Boys Future Stars

The six cards in this set were randomly inserted in both US and Canadian product and featured well-known players who had yet to make their mark in the league by the 1964-65 season, the year which is represented in this set. Card backs include 1963-64 amateur stats, a report on the player's prospects in both French and English, and a merchandise offer. Cards are numbered with an "FS" prefix.

COMPLETE SET (6)	40.00	80.00
FS1 Jacques Lemaire	7.50	15.00
FS2 Gerry Cheevers	12.00	25.00
FS3 Ken Hodge	4.00	10.00
FS4 Bernie Parent	6.00	15.00
FS5 Rogatien Vachon	7.50	15.00
FS6 Derek Sanderson	10.00	20.00

1994 Parkhurst Tall Boys Greats

The 12 cards in this set were split over two distribution channels: cards 1-6 were randomly inserted in Canadian wax, while 7-12 were inserted in American. The cards feature legendary greats from the game's past. These oddly designed cards were the same size as the regular Tall Boys if maintained intact. A large, beige border surrounded the "real card", which approximates the appearance and size of the smaller 1951-52 Parkhurst issue. Although the cards are scored so that they may be punched out from the larger background, collectors are strongly advised against doing this. Card backs are blank. 1,000 copies of each of these cards were circulated.

COMPLETE SET (12)	175.00	250.00
1 Ace Bailey	15.00	30.00
2 Alex Levinsky	6.00	15.00
3 Babe Pratt	6.00	15.00
4 Elmer Lach	6.00	15.00
5 Maurice Richard	25.00	40.00
6 Bill Durnan	15.00	30.00
7 Frank Brimsek	15.00	30.00
8 Dit Clapper	8.00	20.00
9 Tiny Thompson	15.00	30.00
10 Bun Cook	6.00	15.00
11 Ching Johnson	8.00	20.00
12 Lionel Conacher	15.00	30.00

1994 Parkhurst Tall Boys Mail-Ins

Available through a mail-in offer, the cards in these three six-card sets measure 2 1/2" by 4 3/4". To obtain one of the sets, the collector sent in 10 "Tall Boy" wrappers and a check or money order for 12.95. The fronts feature color action cutouts on team color-coded backgrounds. The information on the beige backs varies depending on the particular series. At the bottom, each card carries its serial number out of a total of 1,964. The cards are arranged below as follows: All-Stars, Scoring Leaders, and Trophy Winners.

COMPLETE SET (18)	20.00	50.00
AS1 Roger Crozier	1.00	2.50
AS2 Pierre Pilote	.75	2.00
AS3 Jacques Laperriere	.75	2.00
AS4 Norm Ullman	1.00	2.50
AS5 Bobby Hull	4.00	10.00
AS6 Claude Provost	.40	1.00
SL1 John Bucyk	1.00	2.50
SL2 Stan Mikita	1.50	4.00
SL3 Norm Ullman	1.00	2.50
SL4 Claude Provost	.40	1.00
SL5 Rod Gilbert	1.00	2.50
SL6 Frank Mahovlich	1.50	4.00
TW1 Pierre Pilote	.75	2.00
TW2 Bobby Hull	4.00	10.00
TW3 Stan Mikita	1.50	4.00
TW4 Terry Sawchuk Johnny Bower	3.00	8.00
TW5 Roger Crozier	1.00	2.50
TW6 Bobby Hull	4.00	10.00

1994-95 Parkhurst

This 315-card set was issued in one series. Due to the NHL lockout, series two was not released; therefore, this set does not have a comprehensive player selection. Ten card packs retailed for 99 cents in 36 pack boxes. Sixteen-card jumbo packs also were produced. The design features a nearly full-bleed front, broken only in the lower right corner where a small gray bar features a silver foil hockey player icon. The green Parkhurst logo appears in an upper corner with player name running down either side. Card backs are unique in that they have full career stats and a player photo. Subsets included Rookie Standouts (270-294) and Parkie's Best (295-315). This set is noteworthy for being the last product domestically released by Upper Deck using the Parkhurst name. Although no second series was domestically released, a European-only product - Parkhurst SE - appears to have been the remnants of that planned issue. Prices for that set appear elsewhere.

COMPLETE SET (315)	6.00	15.00
1 Anatoli Semenov	.01	.05
2 Stephan Lebeau	.01	.05
3 Stu Grimson	.01	.05
4 Mikhail Shtalenkov RC	.01	.05
5 Troy Loney	.01	.05
6 Sean Hill UER ('92-93 points total is 54 instead of 8 and career total is 81 instead of 35)	.01	.05
7 Patrik Carnback	.01	.05
8 John Lilley	.01	.05
9 Tim Sweeney	.01	.05
10 Maxim Bets	.01	.05
11 Cam Neely	.07	.20
12 Bryan Smolinski	.01	.05
13 Ray Bourque	.10	.30
14 Vincent Riendeau	.02	.10
15 Al Iafrate	.01	.05
16 Andrew McKim RC	.01	.05
17 Glen Wesley	.01	.05
18 Daniel Marois	.01	.05
19 Jozef Stumpel	.01	.05
20 Mariusz Czerkawski RC	.07	.20
21 Alexander Mogilny	.02	.10
22 Yuri Khmylev	.01	.05
23 Donald Audette	.01	.05
24 Dominik Hasek	.20	.50
25 Randy Wood	.01	.05
26 Brad May	.01	.05
27 Wayne Presley	.01	.05
28 Richard Smehlik	.01	.05
29 Dale Hawerchuk	.02	.10
30 Rob Ray	.01	.05
31 Zarley Zalapski	.01	.05
32 Michael Nylander	.01	.05
33 Joe Nieuwendyk	.02	.10
34 Robert Reichel	.01	.05
35 Al MacInnis	.02	.10
36 Andrei Trefilov	.01	.05
37 Guy Larose	.01	.05
38 Wes Walz	.01	.05
39 Michel Petit	.01	.05
40 James Patrick	.01	.05
41 Ed Belfour	.07	.20
42 Christian Ruuttu	.01	.05
43 Eric Weinrich	.01	.05
44 Joe Murphy	.01	.05
45 Chris Chelios	.07	.20
46 Jeff Shantz	.01	.05
47 Gary Suter	.01	.05
48 Paul Ysebaert	.01	.05
49 Ivan Droppa	.01	.05
50 Keith Carney	.01	.05
51 Andy Moog	.07	.20
52 Russ Courtnall	.01	.05
53 Neal Broten	.02	.10
54 Mike Craig	.01	.05
55 Brent Gilchrist	.01	.05
56 Pelle Eklund	.01	.05
57 Richard Matvichuk	.01	.05
58 Dave Gagner	.02	.10
59 Mark Tinordi	.01	.05
60 Paul Broten	.01	.05
61 Nicklas Lidstrom	.07	.20
62 Shawn Burr	.01	.05
63 Paul Coffey	.07	.20
64 Bob Essensa	.02	.10
65 Dino Ciccarelli	.02	.10
66 Slava Kozlov	.02	.10
67 Keith Primeau	.01	.05
68 Steve Chiasson	.01	.05
69 Terry Carkner	.01	.05
70 Martin Lapointe	.01	.05
71 Bob Probert	.02	.10
72 Bill Ranford	.02	.10
73 Scott Thornton	.01	.05
74 Doug Weight	.02	.10
75 Shayne Corson	.01	.05
76 Zdeno Ciger	.01	.05
77 Adam Bennett	.01	.05
78 Scott Pearson	.01	.05
79 Brent Grieve RC	.01	.05
80 Gordon Mark RC	.01	.05
81 Shjon Podein	.01	.05
82 Geoff Smith	.01	.05
83 Bob Kudelski	.01	.05
84 Andrei Lomakin	.01	.05
85 Scott Mellanby	.02	.10
86 Jesse Belanger	.01	.05
87 Mark Fitzpatrick	.02	.10
88 Peter Andersson	.01	.05
89 Jody Hull	.01	.05
90 Brent Severyn	.01	.05
91 Jim Sandlak	.01	.05
92 Pat Verbeek	.01	.05
93 Ted Crowley	.01	.05
94 Robert Petrovicky	.01	.05
95 Geoff Sanderson	.02	.10
96 Ted Drury	.01	.05
97 Andrew Cassels	.01	.05
98 Igor Chibirev	.01	.05
99 Kevin Smyth	.01	.05
100 Alexander Godynyuk	.01	.05
101 Alexei Zhitnik	.01	.05
102 Dixon Ward	.01	.05
103 Wayne Gretzky	.60	1.50
104 Jari Kurri	.02	.10
105 Rob Blake	.02	.10
106 Marty McSorley	.01	.05
107 Pat Conacher	.01	.05
108 Kevin Todd	.01	.05
109 Robb Stauber	.02	.10
110 Keith Redmond	.01	.05
111 John LeClair	.07	.20
112 Brian Bellows	.01	.05
113 Patrick Roy	.40	1.00
114 Les Kuntar RC	.01	.05
115 Vincent Damphousse	.01	.05
116 Patrice Brisebois	.01	.05
117 Pierre Sevigny	.01	.05
118 Eric Desjardins	.02	.10
119 Oleg Petrov	.01	.05
120 Kevin Haller	.01	.05
121 Christian Proulx RC	.01	.05
122 Corey Millen	.01	.05
123 Jaroslav Modry	.01	.05
124 Valeri Zelepukin	.01	.05
125 John MacLean	.02	.10
126 Martin Brodeur	.20	.50
127 Bill Guerin	.02	.10
128 Bobby Holik	.01	.05
129 Claude Lemieux	.01	.05
130 Jason Smith	.01	.05
131 Ken Daneyko	.01	.05
132 Derek King	.01	.05

133 Darius Kasparaitis .01 .05
134 Ray Ferraro .01 .05
135 Pierre Turgeon .02 .10
136 Ron Hextall .02 .10
137 Travis Green .02 .10
138 Joe Day .01 .05
139 David Volek .01 .05
140 Scott Lachance .01 .05
141 Dennis Vaske .01 .05
142 Alexei Kovalev .01 .05
143 Brian Noonan .01 .05
144 Sergei Zubov .01 .05
145 Craig MacTavish .01 .05
146 Steve Larmer .02 .10
147 Adam Graves .01 .05
148 Jeff Beukeboom .01 .05
149 Corey Hirsch .02 .10
150 Stephane Matteau .01 .05
151 Brian Leetch .07 .20
152 Mattias Norstrom .02 .10
153 Sylvain Turgeon .01 .05
154 Norm Maciver .01 .05
155 Scott Levins .01 .05
156 Derek Mayer .01 .05
157 Dave McLlwain .01 .05
158 Craig Billington .02 .10
159 Claude Boivin .01 .05
160 Troy Mallette .01 .05
161 Evgeny Davydov .01 .05
162 Dmitri Filimonov .01 .05
163 Dimitri Yushkevich .01 .05
164 Rob Zettler .01 .05
165 Mark Recchi .02 .10
166 Josef Beranek .01 .05
167 Rod Brind'Amour .02 .10
168 Yves Racine .01 .05
169 Dominic Roussel .02 .10
170 Brent Fedyk .01 .05
171 Bob Wilkie RC .01 .05
172 Kevin Dineen .01 .05
173 Shawn McEachern .01 .05
174 Jaromir Jagr .10 .30
175 Tomas Sandstrom .01 .05
176 Ron Francis .02 .10
177 Kevin Stevens .01 .05
178 Jim McKenzie .01 .05
179 Larry Murphy .02 .10
180 Joe Mullen .02 .10
181 Greg Hawgood .01 .05
182 Tom Barrasso .02 .10
183 Ulf Samuelsson .01 .05
184 Bob Bassen .01 .05
185 Mats Sundin .07 .20
186 Mike Ricci .01 .05
187 Iain Fraser .01 .05
188 Garth Butcher .01 .05
189 Jocelyn Thibault .07 .20
190 Valeri Kamensky .02 .10
191 Martin Rucinsky .01 .05
192 Ron Sutter .01 .05
193 Rene Corbet .01 .05
194 Reggie Savage .01 .05
195 Alexei Kasatonov .01 .05
196 Brendan Shanahan .07 .20
197 Phil Housley .02 .10
198 Jim Montgomery .01 .05
199 Curtis Joseph .07 .20
200 Craig Janney .02 .10
201 David Roberts .01 .05
202 Dave Mackey .01 .05
203 Peter Stastny .02 .10
204 Terry Hollinger RC .01 .05
205 Steve Duchesne .01 .05
206 Vitali Prokhorov .01 .05
207 Rob Gaudreau .01 .05
208 Sandis Ozolinsh .01 .05
209 Johan Garpenlov .01 .05
210 Todd Elik .01 .05
211 Sergei Makarov .01 .05
212 Jean-Francois Quintin .01 .05
213 Vyacheslav Butsayev .01 .05
214 Jimmy Waite .02 .10
215 Ulf Dahlen .01 .05
216 Andrei Nazarov .01 .05
217 Denis Savard .02 .10
218 Brent Gretzky .01 .05
219 Petr Klima .01 .05
220 Chris Gratton .01 .05
221 Brian Bradley .01 .05
222 Adam Creighton .01 .05
223 Shawn Chambers .01 .05
224 Rob Zamuner .01 .05
225 Daren Puppa .02 .10
226 Mikael Andersson .01 .05
227 Dave Ellett .01 .05
228 Mike Gartner .02 .10
229 Felix Potvin .07 .20
230 Yanic Perreault .01 .05
231 Nikolai Borschevsky .01 .05
232 Dmitri Mironov .01 .05
233 Todd Gill .01 .05
234 Eric Lacroix RC .01 .05
235 Kent Manderville .01 .05
236 Chris Govedaris .01 .05
237 Frank Bialowas RC .01 .05
238 Kirk McLean .02 .10
239 Jimmy Carson .01 .05
240 Geoff Courtnall .01 .05
241 Trevor Linden .02 .10
242 Murray Craven .01 .05
243 Bret Hedican .01 .05
244 Jeff Brown .01 .05
245 Mike Peca .01 .05
246 Yevgeny Namestnikov .01 .05
247 Nathan Lafayette .01 .05
248 Shawn Antoski .01 .05
249 Sergio Momesso .01 .05
250 Mike Ridley .01 .05
251 Peter Bondra .02 .10
252 Dimitri Khristich .01 .05
253 Dave Poulin .01 .05
254 Dale Hunter .01 .05
255 Rick Tabaracci .02 .10
256 Kelly Miller .01 .05
257 John Slaney .01 .05
258 Todd Krygier .01 .05
259 Kevin Hatcher .01 .05
260 Alexei Zhamnov .02 .10
261 Dallas Drake .01 .05
262 Dave Manson .01 .05
263 Thomas Steen .01 .05
264 Keith Tkachuk .07 .20
265 Russ Romaniuk .01 .05
266 Michal Grosek RC .01 .05
267 Nelson Emerson .01 .05
268 Michael O'Neill RC .01 .05
269 Kris King .01 .05
270 Teppo Numminen .01 .05
271 Jason Arnott .01 .05
272 Mikael Renberg .02 .10
273 Alexei Yashin .01 .05
274 Chris Pronger .02 .10
275 Jocelyn Thibault .07 .20
276 Bryan Smolinski .01 .05
277 Derek Plante .01 .05
278 Martin Brodeur RS .07 .20
279 Jim Dowd .01 .05
280 Iain Fraser .01 .05
281 Pat Peake .01 .05
282 Chris Gratton .01 .05
283 Chris Osgood .02 .10
284 Jesse Belanger .01 .05
285 Alexandre Daigle .01 .05
286 Robert Lang .01 .05
287 Markus Naslund .07 .20
288 Trevor Kidd .02 .10
289 Jeff Shantz .01 .05
290 Jaroslav Modry .01 .05
291 Oleg Petrov .01 .05
292 Scott Levins .01 .05
293 Jozef Stumpel .01 .05
294 Rob Niedermayer .02 .10
295 Brent Gretzky .01 .05
296 Mario Lemieux PB .30 .75
297 Pavel Bure .07 .20
298 Brendan Shanahan .07 .20
299 Steve Yzerman .07 .20
300 Teemu Selanne .07 .20
301 Eric Lindros .07 .20
302 Jeremy Roenick .07 .20
303 Dave Andreychuk .02 .10
304 Ray Bourque .07 .20
305 Sergei Fedorov .07 .20
306 Wayne Gretzky .40 1.00
307 Adam Graves .01 .05
308 Mike Modano PB .15 .40
309 Brett Hull .07 .20
310 Pat LaFontaine .02 .10
311 Adam Oates .02 .10
312 Patrick Roy .30 .75
313 Doug Gilmour .02 .10
314 Jaromir Jagr .07 .20
315 Mark Recchi .02 .10

1994-95 Parkhurst Gold

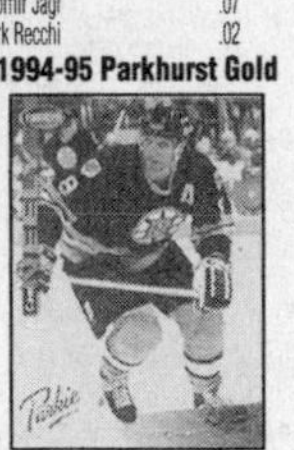

The 315 cards in this parallel version of the '94-95 Parkhurst set were issued 1:47 packs. A gold foil hockey player icon and the addition of the word "Parkie", written in gold foil distinguish this set from the regular Parkhurst set. The Rookie Standout and Parkie's Best subset gold cards were made available for the European marketplace by means other than normal pack distribution, and a sufficient amount of product made its way back into the North American marketplace. With the hockey card market not having absorbed the saturation, multipliers for these subset cards are lower than other cards from this set.

*VETS: 20X TO 50X BASIC CARDS
*ROOKIES: 8X TO 20X BASIC CARDS

1994-95 Parkhurst Crash the Game Green

The 28 cards in this set were randomly inserted into Parkhurst product at a rate of 1:23 packs. There were three variations of each card in this set. Each of the three foil logo colors reflected the different distribution method. Red foil indicated Canadian packaging, blue foil U.S. retail and green foil U.S. hobby. The cards were numbered on the back with a corresponding prefix of C, R, or H. Since the cards were created to be used as an interactive game, the backs contain the rules in extremely fine-print legalese in both English and French, as well as two game dates. If the team featured on the front won on one or both of those dates, the card could be redeemed for a specially foiled set. Unfortunately, the NHL lockout of 1994 prevented the games from being played. As a result, Upper Deck declared all cards winners, enabling each to be redeemed for a 28-card gold-foil version of the set by mail. The expiration date for the exchange was June 30th, 1995.

COMPLETE SET (28) 20.00 40.00
*GOLD: .2X TO .5X GREEN
*BLUE: .4X TO 1X GREEN
*RED: .4X TO 1X GREEN
H1 Stephan Lebeau .25 .60
H2 Ray Bourque .60 1.50
H3 Pat LaFontaine .40 1.00
H4 Joe Nieuwendyk .30 .75
H5 Jeremy Roenick .40 1.00
H6 Mike Modano .50 1.25
H7 Sergei Fedorov .75 2.00
H8 Jason Arnott .30 .75
H9 John Vanbiesbrouck .40 1.00
H10 Geoff Sanderson .25 .60
H11 Wayne Gretzky 2.50 6.00
H12 Patrick Roy 2.00 5.00
H13 Scott Stevens .30 .75
H14 Pierre Turgeon .30 .75
H15 Adam Graves .30 .75
H16 Alexei Yashin .30 .75
H17 Eric Lindros .75 2.00
H18 Mario Lemieux 2.00 5.00
H19 Joe Sakic .75 2.00
H20 Brett Hull .50 1.25
H21 Sandis Ozolinsh .30 .75
H22 Chris Terreri .25 .60
H23 Doug Gilmour .40 1.00
H24 Pavel Bure 1.00 2.50
H25 Joe Juneau .30 .75
H26 Teemu Selanne .40 1.00
H27 Mark Messier 1.25 3.00
Eastern Conference
H28 Wayne Gretzky 4.00 10.00
Western Conference

1994-95 Parkhurst Vintage

The 90 cards in this set were included one per Parkhurst pack and two per jumbo pack. They are printed on heavy white card stock with a design that hearkens back to the style of Parkhurst issues of the '50s and '60s. The player photo is cut out and placed on a white and tan background. The player's name appears in a black bar on the lower portion of the card, alongside the set logo. The card backs are an unfinished cardboard and feature professional statistics, biography and a "Did You Know" section containing interesting trivia. This trivia did not apply to the player pictured. The cards were numbered with a "V" prefix.

COMPLETE SET (90) 15.00 30.00
V1 Dominik Hasek .60 1.50
V2 Mike Modano .40 1.00
V3 Shayne Corson .05 .15
V4 Kirk Muller .05 .15
V5 Mike Richter .20 .50
V6 Mario Lemieux 1.50 4.00
V7 Sandis Ozolinsh .05 .15
V8 Dave Ellett .05 .15
V9 Dave Manson .05 .15
V10 Terry Yake .05 .15
V11 Craig Simpson .05 .15
V12 Paul Cavallini .05 .15
V13 John Vanbiesbrouck .08 .25
V14 Gilbert Dionne .05 .15
V15 Brian Leetch .20 .50
V16 Martin Straka .05 .15
V17 Curtis Joseph .20 .50
V18 Pavel Bure .30 .75
V19 Garry Valk .05 .15
V20 Theo Fleury .08 .25
V21 Brent Gilchrist .05 .15
V22 Rob Niedermayer .05 .15
V23 Vincent Damphousse .05 .15
V24 Alexei Kovalev .05 .15
V25 Rick Tocchet .05 .15
V26 Steve Duchesne .05 .15
V27 Jiri Slegr .05 .15
V28 Patrick Carnback .05 .15
V29 Gary Roberts .05 .15
V30 Derian Hatcher .05 .15
V31 Jesse Belanger .05 .15
V32 Mathieu Schneider .05 .15
V33 Mark Messier .30 .75
V34 Joe Sakic .75 2.00
V35 Brett Hull .30 .75
V36 Martin Gelinas .05 .15
V37 Maxim Bets .05 .15
V38 Joel Otto .05 .15
V39 Sergei Fedorov .30 .75
V40 Chris Pronger .20 .50
V41 Scott Stevens .08 .25
V42 Alexandre Daigle .05 .15
V43 Owen Nolan .08 .25
V44 Nelson Emerson .05 .15
V45 Jeff Brown .05 .15
V46 Adam Oates .08 .25
V47 Robert Reichel .05 .15
V48 Slava Kozlov .08 .25
V49 Geoff Sanderson .05 .15
V50 Stephane Richer .05 .15
V51 Sylvain Turgeon .05 .15
V52 Mike Ricci .08 .25
V53 Roman Hamrlik .05 .15
V54 Kevin Hatcher .05 .15
V55 Mariusz Czerkawski .05 .15
V56 Tony Amonte .08 .25
V57 Steve Yzerman 1.25 3.00
V58 Andrew Cassels .05 .15
V59 Claude Lemieux .05 .15
V60 Derek Mayer .05 .15
V61 Jocelyn Thibault .08 .25
V62 Brent Gretzky .05 .15
V63 Pat Peake .05 .15
V64 Cam Neely .30 .75
V65 Jeremy Roenick .30 .75
V66 Keith Primeau .05 .15
V67 Luc Robitaille .08 .25
V68 Steve Thomas .05 .15
V69 Eric Lindros .30 .75
V70 Pat Falloon .05 .15
V71 Brian Bradley .05 .15
V72 Kelly Miller .05 .15
V73 Pat LaFontaine .20 .50
V74 Gary Suter .05 .15
V75 Bill Ranford .08 .25
V76 Tony Granato .05 .15
V77 Vladimir Malakhov .05 .15
V78 Mikael Renberg .08 .25
V79 Arturs Irbe .08 .25
V80 Doug Gilmour .08 .25
V81 Teemu Selanne .30 .75
V82 Dale Hawerchuk .05 .15
V83 Eric Weinrich .05 .15
V84 Valeri Bure .05 .15
V85 Rob Blake .08 .25
V86 Ray Ferraro .05 .15
V87 Garry Galley .05 .15
V88 Igor Larionov .05 .15
V89 Dave Andreychuk .05 .15
V90 Dallas Drake .05 .15

1994-95 Parkhurst SE

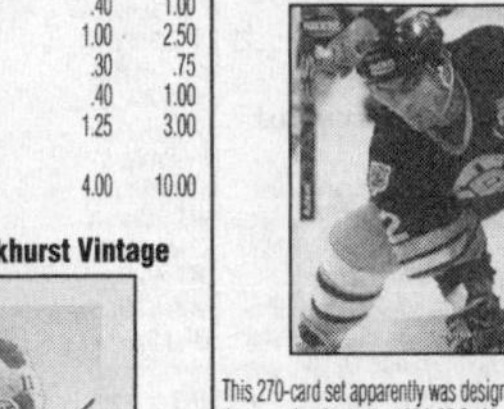

This 270-card set apparently was designed to serve as the second series to the 1994-95 Parkhurst product. In the wake of the NHL lockout of that year, licensing regulations were relaxed, and Upper Deck chose to release the SP line instead. This product subsequently was issued in eleven European countries. However, large quantities eventually made their way to North America. The basic cards have the same design as Parkhurst. Although essentially a companion issue to Parkhurst, this set is numbered from 1-270, with an SE prefix. Subsets include World Junior Championships (206-250) and CAHA Program of Excellence (251-270). Although this set contains the first year cards of many players, they are not recognized as Rookie Cards because of the European-only distribution. A 4" X 6" blowup version of 1994-95 Upper Deck #226, which commemorates Wayne Gretzky's 802 career goals, is inserted at the top of each box.

COMPLETE SET (270) 15.00 30.00
SE1 Guy Hebert .05 .15
SE2 Bob Corkum .02 .10
SE3 Randy Ladouceur .02 .10
SE4 Tom Kurvers .02 .10
SE5 Joe Sacco .02 .10
SE6 Valeri Karpov .02 .10
SE7 Garry Valk .02 .10
SE8 Paul Kariya .10 .30
SE9 Alexei Kasatonov .02 .10
SE10 Sergei Zholtok .02 .10
SE11 Glen Murray .02 .10
SE12 David Reid .02 .10
SE13 Adam Oates .05 .15
SE14 Ted Donato .02 .10
SE15 Don Sweeney .02 .10
SE16 Philippe Boucher .02 .10
SE17 Bob Sweeney .02 .10
SE18 Pat LaFontaine .10 .30
SE19 Derek Plante .05 .15
SE20 Jason Dawe .02 .10
SE21 Petr Svoboda .02 .10
SE22 Craig Simpson .02 .10
SE23 Viktor Gordiouk .02 .10
SE24 Trevor Kidd .05 .15
SE25 Todd Hlushko .02 .10
SE26 German Titov .02 .10
SE27 Gary Roberts .02 .10
SE28 Theo Fleury .05 .15
SE29 Cory Stillman .05 .15
SE30 Phil Housley .05 .15
SE31 Joel Otto .02 .10
SE32 Patrick Poulin .02 .10
SE33 Christian Soucy .05 .15
SE34 Karl Dykhuis .02 .10
SE35 Jeremy Roenick .15 .40
SE36 Tony Amonte .05 .15
SE37 Sergei Krivokrasov .02 .10
SE38 Bernie Nicholls .05 .15
SE39 Todd Harvey .05 .15
SE40 Jarkko Varvio .02 .10
SE41 Shane Churla .02 .10
SE42 Paul Cavallini .02 .10
SE43 Trent Klatt .02 .10
SE44 Darcy Wakaluk .02 .10
SE45 Derian Hatcher .02 .10
SE46 Dean Evason .02 .10
SE47 Mike Modano .20 .50
SE48 Greg Johnson .02 .10
SE49 Ray Sheppard .05 .15
SE50 Sergei Fedorov .20 .50
SE51 Bob Rouse .02 .10
SE52 Mike Vernon .05 .15
SE53 Vladimir Konstantinov .05 .15
SE54 Chris Osgood .05 .15
SE55 Steve Yzerman .60 1.50
SE56 Jason York .05 .15
SE57 Boris Mironov .02 .10
SE58 Igor Kravchuk .02 .10
SE59 Jason Arnott .02 .10
SE60 David Oliver .02 .10
SE61 Todd Marchant .02 .10
SE62 Dean McAmmond .02 .10
SE63 Brian Skrudland .02 .10
SE64 Tom Fitzgerald .02 .10
SE65 Brian Benning .02 .10
SE66 Stu Barnes .02 .10
SE67 John Vanbiesbrouck .05 .15
SE68 Rob Niedermayer .05 .15
SE69 Jimmy Carson .02 .10
SE70 Mark Janssens .02 .10
SE71 Sean Burke .05 .15
SE72 Andrei Nikolishin .02 .10
SE73 Chris Pronger .10 .30
SE74 Jeff Reese .02 .10
SE75 Darren Turcotte .02 .10
SE76 Robert Kron .02 .10
SE77 Kevin Brown .02 .10
SE78 Robert Lang .02 .10
SE79 Rick Tocchet .05 .15
SE80 Jamie Storr .05 .15
SE81 Kelly Hrudey .05 .15
SE82 Darryl Sydor .02 .10
SE83 Tony Granato .02 .10
SE84 Warren Rychel .02 .10
SE85 Gary Shuchuk .02 .10
SE86 Peter Popovic .02 .10
SE87 Valeri Bure .02 .10
SE88 Kirk Muller .05 .15
SE89 Lyle Odelein .02 .10
SE90 Brian Savage .02 .10
SE91 Gilbert Dionne .02 .10
SE92 Mathieu Schneider .02 .10
SE93 Jim Montgomery .02 .10
SE94 Chris Tamer .05 .15
SE95 Scott Niedermayer .05 .15
SE96 Bob Carpenter .02 .10
SE97 Scott Stevens .05 .15
SE98 Jim Dowd .02 .10
SE99 Brian Rolston .05 .15
SE100 Stephane Richer .05 .15
SE101 Mick Vukota .02 .10
SE102 Steve Thomas .02 .10
SE103 Patrick Flatley .02 .10
SE104 Marty McInnis .02 .10
SE105 Rich Pilon .02 .10
SE106 Benoit Hogue .02 .10
SE107 Zigmund Palffy .05 .15
SE108 Vladimir Malakhov .02 .10
SE109 Brett Lindros .02 .10
SE110 Mike Richter .10 .30
SE111 Greg Gilbert .02 .10
SE112 Kevin Lowe .02 .10
SE113 Mark Messier .10 .30
SE114 Alexander Karpovtsev .02 .10
SE115 Sergei Nemchinov .02 .10
SE116 Petr Nedved .05 .15
SE117 Glenn Healy .05 .15
SE118 Dave Archibald .02 .10
SE119 Alexandre Daigle .02 .10
SE120 Darrin Madeley .02 .10
SE121 Pavol Demitra .05 .15
SE122 Brad Shaw .02 .10
SE123 Alexei Yashin .02 .10
SE124 Sean Hill .02 .10
SE125 Vladislav Boulin .02 .10
SE126 Kevin Haller .02 .10
SE127 Chris Therien .02 .10
SE128 Garry Galley .02 .10
SE129 Mikael Renberg .05 .15
SE130 Ron Hextall .05 .15
SE131 Eric Lindros .10 .30
SE132 Craig MacTavish .02 .10
SE133 Patrik Juhlin .05 .15
SE134 Martin Straka .02 .10
SE135 Doug Brown .02 .10
SE136 Markus Naslund .10 .30
SE137 Luc Robitaille .05 .15
SE138 Kjell Samuelsson .02 .10
SE139 Ken Wregget .05 .15
SE140 John Cullen .02 .10
SE141 Peter Taglianetti .02 .10
SE142 Janne Laukkanen .02 .10
SE143 Owen Nolan .05 .15
SE144 Adam Deadmarsh .02 .10
SE145 Dave Karpa .02 .10
SE146 Wendel Clark .05 .15
SE147 Joe Sakic .25 .60
SE148 Alexei Gusarov .02 .10
SE149 Peter Forsberg .50 1.25
SE150 Kevin Miller .02 .10
SE151 Denny Felsner .02 .10
SE152 Al MacInnis .05 .15
SE153 Philippe Bozon .02 .10
SE154 Brett Hull .15 .40
SE155 Guy Carbonneau .02 .10
SE156 Igor Korolev .02 .10
SE157 Esa Tikkanen .05 .15
SE158 Jon Casey .05 .15
SE159 Viktor Kozlov .05 .15
SE160 Mike Rathje .02 .10
SE161 Bob Errey .02 .10
SE162 Arturs Irbe .05 .15
SE163 Ray Whitney .05 .15
SE164 Igor Larionov .05 .15
SE165 Pat Falloon .02 .10
SE166 Jeff Friesen .02 .10
SE167 Vlastimil Kroupa .02 .10
SE168 Chris Joseph .02 .10
SE169 Danton Cole .02 .10
SE170 John Tucker .02 .10
SE171 Roman Hamrlik .05 .15
SE172 Jason Wiemer .02 .10
SE173 Kenny Jonsson .02 .10
SE174 Eric Fichaud XRC .15 .40
SE175 Mats Sundin .10 .30
SE176 Doug Gilmour .05 .15
SE177 Drake Berehowsky .02 .10
SE178 Mike Ridley .02 .10
SE179 Jamie Macoun .02 .10
SE180 Alexei Kudashov .02 .10
SE181 Bill Berg .02 .10
SE182 Dave Andreychuk .05 .15
SE183 Mike Eastwood .02 .10
SE184 Martin Gelinas .02 .10
SE185 Greg Adams .02 .10
SE186 Gino Odjick .02 .10
SE187 Pavel Bure .10 .30
SE188 Cliff Ronning .02 .10
SE189 Jiri Slegr .02 .10
SE190 Jyrki Lumme .02 .10
SE191 Jassen Cullimore .02 .10
SE192 Steve Konowalchuk .02 .10
SE193 Sylvain Cote .02 .10
SE194 Jason Allison .02 .10
SE195 Sergei Gonchar .02 .10
SE196 Pat Peake .02 .10
SE197 Calle Johansson .02 .10
SE198 Joe Juneau .05 .15
SE199 Jeff Nelson .02 .10
SE200 Luciano Borsato .02 .10
SE201 Teemu Selanne .10 .30
SE202 Tie Domi .02 .10
SE203 Tim Cheveldae .05 .15
SE204 Darrin Shannon .02 .10
SE205 Ravil Gusmanov .02 .10
SE206 Todd Harvey .02 .10
SE207 Ed Jovanovski XRC .15 .40
SE208 Jason Allison .02 .10
SE209 Bryan McCabe .02 .10
SE210 Dan Cloutier XRC .30 .75
SE211 Ladislav Kohn XRC .15 .40
SE212 Marek Malik XRC .15 .40
SE213 Jan Hlavac XRC .15 .40
SE214 Petr Cajanek XRC .15 .40
SE215 Jussi Markkanen XRC .75 2.00
SE216 Jere Karalahti XRC .15 .40
SE217 Janne Niinimaa .10 .30
SE218 Kimmo Timonen .05 .15
SE219 Mikko Helisten XRC .15 .40
SE220 Niko Halttunen XRC .15 .40
SE221 Tommi Miettinen .05 .15
SE222 Veli-Pekka Nutikka XRC .15 .40
SE223 Timo Salonen XRC .15 .40
SE224 Tommi Sova XRC .15 .40
SE225 Jussi Tarvainen XRC .15 .40
SE226 Tommi Rajamaki XRC .15 .40
SE227 Antti Aalto XRC .15 .40
SE228 Alexander Korolyuk XRC .15 .40
SE229 Vitali Yachmenev .05 .15
SE230 Nikolai Zavarukhin .05 .15
SE231 Vadim Epantchinsev .05 .15
SE232 Dmitri Klevakin .05 .15
SE233 Anders Eriksson .05 .15
SE234 Anders Soderberg .05 .15
SE235 Per Svartvadet XRC .15 .40
SE236 Johan Davidsson .02 .10
SE237 Niklas Sundstrom .05 .15
SE238 J. Andersson-Junkka XRC .15 .40
SE239 Dick Tarnstrom XRC .15 .40
SE240 P.J. Axelsson XRC .15 .40
SE241 Frederik Johansson .05 .15
SE242 Peter Strom .05 .15
SE243 Mattias Ohlund .05 .15
SE244 Jesper Mattsson .05 .15
SE245 Jonas Forsberg .05 .15
SE246 Adam Deadmarsh .02 .10
SE247 Deron Quint .05 .15
SE248 Jamie Langenbrunner .02 .10
SE249 Richard Park .02 .10
SE250 Bryan Berard XRC .15 .40
SE251 David Belitski XRC .15 .40
SE252 Mike McBain XRC .15 .40
SE253 Hugh Hamilton XRC .15 .40
SE254 Jason Doig XRC .15 .40
SE255 Xavier Delisle XRC .15 .40
SE256 Wade Redden XRC .15 .40
SE257 Jeff Ware XRC .15 .40
SE258 Christian Dube XRC .15 .40
SE259 Louis-Phil.Sevigny XRC .15 .40
SE260 Jarome Iginla XRC 4.00 10.00
SE261 Daniel Briere XRC 3.00 8.00
SE262 Justin Kurtz XRC .15 .40
SE263 Marc Savard XRC .40 1.00
SE264 Alyn McCauley XRC .15 .40
SE265 Brad Mehalko XRC .15 .40
SE266 Jeffrey Ambrosio XRC .15 .40
SE267 Todd Norman XRC .15 .40
SE268 Brian Scott XRC .15 .40
SE269 Brad Larsen XRC .15 .40
SE270 J-S Giguere XRC 2.00 5.00
NNO Wayne Gretzky Large 1.50 4.00

1994-95 Parkhurst SE Gold

This 270-card set parallels the regular Parkhurst SE issue. The distinguishing feature between the two is that the normally silver player icon on the card front is now gold with the word "Parkie" printed alongside it in gold foil. Interestingly, these cards, which were inserted at a rate of one per pack, are significantly easier to find than the gold cards which paralleled the regular Parkhurst set which were inserted 1:35 packs. The cards are grouped alphabetically within teams and checklisted as in the regular set.

COMPLETE SET (270) 50.00 100.00
*VETS: 1X TO 2.5X BASIC CARDS
*ROOKIES: .8X TO 2X BASIC CARDS

1994-95 Parkhurst SE Euro-Stars

The 20 cards in this set were randomly inserted in Parkhurst SE product at an approximate rate of 1:8 packs. The set has some of the top European-born talent in the NHL. The cards feature a horizontal design with an action photo on the right and set logo and European map elements on the left. Card numbers have an "ES" prefix.

COMPLETE SET (20) 8.00 20.00
ES1 Peter Forsberg 2.50 6.00
ES2 Mats Sundin .60 1.50
ES3 Mikael Renberg .30 .75
ES4 Nicklas Lidstrom .60 1.50
ES5 Mariusz Czerkawski .15 .40
ES6 Ulf Dahlen .15 .40
ES7 Kjell Samuelsson .15 .40
ES8 Jyrki Lumme .15 .40
ES9 Jari Kurri .30 .75
ES10 Teppo Numminen .15 .40
ES11 Esa Tikkanen .15 .40
ES12 Christian Ruuttu .15 .40
ES13 Teemu Selanne .60 1.50
ES14 Alexander Mogilny .30 .75
ES15 Pavel Bure .60 1.50
ES16 Sergei Fedorov 1.00 2.50
ES17 Arturs Irbe .30 .75
ES18 Alexei Kovalev .15 .40
ES19 Dominik Hasek 1.25 3.00
ES20 Jaromir Jagr 1.00 2.50

1994-95 Parkhurst SE Vintage

This 45-card standard-size was inserted in Parkhurst SE packs at approximately the rate of 1:6. They are printed on heavy white card stock with a design that hearkens back to the style of Parkhurst issues of the 1950s and 1960s. The player photo is cut out and placed on a white-and-tan background. The player's name appears in a black bar on the lower portion of the card, alongside the set logo. The card backs are an unfinished cardboard and feature professional statistics, biography and a "Did You Know" section containing interesting trivia, which did not apply to the player pictured. The cards were numbered with a "seV" prefix.

COMPLETE SET (45) 15.00 40.00
1 Paul Kariya .60 1.50
2 Dino Ciccarelli .20 .50
3 Patrick Roy 3.00 8.00
4 Markus Naslund .60 1.50
5 Trevor Linden .40 1.00
6 Valeri Karpov .20 .50
7 Pat Verbeek .20 .50
8 Martin Brodeur 1.50 4.00
9 Kevin Stevens .20 .50
10 Kirk McLean .40 1.00
11 Stephan Lebeau .20 .50
12 Scott Niedermayer .20 .50
13 Peter Bondra .40 1.00
14 Ed Belfour .60 1.50
15 Paul Coffey .60 1.50
16 Chris Gratton .20 .50
17 Joe Juneau .40 1.00
18 Ray Bourque .60 1.50
19 Sergei Krivokrasov .20 .50
20 Wayne Gretzky 4.00 10.00
21 Alexei Yashin .20 .50
22 Al Iafrate .20 .50
23 Doug Weight .40 1.00
24 Jari Kurri .20 .50
25 Rod Brind'Amour .40 1.00
26 Bryan Smolinski .20 .50
27 Darius Kasparaitis .20 .50
28 Mark Recchi .20 .50
29 Mike Gartner .40 1.00
30 Russ Courtnall .20 .50
31 Pierre Turgeon .40 1.00
32 Felix Potvin .60 1.50
33 Nelson Emerson .20 .50
34 Alexander Mogilny .40 1.00
35 Bob Kudelski .20 .50
36 Brett Lindros .20 .50
37 Mats Sundin .60 1.50
38 Keith Tkachuk .60 1.50
39 Derek Plante .20 .50
40 Oleg Petrov .20 .50
41 Adam Graves .20 .50
42 Jaromir Jagr 1.00 2.50
43 Viktor Kozlov .20 .50
44 Nathan Lafayette .20 .50
45 Alexei Zhamnov .40 1.00

1995-96 Parkhurst '66-67 Promos

This five-card set was issued to promote the third installment of the Missing Link trilogy. The cards mirror the corresponding regular versions, save for the word PROMO stamped on the back, and a statement which reveals these cards were limited to 1966 copies.

COMPLETE SET (5) 6.00 15.00
16 Gerry Cheevers 1.25 3.00
Boston Bruins
144 Bob Nevin .30 .75
New York Rangers
128 Jacques Laperriere .30 .75
Norris Trophy Winner
125 Jean Beliveau 1.50 4.00
Stan Mikita AS
42 Gordie Howe 4.00 10.00
Detroit Red Wings

1995-96 Parkhurst '66-67

This 150-card set lovingly speculates on what might have been had Parkhurst, the venerable Canadian card manufacturer, been active during Bobby Orr's rookie card season. 2500 numbered 16-box cases were produced of the eight-card packs. The cards utilized period photos and a design element consistent with the time. There were two five-card insert sets honoring "Super Rookie" Orr and "Mr. Hockey" Gordie Howe. Orr and Howe autographed 500 of each card in their respective sets. The five promo cards were issued in set form. They are identical to the regular versions of the cards, save for the bold notation on the back which proclaims them to be prototypes limited to 1966 copies.

COMPLETE SET (150) 12.50 25.00
1 Pit Martin .05 .15
2 Ron Stewart .05 .15
3 Joe Watson .02 .10
4 Ed Westfall .02 .10
5 John Bucyk .08 .25
6 Ted Green .05 .15
7 Bobby Orr 2.50 5.00
8 Bob Woytowich .02 .10
9 Murray Oliver .02 .10
10 John McKenzie .05 .15
11 Tom Williams .02 .10
12 Don Awrey .02 .10
13 Ron Schock .02 .10
14 Bernie Parent .40 1.00
15 Ron Murphy .02 .10
16 Gerry Cheevers .40 1.00
17 Gilles Marotte .02 .10
18 Ed Johnston .05 .15
19 Derek Sanderson .40 1.00
20 Wayne Connelly .02 .10
21 Bobby Hull 1.25 3.00
22 Matt Ravlich .02 .10
23 Ken Hodge .05 .15
24 Stan Mikita .60 1.50
25 Fred Stanfield .02 .10
26 Eric Nesterenko .05 .15
27 Doug Jarrett .02 .10
28 Lou Angotti .02 .10
29 Ken Wharram .02 .10

30 Bill Hay .02 .10
31 Glenn Hall .60 1.50
32 Chico Maki .02 .10
33 Phil Esposito .60 1.50
34 Pierre Pilote .08 .25
35 Doug Mohns .02 .10
36 Ed Van Impe .02 .10
37 Dennis Hull .05 .15
38 Pat Stapleton .02 .10
39 Denis DeJordy .02 .10
40 Paul Henderson .05 .15
41 Gary Bergman .02 .10
42 Gordie Howe 1.50 4.00
43 Bob McCord .02 .10
44 Andy Bathgate .08 .25
45 Norm Ullman .08 .25
46 Peter Mahovlich .05 .15
47 Ted Hampson .02 .10
48 Leo Boivin .08 .25
49 Bruce MacGregor .02 .10
50 Ab McDonald .05 .15
51 Dean Prentice .05 .15
52 Floyd Smith .02 .10
53 Alex Delvecchio .08 .25
54 Pete Goegan .02 .10
55 Parker MacDonald .02 .10
56 Roger Crozier .05 .15
57 Val Fonteyne .02 .10
58 Henri Richard .40 1.00
59 John Ferguson .05 .15
60 Yvan Cournoyer .08 .25
61 Claude Provost .05 .15
62 Dave Balon .02 .10
63 Ted Harris .02 .10
64 Ralph Backstrom .05 .15
65 Jacques Laperriere .08 .25
66 Terry Harper .05 .15
67 J.C. Tremblay .05 .15
68 Jean Guy Talbot .05 .15
69 Claude Larose .05 .15
70 Charlie Hodge .05 .15
71 Gilles Tremblay .02 .10
72 Jim Roberts .02 .10
73 Jean Beliveau .60 1.50
74 Serge Savard .10 .25
75 Rogatien Vachon .30 .75
76 Lorne Worsley .60 1.50
77 Bobby Rousseau .05 .15
78 Dick Duff .05 .15
79 Rod Gilbert .08 .25
80 Harry Howell .08 .25
81 Jim Neilson .02 .10
82 Don Marshall .02 .10
83 Reg Fleming .02 .10
84 Wayne Hillman .02 .10
85 Bob Nevin .02 .10
86 Arnie Brown .02 .10
87 Earl Ingarfield .02 .10
88 Jean Ratelle .08 .25
89 Bernie Geoffrion .40 1.00
90 Orland Kurtenbach .02 .10
91 Bill Hicke .02 .10
92 Red Berenson .05 .15
93 Ed Giacomin .08 .25
94 Al MacNeil .02 .10
95 Rod Seiling .02 .10
96 Doug Robinson .02 .10
97 Cesare Maniago .05 .15
98 Vic Hadfield .02 .10
99 Phil Goyette .02 .10
100 Dave Keon .08 .25
101 Mike Walton .02 .10
102 Frank Mahovlich .60 1.50
103 Tim Horton .60 1.50
104 Larry Hillman .02 .10
105 Kent Douglas .02 .10
106 Ron Ellis .02 .10
107 Jim Pappin .02 .10
108 Marcel Pronovost .08 .25
109 Red Kelly .08 .25
110 Allan Stanley .08 .25
111 Brit Selby .02 .10
112 Pete Stemkowski .02 .10
113 Eddie Shack .40 1.00
114 Bob Pulford .08 .25
115 Larry Jeffrey .02 .10
116 George Armstrong .08 .25
117 Bob Baun .05 .15
118 Bruce Gamble .02 .10
119 Johnny Bower .60 1.50
120 Terry Sawchuk .75 2.00
121 Glenn Hall .30 .75
Gump Worsley AS
122 Jacques Laperriere .05 .15
Allan Stanley AS
123 Pierre Pilote .05 .15
Pat Stapleton AS
124 Bobby Hull .40 1.00
Frank Mahovlich AS
125 Stan Mikita .30 .75
Jean Beliveau AS
126 Gordie Howe/Rousseau AS .60 1.50
127 Alex Delvecchio .05 .15
Lady Byng
128 Jacques Laperriere .05 .15
Norris
129 Bobby Hull .60 1.50
Hart
130 Bobby Hull .60 1.50
Art Ross
131 Worsley/Hodge .20 .50
Vezina
132 Brit Selby .02 .10
Calder
133 Action Card .05 .15
All-Star Game
134 Action Card .05 .15
135 Action Card .05 .15
136 Action Card .05 .15
137 Action Card .05 .15
138 Action Card .05 .15
139 Action Card .05 .15
140 Murray Oliver L .02 .10
141 Bobby Hull L .60 1.50
142 Gordie Howe L .75 2.00
143 Bobby Rousseau L .02 .10
144 Bob Nevin L .02 .10
145 Mahovlich/Pulford L .08 .25
146 Stanley Cup Playoffs .05 .15
Semifinals
147 Stanley Cup Playoffs .05 .15
Semifinals
148 Stanley Cup Playoffs Finals .05 .15
149 Checklist .02 .10
150 Checklist .02 .10
SR1 Bobby Orr 7.50 15.00
SR2 Bobby Orr 7.50 15.00
SR3 Bobby Orr 7.50 15.00
SR4 Bobby Orr 7.50 15.00
SR5 Bobby Orr 7.50 15.00
MHA1 Gordie Howe AU 50.00 100.00
MHA2 Gordie Howe AU 50.00 100.00
MHA3 Gordie Howe AU 50.00 100.00
MHA4 Gordie Howe AU 50.00 100.00
MHA5 Gordie Howe AU 50.00 100.00
MRH1 Gordie Howe 6.00 12.00
MRH2 Gordie Howe 6.00 12.00
MRH3 Gordie Howe 6.00 12.00
MRH4 Gordie Howe 6.00 12.00
MRH5 Gordie Howe 6.00 12.00
SRA1 Bobby Orr AU 125.00 250.00
SRA2 Bobby Orr AU 125.00 250.00
SRA3 Bobby Orr AU 125.00 250.00
SRA4 Bobby Orr AU 125.00 250.00
SRA5 Bobby Orr AU 125.00 250.00

1995-96 Parkhurst '66-67 Coins

In tip of the hat fashion, this 120-coin insert set recreates the popular Shirriff coins of the 1960s. The plastic coins were team color coded, and were inserted one per pack. The coins measure about 1 3/8" in diameter. They are numbered in identical fashion to the card set as the same players are featured. Several collectors and dealers have reported the Paul Henderson coin (#40) as being difficult to locate. Parkhurst officials, however, say no coin was printed in shorter quantity than any other. There also were five black coins randomly inserted honoring Bobby Orr and Gordie Howe.

COMPLETE SET (120) 90.00 175.00
1 Pit Martin .40 1.00
2 Ron Stewart .40 1.00
3 Joe Watson .25 .60
4 Ed Westfall .25 .60
5 John Bucyk .60 1.50
6 Ted Green .40 1.00
7 Bobby Orr 5.00 10.00
8 Bob Woytowich .25 .60
9 Murray Oliver .25 .60
10 John McKenzie .40 1.00
11 Tom Williams .25 .60
12 Don Awrey .25 .60
13 Ron Schock .25 .60
14 Bernie Parent 1.25 3.00
15 Ron Murphy .25 .60
16 Gerry Cheevers 1.25 3.00
17 Gilles Marotte .25 .60
18 Ed Johnston .40 1.00
19 Derek Sanderson 1.25 3.00
20 Wayne Connelly .25 .60
21 Bobby Hull 3.00 6.00
22 Matt Ravlich .25 .60
23 Ken Hodge .40 1.00
24 Stan Mikita 1.50 4.00
25 Fred Stanfield .25 .60
26 Eric Nesterenko .40 1.00
27 Doug Jarrett .25 .60
28 Lou Angotti .25 .60
29 Ken Wharram .25 .60
30 Bill Hay .25 .60
31 Glenn Hall 1.50 4.00
32 Chico Maki .25 .60
33 Phil Esposito 1.50 4.00
34 Pierre Pilote .60 1.50
35 Doug Mohns .25 .60
36 Ed Van Impe .25 .60
37 Dennis Hull .40 1.00
38 Pat Stapleton .25 .60
39 Denis DeJordy .25 .60
40 Paul Henderson 5.00 10.00
41 Gary Bergman .25 .60
42 Gordie Howe 4.00 8.00
43 Bob McCord .25 .60
44 Andy Bathgate .60 1.50
45 Norm Ullman .60 1.50
46 Peter Mahovlich .40 1.00
47 Ted Hampson .25 .60
48 Leo Boivin .60 1.50
49 Bruce MacGregor .25 .60
50 Ab McDonald .40 1.00
51 Dean Prentice .25 .60
52 Floyd Smith .25 .60
53 Alex Delvecchio .60 1.50
54 Pete Goegan .25 .60
55 Parker MacDonald .25 .60
56 Roger Crozier .40 1.00
57 Val Fonteyne .25 .60
58 Henri Richard 1.25 3.00
59 John Ferguson .60 1.50
60 Yvan Cournoyer .60 1.50
61 Claude Provost .40 1.00
62 Dave Balon .25 .60
63 Ted Harris .25 .60
64 Ralph Backstrom .40 1.00
65 Jacques Laperriere .60 1.50
66 Terry Harper .40 1.00
67 J.C. Tremblay .40 1.00
68 Jean Guy Talbot .40 1.00
69 Claude Larose .40 1.00
70 Charlie Hodge .60 1.50
71 Gilles Tremblay .25 .60
72 Jim Roberts .25 .60
73 Jean Beliveau 1.50 4.00
74 Serge Savard .60 1.50
75 Rogatien Vachon 1.25 3.00
76 Lorne Worsley 1.50 4.00
77 Bobby Rousseau .40 1.00
78 Dick Duff .40 1.00
79 Rod Gilbert .60 1.50
80 Harry Howell .60 1.50
81 Jim Neilson .40 1.00
82 Don Marshall .25 .60
83 Reg Fleming .25 .60
84 Wayne Hillman .25 .60
85 Bob Nevin .25 .60
86 Arnie Brown .25 .60
87 Earl Ingarfield .25 .60
88 Jean Ratelle .60 1.50
89 Bernie Geoffrion 1.25 3.00
90 Orland Kurtenbach .25 .60
91 Bill Hicke .25 .60
92 Red Berenson .40 1.00
93 Ed Giacomin .60 1.50
94 Al MacNeil .25 .60
95 Rod Seiling .25 .60
96 Doug Robinson .25 .60
97 Cesare Maniago .40 1.00
98 Vic Hadfield .25 .60
99 Phil Goyette .25 .60
100 Dave Keon .60 1.50
101 Mike Walton .25 .60
102 Frank Mahovlich 1.50 4.00
103 Tim Horton 1.50 4.00
104 Larry Hillman .25 .60
105 Kent Douglas .25 .60
106 Ron Ellis .25 .60
107 Jim Pappin .25 .60
108 Marcel Pronovost .60 1.50
109 Red Kelly .60 1.50
110 Allan Stanley .60 1.50
111 Brit Selby .25 .60
112 Pete Stemkowski .25 .60
113 Eddie Shack 1.25 3.00
114 Bob Pulford .60 1.50
115 Larry Jeffrey .25 .60
116 George Armstrong .60 1.50
117 Bob Baun .40 1.00
118 Bruce Gamble .25 .60
119 Johnny Bower 1.50 4.00
120 Terry Sawchuk 2.50 5.00
BO1 Bobby Orr Black Coin 4.00 10.00
BO2 Bobby Orr Black Coin 4.00 10.00
BO3 Bobby Orr Black Coin 4.00 10.00
BO4 Bobby Orr Black Coin 4.00 10.00
BO5 Bobby Orr Black Coin 4.00 10.00
GH1 Gordie Howe Black Coin 3.00 8.00
GH2 Gordie Howe Black Coin 3.00 8.00
GH3 Gordie Howe Black Coin 3.00 8.00
GH4 Gordie Howe Black Coin 3.00 8.00
GH5 Gordie Howe Black Coin 3.00 8.00

1995-96 Parkhurst International

This two-series issue was produced by Parkhurst in Canada for release in eleven European countries. Interest in the cards, which featured NHL players and were licensed by both the NHL and NHLPA, was such that they became widely available throughout North America. The first series was produced in larger quantities than the second series, which by some estimates was limited to around 900 cases. Each box included 48 14-card packs. The second series is notable for including the first card of Wayne Gretzky in a St. Louis Blues uniform. Two different players autographed cards for insertion in each series: Teemu Selanne and Mikael Renberg each signed 2,500 cards for series 1, while Martin Brodeur and Saku Koivu inked up 2,500 each for series 2. One jumbo Saku Koivu card was inserted in each series 2 box; autographed copies of this jumbo card were randomly inserted as well.

COMPLETE SET (540) 15.00 40.00
COMP.SERIES 1 (270) 8.00 20.00
COMP.SERIES 2 (270) 8.00 20.00
1 Patrik Carnback .02 .10
2 Milos Holan .02 .10
3 Paul Kariya .08 .25
4 Guy Hebert .05 .15
5 Garry Valk .02 .10
6 Mikhail Shtalenkov .02 .10
7 Randy Ladouceur .02 .10
8 Shaun Van Allen .02 .10
9 Oleg Tverdovsky .02 .10
10 Kevin Stevens .02 .10
11 Ray Bourque .15 .40
12 Cam Neely .08 .25
13 Jozef Stumpel .02 .10
14 Blaine Lacher .05 .15
15 Alexei Kasatonov .02 .10
16 Adam Oates .05 .15
17 Ted Donato .02 .10
18 Mariusz Czerkawski .02 .10
19 Alexei Zhitnik .02 .10
20 Pat LaFontaine .08 .25
21 Garry Galley .02 .10
22 Scott Pearson .02 .10
23 Yuri Khmylev .02 .10
24 Jason Dawe .02 .10
25 Robb Stauber .05 .15
26 Wayne Primeau .02 .10
27 Brian Holzinger XRC .08 .25
28 German Titov .02 .10
29 Theo Fleury .02 .10
30 Phil Housley .05 .15
31 Zarley Zalapski .02 .10
32 Rick Tabaracci .05 .15
33 Joe Nieuwendyk .05 .15
34 Michael Nylander .02 .10
35 Trevor Kidd .05 .15
36 Dean Evason .02 .10
37 Bernie Nicholls .02 .10
38 Chris Chelios .08 .25
39 Gary Suter .02 .10
40 Denis Savard .05 .15
41 Ed Belfour .08 .25
42 Patrick Poulin .02 .10
43 Steve Smith .02 .10
44 Jeff Hackett .05 .15
45 Eric Daze .05 .15
46 Joe Sakic .20 .50
47 John Slaney .02 .10
48 Valeri Kamensky .05 .15
49 Owen Nolan .05 .15
50 Uwe Krupp .02 .10
51 Andrei Kovalenko .02 .10
52 Janne Laukkanen .02 .10
53 Jocelyn Thibault .08 .25
54 Adam Deadmarsh .02 .10
55 Mike Modano .15 .40
56 Kevin Hatcher .02 .10
57 Mike Donnelly .02 .10
58 Derian Hatcher .02 .10
59 Andy Moog .08 .25
60 Jamie Langenbrunner .02 .10
61 Shane Churla .05 .15
62 Todd Harvey .05 .15
63 Manny Fernandez .08 .25
64 Nicklas Lidstrom .08 .25
65 Vyacheslav Kozlov .05 .15
66 Paul Coffey .08 .25
67 Chris Osgood .05 .15
68 Slava Fetisov .02 .10
69 Vladimir Konstantinov .05 .15
70 Steve Yzerman .50 1.25
71 Aaron Ward .02 .10
72 Keith Primeau .02 .10
73 Jason Arnott .02 .10
74 Igor Kravchuk .02 .10
75 Boris Mironov .02 .10
76 David Oliver .02 .10
77 Kelly Buchberger .02 .10
78 Bill Ranford .05 .15
79 Zdeno Ciger .02 .10
80 Jason Bonsignore .02 .10
81 Louie DeBrusk .02 .10
82 Rob Niedermayer .05 .15
83 Magnus Svensson .02 .10
84 Robert Svehla .02 .10
85 John Vanbiesbrouck .05 .15
86 Stu Barnes .02 .10
87 Jesse Belanger .02 .10
88 Mark Fitzpatrick .05 .15
89 Jason Woolley .02 .10
90 Johan Garpenlov .02 .10
91 Geoff Sanderson .02 .10
92 Robert Kron .02 .10
93 Darren Turcotte .02 .10
94 Andrei Nikolishin .02 .10
95 Steven Rice .02 .10
96 Sean Burke .05 .15
97 Brendan Shanahan .08 .25
98 Glen Wesley .02 .10
99 Marek Malik .02 .10
100 Wayne Gretzky .75 2.00
101 Robert Lang .02 .10
102 Jari Kurri .08 .25
103 Kelly Hrudey .05 .15
104 Jamie Storr .05 .15
105 Marty McSorley .02 .10
106 Rob Blake .05 .15
107 Eric LaCroix .02 .10
108 Dimitri Khristich .02 .10
109 Pierre Turgeon .05 .15
110 Vincent Damphousse .02 .10
111 Peter Popovic .02 .10
112 Brian Savage .02 .10
113 Patrick Roy .50 1.25
114 Valeri Bure .02 .10
115 Vladimir Malakhov .02 .10
116 Benoit Brunet .02 .10
117 Stephane Quintal .02 .10
118 Stephane Richer .05 .15
119 Sergei Brylin .02 .10
120 Neal Broten .05 .15
121 Scott Stevens .05 .15
122 Martin Brodeur .25 .60
123 John MacLean .05 .15
124 Bill Guerin .05 .15
125 Bobby Holik .05 .15
126 Tommy Albelin .02 .10
127 Tommy Soderstrom .05 .15
128 Tommy Salo .05 .15
129 Kirk Muller .02 .10
130 Mathieu Schneider .02 .10
131 Zigmund Palffy .05 .15
132 Derek King .02 .10
133 Brett Lindros .02 .10
134 Marty McInnis .02 .10
135 Alexander Semak .02 .10
136 Mark Messier .08 .25
137 Adam Graves .05 .15
138 Mike Richter .08 .25
139 Alexei Kovalev .05 .15
140 Luc Robitaille .05 .15
141 Sergei Nemchinov .02 .10
142 Alexander Karpovtsev .02 .10
143 Mattias Norstrom .02 .10
144 Brian Leetch .05 .15
145 Martin Straka .02 .10
146 Sylvain Turgeon .02 .10
147 Radek Bonk .02 .10
148 Stanislav Neckar .02 .10
149 Pavol Demitra .08 .25
150 Alexandre Daigle .02 .10
151 Alexei Yashin .02 .10
152 Don Beaupre .05 .15
153 Steve Duchesne .02 .10
154 Eric Lindros .08 .25
155 Kjell Samuelsson .02 .10
156 Chris Therien .02 .10
157 John LeClair .08 .25
158 Rod Brind'Amour .05 .15
159 Ron Hextall .05 .15
160 Patrik Juhlin .02 .10
161 Mikael Renberg .05 .15
162 Joel Otto .02 .10
163 Markus Naslund .08 .25
164 Ron Francis .05 .15
165 Jaromir Jagr .15 .40
166 Tomas Sandstrom .05 .15
167 Ken Wregget .05 .15
168 Bryan Smolinski .02 .10
169 Richard Park .02 .10
170 Mario Lemieux .50 1.25
171 Norm Maciver .02 .10
172 Brett Hull .10 .30
173 Esa Tikkanen .02 .10
174 Shayne Corson .02 .10
175 Chris Pronger .08 .25
176 Ian Laperriere .02 .10
177 Jon Casey .05 .15
178 Al MacInnis .05 .15
179 David Roberts .02 .10
180 Dale Hawerchuk .08 .25
181 Michal Sykora .02 .10
182 Jeff Friesen .02 .10
183 Ray Whitney .05 .15
184 Igor Larionov .02 .10
185 Sandis Ozolinsh .02 .10
186 Andrei Nazarov .02 .10
187 Viktor Kozlov .05 .15
188 Arturs Irbe .05 .15
189 Wade Flaherty .05 .15
190 Brian Bradley .02 .10
191 Paul Ysebaert .02 .10
192 John Tucker .02 .10
193 Jason Wiemer .02 .10
194 Alexander Selivanov .02 .10
195 Daren Puppa .05 .15
196 Mikael Andersson .02 .10
197 Petr Klima .02 .10
198 Roman Hamrlik .05 .15
199 Doug Gilmour .05 .15
200 Damian Rhodes .05 .15
201 Mats Sundin .08 .25
202 Todd Gill .02 .10
203 Kenny Jonsson .02 .10
204 Felix Potvin .08 .25
205 Tie Domi .05 .15
206 Mike Gartner .05 .15
207 Larry Murphy .05 .15
208 Josef Beranek .02 .10
209 Trevor Linden .05 .15
210 Russ Courtnall .02 .10
211 Roman Oksiuta .02 .10
212 Alexander Mogilny .05 .15
213 Kirk McLean .05 .15
214 Mike Ridley .02 .10
215 Jyrki Lumme .02 .10
216 Bret Hedican .02 .10
217 Keith Jones .05 .15
218 Calle Johansson .02 .10
219 Kelly Miller .02 .10
220 Olaf Kolzig .05 .15
221 Joe Juneau .02 .10
222 Sylvain Cote .02 .10
223 Dale Hunter .05 .15
224 Mark Tinordi .02 .10
225 Sergei Gonchar .02 .10
226 Alexei Zhamnov .05 .15
227 Igor Korolev .02 .10
228 Teppo Numminen .02 .10
229 Craig Martin .02 .10
230 Nikolai Khabibulin .05 .15
231 Michal Grosek .02 .10
232 Teemu Selanne .08 .25
233 Dave Manson .02 .10
234 Tim Cheveldae .05 .15
235 Esa Tikkanen .02 .10
236 Dominik Hasek .08 .25
237 Peter Forsberg .10 .30
238 Sergei Fedorov .08 .25
239 Jari Kurri .08 .25
240 Tommy Soderstrom .05 .15
241 Alexei Zhamnov .05 .15
242 Alexei Yashin .02 .10
243 Mikael Renberg .05 .15
244 Jaromir Jagr .08 .25
245 Ulf Dahlen .02 .10
246 Alexander Mogilny .05 .15
247 Mats Sundin .05 .15
248 Pavel Bure .08 .25
249 Slava Fetisov .02 .10
250 Teemu Selanne .08 .25
251 Arturs Irbe .05 .15
252 Nicklas Lidstrom .08 .25
253 Aki-Petteri Berg .02 .10
254 Zdenek Nedved .02 .10
255 Chad Kilger .02 .10
256 Bryan McCabe .02 .10
257 Daniel Alfredsson XRC .60 1.50
258 Brendan Witt .02 .10
259 Jeff O'Neill .02 .10
260 Radek Dvorak .02 .10
261 Niklas Sundstrom .05 .15
262 Kyle McLaren .02 .10
263 Saku Koivu .08 .25
264 Todd Bertuzzi .08 .25
265 Jere Lehtinen .05 .15
266 Vitali Yachmenev .02 .10
267 Shane Doan .02 .10
268 Marko Kiprusoff .02 .10
269 Deron Quint .02 .10
270 Daymond Langkow XRC .20 .50
271 Alex Hicks .02 .10
272 Steve Rucchin .05 .15
273 David Karpa .02 .10
274 Mike Sillinger .02 .10
275 Teemu Selanne .08 .25
276 Todd Krygier .02 .10
277 Valeri Karpov .02 .10
278 Peter Douris .02 .10
279 Team Checklist .02 .10
280 Shawn McEachern .02 .10
281 Dave Reid .02 .10
282 Bill Ranford .05 .15
283 Don Sweeney .02 .10
284 Stephen Leach .02 .10
285 Craig Billington .05 .15
286 Clayton Beddoes .02 .10
287 Rick Tocchet .05 .15
288 Team Checklist .02 .10
289 Brad May .02 .10
290 Mike Peca .05 .15
291 Dominik Hasek .20 .50
292 Donald Audette .02 .10
293 Randy Burridge .02 .10
294 Derek Plante .02 .10
295 Martin Biron XRC 1.00 2.50
296 Andrei Trefilov .02 .10
297 Team Checklist .02 .10
298 Steve Chiasson .02 .10
299 Cory Stillman .02 .10
300 Mike Sullivan .02 .10
301 Gary Roberts .02 .10
302 Pavel Torgajev .02 .10
303 James Patrick .02 .10
304 Corey Millen .02 .10
305 Ed Ward .02 .10
306 Team Checklist .02 .10
307 Jeremy Roenick .10 .30
308 Mike Prokopec .02 .10
309 Joe Murphy .02 .10
310 Eric Weinrich .02 .10
311 Tony Amonte .05 .15
312 Bob Probert .05 .15
313 Murray Craven .02 .10
314 Sergei Krivokrasov .02 .10
315 Team Checklist .02 .10
316 Peter Forsberg .25 .60
317 Stephane Fiset .05 .15
318 Mike Ricci .05 .15
319 Claude Lemieux .02 .10
320 Sandis Ozolinsh .02 .10
321 Sylvain Lefebvre .02 .10
322 Scott Young .02 .10
323 Patrick Roy .50 1.25
324 Team Checklist .02 .10
325 Brent Fedyk .02 .10
326 Brent Gilchrist .02 .10
327 Greg Adams .02 .10
328 Richard Matvichuk .05 .15
329 Joe Nieuwendyk .05 .15
330 Benoit Hogue .02 .10
331 Darcy Wakaluk .05 .15
332 Guy Carbonneau .08 .25
333 Team Checklist .02 .10
334 Mike Vernon .05 .15
335 Mathieu Dandenault .02 .10
336 Igor Larionov .02 .10
337 Sergei Fedorov .15 .40
338 Greg Johnson .02 .10
339 Dino Ciccarelli .05 .15
340 Martin Lapointe .02 .10
341 Darren McCarty .02 .10
342 Team Checklist .02 .10
343 Joaquin Gage .02 .10
344 Jiri Slegr .02 .10
345 Mariusz Czerkawski .02 .10
346 Doug Weight .05 .15
347 Todd Marchant .02 .10
348 Miroslav Satan XRC .25 .60
349 Jeff Norton .02 .10
350 Curtis Joseph .08 .25
351 Team Checklist .02 .10
352 Tom Fitzgerald .02 .10
353 Jody Hull .02 .10
354 Terry Carkner .02 .10
355 Scott Mellanby .02 .10
356 Bill Lindsay .02 .10
357 Gord Murphy .02 .10
358 Brian Skrudland .02 .10
359 David Nemirovsky .02 .10
360 Team Checklist .02 .10
361 Paul Ranheim .02 .10
362 Jason Muzzatti .05 .15
363 Glen Featherstone .02 .10
364 Andrew Cassels .02 .10
365 Jeff Brown .02 .10
366 Kevin Dineen .02 .10
367 Nelson Emerson .02 .10
368 Gerald Diduck .02 .10
369 Team Checklist .02 .10
370 Kevin Stevens .02 .10
371 Darryl Sydor .05 .15
372 Yanic Perreault .02 .10
373 Arto Blomsten .02 .10
374 Kevin Todd .02 .10
375 Byron Dafoe .05 .15
376 Tony Granato .02 .10
377 Vladimir Tsyplakov XRC .02 .10
378 Team Checklist .02 .10
379 Martin Rucinsky .02 .10
380 Patrice Brisebois .02 .10
381 Lyle Odelein .02 .10
382 Andrei Kovalenko .02 .10
383 Mark Recchi .05 .15
384 Jocelyn Thibault .08 .25
385 Turner Stevenson .02 .10
386 Pat Jablonski .05 .15
387 Team Checklist .02 .10
388 Scott Niedermayer .02 .10
389 Corey Schwab XRC .05 .15
390 Steve Thomas .05 .15
391 Valeri Zelepukin .02 .10
392 Shawn Chambers .02 .10
393 Jocelyn Lemieux .02 .10
394 Brian Rolston .02 .10
395 Denis Pederson .02 .10
396 Team Checklist .02 .10
397 Martin Straka .02 .10
398 Niclas Andersson .02 .10
399 Wendel Clark .05 .15
400 Travis Green .05 .15
401 Chris Marinucci .02 .10
402 Darius Kasparaitis .02 .10
403 Patrick Flatley .02 .10
404 Jamie McLennan .05 .15
405 Team Checklist .02 .10
406 Glenn Healy .05 .15
407 Pat Verbeek .02 .10
408 Ian Laperriere .02 .10
409 Ray Ferraro .02 .10
410 Jeff Beukeboom .02 .10
411 Ulf Samuelsson .02 .10
412 Doug Lidster .02 .10
413 Bruce Driver .02 .10
414 Team Checklist .02 .10
415 Antti Tormanen .02 .10
416 Sean Hill .02 .10
417 Damian Rhodes .05 .15
418 Jaroslav Modry .02 .10
419 Mike Bales .02 .10
420 Trent McCleary .02 .10
421 Randy Cunneyworth .02 .10
422 Ted Drury .02 .10
423 Team Checklist .02 .10
424 Pat Falloon .02 .10
425 Garth Snow .05 .15
426 Shjon Podein .02 .10
427 Petr Svoboda .02 .10
428 Eric Desjardins .05 .15
429 Anatoli Semenov .02 .10
430 Kevin Haller .02 .10
431 Rob Dimaio .02 .10
432 Team Checklist .02 .10
433 Chris Joseph .02 .10
434 Sergei Zubov .02 .10
435 Tom Barrasso .05 .15
436 Chris Tamer .02 .10
437 Dmitri Mironov .02 .10
438 Petr Nedved .05 .15
439 Neil Wilkinson .02 .10
440 Glen Murray .02 .10
441 Team Checklist .02 .10
442 J.J. Daigneault .02 .10
443 Grant Fuhr .08 .25
444 Adam Creighton .02 .10
445 Brian Noonan .02 .10
446 Stephane Matteau .02 .10
447 Roman Vopat .02 .10
448 Geoff Courtnall .02 .10
449 Wayne Gretzky .75 2.00
450 Team Checklist .02 .10
451 Chris Terreri .05 .15
452 Ulf Dahlen .02 .10
453 Owen Nolan .05 .15
454 Doug Bodger .02 .10
455 Craig Janney .02 .10
456 Ville Peltonen .02 .10
457 Ray Sheppard .02 .10
458 Shean Donovan .02 .10
459 Team Checklist .02 .10
460 Jeff Reese .02 .10
461 Shawn Burr .02 .10
462 Chris Gratton .02 .10
463 John Cullen .02 .10
464 Bill Houlder .02 .10
465 J.C. Bergeron .02 .10
466 Brian Bellows .02 .10
467 Drew Bannister .02 .10
468 Team Checklist .02 .10
469 Dimitri Yushkevich .02 .10
470 Dave Andreychuk .05 .15
471 Dave Gagner .02 .10
472 Todd Warriner .02 .10
473 Sergio Momesso .02 .10
474 Kirk Muller .02 .10
475 Dave Ellett .02 .10
476 Ken Baumgartner .02 .10
477 Team Checklist .02 .10
478 Esa Tikkanen .02 .10
479 Cliff Ronning .02 .10
480 Martin Gelinas .02 .10
481 Brian Loney .02 .10
482 Pavel Bure .08 .25
483 Corey Hirsch .05 .15
484 Scott Walker .02 .10
485 Jim Dowd .02 .10
486 Team Checklist .02 .10
487 Michal Pivonka .02 .10
488 Pat Peake .02 .10
489 Martin Gendron .02 .10
490 Peter Bondra .05 .15
491 Nolan Baumgartner .02 .10
492 Jim Carey .05 .15
493 Steve Konowalchuk .02 .10
494 Jason Allison .02 .10
495 Team Checklist .02 .10
496 Oleg Tverdovsky .02 .10
497 Craig Mills .02 .10
498 Darren Turcotte .02 .10
499 Norm Maciver .02 .10
500 Chad Kilger .02 .10
501 Keith Tkachuk .08 .25
502 Kris King .02 .10
503 Dallas Drake .02 .10
504 Team Checklist .02 .10
505 Saku Koivu .08 .25
506 Vitali Yachmenev .02 .10
507 Daniel Alfredsson .05 .15
508 Radek Dvorak .02 .10
509 Miroslav Satan .08 .25
510 Aki Berg .02 .10
511 Valeri Bure .02 .10
512 Petr Sykora .02 .10
513 Andrei Vasilyev .02 .10
514 Niklas Sundstrom .05 .15
515 Viktor Kozlov .05 .15
516 Sami Kapanen .02 .10
517 Anders Myrvold .02 .10
518 Jere Lehtinen .05 .15
519 Marcus Ragnarsson XRC .05 .15
520 Stefan Ustorf .02 .10
521 Ville Peltonen .02 .10
522 Antti Tormanen .02 .10
523 Petr Sykora .02 .10
524 Scott Bailey .02 .10
525 Kevin Hodson XRC .20 .50
526 Landon Wilson .02 .10
527 Aaron Gavey .02 .10
528 Darren Langdon XRC .02 .10
529 Jason Doig .02 .10
530 Marty Murray .02 .10
531 Marcus Ragnarsson .02 .10
532 Peter Ferraro .02 .10
533 Grant Marshall .02 .10
534 Mike Wilson XRC .02 .10
535 Rory Fitzpatrick .02 .10
536 Ed Jovanovski .08 .25
537 Eric Fichaud .05 .15
538 Stefan Ustorf .02 .10
539 Stephane Yelle .02 .10
540 Ethan Moreau XRC .08 .25
NNO1 M.Renberg AU/2500 4.00 10.00
NNO2 T.Selanne AU/2500 12.50 30.00
NNO3 M.Brodeur AU/1500 30.00 80.00
NNO4 S.Koivu AU/1500 8.00 20.00
NNO5 Saku Koivu Jumbo .75 2.00
NNO6 Saku Koivu Jumbo AU 8.00 20.00

1995-96 Parkhurst International Emerald Ice

This 540-card set was issued as a parallel to the regular Parkhurst International series. The cards feature the standard card player photo superimposed on brilliant emerald green foil. The cards were inserted at a rate of 1:3 packs.

*SER.1 VETS: 6X TO 15X BASIC CARDS
*SER.1 XRC's: 4X TO 10X
*SER.2 VETS: 8X TO 20X BASI CARDS
*SER.2 XRC's: 5X TO 12X

1995-96 Parkhurst International All-Stars

These six two-sided cards feature the best foreign-born stars in the NHL at each position. The cards were randomly inserted at a rate of 1:96 first series packs.

COMPLETE SET (6)	6.00	15.00
1 Dominik Hasek / Arturs Irbe	1.00	2.50
2 Nicklas Lidstrom / Sandis Ozolinsh	3.00	8.00
3 Sergei Zubov / Alexei Zhitnik	.40	1.00
4 Sergei Fedorov / Peter Forsberg	1.25	3.00
5 Jaromir Jagr / Teemu Selanne	1.00	2.50
6 Mats Sundin / Mikael Renberg	3.00	8.00

1995-96 Parkhurst International Crown Collection Silver Series 1

This sixteen-card set features some of the most popular players in the game on an attractive silver etched foil background. The cards were inserted 1:16 series 1 packs. A gold parallel version of this set exists as well. These cards were significantly tougher, coming out of 1:96 series 1 packs.

COMPLETE SET (16)	12.00	30.00
*GOLD: 1.2X TO 3X SILVER		
1 Eric Lindros	.50	1.25
2 Felix Potvin	.50	1.25
3 Mario Lemieux	2.50	6.00
4 Paul Kariya	.50	1.25
5 Pavel Bure	.50	1.25
6 Wayne Gretzky	4.00	10.00
7 Mikael Renberg	.30	.75
8 Paul Coffey	.50	1.25
9 Teemu Selanne	.50	1.25
10 Brett Hull	.60	1.50
11 Martin Brodeur	1.25	3.00
12 Doug Gilmour	.30	.75
13 Peter Forsberg	1.25	3.00
14 Sergei Fedorov	.75	2.00
15 Saku Koivu	.50	1.25
16 Jim Carey	.30	.75

1995-96 Parkhurst International Crown Collection Silver Series 2

This 16-card set of the NHL's top stars was randomly inserted in series 2 packs. Although this set echoes the theme of the series 1 Crown Collection, the numbering again is 1-16. There also are several players who make return appearances in this set. As with series one, the silver version come 1:16 packs, while the gold are found 1:96 packs.

COMPLETE SET (16)	12.00	30.00
*GOLD: 1.2X TO 3X SILVER		
1 Jaromir Jagr	.75	2.00
2 Patrick Roy	2.50	6.00
3 Alexander Mogilny	.30	.75
4 Paul Kariya	.50	1.25
5 Dominik Hasek	1.00	2.50
6 Peter Forsberg	1.25	3.00
7 Mark Messier	.50	1.25
8 Mats Sundin	.50	1.25
9 Ray Bourque	.75	2.00
10 Wayne Gretzky	4.00	10.00
11 Eric Lindros	.50	1.25
12 John Vanbiesbrouck	.30	.75
13 Chris Chelios	.50	1.25
14 Brian Leetch	.30	.75
15 Daniel Alfredsson	1.25	3.00
16 Eric Daze	.30	.75

1995-96 Parkhurst International Goal Patrol

This 12-card, horizontally-oriented set salutes the top netminders in the NHL. The cards feature an embossed photo in the Action Packed style, and were inserted 1:24 series 1 packs.

COMPLETE SET (12)	12.00	30.00
1 Martin Brodeur	3.00	8.00
2 Felix Potvin	1.25	3.00
3 Patrick Roy	6.00	15.00
4 Dominik Hasek	2.50	6.00
5 Jim Carey	.75	2.00
6 Ed Belfour	1.25	3.00
7 John Vanbiesbrouck	.75	2.00
8 Trevor Kidd	.75	2.00
9 Bill Ranford	.75	2.00
10 Arturs Irbe	.75	2.00
11 Kirk McLean	.75	2.00
12 Mike Richter	1.25	3.00

1995-96 Parkhurst International NHL All-Stars

These six, two-sided cards feature the NHL's top players by position. The cards were randomly inserted in series 2 packs at a rate of 1:96.

COMPLETE SET (6)	10.00	25.00
1 M.Lemieux/W.Gretzky	4.00	10.00
2 Jaromir Jagr / Brett Hull	1.25	3.00
3 Brendan Shanahan / Pavel Bure	2.50	6.00
4 Scott Stevens / Chris Chelios	2.50	6.00
5 Ray Bourque / Paul Coffey	1.50	4.00
6 Martin Brodeur / Ed Belfour	2.00	5.00

1995-96 Parkhurst International Parkie's Trophy Picks

This 54-card set illustrates Parkhurst's choices for the key individual awards for the 1995-96 NHL season. The cards were noted as being one of 1,000 produced, but were not individually numbered. The odds of pulling one from a second series pack were 1:48.

COMPLETE SET (54)	30.00	80.00
PP1 Eric Lindros	1.00	2.50
PP2 Mario Lemieux	3.00	8.00
PP3 Sergei Fedorov	1.25	3.00
PP4 Peter Forsberg	1.50	4.00
PP5 John Vanbiesbrouck	.60	1.50
PP6 Mark Messier	1.00	2.50
PP7 Jaromir Jagr	1.50	4.00
PP8 Joe Sakic	1.50	4.00
PP9 Grant Fuhr	.60	1.50
PP10 Eric Lindros	1.00	2.50
PP11 Mario Lemieux	3.00	8.00
PP12 Mark Messier	1.00	2.50
PP13 Peter Forsberg	1.50	4.00
PP14 Jaromir Jagr	1.50	4.00
PP15 Paul Kariya	1.00	2.50
PP16 Joe Sakic	1.50	4.00
PP17 Teemu Selanne	1.00	2.50
PP18 Alexander Mogilny	.60	1.50
PP19 Paul Coffey	1.00	2.50
PP20 Chris Chelios	1.00	2.50
PP21 Brian Leetch	.60	1.50
PP22 Ray Bourque	1.00	2.50
PP23 Larry Murphy	.40	1.00
PP24 Nicklas Lidstrom	1.00	2.50
PP25 Roman Hamrlik	.40	1.00
PP26 Gary Suter	.40	1.00
PP27 Sergei Zubov	.40	1.00
PP28 Dominik Hasek	1.50	4.00
PP29 John Vanbiesbrouck	.60	1.50
PP30 Chris Osgood	.60	1.50
PP31 Mike Richter	1.00	2.50
PP32 Martin Brodeur	2.00	5.00
PP33 Ron Hextall	.60	1.50
PP34 Grant Fuhr	1.00	2.50
PP35 Patrick Roy	3.00	8.00
PP36 Jim Carey	.40	1.00
PP37 Vitali Yachmenev	.40	1.00
PP38 Daniel Alfredsson	.60	1.50
PP39 Saku Koivu	1.00	2.50
PP40 Eric Daze	.40	1.00
PP41 Marcus Ragnarsson	.40	1.00
PP42 Ed Jovanovski	.40	1.00
PP43 Petr Sykora	.40	1.00
PP44 Todd Bertuzzi	1.00	2.50
PP45 Radek Dvorak	.40	1.00
PP46 Paul Kariya	1.00	2.50
PP47 Ron Francis	.60	1.50
PP48 Alexander Mogilny	.60	1.50
PP49 Pat LaFontaine	1.00	2.50
PP50 Pierre Turgeon	.40	1.00
PP51 Teemu Selanne	1.00	2.50
PP52 Sergei Fedorov	1.25	3.00
PP53 Adam Oates	.60	1.50
PP54 Brett Hull	1.25	3.00

1995-96 Parkhurst International Trophy Winners

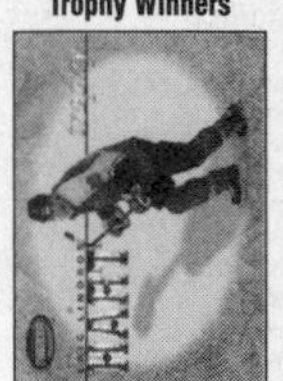

This six-card set recognizes the winners of the key individual trophies from the 1994-95 season. The cards were inserted at a rate of 1:24 series one packs.

COMPLETE SET (6)	3.00	8.00
1 Eric Lindros-Hart	.50	1.25
2 Jaromir Jagr-Art Ross	.75	2.00
3 Peter Forsberg-Calder	1.25	3.00
4 Paul Coffey-Norris	.50	1.25
5 Dominik Hasek-Vezina	1.00	2.50
6 Ron Francis-Lady Byng	.30	.75

1996 Parkhurst Beehive Promos

These cards were available as part of a card show wrapper redemption offer. The five Howe cards were available at the 1996 National in Anaheim in exchange for Parkhurst '66-67 wrappers. The Orr promos were available at several major shows.

COMMON BOBBY ORR	4.00	10.00
COMMON GORDIE HOWE	3.00	8.00

2001-02 Parkhurst

Printed on green foil stock, this 400-card set was originally released in late-November 2001 as a 300 card base set with 50 short prints. Cards 301-400 were available in packs of BAP Update. Cards 251-300 were serial-numbered to 500 copies each.

COMP.SER. 1 SET w/o SP's (250)	40.00	80.00
1 Paul Kariya	.30	.75
2 Patrik Stefan	.10	.25
3 Jeremy Roenick	.40	1.00
4 Patrick Roy	1.50	4.00
5 Jarome Iginla	.40	1.00
6 Jeff O'Neill	.10	.25
7 Sergei Samsonov	.25	.60
8 Peter Forsberg	.75	2.00
9 Scott Gomez	.10	.25
10 Mike Modano	.50	1.25
11 Brendan Shanahan	.30	.75
12 Jean-Sebastien Giguere	.25	.60
13 Pavel Bure	.30	.75
14 Zigmund Palffy	.25	.60
15 Marian Gaborik	.60	1.50
16 Pavol Demitra	.25	.60
17 Alexei Kovalev	.25	.60
18 Patrik Elias	.25	.60
19 Keith Tkachuk	.30	.75
20 Mats Sundin	.30	.75
21 Marian Hossa	.30	.75
22 Mark Recchi	.25	.60
23 John Madden	.10	.25
24 Mario Lemieux	1.50	4.00
25 Teemu Selanne	.30	.75
26 Joe Sakic	.60	1.50
27 Brad Richards	.25	.60
28 Brian Leetch	.25	.60
29 Markus Naslund	.30	.75
30 Peter Bondra	.30	.75
31 Steve Yzerman	1.25	3.00
32 Michael Peca	.10	.25
33 Bill Guerin	.25	.60
34 Jaromir Jagr	.50	1.25
35 Alexei Yashin	.10	.25
36 Theo Fleury	.10	.25
37 Al MacInnis	.25	.60
38 Milan Hejduk	.30	.75
39 Martin Biron	.25	.60
40 Brad Isbister	.10	.25
41 Nicklas Lidstrom	.30	.75
42 Rick DiPietro	.25	.60
43 Roberto Luongo	.40	1.00
44 Tim Connolly	.10	.25
45 Manny Fernandez	.25	.60
46 Scott Niedermayer	.10	.25
47 David Legwand	.25	.60
48 Petr Sykora	.10	.25
49 Ryan Smyth	.10	.25
50 Mark Messier	.30	.75
51 Dave Tanabe	.10	.25
52 Keith Primeau	.10	.25
53 Teppo Numminen	.10	.25
54 Milan Kraft	.25	.60
55 Owen Nolan	.25	.60
56 Alexander Mogilny	.25	.60
57 Brent Johnson	.25	.60
58 Curtis Joseph	.30	.75
59 Felix Potvin	.30	.75
60 Olaf Kolzig	.25	.60
61 Eric Lindros	.30	.75
62 Pierre Turgeon	.25	.60
63 Martin Straka	.10	.25
64 Maxim Afinogenov	.10	.25
65 Oleg Saprykin	.10	.25
66 Shane Willis	.10	.25
67 Brett Hull	.40	1.00
68 Alex Tanguay	.25	.60
69 Marc Denis	.25	.60
70 Ed Belfour	.30	.75
71 Roman Cechmanek	.25	.60
72 Tommy Salo	.25	.60
73 Rob Blake	.25	.60
74 Jose Theodore	.40	1.00
75 Henrik Sedin	.10	.25
76 Tony Amonte	.25	.60
77 Scott Hartnell	.10	.25
78 Brian Rafalski	.10	.25
79 Joe Thornton	.50	1.25
80 Patrick Marleau	.25	.60
81 Daniel Alfredsson	.25	.60
82 Simon Gagne	.30	.75
83 Patrick Lalime	.25	.60
84 Johan Hedberg	.25	.60
85 Adam Oates	.25	.60
86 Chris Pronger	.25	.60
87 Vincent Lecavalier	.30	.75
88 Tomas Kaberle	.10	.25
89 Daniel Sedin	.10	.25
90 Martin Lapointe	.10	.25
91 Chris Drury	.25	.60
92 Dominik Hasek	.60	1.50
93 Evgeni Nabokov	.25	.60
94 Ed Jovanovski	.10	.25
95 John LeClair	.30	.75
96 Sergei Fedorov	.50	1.25
97 Martin Havlat	.25	.60
98 Martin Brodeur	.75	2.00
99 Jason Arnott	.10	.25
100 Mike Comrie	.25	.60
101 Petr Nedved	.10	.25
102 Ray Ferraro	.10	.25
103 Miroslav Satan	.25	.60
104 Rod Brind'Amour	.25	.60
105 Ron Tugnutt	.25	.60
106 Oleg Tverdovsky	.10	.25
107 Anson Carter	.25	.60
108 Wes Walz	.10	.25
109 Andrei Markov	.10	.25
110 Mike Dunham	.25	.60
111 Eric Desjardins	.10	.25
112 Radek Dvorak	.10	.25
113 Pavel Kubina	.10	.25
114 Gary Roberts	.10	.25
115 Andrew Cassels	.10	.25
116 Vitali Vishnevski	.10	.25
117 Byron Dafoe	.25	.60
118 Chris Gratton	.10	.25
119 Marc Savard	.10	.25
120 Shawn McEachern	.10	.25
121 Jocelyn Thibault	.25	.60
122 Joe Nieuwendyk	.25	.60
123 Janne Niinimaa	.10	.25
124 Shane Doan	.10	.25
125 Willie Mitchell	.10	.25
126 Glen Murray	.10	.25
127 Scott Walker	.10	.25
128 Geoff Sanderson	.10	.25
129 Kenny Jonsson	.10	.25
130 Radek Bonk	.10	.25
131 Brad Stuart	.25	.60
132 Scott Young	.10	.25
133 Brendan Morrison	.25	.60
134 Sergei Gonchar	.10	.25
135 Jonathan Girard	.10	.25
136 Arturs Irbe	.25	.60
137 Chris Herperger	.10	.25
138 Brenden Morrow	.25	.60
139 Sergei Zubov	.10	.25
140 Lubomir Visnovsky	.10	.25
141 Aaron Miller	.10	.25
142 Ossi Vaananen	.10	.25
143 Saku Koivu	.30	.75
144 Sean Burke	.25	.60
145 Darryl Sydor	.10	.25
146 Chris Chelios	.30	.75
147 Brian Savage	.10	.25
148 Wade Redden	.10	.25
149 Derian Hatcher	.10	.25
150 Igor Larionov	.10	.25
151 Steve Sullivan	.10	.25
152 Michal Handzus	.10	.25
153 Ron Francis	.25	.60
154 David Vyborny	.10	.25
155 Manny Legace	.25	.60
156 Jeff Friesen	.10	.25
157 Jeff Hackett	.25	.60
158 Marian Cisar	.10	.25
159 Mike York	.10	.25
160 Nikolai Antropov	.10	.25
161 Trevor Linden	.10	.25
162 Bryan Smolinski	.10	.25
163 Janne Laukkanen	.10	.25
164 Dan Cloutier	.25	.60
165 Scott Stevens	.25	.60
166 Jani Hurme	.25	.60
167 Fredrik Modin	.10	.25
168 Steven Reinprecht	.10	.25
169 Kevyn Adams	.10	.25
170 Richard Zednik	.10	.25
171 Viktor Kozlov	.10	.25
172 Cliff Ronning	.10	.25
173 Mariusz Czerkawski	.10	.25
174 Todd Bertuzzi	.30	.75
175 Vincent Damphousse	.10	.25
176 Roman Hamrlik	.10	.25
177 Sandis Ozolinsh	.10	.25
178 Mike Richter	.30	.75
179 Stu Barnes	.10	.25
180 Patric Kjellberg	.10	.25
181 Tomas Holmstrom	.10	.25
182 Sergei Brylin	.10	.25
183 Magnus Arvedson	.10	.25
184 Sami Kapanen	.10	.25
185 Niklas Sundstrom	.10	.25
186 Todd Marchant	.10	.25
187 Mark Parrish	.10	.25
188 Adam Foote	.10	.25
189 Peter Schaefer	.10	.25
190 Mike Ricci	.10	.25
191 Alexei Zhamnov	.10	.25
192 Dainius Zubrus	.10	.25
193 Espen Knutsen	.10	.25
194 Shean Donovan	.10	.25
195 Bobby Holik	.10	.25
196 Tom Poti	.10	.25
197 Marcus Ragnarsson	.10	.25
198 Jozef Stumpel	.10	.25
199 Martin Rucinsky	.10	.25
200 Matt Davidson RC	.30	.75
201 Jan Bulis	.10	.25
202 Matt Pettinger	.10	.25
203 Rob Zamuner	.10	.25
204 Chris Osgood	.25	.60
205 Dan Hinote	.10	.25
206 Travis Green	.10	.25
207 Joe Juneau	.10	.25
208 Mikael Renberg	.10	.25
209 Zdeno Ciger	.10	.25
210 Jochen Hecht	.10	.25
211 Jan Hlavac	.10	.25
212 Jeff Halpern	.10	.25
213 Tom Barrasso	.25	.60
214 Bill Muckalt	.10	.25
215 Luc Robitaille	.25	.60
216 Jason Wiemer	.10	.25
217 Deron Quint	.10	.25
218 Jyrki Lumme	.10	.25
219 Andreas Dackell	.10	.25
220 Tomi Kallio	.10	.25
221 Roman Turek	.25	.60
222 Taylor Pyatt	.10	.25
223 Richard Jackman	.10	.25
224 Michael Nylander	.10	.25
225 Brian Pothier RC	.30	.75
226 Slava Kozlov	.10	.25
227 Kim Johnsson	.10	.25
228 J-P Dumont	.10	.25
229 Marty Reasoner	.10	.25
230 Dimitri Kalinin	.10	.25
231 Damian Rhodes	.10	.25
232 Jason Allison	.10	.25
233 Doug Weight	.25	.60
234 Yanic Perreault	.10	.25
235 Eric Daze	.25	.60
236 Brian Campbell	.10	.25
237 Valeri Bure	.10	.25
238 Adam Deadmarsh	.10	.25
239 Robert Reichel	.10	.25
240 Anders Eriksson	.10	.25
241 Nikolai Khabibulin	.30	.75
242 Sean O'Donnell	.10	.25
243 Bob Essensa	.10	.25
244 Josef Vasicek	.10	.25
245 Donald Audette	.10	.25
246 Steve Heinze	.10	.25
247 Bryan Berard	.10	.25
248 Ville Nieminen	.10	.25
249 Eric Weinrich	.10	.25
250 Adam Graves	.10	.25
251 Jesse Boulerice SP	2.50	6.00
252 Marko Kiprusoff SP	2.50	6.00
253 Ivan Ciernik RC	3.00	8.00
254 Pavel Datsyuk RC	20.00	40.00
255 Jaroslav Bednar RC	3.00	8.00
256 Andreas Salomonsson RC	3.00	8.00
257 Mike Ribeiro SP	2.50	6.00
258 Darcy Hordichuk SP	2.50	6.00
259 Chris Neil RC	3.00	8.00
260 Rostislav Klesla SP	1.00	2.50
261 Kristian Huselius RC	4.00	10.00
262 Brian Sutherby RC	2.00	5.00
263 Jiri Dopita RC	3.00	8.00
264 Radek Martinek RC	2.00	5.00
265 Barrett Heisten SP	2.50	6.00
266 Krystofer Kolanos RC	2.00	5.00
267 Pascal Dupuis RC	3.00	8.00
268 Andreas Lilja SP	2.50	6.00
269 Chris Mason SP	2.50	6.00
270 Mathieu Garon SP	2.00	5.00
271 Andrew Raycroft SP	2.50	6.00
272 Jeff Jillson RC	3.00	8.00
273 Jiri Bicek SP	2.50	6.00
274 Niklas Hagman RC	3.00	8.00
275 Pavel Brendl SP	3.00	8.00
276 Stephen Peat SP	3.00	8.00
277 Sascha Goc SP	2.50	6.00
278 Nick Boynton SP	2.50	6.00
279 Timo Parssinen RC	3.00	8.00
280 Mika Noronen SP	2.50	6.00
281 Scott Clemmensen RC	3.00	8.00
282 Dan Blackburn RC	3.00	8.00
283 Nikita Alexeev RC	3.00	8.00
284 Vaclav Nedorost RC	3.00	8.00
285 Ilja Bryzgalov RC	3.00	8.00
286 Dany Heatley SP	3.00	8.00
287 Niko Kapanen RC	1.00	2.50
288 Rick Berry SP	2.50	6.00
289 Mark Bell SP	2.50	6.00
290 Kamil Piros RC	3.00	8.00
291 Maxime Ouellet SP	3.00	8.00
292 Kris Beech SP	2.50	6.00
293 Miikka Kiprusoff SP	3.00	8.00
294 Martti Jarventie SP	2.50	6.00
295 Ilya Kovalchuk RC	20.00	50.00
296 Nick Schultz RC	3.00	8.00
297 Bryan Allen SP	2.50	6.00
298 Josef Boumedienne RC	3.00	8.00
299 Jason Williams SP	3.00	8.00
300 Daniel Tjarnqvist SP	2.50	6.00
301 Frederic Cassivi RC	.75	2.00
302 Mark Hartigan RC	.75	2.00
303 Pasi Nurminen RC	.75	2.00
304 Ivan Huml RC	.75	2.00
305 Zdenek Kutlak RC	.75	2.00
306 Ales Kotalik RC	1.00	2.50
307 Jukka Hentunen RC	.75	2.00
308 Erik Cole RC	3.00	8.00
309 Tyler Arnason RC	3.00	8.00
310 Jaroslav Obsut RC	.75	2.00
311 Riku Hahl RC	.75	2.00
312 Martin Spanhel RC	.75	2.00
313 Andrej Nedorost RC	.75	2.00
314 Ty Conklin RC	.75	2.00
315 Jason Chimera RC	.75	2.00
316 Kyle Rossiter RC	.75	2.00
317 Lukas Krajicek RC	.75	2.00
318 Stephen Weiss RC	4.00	10.00
319 Tony Virta RC	.75	2.00
320 Marcel Hossa RC	.75	2.00
321 Olivier Michaud RC	.75	2.00
322 Henrik Tallinder RC	.75	2.00
323 Martin Erat RC	.75	2.00
324 Nathan Perrott RC	.75	2.00
325 Pavel Skrbek RC	.75	2.00
326 Robert Schnabel RC	.75	2.00
327 Christian Berglund	.75	2.00
328 Stanislav Gron RC	.75	2.00
329 Raffi Torres RC	.75	2.00
330 Mikael Samuelsson RC	.75	2.00
331 Chris Bala RC	.75	2.00
332 Josh Langfeld RC	.75	2.00
333 Martin Prusek RC	.75	2.00
334 Sean Avery RC	.75	2.00
335 Neil Little RC	.75	2.00
336 Tomas Divisek RC	.75	2.00
337 Vaclav Pletka RC	.75	2.00
338 Guillaume Lefebvre RC	.75	2.00
339 Branko Radivojevic RC	.75	2.00
340 Trent Hunter RC	3.00	8.00
341 Jan Lasak RC	.75	2.00
342 Tom Kostopoulos RC	.75	2.00
343 Hannes Hyvonen RC	.75	2.00
344 Shane Endicott RC	.75	2.00
345 Evgeny Konstantinov RC	.75	2.00
346 Martin Cibak RC	.75	2.00
347 Karel Pilar RC	.75	2.00
348 Sebastien Centomo RC	.75	2.00
349 Mike Farrell RC	.75	2.00
350 Sebastien Charpentier RC	.75	2.00
351 Radim Vrbata	.10	.25
352 Andy McDonald	.10	.25
353 J.P. Vigier	.10	.25
354 Donald Brashear	.10	.25
355 Adrian Aucoin	.10	.25
356 Stephane Richer	.10	.25
357 Byron Ritchie	.10	.25
358 Sergei Berezin	.10	.25
359 Cliff Ronning	.10	.25
360 Tony Hrkac	.10	.25
361 Andre Roy	.10	.25
362 Shjon Podein	.10	.25
363 Andrei Nazarov	.10	.25
364 Marty McInnis	.10	.25
365 Petr Tenkrat	.10	.25
366 Trevor Letowski	.10	.25
367 Randy Robitaille	.10	.25
368 Kim Johnsson	.10	.25
369 Jozef Stumpel	.10	.25
370 P.J. Stock	.10	.25
371 Dean McAmmond	.10	.25
372 Steve Thomas	.10	.25
373 Darius Kasparaitis	.10	.25
374 Mike Sillinger	.10	.25
375 Jason Arnott	.10	.25
376 Alex Auld	.10	.25
377 Mike York	.10	.25
378 Pierre Dagenais	.10	.25
379 Andrew Brunette	.10	.25
380 Sergei Zholtok	.10	.25
381 Donald Audette	.10	.25
382 Doug Gilmour	.10	.25
383 Andy Delmore	.10	.25
384 Martin Rucinsky	.10	.25
385 Jamie Langenbrunner	.10	.25
386 Joe Nieuwendyk	.25	.60
387 John Vanbiesbrouck	.25	.60
388 Shawn Bates	.10	.25
389 Matthew Barnaby	.10	.25
390 Pavel Bure	.30	.75
391 Tom Poti	.10	.25
392 Zdeno Chara	.10	.25
393 Adam Oates	.25	.60
394 Marty Murray	.10	.25
395 Brian Savage	.10	.25
396 Daniil Markov	.10	.25
397 Tom Barrasso	.25	.60
398 Jan Hlavac	.10	.25
399 Trevor Linden	.10	.25
400 Ivan Ciernik	.10	.25

2001-02 Parkhurst Gold

This 300-card set paralleled the base 250 cards but carried gold foil in place of the silver. Cards were numbered out of 50 on the card backs.

*GOLD: 12.5X TO 30X BASIC CARD		
4 Patrick Roy	25.00	60.00
8 Peter Forsberg	20.00	50.00
24 Mario Lemieux	25.00	60.00
31 Steve Yzerman	25.00	60.00

2001-02 Parkhurst Silver

This 300-card set paralleled the first 100 base cards but carried silver foil in place of the silver. Cards were numbered out of 500 on the card backs.

*SILVER: 1.5X TO 4X BASIC CARD

2001-02 Parkhurst Autographs

This 59-card set featured autographs of retired greats. Each card was green in color with a full-color player photo in the center of the card. Underneath the photo was a light area that the featured player signed. Print runs are listed below for each card and cards with less than 25 copies are not priced due to scarcity. Cards PA41-PA59 were only available in BAP Update packs.

PA1 Frank Mahovlich/20		
PA2 Glenn Hall/90	15.00	40.00
PA3 Jean Beliveau/60	25.00	60.00
PA4 Frank Mahovlich/20		
PA5 Henri Richard/90	12.00	30.00
PA6 Jean Beliveau/60	25.00	60.00
PA7 Milt Schmidt/90	12.00	30.00
PA8 Elmer Lach/90	12.00	30.00
PA9 Woody Dumart/20		
PA10 Chuck Rayner/90	25.00	60.00
PA11 Henri Richard/90	15.00	40.00
PA12 Gordie Howe/20	75.00	150.00
PA13 Phil Esposito/60	20.00	50.00
PA14 Bernie Geoffrion/60	25.00	60.00
PA15 Dollard St.Laurent/90	12.00	30.00
PA16 Dickie Moore/90	15.00	40.00
PA17 Jean-Guy Talbot/90	12.00	30.00
PA18 Bill Gadsby/90	12.00	30.00
PA19 Lanny McDonald/80	12.00	30.00
PA20 Gilbert Perreault/60	20.00	50.00
PA21 Johnny Bucyk/90	12.00	30.00
PA22 Dale Hawerchuk/80	12.00	30.00
PA23 Mike Gartner/80	12.00	30.00
PA24 Johnny Bower/90	15.00	40.00
PA25 Butch Bouchard/90	15.00	40.00
PA26 Gordie Howe/20	75.00	150.00
PA27 Jean Beliveau/60	25.00	60.00
PA28 Guy Lafleur/60	40.00	100.00
PA29 Mike Bossy/90	12.00	30.00
PA30 Bryan Trottier/80	12.00	30.00
PA31 Marcel Dionne/60	12.00	30.00
PA32 Jari Kurri/80	30.00	80.00
PA33 Gerry Cheevers/90	15.00	40.00
PA34 Dino Ciccarelli/90	12.00	30.00
PA35 Stan Mikita/60	25.00	60.00
PA36 Gordie Howe/20	75.00	150.00
PA37 Tony Esposito/60	25.00	60.00
PA38 Gump Worsley/90	15.00	40.00
PA39 Ted Lindsay/90	12.00	30.00
PA40 Red Kelly/90	15.00	40.00
PA41 Joe Watson/90	12.00	30.00
PA42 Bobby Clarke/90	15.00	40.00
PA43 Dave Schultz/90	12.00	30.00
PA44 Tiger Williams/90	12.00	30.00
PA45 Serge Savard/90	12.00	30.00
PA46 Jacques Laperriere/90	12.00	30.00
PA47 Peter Mahovlich/90	12.00	30.00
PA48 Denis Potvin/90	12.00	30.00
PA49 Cam Neely/90	20.00	50.00
PA50 Ron Hextall/90	12.00	30.00
PA51 Steve Shutt/90	12.00	30.00
PA52 Yvan Cournoyer/90	20.00	50.00
PA53 Bill Barber/90	12.00	30.00
PA54 Reggie Leach/90	12.00	30.00
PA55 Dennis Hull/90	12.00	30.00
PA56 Bernie Parent/90	12.00	30.00
PA57 Bob Nystrom/90	12.00	30.00
PA58 Guy Lapointe/90	12.00	30.00
PA59 Larry Robinson/90	12.00	30.00

2001-02 Parkhurst 500 Goal Scorers

This 27-card set featured players who hit the milestone of 500 goals in their career. Each card featured an action photo of the given player alongside a game-worn swatch of his jersey on the card front. Print runs are listed below. The Shanahan and Francis cards were available in random packs of BAP Update only.

PGS1 Bobby Hull/30	40.00	100.00
PGS2 Gordie Howe/30	150.00	300.00
PGS3 Marcel Dionne/30	25.00	60.00
PGS4 Phil Esposito/30	25.00	60.00
PGS5 Mike Gartner/80	12.50	30.00
PGS6 Mark Messier/30	40.00	100.00
PGS7 Steve Yzerman/30	75.00	150.00
PGS8 Brett Hull/30	30.00	80.00
PGS9 Mario Lemieux/30	100.00	200.00
PGS10 Dino Ciccarelli/80	10.00	25.00
PGS11 Jari Kurri/80	10.00	25.00
PGS12 Luc Robitaille/30	25.00	60.00
PGS13 Mike Bossy/30	25.00	60.00
PGS14 Dave Andreychuk/80	10.00	25.00
PGS15 Guy Lafleur/30	30.00	80.00
PGS16 John Bucyk/80	10.00	25.00
PGS17 Maurice Richard/80	100.00	250.00
PGS18 Stan Mikita/80	10.00	25.00
PGS19 Frank Mahovlich/80	20.00	50.00
PGS20 Bryan Trottier/80	10.00	25.00
PGS21 Dale Hawerchuk/80	10.00	25.00
PGS22 Gilbert Perreault/80	10.00	25.00
PGS23 Jean Beliveau/80	40.00	100.00
PGS24 Pat Verbeek/80	10.00	25.00
PGS25 Michel Goulet/80	10.00	25.00
PGS26 Joe Mullen/80	10.00	25.00
PGS27 Lanny McDonald/80	10.00	25.00
NNO Ron Francis/25	20.00	50.00
NNO Brendan Shanahan/25	20.00	50.00

2001-02 Parkhurst He Shoots-He Scores Points

Inserted one per pack, these cards carried a value of 1, 2 or 3 points. The points could be redeemed for special memorabilia cards. The cards are unnumbered and are listed below in alphabetical order by point value. The redemption program ended November 31, 2002.

1 Jean Beliveau 1 pt.	.20	.50
2 Doug Harvey 1 pt.	.20	.50
3 Tim Horton 1 pt.	.20	.50
4 Bobby Hull 1 pt.	.20	.50
5 Ted Lindsay 1 pt.	.20	.50
6 Stan Mikita 1 pt.	.20	.50
7 Jacques Plante 1 pt.	.20	.50
8 Chris Pronger 1 pt.	.20	.50
9 Terry Sawchuk 1 pt.	.20	.50
10 Mats Sundin 1 pt.	.20	.50
11 Martin Brodeur 2 pt.	.20	.50
12 Peter Forsberg 2 pt.	.20	.50
13 Patrick Roy 2 pt.	.20	.50
14 Joe Sakic 2 pt.	.20	.50
15 Steve Yzerman 2 pt.	.20	.50
16 Paul Kariya 2 pt.	.20	.50
17 Pavel Bure 3 pt.	.20	.50
18 Gordie Howe 3 pt.	.20	.50
19 Mario Lemieux 3 pt.	.20	.50
20 Rocket Richard 3 pt.	.20	.50

2001-02 Parkhurst He Shoots-He Scores Prizes

Available only by redeeming 400 Parkhurst He Shoots-He Scores points, this 40-card set featured game-used swatches of jersey and a color photo of the player. Each card had a stated print run of 20 serial-numbered sets and each was encased in a clear plastic slab with a descriptive label at the top. This set is unpriced due to scarcity and volatility.

1 Paul Kariya

2 Patrick Roy
3 Jarome Iginla
4 Mike Modano
5 Brendan Shanahan
6 Pavel Bure
7 Mats Sundin
8 Mario Lemieux
9 Teemu Selanne
10 Joe Sakic
11 Denis Potvin
12 Markus Naslund
13 Steve Yzerman
14 John LeClair
15 Sergei Fedorov
16 Martin Brodeur
17 Milan Hejduk
18 Ilya Kovalchuk
19 Saku Koivu
20 Mark Messier
21 Curtis Joseph
22 Alex Tanguay
23 Ed Belfour
24 Rob Blake
25 Tony Amonte
26 Chris Drury
27 Doug Weight
28 Jaromir Jagr
29 Alexander Mogilny
30 Jeremy Roenick
31 Eric Lindros
32 Bobby Clarke
33 Tommy Salo
34 Dominik Hasek
35 Gordie Howe
36 Jacques Plante
37 Ted Lindsay
38 Bobby Hull
39 Terry Sawchuk
40 Jean Beliveau

2001-02 Parkhurst Heroes

This 16-card set featured game-worn jersey swatches of the two players featured on each card. Each card pictured both players, the modern player in color and the vintage player in opaque. Cards from this set were limited to 40 copies each.

H1 Jean Beliveau 15.00 40.00
Vincent Lecavalier
H2 Gordie Howe 75.00 200.00
Steve Yzerman
H3 Terry Sawchuk 100.00 250.00
Patrick Roy
H4 Rocket Richard 40.00 100.00
Pavel Bure
H5 Phil Esposito 15.00 40.00
Joe Thornton
H6 Guy Lafleur 15.00 40.00
Paul Kariya
H7 Doug Harvey 15.00 40.00
Brian Leetch
H8 Stan Mikita 50.00 125.00
Joe Sakic
H9 Jacques Plante 60.00 150.00
Martin Brodeur
H10 Ted Lindsay 20.00 50.00
Owen Nolan
H11 Vladislav Tretiak 60.00 150.00
Ed Belfour
H12 Tim Horton 15.00 40.00
Scott Stevens
H13 Bobby Hull 50.00 125.00
Brett Hull
H14 Gilbert Perreault 30.00 80.00
Mario Lemieux
H15 Henri Richard 15.00 40.00
Scott Gomez
H16 Bill Gadsby 15.00 40.00
Chris Pronger

2001-02 Parkhurst Jerseys

Cards from this 60-card set featured swatches of game-worn jersey from the featured player. Each card carried a player photo and the swatch on a multi-colored card front which included part of the background from the action photo. Cards in this set were limited to 90 copies each.

*MULT.COLOR SWATCH: .5X TO 1.5X
PJ1 Mario Lemieux 25.00 60.00
PJ2 Milan Hejduk 6.00 15.00
PJ3 Vincent Lecavalier 6.00 15.00
PJ4 Mats Sundin 8.00 20.00
PJ5 Mark Recchi 6.00 15.00
PJ6 Mark Messier 8.00 20.00
PJ7 Peter Bondra 8.00 20.00
PJ8 Jeff Friesen 6.00 15.00
PJ9 Scott Gomez 6.00 15.00
PJ10 Daniel Alfredsson 6.00 15.00
PJ11 Nicklas Lidstrom 8.00 20.00
PJ12 Daniel Sedin 6.00 15.00
PJ13 Peter Forsberg 12.00 30.00
PJ14 Ron Francis 6.00 15.00
PJ15 Joe Sakic 15.00 40.00
PJ16 Mike Modano 12.50 30.00
PJ17 Patrik Stefan 6.00 15.00
PJ18 Steve Yzerman 20.00 50.00
PJ19 Pavel Bure 8.00 20.00
PJ20 Al MacInnis 6.00 15.00
PJ21 Joe Thornton 12.50 30.00
PJ22 John LeClair 8.00 20.00
PJ23 Owen Nolan 6.00 15.00
PJ24 Paul Kariya 8.00 20.00
PJ25 Tony Amonte 6.00 15.00
PJ26 Zigmund Palffy 6.00 15.00
PJ27 Brian Leetch 6.00 15.00
PJ28 Scott Stevens 6.00 15.00
PJ29 Sergei Gonchar 6.00 15.00
PJ30 Chris Drury 6.00 15.00
PJ31 Fredrik Modin 6.00 15.00
PJ32 Alexei Zhamnov 6.00 15.00
PJ33 Curtis Joseph 6.00 15.00
PJ34 Patrik Elias 6.00 15.00
PJ35 Roberto Luongo 8.00 20.00
PJ36 Darren McCarty 6.00 15.00
PJ37 Saku Koivu 8.00 20.00
PJ38 Patrick Roy 25.00 60.00
PJ39 Brendan Shanahan 8.00 20.00
PJ40 Chris Pronger 6.00 15.00
PJ41 Martin Straka 6.00 15.00
PJ42 Chris Chelios 8.00 20.00
PJ43 Theo Fleury 6.00 15.00
PJ44 Roman Cechmanek 6.00 15.00
PJ45 Viktor Kozlov 6.00 15.00
PJ46 Martin Brodeur 20.00 50.00
PJ47 Radek Bonk 6.00 15.00
PJ48 Byron Dafoe 6.00 15.00
PJ49 Adam Foote 6.00 15.00
PJ50 Eric Daze 6.00 15.00
PJ51 Ed Belfour 8.00 20.00
PJ52 Milan Kraft 6.00 15.00
PJ53 Arturs Irbe 6.00 15.00
PJ54 Alex Tanguay 6.00 15.00
PJ55 Sergei Fedorov 8.00 20.00
PJ56 Mike Richter 8.00 20.00
PJ57 Marian Hossa 8.00 20.00
PJ58 Joe Nieuwendyk 6.00 15.00
PJ59 Keith Primeau 6.00 15.00
PJ60 Olaf Kolzig 6.00 15.00

2001-02 Parkhurst Jersey and Stick

This set partially paralleled the jersey set but each card carried a jersey swatch and a stick piece from the featured player. Cards in this set were limited to just 70 copies each.

*JSY/STK: .5X TO 1.25X JERSEY CARDS

2001-02 Parkhurst Milestones

This 56-card set featured players who hit the various milestones in their career. Each card featured an action photo of the given player alongside a game-worn swatch of his jersey on the card front. Cards M1-M22 were limited to just 50 cards each. Cards M19U-M52 were limited to just 90 copies each and were available in random BAP Update packs. Due to a printing error, card numbers M19-M22 were used for two different cards each, a "U" suffix is used below to denote the cards available in BAP Update packs.

M1 Chris Osgood 6.00 15.00
200 Wins
M2 Martin Brodeur 15.00 40.00
M3 Jaromir Jagr 12.50 30.00
1000 Points
M4 Jaromir Jagr 12.50 30.00
400 Goals
M5 Ed Belfour 6.00 15.00
50 Shutouts
M6 Brian Leetch 6.00 15.00
600 Assists
M7 Luc Robitaille 6.00 15.00
600 Assists
M8 Jaromir Jagr 12.50 30.00
600 Assists
M9 Mark Recchi 6.00 15.00
Mark Recchi
M10 Curtis Joseph 8.00 20.00
300 Wins
M11 Dominik Hasek 12.00 30.00
50 Shutouts
M12 Mark Messier 12.00 30.00
1500 Games
M13 Scott Stevens 6.00 15.00
1400 Games
M14 Steve Yzerman 20.00 50.00
1300 Games
M15 Doug Gilmour 6.00 15.00
1300 Games
M16 Martin Brodeur 15.00 40.00
M17 Steve Yzerman 20.00 50.00
1600 Points
M18 Patrick Roy 20.00 50.00
50 Shutouts
M19 Ray Bourque 12.00 30.00
1600 Games
M19U Luc Robitaille 8.00 20.00
600 Goals
M20 Mario Lemieux 20.00 50.00
M20U Brett Hull 8.00 20.00
650 Goals
M21 Ray Bourque 12.00 30.00
400 Goals
M21U Mario Lemieux 20.00 50.00
M22 Jeremy Roenick 10.00 25.00
400 Goals
M22U Steve Yzerman 15.00 40.00
650 Goals
M23 Joe Nieuwendyk 5.00 12.00
1000 Games
M24 Ron Francis 5.00 12.00
500 Goals
M25 Brendan Shanahan 8.00 20.00
500 Goals
M26 Pavel Bure 8.00 20.00
400 Goals
M27 Alexander Mogilny 5.00 12.00
400 Goals
M28 Peter Bondra 5.00 12.00
400 Goals
M29 Mats Sundin 5.00 12.00
400 Goals
M30 Mark Recchi 5.00 12.00
400 Goals
M31 Mike Modano 10.00 25.00
M32 Teemu Selanne 8.00 20.00
400 Goals
M33 Steve Yzerman 15.00 40.00
1000 Assists
M34 Adam Oates 5.00 12.00
1000 Assists
M35 Mark Messier 8.00 20.00
1800 Points
M36 Mario Lemieux 20.00 50.00
M37 Patrick Roy 20.00 50.00
500 Wins
M38 Dominik Hasek 12.00 30.00
60 Shutouts
M39 Patrick Roy 20.00 50.00
60 Shutouts
M40 Ed Belfour 6.00 15.00
350 Wins
M41 Curtis Joseph 8.00 20.00
350 Shutouts
M42 Mike Richter 6.00 15.00
300 Wins
M43 Martin Brodeur 20.00 50.00
M44 Ron Francis 5.00 12.00
1700 Points
M45 Adam Oates 5.00 12.00
1300 Points
M46 Brett Hull 10.00 25.00
1200 Points
M47 Joe Sakic 15.00 40.00
1200 Points
M48 Al MacInnis 5.00 12.00
1200 Points
M49 Jaromir Jagr 10.00 25.00
1100 Points
M50 Theo Fleury 5.00 12.00
1000 Points
M51 Brendan Shanahan 6.00 15.00
1000 Points
M52 Jeremy Roenick 8.00 20.00
1000 Points

2001-02 Parkhurst Reprints

This 150-card set featured reprints of vintage Parkhurst cards. Of the 150 cards, 57 were printed with blank backs to form the Parkie Back Checking Contest. Collector's who received a blank back card had to answer a question from the BAP website that could be answered by reading the back of the original card, write the answer on the blank back card and send it to BAP. They would then receive the card back with a printed back. Cards #1, 18, 27, 36, 45, 54, 63, 72, 81, 90, 99, and 108 were originally produced as blank backs in 1951-52 and were not included in the contest.

PR1 Gordie Howe 1.00 5.00
PR2 Maurice Richard 1.00 5.00
PR3 Bernie Geoffrion 1.00 5.00
PR4 Bill Mosienko 1.00 5.00
PR5 Terry Sawchuk 1.00 5.00
PR6 Woody Dumart 1.00 5.00
PR7 Doug Harvey 1.00 5.00
PR8 Frank Mahovlich 1.00 5.00
PR9 Jean Beliveau 1.00 5.00
PR10 Jacques Plante 1.00 5.00
PR11 Jean-Guy Talbot 1.00 5.00
PR12 Gordie Howe 1.00 5.00
PR13 Terry Sawchuk 1.00 5.00
PR14 Maurice Richard 1.00 5.00
PR15 Harry Lumley 1.00 5.00
PR16 Jean Beliveau 1.00 5.00
PR17 Red Kelly 1.00 5.00
PR18 Bernie Geoffrion 1.00 5.00
PR19 Dickie Moore 1.00 5.00
PR20 Dollard St.Laurent 1.00 5.00
PR21 Terry Sawchuk 1.00 5.00
PR22 Harry Lumley 1.00 5.00
PR23 Woody Dumart 1.00 5.00
PR24 Tim Horton 1.00 5.00
PR25 George Hainsworth 1.00 5.00
PR26 Johnny Bower 1.00 5.00
PR27 Doug Harvey 1.00 5.00
PR28 Bill Gadsby 1.00 5.00
PR29 Dickie Moore 1.00 5.00
PR30 Gordie Howe 1.00 5.00
PR31 Red Kelly 1.00 5.00
PR32 Bernie Geoffrion 1.00 5.00
PR33 Jean Beliveau 1.00 5.00
PR34 Jacques Plante 1.00 5.00
PR35 Henri Richard 1.00 5.00
PR36 Chuck Rayner 1.00 5.00
PR37 Henri Richard 1.00 5.00
PR38 Frank Mahovlich 1.00 5.00
PR39 Bill Gadsby 1.00 5.00
PR40 Bernie Geoffrion 1.00 5.00
PR41 Doug Harvey 1.00 5.00
PR42 Maurice Richard 1.00 5.00
PR43 Georges Vezina 1.00 5.00
PR44 Jean-Guy Talbot 1.00 5.00
PR45 Terry Sawchuk 1.00 5.00
PR46 Terry Sawchuk 1.00 5.00
PR47 Jacques Plante 1.00 5.00
PR48 Frank Mahovlich 1.00 5.00
PR49 Bill Gadsby 1.00 5.00
PR50 Butch Bouchard 1.00 5.00
PR51 Bernie Geoffrion 1.00 5.00
PR52 Dollard St. Laurent 1.00 5.00
PR53 Red Kelly 1.00 5.00
PR54 Red Kelly 1.00 5.00
PR55 Johnny Bower 1.00 5.00
PR56 Henri Richard 1.00 5.00
PR57 Bernie Geoffrion 1.00 5.00
PR58 Howe/Lumley 1.00 5.00
PR59 Chuck Rayner 1.00 5.00
PR60 Red Kelly 1.00 5.00
PR61 Dickie Moore 1.00 5.00
PR62 Bernie Geoffrion 1.00 5.00
PR63 Butch Bouchard 1.00 5.00
PR64 Frank Mahovlich 1.00 5.00
PR65 Doug Harvey 1.00 5.00
PR66 Jacques Plante 1.00 5.00
PR67 Tim Horton 1.00 5.00
PR68 Dollard St. Laurent 1.00 5.00
PR69 Bernie Geoffrion 1.00 5.00
PR70 Butch Bouchard 1.00 5.00
PR71 Gordie Howe 1.00 5.00
PR72 Milt Schmidt 1.00 5.00
PR73 Butch Bouchard 1.00 5.00
PR74 Henri Richard 1.00 5.00
PR75 Tim Horton 1.00 5.00
PR76 Gordie Howe 1.00 5.00
PR77 Dickie Moore 1.00 5.00
PR78 Elmer Lach 1.00 5.00
PR79 Bernie Geoffrion 1.00 5.00
PR80 Jean Beliveau 1.00 5.00
PR81 Bill Gadsby 1.00 5.00
PR82 Jean Beliveau 1.00 5.00
PR83 Bill Gadsby 1.00 5.00
PR84 Henri Richard 1.00 5.00
PR85 Plante/Sloan 1.00 5.00
PR86 Frank Mahovlich 1.00 5.00
PR87 Terry Sawchuk 1.00 5.00
PR88 Maurice Richard 1.00 5.00
PR89 Tim Horton 1.00 5.00
PR90 Ted Lindsay 1.00 5.00
PR91 Johnny Bower 1.00 5.00
PR92 Maurice Richard 1.00 5.00
PR93 Red Kelly 1.00 5.00
PR94 Dickie Moore 1.00 5.00
PR95 Bill Gadsby 1.00 5.00
PR96 Ted Lindsay 1.00 5.00
PR97 Tim Horton 1.00 5.00
PR98 Bernie Geoffrion 1.00 5.00
PR99 Woody Dumart 1.00 5.00
PR100 Doug Harvey 1.00 5.00
PR101 Frank Mahovlich 1.00 5.00
PR102 Dickie Moore 1.00 5.00
PR103 Tim Horton 1.00 5.00
PR104 Harry Lumley 1.00 5.00
PR105 Butch Bouchard 1.00 5.00
PR106 Turk Broda 1.00 5.00
PR107 Jean Beliveau 1.00 5.00
PR108 Maurice Richard 1.00 5.00
PR109 Red Kelly 1.00 5.00
PR110 Jean Beliveau 1.00 5.00
PR111 Jean-Guy Talbot 1.00 5.00
PR112 Sawchuk/Geoffrion 1.00 5.00
PR113 Tim Horton 1.00 5.00
PR114 Dollard St. Laurent 1.00 5.00
PR115 Doug Harvey 1.00 5.00
PR116 Gump Worsley 1.00 5.00
PR117 Milt Schmidt 1.00 5.00
PR118 Jean Beliveau 1.00 5.00
PR119 Tim Horton 1.00 5.00
PR120 Dickie Moore 1.00 5.00
PR121 Doug Harvey 1.00 5.00
PR122 Henri Richard 1.00 5.00
PR123 Milt Schmidt 1.00 5.00
PR124 Frank Mahovlich 1.00 5.00
PR125 Johnny Bower 1.00 5.00
PR126 Ted Lindsay 1.00 5.00
PR127 Tim Horton 1.00 5.00
PR128 Jacques Plante 1.00 5.00
PR129 Jean-Guy Talbot 1.00 5.00
PR130 Jean Beliveau 1.00 5.00
PR131 Doug Harvey 1.00 5.00
PR132 Gump Worsley 1.00 5.00
PR133 Terry Sawchuk 1.00 5.00
PR134 Frank Mahovlich 1.00 5.00
PR135 Bill Mosienko 1.00 5.00
PR136 Jean Beliveau 1.00 5.00
PR137 Tim Horton 1.00 5.00
PR138 Jacques Plante 1.00 5.00
PR139 Johnny Bower 1.00 5.00
PR140 Gordie Howe 1.00 5.00
PR141 Chuck Rayner 1.00 5.00
PR142 Henri Richard 1.00 5.00
PR143 Gump Worsley 1.00 5.00
PR144 Red Kelly 1.00 5.00
PR145 Dickie Moore 1.00 5.00
PR146 Frank Mahovlich 1.00 5.00
PR147 Henri Richard 1.00 5.00
PR148 Johnny Bower 1.00 5.00
PR149 Red Kelly 1.00 5.00
PR150 Bill Gadsby 1.00 5.00

2001-02 Parkhurst Sticks

This 70-card set featured pieces of game-used sticks from the featured players alongside color player photos. Cards in this set were limited to 90 copies each.

*SINGLE COLOR SWATCH: .25X TO .75X HI
PS1 Mario Lemieux 30.00 80.00
PS2 Milan Hejduk 8.00 20.00
PS3 Vincent Lecavalier 8.00 20.00
PS4 Mats Sundin 8.00 20.00
PS5 Mark Recchi 6.00 15.00
PS6 Mark Messier 8.00 20.00
PS7 Peter Bondra 6.00 15.00
PS8 Jeff Friesen 6.00 15.00
PS9 Scott Gomez 6.00 15.00
PS10 Daniel Alfredsson 6.00 15.00
PS11 Nicklas Lidstrom 8.00 20.00
PS12 Daniel Sedin 6.00 15.00
PS13 Peter Forsberg 15.00 40.00
PS14 Ron Francis 6.00 15.00
PS15 Joe Sakic 15.00 40.00
PS16 Mike Modano 12.50 30.00
PS17 Patrik Stefan 6.00 15.00
PS18 Steve Yzerman 25.00 60.00
PS19 Pavel Bure 8.00 20.00
PS20 Al MacInnis 6.00 15.00
PS21 Joe Thornton 12.50 30.00
PS22 John LeClair 8.00 20.00
PS23 Owen Nolan 6.00 15.00
PS24 Paul Kariya 8.00 20.00
PS25 Tony Amonte 8.00 20.00
PS26 Zigmund Palffy 6.00 15.00
PS27 Brian Leetch 8.00 20.00
PS28 Scott Stevens 6.00 15.00
PS29 Sergei Gonchar 6.00 15.00
PS30 Chris Drury 6.00 15.00
PS31 Martin Brodeur 20.00 50.00
PS32 Chris Chelios 8.00 20.00
PS33 Rob Blake 6.00 15.00
PS34 Teemu Selanne 8.00 20.00
PS35 Pavol Demitra 6.00 15.00
PS36 Markus Naslund 8.00 20.00
PS37 Alex Tanguay 6.00 15.00
PS38 Keith Primeau 6.00 15.00
PS39 Olaf Kolzig 6.00 15.00
PS40 Sergei Fedorov 12.50 30.00
PS41 Brad Richards 6.00 15.00
PS42 Adam Oates 6.00 15.00
PS43 Darren McCarty 6.00 15.00
PS44 Adam Foote 6.00 15.00
PS45 Sandis Ozolinsh 6.00 15.00
PS46 Chris Pronger 6.00 15.00
PS47 Jason Arnott 6.00 15.00
PS48 Keith Tkachuk 8.00 20.00
PS49 Sergei Samsonov 6.00 15.00
PS50 Kenny Jonsson 6.00 15.00
PS51 Gary Roberts 6.00 15.00
PS52 Marian Hossa 8.00 20.00
PS53 Brendan Shanahan 8.00 20.00
PS54 Patrick Roy 25.00 60.00
PS55 Pierre Turgeon 6.00 15.00
PS56 Roman Turek 6.00 15.00
PS57 Doug Weight 6.00 15.00
PS58 Jaromir Jagr 12.50 30.00
PS59 Brett Hull 10.00 25.00
PS60 Dominik Hasek 15.00 40.00
PS61 Luc Robitaille 6.00 15.00
PS62 Eric Lindros 8.00 20.00
PS63 Stan Mikita 15.00 40.00
PS64 Guy Lafleur 15.00 40.00
PS65 Lanny McDonald 12.50 30.00
PS66 Jari Kurri 15.00 40.00
PS67 Jeremy Roenick 10.00 25.00
PS68 Rick DiPietro 6.00 15.00
PS69 Joe Nieuwendyk 6.00 15.00
PS70 Alexander Mogilny 6.00 15.00

2001-02 Parkhurst Teammates

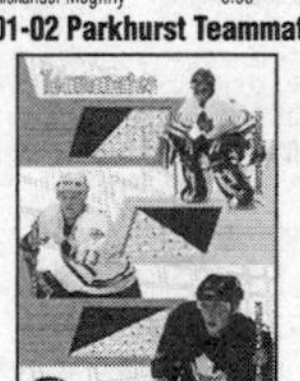

Cards in this 28-card set featured three swatches of game-worn jerseys from the three teammates pictured on the card front. The cards were produced vertically, and the swatches were affixed parallel to a photo of each player. Cards T1-T18 were available in random packs of Parkhurst and were limited to 30 copies each. Cards T19-T28 were available in random packs of BAP Update and were limited to 80 copies each.

T1 Brendan Shanahan 75.00 200.00
Steve Yzerman
Nicklas Lidstrom
T2 Milan Kraft 50.00 125.00
Jean Sebastien Aubin
Mario Lemieux
T3 Theo Fleury 20.00 50.00
Mark Messier
Brian Leetch
T4 Byron Dafoe 12.00 30.00
Joe Thornton
Jason Allison
T5 Adam Foote 20.00 50.00
Joe Sakic
Chris Drury
T6 Olaf Kolzig 20.00 50.00
Sergei Gonchar
Olaf Bondra
T7 Curtis Joseph 20.00 50.00
Mats Sundin
Tomas Kaberle
T8 Patrick Roy 60.00 150.00
Peter Forsberg
Milan Hejduk
T9 Jocelyn Thibault 10.00 25.00
Tony Amonte
Eric Daze
T10 Roberto Luongo 20.00 50.00
Pavel Bure
Viktor Kozlov
T11 Martin Biron 10.00 25.00
Miroslav Satan
Alexei Zhitnik
T12 Bellour/Modano/Sydor 20.00 50.00
T13 Roman Cechmanek 10.00 25.00
Mark Recchi
John LeClair
T14 Martin Brodeur 40.00 100.00
Scott Stevens
Patrik Elias
T15 Bobby Holik 10.00 25.00
Scott Gomez
Jason Arnott
T16 Marion Hossa 25.00
Daniel Alfredsson
Radek Bonk
T17 Daniel Sedin 20.00 50.00
Markus Naslund
Todd Bertuzzi
T18 Ron Francis 10.00 25.00
Arturs Irbe
Sandis Ozolinsh
T19 Sergei Samsonov 25.00 60.00
Joe Thornton
Bill Guerin
T20 Sandis Ozolinsh 12.50 30.00
Pavel Bure
Roberto Luongo
T21 Marty Turco 20.00 50.00
Mike Modano
Ed Belfour
T22 Joe Sakic 40.00 100.00
Patrick Roy
Chris Drury
T23 Steve Yzerman 30.00 80.00
Brendan Shanahan
Dominik Hasek
T24 Eric Lindros 15.00 40.00
Brian Leetch
Mark Messier
T25 Teemu Selanne 12.50 30.00
Jani Hurme
Sami Kapanen
T26 Mats Sundin 12.50 30.00
Tommy Salo
Markus Naslund
T27 Jaromir Jagr 25.00 60.00
Dominik Hasek
Tomas Kaberle
T28 Steve Yzerman 40.00 100.00
Mario Lemieux
Martin Brodeur

2001-02 Parkhurst Vintage Memorabilia

Cards from this 30-card set featured reprints of vintage Parkhurst cards with a piece of game-used memorabilia attached to the card front. Production quantities varied and are listed below beside the card descriptions. Cards with print runs less than 25 are not priced due to scarcity.

MULT.COLOR SWATCH: 1X TO 2X HI
PV1 Rocket Richard GJ/90 60.00 150.00
PV2 Rocket Richard Number/5
PV3 Rocket Richard Emblem/5
PV4 Jacques Plante GJ/90 30.00 80.00
PV5 Jacques Plante Glove/90 30.00 80.00
PV6 Jacques Plante Emblem/5
PV7 Jacques Plante Number/5
PV8 Jacques Plante Stick/90 30.00 80.00
PV9 Bill Gadsby Glove/90 15.00 40.00
PV10 Doug Harvey GJ/90 15.00 40.00
PV11 Doug Harvey Emblem/5
PV12 Doug Harvey Number/5
PV13 Gordie Howe GJ/40 75.00 200.00
PV14 Gordie Howe Emblem/5
PV15 Gordie Howe Number/5
PV16 Bill Mosienko Pants/90 15.00 40.00
PV17 Jean Beliveau GJ/90 20.00 50.00
PV18 Jean Beliveau Number/5
PV19 Jean Beliveau Emblem/5
PV20 Turk Broda Glove/90 25.00 60.00
PV21 Tim Horton 30.00 80.00
PV22 Henri Richard GJ/90 15.00 40.00
PV23 Henri Richard Emblem/5
PV24 Chuck Rayner Glove/90 40.00 100.00
PV25 T.Sawchuk Glove/90 30.00 80.00
PV26 Terry Sawchuk Pad/90 30.00 80.00
PV27 Terry Sawchuk GJ/90 30.00 80.00
PV28 Ted Lindsay GJ/90 15.00 40.00
PV29 Ted Lindsay Emblem/5
PV30 Johnny Bower Pad/90 15.00 40.00

2001-02 Parkhurst World Class Jerseys

This 8-card set featured player photos and game-worn jersey swatches over a background of the national flag of the given player. Each card in this set was limited to just 80 copies each.

WCJ1 Steve Yzerman 20.00 50.00
WCJ2 Teemu Selanne 10.00 25.00
WCJ3 Olaf Kolzig 10.00 25.00
WCJ4 Zigmund Palffy 10.00 25.00
WCJ5 Peter Forsberg 15.00 40.00
WCJ6 Mike Modano 12.50 30.00
WCJ7 Jaromir Jagr 15.00 40.00
WCJ8 Alexei Yashin 10.00 25.00

2001-02 Parkhurst World Class Emblems

This 8-card set paralleled the jersey set but featured swatches of emblems from the player's jersey. Each card was limited to just 20 copies each.

EMBLEMS NOT PRICED DUE TO SCARCITY

2001-02 Parkhurst World Class Numbers

This 8-card set paralleled the jersey set but featured swatches from the numbers on the player's jersey. Each card was limited to just 20 copies each.

NUMBERS NOT PRICED DUE TO SCARCITY

2001-02 Parkhurst Waving the Flag

Inspired by the 1963-64 Parkhurst Design, this set featured a portrait shot of the player with his native flag in the background. Card backs summarize each player's international experience in tournaments. The cards were printed on 20-point foilboard stock and the print run was limited to 2,002 sets. Each set was accompanied by a sequentially-numbered header card to enhance collectibility. The set was available by mail via the Be a Player website.

1 Mario Lemieux 6.00 15.00
2 Joe Sakic 2.00 5.00
3 Steve Yzerman 5.00 12.00
4 Paul Kariya 1.00 2.50
5 Curtis Joseph 1.00 2.50
6 Martin Brodeur 2.50 6.00
7 Eric Lindros 1.00 2.50
8 Chris Pronger .75 2.00
9 Jaromir Jagr 1.50 4.00
10 Milan Hejduk 1.00 2.50
11 Dominik Hasek 2.00 5.00
12 Martin Havlat .75 2.00
13 Teemu Selanne 1.00 2.50
14 Jani Hurme .75 2.00
15 Miikka Kiprusoff .75 2.00
16 Sami Kapanen .75 2.00
17 Mats Sundin 1.00 2.50
18 Nicklas Lidstrom 1.00 2.50
19 Tommy Salo .75 2.00
20 Kristian Huselius .75 2.00
21 Jeremy Roenick 1.25 3.00
22 Doug Weight .75 2.00
23 Tony Amonte .75 2.00
24 Brian Leetch .75 2.00
25 Mike Modano 1.50 4.00
26 Brett Hull 1.25 3.00
27 John LeClair 1.00 2.50
28 Keith Tkachuk 1.00 2.50
29 Alexei Yashin .75 2.00
30 Pavel Bure 1.00 2.50
31 Nikolai Khabibulin 1.00 2.50
32 Darius Kasparaitis .75 2.00

2001-02 Parkhurst Beckett Promos

Inserted into issues of Beckett Hockey collector, this 50-card set paralleled the base Parkhurst set but carried a "Beckett" stamp on the card backs. There is very little secondary market information for these cards, therefore they are unpriced.

COMMON CARD
251 Jesse Boulerice
252 Marko Kiprusoff
253 Ivan Ciernik
254 Pavel Datsyuk
255 Jaroslav Bednar
256 Andreas Salomonsson
257 Mike Ribeiro
258 Darcy Hordichuk
259 Chris Neil
260 Rostislav Klesla
261 Kristian Huselius
262 Brian Sutherby
263 Jiri Dopita
264 Radek Martinek
265 Barrett Heisten
266 Krystofer Kolanos
267 Pascal Dupuis
268 Andreas Lilja
269 Chris Mason
270 Mathieu Garon

271 Andrew Raycroft
272 Jeff Jillson
273 Jiri Bicek
274 Niklas Hagman
275 Pavel Brendl
276 Stephen Peat
277 Sascha Goc
278 Nick Boynton
279 Timo Parssinen
280 Mika Noronen
281 Scott Clemmensen
282 Dan Blackburn
283 Nikita Alexeev
284 Vaclav Nedorost
285 Ilja Bryzgalov
286 Dany Heatley
287 Niko Kapanen
288 Rick Berry
289 Mark Bell
290 Kamil Piros
291 Maxime Ouellet
292 Kris Beech
293 Miikka Kiprusoff
294 Martti Jarventie
295 Ilya Kovalchuk
296 Nick Schultz
297 Bryan Allen
298 Josef Boumedienne
299 Jason Williams
300 Daniel Tjarnqvist

2002-03 Parkhurst

Released in late February, this 250-card set consisted of 200 veteran cards and 50 shortprinted rookie cards. Rookies were serial-numbered out of 500.

Card	Low	High
COMP.SET w/o SP's (200)	25.00	50.00
1 Rod Brind'Amour	.25	.60
2 Alexei Kovalev	.25	.60
3 Brad Richards	.25	.60
4 Milan Hnilicka	.25	.60
5 Arturs Irbe	.25	.60
6 Al MacInnis	.25	.60
7 Pavel Bure	.30	.75
8 Patrick Lalime	.25	.60
9 Vincent Damphousse	.10	.25
10 Bates Battaglia	.10	.25
11 Evgeni Nabokov	.25	.60
12 Glen Murray	.10	.25
13 Chris Osgood	.25	.60
14 Pierre Turgeon	.25	.60
15 Scott Stevens	.25	.60
16 Daniel Briere	.10	.25
17 Patrik Stefan	.10	.25
18 Pavol Demitra	.25	.60
19 Mark Parrish	.10	.25
20 Jason Allison	.10	.25
21 Jaromir Jagr	.50	1.25
22 Mike Modano	.50	1.25
23 Mark Messier	.30	.75
24 Ilya Kovalchuk	.40	1.00
25 Teemu Selanne	.30	.75
26 Marty Turco	.25	.60
27 Keith Tkachuk	.30	.75
28 Simon Gagne	.30	.75
29 Brent Johnson	.25	.60
30 Anson Carter	.25	.60
31 Jeff Jillson	.10	.25
32 Gary Roberts	.10	.25
33 Mike Richter	.30	.75
34 Martin Lapointe	.10	.25
35 Todd Bertuzzi	.30	.75
36 Valeri Bure	.10	.25
37 Marian Hossa	.30	.75
38 Eric Daze	.25	.60
39 Nikolai Khabibulin	.30	.75
40 Miikka Kiprusoff	.25	.60
41 Kevin Weekes	.25	.60
42 Mark Recchi	.25	.60
43 Dan Cloutier	.25	.60
44 Keith Primeau	.10	.25
45 Alex Tanguay	.25	.60
46 Ed Jovanovski	.25	.60
47 Roberto Luongo	.40	1.00
48 Saku Koivu	.30	.75
49 Chris Drury	.25	.60
50 Olaf Kolzig	.25	.60
51 Dan Blackburn	.25	.60
52 Erik Cole	.10	.25
53 Darcy Tucker	.10	.25
54 Chris Chelios	.30	.75
55 Pavel Datsyuk	.30	.75
56 Mike Comrie	.25	.60
57 Paul Kariya	.30	.75
58 Eric Lindros	.30	.75
59 Martin Havlat	.25	.60
60 Scott Niedermayer	.10	.25
61 Krys Kolanos	.10	.25
62 Rostislav Klesla	.10	.25
63 Jocelyn Thibault	.25	.60
64 Mike Dunham	.25	.60
65 Shane Doan	.10	.25
66 John LeClair	.30	.75
67 Tommy Salo	.25	.60
68 Doug Gilmour	.25	.60
69 Johan Hedberg	.25	.60
70 Brett Hull	.40	1.00
71 Alexander Mogilny	.25	.60
72 Chris Pronger	.25	.60
73 Sergei Fedorov	.50	1.25
74 David Legwand	.25	.60
75 Kristian Huselius	.10	.25
76 Manny Fernandez	.25	.60
77 Vincent Lecavalier	.30	.75
78 Rick DiPietro	.25	.60
79 Mike Peca	.10	.25
80 Ryan Smyth	.10	.25
81 Brian Rolston	.25	.60
82 Brian Leetch	.25	.60
83 Steve Sullivan	.10	.25
84 Scott Gomez	.10	.25
85 Adam Foote	.10	.25
86 Scott Hartnell	.10	.25
87 Alexei Zhamnov	.10	.25
88 Marc Denis	.25	.60
89 Joe Nieuwendyk	.25	.60
90 Brad Stuart	.10	.25
91 Patrik Elias	.25	.60
92 Mats Sundin	.30	.75
93 Jose Theodore	.40	1.00
94 Brendan Shanahan	.30	.75
95 Daniel Alfredsson	.25	.60
96 Martin Brodeur	.75	2.00
97 Jarome Iginla	.40	1.00
98 Peter Bondra	.25	.60
99 Peter Forsberg	.60	1.50
100 Steve Yzerman	1.50	4.00
101 Alexei Yashin	.10	.25
102 Patrick Roy	1.50	4.00
103 Markus Naslund	.30	.75
104 Jeremy Roenick	.30	.75
105 Darius Kasparaitis	.10	.25
106 Curtis Joseph	.30	.75
107 Marian Gaborik	.60	1.50
108 Bill Guerin	.25	.60
109 Joe Sakic	.60	1.50
110 Adam Oates	.25	.60
111 Owen Nolan	.25	.60
112 Rob Blake	.25	.60
113 Nicklas Lidstrom	.30	.75
114 Joe Thornton	.50	1.25
115 Mario Lemieux	2.00	5.00
116 Sergei Gonchar	.10	.25
117 Bobby Holik	.10	.25
118 Sandis Ozolinsh	.10	.25
119 Steven Reinprecht	.10	.25
120 Jeff O'Neill	.10	.25
121 Radek Bonk	.10	.25
122 Milan Hejduk	.30	.75
123 Zigmund Palffy	.25	.60
124 Luc Robitaille	.25	.60
125 Dany Heatley	.40	1.00
126 Doug Weight	.25	.60
127 Fredrik Modin	.10	.25
128 Ron Francis	.25	.60
129 Roman Turek	.25	.60
130 Adam Deadmarsh	.10	.25
131 Sami Kapanen	.10	.25
132 Sergei Samsonov	.25	.60
133 Jeff Friesen	.10	.25
134 Martin St. Louis	.25	.60
135 Phil Housley	.10	.25
136 Mark Bell	.10	.25
137 Felix Potvin	.30	.75
138 Ed Belfour	.30	.75
139 Martin Biron	.25	.60
140 Alyn McCauley	.10	.25
141 Miroslav Satan	.25	.60
142 Jan Hrdina	.10	.25
143 Ron Tugnutt	.25	.60
144 Steve Shields	.25	.60
145 Cliff Ronning	.10	.25
146 Wade Redden	.10	.25
147 Patrick Marleau	.25	.60
148 Tony Amonte	.25	.60
149 Byron Dafoe	.25	.60
150 Roman Cechmanek	.25	.60
151 Martin Straka	.10	.25
152 Sergei Zubov	.10	.25
153 Maxim Afinogenov	.10	.25
154 Brian Boucher	.25	.60
155 Jason Arnott	.10	.25
156 Oleg Tverdovsky	.10	.25
157 Daymond Langkow	.10	.25
158 Andrew Brunette	.10	.25
159 Brian Rafalski	.10	.25
160 Mike York	.10	.25
161 Richard Zednik	.10	.25
162 Radim Vrbata	.10	.25
163 Tim Connolly	.10	.25
164 Jamie Storr	.25	.60
165 Henrik Sedin	.10	.25
166 Sean Burke	.25	.60
167 Daniel Sedin	.10	.25
168 Jason Smith	.10	.25
169 Stephen Weiss	.25	.60
170 Bryan McCabe	.10	.25
171 Theo Fleury	.10	.25
172 Jean-Sebastien Giguere	.25	.60
173 Espen Knutsen	.10	.25
174 Mika Noronen	.25	.60
175 Michael Nylander	.10	.25
176 Yanic Perreault	.10	.25
177 Donald Brashear	.10	.25
178 Denis Arkhipov	.10	.25
179 Adrian Aucoin	.10	.25
180 Tie Domi	.10	.25
181 Andrew Cassels	.10	.25
182 Eric Brewer	.10	.25
183 Trevor Linden	.10	.25
184 Brendan Witt	.10	.25
185 Robert Lang	.10	.25
186 Brendan Morrison	.25	.60
187 Mike Fisher	.10	.25
188 Alexei Morozov	.10	.25
189 Martin Erat	.10	.25
190 Jeff Hackett	.25	.60
191 Mariusz Czerkawski	.10	.25
192 Olli Jokinen	.10	.25
193 Brad Isbister	.10	.25
194 Niklas Hagman	.10	.25
195 Jere Lehtinen	.25	.60
196 Igor Larionov	.10	.25
197 Curtis Brown	.10	.25
198 Ray Whitney	.10	.25
199 Grant Marshall	.10	.25
200 Craig Conroy	.10	.25
201 P-M Bouchard RC	8.00	20.00
202 Rick Nash RC	15.00	40.00
203 Dennis Seidenberg RC	2.00	5.00
204 Jay Bouwmeester RC	6.00	15.00
205 Stanislav Chistov RC	2.00	5.00
206 Jared Aulin RC	2.00	5.00
207 Ivan Majesky RC	2.00	5.00
208 Chuck Kobasew RC	4.00	10.00
209 Jordan Leopold RC	4.00	10.00
210 Ryan Miller RC	12.00	30.00
211 Ales Hemsky RC	10.00	25.00
212 Patrick Sharp RC	2.00	5.00
213 Kari Haakana RC	2.00	5.00
214 Dmitri Bykov RC	2.00	5.00
215 Pascal Leclaire RC	6.00	15.00
216 Henrik Zetterberg RC	12.00	30.00
217 Alexander Frolov RC	8.00	20.00
218 Steve Eminger RC	2.00	5.00
219 Scottie Upshall RC	5.00	12.00
220 Tom Koivisto RC	2.00	5.00
221 Shaone Morrisonn RC	2.00	5.00
222 Ron Hainsey RC	2.00	5.00
223 Martin Gerber RC	6.00	15.00
224 Adam Hall RC	2.00	5.00
225 Lasse Pirjeta RC	2.00	5.00
226 Anton Volchenkov RC	2.00	5.00
227 Craig Andersson RC	12.00	30.00
228 Rickard Wallin RC	2.00	5.00
229 Alexander Svitov RC	2.00	5.00
230 Alexei Smirnov RC	2.00	5.00
231 Jeff Taffe RC	2.00	5.00
232 Mikael Tellqvist RC	5.00	12.00
233 Radovan Somik RC	2.00	5.00
234 Dick Tarnstrom RC	2.00	5.00
235 Steve Ott RC	5.00	12.00
236 Brooks Orpik RC	2.00	5.00
237 Eric Bertrand RC	2.00	5.00
238 Sylvain Blouin RC	2.00	5.00
239 Greg Koehler RC	2.00	5.00
240 Stephane Veilleux RC	2.00	5.00
241 Curtis Sanford RC	5.00	12.00
242 Carlo Colaiacovo RC	2.00	5.00
243 Patrick Boileau RC	2.00	5.00
244 Tim Thomas RC	5.00	12.00
245 Mike Cammalleri RC	5.00	12.00
246 Levente Szuper RC	2.00	5.00
247 Jason Spezza RC	15.00	40.00
248 Cody Rudkowsky RC	2.00	5.00
249 Eric Godard RC	2.00	5.00
250 Valeri Kharlamov RC	8.00	20.00

2002-03 Parkhurst Bronze

This 250-card parallel set was serial-numbered to just 100 sets.

*BRONZE: 4X TO 10X BASIC CARDS
*ROOKIES: .25X TO .75X

2002-03 Parkhurst Gold

This 250-card parallel set was serial-numbered to just 10 sets.

GOLD NOT PRICED DUE TO SCARCITY

2002-03 Parkhurst Silver

This 250-card parallel set was serial-numbered to just 50 sets.

*SILVER: 6X TO 15X BASIC CARDS
*ROOKIES: .5X TO 1.25X

2002-03 Parkhurst College Ranks

This 18-card set featured players who played in the NCAA. Cards were limited to 100 copies each.

Card	Low	High
CR1 Chris Drury	4.00	10.00
CR2 Erik Cole	3.00	8.00
CR3 Keith Tkachuk	4.00	10.00
CR4 Rick DiPietro	3.00	8.00
CR5 Rob Blake	3.00	8.00
CR6 Adam Oates	3.00	8.00
CR7 Chris Chelios	4.00	10.00
CR8 Brett Hull	5.00	12.00
CR9 Paul Kariya	4.00	10.00
CR10 Tony Amonte	3.00	8.00
CR11 Doug Weight	3.00	8.00
CR12 Dany Heatley	5.00	12.00
CR13 Steven Reinprecht	3.00	8.00
CR14 Curtis Joseph	4.00	10.00
CR15 Anson Carter	3.00	8.00
CR16 Mike Dunham	3.00	8.00
CR17 Mike Richter	4.00	10.00
CR18 Ed Belfour	4.00	10.00

2002-03 Parkhurst College Ranks Jerseys

This 18-card set paralleled the regular set with the addition of jersey swatches. Cards were limited to 60 copies each.

*MULT.COLOR SWATCH: .5X TO 1.25X

Card	Low	High
CRM1 Chris Drury	8.00	20.00
CRM2 Erik Cole	8.00	20.00
CRM3 Keith Tkachuk	8.00	20.00
CRM4 Rick DiPietro	8.00	20.00
CRM5 Rob Blake	8.00	20.00
CRM6 Adam Oates	8.00	20.00
CRM7 Chris Chelios	8.00	20.00
CRM8 Brett Hull	15.00	40.00
CRM9 Paul Kariya	8.00	20.00
CRM10 Tony Amonte	8.00	20.00
CRM11 Doug Weight	10.00	25.00
CRM12 Dany Heatley	12.50	30.00
CRM13 Steven Reinprecht	8.00	20.00
CRM14 Curtis Joseph	8.00	20.00
CRM15 Anson Carter	8.00	20.00
CRM16 Mike Dunham	10.00	25.00
CRM17 Mike Richter	8.00	20.00
CRM18 Ed Belfour	10.00	25.00

2002-03 Parkhurst Franchise Players

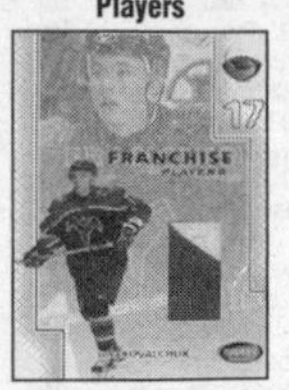

Limited to just 50 copies each, this 30-card set featured game jersey swatches from team leaders.

*MULT.COLOR SWATCH: .5X TO 1.25X

Card	Low	High
FP1 Paul Kariya	8.00	20.00
FP2 Ilya Kovalchuk	12.50	30.00
FP3 Joe Thornton	15.00	40.00
FP4 Miroslav Satan	8.00	20.00
FP5 Jarome Iginla	12.50	30.00
FP6 Jeff O'Neill	8.00	20.00
FP7 Eric Daze	8.00	20.00
FP8 Patrick Roy	25.00	60.00
FP9 Rostislav Klesla	8.00	20.00
FP10 Mike Modano	10.00	25.00
FP11 Steve Yzerman	20.00	50.00
FP12 Mike Comrie	8.00	20.00
FP13 Roberto Luongo	10.00	25.00
FP14 Zigmund Palffy	8.00	20.00
FP15 Marian Gaborik	15.00	40.00
FP16 Jose Theodore	15.00	40.00
FP17 Scott Hartnell	8.00	20.00
FP18 Martin Brodeur	20.00	50.00
FP19 Alexei Yashin	8.00	20.00
FP20 Pavel Bure	8.00	20.00
FP21 Marian Hossa	8.00	20.00
FP22 Simon Gagne	8.00	20.00
FP23 Daniel Briere	8.00	20.00
FP24 Mario Lemieux	25.00	60.00
FP25 Chris Pronger	8.00	20.00
FP26 Owen Nolan	8.00	20.00
FP27 Nikolai Khabibulin	8.00	20.00
FP28 Mats Sundin	8.00	20.00
FP29 Markus Naslund	8.00	20.00
FP30 Jaromir Jagr	12.50	30.00

2002-03 Parkhurst Hardware

These cards were part of a redemption program launched by BAP focusing on the annual NHL awards. Each trophy was represented by 9 hopefuls and a Wild Card. Collectors had the choice of keeping their redemption cards (numbered to just 100 copies each), or sending them in for a chance to win a memorabilia card numbered to just 10. Collectors had to send in the card of the eventual trophy winner in order to be eligible for the random drawing. Winner cards are not priced due to their scarcity. Numbers below correlate to the amount of cards not redeemed.

Card	Low	High
COMMON CARD	4.00	10.00
A1 Eric Lindros/96	4.00	10.00
A2 Jarome Iginla/95	5.00	12.00
A3 Jaromir Jagr/98	4.00	10.00
A4 Joe Sakic/97	4.00	10.00
A5 Markus Naslund/82	4.00	10.00
A6 Pavel Bure/94	4.00	10.00
A7 Peter Forsberg/83	8.00	20.00
A8 Mario Lemieux/88	4.00	10.00
A9 Mats Sundin/98	4.00	10.00
A10 Wildcard/87	4.00	10.00
C1 Chuck Kobasew/95	4.00	10.00
C2 Henrik Zetterberg/78	8.00	20.00
C3 Alexander Svitov/94	4.00	10.00
C4 Jay Bouwmeester/92	4.00	10.00
C5 Jordan Leopold/95	4.00	10.00
C6 Ron Hainsey/96	4.00	10.00
C7 Rick Nash/81	8.00	20.00
C8 Stanislav Chistov/94	4.00	10.00
C9 Stephen Weiss/96	4.00	10.00
C10 Wildcard/85	4.00	10.00
H1 Eric Lindros/92	4.00	10.00
H2 Jarome Iginla/88	5.00	12.00
H3 Jaromir Jagr/85	4.00	10.00
H4 Joe Sakic/82	4.00	10.00
H5 Jose Theodore/91	5.00	12.00
H6 Markus Naslund/78	4.00	10.00
H7 Pavel Bure/91	4.00	10.00
H8 Peter Forsberg/73	8.00	20.00
H9 Mario Lemieux/92	4.00	10.00
H10 Wildcard/80	4.00	10.00
N1 Nicklas Lidstrom/85	6.00	15.00
N2 Sergei Gonchar/95	4.00	10.00
N3 Rob Blake/93	4.00	10.00
N4 Ed Jovanovski/96	4.00	10.00
N5 Brian Rafalski/99	4.00	10.00
N6 Bryan McCabe/98	4.00	10.00
N7 Chris Chelios/95	4.00	10.00
N8 Adrian Aucoin/97	4.00	10.00
N9 Brian Leetch/96	4.00	10.00
N10 Wildcard/77	4.00	10.00
P1 Eric Lindros/94	4.00	10.00
P2 Jarome Iginla/96	5.00	12.00
P3 Jaromir Jagr/88	4.00	10.00
P4 Joe Sakic/89	4.00	10.00
P5 Markus Naslund/79	6.00	15.00
P6 Pavel Bure/98	4.00	10.00
P7 Peter Forsberg/81	4.00	10.00
P8 Mario Lemieux/88	4.00	10.00
P9 Mats Sundin/93	4.00	10.00
P10 Wildcard/77	4.00	10.00
V1 Curtis Joseph/96	4.00	10.00
V2 Evgeni Nabokov/95	4.00	10.00
V3 Jose Theodore/95	5.00	12.00
V4 Martin Brodeur/72	8.00	20.00
V5 Mike Richter/97	4.00	10.00
V6 Patrick Lalime/93	4.00	10.00
V7 Patrick Roy/86	4.00	10.00
V8 Roberto Luongo/97	5.00	12.00
V9 Olaf Kolzig/98	4.00	10.00
V10 Wildcard/86	4.00	10.00
AW1 Peter Forsberg/Hart		
AW2 Barret Jackman/Calder		
AW3 Martin Brodeur/Vezina		
AW4 Peter Forsberg/Art Ross		
AW5 Nicklas Lidstrom/Norris		
AW6 Markus Naslund/Pearson		

2002-03 Parkhurst Heroes

Limited to 25 sets, this 12-card set featured swatches of game jerseys from modern era players and their idols.

Card	Low	High
NH1 Ilya Kovalchuk / Valeri Kharlamov	60.00	150.00
NH2 J.Thornton/S.Yzerman	50.00	125.00
NH3 Jarome Iginla / Mark Messier	30.00	80.00
NH4 S.Yzerman/B.Trottier	60.00	150.00
NH5 S.Gagne/M.Lemieux	50.00	125.00
NH6 Eric Lindros / Mark Messier	30.00	80.00
NH7 M.Lemieux/G.Lafleur	60.00	150.00
NH8 R.Nash/M.Sundin	30.00	80.00
NH9 Chris Pronger / Al MacInnis	30.00	80.00
NH10 J.Bouwmeester/S.Yzerman	30.00	80.00
NH11 Dany Heatley / Brett Hull	60.00	150.00
NH12 Stephen Weiss / Peter Forsberg	50.00	125.00

2002-03 Parkhurst He Shoots-He Scores Points

Inserted one per pack, these cards carried a value of 1, 2 or 3 points. The points could be redeemed for special memorabilia cards. The cards are unnumbered and are listed below in alphabetical order by point value. The redemption program ended January 31, 2004.

Card	Low	High
1 Martin Brodeur 1 pt.	.40	1.00
2 Peter Forsberg 1pt.	.40	1.00
3 Mark Messier 1pt.	.40	1.00
4 Owen Nolan 1 pt.	.40	1.00
5 Jeremy Roenick 1 pt.	.40	1.00
6 Patrick Roy 1 pt.	.40	1.00
7 Joe Sakic 1 pt.	.40	1.00
8 Brendan Shanahan 1 pt.	.40	1.00
9 Mats Sundin 1 pt.	.40	1.00
10 Jose Theodore 1 pt.	.40	1.00
11 Joe Thornton 1 pt.	.40	1.00
12 Pavel Bure 2 pt.	.40	1.00
13 Jaromir Jagr 2 pt.	.40	1.00
14 Paul Kariya 2 pt.	.40	1.00
15 Eric Lindros 2 pt.	.40	1.00
16 Mike Modano 2 pt.	.40	1.00
17 Steve Yzerman 2 pt.	.40	1.00
18 Jarome Iginla 3 pt.	.40	1.00
19 Ilya Kovalchuk 3 pt.	.40	1.00
20 Mario Lemieux 3 pt.	.40	1.00

2002-03 Parkhurst He Shoots-He Scores Prizes

Available only by redeeming 400 Parkhurst He Shoots-He Scores points, this 30-card set featured game-used swatches of jersey and a color photo of the player. Each card had a stated print run of 20 serial-numbered sets and each was encased in a clear plastic slab with a descriptive label at the top. This set is unpriced due to scarcity and volatility.

NOT PRICED DUE TO SCARCITY

1 Mario Lemieux
2 Pavel Bure
3 Jaromir Jagr
4 Eric Lindros
5 Paul Kariya
6 Ilya Kovalchuk
7 Mike Modano
8 Joe Thornton
9 Jose Theodore
10 Jeremy Roenick
11 Martin Brodeur
12 Mats Sundin
13 Mark Messier
14 Steve Yzerman
15 Peter Forsberg
16 Patrick Roy
17 Jarome Iginla
18 Brendan Shanahan
19 Owen Nolan
20 Joe Sakic
21 Teemu Selanne
22 Nicklas Lidstrom
23 John LeClair
24 Dany Heatley
25 Luc Robitaille
26 Eric Daze
27 Keith Tkachuk
28 Brian Leetch
29 Milan Hejduk
30 Rob Blake

2002-03 Parkhurst Jerseys

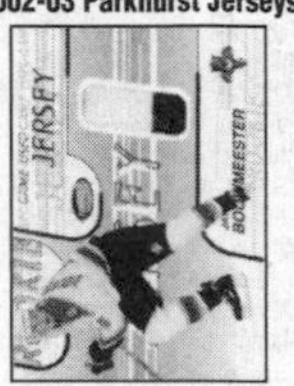

*MULT.COLOR SWATCH: .5X TO 1.25X
STATED PRINT RUN 90 SETS

Card	Low	High
GJ1 Mario Lemieux	20.00	50.00
GJ2 Jose Theodore	10.00	25.00
GJ3 Brian Leetch	6.00	15.00
GJ4 Jaromir Jagr	10.00	25.00
GJ5 Steve Yzerman	20.00	50.00
GJ6 Eric Daze	6.00	15.00
GJ7 Saku Koivu	8.00	20.00
GJ8 John LeClair	8.00	20.00
GJ9 Jeff O'Neill	6.00	15.00
GJ10 Gary Roberts	6.00	15.00
GJ11 Al MacInnis	6.00	15.00
GJ12 Marian Gaborik	12.50	30.00
GJ13 Teemu Selanne	8.00	20.00
GJ14 Alexander Mogilny	6.00	15.00
GJ15 Eric Lindros	8.00	20.00
GJ16 Milan Hejduk	8.00	20.00
GJ17 Zigmund Palffy	8.00	20.00
GJ18 Luc Robitaille	6.00	15.00
GJ19 Ilya Kovalchuk	10.00	25.00
GJ20 Rostislav Klesla	6.00	15.00
GJ21 Mark Messier	8.00	20.00
GJ22 Ron Francis	6.00	15.00
GJ23 Chris Pronger	6.00	15.00
GJ24 Dany Heatley	10.00	25.00
GJ25 Mark Recchi	6.00	15.00
GJ26 Doug Weight	6.00	15.00
GJ27 Alex Tanguay	8.00	20.00
GJ28 Sergei Fedorov	10.00	25.00
GJ29 Todd Bertuzzi	8.00	20.00
GJ30 Sami Kapanen	6.00	15.00
GJ31 Sergei Samsonov	6.00	15.00
GJ32 Jeremy Roenick	10.00	25.00
GJ33 Mike Modano	10.00	25.00
GJ34 Joe Sakic	15.00	40.00
GJ35 Pavel Bure	8.00	20.00
GJ36 Paul Kariya	8.00	20.00
GJ37 Owen Nolan	6.00	15.00
GJ38 Rob Blake	6.00	15.00
GJ39 Nicklas Lidstrom	8.00	20.00
GJ40 Joe Thornton	12.50	30.00
GJ41 Brendan Shanahan	8.00	20.00
GJ42 Daniel Alfredsson	6.00	15.00
GJ43 Martin Brodeur	20.00	50.00
GJ44 Jarome Iginla	10.00	25.00
GJ45 Peter Bondra	6.00	15.00
GJ46 Peter Forsberg	12.00	30.00
GJ47 Mats Sundin	8.00	20.00
GJ48 Alexei Yashin	6.00	15.00
GJ49 Patrick Roy	20.00	50.00
GJ50 Markus Naslund	8.00	20.00
GJ51 Jay Bouwmeester	6.00	15.00
GJ52 Jason Spezza	12.50	30.00
GJ53 Stephen Weiss	6.00	15.00
GJ54 Ron Hainsey	6.00	15.00
GJ55 Jordan Leopold	6.00	15.00
GJ56 Chuck Kobasew	6.00	15.00
GJ57 Rick Nash	12.50	30.00
GJ58 Scottie Upshall	6.00	15.00

2002-03 Parkhurst Magnificent Inserts

This 10-card set featured game-used equipment from the career of Mario Lemieux. Cards MI1-MI5 had a print run of 40 copies each and cards MI6-MI10 were limited to just 10 copies each. Cards MI6-MI10 are not priced due to scarcity.

MI6-MI10 NOT PRICED DUE TO SCARCITY

Card	Low	High
MI1 2000-01 Season Jersey	30.00	80.00
MI2 1985-86 Season Jersey	30.00	80.00
MI3 2002 All-Star Game Jersey	30.00	80.00
MI4 1987 Canada Cup Jersey	30.00	80.00
MI5 Dual Jersey	50.00	125.00
MI6 Number		
MI7 Emblem		
MI8 Triple Jersey		
MI9 Quad Jersey		
MI10 Complete Package		

2002-03 Parkhurst Magnificent Inserts Autographs

This 10-card set paralleled the base Magnificent Inserts but carried certified autographs and each card was hand numbered. Cards MI1-MI5 were serial-numbered to 15 each and cards MI6-MI10 were serial numbered out of 5.

NOT PRICED DUE TO SCARCITY

2002-03 Parkhurst Mario's Mates

Limited to 25 sets, this 10-card set carried dual jersey swatches of Mario Lemieux and other top players.

Card	Low	High
MM1 M.Lemieux/P.Roy	75.00	200.00
MM2 M.Lemieux/S.Yzerman	60.00	150.00
MM3 M.Lemieux/J.Jagr	50.00	125.00
MM4 M.Lemieux/M.Brodeur	60.00	150.00
MM5 M.Lemieux/E.Lindros	40.00	100.00
MM6 M.Lemieux/R.Francis	30.00	80.00
MM7 M.Lemieux/M.Sundin	30.00	80.00
MM8 M.Lemieux/J.Sakic	60.00	150.00
MM9 M.Lemieux/P.Kariya	30.00	80.00
MM10 M.Lemieux/J.Theodore	40.00	100.00

2002-03 Parkhurst Milestones

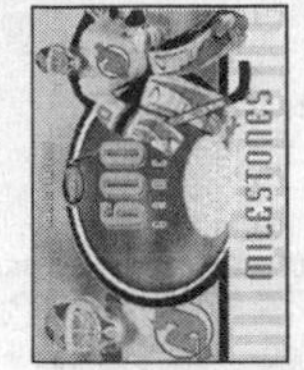

This 11-card set honored career highlights of several veteran players. Cards were limited to 60 copies each (except for the Roy card).

*MULT.COLOR SWATCH: .5X TO 1.25X

Card	Low	High
MS1 Jeremy Roenick 600 Assists	12.50	30.00
MS2 Martin Brodeur	20.00	50.00
MS3 Ed Belfour 60 Shutouts	10.00	25.00
MS4 Mike Richter 300 Wins	10.00	25.00
MS5 Jaromir Jagr 700 Assists	12.50	30.00
MS6 Vincent Damphousse 400 Goals	10.00	25.00
MS7 Ron Francis 1200 Assists	10.00	25.00
MS8 Mats Sundin 400 Goals	10.00	25.00
MS9 Peter Forsberg 600 Points	20.00	50.00
MS10 Pavel Bure 750 Points	10.00	25.00
MS11 Patrick Roy 1000 Games/33	30.00	80.00

2002-03 Parkhurst Patented Power

STATED PRINT RUN 20 SETS
NOT PRICED DUE TO SCARCITY

PP1 M.Lemieux/B.Shanahan
PP2 Steve Yzerman / Mats Sundin
PP3 Jaromir Jagr / Teemu Selanne
PP4 Paul Kariya / Jeremy Roenick
PP5 J.Sakic/M.Modano
PP6 Pavel Bure / Dany Heatley
PP7 Peter Forsberg / Sergei Fedorov
PP8 Eric Lindros / Todd Bertuzzi
PP9 Ilya Kovalchuk / Mark Messier
PP10 Brett Hull / Joe Thornton

2002-03 Parkhurst Reprints

This 150-card set of Parkhurst reprints picks up the numbering where the 2001-02 reprint set left off.

Card	Low	High
151 Floyd Curry	1.00	5.00
152 Billy Reay	1.00	5.00
153 Jim Henry	1.00	5.00
154 Ed Sandford	1.00	5.00
155 Pentti Lund	1.00	5.00
156 Al Dewsbury	1.00	5.00

157 Gerry McNeil 1.00 5.00
The Winning Goal
158 Jack Stewart 1.00 5.00
159 Alex Delvecchio 1.00 5.00
160 Sid Abel 1.00 5.00
161 Ray Timgren 1.00 5.00
162 Ed Kullman 1.00 5.00
163 Billy Reay 1.00 5.00
164 Floyd Curry 1.00 5.00
165 Al Dewsbury 1.00 5.00
166 Allan Stanley 1.00 5.00
167 Paul Ronty 1.00 5.00
168 Gaye Stewart 1.00 5.00
169 Al Rollins 1.00 5.00
170 Leo Boivin 1.00 5.00
171 George Gee 1.00 5.00
172 Ted Kennedy 1.00 5.00
173 Alex Delvecchio 1.00 5.00
174 Marcel Pronovost 1.00 5.00
175 Leo Boivin 1.00 5.00
176 Ted Kennedy 1.00 5.00
177 Ron Stewart 1.00 5.00
178 Bud MacPherson 1.00 5.00
179 Marcel Pronovost 1.00 5.00
180 Alex Delvecchio 1.00 5.00
181 Max Bentley 1.00 5.00
182 Andy Bathgate 1.00 5.00
183 Harry Howell 1.00 5.00
184 Allan Stanley 1.00 5.00
185 Ed Sandford 1.00 5.00
186 Bill Quackenbush 1.00 5.00
187 Eddie Mazur 1.00 5.00
188 Floyd Curry 1.00 5.00
189 Eric Nesterenko 1.00 5.00
190 Ron Stewart 1.00 5.00
191 Leo Boivin 1.00 5.00
192 Ted Kennedy 1.00 5.00
193 Alex Delvecchio 1.00 5.00
194 Bob Armstrong 1.00 5.00
195 Paul Ronty 1.00 5.00
196 Camille Henry 1.00 5.00
197 Al Rollins 1.00 5.00
198 Al Dewsbury 1.00 5.00
199 Netminders nightmare 1.00 5.00
200 Ron Stewart 1.00 5.00
201 Dick Duff 1.00 5.00
202 Lorne Chabot 1.00 5.00
203 Busher Jackson 1.00 5.00
204 Joe Primeau 1.00 5.00
205 Harold Cotton 1.00 5.00
206 King Clancy 1.00 5.00
207 Hap Day 1.00 5.00
208 Newsy Lalonde 1.00 5.00
209 Albert Leduc 1.00 5.00
210 Babe Siebert 1.00 5.00
211 Toe Blake 1.00 5.00
Coach
212 Claude Provost 1.00 5.00
213 Toe Blake 1.00 5.00
214 Charlie Hodge 1.00 5.00
215 Floyd Curry 1.00 5.00
216 Len Broderick 1.00 5.00
Canadiens on guard
217 Ed Chadwick 1.00 5.00
Geoffrion sidesteps Chadwick
218 George Armstrong 1.00 5.00
219 Dick Duff 1.00 5.00
220 Ron Stewart 1.00 5.00
221 Billy Harris 1.00 5.00
222 Bob Baun 1.00 5.00
223 Billy Reay 1.00 5.00
224 Billy Harris 1.00 5.00
225 Toe Blake 1.00 5.00
226 Bob Nevin 1.00 5.00
227 Bob Baun 1.00 5.00
228 Charlie Hodge 1.00 5.00
229 Allan Stanley 1.00 5.00
230 Billy Reay 1.00 5.00
231 Dick Duff 1.00 5.00
232 Marcel Bonin 1.00 5.00
233 Claude Provost 1.00 5.00
234 Canadiens on guard 1.00 5.00
235 E.Lach/R.Richard 1.00 5.00
236 Billy Harris 1.00 5.00
237 Punch Imlach 1.00 5.00
238 Charlie Hodge 1.00 5.00
239 Bob Baun 1.00 5.00
240 Ron Stewart 1.00 5.00
241 Toe Blake 1.00 5.00
242 Action around the net 1.00 5.00
243 Officials intervene 1.00 5.00
244 Frank Selke 1.00 5.00
General Manager
245 King Clancy 1.00 5.00
246 Ron Stewart 1.00 5.00
247 Bob Baun 1.00 5.00
248 Dick Duff 1.00 5.00
249 Billy Harris 1.00 5.00
250 Allan Stanley 1.00 5.00
251 Jacques Plante 1.00 5.00
252 Sid Abel 1.00 5.00
253 Norm Ullman 1.00 5.00
254 Marcel Pronovost 1.00 5.00
255 Alex Delvecchio 1.00 5.00
256 Marcel Bonin 1.00 5.00
257 Claude Provost 1.00 5.00
258 Ron Stewart 1.00 5.00
259 Bob Nevin 1.00 5.00
260 Bob Baun 1.00 5.00
261 Dick Duff 1.00 5.00
262 Billy Harris 1.00 5.00
263 Allan Stanley 1.00 5.00
264 Maurice Richard 1.00 5.00
265 Alex Delvecchio 1.00 5.00
266 Norm Ullman 1.00 5.00
267 Ed Litzenberger 1.00 5.00
268 Marcel Pronovost 1.00 5.00
269 Marcel Bonin 1.00 5.00
270 Billy Harris 1.00 5.00
271 Dick Duff 1.00 5.00
272 Bob Baun 1.00 5.00
273 Maurice Richard 1.00 5.00
274 Allan Stanley 1.00 5.00
275 Bob Nevin 1.00 5.00
276 Ed Litzenberger 1.00 5.00
277 Norm Ullman 1.00 5.00
278 Alex Delvecchio 1.00 5.00
279 Marcel Pronovost 1.00 5.00
280 Sid Abel 1.00 5.00
281 Claude Provost 1.00 5.00
282 J.C. Tremblay 1.00 5.00
283 Allan Stanley 1.00 5.00
284 Ed Litzenberger 1.00 5.00
285 Rocket Roars Through 1.00 5.00
286 Bob Nevin 1.00 5.00
287 Jacques Laperriere 1.00 5.00
288 J.C. Tremblay 1.00 5.00
289 John Ferguson 1.00 5.00
290 Toe Blake 1.00 5.00
291 Mael Pronovost 1.00 5.00
292 Alex Delvecchio 1.00 5.00
293 Allan Stanley 1.00 5.00
294 Dick Duff 1.00 5.00
295 Maurice Richard 1.00 5.00
296 Ron Stewart 1.00 5.00
297 J.C. Tremblay 1.00 5.00
298 John Ferguson 1.00 5.00
299 Toe Blake 1.00 5.00
300 Bill Quackenbush 1.00 5.00

2002-03 Parkhurst Stick and Jerseys

*STK/JSY: .5X TO 1.25X BASIC JERSEY
STATED PRINT RUN 90 SETS

2002-03 Parkhurst Teammates

This 20-card set featured three swatches of game jersey from players who were with the same club. Cards were limited to just 60 copies each.

TT1 Eric Lindros 12.50 30.00
Brian Leetch
Pavel Bure
TT2 John LeClair 12.50 30.00
Mark Recchi
Simon Gagne
TT3 Mats Sundin 12.50 30.00
Alexander Mogilny
Gary Roberts
TT4 Steve Yzerman 50.00 125.00
Brendan Shanahan
Sergei Fedorov
TT5 Brodeur/Stevens/Elias 20.00 50.00
TT6 Felix Potvin 12.50 30.00
Zigmund Palffy
Jason Allison
TT7 Saku Koivu 12.50 30.00
Jose Theodore
Craig Rivet
TT8 Joe Thornton 12.50 30.00
Sergei Samsonov
Kyle McLaren
TT9 Ilya Kovalchuk 20.00 50.00
Dany Heatley
Patrik Stefan
TT10 Mike Dunham 12.50 30.00
David Legwand
Scott Hartnell
TT11 Daniel Alfredsson 25.00 60.00
Marian Havlat
Marian Hossa
TT12 Miroslav Satan 12.50 30.00
Tim Connolly
J-P Dumont
TT13 Eric Daze 12.50 30.00
Jocelyn Thibault
Alexei Zhamnov
TT14 Mario Lemieux 30.00 80.00
Johan Hedberg
Alexei Kovalev
TT15 Owen Nolan 12.50 30.00
Teemu Selanne
Evgeni Nabokov
TT16 Chris Pronger 12.50 30.00
Al MacInnis
Doug Weight
TT17 Jaromir Jagr 12.50 30.00
Olaf Kolzig
Peter Bondra
TT18 Dan Cloutier 12.50 30.00
Todd Bertuzzi
Markus Naslund
TT19 Peter Forsberg 30.00 80.00
Joe Sakic
Patrick Roy
TT20 Sean Burke 12.50 30.00
Daniel Briere
Teppo Numminen

2002-03 Parkhurst Vintage Memorabilia

This 20-card set featured pieces of game-used equipment. Each card was limited to just 20 copies each. This set is not priced due to scarcity.

VM1 John Bucyk
VM2 Gilbert Perreault
VM3 Bobby Hull
VM4 Stan Mikita
VM5 Marcel Dionne
VM6 Jari Kurri
VM7 Jean Beliveau
VM8 Doug Harvey
VM9 Guy Lafleur
VM10 Frank Mahovlich
VM11 Henri Richard
VM12 Maurice Richard
VM13 Tiny Thompson
VM14 Bernie Parent
VM15 Tim Horton
VM16 Terry Sawchuk
VM17 Vladislav Tretiak
VM18 Gerry Cheevers
VM19 Ted Kennedy
VM20 Bill Gadsby

2002-03 Parkhurst Vintage Teammates

Limited to just 20 sets, this 20-card set featured dual game jersey swatches from retired greats who played for the same club. This set is not priced due to scarcity.

VT1 Brett Hull
Dennis Hull
VT2 Phil Esposito
Ed Giacomin
VT3 John Bucyk
Gerry Cheevers
VT4 Serge Savard
Larry Robinson
VT5 Tony Esposito
Stan Mikita
VT6 Terry Sawchuk
Sid Abel
VT7 Frank Mahovlich
Peter Mahovlich
VT8 Jean Beliveau
Doug Harvey
VT9 Guy Lafleur
Henri Richard
VT10 Bryan Trottier
Mike Bossy
VT11 Denis Potvin
Bob Nystrom
VT12 Bobby Clarke
Bill Barber
VT13 Bernie Parent
Dave Schultz
VT14 Tim Horton
Red Kelly
VT15 Valeri Kharlamov
Vladislav Tretiak
VT16 Bill Mosienko
Harry Lumley
VT17 Alex Delvecchio
Roger Crozier
VT18 Ace Bailey
King Clancy
VT19 Eddie Shore
Tiny Thompson
VT20 Lanny McDonald
Tiger Williams

2003-04 Parkhurst Toronto Spring Expo Rookie Preview

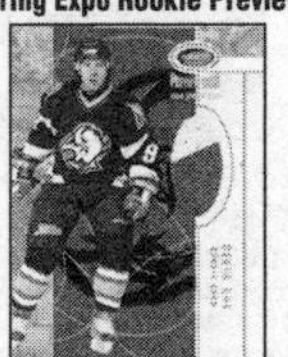

Inserted one in each "Super Box" available at the Toronto Spring Expo, this 20 -card set featured promising prospects and swatches of game-used jerseys.

PRP1 Marc-Andre Fleury 50.00 100.00
PRP2 Jordin Tootoo 15.00 40.00
PRP3 Joni Pitkanen 10.00 25.00
PRP4 Fedor Tyutin 8.00 20.00
PRP5 Derek Roy 15.00 40.00
PRP6 Nathan Horton 15.00 40.00
PRP7 Eric Staal 25.00 60.00
PRP8 Patrice Bergeron 25.00 60.00
PRP9 Dustin Brown 10.00 25.00
PRP10 Dan Hamhuis 10.00 25.00
PRP11 Tim Gleason 8.00 20.00
PRP12 Rastislav Stana 8.00 20.00
PRP13 Matt Stajan 15.00 40.00
PRP14 Matthew Lombardi 8.00 20.00
PRP15 Nikolai Zherdev 20.00 50.00
PRP16 Tuomo Ruutu 20.00 50.00
PRP17 Ryan Malone 15.00 40.00
PRP18 Antoine Vermette 8.00 20.00
PRP19 Kari Lehtonen 30.00 80.00
PRP20 Alexander Semin 25.00 60.00

2003-04 Parkhurst Original Six Boston

This 100-card set featured players from one of the Original Six teams in the NHL, Boston. The set was produced as a stand alone product.

COMPLETE SET (100) 20.00 50.00
1 P.J. Axelsson .15 .40
2 Michal Grosek .15 .40
3 Nick Boynton .15 .40
4 Jeff Jillson .15 .40
5 Felix Potvin .50 1.25
6 Patrick Leahy XRC .40 1.00
7 Joe Thornton .60 1.50
8 Ted Donato .15 .40
9 Hal Gill .15 .40
10 Jonathan Girard .15 .40
11 Rob Zamuner .15 .40
12 Shoane Morrisonn .15 .40
13 Martin Samuelsson .15 .40
14 Doug Doull XRC .15 .40
15 Ivan Huml .15 .40
16 Mike Knuble .15 .40
17 Kris Vernarsky .15 .40
18 Patrice Bergeron XRC 3.00 8.00
19 Sergei Zinovjev XRC .40 1.00
20 Martin Lapointe .15 .40
21 Dan McGillis .15 .40
22 Sandy McCarthy .15 .40
23 Glen Murray .15 .40
24 P.J. Stock .15 .40
25 Sean O'Donnell .15 .40
26 Andrew Raycroft .40 1.00
27 Brian Rolston .15 .40
28 Sergei Samsonov .40 1.00
29 Ian Moran .15 .40
30 Travis Green .15 .40
31 Adam Oates .40 1.00
32 Cam Neely .75 2.00
33 Jason Allison .15 .40
34 Dit Clapper .50 1.25
35 Fern Flaman .15 .40
36 John Bucyk .50 1.25
37 Milt Schmidt .50 1.25
38 Brad Park .50 1.25
39 Terry O'Reilly .50 1.25
40 Wayne Cashman .40 1.00
41 Ray Bourque .75 2.00
42 Allan Stanley .15 .40
43 Bernie Parent .60 1.50
44 Derek Sanderson .50 1.25
45 Bobby Orr 1.50 4.00
46 Tiny Thompson .60 1.50
47 Eddie Shore 1.00 2.50
48 Frank Brimsek .50 1.25
49 Jean Ratelle .50 1.25
50 Ken Hodge .40 1.00
51 Lionel Hitchman .15 .40
52 Phil Esposito .60 1.50
53 Rick Middleton .50 1.25
54 Terry Sawchuk .60 1.50
55 Woody Dumart .15 .40
56 Gerry Cheevers .60 1.50
57 Andy Moog .50 1.25
58 Byron Dafoe .40 1.00
59 Anson Carter .15 .40
60 Bill Guerin .40 1.00
61 Frank Brimsek .50 1.25
62 Bobby Orr 1.50 4.00
63 Eddie Shore 1.00 2.50
64 Dit Clapper .50 1.25
65 Cam Neely .75 2.00
66 Phil Esposito .60 1.50
67 Milt Schmidt .50 1.25
68 Johnny Bucyk .50 1.25
69 Woody Dumart .15 .40
70 Ray Bourque .75 2.00
71 Joe Thornton .60 1.50
72 Dit Clapper .50 1.25
73 Ray Bourque .75 2.00
74 Fern Flaman .15 .40
75 Johnny Bucyk .50 1.25
76 Milt Schmidt .50 1.25
77 Rick Middleton .50 1.25
78 Terry O'Reilly .50 1.25
79 Wayne Cashman .40 1.00
80 Lionel Hitchman .15 .40
81 Bobby Orr 1.50 4.00
82 Johnny Bucyk .50 1.25
83 Phil Esposito .60 1.50
84 Frank Brimsek .50 1.25
85 Fern Flaman .15 .40
86 Gerry Cheevers .60 1.50
87 Dit Clapper .50 1.25
88 Woody Dumart .15 .40
89 Eddie Shore 1.00 2.50
90 Milt Schmidt .50 1.25
91 Bobby Orr 1.50 4.00
92 Johnny Bucyk .50 1.25
93 Terry O'Reilly .50 1.25
94 Ray Bourque .75 2.00
95 Cam Neely .75 2.00
96 Phil Esposito .60 1.50
97 Bobby Orr 1.50 4.00
98 Cam Neely .75 2.00
99 Phil Esposito .60 1.50
100 Ray Bourque .75 2.00

2003-04 Parkhurst Original Six Boston Autographs

This 18-card set featured certified autographs of past Bruins greats. Print runs are listed below.

1 Ray Bourque/30 100.00 200.00
2 Johnny Bucyk/90 25.00 60.00
3 Wayne Cashman/85 25.00 60.00
4 Gerry Cheevers/90 50.00 125.00
5 Phil Esposito/55 75.00 175.00
6 Fern Flaman/85 30.00 80.00
7 Ken Hodge/90 25.00 60.00
8 Stan Jonathan/85 30.00 80.00
9 Rick Middleton/90 20.00 50.00
10 Andy Moog/90 25.00 60.00
11 Cam Neely/90 40.00 100.00
12 Terry O'Reilly/95 60.00 120.00
13 Bobby Orr/30 500.00 700.00
14 Bernie Parent/90 20.00 50.00
15 Brad Park/90 25.00 50.00
16 Jean Ratelle/90 30.00 60.00
17 Derek Sanderson/90 40.00 80.00
18 Milt Schmidt/85 40.00 100.00

2003-04 Parkhurst Original Six Boston Inserts

COMPLETE SET (17) 30.00 60.00
STATED ODDS 1:6
B1 Eddie Shore 2.00 5.00
B2 Milt Schmidt 1.50 4.00
B3 Dit Clapper 1.50 4.00
B4 Phil Esposito 2.00 5.00
B5 Johnny Bucyk 1.50 4.00
B6 Bobby Orr 3.00 8.00
B7 Eddie Shore 2.00 5.00
B8 Phil Esposito 2.00 5.00
B9 Milt Schmidt 1.50 4.00
B10 Phil Esposito 2.00 5.00
B11 Bobby Orr 3.00 8.00
B12 Ray Bourque 2.50 6.00
B13 Derek Sanderson 1.50 4.00
B14 Tiny Thompson 2.00 5.00
B15 Frank Brimsek 1.50 4.00
B16 Joe Thornton 2.00 5.00
B17 Ray Bourque 2.50 6.00

2003-04 Parkhurst Original Six Boston Memorabilia

This 67-card set featured memorabilia from past and present Bruins players. Cards BM1-13 and BM61-62 were single jerseys and were limited to 100 copies each. Cards BM14-18 and BM63 were jersey/stick combos and were limited to 80 sets. Cards BM19-20 were game gear inserts and print runs are listed below. Cards BM21-26, BM58 and BM64 were vintage memorabilia cards and print runs are listed below. Cards BM27-34, BM57 and BM65-67 were vintage jersey cards and were limited to 50 copies each. Cards BM35-39 and BM59 were vintage stick cards and print runs are listed below. Cards BM39-40 and BM60 are retired numbers cards and were limited to 20 copies. Cards BM51-56 were grouped into a subset known as Original Six Shooters, players who have scored high career totals against original six teams. The shooters cards were limited to 100 copies each. Cards BM51-56 were dual-jersey cards and were limited to 100 copies each.

PRINT RUNS UNDER 25 NOT
PRICED DUE TO SCARCITY
BM1 Brian Rolston 10.00 25.00
BM2 Sergei Samsonov 6.00 15.00
BM3 Martin Lapointe 6.00 15.00
BM4 Don Sweeny 6.00 15.00
BM5 Nick Boynton 6.00 15.00
BM6 Joe Thornton 20.00 50.00
BM7 Jeff Hackett 6.00 15.00
BM8 Ivan Huml 6.00 15.00
BM9 Steve Shields 8.00 20.00
BM10 Glen Murray 6.00 15.00
BM11 Shaone Morrisonn 6.00 15.00
BM12 Bryan Berard 8.00 20.00
BM13 Mika Knuble 6.00 15.00
BM14 Bryan Berard J/S 15.00 40.00
BM15 Sergei Samsonov J/S 15.00 40.00
BM16 Joe Thornton J/S/50 30.00 80.00
BM17 Jeff Hackett J/S 10.00 25.00
BM18 Steve Shields J/S 12.50 30.00
BM19 Joe Thornton/20
BM20 S.Samsonov/50 Glove 15.00 40.00
BM21 Tiny Thompson/20
BM22 Gilles Gilbert/50 15.00 40.00
BM23 Gerry Cheevers/50 Pad 30.00 80.00
BM24 Eddie Shore/20 Glove
BM25 Eddie Shore/60 Pants 20.00 50.00
BM26 Frank Brimsek/20
BM27 John Bucyk J 20.00 50.00
BM28 Gerry Cheevers J 20.00 50.00
BM29 Andy Moog J 25.00 60.00
BM30 Gilles Gilbert J 20.00 50.00
BM31 Jason Allison J 20.00 50.00
BM32 Cam Neely J 30.00 80.00
BM33 Phil Esposito J 20.00 50.00
BM34 Adam Oates J 20.00 50.00
BM35 Phil Esposito/30 S 20.00 50.00
BM36 Ray Bourque/50 S 30.00 80.00
BM37 John Bucyk/20 S
BM38 Gerry Cheevers/50 S 15.00 40.00
BM39 Eddie Shore/20 RN J
BM40 Cam Neely/20 RN J
BM41 Mario Lemieux SS 15.00 40.00
BM42 Ron Francis SS 6.00 15.00
BM43 Joe Sakic SS 12.50 30.00
BM44 Brett Hull SS 8.00 20.00
BM45 Jaromir Jagr SS 8.00 20.00
BM46 Mike Modano SS 8.00 20.00
BM47 Teemu Selanne SS 6.00 15.00
BM48 Pavel Bure SS 6.00 15.00
BM49 Paul Kariya SS 8.00 20.00
BM50 Peter Forsberg SS 10.00 25.00
BM51 Gerry Cheevers 20.00 50.00
Felix Potvin
BM52 Phil Esposito 40.00 100.00
Joe Thornton
BM53 Bobby Orr 100.00 250.00
Ray Bourque
BM54 John Bucyk 25.00 60.00
Glen Murray
BM55 Terry O'Reilly 25.00 60.00
Cam Neely
BM56 Tiny Thompson 50.00 125.00
Bernie Parent
BM57 Bobby Orr J 100.00 250.00
BM58 Bobby Orr/50 100.00 250.00
BM59 Bobby Orr/50 S 100.00 250.00
BM60 Bobby Orr/20 RN J
BM61 Felix Potvin 10.00 25.00
BM62 Andrew Raycroft 20.00 50.00
BM63 Felix Potvin J/S 15.00 40.00
BM64 Ray Bourque/50 15.00 40.00
BM65 Brad Park/50 J 20.00 50.00
BM66 Ray Bourque/50 J 20.00 50.00
BM67 Terry O'Reilly/50 J 20.00 50.00

2003-04 Parkhurst Original Six Chicago

This 100-card set featured players from one of the Original Six teams in the NHL, Chicago. The set was produced as a stand alone product.

COMPLETE SET 20.00 50.00
1 Tyler Arnason .40 1.00
2 Mark Bell .15 .40
3 Deron Quint .15 .40
4 Kyle Calder .15 .40
5 Bryan Berard .15 .40
6 Eric Daze .40 1.00
7 Jason Strudwick .15 .40
8 Nathan Dempsey .15 .40
9 Jon Klemm .15 .40
10 Igor Korolev .15 .40
11 Pavel Vorobiev XRC 1.50 4.00
12 Scott Nichol .15 .40
13 Alexander Karpovtsev .15 .40
14 Tuomo Ruutu XRC 3.00 8.00
15 Ville Nieminen .15 .40
16 Steve McCarthy .15 .40
17 Igor Radulov .15 .40
18 Alexei Zhamnov .15 .40
19 Burke Henry .15 .40
20 Craig Andersson .15 .40
21 Steve Passmore .40 1.00
22 Lasse Kukkonen XRC 1.50 4.00
23 Steve Poapst .15 .40
24 Michael Leighton .40 1.00
25 Shawn Thornton .15 .40
26 Brett McLean .15 .40
27 Steve Sullivan .15 .40
28 Jocelyn Thibault .40 1.00
29 Travis Moen XRC 1.50 4.00
30 Ryan Vandenbussche .15 .40
31 Chris Chelios .50 1.25
32 Dominik Hasek .75 2.00
33 Jeremy Roenick .60 1.50
34 Ed Belfour .50 1.25
35 Doug Gilmour .40 1.00
36 Charlie Gardiner .40 1.00
37 Howie Morenz .75 2.00
38 Steve Larmer .15 .40
39 Dirk Graham .15 .40
40 Ken Wharram .40 1.00
41 Pat Stapleton .15 .40
42 Pierre Pilote .40 1.00
43 Bobby Hull 1.25 3.00
44 Tony Amonte .40 1.00
45 Stan Mikita .60 1.50
46 Dennis Hull .60 1.50
47 Denis Savard .75 2.00
48 Doug Wilson .15 .40
49 Bobby Orr 1.50 4.00
50 Glenn Hall .75 2.00
51 Harry Lumley .50 1.25
52 Bill Mosienko .50 1.25
53 Ken Hodge .40 1.00
54 Michel Goulet .50 1.25
55 Keith Magnuson .75 2.00
56 Ted Lindsay .50 1.25
57 Bill Gadsby .40 1.00
58 Darren Pang .50 1.25
59 Tony Esposito .75 2.00
60 Phil Esposito .60 1.50
61 Glenn Hall .75 2.00
62 Ed Belfour .50 1.25
63 Charlie Gardiner .40 1.00
64 Tony Esposito .75 2.00
65 Stan Mikita .60 1.50
66 Bobby Hull 1.25 3.00
67 Pierre Pilote .40 1.00
68 Doug Wilson .15 .40
69 Chris Chelios .50 1.25
70 Ken Wharram .40 1.00
71 Alexei Zhamnov .15 .40
72 Chris Chelios .50 1.25
73 Doug Gilmour .40 1.00
74 Bill Gadsby .40 1.00
75 Denis Savard .75 2.00
76 Tony Amonte .40 1.00
77 Dirk Graham .15 .40
78 Stan Mikita .60 1.50
79 Ed Litzenberger .60 1.50
80 Pierre Pilote .40 1.00
81 Denis Savard .75 2.00
82 Pierre Pilote .40 1.00
83 Stan Mikita .60 1.50
84 Bill Mosienko .50 1.25
85 Glenn Hall .75 2.00
86 Bobby Hull 1.25 3.00
87 Phil Esposito .60 1.50
88 Tony Esposito .75 2.00
89 Bill Gadsby .40 1.00
90 Michel Goulet .50 1.25
91 Bobby Hull MS 1.25 3.00
92 Stan Mikita .60 1.50
93 Stan Mikita .60 1.50
94 Tony Esposito .75 2.00
95 Bobby Hull 1.25 3.00
96 Denis Savard .75 2.00
97 Tony Esposito 1.25 3.00
98 Ed Belfour .50 1.25
99 Chris Chelios .50 1.25
100 Steve Larmer .75 2.00

2003-04 Parkhurst Original Six Chicago Autographs

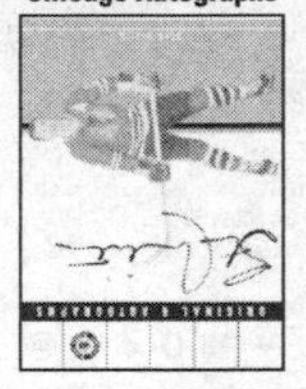

This 18-card set featured certified autographs of past Blackhawks greats. Print runs are listed below.

STATED PRINT RUNS LISTED BELOW
1 Phil Esposito/55 50.00 125.00
2 Tony Esposito/85 30.00 80.00
3 Michel Goulet/90 20.00 50.00
4 Dirk Graham/90 15.00 40.00
5 Glenn Hall/85 60.00 150.00
6 Ken Hodge/89 20.00 50.00
7 Bobby Hull/75 50.00 100.00
8 Steve Larmer/85 40.00 80.00
9 Ted Lindsay/90 20.00 50.00
10 Eddie Litzenberger/90 20.00 50.00
11 Keith Magnuson/99 40.00 80.00
12 Stan Mikita/80 20.00 50.00
13 Darren Pang/90 15.00 40.00
14 Pierre Pilote/85 20.00 50.00
15 Denis Savard/90 25.00 60.00
16 Ken Wharram/90 30.00 80.00
17 Doug Wilson/90 25.00 60.00

2003-04 Parkhurst Original Six Chicago Inserts

COMPLETE SET (16) 30.00 60.00
C1 Stan Mikita 2.50 6.00
C2 Bobby Hull 2.50 6.00
C3 Tony Esposito 2.00 5.00
C4 Glenn Hall 1.50 4.00
C5 Denis Savard 2.00 5.00
C6 Bobby Hull 2.50 6.00
C7 Ed Belfour 1.50 4.00
C8 Tony Esposito 2.00 5.00
C9 Glenn Hall 1.50 4.00
C10 Tony Esposito 2.00 5.00
C11 Stan Mikita 2.50 6.00
C12 Bobby Hull 2.50 6.00
C13 Pierre Pilote 1.50 4.00
C14 Charlie Gardiner 1.50 4.00
C15 Jeremy Roenick 2.00 5.00
C16 Denis Savard 2.00 5.00

2003-04 Parkhurst Original Six Chicago Memorabilia

This 62-card set featured memorabilia from past and present Blackhawks players. Cards CM1-9 were single jerseys and were limited to 100 copies sets. Cards CM10-13 were jersey/stick combos and were limited to 80 sets. Cards CM15-18 were vintage memorabilia cards and were limited to 20 copies each. Cards CM19-30 and CM59-62 were vintage jersey cards and print runs are listed below. Cards CM31-36 were vint age stick cards and print runs are listed below. Cards CM37-40 were retired numbers cards and were limited to 20 copies. Cards CM41-50 were grouped into a subset known as Original Six Shooters; players who have scored high career totals against original six teams. The shooters cards were limited to 100 copies each. Cards CM51-58 were dual-jersey cards and were limited to 100 copies each.

PRINT RUNS UNDER 25 NOT PRICED DUE TO SCARCITY
CM1 Jocelyn Thibault 10.00 25.00
CM2 Steve Sullivan 10.00 25.00
CM3 Eric Daze 6.00 15.00
CM4 Alexei Zhamnov 6.00 15.00
CM5 Mark Bell 6.00 15.00
CM6 Steve McCarthy 6.00 15.00
CM7 Tyler Arnason 6.00 15.00
CM8 Steve Passmore 10.00 25.00
CM9 Ryan Vandenbussche 6.00 15.00
CM10 Jocelyn Thibault J/S 20.00 50.00
CM11 Steve Sullivan J/S 20.00 50.00
CM12 Eric Daze J/S 12.50 30.00
CM13 Alexei Zhamnov J/S 12.50 30.00
CM14 Jocelyn Thibault/50 40.00 100.00
CM15 Tony Esposito
CM16 Bill Mosienko Pants
CM17 Chuck Gardiner Pad
CM18 Harry Lumley
CM19 Frank Brimsek/20 J
CM20 Ed Belfour/100 J 15.00 40.00
CM21 Jeremy Roenick/100 J 15.00 40.00
CM22 Tony Amonte/100 J 15.00 40.00
CM23 Bill Mosienko/60 J 25.00 60.00
CM24 Michel Goulet/100 J 15.00 40.00
CM25 Bobby Hull/50 J 25.00 60.00
CM26 Dennis Hull/60 J 15.00 40.00
CM27 Glenn Hall/50 J 20.00 50.00
CM28 Tony Esposito/50 J 25.00 60.00
CM29 Harry Lumley/50 J 20.00 50.00
CM30 Stan Mikita/50 J 25.00 60.00
CM31 Bobby Hull/50 S 30.00 80.00
CM32 Tony Esposito/60 S 25.00 60.00
CM33 Glenn Hall/60 S 15.00 40.00
CM34 Michel Goulet/70 S 10.00 25.00
CM35 Tony Amonte/70 S 10.00 25.00
CM36 Jeremy Roenick/70 S 10.00 25.00
CM37 Stan Mikita/20 RN
CM38 Bobby Hull/20 RN
CM39 Tony Esposito/20 RN
CM40 Glenn Hall/20 RN
CM41 Mario Lemieux SS 15.00 40.00
CM42 Ron Francis SS 8.00 20.00
CM43 Joe Sakic SS 10.00 25.00
CM44 Brett Hull SS 8.00 20.00
CM45 Jaromir Jagr SS 8.00 20.00
CM46 Mike Modano SS 8.00 20.00
CM47 Teemu Selanne SS 6.00 15.00
CM48 Pavel Bure SS 6.00 15.00
CM49 Paul Kariya SS 8.00 20.00
CM50 Peter Forsberg SS 10.00 25.00
CM51 Glenn Hall 12.50 30.00
Tony Esposito
CM52 Bobby Hull 25.00 60.00
Jeremy Roenick
CM53 Stan Mikita 15.00 40.00
Tony Amonte
CM54 Harry Lumley 12.50 30.00
Jocelyn Thibault
CM55 Michel Goulet 15.00 40.00
Eric Daze
CM56 Bill Mosienko 12.50 30.00
Steve Sullivan
CM57 Frank Brimsek 12.50 30.00
Ed Belfour
CM58 Dennis Hull 15.00 40.00
Alexei Zhamnov
CM59 Chris Chelios/100 J 15.00 40.00
CM60 Jeff Hackett/100 J 15.00 40.00
CM61 Bob Probert/100 J 20.00 50.00
CM62 Denis Savard/100 J 20.00 50.00

2003-04 Parkhurst Original Six Detroit

This 100-card set featured players from one of the Original Six teams in the NHL, Detroit. The set was produced as a stand alone product.

COMPLETE SET (100) 20.00 50.00
1 Mathieu Schneider .15 .40
2 Chris Chelios .40 1.00
3 Mathieu Dandenault .15 .40
4 Pavel Datsyuk .60 1.50
5 Boyd Devereaux .15 .40
6 Kris Draper .15 .40
7 Jason Woolley .15 .40
8 Mark Mowers .15 .40
9 Ray Whitney .15 .40
10 Jiri Fischer .15 .40
11 Tomas Holmstrom .15 .40
12 Brett Hull .60 1.50
13 Curtis Joseph .50 1.25
14 Jamie Rivers .15 .40
15 Dominik Hasek .75 2.00
16 Henrik Zetterberg .60 1.50
17 Steve Thomas .15 .40
18 Manny Legace .40 1.00
19 Nicklas Lidstrom .50 1.25
20 Kirk Maltby .15 .40
21 Darren McCarty .15 .40
22 Jiri Hudler XRC 2.00 5.00
23 Brendan Shanahan .50 1.25
24 Marc Lamothe .40 1.00
25 Derian Hatcher .15 .40
26 Jason Williams .15 .40
27 Steve Yzerman 2.00 4.00
28 Michel Picard .15 .40
29 Derek King .15 .40
30 Dmitri Bykov .15 .40
31 Bob Probert .15 .40
32 Chris Osgood .40 1.00
33 Mike Vernon .40 1.00
34 Adam Oates .40 1.00
35 Terry Sawchuk .50 1.25
36 Alex Delvecchio .50 1.25
37 Danny Gare .15 .40
38 Marcel Dionne .50 1.25
39 Mickey Redmond .40 1.00
40 Ted Lindsay .40 1.00
41 Sid Abel .40 1.00
42 Red Kelly .40 1.00
43 Reed Larson .15 .40
44 Ebbie Goodfellow .15 .40
45 Bill Gadsby .40 1.00
46 Dino Ciccarelli .40 1.00
47 Glenn Hall .50 1.25
48 John Bucyk .50 1.25
49 Brad Smith .40 1.00
50 Norm Ullman .40 1.00
51 Marcel Pronovost .15 .40
52 Roger Crozier .50 1.25
53 Brad Park .50 1.25
54 Keith Primeau .40 1.00
55 Adam Graves .40 1.00
56 Ed Giacomin .50 1.25
57 Pat Verbeek .40 1.00
58 Harry Lumley .40 1.00
59 Gary Bergman .15 .40
60 Gerard Gallant .15 .40
61 Terry Sawchuk AS .50 1.25
62 Glenn Hall AS .50 1.25
63 Red Kelly AS .40 1.00
64 Nicklas Lidstrom AS .50 1.25
65 Marcel Pronovost AS .15 .40
66 Ted Lindsay AS .40 1.00
67 Sid Abel AS .40 1.00
68 Steve Yzerman AS .75 2.00
69 Brendan Shanahan AS .50 1.25
70 Alex Delvecchio AS .50 1.25
71 Steve Yzerman C .75 2.00
72 Alex Delvecchio C .50 1.25
73 Danny Gare C .15 .40
74 Marcel Dionne C .50 1.25
75 Mickey Redmond C .40 1.00
76 Ted Lindsay C .40 1.00
77 Sid Abel C .40 1.00
78 Red Kelly C .40 1.00
79 Reed Larson C .15 .40
80 Ebbie Goodfellow C .15 .40
81 Sid Abel E .40 1.00
82 Alex Delvecchio E .50 1.25
83 Ed Giacomin E .50 1.25
84 Red Kelly E .40 1.00
85 Ted Lindsay E .40 1.00
86 Marcel Pronovost E .15 .40
87 Terry Sawchuk E .50 1.25
88 Norm Ullman E .40 1.00
89 Bill Gadsby E .40 1.00
90 Glenn Hall E .50 1.25
91 Steve Yzerman .75 2.00
goals in a season
92 Steve Yzerman .75 2.00
points in a season
93 Steve Yzerman .75 2.00
assists in a season
94 Terry Sawchuk .50 1.25
career wins
95 Terry Sawchuk .50 1.25
career shutouts
96 Steve Yzerman .75 2.00
career playoff points
97 Sergei Fedorov .30 .75
career playoff assists
98 Nicklas Lidstrom .50 1.25
career points by a defenseman
99 Marcel Dionne .50 1.25
rookie assists in a season
100 Alex Delvecchio .50 1.25
career games by a centerman

2003-04 Parkhurst Original Six Detroit Autographs

This 18-card set featured certified autographs of past Red Wings greats. Print runs are listed below.

PRINT RUNS LISTED BELOW
OSDC Dino Ciccarelli/85 20.00 50.00
OSAD Alex Delvecchio/90 30.00 80.00
OSGH Glenn Hall/80 40.00 100.00
OSBG Bill Gadsby/90 15.00 40.00
OSRK Red Kelly/80 30.00 60.00
OSMP Marcel Pronovost/88 25.00 60.00
OSJB John Bucyk/80 30.00 80.00
OSNU Norm Ullman/85 15.00 40.00
OSDG Danny Gare/90 15.00 40.00
OSRL Reed Larson/98 15.00 40.00
OSTL Ted Lindsay/90 30.00 80.00
OSGG Gerard Gallant/90 20.00 50.00
OSMD Marcel Dionne/75 25.00 60.00
OSBS Brad Smith/90 15.00 40.00

2003-04 Parkhurst Original Six Detroit Inserts

COMPLETE SET (18) 30.00 60.00
STATED ODDS 1:6
D1 Terry Sawchuk 2.00 5.00
D2 Ted Lindsay 1.50 4.00
D3 Alex Delvecchio 2.00 5.00
D4 Sid Abel 1.50 4.00
D5 Ted Lindsay 1.50 4.00
D6 Sid Abel 1.50 4.00
D7 Terry Sawchuk 2.00 5.00
D8 Red Kelly 1.50 4.00
D9 Glenn Hall 2.00 5.00
D10 Roger Crozier 2.00 5.00
D11 Alex Delvecchio 2.00 5.00
D12 Red Kelly 1.50 4.00
D13 Nicklas Lidstrom 2.00 5.00
D14 Steve Yzerman 3.00 8.00
D15 Steve Yzerman 3.00 8.00
D16 Keith Primeau 1.50 4.00
D17 Marcel Dionne 2.00 5.00
D18 Martin Lapointe 1.50 4.00

2003-04 Parkhurst Original Six Detroit Memorabilia

This 63-card set featured memorabilia from past and present Red Wings players. Cards DM1-13 and DM57-59 were single jerseys and were limited to 100 copies sets. Cards DM14-19 and DM60-62 were jersey/stick combos and were limited to 80 sets. Cards DM20-25 were memorabilia cards and were limited to 20 copies each. Cards DM26-33 were vintage jersey cards and print runs are listed below. Cards DM34-36 were vintage stick cards and print runs are listed below. Cards DM37-40 were retired numbers cards and were limited to 20 copies. Cards DM41-50 were grouped into a subset known as Original Six Shooters; players who have scored high career totals against original six teams. The shooters cards were limited to 100 copies each. Cards DM51-56 were dual-jersey cards and were limited to 100 copies each.

PRINT RUNS UNDER 25 NOT PRICE DUE TO SCARCITY
DM1 Nicklas Lidstrom 10.00 25.00
DM2 Brendan Shanahan 10.00 25.00
DM3 Sergei Fedorov 15.00 40.00
DM4 Luc Robitaille 12.50 30.00
DM5 Steve Yzerman 20.00 50.00
DM6 Manny Legace 10.00 25.00
DM7 Mathieu Dandenault 6.00 15.00
DM8 Jiri Fischer 10.00 25.00
DM9 Darren McCarty 12.00 30.00
DM10 Pavel Datsyuk 15.00 40.00
DM11 Brett Hull 12.50 30.00
DM12 Igor Larionov 15.00 40.00
DM13 Chris Chelios 12.50 30.00
DM14 Nicklas Lidstrom J/S 15.00 40.00
DM15 Steve Yzerman J/S 40.00 80.00
DM16 Luc Robitaille J/S 15.00 40.00
DM17 Brendan Shanahan J/S 15.00 40.00
DM18 Sergei Fedorov J/S 20.00 50.00
DM19 Brett Hull J/S 15.00 40.00
DM20 Sergei Fedorov Glove
DM21 Henrik Zetterberg Skate
DM22 Pavel Datsyuk Skate
DM23 Bill Gadsby/50 Glove
DM24 Roger Crozier/20 Pad
DM25 Terry Sawchuk/20 Glove
DM26 Sid Abel/40 J 40.00 100.00
DM27 Dino Ciccarelli/60 J 20.00 50.00
DM28 Alex Delvecchio/60 J 20.00 50.00
DM29 Terry Sawchuk/20 J
DM30 Ted Lindsay/20 J
DM31 Chris Osgood/80 J 12.50 30.00
DM32 Keith Primeau/80 J 12.50 30.00
DM33 Roger Crozier/50 J
DM34 Terry Sawchuk/20 S
DM35 Dino Ciccarelli/60 S 12.50 30.00
DM36 Ed Giacomin/50 S 25.00 60.00
DM37 T.Sawchuk/20 RN J
DM38 A.Delvecchio/20 RN J
DM39 S.Abel/20 RN J
DM40 T.Lindsay/20 RN J
DM41 Mario Lemieux SS 15.00 40.00
DM42 Ron Francis SS 6.00 15.00
DM43 Joe Sakic SS 10.00 25.00
DM44 Brett Hull SS 10.00 25.00
DM45 Jaromir Jagr SS 8.00 20.00
DM46 Mike Modano SS 8.00 20.00
DM47 Teemu Selanne SS 6.00 15.00
DM48 Pavel Bure SS 6.00 15.00
DM49 Paul Kariya SS 8.00 20.00
DM50 Peter Forsberg SS 10.00 25.00
DM51 Lindsay/Hull 20.00 50.00
DM52 Sawchuk/Hasek 30.00 80.00
DM53 Abel/Yzerman 25.00 60.00
DM54 Delvecchio/Shanahan 20.00 50.00
DM55 Ciccarelli/Datsyuk 20.00 50.00
DM56 Crozier/Osgood 15.00 40.00
DM57 Henrik Zetterberg 12.50 30.00
DM58 Dominik Hasek 15.00 40.00
DM59 Manny Legace 15.00 40.00
DM60 Henrik Zetterberg J/S 30.00 80.00
DM61 Pavel Datsyuk J/S 25.00 60.00
DM62 Dominik Hasek J/S 20.00 50.00
DM63 Mike Vernon/100 J 15.00 40.00

2003-04 Parkhurst Original Six He Shoots-He Scores Prizes

Available only by redeeming Parkhurst Original Six HSHS points, this 60-card set featured dual-swatches of players, past and present, who played for the same original six team. The popularity of the program caused ITG to produce an extra 30 cards, different from the original 30 available. Those added cards are denoted by an "A" suffix below.

PRINT RUN 20 SETS
NOT PRICED DUE TO SCARCITY
1 E.Belfour/C.Joseph
1A E.Belfour/C.Joseph
2 M.Sundin/D.Sittler
2A M.Sundin/D.Sittler
3 A.Mogilny/L.McDonald
3A A.Mogilny/L.McDonald
4 O.Nolan/W.Clark
4A O.Nolan/W.Clark
5 B.McCabe/B.Salming
5A B.McCabe/B.Salming
6 T.Domi/T.Williams
6A T.Domi/T.Williams
7 M.Garon/G.Worsley
7A M.Garon/G.Worsley
8 S.Koivu/J.Beliveau
8A S.Koivu/J.Beliveau
9 J.Theodore/P.Roy
9A J.Theodore/P.Roy
10 S.Quintal/D.Harvey
10A S.Quintal/D.Harvey
11 G.Lafleur/M.Richard
11A G.Lafleur/M.Richard
12 P.Roy/J.Plante
12A P.Roy/J.Plante
13 J.Thornton/P.Esposito
13A J.Thornton/P.Esposito
14 A.Raycroft/G.Cheevers
14A A.Raycroft/G.Cheevers
15 S.Samsonov/C.Neely
15A S.Samsonov/C.Neely
16 B.Orr/E.Shore
16A B.Orr/E.Shore
17 R.Bourque/B.Orr
17A R.Bourque/B.Orr
18 P.Bergeron/C.Neely
18A P.Bergeron/C.Neely
19 J.Thibault/T.Esposito
19A J.Thibault/T.Esposito
20 T.Arnason/S.Mikita
20A T. Arnason/S.Mikita
21 E.Daze/Bo.Hull
21A E.Daze/Bo.Hull
22 M.Messier/P.Esposito
22A M.Messier/P.Esposito
23 E.Lindros/R.Gilbert
23A E.Lindros/R.Gilbert
24 A.Kovalev/J.Ratelle
24A A.Kovalev/J.Ratelle
25 Curtis Joseph
Roger Crozier
25A C.Joseph/R.Crozier
26 D.Hasek/T.Sawchuk
26A D.Hasek/T.Sawchuk
27 S.Yzerman/T.Lindsay
27A S.Yzerman/T.Lindsay
28 Br.Hull/A.Delvecchio
28A Br.Hull/A.Delvecchio
29 N.Lidstrom/B.Gadsby
29A N.Lidstrom/B.Gadsby
30 P.Datsyuk/S.Abel
30A P.Datsyuk/S.Abel

2003-04 Parkhurst Original Six Montreal

This 100-card set featured players from one of the Original Six teams in the NHL, Montreal. The set was produced as a stand alone product.

COMPLETE SET (100) 20.00 50.00
COMP. SET w/o SP's
1 Tomas Plekanec XRC .15 .40
2 Jose Theodore .60 1.50
3 Ron Hainsey .15 .40
4 Patrice Brisebois .15 .40
5 Jan Bulis .15 .40
6 Niklas Sundstrom .15 .40
7 Steve Begin .15 .40
8 Andreas Dackell .15 .40
9 Karl Dykhuis .15 .40
10 Michael Ryder .60 1.50
11 Jason Ward .15 .40
12 Benoit Gratton .15 .40
13 Chistopher Higgins XRC .75 2.00
14 Craig Rivet .15 .40
15 Marcel Hossa .50 1.25
16 Joe Juneau .15 .40
17 Chad Kilger .15 .40
18 Saku Koivu .50 1.25
19 Sheldon Souray .15 .40
20 Andrei Markov .15 .40
21 Olivier Michaud .15 .40
22 Mathieu Garon .15 .40
23 Yanic Perreault .15 .40
24 Francis Bouillon .15 .40
25 Mike Ribeiro .15 .40
26 Stephane Quintal .15 .40
27 Richard Zednik .15 .40
28 Darren Langdon .15 .40
29 Mike Komisarek .15 .40
30 Pierre Dagenais .15 .40
31 Chris Chelios .50 1.25
32 John LeClair .50 1.25
33 Mark Recchi .40 1.00
34 Rejean Houle .15 .40
35 Howie Morenz .40 1.00
36 Jacques Laperriere .15 .40
37 Elmer Lach .40 1.00
38 Yvan Cournoyer .50 1.25
39 Larry Robinson .50 1.25
40 Serge Savard .50 1.25
41 Butch Bouchard .15 .40
42 Guy Lafleur 1.00 2.50
43 Henri Richard .50 1.25
44 Jean Beliveau .60 1.50
45 Maurice Richard 1.50 4.00
46 Toe Blake .50 1.25
47 Guy Lapointe .15 .40
48 Gump Worsley .75 2.00
49 Patrick Roy 1.50 4.00
50 Rogie Vachon .40 1.00
51 Bill Durnan .40 1.00
52 John Ferguson .40 1.00
53 Georges Vezina 1.25 3.00
54 Denis Savard .40 1.00
55 Dollard St-Laurent .15 .40
56 Jean-Guy Talbot .15 .40
57 Steve Shutt .40 1.00
58 Frank Mahovlich .50 1.25
59 Jacques Plante 1.00 2.50
60 Dickie Moore .40 1.00
61 Howie Morenz .40 1.00
62 Maurice Richard 1.50 4.00
63 Jean Beliveau .60 1.50
64 Elmer Lach .40 1.00
65 Henri Richard .50 1.25
66 Doug Harvey .50 1.25
67 Jacques Plante 1.00 2.50
68 Larry Robinson .50 1.25
69 Patrick Roy 1.50 4.00
70 Guy Lafleur 1.00 2.50
71 Saku Koivu .50 1.25
72 Butch Bouchard .15 .40
73 Vincent Damphousse .15 .40
74 Henri Richard .50 1.25
75 Jean Beliveau .60 1.50
76 Maurice Richard 1.50 4.00
77 Newsy Lalonde .15 .40
78 Yvan Cournoyer .50 1.25
79 Doug Harvey .50 1.25
80 Serge Savard .50 1.25
81 Howie Morenz .40 1.00
82 Georges Vezina 1.25 3.00
83 Elmer Lach .40 1.00
84 Maurice Richard 1.50 4.00
85 Jean Beliveau .60 1.50
86 Yvan Cournoyer .50 1.25
87 Doug Harvey .50 1.25
88 Guy Lafleur 1.00 2.50
89 Larry Robinson .50 1.25
90 Henri Richard .50 1.25
91 Henri Richard .50 1.25
92 Maurice Richard 1.50 4.00
93 Guy Lafleur 1.00 2.50
94 Guy Lafleur 1.00 2.50
95 Jacques Plante 1.00 2.50
96 Steve Shutt .40 1.00
97 Jean Beliveau .60 1.50
98 Larry Robinson .50 1.25
99 Patrick Roy 1.50 4.00
100 Maurice Richard 1.50 4.00

2003-04 Parkhurst Original Six Montreal Autographs

This 18-card set featured certified autographs of past Canadiens greats. Print runs are listed below.

PRINT RUNS LISTED BELOW
1 Jean Beliveau/85 40.00 80.00
2 Butch Bouchard/85 20.00 50.00
3 Yvan Cournoyer/85 25.00 60.00
4 John Ferguson/90 20.00 50.00
5 Charlie Hodge/85 25.00 60.00
6 Rejean Houle/85 20.00 50.00
7 Elmer Lach/90 25.00 60.00
8 Guy Lafleur/85 40.00 80.00
9 Jacques Laperriere/85 20.00 50.00
10 Frank Mahovlich/90 25.00 60.00
11 Dickie Moore/85 20.00 50.00
12 Henri Richard/85 25.00 60.00
13 Larry Robinson/85 40.00 100.00
14 Denis Savard/90 20.00 50.00
15 Serge Savard/85 25.00 60.00
16 Steve Shutt/85 20.00 50.00
17 Jean-Guy Talbot/85 20.00 50.00
18 Gump Worsley/40 60.00 125.00

2003-04 Parkhurst Original Six Montreal Inserts

COMPLETE SET (16) 25.00 50.00
STATED ODDS 1:6
M1 Jacques Plante 2.00 5.00
M2 Doug Harvey 1.50 4.00
M3 Jean Beliveau 1.50 4.00
M4 Maurice Richard 3.00 8.00
M5 Henri Richard 1.50 4.00
M6 Howie Morenz 1.50 4.00
M7 Guy Lafleur 2.00 5.00
M8 Jean Beliveau 2.00 5.00
M9 Jacques Plante 2.00 5.00
M10 Howie Morenz 1.50 4.00
M11 Doug Harvey 1.50 4.00
M12 Elmer Lach 1.50 4.00
M13 Bill Durnan 1.50 4.00
M14 Patrick Roy 3.00 8.00
M15 Saku Koivu 1.50 4.00
M16 Guy Lafleur 2.00 5.00

2003-04 Parkhurst Original Six Montreal Memorabilia

This 63-card set featured memorabilia from past and present Canadiens players. Cards MM1-10 and MM57-58 were single jerseys and were limited to 100 copies sets. Cards MM11-13 were jersey/stick combos and were limited to 80 sets. Cards MM15-21 were vintage memorabilia cards and print runs are listed below. Cards MM16-30 and MM59-63 were vintage jersey cards and print runs are listed below. Cards MM31-35 were vintage stick cards and print runs are listed below. Cards MM36-40 were retired numbers cards and were limited to 20 copies. Cards MM41-50 were grouped into a subset known as Original Six Shooters; players who have scored high career totals against original six teams. The shooters cards were limited to 100 copies each. Cards MM51-56 were dual-jersey cards and were limited to 100 copies each.

JSY PRINT RUN 100 SETS
JSY/STK PRINT RUN 80 SETS
VIN.MEM PRINT RUNS LISTED BELOW
VIN.JSY PRINT RUNS LISTED BELOW
VIN.STICK PRINT RUNS LISTED BELOW
RET.NMBRS PRINT RUN 20 SETS
SIX SHOOT.PRINT RUN 100 SETS
TIMELINE PRINT RUN 100 SETS
MM1 Jose Theodore 15.00 40.00
MM2 Niklas Sundstrom 6.00 15.00
MM3 Stephane Quintal 6.00 15.00
MM4 Jan Bulis 6.00 15.00
MM5 Saku Koivu 10.00 25.00
MM6 Craig Rivet 6.00 15.00
MM7 Mathieu Garon 10.00 25.00
MM8 Yanic Perreault 8.00 20.00
MM9 Chad Kilger 8.00 20.00
MM10 Marcel Hossa 10.00 25.00
MM11 Jose Theodore J/S 25.00 60.00
MM12 Stephane Quintal J/S 12.50 30.00
MM13 Saku Koivu J/S 25.00 60.00
MM14 Jose Theodore/80 20.00 50.00
MM15 Patrick Roy/80 Pad 30.00 80.00
MM16 Dickie Moore/70 J 30.00 80.00
MM17 Jacques Plante/20
MM18 Guy Lafleur/80 30.00 80.00
MM19 Doug Harvey/60 20.00 50.00
MM20 Charlie Hodge/50 Glove 20.00 50.00
MM21 Newsy Lalonde/60 40.00 100.00
MM22 Aurel Joliat/50 J 40.00 100.00
MM23 Henri Richard/60 J 20.00 50.00
MM24 Jean Beliveau/60 J 20.00 50.00
MM25 Doug Harvey/60 J 20.00 50.00
MM26 Guy Lafleur/50 J 20.00 50.00
MM27 Gump Worsley/70 J 20.00 50.00
MM28 George Hainsworth/20 J
MM29 Maurice Richard/20 J
MM30 Patrick Roy/80 J 30.00 80.00
MM31 Maurice Richard/20 S
MM32 Jean Beliveau/60 S 25.00 60.00
MM33 Guy Lafleur/50 S 30.00 80.00
MM34 Jacques Plante/60 S 30.00 80.00
MM35 Georges Vezina/20 RN J
MM36 Jacques Plante/20 RN J
MM37 Maurice Richard/20 RN J
MM38 Jean Beliveau/20 RN J
MM39 Guy Lafleur/20 RN J
MM40 Doug Harvey/20 RN J
MM41 Mario Lemieux SS 15.00 40.00
MM42 Ron Francis SS 6.00 15.00
MM43 Joe Sakic SS 12.50 30.00
MM44 Brett Hull SS 10.00 25.00
MM45 Jaromir Jagr SS 8.00 20.00
MM46 Mike Modano SS 8.00 20.00
MM47 Teemu Selanne SS 6.00 15.00
MM48 Pavel Bure SS 6.00 15.00
MM49 Paul Kariya SS 8.00 20.00
MM50 Peter Forsberg SS 10.00 25.00
MM51 Jacques Plante 60.00 150.00
Patrick Roy
MM52 Henri Richard 30.00 80.00
Saku Koivu
MM53 Doug Harvey 15.00 40.00
Larry Robinson
MM54 Gump Worsley 40.00 100.00
Jose Theodore
MM55 Jean Beliveau 15.00 40.00
John LeClair
MM56 Aurel Joliat 50.00 100.00
Guy Lafleur
MM57 Mike Komisarek/100 J 10.00 25.00
MM58 Ron Hainsey/100 J 10.00 25.00
MM59 Guy Lapointe/80 J 20.00 50.00
MM60 Serge Savard/100 J 20.00 50.00
MM61 Steve Shutt/100 J 20.00 50.00
MM62 Peter Mahovlich/100 J 20.00 50.00
MM63 Jacques Plante/100 J 30.00 60.00

2003-04 Parkhurst Original Six New York

This 100-card set featured players from one of the Original Six teams in the NHL, New York. The set was produced as a stand alone product.

COMPLETE SET (100) 20.00 50.00
1 Matthew Barnaby .15 .40
2 Alex Kovalev .40 1.00
3 Dan Blackburn .40 1.00
4 Pavel Bure .50 1.25
5 Anson Carter .40 1.00
6 Jussi Markkanen .40 1.00
7 Jamie Lundmark .15 .40
8 Boris Mironov .15 .40
9 Joel Bouchard .15 .40
10 Dale Purinton .15 .40
11 Bobby Holik .15 .40
12 Dan Lacouture .15 .40
13 Mike Dunham .40 1.00
14 Greg de Vries .15 .40
15 Darius Kasparaitis .15 .40
16 Dominic Moore XRC .15 .40
17 Martin Rucinsky .15 .40
18 Brian Leetch .75 2.00
19 Pascal Rheaume .15 .40
20 Eric Lindros .50 1.25
21 Jan Hlavac .15 .40
22 Chris Simon .15 .40
23 Vladimir Malakhov .15 .40
24 Jed Ortmeyer XRC .15 .40
25 Mark Messier 1.50 4.00
26 Jason Labarbera .15 .40
27 Phil Osaer XRC .15 .40
28 Petr Nedved .15 .40
29 Tom Poti .15 .40
30 Jason MacDonald XRC .15 .40
31 Adam Graves .15 .40
32 Doug Weight .40 1.00
33 Tony Amonte .40 1.00
34 Ed Giacomin .60 1.50
35 Mike Gartner 1.50 3.00
36 Phil Esposito 1.50 4.00
37 Dan Cloutier .40 1.00
38 Ron Greschner .40 1.00
39 Luc Robitaille .40 1.00
40 Andy Bathgate .40 1.00
41 Frank Boucher .40 1.00
42 Brad Park .50 1.25
43 Ron Duguay .40 1.00
44 Bill Gadsby .40 1.00
45 Harry Howell .40 1.00
46 Ching Johnson .40 1.00
47 Doug Harvey .50 1.25
48 Guy Lafleur 1.50 3.00
49 John Davidson .60 1.50
50 Jean Ratelle .50 1.25
51 Mike Richter .75 2.00
52 John Vanbiesbrouck .40 1.00
53 Chuck Rayner .40 1.00
54 Lou Fontinato .15 .40
55 Rod Gilbert .50 1.25
56 Lester Patrick .50 1.25
57 Vic Hadfield .50 1.25
58 Walt Tkaczuk .15 .40
59 Gump Worsley .75 2.00
60 Bun Cook .40 1.00
61 Mark Messier 1.50 4.00
62 Brian Leetch .75 2.00
63 Phil Esposito 1.50 4.00
64 Ed Giacomin .60 1.50
65 Brad Park .50 1.25
66 Jean Ratelle .50 1.25
67 Pat Verbeek .15 .40
68 Barry Beck .15 .40
69 Rod Gilbert .50 1.25
70 Chuck Rayner .40 1.00
71 Mark Messier 1.50 4.00
72 Brian Leetch .75 2.00
73 Vic Hadfield .50 1.25
74 Phil Esposito 1.50 4.00
75 Ron Greschner .40 1.00
76 Walt Tkaczuk .15 .40
77 Harry Howell .40 1.00
78 Andy Bathgate .40 1.00
79 Barry Beck .15 .40
80 Brad Park .50 1.25
81 Brad Park .50 1.25
82 Ed Giacomin .60 1.50
83 Jean Ratelle .50 1.25
84 Phil Esposito 1.50 4.00
85 Rod Gilbert .50 1.25
86 Harry Howell .40 1.00
87 Chuck Rayner .40 1.00
88 Ching Johnson .40 1.00
89 Bill Cook .75 2.00
90 Andy Bathgate .40 1.00
91 Rod Gilbert .50 1.25
92 Harry Howell .40 1.00
93 Brian Leetch .75 2.00
94 Mike Richter .75 2.00
95 Ed Giacomin .60 1.50
96 Jean Ratelle .50 1.25
97 Brad Park .50 1.25
98 Mark Messier 1.50 4.00
99 Brian Leetch .75 2.00
100 Adam Graves .15 .40

2003-04 Parkhurst Original Six New York Autographs

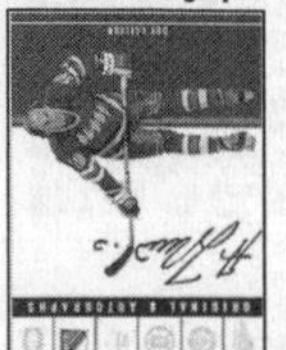

This 18-card set featured certified autographs of past

Rangers greats. Print runs are listed below.
PRINT RUNS LISTED BELOW
1 Andy Bathgate/80 20.00 50.00
2 John Davidson/90 15.00 40.00
3 Ron Duguay/90 15.00 40.00
4 Phil Esposito/55 25.00 60.00
5 Lou Fontinato/95 15.00 40.00
6 Ed Giacomin/90 30.00 80.00
7 Rod Gilbert/85 30.00 80.00
8 Ron Greschner/95 15.00 40.00
9 Vic Hadfield/90 15.00 40.00
10 Harry Howell/95 20.00 50.00
11 Guy Lafleur/80 30.00 80.00
12 Brad Park/90 20.00 50.00
13 Jean Ratelle/90 20.00 50.00
14 Allan Stanley/85 15.00 40.00
15 Walt Tkaczuk/90 15.00 40.00
16 Gump Worsley/80 25.00 60.00

2003-04 Parkhurst Original Six New York Inserts

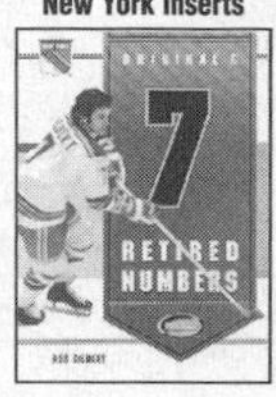

COMPLETE SET (16) 25.00 60.00
STATED ODDS 1:6
N1 Rod Gilbert 1.50 4.00
N2 Ed Giacomin 2.00 5.00
N3 Frank Boucher 1.50 4.00
N4 Rod Gilbert 1.50 4.00
N5 Phil Esposito 3.00 8.00
N6 Gump Worsley 2.00 5.00
N7 Ed Giacomin 2.00 5.00
N8 Doug Harvey 1.50 4.00
N9 Mark Messier 3.00 8.00
N10 Jean Ratelle 1.50 4.00
N11 Andy Bathgate 1.50 4.00
N12 Brian Leetch 2.00 5.00
N13 Chuck Rayner 1.50 4.00
N14 Brian Leetch 1.50 4.00
N15 Alex Kovalev 1.50 4.00
N16 Brad Park 1.50 4.00

2003-04 Parkhurst Original Six New York Memorabilia

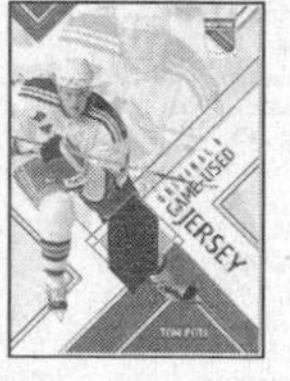

This 63-card set featured memorabilia from past and present Rangers players. Cards NM1-12 and NM56-58 were single jerseys and were limited to 100 copies sets. Cards NM13-19 and NM57 were jersey/stick combos and were limited to 80 sets. Cards NM21-26 were vintage memorabilia cards and were limited to 20 copies each. Cards NM27-33 and NM62-63 were vintage jersey cards and print runs are listed below. Cards NM34-38 and NM59-61 were vintage stick cards and print runs are listed below. Cards NM39-40 were retired numbers cards and were limited to 20 copies. Cards NM411-50 were grouped into a subset known as Original Six Shooters; players who have scored high career totals against original six teams. The shooters cards were limited to 100 copies each. Cards NM51-55 were dual-jersey cards and were limited to 100 copies each.

JSY PRINT RUN 100 SETS
JSY/STK PRINT RUN 80 SETS
VIN MFM PRINT RUN 20 SETS
VIN.STICK PRINT RUNS LISTED BELOW
RET.NMBRS PRINT RUN 20 SETS
SIX SHOOT.PRINT RUN 100 SETS
TIMELINE PRINT RUN 100 SETS
NM1 Mike Dunham 10.00 25.00
NM2 Brian Leetch 15.00 40.00
NM3 Eric Lindros 10.00 25.00
NM4 Mark Messier 10.00 25.00
NM5 Tom Poti 6.00 15.00
NM6 Pavel Bure 10.00 25.00
NM7 Mike Richter 12.50 30.00
NM8 Dan Blackburn 6.00 15.00
NM9 Darius Kasparaitis 6.00 15.00
NM10 Bobby Holik 6.00 15.00
NM11 Vladimir Malakhov 6.00 15.00
NM12 Jamie Lundmark 6.00 15.00
NM13 Brian Leetch J/S 15.00 40.00
NM14 Eric Lindros J/S 15.00 40.00
NM15 Mark Messier J/S 30.00 80.00
NM16 Mike Richter J/S 20.00 50.00
NM17 Pavel Bure J/S 15.00 40.00
NM18 Dan Blackburn J/S 12.50 30.00
NM19 Mike Dunham J/S 15.00 40.00
NM20 Eric Lindros/30 15.00 40.00
NM21 Terry Sawchuk/20
NM22 Jacques Plante/20
NM23 Bill Gadsby/20
NM24 Doug Harvey/20
NM25 Chuck Rayner/20
NM26 Ed Giacomin/20
NM27 Theo Fleury/50 J 10.00 25.00
NM28 Bryan Berard/60 J 10.00 25.00
NM29 Marcel Dionne/60 J 15.00 40.00
NM30 Ed Giacomin/50 J 40.00 100.00
NM31 Phil Esposito/50 J 15.00 40.00
NM32 Rod Gilbert/50 J 30.00 80.00
NM33 Jean Ratelle/50 J 30.00 80.00
NM34 Emile Francis/60 S 15.00 40.00
NM35 Gilles Villemure/60 S 20.00 50.00
NM36 Ed Giacomin/20 S
NM37 Phil Esposito/20 S
NM38 Johnny Bower/20 S
NM39 Ed Giacomin/20 RN
NM40 Rod Gilbert/20 RN
NM41 Mario Lemieux SS 15.00 40.00
NM42 Ron Francis SS 6.00 15.00
NM43 Joe Sakic SS 10.00 25.00
NM44 Brett Hull SS 8.00 20.00
NM45 Jaromir Jagr SS 8.00 20.00
NM46 Mike Modano SS 8.00 20.00
NM47 Teemu Selanne SS 6.00 15.00
NM48 Pavel Bure SS 6.00 15.00
NM49 Paul Kariya SS 8.00 20.00
NM50 Peter Forsberg SS 10.00 25.00
NM51 Ed Giacomin 40.00 100.00
Dan Blackburn
NM52 Phil Esposito 20.00 50.00
Eric Lindros
NM53 Marcel Dionne 12.50 30.00
Alex Kovalev
NM54 Jean Ratelle 50.00 125.00
Mark Messier
NM55 Rod Gilbert 12.50 30.00
Pavel Bure
NM56 Alex Kovalev/100 J 15.00 40.00
NM57 Alex Kovalev/100 J/S 20.00 50.00
NM58 Anson Carter/100 J 12.50 30.00
NM59 John Davidson/100 S 20.00 50.00
NM60 Marcel Dionne/100 S 15.00 40.00
NM61 Adam Graves/100 S 12.50 30.00
NM62 Sergei Zubov/100 J 12.50 30.00
NM63 Dan Cloutier/100 J 12.50 30.00

2003-04 Parkhurst Original Six Shooters

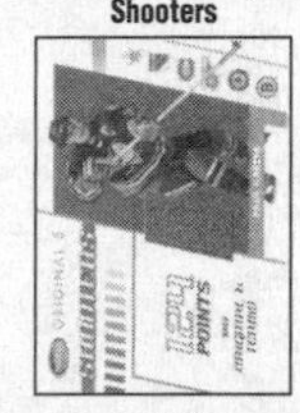

This ten card set paralleled the Shooters cards in each of the Original Six products, but each card carried the total number of points scored against all Original Six team in the player's career. Each card was limited to 10 copies each.

NOT PRICED DUE TO SCARCITY
OSM1 Mario Lemieux
OSM2 Ron Francis
OSM3 Joe Sakic
OSM4 Brett Hull
OSM5 Jaromir Jagr
OSM6 Mike Modano
OSM7 Teemu Selanne
OSM8 Pavel Bure
OSM9 Paul Kariya
OSM10 Peter Forsberg

2003-04 Parkhurst Original Six Toronto

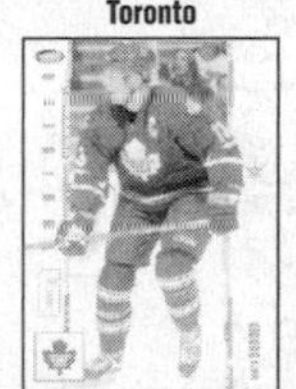

This 100-card set featured players from one of the Original Six teams in the NHL, Toronto. The set was produced as a stand alone product.

COMPLETE SET (100) 20.00 50.00
1 Nikolai Antropov .15 .40
2 Wade Belak .15 .40
3 Ed Belfour .50 1.25
4 Aki Berg .15 .40
5 Maxim Kondratiev XRC 2.00 5.00
6 Owen Nolan .40 1.00
7 Nathan Perrott .15 .40
8 Tie Domi .40 1.00
9 Matt Stajan XRC 4.00 10.00
10 Ken Klee .15 .40
11 Bryan Marchment .15 .40
12 Jamie Hodson .15 .40
13 Carlo Colaiacovo .15 .40
14 Tomas Kaberle .15 .40
15 Joe Nieuwendyk .40 1.00
16 Bryan McCabe .15 .40
17 Ric Jackman .15 .40
18 Alexander Mogilny .40 1.00
19 Karel Pilar .15 .40
20 Alexei Ponikarovsky .15 .40
21 Robert Reichel .15 .40
22 Mikael Renberg .15 .40
23 Gary Roberts .15 .40
24 Mats Sundin .50 1.25
25 Mikael Tellqvist .40 1.00
26 Darcy Tucker .15 .40
27 Aaron Gavey .15 .40
28 Josh Holden .15 .40
29 Trevor Kidd .40 1.00
30 Tom Fitzgerald .15 .40
31 Charlie Conacher .50 1.25
32 Doug Gilmour .40 1.00
33 Felix Potvin .50 1.25
34 Vincent Damphousse .40 1.00
35 Terry Sawchuk .75 2.00
36 Tiger Williams 1.00 2.50
37 Wendel Clark .75 2.00
38 Teeder Kennedy .50 1.25
39 Syl Apps .40 1.00
40 Hap Day .15 .40
41 Rick Vaive .15 .40
42 Curtis Joseph .50 1.25
43 Darryl Sittler .50 1.25
44 Bill Barilko XRC .60 1.50
45 Bobby Baun .40 1.00
46 Borje Salming .50 1.25
47 Harry Lumley .50 1.25
48 Dick Duff .40 1.00
49 Mike Palmateer 1.25 3.00
50 Norm Ullman .50 1.25
51 Frank Mahovlich .50 1.25
52 Red Kelly .50 1.25
53 Sid Smith .40 1.00
54 Mike Gartner 1.00 2.50
55 Dave Andreychuk .15 .40
56 Johnny Bower 2.00 5.00
57 Turk Broda .60 1.50
58 Tim Horton 1.50 4.00
59 King Clancy .50 1.25
60 Ace Bailey .60 1.50
61 Mats Sundin .50 1.25
62 Doug Gilmour .40 1.00
63 Borje Salming .50 1.25
64 Lanny McDonald .50 1.25
65 Darryl Sittler 1.00 2.50
66 King Clancy .50 1.25
67 Turk Broda .60 1.50
68 Felix Potvin .50 1.25
69 Tim Horton 1.50 4.00
70 Sid Smith .40 1.00
71 Mats Sundin .50 1.25
72 Doug Gilmour .40 1.00
73 Wendel Clark .75 2.00
74 Teeder Kennedy .50 1.25
75 Syl Apps .40 1.00
76 Hap Day .15 .40
77 Rick Vaive .15 .40
78 Charlie Conacher .50 1.25
79 Darryl Sittler 1.00 2.50
80 Sid Smith .40 1.00
81 Ace Bailey .60 1.50
82 Johnny Bower 2.00 5.00
83 Turk Broda .60 1.50
84 Tim Horton 1.50 4.00
85 Red Kelly .50 1.25
86 Frank Mahovlich .50 1.25
87 Borje Salming .50 1.25
88 Marcel Pronovost .75 2.00
89 King Clancy .50 1.25
90 Syl Apps .40 1.00
91 Darryl Sittler 1.00 2.50
92 Tim Horton 1.50 4.00
93 Darryl Sittler 1.00 2.50
94 Borje Salming .50 1.25
95 Turk Broda .60 1.50
96 Rick Vaive .15 .40
97 Doug Gilmour .40 1.00
98 Frank Mahovlich .50 1.25
99 Wendel Clark .75 2.00
100 Ed Belfour .50 1.25

2003-04 Parkhurst Original Six Toronto Autographs

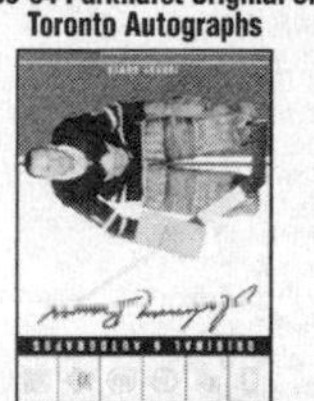

This 18-card set featured certified autographs of past Maple Leafs greats. Print runs are listed below.

COMMON CARD (1-16) 20.00 50.00
1 Bobby Baun/85 30.00 80.00
2 Johnny Bower/90 25.00 60.00
3 Wendel Clark/90 50.00 100.00
4 Dick Duff/85 20.00 50.00
5 Red Kelly/90 25.00 60.00
6 Ted Kennedy/85 20.00 50.00
7 Frank Mahovlich/85 25.00 60.00
8 Eddie Shack/85 25.00 60.00
9 Darryl Sittler/95 25.00 60.00
10 Sid Smith/95 30.00 80.00
11 Ron Stewart/85 20.00 50.00
12 Rick Vaive/95 25.00 60.00
13 Tiger Williams/90 20.00 50.00
14 Mike Palmateer/95 20.00 50.00
15 Mike Gartner/85 20.00 50.00
16 Borje Salming/85 40.00 80.00

2003-04 Parkhurst Original Six Toronto Inserts

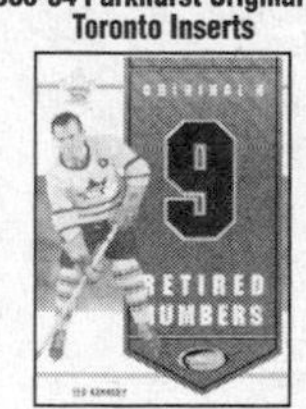

COMPLETE SET (17) 30.00 60.00
STATED ODDS 1:6
T1 Bill Barilko 2.00 5.00
T2 Ace Bailey 2.00 5.00
T3 Tim Horton 3.00 8.00
T4 Syl Apps 1.50 4.00
T5 Ted Kennedy 2.00 5.00
T6 Frank Mahovlich 3.00 8.00
T7 Ted Kennedy 2.00 5.00
T8 Red Kelly 2.00 5.00
T9 Ace Bailey 2.00 5.00
T10 Charlie Conacher 2.00 5.00
T11 Syl Apps 1.50 4.00
T12 Turk Broda 2.00 5.00
T13 Terry Sawchuk 1.50 4.00
T14 Johnny Bower 2.50 6.00
T15 Darryl Sittler 1.50 4.00
T16 Wendel Clark 3.00 8.00
T17 Lanny McDonald 1.50 4.00

2003-04 Parkhurst Original Six Toronto Memorabilia

This 63-card set featured memorabilia from past and present Maple Leafs players. Cards TM1-13 were single jerseys and were limited to 100 copies sets. Cards TM14-19 were jersey/stick combos and were limited to 80 sets. Cards TM20-27 were vintage memorabilia cards and print runs are listed below. Cards TM28-32 and TM59-62 were vintage jersey cards and print runs are listed below. Cards TM33-35 and TM63 were vintage stick cards and print runs are listed below. Cards TM37-40 were retired numbers cards and were limited to 20 copies. Cards TM41-50 were grouped into a subset known as Original Six Shooters; players who have scored high career totals against original six teams. The shooters cards were limited to 100 copies each. Cards tM51-58 were dual-jersey cards and were limited to 100 copies each.

TM1 Mats Sundin 15.00 40.00
TM2 Gary Roberts 10.00 25.00
TM3 Bryan McCabe 8.00 20.00
TM4 Darcy Tucker 10.00 25.00
TM5 Nik Antropov 10.00 25.00
TM6 Tomas Kaberle 10.00 25.00
TM7 Alexander Mogilny 10.00 25.00
TM8 Tie Domi 10.00 25.00
TM9 Ed Belfour 12.50 30.00
TM10 Owen Nolan 8.00 20.00
TM11 Carlo Colaiacovo 6.00 15.00
TM12 Robert Svehla 6.00 15.00
TM13 Trevor Kidd 10.00 25.00
TM14 Mats Sundin J/S 15.00 40.00
TM15 Alexander Mogilny J/S 12.50 30.00
TM16 Darcy Tucker J/S 12.50 30.00
TM17 Bryan McCabe J/S 12.50 30.00
TM18 Tomas Kaberle J/S 20.00 50.00
TM19 Gary Roberts J/S 12.50 30.00
TM20 Johnny Bower/20 Glove
TM21 Terry Sawchuk/20 Glove
TM22 Ted Kennedy/20 Glove
TM23 Charlie Conacher/20
TM24 Tim Horton/60 Pants 40.00 100.00
TM25 Wendel Clark/30 20.00 50.00
TM26 Bill Barilko/20
TM27 Borje Salming/80 15.00 40.00
TM28 Tim Horton/20 J
TM29 Red Kelly/20 J
TM30 Lanny McDonald/60 J 25.00 60.00
TM31 Tiger Williams/60 J 15.00 40.00
TM32 Curtis Joseph/60 J 20.00 50.00
TM33 Frank Mahovlich/50 S 25.00 60.00
TM34 Johnny Bower/50 S 30.00 80.00
TM35 Turk Broda/20 S
TM36 Mats Sundin/50
TM37 Johnny Bower/20 RN J
TM38 T.Kennedy/20 RN Glove
TM39 Ace Bailey/20 RN Glove
TM40 Tim Horton/20 RN Pants
TM41 Mario Lemieux SS 15.00 40.00
TM42 Ron Francis SS 6.00 15.00
TM43 Joe Sakic SS 10.00 25.00
TM44 Brett Hull SS 8.00 20.00
TM45 Jaromir Jagr SS 8.00 20.00
TM46 Mike Modano SS 8.00 20.00
TM47 Teemu Selanne SS 6.00 15.00
TM48 Pavel Bure SS 6.00 15.00
TM49 Paul Kariya SS 8.00 20.00
TM50 Peter Forsberg SS 10.00 25.00
TM51 T.Horton/W.Clark 40.00 100.00
TM52 R.Kelly/O.Nolan 15.00 40.00
TM53 L.McDonald/A.Mogilny 15.00 40.00
TM54 T.Williams/T.Domi 25.00 60.00
TM55 D.Sittler/M.Sundin 30.00 80.00
TM56 M.Gartner/G.Roberts 15.00 40.00
TM57 B.Salming/B.McCabe 15.00 40.00
TM58 R.Vaive/D.Tucker 15.00 40.00
TM59 Felix Potvin/100 J 15.00 40.00
TM60 Wendel Clark/100 J 25.00 60.00
TM61 Mike Gartner/100 J 15.00 40.00
TM62 Rick Vaive/100 J 20.00 50.00
TM63 Mike Gartner/80 S 15.00 40.00

2005-06 Parkhurst

This 700-card set was issued into the hobby in six-card packs, with a $1.59 SRP, which came 36 packs to a box and 20 boxes to a case. Cards numbered 1-499 feature a mix of veterans and Rookie Cards in team alphabetical order while cards 501-530 honor team captains and cards 531-560 are team cards. Cards 561-585 is a Northern Stars subset while cards 586-600 are highlight cards. The set concludes with two more subsets: Rookies (601-670) and Team Checklists (671-700).

COMPLETE SET (700) 75.00 150.00
1 Andy McDonald .15 .40
2 Teemu Selanne .50 1.25
3 Scott Niedermayer .30 .75
4 Joffrey Lupul .30 .75
5 Todd Marchant .15 .40
6 Chris Kunitz .15 .40
7 Jean-Sebastien Giguere .40 1.00
8 Samuel Pahlsson .15 .40
9 Jonathan Hedstrom .15 .40
10 Ilja Bryzgalov .25 .60
11 Jeff Friesen .30 .75
12 Rob Niedermayer .30 .75
13 Francois Beauchemin .15 .40
14 Vitaly Vishnevski .15 .40
15 Ruslan Salei .15 .40
16 Todd Fedoruk .15 .40
17 Dustin Penner 1.50 4.00
18 Ilya Kovalchuk .60 1.50
19 Marc Savard .30 .75
20 Marian Hossa .40 1.00
21 Vyacheslav Kozlov .15 .40
22 Peter Bondra .40 1.00
23 Jaroslav Modry .15 .40
24 Greg de Vries .15 .40
25 Niclas Havelid .15 .40
26 Patrik Stefan .30 .75
27 Serge Aubin .15 .40
28 Andy Sutton .15 .40
29 Kari Lehtonen .50 1.25
30 Garnet Exelby .15 .40
31 Michael Garnett .15 .40
32 Bobby Holik .30 .75
33 Scott Mellanby .15 .40
34 Patrice Bergeron .50 1.25
35 Brad Boyes .15 .40
36 Tim Thomas .15 .40
37 Glen Murray .30 .75
38 Marco Sturm .30 .75
39 Wayne Primeau .15 .40
40 Brad Stuart .30 .75
41 Andrew Raycroft .40 1.00
42 P.J. Axelsson .15 .40
43 Brian Leetch .50 1.25
44 Travis Green .15 .40
45 David Tanabe .15 .40
46 Nick Boynton .30 .75
47 Hal Gill .15 .40
48 Josh Langfeld .15 .40
49 Tom Fitzgerald .15 .40
50 Ales Kotalik .15 .40
51 Maxim Afinogenov .30 .75
52 Chris Drury .40 1.00
53 Tim Connolly .15 .40
54 Ryan Miller .25 .60
55 Brian Campbell .15 .40
56 Jochen Hecht .15 .40
57 Teppo Numminen .15 .40
58 Martin Biron .40 1.00
59 Derek Roy .30 .75
60 Mike Grier .15 .40
61 Paul Gaustad .15 .40
62 Daniel Briere .40 1.00
63 Jason Pominville .15 .40
64 Jay McKee .15 .40
65 J.P. Dumont .30 .75
66 Henrik Tallinder .15 .40
67 Jarome Iginla .40 1.00
68 Daymond Langkow .15 .40
69 Kristian Huselius .15 .40
70 Tony Amonte .40 1.00
71 Andrew Ference .15 .40
72 Chuck Kobasew .30 .75
73 Miikka Kiprusoff .50 1.25
74 Robyn Regehr .30 .75
75 Roman Hamrlik .15 .40
76 Darren McCarty .30 .75
77 Stephane Yelle .15 .40
78 Chris Simon .15 .40
79 Jordan Leopold .30 .75
80 Rhett Warrener .15 .40
81 Shean Donovan .15 .40
82 Marcus Nilson .15 .40
83 Mike LeClerc .15 .40
84 Eric Staal .40 1.00
85 Cory Stillman .30 .75
86 Erik Cole .30 .75
87 Justin Williams .40 1.00
88 Rod Brind'Amour .40 1.00
89 Martin Gerber .40 1.00
90 Doug Weight .40 1.00
91 Ray Whitney .15 .40
92 Matt Cullen .15 .40
93 Frantisek Kaberle .15 .40
94 Bret Hedican .15 .40
95 Oleg Tverdovsky .30 .75
96 Kevyn Adams .15 .40
97 Aaron Ward .15 .40
98 Mark Recchi .40 1.00
99 Glen Wesley .30 .75
100 Josef Vasicek .15 .40
101 Brandon Bochenski RC .75 2.00
102 Kyle Calder .30 .75
103 Mark Bell .30 .75
104 Martin Lapointe .15 .40
105 Pavel Vorobiev .15 .40
106 Nikolai Khabibulin .50 1.25
107 Craig Anderson .15 .40
108 Matthew Barnaby .15 .40
109 Radim Vrbata .15 .40
110 Rene Bourque RC .75 2.00
111 Eric Daze .40 1.00
112 Tuomo Ruutu .30 .75
113 Adrian Aucoin .30 .75
114 Jim Vandermeer .15 .40
115 Milan Bartovic .15 .40
116 Curtis Brown .15 .40
117 Alex Tanguay .40 1.00
118 Joe Sakic 1.00 2.50
119 Marek Svatos .15 .40
120 Jose Theodore .50 1.25
121 Andrew Brunette .15 .40
122 Milan Hejduk .50 1.25
123 John-Michael Liles .30 .75
124 Rob Blake .40 1.00
125 Pierre Turgeon .30 .75
126 Ian Laperriere .15 .40
127 Antti Laaksonen .15 .40
128 Patrice Brisebois .15 .40
129 Brett Clark .15 .40
130 Karlis Skrastins .15 .40
131 Brett McLean .15 .40
132 Dan Hinote .15 .40
133 Steve Konowalchuk .15 .40
134 David Vyborny .15 .40
135 Nikolai Zherdev .40 1.00
136 Bryan Berard .30 .75
137 Rick Nash .60 1.50
138 Sergei Fedorov .50 1.25
139 Jan Hrdina .15 .40
140 Duvie Westcott .15 .40
141 Manny Malhotra .15 .40
142 Marc Denis .40 1.00
143 Jason Chimera .15 .40
144 Trevor Letowski .15 .40
145 Adam Foote .15 .40
146 Rostislav Klesla .30 .75
147 Dan Fritsche .15 .40
148 Pascal LeClaire .25 .60
149 Jody Shelley .15 .40
150 Jaroslav Balastik RC .75 2.00
151 Johan Hedberg .25 .60
152 Trevor Daley .15 .40
153 Jon Klemm .15 .40
154 Willie Mitchell .15 .40
155 Steve Ott .15 .40
156 Antti Miettinen .15 .40
157 Niko Kapanen .15 .40
158 Stu Barnes .15 .40
159 Philippe Boucher .15 .40
160 Bill Guerin .30 .75
161 Jason Arnott .15 .40
162 Mike Modano .50 1.25
163 Marty Turco .40 1.00
164 Brenden Morrow .40 1.00
165 Sergei Zubov .30 .75
166 Jere Lehtinen .40 1.00
167 Pavel Datsyuk .50 1.25
168 Henrik Zetterberg .50 1.25
169 Manny Legace .50 1.25
170 Nicklas Lidstrom .50 1.25
171 Brendan Shanahan .50 1.25
172 Jason Williams .15 .40
173 Steve Yzerman 1.25 3.00
174 Mathieu Schneider .15 .40
175 Robert Lang .15 .40
176 Tomas Holmstrom .15 .40
177 Mikael Samuelsson .15 .40
178 Chris Osgood .25 .60
179 Kris Draper .15 .40
180 Kirk Maltby .15 .40
181 Chris Chelios .50 1.25
182 Johan Franzen RC 6.00 15.00
183 Brett Lebda RC .75 2.00
184 Jiri Fischer .15 .40
185 Shawn Horcoff .15 .40
186 Ty Conklin .40 1.00
187 Ales Hemsky .30 .75
188 Jarret Stoll .15 .40
189 Ryan Smyth .40 1.00
190 Chris Pronger .40 1.00
191 Jaroslav Spacek .15 .40
192 Raffi Torres .30 .75
193 Jussi Markkanen .15 .40
194 Marc-Andre Bergeron .15 .40
195 Fernando Pisani .15 .40
196 Michael Peca .30 .75
197 Jason Smith .15 .40
198 Dwayne Roloson .40 1.00
199 Georges Laraque .15 .40
200 Sergei Samsonov .40 1.00
201 Olli Jokinen .40 1.00
202 Roberto Luongo .75 2.00
203 Nathan Horton .30 .75
204 Joe Nieuwendyk .40 1.00
205 Jozef Stumpel .15 .40
206 Jay Bouwmeester .30 .75
207 Gary Roberts .15 .40
208 Chris Gratton .15 .40
209 Martin Gelinas .15 .40
210 Stephen Weiss .30 .75
211 Mike Van Ryn .15 .40
212 Jamie McLennan .15 .40
213 Lukas Krajicek .15 .40
214 Jon Sim .15 .40
215 Sean Hill .15 .40
216 Juraj Kolnik .15 .40
217 Pavol Demitra .40 1.00
218 Mathieu Garon .40 1.00
219 Lubomir Visnovsky .15 .40
220 Craig Conroy .15 .40
221 Alexander Frolov .40 1.00
222 Mike Cammalleri .15 .40
223 Derek Armstrong .15 .40
224 Joe Corvo .15 .40
225 Eric Belanger .15 .40
226 Sean Avery .15 .40
227 Luc Robitaille .40 1.00
228 Dustin Brown .30 .75
229 Jeremy Roenick .50 1.25
230 Jason Labarbera .25 .60
231 Mattias Norstrom .15 .40
232 Mark Parrish .30 .75
233 Brian Rolston .15 .40
234 Pierre-Marc Bouchard .30 .75
235 Manny Fernandez .40 1.00
236 Marian Gaborik .60 1.50
237 Randy Robitaille .15 .40
238 Todd White .15 .40
239 Alexandre Daigle .30 .75
240 Wes Walz .15 .40
241 Marc Chouinard .15 .40
242 Martin Skoula .15 .40
243 Filip Kuba .30 .75
244 Nick Schultz .15 .40
245 Kurtis Foster .15 .40
246 Derek Boogaard RC .75 2.00
247 Brent Burns .15 .40
248 Pascal Dupuis .15 .40
249 Saku Koivu .50 1.25
250 David Aebischer .40 1.00
251 Alex Kovalev .25 .60
252 Michael Ryder .40 1.00
253 Mike Ribeiro .30 .75
254 Andrei Markov .15 .40
255 Jan Bulis .15 .40
256 Craig Rivet .15 .40
257 Steve Begin .15 .40
258 Sheldon Souray .30 .75
259 Tomas Plekanec .15 .40
260 Richard Zednik .30 .75
261 Cristobal Huet .25 .60
262 Francis Bouillon .15 .40
263 Chris Higgins .15 .40
264 Radek Bonk .15 .40
265 Niklas Sundstrom .15 .40
266 Pierre Dagenais .15 .40
267 Mathieu Dandenault .15 .40
268 Paul Kariya .50 1.25
269 Tomas Vokoun .40 1.00
270 Steve Sullivan .30 .75
271 Yanic Perreault .15 .40
272 Mike Sillinger .15 .40
273 Kimmo Timonen .30 .75
274 Marek Zidlicky .15 .40
275 Scott Hartnell .15 .40
276 Martin Erat .15 .40
277 Dan Hamhuis .15 .40
278 Adam Hall .15 .40
279 Scottie Upshall .15 .40
280 David Legwand .40 1.00
281 Darcy Hordichuk .15 .40
282 Vernon Fiddler .15 .40
283 Scott Walker .30 .75
284 Brendan Witt .30 .75
285 Brian Gionta .15 .40
286 Scott Gomez .40 1.00
287 Martin Brodeur 1.25 3.00
288 Jamie Langenbrunner .15 .40
289 Brian Rafalski .30 .75
290 Sergei Brylin .15 .40
291 Patrik Elias .40 1.00
292 John Madden .30 .75
293 Viktor Kozlov .15 .40
294 Scott Clemmensen .25 .60
295 Grant Marshall .15 .40
296 Jay Pandolfo .15 .40
297 Richard Matvichuk .15 .40
298 Erik Rasmussen .15 .40
299 Colin White .15 .40
300 Paul Martin .15 .40
301 Alexei Yashin .30 .75
302 Miroslav Satan .30 .75
303 Mike York .15 .40
304 Jason Blake .15 .40
305 Robert Nilsson RC 1.00 2.50
306 Trent Hunter .30 .75
307 Alexei Zhitnik .15 .40
308 Eric Godard .15 .40
309 Rick DiPietro .40 1.00
310 Arron Asham .15 .40
311 Denis Grebeshkov .15 .40
312 John Erskine .15 .40
313 Radek Martinek .15 .40
314 Garth Snow .25 .60
315 Shawn Bates .15 .40
316 Sean Bergenheim .15 .40
317 Jaromir Jagr .75 2.00
318 Martin Straka .30 .75
319 Michael Nylander .15 .40
320 Martin Rucinsky .15 .40
321 Kevin Weekes .40 1.00
322 Petr Sykora .30 .75
323 Steve Rucchin .30 .75
324 Jason Ward .15 .40
325 Michal Rozsival .15 .40
326 Fedor Tyutin .15 .40
327 Marek Malik .15 .40
328 Tom Poti .30 .75
329 Dominic Moore .15 .40
330 Darius Kasparaitis .15 .40
331 Jed Ortmeyer .15 .40
332 Marcel Hossa .15 .40
333 Dominik Hasek .60 1.50
334 Daniel Alfredsson .40 1.00
335 Dany Heatley .50 1.25
336 Jason Spezza .50 1.25
337 Wade Redden .30 .75
338 Peter Schaefer .15 .40
339 Bryan Smolinski .15 .40
340 Mike Fisher .15 .40
341 Zdeno Chara .40 1.00
342 Chris Neil .15 .40
343 Antoine Vermette .15 .40
344 Ray Emery .25 .60
345 Patrick Eaves RC 1.50 4.00
346 Vaclav Varada .15 .40
347 Martin Havlat .40 1.00
348 Chris Phillips .15 .40
349 Tyler Arnason .30 .75
350 Antero Niittymaki .25 .60
351 Simon Gagne .50 1.25
352 Peter Forsberg .75 2.00
353 Mike Knuble .15 .40
354 Michal Handzus .15 .40
355 Joni Pitkanen .30 .75
356 Sami Kapanen .30 .75
357 Kim Johnsson .30 .75
358 Mike Rathje .15 .40
359 Eric Desjardins .15 .40
360 Derian Hatcher .15 .40
361 Robert Esche .40 1.00
362 Brian Savage .15 .40
363 Chris Therien .15 .40
364 Keith Primeau .30 .75
365 Petr Nedved .30 .75
366 Donald Brashear .15 .40
367 Curtis Joseph .50 1.25
368 Ladislav Nagy .30 .75
369 Shane Doan .30 .75
370 Mike Comrie .25 .60
371 Mike Johnson .15 .40
372 Paul Mara .15 .40
373 Geoff Sanderson .15 .40
374 Steven Reinprecht .15 .40
375 Dave Scatchard .15 .40
376 Oleg Saprykin .15 .40
377 Zbynek Michalek .15 .40
378 Boyd Devereaux .15 .40
379 Fredrik Sjostrom .15 .40
380 Mike Ricci .30 .75
381 Tyson Nash .15 .40
382 Derek Morris .15 .40
383 Niklas Nordgren RC .75 2.00
384 Sergei Gonchar .15 .40
385 Marc-Andre Fleury .40 1.00

Card	Low	High
386 John LeClair	.50	1.25
387 Richard Jackman	.15	.40
388 Ryan Malone	.30	.75
389 Sebastien Caron	.15	.40
390 Mario Lemieux	2.00	5.00
391 Brooks Orpik	.15	.40
392 Konstantin Koltsov	.15	.40
393 Erik Christensen RC	.75	2.00
394 Josef Melichar	.15	.40
395 Jocelyn Thibault	.40	1.00
396 Tomas Surovy	.15	.40
397 Andre Roy	.15	.40
398 Jani Rita	.15	.40
399 Vesa Toskala	.25	.60
400 Joe Thornton	.75	2.00
401 Patrick Marleau	.40	1.00
402 Jonathan Cheechoo	.50	1.25
403 Evgeni Nabokov	.40	1.00
404 Nils Ekman	.15	.40
405 Tom Preissing	.15	.40
406 Milan Michalek	.15	.40
407 Alyn McCauley	.15	.40
408 Scott Thornton	.15	.40
409 Kyle McLaren	.15	.40
410 Scott Hannan	.15	.40
411 Marcel Goc	.15	.40
412 Grant Stevenson RC	.75	2.00
413 Christian Ehrhoff	.15	.40
414 Mark Smith	.15	.40
415 Scott Young	.15	.40
416 Petr Cajanek	.15	.40
417 Dean McAmmond	.15	.40
418 Curtis Sanford	.15	.40
419 Keith Tkachuk	.50	1.25
420 Dallas Drake	.30	.75
421 Jamal Mayers	.15	.40
422 Jeff Hoggan RC	.75	2.00
423 Christian Backman	.15	.40
424 Barret Jackman	.30	.75
425 Mark Rycroft	.30	.75
426 Jay McClement RC	.75	2.00
427 Patrick Lalime	.40	1.00
428 Kevin Dallman RC	.75	2.00
429 Dennis Wideman RC	.75	2.00
430 Brad Richards	.40	1.00
431 Vaclav Prospal	.15	.40
432 John Grahame	.25	.60
433 Vincent Lecavalier	.50	1.25
434 Martin St. Louis	.40	1.00
435 Dan Boyle	.15	.40
436 Fredrik Modin	.30	.75
437 Ruslan Fedotenko	.30	.75
438 Pavel Kubina	.30	.75
439 Darryl Sydor	.15	.40
440 Sean Burke	.40	1.00
441 Tim Taylor	.15	.40
442 Cory Sarich	.15	.40
443 Nolan Pratt	.15	.40
444 Rob DiMaio	.15	.40
445 Paul Ranger RC	.75	2.00
446 Ryan Craig RC	1.25	3.00
447 Mats Sundin	.50	1.25
448 Ed Belfour	.50	1.25
449 Bryan McCabe	.30	.75
450 Jason Allison	.30	.75
451 Tomas Kaberle	.15	.40
452 Darcy Tucker	.15	.40
453 Kyle Wellwood	.15	.40
454 Jeff O`Neill	.15	.40
455 Alexei Ponikarovsky	.15	.40
456 Eric Lindros	.50	1.25
457 Chad Kilger	.15	.40
458 Mikael Tellqvist	.25	.60
459 Staffan Kronwall RC	.75	2.00
460 Nik Antropov	.30	.75
461 Matt Stajan	.30	.75
462 Tie Domi	.40	1.00
463 Luke Richardson	.15	.40
464 Alexander Khavanov	.15	.40
465 Markus Naslund	.50	1.25
466 Daniel Sedin	.15	.40
467 Henrik Sedin	.15	.40
468 Todd Bertuzzi	.60	1.50
469 Alexander Auld	.15	.40
470 Brendan Morrison	.30	.75
471 Anson Carter	.40	1.00
472 Sami Salo	.15	.40
473 Ed Jovanovski	.40	1.00
474 Nolan Baumgartner	.15	.40
475 Mattias Ohlund	.30	.75
476 Dan Cloutier	.40	1.00
477 Jarkko Ruutu	.15	.40
478 Bryan Allen	.15	.40
479 Ryan Kesler	.30	.75
480 Matt Cooke	.15	.40
481 Trevor Linden	.30	.75
482 Mika Noronen	.40	1.00
483 Brooks Laich	.15	.40
484 Dainius Zubrus	.15	.40
485 Olaf Kolzig	.40	1.00
486 Matt Pettinger	.15	.40
487 Jeff Halpern	.15	.40
488 Brian Willsie	.30	.75
489 Brent Johnson	.15	.40
490 Chris Clark	.15	.40
491 Brian Sutherby	.15	.40
492 Jamie Heward	.15	.40
493 Ben Clymer	.15	.40
494 Bryan Muir	.15	.40
495 Mathieu Biron	.15	.40
496 Shaone Morrisonn	.15	.40
497 Matt Bradley	.15	.40
498 Mike Green RC	1.50	4.00
499 Rico Fata	.15	.40
500 Gordie Howe	1.50	4.00
501 Scott Niedermayer CPT	.30	.75
502 Scott Mellanby CPT	.15	.40
503 Vincent Lecavalier CPT	.50	1.25
504 Chris Drury CPT	.40	1.00
505 Jarome Iginla CPT	.40	1.00
506 Rod Brind`Amour CPT	.40	1.00
507 Adrian Aucoin CPT	.30	.75
508 Joe Sakic CPT	1.00	2.50
509 Adam Foote CPT	.15	.40
510 Mike Modano CPT	.50	1.25
511 Steve Yzerman CPT	1.25	3.00
512 Jason Smith CPT	.15	.40
513 Olli Jokinen CPT	.40	1.00
514 Mattias Norstrom CPT	.15	.40
515 Saku Koivu CPT	.50	1.25
516 Greg Johnson CPT	.15	.40
517 Alexei Yashin CPT	.30	.75
518 Daniel Alfredsson CPT	.40	1.00
519 Keith Primeau CPT	.30	.75
520 Shane Doan CPT	.30	.75
521 Patrick Marleau CPT	.40	1.00
522 Dallas Drake CPT	.30	.75
523 Mats Sundin CPT	.50	1.25
524 Markus Naslund CPT	.50	1.25
525 Jeff Halpern CPT	.15	.40
526 Sidney Crosby CPT	2.50	6.00
527 Brian Leetch CPT	.50	1.25
528 Jaromir Jagr CPT	.75	2.00
529 Wes Walz CPT	.15	.40
530 Patrik Elias CPT	.40	1.00
531 Anaheim Mighty Ducks	.15	.40
532 Atlanta Thrashers	.15	.40
533 Boston Bruins	.15	.40
534 Buffalo Sabres	.15	.40
535 Calgary Flames	.15	.40
536 Carolina Hurricanes	.15	.40
537 Chicago Blackhawks	.15	.40
538 Colorado Colorado Avalanche	.15	.40
539 Columbus Blue Jackets	.15	.40
540 Dallas Stars	.15	.40
541 Detroit Red Wings	.15	.40
542 Edmonton Oilers	.15	.40
543 Florida Panthers	.15	.40
544 Los Angeles Kings	.15	.40
545 Minnesota Wild	.15	.40
546 Montreal Canadiens	.15	.40
547 Nashville Predators	.15	.40
548 New Jersey Devils	.15	.40
549 New York Islanders	.15	.40
550 New York Rangers	.15	.40
551 Ottawa Senators	.15	.40
552 Philadelphia Flyers	.15	.40
553 Phoenix Coyotes	.15	.40
554 Pittsburgh Penguins	.15	.40
555 San Jose Sharks	.15	.40
556 St. Louis Blues	.15	.40
557 Tampa Bay Lightning	.15	.40
558 Toronto Maple Leafs	.15	.40
559 Vancouver Canucks	.15	.40
560 Washington Capitals	.15	.40
561 Martin Brodeur NS	1.50	4.00
562 Roberto Luongo NS	.40	1.00
563 Marty Turco NS	.25	.60
564 Rob Blake NS	.15	.40
565 Adam Foote NS	.15	.40
566 Chris Pronger NS	.15	.40
567 Wade Redden NS	.15	.40
568 Robyn Regehr NS	.15	.40
569 Todd Bertuzzi NS	.15	.40
570 Shane Doan NS	.15	.40
571 Kris Draper NS	.15	.40
572 Simon Gagne NS	.15	.40
573 Dany Heatley NS	.40	1.00
574 Jarome Iginla NS	.40	1.00
575 Vincent Lecavalier NS	.50	1.25
576 Rick Nash NS	.60	1.50
577 Brad Richards NS	.40	1.00
578 Joe Sakic NS	1.00	2.50
579 Ryan Smyth NS	.40	1.00
580 Martin St. Louis NS	.40	1.00
581 Joe Thornton NS	.75	2.00
582 Jay Bouwmeester NS	.30	.75
583 Bryan McCabe NS	.30	.75
584 Ed Jovanovski NS	.40	1.00
585 Scott Niedermayer NS	.30	.75
586 Sidney Crosby HL	2.50	6.00
587 Sidney Crosby HL	2.50	6.00
588 Alexander Ovechkin HL	1.50	4.00
589 Ed Belfour HL	.50	1.25
590 Mario Lemieux HL	2.00	5.00
591 Joe Thornton HL	.75	2.00
592 Teemu Selanne HL	.50	1.25
593 Sidney Crosby HL	2.50	6.00
594 Jaromir Jagr HL	.75	2.00
595 Luc Robitaille HL	.40	1.00
596 Manny Legace HL	.50	1.25
597 Alexander Ovechkin HL	2.00	5.00
598 Daniel Alfredsson HL	.40	1.00
599 Henrik Lundqvist HL	1.50	4.00
600 Alexander Ovechkin HL	2.00	5.00
601 Ryan Getzlaf RC	8.00	20.00
602 Corey Perry RC	3.00	8.00
603 Braydon Coburn RC	2.50	6.00
604 Jim Slater RC	2.50	6.00
605 Andrew Alberts RC	2.00	5.00
606 Hannu Toivonen RC	2.50	6.00
607 Milan Jurcina RC	2.00	5.00
608 Jordan Sigalet RC	1.50	4.00
609 Ben Walter RC	1.00	2.50
610 Thomas Vanek RC	4.00	10.00
611 Daniel Paille RC	1.00	2.50
612 Dion Phaneuf RC	8.00	20.00
613 Eric Nystrom RC	2.50	6.00
614 Cam Ward RC	2.00	5.00
615 Andrew Ladd RC	1.50	4.00
616 Brent Seabrook RC	4.00	10.00
617 Cam Barker RC	2.50	6.00
618 Corey Crawford RC	1.50	4.00
619 Peter Budaj RC	2.50	6.00
620 Wojtek Wolski RC	2.50	6.00
621 Brad Richardson RC	1.00	2.50
622 Gilbert Brule RC	3.00	8.00
623 Alexandre Picard RC	1.50	4.00
624 Jussi Jokinen RC	2.50	6.00
625 Jim Howard RC	4.00	10.00
626 Kyle Quincey RC	1.00	2.50
627 Valtteri Filppula RC	1.00	2.50
628 Matt Greene RC	.75	2.00
629 Jean-Francois Jacques RC	1.00	2.50
630 Rostislav Olesz RC	2.50	6.00
631 Anthony Stewart RC	2.50	6.00
632 Rob Globke RC	1.00	2.50
633 George Parros RC	2.00	5.00
634 Mikko Koivu RC	1.50	4.00
635 Yann Danis RC	2.50	6.00
636 Alexander Perezhogin RC	2.50	6.00
637 Maxim Lapierre RC	1.00	2.50
638 Andrei Kostitsyn RC	1.50	4.00
639 Ryan Suter RC	2.50	6.00
640 Zach Parise RC	6.00	15.00
641 Barry Tallackson RC	3.00	8.00
642 Jeff Tambellini RC	1.00	2.50
643 Chris Campoli RC	2.00	5.00
644 Jeremy Colliton RC	1.00	2.50
645 Bruno Gervais RC	1.00	2.50
646 Henrik Lundqvist RC	8.00	20.00
647 Petr Prucha RC	2.50	6.00
648 Al Montoya RC	1.50	4.00
649 Patrick Eaves RC	1.50	4.00
650 Andrej Meszaros RC	2.00	5.00
651 Christoph Schubert RC	1.00	2.50
652 Mike Richards RC	4.00	10.00
653 Jeff Carter RC	3.00	8.00
654 R.J. Umberger RC	1.50	4.00
655 Ben Eager RC	1.00	2.50
656 Keith Ballard RC	2.00	5.00
657 Sidney Crosby RC	20.00	50.00
658 Maxime Talbot RC	2.00	5.00
659 Ryan Whitney RC	1.50	4.00
660 Colby Armstrong RC	1.50	4.00
661 Ryane Clowe RC	2.00	5.00
662 Steve Bernier RC	1.50	4.00
663 Dimitri Patzold RC	1.00	2.50
664 Lee Stempniak RC	1.00	2.50
665 Evgeny Artyukhin RC	1.00	2.50
666 Jay Harrison RC	1.00	2.50
667 Alexander Steen RC	2.50	6.00
668 Kevin Bieksa RC	1.00	2.50
669 Alexander Ovechkin RC	12.00	30.00
670 Tomas Fleischmann RC	1.00	2.50
671 Jean-Sebastien Giguere NOT	.40	1.00
672 Ilya Kovalchuk TC	.60	1.50
673 Patrice Bergeron TC	.50	1.25
674 Ryan Miller TC	.25	.60
675 Jarome Iginla TC	.40	1.00
676 Eric Staal TC	.40	1.00
677 Nikolai Khabibulin TC	.50	1.25
678 Joe Sakic TC	1.00	2.50
679 Rick Nash TC	.60	1.50
680 Mike Modano TC	.50	1.25
681 Steve Yzerman TC	1.25	3.00
682 Chris Pronger TC	.40	1.00
683 Roberto Luongo TC	.75	2.00
684 Luc Robitaille TC	.40	1.00
685 Marian Gaborik TC	.60	1.50
686 Saku Koivu TC	.50	1.25
687 Paul Kariya TC	.50	1.25
688 Martin Brodeur TC	1.25	3.00
689 Alexei Yashin TC	.30	.75
690 Jaromir Jagr TC	.75	2.00
691 Dominik Hasek TC	.60	1.50
692 Peter Forsberg TC	.75	2.00
693 Shane Doan TC	.30	.75
694 Sidney Crosby TC	2.50	6.00
695 Joe Thornton TC	.75	2.00
696 Keith Tkachuk TC	.50	1.25
697 Vincent Lecavalier TC	.50	1.25
698 Mats Sundin TC	.50	1.25
699 Markus Naslund TC	.50	1.25
700 Alexander Ovechkin TC	2.00	5.00

2005-06 Parkhurst Facsimile Auto Parallel

PRINT RUN 100 #'d SETS

Card	Low	High
526 Sidney Crosby CPT	40.00	80.00
586 Sidney Crosby HL	40.00	80.00
587 Sidney Crosby HL	40.00	80.00
593 Sidney Crosby HL	40.00	80.00
652 Mike Richards	10.00	25.00
657 Sidney Crosby	75.00	125.00
669 Alexander Ovechkin	40.00	80.00
694 Sidney Crosby TC	40.00	80.00

2005-06 Parkhurst Signatures

Card	Low	High
AL Andrew Alberts	5.00	12.00
AB Adam Berkhoel	5.00	12.00
AK Andrei Kostitsyn	6.00	15.00
AL Andrew Ladd	6.00	15.00
AM Andrei Meszaros	3.00	8.00
AM Al Montoya	8.00	20.00
AN Antero Niittymaki	8.00	20.00
AO Alexander Ovechkin SP	150.00	300.00
AP Alexandre Picard SP	8.00	20.00
BA Milan Bartovic	3.00	8.00
BB Brad Boyes	3.00	8.00
BC Braydon Coburn	5.00	12.00
BE Ben Eager	5.00	12.00
BL Brett Lebda	5.00	12.00
BO Brandon Bochenski	5.00	12.00
BS Brent Seabrook	6.00	15.00
BT Barry Tallackson	5.00	12.00
BU Peter Budaj	6.00	15.00
RW Ben Walter	3.00	8.00
CC Chris Campoli	3.00	8.00
CK Chuck Kobasew	3.00	8.00
CS Christoph Schubert	3.00	8.00
CT Chris Thorburn	3.00	8.00
DB Daniel Briere	8.00	20.00
DE Derek Boogaard	5.00	12.00
DK Duncan Keith	10.00	25.00
DL David Leneveu	5.00	12.00
DP Dimitri Patzold	5.00	12.00
DW Dwayne Roloson	6.00	15.00
EA Evgeny Artyukhin	3.00	8.00
FP Fernando Pisani	6.00	15.00
GP George Parros	3.00	8.00
HO Marcel Hossa SP	10.00	25.00
JF Johan Franzen	10.00	25.00
JH Jeff Halpern	3.00	8.00
JH Jim Howard	10.00	25.00
JI Jarome Iginla SP	30.00	60.00
JJ Jussi Jokinen SP	10.00	25.00
JL Jason Labarbera	3.00	8.00
JS Jordan Sigalet	6.00	15.00
JS Jim Slater	5.00	12.00
JT Jeff Tambellini	3.00	8.00
JV Josef Vasicek	3.00	8.00
JW Jeff Woywitka	3.00	8.00
KC Kyle Calder	3.00	8.00
KN Kevin Nastiuk	5.00	12.00
KO Mikko Koivu	8.00	20.00
KQ Kyle Quincey	3.00	8.00
IL Ian Laperriere	5.00	12.00
LJ John-Michael Liles	6.00	15.00
LS Lee Stempniak SP	8.00	20.00
MA Maxim Afinogenov SP	12.00	30.00
MB Martin Biron	6.00	15.00
MC Mike Cammalleri	5.00	12.00
MG Marian Gaborik SP	30.00	60.00
MH Michal Handzus	12.00	30.00
MJ Milan Jurcina SP	8.00	20.00
ML Maxim Lapierre	6.00	15.00
MM Milan Michalek SP	8.00	20.00
MR Mike Richards SP	30.00	60.00
MS Marc Savard	3.00	8.00
MT Mikael Tellqvist	6.00	15.00
NA Nik Antropov SP	10.00	25.00
NN Niklas Nordgren	3.00	8.00
OJ Olli Jokinen SP	10.00	25.00
OK Ole-Kristian Tollefson	3.00	8.00
OK Olaf Kolzig	6.00	15.00
PB Pierre-Marc Bouchard	3.00	8.00
PE Patrick Eaves	6.00	15.00
PN Petteri Nokelainen	3.00	8.00
PP Petr Prucha SP	10.00	25.00
PS Philippe Sauve	3.00	8.00
RC Ryan Craig	5.00	12.00
RE Robert Esche SP	10.00	25.00
RF Ruslan Fedotenko	3.00	8.00
RG Ryan Getzlaf SP	25.00	50.00
RH Ryan Hollweg	5.00	12.00
RM Ryan Malone	5.00	12.00
RN Robert Nilsson	5.00	12.00
RO Rostislav Olesz	5.00	12.00
SB Steve Bernier	6.00	15.00
SC Sidney Crosby SP	600.00	900.00
SH Scott Hartnell	3.00	8.00
TB Todd Bertuzzi SP	25.00	50.00
TC Ty Conklin	3.00	8.00
TF Tomas Fleischmann	5.00	12.00
TG Tim Gleason	3.00	8.00
TS Timofei Shishkanov	3.00	8.00
WI Brad Winchester	5.00	12.00
YD Yann Danis	6.00	15.00
ZM Zbynek Michalek	3.00	8.00
ZP Zach Parise	10.00	25.00

2005-06 Parkhurst True Colors

STATED ODDS 1:432

Card	Low	High
TCANA Teemu Selanne	30.00	80.00
Rob Niedermayer		
Scott Niedermayer		
Sandis Ozolinsh		
Jean-Sebastien Giguere		
Joffrey Lupul		
Corey Perry		
Ryan Getzlaf		
TCATL Peter Bondra	30.00	80.00
Marian Hossa		
Marc Savard		
Scott Mellanby		
Bobby Holik		
Patrik Stefan		
Ilya Kovalchuk		
Kari Lehtonen		
TCBOS Brian Leetch	50.00	100.00
Sergei Samsonov		
Glen Murray		
Andrew Raycroft		
Patrice Bergeron		
Andrew Alberts		
Hannu Toivonen		
Milan Jurcina		
TCBUF Jochen Hecht	40.00	80.00
Tim Connolly		
Maxim Afinogenov		
Chris Drury		
Mike Grier		
Derek Roy		
Ryan Miller		
Thomas Vanek		
TCCAR Doug Weight	40.00	80.00
Cory Stillman		
Justin Williams		
Martin Gerber		
Rod Brind`Amour		
Eric Staal		
Cam Ward		
Andrew Ladd		
TCCGY Tony Amonte	50.00	100.00
Jarome Iginla		
Darren McCarty		
Chuck Kobasew		
Jordan Leopold		
Miikka Kiprusoff		
Matthew Lombardi		
Dion Phaneuf		
TCCHI Kyle Calder	40.00	80.00
Nikolai Khabibulin		
Eric Daze		
Adrian Aucoin		
Tuomo Ruutu		
Brent Seabrook		
Rene Bourque		
Cam Barker		
TCCLB Sergei Fedorov	50.00	125.00
Adam Foote		
Marc Denis		
Rick Nash		
Nikolai Zherdev		
Jaroslav Balastik		
Gilbert Brule		
Alexandre Picard		
TCCOL Pierre Turgeon	40.00	80.00
Joe Sakic		
Rob Blake		
Milan Hejduk		
David Aebischer		
Alex Tanguay		
Marek Svatos		
Peter Budaj		
TCDAL Mike Modano	40.00	80.00
Sergei Zubov		
Bill Guerin		
Marty Turco		
Brenden Morrow		
Trevor Daley		
Steve Ott		
Jussi Jokinen		
TCDET Brendan Shanahan	100.00	200.00
Steve Yzerman		
Nicklas Lidstrom		
Robert Lang		
Manny Legace		
Kris Draper		
Pavel Datsyuk		
Henrik Zetterberg		
TCEDM Chris Pronger	60.00	125.00
Michael Peca		
Ryan Smyth		
Jason Smith		
Shawn Horcoff		
Ty Conklin		
Fernando Pisani		
Ales Hemsky		
TCFLA Roberto Luongo	40.00	80.00
Joe Nieuwendyk		
Olli Jokinen		
Gary Roberts		
Jay Bouwmeester		
Stephen Weiss		
Rostislav Olesz		
Anthony Stewart		
TCLAK Luc Robitaille	40.00	100.00
Pavol Demitra		
Jeremy Roenick		
Mathieu Garon		
Alexander Frolov		
Mike Cammalleri		
Dustin Brown		
George Parros		
TCMIN Manny Fernandez	40.00	100.00
Brian Rolston		
Marian Gaborik		
Dwayne Roloson		
Pierre-Marc Bouchard		
Mikko Koivu		
Matt Foy		
Derek Boogaard		
TCMTL Saku Koivu	50.00	100.00
Mike Ribeiro		
Jose Theodore		
Richard Zednik		
Michael Ryder		
Alexei Kovalev		
Alexander Perezhogin		
Yann Danis		
TCNJD Scott Gomez	50.00	125.00
Martin Brodeur		
Brian Rafalski		
Patrik Elias		
Viktor Kozlov		
Brian Gionta		
Zach Parise		
Barry Tallackson		
TCNSH Paul Kariya	30.00	80.00
Tomas Vokoun		
David Legwand		
Scott Hartnell		
Dan Hamhuis		
Adam Hall		
Scott Upshall		
Ryan Suter		
TCNYI Mark Parrish	75.00	150.00
Miroslav Satan		
Jason Blake		
Alexei Yashin		
Rick DiPietro		
Trent Hunter		
Chris Campoli		
Jeremy Colliton SP		
TCNYR Jaromir Jagr	40.00	80.00
Martin Straka		
Petr Sykora		
Tom Poti		
Ville Nieminen		
Marcel Hossa		
Henrik Lundqvist		
Dominic Moore		
TCOTT Dominik Hasek	30.00	80.00
Daniel Alfredsson		
Wade Redden		
Martin Havlat		
Jason Spezza		
Zdeno Chara		
Dany Heatley		
Andrei Meszaros		
TCPHI Keith Primeau	50.00	120.00
Peter Forsberg		
Robert Esche		
Simon Gagne		
Derian Hatcher		
Joni Pitkanen		
Mike Richards		
Jeff Carter		
TCPHX Curtis Joseph	25.00	60.00
Mike Comrie		
Ladislav Nagy		
Shane Doan		
Steven Reinprecht		
Philippe Sauve		
Keith Ballard		
David Leneveu		
TCPIT Mario Lemieux	125.00	225.00
Jocelyn Thibault		
John LeClair		
Mark Recchi		
Erik Christensen		
Sidney Crosby		
Maxime Talbot		
Ryan Whitney		
TCSJS Patrick Marleau	40.00	80.00
Joe Thornton		
Evgeni Nabokov		
Jonathan Cheechoo		
Milan Michalek		
Ryane Clowe		
Josh Gorges		
Steve Bernier		
TCSTL Keith Tkachuk	25.00	60.00
Patrick Lalime		
Barret Jackman		
Jay McClement		
Jeff Woywitka		
Jeff Hoggan		
Kevin Dallman		
Lee Stempniak		
TCTBL Vincent Lecavalier	50.00	100.00
Brad Richards		
Vaclav Prospal		
Sean Burke		
Martin St. Louis		
Ruslan Fedotenko		
Ryan Craig		
Evgeny Artyukhin		
TCTOR Mats Sundin	40.00	80.00
Bryan McCabe		
Jason Allison		
Carlo Colaiacovo		
Nik Antropov		
Alexander Steen		
Ed Belfour		
Eric Lindros		
TCVAN Dan Cloutier	40.00	80.00
Markus Naslund		
Trevor Linden		
Ed Jovanovski		
Brendan Morrison		
Todd Bertuzzi		
Alex Auld		
Kevin Bieksa		
TCWAS Olaf Kolzig	75.00	150.00
Jeff Friesen		
Jeff Halpern		
Brendan Witt		
Shaone Morrisonn		
Alexander Ovechkin		
Thomas Fleischmann		
Jakub Klepis		
TCCHDE Kyle Calder	50.00	100.00
Nicklas Lidstrom		
Nikolai Khabibulin		
Eric Daze		
Manny Legace		
Kris Draper		
Pavel Datsyuk		
Tuomo Ruutu		
TCDECO Joe Sakic	75.00	125.00
Brendan Shanahan		
Steve Yzerman		
Rob Blake		
Milan Hejduk		
Alex Tanguay		
Pavel Datsyuk#Henrik Zetterberg		
TCEDCA Chris Pronger	40.00	100.00
Jarome Iginla		
Ryan Smyth		
Shawn Horcoff		
Chuck Kobasew		
Ales Hemsky		
Miikka Kiprusoff		
Dion Phaneuf		
TCFLTB Vincent Lecavalier	40.00	100.00
Brad Richards		
Vaclav Prospal		
Roberto Luongo		
Olli Jokinen		
Martin St. Louis		
Jay Bouwmeester		
Stephen Weiss		
TCMIDA Mike Modano	40.00	80.00
Bill Guerin		
Manny Fernandez		
Brian Rolston		
Marian Gaborik		
Marty Turco		
Brenden Morrow		
P-M Bouchard		
TCMOBO Brian Leetch	40.00	100.00
Saku Koivu		
Mike Ribeiro		
Jose Theodore		
Glen Murray		
Andrew Raycroft		
Michael Ryder		
Patrice Bergeron		
TCNJNY Jaromir Jagr	75.00	150.00
Scott Gomez		
Martin Straka		
Martin Brodeur		
Brian Rafalski		
Patrik Elias		
Henrik Lundqvist		
Dominic Moore		
TCNYNY Jaromir Jagr	40.00	100.00
Martin Straka		
Miroslav Satan		
Jason Blake		
Tom Poti		
Alexei Yashin		
Rick DiPietro		
Henrik Lundqvist SP		
TCOTTO Ed Belfour	40.00	100.00
Eric Lindros		
Mats Sundin		
Dominik Hasek		
Daniel Alfredsson		
Bryan McCabe		
Jason Spezza		
Dany Heatley		
TCPHPI Mario Lemieux	100.00	200.00
Keith Primeau		
John LeClair		
Peter Forsberg		
Simon Gagne		
Erik Christensen		
Joni Pitkanen		
Sidney Crosby		
TCSJLA Luc Robitaille	40.00	100.00
Pavol Demitra		
Patrick Marleau		
Jeremy Roenick		
Joe Thornton		
Evgeni Nabokov		
Jonathan Cheechoo		
Alexander Frolov		
TCTOMO Ed Belfour	40.00	80.00
Mats Sundin		
Saku Koivu		
Jose Theodore		
Jason Allison		
Michael Ryder		
Alexei Kovalev		
Alexander Steen		

2006-07 Parkhurst

Card	Low	High
COMPLETE SET w/ SPs (250)	100.00	200.00
COMPLETE SET (160)	12.00	30.00
ENFORCE/CAPT PRINT RUN 3999		
1 Ron MacLean	.40	1.00
2 John Anderson	.20	.50
3 Al Arbour	.20	.50
4 Lou Fontinato	.20	.50
5 Grant Fuhr	.40	1.00
6 Bill Gadsby	.30	.75
7 Danny Gare	.20	.50
8 Ed Giacomin	.40	1.00
9 Andy Bathgate	.30	.75
10 Bob Baun	.30	.75
11 Don Beaupre	.30	.75
12 Barry Beck	.20	.50
13 Jean Beliveau	.60	1.50
14 Rod Gilbert	.30	.75
15 Clark Gillies	.20	.50
16 Doug Gilmour	.60	1.50
17 Danny Grant	.20	.50
18 Ron Greschner	.20	.50
19 Bob Bourne	.20	.50
20 Mike Bossy	.60	1.50
21 Johnny Bower	.60	1.50
22 Scotty Bowman	.60	1.50
23 Stu Grimson	.20	.50
24 Richard Brodeur	.30	.75
25 Aaron Broten	.20	.50
26 Neal Broten	.20	.50
27 Dale Hawerchuk	.40	1.00
28 Johnny Bucyk	.40	1.00
29 Paul Henderson	.30	.75
30 Ron Hextall	.60	1.50
31 Rejean Houle	.20	.50
32 Harry Howell	.30	.75
33 Gerry Cheevers	.40	1.00
34 Don Cherry	1.25	3.00
35 Kelly Hrudey	.30	.75
36 Bobby Hull	.75	2.00
37 Dino Ciccarelli	.30	.75
38 Wendel Clark	.40	1.00
39 Bobby Clarke	.40	1.00
40 Dale Hunter	.20	.50
41 Dick Irvin	.20	.50
42 Tom Johnson	.30	.75
43 Mike Keenan	.20	.50
44 J.P. Kelly	.20	.50
45 Red Kelly	.40	1.00
46 John Davidson	.40	1.00
47 Kelly Kisio	.20	.50
48 Marcel Dionne	.40	1.00
49 Joey Kocur	.20	.50
50 Kevin Dineen	.20	.50
51 Jari Kurri	.40	1.00
52 Elmer Lach	.30	.75
53 Ron Duguay	.20	.50
54 Ron Ellis	.20	.50
55 Guy Lafleur	.75	2.00
56 Phil Esposito	.60	1.50
57 Tony Esposito	.40	1.00
58 Bernie Federko	.20	.50
59 Rod Langway	.20	.50
60 Edgar Laprade	.20	.50
61 Pierre Larouche	.20	.50
62 Mike Foligno	.20	.50
63 Reed Larson	.20	.50
64 Reggie Leach	.20	.50
65 Rejean Lemelin	.30	.75
66 Ted Lindsay	.40	1.00
67 Mike Liut	.30	.75
68 Al MacInnis	.30	.75
69 Clint Malarchuk	.30	.75
70 Cesare Maniago	.30	.75

71 Butch Bouchard .30 .75
72 Brian McFarlane .20 .50
73 Marty McSorley .20 .50
74 Howie Meeker .20 .50
75 Gilles Meloche .30 .75
76 Barry Melrose .20 .50
77 Ray Bourque .60 1.50
78 Brian Mullen .20 .50
79 Joe Mullen .20 .50
80 Cam Neely .60 1.50
81 Eric Nesterenko .20 .50
82 Bernie Nicholls .20 .50
83 Kent Nilsson .20 .50
84 Ulf Nilsson .20 .50
85 Adam Oates .30 .75
86 John Ogrodnick .20 .50
87 Willie O'Ree .40 1.00
88 Terry O'Reilly .40 1.00
89 Bobby Orr 2.00 5.00
90 Greg Millen .30 .75
91 Jim Pappin .20 .50
92 Bernie Parent .40 1.00
93 Brad Park .30 .75
94 Jim Peplinski .20 .50
95 Gilbert Perreault .30 .75
96 Pete Peeters .30 .75
97 Pierre Pilote .20 .50
98 Willi Plett .20 .50
99 Wayne Cashman .20 .50
100 Denis Potvin .30 .75
101 Bob Probert .40 1.00
102 Marcel Pronovost .20 .50
103 Rob Ramage .20 .50
104 Mike Krushelnyski .20 .50
105 Pokey Reddick .30 .75
106 Larry Robinson .30 .75
107 Reijo Ruotsalainen .20 .50
108 Jim Rutherford .30 .75
109 Borje Salming .40 1.00
110 Milt Schmidt .30 .75
111 Jim Schoenfeld .20 .50
112 Dave Schultz .30 .75
113 Dave Semenko .20 .50
114 Eddie Shack .30 .75
115 Claude Lemieux .20 .50
116 Darryl Sittler .40 1.00
117 Dickie Moore .20 .50
118 Bobby Smith .20 .50
119 Clint Smith .30 .75
120 Anton Stastny .20 .50
121 Marian Stastny .20 .50
122 Peter Stastny .30 .75
123 Thomas Steen .20 .50
124 Scott Stevens .20 .50
125 Brent Sutter .20 .50
126 Duane Sutter .20 .50
127 Darryl Sutter .20 .50
128 J.P. Parise .20 .50
129 Ron Sutter .20 .50
130 Brian Sutter .20 .50
131 Walt Tkaczuk .20 .50
132 Denis Savard .20 .50
133 Frank Udvari .20 .50
134 Gump Worsley .30 .75
135 Doug Jarvis .20 .50
136 Jacques Lemaire .20 .50
137 Peter McNab .20 .50
138 Rick Middleton .30 .75
139 Mike Rogers .20 .50
140 Mats Naslund .30 .75
141 Jim Neilson .20 .50
142 Don Metz .20 .50
143 Pat LaFontaine .30 .75
144 Gordie Howe .75 2.00
145 Patrick Roy 1.25 3.00
146 Garry Unger .20 .50
147 Larry Murphy .20 .50
148 Rick Vaive .20 .50
149 Tiger Williams .30 .75
150 Mario Lemieux 1.25 3.00
151 Michel Dion .20 .50
152 Bill Dineen .20 .50
153 Gary Dornhoefer .20 .50
154 Hakan Loob .20 .50
155 Craig MacTavish .20 .50
156 Allan Stanley .20 .50
157 Marc Tardif .20 .50
158 Ryan Walter .20 .50
159 Zigmund Palffy .30 .75
160 Wilf Paiement .20 .50
161 Milt Schmidt 1.25 3.00
162 Johnny Bucyk 1.25 3.00
163 Ray Bourque 1.50 4.00
164 Terry O'Reilly 1.25 3.00
165 Jim Schoenfeld 1.00 2.50
166 Danny Gare 1.00 2.50
167 Gilbert Perreault 1.25 3.00
168 Mike Foligno 1.00 2.50
169 Jim Peplinski 1.00 2.50
170 Pierre Pilote 1.00 2.50
171 Darryl Sutter 1.00 2.50
172 Denis Savard 1.00 2.50
173 Bill Gadsby 1.25 3.00
174 Marc Tardif 1.00 2.50
175 Peter Stastny 1.25 3.00
176 J.P. Parise 1.00 2.50
177 Ted Lindsay 1.25 3.00
178 Red Kelly 1.25 3.00
179 Gordie Howe 2.00 5.00
180 Danny Grant 1.00 2.50
181 Reed Larson 1.00 2.50
182 Wayne Cashman 1.00 2.50
183 Craig MacTavish 1.00 2.50
184 Doug Wilson 1.00 2.50
185 Marcel Dionne 1.25 3.00
186 Butch Bouchard 1.25 3.00
187 Jean Beliveau 1.50 4.00
188 Wilf Paiement 1.00 2.50
189 Scott Stevens 1.00 2.50
190 Clark Gillies 1.00 2.50
191 Denis Potvin 1.25 3.00
192 Brent Sutter 1.00 2.50
193 Allan Stanley 1.25 3.00
194 Andy Bathgate 1.25 3.00
195 Brad Park 1.25 3.00
196 Phil Esposito 1.50 4.00
197 Barry Beck 1.00 2.50
198 Ron Greschner 1.00 2.50
199 Kelly Kisio 1.00 2.50
200 Bobby Clarke 1.50 4.00
201 Ron Sutter 1.00 2.50
202 Dale Hawerchuk 1.50 4.00
203 Thomas Steen 1.00 2.50
204 Mario Lemieux 2.50 6.00
205 Al Arbour 1.00 2.50
206 Brian Sutter 1.00 2.50
207 Bernie Federko 1.00 2.50
208 Scott Stevens 1.00 2.50
209 Darryl Sittler 1.50 4.00
210 Rick Vaive 1.00 2.50
211 Rob Ramage 1.00 2.50
212 Wendel Clark 1.25 3.00
213 Doug Gilmour 1.50 4.00
214 Kevin Dineen 1.00 2.50
215 Rod Langway 1.00 2.50
216 Dale Hunter 1.00 2.50
217 Adam Oates 1.25 3.00
218 Walt Tkaczuk 1.00 2.50
219 Harry Howell 1.00 2.50
220 Rob Ramage 1.00 2.50
221 Clint Smith 1.25 3.00
222 Doug Gilmour 1.50 4.00
223 Mike Rogers 1.00 2.50
224 Pat LaFontaine 1.25 3.00
225 Neal Broten 1.00 2.50
226 Al MacInnis 1.25 3.00
227 Kevin Dineen 1.00 2.50
228 Joey Kocur 1.00 2.50
229 Tiger Williams 1.25 3.00
230 Tiger Williams 1.25 3.00
231 Dale Hunter 1.00 2.50
232 Marty McSorley 1.00 2.50
233 Bob Probert 1.50 4.00
234 Stu Grimson 1.00 2.50
235 Dave Schultz 1.25 3.00
236 Bill Gadsby 1.25 3.00
237 Lou Fontinato 1.00 2.50
238 Joey Kocur 1.00 2.50
239 Ted Lindsay 1.25 3.00
240 Dave Semenko 1.00 2.50
241 Gary Dornhoefer 1.00 2.50
242 Pierre Pilote 1.00 2.50
243 Clark Gillies 1.00 2.50
244 Terry O'Reilly 1.25 3.00
245 Wendel Clark 1.25 3.00
246 Willi Plett 1.00 2.50
247 Wilf Paiement 1.00 2.50
248 Tiger Williams 1.25 3.00
249 Marty McSorley 1.00 2.50
250 Bob Probert 1.50 4.00

2006-07 Parkhurst Autographs

STATED ODDS 1:6 PACKS
2 John Anderson 8.00 20.00
3 Al Arbour 10.00 25.00
4 Lou Fontinato 10.00 25.00
5 Grant Fuhr 10.00 25.00
6 Bill Gadsby 10.00 25.00
7 Danny Gare SP 12.00 30.00
8 Ed Giacomin 8.00 20.00
9 Andy Bathgate 4.00 10.00
10 Bob Baun 15.00 40.00
11 Don Beaupre 6.00 15.00
12 Barry Beck 4.00 10.00
13 Jean Beliveau SP 200.00 300.00
14 Rod Gilbert SP 60.00 100.00
15 Clark Gillies 4.00 10.00
16 Doug Gilmour 40.00 80.00
17 Danny Grant 6.00 15.00
18 Ron Greschner 6.00 15.00
19 Bob Bourne 4.00 10.00
20 Mike Bossy 25.00 60.00
21 Johnny Bower 8.00 20.00
22 Scotty Bowman SP 175.00 250.00
23 Stu Grimson 5.00 12.00
24 Richard Brodeur 4.00 10.00
25 Aaron Broten 4.00 10.00
26 Neal Broten 4.00 10.00
27 Dale Hawerchuk 10.00 25.00
28 Johnny Bucyk SP 50.00 100.00
29 Paul Henderson 8.00 20.00
30 Ron Hextall 10.00 25.00
31 Rejean Houle 10.00 25.00
32 Harry Howell 5.00 12.00
33 Gerry Cheevers 8.00 20.00
34 Don Cherry 30.00 60.00
35 Kelly Hrudey 5.00 12.00
36 Bobby Hull 40.00 80.00
37 Dino Ciccarelli 6.00 15.00
38 Wendel Clark 20.00 40.00
39 Bobby Clarke 8.00 20.00
40 Dale Hunter 8.00 20.00
41 Dick Irvin 6.00 15.00
42 Tom Johnson 25.00 60.00
43 Mike Keenan 8.00 20.00
44 J.P. Kelly 12.00 30.00
45 Red Kelly 6.00 15.00
46 John Davidson 5.00 12.00
47 Kelly Kisio 4.00 10.00
48 Marcel Dionne 10.00 25.00
49 Joey Kocur 25.00 60.00
50 Kevin Dineen 10.00 25.00
51 Jari Kurri 8.00 20.00
52 Elmer Lach 15.00 40.00
53 Ron Duguay 4.00 10.00
54 Ron Ellis 5.00 12.00
55 Guy Lafleur 15.00 40.00
56 Phil Esposito 40.00 80.00
57 Tony Esposito 20.00 50.00
58 Bernie Federko 5.00 12.00
59 Rod Langway 4.00 10.00
60 Edgar Laprade 20.00 50.00
61 Pierre Larouche 8.00 20.00
62 Mike Foligno 4.00 10.00
63 Reed Larson 8.00 20.00
64 Reggie Leach 8.00 20.00
66 Ted Lindsay 8.00 20.00
67 Mike Liut 6.00 15.00
68 Al MacInnis 8.00 20.00
69 Clint Malarchuk 8.00 20.00
70 Cesare Maniago 12.00 30.00
71 Butch Bouchard 30.00 80.00
72 Brian McFarlane 4.00 10.00
73 Marty McSorley 5.00 12.00
74 Howie Meeker 10.00 25.00
75 Gilles Meloche 5.00 12.00
76 Barry Melrose 6.00 15.00
77 Ray Bourque SP 60.00 100.00
78 Brian Mullen 4.00 10.00
79 Joe Mullen 4.00 10.00
80 Cam Neely 12.00 30.00
81 Eric Nesterenko 8.00 20.00
82 Bernie Nicholls 4.00 10.00
84 Ulf Nilsson 5.00 12.00
85 Adam Oates 8.00 20.00
86 John Ogrodnick 4.00 10.00
87 Willie O'Ree 12.00 30.00
88 Terry O'Reilly 8.00 20.00
89 Bobby Orr 175.00 250.00
90 Greg Millen 4.00 10.00
91 Jim Pappin 10.00 25.00
92 Bernie Parent 6.00 15.00
93 Brad Park 5.00 12.00
94 Jim Peplinski 12.00 30.00
95 Gilbert Perreault 20.00 50.00
96 Pete Peeters 6.00 15.00
97 Pierre Pilote 8.00 20.00
98 Willi Plett 4.00 10.00
100 Denis Potvin 5.00 12.00
101 Bob Probert 6.00 15.00
102 Marcel Pronovost 8.00 20.00
103 Rob Ramage 4.00 10.00
104 Mike Krushelnyski 4.00 10.00
106 Larry Robinson 10.00 25.00
107 Reijo Ruotsalainen 8.00 20.00
108 Jim Rutherford 15.00 40.00
109 Borje Salming 10.00 25.00
110 Milt Schmidt 8.00 20.00
111 Jim Schoenfeld 6.00 15.00
112 Dave Schultz 4.00 10.00
113 Dave Semenko 10.00 25.00
114 Eddie Shack 8.00 20.00
115 Claude Lemieux 8.00 20.00
116 Darryl Sittler 20.00 50.00
118 Bobby Smith 4.00 10.00
119 Clint Smith 30.00 60.00
120 Anton Stastny 5.00 12.00
121 Marian Stastny 4.00 10.00
122 Peter Stastny 10.00 25.00
123 Thomas Steen 4.00 10.00
124 Scott Stevens 15.00 40.00
125 Brent Sutter 4.00 10.00
126 Duane Sutter 5.00 12.00
127 Darryl Sutter 5.00 12.00
128 J.P. Parise 4.00 10.00
130 Brian Sutter 8.00 20.00
131 Walt Tkaczuk 6.00 15.00
132 Denis Savard SP 30.00 60.00
133 Frank Udvari 12.00 30.00
135 Doug Jarvis 10.00 25.00
136 Jacques Lemaire 6.00 15.00
137 Peter McNab 10.00 25.00
138 Rick Middleton 10.00 25.00
139 Mike Rogers 6.00 15.00
140 Mats Naslund 6.00 15.00
141 Jim Neilson 6.00 15.00
143 Pat LaFontaine 8.00 20.00
144 Gordie Howe 50.00 100.00
145 Patrick Roy SP
146 Garry Unger 4.00 10.00
148 Rick Vaive 12.00 30.00
149 Tiger Williams 12.00 30.00
150 Mario Lemieux SP 600.00 1000.00
151 Michel Dion 25.00 50.00
152 Bill Dineen 12.00 30.00
153 Gary Dornhoefer 4.00 10.00
154 Hakan Loob 5.00 12.00
155 Craig MacTavish 6.00 15.00
156 Allan Stanley 10.00 25.00
157 Marc Tardif 8.00 20.00
158 Ryan Walter 4.00 10.00
160 Wilf Paiement 4.00 10.00
161 Milt Schmidt CAP 12.00 30.00
162 Johnny Bucyk CAP SP
163 Ray Bourque CAP SP 100.00 175.00
164 Terry O'Reilly CAP 10.00 25.00
165 Jim Schoenfeld CAP 8.00 20.00
166 Danny Gare CAP 12.00 30.00
167 Gilbert Perreault CAP 12.00 30.00
168 Mike Foligno CAP 4.00 10.00
169 Jim Peplinski CAP 12.00 30.00
170 Pierre Pilote CAP 12.00 30.00
171 Darryl Sutter CAP 10.00 25.00
172 Denis Savard CAP 50.00 100.00
173 Bill Gadsby CAP 10.00 25.00
174 Marc Tardif CAP 8.00 20.00
175 Peter Stastny CAP 20.00 50.00
176 J.P. Parise CAP 10.00 25.00
177 Ted Lindsay CAP 12.00 30.00
178 Red Kelly CAP 12.00 30.00
179 Gordie Howe CAP 100.00 175.00
180 Danny Grant CAP 8.00 20.00
181 Reed Larson CAP 6.00 15.00
183 Craig MacTavish CAP 5.00 12.00
185 Marcel Dionne CAP 30.00 60.00
186 Butch Bouchard CAP 25.00 50.00
187 Jean Beliveau CAP SP 25.00 50.00
188 Wilf Paiement CAP 12.00 30.00
189 Scott Stevens CAP 15.00 40.00
190 Clark Gillies CAP 10.00 25.00
191 Denis Potvin CAP 12.00 30.00
192 Brent Sutter CAP 10.00 25.00
193 Allan Stanley CAP 12.00 30.00
194 Andy Bathgate CAP 6.00 15.00
195 Brad Park CAP 6.00 15.00
196 Phil Esposito CAP 15.00 40.00
197 Barry Beck CAP 10.00 25.00
198 Ron Greschner CAP 6.00 15.00
199 Kelly Kisio CAP
200 Bobby Clarke CAP 30.00 60.00
201 Ron Sutter CAP 10.00 25.00
202 Dale Hawerchuk CAP 20.00 50.00
203 Thomas Steen CAP 10.00 25.00
204 Mario Lemieux CAP SP
205 Al Arbour CAP 12.00 30.00
206 Brian Sutter CAP 6.00 15.00
207 Bernie Federko CAP 10.00 25.00
208 Scott Stevens CAP SP 25.00 60.00
209 Darryl Sittler CAP 25.00 60.00
210 Rick Vaive CAP 12.00 30.00
211 Rob Ramage CAP 10.00 25.00
212 Wendel Clark CAP 50.00 100.00
213 Doug Gilmour CAP 12.00 30.00
214 Kevin Dineen CAP
215 Rod Langway CAP 10.00 25.00
216 Dale Hunter CAP 8.00 20.00
217 Adam Oates CAP 12.00 30.00
219 Harry Howell CAP 20.00 40.00
220 Rob Ramage CAP
221 Clint Smith CAP 25.00 60.00
222 Doug Gilmour CAP EXCH 15.00 40.00
223 Mike Rogers CAP 20.00 50.00
224 Pat LaFontaine CAP
225 Neal Broten CAP 12.00 30.00
226 Al MacInnis CAP 15.00 40.00
227 Kevin Dineen CAP 10.00 25.00
228 Joey Kocur ENF 15.00 40.00
229 Tiger Williams ENF EXCH 12.00 30.00
230 Tiger Williams ENF 25.00 50.00
231 Dale Hunter ENF 12.00 30.00
232 Marty McSorley ENF 25.00 50.00
233 Bob Probert ENF 20.00 50.00
234 Stu Grimson ENF 10.00 25.00
235 Dave Schultz ENF 20.00 50.00
236 Bill Gadsby ENF 20.00 50.00
237 Lou Fontinato ENF
238 Joey Kocur ENF 15.00 40.00
239 Ted Lindsay ENF 15.00 40.00
240 Dave Semenko ENF 15.00 40.00
241 Gary Dornhoefer ENF 15.00 30.00
242 Pierre Pilote ENF 12.00 30.00
243 Clark Gillies ENF 4.00 10.00
244 Terry O'Reilly ENF 20.00 50.00
245 Wendel Clark ENF 12.00 30.00
246 Willi Plett ENF 8.00 20.00
247 Wilf Paiement ENF 8.00 20.00
248 Tiger Williams ENF 15.00 40.00
249 Marty McSorley ENF 25.00 50.00
250 Bob Probert ENF 20.00 50.00

2006-07 Parkhurst Autographs Dual

DAAB Al Arbour 60.00 100.00
Scotty Bowman
DABB Neal Broten 60.00 125.00
Aaron Broten
DABG Mike Bossy
Clark Gillies
DABL Butch Bouchard
Elmer Lach
DABM Jean Beliveau
Dickie Moore
DABO Gerry Cheevers
Brad Park
DACB Dino Ciccarelli
Neal Broten
DACL Bobby Clarke 90.00 150.00
Reggie Leach
DACP Bobby Clarke 50.00 100.00
Bernie Parent
DADN Marcel Dionne
Bernie Nicholls
DADR Denis Savard 20.00 50.00
Rick Vaive
DAEB Phil Esposito 60.00 125.00
Johnny Bucyk
DAEE Phil Esposito 30.00 80.00
Tony Esposito
DAES Ron Ellis 25.00 60.00
Eddie Shack
DAFG Lou Fontinato
Bill Gadsby
DAFM Bernie Federko 30.00 80.00
Joe Mullen
DAGB Ron Greschner 30.00 80.00
Barry Beck
DAGC Grant Fuhr 50.00 125.00
Craig MacTavish
DAHE Bobby Hull 50.00 100.00
Tony Esposito
DAHL Gordie Howe 100.00 175.00
Ted Lindsay
DAHP Bobby Hull 25.00 60.00
Jim Pappin
DAHS Dale Hawerchuk
Tomas Steen
DAIM Dick Irvin 15.00 40.00
Brian McFarlane
DALD Mike Liut
Kevin Dineen
DALK Ted Lindsay 30.00 60.00
Red Kelly
DALL Guy Lafleur
Jacques Lemaire
DALS Pat LaFontaine
Brent Sutter
DAMB Gilles Meloche 75.00 150.00
Don Beaupre
DAMM Joe Mullen
Brian Mullen
DAMM Marty McSorley
Bob Probert
DANO Cam Neely 25.00 60.00
Adam Oates
DAOB Bobby Orr 275.00 400.00
Ray Bourque
DAOC Bobby Orr
Phil Esposito
DAOL John Ogrodnick
Reed Larson
DAOM Terry O'Reilly 25.00 50.00
Peter McNab
DAPF Gilbert Perreault 25.00 60.00
Mike Foligno
DAPG Gilbert Perreault 75.00 150.00
Danny Gare
DAPK Bob Probert 30.00 60.00
Joey Kocur
DAPM Pete Peeters 20.00 50.00
Rick Middleton
DAPP Jim Peplinski 30.00 60.00
Willi Plett
DARP Larry Robinson 30.00 60.00
Denis Potvin
DASB Milt Schmidt 60.00 100.00
Johnny Bucyk
DASD Dave Schultz
Gary Dornhoefer
DASV Darryl Sittler 40.00 80.00
Rick Vaive
DATB Tiger Williams 40.00 80.00
Richard Brodeur
DAWS Tiger Williams 75.00 125.00
Dave Semenko
DAST1 Peter Stastny
Anton Stastny
DAST2 Peter Stastny 25.00 60.00
Marian Stastny
DASU1 Darryl Sutter 30.00 60.00
Duane Sutter
DASU2 Brent Sutter
Brian Sutter

2002-03 Parkhurst Retro

Released in mid-April, this 250-card set payed tribute to the look and feel of the 1951-52 Parkhurst set. Card backs were blank. The set consisted of 200 veterans and 50 shorprinted rookies. Rookie cards were serial-numbered to 300 copies each.

COMP.SET w/o SP's (200) 20.00 50.00
1 Mario Lemieux 2.00 5.00
2 Jarome Iginla .40 1.00
3 Jaromir Jagr .50 1.25
4 Alexei Kovalev .25 .60
5 Todd Bertuzzi .30 .75
6 Joe Thornton .50 1.25
7 Jason Allison .10 .25
8 Markus Naslund .30 .75
9 Eric Lindros .30 .75
10 Keith Tkachuk .30 .75
11 Adam Oates .25 .60
12 Mike Modano .50 1.25
13 Pavel Bure .30 .75
14 Ron Francis .25 .60
15 Joe Sakic .60 1.50
16 Brendan Shanahan .30 .75
17 Alexei Yashin .10 .25
18 Patrick Roy 1.50 4.00
19 Dwayne Roloson .25 .60
20 Pavol Demitra .25 .60
21 Sergei Samsonov .25 .60
22 Steve Yzerman 1.50 4.00
23 Mats Sundin .30 .75
24 Peter Bondra .25 .60
25 Daniel Alfredsson .25 .60
26 Jeremy Roenick .40 1.00
27 Zigmund Palffy .25 .60
28 Ray Whitney .10 .25
29 Sami Kapanen .10 .25
30 Alexei Zhamnov .10 .25
31 Radek Bonk .10 .25
32 Eric Daze .25 .60
33 Tommy Salo .25 .60
34 Marian Gaborik .60 1.50
35 Alexander Mogilny .25 .60
36 Glen Murray .10 .25
37 Patrik Elias .25 .60
38 Simon Gagne .30 .75
39 Ryan Smyth .25 .60
40 Bill Guerin .25 .60
41 Jeff Oneill .10 .25
42 Miroslav Satan .25 .60
43 Adam Deadmarsh .10 .25
44 Sergei Fedorov .50 1.25
45 Owen Nolan .25 .60
46 Tony Amonte .25 .60
47 Doug Weight .25 .60
48 Marian Hossa .30 .75
49 Mark Parrish .10 .25
50 Theo Fleury .10 .25
51 Steven Reinprecht .10 .25
52 Dany Heatley .40 1.00
53 Sergei Gonchar .10 .25
54 Ilya Kovalchuk .40 1.00
55 Brett Hull .40 1.00
56 Daniel Briere .10 .25
57 Brad Richards .25 .60
58 Brendan Morrison .25 .60
59 Steve Sullivan .10 .25
60 Mike York .10 .25
61 Nicklas Lidstrom .30 .75
62 Michael Peca .10 .25
63 Mark Recchi .25 .60
64 Daymond Langkow .10 .25
65 Tylor Arnason .25 .60
66 Rob Blake .25 .60
67 Mike Comrie .25 .60
68 Felix Potvin .30 .75
69 Brian Rolston .25 .60
70 Martin Brodeur .75 2.00
71 Anson Carter .25 .60
72 Roberto Luongo .40 1.00
73 Joe Nieuwendyk .25 .60
74 Dean McAmmond .10 .25
75 Niko Kapanen .10 .25
76 Jan Hrdina .10 .25
77 Vincent Damphousse .10 .25
78 Jozef Stumpel .10 .25
79 Milan Hejduk .30 .75
80 Stu Barnes .10 .25
81 Pierre Turgeon .25 .60
82 Marty Turco .25 .60
83 Bryan McCabe .10 .25
84 Gary Roberts .10 .25
85 Martin Havlat .25 .60
86 Kyle Calder .10 .25
87 Paul Kariya .30 .75
88 Martin Straka .10 .25
89 Yanic Perreault .10 .25
90 Brian Boucher .25 .60
91 Darcy Tucker .10 .25
92 Mike Ricci .10 .25
93 Keith Primeau .10 .25
94 Bobby Holik .10 .25
95 Chris Osgood .25 .60
96 Brian Leetch .25 .60
97 Teemu Selanne .30 .75
98 Alex Tanguay .25 .60
99 Rod Brind'Amour .25 .60
100 Petr Sykora .10 .25
101 Jere Lehtinen .25 .60
102 Kevin Weekes .25 .60
103 Jason Arnott .10 .25
104 Al MacInnis .25 .60
105 Scott Gomez .10 .25
106 Byron Dafoe .25 .60
107 Evgeni Nabokov .25 .60
108 Sandis Ozolinsh .10 .25
109 John LeClair .30 .75
110 Mike Dunham .25 .60
111 Manny Fernandez .25 .60
112 Johan Hedberg .25 .60
113 Chris Pronger .25 .60
114 Fredrik Modin .10 .25
115 Rostislav Klesla .10 .25
116 Manny Legace .25 .60
117 Teppo Numminen .10 .25
118 Shane Doan .10 .25
119 Martin Biron .25 .60
120 Luc Robitaille .30 .75
121 Igor Larionov .25 .60
122 Doug Gilmour .25 .60
123 Roman Cechmanek .25 .60
124 Marc Savard .10 .25
125 Scott Stevens .25 .60
126 Steve Rucchin .10 .25
127 Olaf Kolzig .25 .60
128 Ed Jovanovski .25 .60
129 Petr Nedved .10 .25
130 Valeri Bure .10 .25
131 J-P Dumont .10 .25
132 Jocelyn Thibault .25 .60
133 Martin Lapointe .10 .25
134 Tomas Kaberle .10 .25
135 Jose Theodore .40 1.00
136 Bates Battaglia .10 .25
137 Chris Drury .25 .60
138 Patrick Lalime .25 .60
139 Derek Morris .10 .25
140 Sean Burke .25 .60
141 Radek Dvorak .10 .25
142 Ladislav Nagy .10 .25
143 Oleg Petrov .10 .25
144 Kristian Huselius .10 .25
145 Mark Messier .30 .75
146 Curtis Joseph .30 .75
147 Tim Connolly .10 .25
148 Arturs Irbe .25 .60
149 Espen Knutsen .10 .25
150 Ed Belfour .30 .75
151 Jaroslav Modry .10 .25
152 Dan Cloutier .25 .60
153 Jeff Friesen .10 .25
154 Janne Niinimaa .10 .25
155 Nikolai Khabibulin .30 .75
156 Justin Williams .10 .25
157 Kyle McLaren .10 .25
158 Sergei Zubov .10 .25
159 Brian Savage .10 .25
160 Chris Chelios .30 .75
161 Roman Hamrlik .10 .25
162 Scott Niedermayer .10 .25
163 Danny Markov .10 .25
164 Marc Denis .25 .60
165 Scott Hartnell .10 .25
166 Roman Turek .25 .60
167 Brenden Morrow .10 .25
168 David Legwand .25 .60
169 Henrik Sedin .10 .25
170 Oleg Tverdovsky .10 .25
171 Peter Forsberg .75 2.00
172 Vincent Lecavalier .30 .75
173 Pavel Datsyuk .30 .75
174 Dan Blackburn .25 .60
175 Adam Foote .10 .25
176 Joe Juneau .10 .25
177 Mike Richter .25 .60
178 Shawn Bates .10 .25
179 Erik Cole .10 .25
180 Jean-Sebastien Giguere .25 .60
181 Saku Koivu .30 .75
182 Zdeno Chara .10 .25
183 Stephen Weiss .10 .25
184 Robert Svehla .10 .25
185 Patrick Stefan .10 .25
186 Robert Lang .10 .25
187 Olli Jokinen .25 .60
188 Pavel Brendl .10 .25
189 Brent Johnson .25 .60
190 Boris Mironov .10 .25
191 Tomas Vokoun .25 .60
192 Darius Kasparaitis .10 .25
193 Martin St. Louis .25 .60
194 Radim Vrbata .10 .25
195 Jeff Hackett .25 .60
196 Nik Antropov .10 .25
197 Craig Conroy .10 .25
198 Nick Boynton .10 .25
199 Richard Zednik .10 .25
200 Vaclav Prospal .10 .25
201 P-M Bouchard RC 5.00 12.00
202 Rick Nash RC 20.00 40.00
203 Dennis Seidenberg RC 5.00 10.00
204 Jay Bouwmeester RC 8.00 20.00
205 Stanislav Chistov RC 4.00 10.00
206 Pascal Leclaire RC 8.00 20.00
207 Jared Aulin RC 4.00 10.00
208 Chuck Kobasew RC 4.00 10.00
209 Jordan Leopold RC 5.00 12.00
210 Steve Ott RC 5.00 12.00
211 Ales Hemsky RC 10.00 25.00
212 Matt Walker RC 4.00 10.00
213 Tomas Malec RC 4.00 10.00
214 Dmitri Bykov RC 4.00 10.00
215 Michael Leighton RC 6.00 15.00
216 Henrik Zetterberg RC 25.00 50.00
217 Alexander Frolov RC 10.00 25.00
218 Steve Eminger RC 4.00 10.00
219 Scottie Upshall RC 4.00 10.00
220 Rickard Wallin RC 4.00 10.00
221 Alexei Semenov RC 4.00 10.00
222 Ron Hainsey RC 4.00 10.00
223 Martin Gerber RC 5.00 12.00
224 Adam Hall RC 4.00 10.00
225 Ray Emery RC 10.00 25.00
226 Anton Volchenkov RC 4.00 10.00
227 Levente Szuper RC 4.00 10.00
228 Carlo Colaiacovo RC 4.00 10.00
229 Alexander Svitov RC .10 .25
230 Alexei Smirnov RC 4.00 10.00
231 Jeff Taffe RC 4.00 10.00
232 Mikael Tellqvist RC 5.00 12.00
233 Ari Ahonen RC 4.00 10.00
234 Martin Samuelsson RC 4.00 10.00
235 Shaone Morrisonn RC 4.00 10.00
236 Craig Andersson RC 15.00 40.00
237 Jim Fahey RC 4.00 10.00
238 Brooks Orpik RC 4.00 10.00
239 Mike Komisarek RC 5.00 12.00
240 Frederic Cloutier RC 4.00 10.00
241 Curtis Sanford RC 5.00 12.00
242 Jim Vandermeer RC 4.00 10.00
243 Paul Manning RC 4.00 10.00
244 Kris Vernarsky RC 4.00 10.00
245 Dany Sabourin RC 4.00 10.00
246 Mike Cammalleri RC 6.00 15.00
247 Jason Spezza RC 25.00 50.00
248 Cristobal Huet RC 12.00 30.00
249 Ryan Miller RC 25.00 50.00
250 Dick Tarnstrom RC 4.00 10.00

2002-03 Parkhurst Retro Minis

A throwback to the 1951-52 Parkhurst cards, this 250-card set paralleled the base set on cards approximately 2 1/2" X 1 1/2". Cards 201-250 were shortprinted, but no print run was made public.

*STARS: 1.25X TO 3X BASE HI
*SP's (201-250): .2X TO .5X

2002-03 Parkhurst Retro Back In Time

This 15-card set put Mario Lemieux on cards fashioned after Parkhurst designs of the past. Cards carried a swatch of game jersey and were limited to 30 copies each.

*MULT.COLOR SWATCH: .5X TO 1.25X
1 1951-52 Parkhurst 25.00 60.00
2 1952-53 Parkhurst 25.00 60.00
3 1953-54 Parkhurst 25.00 60.00
4 1954-55 Parkhurst 25.00 60.00
5 1955-56 Parkhurst 25.00 60.00
6 1957-58 Parkhurst 25.00 60.00
7 1958-59 Parkhurst 25.00 60.00
8 1959-60 Parkhurst 25.00 60.00
9 1960-61 Parkhurst 25.00 60.00
10 1961-62 Parkhurst 25.00 60.00
11 1962-63 Parkhurst 25.00 60.00
12 1962-63 Parkhurst 25.00 60.00
13 1962-63 Parkhurst 25.00 60.00
14 1963-64 Parkhurst 25.00 60.00
15 1963-64 Parkhurst 25.00 60.00

2002-03 Parkhurst Retro Back In Time SportsFest

13 Mario Lemieux

2002-03 Parkhurst Retro Back In Time Autographs

This 15-card set paralleled the regular insert but included a certified autograph on each card. Cards were serial-numbered to just 10 copies each.

NOT PRICED DUE TO SCARCITY

2002-03 Parkhurst Retro Franchise Players

Limited to just 60 copies each, this 30-card set featured game jersey swatches from team leaders.

*MULT.COLOR SWATCH: .5X TO 1.25X
RF1 Paul Kariya 8.00 20.00
RF2 Dany Heatley 12.50 30.00
RF3 Joe Thornton 15.00 40.00
RF4 Miroslav Satan 8.00 20.00
RF5 Jarome Iginla 12.50 30.00
RF6 Ron Francis 8.00 20.00
RF7 Jocelyn Thibault 8.00 20.00

RF8 Rick Nash 15.00 40.00
RF9 Joe Sakic 15.00 40.00
RF10 Mike Modano 10.00 25.00
RF11 Steve Yzerman 20.00 50.00
RF12 Mike Comrie 8.00 20.00
RF13 Roberto Luongo 15.00 40.00
RF14 Jason Allison 8.00 20.00
RF15 Marian Gaborik 15.00 40.00
RF16 Jose Theodore 15.00 40.00
RF17 David Legwand 8.00 20.00
RF18 Martin Brodeur 20.00 50.00
RF19 Mike Peca 8.00 20.00
RF20 Pavel Bure 8.00 20.00
RF21 Marian Hossa 8.00 20.00
RF22 Jeremy Roenick 10.00 25.00
RF23 Daniel Briere 8.00 20.00
RF24 Mario Lemieux 30.00 80.00
RF25 Teemu Selanne 8.00 20.00
RF26 Chris Pronger 8.00 20.00
RF27 Vincent Lecavalier 8.00 20.00
RF28 Mats Sundin 8.00 20.00
RF29 Markus Naslund 8.00 20.00
RF30 Jaromir Jagr 12.50 30.00

2002-03 Parkhurst Retro He Shoots-He Scores Points

Inserted one per pack, these cards carried a value of 1, 2 or 3 points. The points could be redeemed for special memorabilia cards. The cards are unnumbered and are listed below in alphabetical order by point value. The redemption program ended March 31, 2004.

1 Marian Gaborik 1 pt. .20 .50
2 Dany Heatley 1 pt. .20 .50
3 Marian Hossa 1 pt. .20 .50
4 Mike Modano 1 pt. .20 .50
5 Rick Nash 1 pt. .20 .50
6 Brendan Shanahan 1 pt. .20 .50
7 Joe Thornton 1 pt. .20 .50
8 Marty Turco 1 pt. .20 .50
9 Ed Belfour 2 pts. .20 .50
10 Martin Brodeur 2 pts. .20 .50
11 Pavel Bure 2 pts. .20 .50
12 Peter Forsberg 2 pts. .20 .50
13 Jaromir Jagr 2 pts. .20 .50
14 Paul Kariya 2 pts. .20 .50
15 Ilya Kovalchuk 2 pts. .20 .50
16 Eric Lindros 2 pts. .20 .50
17 Joe Sakic 2 pts. .20 .50
18 Mario Lemieux 3 pts. .20 .50
19 Patrick Roy 3 pts. .20 .50
20 Steve Yzerman 3 pts. .20 .50

2002-03 Parkhurst Retro He Shoots-He Scores Prizes

Available only by redeeming 400 Parkhurst Retro He Shoots-He Scores points, this 30-card set featured game-used swatches of jersey and a color photo of the player. Each card had a stated print run of 20 serial-numbered sets and each was encased in a clear plastic slab with a descriptive label at the top. This set is unpriced due to scarcity and volatility.

1 Steve Yzerman
2 Mario Lemieux
3 Patrick Roy
4 Jaromir Jagr
5 Ilya Kovalchuk
6 Eric Lindros
7 Martin Brodeur
8 Ed Belfour
9 Joe Sakic
10 Peter Forsberg
11 Pavel Bure
12 Paul Kariya
13 Dany Heatley
14 Brendan Shanahan
15 Marian Gaborik
16 Joe Thornton
17 Rick Nash
18 Marian Hossa
19 Marty Turco
20 Mike Modano
21 Roberto Luongo
22 Jose Theodore
23 Todd Bertuzzi
24 Nicklas Lidstrom
25 Jarome Iginla
26 Mats Sundin
27 Markus Naslund
28 Sergei Fedorov
29 Milan Hejduk
30 Teemu Selanne

2002-03 Parkhurst Retro Hopefuls

Limited to just 30 copies each, this 40-card set featured players who were considered contenders for the Calder, Hart, Norris, Richard, or Vezina awards. Each card carried a swatch of game jersey.

*MULT.COLOR SWATCH: .5X TO 1.25X
CH1 Tyler Arnason 12.50 30.00
CH2 Rick Nash 25.00 60.00
CH3 Ryan Miller 15.00 40.00
CH4 Niko Kapanen 10.00 25.00
CH5 Alexander Frolov 12.50 30.00
CH6 Stanislav Chistov 12.50 30.00
CH7 Barret Jackman 12.50 30.00
CH8 Jay Bouwmeester 12.50 30.00
HH1 Mario Lemieux 25.00 60.00
HH2 Joe Thornton 15.00 40.00
HH3 Markus Naslund 12.50 30.00
HH4 Marty Turco 12.50 30.00
HH5 Nicklas Lidstrom 12.50 30.00
HH6 Marian Gaborik 20.00 50.00
HH7 Marian Hossa 12.50 30.00
HH8 Jaromir Jagr 20.00 50.00
NH1 Nicklas Lidstrom 12.50 30.00
NH2 Rob Blake 12.50 30.00
NH3 Adam Foote 12.50 30.00
NH4 Al MacInnis 12.50 30.00
NH5 Sergei Zubov 12.50 30.00
NH6 Ed Jovanovski 12.50 25.00
NH7 Tomas Kaberle 12.50 25.00
NH8 Derian Hatcher 12.50 25.00
RR1 Jaromir Jagr 20.00 50.00
RR2 Marian Hossa 12.50 30.00
RR3 Mats Sundin 12.50 30.00
RR4 Marian Gaborik 20.00 50.00
RR5 Markus Naslund 12.50 30.00
RR6 Ilya Kovalchuk 25.00 60.00
RR7 Joe Thornton 15.00 40.00
RR8 Milan Hejduk 12.50 30.00
VH1 Ed Belfour 25.00 50.00
VH2 Marty Turco 12.50 30.00
VH3 Martin Brodeur 25.00 60.00
VH4 Patrick Lalime 12.50 30.00
VH5 Jean-Sebastien Giguere 12.50 30.00
VH6 Jocelyn Thibault 12.50 30.00
VH7 Patrick Roy 30.00 80.00
VH8 Nikolai Khabibulin 12.50 30.00

2002-03 Parkhurst Retro Jerseys

*MULT.COLOR SWATCH: .5X TO 1.25X
RJ1 Patrick Roy 20.00 50.00
RJ2 Mike Modano 10.00 25.00
RJ3 Peter Forsberg 12.50 30.00
RJ4 Mark Messier 8.00 20.00
RJ5 Brett Hull 12.50 30.00
RJ6 Martin Brodeur 15.00 40.00
RJ7 Joe Thornton 10.00 25.00
RJ8 Ed Belfour 8.00 20.00
RJ9 Pavel Bure 8.00 20.00
RJ10 Rick Nash 12.50 30.00
RJ11 Marty Turco 6.00 15.00
RJ12 Jay Bouwmeester 6.00 15.00
RJ13 Jason Spezza 12.50 30.00
RJ14 Jaromir Jagr 10.00 25.00
RJ15 Mario Lemieux 20.00 50.00
RJ16 Markus Naslund 8.00 20.00
RJ17 Brendan Shanahan 8.00 20.00
RJ18 Paul Kariya 8.00 20.00
RJ19 Roberto Luongo 10.00 25.00
RJ20 Joe Sakic 15.00 40.00
RJ21 Mats Sundin 8.00 20.00
RJ22 Steve Yzerman 15.00 40.00
RJ23 Dany Heatley 10.00 25.00
RJ24 Jose Theodore 10.00 25.00
RJ25 John LeClair 8.00 20.00
RJ26 Marian Hossa 8.00 20.00
RJ27 Eric Lindros 8.00 20.00
RJ28 Sergei Fedorov 10.00 25.00
RJ29 Todd Bertuzzi 8.00 20.00
RJ30 Sergei Samsonov 6.00 15.00
RJ31 Jeremy Roenick 10.00 25.00
RJ32 Nicklas Lidstrom 8.00 20.00
RJ33 Bill Guerin 6.00 15.00
RJ34 Chris Pronger 6.00 15.00
RJ35 Saku Koivu 8.00 20.00
RJ36 Marian Gaborik 12.50 30.00
RJ37 Ilya Kovalchuk 10.00 25.00
RJ38 Jocelyn Thibault 6.00 15.00
RJ39 Vincent Lecavalier 6.00 15.00
RJ40 Teemu Selanne 8.00 20.00

2002-03 Parkhurst Retro Jersey and Sticks

*JSY/STK: .6X TO 1.5X BASIC JERSEY
STATED PRINT RUN 60 SETS

2002-03 Parkhurst Retro Magnificent Inserts

This 10-card set featured game-used equipment from the career of Mario Lemieux. Cards MI1-MI5 had a print run of 40 copies each and cards MI6-MI10 were limited to just 10 copies each. Cards MI6-MI10 are not priced due to scarcity.

MI1 2000-01 Season 30.00 80.00
MI2 1985-86 Season 30.00 80.00
MI3 2002 All-Star 30.00 80.00
MI4 1987 Canada Cup 30.00 80.00
MI5 Dual Jersey 50.00 125.00
MI6 Number
MI7 Emblem
MI8 Triple Jersey
MI9 Quad Jersey
MI10 Complete Package

2002-03 Parkhurst Retro Magnificent Inserts Autographs

This 10-card set paralleled the base Magnificent Inserts but carried certified autographs and each card was hand numbered. Cards MI1-MI5 were serial-numbered to 15 each and cards MI6-MI10 were serial numbered out of 5.

NOT PRICE DUE TO SCARCITY

2002-03 Parkhurst Retro Memorabilia

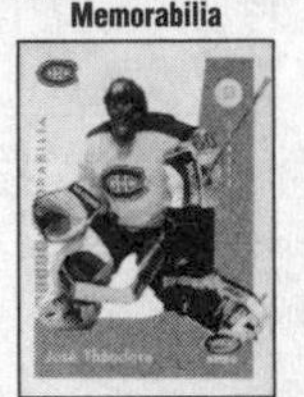

This 30-card set featured swatches of game-used equipment. Print runs for each card are listed below.

RM1 Mario Lemieux/50 20.00 50.00
RM2 Joe Sakic/50 15.00 40.00
RM3 Joe Thornton/60 15.00 40.00
RM4 Marian Hossa/50 10.00 25.00
RM5 Nicklas Lidstrom/50 10.00 25.00
RM6 Patrick Roy/50 20.00 50.00
RM7 Jose Theodore/50 12.50 30.00
RM8 Mario Lemieux/30 25.00 60.00
RM9 Martin Brodeur/50 20.00 50.00
RM10 Dany Heatley/50 12.50 30.00
RM11 Ilya Kovalchuk/60 12.50 30.00
RM12 Marty Turco/50 10.00 25.00
RM13 Sergei Fedorov/50 12.50 30.00
RM14 Steve Yzerman/50 20.00 50.00
RM15 Jason Spezza/60 10.00 25.00
RM16 Pavel Bure/50 10.00 25.00
RM17 Peter Forsberg/50 15.00 40.00
RM18 Brendan Shanahan/50 10.00 25.00
RM19 Joe Thornton/30 15.00 40.00
RM20 Mike Modano/60 12.50 30.00
RM21 Nikolai Khabibulin/30 10.00 25.00
RM22 Jaromir Jagr/60 12.50 30.00
RM23 Joe Sakic/50 15.00 40.00
RM24 Mats Sundin/50 10.00 25.00
RM25 Saku Koivu/60 10.00 25.00
RM26 Jay Bouwmeester/60 15.00 40.00
RM27 Paul Kariya/60 10.00 25.00
RM28 Rick Nash/50 12.50 30.00
RM29 Mario Lemieux/50 20.00 50.00
RM30 Brett Hull/30 15.00 40.00

2002-03 Parkhurst Retro Nicknames

This 30-card set featured game-used memorabilia swatches of the given player on the card fronts beside their "nickname". Individual print runs are listed below.

STAT.PRINT RUNS LISTED BELOW
RN1 Frank Brimsek/35 20.00 50.00
RN2 Henri Richard/40 20.00 50.00
RN3 Ed Giacomin/40 20.00 50.00
RN4 Bobby Hull/35 20.00 50.00
RN5 Bernie Geoffrion/20
RN6 Gerry Cheevers/50 12.50 30.00
RN7 Johnny Bucyk/40 12.50 30.00
RN8 Johnny Bower/40 25.00 60.00
RN9 Gump Worsley/40 30.00 80.00
RN10 Glenn Hall/40 15.00 40.00
RN11 Red Kelly/40 15.00 40.00
RN12 Frank Mahovlich 40.00 100.00
Pete Mahovlich
RN13 Ace Bailey/20
RN14 King Clancy/20
RN15 Roy Worters/20
RN16 Stan Mikita/50 15.00 40.00
RN17 Rocket Richard/20
RN18 Turk Broda/20
RN19 Tony Esposito/35 25.00 60.00
RN20 Jean Beliveau/35 30.00 80.00
RN21 Jacques Plante/35 50.00 125.00
RN22 Steve Yzerman/65 20.00 50.00
RN23 Brett Hull/65 15.00 40.00
RN24 Patrick Roy/65 20.00 50.00
RN25 Nicklas Lidstrom/65 15.00 40.00
RN26 Teemu Selanne/65 12.50 30.00
RN27 Olaf Kolzig/65 12.50 30.00
RN28 Pavel Bure/65 12.50 30.00
RN29 Eric Lindros/65 12.50 30.00
RN30 Mario Lemieux/65 30.00 80.00

2003-04 Parkhurst Rookie

This 200-card set consisted of 60-veteran cards; 18-dual prospect cards; 52-single prospect cards; 25-prospect jersey cards; 30-autographed prospect cards and 25 jersey/autograph prospect cards. Cards 61-130 were serial-numbered out of 500; cards 131-155 were numbered out of 180; cards 156-175 were numbered out of 120 and cards 176-200 were numbered to 100.

*MULT.COLOR SWATCH: .6X TO 1.5X
1 Steve Yzerman 5.00 12.00
2 Joe Sakic 3.00 8.00
3 Jeremy Roenick 2.00 5.00
4 Brian Leetch 1.50 4.00
5 Andrew Raycroft 1.25 3.00
6 Dan Cloutier 1.25 3.00
7 Marty Turco 1.25 3.00
8 Owen Nolan 1.25 3.00
9 Joe Thornton 2.00 5.00
10 Marian Gaborik 3.00 8.00
11 Mario Lemieux 6.00 15.00
12 Zigmund Palffy 1.25 3.00
13 Vincent Lecavalier 1.50 4.00
14 Sean Burke 1.25 3.00
15 Miikka Kiprusoff 1.25 3.00
16 Dominik Hasek 3.00 8.00
17 Nikolai Khabibulin 1.50 4.00
18 Ed Belfour 1.50 4.00
19 Ilya Kovalchuk 2.00 5.00
20 Marian Hossa 1.50 4.00
21 Tommy Salo 1.25 3.00
22 Keith Tkachuk 1.50 4.00
23 Alex Kovalev 1.25 3.00
24 Michael Ryder .75 2.00
25 Steve Sullivan .75 2.00
26 Martin St-Louis 1.25 3.00
27 Al MacInnis 1.25 3.00
28 Sergei Gonchar .75 2.00
29 Jaromir Jagr 2.50 6.00
30 Ron Francis 1.25 3.00
31 Henrik Zetterberg 1.50 4.00
32 Paul Kariya 1.50 4.00
33 Robert Lang .75 2.00
34 Nicklas Lidstrom 1.50 4.00
35 Sergei Fedorov 2.00 5.00
36 Jarome Iginla 2.00 5.00
37 Bill Guerin 1.25 3.00
38 Jose Theodore 2.00 5.00
39 Roberto Luongo 2.00 5.00
40 Alex Tanguay 1.25 3.00
41 Peter Forsberg 4.00 10.00
42 Mike Modano 2.00 5.00
43 Dwayne Roloson 1.25 3.00
44 Martin Brodeur 4.00 10.00
45 Dany Heatley 2.00 5.00
46 Rick Nash 2.00 5.00
47 Jason Spezza 1.50 4.00
48 Chris Pronger 1.25 3.00
49 Brett Hull 2.00 5.00
50 Markus Naslund 1.50 4.00
51 Curtis Joseph 1.50 4.00
52 Olaf Kolzig 1.25 3.00
53 Peter Bondra 1.25 3.00
54 Eric Lindros 1.50 4.00
55 Mats Sundin 1.50 4.00
56 Patrick Roy 5.00 12.00
57 Ray Bourque 3.00 8.00
58 Terry Sawchuk 3.00 8.00
59 Maurice Richard 5.00 12.00
60 Bobby Orr 6.00 15.00
61 M.Bartovic RC/J.Pominville RC 6.00 15.00
62 K.McDonell RC/A.Johnson RC 4.00 10.00
63 A.Hutchinson RC/L.Pivko RC 4.00 10.00
64 K.Gernander RC/P.Osaer RC 4.00 10.00
65 R.Mrozik RC/J.Pollock RC 4.00 10.00
66 S.Meyer RC/D.Verot RC 4.00 10.00
67 M.Yeats RC/D.Zinger RC 4.00 10.00
68 J.DiPenta RC/T.J. Olson RC 4.00 10.00
69 A.Rourke RC/J.MacMillan RC 4.00 10.00
70 M.Underhill RC/D.Salficky RC 4.00 10.00
71 J.Vauclair RC/Z.Michalek RC 4.00 10.00
72 M.Hussey RC/M.Stutzel RC 4.00 10.00
73 B.Lampman RC/T.Pock RC 4.00 10.00
74 G.Mink RC/R.Tvrdon RC 4.00 10.00
75 J.MacDonald RC/M.Morrison RC 4.00 10.00
76 M.Pandolfo RC/G.Mauldin RC 4.00 10.00
77 J.Yablonski RC/C.Larose RC 4.00 10.00
78 C.Brandner RC/E.Perrin RC 4.00 10.00
79 Michal Barinka RC 3.00 8.00
80 Erik Westrum RC 3.00 8.00
81 Gavin Morgan RC 3.00 8.00
82 Matt Ellison RC 3.00 8.00
83 Seamus Kotyk RC 3.00 8.00
84 Andy Chiodo RC 3.00 8.00
85 Mikko Luoma RC 3.00 8.00
86 Jed Ortmeyer RC 3.00 8.00
87 Brad Boyes RC 6.00 15.00
88 Robert Scuderi RC 3.00 8.00
89 Nolan Schaefer RC 3.00 8.00
90 Colton Orr RC 3.00 8.00
91 Travis Moen RC 3.00 8.00
92 Fred Meyer RC 3.00 8.00
93 Joe Motzko RC 3.00 8.00
94 Ryan Barnes RC 3.00 8.00
95 Rob Skrlac RC 3.00 8.00
96 Quintin Laing RC 3.00 8.00
97 Mikhail Kuleshov RC 3.00 8.00
98 Adam Munro RC 3.00 8.00
99 Wade Dubielewicz RC 4.00 10.00
100 Matt Keith RC 3.00 8.00
101 Steve McLaren RC 3.00 8.00
102 Tim Jackman RC 3.00 8.00
103 Doug Doull RC 3.00 8.00
104 Lawrence Nycholat RC 3.00 8.00
105 Aleksander Suglobov RC 3.00 8.00
106 Martin Strbak RC 3.00 8.00
107 Lasse Kukkonen RC 3.00 8.00
108 Gregory Campbell RC 3.00 8.00
109 Tony Martensson RC 3.00 8.00
110 Carl Corazzini RC 3.00 8.00
111 Mike Green RC 3.00 8.00
112 Nathan Robinson RC 3.00 8.00
113 Brent Krahn RC 3.00 8.00
114 Mike Smith RC 4.00 10.00
115 Mike Stuart RC 3.00 8.00
116 Karl Stewart RC 3.00 8.00
117 Jason MacDonald RC 3.00 8.00
118 Brooks Laich RC 3.00 8.00
119 Tom Preissing RC 3.00 8.00
120 Mikhail Yakubov RC 3.00 8.00
121 Benoit Dusablon RC 3.00 8.00
122 Nathan Smith RC 3.00 8.00
123 Goran Bezina RC 3.00 8.00
124 Dan Ellis RC 4.00 10.00
125 Pat Rissmiller RC 3.00 8.00
126 Owen Fussey RC 3.00 8.00
127 Mike Bishai RC 3.00 8.00
128 Matt Murley RC 3.00 8.00
129 Wade Brookbank RC 3.00 8.00
130 Randy Jones RC 3.00 8.00
131 Fedor Tyutin JSY RC 10.00 25.00
132 Niklas Kronwall JSY RC 12.50 30.00
133 Boyd Kane JSY RC 8.00 20.00
134 Sergei Zinovjev JSY RC 8.00 20.00
135 Mark Popovic JSY RC 8.00 20.00
136 Sean Bergenheim JSY RC 8.00 20.00
137 Ryan Kesler JSY RC 8.00 20.00
138 Christian Ehrhoff JSY RC 8.00 20.00
139 Peter Sejna JSY RC 8.00 20.00
140 Denis Grebeshkov JSY RC 8.00 20.00
141 Tuomas Pihlman JSY RC 8.00 20.00
142 Antero Niittymaki JSY RC 20.00 50.00
143 Patrick Leahy JSY RC 8.00 20.00
144 Rastislav Stana JSY RC 8.00 20.00
145 Grant McNeill JSY RC 8.00 20.00
146 Cody McCormick JSY RC 8.00 20.00
147 Boyd Gordon JSY RC 8.00 20.00
148 Garth Murray JSY RC 8.00 20.00
149 Trevor Daley JSY RC 8.00 20.00
150 Marek Svatos JSY RC 20.00 50.00
151 Esa Pirnes JSY RC 8.00 20.00
152 Garrett Burnett JSY RC 8.00 20.00
153 Tony Salmelainen JSY RC 8.00 20.00
154 John Pohl JSY RC 8.00 20.00
155 Dominic Moore JSY RC 8.00 20.00
156 Fredrik Sjostrom AU RC 10.00 25.00
157 Jozef Balej AU RC 10.00 25.00
158 Jiri Hudler AU RC 15.00 40.00
159 Joffrey Lupul AU RC 20.00 50.00
160 Tomas Plekanec AU RC 20.00 50.00
161 Kyle Wellwood AU RC 25.00 60.00
162 Peter Sarno AU RC 10.00 25.00
163 Pavel Vorobiev AU RC 10.00 25.00
164 Andrew Peters AU RC 10.00 25.00
165 Jeff Hamilton AU RC 10.00 25.00
166 Darryl Bootland AU RC 10.00 25.00
167 Noah Clarke AU RC 10.00 25.00
168 Matthew Spiller AU RC 10.00 25.00
169 Milan Michalek AU RC 25.00 60.00
170 Doug Lynch AU RC 10.00 25.00
171 Timofei Shishkanov AU RC 10.00 25.00
172 Maxim Kondratiev AU RC 10.00 25.00
173 Chris Kunitz AU RC 12.50 30.00
174 Jordin Tootoo AU RC 25.00 60.00
175 Anton Babchuk AU RC 10.00 25.00
176 Eric Staal JSY AU RC 75.00 150.00
177 Dan Fritsche JSY AU RC 15.00 40.00
178 Joni Pitkanen JSY AU RC 20.00 50.00
179 Tim Gleason JSY AU RC 15.00 40.00
180 Chris Higgins JSY AU RC 50.00 100.00
181 Nathan Horton JSY AU RC 50.00 100.00
182 Marek Zidlicky JSY AU RC 15.00 40.00
183 Antti Miettinen JSY AU RC 15.00 40.00
184 Patrice Bergeron JSY AU RC 75.00 150.00
185 Ryan Malone JSY AU RC 20.00 50.00
186 Matthew Lombardi JSY AU RC 20.00 50.00
187 Dan Hamhuis JSY AU RC 20.00 50.00
188 J-M Liles JSY AU RC 25.00 50.00
189 David Hale JSY AU RC 15.00 40.00
190 Tuomo Ruutu JSY AU RC 30.00 60.00
191 Derek Roy JSY AU RC 40.00 80.00
192 Paul Martin JSY AU RC 15.00 40.00
193 Kari Lehtonen JSY AU RC 125.00 250.00
194 Dustin Brown JSY AU RC 20.00 50.00
195 Antoine Vermette JSY AU RC 20.00 50.00
196 Alexander Semin JSY AU RC 60.00 120.00
197 Brent Burns JSY AU RC 15.00 40.00
198 Matt Stajan JSY AU RC 40.00 80.00
199 Nikolai Zherdev JSY AU RC 40.00 80.00
200 Marc-Andre Fleury JSY AU RC 125.00 250.00

2003-04 Parkhurst Rookie All-Rookie

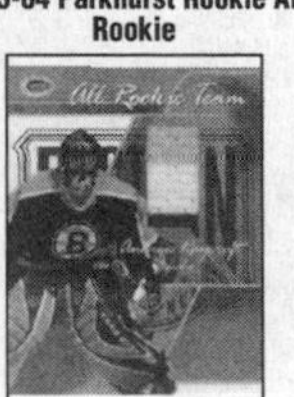

*MULT.COLOR SWATCH: .6X TO 1.5X
PRINT RUN 60 SETS
GOLD PRINT RUN 10 SETS
GOLD NOT PRICED DUE TO SCARCITY
ART1 Andrew Raycroft 8.00 20.00
ART2 Paul Martin 6.00 15.00
ART3 Joni Pitkanen 6.00 15.00
ART4 Eric Staal 12.00 30.00
ART5 Michael Ryder 10.00 25.00
ART6 Ryan Malone 6.00 15.00
ART7 Philippe Sauve 6.00 15.00
ART8 Dan Hamhuis 6.00 15.00
ART9 John-Michael Liles 6.00 15.00
ART10 Tuomo Ruutu 6.00 15.00
ART11 Nikolai Zherdev 8.00 20.00
ART12 Joffrey Lupul 6.00 15.00

2003-04 Parkhurst Rookie All-Rookie Autographs

PRINT RUN 10 SETS
NOT PRICED DUE TO SCARCITY
ARTAR Andrew Raycroft
ARTDH Dan Hamhuis
ARTES Eric Staal
ARTJL John-Michael Liles
ARTJP Joni Pitkanen
ARTMR Michael Ryder
ARTPM Paul Martin
ARTTR Tuomo Ruutu
ARTJLU Joffrey Lupul

2003-04 Parkhurst Rookie Before the Mask

*MULT.COLOR SWATCH: .6X TO 1.5X
PRINT RUN 40 SETS
GOLD PRINT RUN 10 SETS
GOLD NOT PRICED DUE TO SCARCITY
BTM1 Roy Worters 12.50 30.00
BTM2 Frank Brimsek 12.50 30.00
BTM3 Harry Lumley 12.50 30.00
BTM4 Gump Worsley 12.50 30.00
BTM5 Johnny Bower 12.50 30.00
BTM6 Jacques Plante 25.00 60.00
BTM7 Tiny Thompson 12.50 30.00
BTM8 Charlie Gardiner 12.50 30.00
BTM9 Bill Durnan 12.50 30.00
BTM10 George Hainsworth 20.00 50.00
BTM11 Terry Sawchuk 20.00 50.00
BTM12 Glenn Hall 12.50 30.00
BTM13 Ed Giacomin 12.50 30.00
BTM14 Roger Crozier 12.50 30.00
BTM15 Chuck Rayner 12.50 30.00
BTM16 Turk Broda 12.50 30.00

2003-04 Parkhurst Rookie Calder Candidates

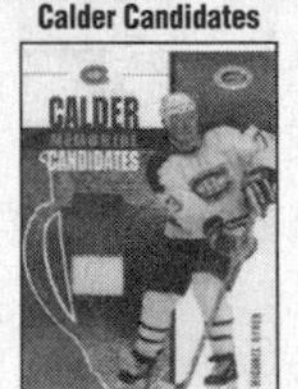

*MULT.COLOR SWATCH: .6X TO 1.5X
PRINT RUN 50 SETS
GOLD PRINT RUN 10 SETS
GOLD NOT PRICED DUE TO SCARCITY
CMC1 Eric Staal 12.50 30.00
CMC2 Michael Ryder 8.00 20.00
CMC3 Marc-Andre Fleury 15.00 40.00
CMC4 Patrice Bergeron 10.00 25.00
CMC5 Ryan Malone 6.00 15.00
CMC6 Joffrey Lupul 6.00 15.00
CMC7 Andrew Raycroft 8.00 20.00
CMC8 Matthew Lombardi 6.00 15.00
CMC9 Joni Pitkanen 6.00 15.00
CMC10 Nikolai Zherdev 8.00 20.00
CMC11 Jordin Tootoo 10.00 25.00
CMC12 Matt Stajan 8.00 20.00
CMC13 Nathan Horton 10.00 25.00
CMC14 Tuomo Ruutu 8.00 20.00
CMC15 Derek Roy 6.00 15.00

2003-04 Parkhurst Rookie Calder Candidate Autographs

PRINT RUN 10 SETS
NOT PRICED DUE TO SCARCITY
CMCAR Andrew Raycroft
CMCDR Derek Roy
CMCES Eric Staal
CMCJL Joffrey Lupul
CMCMR Michael Ryder
CMCMS Matt Stajan

2003-04 Parkhurst Rookie Emblems

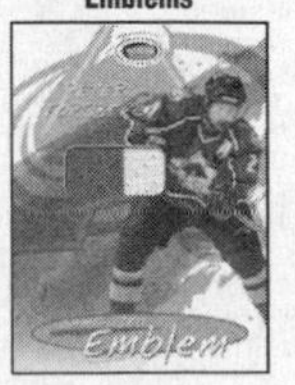

PRINT RUN 9 SETS
NOT PRICED DUE TO SCARCITY
GUE1 Pavel Datsyuk
GUE2 Peter Forsberg
GUE3 Rick Nash
GUE4 Brian Leetch
GUE5 Joe Sakic
GUE6 Dany Heatley
GUE7 Ray Bourque
GUE8 Joe Thornton
GUE9 Ilya Kovalchuk
GUE10 Mario Lemieux

2003-04 Parkhurst Rookie Emblem Autographs

PRINT RUN 10 SETS
NOT PRICED DUE TO SCARCITY

2003-04 Parkhurst Rookie High Expectations

*MULT.COLOR SWATCH: .6X TO 1.5X
PRINT RUN 40 SETS
GOLD PRINT RUN 10 SETS
GOLD NOT PRICED DUE TO SCARCITY
HE1 Ilya Kovalchuk 12.50 30.00
HE2 Rick Nash 10.00 25.00
HE3 Wendel Clark 15.00 40.00
HE4 Mario Lemieux 20.00 50.00
HE5 Guy Lafleur 10.00 25.00
HE6 Gilbert Perreault 12.50 30.00
HE7 Denis Potvin 8.00 20.00
HE8 Mike Modano 12.50 30.00
HE9 Mats Sundin 8.00 20.00
HE10 Joe Thornton 15.00 40.00
HE11 Rick DiPietro 8.00 20.00
HE12 Marc-Andre Fleury 12.50 30.00
HE13 Vincent Lecavalier 8.00 20.00
HE14 Owen Nolan 8.00 20.00

2003-04 Parkhurst Rookie Jerseys

*MULT.COLOR SWATCH: .6X TO 1.5X
PRINT RUN 70 SETS
GOLD PRINT RUN 10 SETS
GOLD NOT PRICED DUE TO SCARCITY
GJ1 Mario Lemieux 20.00 50.00
GJ2 Ilya Kovalchuk 10.00 25.00
GJ3 Joe Thornton 12.00 30.00
GJ4 Bill Guerin 6.00 15.00
GJ5 Jason Spezza 8.00 20.00
GJ6 Peter Forsberg 10.00 25.00
GJ7 Brian Leetch 8.00 20.00
GJ8 Milan Hejduk 8.00 20.00
GJ9 Evgeni Nabokov 6.00 15.00
GJ10 Martin St. Louis 6.00 15.00
GJ11 Rick Nash 10.00 25.00
GJ12 Steve Yzerman 15.00 40.00
GJ13 Pavel Datsyuk 8.00 20.00
GJ14 Henrik Zetterberg 8.00 20.00
GJ15 Joe Sakic 12.00 30.00
GJ16 Jeremy Roenick 10.00 25.00
GJ17 Martin Brodeur 15.00 40.00
GJ18 Mats Sundin 8.00 20.00
GJ19 Keith Tkachuk 8.00 20.00
GJ20 Mike Modano 10.00 25.00
GJ21 Dany Heatley 10.00 25.00
GJ22 Roberto Luongo 10.00 25.00
GJ23 Markus Naslund 8.00 20.00
GJ24 Jose Theodore 10.00 25.00
GJ25 Dominik Hasek 12.00 30.00
GJ26 Paul Kariya 8.00 20.00
GJ27 Teemu Selanne 8.00 20.00
GJ28 Marian Hossa 8.00 20.00
GJ29 Marian Gaborik 12.00 30.00
GJ30 Sergei Fedorov 8.00 20.00
GJ31 Mark Messier 15.00 40.00
GJ32 Jarome Iginla 10.00 25.00
GJ33 Brendan Shanahan 8.00 20.00
GJ34 Ed Belfour 8.00 20.00
GJ35 Curtis Joseph 8.00 20.00
GJ36 Zdeno Chara 8.00 20.00
GJ37 Vincent Lecavalier 8.00 20.00
GJ38 Brett Hull 10.00 25.00
GJ39 Nicklas Lidstrom 8.00 20.00
GJ40 Marty Turco 6.00 15.00
GJ41 Patrick Roy 20.00 50.00
GJ42 Bobby Clarke 10.00 25.00
GJ43 Lanny McDonald 6.00 15.00
GJ44 Marcel Dionne 6.00 15.00
GJ45 Gilbert Perreault 10.00 25.00
GJ46 Ray Bourque 12.00 30.00
GJ47 Mike Bossy 6.00 15.00
GJ48 Vladislav Tretiak 25.00 60.00
GJ49 Bobby Orr 50.00 125.00
GJ50 Cam Neely 10.00 25.00

2003-04 Parkhurst Rookie Jersey Autographs

PRINT RUN 10 SETS
NOT PRICED DUE TO SCARCITY
GUJBG Bill Guerin
GUJBH Brett Hull
GUJCJ Curtis Joseph
GUJDH Dominik Hasek
GUJEN Evgeni Nabokov
GUJHZ Henrik Zetterberg
GUJJS Jason Spezza
GUJJS Joe Sakic
GUJJT Joe Thornton
GUJKT Keith Tkachuk
GUJML Mario Lemieux
GUJMN Markus Naslund
GUJMS Martin St.Louis

GUJPD Pavel Datsyuk
GUJRL Roberto Luongo
GUJRN Rick Nash
GUJSF Sergei Fedorov
GUJSY Steve Yzerman
GUJTHE Jose Theodore

2003-04 Parkhurst Rookie Jersey and Sticks

*JSY/STKS: .6X TO 1.5X JSY
PRINT RUN 80 SETS
GOLD PRINT RUN 10 SETS
GOLD NOT PRICED DUE TO SCARCITY
SJ6 Marc-Andre Fleury 20.00 50.00
SJ7 Eric Lindros 12.50 30.00
SJ15 Chris Pronger 10.00 25.00
SJ21 Andrew Raycroft 12.50 30.00

2003-04 Parkhurst Rookie Records

*MULT.COLOR SWATCH: .6X TO 1.5X
PRINT RUN 40 SETS
GOLD PRINT RUN 10 SETS
GOLD NOT PRICED DUE TO SCARCITY
RRE1 Teemu Selanne 8.00 20.00
RRE2 Teemu Selanne 8.00 20.00
RRE3 Luc Robitaille 8.00 20.00
RRE4 Joe Nieuwendyk 8.00 20.00
RRE5 Brian Leetch 8.00 20.00
RRE6 Tony Esposito 12.50 30.00
RRE7 Patrick Lalime 15.00 40.00
RRE8 Terry Sawchuk 20.00 50.00

2003-04 Parkhurst Rookie Retro Rookies

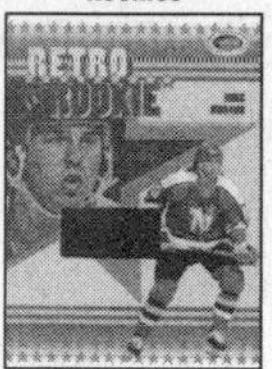

*MULT.COLOR SWATCH: .6X TO 1.5X
PRINT RUN 70 SETS
GOLD PRINT RUN 10 SETS
GOLD NOT PRICED DUE TO SCARCITY
RR1 Mike Modano 10.00 25.00
RR2 Peter Forsberg 15.00 40.00
RR3 Joe Sakic 12.50 30.00
RR4 Patrick Roy 20.00 50.00
RR5 Jaromir Jagr 10.00 25.00
RR6 Rob Blake 8.00 20.00
RR7 Brett Hull 10.00 25.00
RR8 Roberto Luongo 10.00 25.00
RR9 Brian Leetch 8.00 20.00
RR10 Jeremy Roenick 10.00 25.00
RR11 Mats Sundin 8.00 20.00
RR12 Ed Belfour 8.00 20.00
RR13 Curtis Joseph 8.00 20.00
RR14 Sergei Fedorov 10.00 25.00
RR15 Paul Kariya 8.00 20.00
RR16 Mark Messier 12.50 30.00
RR17 Al MacInnis 8.00 20.00
RR18 Felix Potvin 8.00 20.00
RR19 Eric Lindros 8.00 20.00
RR20 Teemu Selanne 8.00 20.00

2003-04 Parkhurst Rookie Retro Rookie Autographs

PRINT RUN 10 SETS
NOT PRICED DUE TO SCARCITY
RRBH Brett Hull
RRJJ Jaromir Jagr
RRJS Joe Sakic
RRMM Mike Modano
RRPR Patrick Roy

2003-04 Parkhurst Rookie Road to the NHL

*MULT.COLOR SWATCH: .75X TO 2X
PRINT RUN 40 SETS
GOLD PRINT RUN 10 SETS
EMBLEM PRINT RUN 9 SETS
GOLD EMBLEM 1/1's EXIST
GOLD/EMBLM NOT PRICED DUE TO SCARCITY
RNJ1 Nick Schultz 6.00 15.00
RNJ2 Jason Spezza 12.50 30.00
RNJ3 Rick Nash 15.00 40.00
RNJ4 Dustin Brown 6.00 15.00
RNJ5 Jay Bouwmeester 6.00 15.00
RNJ6 Jose Theodore 12.00 30.00
RNJ7 Barret Jackman 6.00 15.00
RNJ8 Dany Heatley 15.00 40.00
RNJ9 Eric Staal 15.00 40.00
RNJ10 Scottie Upshall 6.00 15.00
RNJ11 Derek Roy 6.00 15.00
RNJ12 Dan Blackburn 6.00 15.00
RNJ13 Tim Gleason 6.00 15.00
RNJ14 Ron Hainsey 6.00 15.00
RNJ15 Mathieu Garon 6.00 15.00
RNJ16 Steve Ott 12.00 30.00
RNJ17 Dan Hamhuis 6.00 15.00

2003-04 Parkhurst Rookie Road to the NHL Emblems

PRINT RUN 9 SETS
NOT PRICED DUE TO SCARCITY
GOLD 1/1's EXIST

2003-04 Parkhurst Rookie Rookie Emblems

This 50-card set paralleled the Rookie Jerseys set. Cards were limited to just 19 copies each and gold 1/1's were also created.

NOT PRICED DUE TO SCARCITY

2003-04 Parkhurst Rookie Rookie Emblem Autographs

PRINT RUN 10 SETS
NOT PRICED DUE TO SCARCITY
REAM Antti Miettinen
REAP Andrew Peters
REAR Andrew Raycroft
REAS Alexander Semin
REAV Antoine Vermette
REBB Brent Burns
RECH Chris Higgins
REDF Dan Fritsche
REDH Dan Hamhuis
REDR Derek Roy
REDHA David Hale
REES Eric Staal
REJL Joffrey Lupul
REJP Joni Pitkanen
REJLI John-Michael Liles
REKL Kari Lehtonen
REMF Marc-Andre Fleury
REMR Michael Ryder
REMST Matt Stajan
RENH Nathan Horton
RENZ Nikolai Zherdev
REPB Patrice Bergeron
REPM Paul Martin
RERM Ryan Malone
RETR Tuomo Ruutu

2003-04 Parkhurst Rookie Rookie Jerseys

*MULT.COLOR SWATCH: .6X TO 1.5X
PRINT RUN 90 SETS
GOLD PRINT RUN 10 SETS
GOLD NOT PRICED DUE TO SCARCITY
RJ1 Patrice Bergeron 10.00 25.00
RJ2 Fedor Tyutin 6.00 15.00
RJ3 Joffrey Lupul 6.00 15.00
RJ4 Antti Miettinen 6.00 15.00
RJ5 Nathan Horton 10.00 25.00
RJ6 Dustin Brown 6.00 15.00
RJ7 Tim Gleason 6.00 15.00
RJ8 Chris Higgins 10.00 25.00
RJ9 Jordin Tootoo 10.00 25.00
RJ10 Dan Hamhuis 6.00 15.00
RJ11 David Hale 6.00 15.00
RJ12 Garth Murray 6.00 15.00
RJ13 Paul Martin 6.00 15.00
RJ14 Sean Bergenheim 6.00 15.00
RJ15 Joni Pitkanen 6.00 15.00
RJ16 John Pohl 6.00 15.00
RJ17 Libor Pivko 6.00 15.00
RJ18 Marek Svatos 8.00 20.00
RJ19 Dan Fritsche 6.00 15.00
RJ20 Denis Grebeshkov 6.00 15.00
RJ21 Antero Niittymaki 8.00 20.00
RJ22 Tuomo Ruutu 6.00 15.00
RJ23 Kari Lehtonen 12.00 30.00
RJ24 Dominic Moore 6.00 15.00
RJ25 Tony Salmelainen 6.00 15.00
RJ26 Christian Ehrhoff 6.00 15.00
RJ27 Trevor Daley 6.00 15.00
RJ28 Nikolai Zherdev 8.00 20.00
RJ29 Mark Popovic 6.00 15.00
RJ30 Peter Sejna 6.00 15.00
RJ31 Derek Roy 8.00 20.00
RJ32 Trent Hunter 6.00 15.00
RJ33 Cody McCormick 6.00 15.00
RJ34 John-Michael Liles 6.00 15.00
RJ35 Matthew Lombardi 6.00 15.00
RJ36 Marek Zidlicky 6.00 15.00
RJ37 Ryan Malone 6.00 15.00
RJ38 Niklas Kronwall 8.00 20.00
RJ39 Rastislav Stana 6.00 15.00
RJ40 Andrew Raycroft 8.00 20.00
RJ41 Alexander Semin 10.00 25.00
RJ42 Andrew Peters 6.00 15.00
RJ43 Brent Burns 6.00 15.00
RJ44 Matt Stajan 8.00 20.00
RJ45 Antoine Vermette 6.00 15.00
RJ46 Michael Ryder 10.00 25.00
RJ47 Ryan Kesler 6.00 15.00
RJ48 Eric Staal 12.00 30.00
RJ49 Patrick Leahy 6.00 15.00
RJ50 Marc-Andre Fleury 15.00 40.00

2003-04 Parkhurst Rookie Rookie Jersey Autographs

PRINT RUN 10 SETS
NOT PRICED DUE TO SCARCITY
RJAP Andrew Peters
RJAR Andrew Raycroft
RJAS Alexander Semin
RJAV Antoine Vermette
RJBB Brent Burns
RJCH Chris Higgins
RJDF Dan Fritsche
RJDH Dan Hamhuis
RJDR Derek Roy
RJDHA David Hale
RJES Eric Staal
RJJL Joffrey Lupul
RJJP Joni Pitkanen
RJJLI John-Michael Liles
RJKL Kari Lehtonen
RJMF Marc-Andre Fleury
RJMR Michael Ryder
RJMST Matt Stajan
RJNH Nathan Horton
RJPB Patrice Bergeron
RJPM Paul Martin
RJRM Ryan Malone
RJTR Tuomo Ruutu

2003-04 Parkhurst Rookie Rookie Numbers

This 50-card set paralleled the Rookie Jerseys set. Cards were limited to just 19 copies each and gold 1/1's were also created.

NOT PRICED DUE TO SCARCITY

2003-04 Parkhurst Rookie Rookie Number Autographs

STATED PRINT RUN 10 SETS
NOT PRICED DUE TO SCARCITY
RNAP Andrew Peters
RNAR Andrew Raycroft
RNAS Alexander Semin
RNAV Antoine Vermette
RNBB Brent Burns
RNCH Chris Higgins
RNDF Dan Fritsche
RNDH Dan Hamhuis
RNDR Derek Roy
RNDHA David Hale
RNES Eric Staal
RNJL Joffrey Lupul
RNJP Joni Pitkanen
RNJLI John-Michael Liles
RNKL Kari Lehtonen
RNMF Marc-Andre Fleury
RNMR Michael Ryder
RNMST Matt Stajan
RNNH Nathan Horton
RNPB Patrice Bergeron
RNPM Paul Martin
RNRM Ryan Malone
RNTR Tuomo Ruutu

2003-04 Parkhurst Rookie ROYalty

*MULT.COLOR SWATCH: .6X TO 1.5X
PRINT RUN 50 SETS
GOLD PRINT RUN 10 SETS
GOLD NOT PRICED DUE TO SCARCITY
VR1 Dany Heatley 12.50 30.00
VR2 Martin Brodeur 20.00 50.00
VR3 Peter Forsberg 15.00 40.00
VR4 Daniel Alfredsson 10.00 25.00
VR5 Teemu Selanne 10.00 25.00
VR6 Sergei Samsonov 10.00 25.00
VR7 Ray Bourque 15.00 40.00
VR8 Brian Leetch 10.00 25.00
VR9 Mario Lemieux 30.00 80.00
VR10 Bobby Orr 75.00 150.00
VR11 Terry Sawchuk 15.00 40.00
VR12 Jacques Laperriere 10.00 25.00
VR13 Gilbert Perreault 12.50 30.00
VR14 Bryan Trottier 10.00 25.00
VR15 Denis Potvin 10.00 25.00
VR16 Roger Crozier 10.00 25.00
VR17 Pavel Bure 10.00 25.00
VR18 Ed Belfour 10.00 25.00
VR19 Glenn Hall 10.00 25.00
VR20 Evgeni Nabokov 10.00 25.00
VR21 Frank Brimsek 10.00 25.00
VR22 Mike Bossy 12.50 30.00
VR23 Luc Robitaille 10.00 25.00
VR24 Scott Gomez 10.00 25.00
VR25 Bernie Geoffrion 12.50 30.00
VR26 Gump Worsley 10.00 25.00
VR27 Joe Nieuwendyk 10.00 25.00
VR28 Tony Esposito 15.00 40.00

2003-04 Parkhurst Rookie ROYalty Autographs

PRINT RUN 10 SETS
NOT PRICED DUE TO SCARCITY
VRBL Brian Leetch
VRBO Bobby Orr
VRDH Dany Heatley
VRGW Gump Worsley
VRMB Martin Brodeur
VRML Mario Lemieux
VRPF Peter Forsberg
VRRB Ray Bourque
VRTE Tony Esposito

2003-04 Parkhurst Rookie Teammates

*MULT.COLOR SWATCH: .6X TO 1.5X
PRINT RUN 60 SETS
GOLD PRINT RUN 10 SETS
GOLD NOT PRICED DUE TO SCARCITY
RT1 M.Lemieux/M.Fleury 25.00 60.00
RT2 Sergei Fedorov 15.00 40.00
Joffrey Lupul
RT3 Mats Sundin 15.00 40.00
Matt Stajan
RT4 R.Nash/N.Zherdev 15.00 40.00
RT5 Mike Modano 8.00 20.00
Trevor Daley
RT6 Jay Bouwmeester 10.00 25.00
Nathan Horton
RT7 Alexander Frolov 8.00 20.00
Dustin Brown
RT8 Jason Spezza 10.00 25.00
Antoine Vermette
RT9 Jeremy Roenick 8.00 20.00
{Joni Pitkanen
RT10 Joe Sakic 10.00 25.00
Cody McCormick
RT11 Joe Thornton 15.00 40.00
Patrice Bergeron
RT12 Peter Forsberg 20.00 50.00
Marek Svatos
RT13 David Legwand 12.50 30.00
Jordin Tootoo
RT14 Keith Tkachuk 8.00 20.00
Peter Sejna
RT15 Scott Stevens 8.00 20.00
{Paul Martin
RT16 Jose Theodore 15.00 40.00
Michael Ryder
RT17 Rob Blake 8.00 20.00
John-Michael Liles
RT18 Jarome Iginla 10.00 25.00
{Matthew Lombardi
RT19 Miroslav Satan 8.00 20.00
Derek Roy
RT20 Saku Koivu 8.00 20.00
Chris Higgins
RT21 Mark Messier 15.00 40.00
Dominic Moore
RT22 Joceylyn Thibault 8.00 20.00
{Tuomo Ruutu

1971-72 Penguins Postcards

This 22-card set (measuring approximately 3 1/2" by 5 1/2") features full-bleed posed action color player photos. The cards originally came bound together in a flip book, but had perforations at the card top to allow them to be removed. The backs carry the player's name and biography in blue print on a white background. Only the Red Kelly card has a career summary on its back. The cards are unnumbered and checklisted below in alphabetical order. The set is dated by the inclusion of Roy Edwards, whose only season with the Penguins was 1971-72.

COMPLETE SET (22) 20.00 40.00
1 Syl Apps 1.25 2.50
2 Les Binkley 1.25 2.50
3 Dave Burrows 1.00 2.00
4 Darryl Edestrand .75 1.50
5 Roy Edwards 1.00 2.00
6 Val Fonteyne .75 1.50
7 Nick Harbaruk .75 1.50
8 Bryan Hextall 2.00 4.00
9 Sheldon Kannegiesser .75 1.50
10 Red Kelly CO 2.00 4.00
11 Bob Leiter .75 1.50
12 Keith McCreary .75 1.50
13 Joe Noris .75 1.50
14 Greg Polis .75 1.50
15 Jean Pronovost 2.00 4.00
16 Rene Robert 1.25 2.50
17 Jim Rutherford 1.25 2.50
18 Ken Schinkel .75 1.50
19 Ron Schock 1.00 2.00
20 Bryan Watson 1.00 2.00
21 Bob Woytowich .75 1.50
22 Title Card .75 1.50

1974-75 Penguins Postcards

This 22-card set features full-bleed black and white action pictures by photographer Paul Salva. The player's autograph is inscribed across the bottom of the picture. The cards are in the postcard format and measure approximately 3 1/2" by 5 1/2". The horizontal backs are blank. The cards are unnumbered and checklisted below in alphabetical order. The set is dated by the fact that Nelson Debenedet was only with the Penguins during the 1974-75 season. Pierre Larouche appears in this set prior to his Rookie Card appearance.

COMPLETE SET (22) 15.00 30.00
1 Syl Apps 1.25 2.50
2 Chuck Arnason .75 1.50
3 Dave Burrows 1.00 2.00
4 Colin Campbell 1.25 2.50
5 Nelson Debenedet .75 1.50
6 Steve Durbano .75 1.50
7 Vic Hadfield 1.00 2.00
8 Gary Inness 1.00 2.00
9 Bob(B.J.) Johnson .75 1.50
10 Rick Kehoe 1.25 2.50
11 Bob Kelly .75 1.50
12 Jean-Guy Lagace .75 1.50
13 Ron Lalonde .75 1.50
14 Pierre Larouche 2.50 5.00
15 Lowell MacDonald 1.00 2.00
16 Dennis Owchar .75 1.50
17 Bob Paradise .75 1.50
18 Kelly Pratt .75 1.50
19 Jean Pronovost 1.00 2.00
20 Ron Schock 1.00 2.00
21 Ron Stackhouse 1.00 2.00
22 Barry Williams .75 1.50

1977-78 Penguins Puck Bucks

This 18-card set of Pittsburgh Penguins was sponsored by McDonald's restaurants, whose company logo appears at the top of the card face. The cards measure approximately 1 15/16" by 3 1/2" and are perforated so that the bottom tab (measuring 1 15/16" by 1") may be removed. The front of the top portion features a color head shot of the player, with a white border on a mustard-colored background. The back of the top portion has "Hockey Talk," in which a hockey term is explained. The front side of the tab portion shows a hockey puck on an orange background. Its back states that the "puck bucks" are coupons worth 1.00 toward the purchase of any 7.50 Penguins game ticket. These coupons had to be redeemed no later than December 31, 1977.

COMPLETE SET (18) 12.50 25.00
1 Denis Herron 1.50 3.00
3 Ron Stackhouse 1.00 2.00
4 Dave Burrows .75 1.50
6 Colin Campbell 1.25 2.50
7 Russ Anderson .75 1.50
9 Blair Chapman .75 1.50
10 Pierre Larouche 1.50 3.00
12 Greg Malone 1.00 2.00
14 Wayne Bianchin .75 1.50
17 Rick Kehoe 1.50 3.00
18 Lowell MacDonald 1.00 2.00
19 Jean Pronovost 1.25 2.50
23 Jim Hamilton .75 1.50
25 Dennis Owchar .75 1.50
26 Syl Apps 1.00 2.00
27 Mike Corrigan .75 1.50
29 Dunc Wilson 1.00 2.00
NNO Johnny Wilson CO .50 1.00

1983-84 Penguins Coke

This 19-card set of the Pittsburgh Penguins measures approximately 5" by 7". The fronts feature black-and-white player portraits framed in white with the player's name, team name, team logo, and the words "Coke is it!" printed in black in the wide white bottom border. The backs are blank. The cards are unnumbered and checklisted below in alphabetical order. The card of Marty McSorley appears four years before his rookie card.

COMPLETE SET (19) 10.00 25.00
1 Pat Boutette .60 1.50
2 Andy Brickley .40 1.00
3 Mike Bullard .75 2.00
4 Ted Bulley .40 1.00
5 Rod Buskas .40 1.00
6 Randy Carlyle .75 2.00
7 Michel Dion .75 2.00
8 Bob Errey .75 2.00
9 Ron Flockhart .60 1.50
10 Steve Gatzos .40 1.00
11 Jim Hamilton .40 1.00
12 Dave Hannan .40 1.00
13 Denis Herron 1.00 2.50
14 Troy Loney .40 1.00
15 Bryan Maxwell .40 1.00
16 Marty McSorley 2.00 5.00
17 Norm Schmidt .40 1.00
18 Mark Taylor .40 1.00
19 Greg Tebbutt .40 1.00

1983-84 Penguins Heinz Photos

This Pittsburgh Penguins "Photo Pak" was sponsored by Heinz. The cards are unnumbered and checklisted below in alphabetical order. They were giveaways at Pittsburgh Penguins home games. Each photo measures approximately 6" by 9" and they were produced on one large folded sheet.

COMPLETE SET (22) 10.00 25.00
1 Paul Baxter .60 1.50
2 Pat Boutette .60 1.50
3 Randy Boyd .40 1.00
4 Mike Bullard .75 2.00
5 Randy Carlyle .75 2.00
6 Marc Chorney .40 1.00
7 Michel Dion .75 2.00
8 Bill Gardner .40 1.00
9 Pat Graham .40 1.00
10 Anders Hakansson .40 1.00
11 Dave Hannan .40 1.00
12 Denis Herron 1.00 2.50
13 Greg Hotham .40 1.00
14 Stan Jonathan .60 1.50
15 Rick Kehoe .60 1.50
16 Peter Lee .75 2.00
17 Greg Malone .60 1.50
18 Kevin McClelland .40 1.00
19 Ron Meighan .40 1.00
20 Doug Shedden .40 1.00
21 Andre St. Laurent .40 1.00
22 Rich Sutter .60 1.50

1984-85 Penguins Heinz Photos

This Pittsburgh Penguins "Photo Pak" was sponsored by Heinz. The cards are unnumbered and checklisted below in alphabetical order. They were giveaways at Pittsburgh Penguins home games. Each photo measures approximately 6" by 9" and they were produced on one large folded sheet.

COMPLETE SET (22) 10.00 25.00
1 Pat Boutette .60 1.50
2 Andy Brickley .40 1.00
3 Mike Bullard .75 2.00
4 Rod Buskas .40 1.00
5 Randy Carlyle .75 2.00
6 Michel Dion .75 2.00
7 Bob Errey .60 1.50
8 Ron Flockhart .40 1.00
9 Greg Fox .40 1.00
10 Steve Gatzos .40 1.00
11 Denis Herron 1.00 2.50
12 Greg Hotham .40 1.00
13 Rick Kehoe .75 2.00
14 Bryan Maxwell .40 1.00
15 Marty McSorley 2.00 5.00
16 Tom O'Regan .40 1.00
17 Gary Rissling .40 1.00
18 Roberto Romano .60 1.50
19 Tom Roulston .40 1.00
20 Rocky Saganiuk .40 1.00
21 Doug Shedden .60 1.50
22 Mark Taylor .40 1.00

1986-87 Penguins Kodak

The 1986-87 Pittsburgh Penguins Team Photo Album was sponsored by Kodak and commemorates the team's 20 years in the NHL. It consists of three large sheets, each measuring approximately 11" by 8 1/4", joined together to form one continuous sheet. The first panel has a team photo of the 1967 Pittsburgh Penguins. The second panel presents three rows of five cards each. The third panel presents two rows of five cards, with five Kodak coupons completing the left over portion of the panel. After perforation, the cards measure approximately 2 3/16" by 2 1/2". They feature color posed photos bordered in yellow, with player information below the picture. A Kodak film box serving as a logo completes the card face. The back has biographical and statistical information in a horizontal format. We have checklisted the names below in alphabetical order, with the uniform number to the right of the name.

COMPLETE SET (26) 20.00 50.00
1 Bob Berry CO .20 .50
2 Mike Blaisdell 26 .40 1.00
3 Doug Bodger 3 .40 1.00
4 Rod Buskas 7 .30 .75
5 John Chabot 9 .30 .75
6 Randy Cunneyworth 15 .30 .75
7 Ron Duguay 10 .40 1.00
8 Bob Errey 12 .40 1.00
9 Dan Frawley 28 .30 .75
10 Dave Hannan 32 .30 .75
11 Randy Hillier 23 .30 .75
12 Jim Johnson 6 .30 .75
13 Kevin Lavallee 16 .30 .75
14 Mario Lemieux 66 12.00 30.00
15 Willy Lindstrom 19 .30 .75
16 Moe Mantha 20 .30 .75
17 Gilles Meloche 27 .40 1.00
18 Dan Quinn 14 .40 1.00
19 Jim Roberts CO .20 .50
20 Roberto Romano 30 .40 1.00
21 Terry Ruskowski 8 .40 1.00
22 Norm Schmidt 25 .40 1.00
23 Craig Simpson 18 .60 1.50
24 Ville Siren 5 .30 .75
25 Warren Young 35 .40 1.00
NNO '67 Team Photo .75 2.00

1987-88 Penguins Masks

These masks were issued by KDKA and Eagle Food Stores. Mask fronts show top of players head, and backs feature name, stats, and sponsors logos. These masks are unnumbered and checklisted below in alphabetical order.

COMPLETE SET (10) 8.00 20.00
1 Doug Bodger .40 1.00
2 Randy Cunneyworth .40 1.00
3 Bob Errey .40 1.00
4 Dan Frawley .40 1.00
5 Jim Johnson .40 1.00
6 Mario Lemieux 4.00 10.00
7 Gilles Meloche .75 2.00
8 Dan Quinn .40 1.00
9 Craig Simpson .75 2.00
10 Ville Siren .40 1.00

1987-88 Penguins Kodak

The 1987-88 Pittsburgh Penguins Team Photo Album was sponsored by Kodak. It consists of three large sheets, each measuring approximately 11" by 8 1/4", joined together to form one continuous sheet. The first panel has a team photo, with the players' names listed according to rows below the picture. The second panel presents three rows of five cards each. The third panel presents two rows of five cards, with five Kodak coupons completing the left over portion of the panel. After perforation, the cards measure approximately 2 3/16" by 2 1/2". A Kodak film box serves as a logo in the upper right hand corner of the card face. The front features a color head shot inside a thin black border. The picture is set on a Kodak "yellow" background, with white stripes traversing the top of the card. The player's name, number, and position are printed in black lettering below the picture. The back has biographical information and career statistics in a horizontal format. We have checklisted the cards below in alphabetical order, with the player's number to the right of his name.

COMPLETE SET (26) 14.00 35.00
1 Doug Bodger 3 .30 .75
2 Rob Brown 44 .40 1.00
3 Rod Buskas 7 .30 .75
4 Jock Callander 36 .30 .75
5 Paul Coffey 77 .75 2.00
6 Randy Cunneyworth 15 .30 .75
7 Chris Dahlquist 4 .30 .75
8 Bob Errey 12 .30 .75
9 Dan Frawley 28 .30 .75
10 Steve Guenette 30 .40 1.00
11 Randy Hillier 23 .30 .75
12 Dave Hunter 20 .30 .75
13 Jim Johnson 6 .30 .75
14 Mark Kachowski 26 .30 .75
15 Chris Kontos 14 .30 .75
16 Mario Lemieux 66 6.00 15.00
17 Troy Loney 24 .30 .75
18 Dwight Mathiasen 34 .30 .75
19 Dave McLlwain 19 .30 .75
20 Gilles Meloche 27 .40 1.00
21 Dan Quinn 10 .40 1.00
22 Pat Riggin 1 .40 1.00
23 Charlie Simmer 16 .40 1.00
24 Ville Siren 5 .30 .75
25 Wayne Van Dorp .30 .75
NNO Large Team Photo 1.50 4.00

1989-90 Penguins Coke/Elby's

This set measures approximately 4" by 6" and features color action player photos bordered in white with player information at the top and sponsor logos in the bottom margin. The backs are blank except for a coupon for free burger and fries at participating Elby's Big Boy restaurants. The cards are unnumbered and checklisted below in alphabetical order.

COMPLETE SET (5) 4.80 12.00
1 Phil Bourque .20 .50
2 Rob Brown .30 .75
3 Mario Lemieux 4.00 10.00
4 Kevin Stevens .75 2.00
5 Zarley Zalapski .30 .75

1989-90 Penguins Foodland

This 15-card set was sponsored by Foodland in conjunction with the Pittsburgh Penguins and the Crime Prevention Officers of Western Pennsylvania. The Foodland company logo appears on the top and back of each card. The cards measure approximately 2 9/16" by 4 1/8" and could be collected from police officers. The front features a color action photo with a thin black border on white card stock. The player information below the picture is sandwiched between the Penguin and the Crime Dog McGruff logos. The back is dated and presents a Penguins tip and a safety tip (both illustrated with cartoons) in a horizontal format. There were two late issue cards distributed after trades. They are rather scarce and not typically considered part of the complete set.

COMPLETE SET (15) 8.00 20.00
1 Rob Brown .30 .75
2 Jim Johnson .20 .50
3 Zarley Zalapski .30 .75
4 Paul Coffey .75 2.00
5 Phil Bourque .20 .50
6A Dan Quinn .30 .75
6B Gilbert Delorme SP .75 2.00
7 Kevin Stevens .75 2.00
8 Bob Errey .20 .50
9 John Cullen .30 .75
10 Mario Lemieux 4.00 10.00
11 Randy Hillier .20 .50
12 Jay Caufield .20 .50
13A Andrew McBain .20 .50
13B Troy Loney SP .75 2.00
14 Wendell Young .30 .75
15 Tom Barrasso .40 1.00

1990-91 Penguins Foodland

This 15-card set was sponsored by Foodland in conjunction with the Pittsburgh Penguins and the Crime Prevention Officers of Western Pennsylvania. The Foodland company logo appears at the bottom of the card front and the top of the horizontally oriented back. The cards measure approximately 2 11/16" by 4 1/8" and could be collected from police officers. The front features a color action photo with a thin black border surrounded by wide yellow margins on three sides. The team name is printed in white block lettering, running the length of the card on the left side of the picture. The back presents a Penguins tip and a safety tip (both illustrated with cartoons). The set features the appearance of three Penguins, Jaromir Jagr, Mark Recchi, and Kevin Stevens, in their Rookie Card year.

COMPLETE SET (15) 12.00 30.00
1 Phil Bourque 29 .08 .25
2 Paul Coffey 77 .40 1.00
3 Randy Hillier 23 .08 .25
4 Barry Pederson 10 .15 .40
5 Tom Barrasso 35 .30 .75
6 Mark Recchi 8 .75 2.00
7 Bob Johnson CO .75 2.00
8 Joe Mullen 7 .30 .75
9 Kevin Stevens 25 .60 1.50
10 John Cullen 11 .15 .40
11 Jaromir Jagr 68 10.00 25.00
12 Zarley Zalapski 33 .15 .40
13 Mario Lemieux 66 3.00 8.00
14 Tony Tanti 9 .08 .25
15 Bryan Trottier 19 .30 .75

1991-92 Penguins Coke/Elby's

This 24-card set was sponsored by Cola-Cola in conjunction with Elby's Big Boy restaurants. The cards measure approximately 4" by 6" and are printed on thin card stock. The headline "1990-91 Stanley Cup Champions" adorns the top of each front. Immediately below appears the uniform number, player's name, and a twenty-fifth anniversary team logo. The color action player photos are bordered in white, with the two sponsor logos appearing in the bottom white border. The backs are blank. The cards are skip-numbered by uniform number and checklisted below accordingly.

COMPLETE SET (24) 10.00 25.00
1 Wendell Young .30 .75
2 Jim Paek .20 .50
3 Grant Jennings .20 .50
5 Ulf Samuelsson .40 1.00
7 Joe Mullen .40 1.00
8 Mark Recchi .75 2.00
10 Ron Francis 1.00 2.50
16 Jay Caufield .20 .50
18 Ken Priestlay .20 .50
19 Bryan Trottier .40 1.00
20 Jamie Leach .20 .50
22 Paul Stanton .20 .50
24 Troy Loney .20 .50
25 Kevin Stevens .40 1.00
28 Gord Roberts .20 .50
29 Phil Bourque .20 .50
32 Peter Taglianetti .20 .50
40 Frank Pietrangelo .30 .75
43 Jeff Daniels .20 .50
55 Larry Murphy .40 1.00
66 Mario Lemieux 2.50 6.00
68 Jaromir Jagr 3.00 8.00
NNO Scotty Bowman CO .40 1.00

1991-92 Penguins Foodland

This 15-card standard-size set was sponsored by Foodland in conjunction with the Pittsburgh Penguins and the Crime Prevention Officers of Western Pennsylvania. The Foodland logo and McGruff the Crime Dog appear at the bottom of the card face, while a 25th year anniversary emblem appears at the top center. The fronts feature color action player photos on an orangish-yellow card face. The player's name, uniform number, and his position appear in the top silver stripe; the words "1991 Stanley Cup Champions" appears in another silver stripe beneath the picture. The horizontally oriented backs have a "Penguins Tip" and a "Safety Tip," each of which is illustrated by a cartoon.

COMPLETE SET (15) 8.00 20.00
1 Jim Paek .20 .50
2 Ulf Samuelsson .30 .75
3 Ron Francis .75 2.00
4 Mario Lemieux 3.00 8.00
5 Rick Tocchet .40 1.00
6 Joe Mullen .40 1.00
7 Troy Loney .20 .50
8 Kevin Stevens .30 .75
9 Tom Barrasso .40 1.00
10 Larry Murphy .30 .75
11 Jaromir Jagr 3.00 8.00
12 Bryan Trottier .40 1.00
13 Paul Stanton .20 .50
14 Peter Taglianetti .20 .50
15 Phil Bourque .20 .50

1991-92 Penguins Foodland Coupon Stickers

This set of twelve stickers is the result of a unique cross-promotion with Topps and the Foodland stores of Pittsburgh. The stickers, issued in a 3-sticker sheet over a four week period, mimic the 1991-92 Topps card of a Penguin player on the front, with a coupon for Foodland on the peel-off backs. Most feature the player's regular card front; exceptions are Jaromir Jagr (Super Rookie), Mario Lemieux (Award Winner) and Kevin Stevens (All-Star). The stickers are unnumbered, but are listed below in issue of order, top to bottom, per week.

COMPLETE SET (12) 6.00 15.00
1 Bryan Trottier .30 .75
2 Joe Mullen .30 .75
3 Larry Murphy .30 .75
4 Tom Barrasso .30 .75
5 Ron Francis .60 1.50
6 Ulf Samuelsson .30 .75
7 Jaromir Jagr 2.50 6.00
8 Mario Lemieux 2.50 6.00
9 Kevin Stevens .30 .75
10 Mark Recchi .40 1.00
11 Paul Coffey .60 1.50
12 Frank Pietrangelo .30 .75

1992-93 Penguins Coke/Clark

This 26-card set was sponsored by Cola-Cola and Clark. These cards followed the same concept as Coke/Elby's sets of the previous years, i.e., large autograph cards issued to the players for use in personal appearances. The cards measure approximately 4" by 6" and were printed on thin card stock. The backs are blank. The cards are unnumbered and checklisted below in alphabetical order.

COMPLETE SET (26) 10.00 25.00
1 Tom Barrasso .40 1.00
2 Scotty Bowman CO .60 1.50
3 Jay Caufield .20 .50
4 Jeff Daniels .20 .50
5 Bob Errey .20 .50
6 Bryan Fogarty .20 .50
7 Ron Francis .75 2.00
8 Jaromir Jagr 2.50 6.00
9 Grant Jennings .20 .50
10 Mario Lemieux 2.50 6.00
11 Troy Loney .20 .50
12 Shawn McEachern .40 1.00
13 Joe Mullen .40 1.00
14 Larry Murphy .40 1.00
15 Mike Needham .20 .50
16 Jim Paek .20 .50
17 Kjell Samuelsson .20 .50
18 Ulf Samuelsson .30 .75
19 Paul Stanton .20 .50
20 Mike Stapleton .20 .50
21 Kevin Stevens .30 .75
22 Martin Straka .40 1.00
23 Dave Tippett .20 .50
24 Rick Tocchet .50 1.25
25 Ken Wregget .50 1.25
26 Penguins Mascot .08 .25

1992-93 Penguins Foodland

This 18-card standard-size set was sponsored by Foodland in conjunction with the Pittsburgh Penguins and the Crime Prevention Officers of Western Pennsylvania. The cards feature color action player photos with orange-yellow borders on a black card face. The player's name is printed in an orange-yellow stripe below the photo. The words "1991 and 1992 Stanley Cup Champions" are on an orange-yellow bar that overlaps the top of the picture. The Foodland logo and McGruff the Crime Dog appear at the bottom. The horizontal backs have a "Penguins Tip" and a "Safety Tip," each illustrated with a cartoon.

COMPLETE SET (18) 6.00 15.00
1 Mario Lemieux 2.00 5.00
2 Bob Errey .20 .50
3 Jaromir Jagr 1.25 3.00
4 Rick Tocchet .40 1.00
5 Tom Barrasso .40 1.00
6 Joe Mullen .30 .75
7 Ron Francis .75 2.00
8 Troy Loney .20 .50
9 Shawn McEachern .20 .50
10 Larry Murphy .30 .75
11 Jim Paek .20 .50
12 Ulf Samuelsson .20 .50
13 Paul Stanton .20 .50
14 Kjell Samuelsson .20 .50
15 Kevin Stevens .30 .75
16 Dave Tippett .20 .50
17 Martin Straka .40 1.00
18 Penguins Mascot .08 .25

1992-93 Penguins Foodland Coupon Stickers

Sponsored by Foodland and issued in four three-sticker vertical strips, this 12-sticker set features white-bordered color player action photos, with the peel-away backs doubling as manufacturer coupons for different products. Each sticker measures the standard size. The player's name and uniform number appear in a yellow bar under the photo and the words "Back to Back Champs" are printed in a bar alongside the left. The team logo also appears on the front. The strips are numbered as Week 1-4; the stickers themselves are unnumbered. The players are listed below in alphabetical order; W1 to W4 indicates the week the stickers were issued.

COMPLETE SET (12) 6.00 15.00
1 Tom Barrasso W2 .40 1.00
2 Ron Francis W1 .60 1.50
3 Jaromir Jagr W4 2.00 5.00
4 Mario Lemieux W2 2.50 6.00
5 Troy Loney W2 .20 .50
6 Shawn McEachern W4 .20 .50
7 Joe Mullen W3 .30 .75
8 Larry Murphy W4 .30 .75
9 Jim Paek W1 .20 .50
10 Ulf Samuelsson W3 .20 .50
11 Kevin Stevens W1 .30 .75
12 Rick Tocchet W3 .40 1.00

1993-94 Penguins Foodland

Sponsored by Foodland, this 25-card standard-size set features the 1993-94 Pittsburgh Penguins. The fronts have color action player photos with black borders on gray backgrounds. The team name appears in the top part of the card, while the player's name, number and position are printed under the photo. The sponsor's logo on the bottom rounds out the front. The horizontal backs have a "Penguin Tip" and a "Safety Tip," each illustrated with a cartoon.

COMPLETE SET (25) 6.00 15.00
1 Mario Lemieux 1.50 4.00
2 Grant Jennings .15 .40
3 Ulf Samuelsson .20 .50
4 Rick Tocchet .30 .75
5 Marty McSorley .30 .75
6 Rick Kehoe ACO .08 .25
7 Doug Brown .15 .40
8 Martin Straka .20 .50
9 Jim Paek .15 .40
10 Ken Wregget .20 .50
11 Jeff Daniels .15 .40
12 Bryan Trottier .20 .50
13 Larry Murphy .20 .50
14 Ron Francis .40 1.00
15 Mike Needham .15 .40
16 Mike Ramsey .15 .40
17 Kevin Stevens .20 .50
18 Kjell Samuelsson .15 .40
19 Ed Johnston CO .08 .25
20 Markus Naslund .20 .50
21 Mike Stapleton .15 .40
22 Peter Taglianetti .15 .40
23 Jaromir Jagr .75 2.00
24 Tom Barrasso .20 .50
25 Joe Mullen .20 .50

1994-95 Penguins Foodland

Sponsored by Foodland, this 25-card standard-size set features the 1994-1995 Pittsburgh Penguins. The fronts have color action player photos with gray borders on marbleized gray backgrounds. The team name across the top part of the card, while the player's name, number, position, and the team logo are printed under the picture. The horizontal backs carry a "Penguin Tip" and a "Safety Tip", each illustrated with a cartoon.

COMPLETE SET (25) 4.80 12.00
1 Grant Jennings .10 .30
2 Greg Hawgood .10 .30
3 Shawn McEachern .20 .50
4 Len Barrie .10 .30
5 Ulf Samuelsson .20 .50
6 Joe Mullen .20 .50
7 John Cullen .10 .30
8 Mike Hudson .10 .30
9 Ron Francis .40 1.00
10 Tomas Sandstrom .20 .50
11 Eddie Johnston CO .08 .25
12 Chris Tamer .10 .30
13 Francois Leroux .10 .30
14 Luc Robitaille .40 1.00
15 Markus Naslund .20 .50
16 Ken Wregget .20 .50
17 Chris Joseph .10 .30
18 Peter Taglianetti .10 .30
19 Kevin Stevens .20 .50
20 Jim McKenzie .10 .30
21 Kjell Samuelsson .10 .30
22 Tom Barrasso .20 .50
23 Jaromir Jagr 1.50 4.00
24 Larry Murphy .20 .50
25 Martin Straka .10 .30

1995-96 Penguins Foodland

This 25-card set maintains the string of issues released by Foodland, a Pittsburgh-area grocery chain, to honor the hometown Penguins. The cards feature action player photos surrounded by an icy blue border on the front. The backs have two Penguin tips, and the card number. Card number 24 erroneously pictures Ian Moran instead of Bryan Smolinski. The error is not believed to have been corrected.

COMPLETE SET (25) 4.00 10.00
1 Ron Francis .40 1.00
2 Glen Murray .08 .25
3 Chris Wells .08 .25
4 Markus Naslund .10 .30
5 Jaromir Jagr 1.25 3.00
6 Francois Leroux .08 .25
7 Richard Park .08 .25
8 Norm Maciver .08 .25
9 Ken Wregget .20 .50
10 Tom Barrasso .20 .50
11 Rick Kehoe ACO .08 .25
12 Sergei Zubov .20 .50
13 Joe Dziedzic .08 .25
14 Ed Patterson .08 .25
15 Tomas Sandstrom .10 .30
16 Dave Roche .08 .25
17 Petr Nedved .20 .50
18 Chris Tamer .08 .25
19 Chris Joseph .08 .25
20 Ian Moran .08 .25
21 Iceburgh (Mascot) .02 .10
22 Ed Johnston CO .08 .25
23 Mario Lemieux 1.50 4.00
24 Bryan Smolinski .10 .30
UER photo shown Chris Wells
25 Dmitri Mironov .10 .30

1996-97 Penguins Tribune-Review

These oversized 5" x 7" thick stock cards were distributed as inserts in the Penguins game programs to honor the club's two Cup championships of the early '90s. As issued, the cards were folded in half, with the first two "pages" explaining the promotion, the third page actually containing the card/photo, and the fourth page offering biographical info and stats from one of the two seasons.

COMPLETE SET (8) 12.00 30.00
1 Ron Francis 1.50 4.00
2 Joe Mullen .75 2.00
3 Ulf Samuelsson .75 2.00
4 Bryan Trottier 1.25 3.00
5 Tom Barrasso .75 2.00
6 Kevin Stevens 1.25 3.00
7 Jaromir Jagr 3.00 8.00
8 Mario Lemieux 4.00 10.00

1997-98 Penguins USPS Lineup Cards

These oversized issues were inserted in Penguins programs and were sponsored by the post office. The front featured a glossy player photo, while the back listed that night's lineups. This obviously is not a complete listing. Anyone who can help fill it in is encouraged to write hockeymag@beckett.com.

COMPLETE SET (?) 3.00 8.00
NNO Darius Kasparaitis .75 2.00
NNO Jaromir Jagr 2.00 5.00
NNO Ron Francis .75 2.00

1980-81 Pepsi-Cola Caps

This set of 140 bottle caps features 20 players from each of the seven Canadian hockey teams. The bottle caps are written in French and English. There are two sizes of caps depending on whether the cap was from a small or large bottle. The top of the cap displays the Pepsi logo in the familiar red, white, and blue. The sides of the cap were done in blue and white lettering on a pink background. On the inside of the cap is a "black and aluminum" head shot of the player, with his name and the city (from which the team hails) below. We have checklisted the caps in alphabetical order of the teams as follows: Calgary Flames (1-20), Edmonton Oilers (21-40), Montreal Canadiens (41-60), Quebec Nordiques (61-80), Toronto Maple Leafs (81-100), Vancouver Canucks (101-120), and Winnipeg Jets (121-140). Also the players' names have been alphabetized within their teams. Also available through a mail-in offer -- in either English or French -- was a white plastic circular display plaque (approximately 24" by 24") for the caps. The French version sometimes sells for a slight premium. There also are reports that two different size variations exist: a 10 ounce and a 26 ounce size. There does not appear to be a premium on either size cap at this time.

COMPLETE SET (140) 100.00 200.00
1 Dan Bouchard .75 2.00
2 Guy Chouinard .75 2.00
3 Bill Clement .75 2.00
4 Randy Holt .60 1.50
5 Ken Houston .60 1.50
6 Kevin Lavallee .60 1.50
7 Don Lever .60 1.50
8 Bob MacMillan .60 1.50
9 Brad Marsh 1.00 2.50
10 Bob Murdoch .60 1.50
11 Kent Nilsson .75 2.00
12 Willi Plett .75 2.00
13 Jim Peplinski .75 2.00
14 Pekka Rautakillio .60 1.50
15 Paul Reinhart .75 2.00
16 Pat Riggin .75 2.00
17 Phil Russell .60 1.50
18 Brad Smith .60 1.50
19 Eric Vail .60 1.50
20 Bert Wilson .60 1.50
21 Glenn Anderson 1.50 4.00
22 Curt Brackenbury .60 1.50
23 Brett Callighen .60 1.50
24 Paul Coffey 7.50 15.00
25 Lee Fogolin .60 1.50
26 Matti Hagman .60 1.50
27 John Hughes .60 1.50
28 Dave Hunter .60 1.50
29 Jari Kurri 4.00 8.00
30 Ron Low .75 2.00
31 Kevin Lowe 1.00 2.50
32 Dave Lumley .60 1.50
33 Blair MacDonald .60 1.50
34 Mark Messier 12.50 25.00
35 Ed Mio .75 2.00
36 Don Murdoch .60 1.50
37 Pat Price .60 1.50
38 Dave Semenko .75 2.00
39 Risto Siltanen .60 1.50
40 Stan Weir .60 1.50
41 Keith Acton .60 1.50
42 Brian Engblom .60 1.50
43 Bob Gainey 1.25 3.00
44 Gaston Gingras .60 1.50
45 Denis Herron .75 2.00
46 Rejean Houle .60 1.50
47 Doug Jarvis .60 1.50
48 Yvon Lambert .60 1.50
49 Rod Langway 1.25 3.00
50 Guy Lapointe .75 2.00
51 Pierre Larouche 1.00 2.50
52 Pierre Mondou .60 1.50
53 Mark Napier .75 2.00
54 Chris Nilan 1.00 2.50
55 Doug Risebrough .60 1.50
56 Larry Robinson 1.50 4.00
57 Serge Savard .75 2.00
58 Steve Shutt 1.25 3.00
59 Mario Tremblay .75 2.00
60 Doug Wickenheiser .60 1.50
61 Serge Bernier .60 1.50
62 Kim Clackson .75 2.00
63 Real Cloutier .60 1.50
64 Andre Dupont .60 1.50
65 Robbie Ftorek .75 2.00
66 Michel Goulet 2.50 5.00
67 Jamie Hislop .60 1.50
68 Dale Hoganson .60 1.50
69 Dale Hunter 1.50 4.00
70 Pierre Lacroix .60 1.50
71 Garry Lariviere .60 1.50
72 Rich Leduc .60 1.50
73 John Paddock .75 2.00
74 Michel Plasse .75 2.00
75 Jacques Richard .60 1.50
76 Anton Stastny .75 2.00
77 Peter Stastny 3.00 6.00
78 Mark Tardif .75 2.00
79 Wally Weir .60 1.50
80 John Wensink .75 2.00
81 John Anderson .60 1.50
82 Laurie Boschman .60 1.50
83 Jiri Crha .75 2.00
84 Bill Derlago .60 1.50
85 Vitezslav Duris .60 1.50
86 Ron Ellis .75 2.00
87 Dave Farrish .60 1.50
88 Stewart Gavin .75 2.00
89 Pat Hickey .60 1.50
90 Dan Maloney .75 2.00
91 Terry Martin .60 1.50
92 Barry Melrose .75 2.00
93 Wilf Paiement .75 2.00
94 Robert Picard .60 1.50
95 Jim Rutherford 1.00 2.50
96 Rocky Saganiuk .60 1.50
97 Borje Salming 1.25 3.00
98 David Shand .60 1.50
99 Ian Turnbull .75 2.00
100 Rick Vaive 1.00 2.50
101 Brent Ashton .60 1.50
102 Ivan Boldirev .60 1.50
103 Per-Olov Brasar .60 1.50
104 Richard Brodeur 1.00 2.50
105 Jerry Butler .60 1.50
106 Colin Campbell .75 2.00
107 Curt Fraser .60 1.50
108 Thomas Gradin .75 2.00
109 Dennis Kearns .60 1.50
110 Rick Lanz .60 1.50
111 Lars Lindgren .60 1.50
112 Dave Logan .60 1.50
113 Mario Marois .60 1.50
114 Kevin McCarthy .60 1.50
115 Gerald Minor .60 1.50
116 Darcy Rota .60 1.50
117 Bobby Schmautz .60 1.50
118 Stan Smyl .75 2.00
119 Harold Snepsts 1.00 2.50
120 Dave(Tiger) Williams 1.00 2.50
121 Dave Babych .75 2.00
122 Al Cameron .60 1.50
123 Scott Campbell .60 1.50
124 Dave Christian .75 2.00
125 Jude Drouin .60 1.50
126 Norm Dupont .60 1.50
127 Dan Geoffrion .60 1.50
128 Pierre Hamel .60 1.50
129 Barry Legge .60 1.50
130 Willy Lindstrom .60 1.50
131 Barry Long .60 1.50
132 Kris Manery .60 1.50
133 Jimmy Mann .75 2.00
134 Moe Mantha .60 1.50
135 Markus Mattsson .75 2.00
136 Doug Smail .75 2.00
137 Don Spring .60 1.50
138 Anders Steen .60 1.50
139 Peter Sullivan .60 1.50
140 Ron Wilson .60 1.50
NNO Plastic Circular Display 40.00 80.00

2007-08 Pepsi

COMPLETE SET (32) 25.00 50.00
AVAIL. ON CDN PEPSI PACKAGES
1 Sidney Crosby 5.00 12.00
2 Joe Sakic 2.00 5.00
3 Nicklas Lidstrom 1.25 3.00
4 Saku Koivu 1.00 2.50
5 Daniel Alfredsson 1.00 2.50
6 Vincent Lecavalier 1.25 3.00
7 Mats Sundin 1.25 3.00
8 Patrice Bergeron 1.25 3.00
9 Rick Nash 1.25 3.00
10 Marian Gaborik 1.50 4.00
11 Jaromir Jagr 2.00 5.00
12 Simon Gagne 1.25 3.00
13 Doug Weight .75 2.00
14 Duncan Keith 1.25 3.00
15 Jay Bouwmeester .75 2.00
16 Rob Blake 1.00 2.50
17 Shea Weber .75 2.00
18 Ed Jovanovski .75 2.00
19 Ryan Miller 1.25 3.00
20 Miikka Kiprusoff 1.50 4.00
21 Marty Turco 1.25 3.00
22 Dwayne Roloson 1.00 2.50
23 Martin Brodeur 2.50 6.00
24 Rick DiPietro 1.00 2.50
25 Roberto Luongo 2.00 5.00
26 Jean-Sebastien Giguere 1.25 3.00
27 Ilya Kovalchuk 1.50 4.00
28 Cam Ward 1.25 3.00
29 Evgeni Malkin 2.50 6.00
30 Joe Thornton 1.50 4.00
31 Alexander Ovechkin 3.00 8.00
32 Sidney Crosby 5.00 12.00

2007-08 Pepsi 3x5 Stanley Cup Champion

COMPLETE SET (7) 6.00 15.00
1 Jean-Sebastien Giguere 1.00 2.50
2 Patrik Elias .60 1.50
3 Nicklas Lidstrom 1.00 2.50
4 Rob Brind' Amour .75 2.00
5 Chris Drury .75 2.00
6 Ryan Getzlaf .75 2.00
7 Mark Messier 2.00 5.00

1972-73 Philadelphia Blazers

These postcard-like issues feature the short-lived Blazers of the WHA. While we have confirmed just three cards, it is believed that many more exist. The cards are unnumbered and checklisted below in alphabetical order.

COMPLETE SET (3) 15.00 30.00
1 Danny Lawson 5.00 10.00
2 Bernie Parent 10.00 20.00
3 Ron Plumb 5.00 10.00

1974-75 Phoenix Roadrunners WHA Pins

These pins feature color head shots and measure 3 1/2" in diameter. Player name and team name are featured in a black rectangle at the bottom of the pin. Pins are checklisted below in alphabetical order.

COMPLETE SET (9) 20.00 40.00
1 Bob Barlow 2.00 4.00
2 Cam Connor 2.00 4.00
3 Michel Cormier 2.00 4.00
4 Robbie Ftorek 6.00 12.00
5 Dave Gorman 2.00 4.00
6 John Hughes 2.00 4.00
7 Murray Keogan 2.00 4.00
8 Dennis Sobchuk 2.00 4.00
9 Howie Young 2.00 4.00

1975-76 Phoenix Roadrunners WHA

This 22-card set features players of the WHA Phoenix Roadrunners. The cards measure approximately 3" by 4" and the backs are blank. The front features a poor quality black and white head-and-shoulders shot of the player with a white border. The cards are numbered by the uniform number on the front and we have checklisted them below accordingly. The player's position and weight are also given.

COMPLETE SET (22) 25.00 50.00
1 Serge Beaudoin 1.00 2.00
2 Jim Boyd 1.00 2.00
3 Jim Clarke 1.00 2.00
4 Cam Connors 1.00 2.00
5 Michel Cormier 1.00 2.00
6 Barry Dean 1.00 2.00
7 Robbie Ftorek 7.50 15.00
8 Dave Gorman 1.50 3.00
9 John gray 1.00 2.00
10 Del Hall 1.00 2.00
11 Ron Huston 1.00 2.00
12 Murray Keogan 1.00 2.00
13 Gary Kurt 1.00 2.00
14 Garry Lariviere 1.00 2.00
15 Al McLeod 1.00 2.00
16 Peter McNamee 1.00 2.00
17 John Migneault 1.00 2.00
18 Lauri Mononen 1.00 2.00
19 Jim Niekamp 1.00 2.00
20 Jack Norris 1.00 2.00
21 Pekka Rautakallio 2.00 4.00
22 Ron Serafini 1.00 2.00

1976-77 Phoenix Roadrunners WHA

This 18-card set features players of the WHA Phoenix Roadrunners. Each card measures approximately 3 3/8" by 4 5/16". The front features a black and white head shot of the player, enframed by an aqua blue border on white card stock. The top and bottom inner borders are curved, creating space for the basic biographical information as well as the team and league logos that surround the picture. The backs are blank. The cards are unnumbered and we have checklisted them below in alphabetical order.

COMPLETE SET (18) 25.00 50.00
1 Serge Beaudoin 1.00 2.00
2 Michel Cormier 1.00 2.00
3 Robbie Ftorek 7.50 15.00
4 Del Hall 1.00 2.00
5 Clay Hebenton 1.00 2.00
6 Andre Hinse 1.00 2.00
7 Mike Hobin 1.00 2.00
8 Frank Hughes 1.00 2.00
9 Ron Huston 1.00 2.00
10 Gary Kurt 1.00 2.00
11 Garry Lariviere 1.00 2.00
12 Bob Liddington 1.00 2.00
13 Lauri Mononen 1.00 2.00
14 Jim Niekamp 1.00 2.00
15 Pekka Rautakallio 2.00 4.00
16 Seppo Repo 1.00 2.00
17 Jerry Rollins 1.00 2.00
18 Juhani Tamminen 2.00 4.00

1991-92 Pinnacle

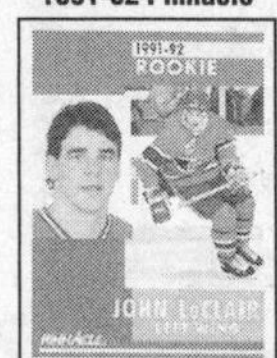

The 1991-92 (Score) Pinnacle Hockey set was issued in English and French editions; each set consists of 420 standard-size cards. The front design of the veteran player cards features two color photos, an action photo and a head shot, on a black background with white borders. The card backs have a color action shot silhouetted against a black background. The rookie cards have the same design, except with green background on the front, and black-and-white head shots rather than action shots on the back. The backs of the veteran player cards include biography, player profile, and statistics, while those of the rookie cards only have a player profile. Rookie Cards include Tony Amonte, Valeri Kamensky, John LeClair, Nicklas Lidstrom, Geoff Sanderson and Doug Weight.

COMPLETE SET (420) 10.00 25.00
1 Mario Lemieux .40 1.00
2 Trevor Linden .05 .15
3 Kirk Muller .02 .10
4 Phil Housley .05 .15
5 Mike Modano .30 .75
6 Adam Oates .05 .15
7 Tom Kurvers .02 .10
8 Doug Bodger .02 .10
9 Rod Brind'Amour .10 .30
10 Mats Sundin .10 .30
11 Gary Suter .02 .10
12 Glenn Anderson .05 .15
13 Doug Wilson .05 .15
14 Stephane Richer .05 .15
15 Ray Bourque .20 .50
16 Adam Graves .05 .15
17 Luc Robitaille .05 .15
18 Steve Smith .02 .10
19 Uwe Krupp .02 .10
20 Rick Tocchet .05 .15
21 Tim Cheveldae .05 .15
22 Kay Whitmore .05 .15
23 Kelly Miller .02 .10
24 Esa Tikkanen .02 .10
25 Pat LaFontaine .10 .30
26 James Patrick .02 .10
27 Daniel Marois .02 .10
28 Denis Savard .05 .15
29 Steve Larmer .05 .15
30 Pierre Turgeon .05 .15
31 Gary Leeman .02 .10
32 Mike Ricci .10 .30
33 Troy Murray .02 .10
34 Sergio Momesso .02 .10
35 Marty McSorley .02 .10
36 Paul Ysebaert .02 .10
37 Gary Roberts .05 .15
38 Mike Hudson .02 .10
39 Kelly Hrudey .05 .15
40 Dale Hunter .05 .15
41 Brendan Shanahan .10 .30
42 Steve Duchesne .02 .10
43 Pat Verbeek .02 .10
44 Tom Barrasso .05 .15
45 Scott Mellanby .05 .15
46 Stephen Leach .02 .10
47 Darren Turcotte .02 .10
48 Jari Kurri .10 .30
49 Michel Petit .02 .10
50 Mark Messier .10 .30
51 Terry Carkner .02 .10
52 Tim Kerr .02 .10
53 Jaromir Jagr .25 .60
54 Joe Nieuwendyk .05 .15
55 Randy Burridge .02 .10
56 Robert Reichel .02 .10
57 Craig Janney .05 .15
58 Chris Chelios .10 .30
59 Bryan Fogarty .02 .10
60 Christian Ruuttu .02 .10
61 Steve Bozek .02 .10
62 Dave Manson .02 .10
63 Bruce Driver .02 .10
64 Mike Ramsey .02 .10
65 Bobby Holik .05 .15
66 Bob Essensa .05 .15
67 Pat Flatley .02 .10
68 Wayne Presley .02 .10
69 Mike Bullard .02 .10
70 Claude Lemieux .02 .10
71 Dave Gagner .02 .10
72 Jeff Brown .02 .10
73 Eric Desjardins .05 .15
74 Fredrik Olausson .02 .10
75 Steve Yzerman .40 1.00
76 Tony Granato .02 .10
77 Adam Burt .02 .10
78 Cam Neely .10 .30
79 Brent Sutter .02 .10
80 Dale Hawerchuk .05 .15
81 Scott Stevens .05 .15
82 Adam Creighton .02 .10
83 Brian Hayward .05 .15
84 Dan Quinn .02 .10
85 Garth Butcher .02 .10
86 Shawn Burr .02 .10
87 Peter Bondra .05 .15
88 Brad Shaw .02 .10
89 Eric Weinrich .02 .10
90 Brian Bradley .02 .10
91 Vincent Damphousse .02 .10
92 Doug Gilmour .05 .15
93 Martin Gelinas .02 .10
94 Mike Ridley .02 .10
95 Ron Sutter .02 .10
96 Mark Osborne .02 .10
97 Mikhail Tatarinov .02 .10
98 Bob McGill .02 .10
99 Bob Carpenter .02 .10
100 Wayne Gretzky .60 1.50
101 Slava Fetisov .02 .10
102 Shayne Corson .02 .10
103 Clint Malarchuk .05 .15
104 Randy Wood .02 .10
105 Curtis Joseph .10 .30
106 Cliff Ronning .02 .10
107 Derek King .02 .10
108 Neil Wilkinson .02 .10
109 Michel Goulet .05 .15
110 Zarley Zalapski .02 .10
111 Dave Ellett .02 .10
112 Glen Wesley .02 .10
113 Bob Kudelski .02 .10
114 Jamie Macoun .02 .10
115 John MacLean .05 .15
116 Steve Thomas .02 .10
117 Pat Elynuik .02 .10
118 Ron Hextall .05 .15
119 Jeff Hackett .05 .15
120 Jeremy Roenick .10 .30
121 John Vanbiesbrouck .05 .15
122 Dave Andreychuk .05 .15
123 Ray Ferraro .02 .10
124 Ron Tugnutt .05 .15
125 John Cullen .02 .10
126 Andy Moog .10 .30
127 Ed Belfour .10 .30
128 Dino Ciccarelli .05 .15
129 Brian Bellows .02 .10
130 Guy Carbonneau .05 .15
131 Kevin Hatcher .02 .10
132 Mike Vernon .05 .15
133 Kevin Miller .02 .10
134 Pelle Eklund .02 .10
135 Brian Mullen .02 .10
136 Brian Leetch .10 .30
137 Daren Puppa .05 .15
138 Steven Finn .02 .10
139 Stephan Lebeau .02 .10
140 Gord Murphy .02 .10
141 Rob Brown .02 .10
142 Ken Daneyko .02 .10
143 Larry Murphy .05 .15
144 Jon Casey .05 .15
145 John Ogrodnick .02 .10
146 Benoit Hogue .02 .10
147 Mike McPhee .02 .10
148 Don Beaupre .05 .15
149 Kjell Samuelsson .02 .10
150 Joe Sakic .30 .75
151 Mark Recchi .10 .30
152 Ulf Dahlen .02 .10
153 Dean Evason .02 .10
154 Keith Brown .02 .10
155 Ray Sheppard .02 .10
156 Owen Nolan .10 .30
157 Sergei Fedorov .25 .60
158 Kirk McLean .05 .15
159 Petr Klima .02 .10
160 Brian Skrudland .02 .10
161 Neal Broten .05 .15
162 Dimitri Khristich .02 .10
163 Alexander Mogilny .10 .30
164 Mike Richter .10 .30
165 Daniel Berthiaume .02 .10
166 Teppo Numminen .02 .10
167 Ron Francis .05 .15
168 Grant Fuhr .10 .30
169 Mike Liut .05 .15
170 Bill Ranford .05 .15
171 Garry Galley .02 .10
172 Jeff Norton .02 .10
173 Jimmy Carson .02 .10
174 Peter Zezel .02 .10
175 Patrick Roy .40 1.00
176 Joe Mullen .05 .15
177 Murray Craven .02 .10
178 Tomas Sandstrom .02 .10
179 Joel Otto .02 .10
180 Steve Konroyd .02 .10
181 Vladimir Ruzicka .02 .10
182 Paul Cavallini .02 .10
183 Bob Probert .05 .15
184 Brian Propp .02 .10
185 Glenn Healy .05 .15
186 Paul Coffey .10 .30
187 Jan Erixon .02 .10
188 Kevin Lowe .05 .15
189 Doug Lidster .02 .10
190 Theo Fleury .02 .10
191 Kevin Stevens .02 .10
192 Petr Nedved .05 .15
193 Ed Olczyk .02 .10
194 Mike Hough .02 .10
195 Rod Langway .02 .10
196 Craig Simpson .02 .10
197 Petr Svoboda .02 .10
198 David Volek .02 .10
199 Mark Tinordi .02 .10
200 Brett Hull .20 .50
201 Rob Blake .05 .15
202 Mike Gartner .05 .15
203 Ken Hodge Jr. .02 .10
204 Murray Baron .02 .10
205 Gerard Gallant .02 .10
206 Joe Murphy .02 .10
207 Al Iafrate .05 .15
208 Larry Robinson .02 .10
209 Mathieu Schneider .02 .10
210 Bobby Smith .05 .15
211 Gerald Diduck .02 .10
212 Luke Richardson .02 .10
213 Rob Zettler .02 .10
214 Brad McCrimmon .02 .10
215 Craig MacTavish .02 .10
216 Gino Cavallini .02 .10
217 Craig Wolanin .02 .10
218 Greg Adams .02 .10
219 Mike Craig .02 .10
220 Al MacInnis .05 .15
221 Sylvain Cote .02 .10
222 Bob Sweeney .02 .10
223 Dave Snuggerud .02 .10
224 Randy Ladouceur .02 .10
225 Charlie Huddy .02 .10
226 Sylvain Turgeon .02 .10
227 Phil Bourque .02 .10
228 Rob Ramage .02 .10
229 Jeff Beukeboom .02 .10
230 Alexei Gusarov RC .05 .15
231 Kelly Kisio .02 .10
232 Calle Johansson .02 .10
233 Yves Racine .02 .10
234 Peter Sidorkiewicz .05 .15
235 Jim Johnson .02 .10
236 Brent Gilchrist .02 .10
237 Jyrki Lumme .02 .10
238 Randy Gilhen .02 .10
239 Ken Baumgartner .02 .10
240 Joey Kocur .05 .15
241 Bryan Trottier .10 .30
242 Todd Krygier .02 .10
243 Darrin Shannon .02 .10
244 Dave Christian .02 .10
245 Stephane Morin .02 .10
246 Kevin Dineen .02 .10
247 Chris Terreri .05 .15
248 Craig Ludwig .02 .10
249 Dave Taylor .05 .15

250 Wendel Clark .05 .15
251 David Shaw .02 .10
252 Paul Ranheim .02 .10
253 Mark Hunter .02 .10
254 Russ Courtnall .02 .10
255 Alexei Kasatonov .02 .10
256 Randy Moller .02 .10
257 Bob Errey .02 .10
258 Curtis Leschyshyn .02 .10
259 Rick Zombo .02 .10
260 Dana Murzyn .02 .10
261 Dirk Graham .02 .10
262 Craig Muni .02 .10
263 Geoff Courtnall .05 .15
264 Todd Elik .02 .10
265 Mike Keane .02 .10
266 Peter Stastny .05 .15
267 Ulf Samuelsson .02 .10
268 Rich Sutter .02 .10
269 Mike Krushelnyski .02 .10
270 Dave Babych .02 .10
271 Sergei Makarov .02 .10
272 David Maley .02 .10
273 Normand Rochefort .02 .10
274 Gordie Roberts .02 .10
275 Thomas Steen .02 .10
276 Dave Lowry .02 .10
277 Michal Pivonka .02 .10
278 Todd Gill .02 .10
279 Paul MacDermid .02 .10
280 Brent Ashton .02 .10
281 Randy Hillier .02 .10
282 Frank Musil .02 .10
283 Geoff Smith .02 .10
284 John Tonelli .02 .10
285 Joe Reekie .02 .10
286 Greg Paslawski .02 .10
287 Perry Berezan .02 .10
288 Randy Carlyle .02 .10
289 Chris Nilan .02 .10
290 Patrik Sundstrom .02 .10
291 Garry Valk .02 .10
292 Mike Foligno .02 .10
293 Igor Larionov .02 .10
294 Jim Sandlak .02 .10
295 Tom Chorske .02 .10
296 Claude Loiselle .02 .10
297 Mark Howe .02 .10
298 Steve Chiasson .02 .10
299 Mike Donnelly RC .02 .10
300 Bernie Nicholls .05 .15
301 Tony Amonte RC .40 1.00
302 Brad May .02 .10
303 Josef Beranek RC .02 .10
304 Rob Pearson RC .02 .10
305 Andrei Lomakin .02 .10
306 Kip Miller .02 .10
307 Kevin Haller RC .02 .10
308 Kevin Todd RC .02 .10
309 Geoff Sanderson RC .10 .30
310 Doug Weight RC .40 1.00
311 Vladimir Konstantinov RC .40 1.00
312 Peter Ahola RC .02 .10
313 Claude Lapointe RC .02 .10
314 Nelson Emerson .02 .10
315 Pavel Bure .10 .30
316 Jimmy Waite .05 .15
317 Sergei Nemchinov .02 .10
318 Alexander Godynyuk RC .02 .10
319 Stu Barnes .02 .10
320 Nicklas Lidstrom RC 1.00 2.50
321 Daryl Sydor .05 .15
322 John LeClair RC .40 1.00
323 Arturs Irbe .10 .30
324 Russ Romaniuk RC .02 .10
325 Ken Sutton RC .02 .10
326 Bob Beers .02 .10
327 Michel Picard RC .02 .10
328 Derian Hatcher .05 .15
329 Pat Falloon .02 .10
330 Donald Audette .02 .10
331 Pat Jablonski RC .05 .15
332 Corey Foster RC .02 .10
333 Tomas Forslund RC .02 .10
334 Steven Rice .02 .10
335 Marc Bureau .02 .10
336 Kimbi Daniels RC .02 .10
337 Adam Foote RC .20 .50
338 Dan Kordic RC .02 .10
339 Link Gaetz .02 .10
340 Valeri Kamensky RC .05 .15
341 Tom Draper RC .05 .15
342 Jay More RC .02 .10
343 Dominic Roussel RC .05 .15
344 Jim Paek RC .02 .10
345 Felix Potvin .30 .75
346 Dan Lambert RC .02 .10
347 Louie DeBrusk RC .02 .10
348 Jamie Baker RC .02 .10
349 Scott Niedermayer .02 .10
350 Paul Dipietro RC .02 .10
351 Chris Winnes RC .02 .10
352 Mark Greig .02 .10
353 Luciano Borsato RC .02 .10
354 Valeri Zelepukin RC .02 .10
355 Martin Lapointe .05 .15
356 Brett Hull GW .10 .30
357 Steve Larmer GW .05 .15
358 Theo Fleury GW .02 .10
359 Jeremy Roenick GW .10 .30
360 Mark Recchi GW .10 .30
361 Brad Marsh .02 .10
362 Kris King .02 .10
363 Doug Brown .02 .10
364 Carey Wilson .02 .10
365 Eric Lindros .10 .30
366 Kevin Dineen GG .02 .10
367 John Vanbiesbrouck GG .05 .15
368 Ray Bourque GG .10 .30
369 Doug Wilson GG .02 .10
370 Keith Brown GG .02 .10
371 Kevin Lowe GG .05 .15
372 Kelly Miller GG .02 .10
373 Dave Taylor GG .05 .15
374 Guy Carbonneau GG .05 .15
375 Tim Hunter GG .02 .10
376 Brett Hull TECH .10 .30
377 Paul Coffey TECH .10 .30
378 Adam Oates TECH .05 .15
379 Andy Moog TECH .05 .15
380 Mario Lemieux TECH .40 1.00
381 Joe Sakic IDOL .40 1.00
(Wayne Gretzky)
382 Rob Blake IDOL .10 .30
(Larry Robinson)
383 Doug Weight IDOL .40 1.00
(Steve Yzerman)
384 Mike Richter IDOL .10 .30
(Bernie Parent)
385 Luc Robitaille IDOL .05 .15
(Marcel Dionne)
386 Ed Olczyk IDOL .02 .10
(Bobby Clarke)
387 Patrick Roy IDOL .40 1.00
(Rogatien Vachon)
388 Ed Belfour IDOL .10 .30
(Tony Esposito)
389 Mats Sundin IDOL .10 .30
(Mats Naslund)
390 Tony Amonte IDOL .05 .15
(Mark Messier)
391 John Cullen IDOL .02 .10
(Ray Cullen)
392 Gary Suter IDOL .30 .75
(Bobby Orr)
393 Rick Zombo IDOL .02 .10
(Glenn Resch)
394 Todd Krygier IDOL .05 .15
(Gilbert Perreault)
395 John Druce IDOL .02 .10
(Bob Gainey)
396 Bob Carpenter SL .02 .10
397 Clint Malarchuk SL .02 .10
398 Jim Kyte SL .02 .10
399 Al MacInnis SL .02 .10
400 Ed Belfour SL .10 .30
401 Brad Marsh SL .02 .10
402 Brian Benning SL .02 .10
403 Larry Robinson SL .05 .15
404 Craig Ludwig SL .02 .10
405 Pat Flatley SL .02 .10
406 Gary Nylund SL .02 .10
407 Kjell Samuelsson SL .02 .10
408 Dan Quinn SL .02 .10
409 Garth Butcher SL .02 .10
410 Rick Zombo SL .02 .10
411 Paul Cavallini SL .02 .10
412 Link Gaetz SL .02 .10
413 Dave Hannan SL .02 .10
414 Peter Zezel SL .02 .10
415 Randy Gregg SL .02 .10
416 Pat Elynuik SL .02 .10
417 Rod Buskas SL .02 .10
418 Mark Howe SL .02 .10
419 Don Sweeney .02 .10
420 Mark Hardy .02 .10

1991-92 Pinnacle French

COMPLETE SET (420) 15.00 30.00
*FRENCH: .4X TO 1X BASIC PINNACLE

1991-92 Pinnacle B

This 12-card standard-size set presents the starting lineup from the 1991 All-Star Game. It features six players each from the Wales Conference (B1-B6) and the Campbell Conference (B7-B12). The cards were inserted into Pinnacle French and English foil packs. The French version has a red name plate, while the English version has a blue name plate. The fronts feature black-and-white head shots, with black borders on three sides and a thicker white border at the bottom. The words "Team Pinnacle" appear in the top black border, while the player's name and team affiliation are listed in the bottom white border. The border design on the back is similar and frames a player profile. The cards are numbered on the back with a "B" prefix.

COMPLETE SET (12) 60.00 125.00
*FRENCH: SAME VALUE
B1 Patrick Roy 20.00 50.00
B2 Ray Bourque 6.00 15.00
B3 Brian Leetch 4.00 10.00
B4 Kevin Stevens 2.50 6.00
B5 Mario Lemieux 20.00 50.00
B6 Cam Neely 4.00 10.00
B7 Bill Ranford 3.00 8.00
B8 Al MacInnis 3.00 8.00
B9 Chris Chelios 4.00 10.00
B10 Luc Robitaille 3.00 8.00
B11 Wayne Gretzky 25.00 60.00
B12 Brett Hull 5.00 12.00

1992-93 Pinnacle American Promo Panel

This promo sheet features six standard-size cards and was issued to promote the U.S. edition of Pinnacle hockey cards. The cards feature color action photos with the players extending beyond the picture background. The card face is black and a thin white line forms a frame around the picture. The player's name appears in a gradated bar at the bottom that matches the team colors. The horizontal backs feature the player's name in a gradated turquoise bar at the top. Close-up player photos are surrounded by biography, statistics, and career highlights on a black background. The backs have white borders. This sheet was intended to remain uncut and the disclaimers "Not For Resale" and "For Promotional Use Only" are printed in the white borders between the rows of cards. The cards are numbered on the back and listed as they appear on the sheet from left to right.

1 Promo Sheet 1.25 3.00
91 Andy Moog
36 Nelson Emerson
61 Denis Savard
6 Owen Nolan
22 Michel Goulet
88 Eric Lindros

1992-93 Pinnacle Canadian Promo Panels

These three promo panels were issued to preview the design of the Canadian version of the 1992-93 Pinnacle hockey series. Measuring approximately 5" by 7", each panel consists of four standard-size cards. The fronts display glossy color action photos framed by black borders. The horizontal backs feature the player's name in a gradated burgundy bar at the top. Close-up photos are surrounded by biography, statistics, and career highlights on a black background. The sheet was intended to remain uncut and the disclaimers "Not For Resale" and "For Promotional Use Only" are printed in the white borders between the rows of cards. The cards on the panels are listed below alphabetically according to player's last name.

COMPLETE SET (3) 2.50 6.00
1 Promo Panel 1.25 3.00
Pavel Bure
Al Iafrate
Mark Recchi
Scott Stevens
2 Promo Panel .75 2.00
Brian Bradley
Kirk Muller
Kevin Stevens
Pierre Turgeon
3 Promo Panel .75 2.00
Doug Gilmour
Alexander Mogilny
Luc Robitaille
Teemu Selanne

1992-93 Pinnacle

The 1992-93 Pinnacle Hockey set was issued in U.S. and Canadian bilingual editions; each set consists of 420 cards. While card numbers 1-220 and 271-398 have different front photography in the U.S. and Canadian versions, the subset cards (221-270) depict the same photos. Rookie Cards in the set include Roman Hamrlik, Andrei Kovalenko, and Martin Straka.

COMPLETE SET (420) 10.00 25.00
1 Mark Messier .10 .30
2 Ray Bourque .25 .60
3 Gary Roberts .02 .10
4 Bill Ranford .07 .20
5 Gilbert Dionne .02 .10
6 Owen Nolan .07 .20
7 Pat LaFontaine .10 .30
8 Nicklas Lidstrom .10 .30
9 Pat Falloon .02 .10
10 Jeremy Roenick .15 .40
11 Kevin Hatcher .02 .10
12 Cliff Ronning .02 .10
13 Jeff Brown .02 .10
14 Kevin Dineen .02 .10
15 Brian Leetch .10 .30
16 Eric Desjardins .07 .20
17 Derek King .02 .10
18 Mark Tinordi .02 .10
19 Kelly Hrudey .07 .20
20 Sergei Fedorov .20 .50
21 Mike Ramsey .02 .10
22 Michel Goulet .07 .20
23 Joe Murphy .02 .10
24 Mark Fitzpatrick .07 .20
25 Cam Neely .10 .30
26 Rod Brind'Amour .07 .20
27 Neil Wilkinson .02 .10
28 Greg Adams .02 .10
29 Thomas Steen .02 .10
30 Calle Johansson .02 .10
31 Joe Nieuwendyk .07 .20
32 Rob Blake .07 .20
33 Darren Turcotte .02 .10
34 Derian Hatcher .02 .10
35 Mikhail Tatarinov .02 .10
36 Nelson Emerson .02 .10
37 Tim Cheveldae .07 .20
38 Donald Audette .07 .20
39 Brent Sutter .02 .10
40 Adam Oates .07 .20
41 Luke Richardson .02 .10
42 Jon Casey .07 .20
43 Guy Carbonneau .07 .20
44 Patrick Flatley .02 .10
45 Brian Benning .02 .10
46 Curtis Leschyshyn .02 .10
47 Trevor Linden .07 .20
48 Don Beaupre .07 .20
49 Troy Murray .02 .10
50 Paul Coffey .10 .30
51 Frank Musil .02 .10
52 Doug Wilson .07 .20
53 Pat Elynuik .02 .10
54 Curtis Joseph .10 .30
55 Tony Amonte .07 .20
56 Bob Probert .07 .20
57 Steve Smith .02 .10
58 Dave Andreychuk .07 .20
59 Vladimir Ruzicka .02 .10
60 Jari Kurri .10 .30
61 Denis Savard .07 .20
62 Benoit Hogue .02 .10
63 Terry Carkner .02 .10
64 Valeri Kamensky .07 .20
65 Jyrki Lumme .02 .10
66 Al Iafrate .07 .20
67 Paul Ranheim .02 .10
68 Ulf Dahlen .02 .10
69 Tony Granato .02 .10
70 Phil Housley .07 .20
71 Brian Lawton .02 .10
72 Garth Butcher .02 .10
73 Steve Leach .02 .10
74 Steve Larmer .07 .20
75 Mike Richter .10 .30
76 Vladimir Konstantinov .10 .30
77 Alexander Mogilny .07 .20
78 Craig MacTavish .02 .10
79 Mathieu Schneider .02 .10
80 Mark Recchi .07 .20
81 Gerald Diduck .02 .10
82 Peter Bondra .07 .20
83 Al MacInnis .07 .20
84 Bob Kudelski .02 .10
85 Dave Gagner .07 .20
86 Uwe Krupp .02 .10
87 Randy Carlyle .02 .10
88 Eric Lindros .10 .30
89 Rob Zettler .02 .10
90 Mats Sundin .10 .30
91 Andy Moog .10 .30
92 Keith Brown .02 .10
93 Paul Ysebaert .02 .10
94 Mike Gartner .07 .20
95 Kelly Buchberger .02 .10
96 Dominic Roussel .07 .20
97 Doug Bodger .02 .10
98 Mike Donnelly .02 .10
99 Mike Craig .02 .10
100 Brett Hull .20 .50
101 Robert Reichel .02 .10
102 Jeff Norton .02 .10
103 Garry Galley .02 .10
104 Dale Hunter .07 .20
105 Jeff Hackett .07 .20
106 Darrin Shannon .02 .10
107 Craig Wolanin .02 .10
108 Adam Graves .02 .10
109 Chris Chelios .10 .30
110 Pavel Bure .10 .30
111 Kirk Muller .02 .10
112 Jeff Beukeboom .02 .10
113 Mike Hough .02 .10
114 Brendan Shanahan .10 .30
115 Randy Burridge .02 .10
116 Dave Poulin .02 .10
117 Petr Svoboda .02 .10
118 Ed Belfour .10 .30
119 Ray Sheppard .02 .10
120 Bernie Nicholls .07 .20
121 Glenn Healy .07 .20
122 Johan Garpenlov .02 .10
123 Mike Lalor .02 .10
124 Brad McCrimmon .02 .10
125 Theo Fleury .02 .10
126 Randy Gilhen .02 .10
127 Petr Nedved .07 .20
128 Steve Thomas .07 .20
129 Rick Zombo .02 .10
130 Patrick Roy .60 1.50
131 Rod Langway .02 .10
132 Gord Murphy .02 .10
133 Randy Wood .02 .10
134 Mike Hudson .02 .10
135 Gerard Gallant .02 .10
136 Brian Glynn .02 .10
137 Jim Johnson .02 .10
138 Corey Millen .02 .10
139 Daniel Marois .02 .10
140 James Patrick .02 .10
141 Claude Lapointe .02 .10
142 Bobby Smith .07 .20
143 Charlie Huddy .02 .10
144 Murray Baron .02 .10
145 Ed Olczyk .02 .10
146 Dimitri Khristich .02 .10
147 Doug Lidster .02 .10
148 Perry Berezan .02 .10
149 Pelle Eklund .02 .10
150 Joe Sakic .25 .60
151 Michal Pivonka .02 .10
152 Joey Kocur .07 .20
153 Patrice Brisebois .02 .10
154 Ray Ferraro .02 .10
155 Mike Modano .20 .50
156 Marty McSorley .02 .10
157 Norm Maciver .02 .10
158 Sergei Nemchinov .02 .10
159 David Bruce .02 .10
160 Kelly Miller .02 .10
161 Alexei Gusarov .02 .10
162 Andrei Lomakin .02 .10
163 Sergio Momesso .02 .10
164 Mike Keane .02 .10
165 Pierre Turgeon .07 .20
166 Martin Gelinas .02 .10
167 Chris Dahlquist .02 .10
168 Kris King .02 .10
169 Dean Evason .02 .10
170 Mike Ridley .02 .10
171 Shawn Burr .02 .10
172 Dana Murzyn .02 .10
173 Dirk Graham .02 .10
174 Trent Yawney .02 .10
175 Luc Robitaille .07 .20
176 Randy Moller .02 .10
177 Vincent Riendeau .07 .20
178 Brian Propp .02 .10
179 Don Sweeney .02 .10
180 Stephane Matteau .02 .10
181 Garry Valk .02 .10
182 Sylvain Cote .02 .10
183 Dave Snuggerud .02 .10
184 Gary Leeman .02 .10
185 John Druce .02 .10
186 John Vanbiesbrouck .07 .20
187 Geoff Courtnall .07 .20
188 David Volek .02 .10
189 Doug Weight .10 .30
190 Bob Essensa .07 .20
191 Jan Erixon .02 .10
192 Geoff Smith .02 .10
193 Dave Christian .02 .10
194 Brian Noonan .02 .10
195 Gary Suter .02 .10
196 Craig Janney .07 .20
197 Brad May .02 .10
198 Gaetan Duchesne .02 .10
199 Adam Creighton .02 .10
200 Wayne Gretzky .75 2.00
201 Dave Babych .02 .10
202 Fredrik Olausson .02 .10
203 Bob Bassen .02 .10
204 Todd Krygier .02 .10
205 Grant Ledyard .02 .10
206 Michel Petit .02 .10
207 Todd Elik .02 .10
208 Josef Beranek .02 .10
209 Neal Broten .07 .20
210 Jim Sandlak .02 .10
211 Kevin Haller .02 .10
212 Paul Broten .02 .10
213 Mark Pederson .02 .10
214 John McIntyre .02 .10
215 Teppo Numminen .02 .10
216 Ken Sutton .02 .10
217 Ronnie Stern .02 .10
218 Luciano Borsato .02 .10
219 Claude Loiselle .02 .10
220 Mark Hardy .02 .10
221 Joe Juneau RK .07 .20
222 Keith Tkachuk RK .10 .30
223 Scott Lachance RK .02 .10
224 Glen Murray RK .02 .10
225 Igor Kravchuk RK .02 .10
226 Evgeny Davydov RK .02 .10
227 Ray Whitney RK RC .20 .50
228 Bret Hedican RK RC .07 .20
229 Keith Carney RK RC .40 1.00
230 Slava Kozlov RK .07 .20
231 Drake Berehowsky RK .02 .10
232 Cam Neely SL .07 .20
233 Al Iafrate SL .02 .10
234 Randy Wood SL .02 .10
235 Luke Richardson SL .02 .10
236 Eric Lindros SL .10 .30
237 Dale Hunter SL .02 .10
238 Pat Falloon SL .02 .10
239 Dean Kennedy SL .02 .10
240 Uwe Krupp SL .02 .10
241 Scott Niedermayer IDOL .30 .75
(Steve Yzerman)
242 Gary Roberts IDOL .07 .20
(Lanny McDonald)
243 Peter Ahola IDOL .10 .30
(Jari Kurri)
244 Scott Lachance IDOL .07 .20
(Mark Howe)
245 Rob Pearson IDOL .15 .40
(Mike Bossy)
246 Kirk McLean IDOL .10 .30
(Bernie Parent)
247 Dmitri Mironov IDOL .07 .20
(Viacheslav Fetisov)
248 Brendan Shanahan IDOL .07 .20
(Darryl Sittler)
249 Petr Nedved IDOL .40 1.00
(Wayne Gretzky)
250 Todd Ewen IDOL .02 .10
(Clark Gillies)
251 Luc Robitaille GG .07 .20
252 Mark Tinordi GG .02 .10
253 Kris King GG .02 .10
254 Pat LaFontaine GG .07 .20
255 Ryan Walter GG .02 .10
256 Jeremy Roenick GW .15 .40
257 Brett Hull GW .08 .25
258 Steve Yzerman GW .30 .75
259 Claude Lemieux GW .07 .20
260 Mike Modano GW .10 .30
261 Vincent Damphousse GW .02 .10
262 Tony Granato GW .02 .10
263 Andy Moog MASK 1.25 3.00
264 Curtis Joseph MASK 1.50 4.00
265 Ed Belfour MASK 1.50 4.00
266 Brian Hayward MASK .75 2.00
267 Grant Fuhr MASK 1.25 3.00
268 Don Beaupre MASK .75 2.00
269 Tim Cheveldae MASK .75 2.00
270 Mike Richter MASK 1.25 3.00
271 Zarley Zalapski .02 .10
272 Kevin Todd .02 .10
273 Dave Ellett .02 .10
274 Chris Terreri .07 .20
275 Jaromir Jagr .20 .50
276 Wendel Clark .07 .20
277 Bobby Holik .07 .20
278 Bruce Driver .02 .10
279 Doug Gilmour .07 .20
280 Scott Stevens .07 .20
281 Murray Craven .02 .10
282 Rick Tocchet .07 .20
283 Peter Zezel .02 .10
284 Claude Lemieux .02 .10
285 John Cullen .02 .10
286 Valeri Zelepukin .02 .10
287 Rob Pearson .02 .10
288 Kevin Stevens .02 .10
289 Alexei Kasatonov .02 .10
290 Todd Gill .02 .10
291 Randy Ladouceur .02 .10
292 Larry Murphy .07 .20
293 Tom Chorske .02 .10
294 Jamie Macoun .02 .10
295 Sean Burke .07 .20
296 Ulf Samuelsson .02 .10
297 Eric Weinrich .02 .10
298 Tom Barrasso .07 .20
299 Slava Fetisov .07 .20
300 Mario Lemieux .60 1.50
301 Grant Fuhr .10 .30
302 Zdeno Ciger .02 .10
303 Ron Francis .07 .20
304 Scott Niedermayer .02 .10
305 Mark Osborne .02 .10
306 Kjell Samuelsson .02 .10
307 Geoff Sanderson .07 .20
308 Paul Stanton .02 .10
309 Frank Pietrangelo .07 .20
310 Bob Errey .02 .10
311 Dino Ciccarelli .07 .20
312 Gordie Roberts .07 .20
313 Kevin Miller .02 .10
314 Mike Ricci .07 .20
315 Bob Carpenter .02 .10
316 Dale Hawerchuk .07 .20
317 Christian Ruuttu .02 .10
318 Mike Vernon .07 .20
319 Paul Cavallini .02 .10
320 Steve Duchesne .02 .10
321 Craig Simpson .02 .10
322 Mark Howe .02 .10
323 Shayne Corson .02 .10
324 Tom Kurvers .02 .10
325 Brian Bellows .02 .10
326 Glen Wesley .02 .10
327 Daren Puppa .07 .20
328 Joel Otto .02 .10
329 Jimmy Carson .02 .10
330 Kirk McLean .07 .20
331 Rob Brown .02 .10
332 Yves Racine .02 .10
333 Brian Mullen .02 .10
334 Dave Manson .02 .10
335 Sergei Makarov .02 .10
336 Esa Tikkanen .02 .10
337 Russ Courtnall .02 .10
338 Kevin Lowe .07 .20
339 Steve Chiasson .02 .10
340 Ron Hextall .07 .20
341 Stephen Lebeau .02 .10
342 Mike McPhee .02 .10
343 David Shaw .02 .10
344 Petr Klima .02 .10
345 Tomas Sandstrom .07 .20
346 Scott Mellanby .02 .10
347 Brian Skrudland .02 .10
348 Pat Verbeek .02 .10
349 Vincent Damphousse .02 .10
350 Steve Yzerman .60 1.50
351 John MacLean .07 .20
352 Steve Konroyd .02 .10
353 Phil Bourque .02 .10
354 Ken Daneyko .02 .10
355 Glenn Anderson .07 .20
356 Ken Wregget .07 .20
357 Brent Gilchrist .02 .10
358 Bob Rouse .02 .10
359 Peter Stastny .07 .20
360 Joe Mullen .07 .20
361 Stephane Richer .07 .20
362 Kelly Kisio .02 .10
363 Keith Acton .02 .10
364 Felix Potvin .10 .30
365 Martin Lapointe .07 .20
366 Ron Tugnutt .07 .20
367 Dave Taylor .07 .20
368 Tim Kerr .07 .20
369 Carey Wilson .02 .10
370 Greg Paslawski .02 .10
371 Peter Sidorkiewicz .07 .20
372 Brad Shaw .02 .10
373 Sylvain Turgeon .02 .10
374 Mark Lamb .02 .10
375 Laurie Boschman .02 .10
376 Mark Osiecki .02 .10
377 Doug Smail .02 .10
378 Brad Marsh .02 .10
379 Mike Peluso .02 .10
380 Steve Weeks .07 .20
381 Wendell Young .07 .20
382 Joe Reekie .02 .10
383 Peter Taglianetti .02 .10
384 Mikael Andersson .02 .10
385 Marc Bergevin .02 .10
386 Anatoli Semenov .02 .10
387 Brian Bradley .02 .10
388 Michel Mongeau .02 .10
389 Rob Ramage .02 .10
390 Ken Hodge Jr. .02 .10
391 Richard Matvichuk RC .15 .40
392 Alexei Zhitnik UER .02 .10
(Drafted in fourth round, not third as bio indicates)
393 Dallas Drake RC .02 .10
394 Dimitri Yushkevich RC .07 .20
395 Andrei Kovalenko RC .07 .20
396 Vladimir Vujtek RC .02 .10
397 Nikolai Borschevsky RC .02 .10
398 Vitali Karamnov RC .02 .10
399 Jim Hiller RC .02 .10
400 Michael Nylander RC .07 .20
401 Tommy Sjodin RC .02 .10
402 Martin Straka RC .07 .20
403 Alexei Kovalev .07 .20
404 Vitali Prokhorov RC .02 .10
405 Dmitri Kvartalnov RC .02 .10
406 Teemu Selanne .60 1.50
407 Darius Kasparaitis .02 .10
408 Roman Hamrlik RC .20 .50
409 Vladimir Malakhov .02 .10
410 Sergei Krivokrasov .02 .10
411 Robert Lang RC .02 .10
412 Jozef Stumpel .02 .10
413 Denny Felsner RC .07 .20
414 Rob Zamuner RC .07 .20
415 Jason Woolley RC .02 .10
416 Alexei Zhamnov .07 .20
417 Igor Korolev RC .07 .20
418 Patrick Poulin .02 .10
419 Dmitri Mironov .02 .10
420 Shawn McEachern .02 .10

1992-93 Pinnacle French

COMPLETE SET (420) 15.00 30.00
*FRENCH: .4X TO 1X BASIC CARDS

1992-93 Pinnacle Team 2000

Inserted two per 27-card super pack, these 30 standard-size cards feature players who Pinnacle predicts will be stars in the NHL in the year 2000. The U.S. version features glossy color action photos that are full-bleed on the top and right and edged by black wedged-shaped borders on the left and bottom. In a gold-foil edged circle, the team logo appears in the lower left corner at the intersection of these two stripes. In gold-foil lettering, the words "Team 2000" are printed vertically in the left stripe while the player's name appears in the bottom stripe. The Canadian version offers different player photos and has a maple leaf following the Team 2000 insignia. The horizontal backs have a black panel with bilingual player profile on the left half and a full-bleed color close-up photo on the right.

COMPLETE SET (30) 8.00 20.00
*FRENCH: 1X TO 1.25X BASIC CARDS
1 Eric Lindros .50 1.25
2 Mike Modano .75 2.00
3 Nicklas Lidstrom .50 1.25
4 Tony Amonte .30 .75
5 Felix Potvin .50 1.25
6 Scott Lachance .15 .40
7 Mats Sundin .50 1.25
8 Pavel Bure .50 1.25
9 Eric Desjardins .30 .75
10 Owen Nolan .30 .75
11 Dominic Roussel .30 .75
12 Scott Niedermayer .15 .40
13 Slava Kozlov .30 .75
14 Patrick Poulin .15 .40
15 Jaromir Jagr .75 2.00
16 Rob Blake .30 .75
17 Pierre Turgeon .30 .75
18 Rod Brind'Amour .30 .75
19 Joe Juneau .30 .75
20 Tim Cheveldae .30 .75
21 Joe Sakic 1.00 2.50
22 Kevin Todd .15 .40
23 Rob Pearson .15 .40
24 Trevor Linden .30 .75
25 Dimitri Khristich .15 .40
26 Pat Falloon .15 .40
27 Jeremy Roenick .60 1.50
28 Alexander Mogilny .30 .75
29 Gilbert Dionne .15 .40
30 Sergei Fedorov .75 2.00

1992-93 Pinnacle Team Pinnacle

Randomly inserted in 1992-93 Pinnacle foil packs, these six double-sided cards feature a top player from the Campbell Conference with his Wales Conference counterpart on the other side. According to Score, the odds of finding a card are not less than 1:125 packs. Painted by Score artist Christopher Greco, the pictures are full-bleed on three sides but edged on the bottom by a gold-foil stripe that features the player's name and position. A black stripe immediately below completes the card face. The words "Team Pinnacle" are printed in turquoise (pink in the Canadian version) vertically near the left edge of both sides of the card, and the conference logo appears below it. The backs of these cards may be distinguished from the fronts by the card number in the lower right corner.

COMPLETE SET (6) 25.00 50.00
*FRENCH: 1X TO 1X BASIC INSERTS
1 Mike Richter 2.00 5.00
Ed Belfour
2 Ray Bourque 2.00 5.00
Chris Chelios
3 Brian Leetch 2.00 5.00
Paul Coffey
4 Kevin Stevens 2.00 5.00
Pavel Bure
5 Eric Lindros 8.00 20.00
Wayne Gretzky
6 Jaromir Jagr 5.00 12.00
Brett Hull

1992-93 Pinnacle Eric Lindros

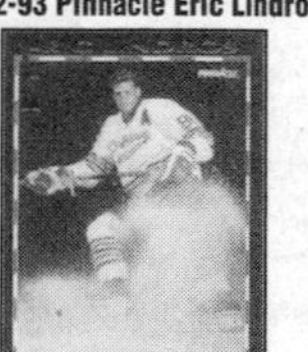

This 30-card boxed standard-size set features posed and action color photos of Eric Lindros as he has progressed from the junior leagues to the NHL. The set begins when Eric Lindros first received attention as a 14-year-old with the St. Michael's Buzzers and ends with his playing for the Philadelphia Flyers. According to Pinnacle, 3,750 numbered cases were produced. The cards have black borders, and his name is printed in gold foil at the top. The backs display a vertical, color photo and Eric's comments about a particular phase of his career.

COMPLETE SET (30) 4.80 12.00
1 St. Michael's Buzzers .30 .75
2 Detroit Compuware .20 .50
3 Oshawa Generals .20 .50
4 Oshawa Generals .20 .50
5 Oshawa Generals .20 .50
6 Oshawa Generals .20 .50
7 Memorial Cup .20 .50
8 World Junior Championship .20 .50
9 World Junior Championship .20 .50
10 World Junior Championship .40 1.00
11 Canada Cup .40 1.00
12 Canada Cup .20 .50
13 Canadian National .40 1.00
14 Canadian National .40 1.00
15 Canadian National .20 .50
16 Canadian National .20 .50
17 First-Round Draft Pick .20 .50
18 Trade To Philadelphia .20 .50
19 Happy Flyer .20 .50
20 Preseason Action .20 .50
21 Preseason Action .20 .50
22 Regular Season Debut .20 .50
23 First NHL Goal .20 .50
24 Winning Home Debut .20 .50
25 First NHL Hat Trick .20 .50
26 Playing Golf .20 .50
27 Backyard Fun .20 .50
28 Fan Favorite .20 .50
29 Welcome To Philly .20 .50
30 Philly Hero .40 1.00

1993-94 Pinnacle I Samples

These six cards were distributed to dealers and media during the summer of 1993 to show the style of the upcoming Pinnacle hockey cards for the 1993-94 season. The cards can be differentiated from regular issues by the presence of dashes rather than stats in the tables on the reverse.

COMPLETE SET (6) 1.50 4.00
1 Tony Amonte .10 .30
2 Tom Barrasso .02 .10
3 Joe Juneau .08 .25
4 Eric Lindros .75 2.00
5 Teemu Selanne .60 1.50
6 Mats Sundin .20 .50

1993-94 Pinnacle II Samples

This 11-card hobby sample set was enclosed in a cello pack. With the exception of the Mogilny "Nifty 50" card, the top right corners of each card have been cut off, apparently to indicate that these are promo cards. The disclaimer "SAMPLE" is stamped across the photo on the back of the Mogilny, WJC card, and the Lindros redemption card.

COMPLETE SEALED SET (11) 4.00 10.00
275 Brian Leetch .01 .05
280 Guy Carbonneau .01 .05
300 Pat LaFontaine .01 .05
320 Pavel Bure .08 .25
340 Terry Yake .01 .05
341 Brian Benning .01 .05
0 World Jr. Championship .30 .75
NF9 Alexander Mogilny 1.25 3.00
SR1 Alexandre Daigle .20 .50
NNO Ad Card .20 .50
NNO You're A Winner (Lindros Instant Winner Game) .60 1.50

1993-94 Pinnacle

Issued in two series of 236 and 275 cards, respectively, the 1993-94 Pinnacle hockey set consists of 511 standard-size cards. On a black background with a thin white border, the fronts feature color action player photos. Both series were offered in a U.S. version as well as a Canadian, bilingual version. Former prospect Brett Lindros is featured on a pair of cards with his talented brother Eric. Inserted at a rate of 1:100 packs, the cards are similar, but feature different photos for the U.S. and Canadian versions; the Canadian card also features bilingual text. A card honoring Wayne Gretzky's 802nd career goal was included in second series jumbo packs. Because of its distribution, the card (No. 512) is not considered part of the set. Rookie Cards include Jason Arnott, Jeff Friesen, Todd Harvey, Chris Osgood, Jamie Storr, Jocelyn Thibault and Oleg Tverdovsky.

COMPLETE SET (511) 12.00 30.00
COMP.SERIES 1 (236) 6.00 15.00
COMP.SERIES 2 (275) 6.00 15.00
1 Eric Lindros .10 .30
2 Mats Sundin .10 .30
3 Tom Barrasso .05 .15
4 Teemu Selanne .10 .30
5 Joe Juneau .05 .15
6 Tony Amonte .05 .15
7 Bob Probert .05 .15
8 Chris Kontos .02 .10
9 Geoff Sanderson .05 .15
10 Alexander Mogilny .05 .15
11 Kevin Lowe .02 .10
12 Nikolai Borschevsky .02 .10
13 Dale Hunter .02 .10
14 Gary Suter .02 .10
15 Curtis Joseph .10 .30
16 Mark Tinordi .02 .10
17 Doug Weight .05 .15
18 Benoit Hogue .02 .10
19 Tommy Soderstrom .05 .15
20 Pat Falloon .02 .10
21 Jyrki Lumme .02 .10
22 Brian Bellows .02 .10
23 Alexei Zhitnik .02 .10
24 Dirk Graham .02 .10
25 Scott Stevens .05 .15
26 Adam Foote .02 .10
27 Mike Gartner .05 .15
28 Dallas Drake RC .02 .10
29 Ulf Samuelsson .02 .10
30 Cam Neely .10 .30
31 Sean Burke .05 .15
32 Petr Svoboda .02 .10
33 Keith Tkachuk .10 .30
34 Roman Hamrlik .05 .15
35 Robert Reichel .02 .10
36 Igor Kravchuk .02 .10
37 Mathieu Schneider .02 .10
38 Bob Kudelski .02 .10
39 Jeff Brown .02 .10
40 Mike Modano .20 .50
41 Rob Gaudreau RC .02 .10
42 Dave Andreychuk .05 .15
43 Trevor Linden .05 .15
44 Dimitri Khristich .02 .10
45 Joe Murphy .02 .10
46 Rob Blake .05 .15
47 Alexander Semak .02 .10
48 Ray Ferraro .02 .10
49 Curtis Leschyshyn .02 .10
50 Mark Recchi .05 .15
51 Sergei Nemchinov .02 .10
52 Larry Murphy .05 .15
53 Steve Heinze .02 .10
54 Sergei Fedorov .20 .50
55 Gary Roberts .02 .10
56 Alexei Zhamnov .05 .15
57 Derian Hatcher .02 .10
58 Kelly Buchberger .02 .10
59 Eric Desjardins .05 .15
60 Brian Bradley .02 .10
61 Patrick Poulin .02 .10
62 Scott Lachance .02 .10
63 Johan Garpenlov .02 .10
64 Sylvain Turgeon .02 .10
65 Grant Fuhr .05 .15
66 Garth Butcher .02 .10
67 Michal Pivonka .02 .10
68 Todd Gill .02 .10
69 Cliff Ronning .02 .10
70 Steve Smith .02 .10
71 Bobby Holik .02 .10
72 Garry Galley .02 .10
73 Steve Leach .02 .10
74 Ron Francis .05 .15
75 Jari Kurri .10 .30
76 Alexei Kovalev .05 .15
77 Dave Gagner .05 .15
78 Steve Duchesne .02 .10
79 Theo Fleury .02 .10
80 Paul Coffey .10 .30
81 Bill Ranford .05 .15
82 Doug Bodger .02 .10
83 Nick Kypreos .02 .10
84 Darius Kasparaitis .02 .10
85 Vincent Damphousse .02 .10
86 Arturs Irbe .05 .15
87 Shawn Chambers .02 .10
88 Murray Craven .02 .10
89 Rob Pearson .02 .10
90 Kevin Hatcher .02 .10
91 Brent Sutter .02 .10
92 Teppo Numminen .02 .10
93 Shawn Burr .02 .10
94 Valeri Zelepukin .02 .10
95 Ron Sutter .02 .10
96 Craig MacTavish .02 .10
97 Dominic Roussel .05 .15
98 Nicklas Lidstrom .10 .30
99 Adam Graves .05 .15
100 Doug Gilmour .05 .15
101 Frank Musil .02 .10
102 Ted Donato .02 .10
103 Andrew Cassels .02 .10
104 Vladimir Malakhov .02 .10
105 Shawn McEachern .02 .10
106 Petr Nedved .05 .15
107 Calle Johansson .02 .10
108 Rich Sutter .02 .10
109 Evgeny Davydov .02 .10
110 Mike Ricci .02 .10
111 Scott Niedermayer .02 .10
112 John LeClair .10 .30
113 Darryl Sydor .02 .10
114 Paul DiPietro .02 .10
115 Stephane Fiset .05 .15
116 Christian Ruuttu .02 .10
117 Doug Zmolek .02 .10
118 Bob Sweeney .02 .10
119 Brent Fedyk .02 .10
120 Norm Maciver .02 .10
121 Rob Zamuner .02 .10
122 Brian Mullen .02 .10
123 Trent Yawney .02 .10
124 David Shaw .02 .10
125 Mark Messier .10 .30
126 Kevin Miller .02 .10
127 Dino Ciccarelli .05 .15
128 Derek King .02 .10
129 Scott Young .02 .10
130 Craig Janney .05 .15
131 Jamie Macoun .02 .10
132 Geoff Courtnall .02 .10
133 Bob Essensa .05 .15
134 Ken Daneyko .02 .10
135 Mike Ridley .02 .10
136 Stephan Lebeau .02 .10
137 Tony Granato .02 .10
138 Kay Whitmore .05 .15
139 Luke Richardson .02 .10
140 Jeremy Roenick .15 .40
141 Brad May .05 .15
142 Sandis Ozolinsh .02 .10
143 Stephane Richer .05 .15
144 John Tucker .02 .10
145 Luc Robitaille .05 .15
146 Dimitri Yushkevich .02 .10
147 Sean Hill .02 .10
148 John Vanbiesbrouck .05 .15
149 Kevin Stevens .02 .10
150 Patrick Roy .60 1.50
151 Owen Nolan .05 .15
152 Richard Smehlik .02 .10
153 Ray Sheppard .05 .15
154 Ed Olczyk .02 .10
155 Al MacInnis .05 .15
156 Sergei Zubov .02 .10
157 Wendel Clark .05 .15
158 Kirk McLean .05 .15
159 Thomas Steen .02 .10
160 Pierre Turgeon .05 .15
161 Dmitri Kvartalnov .02 .10
162 Brian Noonan .02 .10
163 Mike McPhee .02 .10
164 Peter Bondra .05 .15
165 Bernie Nicholls .02 .10
166 Michael Nylander .02 .10
167 Guy Hebert .05 .15
168 Scott Mellanby .05 .15
169 Bob Bassen .02 .10
170 Rod Brind'Amour .05 .15
171 Andrei Kovalenko .02 .10
172 Mike Donnelly .02 .10
173 Steve Thomas .02 .10
174 Rick Tocchet .05 .15
175 Steve Yzerman .60 1.50
176 Dixon Ward .02 .10
177 Randy Wood .02 .10
178 Dean Kennedy .02 .10
179 Joel Otto .02 .10
180 Kirk Muller .02 .10
181 Chris Chelios .10 .30
182 Richard Matvichuk .02 .10
183 John MacLean .05 .15
184 Joe Kocur .02 .10
185 Adam Oates .05 .15
186 Bob Beers .02 .10
187 Ron Tugnutt .05 .15
188 Brian Skrudland .02 .10
189 Al Iafrate .02 .10
190 Felix Potvin .10 .30
191 David Reid .02 .10
192 Jim Johnson .02 .10
193 Kevin Haller .02 .10
194 Steve Chiasson .02 .10
195 Jaromir Jagr .20 .50
196 Martin Rucinsky .02 .10
197 Sergei Bautin .02 .10
198 Joe Nieuwendyk .05 .15
199 Gilbert Dionne .02 .10
200 Brett Hull .15 .40
201 Yuri Khmylev .02 .10
202 Todd Elik .02 .10
203 Patrick Flatley .05 .15
204 Martin Straka .02 .10
205 Brendan Shanahan .10 .30
206 Mark Beaufait RC .02 .10
207 Mike Lenarduzzi RC .02 .10
208 Chris LiPuma .02 .10
209 Andre Faust .02 .10
210 Ben Hankinson RC .02 .10
211 Darrin Madeley RC .02 .10
212 Oleg Petrov .02 .10
213 Philippe Boucher .02 .10
214 Tyler Wright .02 .10
215 Jason Bowen RC .02 .10
216 Matthew Barnaby .05 .15
217 Bryan Smolinski .05 .15
218 Dan Keczmer .02 .10
219 Chris Simon RC .30 .75
220 Corey Hirsch AW .05 .15
221 Mario Lemieux AW .10 .30
222 Teemu Selanne AW .10 .30
223 Chris Chelios AW .05 .15
224 Ed Belfour AW .05 .15
225 Pierre Turgeon AW .05 .15
226 Doug Gilmour AW .05 .15
227 Ed Belfour AW .10 .30
228 Patrick Roy AW .10 .30
229 Dave Poulin AW .02 .10
230 Mario Lemieux AW .10 .30
231 Mike Vernon HH .05 .15
232 Vincent Damphousse HH .02 .10
233 Chris Chelios HH .05 .15
234 Cliff Ronning HH .02 .10
235 Mark Howe HH .02 .10
236 Alexandre Daigle .02 .10
237 Wayne Gretzky .10 .30
238 Mark Messier .10 .30
239 Dino Ciccarelli .05 .15
240 Joe Mullen .05 .15
241 Mike Gartner .05 .15
242 Mike Richter .10 .30
243 Pat Verbeek .02 .10
244 Valeri Kamensky .05 .15
245 Nelson Emerson .02 .10
246 James Patrick .02 .10
247 Greg Adams .02 .10
248 Ulf Dahlen .02 .10
249 Shayne Corson .02 .10
250 Ray Bourque .20 .50
251 Claude Lemieux .05 .15
252 Kelly Hrudey .05 .15
253 Patrice Brisebois .02 .10
254 Mark Howe .02 .10
255 Ed Belfour .10 .30
256 Pelle Eklund .05 .15
257 Zarley Zalapski .02 .10
258 Sylvain Cote .02 .10
259 Uwe Krupp .05 .15
260 Dale Hawerchuk .05 .15
261 Alexei Gusarov .02 .10
262 Dave Ellett .02 .10
263 Tomas Sandstrom .02 .10
264 Vladimir Konstantinov .05 .15
265 Paul Ranheim .02 .10
266 Darrin Shannon .02 .10
267 Chris Terreri .05 .15
268 Russ Courtnall .05 .15
269 Don Sweeney .02 .10
270 Kevin Todd .02 .10
271 Brad Shaw .02 .10
272 Adam Creighton .02 .10
273 Dana Murzyn .02 .10
274 Donald Audette .02 .10
275 Brian Leetch .10 .30
276 Kevin Dineen .02 .10
277 Bruce Driver .02 .10
278 Jim Paek .02 .10
279 Esa Tikkanen .02 .10
280 Guy Carbonneau .02 .10
281 Eric Weinrich .02 .10
282 Tim Cheveldae .05 .15
283 Bryan Marchment .02 .10
284 Kelly Miller .02 .10
285 Jimmy Carson .02 .10
286 Terry Carkner .02 .10
287 Mike Sullivan .02 .10
288 Joe Reekie .02 .10
289 Bob Rouse .02 .10
290 Joe Sakic .25 .60
291 Gerald Diduck .02 .10
292 Don Beaupre .05 .15
293 Kjell Samuelsson .02 .10
294 Claude Lapointe .02 .10
295 Tie Domi .05 .15
296 Charlie Huddy .02 .10
297 Peter Zezel .02 .10
298 Craig Muni .02 .10
299 Rick Tabaracci .05 .15
300 Pat LaFontaine .10 .30
301 Lyle Odelein .02 .10
302 Jocelyn Lemieux .02 .10
303 Craig Ludwig .02 .10
304 Marc Bergevin .02 .10
305 Bill Guerin .02 .10
306 Rick Zombo .02 .10
307 Steven Finn .02 .10
308 Gino Odjick .02 .10
309 Jeff Beukeboom .02 .10
310 Mario Lemieux .60 1.50
311 J.J. Daigneault .02 .10
312 Vincent Riendeau .05 .15
313 Adam Burt .02 .10
314 Mike Craig .02 .10
315 Bret Hedican .02 .10
316 Kris King .02 .10
317 Sylvain Lefebvre .02 .10
318 Troy Murray .02 .10
319 Gordie Roberts .02 .10
320 Pavel Bure .10 .30
321 Marc Bureau .02 .10
322 Randy McKay .02 .10
323 Mark Lamb .02 .10
324 Brian Mullen .02 .10
325 Ken Wregget .05 .15
326 Stephane Quintal .02 .10
327 Robert Dirk .02 .10
328 Mike Krushelnyski .02 .10
329 Mikael Andersson .02 .10
330 Paul Stanton .02 .10
331 Phil Bourque .02 .10
332 Andre Racicot .05 .15
333 Brad Dalgarno .02 .10
334 Neal Broten .05 .15
335 John Blue .05 .15
336 Ken Sutton .02 .10
337 Greg Paslawski .02 .10
338 Robb Stauber .02 .10
339 Mike Keane .02 .10
340 Terry Yake .02 .10
341 Brian Benning .02 .10
342 Brian Propp .02 .10
343 Frank Pietrangelo .05 .15
344 Stephane Matteau .02 .10
345 Steven King .02 .10
346 Joe Cirella .02 .10
347 Andy Moog .05 .15
348 Paul Ysebaert .02 .10
349 Petr Klima .02 .10
350 Corey Millen .02 .10
351 Phil Housley .05 .15
352 Craig Billington .05 .15
353 Jeff Norton .02 .10
354 Neil Wilkinson .02 .10
355 Doug Lidster .02 .10
356 Steve Larmer .05 .15
357 Jon Casey .05 .15
358 Brad McCrimmon .02 .10
359 Alexei Kasatonov .02 .10
360 Andrei Lomakin .02 .10
361 Daren Puppa .05 .15
362 Sergei Makarov .02 .10
363 Dave Manson .02 .10
364 Jim Sandlak .02 .10
365 Glenn Healy .05 .15
366 Martin Gelinas .02 .10
367 Igor Larionov .02 .10
368 Anatoli Semenov .02 .10
369 Mark Fitzpatrick .05 .15
370 Paul Cavallini .02 .10
371 Jimmy Waite .05 .15
372 Yves Racine .02 .10
373 Jeff Hackett .05 .15
374 Marty McSorley .02 .10
375 Scott Pearson .02 .10
376 Ron Hextall .05 .15
377 Gaetan Duchesne .02 .10
378 Jamie Baker .02 .10
379 Troy Loney .02 .10
380 Gord Murphy .02 .10
381 Peter Sidorkiewicz .05 .15
382 Pat Elynuik .02 .10
383 Glen Wesley .02 .10
384 Dean Evason .02 .10
385 Mike Peluso .02 .10
386 Darren Turcotte .02 .10
387 Dave Poulin .02 .10
388 John Cullen .02 .10
389 Randy Ladouceur .02 .10
390 Tom Fitzgerald .02 .10
391 Denis Savard .05 .15
392 Fredrik Olausson .02 .10
393 Sergio Momesso .02 .10
394 Mike Ramsey .02 .10
395 Kelly Kisio .02 .10
396 Craig Simpson .02 .10
397 Slava Fetisov .02 .10
398 Glenn Anderson .05 .15
399 Michel Goulet .05 .15
400 Wayne Gretzky .75 2.00
401 Stu Grimson .02 .10
402 Mike Hough .02 .10
403 Dominik Hasek .40 1.00
404 Gerard Gallant .02 .10
405 Greg Gilbert .02 .10
406 Vladimir Ruzicka .02 .10
407 Jim Hrivnak .05 .15
408 Dave Lowry .02 .10
409 Todd Ewen .02 .10
410 Bob Errey .02 .10
411 Bryan Trottier .05 .15
412 Dave Taylor .05 .15
413 Grant Ledyard .02 .10
414 Chris Dahlquist .02 .10
415 Brent Gilchrist .02 .10
416 Geoff Smith .02 .10
417 Jiri Slegr .02 .10
418 Randy Burridge .02 .10
419 Sergei Krivokrasov .02 .10
420 Keith Primeau .02 .10
421 Robert Kron .02 .10
422 Keith Brown .02 .10
423 David Volek .02 .10
424 Josef Beranek .02 .10
425 Wayne Presley .02 .10
426 Stu Barnes .02 .10
427 Milos Holan RC .02 .10
428 Jeff Shantz .02 .10
429 Brent Gretzky RC .02 .10
430 Jarkko Varvio .02 .10
431 Chris Osgood RC .60 1.50
432 Aaron Ward RC .02 .10
433 Jason Smith RC .02 .10
434 Cam Stewart RC .02 .10
435 Derek Plante RC .02 .10
436 Pat Peake .02 .10
437 Alexander Karpovtsev .02 .10
438 Jim Montgomery RC .02 .10
439 Rob Niedermayer .05 .15
440 Jocelyn Thibault RC .40 1.00
441 Jason Arnott RC .60 1.50
442 Mike Rathje .02 .10
443 Chris Gratton .05 .15
444 Vesa Viitakoski RC .02 .10
445 Alexei Kudashov RC .02 .10
446 Pavol Demitra .05 .15
447 Ted Drury .02 .10
448 Rene Corbet RC .02 .10
449 Markus Naslund .10 .30
450 Dmitri Filimonov .02 .10
451 Roman Oksiuta RC .02 .10
452 Michal Sykora RC .02 .10
453 Greg Johnson .02 .10
454 Mikael Renberg .10 .30
455 Alexei Yashin .02 .10
456 Chris Pronger .15 .40
457 Manny Fernandez RC .40 1.00
458 Jamie Storr RC .25 .60
459 Chris Armstrong RC .02 .10
460 Drew Bannister RC .02 .10
461 Joel Bouchard RC .02 .10
462 Bryan McCabe RC .10 .30
463 Nick Stajduhar RC .02 .10
464 Brent Tully .02 .10
465 Brendan Witt RC .02 .10
466 Jason Allison RC .60 1.50
467 Jason Botterill RC .02 .10
468 Curtis Bowen RC .02 .10
469 Anson Carter RC .30 .75
470 Brandon Convery RC .02 .10
471 Yanick Dube RC .02 .10
472 Jeff Friesen RC .60 1.50
473 Aaron Gavey RC .02 .10
474 Martin Gendron RC .02 .10
475 Rick Girard RC .02 .10
476 Todd Harvey RC .02 .10
477 Marty Murray RC .02 .10
478 Mike Peca RC .40 1.00
479 Aaron Ellis RC .02 .10
480 Toby Kvalevog RC .02 .10
481 Jon Coleman RC .02 .10
482 Ashlin Halfnight RC .02 .10
483 Jason McBain RC .02 .10
484 Chris O'Sullivan RC .02 .10
485 Deron Quint RC .10 .30
486 Blake Sloan RC .05 .15
487 David Wilkie RC .02 .10
488 Kevyn Adams RC .02 .10
489 Jason Bonsignore RC .02 .10
490 Andy Brink RC .02 .10
491 Adam Deadmarsh .02 .10
492 John Emmons .02 .10
493 Kevin Hilton RC .02 .10
494 Jason Karmanos RC .02 .10
495 Bob Lachance RC .02 .10
496 Jamie Langenbrunner RC .40 1.00
497 Jay Pandolfo RC .02 .10
498 Richard Park RC .02 .10
499 Ryan Sittler .02 .10
500 John Varga RC .02 .10
501 Valeri Bure RC .40 1.00
502 Maxim Bets RC .02 .10
503 Vadim Sharifjanov .05 .15
504 Alexander Kharlamov RC .02 .10
505 Pavel Desyatkov RC .02 .10
506 Oleg Tverdovsky RC .25 .60
507 Nikolai Tsulygin .02 .10
508 Evgeni Ryabchikov RC .02 .10
509 Sergei Brylin RC .02 .10
510 Maxim Sushinski RC .05 .15
511 Sergei Kondrashkin RC .02 .10
512 Wayne Gretzky HL SP 3.00 8.00
AU1 Alexandre Daigle Autographed card 6.00 15.00
AU2 Eric Lindros Autographed card 15.00 40.00
NNO Eric Lindros Brett Lindros U.S. version .10 .30
NNO Eric Lindros Expired Redemption .10 .30

1993-94 Pinnacle Canadian

COMPLETE SET (511) 12.00 30.00
COMP.SERIES 1 (236) 6.00 15.00
COMP.SERIES 2 (275) 6.00 15.00
*CANADIAN: .4X TO 1X BASIC CARDS
1 Eric Lindros 1.00 2.50
2 Mats Sundin .15 .40
3 Tom Barrasso .05 .15
4 Teemu Selanne .40 1.00
5 Joe Juneau .15 .40
6 Tony Amonte .02 .10
7 Bob Probert .02 .10
8 Chris Kontos .04 .10
9 Geoff Sanderson .02 .10
10 Alexander Mogilny .15 .40
11 Kevin Lowe .04 .10
12 Nikolai Borschevsky .04 .10
13 Dale Hunter .02 .10
14 Gary Suter .02 .10
15 Curtis Joseph .10 .30
16 Mark Tinordi .04 .10
17 Doug Weight .02 .10
18 Benoit Hogue .04 .10
19 Tommy Soderstrom .02 .10
20 Pat Falloon .04 .10
21 Jyrki Lumme .04 .10
22 Brian Bellows .02 .10
23 Alexei Zhitnik .02 .10
24 Dirk Graham .04 .10
25 Scott Stevens .02 .10
26 Adam Foote .04 .10
27 Mike Gartner .05 .15
28 Dallas Drake RC .07 .20
29 Ulf Samuelsson .04 .10
30 Cam Neely .10 .30
31 Sean Burke .05 .15
32 Petr Svoboda .04 .10
33 Keith Tkachuk .15 .40
34 Roman Hamrlik .04 .10
35 Robert Reichel .02 .10
36 Igor Kravchuk .04 .10
37 Mathieu Schneider .04 .10
38 Bob Kudelski .04 .10
39 Jeff Brown .02 .10
40 Mike Modano .10 .30
41 Rob Gaudreau RC .04 .10
42 Dave Andreychuk .05 .15
43 Trevor Linden .05 .15
44 Dimitri Khristich .04 .10
45 Joe Murphy .02 .10
46 Rob Blake .02 .10
47 Alexander Semak .04 .10
48 Ray Ferraro .02 .10
49 Curtis Leschyshyn .04 .10
50 Mark Recchi .08 .25
51 Sergei Nemchinov .02 .10
52 Larry Murphy .05 .15
53 Steve Heinze .04 .10
54 Sergei Fedorov .40 1.00
55 Gary Roberts .02 .10
56 Alexei Zhamnov .20 .50
57 Derian Hatcher .04 .10
58 Kelly Buchberger .04 .10
59 Eric Desjardins .04 .10
60 Brian Bradley .04 .10
61 Patrick Poulin .04 .10
62 Scott Lachance .04 .10
63 Johan Garpenlov .04 .10
64 Sylvain Turgeon .04 .10
65 Grant Fuhr .05 .15
66 Garth Butcher .04 .10
67 Michal Pivonka .04 .10
68 Todd Gill .04 .10
69 Cliff Ronning .04 .10
70 Steve Smith .04 .10
71 Bobby Holik .04 .10
72 Garry Galley .04 .10
73 Steve Leach .04 .10
74 Ron Francis .05 .15
75 Jari Kurri .05 .15
76 Alexei Kovalev .15 .40
77 Dave Gagner .02 .10
78 Steve Duchesne .02 .10
79 Theo Fleury .05 .15
80 Paul Coffey .07 .20
81 Bill Ranford .05 .15
82 Doug Bodger .04 .10
83 Nick Kypreos .04 .10
84 Darius Kasparaitis .04 .10
85 Vincent Damphousse .02 .10
86 Arturs Irbe .20 .50
87 Shawn Chambers .04 .10
88 Murray Craven .04 .10
89 Rob Pearson .04 .10
90 Kevin Hatcher .02 .10
91 Brent Sutter .02 .10
92 Teppo Numminen .04 .10
93 Shawn Burr .04 .10
94 Valeri Zelepukin .04 .10
95 Ron Sutter .04 .10
96 Craig MacTavish .02 .10
97 Dominic Roussel .02 .10
98 Nicklas Lidstrom .02 .10
99 Adam Graves .08 .25
100 Doug Gilmour .10 .30
101 Frank Musil .04 .10
102 Ted Donato .04 .10
103 Andrew Cassels .04 .10
104 Vladimir Malakhov .02 .10
105 Shawn McEachern .04 .10
106 Petr Nedved .02 .10
107 Calle Johansson .04 .10
108 Rich Sutter .04 .10
109 Evgeny Davydov .04 .10
110 Mike Ricci .02 .10
111 Scott Niedermayer .02 .10
112 John LeClair .15 .40
113 Darryl Sydor .04 .10
114 Paul DiPietro .04 .10
115 Stephane Fiset .05 .15
116 Christian Ruuttu .04 .10
117 Doug Zmolek .04 .10
118 Bob Sweeney .04 .10
119 Brent Fedyk .04 .10
120 Norm Maciver .04 .10
121 Rob Zamuner .04 .10
122 Brian Mullen .05 .15
123 Trent Yawney .04 .10
124 David Shaw .04 .10
125 Mark Messier .07 .20
126 Kevin Miller .04 .10
127 Dino Ciccarelli .05 .15
128 Derek King .04 .10
129 Scott Young .04 .10
130 Craig Janney .02 .10
131 Jamie Macoun .04 .10
132 Geoff Courtnall .02 .10
133 Bob Essensa .02 .10
134 Ken Daneyko .04 .10
135 Mike Ridley .04 .10
136 Stephan Lebeau .04 .10
137 Tony Granato .04 .10
138 Kay Whitmore .02 .10
139 Luke Richardson .04 .10
140 Jeremy Roenick .30 .75
141 Brad May .04 .10
142 Sandis Ozolinsh .02 .10
143 Stephane Richer .02 .10
144 John Tucker .04 .10
145 Luc Robitaille .07 .20
146 Dimitri Yushkevich .04 .10
147 Sean Hill .04 .10
148 John Vanbiesbrouck .04 .10
149 Kevin Stevens .08 .25
150 Patrick Roy .40 1.00
151 Owen Nolan .02 .10
152 Richard Smehlik .04 .10
153 Ray Sheppard .04 .10
154 Ed Olczyk .04 .10
155 Al MacInnis .05 .15
156 Sergei Zubov .20 .50
157 Wendel Clark .05 .15
158 Kirk McLean .05 .15
159 Thomas Steen .04 .10
160 Pierre Turgeon .10 .30
161 Dmitri Kvartalnov .04 .10
162 Brian Noonan .04 .10
163 Mike McPhee .04 .10
164 Peter Bondra .02 .10
165 Bernie Nicholls .05 .15
166 Michael Nylander .04 .10
167 Guy Hebert .07 .20
168 Scott Mellanby .04 .10
169 Bob Bassen .04 .10
170 Rod Brind'Amour .05 .15
171 Andrei Kovalenko .04 .10
172 Mike Donnelly .04 .10
173 Steve Thomas .02 .10
174 Rick Tocchet .05 .15
175 Steve Yzerman .20 .50
176 Dixon Ward .04 .10
177 Randy Wood .04 .10
178 Dean Kennedy .04 .10
179 Joel Otto .04 .10
180 Kirk Muller .04 .10
181 Chris Chelios .05 .15
182 Richard Matvichuk .04 .10
183 John MacLean .02 .10
184 Joe Kocur .04 .10
185 Adam Oates .07 .20
186 Bob Beers .04 .10
187 Ron Tugnutt .02 .10
188 Brian Skrudland .04 .10
189 Al Iafrate .02 .10
190 Felix Potvin .40 1.00
191 David Reid .04 .10
192 Jim Johnson .04 .10
193 Kevin Haller .04 .10
194 Steve Chiasson .04 .10
195 Jaromir Jagr .40 1.00
196 Martin Rucinsky .04 .10
197 Sergei Bautin .02 .10
198 Joe Nieuwendyk .05 .15
199 Gilbert Dionne .04 .10
200 Brett Hull .30 .75
201 Yuri Khmylev .04 .10
202 Todd Elik .04 .10
203 Patrick Flatley .04 .10
204 Martin Straka .02 .10
205 Brendan Shanahan .15 .40
206 Mark Beaufait RC .04 .10
207 Mike Lenarduzzi RC .02 .10
208 Chris LiPuma .04 .10
209 Andre Faust .04 .10
210 Ben Hankinson RC .04 .10
211 Darrin Madeley RC .02 .10
212 Oleg Petrov .04 .10
213 Philippe Boucher .04 .10
214 Tyler Wright .04 .10
215 Jason Bowen RC .04 .10
216 Matthew Barnaby .04 .10
217 Bryan Smolinski .15 .40
218 Dan Keczmer .04 .10
219 Chris Simon RC .07 .20
220 Corey Hirsch AW .04 .10
221 Mario Lemieux AW .15 .40
222 Teemu Selanne AW .15 .40
223 Chris Chelios AW .02 .10
224 Ed Belfour AW .05 .15
225 Pierre Turgeon AW .05 .15
226 Doug Gilmour AW .07 .20
227 Ed Belfour AW .05 .15
228 Patrick Roy AW .15 .40
229 Dave Poulin AW .04 .10
230 Mario Lemieux AW .15 .40
231 Mike Vernon HH .04 .10
232 Vincent Damphousse HH .04 .10
233 Chris Chelios HH .02 .10
234 Cliff Ronning HH .04 .10
235 Mark Howe HH .04 .10
236 Alexandre Daigle .20 .50
237 Wayne Gretzky .60 1.50
238 Mark Messier .08 .25
239 Dino Ciccarelli .04 .10
240 Joe Mullen .05 .15
241 Mike Gartner .05 .15
242 Mike Richter .08 .25
243 Pat Verbeek .04 .10
244 Valeri Kamensky .04 .10
245 Nelson Emerson .04 .10
246 James Patrick .04 .10
247 Greg Adams .04 .10
248 Ulf Dahlen .04 .10
249 Shayne Corson .04 .10
250 Ray Bourque .07 .20
251 Claude Lemieux .02 .10
252 Kelly Hrudey .05 .15
253 Patrice Brisebois .04 .10

1994-95 Pinnacle

254 Mark Howe .02 .10
255 Ed Belfour .15 .40
256 Pelle Eklund .04 .10
257 Zarley Zalapski .04 .10
258 Sylvain Cote .04 .10
259 Uwe Krupp .04 .10
260 Dale Hawerchuk .05 .15
261 Alexei Gusarov .04 .10
262 Dave Ellett .04 .10
263 Tomas Sandstrom .02 .10
264 Vladimir Konstantinov .04 .10
265 Paul Ranheim .04 .10
266 Darrin Shannon .04 .10
267 Chris Terreri .02 .10
268 Russ Courtnall .02 .10
269 Don Sweeney .04 .10
270 Kevin Todd .04 .10
271 Brad Shaw .04 .10
272 Adam Creighton .04 .10
273 Dana Murzyn .04 .10
274 Donald Audette .04 .10
275 Brian Leetch .08 .25
276 Kevin Dineen .04 .10
277 Bruce Driver .04 .10
278 Jim Paek .04 .10
279 Esa Tikkanen .02 .10
280 Guy Carbonneau .02 .10
281 Eric Weinrich .04 .10
282 Tim Cheveldae .02 .10
283 Bryan Marchment .04 .10
284 Kelly Miller .04 .10
285 Jimmy Carson .04 .10
286 Terry Carkner .04 .10
287 Mike Sullivan .04 .10
288 Joe Reekie .04 .10
289 Bob Rouse .04 .10
290 Joe Sakic .15 .40
291 Gerald Diduck .04 .10
292 Don Beaupre .02 .10
293 Kjell Samuelsson .04 .10
294 Claude Lapointe .04 .10
296 Charlie Huddy .04 .10
297 Peter Zezel .04 .10
298 Craig Muni .04 .10
299 Rick Tabaracci .02 .10
300 Pat LaFontaine .07 .20
301 Lyle Odelein .04 .10
302 Jocelyn Lemieux .04 .10
303 Craig Ludwig .04 .10
304 Marc Bergevin .04 .10
305 Bill Guerin .04 .10
306 Rick Zombo .04 .10
307 Steven Finn .04 .10
308 Gino Odjick .04 .10
309 Jeff Beukeboom .04 .10
310 Mario Lemieux .40 1.00
311 J.J. Daigneault .04 .10
312 Vincent Riendeau .02 .10
313 Adam Burt .04 .10
314 Mike Craig .04 .10
315 Bret Hedican .04 .10
316 Kris King .04 .10
317 Sylvain Lefebvre .04 .10
318 Troy Murray .04 .10
319 Gordie Roberts .04 .10
320 Pavel Bure .60 1.50
321 Marc Bureau .04 .10
322 Randy McKay .04 .10
323 Mark Lamb .04 .10
324 Brian Mullen .02 .10
325 Ken Wregget .02 .10
326 Stephane Quintal .04 .10
327 Robert Dirk .04 .10
328 Mike Krushelnyski .04 .10
329 Mikael Andersson .04 .10
330 Paul Stanton .04 .10
331 Phil Bourque .04 .10
332 Andre Racicot .02 .10
333 Brad Dalgarno .04 .10
334 Neal Broten .02 .10
335 John Blue .02 .10
336 Ken Sutton .04 .10
337 Greg Paslawski .04 .10
338 Robb Stauber .02 .10
339 Mike Keane .04 .10
340 Terry Yake .04 .10
341 Brian Benning .04 .10
342 Brian Propp .02 .10
343 Frank Pietrangelo .02 .10
344 Stephane Matteau .04 .10
345 Steven King .04 .10
346 Joe Cirella .04 .10
347 Andy Moog .05 .15
348 Paul Ysebaert .04 .10
349 Petr Klima .04 .10
350 Corey Millen .04 .10
351 Phil Housley .02 .10
352 Craig Billington .02 .10
353 Jeff Norton .04 .10
354 Neil Wilkinson .04 .10
355 Doug Lidster .04 .10
356 Steve Larmer .05 .15
357 Jon Casey .02 .10
358 Brad McCrimmon .04 .10
359 Alexei Kasatonov .04 .10
360 Andrei Lomakin .04 .10
361 Daren Puppa .05 .15
362 Sergei Makarov .05 .15
363 Dave Manson .04 .10
364 Jim Sandlak .04 .10
365 Glenn Healy .02 .10
366 Martin Gelinas .04 .10
367 Igor Larionov .02 .10
368 Anatoli Semenov .04 .10
369 Mark Fitzpatrick .04 .10
370 Paul Cavallini .04 .10
371 Jimmy Waite .02 .10
372 Yves Racine .04 .10
373 Jeff Hackett .02 .10
374 Marty McSorley .02 .10
375 Scott Pearson .04 .10
376 Ron Hextall .02 .10
377 Gaetan Duchesne .04 .10
378 Jamie Baker .04 .10
379 Troy Loney .04 .10
380 Gord Murphy .04 .10
381 Peter Sidorkiewicz .02 .10
382 Pat Elynuik .04 .10
383 Glen Wesley .04 .10
384 Dean Evason .04 .10
385 Mike Peluso .04 .10
386 Darren Turcotte .04 .10
387 Dave Poulin .04 .10
388 John Cullen .04 .10
389 Randy Ladouceur .04 .10
390 Tom Fitzgerald .04 .10
391 Denis Savard .05 .15
392 Fredrik Olausson .04 .10
393 Sergio Momesso .04 .10
394 Mike Ramsey .04 .10
395 Kelly Kisio .04 .10
396 Craig Simpson .04 .10
397 Slava Fetisov .02 .10
398 Glenn Anderson .02 .10
399 Michel Goulet .05 .15
400 Wayne Gretzky .75 2.00
401 Stu Grimson .04 .10
402 Mike Hough .04 .10
403 Dominik Hasek .20 .50
404 Gerard Gallant .04 .10
405 Greg Gilbert .04 .10
406 Vladimir Ruzicka .04 .10
407 Jim Hrivnak .02 .10
408 Dave Lowry .04 .10
409 Todd Ewen .04 .10
410 Bob Errey .04 .10
411 Bryan Trottier .05 .15
412 Dave Taylor .05 .15
413 Grant Ledyard .04 .10
414 Chris Dahlquist .04 .10
415 Brent Gilchrist .04 .10
416 Geoff Smith .04 .10
417 Jiri Slegr .04 .10
418 Randy Burridge .04 .10
419 Sergei Krivokrasov .02 .10
420 Keith Primeau .05 .15
421 Robert Kron .04 .10
422 Keith Brown .04 .10
423 David Volek .04 .10
424 Josef Beranek .04 .10
425 Wayne Presley .04 .10
426 Stu Barnes .04 .10
427 Milos Holan RC .07 .20
428 Jeff Shantz .04 .10
429 Brent Gretzky RC .10 .30
430 Jarkko Varvio .04 .10
431 Chris Osgood RC .25 .60
432 Aaron Ward RC .04 .10
433 Jason Smith RC .04 .10
434 Cam Stewart RC .04 .10
435 Derek Plante RC .08 .25
436 Pat Peake .04 .10
437 Alexander Karpovtsev .04 .10
438 Jim Montgomery RC .04 .10
439 Rob Niedermayer .15 .40
440 Jocelyn Thibault RC .30 .75
441 Jason Arnott RC .75 2.00
442 Mike Rathje .04 .10
443 Chris Gratton .15 .40
444 Vesa Viitakoski RC .04 .10
445 Alexei Kudashov RC .04 .10
447 Ted Drury .04 .10
448 Rene Corbet RC .04 .10
449 Markus Naslund .04 .10
450 Dmitri Filimonov .04 .10
451 Roman Oksiuta RC .08 .25
452 Michal Sykora RC .07 .20
453 Greg Johnson .04 .10
454 Mikael Renberg .30 .75
456 Chris Pronger .15 .40
457 Emmanuel Fernandez RC .25 .60
458 Jamie Storr RC .75 2.00
459 Chris Armstrong RC .05 .15
460 Drew Bannister RC .05 .15
461 Joel Bouchard RC .04 .10
462 Bryan McCabe RC .15 .40
463 Nick Stajduhar RC .10 .30
464 Brent Tully .05 .15
465 Brendan Witt RC .15 .40
466 Jason Allison RC .30 .75
467 Jason Botterill RC .15 .40
468 Curtis Bowen RC .05 .15
469 Anson Carter RC .08 .25
470 Brandon Convery RC .08 .25
471 Yanick Dube RC .15 .40
472 Jeff Friesen RC 1.00 2.50
473 Aaron Gavey RC .20 .50
474 Martin Gendron RC .15 .40
475 Rick Girard RC .05 .15
476 Todd Harvey RC .50 1.25
477 Marty Murray RC .30 .75
478 Mike Peca RC .15 .40
479 Aaron Ellis RC .05 .15
480 Toby Kvalevog RC .05 .15
481 Jon Coleman RC .05 .15
482 Ashlin Halfnight RC .05 .15
483 Jason McBain RC .05 .15
484 Chris O'Sullivan RC .07 .20
485 Deron Quint RC .15 .40
486 Blake Sloan RC .05 .15
487 David Wilkie RC .15 .40
488 Kevyn Adams RC .20 .50
489 Jason Bonsignore RC .30 .75
490 Andy Brink RC .05 .15
491 Adam Deadmarsh .15 .40
492 John Emmons .05 .15
493 Kevin Hilton RC .05 .15
494 Jason Karmanos RC .05 .15
495 Bob Lachance RC .05 .15
496 Jamie Langenbrunner RC .20 .50
497 Jay Pandolfo RC .05 .15
498 Richard Park RC .30 .75
499 Ryan Sittler .05 .15
500 John Varga RC .05 .15
501 Valeri Bure RC .40 1.00
502 Maxim Bets RC .08 .25
503 Vadim Sharifijanov .08 .25
504 Alexander Kharlamov RC .25 .60
505 Pavel Desyatkov RC .05 .15
506 Oleg Tverdovsky RC .50 1.25
507 Nikolai Tsulygin .05 .15
508 Evgeni Ryabchikov RC .15 .40
509 Sergei Brylin RC .15 .40
510 Maxim Sushinski RC .05 .15
511 Sergei Kondrashkin RC .07 .20
NNO Brett Lindros CDN 12.00 30.00
Eric Lindros

1993-94 Pinnacle All-Stars

One bonus Pinnacle All-Star card was inserted in every U.S. and Canadian pack of '93-94 Score series 1 hockey cards. The wrappers from those packs carried a mail-away offer for cards 46-50. These cards feature on their fronts color action shots of players in their All-Star uniforms. The photos of Canadian and U.S. cards differ.

COMPLETE INSERT SET (45) 5.00 10.00
COMP.MAIL-IN SET (5) 10.00 25.00
1 Craig Billington .07 .20
2 Zarley Zalapski .05 .15
3 Kevin Lowe .05 .15
4 Scott Stevens .08 .25
5 Pierre Turgeon .08 .25
6 Mark Recchi .08 .25
7 Kirk Muller .05 .15
8 Mike Gartner .08 .25
9 Adam Oates .08 .25
10 Brad Marsh .05 .15
11 Pat LaFontaine .08 .25
12 Peter Bondra .08 .25
13 Joe Sakic .20 .50
14 Rick Tocchet .08 .25
15 Kevin Stevens .08 .25
16 Steve Duchesne .08 .25
17 Peter Sidorkiewicz .08 .25
18 Patrick Roy .50 1.25
19 Al Iafrate .05 .15
20 Jaromir Jagr .15 .40
21 Ray Bourque .08 .25
22 Alexander Mogilny .08 .25
23 Steve Chiasson .05 .15
24 Garth Butcher .05 .15
25 Phil Housley .07 .20
26 Chris Chelios .08 .25
27 Randy Carlyle .05 .15
28 Mike Modano .15 .40
29 Gary Roberts .05 .15
30 Kelly Kisio .05 .15
31 Pavel Bure .08 .25
32 Teemu Selanne .08 .25
33 Brian Bradley .05 .15
34 Brett Hull .10 .30
35 Jari Kurri .08 .25
36 Steve Yzerman .50 1.25
37 Luc Robitaille .08 .25
38 Dave Manson .05 .15
39 Jeremy Roenick .10 .30
40 Mike Vernon .08 .25
41 Jon Casey .08 .25
42 Ed Belfour .08 .25
43 Paul Coffey .08 .25
44 Doug Gilmour .08 .25
45 Wayne Gretzky .60 1.50
46 Mike Gartner 1.50 4.00
47 Al Iafrate 1.50 4.00
48 Ray Bourque 6.00 15.00
49 Jon Casey 1.50 4.00
50 Campbell Conf. 2.00 5.00

1993-94 Pinnacle Captains

Randomly inserted in second-series jumbo packs at a rate of 1:4, these 27 standard-size cards feature on their fronts two photos of each NHL team captain. The photos of the Canadian and U.S. versions differ. The large borderless photo is a ghosted colour action shot; the smaller image in the center overlays the larger and is a full-contrast color head shot. The player's name in gold-foil lettering appears above the smaller photo. The grayish back carries a color action cutout on the left and a player profile in English (bilingual for the Canadian version) on the right. The cards are numbered on the back with a "CA" prefix.

COMPLETE SET (27) 40.00 100.00
*CANADIAN: .4X TO 1X BASIC INSERTS
1 Troy Loney .75 2.00
2 Ray Bourque 2.50 6.00
3 Pat LaFontaine 1.25 3.00
4 Joe Nieuwendyk 1.25 3.00
5 Dirk Graham .75 2.00
6 Mark Tinordi .75 2.00
7 Steve Yzerman 6.00 15.00
8 Craig MacTavish .75 2.00
9 Brian Skrudland .75 2.00
10 Pat Verbeek .75 2.00
11 Wayne Gretzky 10.00 25.00
12 Guy Carbonneau .75 2.00
13 Scott Stevens .75 2.00
14 Pat Flatley .75 2.00
15 Mark Messier 2.50 6.00
16 Mark Lamb .75 2.00
Brad Shaw
17 Kevin Dineen .75 2.00
18 Mario Lemieux 8.00 20.00
19 Joe Sakic 5.00 12.00
20 Brett Hull 2.50 6.00
21 Bob Errey .75 2.00
22 Marc Bergevin .75 2.00
Denis Savard
John Tucker
23 Wendel Clark 1.25 3.00
24 Trevor Linden 1.25 3.00
25 Kevin Hatcher .75 2.00
26 Keith Tkachuk 1.25 3.00
27 Checklist 2.00 5.00

1993-94 Pinnacle Expansion

Inserted one per series 1 hobby box, this six-card set measures the standard size. One side features a color action shot of a player from the Anaheim Mighty Ducks; the other, his counterpart at that position from the Florida Panthers. Each player's name and position, along with his team's logo, appear in a team color-coded bar below the photo. The cards are numbered on both sides as "X of 6."

COMPLETE SET (6) 5.00 10.00
1 John Vanbiesbrouck 1.25 3.00
Guy Hebert
2 Gord Murphy .75 2.00
Randy Ladouceur
3 Joe Cirella .75 2.00
Sean Hill
4 Dave Lowry .75 2.00
Troy Loney
5 Brian Skrudland .75 2.00
Terry Yake
6 Scott Mellanby .75 2.00
Steven King

1993-94 Pinnacle Masks

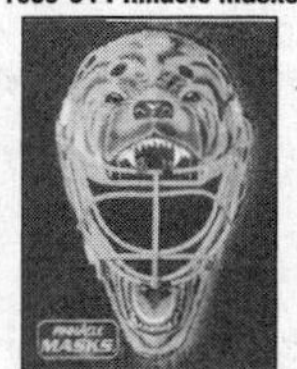

Randomly inserted in first-series packs at a rate of 1:24 packs, this 10-card standard-size set showcases some of the elaborate masks NHL goalies wear. The cards are numbered on the back as "X of 10."

COMPLETE SET (10) 30.00 80.00
1 Grant Fuhr 4.00 10.00
2 Mike Vernon 4.00 10.00
3 Robb Stauber 4.00 10.00
4 Dominic Roussel 4.00 10.00
5 Pat Jablonski 4.00 10.00
6 Stephane Fiset 4.00 10.00
7 Wendell Young 4.00 10.00
8 Ron Hextall 4.00 10.00
9 John Vanbiesbrouck 4.00 10.00
10 Peter Sidorkiewicz 4.00 10.00

1993-94 Pinnacle Nifty Fifty

Randomly inserted in second-series foil packs at a rate of 1:36 and featuring Pinnacle's Dufex process, this 15-card standard-size set spotlights players who scored 50 or more goals. The borderless fronts feature metallic color head shots with a gold-foil Nifty Fifty logo at the lower left. The cards are numbered on the back as "X of 15."

1 Introductory CL Card 2.00 5.00
2 Alexander Mogilny .50 1.25
3 Teemu Selanne 1.00 2.50
4 Mario Lemieux 4.00 10.00
5 Luc Robitaille .50 1.25
6 Pavel Bure 1.00 2.50
7 Pierre Turgeon .50 1.25
8 Steve Yzerman 3.00 8.00
9 Kevin Stevens .30 .75
10 Brett Hull 1.25 3.00
11 Dave Andreychuk .50 1.25
12 Pat LaFontaine 1.00 2.50
13 Mark Recchi .50 1.25
14 Brendan Shanahan 1.00 2.50
15 Jeremy Roenick 1.00 2.50

1993-94 Pinnacle Super Rookies

Randomly inserted in second-series hobby foil packs at a rate of 1:36, this nine-card standard-size set spotlights players who were rookies in 1993-94. The fronts feature color action player shots on darkened backgrounds. The player's name in gold-foil lettering appears at the lower right. On a dark red background, the horizontal backs carry a color player cutout on the left, with career highlights to the right. The set was issued in Canadian and U.S. versions. Each version carries its own front photos and the backs of the Canadian cards are bilingual. The cards are numbered on the back with an "SR" prefix.

COMPLETE SET (9) 2.00 5.00
*CANADIAN: .4X TO 1X BASIC INSERTS
1 Alexandre Daigle .20 .50
2 Chris Pronger .60 1.50
3 Chris Gratton .20 .50
4 Rob Niedermayer .20 .50
5 Alexei Yashin .20 .50
6 Mikael Renberg .20 .50
7 Jason Arnott .60 1.50
8 Markus Naslund .40 1.00
9 Pat Peake .20 .50

1993-94 Pinnacle Team Pinnacle

Randomly inserted in packs at a rate of 1:90, this 12-card set measures the standard size. On the U.S. version, one side features a black-bordered color drawing of a player from the Eastern Conference, the other, one of a player from the Western Conference. The Canadian version carries color photos instead of color drawings. The cards are numbered on both sides as "X of 12."

COMPLETE SET (12) 50.00 100.00
COMP.SERIES 1 (6) 30.00 60.00
COMP.SERIES 2 (6) 20.00 40.00
*CANADIAN: .5X TO 1.2X BASIC INSERTS
1 Patrick Roy 8.00 20.00
Ed Belfour
2 Brian Leetch 8.00 20.00
Chris Chelios
3 Scott Stevens 4.00 10.00
Al MacInnis
4 Kevin Stevens 4.00 10.00
Luc Robitaille
5 Mario Lemieux 10.00 25.00
Wayne Gretzky
6 Jaromir Jagr 5.00 12.00
Brett Hull
7 Tom Barrasso 4.00 10.00
Kirk McLean
8 Ray Bourque 4.00 10.00
Paul Coffey
9 Al Iafrate 4.00 10.00
Phil Housley
10 Vincent Damphousse 4.00 10.00
Pavel Bure
11 Eric Lindros 4.00 10.00
Jeremy Roenick
12 Alexander Mogilny 4.00 10.00
Teemu Selanne

1993-94 Pinnacle Team 2001

Inserted one per first-series jumbo pack, this 30-card set measures the standard size. The fronts feature color action player photos. The words "Team 2001" are printed in gold foil inside a black bar on the left, while the player's name in gold foil appears in a black bar on the bottom, along with the team logo. The horizontal backs carry a color head shot on the right. On a black background to the left of the photo are the player's name in gold foil and career highlights. The Canadian version carries color player drawings instead of photos. The cards are numbered on the back as "X of 30."

COMPLETE SET (30) 12.00 30.00
*CANADIAN: .4X TO 1X BASIC INSERTS
1 Eric Lindros .75 2.00
2 Alexander Mogilny .40 1.00
3 Pavel Bure .75 2.00
4 Joe Juneau .40 1.00
5 Felix Potvin .75 2.00
6 Nicklas Lidstrom .75 2.00
7 Alexei Kovalev .40 1.00
8 Patrick Poulin .20 .50
9 Shawn McEachern .20 .50
10 Teemu Selanne .75 2.00
11 Rod Brind'Amour .40 1.00
12 Jaromir Jagr 1.50 4.00
13 Pierre Turgeon .40 1.00
14 Scott Niedermayer .20 .50
15 Mats Sundin .75 2.00
16 Trevor Linden .40 1.00
17 Mike Modano 1.25 3.00
18 Roman Hamrlik .20 .50
19 Tony Amonte .40 1.00
20 Jeremy Roenick 1.25 3.00
21 Scott Lachance .20 .50
22 Mike Ricci .20 .50
23 Dimitri Khristich .20 .50
24 Sergei Fedorov 1.25 3.00
25 Joe Sakic 2.00 5.00
26 Pat Falloon .20 .50
27 Mathieu Schneider .20 .50
28 Owen Nolan .40 1.00
29 Brendan Shanahan .75 2.00
30 Mark Recchi .40 1.00

1993-94 Pinnacle Daigle Entry Draft

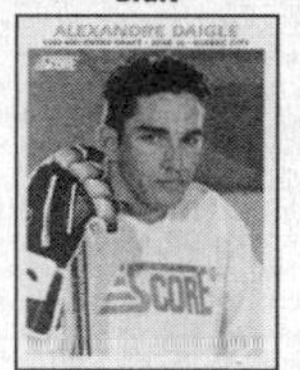

To commemorate Daigle's signing with Score as a spokesperson, Score issued this standard-size card and distributed it to the news media and others who attended the 1993 NHL Draft in Quebec on June 26. The card was also distributed to media at the 1993 National Sports Collectors Convention in Chicago. The front features a color close-up photo with white borders. Daigle is pictured wearing a jersey with "Score" emblazoned across it. The back has a full-bleed action shot with Daigle wearing a "Pinnacle" jersey. A black stripe at the bottom carries the player's name and the anti-counterfeiting device. The card is unnumbered.

1 Alexandre Daigle 4.00 10.00

1994-95 Pinnacle I Hobby Samples

These standard-size cards were issued in a sealed ten-card pack to preview the 1994-95 Pinnacle I regular series. They are identical to the regular issue counterparts, except that the upper right corner has been cut off, and the printing of the names on front is done in the style of Rink Collection, rather than regular, cards. The cards are numbered on the back.

COMPLETE SEALED SET (10) 1.00 2.50
1 Eric Lindros .40 1.00
2 Alexandre Daigle .07 .20
3 Mike Modano .20 .50
Dallas Star
4 Vincent Damphousse .02 .10
5 Dave Andreychuk .02 .10
6 Curtis Joseph .10 .30
7 Joe Juneau .02 .10
246 Mariusz Czerkawski .01 .05
BR1 Al Iafrate .08 .25
(Boomers insert set)
NNO Title Card .20 .50

1994-95 Pinnacle

This 540-card standard-size set was issued in two series of 270 cards. Cards were distributed in 14-card U.S. and Canadian packs, and 17-card jumbo packs. Series 1 packs had exclusive Canadian and U.S. inserts, series 2 did not. Members of the St. Louis Blues and Calgary Flames are posed in front of a locker which displays their newly designed sweaters. Rookie Cards include Mariusz Czerkawski, Eric Daze, Eric Fichaud, Ed Jovanovski, Jeff O'Neill and Wade Redden. A one-per-case (360 packs) insert card was produced for Canadian, and U.S. series 1 packs. Pavel Bure is numbered MVPC, while Dominik Hasek is MVPU. Both cards have MVP printed at top front and utilize a silver Dufex design. The backs feature dual photos over a silver reflective background.

COMPLETE SET (540) 12.50 25.00
COMP.SERIES 1 (270) 7.50 15.00
COMP.SERIES 2 (270) 5.00 10.00
1 Eric Lindros .10 .30
2 Alexandre Daigle .02 .10
3 Mike Modano .20 .50
4 Vincent Damphousse .02 .10
5 Dave Andreychuk .02 .10
6 Curtis Joseph .10 .30
7 Joe Juneau .05 .15
8 Trevor Linden .05 .15
9 Rob Blake .05 .15
10 Mike Richter .10 .30
11 Chris Pronger .10 .30
12 Robert Reichel .02 .10
13 Bryan Smolinski .02 .10
14 Ray Sheppard .05 .15
15 Guy Hebert .05 .15
16 Tony Amonte .05 .15
17 Richard Smehlik .02 .10
18 Doug Weight .05 .15
19 Chris Gratton .02 .10
20 Tom Barrasso .05 .15
21 Brian Skrudland .02 .10
22 Sandis Ozolinsh .02 .10
23 Bill Guerin .05 .15
24 Curtis Leschyshyn .02 .10
25 Teemu Selanne .10 .30
26 Darius Kasparaitis .02 .10
27 Garry Galley .02 .10
28 Alexei Yashin .02 .10
29 Mark Tinordi .02 .10
30 Patrick Roy .60 1.50
31 Mike Gartner .05 .15
32 Brendan Shanahan .10 .30
33 Sylvain Cote .02 .10
34 Jeff Brown .02 .10
35 Jari Kurri .05 .15
36 Sergei Zubov .02 .10
37 Pat Verbeek .02 .10
38 Theo Fleury .02 .10
39 Al Iafrate .02 .10
40 Keith Primeau .02 .10
41 Bobby Dollas .02 .10
42 Ed Belfour .10 .30
43 Dale Hawerchuk .05 .15
44 Shayne Corson .02 .10
45 Danton Cole .02 .10
46 Ulf Samuelsson .02 .10
47 Stu Barnes .02 .10
48 Ulf Dahlen .02 .10
49 Valeri Zelepukin .02 .10
50 Joe Sakic .25 .60
51 Dave Manson .02 .10
52 Steve Thomas .02 .10
53 Mark Recchi .05 .15
54 Dave McLlwain .02 .10
55 Derian Hatcher .02 .10
56 Mathieu Schneider .02 .10
57 Bill Berg .02 .10
58 Petr Nedved .05 .15
59 Dimitri Khristich .02 .10
60 Kirk McLean .05 .15
61 Marty McSorley .02 .10
62 Adam Graves .02 .10
63 Geoff Sanderson .05 .15
64 Frank Musil .02 .10
65 Cam Neely .10 .30
66 Nicklas Lidstrom .10 .30
67 Stephan Lebeau .02 .10
68 Joe Murphy .02 .10
69 Yuri Khmylev .02 .10
70 Zdeno Ciger .02 .10
71 Daren Puppa .05 .15
72 Ron Francis .05 .15
73 Scott Mellanby .05 .15
74 Igor Larionov .02 .10
75 Scott Niedermayer .02 .10
76 Owen Nolan .05 .15
77 Teppo Numminen .02 .10
78 Pierre Turgeon .05 .15
79 Mikael Renberg .05 .15
80 Norm Maciver .02 .10
81 Paul Cavallini .02 .10
82 Kirk Muller .02 .10
83 Felix Potvin .10 .30
84 Craig Janney .05 .15
85 Dale Hunter .02 .10
86 Jyrki Lumme .02 .10
87 Alexei Zhitnik .02 .10
88 Steve Larmer .05 .15
89 Jocelyn Lemieux .02 .10
90 Joe Nieuwendyk .05 .15
91 Don Sweeney .02 .10
92 Slava Kozlov .05 .15
93 Tim Sweeney .02 .10
94 Chris Chelios .10 .30
95 Derek Plante .02 .10
96 Igor Kravchuk .02 .10
97 Shawn Chambers .02 .10
98 Jaromir Jagr .20 .50
99 Jeff Norton .02 .10
100 John Vanbiesbrouck .05 .15
101 John MacLean .05 .15
102 Stephane Fiset .05 .15
103 Keith Tkachuk .10 .30
104 Vladimir Malakhov .02 .10
105 Mike McPhee .02 .10
106 Eric Desjardins .05 .15
107 Alexei Kovalev .02 .10
108 Steve Duchesne .02 .10
109 Peter Zezel .02 .10
110 Randy Burridge .02 .10
111 Jason Bowen .02 .10
112 Phil Bourque .02 .10
113 Cliff Ronning .02 .10
114 Sean Burke .05 .15
115 Gary Roberts .02 .10
116 Vladimir Konstantinov .05 .15
117 Brent Sutter .02 .10
118 Tony Granato .02 .10
119 Garry Valk .02 .10
120 Adam Oates .05 .15
121 Arturs Irbe .05 .15
122 Jesse Belanger .02 .10
123 Roman Hamrlik .05 .15
124 Jason Arnott .02 .10
125 Alexander Mogilny .05 .15
126 Bruce Driver .02 .10
127 Shawn McEachern .02 .10
128 Andrei Kovalenko .02 .10
129 Benoit Hogue .02 .10
130 Tim Cheveldae .05 .15
131 Brian Noonan .02 .10
132 Lyle Odelein .02 .10
133 Russ Courtnall .02 .10
134 Peter Stastny .05 .15
135 Doug Gilmour .05 .15
136 Pat Peake .02 .10
137 Gary Suter .02 .10
138 Paul Ranheim .02 .10
139 Troy Murray .02 .10
140 Pavel Bure .10 .30
141 Gord Murphy .02 .10
142 Michael Nylander .02 .10
143 Craig Muni .02 .10
144 Bob Corkum .02 .10
145 Martin Brodeur .30 .75
146 Ted Donato .02 .10
147 Alexei Zhamnov .05 .15
148 Josef Beranek .02 .10
149 Joe Mullen .05 .15
150 Sergei Fedorov .20 .50
151 Mike Keane .02 .10
152 Sergei Makarov .02 .10
153 Marty McInnis .02 .10
154 Steven Rice .02 .10
155 Brian Leetch .10 .30
156 Chris Joseph .02 .10
157 Darcy Wakaluk .05 .15
158 Kelly Miller .02 .10
159 Jim Montgomery .02 .10
160 Nikolai Borschevsky .02 .10
161 Darren Turcotte .02 .10
162 Brad Shaw .02 .10
163 Mark Lamb .02 .10
164 Alexei Gusarov .02 .10
165 Jeremy Roenick .15 .40
166 Stephane Richer .05 .15
167 German Titov .02 .10
168 Rob Niedermayer .05 .15
169 Glen Murray .02 .10
170 Mario Lemieux .60 1.50
171 Thomas Steen .02 .10
172 Ron Tugnutt .05 .15
173 Pat Falloon .02 .10
174 Esa Tikkanen .02 .10
175 Dominik Hasek .30 .75
176 Patrick Flatley .02 .10
177 Gino Odjick .02 .10
178 Charlie Huddy .02 .10
179 Dave Poulin .02 .10
180 Darren McCarty .02 .10
181 Todd Gill .02 .10
182 Tom Chorske .02 .10
183 Marc Bergevin .02 .10
184 Dave Lowry .02 .10
185 Brent Gilchrist .02 .10
186 Eric Weinrich .02 .10
187 Ted Drury .02 .10
188 Boris Mironov .02 .10
189 Patrik Carnback .02 .10
190 Ray Bourque .20 .50
191 Patrice Brisebois .02 .10
192 Bob Errey .02 .10
193 Scott Lachance .02 .10
194 Brad May .02 .10
195 Jeff Beukeboom .02 .10
196 James Patrick .02 .10
197 Doug Brown .02 .10
198 Dana Murzyn .02 .10
199 Chris Osgood .20 .50
200 Wayne Gretzky .75 2.00
201 Bob Carpenter .02 .10
202 Evgeny Davydov .02 .10
203 Oleg Petrov .02 .10
204 Grant Ledyard .02 .10
205 Jocelyn Thibault .10 .30
206 Bill Houlder .02 .10
207 Tom Fitzgerald .02 .10
208 Dominic Roussel .05 .15
209 Dave Ellett .02 .10
210 Frank Kucera .02 .10
211 Steve Smith .05 .15
212 Vincent Riendeau .05 .15
213 Scott Pearson .02 .10
214 John Slaney .02 .10
215 Larry Murphy .05 .15
216 Travis Green .05 .15
217 Joel Otto .02 .10
218 Randy Wood .02 .10
219 Gaetan Duchesne .02 .10
220 Sergei Nemchinov .02 .10
221 Terry Carkner .02 .10
222 Randy McKay .02 .10
223 Mike Donnelly .02 .10
224 J.J. Daigneault .02 .10
225 Dallas Drake .02 .10
226 John Tucker .02 .10
227 Dimitri Yushkevich .02 .10
228 Mike Stapleton .10 .30
229 Dmitri Mironov .02 .10
230 Ken Wregget .05 .15
231 Claude Lapointe .02 .10
232 Joe Sacco .02 .10
233 Craig Ludwig .02 .10
234 David Reid .02 .10
235 Rich Sutter .02 .10
236 Mark Fitzpatrick .06 .16
237 Jim Storm .02 .10
238 Brad Dalgarno .02 .10
239 Dixon Ward .02 .10
240 Greg Adams .02 .10

241 Dino Ciccarelli .05 .15
242 Vlastimil Kroupa .02 .10
243 Joe Kocur .02 .10
244 Donald Audette .02 .10
245 Trent Yawney .02 .10
246 Mariusz Czerkawski RC .10 .30
247 Jason Allison .02 .10
248 Brian Savage .02 .10
249 Fred Knipscheer .02 .10
250 Jamie McLennan .05 .15
251 Aaron Gavey .02 .10
252 Jeff Friesen .02 .10
253 Adam Deadmarsh .02 .10
254 Jamie Storr .05 .15
255 Brian Rolston .02 .10
256 Zigmund Palffy .05 .15
257 Brett Lindros .02 .10
258 Denis Tsygurov RC .10 .30
259 Chris Tamer RC .10 .30
260 Mike Peca .02 .10
261 Oleg Tverdovsky .05 .15
262 Todd Harvey .02 .10
263 Yan Kaminsky .02 .10
264 Kenny Jonsson .02 .10
265 Paul Kariya .10 .30
266 Peter Forsberg .40 1.00
267 Atlantic Division Checklist .02 .10
268 Northeast Division Checklist .02 .10
269 Central Division Checklist .02 .10
270 Pacific Division Checklist .02 .10
271 Steve Yzerman .60 1.50
272 John LeClair .10 .30
273 Rod Brind'Amour .05 .15
274 Ron Hextall .05 .15
275 Todd Elik .02 .10
276 Geoff Courtnall .02 .10
277 Kjell Samuelsson .02 .10
278 Brian Bradley .02 .10
279 Darrin Shannon .02 .10
280 Mike Ricci .02 .10
281 Peter Bondra .05 .15
282 Terry Yake .02 .10
283 Patrick Poulin .02 .10
284 Bob Kudelski .02 .10
285 Bill Ranford .05 .15
286 Alexander Godynyuk .02 .10
287 Claude Lemieux .02 .10
288 Sylvain Turgeon with young Patrick Kane 6.00 15.00
289 Kevin Miller .02 .10
290 Brian Bellows .02 .10
291 Murray Craven .02 .10
292 Kelly Hrudey .05 .15
293 Neal Broten .05 .15
294 Craig Simpson .02 .10
295 Mark Howe .02 .10
296 Johan Garpenlov .02 .10
297 Jamie Macoun .02 .10
298 Steve Leach .02 .10
299 Kevin Stevens .02 .10
300 Mark Messier .10 .30
301 Paul Ysebaert .02 .10
302 Derek King .02 .10
303 Fredrik Olausson .02 .10
304 John Druce .02 .10
305 Calle Johansson .02 .10
306 Kelly Kisio .02 .10
307 Sergio Momesso .02 .10
308 Joe Cirella .02 .10
309 Tommy Soderstrom .05 .15
310 Scott Stevens .05 .15
311 Petr Klima .02 .10
312 Steven Finn .02 .10
313 Tomas Sandstrom .02 .10
314 Ray Ferraro .02 .10
315 Andy Moog .10 .30
316 Ray Whitney .02 .10
317 Dirk Graham .02 .10
318 Shawn Burr .02 .10
319 Andrew Cassels .02 .10
320 Craig Billington .05 .15
321 Wayne Presley .02 .10
322 Anatoli Semenov .02 .10
323 Michal Pivonka .02 .10
324 Martin Gelinas .02 .10
325 Nelson Emerson .02 .10
326 Brent Fedyk .02 .10
327 Bob Bassen .02 .10
328 Darryl Sydor .02 .10
329 Stephane Matteau .02 .10
330 Ken Daneyko .02 .10
331 Mikhail Shtalenkov RC .10 .30
332 Kelly Buchberger .02 .10
333 Mike Hough .02 .10
334 Dave Gagner .05 .15
335 Chris Terreri .05 .15
336 Robert Kron .02 .10
337 Andrei Lomakin .02 .10
338 Kevin Lowe .02 .10
339 Steve Konroyd .02 .10
340 Denis Savard .05 .15
341 Steve Heinze .02 .10
342 Zarley Zalapski .02 .10
343 Valeri Kamensky .05 .15
344 Tie Domi .05 .15
345 Kevin Hatcher .02 .10
346 Dean Evason .02 .10
347 Bobby Holik .02 .10
348 Steve Konowalchuk .02 .10
349 Rob Gaudreau .02 .10
350 Pat LaFontaine .10 .30
351 Joe Reekie .02 .10
352 Martin Straka .02 .10
353 Dave Babych .02 .10
354 Geoff Smith .02 .10
355 Don Beaupre .05 .15
356 Adam Burt .02 .10
357 Doug Bodger .02 .10
358 Dean McAmmond .02 .10
359 Gerald Diduck .02 .10
360 Rob DiMaio .02 .10
361 Scott Young .02 .10
362 Alexander Semak .02 .10
363 Mike Rathje .02 .10
364 Alexander Karpovtsev .02 .10
365 Trevor Kidd .05 .15
366 Jason Dawe .02 .10
367 Vitali Prokhorov .02 .10
368 Keith Brown .02 .10
369 Bret Hedican .02 .10
370 Markus Naslund .10 .30
371 Rick Tocchet .05 .15
372 Guy Carbonneau .02 .10
373 Kevin Haller .02 .10
374 Bob Rouse .02 .10
375 Rob Pearson .02 .10
376 Steve Chiasson .02 .10
377 Mike Vernon .05 .15
378 Keith Jones .02 .10
379 Sylvain Lefebvre .02 .10
380 Tom Kurvers .02 .10
381 Pat Elynuik .02 .10
382 Uwe Krupp .02 .10
383 Ron Sutter .02 .10
384 Mike Ridley .02 .10
385 Wendel Clark .05 .15
386 Mats Sundin .10 .30
387 Al MacInnis .05 .15
388 Glen Wesley .02 .10
389 Jim Paek .02 .10
390 Rudy Poeschek .02 .10
391 Yves Racine .02 .10
392 Craig MacTavish .02 .10
393 Jon Casey .05 .15
394 Garth Butcher .02 .10
395 Sean Hill .02 .10
396 Troy Loney .02 .10
397 John Cullen .02 .10
398 Alexei Kasatonov .02 .10
399 Mike Craig .02 .10
400 Luc Robitaille .05 .15
401 Randy Moller .02 .10
402 Chris Dahlquist .02 .10
403 Pat Conacher .02 .10
404 Bob Probert .05 .15
405 Robert Dirk .02 .10
406 Randy Cunneyworth .02 .10
407 Bryan Marchment .02 .10
408 Nick Kypreos .02 .10
409 Doug Lidster .02 .10
410 Phil Housley .05 .15
411 Bob Sweeney .02 .10
412 Mike Ramsey .02 .10
413 Robert Lang .02 .10
414 Brian Benning .02 .10
415 Greg Gilbert .02 .10
416 Martin Rucinsky .02 .10
417 Jason Smith .02 .10
418 Jozef Stumpel .02 .10
419 Bob Beers .02 .10
420 Ed Olczyk .02 .10
421 Grant Fuhr .05 .15
422 Gilbert Dionne .02 .10
423 Mike Peluso .02 .10
424 Petr Svoboda .02 .10
425 Corey Millen .02 .10
426 Kevin Dineen .02 .10
427 Brad McCrimmon .02 .10
428 Bob Essensa .05 .15
429 Paul Coffey .10 .30
430 Glenn Healy .05 .15
431 Luke Richardson .02 .10
432 Adam Foote .05 .15
433 Paul Broten .02 .10
434 Christian Ruuttu .02 .10
435 David Shaw .02 .10
436 Jimmy Carson .02 .10
437 Ken Sutton .02 .10
438 Kay Whitmore .05 .15
439 Jim Dowd .02 .10
440 Jim Johnson .02 .10
441 Kirk Maltby .02 .10
442 Trent Klatt .02 .10
443 Paul DiPietro .02 .10
444 Rick Tabaracci .05 .15
445 Craig Wolanin .02 .10
446 Dave Hannan .02 .10
447 Rick Zombo .02 .10
448 Tom Pederson .02 .10
449 Martin Lapointe .02 .10
450 Brett Hull .15 .40
451 Mikael Andersson .02 .10
452 Benoit Brunet .02 .10
453 Nathan Lafayette .02 .10
454 Kent Manderville .02 .10
455 Todd Krygier .02 .10
456 Dennis Vaske .02 .10
457 Peter Popovic .02 .10
458 Jeff Shantz .02 .10
459 Darrin Madeley .02 .10
460 Rene Corbet .02 .10
461 Alexander Daigle IB .02 .10
462 Martin Brodeur IB .30 .75
463 Jason Arnott IB .02 .10
464 Mikael Renberg IB .05 .15
465 Alexei Yashin IB .02 .10
466 Chris Pronger IB .05 .15
467 Mariusz Czerkawski IB .02 .10
468 Chris Gratton IB .02 .10
469 Rob Niedermayer IB .05 .15
470 Bryan Smolinski IB .02 .10
471 Chris Osgood IB .20 .50
472 Derek Plante IB .02 .10
473 Jason Allison IB .02 .10
474 Brian Rolston IB .02 .10
475 Jamie Storr IB .05 .15
476 Kenny Jonsson IB .02 .10
477 Viktor Kozlov IB .02 .10
478 Brett Lindros IB .02 .10
479 Peter Forsberg IB .40 1.00
480 Paul Kariya IB .10 .30
481 Viktor Kozlov .02 .10
482 Michal Grosek RC .10 .30
483 Maxim Bets .02 .10
484 Jason Wiemer RC .10 .30
485 Janne Laukkanen .02 .10
486 Valeri Karpov RC .02 .10
487 Andrei Nikolishin .02 .10
488 Dan Plante RC .10 .30
489 Mattias Norstrom .02 .10
490 David Oliver RC .10 .30
491 Todd Simon RC .10 .30
492 Valeri Bure .02 .10
493 Eric Fichaud RC .10 .30
494 Cory Stillman RC .10 .30
495 Chris Therien .02 .10
496 Matt Johnson RC .10 .30
497 Joby Messier .02 .10
498 Slava Butsayev .02 .10
499 Bernie Nicholls .05 .15
500 Mark Osborne .02 .10
501 Stephane Quintal .02 .10
502 Jamie Baker .02 .10
503 Todd Ewen .02 .10
504 Dan Quinn .02 .10
505 Peter Taglianetti .02 .10
506 Chris Simon .02 .10
507 Jay Wells .02 .10
508 Tommy Albelin .02 .10
509 Warren Rychel .02 .10
510 Brent Hughes .02 .10
511 Greg Johnson .02 .10
512 Stu Grimson .02 .10
513 Iain Fraser .02 .10
514 Rob Ray .02 .10
515 Craig Berube .02 .10
516 Shane Churla .02 .10
517 Checklist .02 .10
518 Checklist .02 .10
519 Checklist .02 .10
520 Checklist .02 .10
521 Jamie Storr .05 .15
522 Dan Cloutier RC .40 1.00
523 Bryan McCabe .02 .10
524 Ed Jovanovski RC .10 .30
525 Nolan Baumgartner RC .10 .30
526 Jamie Rivers RC .10 .30
527 Wade Redden RC .10 .30
528 Lee Sorochan RC .10 .30
529 Eric Daze RC .40 1.00
530 Jason Allison .02 .10
531 Alexandre Daigle .02 .10
532 Jeff Friesen .02 .10
533 Todd Harvey .02 .10
534 Jeff O'Neill RC .10 .30
535 Ryan Smyth RC .50 1.25
536 Marty Murray .02 .10
537 Darcy Tucker RC .10 .30
538 Denis Pederson RC .10 .30
539 Shean Donovan RC .10 .30
540 Larry Courville RC .10 .30
MVPC Pavel Bure .10 .30
MVPU Dominik Hasek 10.00 25.00

1994-95 Pinnacle Artist's Proofs

This set is a parallel version of the standard set. The difference is a reflective gold foil Artist's Proof logo on the front. Series 1 cards also featured an Artist's Proof logo on the back; this logo did not appear on series 2 card backs. The Pinnacle and player name bearing icon, which is gold on normal cards, is printed with a more reflective gold foil on these inserts. Series two production made this feature more bold than in series 1. Cards were inserted at a rate of 1:36 packs in both series 1 and 2, 14 card packs. There are no Artist's Proof versions of the first series checklists, however, there is an Artist's Proof version of the second series checklists. Estimated production of these cards varies; one press release suggests "less than 700 sets", while wrappers state "less than 500".

*VETS: 12X TO 30X BASIC CARDS
*ROOKIES: 4X TO 10X BASIC CARDS
200 Wayne Gretzky 100.00 250.00

1994-95 Pinnacle Rink Collection

This set is a parallel to the Pinnacle set. The cards were inserted in packs at a rate of 1:4. The fronts have a full-color action photo with the player's last name on the left surrounded by the chain for a gold medallion at the bottom. The background consists of silver-foil sunrays. The backs have a color photo with player information and statistics. The bottom has the words "Rink Collection" and the Pinnacle emblem.

*VETS: 4X TO 10X BASIC CARDS
*ROOKIES: 2X TO 5X BASIC CARDS

1994-95 Pinnacle Boomers

This 18-card set could be found randomly inserted at a rate of 1:24 U.S. series 1 hobby packs. These horizontally-oriented cards are notable for their design, which utilizes two-thirds of the space for an action shot of the featured player shooting the puck. The remaining third featured a ghosted goalie image. The player's last name is printed in gold foil down the left side of the card. "Boomers" is written in blue and red on the bottom left portion. The backs are occupied mostly with a player photo, while text assumes the remaining third. Cards are numbered with a "BR" prefix.

COMPLETE SET (18) 25.00 50.00
BR1 Al Iafrate .60 1.50
BR2 Vladimir Malakhov .60 1.50
BR3 Al MacInnis 1.00 2.50
BR4 Chris Chelios 2.00 5.00
BR5 Mike Modano 3.00 8.00
BR6 Brendan Shanahan 2.00 5.00
BR7 Ray Bourque 3.00 8.00
BR8 Geoff Sanderson 1.00 2.50
BR9 Brett Hull 2.50 6.00
BR10 Rob Blake 1.00 2.50
BR11 Steve Thomas .60 1.50
BR12 Cam Neely 2.00 5.00
BR13 Pavel Bure 2.00 5.00
BR14 Stephane Richer 1.00 2.50
BR15 Teemu Selanne 2.00 5.00
BR16 Eric Lindros 2.00 5.00
BR17 Alexander Mogilny 1.00 2.50
BR18 Rick Tocchet 1.00 2.50

1994-95 Pinnacle Gamers

This 18-card set was randomly inserted 1:18 packs of all Pinnacle series 2 product. The cards are enhanced by the Dufex printing technology. Each card is color-coded to the team colors of the player. The player is pictured inside a shape which approximates the design of his team's emblem. The backs are reflective colored, with a photo and paragraph of information. Cards are numbered with a "GR" prefix.

COMPLETE SET (18) 20.00 50.00
GR1 Teemu Selanne 2.00 5.00
GR2 Pat LaFontaine 1.25 3.00
GR3 Sergei Fedorov 2.00 5.00
GR4 Pavel Bure 2.00 5.00
GR5 Jaromir Jagr 3.00 8.00
GR6 Alexandre Daigle .75 2.00
GR7 Kirk Muller .75 2.00
GR8 Mike Modano 2.00 5.00
GR9 Mark Messier 2.00 5.00
GR10 Brendan Shanahan 2.00 5.00
GR11 Doug Gilmour .75 2.00
GR12 Rick Tocchet .75 2.00
GR13 Wendel Clark .75 2.00
GR14 Jeremy Roenick 2.00 5.00
GR15 Adam Graves .75 2.00
GR16 Eric Lindros 2.00 5.00
GR17 Cam Neely 2.00 5.00
GR18 Keith Tkachuk 1.25 3.00

1994-95 Pinnacle Goaltending Greats

Any one of the 18 cards in this set could be found randomly inserted at a rate of 1:9 Pinnacle series 2 jumbo packs. This horizontal set has a full-bleed photo design, with the set logo and player name in gold foil on the left side of the card. Vertical backs have a crowded design, with a small player photo on the lower left, personal information and statistics. Cards are numbered with a "GT" prefix.

COMPLETE SET (18) 40.00 80.00
GT1 Dominik Hasek 5.00 10.00
GT2 Mike Richter 2.50 6.00
GT3 John Vanbiesbrouck 1.50 4.00
GT4 Ed Belfour 3.00 8.00
GT5 Patrick Roy 8.00 20.00
GT6 Bill Ranford 1.50 4.00
GT7 Martin Brodeur 5.00 12.00
GT8 Felix Potvin 3.00 8.00
GT9 Arturs Irbe 1.50 4.00
GT10 Mike Vernon 1.50 4.00
GT11 Kirk McLean 1.50 4.00
GT12 Sean Burke 1.50 4.00
GT13 Curtis Joseph 2.50 6.00
GT14 Andy Moog 1.50 4.00
GT15 Daren Puppa 1.50 4.00
GT16 Chris Osgood 1.50 4.00
GT17 Tom Barrasso 1.50 4.00
GT18 Jocelyn Thibault 1.50 4.00

1994-95 Pinnacle Masks

This popular ten-card insert set was inserted in Canadian series 1 product at the rate of 1:90 packs. The cards feature a photo of a goaltender's mask over a metallic blue Dufex background. No team or player name appears on the front. Backs feature dual photos on a mirror finish and the player and team names. Cards are numbered with an "MA" prefix.

COMPLETE SET (10) 100.00 200.00
MA1 Patrick Roy 30.00 60.00
MA2 John Vanbiesbrouck 12.00 30.00
MA3 Kelly Hrudey 12.00 30.00
MA4 Guy Hebert 10.00 25.00
MA5 Rick Tabaracci 10.00 25.00
MA6 Ron Hextall 12.00 30.00
MA7 Trevor Kidd 10.00 25.00
MA8 Andy Moog 12.00 30.00
MA9 Jimmy Waite 10.00 25.00
MA10 Curtis Joseph 12.00 30.00

1994-95 Pinnacle Northern Lights

This 18-card insert set was randomly inserted 1:24 Canadian series 1 hobby packs. The series highlights the top players from Canadian-based teams. The fronts have a player photo which fades into a sky design with a northern lights image on the left side. The player name is stamped in gold foil above the word "Canada", written in yellow. The horizontal backs have a photo on the left, with some personal information printed over another interpretation of the famous northern lights. Cards are numbered with an "NL" prefix in a red maple leaf.

COMPLETE SET (18) 15.00 40.00
NL1 Patrick Roy 5.00 12.00
NL2 Kirk Muller .75 2.00
NL3 Vincent Damphousse .75 2.00
NL4 Joe Sakic 2.50 6.00
NL5 Wendel Clark 1.25 3.00
NL6 Alexandre Daigle .75 2.00
NL7 Alexei Yashin .75 2.00
NL8 Doug Gilmour 1.25 3.00
NL9 Felix Potvin 1.50 4.00
NL10 Mats Sundin 1.50 4.00
NL11 Teemu Selanne 1.50 4.00
NL12 Keith Tkachuk 1.25 3.00
NL13 Bill Ranford 1.25 3.00
NL14 Jason Arnott .75 2.00
NL15 Theo Fleury .75 2.00
NL16 Gary Roberts .75 2.00
NL17 Pavel Bure 1.50 4.00
NL18 Trevor Linden 1.25 3.00

1994-95 Pinnacle Rookie Team Pinnacle

The 12 cards in this set, featuring a player from each conference on either side, were inserted in Pinnacle series two product at the rate of 1:90 packs. The set focuses on 24 top rookies in the league. Cards are printed using the Gold-line foil technology; either side could be found with the Gold-line foil finish. The cards feature a cutout player photo on a striped background of reds and yellows. The player name is printed on a black border on the top of the card. One side has the card number with an "RTP" prefix and the Pinnacle anti-counterfeiting device.

COMPLETE SET (12) 15.00 40.00
1 Corey Hirsch / Jamie Storr 1.00 2.50
2 Mattias Norstrom / Oleg Tverdovsky 1.00 2.50
3 Denis Tsygurov / Janne Laukkanen 1.00 2.50
4 Chris Tamer / Kenny Jonsson 1.00 2.50
5 Zigmund Palffy / Viktor Kozlov 2.00 5.00
6 Rene Corbet / Maxim Bets 1.00 2.50
7 Jason Allison / Jeff Friesen 2.00 5.00
8 Brian Rolston / Michael Peca 2.00 5.00
9 Peter Forsberg / Paul Kariya 8.00 20.00
10 Brian Savage / Todd Harvey 1.00 2.50
11 Brett Lindros / Valeri Karpov 1.00 2.50
12 Mariusz Czerkawski / Sergei Krivokrasov 1.00 2.50

1994-95 Pinnacle Team Pinnacle

This 12-card set features 24 top players in the league, 12 per conference (one player on either side of the card). These were inserted in series 1 U.S. product at the rate of 1:90 packs. Cards have full-bleed photos on each side. Either side could be found with the Dufex technology, while the other has a mirror finish. The words "Team Pinnacle '94-95" are printed in gold on both sides. The player's last name is printed in an ovoid sphere along the bottom.

COMPLETE SET (12) 75.00 150.00
*DUFEX BACK: .4X TO 1X BASIC INSERTS
TP1 Felix Potvin / Patrick Roy 8.00 20.00
TP2 Curtis Joseph / Mike Richter 5.00 12.00
TP3 Ray Bourque / Chris Chelios 4.00 10.00
TP4 Brian Leetch / Rob Blake 6.00 15.00
TP5 Scott Stevens / Paul Coffey 6.00 15.00
TP6 Adam Graves / Brendan Shanahan 10.00 25.00
TP7 Kevin Stevens / Luc Robitaille 4.00 10.00
TP8 Eric Lindros / Sergei Fedorov 8.00 20.00
TP9 Wayne Gretzky / Mark Messier 10.00 25.00
TP10 Doug Gilmour / Mario Lemieux 8.00 20.00
TP11 Jaromir Jagr / Brett Hull 5.00 12.00
TP12 Pavel Bure / Cam Neely 4.00 10.00

1994-95 Pinnacle World Edition

The 18 cards in this set were randomly inserted at a rate of 1:18 Pinnacle series 2 hobby packs. The cards feature a player photo with his native country's flag as a background. The World Edition logo is stamped in gold foil on the upper left corner. Horizontal backs have a small player photo on the left and a paragraph of information. The cards are numbered with a "WE" prefix. The Pinnacle anti-counterfeiting device also appears on the back.

COMPLETE SET (18) 15.00 40.00
WE1 Teemu Selanne 1.00 2.50
WE2 Doug Gilmour .60 1.50
WE3 Jeremy Roenick 1.00 2.50
WE4 Ulf Dahlen .40 1.00
WE5 Sergei Fedorov 1.00 2.50
WE6 Dominik Hasek 2.00 5.00
WE7 Jari Kurri .60 1.50
WE8 Mario Lemieux 4.00 10.00
WE9 Mike Modano 1.00 2.50
WE10 Mikael Renberg .40 1.00
WE11 Sandis Ozolinsh .40 1.00
WE12 Alexei Kovalev .40 1.00
WE13 Robert Reichel .40 1.00
WE14 Eric Lindros 1.00 2.50
WE15 Brian Leetch 1.00 2.50
WE16 Nicklas Lidstrom 1.00 2.50
WE17 Alexei Yashin .40 1.00
WE18 Petr Nedved .40 1.00

1995-96 Pinnacle

This single-series issue of 225 cards was left incomplete when Pinnacle decided to release the Summit brand in the place of Pinnacle series 2. Nevertheless, most major stars are included. The highlight of the set is a large rookies subset, extending from card #201-220. However, there are no key Rookie Cards in this set.

COMPLETE SET (225) 5.00 12.00
1 Pavel Bure .10 .30
2 Paul Kariya .10 .30
3 Adam Oates .05 .15
4 Garry Galley .02 .10
5 Mark Messier .10 .30
6 Theo Fleury .02 .10
7 Alexandre Daigle .02 .10
8 Joe Murphy .02 .10
9 Eric Lindros .10 .30
10 Kevin Hatcher .02 .10
11 Jaromir Jagr .20 .50
12 Owen Nolan .05 .15
13 Ulf Dahlen .02 .10
14 Paul Coffey .10 .30
15 Brett Hull .15 .40
16 Jason Arnott .02 .10
17 Paul Ysebaert .02 .10
18 Jesse Belanger .02 .10
19 Mats Sundin .10 .30
20 Darren Turcotte .02 .10
21 Dale Hunter .05 .15
22 Jari Kurri .10 .30
23 Alexei Zhamnov .05 .15
24 Mark Recchi .05 .15
25 Dallas Drake .02 .10
26 John MacLean .05 .15
27 Keith Jones .05 .15
28 Mathieu Schneider .02 .10
29 Jeff Brown .02 .10
30 Patrick Flatley .02 .10
31 Dave Andreychuk .05 .15
32 Bill Guerin .05 .15
33 Chris Gratton .05 .15
34 Pierre Turgeon .05 .15
35 Stephane Richer .05 .15
36 Marty McSorley .02 .10
37 Craig Janney .02 .10
38 Geoff Sanderson .02 .10
39 Ron Francis .05 .15
40 Stu Barnes .02 .10
41 Mikael Renberg .05 .15
42 David Oliver .02 .10
43 Radek Bonk .02 .10
44 Sergei Fedorov .20 .50
45 Adam Graves .02 .10
46 Uwe Krupp .02 .10
47 Mike Richter .10 .30
48 Todd Harvey .02 .10
49 Stanislav Neckar .02 .10
50 Chris Chelios .10 .30
51 John LeClair .10 .30
52 German Titov .02 .10
53 Garth Butcher .02 .10
54 Pat LaFontaine .10 .30
55 Jeff Friesen .02 .10
56 Ray Bourque .20 .50
57 Esa Tikkanen .02 .10
58 Steve Rucchin .05 .15
59 Roman Hamrlik .05 .15
60 Oleg Tverdovsky .02 .10
61 Doug Gilmour .05 .15
62 Jocelyn Lemieux .02 .10
63 Roman Oksiuta .02 .10
64 Alexei Zhitnik .02 .10
65 Sylvain Cote .02 .10
66 Paul Kruse .02 .10
67 Teppo Numminen .02 .10
68 Gary Suter .02 .10
69 Darrin Shannon .02 .10
70 Derian Hatcher .02 .10
71 Sergei Gonchar .02 .10
72 Adam Deadmarsh .02 .10
73 Jyrki Lumme .02 .10
74 Dino Ciccarelli .05 .15
75 Mike Gartner .05 .15
76 Todd Marchant .02 .10
77 Jason Wiemer .02 .10
78 Scott Mellanby .05 .15
79 Al MacInnis .05 .15
80 Glen Wesley .02 .10
81 Igor Larionov .02 .10
82 Eric Lacroix .02 .10
83 Mike Keane .02 .10
84 Vincent Damphousse .02 .10
85 Robert Kron .02 .10
86 Scott Stevens .05 .15
87 Don Beaupre .05 .15
88 Zigmund Palffy .05 .15
89 Kevin Lowe .02 .10
90 Tommy Soderstrom .05 .15
91 Glenn Healy .05 .15
92 Randy McKay .02 .10
93 Sean Hill .02 .10
94 Brian Savage .02 .10
95 Ron Hextall .05 .15
96 Darryl Sydor .05 .15
97 Tom Barrasso .05 .15
98 Andrei Nikolishin .02 .10
99 Viktor Kozlov .02 .10
100 Rob Niedermayer .05 .15
101 Wayne Gretzky .75 2.00
102 Shaun Van Allen .02 .10
103 Dave Manson .02 .10
104 Donald Audette .02 .10
105 Daren Puppa .05 .15
106 Jeremy Roenick .15 .40
107 Ken Wregget .05 .15
108 Mike Modano .20 .50
109 Rod Brind'Amour .05 .15
110 Eric Desjardins .05 .15
111 Pat Verbeek .02 .10
112 Jeff Beukeboom .02 .10
113 John Druce .02 .10
114 Andy Moog .10 .30
115 Turner Stevenson .02 .10
116 Alexander Selivanov .02 .10
117 Neal Broten .05 .15
118 Nikolai Khabibulin .05 .15
119 Claude Lemieux .05 .15
120 Sergei Brylin .02 .10
121 Bob Corkum .02 .10
122 Kelly Hrudey .05 .15
123 Jason Dawe .02 .10
124 Sean Burke .05 .15
125 Dave Gagner .02 .10
126 Kirk Maltby .05 .15
127 Ian Laperriere .02 .10
128 Slava Kozlov .05 .15
129 Vladimir Konstantinov .05 .15
130 Kenny Jonsson .02 .10
131 Sylvain Lefebvre .02 .10
132 Kirk McLean .05 .15
133 Brian Leetch .05 .15
134 Olaf Kolzig .05 .15
135 Patrick Poulin .02 .10
136 Tim Cheveldae .05 .15
137 Gary Roberts .02 .10
138 Jim Carey .05 .15
139 Dominik Hasek .25 .60
140 Josef Beranek .02 .10
141 Don Sweeney .02 .10
142 Felix Potvin .10 .30
143 Guy Hebert .05 .15
144 Guy Carbonneau .10 .30
145 Mikhail Shtalenkov .02 .10
146 Kevin Miller .02 .10
147 Blaine Lacher .05 .15
148 Craig MacTavish .05 .15
149 Derek Plante .02 .10
150 Kevin Dineen .02 .10
151 Trevor Kidd .05 .15
152 Sergei Nemchinov .02 .10
153 Ed Belfour .10 .30
154 Sergei Krivokrasov .02 .10
155 Mike Rathje .02 .10
156 Mike Donnelly .02 .10
157 David Roberts .02 .10
158 Jocelyn Thibault .10 .30
159 Tie Domi .05 .15
160 Chris Osgood .05 .15
161 Martin Gelinas .02 .10
162 Scott Thornton .02 .10
163 Bob Rouse .02 .10
164 Randy Wood .02 .10
165 Chris Therien .02 .10
166 Steven Rice .02 .10
167 Scott Lachance .02 .10
168 Petr Svoboda .02 .10
169 Patrick Roy .60 1.50
170 Norm Maciver .02 .10
171 Todd Gill .02 .10
172 Brian Rolston .02 .10
173 Wade Flaherty RC .05 .15
174 Valeri Bure .02 .10
175 Mark Fitzpatrick .05 .15
176 Darren McCarty .02 .10
177 Ken Daneyko .02 .10
178 Yves Racine .02 .10
179 Murray Craven .02 .10
180 Nicklas Lidstrom .10 .30
181 Gord Murphy .02 .10
182 Eric Weinrich .02 .10
183 Todd Krygier .02 .10
184 Cliff Ronning .02 .10
185 Mariusz Czerkawski .02 .10
186 Benoit Hogue .02 .10
187 Richard Smehlik .02 .10
188 Jeff Norton .02 .10
189 Steve Chiasson .02 .10
190 Andrei Nazarov .02 .10
191 Steve Smith .02 .10
192 Mario Lemieux .60 1.50
193 Trent Klatt .02 .10
194 Valeri Zelepukin .02 .10
195 Adam Foote .05 .15
196 Lyle Odelein .02 .10
197 Keith Primeau .05 .15
198 Rob Blake .05 .15
199 Dave Lowry .02 .10
200 Adam Burt .02 .10
201 Martin Gendron .02 .10
202 Tommy Salo RC .40 1.00
203 Eric Daze .05 .15
204 Ryan Smyth .05 .15
205 Brian Holzinger RC .10 .30
206 Chris Marinucci RC .02 .10
207 Jason Bonsignore .02 .10
208 Craig Johnson RC .02 .10
209 Steve Larouche RC .02 .10
210 Chris McAlpine RC .02 .10
211 Shean Donovan .02 .10
212 Cory Stillman RC .02 .10
213 Craig Darby RC .02 .10
214 Philippe DeRouville .02 .10
215 Kevin Brown .02 .10
216 Manny Fernandez .10 .30
217 Radim Bicanek .02 .10
218 Craig Conroy RC .02 .10
219 Todd Warriner RC .02 .10
220 Richard Park .02 .10
221 Checklist .02 .10
222 Checklist .02 .10
223 Checklist .02 .10
224 Checklist .02 .10
225 Checklist .02 .10

1995-96 Pinnacle Artist's Proofs

This 225-card set is a high-end parallel of the standard Pinnacle issue. The cards utilize the same Dufex technology as the Rink Collection cards, but have the Artist's Proof logo embossed on, typically in the lower right corner. On some cards, this can be very difficult to detect: collectors should double check all dufexed cards before buying or selling to ensure which type they are. These cards were inserted at a rate of 1:48 packs.

*VETS: 12X TO 30X BASIC CARDS
*ROOKIES: 4X TO 10X BASIC CARDS

1995-96 Pinnacle Rink Collection

These 225 cards form a low-end parallel version of the Pinnacle set. The cards, which utilize the Dufex process, are difficult to distinguish from the very similar, but much more expensive Artist's Proof cards. Collectors are advised to carefully look for the embossed AP symbol in the lower right corner before buying or selling the 1995-96 Dufexed cards. The Rink Collection cards were inserted at a rate of 1:4 packs.

*VETS: 4X TO 10X BASIC CARDS
*ROOKIES: 2X TO 5X BASIC CARDS

1995-96 Pinnacle Clear Shots

Fifteen veteran superstars are recognized in this set which is distinguished by its use of a clear plastic rainbow holographic printing technology. The cards were inserted at a rate of 1:60 hobby and retail packs.

COMPLETE SET (15) 12.00 30.00
1 Martin Brodeur 2.00 5.00
2 Brett Hull .60 1.50
3 Paul Kariya .50 1.25
4 Eric Lindros .50 1.25
5 Cam Neely .50 1.25
6 Doug Gilmour .25 .60
7 Sergei Fedorov .75 2.00
8 Peter Forsberg 2.00 5.00
9 Wayne Gretzky 3.00 8.00
10 Patrick Roy 2.50 6.00
11 Jaromir Jagr .75 2.00
12 Pavel Bure .50 1.25
13 Mario Lemieux 2.50 6.00
14 Pierre Turgeon .25 .60
15 Dominik Hasek 1.00 2.50

1995-96 Pinnacle First Strike

This 15-card set focusing on game breaking players is enhanced by the use of spot micro-etch technology. The cards were randomly inserted at a rate of 1:24 retail packs only.

COMPLETE SET (15) 10.00 20.00
1 Mark Messier .40 1.00
2 Wayne Gretzky 2.50 6.00
3 Doug Gilmour .20 .50
4 Patrick Roy 2.00 5.00
5 Cam Neely .40 1.00
6 Brian Leetch .20 .50
7 Ed Belfour .40 1.00
8 Wendel Clark .20 .50
9 Chris Chelios .40 1.00
10 Claude Lemieux .10 .30
11 Peter Forsberg .75 2.00
12 Brett Hull .50 1.25
13 Mario Lemieux 2.00 5.00
14 Dominik Hasek .75 2.00
15 Theo Fleury .10 .30

1995-96 Pinnacle Full Contact

This 12-card set used the spot micro-etch technology to bring out the best of the NHL's top bangers and bruisers. The cards were randomly inserted 1:9 retail jumbo packs.

COMPLETE SET (12) 2.00 5.00
STATED ODDS 1:9 JUMBO
1 Cam Neely .30 .75
2 Scott Stevens .15 .40
3 Owen Nolan .15 .40
4 Jeremy Roenick .40 1.00
5 Brendan Shanahan .08 .25
6 Chris Chelios .30 .75
7 Brett Lindros .08 .25
8 Jason Arnott .08 .25
9 Tie Domi .15 .40
10 Mark Tinordi .08 .25
11 Keith Tkachuk .30 .75
12 Mark Messier .30 .75

1995-96 Pinnacle Global Gold

These 25 cards set were randomly inserted into Pinnacle International boxes at a rate of 1:6 packs. These cards are identical to the ones found in the Pinnacle U.S. basic set, save for the circular gold-foil stamp on the front that reads, "Global Gold", and the numbering on the back reading "X of 25" instead of the regular card number.

1 Pavel Bure 2.50 6.00
2 Jaromir Jagr 3.00 8.00
3 Mats Sundin 1.00 2.50
4 Jari Kurri .75 2.00
5 Mikael Renberg .75 2.00
6 Radek Bonk .20 .50
7 Sergei Fedorov 2.00 5.00
8 Uwe Krupp .20 .50
9 German Titov .20 .50
10 Esa Tikkanen .75 2.00
11 Oleg Tverdovsky .20 .50
12 Teppo Numminen .20 .50
13 Jyrki Lumme .20 .50
14 Zigmund Palffy 1.00 2.50
15 Tommy Soderstrom .75 2.00
16 Viktor Kozlov .75 2.00
17 Alexander Selivanov .20 .50
18 Sergei Brylin .20 .50
19 Dominik Hasek 2.00 5.00
20 Sergei Nemchinov .20 .50
21 Petr Svoboda .20 .50
22 Valeri Bure .75 2.00
23 Nicklas Lidstrom 1.00 2.50
24 Mariusz Czerkawski .75 2.00
25 Valeri Zelepukin .20 .50

1995-96 Pinnacle Masks

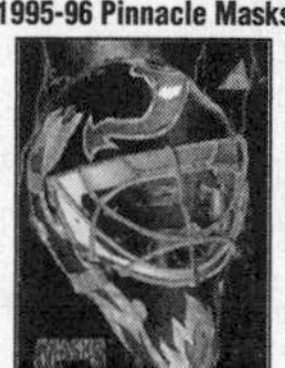

This popular Dufex set returns for the third year to spotlight the unique and colorful world of protection NHL style. No team or player names appear on the front. The cards were randomly inserted at the rate of 1:90 retail and hobby packs.

COMPLETE SET (10) 60.00 100.00
STATED ODDS 1:90 HOB/RET
1 Blaine Lacher 4.00 10.00
2 Martin Brodeur 15.00 40.00
3 Jim Carey 4.00 10.00
4 Felix Potvin 10.00 25.00
5 Andy Moog 4.00 10.00
6 Mike Vernon 4.00 10.00
7 Mark Fitzpatrick 4.00 10.00
8 Ron Hextall 6.00 15.00
9 Sean Burke 4.00 10.00
10 Jocelyn Thibault 10.00 25.00

1995-96 Pinnacle Roaring 20s

This 20-card set highlights the young guns of the NHL. The cards benefit from the use of the spot micro-etch technology and were randomly inserted in 1:19 hobby packs.

COMPLETE SET (20) 20.00 50.00
1 Eric Lindros 1.00 2.50
2 Paul Kariya 1.00 2.50
3 Martin Brodeur 3.00 8.00
4 Jeremy Roenick 1.50 4.00
5 Mike Modano 1.50 4.00
6 Sergei Fedorov 1.50 4.00
7 Mats Sundin 1.00 2.50
8 Pavel Bure 1.00 2.50
9 Jim Carey .60 1.50
10 Felix Potvin 1.25 3.00
11 Alexei Zhamnov .60 1.50
12 Mikael Renberg .60 1.50
13 Jaromir Jagr 2.00 5.00
14 Peter Bondra .60 1.50
15 Peter Forsberg 2.00 5.00
16 John LeClair .60 1.50
17 Joe Sakic 2.50 6.00
18 Brendan Shanahan 1.25 3.00
19 Teemu Selanne 1.25 3.00
20 Pierre Turgeon .60 1.50

1995-96 Pinnacle FANtasy

This 30-card set was distributed as a promotional item at the 1996 All-Star FanFest in Boston and features players from that game as well as four extra Boston Bruins. The cards were available in 2-card packs, free for the asking. Pinnacle later handed out remaining packs at several large sports card conventions in Canada and the U.S. Card #31 features Bobby Orr and injured collegiate player Travis Roy. This tribute card was short printed, and the set is considered complete without it.

COMPLETE SET (30) 15.00 40.00
1 Cam Neely .40 1.00
2 Ray Bourque 1.25 3.00
3 Alexandre Daigle .10 .30
4 Mariusz Czerkawski .10 .25
5 Adam Oates .40 1.00
6 Brendan Shanahan .75 2.00
7 Arturs Irbe .40 1.00
8 Mario Lemieux 3.00 8.00
9 Theo Fleury .40 1.00
10 Patrick Roy 3.00 8.00
11 Roman Hamrlik .20 .50
12 Pavel Bure 1.25 3.00
13 Wayne Gretzky 4.00 10.00
14 Mike Modano .75 2.00
15 Teemu Selanne .75 2.00
16 John Vanbiesbrouck .40 1.00
17 Dominik Hasek .75 2.00
18 Mark Messier .75 2.00
19 Martin Brodeur 1.25 3.00
20 Jim Carey .20 .50
21 Wendel Clark .20 .50
22 Jason Arnott .20 .50
23 Jeremy Roenick .60 1.50
24 Brett Hull .75 2.00
25 Peter Forsberg 1.25 3.00
26 Paul Kariya 2.00 5.00
27 Eric Lindros 1.25 3.00
28 Kevin Stevens .10 .30
29 Felix Potvin .40 1.00
30 Sergei Fedorov .75 2.00
31 Travis Roy 8.00 20.00
Bobby Orr SP

1996-97 Pinnacle

This 250-card set was distributed in 10-card packs with a suggested retail price of $2.49. The set featured color action player photos with player statistics and included a rookie subset plus three numerical checklist cards. Rookies of note include Ethan Moreau and Kevin Hodson.

COMPLETE SET (250) 8.00 20.00
1 Wayne Gretzky .75 2.00
2 Mark Messier .15 .40
3 Kevin Hatcher .02 .10
4 Scott Stevens .08 .25
5 Derek Plante .02 .10
6 Theo Fleury .02 .10
7 Brian Rolston .02 .10
8 Teppo Numminen .02 .10
9 Adam Graves .02 .10
10 Jason Dawe .02 .10
11 Sergei Nemchinov .02 .10
12 Jeff Brown .02 .10
13 Alexei Zhamnov .08 .25
14 Paul Coffey .15 .40
15 Kevin Miller .02 .10
16 Mike Vernon .08 .25
17 Brian Bradley .02 .10
18 Jeff Friesen .02 .10
19 Phil Housley .08 .25
20 Ray Whitney .02 .10
21 Sergei Fedorov .20 .50
22 Pierre Turgeon .08 .25
23 Rick Tocchet .08 .25
24 Uwe Krupp .02 .10
25 Steve Yzerman .60 1.50
26 Tom Chorske .02 .10
27 Pat LaFontaine .15 .40
28 Nicklas Lidstrom .15 .40
29 Ray Ferraro .02 .10
30 Brian Noonan .02 .10
31 Dino Ciccarelli .08 .25
32 Rob Niedermayer .08 .25
33 Stephane Richer .08 .25
34 Chris Chelios .15 .40
35 Mike Gartner .08 .25
36 German Titov .02 .10
37 Sean Burke .08 .25
38 Robert Svehla .02 .10
39 Dave Gagner .08 .25
40 Sergei Gonchar .02 .10
41 Bernie Nicholls .02 .10
42 Yanic Perreault .02 .10
43 Adam Deadmarsh .02 .10
44 Dale Hawerchuk .08 .25
45 Alexei Kovalev .02 .10
46 Esa Tikkanen .02 .10
47 Valeri Kamensky .08 .25
48 Craig Janney .08 .25
49 John LeClair .15 .40
50 Radek Bonk .02 .10
51 David Oliver .02 .10
52 Todd Harvey .02 .10
53 Steve Thomas .02 .10
54 Tony Amonte .08 .25
55 Mikael Renberg .08 .25
56 Brendan Shanahan .15 .40
57 Tom Fitzgerald .02 .10
58 Chris Pronger .08 .25
59 Donald Audette .02 .10
60 Nelson Emerson .02 .10
61 Joe Mullen .08 .25
62 Marty McInnis .02 .10
63 Martin Rucinsky .02 .10
64 Mark Recchi .08 .25
65 Vladimir Konstantinov .08 .25
66 Rick Tabaracci .02 .10
67 Marty McSorley .02 .10
68 Pat Verbeek .02 .10
69 Garry Galley .02 .10
70 Travis Green .08 .25
71 Chris Tancill .02 .10
72 Vincent Damphousse .02 .10
73 Benoit Hogue .02 .10
74 Igor Larionov .02 .10
75 Russ Courtnall .02 .10
76 Mike Hough .02 .10
77 Alexander Selivanov .02 .10
78 Peter Forsberg .30 .75
79 Petr Klima .02 .10
80 Adam Creighton .02 .10
81 Dave Lowry .02 .10
82 Andrew Cassels .02 .10
83 Martin Gelinas .02 .10
84 Bob Probert .08 .25
85 Calle Johansson .02 .10
86 Mario Lemieux .50 1.50
87 Alexander Mogilny .08 .25
88 Guy Hebert .08 .25
89 Bill Ranford .08 .25
90 Kirk McLean .08 .25
91 Kenny Jonsson .02 .10
92 Martin Brodeur .40 1.00
93 Keith Jones .02 .10
94 Ed Belfour .15 .40
95 Tom Barrasso .08 .25
96 Felix Potvin .15 .40
97 Daren Puppa .08 .25
98 Jeremy Roenick .20 .50
99 Chris Osgood UER .08 .25
(Kevin Hodson pictured on back
100 Zigmund Palffy .08 .25
101 Ron Hextall .08 .25
102 Jaromir Jagr .25 .60
103 Chris Terreri .08 .25
104 Shayne Corson .02 .10
105 Jim Carey .15 .40
106 Dominik Hasek .25 .60
107 Eric Lindros .15 .40
108 Petr Nedved .08 .25
109 Peter Bondra .08 .25
110 Jeff Hackett .08 .25
111 Trevor Linden .08 .25
112 Mike Richter .15 .40
113 Claude Lemieux .02 .10
114 Keith Tkachuk .15 .40
115 Pat Falloon .02 .10
116 Brent Fedyk .02 .10
117 Todd Marchant .02 .10
118 Jason Arnott .02 .10
119 Zarley Zalapski .02 .10
120 Kelly Hrudey .08 .25
121 Alexei Yashin .08 .25
122 Sergei Zubov .02 .10
123 Rod Brind'Amour .08 .25
124 Mathieu Schneider .02 .10
125 Bryan Smolinski .02 .10
126 Scott Mellanby .08 .25
127 Doug Gilmour .08 .25
128 Brett Hull .20 .50
129 Vyacheslav Kozlov .02 .10
130 Adam Oates .08 .25
131 Steve Konowalchuk .02 .10
132 Robert Kron .02 .10
133 Alexandre Daigle .02 .10
134 Brian Savage .02 .10
135 Stu Barnes .02 .10
136 Cam Neely .15 .40
137 Steve Rucchin .02 .10
138 Patrick Roy .60 1.50
139 Roman Oksiuta .02 .10
140 Greg Johnson .02 .10
141 Chris Gratton .08 .25
142 Jocelyn Thibault .15 .40
143 Ron Francis .08 .25
144 Mats Sundin .15 .40
145 Oleg Tverdovsky .08 .25
146 Geoff Courtnall .02 .10
147 Kirk Muller .02 .10
148 Zdeno Ciger .02 .10
149 John MacLean .08 .25
150 Damian Rhodes .08 .25
151 Michael Nylander .02 .10
152 Andrei Kovalenko .02 .10
153 Al MacInnis .08 .25
154 Mike Modano .20 .50
155 Teemu Selanne .15 .40
156 Tomas Sandstrom .02 .10
157 Bobby Dollas .02 .10
158 Doug Weight .08 .25
159 Sandis Ozolinsh .02 .10
160 Joe Juneau .02 .10
161 Nikolai Khabibulin .08 .25
162 Murray Craven .02 .10
163 Cliff Ronning .02 .10
164 Curtis Joseph .15 .40
165 Darren Turcotte .02 .10
166 Andy Moog .08 .25
167 Mariusz Czerkawski .02 .10
168 Keith Primeau .02 .10
169 Eric Desjardins .08 .25
170 Bill Guerin .02 .10
171 Glenn Anderson .08 .25
172 Mike Ridley .02 .10
173 Michal Pivonka .02 .10
174 Trevor Kidd .08 .25
175 Pavel Bure .15 .40
176 Todd Gill .02 .10
177 Dave Andreychuk .08 .25
178 Roman Hamrlik .08 .25
179 Andrei Nikolishin .02 .10
180 Alexei Zhitnik .02 .10
181 Grant Fuhr .08 .25
182 Dave Reid .02 .10
183 Joe Nieuwendyk .08 .25
184 Paul Kariya .15 .40
185 Jyrki Lumme .02 .10
186 Owen Nolan .08 .25
187 Geoff Sanderson .08 .25
188 Alexander Semak .02 .10
189 Larry Murphy .08 .25
190 Dimitri Khristich .02 .10
191 Shane Churla .02 .10
192 Bill Lindsay .02 .10
193 Brian Leetch .15 .40
194 Greg Adams .02 .10
195 Gary Suter .02 .10
196 Wendel Clark .08 .25
197 Scott Young .02 .10
198 Randy Burridge .02 .10
199 Ray Bourque .25 .60
200 Joe Murphy .02 .10
201 Joe Sakic .30 .75
202 Saku Koivu .15 .40
203 John Vanbiesbrouck .08 .25
204 Ed Jovanovski .08 .25
205 Daniel Alfredsson .08 .25
206 Vitali Yachmenev .02 .10
207 Marcus Ragnarsson .02 .10
208 Todd Bertuzzi .15 .40
209 Valeri Bure .02 .10
210 Jeff O'Neill .02 .10
211 Corey Hirsch .08 .25
212 Eric Daze .08 .25
213 David Sacco .02 .10
214 Jan Vopat .02 .10
215 Scott Bailey .02 .10
216 Jamie Rivers .02 .10
217 Jose Theodore .20 .50
218 Peter Ferraro .02 .10
219 Anders Eriksson .02 .10
220 Wayne Primeau .02 .10
221 Denis Pederson .02 .10
222 Jay McKee RC .02 .10
223 Sean Pronger .02 .10
224 Martin Biron RC .60 1.50
225 Marek Malik .02 .10
226 Steve Sullivan RC .20 .50
227 Curtis Brown .02 .10
228 Eric Fichaud .08 .25
229 Jan Caloun RC .02 .10
230 Niklas Sundblad .02 .10
231 Steve Staios RC .02 .10
232 Steve Washburn RC .02 .10
233 Chris Ferraro .02 .10
234 Marko Kiprusoff .02 .10
235 Larry Courville .02 .10
236 David Nemirovsky .02 .10
237 Ralph Intranuovo .02 .10
238 Kevin Hodson RC .15 .40
239 Ethan Moreau RC .15 .40
240 Daymond Langkow .08 .25
241 Brandon Convery .02 .10
242 Cale Hulse .02 .10
243 Zdenek Nedved .02 .10
244 Tommy Salo .08 .25
245 Nolan Baumgartner .02 .10
246 Patrick Labrecque .02 .10
247 Jamie Langenbrunner .02 .10
248 Pavel Bure CL (1-126) .15 .40
249 Peter Forsberg CL (127-250) .15 .40
250 Teemu Selanne CL (inserts) .15 .40

1996-97 Pinnacle Artist's Proofs

Randomly inserted in packs at a rate of 1:47 hobby packs and 1:67 magazine packs, this 250-card parallel set was distinguishable from the regular set by the inclusion of a special holographic foil-stamped Artist's Proof logo.

*VETS: 12X TO 30X BASIC CARDS
*ROOKIES: 4X TO 10X

1996-97 Pinnacle Foil

Randomly inserted in retail packs, this set parallels the base set with special foil highlights.

*VETS: .6X TO 1.5X BASIC CARDS
*ROOKIES: .2X TO .5X

1996-97 Pinnacle Premium Stock

This set parallels the base Pinnacle issue of that season, but unlike most parallels, this was a stand-alone brand, rather than an insert. As the name suggests, the cards were printed on thicker paper than the basic brand and utilized additional foil to distinguish them from the other parallels from that season.

*VETS: 1.2X TO 3X BASIC CARDS
*ROOKIES: .4X TO 1X BASIC CARDS

1996-97 Pinnacle Rink Collection

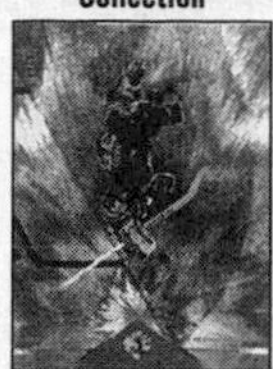

Randomly inserted in packs at a rate of 1:7, this 250-card parallel set was distinguished from the regular set through the use of the all-foil Dufex print technology. A Rink Collection logo is also found on the back of each card.

*VETS: 4X TO 10X BASIC CARDS
*ROOKIES: 2X TO 5X

1996-97 Pinnacle By The Numbers

Randomly inserted in packs at a rate of 1:23, this 15-card, die-cut set honored the league's top statistical standouts. The etched metal, Dufex insert pictured the player with a likeness of his jersey serving as the background. The backs carried the reason for his selection to this insert set. The three confirmed promos were not die-cut like the rest of the set. This design mirrored that which would later be used in the Premium Stock parallel version of this issue inserted at a rate of 1:8 premium stock packs. They are notable for the word PROMO written on the back.

COMPLETE SET (15) 25.00 50.00
*PREM.STOCK: 1X TO 2.5X BASIC INSERTS
1 Teemu Selanne 1.50 4.00
2 Brendan Shanahan 1.50 4.00
3 Sergei Fedorov 2.00 5.00
4 Ed Jovanovski 1.00 2.50
5 Doug Weight 1.00 2.50
6 Brett Hull 2.00 5.00
7 Doug Gilmour 1.00 2.50
8 Jaromir Jagr 2.50 6.00
9 Wayne Gretzky 12.50 30.00
10 Daniel Alfredsson 1.00 2.50
11 Eric Daze 1.00 2.50
12 Mark Messier 1.50 4.00
13 Jocelyn Thibault 1.50 4.00
14 Eric Lindros 1.50 4.00
15 Pavel Bure 1.50 4.00
P1 Teemu Selanne PROMO 1.50 4.00
P11 Eric Daze PROMO 1.50 4.00
P16 Brett Hull PROMO 2.00 5.00

1996-97 Pinnacle Masks

Randomly inserted in packs at a rate of 1:90, this 10-card set spotlighted the most colorful protective headgear worn in the NHL. A die-cut parallel was also created and inserted at a rate of 1:300 hobby packs.

COMPLETE SET (10) 60.00 125.00
*DIE CUTS: .6X TO 1.5X BASIC CARDS
1 Patrick Roy 20.00 50.00
2 Jim Carey 4.00 10.00
3 John Vanbiesbrouck 6.00 15.00
4 Martin Brodeur 12.00 30.00
5 Jocelyn Thibault 4.00 10.00
6 Ron Hextall 6.00 15.00
7 Nikolai Khabibulin 6.00 15.00
8 Stephane Fiset 4.00 10.00
9 Mike Richter 6.00 15.00
10 Kelly Hrudey 4.00 10.00

1996-97 Pinnacle Team Pinnacle

Randomly inserted in packs at a rate of 1:90 hobby packs and 1:127 magazine packs, this 10-card set featured a double-front card design which showcased top players by position from both the Eastern and Western Conferences, back to back. One player from each conference was displayed on opposite sides of the cards, with one side also being enhanced with Dufex technology. Although a small premium might be attached to the card depending upon which side was Dufexed, this premium was not universally applied.

1 Wayne Gretzky 8.00 20.00
Joe Sakic
2 M.Lemieux/P.Forsberg 6.00 15.00
3 Eric Lindros 4.00 10.00
Jeremy Roenick
4 Mark Messier 4.00 10.00
Doug Weight
5 Brendan Shanahan 4.00 10.00
Paul Kariya
6 Jaromir Jagr 5.00 12.00
Brett Hull
7 Ed Jovanovski 4.00 10.00
Paul Coffey
8 John Vanbiesbrouck 6.00 15.00
Patrick Roy
9 Martin Brodeur 5.00 12.00
Chris Osgood
10 Saku Koivu 4.00 10.00
Eric Daze

1996-97 Pinnacle Trophies

Randomly inserted only in specified magazine packs at a rate of 1:33, this 10-card set featured NHL trophies with the previous season's winners on the card backs. Card fronts were printed with Dufex technology and featured the trophy itself. The card backs featured the recipients.

COMPLETE SET (10) 30.00 80.00
1 Mario Lemieux 15.00 40.00
2 Paul Kariya 4.00 10.00
3 Sergei Fedorov 4.00 10.00
4 Daniel Alfredsson 2.00 5.00
5 Jim Carey 1.00 2.50
6 Chris Osgood 4.00 10.00
Mike Vernon
7 Kris King 1.00 2.50
8 Chris Chelios 2.00 5.00
9 Joe Sakic 8.00 20.00
10 Colorado Avalanche 4.00 10.00

1997 Pinnacle Lemieux 600 Goals Commemorative

1 Mario Lemieux

1997-98 Pinnacle

The 1997-98 Pinnacle set was issued in one series totaling 200 cards and was distributed in packs and collectible Mask tins. The fronts feature color action player photos. The backs carry player information.

COMPLETE SET (200) 12.50 25.00
1 Espen Knutsen RC .20 .50
2 Juha Lind RC .02 .10
3 Erik Rasmussen .02 .10
4 Olli Jokinen RC .75 2.00
5 Chris Phillips .02 .10
6 Alexei Morozov .10 .30
7 Chris Dingman RC .10 .30
8 Mattias Ohlund .10 .30
9 Sergei Samsonov .10 .30
10 Daniel Cleary .10 .30
11 Terry Ryan .02 .10
12 Patrick Marleau .25 .60
13 Boyd Devereaux .02 .10
14 Donald MacLean .02 .10
15 Marc Savard .10 .30
16 Magnus Arvedson .02 .10
17 Marian Hossa RC 1.25 3.00
18 Alyn McCauley .10 .30
19 Vaclav Prospal RC .15 .40
20 Brad Isbister .02 .10
21 Robert Dome RC .02 .10
22 Kevyn Adams .02 .10
23 Joe Thornton .40 1.00
24 Jan Bulis RC .02 .10
25 Jaroslav Svejkovsky .10 .30
26 Saku Koivu .15 .40
27 Mark Messier .15 .40
28 Dominik Hasek .30 .75
29 Patrick Roy .75 2.00
30 Jaromir Jagr .25 .60
31 Jarome Iginla .20 .50
32 Joe Sakic .30 .75
33 Jeremy Roenick .20 .50
34 Chris Osgood .10 .30
35 Brett Hull .20 .50
36 Mike Vernon .10 .30
37 John Vanbiesbrouck .10 .30
38 Ray Bourque .25 .60
39 Doug Gilmour .10 .30
40 Keith Tkachuk .15 .40
41 Pavel Bure .15 .40
42 Sean Burke .10 .30
43 Martin Brodeur .40 1.00
44 Damian Rhodes .10 .30
45 Geoff Sanderson .10 .30
46 Bill Ranford .10 .30
47 Kevin Hodson .10 .30
48 Eric Lindros .15 .40
49 Owen Nolan .10 .30
50 Mats Sundin .15 .40
51 Ed Belfour .15 .40
52 Stephane Fiset .10 .30
53 Paul Kariya .15 .40
54 Doug Weight .10 .30
55 Mike Richter .15 .40
56 Zigmund Palffy .10 .30
57 John LeClair .15 .40
58 Alexander Mogilny .10 .30
59 Tommy Salo .10 .30
60 Trevor Kidd .10 .30
61 Jason Arnott .02 .10
62 Adam Oates .10 .30
63 Garth Snow .10 .30
64 Rob Blake .10 .30
65 Chris Chelios .15 .40
66 Eric Fichaud .10 .30
67 Wayne Gretzky 1.00 2.50
68 Dino Ciccarelli .02 .10
69 Pat LaFontaine .15 .40
70 Andy Moog .10 .30
71 Steve Yzerman .75 2.00
72 Jeff Hackett .10 .30
73 Peter Forsberg .40 1.00
74 Arturs Irbe .10 .30
75 Pierre Turgeon .10 .30
76 Tom Barrasso .10 .30
77 Sergei Fedorov .25 .60
78 Ron Francis .10 .30
79 Mike Dunham .10 .30
80 Brendan Shanahan .15 .40
81 Grant Fuhr .10 .30
82 Jamie Storr .10 .30
83 Jim Carey .10 .30
84 Daren Puppa .10 .30
85 Vincent Damphousse .02 .10
86 Teemu Selanne .15 .40
87 Dwayne Roloson .10 .30
88 Kirk McLean .10 .30
89 Olaf Kolzig .10 .30
90 Guy Hebert .10 .30
91 Mike Modano .25 .60
92 Brian Leetch .15 .40
93 Curtis Joseph .15 .40
94 Nikolai Khabibulin .10 .30
95 Felix Potvin .15 .40
96 Ken Wregget .10 .30
97 Steve Shields RC .25 .60
98 Jocelyn Thibault .10 .30
99 Ron Tugnutt .10 .30
100 Ron Hextall .10 .30
101 Mike Peca .02 .10
102 Donald Audette .02 .10
103 Theo Fleury .02 .10
104 Mark Recchi .10 .30
105 Dainius Zubrus .15 .40
106 Trevor Linden .02 .10
107 Joe Juneau .10 .30
108 Matthew Barnaby .02 .10
109 Keith Primeau .02 .10
110 Joe Nieuwendyk .10 .30
111 Rod Brind'Amour .10 .30
112 Daymond Langkow .10 .30
113 Ed Jovanovski .10 .30
114 Adam Deadmarsh .02 .10
115 Scott Niedermayer .02 .10
116 Al MacInnis .10 .30
117 Slava Kozlov .02 .10
118 Jere Lehtinen .02 .10
119 Jeff Friesen .02 .10
120 Alexei Kovalev .02 .10
121 Eric Daze .10 .30
122 Mariusz Czerkawski .02 .10
123 Alexei Zhamnov .02 .10
124 Petr Nedved .10 .30
125 Dmitri Mironov .02 .10
126 Alexei Yashin .02 .10
127 Todd Marchant .02 .10
128 Sandis Ozolinsh .02 .10
129 Igor Larionov .02 .10
130 Jim Campbell .02 .10
131 Dave Andreychuk .02 .10
132 Glen Wesley .02 .10
133 Rem Murray .02 .10
134 Steve Sullivan .02 .10
135 Miroslav Satan .02 .10
136 Bill Guerin .10 .30
137 Mike Gartner .02 .10
138 Jozef Stumpel .10 .30
139 Darryl Sydor .02 .10
140 Darcy Tucker .02 .10
141 Robert Svehla .02 .10
142 Steve Duchesne .02 .10
143 Kevin Stevens .02 .10
144 Mikael Renberg .02 .10
145 Bryan Berard .10 .30
146 Ray Ferraro .02 .10
147 Jason Allison .02 .10
148 Tony Amonte .10 .30
149 Luc Robitaille .02 .10
150 Mathieu Schneider .02 .10
151 Steve Rucchin .02 .10
152 Brian Savage .02 .10
153 Paul Coffey .15 .40
154 Jeff O'Neill .02 .10
155 Daniel Alfredsson .10 .30
156 Dave Gagner .02 .10
157 Rob Niedermayer .02 .10
158 Scott Stevens .10 .30
159 Alexandre Daigle .02 .10
160 Stephane Richer .02 .10
161 Harry York .02 .10
162 Sergei Berezin .02 .10
163 Claude Lemieux .02 .10
164 Ray Sheppard .02 .10
165 Bernie Nicholls .02 .10
166 Oleg Tverdovsky .02 .10
167 Travis Green .02 .10
168 Martin Gelinas .02 .10
169 Derek Plante .02 .10
170 Gary Roberts .02 .10
171 Kevin Hatcher .02 .10
172 Martin Rucinsky .02 .10
173 Pat Verbeek .02 .10
174 Adam Graves .02 .10
175 Roman Hamrlik .02 .10
176 Darren McCarty .02 .10
177 Mike Grier .02 .10
178 Andrew Cassels .02 .10
179 Dimitri Khristich .02 .10
180 Tomas Sandstrom .02 .10
181 Peter Bondra .10 .30
182 Derian Hatcher .02 .10
183 Chris Gratton .10 .30
184 John MacLean .02 .10
185 Wendel Clark .10 .30
186 Valeri Kamensky .10 .30
187 Tony Granato .02 .10
188 Vladimir Vorobiev RC .02 .10
189 Ethan Moreau .02 .10
190 Kirk Muller .02 .10
191 Peter Forsberg SM .15 .40
192 Wayne Gretzky SM .15 .40
193 Jaromir Jagr SM .15 .40
194 Mark Messier SM .15 .40
195 Brian Leetch SM .15 .40
196 John LeClair SM .15 .40
197 Jeremy Roenick SM .10 .30
198 Checklist .02 .10
199 Checklist .02 .10
200 Checklist .02 .10
NNO Paul Kariya 3x5 PROMO .15 .40
NNO J.Vanbiesbrouck 3x5 PROMO .15 .40

1997-98 Pinnacle Artist's Proofs

Randomly inserted in packs at the rate of 1:39 and in tins at the rate of one in 13, this 100-card set is a partial parallel version of the base set. The fronts display the "Artist's Proof" seal.

*ART.PROOF: 12X TO 30X BASIC CARDS

1997-98 Pinnacle Rink Collection

Randomly inserted in packs at the rate of 1:7, this 100-card set is a partial parallel version of the 1997-98 Pinnacle base set printed using Dufex Technology.

*RINK COLL.: 4X TO 10X BASIC CARDS

1997-98 Pinnacle Epix Game Orange

This 24-card set was inserted in various Pinnacle products at the following odds: Certified 1:15; Score 1:121; Pinnacle 1:21 and Zenith 1:11. The set was printed in progressively-scarce three color versions: orange, purple, and emerald and prices for those parallels can be found by using the multipliers below.

COMPLETE SET (24) 40.00 100.00
1-6 INSERTED IN SCORE PACKS
7-12 INSERTED IN PIN.CERT.PACKS
13-18 INSERTED IN ZENITH PACKS
19-24 INSERTED IN PINNACLE PACKS
*PURPLE: .6X TO 1.5X ORANGE
*EMERALD: 1.2X TO 3X ORANGE
PURPLE/EMERALD OVERALL ODDS 1:19
1 Wayne Gretzky 8.00 20.00
2 John Vanbiesbrouck .75 2.00
3 Joe Sakic 2.00 5.00
4 Alexei Yashin .75 2.00
5 Sergei Fedorov 1.50 4.00
6 Keith Tkachuk .75 2.00
7 Patrick Roy 6.00 15.00
8 Martin Brodeur 3.00 8.00
9 Steve Yzerman 6.00 15.00
10 Saku Koivu .75 2.00
11 Felix Potvin .75 2.00
12 Mark Messier 1.25 3.00
13 Eric Lindros 1.25 3.00
14 Peter Forsberg 2.50 6.00
15 Teemu Selanne 1.25 3.00
16 Brendan Shanahan 1.25 3.00
17 Curtis Joseph 1.25 3.00
18 Brett Hull 1.50 4.00
19 Paul Kariya 1.25 3.00
20 Jaromir Jagr 2.00 5.00
21 Pavel Bure 1.25 3.00
22 Dominik Hasek 2.00 5.00
23 John LeClair .75 2.00
24 Doug Gilmour .75 2.00

1997-98 Pinnacle Epix Moment Orange

This 24-card set was inserted in various Pinnacle products at the following odds: Certified 1:15; Score 1:121; Pinnacle 1:21 and Zenith 1:11. The set was printed in progressively-scarce three color versions: orange, purple, and emerald.

COMPLETE SET (24) 100.00 200.00
1-6 INSERTED IN ZENITH PACKS
7-12 INSERTED IN PINNACLE PACKS
13-18 INSERTED IN SCORE PACKS
19-24 INSERTED IN PIN.CERT.PACKS
*PURPLE: .6X TO 1.5X ORANGE
PURPLE STATED ODDS 1:19
*EMERALD: 1.2X TO 3X ORANGE
EMERALD ANNC'D PRINT RUN 30 OR LESS
1 Wayne Gretzky 20.00 50.00
2 John Vanbiesbrouck 2.00 5.00
3 Joe Sakic 6.00 15.00
4 Alexei Yashin 2.00 5.00
5 Sergei Fedorov 4.00 10.00
6 Keith Tkachuk 2.00 5.00
7 Patrick Roy 15.00 40.00
8 Martin Brodeur 10.00 25.00
9 Steve Yzerman 15.00 40.00
10 Saku Koivu 3.00 8.00
11 Felix Potvin 3.00 8.00
12 Mark Messier 3.00 8.00
13 Eric Lindros 3.00 8.00
14 Peter Forsberg 8.00 20.00
15 Teemu Selanne 3.00 8.00
16 Brendan Shanahan 3.00 8.00
17 Curtis Joseph 3.00 8.00
18 Brett Hull 4.00 10.00
19 Paul Kariya 3.00 8.00
20 Jaromir Jagr 5.00 12.00
21 Pavel Bure 3.00 8.00
22 Dominik Hasek 6.00 15.00
23 John LeClair 2.00 5.00
24 Doug Gilmour 2.00 5.00

1997-98 Pinnacle Epix Play Orange

This 24-card set was inserted in various Pinnacle products at the following odds: Certified 1:15; Score 1:121; Pinnacle 1:21 and Zenith 1:11. The set was printed in progressively-scarce three color versions: orange, purple, and emerald and prices for those parallels can be found by using the multipliers below.

COMPLETE SET (24) 40.00 80.00
1-6 INSERTED IN PIN.CERT.PACKS
7-12 INSERTED IN ZENITH PACKS
13-18 INSERTED IN PINNACLE PACKS
19-24 INSERTED IN SCORE PACKS
*PURPLE: .6X TO 1.5X ORANGE
*EMERALD: 1.2X TO 3X ORANGE
PURPLE/EMERALD OVERALL ODDS 1:19
1 Wayne Gretzky 8.00 20.00
2 John Vanbiesbrouck .60 1.50
3 Joe Sakic 1.50 4.00
4 Alexei Yashin .60 1.50
5 Sergei Fedorov 1.25 3.00
6 Keith Tkachuk .75 2.00
7 Patrick Roy 4.00 10.00
8 Martin Brodeur 2.00 5.00
9 Steve Yzerman 4.00 10.00
10 Saku Koivu .75 2.00
11 Felix Potvin .75 2.00
12 Mark Messier .75 2.00
13 Eric Lindros .75 2.00
14 Peter Forsberg 2.00 5.00
15 Teemu Selanne .75 2.00
16 Brendan Shanahan .75 2.00
17 Curtis Joseph .75 2.00
18 Brett Hull 1.00 2.50
19 Paul Kariya .75 2.00
20 Jaromir Jagr 1.25 3.00
21 Pavel Bure .75 2.00
22 Dominik Hasek 1.50 4.00
23 John LeClair .75 2.00
24 Doug Gilmour .60 1.50

1997-98 Pinnacle Epix Season Orange

This 24-card set was inserted in various Pinnacle products at the following odds: Certified 1:15; Score 1:121; Pinnacle 1:21 and Zenith 1:11.

COMPLETE SET (24) 75.00 150.00
1-6 INSERTED IN PINNACLE PACKS
7-12 INSERTED IN SCORE PACKS
13-18 INSERTED IN PIN.CERT.PACKS
19-24 INSERTED IN ZENITH PACKS
*PURPLE: .6X TO 1.5X ORANGE
*EMERALD: 1.2X TO 3X ORANGE
ANNC'D EMERALD PRINT RUN 50 OR LESS
1 Wayne Gretzky 12.00 30.00
2 John Vanbiesbrouck 1.50 4.00
3 Joe Sakic 5.00 12.00
4 Alexei Yashin 1.50 4.00
5 Sergei Fedorov 3.00 8.00
6 Keith Tkachuk 1.50 4.00
7 Patrick Roy 10.00 25.00
8 Martin Brodeur 7.50 15.00
9 Steve Yzerman 10.00 25.00
10 Saku Koivu 2.50 6.00
11 Felix Potvin 2.50 6.00
12 Mark Messier 2.50 6.00
13 Eric Lindros 2.50 6.00
14 Peter Forsberg 6.00 15.00
15 Teemu Selanne 2.50 6.00
16 Brendan Shanahan 2.50 6.00
17 Curtis Joseph 2.50 6.00
18 Brett Hull 3.00 8.00
19 Paul Kariya 2.50 6.00
20 Jaromir Jagr 4.00 10.00
21 Pavel Bure 3.00 8.00
22 Dominik Hasek 5.00 12.00
23 John LeClair 1.50 4.00
24 Doug Gilmour 1.50 4.00

1997-98 Pinnacle Masks

Randomly inserted in packs at the rate of 1:89 and in tins at the rate of 1:30, this ten-card set features color photos of masks worn by the NHL's elite goalies printed on Dufex technology. A die-cut parallel was also produced and inserted at a rate of 1:299 packs and 1:100 tins.

COMPLETE SET (10) 50.00 125.00
*DIE CUT: .5X TO 1.2X BASIC INSERTS
*JUMBOS: .4X TO 1X BASIC INSERTS
*PROMOS: .15X TO .4X BASIC INSERTS
1 John Vanbiesbrouck 4.00 10.00
2 Mike Richter 4.00 10.00
3 Martin Brodeur 10.00 25.00
4 Curtis Joseph 4.00 10.00
5 Patrick Roy 20.00 50.00
6 Guy Hebert 4.00 10.00
7 Jeff Hackett 4.00 10.00
8 Garth Snow 4.00 10.00
9 Nikolai Khabibulin 4.00 10.00
10 Grant Fuhr 4.00 10.00

1997-98 Pinnacle Team Pinnacle

Randomly inserted in packs at the rate of 1:99 and in tins at the rate of 1:33, this 10-card set features color action photos of the game's biggest stars as voted by Hockey fans and printed on double-sided cards with Mylar technology on just one side. A parallel of each card was produced with this special printing on the other side. Finally, mirror parallels were also created of each version (making a total of four different versions of each card) and inserted randomly.

COMPLETE SET (10) 40.00 80.00
*WHITE FRONT PARALLEL: .4X TO 1X
*MIRRORS: 3X TO 8X BASIC INSERTS
1 M.Brodeur/P.Roy 8.00 20.00
2 Dominik Hasek 4.00 10.00
Curtis Joseph
3 Brian Leetch 5.00 12.00
Chris Chelios
4 Wayne Gretzky 8.00 20.00
Paul Kariya
5 Eric Lindros 5.00 12.00
Mark Messier
6 Jaromir Jagr 5.00 12.00
Keith Tkachuk
7 Saku Koivu 4.00 10.00
Peter Forsberg
8 John LeClair 2.50 6.00
Brendan Shanahan
9 Doug Gilmour 6.00 15.00
Steve Yzerman
10 John Vanbiesbrouck 5.00 12.00
Chris Osgood

1997-98 Pinnacle Tins

This set features photos of some of the most distinctive goalie masks in the game printed on collectible tins. Each tin contains 30 cards from the 1997-98 Pinnacle Hockey base set as well as insert sets. The tins are unnumbered and checklisted below in alphabetical order.

COMPLETE SET (10) 6.00 15.00
1 Martin Brodeur 1.25 3.00
2 Grant Fuhr .40 1.00
3 Jeff Hackett .40 1.00
4 Guy Hebert .40 1.00
5 Curtis Joseph .40 1.00
6 Nikolai Khabibulin .40 1.00
7 Mike Richter .50 1.25
8 Patrick Roy 2.00 5.00
9 Garth Snow .40 1.00
10 John Vanbiesbrouck .75 2.00

1997-98 Pinnacle Certified

The 1997-98 Pinnacle Certified set was issued in one series totaling 130 cards and was distributed in five-card hobby packs only with a suggested retail price of $4.99. The fronts feature borderless color action player photos. The backs carry player information.

COMPLETE SET (130) 20.00 40.00
1 Dominik Hasek .60 1.50
2 Patrick Roy 1.50 4.00
3 Martin Brodeur .75 2.00
4 Chris Osgood .20 .50
5 Andy Moog .20 .50
6 John Vanbiesbrouck .20 .50
7 Steve Shields RC .50 1.25
8 Mike Vernon .20 .50
9 Ed Belfour .30 .75
10 Grant Fuhr .20 .50
11 Felix Potvin .30 .75
12 Bill Ranford .20 .50
13 Mike Richter .30 .75
14 Stephane Fiset .20 .50
15 Jim Carey .20 .50
16 Nikolai Khabibulin .20 .50
17 Ken Wregget .20 .50
18 Curtis Joseph .30 .75
19 Guy Hebert .20 .50
20 Damian Rhodes .20 .50
21 Trevor Kidd .20 .50
22 Daren Puppa .20 .50
23 Patrick Lalime .20 .50
24 Tommy Salo .20 .50
25 Sean Burke .20 .50
26 Jocelyn Thibault .20 .50
27 Kirk McLean .20 .50
28 Garth Snow .20 .50
29 Ron Tugnutt .20 .50
30 Jeff Hackett .20 .50
31 Eric Lindros .30 .75
32 Peter Forsberg .75 2.00
33 Mike Modano .50 1.25
34 Paul Kariya .30 .75
35 Jaromir Jagr .50 1.25
36 Brian Leetch .30 .75
37 Keith Tkachuk .30 .75
38 Steve Yzerman 1.50 4.00
39 Teemu Selanne .30 .75
40 Bryan Berard .20 .50
41 Ray Bourque .50 1.25
42 Theo Fleury .07 .20
43 Mark Messier .30 .75
44 Saku Koivu .30 .75
45 Pavel Bure .30 .75
46 Peter Bondra .20 .50
47 Dave Gagner .07 .20
48 Ed Jovanovski .20 .50
49 Adam Oates .20 .50
50 Joe Sakic .60 1.50
51 Doug Gilmour .20 .50
52 Jim Campbell .07 .20
53 Mats Sundin .30 .75
54 Derian Hatcher .07 .20
55 Jarome Iginla .40 1.00
56 Sergei Fedorov .50 1.25
57 Keith Primeau .07 .20
58 Mark Recchi .20 .50
59 Owen Nolan .20 .50
60 Alexander Mogilny .20 .50
61 Brendan Shanahan .30 .75
62 Pierre Turgeon .20 .50
63 Joe Juneau .20 .50
64 Steve Rucchin .07 .20
65 Jeremy Roenick .40 1.00
66 Doug Weight .20 .50
67 Valeri Kamensky .20 .50
68 Tony Amonte .20 .50
69 Dave Andreychuk .07 .20
70 Brett Hull .40 1.00
71 Wendel Clark .20 .50
72 Vincent Damphousse .07 .20
73 Mike Grier .07 .20
74 Chris Chelios .30 .75
75 Nicklas Lidstrom .30 .75
76 Joe Nieuwendyk .20 .50
77 Rob Blake .20 .50
78 Alexei Yashin .07 .20
79 Ryan Smyth .20 .50
80 Pat LaFontaine .30 .75
81 Jeff Friesen .07 .20
82 Ray Ferraro .07 .20
83 Steve Sullivan .07 .20
84 Chris Gratton .20 .50
85 Mike Gartner .20 .50
86 Kevin Hatcher .07 .20
87 Ted Donato .07 .20
88 German Titov .07 .20
89 Sandis Ozolinsh .07 .20
90 Ray Sheppard .07 .20
91 John MacLean .07 .20
92 Luc Robitaille .20 .50
93 Rod Brind'Amour .20 .50
94 Zigmund Palffy .20 .50
95 Petr Nedved .20 .50
96 Adam Graves .07 .20
97 Jozef Stumpel .20 .50
98 Alexandre Daigle .07 .20
99 Mike Peca .07 .20
100 Wayne Gretzky 2.00 5.00
101 Alexei Zhamnov .07 .20
102 Paul Coffey .30 .75
103 Oleg Tverdovsky .07 .20
104 Trevor Linden .20 .50
105 Dino Ciccarelli .07 .20
106 Andrei Kovalenko .07 .20
107 Scott Mellanby .07 .20
108 Bryan Smolinski .07 .20
109 Bernie Nicholls .07 .20
110 Derek Plante .07 .20
111 Pat Verbeek .07 .20
112 Adam Deadmarsh .07 .20
113 Martin Gelinas .07 .20
114 Daniel Alfredsson .20 .50
115 Scott Stevens .20 .50
116 Dainius Zubrus .30 .75
117 Kirk Muller .07 .20
118 Brian Holzinger .07 .20
119 John LeClair .30 .75
120 Al MacInnis .20 .50
121 Ron Francis .20 .50
122 Eric Daze .20 .50
123 Travis Green .07 .20
124 Jason Arnott .07 .20
125 Geoff Sanderson .20 .50
126 Dimitri Khristich .07 .20
127 Sergei Berezin .07 .20
128 Jeff O'Neill .07 .20
129 Claude Lemieux .07 .20
130 Andrew Cassels .07 .20

1997-98 Pinnacle Certified Red

Randomly inserted in packs at the rate of 1:5, this 130-card set is parallel to the Pinnacle Certified base set and is distinguished by the red treatment of the mirror Mylar regular cards.

*RED: 1.2X TO 3X BASIC CARDS

1997-98 Pinnacle Certified Mirror Blue

Randomly inserted in packs at the rate of 1:199, this 130-card set is parallel to the Pinnacle Certified base set. The difference is found in the blue design element on holographic foil.

*MIRROR BLUE: 6X TO 15X BASIC CARDS

1997-98 Pinnacle Certified Mirror Gold

Randomly inserted in packs at the rate of 1:299, this 130-card set is parallel to the Pinnacle Certified base set. The difference is found in the golden holographic mirror Mylar highlights of the set.

*MIRROR GOLD: 12X TO 30X BASIC CARDS
100 Wayne Gretzky 75.00 150.00

1997-98 Pinnacle Certified Mirror Red

Randomly inserted in packs at the rate of 1:99, this 130-card set is parallel to the Pinnacle Certified base set. The difference is found in the holographic red foil design of the set.

*MIRROR RED: 4X TO 10X BASIC CARDS

1997-98 Pinnacle Certified Team

Randomly inserted in packs at the rate of 1:19, this 20-card set features color action photos of 10 Eastern Conference megastars matched with 10 Western Conference superstar counterparts and printed on mirror Mylar all-foil card stock. A gold parallel was also created and randomly inserted at a rate of 1:129. These parallels are distinctive because of the added gold accents and foil stamping. Only 300 of this set were produced and are sequentially numbered.

COMPLETE SET (20) 75.00 150.00
*GOLD TEAM/300: 2X TO 5X BASIC INSERTS
*GT PROMOS: .2X TO .5X BASIC INSERTS
1 Martin Brodeur 5.00 12.00
2 Patrick Roy 10.00 25.00
3 John Vanbiesbrouck 1.25 3.00
4 Dominik Hasek 4.00 10.00
5 Chris Chelios 2.00 5.00
6 Brian Leetch 2.00 5.00
7 Wayne Gretzky 12.50 30.00
8 Eric Lindros 2.00 5.00
9 Paul Kariya 2.00 5.00
10 Peter Forsberg 5.00 12.00
11 Keith Tkachuk 2.00 5.00
12 Mark Messier 2.00 5.00
13 Steve Yzerman 10.00 25.00
14 Jaromir Jagr 3.00 8.00
15 Mats Sundin 2.00 5.00
16 Teemu Selanne 2.00 5.00
17 Brendan Shanahan 2.00 5.00
18 Saku Koivu 2.00 5.00
19 Brett Hull 2.50 6.00
20 John LeClair 2.00 5.00

1997-98 Pinnacle Certified Rookie Redemption

Randomly inserted in packs at the rate of 1:19, this 12-card set was obtained through the mail with the redemption card and features color action player photos printed on super-premium 24-point card stock with an exclusive authenticator bar to protect the set from counterfeiting. Gold and Mirror Gold versions of these cards were also available via redemption. Gold parallels were inserted at a rate of 1:259 and were limited to 250 sets.

COMPLETE SET (12) 25.00 50.00
*GOLD: 2X TO 5X BASIC INSERTS
*MIRROR GOLD: 8X TO 20X BASIC INSERTS
A Joe Thornton 5.00 12.00
B Chris Phillips 1.50 4.00
C Patrick Marleau 4.00 10.00
D Sergei Samsonov 1.50 4.00
E Daniel Cleary 1.50 4.00
F Olli Jokinen 1.50 4.00
G Alyn McCauley 1.50 4.00
H Alexei Morozov 1.50 4.00
I Brad Isbister 1.50 4.00
J Boyd Devereaux 1.50 4.00
K Espen Knutsen 1.50 4.00
L Marc Savard 1.50 4.00

1997-98 Pinnacle Certified Summit Silver

Randomly inserted in packs at the rate of 1:29, this five card set features color action renditions of Paul Henderson by artist Daniel Parry printed on mirror Mylar. The set commemorates Paul Henderson's winning goal at the 1972 Canada-Russia Summit Series. Only 1,000 of each card were produced.

COMMON CARD (1-5) 4.00 10.00
NNO Paul Henderson 20.00 50.00
Black AU/700
NNO Paul Henderson 75.00 200.00
Gold AU/100
NNO Paul Henderson 40.00 100.00
Silver AU/200

1996-97 Pinnacle Fantasy

This 20-card set was made available to attendees of the All-Star FanFest held in San Jose in January, 1997. The cards were distributed in three-card packs, and featured an action photo with a blue foil shark bite design along the top. A 21st card featuring Sharks netminder Kelly Hrudey was available through a redemption card which was randomly inserted in packs. The card had to be redeemed at a San Jose-area card shop. There were, in fact, two variations of the Hrudey card, the more difficult of which featured a refractor-like gloss. Collectors may also run across what appears to be a non-gloss parallel version of this set. The cards are smaller and are in playing card form, with black along the top and a uniform black back with a Pinnacle logo. These were used for a promotion at the show and were not licensed by the NHL or NHLPA. Therefore, these cards will not be listed in the annual.

FC1 Ray Bourque 1.00 2.50
FC2 Paul Coffey .40 1.00
FC3 Eric Lindros 1.50 4.00
FC4 Mario Lemieux 3.00 8.00
FC5 Wayne Gretzky 4.00 10.00
FC6 Mark Messier 1.00 2.50
FC7 Jaromir Jagr 1.50 4.00
FC8 Brendan Shanahan 1.50 4.00
FC9 John Vanbiesbrouck .60 1.50
FC10 Mike Richter .60 1.50
FC11 Chris Chelios .60 1.50
FC12 Nicklas Lidstrom .20 .50
FC13 Sergei Fedorov 1.50 4.00
FC14 Pavel Bure 1.50 4.00
FC15 Peter Forsberg 2.50 6.00
FC16 Brett Hull 1.00 2.50
FC17 Joe Sakic 1.50 4.00
FC18 Owen Nolan .40 1.00
FC19 Patrick Roy 3.00 8.00
FC20 Ed Belfour .60 1.50
NNO1 Kelly Hrudey 10.00 25.00
NNO2 Kelly Hrudey FOIL 15.00 40.00
NNO3 Kelly Hrudey Offer Card 4.00 10.00

1997-98 Pinnacle Inside

The 1997-98 Pinnacle Inside set was issued in one series totaling 190 cards and was distributed inside 24 different collectible player cans with ten cards to a can. The fronts feature color action player photos printed on 20 pt. card stock. The backs carry player information.

COMPLETE SET (190) 20.00 40.00
1 Brendan Shanahan .25 .60
2 Dominik Hasek .50 1.25
3 Wayne Gretzky 1.50 4.00
4 Eric Lindros .25 .60
5 Keith Tkachuk .25 .60
6 Jaromir Jagr .40 1.00
7 Martin Brodeur .60 1.50
8 Peter Forsberg .60 1.50
9 Chris Osgood .20 .50
10 Paul Kariya .25 .60
11 Pavel Bure .25 .60
12 Brett Hull .30 .75
13 Saku Koivu .25 .60
14 Zigmund Palffy .20 .50
15 Mike Modano .40 1.00
16 Ray Bourque .40 1.00
17 Jarome Iginla .30 .75
18 Chris Chelios .25 .60
19 John Vanbiesbrouck .20 .50
20 Brian Leetch .25 .60
21 Mats Sundin .25 .60
22 Ron Hextall .20 .50
23 Stephane Fiset .20 .50
24 Steve Yzerman 1.25 3.00
25 Curtis Joseph .25 .60
26 Daniel Alfredsson .20 .50
27 Owen Nolan .20 .50
28 Adam Oates .20 .50
29 Corey Hirsch .20 .50
30 Sean Burke .20 .50
31 Eric Fichaud .20 .50
32 Ken Wregget .20 .50
33 Dainius Zubrus .25 .60
34 Alexander Mogilny .20 .50
35 Bill Ranford .20 .50
36 Vincent Damphousse .07 .20
37 Patrick Roy 1.25 3.00
38 Teemu Selanne .25 .60
39 Pat LaFontaine .25 .60
40 Theo Fleury .07 .20
41 Jeff Hackett .20 .50
42 Sergei Fedorov .40 1.00
43 Jocelyn Thibault .20 .50
44 Nikolai Khabibulin .20 .50
45 Daren Puppa .20 .50
46 Felix Potvin .25 .60
47 Andy Moog .20 .50
48 Doug Weight .20 .50
49 Tommy Salo .20 .50
50 Mark Messier .25 .60
51 Grant Fuhr .20 .50
52 Ron Francis .20 .50
53 Tony Amonte .20 .50
54 Joe Sakic .50 1.25
55 Jason Arnott .07 .20
56 Jose Theodore .30 .75
57 Alexei Yashin .07 .20
58 John LeClair .25 .60
59 Jeremy Roenick .30 .75
60 Kirk McLean .20 .50
61 Arturs Irbe .20 .50
62 Jim Carey .20 .50
63 Jean-Sebastien Giguere .20 .50
64 Marc Denis .20 .50
65 Damian Rhodes .20 .50
66 Jim Campbell .07 .20
67 Patrick Lalime .20 .50
68 Garth Snow .20 .50
69 Marcel Cousineau .20 .50
70 Guy Hebert .20 .50
71 Rob Blake .20 .50
72 Tomas Vokoun RC .25 .60
73 Doug Gilmour .20 .50
74 Ed Belfour .25 .60
75 Parris Duffus RC .07 .20
76 Mike Fountain .07 .20
77 Steve Shields RC .25 .60
78 Geoff Sanderson .20 .50
79 Roman Turek .20 .50
80 Bryan Berard .20 .50
81 Mike Richter .25 .60
82 Ron Tugnutt .20 .50
83 Peter Bondra .20 .50
84 Mike Vernon .20 .50
85 Mike Grier .07 .20
86 Ed Jovanovski .20 .50
87 Trevor Kidd .20 .50
88 Eric Daze .20 .50
89 Wendel Clark .20 .50
90 Checklist (1-190) .07 .20
91 Nicklas Lidstrom .25 .60
92 Rod Brind'Amour .20 .50
93 Hnat Domenichelli .07 .20
94 Rem Murray .07 .20
95 Scott Niedermayer .07 .20
96 Martin Rucinsky .07 .20
97 Mike Gartner .20 .50
98 Kevin Hatcher .07 .20
99 Daymond Langkow .20 .50
100 Jamie Langenbrunner .07 .20
101 Ted Donato .07 .20
102 Steve Sullivan .07 .20
103 Martin Gelinas .07 .20
104 Adam Graves .07 .20
105 Donald Audette .07 .20
106 Andrew Cassels .07 .20
107 Alexei Zhamnov .07 .20
108 Kirk Muller .07 .20
109 Alexandre Daigle .07 .20
110 Chris Gratton .20 .50
111 Andrew Brunette .20 .50
112 Mark Recchi .20 .50
113 Jari Kurri .20 .50
114 Valeri Kamensky .20 .50
115 Joe Nieuwendyk .20 .50
116 Slava Kozlov .07 .20
117 Steve Kelly .07 .20
118 Dave Andreychuk .07 .20
119 Mikael Renberg .20 .50
120 Sergei Berezin .07 .20
121 Jeff Friesen .07 .20
122 Pierre Turgeon .20 .50
123 Vladimir Vorobiev RC .07 .20
124 Dimitri Khristich .07 .20
125 Jaroslav Svejkovsky .20 .50
126 Vladimir Konstantinov .20 .50
127 Jozef Stumpel .20 .50
128 Mike Peca .07 .20
129 Jonas Hoglund .07 .20
130 Travis Green .07 .20
131 Bill Guerin .20 .50
132 Oleg Tverdovsky .07 .20
133 Petr Nedved .20 .50
134 Dino Ciccarelli .07 .20
135 Brian Savage .07 .20
136 Steve Duchesne .07 .20
137 Sandis Ozolinsh .07 .20
138 Derian Hatcher .07 .20
139 Ray Sheppard .07 .20
140 Brian Bellows .07 .20
141 Paul Brousseau .07 .20
142 Tony Granato .07 .20
143 Vaclav Prospal RC .25 .60
144 Vitali Yachmenev .07 .20
145 John MacLean .07 .20
146 Igor Larionov .07 .20
147 Jason Allison .07 .20
148 Derek Plante .07 .20
149 Jeff O'Neill .07 .20
150 Trevor Linden .20 .50
151 Joe Juneau .20 .50
152 Brandon Convery .07 .20
153 Kevin Stevens .20 .50
154 Scott Stevens .20 .50
155 Niklas Sundstrom .07 .20
156 Claude Lemieux .07 .20
157 Pat Verbeek .07 .20
158 Mariusz Czerkawski .07 .20
159 Robert Svehla .07 .20
160 Paul Coffey .25 .60
161 Al MacInnis .20 .50
162 Roman Hamrlik .20 .50
163 Brian Holzinger .07 .20
164 Cory Stillman .07 .20
165 Scott Mellanby .07 .20
166 Todd Warriner .07 .20
167 Terry Ryan .07 .20
168 Luc Robitaille .20 .50
169 Ed Olczyk .07 .20
170 Adam Deadmarsh .07 .20
171 Anson Carter .20 .50
172 Mike Knuble RC .07 .20
173 Cliff Ronning .07 .20
174 Rick Tocchet .20 .50
175 Chris Pronger .20 .50
176 Matthew Barnaby .07 .20
177 Andrei Kovalenko .07 .20
178 Bryan Smolinski .07 .20
179 Janne Niinimaa .20 .50
180 Ray Ferraro .07 .20
181 Dave Gagner .07 .20
182 Rob Niedermayer .07 .20
183 Vadim Sharifijanov .07 .20
184 Ethan Moreau .07 .20
185 Bernie Nicholls .07 .20
186 Jean-Yves Leroux RC .07 .20
187 Jere Lehtinen .07 .20
188 Steve Rucchin .07 .20
189 Keith Primeau .07 .20
190 Red Wings Stanley .20 .50
Cup Champs CL (inserts)

1997-98 Pinnacle Inside Coach's Collection

Randomly inserted in cans at the rate of 1:7, this 90-card set is a partial parallel version of the base set and highlights some of the NHL's top impact players. The cards are printed entirely on silver foil with bronze foil stamped accents.

*COACH COLL.: 3X TO 8X BASIC CARDS

1997-98 Pinnacle Inside Executive Collection

Randomly inserted in cans at the rate of 1:57, this 90-card set is a partial parallel version of the base set printed on full prismatic foil with foil stamped treatments and an external die-cut card design.

*EXEC.COLL.: 8X TO 20X BASIC CARDS

1997-98 Pinnacle Inside Stand Up Guys

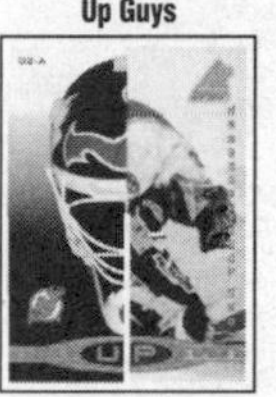

Inserted one per mask can, this 20-card set features color action photos of top goalies on one side with close-up photos of their masks on the flipsides.

COMPLETE SET (20) 15.00 30.00
*PROMOS: .4X TO 1X BASIC INSERTS
1A/B Mike Vernon .60 1.50
Tom Barasso
1C/D M.Vernon/T.Barasso .60 1.50
2A/B John Vanbiesbrouck 2.00 5.00
Martin Brodeur
2C/D J.Vanbiesbrck./M.Brodeur 2.00 5.00
3A/B Jocelyn Thibault .60 1.50
Jim Carey
3C/D J.Thibault/J.Carey .60 1.50
4A/B Garth Snow .60 1.50
Marcel Cousineau
4C/D G.Snow/M.Cousineau .60 1.50
5A/B Patrick Roy 4.00 10.00
Eric Fichaud
5C/D P.Roy/E.Fichaud 4.00 10.00
6A/B Patrick Lalime .60 1.50
Grant Fuhr
6C/D P.Lalime/G.Fuhr .60 1.50
7A/B Olaf Kolzig .60 1.50
Jeff Hackett
7C/D O.Kolzig/J.Hackett .60 1.50
8A/B Trevor Kidd .60 1.50
Guy Hebert
8C/D T.Kidd/G.Hebert .60 1.50
9A/B Nikolai Khabibulin .60 1.50
Corey Hirsch
9C/D N.Khabibulin/C.Hirsch .60 1.50
10A/B Curtis Joseph .60 1.50
Kelly Hrudey
10C/D C.Joseph/K.Hrudey .60 1.50

1997-98 Pinnacle Inside Stoppers

Randomly inserted in cans at the rate of 1:7, this 24-card set features color action photos of the NHL's top goal tenders printed on circular die-cut card stock in 3-D.

COMPLETE SET (24) 30.00 60.00
1 Patrick Roy 8.00 20.00
2 John Vanbiesbrouck 1.00 2.50
3 Dominik Hasek 3.00 8.00
4 Martin Brodeur 4.00 10.00
5 Mike Richter 1.50 4.00
6 Guy Hebert 1.00 2.50
7 Jim Carey 1.00 2.50
8 Jeff Hackett 1.00 2.50
9 Roman Turek 1.00 2.50
10 Kevin Hodson 1.00 2.50
11 Mike Vernon 1.00 2.50
12 Curtis Joseph 1.50 4.00
13 Jean-Sebastien Giguere 1.00 2.50
14 Jose Theodore 2.00 5.00
15 Jocelyn Thibault 1.00 2.50
16 Nikolai Khabibulin 1.00 2.50
17 Garth Snow 1.00 2.50
18 Ron Hextall 1.00 2.50
19 Steve Shields 1.00 2.50
20 Grant Fuhr 1.00 2.50
21 Felix Potvin 1.50 4.00
22 Marcel Cousineau 1.00 2.50
23 Bill Ranford 1.00 2.50
24 Ed Belfour 1.50 4.00

1997-98 Pinnacle Inside Track

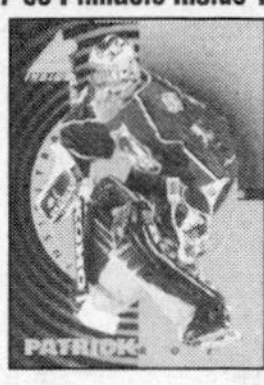

Randomly inserted in cans at the rate of 1:19, this 30-card set features color action photos of some of the game's elite stars with information as to how they became the best players in the NHL.

COMPLETE SET (30) 75.00 200.00
1 Wayne Gretzky 15.00 40.00
2 Patrick Roy 10.00 25.00
3 Eric Lindros 3.00 8.00
4 Paul Kariya 3.00 8.00
5 Peter Forsberg 4.00 10.00
6 Martin Brodeur 6.00 15.00
7 John Vanbiesbrouck 2.00 5.00
8 Joe Sakic 5.00 12.00
9 Steve Yzerman 10.00 25.00
10 Jaromir Jagr 4.00 10.00
11 Teemu Selanne 3.00 8.00
12 Pavel Bure 3.00 8.00
13 Sergei Fedorov 3.00 8.00
14 Brendan Shanahan 3.00 8.00
15 Dominik Hasek 5.00 12.00
16 Saku Koivu 2.00 5.00
17 Jocelyn Thibault 1.00 2.50
18 Mark Messier 2.00 5.00
19 Brett Hull 4.00 10.00
20 Felix Potvin 3.00 8.00
21 Curtis Joseph 3.00 8.00
22 Zigmund Palffy 2.00 5.00
23 Mats Sundin 3.00 8.00
24 Keith Tkachuk 3.00 8.00
25 John LeClair 3.00 8.00
26 Mike Richter 3.00 8.00
27 Alexander Mogilny 2.00 5.00
28 Jarome Iginla 4.00 10.00
29 Mike Grier 1.00 2.50
30 Dainius Zubrus 1.00 2.50

1997-98 Pinnacle Inside Cans

This 24-can set features eight of the most distinctive goalie masks in the game and photos of 16 of the hottest superstars reproduced on the can labels and painted directly on the metal.

COMPLETE SET (24) 8.00 20.00
*GOLD CANS: 2.5X TO 6X BASIC CAN
1 Brendan Shanahan .15 .40
2 Jaromir Jagr .30 .75
3 Saku Koivu .15 .40
4 Mats Sundin .15 .40
5 Mike Vernon .20 .50
6 John LeClair .15 .40
7 Keith Tkachuk .15 .40
8 Joe Sakic .30 .75
9 Steve Yzerman .60 1.50
10 Eric Lindros .15 .40
11 Guy Hebert .20 .50
12 Patrick Roy .75 2.00
13 Pavel Bure .15 .40
14 Jocelyn Thibault .20 .50
15 Paul Kariya .40 1.00
16 Peter Forsberg .40 1.00
17 Martin Brodeur .40 1.00
18 Wayne Gretzky 1.00 2.50
19 Teemu Selanne .30 .75
20 John Vanbiesbrouck .20 .50
21 Mark Messier .15 .40
22 Mike Richter .15 .40
23 Brett Hull .20 .50
24 Curtis Joseph .15 .40

1997-98 Pinnacle Inside Promos

COMPLETE SET
1 Brendan Shanahan PROMO .40 1.00
7 Martin Brodeur/250 .75 2.00
8 Peter Forsberg PROMO .75 2.00
10 Paul Kariya/250 .75 2.00
70 Guy Hebert PROMO .40 1.00
84 Mike Vernon PROMO .40 1.00

1997 Pinnacle Mario's Moments

The Pinnacle Mario Lemieux "Moments" set was issued in one series totaling 18 cards. The set was a Pittsburgh area regional set and was sold over a period of six weeks in three-card packs at Giant Eagle grocery stores. A folder to hold the set, which pictured Lemieux, was available for 99 cents during the first week of the promotion. A gold parallel version of the set also can be found. These cards, issued at a rate of one per ten packs, featured gold foil lettering of Lemieux's name. Authentic autographed cards also were randomly inserted into packs. Reports from the manufacturer suggest approximately 700 of these were available.

COMPLETE SET (18) 10.00 25.00
COMMON CARD (1-18) .60 1.50
*GOLD: 2X to 5X BASIC CARDS
NNO Mario Lemieux AUTO 60.00 120.00

1996-97 Pinnacle Mint

The 1996-97 Pinnacle Mint set was issued in one series totaling 30 cards and was distributed in packs of three cards and two coins for a suggested retail price of $3.99. The challenge was to fit the coins with the die-cut cards that pictured the same player on the minted coin. The fronts feature color action player images on a sepia player portrait background with a cut-out area for the matching coin. Eric Lindros was featured on two promo cards, issued to dealers along with their order

ing forms. The cards are identical to the regular die-cut and bronze cards except for the word "promo" written on the right hand side of the card back.

COMP.DIE CUT SET (30) 8.00 20.00
1 Mario Lemieux .75 2.00
2 Dominik Hasek .30 .75
3 Eric Lindros .40 1.00
4 Jaromir Jagr .50 1.25
5 Paul Kariya .60 1.50
6 Peter Forsberg .40 1.00
7 Pavel Bure .40 1.00
8 Sergei Fedorov .30 .75
9 Saku Koivu .15 .40
10 Daniel Alfredsson .10 .30
11 Joe Sakic .30 .75
12 Steve Yzerman .50 1.25
13 Teemu Selanne .30 .75
14 Brett Hull .20 .50
15 Jeremy Roenick .15 .40
16 Mark Messier .20 .50
17 Mats Sundin .15 .40
18 Brendan Shanahan .20 .50
19 Keith Tkachuk .15 .40
20 Paul Coffey .15 .40
21 Patrick Roy .75 2.00
22 Chris Chelios .15 .40
23 Martin Brodeur .40 1.00
24 Felix Potvin .10 .30
25 Chris Osgood .15 .40
26 John Vanbiesbrouck .15 .40
27 Jocelyn Thibault .10 .30
28 Jim Carey .10 .30
29 Jarome Iginla .10 .30
30 Jim Campbell .10 .30
P3A Eric Lindros Bronze Promo 1.25 3.00
P3B Eric Lindros Die-Cut Promo .40 1.00

1996-97 Pinnacle Mint Bronze

This 30-card version of the 1996-97 Pinnacle Mint set features color action player images on a sepia player portrait background with a bronze foil stamp instead of the die-cut area.

*BRONZE: 1X TO 2X BASIC CARDS
ONE PARALLEL PER PACK

1996-97 Pinnacle Mint Gold

Randomly inserted in packs at a rate of 1:48 (and 1:72 magazine packs), this 30-card set parallels the regular issue version and is distinguished by the use of full Gold-foil Dufex print technologies.

*GOLD: 8X TO 20X BASIC CARDS
ODDS 1:48 HOB/RET, 1:72 MAG

1996-97 Pinnacle Mint Silver

Randomly inserted in packs at a rate of 1:15 (and 1:23 magazine packs), this 30-card set is a parallel to the 1996-97 Pinnacle Mint set and features color action player images on a sepia player portrait background with a silver foil stamp instead of the die-cut area.

*SILVER: 4X TO 10X BASIC CARDS
ODDS 1:15 HOB/RET, 1:23 MAG

1996-97 Pinnacle Mint Coins Brass

This 30-coin set features embossed brass coins designed to be inserted into a die-cut card of the player who is pictured on the coin. Additional quantities of the Eric Lindros coin were mailed out to dealers with their order forms.

COMP.BRASS SET (30) 12.00 30.00
BRASS ODDS 2:1 HOB, 1:1 MAG
*NICKEL: 2X TO 5X BRASS
NICKEL STATED ODDS 1:20
*GOLD PLATED: 5X TO 12X BRASS
GOLD PLATED ODDS 1:48
UNPRICED SILVER ODDS 1:2945
UNPRICED SOLID GOLD ODDS 1:25,621
1 Mario Lemieux 1.50 4.00
2 Dominik Hasek .60 1.50
3 Eric Lindros .75 2.00
4 Jaromir Jagr 1.00 2.50
5 Paul Kariya 1.25 3.00
6 Peter Forsberg .75 2.00
7 Pavel Bure .75 2.00
8 Sergei Fedorov .60 1.50
9 Saku Koivu .30 .75
10 Daniel Alfredsson .25 .60
11 Joe Sakic .60 1.50
12 Steve Yzerman 1.00 2.50
13 Teemu Selanne .60 1.50
14 Brett Hull .40 1.00
15 Jeremy Roenick .30 .75
16 Mark Messier .40 1.00
17 Mats Sundin .30 .75
18 Brendan Shanahan .50 1.25
19 Keith Tkachuk .30 .75
20 Paul Coffey .30 .75
21 Patrick Roy 1.50 4.00
22 Chris Chelios .30 .75
23 Martin Brodeur .75 2.00
24 Felix Potvin .30 .75
25 Chris Osgood .30 .75
26 John Vanbiesbrouck .30 .75
27 Jocelyn Thibault .25 .60
28 Jim Carey .25 .60
29 Jarome Iginla .25 .60
30 Jim Campbell .25 .60

1996 Pinnacle Bobby Orr Autograph

This extremely rare card was produced as a giveaway at a Dallas golf tournament run by Pinnacle. It is believed that fewer than 25 copies of this card exist. The card is an all gold foil laser-etched design using the basic card design from 1996-97 Pinnacle.

NNO Bobby Orr 100.00 200.00

1997-98 Pinnacle Mint

The 1997-98 Pinnacle Mint set was issued in one series totaling 30 cards and was distributed in packs of three cards and two coins with a suggested retail price of $3.99. The challenge was to fit the coins with the die-cut cards that pictured the same player on the minted coin. The fronts feature color player photos with a cut-out area for the matching coin.

1 Eric Lindros .15 .40
2 Paul Kariya .15 .40
3 Peter Forsberg .40 1.00
4 John Vanbiesbrouck .10 .30
5 Steve Yzerman .75 2.00
6 Brendan Shanahan .15 .40
7 Teemu Selanne .15 .40
8 Dominik Hasek .30 .75
9 Jarome Iginla .20 .50
10 Mats Sundin .15 .40
11 Patrick Roy .75 2.00
12 Joe Sakic .30 .75
13 Mark Messier .15 .40
14 Sergei Fedorov .25 .60
15 Saku Koivu .15 .40
16 Martin Brodeur .40 1.00
17 Pavel Bure .15 .40
18 Wayne Gretzky 1.00 2.50
19 Brian Leetch .10 .30
20 John LeClair .15 .40
21 Keith Tkachuk .15 .40
22 Jaromir Jagr .25 .60
23 Brett Hull .20 .50
24 Curtis Joseph .15 .40
25 Jaroslav Svejkovsky .07 .20
26 Sergei Samsonov .10 .30
27 Alexei Morozov .07 .20
28 Alyn McCauley .07 .20
29 Joe Thornton .25 .60
30 Vaclav Prospal RC .10 .30
P3 Peter Forsberg PROMO 3.00 8.00

1997-98 Pinnacle Mint Bronze

This 30-card set is parallel to the base set and is similar in design. The difference is found in the bronze foil stamp instead of the die-cut area. They were inserted at 1:1 hobby and 2:1 retail.

*BRONZE: .8X TO 2X BASIC CARDS

1997-98 Pinnacle Mint Gold Team

Randomly inserted in packs, this 30-card set is parallel version of the Pinnacle Mint base set printed on full gold foil card stock. They were inserted at 1:31 hobby and 1:71 retail.

*GOLD TEAM: 10X TO 25X BASIC CARDS

1997-98 Pinnacle Mint Silver Team

Randomly inserted in packs, this 30-card set is parallel version of the Pinnacle Mint base set printed on full silver foil card stock. They were inserted at 1:15 hobby and 1:23 retail.

*SILVER TEAM: 5X TO 12X BASIC CARDS

1997-98 Pinnacle Mint Coins Brass

Randomly inserted in packs at overall rates of 2:1 hobby and 1:1 retail, this 30-coin set features embossed brass coins designed to be inserted into a die-cut card of the player who is pictured on the coin. A number of parallels were also created and inserted randomly.

COMP.BRASS SET (30) 30.00 60.00
*BRASS PROOF/500: 6X TO 15X BRASS
BRASS PROOF PRINT RUN 500
*NICKEL SILVER: 2X TO 5X BRASS
NICKEL STATED ODDS 1:41 HOB/RET
*NICKEL PROOF: 10X TO 25X BRASS
NICKEL PROOF PRINT RUN 250
*GOLD PLATED: 10X TO 25X BRASS
GOLD PLATED ODDS 1:199 HOB/RET
*GOLD PLT PROOF/100: 25X TO 60X BRASS
GOLD PLATED PROOF PRINT RUN 100
UNPRICED SOLID GOLD PRINT RUN 1
SOLID SILVER TOO SCARCE TO PRICE
1 Eric Lindros .75 2.00
2 Paul Kariya 1.25 3.00
3 Peter Forsberg .75 2.00
4 John Vanbiesbrouck .30 .75
5 Steve Yzerman 1.00 2.50
6 Brendan Shanahan .50 1.25
7 Teemu Selanne .60 1.50
8 Dominik Hasek .60 1.50
9 Jarome Iginla .25 .60
10 Mats Sundin .30 .75
11 Patrick Roy 1.50 4.00
12 Joe Sakic .60 1.50
13 Mark Messier .40 1.00
14 Sergei Fedorov .60 1.50
15 Saku Koivu .30 .75
16 Martin Brodeur .75 2.00
17 Pavel Bure .75 2.00
18 Wayne Gretzky 2.50 5.00
19 Brian Leetch .30 .75
20 John LeClair .50 1.25
21 Keith Tkachuk .30 .75
22 Jaromir Jagr 1.00 2.50
23 Brett Hull .40 1.00
24 Curtis Joseph .40 1.00
25 Jaroslav Svejkovsky .25 .60
26 Sergei Samsonov .30 .75
27 Alexei Morozov .25 .60
28 Alyn McCauley .25 .60
29 Joe Thornton .30 .75
30 Vaclav Prospal .25 .60

1997-98 Pinnacle Mint Minternational

Randomly inserted in hobby packs at the rate of 1:31 and retail packs at the rate of 1:47, this six-card set commemorates the Winter Olympic games with color photos of one player from each nation printed on full silver foil card stock.

COMPLETE SET (6) 15.00 30.00
1 Eric Lindros 6.00 15.00
2 Peter Forsberg 4.00 10.00
3 Brett Hull 2.00 5.00
4 Teemu Selanne 2.50 6.00
5 Dominik Hasek 3.00 8.00
6 Pavel Bure 2.50 6.00

1997-98 Pinnacle Mint Minternational Coins

Randomly inserted in hobby packs only at the rate of 1:31, this six-coin set is parallel to the 1997-98 Pinnacle Mint Minternational set and features the six players on double-sized embossed coins.

COMPLETE SET (6) 30.00 60.00
1 Eric Lindros 8.00 20.00
2 Peter Forsberg 8.00 20.00
3 Brett Hull 3.00 8.00
4 Teemu Selanne 5.00 12.00
5 Dominik Hasek 5.00 12.00
6 Pavel Bure 6.00 12.00

1997-98 Pinnacle Power Pack Blow-Ups

Randomly inserted in packs, this 24-card set features color action photos of some of the hottest players in the NHL printed on 3" X 5" cards.

1 Eric Lindros 1.00 2.50
2 Paul Kariya 1.25 3.00
3 Joe Thornton .40 1.00
4 Dominik Hasek .60 1.50
5 Patrick Roy 1.50 4.00
6 Keith Tkachuk .30 .75
7 Martin Brodeur .75 2.00
8 Brett Hull .40 1.00
9 Mark Messier .40 1.00
10 Saku Koivu .30 .75
11 Jaromir Jagr 1.00 2.50
12 Joe Sakic .60 1.50
13 John Vanbiesbrouck .30 .75
14 Pavel Bure .75 2.00
15 Jarome Iginla .40 1.00
16 Mats Sundin .30 .75
17 Wayne Gretzky 2.00 5.00
18 Steve Yzerman 1.00 2.50
19 Peter Forsberg .75 2.00
20 Brendan Shanahan .60 1.50
21 Sergei Fedorov .60 1.50
22 Curtis Joseph .40 1.00
23 John LeClair .40 1.00
24 Teemu Selanne .60 1.50
P2 Paul Kariya PROMO 1.25 3.00
P13 John Vanbiesbrouck PROMO .60 1.50

1997-98 Pinnacle Totally Certified Platinum Blue

Inserted one in every pack, this 130-card set is parallel to the Totally Certified Platinum Gold and Platinum Red sets. The difference is found in the platinum blue micro-etched holographic foil and foil stamping. Only 2599 goalie cards and 3099 skater cards were printed.

*PLAT.BLUE: .8X TO 2X PLAT.RED

1997-98 Pinnacle Totally Certified Platinum Gold

Randomly inserted in packs at the rate of 1:79, this 130-card set is parallel to the Totally Certified Platinum Blue and Platinum Red sets. The difference is found in the platinum gold micro-etched holographic foil and foil stamping. Only 59 serially numbered goalie cards and 69 serially numbered skater cards were printed. A mirror gold parallel to the gold set was also created and randomly inserted.

*PLAT.GOLD: 6X TO 15X PLAT.RED

1997-98 Pinnacle Totally Certified Platinum Red

Inserted in packs at the rate of two to a pack, this 130-card set was distributed in three card packs with a suggested retail price of $7.99 and featured color player photos printed on 24 pt. card stock with micro-etched holographic foil and platinum red foil stamping. Only 4299 goalie cards and 6199 skater cards were printed and serially numbered.

COMPLETE SET (130) 100.00 250.00
1 Dominik Hasek 5.00 10.00
2 Patrick Roy 12.50 25.00
3 Martin Brodeur 6.00 12.00
4 Chris Osgood 1.50 4.00
5 Andy Moog 1.50 4.00
6 John Vanbiesbrouck 1.50 4.00
7 Steve Shields RC 2.00 5.00
8 Mike Vernon 1.50 4.00
9 Ed Belfour 2.00 5.00
10 Grant Fuhr 1.50 4.00
11 Felix Potvin 2.00 5.00
12 Bill Ranford 1.50 4.00
13 Mike Richter 2.00 5.00
14 Stephane Fiset 1.25 3.00
15 Jim Carey 1.50 4.00
16 Nikolai Khabibulin 1.50 4.00
17 Ken Wregget 1.25 3.00
18 Curtis Joseph 2.00 5.00
19 Guy Hebert 1.50 4.00
20 Damian Rhodes 1.50 4.00
21 Trevor Kidd 1.50 4.00
22 Daren Puppa 1.25 3.00
23 Patrick Lalime 1.50 4.00
24 Tommy Salo 1.50 4.00
25 Sean Burke 1.25 3.00
26 Jocelyn Thibault 1.50 4.00
27 Kirk McLean 1.50 4.00
28 Garth Snow 1.50 4.00
29 Ron Tugnutt 1.50 4.00
30 Jeff Hackett 1.25 3.00
31 Eric Lindros 1.50 4.00
32 Peter Forsberg 5.00 10.00
33 Mike Modano 3.00 6.00
34 Paul Kariya 1.50 4.00
35 Jaromir Jagr 2.50 6.00
36 Brian Leetch 1.50 4.00
37 Keith Tkachuk 1.50 4.00
38 Steve Yzerman 10.00 20.00
39 Teemu Selanne 1.50 4.00
40 Bryan Berard 1.25 3.00
41 Ray Bourque 2.50 5.00
42 Theo Fleury .75 2.00
43 Mark Messier 2.00 5.00
44 Saku Koivu 1.50 4.00
45 Pavel Bure 2.00 5.00
46 Peter Bondra 1.25 3.00
47 Dave Gagner .75 2.00
48 Ed Jovanovski 1.25 3.00
49 Adam Oates 1.25 3.00
50 Joe Sakic 4.00 8.00
51 Doug Gilmour 1.25 3.00
52 Jim Campbell .75 2.00
53 Mats Sundin 1.50 4.00
54 Derian Hatcher .75 2.00
55 Jarome Iginla 2.00 5.00
56 Sergei Fedorov 2.50 6.00
57 Keith Primeau .75 2.00
58 Mark Recchi 1.25 3.00
59 Owen Nolan 1.25 3.00
60 Alexander Mogilny 1.25 3.00
61 Brendan Shanahan 2.00 5.00
62 Pierre Turgeon 1.25 3.00
63 Joe Juneau 1.25 3.00
64 Steve Rucchin .75 2.00
65 Jeremy Roenick 2.00 5.00
66 Doug Weight 1.25 3.00
67 Valeri Kamensky 1.25 3.00
68 Tony Amonte 1.25 3.00
69 Dave Andreychuk .75 2.00
70 Brett Hull 2.50 5.00
71 Wendel Clark 1.25 3.00
72 Vincent Damphousse .75 2.00
73 Mike Grier .75 2.00
74 Chris Chelios 1.50 4.00
75 Nicklas Lidstrom 1.50 4.00
76 Joe Nieuwendyk 1.25 3.00
77 Rob Blake 1.25 3.00
78 Alexei Yashin .75 2.00
79 Ryan Smyth .75 2.00
80 Pat Lafontaine 1.50 4.00
81 Jeff Friesen .75 2.00
82 Ray Ferraro .75 2.00
83 Steve Sullivan .75 2.00
84 Chris Gratton 1.25 3.00
85 Mike Gartner 1.25 3.00
86 Kevin Hatcher .75 2.00
87 Ted Donato .75 2.00
88 German Titov .75 2.00
89 Sandis Ozolinsh .75 2.00
90 Ray Sheppard .75 2.00
91 John MacLean .75 2.00
92 Luc Robitaille 1.25 3.00
93 Rod Brind'Amour 1.25 3.00
94 Zigmund Palffy 1.25 3.00
95 Petr Nedved 1.25 3.00
96 Adam Graves .75 2.00
97 Jozef Stumpel 1.25 3.00
98 Alexandre Daigle .75 2.00
99 Mike Peca .75 2.00
100 Wayne Gretzky 12.50 25.00
101 Alexei Zhamnov .75 2.00
102 Paul Coffey 1.50 4.00
103 Oleg Tverdovsky .75 2.00
104 Trevor Linden 1.25 3.00
105 Dino Ciccarelli .75 2.00
106 Andrei Kovalenko .75 2.00
107 Scott Mellanby .75 2.00
108 Bryan Smolinski .75 2.00
109 Bernie Nicholls .75 2.00
110 Derek Plante .75 2.00
111 Pat Verbeek .75 2.00
112 Adam Deadmarsh .75 2.00
113 Martin Gelinas .75 2.00
114 Daniel Alfredsson 1.25 3.00
115 Scott Stevens .75 2.00
116 Dainius Zubrus 1.50 4.00
117 Kirk Muller .75 2.00
118 Brian Holzinger .75 2.00
119 John LeClair 2.00 5.00
120 Al MacInnis 1.25 3.00
121 Ron Francis 1.25 3.00
122 Eric Daze 1.25 3.00
123 Travis Green .75 2.00
124 Jason Arnott .75 2.00
125 Geoff Sanderson 1.25 3.00
126 Dimitri Khristich .75 2.00
127 Sergei Berezin .75 2.00
128 Jeff O'Neill .75 2.00
129 Claude Lemieux .75 2.00
130 Andrew Cassels .75 2.00

1997-98 Pinnacle Hockey Night in Canada

These cards feature the top on-air personalities from the only hockey broadcast that matters. The cards were produced by Pinnacle, and were given away at autograph signings and other personal appearances.

COMPLETE SET (13) 30.00 75.00
1 Steve Armitage 1.25 3.00
2 Don Cherry 20.00 50.00
3 Bob Cole 2.00 5.00
4 Chris Cuthbert 1.25 3.00
5 John Garrett 2.00 5.00
6 Dick Irvin, Jr. 4.00 10.00
7 Ron Maclean 4.00 10.00
8 Greg Millen 1.25 3.00
9 Harry Neale 2.00 5.00
10 Scott Oake 1.25 3.00
11 Scott Russell 1.25 3.00
12 John Shannon .75 2.00
13 Don Whittman 1.25 3.00

1995-96 Playoff One on One

The 1995-96 Playoff One on One Hockey Challenge is a set of 330 cards which can be used to play a fantasy game. The cards could be found in four different card types: Common (1-110), Uncommon (111-220), Rare, Ultra Rare (found in Booster Packs) and Ultra Rare (found in Starter Packs). The scarcer the card, the higher the point values that can be used during the game. Fifty-card starter decks, including three dice and a rule book, were available for $9.95 ea. Game players could add to the power of their decks by purchasing booster packs for $2.50 ea. Ultra rare cards are designated with suffixes below. UR3 cards were found in starter packs, while URB were hidden in booster packs.

COMPLETE SET (330) 100.00 250.00
1 Guy Hebert .07 .20
2 Paul Kariya .60 1.50
3 Mike Sillinger .02 .10

4 Oleg Tverdovsky .02 .10
5 Ray Bourque .40 1.00
6 Alexei Kasatonov .02 .10
7 Blaine Lacher .02 .10
8 Cam Neely .07 .20
9 Adam Oates .07 .20
10 Kevin Stevens .02 .10
11 Donald Audette .02 .10
12 Dominik Hasek .30 .75
13 Pat LaFontaine .07 .20
14 Alexei Zhitnik .02 .10
15 Steve Chiasson .02 .10
16 Theo Fleury .20 .50
17 Phil Housley .02 .10
18 Joe Nieuwendyk .07 .20
19 Gary Roberts .02 .10
20 German Titov .02 .10
21 Ed Belfour .20 .50
22 Chris Chelios .20 .50
23 Bernie Nicholls .02 .10
24 Jeremy Roenick .20 .50
25 Peter Forsberg .40 1.00
26 Sylvain Lefebvre .02 .10
27 Owen Nolan .07 .20
28 Joe Sakic .40 1.00
29 Jocelyn Thibault .08 .25
30 Dave Gagner .02 .10
31 Mike Modano .30 .75
32 Andy Moog .07 .20
33 Paul Coffey .20 .50
34 Sergei Fedorov .30 .75
35 Keith Primeau .02 .10
36 Ray Sheppard .02 .10
37 Jason Arnott .02 .10
38 David Oliver .02 .10
39 Mike Stapleton .02 .10
40 Jesse Belanger .02 .10
41 Paul Laus .02 .10
42 Rob Niedermayer .02 .10
43 Brian Skrudland .02 .10
44 John Vanbiesbrouck .20 .50
45 Sean Burke .02 .10
46 Andrew Cassels .02 .10
47 Brendan Shanahan .30 .75
48 Rob Blake .02 .10
49 Tony Granato .02 .10
50 Wayne Gretzky 2.00 5.00
51 Marty McSorley .02 .10
52 Jamie Storr .08 .25
53 Vincent Damphousse .07 .20
54 Mark Recchi .07 .20
55 Patrick Roy 1.50 4.00
56 Pierre Turgeon .07 .20
57 Martin Brodeur .40 1.00
58 Bill Guerin .02 .10
59 Scott Niedermayer .02 .10
60 Stephane Richer .02 .10
61 Scott Stevens .02 .10
62 Patrick Flatley .02 .10
63 Brett Lindros .02 .10
64 Mathieu Schneider .02 .10
65 Kirk Muller .02 .10
66 Adam Graves .02 .10
67 Alexei Kovalev .02 .10
68 Brian Leetch .20 .50
69 Mike Richter .20 .50
70 Pat Verbeek .02 .10
71 Luc Robitaille .07 .20
72 Radek Bonk .02 .10
73 Alexandre Daigle .02 .10
74 Alexei Yashin .08 .25
75 Eric Desjardins .02 .10
76 Eric Lindros .30 .75
77 Ron Francis .07 .20
78 Jaromir Jagr .60 1.50
79 Mario Lemieux 1.50 4.00
80 Ken Wregget .02 .10
81 Francois Leroux .02 .10
82 Pat Falloon .02 .10
83 Jeff Friesen .02 .10
84 Arturs Irbe .07 .20
85 Igor Larionov .02 .10
86 Shayne Corson .02 .10
87 Geoff Courtnall .02 .10
88 Steve Duchesne .02 .10
89 Brett Hull .30 .75
90 Al MacInnis .02 .10
91 Brian Bellows .02 .10
92 Chris Gratton .02 .10
93 Dave Andreychuk .07 .20
94 Tie Domi .15 .40
95 Mike Gartner .02 .10
96 Doug Gilmour .20 .50
97 Larry Murphy .02 .10
98 Felix Potvin .20 .50
99 Mats Sundin .20 .50
100 Pavel Bure .40 1.00
101 Kirk McLean .02 .10
102 Alexander Mogilny .05 .15
103 Christian Ruuttu .02 .10
104 Jim Carey .05 .15
105 Joe Juneau .02 .10
106 Jason Allison .05 .15
107 Teppo Numminen .02 .10
108 Teemu Selanne .30 .75
109 Keith Tkachuk .20 .50
110 Alexei Zhamnov .02 .10
111 Patrik Carnback .02 .10
112 Bobby Dollas .02 .10
113 Guy Hebert .20 .50
114 Paul Kariya .60 1.50
115 Shaun Van Allen .02 .10
116 Ray Bourque .40 1.00
117 Mariusz Czerkawski .02 .10
118 Todd Elik .02 .10
119 Blaine Lacher .05 .15
120 Cam Neely .20 .50
121 Adam Oates .08 .25
122 Dave Reid .02 .10
123 Kevin Stevens .02 .10
124 Garry Galley .02 .10
125 Dominik Hasek .40 1.00
126 Brian Holzinger .05 .15
127 Pat LaFontaine .08 .25
128 Mike Peca .20 .50
129 Phil Housley .05 .15
130 Paul Kruse .02 .10
131 Ronnie Stern .02 .10
132 Zarley Zalapski .02 .10
133 Patrick Poulin .02 .10
134 Bob Probert .05 .15
135 Jeremy Roenick .20 .50
136 Adam Deadmarsh .08 .25
137 Peter Forsberg .75 2.00
138 Andrei Kovalenko .02 .10
139 Joe Sakic .40 1.00
140 Derian Hatcher .02 .10
141 Grant Ledyard .02 .10
142 Mike Modano .30 .75
143 Paul Coffey .08 .25
144 Sergei Fedorov .40 1.00
145 Vladimir Konstantinov .20 .50
146 Nicklas Lidstrom .15 .40
147 Steve Yzerman 1.50 4.00
148 Igor Kravchuk .02 .10
149 Kirk Maltby .02 .10
150 Boris Mironov .20 .50
151 Bill Ranford .08 .25
152 Stu Barnes .02 .10
153 Jesse Belanger .02 .10
154 Scott Mellanby .02 .10
155 Adam Burt .02 .10
156 Steven Rice .02 .10
157 Brendan Shanahan .30 .75
158 Glen Wesley .02 .10
159 Wayne Gretzky 2.00 5.00
160 Darryl Sydor .02 .10
161 Rick Tocchet .05 .15
162 Benoit Brunet .02 .10
163 J.J. Daigneault .02 .10
164 Saku Koivu .20 .50
165 Lyle Odelein .02 .10
166 Patrick Roy 1.50 4.00
167 Scott Stevens .05 .15
168 Valeri Zelepukin .02 .10
169 Steve Thomas .07 .20
170 Dennis Vaske .02 .10
171 Brett Lindros .02 .10
172 Zigmund Palffy .08 .25
173 Ray Ferraro .02 .10
174 Brian Leetch .08 .25
175 Mark Messier .30 .75
176 Ulf Samuelsson .02 .10
177 Don Beaupre .05 .15
178 Alexandre Daigle .08 .25
179 Steve Larouche .02 .10
180 Scott Levins .02 .10
181 Ron Hextall .08 .25
182 Eric Lindros .40 1.00
183 Mikael Renberg .08 .25
184 Kjell Samuelsson .02 .10
185 Jaromir Jagr .60 1.50
186 Mario Lemieux 1.50 4.00
187 Sergei Zubov .02 .10
188 Bryan Smolinski .02 .10
189 Dmitri Mironov .02 .10
190 Ulf Dahlen .02 .10
191 Arturs Irbe .20 .50
192 Craig Janney .02 .10
193 Sandis Ozolinsh .05 .15
194 Jon Casey .05 .15
195 Brett Hull .30 .75
196 Esa Tikkanen .02 .10
197 Brian Bradley .07 .20
198 Daren Puppa .05 .15
199 Alexander Selivanov .02 .10
200 Rob Zamuner .02 .10
201 Ken Baumgartner .02 .10
202 Doug Gilmour .08 .25
203 Kenny Jonsson .02 .10
204 Felix Potvin .08 .25
205 Randy Wood .02 .10
206 Jeff Brown .05 .15
207 Pavel Bure .40 1.00
208 Trevor Linden .05 .15
209 Alexander Mogilny .08 .25
210 Roman Oksiuta .02 .10
211 Cliff Ronning .02 .10
212 Peter Bondra .08 .25
213 Jim Carey .08 .25
214 Pat Peake .02 .10
215 Mark Tinordi .02 .10
216 Mike Eastwood .02 .10
217 Nelson Emerson .02 .10
218 Dave Manson .02 .10
219 Teemu Selanne .40 1.00
220 Keith Tkachuk .20 .50
221 Bob Corkum R .08 .25
222 Peter Douris R .08 .25
223 Paul Kariya URB 10.00 25.00
224 Todd Krygier URS .40 1.00
225 Mike Sillinger R .08 .25
226 Ray Bourque URB 6.00 15.00
227 Fred Knipscheer R .08 .25
228 Cam Neely URB 3.00 8.00
229 Adam Oates URB 2.00 5.00
230 Jason Dawe R .08 .25
231 Yuri Khmylev R .08 .25
232 Bob Sweeney URS .40 1.00
233 Trevor Kidd R .20 .50
234 Eric Daze R .30 .75
235 Tony Amonte R .30 .75
236 Jeremy Roenick URB 4.00 10.00
237 Denis Savard R .20 .50
238 Gary Suter R .08 .25
239 Peter Forsberg URB 8.00 20.00
240 Curtis Leschyshyn R .08 .25
241 Owen Nolan URB 2.00 5.00
242 Joe Sakic URS 8.00 20.00
243 Valeri Kamensky R .20 .50
244 Claude Lemieux R .20 .50
245 Bob Bassen R .08 .25
246 Shane Churla R .08 .25
247 Todd Harvey R .08 .25
248 Kevin Hatcher URS .40 1.00
249 Richard Matvichuk R .08 .25
250 Mike Modano URB 3.00 8.00
251 Dino Ciccarelli R .20 .50
252 Paul Coffey URS 3.00 8.00
253 Sergei Fedorov URS 6.00 15.00
254 Vyacheslav Kozlov R .20 .50
255 Mike Vernon R .20 .50
256 Jason Bonsignore R .08 .25
257 Dean McAmmond R .08 .25
258 Bill Ranford R .08 .25
259 Doug Weight URB 2.00 5.00
260 Bob Kudelski R .08 .25
261 Dave Lowry R .08 .25
262 Gord Murphy R .08 .25
263 Rob Niedermayer URS 2.00 5.00
264 Frantisek Kucera R .08 .25
265 Paul Ranheim R .08 .25
266 Geoff Sanderson URS .75 2.00
267 Darren Turcotte R .08 .25
268 Pat Conacher R .08 .25
269 Wayne Gretzky URB 20.00 50.00
270 Kelly Hrudey R .08 .25
271 Jari Kurri R .20 .50
272 Patrice Brisebois R .08 .25
273 Vladimir Malakhov R .08 .25
274 Patrick Roy URB 15.00 40.00
275 Martin Brodeur URB 8.00 20.00
276 Neal Broten R .08 .25
277 Sergei Brylin R .08 .25
278 John MacLean R .08 .25
279 Wendel Clark R .20 .50
280 Travis Green R .08 .25
281 Scott Lachance URS .40 1.00
282 Tommy Salo R .20 .50
283 Brian Leetch URB 3.00 8.00
284 Mark Messier URB 4.00 10.00
285 Sergei Nemchinov R .08 .25
286 Luc Robitaille URS 3.00 8.00
287 Sean Hill R .08 .25
288 Jim Paek URS .40 1.00
289 Martin Straka R .20 .50
290 Sylvain Turgeon R .08 .25
291 Rod Brind'Amour URS 2.00 5.00
292 Kevin Haller R .08 .25
293 John LeClair R .75 2.00
294 Eric Lindros URB 6.00 15.00
295 Joel Otto R .08 .25
296 Chris Therien R .08 .25
297 Jaromir Jagr URS 10.00 25.00
298 Mario Lemieux URB 15.00 40.00
299 Glen Murray R .20 .50
300 Petr Nedved R .20 .50
301 Jamie Baker R .08 .25
302 Arturs Irbe URB 2.00 5.00
303 Jayson More R .08 .25
304 Ray Whitney R .08 .25
305 Geoff Courtnall URS .40 1.00
306 Dale Hawerchuk R .20 .50
307 Brett Hull URB 4.00 10.00
308 Ian Laperriere R .08 .25
309 Chris Pronger R .20 .50
310 Roman Hamrlik R .20 .50
311 Petr Klima URS .40 1.00
312 John Tucker R .08 .25
313 Paul Ysebaert URB .40 1.00
314 Ken Baumgartner R .08 .25
315 Doug Gilmour URB 2.00 5.00
316 Pavel Bure URB 8.00 20.00
317 Bret Hedican R .08 .25
318 Alexander Mogilny URS 2.00 5.00
319 Mike Ridley R .08 .25
320 Peter Bondra R .40 1.00
321 Sylvain Cote R .08 .25
322 Dale Hunter R .08 .25
323 Keith Jones URS .40 1.00
324 Kelly Miller R .08 .25
325 Tim Cheveldae R .08 .25
326 Dallas Drake R .08 .25
327 Igor Korolev R .08 .25
328 Teppo Numminen R .08 .25
329 Teemu Selanne URB 6.00 15.00
330 Alexei Zhamnov URS .40 1.00

1996-97 Playoff One on One

This 110-card set serves as a follow-up to the '95-96 game set of the same name, allowing collectors/players to expand their playing experience. As with the previous set, the cards were available in varying degrees of difficulty. The suffixes below indicate how difficult each is to obtain: C is common, UC is uncommon, R is rare and UR is ultra rare. The cards can also be differentiated quickly be referring to the background color: commons are green, uncommons are violet, rares are silver and ultra rares are gold.

COMPLETE SET (110) 80.00 200.00
331 Mike Sillinger C .02 .10
332 Oleg Tverdovsky C .07 .20
333 Kevin Stevens C .02 .10
334 Joe Nieuwendyk C .07 .20
335 Owen Nolan C .08 .25
336 Jocelyn Thibault C .07 .20
337 Dave Gagner C .02 .10
338 Ray Sheppard C .02 .10
339 Jesse Belanger C .02 .10
340 Tony Granato C .02 .10
341 Daniel Alfredsson C .07 .20
342 Stephane Richer C .02 .10
343 Mathieu Schneider C .02 .10
344 Kirk Muller C .02 .10
345 Arturs Irbe C .08 .25
346 Igor Larionov C .02 .10
347 Steve Duchesne C .02 .10
348 Dave Andreychuk C .02 .10
349 Mike Gartner C .07 .20
350 Teppo Numminen C .02 .10
351 Keith Tkachuk C .20 .50
352 Mike Modano C .20 .50
353 Paul Kariya C .30 .75
354 German Titov C .02 .10
355 Bernie Nicholls C .02 .10
356 Doug Gilmour C .20 .50
357 Peter Forsberg C .30 .75
358 David Oliver C .02 .10
359 Pat Verbeek C .02 .10
360 Ron Francis C .07 .20
361 Pat Falloon C .02 .10
362 Jeff Friesen C .07 .20
363 Todd Krygier C .02 .10
364 Felix Potvin C .20 .50
365 Shane Churla C .02 .10
366 Steve Yzerman C .40 1.00
367 Kelly Hrudey C .02 .10
368 Mariusz Czerkawski U .07 .20
369 Patrick Poulin U .05 .15
370 Chris Chelios U .40 1.00
371 Ray Bourque U .75 2.00
372 Igor Kravchuk U .05 .15
373 Kirk Maltby U .05 .15
374 Bill Ranford U .07 .20
375 Darryl Sydor U .05 .15
376 Rick Tocchet U .07 .20
377 J.J. Daigneault U .05 .15
378 Chris Osgood U .40 1.00
379 Zigmund Palffy U .20 .50
380 Ray Ferraro U .05 .15
381 Don Beaupre U .07 .20
382 Andy Moog U .20 .50
383 Sergei Zubov U .07 .20
384 Craig Janney U .05 .15
385 Sandis Ozolinsh U .07 .20
386 Dave Reid U .05 .15
387 Scott Mellanby U .07 .20
388 Saku Koivu U .40 1.00
389 Bryan Smolinski U .07 .20
390 Alexander Selivanov U .05 .15
391 Peter Bondra U .20 .50
392 Esa Tikkanen U .07 .20
393 Ken Baumgartner U .05 .15
394 Ed Belfour U .40 1.00
395 Randy Wood U .05 .15
396 Jeff Brown U .05 .15
397 Roman Oksiuta U .05 .15
398 Cliff Ronning U .05 .15
399 Mike Eastwood U .05 .15
400 Nelson Emerson U .05 .15
401 Dave Manson U .05 .15
402 Jamie Baker U .05 .15
403 Ian Laperriere U .05 .15
404 Petr Klima U .05 .15
405 Dallas Drake R .07 .20
406 Tim Cheveldae R .20 .50
407 Igor Korolev R .07 .20
408 Kevin Hatcher R .07 .20
409 Dale Hawerchuk R .40 1.00
410 Martin Straka R .30 .75
411 Wendel Clark R .75 2.00
412 Jari Kurri R .75 2.00
413 Darren Turcotte R .07 .20
414 Yuri Khmylev R .07 .20
415 Bob Corkum R .07 .20
416 Roman Hamrlik R .30 .75
417 Jayson More R .07 .20
418 Travis Green R .30 .75
419 Dean McAmmond R .07 .20
420 Valeri Kamensky R .20 .50
421 Jason Dawe R .07 .20
422 Alexander Mogilny R .75 2.00
423 Keith Jones R .07 .20
424 Mark Messier R 3.00 8.00
425 John Vanbiesbrouck R 2.00 5.00
426 Jim Carey R .40 1.00
427 Brett Hull R 4.00 10.00
428 Teemu Selanne UR 6.00 15.00
429 Phil Housley UR 2.00 5.00
430 Wayne Gretzky UR 20.00 50.00
431 Patrick Roy UR 15.00 40.00
432 Joe Sakic UR 8.00 20.00
433 Jaromir Jagr UR 8.00 20.00
434 Doug Weight UR 2.00 5.00
435 Rob Niedermayer UR 2.00 5.00
436 Mario Lemieux UR 15.00 40.00
437 Sergei Fedorov UR 6.00 15.00
438 Pavel Bure UR 6.00 15.00
439 Eric Lindros UR 6.00 15.00
440 Martin Brodeur UR 8.00 20.00

1975-76 Popsicle

This 18-card set presents the teams of the NHL. The cards measure approximately 3 3/8" by 2 1/8" and are printed in the "credit card format", only slightly thinner than an actual credit card. The front has the NHL logo in the upper left hand corner, and the city and team names in the black bar across the top. A colorful team logo appears on the left side of the card face, while a color action shot of the teams' players appears on the right side. The back provides a brief history of the team. The set was issued in two versions (English and bilingual). We have checklisted the cards below in alphabetical order of the team nicknames.

COMPLETE SET (18) 15.00 30.00
1 Chicago Blackhawks 1.50 3.00
2 St. Louis Blues 1.00 2.00
3 Boston Bruins 1.50 3.00
4 Montreal Canadiens 1.50 3.00
5 Vancouver Canucks 1.00 2.00
6 Washington Capitals 1.00 2.00
7 Atlanta Flames 1.50 3.00
8 Philadelphia Flyers 1.00 2.00
9 California Golden Seals 1.50 3.00
10 New York Islanders 1.00 2.00
11 Los Angeles Kings 1.00 2.00
12 Toronto Maple Leafs 1.50 3.00
13 Minnesota North Stars 1.00 2.00
14 Pittsburgh Penguins 1.00 2.00
15 New York Rangers 1.50 3.00
16 Detroit Red Wings 1.50 3.00
17 Buffalo Sabres 1.00 2.00
18 Kansas City Scouts 1.50 3.00

1976-77 Popsicle

This 18-card set presents the teams of the NHL. The cards measure approximately 3 3/8" by 2 1/8" and are printed in the "credit card format", only slightly thinner than an actual credit card. The front has the NHL logo in the upper left hand corner, and the city and team names in the black bar across the top. A colorful team logo appears on the left side of the card face, while a color action shot of the teams' players appears on the right side. The back provides a brief history of the team. The set was issued in two versions (English and bilingual); a bilingual membership card is known to exist. We have checklisted the cards below in alphabetical order of the team nicknames.

COMPLETE SET (19) 20.00 40.00
1 Cleveland Barons 1.50 3.00
2 Chicago Blackhawks 1.50 3.00
3 St. Louis Blues 1.00 2.00
4 Boston Bruins 1.50 3.00
5 Montreal Canadiens 1.50 3.00
6 Vancouver Canucks 1.00 2.00
7 Washington Capitals 1.00 2.00
8 Atlanta Flames 1.50 3.00
9 Philadelphia Flyers 1.00 2.00
10 New York Islanders 1.00 2.00
11 Los Angeles Kings 1.00 2.00
12 Toronto Maple Leafs 1.50 3.00
13 Minnesota North Stars 1.00 2.00
14 Pittsburgh Penguins 1.00 2.00
15 New York Rangers 1.50 3.00
16 Detroit Red Wings 1.50 3.00
17 Colorado Rockies 1.50 3.00
18 Buffalo Sabres 1.00 2.00
19 Membership Card 1.50 3.00

1966-67 Post Cereal Box Backs

These three box backs seem to vary from the 1967-68 set, so we have listed them seperately. The backs picture Pulford and Hall in All-Star uniforms and Worsley in his Canadiens uniform with a notation that Montreal won the Stanley Cup in 1965-66. A "hockey tip" was printed below the pictures in both English and French, though often the picture was cut from the box without the writing underneath. If anyone has any further information about this set, please forward it to hockeymag@beckett.com.

1 Gump Worsley 40.00
2 Bob Pulford 40.00
3 Glenn Hall 40.00

1967-68 Post Cereal Box Backs

These photo premiums were issued on the back of Post cereal boxes. They measure approximately 6 1/2 by 7 1/2 and are blank backed. They are unnumbered and so are listed below in alphabetical order.

COMPLETE SET (13)
1 Gordie Howe 25.00 50.00
(net in background
2 Gordie Howe 25.00 50.00
(no net
3 Harry Howell 10.00 20.00
(passing
4 Harry Howell 10.00 20.00
(kneeling
5 Jacques Laperriere 10.00 20.00
(net in background
6 Jacques Laperriere 10.00 20.00
(no net
7 Stan Mikita 15.00 30.00
(red jersey
8 Stan Mikita 15.00 30.00
(white jersey
9 Bobby Orr 25.00 50.00
(posed
10 Bobby Orr 25.00 50.00
(in action
11 Henri Richard 12.50 25.00
(with puck
12 Henri Richard 12.50 25.00
(no puck
13 checklist 25.00 50.00

1967-68 Post Flip Books

This 1967-68 Post set consists of 12 flip books. They display a Montreal player on one side of the page and a Toronto player on the other side. In the listing below, the Montreal player is listed first.

COMPLETE SET (12) 100.00 200.00
1 Gump Worsley 15.00 30.00
Johnny Bower
2 Rogatien Vachon 17.50 35.00
Johnny Bower
3 J.C. Tremblay 12.50 25.00
Tim Horton
4 Jacques Laperriere 7.50 15.00
Marcel Pronovost
5 Henri Richard 12.50 25.00
Frank Mahovlich
6 Dick Duff 10.00 20.00
Dave Keon
7 Jean Beliveau 15.00 30.00
Jim Pappin
8 Jean Beliveau 15.00 30.00
Ron Ellis
9 Gilles Tremblay 10.00 20.00
George Armstrong
10 J.C. Tremblay 5.00 10.00
Pete Stemkowski
11 Ralph Backstrom 7.50 15.00
Bob Pulford
12 Bobby Rousseau 5.00 10.00
Wayne Hillman

1968-69 Post Marbles

This set of 30 marbles was issued by Post Cereal in Canada and features players of the Montreal Canadiens (MC) and the Toronto Maple Leafs (TML). Also produced was an attractive game board which is rather difficult to find and not included in the complete set price below.

COMPLETE SET (30) 250.00 500.00
1 Ralph Backstrom MC 4.00 8.00
2 Jean Beliveau MC 20.00 40.00
3 Johnny Bower TML 7.50 15.00
4 Wayne Carleton TML 4.00 8.00
5 Yvan Cournoyer MC 10.00 20.00
6 Ron Ellis TML 4.00 8.00
7 John Ferguson MC 4.00 8.00
8 Bruce Gamble TML 4.00 8.00
9 Terry Harper MC 4.00 8.00
10 Ted Harris MC 4.00 8.00
11 Paul Henderson TML 5.00 10.00
12 Tim Horton TML 20.00 40.00
13 Dave Keon TML 12.50 25.00
14 Jacques Laperriere MC 5.00 10.00
15 Jacques Lemaire MC 12.50 25.00
16 Murray Oliver TML 4.00 8.00
17 Mike Pelyk TML 4.00 8.00
18 Pierre Pilote TML 5.00 10.00
19 Marcel Pronovost TML 5.00 10.00
20 Bob Pulford TML 5.00 10.00
21 Henri Richard MC 10.00 20.00
22 Bobby Rousseau MC 4.00 8.00
23 Serge Savard MC 5.00 10.00
24 Floyd Smith TML 4.00 8.00
25 Gilles Tremblay MC 4.00 8.00
26 J.C. Tremblay MC 4.00 8.00
27 Norm Ullman TML 5.00 10.00
28 Rogatien Vachon MC 15.00 30.00
29 Mike Walton TML 4.00 8.00
30 Gump Worsley MC 10.00 20.00
xx Game Board 87.50 175.00

1970-71 Post Shooters

This set of 16 shooters was intended to be used with the hockey game that Post had advertised as a premium. The shooter consists of a plastic figure with a colorful adhesive decal sheet, with stickers that could be applied to the shooter for identification. All players come with home and away, i.e., red or blue shoulders. The figures measure approximately 3 1/2" by 4 1/2". Players are featured in their NHLPA uniform. They are unnumbered and hence are listed below in alphabetical order.

COMPLETE SET (16) 150.00 300.00
1 Johnny Bucyk 7.50 15.00
2 Ron Ellis 5.00 10.00
3 Ed Giacomin 10.00 20.00
4 Paul Henderson 7.50 15.00
5 Ken Hodge 6.25 12.50
6 Dennis Hull 6.25 12.50
7 Orland Kurtenbach 5.00 10.00
8 Jacques Laperriere 6.25 12.50
9 Jacques Lemaire 7.50 15.00
10 Frank Mahovlich 7.50 15.00
11 Peter Mahovlich 6.25 12.50
12 Bobby Orr 50.00 100.00
13 Jacques Plante 20.00 40.00
14 Jean Ratelle 7.50 15.00
15 Dale Tallon 5.00 10.00
16 J.C. Tremblay 6.25 12.50

1972-73 Post Action Transfers

These 12 cards feature two players on each transfer. Each card depicts an important facet of the game. We are listing the players first and then the English title of the card afterwards.

COMPLETE SET (12) 125.00 250.00
1 Garry Unger 30.00 60.00
Bobby Orr
Defense
2 Red Berenson 7.50 15.00
Dale Tallon
In the Corner
3 Gary Dornhoefer 7.50 15.00
Wayne Cashman
Face Off
4 Jim McKenny 10.00 20.00
Ed Giacomin
Power Save
5 Pat Quinn 7.50 15.00
Keith Magnuson
Power Play Goal
6 Paul Shmyr 7.50 15.00
Rod Seiling
Break Away
7 Danny Grant 10.00 20.00
Jacques Plante
Slap Shot
8 Syl Apps Jr. 10.00 20.00
Serge Savard
Rebound
9 Gump Worsley 12.50 25.00
Gary Bergman
Wrist Shot
10 Roger Crozier 10.00 20.00
Ed Westfall
Last Minute
11 Dennis Hull 7.50 15.00
Orland Kurtenbach
Goalmouth Scramble
12 Rogatien Vachon 15.00 30.00
Yvan Cournoyer
Chest Save

1981-82 Post Standups

Each thick card in this 28-card set measures approximately 2 13/16" by 3 3/4" and consists of three panels joined together at one end. The front of the first panel has the logos of Post, the NHL, the NHLPA, and a NHL team, with the title NHL Stars in Action in English and French. The back of the first panel has a full color action photo of a player from the NHL team featured on the card. The second panel is blank backed and features a standup of the player, with his signature at the bottom of the standup. The front of the third panel has the player's name and statistics (from the 1980-81 regular season) in English and French for that player as well as for his entire team, with instructions on the card back in both languages for creating the standup. These three dimensional cards were issued in cellophane packs with one card per specially marked box of Post Sugar-Crisp, Honeycomb, or Alpha-Bits. The set is composed of two players from each Canadian team and one player from each American NHL team. The promotion included a mail-in offer for an official NHL fact chart, which featured the new NHL divisional alignment. Also available, but hard to find, is a two-piece display box; the cover has logos of all NHL teams with two slots inside for cards and space to display one "opened" card.

COMPLETE SET (28) 20.00 50.00
1 Ray Bourque 3.00 8.00
2 Gilbert Perreault 1.00 2.50
3 Denis Savard 1.50 4.00
4 Dale McCourt .40 1.00
5 Bobby Smith .60 1.50
6 Mike Bossy 2.50 6.00
7 Bobby Clarke 1.50 4.00
8 Randy Carlyle .40 1.00
9 Mike Palmateer .75 2.00
10 Dave(Tiger) Williams .60 1.50
11 Mark Howe .75 2.00
12 Marcel Dionne 1.25 3.00
13 Mike Liut .60 1.50
14 Barry Beck .40 1.00
15 Mark Messier 5.00 12.00
16 Larry Robinson 1.25 3.00
17 Real Cloutier .40 1.00
18 Borje Salming .75 2.00
19 Morris Lukowich .40 1.00
20 Brett Callighen .40 1.00
21 Rob Ramage .60 1.50
22 Wilf Paiement .40 1.00
23 Mario Tremblay .60 1.50
24 Robbie Ftorek .40 1.00
25 Stan Smyl .60 1.50
26 Dave Babych .40 1.00
27 Willi Plett .40 1.00
28 Kent Nilsson .75 2.00
xx Display Box 8.00 20.00

1982-83 Post Cereal

This set is composed of panels of 16 mini playing cards, each measuring approximately 1 1/4" by 2" after perforation. The cards were issued in panel form in a cellophane wrapper inside specially marked packages of Post Cereal. The front of each individual card has an action color photo of the player, with uniform number in the upper left-hand corner, and the player's name and uniform number beneath the picture. The back is done in the team's colors and includes the logos of the team, the sponsor (Post), the NHL, and the NHLPA. There were 21 panels produced, one for each NHL team. Game instructions were included in each box so that one could play Shut-out, Face Off, or Hockey Match with the set of 16 hockey playing cards. By mailing in the UPC code or a reasonable hand drawn facsimile, one could enter the sweepstakes for the grand prize of a trip for two to a Stanley Cup Final playoff game. The complete set was available for a limited time through a mail-in offer. Apparently, a salesman's promo kit was produced in conjunction with this offer, which included six oversized sample cards (Dale Hawerchuk, Real Cloutier, Kent Nilsson, Glenn Anderson, Bob Gainey and Rick Vaive). Not enough is known about this kit at this time to assign a value to it or the singles.

COMPLETE SET (21) 30.00 75.00
1 Bruins 2.00 5.00
Rogie Vachon
Ray Bourque
Peter McNab
Steve Kasper
Wayne Cashman
Mike Gillis
Rick Middleton
Stan Jonathan
Mike O'Connell
Brad Park
Terry O'Reilly
Mike Milbury
Tom Fergus
Brad McCrimmon
Bruce Crowder
Larry Melynk
2 Sabres 1.50 4.00
Don Edwards
Richie Dunn
John Van Boxmeer
Mike Ramsey
Dale McCourt
Tony McKegney
Craig Ramsay
Gilbert Perreault
Andre Savard
Yvon Lambert
Ric Seiling
Mike Foligno
J.Francois Sauve
Lindy Ruff
Bill Hajt
Larry Playfair
3 Flames 1.50 4.00
Pat Riggin
Pekka Rautakallio
4 Blackhawks 2.00 5.00
Greg Fox
Dave Hutchison
Terry Ruskowski
Reg Kerr
Tom Lysiak
Bill Gardner
Tim Higgins
Rich Preston
Denis Savard
Al Secord
Grant Mulvey
Doug Crossman
Doug Wilson
Rick Paterson
Ted Bulley
Tony Esposito
5 Red Wings 1.00 2.50
Jim Schoenfeld
John Barrett
Greg Smith
Willie Huber
Walt McKechnie
Paul Woods
Mark Kirton
Danny Gare
Vaclav Nedomansky
Mike Blaisdell
Greg Joly
Mark Osborne
Derek Smith
John Ogrodnick
Reed Larson
Bob Sauve
6 Oilers 8.00 20.00
Grant Fuhr
Lee Fogolin
Kevin Lowe
Garry Lariviere
Paul Coffey
Risto Siltanen
Glenn Anderson
Matti Hagman
Mark Messier
Dave Hunter
Pat Hughes
Jari Kurri
Brett Callighen
Dave Lumley
Dave Semenko
Wayne Gretzky
7 Whalers 1.50 4.00
Paul Shmyr
Ron Francis

Mark Howe
Blake Wesley
Garry Howatt
Jordy Douglas
Dave Keon
George Lyle
Blaine Stoughton
Doug Sulliman
Chris Kotsopoulos
Don Nachbaur
Warren Miller
Pierre Larouche
Greg Millen
8 Kings 1.50 4.00
Mario Lessard
Rick Chartraw
Jerry Korab
Larry Murphy
Charlie Simmer
Dean Hopkins
Marcel Dionne
John P.Kelly
Dave Taylor
Jim Fox
Mark Hardy
Steve Jensen
Doug Smith
Jay Wells
Dave Lewis
Steve Bozek
9 North Stars 1.00 2.50
Curt Giles
Fred Barrett
Craig Hartsburg
Brad Maxwell
K.E. Anderson
Gord Roberts
Tom McCarthy
Brad Palmer
Bobby Smith
Tim Young
Dino Ciccarelli
Gary Sargent
Al MacAdam
Steve Payne
Gilles Meloche
Steve Christoff
10 Canadiens 3.00 8.00
Brian Engblom
Pierre Mondou
Doug Risebrough
Guy Lafleur
Keith Acton
Mario Tremblay
Rod Langway
Larry Robinson
Mark Hunter
Doug Jarvis
Steve Shutt
Bob Gainey
Robert Picard
Craig Laughlin
Mark Napier
Richard Sevigny
11 Devils 1.00 2.50
(Colorado Rockies)
Glenn Resch
12 Islanders 3.00 8.00
Mike McEwen
Tomas Jonsson
Denis Potvin
Ken Morrow
Stefan Persson
Clark Gillies
Wayne Merrick
Bob Bourne
Bryan Trottier
Mike Bossy
Bob Nystrom
Dave Langevin
John Tonelli
Anders Kallur
Billy Smith
Butch Goring
13 Rangers 1.00 2.50
Tom Laidlaw
Barry Beck
Ron Greschner
Steve Vickers
Ron Duguay
Don Maloney
Mike Allison
Ed Johnstone
Nick Fotiu
Dave Maloney
Mike Rogers
Reijo Ruotsalainen
Steve Weeks
Andre Dore
Robbie Florek
Mark Pavelich
14 Flyers 2.00 5.00
Behn Wilson
Fred Arthur
Bill Barber
Brad Marsh
Reid Bailey
Darryl Sittler
Tim Kerr
Kenny Linseman
Bobby Clarke
Paul Holmgren
Jimmy Watson
Ilkka Sinisalo
Brian Propp
Reggie Leach
Glen Cochrane
Pete Peeters
15 Penguins 1.00 2.50
Pat Price
Ron Stackhouse
Paul Baxter
Peter Lee
George Ferguson
Greg Malone
Doug Shedden
Pat Boutette
Marc Chorney
Rick Kehoe
Gregg Sheppard
Paul Gardner
Mike Bullard
Pat Graham
Randy Carlyle
Michel Dion
16 Nordiques 1.50 4.00
John Garrett
Wally Weir
Normand Rochefort
Marc Tardif
Real Cloutier
Jere Gillis
Michel Goulet
Marion Stastny
Alain Cote
Anton Stastny
Mario Marois
Jacques Richard
Peter Stastny
Wilf Paiement
Andre Dupont
Dale Hunter
17 Blues 1.00 2.50
Mike Liut
Guy Lapointe
Larry Patey
Perry Turnbull
Wayne Babych
Brian Sutter
Jack Brownschidle
Ed Kea
Rick Lapointe
Blake Dunlop
Mike Zuke
Jorgen Pettersson
Bernie Federko
Bill Baker
Mike Crombeen
Jim Payese
18 Maple Leafs 1.50 4.00
Michel Larocque
Bob Manno
Bob McGill
Rocky Saganiuk
John Anderson
Fred Boimistruck
Walt Poddubny
Miroslav Frycer
Jim Benning
Stewart Gavin
Bill Derlago
Borje Salming
Rick Vaive
Normand Aubin
Terry Martin
Barry Melrose
19 Canucks 1.00 2.50
Doug Halward
Gary Lupul
Ivan Boldirev
Stan Smyl
Lars Lindgren
Darcy Rota
Ron Delorme
Ivan Hlinka
Tiger Williams
Thomas Gradin
Curt Fraser
Kevin McCarthy
Lars Molin
Harold Snepsts
Marc Crawford
Richard Brodeur
20 Capitals 1.50 4.00
Doug Hicks
Randy Holt
Rick Green
Darren Veitch
Ryan Walter
Bob Carpenter
Mike Gartner
Glen Currie
Gaetan Duchesne
Bengt Gustafsson
Greg Theberge
Dennis Maruk
Bob Gould
Terry Murray
Chris Valentine
Al Jensen
21 Jets 1.50 4.00
Bryan Maxwell
Tim Watters
Dale Hawerchuk
Scott Arniel
Morris Lukowich
Dave Christian
Tim Trimper
Paul MacLean
Serge Savard
Willy Lindstrom
Bengt Lundholm
Lucien DeBlois
Don Spring
Norm Dupont
Ed Staniowski
Dave Babych

1994-95 Post Box Backs

This set of 25 jumbo player cards was issued one per box on the backs of Post Honeycomb and Sugar-Crisp and Alpha-Bits cereals sold in Canada. Each jumbo card measures 8 3/4" by 12 1/4". Inside the box was information on a mail-in offer whereby the collector could receive a complete set by mailing in 4 UPC symbols and 8.00. The offer was valid while supplies lasted, and in no event extended beyond September 30, 1995. The fronts feature posed color photos framed by a black and red border design. The player's name and his number are printed vertically along the lower left edge, while the team's city is printed beneath the picture. On a ghosted version of the front photo, the bilingual backs present biography, statistics, and player profile. The prices below are for cut backs; complete, unopened cereal boxes sell for a premium of about two times the prices listed below. The box backs are unnumbered and checklisted below in alphabetical order.

COMPLETE SET (25) 16.00 40.00
1 Tony Amonte .75 2.00
2 Jason Arnott .60 1.50
3 Ray Bourque 1.25 3.00
4 Martin Brodeur 1.25 3.00
New Jers
5 Pavel Bure 1.25 3.00
6 Chris Chelios .75 2.00
7 Geoff Courtnall .60 1.50
8 Russ Courtnall .60 1.50
9 Steve Duchesne .60 1.50
10 Sergei Fedorov 1.25 3.00
11 Theo Fleury .75 2.00
12 Doug Gilmour .75 2.00
13 Wayne Gretzky 4.00 10.00
14 Jari Kurri .60 1.50
15 Eric Lindros 1.25 3.00
16 Marty McSorley .60 1.50
17 Alexander Mogilny .60 1.50
18 Kirk Muller .60 1.50
19 Rob Niedermayer .60 1.50
20 Felix Potvin .75 2.00
21 Luc Robitaille .75 2.00
22 Joe Sakic 1.50 4.00
23 Teemu Selanne 1.25 3.00
24 Alexei Yashin .60 1.50
25 Title Card .40 1.00

1995-96 Post Upper Deck

This 24-card set features color action photos on the front with the player's name in a black bar at the top. The backs carry a color player portrait, biographical information, and statistics. The cards were inserted one per specially marked box of Post cereals in Canada. Collectors also could get the cards through the mail in complete set form with proofs of purchase and a small charge. These factory sets included the NNO title and checklist cards. Cards still in the original cellophane wrapper from the cereal boxes are somewhat more desirable and can carry a slight premium of up to 1.5X the basic card. There were only 500 copies of the Wayne Gretzky autographed cards randomly inserted into Post cereal boxes. Lucky collectors who found this card could call a toll-free number to have their find certified by Upper Deck. The set is considered complete without the signed card.

COMPLETE FACTORY SET (26) 14.00 35.00
COMPLETE CELLO. BOX SET (24) 20.00 50.00
1 Ray Bourque .75 2.00
2 Martin Brodeur 1.50 4.00
3 Steve Duchesne .08 .25
4 Vincent Damphousse .20 .50
5 Eric Desjardins .08 .25
6 Eric Lindros 2.00 5.00
7 Joe Juneau .20 .50
8 Luc Robitaille .20 .50
9 Mark Recchi .20 .50
10 Patrick Roy 3.00 8.00
11 Brendan Shanahan 1.25 3.00
12 Scott Stevens .08 .25
13 Jason Arnott .20 .50
14 Trevor Linden .08 .25
15 Chris Chelios .60 1.50
16 Paul Coffey .60 1.50
17 Wayne Gretzky 4.00 10.00
18 Doug Gilmour .60 1.50
19 Kelly Hrudey .08 .25
20 Paul Kariya 2.50 6.00
21 Larry Murphy .08 .25
22 Felix Potvin .50 1.25
23 Keith Tkachuk .60 1.50
24 Rob Blake .08 .25
AU17 W.Gretzky AU (500) 175.00 450.00
NNO Title card .08 .25
NNO Checklist .08 .25

1996-97 Post Upper Deck

This 24-card set marks the third consecutive season for Post's collaboration with the NHLPA, and second with Upper Deck. The cards feature action photography on the fronts, with all players pictured in NHLPA togs. The cards were issued one per specially marked box of Post Cereals during the mid-part of the '96-97 season. Unlike the '95-96 product, these cards were actually inserted into the cereal bag itself, making theft from stores more difficult. Because this factor was negated, fewer complete sets hit the market, hence the slightly higher values. The player's name and the logos of Upper Deck and Post also are prominently featured, the latter in the blue or purple border which defines the right side of the card. The backs are noteworthy for including a childhood photo of the player, as well as '95-96 and career totals. The cards are unnumbered, and are listed below in alphabetical order.

COMPLETE SET (24) 18.00 45.00
1 Ray Bourque .75 2.00
2 Chris Chelios .60 1.50
3 Paul Coffey .60 1.50
4 Vincent Damphousse .20 .50
5 Steve Duchesne .10 .30
6 Theo Fleury .60 1.50
7 Doug Gilmour .60 1.50
8 Wayne Gretzky 4.00 10.00
9 Curtis Joseph .75 2.00
10 Ed Jovanovski .20 .50
11 Paul Kariya 1.50 4.00
12 Eric Lindros 1.50 4.00
13 Al MacInnis .40 1.00
14 Felix Potvin .60 1.50
15 Mark Recchi .40 1.00
16 Luc Robitaille .40 1.00
17 Jeremy Roenick .60 1.50
18 Patrick Roy 3.00 8.00
19 Joe Sakic 1.25 3.00
20 Mathieu Schneider .20 .50
21 Brendan Shanahan 1.25 3.00
22 Scott Stevens .10 .30
23 John Vanbiesbrouck .60 1.50
24 Alexei Yashin .40 1.00

1997 Post Pinnacle

Card fronts feature full color photos on the front with jersey number and a Canadian flag also prominently displayed. Backs feature biographical information and 96-97 season stats.

COMPLETE SET (24) 12.00 30.00
1 Eric Lindros 1.00 2.50
2 Patrick Roy 1.50 4.00
3 Joe Sakic .60 1.50
4 Brian Leetch .30 .75
5 Mark Messier .40 1.00
6 Jason Arnott .25 .60
7 Paul Kariya 1.25 3.00
8 Martin Brodeur .75 2.00
9 Vincent Damphousse .25 .60
10 Steve Yzerman 1.00 2.50
11 Brett Hull .40 1.00
12 Chris Chelios .30 .75
13 Sergei Fedorov .60 1.50
14 Nicklas Lidstrom .25 .60
15 Sergei Berezin .15 .40
16 Dominik Hasek .60 1.50
17 Pavel Bure .75 2.00
18 Saku Koivu .30 .75
19 Teemu Selanne .60 1.50
20 Peter Forsberg .75 2.00
21 Jaromir Jagr 1.00 2.50
22 Peter Bondra .30 .75
23 Alexei Yashin .15 .40
24 Slava Fetisov .15 .40
NNO Eric Lindros AUTO

1998-99 Post

1 Wayne Gretzky 2.00 5.00
2 Martin Brodeur .75 2.00
3 Joe Nieuwendyk .20 .50
4 Rick Tocchet .20 .50
5 Theoren Fleury .20 .50
6 Adam Oates .20 .50
7 Mark Recchi .20 .50
8 Eric Lindros .30 .75
9 Steve Yzerman 1.00 2.50
10 Wade Redden .20 .50
11 Glen Murray .20 .50
12 Mike Johnson .20 .50
13 Kelly Buchberger .20 .50
14 Joe Sakic .75 2.00
15 Mark Messier .40 1.00
16 Keith Primeau .20 .50
17 Mike Vernon .20 .50
18 Chris Pronger .20 .50
19 Mike Peca .20 .50
20 Dave Gagner .20 .50
21 Rob Zamuner .20 .50
22 Doug Gilmour .40 1.00
G1 Wayne Gretzky 2.00 5.00
G2 Wayne Gretzky 2.00 5.00
G3 Wayne Gretzky 2.00 5.00
G4 Wayne Gretzky 2.00 5.00
G5 Wayne Gretzky 2.00 5.00
G6 Wayne Gretzky 2.00 5.00

1999-00 Post Wayne Gretzky

These cards were included one per specially marked box of Post Cereals in Canada. The cards were wrapped in cellophane and often sell for slightly less if removed from that original packaging.

COMPLETE SET (14) 12.00 30.00
COMMON CARD (1-14) 1.25 3.00

1993-94 PowerPlay

This 520-card set measures 2 1/2" by 4 3/4". The fronts feature color action shots set within a blended team-colored border. The team name and the player's name appear in team-colored lettering below the photo. The backs carry color player photos at the upper left. The player's name appears above; his number, position, and a short biography are displayed alongside. Statistics are shown below. The cards are checklisted alphabetically according to teams. Rookie Cards include Jason Arnott, Chris Osgood, Damian Rhodes, and Jocelyn Thibault.

COMPLETE SET (520) 30.00 60.00
COMP.SERIES 1 (280) 15.00 30.00
COMP.SERIES 2 (240) 15.00 30.00
1 Stu Grimson .02 .10
2 Guy Hebert .08 .25
3 Sean Hill .02 .10
4 Bill Houlder .02 .10
5 Alexei Kasatonov .02 .10
6 Steven King .02 .10
7 Lonnie Loach .02 .10
8 Troy Loney .02 .10
9 Joe Sacco .02 .10
10 Anatoli Semenov .02 .10
11 Jarrod Skalde .02 .10
12 Tim Sweeney .02 .10
13 Ron Tugnutt .08 .25
14 Terry Yake .02 .10
15 Shaun Van Allen .02 .10
16 Ray Bourque .30 .75
17 Jon Casey .08 .25
18 Ted Donato .02 .10
19 Joe Juneau .08 .25
20 Dimitri Kvartalnov .02 .10
21 Steve Leach .02 .10
22 Cam Neely .20 .50
23 Adam Oates .08 .25
24 Don Sweeney .02 .10
25 Glen Wesley .02 .10
26 Doug Bodger .02 .10
27 Grant Fuhr .08 .25
28 Viktor Gordiouk .02 .10
29 Dale Hawerchuk .08 .25
30 Yuri Khmylev .02 .10
31 Pat LaFontaine .20 .50
32 Alexander Mogilny .08 .25
33 Richard Smehlik .02 .10
34 Bob Sweeney .02 .10
35 Randy Wood .02 .10
36 Theo Fleury .02 .10
37 Kelly Kisio .02 .10
38 Al MacInnis .08 .25
39 Joe Nieuwendyk .08 .25
40 Joel Otto .02 .10
41 Robert Reichel .02 .10
42 Gary Roberts .02 .10
43 Ronnie Stern .02 .10
44 Gary Suter .02 .10
45 Mike Vernon .08 .25
46 Ed Belfour .20 .50
47 Chris Chelios .20 .50
48 Karl Dykhuis .02 .10
49 Michel Goulet .08 .25
50 Dirk Graham .02 .10
51 Sergei Krivokrasov .02 .10
52 Steve Larmer .08 .25
53 Joe Murphy .02 .10
54 Jeremy Roenick .25 .60
55 Steve Smith .02 .10
56 Brent Sutter .02 .10
57 Neal Broten .08 .25
58 Russ Courtnall .02 .10
59 Ulf Dahlen .02 .10
60 Dave Gagner .08 .25
61 Derian Hatcher .02 .10
62 Trent Klatt .02 .10
63 Mike Modano .30 .75
64 Andy Moog .08 .25
65 Tommy Sjodin .02 .10
66 Mark Tinordi .02 .10
67 Tim Cheveldae .08 .25
68 Steve Chiasson .02 .10
69 Dino Ciccarelli .08 .25
70 Paul Coffey .20 .50
71 Dallas Drake RC .02 .10
72 Sergei Fedorov .30 .75
73 Vladimir Konstantinov .08 .25
74 Nicklas Lidstrom .20 .50
75 Keith Primeau .02 .10
76 Ray Sheppard .08 .25
77 Steve Yzerman 1.00 2.50
78 Zdeno Ciger .02 .10
79 Shayne Corson .02 .10
80 Todd Elik .02 .10
81 Igor Kravchuk .02 .10
82 Craig MacTavish .02 .10
83 Dave Manson .02 .10
84 Shjon Podein RC .02 .10
85 Bill Ranford .08 .25
86 Steven Rice .02 .10
87 Doug Weight .08 .25
88 Doug Barrault RC .02 .10
89 Jesse Belanger .02 .10
90 Brian Benning .02 .10
91 Joe Cirella .02 .10
92 Mark Fitzpatrick .08 .25
93 Randy Gilhen .02 .10
94 Mike Hough .02 .10
95 Bill Lindsay .02 .10
96 Andrei Lomakin .02 .10
97 Dave Lowry .02 .10
98 Scott Mellanby .08 .25
99 Gord Murphy .02 .10
100 Brian Skrudland .02 .10
101 Milan Tichy RC .02 .10
102 John Vanbiesbrouck .08 .25
103 Sean Burke .08 .25
104 Andrew Cassels .02 .10
105 Nick Kypreos .02 .10
106 Michael Nylander .02 .10
107 Robert Petrovicky .02 .10
108 Patrick Poulin .02 .10
109 Geoff Sanderson .08 .25
110 Pat Verbeek .02 .10
111 Eric Weinrich .02 .10
112 Zarley Zalapski .02 .10
113 Rob Blake .08 .25
114 Jimmy Carson .02 .10
115 Tony Granato .02 .10
116 Wayne Gretzky 1.25 3.00
117 Kelly Hrudey .08 .25
118 Jari Kurri .20 .50
119 Shawn McEachern .02 .10
120 Luc Robitaille .08 .25
121 Tomas Sandstrom .02 .10
122 Darryl Sydor .02 .10
123 Alexei Zhitnik .02 .10
124 Brian Bellows .02 .10
125 Patrice Brisebois .02 .10
126 Guy Carbonneau .02 .10
127 Vincent Damphousse .02 .10
128 Eric Desjardins .08 .25
129 Mike Keane .02 .10
130 Stephan Lebeau .02 .10
131 Kirk Muller .02 .10
132 Lyle Odelein .02 .10
133 Patrick Roy 1.00 2.50
134 Mathieu Schneider .02 .10
135 Bruce Driver .02 .10
136 Slava Fetisov .02 .10
137 Claude Lemieux .02 .10
138 John MacLean .08 .25
139 Bernie Nicholls .02 .10
140 Scott Niedermayer .02 .10
141 Stephane Richer .08 .25
142 Alexander Semak .02 .10
143 Scott Stevens .08 .25
144 Chris Terreri .08 .25
145 Valeri Zelepukin .02 .10
146 Patrick Flatley .02 .10
147 Ron Hextall .08 .25
148 Benoit Hogue .02 .10
149 Darius Kasparaitis .02 .10
150 Derek King .02 .10
151 Uwe Krupp .02 .10
152 Scott Lachance .02 .10
153 Vladimir Malakhov .02 .10
154 Steve Thomas .02 .10
155 Pierre Turgeon .08 .25
156 Tony Amonte .08 .25
157 Mike Gartner .08 .25
158 Adam Graves .02 .10
159 Alexei Kovalev .08 .25
160 Brian Leetch .20 .50
161 Joby Messier RC .02 .10
162 Mark Messier .20 .50
163 Sergei Nemchinov .02 .10
164 James Patrick .02 .10
165 Mike Richter .20 .50
166 Darren Turcotte .02 .10
167 Sergei Zubov .02 .10
168 Dave Archibald .02 .10
169 Craig Billington .08 .25
170 Bob Kudelski .02 .10
171 Mark Lamb .02 .10
172 Norm Maciver .02 .10
173 Darren Rumble .02 .10
174 Vladimir Ruzicka .02 .10
175 Brad Shaw .02 .10
176 Sylvain Turgeon .02 .10
177 Josef Beranek .02 .10
178 Rod Brind'Amour .08 .25
179 Kevin Dineen .02 .10
180 Pelle Eklund .02 .10
181 Brent Fedyk .02 .10
182 Garry Galley .02 .10
183 Eric Lindros .20 .50
184 Mark Recchi .08 .25
185 Tommy Soderstrom .08 .25
186 Dimitri Yushkevich .02 .10
187 Tom Barrasso .08 .25
188 Ron Francis .08 .25
189 Jaromir Jagr .30 .75
190 Mario Lemieux 1.00 2.50
191 Marty McSorley .02 .10
192 Joe Mullen .08 .25
193 Larry Murphy .08 .25
194 Ulf Samuelsson .02 .10
195 Kevin Stevens .02 .10
196 Rick Tocchet .08 .25
197 Steve Duchesne .02 .10
198 Stephane Fiset .08 .25
199 Valeri Kamensky .08 .25
200 Andrei Kovalenko .02 .10
201 Owen Nolan .08 .25
202 Mike Ricci .02 .10
203 Martin Rucinsky .02 .10
204 Joe Sakic .40 1.00
205 Mats Sundin .20 .50
206 Scott Young .02 .10
207 Jeff Brown .02 .10
208 Garth Butcher .02 .10
209 Nelson Emerson .02 .10
210 Bret Hedican .02 .10
211 Brett Hull .25 .60
212 Craig Janney .08 .25
213 Curtis Joseph .20 .50
214 Igor Korolev .02 .10
215 Kevin Miller .02 .10
216 Brendan Shanahan .20 .50
217 Ed Courtenay .02 .10
218 Pat Falloon .02 .10
219 Johan Garpenlov .02 .10
220 Rob Gaudreau RC .02 .10
221 Artus Irbe .08 .25
222 Sergei Makarov .02 .10
223 Jeff Norton .02 .10
224 Jeff Odgers .02 .10
225 Sandis Ozolinsh .02 .10
226 Tom Pederson .02 .10
227 Bob Beers .02 .10
228 Brian Bradley .02 .10
229 Shawn Chambers .02 .10
230 Gerard Gallant .02 .10
231 Roman Hamrlik .08 .25
232 Petr Klima .02 .10
233 Chris Kontos .02 .10
234 Daren Puppa .08 .25
235 John Tucker .02 .10
236 Rob Zamuner .02 .10
237 Glenn Anderson .08 .25
238 Dave Andreychuk .08 .25
239 Drake Berehowsky .02 .10
240 Nikolai Borschevsky .02 .10
241 Wendel Clark .08 .25
242 John Cullen .02 .10
243 Dave Ellett .02 .10
244 Doug Gilmour .08 .25
245 Dimitri Mironov .02 .10
246 Felix Potvin .20 .50
247 Greg Adams .02 .10
248 Pavel Bure .20 .50
249 Geoff Courtnall .02 .10
250 Gerald Diduck .02 .10
251 Trevor Linden .08 .25
252 Jyrki Lumme .02 .10
253 Kirk McLean .08 .25
254 Petr Nedved .08 .25
255 Cliff Ronning .02 .10
256 Jiri Slegr .02 .10
257 Dixon Ward .02 .10
258 Peter Bondra .08 .25
259 Sylvain Cote .02 .10
260 Pat Elynuik .02 .10
261 Kevin Hatcher .02 .10
262 Dale Hunter .02 .10
263 Al Iafrate .02 .10
264 Dimitri Khristich .02 .10
265 Michal Pivonka .02 .10
266 Mike Ridley .02 .10
267 Rick Tabaracci .08 .25
268 Sergei Bautin .02 .10
269 Evgeny Davydov .02 .10
270 Bob Essensa .08 .25
271 Phil Housley .08 .25
272 Teppo Numminen .02 .10
273 Fredrik Olausson .02 .10
274 Teemu Selanne .20 .50
275 Thomas Steen .02 .10
276 Keith Tkachuk .20 .50
277 Paul Ysebaert .02 .10
278 Alexei Zhamnov .08 .25
279 Checklist .02 .10
280 Checklist .02 .10
281 Patrick Carnback RC .02 .10
282 Bob Corkum .02 .10
283 Bobby Dollas .02 .10
284 Peter Douris .02 .10
285 Todd Ewen .02 .10
286 Garry Valk .02 .10
287 John Blue .08 .25
288 Glen Featherstone .02 .10
289 Steve Heinze .02 .10
290 David Reid .02 .10
291 Bryan Smolinski .02 .10
292 Cam Stewart RC .02 .10
293 Jozef Stumpel .02 .10
294 Sergei Zholtok .02 .10
295 Donald Audette .02 .10
296 Philippe Boucher .02 .10
297 Dominik Hasek .40 1.00
298 Brad May .08 .25
299 Craig Muni .02 .10
300 Derek Plante RC .02 .10
301 Craig Simpson .02 .10
302 Scott Thomas RC .02 .10
303 Ted Drury .02 .10
304 Dan Keczmer RC .02 .10
305 Trevor Kidd .08 .25
306 Sandy McCarthy .02 .10
307 Frank Musil .02 .10
308 Michel Petit .02 .10
309 Paul Ranheim .02 .10
310 German Titov RC .02 .10
311 Andrei Trefilov .02 .10
312 Jeff Hackett .08 .25
313 Stephane Matteau .02 .10
314 Brian Noonan .02 .10
315 Patrick Poulin .02 .10
316 Jeff Shantz RC .02 .10
317 Rich Sutter .02 .10
318 Kevin Todd .02 .10
319 Eric Weinrich .02 .10
320 Dave Barr .02 .10
321 Paul Cavallini .02 .10
322 Mike Craig .02 .10
323 Dean Evason .02 .10
324 Brent Gilchrist .02 .10
325 Grant Ledyard .02 .10
326 Mike McPhee .02 .10
327 Darcy Wakaluk .08 .25
328 Terry Carkner .02 .10
329 Mark Howe .02 .10
330 Greg Johnson .02 .10
331 Slava Kozlov .08 .25
332 Martin Lapointe .02 .10
333 Darren McCarty RC .25 .60
334 Chris Osgood RC 1.25 3.00
335 Bob Probert .08 .25
336 Mike Sillinger .02 .10
337 Jason Arnott RC .75 2.00
338 Bob Beers .02 .10
339 Fred Brathwaite RC .30 .75
340 Kelly Buchberger .02 .10
341 Ilya Byakin RC .02 .10
342 Fredrik Olausson .02 .10
343 Vladimir Vujtek .02 .10
344 Peter White RC .02 .10
345 Stu Barnes .02 .10
346 Mike Foligno .02 .10
347 Greg Hawgood .02 .10
348 Bob Kudelski .02 .10
349 Rob Niedermayer .08 .25
350 Igor Chibirev RC .02 .10
351 Robert Kron .02 .10
352 Bryan Marchment .02 .10
353 James Patrick .02 .10
354 Chris Pronger .25 .60
355 Jeff Reese .02 .10
356 Jim Storm RC .02 .10
357 Darren Turcotte .02 .10
358 Pat Conacher .02 .10
359 Mike Donnelly .02 .10
360 John Druce .02 .10
361 Charlie Huddy .02 .10
362 Warren Rychel .02 .10
363 Robb Stauber .08 .25
364 Dave Taylor .08 .25
365 Dixon Ward .02 .10
366 Benoit Brunet .02 .10
367 J.J. Daigneault .02 .10
368 Gilbert Dionne .02 .10
369 Paul DiPietro .02 .10
370 Kevin Haller .02 .10
371 Oleg Petrov .02 .10
372 Peter Popovic RC .02 .10
373 Ron Wilson .02 .10
374 Martin Brodeur .40 1.00
375 Tom Chorske .02 .10
376 Jim Dowd RC .02 .10
377 David Emma .02 .10
378 Bobby Holik .02 .10
379 Corey Millen .02 .10
380 Jaroslav Modry RC .02 .10
381 Jason Smith RC .02 .10
382 Ray Ferraro .02 .10
383 Travis Green .08 .25
384 Tom Kurvers .02 .10
385 Marty McInnis .02 .10
386 Jamie McLennan RC .08 .25
387 Dennis Vaske .02 .10
388 Dave Volek .02 .10
389 Jeff Beukeboom .02 .10
390 Glenn Healy .08 .25
391 Alexander Karpovtsev .02 .10
392 Steve Larmer .08 .25
393 Kevin Lowe .02 .10
394 Ed Olczyk .02 .10
395 Esa Tikkanen .02 .10
396 Alexandre Daigle .02 .10
397 Evgeny Davydov .02 .10
398 Dmitri Filimonov .02 .10
399 Brian Glynn .02 .10
400 Darrin Madeley RC .02 .10
401 Troy Mallette .02 .10
402 Dave McLlwain .02 .10
403 Alexei Yashin .02 .10
404 Jason Bowen RC .02 .10
405 Jeff Finley .02 .10
406 Yves Racine .02 .10
407 Rob Ramage .02 .10
408 Mikael Renberg .20 .50
409 Dominic Roussel .08 .25
410 Dave Tippett .02 .10

411 Doug Brown .02 .10
412 Markus Naslund .20 .50
413 Pat Neaton RC .02 .10
414 Kjell Samuelsson .02 .10
415 Martin Straka .02 .10
416 Bryan Trottier .08 .25
417 Ken Wregget .08 .25
418 Adam Foote .02 .10
419 Iain Fraser RC .02 .10
420 Alexei Gusarov .02 .10
421 Dave Karpa .02 .10
422 Claude Lapointe .02 .10
423 Curtis Leschyshyn .02 .10
424 Mike McKee RC .02 .10
425 Garth Snow RC .20 .50
426 Jocelyn Thibault RC .50 1.25
427 Phil Housley .08 .25
428 Jim Hrivnak .08 .25
429 Vitali Karamnov .02 .10
430 Basil McRae .02 .10
431 Jim Montgomery RC .02 .10
432 Vitali Prokhorov .02 .10
433 Gaetan Duchesne .02 .10
434 Todd Elik .02 .10
435 Bob Errey .02 .10
436 Igor Larionov .02 .10
437 Mike Rathje .02 .10
438 Jim Waite .08 .25
439 Ray Whitney .02 .10
440 Mikael Anderson .02 .10
441 Danton Cole .02 .10
442 Pat Elynuik .02 .10
443 Chris Gratton .08 .25
444 Pat Jablonski .08 .25
445 Chris Joseph .02 .10
446 Chris LiPuma RC .02 .10
447 Denis Savard .08 .25
448 Ken Baumgartner .02 .10
449 Todd Gill .02 .10
450 Sylvain Lefebvre .02 .10
451 Jamie Macoun .02 .10
452 Mark Osborne .02 .10
453 Rob Pearson .02 .10
454 Damian Rhodes RC .08 .25
455 Peter Zezel .02 .10
456 Dave Babych .02 .10
457 Jose Charbonneau RC .02 .10
458 Murray Craven .02 .10
459 Neil Eisenhut RC .02 .10
460 Dan Kesa RC .02 .10
461 Gino Odjick .02 .10
462 Kay Whitmore .08 .25
463 Don Beaupre .08 .25
464 Randy Burridge .02 .10
465 Calle Johansson .02 .10
466 Keith Jones .02 .10
467 Todd Krygier .02 .10
468 Kelly Miller .02 .10
469 Pat Peake .02 .10
470 Dave Poulin .02 .10
471 Luciano Borsato .02 .10
472 Nelson Emerson .02 .10
473 Randy Gilhen .02 .10
474 Boris Mironov .02 .10
475 Stephane Quintal .02 .10
476 Thomas Steen .02 .10
477 Igor Ulanov .02 .10
478 Adrian Aucoin RC .20 .50
479 Todd Brost RC .02 .10
480 Martin Gendron RC .02 .10
481 David Harlock .02 .10
482 Corey Hirsch .08 .25
483 Todd Hlushko RC .02 .10
484 Fabian Joseph RC .02 .10
485 Paul Kariya 2.00 5.00
486 Brett Lindros RC .02 .10
487 Ken Lovsin RC .02 .10
488 Jason Marshall .02 .10
489 Derek Mayer RC .02 .10
490 Petr Nedved .08 .25
491 Dwayne Norris RC .02 .10
492 Russ Romaniuk .02 .10
493 Brian Savage RC .20 .50
494 Trevor Sim RC .02 .10
495 Chris Therien RC .02 .10
496 Todd Warriner RC .02 .10
497 Craig Woodcroft RC .02 .10
498 Mark Beaufait RC .02 .10
499 Jim Campbell .02 .10
500 Ted Crowley RC .02 .10
501 Mike Dunham .08 .25
502 Chris Ferraro RC .02 .10
503 Peter Ferraro .02 .10
504 Brett Hauer RC .02 .10
505 Darby Hendrickson RC .02 .10
506 Chris Imes RC .02 .10
507 Craig Johnson RC .02 .10
508 Peter Laviolette RC .02 .10
509 Jeff Lazaro .02 .10
510 John Lilley RC .02 .10
511 Todd Marchant .02 .10
512 Ian Moran RC .02 .10
513 Travis Richards RC .08 .25
514 Barry Richter RC .02 .10
515 David Roberts RC .02 .10
516 Brian Rolston .02 .10
517 David Sacco RC .02 .10
518 Checklist .02 .10
519 Checklist .02 .10
520 Checklist .02 .10

1993-94 PowerPlay Gamebreakers

Randomly inserted in series two packs at 1:4, this ten-card set measures 2 1/2" by 4 3/4". The fronts feature color action cutouts on a borderless marbleized background. The player's name in gold foil appears at the lower right, while the word "Gamebreakers" is printed vertically in pastel-colored lettering on the left side. On the same marbleized background, the backs carry another color photo, with the player's name displayed above and career highlights shown below. The cards are numbered on the back as "X of 10."

COMPLETE SET (10) 10.00 20.00
1 Sergei Fedorov .60 1.50
2 Doug Gilmour .20 .50
3 Wayne Gretzky 2.50 6.00
4 Curtis Joseph .40 1.00
5 Mario Lemieux 2.00 5.00
6 Eric Lindros .40 1.00
7 Felix Potvin .40 1.00
8 Jeremy Roenick .50 1.25
9 Patrick Roy 2.00 5.00
10 Steve Yzerman 2.00 5.00

1993-94 PowerPlay Global Greats

Randomly inserted in series two packs at 1:4, this 10-card set measures 2 1/2" by 4 3/4". The borderless fronts feature color action cutouts superimposed on the player's national flag. The player's name and the Global Greats logo in gold foil appear at the bottom. On the same national flag background, the backs carry another color photo with the player's name above and career highlights below. The cards are numbered on the back as "X of 10."

COMPLETE SET (10) 3.00 8.00
1 Pavel Bure .50 1.25
2 Sergei Fedorov .50 1.25
3 Jaromir Jagr .75 2.00
4 Jari Kurri .40 1.00
5 Alexander Mogilny .25 .60
6 Mikael Renberg .10 .30
7 Teemu Selanne .50 1.25
8 Mats Sundin .50 1.25
9 Esa Tikkanen .10 .30
10 Alexei Yashin .10 .30

1993-94 PowerPlay Netminders

Randomly inserted at a rate of 1:8 series one packs, this eight-card set measures 2 1/2" by 4 3/4". On a blue marbleized background, the fronts feature color action photos with the goalie's name in blue-foil lettering under the photo.

COMPLETE SET (8) 10.00 25.00
1 Tom Barrasso .75 2.00
2 Ed Belfour 1.50 4.00
3 Grant Fuhr .75 2.00
4 Curtis Joseph 1.50 4.00
5 Felix Potvin 1.25 3.00
6 Bill Ranford .75 2.00
7 Patrick Roy 4.00 10.00
8 Tommy Soderstrom .75 2.00

1993-94 PowerPlay Point Leaders

Randomly inserted at a rate of 1:2 series one packs, this 20-card set measures 2 1/2" by 4 3/4". The yellow-bordered fronts feature color action cutouts against a yellow-tinted background. The player's name in silver foil appears under the photo. On a yellow background, the backs carry another color photo with the player's name in silver foil above the photo, and career highlights below. The cards are numbered on the back as "X of 20."

COMPLETE SET (20) 8.00 20.00
1 Pavel Bure .40 1.00
2 Doug Gilmour .20 .50
3 Wayne Gretzky 2.00 5.00
4 Brett Hull .50 1.25
5 Jaromir Jagr .60 1.50
6 Joe Juneau .10 .30
7 Pat LaFontaine .20 .50
8 Mario Lemieux 1.50 4.00
9 Mark Messier .40 1.00
10 Alexander Mogilny .20 .50
11 Adam Oates .20 .50
12 Mark Recchi .20 .50
13 Luc Robitaille .20 .50
14 Jeremy Roenick .50 1.25
15 Joe Sakic .75 2.00
16 Teemu Selanne .40 1.00
17 Kevin Stevens .10 .30
18 Mats Sundin .40 1.00
19 Pierre Turgeon .20 .50
20 Steve Yzerman 1.50 4.00

1993-94 PowerPlay Rising Stars

Randomly inserted in series two packs at 1:10, this ten-card set measures 2 1/2" by 4 3/4". Each borderless front features a color action cutout, highlighted with a yellow "aura" and yellow radial lines, set on a stellar background. The player's name and the words "Rising Star" in silver foil appear in a top corner. On a similar background, the borderless horizontal back carries another color cutout on the left, with the player's name and career highlights to the right. The cards are numbered on the back as "X of 10."

COMPLETE SET (10) 4.00 10.00
1 Arturs Irbe .30 .75
2 Slava Kozlov .30 .75
3 Felix Potvin 1.50 4.00
4 Keith Primeau .30 .75
5 Robert Reichel .30 .75
6 Geoff Sanderson .30 .75
7 Martin Straka .30 .75
8 Keith Tkachuk .75 2.00
9 Alexei Zhamnov .30 .75
10 Sergei Zubov .40 1.00

1993-94 PowerPlay Rookie Standouts

Randomly inserted in series two packs at 1:5, this 16-card set measures 2 1/2" by 4 3/4". The borderless fronts feature color player action shots on grainy and ghosted backgrounds. The player's name and the words "Rookie Standouts" in gold foil are printed atop ghosted bars to the right of the player. The cards are numbered on the back as "X of 16."

COMPLETE SET (16) 3.00 8.00
1 Jason Arnott .40 1.00
2 Jesse Belanger .10 .30
3 Alexandre Daigle .10 .30
4 Iain Fraser .10 .30
5 Chris Gratton .10 .30
6 Boris Mironov .10 .30
7 Jaroslav Modry .10 .30
8 Rob Niedermayer .25 .60
9 Chris Osgood .75 2.00
10 Pat Peake .10 .30
11 Derek Plante .10 .30
12 Chris Pronger .75 2.00
13 Mikael Renberg .10 .30
14 Bryan Smolinski .10 .30
15 Jocelyn Thibault .40 1.00
16 Alexei Yashin .10 .30

1993-94 PowerPlay Second Year Stars

Randomly inserted at a rate of 1:3 series one packs, this 12-card set measures 2 1/2" by 4 3/4". The fronts feature color action photos with light blue metallic borders. The player's name in gold foil appears on the bottom, while the words "2nd Year Stars" are printed in gold foil in an upper corner. The cards are numbered on the back as "X of 12."

COMPLETE SET (12) 2.00 5.00
1 Rob Gaudreau .07 .20
2 Joe Juneau .20 .50
3 Darius Kasparaitis .07 .20
4 Dmitri Kvartalnov .07 .20
5 Eric Lindros .40 1.00
6 Vladimir Malakhov .07 .20
7 Shawn McEachern .07 .20
8 Felix Potvin .40 1.00
9 Patrick Poulin .07 .20
10 Teemu Selanne .40 1.00
11 Tommy Soderstrom .20 .50
12 Alexei Zhamnov .20 .50

1993-94 PowerPlay Slapshot Artists

Randomly inserted in series two packs at 1:10, this ten-card set measures 2 1/2" by 4 3/4". On a team-colored tinted background, the fronts feature color action cutouts with a smaller tinted head shot in an upper corner. The player's name and the Slapshot Artist logo in gold foil appear at the bottom. The cards are numbered on the back as "X of 10."

COMPLETE SET (10) 8.00 20.00
1 Dave Andreychuk .40 1.00
2 Ray Bourque 1.50 4.00
3 Sergei Fedorov 1.25 3.00
4 Brett Hull 1.25 3.00
5 Al Iafrate .40 1.00
6 Brian Leetch .60 1.50
7 Al MacInnis .60 1.50
8 Mike Modano 1.50 4.00
9 Teemu Selanne 1.25 3.00
10 Brendan Shanahan 1.25 3.00

1998-99 Predators Team Issue

This set features the Predators of the NHL. The cards were issued on six card sheets at Nashville-area Wendy's restaurants. Each sheet featured five cards and one ad card.

COMPLETE SET (25) 8.00 20.00
1 Blair Atcheynum .30 .75
2 Drake Berehowsky .30 .75
3 Sebastien Bordeleau .30 .75
4 Joel Bouchard .30 .75
5 Bob Boughner .40 1.00
6 Andrew Brunette .40 1.00
7 Patrick Cote .40 1.00
8 Mike Dunham .75 2.00
9 Eric Fichaud .40 1.00
10 Tom Fitzgerald .30 .75
11 Jamie Heward .30 .75
12 Greg Johnson .30 .75
13 Patric Kjellberg .30 .75
14 Sergei Krivokrasov .30 .75
15 Denny Lambert .30 .75
16 Jayson More .30 .75
17 Ville Peltonen .40 1.00
18 Cliff Ronning .40 1.00
19 John Slaney .30 .75
20 Kimmo Timonen .30 .75
21 Darren Turcotte .30 .75
22 Tomas Vokoun .60 1.50
23 Jan Vopat .30 .75
24 Scott Walker .40 1.00
25 Vitali Yachmenev .30 .75

2002-03 Predators Team Issue

These oversized (8X10) blank-backed collectibles were issued by the Predators. It's believed they may have been offered as game program inserts, but that has not been confirmed. We have only listed the cards we have physically confirmed below. Any additional information regarding distribution or checklist should be sent to hockeymag@beckett.com.

COMPLETE SET (?)
1 Brent Gilchrist 3.00
2 Scott Hartnell 6.00
3 Greg Johnson 4.00
4 Domenic Pittis 3.00
5 Kimmo Timonen 4.00
6 Vitali Yachmenev 3.00

2000-01 Private Stock

Released in mid January 2001 as a 152-card set, Pacific Private Stock features 101 base card and 51 Short Prints, card numbers 101-151. Base cards feature a white background with gold highlights. SP's are sequentially numbered to 155. Private Stock came packaged with one memorabilia card per pack and carried a suggested retail price of $14.99.

COMP.SET w/o SP's (101) 25.00 50.00
SP STAT.ODDS 1:10 HOB, 1:49 RET
1 Guy Hebert .25 .60
2 Paul Kariya .30 .75
3 Teemu Selanne .30 .75
4 Ray Ferraro .10 .25
5 Damian Rhodes .10 .25
6 Patrik Stefan .10 .25
7 Byron Dafoe .10 .25
8 Sergei Samsonov .25 .60
9 Joe Thornton .50 1.25
10 Maxim Afinogenov .10 .25
11 Doug Gilmour .25 .60
12 Dominik Hasek .60 1.50
13 Miroslav Satan .25 .60
14 Fred Brathwaite .25 .60
15 Valeri Bure .10 .25
16 Ron Francis .25 .60
17 Arturs Irbe .25 .60
18 Sami Kapanen .10 .25
19 Tony Amonte .25 .60
20 Jocelyn Thibault .25 .60
21 Alexei Zhamnov .10 .25
22 Ray Bourque .50 1.25
23 Peter Forsberg .75 2.00
24 Milan Hejduk .30 .75
25 Patrick Roy 1.50 4.00
26 Joe Sakic .60 1.50
27 Marc Denis .25 .60
28 Ted Drury .10 .25
29 Geoff Sanderson .10 .25
30 Ed Belfour .30 .75
31 Brett Hull .40 1.00
32 Mike Modano .50 1.25
33 Brenden Morrow .25 .60
34 Joe Nieuwendyk .25 .60
35 Sergei Fedorov .50 1.25
36 Chris Osgood .25 .60
37 Brendan Shanahan .30 .75
38 Steve Yzerman 1.50 4.00
39 Tommy Salo .25 .60
40 Ryan Smyth .10 .25
41 Doug Weight .25 .60
42 Pavel Bure .30 .75
43 Trevor Kidd .25 .60
44 Viktor Kozlov .25 .60
45 Stephane Fiset .10 .25
46 Zigmund Palffy .25 .60
47 Luc Robitaille .25 .60
48 Manny Fernandez .25 .60
49 Sergei Krivokrasov .10 .25
50 Stacy Roest .10 .25
51 Saku Koivu .30 .75
52 Trevor Linden .25 .60
53 Jose Theodore .40 1.00
54 Mike Dunham .10 .25
55 David Legwand .25 .60
56 Jason Arnott .10 .25
57 Martin Brodeur .75 2.00
58 Patrik Elias .25 .60
59 Scott Gomez .10 .25
60 Petr Sykora .10 .25
61 Tim Connolly .10 .25
62 Mariusz Czerkawski .10 .25
63 John Vanbiesbrouck .25 .60
64 Theo Fleury .10 .25
65 Brian Leetch .25 .60
66 Mark Messier .30 .75
67 Mike Richter .30 .75
68 Daniel Alfredsson .25 .60
69 Radek Bonk .10 .25
70 Marian Hossa .30 .75
71 Brian Boucher .30 .75
72 Simon Gagne .30 .75
73 John LeClair .30 .75
74 Eric Lindros .30 .75
75 Nikolai Khabibulin .30 .75
76 Jeremy Roenick .40 1.00
77 Keith Tkachuk .30 .75
78 Jean-Sebastien Aubin .25 .60
79 Jan Hrdina .10 .25
80 Jaromir Jagr .50 1.25
81 Martin Straka .10 .25
82 Pavol Demitra .25 .60
83 Al MacInnis .25 .60
84 Chris Pronger .25 .60
85 Roman Turek .25 .60
86 Pierre Turgeon .25 .60
87 Vincent Damphousse .10 .25
88 Jeff Friesen .10 .25
89 Owen Nolan .25 .60
90 Dan Cloutier .10 .25
91 Vincent Lecavalier .30 .75
92 Nikolai Antropov .10 .25
93 Curtis Joseph .30 .75
94 Mats Sundin .30 .75
95 Steve Kariya .10 .25
96 Markus Naslund .30 .75
97 Felix Potvin .30 .75
98 Jeff Halpern .10 .25
99 Olaf Kolzig .25 .60
100 Adam Oates .25 .60
101 Jonas Ronnqvist SP RC 8.00 20.00
102 Samuel Pahlsson SP .75 2.00
103 Andrew Raycroft SP RC 15.00 40.00
104 Eric Boulton SP RC 8.00 20.00
105 Dimitri Kalinin SP .75 2.00
106 Mika Noronen SP .75 2.00
107 Oleg Saprykin SP .75 2.00
108 Josef Vasicek SP RC 8.00 20.00
109 Shane Willis SP .75 2.00
110 Steven McCarthy SP .75 2.00
111 David Aebischer SP RC 15.00 40.00
112 Serge Aubin SP RC 8.00 20.00
113 Rostislav Klesla SP RC 8.00 20.00
114 David Vyborny SP .75 2.00
115 Tyler Bouck SP RC 8.00 20.00
116 Richard Jackman SP .75 2.00
117 Marty Turco SP RC 30.00 80.00
118 Dan Lacouture SP .75 2.00
119 Brian Swanson SP RC 8.00 20.00
120 Denis Shvidki SP .75 2.00
121 Eric Belanger SP RC 8.00 20.00
122 Steven Reinprecht SP RC 8.00 20.00
123 Lubomir Visnovsky SP RC 8.00 20.00
124 Manny Fernandez SP .75 2.00
125 Marian Gaborik RC 125.00 200.00
126 Filip Kuba SP .75 2.00
127 Maxim Sushinski SP .75 2.00
128 Andrei Markov SP .75 2.00
129 Scott Hartnell SP RC 12.00 30.00
130 Colin White SP RC 8.00 20.00
131 Taylor Pyatt SP .75 2.00
132 Martin Havlat SP RC 25.00 60.00
133 Jani Hurme SP RC 8.00 20.00
134 Karel Rachunek SP .75 2.00
135 Maxime Ouellet SP .75 2.00
136 Justin Williams SP RC 15.00 40.00
137 Robert Esche SP .75 2.00
138 Wyatt Smith SP .75 2.00
139 Ossi Vaananen SP RC 8.00 20.00
140 Brent Johnson SP .75 2.00
141 Ladislav Nagy SP .75 2.00
142 Mike Van Ryn SP .75 2.00
143 Bryce Salvador SP RC 8.00 20.00
144 Evgeni Nabokov SP 6.00 15.00
145 Alexander Kharitonov SP RC 8.00 20.00
146 Brad Richards SP 6.00 15.00
147 Petr Svoboda SP RC 8.00 20.00
148 Daniel Sedin SP .10 .25
149 Henrik Sedin SP .10 .25
150 Kris Beech SP .75 2.00
151 Rick DiPietro SP RC 30.00 80.00
152 Mario Lemieux 3.00 8.00

2000-01 Private Stock Gold

Randomly inserted in Hobby packs, this 152-card set parallels the base set enhanced with a gold border and gold foil highlights. Each card is sequentially numbered to 75.

*STARS: 6X TO 15X BASIC CARDS
*SP's: .75X TO 2X BASIC CARDS
*ROOKIE SP's: .4X TO .8X BASIC CARDS

2000-01 Private Stock Premiere Date

Randomly inserted in Hobby packs at the rate of 2:21, this 152-card set parallels the base Private Stock Set enhanced with a foil premiere date box in which cards are sequentially numbered to 60.

*STARS: 8X TO 20X BASIC CARDS
* SP's: 6X TO 15X BASIC CARDS
*ROOKIE SP's: .5X TO 1X BASIC CARDS

2000-01 Private Stock Retail

This 152-card retail set mirrored the hobby set except that base cards featured silver highlights. SP's were sequentially numbered to 230 and were inserted at a rate of 1:49. Retail packs did not contain memorabilia cards in every pack, and carried an SRP of $2.99.

*NON-SP'S: SAME VALUE AS HOBBY
*SP's: .2X TO .5X HOBBY
125 Marian Gaborik RC 50.00 125.00
132 Martin Havlat RC 20.00 50.00

2000-01 Private Stock Silver

Randomly inserted in Retail packs at the rate of three in 25, this 152-card set parallels the main set enhanced with silver borders and silver foil highlights. Each card is sequentially numbered to 120.

*STARS: 4X TO 10X BASIC CARDS
*SP's: 3X TO 8X BASIC CARDS
*ROOKIE SP's: .25X TO .5X BASIC CARDS

2000-01 Private Stock Artist's Canvas

Randomly inserted in Hobby packs at the rate of 1:21 and retail packs at the rate of 1:49, this 20-card set features base card artwork on a card printed on canvas stock. Parallels numbered 1/1 also were created, they are not priced due to scarcity.

COMPLETE SET (20) 50.00 100.00
1 Paul Kariya 2.00 5.00
2 Teemu Selanne 2.00 5.00
3 Joe Thornton 3.00 8.00
4 Maxim Afinogenov 1.50 4.00
5 Dominik Hasek 4.00 10.00
6 Peter Forsberg 5.00 12.00
7 Patrick Roy 10.00 25.00
8 Joe Sakic 4.00 10.00
9 Brett Hull 2.50 6.00
10 Mike Modano 3.00 8.00
11 Brendan Shanahan 3.00 8.00
12 Steve Yzerman 10.00 25.00
13 Pavel Bure 2.00 5.00
14 Martin Brodeur 5.00 12.00
15 Mark Messier 2.50 6.00
16 John LeClair 2.50 6.00
17 Jeremy Roenick 2.50 6.00
18 Jaromir Jagr 3.00 8.00
19 Vincent Lecavalier 2.00 5.00
20 Curtis Joseph 2.00 5.00

2000-01 Private Stock Extreme Action

Randomly inserted in packs at the rate of 2:21, this 20-card set features full color panoramic photography of game action. Cards are enhanced with a colored border along the bottom of the card containing the featured player's name with gold foil highlights.

COMPLETE SET (20) 20.00 40.00
1 Paul Kariya .75 2.00
2 Teemu Selanne .75 2.00
3 Dominik Hasek 1.50 4.00
4 Patrick Roy 4.00 10.00
5 Joe Sakic 1.50 4.00
6 Ed Belfour .75 2.00
7 Brett Hull 1.00 2.50
8 Mike Modano 1.25 3.00
9 Steve Yzerman 4.00 10.00
10 Luc Robitaille .60 1.50
11 Trevor Linden .50 1.25
12 Petr Sykora .50 1.25
13 Martin Brodeur 2.00 5.00
14 Tim Connolly .50 1.25
15 John LeClair 1.00 2.50
16 Eric Lindros 1.25 3.00
17 Jeremy Roenick 1.00 2.50
18 Jaromir Jagr 1.25 3.00
19 Vincent Lecavalier .75 2.00
20 Curtis Joseph .75 2.00

2000-01 Private Stock Game Gear

Inserted one per hobby and 1:49 retail packs, this 105-card set features one or two swatches of game used memorabilia. Included on cards are jersey swatches, stick swatches, or jersey/stick combos. Cards feature a full color action photograph and a circular memorabilia swatch.

*MULT.COLOR SWATCH: 1X TO 2X
1 Guy Hebert J 4.00 10.00
2 Marty McInnis J 2.00 5.00
3 Teemu Selanne J 5.00 12.00
4 Shawn Bates J 2.00 5.00
5 Paul Coffey S 8.00 20.00
6 Paul Coffey J/S 20.00 50.00
7 Bill Guerin S 6.00 15.00
8 Sergei Samsonov J 4.00 10.00
9 Dominik Hasek S 20.00 50.00
10 Jay McKee J 2.00 5.00
11 Jarome Iginla J 6.00 15.00
12 Rod Brind'Amour S 6.00 15.00
13 Kevin Hatcher S 4.00 10.00
14 Sandis Ozolinsh S 4.00 10.00
15 Tony Amonte J 4.00 10.00
16 Eric Daze J 2.00 5.00
17 Alexei Zhamnov J 2.00 5.00
18 Ray Bourque J 15.00 40.00
19 Ray Bourque S 20.00 50.00
20 Greg DeVries J 2.00 5.00
21 Chris Dingman J 2.00 5.00
22 Chris Drury S 6.00 15.00
23 Adam Foote S 4.00 10.00
24 Peter Forsberg S 15.00 40.00
25 Peter Forsberg J/S 15.00 40.00
26 Eric Messier J 2.00 5.00
27 Aaron Miller J 2.00 5.00
28 Patrick Roy S 20.00 50.00
29 Joe Sakic J/S 15.00 40.00
30 Joe Sakic J 10.00 25.00
31 Martin Skoula S 4.00 10.00
32 Alex Tanguay S 6.00 15.00
33 Marc Denis S 6.00 15.00
34 Ed Belfour S 8.00 20.00
35 Derian Hatcher J 2.00 5.00
36 Derian Hatcher J 2.00 5.00
37 Jamie Langenbrunner J 2.00 5.00
38 Jere Lehtinen J 2.00 5.00
39 Mike Modano J 8.00 20.00
40 Darryl Sydor J 2.00 5.00
41 Darryl Sydor J 2.00 5.00
42 Sergei Zubov J 2.00 5.00
43 Chris Chelios S 8.00 20.00
44 Sergei Fedorov J 8.00 20.00
45 Nicklas Lidstrom J 4.00 10.00
46 Chris Osgood J 4.00 10.00
47 Brendan Shanahan J 5.00 12.00
48 Anson Carter J 2.00 5.00
49 Tommy Salo S 4.00 10.00
50 Doug Weight J 4.00 10.00
51 Olli Jokinen S 4.00 10.00
52 Roberto Luongo J 6.00 15.00
53 Scott Mellanby S 4.00 10.00
54 Rob Blake S 6.00 15.00
55 Zigmund Palffy S 6.00 15.00
56 Jeff Hackett J 4.00 10.00
57 Saku Koivu J 5.00 12.00
58 Trevor Linden S 5.00 12.00
59 Brian Savage S 4.00 10.00
60 Eric Weinrich S 4.00 10.00
61 Dainius Zubrus J 2.00 5.00
62 Cliff Ronning S 4.00 10.00
63 Bobby Holik J 2.00 5.00
64 Scott Niedermayer J 2.00 5.00
65 Petr Sykora J 2.00 5.00
66 Chris Terreri J 4.00 10.00
67 Zdeno Chara J 2.00 5.00
68 Tim Connolly S 4.00 10.00
69 Mariusz Czerkawski J 2.00 5.00
70 Claude LaPointe J 2.00 5.00
71 Mats Lindgren J 2.00 5.00
72 John Vanbiesbrouck J 4.00 10.00
73 Adam Graves S 4.00 10.00
74 Valeri Kamensky S 4.00 10.00
75 Brian Leetch J 4.00 10.00
76 Brian Leetch J/S 20.00 50.00
77 Mark Messier J 5.00 12.00
78 Mike Richter J 5.00 12.00
79 Mike Richter J 5.00 12.00
80 Andreas Dackell J 2.00 5.00
81 Eric Desjardins J 2.00 5.00
82 Daymond Langkow J 2.00 5.00
83 John LeClair J 4.00 10.00
84 Eric Lindros J 5.00 12.00
85 Eric Lindros S 8.00 20.00
86 Rick Tocchet S 6.00 15.00
87 Shane Doan J 2.00 5.00
88 Radoslav Suchy J 2.00 5.00
89 Jaromir Jagr J 6.00 15.00
90 Dallas Drake J 2.00 5.00
91 Vincent Damphousse J 2.00 5.00
92 Vincent Damphousse J/S 15.00 40.00
93 Vincent Lecavalier S 8.00 20.00
94 Petr Svoboda J 2.00 5.00
95 Shayne Corson J 2.00 5.00
96 Curtis Joseph S 5.00 12.00
97 Yanic Perreault S 4.00 10.00
98 Gary Roberts S 4.00 10.00
99 Mats Sundin J 5.00 12.00
100 Craig Berube S 4.00 10.00
101 Peter Bondra J 5.00 12.00
102 Sylvain Cote S 4.00 10.00
103 Ulf Dahlen J 2.00 5.00
104 Olaf Kolzig J/S 15.00 40.00
105 Adam Oates S 6.00 15.00

2000-01 Private Stock Game Gear Patches

Randomly inserted in packs, this 62-card set parallels only the jersey portion of the Game Gear insert set. Each card is sequentially numbered and contains a premium swatch of a game jersey emblem or numbers. Card 81 is not priced due to scarcity.

1 Guy Hebert/164 12.50 30.00
2 Marty McInnis/156 10.00 25.00
3 Teemu Selanne/202 15.00 40.00
4 Shawn Bates/156 10.00 25.00
8 Sergei Samsonov/101 15.00 40.00
10 Jay McKee/161 10.00 25.00
11 Jarome Iginla/94 20.00 50.00
15 Tony Amonte/134 12.50 30.00
16 Eric Daze/177 12.50 30.00
17 Alexei Zhamnov/142 10.00 25.00
18 Ray Bourque/39 75.00 200.00
20 Greg DeVries/184 10.00 25.00
21 Chris Dingman/163 10.00 25.00
26 Eric Messier/121 10.00 25.00
27 Aaron Miller/202 10.00 25.00
35 Derian Hatcher/172 10.00 25.00
36 Derian Hatcher/184 10.00 25.00
37 Jamie Langenbrunner/178 10.00 25.00
38 Jere Lehtinen/151 10.00 25.00
39 Mike Modano/417 20.00 50.00
40 Darryl Sydor/40 10.00 25.00
41 Darryl Sydor/88 12.50 30.00
42 Sergei Zubov/220 10.00 25.00
44 Sergei Fedorov/175 20.00 50.00
45 Nicklas Lidstrom/193 15.00 40.00
46 Chris Osgood/143 12.50 30.00
47 Brendan Shanahan/17 150.00 300.00
48 Anson Carter/190 10.00 25.00
50 Doug Weight/162 12.50 30.00
52 Roberto Luongo/183 20.00 50.00
56 Jeff Hackett/149 10.00 25.00
57 Saku Koivu/28 90.00 150.00
61 Dainius Zubrus/172 10.00 25.00
63 Bobby Holik/144 10.00 25.00
64 Scott Niedermayer/119 10.00 25.00
65 Petr Sykora/247 10.00 25.00
66 Chris Terreri/149 10.00 25.00
67 Zdeno Chara/149 10.00 25.00
69 Mariusz Czerkawski/169 10.00 25.00
70 Claude LaPointe/137 10.00 25.00
71 Mats Lindgren/166 10.00 25.00
72 John Vanbiesbrouck/108 12.50 30.00
75 Brian Leetch/122 12.50 30.00

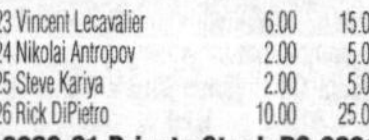

77 Mark Messier/67 15.00 40.00
78 Mike Richter/184 15.00 40.00
79 Mike Richter/193 15.00 40.00
80 Andreas Dackell/175 10.00 25.00
81 Eric Desjardins/20
82 Daymond Langkow/77 12.50 30.00
83 John LeClair/158 15.00 40.00
84 Eric Lindros 15.00 40.00
87 Shane Doan/92 10.00 25.00
88 Radoslav Suchy/125 10.00 25.00
89 Jaromir Jagr/388 20.00 50.00
90 Dallas Drake/180 10.00 25.00
94 Petr Svoboda/227 10.00 25.00
95 Shayne Corson/165 10.00 25.00
99 Mats Sundin/103 15.00 40.00
101 Peter Bondra/190 15.00 40.00
103 Ulf Dahlen/183 10.00 25.00

2000-01 Private Stock PS-2001 Action

Inserted two per pack, this 60-mini card set features top NHL players in action where cards are enhanced with gold foil highlights.

COMPLETE SET (60) 15.00 30.00
1 Paul Kariya .40 1.00
2 Teemu Selanne .40 1.00
3 Sergei Samsonov .30 .75
4 Joe Thornton .60 1.50
5 Maxim Afinogenov .30 .75
6 Doug Gilmour .30 .75
7 Dominik Hasek .75 2.00
8 Ray Bourque .75 2.00
9 Chris Drury .30 .75
10 Peter Forsberg 1.00 2.50
11 Milan Hejduk .40 1.00
12 Patrick Roy 2.00 5.00
13 Joe Sakic .75 2.00
14 Alex Tanguay .30 .75
15 Marc Denis .30 .75
16 Ed Belfour .40 1.00
17 Brett Hull .50 1.25
18 Mike Modano .60 1.50
19 Chris Chelios .40 1.00
20 Sergei Fedorov .75 2.00
21 Chris Osgood .30 .75
22 Brendan Shanahan .60 1.50
23 Steve Yzerman 2.00 5.00
24 Doug Weight .30 .75
25 Pavel Bure .50 1.25
26 Zigmund Palffy .30 .75
27 Luc Robitaille .30 .75
28 Saku Koivu .40 1.00
29 Jose Theodore .50 1.25
30 David Legwand .30 .75
31 Martin Brodeur 1.00 2.50
32 Patrik Elias .30 .75
33 Scott Gomez .30 .75
34 Petr Sykora .30 .75
35 Tim Connolly .30 .75
36 Theo Fleury .30 .75
37 Brian Leetch .30 .75
38 Mark Messier .50 1.25
39 Mike Richter .40 1.00
40 Marian Hossa .40 1.00
41 Brian Boucher .40 1.00
42 John LeClair .50 1.25
43 Eric Lindros .60 1.50
44 Jeremy Roenick .50 1.25
45 Keith Tkachuk .40 1.00
46 Jan Hrdina .30 .75
47 Jaromir Jagr .60 1.50
48 Martin Straka .30 .75
49 Jeff Friesen .30 .75
50 Owen Nolan .30 .75
51 Pavol Demitra .30 .75
52 Chris Pronger .30 .75
53 Pierre Turgeon .30 .75
54 Vincent Lecavalier .40 1.00
55 Curtis Joseph .40 1.00
56 Mats Sundin .40 1.00
57 Steve Kariya .30 .75
58 Markus Naslund .40 1.00
59 Peter Bondra .40 1.00
60 Olaf Kolzig .30 .75

2000-01 Private Stock PS-2001 New Wave

Randomly inserted at the rate of 2 per Hobby case and 1 per Retail case, this 25-card set features mini player cards with player action photograph and bronze foil highlights. Each card is sequentially numbered to 70.

COMPLETE SET (26) 60.00 150.00
1 Patrik Stefan 2.00 5.00
2 Joe Thornton 8.00 20.00
3 Maxim Afinogenov 4.00 10.00
4 Sami Kapanen 2.00 5.00
5 Valeri Bure 2.00 5.00
6 Oleg Saprykin 2.00 5.00
7 Jocelyn Thibault 2.00 5.00
8 Milan Hejduk 4.00 10.00
9 Marc Denis 4.00 10.00
10 Brenden Morrow 4.00 10.00
11 Jose Theodore 8.00 15.00
12 David Legwand 2.00 5.00
13 Patrik Elias 4.00 10.00
14 Scott Gomez 4.00 10.00
15 Tim Connolly 2.00 5.00
16 Marian Hossa 6.00 15.00
17 Brian Boucher 2.00 6.00
18 Simon Gagne 6.00 15.00
19 Jean-Sebastien Aubin 2.00 5.00
20 Roman Turek 2.00 5.00
21 Jeff Friesen 2.00 5.00
22 Dan Cloutier 2.00 5.00
23 Vincent Lecavalier 6.00 15.00
24 Nikolai Antropov 2.00 5.00
25 Steve Kariya 2.00 5.00
26 Rick DiPietro 10.00 25.00

2000-01 Private Stock PS-2001 Rookies

Randomly inserted in packs at the rate of one per Hobby and Retail cases, this 26-card set is comprised of mini cards that feature some of the NHL's brightest prospects. Cards are enhanced with silver foil highlights and are sequentially numbered to 45

1 Samuel Pahlsson 3.00 8.00
2 Andrew Raycroft 12.00 30.00
3 Dimitri Kalinin 3.00 8.00
4 Oleg Saprykin 6.00 15.00
5 Josef Vasicek 6.00 15.00
6 David Aebischer 15.00 40.00
7 David Vyborny 6.00 15.00
8 Marty Turco 20.00 50.00
9 Eric Belanger 3.00 8.00
10 Steven Reinprecht 6.00 15.00
11 Marian Gaborik 30.00 80.00
12 Andrei Markov 6.00 15.00
13 Colin White 3.00 8.00
14 Martin Havlat 20.00 50.00
15 Maxime Ouellet 6.00 15.00
16 Justin Williams 15.00 40.00
17 Wyatt Smith 3.00 8.00
18 Ossi Vaananen 3.00 8.00
19 Brent Johnson 6.00 15.00
20 Ladislav Nagy 6.00 15.00
21 Evgeni Nabokov 15.00 40.00
22 Alexander Kharitonov 3.00 8.00
23 Brad Richards 12.00 30.00
24 Daniel Sedin 15.00 40.00
25 Henrik Sedin 15.00 40.00
26 Rick DiPietro 20.00 50.00

2000-01 Private Stock PS-2001 Stars

Randomly inserted in packs at the rate of three per Hobby case and two per Retail case, this 25-card set features mini cards. Each card is features a portrait style photograph and cards are sequentially numbered to 50.

COMPLETE SET (25) 150.00 300.00
1 Paul Kariya 3.00 8.00
2 Teemu Selanne 3.00 8.00
3 Sergei Samsonov 2.50 6.00
4 Dominik Hasek 8.00 20.00
5 Ray Bourque 8.00 20.00
6 Peter Forsberg 10.00 25.00
7 Patrick Roy 20.00 50.00
8 Joe Sakic 10.00 25.00
9 Brett Hull 4.00 10.00
10 Mike Modano 5.00 12.00
11 Sergei Fedorov 8.00 20.00
12 Brendan Shanahan 6.00 15.00
13 Steve Yzerman 20.00 50.00
14 Pavel Bure 5.00 12.00
15 Luc Robitaille 2.50 6.00
16 Saku Koivu 3.00 8.00
17 Martin Brodeur 12.00 30.00
18 Mark Messier 6.00 15.00
19 John LeClair 4.00 10.00
20 Eric Lindros 5.00 12.00
21 Jeremy Roenick 4.00 10.00
22 Jaromir Jagr 6.00 15.00
23 Pierre Turgeon 2.50 6.00
24 Curtis Joseph 3.00 8.00
25 Mats Sundin 3.00 8.00

2000-01 Private Stock Reserve

Randomly inserted in Hobby packs at the rate of 1:21, this 20-card set features a framed oval portrait style photos of players accented with gold foil highlights.

COMPLETE SET (20) 40.00 80.00
1 Paul Kariya 1.50 4.00
2 Teemu Selanne 1.50 4.00
3 Patrik Stefan 1.25 3.00
4 Dominik Hasek 3.00 8.00
5 Peter Forsberg 4.00 10.00
6 Patrick Roy 8.00 20.00
7 Joe Sakic 3.00 8.00
8 Mike Modano 2.50 6.00
9 Brendan Shanahan 2.50 6.00
10 Steve Yzerman 8.00 20.00
11 Pavel Bure 1.50 4.00
12 Saku Koivu 1.50 4.00
13 Scott Gomez 1.25 3.00
14 Martin Brodeur 4.00 10.00
15 Mark Messier 2.00 5.00
16 John LeClair 2.00 5.00
17 Eric Lindros 2.50 6.00
18 Jaromir Jagr 2.50 6.00
19 Vincent Lecavalier 1.50 4.00
20 Curtis Joseph 1.50 4.00

2001-02 Private Stock

This 140-card set featured player action photos on mat-like finish card fronts with red foil highlights and

white borders. Cards were 101-117 were short-printed and inserted at a rate of 1:17, while cards 111-140 were serial-numbered to 414 copies each.

COMP.SET w/o SP's 30.00 60.00
1 Jeff Friesen .10 .25
2 Paul Kariya .30 .75
3 Milan Hnilicka .25 .60
4 Patrik Stefan .10 .25
5 Bill Guerin .25 .60
6 Sergei Samsonov .25 .60
7 Joe Thornton .50 1.25
8 Martin Biron .25 .60
9 Tim Connolly .10 .25
10 J-P Dumont .10 .25
11 Jarome Iginla .40 1.00
12 Marc Savard .10 .25
13 Roman Turek .25 .60
14 Ron Francis .25 .60
15 Arturs Irbe .25 .60
16 Jeff O'Neill .10 .25
17 Tony Amonte .25 .60
18 Steve Sullivan .10 .25
19 Jocelyn Thibault .25 .60
20 Rob Blake .25 .60
21 Chris Drury .25 .60
22 Milan Hejduk .30 .75
23 Patrick Roy 1.50 4.00
24 Joe Sakic .60 1.50
25 Alex Tanguay .25 .60
26 Espen Knutsen .10 .25
27 Ron Tugnutt .25 .60
28 Ed Belfour .30 .75
29 Mike Modano .50 1.25
30 Joe Nieuwendyk .25 .60
31 Pierre Turgeon .25 .60
32 Sergei Fedorov .50 1.25
33 Dominik Hasek .60 1.50
34 Brett Hull .40 1.00
35 Nicklas Lidstrom .30 .75
36 Luc Robitaille .25 .60
37 Brendan Shanahan .30 .75
38 Steve Yzerman 1.50 4.00
39 Mike Comrie .25 .60
40 Tommy Salo .25 .60
41 Ryan Smyth .10 .25
42 Pavel Bure .30 .75
43 Roberto Luongo .40 1.00
44 Jason Allison .25 .60
45 Zigmund Palffy .25 .60
46 Felix Potvin .30 .75
47 Manny Fernandez .25 .60
48 Marian Gaborik .60 1.50
49 Yanic Perreault .10 .25
50 Brian Savage .10 .25
51 Jose Theodore .40 1.00
52 Mike Dunham .25 .60
53 David Legwand .25 .60
54 Jason Arnott .10 .25
55 Martin Brodeur .75 2.00
56 Patrik Elias .25 .60
57 Scott Gomez .25 .60
58 Chris Osgood .25 .60
59 Michael Peca .10 .25
60 Alexei Yashin .10 .25
61 Theo Fleury .10 .25
62 Brian Leetch .10 .25
63 Eric Lindros .30 .75
64 Mark Messier .30 .75
65 Mike Richter .30 .75
66 Daniel Alfredsson .25 .60
67 Martin Havlat .25 .60
68 Marian Hossa .30 .75
69 Patrick Lalime .25 .60
70 Roman Cechmanek .25 .60
71 Simon Gagne .30 .75
72 John LeClair .30 .75
73 Mark Recchi .25 .60
74 Jeremy Roenick .40 1.00
75 Sean Burke .25 .60
76 Daymond Langkow .25 .60
77 Alexei Kovalev .25 .60
78 Mario Lemieux 3.00 8.00
79 Martin Straka .10 .25
80 Brent Johnson .25 .60
81 Chris Pronger .25 .60
82 Keith Tkachuk .30 .75
83 Doug Weight .25 .60
84 Patrick Marleau .25 .60
85 Evgeni Nabokov .25 .60
86 Owen Nolan .25 .60
87 Teemu Selanne .30 .75
88 Vincent Lecavalier .30 .75
89 Brad Richards .25 .60
90 Curtis Joseph .30 .75
91 Alexander Mogilny .25 .60
92 Mats Sundin .30 .75
93 Dan Cloutier .25 .60
94 Markus Naslund .30 .75
95 Daniel Sedin .10 .25
96 Henrik Sedin .10 .25
97 Peter Bondra .30 .75
98 Jaromir Jagr .50 1.25
99 Olaf Kolzig .25 .60
100 Adam Oates .25 .60
101 Dany Heatley SP 6.00 15.00
102 Mark Bell SP 2.50 6.00
103 Rostislav Klesla SP 4.00 10.00
104 Jason Williams SP 2.50 6.00
105 Rick DiPietro SP 3.00 8.00
106 Pavel Brendl SP 2.50 6.00
107 Kris Beech SP 2.50 6.00
108 Johan Hedberg SP 2.50 6.00
109 Miikka Kiprusoff SP 2.50 6.00
110 Bryan Allen SP 2.50 6.00
111 Ilja Bryzgalov RC 4.00 10.00
112 Timo Parssinen RC 4.00 10.00
113 Ilya Kovalchuk RC 15.00 40.00
114 Kamil Piros RC 4.00 10.00
115 Brian Pothier RC 4.00 10.00
116 Jukka Hentunen RC 4.00 10.00
117 Erik Cole RC 4.00 10.00
118 Vaclav Nedorost RC 4.00 10.00
119 Niko Kapanen RC 4.00 10.00
120 Pavel Datsyuk RC 12.00 30.00
121 Jason Chimera RC 4.00 10.00
122 Niklas Hagman RC 4.00 10.00
123 Kristian Huselius RC 4.00 10.00
124 Jaroslav Bednar RC 4.00 10.00
125 Pascal Dupuis RC 4.00 10.00
126 Nick Schultz RC 4.00 10.00
127 Francis Belanger RC 4.00 10.00
128 Martin Erat RC 4.00 10.00
129 Scott Clemmensen RC 4.00 10.00
130 Radek Martinek RC 4.00 10.00
131 Dan Blackburn RC 4.00 10.00
132 Peter Smrek RC 4.00 10.00
133 Chris Neil RC 4.00 10.00
134 Jiri Dopita RC 4.00 10.00
135 David Cullen RC 4.00 10.00
136 Krystofer Kolanos RC 4.00 10.00
137 Jeff Jillson RC 4.00 10.00
138 Mark Rycroft RC 4.00 10.00
139 Nikita Alexeev RC 4.00 10.00
140 Brian Sutherby RC 4.00 10.00

2001-02 Private Stock Gold

This 140-card hobby only set paralleled the base set but featured gold foil highlights in place of the red. Cards were serial-numbered out of 106.

*GOLD: 5X TO 12X BASIC CARD
*GOLD SP's: 1X TO 3X BASIC CARD
*GOLD ROOKIES: .4X TO .8X BASIC CARD

2001-02 Private Stock Premiere Date

This 140-card hobby only set paralleled the base set but featured a premiere date stamp on the card front. Cards were serial-numbered on the card front out of 100.

*PREM.DATE: 5X TO 12X BASIC CARD
*PREM.DATE SP's: 1X TO 3X BASIC CARD
*PREM.DATE ROOKIES: .4X TO .8X BASIC CARD

2001-02 Private Stock Retail

This 140-card retail set mirrored the hobby set but featured blue foil highlights in place of the red. Cards 111-140 were serial numbered to 450.

*NON-SP's: SAME VALUE AS HOBBY
*SP's: .25X TO .75X HOBBY
*RC'S: SAME VALUE AS HOBBY
113 Ilya Kovalchuk RC 15.00 40.00

2001-02 Private Stock Silver

This 140-card retail only set paralleled the base set but featured silver foil highlights in place of the red. Cards were serial-numbered on the card front out of 108.

*SILVER: 5X TO 12X BASIC CARD
*SILVER SP's: 1X TO 3X BASIC CARD
*SILVER ROOKIES: .4X TO .8X BASIC CARD

2001-02 Private Stock Game Gear

Inserted at one per pack hobby and four per case retail, this 100-card set featured pieces of game-used jerseys or sticks. Stick cards were serial-numbered out of 200. Cards with significantly shorter print runs are noted below with an SP tag. Please note that cards #58, 65 and 72 were not produced in jersey form.

*MULT.COLOR SWATCH: .75X TO 1.5X HI
1 Jean-Sebastien Giguere 5.00 12.00
2 Paul Kariya 5.00 12.00
3 Mike Leclerc SP 3.00 8.00
4 Steve Rucchin 3.00 8.00
5 Oleg Tverdovsky 3.00 8.00
6 Ilya Kovalchuk STK 15.00 40.00
7 P.J. Axelsson 3.00 8.00
8 Byron Dafoe 5.00 12.00
9 Stu Barnes SP 3.00 8.00
10 J-P Dumont 3.00 8.00
11 Jay McKee SP 3.00 8.00
12 Rob Ray 3.00 8.00
13 Richard Smehlik SP 3.00 8.00
14 Craig Conroy 3.00 8.00
15 Jarome Iginla 6.00 15.00
16 Marc Savard 3.00 8.00
17 Roman Turek 5.00 12.00
18 Rod Brind'Amour STK 10.00 25.00
19 Jeff O'Neill STK 10.00 25.00
20 Tony Amonte 5.00 12.00
21 Kyle Calder 3.00 8.00
22 Eric Daze SP 3.00 8.00
23 Boris Mironov 3.00 8.00
24 Michael Nylander 3.00 8.00
25 Steve Sullivan 3.00 8.00
26 Jocelyn Thibault 5.00 12.00
27 Alexei Zhamnov 3.00 8.00
28 Chris Drury STK 10.00 25.00
29 Peter Forsberg SP 15.00 40.00
30 Patrick Roy SP 15.00 40.00
31 Joe Sakic 10.00 25.00
32 Grant Marshall SP 3.00 8.00
33 Blake Sloan SP 3.00 8.00
34 Ed Belfour 5.00 12.00
35 Derian Hatcher 3.00 8.00
36 Jamie Langenbrunner 3.00 8.00
37 Mike Modano 8.00 20.00
38 Joe Nieuwendyk 5.00 12.00
39 Darryl Sydor 3.00 8.00
40 Pierre Turgeon 5.00 12.00
41 Sergei Zubov 3.00 8.00
42 Dominik Hasek SP 12.50 30.00
43 Brett Hull SP 10.00 25.00
44 Brendan Shanahan 5.00 12.00
45 Steve Yzerman 12.50 30.00
46 Anson Carter SP 5.00 12.00
47 Jochen Hecht 3.00 8.00
48 Ryan Smyth SP 3.00 8.00
49 Valeri Bure SP 3.00 8.00
50 Robert Svehla 3.00 8.00
51 Aaron Miller 3.00 8.00
52 Felix Potvin SP 5.00 12.00
53 Jamie McLennan 3.00 8.00
54 Saku Koivu SP 5.00 12.00
55 Jose Theodore 6.00 15.00
56 Mike Dunham 5.00 12.00
57 Tom Fitzgerald 3.00 8.00
59 Cliff Ronning 3.00 8.00
60 Bobby Holik 3.00 8.00
61 Shawn Bates 3.00 8.00
62 Mariusz Czerkawski 3.00 8.00
63 Kenny Jonsson SP 3.00 8.00
64 Chris Osgood 5.00 12.00
66 Rico Fata 3.00 8.00
67 Eric Lindros SP 5.00 12.00
68 Petr Nedved 3.00 8.00
69 Mike Richter 5.00 12.00
70 Pavel Brendl 5.00 12.00
71 John LeClair SP 5.00 12.00
73 Sean Burke 5.00 12.00
74 Shane Doan 3.00 8.00
75 Jean-Sebastien Aubin 5.00 12.00
76 Jan Hrdina 3.00 8.00
77 Alexei Kovalev 5.00 12.00
78 Milan Kraft 5.00 12.00
79 Mario Lemieux SP 20.00 50.00
80 Ian Moran 3.00 8.00
81 Alexei Morozov 3.00 8.00
82 Wayne Primeau SP 3.00 8.00
83 Michal Rozsival 3.00 8.00
84 Kevin Stevens 3.00 8.00
85 Martin Straka 3.00 8.00
86 Fred Brathwaite 5.00 12.00
87 Mike Eastwood 3.00 8.00
88 Cory Stillman 3.00 8.00
89 Doug Weight SP 5.00 12.00
90 Scott Young 3.00 8.00
91 Vincent Damphousse SP 3.00 8.00
92 Teemu Selanne 5.00 12.00
93 Vincent Lecavalier SP 5.00 12.00
94 Tie Domi 5.00 12.00
95 Curtis Joseph SP 8.00 20.00
96 Robert Reichel STK 10.00 25.00
97 Mats Sundin 5.00 12.00
98 Andrew Cassels 3.00 8.00
99 Peter Bondra 5.00 12.00
100 Jaromir Jagr 8.00 20.00

2001-02 Private Stock Game Gear Patches

This 88-card set paralleled the jerseys in the Game Gear set but carried swatches of patches. The set was skip numbered.

*PATCHES: .75X TO 1.5X JERSEY HI
58 David Legwand 10.00 20.00
65 Alexei Yashin 6.00 12.00
72 Jeremy Roenick 12.50 25.00

2001-02 Private Stock Moments in Time

This 10-card hobby only set featured a color action photo combined with a larger silhouette and a blurred effect on the card front. Each card was serial-numbered out of 85.

1 Dany Heatley 15.00 40.00
2 Ilya Kovalchuk 25.00 60.00
3 Vaclav Nedorost 15.00 40.00
4 Rostislav Klesla 10.00 25.00
5 Jaroslav Bednar 10.00 25.00
6 Rick DiPietro 10.00 25.00
7 Dan Blackburn 6.00 15.00
8 Pavel Brendl 10.00 25.00
9 Krystofer Kolanos 10.00 25.00
10 Johan Hedberg 10.00 25.00

2001-02 Private Stock PS-2002

This 102-card set featured small retro styled mini-cards. Card fronts carried a player photo, name, and birthplace. Card backs resembled vintage "tobacco" cards with single color printing. Cards 1-92 were inserted at 2 per pack and cards 93-102 were serial numbered out of 50 and inserted into hobby packs only. Cards 1-92 had red backs and cards 93-102 had blue backs.

1 Paul Kariya .40 1.00
2 Steve Shields .20 .50
3 Ray Ferraro .20 .50
4 Jason Allison .20 .50
5 Byron DaFoe .30 .75
6 Joe Thornton .60 1.50
7 Stu Barnes .20 .50
8 Martin Biron .30 .75
9 Miroslav Satan .30 .75
10 Jarome Iginla .50 1.25
11 Derek Morris .20 .50
12 Sami Kapanen .20 .50
13 Jeff O'Neill .20 .50
14 Eric Daze .30 .75
15 Jocelyn Thibault .30 .75
16 David Aebischer .30 .75
17 Chris Drury .30 .75
18 Peter Forsberg 1.00 2.50
19 Patrick Roy 2.00 5.00
20 Joe Sakic .75 2.00
21 Marc Denis .30 .75
22 Geoff Sanderson .20 .50
23 Ed Belfour .40 1.00
24 Mike Modano .60 1.50
25 Marty Turco .30 .75
26 Pat Verbeek .20 .50
27 Dominik Hasek .75 2.00
28 Brett Hull .50 1.25
29 Brendan Shanahan .60 1.50
30 Steve Yzerman 2.00 5.00
31 Mike Comrie .30 .75
32 Tommy Salo .30 .75
33 Ryan Smyth .30 .75
34 Pavel Bure .60 1.50
35 Roberto Luongo .50 1.25
36 Zigmund Palffy .30 .75
37 Felix Potvin .40 1.00
38 Marian Gaborik .75 2.00
39 Doug Gilmour .30 .75
40 Jeff Hackett .30 .75
41 Joe Juneau .20 .50
42 Cliff Ronning .20 .50
43 Jason Arnott .20 .50
44 Martin Brodeur 1.00 2.50
45 Michael Peca .20 .50
46 Alexei Yashin .20 .50
47 Zdeno Ciger .20 .50
48 Eric Lindros .60 1.50
49 Mark Messier .50 1.25
50 Petr Nedved .20 .50
51 Radek Bonk .20 .50
52 Martin Havlat .30 .75
53 Roman Cechmanek .30 .75
54 John LeClair .50 1.25
55 Jeremy Roenick .50 1.25
56 Sean Burke .30 .75
57 Shane Doan .20 .50
58 Robert Lang .20 .50
59 Mario Lemieux 2.50 6.00
60 Fred Brathwaite .30 .75
61 Chris Pronger .30 .75
62 Keith Tkachuk .40 1.00
63 Doug Weight .30 .75
64 Evgeni Nabokov .30 .75
65 Owen Nolan .30 .75
66 Teemu Selanne .40 1.00
67 Nikolai Khabibulin .40 1.00
68 Vincent Lecavalier .40 1.00
69 Brad Richards .30 .75
70 Curtis Joseph .40 1.00
71 Mats Sundin .40 1.00
72 Andrew Cassels .20 .50
73 Brendan Morrison .30 .75
74 Peter Bondra .40 1.00
75 Jaromir Jagr .60 1.50
76 Ilja Bryzgalov .30 .75
77 Timo Parssinen .20 .50
78 Erik Cole .20 .50
79 Mark Bell .20 .50
80 Pavel Datsyuk 8.00 20.00
81 Jason Williams .20 .50
82 Jaroslav Bednar .20 .50
83 Scott Clemmensen .30 .75
84 Pavel Brendl .30 .75
85 Jiri Dopita .20 .50
86 Kris Beech .20 .50
87 Mark Rycroft .20 .50
88 Jeff Jillson .20 .50
89 Miikka Kiprusoff .30 .75
90 Nikita Alexeev .20 .50
91 Bryan Allen .20 .50
92 Brian Sutherby .20 .50
93 Dany Heatley SP 12.50 30.00
94 Ilya Kovalchuk SP 25.00 60.00
95 Vaclav Nedorost SP 12.50 30.00
96 Rostislav Klesla SP 12.50 30.00
97 Kristian Huselius SP 12.50 30.00
98 Martin Erat SP 12.50 30.00
99 Rick DiPietro SP 12.50 30.00
100 Dan Blackburn SP 12.50 30.00
101 Krystofer Kolanos SP 12.50 30.00
102 Johan Hedberg SP 12.50 30.00

2001-02 Private Stock Reserve

This 40-card set consisted of 3 different subsets; goalies, superstars, and rookies. Goalies and rookies were inserted into packs at a rate of 1:4 boxes for hobby and 1:8 boxes for retail. Superstar cards were inserted at 1:2 boxes for hobby and 1:4 boxes retail. The prefix before each number below is for checklisting only, the letters do not appear on the cards themselves.

G1 Martin Biron .75 2.00
G2 Patrick Roy 8.00 20.00
G3 Ed Belfour 2.00 5.00
G4 Dominik Hasek 4.00 10.00
G5 Tommy Salo .75 2.00
G6 Roberto Luongo 3.00 8.00
G7 Martin Brodeur 5.00 12.00
G8 Roman Cechmanek .75 2.00
G9 Evgeni Nabokov .75 2.00
G10 Curtis Joseph 2.00 5.00
R1 Dany Heatley 6.00 15.00
R2 Ilya Kovalchuk 12.00 30.00
R3 Vaclav Nedorost 1.50 4.00
R4 Pavel Datsyuk 8.00 20.00
R5 Jaroslav Bednar 1.50 4.00
R6 Dan Blackburn 1.50 4.00
R7 Pavel Brendl 1.50 4.00
R8 Krys Kolanos 1.50 4.00
R9 Kris Beech 1.50 4.00
R10 Nikita Alexeev 1.50 4.00
S1 Paul Kariya 2.00 5.00
S2 Joe Thornton 3.00 8.00
S3 Joe Sakic 4.00 10.00
S4 Brendan Shanahan 2.00 5.00
S5 Steve Yzerman 8.00 20.00
S6 Mike Comrie .75 2.00
S7 Pavel Bure 2.50 6.00
S8 Zigmund Palffy .75 2.00
S9 Marian Gaborik 3.00 8.00
S10 Alexei Yashin .75 2.00
S11 Eric Lindros 2.00 5.00
S12 Martin Havlat .75 2.00
S13 John LeClair .75 2.00
S14 Jeremy Roenick 2.50 6.00
S15 Mario Lemieux 12.00 30.00
S16 Keith Tkachuk .75 2.00
S17 Teemu Selanne 2.00 5.00
S18 Vincent Lecavalier 2.00 5.00
S19 Mats Sundin 2.00 5.00
S20 Jaromir Jagr 3.00 8.00

2002-03 Private Stock Reserve

This 185-card set featured full-color player photos on white borderless card fronts accented with gold foil highlights. Cards 101-150 also carried swatches of game-worn jerseys on the card fronts. Cards 151-185 were serial-numbered to just 99 copies each.

COMP.SET w/o SP's (100) 20.00 40.00
1 Jean-Sebastien Giguere .25 .60
2 Paul Kariya .30 .75
3 Petr Sykora .10 .25
4 Milan Hnilicka .25 .60
5 Patrik Stefan .10 .25
6 Glen Murray .10 .25
7 Brian Rolston .10 .25
8 Sergei Samsonov .25 .60
9 Steve Shields .25 .60
10 Martin Biron .25 .60
11 Tim Connolly .10 .25
12 J-P Dumont .10 .25
13 Craig Conroy .10 .25
14 Chris Drury .25 .60
15 Rod Brind'Amour .25 .60
16 Erik Cole .10 .25
17 Arturs Irbe .25 .60
18 Jeff O'Neill .10 .25
19 Mark Bell .10 .25
20 Eric Daze .25 .60
21 Jocelyn Thibault .25 .60
22 Alexei Zhamnov .10 .25
23 Rob Blake .25 .60
24 Peter Forsberg .75 2.00
25 Milan Hejduk .30 .75
26 Dean McAmmond .10 .25
27 Steven Reinprecht .10 .25
28 Alex Tanguay .25 .60
29 Radim Vrbata .10 .25
30 Andrew Cassels .10 .25
31 Espen Knutsen .10 .25
32 Ray Whitney .10 .25
33 Marty Turco .25 .60
34 Pierre Turgeon .25 .60
35 Chris Chelios .30 .75
36 Brett Hull .40 1.00
37 Brendan Shanahan .30 .75
38 Anson Carter .25 .60
39 Ryan Smyth .10 .25
40 Mike York .10 .25
41 Valeri Bure .10 .25
42 Kristian Huselius .10 .25
43 Stephen Weiss .10 .25
44 Jason Allison .10 .25
45 Adam Deadmarsh .10 .25

46 Zigmund Palffy .25 .60
47 Bryan Smolinski .10 .25
48 Andrew Brunette .10 .25
49 Manny Fernandez .25 .60
50 Cliff Ronning .10 .25
51 Mariusz Czerkawski .10 .25
52 Marcel Hossa .10 .25
53 Saku Koivu .30 .75
54 Yanic Perreault .10 .25
55 Richard Zednik .10 .25
56 Denis Arkhipov .10 .25
57 Mike Dunham .25 .60
58 Scott Hartnell .10 .25
59 Greg Johnson .10 .25
60 Christian Berglund .10 .25
61 Jeff Friesen .10 .25
62 Joe Nieuwendyk .25 .60
63 Chris Osgood .25 .60
64 Mark Parrish .10 .25
65 Dan Blackburn .25 .60
66 Pavel Bure .30 .75
67 Bobby Holik .10 .25
68 Brian Leetch .25 .60
69 Mike Richter .30 .75
70 Daniel Alfredsson .25 .60
71 Radek Bonk .10 .25
72 Martin Havlat .25 .60
73 Patrick Lalime .25 .60
74 John LeClair .30 .75
75 Jeremy Roenick .40 1.00
76 Tony Amonte .25 .60
77 Daniel Briere .10 .25
78 Sean Burke .25 .60
79 Johan Hedberg .25 .60
80 Alexei Kovalev .25 .60
81 Alexei Morozov .10 .25
82 Pavol Demitra .25 .60
83 Barret Jackman .25 .60
84 Brent Johnson .25 .60
85 Doug Weight .25 .60
86 Vincent Damphousse .10 .25
87 Patrick Marleau .25 .60
88 Teemu Selanne .30 .75
89 Scott Thornton .10 .25
90 Dave Andreychuk .10 .25
91 Vincent Lecavalier .30 .75
92 Alexander Mogilny .25 .60
93 Gary Roberts .10 .25
94 Darcy Tucker .10 .25
95 Dan Cloutier .25 .60
96 Brendan Morrison .25 .60
97 Markus Naslund .30 .75
98 Sergei Gonchar .10 .25
99 Olaf Kolzig .25 .60
100 Dainius Zubrus .10 .25
101 Adam Oates J 4.00 10.00
102 Dany Heatley J 6.00 15.00
103 Ilya Kovalchuk J SP 8.00 20.00
104 Joe Thornton J 6.00 15.00
105 Miroslav Satan J 4.00 10.00
106 Jarome Iginla J SP 40.00 100.00
107 Roman Turek J 4.00 10.00
108 Ron Francis J 4.00 10.00
109 Theo Fleury J 4.00 10.00
110 Patrick Roy J SP 15.00 40.00
111 Joe Sakic J 10.00 25.00
112 Marc Denis J 4.00 10.00
113 Jason Arnott J 4.00 10.00
114 Bill Guerin J SP 4.00 10.00
115 Mike Modano J 8.00 20.00
116 Sergei Fedorov J 8.00 20.00
117 Dominik Hasek J 8.00 20.00
118 Curtis Joseph J 5.00 12.00
119 Nicklas Lidstrom J 5.00 12.00
120 Luc Robitaille J 4.00 10.00
121 Steve Yzerman J SP 12.50 30.00
122 Mike Comrie J 4.00 10.00
123 Tommy Salo J 4.00 10.00
124 Roberto Luongo J 6.00 15.00
125 Felix Potvin J 5.00 12.00
126 Marian Gaborik J 12.50 30.00
127 Jose Theodore J 6.00 15.00
128 David Legwand J 4.00 10.00
129 Martin Brodeur J 12.50 30.00
130 Patrik Elias J 4.00 10.00
131 Michael Peca J 4.00 10.00
132 Alexei Yashin J 4.00 10.00
133 Eric Lindros J 5.00 12.00
134 Marian Hossa J 5.00 12.00
135 Roman Cechmanek J 4.00 10.00
136 Simon Gagne J 5.00 12.00
137 Daymond Langkow J 4.00 10.00
138 Mario Lemieux J SP 15.00 40.00
139 Chris Pronger J 4.00 10.00
140 Keith Tkachuk J 5.00 12.00
141 Evgeni Nabokov J 4.00 10.00
142 Owen Nolan J 4.00 10.00
143 Nikolai Khabibulin J 5.00 12.00
144 Brad Richards J 4.00 10.00
145 Ed Belfour J SP 5.00 12.00
146 Mats Sundin J 5.00 12.00
147 Todd Bertuzzi J 5.00 12.00
148 Peter Bondra J 5.00 12.00
149 Jaromir Jagr J 10.00 25.00
150 Robert Lang J 4.00 10.00
151 Stanislav Chistov RC 12.00 30.00
152 Martin Gerber RC 12.00 30.00
153 Alexei Smirnov RC 10.00 25.00
154 Tim Thomas RC 12.00 30.00
155 Chuck Kobasew RC 12.00 30.00
156 Jordan Leopold RC 12.00 30.00
157 Rick Nash RC 125.00 250.00
158 Lasse Pirjeta RC 10.00 25.00
159 Dmitri Bykov RC 10.00 25.00
160 Henrik Zetterberg RC 75.00 150.00
161 Kari Haakana RC 10.00 25.00
162 Ales Hemsky RC 25.00 60.00
163 Jay Bouwmeester RC 20.00 50.00
164 Alexander Frolov RC 20.00 50.00
165 P-M Bouchard RC 20.00 50.00
166 Stephane Veilleux RC 12.50 30.00
167 Sylvain Blouin RC 10.00 25.00
168 Ron Hainsey RC 10.00 25.00
169 Adam Hall RC 10.00 25.00
170 Scottie Upshall RC 12.50 30.00
171 Ray Schultz RC 10.00 25.00
172 Mattias Weinhandl SP 10.00 25.00
173 Jason Spezza RC 125.00 300.00
174 Anton Volchenkov RC 12.50 30.00
175 Dennis Seidenberg RC 10.00 25.00
176 Patrick Sharp RC 10.00 25.00
177 Radovan Somik RC 10.00 25.00
178 Jeff Taffe RC 10.00 25.00
179 Dick Tarnstrom RC 10.00 25.00
180 Tom Koivisto RC 10.00 25.00
181 Curtis Sanford RC 12.50 30.00
182 Alexander Svitov RC 10.00 25.00
183 Carlo Colaiacovo RC 12.50 30.00
184 Steve Eminger RC 12.50 30.00
185 Alex Henry RC 10.00 25.00

2002-03 Private Stock Reserve Blue

This 135-card set paralleled the base set without the jersey card subset. Each card carried blue foil highlights. Cards 1-100 were serial-numbered to 499 and cards 151-185 were serial-numbered to 250.

*STARS: .75X TO 2X BASIC CARDS
*SP's: .10X TO .25X

2002-03 Private Stock Reserve Red

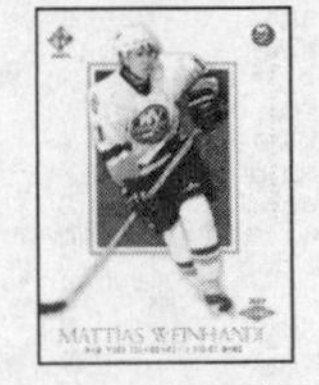

This hobby-only set paralled the base set but was accented with red foil. Cards were serial-numbered to just 50.

*STARS: 8X TO 20X BASIC CARDS
*JERSEYS: .75X TO 2X
*SP's: .15X TO .4X

2002-03 Private Stock Reserve Retail

This 185-card set mirrored the hobby version but with silver foil highlights. Shortprints (151-185) were serial-numbered to 1550.

*BASE/JSY CARDS SAME VALUE
*SP's: .05X TO .12X HBBY HI
157 Rick Nash RC 15.00 40.00
160 Henrik Zetterberg RC 15.00 30.00
173 Jason Spezza RC 12.50 30.00

2002-03 Private Stock Reserve Class Act

COMPLETE SET (10) 30.00 60.00
STATED ODDS 1:9 HBBY/1:49 RETAIL
1 Stanislav Chistov 4.00 10.00
2 Alexei Smirnov 2.50 6.00
3 Ivan Huml 1.50 4.00
4 Chuck Kobasew 3.00 8.00
5 Tyler Arnason 1.50 4.00
6 Rick Nash 6.00 15.00
7 Henrik Zetterberg 6.00 15.00
8 Jay Bouwmeester 5.00 12.00
9 Stephen Weiss 2.00 5.00
10 Barret Jackman 1.50 4.00

2002-03 Private Stock Reserve Elite

COMPLETE SET (6) 30.00 60.00
STATED ODDS 1:17 HBBY/1:49 RETAIL
1 Ilya Kovalchuk 2.50 6.00
2 Peter Forsberg 4.00 10.00
3 Patrick Roy 8.00 20.00
4 Steve Yzerman 8.00 20.00
5 Mario Lemieux 10.00 25.00
6 Jaromir Jagr 2.50 6.00

2002-03 Private Stock Reserve InCrease Security

COMPLETE SET (20) 15.00 30.00
STATED ODDS 1:3 HBBY/1:25 RETAIL
1 Jean-Sebastien Giguere .75 2.00
2 Roman Turek .75 2.00
3 Arturs Irbe .75 2.00
4 Jocelyn Thibault .75 2.00

5 Patrick Roy 3.00 8.00
6 Marc Denis .75 2.00
7 Marty Turco .75 2.00
8 Curtis Joseph 1.50 4.00
9 Tommy Salo .75 2.00
10 Roberto Luongo 2.00 5.00
11 Felix Potvin .75 2.00
12 Jose Theodore 2.00 5.00
13 Martin Brodeur 2.50 6.00
14 Chris Osgood .75 2.00
15 Mike Richter 1.50 4.00
16 Roman Cechmanek .75 2.00
17 Sean Burke .75 2.00
18 Brent Johnson .75 2.00
19 Evgeni Nabokov .75 2.00
20 Ed Belfour 1.50 4.00

2002-03 Private Stock Reserve Moments in Time

COMPLETE SET (8) 20.00 40.00
STATED ODDS 1:9 HBBY/1:49 RETAIL
1 Chuck Kobasew 3.00 8.00
2 Rick Nash 6.00 15.00
3 Jay Bouwmeester 5.00 12.00
4 Stephen Weiss 2.00 5.00
5 Alexander Frolov 4.00 10.00
6 Jamie Lundmark 1.50 4.00
7 Barret Jackman 1.50 4.00
8 Alexander Svitov 2.50 6.00

2002-03 Private Stock Reserve Patches

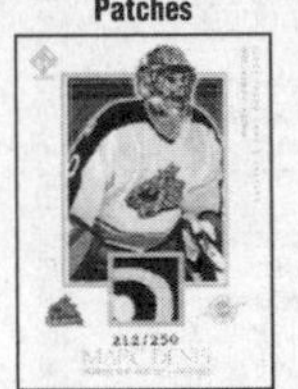

This 39-card hobby only set partially paralleled the jersey cards in the base set but were affixed with jersey patches. Each card was serial-numbered individually. Lower print runs are not priced due to scarcity.

102 Dany Heatley/50 20.00 50.00
103 Ilya Kovalchuk/50 25.00 60.00
104 Joe Thornton/275 15.00 40.00
105 Miroslav Satan/275 10.00 25.00
106 Jarome Iginla/70 20.00 50.00
107 Roman Turek/90 10.00 25.00
109 Theo Fleury/275 10.00 25.00
112 Marc Denis/250 10.00 25.00
113 Jason Arnott/250 10.00 25.00
114 Bill Guerin/100 10.00 25.00
115 Mike Modano/150 20.00 50.00
116 Sergei Fedorov/150 20.00 50.00
119 Nicklas Lidstrom/275 12.50 30.00
121 Steve Yzerman/15
122 Mike Comrie/125 10.00 25.00
123 Tommy Salo/275 10.00 25.00
124 Roberto Luongo/150 15.00 40.00
125 Felix Potvin/250 12.50 30.00
126 Marian Gaborik/100 30.00 80.00
127 Jose Theodore/50 15.00 40.00
128 David Legwand/250 10.00 25.00
129 Martin Brodeur/150 25.00 60.00
130 Patrik Elias/150 10.00 25.00
131 Michael Peca/250 10.00 25.00
133 Eric Lindros/250 12.50 30.00
134 Marian Hossa/250 12.50 30.00
135 Roman Cechmanek/250 10.00 25.00
136 Simon Gagne/200 12.50 30.00
137 Daymond Langkow/150 10.00 25.00
139 Chris Pronger/250 10.00 25.00
140 Keith Tkachuk/150 12.50 30.00
141 Evgeni Nabokov/200 10.00 25.00
142 Owen Nolan/250 10.00 25.00
143 Nikolai Khabibulin/275 12.50 30.00
144 Brad Richards/275 10.00 25.00
145 Ed Belfour/245 12.50 30.00
147 Todd Bertuzzi/275 12.50 30.00
148 Peter Bondra/275 12.50 30.00
150 Robert Lang/250 10.00 25.00

2003-04 Private Stock Reserve

This 212-card set was released in late-January and consisted of 100 base veteran cards; 40 short-printed rookie cards (numbered to 99) and 72 jersey cards with varying print runs. Jersey cards with substantially lower print runs are noted below. Jerseys were one per pack.

COMP.SET w/o SP's (100) 40.00 80.00
*MULT.COLOR SWATCH: .75X TO 2X
1 Stanislav Chistov .10 .25
2 Jean-Sebastien Giguere .25 .60
3 Vaclav Prospal .10 .25
4 Petr Sykora .10 .25
5 Byron Dafoe .25 .60
6 Slava Kozlov .10 .25
7 Pasi Nurminen .25 .60
8 Marc Savard .10 .25
9 Mike Knuble .10 .25
10 Felix Potvin .30 .75
11 Sergei Samsonov .25 .60
12 Daniel Briere .10 .25
13 Ales Kotalik .10 .25
14 Ryan Miller .25 .60
15 Blair Betts .10 .25
16 Chuck Kobasew .10 .25
17 Jordan Leopold .10 .25
18 Ron Francis .25 .60
19 Jeff O'Neill .25 .60
20 Kevin Weekes .25 .60
21 Igor Radulov .10 .25
22 Jocelyn Thibault .25 .60
23 Alexei Zhamnov .10 .25
24 David Aebischer .25 .60
25 Rob Blake .25 .60
26 Andrew Cassels .10 .25
27 Rick Nash .40 1.00
28 Geoff Sanderson .10 .25
29 Niko Kapanen .10 .25
30 Jere Lehtinen .25 .60
31 Steve Ott .10 .25
32 Pavel Datsyuk .30 .75
33 Nicklas Lidstrom .30 .75
34 Dominik Hasek .60 1.50
35 Henrik Zetterberg .30 .75
36 Ales Hemsky .25 .60
37 Georges Laraque .10 .25
38 Tommy Salo .25 .60
39 Mike York .10 .25
40 Jay Bouwmeester .10 .25
41 Valeri Bure .10 .25
42 Viktor Kozlov .10 .25
43 Roberto Luongo .40 1.00
44 Stephen Weiss .10 .25
45 Roman Cechmanek .25 .60
46 Adam Deadmarsh .10 .25
47 Alexander Frolov .10 .25
48 Pierre-Marc Bouchard .10 .25
49 Andrew Brunette .10 .25
50 Marian Gaborik .60 1.50
51 Dwayne Roloson .25 .60
52 Mathieu Garon .10 .25
53 Marcel Hossa .10 .25
54 Yanic Perreault .10 .25
55 Mike Ribeiro .10 .25
56 Andreas Johansson .10 .25
57 Scottie Upshall .10 .25
58 Scott Walker .10 .25
59 Patrik Elias .25 .60
60 Jeff Friesen .10 .25
61 Jamie Langenbrunner .10 .25
62 Scott Stevens .25 .60
63 Jason Blake .10 .25
64 Oleg Kvasha .10 .25
65 Mark Parrish .10 .25
66 Garth Snow .25 .60
67 Mattias Weinhandl .10 .25
68 Mike Dunham .25 .60
69 Alex Kovalev .25 .60
70 Brian Leetch .25 .60
71 Mark Messier .30 .75
72 Radek Bonk .25 .60
73 Vaclav Varada .10 .25
74 Todd White .10 .25
75 Simon Gagne .30 .75
76 John LeClair .30 .75
77 Mark Recchi .25 .60
78 Shane Doan .10 .25
79 Mike Johnson .10 .25
80 Daymond Langkow .25 .60
81 Ladislav Nagy .10 .25
82 Sebastien Caron .25 .60
83 Alexei Morozov .10 .25
84 Brent Johnson .25 .60
85 Al MacInnis .25 .60
86 Chris Pronger .25 .60
87 Keith Tkachuk .30 .75
88 Jonathan Cheechoo .12 .30
89 Vincent Damphousse .10 .25
90 Patrick Marleau .10 .25
91 Evgeni Nabokov .25 .60
92 Dave Andreychuk .10 .25
93 Dan Boyle .10 .25
94 Alexander Mogilny .25 .60
95 Owen Nolan .25 .60
96 Darcy Tucker .10 .25
97 Ed Jovanovski .25 .60
98 Trevor Linden .10 .25
99 Sergei Gonchar .10 .25
100 Olaf Kolzig .25 .60
101 Garrett Burnett RC 8.00 20.00
102 Joffrey Lupul RC 12.00 30.00
103 Joe DiPenta RC 8.00 20.00
104 Patrice Bergeron RC 30.00 60.00
105 Milan Bartovic RC 8.00 20.00
106 Andrew Peters RC 8.00 20.00
107 Brent Krahn RC 8.00 20.00
108 Eric Staal RC 60.00 100.00
109 Lasse Kukkonen RC 8.00 20.00
110 Travis Moen RC 8.00 20.00
111 Tuomo Ruutu RC 20.00 50.00
112 Pavel Vorobiev RC 8.00 20.00
113 Cody McCormick RC 8.00 20.00
114 Dan Fritsche RC 8.00 20.00
115 Kent McDonell RC 8.00 20.00
116 Trevor Daley RC 8.00 20.00
117 Antti Miettinen RC 8.00 20.00
118 Jiri Hudler RC 20.00 50.00
119 Nathan Horton RC 25.00 60.00
120 Dustin Brown RC 12.00 30.00
121 Tim Gleason RC 12.00 30.00
122 Esa Pirnes RC 8.00 20.00
123 Brent Burns RC 12.00 30.00
124 Chris Higgins RC 20.00 50.00
125 Dan Hamhuis RC 12.00 30.00
126 Jordin Tootoo RC 25.00 60.00
127 Marek Zidlicky RC 12.00 30.00
128 David Hale RC 8.00 20.00
129 Paul Martin RC 8.00 20.00
130 Sean Bergenheim RC 8.00 20.00
131 Antoine Vermette RC 12.00 30.00
132 Joni Pitkanen RC 12.00 30.00
133 Matthew Spiller RC 8.00 20.00
134 Marc-Andre Fleury RC 60.00 120.00
135 Matt Murley RC 8.00 20.00
136 Peter Sejna RC 8.00 20.00
137 Milan Michalek RC 20.00 50.00
138 Maxim Kondratiev RC 8.00 20.00
139 Matt Stajan RC 20.00 50.00
140 Boyd Gordon RC 8.00 20.00
141 Sergei Fedorov 5.00 12.00
142 Dany Heatley 5.00 12.00
143 Ilya Kovalchuk 5.00 12.00
144 Glen Murray 3.00 8.00
145 Joe Thornton 6.00 15.00
146 Martin Biron 5.00 12.00
147 Chris Drury 5.00 12.00
148 Miroslav Satan 5.00 12.00
149 Craig Conroy 3.00 8.00
150 Jarome Iginla 5.00 12.00
151 Erik Cole 3.00 8.00
152 Eric Daze 5.00 12.00
153 Theo Fleury 3.00 8.00
154 Peter Forsberg 6.00 15.00
155 Milan Hejduk 4.00 10.00
156 Paul Kariya 4.00 10.00
157 Patrick Roy SP 25.00 60.00
158 Joe Sakic 8.00 20.00
159 Teemu Selanne 4.00 10.00
160 Marc Denis 5.00 12.00
161 Rostislav Klesla 3.00 8.00
162 Bill Guerin 5.00 12.00
163 Mike Modano 5.00 12.00
164 Marty Turco 5.00 12.00
165 Brett Hull 5.00 12.00
166 Steve Yzerman 10.00 25.00
167 Mike Comrie 5.00 12.00
168 Ryan Smyth 3.00 8.00
169 Olli Jokinen 5.00 12.00
170 Jason Allison 3.00 8.00
171 Zigmund Palffy 5.00 12.00
172 Filip Kuba SP 8.00 20.00
173 Saku Koivu 4.00 10.00
174 Jose Theodore 5.00 12.00
175 Richard Zednik 3.00 8.00
176 David Legwand 5.00 12.00
177 Tomas Vokoun 5.00 12.00
178 Martin Brodeur 10.00 25.00
179 Rick DiPietro 5.00 12.00
180 Michael Peca 3.00 8.00
181 Alexei Yashin 3.00 8.00
182 Pavel Bure 4.00 10.00
183 Eric Lindros 4.00 10.00
184 Mike Richter SP
185 Daniel Alfredsson 5.00 12.00
186 Marian Hossa 4.00 10.00
187 Patrick Lalime 5.00 12.00
188 Bryan Smolinski 3.00 8.00
189 Jason Spezza 4.00 10.00
190 Tony Amonte 5.00 12.00
191 Jeff Hackett 5.00 12.00
192 Jeremy Roenick 5.00 12.00
193 Sean Burke 5.00 12.00
194 Mario Lemieux 12.50 30.00
195 Martin Straka 3.00 8.00
196 Pavol Demitra 5.00 12.00
197 Chris Osgood 5.00 12.00
198 Doug Weight 5.00 12.00
199 Nikolai Khabibulin 4.00 10.00
200 Vincent Lecavalier 4.00 10.00
201 Fredrik Modin 5.00 12.00
202 Brad Richards 5.00 12.00
203 Martin St. Louis 5.00 12.00
204 Cory Stillman SP 8.00 20.00
205 Ed Belfour 4.00 10.00
206 Mats Sundin 4.00 10.00
207 Todd Bertuzzi 4.00 10.00
208 Dan Cloutier 5.00 12.00
209 Brendan Morrison 5.00 12.00
210 Markus Naslund 4.00 10.00
211 Jaromir Jagr 6.00 15.00
212 Robert Lang 3.00 8.00

2003-04 Private Stock Reserve Blue

*STARS: .75X TO 2X BASIC CARDS
1-100 PRINT RUN 350 SER.#'d SETS
*ROOKIES: .06X TO .15X
ROOKIE PRINT RUN 250 SER.#'d SETS
*JERSEYS: 1.25X TO 3X
JERSEY PRINT RUN 25 SER.#'d SETS

2003-04 Private Stock Reserve Patches

This 68-card set paralleled the jerseys of the base set but included patch swatches. Please note that cards #151,159 and 161 do not exist. Cards with print runs under 25 were not priced due to scarcity. Known short-prints are listed below.

*PATCHES: 1.25X TO 3X BASE JSY
142 Dany Heatley/50 15.00 40.00
143 Ilya Kovalchuk/25 100.00 200.00
145 Joe Thornton/50 20.00 50.00
154 Peter Forsberg/70 20.00 50.00
157 Patrick Roy 20.00 50.00
164 Marty Turco/50 15.00 40.00
166 Steve Yzerman/19
167 Mike Comrie/25 50.00 100.00
168 Ryan Smyth/25 15.00 40.00
172 Filip Kuba 12.50 30.00
188 Bryan Smolinski/20
189 Jason Spezza/25
193 Sean Burke/65 15.00 40.00
202 Brad Richards/25 25.00 60.00
204 Cory Stillman 8.00 20.00
206 Mats Sundin/50 12.50 30.00
210 Markus Naslund/75 12.50 30.00

2003-04 Private Stock Reserve Red

*STARS: 1.25X TO 3X BASE HI
1-100 PRINT RUN 199 SER.#'d SETS
*ROOKIES: .06X TO .15X
ROOKIE PRINT RUN 225 SER.#'d SETS
*JERSEYS: .75X TO 2X BASE HI
JERSEY PRINT RUN 50 SER.#'d SETS

2003-04 Private Stock Reserve Retail

The retail version of this set carried silver foil highlights. Rookies were serial-numbered out of 1299.

*BASE CARDS SAME VALUE AS HOBBY
*RC: .03X TO .075X BASE HI
*JERSEYS: .6X TO 1.5X
108 Eric Staal 12.50 30.00

2003-04 Private Stock Reserve Class Act

COMPLETE SET (12) 15.00 30.00
STATED ODDS 1:9
1 Joffrey Lupul .75 2.00
2 Eric Staal 1.50 4.00
3 Tuomo Ruutu 1.00 2.50
4 Nathan Horton 1.25 3.00
5 Dustin Brown .50 1.25
6 Chris Higgins 1.00 2.50
7 Jordin Tootoo 1.25 3.00
8 Joni Pitkanen .75 2.00
9 Marc-Andre Fleury 2.00 5.00
10 Peter Sejna .50 1.25
11 Milan Michalek .50 1.25
12 Matt Stajan 1.00 2.50

2003-04 Private Stock Reserve Increase Security

COMPLETE SET (16) 15.00 30.00
STATED ODDS 1:5
1 Jean-Sebastien Giguere .75 2.00
2 Felix Potvin 1.00 2.50
3 Ryan Miller .75 2.00
4 Jocelyn Thibault .75 2.00
5 David Aebischer .75 2.00
6 Marty Turco .75 2.00
7 Dominik Hasek 2.00 5.00
8 Jose Theodore 1.25 3.00
9 Martin Brodeur 3.00 8.00
10 Rick DiPietro .75 2.00
11 Patrick Lalime .75 2.00
12 Sean Burke .75 2.00
13 Marc-Andre Fleury 3.00 8.00
14 Evgeni Nabokov .75 2.00
15 Nikolai Khabibulin 1.00 2.50
16 Ed Belfour 1.00 2.50

2003-04 Private Stock Reserve Moments in Time

COMPLETE SET (10) 20.00 40.00
STATED ODDS 1:17
1 Sergei Fedorov 1.00 2.50
2 Joe Thornton 1.25 3.00
3 Peter Forsberg 2.00 5.00
4 Paul Kariya 2.00 5.00
5 Joe Sakic 1.50 4.00
6 Mike Modano 1.25 3.00
7 Brett Hull 1.00 2.50
8 Steve Yzerman 2.50 6.00
9 Mario Lemieux 3.00 8.00
10 Todd Bertuzzi .75 2.00

2003-04 Private Stock Reserve Rising Stock

COMPLETE SET (12) 10.00 20.00
STATED ODDS 1:9
1 Ilya Kovalchuk 1.25 3.00
2 Ales Kotalik .40 1.00
3 Ryan Miller .40 1.00
4 Chuck Kobasew .40 1.00
5 Rick Nash .75 2.00
6 Henrik Zetterberg .75 2.00
7 Ales Hemsky .40 1.00
8 Jay Bouwmeester .40 1.00
9 Pierre-Marc Bouchard .40 1.00
10 Marcel Hossa .40 1.00
11 Jason Spezza .75 2.00
12 Barret Jackman .40 1.00

1995-96 Pro Magnets

This set of 130 magnets was produced by Chris Martin Enterprises. Each magnet featured a color photo of the player on front, along with his name and team. The backs were simply a black magnetic surface. The checklist to this set mirrors that of the NHL Pro Stamps.

COMPLETE SET (130) 30.00 75.00
1 Stephane Fiset .25 .60
2 Peter Forsberg .75 2.00
3 Claude Lemieux .20 .50
4 Mike Ricci .20 .50
5 Joe Sakic .75 2.00
6 Ed Belfour .40 1.00
7 Chris Chelios .40 1.00
8 Joe Murphy .20 .50
9 Bernie Nicholls .20 .50
10 Jeremy Roenick .40 1.00
11 Geoff Courtnall .20 .50
12 Brett Hull .40 1.00
13 Al MacInnis .20 .50
14 Chris Pronger .20 .50
15 Esa Tikkanen .20 .50
16 Ray Bourque .75 2.00
17 Blaine Lacher .25 .60
18 Cam Neely .30 .75
19 Adam Oates .20 .50
20 Kevin Stevens .20 .50
21 Valeri Bure .20 .50
22 Vincent Damphousse .25 .60
23 Mark Recchi .30 .75
24 Patrick Roy 1.50 4.00
25 Pierre Turgeon .25 .60
26 Pavel Bure .75 2.00
27 Trevor Linden .25 .60
28 Kirk McLean .25 .60
29 Alexander Mogilny .25 .60
30 Cliff Ronning .20 .50
31 Jason Allison .20 .50
32 Jim Carey .25 .60
33 Dale Hunter .20 .50
34 Joe Juneau .20 .50
35 Brendan Witt .20 .50
36 Martin Brodeur .75 2.00
37 John MacLean .20 .50
38 Scott Niedermayer .20 .50
39 Stephane Richer .20 .50
40 Scott Stevens .20 .50
41 Patrik Carnback .20 .50
42 Guy Hebert .25 .60
43 Paul Kariya 1.25 3.00
44 Oleg Tverdovsky .20 .50
45 Garry Valk .20 .50
46 Theo Fleury .25 .60
47 Trevor Kidd .25 .60
48 Joe Nieuwendyk .20 .50
49 Gary Roberts .20 .50
50 German Titov .20 .50
51 Rod Brind'Amour .20 .50
52 Ron Hextall .20 .50
53 John LeClair .40 1.00
54 Eric Lindros .75 2.00
55 Mikael Renberg .25 .60
56 Brett Lindros .20 .50
57 Wendel Clark .20 .50
58 Patrick Flatley .20 .50
59 Kirk Muller .20 .50
60 Mathieu Schneider .20 .50
61 Tim Cheveldae .25 .60
62 Dallas Drake .20 .50
63 Teemu Selanne .60 1.50
64 Keith Tkachuk .30 .75
65 Alexei Zhamnov .20 .50
66 Rob Blake .30 .75
67 Wayne Gretzky 2.00 5.00
68 Jari Kurri .20 .50
69 Jamie Storr .25 .60
70 Rick Tocchet .20 .50
71 Brian Bradley .20 .50
72 Chris Gratton .20 .50
73 Roman Hamrlik .20 .50
74 Paul Ysebaert .20 .50
75 Rob Zamuner .20 .50
76 Dave Andreychuk .20 .50
77 Doug Gilmour .25 .60
78 Kenny Jonsson .20 .50
79 Felix Potvin .40 1.00
80 Mats Sundin .30 .75
81 Jason Arnott .25 .60
82 Jason Bonsignore .20 .50
83 Todd Marchant .20 .50
84 Bill Ranford .25 .60
85 Doug Weight .20 .50
86 Jody Hull .20 .50
87 Bob Kudelski .20 .50
88 Scott Mellanby .20 .50
89 Rob Niedermayer .20 .50
90 John Vanbiesbrouck .30 .75
91 Ron Francis .25 .60
92 Jaromir Jagr .75 2.00
93 Mario Lemieux 1.50 4.00
94 Bryan Smolinski .20 .50
95 Sergei Zubov .20 .50
96 Adam Graves .20 .50
97 Brian Leetch .30 .75
98 Mark Messier .40 1.00
99 Mike Richter .30 .75
100 Luc Robitaille .25 .60
101 Paul Coffey .25 .60
102 Sergei Fedorov .60 1.50
103 Nicklas Lidstrom .30 .75
104 Ray Sheppard .20 .50
105 Steve Yzerman 1.50 4.00
106 Donald Audette .20 .50

107 Dominik Hasek .60 1.50
108 Yuri Khmylev .20 .50
109 Pat LaFontaine .20 .50
110 Alexei Zhitnik .20 .50
111 Radek Bonk .20 .50
112 Randy Cunneyworth .20 .50
113 Alexandre Daigle .20 .50
114 Steve Larouche .20 .50
115 Martin Straka .20 .50
116 Ulf Dahlen .20 .50
117 Pat Falloon .20 .50
118 Jeff Friesen .20 .50
119 Arturs Irbe .25 .60
120 Craig Janney .20 .50
121 Shane Churla .20 .50
122 Todd Harvey .20 .50
123 Derian Hatcher .20 .50
124 Mike Modano .40 1.00
125 Andy Moog .25 .60
126 Sean Burke .25 .60
127 Andrew Cassels .20 .50
128 Geoff Sanderson .20 .50
129 Brendan Shanahan .60 1.50
130 Darren Turcotte .20 .50

1995-96 Pro Magnets Iron Curtain Insert

1 Ed Belfour
2 Martin Brodeur
3 Arturs Irbe
4 Mike Richter
5 Mike Vernon
6 Ron Hextall

1990-91 Pro Set

The inaugural Pro Set issue contains 705 cards measuring the standard size, with the first series containing 405 cards followed by a 300 card second series. The fronts feature a color action photo, banded above and below in the team's colors. The horizontally oriented backs have a head shot of each player and player information sandwiched between color stripes in the team's colors. Many grammatical, statistical and factual errors punctuated this issue.

COMPLETE SET (705) 6.00 15.00
COMP.SERIES 1 (405) 3.00 8.00
COMP.SERIES 2 (300) 3.00 8.00
1A Brett Hull Promo UER .60 1.50
(Born 9/9/64& 85 games in '87-88, height 6-0, TM under Pro Set logos, aqua blue team color)
1B Ray Bourque ERR .10 .30
(Misspelled Borque on card front)
1C Ray Bourque COR .10 .30
2 Randy Burridge .01 .05
3 Lyndon Byers RC .01 .05
4 Bob Carpenter .01 .05
5 John Carter RC .01 .05
6 Dave Christian UER .01 .05
(28 games with Washington& 50 with Boston)
7A Garry Galley ERR RC .01 .05
7B Garry Galley COR RC .01 .05
8 Craig Janney .02 .10
9 Rejean Lemelin UER .02 .10
(Wrong headings, not for goalie; '89-90 stats are Andy Moog's)
10 Andy Moog UER .02 .10
('89-90 stats are Reggie Lemelin's; he was 3rd, not 2nd In Vezina voting)
11 Cam Neely UER .05 .15
(Bruins not capitalized in text)
12 Allen Pedersen .01 .05
13 Dave Poulin UER .01 .05
(Flyers' stats missing from '89-90)
14 Brian Propp .01 .05
15 Bob Sweeney .01 .05
16 Glen Wesley .01 .05
17A Dave Andreychuk ERR .02 .10
(Photo actually Scott Arniel on back)
17B Dave Andreychuk COR .02 .10
18A Scott Arniel ERR .01 .05
(Photo actually Dave Andreychuk on back)
18B Scott Arniel COR .01 .05
19 Doug Bodger .01 .05
20 Mike Foligno .01 .05
21A Phil Housley ERR .02 .10
21B Phil Housley COR .02 .10
22 Dean Kennedy RC .01 .05
23 Uwe Krupp .01 .05
24 Grant Ledyard RC .01 .05
25 Clint Malarchuk UER .02 .10
(Back in action 11 days after hurt& not 2 as said on card)
26 Alexander Mogilny RC .20 .50
27 Daren Puppa .02 .10
28 Mike Ramsey .01 .05
29 Christian Ruuttu .01 .05
30 Dave Snuggerud .01 .05
31 Pierre Turgeon .02 .10
32 Rick Vaive .01 .05
33 Theo Fleury .01 .05
34 Doug Gilmour .02 .10
35 Al MacInnis UER .02 .10
(Misspelled Allan on card back)
36 Brian MacLellan .01 .05
37 Jamie Macoun .01 .05
38 Sergei Makarov RC .01 .05
39A Brad McCrimmon ERR .01 .05
39B Brad McCrimmon COR .01 .05
40A Joe Mullen ERR .02 .10
40B Joe Mullen COR .02 .10
41 Dana Murzyn .01 .05
42A Joe Nieuwendyk ERR .02 .10
(Misspelled Niewendyk on card front)
42B Joe Nieuwendyk COR .02 .10
43 Joel Otto .01 .05
44 Paul Ranheim RC UER .01 .05
(Front LW& Back C)
45 Gary Roberts .01 .05
46 Gary Suter .01 .05
47 Mike Vernon .02 .10
48 Rick Wamsley .02 .10
(Misspelled Rich in bio on card back)
49 Keith Brown .01 .05
50 Adam Creighton .01 .05
51 Dirk Graham UER .01 .05
(Sparking& should be sparkling; season was '88-89& not '89-90)
52 Steve Konroyd .01 .05
53A Steve Larmer ERR .02 .10
(Position and sweater number in white& should be black)
53B Steve Larmer COR .02 .10
54A Dave Manson ERR .01 .05
(Both photos actually Steve Konroyd)
54B Dave Manson COR .01 .05
55A Bob McGill ERR .01 .05
55B Bob McGill COR .01 .05
56 Greg Millen .02 .10
57A Troy Murray .01 .05
(Position and sweater number are white)
57B Troy Murray .01 .05
(Position and sweater number are black)
58 Jeremy Roenick RC .25 .60
59A Denis Savard .02 .10
(No traded stripe; played 70 games in '86-87)
59B Denis Savard .02 .10
(Traded stripe; played 70 games in '86-87)
60A Al Secord .01 .05
60B Al Secord .01 .05
61A Duane Sutter ERR .01 .05
61B Duane Sutter COR .01 .05
62 Steve Thomas .01 .05
63A Doug Wilson .02 .10
(Position and sweater number are white)
63B Doug Wilson .02 .10
(Position and sweater number are black)
64 Trent Yawney .01 .05
65 Dave Barr .01 .05
66 Shawn Burr .01 .05
67 Jimmy Carson .01 .05
68 John Chabot .01 .05
69 Steve Chiasson .01 .05
70 Bernie Federko UER .02 .10
(Says only player from Foam Lake& but Elynuik was too)
71 Gerard Gallant .01 .05
72 Glen Hanlon .02 .10
73 Joey Kocur RC .10 .30
74 Lee Norwood .01 .05
75 Mike O'Connell .01 .05
76 Bob Probert .02 .10
77 Torrie Robertson .01 .05
78 Daniel Shank RC .01 .05
79 Steve Yzerman .25 .60
80 Rick Zombo RC .01 .05
81 Glenn Anderson .02 .10
82 Grant Fuhr .02 .10
83 Martin Gelinas RC UER .01 .05
(Back photo actually Joe Murphy)
84 Adam Graves RC UER .08 .25
(Stats missing '89-90 Detroit info)
85 Charlie Huddy UER .01 .05
(No accent in 1st e in Defenseur)
86 Petr Klima UER .01 .05
(Born Chomulov& should be Chaomutov)
87A Jari Kurri ERR .02 .10
87B Jari Kurri COR .02 .10
88 Mark Lamb .01 .05
89 Kevin Lowe .01 .05
90 Craig MacTavish .01 .05
91 Mark Messier .05 .15
92 Craig Muni .01 .05
93 Joe Murphy RC .01 .05
94 Bill Ranford .02 .10
95 Craig Simpson .01 .05
96 Steve Smith UER .01 .05
(No accent in 1st e in Defenseur)
97 Esa Tikkanen .01 .05
98 Mikael Andersson .01 .05
99 Dave Babych UER .01 .05
(Extra space included after Forum)
100 Yvon Corriveau RC .01 .05
101 Randy Cunneyworth .01 .05
102 Kevin Dineen .01 .05
103 Dean Evason .01 .05
104 Ray Ferraro .02 .10
105 Ron Francis .02 .10
106 Grant Jennings RC .01 .05
107 Todd Krygier RC .01 .05
108 Randy Ladouceur .01 .05
109 Ulf Samuelsson .01 .05
110 Brad Shaw RC .01 .05
111 Dave Tippett .01 .05
112 Pat Verbeek .01 .05
113 Scott Young .01 .05
114 Brian Benning UER .01 .05
(St.Louis and Los Angeles stats not separate)
115 Steve Duchesne .01 .05
116 Todd Elik RC .01 .05
117 Tony Granato UER .01 .05
(Plays RW& not C)
118 Wayne Gretzky .30 .75
119 Kelly Hrudey .02 .10
120 Steve Kasper .01 .05
121A Mike Kushelnyski ERR .01 .05
(No position and number on card front)
121B Mike Kushelnyski COR .01 .05
122 Bob Kudelski RC UER .01 .05
(Born Springfield& not Feeding Hills)
123 Tom Laidlaw .01 .05
124 Marty McSorley .01 .05
125 Larry Robinson .02 .10
126 Luc Robitaille UER .02 .10
(Kings, should be Kings')
127 Tomas Sandstrom UER .01 .05
('89-90 Rangers stats not printed)
128 Dave Taylor .02 .10
129A John Tonelli ERR .01 .05
(Misspelled Tonnelli on card front)
129B John Tonelli COR .01 .05
130A Brian Bellows ERR .01 .05
(Back photo actually Dave Gagner; front LW, back RW)
130B Brian Bellows COR/ERR .01 .05
(Back photo correct, facing forward; front LW, back RW)
131 Aaron Broten UER .01 .05
(New Jersey and Minnesota stats not separate)
132 Neal Broten .02 .10
133 Jon Casey .02 .10
134 Shawn Chambers .01 .05
135 Shane Churla RC .01 .05
136 Ulf Dahlen UER .01 .05
(Rangers and Minnesota stats not separate)
137 Gaetan Duchesne .01 .05
138 Dave Gagner .02 .10
139 Stewart Gavin .01 .05
140 Curt Giles .01 .05
141 Basil McRae .01 .05
142 Mike Modano RC .30 .75
143 Larry Murphy .02 .10
144 Ville Siren RC .01 .05
145 Mark Tinordi RC .01 .05
146 Guy Carbonneau UER .01 .05
(Sep Iles should be Sept-Iles)
147A Chris Chelios ERR .05 .15
147B Chris Chelios COR .05 .15
148 Shayne Corson .01 .05
149 Russ Courtnall .01 .05
150 Brian Hayward .02 .10
151 Mike Keane RC .01 .05
152 Stephan Lebeau RC .01 .05
153 Claude Lemieux UER .01 .05
(Reason is misspelled as reson)
154 Craig Ludwig .01 .05
155 Mike McPhee .01 .05
156 Stephane Richer .02 .10
157 Patrick Roy .25 .60
158 Mathieu Schneider RC .01 .05
159 Brian Skrudland .01 .05
160 Bobby Smith UER .02 .10
(No mention of trade from Montreal to Minnesota)
161 Petr Svoboda .01 .05
162 Tommy Albelin .01 .05
163 Doug Brown .01 .05
164 Sean Burke .02 .10
165 Ken Daneyko .01 .05
166 Bruce Driver .01 .05
167A Slava Fetisov ERR RC .01 .05
167B Slava Fetisov COR RC .01 .05
168 Mark Johnson .01 .05
169 Alexei Kasatonov RC .01 .05
170 John MacLean UER .02 .10
(Should have apostrophe after Devils)
171A David Maley ERR RC .01 .05
171B David Maley COR RC .01 .05
172 Kirk Muller .01 .05
173 Janne Ojanen RC .01 .05
174 Brendan Shanahan .05 .15
175A Peter Stastny ERR .02 .10
(Front photo actually Patrik Sundstrom)
175B Peter Stastny COR .02 .10
176A Patrik Sundstrom ERR .01 .05
(Front photo actually Peter Stastny)
176B Patrik Sundstrom COR .01 .05
177 Sylvain Turgeon .01 .05
178 Ken Baumgartner RC .01 .05
179 Doug Crossman .01 .05
180 Gerald Diduck .01 .05
181 Mark Fitzpatrick RC .02 .10
182 Pat Flatley .01 .05
183 Glenn Healy RC .02 .10
184 Alan Kerr .01 .05
185 Derek King .01 .05
186 Pat LaFontaine .05 .15
187 Don Maloney .01 .05
188 Hubie McDonough RC .01 .05
189 Jeff Norton UER .01 .05
(Born Cambridge& Mass. not Acton)
190 Gary Nylund .01 .05
191 Brent Sutter .01 .05
192 Bryan Trottier UER .02 .10
(Finish the season& not finished)
193 David Volek .01 .05
194 Randy Wood .01 .05
195 Jan Erixon .01 .05
196 Mike Gartner UER .02 .10
(Minnesota and Rangers stats not separate)
197 Ron Greschner .01 .05
198A Miloslav Horava ERR RC .01 .05
198B Miloslav Horava COR RC .01 .05
199 Mark Janssens RC .01 .05
200 Kelly Kisio .01 .05
201 Brian Leetch .05 .15
202 Randy Moller .01 .05
203 Brian Mullen .01 .05
204 Bernie Nicholls UER .02 .10
(Kings and Rangers stats not separate)
205A Chris Nilan ERR .01 .05
205B Chris Nilan COR .01 .05
206 John Ogrodnick .01 .05
207 James Patrick .01 .05
208 Darren Turcotte RC .01 .05
209 John Vanbiesbrouck UER .02 .10
(Front C& back G)
210 Carey Wilson .01 .05
211 Mike Bullard .01 .05
212 Terry Carkner .01 .05
213 Jeff Chychrun RC .01 .05
214 Murray Craven .01 .05
215 Pelle Eklund UER .01 .05
(Centre and previous, not Center and previously)
216 Ron Hextall .02 .10
217 Mark Howe .01 .05
218 Tim Kerr .01 .05
219 Ken Linseman UER .01 .05
(Bruins and Flyers stats not separate)
220 Scott Mellanby .02 .10
221 Gord Murphy .01 .05
222 Kjell Samuelsson UER .01 .05
(Born 10/18/58, not 10/18/56)
223 Ilkka Sinisalo .01 .05
224 Ron Sutter .01 .05
225 Rick Tocchet .02 .10
226 Ken Wregget .02 .10
227 Tom Barrasso .02 .10
228A Phil Bourque ERR .01 .05
(Misspelled Borque on both sides)
228B Phil Bourque COR .01 .05
229 Rob Brown UER .01 .05
(Front RW, back C; actual position is LW)
230 Alain Chevrier UER .02 .10
(Chicago and Pittsburgh stats not separate)
231 Paul Coffey .05 .15
232 John Cullen .01 .05
233 Gord Dineen .01 .05
234 Bob Errey .01 .05
235 Jim Johnson .01 .05
236 Mario Lemieux .30 .75
237 Troy Loney RC .01 .05
238 Barry Pederson .01 .05
239 Mark Recchi RC .20 .50
240 Kevin Stevens RC .01 .05
241 Tony Tanti .01 .05
242 Zarley Zalapski UER .01 .05
(Pittsburgh misspelled as Pittsburg)
243 Joe Cirella .01 .05
244 Lucien DeBlois UER .01 .05
(Front C, back RW; misspelled Deblois in bio on card back)
245A Marc Fortier ERR .01 .05
245B Marc Fortier COR .01 .05
246 Paul Gillis .01 .05
247 Mike Hough .01 .05
248 Tony Hrkac UER .01 .05
(Blues and Nordiques stats not separate)
249 Jeff Johnson RC .01 .05
250 Guy Lafleur .05 .15
251 Curtis Leschyshyn RC .01 .05
252 Claude Loiselle RC .01 .05
253 Mario Marois .01 .05
254 Tony McKegney UER .01 .05
(Red Wings and Nordiques stats not separate)
255 Ken McRae RC .01 .05
256A Michel Petit ERR .01 .05
256B Michel Petit COR .01 .05
257 Joe Sakic UER .15 .40
(Front 88, back 19)
258 Ron Tugnutt .02 .10
259 Rod Brind'Amour RC UER .15 .40
(Misspelled Rob on card back)
260 Jeff Brown UER .01 .05
(Nordiques and Blues stats not separate)
261 Gino Cavallini UER .01 .05
(On back Meagher is misspelled as Meager)
262 Paul Cavallini .01 .05
263 Brett Hull .10 .30
264 Mike Lalor RC .01 .05
265 Dave Lowry RC .01 .05
266 Paul MacLean .01 .05
267 Rick Meagher RC .01 .05
268 Sergio Momesso RC UER .01 .05
(Text has 55 pts. in '89-90& stats 56)
269 Adam Oates .02 .10
270 Vincent Riendeau RC .02 .10
271 Gordie Roberts .01 .05
272 Rich Sutter UER .01 .05
(Canucks and Blues stats not separate)
273 Steve Tuttle .01 .05
274 Peter Zezel .01 .05
275A Allan Bester ERR .02 .10
275B Allan Bester COR .02 .10
276 Wendel Clark .02 .10
277 Brian Curran .01 .05
278 Vincent Damphousse .02 .10
(Name not listed on one line)
279A Tom Fergus ERR .01 .05
(Fourth line in bio has TI& should be that)
279B Tom Fergus COR .01 .05
280 Lou Franceschetti RC .01 .05
281 Al Iafrate .02 .10
282 Tom Kurvers UER .01 .05
(Played for Toronto in 71& not 70)
283 Gary Leeman .01 .05
284 Daniel Marois .01 .05
285 Brad Marsh .01 .05
286 Ed Olczyk .01 .05
287 Mark Osborne .01 .05
288 Rob Ramage .01 .05
289 Luke Richardson .01 .05
290 Gilles Thibaudeau RC .01 .05
291 Greg Adams .01 .05
292 Jim Benning .01 .05
293 Steve Bozek .01 .05
294 Brian Bradley .01 .05
295 Garth Butcher .01 .05
296 Vladimir Krutov RC .02 .10
297 Igor Larionov RC UER .01 .05
(Stats should indicate either Soviet or NHL)
298 Doug Lidster .01 .05
299 Trevor Linden .02 .10
300 Jyrki Lumme RC UER .01 .05
('89-90 Canadiens and Canucks stats not separate)
301A Andrew McBain ERR .01 .05
(Back photo actually Jim Sandlak)
301B Andrew McBain COR .01 .05
302 Kirk McLean UER .02 .10
(Career GAA should be 3.46, not 6.50)
303 Dan Quinn UER .01 .05
(Penguins and Canucks stats not separate)
304 Paul Reinhart .01 .05
305 Jim Sandlak .01 .05
306 Petri Skriko .01 .05
307 Don Beaupre .02 .10
308 Dino Ciccarelli .02 .10
309 Geoff Courtnall .01 .05
310 John Druce RC .01 .05
311 Kevin Hatcher .01 .05
312 Dale Hunter UER .01 .05
(Text has rougish& should be roguish)
313 Calle Johansson UER .01 .05
(No accent in first e in Defenseur)
314 Rod Langway .01 .05
315 Stephen Leach RC .01 .05
316 Mike Liut UER .02 .10
(Capitals and Whalers stats not separate)
317 Alan May RC .01 .05
318 Kelly Miller .01 .05
319 Michal Pivonka RC UER .01 .05
(1988-89 Goals should be 8, not 38)
320A Mike Ridley ERR .01 .05
320B Mike Ridley COR .01 .05
321 Scott Stevens UER .02 .10
(No accent in first e in Defenseur; 1987-886)
322 John Tucker UER .01 .05
(1989-90 Buffalo Sabres team affiliation and stats missing 8 games; Ottawa misspelled Ottowa)
323 Brent Ashton .01 .05
324 Laurie Boschman .01 .05
325 Randy Carlyle .01 .05
326 Dave Ellett .01 .05
327 Pat Elynuik .01 .05
328 Bob Essensa RC .08 .25
329 Paul Fenton .01 .05
330A Dale Hawerchuk .02 .10
(No traded stripe; 19089-90; Center should be Centre)
330B Dale Hawerchuk .02 .10
(Traded stripe on front; 19089-90; Center should be Centre)
331 Paul MacDermid .01 .05
332 Moe Mantha .01 .05
333 Dave McLlwain .01 .05
334 Teppo Numminen RC .01 .05
335A Fredrik Olausson ERR .01 .05
(Misspelled Frederik on both sides)
335B Fredrik Olausson COR .01 .05
336 Greg Paslawski .01 .05
(TM after Jets is larger than other TM symbols)
337 Al MacInnis AS .02 .10
338 Mike Vernon AS .02 .10
339 Kevin Lowe AS .01 .05
340 Wayne Gretzky AS .08 .25
341 Luc Robitaille AS UER .02 .10
(Fewest shots by Eastern AS's, not Boston)
342 Brett Hull AS .05 .15
343 Joe Mullen AS .02 .10
344 Joe Nieuwendyk AS .02 .10
345 Steve Larmer AS .02 .10
346 Doug Wilson AS .02 .10
347 Steve Yzerman AS .05 .15
348A Jari Kurri AS ERR .02 .10
348B Jari Kurri AS COR .02 .10
349 Mark Messier AS .05 .15
350 Steve Duchesne AS UER .01 .05
(Shot record held by Boston, not East)
351 Mike Gartner AS .02 .10
352 Bernie Nicholls AS .02 .10
353 Paul Cavallini AS .01 .05
354 Al Iafrate AS .02 .10
355 Kirk McLean AS .02 .10
356 Thomas Steen AS .01 .05
357 Ray Bourque AS .05 .15
358 Cam Neely AS .02 .10
359 Patrick Roy AS .08 .25
360 Brian Propp AS .01 .05
361 Paul Coffey AS .05 .15
362 Mario Lemieux AS .08 .25
363 Dave Andreychuk AS .02 .10
364 Phil Housley AS .02 .10
365 Daren Puppa AS .02 .10
366 Pierre Turgeon AS .02 .10
367 Ron Francis AS .02 .10
368 Chris Chelios AS .02 .10
369A Shayne Corson AS ERR .01 .05
369B Shayne Corson AS COR .01 .05
370 Stephane Richer AS .02 .10
371 Kirk Muller AS .01 .05
372 Pat LaFontaine AS .02 .10
373 Brian Leetch AS .05 .15
374 Rick Tocchet AS .02 .10
375 Joe Sakic AS .05 .15
376 Kevin Hatcher AS .01 .05
377 Bob Murdoch Adams .01 .05
378 Brett Hull Byng UER .05 .15
(Should be Lady Byng Memorial Trophy)
379 Sergei Makarov Calder .01 .05
380 Kevin Lowe Clancy .01 .05
381 Mark Messier Hart .05 .15
382 Moog/Lemelin Jennings .01 .05
383 Gord Kluzak Mast UER .01 .05
(Should be Bill Masterton Memorial Trophy)
384 Ray Bourque Norris .05 .15
385A Len Ceglarski Patrick ERR .01 .05
385B Len Ceglarski Patrick COR .01 .05
386 Mark Messier Pearson .05 .15
387 Boston Bruins .01 .05
388 Wayne Gretzky Ross UER .08 .25
(Gretzky has won eight Art Ross Trophies)
389 Rick Meagher Selke .01 .05
390 Bill Ranford Smythe .01 .05
391 Patrick Roy Vezina .08 .25
392 Edmonton Oilers UER .01 .05
(Should be Clarence S. Campbell Bowl)
393 Boston Bruins .01 .05
394 Wayne Gretzky LL UER .08 .25
(Lemieux and Dionne, should read Lemieux only)
395 Brett Hull LL UER .05 .15
(Born 8/9/64, not 9/9/64)
396 Sergei Makarov ROY .01 .05
397 Mark Messier MVP .05 .15
398 Mike Richter RLL UER .05 .15
(Plays, not lays)
399 Patrick Roy LL .08 .25
400 Darren Turcotte RLL .01 .05
UER (Front RW, back C)
401 Owen Nolan RC .20 .50
402 Petr Nedved RC .08 .25
403 Phil Esposito HOF .02 .10
404 Darryl Sittler HOF UER .02 .10
(Career: 15 seasons, not stats)
405 Stan Mikita HOF .02 .10
406 Andy Brickley .01 .05
407 Peter Douris .01 .05
408 Nevin Markwart .01 .05
409 Chris Nilan .01 .05
410 Stephane Quintal RC .01 .05
411 Bruce Shoebottom RC .01 .05
412 Don Sweeney RC .01 .05
413 Jim Wiemer RC .01 .05
414 Mike Hartman RC .01 .05
415 Dale Hawerchuk .02 .10
416 Benoit Hogue .01 .05
417 Bill Houlder RC .01 .05
418 Mikko Makela .01 .05
419 Robert Ray RC .08 .25
420 John Tucker .01 .05
421 Jiri Hrdina RC .01 .05
422 Mark Hunter .01 .05
423 Tim Hunter RC .01 .05
424 Roger Johansson RC .01 .05
425 Frank Musil .01 .05
426 Ric Nattress .01 .05
427 Chris Chelios .05 .15
428 Jacques Cloutier RC .02 .10
429 Greg Gilbert .01 .05
430 Michel Goulet .02 .10
(White position and number on front, not black)
431 Mike Hudson .01 .05
432 Jocelyn Lemieux RC .01 .05
433 Brian Noonan .01 .05
434 Wayne Presley .01 .05
435 Brent Fedyk RC .01 .05
436 Rick Green .01 .05
437 Marc Habscheid .01 .05
438 Brad McCrimmon .01 .05
439 Jeff Beukeboom RC .01 .05
440 Dave Brown RC .01 .05
441 Kelly Buchberger RC .01 .05
442 Greg Hawgood .01 .05
443 Chris Joseph .01 .05
444 Ken Linseman .01 .05
445 Eldon Reddick RC .02 .10
446 Geoff Smith RC .01 .05
447 Adam Burt RC .01 .05
448 Sylvain Cote .01 .05
449 Paul Cyr .01 .05
450 Ed Kastelic RC .01 .05
451 Peter Sidorkiewicz .02 .10
452 Mike Tomlak RC .01 .05
453 Carey Wilson .01 .05
454 Daniel Berthiaume .02 .10
455 Scott Bjugstad .01 .05
456 Rod Buskas RC .01 .05
457 John McIntyre .01 .05
458 Tim Watters .01 .05
459 Perry Berezan RC .01 .05
460 Brian Propp .01 .05
461 Ilkka Sinisalo .01 .05
462 Doug Smail .01 .05
463 Bobby Smith .02 .10
464 Chris Dahlquist .01 .05
465 Neil Wilkinson RC .01 .05
466 J.J. Daigneault .01 .05
467 Eric Desjardins RC .08 .25
468 Gerald Diduck .01 .05
469 Donald Dufresne RC .01 .05
470A Todd Ewen ERR RC .01 .05
470B Todd Ewen COR RC .01 .05
471 Brent Gilchrist RC .01 .05
472 Sylvain Lefebvre RC .01 .05
473 Denis Savard .02 .10
474 Sylvain Turgeon .01 .05
475 Ryan Walter .01 .05
476 Laurie Boschman .01 .05
477 Pat Conacher RC .01 .05
478 Claude Lemieux .01 .05
479 Walt Poddubny .01 .05
480 Alan Stewart RC .01 .05
481 Chris Terreri RC .02 .10
482 Brad Dalgarno .01 .05
483 Dave Chyzowski RC .01 .05
484 Craig Ludwig .01 .05
485 Wayne McBean RC .01 .05
486 Rich Pilon RC .01 .05
487 Joe Reekie RC .01 .05
488 Mick Vukota RC .01 .05
489 Mark Hardy .01 .05
490 Jody Hull RC .01 .05
491 Kris King RC .01 .05
492 Troy Mallette RC .01 .05
493 Kevin Miller RC .01 .05
494 Normand Rochefort .01 .05
495 David Shaw .01 .05
496 Ray Sheppard .02 .10
497 Keith Acton .01 .05
498 Craig Berube RC .01 .05
499 Tony Horacek RC .01 .05
500 Normand Lacombe RC .01 .05
501 Jiri Latal RC .01 .05
502 Pete Peeters .02 .10
503 Derrick Smith RC .01 .05
504 Jay Caufield .01 .05
505 Peter Taglianetti .01 .05
506 Randy Gilhen RC .01 .05
507 Randy Hillier .01 .05
508 Joe Mullen .02 .10
509 Frank Pietrangelo RC .02 .10
510 Gordie Roberts .01 .05
511 Bryan Trottier .02 .10
512 Wendell Young .02 .10
513 Shawn Anderson RC .01 .05
514 Steven Finn RC .01 .05
515 Bryan Fogarty RC .01 .05
516 Mike Hough .01 .05
517 Darin Kimble .01 .05
518 Randy Velischek .01 .05
519 Craig Wolanin RC .01 .05
520 Bob Bassen RC .01 .05
521 Geoff Courtnall .01 .05
522 Robert Dirk RC .01 .05
523 Glen Featherstone RC .01 .05
524 Mario Marois .01 .05
525 Herb Raglan RC .01 .05
526 Cliff Ronning .01 .05
527 Harold Snepsts .01 .05
528 Scott Stevens .02 .10
529 Ron Wilson .01 .05
530 Aaron Broten .01 .05
531 Lucien DeBlois .01 .05
532 Dave Ellett .01 .05
533A Paul Fenton ERR .01 .05
(Trademark on front next to name)
533B Paul Fenton COR .01 .05
534 Todd Gill RC .01 .05
535 Dave Hannan .01 .05
536 John Kordic .01 .05
537 Mike Krushelnyski .01 .05
538 Kevin Maguire RC .01 .05
539 Michel Petit .01 .05
540 Jeff Reese RC .01 .05
541 David Reid RC .01 .05
542 Doug Shedden .01 .05
543 Dave Capuano RC .01 .05
544 Craig Coxe RC .01 .05
545 Kevan Guy .01 .05
546 Rob Murphy RC .01 .05
547 Robert Nordmark RC .01 .05
548 Stan Smyl .01 .05
549 Ronnie Stern RC .01 .05
550 Tim Bergland RC .01 .05
551 Nick Kypreos RC .01 .05
552 Mike Lalor RC .01 .05
553 Rob Murray RC .01 .05
554 Bob Rouse .01 .05
555 Dave Tippett .01 .05
556 Peter Zezel UER .01 .05
(Card says number 25, sweater shows 9)
557 Scott Arniel .01 .05
558 Don Barber .01 .05
559 Shawn Cronin RC .01 .05
560 Gord Donnelly .01 .05
561 Doug Evans RC .01 .05
562 Phil Housley .02 .10
563 Ed Olczyk .01 .05
564 Mark Osborne .01 .05
565 Thomas Steen .01 .05
566 Boston Bruins Logo .01 .05
567 Buffalo Sabres Logo .01 .05
568 Calgary Flames Logo .01 .05
569 Chicago Blackhawks Logo .01 .05
570 Detroit Red Wings Logo .01 .05

571 Edmonton Oilers Logo .01 .05
572 Hartford Whalers Logo .01 .05
573A Los Angeles Kings .01 .05
Logo ERR
(Registration mark
missing from Kings
on card front)
573B Los Angeles Kings Logo COR .01 .05
574 Minn. North Stars Logo .01 .05
575 Montreal Canadiens Logo .01 .05
576 New Jersey Devils Logo .01 .05
577 New York Islanders Logo .01 .05
578 New York Rangers Logo .01 .05
579 Philadelphia Flyers Logo .01 .05
580 Pittsburgh Penguins Logo .01 .05
581 Quebec Nordiques Logo .01 .05
582 St. Louis Blues Logo .01 .05
583 Toronto Maple Leafs Logo .01 .05
584 Vancouver Canucks Logo .01 .05
585 Washington Capitals Logo .01 .05
586 Winnipeg Jets Logo .01 .05
587 Ken Hodge Jr. RC .01 .05
588 Vladimir Ruzicka RC .01 .05
589 Wes Walz RC .01 .05
590 Greg Brown RC .01 .05
591 Brad Miller .01 .05
592 Darrin Shannon RC .01 .05
593 Stephane Matteau RC UER .01 .05
(Front RW& back LW)
594 Sergei Priakin RC .01 .05
595 Robert Reichel RC .07 .20
596 Ken Sabourin RC .01 .05
597 Tim Sweeney .01 .05
598 Ed Belfour RC .40 1.00
599 Frantisek Kucera RC .01 .05
600 Mike McNeil .01 .05
601 Mike Peluso RC .01 .05
602 Tim Cheveldae RC .02 .10
603 Per Djoos RC .01 .05
604 Sergei Fedorov RC .30 .75
605 Johan Garpenlov RC .01 .05
606 Keith Primeau RC .01 .05
607 Paul Ysebaert RC .01 .05
608 Anatoli Semenov RC .01 .05
609 Bobby Holik RC .07 .20
610 Kay Whitmore RC .02 .10
611 Rob Blake RC .10 .30
612 Francois Breault RC .01 .05
613 Mike Craig RC UER .01 .05
(Wearing 50&
card says 20)
614 J.C. Bergeron RC UER .01 .05
(Front J.C.&
back Jean Claude)
615 Andrew Cassels .01 .05
616 Tom Chorske RC .01 .05
617 Lyle Odelein RC .01 .05
618 Mark Pederson RC .01 .05
619 Zdeno Ciger .01 .05
620 Troy Crowder RC .01 .05
621 Jon Morris RC .01 .05
622 Eric Weinrich RC .01 .05
623 David Marcinyshyn RC .01 .05
624 Jeff Hackett RC .02 .10
625 Rob DiMaio RC .01 .05
626 Steven Rice RC .01 .05
627 Mike Richter RC .20 .50
628 Dennis Vial RC .01 .05
629 Martin Hostak RC .01 .05
630 Pat Murray RC .01 .05
631 Mike Ricci RC .07 .20
632 Jaromir Jagr RC .50 1.25
632B Jaromir Jagr RC COR .50 1.25
633 Paul Stanton RC .01 .05
634 Scott Gordon RC .01 .05
635 Owen Nolan .02 .10
636 Mats Sundin RC .25 .60
637 John Tanner RC .01 .05
638 Curtis Joseph RC .30 .75
639 Peter Ing RC .02 .10
640 Scott Thornton RC .01 .05
641 Troy Gamble RC .02 .10
642 Robert Kron RC .01 .05
643 Petr Nedved .01 .05
644 Adrien Plavsic .01 .05
645 Peter Bondra RC .20 .50
646 Jim Hrivnak RC .02 .10
647 Mikhail Tatarinov RC .01 .05
648 Stephane Beauregard RC .02 .10
649 Rick Tabaracci RC .02 .10
650 Mike Bossy CPL .02 .10
651 Bobby Clarke CPL .02 .10
652 Alex Delvecchio CPL .02 .10
653 Marcel Dionne CPL .02 .10
654 Gordie Howe CPL .08 .25
655 Stan Mikita CPL .02 .10
656 Denis Potvin CPL .02 .10
657 Bobby Clarke HOF .02 .10
658 Alex Delvecchio HOF .02 .10
659 Tony Esposito HOF .02 .10
660 Gordie Howe HOF .08 .25
661 Mike Milbury CO .01 .05
662 Rick Dudley CO .01 .05
663 Doug Risebrough CO .01 .05
664 Bryan Murray CO RC .01 .05
665 John Muckler CO .01 .05
666 Rick Ley CO .01 .05
667 Tom Webster CO .01 .05
668 Bob Gainey CO UER .01 .05
(Stats and bio are
Bob McCammon's)
669 Pat Burns CO RC .01 .05
670 John Cunniff CO .01 .05
671 Al Arbour CO .01 .05
672 Roger Neilson CO RC .01 .05
673 Paul Holmgren CO .01 .05
674 Bob Johnson CO RC .01 .05
675 Dave Chambers CO RC .01 .05
676 Brian Sutter CO UER .01 .05
(Coaching totals say
0-69-21& should
be 70-69-21)
677 Tom Watt CO RC .01 .05
678 Bob McCammon CO UER .01 .05
(Stats and bio are
Bob Gainey's)
679 Terry Murray CO .01 .05
680 Bob Murdoch CO .01 .05
681 Ron Asselstine REF .01 .05
682 Wayne Bonney REF .01 .05
683 Kevin Collins REF .01 .05
684 Pat Dapuzzo REF .01 .05
685 Ron Finn REF .01 .05
686 Kerry Fraser REF .01 .05
687 Gerard Gauthier REF .01 .05
688 Terry Gregson REF .01 .05
689 Bob Hodges REF .01 .05
690 Ron Hoggarth REF .01 .05
691 Don Koharski REF .01 .05
692 Dan Marouelli REF .01 .05
693 Danny McCourt REF .01 .05
694 Bill McCreary REF .01 .05
695 Denis Morel REF .01 .05
696 Jerry Pateman REF .01 .05
697 Ray Scapinello REF .01 .05
698 Rob Shick REF .01 .05
699 Paul Stewart REF .01 .05
700 Leon Stickle REF .01 .05
701 Andy van Hellemond REF .01 .05
702 Mark Vines REF .01 .05
703 Wayne Gretzky 2000th .08 .25
(2.33 goals per game&
should be points) UER
704 Stanley Cup Champs .01 .05
705 The Puck-La Rondelle .01 .05
NNO Stanley Cup Hologram 40.00 100.00

1990-91 Pro Set Player of the Month

This four-card set features the NHL player of the month for four consecutive months (the month for which the player won the award is listed below his name). All cards feature the basic 1990-91 Pro Set design, and say NHL Pro Set Player of the Month and the date at the bottom of each obverse. The cards are numbered on the back; note that the Peeters card has no number. The cards were issued in the home rink of the winner each month after announcement of the winner. Pro Set sponsored the Player of the Week/Month/Year Awards for the NHL. Reportedly less than 25,000 of each POM card were produced.

COMPLETE SET (4) 8.00 20.00
P1 Tom Barrasso 1.50 4.00
POM December 1990
P2 Wayne Gretzky 4.00 10.00
POM January 1991
P3 Brett Hull 2.50 6.00
POM February 1991
NNO Pete Peeters 1.50 4.00
POM November 1990

1991-92 Pro Set Preview

This six-card standard-size set was given to dealers to show what the 1991-92 Pro Set hockey set would look like. There is really not that much interest in the set due to the egregiously poor player selection, i.e., no superstars in the set. The setup of the text on the card backs of these preview cards is different from the regular issue cards; cards are labeled "Promo" on the back where the card number is in the regular issue cards. The David Reid card has an entirely different photo. Even though the cards are unnumbered, they are assigned reference numbers below according to their numbers in the 1991-92 Pro Set regular issue.

COMPLETE SET (6) .60 1.50
151 Randy Wood NNO .08 .25
171 Gord Murphy NNO .08 .25
203 Craig Wolanin NNO .08 .25
229 David Reid NNO .08 .25
266 Bob Essensa NNO .08 .25
NNO Title Card .02 .10

1991-92 Pro Set

The Pro Set hockey issue contains 615 numbered cards. The set was released in two series of 345 and 270 cards, respectively. Pro Set also issued a French version which carries the same value. French wax boxes contained randomly inserted Patrick Roy personally autographed cards signed and numbered on the back; 1,000 of card number 125 (first series) and 1,000 of card number 599 numbered 1001 to 2000 (second series). Roy also signed 500 cards for distribution in Canadian collector's kits. Randomly inserted in U.S. packs were a limited quantity of Kirk McLean autographed cards. Ten thousand hand-numbered 3-D hologram cards were inserted in second series foil packs to commemorate the NHL's Diamond Anniversary.

COMPLETE SET (615) 7.50 15.00
COMP.SERIES 1 (345) 3.00 8.00
COMP.SERIES 2 (270) 3.00 8.00
1 Glen Wesley .01 .05
2 Craig Janney .02 .10
3 Ken Hodge Jr. .01 .05
4 Randy Burridge .01 .05
5 Cam Neely .05 .15
6 Bob Sweeney .01 .05
7 Garry Galley .01 .05
8 Petri Skriko .01 .05
9 Ray Bourque .10 .30
10 Andy Moog UER .02 .10
(4.0 record
should be 4-0)
11 Dave Christian .01 .05
12 Dave Poulin .01 .05
13 Jeff Lazaro RC .01 .05
14 Darrin Shannon .01 .05
15 Pierre Turgeon UER .02 .10
(Born 8/29 not 8/28)
16 Alexander Mogilny .05 .15
17 Benoit Hogue UER .01 .05
(Stats show two seasons
with Winnipeg& should
say Buffalo)
18 Dave Snuggerud .01 .05
19 Doug Bodger UER .01 .05
(Second highest offens-
ive total of his career&
should say third highest)
20 Uwe Krupp .01 .05
21 Daren Puppa .02 .10
22 Christian Ruuttu .01 .05
23 Dave Andreychuk .02 .10
24 Dale Hawerchuk .02 .10
25 Mike Ramsey .01 .05
26 Rick Vaive .01 .05
27 Stephane Matteau .01 .05
28 Theo Fleury .01 .05
29 Joe Nieuwendyk .02 .10
30 Gary Roberts .02 .10
31 Paul Ranheim .01 .05
32 Gary Suter .01 .05
33 Al MacInnis .02 .10
34 Doug Gilmour .02 .10
35 Mike Vernon .02 .10
36 Carey Wilson .01 .05
37 Joel Otto .01 .05
38 Jamie Macoun .01 .05
39 Sergei Makarov .01 .05
40 Jeremy Roenick .08 .25
41 Dave Manson .01 .05
42 Adam Creighton .01 .05
43 Ed Belfour .10 .30
44 Wayne Presley .01 .05
45 Steve Thomas .01 .05
46 Troy Murray .01 .05
47 Bob McGill .01 .05
48 Chris Chelios .05 .15
49 Steve Larmer .02 .10
50 Michel Goulet .02 .10
51 Dirk Graham .01 .05
52 Doug Wilson .02 .10
53 Sergei Fedorov .08 .25
54 Yves Racine .01 .05
55 Jimmy Carson .01 .05
56 Johan Garpenlov .01 .05
57 Tim Cheveldae .02 .10
58 Shawn Burr .01 .05
59 Paul Ysebaert .01 .05
60 Kevin Miller .01 .05
61 Bob Probert .02 .10
62 Steve Yzerman .25 .60
63 Gerard Gallant .01 .05
64 Rick Zombo .01 .05
65 Dave Barr .01 .05
66 Martin Gelinas .01 .05
67 Adam Graves UER .02 .10
(Kid Line included
Gelinas not Simpson)
68 Joe Murphy .01 .05
69 Craig Simpson .01 .05
70 Bill Ranford .02 .10
71 Esa Tikkanen .01 .05
72 Petr Klima .01 .05
73 Steve Smith .01 .05
74 Mark Messier .05 .15
75 Glenn Anderson .02 .10
76 Kevin Lowe .02 .10
77 Craig MacTavish .01 .05
78 Grant Fuhr .05 .15
79 Bobby Holik .02 .10
80 Rob Brown .01 .05
81 Doug Houda .01 .05
82 Sylvain Cote .01 .05
83 Todd Krygier .01 .05
84 Dean Evason .01 .05
85 John Cullen .01 .05
86 Pat Verbeek .01 .05
87 Brad Shaw .01 .05
88 Paul Cyr UER .01 .05
(Stats show New York,
should say NY Rangers)
89 Kevin Dineen .01 .05
90 Peter Sidorkiewicz .02 .10
91 Zarley Zalapski .01 .05
92 Rob Blake .02 .10
93 Jari Kurri UER .05 .15
(No transaction
line on front, al-
though back says Kings)
94 Todd Elik .01 .05
95 Luc Robitaille .02 .10
96 Steve Duchesne .02 .10
97 Tomas Sandstrom .01 .05
98 Tony Granato .01 .05
99 Bob Kudelski .01 .05
100 Marty McSorley .01 .05
101 Wayne Gretzky .30 .75
102 Kelly Hrudey .02 .10
103 Dave Taylor .02 .10
104 Larry Robinson .02 .10
105 Mike Modano .10 .30
106 Ulf Dahlen .01 .05
107 Mark Tinordi .01 .05
108 Dave Gagner .01 .05
109 Brian Bellows .01 .05
110 Gaetan Duchesne .01 .05
111 Jon Casey .02 .10
112 Neal Broten .02 .10
113 Brian Propp .01 .05
114 Curt Giles .01 .05
115 Bobby Smith .02 .10
116 Jim Johnson .01 .05
117 Doug Smail .01 .05
118 Eric Desjardins .02 .10
119 Mathieu Schneider .01 .05
120 Stephan Lebeau .01 .05
121 Mike Keane .01 .05
122 Stephane Richer .02 .10
123 Petr Svoboda .01 .05
124 J.J. Daigneault .01 .05
125 Patrick Roy .25 .60
126 Russ Courtnall .01 .05
127 Brian Skrudland .01 .05
128 Denis Savard .02 .10
129 Mike McPhee .01 .05
130 Guy Carbonneau .02 .10
131 Brendan Shanahan .05 .15
132 Sean Burke .02 .10
133 Eric Weinrich .01 .05
134 Kirk Muller .01 .05
135 Claude Lemieux .01 .05
136 John MacLean .02 .10
137 Chris Terreri .02 .10
138 Doug Brown .01 .05
139 Ken Daneyko .01 .05
140 Bruce Driver .01 .05
141 Patrik Sundstrom .01 .05
142 Slava Fetisov .01 .05
143 Peter Stastny .02 .10
144 Wayne McBean .01 .05
145 Bill Berg .01 .05
146 Derek King .01 .05
147 David Volek .01 .05
148 Jeff Norton .01 .05
149 Pat LaFontaine .05 .15
150 Gary Nylund .01 .05
151 Randy Wood .01 .05
152 Pat Flatley .01 .05
153 Glenn Healy .02 .10
154 Brent Sutter .01 .05
155 Craig Ludwig .01 .05
156 Ray Ferraro .01 .05
157 Troy Mallette .01 .05
158 Mark Janssens .01 .05
159 Brian Leetch UER .05 .15
(Career points total
329 should be 229)
160 Darren Turcotte .01 .05
161 Mike Richter .05 .15
162 Ray Sheppard .01 .05
163 Randy Moller .01 .05
164 James Patrick .01 .05
165 Brian Mullen UER .01 .05
(Transaction says
drafted by San Jose&
was actually traded)
166 Bernie Nicholls .02 .10
167 Mike Gartner .02 .10
168 Kelly Kisio UER .01 .05
(Transaction says
drafted by Minnesota,
was actually traded
to San Jose)
169 John Ogrodnick .01 .05
170 Mike Ricci .05 .15
171 Gord Murphy .01 .05
172 Scott Mellanby .01 .05
173 Terry Carkner .01 .05
174 Derrick Smith .01 .05
175 Murray Craven .01 .05
176 Ron Hextall .02 .10
177 Rick Tocchet .02 .10
178 Ron Sutter .01 .05
179 Pelle Eklund .01 .05
180 Tim Kerr UER .01 .05
(Only transaction
line to show a date)
181 Kjell Samuelsson .01 .05
182 Mark Howe .01 .05
183 Jaromir Jagr .08 .25
184 Mark Recchi .05 .15
185 Kevin Stevens .01 .05
186 Tom Barrasso .02 .10
187 Bob Errey .01 .05
188 Ron Francis .02 .10
189 Phil Bourque .01 .05
190 Paul Coffey .05 .15
191 Joe Mullen .02 .10
192 Bryan Trottier .05 .15
193 Larry Murphy .02 .10
194 Mario Lemieux .25 .60
195 Scott Young .01 .05
196 Owen Nolan .05 .15
197 Mats Sundin .02 .10
198 Curtis Leschyshyn .01 .05
199 Joe Sakic .10 .30
200 Bryan Fogarty .01 .05
201 Stephane Morin .01 .05
202 Ron Tugnutt .02 .10
203 Craig Wolanin .01 .05
204 Steven Finn .01 .05
205 Tony Hrkac .01 .05
206 Randy Velischek .01 .05
207 Alexei Gusarov RC .02 .10
208 Scott Pearson .01 .05
209 Dan Quinn .01 .05
210 Garth Butcher .01 .05
211 Rod Brind'Amour UER .05 .15
(Type in stat box is
smaller than others)
212 Jeff Brown .01 .05
213 Vincent Riendeau .02 .10
214 Paul Cavallini .01 .05
215 Brett Hull .08 .25
216 Scott Stevens .02 .10
217 Rich Sutter .01 .05
218 Gino Cavallini .01 .05
219 Adam Oates UER .02 .10
(Stats are off-line
from top to bottom)
220 Ron Wilson .01 .05
221 Bob Bassen .01 .05
222 Peter Ing .02 .10
223 Daniel Marois .01 .05
224 Vincent Damphousse .01 .05
225 Wendel Clark UER .02 .10
(Connecticut not cap-
italized in last line)
226 Todd Gill .01 .05
227 Peter Zezel .01 .05
228 Bob Rouse .01 .05
229 David Reid .01 .05
230 Dave Ellett .01 .05
231 Gary Leeman .01 .05
232 Grant Fuhr .05 .15
233 Mike Krushelnyski .01 .05
234 Tom Fergus .01 .05
235 Petr Nedved .02 .10
236 Trevor Linden .02 .10
237 Dave Capuano .01 .05
238 Troy Gamble .02 .10
239 Robert Kron UER .01 .05
(Type in stat box is
smaller than others)
240 Jyrki Lumme .01 .05
241 Cliff Ronning .01 .05
242 Sergio Momesso .01 .05
243 Greg Adams .01 .05
244 Tom Kurvers .01 .05
245 Geoff Courtnall .02 .10
246 Igor Larionov .01 .05
247 Doug Lidster UER .01 .05
(No space between 51
and assist in last
line of text)
248 Calle Johansson .01 .05
249 Kevin Hatcher .02 .10
250 Al Iafrate .02 .10
251 John Druce .01 .05
252 Michal Pivonka .01 .05
253 Stephen Leach .01 .05
254 Mike Ridley .01 .05
255 Mike Lalor .01 .05
256 Kelly Miller .01 .05
257 Don Beaupre .02 .10
258 Dino Ciccarelli .02 .10
259 Rod Langway .01 .05
260 Dimitri Khristich .01 .05
261 Teppo Numminen .01 .05
262 Pat Elynuik .01 .05
263 Danton Cole .01 .05
264 Fredrik Olausson UER .01 .05
(Fifth line of text&
the word the is missing
between in and 10th)
265 Ed Olczyk .01 .05
266 Bob Essensa .02 .10
267 Phil Housley .02 .10
268 Shawn Cronin .01 .05
269 Paul MacDermid .01 .05
270 Mark Osborne .01 .05
271 Thomas Steen .01 .05
272 Brent Ashton .01 .05
273 Randy Carlyle .01 .05
274 Theo Fleury AS .01 .05
275 Al MacInnis AS .01 .05
276 Gary Suter AS .01 .05
277 Mike Vernon AS .02 .10
278 Chris Chelios AS .02 .10
279 Steve Larmer AS .01 .05
280 Jeremy Roenick AS .05 .15
281 Steve Yzerman AS .10 .30
282 Mark Messier AS .05 .15
283 Bill Ranford AS .02 .10
284 Steve Smith AS .01 .05
285 Wayne Gretzky AS .10 .30
286 Luc Robitaille AS .02 .10
287 Tomas Sandstrom AS .01 .05
288 Dave Gagner AS .01 .05
289 Bobby Smith AS .01 .05
290 Brett Hull AS .05 .15
291 Adam Oates AS .01 .05
292 Scott Stevens AS .01 .05
293 Vincent Damphousse AS .01 .05
294 Trevor Linden AS .01 .05
295 Phil Housley AS .01 .05
296 Ray Bourque AS .05 .15
297 Dave Christian AS .01 .05
298 Garry Galley AS .01 .05
299 Andy Moog AS .02 .10
300 Cam Neely AS .02 .10
301 Uwe Krupp AS .01 .05
302 John Cullen AS .01 .05
303 Pat Verbeek AS .01 .05
304 Patrick Roy AS .10 .30
305 Denis Savard AS .01 .05
306 Brian Skrudland AS .01 .05
307 John MacLean AS .01 .05
308 Pat LaFontaine AS .05 .15
309 Brian Leetch AS .02 .10
310 Darren Turcotte AS .01 .05
311 Rick Tocchet AS .01 .05
312 Paul Coffey AS .02 .10
313 Mark Recchi AS .02 .10
314 Kevin Stevens AS .01 .05
315 Joe Sakic AS .05 .15
316 Kevin Hatcher AS .01 .05
317 Guy Lafleur AS .05 .15
318 Mario Lemieux Smythe .10 .30
319 Pittsburgh Penguins .01 .05
Stanley Cup Champs UER
(On fourth line says
won in 5 games& should
say 6 games)
320 Brett Hull .05 .15
Hart Trophy
321 Ed Belfour .05 .15
Vezina/Jennings
322 Ray Bourque .05 .15
Norris
323 Dirk Graham .01 .05
Selke
324 Wayne Gretzky .10 .30
Ross/Lady Byng
325 Dave Taylor .01 .05
King Clancy Trophy
326 Brett Hull .05 .15
PS Player of the Year
327 Brian Hayward .02 .10
328 Neil Wilkinson UER .01 .05
(Born Manitoba
not Minnesota)
329 Craig Coxe .01 .05
330 Rob Zettler .01 .05
331 Jeff Hackett .02 .10
332 Joe Malone .01 .05
333 Georges Vezina .05 .15
334 The Modern Arena .01 .05
335 Ace Bailey Benefit .05 .15
336 Howie Morenz .02 .10
337 The Punch Line .01 .05
338 The Kid Line .01 .05
339 Before the Zamboni .05 .15
340 Bill Barilko .02 .10
341 Jacques Plante .05 .15
342 Arena Designs .01 .05
343 Terry Sawchuk .05 .15
344 Gordie Howe .08 .25
345 Guy Carbonneau .02 .10
Play Smart
346 Stephen Leach .01 .05
347 Peter Douris .01 .05
348 David Reid .01 .05
349 Bob Carpenter .01 .05
350 Stephane Quintal .01 .05
351 Barry Pederson .01 .05
352 Brent Ashton .01 .05
353 Vladimir Ruzicka .01 .05
354 Brad Miller .01 .05
355 Robert Ray .01 .05
356 Colin Patterson .01 .05
357 Gord Donnelly .01 .05
358 Pat LaFontaine .05 .15
359 Randy Wood .01 .05
360 Randy Hillier .01 .05
361 Robert Reichel .01 .05
362 Ronnie Stern .01 .05
363 Ric Nattress .01 .05
364 Tim Sweeney .01 .05
365 Marc Habscheid .01 .05
366 Tim Hunter .01 .05
367 Rick Wamsley .02 .10
368 Frank Musil .01 .05
369 Mike Hudson .01 .05
370 Steve Smith .01 .05
371 Keith Brown .01 .05
372 Greg Gilbert .01 .05
373 John Tonelli .01 .05
374 Brent Sutter .01 .05
375 Brad Lauer .01 .05
376 Alan Kerr .01 .05
377 Brad McCrimmon .01 .05
378 Brad Marsh .01 .05
379 Brent Fedyk .01 .05
380 Ray Sheppard .01 .05
381 Vincent Damphousse .01 .05
382 Craig Muni .01 .05
383 Scott Mellanby .01 .05
384 Geoff Smith .01 .05
385 Kelly Buchberger .01 .05
386 Bernie Nicholls .02 .10
387 Luke Richardson .01 .05
388 Peter Ing .02 .10
389 Dave Manson .01 .05
390 Mark Hunter .01 .05
391 Jim McKenzie .01 .05
392 Randy Cunneyworth .01 .05
393 Murray Craven .01 .05
394 Mikael Andersson .01 .05
395 Andrew Cassels .01 .05
396 Randy Ladouceur .01 .05
397 Marc Bergevin .01 .05
398 Brian Benning .01 .05
399 Mike Donnelly RC .01 .05
400 Charlie Huddy .01 .05
401 John McIntyre .01 .05
402 Jay Miller .01 .05
403 Randy Gilhen .01 .05
404 Stewart Gavin .01 .05
405 Mike Craig .01 .05
406 Brian Glynn .01 .05
407 Rob Ramage .01 .05
408 Chris Dahlquist .01 .05
409 Basil McRae .01 .05
410 Todd Elik .01 .05
411 Craig Ludwig .01 .05
412 Kirk Muller .01 .05
413 Shayne Corson .01 .05
414 Brent Gilchrist .01 .05
415 Mario Roberge .01 .05
416 Sylvain Turgeon .01 .05
417 Alain Cote .01 .05
418 Donald Dufresne .01 .05
419 Todd Ewen .01 .05
420 Stephane Richer .02 .10
421 David Maley .01 .05
422 Randy McKay .01 .05
423 Scott Stevens .02 .10
424 Jon Morris .01 .05
425 Claude Vilgrain .01 .05
426 Laurie Boschman .01 .05
427 Pat Conacher .01 .05
428 Tom Kurvers .01 .05
429 Joe Reekie .01 .05
430 Rob DiMaio .01 .05
431 Tom Fitzgerald .01 .05
432 Ken Baumgartner .01 .05
433 Pierre Turgeon .02 .10
434 Dave McLlwain .01 .05
435 Benoit Hogue .01 .05
436 Uwe Krupp .01 .05
437 Adam Creighton .01 .05
438 Steve Thomas .01 .05
439 Mark Messier .05 .15
440 Tie Domi .01 .05
441 Sergei Nemchinov .01 .05
442 Mark Hardy .01 .05
443 Adam Graves .02 .10
444 Jeff Beukeboom .01 .05
445 Kris King .01 .05
446 Tim Kerr .01 .05
447 John Vanbiesbrouck .02 .10
448 Steve Duchesne .01 .05
449 Steve Kasper .01 .05
450 Ken Wregget .02 .10
451 Kevin Dineen .01 .05
452 Dave Brown .01 .05
453 Rod Brind'Amour .05 .15
454 Jiri Latal .01 .05
455 Tony Horacek .01 .05
456 Brad Jones .01 .05
457 Paul Stanton .01 .05
458 Gordie Roberts .01 .05
459 Ulf Samuelsson .01 .05
460 Ken Priestlay .01 .05
461 Jiri Hrdina .01 .05
462 Mikhail Tatarinov .01 .05
463 Mike Hough .01 .05
464 Don Barber .01 .05
465 Greg Smyth RC .01 .05
466 Jacques Cloutier .01 .05
467 Mike McNeill .01 .05
468 John Kordic .01 .05
469 Greg Paslawski .01 .05
470 Herb Raglan .01 .05
471 Dave Christian .01 .05
472 Murray Baron .01 .05
473 Curtis Joseph .05 .15
474 Rick Zombo .01 .05
475 Brendan Shanahan .05 .15
476 Ron Sutter .01 .05
477 Mario Marois .01 .05
478 Doug Wilson .02 .10
479 Kelly Kisio .01 .05
480 Bob McGill .01 .05
481 Perry Anderson .01 .05
482 Brian Lawton .01 .05
483 Neil Wilkinson .01 .05
484 Ken Hammond RC .01 .05
485 David Bruce RC .01 .05
486 Steve Bozek .01 .05
487 Perry Berezan .01 .05
488 Wayne Presley .01 .05
489 Brian Bradley .01 .05
490 Darryl Shannon .01 .05
491 Lucien DeBlois .01 .05
492 Michel Petit .01 .05
493 Claude Loiselle .01 .05
494 Grant Fuhr .05 .15
495 Craig Berube .01 .05
496 Mike Bullard .01 .05
497 Jim Sandlak .01 .05
498 Dana Murzyn .01 .05
499 Garry Valk .01 .05
500 Andrew McBain .01 .05
501 Kirk McLean .02 .10
502 Gerald Diduck .01 .05
503 Dave Babych .01 .05
504 Ryan Walter .01 .05
505 Gino Odjick .01 .05
506 Dale Hunter .01 .05
507 Tim Bergland .01 .05
508 Alan May .01 .05
509 Jim Hrivnak .02 .10
510 Randy Burridge .01 .05
511 Peter Bondra .02 .10
512 Sylvain Cote .01 .05
513 Nick Kypreos .01 .05
514 Troy Murray .01 .05
515 Darrin Shannon .01 .05
516 Bryan Erickson .01 .05
517 Petri Skriko .01 .05
518 Mike Eagles .01 .05
519 Mike Hartman .01 .05
520 Bob Beers .01 .05
521 Matt DelGuidice RC .01 .05
522 Chris Winnes .01 .05
523 Brad May .01 .05
524 Donald Audette .01 .05
525 Kevin Haller RC .01 .05
526 Martin Simard .01 .05
527 Tomas Forslund RC .01 .05
528 Mark Osiecki .01 .05
529 Dominik Hasek RC .60 1.50
530 Jimmy Waite .02 .10
531 Nicklas Lidstrom RC .30 .75
532 Martin Lapointe .02 .10
533 Vladimir Konstantinov RC .15 .40
534 Josef Beranek RC .01 .05
535 Louie DeBrusk RC .01 .05
536 Geoff Sanderson RC .02 .10
537 Mark Greig .01 .05
538 Michel Picard RC .01 .05
539 Chris Tancill RC .01 .05
540 Peter Ahola RC .01 .05
541 Francois Breault .01 .05
542 Darryl Sydor .02 .10
543 Derian Hatcher .02 .10
544 Marc Bureau .01 .05
545 John LeClair RC .30 .75
546 Paul DiPietro RC .01 .05
547 Scott Niedermayer UER .01 .05
(Misspelled on front
as Neidermayer)
548 Kevin Todd RC .01 .05
549 Doug Weight RC .25 .60
550 Tony Amonte RC .30 .75
551 Corey Foster RC .01 .05
552 Dominic Roussel RC .02 .10
553 Dan Kordic RC .01 .05
554 Jim Paek RC .01 .05
555 Kip Miller .01 .05
556 Claude Lapointe RC .01 .05
557 Nelson Emerson .01 .05
558 Pat Falloon .01 .05
559 Pat MacLeod RC .01 .05
560 Rick Lessard RC .01 .05
561 Link Gaetz .01 .05
562 Rob Pearson RC .01 .05
563 Alexander Godynyuk RC .01 .05
564 Pavel Bure .05 .15
565 Russell Romaniuk RC .01 .05
566 Stu Barnes .01 .05
567 Ray Bourque CAP .05 .15
568 Mike Ramsey CAP .01 .05
569 Joe Nieuwendyk CAP .01 .05
570 Dirk Graham CAP .01 .05
571 Steve Yzerman CAP .10 .30
572 Kevin Lowe CAP .01 .05
573 Randy Ladouceur CAP .01 .05
574 Wayne Gretzky CAP .10 .30
575 Mark Tinordi CAP .01 .05
576 Guy Carbonneau CAP .02 .10
577 Bruce Driver CAP .01 .05
578 Pat Flatley CAP .01 .05
579 Mark Messier CAP .05 .15
580 Rick Tocchet CAP .01 .05
581 Mario Lemieux CAP .10 .30
582 Mike Hough CAP .01 .05
583 Garth Butcher CAP .01 .05
584 Doug Wilson CAP .01 .05
585 Wendel Clark CAP .02 .10
586 Trevor Linden CAP .01 .05
587 Rod Langway CAP .01 .05
588 Troy Murray CAP .01 .05
589 Practicing Outdoors .01 .05
590 Shape Up .01 .05
591 Boston Bruins Cartoon .01 .05

592 Opening Night .01 .05
593 Rod Gilbert .01 .05
594 Phil Esposito .05 .15
595 Dale Tallon .01 .05
596 Gilbert Perreault .01 .05
597 Bernie Federko .01 .05
598 All-Star Game .02 .10
599 Patrick Roy LL .10 .30
600 Ed Belfour LL .05 .15
601 Don Beaupre LL .01 .05
602 Bob Essensa LL .01 .05
603 Kirk McLean UER LL .02 .10
(Leader logo shows
PPG should be GAA)
604 Mike Gartner LL .01 .05
605 Jeremy Roenick LL .05 .15
606 Rob Brown LL .01 .05
607 Ulf Dahlen LL .01 .05
608 Paul Ysebaert LL .01 .05
609 Brad McCrimmon LL .01 .05
610 Nicklas Lidstrom LL .10 .30
611 Kelly Miller LL .01 .05
612 Jim Kyte SMART .01 .05
613 Patrick Roy SMART .10 .30
614 Alan May SMART .01 .05
615 Kelly Miller SMART .01 .05
AU125 Patrick Roy AU/1000 100.00 200.00
AU501 Kirk McLean AU/500 15.00 30.00
AU599 Patrick Roy LL AU/1000 50.00 125.00
NNO 75th Anniv.HOLO/10,000 20.00 50.00

1991-92 Pro Set French

COMPLETE SET (615) 6.00 15.00
COMP.SERIES 1 (345) 3.00 8.00
COMP.SERIES 2 (270) 3.00 8.00
*FRENCH: .4X TO 1X BASIC PRO SET

1991-92 Pro Set CC

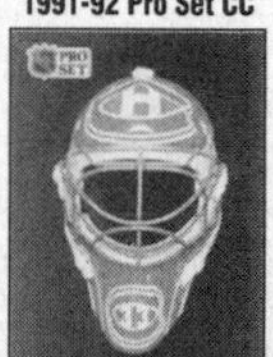

These standard-size cards were issued as random inserts in French and English Pro Set 15-card foil packs. The first four were in the first series and the last five were inserted in with the second series. The Pat Falloon and Scott Niedermayer cards were withdrawn early in the first series print run. This was due to the cards being released prior to the players having appeared in an NHL game; a contravention of licensing regulations. The cards are numbered on the back with a "CC" prefix.

COMPLETE SET (9) 6.00 15.00
*FRENCH: .5X TO 1.2X BASIC INSERTS
CC1 Entry Draft .40 1.00
CC2 The Mask 1.00 2.50
CC3 Pat Falloon UER SP 1.25 3.00
(Born Birtle&
not Foxwarren)
CC4 Scott Niedermayer SP 2.00 5.00
CC5 Wayne Gretzky 2.00 5.00
CC6 Brett Hull .60 1.50
CC7 Adam Oates .50 1.25
CC8 Mark Recchi .60 1.50
CC9 John Cullen .40 1.00

1991-92 Pro Set Gazette

These standard-size cards were issued in cello packs. The front of card number 2 had the words "Pro Set Gazette" in the upper left corner and the player's name in a blue stripe near the bottom of the card. The SC1 Roy card has his name appearing in a red stripe at the bottom with the words "Goalie of the Year" in a blue stripe. The card is numbered "Special Collectible 1" on the back.

COMPLETE SET (2) 2.00 5.00
2 Patrick Roy 1.25 3.00
(Gazette Collectible)
SC1 Patrick Roy 1.25 3.00
(Special Collectible 1)

1991-92 Pro Set HOF Induction

This 14-card set was issued by Pro Set to commemorate the 1991 Hockey Hall of Fame Induction Dinner and Ceremonies in September, 1991 held in Ottawa. The standard-size cards feature borderless glossy sepia-toned player or team photos on the fronts. A colorful insignia with the words "Hockey Hall of Fame and Museum" appears on the front of each card. The team cards represent the past Ottawa Stanley Cup winning teams.

COMPLETE SET (14) 30.00 75.00
1 Mike Bossy 6.00 15.00
1991 HOF Inductee
2 Denis Potvin 5.00 12.00
1991 HOF Inductee
3 Bob Pulford 3.00 8.00
1991 HOF Inductee
4 William Scott Bowman 6.00 15.00
1991 HOF Inductee
5 Neil P. Armstrong 2.50 6.00
1991 HOF Inductee
6 Clint Smith 2.50 6.00
1991 HOF Inductee
7 1903-04 Ottawa Silver 2.00 5.00
Seven
8 1905 Ottawa Silver 2.00 5.00
Seven
9 1909 Ottawa Senators 2.00 5.00
10 1911 Ottawa Senators 2.00 5.00
11 1920-21 Ottawa 2.00 5.00
Senators
12 1923 Ottawa Senators 2.00 5.00
13 1927 Ottawa Senators 2.00 5.00
14 Title Card 2.00 5.00
1991 Hockey Hall of Fame
Dinner and Ceremonies

1991-92 Pro Set Awards Special

This 17-card standard-size set features NHL players who were All-Stars, nominees, or winners of prestigious trophies. The fronts feature a borderless color action photo, with the team logo in the lower left corner, and the player's name in the black wedge below the logo. The backs present player information and the award which the player won or was nominated for, on a white and gray hockey puck background. The cards are numbered on the back and also have a star logo with the words "A Celebration of Excellence". The cards have the 1991-92 Pro Set style of design.

AC1 Ed Belfour 12.00 30.00
AC2 Mike Richter 12.00 30.00
AC3 Patrick Roy 75.00 200.00
AC4 Wayne Gretzky 125.00 300.00
AC5 Joe Sakic 30.00 75.00
AC6 Brett Hull 25.00 60.00
AC7 Ray Bourque 25.00 60.00
AC8 Al MacInnis 6.00 15.00
AC9 Luc Robitaille 10.00 25.00
AC10 Sergei Fedorov 40.00 100.00
AC11 Ken Hodge Jr. .75 2.00
AC12 Dirk Graham .75 2.00
AC13 Steve Larmer 2.00 5.00
AC14 Esa Tikkanen 4.00 10.00
AC15 Chris Chelios 15.00 40.00
AC16 Dave Taylor 1.50 4.00
NNO Title Card .40 1.00

1991-92 Pro Set NHL Sponsor Awards

This eight-card standard-size set is numbered as an extension of the 1991-92 Pro Set NHL Awards Special. The cards feature the same glossy color player photos as does the regular issue. The fronts differ in having the name of the award inscribed across the bottom of the card face. Also the backs differ in that they omit the head and shoulders photo and have only a player profile. The cards were distributed at The Hockey News Sponsor Awards luncheon in Toronto on June 6, 1991.

AC17 Kevin Dineen 2.50 6.00
Bud Light/NHL Man
of the Year Award
AC18 Brett Hull 25.00 60.00
NHL Pro Set Player
of the Year Award
AC19 Ed Belfour 10.00 25.00
Trico Goaltender Award
AC20 Theo Fleury 10.00 25.00
Alka-Seltzer
Plus Award
AC21 Marty McSorley 2.50 6.00
Alka-Seltzer
Plus Award
AC22 Mike Ilitch 1.50 4.00
Detroit Red Wings OWN
Lester Patrick Award
AC23 Rod Gilbert 2.50 6.00
Lester Patrick Award
NNO Title Card .40 1.00
1990-91 NHL
Sponsor Awards

1991-92 Pro Set Opening Night

This six-card promo set was issued by Pro Set to commemorate the opening night of the 1991-92 NHL season. The standard-size player cards are the same as the regular issue, with borderless glossy color player photos on the fronts, and a color headshot and player information on the backs. Four (different each time) regular issue cards were included in each promo pack.

COMPLETE SET (2) 3.00 8.00
NNO NHL 75th Anniversary 1.50 4.00
Opening Night
NNO 1991-92 Opening Night 1.50 4.00

1991-92 Pro Set Platinum

The 1991-92 Pro Set Platinum hockey set was released in two series of 150 standard-size cards. The front design features full-bleed glossy color action player photos, with the Pro Set Platinum icon superimposed at the lower right corner. Player names do not appear on the front.

COMPLETE SET (300) 3.00 8.00
COMP.SERIES 1 (150) 1.50 4.00
COMP.SERIES 2 (150) 1.50 4.00
1 Cam Neely .07 .20
2 Ray Bourque .15 .40
3 Craig Janney .02 .10
4 Andy Moog .07 .20
5 Dave Poulin .01 .05
6 Ken Hodge Jr. .01 .05
7 Glen Wesley .01 .05
8 Dave Andreychuk .02 .10
9 Daren Puppa .02 .10
10 Pierre Turgeon .02 .10
11 Dale Hawerchuk .02 .10
12 Doug Bodger .01 .05
13 Mike Ramsey .01 .05
14 Alexander Mogilny .07 .20
15 Sergei Makarov .01 .05
16 Theo Fleury .01 .05
17 Joel Otto .01 .05
18 Joe Nieuwendyk .02 .10
19 Al MacInnis .02 .10
20 Gary Suter .01 .05
21 Mike Vernon .02 .10
22 John Tonelli .01 .05
23 Dirk Graham .01 .05
24 Jeremy Roenick .15 .40
25 Chris Chelios .07 .20
26 Ed Belfour .20 .50
27 Steve Smith .01 .05
28 Steve Larmer .02 .10
29 Johan Garpenlov .01 .05
30 Sergei Fedorov .15 .40
31 Tim Cheveldae .02 .10
32 Steve Yzerman .40 1.00
33 Jimmy Carson .01 .05
34 Bob Probert .02 .10
35 Vincent Damphousse .02 .10
36 Bill Ranford .02 .10
37 Petr Klima .01 .05
38 Kevin Lowe .02 .10
39 Esa Tikkanen .01 .05
40 Craig Simpson .01 .05
41 Peter Ing .01 .05
42 Rob Brown .01 .05
43 Bobby Holik .02 .10
44 Pat Verbeek .01 .05
45 Brad Shaw .01 .05
46 Kevin Dineen .01 .05
47 Zarley Zalapski .01 .05
48 Jari Kurri .07 .20
49 Tony Granato .01 .05
50 Luc Robitaille .02 .10
51 Rob Blake .02 .10
52 Wayne Gretzky .50 1.25
53 Tomas Sandstrom .01 .05
54 Kelly Hrudey .02 .10
55 Mike Modano .20 .50
56 Jon Casey .02 .10
57 Todd Elik .01 .05
58 Mark Tinordi .01 .05
59 Brian Bellows .01 .05
60 Dave Gagner .01 .05
61 Patrick Roy .40 1.00
62 Russ Courtnall .01 .05
63 Guy Carbonneau .02 .10
64 Stephan Lebeau .01 .05
65 Petr Svoboda .01 .05
66 Kirk Muller .01 .05
67 Stephane Richer .02 .10
68 Chris Terreri .02 .10
69 Bruce Driver .01 .05
70 John MacLean .02 .10
71 Patrik Sundstrom .01 .05
72 Scott Stevens .02 .10
73 Glenn Healy .02 .10
74 Brent Sutter .01 .05
75 David Volek .01 .05
76 Ray Ferraro .01 .05
77 Pat Flatley .01 .05
78 Jeff Norton .01 .05
79 Brian Leetch .07 .20
80 Tim Kerr .01 .05
81 Mark Messier .07 .20
82 James Patrick .01 .05
83 Mike Richter .07 .20
84 Mike Gartner .07 .20
85 Mike Ricci .07 .20
86 Steve Duchesne .01 .05
87 Ron Hextall .02 .10
88 Rick Tocchet .02 .10
89 Pelle Eklund .01 .05
90 Rod Brind'Amour .02 .10
91 Mario Lemieux .40 1.00
92 Jaromir Jagr .15 .40
93 Kevin Stevens .01 .05
94 Paul Coffey .07 .20
95 Ulf Samuelsson .01 .05
96 Tom Barrasso .02 .10
97 Mark Recchi .07 .20
98 Ron Tugnutt .02 .10
99 Mats Sundin .07 .20
100 Stephane Morin .01 .05
101 Owen Nolan .07 .20
102 Joe Sakic .20 .50
103 Bryan Fogarty .01 .05
104 Kelly Kisio .01 .05
105 Tony Hrkac .01 .05
106 Brian Mullen .01 .05
107 Doug Wilson .02 .10
108 Rich Sutter .01 .05
109 Brett Hull .15 .40
110 Dave Christian .01 .05
111 Brendan Shanahan .07 .20
112 Vincent Riendeau .02 .10
113 Adam Oates .07 .20
114 Jeff Brown .01 .05
115 Gary Leeman .01 .05
116 Dave Ellett .01 .05
117 Grant Fuhr .07 .20
118 Daniel Marois .01 .05
119 Mike Krushelnyski .01 .05
120 Wendel Clark .02 .10
121 Troy Gamble .02 .10
122 Robert Kron .01 .05
123 Geoff Courtnall .02 .10
124 Trevor Linden .02 .10
125 Greg Adams .01 .05
126 Igor Larionov .01 .05
127 Kevin Hatcher .02 .10
128 Mike Ridley .02 .10
129 John Druce .01 .05
130 Al Iafrate .02 .10
131 Dino Ciccarelli .02 .10
132 Michal Pivonka .01 .05
133 Fredrik Olausson .01 .05
134 Ed Olczyk .01 .05
135 Bob Essensa .02 .10
136 Pat Elynuik .01 .05
137 Phil Housley .02 .10
138 Thomas Steen .01 .05
139 Don Beaupre .02 .10
140 Boston Bruins .01 .05
141 Chicago Blackhawks .01 .05
142 Los Angeles Kings .01 .05
143 Minnesota North Stars .01 .05
144 Pittsburgh Penguins .01 .05
145 Boston Bruins .01 .05
146 Chicago Blackhawks .01 .05
147 Detroit Red Wings .01 .05
148 Montreal Canadiens .01 .05
149 New York Rangers .01 .05
150 Toronto Maple Leafs .01 .05
151 Stephen Leach .01 .05
152 Vladimir Ruzicka .01 .05
153 Don Sweeney .01 .05
154 Bob Carpenter .01 .05
155 Brent Ashton .01 .05
156 Gord Murphy .01 .05
157 Pat LaFontaine .07 .20
158 Randy Hillier .01 .05
159 Clint Malarchuk .02 .10
160 Randy Wood .01 .05
161 Gary Roberts .02 .10
162 Gary Leeman .01 .05
163 Robert Reichel .01 .05
164 Brent Sutter .01 .05
165 Brian Noonan .01 .05
166 Michel Goulet UER .01 .05
(Prospect on front)
167 Paul Ysebaert .01 .05
168 Kevin Miller .01 .05
169 Ray Sheppard .01 .05
170 Brad McCrimmon .01 .05
171 Joe Murphy .01 .05
172 Dave Manson .01 .05
173 Scott Mellanby .01 .05
174 Bernie Nicholls .02 .10
175 John Cullen .01 .05
176 Marc Bergevin .01 .05
177 Steve Konroyd .01 .05
178 Kay Whitmore .02 .10
179 Murray Craven .01 .05
180 Mikael Andersson .01 .05
181 Bob Kudelski .01 .05
182 Brian Benning .01 .05
183 Mike Donnelly .01 .05
184 Marty McSorley .01 .05
185 Corey Millen RC .01 .05
186 Ulf Dahlen .01 .05
187 Brian Propp .01 .05
188 Neal Broten .02 .10
189 Mike Craig .01 .05
190 Stephan Lebeau .01 .05
191 Mike Keane .01 .05
192 Brent Gilchrist .01 .05
193 Eric Desjardins .02 .10
194 Peter Stastny .01 .05
195 Claude Vilgrain .01 .05
196 Claude Lemieux .01 .05
197 Craig Billington RC .02 .10
198 Alexei Kasatonov .01 .05
199 Slava Fetisov .01 .05
200 Benoit Hogue .01 .05
201 Derek King .01 .05
202 Uwe Krupp .01 .05
203 Steve Thomas .01 .05
204 John Ogrodnick .01 .05
205 Sergei Nemchinov .01 .05
206 Jeff Beukeboom .01 .05
207 Adam Graves .02 .10
208 Andrei Lomakin .01 .05
209 Dan Quinn .01 .05
210 Ken Wregget .02 .10
211 Garry Galley .01 .05
212 Terry Carkner .01 .05
213 Larry Murphy .02 .10
214 Ron Francis .02 .10
215 Bob Errey .01 .05
216 Bryan Trottier .07 .20
217 Mike Hough .01 .05
218 Mikhail Tatarinov .01 .05
219 Jacques Cloutier .02 .10
220 Greg Paslawski .01 .05
221 Alexei Gusarov RC .02 .10
222 Ron Sutter .01 .05
223 Garth Butcher .01 .05
224 Paul Cavallini .01 .05
225 Curtis Joseph .07 .20
226 Jeff Hackett .02 .10
227 David Bruce RC .01 .05
228 Wayne Presley .01 .05
229 Neil Wilkinson .01 .05
230 Dean Evason .01 .05
231 Brian Bradley .01 .05
232 Peter Zezel .01 .05
233 Mike Bullard .01 .05
234 Doug Gilmour .02 .10
235 Jamie Macoun .01 .05
236 Cliff Ronning .01 .05
237 Jyrki Lumme .01 .05
238 Tom Fergus .01 .05
239 Kirk McLean .02 .10
240 Sergio Momesso .01 .05
241 Randy Burridge .01 .05
242 Dimitri Khristich .01 .05
243 Calle Johansson .01 .05
244 Peter Bondra .02 .10
245 Dale Hunter .01 .05
246 Darrin Shannon .01 .05
247 Troy Murray .01 .05
248 Teppo Numminen .01 .05
249 Donald Audette .01 .05
250 Kevin Haller RC .01 .05
251 Alexander Godynyuk .01 .05
252 Dominik Hasek RC 1.00 2.50
253 Nicklas Lidstrom RC .50 1.25
254 Vladimir Konstantinov RC .25 .60
255 Josef Beranek RC .02 .10
256 Geoff Sanderson RC .02 .10
257 Peter Ahola RC .01 .05
258 Derian Hatcher .02 .10
259 John LeClair RC .50 1.25
260 Kevin Todd RC .01 .05
261 Valeri Zelepukin RC .01 .05
262 Tony Amonte RC .50 1.25
263 Doug Weight RC .40 1.00
264 Claude Boivin RC .01 .05
265 Corey Foster RC .01 .05
266 Jim Paek RC .01 .05
267 Claude Lapointe RC .01 .05
268 Adam Foote RC .08 .25
269 Nelson Emerson .01 .05
270 Arturs Irbe .07 .20
271 Pat Falloon .01 .05
272 Pavel Bure .07 .20
273 Stu Barnes .01 .05
274 Russ Romaniuk RC .01 .05
275 Luciano Borsato RC .01 .05
276 Al MacInnis AS .01 .05
277 Sergei Fedorov AS .07 .20
278 Ray Bourque AS .07 .20
279 Mike Richter AS .02 .10
280 Campbell Conference .01 .05
281 Wales Conference .01 .05
282 Brett Hull PP .07 .20
283 Alexander Mogilny PP .02 .10
284 Brian Leetch PP .02 .10
285 Bob Essensa PP .01 .05
286 Derek King PP .01 .05
287 Steve Larmer PP .01 .05
288 Chris Terreri PP .02 .10
289 Terry O'Reilly CAP .01 .05
290 Burton Cummings CAP .01 .05
291 Marv Albert CAP .01 .05
292 Larry King CAP .01 .05
293 Jim Kelly CAP .07 .20
294 David Wheaton CAP .01 .05
295 Ralph Macchio CAP .01 .05
296 Rick Hansen CAP .01 .05
297 Fred Rogers CAP .01 .05
298 Gaetan Boucher CAP .01 .05
299 Susan Saint James CAP .01 .05
300 James Belushi CAP .01 .05

1991-92 Pro Set Platinum PC

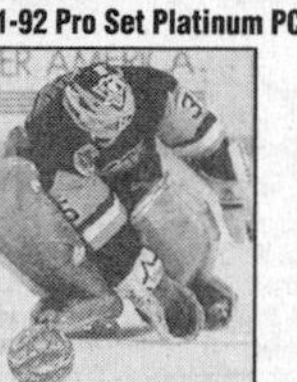

The 1991-92 Pro Set Platinum PC set consists of 20 standard size cards randomly inserted in Platinum foil packs. The first series inserts were a ten-card Platinum Collectibles subset featuring Players of the Month (PC1-PC6) and Sensational Sophomores (PC7-PC10). The second series inserts were subtitled Platinum Milestones (PC11-PC20).

COMPLETE SET (20) 12.50 25.00
PC1 John Vanbiesbrouck .50 1.25
PC2 Pete Peeters .30 .75
PC3 Tom Barrasso .30 .75
PC4 Wayne Gretzky 2.00 5.00
PC5 Brett Hull .75 2.00
PC6 Kelly Hrudey .30 .75
PC7 Sergei Fedorov .75 2.00
PC8 Rob Blake .30 .75
PC9 Ken Hodge Jr. .20 .50
PC10 Eric Weinrich .20 .50
PC11 Mike Gartner .30 .75
PC12 Paul Coffey .50 1.25
PC13 Bobby Smith .30 .75
PC14 Wayne Gretzky 2.00 5.00
PC15 Michel Goulet .40 1.00
PC16 Mike Liut .30 .75
PC17 Brian Propp .20 .50
PC18 Denis Savard .30 .75
PC19 Bryan Trottier .40 1.00
PC20 Mark Messier .60 1.50

1991-92 Pro Set Platinum HOF 75th

This eight-card standard-size set was issued in a cello pack to pay tribute to the NHL's 75th Anniversary. The set includes the Original Six team cards (indistinguishable from cards 145-150 in the regular set) from the 1991-92 Pro Set Platinum hockey set and two special cards. The Hockey Hall of Fame Collectible features on the front a full-bleed sepia-toned picture of Exhibition Place, where the Hockey Hall of Fame has been located since 1961. In addition to commentary, the back features a small color picture of BCE Place, its new location beginning in the fall of 1992. On a black background, the title card features the Hockey Hall of Fame and Museum logo at the top as well as the NHL and Pro Set logos at the bottom. The title card has a blank back. The actual numbering of the cards is reflected in the listing below.

COMPLETE SET (8) 3.00 8.00
145 Boston Bruins .02 .10
146 Chicago Blackhawks .02 .10
147 Detroit Red Wings .02 .10
148 Montreal Canadiens .02 .10
149 New York Rangers .02 .10
150 Toronto Maple Leafs .02 .10
NNO Title Card 1.25 3.00
(Blank back)
HHOF1 Hockey Hall of Fame 2.00 5.00
Collectible; Excellence,
Education, Entertainment
(Pictures the opening
of the Hall of Fame
in 1961 in Toronto)

1991-92 Pro Set Player of the Month

This six-card set was issued by Pro Set to honor hockey players for their outstanding performances during the season. The cards were distributed to all ticket holders at home games the evening of the presentation. Another feature of the presentation was a $1200 donation on behalf of the winning player to the youth hockey organization of his choice. Measuring the standard 2 1/2" by 3 1/2", card fronts feature borderless four-color action photographs. The player's team emblem appears in the lower left corner while the player's name is reversed-out white in a black wedge. On a screened hockey puck design, the horizontally oriented backs have a head shot in a circular format, biography, career statistics, and a summary of the outstanding achievement. The card number and team position appears in the upper right corner.

COMPLETE SET (6) 28.00 70.00
P1 Kirk McLean 2.00 5.00
POM October 1991
(Issued 11/19/91)
P2 Kevin Stevens 2.00 5.00
POM November 1991
(Issued 12/26/91)
P3 Mario Lemieux 12.00 30.00
Pittsburg
P4 Andy Moog 4.00 10.00
POM January 1991
P5 Pat LaFontaine 4.00 10.00
POM January 1991
P6 Luc Robitaille 4.00 10.00
POM February 1991

1991-92 Pro Set Puck Candy Promos

This set of three standard-size hockey cards was distributed in a cello pack to show the design of the upcoming Puck cards. The fronts of the promos are identical to the regular issue. Their backs differ in two respects: 1) instead of a card number, the promos have the words "Prototype For Review Only" in an aqua box; and 2) The "Puck Note" on the promos differs from that found on the regular cards. The cards are unnumbered and checklisted below in alphabetical order.

COMPLETE SET (3) 1.50 4.00
1 Kirk McLean .40 1.00
2 Andy Moog .75 2.00
3 Pat Verbeek .40 1.00

1991-92 Pro Set Puck Candy

This set of thirty standard-size hockey cards was created for a new product, the NHL Pro Set Puck, a combination chocolate, peanut vanilla nougat, and caramel confection. This test product was available in all U.S. NHL and Northeast markets, and each candy package contained three Puck hockey cards. The fronts feature a borderless four-color action player photo with the Pro Set logo and player's name in the bottom border. The horizontally oriented backs have a head shot, biography, and a "Puck Note" that consists of personal information about the player. Pro Set advertised this 30-card set as Series 1; however no Series 2 was ever issued.

COMPLETE SET (30) 16.00 40.00
1 Ray Bourque .75 2.00
2 Andy Moog .30 .75
3 Doug Bodger .15 .40
4 Theo Fleury .30 .75
5 Al MacInnis .30 .75
6 Jeremy Roenick .60 1.50
7 Tim Cheveldae .15 .40
8 Steve Yzerman 1.50 4.00
9 Craig Simpson .15 .40
10 Pat Verbeek .15 .40
11 Wayne Gretzky 15.00 40.00
12 Luc Robitaille .30 .75
13 Brian Bellows .15 .40
14 Patrick Roy 3.00 8.00
15 Guy Carbonneau .15 .40
16 Peter Stastny .30 .75
17 Adam Creighton .15 .40
18 Glenn Healy .30 .75
19 Mark Messier .75 2.00
20 Rod Brind'Amour .30 .75
21 Paul Coffey .60 1.50
22 Tom Barrasso .30 .75
23 Joe Sakic 1.25 3.00
24 Brett Hull .75 2.00
25 Adam Oates .30 .75
26 Kelly Kisio .15 .40
27 Grant Fuhr .30 .75
28 Kirk McLean .30 .75
29 Kevin Hatcher .15 .40
30 Phil Housley .15 .40

1991-92 Pro Set Rink Rat

These standard-size cards were produced by Pro Set to promote education. On card number 2 the front cartoon portrays the Rink Rat shooting the puck through a defenseman's legs right toward the viewer of the card; on a screen design with miniature hockey pucks, the horizontally oriented back has another circular-shaped cartoon picture of the Rink Rat reading and a "stay in school/study hard" message.

COMPLETE SET (2) 3.00 8.00
RR1 Rink Rat 1.50 4.00
(Holding stick over
head; copyright 1991)
RR2 Rink Rat 1.50 4.00
(Shooting puck)

1991-92 Pro Set St. Louis Midwest

This four-card standard-size set was available at the Midwest Sports Collectors Show in St. Louis in November 1991. The cards were a special issue for the card show; in fact, Pro Set did not even issue a Meagher card in its regular set. All four cards show explicitly on the front that they were a special issue from this show. The fronts of these cards differ from the regular issue in two respects: 1) a royal blue border stripe runs the length of the card on the right side; and 2) the cards are numbered in the stripe "X of Four Midwest Collectors Show". The card backs are the same as the regular issue cards.

COMPLETE SET (4) 4.00 10.00
1 Adam Oates 1.25 3.00
2 Paul Cavallini .40 1.00
3 Rick Meagher .40 1.00
4 Brett Hull 3.00 8.00

1992-93 Pro Set

The 1992-93 Pro Set hockey set consists of 270 cards. The production run was 8,000 numbered 20-box foil cases and 2,000 20-box jumbo cases. One thousand Kirk McLean autographed cards were randomly inserted. The McLean cards have No. 239 on the back; his regular card is #193. The most noteworthy Rookie Card in the set is Bill Guerin.

COMPLETE SET (270) 5.00 15.00
1 Mario Lemieux PS-POY .20 .50
2 Patrick Roy .20 .50
Hockey News POY
3 Adam Oates .02 .10
4 Ray Bourque .15 .40
5 Vladimir Ruzicka .01 .05
6 Stephen Leach .01 .05
7 Andy Moog .08 .25
8 Cam Neely .08 .25
9 Dave Poulin .01 .05
10 Glen Wesley .01 .05
11 Gord Murphy .01 .05
12 Dale Hawerchuk .02 .10
13 Pat LaFontaine .08 .25
14 Tom Draper .01 .05
15 Dave Andreychuk .02 .10
16 Petr Svoboda .01 .05
17 Doug Bodger .01 .05
18 Donald Audette .01 .05
19 Alexander Mogilny .02 .10
20 Randy Wood .01 .05
21 Gary Roberts .01 .05
22 Al MacInnis .02 .10
23 Theo Fleury .01 .05
24 Sergei Makarov .01 .05
25 Mike Vernon .02 .10
26 Joe Nieuwendyk .02 .10
27 Gary Suter .01 .05
28 Joel Otto .01 .05
29 Paul Ranheim .01 .05
30 Jeremy Roenick .10 .30
31 Steve Larmer .02 .10
32 Michel Goulet .02 .10
33 Ed Belfour .08 .25
34 Chris Chelios .08 .25
35 Igor Kravchuk .01 .05
36 Brent Sutter .01 .05
37 Steve Smith .01 .05
38 Dirk Graham .01 .05
39 Steve Yzerman .40 1.00
40 Sergei Fedorov .10 .30
41 Paul Ysebaert .01 .05
42 Nicklas Lidstrom .08 .25
43 Tim Cheveldae .02 .10
44 Vladimir Konstantinov .08 .25
45 Shawn Burr .01 .05
46 Bob Probert .02 .10
47 Ray Sheppard .01 .05
48 Kelly Buchberger .01 .05
49 Joe Murphy .01 .05
50 Norm Maciver .01 .05
51 Bill Ranford .02 .10
52 Bernie Nicholls .02 .10
53 Esa Tikkanen .01 .05
54 Scott Mellanby .01 .05
55 Dave Manson .01 .05
56 Craig Simpson .01 .05
57 John Cullen .01 .05
58 Pat Verbeek .01 .05
59 Zarley Zalapski .01 .05
60 Murray Craven .01 .05
61 Bobby Holik .02 .10
62 Steve Konroyd .01 .05
63 Geoff Sanderson .02 .10
64 Frank Pietrangelo .01 .05
65 Mikael Andersson UER .01 .05
66 Wayne Gretzky .50 1.25
67 Rob Blake .02 .10
68 Jari Kurri .08 .25
69 Marty McSorley .01 .05
70 Kelly Hrudey .02 .10
71 Paul Coffey .08 .25
72 Luc Robitaille .02 .10
73 Peter Ahola .01 .05
74 Tony Granato .01 .05
75 Derian Hatcher .01 .05
76 Mike Modano .15 .40
77 Dave Gagner .02 .10
78 Mark Tinordi .01 .05
79 Craig Ludwig .01 .05
80 Ulf Dahlen .01 .05
81 Bobby Smith .02 .10
82 Jon Casey .02 .10
83 Jim Johnson .01 .05
84 Denis Savard .02 .10
85 Patrick Roy .40 1.00
86 Eric Desjardins .02 .10
87 Kirk Muller .01 .05
88 Guy Carbonneau .02 .10
89 Shayne Corson .01 .05
90 Brent Gilchrist .01 .05
91 Mathieu Schneider UER .01 .05
92 Gilbert Dionne .01 .05
93 Stephane Richer .02 .10
94 Kevin Todd .01 .05
95 Scott Stevens .02 .10
96 Slava Fetisov .01 .05
97 Chris Terreri .02 .10
98 Claude Lemieux .01 .05
99 Bruce Driver .01 .05
100 Peter Stastny .02 .10
101 Alexei Kasatonov .01 .05

102 Patrick Flatley	.01	.05
103 Adam Creighton UER	.01	.05
104 Pierre Turgeon	.02	.10
105 Ray Ferraro	.01	.05
106 Steve Thomas	.02	.10
107 Mark Fitzpatrick	.02	.10
108 Benoit Hogue	.01	.05
109 Uwe Krupp	.01	.05
110 Derek King	.01	.05
111 Mark Messier	.08	.25
112 Brian Leetch	.08	.25
113 Mike Gartner	.02	.10
114 Darren Turcotte	.01	.05
115 Adam Graves	.01	.05
116 Mike Richter	.08	.25
117 Sergei Nemchinov	.01	.05
118 Tony Amonte	.02	.10
119 James Patrick	.01	.05
120 Andrew McBain	.01	.05
121 Rob Murphy	.01	.05
122 Mike Peluso	.01	.05
123 Sylvain Turgeon	.01	.05
124 Brad Shaw	.01	.05
125 Peter Sidorkiewicz	.02	.10
126 Brad Marsh	.01	.05
127 Mark Freer	.01	.05
128 Marc Fortier	.01	.05
129 Ron Hextall	.02	.10
130 Claude Boivin	.01	.05
131 Mark Recchi	.02	.10
132 Rod Brind'Amour	.02	.10
133 Mike Ricci	.02	.10
134 Kevin Dineen	.01	.05
135 Brian Benning	.01	.05
136 Kerry Huffman	.01	.05
137 Steve Duchesne	.01	.05
138 Rick Tocchet	.02	.10
139 Mario Lemieux	.40	1.00
140 Kevin Stevens	.01	.05
141 Jaromir Jagr	.10	.30
142 Joe Mullen	.02	.10
143 Ulf Samuelsson	.01	.05
144 Ron Francis	.02	.10
145 Tom Barrasso	.02	.10
146 Larry Murphy	.02	.10
147 Alexei Gusarov	.01	.05
148 Valeri Kamensky	.01	.05
149 Mats Sundin	.08	.25
150 Joe Sakic	.15	.40
151 Claude Lapointe	.01	.05
152 Stephane Fiset	.02	.10
153 Owen Nolan	.02	.10
154 Mike Hough	.01	.05
155 Greg Paslawski	.01	.05
156 Brett Hull	.10	.30
157 Craig Janney	.02	.10
158 Jeff Brown	.01	.05
159 Paul Cavallini	.01	.05
160 Garth Butcher	.01	.05
161 Nelson Emerson	.01	.05
162 Ron Sutter	.01	.05
163 Brendan Shanahan	.08	.25
164 Curtis Joseph	.08	.25
165 Doug Wilson	.02	.10
166 Pat Falloon	.01	.05
167 Kelly Kisio	.01	.05
168 Neil Wilkinson	.01	.05
169 Jay More	.01	.05
170 David Bruce	.01	.05
171 Jeff Hackett	.02	.10
172 David Williams RC	.01	.05
173 Brian Lawton	.01	.05
174 Brian Bradley	.01	.05
175 Jock Callander RC	.01	.05
176 Basil McRae	.01	.05
177 Rob Ramage	.01	.05
178 Pat Jablonski	.02	.10
179 Joe Reekie	.01	.05
180 Doug Crossman	.01	.05
181 Jim Benning	.01	.05
182 Ken Hodge Jr.	.01	.05
183 Grant Fuhr	.08	.25
184 Doug Gilmour	.02	.10
185 Glenn Anderson	.02	.10
186 Dave Ellett	.01	.05
187 Peter Zezel	.01	.05
188 Jamie Macoun	.01	.05
189 Wendel Clark	.02	.10
190 Bob Halkidis	.01	.05
191 Rob Pearson	.01	.05
192 Pavel Bure	.08	.25
193 Kirk McLean	.02	.10
194 Sergio Momesso	.01	.05
195 Cliff Ronning	.01	.05
196 Jyrki Lumme	.01	.05
197 Trevor Linden	.02	.10
198 Geoff Courtnall	.01	.05
199 Doug Lidster	.01	.05
200 Dave Babych	.01	.05
201 Michal Pivonka	.01	.05
202 Dale Hunter	.02	.10
203 Calle Johansson	.01	.05
204 Kevin Hatcher	.01	.05
205 Al Iafrate	.02	.10
206 Don Beaupre	.02	.10
207 Randy Burridge	.01	.05
208 Dimitri Khristich	.01	.05
209 Peter Bondra	.02	.10
210 Teppo Numminen	.01	.05
211 Bob Essensa	.02	.10
212 Phil Housley	.02	.10
213 Ed Olczyk	.01	.05
214 Pat Elynuik	.01	.05
215 Troy Murray	.01	.05
216 Igor Ulanov	.01	.05
217 Thomas Steen	.01	.05
218 Darrin Shannon	.01	.05
219 Joe Juneau	.02	.10
220 Stephen Heinze	.01	.05
221 Ted Donato	.01	.05
222 Glen Murray	.01	.05
223 Keith Carney RC	.30	.75
224 Dean McAmmond RC	.01	.05
225 Slava Kozlov	.02	.10
226 Martin Lapointe	.02	.10
227 Patrick Poulin	.01	.05
228 Darryl Sydor	.01	.05
229 Trent Klatt RC	.02	.10
230 Bill Guerin RC	.10	.30
231 Jarrod Skalde	.01	.05
232 Scott Niedermayer	.01	.05
233 Marty McInnis	.01	.05
234 Scott LaChance	.01	.05
235 Dominic Roussel	.02	.10
236 Eric Lindros	.08	.25
237 Shawn McEachern	.01	.05
238 Martin Rucinsky	.01	.05
239 Bill Lindsay RC	.01	.05
240 Bret Hedican RC	.02	.10
241 Ray Whitney RC	.15	.40
242 Felix Potvin	.08	.25
243 Keith Tkachuk	.08	.25
244 Evgeny Davydov	.01	.05
245 Brett Hull SL	.08	.25
246 Wayne Gretzky SL	.25	.60
247 Steve Yzerman SL	.20	.50
248 Paul Ysebaert SL	.01	.05
249 Dave Andreychuk SL	.01	.05
250 Kirk McLean SL	.01	.05
251 Tim Cheveldae SL	.01	.05
252 Jeremy Roenick SL	.10	.30
253 NHL Pro Set NR	.01	.05
Youth Parade		
254 NHL Pro Set NR	.01	.05
Youth Clinics		
255 NHL Pro Set NR	.01	.05
All-Time Team		
256 Mike Gartner MS	.01	.05
257 Brian Propp MS	.01	.05
258 Dave Taylor MS	.02	.10
259 Bobby Smith MS	.02	.10
260 Denis Savard MS	.01	.05
261 Ray Bourque MS	.07	.20
262 Joe Mullen MS	.01	.05
263 John Tonelli MS	.01	.05
264 Brad Marsh MS	.01	.05
265 Randy Carlyle MS	.01	.05
266 Mike Hough PS	.01	.05
Power		
267 Bob Essensa PS	.02	.10
Achieve		
268 Mike Lalor PS	.01	.05
Motivate		
269 Terry Carkner PS	.01	.05
Attitude		
270 Todd Krygier PS	.01	.05
Responsibility		
AU239 Kirk McLean AU/100	20.00	40.00

1992-93 Pro Set Award Winners

Randomly inserted in 1992-93 Pro Set packs, these five standard-size cards capture five NHL players who were honored with trophies for their outstanding play. The fronts feature full-bleed color action player photos. A gold-foil stamped "Award Winner" emblem is superimposed at the upper right corner. The player's name, team name, and trophy awarded appear in two bars toward the bottom of the picture. The backs carry a color headshot and a career summary.

COMPLETE SET (5)	8.00	15.00
CC1 Mark Messier	1.00	2.50
Hart/Pearson Trophies		
CC2 Patrick Roy	4.00	10.00
Vezina/Jennings Trophies		
CC3 Pavel Bure	1.00	2.50
Calder Trophy		
CC4 Brian Leetch	1.00	2.50
Norris Trophy		
CC5 Guy Carbonneau	.40	1.00
Selke Trophy		

1992-93 Pro Set Gold Team Leaders

Inserted one per jumbo pack, this 15-card standard-size set spotlights team scoring leaders from the Campbell Conference. The color action player photos on the fronts are full-bleed with "1991-92 Team Leader" gold foil stamped on the picture at the upper right corner. Toward the bottom of the picture the player's name appears on a rust-colored bar that overlays a jagged design. Bordered by a dark brown screened background with Campbell Conference logos, the back carries career summary on a rust-colored panel. The cards are numbered on the back "X of 15."

COMPLETE SET (15)	10.00	25.00
1 Gary Roberts	.20	.50
2 Jeremy Roenick	1.25	3.00
3 Steve Yzerman	2.00	5.00
4 Nicklas Lidstrom	.75	2.00
5 Vincent Damphousse	.40	1.00
6 Wayne Gretzky	3.00	8.00
7 Mike Modano	1.25	3.00
8 Brett Hull	1.25	3.00
9 Nelson Emerson	.20	.50
10 Pat Falloon	.20	.50
11 Doug Gilmour	.40	1.00
12 Trevor Linden	.40	1.00
13 Pavel Bure	.75	2.00
14 Phil Housley	.40	1.00
15 Luciano Borsato	.20	.50

1992-93 Pro Set Rookie Goal Leaders

This 12-card Rookie Goal Leader standard-size set features the top rookie goal scorers from the 1991-92 season. The cards were randomly inserted in 1992-93 Pro Set packs. The player's name appears in a white bar above the picture, while the words "1991-92 Rookie Goal Leader" are gold foil-stamped across the bottom of the picture.

COMPLETE SET (12)	2.50	6.00
1 Tony Amonte	.40	1.00
2 Pavel Bure	1.25	3.00
3 Donald Audette	.20	.50
4 Pat Falloon	.20	.50
5 Nelson Emerson	.20	.50
6 Gilbert Dionne	.20	.50
7 Kevin Todd	.20	.50
8 Luciano Borsato	.20	.50
9 Rob Pearson	.20	.50
10 Valeri Zelepukin	.20	.50
11 Geoff Sanderson	.40	1.00
12 Claude Lapointe	.20	.50

1987 Pro-Sport All-Stars

Issued in Canadian retail packs that included an LCD quartz watch, each of these red, white, and blue oversized cards measures approximately 11 3/4" by 10 1/2" when unfolded and features a color player action shot at the lower right. The player's name, along with his career highlights in English and French, are shown at the lower left. A middle section is cut away to accommodate the watch. The cards are numbered on the front with a "CW" prefix. These cards are priced below without the watches. Number 4 was apparently not issued.

COMPLETE SET (17)	20.00	50.00
1 Larry Robinson	1.25	3.00
2 Guy Carbonneau	.75	2.00
3 Chris Chelios	2.00	5.00
5 Mario Lemieux	6.00	15.00
Pittsburg		
6 Mike Bossy	1.50	4.00
7 Dale Hawerchuk	1.25	3.00
8 Joe Mullen	1.25	3.00
9 Rick Vaive	.75	2.00
10 Wendel Clark	1.50	4.00
11 Michel Goulet	1.25	3.00
12 Peter Stastny	1.25	3.00
13 Mark Messier	2.50	6.00
14 Paul Coffey	2.00	5.00
15 Tony Tanti	.75	2.00
16 Borje Salming	1.25	3.00
17 Chris Nilan	.75	2.00
18 Mats Naslund	1.25	3.00

1983-84 Puffy Stickers

This set of 150 puffy stickers was issued in panels of six stickers each. The panels measure approximately 3 1/2" by 6". There are 21 player panels and four logo panels. The NHL and NHLPA logos appear in the center of each panel. The stickers are oval-shaped and measure approximately 1 1/4" by 1 3/4". In the top portion of the oval they feature a color head shot of the player, with the team name above the head and the player name below the picture in a white box. The sticker background is wood-grain in design. The 21 player panels are numbered and we have checklisted them below accordingly. The logo panels are unnumbered and they are listed after the player panels. The backs are blank. There was also an album produced for this set; the album is not included in the complete set price below.

COMPLETE SET (25)	30.00	75.00
1 Doug Risebrough	6.00	15.00
Wayne Gretzky		
Mats Naslund		
Bill Derlago		
Richard Brodeur		
Dave Babych		
2 Glenn Anderson	1.50	4.00
Larry Robinson		
Rick Vaive		
Stan Smyl		
Scott Arniel		
Don Edwards		
3 Ryan Walter	1.25	3.00
Peter Ihnacak		
Thomas Gradin		
Morris Lukowich		
Kent Nilsson		
Paul Coffey		
4 John Anderson	2.50	6.00
Dave(Tiger) Williams		
Brian Mullen		
Steve Tambellini		
Mark Messier		
Guy Lafleur		
5 Darcy Rota	1.25	3.00
Dale Hawerchuk		
Paul Reinhart		
Jari Kurri		
Mario Tremblay		
Mike Palmateer		
6 Paul MacLean	1.50	4.00
Lanny McDonald		
Ken Linseman		
Steve Shutt		
Borje Salming		
Kevin McCarthy		
7 Barry Pederson	1.25	3.00
Mike Foligno		
Jim Fox		
Don Lever		
Bobby Clarke		
Greg Malone		
8 Gilbert Perreault	1.25	3.00
Charlie Simmer		
Hector Marini		
Mark Howe		
Rick Kehoe		
Jim Schoenfeld		
9 Larry Murphy	1.25	3.00
Phil Russell		
Bill Barber		
Mike Bullard		
Pete Peeters		
John Van Boxmeer		
10 Tapio Levo	1.50	4.00
Darryl Sittler		
Paul Gardner		
Rick Middleton		
Real Cloutier		
Bernie Nicholls		
11 Brian Propp	1.50	4.00
Michel Dion		
Ray Bourque		
Dale McCourt		
Marcel Dionne		
Bob MacMillan		
12 Randy Carlyle	1.25	3.00
Terry O'Reilly		
Phil Housley		
Dave Taylor		
Glenn Resch		
Behn Wilson		
13 Tony Esposito	1.50	4.00
Ron Duguay		
Pierre Larouche		
Neal Broten		
Peter Stastny		
Blake Dunlop		
14 Walt McKechnie	1.00	2.50
Risto Siltanen		
Bobby Smith		
Anton Stastny		
Mike Liut		
Doug Wilson		
15 Blaine Stoughton	1.25	3.00
Dino Ciccarelli		
Michel Goulet		
Jorgen Pettersson		
Tom Lysiak		
Brad Park		
16 Craig Hartsburg	1.00	2.50
Marian Stastny		
Rob Ramage		
Al Secord		
John Ogrodnick		
Greg Millen		
17 Tony McKegney	1.00	2.50
Brian Sutter		
Steve Larmer		
Danny Gare		
Mark Johnson		
Brian Bellows		
18 Bernie Federko	1.25	3.00
Denis Savard		
Reed Larson		
Ron Francis		
Dennis Maruk		
Dan Bouchard		
19 Mike Bossy	1.50	4.00
Anders Hedberg		
Rod Langway		
Billy Smith		
Reijo Ruotsalainen		
Milan Novy		
20 Barry Beck	1.25	3.00
Bob Carpenter		
Clark Gillies		
Rob McClanahan		
Brian Engblom		
Denis Potvin		
21 Mike Gartner	1.50	4.00
John Tonelli		
Willie Huber		
Pat Riggin		
Bryan Trottier		
Don Maloney		
22 Norris Division	2.00	5.00
Blackhawks logo		
Red Wings logo		
North Stars logo		
Blues logo		
Maple Leafs logo		
NHL logo		
23 Patrick Division	2.00	5.00
Devils logo		
Islanders logo		
Rangers logo		
Flyers logo		
Penguins logo		
Capitals logo		
24 Adams Division	2.00	5.00
Bruins logo		
Sabres logo		
Whalers logo		
Canadiens logo		
Nordiques logo		
NHL logo		
25 Smythe Division	2.00	5.00
Flames logo		
Oilers logo		
Kings logo		
Canucks logo		
Jets logo		
NHL logo		
xx Album	10.00	25.00

1938-39 Quaker Oats Photos

This 30-card set of Toronto Maple Leafs and Montreal Canadiens was sponsored by Quaker Oats. The photos were obtainable by mail with the redemption of proofs of purchase. These oversized cards (approximately 6 1/4" by 7 3/8") are unnumbered and hence are listed below alphabetically. Facsimile autographs are printed in white on the fronts of these blank-backed cards.

COMPLETE SET (30)	750.00	1500.00
1 Syl Apps	62.50	125.00
2 Toe Blake	125.00	250.00
3 Buzz Boll	25.00	50.00
4 Turk Broda	87.50	175.00
5 Walter Buswell	25.00	50.00
6 Herb Cain	30.00	60.00
7 Murph Chamberlain	25.00	50.00
8 Wilf Cude	30.00	60.00
9 Bob Davidson	25.00	50.00
10 Gordie Drillon	50.00	100.00
11 Paul Drouin	25.00	50.00
12 Stew Evans	25.00	50.00
13 James Fowler	25.00	50.00
14 Johnny Gagnon	25.00	50.00
15 Robert Gracie	25.00	50.00
16 Reg Hamilton	25.00	50.00
17 Paul Haynes	25.00	50.00
18 Foster Hewitt	50.00	100.00
19 Red Horner	50.00	100.00
20 Harvey(Busher) Jackson	62.50	125.00
21 Bingo Kampman	25.00	50.00
22 Pep Kelly	25.00	50.00
23 Rod Lorrain	25.00	50.00
24 Georges Mantha	25.00	50.00
25 Nick Metz	25.00	50.00
26 George Parsons	25.00	50.00
27 Babe Siebert	50.00	100.00
28 Bill Thoms	25.00	50.00
29 James Ward	25.00	50.00
30 Cy Wentworth	30.00	60.00

1945-54 Quaker Oats Photos

Quaker Oats of Canada continued its tradition of redeeming proofs of purchase for photos of Montreal Canadiens and Toronto Maple Leafs in this nine-year series. Many players are featured in multiple versions, as their photos were updated over the years. The photos themselves are black and white with a thin white border and measure 8" X 10". Because of the numerous variations and the potential for more to be unearthed, no complete set price is listed below. Currently, 113 players are featured on 200 different photos. Anyone with information regarding other photos or variations is encouraged to contact Beckett Publications. The photos are blank-backed and unnumbered and are listed below in alphabetical order within their team (Toronto first, then Montreal).

1A Syl Apps	15.00	30.00
Home Still, CJS Apps auto.		
1B Syl Apps	12.50	25.00
Home Still, Syl Apps auto.		
1C Syl Apps	75.00	150.00
Away With Stanley Cup		
2 George Armstrong	12.50	25.00
Home Action		
3 Doug Baldwin	50.00	100.00
Home Still		
4A Bill Barilko	12.50	25.00
Home Action		
auto. 1/4-inch from border		
4B Bill Barilko	12.50	25.00
Home Action		
auto. 3/4-inch from border		
4C Bill Barilko	12.50	25.00
Away Action		
5 Baz Bastien	62.50	125.00
Home Still		
6 Gordon Bell	62.50	125.00
Home Still		
7A Max Bentley	10.00	20.00
Home Still		
7B Max Bentley	75.00	150.00
Home Dressing Room		
7C Max Bentley	10.00	20.00
Away Action		
8 Gus Bodnar	20.00	40.00
Home Still		
9A Garth Boesch	7.50	15.00
Home Still, closed B in auto.		
9B Garth Boesch	7.50	15.00
Home Still, open B in auto.		
9C Garth Boesch	50.00	100.00
Away Action		
10 Hugh Bolton	6.00	12.00
Home Action		
11 Leo Boivin	15.00	30.00
Home Action		
12A Turk Broda	25.00	50.00
Away Splits, W.E. auto.		
12B Turk Broda	20.00	40.00
Away Splits, Turk auto.		
12C Turk Broda	20.00	40.00
Away Action		
13 Lorne Carr	15.00	30.00
Home Still		
14 Les Costello	15.00	30.00
Home Still		
15 Bob Davidson	12.50	25.00
Home Still		
16A Bill Ezinicki	10.00	20.00
cropped William auto., blue tint		
16B Bill Ezinicki	6.00	12.00
entire William auto.		
16C Bill Ezinicki	6.00	12.00
Home Still, Bill auto.		
16D Bill Ezinicki	6.00	12.00
Away Action		
17 Fernie Flaman	7.50	15.00
Home Action		
18A Cal Gardner	6.00	12.00
Home Still		
18B Cal Gardner	6.00	12.00
Away Action		
19A Bob Goldham	6.00	12.00
sweeping G in auto.		
19B Bob Goldham	6.00	12.00
normal G, entire blade		
19C Bob Goldham	75.00	150.00
normal G, blade cropped		
20 Gord Hannigan	15.00	30.00
Home Action		
21 Bob Hassard	25.00	50.00
Away Action		
22 Mel Hill	40.00	80.00
Home Still		
23 Tim Horton	50.00	100.00
Home Action		
24A Bill Judza	6.00	12.00
Home Still		
24B Bill Judza	6.00	12.00
Away Action		
25A Ted Kennedy	25.00	50.00
Home Still, blade in corner		
25B Ted Kennedy	25.00	50.00
Home Still		
25C Ted Kennedy	50.00	100.00
Home Still		
25D Ted Kennedy	10.00	20.00
Home Still, C on jersey		
25E Ted Kennedy	87.50	175.00
Home With Stanley Cup		
25F Ted Kennedy	10.00	20.00
Away Action		
26A Joe Klukay	6.00	12.00
Home Still		
26B Joe Klukay	6.00	12.00
Away Action		
27 Danny Lewicki	7.50	15.00
Home Action		
28 Harry Lumley	30.00	60.00
Home Action		
29A Vic Lynn	6.00	12.00
Home Still		
head 3/8-inch from border		
29B Vic Lynn	15.00	30.00
Home Still		
head 1/8-inch from border		
29C Vic Lynn	6.00	12.00
Away Action		
30A Fleming Mackell	6.00	12.00
Home Still		
30B Fleming Mackell	7.50	15.00
Away Action		
31 Phil Maloney	40.00	80.00
Home Action		
32 Frank Mathers	20.00	40.00
Home Still		
33 Frank McCool	62.50	125.00
Home Still		
34 John McCormick	15.00	30.00
Away Action		
35A Howie Meeker	10.00	20.00
Home Still, large image		
35B Howie Meeker	10.00	20.00
Home Still, small image		
35C Howie Meeker	10.00	20.00
Away Action		
36A Don Metz	6.00	12.00
Home, posed to right		
36B Don Metz	12.50	25.00
Home, center pose, b&w tint		
36C Don Metz	40.00	80.00
Home, center pose, blue tint		
37A Nick Metz	6.00	12.00
Home Still, original stick		
37B Nick Metz	12.50	25.00
Home Still		
37C Nick Metz	25.00	50.00
Home Still		
38 Rudy Migay	30.00	60.00
Home Action		
39 Elwyn Morris	40.00	80.00
Home Still		
40 Jim Morrison	6.00	12.00
Home Action		
41A Gus Mortson	6.00	12.00
Home Still		
41B Gus Mortson	6.00	12.00
Away Action		
42 Eric Nesterenko	40.00	80.00
Home Action		
43 Bud Poile	15.00	30.00
Home Still		
44 Babe Pratt	50.00	100.00
Home Still		
45 Al Rollins	12.50	25.00
Home Action		
46 Dave Schriner	30.00	60.00
Home Still		
47A Tod Sloan	12.50	25.00
Home Still		
47B Tod Sloan	6.00	12.00
Home Action		
48A Sid Smith	12.50	25.00
Home Still		
48B Sid Smith	6.00	12.00
Away Action		
49 Bob Solinger	15.00	30.00
50A Wally Stanowski	12.50	25.00
Home Still, entire blade		
50B Wally Stanowski	6.00	12.00
Home Still, blade cropped		
51A Gaye Stewart	50.00	100.00
Home Action		
51B Gaye Stewart	6.00	12.00
Home Still, blue tint		
52 Ron Stewart	50.00	100.00
Home Action		
53 Harry Taylor	7.50	15.00
Home Still		
54 Billy Taylor	25.00	50.00
Home Still		
55 Cy Thomas	25.00	50.00
Home Still		
56A Jim Thomson	30.00	60.00
Home Still, stick cropped		
56B Jim Thomson	6.00	12.00
Home Still		
stick touching border		
56C Jim Thomson	30.00	60.00
Home Still		
stick away from border		
56D Jim Thomson	6.00	12.00
Away Action		
57A Ray Timgren	7.50	15.00
Home Still		
57B Ray Timgren	6.00	12.00
Away Action		
58A Harry Watson	6.00	12.00
Home Still, tape on stick		
58B Harry Watson	6.00	12.00
Home Still, no tape visible		
58C Harry Watson	6.00	12.00
Away Action		
59 1947-49 Toronto Team Picture	30.00	60.00
60A Leafs Attack McNeil	87.50	175.00
60B Gardner attacks Harvey	100.00	200.00
60C Rollins, Judza stop Curry	100.00	200.00
60D McNeil Saves on Gardner	100.00	200.00
61 George Allen	6.00	12.00
Home Still		
62 Jean Beliveau	87.50	175.00
Home Action		
63 Joe Benoit	10.00	20.00
Home Still		
64A Toe Blake	75.00	150.00
Hector Toe Blake auto.		
64B Toe Blake	10.00	20.00
Toe Blake auto. above skates		
64C Toe Blake	10.00	20.00
Toe Blake auto. below skate		
65A Butch Bouchard	6.00	12.00
Home Still, entire skate		
65B Butch Bouchard	6.00	12.00
Home Still, skate cropped		
65C Butch Bouchard	7.50	15.00
Home Action		
66 Todd Campeau	6.00	12.00
Home Still		
67 Bob Carse	6.00	12.00
Home Still		
68 Joe Carveth	6.00	12.00
Home Portrait		
69A Murph Chamberlain	10.00	20.00
facing sideways, entire skates		
69B Murph Chamberlain	10.00	20.00
Home Still		
69C Murph Chamberlain	15.00	30.00
Home Still, facing forward		
70 Gerry Couture	6.00	12.00
Home Action		
71A Floyd Curry	62.50	125.00
Home Still		
71B Floyd Curry	6.00	12.00
Home Action		
72 Ed Dorohoy	6.00	12.00
Home Action		
73A Bill Durnan	12.50	25.00
Home Still		
stick handle cropped		
73B Bill Durnan	25.00	50.00
Home Still		
73C Bill Durnan	87.50	175.00
Home Still		
73D Bill Durnan	15.00	30.00
Home Action		
74A Norm Dussault	6.00	12.00
Home Portrait		
74B Norm Dussault	15.00	30.00
Home Action		
75 Frank Eddolls	10.00	20.00
Home Action		
76A Bob Fillion	25.00	50.00
Home Still		
small image		
76B Bob Fillion	6.00	12.00
Home Still		
76C Bob Fillion	12.50	25.00
Home Still		
test		
76D Bob Fillion	6.00	12.00
Home Action(teststesttees		
testst		
77 Dick Gamble	10.00	20.00
Away Action		
78 Bernie Geoffrion	15.00	30.00
Home Action		
79A Leo Gravelle	6.00	12.00
Home Still		
79B Leo Gravelle	25.00	50.00
Away Still		
79C Leo Gravelle	6.00	12.00
Home Action		
80A Glen Harmon	6.00	12.00
Home Still, entire puck		
80B Glen Harmon	6.00	12.00
Home Still, no puck		
80C Glen Harmon	12.50	25.00
Home Action		
81A Doug Harvey	12.50	25.00
Home Still		
81B Doug Harvey	10.00	20.00
Home Action		
82 Dutch Hiller	10.00	20.00
Home Still		
83 Bert Hirschfield	10.00	20.00
Home Action		
Testtestestsetstset		
84 Tom Johnson	10.00	20.00
Home Action		
sdfsdfsdfsdfsdfsdfsdf		
85 Vern Kaiser	10.00	20.00
Home Action		
86A Elmer Lach	10.00	20.00
Home Still, stick in corner		
86B Elmer Lach	10.00	20.00
Home Still, stick cropped		
86C Elmer Lach	40.00	80.00
Home Still		
stick 1/2-inch up from corner		
86D Elmer Lach	10.00	20.00
Home Action		
87A Leo Lamoureaux	12.50	25.00
Home Still, entire blade		
87B Leo Lamoureaux	10.00	20.00
Home Still, blade cropped		
88A Hal Laycoe	50.00	100.00
Home Portrait		
88B Hal Laycoe	6.00	12.00
Home Action		
89A Roger Leger	6.00	12.00
Home Still		
light background		
89B Roger Leger	6.00	12.00
Home Still		
dark background		
89C Roger Leger	25.00	50.00

Home Action
90 Jacques Locas 10.00 20.00
Home Still
91 Ross Lowe 10.00 20.00
Away Action
92 Calum MacKay 6.00 12.00
Home Action
93 Murdo MacKay 6.00 12.00
Home Portrait
94 James MacPherson 6.00 12.00
Home Action
95 Paul Masnick 6.00 12.00
Home Action
96A John McCormick 50.00 100.00
Home Action, vertical
96B John McCormick 30.00 60.00
Home Action, horizontal
97 Mike McMahon 50.00 100.00
Home Still
98 Gerry McNeil 12.50 25.00
Home Action
99 Paul Meger 7.50 15.00
Home Action
100 Dickie Moore 15.00 30.00
Home Action
101A Ken Mosdell 6.00 12.00
Home Still, small image
101B Ken Mosdell 25.00 50.00
Home Still, large image
auto. croppe
101C Ken Mosdell 25.00 50.00
Home Still, large image
auto. not cr
101D Ken Mosdell 6.00 12.00
Home Action
102A Buddy O'Connor 20.00 40.00
Home Still, entire blade
102B Buddy O'Connor 10.00 20.00
Home Still, blade cropped
103 Bert Olmstead 12.50 25.00
Home Action
104A Jim Peters 6.00 12.00
Home Still, large image
104B Jim Peters 6.00 12.00
Home Still, small image
105 Gerry Plamondon 7.50 15.00
Home Action
106 Johnny Quilty 7.50 15.00
Home Portrait
107A Ken Reardon 10.00 20.00
Home Still, large image
107B Ken Reardon 15.00 30.00
Home Still, small image
107C Kenny Reardon 10.00 20.00
Home Action
108A Billy Reay 6.00 12.00
Home Still, large image
stick touchin
108B Billy Reay 6.00 12.00
Home Still, large image
stick away fr
108C Billy Reay 62.50 125.00
Home Still, small image
108D Billy Reay 6.00 12.00
Home Action
109A Maurice Richard 150.00 300.00
Home, screen background
109B Maurice Richard 15.00 30.00
Home, large image
auto. cropped
109C Maurice Richard 15.00 30.00
Home, large image
entire auto.
109D Maurice Richard 30.00 60.00
Home Action
110A Howie Riopelle 10.00 20.00
Home Still
110B Howie Riopelle 10.00 20.00
Home Action
111 George Robertson 20.00 40.00
Home Action
112 Dollard St. Laurent 30.00 60.00
Home Action
113 Grant Warwick 40.00 80.00
Home Action

1973-74 Quaker Oats WHA

This set of 50 cards features players of the World Hockey Association. The cards were issued in strips (panels) of five in Quaker Oats products. The cards measure approximately 2 1/4" by 3 1/4" and are numbered on the back. The information on the card backs is written in English and French. The value of unseparated panels would be approximately 20 percent greater than the sum of the individual values listed below.

COMPLETE SET (50) 137.50 275.00
1 Jim Wiste 2.50 5.00
2 Al Smith 3.00 6.00
3 Rosaire Paiement 2.50 5.00
4 Ted Hampson 2.00 4.00
5 Gavin Kirk 2.00 4.00
6 Andre Lacroix 3.00 6.00
7 John Schella 2.00 4.00
8 Gerry Cheevers 10.00 20.00
9 Norm Beaudin 2.00 4.00
10 Jim Harrison 2.00 4.00
11 Gerry Pinder 2.50 5.00
12 Bob Sicinski 2.00 4.00
13 Bryan Campbell 2.00 4.00
14 Murray Hall 2.00 4.00
15 Chris Bordeleau 2.50 5.00
16 Al Hamilton 3.00 6.00
17 Jimmy McLeod 2.00 4.00
18 Larry Pleau 2.50 5.00
19 Larry Lund 2.00 4.00
20 Bobby Sheehan 2.50 5.00
21 Jan Popiel 2.00 4.00
22 Andre Gaudette 2.00 4.00
23 Bob Charlebois 2.00 4.00
24 Gene Peacosh 2.00 4.00
25 Rick Ley 2.50 5.00
26 Larry Hornung 2.00 4.00
27 Gary Jarrett 2.00 4.00
28 Ted Taylor 2.00 4.00
29 Pete Donnelly 2.00 4.00
30 J.C. Tremblay 3.00 6.00
31 Jim Cardiff 2.00 4.00
32 Gary Veneruzzo 2.00 4.00
33 John French 2.00 4.00
34 Ron Ward 2.50 5.00
35 Wayne Connelly 2.50 5.00
36 Ron Buchanan 2.00 4.00
37 Ken Block 2.00 4.00
38 Alain Caron 2.00 4.00
39 Brit Selby 2.50 5.00
40 Guy Trottier 2.00 4.00
41 Ernie Wakely 3.00 6.00
42 J.P. LeBlanc 2.00 4.00
43 Michel Parizeau 2.00 4.00
44 Wayne Rivers 2.00 4.00
45 Reg Fleming 2.50 5.00
46 Don Herriman 2.00 4.00
47 Jim Dorey 2.00 4.00
48 Danny Lawson 3.00 6.00
49 Dick Paradise 2.00 4.00
50 Bobby Hull 30.00 60.00

1989-90 Rangers Marine Midland Bank

This 30-card set of New York Rangers was sponsored by Marine Midland Bank; the card backs have the bank's logo and name at the bottom. The cards measure approximately 2 5/8" by 3 5/8". The fronts feature color action photos of the players, with a thin red border on the left and bottom of the picture. Outside the red border appears a blue margin, with the player's name, position, and jersey number printed at right angles to one another. The Rangers' logo in the lower right hand corner completes the face of the card. The back has biographical information and career statistics. The cards have been listed below according to sweater number. The key cards in the set are early cards of Brian Leetch and Mike Richter.

COMPLETE SET (30) 14.00 35.00
2 Brian Leetch 3.00 8.00
3 James Patrick .30 .75
4 Ron Greschner .40 1.00
5 Normand Rochefort .20 .50
6 Miloslav Horava .20 .50
8 Darren Turcotte .30 .75
9 Bernie Nicholls .40 1.00
11 Kelly Kisio .30 .75
12 Kris King .40 1.00
14 Mark Hardy .20 .50
15 Mark Janssens .20 .50
16 Ulf Dahlen .30 .75
17 Carey Wilson .20 .50
19 Brian Mullen .30 .75
20 Jan Erixon .20 .50
21 David Shaw .20 .50
23 Corey Millen .20 .50
24 Randy Moller .20 .50
25 John Ogrodnick .40 1.00
26 Troy Mallette .20 .50
29 Rudy Poeschek .40 1.00
30 Chris Nilan .40 1.00
33 Bob Froese .40 1.00
34 John Vanbiesbrouck 1.50 4.00
35 Mike Richter 3.00 8.00
37 Paul Broten .20 .50
38 Jeff Bloemberg .20 .50
44 Lindy Ruff .20 .50
NNO Roger Neilson CO .20 .50
NNO Rangers MasterCard .02 .10

2002-03 Rangers Team Issue

This unusual team issue features two different sizes. The player cards measure 6 X 9.5, while the coach cards measure approx. 5 X 6. The fronts feature different designs, but the backs are similar. Information on distribution and any additional cards in the checklist can be forwarded to hockeymag@beckett.com.

COMPLETE SET (?)
1 Matthew Barnaby .60 1.50
2 Dan Blackburn .60 1.50
3 Pavel Bure 2.00 5.00
4 Ted Green ACO .20 .50
5 Bobby Holik .40 1.00
6 Dave Karpa .40 1.00
7 Darius Kasparaitis .40 1.00
8 Sylvain Lefebvre .40 1.00
9 Vladimir Malakhov .40 1.00
10 Sandy McCarthy .60 1.50
11 Mark Messier 2.00 5.00
12 Terry O'Reilly ACO .40 1.00
13 Mike Richter .75 2.00
14 Jim Schoenfeld ACO .20 .50

2003-04 Rangers Team Issue

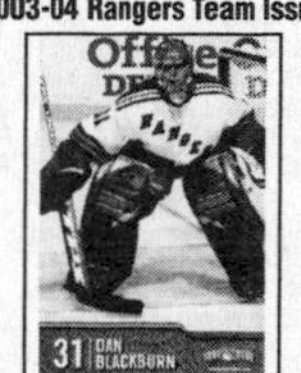

These oversized cards measure 6x9 and were available only at team events. This checklist is possibly incomplete. Please forward additional information to hockeymag@beckett.com.

COMPLETE SET (24) 15.00 30.00
1 Matthew Barnaby .75 2.00
2 Dan Blackburn .60 1.50
3 Anson Carter .60 1.50
4 Greg deVries .40 1.00
5 Mike Dunham .60 1.50
6 Jan Hlavac .40 1.00
7 Bobby Holik .40 1.00
8 Darius Kasparaitis .40 1.00
9 Alexei Kovalev .40 1.00
10 Dan Lacouture .40 1.00
11 Brian Leetch .75 2.00
12 Eric Lindros 1.25 3.00
13 Jamie Lundmark .40 1.00
14 Vladimir Malakhov .40 1.00
15 Jussi Markkanen .75 2.00
16 Mark Messier .75 2.00
17 Boris Mironov .40 1.00
18 Petr Nedved .40 1.00
19 Tom Poti .40 1.00
20 Dale Purinton .75 2.00
21 Martin Rucinsky .40 1.00
22 Glen Sather HCO .20 .50
23 Chris Simon .60 1.50
24 Glen Sather .20 .50
Tom Renney
Terry O'Reilly
Ted Green

1970-71 Red Wings Marathon

This 11-card (artistic) portrait set of Detroit Red Wings was part of a (Pro Star Portraits) promotion by Marathon Oil. The cards measure approximately 7 1/2" by 14"; the bottom portion, which measures 7 1/2" by 4 1/16", was a tear-off postcard in the form of a credit card application. The front features a full color portrait by Nicholas Volpe, with a facsimile autograph of the player inscribed across the bottom of the painting. The back included an offer for other sports memorabilia on the upper portion.

COMPLETE SET (11) 40.00 80.00
1 Gary Bergman 2.50 5.00
2 Wayne Connelly 2.00 4.00
3 Alex Delvecchio 5.00 10.00
4 Roy Edwards 2.50 5.00
5 Gordie Howe 25.00 50.00
6 Bruce MacGregor 2.00 4.00
7 Frank Mahovlich 6.00 12.00
8 Dale Rolfe 2.00 4.00
9 Jim Rutherford 3.00 6.00
10 Garry Unger 2.50 5.00
11 Tom Webster 2.50 5.00

1971 Red Wings Citgo Tumblers

These tumblers were available at Citgo gas stations and measure approximately 8" high. Tumblers feature color head shots, a facsimile autograph, and a color artwork action shot. They are made by Cinemac Inc, and feature a copyright of 1971.

COMPLETE SET 100.00 200.00
1 Wayne Connelly 12.50 25.00
2 Alex Delvecchio 20.00 40.00
3 Don Edwards 10.00 20.00
4 Garry Unger 10.00 20.00
5 Gordie Howe 37.50 75.00
6 Frank Mahovlich 15.00 30.00

1973-74 Red Wings Team Issue

Cards measure 8 3/4" x 10 3/4". Fronts feature color photos, and backs are blank. Cards are unnumbered and checklisted below in alphabetical order.

COMPLETE SET (18) 50.00 100.00
1 Ace Bailey 2.50 5.00
2 Red Berenson 4.00 8.00
3 Gary Bergman 2.50 5.00
4 Thommie Bergman 4.00 8.00
5 Guy Charron 2.50 5.00
6 Bill Collins 2.50 5.00
7 Denis Dejordy 4.00 8.00
8 Alex Delvecchio 7.50 15.00
9 Marcel Dionne 7.50 15.00
10 Gary Doak 2.50 5.00
11 Tim Ecclestone 2.50 5.00
12 Larry Johnston 2.50 5.00
13 Al Karlander 2.50 5.00
14 Brian Lavender 2.50 5.00
15 Nick Libett 2.50 5.00
16 Ken Murphy 2.50 5.00
17 Mickey Redmond 7.50 15.00
18 Ron Stackhouse 2.50 5.00

1973-75 Red Wings McCarthy Postcards

Measuring approximately 3 1/4" by 5 1/2", these postcards display color posed action shots on their fronts. The backs are blank. Since there is no Marcel Dionne or Alex Delvecchio (the latter played 11 games in 1973-74 before coaching), it is doubtful that this is a complete set. The date is established by two players: Brent Hughes (1973-74 was his only season with the Red Wings) and Tom Mellor (1974-75). The cards are unnumbered and checklisted below in alphabetical order. The photos and cards were produced by noted photographer J.D. McCarthy.

COMPLETE SET (15) 12.50 25.00
1 Garnet Bailey 1.00 2.00
2 Thommie Bergman 1.00 2.00
3 Henry Boucha 1.25 2.50
4 Guy Charron 1.00 2.00
5 Bill Collins 1.00 2.00
6 Doug Grant 1.00 2.00
7 Ted Harris 1.00 2.00
8 Bill Hogaboam 1.00 2.00
9 Brent Hughes 1.00 2.00
10 Pierre Jarry 1.00 2.00
11 Larry Johnston 1.00 2.00
12 Nick Libett 1.00 2.00
13 Tom Mellor 1.00 2.00
14 Doug Roberts 1.00 2.00
15 Ron Stackhouse 1.00 2.00

1979 Red Wings Postcards

This set features borderless color fronts and was issued by the Red Wings during the 1979 season.

COMPLETE SET (18) 7.50 15.00
1 Thommie Bergman .38 .75
2 Dan Bolduc .38 .75
3 Mike Foligno .38 .75
4 Jean Hamel .38 .75
5 Glen Hicks .38 .75
6 Greg Joly .38 .75
7 Willie Huber .38 .75
8 Jim Korn .38 .75
9 Dan Labraaten .38 .75
10 Barry Long .38 .75
11 Reed Larson .38 .75
12 Dale McCourt .38 .75
13 Vaclav Nedomansky .38 .75
14 Jim Rutherford .38 .75
15 Dennis Polonich .38 .75
16 Errol Thompson .38 .75
17 Rogie Vachon .38 .75
18 Paul Woods .38 .75

1981-82 Red Wings Oldtimers

This set of slightly undersized cards features black and white head shots of former players with the Detroit Red Wings. The backs are blank. It is not known how these were distributed. Any additional information can be forwarded to hockeymag@beckett.com.

COMPLETE SET (24) 10.00 25.00
1 Bob Johnson .40 1.00
2 Ed Giacomin .75 2.00
3 Gary Bergman .40 1.00
4 Bill Gadsby .40 1.00
5 Larry Johnston .40 1.00
6 Jim Peters .40 1.00
7 Bobby Kromm .40 1.00
8 Marcel Pronovost .75 2.00
9 Gerry Abel .40 1.00
10 Bill Collins .40 1.00
11 Billy Dea .40 1.00
12 Nelson DeBenedet .40 1.00
13 Alex Delvecchio .75 2.00
14 Dennis Hextall .60 1.50
15 Nick Libett .40 1.00
16 Mickey Redmond 1.25 3.00
17 John Wilson .40 1.00
18 Joe Klukay .40 1.00
19 Art Skov .40 1.00
20 Art Bouge .40 1.00
21 Rollie Roulston .40 1.00
22 Gordie Howe 2.00 5.00
23 Dr.C Boone .40 1.00
24 Checklist .40 1.00

1987-88 Red Wings Little Caesars

This 30-card set was sponsored by Little Caesars Pizza and measures approximately 3 3/4" by 6". The fronts have color action player photos with white borders. The player's name appears below the photo, along with the team and sponsor logos. The backs are blank. The cards are unnumbered and checklisted below in alphabetical order.

COMPLETE SET (30) 18.00 45.00
1 Brent Ashton .40 1.00
2 Dave Barr .40 1.00
3 Mel Bridgman .40 1.00
4 Shawn Burr .40 1.00
5 John Chabot .40 1.00
6 Steve Chiasson .60 1.50
7 Gilbert Delorme .40 1.00
8 Jacques Demers CO .75 2.00
9 Ron Duguay .40 1.00
10 Dwight Foster .40 1.00
11 Gerard Gallant .40 1.00
12 Adam Graves 1.50 4.00
13 Doug Halward .40 1.00
14 Glen Hanlon .60 1.50
15 Tim Higgins .40 1.00
16 Petr Klima .60 1.50
17 Joe Kocur .75 2.00
18 Lane Lambert .40 1.00
19 Joe Murphy .40 1.00
20 Lee Norwood .40 1.00
21 Adam Oates 4.00 10.00
22 Mike O'Connell .40 1.00
23 John Ogrodnick .60 1.50
24 Bob Probert 1.50 4.00
25 Jeff Sharples .40 1.00
26 Greg Smith .40 1.00
27 Greg Stefan .60 1.50
28 Darren Veitch .40 1.00
29 Steve Yzerman 5.00 12.00
30 Rick Zombo .40 1.00

1988-89 Red Wings Little Caesars

Set features color action photos with a white border. Players name and team logo are also visible on the front. Cards are blank backed and checklisted below in alphabetical order.

COMPLETE SET (24) 10.00 25.00
1 David Barr .40 1.00
2 Shawn Burr .40 1.00
3 John Chabot .40 1.00
4 Steve Chiasson .75 2.00
5 Gilbert Delorme .40 1.00
6 Jacques Demers .40 1.00
7 Gerard Gallant .40 1.00
8 Adam Graves .75 2.00
9 Doug Houda .40 1.00
10 Glen Hanlon .60 1.50
11 Kris King .40 1.00
12 Petr Klima .40 1.00
13 Joe Kocur .60 1.50
14 Paul MacLean .40 1.00
15 Jim Nill .40 1.00
16 Lee Norwood .40 1.00
17 Adam Oates 1.25 3.00
18 Mike O'Connell .40 1.00
19 Jim Pavese .40 1.00
20 Bob Probert .75 2.00
21 Jeff Sharples .40 1.00
22 Greg Stefan .60 1.50
23 Steve Yzerman 2.50 6.00
24 Rick Zombo .40 1.00

1989-90 Red Wings Little Caesars

This elongated postcard-sized set features color action photos with a white border. Players name and team logo are also visible on the front. Cards are blank backed and are checklisted below in alphabetical order, save for the recently confirmed team personnel cards that are lumped in at the end.

COMPLETE SET (24) 10.00 25.00
1 Dave Barr .40 1.00
2 Shawn Burr .40 1.00
3 Jim Carson .40 1.00
4 John Chabot .40 1.00
5 Steve Chiasson .40 1.00
6 Bernie Federko .40 1.00
7 Gerard Gallant .40 1.00
8 Marc Habscheid .40 1.00
9 Glen Hanlon .40 1.00
10 Doug Houda .40 1.00
11 Joey Kocur .40 1.00
12 Kevin McLelland .40 1.00
13 Lee Norwood .40 1.00
14 Mike O'Connell .40 1.00
15 Borje Salming .40 1.00
16 Greg Stefan .40 1.00
17 Steve Yzerman .40 1.00
18 Rick Zombo .40 1.00
19 Jacques Demers CO .40 1.00
20 Team Photo .40 1.00
21 Mickey Redmond .20 .50
22 Dave Lewis .20 .50
Phil Myre
Jacques Demers
Colin Campbell
23 Bruce Martin .20 .50
Paul Woods
24 Dave Strader .20 .50
Mickey Redmond

1990-91 Red Wings Little Caesars

Set features color action photos with a white border. Players name and team logo are also visible on the front. Cards are blank backed and checklisted below in alphabetical order.

COMPLETE SET (20) 16.00 40.00
1 Dave Barr .40 1.00
2 Shawn Burr .40 1.00
3 John Chabot .40 1.00
4 Tim Cheveldae .60 1.50
5 Per Djoos .40 1.00
6 Bobby Dollas .40 1.00
7 Sergei Fedorov 4.00 10.00
8 Brent Fedyk .40 1.00
9 Johan Garpenlov .40 1.00
10 Rick Green .40 1.00
11 Sheldon Kennedy .75 2.00
12 Kevin McClelland .40 1.00
13 Brad McCrimmon .40 1.00
14 Randy McKay .40 1.00
15 Keith Primeau 1.50 4.00
16 Bob Probert 1.25 3.00
17 Steve Yzerman 2.00 5.00
18 Rick Zombo .40 1.00
19 Bryan Murray CO .40 1.00
20 Team Photo .75 2.00

1991-92 Red Wings Little Caesars

Sponsored by Little Caesars, this 19-card set measures approximately 8 1/2" by 3 5/8" and features a color, action player photo on the left half of the card. The right half displays the player's name, position, biographical information, early career history, and jersey number, along with a close-up player photo. The backs are blank. The cards are unnumbered and checklisted below in alphabetical order.

COMPLETE SET (19) 16.00 40.00
1 Shawn Burr .40 1.00
2 Jimmy Carson .40 1.00
3 Steve Chiasson .40 1.00
4 Sergei Fedorov 3.00 8.00
5 Gerard Gallant .40 1.00
6 Johan Garpenlov .40 1.00
7 Rick Green .40 1.00
8 Marc Habscheid .40 1.00
9 Sheldon Kennedy .40 1.00
10 Martin Lapointe .75 2.00
11 Nicklas Lidstrom 1.25 3.00
12 Brad McCrimmon .40 1.00
13 Bryan Murray CO/MG .20 .50
14 Keith Primeau .60 1.50
15 Bob Probert 1.25 3.00
16 Dennis Vial .40 1.00
17 Paul Ysebaert .40 1.00
18 Steve Yzerman 4.00 10.00
19 Team Card .75 2.00

1996-97 Red Wings Detroit News/Free Press

These five posters were issued one per week in the Sunday editions of the Detroit News/Free Press. They measure approximately 12 by 18 inches and feature a full color photo on the front. The backs feature an ad for the issuing paper.

COMPLETE SET (5) 8.00 20.00
1 Darren McCarty 1.50 4.00
Kris Draper
Kirk Maltby
Joe Kocur
2 Sergei Fedorov 2.50 6.00
3 Mike Vernon 1.50 4.00
4 Mike Vernon 1.50 4.00
5 Sergei Fedorov 2.50 6.00

1932 Reemstma Olympia

This colorful set was produced by Reemstma for the 1932 winter Olympics. Cards measure approximately 6 3/4 by 4 3/4 and are in full color. Backs are in German. Smaller versions of the cards also exist and are in black and white.

188 Dutch hockey player 10.00 20.00
191 USA vs. Canada 25.00 50.00

1936 Reemstma Olympia

This group of cards may or may not make up a complete set of Reemstma Olympia. These undersized issues picture international hockey players and matches from the early 1930s. It is believed they were issued as some sort of premium -- perhaps with cigarettes -- and it's likely that they were issued in Germany.

30 Team Canada 20.00 40.00
(6 3/4 x 4 3/4
31 Ice Hockey Spectators 20.00 40.00
32 Hockey Action Photo 20.00 40.00
33 Goalie making sliding save 20.00 40.00
34 Hockey Action Photo 20.00 40.00
35 Hockey Action Photo 20.00 40.00
Canada player in crease
36 Team Canada Photo 20.00 40.00
37 Team USA Photo 20.00 40.00
38 Gustav Jaenecke 20.00 40.00
39 Teiji Homna 20.00 40.00
Japan Goalie
40 Clearing the Ice 20.00 40.00

1997-98 Revolution

The 1997-98 Pacific Revolution set was issued in one series totaling 150 cards and distributed in three-card packs. The fronts feature color player images printed with etched gold and holographic silver foils on the circular design background. The backs carry another player photo and career statistics.

COMPLETE SET (150) 30.00 60.00
1 Guy Hebert .30 .75
2 Paul Kariya .40 1.00
3 Dmitri Mironov .20 .50
4 Ruslan Salei .20 .50
5 Teemu Selanne .40 1.00
6 Jason Allison .20 .50
7 Ray Bourque .75 2.00
8 Byron Dafoe .30 .75
9 Ted Donato .20 .50
10 Dimitri Khristich .20 .50
11 Joe Thornton .60 1.50
12 Matthew Barnaby .20 .50
13 Jason Dawe .20 .50
14 Dominik Hasek .75 2.00
15 Michael Peca .20 .50
16 Miroslav Satan .20 .50
17 Theo Fleury .20 .50
18 Jarome Iginla .50 1.25
19 Marty McInnis .20 .50
20 Cory Stillman .20 .50
21 Rick Tabaracci .30 .75
22 Martin Gelinas .20 .50
23 Sami Kapanen .20 .50
24 Trevor Kidd .30 .75
25 Keith Primeau .20 .50
26 Gary Roberts .20 .50
27 Tony Amonte .20 .50
28 Chris Chelios .40 1.00
29 Eric Daze .30 .75
30 Jeff Hackett .30 .75
31 Dmitri Nabokov .20 .50
32 Peter Forsberg 1.00 2.50
33 Valeri Kamensky .30 .75
34 Jari Kurri .30 .75
35 Claude Lemieux .20 .50
36 Eric Messier RC .30 .75
37 Sandis Ozolinsh .30 .75
38 Patrick Roy 1.50 4.00
39 Joe Sakic .75 2.00
40 Ed Belfour .40 1.00
41 Jamie Langenbrunner .20 .50
42 Jere Lehtinen .20 .50
43 Mike Modano .60 1.50
44 Joe Nieuwendyk .30 .75
45 Sergei Zubov .20 .50
46 Slava Fetisov .20 .50
47 Nicklas Lidstrom .40 1.00
48 Darren McCarty .20 .50
49 Larry Murphy .20 .50
50 Chris Osgood .30 .75
51 Brendan Shanahan .40 1.00
52 Steve Yzerman 1.50 4.00
53 Roman Hamrlik .30 .75
54 Bill Guerin .30 .75
55 Curtis Joseph .40 1.00
56 Ryan Smyth .30 .75
57 Doug Weight .30 .75
58 Dino Ciccarelli .30 .75
59 Dave Gagner .20 .50
60 Ed Jovanovski .30 .75
61 Paul Laus .20 .50
62 John Vanbiesbrouck .30 .75
63 Ray Whitney .20 .50
64 Russ Courtnall .20 .50
65 Yanic Perreault .20 .50
66 Luc Robitaille .30 .75
67 Jozef Stumpel .30 .75
68 Vladimir Tsyplakov .20 .50
69 Shayne Corson .20 .50
70 Vincent Damphousse .20 .50
71 Saku Koivu .40 1.00
72 Andy Moog .30 .75
73 Mark Recchi .30 .75
74 Jocelyn Thibault .30 .75
75 Martin Brodeur 1.00 2.50
76 Patrik Elias RC 2.00 5.00
77 Doug Gilmour .30 .75
78 Bobby Holik .20 .50
79 Scott Niedermayer .20 .50
80 Bryan Berard .30 .75
81 Travis Green .20 .50
82 Zigmund Palffy .30 .75
83 Robert Reichel .20 .50
84 Tommy Salo .30 .75
85 Dan Cloutier .20 .50
86 Adam Graves .20 .50
87 Wayne Gretzky 2.00 5.00
88 Pat LaFontaine .40 1.00
89 Brian Leetch .40 1.00
90 Mike Richter .40 1.00
91 Kevin Stevens .30 .75
92 Daniel Alfredsson .30 .75
93 Shawn McEachern .20 .50
94 Damian Rhodes .30 .75
95 Ron Tugnutt .30 .75
96 Alexei Yashin .20 .50
97 Rod Brind'Amour .30 .75
98 Paul Coffey .40 1.00
99 Alexandre Daigle .20 .50
100 Chris Gratton .20 .50
101 Ron Hextall .30 .75
102 John LeClair .40 1.00
103 Eric Lindros .40 1.00
104 Dainius Zubrus .40 1.00
105 Mike Gartner .30 .75
106 Craig Janney .20 .50
107 Nikolai Khabibulin .30 .75
108 Jeremy Roenick .50 1.25
109 Keith Tkachuk .40 1.00
110 Stu Barnes .20 .50
111 Tom Barrasso .30 .75
112 Ron Francis .30 .75
113 Jaromir Jagr .60 1.50
114 Peter Skudra RC .20 .50
115 Martin Straka .20 .50
116 Blair Atcheynum RC .20 .50
117 Jim Campbell .20 .50
118 Geoff Courtnall .20 .50
119 Steve Duchesne .20 .50
120 Grant Fuhr .30 .75
121 Brett Hull .50 1.25
122 Pierre Turgeon .30 .75
123 Jeff Friesen .20 .50
124 John MacLean .20 .50
125 Patrick Marleau .30 .75
126 Owen Nolan .30 .75
127 Marco Sturm RC 1.00 2.50
128 Mike Vernon .30 .75
129 Daren Puppa .30 .75
130 Mikael Renberg .30 .75
131 Paul Ysebaert .20 .50
132 Rob Zamuner .20 .50
133 Wendel Clark .30 .75
134 Tie Domi .30 .75
135 Igor Korolev .20 .50
136 Felix Potvin .40 1.00
137 Mats Sundin .40 1.00
138 Donald Brashear .20 .50
139 Pavel Bure .40 1.00
140 Sean Burke .30 .75
141 Trevor Linden .30 .75
142 Mark Messier .40 1.00
143 Alexander Mogilny .30 .75
144 Mattias Ohlund .30 .75
145 Peter Bondra .30 .75
146 Phil Housley .20 .50
147 Dale Hunter .20 .50
148 Joe Juneau .30 .75
149 Olaf Kolzig .30 .75
150 Adam Oates .30 .75

1997-98 Revolution Copper

*VETS: 2X TO 8X BASIC CARDS
*ROOKIES: 1.5X TO 4X BASIC CARDS
STATED ODDS 2:25 HOBBY

1997-98 Revolution Emerald

*VETS: 3X TO 8X BASIC CARDS
*ROOKIES: 1.5X TO 4X BASIC CARDS
STATED ODDS 2:25 CANADIAN

1997-98 Revolution Ice Blue

*VETS: 5X TO 12X BASIC CARDS
*ROOKIES: 2X TO 4X BASIC CARDS
STATED ODDS 1:49

1997-98 Revolution Red

Randomly inserted in special Treat Entertainment retail and hobby packs at the rate of two in 25, this 150-card set is parallel to the base set and is similar in design. The difference is seen in the red foil design element.

*VETS: 3X TO 8X BASIC CARDS
*ROOKIES: 2X TO 4X BASIC CARDS
STATED ODDS 2:25 SPECIAL RETAIL
1 Guy Hebert 2.50 6.00
2 Paul Kariya 3.00 8.00
3 Dmitri Mironov 1.50 4.00
4 Ruslan Salei 1.50 4.00
5 Teemu Selanne 3.00 8.00
6 Jason Allison 1.50 4.00
7 Ray Bourque 6.00 15.00
8 Byron Dafoe 2.50 6.00
9 Ted Donato 1.50 4.00
10 Dimitri Khristich 1.50 4.00
11 Joe Thornton 5.00 12.00
12 Matthew Barnaby 1.50 4.00
13 Jason Dawe 1.50 4.00
14 Dominik Hasek 6.00 15.00
15 Michael Peca 1.50 4.00
16 Miroslav Satan 1.50 4.00
17 Theoren Fleury 1.50 4.00
18 Jarome Iginla 4.00 10.00
19 Marty McInnis 1.50 4.00
20 Cory Stillman 1.50 4.00
21 Rick Tabaracci 2.50 6.00
22 Martin Gelinas 1.50 4.00
23 Sami Kapanen 1.50 4.00
24 Trevor Kidd 2.50 6.00
25 Keith Primeau 1.50 4.00
26 Gary Roberts 1.50 4.00
27 Tony Amonte 2.50 6.00
28 Chris Chelios 3.00 8.00
29 Eric Daze 2.50 6.00
30 Jeff Hackett 2.50 6.00
31 Dmitri Nabokov 1.50 4.00
32 Peter Forsberg 8.00 20.00
33 Valeri Kamensky 2.50 6.00
34 Jari Kurri 2.50 6.00
35 Claude Lemieux 1.50 4.00
36 Eric Messier 2.00 5.00
37 Sandis Ozolinsh 1.50 4.00

38 Patrick Roy 12.00 30.00
39 Joe Sakic 6.00 15.00
40 Ed Belfour 3.00 8.00
41 Jamie Langenbrunner 1.50 4.00
42 Jere Lehtinen 1.50 4.00
43 Mike Modano 5.00 12.00
44 Joe Nieuwendyk 2.50 6.00
45 Sergei Zubov 1.50 4.00
46 Viacheslav Fetisov 1.50 4.00
47 Nicklas Lidstrom 3.00 8.00
48 Darren McCarty 1.50 4.00
49 Larry Murphy 1.50 4.00
50 Chris Osgood 2.50 6.00
51 Brendan Shanahan 3.00 8.00
52 Steve Yzerman 12.00 30.00
53 Roman Hamrlik 2.50 6.00
54 Bill Guerin 2.50 6.00
55 Curtis Joseph 3.00 8.00
56 Ryan Smyth 2.50 6.00
57 Doug Weight 2.50 6.00
58 Dino Ciccarelli 1.50 4.00
59 Dave Gagner 1.50 4.00
60 Ed Jovanovski 2.50 6.00
61 Paul Laus 1.50 4.00
62 John Vanbiesbrouck 2.50 6.00
63 Ray Whitney 1.50 4.00
64 Russ Courtnall 1.50 4.00
65 Yanic Perreault 1.50 4.00
66 Luc Robitaille 2.50 6.00
67 Jozef Stumpel 2.50 6.00
68 Vladimir Tsyplakov 1.50 4.00
69 Shayne Corson 1.50 4.00
70 Vincent Damphousse 1.50 4.00
71 Saku Koivu 3.00 8.00
72 Andy Moog 2.50 6.00
73 Mark Recchi 2.50 6.00
74 Jocelyn Thibault 2.50 6.00
75 Martin Brodeur 8.00 20.00
76 Patrik Elias 12.00 30.00
77 Doug Gilmour 2.50 6.00
78 Bobby Holik 1.50 4.00
79 Scott Niedermayer 1.50 4.00
80 Bryan Berard 2.50 6.00
81 Travis Green 1.50 4.00
82 Zigmund Palffy 2.50 6.00
83 Robert Reichel 1.50 4.00
84 Tommy Salo 2.50 6.00
85 Dan Cloutier 1.50 4.00
86 Adam Graves 1.50 4.00
87 Wayne Gretzky 15.00 40.00
88 Pat LaFontaine 3.00 8.00
89 Brian Leetch 3.00 8.00
90 Mike Richter 3.00 8.00
91 Kevin Stevens 2.50 6.00
92 Daniel Alfredsson 2.50 6.00
93 Shawn McEachern 1.50 4.00
94 Damian Rhodes 2.50 6.00
95 Ron Tugnutt 2.50 6.00
96 Alexei Yashin 1.50 4.00
97 Rod Brind'Amour 2.50 6.00
98 Paul Coffey 3.00 8.00
99 Alexandre Daigle 1.50 4.00
100 Chris Gratton 2.50 6.00
101 Ron Hextall 2.50 6.00
102 John LeClair 3.00 8.00
103 Eric Lindros 3.00 8.00
104 Dainius Zubrus 3.00 8.00
105 Mike Gartner 2.50 6.00
106 Craig Janney 1.50 4.00
107 Nikolai Khabibulin 2.50 6.00
108 Jeremy Roenick 4.00 10.00
109 Keith Tkachuk 3.00 8.00
110 Stu Barnes 1.50 4.00
111 Tom Barrasso 2.50 6.00
112 Ron Francis 2.50 6.00
113 Jaromir Jagr 5.00 12.00
114 Peter Skudra 1.25 3.00
115 Martin Straka 1.50 4.00
116 Blair Atcheynum 1.25 3.00
117 Jim Campbell 1.50 4.00
118 Geoff Courtnall 1.50 4.00
119 Steve Duchesne 1.50 4.00
120 Grant Fuhr 2.50 6.00
121 Brett Hull 4.00 10.00
122 Pierre Turgeon 2.50 6.00
123 Jeff Friesen 1.50 4.00
124 John MacLean 1.50 4.00
125 Patrick Marleau 2.50 6.00
126 Owen Nolan 2.50 6.00
127 Marco Sturm 6.00 15.00
128 Mike Vernon 2.50 6.00
129 Daren Puppa 2.50 6.00
130 Mikael Renberg 2.50 6.00
131 Paul Ysebaert 1.50 4.00
132 Rob Zamuner 1.50 4.00
133 Wendel Clark 2.50 6.00
134 Tie Domi 2.50 6.00
135 Igor Korolev 1.50 4.00
136 Felix Potvin 3.00 8.00
137 Mats Sundin 3.00 8.00
138 Donald Brashear 1.50 4.00
139 Pavel Bure 3.00 8.00
140 Sean Burke 2.50 6.00
141 Trevor Linden 2.50 6.00
142 Mark Messier 3.00 8.00
143 Alexander Mogilny 2.50 6.00
144 Mattias Ohlund 2.50 6.00
145 Peter Bondra 2.50 6.00
146 Phil Housley 1.50 4.00
147 Dale Hunter 1.50 4.00
148 Joe Juneau 2.50 6.00
149 Olaf Kolzig 2.50 6.00
150 Adam Oates 2.50 6.00

1997-98 Revolution Silver

*VETS: 3X TO 8X BASIC CARDS
*ROOKIES: 1.5X TO 4X BASIC CARDS
STATED ODDS 2:25 RETAIL

1997-98 Revolution 1998 All-Star Game Die-Cuts

Randomly inserted in packs at the rate of 1:49, this 20-card set features color photos of the hottest players named to the 1998 NHL All-Star game printed on a die-cut star-background card and appearing in their All-Star uniform from the game in Vancouver.

COMPLETE SET (20) 40.00 80.00
1 Teemu Selanne 1.50 4.00
2 Ray Bourque 3.00 8.00
3 Dominik Hasek 3.00 8.00
4 Theo Fleury .75 2.00
5 Chris Chelios 1.50 4.00
6 Peter Forsberg 4.00 10.00
7 Patrick Roy 6.00 15.00
8 Joe Sakic 3.00 8.00
9 Ed Belfour 1.50 4.00
10 Mike Modano 2.50 6.00
11 Brendan Shanahan 1.50 4.00
12 Saku Koivu 1.50 4.00
13 Martin Brodeur 4.00 10.00
14 Wayne Gretzky 8.00 20.00
15 John LeClair 1.50 4.00
16 Eric Lindros 1.50 4.00
17 Jaromir Jagr 2.50 6.00
18 Pavel Bure 1.50 4.00
19 Mark Messier 1.50 4.00
20 Peter Bondra 1.25 3.00

1997-98 Revolution NHL Icons

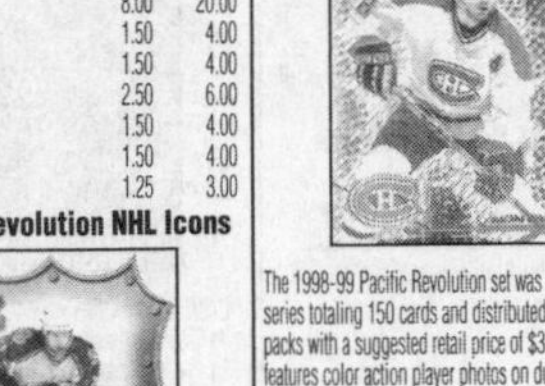

Randomly inserted in packs at the rate of 1:121, this 10-card set features color photos of today's living legends of hockey printed on a die-cut card.

COMPLETE SET (10) 30.00 60.00
1 Paul Kariya 1.50 4.00
2 Teemu Selanne 1.50 4.00
3 Peter Forsberg 4.00 10.00
4 Patrick Roy 6.00 15.00
5 Steve Yzerman 6.00 15.00
6 Martin Brodeur 4.00 10.00
7 Wayne Gretzky 8.00 20.00
8 Eric Lindros 1.50 4.00
9 Jaromir Jagr 2.50 6.00
10 Pavel Bure 1.50 4.00

1997-98 Revolution Return to Sender Die-Cuts

Randomly inserted in packs at the rate of 1:25, this 20-card set features color photos of the top goalies printed on a postage stamp shaped die-cut card.

COMPLETE SET (20) 20.00 40.00
1 Guy Hebert 1.00 2.50
2 Byron Dafoe 1.00 2.50
3 Dominik Hasek 2.50 6.00
4 Jeff Hackett 1.00 2.50
5 Patrick Roy 5.00 12.00
6 Ed Belfour 1.25 3.00
7 Chris Osgood 1.00 2.50
8 Curtis Joseph 1.25 3.00
9 John Vanbiesbrouck 1.00 2.50
10 Andy Moog 1.00 2.50
11 Martin Brodeur 3.00 8.00
12 Tommy Salo 1.00 2.50
13 Mike Richter 1.25 3.00
14 Ron Hextall 1.00 2.50
15 Nikolai Khabibulin 1.00 2.50
16 Tom Barrasso 1.00 2.50
17 Grant Fuhr 1.00 2.50
18 Mike Vernon 1.00 2.50
19 Felix Potvin 1.25 3.00
20 Olaf Kolzig 1.00 2.50

1997-98 Revolution Team Checklist Laser Cuts

Randomly inserted in packs at the rate of 1:25, this 26-card set features color action photos of top players with his laser-cut team logo beside the player image. The backs carry a Revolution main set checklist.

COMPLETE SET (26) 40.00 80.00
1 Paul Kariya 1.25 3.00
2 Joe Thornton 2.00 5.00
3 Michael Peca .60 1.50
4 Theo Fleury .60 1.50
5 Keith Primeau .60 1.50
6 Chris Chelios 1.25 3.00
7 Patrick Roy 5.00 12.00
8 Mike Modano 2.00 5.00
9 Steve Yzerman 4.00 10.00
10 Ryan Smyth 1.00 2.50
11 John Vanbiesbrouck 1.00 2.50
12 Jozef Stumpel 1.00 2.50
13 Saku Koivu 1.25 3.00
14 Martin Brodeur 3.00 8.00
15 Zigmund Palffy 1.00 2.50
16 Wayne Gretzky 6.00 15.00
17 Daniel Alfredsson 1.00 2.50
18 Eric Lindros 1.25 3.00
19 Keith Tkachuk 1.25 3.00
20 Jaromir Jagr 2.00 5.00
21 Brett Hull 1.50 4.00
22 Mike Vernon 1.00 2.50
23 Rob Zamuner .60 1.50
24 Mats Sundin 1.25 3.00
25 Pavel Bure 1.25 3.00
26 Peter Bondra 1.00 2.50

1998-99 Revolution

The 1998-99 Pacific Revolution set was issued in one series totaling 150 cards and distributed in three-card packs with a suggested retail price of $3.99. The set features color action player photos on dual-foiled, etched and embossed cards. The backs carry another player photos, biographical information, and career statistics.

COMPLETE SET (150) 50.00 100.00
1 Guy Hebert .30 .75
2 Paul Kariya .40 1.00
3 Marty McInnis .20 .50
4 Steve Rucchin .20 .50
5 Teemu Selanne .40 1.00
6 Jason Allison .20 .50
7 Ray Bourque .75 2.00
8 Anson Carter .30 .75
9 Byron Dafoe .30 .75
10 Dimitri Khristich .20 .50
11 Sergei Samsonov .30 .75
12 Matthew Barnaby .20 .50
13 Michal Grosek .20 .50
14 Dominik Hasek .75 2.00
15 Michael Peca .20 .50
16 Miroslav Satan .30 .75
17 Dixon Ward .20 .50
18 Theo Fleury .30 .75
19 Jean-Sebastien Giguere .30 .75
20 Jarome Iginla .50 1.25
21 Tyler Moss .20 .50
22 Cory Stillman .20 .50
23 Ron Francis .30 .75
24 Arturs Irbe .30 .75
25 Trevor Kidd .30 .75
26 Keith Primeau .20 .50
27 Ray Sheppard .20 .50
28 Tony Amonte .30 .75
29 Chris Chelios .40 1.00
30 Eric Daze .30 .75
31 Doug Gilmour .30 .75
32 Jocelyn Thibault .30 .75
33 Adam Deadmarsh .20 .50
34 Chris Drury .30 .75
35 Peter Forsberg 1.00 2.50
36 Milan Hejduk RC 2.00 5.00
37 Claude Lemieux .20 .50
38 Patrick Roy 1.50 4.00
39 Joe Sakic .75 2.00
40 Ed Belfour .40 1.00
41 Brett Hull .50 1.25
42 Jamie Langenbrunner .20 .50
43 Jere Lehtinen .20 .50
44 Mike Modano .60 1.50
45 Joe Nieuwendyk .30 .75
46 Darryl Sydor .20 .50
47 Sergei Fedorov .50 1.25
48 Nicklas Lidstrom .40 1.00
49 Norm Maracle RC .40 1.00
50 Darren McCarty .20 .50
51 Chris Osgood .30 .75
52 Brendan Shanahan .40 1.00
53 Steve Yzerman 1.25 3.00
54 Bill Guerin .30 .75
55 Andrei Kovalenko .20 .50
56 Mikhail Shtalenkov .20 .50
57 Ryan Smyth .30 .75
58 Doug Weight .30 .75
59 Pavel Bure .40 1.00
60 Sean Burke .30 .75
61 Dino Ciccarelli .30 .75
62 Viktor Kozlov .20 .50
63 Rob Niedermayer .20 .50
64 Mark Parrish RC .40 1.00
65 Rob Blake .30 .75
66 Stephane Fiset .30 .75
67 Olli Jokinen .30 .75
68 Luc Robitaille .30 .75
69 Pavel Rosa RC .20 .50
70 Jozef Stumpel .20 .50
71 Shayne Corson .20 .50
72 Vincent Damphousse .20 .50
73 Jeff Hackett .30 .75
74 Saku Koivu .40 1.00
75 Mark Recchi .30 .75
76 Brian Savage .20 .50
77 Andrew Brunette .30 .75
78 Mike Dunham .30 .75
79 Sergei Krivokrasov .20 .50
80 Cliff Ronning .20 .50
81 Tomas Vokoun .20 .50
82 Jason Arnott .20 .50
83 Martin Brodeur 1.00 2.50
84 Patrik Elias .30 .75
85 Bobby Holik .20 .50
86 Brendan Morrison .30 .75
87 Kenny Jonsson .20 .50
88 Trevor Linden .30 .75
89 Zigmund Palffy .30 .75
90 Tommy Salo .30 .75
91 Mike Watt .20 .50
92 Wayne Gretzky 2.00 5.00
93 Todd Harvey .20 .50
94 Brian Leetch .40 1.00
95 Manny Malhotra .30 .75
96 Petr Nedved .30 .75
97 Mike Richter .40 1.00
98 Daniel Alfredsson .30 .75
99 Marian Hossa .40 1.00
100 Shawn McEachern .20 .50
101 Damian Rhodes .30 .75
102 Alexei Yashin .20 .50
103 Rod Brind'Amour .30 .75
104 Ron Hextall .30 .75
105 John LeClair .40 1.00
106 Eric Lindros .40 1.00
107 John Vanbiesbrouck .30 .75
108 Dainius Zubrus .20 .50
109 Daniel Briere .20 .50
110 Nikolai Khabibulin .30 .75
111 Jeremy Roenick .50 1.25
112 Keith Tkachuk .40 1.00
113 Rick Tocchet .30 .75
114 Jim Waite .30 .75
115 Jean-Sebastien Aubin RC .40 1.00
116 Stu Barnes .20 .50
117 Tom Barrasso .30 .75
118 Jaromir Jagr .60 1.50
119 Alexei Kovalev .20 .50
120 Martin Straka .20 .50
121 Pavol Demitra .30 .75
122 Grant Fuhr .30 .75
123 Al MacInnis .30 .75
124 Chris Pronger .30 .75
125 Pierre Turgeon .30 .75
126 Jeff Friesen .20 .50
127 Patrick Marleau .30 .75
128 Owen Nolan .30 .75
129 Marco Sturm .20 .50
130 Mike Vernon .30 .75
131 Wendel Clark .30 .75
132 Daren Puppa .30 .75
133 Vincent Lecavalier .40 1.00
134 Stephane Richer .30 .75
135 Rob Zamuner .20 .50
136 Tie Domi .30 .75
137 Mike Johnson .20 .50
138 Curtis Joseph .40 1.00
139 Tomas Kaberle RC .75 2.00
140 Mats Sundin .40 1.00
141 Mark Messier .40 1.00
142 Alexander Mogilny .30 .75
143 Bill Muckalt RC .20 .50
144 Mattias Ohlund .30 .75
145 Garth Snow .30 .75
146 Peter Bondra .30 .75
147 Joe Juneau .30 .75
148 Olaf Kolzig .30 .75
149 Adam Oates .30 .75
150 Richard Zednik .20 .50
S83 Martin Brodeur SAMPLE

1998-99 Revolution Ice Shadow

Randomly inserted into hobby packs only, this 150-card set is a limited blue foil hobby parallel version of the base set. Only 99 serial-numbered sets were made.

*VETERANS: 6X TO 15X BASIC CARDS
*ROOKIES: 1.5X TO 4X BASIC CARDS

1998-99 Revolution Red

*VETERANS: 2.5X TO 6X BASIC CARDS
*ROOKIES: 1.5X TO 4X BASIC CARDS
RED PRINT RUN 299 SER.#'d SETS

1998-99 Revolution All-Star Die Cuts

Randomly inserted in packs at the rate of 1:25, this 30-card set features color images of players from the 1999 World and North America All-Star teams printed on full-foil die-cut cards with a jagged star design at the top.

COMPLETE SET (30) 40.00 80.00
1 Tony Amonte .75 2.00
2 Ed Belfour 1.25 3.00
3 Peter Bondra .75 2.00
4 Ray Bourque 2.00 5.00
5 Martin Brodeur 3.00 8.00
6 Theo Fleury .75 2.00
7 Peter Forsberg 2.50 6.00
8 Wayne Gretzky 6.00 15.00
9 Dominik Hasek 2.50 6.00
10 Bobby Holik .40 1.00
11 Arturs Irbe .75 2.00
12 Jaromir Jagr 2.00 5.00
13 Paul Kariya 1.25 3.00
14 Nikolai Khabibulin 1.25 3.00
15 Sergei Krivokrasov .40 1.00
16 John LeClair .40 1.00
17 Nicklas Lidstrom .75 2.00
18 Eric Lindros 1.25 3.00
19 Al MacInnis .75 2.00
20 Mike Modano 2.00 5.00
21 Mattias Ohlund .40 1.00
22 Keith Primeau .75 2.00
23 Chris Pronger .75 2.00
24 Mark Recchi .75 2.00
25 Jeremy Roenick 1.50 4.00
26 Teemu Selanne 1.25 3.00
27 Brendan Shanahan 1.25 3.00
28 Mats Sundin 1.25 3.00
29 Keith Tkachuk .75 2.00
30 Alexei Yashin .40 1.00

1998-99 Revolution Chalk Talk Laser-Cuts

Randomly inserted into packs at the rate of 1:49, this 20-card set features color action player photos printed on full-foil horizontal cards alongside plays diagramed on a laser cut chalkboard.

COMPLETE SET (20) 40.00 80.00
1 Paul Kariya 1.50 4.00
2 Teemu Selanne 1.50 4.00
3 Theo Fleury .75 2.00
4 Peter Forsberg 4.00 10.00
5 Joe Sakic 3.00 8.00
6 Brett Hull 2.00 5.00
7 Mike Modano 2.50 6.00
8 Sergei Fedorov 2.00 5.00
9 Brendan Shanahan 1.50 4.00
10 Steve Yzerman 6.00 15.00
11 Wayne Gretzky 8.00 20.00
12 Alexei Yashin .75 2.00
13 John LeClair 1.50 4.00
14 Eric Lindros 1.50 4.00
15 Keith Tkachuk 1.50 4.00
16 Jaromir Jagr 2.50 6.00
17 Vincent Lecavalier 1.50 4.00
18 Mats Sundin 1.50 4.00
19 Mark Messier 1.50 4.00
20 Peter Bondra 1.25 3.00

1998-99 Revolution NHL Icons

Randomly inserted into packs at the rate of 1:121, this 10-card set features color images of some of the most renown players in hockey printed on die-cut silver foil cards.

COMPLETE SET (10) 30.00 60.00
1 Paul Kariya 1.50 4.00
2 Dominik Hasek 3.00 8.00
3 Peter Forsberg 4.00 10.00
4 Patrick Roy 6.00 15.00
5 Mike Modano 2.50 6.00
6 Steve Yzerman 6.00 15.00
7 Martin Brodeur 4.00 10.00
8 Wayne Gretzky 8.00 20.00
9 Eric Lindros 1.50 4.00
10 Jaromir Jagr 2.50 6.00

1998-99 Revolution Showstoppers

Randomly inserted in packs at the rate of 2:25, this 36-card set features color action photos of players known for their game-winning heroics printed on holographic silver foil cards.

COMPLETE SET (36) 20.00 50.00
1 Paul Kariya 1.00 2.50
2 Teemu Selanne 1.00 2.50
3 Ray Bourque 1.25 3.00
4 Dominik Hasek 2.00 5.00
5 Michael Peca .40 1.00
6 Theo Fleury .40 1.00
7 Tony Amonte .60 1.50
8 Chris Chelios .60 1.50
9 Doug Gilmour .60 1.50
10 Peter Forsberg 1.50 4.00
11 Patrick Roy 3.00 8.00
12 Joe Sakic 2.00 5.00
13 Ed Belfour 1.00 2.50
14 Brett Hull 1.25 3.00
15 Mike Modano 1.25 3.00
16 Sergei Fedorov 1.25 3.00
17 Brendan Shanahan 1.00 2.50
18 Steve Yzerman 3.00 8.00
19 Mark Parrish .40 1.00
20 Saku Koivu 1.00 2.50
21 Martin Brodeur 2.50 6.00
22 Zigmund Palffy .60 1.50
23 Wayne Gretzky 4.00 10.00
24 Alexei Yashin .40 1.00
25 John LeClair .60 1.50
26 Eric Lindros 1.00 2.50
27 John Vanbiesbrouck .60 1.50
28 Nikolai Khabibulin .60 1.50
29 Jeremy Roenick 1.25 3.00
30 Keith Tkachuk .60 1.50
31 Jaromir Jagr 1.50 4.00
32 Vincent Lecavalier 1.00 2.50
33 Curtis Joseph 1.00 2.50
34 Mats Sundin 1.00 2.50
35 Mark Messier 1.25 3.00
36 Peter Bondra .60 1.50

1998-99 Revolution Three Pronged Attack

Randomly inserted into hobby packs only at the rate of 4:25, this 30-card set features color action photos of some of the NHL's top players. A parallel version of this set was also produced and inserted only in hobby packs. The parallel consists of three separate tiers of 10 cards each with each tier serially numbered in varying amounts. Only 99 serial-numbered Tier 1 (cards #1-10) sets were made; 199 Tier 2 (11-20) serial-numbered sets were made; and 299 serial-numbered Tier 3 (21-30) sets were produced.

COMPLETE SET (30) 15.00 30.00
*1-10 PARALLEL/99: 5X TO 12X BASIC INSERT
*11-20 PARALLEL/199: 3X TO 8X BASIC INSERT
*21-30 PARALLEL/299: 2X TO 5X BASIC INSERT
1 Matthew Barnaby .30 .75
2 Theo Fleury .30 .75
3 Chris Chelios .50 1.25
4 Darren McCarty .30 .75
5 Brendan Shanahan .50 1.25
6 Eric Lindros .50 1.25
7 Keith Tkachuk .50 1.25
8 Tony Twist .30 .75
9 Tie Domi .30 .75
10 Donald Brashear .30 .75
11 Dominik Hasek .75 2.00
12 Patrick Roy 1.25 3.00
13 Ed Belfour .40 1.00
14 Chris Osgood .40 1.00
15 Martin Brodeur 1.00 2.50
16 Mike Richter .50 1.25
17 John Vanbiesbrouck .40 1.00
18 Nikolai Khabibulin .40 1.00
19 Curtis Joseph .50 1.25
20 Olaf Kolzig .40 1.00
21 Paul Kariya .50 1.25
22 Teemu Selanne .50 1.25
23 Peter Forsberg 1.00 2.50
24 Joe Sakic .75 2.00
25 Mike Modano .30 .75
26 Steve Yzerman 1.25 3.00
27 Wayne Gretzky 1.50 4.00
28 John LeClair .50 1.25
29 Jaromir Jagr .60 1.50
30 Pavel Bure .50 1.25

1999-00 Revolution

Released as a 150-card set, Revolution features holographic foil base cards with gold foil highlights. Packaged in 24-pack boxes, each pack contained three cards and carried a suggested retail price of $3.99.

COMPLETE SET (150) 40.00 80.00
1 Guy Hebert .30 .75
2 Paul Kariya .40 1.00
3 Marty McInnis .20 .50
4 Teemu Selanne .40 1.00
5 Steve Rucchin .30 .75
6 Kelly Buchberger .20 .50
7 Ray Ferraro .20 .50
8 Damian Rhodes .20 .50
9 Johan Garpenlov .20 .50
10 Jason Allison .20 .50
11 Ray Bourque .75 2.00
12 Anson Carter .30 .75
13 Byron Dafoe .30 .75
14 Sergei Samsonov .30 .75
15 Joe Thornton .60 1.50
16 Martin Biron .30 .75
17 Curtis Brown .20 .50
18 Dominik Hasek .75 2.00
19 Michael Peca .20 .50
20 Miroslav Satan .20 .50
21 Dixon Ward .20 .50
22 Valeri Bure .20 .50
23 Fred Brathwaite .30 .75
24 Phil Housley .30 .75
25 Jarome Iginla .50 1.25
26 Cory Stillman .20 .50
27 Ron Francis .30 .75
28 Arturs Irbe .30 .75
29 Sami Kapanen .20 .50
30 Keith Primeau .20 .50
31 Gary Roberts .20 .50
32 Tony Amonte .30 .75
33 J-P Dumont .30 .75
34 Doug Gilmour .30 .75
35 Jocelyn Thibault .30 .75
36 Alexei Zhamnov .20 .50
37 Adam Deadmarsh .20 .50
38 Chris Drury .30 .75
39 Peter Forsberg 1.00 2.50
40 Milan Hejduk .40 1.00
41 Claude Lemieux .20 .50
42 Patrick Roy 1.50 4.00
43 Joe Sakic .75 2.00
44 Ed Belfour .40 1.00
45 Brett Hull .50 1.25
46 Jamie Langenbrunner .20 .50
47 Jere Lehtinen .30 .75
48 Mike Modano .60 1.50
49 Joe Nieuwendyk .30 .75
50 Chris Chelios .40 1.00
51 Sergei Fedorov .50 1.25
52 Vyacheslav Kozlov .30 .75
53 Nicklas Lidstrom .40 1.00
54 Chris Osgood .30 .75
55 Brendan Shanahan .40 1.00
56 Steve Yzerman 1.50 4.00
57 Mike Grier .20 .50
58 Bill Guerin .20 .50
59 Tommy Salo .30 .75
60 Ryan Smyth .30 .75
61 Doug Weight .30 .75
62 Pavel Bure .40 1.00
63 Sean Burke .30 .75
64 Viktor Kozlov .20 .50
65 Mark Parrish .20 .50
66 Ray Whitney .30 .75
67 Donald Audette .20 .50
68 Rob Blake .30 .75
69 Stephane Fiset .30 .75
70 Zigmund Palffy .30 .75
71 Luc Robitaille .30 .75
72 Jamie Storr .30 .75
73 Shayne Corson .20 .50
74 Jeff Hackett .30 .75
75 Saku Koivu .40 1.00
76 Vladimir Malakhov .20 .50
77 Martin Rucinsky .20 .50
78 Mike Dunham .30 .75
79 Greg Johnson .20 .50
80 Sergei Krivokrasov .20 .50
81 Cliff Ronning .30 .75
82 Scott Walker .20 .50
83 Jason Arnott .20 .50
84 Martin Brodeur 1.00 2.50
85 Patrik Elias .30 .75
86 Bobby Holik .20 .50
87 Brendan Morrison .30 .75
88 Scott Niedermayer .20 .50
89 Petr Sykora .20 .50
90 Mariusz Czerkawski .20 .50
91 Kenny Jonsson .20 .50
92 Mats Lindgren .20 .50
93 Felix Potvin .40 1.00
94 Mike Watt .20 .50
95 Theo Fleury .20 .50
96 Adam Graves .20 .50
97 Brian Leetch .40 1.00
98 John MacLean .20 .50
99 Petr Nedved .30 .75
100 Mike Richter .40 1.00
101 Magnus Arvedson .20 .50
102 Marian Hossa .40 1.00
103 Shawn McEachern .20 .50
104 Ron Tugnutt .30 .75
105 Alexei Yashin .20 .50
106 Rod Brind'Amour .30 .75
107 Eric Lindros .40 1.00
108 John LeClair .40 1.00
109 Mark Recchi .30 .75
110 John Vanbiesbrouck .30 .75
111 Nikolai Khabibulin .30 .75
112 Teppo Numminen .20 .50
113 Jeremy Roenick .50 1.25
114 Keith Tkachuk .40 1.00
115 Rick Tocchet .30 .75
116 Tom Barrasso .30 .75
117 Jan Hrdina .20 .50
118 Jaromir Jagr .60 1.50
119 Alexei Kovalev .20 .50
120 Martin Straka .20 .50
121 Pavol Demitra .30 .75
122 Jochen Hecht RC .75 2.00
123 Al MacInnis .30 .75
124 Chris Pronger .30 .75
125 Pierre Turgeon .30 .75
126 Vincent Damphousse .20 .50
127 Jeff Friesen .20 .50
128 Patrick Marleau .30 .75
129 Steve Shields .30 .75
130 Mike Vernon .30 .75
131 Chris Gratton .20 .50
132 Collin Forbes .20 .50
133 Vincent Lecavalier .40 1.00
134 Darcy Tucker .20 .50
135 Sergei Berezin .20 .50
136 Tie Domi .20 .50
137 Mike Johnson .30 .75
138 Curtis Joseph .40 1.00
139 Derek King .20 .50
140 Mats Sundin .40 1.00
141 Steve Thomas .20 .50
142 Mark Messier .40 1.00
143 Bill Muckalt .30 .75
144 Markus Naslund .40 1.00
145 Mattias Ohlund .30 .75
146 Garth Snow .30 .75
147 Peter Bondra .30 .75
148 Sergei Gonchar .20 .50
149 Olaf Kolzig .30 .75
150 Adam Oates .30 .75

1999-00 Revolution Premiere Date

Randomly inserted in Hobby packs at 1:25, this 150-card set parallels the base Revolution set with a foil Premier Date stamp. Each card is sequentially numbered to 42.

*PREM.DATE: 15X TO 40X BASIC CARDS

1999-00 Revolution Red

Randomly inserted in retail packs, this 150-card set parallels the base Revolution set in a red foil version. Each card is sequentially numbered to 299.

*RED: 4X TO 10X BASIC CARDS

1999-00 Revolution Shadow Series

Randomly inserted in Hobby packs, this 150-card set parallels the base Revolution set. Each card has a Shadow Series stamp and is sequentially numbered to 99.

*SHADOWS: 10X TO 25X BASIC CARDS

1999-00 Revolution Ice Sculptures

Randomly inserted in packs at the rate of 1:49, this 10-card set features top NHL players on an embossed silver foil card giving the effect of an ice carving.

COMPLETE SET (10) 50.00 100.00
1 Paul Kariya 2.00 5.00
2 Dominik Hasek 4.00 10.00

3 Patrick Roy 10.00 25.00
4 Joe Sakic 4.00 10.00
5 Steve Yzerman 10.00 25.00
6 Pavel Bure 2.50 6.00
7 Martin Brodeur 5.00 12.00
8 Theo Fleury 2.00 5.00
9 Eric Lindros 3.00 8.00
10 Jaromir Jagr 3.00 8.00

1999-00 Revolution NHL Icons

Randomly inserted in packs at the rate of 1:121, this 20-card set features close up action photography on a die cut card stock.

COMPLETE SET (20) 30.00 80.00
1 Teemu Selanne 1.50 4.00
2 Ray Bourque 3.00 8.00
3 Dominik Hasek 3.00 8.00
4 Doug Gilmour 1.25 3.00
5 Peter Forsberg 4.00 10.00
6 Patrick Roy 6.00 15.00
7 Joe Sakic 3.00 8.00
8 Brett Hull 2.00 5.00
9 Mike Modano 2.50 6.00
10 Brendan Shanahan 1.50 4.00
11 Steve Yzerman 6.00 15.00
12 Martin Brodeur 4.00 10.00
13 John LeClair 1.50 4.00
14 Eric Lindros 1.50 4.00
15 John Vanbiesbrouck 1.25 3.00
16 Keith Tkachuk 1.50 4.00
17 Jaromir Jagr 2.50 6.00
18 Curtis Joseph 1.50 4.00
19 Mats Sundin 1.50 4.00
20 Mark Messier 1.50 4.00

1999-00 Revolution Ornaments

Randomly seeded in packs at the rate of 1:25, this 20-card set features color player photos on a die-cut Christmas tree ornament.

COMPLETE SET (20) 40.00 80.00
1 Paul Kariya 1.25 3.00
2 Teemu Selanne 1.25 3.00
3 Sergei Samsonov 1.00 2.50
4 Dominik Hasek 2.50 6.00
5 Jarome Iginla 1.50 4.00
6 Peter Forsberg 3.00 8.00
7 Patrick Roy 5.00 12.00
8 Ed Belfour 1.25 3.00
9 Mike Modano 2.00 5.00
10 Brendan Shanahan 1.25 3.00
11 Steve Yzerman 5.00 12.00
12 Pavel Bure 1.25 3.00
13 Martin Brodeur 3.00 8.00
14 John LeClair 1.25 3.00
15 Eric Lindros 1.25 3.00
16 Jaromir Jagr 2.00 5.00
17 Vincent Lecavalier 1.25 3.00
18 Curtis Joseph 1.25 3.00
19 Mats Sundin 1.25 3.00
20 Mark Messier 1.25 3.00

1999-00 Revolution Showstoppers

Randomly seeded in packs at the rate of 2:25, this 36-card set features top NHL players on an all foil insert card.

COMPLETE SET (36) 30.00 70.00
1 Paul Kariya 1.00 2.50
2 Teemu Selanne 1.00 2.50
3 Ray Bourque 1.50 4.00
4 Byron Dafoe .40 1.00
5 Dominik Hasek 1.50 4.00
6 Michael Peca .40 1.00
7 Tony Amonte .75 2.00
8 Chris Drury .75 2.00
9 Peter Forsberg 1.50 4.00
10 Patrick Roy 4.00 10.00
11 Joe Sakic 2.00 5.00
12 Ed Belfour 1.00 2.50
13 Brett Hull 1.00 2.50
14 Mike Modano 1.00 2.50
15 Joe Nieuwendyk .75 2.00
16 Sergei Fedorov 1.00 2.50
17 Brendan Shanahan 1.00 2.50
18 Doug Weight .40 1.00
19 Pavel Bure 1.00 2.50
20 Mark Parrish .40 1.00
21 Martin Brodeur 2.50 6.00
22 Felix Potvin 1.00 2.50
23 Mike Richter 1.00 2.50
24 Marian Hossa .75 2.00
25 Alexei Yashin .40 1.00
26 John LeClair .75 2.00
27 John Vanbiesbrouck .75 2.00
28 Jeremy Roenick 1.00 2.50
29 Keith Tkachuk .75 2.00
30 Pavol Demitra .40 1.00
31 Patrick Marleau .75 2.00
32 Vincent Lecavalier 1.00 2.50
33 Curtis Joseph 1.00 2.50
34 Mats Sundin 1.00 2.50
35 Mark Messier 1.00 2.50
36 Peter Bondra .40 1.00

1999-00 Revolution Top of the Line

Randomly inserted in packs, this 30-card set was released as a three tier issue. Card numbers 1-10 are serial numbered out of 99, card numbers 11-20 are serial numbered out of 199, and card numbers 21-30 are serial numbered out of 299.

1 Paul Kariya/99 12.00 30.00
2 Sergei Samsonov/99 10.00 25.00
3 Brendan Shanahan/99 12.00 30.00
4 Pavel Bure/99 12.00 30.00
5 Luc Robitaille/99 10.00 25.00
6 Marian Hossa/99 10.00 25.00
7 John LeClair/99 8.00 20.00
8 Keith Tkachuk/99 12.00 30.00
9 Pavol Demitra/99 8.00 20.00
10 Jeff Friesen/99 8.00 20.00
11 Chris Drury/199 4.00 10.00
12 Peter Forsberg/199 12.00 30.00
13 Joe Sakic/199 12.00 30.00
14 Steve Yzerman/199 25.00 60.00
15 Mike Modano/199 10.00 25.00
16 Joe Nieuwendyk/199 6.00 15.00
17 Alexei Yashin/199 4.00 10.00
18 Eric Lindros/199 5.00 12.00
19 Mats Sundin/199 6.00 15.00
20 Mark Messier/199 6.00 15.00
21 Teemu Selanne/299 4.00 10.00
22 Miroslav Satan/299 3.00 8.00
23 Jarome Iginla/299 6.00 15.00
24 Tony Amonte/299 3.00 8.00
25 Milan Hejduk/299 3.00 8.00
26 Brett Hull/299 6.00 15.00
27 Theo Fleury/299 3.00 8.00
28 Mark Recchi/299 3.00 8.00
29 Jaromir Jagr/299 8.00 20.00
30 Peter Bondra/299 3.00 8.00

1999-00 Revolution Copper

Randomly inserted in packs, this 75-card set is skip numbered and parallels half of the base set with cards sequentially numbered to 10. This set is not priced due to scarcity.

UNPRICED COPPER PRINT RUN 10

1999-00 Revolution Gold

Randomly inserted in packs, this 75-card set is skip numbered and parallels half of the base set with cards numbered one of one. The checklist parallels the copper set. This set not priced due to scarcity.

UNPRICED GOLD PRINT RUN 1

1999-00 Revolution CSC Silver

These cards were not available in packs nor in boxed form. They were only available to dealers who dealt with Continental Sports Cards, a distributor in Canada. The checklist parallels the copper set.

*CSC SILVER: 20X TO 50X BASIC CARDS

2000-01 Revolution

Released as a 150-card set in late September 2000, Revolution base cards featured a centered player action photo set against holographic and gold foil accented blue card stock. Revolution was packaged in 24-pack boxes with each pack contained three cards.

COMPLETE SET (150) 50.00 100.00
1 Guy Hebert .50 1.25
2 Paul Kariya .60 1.50
3 Steve Rucchin .20 .50
4 Teemu Selanne .60 1.50
5 Andrew Brunette .50 1.25
6 Ray Ferraro .20 .50
7 Damian Rhodes .50 1.25
8 Patrik Stefan .20 .50
9 Anson Carter .50 1.25
10 Byron Dafoe .50 1.25
11 John Grahame .50 1.25
12 Sergei Samsonov .50 1.25
13 Joe Thornton 1.00 2.50
14 Maxim Afinogenov .20 .50
15 Martin Biron .50 1.25
16 Doug Gilmour .50 1.25
17 Dominik Hasek 1.25 3.00
18 Michael Peca .50 1.25
19 Miroslav Satan .50 1.25
20 Fred Brathwaite .50 1.25
21 Valeri Bure .20 .50
22 Phil Housley .50 1.25
23 Jarome Iginla .75 2.00
24 Oleg Saprykin .20 .50
25 Rod Brind'Amour .50 1.25
26 Ron Francis .50 1.25
27 Arturs Irbe .50 1.25
28 Sami Kapanen .20 .50
29 Tony Amonte .50 1.25
30 Michal Grosek .20 .50
31 Steve Sullivan .20 .50
32 Jocelyn Thibault .50 1.25
33 Alexei Zhamnov .50 1.25
34 Ray Bourque 1.25 3.00
35 Chris Drury .50 1.25
36 Peter Forsberg 1.50 4.00
37 Milan Hejduk .60 1.50
38 Patrick Roy 3.00 8.00
39 Joe Sakic 1.25 3.00
40 Alex Tanguay .50 1.25
41 Kevyn Adams .20 .50
42 Marc Denis .50 1.25
43 Krzysztof Oliwa .20 .50
44 Geoff Sanderson .20 .50
45 Ed Belfour .60 1.50
46 Brett Hull .75 2.00
47 Mike Modano 1.00 2.50
48 Brenden Morrow .50 1.25
49 Joe Nieuwendyk .50 1.25
50 Chris Chelios .60 1.50
51 Sergei Fedorov 1.00 2.50
52 Nicklas Lidstrom .60 1.50
53 Chris Osgood .60 1.50
54 Brendan Shanahan .60 1.50
55 Steve Yzerman 3.00 8.00
56 Bill Guerin .50 1.25
57 Todd Marchant .20 .50
58 Tommy Salo .50 1.25
59 Ryan Smyth .50 1.25
60 Doug Weight .50 1.25
61 Pavel Bure .60 1.50
62 Trevor Kidd .50 1.25
63 Viktor Kozlov .50 1.25
64 Scott Mellanby .20 .50
65 Ray Whitney .20 .50
66 Rob Blake .60 1.50
67 Stephane Fiset .50 1.25
68 Zigmund Palffy .50 1.25
69 Luc Robitaille .60 1.50
70 Jamie Storr .50 1.25
71 Manny Fernandez .50 1.25
72 Jamie McLennan .50 1.25
73 Sean O'Donnell .20 .50
74 Stacy Roest .20 .50
75 Jeff Hackett .50 1.25
76 Saku Koivu .60 1.50
77 Trevor Linden .50 1.25
78 Martin Rucinsky .20 .50
79 Jose Theodore .75 2.00
80 Mike Dunham .50 1.25
81 David Gosselin RC .60 1.50
82 David Legwand .20 .50
83 Cliff Ronning .20 .50
84 Jason Arnott .20 .50
85 Martin Brodeur 1.50 4.00
86 Patrik Elias .50 1.25
87 Scott Gomez .20 .50
88 Scott Stevens .50 1.25
89 Petr Sykora .20 .50
90 Tim Connolly .20 .50
91 Mariusz Czerkawski .20 .50
92 Brad Isbister .20 .50
93 Steve Valiquette RC .60 1.50
94 Theo Fleury .20 .50
95 Adam Graves .20 .50
96 Brian Leetch .50 1.25
97 Mark Messier .60 1.50
98 Petr Nedved .50 1.25
99 Mike Richter .60 1.50
100 Mike York .20 .50
101 Daniel Alfredsson .50 1.25
102 Radek Bonk .20 .50
103 Marian Hossa .60 1.50
104 Patrick Lalime .50 1.25
105 Shawn McEachern .20 .50
106 Brian Boucher .60 1.50
107 Eric Desjardins .50 1.25
108 Simon Gagne .60 1.50
109 John LeClair .60 1.50
110 Eric Lindros .60 1.50
111 Mark Recchi .50 1.25
112 Shane Doan .50 1.25
113 Nikolai Khabibulin .50 1.25
114 Jeremy Roenick .75 2.00
115 Keith Tkachuk .60 1.50
116 Jean-Sebastien Aubin .50 1.25
117 Jan Hrdina .20 .50
118 Jaromir Jagr 1.00 2.50
119 Alexei Kovalev .50 1.25
120 Martin Straka .20 .50
121 Pavol Demitra .50 1.25
122 Michal Handzus .50 1.25
123 Al MacInnis .50 1.25
124 Chris Pronger .50 1.25
125 Roman Turek .50 1.25
126 Pierre Turgeon .50 1.25
127 Vincent Damphousse .20 .50
128 Jeff Friesen .20 .50
129 Patrick Marleau .50 1.25
130 Owen Nolan .50 1.25
131 Steve Shields .50 1.25
132 Dan Cloutier .50 1.25
133 Mike Johnson .20 .50
134 Dieter Kochan RC .50 1.25
135 Vincent Lecavalier .60 1.50
136 Nikolai Antropov .20 .50
137 Tie Domi .50 1.25
138 Jeff Farkas .50 1.25
139 Curtis Joseph .60 1.50
140 Mats Sundin .60 1.50
141 Darcy Tucker .20 .50
142 Todd Bertuzzi .60 1.50
143 Steve Kariya .20 .50
144 Markus Naslund .60 1.50
145 Felix Potvin .60 1.50
146 Peter Bondra .60 1.50
147 Jeff Halpern .50 1.25
148 Olaf Kolzig .50 1.25
149 Adam Oates .50 1.25
150 Chris Simon .20 .50

2000-01 Revolution Blue

Randomly inserted in Hobby packs, this 150-card set parallels the base set with an embossed stamp in the middle of the card, and each card is sequentially numbered to 85.

*STARS: 6X TO 15X BASIC CARDS
*ROOKIES: 3X TO 8X BASIC CARDS

2000-01 Revolution Premiere Date

Randomly inserted in Hobby packs, this 150-card set parallels the base set where each card is sequentially numbered to 60.

*STARS: 6X TO 15X HI COL.
*ROOKIES: 3X TO 8X HI COL.

2000-01 Revolution Red

Randomly inserted in Retail packs, this 150-card set parallels the base set enhanced with red highlights where each card is sequentially numbered to 99.

*STARS: 4X TO 10X BASIC CARDS
*ROOKIES: 2.5X TO 6X BASIC CARDS

2000-01 Revolution Game-Worn Jerseys

Randomly inserted in packs, this 10-card set features a player action photo on the right side of the card front with circular swatches of game worn jerseys on the left. A gold foil serial number box appears right below the jersey swatch, and each card is sequentially numbered to 400.

1 Marty McInnis 4.00 10.00
2 Anson Carter 6.00 15.00
3 Jarome Iginla 10.00 25.00
4 Tony Amonte 6.00 15.00
5 Jamie Langenbrunner 4.00 10.00
6 Saku Koivu 8.00 20.00
7 Zdeno Chara 6.00 15.00
8 Brian Leetch 6.00 15.00
9 Andreas Dackell 4.00 10.00
10 Petr Svoboda 4.00 10.00

2000-01 Revolution Game-Worn Jersey Patches

Randomly inserted in packs, this 10-card set parallels the base Game Worn Jerseys insert with premium swatches of game worn jerseys. Each card is sequentially numbered to 50.

*PATCHES: 1.25X TO 3X JERSEY CARD

2000-01 Revolution HD NHL

This 36-card set was randomly inserted in packs at the rate of 2:25.

COMPLETE SET (36) 30.00 60.00
1 Paul Kariya 1.00 2.50
2 Teemu Selanne 1.00 2.50
3 Patrik Stefan .30 .75
4 Joe Thornton 1.50 4.00
5 Dominik Hasek 2.00 5.00
6 Jarome Iginla 1.25 3.00
7 Tony Amonte .75 2.00
8 Peter Forsberg 2.50 6.00
9 Milan Hejduk 1.00 2.50
10 Joe Sakic 2.00 5.00
11 Patrick Roy 5.00 12.00
12 Ed Belfour 1.00 2.50
13 Brett Hull 1.25 3.00
14 Sergei Fedorov 1.50 4.00
15 Brendan Shanahan 1.00 2.50
16 Pavel Bure 1.00 2.50
17 Zigmund Palffy .75 2.00
18 Luc Robitaille .75 2.00
19 Saku Koivu 1.00 2.50
20 Martin Brodeur 2.50 6.00
21 Patrik Elias .75 2.00
22 Scott Gomez .30 .75
23 Marian Hossa 1.00 2.50
24 Brian Boucher 1.00 2.50
25 John LeClair 1.00 2.50
26 Mark Recchi .75 2.00
27 Jeremy Roenick 1.25 3.00
28 Keith Tkachuk 1.00 2.50
29 Chris Pronger .75 2.00
30 Roman Turek .75 2.00
31 Owen Nolan .75 2.00
32 Vincent Lecavalier 1.00 2.50
33 Nikolai Antropov .30 .75
34 Mats Sundin 1.00 2.50
35 Curtis Joseph 1.00 2.50
36 Olaf Kolzig .75 2.00

2000-01 Revolution Ice Immortals

Randomly inserted in packs at the rate of 1:25, this 20-card set features gray borders and a "snow" effect in front of player action photography on a blue and white background.

COMPLETE SET (20) 30.00 60.00
1 Paul Kariya 1.25 3.00
2 Teemu Selanne 1.25 3.00
3 Dominik Hasek 2.50 6.00
4 Ray Bourque 2.50 6.00
5 Peter Forsberg 3.00 8.00
6 Patrick Roy 6.00 15.00
7 Ed Belfour 1.25 3.00
8 Brett Hull 1.50 4.00
9 Mike Modano 2.00 5.00
10 Brendan Shanahan 1.25 3.00
11 Steve Yzerman 6.00 15.00
12 Pavel Bure 1.25 3.00
13 Martin Brodeur 3.00 8.00
14 Scott Gomez .40 1.00
15 John LeClair 1.25 3.00
16 Mark Recchi 1.00 2.50
17 Jeremy Roenick 1.50 4.00
18 Jaromir Jagr 2.00 5.00
19 Curtis Joseph 1.25 3.00
20 Olaf Kolzig 1.00 2.50

2000-01 Revolution NHL Game Gear

Randomly inserted in packs, this 10-card set features swatches of game worn jerseys and game used sticks. A player photo appears on the right side of the card front while two circular swatches of memorabilia, jersey on top and stick on bottom are separated by a gold serial number box. Each card is sequentially numbered to 200.

1 Peter Forsberg 15.00 40.00
2 Joe Sakic 15.00 40.00
3 Mike Modano 12.50 30.00
4 Sergei Fedorov 12.50 30.00
5 Nicklas Lidstrom 8.00 20.00
6 Steve Yzerman 20.00 50.00
7 Mark Messier 8.00 20.00
8 Nikolai Khabibulin 8.00 20.00
9 Jaromir Jagr 12.50 30.00
10 Peter Bondra 6.00 15.00

2000-01 Revolution NHL Icons

Randomly inserted in packs at the rate of 1:121, this 20-card set features a die-cut card stock in the shape of the NHL logo. Each card features gray borders around full color player photography.

COMPLETE SET (20) 50.00 100.00
1 Paul Kariya 1.50 4.00
2 Teemu Selanne 1.50 4.00
3 Doug Gilmour 1.25 3.00
4 Dominik Hasek 3.00 8.00
5 Ray Bourque 3.00 8.00
6 Peter Forsberg 4.00 10.00
7 Patrick Roy 8.00 20.00
8 Joe Sakic 3.00 8.00
9 Brett Hull 2.00 5.00
10 Mike Modano 2.50 6.00
11 Brendan Shanahan 1.50 4.00
12 Steve Yzerman 8.00 20.00
13 Pavel Bure 1.50 4.00
14 Luc Robitaille 1.25 3.00
15 Martin Brodeur 4.00 10.00
16 John LeClair 1.50 4.00
17 Jaromir Jagr 2.50 6.00
18 Curtis Joseph 1.50 4.00
19 Mats Sundin 1.50 4.00
20 Olaf Kolzig 1.25 3.00

2000-01 Revolution Stat Masters

Randomly inserted in packs, this 30-card set is a three tier issue. Tier one features top goal scorers and cards are sequentially numbered to 99, tier two features the NHL's leaders in shutouts and cards are sequentially numbered to 199, and tier three features assist leaders and cards are sequentially numbered to 299.

COMPLETE SET (30) 100.00 200.00
1 Teemu Selanne/99 6.00 15.00
2 Tony Amonte/99 5.00 12.00
3 Milan Hejduk/99 5.00 12.00
4 Brett Hull/99 6.00 15.00
5 Brendan Shanahan/99 5.00 12.00
6 Pavel Bure/99 5.00 12.00
7 Luc Robitaille/99 5.00 12.00
8 John LeClair/99 5.00 12.00
9 Jaromir Jagr/99 10.00 25.00
10 Owen Nolan/99 5.00 12.00
11 Martin Biron/199 2.50 6.00
12 Dominik Hasek/199 6.00 15.00
13 Patrick Roy/199 10.00 25.00
14 Ed Belfour/199 2.50 6.00
15 Jose Theodore/199 3.00 8.00
16 Martin Brodeur/199 6.00 15.00
17 Brian Boucher/199 2.50 6.00
18 Roman Turek/199 2.50 6.00
19 Curtis Joseph/199 2.50 6.00
20 Olaf Kolzig/199 2.50 6.00
21 Paul Kariya/299 5.00 12.00
22 Doug Gilmour/299 2.00 5.00
23 Ray Bourque/299 4.00 10.00
24 Joe Sakic/299 4.00 10.00
25 Mike Modano/299 3.00 8.00
26 Steve Yzerman/299 8.00 20.00
27 Scott Gomez/299 2.00 5.00
28 Mark Recchi/299 2.00 5.00
29 Mats Sundin/299 2.00 5.00
30 Adam Oates/299 2.00 5.00

2006-07 Rochester Americans

COMPLETE SET (25) 10.00 18.00
1 Craig Anderson .30 .75
2 David Booth .20 .50
3 Mike Card .20 .50
4 Adam Dennis .40 1.00
5 Mike Funk .20 .50
6 Rob Globke .40 1.00
7 Dylan Hunter .40 1.00
8 Greg Jacina .20 .50
9 Patrick Kaleta .20 .50
10 Kamil Kreps .20 .50
11 Drew Larman .20 .50
12 Martin Lojek .20 .50
13 Clarke MacArthur .40 1.00
14 Mark Mancari .40 1.00
15 Stefan Meyer .20 .50
16 Daniel Paille .40 1.00
17 Michael Ryan .40 1.00
18 Andrej Sekera .20 .50
19 Brandon Smith .20 .50
20 Janis Sprukts .20 .50
21 Drew Stafford .75 2.00
22 Anthony Stewart .30 .75
23 Marek Zagrapan .30 .75
24 Coaches .10 .25
NNO Cover Card .01 .01

1976-77 Rockies Puck Bucks

This 20-card set measures approximately 2 9/16" by 2 1/8" (after perforation) and features members of the then-expansion Colorado Rockies team. The set was issued in the Greater Denver area as part of a regional promotion for the Rockies. The cards feature a horizontal format on the front which has the player's photo. The cards were issued two to a panel (they could be separated, but then one couldn't compete in contest). Left side and right side in the rules refers to the two different cards that were joined: an action scene on the left side and a posed head shot in a circle on the right side). If the same player appeared in the action scene and in the circle, and if the ticket values and the color bars below both pictures matched, the contestant became an instant winner of two Colorado Rockies' hockey tickets, whose value is shown in the color bar. One could also save all player pictures until one had the same player appearing in the action scene and in the circle both with matching ticket values and matching color bars. The color bars at the bottom appeared in four different colors (yellow, blue, green, or orange). The cards feature either a "Play Puck Bucks" logo on the back, which also features a skeletal-like picture of a player, or a rules definition. Winners had to claim prizes by February 20, 1977. Since there is no numerical designation for the cards, they are checklisted alphabetically below.

COMPLETE SET (20) 37.50 75.00
1 Ron Andruff 2.00 4.00
2 Chuck Arnason 2.00 4.00
3 Henry Boucha 2.50 5.00
4 Colin Campbell 3.00 6.00
5 Gary Croteau 2.00 4.00
6 Guy Delparte 2.00 4.00
7 Steve Durbano 2.50 5.00
8 Tom Edur 2.00 4.00
9 Doug Favell [illegible] [illegible]
10 Dave Hudson 2.00 4.00
11 Bryan Lefley 2.00 4.00
12 Roger Lemelin 2.00 4.00
13 Simon Nolet 2.00 4.00
14 Wilf Paiement 2.50 5.00
15 Michel Plasse 3.00 6.00
16 Tracy Pratt 2.00 4.00
17 Nelson Pyatt 2.00 4.00
18 Phil Roberto 2.00 4.00
19 Sean Shanahan 2.00 4.00
20 Larry Skinner 2.00 4.00

1979-80 Rockies Team Issue

This 23-card set of the Colorado Rockies measures approximately 4" by 6". The fronts feature black-and-white action player photos. The backs are blank. The cards are unnumbered and checklisted below in alphabetical order.

COMPLETE SET (23) 20.00 40.00
1 Hardy Astrom 1.50 3.00
2 Doug Berry .75 1.50
3 Nick Beverley 1.00 2.00
4 Mike Christie .75 1.50
5 Gary Croteau 1.00 2.00
6 Lucien Deblois 1.00 2.00
7 Ron Delorme .75 1.50
8 Mike Gillis .75 1.50
9 Trevor Johansen .75 1.50
10 Mike Kitchen .75 1.50
11 Lanny McDonald 2.50 5.00
12 Mike McEwen .75 1.50
13 Bill McKenzie .75 1.50
14 Kevin Morrison .75 1.50
15 Bill Oleschuk .75 1.50
16 Randy Pierce .75 1.50
17 Michel Plasse 1.50 3.00
18 Joel Quenneville 1.00 2.00
19 Rob Ramage 2.50 5.00
20 Rene Robert 1.00 2.00
21 Don Saleski 1.00 2.00
22 Barry Smith 1.00 2.00
23 Jack Valiquette .75 1.50

1981-82 Rockies Postcards

This 30-card postcard set measures 3 1/2" by 5 1/2" and features borderless black-and-white action player photos of the Colorado Rockies. The backs have the standard white postcard design with the player's name and biographical information in the upper left corner. The team emblem is printed in light gray on the left side. The cards are unnumbered and checklisted below in alphabetical order.

COMPLETE SET (30) 14.00 35.00
1 Brent Ashton .75 2.00
2 Aaron Broten .40 1.00
3 Dave Cameron .40 1.00
4 Joe Cirella .75 2.00
5 Dwight Foster .40 1.00
6 Paul Gagne .40 1.00
7 Marshall Johnston CO .40 1.00
8 Veli-Pekka Ketola .60 1.50
9 Mike Kitchen .40 1.00
10 Rick Laferriere .40 1.00
11 Don Lever .60 1.50
12 Tapio Levo .40 1.00
13 Bob Lorimer .40 1.00
14 Bill MacMillan .40 1.00
15 Bob MacMillan VP .60 1.50
16 Merlin Malinowski .60 1.50
17 Bert Marshall GM .40 1.00
18 Kevin Maxwell .40 1.00
19 Joe Micheletti .75 2.00
20 Bobby Miller .40 1.00
21 Phil Myre .75 2.00
22 Graeme Nicolson .40 1.00
23 Jukka Porvari .40 1.00
24 Joel Quenneville .60 1.50
25 Rob Ramage 1.25 3.00
26 Glenn Resch 1.25 3.00
27 Steve Tambellini .60 1.50
28 Yvon Vautour .40 1.00
29 John Wensink .60 1.50
30 Title Card .75 2.00
(Team logo)

1952 Royal Desserts

The 1952 Royal Desserts Hockey set contains eight cards. The cards measure approximately 2 5/8" by 3 1/4". The set is cataloged as F219-2. The cards formed the backs of Royal Desserts packages of the period; consequently many cards are found with uneven edges stemming from the method of cutting the cards off the box. Each card has its number and the statement "Royal Stars of Hockey" in a red rectangle at the top. The blue tinted picture also features a facsimile autograph of the player. An album was presumably available as it is advertised on the card. The exact year (or years) of issue of these cards is not verified at this time.

COMPLETE SET (8) 6500.00 13000.00
1 Tony Leswick 300.00 750.00
2 Chuck Rayner 400.00 800.00
3 Edgar Laprade 300.00 750.00
4 Sid Abel 600.00 1200.00
5 Ted Lindsay 600.00 1200.00
6 Leo Reise 300.00 750.00
7 Red Kelly 600.00 1200.00
8 Gordie Howe 3750.00 7500.00

1971-72 Sabres Postcards

These standard-sized postcards feature borderless color photos. The backs feature player name, position, uniform number, and biographical information. These postcards were issued in bound form, with perforated top edges so as to be separated if necessary. The postcards are numbered in a long code format (for example, Punch Imlach is 82269-C). For space reasons, the 822 prefix and -C suffix have been deleted in the checklist below. Thanks to collector Edward Morse for updating the information seen below.

COMPLETE SET (22) 15.00 30.00
69 Punch Imlach CO 1.00 2.00
70 Roger Crozier 1.50 3.00
71 Jim Watson .50 1.00
72 Mike Robitaille .50 1.00
73 Tracy Pratt .50 1.00
74 Doug Barrie .50 1.00
75 Al Hamilton .50 1.00
76 Richard Martin 1.50 3.00
77 Dick Duff .75 1.50
78 Danny Lawson .50 1.00
79 Phil Goyette .50 1.00

80 Gil Perreault	4.00	8.00
81 Rod Zaine	.50	1.00
82 Gerry Meehan	.75	1.50
83 Ron Anderson	.50	1.00
84 Floyd Smith	.75	1.50
85 Kevin O'Shea	.50	1.00
86 Steve Atkinson	.50	1.00
87 Don Luce		
88 Ray McKay	.50	1.00
89 Eddie Shack	1.00	2.00
90 Dave Dryden	1.50	3.00

1972-73 Sabres Pepsi Pinback Buttons

These smallish buttons were apparently given away with the purchase of Pepsi products in the Buffalo area. The photos are black and white and feature early heroes of the Sabres history.

COMPLETE SET (9)	25.00	50.00
1 Roger Crozier	2.50	5.00
2 Don Luce	2.00	4.00
3 Rick Martin (action)	2.50	5.00
4 Rick Martin (head)	2.50	5.00
5 Gilbert Perreault (action)	5.00	10.00
6 Gilbert Perreault (head)	5.00	10.00
7 Rene Robert	2.50	5.00
8 Jim Schoenfeld	2.50	5.00
9 French Connection	5.00	10.00

1972-73 Sabres Postcards

This set of color postcards was issued by the team in response to autograph requests. It is not known whether they were actually sold in set form at any point, but given the difficulty in completing a set, it seems unlikely.

COMPLETE SET (20)	30.00	60.00
1 Steve Atkinson	1.00	2.00
2 Larry Carriere	1.00	2.00
3 Roger Crozier	4.00	8.00
4 Butch Deadmarsh	1.00	2.00
5 Dave Dryden	1.50	3.00
6 Larry Hillman	1.00	2.00
7 Tim Horton	5.00	10.00
8 Jim Lorentz	1.00	2.00
9 Don Luce	1.50	3.00
10 Richard Martin	3.00	6.00
11 Gerry Meehan	1.50	3.00
12 Larry Mickey	1.00	2.00
13 Gilbert Perreault	5.00	10.00
14 Tracy Pratt	1.50	3.00
15 Craig Ramsay	1.50	3.00
16 Rene Robert	1.50	3.00
17 Mike Robitaille	1.00	2.00
18 Jim Schoenfeld	3.00	6.00
19 Paul Terbenche	1.00	2.00
20 Randy Wyrozub	1.00	2.00

1973-74 Sabres Bells

This set of four photos of Buffalo Sabres players was sponsored by Bells Markets. The photos measure approximately 3 15/16" by 5 1/2" and were sold for 10 cents each. The front has a color action photo. These blank-backed cards are unnumbered and listed alphabetically in the checklist below. The team card was issued and cost 50 cents apiece.

COMPLETE SET (4)	15.00	30.00
1 Roger Crozier	4.00	8.00
2 Jim Lorentz	2.50	5.00
3 Richard Martin	4.00	8.00
4 Gilbert Perreault	6.00	12.00
5 Team Photo		

1973-74 Sabres Postcards

This 13-card set was published by Robert B. Shaver of Kenmore, New York. The cards are in the postcard format and measure approximately 3 1/2" by 5 1/2". The fronts feature a black-and-white action shot with white borders. The backs carry the player's name, position, and team name at the upper left and are divided in the middle. The set is dated by the inclusion of Joe Noris, who played with the Sabres only during the 1973-74 season. The cards are unnumbered and checklisted below in alphabetical order.

COMPLETE SET (13)	20.00	40.00
1 Roger Crozier	2.00	4.00
2 Dave Dryden	2.00	4.00
3 Tim Horton	5.00	10.00
4 Jim Lorentz	1.00	2.00
5 Don Luce	1.25	2.50
6 Rick Martin	2.00	4.00
7 Gerry Meehan	1.50	3.00
8 Larry Mickey	1.00	2.00
9 Joe Noris	1.00	2.00
10 Gilbert Perreault	4.00	8.00
11 Mike Robitaille	1.00	2.00
12 Jim Schoenfeld	2.00	4.00
13 Paul Terbenche	1.00	2.00

1974-75 Sabres Postcards

This set of color postcards was issued by the team in response to autograph requests. It is not known whether they were actually sold in set form at any point, but given the difficulty in completing a set, it seems unlikely.

COMPLETE SET (21)	30.00	60.00
1 Gary Bromley	2.00	4.00
2 Larry Carriere	1.00	2.00
3 Roger Crozier	4.00	8.00
4 Rick Dudley	2.00	4.00
5 Rocky Farr	1.00	2.00
6 Lee Fogolin	2.00	4.00
7 Danny Gare	2.00	4.00
8 Norm Gratton	1.00	2.00
9 Jocelyn Guevremont	1.00	2.00
10 Bill Hajt	1.00	2.00
11 Jerry Korab	2.00	4.00
12 Jim Lorentz	1.00	2.00
13 Don Luce	1.25	2.50
14 Richard Martin	2.00	4.00
15 Peter McNab	1.25	2.50
16 Larry Mickey	1.00	2.00
17 Gilbert Perreault	4.00	8.00
18 Craig Ramsay	1.50	3.00
19 Rene Robert	1.50	3.00
20 Jim Schoenfeld	2.00	4.00
21 Brian Spencer	2.50	5.00

1975-76 Sabres Linnett

Produced by Linnett Studios, this 12-card set featured Buffalo Sabres players from the 1975-76 season.

COMPLETE SET (12)	15.00	30.00
1 Roger Crozier	2.00	4.00
2 Gerry Desjardins	1.50	3.00
3 Dave Dryden	1.50	3.00
4 Jim Lorentz	1.00	2.00
5 Don Luce	1.25	2.50
6 Richard Martin	2.00	4.00
7 Peter McNab	1.25	2.50
8 Gerry Meehan	1.00	2.00
9 Gilbert Perreault	4.00	8.00
10 Rene Robert	1.50	3.00
11 Jim Schoenfeld	2.00	4.00
12 Fred Stanfield	1.50	3.00

1976-77 Sabres Glasses

Glasses feature a black and white portrait of the player. Glasses were available at Your Host restaurants.

COMPLETE SET (4)	12.50	25.00
1 Jerry Korab	3.00	6.00
2 Rick Martin	3.00	6.00
3 Gilbert Perreault	3.00	6.00
4 Jim Schoenfeld	3.00	6.00

1979-80 Sabres Bells

This set of nine photos of Buffalo Sabres players was sponsored by Bells Markets. The photos measure approximately 7 5/8" by 10". The front has a color action photo, with the player's name and team name in the white border at the lower right hand corner. The back is printed in blue and has the Sabres' logo, a head shot of the player, biographical information, and career statistics.

COMPLETE SET (9)	10.00	20.00
1 Don Edwards	2.00	4.00
2 Danny Gare	1.25	2.50
3 Jerry Korab	1.00	2.00
4 Richard Martin	2.00	4.00
5 Tony McKegney	1.25	2.50
6 Craig Ramsay	1.00	2.00
7 Bob Sauve	2.00	4.00
8 Jim Schoenfeld	1.50	3.00
9 John Van Boxmeer	1.00	2.00

1979-80 Sabres Milk Panels

This set of four confirmed panels feature singles that are approximately 3 1/2 by 1 1/2. The top portion features a blue-toned head shot, while the bottom includes player bio information. The backs are blank.

COMPLETE SET (4)	3.00	6.00
1 Don Edwards	.50	1.00
2 Ric Seiling	.50	1.00
3 Jerry Korab	.50	1.00
4 Gil Perreault	.50	1.00

1980-81 Sabres Milk Panels

This set of Buffalo Sabres was issued on the side of half gallon milk cartons. After cutting, the panels measure approximately 3 3/4" by 7 1/2", with two players per panel. The picture and text of the player panels are printed in red; the set can also be found in blue print. The top of the panel reads "Kids, Collect a Complete Set of Buffalo Sabres Players". Arranged alongside each other, the panel features for each player a head shot, biographical information, and player profile. The panels are subtly dated and numbered below the photo area in the following way. Perreault/Seiling is M325-80-4H (M325 is the product code, the number 80 gives the last two digits of the year, and 4 is the card number perhaps also indicating release week).

COMPLETE SET (2)	15.00	30.00
4 Gilbert Perreault and Ric Seiling	10.00	20.00
8 Bob Sauve and Richard Martin	6.00	12.00

1981-82 Sabres Milk Panels

This sixteen-panel set of Buffalo Sabres was issued by Wilson Farms Dairy on the side of 2 percent milk fat and homogenized Vitamin D half gallon milk cartons. After cutting, the panels measure approximately 3 3/4" by 7 1/2". Although the 2 percent milk fat cartons have some lime green lettering and a lime green stripe, the picture and text of the player panels are printed in red on both cartons. The top of the panel reads "Kids, Collect Action Photos of the 1981-82 Buffalo Sabres." Inside a red broken border, the panel has a action player photo, with player information and career summary beneath the picture. The panels are subtly dated and numbered below the photo area in the following way, Gilbert Perreault is M325-81-4H (M325 is the product code, the number 81 gives the last two digits of year, and 4 is the card number perhaps also indicating release week). The set can also be found in blue print.

COMPLETE SET (17)	60.00	150.00
1 Craig Ramsay	4.00	10.00
2 John Van Boxmeer	4.00	10.00
3 Don Edwards	5.00	12.00
4 Gilbert Perreault	8.00	20.00
5 Alan Haworth	4.00	10.00
6 Jim Schoenfeld	6.00	15.00
7 Richie Dunn	4.00	10.00
8 Bob Sauve	5.00	12.00
9 Bill Hajt	4.00	10.00
10 Larry Playfair	4.00	10.00
11 Tony McKegney	5.00	12.00
12 Mike Ramsey	5.00	12.00
13 Andre Savard	4.00	10.00
14 Derek Smith	4.00	10.00
15 Ric Seiling	4.00	10.00
16 Yvon Lambert	4.00	10.00
17 Dale McCourt	4.00	10.00

1982-83 Sabres Milk Panels

This seventeen-panel set of Buffalo Sabres was issued on the side of half gallon milk cartons. After cutting, the panels measure approximately 3 3/4" by 7 1/2". The picture and text of the player panels are printed in blue. The top of the panel reads "Kids, Clip and Save Exciting Tips and Pictures of Buffalo Sabres." Inside a blue broken border, the panel has a posed head and shoulders shot, with the player's name, position, and a hockey tip beneath the picture. The panels are subtly dated and numbered below the photo area in the following way, Gilbert Perreault is M325-82-7H. Phil Housley's card predates his Rookie Card.

COMPLETE SET (17)	60.00	150.00
2 1982-83 Home Schedule	6.00	15.00
3 Craig Ramsay	4.00	10.00
4 John Van Boxmeer	4.00	10.00
5 Larry Ruff	4.00	10.00
6 Bob Sauve	5.00	12.00
7 Gilbert Perreault	8.00	20.00
8 Ric Seiling	4.00	10.00
9 Jacques Cloutier	5.00	12.00
10 Larry Playfair	4.00	10.00
11 Phil Housley	8.00	20.00
12 Mike Foligno	5.00	12.00
13 Tony McKegney	5.00	12.00
14 Dale McCourt	4.00	10.00
15 Mike Ramsey	4.00	10.00
16 Hannu Virta	4.00	10.00
17 Brent Peterson	4.00	10.00
18 Scott Bowman GM	8.00	20.00

1984-85 Sabres Blue Shield

This 21-card set was issued by the Buffalo Sabres in conjunction with Blue Shield of Western New York. The cards measure approximately 2 1/2" by 3 3/4". It has been reported that only 500 sets were printed as a test for future issues. The fronts feature a head and shoulder color photo with player information below the picture. The card backs have the Blue Shield logo and the words "The Caring Card -- The Blue Shield of Western New York, Inc." We have checklisted the cards below in alphabetical order. Dave Andreychuk and Tom Barrasso appear in their Rookie Card year.

COMPLETE SET (21)	40.00	100.00
1 Dave Andreychuk	8.00	20.00
2 Tom Barrasso	8.00	20.00
3 Adam Creighton	2.00	5.00
4 Paul Cyr	1.25	3.00
5 Malcolm Davis	1.25	3.00
6 Mike Foligno	2.00	5.00
7 Bill Hajt	1.25	3.00
8 Gilles Hamel	1.25	3.00
9 Phil Housley	4.00	10.00
10 Sean McKenna	1.25	3.00
11 Mike Moller	1.25	3.00
12 Gilbert Perreault	6.00	15.00
13 Brent Peterson	1.25	3.00
14 Larry Playfair	1.25	3.00
15 Craig Ramsay	2.00	5.00
16 Mike Ramsey	2.00	5.00
17 Lindy Ruff	2.00	5.00
18 Bob Sauve	2.00	5.00
19 Ric Seiling	1.25	3.00
20 John Tucker	2.00	5.00
21 Hannu Virta	1.25	3.00

1985-86 Sabres Blue Shield

This 28-card set was issued by the Buffalo Sabres in conjunction with Blue Shield of Western New York. The cards were printed in two different sizes: large (4" by 6" with postcard backs) and small (2 1/2" by 3 1/2"). Both sizes have the Blue Shield logo on the backs. Though both sizes are scarce, the small cards are considered harder to obtain. The front of the large card features a color action photo of the player, with his name as well as biographical and statistical information below the picture. The front of the small card is identical except for the omission of the statistical information. The firing of Sabres' coach Jim Schoenfeld at the time the cards were issued makes his card rare as he was removed from the set. The set is priced below as complete without the Schoenfeld card. Daren Puppa's card predates his Rookie Card by three years.

COMPLETE SET (27)	16.00	40.00
1 Mikael Andersson	.40	1.00
2 Dave Andreychuk	2.00	5.00
3 Tom Barrasso	1.25	3.00
4 Adam Creighton	.40	1.00
5 Paul Cyr	.40	1.00
6 Malcolm Davis	.40	1.00
7 Steve Dykstra	.40	1.00
8 Dave Fenyves	.40	1.00
9 Mike Foligno	.40	1.00
10 Bill Hajt	.40	1.00
11 Bob Halkidis	.40	1.00
12 Gilles Hamel	.40	1.00
13 Phil Housley	1.25	3.00
14 Pat Hughes	.40	1.00
15 Normand Lacombe	.40	1.00
16 Chris Langevin	.40	1.00
17 Sean McKenna	.40	1.00
18 Gates Orlando	.75	2.00
19 Gilbert Perreault	2.00	5.00
20 Larry Playfair	.40	1.00
21 Daren Puppa	1.00	2.50
22 Craig Ramsay ACO	.20	.50
23 Mike Ramsey	.40	1.00
24 Lindy Ruff	.40	1.00
25 Jim Schoenfeld CO SP	6.00	15.00
26 Ric Seiling	.40	1.00
27 John Tucker	.60	1.50
28 Hannu Virta	.40	1.00

1985-86 Sabres Blue Shield Small

This set is the same as the regular Sabres Blue Shield set, only in a smaller format.

COMPLETE SET (27)	16.00	40.00
1 Mikael Andersson	.40	1.00
2 Dave Andreychuk	1.50	4.00
3 Tom Barrasso	.75	2.00
4 Adam Creighton	.40	1.00
5 Paul Cyr	.40	1.00
6 Malcolm Davis	.40	1.00
7 Steve Dykstra	.40	1.00
8 Dave Fenyves	.40	1.00
9 Mike Foligno	.40	1.00
10 Bill Hajt	.40	1.00
11 Bob Halkidis	.40	1.00
12 Gilles Hamel	.40	1.00
13 Phil Housley	.75	2.00
14 Pat Hughes	.40	1.00
15 Normand Lacombe	.40	1.00
16 Chris Langevin	.40	1.00
17 Sean McKenna	.40	1.00
18 Gates Orlando	.60	1.50
19 Gilbert Perreault	1.50	4.00
20 Larry Playfair	.40	1.00
21 Daren Puppa	.75	2.00
22 Craig Ramsay ACO	.20	.50
23 Mike Ramsey	.40	1.00
24 Lindy Ruff	.40	1.00
25 Jim Schoenfeld CO SP	4.00	10.00
26 Ric Seiling	.40	1.00
27 John Tucker	.60	1.50
28 Hannu Virta	.40	1.00

1986-87 Sabres Blue Shield

This 28-card set was issued by the Buffalo Sabres in conjunction with Blue Shield of Western New York. In contrast to the previous year's issue, the cards were printed only in one size, the approximately 4" by 6" postcard type with the Blue Shield logo on the backs. The front of the cards can be distinguished from the previous year's issue by the addition of the player's uniform number (inadvertently omitted on the Creighton and Fenyves cards) and updated statistics.

COMPLETE SET (28)	12.00	30.00
1 Shawn Anderson	.30	.75
2 Dave Andreychuk	2.50	6.00
3 Scott Arniel	.30	.75
4 Tom Barrasso	1.25	3.00
5 Jacques Cloutier	.40	1.00
6 Adam Creighton	.40	1.00
7 Paul Cyr	.30	.75
8 Steve Dykstra	.30	.75
9 Dave Fenyves	.30	.75
10 Mike Foligno	.60	1.50
11 Clark Gillies	.75	2.00
12 Bill Hajt	.30	.75
13 Bob Halkidis	.30	.75
14 Jim Hofford	.30	.75
15 Phil Housley	1.00	2.50
16 Jim Korn	.30	.75
17 Uwe Krupp	.60	1.50
18 Tom Kurvers	.30	.75
19 Norm Lacombe	.30	.75
20 Gates Orlando	.30	.75
21 Wilf Paiement	.40	1.00
22 Gilbert Perreault	2.00	5.00
23 Daren Puppa	1.25	3.00
24 Mike Ramsey	.40	1.00
25 Lindy Ruff	.30	.75
26 Christian Ruuttu	.30	.75
27 Doug Smith	.30	.75
28 John Tucker	.40	1.00

1986-87 Sabres Blue Shield Small

Same as the regular Sabres Shield set only in a smaller format.

COMPLETE SET (28)	14.00	35.00
1 Shawn Anderson	.30	.75
2 Dave Andreychuk	2.50	6.00
3 Scott Arniel	.30	.75
4 Tom Barrasso	1.25	3.00
5 Jacques Cloutier	.40	1.00
6 Adam Creighton	.40	1.00
7 Paul Cyr	.30	.75
8 Steve Dykstra	.30	.75
9 Dave Fenyves	.30	.75
10 Mike Foligno	.60	1.50
11 Clark Gillies	.75	2.00
12 Bill Hajt	.30	.75
13 Bob Halkidis	.30	.75
14 Jim Hofford	.30	.75
15 Phil Housley	1.25	3.00
16 Jim Korn	.30	.75
17 Uwe Krupp	.60	1.50
18 Tom Kurvers	.30	.75
19 Norm Lacombe	.30	.75
20 Gates Orlando	.30	.75
21 Wilf Paiement	.40	1.00
22 Gilbert Perreault	2.00	5.00
23 Daren Puppa	1.25	3.00
24 Mike Ramsey	.40	1.00
25 Lindy Ruff	.30	.75
26 Christian Ruuttu	.30	.75
27 Doug Smith	.30	.75
28 John Tucker	.40	1.00

1987-88 Sabres Blue Shield

This 28-card set was issued by the Buffalo Sabres in conjunction with Blue Shield of Western New York. In contrast to the previous year's issue, the cards are a different size, approximately 4" by 5", again in the postcard format with the Blue Shield logo on the backs. The front of the cards feature a color action photo of the player, with the player's name, team name, and team logo in a yellow stripe at the top. The player's number and a facsimile autograph appear in blue at the bottom on the front. Supposedly there exists a rare variation on the Phil Housley card which has his last name misspelled "Housely". The card of Pierre Turgeon predates his Rookie Card by one year.

COMPLETE SET (28)	10.00	25.00
1 Mikael Andersson 14	.30	.75
2 Dave Andreychuk 25	1.25	3.00
3 Scott Arniel 9	.30	.75
4 Tom Barrasso 30	.60	1.50
5 Jacques Cloutier 1	.40	1.00
6 Adam Creighton 38	.40	1.00
7 Mike Donnelly 16	.30	.75
8 Mike Foligno 17	.40	1.00
9 Clark Gillies 90	.40	1.00
10 Bob Halkidis 18	.30	.75
11 Mike Hartman 20	.30	.75
12 Ed Hospodar 24	.30	.75
13 Phil Housley 6	.60	1.50
14 Calle Johansson 3	.40	1.00
15 Uwe Krupp 40	.40	1.00
16 Jan Ludvig 36	.30	.75
17 Kevin Maguire 19	.30	.75
18 Mark Napier 65	.30	.75
19 Ken Priestlay 12	.30	.75
20 Daren Puppa 35	.60	1.50
21 Mike Ramsey 5	.40	1.00
22 Joe Reekie 27	.30	.75
23 Lindy Ruff 22	.30	.75
24 Christian Ruuttu 21	.40	1.00
25 Ray Sheppard 23	1.25	3.00
26 Doug Smith 15	.30	.75
27 John Tucker 7	.40	1.00
28 Pierre Turgeon 77	4.00	10.00

1987-88 Sabres Wonder Bread/Hostess

The 1987-88 Buffalo Sabres Team Photo Album was sponsored by Wonder Bread and Hostess Cakes. It consists of three large sheets, each measuring approximately 13 1/2" by 10 1/4" and joined together to form one continuous sheet. The first panel has a team photo of the Buffalo Sabres. The second and third panels present three rows of five cards each. After perforation, the cards measure approximately 2 5/8" by 3 3/8". They feature color posed photos bordered in various color dots, with player information below the picture sandwiched between the Sabres' and sponsors' logos. The back has biographical and statistical information in a horizontal format. We have checklisted the names below in alphabetical order, with the uniform number to the right of the name. The set features an early card of Pierre Turgeon pre-dating his Rookie Cards by one year.

COMPLETE SET (31)	8.00	20.00
1 Mikael Andersson 14	.20	.50
2 Shawn Anderson 37	.20	.50
3 Dave Andreychuk 25	1.00	2.50
4 Scott Arniel 9	.20	.50
5 Tom Barrasso 30	.75	2.00
6 Jacques Cloutier 1	.30	.75
7 Adam Creighton 38	.30	.75
8 Steve Dykstra 4	.20	.50
9 Mike Foligno 17	.30	.75
10 Clark Gillies 90	.30	.75
11 Ed Hospodar 24	.20	.50
12 Phil Housley 6	.50	1.25
13 Calle Johansson 3	.30	.75
14 Uwe Krupp 40	.30	.75
15 Don Lever CO	.20	.50
16 Bob Logan 26	.20	.50
17 Jan Ludvig 36	.20	.50
18 Kevin Maguire 19	.20	.50
19 Mark Napier 65	.30	.75
20 Daren Puppa 31	.60	1.50
21 Mike Ramsey 5	.30	.75
22 Joe Reekie 27	.30	.75
23 Lindy Ruff 22	.20	.50
24 Christian Ruuttu 21	.30	.75
25 Ted Sator CO	.20	.50
26 Ray Sheppard 23	.75	2.00
27 Barry Smith CO	.20	.50
28 Doug Smith 15	.20	.50
29 John Tucker 7	.30	.75
30 Pierre Turgeon 77	3.00	8.00
NNO Large Team Photo	1.25	3.00

1988-89 Sabres Blue Shield

This 28-card set was issued by the Buffalo Sabres in conjunction with Blue Shield of Western New York. The cards measure approximately 4" by 6" and are in the postcard format, with the Blue Shield logo on the backs. The fronts feature a color action photo of the player. The picture is sandwiched between yellow stripes, with team logo and player's name above, and player information below. The cards are unnumbered and we have checklisted them below in alphabetical order, with the uniform number next to the player's name. The cards of Benoit Hogue, Jan Ludvig, Mark Napier, and Joe Reekie were apparently late additions to the set; they are marked as SP in the checklist below.

COMPLETE SET (28)	10.00	25.00
1 Mikael Andersson 14	.20	.50
2 Dave Andreychuk 25	.60	1.50
3 Scott Arniel 9	.08	.25
4 Doug Bodger 8	.30	.75
5 Jacques Cloutier 1	.30	.75
6 Mike Donnelly 16	.20	.50
7 Mike Foligno 17	.30	.75
8 Bob Halkidis 18	.08	.25
9 Mike Hartman 20	.08	.25
10 Benoit Hogue 33 SP	1.25	3.00
11 Phil Housley 6	.40	1.00
12 Calle Johansson 3	.30	.75
13 Uwe Krupp 4	.30	.75
14 Jan Ludvig 36 SP	.75	2.00
15 Kevin Maguire 19	.08	.25
16 Mark Napier 65 SP	.75	2.00
17 Jeff Parker 29	.08	.25
18 Larry Playfair 27	.08	.25
19 Daren Puppa 31	.75	2.00
20 Mike Ramsey 5	.30	.75
21 Joe Reekie 55 SP	.75	2.00
22 Lindy Ruff 22	.08	.25
23 Christian Ruuttu 21	.08	.25
24 Sabretooth Mascot	.08	.25
25 Ray Sheppard 23	.60	1.50
26 John Tucker 7	.30	.75
27 Pierre Turgeon 77	2.50	6.00
28 Rick Vaive 12	.30	.75

1988-89 Sabres Wonder Bread/Hostess

The 1988-89 Buffalo Sabres Team Photo Album was sponsored by Wonder Bread and Hostess Cakes. It consists of three large sheets, each measuring approximately 13 1/2" by 10 1/4" and joined together to form one continuous sheet. The first panel has a team photo of the Sabres in civilian clothing. The second and third panels present three rows of five cards each. After perforation, the cards measure approximately 2 5/8" by 3 3/8". They feature color posed photos on white card stock. The top half has thin diagonal blue lines traversing the white background. Player information appears below the picture, between the Sabres' and sponsors' logos. The back has biographical and statistical information in a horizontal format. The cards are unnumbered and we have checklisted them below in alphabetical order, with the uniform number to the right of the player's name.

COMPLETE SET (31)	8.00	20.00
1 Mikael Andersson 14	.20	.50
2 Dave Andreychuk 25	.60	1.50
3 Scott Arniel 9	.20	.50
4 Doug Bodger 8	.20	.50
5 Jacques Cloutier 1	.30	.75
6 Adam Creighton 38	.25	.60
7 Mike Foligno 17	.30	.75
8 Bob Halkidis 18	.20	.50
9 Mike Hartman 20	.20	.50
10 Benoit Hogue 33	.40	1.00
11 Phil Housley 6	.40	1.00
12 Calle Johansson 3	.30	.75
13 Uwe Krupp 4	.30	.75
14 Don Lever CO	.20	.50
15 Jan Ludvig 36	.20	.50
16 Kevin Maguire 19	.20	.50
17 Brad Miller 44	.20	.50
18 Mark Napier 65	.20	.50
19 Jeff Parker 29	.20	.50
20 Larry Playfair 27	.20	.50
21 Daren Puppa 31	.75	2.00
22 Mike Ramsey 5	.20	.50
23 Joe Reekie 55	.20	.50
24 Lindy Ruff 22	.20	.50
25 Christian Ruuttu 21	.20	.50
26 Ted Sator CO	.20	.50
27 Ray Sheppard 23	.60	1.50
28 Barry Smith CO	.20	.50
29 John Tucker 7	.20	.50
30 Pierre Turgeon 77	2.50	6.00
xx Large Team Photo	.40	1.00

1989-90 Sabres Blue Shield

This 24-card set was issued by the Buffalo Sabres in conjunction with Blue Shield of Western New York. The cards measure approximately 4" by 6" and are in the postcard format, with the Blue Shield logo on the backs. The fronts feature a color action photo of the player. The picture is sandwiched between yellow stripes, with team logo and player's name above, and player information below. The cards are unnumbered and we have checklisted them below in alphabetical order, with the uniform number next to the player's name. The card of Alexander Mogilny predates his Rookie Card by one year.

COMPLETE SET (24)	8.00	20.00
1 Dave Andreychuk 25	.60	1.50
2 Scott Arniel 9	.20	.50
3 Doug Bodger 8	.20	.50
4 Mike Foligno 17	.30	.75
5 Mike Hartman 20	.20	.50
6 Benoit Hogue 33	.40	1.00
7 Phil Housley 6	.40	1.00
8 Dean Kennedy 26	.20	.50
9 Uwe Krupp 4	.30	.75
10 Grant Ledyard 3	.20	.50
11 Kevin Maguire 19	.20	.50
12 Clint Malarchuk 30	.30	.75
13 Alexander Mogilny 89	2.00	5.00
14 Jeff Parker 29	.20	.50
15 Larry Playfair 27	.20	.50
16 Ken Priestlay 56	.20	.50
17 Daren Puppa 31	.60	1.50
18 Mike Ramsey 5	.20	.50
19 Christian Ruuttu 21	.20	.50
20 Ray Sheppard 23	.40	1.00
21 Dave Snuggerud 18	.20	.50
22 Sabretooth Mascot	.08	.25
23 Pierre Turgeon 77	1.25	3.00
24 Rick Vaive 22	.30	.75

1989-90 Sabres Campbell's

The 1989-90 Buffalo Sabres Team Photo Album was sponsored by Campbell's and commemorates 20 years in the NHL. It consists of three large sheets (the first two measuring approximately 10" by 13 1/2" and the third smaller), all joined together to form one continuous sheet. The first panel has three color action shots superimposed on a large black and white picture of the Sabres. While the second panel presents four rows of four cards each (16 player cards), the third panel presents four rows of three cards each (11 player cards and a 20th year card). After perforation, the cards measure approximately 2 1/2" by 3 3/8". They feature color posed photos bordered in yellow (on three sides), on a dark blue background interspersed with Sabres' logos in light blue. Player information appears below the picture in a yellow diamond, sandwiched between the Sabres' and the Franco-American logos. The back has biographical and statistical information in a horizontal format. We have checklisted the names below in alphabetical order, with the uniform number to the right of the name. The card of Alexander Mogilny predates his Rookie Card by one year.

COMPLETE SET (28)	8.00	20.00
1 Shawn Anderson 37	.20	.50
2 Dave Andreychuk 25	.60	1.50
3 Scott Arniel 9	.20	.50
4 Doug Bodger 8	.20	.50
5 Rick Dudley CO	.30	.75
6 Mike Foligno 17	.30	.75
7 Mike Hartman 20	.20	.50
8 Benoit Hogue 33	.40	1.00
9 Phil Housley 6	.40	1.00
10 Dean Kennedy 26	.20	.50
11 Uwe Krupp 4	.30	.75
12 Grant Ledyard 3	.20	.50
13 Kevin Maguire 19	.20	.50
14 Clint Malarchuk 39	.30	.75
15 Alexander Mogilny 89	2.00	5.00
16 Mark Napier 65	.20	.50
17 Jeff Parker 29	.20	.50
18 Larry Playfair 27	.20	.50
19 Daren Puppa 31	.60	1.50
20 Mike Ramsey 5	.20	.50
21 Robert Ray 32	.40	1.00
22 Christian Ruuttu 21	.20	.50
23 Ray Sheppard 23	.40	1.00
24 Dave Snuggerud 18	.20	.50
25 John Tortorella CO	.20	.50
26 Pierre Turgeon 77	1.25	3.00
27 Rick Vaive 22	.30	.75
xx Large Team Photo	.40	1.00

1990-91 Sabres Blue Shield

This 26-card set was issued by the Buffalo Sabres in conjunction with Blue Shield of Western New York. The cards measure approximately 4" by 6" and are in the postcard format, with the Blue Shield logo on the backs. The fronts feature a color action photo of the player. The picture is sandwiched between yellow stripes, with team logo and player's name above, and player information below. These cards may be distinguished from the previous year's issue by the "medical shield logo" in the upper right corner. The cards are unnumbered and we have checklisted them below in alphabetical order, with the uniform number next to the player's name.

COMPLETE SET (26)	6.00	15.00
1 Dave Andreychuk 25	.30	.75
2 Donald Audette 28	.40	1.00
3 Doug Bodger 8	.20	.50
4 Greg Brown 9	.20	.50
5 Brian Curran 39	.20	.50
6 Lou Franceschetti 15	.20	.50
7 Mike Hartman 20	.20	.50
8 Dale Hawerchuk 10	.40	1.00
9 Benoit Hogue 33	.25	.60
10 Dean Kennedy 26	.20	.50
11 Uwe Krupp 4	.30	.75
12 Grant Ledyard 3	.20	.50
13 Mikko Makela 42	.20	.50
14 Clint Malarchuk 30	.30	.75
15 Alexander Mogilny 89	1.25	3.00
16 Daren Puppa 31	.40	1.00
17 Mike Ramsey 5	.20	.50
18 Robert Ray 32	.30	.75
19 Christian Ruuttu 21	.20	.50
20 Sabretooth Mascot	.08	.25
21 Jiri Sejba 23	.20	.50
22 Dave Snuggerud 18	.20	.50
23 John Tucker 7	.20	.50
24 Pierre Turgeon 77	.60	1.50
25 Rick Vaive 22	.20	.50
26 Jay Wells 24	.20	.50

1990-91 Sabres Campbell's

The 1990-91 Buffalo Sabres Team Photo Album was sponsored by Campbell's. It consists of three large sheets, each measuring approximately 10" by 13 1/2" and joined together to form one continuous sheet. The first panel has a team photo of the Sabres in street clothing. The second and third panels present four rows of four cards each (31 player cards plus a Sabres' logo card). After perforation, the cards measure approximately 2 1/2" by 3 3/8". They feature color posed photos bordered in white, on a dark blue background. The player's name is given above the picture, with the Sabres' logo, uniform number, and Franco-American logo below the picture. The back has biographical and statistical information in a horizontal format. We have checklisted the names below in alphabetical order, with the uniform number to the right of the name.

COMPLETE SET (32)	6.00	15.00
1 Dave Andreychuk 25	.30	.75
2 Donald Audette 28	.40	1.00
3 Doug Bodger 8	.20	.50
4 Greg Brown 9	.20	.50
5 Bob Corkum 19	.20	.50
6 Rick Dudley CO	.08	.25
7 Mike Foligno 17	.30	.75
8 Mike Hartman 20	.20	.50
9 Dale Hawerchuk 10	.40	1.00
10 Benoit Hogue 33	.25	.60
11 Dean Kennedy 26	.20	.50
12 Uwe Krupp 4	.30	.75
13 Grant Ledyard 3	.20	.50
14 Darcy Loewen 36	.20	.50
15 Mikko Makela 42	.20	.50
16 Clint Malarchuk 30	.30	.75
17 Brad Miller 44	.20	.50
18 Alexander Mogilny 89	1.25	3.00
19 Daren Puppa 31	.40	1.00
20 Mike Ramsey 5	.20	.50
21 Robert Ray 32	.30	.75
22 Christian Ruuttu 17	.20	.50
23 Jiri Sejba 23	.20	.50
24 Darrin Shannon 16	.20	.50
25 Dave Snuggerud 18	.20	.50
26 John Tortorella CO	.08	.25
27 John Tucker 7	.20	.50
28 Pierre Turgeon 77	.60	1.50
29 Rick Vaive 22	.20	.50
30 John Van Boxmeer CO	.08	.25
31 Jay Wells 24	.20	.50
xx Large Team Photo (In street clothes)	.40	1.00

1991-92 Sabres Blue Shield

This 26-card postcard set of Buffalo Sabres measuring approximately 4" by 6" features an action photograph enclosed in white and blue borders. The player's name, date, and team name appear in blue lettering on a gold background and are flanked on the right and left by the team logo and Blue Shield of Western New York's logo. Biographical information and the player's jersey number appear in blue over gold within a blue border at the bottom. Card backs carry a large Blue Shield logo and motto on the left side. The cards are unnumbered and checklisted below in alphabetical order, with the jersey number to the right of the name.

COMPLETE SET (26)	6.00	15.00
1 Dave Andreychuk 25	.40	1.00
2 Donald Audette 28	.30	.75
3 Doug Bodger 8	.25	.60
4 Gord Donnelly 34	.20	.50
5 Tom Draper 35	.25	.60
6 Kevin Haller 7	.20	.50
7 Dale Hawerchuk 10	.60	1.50
8 Randy Hillier 23	.20	.50
9 Pat LaFontaine 16	1.25	3.00
10 Grant Ledyard 3	.20	.50
11 Clint Malarchuk 30	.30	.75
12 Brad May 27	.40	1.00
13 Brad Miller 44	.20	.50
14 Alexander Mogilny 89	.75	2.00
15 Colin Patterson 17	.20	.50
16 Daren Puppa 31	.40	1.00
17 Mike Ramsey 5	.20	.50
18 Robert Ray 32	.30	.75
19 Christian Ruuttu 21	.20	.50
20 Dave Snuggerud 18	.20	.50
21 Ken Sutton 41	.20	.50
22 Tony Tanti 19	.20	.50
23 Rick Vaive 22	.25	.60
24 Jay Wells 24	.20	.50
25 Randy Wood 15	.20	.50
26 Sabretooth (Mascot)	.08	.25

1991-92 Sabres Pepsi/Campbell's

e 1991-92 Buffalo Sabres Team Photo Album was onsored in two different varieties. One version was onsored by Pepsi in conjunction with the Sheriff's fice of Erie County. The Pepsi logo appears on both des of each card. A second version was sponsored by ampbell's; the card fronts have the Campbell's unky soup logo and the flipside carries the Franco-merican emblem. The set consists of three large eets, joined together to form one continuous sheet. e first panel has a team photo of the Sabres in street othing, superimposed over lightning streaks on the t side. The second (10" by 13") and third (7 1/2" by ") panels present 28 cards; after perforation, the rds measure 2 1/2" by 3 1/4". The color action phos are full-bleed on three sides; the blue border runng down their right side carries the jersey number, m logo, player's name (on a gold band which jets t into the photo), and the Pepsi logo. The backs list ographical and statistical information. The cards are numbered and checklisted below in alphabetical der, with the jersey number to the right of the name.

OMPLETE SET (29)	6.00	15.00
Dave Andreychuk 25	.40	1.00
Donald Audette 28	.30	.75
Doug Bodger 8	.25	.60
Gord Donnelly 34	.20	.50
Tom Draper 35	.25	.60
Kevin Haller 7	.20	.50
Dale Hawerchuk 10	.60	1.50
Randy Hillier 23	.20	.50
Pat LaFontaine 16	.75	2.00
Grant Ledyard 3	.20	.50
Clint Malarchuk 30	.30	.75
Brad May 27	.40	1.00
Brad Miller 44	.20	.50
Alexander Mogilny 89	1.25	3.00
Colin Patterson 17	.20	.50
Daren Puppa 31	.40	1.00
Mike Ramsey 5	.20	.50
Robert Ray 32	.30	.75
Christian Ruuttu 21	.20	.50
Dave Snuggerud 18	.20	.50
Ken Sutton 41	.20	.50
Tony Tanti 9	.20	.50
Rick Vaive 22	.20	.50
Jay Wells 24	.20	.50
Randy Wood 15	.20	.50
Sabretooth (Mascot)	.08	.25
Team Logo	.08	.25
NHL Logo	.08	.25
Large Team Photo (In street clothes)	.40	1.00

1992-93 Sabres Blue Shield

onsored by Blue Shield of Western New York, this -card postcard set measures approximately 4" by 6" d features color action player photos. In a mustardlored box at the top are printed the player's name, the ar and team name, and the team and sponsor logos. a mustard-colored box at the bottom is biographical formation. These boxes and the photo are outlined by thin royal blue line. The horizontal backs have a light ue postcard design with the sponsor logo and a ellness Goal." The cards are unnumbered and ecklisted below in alphabetical order.

OMPLETE SET (26)	6.00	15.00
Dave Andreychuk	.30	.75
Donald Audette	.30	.75
Doug Bodger	.15	.40
Bob Corkum	.15	.40
Gord Donnelly	.15	.40
Dave Hannan	.15	.40
Dominik Hasek	2.50	6.00
Dale Hawerchuk	.40	1.00
Yuri Khmylev	.15	.40
Pat LaFontaine	.60	1.50
Grant Ledyard	.15	.40
Brad May	.20	.50
Alexander Mogilny	.60	1.50
Randy Moller	.15	.40
John Muckler CO	.15	.40
Colin Patterson	.15	.40
Wayne Presley	.15	.40
Daren Puppa	.30	.75
Mike Ramsey	.15	.40
Rob Ray	.30	.75
Richard Smehlik	.15	.40
Ken Sutton	.15	.40
Petr Svoboda	.20	.50
Bob Sweeney	.15	.40
Randy Wood	.15	.40
Sabretooth (Mascot)	.02	.10

1992-93 Sabres Jubilee Foods

rinted on thin white stock, the cards of this set, which e subtitled "Junior Fan Club," measure approximately " by 7" and feature color action shots of Sabres plays on their fronts. These photos are borderless, except cross the bottom, where a half-inch wide, mustardolored stripe carries the sponsor's name. A thin blue ripe edges the card at the very bottom. The player's ame appears vertically in blue lettering down one de. The Junior Fan Club logo in the lower left stradles the bottom of the photo and the two stripes. The acks have the player's name and biography in the pper left and the Sabres logo in the upper right. Beeath are highlights and stats from the 1991-92 seaon. The Stanley Cup logo at the bottom rounds out the ard. The cards are unnumbered and checklisted below alphabetical order.

OMPLETE SET (16)	4.80	12.00
Dave Andreychuk	.30	.75
Doug Bodger	.15	.40
Gord Donnelly	.40	1.00
Rob Ray		
Dominik Hasek	2.50	6.00
Daren Puppa		
Dale Hawerchuk	.40	1.00
Yuri Khmylev	.15	.40
Viktor Gordijuk		
Pat LaFontaine	.60	1.50
Brad May	.30	.75
Alexander Mogilny	.60	1.50
Randy Moller	.15	.40
Ken Sutton		
11 Wayne Presley	.30	.75
Donald Audette		
12 Mike Ramsey	.15	.40
13 Richard Smehlik	.15	.40
Bob Corkum		
14 Petr Svoboda	.20	.50
15 Bob Sweeney	.15	.40
16 Randy Wood	.15	.40

1993-94 Sabres Limited Edition Team Issue

Given out one per fan at a Sabres home game during the 93-94 season, these blank back cards with color action photos on the front are limited to 5,000 sets. There is a yellow stripe at the bottom of the card with the players name, and Sabres logo. Cards are unnumbered and checklisted below in alphabetical order.

COMPLETE SET (4)	4.00	10.00
1 Doug Bodger	.40	1.00
2 Dominik Hasek	2.00	5.00
3 Dale Hawerchuk	.75	2.00
4 Alexander Mogilny	1.25	3.00

1993-94 Sabres Noco

Subtitled Sabres Stars and issued in five-card perforated strips, these 20 standard-size cards feature on their fronts white-bordered color player action shots framed by a yellow line. The player's name and the team logo appear in the white margin below the photo. The white back carries the player's name and number at the top, followed below by statistics and career highlights. The logo for the set's sponsor, Noco Express Shop, rounds out the card at the bottom. The cards are unnumbered and checklisted below in alphabetical order.

COMPLETE SET (20)	4.80	12.00
1 Roger Crozier	.25	.60
2 Rick Dudley	.20	.50
3 Mike Foligno	.20	.50
4 Grant Fuhr	.40	1.00
5 Danny Gare	.20	.50
6 Dominik Hasek	2.00	5.00
7 Dale Hawerchuk	.30	.75
8 Tim Horton	.75	2.00
9 Pat LaFontaine	.50	1.25
10 Don Luce	.20	.50
11 Rick Martin	.30	.75
12 Brad May	.25	.60
13 Alexander Mogilny	.50	1.25
14 Gilbert Perreault	.40	1.00
15 Craig Ramsay	.20	.50
16 Mike Ramsey	.20	.50
17 Rene Robert	.25	.60
18 Sabretooth Mascot	.15	.40
19 Jim Schoenfeld	.30	.75
20 Knoxes Unveil Sabres Uniform Northrup Knox Punch Imlach Seymour Knox	.15	.40

2002-03 Sabres Team Issue

This oversized (5X7) set features action photos on the front and blank backs. It was printed on very thin stock. The cards likely were handed out as promotional items at signing appearances. It's possible the checklist is not complete. Internal documents revealed that just 500 copies were printed for Mair, Hecht, Noronen, Patrick and Campbell. 1,000 copies of each were printed of the remaining players.

COMPLETE SET (14)	10.00	20.00
1 Stu Barnes	.75	2.00
2 Martin Biron	.75	2.00
3 Eric Boulton	.75	2.00
4 Brian Campbell	.75	2.00
5 Tim Connolly	.40	1.00
6 Jochen Hecht	.75	2.00
7 Dmitri Kalinin	.40	1.00
8 Adam Mair	.75	2.00
9 Jay McKee	.40	1.00
10 Mika Noronen	.75	2.00
11 James Patrick	.75	2.00
12 Taylor Pyatt	.40	1.00
13 Rob Ray	.75	2.00
14 Rhett Warrener	.40	1.00

1974-75 San Diego Mariners WHA

Sponsored by Dean's Photo Service Inc., this set of seven photos measured approximately 5 3/8" by 8 1/2" and featured black-and-white action pictures against a white background on thin paper stock. The player's name appeared in the white margin below the photo along with the team and sponsor logos. The backs featured biographical information, career highlights, and statistics. The cards came in a light blue paper "picture pack" with the team and sponsor logos and game dates suggested for acquiring autographs. The cards were unnumbered and checklisted below in alphabetical order. This set may be incomplete; additions to the checklist would be welcome.

COMPLETE SET (7)	20.00	40.00
1 Andre Lacroix	5.00	10.00
2 Mike Laughton	2.50	5.00
3 Brian Morenz	2.50	5.00
4 Kevin Morrison	2.50	5.00
5 Gene Peacosh	2.50	5.00
6 Ron Plumb	4.00	8.00
7 Craig Reichmuth	2.50	5.00

1976-77 San Diego Mariners WHA

These cards measure 5" x 8" and were issued in two sheets of seven players each. Card fronts feature black and white photos with a white border. Backs feature player statistics. Cards are unnumbered and checklisted below alphabetically. Prices below are for individual cards.

COMPLETE SET (14)	20.00	40.00
1 Kevin Devine	1.25	2.50
2 Bob Dobek	1.25	2.50
3 Norm Ferguson	1.25	2.50
4 Brent Hughes	1.25	2.50
5 Randy Legge	1.25	2.50
6 Ken Lockett	1.25	2.50
7 Kevin Morrison	1.25	2.50
8 Joe Norris	1.25	2.50
9 Gerry Pinder	2.00	4.00
10 Brad Rhiness	1.25	2.50
11 Wayne Rivers	2.00	4.00
12 Paul Shmyr	1.50	3.00
13 Gary Veneruzzo	1.50	3.00
14 Ernie Wakely	2.50	5.00

1994 Santa Fe Hotel and Casino Manon Rheaume Postcard

Card is full color, and measures 3" x 5". Was given out as promotional piece for the Santa Fe Hotel and Casino in Las Vegas. Item is limited to 10,000 pieces.

NNO Manon Rheaume	2.00	5.00

1970-71 Sargent Promotions Stamps

This set consists of 224 total stamps, 16 for each NHL team. Individual stamps measure approximately 2" by 2 1/2". The set could be put into a album featuring Bobby Orr on the cover. Stamp fronts feature a full-color head shot of the player, player's name, and team. The stamp number is located in the upper left corner. The 1970-71 set features one-time appearances in Eddie Sargent Promotions sets by Hall of Famers Gordie Howe, Jean Beliveau, Andy Bathgate. The set also features first appearances of Gil Perreault, Brad Park, and Bobby Clarke. The three have Rookie Cards in both Topps and O-Pee-Chee for the same year.

COMPLETE SET (224)	325.00	650.00
1 Bobby Orr	62.50	125.00
2 Don Awrey	.50	1.00
3 Derek Sanderson	5.00	10.00
4 Ted Green	.63	1.25
5 Eddie Johnston	1.25	2.50
6 Wayne Carleton	.50	1.00
7 Ed Westfall	.75	1.50
8 Johnny Bucyk	2.50	5.00
9 John McKenzie	.50	1.00
10 Ken Hodge	1.00	2.00
11 Rick Smith	.50	1.00
12 Fred Stanfield	.50	1.00
13 Garnet Bailey	.50	1.00
14 Phil Esposito	10.00	20.00
15 Gerry Cheevers	5.00	10.00
16 Dallas Smith	.50	1.00
17 Joe Daley	1.00	2.00
18 Ron Anderson	.50	1.00
19 Tracy Pratt	.50	1.00
20 Gerry Meehan	.75	1.50
21 Reg Fleming	.50	1.00
22 Al Hamilton	.63	1.25
23 Gil Perreault	12.50	25.00
24 Skip Krake	.50	1.00
25 Kevin O'Shea	.50	1.00
26 Roger Crozier	1.50	3.00
27 Bill Inglis	.50	1.00
28 Mike McMahon	.50	1.00
29 Cliff Schmautz	.50	1.00
30 Floyd Smith	.50	1.00
31 Randy Wyrozub	.50	1.00
32 Jim Watson	.50	1.00
33 Tony Esposito	15.00	30.00
34 Doug Jarrett	.50	1.00
35 Keith Magnuson	.63	1.25
36 Dennis Hull	1.00	2.00
37 Cliff Koroll	.50	1.00
38 Eric Nesterenko	.75	1.50
39 Pit Martin	.63	1.25
40 Lou Angotti	.50	1.00
41 Jim Pappin	.63	1.25
42 Gerry Pinder	.50	1.00
43 Bobby Hull	25.00	50.00
44 Pat Stapleton	.63	1.25
45 Gerry Desjardins	1.00	2.00
46 Chico Maki	.63	1.25
47 Doug Mohns	.63	1.25
48 Stan Mikita	10.00	20.00
49 Gary Bergman	.63	1.25
50 Pete Stemkowski	.63	1.25
51 Bruce MacGregor	.50	1.00
52 Ron Harris	.50	1.00
53 Billy Dea	.50	1.00
54 Wayne Connelly	.50	1.00
55 Dale Rolfe	.50	1.00
56 Gordie Howe	40.00	80.00
57 Tom Webster	.63	1.25
58 Al Karlander	.50	1.00
59 Alex Delvecchio	2.50	5.00
60 Nick Libett	.63	1.25
61 Garry Unger	1.00	2.00
62 Roy Edwards	1.00	2.00
63 Frank Mahovlich	5.00	10.00
64 Bob Baun	1.25	2.50
65 Dick Duff	1.00	2.00
66 Ross Lonsberry	.50	1.00
67 Ed Joyal	.50	1.00
68 Dale Hoganson	.50	1.00
69 Eddie Shack	2.50	5.00
70 Real Lemieux	.50	1.00
71 Matt Ravlich	.50	1.00
72 Bob Pulford	1.50	3.00
73 Denis DeJordy	1.25	2.50
74 Larry Mickey	.50	1.00
75 Bill Flett	.50	1.00
76 Juha Widing	.75	1.50
77 Jim Peters	.63	1.25
78 Gilles Marotte	.63	1.25
79 Larry Cahan	.50	1.00
80 Howie Hughes	.50	1.00
81 Cesare Maniago	1.25	2.50
82 Ted Harris	.50	1.00
83 Tom Williams	.50	1.00
84 Gump Worsley	5.00	10.00
85 Tom Reid	.50	1.00
86 Murray Oliver	.50	1.00
87 Charlie Burns	.50	1.00
88 Jude Drouin	.50	1.00
89 Walt McKechnie	.50	1.00
90 Danny O'Shea	.50	1.00
91 Barry Gibbs	.50	1.00
92 Danny Grant	.63	1.25
93 Bob Barlow	.50	1.00
94 J.P. Parise	.63	1.25
95 Bill Goldsworthy	.75	1.50
96 Bobby Rousseau	.63	1.25
97 Jacques Laperriere	1.00	2.00
98 Henri Richard	5.00	10.00
99 J.C. Tremblay	.75	1.50
100 Rogie Vachon	4.00	8.00
101 Claude Larose	.50	1.00
102 Pete Mahovlich	.75	1.50
103 Jacques Lemaire	4.00	8.00
104 Bill Collins	.50	1.00
105 Guy Lapointe	1.50	3.00
106 Mickey Redmond	2.50	5.00
107 Larry Pleau	.63	1.25
108 Jean Beliveau	12.50	25.00
109 Yvan Cournoyer	4.00	8.00
110 Serge Savard	4.00	8.00
111 Terry Harper	.63	1.25
112 Phil Myre	1.00	2.00
113 Syl Apps	.63	1.25
114 Ted Irvine	.50	1.00
115 Ed Giacomin	5.00	10.00
116 Arnie Brown	.50	1.00
117 Walt Tkaczuk	.63	1.25
118 Jean Ratelle	2.50	5.00
119 Dave Balon	.50	1.00
120 Ron Stewart	.50	1.00
121 Jim Neilson	.50	1.00
122 Rod Gilbert	2.50	5.00
123 Bill Fairbairn	.50	1.00
124 Brad Park	10.00	20.00
125 Tim Horton	7.50	15.00
126 Vic Hadfield	.75	1.50
127 Bob Nevin	.50	1.00
128 Rod Seiling	.50	1.00
129 Gary Smith	1.25	2.50
130 Carol Vadnais	.50	1.00
131 Bert Marshall	.50	1.00
132 Earl Ingarfield	.50	1.00
133 Dennis Hextall	.63	1.25
134 Harry Howell	1.50	3.00
135 Wayne Muloin	.50	1.00
136 Mike Laughton	.50	1.00
137 Ted Hampson	.50	1.00
138 Doug Roberts	.50	1.00
139 Dick Mattiussi	.50	1.00
140 Gary Jarrett	.50	1.00
141 Gary Croteau	.50	1.00
142 Norm Ferguson	.50	1.00
143 Bill Hicke	.50	1.00
144 Gerry Ehman	.50	1.00
145 Ralph McSweyn	.50	1.00
146 Bernie Parent	7.50	15.00
147 Brent Hughes	.50	1.00
148 Bobby Clarke	20.00	40.00
149 Gary Dornhoefer	.63	1.25
150 Simon Nolet	.50	1.00
151 Garry Peters	.50	1.00
152 Doug Favell	1.25	2.50
153 Jim Johnson	.50	1.00
154 Andre Lacroix	.75	1.50
155 Larry Hale	.50	1.00
156 Joe Watson	.50	1.00
157 Jean-Guy Gendron	.50	1.00
158 Larry Hillman	.50	1.00
159 Ed Van Impe	.50	1.00
160 Wayne Hillman	.50	1.00
161 Al Smith	1.00	2.00
162 Jean Pronovost	.63	1.25
163 Bob Woytowich	.50	1.00
164 Bryan Watson	.63	1.25
165 Dean Prentice	.75	1.50
166 Duane Rupp	.50	1.00
167 Glen Sather	1.00	2.00
168 Keith McCreary	.50	1.00
169 Jim Morrison	.50	1.00
170 Ron Schock	.50	1.00
171 Wally Boyer	.50	1.00
172 Nick Harbaruk	.50	1.00
173 Andy Bathgate	2.50	5.00
174 Ken Schinkel	.50	1.00
175 Les Binkley	1.00	2.00
176 Val Fonteyne	.50	1.00
177 Red Berenson	.75	1.50
178 Ab McDonald	.50	1.00
179 Jim Roberts	.50	1.00
180 Frank St. Marseille	.50	1.00
181 Ernie Wakely	1.25	2.50
182 Terry Crisp	.63	1.25
183 Bob Plager	.75	1.50
184 Barclay Plager	.75	1.50
185 Chris Bordeleau	.50	1.00
186 Gary Sabourin	.50	1.00
187 Bill Plager	.63	1.25
188 Tim Ecclestone	.50	1.00
189 Jean-Guy Talbot	.75	1.50
190 Noel Picard	.50	1.00
191 Bob Wall	.50	1.00
192 Jim Lorentz	.50	1.00
193 Bruce Gamble	1.50	3.00
194 Jim Harrison	.50	1.00
195 Paul Henderson	1.50	3.00
196 Brian Glennie	.50	1.00
197 Jim Dorey	.50	1.00
198 Rick Ley	.63	1.25
199 Jacques Plante	12.50	25.00
200 Ron Ellis	.75	1.50
201 Jim McKenny	.50	1.00
202 Brit Selby	.50	1.00
203 Mike Pelyk	.50	1.00
204 Norm Ullman	2.50	5.00
205 Bill MacMillan	.50	1.00
206 Mike Walton	.63	1.25
207 Garry Monahan	.50	1.00
208 Dave Keon	2.50	5.00
209 Pat Quinn	1.00	2.00
210 Wayne Maki	.50	1.00
211 Charlie Hodge	1.25	2.50
212 Orland Kurtenbach	.63	1.25
213 Paul Popiel	.63	1.25
214 Dan Johnson	.50	1.00
215 Dale Tallon	.63	1.25
216 Ray Cullen	.63	1.25
217 Bob Dillabough	.50	1.00
218 Gary Doak	.50	1.00
219 Andre Boudrias	.75	1.50
220 Rosaire Paiement	.63	1.25
221 Darryl Sly	.50	1.00
222 George Gardner	.50	1.00
223 Jim Wiste	.50	1.00
224 Murray Hall	.50	1.00
xx Stamp Album (Bobby Orr on cover)	17.50	35.00

1971-72 Sargent Promotions Stamps

Issued by Eddie Sargent Promotions in a series of 16 ten-cent sheets of 14 NHL players each, this 224-stamp set featured posed color photos of players in their NHLPA jerseys. The pictures are framed on their tops and sides in different color borders with the players' names and teams appearing along the bottom. Each sheet measured approximately 7 7/8" by 10" and was divided into four rows, with four 2" by 2 1/2" stamps per row. Two of these 16 sections gave the series number (e.g., Series 1), resulting in a total of 14 players per sheet. The sections are perforated and the backs are blank. There was a stamp album (approximately 9 1/2" by 13") which featured information on the team history and individual players. The stamps are numbered in the upper left corner and they are grouped into 14 teams of 16 players each as follows: Boston Bruins (1-16), Buffalo Sabres (17-32), Chicago Blackhawks (33-48), Detroit Red Wings (49-64), Los Angeles Kings (65-80), Minnesota North Stars (81-96), Montreal Canadiens (97-112), New York Rangers (113-128), California Golden Seals (129-144), Philadelphia Flyers (145-160), Pittsburgh Penguins (161-176), St. Louis Blues (177-192), Toronto Maple Leafs (193-208), and Vancouver Canucks (209-224).

COMPLETE SET (224)	225.00	450.00
1 Fred Stanfield	.50	1.00
2 Ed Westfall	.75	1.50
3 John McKenzie	.50	1.00
4 Derek Sanderson	4.00	8.00
5 Rick Smith	.50	1.00
6 Teddy Green	.63	1.25
7 Phil Esposito	7.50	15.00
8 Ken Hodge	1.00	2.00
9 Johnny Bucyk	4.00	8.00
10 Bobby Orr	50.00	100.00
11 Dallas Smith	.50	1.00
12 Mike Walton	.63	1.25
13 Don Awrey	.50	1.00
14 Unknown	.50	1.00
15 Eddie Johnston	1.00	2.00
16 Gerry Cheevers	4.00	8.00
17 Gerry Meehan	.75	1.50
18 Ron Anderson	.50	1.00
19 Gilbert Perreault	6.00	12.00
20 Eddie Shack	2.00	4.00
21 Jim Watson	.50	1.00
22 Kevin O'Shea	.50	1.00
23 Al Hamilton	.50	1.00
24 Dick Duff	.75	1.50
25 Tracy Pratt	.50	1.00
26 Don Luce	.50	1.00
27 Roger Crozier	1.00	2.00
28 Doug Barrie	.50	1.00
29 Mike Robitaille	.50	1.00
30 Phil Goyette	.50	1.00
31 Larry Keenan	.50	1.00
32 Dave Dryden	1.00	2.00
33 Stan Mikita	6.00	12.00
34 Bobby Hull	20.00	40.00
35 Cliff Koroll	.50	1.00
36 Chico Maki	.63	1.25
37 Danny O'Shea	.50	1.00
38 Lou Angotti	.50	1.00
39 Andre Lacroix	.63	1.25
40 Jim Pappin	.50	1.00
41 Doug Jarrett	.50	1.00
42 Pit Martin	.63	1.25
43 Gary Smith	1.00	2.00
44 Tony Esposito	7.50	15.00
45 Pat Stapleton	.50	1.00
46 Dennis Hull	1.00	2.00
47 Bill White	.50	1.00
48 Keith Magnuson	.63	1.25
49 Bill Collins	.50	1.00
50 Bob Wall	.50	1.00
51 Red Berenson	.75	1.50
52 Mickey Redmond	1.50	3.00
53 Nick Libett	.50	1.00
54 Gary Bergman	.63	1.25
55 Alex Delvecchio	2.50	5.00
56 Tim Ecclestone	.50	1.00
57 Arnie Brown	.50	1.00
58 Ron Harris	.50	1.00
59 Ab McDonald	.50	1.00
60 Guy Charron	.63	1.25
61 Al Smith	1.00	2.00
62 Joe Daley	1.00	2.00
63 Leon Rochefort	.50	1.00
64 Ron Stackhouse	.50	1.00
65A Larry Johnston	.75	1.50
65B Juha Widing	.50	1.00
66 Bob Pulford	1.00	2.00
67 Bill Flett	.50	1.00
68 Rogie Vachon	2.50	5.00
69 Ross Lonsberry	.50	1.00
70 Gilles Marotte	.50	1.00
71 Harry Howell	1.00	2.00
72 Real Lemieux	.50	1.00
73 Butch Goring	.50	1.00
74 Ed Joyal	.50	1.00
75 Larry Hillman	.50	1.00
76 Lucien Grenier	.50	1.00
77 Paul Curtis	.50	1.00
78 Unknown	.50	1.00
79 Unknown	.50	1.00
80 Unknown	.50	1.00
81 Jude Drouin	.50	1.00
82 Tom Reid	.50	1.00
83 J.P. Parise	.63	1.25
84 Doug Mohns	.63	1.25
85 Danny Grant	.63	1.25
86 Bill Goldsworthy	.75	1.50
87 Charlie Burns	.50	1.00
88 Murray Oliver	.50	1.00
89 Dean Prentice	.75	1.50
90 Bob Nevin	.63	1.25
91 Ted Harris	.63	1.25
92 Cesare Maniago	1.00	2.00
93 Lou Nanne	.63	1.25
94 Ted Hampton	.50	1.00
95 Barry Gibbs	.50	1.00
96 Gump Worsley	4.00	8.00
97 J.C. Tremblay	.75	1.50
98 Guy Lapointe	1.00	2.00
99 Pete Mahovlich	.75	1.50
100 Larry Pleau	.63	1.25
101 Phil Myre	1.00	2.00
102 Yvan Cournoyer	2.50	5.00
103 Henri Richard	5.00	10.00
104 Frank Mahovlich	5.00	10.00
105 Jacques Lemaire	2.00	4.00
106 Claude Larose	.50	1.00
107 Terry Harper	.63	1.25
108 Jacques Laperriere	1.00	2.00
109 Phil Roberto	.50	1.00
110 Serge Savard	2.00	4.00
111 Marc Tardif	.63	1.25
112 Pierre Bouchard	.63	1.25
113 Rod Gilbert	2.50	5.00
114 Jean Ratelle	2.50	5.00
115 Pete Stemkowski	.50	1.00
116 Brad Park	4.00	8.00
117 Bobby Rousseau	.50	1.00
118 Dale Rolfe	.50	1.00
119 Rod Seiling	.50	1.00
120 Walt Tkaczuk	.50	1.00
121 Vic Hadfield	.63	1.25
122 Jim Neilson	.50	1.00
123 Bill Fairbairn	.50	1.00
124 Bruce MacGregor	.50	1.00
125 Dave Balon	.50	1.00
126 Ted Irvine	.50	1.00
127 Gilles Villemure	1.00	2.00
128 Ed Giacomin	4.00	8.00
129 Walt McKechnie	.50	1.00
130 Tom Williams	.50	1.00
131 Wayne Carleton	.63	1.25
132 Gerry Pinder	.50	1.00
133 Gary Croteau	.50	1.00
134 Bert Marshall	.50	1.00
135 Tom Webster	.50	1.00
136 Norm Ferguson	.50	1.00
137 Carol Vadnais	.50	1.00
138 Gary Jarrett	.50	1.00
139 Ernie Hicke	.50	1.00
140 Paul Shmyr	.50	1.00
141 Marshall Johnston	.50	1.00
142 Don O'Donoghue	.50	1.00
143 Joey Johnston	.50	1.00
144 Dick Redmond	.50	1.00
145 Simon Nolet	.50	1.00
146 Wayne Hillman	.50	1.00
147 Brent Hughes	.50	1.00
148 Jim Johnson	.50	1.00
149 Larry Mickey	.50	1.00
150 Ed Van Impe	.50	1.00
151 Gary Dornhoefer	.63	1.25
152 Bobby Clarke	12.50	25.00
153 Jean-Guy Gendron	.50	1.00
154 Larry Hale	.50	1.00
155 Serge Bernier	.50	1.00
156 Doug Favell	1.00	2.00
157 Bob Kelly	.50	1.00
158 Joe Watson	.50	1.00
159 Larry Brown	.50	1.00
160 Bruce Gamble	1.00	2.00
161 Syl Apps	.63	1.25
162 Ken Schinkel	.50	1.00
163 Val Fonteyne	.50	1.00
164 Bryan Watson	.75	1.50
165 Bob Woytowich	.50	1.00
166 Les Binkley	1.00	2.00
167 Roy Edwards	1.00	2.00
168 Jean Pronovost	.63	1.25
169 Tim Horton	6.00	12.00
170 Ron Schock	.50	1.00
171 Nick Harbaruk	.50	1.00
172 Greg Polis	.50	1.00
173 Bryan Hextall	.63	1.25
174 Keith McCreary	.50	1.00
175 Bill Hicke	.50	1.00
176 Jim Rutherford	1.00	2.00
177 Gary Sabourin	.50	1.00
178 Garry Unger	1.00	2.00
179 Terry Crisp	.63	1.25
180 Noel Picard	.50	1.00
181 Jim Roberts	.50	1.00
182 Barclay Plager	.75	1.50
183 Brit Selby	.50	1.00
184 Frank St. Marseille	.50	1.00
185 Ernie Wakely	1.00	2.00
186 Wayne Connelly	.50	1.00
187 Chris Bordeleau	.50	1.00
188 Bill Sutherland	.50	1.00
189 Bob Plager	.75	1.50
190 Bill Plager	.63	1.25
191 George Morrison	.50	1.00
192 Jim Lorentz	.50	1.00
193 Norm Ullman	2.50	5.00
194 Jim McKenny	.50	1.00
195 Rick Ley	.50	1.00
196 Bob Baun	1.00	2.00
197 Mike Pelyk	.50	1.00
198 Bill MacMillan	.50	1.00
199 Garry Monahan	.50	1.00
200 Paul Henderson	1.50	3.00
201 Jim Dorey	.50	1.00
202 Jim Harrison	.50	1.00
203 Ron Ellis	.75	1.50
204 Darryl Sittler	3.00	6.00
205 Bernie Parent	2.50	5.00
206 Dave Keon	2.50	5.00
207 Brad Selwood	.50	1.00
208 Don Marshall	.50	1.00
209 Dale Tallon	.63	1.25
210 Dan Johnson	.50	1.00
211 Murray Hall	.50	1.00
212 Paul Popiel	.63	1.25
213 George Gardner	.50	1.00
214 Gary Doak	.50	1.00
215 Andre Boudrias	.63	1.25
216 Orland Kurtenbach	.63	1.25
217 Wayne Maki	.50	1.00
218 Rosaire Paiement	.63	1.25
219 Pat Quinn	1.00	2.00
220 Fred Speck	.50	1.00
221 Barry Wilkins	.50	1.00
222 Dunc Wilson	1.00	2.00
223 Ted Taylor	.50	1.00
224 Mike Corrigan	.50	1.00
xx Stamp Album (Bobby Orr on cover)	12.50	25.00

1972-73 Sargent Promotions Stamps

During the 1972-73 hockey season, Eddie Sargent Promotions produced a set of 224 stamps. They were issued in cello packages in a series of 16 sheets and, at that time, sold for ten cents per sheet with one sheet being available each week of the promotion. Each sheet measures approximately 7 7/8" by 10" and was divided into four rows, with four 2" by 2 1/2" sections per row. Since two of the 16 sections gave the series number (e.g., Series 1), color photos of fourteen NHL players were featured in each series. The set features 224 players from sixteen NHL teams. The pictures were numbered in the upper left hand corner and are checklisted below accordingly. The pictures are framed on their top and sides in different color borders, with the player's name and the team's city name given below. There are two sticker albums (approximately 11 1/4" by 12") available for the set, both of which are bilingual. After a general introduction, the album is divided into team sections, with two pages devoted to each team. A brief history of each team is presented, followed by 14 numbered sticker slots. Biographical information and career summary appear below each stamp slot on the page itself. The typically found album has Bobby Orr on the cover. Another album is the more difficult Paul Henderson Team Canada cover. The toughest of the three is the Richard Martin cover. The stamps are numbered on the front and checklisted below alphabetically according to teams as follows: Atlanta Flames (1-14), Boston Bruins (15-28), Buffalo Sabres (29-42), California Seals (43-56), Chicago Blackhawks (57-70), Detroit Red Wings (71-84), Los Angeles Kings (85-98), Minnesota North Stars (99-112), Montreal Canadiens (113-126), New York Islanders (127-140), New York Rangers (141-154), Philadelphia Flyers (155-168), Pittsburgh Penguins (169-182), St. Louis Blues (183-196), Toronto Maple Leafs (197-210), and Vancouver Canucks (211-224).

COMPLETE SET (224)	112.50	225.00
1 Lucien Grenier	.25	.50
2 Phil Myre	.50	1.00
3 Ernie Hicke	.25	.50
4 Keith McCreary	.25	.50
5 Bill MacMillan	.25	.50
6 Pat Quinn	.50	1.00
7 Bill Plager	.38	.75
8 Noel Price	.25	.50
9 Bob Leiter	.25	.50
10 Randy Manery	.25	.50
11 Bob Paradise	.25	.50
12 Larry Romanchych	.25	.50
13 Lew Morrison	.25	.50
14 Dan Bouchard	.50	1.00
15 Fred Stanfield	.25	.50
16 Johnny Bucyk	1.50	3.00
17 Bobby Orr	20.00	40.00
18 Wayne Cashman	.38	.75
19 Dallas Smith	.25	.50
20 Ed Johnston	.75	1.50
21 Phil Esposito	5.00	10.00
22 Ken Hodge	.50	1.00
23 Don Awrey	.25	.50
24 Mike Walton	.25	.50
25 Carol Vadnais	.25	.50
26 Doug Roberts	.25	.50
27 Don Marcotte	.25	.50
28 Garnet Bailey	.25	.50
29 Gerry Meehan	.25	.50
30 Tracy Pratt	.25	.50
31 Gilbert Perreault	2.00	4.00
32 Roger Crozier	1.00	2.00
33 Don Luce	.25	.50
34 Dave Dryden	.50	1.00
35 Richard Martin	.50	1.00
36 Jim Lorentz	.25	.50
37 Tim Horton	4.00	8.00
38 Craig Ramsay	.25	.50
39 Larry Hillman	.25	.50
40 Steve Atkinson	.25	.50
41 Jim Schoenfeld	.38	.75
42 Rene Robert	.38	.75
43 Walt McKechnie	.25	.50
44 Marshall Johnston	.25	.50
45 Joey Johnston	.25	.50
46 Dick Redmond	.25	.50
47 Bert Marshall	.25	.50
48 Gary Croteau	.25	.50
49 Marv Edwards	.50	1.00
50 Gilles Meloche	.50	1.00
51 Ivan Boldirev	.25	.50
52 Stan Gilbertson	.25	.50
53 Peter Laframboise	.25	.50
54 Reggie Leach	.50	1.00
55 Craig Patrick	.50	1.00
56 Bob Stewart	.25	.50
57 Keith Magnuson	.38	.75
58 Doug Jarrett	.25	.50
59 Cliff Koroll	.25	.50
60 Chico Maki	.25	.50
61 Gary Smith	.50	1.00
62 Bill White	.25	.50
63 Stan Mikita	3.00	6.00
64 Jim Pappin	.25	.50
65 Lou Angotti	.25	.50
66 Tony Esposito	4.00	8.00

67 Dennis Hull .50 1.00
68 Pit Martin .25 .50
69 Pat Stapleton .25 .50
70 Dan Maloney .25 .50
71 Bill Collins .25 .50
72 Arnie Brown .25 .50
73 Red Berenson .38 .75
74 Mickey Redmond 1.00 2.00
75 Nick Libett .25 .50
76 Alex Delvecchio 1.25 2.50
77 Ron Stackhouse .25 .50
78 Tim Ecclestone .25 .50
79 Gary Bergman .25 .50
80 Guy Charron .25 .50
81 Leon Rochefort .25 .50
82 Larry Johnston .25 .50
83 Andy Brown .25 .50
84 Henry Boucha .38 .75
85 Paul Curtis .25 .50
86 Jim Stanfield .25 .50
87 Rogatien Vachon 1.50 3.00
88 Ralph Backstrom .38 .75
89 Gilles Marotte .25 .50
90 Harry Howell .75 1.50
91 Real Lemieux .25 .50
92 Butch Goring .38 .75
93 Juha Widing .25 .50
94 Mike Corrigan .25 .50
95 Larry Brown .25 .50
96 Terry Harper .38 .75
97 Serge Bernier .25 .50
98 Bob Berry .25 .50
99 Tom Reid .25 .50
100 Jude Drouin .25 .50
101 Jean-Paul Parise .38 .75
102 Doug Mohns .38 .75
103 Danny Grant .38 .75
104 Bill Goldsworthy .50 1.00
105 Gump Worsley 2.50 5.00
106 Charlie Burns .25 .50
107 Murray Oliver .25 .50
108 Barry Gibbs .25 .50
109 Ted Harris .25 .50
110 Cesare Maniago 1.00 2.00
111 Lou Nanne .38 .75
112 Bob Nevin .25 .50
113 Guy Lapointe .75 1.50
114 Peter Mahovlich .38 .75
115 Jacques Lemaire 1.00 2.00
116 Pierre Bouchard .25 .50
117 Yvan Cournoyer 1.25 2.50
118 Marc Tardif .25 .50
119 Henri Richard 2.50 5.00
120 Frank Mahovlich 2.50 5.00
121 Jacques Laperriere .75 1.50
122 Claude Larose .25 .50
123 Serge Savard 1.00 2.00
124 Ken Dryden 10.00 20.00
125 Rejean Houle .38 .75
126 Jim Roberts .25 .50
127 Ed Westfall .38 .75
128 Terry Crisp .38 .75
129 Gerry Desjardins .50 1.00
130 Denis DeJordy .75 1.50
131 Billy Harris .25 .50
132 Brian Spencer .50 1.00
133 Germaine Gagnon UER .25 .50
134 David Hedson .25 .50
135 Lorne Henning .25 .50
136 Brian Marchinko .25 .50
137 Tom Miller .25 .50
138 Gerry Hart .25 .50
139 Bryan Lefley .25 .50
140 James Mair .25 .50
141 Rod Gilbert 1.25 2.50
142 Jean Ratelle 1.25 2.50
143 Pete Stemkowski .25 .50
144 Brad Park 1.50 3.00
145 Bobby Rousseau .25 .50
146 Dale Rolfe .25 .50
147 Ed Giacomin 1.50 3.00
148 Rod Seiling .25 .50
149 Walt Tkaczuk .25 .50
150 Bill Fairbairn .25 .50
151 Vic Hadfield .38 .75
152 Ted Irvine .25 .50
153 Bruce MacGregor .25 .50
154 Jim Neilson .25 .50
155 Brent Hughes .25 .50
156 Wayne Hillman .25 .50
157 Doug Favell .75 1.50
158 Simon Nolet .25 .50
159 Joe Watson .25 .50
160 Ed Van Impe .25 .50
161 Gary Dornhoefer .38 .75
162 Bobby Clarke 5.00 10.00
163 Bob Kelly .25 .50
164 Bill Flett .25 .50
165 Rick Foley .25 .50
166 Ross Lonsberry .25 .50
167 Rick MacLeish .50 1.00
168 Bill Clement .50 1.00
169 Syl Apps .38 .75
170 Ken Schinkel .25 .50
171 Nick Harbaruk .25 .50
172 Bryan Watson .38 .75
173 Bryan Hextall .38 .75
174 Roy Edwards .50 1.00
175 Jim Rutherford .75 1.50
176 Jean Pronovost .38 .75
177 Rick Kessell .25 .50
178 Greg Polis .25 .50
179 Ron Schock .25 .50
180 Duane Rupp .25 .50
181 Darryl Edestrand .25 .50
182 Dave Burrows .25 .50
183 Gary Sabourin .25 .50
184 Garry Unger .50 1.00
185 Noel Picard .25 .50
186 Bob Plager .38 .75
187 Barclay Plager .38 .75
188 Frank St. Marseille .25 .50
189 Danny O'Shea .25 .50
190 Kevin O'Shea .25 .50
191 Wayne Stephenson .50 1.00
192 Chris Evans .25 .50
193 Jacques Caron .25 .50
194 Andre Dupont .25 .50
195 Mike Murphy .25 .50
196 Jack Egers .25 .50
197 Norm Ullman 1.25 2.50
198 Jim McKenny .25 .50
199 Bob Baun .50 1.00
200 Mike Pelyk .25 .50
201 Ron Ellis .38 .75
202 Garry Monahan .25 .50
203 Paul Henderson 1.00 2.00
204 Darryl Sittler 1.75 3.50
205 Brian Glennie .25 .50
206 Dave Keon 1.25 2.50
207 Jacques Plante 5.00 10.00
208 Pierre Jarry .25 .50
209 Rick Kehoe .38 .75
210 Denis Dupere .25 .50
211 Dale Tallon .38 .75
212 Murray Hall .25 .50
213 Dunc Wilson .50 1.00
214 Andre Boudrias .38 .75
215 Orland Kurtenbach .38 .75
216 Wayne Maki .25 .50
217 Barry Wilkins .25 .50
218 Richard Lemieux .25 .50
219 Bobby Schmautz .25 .50
220 Dave Balon .25 .50
221 Robert Lalonde .25 .50
222 Jocelyn Guevremont .25 .50
223 Gregg Boddy .25 .50
224 Dennis Kearns .25 .50
xx Stamp Album 10.00 20.00
(Bobby Orr on cover)
XX Stamp Album 25.00 50.00
Richard Martin
xx Stamp Album 17.50 35.00
(Paul Henderson on cover)

1990-91 Score Promos

The 1990-91 Score Promo set contains six different player standard-size cards. The promos were issued in both a Canadian and an American version. Three (10 Patrick Roy, 40 Gary Leeman, and 100 Mark Messier) were distributed as Canadian promos and the other three were given to U.S. card dealer accounts. Though all these promo versions have the same numbering as the regular issues, several of them are easily distinguished from their regular issue counterparts. The Roy and Messier promos have different player photos on their fronts (Roy promo also has a different photo on its back). The photo on the front of the Roenick promo is cropped differently, and the blurb on its back is also slightly different. Even for those promos that appear to be otherwise identical with the regular cards, close inspection reveals the following distinguishing marks: 1) on the backs, the promos have the registered mark (circle R) by the Score logo, whereas the regular issues have instead the trademark (TM); and 2) on the back, the NHL logo is slightly larger on the promos and the text around it is only in English (the regular issues also have a French translation).

1A Wayne Gretzky ERR 25.00 60.00
(Catches Left)
1B Wayne Gretzky COR 10.00 25.00
(Shoots Left)
10 Patrick Roy 8.00 20.00
40 Gary Leeman .30 .75
100A Mark Messier ERR 6.00 15.00
(Won Smythe in 1990)
100B Mark Messier COR 2.50 6.00
(Won Smythe in 1984)
179 Jeremy Roenick 2.00 5.00
200 Ray Bourque 2.50 6.00

1990-91 Score

The 1990-91 Score hockey set contains 440 standard-size cards. The fronts feature a color action photo, superimposed over blue and red stripes on a white background. The team logo appears in the upper left hand corner, while an image of a hockey player (in various colors) appears in the lower right hand corner. The backs are outlined in a blue border and show a head shot of the player on the upper half. The career statistics and highlights on the lower half are printed on a pale yellow background. The complete factory set price includes the five Eric Lindros bonus cards (B1-B5) that were only available in the factory sets sold to hobby dealers.

COMPLETE SET (440) 5.00 15.00
COMP.FACT.SET (445) 10.00 18.00
1 Wayne Gretzky .50 1.25
2 Mario Lemieux .50 1.25
3 Steve Yzerman .40 1.00
4 Cam Neely .05 .15
5 Al MacInnis .02 .10
6 Paul Coffey .08 .25
7 Brian Bellows .01 .05
8 Joe Sakic .25 .60
9 Bernie Nicholls .02 .10
10 Patrick Roy .40 1.00
11 Doug Houda RC .01 .05
12 David Volek .01 .05
13 Esa Tikkanen .01 .05
14 Thomas Steen .01 .05
15 Chris Chelios .08 .25
16 Bob Carpenter .01 .05
17 Dirk Graham .01 .05
18 Garth Butcher .01 .05
19 Patrik Sundstrom .01 .05
20 Rod Langway .01 .05
21 Scott Young .01 .05
22 Ulf Dahlen .01 .05
23 Mike Ramsey .01 .05
24 Peter Zezel .01 .05
25 Ron Hextall .02 .10
26 Steve Duchesne .01 .05
27 Allan Bester .02 .10
28 Everett Sanipass RC .01 .05
29 Steve Konroyd .01 .05
30A Joe Nieuwendyk ERR .02 .10
30B Joe Nieuwendyk COR .02 .10
31A Brent Ashton ERR .01 .05
31B Brent Ashton COR .01 .05
32 Trevor Linden .02 .10
33 Mike Ridley .01 .05
34 Sean Burke .02 .10
35 Pat Verbeek .01 .05
36 Rob Ramage .01 .05
37 Kelly Kisio .01 .05
38A Craig Muni ERR .01 .05
38B Craig Muni COR .01 .05
39 Brent Sutter .01 .05
40 Gary Leeman .01 .05
41 Jeff Brown .01 .05
42 Greg Millen .02 .10
43 Alexander Mogilny RC .30 .75
44 Dale Hunter .01 .05
45 Randy Moller .01 .05
46 Peter Sidorkiewicz .02 .10
47 Terry Carkner .01 .05
48 Tony Granato .01 .05
49 Shawn Burr .01 .05
50 Dale Hawerchuk .02 .10
51A Don Sweeney ERR RC .01 .05
51B Don Sweeney COR RC .01 .05
52 Mike Vernon UER .02 .10
53 Kevin Stevens RC .02 .10
54 Bryan Fogarty RC .01 .05
55 Dan Quinn .01 .05
56 Murray Craven .01 .05
57 Shawn Chambers .01 .05
58 Craig Simpson .01 .05
59 Doug Crossman .01 .05
60 Daren Puppa .02 .10
61 Bobby Smith .02 .10
62 Slava Fetisov RC .02 .10
63 Gino Cavallini .01 .05
64 Jimmy Carson .01 .05
65 Dave Ellett .01 .05
66 Steve Thomas .01 .05
67 Mike Lalor RC .01 .05
68 Mike Liut .02 .10
69 Tom Laidlaw .01 .05
70 Ron Francis .02 .10
71 Sergei Makarov RC .02 .10
72 Randy Burridge .01 .05
73 Doug Lidster .01 .05
74 Mike Richter RC .40 1.00
75 Stephane Richer .02 .10
76 Randy Hillier .01 .05
77 Christian Ruuttu .01 .05
78 Marc Fortier .01 .05
79 Bill Ranford .02 .10
80 Rick Tocchet .02 .10
81 Fredrik Olausson .01 .05
82 Adam Creighton .01 .05
83 Sylvain Cote .01 .05
84 Brian Mullen .01 .05
85 Adam Oates .02 .10
86 Gary Nylund .01 .05
87 Tim Cheveldae RC .02 .10
88 Gary Suter .01 .05
89 John Tonelli .01 .05
90 Kevin Hatcher .01 .05
91 Guy Carbonneau .02 .10
92 Curtis Leschyshyn RC .01 .05
93 Kirk McLean .02 .10
94 Curt Giles .01 .05
95 Vincent Damphousse .01 .05
96 Peter Stastny .02 .10
97 Glen Wesley .01 .05
98 David Shaw .01 .05
99 Brad Shaw RC .01 .05
100 Mark Messier .08 .25
101 Rick Zombo RC .01 .05
102A Mark Fitzpatrick ERR RC .02 .10
102B Mark Fitzpatrick COR RC .02 .10
103 Rick Vaive .01 .05
104 Mark Osborne .01 .05
105 Rob Brown .01 .05
106 Gary Roberts .01 .05
107 Vincent Riendeau RC .02 .10
108 Dave Gagner .02 .10
109 Bruce Driver .01 .05
110 Pierre Turgeon .02 .10
111 Claude Lemieux .01 .05
112 Bob Essensa RC .15 .40
113 John Ogrodnick .01 .05
114 Glenn Anderson .02 .10
115 Kelly Hrudey .02 .10
116 Sylvain Turgeon .01 .05
117 Gord Murphy RC .01 .05
118 Craig Janney .02 .10
119 Randy Wood .01 .05
120 Mike Modano RC .50 1.25
121 Tom Barrasso .02 .10
122 Daniel Marois .01 .05
123 Igor Larionov RC .15 .40
124 Geoff Courtnall .01 .05
125 Denis Savard .02 .10
126 Ron Tugnutt .02 .10
127 Mathieu Schneider RC .01 .05
128 Joel Otto .01 .05
129 Steve Smith .01 .05
130 Mike Gartner .02 .10
131 Rod Brind'Amour RC .30 .75
132 Jyrki Lumme RC .01 .05
133 Mike Foligno .01 .05
134 Ray Ferraro .01 .05
135 Steve Larmer .02 .10
136 Randy Carlyle .01 .05
137 Tony Tanti .01 .05
138 Jeff Chychrun RC .01 .05
139 Gerald Diduck .01 .05
140 Andy Moog .02 .10
141 Paul Gillis .01 .05
142 Tom Kurvers .01 .05
143 Bob Probert .02 .10
144 Neal Broten .02 .10
145 Phil Housley .02 .10
146 Brendan Shanahan .08 .25
147 Bob Rouse .01 .05
148 Russ Courtnall .01 .05
149 Normand Rochefort .01 .05
150 Luc Robitaille .02 .10
151 Curtis Joseph RC .60 1.50
152 Ulf Samuelsson .01 .05
153 Ron Sutter .01 .05
154 Petri Skriko .01 .05
155 Doug Gilmour .02 .10
156 Paul Fenton .01 .05
157 Jeff Norton .01 .05
158 Jari Kurri .02 .10
159 Rejean Lemelin .02 .10
160 Kirk Muller .01 .05
161 Keith Brown .01 .05
162 Aaron Broten .01 .05
163 Adam Graves RC .15 .40
164 John Cullen .01 .05
165 Craig Ludwig .01 .05
166 Dave Taylor .02 .10
167 Craig Wolanin RC .01 .05
168 Kelly Miller .01 .05
169 Uwe Krupp .01 .05
170 Kevin Lowe .01 .05
171 Wendel Clark .02 .10
172 Dave Babych .01 .05
173 Paul Reinhart .01 .05
174 Pat Flatley .01 .05
175 John Vanbiesbrouck .02 .10
176 Teppo Numminen RC .01 .05
177 Tim Kerr .01 .05
178 Ken Daneyko .01 .05
179 Jeremy Roenick RC .40 1.00
180 Gerard Gallant .01 .05
181 Allen Pederson .01 .05
182 Jon Casey .02 .10
183 Tomas Sandstrom .01 .05
184 Brad McCrimmon .01 .05
185 Paul Cavallini .01 .05
186 Mark Recchi RC .40 1.00
187 Michel Petit .01 .05
188 Scott Stevens .02 .10
189 Dave Andreychuk .02 .10
190 John MacLean .02 .10
191 Petr Svoboda .01 .05
192 Dave Tippett .01 .05
193 Dave Manson .01 .05
194 James Patrick .01 .05
195 Al Iafrate .02 .10
196 Doug Smail .01 .05
197 Kjell Samuelsson .01 .05
198 Brian Bradley .01 .05
199 Charlie Huddy .01 .05
200 Ray Bourque .15 .40
201 Joey Kocur RC .15 .40
202 Jim Johnson .01 .05
203 Paul MacLean .01 .05
204 Tim Watters .01 .05
205 Pat Elynuik .01 .05
206 Larry Murphy .02 .10
207 Claude Loiselle RC .01 .05
208 Joe Mullen .02 .10
209 Alexei Kasatonov RC .01 .05
210 Ed Olczyk .01 .05
211 Doug Bodger .01 .05
212 Kevin Dineen .01 .05
213 Shayne Corson .01 .05
214 Steve Chiasson .01 .05
215 Don Beaupre .02 .10
216 Jamie Macoun .01 .05
217 Dave Poulin .01 .05
218 Zarley Zalapski .01 .05
219 Brad Marsh .01 .05
220 Mark Howe .01 .05
221 Michel Goulet .02 .10
222 Hubie McDonough RC .01 .05
223 Frank Musil .01 .05
224 Sergio Momesso RC .01 .05
225 Brian Leetch .10 .30
226 Theo Fleury .01 .05
227 Mike Krushelnyski .01 .05
228 Glen Hanlon .02 .10
229 Mario Marois .01 .05
230 Dino Ciccarelli .02 .10
231A Dave McLlwain ERR .01 .05
231B Dave McLlwain COR .01 .05
232 Petr Klima .01 .05
233 Grant Ledyard RC .01 .05
234 Phil Bourque .01 .05
235 Rob Sweeney .01 .05
236 Luke Richardson .01 .05
237 Todd Krygier RC .01 .05
238 Brian Skrudland .01 .05
239 Chris Terreri RC .02 .10
240 Greg Adams .01 .05
241 Darren Turcotte RC .01 .05
242 Scott Mellanby .02 .10
243 Troy Murray .01 .05
244 Stewart Gavin .01 .05
245 Gordie Roberts .01 .05
246 John Druce RC .01 .05
247 Steve Kasper .01 .05
248 Paul Ranheim RC .01 .05
249 Greg Paslawski .01 .05
250 Pat LaFontaine .08 .25
251 Scott Arniel .01 .05
252 Bernie Federko .02 .10
253 Garry Galley RC .01 .05
254 Carey Wilson .01 .05
255 Bob Errey .01 .05
256 Tony Hrkac .01 .05
257 Andrew McBain .01 .05
258 Craig MacTavish .01 .05
259A Dean Evason ERR .01 .05
259B Dean Evason COR .01 .05
260 Larry Robinson .02 .10
261 Basil McRae .01 .05
262 Stephan Lebeau RC .01 .05
263 Ken Wregget .02 .10
264 Greg Gilbert .01 .05
265 Ken Baumgartner RC .01 .05
266 Lou Franceschetti RC .01 .05
267 Rick Meagher .01 .05
268 Michal Pivonka RC .01 .05
269 Brian Propp .01 .05
270 Bryan Trottier .02 .10
271 Marty McSorley .01 .05
272 Jan Erixon .01 .05
273 Vladimir Krutov RC .02 .10
274 Dana Murzyn .01 .05
275 Grant Fuhr .02 .10
276 Randy Cunneyworth .01 .05
277 John Chabot .01 .05
278 Walt Poddubny .01 .05
279 Stephen Leach RC .01 .05
280 Doug Wilson .02 .10
281 Rich Sutter .01 .05
282 Stephane Beauregard .02 .10
283 John Carter RC .01 .05
284 Don Barber RC .01 .05
285 Tom Fergus .01 .05
286 Ilkka Sinisalo .01 .05
287 Kevin McClelland .01 .05
288 Troy Mallette RC .01 .05
289 Clint Malarchuk .02 .10
290 Guy Lafleur .08 .25
291 Bob Joyce .01 .05
292 Trent Yawney .01 .05
293 Joe Murphy RC .01 .05
294 Glenn Healy RC .02 .10
295 Dave Christian .01 .05
296 Paul MacDermid .01 .05
297 Todd Elik RC .01 .05
298 Wendell Young .02 .10
299 Dean Kennedy RC .01 .05
300 Brett Hull .20 .50
301 Keith Acton .01 .05
302 Yvon Corriveau RC .01 .05
303 Don Maloney .01 .05
304 Mark Tinordi RC .01 .05
305 Bob Kudelski RC .01 .05
306 Brian Benning .01 .05
307 Alan Kerr .01 .05
308 Pelle Eklund .01 .05
309 Calle Johansson .01 .05
310 David Maley RC .01 .05
311 Chris Nilan .01 .05
312 Patrick Roy AS1 .10 .30
313 Ray Bourque AS1 .08 .25
314 Al MacInnis AS1 .02 .10
315 Mark Messier AS1 .08 .25
316 Luc Robitaille AS1 .01 .05
317 Brett Hull AS1 .08 .25
318 Daren Puppa AS2 .02 .10
319 Paul Coffey AS2 .08 .25
320 Doug Wilson AS2 .02 .10
321 Wayne Gretzky AS2 .15 .40
322 Brian Bellows AS2 .01 .05
323 Cam Neely AS2 .02 .10
324 Bob Essensa ART .02 .10
325 Brad Shaw ART .01 .05
326 Geoff Smith ART .01 .05
327 Mike Modano ART .02 .10
328 Rod Brind'Amour ART .02 .10
329 Sergei Makarov ART .01 .05
330A Kip Miller Hob ERR RC .01 .05
330B Kip Miller Hob COR RC .01 .05
331 Edmonton Oilers Champs .01 .05
332 Paul Coffey Speed .08 .25
333 Mike Gartner Speed .02 .10
334 Al Iafrate Blaster .02 .10
335 Al MacInnis Blaster .02 .10
336 Wayne Gretzky Sniper .15 .40
337 Mario Lemieux Sniper .20 .50
338 Wayne Gretzky Magic .15 .40
339 Steve Yzerman Magic .08 .25
340 Cam Neely Banger .02 .10
341 Scott Stevens Banger .02 .10
342 Esa Tikkanen Shadow .01 .05
343 Jan Erixon Shadow .01 .05
344 Patrick Roy Stopper .10 .30
345 Bill Ranford Stopper .02 .10
346 Brett Hull RB .08 .25
347 Wayne Gretzky RB .15 .40
348 Jari Kurri LL .02 .10
349 Paul Cavallini LL .01 .05
350 Sergei Makarov RLL .01 .05
351 Brett Hull LL .08 .25
352 Wayne Gretzky LL .15 .40
353 Wayne Gretzky LL .15 .40
354 P.Roy/Liut LL .10 .30
355 Gilbert Perreault HOF .01 .05
356 Bill Barber HOF .01 .05
357 Fern Flaman HOF .01 .05
358 Bill Ranford Smythe .02 .10
359 Rick Meagher Selke .01 .05
360 Mark Messier Hart .08 .25
361 Wayne Gretzky Ross .15 .40
362 Sergei Makarov Calder .01 .05
363 Ray Bourque Norris .08 .25
364 Patrick Roy Vezina .10 .30
365 Moog/Lemelin Jennings .01 .05
366 Brett Hull Byng .08 .25
367 Gord Kluzak Mast .01 .05
368 Boston/Washington .01 .05
369 Edmonton/Chicago .01 .05
370 Adam Burt RC .01 .05
371 Troy Loney RC .01 .05
372 Dave Chyzowski RC .01 .05
373 Geoff Smith RC .01 .05
374 Stan Smyl .01 .05
375 Gaetan Duchesne .01 .05
376 Bob Murray .01 .05
377 Daniel Shank RC .01 .05
378 Tommy Albelin .01 .05
379 Perry Berezan RC .01 .05
380 Ken Linseman .01 .05
381 Stephane Matteau RC .01 .05
382 Mario Thyer RC .01 .05
383 Nelson Emerson RC .01 .05
384 Kory Kocur RC .01 .05
385 Bob Beers RC .01 .05
386 Jim Hrivnak RC .02 .10
387 Mark Pederson RC .01 .05
388 Jeff Hackett RC .15 .40
389 Eric Weinrich RC .01 .05
390 Steven Rice RC .01 .05
391 Stu Barnes RC .01 .05
392 Olaf Kolzig RC .40 1.00
393 Francois Leroux RC .01 .05
394 Adrien Plavsic .01 .05
395 Michel Mongeau RC .01 .05
396 Rick Corriveau RC .01 .05
397 Wayne Doucet RC .01 .05
398 Mats Sundin RC .40 1.00
399 Murray Baron RC .01 .05
400 Rick Bennett RC .01 .05
401 Jon Morris RC .01 .05
402 Kay Whitmore RC .02 .10
403 Peter Lappin RC .01 .05
404 Kris Draper RC .15 .40
405 Shayne Stevenson RC .01 .05
406 Paul Ysebaert RC .01 .05
407A Jim Waite ERR RC .02 .10
407B Jim Waite COR RC .02 .10
408 Cam Russell RC .01 .05
409 Kim Issel RC .01 .05
410 Darrin Shannon RC .01 .05
411 Link Gaetz RC .01 .05
412 Craig Fisher RC .01 .05
413 Bruce Hoffort RC .01 .05
414 Peter Ing RC .02 .10
415 Stephane Fiset RC .15 .40
416 Dominic Lavoie RC .01 .05
417 Steve Maltais RC .01 .05
418 Wes Walz RC .01 .05
419 Terry Yake RC .01 .05
420 Jamie Leach RC .01 .05
421 Rob Blake RC .20 .50
422 Andrew Cassels RC .01 .05
423 Marc Bureau RC .01 .05
424 Scott Allison RC .01 .05
425 Darryl Sydor RC .15 .40
426 Turner Stevenson RC .01 .05
427 Brad May RC .02 .10
428 Jaromir Jagr RC .75 2.00
429 Shawn Antoski RC .01 .05
430 Derian Hatcher RC .15 .40
431 Mark Greig RC .01 .05
432 Scott Scissons RC .01 .05
433 Mike Ricci RC .10 .30
434 Drake Berehowsky RC .01 .05
435 Owen Nolan RC .40 1.00
436 Keith Primeau RC .30 .75
437 Karl Dykhuis RC .01 .05
438 Trevor Kidd RC .25 .60
439 Martin Brodeur RC 6.00 15.00
440 Eric Lindros RC 1.25 3.00
B1 Eric Lindros .40 1.00
B2 Eric Lindros .40 1.00
B3 Eric Lindros .40 1.00
B4 Eric Lindros .40 1.00
B5 Eric Lindros .40 1.00

1990-91 Score Canadian

COMPLETE SET (440) 7.00 14.00
COMP.FACT.SET (445) 10.00 18.00
COMMON LINDROS (B1-B5) .40 1.00
LINDROS B1-B5 IN FACTORY SET ONLY
BEWARE LINDROS COUNTERFEITS
*CANADIAN: .4X TO 1X EXCEPT WHERE NOTED
1 Wayne Gretzky .40 1.00
2 Mario Lemieux .30 .75
3 Steve Yzerman .15 .40
4 Cam Neely .08 .25
5 Al MacInnis .02 .10
6 Paul Coffey .07 .20
7 Brian Bellows .04 .10
8 Joe Sakic .15 .40
9 Bernie Nicholls .02 .10
10 Patrick Roy .30 .75
11 Doug Houda RC .01 .05
12 David Volek .01 .05
13 Esa Tikkanen .04 .10
14 Thomas Steen .04 .10
15 Chris Chelios .02 .10
16 Bob Carpenter .01 .05
17 Dirk Graham .04 .10
18 Garth Butcher .04 .10
19 Patrik Sundstrom .01 .05
20 Rod Langway .04 .10
21 Scott Young .04 .10
22 Ulf Dahlen .04 .10
23 Mike Ramsey .01 .05
24 Peter Zezel .01 .05
25 Ron Hextall .02 .10
26 Steve Duchesne .04 .10
27 Allan Bester .04 .10
28 Everett Sanipass RC .01 .05
29 Steve Konroyd .01 .05
30A Joe Nieuwendyk ERR .20 .50
(Text says& now I fell& should say feel)
30B Joe Nieuwendyk COR .02 .10
31A Brent Ashton ERR .05 .15
(No position on card front)
31B Brent Ashton COR .05 .15
(LW on card front)
32 Trevor Linden .08 .25
33 Mike Ridley .04 .10
34 Sean Burke .02 .10
35 Pat Verbeek .02 .10
36 Rob Ramage .01 .05
37 Kelly Kisio .01 .05
38A Craig Muni ERR .05 .15
(Back photo actually Craig Simpson)
38B Craig Muni COR .01 .05
39 Brent Sutter .04 .10
40 Gary Leeman .01 .05
41 Jeff Brown .04 .10
42 Greg Millen .04 .10
43 Alexander Mogilny RC .30 .75
44 Dale Hunter .04 .10
45 Randy Moller .01 .05
46 Peter Sidorkiewicz .04 .10
47 Terry Carkner .01 .05
48 Tony Granato .04 .10
49 Shawn Burr .01 .05
50 Dale Hawerchuk .02 .10
51A Don Sweeney ERR RC .01 .05
51B Don Sweeney COR RC .01 .05
52 Mike Vernon UER .02 .10
(Text says won WHL MVP twice& should be once)
53 Kevin Stevens RC .25 .60
54 Bryan Fogarty RC .01 .05
55 Dan Quinn .01 .05
56 Murray Craven .01 .05
57 Shawn Chambers .01 .05
58 Craig Simpson .04 .10
59 Doug Crossman .01 .05
60 Daren Puppa .02 .10
61 Bobby Smith .04 .10
62 Slava Fetisov RC .02 .10
63 Gino Cavallini .01 .05
64 Jimmy Carson .04 .10
65 Dave Ellett .01 .05
66 Steve Thomas .04 .10
67 Mike Lalor RC .01 .05
68 Mike Liut .04 .10
69 Tom Laidlaw .01 .05
70 Ron Francis .02 .10
71 Sergei Makarov RC .10 .30
72 Randy Burridge .01 .05
73 Doug Lidster .01 .05
74 Mike Richter RC .20 .50
75 Stephane Richer .04 .10
76 Randy Hillier .01 .05
77 Christian Ruuttu .01 .05
78 Marc Fortier .01 .05
79 Bill Ranford .02 .10
80 Rick Tocchet .02 .10
81 Fredrik Olausson .04 .10
82 Adam Creighton .01 .05
83 Sylvain Cote .01 .05
84 Brian Mullen .04 .10
85 Adam Oates .07 .20
86 Gary Nylund .01 .05
87 Tim Cheveldae RC .07 .20
88 Gary Suter .04 .10
89 John Tonelli .04 .10
90 Kevin Hatcher .04 .10
91 Guy Carbonneau .04 .10
92 Curtis Leschyshyn RC .01 .05
93 Kirk McLean .02 .10
94 Curt Giles .01 .05
95 Vincent Damphousse .02 .10
96 Peter Stastny .02 .10
97 Glen Wesley .04 .10
98 David Shaw .01 .05
99 Brad Shaw RC .01 .05
100 Mark Messier .08 .25
101 Rick Zombo RC .01 .05
102A Mark Fitzpatrick ERR RC .04 .10
102B Mark Fitzpatrick COR RC .04 .10
103 Rick Vaive .01 .05
104 Mark Osborne .01 .05
105 Rob Brown .01 .05
106 Gary Roberts .04 .10
107 Vincent Riendeau RC .04 .10
108 Dave Gagner .04 .10
109 Bruce Driver .01 .05
110 Pierre Turgeon .08 .25
111 Claude Lemieux .04 .10
112 Bob Essensa RC .04 .10
113 John Ogrodnick .01 .05
114 Glenn Anderson .02 .10
115 Kelly Hrudey .02 .10
116 Sylvain Turgeon .01 .05
117 Gord Murphy RC .01 .05
118 Craig Janney .02 .10
119 Randy Wood .01 .05
120 Mike Modano RC .30 .75
121 Tom Barrasso .02 .10
122 Daniel Marois .01 .05
123 Igor Larionov RC .10 .30
124 Geoff Courtnall .04 .10
125 Denis Savard .04 .10
126 Ron Tugnutt .04 .10
127 Mathieu Schneider RC .02 .10
128 Joel Otto .01 .05
129 Steve Smith .04 .10
130 Mike Gartner .02 .10
131 Rod Brind'Amour RC .15 .40
132 Jyrki Lumme RC .01 .05
133 Mike Foligno .04 .10
134 Ray Ferraro .04 .10
135 Steve Larmer .02 .10
136 Randy Carlyle .01 .05
137 Tony Tanti .01 .05
138 Jeff Chychrun RC .01 .05
139 Gerald Diduck .01 .05
140 Andy Moog .02 .10
141 Paul Gillis .01 .05
142 Tom Kurvers .01 .05
143 Bob Probert .04 .10
144 Neal Broten .04 .10
145 Phil Housley .04 .10
146 Brendan Shanahan .08 .25
147 Bob Rouse .01 .05
148 Russ Courtnall .04 .10
149 Normand Rochefort UER .01 .05
(RW& should be D)
150 Luc Robitaille .08 .25
151 Curtis Joseph RC .25 .60
152 Ulf Samuelsson .04 .10
153 Ron Sutter .01 .05
154 Petri Skriko .01 .05
155 Doug Gilmour .08 .25
156 Paul Fenton .01 .05
157 Jeff Norton .01 .05
158 Jari Kurri .02 .10
159 Rejean Lemelin .02 .10
160 Kirk Muller .04 .10
161 Keith Brown .01 .05
162 Aaron Broten UER .01 .05
(Photo actually Dave Archibald)

1990-91 Score Promos

163 Adam Graves RC .25 .60
164 John Cullen UER .04 .10
(Birthdate 1/6/6&
should be 1/9/64)
165 Craig Ludwig .01 .05
166 Dave Taylor .02 .10
167 Craig Wolanin RC .01 .05
168 Kelly Miller .01 .05
169 Uwe Krupp .04 .10
170 Kevin Lowe .04 .10
171 Wendel Clark .07 .20
172 Dave Babych .01 .05
173 Paul Reinhart .01 .05
174 Pat Flatley .01 .05
175 John Vanbiesbrouck .07 .20
176 Teppo Numminen RC .01 .05
177 Tim Kerr .04 .10
178 Ken Daneyko .01 .05
179 Jeremy Roenick RC .40 1.00
180 Gerard Gallant .01 .05
181 Allen Pederson .01 .05
182 Jon Casey .04 .10
183 Tomas Sandstrom .04 .10
184 Brad McCrimmon .01 .05
185 Paul Cavallini .01 .05
186 Mark Recchi RC .20 .50
187 Michel Petit .01 .05
188 Scott Stevens .02 .10
189 Dave Andreychuk .02 .10
190 John MacLean .04 .10
191 Petr Svoboda .01 .05
192 Dave Tippett .01 .05
193 Dave Manson .04 .10
194 James Patrick .01 .05
195 Al Iafrate .04 .10
196 Doug Smail .01 .05
197 Kjell Samuelsson .01 .05
198 Brian Bradley .04 .10
199 Charlie Huddy .01 .05
200 Ray Bourque .07 .20
201 Joey Kocur .01 .05
202 Jim Johnson UER .01 .05
(Born Michigan&
not Minnesota)
203 Paul MacLean .01 .05
204 Tim Watters .01 .05
205 Pat Elynuik .01 .05
206 Larry Murphy .02 .10
207 Claude Loiselle RC .01 .05
208 Joe Mullen .02 .10
209 Alexei Kasatonov RC .01 .05
210 Ed Olczyk .01 .05
211 Doug Bodger .01 .05
212 Kevin Dineen .04 .10
213 Shayne Corson .04 .10
214 Steve Chiasson .04 .10
215 Don Beaupre .04 .10
216 Jamie Macoun .01 .05
217 Dave Poulin .04 .10
218 Zarley Zalapski .04 .10
219 Brad Marsh .04 .10
220 Mark Howe .04 .10
221 Michel Goulet .02 .10
222 Hubie McDonough RC .01 .05
223 Frank Musil .01 .05
224 Sergio Momesso RC .01 .05
225 Brian Leetch .15 .40
226 Theo Fleury .08 .25
227 Mike Krushelnyski .01 .05
228 Glen Hanlon .04 .10
229 Mario Marois .01 .05
230 Dino Ciccarelli .02 .10
231A Dave McLlwain ERR .05 .15
(Shoots right)
231B Dave McLlwain COR .01 .05
(Shoots left)
232 Petr Klima .04 .10
233 Grant Ledyard RC .01 .05
234 Phil Bourque .01 .05
235 Rob Sweeney .01 .05
236 Luke Richardson .01 .05
237 Todd Krygier RC .01 .05
238 Brian Skrudland .01 .05
239 Chris Terreri RC .07 .20
240 Greg Adams .01 .05
241 Darren Turcotte RC .02 .10
242 Scott Mellanby .04 .10
243 Troy Murray .01 .05
244 Stewart Gavin .01 .05
245 Gordie Roberts .01 .05
246 John Druce RC .01 .05
247 Steve Kasper .01 .05
248 Paul Ranheim RC .01 .05
249 Greg Paslawski .01 .05
250 Pat LaFontaine .07 .20
251 Scott Arniel .01 .05
252 Bernie Federko .04 .10
253 Garry Galley RC .01 .05
254 Carey Wilson .01 .05
255 Bob Errey .01 .05
256 Tony Hrkac .01 .05
257 Andrew McBain .01 .05
258 Craig MacTavish .04 .10
259A Dean Evason ERR .05 .15
(Reversed negative)
259B Dean Evason COR .01 .05
260 Larry Robinson .04 .10
261 Basil McRae .01 .05
262 Stephan Lebeau RC .01 .05
263 Ken Wregget .04 .10
264 Greg Gilbert .01 .05
265 Ken Baumgartner RC .01 .05
266 Lou Franceschetti RC .01 .05
267 Rick Meagher .01 .05
268 Michal Pivonka RC .07 .20
269 Brian Propp .04 .10
270 Bryan Trottier .02 .10
271 Marty McSorley .04 .10
272 Jan Erixon .01 .05
273 Vladimir Krutov RC .02 .10
274 Dana Murzyn .01 .05
275 Grant Fuhr .02 .10
276 Randy Cunneyworth .01 .05
277 John Chabot .01 .05
278 Walt Poddubny .01 .05
279 Stephen Leach RC .01 .05
280 Doug Wilson .04 .10
281 Rich Sutter .01 .05
282 Steph Beauregard RC .04 .10
283 John Carter RC .01 .05
284 Don Barber .01 .05
285 Tom Fergus .01 .05
286 Ilkka Sinisalo .01 .05
287 Kevin McClelland UER .01 .05
(Back has shoots&
but no side indicated)
288 Troy Mallette RC .01 .05
289 Clint Malarchuk UER .04 .10
(Photo actually
Tom Barrasso)
290 Guy Lafleur .07 .20
291 Bob Joyce .01 .05
292 Trent Yawney .01 .05
293 Joe Murphy RC .10 .30
294 Glenn Healy RC .04 .10
295 Dave Christian .01 .05
296 Paul MacDermid .01 .05
297 Todd Elik RC .01 .05
298 Wendell Young .04 .10
299 Dean Kennedy RC .01 .05
300 Brett Hull .25 .60
301 Martin Gelinas RC .01 .05
302 Ric Nattress .01 .05
303 Jim Sandlak .01 .05
304 Brian Hayward .04 .10
305 Joe Cirella .01 .05
306 Randy Gregg .01 .05
307 Sylvain Lefebvre RC .01 .05
308 Mark Lamb .01 .05
309 Rick Wamsley .04 .10
310 Moe Mantha .01 .05
311 Tony McKegney .01 .05
312 Patrick Roy AS1 .08 .25
313 Ray Bourque AS1 .04 .10
314 Al MacInnis AS1 .04 .10
315 Mark Messier AS1 .02 .10
316 Luc Robitaille AS1 .04 .10
317 Brett Hull AS1 .08 .25
318 Daren Puppa AS2 .04 .10
319 Paul Coffey AS2 .04 .10
320 Doug Wilson AS2 .01 .05
321 Wayne Gretzky AS2 .15 .40
322 Brian Bellows AS2 .01 .05
323 Cam Neely AS2 .02 .10
324 Bob Essensa ART .04 .10
325 Brad Shaw ART .01 .05
326 Geoff Smith ART .01 .05
327 Mike Modano ART .02 .10
328 Rod Brind'Amour ART .04 .10
329 Sergei Makarov ART .04 .10
330 Memorial Cup .20 .50
331 Edmonton Oilers Champs .04 .10
332 Paul Coffey Speed .02 .10
333 Mike Gartner Speed .04 .10
334 Al Iafrate Blaster .01 .05
335 Al MacInnis Blaster .04 .10
336 Wayne Gretzky Sniper .15 .40
337 Mario Lemieux Sniper .08 .25
338 Wayne Gretzky Magic .15 .40
339 Steve Yzerman Magic .02 .10
340 Cam Neely Banger .02 .10
341 Scott Stevens Banger .04 .10
342 Esa Tikkanen Shadow .01 .05
343 Jan Erixon Shadow .01 .05
344 Patrick Roy Stopper .08 .25
345 Bill Ranford Stopper .04 .10
346 Brett Hull RB .08 .25
347 Wayne Gretzky RB .15 .40
348 Jari Kurri LL .04 .10
349 Paul Cavallini LL .01 .05
350 Sergei Makarov RLL .04 .10
351 Brett Hull LL .08 .25
352 Wayne Gretzky LL .15 .40
353 Wayne Gretzky LL .15 .40
354 P.Roy/Liut LL .08 .25
355 Gilbert Perreault HOF .01 .05
356 Bill Barber HOF .01 .05
357 Fern Flaman HOF .01 .05
358 Bill Ranford Smythe .04 .10
359 Rick Meagher Selke .01 .05
360 Mark Messier Hart .04 .10
361 Wayne Gretzky Ross .15 .40
362 Sergei Makarov Calder .04 .10
363 Ray Bourque Norris .04 .10
364 Patrick Roy Vezina .08 .25
365 Moog/Lemelin Jennings .04 .10
366 Brett Hull Byng .08 .25
367 Gord Kluzak Mast .01 .05
368 Boston/Washington UER .01 .05
(Janney misspelled Janny on back)
369 Edmonton/Chicago .01 .05
370 Adam Burt RC .01 .05
371 Troy Loney RC .01 .05
372 Dave Chyzowski RC .01 .05
373 Geoff Smith RC .01 .05
374 Stan Smyl .01 .05
375 Gaetan Duchesne .01 .05
376 Bob Murray .01 .05
377 Daniel Shank RC .01 .05
378 Tommy Albelin .01 .05
379 Perry Berezan RC .01 .05
380 Ken Linseman .01 .05
381 Stephane Matteau RC .01 .05
382 Mario Thyer RC .01 .05
383 Nelson Emerson RC .10 .30
384 Kory Kocur RC .01 .05
385 Bob Beers RC .01 .05
386 Jim Hrivnak RC .04 .10
387 Mark Pederson RC .01 .05
388 Jeff Hackett RC .04 .10
389 Eric Weinrich RC .01 .05
390 Steven Rice RC .01 .05
391 Stu Barnes RC .02 .10
392 Olaf Kolzig RC .04 .10
393 Francois Leroux RC .01 .05
394 Adrien Plavsic RC .01 .05
395 Michel Mongeau RC .01 .05
396 Rick Corriveau RC .01 .05
397 Wayne Doucet RC .01 .05
398 Mats Sundin RC .30 .75
399 Murray Baron RC .01 .05
400 Rick Bennett RC .01 .05
401 Jon Morris RC .01 .05
402 Kay Whitmore RC .04 .10
403 Peter Lappin RC .01 .05
404 Kris Draper RC .01 .05
405 Shayne Stevenson RC .01 .05
406 Paul Ysebaert RC .01 .05
407A Jim Waite ERR RC .10 .30
407B Jim Waite COR RC .04 .10
408 Cam Russell RC .01 .05
409 Kim Issel RC .01 .05
410 Darrin Shannon RC .01 .05
411 Link Gaetz RC .01 .05
412 Craig Fisher RC .01 .05
413 Bruce Hoffort RC .04 .10
414 Peter Ing RC .04 .10
415 Stephane Fiset RC .25 .60
416 Dominic Lavoie RC .01 .05
417 Steve Maltais RC .01 .05
418 Wes Walz RC .01 .05
419 Terry Yake RC .01 .05
420 Jamie Leach RC .01 .05
421 Rob Blake RC .20 .50
422 Andrew Cassels RC .07 .20
423 Marc Bureau RC .01 .05
424 Scott Allison RC .01 .05
425 Darryl Sydor RC .07 .25
426 Turner Stevenson RC .01 .05
427 Brad May RC .04 .10
428 Jaromir Jagr RC .75 2.00
429 Shawn Antoski RC .01 .05
430 Derian Hatcher RC .04 .10
431 Mark Greig RC .01 .05
432 Scott Scissons RC .01 .05
433 Mike Ricci RC .10 .30
434 Drake Berehowsky RC .01 .05
435 Owen Nolan RC .25 .60
436 Keith Primeau RC .20 .50
437 Karl Dykhuis RC .01 .05
438 Trevor Kidd RC .20 .50
439 Martin Brodeur RC 7.50 15.00
440 Eric Lindros RC 1.25 3.00
B1 Eric Lindros .75 2.00
Junior B Team
B2 Eric Lindros .75 2.00
Regular Junior OHL
B3 Eric Lindros .75 2.00
OHL All-Star
B4 Eric Lindros .75 2.00
Oshawa Generals
(Non-action pose;
head shot with his
gloves over his mouth)
B5 Eric Lindros .75 2.00
Oshawa Generals
(Non-action pose;
shot from waist up&
arms draped over hockey
stick across his back)

1990-91 Score Hottest/Rising Stars

This 100-card standard-size set was released along with a special book. The book provided further information about the players. The fronts of the cards have the same photos as the regular Score issue but the numbers are different on the back.

COMP.FACT.SET (100) 6.00 15.00
1 Wayne Gretzky 2.00 5.00
2 Craig Simpson .02 .10
3 Brian Bellows .02 .10
4 Steve Yzerman 1.00 2.50
5 Bernie Nicholls .02 .10
6 Esa Tikkanen .02 .10
7 Joe Sakic .75 2.00
8 Thomas Steen .02 .10
9 Chris Chelios .30 .75
10 Patrik Sundstrom .02 .10
11 Rod Langway .02 .10
12 Scott Young .02 .10
13 Mike Ramsey .02 .10
14 Ron Hextall .20 .50
15 Steve Duchesne .08 .25
16 Trevor Linden .20 .50
17 Sean Burke .20 .50
18 Pat Verbeek .08 .25
19 Brent Sutter .02 .10
20 Gary Leeman .02 .10
21 Shawn Burr .02 .10
22 Dale Hawerchuk .08 .25
23 Mike Vernon .08 .25
24 Dan Quinn .02 .10
25 Patrick Roy 1.50 4.00
26 Daren Puppa .08 .25
27 Gino Cavallini .02 .10
28 Jimmy Carson .02 .10
29 Dave Ellett .02 .10
30 Steve Thomas .02 .10
31 Jeremy Roenick .75 2.00
32 Mike Liut .02 .10
33 Mark Messier .40 1.00
34 Mario Lemieux 1.50 4.00
35 Ray Bourque .40 1.00
36 Al MacInnis .20 .50
37 Ron Francis .20 .50
38 Stephane Richer .02 .10
39 Bill Ranford .20 .50
40 Rick Tocchet .08 .25
41 Adam Oates .20 .50
42 Kevin Hatcher .02 .10
43 Guy Carbonneau .02 .10
44 Curtis Leschyshyn .02 .10
45 Joe Nieuwendyk .20 .50
46 Kirk McLean .20 .50
47 Vincent Damphousse .20 .50
48 Peter Stastny .08 .25
49 Rick Zombo .02 .10
50 Mark Fitzpatrick .08 .25
51 Rob Brown .02 .10
52 Dave Gagner .02 .10
53 Pierre Turgeon .20 .50
54 Glenn Anderson .02 .10
55 Kelly Hrudey .20 .50
56 Gord Murphy .02 .10
57 Glen Wesley .02 .10
58 Craig Janney .08 .25
59 Denis Savard .08 .25
60 Mike Gartner .20 .50
61 Steve Larmer .02 .10
62 Andy Moog .20 .50
63 Phil Housley .02 .10
64 Ulf Samuelsson .02 .10
65 Paul Coffey .30 .75
66 Luc Robitaille .20 .50
67 Cam Neely .30 .75
68 Doug Wilson .02 .10
69 Doug Gilmour .30 .75
70 Jeff Norton .02 .10
71 Kirk Muller .02 .10
72 Aaron Broten .02 .10
73 John Cullen .02 .10
74 Craig Ludwig .02 .10
75 Kevin Lowe .02 .10
76 John Vanbiesbrouck .30 .75
77 Tim Kerr .02 .10
78 Gerard Gallant .02 .10
79 Tomas Sandstrom .02 .10
80 Jon Casey .20 .50
81 Mark Recchi .40 1.00
82 Scott Stevens .08 .25
83 John MacLean .02 .10
84 James Patrick .02 .10
85 Al Iafrate .02 .10
86 Pat Elynuik .02 .10
87 Dave Andreychuk .02 .10
88 Joe Mullen .02 .10
89 Ed Olczyk .02 .10
90 Kevin Dineen .02 .10
91 Shayne Corson .08 .25
92 Mark Howe .02 .10
93 Brian Leetch .20 .50
94 Dino Ciccarelli .08 .25
95 Pat LaFontaine .20 .50
96 Guy Lafleur .20 .50
97 Mike Modano .75 2.00
98 Rod Brind'Amour .40 1.00
99 Sergei Makarov .08 .25
100 Brett Hull .40 1.00

1990-91 Score Rookie/Traded

The 1990-91 Score Rookie and Traded hockey set contains 110 standard-size cards. The cards were issued as a complete set in a factory box. The fronts feature a color action photo, superimposed over blue and red stripes on a white background. The team logo appears in the upper left hand corner, while an image of a hockey player (in various colors) appears in the lower right hand corner. Yellow strips appear at the top and bottom of the card front. The backs are outlined in a yellow border and show a head shot of the player on the upper half. The career statistics and highlights on the lower half are printed on a pale blue background. Rookie Cards include Ed Belfour, Peter Bondra, Sergei Fedorov, Petr Nedved and Robert Reichel. The back of the set's custom box contains the set checklist. The cards are numbered with a "T" suffix.

COMP. FACT SET (110) 4.00 10.00
1T Denis Savard .05 .15
2T Dale Hawerchuk .05 .15
3T Phil Housley .01 .05
4T Chris Chelios .15 .40
5T Geoff Courtnall .01 .05
6T Peter Zezel .01 .05
7T Joe Mullen .05 .15
8T Craig Ludwig .01 .05
9T Claude Lemieux .01 .05
10T Bobby Holik RC .15 .40
11T Peter Ing .05 .15
12T Rod Buskas RC .01 .05
13T Tim Sweeney RC .01 .05
14T Don Barber RC .01 .05
15T Ray Ferraro .01 .05
16T Peter Taglianetti .01 .05
17T Johan Garpenlov RC .01 .05
18T Kevin Miller RC .01 .05
19T Frank Musil .01 .05
20T Sergei Fedorov RC .60 1.50
21T Aaron Broten .01 .05
22T Chris Nilan .01 .05
23T Gerald Diduck .01 .05
24T Marc Habscheid .01 .05
25T Glen Featherstone RC .01 .05
26T Mikko Makela .01 .05
27T Paul Stanton .01 .05
28T Mark Osborne .01 .05
29T Dave Tippett .01 .05
30T Robert Reichel RC .05 .15
31T Grant Jennings RC .01 .05
32T Troy Gamble .05 .15
33T Mark Janssens .01 .05
34T Brian Propp .01 .05
35T Donald Dufresne RC .01 .05
36T Martin Hostak RC .01 .05
37T Brad McCrimmon .01 .05
38T Dave Lowry RC .01 .05
39T Anatoli Semenov RC .01 .05
40T Scott Stevens .05 .15
41T Paul Broten .01 .05
42T Carey Wilson .01 .05
43T Troy Crowder RC .01 .05
44T Vladimir Ruzicka RC .01 .05
45T Rich Pilon .01 .05
46T John McIntyre RC .01 .05
47T Mike Krushelnyski .01 .05
48T Dave Snuggerud .01 .05
49T Bob McGill .01 .05
50T Petr Nedved RC .25 .60
51T Ed Olczyk .01 .05
52T Doug Crossman .01 .05
53T Mikhail Tatarinov RC .01 .05
54T Michel Petit .01 .05
55T Frank Pietrangelo RC .05 .15
56T Brian MacLellan .01 .05
57T Paul Fenton .01 .05
58T Eric Desjardins RC .25 .60
59T Mike Craig RC .01 .05
60T Mike Ricci .05 .15
61T Harold Snepsts .01 .05
62T John Byce .01 .05
63T Laurie Boschman .01 .05
64T Randy Velischek .01 .05
65T Robert Kron .01 .05
66T Jocelyn Lemieux .01 .05
67T Dave Ellett .01 .05
68T Scott Arniel .01 .05
69T Doug Smail .01 .05
70T Jaromir Jagr .75 2.00
71T Peter Bondra RC .30 .75
72T Paul Cyr .01 .05
73T Daniel Berthiaume .05 .15
74T Lee Norwood .01 .05
75T Bobby Smith .05 .15
76T Kris King RC .01 .05
77T Mark Hunter .01 .05
78T Brian Hayward .05 .15
79T Greg Hawgood .01 .05
80T Owen Nolan .40 1.00
81T Cliff Ronning .05 .15
82T Zdeno Ciger RC .01 .05
83T Gordie Roberts .01 .05
84T Rick Green .01 .05
85T Ken Hodge Jr. RC .01 .05
86T Derek King .01 .05
87T Brent Gilchrist RC .01 .05
88T Eric Lindros .75 2.00
89T Steve Bozek .01 .05
90T Keith Primeau .15 .40
91T Roger Johansson RC .01 .05
92T Wayne Presley .01 .05
93T Ilkka Sinisalo .01 .05
94T Mario Marois .01 .05
95T Ken Linseman .01 .05
96T Greg Brown RC .01 .05
97T Ray Sheppard .05 .15
98T Mike Lalor .01 .05
99T Normand Lacombe .01 .05
100T Mats Sundin .40 1.00
101T Jergus Baca RC .01 .05
102T Mike Keane RC .01 .05
103T Ed Belfour RC 1.00 2.50
104T Mark Hardy .01 .05
105T Dave Capuano RC .01 .05
106T Bryan Trottier .05 .15
107T Per Djoos RC .01 .05
108T Sylvain Turgeon .01 .05
109T David Reid .01 .05
110T Gretzky's 2000th Point .40 1.00

1990-91 Score Young Superstars

This 40-card standard-size set was issued by Score to honor some of the leading young players active in hockey. The set has a glossy sheen to it with an action shot of the player, while the back of the card has a portrait color shot on the back along with biographical and statistical information. The set was available only in this special box format. The set was also available direct to collectors through an offer detailed on certain wax wrappers.

COMP.FACT.SET (40) 8.00 20.00
1 Pierre Turgeon .30 .75
2 Brian Leetch .40 1.00
3 Daniel Marois .02 .10
4 Peter Sidorkiewicz .20 .50
5 Rob Brown .02 .10
6 Theo Fleury .40 1.00
7 Mats Sundin 1.25 3.00
8 Glen Wesley .02 .10
9 Sergei Fedorov 1.25 3.00
10 Joe Sakic .75 2.00
11 Sean Burke .20 .50
12 Dave Chyzowski .02 .10
13 Gord Murphy .02 .10
14 Scott Young .02 .10
15 Curtis Joseph 1.25 3.00
16 Darren Turcotte .20 .50
17 Kevin Stevens .20 .50
18 Mathieu Schneider .02 .10
19 Trevor Linden .20 .50
20 Mike Modano 1.25 3.00
21 Martin Gelinas .02 .10
22 Stephane Fiset .20 .50
23 Brendan Shanahan .75 2.00
24 Jeremy Roenick 1.25 3.00
25 John Druce .02 .10
26 Alexander Mogilny .40 1.00
27 Mike Richter 1.25 3.00
28 Pat Elynuik .02 .10
29 Robert Reichel .02 .10
30 Craig Janney .02 .10
31 Rod Brind'Amour .60 1.50
32 Mark Fitzpatrick .20 .50
33 Tony Granato .02 .10
34 Bobby Holik .02 .10
35 Mark Recchi .75 2.00
36 Owen Nolan .75 2.00
37 Petr Nedved .60 1.50
38 Keith Primeau .60 1.50
39 Mike Ricci .40 1.00
40 Eric Lindros 2.00 5.00

1991 Score National

This ten-card standard-size set features outstanding hockey players. The cards were given out as a cello-wrapped complete set by Score at the National Sports Collectors Convention in Anaheim, at the Fanfest in Toronto, and at the National Candy Wholesalers Convention in St. Louis. Some dealers have reported selling the cards with the NCWA imprint and no imprint (FanFest) for a premium above the prices listed below. The front has an action photo of the player, bounded by diagonal green borders above and below the picture. The player's name and team name appear in the top green border. The light blue background shows through above and below the green borders, and it is decorated with hockey pucks and player icons. The back presents player information and career summary in a diagonal format similar to the design of the front. Some dealers have reported getting premiums of 2-3 times the values below for the Toronto FanFest versions.

COMPLETE SET (10) 12.00 30.00
1 Wayne Gretzky 4.00 10.00
2 Brett Hull .75 2.00
3 Ray Bourque .75 2.00
4 Al MacInnis .50 1.25
5 Luc Robitaille .50 1.25
6 Ed Belfour .60 1.50
7 Steve Yzerman 2.00 5.00
8 Cam Neely .50 1.25
9 Paul Coffey .60 1.50
10 Patrick Roy 3.00 8.00

1991 Score Fanfest

COMPLETE SET (10)
1 Wayne Gretzky 4.00 10.00
2 Brett Hull .75 2.00
3 Ray Bourque .75 2.00
4 Al MacInnis .50 1.25
5 Luc Robitaille .50 1.25
6 Ed Belfour .60 1.50
7 Steve Yzerman 2.00 5.00
8 Cam Neely .50 1.25
9 Paul Coffey .60 1.50
10 Patrick Roy 3.00 8.00

1991-92 Score American

The 1991-92 Score American hockey set features 440 standard-size cards. As one moves down the card face, the fronts shade from purple to white. The color action player photo is enclosed by an thin red border, with a shadow border on the right and below. At the card top, the player's name is written over a hockey puck, and the team name is printed below the picture in the lower right corner. A purple border stripe at the bottom completes the front. In a horizontal format, the backs have biography, statistics, player profile, and a color close-up photo.

COMPLETE SET (440) 4.00 10.00
COMP.FACT.SET (440) 4.00 10.00
1 Brett Hull .08 .25
2 Al MacInnis .02 .10
3 Luc Robitaille .02 .10
4 Pierre Turgeon .02 .10
5 Brian Leetch .07 .20
6 Cam Neely .07 .20
7 John Cullen .01 .05
8 Trevor Linden .02 .10
9 Rick Tocchet .02 .10
10 John Vanbiesbrouck .02 .10
11 Steve Smith .01 .05
12 Doug Smail .01 .05
13 Craig Ludwig .01 .05
14 Paul Fenton .01 .05
15 Dirk Graham .01 .05
16 Brad McCrimmon .01 .05
17 Dean Evason .01 .05
18 Fredrik Olausson .01 .05
19 Guy Carbonneau .02 .10
20 Kevin Hatcher .02 .10
21 Paul Ranheim .01 .05
22 Claude Lemieux .01 .05
23 Vincent Riendeau .02 .10
24 Garth Butcher .01 .05
25 Joe Sakic .15 .40
26 Rick Vaive .01 .05
27 Rob Blake .02 .10
28 Mike Ricci .07 .20
29 Pat Flatley .01 .05
30 Bill Ranford .02 .10
31 Larry Murphy .02 .10
32 Bobby Smith .02 .10
33 Mike Krushelnyski .01 .05
34 Gerard Gallant .01 .05
35 Doug Wilson .02 .10
36 John Ogrodnick .01 .05
37 Mikhail Tatarinov .01 .05
38 Doug Crossman .01 .05
39 Mark Osborne .01 .05
40 Scott Stevens .02 .10
41 Ron Tugnutt .02 .10
42 Russ Courtnall .02 .10
43 Gord Murphy .01 .05
44 Greg Adams .01 .05
45 Christian Ruuttu .01 .05
46 Ken Daneyko .01 .05
47 Glenn Anderson .02 .10
48 Ray Ferraro .01 .05
49 Tony Tanti .01 .05
50 Ray Bourque .10 .30
51 Sergei Makarov .01 .05
52 Jim Johnson .01 .05
53 Troy Murray .01 .05
54 Shawn Burr .01 .05
55 Peter Ing .02 .10
56 Dale Hunter .01 .05
57 Tony Granato .01 .05
58 Curtis Leschyshyn .01 .05
59 Brian Mullen .01 .05
60 Ed Olczyk .01 .05
61 Mike Ramsey .01 .05
62 Dan Quinn .01 .05
63 Rich Sutter .01 .05
64 Terry Carkner .01 .05
65 Shayne Corson .01 .05
66 Peter Stastny .02 .10
67 Craig Muni .01 .05
68 Glenn Healy .02 .10
69 Phil Bourque .01 .05
70 Pat Verbeek .01 .05
71 Garry Galley .01 .05
72 Dave Gagner .01 .05
73 Bob Probert .02 .10
74 Craig Wolanin .01 .05
75 Patrick Roy .40 1.00
76 Keith Brown .01 .05
77 Gary Leeman .01 .05
78 Brent Ashton .01 .05
79 Randy Moller .01 .05
80 Mike Vernon .02 .10
81 Kelly Miller .01 .05
82 Ulf Samuelsson .01 .05
83 Todd Elik .01 .05
84 Uwe Krupp .01 .05
85 Rod Brind'Amour .07 .20
86 Dave Capuano .01 .05
87 Geoff Smith .01 .05
88 David Volek .01 .05
89 Bruce Driver .01 .05
90 Andy Moog .07 .20
91 Pelle Eklund .01 .05
92 Joey Kocur .02 .10
93 Mark Tinordi .01 .05
94 Steve Thomas .01 .05
95 Petr Svoboda .01 .05
96 Joel Otto .01 .05
97 Todd Krygier .01 .05
98 Jaromir Jagr .10 .30
99 Mike Liut .02 .10
100 Wayne Gretzky .50 1.25
101 Teppo Numminen .01 .05
102 Randy Burridge .01 .05
103 Michel Petit .01 .05
104 Tony McKegney .01 .05
105 Mathieu Schneider .01 .05
106 Daren Puppa .02 .10
107 Paul Cavallini .01 .05
108 Tim Kerr .01 .05
109 Kevin Lowe .01 .05
110 Kirk Muller .01 .05
111 Zarley Zalapski .01 .05
112 Mike Hough .01 .05
113 Ken Hodge Jr. .01 .05
114 Grant Fuhr .07 .20
115 Paul Coffey .07 .20
116 Wendel Clark .02 .10
117 Patrik Sundstrom .01 .05
118 Kevin Dineen .01 .05
119 Eric Desjardins .01 .05
120 Mike Richter .07 .20
121 Sergio Momesso .01 .05
122 Tony Hrkac .01 .05
123 Joe Reekie .01 .05
124 Petr Nedved .01 .05
125 Randy Carlyle .01 .05
126 Kevin Miller .01 .05
127 Rejean Lemelin .02 .10
128 Dino Ciccarelli .02 .10
129 Sylvain Cote .01 .05
130 Mats Sundin .07 .20
131 Eric Weinrich .01 .05
132 Daniel Berthiaume .02 .10
133 Keith Acton .01 .05
134 Benoit Hogue .01 .05
135 Mike Gartner .02 .10
136 Petr Klima .01 .05
137 Curt Giles .01 .05
138 Scott Pearson .01 .05
139 Luke Richardson .01 .05
140 Steve Larmer .02 .10
141 Ken Wregget .01 .05
142 Frank Musil .01 .05
143 Owen Nolan .07 .20
144 Keith Primeau .01 .05
145 Mark Recchi .07 .20
146 Don Sweeney .01 .05
147 Mike McPhee .01 .05
148 Ken Baumgartner .01 .05
149 Dave Lowry .01 .05
150 Geoff Courtnall .02 .10
151 Chris Terreri .02 .10
152 Dave Manson .01 .05
153 Bobby Holik .01 .05
154 Bob Kudelski .01 .05
155 Calle Johansson .01 .05
156 Mark Hunter .01 .05
157 Randy Gilhen .01 .05
158 Yves Racine .01 .05
159 Martin Gelinas .01 .05
160 Brian Bellows .01 .05
161 David Shaw .01 .05
162 Bob Carpenter .01 .05
163 Doug Brown .01 .05
164 Ulf Dahlen .01 .05
165 Denis Savard .02 .10
166 Paul Ysebaert .01 .05
167 Derek King .01 .05
168 Igor Larionov .01 .05
169 Bob Errey .01 .05
170 Joe Nieuwendyk .02 .10
171 Normand Rochefort .01 .05
172 John Tonelli .01 .05
173 David Reid .01 .05
174 Tom Kurvers .01 .05
175 Dimitri Khristich .01 .05
176 Bob Sweeney .01 .05
177 Rick Zombo .01 .05
178 Troy Mallette .01 .05
179 Bob Bassen .01 .05
180 John Druce .01 .05
181 Mike Craig .01 .05
182 John McIntyre .01 .05
183 Murray Baron .01 .05
184 Slava Fetisov .01 .05
185 Don Beaupre .02 .10
186 Brian Benning .01 .05
187 Dave Barr .01 .05

188 Petri Skriko .01 .05
189 Steve Konroyd .01 .05
190 Steve Yzerman .30 .75
191 Jon Casey .02 .10
192 Gary Nylund .01 .05
193 Michal Pivonka .01 .05
194 Alexei Kasatonov .01 .05
195 Garry Valk .01 .05
196 Darren Turcotte .01 .05
197 Chris Nilan .01 .05
198 Thomas Steen .01 .05
199 Gary Roberts .02 .10
200 Mario Lemieux .50 1.25
201 Michel Goulet .02 .10
202 Craig MacTavish .01 .05
203 Peter Sidorkiewicz .02 .10
204 Johan Garpenlov .01 .05
205 Steve Duchesne .01 .05
206 Dave Snuggerud .01 .05
207 Kjell Samuelsson .01 .05
208 Sylvain Turgeon .01 .05
209 Al Iafrate .02 .10
210 John MacLean .02 .10
211 Brian Hayward .02 .10
212 Cliff Ronning .01 .05
213 Ray Sheppard .01 .05
214 Dave Taylor .02 .10
215 Doug Lidster .01 .05
216 Peter Bondra .02 .10
217 Marty McSorley .01 .05
218 Doug Gilmour .02 .10
219 Paul MacDermid .01 .05
220 Jeremy Roenick .08 .25
221 Wayne Presley .01 .05
222 Jeff Norton .01 .05
223 Brian Propp .01 .05
224 Jimmy Carson .01 .05
225 Tom Barrasso .02 .10
226 Theo Fleury .01 .05
227 Carey Wilson .01 .05
228 Rod Langway .01 .05
229 Bryan Trottier .07 .20
230 James Patrick .01 .05
231 Kelly Hrudey .02 .10
232 Dave Poulin .01 .05
233 Rob Ramage .01 .05
234 Stephane Richer .02 .10
235 Chris Chelios .07 .20
236 Alexander Mogilny .07 .20
237 Bryan Fogarty .01 .05
238 Adam Oates .02 .10
239 Ron Hextall .02 .10
240 Bernie Nicholls .02 .10
241 Esa Tikkanen .01 .05
242 Jyrki Lumme .01 .05
243 Brent Sutter .01 .05
244 Gary Suter .01 .05
245 Sean Burke .02 .10
246 Rob Brown .01 .05
247 Mike Modano .15 .40
248 Kevin Stevens .01 .05
249 Mike Lalor .01 .05
250 Sergei Fedorov .10 .30
251 Bob Essensa .02 .10
252 Mark Howe .01 .05
253 Craig Janney .02 .10
254 Daniel Marois .01 .05
255 Craig Simpson .01 .05
256 Steve Kasper .01 .05
257 Randy Velischek .01 .05
258 Gino Cavallini .01 .05
259 Dale Hawerchuk .02 .10
260 Pat LaFontaine .07 .20
261 Kirk McLean .02 .10
262 Murray Craven .01 .05
263 Robert Reichel .01 .05
264 Jan Erixon .01 .05
265 Adam Creighton .01 .05
266 Mark Fitzpatrick .02 .10
267 Ron Francis .02 .10
268 Joe Mullen .02 .10
269 Peter Zezel .01 .05
270 Tomas Sandstrom .01 .05
271 Phil Housley .02 .10
272 Tim Cheveldae .02 .10
273 Glen Wesley .01 .05
274 Stephan Lebeau .01 .05
275 Dave Ellett .01 .05
276 Jeff Brown .01 .05
277 Dave Andreychuk .02 .10
278 Steven Finn .01 .05
279 Scott Mellanby .01 .05
280 Neal Broten .02 .10
281 Randy Wood .01 .05
282 Troy Gamble .02 .10
283 Mike Ridley .01 .05
284 Jamie Macoun .01 .05
285 Mark Messier .07 .20
286 Brendan Shanahan .07 .20
287 Scott Young .01 .05
288 Kelly Kisio .01 .05
289 Brad Shaw .01 .05
290 Ed Belfour .07 .20
291 Larry Robinson .02 .10
292 Dave Christian .01 .05
293 Steve Chiasson .01 .05
294 Brian Skrudland .01 .05
295 Pat Elynuik .01 .05
296 Curtis Joseph .07 .20
297 Doug Bodger .01 .05
298 Ron Sutter .01 .05
299 Joe Murphy .01 .05
300 Vincent Damphousse .01 .05
301 Cam Neely CC .02 .10
302 Rick Tocchet CC .01 .05
303 Scott Stevens CC .01 .05
304 Ulf Samuelsson CC .01 .05
305 Jeremy Roenick CC .08 .25
306 The Hunter Brothers .01 .05
Dale Hunter
Mark Hunter
307 The Broten Brothers .01 .05
Aaron Broten
Neal Broten
308 The Cavallini Brothers .01 .05
Gino Cavallini
Paul Cavallini
309 The Miller Brothers .01 .05
Kelly Miller
Kevin Miller
310 Dennis Vaske TP .01 .05
311 Rob Pearson RC .01 .05
312 Jason Miller TP .01 .05
313 John LeClair RC .50 1.25
314 Bryan Marchment TP RC .02 .10
315 Gary Shuchuk TP .01 .05
316 Dominik Hasek RC 1.50 4.00
317 Michel Picard TP RC .01 .05
318 Corey Millen RC .01 .05
319 Joe Sacco RC .01 .05
320 Reggie Savage RC .01 .05
321 Pat Murray TP .01 .05
322 Myles O'Connor TP .01 .05
323 Shawn Antoski TP .01 .05
324 Geoff Sanderson RC .02 .10
325 Chris Govedaris TP .01 .05
326 Alexei Gusarov RC .02 .10
327 Mike Sillinger TP .01 .05
328 Bob Wilkie TP .01 .05
329 Pat Jablonski RC .02 .10
330 David Emma RC .01 .05
331 Kirk Muller FP .01 .05
332 Pat LaFontaine FP .02 .10
333 Brian Leetch FP .02 .10
334 Rick Tocchet FP .01 .05
335 Mario Lemieux FP .10 .30
336 Joe Sakic FP .07 .20
337 Brett Hull FP .07 .20
338 Vincent Damphousse FP .01 .05
339 Trevor Linden FP .01 .05
340 Kevin Hatcher FP .01 .05
341 Pat Elynuik FP .01 .05
342 Patrick Roy DT .10 .30
343 Brian Leetch DT .02 .10
344 Ray Bourque DT .07 .20
345 Luc Robitaille DT .02 .10
346 Wayne Gretzky DT .20 .50
347 Brett Hull DT .07 .20
348 Ed Belfour ART .07 .20
349 Rob Blake ART .01 .05
350 Eric Weinrich ART .01 .05
351 Jaromir Jagr ART .07 .20
352 Sergei Fedorov ART .07 .20
353 Ken Hodge Jr. ART .01 .05
354 Eric Lindros Art .07 .20
355 Eric Lindros .07 .20
Awards and Honors
356 Eric Lindros .07 .20
'91 1st Rd Draft Choice
357 Dana Murzyn .01 .05
358 Adam Graves .02 .10
359 Ken Linseman .01 .05
360 Mike Keane .01 .05
361 Stephane Morin .01 .05
362 Grant Ledyard .01 .05
363 Kris King .01 .05
364 Paul Gillis .01 .05
365 Chris Dahlquist .01 .05
366 Paul Stanton .01 .05
367 Jeff Hackett .02 .10
368 Bob McGill .01 .05
369 Neil Wilkinson .01 .05
370 Rob Zettler .01 .05
371 Brett Hull MOY .07 .20
372 Paul Coffey 1000 .02 .10
373 Mark Messier 1000 .07 .20
374 Dave Taylor 1000 .01 .05
375 Michel Goulet 1000 .01 .05
376 Dale Hawerchuk 1000 .01 .05
377 The Turgeon Brothers .02 .10
Pierre Turgeon
Sylvain Turgeon
378 The Sutter Brothers .01 .05
Rich Sutter
Brian Sutter
Ron Sutter
379 The Mullen Brothers .02 .10
Brian Mullen
Joe Mullen
380 The Courtnall Brothers .01 .05
Geoff Courtnall
Russ Courtnall
381 Trevor Kidd TP .02 .10
382 Patrice Brisebois TP .01 .05
383 Mark Greig TP .01 .05
384 Kip Miller TP .01 .05
385 Drake Berehowsky TP .01 .05
386 Kevin Haller RC .01 .05
387 Dave Gagnon TP .01 .05
388 Jason Marshall TP .01 .05
389 Donald Audette TP .01 .05
390 Patrick Lebeau RC .01 .05
391 Alexander Godynyuk TP .01 .05
392 Jarrod Skalde TP RC .01 .05
393 Ken Sutton RC .01 .05
394 Sergei Kharin TP .01 .05
395 Andre Racicot TP RC .02 .10
396 Doug Weight RC .30 .75
397 Kevin Todd RC .01 .05
398 Tony Amonte TP RC .50 1.25
399 Kimbi Daniels TP .01 .05
400 Jeff Daniels RC .01 .05
401 Guy Lafleur .07 .20
Speed and Grace
402 Guy Lafleur .07 .20
Awards and Achievements
403 Guy Lafleur .07 .20
A Hall of Famer
404 Brett Hull SL .07 .20
405 Wayne Gretzky SL .20 .50
406 Wayne Gretzky SL .20 .50
407 Theo Fleury SL and .01 .05
Marty McSorley SL
408 Sergei Fedorov SL .07 .20
409 Al MacInnis SL .01 .05
410 Ed Belfour SL .07 .20
411 Ed Belfour SL .07 .20
412 Brett Hull HL .07 .20
(50 goals in 50 games)
413 Wayne Gretzky HL .20 .50
(700th goal)
414 San Jose Sharks .01 .05
415 Ray Bourque FP .07 .20
416 Pierre Turgeon FP .01 .05
417 Al MacInnis FP .01 .05
418 Jeremy Roenick FP .08 .25
419 Steve Yzerman FP .10 .30
420 Mark Messier FP .07 .20
421 John Cullen FP .01 .05
422 Wayne Gretzky FP .20 .50
423 Mike Modano FP .07 .20
424 Patrick Roy FP .10 .30
425 Stanley Cup Champs .02 .10
426 Mario Lemieux Smythe .10 .30
427 Wayne Gretzky .20 .50
Art Ross Trophy
428 Brett Hull .07 .20
Hart Memorial Trophy
429 Ray Bourque .07 .20
Norris Trophy
430 Ed Belfour .07 .20
Calder Trophy
431 Ed Belfour .07 .20
Vezina Trophy
432 Dirk Graham .01 .05
Frank J. Selke Trophy
433 Ed Belfour .07 .20
Jennings Trophy
434 Wayne Gretzky .20 .50
Lady Byng Trophy
435 Dave Taylor .01 .05
Bill Masterton Trophy
436 Randy Ladouceur .01 .05
437 Dave Tippett .01 .05
438 Clint Malarchuk .02 .10
439 Gordie Roberts .01 .05
440 Frank Pietrangelo .01 .05

1991-92 Score Canadian Bilingual

The 1991-92 Score Canadian hockey set features 660 standard-size cards. The set was released in two series of 330 cards each. The borders on the front of first series cards shade from red to white, top to bottom. The fronts of the second series cards shade from bright blue to white. The two series also differ in that first series cards have the player enclosed by a thin purple border and second series cards have a red border. At the top, the player's name is written over a hockey puck and the team name is printed below the picture in the lower right corner. A red border stripe at the bottom completes the front. In a horizontal format, the bilingual backs have biography, statistics, player profile, and a color close-up photo. An identical version (Score Canadian-English) to this set exists, with the difference being that the text on each card is strictly in English.

COMPLETE SET (660) 5.00 12.00
COMP.FACT.SET (660) 5.00 12.00
COMP.SERIES 1 (330) 2.50 6.00
COMP.SERIES 2 (330) 2.50 6.00
1 Brett Hull .08 .25
2 Al MacInnis .02 .10
3 Luc Robitaille .02 .10
4 Pierre Turgeon .02 .10
5 Brian Leetch .07 .20
6 Cam Neely .07 .20
7 John Cullen .01 .05
8 Trevor Linden .02 .10
9 Rick Tocchet .02 .10
10 John Vanbiesbrouck .02 .10
11 Steve Smith .01 .05
12 Doug Smail .01 .05
13 Craig Ludwig .01 .05
14 Paul Fenton .01 .05
15 Dirk Graham .01 .05
16 Brad McCrimmon .01 .05
17 Dean Evason .01 .05
18 Fredrik Olausson .01 .05
19 Guy Carbonneau .02 .10
20 Kevin Hatcher .02 .10
21 Paul Ranheim .01 .05
22 Claude Lemieux .02 .10
23 Vincent Riendeau .02 .10
24 Garth Butcher .01 .05
25 Joe Sakic .15 .40
26 Rick Vaive .01 .05
27 Rob Blake .02 .10
28 Mike Ricci .07 .20
29 Pat Flatley .01 .05
30 Bill Ranford .02 .10
31 Larry Murphy .02 .10
32 Bobby Smith .02 .10
33 Mike Krushelnyski .01 .05
34 Gerard Gallant .01 .05
35 Doug Wilson .02 .10
36 John Ogrodnick .01 .05
37 Mikhail Tatarinov .01 .05
38 Doug Crossman .01 .05
39 Mark Osborne .01 .05
40 Scott Stevens .02 .10
41 Ron Tugnutt .02 .10
42 Russ Courtnall .02 .10
43 Gord Murphy .01 .05
44 Greg Adams .01 .05
45 Christian Ruuttu .01 .05
46 Ken Daneyko .01 .05
47 Glenn Anderson .02 .10
48 Ray Ferraro .01 .05
49 Tony Tanti .01 .05
50 Ray Bourque .10 .30
51 Sergei Makarov .01 .05
52 Jim Johnson .01 .05
53 Troy Murray .01 .05
54 Shawn Burr .01 .05
55 Peter Ing .02 .10
56 Dale Hunter .01 .05
57 Tony Granato .01 .05
58 Curtis Leschyshyn .01 .05
59 Brian Mullen .01 .05
60 Ed Olczyk .01 .05
61 Mike Ramsey .01 .05
62 Dan Quinn .01 .05
63 Rich Sutter .01 .05
64 Terry Carkner .01 .05
65 Shayne Corson .01 .05
66 Peter Stastny .02 .10
67 Craig Muni .01 .05
68 Glenn Healy .02 .10
69 Phil Bourque .01 .05
70 Pat Verbeek .01 .05
71 Garry Galley .01 .05
72 Dave Gagner .01 .05
73 Bob Probert .02 .10
74 Craig Wolanin .01 .05
75 Patrick Roy .40 1.00
76 Keith Brown .01 .05
77 Gary Leeman .01 .05
78 Brent Ashton .01 .05
79 Randy Moller .01 .05
80 Mike Vernon .02 .10
81 Kelly Miller .01 .05
82 Ulf Samuelsson .01 .05
83 Todd Elik .01 .05
84 Uwe Krupp .01 .05
85 Rod Brind'Amour .07 .20
86 Dave Capuano .01 .05
87 Geoff Smith .01 .05
88 David Volek .01 .05
89 Bruce Driver .01 .05
90 Andy Moog .07 .20
91 Pelle Eklund .01 .05
92 Joey Kocur .02 .10
93 Mark Tinordi .01 .05
94 Steve Thomas .01 .05
95 Petr Svoboda .01 .05
96 Joel Otto .01 .05
97 Todd Krygier .01 .05
98 Jaromir Jagr .10 .30
99 Mike Liut .02 .10
100 Wayne Gretzky .50 1.25
101 Teppo Numminen .01 .05
102 Randy Burridge .01 .05
103 Michel Petit .01 .05
104 Tony McKegney .01 .05
105 Mathieu Schneider .01 .05
106 Daren Puppa .02 .10
107 Paul Cavallini .01 .05
108 Tim Kerr .01 .05
109 Kevin Lowe .02 .10
110 Kirk Muller .01 .05
111 Zarley Zalapski .01 .05
112 Mike Hough .01 .05
113 Ken Hodge Jr. .01 .05
114 Grant Fuhr .07 .20
115 Paul Coffey .07 .20
116 Wendel Clark .02 .10
117 Patrick Sundstrom .01 .05
118 Kevin Dineen .01 .05
119 Eric Desjardins .02 .10
120 Mike Richter .07 .20
121 Sergio Momesso .01 .05
122 Tony Hrkac .01 .05
123 Joe Reekie .01 .05
124 Petr Nedved .02 .10
125 Randy Carlyle .01 .05
126 Kevin Miller .01 .05
127 Rejean Lemelin .02 .10
128 Dino Ciccarelli .02 .10
129 Sylvain Cote .01 .05
130 Mats Sundin .07 .20
131 Eric Weinrich .01 .05
132 Daniel Berthiaume .02 .10
133 Keith Acton .01 .05
134 Benoit Hogue .01 .05
135 Mike Gartner .02 .10
136 Petr Klima .01 .05
137 Curt Giles .01 .05
138 Scott Pearson .01 .05
139 Luke Richardson .01 .05
140 Steve Larmer .02 .10
141 Ken Wreggel .02 .10
142 Frank Musil .01 .05
143 Owen Nolan .07 .20
144 Keith Primeau .01 .05
145 Mark Recchi .07 .20
146 Don Sweeney .01 .05
147 Mike McPhee .01 .05
148 Ken Baumgartner .01 .05
149 Dave Lowry .01 .05
150 Geoff Courtnall .01 .05
151 Chris Terreri .02 .10
152 Dave Manson .01 .05
153 Bobby Holik .02 .10
154 Bob Kudelski .01 .05
155 Calle Johansson .01 .05
156 Mark Hunter .01 .05
157 Randy Gilhen .01 .05
158 Yves Racine .01 .05
159 Martin Gelinas .01 .05
160 Brian Bellows .01 .05
161 David Shaw .01 .05
162 Bob Carpenter .01 .05
163 Doug Brown .01 .05
164 Ulf Dahlen .01 .05
165 Denis Savard .02 .10
166 Paul Ysebaert .01 .05
167 Derek King .01 .05
168 Igor Larionov .01 .05
169 Bob Errey .01 .05
170 Joe Nieuwendyk .02 .10
171 Normand Rochefort .01 .05
172 John Tonelli .01 .05
173 David Reid .01 .05
174 Tom Kurvers .01 .05
175 Dimitri Khristich .01 .05
176 Bob Sweeney .01 .05
177 Rick Zombo .01 .05
178 Troy Mallette .01 .05
179 Bob Bassen .01 .05
180 John Druce .01 .05
181 Mike Craig .01 .05
182 John McIntyre .01 .05
183 Murray Baron .01 .05
184 Slava Fetisov .01 .05
185 Don Beaupre .02 .10
186 Brian Benning .01 .05
187 Dave Barr .01 .05
188 Petri Skriko .01 .05
189 Steve Konroyd .01 .05
190 Steve Yzerman .30 .75
191 Jon Casey .02 .10
192 Gary Nylund .01 .05
193 Michal Pivonka .01 .05
194 Alexei Kasatonov .01 .05
195 Garry Valk .01 .05
196 Darren Turcotte .01 .05
197 Chris Nilan .01 .05
198 Thomas Steen .01 .05
199 Gary Roberts .02 .10
200 Mario Lemieux .50 1.25
201 Michel Goulet .02 .10
202 Craig MacTavish .01 .05
203 Peter Sidorkiewicz .02 .10
204 Johan Garpenlov .01 .05
205 Steve Duchesne .01 .05
206 Dave Snuggerud .01 .05
207 Kjell Samuelsson .01 .05
208 Sylvain Turgeon .01 .05
209 Al Iafrate .02 .10
210 John MacLean .02 .10
211 Brian Hayward .02 .10
212 Cliff Ronning .01 .05
213 Ray Sheppard .01 .05
214 Dave Taylor .02 .10
215 Doug Lidster .01 .05
216 Peter Bondra .02 .10
217 Marty McSorley .01 .05
218 Doug Gilmour .02 .10
219 Paul MacDermid .01 .05
220 Jeremy Roenick .10 .30
221 Wayne Presley .01 .05
222 Jeff Norton .01 .05
223 Brian Propp .01 .05
224 Jimmy Carson .01 .05
225 Tom Barrasso .02 .10
226 Theo Fleury .01 .05
227 Carey Wilson .01 .05
228 Rod Langway .01 .05
229 Bryan Trottier .07 .20
230 James Patrick .01 .05
231 Dana Murzyn .01 .05
232 Rick Wamsley .02 .10
233 Dave McLlwain .01 .05
234 Tom Fergus .01 .05
235 Adam Graves .02 .10
236 Jacques Cloutier .02 .10
237 Gino Odjick .01 .05
238 Andrew Cassels .01 .05
239 Ken Linseman .01 .05
240 Danton Cole .01 .05
241 Dave Hannan .01 .05
242 Stephane Matteau .01 .05
243 Gerald Diduck .01 .05
244 Rick Tabaracci .02 .10
245 Sylvain Lefebvre .01 .05
246 Bob Rouse .01 .05
247 Charlie Huddy .01 .05
248 Mike Foligno .01 .05
249 Ric Nattress .01 .05
250 Aaron Broten .01 .05
251 Mike Keane .01 .05
252 Steve Bozek .01 .05
253 Jeff Beukeboom .01 .05
254 Stephane Morin .01 .05
255 Brian Bradley .01 .05
256 Scott Arniel .01 .05
257 Robert Kron .01 .05
258 Anatoli Semenov .01 .05
259 Brent Gilchrist .01 .05
260 Jim Sandlak .01 .05
261 Brett Hull (Man of Year) .07 .20
262 Paul Coffey 1000 PTS .02 .10
263 Mark Messier 1000 PTS .07 .20
264 Dave Taylor 1000 PTS .01 .05
265 Michel Goulet 1000 PTS .01 .05
266 Dale Hawerchuk 1000 PTS .01 .05
267 The Turgeon Brothers .02 .10
Pierre Turgeon
Sylvain Turgeon
268 The Sutter Brothers .01 .05
Rich Sutter
Brian Sutter
Ron Sutter
269 The Mullen Brothers .02 .10
Brian Mullen
Joe Mullen
270 The Courtnall Brothers .01 .05
Geoff Courtnall
Russ Courtnall
271 Trevor Kidd TP .02 .10
272 Patrice Brisebois TP .01 .05
273 Mark Greig TP .01 .05
274 Kip Miller TP .01 .05
275 Drake Berehowsky TP .01 .05
276 Kevin Haller RC .01 .05
277 Dave Gagnon TP .01 .05
278 Jason Marshall TP .01 .05
279 Donald Audette TP .01 .05
280 Patrick Lebeau RC .01 .05
281 Alexander Godynyuk TP .01 .05
282 Jarrod Skalde TP RC .01 .05
283 Ken Sutton RC .01 .05
284 Sergei Kharin TP .01 .05
285 Andre Racicot TP RC .02 .10
286 Doug Weight RC .30 .75
287 Kevin Todd RC .01 .05
288 Tony Amonte TP RC .50 1.25
289 Kimbi Daniels TP .01 .05
290 Jeff Daniels RC .01 .05
291 Guy Lafleur .07 .20
Speed and Grace
292 Guy Lafleur .07 .20
Awards and Achievements
293 Guy Lafleur .07 .20
A Hall of Famer
294 Brett Hull SL .07 .20
295 Wayne Gretzky SL .20 .50
296 Wayne Gretzky SL .20 .50
297 Theo Fleury and .01 .05
Marty McSorley SL
298 Sergei Fedorov SL .07 .20
299 Al MacInnis SL .01 .05
300 Ed Belfour SL .07 .20
301 Ed Belfour SL .07 .20
302 Brett Hull 50/50 .07 .20
303 Wayne Gretzky .20 .50
700th Career Goal
304 San Jose Sharks Logo .01 .05
305 Cam Neely Crunch .02 .10
306 Rick Tocchet Crunch .01 .05
307 Scott Stevens Crunch .01 .05
308 Ulf Samuelsson Crunch .01 .05
309 Jeremy Roenick Crunch .08 .25
310 Mark Messier FRAN .07 .20
311 John Cullen FRAN .01 .05
312 Wayne Gretzky FRAN .20 .50
313 Mike Modano FRAN .07 .20
314 Patrick Roy FRAN .10 .30
315 Stanley Cup Champs .02 .10
316 Mario Lemieux Smythe .10 .30
317 Wayne Gretzky .20 .50
Art Ross Trophy
318 Brett Hull .07 .20
Hart Memorial Trophy
319 Ray Bourque .07 .20
Norris Trophy
320 Ed Belfour .07 .20
Calder Trophy
321 Ed Belfour .07 .20
Vezina Trophy
322 Dirk Graham .01 .05
Frank J. Selke Trophy
323 Ed Belfour .07 .20
Jennings Trophy
324 Wayne Gretzky .20 .50
Lady Byng Trophy
325 Dave Taylor .01 .05
Bill Masterton Trophy
326 Jeff Hackett .02 .10
327 Bob McGill .01 .05
328 Neil Wilkinson .01 .05
329 Eric Lindros .07 .20
1st Rd Draft Choice
330 Eric Lindros .07 .20
Awards and Honors
331 Ray Bourque FP .07 .20
332 Pierre Turgeon FP .01 .05
333 Al MacInnis FP .01 .05
334 Jeremy Roenick FP .08 .25
335 Steve Yzerman FP .10 .30
336 The Hunter Brothers .01 .05
Dale Hunter
Mark Hunter
337 The Broten Brothers .01 .05
Neal Broten
Aaron Broten
338 The Cavallini Brothers .01 .05
Gino Cavallini
Paul Cavallini
339 The Miller Brothers .01 .05
Kelly Miller
Kevin Miller
340 Dennis Vaske TP .01 .05
341 Rob Pearson RC .01 .05
342 Jason Miller TP .01 .05
343 John LeClair RC .50 1.25
344 Bryan Marchment TP RC .02 .10
345 Gary Shuchuk TP .01 .05
346 Dominik Hasek RC .75 2.00
347 Michel Picard TP RC .01 .05
348 Corey Millen RC .01 .05
349 Joe Sacco RC .01 .05
350 Reggie Savage RC .01 .05
351 Pat Murray TP .01 .05
352 Myles O'Connor TP .01 .05
353 Shawn Antoski TP .01 .05
354 Geoff Sanderson RC .08 .25
355 Chris Govedaris TP .01 .05
356 Alexei Gusarov RC .02 .10
357 Mike Sillinger TP .01 .05
358 Bob Wilkie TP .01 .05
359 Pat Jablonski RC .02 .10
360 Memorial Cup .01 .05
Spokane Chiefs
361 Kirk Muller FP .01 .05
362 Pat LaFontaine FP .02 .10
363 Brian Leetch FP .02 .10
364 Rick Tocchet FP .01 .05
365 Mario Lemieux FP .10 .30
366 Joe Sakic FP .07 .20
367 Brett Hull FP .07 .20
368 Vincent Damphousse FP .01 .05
369 Trevor Linden FP .01 .05
370 Kevin Hatcher FP .01 .05
371 Pat Elynuik FP .01 .05
372 Patrick Roy DT .10 .30
373 Brian Leetch DT .02 .10
374 Ray Bourque DT .07 .20
375 Luc Robitaille DT .02 .10
376 Wayne Gretzky DT .20 .50
377 Brett Hull DT .07 .20
378 Ed Belfour ART .07 .20
379 Rob Blake ART .01 .05
380 Eric Weinrich ART .01 .05
381 Jaromir Jagr ART .07 .20
382 Sergei Fedorov ART .07 .20
383 Ken Hodge Jr. ART .01 .05
384 Eric Lindros Art .07 .20
385 Eric Lindros .07 .20
with Rob Pearson
386 Ottawa/Tampa Bay .07 .20
Logo Card
387 Mick Vukota .01 .05
388 Lou Franceschetti .01 .05
389 Mike Hudson .01 .05
390 Frantisek Kucera .01 .05
391 Basil McRae .01 .05
392 Donald Dufresne .01 .05
393 Tommy Albelin .01 .05
394 Normand Lacombe .01 .05
395 Lucien DeBlois .01 .05
396 Tony Twist RC .07 .20
397 Rob Murphy .01 .05
398 Ken Sabourin .01 .05
399 Doug Evans .01 .05
400 Walt Poddubny .01 .05
401 Grant Ledyard .01 .05
402 Kris King .01 .05
403 Paul Gillis .01 .05
404 Chris Dahlquist .01 .05
405 Zdeno Ciger .01 .05
406 Paul Stanton .01 .05
407 Randy Ladouceur .01 .05
408 Ronnie Stern .01 .05
409 Dave Tippett .01 .05
410 Jeff Reese .01 .05
411 Vladimir Ruzicka .01 .05
412 Brent Fedyk .01 .05
413 Paul Cyr .01 .05
414 Mike Eagles .01 .05
415 Chris Joseph .01 .05
416 Brad Marsh .01 .05
417 Rich Pilon .01 .05
418 Jiri Hrdina .01 .05
419 Clint Malarchuk .02 .10
420 Steven Rice .01 .05
421 Mark Janssens .01 .05
422 Gordie Roberts .01 .05
423 Shawn Cronin .01 .05
424 Randy Cunneyworth .01 .05
425 Frank Pietrangelo .01 .05
426 David Maley .01 .05
427 Rod Buskas .01 .05
428 Dennis Vial .01 .05
429 Kelly Buchberger .01 .05
430 Wes Walz .01 .05
431 Dean Kennedy .01 .05
432 Nick Kypreos .01 .05
433 Stewart Gavin .01 .05
434 Norm Maciver RC .01 .05
435 Mark Pederson .01 .05
436 Laurie Boschman .01 .05
437 Stephane Quintal .01 .05
438 Darrin Shannon .01 .05
439 Trent Yawney .01 .05
440 Gaetan Duchesne .01 .05
441 Joe Cirella .01 .05
442 Doug Houda .01 .05
443 Dave Chyzowski .01 .05
444 Derrick Smith .01 .05
445 Jeff Lazaro .01 .05
446 Brian Glynn .01 .05
447 Jocelyn Lemieux .01 .05
448 Peter Taglianetti .01 .05
449 Adam Burt .01 .05
450 Hubie McDonough .01 .05
451 Kelly Hrudey .02 .10
452 Dave Poulin .01 .05
453 Mark Hardy .01 .05
454 Mike Hartman .01 .05
455 Chris Chelios .07 .20
456 Alexander Mogilny .07 .20
457 Bryan Fogarty .01 .05
458 Adam Oates .02 .10
459 Ron Hextall .02 .10
460 Bernie Nicholls .02 .10
461 Esa Tikkanen .01 .05
462 Jyrki Lumme .01 .05
463 Brent Sutter .01 .05
464 Gary Suter .01 .05
465 Sean Burke .02 .10
466 Rob Brown .01 .05
467 Mike Modano .15 .40
468 Kevin Stevens .01 .05
469 Mike Lalor .01 .05
470 Sergei Fedorov .10 .30
471 Bob Essensa .02 .10
472 Mark Howe .01 .05
473 Craig Janney .02 .10
474 Daniel Marois .01 .05
475 Craig Simpson .01 .05
476 Marc Bureau .01 .05
477 Randy Velischek .01 .05
478 Gino Cavallini .01 .05
479 Dale Hawerchuk .02 .10
480 Pat LaFontaine .07 .20
481 Kirk McLean .02 .10
482 Murray Craven .01 .05
483 Robert Reichel .01 .05
484 Jan Erixon .01 .05
485 Adam Creighton .01 .05
486 Mark Fitzpatrick .02 .10
487 Ron Francis .02 .10
488 Joe Mullen .02 .10
489 Peter Zezel .01 .05
490 Tomas Sandstrom .01 .05
491 Phil Housley .02 .10
492 Tim Cheveldae .02 .10
493 Glen Wesley .01 .05
494 Stephan Lebeau .01 .05
495 Dave Ellett .01 .05
496 Jeff Brown .01 .05
497 Dave Andreychuk .02 .10
498 Steven Finn .01 .05
499 Mike Donnelly RC .01 .05
500 Neal Broten .02 .10
501 Randy Wood .01 .05
502 Troy Gamble .02 .10
503 Mike Ridley .01 .05
504 Jamie Macoun .01 .05
505 Mark Messier .07 .20
506 Moe Mantha .01 .05
507 Scott Young .01 .05
508 Robert Dirk .01 .05
509 Brad Shaw .01 .05
510 Ed Belfour .07 .20
511 Larry Robinson .02 .10
512 Dale Kushner .01 .05
513 Steve Chiasson .01 .05
514 Brian Skrudland .01 .05
515 Pat Elynuik .01 .05
516 Curtis Joseph .07 .20
517 Doug Bodger .01 .05
518 Greg Brown .01 .05
519 Joe Murphy .01 .05
520 J.J. Daigneault .01 .05
521 Todd Gill .01 .05
522 Troy Loney .01 .05
523 Tim Walters .01 .05
524 Jody Hull .01 .05

525 Colin Patterson .01 .05
526 Darin Kimble .01 .05
527 Perry Berezan .01 .05
528 Lee Norwood .01 .05
529 Mike Peluso .01 .05
530 Wayne McBean .01 .05
531 Grant Jennings .01 .05
532 Claude Loiselle .01 .05
533 Ron Wilson .01 .05
534 Phil Sykes .01 .05
535 Jim Wiemer .01 .05
536 Herb Raglan .01 .05
537 Tim Hunter .01 .05
538 Mike Tomlak .01 .05
539 Greg Gilbert .01 .05
540 Jiri Latal .01 .05
541 Bill Berg .01 .05
542 Shane Churla .01 .05
543 Jay Miller .01 .05
544 Pete Peeters .02 .10
545 Alan May .01 .05
546 Mario Marois .01 .05
547 Jim Kyte .01 .05
548 Jon Morris .01 .05
549 Mikko Makela .01 .05
550 Nelson Emerson .01 .05
551 Doug Wilson .02 .10
552 Brian Mullen .01 .05
553 Kelly Kisio .01 .05
554 Brian Hayward .02 .10
555 Tony Hrkac .01 .05
556 Steve Bozek .01 .05
557 John Carter .01 .05
558 Neil Wilkinson .01 .05
559 Wayne Presley .01 .05
560 Bob McGill .01 .05
561 Craig Ludwig .01 .05
562 Mikhail Tatarinov .01 .05
563 Todd Elik .01 .05
564 Randy Burridge .01 .05
565 Tim Kerr .01 .05
566 Randy Gilhen .01 .05
567 John Tonelli .01 .05
568 Tom Kurvers .01 .05
569 Steve Duchesne .01 .05
570 Charlie Huddy .01 .05
571 Alan Kerr .01 .05
572 Shawn Chambers .01 .05
573 Rob Ramage .01 .05
574 Steve Kasper .01 .05
575 Scott Mellanby .01 .05
576 Stephen Leach .01 .05
577 Scott Niedermayer .01 .05
578 Craig Berube .01 .05
579 Greg Paslawski .01 .05
580 Randy Hillier .01 .05
581 Stephane Richer .02 .10
582 Brian MacLellan .01 .05
583 Marc Habscheid .01 .05
584 Dave Babych .01 .05
585 Troy Murray .01 .05
586 Ray Sheppard .01 .05
587 Glen Featherstone .01 .05
588 Brendan Shanahan .07 .20
589 Dave Christian .01 .05
590 Mike Bullard .01 .05
591 Ryan Walter .01 .05
592 Doug Smail .01 .05
593 Paul Fenton .01 .05
594 Adam Graves .02 .10
595 Scott Stevens .02 .10
596 Sylvain Cote .01 .05
597 Dave Barr .01 .05
598 Randy Gregg .01 .05
599 Allen Pedersen .01 .05
600 Jari Kurri .07 .20
601 Troy Mallette .01 .05
602 Troy Crowder .01 .05
603 Brad Jones .01 .05
604 Randy McKay .01 .05
605 Scott Thornton .01 .05
606 Bryan Marchment RC .02 .10
607 Andrew Cassels .01 .05
608 Grant Fuhr .07 .20
609 Vincent Damphousse .01 .05
610 Robert Ray .01 .05
611 Glenn Anderson .02 .10
612 Peter Ing .02 .10
613 Tom Chorske .01 .05
614 Kirk Muller .01 .05
615 Dan Quinn .01 .05
616 Murray Baron .01 .05
617 Sergei Nemchinov .01 .05
618 Rod Brind'Amour .07 .20
619 Ron Sutter .01 .05
620 Luke Richardson .01 .05
621 Nicklas Lidstrom RC .40 1.00
622 Ken Linseman .01 .05
623 Steve Smith .01 .05
624 Dave Manson .01 .05
625 Kay Whitmore .02 .10
626 Jeff Chychrun .01 .05
627 Russ Romaniuk RC .01 .05
628 Brad May .01 .05
629 Tomas Forslund RC .01 .05
630 Stu Barnes .01 .05
631 Darryl Sydor .02 .10
632 Jimmy Waite .02 .10
633 Peter Douris .01 .05
634 Dave Brown .01 .05
635 Mark Messier .07 .20
636 Neil Sheehy .01 .05
637 Todd Krygier .01 .05
638 Stephane Beauregard .02 .10
639 Barry Pederson .01 .05
640 Pat Falloon .01 .05
641 Dean Evason .01 .05
642 Jeff Hackett .02 .10
643 Rob Zettler .01 .05
644 David Bruce RC .01 .05
645 Pat MacLeod RC .01 .05
646 Craig Coxe .01 .05
647 Ken Hammond RC .01 .05
648 Brian Lawton .01 .05
649 Perry Anderson .01 .05
650 Kevin Evans .01 .05
651 Mike McHugh .01 .05
652 Mark Lamb .01 .05
653 Darcy Wakaluk RC .02 .10
654 Pat Conacher .01 .05
655 Martin Lapointe .02 .10
656 Derian Hatcher .02 .10
657 Bryan Erickson .01 .05
658 Ken Priestlay .01 .05
659 Vladimir Konstantinov RC .20 .50
660 Andrei Lomakin .01 .05

1991-92 Score Canadian English

*CANADIAN ENGLISH: .4X TO 1X BASIC CARDS

1991-92 Score Bobby Orr

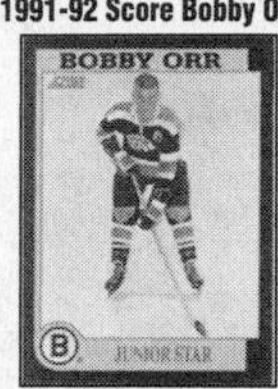

This six-card standard-size set highlights the career of Bobby Orr, one of hockey's all-time greats. The cards were inserted in 1991-92 Score hockey poly packs. Cards 1 and 2 were inserted in both American and Canadian editions. Cards 3 and 4 were inserted in Canadian packs, while cards 5 and 6 were inserted in American packs. On a black card face, the fronts feature color player photos enclosed by a thin red border and accented by yellow borders on three sides. The backs carry a close-up color photo and biographical comments on Orr's career. The cards are not numbered on the back. It is claimed that 270,000 of these Orr cards were produced, and that Orr personally signed 2,500 of each of these cards. The personally autographed cards are autographed on the card back. They are slightly different in design.

COMPLETE SET (6) 20.00 40.00
COMMON ORR (1-6) 3.00 8.00
AU Bobby Orr AU/2500* 125.00 250.00

1991-92 Score Eric Lindros

This three-card standard-size set was produced by Score and distributed in a cello pack with the first printing of Eric Lindros' autobiography "Fire on Ice". The cards feature on the fronts color photos that capture three different moments in Lindros' life (childhood, adolescence, and NHL Entry Draft). The pictures are bordered on all sides by light blue, with the player's name in block lettering between two red stripes at the card top. A red stripe at the bottom separates the picture from its title line. The backs have relevant biographical comments as well as a second color photo. The cards are unnumbered and checklisted below in chronological order.

COMPLETE SET (3) 6.00 15.00
COMMON LINDROS (1-3) 2.00 5.00

1991-92 Score Hot Cards

The 1991-92 Score Hot cards were inserted in American and Canadian English 100-card blister packs at a rate of one per pack. The standard size cards feature on the fronts color action player photos bordered in bright red. Thin yellow stripes accent the photos, and the player's name appears beneath the picture in a purple stripe. The back design reflects the same three colors as the front and features a color head shot, team logo, and player profile. The cards are numbered on the back. Hot Cards differ in design, photos, and text from the regular issues.

COMPLETE SET (10) 6.00 15.00
1 Eric Lindros .75 2.00
2 Wayne Gretzky 3.00 8.00
3 Brett Hull 1.00 2.50
4 Sergei Fedorov 1.00 2.50
5 Mario Lemieux 2.50 6.00
6 Adam Oates .40 1.00
7 Theo Fleury .20 .50
8 Jaromir Jagr 1.00 2.50
9 Ed Belfour .75 2.00
10 Jeremy Roenick .75 2.00

1991-92 Score Rookie/Traded

The 1991-92 Score Rookie and Traded hockey set contains 110 standard-size cards. It was issued only as a factory set. As one moves down the card face, the fronts shade from dark green to white. The color action player photo is enclosed by an thin red border, with a shadow border on the right and below. At the card top the player's name is written over a hockey puck, and the team name is printed below the picture in the lower right corner. A dark green border stripe at the bottom rounds out the front. In a horizontal format, the backs present biography, statistics, player profile, and a color close-up photo. The cards are numbered on the back with a "T" suffix. The set includes Eric Lindros pictured in his World Junior uniform. The back of the set's custom box contains the set checklist. The key Rookie Cards in this set are Valeri Kamensky and Nicklas Lidstrom.

COMP. FACT SET (110) 1.50 4.00
1T Doug Wilson .02 .10
2T Brian Mullen .01 .05
3T Kelly Kisio .01 .05
4T Brian Hayward .02 .10
5T Tony Hrkac .01 .05
6T Steve Bozek .01 .05
7T John Carter .01 .05
8T Neil Wilkinson .01 .05
9T Wayne Presley .01 .05
10T Bob McGill .01 .05
11T Craig Ludwig .01 .05
12T Mikhail Tatarinov .01 .05
13T Todd Elik .01 .05
14T Randy Burridge .01 .05
15T Tim Kerr .01 .05
16T Randy Gilhen .01 .05
17T John Tonelli .01 .05
18T Tom Kurvers .01 .05
19T Steve Duchesne .01 .05
20T Charlie Huddy .01 .05
21T Adam Creighton .01 .05
22T Brent Ashton .01 .05
23T Rob Ramage .01 .05
24T Steve Kasper .01 .05
25T Scott Mellanby .01 .05
26T Stephen Leach .01 .05
27T Scott Niedermayer .01 .05
28T Craig Berube .01 .05
29T Greg Paslawski .01 .05
30T Randy Hillier .01 .05
31T Stephane Richer .02 .10
32T Brian MacLellan .01 .05
33T Marc Habscheid .01 .05
34T Dave Babych .01 .05
35T Troy Murray .01 .05
36T Ray Sheppard .01 .05
37T Glen Featherstone .01 .05
38T Brendan Shanahan .08 .25
39T Dave Christian .01 .05
40T Mike Bullard .01 .05
41T Ryan Walter .01 .05
42T Randy Wood .01 .05
43T Vincent Riendeau .02 .10
44T Adam Graves .02 .10
45T Scott Stevens .02 .10
46T Sylvain Cote .01 .05
47T Dave Barr .01 .05
48T Randy Gregg .01 .05
49T Pavel Bure .08 .25
50T Jari Kurri .08 .25
51T Steve Thomas .01 .05
52T Troy Crowder .01 .05
53T Brad Jones .01 .05
54T Randy McKay .01 .05
55T Scott Thornton .01 .05
56T Bryan Marchment .02 .10
57T Andrew Cassels .01 .05
58T Grant Fuhr .08 .25
59T Vincent Damphousse .01 .05
60T Rick Zombo .01 .05
61T Glenn Anderson .02 .10
62T Peter Ing .02 .10
63T Tom Chorske .01 .05
64T Kirk Muller .01 .05
65T Dan Quinn .01 .05
66T Murray Baron .01 .05
67T Sergei Nemchinov .01 .05
68T Rod Brind'Amour .08 .25
69T Ron Sutter .01 .05
70T Luke Richardson .01 .05
71T Nicklas Lidstrom RC .40 1.00
72T Petri Skriko .01 .05
73T Steve Smith .01 .05
74T Dave Manson .01 .05
75T Kay Whitmore .02 .10
76T Valeri Kamensky RC .02 .10
77T Russ Romaniuk RC .01 .05
78T Brad May .01 .05
79T Tomas Forslund RC .01 .05
80T Stu Barnes .01 .05
81T Darryl Sydor .02 .10
82T Jimmy Waite .02 .10
83T Vladimir Ruzicka .01 .05
84T Dave Brown .01 .05
85T Mark Messier .08 .25
86T Neil Sheehy .01 .05
87T Todd Krygier .01 .05
88T Eric Lindros .08 .25
89T Nelson Emerson .01 .05
90T Pat Falloon .01 .05
91T Dean Evason .01 .05
92T Jeff Hackett .02 .10
93T Rob Zettler .01 .05
94T Perry Berezan .01 .05
95T Pat MacLeod RC .01 .05
96T Craig Coxe .01 .05
97T Ken Hammond RC .01 .05
98T Brian Lawton .01 .05
99T Perry Anderson .01 .05
100T Pat LaFontaine .08 .25
101T Pierre Turgeon .02 .10
102T Dave McLlwain .01 .05
103T Brent Sutter .01 .05
104T Uwe Krupp .01 .05
105T Martin Lapointe .02 .10
106T Derian Hatcher .02 .10
107T Darrin Shannon .01 .05
108T Benoit Hogue .01 .05
109T Vladimir Konstantinov RC .20 .50
110T Andrei Lomakin .01 .05

1991-92 Score Kellogg's

This 24-card standard-size set was produced by Score as a promotion for Kellogg's Canada. Two-card poly packs were inserted in specially marked 675-gram Kellogg's Corn Flakes cereals. The side panel of the cereal boxes presented a mail-in offer for the complete set and a card binder for 5.99 plus three proof of purchase tokens (one token featured per side panel). Card fronts have player action photos enclosed in a small red border, player's name in white reverse-out lettering, and team logo in bottom portion of the purple border. Card backs, also in purple, red, and white, carry the card number, Kellogg's Limited Edition Collector's Set logo, biography, statistics, and player profile in English and French.

COMPLETE SET (24) 14.00 35.00
1 Patrick Roy 3.00 8.00
2 Rick Tocchet .40 1.00
3 Wendel Clark .40 1.00
4 Mike Modano .75 2.00
5 Jeremy Roenick .60 1.50
6 Pierre Turgeon .40 1.00
7 Kevin Hatcher .20 .50
8 Brian Leetch .60 1.50
9 Mark Recchi .40 1.00
10 Andy Moog .40 1.00
11 Kevin Dineen .20 .50
12 Joe Sakic 1.25 3.00
13 John MacLean .20 .50
14 Steve Yzerman 2.00 5.00
15 Pat LaFontaine .40 1.00
16 Al MacInnis .40 1.00
17 Petr Klima .20 .50
18 Ed Olczyk .20 .50
19 Doug Wilson .20 .50
20 Trevor Linden .20 .50
21 Brett Hull .75 2.00
22 Rob Blake .20 .50
23 Dave Ellett .20 .50
24 Cornelius Rooster SP .75 2.00
Kellogg's mascot
NNO Card Binder 2.00 5.00

1991-92 Score Young Superstars

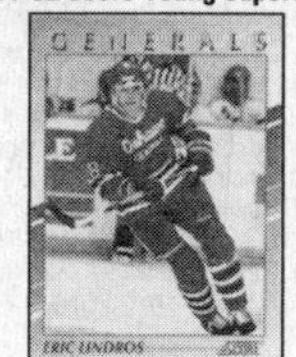

This 40-card standard-size set was issued by Score to showcase some of the leading young hockey players. The color action player photos on the fronts are framed in green on a card face consisting of blended diagonal taupe stripes. In a horizontal format, the backs have a color head shot on the left half while the right half carries his biography, "Rink Report," and career statistics.

COMP. FACT SET (40) 4.00 10.00
1 Sergei Fedorov .60 1.50
2 Mike Richter .30 .75
3 Mats Sundin .30 .75
4 Theo Fleury .30 .75
5 John Cullen .05 .15
6 Dimitri Khristich .05 .15
7 Stephan Lebeau .05 .15
8 Rob Blake .30 .75
9 Ken Hodge Jr. .05 .15
10 Mike Ricci .15 .40
11 Trevor Linden .15 .40
12 Peter Ing .15 .40
13 Alexander Mogilny .15 .40
14 Martin Gelinas .05 .15
15 Chris Terreri .15 .40
16 Jeff Norton .05 .15
17 Bob Essensa .15 .40
18 Mark Tinordi .05 .15
19 Curtis Joseph .30 .75
20 Joe Sakic .60 1.50
21 Jeremy Roenick .30 .75
22 Mark Recchi .15 .40
23 Eric Desjardins .15 .40
24 Robert Reichel .05 .15
25 Tim Cheveldae .15 .40
26 Eric Weinrich .05 .15
27 Murray Baron .05 .15
28 Darren Turcotte .05 .15
29 Troy Gamble .15 .40
30 Eric Lindros 1.00 2.50
31 Benoit Hogue .05 .15
32 Ed Belfour .30 .75
33 Ron Tugnutt .15 .40
34 Pat Elynuik .05 .15
35 Mike Modano .30 .75
36 Bobby Holik .15 .40
37 Yves Racine .05 .15
38 Jaromir Jagr 1.00 2.50
39 Stephane Morin .05 .15
40 Kevin Miller .05 .15

1992-93 Score Canadian Promo Sheets

These two 5" by 7" promotional sheets each feature four uncut cards. If the cards were cut, they would measure the standard size. The fronts feature color action player photos bordered at the top and bottom by black stripes containing the player's name and position. The outer borders are metallic-blue with diagonal stripes formed by an alternating matte and glossy finish. The backs have the disclaimers "For Promotional Purposes Only" and "Not For Resale" overprinted in magenta. They show a white background with a narrow color player photo running along the left edge. Biography and career highlights are contained in a graded blue panel with black borders. Statistical information appears at the bottom. The cards are numbered on the back and are listed below as the appear on the sheets from left to right starting with the top row.

COMPLETE SET (2) 2.00 5.00
1 Promo Sheet 1 .75 2.00
6 Pat LaFontaine
25 Kevin Stevens
2 Chris Chelios
16 Esa Tikkanen
2 Promo Sheet 2 1.50 4.00
5 Mike Richter
14 Pavel Bure
6 Pat LaFontaine
25 Kevin Stevens

1992-93 Score

The 1992-93 Score hockey set contains 550 standard-size cards. The American and Canadian sets are identical in terms of player selection (except for card numbers 548-549) but feature different insert subsets (USA Greats in the American and Canadian Olympic Heroes in the Canadian). Moreover, the player photos and card design differ in each set. In the American set, the color action photos on the fronts have two-toned borders on three sides (icy gray diagonal stripes accented by either red, blue, or black); in the Canadian, the front borders are metallic blue with diagonally varnished stripes. The American backs are horizontally oriented and include biography, statistics, career summary, and a close-up photo; the Canadian backs are vertically oriented, bilingual, and have the same features in a different layout. A special Eric Lindros card, unnumbered and featuring his first photo in a Philadelphia Flyers uniform, was randomly inserted into packs. Reportedly more than 500 of these special Lindros "Press Conference" cards were given away to news media, members of the Flyers organization, and other guests attending the July 15 news conference which marked Lindros' signing with the Flyers. It is claimed that the odds of finding one of these cards are no less than one in 500 packs. Rookie Cards include Guy Hebert and Yanic Perrault.

COMPLETE SET (550) 6.00 15.00
1 Wayne Gretzky .50 1.25
2 Chris Chelios .08 .25
3 Joe Mullen .02 .10
4 Russ Courtnall .01 .05
5 Mike Richter .08 .25
6 Pat LaFontaine .08 .25
7 Mark Tinordi .01 .05
8 Claude Lemieux .01 .05
9 Jimmy Carson .01 .05
10 Cam Neely .08 .25
11 Al Iafrate .02 .10
12 Steve Thomas .02 .10
13 Fredrik Olausson .01 .05
14 Pavel Bure .08 .25
15 Doug Wilson .02 .10
16 Esa Tikkanen .01 .05
17 Gary Suter .01 .05
18 Murray Craven .01 .05
19 Garry Galley .01 .05
20 Grant Fuhr .08 .25
21 Craig Wolanin .01 .05
22 Paul Cavallini .01 .05
23 Eric Desjardins .02 .10
24 Joey Kocur .02 .10
25 Kevin Stevens .01 .05
26 Marty McSorley .01 .05
27 Dirk Graham .01 .05
28 Mike Ramsey .01 .05
29 Gord Murphy .01 .05
30 John MacLean .02 .10
31 Vladimir Konstantinov .08 .25
32 Neal Broten .02 .10
33 Dimitri Khristich .01 .05
34 Gerald Diduck .01 .05
35 Ken Baumgartner .01 .05
36 Darrin Shannon .01 .05
37 Steve Bozek .01 .05
38 Michel Petit .01 .05
39 Kevin Lowe .02 .10
40 Doug Gilmour .02 .10
41 Peter Sidorkiewicz .02 .10
42 Gino Cavallini .01 .05
43 Dan Quinn .02 .10
44 Steven Finn .01 .05
45 Larry Murphy .02 .10
46 Brent Gilchrist .01 .05
47 Daren Puppa .02 .10
48 Steve Smith .01 .05
49 Dave Taylor .02 .10
50 Mike Gartner .02 .10
51 Derian Hatcher .01 .05
52 Bob Probert .02 .10
53 Ken Daneyko .01 .05
54 Steve Leach .01 .05
55 Kelly Miller .01 .05
56 Jeff Norton .01 .05
57 Kelly Kisio .01 .05
58 Igor Larionov .01 .05
59 Paul MacDermid .01 .05
60 Mike Vernon .02 .10
61 Randy Ladouceur .01 .05
62 Luke Richardson .01 .05
63 Daniel Marois .01 .05
64 Mike Hough .01 .05
65 Garth Butcher .01 .05
66 Terry Carkner .01 .05
67 Mike Donnelly .01 .05
68 Keith Brown .01 .05
69 Mathieu Schneider .01 .05
70 Tom Barrasso .02 .10
71 Adam Graves .01 .05
72 Brian Propp .01 .05
73 Randy Wood .01 .05
74 Yves Racine .01 .05
75 Scott Stevens .02 .10
76 Chris Nilan .01 .05
77 Uwe Krupp .01 .05
78 Sylvain Cote .01 .05
79 Sergio Momesso .01 .05
80 Thomas Steen .01 .05
81 Craig Muni .01 .05
82 Jeff Hackett .02 .10
83 Frank Musil .01 .05
84 Mike Ricci .02 .10
85 Brad Shaw .01 .05
86 Ron Sutter .01 .05
87 Curtis Leschyshyn .01 .05
88 Jamie Macoun .01 .05
89 Brian Noonan .01 .05
90 Ulf Samuelsson .01 .05
91 Mike McPhee .01 .05
92 Charlie Huddy .01 .05
93 Tim Kerr .01 .05
94 Craig Ludwig .01 .05
95 Paul Ysebaert .01 .05
96 Brad May .01 .05
97 Slava Fetisov .01 .05
98 Todd Krygier .01 .05
99 Patrick Flatley .01 .05
100 Ray Bourque .15 .40
101 Petr Nedved .02 .10
102 Teppo Numminen .01 .05
103 Dean Evason .01 .05
104 Ron Hextall .02 .10
105 Josef Beranek .01 .05
106 Robert Reichel .01 .05
107 Mikhail Tatarinov .01 .05
108 Geoff Sanderson .02 .10
109 Dave Lowry .01 .05
110 Wendel Clark .02 .10
111 Corey Millen UER .01 .05
(Mike Donnelly pictured on front)
112 Brent Sutter .01 .05
113 Jaromir Jagr .10 .30
114 Petr Svoboda .01 .05
115 Sergei Nemchinov .01 .05
116 Tony Tanti .01 .05
117 Stewart Gavin .01 .05
118 Doug Brown .01 .05
119 Gerard Gallant .01 .05
120 Andy Moog .08 .25
121 John Druce .01 .05
122 Dave McLlwain .01 .05
123 Bob Essensa .02 .10
124 Doug Lidster .01 .05
125 Pat Falloon .01 .05
126 Kelly Buchberger .01 .05
127 Carey Wilson .01 .05
128 Bobby Holik .02 .10
129 Andrei Lomakin .01 .05
130 Bob Rouse .01 .05
131 Adam Foote .02 .10
132 Bob Bassen .01 .05
133 Brian Benning .01 .05
134 Greg Gilbert .01 .05
135 Paul Stanton .01 .05
136 Brian Skrudland .01 .05
137 Jeff Beukeboom .01 .05
138 Clint Malarchuk .02 .10
139 Mike Modano .10 .30
140 Stephane Richer .02 .10
141 Brad McCrimmon .01 .05
142 Bob Carpenter .01 .05
143 Rod Langway .01 .05
144 Adam Creighton .01 .05
145 Ed Olczyk .01 .05
146 Greg Adams .01 .05
147 Jay More .01 .05
148 Scott Mellanby .01 .05
149 Paul Ranheim .01 .05
150 John Cullen .01 .05
151 Steve Duchesne .01 .05
152 Dave Ellett .01 .05
153 Mats Sundin .08 .25
154 Rick Zombo .01 .05
155 Kelly Hrudey .02 .10
156 Mike Hudson .01 .05
157 Bryan Trottier .02 .10
158 Shayne Corson .01 .05
159 Kevin Haller .01 .05
160 John Vanbiesbrouck .02 .10
161 Jim Johnson .01 .05
162 Kevin Todd .01 .05
163 Ray Sheppard .01 .05
164 Brent Ashton .01 .05
165 Peter Bondra .02 .10
166 David Volek .01 .05
167 Randy Carlyle .01 .05
168 Dana Murzyn .01 .05
169 Perry Berezan .01 .05
170 Vincent Damphousse .01 .05
171 Gary Leeman .01 .05
172 Steve Konroyd .01 .05
173 Pelle Eklund .01 .05
174 Peter Zezel .01 .05
175 Greg Paslawski .01 .05
176 Murray Baron .01 .05
177 Rob Blake .02 .10
178 Ed Belfour .08 .25
179 Mike Keane .01 .05
180 Mark Recchi .02 .10
181 Kris King .01 .05
182 Dave Snuggerud .01 .05
183 David Shaw .01 .05
184 Tom Chorske .01 .05
185 Steve Chiasson .01 .05
186 Don Sweeney .01 .05
187 Mike Ridley .01 .05
188 Glenn Healy .02 .10
189 Troy Murray .01 .05
190 Tom Fergus .01 .05
191 Rob Zettler .01 .05
192 Geoff Smith .01 .05
193 Joe Nieuwendyk .02 .10
194 Mark Hunter .01 .05
195 Kjell Samuelsson .01 .05
196 Todd Gill .01 .05
197 Doug Smail .01 .05
198 Dave Christian .01 .05
199 Tomas Sandstrom .02 .10
200 Jeremy Roenick .10 .30
201 Gordie Roberts .01 .05
202 Denis Savard .02 .10
203 James Patrick .01 .05
204 Dave Andreychuk .02 .10
205 Bobby Smith .02 .10
206 Valeri Zelepukin .01 .05
207 Shawn Burr .01 .05
208 Vladimir Ruzicka .01 .05
209 Calle Johansson .01 .05
210 Mark Fitzpatrick .02 .10
211 Dean Kennedy .01 .05
212 Dave Babych .01 .05
213 Wayne Presley .01 .05
214 Dave Manson .01 .05
215 Mikael Andersson .01 .05
216 Trent Yawney .01 .05
217 Mark Howe .01 .05
218 Mike Bullard .01 .05
219 Claude Lapointe .01 .05
220 Jeff Brown .01 .05
221 Bob Kudelski .01 .05
222 Michel Goulet .02 .10
223 Phil Bourque .01 .05
224 Darren Turcotte .01 .05
225 Kirk Muller .01 .05
226 Doug Bodger .01 .05
227 Dave Gagner .02 .10
228 Craig Billington .02 .10
229 Kevin Miller .01 .05
230 Glen Wesley .01 .05
231 Dale Hunter .02 .10
232 Tom Kurvers .01 .05
233 Pat Elynuik .01 .05
234 Geoff Courtnall .01 .05
235 Neil Wilkinson .01 .05
236 Bill Ranford .02 .10
237 Ronnie Stern .01 .05
238 Zarley Zalapski .01 .05
239 Kerry Huffman .01 .05
240 Joe Sakic .15 .40
241 Glenn Anderson .02 .10
242 Stephane Quintal .01 .05
243 Tony Granato .01 .05
244 Rob Brown .01 .05
245 Rick Tocchet .02 .10
246 Stephan Lebeau .01 .05
247 Mark Hardy .01 .05
248 Alexander Mogilny .02 .10
249 Jon Casey .02 .10
250 Adam Oates .02 .10
251 Bruce Driver .01 .05
252 Sergei Fedorov .10 .30
253 Michal Pivonka .01 .05
254 Cliff Ronning .01 .05
255 Derek King .01 .05
256 Luciano Borsato .01 .05
257 Paul Fenton .01 .05
258 Craig Berube .01 .05
259 Brian Bradley .01 .05
260 Craig Simpson .01 .05
261 Adam Burt .01 .05
262 Curtis Joseph .08 .25
263 Mark Pederson .01 .05
264 Alexei Gusarov .01 .05
265 Paul Coffey .08 .25
266 Steve Larmer .02 .10
267 Ron Francis .02 .10
268 Randy Gilhen .01 .05
269 Guy Carbonneau .02 .10
270 Chris Terreri .02 .10
271 Mike Craig .01 .05
272 Dale Hawerchuk .02 .10
273 Kevin Hatcher .01 .05
274 Ken Hodge Jr. .01 .05
275 Tim Cheveldae .02 .10
276 Benoit Hogue .01 .05
277 Mark Osborne .01 .05
278 Brian Mullen .01 .05
279 Robert Dirk .01 .05
280 Theo Fleury .01 .05
281 Martin Gelinas .01 .05
282 Pat Verbeek .01 .05
283 Mike Krushelnyski .01 .05
284 Kevin Dineen .01 .05
285 Craig Janney .02 .10
286 Owen Nolan .02 .10
287 Bob Errey .01 .05
288 Bryan Marchment .01 .05
289 Randy Moller .01 .05
290 Luc Robitaille .02 .10
291 Peter Stastny .02 .10
292 Ken Sutton .01 .05
293 Brad Marsh .01 .05
294 Chris Dahlquist .01 .05
295 Patrick Roy .40 1.00
296 Andy Brickley .01 .05
297 Randy Burridge .01 .05
298 Ray Ferraro .01 .05
299 Phil Housley .01 .05
300 Mark Messier .08 .25
301 David Bruce .01 .05
302 Al MacInnis .02 .10
303 Craig MacTavish .01 .05
304 Kay Whitmore .02 .10
305 Trevor Linden .02 .10
306 Steve Kasper .01 .05
307 Todd Elik .01 .05
308 Eric Weinrich .01 .05
309 Jocelyn Lemieux .01 .05
310 Peter Ahola .01 .05
311 J.J. Daigneault .01 .05
312 Colin Patterson .01 .05
313 Darcy Wakaluk .02 .10
314 Doug Weight .08 .25
315 Dave Barr .01 .05
316 Keith Primeau .02 .10
317 Bob Sweeney .01 .05
318 Jyrki Lumme .01 .05
319 Stu Barnes .01 .05
320 Don Beaupre .02 .10
321 Joe Murphy .01 .05
322 Gary Roberts .01 .05
323 Andrew Cassels .01 .05
324 Rod Brind'Amour .02 .10
325 Pierre Turgeon .02 .10

326 Claude Vilgrain .01 .05
327 Rich Sutter .01 .05
328 Claude Loiselle .01 .05
329 John Ogrodnick .01 .05
330 Ulf Dahlen .01 .05
331 Gilbert Dionne .01 .05
332 Joel Otto .01 .05
333 Rob Pearson .01 .05
334 Christian Ruuttu .01 .05
335 Brian Bellows .01 .05
336 Anatoli Semenov .01 .05
337 Brent Fedyk .01 .05
338 Gaetan Duchesne .01 .05
339 Randy McKay .01 .05
340 Bernie Nicholls .02 .10
341 Keith Acton .01 .05
342 John Tonelli .01 .05
343 Brian Lawton .01 .05
344 Ric Nattress .01 .05
345 Mike Eagles .01 .05
346 Frantisek Kucera .01 .05
347 John McIntyre .01 .05
348 Troy Loney .01 .05
349 Norm Maciver .01 .05
350 Brett Hull .10 .30
351 Rob Ramage .01 .05
352 Claude Boivin .01 .05
353 Paul Broten .01 .05
354 Stephane Fiset .02 .10
355 Garry Valk .01 .05
356 Basil McRae .01 .05
357 Alan May .01 .05
358 Grant Ledyard .01 .05
359 Dave Poulin .01 .05
360 Valeri Kamensky .01 .05
361 Brian Glynn .01 .05
362 Jan Erixon .01 .05
363 Mike Lalor .01 .05
364 Jeff Chychrun .01 .05
365 Ron Wilson .01 .05
366 Shawn Cronin .01 .05
367 Sylvain Turgeon .01 .05
368 Mike Liut .02 .10
369 Joe Cirella .01 .05
370 David Maley .01 .05
371 Lucien Deblois .01 .05
372 Per Djoos .01 .05
373 Dominik Hasek .30 .75
374 Laurie Boschman .01 .05
375 Brian Leetch .08 .25
376 Nelson Emerson .01 .05
377 Normand Rochefort .01 .05
378 Jacques Cloutier .02 .10
379 Jim Sandlak .01 .05
380 David Reid .01 .05
381 Gary Nylund .01 .05
382 Sergei Makarov .01 .05
383 Petr Klima .01 .05
384 Peter Douris .01 .05
385 Kirk McLean .02 .10
386 Bob McGill .01 .05
387 Ron Tugnutt .02 .10
388 Patrice Brisebois .01 .05
389 Tony Amonte .02 .10
390 Mario Lemieux .40 1.00
391 Nicklas Lidstrom .08 .25
392 Brendan Shanahan .08 .25
393 Donald Audette .01 .05
394 Alexei Kasatonov .01 .05
395 Dino Ciccarelli .02 .10
396 Vincent Riendeau .02 .10
397 Joe Reekie .01 .05
398 Jari Kurri .08 .25
399 Ken Wregget .02 .10
400 Steve Yzerman .40 1.00
401 Scott Niedermayer .01 .05
402 Stephane Beauregard .02 .10
403 Tim Hunter .01 .05
404 Marc Bergevin .01 .05
405 Sylvain Lefebvre .01 .05
406 Johan Garpenlov .01 .05
407 Tony Hrkac .01 .05
408 Tie Domi .08 .25
409 Martin Lapointe .02 .10
410 Darryl Sydor .01 .05
411 Brett Hull SL .08 .25
412 Wayne Gretzky SL .25 .60
413 Mario Lemieux SL .20 .50
414 Paul Ysebaert SL .01 .05
415 Tony Amonte SL .02 .10
416 Brian Leetch SL .02 .10
417 Tim Cheveldae SL .01 .05
Kirk McLean SL
418 Patrick Roy SL .20 .50
419 Ray Bourque FP .07 .20
420 Pat LaFontaine FP .02 .10
421 Al MacInnis FP .02 .10
422 Jeremy Roenick FP .02 .10
423 Steve Yzerman FP .20 .50
424 Bill Ranford FP .01 .05
425 John Cullen FP .01 .05
426 Wayne Gretzky FP .25 .60
427 Mike Modano FP .02 .10
428 Patrick Roy FP .20 .50
429 Scott Stevens FP .01 .05
430 Pierre Turgeon FP .01 .05
431 Mark Messier FP .05 .15
432 Eric Lindros FP .08 .25
433 Mario Lemieux FP .20 .50
434 Joe Sakic FP .08 .25
435 Brett Hull FP .08 .25
436 Pat Falloon FP .01 .05
437 Grant Fuhr FP .02 .10
438 Trevor Linden FP .01 .05
439 Kevin Hatcher FP .01 .05
440 Phil Housley FP .01 .05
441 Paul Coffey SH .02 .10
442 Brett Hull SH .08 .25
443 Mike Gartner SH .01 .05
444 Michel Goulet SH .01 .05
445 Mike Gartner SH .01 .05
446 Bobby Smith SH .02 .10
447 Ray Bourque SH .07 .20
448 Mario Lemieux HL .20 .50
449 Scott Lachance TP .01 .05
450 Keith Tkaczuk TP .08 .25
451 Alexander Semak TP .01 .05
452 John Tanner TP .01 .05
453 Joe Juneau TP .01 .05
454 Igor Kravchuk TP .01 .05
455 Brent Thompson TP .01 .05
456 Evgeny Davydov TP .01 .05
457 Arturs Irbe TP .02 .10
458 Kent Manderville TP .01 .05
459 Shawn McEachern TP .01 .05
460 Guy Hebert RC .25 .60
461 Keith Carney TP RC .30 .75
462 Karl Dykhuis TP .01 .05
463 Bill Lindsay TP RC .01 .05
464 Dominic Roussel TP .01 .05
465 Marty McInnis TP .01 .05
466 Dale Craigwell TP .01 .05
467 Igor Ulanov TP .01 .05
468 Dmitri Mironov TP .01 .05
469 Dean McAmmond TP RC .01 .05
470 Bill Guerin TP RC .50 1.25
471 Bret Hedican TP RC .02 .10
472 Felix Potvin TP .08 .25
473 Slava Kozlov TP .01 .05
474 Martin Rucinsky TP .01 .05
475 Ray Whitney TP RC .15 .40
476 Stephen Heinze TP .01 .05
477 Brad Schlegel TP .01 .05
478 Patrick Poulin TP .01 .05
479 Ted Donato TP .01 .05
480 Martin Brodeur .30 .75
481 Denny Felsner TP RC .02 .10
482 Trent Klatt TP RC .02 .10
483 Gord Hynes TP .01 .05
484 Glen Murray TP .01 .05
485 Chris Lindberg TP .01 .05
486 Ray LeBlanc TP .01 .05
487 Yanic Perreault TP RC .10 .30
488 J.F. Quintin TP RC .01 .05
489 Patrick Roy DT .20 .50
490 Ray Bourque DT .07 .20
491 Brian Leetch DT .02 .10
492 Kevin Stevens DT .01 .05
493 Mark Messier DT .05 .15
494 Jaromir Jagr DT .08 .25
495 Bill Ranford DT .01 .05
496 Al MacInnis DT .01 .05
497 Chris Chelios DT .08 .25
498 Luc Robitaille DT .02 .10
499 Jeremy Roenick DT .05 .15
500 Brett Hull DT .08 .25
501 Felix Potvin RDT .02 .10
502 Nicklas Lidstrom RDT .02 .10
503 Vladimir Konstantinov RDT .08 .25
504 Pavel Bure RDT .05 .15
505 Nelson Emerson RDT .01 .05
506 Tony Amonte RDT .02 .10
507 Tampa Bay Lightning Logo .01 .05
508 Shawn Chambers .01 .05
509 Basil McRae .01 .05
510 Joe Reekie .01 .05
511 Wendell Young .02 .10
512 Ottawa Senators Logo .08 .25
513 Laurie Boschman .01 .05
514 Mark Lamb .01 .05
515 Peter Sidorkiewicz .02 .10
516 Sylvain Turgeon .01 .05
517 Bill Dineen .01 .05
Kevin Dineen
518 Stanley Cup .02 .10
Champions
519 Mario Lemieux AW .20 .50
520 Ray Bourque AW .07 .20
King Clancy
521 Mark Messier AW .05 .15
Hart Trophy
522 Brian Leetch AW .02 .10
Norris Trophy
523 Pavel Bure AW .05 .15
Calder Trophy
524 Guy Carbonneau AW .02 .10
Selke Trophy
525 Wayne Gretzky AW .25 .60
Lady Byng Trophy
526 Mark Fitzpatrick AW .02 .10
Masterton Trophy
527 Patrick Roy AW .20 .50
Vezina Trophy
528 Memorial Cup .01 .05
Kamloops Blazers
529 Rick Tabaracci .02 .10
530 Tom Draper .01 .05
531 Adrien Plavsic .01 .05
532 Joe Sacco .01 .05
533 Mike Sullivan .01 .05
534 Zdeno Ciger .01 .05
535 Frank Pietrangelo .02 .10
536 Mike Peluso .01 .05
537 Jim Paek .01 .05
538 Dave Hannan .01 .05
539 David Williams RC .01 .05
540 Gino Odjick .01 .05
541 Yvon Corriveau .01 .05
542 Grant Jennings .01 .05
543 Stephane Matteau .01 .05
544 Pat Conacher .01 .05
545 Steven Rice .01 .05
546 Marc Habscheid .01 .05
547 Steve Weeks .02 .10
548A Jay Wells USA .01 .05
548C Maurice Richard CAN .08 .25
549A Mick Vukota USA .01 .05
549C Maurice Richard CAN .08 .25
550 Eric Lindros UER .08 .25
(Acquired 6-30-92&
not 6-20-92)
NNO Eric Lindros 4.00 10.00
(Press Conference Card

1992-93 Score Canadian

COMPLETE SET (550) 6.00 15.00
*US AND CDN: SAME VALUE

1992-93 Score Canadian Olympians

This 13-card standard-size set showcases Canadian hockey players who participated in the '92 Olympics in Albertville, France. The cards were randomly inserted at the rate of 1:24 '92-93 Score Canadian hockey packs. The color action photos on the fronts are highlighted by a red border with a diagonal white stripe. The year appears in a maple leaf at the upper left. The player's name and position are printed in the borders above and below the picture respectively. The backs feature the same red border design as the front with a player profile printed on a ghosted photo of the Canadian flag. The cards are numbered on the back. Not part of the set, but inserted in Canadian foil packs are two Maurice Richard cards and one autographed card of The Rocket.

COMPLETE SET (13) 20.00 40.00
1 Eric Lindros 2.50 5.00
2 Joe Juneau 1.00 2.50
3 Dave Archibald 1.00 2.50
4 Randy Smith 1.00 2.50
5 Gord Hynes 1.00 2.50
6 Chris Lindberg 1.00 2.50
7 Jason Woolley 1.00 2.50
8 Fabian Joseph 1.00 2.50
9 Brad Schlegel 1.00 2.50
10 Kent Manderville 1.00 2.50
11 Adrien Plavsic 1.00 2.50
12 Trevor Kidd 1.00 2.50
13 Sean Burke 1.00 2.50
NNO1 Maurice Richard 2.00 5.00
The Rocket
NNO2 Maurice Richard 2.00 5.00
AU1 Maurice Richard AU/1250 75.00 150.00

1992-93 Score Sharpshooters

This 30-card standard-size set showcases the most accurate shooters during the 1991-92 season. Two cards were inserted in each 1992-93 Score jumbo pack. The cards feature full-bleed color action photos. A black border at the bottom contains the player's name in red and the words "Sharp Shooters" in gold foil lettering. A puck and target icon fills out the card front at the lower left corner. The horizontal backs carry close-up player photos with statistics and the team logo on either side against a gray background. A black border, nearly identical to the front, runs across the bottom. The cards are numbered on the back and arranged in descending order of 1991-92 shooting percentage ranking.

COMPLETE SET (30) 5.00 12.00
*CANADIAN: .4X TO 1X US INSERTS
1 Gary Roberts .08 .25
2 Sergei Makarov .08 .25
3 Ray Ferraro .08 .25
4 Dale Hunter .40 1.00
5 Sergei Nemchinov .08 .25
6 Mike Ridley .08 .25
7 Gilbert Dionne .08 .25
8 Pat LaFontaine .50 1.25
9 Jimmy Carson .08 .25
10 Jeremy Roenick .60 1.50
11 Kelly Buchberger .08 .25
12 Owen Nolan .40 1.00
13 Igor Larionov .08 .25
14 Claude Vilgrain .08 .25
15 Derek King .08 .25
16 Greg Paslawski .08 .25
17 Bob Probert .40 1.00
18 Mark Recchi .40 1.00
19 Donald Audette .08 .25
20 Ray Sheppard .08 .25
21 Benoit Hogue .08 .25
22 Rob Brown .08 .25
23 Pat Elynuik .08 .25
24 Petr Klima .08 .25
25 Pierre Turgeon .40 1.00
26 Corey Millen .08 .25
27 Dimitri Khristich .08 .25
28 Anatoli Semenov .08 .25
29 Kirk Muller .08 .25
30 Craig Simpson .08 .25

1992-93 Score USA Greats

This 15-card set showcases outstanding United States-born players. The standard-size cards were randomly inserted at the rate of 1:24 '92-93 Score American hockey packs. The color action photos on the fronts are full-bleed on the right side only and framed on the other three sides by a red foil stripe and a blue outer border. The backs feature a close-up photo and a player profile.

COMPLETE SET (15) 15.00 40.00
1 Pat LaFontaine 1.50 4.00
2 Chris Chelios 1.50 4.00
3 Jeremy Roenick 1.50 4.00
4 Tony Granato 1.00 2.50
5 Mike Modano 2.00 5.00
6 Mike Richter 1.50 4.00
7 John Vanbiesbrouck 1.50 4.00
8 Brian Leetch 1.50 4.00
9 Joe Mullen 1.00 2.50
10 Kevin Stevens 1.00 2.50
11 Craig Janney 1.00 2.50
12 Brian Mullen 1.00 2.50
13 Kevin Hatcher 1.00 2.50
14 Kelly Miller 1.00 2.50
15 Ed Olczyk 1.00 2.50

1992-93 Score Young Superstars

This 40-card, boxed standard-size set was issued to showcase some of the leading young hockey players. The fronts feature glossy color player photos with white and bluish-gray streaked borders. The player's team name is printed in the top border, while the player's name is printed in the bottom border. The horizontal backs carry a close-up color photo, biography, "Rink Report," and statistics.

COMP.FACT SET (40) 3.00 8.00
1 Eric Lindros 1.00 2.50
2 Tony Amonte .10 .30
3 Mats Sundin .20 .50
4 Jaromir Jagr 1.00 2.50
5 Sergei Fedorov .60 1.50
6 Gilbert Dionne .02 .10
7 Mark Recchi .10 .30
8 Alexander Mogilny .10 .30
9 Mike Richter .20 .50
10 Jeremy Roenick .20 .50
11 Nicklas Lidstrom .20 .50
12 Scott Lachance .02 .10
13 Nelson Emerson .02 .10
14 Pat Falloon .02 .10
15 Dimitri Khristich .02 .10
16 Trevor Linden .10 .30
17 Curtis Joseph .40 1.00
18 Rob Pearson .02 .10
19 Kevin Todd .02 .10
20 Joe Sakic .60 1.50
21 Tim Cheveldae .10 .30
22 Joe Juneau .10 .30
23 Vladimir Konstantinov .10 .30
24 Valeri Kamensky .10 .30
25 Ed Belfour .20 .50
26 Rod Brind'Amour .10 .30
27 Pierre Turgeon .10 .30
28 Eric Desjardins .10 .30
29 Keith Tkachuk .20 .50
30 Pavel Bure .75 2.00
31 Patrick Poulin .02 .10
32 Viacheslav Kozlov .10 .30
33 Scott Niedermayer .10 .30
34 Jyrki Lumme .02 .10
35 Paul Ysebaert .02 .10
36 Dominic Roussel .10 .30
37 Owen Nolan .10 .30
38 Rob Blake .10 .30
39 Felix Potvin .20 .50
40 Mike Modano .20 .50

1993-94 Score Promo Panel

This promo panel was issued to promote the second series of the 1993-94 Score hockey series. Measuring approximately 5" by 2 1/2", the panel is actually the size of two standard-size cards. The left front features a Gold Rush version of the Alexandre Daigle card. On a purple foil background, the right front presents an advertisement for the second series. The reverse of the left front is the expected card back as with a regular card; the reverse of the right front is the front of the regular issue Daigle card.

587 Alexandre Daigle .75 2.00

1993-94 Score Samples

This six-card standard-size set was issued by Score as a preview of the design of the 1993-94 Score hockey set. The fronts display color action shots within a white border. The team name is printed on a team color-coded stripe along the left side. The player's position and name is printed across the bottom of the picture. The backs have team color-coded backgrounds with a head shot on the upper half and biography, statistics, and player profile. The words "sample card" are printed in the lower right corner.

COMPLETE SET (6) 1.50 4.00
1 Eric Lindros .75 2.00
2 Mike Gartner .20 .50
3 Steve Larmer .08 .25
4 Brian Bellows .08 .25
5 Felix Potvin .40 1.00
6 Pierre Turgeon .30 .75

1993-94 Score

The 1993-94 Score hockey set consists of 661 standard-size cards. The first series contains 495 cards and the second series 166. The fronts of the first series feature white-bordered color player action shots. The player's name and position appear at the bottom, with his team name displayed vertically on the left within a team color-coded stripe. The second series was redesigned and consists of traded players in new uniforms, rookies and individual highlights. Blue borders surround the card with player name and team logo at the bottom. Card 496, Alexandre Daigle, is the card received after mailing in the unnumbered Daigle redemption card. The set is considered complete without it. The redemption card was randomly inserted in first series packs. An Eric Lindros All-Star card was the SP insert in series two, at a rate of 1:360 packs.

COMPLETE SET (661) 8.00 20.00
COMP.SERIES 1 (495) 6.00 15.00
COMP.SERIES 2 (166) 2.00 5.00
1 Eric Lindros .07 .20
2 Mike Gartner .02 .10
3 Steve Larmer .02 .10
4 Brian Bellows .01 .05
5 Felix Potvin .07 .20
6 Pierre Turgeon .02 .10
7 Joe Mullen .02 .10
8 Craig MacTavish .01 .05
9 Mats Sundin .07 .20
10 Pat Verbeek .01 .05
11 Andy Moog .02 .10
12 Dirk Graham .01 .05
13 Gary Suter .01 .05
14 Brent Fedyk .01 .05
15 Brad Shaw .01 .05
16 Benoit Hogue .01 .05
17 Cliff Ronning .01 .05
18 Mathieu Schneider .01 .05
19 Bernie Nicholls .01 .05
20 Vladimir Konstantinov .02 .10
21 Doug Bodger .01 .05
22 Peter Stastny .02 .10
23 Larry Murphy .02 .10
24 Darren Turcotte .01 .05
25 Doug Crossman .01 .05
26 Bob Essensa .02 .10
27 Kelly Kisio .01 .05
28 Nelson Emerson .01 .05
29 Ray Bourque .10 .30
30 Kelly Miller .01 .05
31 Peter Zezel .01 .05
32 Owen Nolan .02 .10
33 Sergei Makarov .01 .05
34 Stephane Richer .02 .10
35 Adam Graves .01 .05
36 Rob Ramage .01 .05
37 Ed Olczyk .01 .05
38 Jeff Hackett .02 .10
39 Ron Sutter .01 .05
40 Dale Hunter .01 .05
41 Nikolai Borschevsky .01 .05
42 Curtis Leschyshyn .01 .05
43 Mike Vernon .02 .10
44 Brent Sutter .01 .05
45 Rod Brind'Amour .02 .10
46 Sylvain Turgeon .01 .05
47 Kirk McLean .02 .10
48 Derek King .01 .05
49 Murray Craven .01 .05
50 Jaromir Jagr .10 .30
51 Guy Carbonneau .01 .05
52 Tony Granato .01 .05
53 Mark Tinordi .01 .05
54 Brad McCrimmon .01 .05
55 Randy Wood .01 .05
56 Scott Young .01 .05
57 Jamie Baker .01 .05
58 Don Beaupre .02 .10
59 Bob Probert .02 .10
60 Ray Ferraro .01 .05
61 Alexei Kasatonov .01 .05
62 Corey Millen .01 .05
63 Scott Mellanby .02 .10
64 Brian Benning .01 .05
65 Doug Lidster .01 .05
66 Doug Gilmour .02 .10
67 Shawn McEachern .01 .05
68 Tim Cheveldae .02 .10
69 Jeff Norton .01 .05
70 Ed Belfour .07 .20
71 Thomas Steen .01 .05
72 Stephan Lebeau .01 .05
73 James Patrick .01 .05
74 Joel Otto .01 .05
75 Grant Fuhr .02 .10
76 Calle Johansson .01 .05
77 Donald Audette .01 .05
78 Geoff Courtnall .01 .05
79 Fredrik Olausson .01 .05
80 Dimitri Khristich .01 .05
81 John MacLean .02 .10
82 Dominic Roussel .02 .10
83 Ray Sheppard .02 .10
84 Christian Ruuttu .01 .05
85 Mike McPhee .01 .05
86 Adam Creighton .01 .05
87 Uwe Krupp .01 .05
88 Steve Leach .01 .05
89 Kevin Miller .01 .05
90 Charlie Huddy .01 .05
91 Mark Howe .01 .05
92 Sylvain Cote .01 .05
93 Anatoli Semenov .01 .05
94 Jeff Beukeboom .01 .05
95 Gord Murphy .01 .05
96 Rob Pearson .01 .05
97 Esa Tikkanen .01 .05
98 Dave Gagner .02 .10
99 Mike Richter .07 .20
100 Jari Kurri .07 .20
101 Chris Chelios .07 .20
102 Peter Sidorkiewicz .02 .10
103 Scott Lachance .01 .05
104 Zarley Zalapski .01 .05
105 Denis Savard .02 .10
106 Paul Coffey .07 .20
107 Ulf Dahlen .01 .05
108 Shayne Corson .01 .05
109 Jimmy Carson .01 .05
110 Petr Svoboda .01 .05
111 Scott Stevens .02 .10
112 Kevin Lowe .01 .05
113 Chris Kontos .01 .05
114 Evgeny Davydov .01 .05
115 Doug Wilson .02 .10
116 Curtis Joseph .07 .20
117 Trevor Linden .02 .10
118 Michal Pivonka .01 .05
119 Dave Ellett .01 .05
120 Mike Ricci .01 .05
121 Al MacInnis .02 .10
122 Kevin Dineen .01 .05
123 Norm Maciver .01 .05
124 Darius Kasparaitis .01 .05
125 Adam Oates .02 .10
126 Sean Burke .02 .10
127 Dave Manson .01 .05
128 Eric Desjardins .02 .10
129 Tomas Sandstrom .01 .05
130 Russ Courtnall .01 .05
131 Roman Hamrlik .02 .10
132 Teppo Numminen .01 .05
133 Pat Falloon .01 .05
134 Jyrki Lumme .01 .05
135 Joe Sakic .15 .40
136 Kevin Hatcher .01 .05
137 Wendel Clark .02 .10
138 Neil Wilkinson .01 .05
139 Craig Simpson .01 .05
140 Kelly Hrudey .02 .10
141 Steve Thomas .01 .05
142 Mike Modano .10 .30
143 Garry Galley .01 .05
144 Jim Johnson .01 .05
145 Rod Langway .01 .05
146 Bob Sweeney .01 .05
147 Gary Leeman .01 .05
148 Alexei Zhitnik .01 .05
149 Adam Foote .01 .05
150 Mark Recchi .02 .10
151 Ron Francis .02 .10
152 Ron Hextall .02 .10
153 Michel Goulet .02 .10
154 Vladimir Ruzicka .01 .05
155 Bill Ranford .02 .10
156 Mike Craig .01 .05
157 Vladimir Malakhov .01 .05
158 Nicklas Lidstrom .07 .20
159 Dale Hawerchuk .02 .10
160 Claude Lemieux .01 .05
161 Ulf Samuelsson .01 .05
162 John Vanbiesbrouck .02 .10
163 Patrice Brisebois .01 .05
164 Andrew Cassels .01 .05
165 Paul Ranheim .01 .05
166 Neal Broten .02 .10
167 Joe Reekie .01 .05
168 Derian Hatcher .01 .05
169 Don Sweeney .01 .05
170 Mike Keane .01 .05
171 Mark Fitzpatrick .02 .10
172 Paul Cavallini .01 .05
173 Garth Butcher .01 .05
174 Andrei Kovalenko .01 .05
175 Shawn Burr .01 .05
176 Mike Donnelly .01 .05
177 Glenn Healy .02 .10
178 Gilbert Dionne .01 .05
179 Mike Ramsey .01 .05
180 Glenn Anderson .02 .10
181 Pelle Eklund .01 .05
182 Kerry Huffman .01 .05
183 Johan Garpenlov .01 .05
184 Kjell Samuelsson .01 .05
185 Todd Elik .01 .05
186 Craig Janney .02 .10
187 Dmitri Kvartalnov .01 .05
188 Al Iafrate .01 .05
189 John Cullen .01 .05
190 Steve Duchesne .01 .05
191 Theo Fleury .01 .05
192 Steve Smith .01 .05
193 Jon Casey .02 .10
194 Jeff Brown .01 .05
195 Keith Tkachuk .07 .20
196 Greg Adams .01 .05
197 Mike Ridley .01 .05
198 Bobby Holik .01 .05
199 Joe Nieuwendyk .02 .10
200 Mark Messier .07 .20
201 Jim Hrivnak .02 .10
202 Patrick Poulin .01 .05
203 Alexei Kovalev .02 .10
204 Robert Reichel .01 .05
205 David Shaw .01 .05
206 Brent Gilchrist .01 .05
207 Craig Billington .02 .10
208 Bob Errey .01 .05
209 Dmitri Mironov .01 .05
210 Dixon Ward .01 .05
211 Rick Zombo .01 .05
212 Marty McSorley .01 .05
213 Geoff Sanderson .02 .10
214 Dino Ciccarelli .02 .10
215 Tony Amonte .02 .10
216 Dimitri Yushkevich .01 .05
217 Scott Niedermayer .01 .05
218 Sergei Nemchinov .01 .05
219 Steve Konroyd .01 .05
220 Patrick Flatley .01 .05
221 Steve Chiasson .01 .05
222 Alexander Mogilny .02 .10
223 Pat Elynuik .01 .05
224 Jamie Macoun .01 .05
225 Tom Barrasso .02 .10
226 Gaetan Duchesne .01 .05
227 Eric Weinrich .01 .05
228 Dave Poulin .01 .05
229 Slava Fetisov .01 .05
230 Brian Bradley .01 .05
231 Petr Nedved .02 .10
232 Phil Housley .02 .10
233 Terry Carkner .01 .05
234 Kirk Muller .01 .05
235 Brian Leetch .07 .20
236 Rob Blake .02 .10
237 Chris Terreri .02 .10
238 Brendan Shanahan .07 .20
239 Paul Ysebaert .01 .05
240 Jeremy Roenick .08 .25
241 Gary Roberts .01 .05
242 Petr Klima .01 .05
243 Glen Wesley .01 .05
244 Vincent Damphousse .01 .05
245 Luc Robitaille .02 .10
246 Dallas Drake RC .01 .05
247 Rob Gaudreau RC .01 .05
248 Tommy Sjodin .01 .05
249 Richard Smehlik .01 .05
250 Sergei Fedorov .10 .30
251 Steve Heinze .01 .05
252 Luke Richardson .01 .05
253 Doug Weight .02 .10
254 Martin Rucinsky .01 .05
255 Sergio Momesso .01 .05
256 Alexei Zhamnov .02 .10
257 Bob Kudelski .01 .05
258 Brian Skrudland .01 .05
259 Terry Yake .01 .05
260 Alexei Gusarov .01 .05
261 Sandis Ozolinsh .01 .05
262 Ted Donato .01 .05
263 Bruce Driver .01 .05
264 Yves Racine .01 .05
265 Mike Peluso .01 .05
266 Craig Muni .01 .05
267 Bob Carpenter .01 .05
268 Kevin Haller .01 .05
269 Brad May .02 .10
270 Joe Kocur .01 .05
271 Igor Korolev .01 .05
272 Troy Murray .01 .05
273 Daren Puppa .02 .10
274 Gordie Roberts .01 .05
275 Michel Petit .01 .05
276 Vincent Riendeau .02 .10
277 Robert Petrovicky .01 .05
278 Valeri Zelepukin .01 .05
279 Bob Bassen .01 .05
280 Darrin Shannon .01 .05
281 Dominik Hasek .20 .50
282 Craig Ludwig .01 .05
283 Lyle Odelein .01 .05
284 Alexander Semak .01 .05
285 Richard Matvichuk .01 .05
286 Ken Daneyko .01 .05
287 Jan Erixon .01 .05
288 Robert Dirk .01 .05
289 Laurie Boschman .01 .05
290 Greg Paslawski .01 .05
291 Rob Zamuner .01 .05
292 Todd Gill .01 .05
293 Neil Brady .01 .05
294 Murray Baron .01 .05
295 Peter Taglianetti .01 .05
296 Wayne Presley .01 .05
297 Paul Broten .01 .05
298 Dana Murzyn .01 .05
299 J.J. Daigneault .01 .05
300 Wayne Gretzky .50 1.25
301 Keith Acton .01 .05
302 Yuri Khmylev .01 .05
303 Frank Musil .01 .05
304 Bob Rouse .01 .05
305 Greg Gilbert .01 .05
306 Geoff Smith .01 .05
307 Adam Burt .01 .05
308 Phil Bourque .01 .05
309 Igor Kravchuk .01 .05
310 Steve Yzerman .40 1.00
311 Darryl Sydor .01 .05
312 Tie Domi .02 .10
313 Sergei Zubov .01 .05
314 Chris Dahlquist .01 .05
315 Patrick Roy .40 1.00
316 Mark Osborne .01 .05
317 Kelly Buchberger .01 .05
318 John LeClair .07 .20
319 Randy McKay .01 .05
320 Jody Hull .01 .05
321 Paul Stanton .01 .05
322 Steven Finn .01 .05
323 Rich Sutter .01 .05
324 Ray Whitney .01 .05
325 Kevin Stevens .01 .05
326 Valeri Kamensky .02 .10
327 Doug Zmolek .01 .05
328 Mikhail Tatarinov .01 .05
329 Ken Wregget .02 .10
330 Joe Juneau .02 .10
331 Teemu Selanne .07 .20
332 Trent Yawney .01 .05
333 Pavel Bure .07 .20
334 Jim Paek .01 .05
335 Brett Hull .08 .25
336 Tommy Soderstrom .02 .10
337 Grigori Panteleyev .01 .05
338 Kevin Todd .01 .05
339 Mark Janssens .01 .05
340 Rick Tocchet .02 .10
341 Wendell Young .02 .10
342 Cam Neely .07 .20
343 Dave Andreychuk .02 .10
344 Peter Bondra .02 .10
345 Pat LaFontaine .07 .20
346 Robb Stauber .02 .10
347 Brian Mullen .01 .05
348 Joe Murphy .01 .05
349 Pat Jablonski .02 .10
350 Mario Lemieux .40 1.00
351 Sergei Bautin .01 .05
352 Claude Lapointe .01 .05
353 Dean Evason .01 .05
354 John Tucker .01 .05
355 Drake Berehowsky .01 .05
356 Gerald Diduck .01 .05
357 Todd Krygier .01 .05
358 Adrien Plavsic .01 .05
359 Sylvain Lefebvre .01 .05
360 Kay Whitmore .02 .10
361 Sheldon Kennedy .01 .05
362 Kris King .01 .05
363 Marc Bergevin .01 .05
364 Keith Primeau .01 .05
365 Jimmy Waite .02 .10
366 Dean Kennedy .01 .05
367 Mike Krushelnyski .01 .05
368 Ron Tugnutt .02 .10
369 Bob Beers .01 .05
370 Randy Burridge .01 .05
371 David Reid .01 .05
372 Frantisek Kucera .01 .05
373 Scott Pellerin RC .01 .05
374 Brad Dalgarno .01 .05
375 Martin Straka .01 .05
376 Scott Pearson .01 .05
377 Arturs Irbe .02 .10
378 Jiri Slegr .01 .05
379 Stephane Fiset .02 .10
380 Stu Barnes .01 .05
381 Ric Nattress .01 .05
382 Steven King .01 .05
383 Michael Nylander .01 .05
384 Keith Brown .01 .05
385 Gino Odjick .01 .05
386 Bryan Marchment .01 .05
387 Mike Foligno .01 .05
388 Zdeno Ciger .01 .05
389 Dave Taylor .02 .10
390 Mike Sullivan .01 .05
391 Shawn Chambers .01 .05
392 Brad Marsh .01 .05
393 Mike Hough .01 .05

394 Jeff Reese .01 .05
395 Bill Guerin .01 .05
396 Greg Hawgood .01 .05
397 Jim Sandlak .01 .05
398 Stephane Matteau .01 .05
399 John Blue .02 .10
400 Tony Twist .01 .05
401 Luciano Borsato .01 .05
402 Gerard Gallant .01 .05
403 Rick Tabaracci .02 .10
404 Nick Kypreos .01 .05
405 Marty McInnis .01 .05
406 Craig Wolanin .01 .05
407 Mark Lamb .01 .05
408 Martin Gelinas .01 .05
409 Ronnie Stern .01 .05
410 Ken Sutton .01 .05
411 Brian Noonan .01 .05
412 Stephane Quintal .01 .05
413 Rob Zettler .01 .05
414 Gino Cavallini .01 .05
415 Mark Hardy .01 .05
416 Jay Wells .01 .05
417 Keith Jones .01 .05
418 Dave McLlwain .01 .05
419 Frank Pietrangelo .02 .10
420 Jocelyn Lemieux .01 .05
421 Slava Kozlov .02 .10
422 Randy Moller .01 .05
423 Kevin Dahl .01 .05
424 Shjon Podein RC .01 .05
425 Shane Churla .01 .05
426 Guy Hebert .02 .10
427 Mikael Andersson .01 .05
428 Robert Kron .01 .05
429 Mike Eagles .01 .05
430 Alan May .01 .05
431 Ron Wilson .01 .05
432 Darcy Wakaluk .02 .10
433 Rob Ray .01 .05
434 Brent Ashton .01 .05
435 Jason Woolley .01 .05
436 Basil McRae .01 .05
437 Andre Racicot .02 .10
438 Brad Werenka .01 .05
439 Josef Beranek .01 .05
440 Dave Christian .01 .05
441 Theo Fleury LBM .01 .05
442 Mark Recchi LBM .02 .10
443 Cliff Ronning LBM .01 .05
444 Tony Granato LBM .01 .05
445 John Vanbiesbrouck LBM .02 .10
446 Jari Kurri HL .02 .10
500th goal
447 Mike Gartner HL .02 .10
14th Straight
30-goal season
448 Steve Yzerman HL .07 .20
1,000th Point
449 Glenn Anderson HL .02 .10
1,000th Point
450 Washington Caps HL .01 .05
Al Iafrate
Sylvain Cote
Kevin Hatcher
Highest Scoring Defense
in NHL History
451 Luc Robitaille HL .02 .10
Most Goals by
left winger
452 Pittsburgh Penguins HL .01 .05
17-Game Winning Streak
453 Corey Hirsch .02 .10
454 Jesse Belanger .01 .05
455 Philippe Boucher .01 .05
456 Robert Lang .01 .05
457 Doug Barrault RC .01 .05
458 Steve Konowalchuk .01 .05
459 Oleg Petrov .01 .05
460 Niclas Andersson .01 .05
461 Milan Tichy RC .01 .05
462 Darrin Madeley RC .01 .05
463 Tyler Wright .01 .05
464 Sergei Krivokrasov .01 .05
465 Vladimir Vujtek .01 .05
466 Rick Knickle RC .02 .10
467 Gord Kruppke RC .01 .05
468 David Emma .01 .05
469 Scott Thomas RC .01 .05
470 Shawn Rivers RC .01 .05
471 Jason Bowen RC .01 .05
472 Bryan Smolinski .01 .05
473 Chris Simon RC .20 .50
474 Peter Ciavaglia RC .01 .05
475 Sergei Zholtok .01 .05
476 Radek Hamr RC .01 .05
477 Teemu Selanne .07 .20
(Alexander Mogilny
SL Goals
478 Adam Oates SL .02 .10
Assists
479 Mario Lemieux SL .20 .50
480 Mario Lemieux SL .20 .50
481 Dave Andreychuk SL .02 .10
Power-Play Goals
482 Phil Housley SL .02 .10
Defenseman Scoring
483 Tom Barrasso SL .02 .10
Wins
484 Felix Potvin SL .07 .20
GAA
485 Ed Belfour SL .07 .20
486 Sault Ste. Marie .02 .10
Greyhounds
Memorial Cup Champions
487 Montreal Canadiens .02 .10
Stanley Cup Champions
488 Anaheim Mighty Ducks .07 .20
Logo
489 Guy Hebert .02 .10
490 Sean Hill .01 .05
491 Florida Panthers Logo .07 .20
492 John Vanbiesbrouck .02 .10
493 Tom Fitzgerald .01 .05
494 Paul DiPietro .01 .05
495 David Volek .01 .05
496 Alexandre Daigle SP .40 1.00
(issued via mail redemption)
497 Shawn McEachern .01 .05
498 Rich Sutter .01 .05
499 Evgeny Davydov .01 .05
500 Sean Hill .01 .05
501 John Vanbiesbrouck .02 .10
502 Guy Hebert .02 .10
503 Scott Mellanby .02 .10
504 Ron Tugnutt .02 .10
505 Brian Skrudland .01 .05
506 Nelson Emerson .01 .05
507 Kevin Todd .01 .05
508 Terry Carkner .01 .05
509 Stephane Quintal .01 .05
510 Paul Stanton .01 .05
511 Terry Yake .01 .05
512 Brian Benning .01 .05
513 Brian Propp .01 .05
514 Steven King .01 .05
515 Joe Cirella .01 .05
516 Andy Moog .02 .10
517 Paul Ysebaert .01 .05
518 Petr Klima .01 .05
519 Corey Millen .01 .05
520 Phil Housley .02 .10
521 Craig Billington .02 .10
522 Jeff Norton .01 .05
523 Neil Wilkinson .01 .05
524 Doug Lidster .01 .05
525 Steve Larmer .02 .10
526 Jon Casey .02 .10
527 Brad McCrimmon .01 .05
528 Alexei Kasatonov .01 .05
529 Andrei Lomakin .01 .05
530 Daren Puppa .02 .10
531 Sergei Makarov .01 .05
532 Jim Sandlak .01 .05
533 Glenn Healy .02 .10
534 Martin Gelinas .01 .05
535 Igor Larionov .01 .05
536 Anatoli Semenov .01 .05
537 Mark Fitzpatrick .02 .10
538 Paul Cavallini .01 .05
539 Jimmy Waite .02 .10
540 Yves Racine .01 .05
541 Jeff Hackett .02 .10
542 Marty McSorley .01 .05
543 Scott Pearson .01 .05
544 Ron Hextall .02 .10
545 Gaetan Duchesne .01 .05
546 Jamie Baker .01 .05
547 Troy Loney .01 .05
548 Gord Murphy .01 .05
549 Bob Kudelski .01 .05
550 Dean Evason .01 .05
551 Mike Peluso .01 .05
552 Dave Poulin .01 .05
553 Randy Ladouceur .01 .05
554 Tom Fitzgerald .01 .05
555 Denis Savard .02 .10
556 Kelly Kisio .01 .05
557 Craig Simpson .01 .05
558 Stu Grimson .01 .05
559 Mike Hough .01 .05
560 Gerard Gallant .01 .05
561 Greg Gilbert .01 .05
562 Vladimir Ruzicka .01 .05
563 Jim Hrivnak .02 .10
564 Dave Lowry .01 .05
565 Todd Ewen .01 .05
566 Bob Errey .01 .05
567 Bryan Trottier .02 .10
568 Grant Ledyard .01 .05
569 Keith Brown .01 .05
570 Darren Turcotte .01 .05
571 Patrick Poulin .01 .05
572 Jimmy Carson .01 .05
573 Eric Weinrich .01 .05
574 James Patrick .01 .05
575 Bob Beers .01 .05
576 Chris Joseph .01 .05
577 Bryan Marchment .01 .05
578 Bob Carpenter .01 .05
579 Craig Muni .01 .05
580 Pat Elynuik .01 .05
581 Todd Elik .01 .05
582 Doug Brown .01 .05
583 Dave McLlwain .01 .05
584 Dave Tippett .01 .05
585 Jesse Belanger .01 .05
586 Chris Pronger .08 .25
587 Alexandre Daigle .01 .05
588 Cam Stewart RC .01 .05
589 Derek Plante RC .01 .05
590 Pat Peake .01 .05
591 Alexander Karpovtsev .01 .05
592 Rob Niedermayer .02 .10
593 Jocelyn Thibault RC .25 .60
594 Jason Arnott RC .40 1.00
595 Mike Rathje .01 .05
596 Chris Gratton .02 .10
597 Markus Naslund .07 .20
598 Dmitri Filimonov .01 .05
599 Andrei Trefilov .01 .05
600 Michal Sykora RC .01 .05
601 Greg Johnson .01 .05
602 Mikael Renberg .07 .20
603 Alexei Yashin .01 .05
604 Damian Rhodes RC .02 .10
605 Jeff Shantz RC .01 .05
606 Brent Gretzky RC .01 .05
607 Boris Mironov .01 .05
608 Ted Drury .01 .05
609 Chris Osgood RC .60 1.50
610 Jim Storm RC .01 .05
611 Dave Karpa .01 .05
612 Stewart Malgunas RC .01 .05
613 Jason Smith RC .01 .05
614 German Titov RC .01 .05
615 Patrick Carnback RC .01 .05
616 Jaroslav Modry RC .01 .05
617 Scott Levins RC .01 .05
618 Fred Brathwaite RC .10 .30
619 Ilya Byakin RC .01 .05
620 Jarkko Varvio .01 .05
621 Jim Montgomery RC .01 .05
622 Vesa Viitakoski RC .01 .05
623 Alexei Kudashov RC .01 .05
624 Pavol Demitra .02 .10
625 Iain Fraser RC .01 .05
626 Peter Popovic RC .01 .05
627 Kirk Maltby RC .01 .05
628 Garth Snow RC .02 .10
629 Peter White RC .01 .05
630 Mike McKee RC .01 .05
631 Darren McCarty RC .15 .40
632 Pat Neaton RC .01 .05
633 Sandy McCarthy .01 .05
634 Pierre Sevigny .01 .05
635 Matt Martin RC .01 .05
636 John Slaney .01 .05
637 Bob Corkum .01 .05
638 Mike Stapleton RC .01 .05
639 Bill Houlder .01 .05
640 Warren Rychel .01 .05
641 Garry Valk .01 .05
642 Greg Hawgood .01 .05
643 Randy Gilhen .01 .05
644 Stu Barnes .01 .05
645 Fredrik Olausson .01 .05
646 Geoff Smith .01 .05
647 Mike Foligno .01 .05
648 Martin Brodeur .20 .50
649 Ryan McGill .01 .05
650 Jeff Reese .01 .05
651 Mike Sillinger .01 .05
652 Brent Severyn RC .01 .05
653 Rob Ramage .01 .05
654 Dixon Ward .01 .05
655 Danton Cole .01 .05
656 Viacheslav Butsayev .01 .05
657 Ron Wilson .01 .05
658 Paul Broten .01 .05
659 Mike Hudson .01 .05
660 Trevor Kidd .02 .10
661 Travis Green .02 .10
662 Wayne Gretzky 1.00 2.50
NNO Alexandre Daigle .20 .50
Redemption card
NNO Eric Lindros AS SP 4.00 10.00

1993-94 Score Gold

The 1993-94 Score Gold Rush set consists of 166 standard-size cards. The fronts are identical in design with the regular second-series Score cards, except for the metallic finish and gold marbleized borders. The backs are nearly identical to the regular issue cards, the Gold Rush logo at the top being the only difference. No Gold Rush parallels were produced for first series cards.

COMPLETE SET (166) 15.00 40.00
*VETS: 2.5X TO 6X BASIC CARDS
*ROOKIES: 1.2X TO 3X BASIC CARDS

1993-94 Score Canadian

COMPLETE SET (661) 8.00 20.00
COMP.SERIES 1 (495) 6.00 15.00
COMP.SERIES 2 (166) 2.00 5.00
*CANADIAN: .4X TO 1X BASIC CARDS

1993-94 Score Canadian Gold

COMPLETE SET (166) 15.00 40.00
*VETS: 2.5X TO 6X BASIC CARDS
*ROOKIES: 1.2X TO 3X BASIC CARDS
ONE GOLD PER SER.2 FOIL PACK

1993-94 Score Dream Team

Randomly inserted at the rate of 1:24 first series Canadian packs, this 24 card standard-size set features Score's Dream Team selections. Horizontal fronts feature an action photo and a head shot at lower right. The player's name and position appear in beneath the large photo. The backs contain career highlights and are numbered "X of 24".

COMPLETE SET (24) 50.00 100.00
1 Tom Barrasso .75 2.00
2 Patrick Roy 8.00 20.00
3 Chris Chelios 1.50 4.00
4 Al MacInnis .75 2.00
5 Scott Stevens .75 2.00
6 Brian Leetch 1.50 4.00
7 Ray Bourque 2.50 6.00
8 Paul Coffey 1.50 4.00
9 Al Iafrate .40 1.00
10 Mario Lemieux 8.00 20.00
11 Wayne Gretzky 10.00 25.00
12 Eric Lindros 1.50 4.00
13 Pat LaFontaine 1.50 4.00
14 Joe Sakic 3.00 8.00
15 Pierre Turgeon .75 2.00
16 Steve Yzerman 8.00 20.00
17 Adam Oates .75 2.00
18 Brett Hull 2.00 5.00
19 Pavel Bure 1.50 4.00
20 Alexander Mogilny .75 2.00
21 Teemu Selanne 1.50 4.00
22 Steve Larmer .75 2.00
23 Kevin Stevens .40 1.00
24 Luc Robitaille .75 2.00

1993-94 Score Dynamic Duos Canadian

Randomly inserted at a rate of 1:48 Canadian second-series packs, this nine-card standard-size set highlights two team members on each card. Both the front and back of each card features a color player action shot. The player's name appears in red lettering within the team-colored bottom margin. The words "Dynamic Duos" appears in gold foil along the right side. A red maple leaf is placed at the upper left. The cards are numbered on the back with a "DD" prefix.

COMPLETE SET (9) 20.00 50.00
1 Doug Gilmour 2.00 5.00
Dave Andreychuk
2 Teemu Selanne 2.00 5.00
Alexei Zhamnov
3 Alexandre Daigle 1.50 4.00
Alexei Yashin
4 Gary Roberts 1.50 4.00
Joe Nieuwendyk
5 Joe Sakic 6.00 15.00
Mats Sundin
6 Brian Bellows 1.50 4.00
Kirk Muller
7 Shayne Corson 1.50 4.00
Jason Arnott
8 Mario Lemieux 10.00 25.00
Kevin Stevens
9 Pierre Turgeon 1.50 4.00
Derek King

1993-94 Score Dynamic Duos U.S.

Randomly inserted at a rate of 1:48 U.S. second series packs, this nine-card standard-size set highlights two team members on each card. Both the front and back of each card features a color player action shot. The player's name appears in red lettering within the team-colored bottom margin. The words "Dynamic Duos" appear in gold foil along the right side. A blue star is placed at the upper left. The cards are numbered on the back with a "DD" prefix.

COMPLETE SET (9) 25.00 60.00
1 Mark Recchi 2.00 5.00
Eric Lindros
2 Pat LaFontaine 2.00 5.00
Alexander Mogilny
3 Adam Oates 2.00 5.00
Joe Juneau
4 Brett Hull 3.00 8.00
Craig Janney
5 Mark Messier 3.00 8.00
Adam Graves
6 Jeremy Roenick 2.00 5.00
Joe Murphy
7 Jari Kurri 10.00 25.00
Wayne Gretzky
8 Sergei Makarov 1.50 4.00
Igor Larionov
9 Steve Yzerman 8.00 20.00
Sergei Fedorov

1993-94 Score Franchise

Randomly inserted at a rate of 1:24 U.S. first series packs, this 24-card set features borderless color player action shots on the fronts, the backgrounds of which are ghosted and darkened. The cards are numbered "X of 24" on the back.

COMPLETE SET (24) 40.00 80.00
1 Ray Bourque 2.50 6.00
2 Pat LaFontaine 1.50 4.00
3 Al MacInnis .75 2.00
4 Jeremy Roenick 2.00 5.00
5 Mike Modano 2.00 5.00
6 Steve Yzerman 5.00 12.00
7 Bill Ranford .75 2.00
8 Sean Burke .75 2.00
9 Wayne Gretzky 8.00 20.00
10 Patrick Roy 6.00 15.00
11 Scott Stevens .75 2.00
12 Pierre Turgeon .75 2.00
13 Brian Leetch 1.50 4.00
14 Peter Sidorkiewicz .75 2.00
15 Eric Lindros 1.50 4.00
16 Mario Lemieux 6.00 15.00
17 Joe Sakic 3.00 8.00
18 Brett Hull 2.00 5.00
19 Pat Falloon .40 1.00
20 Brian Bradley .40 1.00
21 Doug Gilmour .75 2.00
22 Pavel Bure 1.50 4.00
23 Kevin Hatcher .40 1.00
24 Teemu Selanne 1.50 4.00

1993-94 Score International Stars

Inserted one per series one jumbo pack, this 22-card standard-size set highlights some of the NHL's hottest international stars. The fronts feature full-bleed color action shots, with the player's name and nationality appearing in a banner at the bottom that bears the colors of his national flag. The words "International Stars" in gold foil are printed at the top. On purplish backgrounds, the backs carry a color headshot at the upper left, with the player's national flag to the right and his name and country in his flag's colors below. Career highlights at the bottom round out the card. The cards are numbered on the back as "X of 22." Multipliers to determine values for the French version can be found in the header below.

COMPLETE SET (22) 8.00 20.00
*CANADIAN: .4X TO 1X BASIC INSERTS
1 Pavel Bure .75 2.00
2 Teemu Selanne .75 2.00
3 Sergei Fedorov 1.25 3.00
4 Peter Bondra .40 1.00
5 Tommy Soderstrom .20 .50
6 Robert Reichel .20 .50
7 Jari Kurri .75 2.00
8 Alexander Mogilny .40 1.00
9 Jaromir Jagr 1.25 3.00
10 Mats Sundin .75 2.00
11 Uwe Krupp .20 .50
12 Nikolai Borschevsky .20 .50
13 Ulf Dahlen .20 .50
14 Alexander Semak .20 .50
15 Michal Pivonka .20 .50
16 Sergei Nemchinov .20 .50
17 Darius Kasparaitis .20 .50
18 Sandis Ozolinsh .20 .50
19 Alexei Kovalev .40 1.00
20 Dimitri Khristich .20 .50
21 Tomas Sandstrom .20 .50
22 Petr Nedved .20 .50

1994-95 Score Samples

Issued in packs of 12, the 1994 Score hockey Hobby Sample cards measure the standard-size and preview the 1994 Score hockey issue. The top right and left corners have been cut off of some cards. The fronts feature color action player photos with white borders, and a small headshot in the left bottom corner. The player's name appears in colorful letters at the bottom of the picture. The horizontal backs carry another player photo on the left, along with the player's name, biography, career highlights and stats on the right.

COMPLETE SEALED SET (12) 1.50 4.00
1 Eric Lindros .20 .50
2 Pat LaFontaine .01 .05
3 Wendel Clark .01 .05
4 Cam Neely .01 .05
5 Larry Murphy .01 .05
6 Patrick Poulin .01 .05
7 Bob Beers .01 .05
254 Jason Arnott .02 .10
C13 Darius Kasparaitis .75 2.00
Check-It
TF16 Alexandre Daigle .40 1.00
The Franchise
NNO Pro Debut Rookie .20 .50
Redemption Card
NNO Title Card .01 .05

1994-95 Score

This 275-card standard-size set was issued in one series and does not have a comprehensive player selection. Due to the NHL lock-out, series two was replaced on the production schedule by Select; therefore many stars such as Patrick Roy and Wayne Gretzky were not featured in this set. The unique design features a full color player photo, surrounded by a white border. The Score logo appears in the top right corner, while a player head shot and team logo dominate the lower left. The upper right corner displays five globes; player name appears in a multi-hued strip along the card bottom. Cards were issued in 14-card U.S. and Canadian packs that included one Gold Line parallel card. Retail jumbo packs contained 30 cards and two Gold Line cards for $1.79. Subsets include World Junior Championships (201-215), Season Highlights (241-247), Young Stars (248-262), and Team Checklists (263-275). The only Rookie Card of note in the set is Mariusz Czerkawski.

COMPLETE SET (275) 5.00 12.00
1 Eric Lindros .07 .20
2 Pat LaFontaine .07 .20
3 Wendel Clark .02 .10
4 Cam Neely .07 .20
5 Larry Murphy .02 .10
6 Patrick Poulin .01 .05
7 Bob Beers .01 .05
8 James Patrick .01 .05
9 Gino Odjick .01 .05
10 Arturs Irbe .02 .10
11 Darius Kasparaitis .01 .05
12 Peter Bondra .02 .10
13 Garth Butcher .01 .05
14 Sergei Nemchinov .01 .05
15 Doug Brown .01 .05
16 Anatoli Semenov .01 .05
17 Mike McPhee .01 .05
18 Joel Otto .01 .05
19 Dino Ciccarelli .02 .10
20 Marty McSorley .01 .05
21 Ron Tugnutt .02 .10
22 Scott Niedermayer .01 .05
23 John Tucker .01 .05
24 Norm Maciver .01 .05
25 Kevin Miller .01 .05
26 Garry Galley .01 .05
27 Ted Donato .01 .05
28 Bob Kudelski .01 .05
29 Craig Muni .01 .05
30 Nikolai Borschevsky .01 .05
31 Tom Barrasso .02 .10
32 Brent Sutter .01 .05
33 Igor Kravchuk .01 .05
34 Andrew Cassels .01 .05
35 Jyrki Lumme .01 .05
36 Sandis Ozolinsh .01 .05
37 Steve Thomas .01 .05
38 Dave Poulin .01 .05
39 Andrei Kovalenko .01 .05
40 Steve Larmer .02 .10
41 Nelson Emerson .01 .05
42 Guy Hebert .02 .10
43 Russ Courtnall .01 .05
44 Gary Suter .01 .05
45 Steve Chiasson .01 .05
46 Guy Carbonneau .01 .05
47 Rob Blake .02 .10
48 Roman Hamrlik .02 .10
49 Valeri Zelepukin .01 .05
50 Mark Recchi .02 .10
51 Darrin Madeley .01 .05
52 Steve Duchesne .01 .05
53 Brian Skrudland .01 .05
54 Craig Simpson .01 .05
55 Todd Gill .01 .05
56 Dirk Graham .01 .05
57 Joe Mullen .02 .10
58 Doug Weight .02 .10
59 Michael Nylander .01 .05
60 Kirk McLean .02 .10
61 Igor Larionov .01 .05
62 Vladimir Malakhov .01 .05
63 Kelly Miller .01 .05
64 Curtis Leschyshyn .01 .05
65 Thomas Steen .01 .05
66 Jeff Beukeboom .01 .05
67 Troy Loney .01 .05
68 Mark Tinordi .01 .05
69 Theo Fleury .02 .10
70 Slava Kozlov .02 .10
71 Tony Granato .01 .05
72 Daren Puppa .02 .10
73 Brian Bellows .01 .05
74 Bernie Nicholls .01 .05
75 Rick Zombo .01 .05
76 Brad Shaw .01 .05
77 Josef Beranek .01 .05
78 Dominik Hasek .08 .25
79 Steve Leach .01 .05
80 David Reid .01 .05
81 Dave Lowry .01 .05
82 Martin Straka .01 .05
83 Dave Ellett .01 .05
84 Sean Burke .02 .10
85 Craig MacTavish .01 .05
86 Cliff Ronning .01 .05
87 Bob Errey .01 .05
88 Marty McInnis .01 .05
89 Mats Sundin .07 .20
90 Randy Burridge .01 .05
91 Teppo Numminen .01 .05
92 Tony Amonte .02 .10
93 Terry Yake .01 .05
94 Paul Cavallini .01 .05
95 German Titov .01 .05
96 Vladimir Konstantinov .02 .10
97 Darryl Sydor .01 .05
98 Chris Joseph .01 .05
99 Corey Millen .01 .05
100 Brett Hull .10 .30
101 Don Sweeney .01 .05
102 Scott Mellanby .02 .10
103 Mathieu Schneider .01 .05
104 Brad May .01 .05
105 Dominic Roussel .02 .10
106 Jamie Macoun .01 .05
107 Bryan Marchment .01 .05
108 Shawn McEachern .01 .05
109 Murray Craven .01 .05
110 Eric Desjardins .02 .10
111 Jon Casey .02 .10
112 Mike Gartner .02 .10
113 Neal Broten .02 .10
114 Jari Kurri .02 .10
115 Bruce Driver .01 .05
116 Patrick Flatley .01 .05
117 Gord Murphy .01 .05
118 Dimitri Khristich .01 .05
119 Nicklas Lidstrom .07 .20
120 Al MacInnis .02 .10
121 Steve Smith .01 .05
122 Zdeno Ciger .01 .05
123 Tie Domi .02 .10
124 Joe Juneau .02 .10
125 Todd Elik .01 .05
126 Stephane Fiset .02 .10
127 Craig Janney .02 .10
128 Stephan Lebeau .01 .05
129 Richard Smehlik .01 .05
130 Mike Richter .07 .20
131 Danton Cole .01 .05
132 Rod Brind'Amour .02 .10
133 Dave Archibald .01 .05
134 Dana Murzyn .01 .05
135 Jaromir Jagr .10 .30
136 Esa Tikkanen .01 .05
137 Rob Pearson .01 .05
138 Stu Barnes .01 .05
139 Frank Musil .01 .05
140 Ron Hextall .02 .10
141 Adam Oates .02 .10
142 Ken Daneyko .01 .05
143 Dale Hunter .01 .05
144 Geoff Sanderson .02 .10
145 Kelly Hrudey .02 .10
146 Kirk Muller .01 .05
147 Fredrik Olausson .01 .05
148 Derian Hatcher .01 .05
149 Ed Belfour .07 .20
150 Steve Yzerman .40 1.00
151 Adam Foote .02 .10
152 Pat Falloon .01 .05
153 Shawn Chambers .01 .05
154 Alexei Zhamnov .02 .10
155 Brendan Shanahan .07 .20
156 Ulf Samuelsson .01 .05
157 Donald Audette .01 .05
158 Bob Corkum .01 .05
159 Joe Nieuwendyk .02 .10
160 Felix Potvin .07 .20
161 Geoff Courtnall .01 .05
162 Yves Racine .01 .05
163 Tom Fitzgerald .01 .05
164 Adam Graves .01 .05
165 Vincent Damphousse .01 .05
166 Pierre Turgeon .02 .10
167 Craig Billington .02 .10
168 Al Iafrate .01 .05
169 Darren Turcotte .01 .05
170 Joe Murphy .01 .05
171 Alexei Zhitnik .01 .05
172 John MacLean .02 .10
173 Andy Moog .07 .20
174 Shayne Corson .02 .10
175 Ray Sheppard .02 .10
176 Johan Garpenlov .01 .05
177 Ron Sutter .01 .05
178 Teemu Selanne .07 .20
179 Brian Bradley .01 .05
180 Ray Bourque .15 .40
181 Curtis Joseph .07 .20
182 Kevin Stevens .01 .05
183 Alexei Kasatonov .01 .05
184 Brian Leetch .07 .20
185 Doug Gilmour .07 .20
186 Gary Roberts .02 .10
187 Mike Keane .01 .05
188 Mike Modano .15 .40
189 Chris Chelios .07 .20
190 Pavel Bure .07 .20
191 Bob Essensa .02 .10
192 Dale Hawerchuk .02 .10
193 Scott Stevens .02 .10
194 Claude Lapointe .01 .05
195 Scott Lachance .01 .05
196 Gaetan Duchesne .01 .05
197 Kevin Dineen .01 .05
198 Doug Bodger .01 .05
199 Mike Ridley .01 .05
200 Alexander Mogilny .02 .10
201 Jamie Storr .01 .05
202 Jason Botterill .01 .05
203 Jeff Friesen .01 .05
204 Todd Harvey .01 .05
205 Brendan Witt .01 .05
206 Jason Allison .01 .05
207 Aaron Gavey .01 .05
208 Deron Quint .01 .05
209 Jason Bonsignore .01 .05
210 Richard Park .01 .05
211 Jamie Langenbrunner .01 .05
212 Vadim Sharifjanov .02 .10
213 Alexander Kharlamov .01 .05
214 Oleg Tverdovsky .02 .10
215 Valeri Bure .01 .05
216 Dane Jackson RC .01 .05
217 Josef Cierny RC .01 .05
218 Yevgeny Namestnikov .01 .05
219 Dan Laperriere RC .01 .05
220 Fred Knipscheer .01 .05
221 Yan Kaminsky .01 .05
222 David Roberts .01 .05
223 Derek Mayer .01 .05
224 Jamie McLennan .02 .10
225 Kevin Smyth .01 .05
226 Todd Marchant .01 .05
227 Mariusz Czerkawski RC .08 .25
228 John Lilley .01 .05
229 Aaron Ward .01 .05
230 Brian Savage .01 .05
231 Jason Allison .01 .05
232 Maxim Bets .01 .05
233 Ted Crowley .01 .05
234 Todd Simon RC .01 .05
235 Zigmund Palffy .02 .10
236 Rene Corbet .01 .05
237 Mike Peca .01 .05
238 Dwayne Norris .01 .05
239 Andrei Nazarov .01 .05
240 David Sacco .01 .05
241 Wayne Gretzky .40 1.00
242 Mike Gartner .02 .10
243 Dino Ciccarelli .02 .10
244 Ron Francis .02 .10
245 Bernie Nicholls .02 .10
246 Dino Ciccarelli .02 .10
247 Brian Propp .01 .05
248 Alexandre Daigle .01 .05
249 Mikael Renberg .02 .10
250 Jocelyn Thibault .07 .20
251 Derek Plante .01 .05
252 Chris Pronger .02 .10
253 Alexei Yashin .01 .05
254 Jason Arnott .01 .05
255 Boris Mironov .01 .05
256 Chris Osgood .10 .30
257 Jesse Belanger .01 .05
258 Darren McCarty .01 .05
259 Trevor Kidd .02 .10
260 Oleg Petrov .01 .05
261 Mike Rathje .01 .05
262 John Slaney .01 .05
263 Anaheim Mighty Ducks .01 .05
Boston Bruins CL
264 Buffalo Sabres .01 .05
Calgary Flames CL
265 Chicago Blackhawks .01 .05
Dallas Stars CL
266 Detroit Red Wings .01 .05
Edmonton Oilers CL
267 Florida Panthers .01 .05
Hartford Whalers CL
268 Los Angeles Kings .01 .05
Montreal Canadiens CL
269 New Jersey Devils .01 .05
New York Islanders CL
270 New York Rangers .01 .05
Ottawa Senators CL
271 Philadelphia Flyers .01 .05
Pittsburgh Penguins CL
272 Quebec Nordiques .01 .05
St.Louis Blues CL
273 San Jose Sharks .01 .05
Tampa Bay Lightning CL
274 Toronto Maple Leafs .01 .05
Vancouver Canucks CL
275 Washington Capitals .01 .05
Winnipeg Jets CL

1994-95 Score Gold

These parallel cards were issued one per regular or jumbo pack. These differ from the basic cards through the usage of a gold foil coating. In a unique offer designed to promote set building, Score offered collectors who submitted complete team sets a limited Platinum foil team set in return. Redeemed gold cards were returned with a Pinnacle brand logo hole-punched through them. Hole-punched gold cards have a value of roughly 2X to 3X that of the basic cards.

*VETS: 4X TO 10X BASIC CARDS
*ROOKIES: 2.5X TO 6X BASIC CARDS

1994-95 Score Platinum

This set was a partial parallel set to Score. Platinum cards could only be obtained through a mail-in offer via the trading of complete Score Gold Line team sets. The cards feature a platinum reflective mirror finish. Because the cards are almost invariably traded in complete team set form, that is how they are listed below. Score reportedly made 1,994 of each team set available for redemption. Pinnacle officials report very few sets were redeemed.

COMP.BLACKHAWKS (9) 15.00 30.00
COMP.BLUES (10) 15.00 30.00
COMP.BRUINS (11) 12.50 25.00
COMP.CANADIENS (10) 12.50 25.00
COMP.CANUCKS (11) 20.00 40.00
COMP.CAPITALS (10) 7.50 15.00
COMP.DEVILS (9) 7.50 15.00

COMP.FLAMES (10) 12.50 25.00
COMP.FLYERS (9) 30.00 60.00
COMP.ISLANDERS (11) 7.50 15.00
COMP.JETS (6) 12.50 25.00
COMP.KINGS (8) 50.00 75.00
COMP.LIGHTNING (7) 7.50 15.00
COMP.MAPLE LEAFS (11) 15.00 30.00
COMP.MIGHTY DUCKS (8) 7.50 15.00
COMP.NORDIQUES (11) 15.00 30.00
COMP.OILERS (10) 12.50 25.00
COMP.PANTHERS (8) 7.50 15.00
COMP.PENGUINS (10) 17.50 35.00
COMP.RANGERS (6) 15.00 30.00
COMP.RED WINGS (13) 20.00 40.00
COMP.SABRES (12) 10.00 20.00
COMP.SENATORS (8) 7.50 15.00
COMP.SHARKS (10) 10.00 20.00
COMP.STARS (8) 7.50 15.00
COMP.WHALERS (9) 7.50 15.00
*VETS: 20X TO 40X BASIC CARDS
*ROOKIES: 10X TO 20X BASIC CARDS

1994-95 Score Check It

The 18 cards in this set were randomly inserted into Score Canadian hobby product at the rate of 1:72 packs.

COMPLETE SET (18) 40.00 100.00
CI1 Eric Lindros 4.00 10.00
CI2 Scott Stevens 1.50 4.00
CI3 Darius Kasparaitis 1.50 4.00
CI4 Kevin Stevens 1.50 4.00
CI5 Brendan Shanahan 6.00 15.00
CI6 Jeremy Roenick 6.00 15.00
CI7 Ulf Samuelsson 1.50 4.00
CI8 Cam Neely 6.00 15.00
CI9 Adam Graves 1.50 4.00
CI10 Kirk Muller 1.50 4.00
CI11 Rick Tocchet 1.50 4.00
CI12 Gary Roberts 1.50 4.00
CI13 Wendel Clark 3.00 8.00
CI14 Keith Tkachuk 3.00 8.00
CI15 Theo Fleury 1.50 4.00
CI16 Claude Lemieux 1.50 4.00
CI17 Chris Chelios 3.00 8.00
CI18 Pat Verbeek 1.50 4.00

1994-95 Score Dream Team

The 24 cards in this set were randomly inserted into all Score U.S. product at the rate of 1:36 packs. The cards feature a holographic image on the front which must be angled properly in the light, along with player name and the 1994 Dream Team logo. A full color photo and player information appear on the back. The cards are numbered with an "DT" prefix.

COMPLETE SET (24) 50.00 100.00
DT1 Patrick Roy 6.00 15.00
DT2 Felix Potvin 2.00 5.00
DT3 Ray Bourque 2.50 6.00
DT4 Brian Leetch 2.00 5.00
DT5 Scott Stevens 1.50 4.00
DT6 Paul Coffey 2.00 5.00
DT7 Al MacInnis 1.50 4.00
DT8 Chris Chelios 2.00 5.00
DT9 Adam Graves 1.00 2.50
DT10 Luc Robitaille 1.00 2.50
DT11 Dave Andreychuk 1.00 2.50
DT12 Sergei Fedorov 2.50 6.00
DT13 Doug Gilmour 1.00 2.50
DT14 Wayne Gretzky 10.00 25.00
DT15 Mario Lemieux 6.00 15.00
DT16 Mark Messier 2.00 5.00
DT17 Mike Modano 2.50 6.00
DT18 Jeremy Roenick 2.50 6.00
DT19 Eric Lindros 2.00 5.00
DT20 Steve Yzerman 5.00 12.00
DT21 Alexandre Daigle 1.00 2.50
DT22 Brett Hull 2.50 6.00
DT23 Cam Neely 2.00 5.00
DT24 Pavel Bure 2.00 5.00

1994-95 Score Franchise

The 26 cards in this set were randomly inserted into Score U.S. hobby product at the rate of 1:72 packs. The cards feature red printing and gold foil on the card face. A largely black and white action shot, with the player's head and torso punched out in full color, dominates the card front. Cards are numbered with a TF prefix on the back. The backs also feature a color photo with text information.

COMPLETE SET (26) 75.00 200.00
TF1 Guy Hebert 2.00 5.00
TF2 Cam Neely 4.00 10.00
TF3 Pat LaFontaine 4.00 10.00
TF4 Theo Fleury 2.00 5.00
TF5 Jeremy Roenick 4.00 10.00
TF6 Mike Modano 4.00 10.00
TF7 Sergei Fedorov 5.00 12.00
TF8 Jason Arnott 2.00 5.00
TF9 John Vanbiesbrouck 2.00 5.00
TF10 Geoff Sanderson 2.00 5.00
TF11 Wayne Gretzky 15.00 40.00
TF12 Patrick Roy 10.00 25.00
TF13 Scott Stevens 2.00 5.00
TF14 Pierre Turgeon 2.00 5.00
TF15 Mark Messier 4.00 10.00
TF16 Alexandre Daigle 2.00 5.00
TF17 Eric Lindros 4.00 10.00
TF18 Mario Lemieux 10.00 25.00
TF19 Joe Sakic 6.00 15.00
TF20 Brett Hull 5.00 12.00
TF21 Arturs Irbe 2.00 5.00
TF22 Daren Puppa 2.00 5.00
TF23 Doug Gilmour 2.00 5.00
TF24 Pavel Bure 4.00 10.00
TF25 Joe Juneau 2.00 5.00
TF26 Teemu Selanne 4.00 10.00

1994-95 Score 90 Plus Club

The 21 cards in this set were randomly inserted into Score retail jumbo packs at the rate of 1:4. The set features all players who tallied more than 90 points in the previous season. The cards have a full tan border. A simple round set logo is on the lower portion of the card. The player name is in gold foil. The backs are team color coordinated, with a player photo, and short text information. The cards are numbered with an "NP" prefix.

COMPLETE SET (21) 30.00 60.00
1 Wayne Gretzky 8.00 20.00
2 Sergei Fedorov 2.00 5.00
3 Adam Oates 1.00 2.50
4 Doug Gilmour 1.00 2.50
5 Pavel Bure 1.50 4.00
6 Jeremy Roenick 2.00 5.00
7 Mark Recchi 1.00 2.50
8 Brendan Shanahan 1.50 4.00
9 Jaromir Jagr 3.00 8.00
10 Dave Andreychuk .40 1.00
11 Brett Hull 2.00 5.00
12 Eric Lindros 1.50 4.00
13 Rod Brind'Amour 1.00 2.50
14 Pierre Turgeon 1.00 2.50
15 Ray Sheppard .40 1.00
16 Mike Modano 2.00 5.00
17 Robert Reichel .40 1.00
18 Ron Francis 1.00 2.50
19 Joe Sakic 4.00 10.00
20 Vincent Damphousse .40 1.00
21 Ray Bourque 2.00 5.00

1994-95 Score Team Canada

The 24 cards in this set were randomly inserted into Score Canadian retail and hobby product at the rate of 1:36 packs. The cards feature a holographic player photo front with a background that reads Lillehammer. The set highlights players from the Canadian Olympic team which took home the silver in the 1994 Games. Although included in this set, Brett Lindros actually did not play in Norway due to an injury. The backs have a full color player portrait over a maple leaf background. The cards are numbered with a CT prefix.

COMPLETE SET (24) 30.00 60.00
CT1 Paul Kariya 5.00 12.00
CT2 Petr Nedved 1.50 4.00
CT3 Todd Warriner 1.25 3.00
CT4 Corey Hirsch 1.50 4.00
CT5 Greg Johnson 1.25 3.00
CT6 Chris Kontos 1.25 3.00
CT7 Dwayne Norris 1.25 3.00
CT8 Brian Savage 1.50 4.00
CT9 Todd Hlushko 1.25 3.00
CT10 Fabian Joseph 1.25 3.00
CT11 Greg Parks 1.25 3.00
CT12 Jean-Yves Roy 1.25 3.00
CT13 Mark Astley 1.25 3.00
CT14 Adrian Aucoin 1.25 3.00
CT15 David Harlock 1.25 3.00
CT16 Ken Lovsin 1.25 3.00
CT17 Derek Mayer 1.25 3.00
CT18 Brad Schlegel 1.25 3.00
CT19 Chris Therien 1.50 4.00
CT20 Manny Legace 2.00 5.00
CT21 Brad Werenka 1.25 3.00
CT22 Wally Schreiber 1.25 3.00
CT23 Allain Roy 1.25 3.00
CT24 Brett Lindros 1.25 3.00

1994-95 Score Top Rookie Redemption

The 10 cards in this set were available only through a redemption card offer. Redemption cards were inserted at the rate of 1:48 Score packs. The redemption cards were individually numbered 1-10, but do not mention the player for whom they are redeemable. The mail-in offer expired April 1, 1995. These redemption cards are priced in the header below. Top Rookie redeemed cards have a cut-out photo of the player over a silver foil background. The Top Rookie logo runs down the right side of the card; the player name, position and team logo are on the bottom of the card. The back has a color photo with text information and is numbered with a "TR" prefix.

COMPLETE SET (10) 20.00 40.00
1 Paul Kariya 8.00 20.00
2 Peter Forsberg 8.00 20.00
3 Brett Lindros 1.25 3.00
4 Oleg Tverdovsky 1.25 3.00
5 Jamie Storr 1.25 3.00
6 Kenny Jonsson 1.25 3.00
7 Brian Rolston 1.25 3.00
8 Jeff Friesen 1.25 3.00
9 Todd Harvey 1.25 3.00
10 Victor Kozlov 1.25 3.00

1995-96 Score Promos

Enclosed in a cello pack, this nine-card standard-size set was issued to preview the 1995-96 Score hockey series. The cards are identical in design to their regular issue counterparts, save for the way the player's name is presented on the back and the hole punched into the upper right corner. On the promos, it is last name only, while the regular cards include Christian name as well.

COMPLETE SEALED SET (9) .75 2.00
3 Chris Chelios .08 .25
8 Jason Arnott .02 .10
10 Mark Recchi .05 .15
19 Trevor Kidd .05 .15
25 Martin Brodeur .20 .50
33 Keith Tkachuk .15 .40
313 Jamie Linden .01 .05
3 Cam Neely .40 1.00
Border Battle
NNO Ad Card .01 .05

1995-96 Score

This 330 card standard-size set was issued in one series in packs of 12-card hobby, 12-card retail and 24-card retail jumbo. Canadian packs of 5-cards each also were available. These packs also held chase cards, but because of the pack size, the odds were considerably more difficult. The fronts feature a full-color action photo on a white background with the player's last

name at the bottom and the team name at the top both in team colors. The backs have a color photo with the player's name at the top. Player information, statistics and the team emblem are also on the back of the card. Subsets are Rookies (291-315) and Stoppers (316-325). The Ron Hextall Contest Winner card (#AD4) was awarded to collectors who correctly spotted four errors in a photograph in a contest sponsored by Score. The card back approximates the standard Score issue, but the front uses a silver prismatic foil background.

COMPLETE SET (330) 6.00 15.00
1 Jaromir Jagr .10 .30
2 Adam Graves .01 .05
3 Chris Chelios .07 .20
4 Felix Potvin .07 .20
5 Joe Sakic .15 .40
6 Chris Pronger .07 .20
7 Teemu Selanne .07 .20
8 Jason Arnott .01 .05
9 John LeClair .07 .20
10 Mark Recchi .02 .10
11 Rob Blake .02 .10
12 Kevin Hatcher .01 .05
13 Shawn Burr .01 .05
14 Brett Lindros .01 .05
15 Craig Janney .01 .05
16 Oleg Tverdovsky .01 .05
17 Blaine Lacher .02 .10
18 Alexandre Daigle .01 .05
19 Trevor Kidd .02 .10
20 Brendan Shanahan .07 .20
21 Alexander Mogilny .02 .10
22 Stu Barnes .01 .05
23 Jeff Brown .01 .05
24 Paul Coffey .07 .20
25 Martin Brodeur .20 .50
26 Darryl Sydor .02 .10
27 Steve Smith .01 .05
28 Ted Donato .01 .05
29 Bernie Nicholls .01 .05
30 Kenny Jonsson .01 .05
31 Peter Forsberg .20 .50
32 Sean Burke .02 .10
33 Keith Tkachuk .07 .20
34 Todd Marchant .01 .05
35 Mikael Renberg .02 .10
36 Vincent Damphousse .01 .05
37 Rick Tocchet .02 .10
38 Todd Harvey .02 .10
39 Chris Gratton .01 .05
40 Darius Kasparaitis .01 .05
41 Sergei Nemchinov .01 .05
42 Bob Corkum .01 .05
43 Bryan Smolinski .01 .05
44 Kevin Stevens .01 .05
45 Phil Housley .02 .10
46 Al MacInnis .02 .10
47 Alexei Zhitnik .01 .05
48 Rob Niedermayer .02 .10
49 Kirk McLean .02 .10
50 Mark Messier .07 .20
51 Nicklas Lidstrom .07 .20
52 Scott Niedermayer .01 .05
53 Peter Bondra .02 .10
54 Luc Robitaille .02 .10
55 Jeremy Roenick .08 .25
56 Mats Sundin .07 .20
57 Wendel Clark .02 .10
58 Todd Elik .01 .05
59 Dave Manson .01 .05
60 David Oliver .01 .05
61 Yuri Khmylev .01 .05
62 Sergei Krivokrasov .01 .05
63 Randy Wood .01 .05
64 Andy Moog .07 .20
65 Petr Klima .01 .05
66 Ray Ferraro .01 .05
67 Sandis Ozolinsh .01 .05
68 Joe Sacco .01 .05
69 Zarley Zalapski .01 .05
70 Ron Tugnutt .07 .20
71 German Titov .01 .05
72 Ian Laperriere .01 .05
73 Doug Gilmour .02 .10
74 Brian Skrudland .01 .05
75 Cliff Ronning .01 .05
76 Brian Savage .01 .05
77 John MacLean .02 .10
78 Jim Carey .02 .10
79 Alexei Kovalev .01 .05
80 Brian Rolston .01 .05
81 Shawn McEachern .01 .05
82 Gary Suter .01 .05
83 Owen Nolan .02 .10
84 Ray Whitney .02 .10
85 Alexei Zhamnov .02 .10
86 Shawn Chambers .01 .05
87 Ed Belfour .07 .20
88 Patrice Tardif .01 .05
89 Greg Adams .01 .05
90 Pierre Turgeon .02 .10
91 Jeff Friesen .01 .05
92 Marty McSorley .01 .05
93 Dave Gagner .01 .05
94 Guy Hebert .02 .10
95 Keith Jones .02 .10
96 Kirk Muller .01 .05
97 Gary Roberts .01 .05
98 Chris Therien .01 .05
99 Steve Duchesne .01 .05
100 Sergei Fedorov .10 .30
101 Donald Audette .01 .05
102 Jyrki Lumme .01 .05
103 Darrin Shannon .01 .05
104 Gord Murphy .01 .05
105 John Cullen .01 .05
106 Bill Guerin .01 .05
107 Dale Hunter .02 .10
108 Uwe Krupp .01 .05
109 Dave Andreychuk .02 .10
110 Joe Murphy .01 .05
111 Geoff Sanderson .02 .10
112 Garry Galley .01 .05
113 Ron Sutter .01 .05
114 Viktor Kozlov .02 .10
115 Jari Kurri .07 .20
116 Paul Ysebaert .01 .05
117 Vladimir Malakhov .01 .05
118 Josef Beranek .01 .05
119 Adam Oates .02 .10
120 Mike Modano .10 .30
121 Theo Fleury .01 .05
122 Pat Verbeek .01 .05
123 Esa Tikkanen .01 .05
124 Brian Leetch .02 .10
125 Paul Kariya .07 .20
126 Ken Wregget .02 .10
127 Ray Sheppard .01 .05
128 Jason Allison .01 .05
129 Dave Ellett .01 .05
130 Stephane Richer .02 .10
131 Jocelyn Thibault .07 .20
132 Martin Straka .01 .05
133 Tony Amonte .02 .10
134 Scott Mellanby .01 .05
135 Pavel Bure .07 .20
136 Andrew Cassels .01 .05
137 Ulf Dahlen .01 .05
138 Valeri Bure .01 .05
139 Teppo Numminen .01 .05
140 Mike Richter .07 .20
141 Rob Gaudreau .01 .05
142 Nikolai Khabibulin .02 .10
143 Mariusz Czerkawski .01 .05
144 Mark Tinordi .01 .05
145 Patrick Roy .40 1.00
146 Steve Chiasson .01 .05
147 Mike Donnelly .01 .05
148 Patrice Brisebois .01 .05
149 Jason Wiemer .01 .05
150 Eric Lindros .07 .20
151 Dimitri Khristich .01 .05
152 Tom Barrasso .02 .10
153 Curtis Leschyshyn .01 .05
154 Robert Kron .01 .05
155 Jesse Belanger .01 .05
156 Brian Noonan .01 .05
157 Mike Peca .02 .10
158 Patrick Poulin .01 .05
159 Sergei Makarov .01 .05
160 Scott Stevens .02 .10
161 Sergio Momesso .01 .05
162 Todd Gill .01 .05
163 Don Sweeney .01 .05
164 Randy Burridge .01 .05
165 Slava Kozlov .02 .10
166 Shaun Van Allen .01 .05
167 Steven Rice .01 .05
168 Adam Deadmarsh .01 .05
169 Andrei Nikolishin .01 .05
170 Valeri Karpov .01 .05
171 Doug Bodger .01 .05
172 Corey Millen .01 .05
173 Mark Fitzpatrick .02 .10
174 Bob Errey .01 .05
175 Dan Quinn .01 .05
176 Vladimir Konstantinov .02 .10
177 Scott Lachance .01 .05
178 Jeff Norton .01 .05
179 Valeri Zelepukin .01 .05
180 Dmitri Mironov .01 .05
181 Pat Peake .01 .05
182 Dominic Roussel .02 .10
183 Sylvain Cote .01 .05
184 Pat Falloon .01 .05
185 Roman Hamrlik .02 .10
186 Joel Otto .01 .05
187 Ron Francis .02 .10
188 Sergei Zubov .01 .05
189 Arturs Irbe .02 .10
190 Radek Bonk .01 .05
191 John Tucker .01 .05
192 Sylvain Lefebvre .01 .05
193 Doug Brown .01 .05
194 Glen Wesley .01 .05
195 Ron Hextall .02 .10
196 Patrick Flatley .01 .05
197 Darcy Wakaluk .02 .10
198 Kelly Hrudey .02 .10
199 Ray Bourque .10 .30
200 Dominik Hasek .15 .40
201 Pat LaFontaine .07 .20
202 Chris Osgood .08 .25
203 Ulf Samuelsson .01 .05
204 Mike Gartner .02 .10
205 Stephane Fiset .02 .10
206 Mathieu Schneider .01 .05
207 Eric Desjardins .02 .10
208 Trevor Linden .02 .10
209 Cam Neely .07 .20
210 Daren Puppa .02 .10
211 Steve Larmer .02 .10
212 Tim Cheveldae .02 .10
213 Derek Plante .01 .05
214 Murray Craven .01 .05
215 Tommy Soderstrom .02 .10
216 Bob Bassen .01 .05
217 Marty McInnis .01 .05
218 Dave Lowry .01 .05
219 Mike Vernon .02 .10
220 Petr Nedved .02 .10
221 Yves Racine .01 .05
222 Dale Hawerchuk .07 .20
223 Wayne Presley .01 .05
224 Darren Turcotte .01 .05
225 Derian Hatcher .01 .05
226 Steve Thomas .02 .10
227 Stephane Matteau .01 .05
228 Grant Fuhr .07 .20
229 Joe Nieuwendyk .02 .10
230 Alexei Yashin .01 .05
231 Brian Bellows .01 .05
232 Brian Bradley .01 .05
233 Tony Granato .01 .05
234 Mike Ricci .02 .10
235 Brett Hull .08 .25
236 Mike Ridley .01 .05
237 Al Iafrate .02 .10
238 Derek King .01 .05
239 Bill Ranford .02 .10
240 Steve Yzerman .40 1.00
241 John Vanbiesbrouck .07 .20
242 Russ Courtnall .01 .05
243 Chris Terreri .02 .10
244 Rod Brind'Amour .02 .10
245 Shayne Corson .01 .05
246 Don Beaupre .02 .10
247 Dino Ciccarelli .02 .10
248 Kevin Lowe .02 .10
249 Craig MacTavish .02 .10
250 Wayne Gretzky .50 1.25
251 Curtis Joseph .07 .20
252 Joe Mullen .02 .10
253 Andrei Kovalenko .01 .05
254 Igor Larionov .01 .05
255 Geoff Courtnall .01 .05
256 Joe Juneau .02 .10
257 Bruce Driver .01 .05
258 Michal Pivonka .01 .05
259 Nelson Emerson .01 .05
260 Larry Murphy .02 .10
261 Brent Gilchrist .01 .05
262 Benoit Hogue .01 .05
263 Doug Weight .02 .10
264 Keith Primeau .01 .05
265 Neal Broten .02 .10
266 Mike Keane .01 .05
267 Zigmund Palffy .02 .10
268 Valeri Kamensky .02 .10
269 Claude Lemieux .01 .05
270 Bryan Marchment .01 .05
271 Kelly Miller .01 .05
272 Brent Sutter .01 .05
273 Glenn Healy .02 .10
274 Sergei Brylin .01 .05
275 Tie Domi .02 .10
276 Norm Maciver .01 .05
277 Kevin Dineen .01 .05
278 Scott Young .01 .05
279 Tomas Sandstrom .01 .05
280 Guy Carbonneau .07 .20
281 Denis Savard .02 .10
282 Ed Olczyk .01 .05
283 Adam Creighton .01 .05
284 Tom Chorske .01 .05
285 Roman Oksiuta .01 .05
286 David Roberts .01 .05
287 Petr Svoboda .01 .05
288 Brad May .01 .05
289 Michael Nylander .01 .05
290 Jon Casey UER .02 .10
(back photo depicts Curtis Joseph)
291 Philippe DeRouville .01 .05
292 Craig Johnson .01 .05
293 Chris McAlpine RC .01 .05
294 Ralph Intranuovo .01 .05
295 Richard Park .01 .05
296 Todd Warriner .01 .05
297 Craig Conroy RC .01 .05
298 Marek Malik .01 .05
299 Manny Fernandez .07 .20
300 Cory Stillman .01 .05
301 Kevin Brown .01 .05
302 Steve Larouche RC .01 .05
303 Chris Taylor .01 .05
304 Ryan Smyth .02 .10
305 Craig Darby RC .01 .05
306 Radim Bicanek .01 .05
307 Shean Donovan .01 .05
308 Jason Bonsignore .01 .05
309 Chris Marinucci RC .01 .05
310 Brian Holzinger RC .07 .20
311 Mike Torchia RC .02 .10
312 Eric Daze .02 .10
313 Jamie Linden .01 .05
314 Tommy Salo RC .30 .75
315 Martin Gendron .01 .05
316 Felix Potvin ST .02 .10
317 Jim Carey ST .01 .05
318 Ed Belfour ST .07 .20
319 Mike Vernon ST .02 .10
320 Sean Burke ST .02 .10
321 Mike Richter ST .07 .20
322 John Vanbiesbrouck ST .02 .10
323 Martin Brodeur ST .07 .20
324 Patrick Roy ST .20 .50
325 Dominik Hasek ST .07 .20
326 Checklist .01 .05
Pacific Division
327 Checklist .01 .05
Central Division
328 Checklist .01 .05
Atlantic Division
329 Checklist .01 .05
Northeast Division
330 Checklist - Chase .01 .05
AD4 Ron Hextall Contest Winner 2.50 5.00

1995-96 Score Black Ice Artist's Proofs

This 330-card set is a high-end parallel of the basic Score issue. The cards can be differentiated from the standard issue by a black foil background with the words "Artist's Proof" written throughout. The cards were randomly inserted 1:36 packs.

*VETS: 40X TO 100X BASIC CARDS

1995-96 Score Black Ice

This 330-card set is a parallel version of the basic set. Card fronts differ in that they feature a silver, metallic background surrounded by a grayish border. The words "Black Ice" are stamped on the back in a gray block. They were inserted one in every three packs.

*VETS: 4X TO 10X BASIC CARDS

1995-96 Score Border Battle

This 15-card standard-size set was inserted in 12-card hobby and retail packs at a rate of one in 12 and retail jumbos at a rate of one in 9. The set features the top players from different countries. The fronts have a color action photo with the background in the color of the player's home country. The left side of the card has a gold foil triangle jutting out with a red circle in it that has the words "Border Battle" and the country's flag. The backs have a color head shot and an action photo tinted in the color of the player's country. The backs also state the player's home country and have information on him. The cards are numbered "X of 15" at the bottom.

COMPLETE SET (15) 10.00 20.00
1 Pierre Turgeon .25 .60
2 Wayne Gretzky 3.00 8.00
3 Cam Neely .50 1.25
4 Joe Sakic 1.00 2.50
5 Doug Gilmour .25 .60
6 Brett Hull .60 1.50
7 Pat LaFontaine .50 1.25
8 Joe Mullen .25 .60
9 Mike Modano .75 2.00
10 Jeremy Roenick .60 1.50
11 Pavel Bure .50 1.25
12 Alexei Zhamnov .25 .60
13 Sergei Fedorov UER .75 2.00
14 Jaromir Jagr .75 2.00
15 Mats Sundin .50 1.25

1995-96 Score Check It

This 12-card standard-size set was inserted in 12-card retail packs at a rate of 1:36, and in 1:86 Canadian packs. Cards were numbered "X of 12" at the topof the card backs.

COMPLETE SET (12) 15.00 40.00
1 Eric Lindros 4.00 10.00
2 Owen Nolan .75 2.00
3 Brett Lindros .75 2.00
4 Chris Gratton .75 2.00
5 Chris Pronger 2.00 5.00
6 Adam Deadmarsh .75 2.00
7 Peter Forsberg 6.00 15.00
8 Derian Hatcher .75 2.00
9 Rob Blake .75 2.00
10 Jeff Friesen .75 2.00
11 Keith Tkachuk 1.50 4.00
12 Mike Ricci .75 2.00

1995-96 Score Dream Team

This 12-card standard-size set was inserted in 12-card hobby and retail packs at a rate of 1:72. The cards are numbered "X of 12" at the top.

COMPLETE SET (12) 30.00 60.00
1 Wayne Gretzky 12.50 30.00
2 Sergei Fedorov 1.25 3.00
3 Eric Lindros 1.00 2.50
4 Mark Messier 1.25 3.00
5 Peter Forsberg 3.00 8.00
6 Doug Gilmour .60 1.50
7 Paul Kariya 1.00 2.50
8 Jaromir Jagr 2.00 5.00
9 Brett Hull 1.25 3.00
10 Pavel Bure 1.00 2.50
11 Patrick Roy 6.00 15.00
12 Jim Carey .40 1.00

1995-96 Score Golden Blades

This 20-card set was randomly inserted in 1:18 retail jumbo packs. The cards, which feature the fastest skaters in the game, are printed on gold prismatic foil.

COMPLETE SET (20) 25.00 50.00
1 Joe Sakic 3.00 8.00
2 Teemu Selanne 1.50 4.00
3 Alexander Mogilny .40 1.00
4 Peter Bondra .40 1.00
5 Paul Coffey .75 2.00
6 Mike Modano 2.00 5.00
7 Alexei Yashin .40 1.00
8 Pat LaFontaine .75 2.00
9 Paul Kariya 2.00 5.00
10 Peter Forsberg 3.00 8.00
11 Jeff Friesen .40 1.00
12 Steve Yzerman 5.00 12.00
13 Theo Fleury .75 2.00
14 Stephane Richer .40 1.00
15 Mark Messier 2.00 5.00
16 Mats Sundin 1.50 4.00
17 Brendan Shanahan 1.50 4.00
18 Mark Recchi .75 2.00
19 Jeremy Roenick 1.50 4.00
20 Jason Arnott .40 1.00

1995-96 Score Lamplighters

This 15-card standard-size set was inserted in 12-card hobby packs at a rate of 1:36. The cards, which feature the top goal scorers in the game, are printed on a silver prismatic foil card stock.

COMPLETE SET (15) 25.00 50.00
1 Wayne Gretzky 8.00 20.00
2 Pavel Bure 1.25 3.00
3 Cam Neely 1.25 3.00
4 Owen Nolan .60 1.50
5 Sergei Fedorov 1.25 3.00
6 Pierre Turgeon .60 1.50
7 Peter Bondra .60 1.50
8 Mikael Renberg .60 1.50
9 Luc Robitaille .60 1.50
10 Alexei Zhamnov .60 1.50
11 Brett Hull 1.50 3.00
12 Jaromir Jagr 2.00 5.00
13 Theo Fleury .60 1.50
14 Teemu Selanne 1.25 3.00
15 Eric Lindros 1.25 3.00

1996-97 Score Samples

This eight-card set features samples of the 1996-97 Score hockey issue. Interestingly, all samples mirror the linen-stock Golden Blades parallel set rather than the basic issue. The cards are identical in design to their regular counterparts with the exception of the word "sample" printed on the backs at the bottom. The cards are listed below according to their regular issue numbers.

COMPLETE SET (8) 3.00 8.00
1 Patrick Roy 1.00 2.50
10GBW Martin Brodeur .50 1.25
Golden Blades WINNER
10W Martin Brodeur WINNER .50 1.25
10 Martin Brodeur .50 1.25
16 Alexander Mogilny .20 .50
19 Brett Hull .25 .60
63 John Vanbiesbrouck .30 .75
77 Sergei Fedorov .40 1.00
236 Eric Daze .20 .50
238 Saku Koivu .20 .50

1996-97 Score

The 1996-97 Score set -- the first release of that season -- was issued in one series totalling 275 cards. The 10-card packs retailed for $.99 each. The cards featured action photography on the front complemented by simple white borders, while the backs were highlighted by another photograph and complete career stats. The only rookie of note is Ethan Moreau.

COMPLETE SET (275) 5.00 10.00
1 Patrick Roy .50 1.25
2 Brendan Shanahan .08 .25
3 Rob Niedermayer .02 .10
4 Jeff Friesen .01 .05
5 Teppo Numminen .01 .05
6 Mario Lemieux .50 1.25
7 Eric Lindros .08 .25
8 Paul Kariya .08 .25
9 Joe Sakic .20 .50
10 Martin Brodeur .25 .60
11 Mark Tinordi .01 .05
12 Theo Fleury .01 .05
13 Guy Hebert .02 .10
14 Dave Gagner .02 .10
15 Travis Green .02 .10
16 Alexander Mogilny .02 .10
17 Stephane Fiset .02 .10
18 Dominik Hasek .20 .50
19 Brett Hull .10 .30
20 Zdeno Ciger .01 .05
21 Pat Falloon .01 .05
22 Jyrki Lumme .01 .05
23 Rick Tabaracci .02 .10
24 Mark Messier .08 .25
25 Yanic Perreault .01 .05
26 Mark Recchi .02 .10
27 Alexander Selivanov .01 .05
28 Chris Terreri .02 .10
29 Jaromir Jagr .15 .40
30 Ted Donato .01 .05
31 Scott Mellanby .02 .10
32 Geoff Courtnall .01 .05
33 Michal Pivonka .01 .05
34 Glenn Healy .02 .10
35 Pavel Bure .08 .25
36 Chris Chelios .08 .25
37 Nelson Emerson .01 .05
38 Petr Nedved .02 .10
39 Greg Adams .01 .05
40 Bill Ranford .02 .10
41 Wayne Gretzky .60 1.50
42 Wendel Clark .02 .10
43 Sandis Ozolinsh .01 .05
44 Dave Andreychuk .02 .10
45 Brian Bradley .01 .05
46 Sean Burke .02 .10
47 Keith Tkachuk .08 .25
48 Brad May .02 .10
49 Brent Gilchrist .01 .05
50 Vincent Damphousse .01 .05
51 Dale Hawerchuk .01 .05
52 Randy Burridge .01 .05
53 Ray Bourque .15 .40
54 Keith Primeau .01 .05
55 Jason Arnott .01 .05
56 Ron Francis .02 .10
57 Craig Janney .02 .10
58 Trevor Kidd .02 .10
59 Jason Dawe .01 .05
60 Steve Yzerman .50 1.25
61 Alexei Kovalev .01 .05
62 Steve Duchesne .01 .05
63 John Vanbiesbrouck .02 .10
64 Steve Thomas .01 .05
65 Bernie Nicholls .01 .05
66 Alexandre Daigle .01 .05
67 Pat Peake .01 .05
68 Kelly Hrudey .02 .10
69 Owen Nolan .02 .10
70 Alexei Zhitnik .01 .05
71 Pierre Turgeon .02 .10
72 Mike Modano .15 .40
73 Slava Fetisov .01 .05
74 Jim Carey .08 .25
75 Larry Murphy .02 .10
76 Roman Oksiuta .01 .05
77 Sergei Fedorov .10 .30
78 Shayne Corson .01 .05
79 Michael Nylander .01 .05
80 Ron Hextall .02 .10

81 Adam Graves .01 .05
82 Tommy Soderstrom .02 .10
83 Robert Svehla .01 .05
84 Vladimir Konstantinov .02 .10
85 Jeff Hackett .01 .05
86 Todd Harvey .01 .05
87 Jeff Brown .01 .05
88 Bryan Smolinski .01 .05
89 Oleg Tverdovsky .02 .10
90 Curtis Joseph .08 .25
91 Grant Fuhr .02 .10
92 Rick Tocchet .02 .10
93 Adam Deadmarsh .01 .05
94 Pat Verbeek .01 .05
95 Doug Gilmour .02 .10
96 Jocelyn Thibault .08 .25
97 Radek Bonk .01 .05
98 Martin Gelinas .01 .05
99 Peter Forsberg .25 .60
100 Joe Murphy .01 .05
101 Dino Ciccarelli .02 .10
102 Rod Brind'Amour .02 .10
103 Kirk Muller .01 .05
104 Andy Moog .02 .10
105 Nikolai Khabibulin .02 .10
106 Mike Ricci .01 .05
107 Ray Ferraro .01 .05
108 Scott Niedermayer .01 .05
109 Russ Courtnall .01 .05
110 Dale Hunter .01 .05
111 Cam Neely .08 .25
112 Ray Sheppard .02 .10
113 Luc Robitaille .02 .10
114 Al MacInnis .02 .10
115 Mathieu Schneider .01 .05
116 Claude Lemieux .01 .05
117 Kevin Hatcher .01 .05
118 Daren Puppa .02 .10
119 Geoff Sanderson .02 .10
120 Zigmund Palffy .02 .10
121 Denis Savard .02 .10
122 Dimitri Khristich .01 .05
123 Ed Belfour .08 .25
124 Tom Barrasso .02 .10
125 Bob Rouse .01 .05
126 Tomas Sandstrom .01 .05
127 Roman Hamrlik .02 .10
128 Alexei Zhamnov .02 .10
129 Chris Osgood .08 .25
130 Rob Blake .02 .10
131 Garry Galley .01 .05
132 Greg Johnson .01 .05
133 Brian Skrudland .01 .05
134 Martin Rucinsky .01 .05
135 Steve Konowalchuk .01 .05
136 Damian Rhodes .02 .10
137 Jeremy Roenick .10 .30
138 Scott Stevens .02 .10
139 Pat LaFontaine .08 .25
140 Scott Young .01 .05
141 Benoit Hogue .01 .05
142 Paul Coffey .08 .25
143 John MacLean .02 .10
144 Joe Juneau .01 .05
145 Teemu Selanne .08 .25
146 Andrew Cassels .01 .05
147 Brian Savage .01 .05
148 Chris Gratton .02 .10
149 Corey Hirsch .02 .10
150 Mike Richter .08 .25
151 Shawn McEachern .01 .05
152 Joe Nieuwendyk .02 .10
153 Phil Housley .02 .10
154 Mike Gartner .02 .10
155 Kirk McLean .02 .10
156 Bob Probert .02 .10
157 Valeri Kamensky .02 .10
158 Vyacheslav Kozlov .01 .05
159 Eric Desjardins .02 .10
160 Mats Sundin .08 .25
161 John LeClair .08 .25
162 Adam Oates .02 .10
163 Cliff Ronning .01 .05
164 Mike Vernon .02 .10
165 German Titov .01 .05
166 Chris Pronger .02 .10
167 Norm Maciver .01 .05
168 Kenny Jonsson .01 .05
169 Tony Amonte .02 .10
170 Doug Weight .02 .10
171 Sergei Zubov .01 .05
172 Felix Potvin .08 .25
173 Trevor Linden .02 .10
174 Derek Plante .01 .05
175 Uwe Krupp .01 .05
176 Nicklas Lidstrom .08 .25
177 Mikael Renberg .02 .10
178 Igor Larionov .01 .05
179 Brian Leetch .08 .25
180 Stu Barnes .01 .05
181 Alexei Yashin .01 .05
182 Gary Suter .01 .05
183 Ken Wregget .02 .10
184 Mike Ridley .01 .05
185 Peter Bondra .02 .10
186 Steve Rucchin .01 .05
187 Jozef Stumpel .01 .05
188 Matthew Barnaby .02 .10
189 James Patrick .01 .05
190 Chris Simon .01 .05
191 Brent Fedyk .01 .05
192 Kris Draper .01 .05
193 David Oliver .01 .05
194 Dave Lowry .01 .05
195 Robert Kron .01 .05
196 Andrei Kovalenko .01 .05
197 Bill Guerin .01 .05
198 Ed Olczyk .01 .05
199 Yuri Khmylev .01 .05
200 Rob Ray .01 .05
201 Joe Mullen .02 .10
202 Petr Klima .01 .05
203 Todd Krygier .01 .05
204 Garth Snow .02 .10
205 Zarley Zalapski .01 .05
206 Ken Baumgartner .01 .05
207 Tony Twist .01 .05
208 Todd Gill .01 .05
209 Mike Peca .01 .05
210 Darcy Wakaluk .02 .10
211 Milos Holan .01 .05
212 Alexander Semak .01 .05
213 Jeff Reese .01 .05
214 Jon Casey .02 .10
215 Sandy McCarthy .01 .05
216 Curtis Leschyshyn .01 .05
217 Todd Marchant .01 .05
218 Bob Bassen .01 .05
219 Darren Turcotte .01 .05
220 David Reid .01 .05
221 Brian Bellows .01 .05
222 Jesse Belanger .01 .05
223 Bill Lindsay .01 .05
224 Lyle Odelein .01 .05
225 Keith Jones .01 .05
226 Sylvain Lefebvre .01 .05
227 Shaun Van Allen .01 .05
228 Dan Quinn .01 .05
229 Richard Matvichuk .01 .05
230 Craig MacTavish .01 .05
231 Craig Billington .02 .10
232 Stephane Richer .02 .10
233 Donald Audette .01 .05
234 Ulf Dahlen .01 .05
235 Steve Chiasson .01 .05
236 Eric Daze .02 .10
237 Petr Sykora .01 .05
238 Saku Koivu .08 .25
239 Ed Jovanovski .02 .10
240 Daniel Alfredsson .02 .10
241 Vitali Yachmenev .01 .05
242 Marcus Ragnarsson .01 .05
243 Cory Stillman .01 .05
244 Todd Bertuzzi .08 .25
245 Valeri Bure .01 .05
246 Jere Lehtinen .01 .05
247 Radek Dvorak .01 .05
248 Niclas Andersson .01 .05
249 Miroslav Satan .01 .05
250 Jeff O'Neill .01 .05
251 Nolan Baumgartner .01 .05
252 Roman Vopat .01 .05
253 Bryan McCabe .01 .05
254 Jamie Langenbrunner .01 .05
255 Chad Kilger .01 .05
256 Eric Fichaud .02 .10
257 Landon Wilson .01 .05
258 Kyle McLaren .01 .05
259 Aaron Gavey .01 .05
260 Byron Dafoe .02 .10
261 Grant Marshall .01 .05
262 Shane Doan .01 .05
263 Ralph Intranuovo .01 .05
264 Aki Berg .01 .05
265 Antti Tormanen .01 .05
266 Brian Holzinger .02 .10
267 Jose Theodore .10 .30
268 Ethan Moreau RC .08 .25
269 Niklas Sundstrom .01 .05
270 Brendan Witt .01 .05
271 Checklist (1-70) .01 .05
272 Checklist (71-140) .01 .05
273 Checklist (141-210) .01 .05
274 Checklist (211-275) .01 .05
275 Checklist (Chase Program) .01 .05

1996-97 Score Artist's Proofs

This 275-card parallel of the 1996-97 Score set could be differentiated from the regular cards by the bronze foil circular Artist's Proof logo on the card front. These chase cards were inserted 1:55 hobby and retail packs, and 1:27 magazine packs.

*SINGLES: 30X TO 80X BASIC CARDS

1996-97 Score Dealer's Choice Artist's Proofs

Another parallel to the Score set, these cards were sent to dealers whose customers pulled winning Golden Blades cards. The dealer mailed in the winning card and was given two cards in exchange. The customer received the Special Artist Proof while the dealer received this version. Identical to regular Artist Proofs, only the words 'Dealers Choice' were added around the circular AP logo.

*SINGLES: 75X TO 150X BASIC CARDS
TWO PER MAIL REDEMPTION

1996-97 Score Special Artist's Proofs

A parallel to the Score set, these cards were redemptions of winning Golden Blades cards, which had blacked out boxes readable only with a special lens available at hobby shops. Customers received a Special Artist Proof card while the dealers who sent in the cards for the customers received similar versions called Dealer's Choice Artist Proofs. The only difference is on the Artist Proof logo, which adds the word 'Special' on these versions.

*SINGLES: 60X TO 120X BASIC CARDS
ISSUED ONE PER GOLDEN BLADE EXCH

1996-97 Score Check It

Randomly inserted in magazine packs at a rate of 1:35, this 16-card set features some of the toughest hitters in the game.

COMPLETE SET (16) 4.00 10.00
1 Eric Lindros .30 .75
2 Peter Forsberg 2.00 5.00
3 Keith Tkachuk .30 .75
4 Cam Neely .30 .75
5 Jeremy Roenick .40 1.00
6 Brendan Shanahan .30 .75
7 Wendel Clark .30 .75
8 Owen Nolan .20 .50
9 Doug Gilmour .20 .50
10 Trevor Linden .20 .50
11 Saku Koivu .30 .75
12 Ed Jovanovski .20 .50
13 Theo Fleury .20 .50
14 Doug Weight .20 .50
15 Chris Chelios .30 .75
16 Eric Daze .20 .50

1996-97 Score Golden Blades

This 275-card set was a parallel to the basic issue. The cards were inserted at rates of 1:7 hobby and retail packs, and 1:3 magazine packs. The cards were printed on linen stock and featured the Golden Blades logo superimposed over the stat package on the card backs. Each Golden Blades card has a rectangular box within the player's picture on the back which to the naked eye, resembles television snow. But placing a special Pinnacle device over the rectangle revealed (for one out of every eight Golden Blades) the words "Special Artist's Proof". These cards were eligible to be redeemed for two more parallel cards: a Special Artist's Proof for the collector and a Dealer's Choice Artist Proof for the redeeming hobby store owner. These SAP winner cards were inserted at approximately the same rate as standard Artist Proof cards, but because of the limited redemption period, are in somewhat shorter supply. This checklist represents the Score Golden Blades cards that have Sorry Try Again in the decoder window and were not redeemable for Special Artist Proofs.

COMPLETE SET (275) 100.00 200.00
*SINGLES: 5X TO 12X BASIC CARDS

1996-97 Score Golden Blades Winners

This checklist represents the Score Golden Blades cards that are noted as Special Artist Proof winners in the decoder box. These cards were eligible to be redeemed for two more parallel cards: a Special Artist's Proof for the collector and a Dealer's Choice Artist Proof for the redeeming hobby store owner. These Special Artist Proof winner cards were inserted at approximately the same rate as standard Artist Proof cards, but because of the limited redemption period, are in somewhat shorter supply.

*SINGLES: 5X TO 12X BASIC CARDS
ISSUED VIA MAIL REDEMPTION

1 Patrick Roy 8.00 20.00
2 Brendan Shanahan 1.50 4.00
3 Rob Niedermayer .60 1.50
4 Jeff Friesen .30 .75
5 Teppo Numminen .30 .75
6 Mario Lemieux 8.00 20.00
7 Eric Lindros 1.50 4.00
8 Paul Kariya 1.50 4.00
9 Joe Sakic 3.00 8.00
10 Martin Brodeur 4.00 10.00
11 Mark Tinordi .30 .75
12 Theo Fleury .30 .75
13 Guy Hebert .60 1.50
14 Dave Gagner .60 1.50
15 Travis Green .60 1.50
16 Alexander Mogilny .60 1.50
17 Stephane Fiset .60 1.50
18 Dominik Hasek 3.00 8.00
19 Brett Hull 2.00 5.00
20 Zdeno Ciger .30 .75
21 Pat Falloon .30 .75
22 Jyrki Lumme .30 .75
23 Rick Tabaracci .60 1.50
24 Mark Messier 1.50 4.00
25 Yanic Perreault .30 .75
26 Mark Recchi .60 1.50
27 Alexander Selivanov .30 .75
28 Chris Terreri .60 1.50
29 Jaromir Jagr 2.50 6.00
30 Ted Donato .30 .75
31 Scott Mellanby .60 1.50
32 Geoff Courtnall .30 .75
33 Michal Pivonka .30 .75
34 Glenn Healy .60 1.50
35 Pavel Bure 1.50 4.00
36 Chris Chelios 1.50 4.00
37 Nelson Emerson .30 .75
38 Petr Nedved .60 1.50
39 Greg Adams .30 .75
40 Bill Ranford .60 1.50
41 Wayne Gretzky 10.00 25.00
42 Wendel Clark .60 1.50
43 Sandis Ozolinsh .30 .75
44 Dave Andreychuk .60 1.50
45 Brian Bradley .30 .75
46 Sean Burke .60 1.50
47 Keith Tkachuk 1.50 4.00
48 Brad May .30 .75
49 Brent Gilchrist .30 .75
50 Vincent Damphousse .30 .75
51 Dale Hawerchuk .60 1.50
52 Randy Burridge .30 .75
53 Ray Bourque 2.50 6.00
54 Keith Primeau .30 .75
55 Jason Arnott .30 .75
56 Ron Francis .60 1.50
57 Craig Janney .60 1.50
58 Trevor Kidd .60 1.50
59 Jason Dawe .30 .75
60 Steve Yzerman 8.00 20.00
61 Alexei Kovalev .30 .75
62 Steve Duchesne .30 .75
63 John Vanbiesbrouck .60 1.50
64 Steve Thomas .30 .75
65 Bernie Nicholls .30 .75
66 Alexandre Daigle .30 .75
67 Pat Peake .30 .75
68 Kelly Hrudey .60 1.50
69 Owen Nolan .60 1.50
70 Alexei Zhitnik .30 .75
71 Pierre Turgeon .60 1.50
72 Mike Modano 2.50 6.00
73 Slava Fetisov .30 .75
74 Jim Carey 1.50 4.00
75 Larry Murphy .60 1.50
76 Roman Oksiuta .30 .75
77 Sergei Fedorov 2.00 5.00
78 Shayne Corson .30 .75
79 Michael Nylander .30 .75
80 Ron Hextall .60 1.50
81 Adam Graves .30 .75
82 Tommy Soderstrom .60 1.50
83 Robert Svehla .30 .75
84 Vladimir Konstantinov .60 1.50
85 Jeff Hackett .60 1.50
86 Todd Harvey .30 .75
87 Jeff Brown .30 .75
88 Bryan Smolinski .30 .75
89 Oleg Tverdovsky .60 1.50
90 Curtis Joseph 1.50 4.00
91 Grant Fuhr .60 1.50
92 Rick Tocchet .60 1.50
93 Adam Deadmarsh .30 .75
94 Pat Verbeek .30 .75
95 Doug Gilmour .60 1.50
96 Jocelyn Thibault 1.50 4.00
97 Radek Bonk .30 .75
98 Martin Gelinas .30 .75
99 Peter Forsberg 4.00 10.00
100 Joe Murphy .30 .75
101 Dino Ciccarelli .60 1.50
102 Rod Brind'Amour .60 1.50
103 Kirk Muller .30 .75
104 Andy Moog .60 1.50
105 Nikolai Khabibulin .60 1.50
106 Mike Ricci .30 .75
107 Ray Ferraro .30 .75
108 Scott Niedermayer .30 .75
109 Russ Courtnall .30 .75
110 Dale Hunter .30 .75
111 Cam Neely 1.50 4.00
112 Ray Sheppard .60 1.50
113 Luc Robitaille .60 1.50
114 Al MacInnis .60 1.50
115 Mathieu Schneider .30 .75
116 Claude Lemieux .30 .75
117 Kevin Hatcher .30 .75
118 Daren Puppa .60 1.50
119 Geoff Sanderson .60 1.50
120 Zigmund Palffy .60 1.50
121 Denis Savard .60 1.50
122 Dimitri Khristich .30 .75
123 Ed Belfour 1.50 4.00
124 Tom Barrasso .60 1.50
125 Bob Rouse .30 .75
126 Tomas Sandstrom .30 .75
127 Roman Hamrlik .60 1.50
128 Alexei Zhamnov .60 1.50
129 Chris Osgood .60 1.50
130 Rob Blake .60 1.50
131 Garry Galley .30 .75
132 Greg Johnson .30 .75
133 Brian Skrudland .30 .75
134 Martin Rucinsky .30 .75
135 Steve Konowalchuk .30 .75
136 Damian Rhodes .60 1.50
137 Jeremy Roenick 2.00 5.00
138 Scott Stevens .60 1.50
139 Pat LaFontaine 1.50 4.00
140 Scott Young .30 .75
141 Benoit Hogue .30 .75
142 Paul Coffey 1.50 4.00
143 John MacLean .60 1.50
144 Joe Juneau .30 .75
145 Teemu Selanne 1.50 4.00
146 Andrew Cassels .30 .75
147 Brian Savage .30 .75
148 Chris Gratton .60 1.50
149 Corey Hirsch .60 1.50
150 Mike Richter 1.50 4.00
151 Shawn McEachern .30 .75
152 Joe Nieuwendyk .60 1.50
153 Phil Housley .60 1.50
154 Mike Gartner .60 1.50
155 Kirk McLean .60 1.50
156 Bob Probert .60 1.50
157 Valeri Kamensky .60 1.50
158 Vyacheslav Kozlov .30 .75
159 Eric Desjardins .60 1.50
160 Mats Sundin 1.50 4.00
161 John LeClair 1.50 4.00
162 Adam Oates .60 1.50
163 Cliff Ronning .30 .75
164 Mike Vernon .60 1.50
165 German Titov .30 .75
166 Chris Pronger .60 1.50
167 Norm Maciver .30 .75
168 Kenny Jonsson .30 .75
169 Tony Amonte .60 1.50
170 Doug Weight .60 1.50
171 Sergei Zubov .30 .75
172 Felix Potvin 1.50 4.00
173 Trevor Linden .60 1.50
174 Derek Plante .30 .75
175 Uwe Krupp .30 .75
176 Nicklas Lidstrom 1.50 4.00
177 Mikael Renberg .60 1.50
178 Igor Larionov .30 .75
179 Brian Leetch 1.50 4.00
180 Stu Barnes .30 .75
181 Alexei Yashin .30 .75
182 Gary Suter .30 .75
183 Ken Wregget .60 1.50
184 Mike Ridley .30 .75
185 Peter Bondra .60 1.50
186 Steve Rucchin .30 .75
187 Jozef Stumpel .30 .75
188 Matthew Barnaby .60 1.50
189 James Patrick .30 .75
190 Chris Simon .30 .75
191 Brent Fedyk .30 .75
192 Kris Draper .30 .75
193 David Oliver .30 .75
194 Dave Lowry .30 .75
195 Robert Kron .30 .75
196 Andrei Kovalenko .30 .75
197 Bill Guerin .30 .75
198 Ed Olczyk .30 .75
199 Yuri Khmylev .30 .75
200 Rob Ray .30 .75
201 Joe Mullen .60 1.50
202 Petr Klima .30 .75
203 Todd Krygier .30 .75
204 Garth Snow .60 1.50
205 Zarley Zalapski .30 .75
206 Ken Baumgartner .30 .75
207 Tony Twist .30 .75
208 Todd Gill .30 .75
209 Mike Peca .30 .75
210 Darcy Wakaluk .60 1.50
211 Milos Holan .30 .75
212 Alexander Semak .30 .75
213 Jeff Reese .30 .75
214 Jon Casey .60 1.50
215 Sandy McCarthy .30 .75
216 Curtis Leschyshyn .30 .75
217 Todd Marchant .30 .75
218 Bob Bassen .30 .75
219 Darren Turcotte .30 .75
220 David Reid .30 .75
221 Brian Bellows .30 .75
222 Jesse Belanger .30 .75
223 Bill Lindsay .30 .75
224 Lyle Odelein .30 .75
225 Keith Jones .30 .75
226 Sylvain Lefebvre .30 .75
227 Shaun Van Allen .30 .75
228 Dan Quinn .30 .75
229 Richard Matvichuk .30 .75
230 Craig MacTavish .30 .75
231 Craig Billington .60 1.50
232 Stephane Richer .60 1.50
233 Donald Audette .30 .75
234 Ulf Dahlen .30 .75
235 Steve Chiasson .30 .75
236 Eric Daze .60 1.50
237 Petr Sykora .30 .75
238 Saku Koivu 1.50 4.00
239 Ed Jovanovski .60 1.50
240 Daniel Alfredsson .60 1.50
241 Vitali Yachmenev .30 .75
242 Marcus Ragnarsson .30 .75
243 Cory Stillman .30 .75
244 Todd Bertuzzi 1.50 4.00
245 Valeri Bure .30 .75
246 Jere Lehtinen .30 .75
247 Radek Dvorak .30 .75
248 Niclas Andersson .30 .75
249 Miroslav Satan .30 .75
250 Jeff O'Neill .30 .75
251 Nolan Baumgartner .30 .75
252 Roman Vopat .30 .75
253 Bryan McCabe .30 .75
254 Jamie Langenbrunner .30 .75
255 Chad Kilger .30 .75
256 Eric Fichaud .60 1.50
257 Landon Wilson .30 .75
258 Kyle McLaren .30 .75
259 Aaron Gavey .30 .75
260 Byron Dafoe .60 1.50
261 Grant Marshall .30 .75
262 Shane Doan .30 .75
263 Ralph Intranuovo .30 .75
264 Aki Berg .30 .75
265 Antti Tormanen .30 .75
266 Brian Holzinger .60 1.50
267 Jose Theodore 2.00 5.00
268 Ethan Moreau 1.50 4.00
269 Niklas Sundstrom .30 .75
270 Brendan Witt .30 .75
271 Checklist
272 Checklist
273 Checklist
274 Checklist
275 Checklist

1996-97 Score Golden Blades Winners Punched

This checklist represents the version of the card that was sent back to collectors once they were redeemed for the Platinum version. Pinnacle punched their logo into the card over the Score logo to indicate the card has already been redeemed.

*SINGLES: 5X TO 12X BASIC CARDS
ISSUED VIA MAIL REDEMPTION

1 Patrick Roy 6.00 15.00
2 Brendan Shanahan 1.25 3.00
3 Rob Niedermayer .50 1.25
4 Jeff Friesen .25 .60
5 Teppo Numminen .25 .60
6 Mario Lemieux 6.00 15.00
7 Eric Lindros 1.25 3.00
8 Paul Kariya 1.25 3.00
9 Joe Sakic 2.50 6.00
10 Martin Brodeur 3.00 8.00
11 Mark Tinordi .25 .60
12 Theo Fleury .25 .60
13 Guy Hebert .50 1.25
14 Dave Gagner .50 1.25
15 Travis Green .50 1.25
16 Alexander Mogilny .50 1.25
17 Stephane Fiset .50 1.25
18 Dominik Hasek 2.50 6.00
19 Brett Hull 1.50 4.00
20 Zdeno Ciger .25 .60
21 Pat Falloon .25 .60
22 Jyrki Lumme .25 .60
23 Rick Tabaracci .50 1.25
24 Mark Messier 1.25 3.00
25 Yanic Perreault .25 .60
26 Mark Recchi .50 1.25
27 Alexander Selivanov .25 .60
28 Chris Terreri .50 1.25
29 Jaromir Jagr 2.00 5.00
30 Ted Donato .25 .60
31 Scott Mellanby .50 1.25
32 Geoff Courtnall .25 .60
33 Michal Pivonka .25 .60
34 Glenn Healy .50 1.25
35 Pavel Bure 1.25 3.00
36 Chris Chelios 1.25 3.00
37 Nelson Emerson .25 .60
38 Petr Nedved .50 1.25
39 Greg Adams .25 .60
40 Bill Ranford .50 1.25
41 Wayne Gretzky 8.00 20.00
42 Wendel Clark .50 1.25
43 Sandis Ozolinsh .25 .60
44 Dave Andreychuk .50 1.25
45 Brian Bradley .25 .60
46 Sean Burke .50 1.25
47 Keith Tkachuk 1.25 3.00
48 Brad May .25 .60
49 Brent Gilchrist .25 .60
50 Vincent Damphousse .25 .60
51 Dale Hawerchuk .50 1.25
52 Randy Burridge .25 .60
53 Ray Bourque 2.00 5.00
54 Keith Primeau .25 .60
55 Jason Arnott .25 .60
56 Ron Francis .50 1.25
57 Craig Janney .50 1.25
58 Trevor Kidd .50 1.25
59 Jason Dawe .25 .60
60 Steve Yzerman 6.00 15.00
61 Alexei Kovalev .25 .60
62 Steve Duchesne .25 .60
63 John Vanbiesbrouck .50 1.25
64 Steve Thomas .25 .60
65 Bernie Nicholls .25 .60
66 Alexandre Daigle .25 .60
67 Pat Peake .25 .60
68 Kelly Hrudey .50 1.25
69 Owen Nolan .50 1.25
70 Alexei Zhitnik .25 .60
71 Pierre Turgeon .50 1.25
72 Mike Modano 2.00 5.00
73 Slava Fetisov .25 .60
74 Jim Carey 1.25 3.00
75 Larry Murphy .50 1.25
76 Roman Oksiuta .25 .60
77 Sergei Fedorov 1.50 4.00
78 Shayne Corson .25 .60
79 Michael Nylander .25 .60
80 Ron Hextall .50 1.25
81 Adam Graves .25 .60
82 Tommy Soderstrom .50 1.25
83 Robert Svehla .25 .60
84 Vladimir Konstantinov .50 1.25
85 Jeff Hackett .50 1.25
86 Todd Harvey .25 .60
87 Jeff Brown .25 .60
88 Bryan Smolinski .25 .60
89 Oleg Tverdovsky .50 1.25
90 Curtis Joseph 1.25 3.00
91 Grant Fuhr .50 1.25
92 Rick Tocchet .50 1.25
93 Adam Deadmarsh .25 .60
94 Pat Verbeek .25 .60
95 Doug Gilmour .50 1.25
96 Jocelyn Thibault 1.25 3.00
97 Radek Bonk .25 .60
98 Martin Gelinas .25 .60
99 Peter Forsberg 3.00 8.00
100 Joe Murphy .25 .60
101 Dino Ciccarelli .50 1.25
102 Rod Brind'Amour .50 1.25
103 Kirk Muller .25 .60
104 Andy Moog .50 1.25
105 Nikolai Khabibulin .50 1.25
106 Mike Ricci .25 .60
107 Ray Ferraro .25 .60
108 Scott Niedermayer .25 .60
109 Russ Courtnall .25 .60
110 Dale Hunter .25 .60
111 Cam Neely 1.25 3.00
112 Ray Sheppard .50 1.25
113 Luc Robitaille .50 1.25
114 Al MacInnis .50 1.25
115 Mathieu Schneider .25 .60
116 Claude Lemieux .25 .60
117 Kevin Hatcher .25 .60
118 Daren Puppa .50 1.25
119 Geoff Sanderson .50 1.25
120 Zigmund Palffy .50 1.25
121 Denis Savard .50 1.25
122 Dimitri Khristich .25 .60
123 Ed Belfour 1.25 3.00
124 Tom Barrasso .50 1.25
125 Bob Rouse .25 .60
126 Tomas Sandstrom .25 .60
127 Roman Hamrlik .50 1.25
128 Alexei Zhamnov .50 1.25
129 Chris Osgood .50 1.25
130 Rob Blake .50 1.25
131 Garry Galley .25 .60
132 Greg Johnson .25 .60
133 Brian Skrudland .25 .60
134 Martin Rucinsky .25 .60
135 Steve Konowalchuk .25 .60
136 Damian Rhodes .50 1.25
137 Jeremy Roenick 1.50 4.00
138 Scott Stevens .50 1.25
139 Pat LaFontaine 1.25 3.00
140 Scott Young .25 .60
141 Benoit Hogue .25 .60
142 Paul Coffey 1.25 3.00
143 John MacLean .50 1.25
144 Joe Juneau .25 .60
145 Teemu Selanne 1.25 3.00
146 Andrew Cassels .25 .60
147 Brian Savage .25 .60
148 Chris Gratton .50 1.25
149 Corey Hirsch .50 1.25
150 Mike Richter 1.25 3.00
151 Shawn McEachern .25 .60
152 Joe Nieuwendyk .50 1.25
153 Phil Housley .50 1.25
154 Mike Gartner .50 1.25
155 Kirk McLean .50 1.25
156 Bob Probert .50 1.25
157 Valeri Kamensky .50 1.25
158 Vyacheslav Kozlov .25 .60
159 Eric Desjardins .50 1.25
160 Mats Sundin 1.25 3.00
161 John LeClair 1.25 3.00
162 Adam Oates .50 1.25
163 Cliff Ronning .25 .60
164 Mike Vernon .50 1.25
165 German Titov .25 .60
166 Chris Pronger .50 1.25
167 Norm Maciver .25 .60
168 Kenny Jonsson .25 .60
169 Tony Amonte .50 1.25
170 Doug Weight .50 1.25
171 Sergei Zubov .25 .60
172 Felix Potvin 1.25 3.00
173 Trevor Linden .50 1.25
174 Derek Plante .25 .60
175 Uwe Krupp .25 .60
176 Nicklas Lidstrom 1.25 3.00
177 Mikael Renberg .50 1.25
178 Igor Larionov .25 .60
179 Brian Leetch 1.25 3.00
180 Stu Barnes .25 .60
181 Alexei Yashin .25 .60
182 Gary Suter .25 .60
183 Ken Wregget .50 1.25
184 Mike Ridley .25 .60
185 Peter Bondra .50 1.25
186 Steve Rucchin .25 .60
187 Jozef Stumpel .25 .60
188 Matthew Barnaby .50 1.25
189 James Patrick .25 .60
190 Chris Simon .25 .60
191 Brent Fedyk .25 .60
192 Kris Draper .25 .60
193 David Oliver .25 .60
194 Dave Lowry .25 .60
195 Robert Kron .25 .60
196 Andrei Kovalenko .25 .60
197 Bill Guerin .25 .60
198 Ed Olczyk .25 .60
199 Yuri Khmylev .25 .60
200 Rob Ray .25 .60
201 Joe Mullen .50 1.25
202 Petr Klima .25 .60
203 Todd Krygier .25 .60
204 Garth Snow .50 1.25
205 Zarley Zalapski .25 .60
206 Ken Baumgartner .25 .60
207 Tony Twist .25 .60
208 Todd Gill .25 .60
209 Mike Peca .25 .60
210 Darcy Wakaluk .50 1.25
211 Milos Holan .25 .60
212 Alexander Semak .25 .60
213 Jeff Reese .25 .60
214 Jon Casey .50 1.25
215 Sandy McCarthy .25 .60
216 Curtis Leschyshyn .25 .60
217 Todd Marchant .25 .60
218 Bob Bassen .25 .60
219 Darren Turcotte .25 .60
220 David Reid .25 .60
221 Brian Bellows .25 .60
222 Jesse Belanger .25 .60
223 Bill Lindsay .25 .60
224 Lyle Odelein .25 .60
225 Keith Jones .25 .60
226 Sylvain Lefebvre .25 .60
227 Shaun Van Allen .25 .60
228 Dan Quinn .25 .60
229 Richard Matvichuk .25 .60
230 Craig MacTavish .25 .60
231 Craig Billington .50 1.25
232 Stephane Richer .50 1.25
233 Donald Audette .25 .60
234 Ulf Dahlen .25 .60
235 Steve Chiasson .25 .60
236 Eric Daze .50 1.25
237 Petr Sykora .25 .60
238 Saku Koivu 1.25 3.00
239 Ed Jovanovski .50 1.25
240 Daniel Alfredsson .50 1.25
241 Vitali Yachmenev .25 .60
242 Marcus Ragnarsson .25 .60
243 Cory Stillman .25 .60
244 Todd Bertuzzi 1.25 3.00
245 Valeri Bure .25 .60
246 Jere Lehtinen .25 .60
247 Radek Dvorak .25 .60
248 Niclas Andersson .25 .60
249 Miroslav Satan .25 .60
250 Jeff O'Neill .25 .60
251 Nolan Baumgartner .25 .60
252 Roman Vopat .25 .60
253 Bryan McCabe .25 .60
254 Jamie Langenbrunner .25 .60
255 Chad Kilger .25 .60
256 Eric Fichaud .50 1.25
257 Landon Wilson .25 .60
258 Kyle McLaren .25 .60
259 Aaron Gavey .25 .60
260 Byron Dafoe .50 1.25
261 Grant Marshall .25 .60
262 Shane Doan .25 .60
263 Ralph Intranuovo .25 .60
264 Aki Berg .25 .60
265 Antti Tormanen .25 .60
266 Brian Holzinger .50 1.25
267 Jose Theodore 1.50 4.00
268 Ethan Moreau 1.25 3.00
269 Niklas Sundstrom .25 .60
270 Brendan Witt .25 .60
271 Checklist
272 Checklist
273 Checklist
274 Checklist
275 Checklist

1996-97 Score Dream Team

Randomly inserted in packs at a rate of 1:71 hobby and retail packs, this 12-card set features the top players at each position in the NHL today on an all-rainbow holographic foil card stock.

COMPLETE SET (12) 10.00 25.00
1 Eric Lindros .60 1.50
2 Paul Kariya .60 1.50
3 Joe Sakic 1.25 3.00
4 Peter Forsberg 1.50 4.00
5 Mark Messier .60 1.50
6 Mario Lemieux 3.00 8.00
7 Jaromir Jagr 1.00 2.50
8 Wayne Gretzky 4.00 10.00
9 Alexander Mogilny .25 .60
10 Pavel Bure .60 1.50
11 Sergei Fedorov .75 2.00
12 Patrick Roy 3.00 8.00

1996-97 Score Net Worth

Inserted exclusively into retail packs at a rate of 1:35, these cards feature the top netminders in the NHL today. Two photos grace the front of each card, with one being a black and silver metallic image.

COMPLETE SET (18)	10.00	20.00
1 Patrick Roy	2.00	5.00
2 Martin Brodeur	2.00	5.00
3 Jim Carey	.40	1.00
4 Dominik Hasek	1.25	3.00
5 Ed Belfour	.40	1.00
6 Chris Osgood	.40	1.00
7 Curtis Joseph	.40	1.00
8 John Vanbiesbrouck	.40	1.00
9 Jocelyn Thibault	.40	1.00
10 Stephane Fiset	.40	1.00
11 Ron Hextall	.40	1.00
12 Tom Barrasso	.40	1.00
13 Daren Puppa	.40	1.00
14 Mike Vernon	.40	1.00
15 Bill Ranford	.40	1.00
16 Corey Hirsch	.40	1.00
17 Damian Rhodes	.40	1.00
18 Nikolai Khabibulin	.40	1.00

1996-97 Score Sudden Death

Randomly inserted in hobby packs only at a rate of 1:35, this 15-card holofoil set features two action photos simulating matchups of some of the deadliest snipers against the stingiest netminders.

COMPLETE SET (15)	12.00	25.00
1 Martin Brodeur	.75	2.00
Pierre Turgeon		
2 Jim Carey	1.00	2.50
Steve Yzerman		
3 Dominik Hasek	.40	1.00
Brendan Shanahan		
4 Ed Belfour	.40	1.00
Brett Hull		
5 Chris Osgood	.40	1.00
Jeremy Roenick		
6 Curtis Joseph	.40	1.00
Pavel Bure		
7 John Vanbiesbrouck	3.00	8.00
Mario Lemieux		
8 Jocelyn Thibault	.40	1.00
Alexander Mogilny		
9 Mike Richter	.40	1.00
Jaromir Jagr		
10 Tom Barrasso	.40	1.00
Mark Messier		
11 Darren Puppa	.75	2.00
Joe Sakic		
12 Felix Potvin	3.00	8.00
Wayne Gretzky		
13 Corey Hirsch	.40	1.00
Paul Kariya		
14 Ron Hextall	.40	1.00
Sergei Fedorov		
15 Nikolai Khabibulin	.40	1.00
Teemu Selanne		

1996-97 Score Superstitions

The 13-cards in this set (note the foolhardy use of this unlucky number!) highlight some of the unusual pre-game rituals and neuroses of some of the NHL's most successful players. The cards were randomly inserted 1:19 hobby and retail packs and 1:10 magazine packs.

COMPLETE SET (13)	3.00	8.00
1 Teemu Selanne	.30	.75
2 Doug Weight	.25	.60
3 Mats Sundin	.30	.75
4 Mike Modano	.40	1.00
5 Felix Potvin	.30	.75
6 Paul Coffey	.30	.75
7 Ray Bourque	.50	1.25
8 Chris Chelios	.30	.75
9 Ron Hextall	.25	.60
10 Alexander Selivanov	.25	.60
11 Brett Hull	.40	1.00
12 Mike Richter	.30	.75
13 Scott Mellanby	.25	.60

1997-98 Score

The 1997-98 Score set was issued in one series totaling 270 cards and was distributed in packs with a suggested retail price of $.99. The fronts feature color player photos in white borders. The backs carry player information.

COMPLETE SET (270)	7.50	15.00
1 Sean Burke	.05	.15
2 Chris Osgood	.05	.15
3 Garth Snow	.05	.15
4 Mike Vernon	.05	.15
5 Grant Fuhr	.05	.15
6 Guy Hebert	.05	.15
7 Arturs Irbe	.05	.15
8 Andy Moog	.05	.15
9 Tommy Salo	.05	.15
10 Nikolai Khabibulin	.05	.15
11 Mike Richter	.08	.25
12 Corey Hirsch	.05	.15
13 Bill Ranford	.05	.15
14 Jim Carey	.05	.15
15 Jeff Hackett	.05	.15
16 Damian Rhodes	.05	.15
17 Tom Barrasso	.05	.15
18 Daren Puppa	.05	.15
19 Craig Billington	.05	.15
20 Ed Belfour	.08	.25
21 Mikhail Shtalenkov	.01	.05
22 Glenn Healy	.05	.15
23 Marcel Cousineau	.05	.15
24 Kevin Hodson	.05	.15
25 Olaf Kolzig	.05	.15
26 Eric Fichaud	.05	.15
27 Ron Hextall	.05	.15
28 Rick Tabaracci	.05	.15
29 Felix Potvin	.08	.25
30 Martin Brodeur	.25	.60
31 Curtis Joseph	.08	.25
32 Ken Wregget	.05	.15
33 Patrick Roy	.50	1.25
34 John Vanbiesbrouck	.05	.15
35 Stephane Fiset	.05	.15
36 Roman Turek	.05	.15
37 Trevor Kidd	.05	.15
38 Dwayne Roloson	.01	.05
39 Dominik Hasek	.20	.50
40 Patrick Lalime	.05	.15
41 Jocelyn Thibault	.05	.15
42 Jose Theodore	.10	.30
43 Kirk McLean	.05	.15
44 Steve Shields RC	.15	.40
45 Mike Dunham	.05	.15
46 Jamie Storr	.05	.15
47 Byron Dafoe	.05	.15
48 Chris Terreri	.05	.15
49 Ron Tugnutt	.05	.15
50 Kelly Hrudey	.05	.15
51 Vaclav Prospal RC	.08	.25
52 Alyn McCauley	.05	.15
53 Jaroslav Svejkovsky	.05	.15
54 Steve Shields	.25	.60
55 Chris Dingman RC	.01	.05
56 Vadim Sharifijanov	.01	.05
57 Larry Courville	.01	.05
58 Erik Rasmussen	.01	.05
59 Sergei Samsonov	.05	.15
60 Kevyn Adams	.01	.05
61 Daniel Cleary	.05	.15
62 Martin Prochazka RC	.01	.05
63 Mattias Ohlund	.05	.15
64 Juha Lind RC	.01	.05
65 Olli Jokinen RC	.30	.75
66 Espen Knutsen RC	.20	.50
67 Marc Savard	.05	.15
68 Hnat Domenichelli	.01	.05
69 Warren Luhning RC	.01	.05
70 Magnus Arvedson RC	.01	.05
71 Chris Phillips	.01	.05
72 Brad Isbister	.01	.05
73 Boyd Devereaux	.01	.05
74 Alexei Morozov	.05	.15
75 Vladimir Vorobiev RC	.01	.05
76 Steven Rice	.01	.05
77 Tony Granato	.01	.05
78 Lonny Bohonos	.01	.05
79 Dave Gagner	.01	.05
80 Brendan Shanahan	.08	.25
81 Brett Hull	.10	.30
82 Jaromir Jagr	.15	.40
83 Peter Forsberg	.25	.60
84 Paul Kariya	.08	.25
85 Mark Messier	.08	.25
86 Steve Yzerman	.50	1.25
87 Keith Tkachuk	.08	.25
88 Eric Lindros	.08	.25
89 Ray Bourque	.15	.40
90 Chris Chelios	.08	.25
91 Sergei Fedorov	.15	.40
92 Mike Modano	.15	.40
93 Doug Gilmour	.05	.15
94 Saku Koivu	.08	.25
95 Mats Sundin	.08	.25
96 Pavel Bure	.08	.25
97 Theo Fleury	.01	.05
98 Keith Primeau	.01	.05
99 Wayne Gretzky	.60	1.50
100 Doug Weight	.05	.15
101 Alexandre Daigle	.01	.05
102 Owen Nolan	.05	.15
103 Peter Bondra	.05	.15
104 Pat LaFontaine	.08	.25
105 Kirk Muller	.01	.05
106 Zigmund Palffy	.05	.15
107 Jeremy Roenick	.10	.30
108 John LeClair	.08	.25
109 Derek Plante	.01	.05
110 Geoff Sanderson	.05	.15
111 Dimitri Khristich	.01	.05
112 Vincent Damphousse	.01	.05
113 Teemu Selanne	.08	.25
114 Tony Amonte	.05	.15
115 Dave Andreychuk	.01	.05
116 Alexei Yashin	.01	.05
117 Adam Oates	.05	.15
118 Pierre Turgeon	.05	.15
119 Dino Ciccarelli	.01	.05
120 Ryan Smyth	.05	.15
121 Ray Sheppard	.01	.05
122 Jozef Stumpel	.01	.05
123 Jarome Iginla	.10	.30
124 Pat Verbeek	.01	.05
125 Joe Sakic	.20	.50
126 Brian Leetch	.08	.25
127 Rod Brind'Amour	.05	.15
128 Wendel Clark	.05	.15
129 Alexander Mogilny	.05	.15
130 Mark Recchi	.05	.15
131 Daniel Alfredsson	.05	.15
132 Ron Francis	.05	.15
133 Martin Gelinas	.01	.05
134 Andrew Cassels	.01	.05
135 Joe Nieuwendyk	.05	.15
136 Jason Arnott	.01	.05
137 Bryan Berard	.05	.15
138 Mikael Renberg	.05	.15
139 Mike Gartner	.05	.15
140 Joe Juneau	.05	.15
141 John MacLean	.01	.05
142 Adam Graves	.01	.05
143 Petr Nedved	.05	.15
144 Trevor Linden	.05	.15
145 Sergei Berezin	.01	.05
146 Adam Deadmarsh	.01	.05
147 Jeff O'Neill	.01	.05
148 Rob Blake	.05	.15
149 Luc Robitaille	.05	.15
150 Markus Naslund	.08	.25
151 Ethan Moreau	.01	.05
152 Martin Rucinsky	.01	.05
UER front Ruckinski		
153 Mike Grier	.01	.05
154 Craig Janney	.01	.05
155 John Cullen	.01	.05
156 Alexei Kovalev	.01	.05
157 Tony Twist	.05	.15
158 Claude Lemieux	.01	.05
159 Kevin Stevens	.05	.15
160 Mathieu Schneider	.01	.05
161 Randy Cunneyworth	.01	.05
162 Darius Kasparaitis	.01	.05
163 Joe Murphy	.01	.05
164 Brandon Convery	.01	.05
165 Janne Niinimaa	.05	.15
166 Paul Coffey	.08	.25
167 Daymond Langkow	.05	.15
168 Chris Gratton	.05	.15
169 Ray Ferraro	.01	.05
170 Jeff Friesen	.01	.05
171 Ted Donato	.01	.05
172 Brian Holzinger	.01	.05
173 Travis Green	.01	.05
174 Sandis Ozolinsh	.01	.05
175 Alexei Zhamnov	.01	.05
176 Steve Rucchin	.01	.05
177 Scott Mellanby	.01	.05
178 Andrei Kovalenko	.01	.05
179 Donald Audette	.01	.05
180 Bernie Nicholls	.01	.05
181 Jonas Hoglund	.01	.05
182 Nicklas Lidstrom	.08	.25
183 Bobby Holik	.01	.05
184 Geoff Courtnall	.01	.05
185 Steve Sullivan	.01	.05
186 Valeri Kamensky	.05	.15
187 Mike Peca	.01	.05
188 Jere Lehtinen	.01	.05
189 Robert Svehla	.01	.05
190 Darren McCarty	.01	.05
191 Brian Savage	.01	.05
192 Harry York	.01	.05
193 Eric Daze	.05	.15
194 Niklas Sundstrom	.01	.05
195 Oleg Tverdovsky	.01	.05
196 Eric Desjardins	.05	.15
197 German Titov	.01	.05
198 Derian Hatcher	.01	.05
199 Bill Guerin	.05	.15
200 Rob Zamuner	.01	.05
201 Dale Hunter	.01	.05
202 Darcy Tucker	.01	.05
203 Andreas Dackell	.01	.05
204 Jason Dawe	.01	.05
205 Brian Rolston	.01	.05
206 Ed Olczyk	.01	.05
207 Todd Warriner	.01	.05
208 Mariusz Czerkawski	.01	.05
209 Slava Kozlov	.01	.05
210 Marty McInnis	.01	.05
211 Jamie Langenbrunner	.01	.05
212 Vitali Yachmenev	.01	.05
213 Stephane Richer	.01	.05
214 Roman Hamrlik	.05	.15
215 Jim Campbell	.01	.05
216 Matthew Barnaby	.01	.05
217 Benoit Hogue	.01	.05
218 Robert Reichel	.01	.05
219 Tie Domi	.05	.15
220 Steve Konowalchuk	.01	.05
221 Radek Dvorak	.01	.05
222 Kevin Hatcher	.01	.05
223 Viktor Kozlov	.01	.05
224 Scott Stevens	.05	.15
225 Cory Stillman	.01	.05
226 Anson Carter	.05	.15
227 Rem Murray	.01	.05
228 Vladimir Konstantinov	.05	.15
229 Scott Niedermayer	.05	.15
230 Steve Duchesne	.01	.05
231 Valeri Bure	.01	.05
232 Miroslav Satan	.01	.05
233 Jason Allison	.01	.05
234 Mark Fitzpatrick	.05	.15
235 Ed Jovanovski	.05	.15
236 Esa Tikkanen	.01	.05
237 Stu Barnes	.01	.05
238 Darryl Sydor	.01	.05
239 Ulf Samuelsson	.01	.05
240 Dmitri Mironov	.01	.05
241 Bryan Smolinski	.01	.05
242 Rob Ray	.01	.05
243 Todd Marchant	.01	.05
244 Cliff Ronning	.01	.05
245 Alexander Selivanov	.01	.05
246 Rick Tocchet	.05	.15
247 Vladimir Malakhov	.01	.05
248 Al MacInnis	.05	.15
249 Dainius Zubrus	.08	.25
250 Keith Jones	.01	.05
251 Darren Turcotte	.01	.05
252 Ulf Dahlen	.01	.05
253 Rob Niedermayer	.01	.05
254 J.J. Daigneault	.01	.05
255 Michal Grosek	.01	.05
256 Chris Therien	.01	.05
257 Adam Foote	.01	.05
258 Tomas Sandstrom	.01	.05
259 Scott Lachance	.01	.05
260 Paul Kariya SM	.08	.25
261 Pavel Bure SM	.08	.25
262 Mike Modano SM	.08	.25
263 Steve Yzerman SM	.08	.25
264 Sergei Fedorov SM	.08	.25
265 Eric Lindros SM	.08	.25
266 Dominik Hasek CL (1-66)	.05	.15
267 Bryan Berard CL (67-132)	.01	.05
268 Mike Peca CL (133-201)	.01	.05
269 Martin Brodeur	.01	.05
Mike Dunham CL (202-270)		
270 Paul Kariya CL (inserts)	.08	.25
PR82 Jaromir Jagr PROMO	1.00	2.50
PR83 Peter Forsberg PROMO	1.25	3.00
PR84 Paul Kariya PROMO	1.50	4.00
PR86 Steve Yzerman PROMO	1.50	4.00

1997-98 Score Artist's Proofs

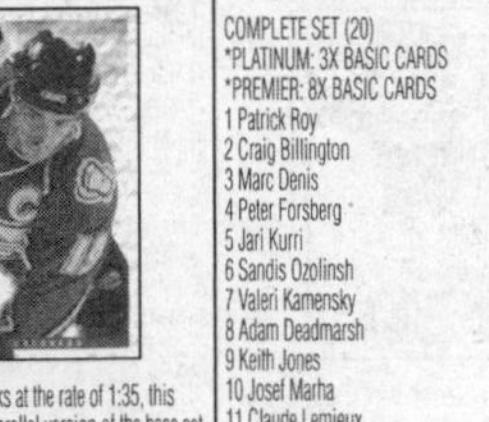

Randomly inserted in packs at the rate of 1:35, this 160-card set is a partial parallel version of the base set and is printed on prismatic foil board with the "Artist's Proof" seal on the front.

*ART.PROOF: 25X TO 60X BASIC CARDS

1997-98 Score Golden Blades

Randomly inserted in packs at the rate of 1:7, this 160-card set is a partial parallel version of the base set printed on silver gloss foil board.

*GOLDEN BLADES: 1.2X TO 3X BASIC CARDS

1997-98 Score Check It

Randomly inserted in packs at the rate of 1:18, this 18-card set features action color photos of some of the toughest hitters in the game.

COMPLETE SET (18)	3.00	6.00
1 Eric Lindros	.30	.75
2 Mark Recchi	.20	.50
3 Brendan Shanahan	.30	.75
4 Keith Tkachuk	.30	.75
5 John LeClair	.30	.75
6 Doug Gilmour	.20	.50
7 Jarome Iginla	.40	1.00
8 Ryan Smyth	.20	.50
9 Chris Chelios	.30	.75
10 Mike Grier	.05	.15
11 Vincent Damphousse	.05	.15
12 Bryan Berard	.20	.50
13 Jaromir Jagr	.50	1.25
14 Mike Peca	.05	.15
15 Dino Ciccarelli	.05	.15
16 Rod Brind'Amour	.20	.50
17 Owen Nolan	.20	.50
18 Pat Verbeek	.05	.15

1997-98 Score Net Worth

Randomly inserted in packs at the rate of 1:35, this 18-card set features color action photos of the NHL's best goalies.

COMPLETE SET (18)	8.00	15.00
1 Guy Hebert	.25	.60
2 Jim Carey	.25	.60
3 Trevor Kidd	.25	.60
4 Chris Osgood	.25	.60
5 Curtis Joseph	.40	1.00
6 Mike Richter	.40	1.00
7 Damian Rhodes	.25	.60
8 Garth Snow	.25	.60
9 Nikolai Khabibulin	.25	.60
10 Grant Fuhr	.25	.60
11 Jocelyn Thibault	.25	.60
12 Tommy Salo	.25	.60
13 Patrick Roy	2.00	5.00
14 Martin Brodeur	1.00	2.50
15 John Vanbiesbrouck	.25	.60
16 Felix Potvin	.40	1.00
17 Dominik Hasek	.75	2.00
18 Ed Belfour	.40	1.00

1997-98 Score Avalanche

This 20-card team set of the Colorado Avalanche was produced by Pinnacle and features bordered color action player photos. The backs carry player information.

COMPLETE SET (20)	4.00	10.00
*PLATINUM: 3X BASIC CARDS		
*PREMIER: 8X BASIC CARDS		
1 Patrick Roy	1.50	4.00
2 Craig Billington	.25	.60
3 Marc Denis	.25	.60
4 Peter Forsberg	1.00	2.50
5 Jari Kurri	.25	.60
6 Sandis Ozolinsh	.25	.60
7 Valeri Kamensky	.25	.60
8 Adam Deadmarsh	.25	.60
9 Keith Jones	.10	.30
10 Josef Marha	.08	.25
11 Claude Lemieux	.25	.60
12 Adam Foote	.10	.30
13 Eric Lacroix	.08	.25
14 Rene Corbet	.08	.25
15 Uwe Krupp	.08	.25
16 Sylvain Lefebvre	.08	.25
17 Mike Ricci	.25	.60
18 Joe Sakic	.75	2.00
19 Stephane Yelle	.08	.25
20 Yves Sarault	.08	.25

1997-98 Score Blues

This 20-card team set of the St. Louis Blues was produced by Pinnacle and features bordered color action player photos. The backs carry player information.

COMPLETE SET (20)	3.00	8.00
*PLATINUM: 3X BASIC CARDS		
*PREMIER: 8X BASIC CARDS		
1 Brett Hull	.40	1.00
2 Pierre Turgeon	.25	.60
3 Joe Murphy	.08	.25
4 Jim Campbell	.08	.25
5 Harry York	.08	.25
6 Al MacInnis	.25	.60
7 Chris Pronger	.25	.60
8 Darren Turcotte	.08	.25
9 Robert Petrovicky	.08	.25
10 Tony Twist	.30	.75
11 Grant Fuhr	.25	.60
12 Scott Pellerin	.08	.25
13 Jamie Rivers	.10	.25
14 Chris McAlpine	.08	.25
15 Geoff Courtnall	.25	.60
16 Steve Duchesne	.20	.50
17 Libor Zabransky	.08	.25
18 Pavol Demitra	.25	.60
19 Marc Bergevin	.08	.25
20 Jamie McLennan	.08	.25

1997-98 Score Bruins

This 20-card team set of the Boston Bruins was produced by Pinnacle and features bordered color action player photos. The backs carry player information.

COMPLETE SET (20)	2.50	6.00
*PLATINUM: 3X BASIC CARDS		
*PREMIER: 8X BASIC CARDS		
1 Shawn Bates	.08	.25
2 Jim Carey	.15	.40
3 Rob Tallas	.08	.25
4 Ray Bourque	.30	.75
5 Dimitri Khristich	.08	.25
6 Ted Donato	.08	.25
7 Jason Allison	.25	.60
8 Anson Carter	.15	.40
9 Rob Dimaio	.08	.25
10 Steve Heinze	.08	.25
11 Jean Yves Roy	.08	.25
12 Randy Robitaille	.08	.25
13 Byron Dafoe	.30	.75
14 Sergei Samsonov	.75	2.00
15 Ken Baumgartner	.08	.25
16 Dave Ellett	.08	.25
17 Joe Thornton	.75	2.00
18 Jeff Odgers	.08	.25
19 Kyle McLaren	.08	.25
20 Don Sweeney	.08	.25

1997-98 Score Canadiens

This 20-card team set of the Montreal Canadiens was produced by Pinnacle and features bordered color action player photos. The backs carry player information.

COMPLETE SET (20)	3.00	8.00
*PLATINUM: 3X BASIC CARDS		
*PREMIER: 8X BASIC CARDS		
1 Andy Moog	.25	.60
2 Jocelyn Thibault	.25	.60
3 Jose Theodore	.25	.60
4 Vincent Damphousse	.25	.60
5 Mark Recchi	.25	.60
6 Brian Savage	.08	.25
7 Saku Koivu	.60	1.50
8 Stephane Richer	.25	.60
9 Martin Rucinsky	.08	.25
10 Valeri Bure	.08	.25
11 Vladimir Malakhov	.08	.25
12 Shayne Corson	.25	.60
13 Darcy Tucker	.08	.25
14 Sebastien Bordeleau	.08	.25
15 Terry Ryan	.08	.25
16 David Ling	.08	.25
17 Dave Manson	.08	.25
18 Benoit Brunet	.08	.25
19 Marc Bureau	.08	.25
20 Patrice Brisebois	.08	.25

1997-98 Score Canucks

This 20-card team set of the Vancouver Canucks was produced by Pinnacle and features bordered color action player photos. The backs carry player information.

COMPLETE SET (20)	3.00	8.00
*PLATINUM: 3X BASIC CARDS		
*PREMIER: 8X BASIC CARDS		
1 Pavel Bure	.60	1.50
2 Alexander Mogilny	.25	.60
3 Mark Messier	.40	1.00
4 Trevor Linden	.25	.60
5 Martin Gelinas	.08	.25
6 Mattias Ohlund	.15	.40
7 Markus Naslund	.08	.25
8 Jyrki Lumme	.08	.25
9 Lonny Bohonos	.08	.25
10 Kirk McLean	.25	.60
11 Corey Hirsch	.25	.60
12 Arturs Irbe	.25	.60
13 Larry Courville	.08	.25
14 Adrian Aucoin	.08	.25
15 Grant Ledyard	.08	.25
16 Gino Odjick	.08	.25
17 Donald Brashear	.08	.25
18 Brian Noonan	.08	.25
19 David Roberts	.08	.25
20 Dave Babych	.08	.25

1997-98 Score Devils

This 20-card team set of the New Jersey Devils was produced by Pinnacle and features bordered color action player photos. The backs carry player information.

COMPLETE SET (20)	3.00	8.00
*PLATINUM: 3X BASIC CARDS		
*PREMIER: 8X BASIC CARDS		
1 Doug Gilmour	.30	.75
2 Bobby Holik	.08	.25
3 Dave Andreychuk	.25	.60
4 John MacLean	.08	.25
5 Bill Guerin	.08	.25
6 Brian Rolston	.08	.25
7 Scott Niedermayer	.08	.25
8 Scott Stevens	.08	.25
9 Valeri Zelepukin	.08	.25
10 Steve Thomas	.08	.25
11 Denis Pederson	.08	.25
12 Randy McKay	.08	.25
13 Mike Dunham	.25	.60
14 Petr Sykora	.15	.40
15 Lyle Odelein	.08	.25
16 Martin Brodeur	.75	2.00
17 Vadim Sharifijanov	.08	.25
18 Bob Carpenter	.08	.25
19 Sergei Brylin	.08	.25
20 Ken Daneyko	.08	.25

1997-98 Score Flyers

This 20-card team set of the Philadelphia Flyers was produced by Pinnacle and features bordered color action player photos. The backs carry player information.

COMPLETE SET (20)	4.00	10.00
*PLATINUM: 3X BASIC CARDS		
*PREMIER: 8X BASIC CARDS		
1 Ron Hextall	.25	.60
2 Garth Snow	.25	.60
3 Eric Lindros	1.25	3.00
4 John LeClair	.60	1.50
5 Rod Brind'Amour	.25	.60
6 Chris Gratton	.15	.40
7 Eric Desjardins	.08	.25
8 Trent Klatt	.08	.25
9 Janne Niinimaa	.25	.60
10 Luke Richardson	.08	.25
11 Paul Coffey	.30	.75
12 Dainius Zubrus	.30	.75
13 Shjon Podein	.08	.25
14 Joel Otto	.08	.25
15 Chris Therien	.08	.25
16 Pat Falloon	.08	.25
17 Petr Svoboda	.08	.25
18 Vaclav Prospal	.30	.75
19 John Druce	.08	.25
20 Daniel Lacroix	.08	.25

1997-98 Score Maple Leafs

This 20-card team set of the Toronto Maple Leafs was produced by Pinnacle and features bordered color action player photos. The backs carry player information.

COMPLETE SET (20)	3.00	8.00
*PLATINUM: 3X BASIC CARDS		
*PREMIER: 8X BASIC CARDS		
1 Felix Potvin	.30	.75
2 Glenn Healy	.25	.60
3 Marcel Cousineau	.25	.60
4 Mats Sundin	.30	.75
5 Wendel Clark	.25	.60
6 Sergei Berezin	.25	.60
7 Steve Sullivan	.08	.25
8 Tie Domi	.10	.30
9 Todd Warriner	.08	.25
10 Mathieu Schneider	.08	.25
11 Mike Craig	.08	.25
12 Darby Hendrickson	.08	.25
13 Fredrik Modin	.08	.25
14 Brandon Convery	.08	.25
15 Kevyn Adams	.08	.25
16 Dimitri Yushkevich	.08	.25
17 Alyn McCauley	.08	.25
18 Derek King	.08	.25
19 Jamie Baker	.08	.25
20 Martin Prochazka	.08	.25

1997-98 Score Mighty Ducks

This 20-card team set of the Mighty Ducks of Anaheim was produced by Pinnacle and features bordered color action player photos. The backs carry player information.

COMPLETE SET (20)	4.00	10.00
*PLATINUM: 3X BASIC CARDS		
*PREMIER: 8X BASIC CARDS		
1 Paul Kariya	1.25	3.00
2 Teemu Selanne	.75	2.00
3 Steve Rucchin	.08	.25
4 Dmitri Mironov	.08	.25
5 Matt Cullen	.08	.25
6 Kevin Todd	.08	.25
7 Joe Sacco	.08	.25
8 J.J. Daigneault	.08	.25
9 Darren Van Impe	.08	.25
10 Scott Young	.08	.25
11 Ted Drury	.08	.25
12 Tomas Sandstrom	.08	.25
13 Warren Rychel	.08	.25
14 Guy Hebert	.25	.60
15 Shawn Antoski	.08	.25
16 Mikhail Shtalenkov	.25	.60
17 Peter Leboutillier	.08	.25
18 Sean Pronger	.08	.25
19 Dave Karpa	.08	.25
20 Espen Knutsen	.20	.50

1997-98 Score Penguins

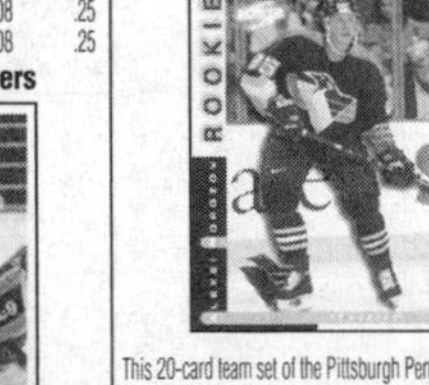

This 20-card team set of the Pittsburgh Penguins was produced by Pinnacle and features bordered color action player photos. The backs carry player information.

COMPLETE SET (20)	3.60	9.00
*PLATINUM: 3X BASIC CARDS		
*PREMIER: 8X BASIC CARDS		
1 Tom Barrasso	.08	.25
2 Ken Wregget	.25	.60
3 Patrick Lalime	.25	.60
4 Jaromir Jagr	1.00	2.50
5 Ron Francis	.25	.60
6 Petr Nedved	.25	.60
7 Ed Olczyk	.08	.25
8 Kevin Hatcher	.08	.25
9 Stu Barnes	.08	.25
10 Darius Kasparaitis	.08	.25

11 Greg Johnson .08 .25
12 Garry Valk .08 .25
13 Roman Oksiuta .08 .25
14 Dan Quinn .08 .25
15 Alex Hicks .08 .25
16 Robert Dome .08 .25
17 Dave Roche .08 .25
18 Alexei Morozov .25 .60
19 Rob Brown .08 .25
20 Domenic Pittis .08 .25

1997-98 Score Rangers

This 20-card team set of the New York Rangers was produced by Pinnacle and features bordered color action player photos. The backs carry player information.

COMPLETE SET (20) 4.00 10.00
*PLATINUM: 3X BASIC CARDS
*PREMIER: 8X BASIC CARDS
1 Wayne Gretzky 2.00 5.00
2 Brian Leetch .30 .75
3 Mike Keane .08 .25
4 Adam Graves .25 .60
5 Niklas Sundstrom .08 .25
6 Kevin Stevens .08 .25
7 Alexei Kovalev .08 .25
8 Alexander Karpovtsev .08 .25
9 Bill Berg .08 .25
10 Pat Lafontaine .25 .60
11 Bruce Driver .08 .25
12 Pat Flatley .08 .25
13 Vladimir Vorobiev .08 .25
14 Christian Dube .08 .25
15 Ulf Samuelsson .08 .25
16 Mike Richter .30 .75
17 Jason Muzzatti .08 .25
18 Daniel Goneau .08 .25
19 Marc Savard .08 .25
20 Jeff Beukeboom .08 .25

1997-98 Score Red Wings

This 20-card team set of the Detroit Red Wings was produced by Pinnacle and features bordered color action player photos. The backs carry player information.

COMPLETE SET (20) 4.00 10.00
*PLATINUM: 3X BASIC CARDS
*PREMIER: 8X BASIC CARDS
1 Brendan Shanahan .60 1.50
2 Steve Yzerman 1.00 2.50
3 Sergei Fedorov .60 1.50
4 Nicklas Lidstrom .25 .60
5 Igor Larionov .15 .40
6 Darren McCarty .25 .60
7 Slava Kozlov .25 .60
8 Larry Murphy .25 .60
9 Vladimir Konstantinov .25 .60
10 Martin Lapointe .10 .30
11 Slava Fetisov .10 .30
12 Kris Draper .10 .30
13 Doug Brown .08 .25
14 Brent Gilchrist .08 .25
15 Kirk Maltby .08 .25
16 Tomas Holmstrom .08 .25
17 Chris Osgood .30 .75
18 Kevin Hodson .30 .75
19 Jamie Pushor .08 .25
20 Mike Knuble .25 .60

1997-98 Score Sabres

This 20-card team set of the Buffalo Sabres was produced by Pinnacle and features bordered color action player photos. The backs carry player information.

COMPLETE SET (20) 3.00 8.00
*PLATINUM: 3X BASIC CARDS
*PREMIER: 8X BASIC CARDS
1 Dominik Hasek .75 2.00
2 Steve Shields .25 .60
3 Dixon Ward .08 .25
4 Donald Audette .08 .25
5 Matthew Barnaby .08 .25
6 Randy Burridge .08 .25
7 Jason Dawe .08 .25
8 Michael Grosek .08 .25
9 Brian Holzinger .25 .60
10 Brad May .08 .25
11 Mike Peca .30 .75
12 Derek Plante .08 .25
13 Wayne Primeau .08 .25
14 Rob Ray .25 .60
15 Miroslav Satan .25 .60
16 Erik Rasmussen .08 .25
17 Jason Wooley .08 .25
18 Alexei Zhitnik .08 .25
19 Darryl Shannon .08 .25
20 Mike Wilson .08 .25

1967-68 Seals Team Issue

Produced as a first year team issue of the expansion Oakland Seals, this 19-piece set features 8x10 individual player cards on thin cardboard stock. They are not numbered and are listed below in alphabetical order.

1 Bobby Baun 10.00 20.00
2 Ron Boehm 2.00 4.00
3 Wally Boyer 3.00 6.00
4 Charlie Burns 4.00 8.00
5 Larry Cahan 2.00 4.00
6 Alain Caron 2.00 4.00
7 Terry Clancy 2.00 4.00
8 Kent Douglas 4.00 8.00
9 Gerry Ehman 3.00 6.00
10 Autry Erickson 3.00 6.00
11 Billy Harris 3.00 6.00
12 Ron Harris 3.00 6.00
13 Bill Hicke 3.00 6.00
14 Charlie Hodge 7.50 15.00
15 Mike Laughton 2.00 4.00
16 Bob Lemieux 2.00 4.00
17 Gary Smith 6.00 12.00
18 George Swarbrick 3.00 6.00
19 Joe Szura 3.00 6.00

1992-93 Seasons Patches

Each measuring approximately 3 1/8" by 4 1/4", these 70 patches were licensed by the NHL/NHLPA and feature color action player photos on black fabric. The player's team appears above the photo and his name, position, and sweater number are below. An embroidered border in the team color edges the patch. The patches come in a poly-wrap sleeve attached to a teal cardboard rack display. These displays were pegged on team customized counter display easels, showcasing four different players (six patches per player), for a total of 24 patches per team display. Two versions are available. The bilingual version has both French and English printed on the package. The other version is printed in English only. A checklist of 71 patches is printed on the back of the display. In the checklist, patch 22, an unnamed prototype, features ex-NHL star and Seasons President Grant Mulvey. Mulvey's patch was only available through him as a handout and could not be purchased by the public; it is not considered part of the complete set.

COMPLETE SET (70) 60.00 150.00
1 Jeremy Roenick 1.25 3.00
2 Steve Larmer 1.00 2.50
3 Ed Belfour 1.25 3.00
4 Chris Chelios 1.25 3.00
5 Sergei Fedorov 1.25 3.00
6 Steve Yzerman 2.00 5.00
7 Tim Cheveldae .40 1.00
8 Bob Probert 1.00 2.50
9 Wayne Gretzky 4.00 10.00
10 Luc Robitaille 1.00 2.50
11 Tony Granato .40 1.00
12 Kelly Hrudey 1.00 2.50
13 Brett Hull 1.25 3.00
14 Curtis Joseph 1.25 3.00
15 Brendan Shanahan 1.25 3.00
16 Nelson Emerson .40 1.00
17 Ray Bourque 1.25 3.00
18 Joe Juneau 1.00 2.50
19 Andy Moog 1.00 2.50
20 Adam Oates 1.00 2.50
21 Patrick Roy 3.00 8.00
22 Grant Mulvey (Prototype) 8.00 20.00
23 Denis Savard 1.00 2.50
24 Gilbert Dionne .40 1.00
25 Kirk Muller 1.00 2.50
26 Mark Messier 1.25 3.00
27 Tony Amonte 1.00 2.50
28 Brian Leetch 1.25 3.00
29 Mike Richter 1.25 3.00
30 Trevor Linden 1.00 2.50
31 Pavel Bure 1.25 3.00
32 Cliff Ronning .40 1.00
33 Russ Courtnall .40 1.00
34 Mario Lemieux 3.00 8.00
35 Jaromir Jagr 2.00 5.00
36 Tom Barrasso 1.00 2.50
37 Rick Tocchet 1.00 2.50
38 Eric Lindros 2.00 5.00
39 Rod Brind'Amour 1.00 2.50
40 Dominic Roussel .40 1.00
41 Mark Recchi 1.00 2.50
42 Pat LaFontaine 1.00 2.50
43 Donald Audette .40 1.00
44 Pat Verbeek 1.00 2.50
45 John Cullen .40 1.00
46 Owen Nolan 1.00 2.50
47 Joe Sakic 1.25 3.00
48 Kevin Hatcher .40 1.00
49 Don Beaupre .40 1.00
50 Scott Stevens 1.00 2.50
51 Chris Terreri .40 1.00
52 Scott Lachance .40 1.00
53 Pierre Turgeon 1.00 2.50
54 Grant Fuhr 1.00 2.50
55 Doug Gilmour 1.25 3.00
56 Dave Manson .40 1.00
57 Bill Ranford 1.00 2.50
58 Troy Murray .40 1.00
59 Phil Housley .40 1.00
60 Al MacInnis 1.00 2.50
61 Mike Vernon 1.00 2.50
62 Pat Falloon .40 1.00
63 Doug Wilson 1.00 2.50
64 Jon Casey .40 1.00
65 Mike Modano 1.25 3.00
66 Kevin Stevens .40 1.00
67 Al Iafrate .40 1.00
68 Dale Hawerchuk 1.00 2.50
69 Igor Kravchuk .40 1.00
70 Wendel Clark 1.00 2.50
71 Kirk McLean 1.00 2.50

1993-94 Seasons Patches

Each measuring approximately 3 1/8" by 4 1/4", these 20 patches were licensed by the NHL/NHLPA and feature color action player photos on black fabric. The player's team appears above the photo and his name, position, and jersey number are below. An embroidered border in the team color edges the patch. The team logo and year of issue in the lower right corner round out the front. The patches were encased in a hard plastic sleeve attached to a black cardboard rack display. A checklist was printed on the back of the display. The patches are unnumbered but are checklisted below according to the numbering of the checklist card.

COMPLETE SET (20) 24.00 60.00
1 Ed Belfour .60 1.50
2 Pavel Bure 1.25 3.00
3 Paul Coffey .60 1.50
4 Doug Gilmour .60 1.50
5 Wayne Gretzky 4.00 10.00
6 Brett Hull .75 2.00
7 Jaromir Jagr 2.00 5.00
8 Joe Juneau .40 1.00
9 Mario Lemieux 3.00 8.00
10 Eric Lindros 2.00 5.00
11 Shawn McEachern .40 1.00
12 Alexander Mogilny .50 1.25
13 Adam Oates .50 1.25
14 Felix Potvin .60 1.50
15 Jeremy Roenick .60 1.50
16 Patrick Roy 3.00 8.00
17 Joe Sakic 1.25 3.00
18 Teemu Selanne 1.25 3.00
19 Kevin Stevens .40 1.00
20 Steve Yzerman 2.00 5.00

1994-95 Select Promos

These nine standard-size cards were issued to herald the release of the 1994-95 Select hockey series. The fronts feature borderless color action player photos. The player's last name and position, the team logo and a small, sepia-toned player portrait appear on gold-foil background in the lower left corner. The backs carry another color action player photo with player biography, profile and stats next to it. The top right corner of these cards has been cut off to mark them as sample cards. The Jamie Storr YE1 card is a sample of the Youth Explosion insert set.

COMPLETE SEALED SET (9) .40 1.00
7 John Vanbiesbrouck .05 .15
90 Felix Potvin .05 .15
108 Stephane Richer .01 .05
118 Dino Ciccarelli .01 .05
128 Sylvain Cote .01 .05
142 Kevin Dineen .01 .05
194 Mattias Norstrom .01 .05
YE1 Jamie Storr .40 1.00
NNO Title Card .02 .10

1994-95 Select

This 200-card set had an announced print run of 3,950, 24-box hobby-only cases. The design resembled a modernized version of the 1984-85 OPC set with a main action shot complemented by a corner head shot. The set is notable for the inclusion of 20 cards of players who competed in the 1994 Mexico Cup for 17-year-olds. One 4" by 6" bonus Mike Modano card featuring Sportflics technology was included in every box.

COMPLETE SET (200) 10.00 25.00
1 Mark Messier .08 .25
2 Rick Tocchet .02 .10
3 Alexandre Daigle .02 .10
4 Owen Nolan .05 .15
5 Bill Ranford .05 .15
6 Dave Gagner .05 .15
7 John Vanbiesbrouck .05 .15
8 Sergei Makarov .02 .10
9 Derek King .02 .10
10 Sergei Fedorov .20 .50
11 Trevor Linden .05 .15
12 Don Beaupre .02 .10
13 Dave Manson .02 .10
14 Sergei Zubov .02 .10
15 Keith Primeau .02 .10
16 Joe Mullen .05 .15
17 Bernie Nicholls .05 .15
18 Ray Bourque .20 .50
19 Mike Ridley .02 .10
20 Wendel Clark .05 .15
21 Mats Sundin .08 .25
22 Alexander Mogilny .05 .15
23 Mathieu Schneider .02 .10
24 Brian Leetch .08 .25
25 Rob Niedermayer .02 .10
26 Donald Audette .02 .10
27 Doug Weight .05 .15
28 Al MacInnis .05 .15
29 Jeremy Roenick .15 .40
30 Mark Recchi .05 .15
31 Chris Chelios .08 .25
32 Luc Robitaille .05 .15
33 Dale Hunter .02 .10
34 Kelly Hrudey .05 .15
35 Steve Yzerman .50 1.25
36 Martin Straka .02 .10
37 Arturs Irbe .05 .15
38 Mike Modano .20 .50
39 Cam Neely .08 .25
40 Igor Larionov .02 .10
41 Ray Ferraro .02 .10
42 Dale Hawerchuk .05 .15
43 Brian Bradley .02 .10
44 Joe Murphy .02 .10
45 Daren Puppa .05 .15
46 Pierre Turgeon .05 .15
47 Shayne Corson .02 .10
48 Adam Graves .02 .10
49 Craig Billington .05 .15
50 Derian Hatcher .02 .10
51 Alexei Zhamnov .05 .15
52 Dominik Hasek .25 .60
53 Ed Belfour .08 .25
54 Mike Vernon .05 .15
55 Bob Kudelski .02 .10
56 Ray Sheppard .05 .15
57 Pat LaFontaine .08 .25
58 Adam Oates .05 .15
59 Vincent Damphousse .02 .10
60 Jaromir Jagr .20 .50
61 Mikael Renberg .05 .15
62 Joe Sakic .25 .60
63 Sandis Ozolinsh .02 .10
64 Kirk McLean .05 .15
65 Stephan Lebeau .02 .10
66 Alexei Kovalev .02 .10
67 Ron Hextall .05 .15
68 Geoff Sanderson .05 .15
69 Doug Gilmour .05 .15
70 Russ Courtnall .02 .10
71 Jari Kurri .05 .15
72 Paul Coffey .08 .25
73 Claude Lemieux .02 .10
74 Teemu Selanne .08 .25
75 Keith Tkachuk .08 .25
76 Pat Verbeek .02 .10
77 Chris Gratton .02 .10
78 Martin Brodeur .30 .75
79 Guy Hebert .05 .15
80 Al Iafrate .02 .10
81 Glen Wesley .02 .10
82 Scott Stevens .05 .15
83 Wayne Gretzky .75 2.00
84 Ron Francis .05 .15
85 Scott Mellanby .05 .15
86 Joe Juneau .05 .15
87 Jason Arnott .05 .15
88 Tom Barrasso .05 .15
89 Peter Bondra .08 .25
90 Felix Potvin .05 .15
91 Brian Bellows .02 .10
92 Pavel Bure .08 .25
93 Grant Fuhr .05 .15
94 Andy Moog .08 .25
95 Mike Gartner .05 .15
96 Patrick Roy .60 1.50
97 Brett Hull .15 .40
98 Rob Blake .05 .15
99 Dave Andreychuk .05 .15
100 Eric Lindros .08 .25
101 Scott Niedermayer .02 .10
102 Tim Cheveldae .05 .15
103 Slava Kozlov .05 .15
104 Dimitri Khristich .02 .10
105 Steve Thomas .02 .10
106 Kevin Stevens .02 .10
107 Kirk Muller .02 .10
108 Stephane Richer .05 .15
109 Theo Fleury .05 .15
110 Jeff Brown .02 .10
111 Chris Pronger .08 .25
112 Steve Larmer .05 .15
113 Eric Desjardins .05 .15
114 Mike Ricci .02 .10
115 Tony Amonte .05 .15
116 Pat Falloon .02 .10
117 Garry Galley .02 .10
118 Dino Ciccarelli .05 .15
119 Rod Brind'Amour .05 .15
120 Kevin Hatcher .02 .10
121 Curtis Joseph .08 .25
122 Cliff Ronning .02 .10
123 Ulf Dahlen .02 .10
124 Marty McSorley .02 .10
125 Nelson Emerson .02 .10
126 Brian Skrudland .02 .10
127 Sean Burke .05 .15
128 Sylvain Cote .02 .10
129 Brendan Shanahan .08 .25
130 Benoit Hogue .02 .10
131 Joe Nieuwendyk .05 .15
132 Bryan Smolinski .02 .10
133 Mike Richter .08 .25
134 Nicklas Lidstrom .08 .25
135 Alexei Yashin .02 .10
136 John MacLean .05 .15
137 Geoff Courtnall .02 .10
138 Robert Reichel .02 .10
139 Craig Janney .05 .15
140 Zarley Zalapski .02 .10
141 Andrew Cassels .02 .10
142 Kevin Dineen .02 .10
143 Larry Murphy .05 .15
144 Valeri Kamensky .05 .15
145 Steve Duchesne .02 .10
146 Phil Housley .05 .15
147 Gary Roberts .02 .10
148 Kevin Hatcher .02 .10
149 Bryan Berard RC .30 .75
150 Marty Reasoner RC .25 .60
151 Andrew Berenzweig RC .02 .10
152 Erik Rasmussen RC .25 .60
153 Luke Curtin RC .02 .10
154 Dan Lacouture RC .02 .10
155 Brian Boucher RC 1.25 3.00
156 Wyatt Smith RC .10 .30
157 Maxim Kuznetsov RC .05 .15
158 Alexei Morozov RC .60 1.50
159 Dmitri Nabokov RC .02 .10
160 Wade Redden RC .20 .50
161 Jason Doig RC .02 .10
162 Alyn McCauley RC .20 .50
163 Jeff Ware RC .05 .15
164 Brad Larsen RC .02 .10
165 Jarome Iginla RC 3.00 8.00
166 Christian Dube RC .05 .15
167 Mike McBain RC .02 .10
168 Todd Norman RC .02 .10
169 Oleg Tverdovsky .08 .25
170 Jamie Storr .08 .25
171 Jason Wiemer RC .08 .25
172 Kenny Jonsson .02 .10
173 Paul Kariya .08 .25
174 Viktor Kozlov .08 .25
175 Peter Forsberg .50 1.25
176 Jeff Friesen .02 .10
177 Brian Rolston .08 .25
178 Brett Lindros .05 .15
179 Adam Deadmarsh .05 .15
180 Aaron Gavey .02 .10
181 Janne Laukkanen .02 .10
182 Todd Harvey .02 .10
183 Valeri Karpov RC .05 .15
184 Andrei Nikolishin .02 .10
185 Pavol Demitra .08 .25
186 Radek Bonk RC .30 .75
187 Valeri Bure .02 .10
188 Eric Fichaud RC .05 .15
189 Jamie McLennan .05 .15
190 Mariusz Czerkawski RC .10 .30
191 John Lilley .02 .10
192 Brian Savage .02 .10
193 Jason Allison .10 .30
194 Mattias Norstrom .02 .10
195 Todd Simon RC .02 .10
196 Zigmund Palffy .05 .15
197 Rene Corbet .02 .10
198 Mike Peca .02 .10
199 Checklist (1-100) .02 .10
200 Checklist (101-198) .02 .10
NNO Mike Modano Large 1.00 2.50

1994-95 Select Gold

This 200-card set is a parallel version of the regular Select issue. These cards feature a gold foil printing process on the front, as well as a Certified Gold logo printed on the back. These were inserted at a rate of 1:3 packs.

COMPLETE SET (200) 25.00 60.00
*VETS: 1X TO 2.5X BASIC CARDS
*ROOKIES: .75X TO 2X BASIC CARDS

1994-95 Select First Line

The 12 cards in this set utilize the Dufex printing technology and were inserted at a rate of 1:48 packs. The player's name, team affiliation and "1st Line" logo appear along the left card front. Cards are numbered with an "FL" prefix.

COMPLETE SET (12) 15.00 30.00
FL1 Patrick Roy 5.00 12.00
FL2 Ray Bourque 1.50 4.00
FL3 Brian Leetch .75 2.00
FL4 Brendan Shanahan .75 2.00
FL5 Eric Lindros .75 2.00
FL6 Pavel Bure .75 2.00
FL7 Mike Richter .75 2.00
FL8 Scott Stevens .50 1.25
FL9 Chris Chelios .75 2.00
FL10 Luc Robitaille .50 1.25
FL11 Wayne Gretzky 6.00 15.00
FL12 Brett Hull 1.25 3.00

1994-95 Select Youth Explosion

The 12 cards in this set were randomly inserted in Select product at the rate of 1:24 packs. The striking design benefits from the use of a special holographic silver foil printing. The borders are blue and silver with player name and position above the set title located near the bottom. The cards are numbered with a "YE" prefix.

COMPLETE SET (12) 8.00 15.00
YE1 Jamie Storr .50 1.25
YE2 Oleg Tverdovsky .50 1.25
YE3 Janne Laukkanen .20 .50
YE4 Kenny Jonsson .20 .50
YE5 Paul Kariya .50 1.25
YE6 Viktor Kozlov .50 1.25
YE7 Peter Forsberg 2.50 6.00
YE8 Jason Allison .60 1.50
YE9 Jeff Friesen .20 .50
YE10 Brian Rolston .50 1.25
YE11 Mariusz Czerkawski .60 1.50
YE12 Brett Lindros .30 .75

1995-96 Select Certified Promos

These cards are samples of the 1995-96 Select Certified series. Their description is the same as the regular series with the exception of the word "Sample" printed on the back of each one. The cards are listed below according to their number in their regular series. The Pavel Bure card is from the Gold Team insert series. It is identical to the expensive insert save for the word "sample" written on the card back.

COMPLETE SET (9) 12.00 30.00
5 Pavel Bure Gold Team 6.00 15.00
12 Jim Carey .60 1.50
13 Paul Kariya 4.00 10.00
17 Mike Modano 1.25 3.00
19 Owen Nolan .75 2.00
43 Alexander Mogilny .75 2.00
68 Peter Forsberg 3.00 8.00
69 Felix Potvin .75 2.00
NNO Title Card .08 .25

1995-96 Select Certified

The 1995-96 Select Certified set was issued in one series totaling 144 cards. The 6-card packs retailed for $4.00. The cards featured a smart, silver mirror finish, which was protected from routine scratching by a "Pinnacle Peel", which collectors could remove if they so wished. Although collectors are free to do so, cards without the foil may be slightly harder to resell, although they will be more sightly. The card stock was 24-point, double that of a normal card. Rookie Cards in this set include Daniel Alfredsson and Petr Sykora.

COMPLETE SET (144) 25.00 50.00
1 Mario Lemieux 2.50 6.00
2 Chris Chelios .40 1.00
3 Scott Mellanby .08 .25
4 Brett Hull .60 1.50
5 Theo Fleury .08 .25
6 Alexei Zhamnov .20 .50
7 Mats Sundin .40 1.00
8 Mathieu Schneider .08 .25
9 Jason Arnott .08 .25
10 Mark Recchi .20 .50
11 Adam Oates .20 .50
12 Jim Carey .20 .50
13 Paul Kariya .40 1.00
14 Mark Messier .40 1.00
15 Eric Lindros .40 1.00
16 Pavel Bure .40 1.00
17 Mike Modano .60 1.50
18 Pat LaFontaine .40 1.00
19 Owen Nolan .20 .50
20 Roman Hamrlik .20 .50
21 Paul Coffey .40 1.00
22 Alexandre Daigle .08 .25
23 Wayne Gretzky 3.00 8.00
24 Martin Brodeur 1.25 3.00
25 Ulf Dahlen .08 .25
26 Geoff Sanderson .08 .25
27 Brian Leetch .20 .50
28 Dave Andreychuk .20 .50
29 Sergei Fedorov .60 1.50
30 Jocelyn Thibault .40 1.00
31 Mikael Renberg .20 .50
32 Joe Nieuwendyk .20 .50
33 Craig Janney .08 .25
34 Ray Bourque .75 2.00
35 Jari Kurri .40 1.00
36 Alexei Yashin .08 .25
37 Keith Tkachuk .40 1.00
38 Jaromir Jagr .75 2.00
39 Stephane Richer .20 .50
40 Trevor Kidd .20 .50
41 Kevin Hatcher .08 .25
42 Mike Vernon .20 .50
43 Alexander Mogilny .20 .50
44 John LeClair .40 1.00
45 Joe Sakic 1.00 2.50
46 Kevin Stevens .08 .25
47 Adam Graves .08 .25
48 Doug Gilmour .20 .50
49 Pierre Turgeon .20 .50
50 Joe Murphy .08 .25
51 Peter Bondra .20 .50
52 Ron Francis .20 .50
53 Luc Robitaille .20 .50
54 Mike Gartner .20 .50
55 Bill Ranford .20 .50
56 Jeff Friesen .08 .25
57 Cam Neely .40 1.00
58 Daren Puppa .20 .50
59 Rod Brind'Amour .20 .50
60 Jeremy Roenick .50 1.25
61 Brett Lindros .08 .25
62 Todd Harvey .20 .50
63 Kirk McLean .20 .50
64 Brendan Shanahan .40 1.00
65 Kelly Hrudey .20 .50
66 Scott Stevens .20 .50
67 Sergei Zubov .08 .25
68 Peter Forsberg 1.25 3.00
69 Felix Potvin .40 1.00
70 Scott Niedermayer .20 .50
71 Keith Primeau .08 .25
72 Al MacInnis .20 .50
73 Mike Richter .40 1.00
74 Rob Blake .20 .50
75 Vincent Damphousse .08 .25
76 Teemu Selanne .40 1.00
77 Andy Moog .40 1.00
78 Ron Hextall .20 .50
79 Oleg Tverdovsky .08 .25
80 Joe Juneau .08 .25
81 Patrick Roy 2.50 6.00
82 Wendel Clark .20 .50
83 Brian Bradley .08 .25
84 Curtis Joseph .40 1.00
85 John Vanbiesbrouck .20 .50
86 Phil Housley .20 .50
87 Trevor Linden .20 .50
88 Alexei Kovalev .08 .25
89 Dominik Hasek 1.00 2.50
90 Larry Murphy .20 .50
91 Arturs Irbe .20 .50
92 John MacLean .20 .50
93 Ed Belfour .40 1.00
94 Steve Yzerman 2.50 6.00
95 Tom Barrasso .20 .50
96 Rob Niedermayer .20 .50
97 Dale Hawerchuk .40 1.00
98 Rick Tocchet .20 .50
99 Claude Lemieux .08 .25
100 Sean Burke .20 .50
101 Shayne Corson .20 .50
102 Dino Ciccarelli .08 .25
103 Kirk Muller .08 .25
104 Don Beaupre .20 .50
105 Valeri Kamensky .20 .50
106 Markus Naslund .40 1.00
107 Tomas Sandstrom .08 .25
108 Pat Verbeek .08 .25
109 Doug Weight .20 .50
110 Brian Holzinger RC .40 1.00
111 Antti Tormanen .08 .25
112 Tommy Salo RC 1.50 4.00
113 Jason Bonsignore .08 .25
114 Shane Doan RC 1.25 3.00
115 Robert Svehla RC .08 .25
116 Chad Kilger RC .08 .25
117 Saku Koivu .40 1.00
118 Jeff O'Neill .08 .25
119 Brendan Witt .08 .25
120 Byron Dafoe .20 .50
121 Ryan Smyth .20 .50
122 Daniel Alfredsson RC 1.25 3.00
123 Todd Bertuzzi RC 1.50 4.00
124 Daymond Langkow RC .60 1.50
125 Miroslav Satan RC 1.25 3.00
126 Bryan McCabe .08 .25
127 Aki Berg RC .20 .50
128 Cory Stillman .20 .50
129 Deron Quint .08 .25
130 Vitali Yachmenev .08 .25
131 Valeri Bure .08 .25
132 Eric Daze .20 .50
133 Radek Dvorak RC .60 1.50
134 Landon Wilson RC .08 .25
135 Niklas Sundstrom .20 .50
136 Jamie Storr .20 .50
137 Ed Jovanovski .40 1.00
138 Marcus Ragnarsson RC .20 .50
139 Kyle McLaren RC .08 .25
140 Sandy Moger .08 .25
141 Marty Murray .08 .25
142 Darby Hendrickson .08 .25
143 Corey Hirsch .20 .50
144 Petr Sykora RC 1.25 3.00

1995-96 Select Certified Mirror Gold

The cards from this high-end parallel set of the base Select Certified issue were randomly inserted 1:5 packs. Instead of the typical silver finish, these, as the title suggests, had a golden background.

*VETS: 2X TO 5X BASIC CARDS
*ROOKIES: .8X TO 2X

1995-96 Select Certified Double Strike

Randomly inserted in packs at a rate of 1:32, this 20-card set shines the spotlight on players whose abilities make them an imposing threat both offensively and defensively. The cards feature a rainbow silver foil background on the front, while the backs contain a note stating that no more than 1,975 complete sets were produced. There also was a Gold version of this set, with singles issued in black packs as inserts in roughly every 3.5 boxes. The fronts are essentially the same, save for the use of a gold foil background. The backs contain a small box reading "Case Chase" and "No more than 903 sets produced."

COMPLETE SET (20) 15.00 40.00
*GOLD: 1X TO 2.5X BASIC INSERTS
GOLD STATED ODDS 1:3.5 BOXES
1 Doug Gilmour .75 2.00
2 Ron Francis .75 2.00
3 Ray Bourque 1.50 4.00
4 Chris Chelios 1.25 3.00
5 Adam Oates .75 2.00
6 Mike Ricci .75 2.00
7 Jeremy Roenick 1.25 3.00
8 Jason Arnott .75 2.00
9 Brendan Shanahan 1.25 3.00
10 Joe Nieuwendyk .75 2.00
11 Trevor Linden .75 2.00
12 Mikael Renberg .75 2.00
13 Theo Fleury .75 2.00
14 Sergei Fedorov 1.50 4.00
15 Mark Messier 1.50 4.00
16 Keith Primeau .75 2.00
17 Keith Tkachuk 1.25 3.00
18 Scott Stevens .75 2.00
19 Claude Lemieux .75 2.00
20 Alexei Zhamnov .75 2.00

1995-96 Select Certified Future

Randomly inserted in packs at a rate of 1:19, this 10-card set features some of the league's brightest future stars in silver rainbow holographic foil print technology.

COMPLETE SET (10) 15.00 30.00
1 Peter Forsberg 6.00 15.00
2 Jim Carey .75 2.00
3 Paul Kariya 2.00 5.00
4 Jocelyn Thibault 1.25 3.00
5 Saku Koivu 2.00 5.00
6 Brian Holzinger .75 2.00
7 Todd Harvey .75 2.00
8 Jeff O'Neill .75 2.00
9 Oleg Tverdovsky .75 2.00
10 Ed Jovanovski .75 2.00

1995-96 Select Certified Gold Team

Randomly inserted in packs at a rate of 1:41, this 10-card set honors some of the league's top players, bestowing best-of-the-best honors with a Dufexed gold-foil design element. The presence of a Pavel Bure Gold Team sample card in the Promo set led to some softening of demand for the insert version of the card found in this set.

COMPLETE SET (10) 50.00 125.00
1 Eric Lindros 3.00 8.00
2 Wayne Gretzky 15.00 40.00
3 Mario Lemieux 10.00 25.00
4 Jaromir Jagr 4.00 10.00
5 Pavel Bure 3.00 8.00
6 Brett Hull 3.00 8.00
7 Cam Neely 3.00 8.00
8 Joe Sakic 6.00 15.00
9 Martin Brodeur 6.00 15.00
10 Patrick Roy 10.00 25.00

1996-97 Select Certified

The 1996-97 Select Certified set was issued in one series totaling 120 cards. The cards featured a silver mirror like background with player names scripted horizontally in gold foil on the front and complete stats on the reverse against each opposing team.

COMPLETE SET (120) 15.00 40.00
1 Eric Lindros .30 .75
2 Mike Modano .40 1.00

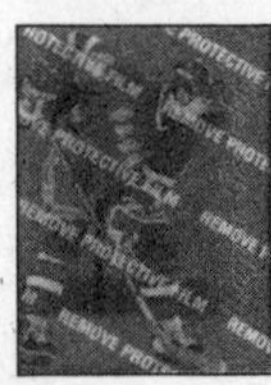

3 Jocelyn Thibault .30 .75
4 Wayne Gretzky 2.00 5.00
5 Ray Bourque .50 1.25
6 Martin Brodeur .75 2.00
7 Rob Niedermayer .15 .40
8 Stephane Fiset .15 .40
9 Pat LaFontaine .30 .75
10 Mario Lemieux 1.50 4.00
11 Ed Belfour .30 .75
12 Ron Francis .15 .40
13 Luc Robitaille .15 .40
14 Paul Kariya .30 .75
15 Doug Gilmour .15 .40
16 Joe Sakic .60 1.50
17 Nikolai Khabibulin .15 .40
18 Valeri Bure .07 .20
19 Brett Hull .40 1.00
20 Chris Osgood .15 .40
21 Trevor Kidd .15 .40
22 Kirk McLean .15 .40
23 Zigmund Palffy .15 .40
24 Keith Tkachuk .30 .75
25 Andy Moog .15 .40
26 Bill Guerin .07 .20
27 Chris Chelios .30 .75
28 Damian Rhodes .15 .40
29 Jim Carey .30 .75
30 Ed Jovanovski .15 .40
31 Felix Potvin .30 .75
32 Teemu Selanne .30 .75
33 John LeClair .30 .75
34 Pavel Bure .30 .75
35 Grant Fuhr .15 .40
36 Mark Messier .30 .75
37 Vincent Damphousse .07 .20
38 Jason Arnott .07 .20
39 Mike Richter .30 .75
40 Keith Primeau .07 .20
41 Steve Yzerman 1.50 4.00
42 Trevor Linden .15 .40
43 Jaromir Jagr .50 1.25
44 Sean Burke .15 .40
45 Alexei Zhitnik .07 .20
46 Dimitri Khristich .07 .20
47 Daniel Alfredsson .15 .40
48 Roman Hamrlik .15 .40
49 Pat Verbeek .07 .20
50 Doug Weight .15 .40
51 Adam Graves .07 .20
52 Michal Pivonka .07 .20
53 Claude Lemieux .07 .20
54 Scott Stevens .15 .40
55 Sergei Fedorov .40 1.00
56 Owen Nolan .15 .40
57 Niklas Andersson .07 .20
58 Cory Stillman .07 .20
59 John Vanbiesbrouck .15 .40
60 Craig Janney .15 .40
61 Jeff Friesen .07 .20
62 Igor Larionov .07 .20
63 Ron Hextall .15 .40
64 Saku Koivu .30 .75
65 Wendel Clark .15 .40
66 Curtis Joseph .30 .75
67 Valeri Kamensky .15 .40
68 Adam Oates .15 .40
69 Daren Puppa .15 .40
70 Alexander Mogilny .15 .40
71 Corey Hirsch .15 .40
72 Brendan Shanahan .30 .75
73 Shayne Corson .07 .20
74 Dominik Hasek .50 1.25
75 Theo Fleury .07 .20
76 Brian Leetch .30 .75
77 Jeremy Roenick .40 1.00
78 Peter Bondra .15 .40
79 Eric Daze .15 .40
80 Todd Bertuzzi .30 .75
81 Patrick Roy 1.50 4.00
82 Pierre Turgeon .15 .40
83 Alexei Yashin .07 .20
84 Scott Mellanby .15 .40
85 Mats Sundin .30 .75
86 Jari Kurri .40 1.00
87 Kelly Hrudey .15 .40
88 Joe Nieuwendyk .15 .40
89 Paul Coffey .30 .75
90 Jeff O'Neill .07 .20
91 Kai Nurminen RC .07 .20
92 Anders Eriksson .07 .20
93 Jarome Iginla .40 1.00
94 Anson Carter .15 .40
95 Christian Dube .07 .20
96 Harry York RC .30 .75
97 Tomas Holmstrom RC 1.00 2.50
98 Sergei Berezin RC .40 1.00
99 Mattias Timander RC .07 .20
100 Wade Redden .07 .20
101 Mike Grier RC .60 1.50
102 Jonas Hoglund .07 .20
103 Eric Fichaud .15 .40
104 Janne Niinimaa .30 .75
105 Tuomas Gronman .07 .20
106 Jim Campbell .07 .20
107 Daniel Goneau RC .15 .40
108 Patrick Lalime RC .75 2.00
109 Ruslan Salei RC .07 .20
110 Richard Zednik RC .40 1.00
111 Chris O'Sullivan .07 .20
112 Fredrik Modin RC .40 1.00
113 Brad Smyth RC .07 .20
114 Bryan Berard .30 .75
115 Jamie Langenbrunner .07 .20
116 Ethan Moreau RC .30 .75
117 Daymond Langkow .15 .40
118 Andreas Dackell RC .07 .20
119 Rem Murray RC .15 .40
120 Dainius Zubrus RC .40 1.00
P60 Craig Janney PROMO .40 1.00
P65 Wendel Clark PROMO .40 1.00

1996-97 Select Certified Artist's Proofs

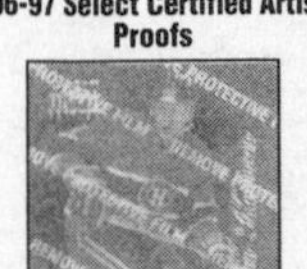

Inserted 1:48 packs, this insert parallels the base set. The cards can be distinguished by an Artist Proof logo stamped on the front of the card. Although the cards suggest that 500 were printed, there were, in fact, just 150 of each card made.

*VETS: 3X TO 8X BASIC CARDS
*ROOKIES: 1.5X TO 4X
P60 Craig Janney PROMO 2.50 6.00
P65 Wendel Clark PROMO 2.50 6.00

1996-97 Select Certified Blue

Inserted at 1:50 packs, these cards can be differentiated from the base cards by the blue foil background on the front of the card.

*VETS: 3X TO 8X BASIC CARDS
*ROOKIES: 1.5X TO 4X

1996-97 Select Certified Mirror Blue

Inserted at 1:200 packs, these cards are differentiated by a blue holographic foil background on the front of the card and the words 'Mirror Blue' on the reverse. Though the actual number of cards printed is not known, sources estimate that only 36 copies of each Mirror Blue card exists.

*VETS: 8X TO 20X BASIC CARDS
*ROOKIES: 4X TO 10X

1996-97 Select Certified Mirror Gold

Inserted at 1:300, this 120-card parallel set could be differentiated from the base set by a gold holographic foil background on the front of the card and the words 'Mirror Gold' on the reverse. Though the actual number of cards printed is not known, sources estimate that only 24 copies of each Mirror Gold card exists.

*VETS: 12X TO 30X BASIC CARDS
*ROOKIES: 6X TO 15X

1996-97 Select Certified Mirror Red

Inserted at 1:100 packs, these cards can be differentiated from the base set by a red holographic foil background on the front of the card and the words 'Mirror Red' on the reverse. Though the actual number of cards printed is not known, sources estimate that just 72 copies of each Mirror Red card exists.

*VETS: 4X TO 10X BASIC CARDS
*ROOKIES: 2X TO 5X

1996-97 Select Certified Red

A 1:8 pack parallel insert, these cards are differentiated from those in the base set by a red foil background on the front of the card.

*VETS: 2.5X TO 6X BASIC CARDS
*ROOKIES: 1.2X TO 3X

1996-97 Select Certified Cornerstones

Randomly inserted in packs at a rate of 1:38, these cards feature a player photo framed in silver and black etched metal Dufex foil. The text on the card backs describe why each of the 15 players is considered his team's cornerstone player.

COMPLETE SET (15) 30.00 80.00
1 Eric Lindros 2.50 6.00
2 Mario Lemieux 6.00 15.00
3 Jaromir Jagr 3.00 8.00
4 Wayne Gretzky 8.00 20.00
5 Mark Messier 2.50 6.00
6 Brett Hull 2.50 6.00
7 Pavel Bure 2.50 6.00
8 Saku Koivu 2.00 5.00
9 Joe Sakic 4.00 10.00
10 Keith Tkachuk 2.00 5.00
11 Paul Kariya 2.50 6.00
12 Teemu Selanne 2.50 6.00
13 Sergei Fedorov 2.50 6.00
14 Steve Yzerman 6.00 15.00
15 Peter Forsberg 3.00 8.00

1996-97 Select Certified Freezers

Randomly inserted in packs at a rate of 1:41, this set features silver holofoil cards of 15 highly regarded NHL goaltenders.

COMPLETE SET (15) 50.00 100.00
1 Martin Brodeur 6.00 15.00
2 Patrick Roy 10.00 25.00
3 Jim Carey 2.00 5.00
4 John Vanbiesbrouck 2.50 6.00
5 Dominik Hasek 4.00 10.00
6 Ed Belfour 2.50 6.00
7 Curtis Joseph 2.50 6.00
8 Felix Potvin 2.50 6.00
9 Daren Puppa 2.00 5.00
10 Chris Osgood 2.50 6.00
11 Mike Richter 2.50 6.00
12 Jocelyn Thibault 2.00 5.00
13 Ron Hextall 2.00 5.00
14 Nikolai Khabibulin 2.00 5.00
15 Damian Rhodes 2.00 5.00

1992-93 Senators Team Issue

This 15-postcard set commemorates the inaugural season of the Ottawa Senators. The postcards feature full-bleed action photography, along with the logos of the set's two sponsors, CFRA Radio and Colonial Furniture. There is no indication of the player's identity anywhere on the card, so knowledge of obscure expansion draft-caliber players is a must to truly appreciate this set. The backs are blank. The cards are unnumbered, and are listed below alphabetically.

COMPLETE SET (15) 6.00 15.00
1 Jamie Baker .40 1.00
2 Daniel Berthiaume .60 1.50
3 Neil Brady .40 1.00
4 Ken Hammond .40 1.00
5 Dave Hannan .40 1.00
6 Jody Hull .40 1.00
7 Mark Lamb .40 1.00
8 Darcy Loewen .40 1.00
9 Norm Maciver .40 1.00
10 Brad Marsh .60 1.50
11 Andrew McBain .40 1.00
12 Mike Peluso .50 1.25
13 Darren Rumble .40 1.00
14 Brad Shaw .40 1.00
15 Sylvain Turgeon .40 1.00

1993-94 Senators Kraft Sheets

These 27 blank-backed photo sheets of the 1993-94 Ottawa Senators measure approximately 8 1/2" by 11" and feature color player action shots bordered in team colors (red, white, and gold). The player's name and uniform number, along with the Senators' logo, appear near the top. The logo for Kraft appears at the lower right; the logo for Loeb appears at the lower left. The production number out of the total produced for each sheet is shown within the white rectangle immediately above the Kraft logo. The sheets were produced in differing quantities. These production figures are shown in the checklist below. A special storage album was also available for the sheets. The sheets are unnumbered and checklisted below in alphabetical order.

COMPLETE SET (27) 60.00 150.00
1 Dave Archibald 3,500 2.00 5.00
2 Craig Billington 6,500 2.50 6.00
3 Rick Bowness CO 6,500 2.00 5.00
4 Robert Burakovsky 1,500 3.00 8.00
5 Alexandre Daigle 6,500 2.00 5.00
6 Pavol Demitra 1,500 4.00 10.00
7 Gord Dineen 3,500 2.00 5.00
8 Dmitri Filimonov 1,500 3.00 8.00
9 Brian Glynn 1,500 3.00 8.00
10 Bill Huard 1,500 3.00 8.00
11 Jarmo Kekalainen 1,500 3.00 8.00
12 Bob Kudelski 1,500 3.00 8.00
13 Mark Lamb 1,500 3.00 8.00
14 Darcy Loewen 3,500 2.00 5.00
15 Norm Maciver 3,500 2.00 5.00
16 Darrin Madeley 1,500 3.00 8.00
17 Troy Mallette 3,500 2.00 5.00
18 Brad Marsh 6,500 3.00 8.00
19 Dave McLlwain 3,500 2.00 5.00
20 Darren Rumble 1,500 3.00 8.00
21 Vladimir Ruzicka 1,500 3.00 8.00
22 Brad Shaw 6,500 2.00 5.00
23 Graeme Townshend 1,500 3.00 8.00
24 Sylvain Turgeon 6,500 2.50 6.00
25 Dennis Vial 1,500 3.00 8.00
26 Alexei Yashin 6,500 2.00 5.00
27 Team Photo 12,500 2.00 5.00
xx Album 6.00 15.00
NNO Team Photo 2.00 5.00

1994-95 Senators Team Issue

Sponsored by Bell Mobility, this 28-card sets measures approximately 4" by 6" and features members of the 1994-95 Ottawa Senators. The fronts have full-bleed color action player photos with a fading team color-coded inside border. The player's name appears alongside the left, while his uniform number is on the bottom. The team logo in the upper right corner and sponsor logos in English and French on the bottom round out the card face. The backs are blank. The cards are unnumbered and checklisted below in alphabetical order.

COMPLETE SET (28) 6.00 15.00
1 Dave Archibald .20 .50
2 Don Beaupre .30 .75
3 Radim Bicanek .20 .50
4 Craig Billington .30 .75
5 Claude Boivin .20 .50
6 Radek Bonk .40 1.00
7 Phil Bourque .20 .50
8 Rick Bowness CO .20 .50
9 Randy Cunneyworth .20 .50
10 Chris Dahlquist .20 .50
11 Alexandre Daigle .40 1.00
12 Pat Elynuik .20 .50
13 Rob Gaudreau .20 .50
14 Sean Hill .20 .50
15 Bill Huard .20 .50
16 Kerry Huffman .20 .50
17 Scott Levins .20 .50
18 Norm Maciver .20 .50
19 Darrin Madeley .30 .75
20 Troy Mallette .20 .50
21 Brad Marsh CO .30 .75
22 Dave McLlwain .20 .50
23 Troy Murray .20 .50
24 Stanislav Neckar .25 .60
25 Jim Paek .20 .50
26 Sylvain Turgeon .20 .50
27 Dennis Vial .20 .50
28 Alexei Yashin .75 2.00

1995-96 Senators Team Issue

This 24-postcard set was produced by the Senators as a promotional giveaway. The cards feature full-bleed action photography with the club's name in both English and French inscribed along three borders. The fourth border displays the player's name. The backs are blank. As the cards are unnumbered, they are listed below in alphabetical order.

COMPLETE SET (24) 6.00 15.00
1 Daniel Alfredsson 1.25 3.00
2 Dave Archibald .20 .50
3 Mike Bales .25 .60
4 Don Beaupre .30 .75
5 Radek Bonk .25 .60
6 Tom Chorske .20 .50
7 Randy Cunneyworth .20 .50
8 Alexandre Daigle .20 .50
9 Ted Drury .20 .50
10 Steve Duchesne .25 .60
11 Rob Gaudreau .20 .50
12 Sean Hill .20 .50
13 Kerry Huffman .20 .50
14 Scott Levins .20 .50
15 Troy Mallette .20 .50
16 Brad Marsh .40 1.00
17 Trent McCleary .20 .50
18 Jaroslav Modry .20 .50
19 Frank Musil .20 .50
20 Stan Neckar .25 .60
21 Martin Straka .40 1.00
22 Antti Tormanen .20 .50
23 Dennis Vial .20 .50
24 Alexei Yashin .40 1.00

1996-97 Senators Pizza Hut

This 30-card set of the Ottawa Senators was produced in conjunction with Pizza Hut as a promotional giveaway. This standard postcard size set features glossy fronts and full-bleed action photography, with the player's name on the right side, and the Pizza Hut Canada logo in the bottom left corner. The backs are blank. As the cards are unnumbered, they are listed below in alphabetical order.

COMPLETE SET (32) 6.00 15.00
1 Daniel Alfredsson .75 2.00
2 Radek Bonk .30 .75
3 Tom Chorske .20 .50
4 Randy Cunneyworth .20 .50
5 Andreas Dackell .20 .50
6 Alexandre Daigle .20 .50
7 Steve Duchesne .30 .75
8 Bruce Gardiner .20 .50
9 Dave Hannan .20 .50
10 Sean Hill .20 .50
11 Denny Lambert .20 .50
12 Janne Laukkanen .30 .75
13 Jacques Martin CO .08 .25
14 Shawn Mceachern .20 .50
15 Frank Musil .20 .50
16 Phil Myre ACO .08 .25
17 Stan Neckar .20 .50
18 Christer Olsson .20 .50
19 Perry Pearn ACO .08 .25
20 Lance Pitlick .20 .50
21 Craig Ramsay .20 .50
22 Wade Redden .40 1.00
23 Damian Rhodes .40 1.00
24 Ron Tugnutt .40 1.00
25 Shaun Van Allen .20 .50
26 Dennis Vial .20 .50
27 Alexei Yashin .40 1.00
28 Jason York .20 .50
29 Jason Zent .20 .50
30 Sergei Zholtok .20 .50

1998-99 Senators Team Issue

This set features the Senators of the NHL. These oversized cards were sold in set form by the team at home games. The backs are blank and the cards unnumbered. Therefore, they are listed in alphabetical order.

COMPLETE SET (26) 6.00 15.00
1 Daniel Alfredsson .40 1.00
2 Magnus Arvedson .20 .50
3 Bill Berg .20 .50
4 Radek Bonk .20 .50
5 Andreas Dackell .20 .50
6 Bruce Gardiner .20 .50
7 Marian Hossa .75 2.00
8 Andreas Johansson .20 .50
9 Igor Kravchuk .20 .50
10 Janne Laukkanen .20 .50
11 Jacques Martin CO .20 .50
12 Steve Martins .20 .50
13 Shawn McEachern .20 .50
14 Chris Murray .20 .50
15 Chris Phillips .20 .50
16 Lance Pitlick .20 .50
17 Vaclav Prospal .20 .50
18 Wade Redden .40 1.00
19 Damian Rhodes .30 .75
20 Sami Salo .20 .50
21 Patrick Traverse .20 .50
22 Ron Tugnutt .40 1.00
23 Shaun Van Allen .20 .50
24 Alexei Yashin .20 .50
25 Ottawa Senators .20 .50
26 Spartacat MASCOT .08 .25

1999-00 Senators Team Issue

This team-issued set measures approximately 4 1/2" x 8 1/2". The cards carry an action photo of each player on the front accompanied by their jersey number, the CCM logo and the team logo. The back of each card carries the Senators 1999-00 game schedule. The card are not numbered and are listed below in alphabetical order.

COMPLETE SET (26) 8.00 20.00
1 Daniel Alfredsson .40 1.00
2 Magnus Arvedson .20 .50
3 Radek Bonk .30 .75
4 Andreas Dackell .20 .50
5 Kevin Dineen .20 .50
6 Mike Fisher .40 1.00
7 Bruce Gardiner .20 .50
8 Marian Hossa 2.00 5.00
9 Joe Juneau .20 .50
10 Igor Kravchuk .20 .50
11 Patrick Lalime .60 1.50
12 Janne Laukkanen .20 .50
13 Shawn McEachern .30 .75
14 Chris Phillips .30 .75
15 Vaclav Prospal .20 .50
16 Wade Redden .40 1.00
17 Andre Roy .20 .50
18 Sami Salo .20 .50
19 Patrick Traverse .20 .50
20 Ron Tugnutt .40 1.00
21 Shaun Van Allen .20 .50
22 Jason York .20 .50
23 Rob Zamuner .20 .50
24 Jacques Martin HCO .08 .25
25 Spartacat MASCOT .02 .10
26 Team Photo .20 .50

2000-01 Senators Team Issue

This set features the Senators of the NHL. The slightly oversized cards were issued as a promotional giveaway early in the season. The cards feature an action photo on the front and a complete season schedule on the back.

COMPLETE SET (26)
1 Daniel Alfredsson .40 1.00
2 Magnus Arvedson .20 .50
3 Radek Bonk .30 .75
4 Andreas Dackell .20 .50
5 Mike Fisher .30 .75
6 Colin Forbes .20 .50
7 Martin Havlat 1.60 4.00
8 Marian Hossa 2.00 5.00
9 Jani Hurme .60 1.50
10 Patrick Lalime .60 1.50
11 Jacques Martin CO .10 .25
12 Shawn McEachern .20 .50
13 Roger Neilson ACO .10 .25
14 Perry Pearn ACO .10 .25
15 Ricard Persson .20 .50
16 Chris Phillips .20 .50
17 Vaclav Prospal .20 .50
18 Karel Rachunek .20 .50
19 Wade Redden .30 .75
20 Jamie Rivers .20 .50
21 Andre Roy .30 .75
22 Sami Salo .20 .50
23 Spartacat MASCOT .04 .10
24 Alexei Yashin .40 1.00
25 Jason York .20 .50
26 Rob Zamuner .20 .50
27 Team Photo

2001-02 Senators Team Issue

This 29-card set was issued by the NHL Senators. The cards measure and oversized 3 X 5 inches, and feature a stylized color photo on the front, with a black and white team schedule on the back. It is not known how they were distributed, but evidence suggests they were a giveaway item. The cards are not numbered, so are listed below alphabetically. Note: the autograph card is not signed: it is a blank front with room for autographs.

COMPLETE SET (29)
1 Daniel Alfredsson .62 1.56
2 Magnus Arvedson .20 .50
3 Radek Bonk .20 .50
4 Zdeno Chara .20 .50
5 Ivan Ciernik .31 .78
6 Mike Fisher .31 .78
7 Martin Havlat 1.20 3.00
8 Chris Herperger .20 .50
9 Shane Hnidy .20 .50
10 Marian Hossa .80 2.00
11 Jani Hurme .62 1.56
12 Don Jackson ACO .04 .11
13 Patrick Lalime .40 1.00
14 Curtis Leschyshyn .20 .50
15 Jacques Martin CO .04 .11
16 Shawn McEachern .20 .50
17 Bill Muckalt .20 .50
18 Chris Neil .40 1.00
19 Roger Neilson ACO .04 .11
20 Perry Pearn ACO .04 .11
21 Ricard Persson .20 .50
22 Chris Phillips .20 .50
23 Karel Rachunek .20 .50
24 Wade Redden .31 .78
25 Andre Roy .31 .78
26 Sami Salo .20 .50
27 Todd White .20 .50
28 SpartaCat .04 .11
29 Autograph Card .04 .11

2002-03 Senators Team Issue

This 15-card set was issued by the team and given away as promotions. The cards measured approximately 3 1/2" X 4 1/2". Card backs carried the 02-03 schedule.

COMPLETE SET (15) 12.00 20.00
1 Daniel Alfredsson .75 2.00
2 Magnus Arvedson .40 1.00
3 Radek Bonk .40 1.00
4 Zdeno Chara .60 1.50
5 Mike Fisher .60 1.50
6 Martin Havlat 1.25 3.00
7 Marian Hossa 1.25 3.00
8 Jody Hull .40 1.00
9 Patrick Lalime .60 1.50
10 Curtis Leschyshyn .40 1.00
11 Chris Neil .40 1.00
12 Chris Phillips .40 1.00
13 Martin Prusek .60 1.50
14 Wade Redden .60 1.50
15 Anton Volchenkov .40 1.00

2003-04 Senators Postcards

COMPLETE SET (28) 10.00 20.00
1 Brian Pothier .20 .50
2 Zdeno Chara .40 1.00
3 Chris Phillips .20 .50
4 Wade Redden .40 1.00
5 Curtis Leschyshyn .20 .50
6 Martin Havlat .60 1.50
7 Daniel Alfredsson .75 2.00
8 Mike Fisher .40 1.00
9 Radek Bonk .20 .50
10 Peter Schaefer .20 .50
11 Jody Hull .20 .50
12 Marian Hossa .60 1.50
13 Petr Schastlivy .20 .50
14 Bryan Smolinski .20 .50
15 Shaun Van Allen .20 .50
16 Karel Rachunek .20 .50
17 Anton Volchenkov .20 .50
18 Chris Neil .20 .50
19 Vaclav Varada .20 .50
20 Todd White .20 .50
21 Martin Prusek .30 .75
22 Shane Hnidy .20 .50
23 Jason Spezza 1.25 3.00
24 Patrick Lalime .40 1.00
25 Jacques Martin CO .10 .25
26 Don Jackson ACO .10 .25
27 Perry Pearn ACO .10 .25
28 Spartacat MASCOT .02 .10

2006-07 Senators Postcards

This listing is believed to be incomplete. If you can confirm other singles from this set, please email us at hockeymag@beckett.com.

3 Daniel Alfredsson 1.25 3.00
4 Joe Corvo .40 1.00
5 Denis Hamel .40 1.00
6 Dany Heatley 1.25 3.00
7 Chris Kelly .40 1.00
8 Brian McGrattan .75 2.00
9 Andrej Meszaros .40 1.00
10 Chris Phillips .40 1.00
11 Jason Spezza 1.25 3.00
12 Peter Schaefer .40 1.00
13 Christoph Schubert .40 1.00
14 Wade Redden .75 2.00
15 Logo Card .10 .25

1972-73 7-Eleven Slurpee Cups WHA

This 20-cup set features a color head shot and facsimile autograph on the front, and a 7-11 logo, team logo, players name, and biographical information on the back. Cups are unnumbered and checklisted below alphabetically.

COMPLETE SET (20) 125.00 250.00
1 Norm Beaudin 5.00 10.00
2 Chris Bordeleau 5.00 10.00
3 Carl Brewer 5.00 10.00
4 Wayne Carleton 6.00 12.00
5 Gerry Cheevers 12.50 25.00
6 Wayne Connelly 7.50 15.00
7 Jean-Guy Gendron 5.00 10.00
8 Ted Green 5.00 10.00
9 Al Hamilton 5.00 10.00
10 Jim Harrison 5.00 10.00
11 Bobby Hull 25.00 50.00
12 Andre Lacroix 6.00 12.00
13 Danny Lawson 5.00 10.00
14 John McKenzie 5.00 10.00
15 Jim Mcleod 5.00 10.00
16 Jack Norris 5.00 10.00
17 John Schella 5.00 10.00
18 J.C. Tremblay 7.50 15.00
19 Ron Ward 5.00 10.00
20 Jim Watson 5.00 10.00

1984-85 7-Eleven Discs

This set of 60 discs was sponsored by 7-Eleven. Each disc or coin measures approximately 2" in diameter and features an alternating portrait of the player and the team's logo. The coins are quite colorful and have adhesive backing. We have checklisted the coins below in alphabetical order of team name. Also the player's names have been alphabetized within their teams, and their uniform numbers placed to the right of their names. In addition, 7-Eleven also issued a large 4 1/2" diameter Wayne Gretzky disc which is not considered an essential part of the complete set. There is also a paper checklist sheet produced which pictured (in red, white, and blue) some of the coins and listed the players in the set.

COMPLETE SET (60) 50.00 125.00
1 Ray Bourque 7 2.00 5.00
2 Rick Middleton 16 .60 1.50
3 Tom Barrasso 30 1.00 2.50
4 Gilbert Perreault 11 .75 2.00
5 Rejean Lemelin 31 .60 1.50
6 Lanny McDonald 9 1.00 2.50
7 Paul Reinhart 23 .40 1.00
8 Doug Risebrough 8 .40 1.00
9 Denis Savard 18 1.00 2.50
10 Al Secord 20 .40 1.00
11 Steve Yzerman 19 6.00 15.00
12 Dave(Tiger) Williams 55 .60 1.50
13 Glenn Anderson 9 .75 2.00
14 Paul Coffey 7 2.00 5.00
15 Michel Goulet 16 .75 2.00
16 Wayne Gretzky 99 8.00 20.00
17 Charlie Huddy 22 .40 1.00
18 Pat Hughes 16 .40 1.00
19 Jari Kurri 17 1.25 3.00
20 Kevin Lowe 4 .40 1.00
21 Mark Messier 11 3.00 8.00
22 Ron Francis 10 1.50 4.00
23 Sylvain Turgeon 16 .40 1.00
24 Marcel Dionne 16 .75 2.00
25 Dave Taylor 18 .60 1.50
26 Brian Bellows 23 .40 1.00
27 Dino Ciccarelli 20 .60 1.50
28 Harold Snepsts 28 .60 1.50
29 Bob Gainey 23 .75 2.00
30 Larry Robinson 19 1.00 2.50
31 Mel Bridgman 18 .40 1.00
32 Chico Resch 1 .60 1.50
33 Mike Bossy 22 1.25 3.00
34 Bryan Trottier 19 1.00 2.50
35 Barry Beck 5 .40 1.00
36 Don Maloney 12 .40 1.00
37 Tim Kerr 12 .60 1.50
38 Darryl Sittler 27 1.00 2.50
39 Mike Bullard 22 .40 1.00
40 Rick Kehoe 17 .60 1.50
41 Peter Stastny 26 1.25 3.00
42 Bernie Federko 24 .60 1.50
43 Rob Ramage 5 .40 1.00
44 John Anderson 10 .40 1.00
45 Bill Derlago 19 .40 1.00
46 Gary Nylund 2 .40 1.00
47 Rick Vaive 22 .40 1.00
48 Richard Brodeur 35 .60 1.50
49 Gary Lupul 7 .40 1.00
50 Darcy Rota 18 .40 1.00
51 Stan Smyl 12 .60 1.50
52 Tony Tanti 9 .40 1.00
53 Mike Gartner 11 1.25 3.00
54 Rod Langway 5 .60 1.50
55 Scott Arniel 11 .40 1.00
56 Dave Babych 44 .40 1.00
57 Laurie Boschman 16 .40 1.00
58 Dale Hawerchuk 10 1.00 2.50
59 Paul MacLean 15 .40 1.00
60 Brian Mullen 19 .40 1.00
NNO Wayne Gretzky Large 10.00 25.00
NNO Paper Checklist Sheet 2.00 5.00

1985-86 7-Eleven Credit Cards

This 25-card set was sponsored by 7-Eleven. The cards measure approximately 3 3/8" by 2 1/8" and were issued in the "credit card" format. The front features color head and shoulder shots of two players from the same NHL team. These pictures are enframed by a black background, with the player's name, position, and uniform number in blue lettering below the photo. The information on the card back is framed in red boxes. In the smaller box on the left appears the 7-Eleven logo, card number, and the team logo. The right-hand box gives a brief history of the team. The key card in the set is Mario Lemieux, shown during his Rookie Card year.

COMPLETE SET (25) 14.00 35.00
1 Ray Bourque and Rick Middleton .75 2.00
2 Tom Barrasso and Gilbert Perreault .60 1.50
3 Paul Reinhart and Lanny McDonald .40 1.00
4 Denis Savard and Doug Wilson .60 1.50
5 Ron Duguay and Steve Yzerman 3.00 8.00
6 Paul Coffey and Jari Kurri 1.00 2.50
7 Ron Francis and Mike Liut .75 2.00
8 Marcel Dionne and Dave Taylor .50 1.25
9 Brian Bellows and Dino Ciccarelli .60 1.50
10 Larry Robinson and Guy Carbonneau .60 1.50

11 Mel Bridgman and Chico Resch .30 .75
12 Mike Bossy and Bryan Trottier 1.00 2.50
13 Reijo Ruotsalainen and Barry Beck .30 .75
14 Tim Kerr and Mark Howe .30 .75
15 Mario Lemieux and Mike Bullard 8.00 20.00
16 Peter Stastny and Michel Goulet 1.00 2.50
17 Rob Ramage and Brian Sutter .30 .75
18 Rick Vaive and Borje Salming .40 1.00
19 Patrik Sundstrom and Stan Smyl .30 .75
20 Rod Langway and Mike Gartner .50 1.25
21 Dale Hawerchuk and Paul MacLean .40 1.00
22 Stanley Cup Winners .30 .75
23 Prince of Wales Trophy Winners .30 .75
24 Clarence S. Campbell Bowl Winners .30 .75
25 Title Card .08 .25

1991-92 Sharks Sports Action

This 22-card standard-size set was issued by Sports Action and features members of the 1991-92 San Jose Sharks. The cards are printed on thin card stock. The fronts feature full-bleed glossy color action photos. The backs carry brief biography, career summary, and the team logo. The cards are unnumbered and checklisted below in alphabetical order.

COMPLETE SET (22) 4.00 10.00
1 Perry Anderson .20 .50
2 Perry Berezan .20 .50
3 Steve Bozek .20 .50
4 Dean Evason .20 .50
5 Pat Falloon .30 .75
6 Paul Fenton .20 .50
7 Link Gaetz .20 .50
8 Jeff Hackett .40 1.00
9 Ken Hammond .20 .50
10 Brian Hayward .30 .75
11 Tony Hrkac .20 .50
12 Kelly Kisio .25 .60
13 Brian Lawton .20 .50
14 Pat MacLeod .20 .50
15 Bob McGill .20 .50
16 Brian Mullen .20 .50
17 Jarmo Myllys .25 .60
18 Wayne Presley .20 .50
19 Neil Wilkinson .25 .60
20 Doug Wilson .40 1.00
21 Rob Zettler .20 .50
22 San Jose Sharks Game action .30 .75

1997 Sharks Fleer All-Star Sheet

This odd-sized sheet was handed out to attendees of the '97 NHL All-Star Game to promote the '96-'97 line of Fleer hockey products. The sheet also was available at the All-Star Fanfest card show. It features eight members of the hometown San Jose Sharks on three different types of Fleer cards; the brand pictured is listed after each player's name.

1 Sharks Sheet 1.50 4.00
Doug Bodger Fleer Picks
Kelly Hrudey Metal Universe
Al Iafrate Metal Universe
Bernie Nicholls Metal Universe
Owen Nolan Fleer
Marcus Ragnarsson Fleer
Chris Terreri Fleer
Alexei Yegorov Fleer Picks

2001-02 Sharks Postcards

This set was given away by the team during the 2001-02 season. The checklist below is not believed to be complete. Please forward any info to hockeymag@beckett.com. Special thanks to Sgt. Randy Garcia of the Humboldt County Sheriff's Dept. for the checklist and image.

1 Adam Graves .75 2.00
2 Vincent Damphousse .40 1.00
3 Matt Bradley .40 1.00
4 Brad Stuart .75 2.00
5 Owen Nolan .75 2.00
6 Patrick Marleau .75 2.00
7 Gary Suter .40 1.00
8 Niklas Sundstrom .40 1.00
9 Marco Sturm .40 1.00
10 Mike Ricci .40 1.00
11 Marcus Ragnarsson .40 1.00
12 Scott Thornton .40 1.00
13 Scott Hannan .40 1.00
14 Todd Harvey .40 1.00
15 Bryan Marchment .40 1.00
16 Teemu Selanne 1.25 3.00

2002-03 Sharks Team Issue

These 4X 7 blank backs were issued by the team at promotional events. It's likely more exist in the set. If you can confirm this, please contact us at hockeymag@beckett.com.

COMPLETE SET (?)
1 Vincent Damphousse 1.00
2 Adam Graves 1.00
3 Patrick Marleau 1.00
4 Evgeni Nabokov 2.00
5 Mike Rathje 1.00
6 Mike Ricci 1.00
7 Teemu Selanne 3.00
8 Marco Sturm 1.00

2003-04 Sharks Postcards

The checklist is likely incomplete. Please send additional info to hockeymag@beckett.com.

COMPLETE SET (?)
1 Jonathan Cheechoo 1.25 3.00
2 Vincent Damphousse .40 1.00
3 Rob Davidson .40 1.00
4 Nils Ekman .40 1.00
5 Jim Fahey .40 1.00
6 Scott Hannan .40 1.00
7 Todd Harvey .40 1.00
8 Alexander Korolyuk .40 1.00
9 Patrick Marleau .75 2.00
10 Alyn McCauley .40 1.00
11 Kyle McLaren .40 1.00
12 Evgeni Nabokov .75 2.00
13 Tom Preissing .40 1.00
14 Wayne Primeau .40 1.00
15 Mike Rathje .40 1.00
16 Mike Ricci .40 1.00
17 Brad Stuart .40 1.00
18 Marco Sturm .40 1.00
19 Scott Thornton .40 1.00

1960-61 Shirriff Coins

This set of 120 coins (each measuring approximately 1 3/8" in diameter) features players from all six NHL teams. These plastic coins are in color and numbered on the front. The coins are checklisted below according to teams as follows: Toronto Maple Leafs (1-20), Montreal Canadiens (21-40), Detroit Red Wings (41-60), Chicago Blackhawks (61-80), New York Rangers (81-100), and Boston Bruins (101-120). The set was also issued on a limited basis as a factory set in a black presentation box.

COMPLETE SET (120) 250.00 500.00
1 Johnny Bower 5.00 10.00
2 Dick Duff 2.50 5.00
3 Carl Brewer 2.50 5.00
4 Red Kelly 5.00 10.00
5 Tim Horton 7.50 15.00
6 Allan Stanley 2.50 5.00
7 Bob Baun 2.50 5.00
8 Billy Harris 1.50 3.00
9 George Armstrong 3.00 6.00
10 Ron Stewart 1.50 3.00
11 Bert Olmstead 2.50 5.00
12 Frank Mahovlich 7.50 15.00
13 Bob Pulford 2.50 5.00
14 Gary Edmundson 1.50 3.00
15 Johnny Wilson 1.50 3.00
16 Larry Regan 1.50 3.00
17 Gerry James 2.00 4.00
18 Rudy Migay 1.50 3.00
19 Gerry Ehman 1.50 3.00
20 Punch Imlach CO 2.00 4.00
21 Jacques Plante 12.50 25.00
22 Dickie Moore 3.00 6.00
23 Don Marshall 1.50 3.00
24 Albert Langlois 1.50 3.00
25 Tom Johnson 2.50 5.00
26 Doug Harvey 5.00 10.00
27 Phil Goyette 1.50 3.00
28 Boom Boom Geoffrion 6.00 12.00
29 Marcel Bonin 1.50 3.00
30 Jean Beliveau 10.00 20.00
31 Ralph Backstrom 2.00 4.00
32 Andre Pronovost 1.50 3.00
33 Claude Provost 2.00 4.00
34 Henri Richard 7.50 15.00
35 Jean-Guy Talbot 2.00 4.00
36 J.C. Tremblay 2.00 4.00
37 Bob Turner 1.50 3.00
38 Bill Hicke 1.50 3.00
39 Charlie Hodge 4.00 8.00
40 Toe Blake CO 2.50 5.00
41 Terry Sawchuk 10.00 20.00
42 Gordie Howe 25.00 50.00
43 John McKenzie 1.50 3.00
44 Alex Delvecchio 5.00 10.00
45 Norm Ullman 3.00 6.00
46 Jack McIntyre 1.50 3.00
47 Barry Cullen 2.00 4.00
48 Val Fonteyne 2.00 4.00
49 Warren Godfrey 1.50 3.00
50 Pete Goegan 1.50 3.00
51 Gerry Melnyk 1.50 3.00
52 Marc Reaume 1.50 3.00
53 Gary Aldcorn 1.50 3.00
54 Len Lunde 1.50 3.00
55 Murray Oliver 1.50 3.00
56 Marcel Pronovost 2.50 5.00
57 Howie Glover 1.50 3.00
58 Gerry Odrowski 1.50 3.00
59 Parker MacDonald 1.50 3.00
60 Sid Abel CO 2.50 5.00
61 Glenn Hall 6.00 12.00
62 Ed Litzenberger 2.00 4.00
63 Bobby Hull 20.00 40.00
64 Tod Sloan 1.50 3.00
65 Murray Balfour 1.50 3.00
66 Pierre Pilote 2.50 5.00
67 Al Arbour 2.50 5.00
68 Earl Balfour 1.50 3.00
69 Eric Nesterenko 2.00 4.00
70 Ken Wharram 2.50 5.00
71 Stan Mikita 12.50 25.00
72 Ab McDonald 1.50 3.00
73 Elmer Vasko 2.00 4.00
74 Dollard St.Laurent 2.00 4.00
75 Ron Murphy 1.50 3.00
76 Jack Evans 1.50 3.00
77 Bill(Red) Hay 1.50 3.00
78 Reg Fleming 2.00 4.00
79 Cecil Hoekstra 1.50 3.00
80 Tommy Ivan CO 2.00 4.00
81 Jack McCartan 4.00 8.00
82 Red Sullivan 1.50 3.00
83 Camille Henry 2.00 4.00
84 Larry Popein 1.50 3.00
85 John Hanna 1.50 3.00
86 Harry Howell 2.50 5.00
87 Eddie Shack 5.00 10.00
88 Irv Spencer 1.50 3.00
89 Andy Bathgate 3.00 6.00
90 Bill Gadsby 2.50 5.00
91 Andy Hebenton 1.50 3.00
92 Earl Ingarfield 1.50 3.00
93 Don Johns 1.50 3.00
94 Dave Balon 1.50 3.00
95 Jim Morrison 1.50 3.00
96 Ken Schinkel 1.50 3.00
97 Lou Fontinato 1.50 3.00
98 Ted Hampson 1.50 3.00
99 Brian Cullen 2.00 4.00
100 Alf Pike CO 1.50 3.00
101 Don Simmons 2.50 5.00
102 Fern Flaman 2.50 5.00
103 Vic Stasiuk 2.00 4.00
104 Johnny Bucyk 5.00 10.00
105 Bronco Horvath 2.00 4.00
106 Doug Mohns 4.00 8.00
107 Leo Boivin 2.50 5.00
108 Don McKenney 1.50 3.00
109 Jean-Guy Gendron 1.50 3.00
110 Jerry Toppazzini 1.50 3.00
111 Dick Meissner 1.50 3.00
112 Autry Erickson 1.50 3.00
113 Jim Bartlett 1.50 3.00
114 Orval Tessier 2.00 4.00
115 Billy Carter 1.50 3.00
116 Dallas Smith 2.00 4.00
117 Leo Labine 1.50 3.00
118 Bob Armstrong 1.50 3.00
119 Bruce Gamble 2.50 5.00
120 Milt Schmidt CO 3.00 6.00

1961-62 Shirriff/Salada Coins

This set of 120 coins (each measuring approximately 1 3/8" in diameter) features players of the NHL, all six teams. These plastic coins are in color and numbered on the front. The coins are numbered according to teams as follows: Boston Bruins (1-20), Chicago Blackhawks (21-40), Toronto Maple Leafs (41-60), Detroit Red Wings (61-80), New York Rangers (81-100), and Montreal Canadiens (101-120). The coins were also produced in identical fashion for Salada with a Salada imprint; the Salada version has the same values as listed below. This was the only year of Shirriff coins where collectors could obtain plastic shields for displaying their collection. These shields are not considered part of the complete set.

COMPLETE SET (120) 200.00 400.00
1 Cliff Pennington 1.25 2.50
2 Dallas Smith 2.00 4.00
3 Andre Pronovost 1.25 2.50
4 Charlie Burns 1.25 2.50
5 Leo Boivin 2.50 5.00

1961-62 Shirriff/Salada Coins

This set of 120 coins (each measuring approximately 1 3/8" in diameter) features players of the NHL, all six teams. These plastic coins are in color and numbered on the front. The coins are numbered according to teams as follows: Boston Bruins (1-20), Chicago Blackhawks (21-40), Toronto Maple Leafs (41-60), Detroit Red Wings (61-80), New York Rangers (81-100), and Montreal Canadiens (101-120). The coins were also produced in identical fashion for Salada with a Salada imprint; the Salada version has the same values as listed below. This was the only year of Shirriff coins where collectors could obtain plastic shields for displaying their collection. These shields are not considered part of the complete set.

COMPLETE SET (120) 200.00 400.00
1 Cliff Pennington 1.25 2.50
2 Dallas Smith 2.00 4.00
3 Andre Pronovost 1.25 2.50
4 Charlie Burns 1.25 2.50
5 Leo Boivin 2.50 5.00

6 Don McKenney 1.25 2.50
7 Johnny Bucyk 4.00 8.00
8 Murray Oliver 1.25 2.50
9 Jerry Toppazzini 1.25 2.50
10 Doug Mohns 2.00 4.00
11 Don Head 2.00 4.00
12 Bob Armstrong 1.25 2.50
13 Pat Stapleton 2.00 4.00
14 Orland Kurtenbach 2.00 4.00
15 Dick Meissner 1.25 2.50
16 Ted Green 2.00 4.00
17 Tom Williams 1.25 2.50
18 Autry Erickson 1.25 2.50
19 Phil Watson CO 2.50 5.00
20 Ed Chadwick 2.50 5.00
21 Wayne Hillman 5.00 10.00
22 Stan Mikita 6.00 12.00
23 Eric Nesterenko 2.00 4.00
24 Reg Fleming 1.25 2.50
25 Bobby Hull 12.50 25.00
26 Elmer Vasko 1.25 2.50
27 Pierre Pilote 2.50 5.00
28 Chico Maki 2.00 4.00
29 Glenn Hall 5.00 10.00
30 Murray Balfour 1.25 2.50
31 Bronco Horvath 1.50 3.00
32 Ken Wharram 2.00 4.00
33 Ab McDonald 1.25 2.50
34 Bill(Red) Hay 1.25 2.50
35 Dollard St.Laurent 2.00 4.00
36 Ron Murphy 1.25 2.50
37 Bob Turner 1.25 2.50
38 Gerry Melnyk 1.25 2.50
39 Jack Evans 1.25 2.50
40 Rudy Pilous CO 2.50 5.00
41 Johnny Bower 5.00 10.00
42 Allan Stanley 3.00 6.00
43 Frank Mahovlich 5.00 10.00
44 Tim Horton 7.50 15.00
45 Carl Brewer 2.00 4.00
46 Bob Pulford 2.50 5.00
47 Bob Nevin 2.00 4.00
48 Eddie Shack 4.00 8.00
49 Red Kelly 4.00 8.00
50 Bob Baun 2.00 4.00
51 George Armstrong 3.00 6.00
52 Bert Olmstead 2.50 5.00
53 Dick Duff 2.00 4.00
54 Billy Harris 2.00 4.00
55 Larry Keenan 1.25 2.50
56 Johnny MacMillan 1.25 2.50
57 Punch Imlach CO 2.00 4.00
58 Dave Keon 7.50 15.00
59 Larry Hillman 1.25 2.50
60 Al Arbour 2.50 5.00
61 Sid Abel CO 2.50 5.00
62 Warren Godfrey 1.25 2.50
63 Vic Stasiuk 1.25 2.50
64 Leo Labine 1.25 2.50
65 Howie Glover 1.25 2.50
66 Gordie Howe 20.00 40.00
67 Val Fonteyne 1.25 2.50
68 Marcel Pronovost 2.50 5.00
69 Parker MacDonald 1.25 2.50
70 Alex Delvecchio 4.00 8.00
71 Ed Litzenberger 1.25 2.50
72 Al Johnson 1.25 2.50
73 Bruce MacGregor 1.25 2.50
74 Howie Young 1.25 2.50
75 Pete Goegan 1.25 2.50
76 Norm Ullman 3.00 6.00
77 Terry Sawchuk 12.50 25.00
78 Gerry Odrowski 1.25 2.50
79 Bill Gadsby 2.50 5.00
80 Hank Bassen 2.00 4.00
81 Doug Harvey 4.00 8.00
82 Earl Ingarfield 1.25 2.50
83 Pat Hannigan 1.25 2.50
84 Dean Prentice 2.00 4.00
85 Gump Worsley 5.00 10.00
86 Irv Spencer 1.25 2.50
87 Camille Henry 2.00 4.00
88 Andy Bathgate 3.00 6.00
89 Harry Howell 2.50 5.00
90 Andy Hebenton 1.25 2.50
91 Red Sullivan 1.25 2.50
92 Ted Hampson 1.25 2.50
93 Jean-Guy Gendron 1.25 2.50
94 Albert Langlois 1.25 2.50
95 Larry Cahan 1.25 2.50
96 Bob Cunningham 1.25 2.50
97 Vic Hadfield 2.00 4.00
98 Jean Ratelle 5.00 10.00
99 Ken Schinkel 1.25 2.50
100 Johnny Wilson 1.25 2.50
101 Toe Blake CO 2.50 5.00
102 Jean Beliveau 10.00 20.00
103 Don Marshall 1.25 2.50
104 Boom Boom Geoffrion 6.00 12.00
105 Claude Provost 2.00 4.00
106 Tom Johnson 2.50 5.00
107 Dickie Moore 4.00 8.00
108 Bill Hicke 1.25 2.50
109 Jean-Guy Talbot 2.00 4.00
110 Henri Richard 5.00 10.00
111 Lou Fontinato 1.50 3.00
112 Gilles Tremblay 1.25 2.50
113 Jacques Plante 10.00 20.00
114 Ralph Backstrom 2.00 4.00
115 Marcel Bonin 1.25 2.50
116 Phil Goyette 1.25 2.50
117 Bobby Rousseau 2.00 4.00
118 J.C. Tremblay 1.25 2.50
119 Al MacNeil 1.25 2.50
120 Jean Gauthier 1.25 2.50
S1 Boston Bruins Shield 30.00 60.00
S2 Chicago Blackhawks Shield 30.00 60.00
S3 Detroit Red Wings Shield 30.00 60.00
S4 Montreal Canadiens Shield 30.00 60.00
S5 New York Rangers Shield 30.00 60.00
S6 Toronto Maple Leafs Shield 30.00 60.00

1962-63 Shirriff Coins

This set of 60 coins (each measuring approximately 1 1/2" in diameter) features 12 All-Stars, six Trophy winners, and players from Montreal (20) and Toronto (22). The four American teams in the NHL were not included in this set except where they appeared as All-Stars or Trophy winners. These metal coins are in color and numbered on the front. The backs are written in French and English.

COMPLETE SET (60) 200.00 400.00
1 Johnny Bower 5.00 10.00
2 Allan Stanley 4.00 8.00
3 Frank Mahovlich 10.00 20.00
4 Tim Horton 10.00 20.00
5 Carl Brewer 2.50 5.00
6 Bob Pulford 4.00 8.00
7 Bob Nevin 2.50 5.00
8 Eddie Shack 4.00 8.00
9 Red Kelly 4.00 8.00
10 George Armstrong 4.00 8.00
11 Bert Olmstead 3.00 6.00
12 Dick Duff 2.50 5.00
13 Billy Harris 2.00 4.00
14 Johnny MacMillan 2.00 4.00
15 Punch Imlach CO 2.50 5.00
16 Dave Keon 7.50 15.00
17 Larry Hillman 2.00 4.00
18 Ed Litzenberger 2.00 4.00
19 Bob Baun 3.00 6.00
20 Al Arbour 4.00 8.00
21 Ron Stewart 2.00 4.00
22 Don Simmons 3.00 6.00
23 Lou Fontinato 2.00 4.00
24 Gilles Tremblay 2.00 4.00
25 Jacques Plante 12.50 25.00
26 Ralph Backstrom 2.50 5.00
27 Marcel Bonin 2.00 4.00
28 Phil Goyette 2.00 4.00
29 Bobby Rousseau 2.50 5.00
30 J.C. Tremblay 2.50 5.00
31 Toe Blake CO 4.00 8.00
32 Jean Beliveau 10.00 20.00
33 Don Marshall 2.00 4.00
34 Boom Boom Geoffrion 6.00 12.00
35 Claude Provost 2.50 5.00
36 Tom Johnson 3.00 6.00
37 Dickie Moore 5.00 10.00
38 Bill Hicke 2.00 4.00
39 Jean-Guy Talbot 2.50 5.00
40 Al MacNeil 2.50 5.00
41 Henri Richard 7.50 15.00
42 Red Berenson 2.50 5.00
43 Jacques Plante AS 12.50 25.00
44 Jean-Guy Talbot AS 2.50 5.00
45 Doug Harvey AS 5.00 10.00
46 Stan Mikita AS 5.00 10.00
47 Bobby Hull AS 12.50 25.00
48 Andy Bathgate AS 4.00 8.00
49 Glenn Hall AS 5.00 10.00
50 Pierre Pilote AS 4.00 8.00
51 Carl Brewer AS 2.50 5.00
52 Dave Keon AS 7.50 15.00
53 Frank Mahovlich AS 7.50 15.00
54 Gordie Howe AS 20.00 40.00
55 Dave Keon Byng 7.50 15.00
56 Bobby Rousseau Calder 2.50 5.00
57 Bobby Hull Ross 12.50 25.00
58 Jacques Plante Vezina 12.50 25.00
59 Jacques Plante Hart 12.50 25.00
60 Doug Harvey Norris 5.00 10.00

1968-69 Shirriff Coins

This set of 176 coins (each measuring approximately 1 3/8" in diameter) features players from all of the teams in the NHL. These plastic coins are in color and numbered on the front. However the coins are numbered by Shirriff within each team and not for the whole set. The correspondence between the actual coin numbers and the numbers assigned below should be apparent. For those few situations where two coins from the same team have the same number, that number is listed in the checklist below next to the name. The coins are checklisted below according to teams as follows: Boston Bruins (1-16), Chicago Blackhawks (17-33), Detroit Red Wings (34-49), Los Angeles Kings (50-61), Minnesota North Stars (62-74), Montreal Canadiens (75-92), New York Rangers (93-108), Oakland Seals (109-121), Philadelphia Flyers (122-134), Pittsburgh Penguins (135-146), St. Louis Blues (147-158), and Toronto Maple Leafs (159-176). Some of the coins are quite challenging to find. It seems the higher numbers within each team and the coins from the players on the expansion teams are more difficult to find; these are marked by SP in the list below.

COMPLETE SET (176) 3000.00 6000.00
1 Eddie Shack 5.00 10.00
2 Ed Westfall 2.50 5.00
3 Don Awrey 2.00 4.00
4 Gerry Cheevers 6.00 12.00
5 Bobby Orr 50.00 100.00
6 Johnny Bucyk 5.00 10.00
7 Derek Sanderson 10.00 20.00
8 Phil Esposito 10.00 20.00
9 Fred Stanfield 2.00 4.00
10 Ken Hodge 3.00 6.00
11 John McKenzie 2.00 4.00
12 Ted Green 2.50 5.00
13 Dallas Smith SP 50.00 100.00
14 Gary Doak SP 50.00 100.00
15 Glen Sather SP 50.00 100.00
16 Tom Williams SP 37.50 75.00
17 Bobby Hull 25.00 50.00
18 Pat Stapleton 2.00 4.00
19 Wayne Maki 2.00 4.00
20 Denis DeJordy 4.00 8.00
21 Ken Wharram 2.50 5.00
22 Pit Martin 2.00 4.00
23 Chico Maki 2.00 4.00
24 Doug Mohns 2.50 5.00
25 Stan Mikita 7.50 15.00
26 Doug Jarrett 2.00 4.00
27 Dennis Hull 11 SP (small portrait) 50.00 100.00
28 Dennis Hull 11 (large portrait) 12.50 25.00
29 Matt Ravlich 2.00 4.00
30 Dave Dryden SP 40.00 80.00
31 Eric Nesterenko SP 40.00 80.00
32 Gilles Marotte SP 40.00 80.00
33 Jim Pappin SP 40.00 80.00
34 Gary Bergman 2.00 4.00
35 Roger Crozier 4.00 8.00
36 Peter Mahovlich 3.00 6.00
37 Alex Delvecchio 4.00 8.00
38 Dean Prentice 2.50 5.00
39 Kent Douglas 2.00 4.00
40 Roy Edwards 3.00 6.00
41 Bruce MacGregor 2.00 4.00
42 Garry Unger 3.00 6.00
43 Pete Stemkowski 2.00 4.00
44 Gordie Howe 40.00 80.00
45 Frank Mahovlich 6.00 12.00
46 Bob Baun SP 40.00 80.00
47 Brian Conacher SP 40.00 80.00
48 Jim Watson SP 40.00 80.00
49 Nick Libett SP 40.00 80.00
50 Real Lemieux 2.50 5.00
51 Ted Irvine 2.50 5.00
52 Bob Wall 2.50 5.00
53 Bill White 2.50 5.00
54 Gord Labossiere 2.50 5.00
55 Eddie Joyal 2.00 4.00
56 Lowell MacDonald 2.50 5.00
57 Bill Flett 2.50 5.00
58 Wayne Rutledge 3.00 6.00
59 Dave Amadio 2.00 4.00
60 Skip Krake SP 25.00 50.00
61 Doug Robinson SP 25.00 50.00
62 Wayne Connelly 2.50 5.00
63 Bob Woytowich 2.50 5.00
64 Andre Boudrias 2.50 5.00
65 Bill Goldsworthy 3.00 6.00
66 Cesare Maniago 4.00 8.00
67 Milan Marcetta 2.50 5.00
68 Bill Collins SP 7 25.00 50.00
69 Claude Larose SP 7 50.00 100.00
70 Parker MacDonald 2.50 5.00
71 Ray Cullen 2.50 5.00
72 Mike McMahon 2.50 5.00
73 Bob McCord SP 25.00 50.00
74 Larry Hillman SP 25.00 50.00
75 Gump Worsley 5.00 10.00
76 Rogatien Vachon 7.50 15.00
77 Ted Harris 2.00 4.00
78 Jacques Laperriere 3.00 6.00
79 J.C. Tremblay 2.50 5.00
80 Jean Beliveau 15.00 30.00
81 Gilles Tremblay 2.00 4.00
82 Ralph Backstrom 2.50 5.00
83 Bobby Rousseau 2.00 4.00
84 John Ferguson 3.00 6.00
85 Dick Duff 3.00 6.00
86 Terry Harper 3.00 6.00
87 Yvan Cournoyer 4.00 8.00
88 Jacques Lemaire 6.00 12.00
89 Henri Richard 6.00 12.00
90 Claude Provost SP 50.00 100.00
91 Serge Savard SP 75.00 150.00
92 Mickey Redmond SP 75.00 150.00
93 Rod Seiling 2.00 4.00
94 Jean Ratelle 4.00 8.00
95 Ed Giacomin 7.50 15.00
96 Reg Fleming 2.00 4.00
97 Phil Goyette 2.00 4.00
98 Arnie Brown 2.00 4.00
99 Don Marshall 2.00 4.00
100 Orland Kurtenbach 3.00 6.00
101 Bob Nevin 2.00 4.00
102 Rod Gilbert 4.00 8.00
103 Harry Howell 3.00 6.00
104 Jim Neilson 2.00 4.00
105 Vic Hadfield SP 150.00 400.00
106 Larry Jeffrey SP 125.00 250.00
107 Dave Balon SP 75.00 150.00
108 Ron Stewart SP 75.00 150.00
109 Gerry Ehman 2.00 4.00
110 John Brenneman 2.50 5.00
111 Ted Hampson 2.50 5.00
112 Billy Harris 2.50 5.00
113 George Swarbrick SP 5 50.00 100.00
114 Carol Vadnais SP 5 250.00 500.00
115 Gary Smith 4.00 8.00
116 Charlie Hodge 4.00 8.00
117 Bert Marshall 2.50 5.00
118 Bill Hicke 2.50 5.00
119 Tracy Pratt 2.50 5.00
120 Gary Jarrett SP 250.00 500.00
121 Howie Young SP 250.00 500.00
122 Bernie Parent 20.00 40.00
123 John Miszuk 2.50 5.00
124 Ed Hoekstra SP 3 50.00 100.00
125 Allan Stanley SP 3 50.00 100.00
126 Gary Dornhoefer 3.00 6.00
127 Doug Favell 4.00 8.00
128 Andre Lacroix 2.50 5.00
129 Brit Selby 2.50 5.00
130 Don Blackburn 2.50 5.00
131 Leon Rochefort 2.50 5.00
132 Forbes Kennedy 2.50 5.00
133 Claude Laforge SP 40.00 80.00
134 Pat Hannigan SP 40.00 80.00
135 Ken Schinkel 2.50 5.00
136 Earl Ingarfield 2.50 5.00
137 Val Fonteyne 2.00 4.00
138 Noel Price 2.00 4.00
139 Andy Bathgate 4.00 8.00
140 Les Binkley 4.00 8.00
141 Leo Boivin 2.50 5.00
142 Paul Andrea 2.00 4.00
143 Dunc McCallum 3.00 6.00
144 Keith McCreary 2.50 5.00
145 Lou Angotti SP 40.00 80.00
146 Wally Boyer SP 40.00 80.00
147 Ron Schock 2.50 5.00
148 Bob Plager 3.00 6.00
149 Al Arbour 4.00 8.00
150 Red Berenson 3.00 6.00
151 Glenn Hall 7.50 15.00
152 Jim Roberts 2.50 5.00
153 Noel Picard 2.50 5.00
154 Barclay Plager 3.00 6.00
155 Larry Keenan 2.50 5.00
156 Terry Crisp 3.00 6.00
157 Gary Sabourin SP 40.00 80.00
158 Ab McDonald SP 40.00 80.00
159 George Armstrong 4.00 8.00
160 Wayne Carleton 2.00 4.00
161 Paul Henderson 3.00 6.00
162 Bob Pulford 3.00 6.00
163 Mike Walton 2.50 5.00
164 Johnny Bower 4.00 8.00
165 Ron Ellis 2.50 5.00
166 Mike Pelyk 2.00 4.00
167 Murray Oliver 2.00 4.00
168 Norm Ullman 4.00 8.00
169 Dave Keon 4.00 8.00
170 Floyd Smith 2.00 4.00
171 Marcel Pronovost 3.00 6.00
172 Tim Horton 7.50 15.00
173 Bruce Gamble 3.00 6.00
174 Jim McKenny SP 50.00 100.00
175 Mike Byers SP 50.00 100.00
176 Pierre Pilote SP 75.00 150.00

1995-96 SkyBox Impact Promo Panel

Measuring 7" by 7", this perforated promo panel was issued by SkyBox to celebrate the inaugural edition of the SkyBox Impact hockey series. The left strip consists of ad copy, with four standard-size player cards filling out the rest of the panel. As indicated in the listing below, Blaine Lacher is featured on two cards: a regular card as well as a Deflector insert card. The only difference from their regular issue counterparts is that these cards have the word "SAMPLE" on a black rectangle in place of card number.

1 Theo Fleury .40 1.00
Blaine Lacher
Blaine Lacher
Jeremy Roenick

1995-96 SkyBox Impact

The 1996 Skybox Impact set was issued in one series totaling 250 cards. The 10-card packs retailed for $1.29. Each pack included an NHL on Fox Slapshot Instant Win Game Card, offering a chance at more than 20,000 prizes. The unused game cards sell for about ten cents. The Blaine Lacher SkyMotion exchange card was randomly inserted at a rate of 1:360 packs. The exchange deadline for the Lacher SkyMotion card was December 31st, 1996. Prices for the expired card and the redeemed card are listed below.

COMPLETE SET (250) 6.00 15.00
1 Bobby Dollas .01 .05
2 Guy Hebert .02 .10
3 Paul Kariya .07 .20
4 Todd Krygier .01 .05
5 Oleg Tverdovsky .01 .05
6 Shaun Van Allen .01 .05
7 Ray Bourque .10 .30
8 Al Iafrate .02 .10
9 Blaine Lacher .02 .10
10 Joe Mullen .02 .10
11 Cam Neely .07 .20
12 Adam Oates .02 .10
13 Kevin Stevens .01 .05
14 Donald Audette .01 .05
15 Garry Galley .01 .05
16 Dominik Hasek .15 .40
17 Pat LaFontaine .07 .20
18 Derek Plante .01 .05
19 Alexei Zhitnik .01 .05
20 Steve Chiasson .01 .05
21 Theo Fleury .01 .05
22 Phil Housley .02 .10
23 Trevor Kidd .02 .10
24 Joe Nieuwendyk .02 .10
25 German Titov .01 .05
26 Zarley Zalapski .01 .05
27 Ed Belfour .07 .20
28 Chris Chelios .07 .20
29 Sergei Krivokrasov .01 .05
30 Joe Murphy .01 .05
31 Bernie Nicholls .01 .05
32 Patrick Poulin .01 .05
33 Jeremy Roenick .08 .25
34 Gary Suter .01 .05
35 Peter Forsberg .20 .50
36 Valeri Kamensky .02 .10
37 Claude Lemieux .01 .05
38 Curtis Leschyshyn .01 .05
39 Sandis Ozolinsh .01 .05
40 Mike Ricci .02 .10
41 Joe Sakic .15 .40
42 Jocelyn Thibault .07 .20
43 Bob Bassen .01 .05
44 Dave Gagner .01 .05
45 Todd Harvey .02 .10
46 Derian Hatcher .01 .05
47 Kevin Hatcher .01 .05
48 Mike Modano .10 .30
49 Andy Moog .07 .20
50 Dino Ciccarelli .02 .10
51 Paul Coffey .07 .20
52 Sergei Fedorov .10 .30
53 Vladimir Konstantinov .02 .10
54 Slava Kozlov .02 .10
55 Nicklas Lidstrom .07 .20
56 Chris Osgood .02 .10
57 Keith Primeau .01 .05
58 Steve Yzerman .40 1.00
59 Jason Arnott .01 .05
60 Curtis Joseph .07 .20
61 Igor Kravchuk .01 .05
62 Todd Marchant .01 .05
63 David Oliver .01 .05
64 Bill Ranford .02 .10
65 Doug Weight .02 .10
66 Stu Barnes .01 .05
67 Jesse Belanger .01 .05
68 Gord Murphy .01 .05
69 Magnus Svensson .01 .05
70 John Vanbiesbrouck .02 .10
71 Sean Burke .02 .10
72 Andrew Cassels .01 .05
73 Nelson Emerson .01 .05
74 Andrei Nikolishin .01 .05
75 Geoff Sanderson .01 .05
76 Brendan Shanahan .07 .20
77 Glen Wesley .01 .05
78 Rob Blake .02 .10
79 Wayne Gretzky .60 1.50
80 Dimitri Khristich .01 .05
81 Jari Kurri .07 .20
82 Darryl Sydor .02 .10
83 Rick Tocchet .02 .10
84 Vincent Damphousse .01 .05
85 Vladimir Malakhov .01 .05
86 Mark Recchi .02 .10
87 Patrick Roy .40 1.00
88 Brian Savage .01 .05
89 Pierre Turgeon .02 .10
90 Martin Brodeur .20 .50
91 Neal Broten .01 .05
92 Shawn Chambers .01 .05
93 John MacLean .02 .10
94 Randy McKay .01 .05
95 Scott Niedermayer .01 .05
96 Stephane Richer .02 .10
97 Scott Stevens .02 .10

98 Steve Thomas .02 .10
99 Wendel Clark .02 .10
100 Patrick Flatley .01 .05
101 Scott Lachance .01 .05
102 Brett Lindros .01 .05
103 Kirk Muller .01 .05
104 Tommy Salo RC .30 .75
105 Mathieu Schneider .01 .05
106 Dennis Vaske .01 .05
107 Ray Ferraro .01 .05
108 Adam Graves .01 .05
109 Alexei Kovalev .01 .05
110 Brian Leetch .02 .10
111 Mark Messier .07 .20
112 Mike Richter .07 .20
113 Luc Robitaille .02 .10
114 Ulf Samuelsson .01 .05
115 Pat Verbeek .01 .05
116 Don Beaupre .02 .10
117 Radek Bonk .01 .05
118 Alexandre Daigle .01 .05
119 Steve Duchesne .01 .05
120 Dan Quinn .01 .05
121 Martin Straka .01 .05
122 Alexei Yashin .01 .05
123 Rod Brind'Amour .02 .10
124 Eric Desjardins .02 .10
125 Ron Hextall .02 .10
126 John LeClair .07 .20
127 Eric Lindros .07 .20
128 Mikael Renberg .02 .10
129 Chris Therien .01 .05
130 Ron Francis .02 .10
131 Jaromir Jagr .10 .30
132 Mario Lemieux .40 1.00
133 Petr Nedved .02 .10
134 Tomas Sandstrom .01 .05
135 Bryan Smolinski .01 .05
136 Ken Wregget .02 .10
137 Sergei Zubov .01 .05
138 Shayne Corson .01 .05
139 Geoff Courtnall .01 .05
140 Dale Hawerchuk .07 .20
141 Brett Hull .08 .25
142 Ian Laperriere .01 .05
143 Al MacInnis .02 .10
144 Chris Pronger .07 .20
145 Esa Tikkanen .01 .05
146 Ulf Dahlen .01 .05
147 Jeff Friesen .01 .05
148 Arturs Irbe .02 .10
149 Craig Janney .01 .05
150 Owen Nolan .02 .10
151 Mike Rathje .01 .05
152 Ray Sheppard .01 .05
153 Brian Bradley .01 .05
154 Chris Gratton .01 .05
155 Roman Hamrlik .02 .10
156 Petr Klima .01 .05
157 Daren Puppa .02 .10
158 Dave Andreychuk .02 .10
159 Mike Gartner .02 .10
160 Todd Gill .01 .05
161 Doug Gilmour .02 .10
162 Kenny Jonsson .01 .05
163 Larry Murphy .02 .10
164 Felix Potvin .07 .20
165 Mats Sundin .07 .20
166 Jeff Brown .01 .05
167 Pavel Bure .07 .20
168 Russ Courtnall .01 .05
169 Trevor Linden .02 .10
170 Kirk McLean .02 .10
171 Alexander Mogilny .02 .10
172 Roman Oksiuta .01 .05
173 Mike Ridley .01 .05
174 Peter Bondra .02 .10
175 Jim Carey .02 .10
176 Sergei Gonchar .01 .05
177 Dale Hunter .02 .10
178 Calle Johansson .01 .05
179 Joe Juneau .01 .05
180 Michal Pivonka .01 .05
181 Nikolai Khabibulin .02 .10
182 Dave Manson .01 .05
183 Teppo Numminen .01 .05
184 Teemu Selanne .07 .20
185 Keith Tkachuk .07 .20
186 Darren Turcotte .01 .05
187 Alexei Zhamnov .02 .10
188 Chad Kilger RC .01 .05
189 Kyle McLaren RC .01 .05
190 Brian Holzinger RC .07 .20
191 Wayne Primeau RC .01 .05
192 Marty Murray RC .01 .05
193 Eric Daze .02 .10
194 Jon Klemm RC .01 .05
195 Jere Lehtinen .01 .05
196 Jason Bonsignore RC .01 .05
197 Miroslav Satan RC .30 .75
198 Ryan Smyth .02 .10
199 Tyler Wright RC .01 .05
200 Radek Dvorak RC .15 .40
201 Ed Jovanovski .07 .20
202 Jeff O'Neill .01 .05
203 Aki Berg RC .02 .10
204 Jamie Storr .02 .10
205 Vitali Yachmenev .01 .05
206 Saku Koivu .07 .20
207 Denis Pederson RC .01 .05
208 Todd Bertuzzi RC .50 1.25
209 Bryan McCabe RC .01 .05
210 Dan Plante RC .08 .25
211 Peter Ferraro .01 .05
212 Darren Langdon RC .01 .05
213 Niklas Sundstrom .01 .05
214 Daniel Alfredsson RC .30 .75
215 Garth Snow RC .02 .10
216 Ian Moran RC .01 .05
217 Richard Park RC .01 .05
218 Jamie Rivers RC .01 .05
219 Roman Vopat RC .01 .05
220 Marcus Ragnarsson RC .02 .10
221 Aaron Gavey .01 .05
222 Daymond Langkow RC .15 .40
223 Darby Hendrickson RC .01 .05
224 Martin Gendron RC .01 .05
225 Brendan Witt .01 .05
226 Shane Doan RC .25 .60
227 Deron Quint RC .01 .05
228 Jim Carey HH .01 .05
229 Peter Forsberg HH .10 .30
230 Paul Kariya HH .07 .20
231 David Oliver HH .01 .05
232 Blaine Lacher HH .02 .10
233 Todd Harvey HH .01 .05
234 Todd Marchant HH .01 .05
235 Jeff Friesen HH .01 .05
236 Oleg Tverdovsky HH .01 .05
237 Jason Arnott HH .01 .05
238 Cam Neely PP .02 .10
239 Keith Tkachuk PP .07 .20
240 Owen Nolan PP .02 .10
241 Keith Primeau PP .01 .05
242 Peter Bondra PP .02 .10
243 Jeremy Roenick PP .08 .25
244 John LeClair PP .07 .20
245 Mikael Renberg PP .02 .10
246 Dave Andreychuk PP .02 .10
247 Rick Tocchet PP .02 .10
NNO Blaine Lacher .02 .10
Exchange card
NNO Blaine Lacher 4.00 10.00
SkyMotion card

1995-96 SkyBox Impact Deflectors

Randomly inserted in packs at a rate of 1:10, this 12-card set features top NHL goalies.

COMPLETE SET (12) 3.00 8.00
1 Dominik Hasek .50 1.25
2 Jim Carey .10 .30
3 Felix Potvin .25 .60
4 Sean Burke .10 .30
5 Blaine Lacher .10 .30
6 John Vanbiesbrouck .10 .30
7 Jocelyn Thibault .25 .60
8 Patrick Roy 1.25 3.00
9 Ed Belfour .25 .60
10 Trevor Kidd .10 .30
11 Martin Brodeur .60 1.50
12 Kirk McLean .10 .30

1995-96 SkyBox Impact Countdown to Impact

Randomly inserted in hobby packs only at a rate of 1:60, this set features nine explosive stars whose names can be found on the backs of many fans jerseys at NHL arenas across North America. The card fronts also point to statistical milestones that are within range for that player.

COMPLETE SET (9) 12.00 30.00
1 Eric Lindros 1.50 4.00
2 Jaromir Jagr 2.50 5.00
3 Mario Lemieux 4.00 10.00
4 Wayne Gretzky 6.00 15.00
5 Mark Messier 1.50 4.00
6 Sergei Fedorov 1.50 4.00
7 Paul Kariya 1.50 4.00
8 Doug Gilmour 1.00 2.50
9 Pavel Bure 1.50 4.00

1995-96 SkyBox Impact Ice Quake

Randomly inserted in packs at a rate of 1:20, this 15-card set delivers the rumble that goalies feel when the NHL's best forwards have the puck on their sticks and start skating towards the net.

COMPLETE SET (15) 15.00 40.00
1 Jaromir Jagr 2.50 6.00
2 Brett Hull 1.50 4.00
3 Pavel Bure 1.00 2.50
4 Eric Lindros 1.00 2.50
5 Mark Messier 1.50 4.00
6 Wayne Gretzky 6.00 15.00
7 Mario Lemieux 5.00 12.00
8 Peter Forsberg 2.50 6.00
9 Sergei Fedorov 1.50 4.00
10 Cam Neely 1.00 2.50
11 Owen Nolan .40 1.00
12 Alexei Zhamnov .40 1.00
13 Theo Fleury .40 1.00
14 Luc Robitaille .40 1.00
15 Teemu Selanne 1.00 2.50

1995-96 SkyBox Impact NHL On Fox

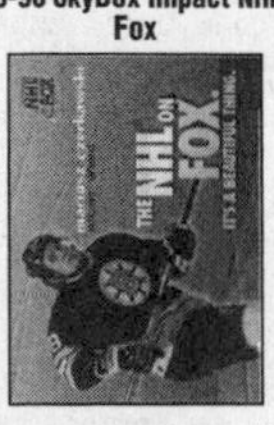

Randomly inserted in packs at a rate of 1:3, this 18-card set showcases both bright young stars and the company's strong affiliation with the NHL broadcasts on the Fox television network in the States.

COMPLETE SET (18) 2.00 5.00
1 Mariusz Czerkawski .20 .50
2 Roman Oksiuta .20 .50
3 David Oliver .20 .50
4 Adam Deadmarsh .20 .50
5 Denis Chasse .20 .50
6 Sergei Krivokrasov .20 .50
7 Ian Laperriere .20 .50
8 Chris Therien .20 .50
9 Brian Savage .20 .50
10 Todd Marchant .20 .50
11 Jeff O'Neill .20 .50
12 Brett Lindros .20 .50
13 Kenny Jonsson .20 .50
14 Manny Fernandez .40 1.00
15 Brian Holzinger .20 .50
16 Niklas Sundstrom .20 .50
17 Eric Daze .20 .50
18 Chad Kilger .20 .50

1996-97 SkyBox Impact

This 175-card set featured color action player photos of 118 seasoned stars plus a 20-card Rookies subset (#119-#138) and a 10-card Power Play subset (#139-#146). These ten Power Play cards had front designs that actually looked like miniature magazine covers. A special Stanley Cup logo appeared on all Colorado Avalanche player cards. The backs carried player stats, bio information, and a statement about the player as written by hockey HOF and Fox broadcaster Denis Potvin. A "John LeClair SkyPin Exchange" card, inserted at the rate of one in every 180 packs, entitled the collector to send for a John LeClair "preview card" from the proposed -- but never materialized -- SkyPin trading card line. One "SkyBox/Fox Game" card was inserted in every pack which enabled the holder to win big prizes from SkyBox, Fox, and the NHL.

COMPLETE SET (175) 5.00 12.00
1 Guy Hebert .05 .15
2 Paul Kariya .08 .25
3 Roman Oksiuta .02 .10
4 Teemu Selanne .08 .25
5 Ray Bourque .15 .40
6 Kyle McLaren .02 .10
7 Adam Oates .05 .15
8 Bill Ranford .05 .15
9 Rick Tocchet .05 .15
10 Dominik Hasek .20 .50
11 Pat LaFontaine .08 .25
12 Mike Peca .02 .10
13 Theo Fleury .02 .10
14 Trevor Kidd .05 .15
15 German Titov .02 .10
16 Tony Amonte .05 .15
17 Ed Belfour .08 .25
18 Chris Chelios .08 .25
19 Eric Daze .05 .15
20 Gary Suter .02 .10
21 Alexei Zhamnov .05 .15
22 Peter Forsberg .25 .60
23 Valeri Kamensky .05 .15
24 Uwe Krupp .02 .10
25 Claude Lemieux .02 .10
26 Sandis Ozolinsh .02 .10
27 Patrick Roy .50 1.25
28 Joe Sakic .20 .50
29 Derian Hatcher .02 .10
30 Mike Modano .15 .40
31 Joe Nieuwendyk .05 .15
32 Sergei Zubov .02 .10
33 Paul Coffey .08 .25
34 Sergei Fedorov .15 .40
35 Vladimir Konstantinov .05 .15
36 Slava Kozlov .05 .15
37 Nicklas Lidstrom .08 .25
38 Chris Osgood .08 .25
39 Keith Primeau .02 .10
40 Steve Yzerman .50 1.25
41 Jason Arnott .02 .10
42 Curtis Joseph .08 .25
43 Doug Weight .05 .15
44 Radek Dvorak .02 .10
45 Ed Jovanovski .05 .15
46 Scott Mellanby .05 .15
47 Rob Niedermayer .05 .15
48 Ray Sheppard .05 .15
49 Robert Svehla .02 .10
50 John Vanbiesbrouck .05 .15
51 Jeff Brown .02 .10
52 Sean Burke .05 .15
53 Andrew Cassels .02 .10
54 Geoff Sanderson .05 .15
55 Brendan Shanahan .08 .25
56 Byron Dafoe .05 .15
57 Ray Ferraro .02 .10
58 Dimitri Khristich .02 .10
59 Vitali Yachmenev .02 .10
60 Valeri Bure .02 .10
61 Vincent Damphousse .02 .10
62 Saku Koivu .08 .25
63 Mark Recchi .05 .15
64 Martin Rucinsky .02 .10
65 Jocelyn Thibault .08 .25
66 Pierre Turgeon .05 .15
67 Dave Andreychuk .02 .10
68 Martin Brodeur .25 .60
69 Bill Guerin .02 .10
70 Scott Niedermayer .02 .10
71 Scott Stevens .02 .10
72 Petr Sykora .02 .10
73 Steve Thomas .02 .10
74 Todd Bertuzzi .08 .25
75 Travis Green .05 .15
76 Kenny Jonsson .02 .10
77 Zigmund Palffy .05 .15
78 Adam Graves .02 .10
79 Wayne Gretzky .60 1.50
80 Alexei Kovalev .02 .10
81 Brian Leetch .08 .25
82 Mark Messier .08 .25
83 Mike Richter .08 .25
84 Ulf Samuelsson .02 .10
85 Niklas Sundstrom .02 .10
86 Daniel Alfredsson .05 .15
87 Radek Bonk .02 .10
88 Alexandre Daigle .02 .10
89 Steve Duchesne .02 .10
90 Damian Rhodes .05 .15
91 Alexei Yashin .02 .10
92 Rod Brind'Amour .05 .15
93 Eric Desjardins .05 .15
94 Dale Hawerchuk .05 .15
95 Ron Hextall .05 .15
96 John LeClair .08 .25
97 Eric Lindros .08 .25
98 Mikael Renberg .05 .15
99 Tom Barrasso .05 .15
100 Ron Francis .05 .15
101 Jaromir Jagr .15 .40
102 Mario Lemieux .50 1.25
103 Petr Nedved .05 .15
104 Bryan Smolinski .02 .10
105 Nikolai Khabibulin .05 .15
106 Teppo Numminen .02 .10
107 Keith Tkachuk .08 .25
108 Jeremy Roenick .10 .30
109 Oleg Tverdovsky .05 .15
110 Shayne Corson .02 .10
111 Geoff Courtnall .02 .10
112 Grant Fuhr .05 .15
113 Brett Hull .10 .30
114 Al MacInnis .05 .15
115 Chris Pronger .05 .15
116 Jeff Friesen .02 .10
117 Owen Nolan .05 .15
118 Marcus Ragnarsson .02 .10
119 Chris Terreri .05 .15
120 Brian Bradley .02 .10
121 Chris Gratton .05 .15
122 Roman Hamrlik .05 .15
123 Daren Puppa .05 .15
124 Alexander Selivanov .02 .10
125 Wendel Clark .05 .15
126 Doug Gilmour .05 .15
127 Kirk Muller .02 .10
128 Larry Murphy .05 .15
129 Felix Potvin .08 .25
130 Mats Sundin .08 .25
131 Pavel Bure .08 .25
132 Russ Courtnall .02 .10
133 Trevor Linden .05 .15
134 Kirk McLean .05 .15
135 Alexander Mogilny .05 .15
136 Peter Bondra .05 .15
137 Jim Carey .08 .25
138 Sylvain Cote .02 .10
139 Sergei Gonchar .02 .10
140 Phil Housley .05 .15
141 Joe Juneau .02 .10
142 Michal Pivonka .02 .10
143 Brendan Witt .02 .10
144 Nolan Baumgartner .02 .10
145 Martin Biron RC .60 1.50
146 Jason Bonsignore .02 .10
147 Andrew Brunette RC .15 .40
148 Jason Doig .02 .10
149 Peter Ferraro .02 .10
150 Eric Fichaud .05 .15
151 Ladislav Kohn .02 .10
152 Jamie Langenbrunner .02 .10
153 Daymond Langkow .05 .15
154 Jay McKee RC .02 .10
155 Marty Murray .02 .10
156 Wayne Primeau .02 .10
157 Jamie Pushor .02 .10
158 Jamie Rivers .02 .10
159 Jamie Storr .05 .15
160 Steve Sullivan RC .15 .40
161 Jose Theodore .10 .30
162 Roman Vopat .02 .10
163 Alexei Yegorov RC .02 .10
164 Daniel Alfredsson PP .05 .15
165 Niklas Andersson PP .02 .10
166 Todd Bertuzzi PP .08 .25
167 Valeri Bure PP .02 .10
168 Eric Daze PP .05 .15
169 Saku Koivu PP .08 .25
170 Miroslav Satan PP .02 .10
171 Petr Sykora PP .02 .10
172 Cory Stillman PP .02 .10
173 Vitali Yachmenev PP .02 .10
174 Checklist 1 .02 .10
175 Checklist 2 UER .02 .10
Pavel Bure misidentified as Paul
Palffy misspelled with one F
Lafontaine, not Lafontanine
Selanne, not Selanna
S1 John LeClair PROMO .10 .30

1996-97 SkyBox Impact BladeRunners

Randomly inserted at the rate of 1:3 packs, this 25-card set featured some of the fastest hockey players on ice. The fronts carried a color action player photo while the backs displayed player information.

COMPLETE SET (25) 15.00 40.00
1 Brian Bradley .30 .75
2 Chris Chelios .75 2.00
3 Peter Forsberg 2.50 5.00
4 Ron Francis .50 1.25
5 Mike Gartner .50 1.25
6 Doug Gilmour .50 1.25
7 Phil Housley .50 1.25
8 Brett Hull 1.00 2.50
9 Valeri Kamensky .50 1.25
10 Pat LaFontaine .75 2.00
11 John LeClair .75 2.00
12 Claude Lemieux .30 .75
13 Nicklas Lidstrom .75 2.00
14 Mark Messier .75 2.00
15 Alexander Mogilny .50 1.25
16 Petr Nedved .50 1.25
17 Adam Oates .50 1.25
18 Zigmund Palffy .50 1.25
19 Jeremy Roenick 1.00 2.50
20 Teemu Selanne .75 2.00
21 Brendan Shanahan .75 2.00
22 Keith Tkachuk .75 2.00
23 Pierre Turgeon .50 1.25
24 Doug Weight .50 1.25
25 Steve Yzerman 5.00 10.00

1996-97 SkyBox Impact Countdown to Impact

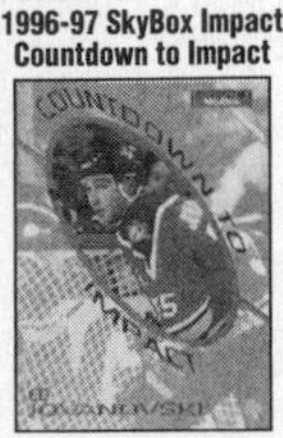

Randomly inserted in hobby packs only at the rate of 1:30, this 10-card insert set focused on the superstars of the game. The fronts displayed color player photos while the backs carried player information.

COMPLETE SET (10) 20.00 50.00
1 Pavel Bure 1.25 3.00
2 Sergei Fedorov 1.25 3.00
3 Wayne Gretzky 8.00 20.00
4 Jaromir Jagr 2.00 5.00
5 Ed Jovanovski .75 2.00
6 Paul Kariya 1.25 3.00
7 Mario Lemieux 6.00 15.00
8 Eric Lindros 1.25 3.00
9 Patrick Roy 6.00 15.00
10 Joe Sakic 3.00 8.00

1996-97 SkyBox Impact NHL on Fox

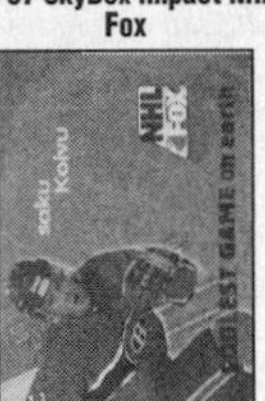

Randomly inserted at the rate of 1:10 packs, this 20-card set was a joint venture with Fox TV.

COMPLETE SET (20) 5.00 12.00
1 Daniel Alfredsson .40 1.00
2 Todd Bertuzzi .40 1.00
3 Ray Bourque 1.25 3.00
4 Valeri Bure .20 .50
5 Chris Chelios .75 2.00
6 Paul Coffey .75 2.00
7 Eric Daze .20 .50
8 Eric Desjardins .20 .50
9 Sergei Gonchar .20 .50
10 Phil Housley .20 .50
11 Ed Jovanovski .20 .50
12 Vladimir Konstantinov .75 2.00
13 Saku Koivu .75 2.00
14 Brian Leetch .40 1.00
15 Larry Murphy .20 .50
16 Teppo Numminen .20 .50
17 Sandis Ozolinsh .20 .50
18 Marcus Ragnarsson .20 .50
19 Petr Sykora .20 .50
20 Vitali Yachmenev .20 .50

1996-97 SkyBox Impact VersaTeam

Randomly inserted at the rate of 1:120 packs, this 10-card set featured the NHL's best multi-skilled players. The fronts displayed color player photos while the backs carried player information.

COMPLETE SET (10) 40.00 100.00
1 Pavel Bure 2.50 6.00
2 Sergei Fedorov 2.50 6.00
3 Peter Forsberg 4.00 10.00
4 Wayne Gretzky 15.00 40.00
5 Jaromir Jagr 4.00 10.00
6 Paul Kariya 2.50 6.00
7 Mario Lemieux 12.00 30.00
8 Eric Lindros 2.50 6.00
9 Joe Sakic 6.00 15.00
10 Teemu Selanne 2.50 6.00

1996-97 SkyBox Impact Zero Heroes

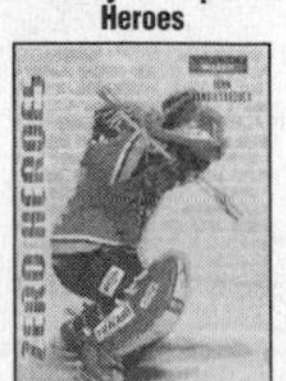

Randomly inserted in retail packs only at the rate of 1:30, this 10-card set featured the stingiest goaltenders in the league. The fronts displayed color player photos while the backs carried player information.

COMPLETE SET (10) 20.00 50.00
1 Ed Belfour 2.50 6.00
2 Sean Burke 1.25 3.00
3 Jim Carey 1.25 3.00
4 Dominik Hasek 4.00 10.00
5 Ron Hextall 2.50 6.00
6 Chris Osgood 2.50 6.00
7 Felix Potvin 2.50 6.00
8 Daren Puppa 1.25 3.00
9 Patrick Roy 10.00 25.00
10 John Vanbiesbrouck 2.50 6.00

1995-96 Slapshot

The 1995-96 Slapshot set features the players of the OHL and was issued in foil packs in one series totaling 440 cards. Randomly inserted into packs were promo cards and an autographed card of Zac Bierk. The set is notable for the inclusion of several top prospects, including Alexandre Volchkov, Boyd Devereaux, Joe Thornton, Daniel Cleary and Rico Fata.

COMPLETE SET (440) 20.00 50.00
1 Checklist .01 .05
2 Checklist .01 .05
3 Checklist .01 .05
4 Checklist .01 .05
5 David E. Branch .01 .05
6 Bert Templeton .01 .05
7 Chris George .01 .05
8 Chris Thompson .08 .25
9 Quade Lightbody .01 .05
10 Shane Delaronde .01 .05
11 Justin Robinson .01 .05
12 Shawn Frappier .01 .05
13 Lucio Nasato .08 .25
14 Jason Payne .01 .05
15 Jason Cannon .01 .05
16 Alexandre Volchkov .08 .25
17 Daniel Tkaczuk .20 .50
18 Gerry Lanigan .01 .05
19 Darrell Woodley .01 .05
20 Brian Barker .01 .05
21 Mauricio Alvarez .01 .05
22 Brock Boucher .01 .05
23 Jeff Cowan .15 .40
24 Jan Bulis .20 .50
25 Jeff Tetzlaff .01 .05
26 Caleb Ward .05 .15
27 Mike White .01 .05
28 Jeremy Miculinic .01 .05
29 Andrew Morrison .01 .05
30 Robert Dubois .01 .05
31 Kory Cooper .08 .25
32 Jason Gaggi .08 .25
33 Mike Van Volsen .01 .05
34 Paul McInness .01 .05
35 Harkie Singh .01 .05
36 Robin Lacour .01 .05
37 Jamie Sokolsky .01 .05
38 Marc Dupuis .01 .05
39 Daniel Cleary .20 .50
40 David Peca .01 .05
41 Adam Robbins .01 .05
42 Steve Tracze .01 .05
43 James Boyd .01 .05
44 Jake Irsag .01 .05
45 Ryan Ready .01 .05
46 Walker McDonald .01 .05
47 Rob Guinn .01 .05
48 Rob Fitzgerald .01 .05
49 Joe Coombs .01 .05
50 Daniel Reja .01 .05
51 Joe Van Volsen .02 .10
52 Craig Mills .08 .25
53 Murray Hogg .01 .05
54 Andrei Shurupov .08 .25
55 Andrew Williamson .01 .05
56 Mike Minard .08 .25
57 Robert Esche .75 2.00
58 Lee Jinman .08 .25
59 Corey Neilson .07 .20
60 Troy Smith .01 .05
61 Mike Rucinski .07 .20
62 Colin Beardsmore .01 .05
63 Dan Pawlaczyk .01 .05
64 Scott Blair .01 .05
65 Mike Morrone .01 .05
66 Matt Ball .01 .05
67 Steve Dumonski .01 .05
68 Murray Sheehan .01 .05
69 Sean Haggerty .08 .25
70 Andrew Taylor .01 .05
71 Steve Wasylko .02 .10
72 Jan Vodrazka .01 .05
73 Dan Preston .01 .05
74 Jesse Boulerice .20 .50
75 Bryan Berard .30 .75
76 Nicolas Beaudoin .08 .25
77 Tom Buckley .02 .10
78 Mark Cadotte .07 .20
79 Greg Stephan .01 .05
80 Peter DeBoer .02 .10
81 Regan Stocco .01 .05
82 Andy Adams .08 .25
83 Brett Thompson .08 .25
84 Darryl McArthur .01 .05
85 Ryan Risidore .07 .20
86 Joel Cort .02 .10
87 Chris Hajt .08 .25
88 Bryan McKinney .01 .05
89 Dwayne Hay .20 .50
90 Andrew Clark .01 .05
91 Ryan Robichaud .01 .05
92 Mike Vellinga .01 .05
93 Jamie Wright .01 .05
94 Herbert Vasilijevs .01 .05
95 Dan Cloutier .75 2.00
96 Brian Wesenberg .08 .25
97 Michael Pittman .01 .05
98 Jeff Williams .01 .05
99 Todd Norman .08 .25
100 Brian Willsie .01 .05
101 Jason Jackman .07 .20
102 Mike Lankshear .05 .15
103 Andrew Long .07 .20
104 Nick Bootland .02 .10
105 E.J. McGuire .01 .05
106 Bujar Amidovski .20 .50
107 John Hultberg .08 .25
108 Eric Olsen .01 .05
109 Chris Allen .20 .50
110 Michael Tilson .01 .05
111 Jeff DaCosta .01 .05
112 Gord Walsh .01 .05
113 Matt Bradley .01 .05
114 Robert Mailloux .01 .05
115 Justin Davis .01 .05
116 Marc Moro .15 .40
117 Cail MacLean .01 .05
118 Jason Sands .01 .05
119 Matt Price .01 .05
120 Zdenek Skorepa .02 .10
121 Jason Morgan .01 .05
122 Mike Oliveira .08 .25
123 Colin Chaulk .01 .05
124 Dylan Taylor .01 .05
125 Kurt Johnston .01 .05
126 Bill Minkhorst .01 .05
127 Wes Swinson .08 .25
128 Adam Fleming .01 .05
129 Chris MacDonald .01 .05
130 Gary Agnew .01 .05
131 David Belitski .08 .25
132 Jarrett Rose .01 .05
133 Ryan Mougenel .01 .05
134 Rob Stanfield .01 .05
135 Duncan Fader .01 .05
136 Rob Maric .01 .05
137 Mark McMahon .01 .05
138 Serge Payer .01 .05
139 Paul Traynor .01 .05
140 Bogdan Rudenko .01 .05
141 Robert DeCiantis .05 .15
142 Andrew Dale .08 .25
143 Jeff Ambrosio .02 .10
144 Paul Doyle .07 .20
145 Bryan Duce .01 .05
146 Jason Byrnes .01 .05
147 Ryan Pepperall .08 .25
148 Wes Vander Wal .01 .05
149 Boyd Devereaux .20 .50
150 Keith Walsh .01 .05
151 Joe Birch .01 .05
152 Craig Nelson .01 .05
153 Brian Hayden .01 .05
154 Matt O'Dette .01 .05
155 Geoff Ward .01 .05
156 Frank Ivankovic .08 .25
157 Eoin McInerney .20 .50
158 Joel Dezainde .01 .05
159 Duncan Dalmao .01 .05
160 Brandon Sugden .20 .50
161 Jamie Wentzell .01 .05
162 Ryan Burgoyne .01 .05
163 Todd Crane .01 .05
164 Chad Cavanagh .01 .05
165 Andrew Fagan .01 .05
166 Ryan Gardner .01 .05
167 Kevin Boyd .01 .05
168 Kevin Barry .01 .05
169 Richard Pitirri .01 .05
170 Adam Colagiacomo .20 .50
171 Jason Brooks .01 .05
172 Justin McPolin .01 .05
173 Travis Riggin .01 .05
174 Steve Lowe .01 .05
175 Todd St. Louis .01 .05
176 Kevin Slota .01 .05
177 Ryan McKie .01 .05
178 Corey Isen .01 .05
179 Sasha Cucuz .01 .05
180 Tom Barrett .01 .05
181 Ken Carroll .01 .05
182 Ryan Penney .08 .25
183 Jay McKee .30 .75
184 Ryan Taylor .01 .05
185 Jeff Paul .01 .05
186 Jason Ward .20 .50
187 Jesse Black .02 .10
188 Steve Nimigon .07 .20
189 Chris Haskett .01 .05
190 Geoff Peters .08 .25
191 Ryan Cirillo .01 .05
192 David Froh .01 .05
193 Jeff Johnstone .01 .05
194 Shane Nash .07 .20
195 Jason Robinson .01 .05
196 Rich Vrataric .01 .05
197 Colin Pepperall .01 .05
198 Craig Jalbert .01 .05
199 Andrew Williamson .01 .05
200 Greg Tymchuk .01 .05
201 Chester Gallant .01 .05
202 Mike Perna .01 .05
203 Adam Nitel .20 .50
204 Dave Burkholder .01 .05
205 Chris Johnstone .01 .05
206 Elliott Faust .08 .25
207 Scott Roche .08 .25
208 Kam White .01 .05
209 Scott Atkins .01 .05
210 Luc Belliveau .01 .05
211 Jamie Vossen .01 .05
212 Ryan MacDonald .01 .05
213 Jim Midgley .01 .05
214 Steven Carpenter .01 .05
215 Jake Martel .01 .05
216 Alex Matvichuk .01 .05
217 Trevor Gallant .08 .25
218 Ryan Gillis .01 .05
219 Kris Cantu .01 .05
220 Mark Provenzano .01 .05
221 Brian Whitley .01 .05
222 Dustin Virag .01 .05
223 Lee Jinman .08 .25
224 Peter McCague .01 .05
225 Herb Bonvie .01 .05
226 Philippe Poirier .01 .05
227 Greg Labanski .01 .05
228 Milan Kostolny .08 .25
229 Ryan Power .01 .05
230 Shane Parker .01 .05
231 Travis Scott .08 .25
232 Tyrone Garner .08 .25
233 Marty Wilford .08 .25
234 Ole Anderson .01 .05

235 Ryan Tocher .01 .05
236 Nathan Perrott .30 .75
237 Brandon Coalter .01 .05
238 John Tripp .08 .25
239 Jay Legault .20 .50
240 Wayne Primeau .20 .50
241 Trevor Edgar .01 .05
242 Peter Hogan .01 .05
243 Warren Holmes .01 .05
244 Jason Metcalfe .01 .05
245 Mike Zanutto .01 .05
246 Jeff Ware .08 .25
247 Ian MacNeil .01 .05
248 Jan Snopek .07 .20
249 Kurt Walsh .01 .05
250 Marc Savard .30 .75
251 Darcy O'Shea .01 .05
252 Jason Sweitzer .01 .05
253 Ryan Lindsay .01 .05
254 Scott Seiling .01 .05
255 Stan Butler .08 .25
256 Tim Keyes .08 .25
257 Craig Hillier .08 .25
258 Craig Whynot .01 .05
259 David Bell .01 .05
260 Rich Bronilla .01 .05
261 Roy Gray .01 .05
262 Nick Boynton .40 1.00
263 Mike Sim .08 .25
264 B.J. Johnston .01 .05
265 Niall Maynard .01 .05
266 Dan Tudin .08 .25
267 Jure Kovacavic .01 .05
268 Ben Gustavson .01 .05
269 Steve Zaryk .01 .05
270 Darren Debrie .01 .05
271 Troy Stonier .01 .05
272 David Nemirovsky .08 .25
273 Joel Trottier .08 .25
274 Mike Lavell .01 .05
275 Brian Campbell .20 .50
276 Chris Despatis .01 .05
277 Sean Blanchard .08 .25
278 Alyn McCauley .30 .75
279 Chris Pittman .07 .20
280 Daryl Rivers .01 .05
281 Brent Johnson .75 2.00
282 Shawn Gallant .01 .05
283 Shane Kenny .01 .05
284 Chris Biagini .01 .05
285 Jim Ensom .02 .10
286 Marek Babic .01 .05
287 Oleg Tsyrkunov .01 .05
288 Mike Loach .01 .05
289 Peter MacKellar .01 .05
290 Ryan Davis .01 .05
291 John Argiropoulos .01 .05
292 Jason Campbell .01 .05
293 Ryan Christie .20 .50
294 Dan Snyder .40 1.00
295 Steve Gallace .01 .05
296 Scott Seiling .01 .05
297 Jeremy Rebek .01 .05
298 Adam Mair .20 .50
299 Matt Osborne .01 .05
300 Mike Gelati .01 .05
301 Wayne Primeau .20 .50
302 Chris Wismer .01 .05
303 Larry Paleczny .08 .25
304 Kurt Walsh .01 .05
305 John Lovell .01 .05
306 Allan Hitchen .08 .25
307 Zac Bierk .20 .50
308 Mike Martone .01 .05
309 Jonathan Murphy .01 .05
310 Adrian Murray .01 .05
311 Rob Giffin .01 .05
312 Corey Crocker .08 .25
313 Cameron Mann .20 .50
314 Ryan Pawluk .01 .05
315 Jason MacMillan .01 .05
316 Shawn Thornton .40 1.00
317 Wade Dawe .01 .05
318 Eric Landry .01 .05
319 Steve Hogg .01 .05
320 Kevin Bolibruck .01 .05
321 Dave Duerden .08 .25
322 Mike Williams .01 .05
323 Andy Johnson .01 .05
324 Jaret Nixon .01 .05
325 Evgeny Korolev .08 .25
326 Matthew Lahey .01 .05
327 Ryan Schmidt .01 .05
328 Scott Barney .08 .25
329 Steve Jones .01 .05
330 Dave McQueen .01 .05
331 Jeff Salajko .08 .25
332 Patrick DesRochers .20 .50
333 Gerald Moriarity .01 .05
334 Allan Carr .01 .05
335 Tom Brown .01 .05
336 Andy Delmore .20 .50
337 Darren Mortier .01 .05
338 Aaron Brand .08 .25
339 Eric Boulton .40 1.00
340 Jonathan Sim .20 .50
341 Trevor Letowski .20 .50
342 Michael Hanson .01 .05
343 Todd Miller .01 .05
344 Brendan Yarema .01 .05
345 Brad Simms .01 .05
346 David Nemirovsky .08 .25
347 Jeff Brown .08 .25
348 Andrew Proskurnicki .01 .05
349 Wes Mason .08 .25
350 Scott Corbett .01 .05
351 Dave Bourque .01 .05
352 Sean Brown .20 .50
353 Marcin Snita .01 .05
354 Rich Brown .01 .05
355 Mark Hunter .01 .05
356 Michal Podolka .08 .25
357 Dan Cloutier .75 2.00
358 Cory Murphy .01 .05
359 Kevin Murnaghan .01 .05
360 Andre Payette .01 .05
361 Richard Uniacke .07 .20
362 Joe Veroski .05 .15
363 Joe Thornton 4.00 10.00
364 Ben Schust .01 .05
365 Peter Cava .01 .05
366 Darryl Green .01 .05
367 Trevor Tokarczyk .01 .05
368 Jeff Gies .01 .05
369 Rico Fata .20 .50
370 Brian Secord .01 .05
371 Scott Cherrey .05 .15
372 Brian Stacey .01 .05
373 Lee Cole .01 .05
374 Richard Jackman .20 .50
375 Jason Doyle .08 .25
376 Brian Stewart .02 .10
377 Blaine Fitzpatrick .01 .05
378 Robert Mulick .01 .05
379 Andy Adams .08 .25
380 Joe Paterson .01 .05
381 Dave MacDonald .08 .25
382 Stephan Valiquette .40 1.00
383 Tim Swartz .01 .05
384 Gregg Lalonde .01 .05
385 Tyson Flinn .01 .05
386 Ryan Sly .01 .05
387 Neal Martin .01 .05
388 Kevin Hansen .01 .05
389 Joe Lombardo .01 .05
390 Darryl Moxam .01 .05
391 Jeremy Adduono .05 .15
392 Ryan Shanahan .01 .05
393 Sean Venedam .05 .15
394 Andrew Dale .08 .25
395 Rob Butler .01 .05
396 Brian Scott .01 .05
397 Liam MacEachern .01 .05
398 Luc Gagne .01 .05
399 Richard Rochefort .01 .05
400 Noel Burkitt .01 .05
401 Simon Sherry .01 .05
402 Brad Domonsky .08 .25
403 Ron Newhook .15 .40
404 Serge Dunphy .01 .05
405 Todd Lalonde .01 .05
406 Ryan Gelinas .08 .25
407 Terry Joss .07 .20
408 Mike Martin .07 .20
409 Chris Van Dyk .07 .20
410 D.J. Smith .20 .50
411 Glenn Crawford .07 .20
412 Robert Blain .01 .05
413 Matt Masterson .01 .05
414 Adam Young .01 .05
415 Matt Cooke .40 1.00
416 Jeff Zehr .20 .50
417 Wes Ward .07 .20
418 Matt Elich .15 .40
419 Rob Shearer .15 .40
420 Dean Mando .01 .05
421 Chris Kerr .01 .05
422 Vladimir Kretchine .01 .05
423 Jeff Martin .01 .05
424 Valeri Svoboda .01 .05
425 Dave Geris .07 .20
426 Ryan Pawluk .01 .05
427 Ryan Shaver .01 .05
428 Cameron Kincaid .01 .05
429 Tim Findlay .08 .25
430 Tim Bryan .01 .05
431 Alexandre Volchkov .20 .50
432 Boyd Devereaux .40 1.00
433 Chris Allen .08 .25
434 Paul Doyle .07 .20
435 Wes Mason .08 .25
436 Chris Hajt .08 .25
437 Kurt Walsh .01 .05
438 Glenn Crawford .07 .20
439 Jeff Brown .08 .25
440 Geoff Peters .08 .25
NNO Sean Haggerty promo .20 .50
NNO Jay McKee promo .20 .50
NNO Ryan Pepperall promo .20 .50
NNO Mike Martin promo .20 .50
NNO Nick Boynton promo .40 1.00
NNO Zac Bierk promo .20 .50
NNO Cameron Mann promo .20 .50
NNO Scott Roche promo .20 .50
NNO Adam Colagiacomo promo .20 .50
NNO Zac Bierk autograph 2.00 5.00

1994-95 SP

Wayne Gretzky's card number 54 was released as a promo. The only discernible difference between the two versions is that the foil on the promo is a brighter gold than the regular issue card. A special Wayne Gretzky 2500 point card was inserted one per case. This card is designed horizontally with die-cutting of the top corners. Wayne appears on a gold background with "2500" in block numbers on the front of the card.

COMPLETE SET (195) 10.00 25.00
1 Paul Kariya .25 .60
2 Oleg Tverdovsky .05 .15
3 Stephan Lebeau .05 .15
4 Bob Corkum .05 .15
5 Guy Hebert .10 .30
6 Ray Bourque .40 1.00
7 Blaine Lacher RC .10 .30
8 Adam Oates .10 .30
9 Cam Neely .25 .60
10 Mariusz Czerkawski RC .20 .50
11 Bryan Smolinski .05 .15
12 Pat LaFontaine .25 .60
13 Alexander Mogilny .10 .30
14 Dominik Hasek .50 1.25
15 Dale Hawerchuk .10 .30
16 Alexei Zhitnik .05 .15
17 Theo Fleury .05 .15
18 German Titov .05 .15
19 Phil Housley .10 .30
20 Joe Nieuwendyk .10 .30
21 Trevor Kidd .10 .30
22 Jeremy Roenick .30 .75
23 Chris Chelios .25 .60
24 Ed Belfour .25 .60
25 Bernie Nicholls .05 .15
26 Tony Amonte .10 .30
27 Joe Murphy .05 .15
28 Mike Modano .40 1.00
29 Trent Klatt .05 .15
30 Dave Gagner .05 .15
31 Kevin Hatcher .05 .15
32 Andy Moog .25 .60
33 Sergei Fedorov .40 1.00
34 Steve Yzerman 1.00 2.50
35 Slava Kozlov .05 .15
36 Paul Coffey .25 .60
37 Keith Primeau .05 .15
38 Ray Sheppard .05 .15
39 Doug Weight .10 .30
40 Jason Arnott .05 .15
41 Bill Ranford .10 .30
42 Shayne Corson .05 .15
43 Stu Barnes .05 .15
44 John Vanbiesbrouck .10 .30
45 Johan Garpenlov .05 .15
46 Bob Kudelski .05 .15
47 Scott Mellanby .05 .15
48 Chris Pronger .25 .60
49 Darren Turcotte .05 .15
50 Andrew Cassels .05 .15
51 Sean Burke .10 .30
52 Geoff Sanderson .05 .15
53 Rob Blake .10 .30
54A Wayne Gretzky 1.50 4.00
54B Wayne Gretzky PROMO 2.00 5.00
55 Rick Tocchet .10 .30
56 Tony Granato .05 .15
57 Jari Kurri .25 .60
58 Vincent Damphousse .05 .15
59 Patrick Roy 1.25 3.00
60 Vladimir Malakhov .05 .15
61 Pierre Turgeon .10 .30
62 Mark Recchi .10 .30
63 Martin Brodeur .60 1.50
64 Stephane Richer .10 .30
65 John MacLean .05 .15
66 Scott Stevens .10 .30
67 Scott Niedermayer .05 .15
68 Kirk Muller .05 .15
69 Ray Ferraro .05 .15
70 Brett Lindros .05 .15
71 Steve Thomas .05 .15
72 Pat Verbeek .05 .15
73 Mark Messier .25 .60
74 Brian Leetch .10 .30
75 Mike Richter .25 .60
76 Alexei Kovalev .05 .15
77 Adam Graves .05 .15
78 Sergei Zubov .05 .15
79 Alexei Yashin .05 .15
80 Radek Bonk RC .20 .50
81 Alexandre Daigle .05 .15
82 Don Beaupre .10 .30
83 Mikael Renberg .05 .15
84 Eric Lindros .25 .60
85 John LeClair .25 .60
86 Rod Brind'Amour .10 .30
87 Ron Hextall .10 .30
88 Ken Wregget .10 .30
89 Jaromir Jagr .40 1.00
90 Tomas Sandstrom .05 .15
91 John Cullen .05 .15
92 Ron Francis .10 .30
93 Luc Robitaille .10 .30
94 Joe Sakic .50 1.25
95 Owen Nolan .10 .30
96 Peter Forsberg 1.00 2.50
97 Wendel Clark .10 .30
98 Mike Ricci .05 .15
99 Stephane Fiset .10 .30
100 Brett Hull .30 .75
101 Brendan Shanahan .25 .60
102 Curtis Joseph .25 .60
103 Esa Tikkanen .05 .15
104 Al MacInnis .10 .30
105 Arturs Irbe .10 .30
106 Ray Whitney .05 .15
107 Sergei Makarov .05 .15
108 Sandis Ozolinsh .05 .15
109 Craig Janney .05 .15
110 Petr Klima .05 .15
111 Chris Gratton .05 .15
112 Roman Hamrlik .10 .30
113 Alexander Selivanov RC .25 .60
114 Brian Bradley .05 .15
115 Doug Gilmour .10 .30
116 Mats Sundin .25 .60
117 Felix Potvin .25 .60
118 Mike Ridley .05 .15
119 Dave Andreychuk .10 .30
120 Dmitri Mironov .05 .15
121 Pavel Bure .25 .60
122 Trevor Linden .10 .30
123 Jeff Brown .05 .15
124 Kirk McLean .10 .30
125 Geoff Courtnall .05 .15
126 Joe Juneau .05 .15
127 Dale Hunter .05 .15
128 Jim Carey RC .25 .60
129 Peter Bondra .25 .60
130 Dimitri Khristich .05 .15
131 Teemu Selanne .25 .60
132 Keith Tkachuk .25 .60
133 Alexei Zhamnov .10 .30
134 Dave Manson .05 .15
135 Nelson Emerson .05 .15
136 Alexandre Daigle .05 .15
137 Jamie Storr .10 .30
138 Todd Harvey .05 .15
139 Wade Redden RC .20 .50
140 Ed Jovanovski RC .30 .75
141 Jamie Rivers RC .05 .15
142 Ryan Smyth RC .75 2.00
143 Jason Botterill .05 .15
144 Denis Pederson RC .05 .15
145 Jeff Friesen .05 .15
146 Dan Cloutier RC .30 .75
147 Lee Sorochan RC .05 .15
148 Marty Murray .05 .15
149 Shean Donovan RC .05 .15
150 Larry Courville RC .05 .15
151 Jason Allison .05 .15
152 Jeff O'Neill RC .30 .75
153 Bryan McCabe .05 .15
154 Miloslav Guren RC .10 .30
155 Petr Buzek RC .10 .30
156 Tomas Blazek .05 .15
157 Josef Marha .05 .15
158 Jan Hlavac RC .20 .50
159 Veli-Pekka Nutikka RC .10 .30
160 Kimmo Timonen .10 .30
161 Antti Aalto RC .10 .30
162 Janne Niinimaa .10 .30
163 Nikolai Zavarukhin .05 .15
164 Vadim Epantchinsev RC .05 .15
165 Alexander Korolyuk RC .20 .50
166 Dmitri Klevakin RC .10 .30
167 Vitali Yachmenev RC .05 .15
168 Niklas Sundstrom .05 .15
169 Anders Soderberg RC .10 .30
170 Anders Eriksson .10 .30
171 Jesper Mattsson RC .10 .30
172 Mattias Ohlund RC .30 .75
173 Jason Bonsignore .05 .15
174 Bryan Berard RC .20 .50
175 Richard Park .05 .15
176 Mike McBain RC .05 .15
177 Jason Doig RC .05 .15
178 Xavier Delisle RC .10 .30
179 Christian Dube RC .25 .60
180 Louis-Philippe Sevigny RC .05 .15
181 Jarome Iginla RC 3.00 8.00
182 Marc Savard RC 1.00 2.50
183 Alyn McCauley RC .30 .75
184 Brad Mehalko RC .10 .30
185 Todd Norman RC .05 .15
186 Brian Scott RC .05 .15
187 Brad Larsen RC .05 .15
188 Jeffrey Ware RC .25 .60
189 Sergei Samsonov RC .75 2.00
190 Andrei Petrunin RC .25 .60
191 Jason Holland RC .10 .30
192 Rory Fitzpatrick RC .05 .15
193 Deron Quint .05 .15
194 Jamie Langenbrunner .25 .60
195 Jeff Mitchell RC .05 .15
SP1 Wayne Gretzky 2500 10.00 25.00

1994-95 SP Die Cuts

This 195-card set is a parallel version of the regular issue. These were inserted at a rate of one per pack. They are distinguished by the die-cutting of the top and bottom right corners of the card, and the use of a silver instead of gold hologram. The numbering of the cards is consistent with the regular issue.

COMPLETE SET (195) 20.00 50.00
*VETS: .8X TO 2X BASIC CARDS
*ROOKIES: .8X TO 2X BASIC CARDS

1994-95 SP Premier

The 30 cards in this set were randomly inserted in SP at the rate of 1:9 packs. The cards are printed on white paper stock and have a full white border. The action photo has a ghosted background, making the picture look slightly out of focus. The set name is embossed on the lower card front. Player name and position are printed above and below the set name. Player photo and limited text are the back. A gold rectangular hologram is used on this version.

COMPLETE SET (30) 20.00 40.00
*DIE CUT: 4X TO 10X BASIC INSERTS
1 Paul Kariya .60 1.50
2 Peter Forsberg 2.50 6.00
3 Viktor Kozlov .30 .75
4 Todd Marchant .30 .75
5 Oleg Tverdovsky .15 .40
6 Todd Harvey .15 .40
7 Kenny Jonsson .30 .75
8 Blaine Lacher .30 .75
9 Radek Bonk .75 2.00
10 Brett Lindros .30 .75
11 Valeri Bure .30 .75
12 Brian Rolston .15 .40
13 David Oliver .15 .40
14 Ian Laperriere .15 .40
15 Adam Deadmarsh .30 .75
16 Pavel Bure .60 1.50
17 Wayne Gretzky 4.00 10.00
18 Jeremy Roenick .75 2.00
19 Dominik Hasek 1.25 3.00
20 Ray Bourque 1.00 2.50
21 Doug Gilmour .30 .75
22 Teemu Selanne .60 1.50
23 Cam Neely .60 1.50
24 Sergei Fedorov 1.00 2.50
25 Bernie Nicholls .15 .40
26 Jaromir Jagr 1.00 2.50
27 Joe Sakic 1.25 3.00
28 Mark Messier .60 1.50
29 Brett Hull .75 2.00
30 Eric Lindros .60 1.50

1995-96 SP

The 1995-96 Upper Deck SP set was issued in one series totaling 188 cards. The 8-card packs had an SRP of $4.39 each. The Great Connections inserts (GC1and GC2), were randomly inserted at the rate of 1:381 packs. There are two versions of card number 66. The first features Wayne Gretzky in an All-Star sweater. This was used as a promotional card and was issued with the dealer solicitation. The second is the regular number 66 found in packs and features Craig Johnson, a player acquired by the Kings in the Gretzky trade.

COMPLETE SET (188) 20.00 40.00
1 Paul Kariya .25 .60
2 Teemu Selanne .25 .60
3 Guy Hebert .10 .30
4 Steve Rucchin .10 .30
5 Ray Bourque .40 1.00
6 Cam Neely .25 .60
7 Adam Oates .10 .30
8 Kyle McLaren RC .05 .15
9 Bill Ranford .10 .30
10 Shawn McEachern .05 .15
11 Don Sweeney .05 .15
12 Pat LaFontaine .25 .60
13 Dominik Hasek .50 1.25
14 Brian Holzinger RC .05 .15
15 Alexei Zhitnik .05 .15
16 Theo Fleury .05 .15
17 Cory Stillman .05 .15
18 German Titov .05 .15
19 Phil Housley .10 .30
20 Michael Nylander .05 .15
21 Trevor Kidd .10 .30
22 Eric Daze .10 .30
23 Chris Chelios .25 .60
24 Jeremy Roenick .30 .75
25 Gary Suter .05 .15
26 Bernie Nicholls .05 .15
27 Ed Belfour .25 .60
28 Tony Amonte .10 .30
29 Peter Forsberg .60 1.50
30 Patrick Roy 1.25 3.00
31 Joe Sakic .50 1.25
32 Sandis Ozolinsh .05 .15
33 Adam Deadmarsh .05 .15
34 Stephane Fiset .10 .30
35 Claude Lemieux .05 .15
36 Mike Modano .40 1.00
37 Kevin Hatcher .05 .15
38 Joe Nieuwendyk .10 .30
39 Todd Harvey .10 .30
40 Derian Hatcher .05 .15
41 Jere Lehtinen .10 .30
42 Nicklas Lidstrom .25 .60
43 Mathieu Dandenault .05 .15
44 Sergei Fedorov .40 1.00
45 Paul Coffey .25 .60
46 Steve Yzerman 1.25 3.00
47 Keith Primeau .05 .15
48 Chris Osgood .10 .30
49 Vyacheslav Kozlov .10 .30
50 Doug Weight .10 .30
51 Jason Arnott .05 .15
52 Miroslav Satan RC 1.00 2.50
53 Zdeno Ciger .05 .15
54 Curtis Joseph .25 .60
55 Scott Mellanby .05 .15
56 John Vanbiesbrouck .10 .30
57 Jody Hull .05 .15
58 Ed Jovanovski .25 .60
59 Radek Dvorak RC .40 1.00
60 Rob Niedermayer .05 .15
61 Andrew Cassels .05 .15
62 Brendan Shanahan .25 .60
63 Nelson Emerson .05 .15
64 Jeff O'Neill .05 .15
65 Sean Burke .10 .30
66A Wayne Gretzky promo card 4.00 10.00
66B Craig Johnson .05 .15
67 Dimitri Khristich .05 .15
68 Vitali Yachmenev .05 .15
69 Aki Berg RC .10 .30
70 Byron Dafoe .10 .30
71 Pierre Turgeon .10 .30
72 Mark Recchi .10 .30
73 Saku Koivu .25 .60
74 Valeri Bure .05 .15
75 Vincent Damphousse .05 .15
76 Jocelyn Thibault .25 .60
77 Patrice Brisebois .05 .15
78 John MacLean .10 .30
79 Martin Brodeur .60 1.50
80 Steve Thomas .10 .30
81 Scott Stevens .10 .30
82 Bill Guerin .10 .30
83 Petr Sykora RC 1.00 2.50
84 Scott Niedermayer .05 .15
85 Stephane Richer .10 .30
86 Zigmund Palffy .10 .30
87 Travis Green .10 .30
88 Todd Bertuzzi RC 2.00 5.00
89 Mathieu Schneider .05 .15
90 Eric Fichaud .10 .30
91 Bryan McCabe .05 .15
92 Mark Messier .25 .60
93 Pat Verbeek .05 .15
94 Brian Leetch .10 .30
95 Mike Richter .25 .60
96 Niklas Sundstrom .10 .30
97 Luc Robitaille .10 .30
98 Adam Graves .05 .15
99 Alexei Kovalev .05 .15
100 Daniel Alfredsson RC 2.00 5.00
101 Alexei Yashin .05 .15
102 Radek Bonk .05 .15
103 Alexandre Daigle .05 .15
104 Damian Rhodes .10 .30
105 Antti Tormanen .05 .15
106 Eric Lindros .25 .60
107 Mikael Renberg .10 .30
108 John LeClair .25 .60
109 Ron Hextall .10 .30
110 Rod Brind'Amour .10 .30
111 Joel Otto .05 .15
112 Eric Desjardins .10 .30
113 Mario Lemieux 1.25 3.00
114 Jaromir Jagr .40 1.00
115 Ron Francis .10 .30
116 Markus Naslund .25 .60
117 Sergei Zubov .05 .15
118 Tomas Sandstrom .05 .15
119 Tom Barrasso .10 .30
120 Richard Park .05 .15
121 Brett Hull .30 .75
122 Shayne Corson .05 .15
123 Dale Hawerchuk .25 .60
124 Chris Pronger .25 .60
125 Al MacInnis .10 .30
126 Grant Fuhr .25 .60
127 Wayne Gretzky 1.50 4.00
128 Geoff Courtnall .05 .15
129 Owen Nolan .10 .30
130 Ray Sheppard .10 .30
131 Chris Terreri .10 .30
132 Marcus Ragnarsson RC .05 .15
133 Jeff Friesen .05 .15
134 Doug Bodger .05 .15
135 Roman Hamrlik .10 .30
136 Petr Klima .05 .15
137 Daren Puppa .10 .30
138 Aaron Gavey .05 .15
139 Daymond Langkow RC .40 1.00
140 Alexander Selivanov .05 .15
141 Mats Sundin .25 .60
142 Kirk Muller .05 .15
143 Larry Murphy .10 .30
144 Doug Gilmour .10 .30
145 Darby Hendrickson .05 .15
146 Felix Potvin .25 .60
147 Kenny Jonsson .05 .15
148 Alexander Mogilny .10 .30
149 Pavel Bure .25 .60
150 Trevor Linden .10 .30
151 Corey Hirsch .10 .30
152 Kirk McLean .10 .30
153 Esa Tikkanen .05 .15
154 Cliff Ronning .05 .15
155 Peter Bondra .10 .30
156 Jim Carey .10 .30
157 Michal Pivonka .05 .15
158 Joe Juneau .05 .15
159 Dale Hunter .10 .30
160 Steve Konowalchuk .05 .15
161 Stefan Ustorf .05 .15
162 Brendan Witt .05 .15
163 Chad Kilger RC .05 .15
164 Keith Tkachuk .25 .60
165 Deron Quint .05 .15
166 Oleg Tverdovsky .05 .15
167 Alexei Zhamnov .10 .30
168 Igor Korolev .05 .15
169 Wade Redden .05 .15
170 Jarome Iginla .30 .75
171 Christian Dube .05 .15
172 Jason Podollan .05 .15
173 Alyn McCauley .10 .30
174 Nolan Baumgartner .05 .15
175 Jason Botterill .05 .15
176 Chris Phillips RC .30 .75
177 Dmitri Nabokov .10 .30
178 Andrei Petrunin .05 .15
179 Alexander Korolyuk .10 .30
180 Sergei Samsonov .60 1.50
181 Ilja Gorokhov RC .10 .30
182 Alexei Kolkunov RC .10 .30
183 Samuel Pahlsson RC .05 .15
184 Mattias Ohlund .05 .15
185 Marcus Nilsson RC .25 .60
186 Daniel Tjarnqvist RC .05 .15
187 Per Anton Lundstrom RC .05 .15
188 Fredrik Loven RC .05 .15
GC1 Wayne Gretzky 15.00 40.00
GC2 Sergei Samsonov 8.00 20.00

1995-96 SP Holoviews

Randomly inserted in packs at a rate of 1:5, this 20-card set utilizes UD's Holoview technology to great effect. There also exists a die-cut parallel version of this set (known as Special FX), issued 1:75 packs. Special FX cards are enhanced by rainbow foil, as well as the die-cutting. Multipliers to determine the value of these cards are listed below.

COMPLETE SET (20) 25.00 50.00
*SPECIAL FX: 1.25X TO 3X BASIC INSERTS
FX1 Teemu Selanne .60 1.50
FX2 Paul Kariya .60 1.50
FX3 Chris Chelios .60 1.50
FX4 Peter Forsberg 1.50 4.00
FX5 Sergei Fedorov 1.00 2.50
FX6 Paul Coffey .60 1.50
FX7 Steve Yzerman 3.00 8.00
FX8 Jason Arnott .15 .40
FX9 Doug Weight .30 .75
FX10 Wayne Gretzky 4.00 10.00
FX11 Vitali Yachmenev .15 .40
FX12 Martin Brodeur 1.50 4.00
FX13 Scott Stevens .30 .75
FX14 Mark Messier .60 1.50
FX15 Daniel Alfredsson 6.00 15.00
FX16 Eric Lindros .60 1.50
FX17 Mario Lemieux 3.00 8.00
FX18 Jaromir Jagr 1.00 2.50
FX19 Shayne Corson .15 .40
FX20 Pavel Bure .60 1.50

1995-96 SP Stars/Etoiles

Randomly inserted in packs at a rate of 1:3, this 30-card set uses a double die-cut design to highlight the top athletes in the NHL. This version uses silver foil as it's primary element. There also is a gold foil parallel version, which is significantly tougher to pull. These cards were randomly inserted 1:61 packs.

COMPLETE SET (30) 25.00 50.00
*GOLD: 3X TO 8X BASIC INSERTS
GOLD STATED ODDS 1:61
E1 Paul Kariya .50 1.25
E2 Teemu Selanne .50 1.25
E3 Ray Bourque .75 2.00
E4 Cam Neely .50 1.25
E5 Pat LaFontaine .50 1.25
E6 Theo Fleury .10 .30
E7 Jeremy Roenick .60 1.50
E8 Joe Sakic 1.00 2.50
E9 Patrick Roy 2.50 6.00
E10 Peter Forsberg 1.25 3.00
E11 Mike Modano .75 2.00
E12 Sergei Fedorov .75 2.00
E13 Paul Coffey .50 1.25
E14 Steve Yzerman 2.50 6.00
E15 Pierre Turgeon .25 .60
E16 Brendan Shanahan .50 1.25
E17 Wayne Gretzky 3.00 8.00
E18 Martin Brodeur 1.25 3.00
E19 Mark Messier .50 1.25
E20 Brian Leetch .25 .60
E21 Eric Lindros .50 1.25
E22 Mario Lemieux 2.50 6.00
E23 Jaromir Jagr .75 2.00
E24 Brett Hull .60 1.50
E25 Roman Hamrlik .25 .60
E26 Mats Sundin .50 1.25
E27 Felix Potvin .50 1.25
E28 Alexander Mogilny .25 .60
E29 Pavel Bure .50 1.25
E30 Keith Tkachuk .50 1.25

1996-97 SP

The 1996-97 SP set was issued in one series totaling 188 cards. The eight-card packs had a suggested retail price of $3.49 each. Printed on 20 pt. card stock, this set featured color action photos of 168 regular players from all 26 NHL teams and included a subset of 20 premier prospects. The backs carried player information and statistics. The Gretzky promo was distributed to dealers; it mirrored the regular issue save for the word SAMPLE written across the back.

COMPLETE SET (188) 15.00 40.00
1 Paul Kariya .30 .75
2 Teemu Selanne .30 .75
3 Jari Kurri .15 .40
4 Darren Van Impe .07 .20
5 Guy Hebert .15 .40
6 Steve Rucchin .07 .20
7 Ray Bourque .50 1.25
8 Kyle McLaren .07 .20
9 Bill Ranford .15 .40
10 Don Sweeney .07 .20
11 Adam Oates .15 .40
12 Rick Tocchet .15 .40
13 Ted Donato .07 .20
14 Curtis Brown .07 .20
15 Pat LaFontaine .30 .75
16 Derek Plante .07 .20
17 Dominik Hasek .50 1.25
18 Brian Holzinger .15 .40
19 Alexei Zhitnik .07 .20
20 Theo Fleury .07 .20
21 Trevor Kidd .15 .40
22 Steve Chiasson .07 .20
23 Jarome Iginla .40 1.00
24 German Titov .07 .20
25 Zarley Zalapski .07 .20
26 Eric Daze .15 .40
27 Chris Chelios .30 .75
28 Ed Belfour .30 .75
29 Gary Suter .07 .20
30 Alexei Zhamnov .15 .40
31 Ethan Moreau RC .30 .75
32 Tony Amonte .15 .40
33 Peter Forsberg .50 1.25
34 Joe Sakic .60 1.50
35 Patrick Roy 1.50 4.00
36 Adam Deadmarsh .07 .20
37 Mike Ricci .07 .20
38 Adam Foote .07 .20
39 Claude Lemieux .07 .20
40 Mike Modano .40 1.00
41 Pat Verbeek .07 .20
42 Todd Harvey .07 .20
43 Sergei Zubov .07 .20
44 Andy Moog .15 .40
45 Derian Hatcher .07 .20
46 Jamie Langenbrunner .07 .20
47 Steve Yzerman 1.50 4.00
48 Sergei Fedorov .40 1.00
49 Slava Kozlov .07 .20
50 Brendan Shanahan .30 .75
51 Chris Osgood .15 .40
52 Nicklas Lidstrom .30 .75
53 Vladimir Konstantinov .15 .40
54 Curtis Joseph .30 .75
55 Jason Arnott .07 .20
56 Ryan Smyth .30 .75
57 Doug Weight .15 .40
58 Andrei Kovalenko .07 .20
59 Mariusz Czerkawski .07 .20
60 Ed Jovanovski .15 .40
61 John Vanbiesbrouck .15 .40
62 Rob Niedermayer .15 .40
63 Robert Svehla .07 .20
64 Brian Skrudland .07 .20
65 Scott Mellanby .15 .40
66 Ray Sheppard .15 .40

67 Jeff O'Neill .07 .20
68 Keith Primeau .07 .20
69 Geoff Sanderson .15 .40
70 Sean Burke .15 .40
71 Kevin Dineen .07 .20
72 Andrew Cassels .07 .20
73 Kevin Stevens .07 .20
74 Rob Blake .15 .40
75 Ed Olczyk .07 .20
76 Mattias Norstrom .07 .20
77 Stephane Fiset .15 .40
78 Vitali Yachmenev .07 .20
79 Saku Koivu .30 .75
80 Valeri Bure .07 .20
81 Jocelyn Thibault .30 .75
82 David Wilkie .07 .20
83 Stephane Richer .15 .40
84 Shayne Corson .07 .20
85 Mark Recchi .15 .40
86 Martin Brodeur .75 2.00
87 Bobby Holik .07 .20
88 Petr Sykora .07 .20
89 Scott Stevens .15 .40
90 Scott Niedermayer .07 .20
91 Bill Guerin .07 .20
92 Eric Fichaud .15 .40
93 Kenny Jonsson .07 .20
94 Travis Green .15 .40
95 Derek King .07 .20
96 Todd Bertuzzi .30 .75
97 Zigmund Palffy .15 .40
98 Mark Messier .30 .75
99 Wayne Gretzky 2.00 5.00
100 Mike Richter .30 .75
101 Brian Leetch .30 .75
102 Luc Robitaille .15 .40
103 Adam Graves .07 .20
104 Alexei Kovalev .07 .20
105 Radek Bonk .07 .20
106 Alexandre Daigle .07 .20
107 Daniel Alfredsson .15 .40
108 Alexei Yashin .15 .40
109 Andreas Dackell RC .07 .20
110 Damian Rhodes .15 .40
111 Petr Svoboda .07 .20
112 John LeClair .30 .75
113 Eric Desjardins .15 .40
114 Eric Lindros .30 .75
115 Mikael Renberg .15 .40
116 Ron Hextall .15 .40
117 Dainius Zubrus RC .40 1.00
118 Keith Tkachuk .30 .75
119 Jeremy Roenick .40 1.00
120 Nikolai Khabibulin .15 .40
121 Oleg Tverdovsky .15 .40
122 Teppo Numminen .07 .20
123 Mike Gartner .15 .40
124 Cliff Ronning .07 .20
125 Mario Lemieux 1.50 4.00
126 Jaromir Jagr .50 1.25
127 Ron Francis .15 .40
128 Petr Nedved .15 .40
129 Darius Kasparaitis .07 .20
130 Kevin Hatcher .07 .20
131 Joe Mullen .15 .40
132 Joe Murphy .07 .20
133 Grant Fuhr .15 .40
134 Harry York RC .30 .75
135 Chris Pronger .15 .40
136 Brett Hull .40 1.00
137 Pierre Turgeon .15 .40
138 Owen Nolan .15 .40
139 Bernie Nicholls .07 .20
140 Tony Granato .07 .20
141 Kelly Hrudey .15 .40
142 Darren Turcotte .07 .20
143 Jeff Friesen .07 .20
144 Roman Hamrlik .15 .40
145 Chris Gratton .15 .40
146 Daymond Langkow .15 .40
147 Dino Ciccarelli .15 .40
148 Alexander Selivanov .07 .20
149 Brian Bradley .07 .20
150 Wendel Clark .15 .40
151 Mats Sundin .30 .75
152 Doug Gilmour .15 .40
153 Felix Potvin .30 .75
154 Larry Murphy .15 .40
155 Mathieu Schneider .07 .20
156 Kirk Muller .07 .20
157 Pavel Bure .30 .75
158 Alexander Mogilny .15 .40
159 Corey Hirsch .15 .40
160 Jyrki Lumme .07 .20
161 Russ Courtnall .07 .20
162 Mike Fountain RC .07 .20
163 Peter Bondra .15 .40
164 Jim Carey .30 .75
165 Sergei Gonchar .07 .20
166 Joe Juneau .07 .20
167 Phil Housley .15 .40
168 Jason Allison .07 .20
169 Ruslan Salei RC .07 .20
170 Mattias Timander RC .07 .20
171 Vaclav Varada RC .15 .40
172 Jonas Hoglund .07 .20
173 Jason Podollan .15 .40
174 Jose Theodore .30 .75
175 Roman Turek RC .40 1.00
176 Anders Eriksson .07 .20
177 Mike Grier RC .40 1.00
178 Rem Murray RC .15 .40
179 Per Gustafsson RC .07 .20
180 Jay Pandolfo UER .07 .20
181 Kai Nurminen RC .07 .20
182 Bryan Berard .30 .75
183 Christian Dube .07 .20
184 Daniel Goneau RC .15 .40
185 Wade Redden .07 .20
186 Janne Niinimaa .30 .75
187 Jim Campbell .07 .20
188 Sergei Berezin RC .40 1.00
P99 Wayne Gretzky PROMO .07 .20

1996-97 SP Clearcut Winner

Randomly inserted in packs at a rate of 1:91, this 20-card set featured color player images in a chiseled-out ice block, die-cut card displaying a full body transparent Hologram.

CW1 Wayne Gretzky 15.00 40.00
CW2 Saku Koivu 2.50 6.00
CW3 Mario Lemieux 10.00 25.00
CW4 Sergei Fedorov 3.00 8.00
CW5 Paul Kariya 2.50 6.00
CW6 Patrick Roy 10.00 25.00
CW7 Jeremy Roenick 3.00 8.00
CW8 Brendan Shanahan 2.50 6.00
CW9 John Vanbiesbrouck 2.00 5.00
CW10 Doug Weight 2.00 5.00
CW11 Mark Messier 2.50 6.00
CW12 Mats Sundin 2.50 6.00
CW13 Paul Coffey 2.00 5.00
CW14 Theo Fleury 2.00 5.00
CW15 Steve Yzerman 8.00 20.00
CW16 Pavel Bure 2.50 6.00
CW17 Adam Deadmarsh 1.00 2.50
CW18 Chris Chelios 2.00 5.00
CW19 Joe Sakic 6.00 15.00
CW20 Eric Daze 1.00 2.50

1996-97 SP Holoview Collection

Randomly inserted in packs at a rate of 1:9, this 30-card set featured color player photos of some of the NHL's most elite stars printed on an all new design Holoview die-cut card.

COMPLETE SET (30) 20.00 50.00
HC1 Wayne Gretzky 6.00 15.00
HC2 Eric Daze .40 1.00
HC3 Doug Gilmour .60 1.50
HC4 Jason Arnott .60 1.50
HC5 Sergei Fedorov 1.50 4.00
HC6 Chris Chelios 1.00 2.50
HC7 Alexei Kovalev .60 1.50
HC8 Pat LaFontaine .40 1.00
HC9 Daniel Alfredsson .60 1.50
HC10 Chris Pronger .60 1.50
HC11 Jocelyn Thibault .60 1.50
HC12 Chris Gratton .40 1.00
HC13 Alexei Yashin .40 1.00
HC14 Peter Bondra .60 1.50
HC15 Saku Koivu 1.00 2.50
HC16 Valeri Bure .40 1.00
HC17 John LeClair 1.00 2.50
HC18 Tony Amonte 1.00 2.50
HC19 Brian Holzinger .40 1.00
HC20 Mats Sundin 1.00 2.50
HC21 Chris Osgood .60 1.50
HC22 Roman Hamrlik .40 1.00
HC23 Ray Bourque 2.00 5.00
HC24 Doug Weight .60 1.50
HC25 Mike Modano 1.50 4.00
HC26 Niklas Sundstrom .40 1.00
HC27 Mike Richter 1.00 2.50
HC28 Zigmund Palffy .60 1.50
HC29 Adam Oates .60 1.50
HC30 Dominik Hasek 2.00 5.00

1996-97 SP Inside Info

Inserted at the rate of one per box, this eight-card set featured color action player photos with a special pull-out panel that displayed another photo of the same player and statistics. A gold version was also available and was seeded one in every two cases. Values for these cards can be determined by using the multipliers listed below.

COMPLETE SET (8) 20.00 50.00
*GOLDS: 2X TO 5X BASIC INSERTS
IN1 Wayne Gretzky 10.00 25.00
IN2 Keith Tkachuk 2.00 5.00
IN3 Brendan Shanahan 2.00 5.00
IN4 Teemu Selanne 2.00 5.00
IN5 Ray Bourque 3.00 8.00
IN6 Joe Sakic 4.00 10.00
IN7 Felix Potvin 2.00 5.00
IN8 Steve Yzerman 6.00 15.00

1996-97 SP Game Film

Randomly inserted in packs at a rate of 1:30, this 20-card set carried actual game photography featuring film footage of favorite NHL players.

COMPLETE SET (20) 40.00 100.00
GF1 Wayne Gretzky 15.00 40.00
GF2 Peter Forsberg 4.00 10.00
GF3 Patrick Roy 10.00 25.00
GF4 Brett Hull 2.50 6.00
GF5 Keith Tkachuk 1.00 2.50
GF6 Eric Lindros 2.50 6.00
GF7 Felix Potvin 2.50 6.00
GF8 John Vanbiesbrouck 1.50 4.00
GF9 Paul Kariya 2.50 6.00
GF10 Mark Messier 2.50 6.00
GF11 Ed Belfour 2.50 6.00
GF12 Alexander Mogilny 1.00 2.50
GF13 Jim Carey 1.50 4.00
GF14 Ed Jovanovski 1.00 2.50
GF15 Theo Fleury 1.00 2.50
GF16 Doug Gilmour 1.50 4.00
GF17 John LeClair 1.00 2.50
GF18 Pat LaFontaine 1.00 2.50
GF19 Paul Coffey 1.50 4.00
GF20 Daniel Alfredsson 1.50 4.00

1996-97 SP SPx Force

Randomly inserted in packs at a rate of 1:360, this five-card set featured top NHL players on a multi-image Holoview card. Each of the first four cards displayed a center, winger, goalie and rookie. The last card carried the top player from each of the previous cards.

COMPLETE SET (5) 60.00 150.00
1 Eric Lindros 25.00 60.00
Mario Lemieux

Peter Forsberg
Wayne Gretzky
2 Brett Hull 12.00 30.00
Jaromir Jagr
Pavel Bure
Teemu Selanne
3 Chris Osgood 12.00 30.00
Dominik Hasek
Martin Brodeur
Mike Richter
4 Anders Eriksson 8.00 20.00
Bryan Berard
Jarome Iginla
Sergei Berezin
5 Jarome Iginla 20.00 50.00
Jaromir Jagr
Wayne Gretzky
Martin Brodeur

1996-97 SP SPx Force Autographs

These four different autograph cards were randomly inserted one in 2,500 packs of 1996-97 SP. Besides the player's signature, the cards are parallel to the more common, unsigned SPx Force inserts. Only 100 cards were signed by each player.

1 Wayne Gretzky AU 200.00 400.00
2 Jaromir Jagr AU 50.00 125.00
3 Martin Brodeur AU 60.00 150.00
4 Jarome Iginla AU 30.00 80.00

1997-98 SP Authentic

The 1997-98 SP Authentic set was issued in one series totaling 198 cards and was distributed in five-card packs with a suggested retail price of $4.99. The fronts features color player photos printed on 24 pt. card stock. The backs carry player information. The set contains the topical subset: Future Watch (169-198).

COMPLETE SET (198) 30.00 60.00
1 Teemu Selanne .30 .75
2 Sean Pronger .08 .25
3 Joe Sacco .08 .25
4 Tomas Sandstrom .08 .25
5 Steve Rucchin .08 .25
6 Paul Kariya .30 .75
7 Ted Donato .08 .25
8 Ray Bourque .50 1.25
9 Tim Taylor .08 .25
10 Jason Allison .08 .25
11 Kyle McLaren .08 .25
12 Dimitri Khristich .08 .25
13 Jason Dawe .08 .25
14 Dominik Hasek .60 1.50
15 Miroslav Satan .08 .25
16 Brian Holzinger .08 .25
17 Alexei Zhitnik .08 .25
18 Theo Fleury .08 .25
19 Cory Stillman .08 .25
20 Jarome Iginla .40 1.00
21 Sandy McCarthy .08 .25
22 German Titov .08 .25
23 Glen Wesley .08 .25
24 Keith Primeau .08 .25
25 Geoff Sanderson .25 .60
26 Gary Roberts .08 .25
27 Sami Kapanen .08 .25
28 Jeff O'Neill .08 .25
29 Tony Amonte .25 .60
30 Chris Chelios .30 .75
31 Eric Daze .25 .60
32 Alexei Zhamnov .08 .25
33 Chris Terreri .25 .60
34 Sergei Krivokrasov .08 .25
35 Joe Sakic .60 1.50
36 Peter Forsberg .75 2.00
37 Patrick Roy 1.50 4.00
38 Claude Lemieux .08 .25
39 Valeri Kamensky .25 .60
40 Adam Deadmarsh .08 .25
41 Sandis Ozolinsh .08 .25
42 Jari Kurri .25 .60
43 Mike Modano .50 1.25
44 Ed Belfour .30 .75
45 Derian Hatcher .08 .25
46 Sergei Zubov .08 .25
47 Jamie Langenbrunner .08 .25
48 Jere Lehtinen .08 .25
49 Joe Nieuwendyk .25 .60
50 Vyacheslav Kozlov .08 .25
51 Chris Osgood .25 .60
52 Steve Yzerman 1.50 4.00
53 Nicklas Lidstrom .30 .75
54 Igor Larionov .08 .25
55 Brendan Shanahan .30 .75
56 Anders Eriksson .08 .25
57 Darren McCarty .08 .25
58 Doug Weight .25 .60
59 Jason Arnott .08 .25
60 Curtis Joseph .30 .75
61 Ryan Smyth .08 .25
62 Dean McAmmond .08 .25
63 Mike Grier .08 .25
64 Kelly Buchberger .08 .25
65 Ed Jovanovski .08 .25
66 Ray Whitney .08 .25
67 Rob Niedermayer .08 .25
68 Scott Mellanby .08 .25
69 John Vanbiesbrouck .25 .60
70 Viktor Kozlov .08 .25
71 Jozef Stumpel .25 .60
72 Rob Blake .25 .60
73 Garry Galley .08 .25
74 Vladimir Tsyplakov .08 .25
75 Yanic Perreault .08 .25
76 Stephane Fiset .25 .60
77 Luc Robitaille .25 .60
78 Valeri Bure .08 .25
79 Mark Recchi .25 .60
80 Saku Koivu .30 .75
81 Andy Moog .25 .60
82 Vincent Damphousse .08 .25
83 Vladimir Malakhov .08 .25
84 Shayne Corson .08 .25
85 Scott Stevens .25 .60
86 Bill Guerin .25 .60
87 Martin Brodeur .75 2.00
88 Doug Gilmour .25 .60
89 Bobby Holik .08 .25
90 Petr Sykora .08 .25
91 Zigmund Palffy .25 .60
92 Bryan Berard .25 .60
93 Tommy Salo .25 .60
94 Travis Green .08 .25
95 Kenny Jonsson .08 .25
96 Todd Bertuzzi .30 .75
97 Robert Reichel .08 .25
98 Pat LaFontaine .30 .75
99 Wayne Gretzky 2.00 5.00
100 Brian Leetch .30 .75
101 Mike Richter .30 .75
102 Alexei Kovalev .08 .25
103 Adam Graves .08 .25
104 Niklas Sundstrom .08 .25
105 Alexei Yashin .08 .25
106 Daniel Alfredsson .25 .60
107 Alexandre Daigle .08 .25
108 Wade Redden .08 .25
109 Andreas Dackell .08 .25
110 Shawn McEachern .08 .25
111 Eric Lindros .30 .75
112 Chris Gratton .25 .60
113 Paul Coffey .30 .75
114 John LeClair .30 .75
115 Rod Brind'Amour .25 .60
116 Ron Hextall .25 .60
117 Dainius Zubrus .30 .75
118 Jeremy Roenick .40 1.00
119 Keith Tkachuk .30 .75
120 Nikolai Khabibulin .25 .60
121 Rick Tocchet .25 .60
122 Teppo Numminen .08 .25
123 Craig Janney .08 .25
124 Mike Gartner .25 .60
125 Jaromir Jagr .50 1.25
126 Ron Francis .25 .60
127 Kevin Hatcher .08 .25
128 Robert Dome RC .08 .25
129 Martin Straka .08 .25
130 Peter Skudra RC .08 .25
131 Owen Nolan .25 .60
132 Bernie Nicholls .08 .25
133 Mike Vernon .25 .60
134 Jeff Friesen .25 .60
135 Tony Granato .08 .25
136 Mike Ricci .08 .25
137 Jim Campbell .08 .25
138 Brett Hull .40 1.00
139 Chris Pronger .25 .60
140 Al MacInnis .25 .60
141 Pierre Turgeon .25 .60
142 Pavol Demitra .25 .60
143 Grant Fuhr .25 .60
144 Steve Duchesne .08 .25
145 Daymond Langkow .08 .25
146 Alexander Selivanov .08 .25
147 Daren Puppa .25 .60
148 Dino Ciccarelli .08 .25
149 Roman Hamrlik .25 .60
150 Mats Sundin .30 .75
151 Felix Potvin .30 .75
152 Wendel Clark .25 .60
153 Sergei Berezin .25 .60
154 Steve Sullivan .08 .25
155 Alexander Mogilny .25 .60
156 Pavel Bure .30 .75
157 Mark Messier .30 .75
158 Bret Hedican .08 .25
159 Kirk McLean .25 .60
160 Trevor Linden .25 .60
161 Dave Scatchard RC .08 .25
162 Adam Oates .25 .60
163 Joe Juneau .25 .60
164 Peter Bondra .25 .60
165 Bill Ranford .25 .60
166 Sergei Gonchar .08 .25
167 Calle Johansson .08 .25
168 Phil Housley .25 .60
169 Espen Knutsen RC .75 2.00
170 Pavel Trnka RC .25 .60
171 Joe Thornton 1.00 2.50
172 Sergei Samsonov .40 1.00
173 Erik Rasmussen .25 .60
174 Tyler Moss RC .25 .60
175 Derek Morris RC .40 1.00
176 Craig Mills .25 .60
177 Daniel Cleary .25 .60
178 Eric Messier RC .30 .75
179 Kevin Hodson .25 .60
180 Mike Knuble RC .25 .60
181 Boyd Devereaux .25 .60
182 Craig Millar RC .08 .25
183 Kevin Weekes RC 2.00 5.00
184 Donald MacLean RC .25 .60
185 Patrik Elias RC 3.00 8.00
186 Zdeno Chara RC 4.00 10.00
187 Chris Phillips .25 .60
188 Vaclav Prospal RC .30 .75
189 Brad Isbister .25 .60
190 Alexei Morozov .25 .60
191 Patrick Marleau .60 1.50
192 Marco Sturm RC .50 1.25
193 Brendan Morrison RC 1.25 3.00
194 Mike Johnson RC .30 .75
195 Alyn McCauley .25 .60
196 Mattias Ohlund .25 .60
197 Richard Zednik .25 .60
198 Jan Bulis RC .25 .60

1997-98 SP Authentic Authentics

Randomly inserted in packs at the rate of 1:288, these special "trade" cards could be redeemed for an assortment of Wayne Gretzky's signed memorabilia from Upper Deck Authenticated such as autographed jerseys, pucks, sticks and other items. Only three "SP Authentics Collection" cards were produced that could be redeemed for Wayne Gretzky's entire collection of autographed memorabilia. We have listed and priced only the autographed trading card below.

STATED ODDS 1:288
10 W.Gretzky 802 Card/184 25.00 50.00

1997-98 SP Authentic Icons

Randomly inserted in packs at the rate of 1:5, this 40-card set features color action photos of the most respected players of the NHL. Embossed and die cut parallels were also created and inserted randomly.

COMPLETE SET (40) 40.00 80.00
*EMBOSSED: .8X TO 2X BASIC INSERTS
*DIE CUT: 4X TO 10X BASIC INSERTS
I1 Pat LaFontaine .75 2.00
I2 Brett Hull 1.00 2.50
I3 Chris Chelios .75 2.00
I4 Joe Sakic 1.50 4.00
I5 John Vanbiesbrouck .60 1.50
I6 Patrik Elias .75 2.00
I7 Eric Lindros .75 2.00
I8 Jaromir Jagr 1.25 3.00
I9 Joe Thornton 1.50 4.00
I10 Brendan Shanahan .75 2.00
I11 Paul Kariya .75 2.00
I12 Peter Forsberg 2.00 5.00
I13 Ed Belfour .75 2.00
I14 Martin Brodeur 2.00 5.00
I15 Alexei Morozov .60 1.50
I16 Mark Messier .75 2.00
I17 John LeClair .75 2.00
I18 Luc Robitaille .60 1.50
I19 Teemu Selanne .75 2.00
I20 Theo Fleury .25 .60
I21 Steve Yzerman 2.00 5.00
I22 Chris Phillips .25 .60
I23 Keith Tkachuk .75 2.00
I24 Patrick Roy 2.00 5.00
I25 Mark Recchi .60 1.50
I26 Wayne Gretzky 3.00 8.00
I27 Dino Ciccarelli .25 .60
I28 Ray Bourque 1.25 3.00
I29 Tony Amonte .60 1.50
I30 Daniel Alfredsson .60 1.50
I31 Saku Koivu .75 2.00
I32 Doug Weight .60 1.50
I33 Mats Sundin .75 2.00
I34 Dominik Hasek 1.50 4.00
I35 Scott Stevens .60 1.50
I36 Pavel Bure .75 2.00
I37 Mike Modano 1.25 3.00
I38 Zigmund Palffy .60 1.50
I39 Brian Leetch .75 2.00
I40 Marco Sturm .75 2.00

1997-98 SP Authentic Mark of a Legend

Randomly inserted in packs at the rate of 1:198, this six-card set features autographed color portraits of six of the NHL's greatest all-time players.

M1 Gordie Howe/112 125.00 250.00
M2 Billy Smith/560 10.00 25.00
M3 Cam Neely/560 15.00 40.00
M4 Bryan Trottier/560 12.00 30.00
M5 Bobby Hull/560 25.00 60.00
M6 Wayne Gretzky/560 100.00 200.00

1997-98 SP Authentic Sign of the Times

Randomly inserted in packs at the rate of 1:23, this 29-card set features autographed color action photos of top players in the NHL. Exchange card expired 3/16/99.

BB Bryan Berard 2.00 5.00
BH Brian Holzinger 2.00 5.00
BH Brett Hull 10.00 25.00
CC Chris Chelios 6.00 15.00
DM Darren McCarty 4.00 10.00
DW Doug Weight 4.00 10.00
DZ Dainius Zubrus 4.00 10.00
GF Grant Fuhr 4.00 10.00
GH Guy Hebert 4.00 10.00
JI Jarome Iginla 10.00 25.00
JS Jaroslav Svejkovsky 2.00 5.00
JLA Jamie Langenbrunner 4.00 10.00
JT Joe Thornton 10.00 25.00
JTH Jose Theodore 10.00 25.00
MB Martin Brodeur 50.00 100.00
MG Mike Grier 4.00 10.00
MS Mats Sundin 20.00 50.00
NK Nikolai Khabibulin 6.00 15.00
NL Nicklas Lidstrom 8.00 20.00
PB Peter Bondra 4.00 10.00
PR Patrick Roy 50.00 100.00
RB Ray Bourque 20.00 50.00
RN Rob Niedermayer 4.00 10.00
SB Sergei Berezin 2.00 5.00
SS Sergei Samsonov 4.00 10.00
SY Steve Yzerman 50.00 100.00
TA Tony Amonte 4.00 10.00
WG Wayne Gretzky 75.00 150.00
YP Yanic Perreault 4.00 10.00

1997-98 SP Authentic Tradition

Randomly inserted in packs at the rate of 1:340, this six-card set features color action dual photos and autographs of a current star and an NHL legend.

T1 Wayne Gretzky 200.00 500.00
Gordie Howe
T2 Patrick Roy 40.00 100.00
Billy Smith/333
T3 Joe Thornton 25.00 60.00
Cam Neely/352
T4 Bryan Berard 8.00 20.00
Bryan Trottier/352
T5 Brett Hull 40.00 100.00
Bobby Hull/352
T6 Ray Bourque 50.00 125.00
Cam Neely/140

1998-99 SP Authentic

The 1998-99 SP Authentic set was issued in one series totaling 135 cards and was distributed in five-card packs with a suggested retail price of $4.99. The set features action color photos of 90 superstars of the NHL (1-90) and 45 top prospects (91-135) which are numbered to just 2000.

COMPLETE SET (135) 125.00 300.00
COMP.SET w/o SP's (90) 10.00 25.00
1 Paul Kariya .30 .75
2 Teemu Selanne .30 .75
3 Guy Hebert .25 .60
4 Sergei Samsonov .25 .60
5 Joe Thornton .50 1.25
6 Jason Allison .08 .25
7 Ray Bourque .50 1.25
8 Dominik Hasek .60 1.50
9 Michael Peca .08 .25
10 Michal Grosek .08 .25
11 Derek Morris .08 .25
12 Theo Fleury .08 .25
13 Jarome Iginla .40 1.00
14 Ron Francis .25 .60
15 Keith Primeau .08 .25
16 Sami Kapanen .08 .25
17 Tony Amonte .25 .60
18 Doug Gilmour .25 .60
19 Chris Chelios .30 .75
20 Peter Forsberg .75 2.00
21 Patrick Roy 1.50 4.00
22 Joe Sakic .60 1.50
23 Adam Deadmarsh .08 .25
24 Brett Hull .40 1.00
25 Mike Modano .50 1.25
26 Ed Belfour .30 .75
27 Jere Lehtinen .08 .25
28 Sergei Fedorov .50 1.25
29 Brendan Shanahan .30 .75
30 Chris Osgood .25 .60
31 Steve Yzerman 1.50 4.00
32 Nicklas Lidstrom .30 .75
33 Doug Weight .25 .60
34 Bill Guerin .25 .60
35 Tom Poti .08 .25
36 Rob Niedermayer .08 .25
37 Ed Jovanovski .08 .25
38 Luc Robitaille .25 .60
39 Rob Blake .25 .60
40 Glen Murray .08 .25
41 Saku Koivu .30 .75
42 Mark Recchi .25 .60
43 Vincent Damphousse .08 .25
44 Mike Dunham .25 .60
45 Sergei Krivokrasov .08 .25
46 Andrew Brunette .25 .60
47 Brendan Morrison .25 .60
48 Martin Brodeur .75 2.00
49 Scott Stevens .25 .60
50 Patrik Elias .25 .60
51 Trevor Linden .25 .60
52 Zigmund Palffy .25 .60
53 Bryan Berard .08 .25
54 Robert Reichel .08 .25
55 Mike Richter .30 .75
56 Wayne Gretzky 2.00 5.00
57 Brian Leetch .25 .60
58 Wade Redden .08 .25
59 Alexei Yashin .08 .25
60 Daniel Alfredsson .25 .60
61 Eric Lindros .30 .75
62 John Vanbiesbrouck .25 .60
63 John LeClair .30 .75
64 Rod Brind'Amour .25 .60
65 Jeremy Roenick .40 1.00
66 Keith Tkachuk .30 .75
67 Nikolai Khabibulin .25 .60
68 German Titov .08 .25
69 Martin Straka .08 .25
70 Jaromir Jagr .50 1.25
71 Chris Pronger .25 .60
72 Al MacInnis .25 .60
73 Pierre Turgeon .25 .60
74 Pavol Demitra .25 .60
75 Patrick Marleau .08 .25
76 Jeff Friesen .08 .25
77 Owen Nolan .08 .25
78 Bill Ranford .08 .25
79 Wendel Clark .25 .60
80 Craig Janney .08 .25
81 Mike Johnson .08 .25
82 Curtis Joseph .30 .75
83 Mats Sundin .30 .75
84 Mattias Ohlund .25 .60
85 Mark Messier .30 .75
86 Pavel Bure .30 .75
87 Olaf Kolzig .25 .60
88 Peter Bondra .25 .60
89 Joe Juneau .25 .60
90 Adam Oates .25 .60
91 Johan Davidsson 1.50 4.00
92 Rico Fata 1.50 4.00
93 Mike Maneluk RC 2.00 5.00
94 J-P Dumont 1.50 4.00
95 Milan Hejduk RC 15.00 30.00
96 Chris Drury 1.50 4.00
97 Mark Parrish RC 4.00 10.00
98 Oleg Kvasha RC 2.00 5.00
99 Josh Green RC 2.00 5.00
100 Olli Jokinen 1.50 4.00
101 Manny Malhotra 1.50 4.00
102 Eric Brewer 1.50 4.00
103 Mike Watt 1.50 4.00
104 Daniel Briere 6.00 15.00
105 Jean-Sebastien Aubin RC 4.00 10.00
106 Jan Hrdina RC 2.00 5.00
107 Marty Reasoner 1.50 4.00
108 Michal Handzus RC 4.00 10.00
109 Vincent Lecavalier 4.00 10.00
110 Tomas Kaberle RC 4.00 10.00
111 Bill Muckalt RC 2.00 5.00
112 Josh Holden 1.50 4.00
113 Matt Herr RC 2.00 5.00
114 Brian Finley RC 3.00 8.00
115 Maxime Ouellet RC 2.00 5.00
116 Kurtis Foster RC 2.00 5.00
117 Barret Jackman RC 4.00 10.00
118 Ross Lupaschuk RC 2.00 5.00
119 Steven McCarthy RC 2.00 5.00
120 Peter Reynolds RC 2.00 5.00
121 Bart Rushmer RC 2.00 5.00
122 Jonathon Zion RC 2.00 5.00
123 Kris Beech RC 3.00 8.00
124 Brandin Cote RC 2.00 5.00
125 Scott Kelman RC 2.00 5.00
126 Jamie Lundmark RC 3.00 8.00
127 Derek MacKenzie RC 2.00 5.00
128 Rory McDade RC 2.00 5.00
129 David Morisset RC 2.00 5.00
130 Mirko Murovic RC 2.00 5.00
131 Taylor Pyatt RC 4.00 10.00
132 Charlie Stephens 2.00 5.00
133 Kyle Wanvig RC 2.00 5.00
134 Krzystof Wieckowski RC 2.00 5.00
135 Michael Zigomanis RC 2.00 5.00

1998-99 SP Authentic Power Shift

Randomly inserted into packs, this 135-card set is parallel to the base set. Only 500 sets were made.

*1-90 POWER SHIFT: 4X TO 10X BAIC CARDS
*91-135 POWER SHIFT: .3X TO .8X BASIC SP

1998-99 SP Authentic Authentics

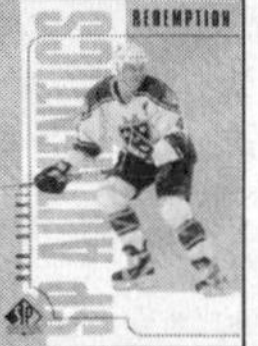

Randomly inserted into packs at the rate of 1:697, this set features hand numbered redemption cards for autographed merchandise and game used memorabilia. We have listed and priced only the autographed trading cards. The number of each item available is indicated below. The cards expired on February 23, 2000.

6 R.Blake Puck/75 12.50 25.00
7 R.Blake Photo/100 12.50 25.00
8 C.Chelios Photo/75 30.00 60.00
9 C.Chelios Puck/75 30.00 60.00
10 W.Gretzky Puck/50 125.00 250.00
11 W.Gretzky Photo/50 125.00 250.00
12 B.Hull Puck/90 30.00 60.00
13 K.Tkachuk Photo/75 30.00 60.00
14 K.Tkachuk Puck/75 30.00 60.00
15 S.Yzerman Card/50 50.00 100.00
16 S.Yzerman 2-card 75.00 150.00
17 S.Yzerman '98 BD Card/50 75.00 150.00

1998-99 SP Authentic Sign of the Times

Randomly inserted into packs at the rate of 1:23, this 50-card set features autographed color photos of top players and future stars of the NHL. Some of the autographs were obtained through redemption cards.

AD Adam Deadmarsh 2.00 5.00
AM Alexander Mogilny 4.00 10.00
AS Alex Selivanov 3.00 8.00
BB Bates Battaglia 2.00 5.00
BD Byron Dafoe 4.00 10.00
BF Brian Finley 2.00 5.00
BH Brett Hull 12.50 30.00
BJ Barret Jackman 8.00 20.00
CJ Curtis Joseph 8.00 20.00
CS Charlie Stephens 2.00 5.00
DA Daniel Alfredsson 4.00 10.00
DM David Morisset 2.00 5.00
(unconfirmed)
DW Doug Weight 5.00 12.00
EJ Ed Jovanovski 4.00 10.00
JA Jason Allison 2.00 5.00
JJ Joe Juneau 4.00 10.00
JS Jozef Stumpel 2.00 5.00
JT Joe Thornton 10.00 25.00
KB Kris Beech 2.00 5.00
KF Kurtis Foster 3.00 8.00
KT Keith Tkachuk 8.00 20.00
MB Matthew Barnaby 2.00 5.00
MH Marian Hossa 8.00 20.00
MM Manny Malhotra 4.00 10.00
MO Mattias Ohlund 2.00 5.00
MS Mats Sundin 25.00 50.00
MZ Michael Zigomanis 2.00 5.00
NL Nicklas Lidstrom 8.00 20.00
ON Owen Nolan 4.00 10.00
PR Patrick Roy 40.00 80.00
RB Rob Blake 4.00 10.00
RL Ross Lupaschuk 2.00 5.00
RM Rory McDade 2.00 5.00
RN Rumun Ndur 2.00 5.00
RS Ryan Smyth 4.00 10.00
SG Sergei Gonchar 2.00 5.00
SK Scott Kelman 3.00 8.00
SM Steven McCarthy 2.00 5.00
SY Steve Yzerman 40.00 80.00
TH Tomas Holmstrom 4.00 10.00
TP Taylor Pyatt 5.00 12.00
VL Vincent Lecavalier 8.00 20.00
WG Wayne Gretzky 100.00 200.00
DMA Derek Mackenzie 2.00 5.00
MAO Maxime Ouellet 2.00 5.00
MIM Mirko Murovic 2.00 5.00
MMC Marty McSorley 4.00 10.00
PBO Peter Bondra 4.00 10.00
PRE Peter Reynolds 2.00 5.00
PB Pavel Bure 8.00 20.00

1998-99 SP Authentic Sign of the Times Gold

Randomly inserted into packs, this set is a parallel version of the regular SP Authentic Sign of the Times insert set with each card hand-numbered to the pictured player's jersey number. These numbers follow the player's name in the checklist below. Cards with print runs less than 25 are not priced due to scarcity.

AD Adam Deadmarsh/18
AM A.Mogilny/89 25.00 50.00
AS Alex Selivanov/29 12.50 30.00
BB Bates Battaglia/13
BD Byron Dafoe/34 20.00 50.00
BF Brian Finley/100 10.00 25.00
BH Brett Hull/22
BJ Barret Jackman/100 10.00 25.00
CJ Curtis Joseph/31 50.00 125.00
CS Charlie Stephens/100 6.00 15.00
DA Daniel Alfredsson/11
DM David Morisset/100 6.00 15.00
DW Doug Weight/39 25.00 50.00
EJ E.Jovanovski/55 25.00 50.00
JA Jason Allison/41 10.00 25.00
JJ Joe Juneau/49 10.00 25.00
JS Jozef Stumpel/16
JT Joe Thornton/19
KB Kris Beech/100 6.00 15.00
KF Kurtis Foster/100 6.00 15.00
KT Keith Tkachuk/7
MB Matthew Barnaby/36 10.00 25.00
MH Marian Hossa/18
MM Manny Malhotra/10
MO Mattias Ohlund/10
MS Mats Sundin/13
MZ Michael Zigomanis/100 8.00 20.00
NL Nicklas Lidstrom/10
ON Owen Nolan/11
PR Patrick Roy/33 200.00 350.00
RB Rob Blake/10
RL Ross Lupaschuk/100 6.00 15.00
RM Rory McDade/100 6.00 15.00
RN Rumun Ndur/40 10.00 25.00
RS Ryan Smyth/94 12.50 30.00
SG Sergei Gonchar/55 12.50 30.00
SK Scott Kelman/100 6.00 15.00
SM Steven McCarthy/100 6.00 15.00
SY Steve Yzerman/19
TH Tomas Holmstrom/96 10.00 25.00
TP Taylor Pyatt/100 15.00 30.00
VL Vincent Lecavalier/14
WG Wayne Gretzky/99 200.00 300.00
DMA Derek Mackenzie/100 6.00 15.00
MAO Maxime Ouellet/100 10.00 25.00
MIM Mirko Murovic/100 6.00 15.00
MMC Marty McSorley/33 10.00 25.00
PBO Peter Bondra/12
PRE Peter Reynolds/100 6.00 15.00
PB Pavel Bure/10

1998-99 SP Authentic Snapshots

Randomly inserted in packs at the rate of 1:11, this 30-card set features unique images of the NHL's most exciting players. The backs carry player information.

COMPLETE SET (30) 30.00 60.00
SS1 Wayne Gretzky 4.00 10.00
SS2 Patrick Roy 3.00 8.00
SS3 Steve Yzerman 3.00 8.00
SS4 Brett Hull .75 2.00
SS5 Jaromir Jagr 1.00 2.50
SS6 Peter Forsberg 1.50 4.00
SS7 Dominik Hasek 1.25 3.00
SS8 Paul Kariya .60 1.50
SS9 Eric Lindros .60 1.50
SS10 Teemu Selanne .60 1.50
SS11 John LeClair .60 1.50
SS12 Mike Modano 1.00 2.50
SS13 Martin Brodeur 1.50 4.00
SS14 Brendan Shanahan .60 1.50
SS15 Ray Bourque 1.00 2.50
SS16 John Vanbiesbrouck .50 1.25
SS17 Brian Leetch .50 1.25
SS18 Vincent Lecavalier 4.00 10.00
SS19 Joe Sakic 1.25 3.00
SS20 Chris Drury .75 2.00
SS21 Eric Brewer 1.00 2.50
SS22 Jeremy Roenick .75 2.00
SS23 Mats Sundin .60 1.50
SS24 Zigmund Palffy .50 1.25
SS25 Keith Tkachuk .60 1.50
SS26 Sergei Samsonov .50 1.25
SS27 Curtis Joseph .60 1.50
SS28 Peter Bondra .50 1.25
SS29 Sergei Fedorov 1.00 2.50
SS30 Doug Gilmour .50 1.25

1998-99 SP Authentic Stat Masters

Randomly inserted into packs, this 30-card set features color photos of the NHL's best players printed on sequentially numbered cards based on the achievements of the player featured. Each player's card is sequentially numbered to the player's key accomplishment. These numbers follow the player's name in the checklist below.

COMPLETE SET (30) 200.00 400.00
STATED PRINT RUN 92-2000
S1 Brendan Shanahan/400 2.50 6.00
S2 Brett Hull/1000 3.00 8.00
S3 Dominik Hasek/200 10.00 25.00
S4 Doug Gilmour/1200 2.50 6.00
S5 Doug Weight/500 2.50 6.00
S6 Eric Lindros/115 8.00 20.00
S7 Jaromir Jagr/301 8.00 20.00
S8 Joe Sakic/900 3.00 8.00
S9 John LeClair/500 3.00 8.00
S10 John Vanbiesbrouck/306 2.50 6.00
S11 Keith Tkachuk/250 2.50 6.00
S12 Mark Messier/600 2.50 6.00
S13 Martin Brodeur/200 12.50 30.00
S14 Mike Modano/650 3.00 8.00
S15 Patrick Roy/400 10.00 25.00
S16 Paul Kariya/108 30.00 80.00
S17 Pavel Bure/500 2.50 6.00
S18 Peter Bondra/900 2.50 6.00
S19 Peter Forsberg/400 5.00 12.00
S20 Ray Bourque/1500 3.00 8.00
S21 Ron Francis/1500 2.50 6.00
S22 Sergei Fedorov/600 3.00 8.00
S23 Steve Yzerman/1500 5.00 12.00
S24 Steve Yzerman/900 6.00 15.00
S25 Steve Yzerman/500 10.00 25.00
S26 Teemu Selanne/300 2.50 6.00
S27 Vincent Lecavalier/1998 2.50 6.00
S28 Wayne Gretzky/92 75.00 200.00
S29 Wayne Gretzky/900 5.00 12.00
S30 Wayne Gretzky/2000 3.00 8.00

1999-00 SP Authentic

Released as a 135-card set, the 1999-00 SP Authentic base set is composed of 90-regular issue cards and 45-short printed Future Watch cards which are serial numbered out of 2000. This subset features some of the NHL's most promising prospects. Base cards have a white border and are enhanced by an embossed SP Authentic logo towards the bottom, and embossed framing along the top and bottom. The Future Watch subset contains a foil SP Authentic logo in the lower left front corner, and players are set against a green grid-line background. SP Authentic was released as 24-pack boxes containing 5-card packs that carried a suggested retail price of $4.99.

COMPLETE SET (135) 150.00 300.00
COMP.SET w/o SP's (90) 15.00 40.00
1 Paul Kariya .30 .75
2 Teemu Selanne .30 .75
3 Guy Hebert .25 .60
4 Ray Ferraro .08 .25
5 Andrew Brunette .25 .60
6 Joe Thornton .50 1.25
7 Ray Bourque .50 1.25
8 Sergei Samsonov .25 .60
9 Michael Peca .08 .25
10 Dominik Hasek .60 1.50
11 Miroslav Satan .08 .25
12 Maxim Afinogenov .08 .25
13 Valeri Bure .08 .25
14 Marc Savard .25 .60
15 Fred Brathwaite .25 .60
16 Ron Francis .25 .60
17 Arturs Irbe .25 .60
18 Sami Kapanen .08 .25
19 Tony Amonte .25 .60
20 Steve Passmore RC .40 1.00
21 Doug Gilmour .25 .60
22 Milan Hejduk .30 .75
23 Joe Sakic .60 1.50
24 Patrick Roy 1.50 4.00
25 Chris Drury .25 .60
26 Peter Forsberg .75 2.00
27 Mike Modano .50 1.25
28 Brett Hull .40 1.00
29 Ed Belfour .30 .75
30 Steve Yzerman 1.50 4.00
31 Chris Osgood .25 .60
32 Brendan Shanahan .30 .75
33 Sergei Fedorov .50 1.25
34 Doug Weight .25 .60
35 Bill Guerin .08 .25
36 Alexander Selivanov .08 .25
37 Pavel Bure .30 .75
38 Trevor Kidd .25 .60
39 Viktor Kozlov .08 .25
40 Luc Robitaille .25 .60
41 Zigmund Palffy .25 .60
42 Rob Blake .25 .60
43 Saku Koivu .30 .75
44 Mike Ribeiro .25 .60
45 Jose Theodore .40 1.00
46 David Legwand .25 .60
47 Mike Dunham .25 .60
48 Robert Valicevic RC .08 .25
49 Martin Brodeur .75 2.00
50 Claude Lemieux .08 .25
51 Scott Gomez .08 .25
52 Tim Connolly .08 .25
53 Roberto Luongo .40 1.00
54 Kenny Jonsson .08 .25
55 Mike Richter .30 .75
56 Theo Fleury .08 .25
57 Mike York .08 .25
58 Brian Leetch .30 .75
59 Radek Bonk .08 .25
60 Marian Hossa .30 .75
61 Patrick Lalime .25 .60
62 Keith Primeau .08 .25
63 Eric Lindros .30 .75
64 John LeClair .30 .75
65 Trevor Letowski .08 .25
66 Keith Tkachuk .30 .75
67 Jeremy Roenick .40 1.00
68 Jaromir Jagr .50 1.25
69 Alexei Kovalev .08 .25
70 Martin Straka .08 .25
71 Brad Stuart .08 .25
72 Steve Shields .25 .60
73 Owen Nolan .25 .60
74 Jeff Friesen .08 .25
75 Pavol Demitra .25 .60
76 Roman Turek .25 .60
77 Pierre Turgeon .25 .60
78 Vincent Lecavalier .30 .75
79 Dan Cloutier .25 .60
80 Chris Gratton .25 .60
81 Mats Sundin .30 .75
82 Bryan Berard .25 .60
83 Curtis Joseph .30 .75
84 Jonas Hoglund .08 .25
85 Mark Messier .30 .75
86 Peter Schaefer .08 .25
87 Alexander Mogilny .25 .60
88 Olaf Kolzig .25 .60
89 Adam Oates .25 .60
90 Peter Bondra .25 .60
91 Patrik Stefan RC 3.00 8.00
92 Dean Sylvester RC 2.00 5.00
93 Scott Fankhouser RC 2.00 5.00
94 Brian Campbell RC 2.00 5.00
95 Byron Ritchie RC 2.00 5.00
96 John Grahame RC 3.00 8.00
97 Andre Savage RC 2.00 5.00
98 Oleg Saprykin RC 3.00 8.00
99 Kyle Calder RC 3.00 8.00
100 Dan Hinote RC 3.00 8.00
101 Jonathan Sim RC 2.00 5.00
102 Marc Rodgers RC 2.00 5.00
103 Paul Comrie RC 2.00 5.00
104 Ivan Novoseltsev RC 2.00 5.00
105 Jason Blake RC 2.00 5.00
106 Brian Rafalski RC 3.00 8.00
107 John Madden RC 3.00 8.00
108 Jason Krog RC 3.00 8.00
109 Jorgen Jonsson RC 2.00 5.00
110 Kim Johnsson RC 2.00 5.00
111 Mike Fisher RC 3.00 8.00
112 Michal Rozsival RC 2.00 5.00
113 Mika Alatalo RC 2.00 5.00
114 Tyson Nash RC 2.00 5.00
115 Ladislav Nagy RC 6.00 15.00
116 Jochen Hecht RC 3.00 8.00
117 Adam Mair RC 2.00 5.00
118 Nikolai Antropov RC 5.00 12.00
119 Steve Kariya RC 2.00 5.00
120 Jeff Halpern RC 2.00 5.00
121 Alexandre Volchkov RC 2.00 5.00
122 Pavel Brendl RC 2.00 5.00
123 Sheldon Keefe RC 2.00 5.00
124 Branislav Mezei RC 2.00 5.00
125 Milan Kraft RC 2.00 5.00
126 Kristian Kudroc RC 2.00 5.00
127 Jaroslav Kristek RC 2.00 5.00
128 Alexander Buturlin RC 2.00 5.00
129 Andrei Shefer RC 2.00 5.00
130 Brad Moran RC 2.00 5.00
131 Ryan Jardine RC 2.00 5.00
132 Brett Lysak RC 2.00 5.00
133 Michal Sivek RC 2.00 5.00
134 Luke Sellars RC 2.00 5.00
135 Brad Ralph RC 2.00 5.00

1999-00 SP Authentic Buyback Signatures

Randomly inserted in packs at 1:287, this 66-card set features some of the NHL's most sought after autographs on Upper Deck and Upper Deck SP (Authentic) dating back to 1993-94. Each card is serial numbered out of how many were signed. Lower print runs are unpriced due to scarcity.

SERIAL #'d UNDER 25 NOT PRICED
1 P.Bure 94SP/65 30.00 80.00
2 P.Bure 94SPDC/4
3 P.Bure 94UDSPI/60 30.00 80.00
4 P.Bure 94UDSPIDC/2
5 P.Bure 94SP/1
6 P.Bure 95SP/3
7 P.Bure 95SPHol/1
8 P.Bure 96SP/10
9 P.Bure 97SPAIcon/3
10 P.Bure 98SPA/30 100.00 200.00
11 W.Gretzky 94SP/56 150.00 400.00
12 W.Gretzky 94SPDC/1
13 W.Gretzky 94UDSPI/16
14 W.Gretzky 94UDSPIDC/5
15 W.Gretzky 95SP/1
16 W.Gretzky 95SPPromo/2
17 W.Gretzky 96SP/13
18 W.Gretzky 97SPAIcon/2
19 W.Gretzky 98SPA/101 200.00 300.00
21 B.Hull 94SP/92
22 B.Hull 94UDSPI/17
23 B.Hull 94UDSPIDC/3
24 B.Hull 95SP/2
25 B.Hull 95SPStars/4
26 B.Hull 97SPA/4
27 B.Hull 97SPAIcon/1
28 B.Hull 98SPA/100 25.00 60.00
30 M.Johnson 97SPA/25 8.00 20.00
31 M.Johnson 98SPA/300 5.00 12.00
32 C.Joseph 94SP/65 15.00 40.00
33 C.Joseph 94SPDC/9
34 C.Joseph 94UDSPI/34 12.00 30.00
35 C.Joseph 94UDSPIDC/4
36 C.Joseph 96SP/29 12.00 30.00
37 C.Joseph 98SPA/200 12.00 30.00
39 J.LeClair 94SP/150 12.00 30.00
40 J.LeClair 94SPDC/10
41 J.LeClair 96SP/130 15.00 40.00
42 J.LeClair 98SPA/100 20.00 50.00
43 Z.Palffy 94UDSPI/75 20.00 50.00
44 Z.Palffy 94UDSPI/10
45 Z.Palffy 96SP/33 20.00 50.00
46 Z.Palffy 97SPA/3
47 Z.Palffy 98SPA/100 12.00 30.00
48 L.Robitaille 93SPI/16
49 L.Robitaille 94SP/20
50 L.Robitaille 94SPDC/19
51 L.Robitaille 94UDSPI/60 20.00 50.00
52 L.Robitaille 94UDSPIDC/9
53 L.Robitaille 98SPA/65 20.00 50.00
54 J.Roenick 93SPI/11
55 J.Roenick 94SP/70 25.00 60.00
56 J.Roenick 94SPDC/14
57 J.Roenick 94UDSPI/40 40.00 80.00
58 J.Roenick 94UDSPIDC/13
59 J.Roenick 95SP/3
60 J.Roenick 96SP/32 50.00 100.00
61 J.Roenick 98SPA/97 25.00 60.00
62 S.Samsonov 94SP/65 30.00 80.00
63 S.Samsonov 94SPDC/15
64 S.Samsonov 95SP/10
65 S.Samsonov 98SPA/255 8.00 20.00
66 S.Yzerman 93SPI/3
67 S.Yzerman 94SP/65 60.00 150.00
68 S.Yzerman 96SP/21
69 S.Yzerman 98SPA/77 60.00 150.00

1999-00 SP Authentic Honor Roll

Randomly seeded in packs at 1:24, this 6-card set places some of hockey's most dominating on a grey card with a centered foil background. Card backs carry an "HR" prefix.

COMPLETE SET (6) 15.00 30.00
HR1 Paul Kariya 2.50 6.00
HR2 Patrick Roy 5.00 12.00
HR3 Steve Yzerman 5.00 12.00
HR4 Martin Brodeur 2.50 6.00
HR5 Eric Lindros 1.50 4.00
HR6 Jaromir Jagr 1.50 4.00

1999-00 SP Authentic Legendary Heroes

Randomly inserted in packs at 1:72, this 5-card set pays homage to the NHL's past superstars. Card backs carry an "LH" prefix.

COMPLETE SET (5) 20.00 40.00
LH1 Wayne Gretzky 5.00 12.00
LH2 Bobby Orr 5.00 12.00
LH3 Gordie Howe 4.00 10.00
LH4 Maurice Richard 4.00 10.00
LH5 Bobby Hull 3.00 8.00

1999-00 SP Authentic Sign of the Times

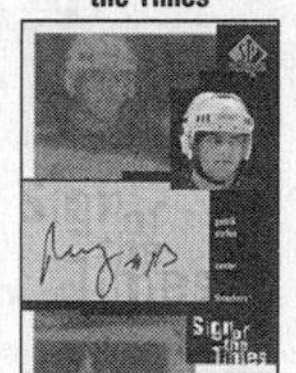

Randomly seeded in packs at 1:23, this 32-card set features autographs from past superstars, current veteran players, and top prospects. Each card is set with a white box in the middle containing the player's autograph.

AT Alex Tanguay 5.00 12.00
BC Brian Campbell 3.00 8.00
BH Bobby Hull 15.00 40.00
BM Bill Muckalt 3.00 8.00
BO Bobby Orr 100.00 200.00
BS Brad Stuart 3.00 8.00
CJ Curtis Joseph 8.00 20.00
DL David Legwand 3.00 8.00
DT Dave Tanabe 3.00 8.00
HG Gordie Howe 40.00 80.00
JH Jochen Hecht 3.00 8.00
JL John LeClair 5.00 12.00
JR Jeremy Roenick 8.00 20.00
LR Luc Robitaille 5.00 12.00
MH Marian Hossa 6.00 15.00
OS Oleg Saprykin 3.00 8.00
PB Pavel Bure 6.00 15.00
PM Paul Mara 3.00 8.00
PS Patrik Stefan 3.00 8.00
SF Sergei Fedorov 12.50 30.00
SG Simon Gagne 5.00 12.00
SS Sergei Samsonov 5.00 12.00
SY Steve Yzerman 40.00 80.00
TC Tim Connolly 3.00 8.00
TF Theo Fleury 5.00 12.00
WG Wayne Gretzky 75.00 200.00
ZP Zigmund Palffy 5.00 12.00
BHU Brett Hull 12.50 30.00
JST Jozef Stumpel 3.00 8.00
MRC Maurice Richard 150.00 300.00
MRI Mike Ribeiro 3.00 8.00
SGO Scott Gomez 3.00 8.00

1999-00 SP Authentic Sign of the Times Gold

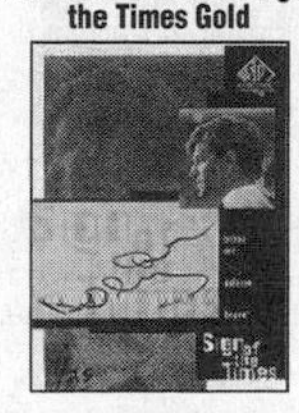

Randomly inserted in packs, this 32-card set parallels the base Sign of the Times insert set. Each card is serial numbered out of 25. Cards # CJ, PM, and WG were inserted in packs as redemption cards.

*UNLISTED GOLD: 2.5X TO 6X BASIC AU
HG Gordie Howe 250.00 500.00
WG Wayne Gretzky 300.00 600.00
MRC Maurice Richard 150.00 300.00

1999-00 SP Authentic Special Forces

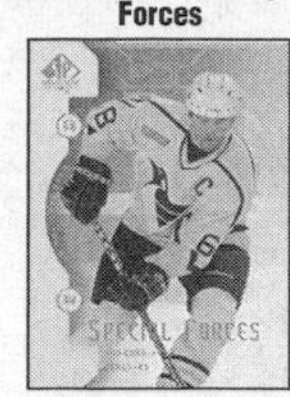

Randomly inserted in packs at 1:12, this 10-card set showcases top players set against an all foil true-life background. Card backs carry an "SF" prefix.

COMPLETE SET (10) 12.00 25.00
SF1 Paul Kariya .60 1.50
SF2 Joe Sakic 1.25 3.00
SF3 Patrick Roy 3.00 8.00
SF4 Steve Yzerman 3.00 8.00
SF5 Mike Modano 1.00 2.50
SF6 Pavel Bure .75 2.00
SF7 Jaromir Jagr 1.00 2.50
SF8 Eric Lindros 1.00 2.50
SF9 Curtis Joseph .60 1.50
SF10 Steve Kariya .60 1.50

1999-00 SP Authentic Supreme Skill

Randomly seeded in packs at 1:4, this 11-card set places NHL's most dominating against an all-foil true to life background. Card backs carry an "SS" prefix.

COMPLETE SET (11) 6.00 12.00
SS1 Paul Kariya .40 1.00
SS2 Teemu Selanne .40 1.00
SS3 Peter Forsberg 1.00 2.50
SS4 Brett Hull .50 1.25
SS5 Sergei Fedorov .75 2.00
SS6 Pavel Bure .50 1.25
SS7 Martin Brodeur 1.00 2.50
SS8 Theo Fleury .40 1.00
SS9 John LeClair .50 1.25
SS10 Keith Tkachuk .40 1.00
SS11 Jaromir Jagr .75 2.00

1999-00 SP Authentic Tomorrow's Headliners

Randomly inserted in packs at 1:10, this 10-card set features top prospects and young stars on an all-foil background. Card backs carry a "TH" prefix and contain a brief blurb about each player's standout skills.

COMPLETE SET (10) 8.00 20.00
TH1 Patrik Stefan 1.00 2.50
TH2 Joe Thornton 1.50 4.00
TH3 Maxim Afinogenov 1.00 2.50
TH4 Milan Hejduk 1.00 2.50
TH5 David Legwand 1.00 2.50
TH6 Scott Gomez 1.00 2.50
TH7 Marian Hossa 1.00 2.50
TH8 Jochen Hecht 1.00 2.50
TH9 Vincent Lecavalier 1.50 4.00
TH10 Steve Kariya 1.00 2.50

2000-01 SP Authentic

SP Authentic released these cards as a 165-card set with 75 short-printed rookies. The bas set design had white with blue and grey borders. The card fronts were highlighted with silver-foil lettering and logo. The card backs had a short summary about the player along with his statistics and a small photo. The short-printed rookies were serial numbered to 900.

COMPLETE SET w/o SP's 10.00 25.00
1 Paul Kariya .30 .75
2 Jean-Sebastien Giguere .25 .60
3 Oleg Tverdovsky .10 .25
4 Patrik Stefan .10 .25
5 Donald Audette .10 .25
6 Damian Rhodes .10 .25
7 Joe Thornton .50 1.25
8 Jason Allison .10 .25
9 Bill Guerin .25 .60
10 Dominik Hasek .60 1.50
11 Maxim Afinogenov .10 .25
12 Doug Gilmour .25 .60
13 Valeri Bure .10 .25
14 Marc Savard .10 .25
15 Jarome Iginla .40 1.00
16 Ron Francis .25 .60
17 Jeff O'Neill .10 .25
18 Sandis Ozolinsh .10 .25
19 Steve Sullivan .10 .25
20 Tony Amonte .25 .60
21 Rob Blake .25 .60
22 Ray Bourque .50 1.25
23 Patrick Roy 1.50 4.00
24 Peter Forsberg .60 1.50
25 Joe Sakic .60 1.50
26 Ron Tugnutt .25 .60
27 Geoff Sanderson .10 .25
28 Ed Belfour .30 .75
29 Mike Modano .50 1.25
30 Brett Hull .40 1.00
31 Steve Yzerman 1.50 4.00
32 Brendan Shanahan .30 .75
33 Nicklas Lidstrom .30 .75
34 Sergei Fedorov .50 1.25
35 Doug Weight .25 .60
36 Ryan Smyth .10 .25
37 Tommy Salo .25 .60
38 Pavel Bure .30 .75
39 Ray Whitney .10 .25
40 Ivan Novoseltsev .10 .25
41 Adam Deadmarsh .10 .25
42 Zigmund Palffy .25 .60
43 Luc Robitaille .25 .60
44 Darby Hendrickson .10 .25
45 Manny Fernandez .25 .60
46 Jose Theodore .40 1.00
47 Andrei Markov .10 .25
48 Trevor Linden .25 .60
49 David Legwand .25 .60
50 Mike Dunham .25 .60
51 Cliff Ronning .10 .25
52 Scott Gomez .10 .25
53 Martin Brodeur .75 2.00
54 Jason Arnott .10 .25
55 Mark Messier .30 .75
56 Theo Fleury .10 .25
57 Brian Leetch .25 .60
58 Tim Connolly .10 .25
59 Brad Isbister .10 .25
60 Taylor Pyatt .10 .25
61 Alexei Yashin .10 .25
62 Marian Hossa .30 .75
63 Patrick Lalime .25 .60
64 John LeClair .30 .75
65 Simon Gagne .30 .75
66 Mark Recchi .25 .60
67 Jeremy Roenick .40 1.00
68 Keith Tkachuk .30 .75
69 Shane Doan .10 .25
70 Jaromir Jagr .50 1.25
71 Alexei Kovalev .25 .60
72 Mario Lemieux 2.00 5.00
73 Owen Nolan .25 .60
74 Patrick Marleau .25 .60
75 Evgeni Nabokov 1.25 3.00
76 Pierre Turgeon .25 .60
77 Chris Pronger .25 .60
78 Roman Turek .25 .60
79 Brad Richards .25 .60
80 Vincent Lecavalier .30 .75
81 Fredrik Modin .10 .25
82 Mats Sundin .30 .76
83 Curtis Joseph .30 .75
84 Gary Roberts .10 .25
85 Daniel Sedin .10 .25
86 Henrik Sedin .10 .25
87 Markus Naslund .30 .75
88 Peter Bondra .30 .75
89 Olaf Kolzig .25 .60
90 Adam Oates .25 .60
91 Petr Tenkrat RC 2.00 5.00
92 Andy McDonald RC 4.00 10.00
93 Brad Tapper RC 2.00 5.00
94 Andrew Raycroft RC 8.00 20.00
95 Lee Goren RC 2.00 5.00
96 Josef Vasicek RC 2.00 5.00
97 Reto Von Arx RC 2.00 5.00
98 David Aebischer RC 8.00 20.00
99 Ville Nieminen RC 2.00 5.00
100 Serge Aubin RC 2.00 5.00
101 Rostislav Klesla RC 3.00 8.00
102 Marty Turco RC 8.00 20.00
103 Tyler Bouck RC 2.00 5.00
104 Jason Williams RC 3.00 8.00
105 Shawn Horcoff RC 4.00 10.00
106 Mike Comrie RC 8.00 20.00
107 Eric Belanger RC 2.00 5.00
108 Steven Reinprecht RC 3.00 8.00
109 Lubomir Visnovsky RC 2.00 5.00
110 Marian Gaborik RC 30.00 80.00
111 Peter Bartos RC 2.00 5.00
112 Scott Hartnell RC 5.00 12.00
113 Chris Mason RC 6.00 15.00
114 Rick DiPietro RC 10.00 25.00
115 Martin Havlat RC 10.00 25.00
116 Jani Hurme RC 2.00 5.00
117 Petr Hubacek RC 2.00 5.00
118 Justin Williams RC 6.00 15.00
119 Roman Cechmanek RC 2.00 5.00
120 Ruslan Fedotenko RC 2.00 5.00
121 Roman Simicek RC 2.00 5.00
122 Mark Smith RC 2.00 5.00
123 Alexander Kharitonov RC 2.00 5.00
124 Alexei Ponikarovsky RC 2.00 5.00
125 Matt Pettinger RC 2.00 5.00
126 Zdenek Blatny RC 2.00 5.00
127 Damian Surma RC 2.00 5.00
128 Marc-Andre Thinel RC 2.00 5.00
129 Fedor Fedorov RC 2.00 5.00
130 Jason Jaspers RC 2.00 5.00
131 Jordan Krestanovich RC 2.00 5.00
132 Jeff Bateman RC 2.00 5.00
133 Marc Chouinard RC 2.00 5.00
134 Darcy Hordichuk RC 2.00 5.00
135 Bryan Adams RC 2.00 5.00
136 Jarno Kultanen RC 2.00 5.00
137 Eric Boulton RC 2.00 5.00
138 Ronald Petrovicky RC 2.00 5.00
139 Martin Brochu RC 2.00 5.00
140 Craig Adams RC 2.00 5.00

141 Chris Nielsen RC 2.00 5.00
142 Petteri Nummelin RC 2.00 5.00
143 Brian Swanson RC 2.00 5.00
144 Michel Riesen RC 2.00 5.00
145 Lance Ward RC 2.00 5.00
146 Travis Scott RC 2.00 5.00
147 Lubomir Sekeras RC 2.00 5.00
148 Eric Landry RC 2.00 5.00
149 Greg Classen RC 2.00 5.00
150 Sascha Goc RC 2.00 5.00
151 Mike Commodore RC 2.00 5.00
152 Johan Holmqvist RC 3.00 8.00
153 Vitali Yeremeyev RC 2.00 5.00
154 Tomas Kloucek RC 2.00 5.00
155 Dale Purinton RC 2.00 5.00
156 Shane Hnidy RC 2.00 5.00
157 Todd Fedoruk RC 2.00 5.00
158 Jean-Guy Trudel RC 2.00 5.00
159 Ossi Vaananen RC 2.00 5.00
160 Greg Andrusak RC 2.00 5.00
161 Alexander Khavanov RC 2.00 5.00
162 Bryce Salvador RC 2.00 5.00
163 Reed Low RC 2.00 5.00
164 Petr Svoboda RC 2.00 5.00
165 Brent Sopel RC 2.00 5.00

2000-01 SP Authentic BuyBacks

Randomly inserted in packs of 2000-01 SP Authentic at a rate of 1:144, this 114 card set featured original SP cards that were purchased from the secondary market and autographed. Cards with lower print runs are unpriced due to scarcity.

1 B.Orr 99SPALH/49 150.00 300.00
2 S.Samsonov 94SP/3
3 S.Samsonov 95SP/2
4 S.Samsonov 97SPA/3
5 S.Samsonov 98SPA/26
6 S.Samsonov 99SPA/184 8.00 20.00
7 B.Dafoe 95SP/7
8 M.Satan 95SP/6
9 M.Satan 97SPA/3
10 M.Satan 99SPA/145 20.00 40.00
11 P.Brendl 99SPA/3
12 Bo.Hull 99SPALH/98 25.00 60.00
13 M.Hejduk 99SPA/200 10.00 25.00
14 M.Hejduk 99SPATH/143 12.50 30.00
15 R.Bourque 98SPASS/1
16 R.Bourque 98SPA/24 75.00 200.00
17 R.Bourque 99SPA/122 40.00 80.00
18 M.Modano 94SP/61 20.00 50.00
19 M.Modano 95SP/10
20 M.Modano 96SP/5
21 M.Modano 97SPA/2
22 M.Modano 97SPASM/1
23 M.Modano 98SPA/40 25.00 60.00
24 M.Modano 99SPA/168 12.50 30.00
25 M.Modano 99SPASF/155 12.50 30.00
26 N.Lidstrom 94SP/6
27 N.Lidstrom 95SP/11
28 N.Lidstrom 96SP/14
29 N.Lidstrom 97SPA/1
30 N.Lidstrom 98SPA/19
31 Br.Hull 94SPDC/1
32 Br.Hull 94SP/7
33 Br.Hull 97SPA/3
34 Br.Hull 97SPAIC/2
35 Br.Hull 98SPA/16
36 Br.Hull 99SPA/119 20.00 50.00
37 T.Salo 97SPA/12
38 P.Bure 94SP/2
39 P.Bure 96SP/16
40 P.Bure 97SPA/6
41 P.Bure 97SPAIC/2
42 P.Bure 98SPA/1
43 P.Bure 99SPA/225 10.00 25.00
44 P.Bure 99SPASF/154 15.00 40.00
45 P.Bure 99SPASS/69 20.00 50.00
46 I.Novoseltsev 99SPA/1
47 L.Robitaille 94SP/36 25.00 60.00
48 L.Robitaille 94SPPRE/8
49 L.Robitaille 95SP/1
50 L.Robitaille 97SPA/6
51 L.Robitaille 97SPAIC/6
52 L.Robitaille 99SPA/97 15.00 40.00
53 M.Ribeiro 99SPA/117 12.50 30.00
54 D.Legwand 99SPA/214 6.00 15.00
55 D.Legwand 99SPATH/130 12.50 25.00
56 S.Gomez 99SPA/243 10.00 25.00
57 S.Gomez 99SPATH/157 12.50 30.00
58 P.Elias 97SPA/1
59 P.Elias 98SPA/43 15.00 40.00
60 M.Brodeur 94SPDC/3
61 M.Brodeur 95SP/11
62 M.Brodeur 96SP/21
63 M.Brodeur 98SPA/5
64 W.Gretzky 94SP/4
65 W.Gretzky 94SPDC/1
66 W.Gretzky 96SP/2
67 W.Gretzky 98SPA/4
68 W.Gretzky 99SPALH/9
69 M.Messier 94SP/50 60.00 125.00
70 M.Messier 95SP/9
71 M.Messier 96SP/3
72 M.Messier 97SPA/10
73 M.Messier 98SPA/26 60.00 125.00
74 M.Messier 99SPA/147 40.00 100.00
75 M.Richter 94SP/5
76 M.Richter 94SPPRE/8
77 M.Richter 95SP/21
78 M.Richter 96SP/21
79 M.Richter 97SPA/8
80 M.Richter 98SPA/48 15.00 30.00
81 M.Richter 99SPA/214 8.00 20.00
82 M.York 99SPA/212 8.00 20.00
83 J.LeClair 94SP/12
84 J.LeClair 95SP/24
85 J.LeClair 96SP/14
86 J.LeClair 97SPA/10
87 J.LeClair 97SPAIC/6
88 J.LeClair 98SPA/100 8.00 20.00
89 J.LeClair 99SPA/207 8.00 20.00
90 J.LeClair 99SPASS/116 15.00 40.00
91 J.Roenick 99SPA/98 15.00 40.00
92 M.Lemieux 95SP/19
93 M.Lemieux 96SP/1
94 M.Kraft 99SPA/3
95 S.Shields 99SPA/195 6.00 15.00
96 C.Joseph 98SPA/14
97 C.Joseph 99SPA/187 20.00 40.00
98 C.Joseph 99SPASF/135 20.00 40.00
99 F.Potvin 95SP/10
100 F.Potvin 96SP/2
101 F.Potvin 97SPA/5
102 S.Yzerman 93UDSP/3
103 S.Yzerman 94SP/22
104 S.Yzerman 94SPDC/2
105 S.Yzerman 94SPPRE/34 50.00 125.00
106 S.Yzerman 94SPPREDC/4
107 S.Yzerman 95SPHOL/1
108 S.Yzerman 95SP/2
109 S.Yzerman 96SP/9
110 S.Yzerman 98SPASS/1
111 S.Yzerman 98SPA/5
112 S.Yzerman 99SPA/152 30.00 80.00
113 S.Yzerman 99SPASF/35 50.00 125.00

2000-01 SP Authentic Honor

These cards were inserted into packs of SP Authentic at a rate of 1:24. The 7-card set featured the hottest players from the NHL. The cards carried a 'SP' prefix for their numbering.

COMPLETE SET (7) 12.00 25.00
SP1 Paul Kariya .75 2.00
SP2 Patrick Roy 3.00 8.00
SP3 Pavel Bure .75 2.00
SP4 Martin Brodeur 1.50 4.00
SP5 Mark Messier .75 2.00
SP6 Mario Lemieux 4.00 10.00
SP7 Jaromir Jagr 1.00 2.50

2000-01 SP Authentic Parents' Scrapbook

These cards were inserted into packs of SP Authentic at a rate of 1:24. The 7-card set featured the hottest players from the NHL. The cards carried a 'PS' prefix for their numbering.

COMPLETE SET (7) 5.00 10.00
PS1 Paul Kariya .50 1.25
PS2 Joe Thornton .75 2.00
PS3 Mike Modano .75 2.00
PS4 Scott Gomez .50 1.25
PS5 Martin Brodeur 1.25 3.00
PS6 John LeClair .36 1.50
PS7 Vincent Lecavalier .50 1.25

2000-01 SP Authentic Power Skaters

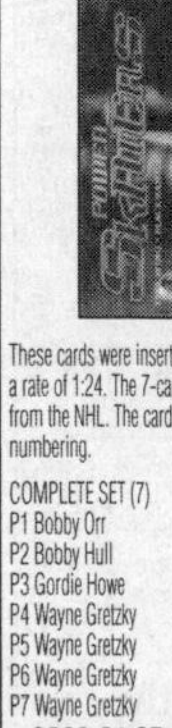

These cards were inserted into packs of SP Authentic at a rate of 1:24. The 7-card set featured Hall of Famers from the NHL. The cards carried a 'P' prefix for their numbering.

COMPLETE SET (7) 20.00 40.00
P1 Bobby Orr 3.00 8.00
P2 Bobby Hull 2.50 6.00
P3 Gordie Howe 2.50 6.00
P4 Wayne Gretzky 3.00 8.00
P5 Wayne Gretzky 3.00 8.00
P6 Wayne Gretzky 3.00 8.00
P7 Wayne Gretzky 3.00 8.00

2000-01 SP Authentic Sign of the Times

These cards were inserted into packs of SP Authentic at a rate of 1:23 for the single player autographs, 1:287 for the double autographs, and the triple autographs are serial numbered to 25.. The 68-card set featured some of the hottest players from the NHL. The cards used the player's initials for their numbering. Please note that there were 5 cards that were issued as exchange/redemption cards at time of release. Upper Deck has reported that only 19 of the Ray Bourque cards were produced.

AC Anson Carter 3.00 8.00

AE Anders Eriksson 3.00 8.00
AU Serge Aubin 3.00 8.00
BD Byron Dafoe 3.00 8.00
BH Bobby Hull 25.00 60.00
BI Martin Biron 3.00 8.00
BO Bobby Orr SP 125.00 250.00
BR Pavel Brendl 3.00 8.00
CJ Curtis Joseph 8.00 20.00
DG David Gosselin 3.00 8.00
DL David Legwand 3.00 8.00
DS Daniel Sedin 4.00 10.00
FP Felix Potvin 8.00 20.00
GH Gordie Howe 75.00 150.00
HA Martin Havlat 6.00 15.00
HS Henrik Sedin 4.00 10.00
IN Ivan Novoseltsev 3.00 8.00
JA Jean-Sebastien Aubin 3.00 8.00
JH Jani Hurme 3.00 8.00
JL John LeClair 8.00 20.00
JT Jose Theodore 10.00 25.00
LB Lubos Bartecko 10.00 25.00
LR Luc Robitaille 6.00 15.00
MB Martin Brodeur 30.00 80.00
MD Marc Denis 3.00 8.00
MG Marian Gaborik 12.00 30.00
MH Milan Hejduk SP 40.00 100.00
MK Milan Kraft 3.00 8.00
ML Mario Lemieux SP 150.00 300.00
MM Mark Messier SP 100.00 200.00
MO Mike Modano 10.00 25.00
MR Mike Richter 10.00 25.00
MS Miroslav Satan 3.00 8.00
MT Marty Turco 8.00 20.00
MY Mike York 3.00 8.00
NL Nicklas Lidstrom 8.00 20.00
PB Pavel Bure 8.00 20.00
PE Patrik Elias 3.00 8.00
PS Petr Sykora 3.00 8.00
RB Ray Bourque SP 200.00 400.00
RD Rick DiPietro 8.00 20.00
RI Michel Riesen 3.00 8.00
RK Rostislav Klesla 3.00 8.00
RO Mike Ribeiro 3.00 8.00
RT Ron Tugnutt 3.00 8.00
SA Sergei Samsonov 6.00 15.00
SG Scott Gomez 3.00 8.00
SH Scott Hartnell 3.00 8.00
SR Steven Reinprecht 3.00 8.00
SS Steve Shields 3.00 8.00
SY Steve Yzerman 50.00 125.00
TS Tommy Salo 3.00 8.00
WG Wayne Gretzky SP 250.00 500.00
B/S Martin Brodeur 40.00 80.00
Petr Sykora
B/N Pavel Bure 10.00 25.00
Ivan Novoseltsev
B/Y Pavel Brendl 8.00 20.00
Mike York
E/G Patrik Elias 10.00 25.00
Scott Gomez
H/G Gordie Howe 300.00 600.00
Wayne Gretzky
H/H Brett Hull 60.00 150.00
Bobby Hull
L/K Mario Lemieux 75.00 200.00
Milan Kraft
M/G Mark Messier 300.00 600.00
Wayne Gretzky
O/B Bobby Orr 200.00 400.00
Ray Bourque
S/S Daniel Sedin 12.00 30.00
Henrik Sedin
Y/L Steve Yzerman 100.00 200.00
Nicklas Lidstrom
BGE Martin Brodeur 100.00 200.00
Scott Gomez
Patrik Elias
GMF Wayne Gretzky 700.00 1200.00
Mark Messier
Grant Fuhr
HLY Hull/Lemieux/Yzerman 400.00 600.00
HOG Gordie Howe 1200.00 2500.00
Wayne Gretzky
Bobby Orr
LMB John LeClair 50.00 100.00
Mike Modano
Pavel Bure

2000-01 SP Authentic Significant Stars

These cards were inserted into packs of SP Authentic at a rate of 1:24. The 7-card set featured the hottest players from the NHL. The cards carried a 'ST' prefix for their numbering.

COMPLETE SET (7) 8.00 15.00
ST1 Peter Forsberg 1.25 3.00
ST2 Brett Hull .60 1.50
ST3 Steve Yzerman 2.50 6.00
ST4 Pavel Bure .60 1.50
ST5 Mark Messier .60 1.50
ST6 Jaromir Jagr .75 2.00
ST7 Mario Lemieux 3.00 8.00

2000-01 SP Authentic Special Forces

These cards were inserted into packs of SP Authentic at a rate of 1:24. The 7-card set featured the hottest players from the NHL. The cards carried a 'SF' prefix for their numbering.

COMPLETE SET (7) 4.00 8.00
SF1 Teemu Selanne .50 1.25
SF2 Mike Modano .75 2.00
SF3 Brendan Shanahan .50 1.25
SF4 Pavel Bure .50 1.25
SF5 John LeClair .50 1.25
SF6 Keith Tkachuk .50 1.25
SF7 Jaromir Jagr .75 2.00

2000-01 SP Authentic Super Stoppers

These cards were inserted into packs of SP Authentic at a rate of 1:24. The 7-card set featured the to goalies from the NHL. The cards carried a 'SS' prefix for their numbering.

COMPLETE SET (7) 4.00 8.00
SS1 Dominik Hasek 1.00 2.50
SS2 Patrick Roy 2.50 6.00
SS3 Ed Belfour .50 1.25
SS4 Martin Brodeur 1.25 3.00
SS5 Roman Turek .40 1.00
SS6 Curtis Joseph .50 1.25
SS7 Olaf Kolzig .40 1.00

2001-02 SP Authentic

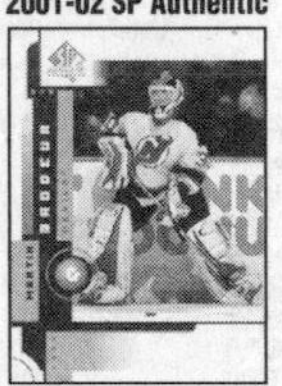

This 180-card set was released in mid-February with an SRP of $4.99 for a 5-card pack. The set consisted of 90 base cards, 50 Future Watch subset rookie cards (6 of which were autographed), 20 Future Greats subset cards and 20 All-Time Greats subset cards. Future Greats and All-Time Greats were serial-numbered out of 3500 while the Future Watch cards were serial-numbered to 900.

COMP.SET w/o SP's (90) 20.00 40.00
1 Jeff Friesen .10 .30
2 Paul Kariya .30 .75
3 Dany Heatley .40 1.00
4 Milan Hnilicka .25 .60
5 Bill Guerin .25 .60
6 Joe Thornton .50 1.25
7 Sergei Samsonov .25 .60
8 Miroslav Satan .25 .60
9 Martin Biron .25 .60
10 J-P Dumont .10 .30
11 Jarome Iginla .40 1.00
12 Roman Turek .25 .60
13 Craig Conroy .10 .30
14 Tony Amonte .25 .60
15 Steve Sullivan .10 .30
16 Joe Sakic .60 1.50
17 Milan Hejduk .30 .75
18 Patrick Roy 1.50 4.00
19 Rob Blake .25 .60
20 Chris Drury .25 .60
21 Ron Tugnutt .25 .60
22 Geoff Sanderson .10 .30
23 Mike Modano .50 1.25
24 Ed Belfour .30 .75
25 Pierre Turgeon .25 .60
26 Brett Hull .40 1.00
27 Dominik Hasek .60 1.50
28 Steve Yzerman 1.50 4.00
29 Sergei Fedorov .50 1.25
30 Luc Robitaille .25 .60
31 Brendan Shanahan .30 .75
32 Tommy Salo .25 .60
33 Ryan Smyth .10 .30
34 Mike Comrie .25 .60
35 Pavel Bure .30 .75
36 Valeri Bure .10 .30
37 Roberto Luongo .40 1.00
38 Jason Allison .10 .30
39 Zigmund Palffy .25 .60
40 Felix Potvin .30 .75
41 Manny Fernandez .25 .60
42 Marian Gaborik .60 1.50
43 Jose Theodore .40 1.00
44 Brian Savage .10 .30
45 David Legwand .25 .60
46 Mike Dunham .25 .60
47 Patrik Elias .25 .60
48 Martin Brodeur .75 2.00
49 Jason Arnott .10 .30
50 Scott Stevens .25 .60
51 Chris Osgood .25 .60
52 Alexei Yashin .10 .30
53 Mark Parrish .10 .30
54 Mark Messier .30 .75
55 Eric Lindros .30 .75
56 Petr Nedved .10 .30
57 Marian Hossa .30 .75
58 Radek Bonk .10 .30
59 Daniel Alfredsson .25 .60
60 Jeremy Roenick .40 1.00
61 John LeClair .30 .75
62 Keith Primeau .10 .30
63 Mark Recchi .25 .60
64 Roman Cechmanek .25 .60
65 Sean Burke .25 .60
66 Michal Handzus .10 .30
67 Shane Doan .10 .30
68 Mario Lemieux 2.00 5.00
69 Alexei Kovalev .25 .60
70 Johan Hedberg .25 .60
71 Teemu Selanne .30 .75
72 Owen Nolan .25 .60
73 Evgeni Nabokov .25 .60
74 Vincent Damphousse .10 .30
75 Pavol Demitra .25 .60
76 Doug Weight .25 .60
77 Keith Tkachuk .30 .75
78 Chris Pronger .25 .60
79 Brad Richards .25 .60
80 Vincent Lecavalier .30 .75
81 Nikolai Khabibulin .30 .75
82 Curtis Joseph .30 .75
83 Mats Sundin .30 .75
84 Alexander Mogilny .25 .60
85 Markus Naslund .30 .75
86 Daniel Sedin .10 .30
87 Henrik Sedin .10 .30
88 Peter Bondra .30 .75
89 Olaf Kolzig .25 .60
90 Jaromir Jagr .50 1.25
91 Paul Kariya ATG 1.25 3.00
92 Ray Bourque ATG 2.50 6.00
93 Patrick Roy ATG 5.00 12.00
94 Joe Sakic ATG 2.50 6.00
95 Mike Modano ATG 2.00 5.00
96 Ed Belfour ATG 1.25 3.00
97 Steve Yzerman ATG 5.00 12.00
98 Dominik Hasek ATG 2.50 6.00
99 Gordie Howe ATG 5.00 12.00
100 Brett Hull ATG 1.50 4.00
101 Wayne Gretzky ATG 6.00 15.00
102 Martin Brodeur ATG 3.00 8.00
103 Mark Messier ATG 1.50 4.00
104 John LeClair ATG 1.50 4.00
105 Jeremy Roenick ATG 1.50 4.00
106 Mario Lemieux ATG 5.00 12.00
107 Teemu Selanne ATG 1.25 3.00
108 Al MacInnis ATG 1.00 2.50
109 Curtis Joseph ATG 1.25 3.00
110 Jaromir Jagr ATG 2.00 5.00
111 Dany Heatley FG 2.50 6.00
112 Mike Comrie FG 1.00 2.50
113 David Legwand FG 1.00 2.50
114 Justin Williams FG .75 2.00
115 Mike Van Ryn FG .75 2.00
116 Alex Tanguay FG 3.00 8.00
117 Manny Fernandez FG 1.00 2.50
118 Martin Havlat FG 1.00 2.50
119 Kris Beech FG .75 2.00
120 Nikolai Antropov FG .75 2.00
121 Patrik Stefan FG .75 2.00
122 Steven Reinprecht FG .75 2.00
123 Marian Gaborik FG 4.00 10.00
124 Pavel Brendl FG 1.00 2.50
125 Brad Stuart FG .75 2.00
126 Martin Biron FG 1.00 2.50
127 Eric Belanger FG .75 2.00
128 Rick DiPietro FG 1.00 2.50
129 Ladislav Nagy FG .75 2.00
130 Brad Richards FG 1.00 2.50
131 Ilja Bryzgalov RC 4.00 10.00
132 Timo Parssinen RC 2.00 5.00
133 Kevin Sawyer RC 2.00 5.00
134 Brian Pothier RC 2.00 5.00
135 Kamil Piros RC 2.00 5.00
136 Ivan Huml RC .10 .30
137 Scott Nichol RC 2.00 5.00
138 Jukka Hentunen RC 2.00 5.00
139 Erik Cole RC 4.00 10.00
140 Casey Hankinson RC 2.00 5.00
141 Jaroslav Obsut RC 2.00 5.00
142 Jody Shelley RC 2.00 5.00
143 Matt Davidson RC 2.00 5.00
144 Niko Kapanen RC 2.00 5.00
145 Pavel Datsyuk RC 30.00 60.00
146 Ty Conklin RC 2.00 5.00
147 Sean Selmser RC 2.00 5.00
148 Jason Chimera RC 2.00 5.00
149 Andrej Podkonicky RC 2.00 5.00
150 Niklas Hagman RC 2.00 5.00
151 Jaroslav Bednar RC 2.00 5.00
152 Mike Matteucci RC 2.00 5.00
153 Pascal Dupuis RC 2.00 5.00
154 Francis Belanger RC 2.00 5.00
155 Martti Jarventie SP 2.00 5.00
156 Pavel Skrbek RC 2.00 5.00
157 Martin Erat RC 2.00 5.00
158 Andreas Salomonsson RC 2.00 5.00
159 Scott Clemmensen RC 2.00 5.00
160 Josef Boumedienne RC 2.00 5.00
161 Peter Smrek RC 2.00 5.00
162 Mikael Samuelsson RC 2.00 5.00
163 Radek Martinek RC 2.00 5.00
164 Joel Kwiatkowski RC 2.00 5.00
165 Ivan Ciernik RC 2.00 5.00
166 Chris Neil RC 2.00 5.00
167 Jiri Dopita RC 2.00 5.00
168 Vaclav Pletka RC 2.00 5.00
169 David Cullen RC 2.00 5.00
170 Jeff Jillson RC 2.00 5.00
171 Mark Rycroft RC 2.00 5.00
172 Nikita Alexeev RC 2.00 5.00
173 Ryan Tobler RC 2.00 5.00
174 Bob Wren RC 2.00 5.00
175 Ilya Kovalchuk AU RC 100.00 175.00
176 Vaclav Nedorost RC AU 6.00 15.00
177 Kristian Huselius AU RC 10.00 25.00
178 Dan Blackburn AU RC 6.00 15.00
179 Krys Kolanos AU RC 5.00 12.00
180 Raffi Torres 12.00 30.00
NNO Pavel Bure SAMPLE 1.00 2.50

2001-02 SP Authentic Limited

This 150-card set paralleled the base set but each cards was serial-numbered out of 150.

*LIMITED: 1.5X TO 4X BASIC CARD
*LTD SP's: .75X TO 2X BASIC CARD
*LTD ROOKIES: .3X TO .75X BASIC CARD
175 Ilya Kovalchuk AU 125.00 250.00
176 Vaclav Nedorost AU 6.00 15.00
177 Kristian Huselius AU 10.00 25.00
178 Dan Blackburn AU 8.00 20.00
179 Krys Kolanos AU 5.00 12.00
180 Raffi Torres AU 12.50 30.00

2001-02 SP Authentic Limited Gold

This 150-card set paralleled the base set but each card was serial-numbered out of 25.

*LTD.GOLD: 10X TO 25X BASIC CARD
*SP's: 6X TO 15X
*ROOKIES: .75X TO 2X
*ROOKIE AU: .5X TO 1.25X
175 Ilya Kovalchuk AU 300.00 500.00

2001-02 SP Authentic Buybacks

Randomly inserted into packs, this 41-card set featured original Upper Deck cards that were purchased from the secondary market and autographed. Print runs for each card are listed below. Cards with a stated print run of less than 20 are not priced due to scarcity.

1 A.Irbe 00SPGU/8
2 B.Orr 98UDCL/2
3 B.Orr 99UDR/4
4 C.Joseph 00BDGG/4
5 C.Joseph 99WGTOG/3
6 C.Joseph 99UDMVPSC/31 40.00 100.00
7 D.Heatley 00UD/50 200.00 400.00
8 G.Howe 00UDLGJ/9
9 D.Weight 91UD/20
10 G.Howe 98UDCL/3
11 J.LeClair 00UDGJ/5
12 J.LeClair 99UDLJ/10
13 M.Biron 00BDGG/41 25.00 60.00
14 M.Brodeur 00UDLGJ/30 60.00 150.00
15 M.Comrie 00SPA/1
16 M.Comrie 00BD/37 30.00 80.00
17 M.Gaborik 00UD/32 50.00 125.00
18 M.Havlat 00UD/37 60.00 150.00
19 M.Modano 00UDLGJ/9
20 M.Modano 90UD/75 20.00 50.00
21 M.Turco 00UD/37 30.00 80.00
22 O.Kolzig 00BDGG/20
23 P.Bondra 90UD/10
24 P.Bure 90UD/6
25 R.Blake 90UD/4
26 R.Bourque 99MVPSCGS/20
27 R.Bourque 00UDLGJ/7
28 R.DiPietro 00UD/31 25.00 60.00
29 R.Brind'Amour 90UD/95 12.50 30.00
30 R.Klesla 00UD/46 25.00 60.00
31 S.Hartnell 00UD/84 15.00 40.00
32 S.Yzerman 99UDGJ/1
33 S.Yzerman 99UDGJP/1
34 S.Yzerman 99MVPSCGS/7
35 T.Salo 00BDGG/5
36 T.Salo 00BDGG/8
37 T.Selanne 00UDGJ/8
38 T.Selanne BDGG/3
39 Teemu Selanne 99MVPSCGS/13
40 W.Gretzky 00UDGJ/3
41 W.Gretzky 98UDCL/1

2001-02 SP Authentic Jerseys

This 30-card set featured game-worn jersey swatches and were divided between two different subsets: Notable Numbers and Personal Prolifics. Each card was serial-numbered to an individual statistic for the featured player. All print runs are listed below.

*MULT.COLOR SWATCH: .75X TO 1.5X HI
NNBP Bob Probert/1034 8.00 20.00
NNBS Brendan Shanahan/955 4.00 10.00
NNCC Chris Chelios/1181 4.00 10.00
NNEL Eric Lindros/659 4.00 10.00
NNJK Jari Kurri/601 12.50 30.00
NNJL John LeClair/627 4.00 10.00
NNJS Joe Sakic/1178 12.50 30.00
NNKP Keith Primeau/496 4.00 10.00
NNMC Sandy McCarthy/1252 4.00 10.00
NNMG Mike Gartner/102 12.50 30.00
NNML Mario Lemieux/648 10.00 25.00
NNMM Mark Messier/651 4.00 10.00
NNMO Mike Modano/900 5.00 12.00
NNMR Mark Recchi/1010 4.00 10.00
NNPK Paul Kariya/531 4.00 10.00
NNRB Ray Bourque/1169 6.00 15.00
NNRT Rick Tocchet/950 4.00 10.00
NNSS Scott Stevens/1434 4.00 10.00
NNSY Steve Yzerman/1614 8.00 20.00
NNTD Tie Domi/1620 4.00 10.00
PPBH Brett Hull/86 20.00 50.00
PPJJ Jaromir Jagr/87 20.00 50.00
PPJS Joe Sakic/75 30.00 80.00
PPLR Luc Robitaille/63 15.00 40.00
PPMB Martin Brodeur/43 30.00 80.00
PPML Mario Lemieux/38 75.00 150.00
PPPR Patrick Roy/52 40.00 100.00
PPRB Ray Bourque/77 25.00 60.00
PPTS Teemu Selanne/76 20.00 50.00
PPWG Wayne Gretzky/92 60.00 150.00

2001-02 SP Authentic Sign of the Times

Randomly inserted into packs at overall odds of 1:24, this 82-card set featured autographs of one, two or three NHL players. Two player cards were serial-numbered out of 150 and triple player cards were serial-numbered to 25.

AI Arturs Irbe 6.00 15.00
AK Alexei Kovalev 4.00 10.00
AM Al MacInnis 6.00 15.00
BG Bill Guerin 4.00 10.00
BO Bobby Orr 125.00 250.00
BR Martin Brodeur 40.00 100.00
BS Brent Sopel 4.00 10.00
CJ Curtis Joseph 8.00 20.00
DH Dany Heatley 12.00 30.00
DS Daniel Sedin 6.00 15.00
DW Doug Weight 4.00 10.00
EB Ed Belfour 10.00 25.00
FP Felix Potvin 8.00 20.00
GH Gordie Howe 75.00 150.00
HA Martin Havlat 4.00 10.00
HE Johan Hedberg 4.00 10.00
HO Marian Hossa 6.00 15.00
HS Henrik Sedin 6.00 15.00
IK Ilya Kovalchuk 20.00 50.00
JA Jason Allison 4.00 10.00
JH Jochen Hecht 4.00 10.00
JI Jarome Iginla 10.00 25.00
JL John LeClair 8.00 20.00
JN Jeff O'Neill 4.00 10.00
JT Joe Thornton 12.50 30.00
KP Keith Primeau 4.00 10.00
MB Martin Biron 4.00 10.00
MC Mike Comrie 4.00 10.00
MF Manny Fernandez 6.00 15.00
MG Marian Gaborik 12.00 30.00
MH Milan Hejduk 8.00 20.00
MK Milan Kraft 4.00 10.00
MM Mike Modano 10.00 25.00
MN Markus Naslund 10.00 25.00
MR Mike Ribeiro 4.00 10.00
OK Olaf Kolzig 5.00 20.00
PB Pavel Bure 8.00 20.00
PR Patrick Roy/33 100.00 250.00
PS Patrik Stefan 4.00 10.00
RB Rod Brind'Amour 4.00 10.00
RB Rob Blake 4.00 10.00
RD Rick DiPietro 6.00 15.00
RK Rostislav Klesla 4.00 10.00
RL Roberto Luongo 20.00 50.00
SG Simon Gagne 8.00 20.00
SH Scott Hartnell 4.00 10.00
SY Steve Yzerman 30.00 80.00
TA Tony Amonte 4.00 10.00
TS Teemu Selanne 8.00 20.00
TS Tommy Salo 4.00 10.00
VL Vincent Lecavalier 8.00 20.00
WG Wayne Gretzky 125.00 250.00
ZP Zigmund Palffy 6.00 15.00
TRL Trevor Letowski 4.00 10.00
BB Martin Brodeur 40.00 100.00
Ed Belfour
BL Pavel Bure 12.50 30.00
Roberto Luongo
CH Mike Comrie 10.00 25.00
Jochen Hecht
DL Rick DiPietro 20.00 50.00
Roberto Luongo
ET Phil Esposito 30.00 80.00
Joe Thornton
FG Manny Fernandez 15.00 40.00
Marian Gaborik
GO Gordie Howe 200.00 400.00
Bobby Orr
HH Martin Havlat 12.00 30.00
Marian Hossa
HS Johan Hedberg 12.50 30.00
Tommy Salo
HT Marian Hossa 20.00 50.00
Joe Thornton
HY Gordie Howe 125.00 250.00
Steve Yzerman
IH Jarome Iginla 15.00 40.00
Milan Hejduk
LR John LeClair 10.00 25.00
Mark Recchi
PP Zigmund Palffy 12.50 30.00
Felix Potvin
SS Daniel Sedin 15.00 40.00
Henrik Sedin
TL Joe Thornton 25.00 60.00
Vincent Lecavalier
WM Doug Weight 10.00 25.00
Al MacInnis
YA S.Yzerman/J.Allison 30.00 80.00
BKK Pavel Bure 100.00 250.00

Ilya Kovalchuk
Alexei Kovalev
BOB Ray Bourque 250.00 450.00
Bobby Orr
Rob Blake
GWA Bill Guerin 40.00 100.00
Doug Weight
Tony Amonte
HBB Milan Hejduk 100.00 250.00
Ray Bourque
Rob Blake
HGY Gordie Howe 700.00 1500.00
Wayne Gretzky
Steve Yzerman
HHS Martin Havlat 40.00 100.00
Milan Hejduk
Petr Sykora
JBB Curtis Joseph 125.00 250.00
Martin Brodeur
Ed Belfour
PHG Zigmund Palffy 60.00 150.00
Marian Hossa
Marian Gaborik
SDP Tommy Salo 40.00 100.00
Rick DiPietro
Felix Potvin
SSN Daniel Sedin 40.00 100.00
Henrik Sedin
Markus Naslund

2002-03 SP Authentic

Released in late February, this 219-card set consisted of 90 veteran base cards, 15 shortprinted "Hat Trick" subset cards (serial-numbered to 1499), 30 short-printed "Future Great" subset cards (serial numbered to 2003), 60 shortprinted rookies (serial-numbered to 900) and 20 shortprinted rookie autographs (serial-numbered to 999). Cards 202-218 were available only in packs of UD Rookie Update.

COMP.SET w/o SP's (90) 15.00 40.00
1 Jean-Sebastien Giguere .25 .60
2 Paul Kariya .30 .75
3 Adam Oates .25 .60
4 Dany Heatley .40 1.00
5 Ilya Kovalchuk .40 1.00
6 Joe Thornton .50 1.25
7 Sergei Samsonov .25 .60
8 Steve Shields .25 .60
9 Martin Biron .25 .60
10 Miroslav Satan .25 .60
11 Tim Connolly .10 .30
12 Jarome Iginla .40 1.00
13 Roman Turek .25 .60
14 Arturs Irbe .25 .60
15 Rod Brind'Amour .25 .60
16 Ron Francis .25 .60
17 Alexei Zhamnov .10 .30
18 Eric Daze .25 .60
19 Jocelyn Thibault .25 .60
20 Chris Drury .25 .60
21 Joe Sakic .60 1.50
22 Patrick Roy 1.50 4.00
23 Peter Forsberg .75 2.00
24 Rob Blake .25 .60
25 Ray Whitney .10 .30
26 Marc Denis .25 .60
27 Rostislav Klesla .10 .30
28 Bill Guerin .25 .60
29 Marty Turco .25 .60
30 Mike Modano .50 1.25
31 Brendan Shanahan .30 .75
32 Brett Hull .40 1.00
33 Curtis Joseph .30 .75
34 Nicklas Lidstrom .30 .75
35 Sergei Fedorov .50 1.25
36 Steve Yzerman 1.50 4.00
37 Mike Comrie .25 .60
38 Tommy Salo .25 .60
39 Anson Carter .25 .60
40 Roberto Luongo .40 1.00
41 Olli Jokinen .25 .60
42 Felix Potvin .30 .75
43 Zigmund Palffy .25 .60
44 Jason Allison .10 .30
45 Manny Fernandez .25 .60
46 Marian Gaborik .60 1.50
47 Jose Theodore .40 1.00
48 Saku Koivu .30 .75
49 Yanic Perreault .10 .30
50 Tomas Vokoun .25 .60
51 David Legwand .25 .60
52 Scott Hartnell .10 .30
53 Martin Brodeur .75 2.00
54 Patrik Elias .25 .60
55 Jeff Friesen .10 .30
56 Alexei Yashin .10 .30
57 Chris Osgood .25 .60
58 Michael Peca .10 .30
59 Eric Lindros .30 .75
60 Bobby Holik .10 .30
61 Pavel Bure .30 .75
62 Daniel Alfredsson .25 .60
63 Marian Hossa .30 .75
64 Patrick Lalime .25 .60
65 Jeremy Roenick .30 .75
66 Roman Cechmanek .25 .60
67 Simon Gagne .30 .75
68 John LeClair .30 .75
69 Sean Burke .25 .60
70 Tony Amonte .25 .60
71 Daniel Briere .10 .30
72 Alexei Kovalev .25 .60
73 Mario Lemieux 2.00 5.00
74 Evgeni Nabokov .25 .60
75 Owen Nolan .25 .60
76 Teemu Selanne .30 .75
77 Doug Weight .25 .60
78 Pavol Demitra .10 .30
79 Keith Tkachuk .30 .75
80 Nikolai Khabibulin .30 .75
81 Vincent Lecavalier .30 .75
82 Alexander Mogilny .25 .60
83 Ed Belfour .30 .75
84 Mats Sundin .30 .75
85 Markus Naslund .30 .75
86 Ed Jovanovski .25 .60
87 Todd Bertuzzi .30 .75
88 Jaromir Jagr .50 1.25
89 Olaf Kolzig .25 .60
90 Peter Bondra .25 .60
91 Paul Kariya HT 1.25 3.00
92 Joe Thornton HT 2.00 5.00
93 Jarome Iginla HT 1.50 4.00
94 Joe Sakic HT 2.50 6.00
95 Peter Forsberg HT 3.00 8.00
96 Steve Yzerman HT 6.00 15.00
97 Brendan Shanahan HT 2.00 5.00
98 Brett Hull HT 1.50 4.00
99 Wayne Gretzky HT 6.00 15.00
100 Eric Lindros HT 2.00 5.00
101 Pavel Bure HT 1.50 4.00
102 Mario Lemieux HT 8.00 20.00
103 Keith Tkachuk HT 1.25 3.00
104 Todd Bertuzzi HT 1.00 2.50
105 Peter Bondra HT 1.00 2.50
106 Andy McDonald FG 1.50 4.00
107 Dany Heatley FG 2.50 6.00
108 Ilya Kovalchuk FG 2.00 5.00
109 Ivan Huml FG 1.50 4.00
110 Maxim Afinogenov FG 1.50 4.00
111 Jaroslav Svoboda FG 1.50 4.00
112 Kyle Calder FG 1.50 4.00
113 Radim Vrbata FG 1.50 4.00
114 Rostislav Klesla FG 1.50 4.00
115 Pavel Datsyuk FG 2.50 6.00
116 Mike Comrie FG 1.50 4.00
117 Marcus Nilsson FG 1.50 4.00
118 Kristian Huselius FG 1.50 4.00
119 Marian Gaborik FG 2.00 5.00
120 Mike Ribeiro FG 1.50 4.00
121 Scott Hartnell FG 1.50 4.00
122 Brian Gionta FG 1.50 4.00
123 Raffi Torres FG 1.50 4.00
124 Dan Blackburn FG 2.00 5.00
125 Tom Poti FG 1.50 4.00
126 Petr Schastlivy FG 1.50 4.00
127 Pavel Brendl FG 1.50 4.00
128 Brian Boucher FG 2.00 5.00
129 Ville Nieminen FG 1.50 4.00
130 Jeff Jillson FG 1.50 4.00
131 Justin Papineau FG 1.50 4.00
132 Brad Richards FG 2.00 5.00
133 Nikita Alexeev FG 1.50 4.00
134 Nikolai Antropov FG 1.50 4.00
135 Matt Pettinger FG 1.50 4.00
136 Martin Gerber RC 6.00 15.00
137 Tim Thomas RC 6.00 15.00
138 Micki Dupont RC 2.00 5.00
139 Shawn Thornton RC 2.00 5.00
140 Matt Henderson RC 2.00 5.00
141 Jeff Paul RC 2.00 5.00
142 Lasse Pirjeta RC 2.00 5.00
143 Dmitri Bykov RC 2.00 5.00
144 Alex Henry RC 2.00 5.00
145 Kari Haakana RC 2.00 5.00
146 Ivan Majesky RC 2.00 5.00
147 Sylvain Blouin RC 2.00 5.00
148 Stephane Veilleux RC 2.00 5.00
149 Greg Koehler RC 2.00 5.00
150 Ray Schultz RC 2.00 5.00
151 Tomi Pettinen RC 2.00 5.00
152 Eric Godard RC 2.00 5.00
153 Dennis Seidenberg RC 2.00 5.00
154 Radovan Somik RC 2.00 5.00
155 Patrick Sharp RC 2.00 5.00
156 Lynn Loyns RC 2.00 5.00
157 Tom Koivisto RC 2.00 5.00
158 Curtis Sanford RC 5.00 12.00
159 Cody Rudkowsky RC 2.00 5.00
160 Steve Eminger RC 2.00 5.00
161 Shaone Morrisonn RC 2.00 5.00
162 Anton Volchenkov RC 2.00 5.00
163 Carlo Colaiacovo RC 2.00 5.00
164 Rickard Wallin RC 2.00 5.00
165 Matt Walker RC 2.00 5.00
166 Ryan Miller RC 15.00 40.00
167 Levente Szuper RC 2.00 5.00
168 Tomas Malec RC 2.00 5.00
169 Jim Fahey RC 2.00 5.00
170 Jonathan Hedstrom RC 2.00 5.00
171 Michael Leighton RC 10.00 25.00
172 Dany Sabourin RC 2.00 5.00
173 Mike Cammalleri RC 8.00 20.00
174 Craig Andersson RC 15.00 40.00
175 Darren Haydar RC 3.00 8.00
176 Vernon Fiddler RC 2.00 5.00
177 Curtis Murphy RC 2.00 5.00
178 Jared Aulin RC 2.00 5.00
179 Ian MacNeil RC 2.00 5.00
180 Dick Tarnstrom RC 2.00 5.00
181 Alexei Smirnov AU RC 6.00 15.00
182 Stanislav Chistov AU RC 6.00 15.00
183 Chuck Kobasew AU RC 6.00 15.00
184 Rick Nash AU RC 50.00 100.00
185 Pascal LeClaire AU RC 15.00 40.00
186 Henrik Zetterberg AU RC 75.00 125.00
187 Jay Bouwmeester AU RC 30.00 80.00
188 Alexander Frolov AU RC 15.00 40.00
189 Ron Hainsey AU RC 6.00 15.00
190 Adam Hall AU RC 6.00 15.00
191 Jason Spezza AU RC 75.00 150.00
192 Jeff Taffe AU RC 6.00 15.00
193 Kurt Sauer AU RC 6.00 15.00
194 Alexander Svitov AU RC 6.00 15.00
195 Mikael Tellqvist AU RC 10.00 25.00
196 Jordan Leopold AU RC 6.00 15.00
197 Ales Hemsky AU RC 15.00 40.00
198 P-M Bouchard AU RC 8.00 20.00
199 Scottie Upshall AU RC 8.00 20.00
200 Brooks Orpik AU RC 6.00 15.00
201 Steve Ott AU RC 6.00 15.00
202 Igor Radulov RC 2.00 5.00
203 Alexei Semenov RC 2.00 5.00
204 Mike Komisarek RC 5.00 12.00
205 Tomas Surovy RC 2.00 5.00
206 Jason Bacashihua RC 5.00 12.00
207 Ray Emery RC 8.00 20.00
208 Fernando Pisani RC 6.00 15.00
209 Simon Gamache RC 3.00 8.00
210 Ari Ahonen RC 3.00 8.00
211 Brandon Reid RC 3.00 8.00
212 Ryan Bayda RC 2.00 5.00
213 Niko Dimitrakos RC 3.00 8.00
214 Rob Davison RC 2.00 5.00
215 Konstantin Koltsov RC 6.00 15.00
216 Jarret Stoll RC 6.00 15.00
217 Cristobal Huet RC 12.00 30.00
218 Jason King RC 3.00 5.00
219 Tomas Kurka RC 2.00 5.00

2002-03 SP Authentic Beckett Promos

Inserted into copies of the April 2003 issue of Beckett Hockey Collector, this 90-card set parallels the base SP Authentic set but carried a silver foil "UD Promo" stamp across the card fronts. Due to the type of distribution and the wide range of prices realized by these cards in the secondary market, they are not priced.

NOT PRICED DUE TO SCARCITY
1 Jean-Sebastien Giguere 2.00 5.00
2 Paul Kariya 2.50 6.00
3 Adam Oates 2.00 5.00
4 Dany Heatley 2.00 5.00
5 Ilya Kovalchuk 2.00 5.00
6 Joe Thornton 2.00 5.00
7 Sergei Samsonov 2.00 5.00
8 Steve Shields 2.00 5.00
9 Martin Biron 2.00 5.00
10 Miroslav Satan 2.00 5.00
11 Tim Connolly 2.00 5.00
12 Jarome Iginla 2.00 5.00
13 Roman Turek 2.00 5.00
14 Arturs Irbe 2.00 5.00
15 Rod Brind'Amour 2.00 5.00
16 Ron Francis 2.00 5.00
17 Alexei Zhamnov 2.00 5.00
18 Eric Daze 2.00 5.00
19 Jocelyn Thibault 2.00 5.00
20 Chris Drury 2.00 5.00
21 Joe Sakic 2.50 6.00
22 Patrick Roy 4.00 10.00
23 Peter Forsberg 2.50 6.00
24 Rob Blake 2.00 5.00
25 Ray Whitney 2.00 5.00
26 Marc Denis 2.00 5.00
27 Rostislav Klesla 2.00 5.00
28 Bill Guerin 2.00 5.00
29 Marty Turco 2.00 5.00
30 Mike Modano 2.00 5.00
31 Brendan Shanahan 2.00 5.00
32 Brett Hull 2.00 5.00
33 Curtis Joseph 2.00 5.00
34 Nicklas Lidstrom 2.00 5.00
35 Sergei Fedorov 2.00 5.00
36 Steve Yzerman 4.00 10.00
37 Mike Comrie 2.00 5.00
38 Tommy Salo 2.00 5.00
39 Anson Carter 2.00 5.00
40 Roberto Luongo 2.00 5.00
41 Olli Jokinen 2.00 5.00
42 Felix Potvin 2.00 5.00
43 Zigmund Palffy 2.00 5.00
44 Jason Allison 2.00 5.00
45 Manny Fernandez 2.00 5.00
46 Marian Gaborik 2.00 5.00
47 Jose Theodore 2.00 5.00
48 Saku Koivu 2.00 5.00
49 Yanic Perreault 2.00 5.00
50 Tomas Vokoun 2.00 5.00
51 David Legwand 2.00 5.00
52 Scott Hartnell 2.00 5.00
53 Martin Brodeur 3.00 8.00
54 Patrik Elias 2.00 5.00
55 Jeff Friesen 2.00 5.00
56 Alexei Yashin 2.00 5.00
57 Chris Osgood 2.00 5.00
58 Michael Peca 2.00 5.00
59 Eric Lindros 2.00 5.00
60 Bobby Holik 2.00 5.00
61 Pavel Bure 2.00 5.00
62 Daniel Alfredsson 2.00 5.00
63 Marian Hossa 2.00 5.00
64 Patrick Lalime 2.00 5.00
65 Jeremy Roenick 2.00 5.00
66 Roman Cechmanek 2.00 5.00
67 Simon Gagne 2.00 5.00
68 John LeClair 2.00 5.00
69 Sean Burke 2.00 5.00
70 Tony Amonte 2.00 5.00
71 Daniel Briere 2.00 5.00
72 Alex Kovalev 2.00 5.00
73 Mario Lemieux 4.00 10.00
74 Evgeni Nabokov 2.00 5.00
75 Owen Nolan 2.00 5.00
76 Teemu Selanne 2.00 5.00
77 Doug Weight 2.00 5.00
78 Pavol Demitra 2.00 5.00
79 Keith Tkachuk 2.00 5.00
80 Nikolai Khabibulin 2.00 5.00
81 Vincent Lecavalier 2.00 5.00
82 Alexander Mogilny 2.00 5.00
83 Ed Belfour 2.00 5.00
84 Mats Sundin 2.00 5.00
85 Markus Naslund 2.00 5.00
86 Ed Jovanovski 2.00 5.00
87 Todd Bertuzzi 2.00 5.00
88 Jaromir Jagr 3.00 8.00
89 Olaf Kolzig 2.00 5.00
90 Peter Bondra 2.00 5.00

2002-03 SP Authentic Legendary Cuts

This three card set featured cut autographs of some of the pioneers of the sport. Only one card was produced of Brimsek and two were produced of Abel and Adams. Please note that there is some controversy surrounding the authenticity of one of the Jack Adams cuts. These cards are not priced due to scarcity.

LCFB Frank Brimsek/1
LCJA Jack Adams/2
LCSA Sid Abel/2

2002-03 SP Authentic Sign of the Times

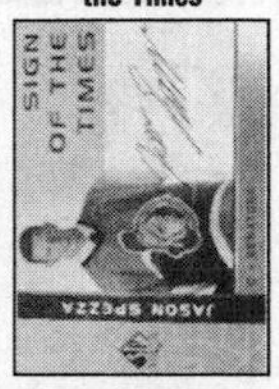

This 33-card set carried authentic player autographs of one, two or three NHL players. Single autographs were inserted at 1:96 packs, Dual autographs were serial-numbered to 99 sets and triple autographs were serial-numbered to 25 sets.

AF Alexander Frolov 10.00 25.00
BE Pavel Brendl 4.00 10.00
BO Bobby Orr SP 125.00 200.00
CJ Curtis Joseph SP 15.00 40.00
DH Dany Heatley 15.00 40.00
EC Erik Cole 4.00 10.00
EN Evgeni Nabokov SP 5.00 12.00
GH Gordie Howe 60.00 150.00
HE Ales Hemsky 8.00 20.00
HZ Henrik Zetterberg 20.00 50.00
JB Jay Bouwmeester 12.00 30.00
JI Jarome Iginla 10.00 25.00
JL John LeClair 4.00 10.00
JT Joe Thornton 12.00 30.00
JW Justin Williams 4.00 10.00
MA Maxim Afinogenov 4.00 10.00
MB Martin Brodeur SP 75.00 200.00
MC Mike Comrie 8.00 20.00
MF Manny Fernandez 4.00 10.00
MH Martin Havlat 4.00 10.00
MK Milan Kraft 4.00 10.00
MN Markus Naslund 6.00 15.00
NK Nikolai Khabibulin SP 20.00 50.00
PB Pavel Bure 6.00 15.00
PR Patrick Roy 75.00 200.00
RB Ray Bourque 20.00 50.00
RN Rick Nash SP 40.00 100.00
SG Simon Gagne 6.00 15.00
SP Jason Spezza 20.00 50.00
SS Sergei Samsonov 4.00 10.00
SY Steve Yzerman 30.00 80.00
TS Teemu Selanne 6.00 15.00
WG Wayne Gretzky 125.00 250.00
BB Bobby Orr 75.00 175.00
Jay Bouwmeester
BR Patrick Roy 75.00 200.00
Ray Bourque
CI Mike Comrie 15.00 40.00
Jarome Iginla
GB Simon Gagne 12.00 30.00
Pavel Brendl
GC Wayne Gretzky 100.00 200.00
Mike Comrie
GL Simon Gagne 20.00 50.00
John LeClair
GW Wayne Gretzky 300.00 500.00
Gordie Howe
KA Ilya Kovalchuk 15.00 40.00
Maxim Afinogenov
KH Ilya Kovalchuk 30.00 80.00
Dany Heatley
KN Evgeni Nabokov 12.00 30.00
Nikolai Khabibulin
LW John Leclair 12.00 30.00
Justin Williams
MM Martin Brodeur 30.00 80.00
Maxime Ouellet
OB Bobby Orr 175.00 350.00
Ray Bourque
SN Teemu Selanne 12.00 30.00
Evgeni Nabokov
ST Joe Thornton 12.00 30.00
Sergei Samsonov
SZ Jason Spezza 60.00 125.00
Henrik Zetterberg
YH S.Yzerman/G.Howe 150.00 300.00
YZ S.Yzerman/H.Zetterberg 75.00 200.00
GHO Wayne Gretzky 1000.00 1500.00
Gordie Howe
Bobby Orr
HCI Dany Heatley 75.00 200.00
Mike Comrie
Jarome Iginla
OBT Bobby Orr 200.00 500.00
Ray Bourque
Joe Thornton
SZB Jason Spezza 125.00 250.00
Henrik Zetterberg
Jason Bouwmeester
TSB Joe Thornton 100.00 250.00
Sergei Samsonov
Ray Bourque

2002-03 SP Authentic Signed Patches

Limited to just 100 copies each, this 15-card set featured swatches of game jersey patches and authentic polayer autographs from some of the hottest rookies of the year.

*SINGLE COLOR: .25X TO .75X HI
PAF Alexander Frolov 100.00 200.00
PAH Ales Hemsky 100.00 200.00
PAS Alexander Svitov 30.00 80.00
PCK Chuck Kobasew 50.00 100.00
PHA Adam Hall 30.00 80.00
PHZ Henrik Zetterberg 175.00 350.00
PJB Jay Bouwmeester 75.00 150.00
PJL Jordan Leopold 30.00 80.00
PJS Jason Spezza 200.00 400.00
PPB P-M Bouchard 60.00 120.00
PRH Ron Hainsey 30.00 80.00
PRN Rick Nash 175.00 350.00
PSC Stanislav Chistov 30.00 80.00
PSM Alexei Smirnov 30.00 80.00
PSU Scottie Upshall 75.00 150.00

2002-03 SP Authentic Super Premiums

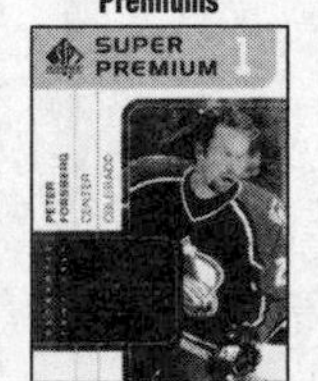

Randomly inserted, this memorabilia card set featured single, double or triple swatches of game used jerseys. Singles cards were serial-numbered to 599, doubles were numbered to 299 and triples were numbered to just 15. Triples are not priced due to scarcity.

SPAM Alexei Morozov 3.00 8.00
SPBG Bill Guerin 3.00 8.00
SPBI Martin Biron 3.00 8.00
SPBL Brian Leetch 3.00 8.00
SPBS Brendan Shanahan 5.00 12.00
SPDB Daniel Briere 3.00 8.00
SPDH Dan Hinote 3.00 8.00
SPEJ Ed Jovanovski 3.00 8.00
SPJA Jason Allison 3.00 8.00
SPJI Jarome Iginla 6.00 15.00
SPJJ Jaromir Jagr 6.00 15.00
SPJR Jeremy Roenick 6.00 15.00
SPJS Joe Sakic 8.00 20.00
SPJT Joe Thornton 6.00 15.00
SPMB Martin Brodeur 10.00 25.00
SPMD Marc Denis 3.00 8.00
SPML Mario Lemieux 10.00 25.00
SPMM Mike Modano 6.00 15.00
SPMN Markus Naslund 5.00 12.00
SPMS Mats Sundin 5.00 12.00
SPOK Olaf Kolzig 3.00 8.00
SPPF Peter Forsberg 6.00 15.00
SPPK Paul Kariya 5.00 12.00
SPPR Patrick Roy 10.00 25.00
SPSF Sergei Fedorov 6.00 15.00
SPSG Simon Gagne 5.00 12.00
SPSS Sergei Samsonov 3.00 8.00
SPSY Steve Yzerman 10.00 25.00
SPTH Jose Theodore 6.00 15.00
SPZP Zigmund Palffy 3.00 8.00
DPDS Chris Drury 6.00 15.00
Joe Sakic
DPFR Peter Forsberg 15.00 40.00
Patrick Roy
DPGL M.Lemieux/W.Gretzky 40.00 100.00
DPKJ Olaf Kolzig 8.00 20.00
Jaromir Jagr
DPMG M.Modano/B.Guerin 6.00 15.00
DPRG Jeremy Roenick 8.00 20.00
Simon Gagne
DPST Sergei Samsonov 10.00 25.00
Joe Thornton
DPTK Jose Theodore 12.50 30.00
Saku Koivu
DPYS S.Yzerman/B.Shanahan 15.00 40.00
TPGLY Lemieux/Gretzky/Yzerman
TPRBB Roy/Brodeur/Belfour
TPTBN Joe Thornton
Ray Bourque
Cam Neely

2003-04 SP Authentic

This 166-card set consisted of 90 veteran cards, 53 short-printed rookie cards (91-135 and 159-166) and 23 rookie autograph cards (136-158). Rookie cards were serial-numbered out of 900 and cards 159-166 were available in packs of UD Rookie Update.

COMPLETE SET (158)
COMP.SET w/o SP's (90) 15.00 30.00
1 Jean-Sebastien Giguere .25 .60
2 Sergei Fedorov .40 1.00
3 Stanislav Chistov .12 .30
4 Dany Heatley .40 1.00
5 Ilya Kovalchuk .40 1.00
6 Felix Potvin .30 .75
7 Joe Thornton .50 1.25
8 Sergei Samsonov .25 .60
9 Chris Drury .25 .60
10 Daniel Briere .12 .30
11 Martin Biron .25 .60
12 Jarome Iginla .40 1.00
13 Roman Turek .25 .60
14 Jamie Storr .25 .60
15 Ron Francis .25 .60
16 Alexei Zhamnov .12 .30
17 Jocelyn Thibault .25 .60
18 Tyler Arnason .25 .60
19 David Aebischer .25 .60
20 Joe Sakic .60 1.50
21 Paul Kariya .30 .75
22 Peter Forsberg .60 1.50
23 Marc Denis .25 .60
24 Rick Nash .40 1.00
25 Todd Marchant .12 .30
26 Bill Guerin .25 .60
27 Marty Turco .25 .60
28 Mike Modano .50 1.25
29 Dominik Hasek .60 1.50
30 Henrik Zetterberg .30 .75
31 Steve Yzerman 1.50 4.00
32 Ales Hemsky .25 .60
33 Raffi Torres .12 .30
34 Adam Oates .25 .60
35 Tommy Salo .25 .60
36 Jay Bouwmeester .12 .30
37 Olli Jokinen .25 .60
38 Roberto Luongo .40 1.00
39 Luc Robitaille .25 .60
40 Roman Cechmanek .25 .60
41 Zigmund Palffy .25 .60
42 Manny Fernandez .25 .60
43 Marian Gaborik .60 1.50
44 Pierre-Marc Bouchard .12 .30
45 Jose Theodore .40 1.00
46 Marcel Hossa .12 .30
47 Michael Ryder .40 1.00
48 Saku Koivu .25 .60
49 David Legwand .25 .60
50 Tomas Vokoun .25 .60
51 Martin Brodeur .75 2.00
52 Patrik Elias .25 .60
53 Scott Gomez .12 .30
54 Scott Stevens .25 .60
55 Alexei Yashin .12 .30
56 Michael Peca .12 .30
57 Rick DiPietro .25 .60
58 Eric Lindros .30 .75
59 Mark Messier .30 .75
60 Mike Dunham .25 .60
61 Jason Spezza .30 .75
62 Marian Hossa .30 .75
63 Patrick Lalime .25 .60
64 Jeff Hackett .25 .60
65 Jeremy Roenick .30 .75
66 Simon Gagne .30 .75
67 Mike Johnson .12 .30
68 Sean Burke .25 .60
69 Mario Lemieux 2.00 5.00
70 Martin Straka .12 .30
71 Evgeni Nabokov .25 .60
72 Patrick Marleau .25 .60
73 Vincent Damphousse .12 .30
74 Chris Osgood .25 .60
75 Doug Weight .25 .60
76 Keith Tkachuk .30 .75
77 Pavol Demitra .25 .60
78 Nikolai Khabibulin .30 .75
79 Vincent Lecavalier .30 .75
80 Alexander Mogilny .25 .60
81 Ed Belfour .30 .75
82 Mats Sundin .30 .75
83 Owen Nolan .25 .60
84 Ed Jovanovski .25 .60
85 Jason King .12 .30
86 Markus Naslund .30 .75
87 Todd Bertuzzi .30 .75
88 Jaromir Jagr .60 1.50
89 Olaf Kolzig .25 .60
90 Peter Bondra .25 .60
91 Andrew Hutchinson RC 2.00 5.00
92 Phil Osaer RC 2.00 5.00
93 Boyd Kane RC 2.00 5.00
94 Brent Krahn RC 4.00 10.00
95 Cody McCormick RC 2.00 5.00
96 Christoph Brandner RC 2.00 5.00
97 Dan Fritsche RC 2.00 5.00
98 David Hale RC 2.00 5.00
99 Esa Pirnes RC 2.00 5.00
100 Libor Pivko RC 2.00 5.00
101 Greg Campbell RC 2.00 5.00
102 John-Michael Liles RC 4.00 10.00
103 Mikhail Yakubov RC 2.00 5.00
104 Marek Svatos RC 10.00 25.00
105 Marek Zidlicky RC 4.00 10.00
106 Nathan Robinson RC 2.00 5.00
107 Matthew Lombardi RC 4.00 10.00
108 Matthew Spiller RC 2.00 5.00
109 Matt Murley RC 2.00 5.00
110 Maxim Kondratiev RC 2.00 5.00
111 Ryan Kesler RC 6.00 15.00
112 Paul Martin RC 2.00 5.00
113 Ryan Malone RC 8.00 20.00
114 Tim Gleason RC 2.00 5.00
115 Tom Preissing RC 2.00 5.00
116 Fredrik Sjostrom RC 2.00 5.00
117 Tony Martensson RC 2.00 5.00
118 Aaron Johnson RC 2.00 5.00
119 Seamus Kotyk RC 2.00 5.00
120 Pat Rissmiller RC 2.00 5.00
121 Jeff Hamilton RC 2.00 5.00
122 Sergei Zinovjev RC 2.00 5.00
123 Julien Vauclair RC 2.00 5.00
124 Nikolai Zherdev RC 8.00 20.00
125 Brent Burns RC 4.00 10.00
126 John Pohl RC 4.00 10.00
127 Dominic Moore RC 2.00 5.00
128 Rastislav Stana RC 2.00 5.00
129 Gavin Morgan RC 2.00 5.00
130 Darryl Bootland RC 2.00 5.00
131 Trevor Daley RC 2.00 5.00
132 Peter Sarno RC 2.00 5.00
133 Jed Ortmeyer RC 2.00 5.00
134 Nathan Smith RC 2.00 5.00
135 Grant McNeill RC 2.00 5.00
136 Joffrey Lupul AU RC 10.00 25.00
137 Eric Staal AU RC 40.00 80.00
138 Pavel Vorobiev AU RC 6.00 15.00
139 Tuomo Ruutu AU RC 10.00 25.00
140 Antoine Vermette AU RC 8.00 20.00
141 Antti Miettinen AU RC 6.00 15.00
142 Boyd Gordon AU RC 6.00 15.00
143 Nathan Horton AU RC 20.00 50.00
144 Tony Salmelainen AU RC 6.00 15.00
145 Christian Ehrhoff AU RC 6.00 15.00
146 Patrice Bergeron AU RC 25.00 60.00
147 Dan Hamhuis AU RC 6.00 15.00
148 Jordin Tootoo AU RC 12.00 30.00
149 Joni Pitkanen AU RC 8.00 20.00
150 Dustin Brown AU RC 8.00 20.00
151 Chris Higgins AU RC 15.00 40.00
152 Sean Bergenheim AU RC 6.00 15.00
153 Marc-Andre Fleury AU RC 60.00 120.00
154 Jiri Hudler AU RC 10.00 25.00
155 Milan Michalek AU RC 15.00 40.00
156 Peter Sejna AU RC 6.00 15.00
157 Matt Stajan AU RC 15.00 40.00
158 Alexander Semin AU RC 25.00 60.00
159 Niklas Kronwall RC 6.00 15.00
160 Derek Roy RC 8.00 20.00
161 Kyle Wellwood RC 8.00 20.00
162 Brad Boyes RC 6.00 15.00
163 Timofei Shishkanov RC 2.00 5.00
164 Jason Pominville RC 10.00 25.00
165 Aleksander Suglobov RC 2.00 5.00
166 Carl Corazzini RC 2.00 5.00

2003-04 SP Authentic Limited

*STARS: 4X TO 10X BASE HI
PRINT RUN 99 SER.#'d SETS
*ROOKIES: .75X TO 2X
*ROOKIE AUTOS: .6X TO 1.5X
ROOKIE PRINT RUN 50 SER.#'d SETS

2003-04 SP Authentic 10th Anniversary

COMPLETE SET (20) 10.00 20.00
PRINT RUN 1994 SER.#'d SETS
*LIMITED: 1X TO 2.5X BASIC INSERTS
LTD PRINT RUN 99 SER.#'d SETS
SP1 Wayne Gretzky 2.50 6.00
SP2 Patrick Roy 1.60 4.00
SP3 Steve Yzerman 1.50 4.00
SP4 Mario Lemieux 2.00 5.00
SP5 Teemu Selanne .50 1.25
SP6 Joe Sakic 1.00 2.50
SP7 Jaromir Jagr .75 2.00
SP8 Sergei Fedorov .60 1.50
SP9 Mike Modano .75 2.00
SP10 Brett Hull .60 1.50
SP11 Jason Spezza .50 1.25
SP12 Joe Thornton .75 2.00
SP13 Rick Nash .60 1.50
SP14 Marian Gaborik 1.00 2.50
SP15 Ales Hemsky .40 1.00
SP16 Marian Hossa .50 1.25
SP17 Jean-Sebastien Giguere .40 1.00
SP18 Martin Brodeur 1.25 3.00
SP19 Todd Bertuzzi .50 1.25
SP20 Markus Naslund .50 1.25

2003-04 SP Authentic Breakout Seasons

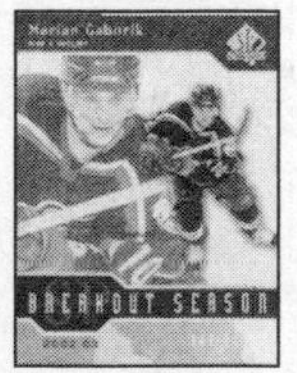

PRINT RUN 500 SER.#'d SETS
*LIMITED: .75X TO 2X BASIC INSERTS
LTD PRINT RUN 99 SER.#'d SETS
B1 Steve Yzerman 5.00 12.00
B2 Martin Brodeur 5.00 12.00
B3 Nicklas Lidstrom 1.50 4.00
B4 Joe Thornton 1.50 4.00
B5 Jeremy Roenick 1.25 3.00
B6 Todd Bertuzzi 1.00 2.50
B7 Markus Naslund 1.00 2.50
B8 Sergei Fedorov 1.25 3.00
B9 Chris Pronger .75 2.00
B10 Zigmund Palffy .75 2.00
B11 Marian Gaborik 2.50 6.00
B12 Jose Theodore 1.25 3.00
B13 Mike Modano 1.50 4.00
B14 Vincent Lecavalier 1.00 2.50
B15 Jean-Sebastien Giguere .75 2.00
B16 Keith Tkachuk 1.00 2.50
B17 Mats Sundin 1.00 2.50
B18 Paul Kariya 1.00 2.50
B19 Jarome Iginla 1.25 3.00
B20 Jaromir Jagr 1.50 4.00
B21 Dominik Hasek 2.00 5.00
B22 Teemu Selanne 1.00 2.50

B23 Jocelyn Thibault .75 2.00
B24 Alexei Yashin .75 2.00
B25 Ilya Kovalchuk 1.25 3.00
B26 Marian Hossa 1.00 2.50
B27 Ed Belfour 1.00 2.50
B28 Peter Forsberg 3.00 8.00
B29 Mario Lemieux 6.00 15.00
B30 Saku Koivu 1.00 2.50

2003-04 SP Authentic Foundations

PRINT RUN 250 SER.#'d SETS
*LIMITED: .6X TO 1.5X BASIC INSERTS
LTD PRINT RUN 99 SER.#'d SETS
F1 S.Fedorov/J.Giguere 3.00 8.00
F2 J.Thornton/S.Samsonov 2.50 6.00
F3 P.Kariya/T.Selanne 2.50 6.00
F4 P.Forsberg/J.Sakic 5.00 12.00
F5 S.Yzerman/D.Hasek 3.00 8.00
F6 T.Bertuzzi/M.Naslund 2.50 6.00
F7 M.Modano/M.Turco 2.50 6.00
F8 M.Brodeur/S.Stevens 3.00 8.00
F9 M.Sundin/E.Belfour 4.00 10.00
F10 S.Koivu/J.Theodore 2.50 6.00

2003-04 SP Authentic Honors

PRINT RUN 900 SER.#'d SETS
*LIMITED: 1X TO 2.5X BASIC INSERTS
LTD PRINT RUN 99 SER.#'d SETS
H1 Wayne Gretzky 5.00 12.00
H2 Wayne Gretzky 5.00 12.00
H3 Wayne Gretzky 5.00 12.00
H4 Gordie Howe 2.50 6.00
H5 Gordie Howe 2.50 6.00
H6 Gordie Howe 2.50 6.00
H7 Scotty Bowman 1.00 2.50
H8 Scotty Bowman 1.00 2.50
H9 Scotty Bowman 1.00 2.50
H10 Don Cherry 1.00 2.50
H11 Don Cherry 1.00 2.50
H12 Patrick Roy 4.00 10.00
H13 Patrick Roy 4.00 10.00
H14 Bobby Clarke .60 1.50
H15 Marcel Dionne .60 1.50
H16 Guy Lafleur .75 2.00
H17 Mario Lemieux 4.00 10.00
H18 Jason Spezza .75 2.00
H19 Jean-Sebastien Giguere .60 1.50
H20 Mike Modano 1.25 3.00
H21 Rick Nash 1.00 2.50
H22 Todd Bertuzzi .75 2.00
H23 Marian Gaborik 1.50 4.00
H24 Martin Brodeur 2.00 5.00
H25 Joe Thornton 1.25 3.00
H26 Ed Belfour .75 2.00
H27 Saku Koivu .75 2.00
H28 Steve Yzerman 3.00 8.00
H29 Markus Naslund .75 2.00
H30 Marian Hossa .75 2.00

2003-04 SP Authentic Sign of the Times

This 77-card set featured certified autographs. Overall odds were stated at 1:24. Single player autos were inserted at 1:26, dual player autos were serial-numbered to 99 copies and triple player autos were serial-numbered to 25.

AF Alexander Frolov 6.00 15.00
AH Adam Hall 4.00 10.00
AS Alexei Smirnov 4.00 10.00
BC Bobby Clarke SP 25.00 60.00
BO Bobby Orr 100.00 200.00
CK Chuck Kobasew 4.00 10.00
DA David Aebischer 4.00 10.00
DC Don Cherry 15.00 40.00
EL Eric Lindros SP 20.00 50.00
GL Guy Lafleur SP 20.00 50.00
HZ Henrik Zetterberg 10.00 25.00
IK Ilya Kovalchuk 10.00 25.00
JI Jarome Iginla 12.50 30.00
JK Jari Kurri 8.00 20.00
JL Jordan Leopold 4.00 10.00
JN Joe Nieuwendyk 4.00 10.00
JP Joni Pitkanen 4.00 10.00
JR Jeremy Roenick 10.00 25.00
JS Jason Spezza 12.50 30.00
JT Jose Theodore 10.00 25.00
KL Eric Staal SP 25.00 60.00
LM Lanny McDonald 10.00 25.00
MB Martin Brodeur 50.00 100.00
MC Mike Comrie 4.00 10.00
MG Marian Gaborik 10.00 25.00
MH Gordie Howe 40.00 80.00
MT Marty Turco 5.00 12.00
MT Mikael Tellqvist SP 15.00 40.00
PE Phil Esposito SP 30.00 80.00
PL Pascal Leclaire 4.00 10.00
PR Patrick Roy SP 75.00 150.00
RN Rick Nash 12.00 30.00
SB Scotty Bowman SP 25.00 60.00
SC Stanislav Chistov 4.00 10.00
SF Sergei Fedorov 10.00 25.00
SG Curtis Joseph 6.00 15.00
SH Scott Hartnell 4.00 10.00
SK Saku Koivu SP 25.00 60.00
SM Stan Mikita 15.00 40.00
SS Sergei Samsonov 4.00 10.00
TB Todd Bertuzzi 8.00 20.00
TR Tuomo Ruutu 8.00 20.00
WG Wayne Gretzky 100.00 200.00
ZP Zigmund Palffy 5.00 12.00
AHY Ales Hemsky 5.00 12.00
JLC John LeClair 4.00 10.00
JSG Jean-Sebastien Giguere 5.00 12.00
JTH Joe Thornton 12.50 30.00
MAF Marc-Andre Fleury 25.00 50.00
MHA Marian Hossa 6.00 15.00
BL P.Bure/E.Lindros 15.00 40.00
CF S.Chistov/S.Fedorov 15.00 40.00
CH M.Comrie/A.Hemsky 10.00 25.00
CR B.Clarke/J.Roenick 20.00 50.00
ET P.Esposito/J.Thornton 30.00 80.00
FG S.Fedorov/J.Giguere 20.00 50.00
FS E.Staal/M.Fleury 60.00 120.00
GK W.Gretzky/J.Kurri 125.00 250.00
GR J.Giguere/P.Roy 50.00 125.00
HS M.Hossa/J.Spezza 25.00 60.00
IM J.Iginla/L.McDonald 20.00 50.00
NB M.Naslund/T.Bertuzzi 20.00 50.00
NL R.Nash/P.Leclaire 25.00 60.00
TK J.Theodore/S.Koivu 15.00 40.00
BCY S.Bowman/D.Cherry 60.00 125.00
BTG Bossy/Trottier/Gillies 100.00 250.00
CRG Clarke/Roenick/Gagne 75.00 200.00
GCF Giggy/Chistov/Fedrv 40.00 100.00
GKF Gretzky/Kurri/Fuhr 400.00 700.00
GMM Howe/Howe/Howe 250.00 400.00
GTS Gretzky/Thornton/Spezza 250.00 500.00
LFR Staal/Fleury/Ruutu 150.00 250.00
NSZ Nash/Spezza/Zetterberg 150.00 250.00
PAF Palffy/Aulin/Frolov 40.00 100.00
RGB Roy/Giguere/Brodeur 250.00 500.00

2003-04 SP Authentic Signed Patches

This 18-card set featured autographs as well as jersey patches from some of the hottest rookies of the 2003-04 season. Each card was serial-numbered to 100.

*SINGLE COLOR: .25X TO .75X
AM Antti Miettinen 25.00 60.00
AS Alexander Semin 100.00 200.00
CH Chris Higgins 60.00 150.00
DB Dustin Brown 60.00 150.00
DH Dan Hamhuis 40.00 100.00
ES Eric Staal 125.00 250.00
JH Jiri Hudler 60.00 120.00
JL Joffrey Lupul 40.00 100.00
JP Joni Pitkanen 40.00 100.00
JT Jordin Tootoo 75.00 200.00
MF Marc-Andre Fleury 175.00 300.00
MS Matt Stajan 75.00 150.00
NH Nathan Horton 75.00 150.00
PB Patrice Bergeron 125.00 250.00
PS Peter Sejna 25.00 60.00
SB Sean Bergenheim 25.00 60.00
TR Tuomo Ruutu 60.00 120.00
TS Tony Salmelainen 25.00 60.00

2003-04 SP Authentic Special Cuts

This 5-card set featured cut signatures of legendary players. Each card was serial-numbered 1/1.

NOT PRICED DUE TO SCARCITY
AC Alex Connell
AR Art Ross
HL Harry Lumley
TB Turk Broda
PROD Lindsay/Abel/Howe

2004-05 SP Authentic

This 150-card set was released in late May 2005, it consisted of 90 veteran player cards, 6 rookie cards and 54 All-World subset cards which were inserted at one per pack.

COMPLETE SET (150) 30.00 80.00
COMP.SET w/o SP's (90) 8.00 20.00
1 Jean-Sebastien Giguere .25 .60
2 Joffrey Lupul .12 .30
3 Sergei Fedorov .40 1.00
4 Dany Heatley .40 1.00
5 Ilya Kovalchuk .40 1.00
6 Kari Lehtonen .25 .60
7 Andrew Raycroft .25 .60
8 Joe Thornton .50 1.25
9 Patrice Bergeron .25 .60
10 Glen Murray .12 .30
11 Mika Noronen .25 .60
12 Miroslav Satan .25 .60
13 Maxim Afinogenov .12 .30
14 Jarome Iginla .40 1.00
15 Matthew Lombardi .12 .30
16 Miikka Kiprusoff .25 .60
17 Eric Staal .25 .60
18 Erik Cole .12 .30
19 Tyler Arnason .25 .60
20 Tuomo Ruutu .25 .60
21 David Aebischer .25 .60
22 Joe Sakic .60 1.50
23 Peter Forsberg .60 1.50
24 Milan Hejduk .30 .75
25 Alex Tanguay .25 .60
26 Rick Nash .40 1.00
27 Nikolai Zherdev .12 .30
28 Mike Modano .50 1.25
29 Bill Guerin .25 .60
30 Marty Turco .25 .60
31 Manny Legace .25 .60
32 Pavel Datsyuk .30 .75
33 Brendan Shanahan .30 .75
34 Steve Yzerman 1.25 3.00
35 Henrik Zetterberg .30 .75
36 Jason Smith .12 .30
37 Ryan Smyth .12 .30
38 Ty Conklin .25 .60
39 Nathan Horton .12 .30
40 Roberto Luongo .40 1.00
41 Olli Jokinen .25 .60
42 Alexander Frolov .12 .30
43 Zigmund Palffy .25 .60
44 Marian Gaborik .50 1.25
45 Manny Fernandez .25 .60
46 Michael Ryder .12 .30
47 Jose Theodore .30 .75
48 Saku Koivu .30 .75
49 Steve Sullivan .30 .75
50 Jordin Tootoo .12 .30
51 Tomas Vokoun .25 .60
52 Martin Brodeur .75 2.00
53 Patrik Elias .25 .60
54 Scott Stevens .25 .60
55 Eric Lindros .30 .75
56 Mark Messier .30 .75
57 Jaromir Jagr .50 1.25
58 Michael Peca .12 .30
59 Rick DiPietro .25 .60
60 Daniel Alfredsson .25 .60
61 Marian Hossa .30 .75
62 Jason Spezza .30 .75
63 Martin Havlat .25 .60
64 Dominik Hasek .60 1.50
65 Jeremy Roenick .40 1.00
66 Robert Esche .25 .60
67 Simon Gagne .30 .75
68 Brett Hull .40 1.00
69 Mike Comrie .25 .60
70 Shane Doan .12 .30
71 Marc-Andre Fleury .25 .60
72 Mario Lemieux 2.00 5.00
73 Mark Recchi .25 .60
74 Evgeni Nabokov .25 .60
75 Patrick Marleau .25 .60
76 Chris Pronger .25 .60
77 Doug Weight .25 .60
78 Keith Tkachuk .30 .75
79 Brad Richards .25 .60
80 Nikolai Khabibulin .30 .75
81 Martin St. Louis .25 .60
82 Vincent Lecavalier .30 .75
83 Owen Nolan .25 .60
84 Ed Belfour .30 .75
85 Mats Sundin .30 .75
86 Gary Roberts .12 .30
87 Ed Jovanovski .25 .60
88 Markus Naslund .30 .75
89 Trevor Linden .12 .30
90 Olaf Kolzig .25 .60
91 Brad Fast RC 1.25 3.00
92 Brennan Evans RC 1.25 3.00
93 Layne Ulmer RC 1.25 3.00
94 Mel Angelstad RC 1.25 3.00
95 Garret Stroshein RC 1.25 3.00
96 Marcel Goc RC 1.50 4.00
97 Sergei Fedorov AW 1.00 2.50
98 Dany Heatley AW 1.00 2.50
99 Joe Thornton AW 1.25 3.00
100 Glen Murray AW .60 1.50
101 Ilya Kovalchuk AW 1.00 2.50
102 Miroslav Satan AW .60 1.50
103 Jarome Iginla AW 1.00 2.50
104 Eric Daze AW .60 1.50
105 Paul Kariya AW .75 2.00
106 Peter Forsberg AW 1.25 3.00
107 Joe Sakic AW 1.50 4.00
108 Patrick Roy AW 3.00 8.00
109 Milan Hejduk AW .75 2.00
110 Mike Modano AW 1.25 3.00
111 Bill Guerin AW .60 1.50
112 Nicklas Lidstrom AW .75 2.00
113 Steve Yzerman AW 2.50 6.00
114 Brendan Shanahan AW .75 2.00
115 Martin St. Louis AW .60 1.50
116 Roberto Luongo AW 1.00 2.50
117 Zigmund Palffy AW .60 1.50
118 Luc Robitaille AW .60 1.50
119 Marian Gaborik AW 1.25 3.00
120 Saku Koivu AW .75 2.00
121 Jose Theodore AW .75 2.00
122 Martin Brodeur AW 1.50 4.00
123 Scott Niedermayer AW .60 1.50
124 Scott Stevens AW .60 1.50
125 Patrik Elias AW .60 1.50
126 Alexei Yashin AW .60 1.50
127 Pavel Bure AW .75 2.00
128 Jaromir Jagr AW 1.25 3.00
129 Wayne Gretzky AW 4.00 10.00
130 Dominik Hasek AW 1.25 3.00
131 Marian Hossa AW .75 2.00
132 Daniel Alfredsson AW .60 1.50
133 Jeremy Roenick AW 1.00 2.50
134 Keith Primeau AW .60 1.50
135 John LeClair AW .75 2.00
136 Tony Amonte AW .60 1.50
137 Brett Hull AW 1.00 2.50
138 Mario Lemieux AW 3.00 8.00
139 Vincent Damphousse AW .60 1.50
140 Keith Tkachuk AW .75 2.00
141 Doug Weight AW .60 1.50
142 Chris Pronger AW .60 1.50
143 Vincent Lecavalier AW .75 2.00
144 Nikolai Khabibulin AW .75 2.00
145 Mats Sundin AW .75 2.00
146 Ed Belfour AW .75 2.00
147 Joe Nieuwendyk AW .60 1.50
148 Brian Leetch AW .75 2.00
149 Markus Naslund AW .75 2.00
150 Olaf Kolzig AW .60 1.50

2004-05 SP Authentic Limited

This skip-numbered parallel set featured certified autographs. Cards 1-90 were serial-numbered out of 10 and cards 97-150 were serial-numbered out of 25.

1-90 NOT PRICED DUE TO SCARCITY
1 Jean-Sebastien Giguere
2 Joffrey Lupul
4 Dany Heatley
5 Ilya Kovalchuk
6 Kari Lehtonen
7 Andrew Raycroft
8 Joe Thornton
9 Patrice Bergeron
11 Mika Noronen
13 Maxim Afinogenov
14 Jarome Iginla
15 Matthew Lombardi
17 Eric Staal
18 Erik Cole
19 Tyler Arnason
20 Tuomo Ruutu
21 David Aebischer
24 Milan Hejduk
25 Alex Tanguay
26 Rick Nash
27 Nikolai Zherdev
30 Marty Turco
31 Manny Legace
35 Henrik Zetterberg
37 Ryan Smyth
39 Nathan Horton
40 Roberto Luongo
42 Alexander Frolov
43 Zigmund Palffy
44 Marian Gaborik
46 Michael Ryder
47 Jose Theodore
49 Steve Sullivan
52 Martin Brodeur
58 Michael Peca
60 Daniel Alfredsson
61 Marian Hossa
62 Jason Spezza
63 Martin Havlat
64 Dominik Hasek
65 Jeremy Roenick
66 Robert Esche
67 Simon Gagne
70 Shane Doan
71 Marc-Andre Fleury
74 Evgeni Nabokov
76 Chris Pronger
77 Doug Weight
79 Brad Richards
80 Nikolai Khabibulin
81 Martin St. Louis
82 Vincent Lecavalier
84 Ed Belfour
87 Ed Jovanovski
88 Markus Naslund
98 Dany Heatley AW 20.00 50.00
99 Joe Thornton AW 30.00 80.00
101 Ilya Kovalchuk AW 25.00 60.00
103 Jarome Iginla AW 30.00 80.00
109 Milan Hejduk AW 20.00 50.00
115 Martin St. Louis AW 20.00 50.00
116 Roberto Luongo AW 30.00 80.00
117 Zigmund Palffy AW 20.00 50.00
118 Luc Robitaille AW 20.00 50.00
119 Marian Gaborik AW 30.00 80.00
120 Saku Koivu AW 25.00 60.00
121 Jose Theodore AW 30.00 80.00
129 Wayne Gretzky AW 200.00 400.00
130 Dominik Hasek AW 60.00 150.00
131 Marian Hossa AW 20.00 50.00
132 Daniel Alfredsson AW
133 Jeremy Roenick AW 25.00 60.00
134 Keith Primeau AW 20.00 50.00
141 Doug Weight AW 20.00 50.00
142 Chris Pronger AW 20.00 50.00
144 Nikolai Khabibulin AW 20.00 50.00
146 Ed Belfour AW 25.00 60.00
148 Brian Leetch AW 20.00 50.00
149 Markus Naslund AW 20.00 50.00

2004-05 SP Authentic Buybacks

This 201-card set followed the historical notion of "Buybacks" as being previously issued cards that were bought back by Upper Deck, autographed by the player and then serial-numbered for inclusion into SP Authentic. For 2004-05 SP Authentic, Upper Deck also bought back rookie cards and previously signed cards for inclusion in packs. Since those cards were not altered from their previous form, they are not listed seperately.

PRINT RUNS UNDER 25 NOT PRICED DUE TO SCARCITY
1 Ales Hemsky
03UD Ice/2
2 Ales Hemsky
03UD Rookie Update/32
3 Ales Hemsky
03SPx/1
4 Alex Tanguay
01UD Classic Portraits Starring Cast/2
5 Alex Tanguay
02SP Game Used Authentic Fabrics/4
6 Alex Tanguay
02SP Game Used Authentic Fabrics/7
7 Alex Tanguay
02SP Game Used First Rounders/4
8 Alex Tanguay
02SP Game Used Future Fabrics/8
9 Alex Tanguay
03Black Diamond Threads/10
10 Alexander Frolov
03Black Diamond Threads/12
11 Alexander Frolov
03SPx/1
12 Andrew Raycroft
03UD Ice/2
13 Andrew Raycroft 12.50 30.00
03UD Rookie Update/51
14 Bobby Clarke
99UD Century Legends Jerseys of the Century/3
15 Bobby Hull 25.00 60.00
04UD Legendary Signatures/38
16 Brian Leetch
02SP Authentic Super Premium/11
17 Brian Leetch
02SP Game Used Authentic Fabrics/6
18 Brian Leetch
02SP Game Used First Rounders/2
19 Brian Leetch
02UD Specialists/8
20 Brian Leetch
03UD Ice Icons/1
21 Chris Drury
01UD Classic Portraits Classic Stitches/16
22 Chris Drury
02SP Game Used Authentic Fabrics/11
23 Chris Drury
02SP Game Used Piece of History/7
24 Chris Drury
02SP Game Used Piece of History/4
25 Chris Drury
03UD Ice/2
26 Chris Drury
03UD Rookie Update/23
27 Daniel Briere
02SP Authentic Super Premium/16
28 Daniel Briere
02SP Game Used First Rounders/1
29 Daniel Briere
02SP Game Used Future Fabrics/10
30 Daniel Briere
02UD CHL Graduates/11
31 Daniel Briere
02UD Hot Spot/8
32 Daniel Briere
02UD Speed Demon/18
33 Daniel Briere
03Black Diamond Threads/12
34 Daniel Briere
03UD Ice/5
35 Daniel Briere 15.00 40.00
03UD Rookie Update/48
36 Dany Heatley
03UD Rookie Update/15
37 David Aebischer
02SP Game Used Future Fabrics/9
38 David Aebischer
03Beehive Red Sticks/5
39 David Aebischer
03Black Diamond Threads/9
40 David Aebischer
03UD Ice/5
41 David Aebischer 12.50 30.00
03UD Rookie Update/52
42 David Aebischer
03SP Game Used Authentic Fabrics/16
43 Dominik Hasek
01SP Game Used Authentic Fabrics/1
44 Doug Weight
03Beehive Game Jerseys/23
45 Doug Weight
03Black Diamond Threads/12
46 Doug Weight
03UD Ice/1
47 Doug Weight
03UD Rookie Update/39
48 Ed Belfour
01SP Game Used Authentic Fabrics/1
49 Ed Belfour
03UD Rookie Update/6
50 Ed Jovanovski
02SP Authentic Super Premium/21
51 Ed Jovanovski
02UD All Stars/7
52 Ed Jovanovski
03Beehive Beige Sticks/8
53 Ed Jovanovski
03Black Diamond Threads/10
54 Ed Jovanovski
03UD Ice/5
55 Ed Jovanovski 10.00 25.00
03UD Rookie Update/55
56 Evgeni Nabokov
03UD Ice/1
57 Evgeni Nabokov
03SPx/1
58 Gerry Cheevers 20.00 50.00
04UD Legendary Signatures/45
59 Gilbert Perreault
04UD Legendary Signatures/22
60 Glenn Hall
04UD Legendary Signatures/19
61 Gordie Howe
01SP Authentic All Stars/7
62 Grant Fuhr
04UD Legendary Signatures/16
63 Henrik Zetterberg
03UD Ice/1
64 Henrik Zetterberg 15.00 40.00
03UD Rookie Update/40
65 Henrik Zetterberg
03SP Game Used Jsy/18
66 Henrik Zetterberg
03SPx/1
67 Ilya Kovalchuk
02SP Game Used Authentic Fabrics/5
68 Ilya Kovalchuk
02SP Game Used First Rounders/2
69 Ilya Kovalchuk
03UD Rookie Update/17
70 Jari Kurri
01SP Authentic Notable Numbers/7
71 Jarome Iginla
02SP Authentic Super Premium/8
72 Jarome Iginla
03UD Rookie Update/12
73 Jason Spezza
03Black Diamond Threads/7
74 Jason Spezza
03UD Ice/2
75 Jason Spezza
03UD Rookie Update/39
76 Jason Spezza
03SPx/1
77 Jason Spezza
03UD Highlight Heroes/1
78 Jay Bouwmeester
03Black Diamond Threads/7
79 Jay Bouwmeester
03UD Ice/4
80 Jay Bouwmeester 10.00 25.00
03UD Rookie Update/48
81 Jay Bouwmeester
03SPx/1
82 Jean Beliveau
03UD Trilogy/12
83 Jean Beliveau
03UD Trilogy Crest Variations/1
84 Jean Beliveau 20.00 50.00
04UD Legendary Signatures/49
85 Jean-Sebastien Giguere
02SP Game Used Authentic Fabrics/14
86 Jean-Sebastien Giguere
02SP Game Used Authentic Fabrics/3
87 Jean-Sebastien Giguere
02SP Game Used Future Fabrics/8
88 Jean-Sebastien Giguere
03Beehive Blue Sticks/2
89 Jean-Sebastien Giguere
03UD Ice/2
90 Jean-Sebastien Giguere
03UD Rookie Update/19
91 Jeremy Roenick
02SP Game Used First Rounders/4
92 Jeremy Roenick
02SP Game Used Tools of the Game/7
93 Jeremy Roenick
03UD Rookie Update/20
94 Joe Thornton
01UD Classic Portraits Classic Stitches/13
95 Joe Thornton
02SP Authentic Super Premium/15
96 Joe Thornton
02SP Game Used Authentic Fabrics/6
97 Joe Thornton
03UD Rookie Update/19
98 Johnny Bucyk
03UD Trilogy/14
99 Johnny Bucyk
03UD Trilogy Crest Variations/1
100 Jose Theodore 30.00 80.00
03UD Rookie Update/29
101 Keith Primeau
01SP Authentic Notable Numbers/7
102 Ladislav Nagy
03UD Ice/3
103 Lanny McDonald
03UD Trilogy/14
104 Lanny McDonald 15.00 40.00
04UD Legendary Signatures/48
105 Luc Robitaille
03Beehive Beige Sticks/3
106 Marcel Dionne
03Beehive Beige Sticks/3
107 Marcel Dionne
03Beehive Red Sticks/8
108 Marcel Dionne
03UD Trilogy Crest Variations/1
109 Marcel Dionne
03UD Trilogy/13
110 Marcel Hossa
03SPx Prospects/1
111 Marcel Hossa
03UD Classic Portraits Hockey Headliners/16
112 Marian Hossa
03Black Diamond Threads/11
113 Marian Hossa
03UD Ice/2
114 Marian Hossa
03UD Rookie Update/18
115 Markus Naslund
03UD Rookie Update/19
116 Markus Naslund
01UD Classic Portraits Starring Cast/8
117 Markus Naslund
01SP Game Used Authentic Fabrics/2
118 Markus Naslund
02SP Authentic Super Premium/15
119 Markus Naslund
02SP Game Used Authentic Fabrics/5
120 Markus Naslund
02SP Game Used Authentic Fabrics/5
121 Markus Naslund
02SP Game Used First Rounders/1
122 Markus Naslund
02UD All Stars/9
123 Markus Naslund
03Beehive Game Jerseys/9
124 Markus Naslund
03Black Diamond Threads/11
125 Markus Naslund
03UD Ice/4
126 Markus Naslund
03SPx/1
127 Martin Biron
01SP Authentic All Stars/2
128 Martin Biron
02SP Game Used Authentic Fabrics/6
129 Martin Biron
02SP Game Used First Rounders/4
130 Martin Biron
02SP Game Used Piece of History/3
131 Martin Biron
02UD Saviours/12
132 Martin Biron
03SP Game Used Authentic Fabrics/19
133 M.Brodeur 03Rookie Upd/3
134 Martin St. Louis
03SP Game Used Authentic Fabrics/17
135 Marty Turco
02SP Game Used Future Fabrics/5
136 Marty Turco
03Beehive Game Jerseys/12
137 Marty Turco
03Black Diamond Threads/11
138 Marty Turco
03UD Ice/3
139 Marty Turco 15.00 40.00
03UD Rookie Update/35
140 Marty Turco
03SP Game Used Authentic Fabrics/12
141 Maxim Afinogenov
01SP Game Used Authentic Fabrics Gold/1
142 Maxim Afinogenov
02SP Game Used Future Fabrics/6
143 Maxim Afinogenov
03Black Diamond Threads/11
144 Maxim Afinogenov
03UD Classic Portraits Classic Stitches/16
145 Michael Peca
03SPx/1
146 Mika Noronen
02SP Game Used First Rounders/4
147 Mika Noronen 10.00 25.00
03UD Rookie Update/35
148 Mika Noronen
01SP Game Used Authentic Fabrics/2
149 Mika Noronen
03Beehive Beige Sticks/15
150 Mika Noronen
03UD Ice/2
151 Mike Bossy
03SPx/1
152 Mike Bossy
99UD Century Legends Jerseys of the Century/4
153 Mike Bossy 12.50 30.00
04UD Legendary Signatures/47
154 Mike Ribeiro
02SP Game Used Future Fabrics/10
155 Mike Ribeiro
03UD Ice/2
156 Mike Ribeiro 10.00 25.00
03UD Rookie Update/53
157 Milan Hejduk
02SP Game Used Authentic Fabrics/7
158 Milan Hejduk
03Beehive Beige Sticks/2
159 Milan Hejduk
03SP Game Used Authentic Fabrics/17
160 Nikolai Khabibulin
03UD Ice/1
161 Nikolai Khabibulin 25.00 60.00
03UD Rookie Update/26
162 Phil Esposito
04UD Legendary Signatures/17
163 Ray Bourque
99UD Century Legends Jerseys of the Century/5
164 Reggie Leach
04UD Legendary Signatures/24
165 Rene Robert
04UD Legendary Signatures/24
166 R.Nash 03Beehive Jsy/11
167 R.Nash 03Blk Diam Threads/10
168 R.Nash 03Ice/2
169 R.Nash 03Rookie Upd/41 25.00 60.00
170 R.Nash 03UD Highlight Heroes/1
171 Roberto Luongo
03Black Diamond Threads/11
172 Roberto Luongo
03UD Ice/2
173 Roberto Luongo 15.00 40.00
03UD Rookie Update/45
174 Ryan Smyth
03Beehive Game Jerseys/20
175 Saku Koivu
03UD Rookie Update/11
176 Scotty Bowman
03UD Trilogy/4
177 Shane Doan
02SP Game Used Authentic Fabrics/6
178 Shane Doan
02SP Game Used Authentic Fabrics Gold/4
179 Shane Doan
02SP Game Used First Rounders/2
180 Shane Doan
02UD Hot Spots/8
181 Simon Gagne
01Honor Roll Grade A Jerseys/2
182 Simon Gagne
02SP Authentic Super Premium/13
183 Simon Gagne
02SP Game Used First Rounders/4
184 Simon Gagne
02SP Game Used Future Fabrics/7
185 Stan Mikita
03UD Trilogy/14
186 Stan Mikita
03UD Trilogy Crest Variations/1
187 Stan Mikita 10.00 25.00
04UD Legendary Signatures/30
188 Stanislav Chistov
03SPx/1
189 Stephen Weiss
03SPx/1
190 Steve Sullivan
02SP Game Used Authentic Fabrics/15
191 Steve Sullivan

02UD CHL Graduates/6
192 Steve Sullivan
02UD Speed Demon/20
193 Steve Sullivan 10.00 25.00
03UD Rookie Update/26
194 Tony Esposito
04UD Legendary Signatures/18
195 Trent Hunter
03UD Ice/4
196 Trent Hunter
03UD Rookie Update/7
197 Vincent Lecavalier
03UD Ice/1
198 Zigmund Palffy
01SP Game Used Authentic FabricsGold/1
199 Zigmund Palffy
02SP Authentic Super Premium/17
200 Zigmund Palffy 10.00 25.00
03UD Rookie Update/32

2004-05 SP Authentic Octographs

A first in the hockey market, this insert set featured certified autographs of eight different players. Four autographs were placed on the card fronts and four on the backs. This set was serial-numbered out of 5 and not priced due to scarcity.

PRINT RUN 5 SER.#'d SETS
NOT PRICED DUE TO SCARCITY
OSGOA
Roy/Hall/T.Espo/Cheevers/Brodeur/Theodore/Luongo/Lehtonen
OSROK Fleury/Staal/Horton/Zherdev/Nash/Lehtonen/J-Bo/Pitkanen
OSCAP Wayne Gretzky/Bryan Trottier/Bobby Clarke/Phil Esposito/Jarome Iginla/Joe Thornton/Markus Naslund/Saku Koivu
OSART Wayne Gretzky/Gordie Howe/Guy Lafleur/Jarome Iginla/Stan Mikita/Marcel Dionne/Bryan Trottier/Martin St. Louis
OSCUP Jarome Iginla/Matthew Lombardi/Robyn Regehr/Chuck Kobasew/Brad Richards/Martin St. Louis/Vincent Lecavalier/Nikolai Khabibulin

2004-05 SP Authentic Rookie Redemptions

This 51-card set was issued in packs as redemption cards redeemable for rookies who first skated in the 2005-06 season. Cards RR1-RR30 are team specific and cards RR31-RR51 were "Wild" cards. Print run was limited to 399 copies each. Please note that due to a printing error, cards 41 and 42 have a "PP" prefix.

RR1 Corey Perry 12.00 30.00
RR2 Braydon Coburn 4.00 10.00
RR3 Hannu Toivonen 5.00 12.00
RR4 Thomas Vanek 12.00 30.00
RR5 Dion Phaneuf 20.00 60.00
RR6 Cam Ward 10.00 25.00
RR7 Brent Seabrook 8.00 20.00
RR8 Wojtek Wolski 10.00 25.00
RR9 Gilbert Brule 10.00 25.00
RR10 Jussi Jokinen 6.00 15.00
RR11 Jim Howard 8.00 20.00
RR12 Brad Winchester 4.00 10.00
RR13 Rostislav Olesz 4.00 10.00
RR14 George Parros 4.00 10.00
RR15 Matt Foy 4.00 10.00
RR16 Alexander Perezhogin 4.00 10.00
RR17 Ryan Suter 4.00 10.00
RR18 Zach Parise 10.00 25.00
RR19 Robert Nilsson 4.00 10.00
RR20 Henrik Lundqvist 25.00 60.00
RR21 Andrej Meszaros 4.00 10.00
RR22 Jeff Carter 8.00 20.00
RR23 David Leneveu 4.00 10.00
RR24 Sidney Crosby 175.00 350.00
RR25 Ryane Clowe 4.00 10.00
RR26 Jeff Woywitka 4.00 10.00
RR27 Evgeny Artyukhin 4.00 10.00
RR28 Alexander Steen 6.00 15.00
RR29 Rob McVicar 4.00 10.00
RR30 Alexander Ovechkin 125.00 200.00
RR31 Peter Budaj 5.00 12.00
RR32 Rene Bourque 4.00 10.00
RR33 Duncan Keith 8.00 20.00
RR34 Lee Stempniak 5.00 12.00
RR35 Andrew Alberts 4.00 10.00
RR36 Milan Jurcina 4.00 10.00
RR37 Yann Danis 4.00 10.00
RR38 Keith Ballard 4.00 10.00
RR39 Eric Nystrom 4.00 10.00
RR40 Mike Richards 10.00 25.00
PP41 Kevin Nastiuk 4.00 10.00
PP42 Petteri Nokelainen 4.00 10.00
RR43 Chris Campoli 4.00 10.00
RR44 Andrew Wozniewski 4.00 10.00
RR45 Ryan Getzlaf 20.00 30.00
RR46 Maxime Talbot 4.00 10.00
RR47 Petr Prucha 5.00 12.00
RR48 Johan Franzen 10.00 25.00
RR49 Brandon Bochenski 4.00 10.00
RR50 Patrick Eaves 5.00 12.00
RR51 Jim Slater 4.00 10.00

2004-05 SP Authentic Rookie Review

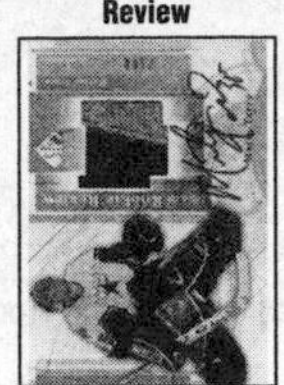

This 42-card set featured certified player autographs along with jersey patch swatches. Each card was serial-numbered out of 100.

PRINT RUN 100 SER.#'d SETS
RRJB Jay Bouwmeester 20.00 50.00
RRWG Wayne Gretzky/12
RRDA Daniel Briere 25.00 60.00
RREJ Ed Jovanovski 15.00 40.00
RRZC Zdeno Chara 20.00 50.00
RRRS Ryan Smyth 15.00 40.00
RRMH Marcel Hossa 15.00 40.00
RRNS Nathan Smith 15.00 40.00
RRJT Joe Thornton 50.00 125.00
RRMT Marty Turco 20.00 50.00
RRRN Rick Nash 40.00 100.00
RRPB Patrice Bergeron/90 30.00 80.00
RRCD Chris Drury 20.00 50.00
RRDB Dustin Brown 15.00 40.00
RRRL Roberto Luongo 30.00 80.00
RRDL David Legwand 15.00 40.00
RRMN Markus Naslund 25.00 60.00
RRPS Philippe Sauve 15.00 40.00
RRMG Marian Gaborik 50.00 125.00
RRJR Jeremy Roenick 20.00 50.00
RRHV Martin Havlat 25.00 60.00
RRMA Maxim Afinogenov 15.00 40.00
RRMR Michael Ryder 30.00 80.00
RRMP Mark Parrish 20.00 50.00
RRKL Kari Lehtonen 40.00 80.00
RRSG Simon Gagne 15.00 40.00
RRIK Ilya Kovalchuk 75.00 150.00
RRAB David Aebischer 20.00 50.00
RRSW Stephen Weiss 15.00 40.00
RRJL Joffrey Lupul 20.00 50.00
RRRE Robert Esche 15.00 40.00
RRHZ Henrik Zetterberg 50.00 100.00
RRAF Alexander Frolov 25.00 60.00
RRSP Jason Spezza 40.00 80.00
RRJG Jarome Iginla 50.00 125.00
RRKP Keith Primeau 15.00 40.00
RRHE Milan Hejduk 50.00 100.00
RRDW Doug Weight 15.00 40.00
RRSC Stanislav Chistov 15.00 40.00
RRBR Martin Brodeur 125.00 200.00
RRJK Jari Kurri 60.00 120.00

2004-05 SP Authentic Sign of the Times

For 2004-05, the Sign of the Times set featured autograph cards carrying 1, 2, 3, 4, 5 and 6 player autographs. Single autographs were inserted at 1:20. Dual-player autos were serial-numbered to 100 (unless otherwise noted below). Triple-player autos were serial-numbered out of 25. Quad-player autos were serial-numbered out of 20. Five player-autos were serial numbered out of 15 and six player autos were serial numbered to just 10 copies each. Please note that card #SS-AWS contained two autographs of each of the three players depicted and was a 1/1.

UNDER 25 NOT PRICED DUE TO SCARCITY
STAB David Aebischer 6.00 15.00
STAF Maxim Afinogenov 15.00 40.00
STAH Ales Hemsky 6.00 15.00
STAR Andrew Raycroft 8.00 20.00
STAT Alex Tanguay 6.00 15.00
STBA Milan Bartovic 4.00 10.00
STBB Brad Boyes 6.00 15.00
STBI Martin Biron 6.00 15.00
STBL Brian Leetch SP 30.00 80.00
STBM Brenden Morrow 6.00 15.00
STBO Scotty Bowman SP 30.00 80.00
STBR Brad Richards 8.00 20.00
STCD Chris Drury 4.00 10.00
STCH Chris Higgins 8.00 20.00
STCP Chris Pronger 6.00 15.00
STDB Daniel Briere 6.00 15.00
STDC Don Cherry 15.00 40.00
STDH Dany Heatley SP 15.00 40.00
STDL David Legwand 4.00 10.00
STDR Dwayne Roloson 6.00 15.00
STDU Dustin Brown 4.00 10.00
STDW Doug Weight SP 10.00 25.00
STEC Erik Cole 4.00 10.00
STEJ Ed Jovanovski 4.00 10.00
STES Eric Staal 12.00 30.00
STFL Marc-Andre Fleury 12.00 30.00
STFM Frank Mahovlich SP 30.00 80.00
STFR Alexander Frolov 4.00 10.00
STFS Fredrik Sjostrom 4.00 10.00
STGA Marian Gaborik 12.00 30.00
STGE Georges Laraque 4.00 10.00
STGH Gordie Howe 40.00 80.00
STGI Gilbert Perreault SP 30.00 80.00
STGL Guy Lafleur SP 75.00 150.00
STHA Dominik Hasek SP 20.00 50.00
STHO Nathan Horton 4.00 10.00
STHZ Henrik Zetterberg 10.00 25.00
STIK Ilya Kovalchuk 15.00 40.00
STJB Jay Bouwmeester 4.00 10.00
STJG Jean-Sebastien Giguere 6.00 15.00
STJI Jarome Iginla 15.00 40.00
STJL Joffrey Lupul 6.00 15.00
STJO Jose Theodore SP 20.00 50.00
STJR Jeremy Roenick 10.00 25.00
STJT Joe Thornton 12.50 30.00
STKL Kari Lehtonen 10.00 25.00
STKU Jari Kurri 10.00 25.00
STLE Manny Legace 4.00 10.00
STLM Lanny McDonald 8.00 20.00
STLN Ladislav Nagy 4.00 10.00
STLO Matthew Lombardi 4.00 10.00
STMA Marcel Hossa 4.00 10.00
STMB Martin Brodeur SP 75.00 200.00
STMH Milan Hejduk 8.00 20.00
STMJ Matt Stajan 6.00 15.00
STML John-Michael Liles 4.00 10.00
STMN Markus Naslund 8.00 20.00
STMO Brendan Morrison 4.00 10.00
STMP Michael Peca 4.00 10.00
STMT Marty Turco 6.00 15.00
STNK Nikolai Khabibulin 10.00 25.00
STNS Nathan Smith 4.00 10.00
STNZ Nikolai Zherdev 6.00 15.00
STPA Mark Parrish 4.00 10.00
STPB Patrice Bergeron 8.00 20.00
STPR Patrick Roy SP 200.00 400.00
STPS Philippe Sauve 4.00 10.00
STPW Peter Worrell 4.00 10.00
STRE Robert Esche 4.00 10.00
STRL Roberto Luongo 12.50 30.00
STRN Rick Nash 15.00 40.00
STRR Robyn Regehr 4.00 10.00
STRS Ryan Smyth 6.00 15.00
STRY Michael Ryder 6.00 15.00
STSC Stanislav Chistov 6.00 15.00
STSD Shane Doan 4.00 10.00
STSG Simon Gagne 8.00 20.00
STSK Saku Koivu 10.00 25.00
STSP Jason Spezza SP 30.00 80.00
STST Martin St. Louis 8.00 20.00
STSU Steve Sullivan 4.00 10.00
STSW Stephen Weiss 4.00 10.00
STTA Tyler Arnason 4.00 10.00
STTH Trent Hunter 4.00 10.00
STTU Tuomo Ruutu 6.00 15.00
STVL Vincent Lecavalier SP 250.00 400.00
STWG Wayne Gretzky SP 200.00 400.00
STZC Zdeno Chara 6.00 15.00
DSPR Perreault/Robert/25 25.00 60.00
DSAH D.Alfredsson/M.Hossa 15.00 40.00
DSBC Bowman/Cherry/25 75.00 150.00
DSBD M.Biron/C.Drury 10.00 25.00
DSBR Brodeur/Roy/25 300.00 450.00
DSBT Bossy/Trottier/25 50.00 125.00
DSCR R.Esche/J.Roenick 12.50 30.00
DSDS S.Doan/F.Sjostrom 10.00 25.00
DSEE T.Espo/P.Espo/25 75.00 125.00
DSFH G.Fuhr/G.Hall/25 50.00 100.00
DSHG Howe/Gretzky/25 400.00 650.00
DSHH M.Hossa/M.Hossa 15.00 40.00
DSHS D.Hasek/J.Spezza 30.00 60.00
DSIR J.Iginla/R.Regehr 20.00 50.00
DSKL N.Khabibulin/R.Luongo 25.00 60.00
DSKN I.Kovalchuk/K.Lehtonen 40.00 80.00
DSLB B.Leetch/E.Belfour 25.00 60.00
DSLK M.St.Louis/I.Kovalchuk 40.00 80.00
DSLL St. Louis/Lecavalier/25 60.00 120.00
DSLW G.Laraque/P.Worrell 15.00 40.00
DSMJ M.Ryder/J.Theodore 15.00 40.00
DSMT B.Morrow/M.Turco 15.00 40.00
DSMZ M.Naslund/H.Zetterberg 15.00 40.00
DSNH C.Neely/G.Howe/25 50.00 125.00
DSNJ M.Naslund/E.Jovanovski 15.00 40.00
DSNK E.Nabokov/N.Khabibulin 15.00 40.00
DSNZ R.Nash/N.Zherdev 30.00 80.00
DSPH M.Peca/T.Hunter 10.00 25.00
DSPM P.Bergeron/M.Ryder 12.00 30.00
DSPW C.Pronger/D.Weight 12.50 30.00
DSRA R.Smyth/A.Hemsky 15.00 40.00
DSRL A.Raycroft/K.Lehtonen 15.00 40.00
DSRP R.Bourque/C.Neely 40.00 100.00
DSRR M.Ryder/M.Ribeiro 12.00 30.00
DSRT A.Raycroft/J.Thornton 20.00 50.00
DSSH J.Spezza/M.Havlat 15.00 40.00
DSST E.Staal/J.Thornton 25.00 60.00
DSTN J.Thornton/C.Neely 30.00 80.00
DSWL S.Weiss/R.Luongo 15.00 40.00
TSBNT Bourque/Neely/Thornton 75.00 150.00
TSBTG Bossy/Trottier/Gillies 50.00 125.00
TSCLR Clarke/Leach/Roenick 75.00 150.00
TSGKF Gretzky/Kurri/Fuhr 400.00 700.00
TSGRE Gagne/Roenick/Esche 50.00 125.00
TSHLK Heatly/Lehtnen/Kovlchk 100.00 200.00
TSHTA Hejduk/Tanguay/Aebischer 40.00 80.00
TSIKN Iginla/Kovalchuk/Nash 100.00 250.00
TSILN Iginla/St. Louis/Nash 75.00 200.00
TSKLL Khabiblin/Luongo/Lehtnen 50.00 125.00
TSLPJ Leetch/Pronger/Jovo 40.00 80.00
TSLRZ Lupul/Ruutu/Zherdev 25.00 60.00
TSLWH Luongo/Weiss/Horton 60.00 150.00
TSNSS Nash/Spezza/Staal 150.00 300.00
TSPBF Palffy/Brown/Frolov 30.00 80.00
TSRBT Raycroft/Belfour/Turco 75.00 200.00
TSRKR Ribeiro/Koivu/Ryder 50.00 100.00
TSRLB Roy/Luongo/Brodeur 250.00 500.00
TSSHZ Staal/Horton/Zherdev 60.00 150.00
TSTRB Thornton/Raycrft/Bergern 60.00 125.00
QSHRBG Bo.Hull/Robitaille/Bucyk/Gillies
QSBBLK Patrice Bergeron/Dustin Brown/Joffrey Lupul/Ryan Kesler
QSBDPB Jean Beliveau/Marcel Dionne/Gilbert Perreault/Mike Bossy
QSBPBP Ray Bourque/Chris Pronger/Jay Bouwmeester/Joni Pitkanen
QSBTCR Johnny Bucyk/Joe Thornton/Gerry Cheevers/Andrew Raycroft
QSFBRE Grant Fuhr/Martin Brodeur/Patrick Roy/Tony Esposito
QSFSHZ Marc-Andre Fleury/Eric Staal/Nathan Horton/Nikolai Zherdev
QSGPRE Simon Gagne/Keith Primeau/Jeremy Roenick/Robert Esche
QSGTDC Wayne Gretzky/Joe Thornton/Marcel Dionne/Bobby Clarke
QSHINS Hejduk/Iginla/Nash/St. Louis
QSIKHL Jarome Iginla/Chuck Kobasew/Milan Hejduk/Jon-Michael Liles
QSLKSN Martin St. Louis/Ilya Kovalchuk/Marian Hossa/Markus Naslund
QSLRLK Martin St. Louis/Brad Richards/Vincent Lecavalier/Nikolai Khabibulin
QSMHCL Stan Mikita/Bobby Hull/Bobby Clarke/Reggie Leach
QSNHKS Nash/Heatley/Kovalchuk/Bergeron
QSTAHS Alex Tanguay/David Aebischer/Milan Hejduk/Philippe Sauve
QSTPLS Thornton/Primeau/Lecavalier/Eric Staal
QSVANC Markus Naslund/Brendan Morrison/Ed Jovanovski/Ryan Kesler
FSBOS Johnny Bucyk/Cam Neely/Ray Bourque/Joe Thornton/Andrew Raycroft
FSCTR Phil Esposito/Marcel Dionne/Gilbert Perreault/Johnny Bucyk/Brian Trottier
FSGOL Marc-Andre Fleury/Kari Lehtonen/Martin Brodeur/David Aebischer/Jose Theodore
FSMON Marcel Hossa/Guy Lafleur/Jose Theodore/Michael Ryder/Jean Beliveau
FSNED Brad Boyes/Michael Ryder/Jason Spezza/Chris Drury/Matt Stajan
FSPAC Alexander Frolov/Dustin Brown/Shane Doan/Joffrey Lupul/Brendan Morrow
FSRGT Markus Naslund/Simon Gagne/Dany Heatley/Milan Hejduk/Daniel Alfredsson
FSSEN Marian Hossa/Daniel Alfredsson/Jason Spezza/Martin Havlat/Dominik Hasek
FSSES Ilya Kovalchuk/Dany Heatley/Kari Lehtonen/Roberto Luongo/Stephen Weiss
FSVAN Markus Naslund/Ryan Kesler/Ed Jovanovski/Brendan Morrison/Nathan Smith
SSAWS Wayne Gretzky/Jari Kurri/Luc Robitaille/Wayne Gretzky/Jari Kurri/Luc Robitaille/1
SSALS Gordie Howe/Guy Lafleur/Joe Thornton/Patrick Roy/Grant Fuhr/Martin Brodeur
SSCAN Jacques Plante
Jean Sebastien Giguere
Leland Irving
SSCNP Smyth/Spezza/Ribeiro/Iginla/Brodeur/Jovanovski
SSDEE Ray Bourque/Chris Pronger/Jay Bouwmeester/Brian Leetch/Joni Pitkanen/Ed Jovanovski
SSFIN Kari Lehtonen/Joni Pitkanen/Jari Kurri/Mika Noronen/Tuomo Ruutu/Saku Koivu
SSORG Gordie Howe/Wayne Gretzky/Frank Mahovlich/Guy Lafleur/Phil Esposito/Bobby Hull
SSRLW Gordie Howe/Mike Bossy/Jari Kurri/Bobby Hull/Luc Robitaille/Johnny Bucyk
SSUSA Jeremy Roenick/Brian Leetch/Robert Esche/Chris Drury/Doug Weight/David Legwand

2004-05 SP Authentic UD Promos

1 Jean-Sebastien Giguere
2 Joffrey Lupul
3 Sergei Fedorov
4 Dany Heatley
5 Ilya Kovalchuk
6 Kari Lehtonen
7 Andrew Raycroft
8 Joe Thornton
9 Patrice Bergeron
10 Glen Murray
11 Mika Noronen
12 Miroslav Satan
13 Maxim Afinogenov
14 Jarome Iginla
15 Matthew Lombardi
16 Miikka Kiprusoff
17 Eric Staal
18 Erik Cole
19 Tyler Arnason
20 Tuomo Ruutu
21 David Aebischer
22 Joe Sakic
23 Peter Forsberg
24 Milan Hejduk
25 Alex Tanguay
26 Rick Nash
27 Nikolai Zherdev
28 Mike Modano
29 Bill Guerin
30 Marty Turco
31 Manny Legace
32 Pavel Datsyuk
33 Brendan Shanahan
34 Steve Yzerman
35 Henrik Zetterberg
36 Jason Smith
37 Ryan Smyth
38 Ty Conklin
39 Nathan Horton
40 Roberto Luongo
41 Olli Jokinen
42 Alexander Frolov
43 Zigmund Palffy
44 Marian Gaborik
45 Manny Fernandez
46 Michael Ryder
47 Jose Theodore
48 Saku Koivu
49 Steve Sullivan
50 Jordin Tootoo
51 Tomas Vokoun
52 Martin Brodeur
53 Patrik Elias
54 Scott Stevens
55 Eric Lindros
56 Mark Messier
57 Jaromir Jagr
58 Michael Peca
59 Rick DiPietro
60 Daniel Alfredsson
61 Marian Hossa
62 Jason Spezza
63 Martin Havlat
64 Dominik Hasek
65 Jeremy Roenick
66 Robert Esche
67 Simon Gagne
68 Brett Hull
69 Mike Comrie
70 Shane Doan
71 Marc-Andre Fleury
72 Mario Lemieux
73 Mark Recchi
74 Evgeni Nabokov
75 Patrick Marleau
76 Chris Pronger
77 Doug Weight
78 Keith Tkachuk
79 Brad Richards
80 Nikolai Khabibulin
81 Martin St. Louis
82 Vincent Lecavalier
83 Owen Nolan
84 Ed Belfour
85 Mats Sundin
86 Gary Roberts
87 Ed Jovanovski
88 Markus Naslund
89 Trevor Linden
90 Olaf Kolzig

2005-06 SP Authentic

COMP.SET w/o SP's (100) 12.50 30.00
101-130 PRINT RUN 999 SER. #'d SETS
131-220 PRINT RUN 999 SER. #'d SETS
221-287 PRINT RUN 1,999 SER. #'d SETS
288-290 ONLY IN ROOKIE UPD. PACKS
1 Jean-Sebastien Giguere .40 1.00
2 Joffrey Lupul .30 .75
3 Teemu Selanne .50 1.25
4 Scott Niedermayer .30 .75
5 Ilya Kovalchuk .60 1.50
6 Kari Lehtonen .50 1.25
7 Marian Hossa .40 1.00
8 Sergei Samsonov .40 1.00
9 Brian Leetch .50 1.25
10 Andrew Raycroft .40 1.00
11 Patrice Bergeron .50 1.25
12 Glen Murray .30 .75
13 Chris Drury .40 1.00
14 Martin Biron .40 1.00
15 Daniel Briere .40 1.00
16 Jarome Iginla .60 1.50
17 Miikka Kiprusoff .50 1.25
18 Doug Weight .40 1.00
19 Martin Gerber .40 1.00
20 Eric Staal .40 1.00
21 Nikolai Khabibulin .50 1.25
22 Tuomo Ruutu .30 .75
23 Eric Daze .40 1.00
24 Joe Sakic 1.00 2.50
25 Alex Tanguay .40 1.00
26 Milan Hejduk .50 1.25
27 David Aebischer .40 1.00
28 Rob Blake .40 1.00
29 Rick Nash .60 1.50
30 Sergei Fedorov .50 1.25
31 Mike Modano .50 1.25
32 Marty Turco .40 1.00
33 Bill Guerin .30 .75
34 Brendan Shanahan .50 1.25
35 Steve Yzerman 1.25 3.00
36 Henrik Zetterberg .50 1.25
37 Pavel Datsyuk .50 1.25
38 Gordie Howe 1.50 4.00
39 Chris Pronger .40 1.00
40 Michael Peca .30 .75
41 Ryan Smyth .40 1.00
42 Wayne Gretzky 2.00 5.00
43 Roberto Luongo .75 2.00
44 Olli Jokinen .40 1.00
45 Luc Robitaille .40 1.00
46 Jeremy Roenick .50 1.25
47 Alexander Frolov .40 1.00
48 Pavol Demitra .40 1.00
49 Marian Gaborik .60 1.50
50 Dwayne Roloson .40 1.00
51 Jose Theodore .50 1.25
52 Saku Koivu .50 1.25
53 Mike Ribeiro .30 .75
54 Michael Ryder .40 1.00
55 Paul Kariya .50 1.25
56 Tomas Vokoun .40 1.00
57 Martin Brodeur 1.25 3.00
58 Patrik Elias .40 1.00
59 Scott Gomez .40 1.00
60 Brian Gionta .15 .40
61 Miroslav Satan .30 .75
62 Alexei Yashin .30 .75
63 Rick DiPietro .40 1.00
64 Mark Parrish .30 .75
65 Jaromir Jagr .75 2.00
66 Martin Straka .15 .40
67 Dominik Hasek .60 1.50
68 Dany Heatley .50 1.25
69 Wade Redden .30 .75
70 Martin Havlat .40 1.00
71 Daniel Alfredsson .40 1.00
72 Jason Spezza .50 1.25
73 Peter Forsberg .75 2.00
74 Keith Primeau .30 .75
75 Simon Gagne .50 1.25
76 Robert Esche .40 1.00
77 Shane Doan .30 .75
78 Curtis Joseph .50 1.25
79 Mario Lemieux 2.00 5.00
80 Zigmund Palffy .10 1.00
81 Mark Recchi .40 1.00
82 Jonathan Cheechoo .50 1.25
83 Evgeni Nabokov .40 1.00
84 Patrick Marleau .40 1.00
85 Joe Thornton .75 2.00
86 Barret Jackman .30 .75
87 Keith Tkachuk .50 1.25
88 Martin St. Louis .40 1.00
89 Vincent Lecavalier .50 1.25
90 Brad Richards .40 1.00
91 Sean Burke .40 1.00
92 Eric Lindros .50 1.25
93 Mats Sundin .50 1.25
94 Ed Belfour .50 1.25
95 Matt Stajan .30 .75
96 Jason Allison .30 .75
97 Todd Bertuzzi .60 1.50
98 Markus Naslund .50 1.25
99 Brendan Morrison .30 .75
100 Olaf Kolzig .40 1.00
101 Mario Lemieux/999 5.00 12.00
102 Joe Sakic/999 8.00 20.00
103 Jaromir Jagr/999 6.00 15.00
104 Mike Modano/999 3.00 8.00
105 Dominik Hasek/999 4.00 10.00
106 Ilya Kovalchuk/999 5.00 12.00
107 Steve Yzerman/999 5.00 12.00
108 Nikolai Khabibulin/999 4.00 10.00
109 Joe Thornton/999 6.00 15.00
110 Jarome Iginla/999 3.00 8.00
111 Martin St. Louis/999 3.00 8.00
112 Paul Kariya/999 4.00 10.00
113 Martin Brodeur/999 4.00 10.00
114 Mats Sundin/999 4.00 10.00
115 Peter Forsberg/999 5.00 12.00
116 Jean-Sebastien Giguere/999 3.00 8.00
117 Marian Hossa/999 3.00 8.00
118 Alex Tanguay/999 3.00 8.00
119 Rick Nash/999 4.00 10.00
120 Jeremy Roenick/999 4.00 10.00
121 Dany Heatley/999 4.00 10.00
122 Brendan Shanahan/999 4.00 10.00
123 Jose Theodore/999 3.00 8.00
124 Patrik Elias/999 3.00 8.00
125 Curtis Joseph/999 4.00 10.00
126 Evgeni Nabokov/999 3.00 8.00
127 Vincent Lecavalier/999 4.00 10.00
128 Markus Naslund/999 4.00 10.00
129 Olaf Kolzig/999 3.00 8.00
130 Doug Weight/999 3.00 8.00
131 Ryan Getzlaf AU RC/999 30.00 60.00
132 Corey Perry AU RC/999 12.00 30.00
133 Braydon Coburn AU RC/999 5.00 12.00
134 Jim Slater AU RC/999 4.00 10.00
135 Hannu Toivonen AU RC/999 6.00 15.00
136 Andrew Alberts AU RC/999 4.00 10.00
137 Milan Jurcina AU RC/999 4.00 10.00
138 Kevin Dallman AU RC/999 4.00 10.00
139 Thomas Vanek AU RC/999 25.00 60.00
140 Dion Phaneuf AU RC/999 40.00 80.00
141 Eric Nystrom AU RC/999 5.00 12.00
142 Cam Ward AU RC/999 15.00 40.00
143 Kevin Nastiuk AU RC/999 4.00 10.00
144 Niklas Nordgren AU RC/999 4.00 10.00
145 Brent Seabrook AU RC/999 10.00 25.00
146 Cam Barker AU RC/999 8.00 20.00
147 Duncan Keith AU RC/999 12.00 30.00
148 Rene Bourque AU RC/999 4.00 10.00
149 Wojtek Wolski AU RC/999 15.00 40.00
150 Peter Budaj AU RC/999 8.00 20.00
151 Gilbert Brule AU RC/999 10.00 25.00
152 Jaroslav Balastik AU RC/999 4.00 10.00
153 Jussi Jokinen AU RC/999 8.00 20.00
154 Johan Franzen AU RC/999 20.00 50.00
155 Jim Howard AU RC/999 15.00 40.00
156 Brett Lebda AU RC/999 5.00 12.00
157 Brad Winchester AU RC/999 4.00 10.00
158 Rostislav Olesz AU RC/999 6.00 15.00
159 Anthony Stewart AU RC/999 4.00 10.00
160 George Parros AU RC/999 4.00 10.00
161 Matt Foy AU RC/999 4.00 10.00
162 Derek Boogaard AU RC/999 4.00 10.00
163 Alexander Perezhogin AU RC/999 6.00 15.00
164 Yann Danis AU RC/999 5.00 12.00
165 Raitis Ivanans AU RC/999 4.00 10.00
166 Ryan Suter AU RC/999 6.00 15.00
167 Zach Parise AU RC/999 40.00 80.00
168 Robert Nilsson AU RC/999 5.00 12.00
169 Petteri Nokelainen AU RC/999 4.00 10.00
170 Al Montoya AU RC/999 10.00 25.00
171 Henrik Lundqvist AU RC/999 40.00 80.00
172 Petr Prucha AU RC/999 10.00 25.00
173 Ryan Hollweg AU RC/999 5.00 12.00
174 Patrick Eaves AU RC/999 8.00 20.00
175 Brandon Bochenski AU RC/999 5.00 12.00
176 Andrej Meszaros AU RC/999 8.00 20.00
177 Jeff Carter AU RC/999 25.00 60.00
178 Mike Richards AU RC/999 30.00 80.00
179 David Leneveu AU RC/999 5.00 12.00
180 Keith Ballard AU RC/999 4.00 10.00
181 Sidney Crosby AU RC/999 450.00 700.00
182 Maxime Talbot AU RC/999 10.00 25.00
183 Josh Gorges AU RC/999 4.00 10.00
184 Ryane Clowe AU RC/999 5.00 12.00
185 Jay McClement AU RC/999 4.00 10.00
186 Jeff Hoggan AU RC/999 4.00 10.00
187 Jeff Woywitka AU RC/999 4.00 10.00
188 Alexander Steen AU RC/999 10.00 25.00
189 Andy Wozniewski AU RC/999 4.00 10.00
190 Alexander Ovechkin AU RC/999 350.00 600.00
191 Ryan Whitney AU RC/999 8.00 20.00
192 R.J. Umberger AU RC/999 10.00 25.00
193 Mikko Koivu AU RC/999 8.00 20.00
194 Steve Bernier AU RC/999 8.00 20.00
195 Timo Helbling AU RC/999 4.00 10.00
196 Ryan Craig AU RC/999 4.00 10.00
197 Valtteri Filppula AU RC/999 10.00 25.00
198 Daniel Paille AU RC/999 5.00 12.00
199 Danny Richmond AU RC/999 4.00 10.00
200 Maxim Lapierre AU RC/999 8.00 20.00
201 Barry Tallackson AU RC/999 5.00 12.00
202 Chris Campoli AU RC/999 4.00 10.00
203 Jeremy Colliton AU RC/999 4.00 10.00
204 Christoph Schubert AU RC 4.00 10.00
205 Kevin Bieksa AU RC/999 6.00 15.00
206 Jordan Sigalet AU RC/999 6.00 15.00
207 Adam Berkhoel AU RC/999 4.00 10.00
208 Erik Christensen AU RC/999 8.00 20.00
209 Ole-Kristian Tollefsen AU RC/999 4.00 10.00
210 Dimitri Patzold AU RC/999 4.00 10.00
211 Brad Richardson AU RC/999 4.00 10.00
212 Lee Stempniak AU RC/999 6.00 15.00
213 Andrei Kostitsyn AU RC/999 25.00 60.00
214 Evgeny Artyukhin AU RC/999 4.00 10.00
215 Ben Eager AU RC/999 4.00 10.00
216 Andrew Ladd AU RC/999 6.00 15.00
217 Jeff Tambellini AU RC/999 5.00 12.00
218 Kyle Quincey AU RC/999 6.00 15.00
219 Tomas Fleischmann AU RC/999 4.00 10.00
220 Jakub Klepis AU RC/999 6.00 12.00
221 Michael Wall RC/1999 2.00 5.00
222 Zenon Konopka RC/1999 2.00 5.00
223 Vojtech Polak RC/1999 2.00 5.00
224 Martin St. Pierre RC/1999 2.00 5.00
225 Steve Goertzen RC 2.00 5.00
226 Andrew Penner RC/1999 2.00 5.00
227 Danny Syvret RC/1999 2.00 5.00
228 Jeff Giuliano RC/1999 2.00 5.00
229 Adam Hauser RC/1999 2.00 5.00
230 Kyle Brodziak RC/1999 2.00 5.00
231 Cam Janssen RC/1999 2.00 5.00
232 Kevin Colley RC/1999 2.00 5.00
233 Chris Holt RC/1999 2.00 5.00
234 Greg Jacina RC/1999 2.00 5.00
235 Yanick Lehoux RC/1999 2.00 5.00
236 Brian McGrattan RC/1999 2.00 5.00
237 Colin Hemingway RC/1999 2.00 5.00
238 Paul Ranger RC/1999 2.00 5.00
239 Gerald Coleman RC/1999 2.00 5.00
240 Dennis Wideman RC/1999 2.00 5.00
241 Junior Lessard RC/1999 2.00 5.00
242 Matt Jones RC/1999 2.00 5.00
243 Brian Eklund RC/1999 2.00 5.00
244 Nick Tarnasky RC/1999 2.00 5.00
245 Bruno Gervais RC/1999 2.00 5.00
246 Staffan Kronwall RC/1999 2.00 5.00
247 Dustin Penner RC/1999 3.00 8.00
248 Kevin Klein RC/1999 2.00 5.00
249 Rob McVicar RC/1999 2.00 5.00
250 Eric Healey RC/1999 2.00 5.00
251 Ben Guite RC/1999 2.00 5.00
252 Nathan Paetsch RC/1999 2.00 5.00
253 Jiri Novotny RC/1999 2.00 5.00
254 Richie Regehr RC/1999 2.00 5.00
255 Mark Giordano RC/1999 2.00 5.00
256 Chad Larose RC/1999 2.00 5.00
257 Corey Crawford RC/1999 2.00 5.00
258 Vitaly Kolesnik RC/1999 2.00 5.00
259 Geoff Platt RC/1999 2.00 5.00
260 Matt Greene RC/1999 2.00 5.00
261 Jean-Francois Jacques RC/1999 2.00 5.00
262 Rob Globke RC 2.00 5.00
263 Petr Taticek RC/1999 2.00 5.00
264 Petr Kanko RC/1999 2.00 5.00
265 Matt Ryan RC/1999 2.00 5.00
266 Connor James RC/1999 2.00 5.00
267 Richard Petiot RC/1999 2.00 5.00
268 Mark Streit RC/1999 2.00 5.00
269 Jean-Philippe Cote RC/1999 2.00 5.00
270 Jonathan Ferland RC/1999 2.00 5.00
271 Pekka Rinne RC/1999 2.00 5.00
272 Jason Ryznar RC/1999 2.00 5.00
273 Josh Gratton RC/1999 2.00 5.00
274 Alexandre Picard RC/1999 2.00 5.00
275 Colby Armstrong RC/1999 4.00 10.00
276 Grant Stevenson RC/1999 2.00 5.00
277 Doug Murray RC/1999 2.00 5.00
278 Chris Beckford-Tseu RC/1999 3.00 8.00
279 Jon DiSalvatore RC/1999 2.00 5.00
280 Mike Glumac RC/1999 2.00 5.00
281 Darren Reid RC/1999 2.00 5.00
282 Doug O'Brien RC/1999 2.00 5.00
283 Jay Harrison RC/1999 2.00 5.00
284 Rick Rypien RC/1999 2.00 5.00
285 Alexandre Burrows RC/1999 2.00 5.00
286 David Steckel RC/1999 2.00 5.00
287 Mike Green RC/1999 6.00 15.00
288 Ben Walter AU RC 4.00 10.00
289 Alexandre Picard AU RC 6.00 15.00
290 Chris Thorburn AU RC 4.00 10.00

2005-06 SP Authentic Limited

COMMON LIMITED (1-100) 1.50 4.00
STARS 5X TO 12X BASE HI
131 Ryan Getzlaf PATCH AU 100.00 250.00
132 Corey Perry PATCH AU 60.00 150.00
133 Braydon Coburn PATCH AU 25.00 60.00
134 Jim Slater PATCH AU 60.00 120.00
135 Hannu Toivonen PATCH AU 30.00 80.00
136 Andrew Alberts PATCH AU 25.00 60.00
137 Milan Jurcina PATCH AU 25.00 60.00
138 Kevin Dallman PATCH AU 25.00 60.00
139 Thomas Vanek PATCH AU 100.00 250.00
140 Dion Phaneuf PATCH AU 175.00 350.00
141 Eric Nystrom PATCH AU 40.00 100.00
142 Cam Ward PATCH AU 50.00 100.00
143 Kevin Nastiuk PATCH AU 30.00 80.00
144 Niklas Nordgren PATCH AU 25.00 60.00
145 Brent Seabrook PATCH AU 60.00 120.00
146 Cam Barker PATCH AU 40.00 80.00
147 Duncan Keith PATCH AU 100.00 200.00
148 Rene Bourque PATCH AU 50.00 150.00
149 Wojtek Wolski PATCH AU 60.00 120.00

150 Peter Budaj PATCH AU 40.00 100.00
151 Gilbert Brule PATCH AU 75.00 200.00
152 Jaroslav Balastik PATCH AU 60.00 120.00
153 Jussi Jokinen PATCH AU 40.00 100.00
154 Johan Franzen PATCH AU 50.00 100.00
155 Jim Howard PATCH AU 60.00 120.00
156 Brett Lebda PATCH AU 25.00 60.00
157 Brad Winchester PATCH AU 40.00 100.00
158 Rostislav Olesz PATCH AU 60.00 120.00
159 Anthony Stewart PATCH AU 40.00 100.00
160 George Parros PATCH AU 25.00 60.00
161 Matt Foy PATCH AU 25.00 60.00
162 Derek Boogaard PATCH AU 30.00 80.00
163 Alexander Perezhogin PATCH AU 60.00 120.00
164 Yann Danis PATCH AU 40.00 100.00
165 Raitis Ivanans PATCH AU 25.00 60.00
166 Ryan Suter PATCH AU 60.00 120.00
167 Zach Parise PATCH AU 100.00 200.00
168 Robert Nilsson PATCH AU 40.00 100.00
169 Petteri Nokelainen PATCH AU 25.00 60.00
170 Al Montoya PATCH AU 50.00 150.00
171 Henrik Lundqvist PATCH AU 125.00 300.00
172 Petr Prucha PATCH AU 50.00 150.00
173 Ryan Hollweg PATCH AU 25.00 60.00
174 Patrick Eaves PATCH AU 40.00 100.00
175 Brandon Bochenski PATCH AU 30.00 80.00
176 Andrej Meszaros PATCH AU 50.00 100.00
177 Jeff Carter PATCH AU 125.00 250.00
178 Mike Richards PATCH AU 75.00 200.00
179 David Leneveu PATCH AU 40.00 100.00
180 Keith Ballard PATCH AU 25.00 60.00
181 Sidney Crosby PATCH AU 1000.00 1500.00
182 Maxime Talbot PATCH AU 40.00 100.00
183 Josh Gorges PATCH AU 25.00 60.00
184 Ryane Clowe PATCH AU 25.00 60.00
185 Jay McClement PATCH AU 25.00 60.00
186 Jeff Hoggan PATCH AU 30.00 80.00
187 Jeff Woywitka PATCH AU 25.00 60.00
188 Alexander Steen PATCH AU 50.00 100.00
189 Andy Wozniewski PATCH AU 25.00 60.00
190 Alexander Ovechkin PATCH AU 600.00 1000.00
192 R.J. Umberger PATCH AU 25.00 60.00
193 Mikko Koivu PATCH AU 60.00 120.00
194 Steve Bernier PATCH AU 125.00 250.00
195 Timo Helbling PATCH AU 25.00 60.00
201 Barry Tallackson PATCH AU
202 Chris Campoli PATCH AU 25.00 60.00
204 Christoph Schubert PATCH AU
206 Jordan Sigalet PATCH AU
210 Dimitri Patzold PATCH AU
211 Brad Richardson PATCH AU 25.00 60.00
212 Lee Stempniak PATCH AU 25.00 60.00
214 Evgeny Artyukhin PATCH AU EXCH
216 Andrew Ladd PATCH AU 25.00 60.00
217 Jeff Tambellini PATCH AU
219 Tomas Fleischmann PATCH AU
220 Jakub Klepis PATCH AU

2005-06 SP Authentic Chirography

PRINT RUN 50 SER. #'d SETS
SPAR Andrew Raycroft 10.00 25.00
SPAT Alex Tanguay 10.00 25.00
SPAY Alexei Yashin 8.00 20.00
SPCP Chris Pronger 12.00 30.00
SPDH Dany Heatley 15.00 40.00
SPEB Ed Belfour 10.00 25.00
SPEN Evgeni Nabokov 10.00 25.00
SPHK Dominik Hasek 20.00 50.00
SPHV Martin Havlat 10.00 25.00
SPIK Ilya Kovalchuk 20.00 50.00
SPJG Jean-Sebastien Giguere 10.00 25.00
SPJI Jarome Iginla 20.00 50.00
SPJO Joe Thornton 25.00 50.00
SPJR Jeremy Roenick 20.00 50.00
SPJT Jose Theodore 12.00 30.00
SPMB Martin Brodeur 75.00 125.00
SPMG Marian Gaborik 20.00 50.00
SPMH Milan Hejduk 8.00 20.00
SPML Manny Legace 8.00 20.00
SPMM Mike Modano 15.00 40.00
SPMN Markus Naslund 10.00 25.00
SPOK Olaf Kolzig 15.00 40.00
SPPB Patrice Bergeron 10.00 25.00
SPRL Roberto Luongo 20.00 50.00
SPRN Rick Nash 15.00 40.00
SPSL Martin St. Louis 10.00 25.00
SPTV Tomas Vokoun 10.00 25.00
SPVL Vincent Lecavalier 25.00 60.00

2005-06 SP Authentic Exquisite Endorsements

EEAO Alexander Ovechkin
EEAP Alexander Perezhogin
EEAR Andrew Raycroft
EEAS Alexander Steen
EEBH Bobby Hull
EEBS Borje Salming
EEBT Bryan Trottier
EECN Cam Neely
EECP Corey Perry
EEDH Dany Heatley
EEDS Darryl Sittler
EEDT Dave Taylor
EEEB Ed Belfour
EEGB Gilbert Brule
EEGC Gerry Cheevers
EEGF Grant Fuhr
EEGH Gordie Howe
EEGL Guy Lapointe
EEHK Dominik Hasek
EEHL Henrik Lundqvist
EEHT Hannu Toivonen
EEIK Ilya Kovalchuk
EEJC Jeff Carter
EEJG Jean-Sebastien Giguere
EEJI Jarome Iginla
EEJK Jari Kurri
EEJO Joe Thornton
EEJR Jeremy Roenick
EEJS Jason Spezza
EEJT Jose Theodore
EEKL Kari Lehtonen
EELF Guy Lafleur
EELU Luc Robitaille
EEMB Mike Bossy
EEMD Marcel Dionne
EEMK Mikko Koivu
EEMM Mike Modano
EEMS Mats Sundin
EEPB Patrice Bergeron
EEPR Patrick Roy
EERB Ray Bourque
EERL Roberto Luongo
EESC Sidney Crosby
EESK Saku Koivu
EESL Martin St. Louis
EETE Tony Esposito
EETV Thomas Vanek
EEVL Vincent Lecavalier
EEWC Wayne Cashman
EEWG Wayne Gretzky

2005-06 SP Authentic Immortal Inks

PRINT RUN 10 SER.#'d SETS
NOT PRICED DUE TO SCARCITY
IIBT Bryan Trottier
IICN Cam Neely
IIFM Frank Mahovlich
IIGH Gordie Howe
IIGL Guy Lafleur
IIMB Mike Bossy
IIPR Patrick Roy
IIRB Ray Bourque
IIWG Wayne Gretzky

2005-06 SP Authentic Marks of Distinction

COMMON CARD 8.00 20.00
PRINT RUN 25 SERIAL #'d SETS
MDAO Alexander Ovechkin 200.00 300.00
MDAR Andrew Raycroft 15.00 40.00
MDAT Alex Tanguay 20.00 50.00
MDAY Alexei Yashin 8.00 20.00
MDBL Brian Leetch 20.00 50.00
MDBO Ray Bourque 60.00 120.00
MDBR Brad Richards 25.00 60.00
MDCP Chris Pronger 20.00 50.00
MDDH Dany Heatley 25.00 60.00
MDDW Doug Weight
MDEB Ed Belfour EXCH 50.00 100.00
MDGH Gordie Howe 100.00 200.00
MDGL Guy Lafleur 75.00 125.00
MDHV Martin Havlat 12.00 30.00
MDIK Ilya Kovalchuk 50.00 100.00
MDJC Jonathan Cheechoo 30.00 60.00
MDJG Jean-Sebastien Giguere 20.00 40.00
MDJI Jarome Iginla 50.00 100.00
MDJO Joe Thornton 60.00 100.00
MDJR Jeremy Roenick 30.00 60.00
MDJS Jason Spezza 30.00 60.00
MDJT Jose Theodore 30.00 60.00
MDKL Kari Lehtonen 25.00 60.00
MDKP Keith Primeau 8.00 20.00
MDMD Marcel Dionne
MDMH Milan Hejduk 12.00 30.00
MDMM Mike Modano 40.00 80.00
MDMN Markus Naslund 15.00 40.00
MDMS Mats Sundin
MDPB Patrice Bergeron 25.00 50.00
MDPE Phil Esposito 30.00 60.00
MDPR Patrick Roy 150.00 250.00
MDRB Rob Blake 12.00 30.00
MDRL Roberto Luongo 50.00 100.00
MDRN Rick Nash 50.00 100.00
MDSC Sidney Crosby 650.00 900.00
MDSG Simon Gagne 12.00 30.00
MDSK Saku Koivu 40.00 80.00
MDSL Martin St. Louis 20.00 50.00
MDSN Scott Niedermayer 12.00 30.00
MDVL Vincent Lecavalier 40.00 80.00

2005-06 SP Authentic Octographs

PRINT RUN 3 SER. #'d SETS
NOT PRICED DUE TO SCARCITY
OF Jarome Iginla
Martin St. Louis
Rick Nash
Dany Heatley
Ilya Kovalchuk
Patrice Bergeron
Marion Hossa
Markus Naslund
OG Patrick Roy
Dominik Hasek
Martin Brodeur
Ed Belfour
Olaf Kolzig
Jose Theodore
Jean-Sebastien Giguere
Evgeni Nabokov
OH Gordie Howe
Wayne Gretzky
Marcel Dionne
Guy Lafleur
Bryan Trottier
Bobby Hull
Phil Esposito
Mike Bossy
OR Dion Phaneuf
Alexander Ovechkin
Corey Perry
Jeff Carter
Gilbert Brule
Thomas Vanek
Alexander Steen
Alexander Perezhogin

2005-06 SP Authentic Prestigious Pairings

PPAH Daniel Alfredsson 20.00 50.00
Dany Heatley/100
PPBN Ray Bourqe 40.00 80.00
Cam Neely/50
PPBP Rob Blake 15.00 40.00
Chris Pronger/100
PPBS Ed Belfour
Mats Sundin/50
PPCE Gerry Cheevers
Phil Esposito/50
PPCR Jeff Carter 40.00 100.00
Mike Richards/100
PPDT Marcel Dionne 40.00 80.00
Dave Taylor/100
PPEP Robert Esche 5.00 12.00
Joni Pitkanen/100
PPFK Grant Fuhr 30.00 60.00
Jarri Kurri/50
PPGR Marian Gaborik 12.00 30.00
Dwayne Roloson/100
PPGS Guy Lafleur 25.00 60.00
Saku Koivu/50
PPHB Nathan Horton
Jay Bouwmeester/100
PPHE Bobby Hull 125.00 200.00
Tony Esposito/50
PPHG Gordie Howe 275.00 400.00
Wayne Gretzky/50
PPHV Dominik Hasek 15.00 40.00
Tomas Vokoun/100
PPIS Jarome Iginla 20.00 50.00
Martin St. Louis/50
PPKN Nikolai Khabibulin 8.00 20.00
Evgeni Nabokov/100
PPLH Manny Legace 15.00 40.00
Jim Howard/100
PPLK Kari Lehtonen 15.00 40.00
Ilya Kovalchuk/100
PPLM Henrik Lundqvist 25.00 60.00
Alvaro Montoya/100
PPLR Vincent Lecavalier 30.00 60.00
Brad Richards/100
PPMB Ryan Miller 20.00 50.00
Martin Biron/100
PPNL Markus Naslund 25.00 60.00
Trevor Linden/100
PPNZ Rick Nash 15.00 40.00
Nikolai Zherdev/100
PPOS Rostislav Olesz 5.00 12.00
Anthony Stewart/100
PPPG Corey Perry 25.00 60.00
Ryan Getzlaf/100
PPPH Mark Parrish 5.00 12.00
Trent Hunter/100
PPPN Dion Phaneuf 30.00 80.00
Eric Nystrom/100
PPPO Dion Phaneuf 125.00 250.00
Alexander Ovechkin/50
PPPV Gilbert Perreault 20.00 50.00
Thomas Vanek/100
PPRA Tuomo Ruutu 5.00 12.00
Tyler Arnason/100
PPRB Patrick Roy 150.00 250.00
Martin Brodeur/50
PPRP Mark Recchi
Zigmund Palffy/100
PPRR Michael Ryder 8.00 20.00
Mike Ribeiro/100
PPTB Bryan Trottier 15.00 40.00
Mike Bossy/50
PPTC Joe Thornton 25.00 60.00
Jonathan Cheechoo/100
PPTF Jocelyn Thibault 20.00 50.00
Marc-Andre Fleury/100
PPTW Keith Tkachuk
Doug Weight/100
PPTZ Marty Turco 8.00 20.00
Sergei Zubov/100

2005-06 SP Authentic Rarefied Rookies

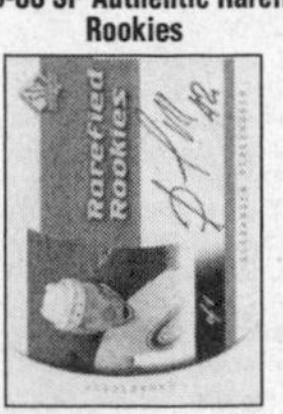

PRINT RUN 1 SER.#'d SET
NOT PRICED DUE TO SCARCITY
RRAA Andrew Alberts
RRAL Alexander Steen
RRAM Andrej Meszaros
RRAO Alexander Ovechkin
RRAP Alexander Perezhogin
RRAS Anthony Stewart
RRAW Andrew Wozniewski
RRBC Braydon Coburn
RRBS Brent Seabrook
RRBW Brad Winchester
RRCB Cam Barker
RRCP Corey Perry
RRCW Cam Ward
RRDL David Leneveu
RRDP Dion Phaneuf
RREN Eric Nystrom
RRGB Gilbert Brule
RRHL Henrik Lundqvist
RRHT Hannu Toivonen
RRJC Jeff Carter
RRJF Johan Franzen
RRJH Jim Howard
RRJJ Jussi Jokinen
RRJM Jay McClement
RRJS Jim Slater
RRJW Jeff Woywitka
RRKB Keith Ballard
RRMF Matt Foy
RRMJ Milan Jurcina
RRMK Mikko Koivu
RRMO Al Montoya
RRMR Mike Richards
RRMT Maxime Talbot
RRPB Peter Budaj
RRPE Patrick Eaves
RRPP Petr Prucha
RRRB Rene Bourque
RRRC Ryane Clowe
RRRG Ryan Getzlaf
RRRJ R.J. Umberger
RRRN Robert Nilsson
RRRO Rostislav Olesz
RRRS Ryan Suter
RRRW Ryan Whitney
RRSB Steve Bernier
RRSC Sidney Crosby
RRTV Thomas Vanek
RRWW Wojtek Wolski
RRYD Yann Danis
RRZP Zach Parise

2005-06 SP Authentic Rookie Authentics

PRINT RUN 250 SER.#'d SETS
RAAM Andrej Meszaros 8.00 20.00
RAAO Alexander Ovechkin 125.00 200.00
RAAP Alexander Perezhogin 8.00 20.00
RAAS Alexander Steen 10.00 25.00
RABC Braydon Coburn 8.00 20.00
RABS Brent Seabrook 8.00 20.00
RABW Brad Winchester 8.00 20.00
RACB Cam Barker
RACP Corey Perry 12.00 30.00
RACW Cam Ward 12.00 30.00
RADP Dion Phaneuf
RAEN Eric Nystrom 8.00 20.00
RAGB Gilbert Brule 10.00 25.00
RAHL Henrik Lundqvist 20.00 50.00
RAHT Hannu Toivonen 8.00 20.00
RAJC Jeff Carter 15.00 40.00
RAJH Jim Howard 15.00 40.00
RAJJ Jussi Jokinen 8.00 20.00
RAJW Jeff Woywitka 8.00 20.00
RAKB Keith Ballard 8.00 20.00
RAMR Mike Richards 12.00 30.00
RARG Ryan Getzlaf 15.00 40.00
RARN Robert Nilsson 8.00 20.00
RARO Rostislav Olesz 10.00 25.00
RARS Ryan Suter 8.00 20.00
RAST Anthony Stewart 8.00 20.00
RATV Thomas Vanek 15.00 40.00
RAWW Wojtek Wolski 10.00 25.00
RAYD Yann Danis 8.00 20.00
RAZP Zach Parise 20.00 50.00

2005-06 SP Authentic Scripts to Success

PRINT RUN 100 SER.#'d SETS
SSAF Alexander Frolov 6.00 15.00
SSAH Ales Hemsky 6.00 15.00
SSAR Andrew Raycroft 6.00 15.00
SSCB Christian Backman 4.00 10.00
SSCC Carlo Colaiacovo 4.00 10.00
SSDB Dustin Brown 4.00 10.00
SSDF Dan Fritsche 4.00 10.00
SSES Eric Staal 12.00 30.00
SSFT Fedor Tjutin 4.00 10.00
SSHZ Henrik Zetterberg 10.00 25.00
SSJB Jay Bouwmeester 6.00 15.00
SSJC Jonathan Cheechoo 8.00 20.00
SSJL Jamie Lundmark 4.00 10.00
SSJM John-Michael Liles 4.00 10.00
SSJP Joni Pitkanen 4.00 10.00
SSJR Jani Rita 4.00 10.00
SSKL Kari Lehtonen 10.00 25.00
SSLU Joffrey Lupul 4.00 10.00
SSMF Marc-Andre Fleury 12.00 30.00
SSMH Marcel Hossa 4.00 10.00
SSMR Mike Ribeiro 4.00 10.00
SSMS Matt Stajan 6.00 15.00
SSPB Patrice Bergeron 12.00 30.00
SSPL Pascal Leclaire 4.00 10.00
SSPS Philippe Sauve 4.00 10.00
SSRK Ryan Kesler 4.00 10.00
SSRM Ryan Miller 12.00 30.00
SSRY Michael Ryder 8.00 20.00
SSTA Tyler Arnason 4.00 10.00
SSTR Tuomo Ruutu 10.00 25.00

2005-06 SP Authentic Sign of the Times

STATED ODDS 1:24
AF Alexander Frolov 4.00 10.00
AR Andrew Raycroft 4.00 10.00
AT Jason Arnott 4.00 10.00
AY Alexei Yashin 3.00 8.00
BL Brett Lebda 3.00 8.00
BO Derek Boogaard 4.00 10.00
BR Brian Rafalski 3.00 8.00
BW Jay Bouwmeester 3.00 8.00
CB Christian Backman 3.00 8.00
CC Carlo Colaiacovo 3.00 8.00
CO Craig Conroy 3.00 8.00
CP Chris Pronger SP 8.00 20.00
DB Dustin Brown 3.00 8.00
DC Dan Cloutier 4.00 10.00
DF Dan Fritsche 3.00 8.00
DH Dany Heatley SP 15.00 40.00
DK Duncan Keith 10.00 25.00
DW Doug Weight 4.00 10.00
ED Eric Daze 3.00 8.00
ES Eric Staal EXCH 10.00 25.00
FT Fedor Tjutin 3.00 8.00
GL Georges Laraque 4.00 10.00
GM Glen Murray SP 15.00 40.00
GP George Parros 4.00 10.00
HE Timo Helbling 3.00 8.00
HG Jeff Hoggan 3.00 8.00
HO Marcel Hossa 3.00 8.00
HV Martin Havlat 3.00 8.00
HZ Henrik Zetterberg 8.00 20.00
IL Ian Laperriere 3.00 8.00
JA Jani Rita 3.00 8.00
JB Jaroslav Balastik 3.00 8.00
JC Jonathan Cheechoo 6.00 15.00
JH Jochen Hecht 3.00 8.00
JI Jarome Iginla SP 25.00 60.00
JL Jamie Lundmark 3.00 8.00
JM John-Michael Liles 3.00 8.00
JO Jeff O'Neill 3.00 8.00
JP Joni Pitkanen 3.00 8.00
JR Jeremy Roenick SP 20.00 50.00
JS Jim Slater 3.00 8.00
JT Jocelyn Thibault
KD Kris Draper 4.00 10.00
KE Kevin Dallman 3.00 8.00
KH Kristian Huselius 3.00 8.00
KL Kari Lehtonen 6.00 15.00
KP Keith Primeau 3.00 8.00
KW Kevin Weekes 4.00 10.00
LU Joffrey Lupul 3.00 8.00
MA Marc-Andre Fleury 10.00 25.00
MB Matthew Barnaby
MG Martin Gerber EXCH 4.00 10.00
MR Mike Ribeiro 3.00 8.00
MS Matt Stajan
MT Maxime Talbot 4.00 10.00
MW Brenden Morrow 4.00 10.00
NN Niklas Nordgren 3.00 8.00
NY Michael Nylander 3.00 8.00
OS Chris Osgood 6.00 15.00
PB Patrice Bergeron 6.00 15.00
PL Pascal Leclaire 4.00 10.00
PM Pierre-Marc Bouchard 4.00 10.00
PS Philippe Sauve 3.00 8.00
RA Raitis Ivanans 3.00 8.00
RH Ryan Hollweg 3.00 8.00
RI Brad Richards
RK Ryan Kesler 3.00 8.00
RL Roberto Luongo SP 20.00 50.00
RM Ryan Miller 10.00 25.00
RN Rob Niedermayer 3.00 8.00
RO Dwayne Roloson 4.00 10.00
RS Ryan Smith 6.00 15.00
RY Michael Ryder 6.00 15.00
RZ Richard Zednik 3.00 8.00
SA Miroslav Satan 4.00 10.00
SB Sean Burke 4.00 10.00
SC Sidney Crosby 150.00 300.00
SL Martin St. Louis SP 15.00 40.00
SN Scott Niedermayer 4.00 10.00
SP Jason Spezza 10.00 25.00
SS Sheldon Souray 3.00 8.00
ST Marco Sturm 3.00 8.00
SZ Sergei Zubov 3.00 8.00
TA Tyler Arnason 3.00 8.00
TG Tim Gleason 3.00 8.00
TH Trent Hunter 3.00 8.00
TL Trevor Linden 6.00 15.00
TP Tom Poti 3.00 8.00
TU Tuomo Ruutu 4.00 10.00
VL Vincent Lecavalier 12.00 30.00
VP Vaclav Prospal 3.00 8.00
WG Wayne Gretzky/15 SP 250.00 400.00

2005-06 SP Authentic Sign of the Times Duals

STATED ODDS 1:288
DAS Nik Antropov 6.00 15.00
Matt Stajan
DBM Patrice Bergeron 8.00 20.00
Glen Murray
DBR Martin Brodeur 12.00 30.00
Brian Rafalski
DBS Cam Barker EXCH 10.00 25.00
Brent Seabrook
DCS Erik Cole 10.00 25.00
Eric Staal
DDV Chris Drury 12.00 30.00
Thomas Vanek
DGW Martin Gerber 10.00 25.00
Cam Ward
DHK Marian Hossa 12.00 30.00
Ilya Kovalchuk
DKO Olaf Kolzig 50.00 100.00
Alexander Ovechkin
DKP Saku Koivu 12.00 30.00
Alexander Perezhogin
DLO Manny Legace 8.00 20.00
Chris Osgood
DLP Joffrey Lupul 8.00 20.00
Corey Perry
DMA Mike Modano 12.00 30.00
Jason Arnott
DMC Brendan Morrison 6.00 15.00
Dan Cloutier
DNB Rick Nash 40.00 80.00
Gilbert Brule
DNC Evgeni Nabokov 12.00 30.00
Jonathan Cheechoo
DNN Scott Niedermayer 12.00 30.00
Rob Niedermayer
DPH Michael Peca 6.00 15.00
Ales Hemsky
DPR Keith Primeau 10.00 25.00
Mike Richards
DPS Chris Pronger 12.00 30.00
Ryan Smyth
DRR Jeremy Roenick 20.00 50.00
Luc Robitaille
DRT Andrew Raycroft 6.00 15.00
Hannu Toivonen
DSH Jason Spezza 40.00 80.00
Dany Heatley
DSL Martin St. Louis EXCH 20.00 50.00
Vincent Lecavalier
DSO Mats Sundin EXCH 15.00 40.00
Jeff O'Neill
DSS Thomas Steen 10.00 25.00
Alexander Steen
DTD Jose Theodore 8.00 20.00
Yann Danis
DWL Kevin Weekes 10.00 25.00
Henrik Lundqvist
DYS Alexei Yashin 6.00 15.00
Miroslav Satan
DZF Henrik Zetterberg 15.00 40.00
Johan Franzen

2005-06 SP Authentic Sign of the Times Triples

PRINT RUN 15 SER.#'d SETS
NOT PRICED DUE TO SCARCITY
TBSO Ed Belfour
Mats Sundin
Jeff O'Neill
TDBV Chris Drury
Daniel Briere
Thomas Vanek
THAS Dany Heatley
Daniel Alfredsson
Jason Spezza
THHC Dominik Hasek
Martin Havlat
Zdeno Chara
TIPN Jarome Iginla
Dion Phaneuf
Eric Nystrom
TKHL Ilya Kovalchuk
Marian Hossa
Kari Lehtonen
TKRB Nikolai Khabibulin
Tuomo Ruutu
Cam Barker
TLOH Manny Legace
Chris Osgood
Jim Howard
TLPG Joffrey Lupul
Corey Perry
Ryan Getzlaf
TNMB Markus Naslund
Brendan Morrison
Todd Bertuzzi
TPGC Keith Primeau
Simon Gagne
Jeff Carter
TRBL Andrew Raycroft EXCH
Patrice Bergeron
Brian Leetch
TRRP Michael Ryder EXCH
Mike Ribeiro
Alexander Perezhogin
TRTD Patrick Roy
Jose Theodore
Yann Danis
TSAS Matt Stajan
Nik Antropov
Alexander Steen
TSLR Martin St. Louis
Vincent Lecavalier
Brad Richards
TSOC Alexander Steen
Alexander Ovechkin
Jeff Carter
TTHW Alex Tanguay EXCH
Milan Hejduk
Wojtek Wolski
TYPN Alexei Yashin
Mark Parrish
Robert Nilsson
TZFD Henrik Zetterberg EXCH
Johan Franzen
Kris Draper

2005-06 SP Authentic Sign of the Times Quads

PRINT RUN 10 SER.#'d SETS
NOT PRICED DUE TO SCARCITY
QCECS Gerry Cheevers
Phil Esposito
Wayne Cashman
Derek Sanderson
QGTVD Wayne Gretzky
Dave Taylor
Rogie Vachon
Marcel Dionne
QPSCW Chris Pronger
Ryan Smyth
Ty Conklin
Brad Winchester
QRCEB Patrick Roy
Gerry Cheevers
Tony Esposito
Martin Brodeur
QSHAH Jason Spezza
Dany Heatley
Daniel Alfredsson
Martin Havlat
QSOPC Alexander Steen
Alexander Ovechkin
Corey Perry
Jeff Carter
QSSOS Mats Sundin
Matt Stajan
Jeff O'Neill
Alexander Steen
QTBNP Bryan Trottier
Mike Bossy
Bob Nystrom
Denis Potvin
QTNBB Joe Thornton
Cam Neely
Patrice Bergeron
Ray Bourque
QTRRK Jose Theodore
Michael Ryder
Mike Ribeiro
Saku Koivu

2005-06 SP Authentic Sign of the Times Fives

PRINT RUN 6 SER.#'d SETS
NOT PRICED DUE TO SCARCITY
ISNKN Jarome Iginla
Martin St. Louis
Rick Nash
Ilya Kovalchuk
Markus Naslund
LRMMG Guy Lafleur
Patrick Roy
Frank Mahovlich
Dickie Moore
Bernie Geoffrion
MMZTJ Mike Modano
Brenden Morrow
Sergei Zubov
Marty Turco
Jussi Jokinen
PEGCR Keith Primeau
Robert Esche
Simon Gagne
Jeff Carter
Mike Richards
POCLS Dion Phaneuf
Alexander Ovechkin
Jeff Carter
Henrik Lundqvist
Alexander
SMSMK Darryl Sittler
Frank Mahovlich
Borje Salming
Lanny McDonald
Red Kelly
TNCMC Joe Thornton
Evgeni Nabokov
Jonathan Cheechoo
Patrick Marleau
Ryane Clo
TWLDH Hannu Toivonen
Cam Ward
Henrik Lundqvist

Yann Danis
Jim Howard

2005-06 SP Authentic Six Star Signatures

PRINT RUN 5 SER.#'d SETS
NOT PRICED DUE TO SCARCITY
SSBO Gerry Cheevers
Ray Bourque
Cam Neely
Wayne Cashman
Phil Esposito
Johnny Bucyk
SSGO Patrick Roy
Martin Brodeur
Jose Theodore
Roberto Luongo
Jean-Sebastien Giguere
Yann Danis
SSHF Wayne Gretzky
Gordie Howe
Marcel Dionne
Guy Lafleur
Bryan Trottier
Bobby Hull
SSMO Bernie Geoffrion
Guy Lafleur
Guy Lapointe
Steve Shutt
Frank Mahovlich
Dickie Moore
SSRO Dion Phaneuf
Alexander Ovechkin
Corey Perry
Jeff Carter
Gilbert Brule
Thomas Vanek
SSTO Darryl Sittler
Lanny McDonald
Red Kelly
Borje Salming
Frank Mahovlich
Mats Sundin

2006-07 SP Authentic

NOTABLE PRINT RUN 999 #'d SETS
RC PRINT RUN 999 #'d SETS
1 Alexander Ovechkin 1.00 2.50
2 Olaf Kolzig .30 .75
3 Markus Naslund .30 .75
4 Roberto Luongo .40 1.00
5 Brendan Morrison .15 .40
6 Mats Sundin .30 .75
7 Michael Peca .15 .40
8 Alexander Steen .25 .60
9 Andrew Raycroft .25 .60
10 Vincent Lecavalier .30 .75
11 Martin St. Louis .25 .60
12 Brad Richards .25 .60
13 Doug Weight .15 .40
14 Keith Tkachuk .25 .60
15 Manny Legace .25 .60
16 Joe Thornton .50 1.25
17 Patrick Marleau .25 .60
18 Jonathan Cheechoo .30 .75
19 Vesa Toskala .25 .60
20 Sidney Crosby 2.00 5.00
21 Marc-Andre Fleury .30 .75
22 Mark Recchi .15 .40
23 Mario Lemieux 1.25 3.00
24 Shane Doan .15 .40
25 Jeremy Roenick .40 1.00
26 Owen Nolan .25 .60
27 Curtis Joseph .30 .75
28 Peter Forsberg .50 1.25
29 Simon Gagne .30 .75
30 Jeff Carter .30 .75
31 Mike Richards .15 .40
32 Jason Spezza .30 .75
33 Daniel Alfredsson .25 .60
34 Dany Heatley .40 1.00
35 Martin Gerber .30 .75
36 Jaromir Jagr .50 1.25
37 Brendan Shanahan .30 .75
38 Henrik Lundqvist .40 1.00
39 Petr Prucha .15 .40
40 Miroslav Satan .15 .40
41 Rick DiPietro .25 .60
42 Alexei Yashin .15 .40
43 Martin Brodeur 1.00 2.50
44 Patrik Elias .15 .40
45 Brian Gionta .15 .40
46 Paul Kariya .30 .75
47 Tomas Vokoun .25 .60
48 Saku Koivu .30 .75
49 Michael Ryder .25 .60
50 Cristobal Huet .30 .75
51 Chris Higgins .15 .40
52 Pavol Demitra .15 .40
53 Marian Gaborik .40 1.00
54 Manny Fernandez .25 .60
55 Wayne Gretzky 1.50 4.00
56 Rob Blake .25 .60
57 Alexander Frolov .15 .40
58 Ed Belfour .30 .75
59 Olli Jokinen .15 .40
60 Todd Bertuzzi .25 .60
61 Ryan Smyth .25 .60
62 Ales Hemsky .15 .40
63 Joffrey Lupul .15 .40
64 Gordie Howe .75 2.00
65 Henrik Zetterberg .30 .75
66 Dominik Hasek .50 1.25
67 Pavel Datsyuk .25 .60
68 Nicklas Lidstrom .30 .75
69 Marty Turco .25 .60
70 Mike Modano .30 .75
71 Eric Lindros .30 .75
72 Rick Nash .30 .75
73 Pascal LeClaire .25 .60
74 Sergei Fedorov .30 .75
75 Joe Sakic .60 1.50
76 Jose Theodore .30 .75
77 Milan Hejduk .25 .60
78 Marek Svatos .15 .40
79 Martin Havlat .25 .60
80 Tuomo Ruutu .15 .40
81 Nikolai Khabibulin .30 .75
82 Eric Staal .30 .75
83 Cam Ward .30 .75
84 Rod Brind'Amour .25 .60
85 Miikka Kiprusoff .30 .75
86 Alex Tanguay .25 .60
87 Jarome Iginla .40 1.00
88 Dion Phaneuf .40 1.00
89 Ryan Miller .30 .75
90 Chris Drury .25 .60
91 Daniel Briere .25 .60
92 Patrice Bergeron .30 .75
93 Brad Boyes .15 .40
94 Zdeno Chara .15 .40
95 Bobby Orr 1.25 3.00
96 Marian Hossa .25 .60
97 Kari Lehtonen .30 .75
98 Ilya Kovalchuk .40 1.00
99 Chris Pronger .25 .60
100 Teemu Selanne .30 .75
101 Ales Hemsky 1.25 3.00
102 Alexander Frolov 1.25 3.00
103 Alexander Ovechkin 3.00 8.00
104 Alexander Steen 1.50 4.00
105 Bobby Orr 3.00 8.00
106 Brendan Shanahan 2.00 5.00
107 Cam Ward 2.00 5.00
108 Dany Heatley 2.00 5.00
109 Dion Phaneuf 2.00 5.00
110 Dominik Hasek 3.00 8.00
111 Doug Weight 1.25 3.00
112 Ed Belfour 2.00 5.00
113 Eric Staal 2.00 5.00
114 Gordie Howe 2.00 5.00
115 Henrik Lundqvist 2.00 5.00
116 Henrik Zetterberg 2.00 5.00
117 Ilya Kovalchuk 2.00 5.00
118 Jarome Iginla 2.50 6.00
119 Jaromir Jagr 2.50 6.00
120 Larry Robinson 1.50 4.00
121 Jason Spezza 2.00 5.00
122 Jay Bouwmeester 1.25 3.00
123 Jeremy Roenick 2.00 5.00
124 Joe Sakic 3.00 8.00
125 Joe Thornton 2.50 6.00
126 Jonathan Cheechoo 1.50 4.00
127 Jose Theodore 1.50 4.00
128 Kari Lehtonen 1.50 4.00
129 Marc-Andre Fleury 1.50 4.00
130 Marian Gaborik 2.50 6.00
131 Mario Lemieux 4.00 10.00
132 Markus Naslund 1.50 4.00
133 Martin Brodeur 3.00 8.00
134 Scott Stevens 1.25 3.00
135 Martin Havlat 2.00 5.00
136 Martin St. Louis 2.00 5.00
137 Mats Sundin 2.00 5.00
138 Michael Ryder 1.50 4.00
139 Miikka Kiprusoff 2.00 5.00
140 Mike Modano 2.00 5.00
141 Milan Hejduk 1.50 4.00
142 Nicklas Lidstrom 2.00 5.00
143 Patrice Bergeron 2.00 5.00
144 Patrick Roy 4.00 10.00
145 Paul Kariya 2.00 5.00
146 Peter Forsberg 2.50 6.00
147 Bobby Clarke 1.50 4.00
148 Ray Bourque 2.00 5.00
149 Rick Nash 2.00 5.00
150 Rob Blake 1.50 4.00
151 Roberto Luongo 2.50 6.00
152 Ryan Miller 2.00 5.00
153 Saku Koivu 2.00 5.00
154 Shane Doan 1.25 3.00
155 Sidney Crosby 8.00 20.00
156 Simon Gagne 2.00 5.00
157 Teemu Selanne 2.00 5.00
158 Tomas Vokoun 2.00 5.00
159 Vincent Lecavalier 2.00 5.00
160 Wayne Gretzky 6.00 15.00
161 Ryan Shannon AU RC 5.00 12.00
162 Shane O'Brien AU RC 5.00 12.00
163 Phil Kessel AU RC 25.00 60.00
164 Mark Stuart AU RC 5.00 12.00
165 Matt Lashoff AU RC 5.00 12.00
166 Yan Stastny AU RC 5.00 12.00
167 Nate Thompson AU RC 5.00 12.00
168 Drew Stafford AU RC 8.00 20.00
169 Dustin Boyd AU RC 6.00 15.00
170 Brandon Prust AU RC 5.00 12.00
171 Dave Bolland AU RC 12.00 30.00
172 Michael Blunden AU RC 5.00 12.00
173 Dustin Byfuglien AU RC 15.00 40.00
174 Paul Stastny AU RC 30.00 60.00
175 Karri Ramo AU RC 5.00 12.00
176 Loui Eriksson AU RC 5.00 12.00
177 Tomas Kopecky AU RC 8.00 20.00
178 Ladislav Smid AU RC 5.00 12.00
179 Marc-Antoine Pouliot AU RC 6.00 15.00
180 Niklas Grossman AU RC 5.00 12.00
181 Patrick Thoresen AU RC 6.00 15.00
182 Janis Sprukts AU RC 5.00 12.00
183 Patrick O'Sullivan AU RC 8.00 20.00
184 Anze Kopitar AU RC 25.00 60.00
185 Konstantin Pushkaryov AU RC 5.00 12.00
186 Guillaume Latendresse AU RC 12.00 40.00
187 Shea Weber AU RC 6.00 15.00
188 Alexander Radulov AU RC 20.00 40.00
189 Travis Zajac AU RC 8.00 20.00
190 Jarkko Immonen AU RC 5.00 12.00
191 Nigel Dawes AU RC 6.00 15.00
192 Kelly Guard AU RC 5.00 12.00
193 Ryan Potulny AU RC 6.00 15.00
194 Benoit Pouliot AU RC 6.00 15.00
195 Keith Yandle AU RC 5.00 12.00
196 Evgeni Malkin AU RC 125.00 200.00
197 Noah Welch AU RC 5.00 12.00
198 Jordan Staal AU RC 30.00 60.00
199 Michel Ouellet AU RC 6.00 15.00
200 Kristopher Letang AU RC 10.00 25.00
201 Matt Carle AU RC 6.00 15.00
202 Marc-Edouard Vlasic AU RC 5.00 12.00
203 Roman Polak AU RC 5.00 12.00
204 Jeremy Williams AU RC 5.00 12.00
205 Ian White AU RC 5.00 12.00
206 Jesse Schultz AU RC 5.00 12.00
207 Brendan Bell AU RC 5.00 12.00
208 Luc Bourdon AU RC 6.00 15.00
209 Alexander Edler AU RC 5.00 12.00
210 Eric Fehr AU RC 6.00 15.00
211 Daren Machesney RC 2.00 5.00
212 Nathan McIver RC 2.00 5.00
213 Patrick Coulombe RC 2.00 5.00
214 Alexei Mikhnov RC 2.00 5.00
215 Kris Newbury RC 2.00 5.00
216 Blair Jones RC 2.00 5.00
217 Marek Schwarz RC 3.00 8.00
218 David Backes RC 3.00 8.00
219 Joe Pavelski RC 6.00 15.00
220 Patrick Fischer RC 2.00 5.00
221 Bill Thomas RC 2.00 5.00
222 Triston Grant RC 2.00 5.00
223 Lars Jonsson RC 2.00 5.00
224 David Printz RC 2.00 5.00
225 Jussi Timonen RC 2.00 5.00
226 Martin Houle RC 2.00 5.00
227 Josh Hennessy RC 2.00 5.00
228 Blake Comeau RC 2.00 5.00
229 Masi Marjamaki RC 2.00 5.00
230 Ben Ondrus RC 2.00 5.00
231 Fredrik Norrena RC 3.00 8.00
232 Johnny Oduya RC 2.00 5.00
233 Enver Lisin RC 2.00 5.00
234 Mikhail Grabovski RC 2.00 5.00
235 Mikko Lehtonen RC 2.00 5.00
236 Niklas Backstrom RC 8.00 20.00
237 Miroslav Kopriva RC 2.00 6.00
238 Benoit Pouliot RC 4.00 10.00
239 Peter Harrold RC 2.00 5.00
240 David Booth RC 2.00 5.00
241 Drew Larman RC 2.00 5.00
242 Jan Hejda RC 2.00 5.00
243 Jeff Deslauriers RC 2.00 5.00
244 Stefan Liv RC 3.00 8.00
245 Adam Burish RC 2.00 5.00
246 Michael Funk RC 2.00 5.00
247 Mike Card RC 2.00 5.00
248 Adam Dennis RC 2.00 5.00
249 Clarke MacArthur RC 2.00 5.00
250 David McKee RC 3.00 8.00

2006-07 SP Authentic Chirography

STATED PRINT RUN 75 #'d SETS
AF Alexander Frolov 8.00 20.00
AH Ales Hemsky 6.00 15.00
AK Anze Kopitar 20.00 50.00
BB Brad Boyes 4.00 10.00
CP Corey Perry 8.00 20.00
DH Dany Heatley 12.00 30.00
DR Dwayne Roloson 4.00 10.00
DT Darcy Tucker 8.00 20.00
EM Evgeni Malkin 30.00 80.00
ES Eric Staal 8.00 20.00
GE Martin Gerber 8.00 20.00
HA Dominik Hasek 20.00 50.00
HE Milan Hejduk 6.00 15.00
JC Jonathan Cheechoo 8.00 20.00
JI Jarome Iginla 20.00 50.00
JS Jordan Staal 20.00 50.00
KD Kris Draper 6.00 15.00
MC Mike Cammalleri 8.00 20.00
MF Marc-Andre Fleury 15.00 40.00
MG Marian Gaborik 12.00 30.00
MH Martin Havlat 6.00 15.00
MM Mike Modano 10.00 25.00
MP Michael Peca 8.00 20.00
MS Marek Svatos 6.00 15.00
MT Marty Turco 8.00 20.00
NL Nicklas Lidstrom 15.00 30.00
PE Patrik Elias 6.00 15.00
PM Patrick Marleau 8.00 20.00
PO Patrick O'Sullivan 12.00 30.00
PP Petr Prucha 4.00 10.00
RM Ryan Miller 15.00 40.00
RN Rick Nash 15.00 40.00
RS Matt Carle 6.00 15.00
SC Sidney Crosby 100.00 200.00
TV Tomas Vokoun 8.00 20.00

2006-07 SP Authentic Limited

*LIMITED: 4X TO 10X BASE HI
*LTD NOTABLES: 1X TO 2X HI
STATED PRINT RUN 100 #'d SETS
1 Alexander Ovechkin 8.00 20.00
2 Olaf Kolzig 2.50 6.00
3 Markus Naslund 2.50 6.00
4 Roberto Luongo 4.00 10.00
5 Brendan Morrison 1.50 4.00
6 Mats Sundin 3.00 8.00
7 Michael Peca 3.00 8.00
8 Alexander Steen 4.00 10.00
9 Andrew Raycroft 4.00 10.00
10 Vincent Lecavalier 5.00 12.00
11 Martin St. Louis 5.00 12.00
12 Brad Richards 5.00 12.00
13 Doug Weight 3.00 8.00
14 Keith Tkachuk 4.00 10.00
15 Manny Legace 4.00 10.00
16 Joe Thornton 6.00 15.00
17 Patrick Marleau 4.00 10.00
18 Jonathan Cheechoo 5.00 12.00
19 Vesa Toskala 4.00 10.00
20 Sidney Crosby 15.00 40.00
21 Marc-Andre Fleury 5.00 12.00
22 Mark Recchi 3.00 8.00
23 Mario Lemieux 12.00 30.00
24 Shane Doan 4.00 10.00
25 Jeremy Roenick 5.00 12.00
26 Owen Nolan 4.00 10.00
27 Curtis Joseph 5.00 12.00
28 Peter Forsberg 6.00 15.00
29 Simon Gagne 5.00 12.00
30 Jeff Carter 5.00 12.00
31 Mike Richards 5.00 12.00
32 Jason Spezza 5.00 12.00
33 Daniel Alfredsson 4.00 10.00
34 Dany Heatley 5.00 12.00
35 Martin Gerber 5.00 12.00
36 Jaromir Jagr 6.00 15.00
37 Brendan Shanahan 5.00 12.00
38 Henrik Lundqvist 8.00 20.00
39 Petr Prucha 3.00 8.00
40 Miroslav Satan 3.00 8.00
41 Rick DiPietro 5.00 12.00
42 Alexei Yashin 3.00 8.00
43 Martin Brodeur 10.00 25.00
44 Patrik Elias 3.00 8.00
45 Brian Gionta 3.00 8.00
46 Paul Kariya 5.00 12.00
47 Tomas Vokoun 4.00 10.00
48 Saku Koivu 5.00 12.00
49 Michael Ryder 4.00 10.00
50 Cristobal Huet 4.00 10.00
51 Chris Higgins 3.00 8.00
52 Pavol Demitra 3.00 8.00
53 Marian Gaborik 8.00 20.00
54 Manny Fernandez 5.00 12.00
55 Wayne Gretzky 12.00 30.00
56 Rob Blake 4.00 10.00
57 Alexander Frolov 3.00 8.00
58 Ed Belfour 12.00 30.00
59 Olli Jokinen 3.00 8.00
60 Todd Bertuzzi 4.00 10.00
61 Ryan Smyth 4.00 10.00
62 Ales Hemsky 3.00 8.00
63 Joffrey Lupul 3.00 8.00
64 Gordie Howe 4.00 10.00
65 Henrik Zetterberg 5.00 12.00
66 Dominik Hasek 5.00 12.00
67 Pavel Datsyuk 5.00 12.00
68 Nicklas Lidstrom 5.00 12.00
69 Marty Turco 4.00 10.00
70 Mike Modano 5.00 12.00
71 Eric Lindros 5.00 12.00
72 Rick Nash 5.00 12.00
73 Pascal LeClaire 5.00 12.00
74 Sergei Fedorov 5.00 12.00
75 Joe Sakic 8.00 20.00
76 Jose Theodore 5.00 12.00
77 Milan Hejduk 4.00 10.00
78 Marek Svatos 3.00 8.00
79 Martin Havlat 4.00 10.00
80 Tuomo Ruutu 3.00 8.00
81 Nikolai Khabibulin 5.00 12.00
82 Eric Staal 4.00 10.00
83 Cam Ward 0.00 20.00
84 Rod Brind'Amour 4.00 10.00
85 Miikka Kiprusoff 5.00 12.00
86 Alex Tanguay 4.00 10.00
87 Jarome Iginla 8.00 20.00
88 Dion Phaneuf 6.00 15.00
89 Ryan Miller 5.00 12.00
90 Chris Drury 4.00 10.00
91 Daniel Briere 4.00 10.00
92 Patrice Bergeron 4.00 10.00
93 Brad Boyes 3.00 8.00
94 Zdeno Chara 3.00 8.00
95 Bobby Orr 10.00 25.00
96 Marian Hossa 4.00 10.00
97 Kari Lehtonen 5.00 12.00
98 Ilya Kovalchuk 6.00 15.00
99 Chris Pronger 4.00 10.00
100 Teemu Selanne 5.00 12.00
101 Ales Hemsky 5.00 12.00
102 Alexander Frolov 5.00 12.00
103 Alexander Ovechkin 12.00 30.00
104 Alexander Steen 6.00 15.00
105 Bobby Orr 10.00 25.00
106 Brendan Shanahan 8.00 20.00
107 Cam Ward 12.00 30.00
108 Dany Heatley 6.00 15.00
109 Dion Phaneuf 8.00 20.00
110 Dominik Hasek 8.00 20.00
111 Doug Weight 5.00 12.00
112 Ed Belfour 20.00 50.00
113 Eric Staal 6.00 15.00
114 Gordie Howe 6.00 15.00
115 Henrik Lundqvist 10.00 25.00
116 Henrik Zetterberg 6.00 15.00
117 Ilya Kovalchuk 8.00 20.00
118 Jarome Iginla 10.00 25.00
119 Jaromir Jagr 10.00 25.00
120 Larry Robinson 4.00 10.00
121 Jason Spezza 6.00 15.00
122 Jay Bouwmeester 5.00 12.00
123 Jeremy Roenick 6.00 15.00
124 Joe Sakic 12.00 30.00
125 Joe Thornton 10.00 25.00
126 Jonathan Cheechoo 6.00 15.00
127 Jose Theodore 6.00 15.00
128 Kari Lehtonen 6.00 15.00
129 Marc-Andre Fleury 6.00 15.00
130 Marian Gaborik 10.00 25.00
131 Mario Lemieux 10.00 25.00
132 Markus Naslund 6.00 15.00
133 Martin Brodeur 12.00 30.00
134 Scott Stevens 2.50 6.00
135 Martin Havlat 6.00 15.00
136 Martin St. Louis 6.00 15.00
137 Mats Sundin 6.00 15.00
138 Michael Ryder 6.00 15.00
139 Miikka Kiprusoff 6.00 15.00
140 Mike Modano 6.00 15.00
141 Milan Hejduk 5.00 12.00
142 Nicklas Lidstrom 6.00 15.00
143 Patrice Bergeron 5.00 12.00
144 Patrick Roy 10.00 25.00
145 Paul Kariya 6.00 15.00
146 Peter Forsberg 10.00 25.00
147 Bobby Clarke 6.00 15.00
148 Ray Bourque 6.00 15.00
149 Rick Nash 6.00 15.00
150 Rob Blake 6.00 15.00
151 Roberto Luongo 12.00 30.00
152 Ryan Miller 6.00 15.00
153 Saku Koivu 6.00 15.00
154 Shane Doan 5.00 12.00
155 Sidney Crosby 20.00 50.00
156 Simon Gagne 6.00 15.00
157 Teemu Selanne 6.00 15.00
158 Tomas Vokoun 5.00 12.00
159 Vincent Lecavalier 6.00 15.00
160 Wayne Gretzky 12.00 30.00
161 Ryan Shannon 25.00 60.00
162 Shane O'Brien 20.00 50.00
163 Phil Kessel 75.00 150.00
164 Mark Stuart 20.00 50.00
165 Matt Lashoff 25.00 60.00
166 Yan Stastny 25.00 60.00
167 Nate Thompson
168 Drew Stafford 40.00 100.00
169 Dustin Boyd 30.00 80.00
170 Brandon Prust 25.00 60.00
171 Dave Bolland 30.00 80.00
172 Michael Blunden 20.00 50.00
173 Dustin Byfuglien 40.00 100.00
174 Paul Stastny 150.00 300.00
175 Karri Ramo 25.00 60.00
176 Loui Eriksson 25.00 80.00
177 Tomas Kopecky 30.00 80.00
178 Ladislav Smid 20.00 50.00
179 Marc-Antoine Pouliot 25.00 60.00
180 Niklas Grossman 20.00 50.00
181 Patrick Thoresen 20.00 50.00
182 Janis Sprukts 20.00 50.00
183 Patrick O'Sullivan 40.00 100.00
184 Anze Kopitar 125.00 250.00
185 Konstantin Pushkaryov 20.00 50.00
186 Guillaume Latendresse 40.00 150.00
187 Shea Weber 30.00 80.00
188 Alexander Radulov 40.00 175.00
189 Travis Zajac 30.00 80.00
190 Jarkko Immonen 25.00 60.00
191 Nigel Dawes 20.00 50.00
192 Kelly Guard
193 Ryan Potulny 25.00 80.00
194 Benoit Pouliot 25.00 80.00
195 Keith Yandle 20.00 50.00
196 Evgeni Malkin 275.00 400.00
197 Noah Welch 20.00 50.00
198 Jordan Staal 125.00 250.00
199 Michel Ouellet 25.00 60.00
200 Kristopher Letang 40.00 100.00
201 Matt Carle 25.00 60.00
202 Marc-Edouard Vlasic 25.00 80.00
203 Roman Polak 15.00 40.00
204 Jeremy Williams 25.00 60.00
205 Ian White 15.00 40.00
206 Jesse Schultz 25.00 60.00
207 Brendan Bell 15.00 40.00
208 Luc Bourdon 25.00 80.00
209 Alexander Edler 30.00 80.00
210 Eric Fehr 30.00 80.00
211 Daren Machesney 6.00 15.00
212 Nathan McIver 3.00 8.00
213 Patrick Coulombe 3.00 8.00
214 Alexei Mikhnov 6.00 15.00
215 Kris Newbury 6.00 15.00
216 Blair Jones 6.00 15.00
217 Marek Schwarz 15.00 40.00
218 David Backes 5.00 12.00
219 Joe Pavelski 25.00 60.00
220 Patrick Fischer 3.00 8.00
221 Bill Thomas 6.00 15.00
222 Triston Grant 3.00 8.00
223 Lars Jonsson 3.00 8.00
224 David Printz 6.00 15.00
225 Jussi Timonen 3.00 8.00
226 Martin Houle 8.00 20.00
227 Josh Hennessy 6.00 15.00
228 Blake Comeau 6.00 15.00
229 Masi Marjamaki 6.00 15.00
230 Ben Ondrus 6.00 15.00
231 Fredrik Norrena 6.00 15.00
232 Johnny Oduya 6.00 15.00
233 Enver Lisin 6.00 15.00
234 Mikhail Grabovski 6.00 15.00
235 Mikko Lehtonen 3.00 8.00
236 Niklas Backstrom 6.00 15.00
237 Miroslav Kopriva 6.00 15.00
238 Benoit Pouliot 8.00 20.00
239 Peter Harrold 6.00 15.00
240 David Booth 6.00 15.00
241 Drew Larman 3.00 8.00
242 Jan Hejda 3.00 8.00
243 Jeff Deslauriers 8.00 20.00
244 Stefan Liv 8.00 20.00
245 Adam Burish 3.00 8.00
246 Michael Funk 3.00 8.00
247 Mike Card 3.00 8.00
248 Adam Dennis 3.00 8.00
249 Clarke MacArthur 6.00 15.00
250 David McKee 8.00 20.00

2006-07 SP Authentic Sign of the Times

The Phaneuf single was not part of the original checklist and may not have been issued in packs. However, a handful of copies were circulated, apparently by company employees, and thus it is included in this listing but without a price. The Bernier single was not included in packs, but was released later as a redemption replacement single.

STATED ODDS 1:24
STAF Alexander Frolov 4.00 10.00
STAH Ales Hemsky 4.00 10.00
STAR Andrew Raycroft 6.00 15.00
STBG Brian Gionta 4.00 10.00
STBH Bobby Hull SP 20.00 50.00
STBO Bobby Orr 100.00 200.00
STBU Johnny Bucyk 8.00 20.00
STCA Colby Armstrong SP 10.00 25.00
STCP Corey Perry 8.00 20.00
STCW Cam Ward 6.00 15.00
STDC Don Cherry 10.00 25.00
STDH Dominik Hasek 12.00 30.00
STDP Dion Phaneuf 25.00 50.00
STDR Dwayne Roloson 4.00 10.00
STDS Denis Savard 6.00 15.00
STEL Patrik Elias 4.00 10.00
STEM Evgeni Malkin 40.00 80.00
STES Eric Staal 8.00 20.00
STGB Gilbert Brule 6.00 15.00
STGE Martin Gerber SP 6.00 15.00
STGH Gordie Howe 40.00 80.00
STGO Scott Gomez 4.00 10.00
STHE Dany Heatley 10.00 25.00
STHJ Milan Hejduk 4.00 10.00
STJB Ray Bourque SP 40.00 80.00
STJB Jean Beliveau SP 150.00 250.00
STJC Jonathan Cheechoo 6.00 15.00
STJE Jeff Carter 4.00 10.00
STJG Jean-Sebastien Giguere 6.00 15.00
STJI Jarome Iginla 10.00 25.00
STJK Jari Kurri 8.00 20.00
STJM Joe Mullen 4.00 10.00
STJS Jarret Stoll 4.00 10.00
STJT Jose Theodore 6.00 15.00
STJW Justin Williams 4.00 10.00
STKD Kris Draper 4.00 10.00
STLR Luc Robitaille SP 150.00 250.00
STMA Matt Carle 4.00 10.00
STMB Martin Brodeur 40.00 80.00
STMF Marc-Andre Fleury 10.00 25.00
STMH Martin Havlat 6.00 15.00
STMI Ryan Miller 8.00 20.00
STML Mario Lemieux SP 125.00 250.00
STMM Mike Modano 8.00 20.00
STMO Brenden Morrow 6.00 15.00
STMT Marty Turco 6.00 15.00
STNL Nicklas Lidstrom 6.00 15.00
STPB Pierre-Marc Bouchard SP 4.00 10.00
STPE Michael Peca 4.00 10.00
STPK Phil Kessel 8.00 20.00
STPM Patrick Marleau SP 6.00 15.00
STPP Petr Prucha SP 10.00 25.00
STRN Rick Nash 10.00 25.00
STRY Michael Ryder 6.00 15.00
STSB Steve Bernier 12.00 30.00
STSC Sidney Crosby 100.00 175.00
STSK Saku Koivu SP 12.00 30.00
STSV Marek Svatos 4.00 10.00
STTE Tony Esposito 15.00 40.00
STTV Tomas Vokoun 6.00 15.00
STVT Vesa Toskala 6.00 15.00
STWC Wendel Clark 10.00 25.00
STWG Wayne Gretzky 100.00 200.00
STWO Willie O'Ree SP 15.00 40.00

2006-07 SP Authentic Sign of the Times Duals

STAS Glenn Anderson 20.00 50.00
Ryan Smyth
STBE Ron Ellis 15.00 40.00
Johnny Bower
STBG Mike Bossy 15.00 40.00
Clark Gillies
STBM Rob Blake 10.00 25.00
Larry Murphy
STBW Martin Brodeur 50.00 100.00
Cam Ward
STCB Jonathan Cheechoo 10.00 25.00
Steve Bernier
STCC Bobby Clarke 15.00 40.00
Jeff Carter
STCG Dino Ciccarelli 20.00 50.00
Marian Gaborik
STCT Gerry Cheevers 20.00 50.00
Hannu Toivonen
STDS Saku Koivu 20.00 50.00
Denis Savard
STDV Marcel Dionne 15.00 40.00
Rogie Vachon
STEG Patrik Elias 12.00 30.00
Brian Gionta
STET Tony Esposito 20.00 50.00
Marty Turco
STFK Alexander Frolov 15.00 40.00
Anze Kopitar
STFM Bernie Federko 8.00 20.00
Joe Mullen
STGL Mario Lemieux 350.00 500.00
Wayne Gretzky SP
STGR Grant Fuhr 20.00 50.00
Ryan Miller
STHA David Aebischer 15.00 40.00
Cristobal Huet
STHE Dany Heatley 12.00 30.00
Patrick Eaves
STHK Martin Havlat 12.00 30.00
Nikolai Khabibulin
STHO Bobby Orr 200.00 300.00
Gordie Howe
STHS Milan Hejduk 8.00 20.00
Marek Svatos
STIT Jarome Iginla 25.00 60.00
Alex Tanguay
STKB Patrice Bergeron 12.00 30.00
Phil Kessel
STKL Ilya Kovalchuk 20.00 40.00
Kari Lehtonen
STLB Roberto Luongo 25.00 60.00
Richard Brodeur
STLG Simon Gagne 12.00 30.00
Reggie Leach
STLM Mario Lemieux 150.00 250.00
Evgeni Malkin SP
STLR Guy Lafleur 20.00 50.00
Michael Ryder
STLS Nicklas Lidstrom 20.00 50.00
Borje Salming
STLT Vincent Lecavalier 30.00 80.00
Joe Thornton
STMC Guy Lafleur 20.00 50.00
Larry Robinson
STMM Mike Modano 12.00 30.00
Brenden Morrow
STMR Mike Modano 12.00 30.00
Mike Ribeiro
STNB Rick Nash 12.00 30.00
Gilbert Brule
STNK Cam Neely 25.00 60.00
Phil Kessel
STOB Bobby Orr 200.00 350.00
Ray Bourque
STPJ Patrick Marleau 12.00 30.00
Jonathan Cheechoo
STPP Zach Parise 20.00 50.00
J.P. Parise
STQC Peter Stastny 25.00 60.00
Paul Stastny
STRB Patrick Roy 250.00 350.00
Martin Brodeur SP
STRL Michael Ryder 15.00 40.00
Guillaume Latendresse
STRP Denis Potvin 10.00 25.00
Larry Robinson
STRR Dwayne Roloson 10.00 25.00
Bill Ranford
STRT Luc Robitaille 15.00 40.00
Dave Taylor
STSA Colby Armstrong 15.00 40.00
Jordan Staal
STSS Eric Staal 40.00 80.00
Jordan Staal
STSW Eric Staal 15.00 40.00
Cam Ward
STVA Tomas Vokoun 8.00 20.00
Jason Arnott
STVH Tomas Vokoun 20.00 50.00
Dominik Hasek
STWR Shea Weber 20.00 50.00
Alexander Radulov

2006-07 SP Authentic Sign of the Times Triples

STATED PRINT RUN 25 #'d SETS
ST3BBK Brad Boyes 30.00 80.00
Patrice Bergeron
Phil Kessel
ST3BEK Ron Ellis 50.00 100.00
Johnny Bower
Red Kelly
ST3COS Gerry Cheevers
Terry O'Reilly
Derek Sanderson
ST3DBM Chris Drury 60.00 125.00
Daniel Briere
Ryan Miller
ST3HNS Dany Heatley 100.00 175.00
Rick Nash
Eric Staal
ST3HTS Milan Hejduk 30.00 80.00
Jose Theodore
Marek Svatos
ST3ITK Jarome Iginla 50.00 100.00
Alex Tanguay
Miikka Kiprusoff
ST3LFM Mario Lemieux 200.00 350.00
Marc-Andre Fleury
Evgeni Malkin
ST3LGH Mario Lemieux 700.00 1000.00
Wayne Gretzky
Gordie Howe
ST3LHZ Nicklas Lidstrom 75.00 150.00
Tomas Holmstrom
Henrik Zetterberg
ST3LRS Guy Lafleur
Steve Shutt
Larry Robinson
ST3MTC Patrick Marleau 60.00 125.00
Joe Thornton
Jonathan Cheechoo
ST3MTM Mike Modano 30.00 60.00
Marty Turco
Brenden Morrow
ST3NLM Markus Naslund 50.00 100.00
Roberto Luongo
Brendan Morrison
ST3OBE Phil Esposito 400.00 500.00
Bobby Orr
Ray Bourque
ST3PGB Mark Parrish 60.00 125.00
Marian Gaborik
Pierre-Marc Bouchard
ST3RBW Patrick Roy 250.00 350.00
Martin Brodeur
Cam Ward
ST3RHG Wade Redden
Dany Heatley
Martin Gerber
ST3RKH Chris Higgins 50.00 100.00
Saku Koivu
Michael Ryder
ST3APT Andrew Raycroft 30.00 80.00
Mike Peca
Darcy Tucker
ST3SSH Ryan Smyth 30.00 80.00
Jarret Stoll

Ales Hemsky
ST3SSS Peter Stastny
Yan Stastny
Paul Stastny
ST3WSW Justin Williams 50.00 125.00
Eric Staal
Cam Ward
ST3SUT1 Brent Sutter 30.00 80.00
Darryl Sutter
Duane Sutter
ST3SUT2 Brian Sutter 30.00 80.00
Rich Sutter
Ron Sutter

2006-07 SP Authentic Sign of the Times Quads

PRINT RUN 10 #'d SETS
NOT PRICED DUE TO SCARCITY
ST4BCTS Mike Bossy
Bobby Clarke
Dave Taylor
Darryl Sittler
ST4BLSR Guy Lafleur
Steve Shutt
Scotty Bowman
Larry Robinson
ST4EBOC Phil Esposito
Johnny Bucyk
Bobby Orr
Don Cherry
ST4ECVP Tony Esposito
Gerry Cheevers
Rogie Vachon
Bernie Parent
ST4EHSW Tony Esposito
Bobby Hull
Denis Savard
Doug Wilson
ST4IKPT Jarome Iginla
Alex Tanguay
Miikka Kiprusoff
Dion Phaneuf
ST4LOGH Mario Lemieux
Bobby Orr
Wayne Gretzky
Gordie Howe
ST4MKSL Evgeni Malkin
Phil Kessel
Jordan Staal
Guillaume Latendresse
ST4RBLF Patrick Roy
Martin Brodeur
Roberto Luongo
Marc-Andre Fleury
ST4SSSS Peter Stastny
Anton Stastny
Yan Stastny
Paul Stastny

2007-08 SP Authentic

COMP.SET w/o SP's (100)
NOTABLES STATED PRINT RUN 1999
RC STATED PRINT RUN 999
AU RC STATED PRINT RUN 999
1 Daniel Briere .40 1.00
2 Simon Gagne .40 1.00
3 Jeff Carter .25 .60
4 Alexander Ovechkin 1.25 3.00
5 Olaf Kolzig .40 1.00
6 Alexander Semin .40 1.00
7 Patrice Bergeron .40 1.00
8 Marc Savard .25 .60
9 Phil Kessel .40 1.00
10 Tomas Vokoun .40 1.00
11 Nathan Horton .25 .60
12 Olli Jokinen .25 .60
13 Eric Staal .40 1.00
14 Cam Ward .40 1.00
15 Rod Brind'Amour .30 .75
16 Saku Koivu .30 .75
17 Michael Ryder .25 .60
18 Guillaume Latendresse .30 .75
19 Cristobal Huet .30 .75
20 Mats Sundin .40 1.00
21 Vesa Toskala .30 .75
22 Darcy Tucker .30 .75
23 Alexander Steen .25 .60
24 Rick DiPietro .30 .75
25 Bill Guerin .25 .60
26 Miroslav Satan .25 .60
27 Vincent Lecavalier .40 1.00
28 Brad Richards .30 .75
29 Martin St. Louis .30 .75
30 Jaromir Jagr .60 1.50
31 Henrik Lundqvist .50 1.25
32 Brendan Shanahan .40 1.00
33 Chris Drury .30 .75
34 Sidney Crosby 2.00 5.00
35 Evgeni Malkin 1.00 2.50
36 Marc-Andre Fleury .40 1.00
37 Jordan Staal .50 1.25
38 Dany Heatley .50 1.25
39 Ray Emery .30 .75
40 Jason Spezza .40 1.00
41 Daniel Alfredsson .30 .75
42 Ilya Kovalchuk .50 1.25
43 Kari Lehtonen .40 1.00
44 Marian Hossa .40 1.00
45 Martin Brodeur 1.00 2.50
46 Patrik Elias .25 .60
47 Zach Parise .30 .75
48 Ryan Miller .40 1.00
49 Thomas Vanek .30 .75
50 Jason Pominville .25 .60
51 Shane Doan .25 .60
52 Ilya Bryzgalov .40 1.00
53 Ed Jovanovski .25 .60
54 Anze Kopitar .40 1.00
55 Rob Blake .30 .75
56 Alexander Frolov .25 .60
57 Martin Havlat .30 .75
58 Nikolai Khabibulin .40 1.00
59 Tuomo Ruutu .25 .60
60 Ales Hemsky .25 .60
61 Joni Pitkanen .25 .60
62 Dwayne Roloson .30 .75
63 Rick Nash .40 1.00
64 Sergei Fedorov .40 1.00
65 David Vyborny .25 .60
66 Paul Kariya .40 1.00
67 Manny Legace .30 .75
68 Keith Tkachuk .30 .75
69 Joe Sakic .75 2.00
70 Ryan Smyth .30 .75
71 Paul Stastny .40 1.00
72 Milan Hejduk .30 .75
73 Jarome Iginla .60 1.50
74 Miikka Kiprusoff .50 1.25
75 Alex Tanguay .30 .75
76 Dion Phaneuf .40 1.00
77 Marian Gaborik .50 1.25
78 Mikko Koivu .25 .60
79 Niklas Backstrom .30 .75
80 Mike Modano .40 1.00
81 Marty Turco .40 1.00
82 Mike Ribeiro .25 .60
83 Joe Thornton .50 1.25
84 Jonathan Cheechoo .30 .75
85 Patrick Marleau .30 .75
86 Chris Mason .30 .75
87 Alexander Radulov .40 1.00
88 Jason Arnott .25 .60
89 Roberto Luongo .60 1.50
90 Markus Naslund .40 1.00
91 Henrik Sedin .25 .60
92 Daniel Sedin .25 .60
93 Ryan Getzlaf .30 .75
94 Jean-Sebastien Giguere .40 1.00
95 Doug Weight .25 .60
96 Chris Pronger .40 1.00
97 Pavel Datsyuk .40 1.00
98 Nicklas Lidstrom .40 1.00
99 Henrik Zetterberg .40 1.00
100 Dominik Hasek .50 1.25
101 Alexander Ovechkin NOT 5.00 12.00
102 Markus Naslund NOT 1.50 4.00
103 Roberto Luongo NOT 2.50 6.00
104 Frank Mahovlich NOT 2.50 6.00
105 Mats Sundin NOT 1.50 4.00
106 Martin St. Louis NOT 1.25 3.00
107 Vincent Lecavalier NOT 1.50 4.00
108 Paul Kariya NOT 1.50 4.00
109 Brad Boyes NOT 1.25 3.00
110 Patrick Marleau NOT 1.25 3.00
111 Joe Thornton NOT 2.00 5.00
112 Evgeni Malkin NOT 4.00 10.00
113 Marc-Andre Fleury NOT 1.50 4.00
114 Mario Lemieux NOT 5.00 12.00
115 Sidney Crosby NOT 8.00 20.00
116 Shane Doan NOT 1.00 2.50
117 Bernie Parent NOT 2.00 5.00
118 Bobby Clarke NOT 1.50 4.00
119 Daniel Briere NOT 1.50 4.00
120 Ron Hextall NOT 2.50 6.00
121 Simon Gagne NOT 1.50 4.00
122 Dany Heatley NOT 2.00 5.00
123 Ray Emery NOT 1.25 3.00
124 Brendan Shanahan NOT 1.50 4.00
125 Jaromir Jagr NOT 2.50 6.00
126 Mark Messier NOT 3.00 8.00
127 Rick DiPietro NOT 1.25 3.00
128 Zach Parise NOT 1.25 3.00
129 Martin Brodeur NOT 4.00 10.00
130 Guy Lafleur NOT 4.00 10.00
131 Larry Robinson NOT 2.00 5.00
132 Saku Koivu NOT 1.25 3.00
133 Marian Gaborik NOT 2.00 5.00
134 Luc Robitaille NOT 1.25 3.00
135 Tomas Vokoun NOT 1.25 3.00
136 Grant Fuhr NOT 2.50 6.00
137 Jari Kurri NOT 1.50 4.00
138 Wayne Gretzky NOT 8.00 20.00
139 Henrik Zetterberg NOT 1.50 4.00
140 Dominik Hasek NOT 2.00 5.00
141 Gordie Howe NOT 4.00 10.00
142 Nicklas Lidstrom NOT 1.50 4.00
143 Mike Modano NOT 1.50 4.00
144 Rick Nash NOT 1.50 4.00
145 Paul Stastny NOT 1.50 4.00
146 Joe Sakic NOT 3.00 8.00
147 Bobby Hull NOT 2.50 6.00
148 Stan Mikita NOT 1.50 4.00
149 Tony Esposito NOT 2.50 6.00
150 Jarome Iginla NOT 2.50 6.00
151 Miikka Kiprusoff NOT 2.00 5.00
152 Gilbert Perreault NOT 1.25 3.00
153 Thomas Vanek NOT 1.25 3.00
154 Bobby Orr NOT 6.00 15.00
155 Johnny Bucyk NOT 1.00 2.50
156 Patrice Bergeron NOT 1.50 4.00
157 Phil Esposito NOT 2.50 6.00
158 Ray Bourque NOT 2.00 5.00
159 Jean-Sebastien Giguere HK 1.50 4.00
160 Ryan Getzlaf NOT 1.25 3.00
161 Petteri Wirtanen RC 2.50 6.00
162 Kent Huskins RC 2.50 6.00
163 Mike Weber RC 2.50 6.00
164 Mark Mancari RC 3.00 8.00
165 Kris Russell RC 4.00 10.00
166 Matt Keetley RC 3.00 8.00
167 David Moss RC 4.00 10.00
168 Magnus Johansson RC 2.50 6.00
169 David Koci RC 2.50 6.00
170 Jeff Finger RC 2.50 6.00
171 Tomas Popperle RC 3.00 8.00
172 Chris Conner RC 2.50 6.00
173 Joel Lundqvist RC 2.50 6.00
174 Matt Ellis RC 2.50 6.00
175 Bryan Young RC 2.50 6.00
176 Liam Reddox RC 2.50 6.00
177 Jonathan Quick RC 10.00 25.00
178 Cal Clutterbuck RC 2.50 6.00
179 Sergei Kostitsyn RC 8.00 20.00
180 Ryan O'Byrne RC 4.00 10.00
181 Mark Fraser RC 2.50 6.00
182 Cody Bass RC 3.00 8.00
183 Riley Cote RC 3.00 8.00
184 Craig Weller RC 2.50 6.00
185 Daniel Winnik RC 2.50 6.00
186 Tyler Kennedy RC 4.00 10.00
187 Lukas Kaspar RC 2.50 6.00
188 Tomas Plihal RC 3.00 8.00
189 Mike Lundin RC 2.50 6.00
190 Chris Bourque RC 3.00 8.00
191 Jonas Hiller AU RC 10.00 25.00
192 Drew Miller AU RC 4.00 10.00
193 Bobby Ryan AU RC 20.00 50.00
194 Ryan Carter AU RC 5.00 12.00
195 Bryan Little AU RC 6.00 15.00
196 Brett Sterling AU RC 4.00 10.00
197 Tobias Enstrom AU RC 6.00 15.00
198 Ondrej Pavelec AU RC 6.00 15.00
199 Milan Lucic AU RC 10.00 25.00
200 David Krejci AU RC 8.00 20.00
201 Tuukka Rask AU RC EXCH 75.00 150.00
202 Curtis McElhinney AU RC 5.00 12.00
203 Jonathan Toews AU RC 60.00 120.00
204 Patrick Kane AU RC 50.00 100.00
205 Jaroslav Hlinka AU RC 5.00 12.00
206 Tyler Weiman AU RC 5.00 12.00
207 Jonathan Sigalet AU RC 4.00 10.00
208 Jared Boll AU RC 4.00 10.00
209 Marc Methot AU RC 4.00 10.00
210 Matt Niskanen AU RC 4.00 10.00
211 Tobias Stephan AU RC 5.00 12.00
212 Andrew Cogliano AU RC 10.00 25.00
213 Sam Gagner AU RC 8.00 20.00
214 Tom Gilbert AU RC 5.00 12.00
215 Rob Schremp AU RC 5.00 12.00
216 Cory Murphy AU RC 4.00 10.00
217 Stefan Meyer AU RC 4.00 10.00
218 Jack Johnson AU RC 6.00 15.00
219 Jonathan Bernier AU RC 10.00 25.00
220 Lauri Tukonen AU RC 4.00 10.00
221 Petr Kalus AU RC 4.00 10.00
222 James Sheppard AU RC 4.00 10.00
223 Jaroslav Halak AU RC 30.00 60.00
224 Kyle Chipchura AU RC 6.00 15.00
225 Carey Price AU RC 50.00 100.00
226 Ville Koistinen AU RC 4.00 10.00
227 Nicklas Bergfors AU RC 5.00 12.00
228 Andy Greene AU RC 4.00 10.00
229 Frans Nielsen AU RC 4.00 10.00
230 Ryan Callahan AU RC 6.00 15.00
231 Marc Staal AU RC 10.00 25.00
232 Brandon Dubinsky AU RC 6.00 15.00
233 Daniel Girardi AU RC 4.00 10.00
234 Brian Elliott AU RC 6.00 15.00
235 Nick Foligno AU RC 6.00 15.00
236 Ryan Parent AU RC 5.00 12.00
237 Peter Mueller AU RC 12.00 30.00
238 Martin Hanzal AU RC 5.00 12.00
239 Daniel Carcillo AU RC 5.00 12.00
240 Torrey Mitchell AU RC 5.00 12.00
241 Devin Setoguchi AU RC 8.00 20.00
242 Erik Johnson AU RC 8.00 20.00
243 David Perron AU RC 6.00 15.00
244 Steve Wagner AU RC 4.00 10.00
245 Matt Smaby AU RC 4.00 10.00
246 Anton Stralman AU RC 5.00 12.00
247 Jiri Tlusty AU RC 10.00 25.00
248 Jannik Hansen AU RC 4.00 10.00
249 Mason Raymond AU RC 10.00 25.00
250 Nicklas Backstrom AU RC 25.00 60.00

2007-08 SP Authentic Limited

*LIMITED (1-100): 1.2X TO 3X
*LIMITED NOT (101-160): .6X TO 1.5X
*LIMITED RC (161-190): .8X TO 2X
191 Jonas Hiller AU PATCH 50.00 100.00
192 Drew Miller AU PATCH 12.00 30.00
193 Bobby Ryan AU PATCH 50.00 100.00
194 Ryan Carter AU PATCH 12.00 30.00
195 Bryan Little AU PATCH 20.00 50.00
196 Brett Sterling AU PATCH 15.00 40.00
197 Tobias Enstrom AU PATCH 30.00 60.00
198 Ondrej Pavelec AU PATCH 15.00 40.00
199 Milan Lucic AU PATCH 75.00 150.00
200 David Krejci AU PATCH 15.00 40.00
201 Tuukka Rask AU PATCH
202 Curtis McElhinney AU PATCH 12.00 30.00
203 Jonathan Toews AU PATCH 200.00 350.00
204 Patrick Kane AU PATCH 200.00 350.00
205 Jaroslav Hlinka AU PATCH 12.00 30.00
206 Tyler Weiman AU PATCH 25.00 60.00
207 Jonathan Sigalet AU PATCH 10.00 25.00
208 Jared Boll AU PATCH 12.00 30.00
209 Marc Methot AU PATCH 15.00 40.00
210 Matt Niskanen AU PATCH 20.00 50.00
211 Tobias Stephan AU PATCH 15.00 40.00
212 Andrew Cogliano AU PATCH 40.00 80.00
213 Sam Gagner AU PATCH 60.00 120.00
214 Tom Gilbert AU PATCH 40.00 80.00
215 Rob Schremp AU PATCH 20.00 50.00
216 Cory Murphy AU PATCH
217 Stefan Meyer AU PATCH
218 Jack Johnson AU PATCH 50.00 100.00
219 Jonathan Bernier AU PATCH 60.00 120.00
220 Lauri Tukonen AU PATCH 12.00 30.00
221 Petr Kalus AU PATCH 15.00 40.00
222 James Sheppard AU PATCH 20.00 50.00
223 Jaroslav Halak AU PATCH 40.00 80.00
224 Kyle Chipchura AU PATCH 15.00 40.00
225 Carey Price AU PATCH 250.00 400.00
226 Ville Koistinen AU PATCH 20.00 50.00
227 Nicklas Bergfors AU PATCH 20.00 50.00
228 Andy Greene AU PATCH 15.00 40.00
229 Frans Nielsen AU PATCH 15.00 40.00
230 Ryan Callahan AU PATCH 20.00 50.00
231 Marc Staal AU PATCH 30.00 60.00
232 Brandon Dubinsky AU PATCH 40.00 80.00
233 Daniel Girardi AU PATCH 15.00 40.00
234 Brian Elliott AU PATCH 15.00 40.00
235 Nick Foligno AU PATCH 15.00 40.00
236 Ryan Parent AU PATCH 15.00 40.00
237 Peter Mueller AU PATCH 75.00 150.00
238 Martin Hanzal AU PATCH 15.00 40.00
239 Daniel Carcillo AU PATCH 12.00 30.00
240 Torrey Mitchell AU PATCH 20.00 50.00
241 Devin Setoguchi AU PATCH 40.00 80.00
242 Erik Johnson AU PATCH 60.00 120.00
243 David Perron AU PATCH 50.00 100.00
244 Steve Wagner AU PATCH 15.00 40.00
245 Matt Smaby AU PATCH 12.00 30.00
246 Anton Stralman AU PATCH 12.00 30.00
247 Jiri Tlusty AU PATCH 30.00 60.00
248 Jannik Hansen AU PATCH 15.00 40.00
249 Mason Raymond AU PATCH 30.00 60.00
250 Nicklas Backstrom AU PATCH 100.00 200.00

2007-08 SP Authentic Chirography

STATED PRINT RUN 75 SERIAL #'d SETS
AO Alexander Ovechkin 60.00 120.00
AR Alexander Radulov 15.00 40.00
DH Dany Heatley 12.00 30.00
IK Ilya Kovalchuk 25.00 50.00
JG Jean-Sebastien Giguere 10.00 25.00
JI Jarome Iginla 15.00 40.00
JT Joe Thornton 15.00 40.00
MB Martin Brodeur 40.00 80.00
MG Marian Gaborik 10.00 25.00
MM Mike Modano 15.00 40.00
MN Markus Naslund 12.00 30.00
NL Nicklas Lidstrom 15.00 40.00
PB Patrice Bergeron 10.00 25.00
RM Ryan Miller 12.00 30.00
RN Rick Nash 12.00 30.00
SC Sidney Crosby 100.00 200.00
SD Shane Doan EXCH 12.00 30.00
SG Simon Gagne 15.00 40.00
SK Saku Koivu 15.00 40.00
VL Vincent Lecavalier 25.00 50.00

2007-08 SP Authentic Holoview FX

COMPLETE SET (42) 50.00 100.00
STATED ODDS 1:12
FX1 Alexander Ovechkin 4.00 10.00
FX2 Alexander Radulov 1.25 3.00
FX3 Patrick Kane 5.00 12.00
FX4 Brendan Shanahan 1.25 3.00
FX5 Dany Heatley 1.50 4.00
FX6 Dwayne Roloson 1.00 2.50
FX7 Eric Staal 1.25 3.00
FX8 Evgeni Malkin 3.00 8.00
FX9 Henrik Zetterberg 1.25 3.00
FX10 Ilya Kovalchuk 1.50 4.00
FX11 Jarome Iginla 2.00 5.00
FX12 Jaromir Jagr 2.00 5.00
FX13 Jason Spezza 1.25 3.00
FX14 Jean-Sebastien Giguere 1.25 3.00
FX15 Joe Sakic 2.50 6.00
FX16 Joe Thornton 1.50 4.00
FX17 Marian Gaborik 1.50 4.00
FX18 Markus Naslund 1.25 3.00
FX19 Martin Brodeur 3.00 8.00
FX20 Martin St. Louis 1.00 2.50
FX21 Marty Turco 1.25 3.00
FX22 Mats Sundin 1.25 3.00
FX23 Michael Ryder .75 2.00
FX24 Miikka Kiprusoff 1.50 4.00
FX25 Mike Modano 1.25 3.00
FX26 Nicklas Lidstrom 1.25 3.00
FX27 Patrice Bergeron 1.25 3.00
FX28 Patrick Marleau 1.00 2.50
FX29 Paul Kariya 1.25 3.00
FX30 Phil Kessel 1.25 3.00
FX31 Rick Nash 1.25 3.00
FX32 Roberto Luongo 2.00 5.00
FX33 Ryan Getzlaf 1.00 2.50
FX34 Ryan Smyth 1.00 2.50
FX35 Saku Koivu 1.00 2.50
FX36 Jonathan Toews 5.00 12.00
FX37 Sidney Crosby 6.00 15.00
FX38 Simon Gagne 1.25 3.00
FX39 Thomas Vanek 1.00 2.50
FX40 Carey Price 4.00 10.00
FX41 Vincent Lecavalier 1.25 3.00
FX42 Zach Parise 1.00 2.50

2007-08 SP Authentic Holoview FX Die Cuts

*DIE CUTS: .8X TO 2X BASIC
STATED ODDS 1:144

2007-08 SP Authentic Prestigious Pairings

STATED PRINT RUN 100 SER.#'d SETS
PPCR Jonathan Cheechoo 8.00 20.00
Michael Ryder
PPDH Dany Heatley 12.00 30.00
Shane Doan
PPGS Martin St. Louis 12.00 30.00
Simon Gagne
PPGT Jean-Sebastien Giguere 12.00 30.00
Marty Turco
PPHG Marian Gaborik 8.00 20.00
Marian Hossa EXCH
PPIN Jarome Iginla 15.00 40.00
Rick Nash
PPJJ Erik Johnson 12.00 30.00
Jack Johnson
PPKR Ilya Kovalchuk 25.00 50.00
Alexander Radulov EXCH
PPKS Paul Stastny 15.00 40.00
Anze Kopitar EXCH
PPLS Nicklas Lidstrom 10.00 25.00
Borje Salming EXCH
PPLT Joe Thornton 15.00 40.00
Vincent Lecavalier EXCH
PPMM Mike Modano 12.00 30.00
Joe Mullen
PPOM Alexander Ovechkin 125.00 250.00
Evgeni Malkin
PPRP Corey Perry 12.00 30.00
Mike Richards EXCH
PPTB Patrice Bergeron 8.00 20.00
Alex Tanguay
PPVH Dominik Hasek 12.00 30.00
Tomas Vokoun EXCH
PPVL Thomas Vanek 12.00 30.00
Guillaume Latendresse

2007-08 SP Authentic Rookie Review Autographed Patches

STATED PRINT RUN 100 SERIAL #'d SETS
RRAK Anze Kopitar 25.00 60.00
RRAO Alexander Ovechkin 150.00 250.00
RRAR Andrew Raycroft 20.00 50.00
RRAT Alex Tanguay 20.00 50.00
RRBL Brian Leetch 25.00 60.00
RRCD Chris Drury 20.00 50.00
RRCW Cam Ward 25.00 60.00
RRDC Dino Ciccarelli 20.00 50.00
RRDH Dale Hawerchuk 20.00 50.00
RREM Evgeni Malkin 100.00 200.00
RREN Evgeni Nabokov 20.00 50.00
RRHE Dany Heatley 30.00 80.00
RRJC Jonathan Cheechoo 20.00 50.00
RRJI Jarome Iginla
RRJP Joni Pitkanen 15.00 40.00
RRJT Joe Thornton 30.00 80.00
RRJW Justin Williams
RRKB Kevin Bieksa 15.00 40.00
RRKD Kris Draper 20.00 50.00
RRMG Marian Gaborik 30.00 80.00
RRMH Marian Hossa 25.00 60.00
RRMM Mike Modano 25.00 60.00
RRMR Mike Ribeiro
RRMS Marc Savard 15.00 40.00
RRMT Marty Turco 25.00 60.00
RRNL Nicklas Lidstrom
RRPB Patrice Bergeron 25.00 60.00
RRPS Paul Stastny 25.00 60.00
RRRB Ray Bourque 30.00 80.00
RRRN Rick Nash 25.00 60.00
RRSC Sidney Crosby 150.00 300.00
RRSG Scott Gomez 15.00 40.00
RRST Peter Stastny
RRTH Jose Theodore 25.00 60.00

2007-08 SP Authentic Sign of the Times

STATED ODDS 1:14
STAC Andrew Cogliano 10.00 25.00
STAF Alexander Frolov 4.00 10.00
STAM Andy McDonald 4.00 10.00
STAO Adam Oates 4.00 10.00
STAT Alex Tanguay 5.00 12.00
STBA Nicklas Backstrom 10.00 25.00
STBB Brad Boyes 5.00 12.00
STBC Bobby Clarke 10.00 25.00
STBE Steve Bernier 8.00 20.00
STBF Bernie Federko 4.00 10.00
STBG Brian Gionta 4.00 10.00
STBI Kevin Bieksa 4.00 10.00
STBL Bryan Little 5.00 12.00
STBO Bobby Orr SP 175.00 300.00
STBP Bob Probert 8.00 20.00
STBR Dustin Brown 4.00 10.00
STCG Clark Gillies 5.00 12.00
STCK Chuck Kobasew 4.00 10.00
STCP Carey Price 30.00 60.00
STDB Dustin Boyd 4.00 10.00
STDG Doug Gilmour 8.00 20.00
STDH Dominik Hasek 12.00 30.00
STDT Darcy Tucker 5.00 12.00
STDW Doug Wilson 8.00 20.00
STEJ Erik Johnson 8.00 20.00
STEM Evgeni Malkin 40.00 80.00
STER Loui Eriksson 4.00 10.00
STES Eric Staal 6.00 15.00
STFP Fernando Pisani 4.00 10.00
STGB Gilbert Brule 4.00 10.00
STGF Grant Fuhr 10.00 25.00
STGH Gordie Howe SP 100.00 175.00
STHL Hakan Loob 6.00 15.00
STJA Jason Arnott 4.00 10.00
STJB Jonathan Bernier 8.00 20.00
STJC Jonathan Cheechoo 5.00 12.00
STJG Jean-Sebastien Giguere 6.00 15.00
STJI Jarome Iginla 10.00 25.00
STJJ Jack Johnson 6.00 15.00
STJK Jari Kurri SP
STJP Joni Pitkanen 4.00 10.00
STJS Jordan Staal 15.00 40.00
STJT Jonathan Toews 30.00 60.00
STJW Justin Williams 4.00 10.00
STKA Petr Kalus 4.00 10.00
STKB Keith Ballard 4.00 10.00
STKD Kris Draper 5.00 12.00
STKE Ryan Kesler 4.00 10.00
STKH Kelly Hrudey 5.00 12.00
STLE Brian Leetch 8.00 20.00
STLM Lanny McDonald 5.00 12.00
STMB Martin Brodeur SP 175.00 300.00
STMC Mike Cammalleri 5.00 12.00
STMD Marcel Dionne 30.00 60.00
STMF Marc-Andre Fleury 15.00 40.00
STMG Marian Gaborik 8.00 20.00
STMH Marian Hossa 6.00 15.00
STML Mario Lemieux SP
STMM Mark Messier 75.00 150.00
STMN Markus Naslund 6.00 15.00
STMO Mike Modano 15.00 40.00
STMP Marc-Antoine Pouliot 4.00 10.00
STMR Michael Ryder 4.00 10.00
STMS Marc Savard 4.00 10.00
STMT Marty Turco 8.00 20.00
STNB Nicklas Backstrom 15.00 40.00
STNF Nick Foligno 10.00 25.00
STNG Niklas Grossman 4.00 10.00
STNO Fredrik Norrena 5.00 12.00
STNZ Nikolai Zherdev 4.00 10.00
STOV Alexander Ovechkin 60.00 120.00
STPK Patrick Kane 30.00 60.00
STPM Peter Mueller 12.00 30.00
STPO Patrick O'Sullivan 5.00 12.00
STPP Petr Prucha 4.00 10.00
STPR Brandon Prust 4.00 10.00
STPS Paul Stastny 6.00 15.00
STRA Andrew Raycroft 5.00 12.00
STRI Mike Richards 8.00 20.00
STRK Red Kelly 8.00 20.00
STRP Ryan Parent 8.00 20.00
STRS Rob Schremp 5.00 12.00
STRY Ryan Potulny 4.00 10.00
STSA Miroslav Satan 4.00 10.00
STSB Scotty Bowman 8.00 20.00
STSC Sidney Crosby SP 200.00 400.00
STSD Shane Doan
STSS Steve Shutt 5.00 12.00
STST Martin St. Louis 5.00 12.00
STTK Tomas Kopecky 5.00 12.00
STTV Tomas Vokoun 6.00 15.00
STVF Valtteri Filppula 4.00 10.00
STVL Vincent Lecavalier 10.00 25.00
STWG Wayne Gretzky SP 300.00 400.00

2007-08 SP Authentic Sign of the Times Duals

STATED ODDS 1:288
ST2AN Alexander Ovechkin 75.00 150.00
Nicklas Backstrom
ST2BC Bobby Clarke 12.00 30.00
Johnny Bucyk
ST2BG Mike Bossy 10.00 25.00
Clark Gillies
ST2BK Patrice Bergeron 12.00 30.00
Phil Kessel EXCH
ST2CB Jonathan Cheechoo 10.00 25.00
Steve Bernier EXCH
ST2CG Andrew Cogliano 20.00 50.00
Sam Gagner EXCH
ST2CH Bobby Clarke 20.00 50.00
Ron Hextall
ST2DH Dany Heatley 15.00 40.00
Shane Doan EXCH
ST2FK Alexander Frolov 12.00 30.00
Anze Kopitar
ST2FR Grant Fuhr 20.00 50.00
Bill Ranford EXCH
ST2FS Marc-Andre Fleury 15.00 40.00
Jordan Staal EXCH
ST2GS Marian Gaborik 15.00 40.00
James Sheppard
ST2HM Gordie Howe 150.00 250.00
Mark Messier
ST2IT Jarome Iginla 20.00 50.00
Alex Tanguay EXCH
ST2KL Ilya Kovalchuk 15.00 40.00
Bryan Little
ST2LH Nicklas Lidstrom 12.00 30.00
Tomas Holmstrom
ST2LS Vincent Lecavalier 12.00 30.00
Martin St. Louis
ST2MM Mike Modano 12.00 30.00
Brenden Morrow
ST2MP Andy McDonald 8.00
Corey Perry
ST2MR Evgeni Malkin 40.00 80.00
Alexander Radulov EXCH
ST2NB Rick Nash 12.00 30.00
Gilbert Brule EXCH
ST2NK Markus Naslund 12.00 30.00
Ryan Kesler EXCH
ST2OB Bobby Orr 150.00 300.00
Ray Bourque EXCH
ST2RL Michael Ryder 10.00 25.00
Guillaume Latendresse EXCH
ST2SS Eric Staal 15.00 40.00
Jordan Staal
ST2TK Jonathan Toews 125.00 250.00
Patrick Kane
ST2VS Thomas Vanek 10.00 25.00
Drew Stafford EXCH
ST2VT Valtteri Filppula 10.00 25.00
Tomas Kopecky EXCH
ST2WS Paul Stastny 12.00 30.00
Wojtek Wolski EXCH

2007-08 SP Authentic Sign of the Times Triples

Six cards were released in packs as redemption cards: Malkin/Fleury/Staal, Hasek/Lidstrom/Draper, Nash/Brule/Zherdev, Price/Ryder/Latendresse, Staal/Staal/Staal and Stastny/Wolski/Svatos.

STATED PRIN RUN 25 SERIAL #'d SETS
ST3FMS Evgeni Malkin 100.00 200.00
Marc-Andre Fleury
Jordan Staal EXCH
ST3GPR Ryan Getzlaf 75.00 150.00
Corey Perry
Bobby Ryan
ST3GRL Simon Gagne
Mike Richards
Joffrey Lupul
ST3HLD Dominik Hasek 60.00 120.00
Nicklas Lidstrom
Kris Draper
ST3KJB Anze Kopitar 175.00 300.00
Jack Johnson
Jonathan Bernier
ST3MRT Mike Modano 50.00 100.00
Marty Turco
Mike Ribeiro
ST3MSS Darryl Sittler
Borje Salming
Frank Mahovlich
ST3MVS Ryan Miller
Thomas Vanek
Drew Stafford
ST3NZB Rick Nash 40.00 80.00
Gilbert Brule
Nikolai Zherdev
ST3OJK Alexander Ovechkin 100.00 200.00
Erik Johnson
Patrick Kane
ST3PHP Patrick Roy 125.00 250.00
Martin Brodeur
Carey Price
ST3PRL Carey Price 75.00 150.00
Michael Ryder
Guillaume Latendresse
ST3RGP Dwayne Roloson
Sam Gagner
Joni Pitkanen
ST3SBK Patrice Bergeron 40.00 80.00
Phil Kessel
Marc Savard
ST3SSS Eric Staal 125.00 250.00
Jordan Staal
Marc Staal
ST3SWS Paul Stastny 50.00 100.00
Wojtek Wolski
Marek Svatos EXCH

2007-08 SP Authentic Sign of the Times Quads

STATED PRIN RUN 10 SERIAL #'d SETS
NOT PRICED DUE TO SCARCITY
ST4BYN Jari Kurri
Mike Bossy
Joe Mullen
Mats Naslund
ST4CHI Tony Esposito
Bobby Hull
Stan Mikita
Pierre Pilote
ST4CNG Wayne Gretzky
Marcel Dionne
Phil Esposito
Mark Messier
ST4HRT Guy Lafleur
Phil Esposito
Bobby Clarke
Stan Mikita
ST4JAA Scotty Bowman
Al Arbour
Brian Sutter
Mike Keenan
ST4LWG Bobby Hull
Luc Robitaille
Johnny Bucyk
Steve Shutt
ST4RWG Gordie Howe
Guy Lafleur
Jari Kurri
Mike Bossy
ST4STY Peter Stastny
Marian Stastny
Paul Stastny
Yan Stastny

2007-08 SP Authentic Sign of the Times Fives

STATED PRIN RUN 6 SERIAL #'d SETS
NOT PRICED DUE TO SCARCITY
ST5CPT Nicklas Lidstrom
Jarome Iginla
Patrick Marleau
Markus Naslund
Saku Koivu
ST5EUR Alexander Ovechkin
Alexander Radulov
Evgeni Malkin
Anze Kopitar
Marek Svatos
ST5LEG Wayne Gretzky
Gordie Howe
Bobby Orr
Mario Lemieux
Mark Messier
ST5NET Ryan Miller
Marc-Andre Fleury
Henrik Lundqvist
Cam Ward
Andrew Raycroft
ST5ROK Jonathan Toews
Carey Price
Jack Johnson
Patrick Kane
Nicklas Backstrom
ST5STR Joe Thornton
Vincent Lecavalier
Jarome Iginla
Dany Heatley
Patrice Bergeron
ST5WIN Patrick Roy
Martin Brodeur
Ed Belfour
Tony Esposito
Grant Fuhr
ST5YNG Zach Parise
Drew Stafford
Jordan Staal
Mike Richards
Paul Stastny

2007-08 SP Authentic Sign of the Times Sixes

STATED PRIN RUN 5 SERIAL #'d SETS
NOT PRICED DUE TO SCARCITY
ST6CGY Al MacInnis
Lanny McDonald
Joe Mullen
Hakan Loob
Doug Gilmour
Jim Peplinski
ST6EDM Wayne Gretzky

Mark Messier
Jari Kurri
Grant Fuhr
Marty McSorley
Craig MacTavish
ST6MTL Guy Lafleur
Larry Robinson
Elmer Lach
Frank Mahovlich
Steve Shutt
Scotty Bowman
ST6TOR Frank Mahovlich
Ron Ellis
Red Kelly
Bob Baun
Johnny Bower
Darryl Sittler

2007-08 SP Authentic Sign of the Times Eights

STATED PRINT RUN 3 SER.#'d SETS
NOT PRICED DUE TO SCARCITY
ST8CAN Martin Brodeur
Joe Thornton
Jarome Iginla
Jean-Sebastien Giguere
Dany Heatley
Vincent Lecavalier
Simon Gagne
Patrick Marleau
ST8USA Mike Modano
Zach Parise
Ryan Miller
Chris Drury
Brian Gionta
John-Michael Liles
Ryan Whitney
Scott Gomez
ST8WLD Alexander Ovechkin
Ilya Kovalchuk
Nicklas Lidstrom
Henrik Lundqvist
Marian Gaborik
Dominik Hasek
Saku Koivu
Evgeni Malkin

2008-09 SP Authentic

This set was released on April 1, 2009. The base set consists of 250 cards.

COMP.SET w/o SPs (160) 12.00 30.00
NOTABLES STATED ODDS 1:18
NOTABLES STATED PRINT RUN 999
FW ROOKIE STATED ODDS 1:24
FW ROOKIE PRINT RUN 999 SERIAL #'d SETS
FW AU ROOKIE STATED ODDS 1:48
FW AU ROOKIE PRINT RUN 999 SERIAL #'d SETS
1 Zach Parise .40 1.00
2 Wayne Gretzky 2.00 5.00
3 Vincent Lecavalier .40 1.00
4 Vesa Toskala .40 1.00
5 Mike Cammalleri .40 1.00
6 Tomas Vokoun .40 1.00
7 Tomas Kaberle .25 .60
8 Thomas Vanek .40 1.00
9 Simon Gagne .30 .75
10 Sidney Crosby 2.00 5.00
11 Sam Gagner .60 1.50
12 Shane Doan .25 .60
13 Scott Niedermayer .25 .60
14 Saku Koivu .40 1.00
15 Ryan Miller .40 1.00
16 Ryan Getzlaf .50 1.25
17 Rod Brind'Amour .30 .75
18 Roberto Luongo .60 1.50
19 Rick Nash .40 1.00
20 Rick DiPietro .40 1.00
21 Phil Kessel .40 1.00
22 Peter Mueller .50 1.25
23 Pavel Datsyuk .40 1.00
24 Paul Stastny .40 1.00
25 Paul Kariya .40 1.00
26 Patrik Elias .25 .60
27 Patrick Sharp .25 .60
28 Mikko Koivu .40 1.00
29 Patrick Kane 1.00 2.50
30 Pascal Leclaire .30 .75
31 Olli Jokinen .25 .60
32 Nikolai Zherdev .25 .60
33 Niklas Backstrom .40 1.00
34 Nicklas Lidstrom .40 1.00
35 Nicklas Backstrom .75 2.00
36 Nathan Horton .25 .60
37 Milan Hejduk .30 .75
38 Mike Richards .60 1.50
39 Andrew Cogliano .60 1.50
40 Mike Modano .40 1.00
41 Miikka Kiprusoff .40 1.00
42 Mikhail Grabovski .60 1.50
43 Marty Turco .30 .75
44 Martin St. Louis .40 1.00
45 Martin Brodeur .75 2.00
46 Martin Biron .30 .75
47 Doug Weight .25 .60
48 Miroslav Satan .25 .60
49 Marian Hossa .60 1.50
50 Marian Gaborik .60 1.50
51 Marc-Andre Fleury .40 1.00
52 Marc Savard .25 .60
53 Kari Lehtonen .25 .60
54 Jordan Staal .60 1.50
55 Jonathan Toews 1.25 3.00
56 Jonathan Cheechoo .40 1.00
57 Johan Franzen .25 .60
58 Joe Thornton .60 1.50
59 Joe Sakic .60 1.50
60 Jean-Sebastien Giguere .40 1.00
61 Jason Spezza .50 1.25
62 Jason Pominville .30 .75
63 Jason Arnott .25 .60
64 Jarome Iginla .75 2.00
65 Dustin Brown .25 .60
66 Ilya Kovalchuk .50 1.25
67 Henrik Zetterberg .75 2.00
68 Henrik Sedin .40 1.00
69 Henrik Lundqvist .75 2.00
70 Tomas Plekanec .25 .60
71 Gordie Howe 1.50 4.00
72 Evgeni Nabokov .40 1.00
73 Evgeni Malkin 1.00 2.50
74 Eric Staal .60 1.50
75 Dion Phaneuf .40 1.00
76 Derek Roy .25 .60
77 Dany Heatley .50 1.25
78 Daniel Sedin .40 1.00
79 Daniel Briere .40 1.00
80 Daniel Alfredsson .30 .75
81 Dan Ellis .25 .60
82 Cristobal Huet .40 1.00
83 Alexander Semin .40 1.00
84 Teemu Selanne .40 1.00
85 Chris Osgood .40 1.00
86 Chris Drury .40 1.00
87 Carey Price 1.25 3.00
88 Cam Ward .40 1.00
89 Markus Naslund .40 1.00
90 Brian Campbell .60 1.50
91 Brad Richards .30 .75
92 Brad Boyes .30 .75
93 Patrice Bergeron .40 1.00
94 Mats Sundin .40 1.00
95 Anze Kopitar .40 1.00
96 Alexander Ovechkin 1.50 4.00
97 Alexander Frolov .25 .60
98 Alex Tanguay .30 .75
99 Alex Kovalev .40 1.00
100 Ales Hemsky .25 .60
101 Alexander Ovechkin NOT 5.00 12.00
102 Bernie Parent NOT 1.25 3.00
103 Bobby Clarke NOT 1.25 3.00
104 Bobby Hull NOT 2.50 6.00
105 Bobby Orr NOT 4.00 10.00
106 Mike Bossy NOT 1.25 3.00
107 Carey Price NOT 4.00 10.00
108 Chris Chelios NOT 1.50 4.00
109 Daniel Briere NOT 1.25 3.00
110 Dany Heatley NOT 1.50 4.00
111 Evgeni Malkin NOT 3.00 8.00
112 Guy Carbonneau NOT 1.50 4.00
113 Gordie Howe NOT 5.00 12.00
114 Grant Fuhr NOT 1.25 3.00
115 Guy Lafleur NOT 2.50 6.00
116 Henrik Lundqvist NOT 2.50 6.00
117 Henrik Zetterberg NOT 2.50 6.00
118 Jarome Iginla NOT 2.50 6.00
119 Jason Spezza NOT 1.50 4.00
120 Jean-Sebastien Giguere NOT 1.25 3.00
121 Joe Sakic NOT 2.00 5.00
122 Joe Thornton NOT 2.00 5.00
123 Johnny Bucyk NOT 1.25 3.00
124 Jonathan Toews NOT 4.00 10.00
125 Luc Robitaille NOT 1.00 2.50
126 Marc-Andre Fleury NOT 1.25 3.00
127 Marian Gaborik NOT 2.00 5.00
128 Mario Lemieux NOT 3.00 8.00
129 Mark Messier NOT 2.50 6.00
130 Markus Naslund NOT 1.25 3.00
131 Martin Brodeur NOT 2.50 6.00
132 Martin St. Louis NOT 1.25 3.00
133 Keith Tkachuk NOT 1.00 2.50
134 Mike Modano NOT 1.25 3.00
135 Nicklas Lidstrom NOT 1.25 3.00
136 Patrick Kane NOT 3.00 8.00
137 Paul Kariya NOT 1.25 3.00
138 Peter Forsberg NOT 2.00 5.00
139 Phil Esposito NOT 2.00 5.00
140 Ray Bourque NOT 2.50 6.00
141 Rick DiPietro NOT 1.25 3.00
142 Rick Nash NOT 1.25 3.00
143 Jeremy Roenick NOT 1.25 3.00
144 Roberto Luongo NOT 2.00 5.00
145 Mike Richards NOT 2.00 5.00
146 Miikka Kiprusoff NOT 1.25 3.00
147 Ryan Miller NOT 1.25 3.00
148 Saku Koivu NOT 1.25 3.00
149 Shane Doan NOT .75 2.00
150 Sidney Crosby NOT 6.00 15.00
151 Simon Gagne NOT 1.00 2.50
152 Stan Mikita NOT 1.25 3.00
153 Teemu Selanne NOT 1.25 3.00
154 Patrick Roy NOT 4.00 10.00
155 Thomas Vanek NOT 1.25 3.00
156 Tomas Vokoun NOT 1.25 3.00
157 Tony Esposito NOT 1.25 3.00
158 Vincent Lecavalier NOT 1.25 3.00
159 Wayne Gretzky NOT 6.00 15.00
160 Zach Parise NOT 1.25 3.00
161 Adam Pardy FW RC 4.00 10.00
162 Matthew Halischuk FW RC 5.00 12.00
163 Karl Alzner FW RC 6.00 15.00
164 Brendan Mikkelson FW RC 2.50 6.00
165 Trevor Lewis FW RC 4.00 10.00
166 Michal Repik FW RC 5.00 12.00
167 Chris Porter FW RC 4.00 10.00
168 Brad Staubitz FW RC 3.00 8.00
169 Cam Paddock FW RC 2.50 6.00
170 Jonas Frogren FW RC 5.00 12.00
171 Ben Bishop FW RC 6.00 15.00
172 Ben Maxwell FW RC 6.00 15.00
173 Nathan Gerbe FW RC 8.00 20.00
174 Tim Kennedy FW RC 6.00 15.00
175 Jesse Winchester FW RC 4.00 10.00
176 Simeon Varlamov FW RC 20.00 50.00
177 John Mitchell FW RC 4.00 10.00
178 Max Pacioretty FW RC 10.00 25.00
179 Chris Stewart FW RC 5.00 12.00
180 Brett Festerling FW RC 3.00 8.00
181 Mike Brown FW RC 5.00 12.00
182 Kenndal McArdle FW RC 4.00 10.00
183 Cory Schneider FW RC 8.00 20.00
184 Derek Dorsett FW RC 5.00 12.00
185 Ryan Jones FW RC 5.00 12.00
186 Ty Wishart FW RC 4.00 10.00
187 Theo Peckham FW RC 4.00 10.00
188 Tom Cavanagh FW RC 3.00 8.00
189 Wayne Simmonds FW RC 4.00 10.00
190 Janne Pesonen FW RC 3.00 8.00
191 Luke Schenn FW AU RC 20.00 50.00
192 Zach Bogosian FW AU RC 12.00 30.00
193 Justin Abdelkader FW AU RC 12.00 30.00
194 Ryan Jones FW AU RC 8.00 20.00
195 Brandon Sutter FW AU RC 8.00 20.00
196 Derick Brassard FW AU RC 12.00 30.00
197 Marc-Andre Gragnani FW RC 3.00 8.00
198 James Neal FW AU RC 10.00 25.00
199 Colton Gillies FW AU RC 6.00 15.00
200 Kyle Okposo FW AU RC 12.00 30.00
201 Brian Boyle FW AU RC 6.00 15.00
202 Petr Vrana FW AU RC 8.00 20.00
203 Zach Boychuk FW AU RC 10.00 25.00
204 Kevin Porter FW RC 3.00 8.00
205 Patric Hornqvist FW AU RC 6.00 15.00
206 Nikita Filatov FW AU RC 25.00 60.00
207 Mark Fistric FW AU RC 5.00 12.00
208 Dan LaCosta FW AU RC 5.00 12.00
209 Steve Mason FW AU RC 40.00 80.00
210 Erik Ersberg FW AU RC 6.00 15.00
211 Ryan Stone FW AU RC 6.00 15.00
212 Jon Filewich FW AU RC 5.00 12.00
213 Tyler Plante FW RC 4.00 10.00
214 Matt D'Agostini FW AU RC 10.00 25.00
215 Adam Pineault FW AU RC 4.00 10.00
216 Shawn Matthias FW AU RC 6.00 15.00
217 Viktor Tikhonov FW AU RC 6.00 15.00
218 Nikolai Kulemin FW AU RC 6.00 15.00
219 Blake Wheeler FW AU RC 25.00 60.00
220 Mattias Ritola FW AU RC 8.00 20.00
221 Tom Sestito FW RC 3.00 8.00
222 Darren Helm FW AU RC 10.00 25.00
223 Danny Taylor FW RC 4.00 10.00
224 Josh Bailey FW AU RC 10.00 25.00
225 Luca Sbisa FW AU RC 10.00 25.00
226 Jamie McGinn FW AU RC 6.00 15.00
227 Andrew Ebbett FW RC 4.00 10.00
228 Boris Valabik FW RC 5.00 12.00
229 Oscar Moller FW AU RC 6.00 15.00
230 Jonathan Ericsson FW AU RC 10.00 25.00
231 Alex Pietrangelo FW AU RC 10.00 25.00
232 Robbie Earl FW AU RC 5.00 12.00
233 Ilya Zubov FW AU RC 6.00 15.00
234 Teddy Purcell FW AU RC 6.00 15.00
235 Justin Pogge FW RC 8.00 20.00
236 Brian Lee FW AU RC 6.00 15.00
237 Claude Giroux FW AU RC 20.00 50.00
238 Vladimir Mihalik FW AU RC 6.00 15.00
239 Patrik Berglund FW AU RC 15.00 40.00
240 Lauri Korpikoski FW AU RC 6.00 15.00
241 Michael Frolik FW AU RC 12.00 30.00
242 Alex Goligoski FW AU RC 12.00 30.00
243 T.J. Oshie FW AU RC 15.00 40.00
244 Drew Doughty FW AU RC 20.00 50.00
245 Mikkel Boedker FW AU RC 10.00 25.00
246 Kyle Turris FW AU RC 12.00 30.00
247 Steven Stamkos FW AU RC 75.00 150.00
248 Jakub Voracek FW AU RC 12.00 30.00
249 Fabian Brunnstrom FW AU RC 10.00 25.00
250 Andreas Nodl FW AU RC 6.00 15.00

2008-09 SP Authentic Limited

*LIMITED (1-100): 2X TO 5X BASE
*LIMITED NOT (101-160): 1.2X TO 3X BASIC NOT.
*LIMITED FW (161-250): .6X TO 1.5X BASE FW
STATED PRINT RUN 100 SER.#'d SETS
200 CARD SKIP-NUMBERED SET

2008-09 SP Authentic Holoview FX

COMPLETE SET (42) 60.00 120.00
STATED ODDS 1:12
FX43 Colton Gillies 1.25 3.00
FX44 Teemu Selanne 1.25 3.00
FX45 Ilya Kovalchuk 1.50 4.00
FX46 Marc Savard .75 2.00
FX47 Ryan Miller 1.25 3.00
FX48 Jarome Iginla 2.50 6.00
FX49 Dion Phaneuf 1.25 3.00
FX50 Eric Staal 2.00 5.00
FX51 Patrick Kane 3.00 8.00
FX52 Jonathan Toews 4.00 10.00
FX53 Paul Stastny 1.25 3.00
FX54 Rick Nash 1.25 3.00
FX55 Brenden Morrow 1.00 2.50
FX56 Brad Richards 1.00 2.50
FX57 Henrik Zetterberg 2.50 6.00
FX58 Marian Hossa 2.00 5.00
FX59 Nicklas Lidstrom 1.25 3.00
FX60 Shawn Horcoff .75 2.00
FX61 Sam Gagner 2.00 5.00
FX62 Fabian Brunnstrom 2.00 5.00
FX63 Anze Kopitar 1.25 3.00
FX64 Marian Gaborik 2.00 5.00
FX65 Saku Koivu 1.25 3.00
FX66 Carey Price 4.00 10.00
FX67 Steven Stamkos 10.00 25.00
FX68 Martin Brodeur 2.50 6.00
FX69 Rick DiPietro 1.25 3.00
FX70 Dany Heatley 1.50 4.00
FX71 Mike Richards 2.00 5.00
FX72 Peter Mueller 1.50 4.00
FX73 Evgeni Malkin 3.00 8.00
FX74 Marc-Andre Fleury 1.25 3.00
FX75 Sidney Crosby 6.00 15.00
FX76 Jonathan Cheechoo 1.25 3.00
FX77 Joe Thornton 2.00 5.00
FX78 Blake Wheeler 3.00 8.00
FX79 Vincent Lecavalier 1.25 3.00
FX80 Kyle Turris 2.50 6.00
FX81 Jakub Voracek 2.50 6.00
FX82 Roberto Luongo 2.50 6.00
FX83 Alexander Ovechkin 5.00 12.00
FX84 Nicklas Backstrom 2.50 6.00

2008-09 SP Authentic Holoview FX Die Cuts

*SINGLES: 1.2X TO 3X BASIC INSERTS
STATED ODDS 1:288

2008-09 SP Authentic Limited Patches

STATED PRINT RUN 100 SER.#'d SETS
191 Luke Schenn 60.00 150.00
192 Zach Bogosian 40.00 100.00
193 Justin Abdelkader 40.00 100.00
194 Ryan Jones 25.00 60.00
195 Brandon Sutter 25.00 60.00
196 Derick Brassard 40.00 100.00
197 Marc-Andre Gragnani
198 James Neal 30.00 80.00
199 Colton Gillies 20.00 50.00
200 Kyle Okposo
201 Brian Boyle 20.00 50.00
202 Petr Vrana 25.00 60.00
203 Zach Boychuk 30.00 80.00
204 Kevin Porter
205 Patric Hornqvist 20.00 50.00
206 Nikita Filatov 80.00 200.00
207 Mark Fistric 15.00 40.00
208 Dan LaCosta
209 Steve Mason 175.00 350.00
210 Erik Ersberg 20.00 50.00
211 Ryan Stone 20.00 50.00
212 Jon Filewich 15.00 40.00
213 Tyler Plante
214 Matt D'Agostini 30.00 80.00
215 Adam Pineault
216 Shawn Matthias 20.00 50.00
217 Viktor Tikhonov 20.00 50.00
218 Nikolai Kulemin 20.00 50.00
219 Blake Wheeler 40.00 100.00
220 Mattias Ritola 25.00 60.00
221 Tom Sestito
222 Darren Helm 30.00 80.00
223 Danny Taylor
224 Josh Bailey 30.00 80.00
225 Luca Sbisa
226 Jamie McGinn 20.00 50.00
227 Andrew Ebbett
228 Boris Valabik
229 Oscar Moller 20.00 50.00
230 Jonathan Ericsson 30.00 80.00
231 Alex Pietrangelo 30.00 80.00
232 Robbie Earl 15.00 40.00
233 Ilya Zubov 20.00 50.00
234 Teddy Purcell 20.00 50.00
235 Nathan Oystrick
236 Brian Lee 20.00 50.00
237 Claude Giroux 40.00 100.00
238 Vladimir Mihalik 20.00 50.00
239 Patrik Berglund 50.00 120.00
240 Lauri Korpikoski 20.00 50.00
241 Michael Frolik 40.00 100.00
242 Alex Goligoski 40.00 100.00
243 T.J. Oshie 50.00 120.00
244 Drew Doughty 100.00 200.00
245 Mikkel Boedker 30.00 80.00
246 Kyle Turris 40.00 100.00
247 Steven Stamkos 175.00 350.00
248 Jakub Voracek 40.00 100.00
249 Fabian Brunnstrom 30.00 80.00
250 Andreas Nodl 20.00 50.00

2008-09 SP Authentic Marks of Distinction

STATED PRINT RUN 25 SER.#'d SETS
MDBH Bobby Hull 75.00 150.00
MDBO Bobby Orr
MDGH Gordie Howe 125.00 200.00
MDMB Martin Brodeur 125.00 200.00
MDMM Mark Messier
MDPR Patrick Roy 125.00 200.00
MDSC Sidney Crosby 150.00 250.00
MDWG Wayne Gretzky 200.00 350.00

2008-09 SP Authentic Penned Perfection

STATED PRINT RUN 50 SERIAL #'d SETS
PPCP Carey Price 30.00 80.00
PPDH Dany Heatley
PPES Eric Staal 15.00 40.00
PPHZ Henrik Zetterberg
PPJG Jean-Sebastien Giguere 10.00 25.00
PPJI Jarome Iginla 20.00 50.00
PPJT Joe Thornton 15.00 40.00
PPMG Nicklas Backstrom 20.00 50.00
PPMN Markus Naslund 10.00 25.00
PPMR Mike Richards 40.00 80.00
PPNL Nicklas Lidstrom 20.00 50.00
PPPB Patrice Bergeron 10.00 25.00
PPPK Patrick Kane 25.00 60.00
PPPM Peter Mueller 12.00 30.00
PPRM Ryan Miller 10.00 25.00
PPRN Rick Nash
PPSK Saku Koivu
PPTO Jonathan Toews 30.00 80.00

2008-09 SP Authentic Rookie Review Autographed Patches

STATED PRINT RUN 100 SERIAL #'d SETS
RRBM Brenden Morrow 12.00 30.00
RRCD Chris Drury 15.00 40.00
RRCP Carey Price 50.00 120.00
RRCW Cam Ward 15.00 40.00
RRDH Dany Heatley 20.00 50.00
RRDK Dominik Hasek 25.00 60.00
RREM Evgeni Malkin 50.00 100.00
RRES Eric Staal 25.00 60.00
RRHZ Henrik Zetterberg 30.00 80.00
RRJI Jarome Iginla 30.00 80.00
RRJS Jordan Staal 25.00 60.00
RRJT Jonathan Toews 50.00 120.00
RRMB Martin Brodeur 50.00 100.00
RRMF Marc-Andre Fleury 40.00 80.00
RRMH Marian Hossa 25.00 60.00
RRMM Mike Modano 15.00 40.00
RRMR Mike Richards 25.00 60.00
RRMT Marty Turco 12.00 30.00
RRNL Nicklas Lidstrom 15.00 40.00
RRPK Patrick Kane 40.00 100.00
RRPS Paul Stastny 15.00 40.00
RRRG Ryan Getzlaf 20.00 50.00
RRRM Ryan Miller 20.00 50.00
RRRN Rick Nash 15.00 40.00
RRSC Sidney Crosby 100.00 200.00
RRSG Scott Gomez 12.00 30.00
RRTH Joe Thornton 20.00 50.00
RRVL Vincent Lecavalier 20.00 50.00

2008-09 SP Authentic Sign of the Times

STATED ODDS 1:14
STAP Alex Pietrangelo 10.00 25.00
STBB Brian Boyle 6.00 15.00
STBD Mikkel Boedker 10.00 25.00
STBH Bobby Hull 12.00 30.00
STBO Ray Bourque
STBS Brandon Sutter 8.00 20.00
STCA Carey Price 20.00 50.00
STCW Cam Ward 6.00 15.00
STDC Daniel Carcillo 4.00 10.00
STDD Drew Doughty 20.00 50.00
STDH Darren Helm 10.00 25.00
STDS Drew Stafford 6.00 15.00
STEM Evgeni Malkin 20.00 50.00
STES Eric Staal 10.00 25.00
STFL Marc-Andre Fleury 15.00 40.00
STGH Gordie Howe 75.00 150.00
STHE T.J. Hensick 5.00 12.00
STHZ Henrik Zetterberg
STJF Jon Filewich 5.00 12.00
STJH Josh Harding 5.00 12.00
STJI Jarome Iginla 12.00 30.00
STJK Jari Kurri 12.00 30.00
STJM Joe Mullen 6.00 15.00
STJO Joe Thornton 10.00 25.00
STJT Jonathan Toews 20.00 50.00
STJV Jakub Voracek 12.00 30.00
STKA Patrick Kane 15.00 40.00
STKO Kyle Okposo 12.00 30.00
STKT Kyle Turris 15.00 40.00
STLS Luke Schenn 20.00 50.00
STMB Martin Brodeur 75.00 150.00
STME Mark Messier
STMI Mike Iggulden 5.00 12.00
STMK Mike Richards 10.00 25.00
STOR Bobby Orr 75.00 150.00
STPK Phil Kessel 6.00 15.00
STRE Robbie Earl 5.00 12.00
STRM Ryan Miller 6.00 15.00
STRN Rick Nash 15.00 40.00
STRS Ryan Stone 6.00 15.00
STSA Denis Savard 6.00 15.00
STSC Sidney Crosby 75.00 150.00
STSH James Sheppard 6.00 15.00
STSM Steve Mason 30.00 60.00
STSS Steven Stamkos 40.00 80.00
STST Paul Stastny 6.00 15.00
STTE Tobias Enstrom 6.00 15.00
STTJ T.J. Oshie 15.00 40.00
STTV Tomas Vokoun 6.00 15.00
STVA Thomas Vanek 6.00 15.00
STVL Vincent Lecavalier 25.00 60.00
STWG Wayne Gretzky 175.00 300.00
STZB Zach Bogosian 12.00 30.00
STZH Zach Boychuk 10.00 25.00

2008-09 SP Authentic Sign of the Times Duals

STATED ODDS 1:288
ST2BF Martin Brodeur
Marc-Andre Fleury
ST2BM Steve Mason 25.00 60.00
Derick Brassard
ST2EE Tony Esposito 15.00 40.00
Phil Esposito
ST2GM Wayne Gretzky 250.00 400.00
Mark Messier
ST2HT Bobby Hull 50.00 100.00
Jonathan Toews
ST2HZ Dany Heatley 12.00 30.00
Ilya Zubov
ST2KP Kyle Okposo 20.00 50.00
Phil Kessel
ST2KS Patrick Kane 25.00 60.00
Jack Skille
ST2KT Saku Koivu
Alex Tanguay
ST2LM Mario Lemieux
Evgeni Malkin
ST2LT Joe Thornton 15.00 40.00
Vincent Lecavalier
ST2MT Mike Modano 10.00 25.00
Marty Turco
ST2OB Bobby Orr 100.00 200.00
Ray Bourque
ST2PK Carey Price 30.00 80.00
Patrick Kane
ST2PP Peter Stastny 15.00 40.00
Paul Stastny
ST2PT Peter Mueller 25.00 60.00
Kyle Turris
ST2RC Mike Richards 25.00 60.00
Jeff Carter
ST2RK Luc Robitaille 20.00 50.00
Jari Kurri
ST2SS Jordan Staal 15.00 40.00
Marc Staal
ST2SW Eric Staal 15.00 40.00
Cam Ward
ST2ZH Gordie Howe 60.00 120.00
Henrik Zetterberg

2008-09 SP Authentic Sign of the Times Triples

STATED PRINT RUN 25 SER.#'d SETS
SOME NOT PRICED DUE TO SCARCITY
ST3BHS Josh Harding
James Sheppard
Pierre-Marc Bouchard
ST3BTK Patrick Kane
Jonathan Toews
Nicklas Backstrom
ST3CHS Ron Hextall
Bobby Clarke
Dave Schultz
ST3GND Markus Naslund
Scott Gomez
Chris Drury
ST3GNT Marty Turco
Evgeni Nabokov
Jean-Sebastien Giguere
ST3HN Dany Heatley
Jarome Iginla
Rick Nash
ST3KTI Saku Koivu
Alex Tanguay
Chris Higgins
ST3LBC Butch Bouchard
Guy Carbonneau
Guy Lafleur
ST3LBM Mark Messier
Mario Lemieux
Ray Bourque
ST3MCT Peter Mueller
Kyle Turris
Daniel Carcillo
ST3MRM Mike Modano
Brenden Morrow
Mike Ribeiro
ST3MSG Doug Gilmour
Frank Mahovlich
Borje Salming
ST3OGH Wayne Gretzky
Gordie Howe
Bobby Orr
ST3PMV Ryan Miller
Thomas Vanek
Jason Pominville
ST3RBP Patrick Roy
Martin Brodeur
Carey Price
ST3SSS Eric Staal
Jordan Staal
Marc Staal

2008-09 SP Authentic Sign of the Times Quads

STATED PRINT RUN 10 SERIAL #'d SETS
NOT PRICED DUE TO SCARCITY
ST4500G Jari Kurri
Dino Ciccarelli
Luc Robitaille
Gilbert Perreault
ST4BROS Tony Esposito
Phil Esposito
Eric Staal
Jordan Staal
ST4CNDN Vincent Lecavalier
Jarome Iginla
Joe Thornton
Dany Heatley
ST4FUTR Kyle Turris
Kyle Okposo
Derick Brassard
Claude Giroux
ST4GR8D Ray Bourque
Bobby Orr
Larry Robinson
Brian Leetch
ST4HALL Wayne Gretzky
Gordie Howe
Mario Lemieux
Mark Messier
ST4HAWK Bobby Hull
Patrick Kane
Jonathan Toews
Denis Savard
ST4QBCG Patrick Roy
Martin Brodeur
Marc-Andre Fleury
Jean-Sebastien Giguere

2008-09 SP Authentic Sign of the Times Fives

STATED PRINT RUN 7 SERIAL #'d SETS
NOT PRICED DUE TO SCARCITY
ST5PTS Wayne Gretzky
Gordie Howe
Marcel Dionne
Phil Esposito
Mark Messier
ST52WAY Bobby Orr
Ray Bourque
Larry Robinson
Al MacInnis
Nicklas Lidstrom
ST5600G Mario Lemieux
Bobby Hull
Luc Robitaille
Dino Ciccarelli
Jari Kurri
ST5NEXT Carey Price
Jonathan Toews
Patrick Kane
Nicklas Backstrom
Peter Mueller
ST5QUEBC Patrick Roy
Martin Brodeur
Marc-Andre Fleury
Jean-Sebastien Giguere
Rogie Vachon

2008-09 SP Authentic Sign of the Times Sixes

STATED PRINT RUN 5 SERIAL #'d SETS
NOT PRICED DUE TO SCARCITY
ST6CNDN Joe Thornton
Dany Heatley
Rick Nash
Jonathan Toews
Vincent Lecavalier
Martin St. Louis
ST6CUPG Patrick Roy
Martin Brodeur
Grant Fuhr
Ron Hextall
Jean-Sebastien Giguere
Cam Ward
ST6STAR Wayne Gretzky
Gordie Howe
Bobby Orr
Mark Messier
Mario Lemieux
Bobby Hull
ST6SWDN Henrik Zetterberg
Nicklas Lidstrom
Nicklas Backstrom
Markus Naslund
Henrik Sedin
Daniel Sedin

2008-09 SP Authentic Sign of the Times Sevens

STATED PRINT RUN 3 SERIAL #'d SETS
NOT PRICED DUE TO SCARCITY
ST7HOF Wayne Gretzky
Gordie Howe
Bobby Orr
Mark Messier
Mario Lemieux
Guy Lafleur
Bobby Hull
ST7VEZINA Patrick Roy
Martin Brodeur
Tony Esposito
Grant Fuhr
Ron Hextall
Rogie Vachon
Dominik Hasek

2008-09 SP Authentic Sign of the Times Eights

STATED PRINT RUN 3 SERIAL #'d SETS
NOT PRICED DUE TO SCARCITY
ST8MASKED Patrick Roy
Martin Brodeur
Ron Hextall
Tony Esposito
Grant Fuhr
Dominik Hasek
Rogie Vachon
Carey Price
ST8RIVALS Wayne Gretzky
Mark Messier
Jari Kurri
Glenn Anderson
Lanny McDonald
Joe Mullen
Al MacInnis
Theoren Fleury

2009-10 SP Authentic

ESS PRINT RUN 1999 SER.#'d SETS
(161-200) PRINT RUN 999 SER.#'d SETS
(201-260) PRINT RUN 999 SER.#'d SETS
1 Phil Kessel .40 1.00
2 Luke Schenn .60 1.50
3 Doug Weight .25 .60
4 Drew Doughty .75 2.00
5 Carey Price 1.00 2.50
6 Vincent Lecavalier .50 1.25
7 Joe Thornton .75 2.00
8 Alexander Ovechkin 1.50 4.00
9 Steve Mason .60 1.50
10 Dany Heatley .75 2.00
11 Peter Mueller .50 1.25
12 Henrik Zetterberg .75 2.00
13 Ryan Getzlaf .60 1.50
14 Claude Giroux .75 2.00
15 Tomas Vokoun .40 1.00
16 Roberto Luongo 1.00 2.50
17 Ilya Kovalchuk .50 1.25
18 Mike Richards .75 2.00
19 Jonathan Toews 1.00 2.50
20 Marian Gaborik .60 1.50
21 Mike Modano .40 1.00
22 Eric Staal .50 1.25
23 Pekka Rinne .30 .75
24 Miikka Kiprusoff .40 1.00
25 Jason Pominville .40 1.00
26 Paul Stastny .40 1.00
27 Paul Kariya .40 1.00
28 Mikko Koivu .40 1.00
29 Marc-Andre Fleury .40 1.00
30 Martin Brodeur 1.00 2.50
31 Sam Gagner .50 1.25
32 Nicklas Lidstrom .50 1.25
33 Jakub Voracek .40 1.00
34 Chris Pronger .30 .75
35 Marc Staal .50 1.25
36 Kris Versteeg .50 1.25
37 Martin St. Louis .40 1.00
38 Olli Jokinen .25 .60
39 Martin Havlat .30 .75
40 Jason Spezza .50 1.25
41 Chris Stewart .40 1.00
42 Brad Richards .30 .75
43 Bryan Little .40 1.00
44 Nikolai Khabibulin .40 1.00
45 Derek Roy .40 1.00
46 Bobby Ryan .50 1.25
47 Scott Gomez .40 1.00
48 Shea Weber .30 .75
49 Henrik Lundqvist .75 2.00
50 Johan Franzen .25 .60
51 Tim Thomas .40 1.00
52 Patrick Marleau .40 1.00
53 Evgeni Malkin 1.00 2.50
54 Anze Kopitar .40 1.00
55 Jeff Carter .40 1.00
56 Mike Ribeiro .25 .60
57 Tomas Kaberle .25 .60
58 Shane Doan .30 .75
59 Zach Parise .40 1.00
60 Alex Kovalev .40 1.00
61 Rick Nash .40 1.00
62 Mike Green .75 2.00
63 Andrei Markov .30 .75
64 Marian Hossa .60 1.50
65 Nathan Horton .25 .60
66 Daniel Sedin .50 1.25
67 Kyle Okposo .40 1.00
68 Dion Phaneuf .60 1.50
69 Cam Ward .40 1.00
70 Milan Hejduk .40 1.00
71 Blake Wheeler .50 1.25
72 Patrik Berglund .75 2.00
73 Ales Hemsky .30 .75
74 Kari Lehtonen .40 1.00
75 Niklas Backstrom .40 1.00
76 Thomas Vanek .40 1.00
77 Scott Niedermayer .25 .60
78 Simon Gagne .40 1.00
79 Steven Stamkos 1.00 2.50
80 Jason Arnott .25 .60
81 Chris Drury .30 .75
82 Pavel Datsyuk .40 1.00
83 Nikolai Kulemin .30 .75
84 Ryan Smyth .40 1.00
85 Marty Turco .30 .75
86 Mike Cammalleri .30 .75
87 Sidney Crosby 2.00 5.00
88 Patrick Kane .75 2.00
89 Patrik Elias .30 .75
90 Devin Setoguchi .30 .75
91 Zdeno Chara .25 .60
92 Andrew Cogliano .50 1.25
93 Josh Bailey .30 .75
94 Derick Brassard .40 1.00
95 Daniel Alfredsson .40 1.00
96 Jarome Iginla .75 2.00
97 Rod Brind'Amour .30 .75

98 Semyon Varlamov .75 2.00
99 Henrik Sedin .60 1.50
100 Ryan Miller .40 1.00
101 Alexander Ovechkin ESS 3.00 8.00
102 Bobby Hull ESS 2.00 5.00
103 Bobby Orr ESS 3.00 8.00
104 Bobby Ryan ESS 1.00 2.50
105 Bryan Little ESS .75 2.00
106 Cam Neely ESS 1.25 3.00
107 Cam Ward ESS .75 2.00
108 Carey Price ESS 2.00 5.00
109 Dany Heatley ESS 1.50 4.00
110 Drew Doughty ESS 1.50 4.00
111 Eric Staal ESS 1.00 2.50
112 Evgeni Malkin ESS 2.00 5.00
113 Gordie Howe ESS 3.00 8.00
114 Henrik Lundqvist ESS 1.50 4.00
115 Henrik Zetterberg ESS 1.50 4.00
116 Ilya Kovalchuk ESS 1.00 2.50
117 Jarome Iginla ESS 1.50 4.00
118 Jason Spezza ESS 1.00 2.50
119 Jean Beliveau ESS 1.25 3.00
120 Jeff Carter ESS .75 2.00
121 Joe Thornton ESS 1.50 4.00
122 Johan Franzen ESS .50 1.25
123 Jonathan Toews ESS 2.00 5.00
124 Luke Schenn ESS 1.25 3.00
125 Marc-Andre Fleury ESS .75 2.00
126 Marian Gaborik ESS 1.25 3.00
127 Marian Hossa ESS 1.25 3.00
128 Mario Lemieux ESS 2.00 5.00
129 Mark Messier ESS 1.50 4.00
130 Martin Brodeur ESS 2.00 5.00
131 Martin St. Louis ESS .75 2.00
132 Marty Turco ESS .60 1.50
133 Miikka Kiprusoff ESS .75 2.00
134 Mike Richards ESS 1.50 4.00
135 Mikko Koivu ESS .75 2.00
136 Nicklas Backstrom ESS 1.50 4.00
137 Niklas Backstrom ESS .75 2.00
138 Nikolai Khabibulin ESS .75 2.00
139 Patrick Kane ESS 1.50 4.00
140 Patrick Marleau ESS .75 2.00
141 Patrick Roy ESS 2.50 6.00
142 Paul Kariya ESS .75 2.00
143 Paul Stastny ESS .75 2.00
144 Pavel Datsyuk ESS .75 2.00
145 Rick Nash ESS .75 2.00
146 Roberto Luongo ESS 2.00 5.00
147 Ryan Getzlaf ESS 1.25 3.00
148 Ryan Miller ESS .75 2.00
149 Sam Gagner ESS 1.00 2.50
150 Shane Doan ESS .60 1.50
151 Shea Weber ESS .60 1.50
152 Sidney Crosby ESS 4.00 10.00
153 Steve Mason ESS 1.25 3.00
154 Steve Yzerman ESS 2.50 6.00
155 Thomas Vanek ESS .75 2.00
156 Tim Thomas ESS .75 2.00
157 Vincent Lecavalier ESS 1.00 2.50
158 Wayne Gretzky ESS 4.00 10.00
159 Zach Parise ESS .75 2.00
160 Zdeno Chara ESS .50 1.25
161 Lars Eller FW RC 6.00 15.00
162 Ryan Wilson FW RC 4.00 10.00
163 Aaron Gagnon FW RC 2.50 6.00
164 James Reimer FW RC 4.00 10.00
165 Anton Khudobin FW RC 4.00 10.00
166 Scott Parse FW RC 4.00 10.00
167 Mathieu Carle FW RC 5.00 12.00
168 Alexander Salak FW RC 4.00 10.00
169 Mario Bliznak FW RC 4.00 10.00
170 Steven Zalewski FW RC 3.00 8.00
171 Peter Olvecky FW RC 4.00 10.00
172 Tom Pyatt FW RC 5.00 12.00
173 Ryan O'Marra FW RC 3.00 8.00
174 Deryk Engelland FW RC 5.00 12.00
175 Mathieu Perreault FW RC 5.00 12.00
176 Francis Wathier FW RC 3.00 8.00
177 Philippe Dupuis FW RC 4.00 10.00
178 David Laliberte FW RC 4.00 10.00
179 Shaun Heshka FW RC 5.00 12.00
180 Teemu Laakso FW RC 2.50 6.00
181 Ryan White FW RC 5.00 12.00
182 Victor Oreskovich FW RC 3.00 8.00
183 Davis Drewiske FW RC 4.00 10.00
184 Ryan Vesce FW RC 3.00 8.00
185 Peter Regin FW RC 5.00 12.00
186 Bobby Sanguinetti FW RC 3.00 8.00
187 Tyson Strachan FW RC 2.50 6.00
188 Guillaume Desbiens FW RC 4.00 10.00
189 Mika Pyorala FW RC 4.00 10.00
190 Devan Dubnyk FW RC 5.00 12.00
191 Phil Oreskovic FW RC 4.00 10.00
192 Andreas Thuresson FW RC 3.00 8.00
193 Jakub Kindl FW RC 5.00 12.00
194 Drayson Bowman FW RC 5.00 12.00
195 Johan Backlund FW RC 4.00 10.00
196 Ryan Stoa FW RC 4.00 10.00
197 Braden Holtby FW RC 5.00 12.00
198 Keaton Ellerby FW RC 6.00 15.00
199 Matthew Corrente FW RC 4.00 10.00
200 Alexander Sulzer FW RC 2.50 6.00
201 John Tavares FW AU RC 75.00 150.00
202 Victor Hedman FW AU RC 15.00 40.00
203 Matt Duchene FW AU RC 50.00 100.00
204 Colin Wilson FW AU RC 12.00 30.00
205 Tyler Bozak FW AU RC 15.00 40.00
206 James van Riemsdyk FW AU RC 15.00 40.00
207 Evander Kane FW AU RC 15.00 40.00
208 Michael Grabner FW AU RC 8.00 20.00
209 Erik Karlsson FW AU RC 20.00 50.00
210 Matt Gilroy FW AU RC 8.00 20.00
211 Tyler Myers FW AU RC 25.00 60.00
212 Antti Niemi FW AU RC 25.00 60.00
213 Ville Leino FW AU RC 8.00 20.00
214 Yannick Weber FW AU RC 8.00 20.00
215 Jonas Gustavsson FW AU RC 20.00 50.00
216 Brian Salcido FW AU RC 5.00 12.00
217 Spencer Machacek FW AU RC 5.00 12.00
218 Chris Butler FW AU RC 6.00 15.00
219 Lars Eller FW AU RC 10.00 25.00
220 Benn Ferriero FW AU RC 6.00 15.00
221 Alec Martinez FW AU RC 4.00 10.00
222 Ryan O'Reilly FW AU RC 12.00 30.00
223 Jamie Benn FW AU RC 10.00 25.00
224 Byron Bitz FW AU RC 5.00 12.00
225 John Scott FW AU RC 6.00 15.00
226 Riku Helenius FW AU RC 6.00 15.00
227 Jesse Joensuu FW AU RC 8.00 20.00
228 Cody Franson FW AU RC 6.00 15.00
229 Matt Beleskey FW AU RC 6.00 15.00
230 Dmitry Kulikov FW AU RC 6.00 15.00
231 Michael Del Zotto FW AU RC 12.00 30.00
232 Ivan Vishnevskiy FW AU RC 8.00 20.00
233 Jhonas Enroth FW AU RC 8.00 20.00
234 Christian Hanson FW AU RC 8.00 20.00
235 Mikael Backlund FW AU RC 10.00 25.00
236 Michal Neuvirth FW AU RC 15.00 40.00
237 Ray Macias FW AU RC 6.00 15.00
238 Cal O'Reilly FW AU RC 6.00 15.00
239 Taylor Chorney FW AU RC 6.00 15.00
240 Oskars Bartulis FW AU RC 10.00 25.00
241 Mike Santorelli FW AU RC 4.00 10.00
242 Tom Wandell FW AU RC 20.00 50.00
243 Andrew MacDonald FW AU RC 5.00 12.00
244 Artem Anisimov FW AU RC 8.00 20.00
245 Matt Pelech FW AU RC 8.00 20.00
246 Peter Regin FW AU RC 6.00 15.00
247 Ryan O'Marra FW AU RC 5.00 12.00
248 Joel Rechlicz FW AU RC 6.00 15.00
249 Jason Demers FW AU RC 5.00 12.00
250 Sergei Shirokov FW AU RC 10.00 25.00
251 Jay Rosehill FW AU RC 4.00 10.00
252 Frazer McLaren FW AU RC 4.00 10.00
253 Michael Sauer FW AU RC 5.00 12.00
254 Kris Chucko FW AU RC 5.00 12.00
255 T.J. Galiardi FW AU RC 8.00 20.00
256 Luca Caputi FW AU RC 8.00 20.00
257 Viktor Stalberg FW AU RC 10.00 25.00
258 Perttu Lindgren FW AU RC 6.00 15.00
259 Logan Couture FW AU RC 12.00 30.00
260 Brad Marchand FW AU RC 8.00 20.00

2009-10 SP Authentic Limited Patches

STATED PRINT RUN 100 SER.#'d SETS
201 John Tavares 300.00 450.00
202 Victor Hedman 75.00 150.00
203 Matt Duchene 150.00 300.00
204 Colin Wilson 30.00 80.00
205 Tyler Bozak 40.00 100.00
206 James van Riemsdyk 60.00 120.00
207 Evander Kane 75.00 150.00
208 Michael Grabner 25.00 60.00
209 Erik Karlsson 50.00 120.00
210 Matt Gilroy 20.00 50.00
211 Tyler Myers 75.00 150.00
212 Antti Niemi 100.00 200.00
213 Ville Leino 20.00 50.00
214 Yannick Weber 30.00 80.00
215 Jonas Gustavsson 75.00 150.00
216 Brian Salcido 12.00 30.00
217 Spencer Machacek 20.00 50.00
218 Chris Butler 15.00 40.00
219 Lars Eller 30.00 80.00
220 Benn Ferriero 15.00 40.00
221 Alec Martinez 20.00 50.00
222 Ryan O'Reilly 30.00 80.00
223 Jamie Benn 25.00 60.00
224 Byron Bitz 12.00 30.00
225 John Scott 15.00 40.00
226 Riku Helenius 15.00 40.00
227 Jesse Joensuu 25.00 60.00
228 Cody Franson 20.00 50.00
229 Matt Beleskey 15.00 40.00
230 Dmitry Kulikov 25.00 60.00
231 Michael Del Zotto 30.00 80.00
232 Ivan Vishnevskiy 20.00 50.00
233 Jhonas Enroth 20.00 50.00
234 Christian Hanson 20.00 50.00
235 Mikael Backlund 25.00 60.00
236 Michal Neuvirth 75.00 150.00
237 Ray Macias 15.00 40.00
238 Cal O'Reilly 15.00 40.00
240 Oskars Bartulis 25.00 60.00
241 Mike Santorelli 10.00 25.00
243 Andrew MacDonald 20.00 50.00
244 Artem Anisimov 30.00 80.00
245 Matt Pelech 15.00 40.00
247 Ryan O'Marra 25.00 60.00
248 Joel Rechlicz 15.00 40.00
249 Jason Demers 20.00 50.00
250 Sergei Shirokov 25.00 60.00
251 Jay Rosehill 10.00 25.00
252 Frazer McLaren 20.00 50.00
253 Michael Sauer 12.00 30.00
254 Kris Chucko 12.00 30.00
255 T.J. Galiardi 40.00 100.00
257 Viktor Stalberg 30.00 80.00
258 Perttu Lindgren 15.00 40.00
259 Logan Couture 50.00 100.00
260 Brad Marchand 20.00 50.00

2009-10 SP Authentic Chirography

STATED PRINT RUN 50 SER.#'d SETS
AM Andrei Markov 8.00 20.00
AO Alexander Ovechkin 75.00 150.00
AZ Anze Kopitar 10.00 25.00
BR Bobby Ryan 12.00 30.00
CD Chris Drury 8.00 20.00
CG Claude Giroux 20.00 50.00
DE Derick Brassard 10.00 25.00
EN Evgeni Nabokov 10.00 25.00
ES Eric Staal
JS James Sheppard 10.00 25.00
JT Jonathan Toews 25.00 60.00
MF Marc-Andre Fleury 15.00 40.00
MM Mike Modano 10.00 25.00
MR Mike Ribeiro 6.00 15.00
PD Pavel Datsyuk 10.00 25.00
PK Phil Kessel 10.00 25.00
PM Peter Mueller 12.00 30.00
PS Paul Stastny 10.00 25.00
RI Mike Richards 25.00 60.00
RM Ryan Miller 10.00 25.00
SC Sidney Crosby 100.00 200.00
SS Steven Stamkos 25.00 60.00
ST Jordan Staal 12.00 30.00
SW Shea Weber 8.00 20.00
VF Valtteri Filppula 10.00 25.00

2009-10 SP Authentic Holoview FX

STATED ODDS 1:12
FX1 Alexander Ovechkin 5.00 12.00
FX2 Anze Kopitar 1.25 3.00
FX3 Bobby Orr 5.00 12.00
FX4 Carey Price 3.00 8.00
FX5 Dany Heatley 2.50 6.00
FX6 Eric Staal 1.50 4.00
FX7 Evgeni Malkin 3.00 8.00
FX8 Gordie Howe 5.00 12.00
FX9 Henrik Zetterberg 2.50 6.00
FX10 Ilya Kovalchuk 1.50 4.00
FX11 Jarome Iginla 2.50 6.00
FX12 Jason Spezza 1.50 4.00
FX13 Jeff Carter 1.25 3.00
FX14 Joe Thornton 2.50 6.00
FX15 John Tavares 6.00 15.00
FX16 Jonathan Toews 3.00 8.00
FX17 Marc-Andre Fleury 1.25 3.00
FX18 Marian Gaborik 2.00 5.00
FX19 Mario Lemieux 3.00 8.00
FX20 Mark Messier 2.50 6.00
FX21 Martin Brodeur 3.00 8.00
FX22 Matt Duchene 5.00 12.00
FX23 Mike Modano 1.25 3.00
FX24 Mikko Koivu 1.25 3.00
FX25 Patrick Kane 2.50 6.00
FX26 Patrick Roy 4.00 10.00
FX27 Paul Kariya 1.25 3.00
FX28 Paul Stastny 1.25 3.00
FX29 Pavel Datsyuk 1.25 3.00
FX30 Phil Kessel 1.25 3.00
FX31 Rick Nash 1.25 3.00
FX32 Roberto Luongo 3.00 8.00
FX33 Ryan Getzlaf 2.00 5.00
FX34 Ryan Miller 1.25 3.00
FX35 Sam Gagner 1.50 4.00
FX36 Shane Doan 1.00 2.50
FX37 Sidney Crosby 6.00 15.00
FX38 Steve Yzerman 4.00 10.00
FX39 Tim Thomas 1.25 3.00
FX40 Victor Hedman 2.50 6.00
FX41 Vincent Lecavalier 1.50 4.00
FX42 Wayne Gretzky 6.00 15.00

2009-10 SP Authentic Holoview FX Die Cuts

*SINGLES: 1.5X TO 4X HOLOVIEW
STATED ODDS 1:288

2009-10 SP Authentic Immortal Inks

STATED PRINT RUN 10 SER.#'d SETS
NOT PRICED DUE TO SCARCITY
IIBH Bobby Hull
IIBL Brian Leetch
IIBO Bobby Orr
IICN Cam Neely
IIDC Don Cherry
IIGF Grant Fuhr
IIGP Gilbert Perreault
IILR Luc Robitaille
IIME Mark Messier
IIML Mario Lemieux
IIPE Phil Esposito
IIPR Patrick Roy
IISY Steve Yzerman
IITE Tony Esposito
IIWG Wayne Gretzky

2009-10 SP Authentic Marks of Distinction

STATED PRINT RUN 25 SER.#'d SETS
MDAK Anze Kopitar 20.00 50.00
MDAO Alexander Ovechkin 75.00 150.00
MDBL Brian Lee 12.00 30.00
MDCP Carey Price 30.00 80.00
MDCW Cam Ward 12.00 30.00
MDDH Dany Heatley 25.00 60.00
MDES Eric Staal 15.00 40.00
MDGA Simon Gagne 12.00 30.00
MDHL Henrik Lundqvist
MDJA Jason Arnott 8.00 20.00
MDJB Josh Bailey
MDJC Jeff Carter 15.00 40.00
MDJI Jarome Iginla 25.00 60.00
MDJT Jonathan Toews 30.00 80.00
MDKA Karl Alzner 12.00 30.00
MDMB Martin Brodeur EXCH 60.00 120.00
MDMG Marian Gaborik 20.00 50.00
MDMS Martin St. Louis 12.00 30.00
MDMT Marty Turco 10.00 25.00
MDNL Nicklas Lidstrom 15.00 40.00
MDPD Pavel Datsyuk 15.00 40.00
MDSC Sidney Crosby 175.00 300.00
MDSD Shane Doan 10.00 25.00
MDSG Scott Gomez 12.00 30.00
MDSS Steven Stamkos 40.00 80.00
MDTH Joe Thornton 25.00 60.00

2009-10 SP Authentic Prestigious Pairings

STATED PRINT RUN 100 SER.#'d SETS
PPBS Steven Stamkos 25.00 60.00
Derick Brassard
PPEG Patrik Elias 15.00 40.00
Marian Gaborik EXCH
PPFS Jordan Staal 20.00 50.00
Marc-Andre Fleury
PPGP Carey Price 25.00 60.00
Scott Gomez
PPHH Mark Howe 40.00 100.00
Gordie Howe
PPIS Jarome Iginla 20.00 50.00
Eric Staal
PPKK Phil Kessel
Patrick Kane
PPLD Alex Delvecchio
Ted Lindsay
PPLS Nicklas Lidstrom
Borje Salming
PPMJ Jordan Staal 20.00 50.00
Mike Richards
PPMR Mike Modano 10.00 25.00
Mike Ribeiro
PPMT Kyle Turris 12.00 30.00
Peter Mueller
PPNB Derick Brassard
Rick Nash
PPOB Alexander Ovechkin 40.00 100.00
Nicklas Backstrom
PPPB Patrik Berglund 20.00 50.00
David Perron
PPPV Thomas Vanek
Jason Pominville
PPPW Dion Phaneuf
Shea Weber
PPRS Devin Setoguchi
Bobby Ryan
PPTH Dany Heatley 20.00 50.00
Joe Thornton
PPTT Joe Thornton 25.00 60.00
Jonathan Toews
PPTW Cam Ward 10.00 25.00
Marty Turco
PPVS Vincent Lecavalier 25.00 60.00
Steven Stamkos
PPYM Steve Yzerman 100.00 175.00
Mark Messier

2009-10 SP Authentic Rookie Review Autographed Patches

STATED PRINT RUN 100 SER.#'d SETS
SP STATED PRINT RUN 25 SER.#'d SETS
RRAK Anze Kopitar 40.00 100.00
RRAO Alexander Ovechkin SP 200.00 300.00
RRBL Brian Leetch SP 20.00 50.00
RRCD Chris Drury 15.00 40.00
RRCW Cam Ward 15.00 40.00
RRDH Dany Heatley SP 40.00 100.00
RREM Evgeni Malkin SP
RRES Eric Staal 20.00 50.00
RRHL Henrik Lundqvist 30.00 80.00
RRHS Henrik Sedin 25.00 60.00
RRJA Jason Arnott 10.00 25.00
RRJC Jeff Carter 15.00 40.00
RRJD J.P. Dumont 10.00 25.00
RRJI Jarome Iginla SP 40.00 100.00
RRJT Joe Thornton SP 40.00 100.00
RRLM Lanny McDonald 15.00 40.00
RRLR Luc Robitaille 15.00 40.00
RRMG Marian Gaborik SP 40.00 100.00
RRMH Milan Hejduk 15.00 40.00
RRMM Mike Modano 25.00 60.00
RRMS Martin St. Louis 15.00 40.00
RRMT Marty Turco 20.00 50.00
RRMV Andrei Markov 15.00 40.00
RRNB Nicklas Backstrom SP 50.00 100.00
RRPD Pavel Datsyuk 40.00 80.00
RRPL Pascal Leclaire 15.00 40.00
RRPR Patrick Roy SP 100.00 200.00
RRPS Peter Stastny 15.00 40.00
RRRI Mike Ribeiro 10.00 25.00
RRRO Larry Robinson SP 40.00 100.00
RRRS Ryan Smyth 15.00 40.00
RRSG Scott Gomez 15.00 40.00
RRSI Simon Gagne 25.00 60.00
RRSS Steve Shutt 15.00 40.00
RRSY Steve Yzerman SP
RRTV Thomas Vanek 15.00 40.00
RRVL Vincent Lecavalier SP 20.00 50.00

2009-10 SP Authentic Sign of the Times

OVERALL AU ODDS 1:8
STAC Andrew Cogliano 8.00 20.00
STAE Andrew Ebbett 5.00 12.00
STAK Anze Kopitar 6.00 15.00
STAL Andrew Ladd 6.00 15.00
STAO Adam Oates 6.00 15.00
STAP Alex Pietrangelo 5.00 12.00
STBA Mikael Backlund 10.00 25.00
STBH Bobby Hull 25.00 50.00
STBL Brian Leetch 6.00 15.00
STBM Ben Maxwell 10.00 25.00
STBO Bobby Orr 100.00 200.00
STBR Bobby Ryan 8.00 20.00
STBS Brandon Sutter 6.00 15.00
STCG Colton Gillies 8.00 20.00
STCH Christian Hanson 8.00 20.00
STCP Carey Price 15.00 40.00
STDB David Backes 5.00 12.00
STDC Daniel Carcillo 6.00 15.00
STDS Darryl Sutter 5.00 12.00
STDU Matt Duchene 25.00 60.00
STEE Erik Ersberg 5.00 12.00
STEJ Jhonas Enroth 8.00 20.00
STEK Evander Kane 12.00 30.00
STEN Eric Nystrom 5.00 12.00
STES Eric Staal 8.00 20.00
STFB Fabian Brunnstrom 6.00 15.00
STFO Nick Foligno 6.00 15.00
STGA Simon Gagne 6.00 15.00
STGU Jonas Gustavsson 15.00 40.00
STHL Henrik Lundqvist 12.00 30.00
STIV Ivan Vishnevskiy 8.00 20.00
STJA Jason Arnott 4.00 10.00
STJB Josh Bailey 5.00 12.00
STJD J.P. Dumont 4.00 10.00
STJE Jonathan Ericsson 6.00 15.00
STJH Josh Harding 5.00 12.00
STJI Jarome Iginla SP 50.00 100.00
STJJ Jack Johnson 5.00 12.00
STJS James Sheppard 6.00 15.00
STJT Jonathan Toews 15.00 40.00
STKA Karl Alzner 6.00 15.00
STMA Andrei Markov 5.00 12.00
STMG Marian Gaborik 10.00 25.00
STMI Mikkel Boedker 5.00 12.00
STML Maxim Lapierre 4.00 10.00
STMP Max Pacioretty 6.00 15.00
STMS Mark Streit 4.00 10.00
STMT Maxime Talbot 6.00 15.00
STNB Nicklas Backstrom 12.00 30.00
STNG Nathan Gerbe 8.00 20.00
STOM Oscar Moller 5.00 12.00
STOV Alexander Ovechkin 60.00 120.00
STPD Pavel Datsyuk 15.00 40.00
STPK Phil Kessel 6.00 15.00
STPM Peter Mueller 8.00 20.00
STRI Mike Richards 12.00 30.00
STRM Ryan Miller 15.00 40.00
STSC Sidney Crosby SP EXCH 350.00
STSG Scott Gomez 6.00 15.00
STSM Martin St. Louis 6.00 15.00
STSS Steven Stamkos 15.00 40.00
STST Jordan Staal 8.00 20.00
STSY Steve Yzerman SP 175.00 300.00
STTA John Tavares 30.00 80.00
STTK Tim Kennedy 6.00 15.00
STTV Thomas Vanek 6.00 15.00
STTW Ty Wishart 6.00 15.00
STVF Valtteri Filppula 6.00 15.00
STVH Victor Hedman 12.00 30.00
STVL Ville Leino 8.00 20.00
STVR James van Riemsdyk 15.00 40.00
STWE Shea Weber 5.00 12.00

2009-10 SP Authentic Sign of the Times Duals

OVERALL AU ODDS 1:8
ST2AW Jason Arnott
Colin Wilson
ST2BH Josh Harding
Niklas Backstrom
ST2BL Luca Sbisa
Brian Salcido
ST2BO David Backes
T.J. Oshie
ST2BW Patrice Bergeron
Blake Wheeler
ST2DC Matt Duchene 40.00 100.00
Paul Stastny
ST2DM Peter Mueller 12.00 30.00
Shane Doan
ST2DW Shea Weber 8.00 20.00
J.P. Dumont
ST2EO Phil Esposito 75.00 150.00
Bobby Orr
ST2EZ Eric Staal
Zach Boychuk
ST2FF Mike Foligno 10.00 25.00
Nick Foligno
ST2FK Jari Kurri 60.00 120.00
Grant Fuhr
ST2FL Valtteri Filppula 12.00 30.00
Ville Leino
ST2FM Nikita Filatov
Maxsim Mayorov
ST2FV Ivan Vishnevskiy
Mark Fistric
ST2GA Mike Green
Karl Alzner
ST2GG Colton Gillies
Clark Gillies
ST2GL Marian Gaborik
Henrik Lundqvist
ST2GS Luke Schenn
Jonas Gustavsson
ST2HB Tyler Bozak 25.00 60.00
Christian Hanson
ST2HD Alex Delvecchio
Gordie Howe
ST2HT Jonathan Toews 40.00 100.00
Bobby Hull
ST2IB Jarome Iginla 15.00 40.00
Mikael Backlund
ST2JD Drew Doughty
Jack Johnson
ST2KM Anze Kopitar
Oscar Moller
ST2LE Jonathan Ericsson 12.00 30.00
Nicklas Lidstrom
ST2LF Nick Foligno 10.00 25.00
Pascal Leclaire
ST2LG Scott Gomez
Maxim Lapierre
ST2LM Brian Leetch
Mark Messier
ST2LP Max Pacioretty
Maxim Lapierre
ST2MA Artem Anisimov
Marian Gaborik
ST2MM Tyler Myers 40.00 100.00
Ryan Miller
ST2MP Carey Price 25.00 60.00
Andrei Markov
ST2MW Andrei Markov
Yannick Weber
ST2NC Kris Chucko
Eric Nystrom
ST2NV Michal Neuvirth
Semyon Varlamov
ST2NW Cam Neely
Blake Wheeler
ST2OC Patrick O'Sullivan
Andrew Cogliano
ST2OM Alexander Ovechkin 100.00 200.00
Evgeni Malkin
ST2PL Chris Phillips
Brian Lee
ST2PP Dion Phaneuf
Matt Pelech
ST2RB Matt Beleskey
Bobby Ryan
ST2RC Daniel Carcillo
Mike Richards
ST2SB Mark Streit 15.00 40.00
Josh Bailey
ST2SG James Sheppard
Colton Gillies
ST2SM Matt Stajan 8.00 20.00
John Mitchell
ST2SS Peter Stastny 10.00 25.00
Paul Stastny
ST2ST Steven Stamkos 25.00 60.00
Martin St. Louis
ST2SU Brandon Sutter 10.00 25.00
Brent Sutter
ST2TC Luca Caputi 12.00 30.00
Maxime Talbot
ST2TS Maxime Talbot 20.00 50.00
Jordan Staal
ST2VB Zach Bogosian
Boris Valabik
ST2VK Tim Kennedy
Thomas Vanek
ST2VW Tomas Vokoun
Stephen Weiss
ST2YB Steve Yzerman 75.00 150.00
Scotty Bowman

2009-10 SP Authentic Sign of the Times Eights

STATED PRINT RUN 5 SER.#'d SETS
NOT PRICED DUE TO SCARCITY
ST8BOS Blake Wheeler
Cam Neely
Bobby Orr
Johnny Bucyk
Phil Esposito
Michael Ryder
Ray Bourque
Patrice Bergeron
ST8CHI Tony Esposito
Denis Savard
Bobby Hull
Andrew Ladd
Doug Wilson
Cam Barker
Jonathan Toews
Patrick Kane
ST8DET Pavel Datsyuk
Tomas Holmstrom
Ted Lindsay
Henrik Zetterberg
Steve Yzerman
Nicklas Lidstrom
Gordie Howe
Valtteri Filppula
ST8MTL Patrick Roy
Scott Gomez
Jean Beliveau
Steve Shutt
Andrei Markov
Butch Bouchard
Larry Robinson
Carey Price
ST8NYR Brian Leetch
Marian Gaborik
Harry Howell
Chris Drury
Henrik Lundqvist
Mark Messier
Marc Staal
Artem Anisimov
ST8TOR Luke Schenn
Borje Salming
Lanny McDonald
Matt Stajan
Doug Gilmour
Johnny Bower
Phil Kessel
Ron Ellis

2009-10 SP Authentic Sign of the Times Fives

STATED PRINT RUN 8 SER.#'d SETS
NOT PRICED DUE TO SCARCITY
ST52002 Chris Higgins
Pierre-Marc Bouchard
Eric Nystrom
Cam Ward
Rick Nash
ST5QUE1 Gilbert Perreault
Guy Lafleur
Vincent Lecavalier
Marc-Andre Fleury
Mario Lemieux
ST52003A Marc-Andre Fleury
Thomas Vanek
Eric Staal
Dion Phaneuf
Nathan Horton
ST52003B Ryan Kesler
Dion Phaneuf
Steve Bernier
Jeff Carter
Mike Richards
ST52004A Blake Wheeler
Alexander Ovechkin
Cam Barker
Andrew Ladd
Evgeni Malkin
ST52004B Kris Chucko
Drew Stafford
Cory Schneider
Boris Valabik
Mike Green
ST52005A Kenndal McArdle
Anze Kopitar
T.J. Oshie
Devin Setoguchi
Bobby Ryan
ST52005B Brian Lee
Matt Pelech
Jack Johnson
Matt Niskanen
Marc Staal
ST52006A Jonathan Toews
Nicklas Backstrom
Phil Kessel
Jordan Staal
Derick Brassard
ST52006B Peter Mueller
Jonathan Bernier
Michael Frolik
Riku Helenius
Kyle Okposo
ST52006C Nick Foligno
Ty Wishart
Claude Giroux
Trevor Lewis
Chris Stewart
ST52007A Kyle Turris
Jakub Voracek
Karl Alzner
Patrick Kane
Sam Gagner
ST52007B Max Pacioretty
Mikael Backlund
Brandon Sutter
David Perron
Colton Gillies
ST52008A Zach Boychuk
Nikita Filatov
Mikkel Boedker
Steven Stamkos
Josh Bailey
ST52008B Luca Sbisa
Zach Bogosian
Alex Pietrangelo
Luke Schenn
Drew Doughty
ST5FIRST Steven Stamkos
Dale Hawerchuk
Mike Modano
Joe Thornton
Mario Lemieux

2009-10 SP Authentic Sign of the Times Quads

STATED PRINT RUN 10 SER.#'d SETS
NOT PRICED DUE TO SCARCITY
ST4SC07 Ryan Getzlaf
Jean-Sebastien Giguere
Chris Phillips
Dany Heatley
ST4SC09 Pavel Datsyuk
Nicklas Lidstrom
Maxime Talbot
Marc-Andre Fleury
ST4SC71 Rogie Vachon
Jean Beliveau
Tony Esposito
Bobby Hull
ST4SC74 Rick MacLeish
Bobby Orr
Bobby Clarke
Phil Esposito
ST4SC77 Johnny Bucyk
Terry O'Reilly
Steve Shutt
Larry Robinson
ST4SC80 Bobby Clarke
Rick MacLeish
Mike Bossy
Denis Potvin
ST4SC84 Denis Potvin
Bob Bourne
Grant Fuhr
Wayne Gretzky
ST4SC87 Jari Kurri
Grant Fuhr
Ron Hextall
Ron Sutter
ST4SC89 Patrick Roy
Guy Carbonneau
Doug Gilmour
Al MacInnis
ST4SC90 Jari Kurri
Mark Messier
Cam Neely
Ray Bourque
ST4SC91 Mike Modano
Larry Murphy
Mario Lemieux
Joe Mullen
ST4SC97 Nicklas Lidstrom
Steve Yzerman
Dale Hawerchuk
Ron Hextall

2009-10 SP Authentic Sign of the Times Sevens

STATED PRINT RUN 6 SER.#'d SETS
NOT PRICED DUE TO SCARCITY
ST7BYNG Joe Mullen
Gilbert Perreault
Marcel Dionne
Alex Delvecchio
Pavel Datsyuk
Johnny Bucyk
Mike Bossy
ST7CLDR Alexander Ovechkin
Patrick Kane
Dany Heatley
Scott Gomez
Chris Drury
Evgeni Malkin
Steve Mason
ST7CONN Evgeni Malkin
Cam Ward
Patrick Roy
Jean-Sebastien Giguere
Henrik Zetterberg
Nicklas Lidstrom
Steve Yzerman
ST7HART Alexander Ovechkin
Martin St. Louis
Wayne Gretzky
Mark Messier
Gordie Howe
Joe Thornton
Mario Lemieux
ST7RCRD Jonathan Cheechoo
Milan Hejduk
Rick Nash
Jarome Iginla
Ilya Kovalchuk
Alexander Ovechkin
Vincent Lecavalier
ST7ROSS Alexander Ovechkin
Martin St. Louis
Wayne Gretzky
Jarome Iginla
Evgeni Malkin
Joe Thornton
Mario Lemieux
ST7SLKE Michael Peca
Doug Gilmour
Guy Carbonneau
Steve Yzerman
Kris Draper
Pavel Datsyuk
Bobby Clarke
ST7VZNA Ron Hextall
Rogie Vachon
Patrick Roy
Grant Fuhr
Tony Esposito
Johnny Bower
Martin Brodeur

2009-10 SP Authentic Sign of the Times Sixes

STATED PRINT RUN 7 SER.#'d SETS
NOT PRICED DUE TO SCARCITY
ST600S1 Ryan Smyth
Joe Thornton
Jarome Iginla
Dion Phaneuf
Shea Weber
Marc-Andre Fleury
ST600S2 Semyon Varlamov
Alexander Ovechkin
Andrei Markov
Evgeni Malkin
Ivan Vishnevskiy
Pavel Datsyuk
ST600S3 Henrik Lundqvist
Nicklas Backstrom
Nicklas Lidstrom
Johan Franzen
Henrik Zetterberg
Niklas Kronwall
ST600S5 Ryan Miller
Phil Kessel
Jack Johnson
Patrick Kane
Zach Bogosian
Patrick O'Sullivan
ST670S1 Tony Esposito
Larry Robinson
Steve Shutt
Bobby Orr
Phil Esposito
Mike Bossy
ST670S2 Johnny Bucyk
Brad Park
Bobby Clarke
Guy Lafleur
Borje Salming
Rogie Vachon
ST680S1 Patrick Roy
Wayne Gretzky
Jari Kurri
Glenn Anderson
Ray Bourque
Rod Langway
ST690S1 Patrick Roy
Luc Robitaille
Brian Leetch
Mark Messier
Ray Bourque
Cam Neely

2009-10 SP Authentic Sign of the Times Triples

STATED PRINT RUN 25 SER.#'d SETS
ST3CGR Mike Richards
Simon Gagne
Bobby Clarke
ST3DOM Pavel Datsyuk 200.00 300.00
Alexander Ovechkin
Evgeni Malkin
ST3FME Grant Fuhr 60.00 120.00
Ryan Miller
Jhonas Enroth
ST3GSP Max Pacioretty 40.00 100.00
Scott Gomez
Steve Shutt
ST3LPM Steve Mason 50.00 100.00
Carey Price
Pascal Leclaire
ST3LSS Vincent Lecavalier 60.00 120.00
Martin St. Louis
Steven Stamkos
ST3LYG Wayne Gretzky 350.00 500.00
Steve Yzerman
Mario Lemieux
ST3LYR Steve Yzerman
Brian Leetch
Luc Robitaille
ST3MRW Yannick Weber 40.00 100.00
Larry Robinson
Andrei Markov
ST3YZH Gordie Howe 125.00 250.00
Steve Yzerman
Henrik Zetterberg

2000-01 SP Game Used

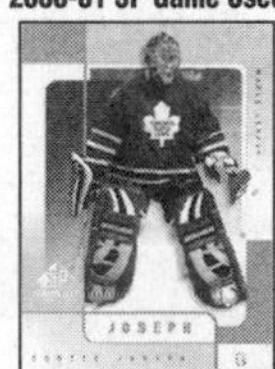

The SP Game-Used set was released as a 90-card set with 30 short-printed rookies, serial numbered to 500. The card fronts featured a full color photo of the featured player. The card design had grey and white boarders, along with silver-foil highlights. The card backs had a small color photo of the featured player along with his statistics and a brief summary of his 2000-01 season.

COMP.SET w/o SP's (60) 40.00 100.00
1 Paul Kariya 1.25 3.00
2 Teemu Selanne 1.25 3.00
3 Patrik Stefan .40 1.00
4 Byron Dafoe .60 1.50
5 Joe Thornton 2.00 5.00
6 Dominik Hasek 2.50 6.00
7 Maxim Afinogenov .40 1.00
8 Valeri Bure .40 1.00
9 Ron Francis .60 1.50
10 Arturs Irbe .60 1.50
11 Tony Amonte .60 1.50
12 Steve Sullivan .40 1.00
13 Patrick Roy 6.00 15.00
14 Joe Sakic 2.50 6.00
15 Peter Forsberg 3.00 8.00
16 Ray Bourque 1.50 4.00
17 Ron Tugnutt .60 1.50
18 Mike Modano 2.00 5.00
19 Brett Hull 1.50 4.00
20 Ed Belfour 1.25 3.00
21 Steve Yzerman 5.00 12.00
22 Brendan Shanahan 1.25 3.00
23 Sergei Fedorov 1.50 4.00
24 Nicklas Lidstrom 1.25 3.00
25 Doug Weight .60 1.50
26 Tommy Salo .60 1.50
27 Pavel Bure 1.25 3.00
28 Trevor Kidd .60 1.50
29 Luc Robitaille .60 1.50
30 Zigmund Palffy .60 1.50
31 Manny Fernandez .60 1.50
32 Jose Theodore 1.25 3.00
33 Trevor Linden .60 1.50
34 Mike Dunham .40 1.00
35 David Legwand .60 1.50
36 Martin Brodeur 3.00 8.00
37 Scott Gomez .40 1.00
38 Tim Connolly .40 1.00
39 John Vanbiesbrouck .60 1.50
40 Mike Richter 1.25 3.00
41 Mark Messier 1.25 3.00
42 Marian Hossa .75 2.00
43 Alexei Yashin .40 1.00
44 Brian Boucher .60 1.50
45 John LeClair .75 2.00
46 Jeremy Roenick 1.50 4.00
47 Keith Tkachuk .75 2.00
48 Jaromir Jagr 2.00 5.00
49 Mario Lemieux 6.00 15.00
50 Steve Shields .60 1.50
51 Owen Nolan .60 1.50
52 Roman Turek .60 1.50
53 Pavol Demitra .60 1.50
54 Vincent Lecavalier 1.25 3.00
55 Curtis Joseph 1.25 3.00
56 Mats Sundin 1.25 3.00
57 Daniel Sedin .40 1.00
58 Henrik Sedin .40 1.00
59 Olaf Kolzig .60 1.50
60 Chris Simon .40 1.00
61 Jonas Ronnqvist RC 2.00 5.00
62 Andy McDonald RC 3.00 8.00
63 Andrew Raycroft RC 5.00 12.00
64 Josef Vasicek RC 2.00 5.00
65 David Aebischer RC 5.00 12.00
66 Rostislav Klesla RC 3.00 8.00
67 Marty Turco RC 6.00 15.00
68 Tyler Bouck RC 2.00 5.00
69 Steven Reinprecht RC 2.50 6.00
70 Marian Gaborik RC 20.00 50.00
71 Scott Hartnell RC 4.00 10.00
72 Greg Classen RC 2.00 5.00
73 Rick DiPietro RC 10.00 25.00
74 Jason LaBarbera RC 3.00 8.00
75 Martin Havlat RC 6.00 15.00
76 Jani Hurme RC 2.50 6.00
77 Roman Cechmanek RC 2.50 6.00
78 Ruslan Fedotenko RC 2.00 5.00
79 Justin Williams RC 4.00 10.00
80 Roman Simicek RC 2.00 5.00
81 Mark Smith RC 2.00 5.00
82 Matt Elich RC 2.00 5.00
83 Alexander Kharitonov RC 2.00 5.00
84 Fedor Fedorov RC 2.00 5.00
85 Marc-Andre Thinel RC 2.00 5.00
86 Zdenek Blatny RC 2.00 5.00
87 Jeff Bateman RC 2.00 5.00
88 Jason Jaspers RC 2.00 5.00
89 Jordan Krestanovich RC 2.00 5.00
90 Damian Surma RC 2.00 5.00

2000-01 SP Game Used Patch Cards

Randomly inserted in SP Game-Used Edition packs, the 29-card set featured jersey patch swatches. The set had 5 combo player swatches. The card numbers carried a 'P' prefix and a 'D' prefix on the combo cards. The cards were serial numbered to 50.

DFR Peter Forsberg 75.00 200.00
Patrick Roy
DJL Jaromir Jagr 150.00 400.00
Mario Lemieux
DKG Paul Kariya 200.00 400.00
Wayne Gretzky
DMG Mark Messier 200.00 500.00
Wayne Gretzky
DOB Bobby Orr 200.00 500.00
Ray Bourque
PBB Brian Boucher 20.00 50.00
PBH Brett Hull 30.00 80.00
PBO Bobby Orr 150.00 400.00
PGH Gordie Howe 100.00 250.00
PJJ Jaromir Jagr 40.00 100.00
PJL John LeClair 25.00 60.00
PJR Jeremy Roenick 40.00 100.00
PJS Joe Sakic 50.00 125.00
PKT Keith Tkachuk 25.00 60.00
PMB Martin Brodeur 60.00 150.00
PML Mario Lemieux 125.00 300.00
PMM Mark Messier 60.00 150.00
PMO Mike Modano 30.00 80.00
PMS Mats Sundin 25.00 60.00
PPB Pavel Bure 25.00 60.00
PPF Peter Forsberg 50.00 125.00
PPK Paul Kariya 25.00 60.00
PPR Patrick Roy 75.00 200.00
PRB Ray Bourque 50.00 125.00
PSF Sergei Fedorov 25.00 60.00
PSY Steve Yzerman 75.00 200.00
PTA Tony Amonte 20.00 50.00
PTS Teemu Selanne 25.00 60.00
PWG Wayne Gretzky 150.00 350.00

2000-01 SP Game Used Tools of the Game

Randomly inserted in SP Game-Used Edition packs, the 38-card set featured game-used jersey swatches. The card numbers had the player's initials in place of the number. The cards were serial numbered to 350.

*MULT.COLOR SWATCH 1.5X TO 2X HI
*EXCL.STARS: 1X TO 1.5X HI COLUMN
EXCL.STAT.PRINT RUN 350 SER.#'d SETS

2000-01 SP Game Used Tools of the Game Combos

Randomly inserted in SP Game-Used Edition packs, the 21-card set featured combo game-used jersey swatches. The cards were serial numbered to 100.

CBF Pavel Bure 20.00 50.00
Sergei Fedorov
CBR Martin Brodeur 25.00 60.00
Mike Richter
CDM Pavol Demitra 15.00 40.00
Al MacInnis
CGS Doug Gilmour 20.00 50.00
Mats Sundin
CGY Scott Gomez 15.00 40.00
Mike York
CHB Brett Hull 15.00 40.00
Ed Belfour
CHG Gordie Howe 75.00 200.00
Wayne Gretzky
CHP Dominik Hasek 15.00 40.00
Michael Peca
CKS Paul Kariya 15.00 40.00
Teemu Selanne
CLB Brian Boucher 15.00 40.00
John LeClair
CLG M.Lemieux/W.Gretzky 125.00 300.00
CLJ Mario Lemieux 75.00 200.00
Jaromir Jagr
CMG Mark Messier 125.00 300.00
Wayne Gretzky
CMN Mike Modano 15.00 40.00
Joe Nieuwendyk
COL Chris Osgood 15.00 40.00
Nicklas Lidstrom
CRF Patrick Roy 30.00 80.00
Peter Forsberg
CRT Jeremy Roenick 15.00 40.00
Keith Tkachuk
CSD Byron Dafoe 15.00 40.00
Sergei Samsonov
CSH Brendan Shanahan 50.00 125.00
Gordie Howe
CSS Joe Sakic 40.00 100.00
Joe Sakic
CYH Steve Yzerman 100.00 250.00
Gordie Howe

2000-01 SP Game Used Tools of the Game Autographed Bronze

Randomly inserted in SP Game-Used Edition packs, the 8-card set featured game-used jersey swatches and the individual player's autograph. The cards were serial numbered to 300.

*SILVER: .5X TO 1.25X HI
SILV.STAT.PRINT RUN 100 SER.#'d SETS
*GOLD: .75X TO 2X HI
GOLD STAT.PRINT RUN 25 SER.#'d SETS
ABR Brett Hull 20.00 50.00
AJL John LeClair 12.50 30.00
APB Pavel Bure 12.50 30.00
ARB Ray Bourque 30.00 80.00
ARL Roberto Luongo 20.00 50.00
ASG Scott Gomez 12.50 30.00
ASY Steve Yzerman 50.00 125.00
AWG Wayne Gretzky 125.00 250.00

2001-02 SP Game Used

Released in mid January 2001, this 100-card set carried an SRP of $29.99 per pack. Each pack contained three cards with a game-used insert card in every pack. The base set consisted of 60 veteran player cards. In addition; there were Rookie Cards numbered 61-100 which were serial numbered to 499.

1 Paul Kariya 1.25 3.00
2 Dany Heatley 1.00 2.50
3 Joe Thornton 2.00 5.00
4 Bill Guerin 1.00 2.50
5 Miroslav Satan 1.00 2.50
6 Roman Turek 1.00 2.50
7 Jeff O'Neill .60 1.50
8 Tony Amonte 1.00 2.50
9 Rob Blake 1.00 2.50
10 Joe Sakic 2.00 5.00
11 Chris Drury 1.00 2.50
12 Patrick Roy 6.00 15.00
13 Ron Tugnutt 1.00 2.50
14 Mike Modano 2.00 5.00
15 Ed Belfour 1.25 3.00
16 Pierre Turgeon 1.00 2.50
17 Brendan Shanahan 1.25 3.00
18 Steve Yzerman 6.00 15.00
19 Brett Hull 2.00 2.50
20 Dominik Hasek 2.00 5.00
21 Luc Robitaille 1.00 2.50
22 Mike Comrie 1.00 2.50
23 Pavel Bure 1.25 3.00
24 Valeri Bure .60 1.50
25 Adam Deadmarsh .60 1.50
26 Zigmund Palffy 1.00 2.50
27 Marian Gaborik 2.00 5.00
28 Jose Theodore 1.00 2.50
29 Mike Dunham 1.00 2.50
30 Patrik Elias 1.00 2.50
31 Martin Brodeur 3.00 5.00
32 Rick DiPietro 1.00 2.50
33 Alexei Yashin .60 1.50
34 Eric Lindros 1.25 3.00
35 Mark Messier 1.25 3.00
36 Marian Hossa 1.25 3.00
37 Radek Bonk .60 1.50
38 John LeClair 1.00 2.50
39 Jeremy Roenick 2.00 2.50
40 Pavel Brendl .60 1.50
41 Roman Cechmanek .60 1.50
42 Sean Burke 1.00 2.50
43 Mario Lemieux 8.00 20.00
44 Johan Hedberg 1.00 2.50
45 Alexei Kovalev 1.00 2.50
46 Teemu Selanne 1.25 3.00
47 Evgeni Nabokov 1.00 2.50
48 Keith Tkachuk 1.00 2.50
49 Chris Pronger 1.00 2.50
50 Pavol Demitra 1.00 2.50
51 Doug Weight 1.00 2.50
52 Vincent Lecavalier 1.25 3.00
53 Curtis Joseph 1.25 3.00
54 Alexander Mogilny 1.00 2.50
55 Mats Sundin 1.25 3.00
56 Markus Naslund 1.25 3.00
57 Daniel Sedin .60 1.50
58 Jaromir Jagr 2.00 5.00
59 Olaf Kolzig 1.00 2.50
60 Peter Bondra 1.00 2.50
61 Ilja Bryzgalov RC 4.00 10.00
62 Timo Parssinen RC 2.00 5.00
63 Kevin Sawyer RC 2.00 5.00
64 Brian Pothier RC 2.00 5.00
65 Kamil Piros RC 2.00 5.00
66 Ilya Kovalchuk RC 30.00 80.00
67 Zdenek Kutlak RC 2.00 5.00
68 Scott Nichol RC 2.00 5.00
69 Erik Cole RC 4.00 10.00
70 Jaroslav Obsut RC 2.00 5.00
71 Vaclav Nedorost RC 2.00 5.00
72 Mathieu Darche RC 2.00 5.00
73 Matt Davidson RC 2.00 5.00
74 Niko Kapanen RC 2.00 5.00
75 Pavel Datsyuk RC 25.00 50.00
76 Ty Conklin RC 4.00 10.00
77 Jason Chimera RC 2.00 5.00
78 Niklas Hagman RC 2.00 5.00
79 Kristian Huselius RC 5.00 12.00
80 Jaroslav Bednar RC 2.00 5.00
81 Nick Schultz RC 2.00 5.00
82 Travis Roche RC 2.00 5.00
83 Martin Erat RC 2.00 5.00
84 Scott Clemmensen RC 2.00 5.00
85 Josef Boumedienne RC 2.00 5.00
86 Raffi Torres RC 5.00 12.00
87 Radek Martinek RC 2.00 5.00
88 Dan Blackburn RC 3.00 8.00
89 Peter Smrek RC 2.00 5.00
90 Ivan Ciernik RC 2.00 5.00
91 Chris Neil RC 2.00 5.00
92 Vaclav Pletka RC 2.00 5.00
93 Jiri Dopita RC 2.00 5.00
94 Krys Kolanos RC 2.00 5.00
95 Jeff Jillson RC 2.00 5.00
96 Mark Rycroft RC 2.00 5.00
97 Ryan Tobler RC 2.00 5.00
98 Nikita Alexeev RC 2.00 5.00
99 Chris Corrinet RC 2.00 5.00
100 Brian Sutherby RC 2.00 5.00

2001-02 SP Game Used Authentic Fabric

Inserted one per pack, this 77-card set featured game-worn jersey swatches from one, two, three or four players. Dual player cards were serial-numbered to 100 each, triple player cards were serial-numbered to 25, and quadruple player cards were serial-numbered to 10. Quadruple player cards are not priced due to scarcity.

*MULT.COLOR SWATCH: 1X TO 1.5X HI
AFAK Alexei Kovalev 3.00 8.00
AFBB Brian Boucher 3.00 8.00
AFBG Bill Guerin 3.00 8.00
AFBJ Brent Johnson 3.00 8.00
AFBN Radek Bonk 3.00 8.00
AFBS Brendan Shanahan 4.00 10.00
AFBU Pavel Bure SP 10.00 25.00
AFCO Chris Osgood 3.00 8.00
AFDH Dominik Hasek 6.00 15.00
AFEB Ed Belfour 4.00 10.00
AFFP Felix Potvin 4.00 10.00
AFGE Wayne Gretzky SP 20.00 50.00
AFGH Gordie Howe 15.00 40.00
AFGR Wayne Gretzky SP 20.00 50.00
AFJB Jaroslav Bednar 3.00 8.00
AFJD J-P Dumont 3.00 8.00
AFJH Jan Hlavac 3.00 8.00
AFJI Jarome Iginla 6.00 15.00
AFJJ Jaromir Jagr SP 12.50 30.00
AFJL John LeClair 4.00 10.00
AFJN Joe Nieuwendyk 3.00 8.00
AFJO Jose Theodore 6.00 15.00
AFJS Joe Sakic 6.00 15.00
AFJT Joe Thornton 10.00 25.00
AFKA Paul Kariya SP 15.00 40.00
AFKP Keith Primeau 3.00 8.00
AFLR Luc Robitaille 3.00 8.00
AFMA Maxim Afinogenov 3.00 8.00
AFMB Martin Brodeur 10.00 25.00
AFML Mario Lemieux 15.00 40.00
AFMM Mike Modano 5.00 12.00
AFMN Markus Naslund 4.00 10.00
AFMN Mika Noronen 3.00 8.00
AFMO Mike Modano SP 10.00 25.00
AFMR Mark Recchi 3.00 8.00
AFMS Miroslav Satan 3.00 8.00
AFMY Mike York 3.00 8.00
AFON Owen Nolan 3.00 8.00
AFPB Peter Bondra 4.00 10.00
AFPD Pavol Demitra 3.00 8.00
AFPF Peter Forsberg 6.00 15.00
AFPK Paul Kariya 4.00 10.00
AFPM Patrick Marleau 3.00 8.00
AFPR Patrick Roy 12.50 30.00
AFRB Ray Bourque 6.00 15.00
AFRD Radek Dvorak 3.00 8.00
AFRF Ruslan Fedotenko 3.00 8.00
AFRF Rico Fata 3.00 8.00
AFRL Robert Lang 3.00 8.00
AFSA Joe Sakic SP 12.50 30.00
AFSF Sergei Fedorov 5.00 12.00
AFSK Saku Koivu 4.00 10.00
AFSS Scott Stevens SP 10.00 25.00
AFSV Marc Savard 3.00 8.00
AFSY Steve Yzerman 10.00 25.00
AFTF Theo Fleury 3.00 8.00
AFTS Teemu Selanne SP 4.00 10.00
AFWG Wayne Gretzky SP 20.00 50.00
AFZP Zigmund Palffy 3.00 8.00
DFAB Maxim Afinogenov 8.00 20.00
Martin Biron
DFBR M.Brodeur/P.Roy 30.00 80.00
DFDS J-P Dumont/M.Satan 10.00 25.00
DFFD Theo Fleury 10.00 25.00
Radek Dvorak
DFFS Sergei Fedorov 20.00 50.00
Brendan Shanahan
DFFS Peter Forsberg 25.00 60.00
Joe Sakic
DFIS Jarome Iginla 10.00 25.00
Marc Savard
DFLB John LeClair 10.00 25.00
Brian Boucher
DFLG M.Lemieux/W.Gretzky 75.00 200.00
DFLK Mario Lemieux 25.00 60.00
Alexei Kovalev
DFMB Mike Modano 15.00 40.00
Ed Belfour
DFNB Markus Naslund 10.00 25.00
Peter Bondra
DFPK Paul Kariya 10.00 25.00
Paul Kariya
DFPL Keith Primeau 10.00 25.00
John LeClair
DFPP Zigmund Palffy 10.00 25.00
Felix Potvin
DFPT Felix Potvin 15.00 40.00
Jose Theodore
DFRF Mark Recchi 10.00 25.00
Ruslan Fedotenko
DFTG Joe Thornton 15.00 40.00
Bill Guerin
DFYO Steve Yzerman 30.00 80.00
Chris Osgood
TFFSR Peter Forsberg 125.00 250.00
Joe Sakic
Patrick Roy
TFLKL Mario Lemieux 125.00 200.00
Alexei Kovalev
Robert Lang
TFLRP John LeClair 30.00 80.00
Mark Recchi
Keith Primeau
TFMNB Mike Modano 40.00 100.00
Joe Nieuwendyk
Ed Belfour
TFYSF Steve Yzerman 125.00 250.00
Brendan Shanahan
Sergei Fedorov
FSRB Peter Forsberg
Joe Sakic
Patrick Roy
Ray Bourque
GYSL Gretz./Yze./Sakic/Lemieux
HGBL Howe/Gretz./Bout./Lem.
YSFO Steve Yzerman
Brendan Shanahan
Sergei Fedorov
Chris Osgood

2001-02 SP Game Used Authentic Fabric Gold

This 55-card set paralleled the single-player cards of the base jersey set but were gold on the card fronts. Cards denoted as short prints in the base set were serial-numbered out of 50 in this parallel. All other cards in this set were serial-numbered out of 300.

*GOLD NON-SP's: .5X TO 1.25X BASIC CARDS
*GOLD SP's: .6X TO 1.5X BASIC CARDS

2001-02 SP Game Used Inked Sweaters

Randomly inserted, this 40-card set featured swatches of game-worn jerseys and player autographs. Single player cards were serial-numbered to 100 unless otherwise noted below. Dual player cards were serial-numbered to just 10 and are not priced due to scarcity.

SCJ Curtis Joseph/50 25.00 60.00
SEB Ed Belfour/50 25.00 60.00
SGA Simon Gagne/50 25.00 60.00
SGH Gordie Howe/50 100.00 200.00
SJL John LeClair/50 15.00 40.00
SMB Martin Brodeur/50 75.00 150.00
SRB Ray Bourque/50 50.00 100.00
SSY Steve Yzerman/50 100.00 200.00
SWG Wayne Gretzky/50 200.00 400.00
ISAK Alexei Kovalev 10.00 25.00
ISCJ Curtis Joseph 15.00 40.00
ISHS Henrik Sedin 10.00 25.00
ISJI Jarome Iginla 25.00 60.00
ISJL John LeClair 15.00 40.00
ISJT Joe Thornton 40.00 80.00
ISMB Martin Biron 10.00 25.00
ISMB Martin Brodeur 75.00 150.00
ISMH Marian Hossa 15.00 40.00
ISMM Mike Modano 25.00 60.00
ISOK Olaf Kolzig 10.00 25.00
ISRB Ray Bourque 50.00 100.00
ISSG Simon Gagne 15.00 40.00
ISSY Steve Yzerman 75.00 150.00
ISVL Vincent Lecavalier 15.00 40.00
ISZP Zigmund Palffy 10.00 25.00
DSBH Ray Bourque
Milan Hejduk
DSBO Martin Biron
Maxime Ouellet
DSGO Simon Gagne
Maxime Ouellet
DSGP Wayne Gretzky
Zigmund Palffy
DSHG Gordie Howe
Wayne Gretzky
DSIG Jarome Iginla
Simon Gagne
DSJT Curtis Joseph
Jose Theodore
DSKB Olaf Kolzig
Peter Bondra
DSLG John LeClair
Simon Gagne
DSLK John LeClair
Alexei Kovalev
DSMA M.Modano/T.Amonte EXCH
DSPB Zigmund Palffy
Peter Bondra
DSST Sergei Samsonov
Joe Thornton
DSWM Doug Weight
Al MacInnis
DSYH Gordie Howe
Steve Yzerman

2001-02 SP Game Used Patches

Randomly inserted, this 55-card set featured patch swatches from one, two or three different players' jerseys. Single player cards were serial-numbered out of 50, dual player cards were serial-numbered out of 25, and triple player cards were serial-numbered to just 10 copies each. Triple player cards are not priced due to scarcity.

PBI Martin Biron 10.00 25.00
PBO Peter Bondra 10.00 25.00
PBS Brendan Shanahan 15.00 40.00
PCJ Curtis Joseph 25.00 60.00
PEB Ed Belfour 20.00 50.00
PJH Jani Hurme 10.00 25.00
PJI Jarome Iginla 20.00 50.00
PJJ Jaromir Jagr 25.00 60.00
PJL John LeClair 10.00 25.00
PJS Joe Sakic 30.00 80.00
PJT Joe Thornton 30.00 80.00
PKP Keith Primeau 10.00 25.00
PMB Martin Brodeur 40.00 100.00
PMH Marian Hossa 15.00 40.00
PML Mario Lemieux 60.00 150.00
PMM Mike Modano 20.00 50.00
PMS Mats Sundin 15.00 40.00
POK Olaf Kolzig 15.00 40.00
PPB Pavel Bure 15.00 40.00
PPF Peter Forsberg 25.00 60.00
PPK Paul Kariya 15.00 40.00
PPR Patrick Roy 60.00 150.00
PPS Patrik Stefan 10.00 25.00
PSA Miroslav Satan 15.00 40.00
PSF Sergei Fedorov 20.00 50.00
PSG Simon Gagne 15.00 40.00
PSS Sergei Samsonov 15.00 40.00
PSY Steve Yzerman 40.00 100.00
PTA Tony Amonte 15.00 40.00
PWG Wayne Gretzky 75.00 200.00
CPAI Tony Amonte 30.00 80.00
Jarome Iginla
CPBA Peter Bondra 20.00 50.00
Tony Amonte
CPBJ Martin Brodeur 75.00 200.00
Curtis Joseph
CPGK Simon Gagne 15.00 40.00
Paul Kariya
CPHB Jani Hurme 60.00 150.00
Martin Brodeur
CPHH Jani Hurme 25.00 60.00
Marian Hossa
CPHL Marian Hossa 25.00 60.00
John LeClair
CPJB Jaromir Jagr 50.00 100.00
Peter Bondra
CPKB Olaf Kolzig 30.00 80.00
Peter Bondra
CPKR Olaf Kolzig 75.00 200.00
Patrick Roy
CPKS Paul Kariya 30.00 80.00
Sergei Samsonov
CPLJ Mario Lemieux 150.00 300.00
Jaromir Jagr
CPLP John LeClair 25.00 60.00
Keith Primeau
CPPG Keith Primeau 30.00 80.00
Simon Gagne
CPSB Brendan Shanahan 30.00 80.00
Pavel Bure
CPSJ Mats Sundin 15.00 40.00
Curtis Joseph
CPSK Miroslav Satan 15.00 40.00
Paul Kariya
CPSR Joe Sakic 150.00 400.00
Patrick Roy
CPSY Brendan Shanahan 100.00 250.00
Steve Yzerman
CPYF Steve Yzerman 75.00 200.00
Sergei Fedorov
TPJBB Curtis Joseph
Martin Brodeur
Ed Belfour
TPKYB Paul Kariya
Steve Yzerman
Pavel Bure
TPLGY Lemieux/Gretzky/Yzerman
TPSLS Sergei Samsonov
John LeClair
Brendan Shanahan
TPSSP Patrik Stefan
Joe Sakic
Keith Primeau

2001-02 SP Game Used Patches Signed

This 20-card set partially paralleled the regular patch set, but included authentic autographs of the featured player(s). Single player cards were serial-numbered out of 50 and dual player cards were serial-numbered to just 10 copies each. Dual player cards are not priced due to scarcity. Please note that not all cards in this set have a parent card in the base patches set.

SPCJ Curtis Joseph 60.00 150.00
SPEB Ed Belfour 40.00 100.00
SPJI Jarome Iginla 40.00 100.00
SPJL John LeClair 30.00 80.00
SPJT Joe Thornton 60.00 150.00
SPKP Keith Primeau 30.00 80.00
SPMB Martin Brodeur 100.00 250.00
SPMB Martin Biron 30.00 80.00
SPMH Marian Hossa 30.00 80.00
SPOK Olaf Kolzig 30.00 80.00
SPPB Pavel Bure 30.00 80.00
SPPB Peter Bondra 30.00 80.00
SPPS Patrik Stefan 30.00 80.00
SPSG Simon Gagne 30.00 80.00
SPSS Sergei Samsonov 30.00 80.00
SPSY Steve Yzerman 75.00 200.00
SPTA Tony Amonte 30.00 80.00
SPTH Jose Theodore 40.00 100.00
SPTS Teemu Selanne 40.00 100.00
SPWG Wayne Gretzky 300.00 600.00
DSPAB Peter Bondra
Tony Amonte
DSPBJ Martin Brodeur
Curtis Joseph
DSPBK Olaf Kolzig
Martin Biron
DSPBL Pavel Bure
John LeClair
DSPGB Wayne Gretzky

Card	Low	High
Pavel Bure		
DSPGP Simon Gagne Keith Primeau		
DSPHI Marian Hossa Jarome Iginla		
DSPKB Olaf Kolzig Ed Belfour		
DSPKBO Olaf Kolzig Peter Bondra		
DSPTB Joe Thornton Martin Biron		

2001-02 SP Game Used Signs of Tradition

This 5-card set ultra short printed set featured "cut" autographs from legendary figures in hockey's history. Actual print runs for each card are listed below and this set is not priced due to scarcity.

LCCC Clarence Campbell/2
LCDH Doug Harvey/2
LCLS Lord Stanley/1
LCSA Sid Abel/2
LCTH Tim Horton/2

2001-02 SP Game Used Tools of the Game

Randomly inserted, this 52-card set featured one, two or three swatches of game-used gear from the player(s) featured. Single player cards were serial-numbered out of 100 (unless otherwise noted below), dual player cards were serial numbered out of 50 and triple player cards were serial numbered out of 35. As of press time, not all cards have been verified.

*MULT.COLOR SWATCH: .5X TO 1.25X HI

Card	Low	High
TAC Anson Carter	12.50	30.00
TBB Brian Boucher	12.50	30.00
TBD Byron Dafoe	12.50	30.00
TCO Chris Osgood	12.50	30.00
TDA Byron Dafoe	12.50	30.00
TDF Byron Dafoe	12.50	30.00
TGF Grant Fuhr	15.00	40.00
TGP Gilbert Perreault/92	20.00	50.00
TJA Jaromir Jagr	15.00	40.00
TJF Jeff Friesen	8.00	20.00
TJH Johan Hedberg	8.00	20.00
TJJ Jaromir Jagr	15.00	40.00
TJT Joe Thornton/36	40.00	100.00
TLE John LeClair	10.00	25.00
TMM Mark Messier	12.50	30.00
TOK Olaf Kolzig	12.50	30.00
TPR Patrick Roy	30.00	80.00
TRA Bill Ranford	8.00	20.00
TRC Roman Cechmanek	12.50	30.00
TRD Rick DiPietro EXISTS?		
TSA Sergei Samsonov/83	12.50	30.00
TSF Sergei Fedorov	12.50	30.00
TSS Sergei Samsonov	12.50	30.00
TSY Steve Yzerman/30	75.00	200.00
TTE Tony Esposito	25.00	60.00
TTH Jose Theodore	20.00	50.00
TWG Wayne Gretzky/71	100.00	250.00
CTCB Roman Cechmanek Brian Boucher	20.00	50.00
CTCH Roman Cechmanek Johan Hedberg	20.00	50.00
CTCS Anson Carter Sergei Samsonov	20.00	50.00
CTDB Byron Dafoe Brian Boucher	20.00	50.00
CTDC Byron Dafoe Gerry Cheevers	20.00	50.00
CTEC Tony Esposito Gerry Cheevers	25.00	60.00
CTFC Grant Fuhr Roman Cechmanek	20.00	50.00
CTFF Sergei Fedorov Jeff Friesen	20.00	50.00
CTFR Sergei Fedorov Patrick Roy	25.00	60.00
CTHD Johan Hedberg Byron Dafoe	20.00	50.00
CTKB Olaf Kolzig Brian Boucher	20.00	50.00
CTKT Olaf Kolzig Jose Theodore	20.00	50.00
CTLJ John LeClair Jaromir Jagr	25.00	60.00
CTRC Patrick Roy Roman Cechmanek	25.00	60.00
CTRF Bill Ranford Grant Fuhr	20.00	50.00
CTRF Patrick Roy Grant Fuhr	30.00	80.00
CTSF Sergei Samsonov Sergei Fedorov	20.00	50.00
CTTD Jose Theodore Byron Dafoe	20.00	50.00
TTDER Byron Dafoe Tony Esposito Patrick Roy	100.00	200.00
TTFCF Jeff Friesen Anson Carter Sergei Fedorov	30.00	80.00
TTFSL Sergei Fedorov Sergei Samsonov John LeClair	40.00	100.00
TTHCR Johan Hedberg Gerry Cheevers Patrick Roy	60.00	150.00
TTKCH Olaf Kolzig Roman Cechmanek Johan Hedberg	40.00	100.00
TTRBK Patrick Roy Brian Boucher Olaf Kolzig	75.00	200.00
TTRFE Bill Ranford Grant Fuhr Tony Esposito	40.00	100.00

2001-02 SP Game Used Tools of the Game Signed

This 22-card set featured swatches of game-worn gear as well as authentic player autographs of the player(s) featured. Single player cards were serial-numbered out of 100 while dual player cards were serial-numbered out of 35.

Card	Low	High
STBR Bill Ranford	40.00	80.00
STGF Grant Fuhr	40.00	80.00
STGP Gilbert Perrault	40.00	100.00
STJH Johan Hedberg	15.00	40.00
STJL John LeClair	20.00	50.00
STJT Jose Theodore	40.00	100.00
STJT Joe Thornton	25.00	60.00
STKP Keith Primeau	20.00	50.00
STLE John LeClair	20.00	50.00
STPB Peter Bondra	25.00	60.00
STRB Ray Bourque	40.00	100.00
STSA Sergei Samsonov	25.00	60.00
STSM Sergei Samsonov	25.00	60.00
STSY Steve Yzerman	75.00	200.00
STTS Teemu Selanne	20.00	50.00
SCBS Ray Bourque Sergei Samsonov	100.00	200.00
SCLT John LeClair Joe Thornton	75.00	200.00
SCPS Keith Primeau Sergei Samsonov	25.00	60.00
SCPY Keith Primeau Steve Yzerman	60.00	150.00
SCRF Bill Ranford Grant Fuhr	40.00	100.00
SCRH Bill Ranford Johan Hedberg	40.00	100.00
SCTY J.Thornton/S.Yzerman	125.00	250.00

2002-03 SP Game Used

Released in March of 2003, this 103-card set carried an SRP of $29.99. There were two subsets; All-Star Flashbacks (51-65) and New Grooves (66-103). The All-Star Flashbacks were serial-numbered out of 999 and the New Grooves rookie cards were serial-numbered out of 750.

Card	Low	High
COMP.SET w/o SP's (50)	60.00	125.00
1 Paul Kariya	1.00	2.50
2 Ilya Kovalchuk	1.25	3.00
3 Dany Heatley	1.25	3.00
4 Joe Thornton	1.50	4.00
5 Sergei Samsonov	.75	2.00
6 Martin Biron	.75	2.00
7 Jarome Iginla	1.25	3.00
8 Jeff O'Neill	.75	2.00
9 Ron Francis	.75	2.00
10 Eric Daze	.75	2.00
11 Peter Forsberg	2.00	5.00
12 Joe Sakic	2.00	5.00
13 Patrick Roy	5.00	12.00
14 Marc Denis	.75	2.00
15 Bill Guerin	.75	2.00
16 Mike Modano	1.50	4.00
17 Steve Yzerman	5.00	12.00
18 Brendan Shanahan	1.00	2.50
19 Curtis Joseph	1.00	2.50
20 Mike Comrie	.75	2.00
21 Roberto Luongo	1.25	3.00
22 Felix Potvin	1.00	2.50
23 Zigmund Palffy	1.00	2.50
24 Marian Gaborik	2.00	5.00
25 Jose Theodore	1.25	3.00
26 Saku Koivu	1.00	2.50
27 Mike Dunham	.75	2.00
28 Martin Brodeur	2.50	6.00
29 Patrik Elias	.75	2.00
30 Mike Peca	.75	2.00
31 Alexei Yashin	.75	2.00
32 Eric Lindros	1.00	2.50
33 Pavel Bure	1.00	2.50
34 Martin Havlat	.75	2.00
35 Daniel Alfredsson	.75	2.00
36 Simon Gagne	1.00	2.50
37 Jeremy Roenick	1.25	3.00
38 Sean Burke	.75	2.00
39 Tony Amonte	.75	2.00
40 Mario Lemieux	6.00	15.00
41 Owen Nolan	.75	2.00
42 Evgeni Nabokov	.75	2.00
43 Chris Pronger	.75	2.00
44 Keith Tkachuk	1.00	2.50
45 Vincent Lecavalier	1.00	2.50
46 Mats Sundin	1.00	2.50
47 Ed Belfour	1.00	2.50
48 Markus Naslund	1.00	2.50
49 Olaf Kolzig	.75	2.00
50 Jaromir Jagr	1.50	4.00
51 Gordie Howe AF	6.00	15.00
52 Mario Lemieux AF	8.00	20.00
53 Wayne Gretzky AF	12.50	30.00
54 Mario Lemieux AF	8.00	20.00
55 Wayne Gretzky AF	8.00	20.00
56 Vincent Damphousse AF	2.00	5.00
57 Brett Hull AF	3.00	8.00
58 Mike Richter AF	2.00	5.00
59 Ray Bourque AF	5.00	12.00
60 Mark Recchi AF	2.00	5.00
61 Teemu Selanne AF	2.00	5.00
62 Wayne Gretzky AF	8.00	20.00
63 Pavel Bure AF	2.00	5.00
64 Bill Guerin AF	2.00	5.00
65 Eric Daze AF	2.00	5.00
66 Alexei Smirnov RC	2.00	5.00
67 Stanislav Chistov RC	4.00	10.00
68 Martin Gerber RC	4.00	10.00
69 Kurt Sauer RC	2.00	5.00
70 Chuck Kobasew RC	4.00	10.00
71 Jordan Leopold RC	2.00	5.00
72 Jeff Paul RC	2.00	5.00
73 Rick Nash RC	15.00	40.00
74 Lasse Pirjeta RC	2.00	5.00
75 Henrik Zetterberg RC	12.50	30.00
76 Dmitri Bykov RC	2.00	5.00
77 Ales Hemsky RC	8.00	20.00
78 Jay Bouwmeester RC	6.00	15.00
79 Alexander Frolov RC	8.00	20.00
80 Sylvain Blouin RC	2.00	5.00
81 P-M Bouchard RC	6.00	15.00
82 Jason Spezza RC	15.00	40.00
83 Ron Hainsey RC	2.00	5.00
84 Adam Hall RC	2.00	5.00
85 Scottie Upshall RC	4.00	10.00
86 Anton Volchenkov RC	2.00	5.00
87 Dennis Seidenberg RC	2.00	5.00
88 Patrick Sharp RC	2.00	5.00
89 Jeff Taffe RC	2.00	5.00
90 Cody Rudkowsky RC	2.00	5.00
91 Tom Koivisto RC	2.00	5.00
92 Curtis Sanford RC	4.00	10.00
93 Alexander Svitov RC	2.00	5.00
94 Carlo Colaiacovo RC	2.00	5.00
95 Steve Eminger RC	2.00	5.00
96 Shaone Morrisonn RC	2.00	5.00
97 Ryan Miller RC	15.00	30.00
98 Levente Szuper RC	2.00	5.00
99 Mike Cammalleri RC	4.00	10.00
100 Stephane Veilleux RC	2.00	5.00
101 Darren Haydar RC	2.00	5.00
102 Lynn Loyns RC	2.00	5.00
103 Mikael Tellqvist RC	4.00	10.00

2002-03 SP Game Used Authentic Fabrics

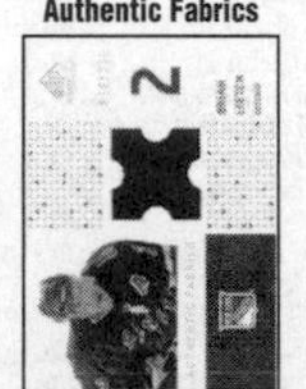

Randomly inserted, this 102-card set featured single or dual swatches of game-worn jerseys on the card fronts. Each card was serial-numbered in silver foil out of 225.

Card	Low	High
AFAM Tony Amonte	3.00	8.00
AFAT Alex Tanguay	3.00	8.00
AFAY Alexei Yashin	3.00	8.00
AFBB Brian Boucher	3.00	8.00
AFBD Peter Bondra	3.00	8.00
AFBG Bill Guerin	3.00	8.00
AFBH Brett Hull	6.00	15.00
AFBI Martin Biron	3.00	8.00
AFBL Brian Leetch	3.00	8.00
AFBO Peter Bondra	3.00	8.00
AFBQ Ray Bourque	8.00	20.00
AFBS Brendan Shanahan	4.00	10.00
AFCD Chris Drury	3.00	8.00
AFCK Roman Cechmanek	3.00	8.00
AFDA Eric Daze	3.00	8.00
AFDB Donald Brashear	3.00	8.00
AFDR Chris Drury	3.00	8.00
AFED Eric Daze	3.00	8.00
AFFO Peter Forsberg	8.00	20.00
AFFP Felix Potvin	4.00	10.00
AFFV Sergei Fedorov	5.00	12.00
AFGI Jean-Sebastien Giguere	3.00	8.00
AFGM Glen Murray	3.00	8.00
AFGU Bill Guerin	3.00	8.00
AFGY Wayne Gretzky	25.00	60.00
AFHE Milan Hejduk	4.00	10.00
AFHO Marian Hossa	4.00	10.00
AFHU Brett Hull	5.00	12.00
AFIK Ilya Kovalchuk	8.00	20.00
AFJA Jason Allison	3.00	8.00
AFJF Jeff Friesen	3.00	8.00
AFJG Jean-Sebastien Giguere	3.00	8.00
AFJI Jarome Iginla	8.00	20.00
AFJJ Jaromir Jagr	6.00	15.00
AFJL John LeClair	4.00	10.00
AFJR Jeremy Roenick	6.00	15.00
AFJS Joe Sakic	8.00	20.00
AFJT Joe Thornton	6.00	15.00
AFJW Justin Williams	3.00	8.00
AFKA Paul Kariya	4.00	10.00
AFKK Ilya Kovalchuk	8.00	20.00
AFKO Alexei Kovalev	3.00	8.00
AFKP Keith Primeau	3.00	8.00
AFKV Alexei Kovalev	3.00	8.00
AFMB Martin Brodeur	15.00	40.00
AFMD Marc Denis	3.00	8.00
AFMH Marian Hossa	4.00	10.00
AFML Mario Lemieux	15.00	40.00
AFMM Mike Modano	5.00	12.00
AFMN Markus Naslund	4.00	10.00
AFMO Mike Modano	8.00	20.00
AFMR Mark Recchi	3.00	8.00
AFMS Mats Sundin	4.00	10.00
AFMT Mats Sundin	4.00	10.00
AFNA Markus Naslund	4.00	10.00
AFOK Olaf Kolzig	3.00	8.00
AFPB Pavel Bure	4.00	10.00
AFPD Pavol Demitra	3.00	8.00
AFPK Paul Kariya	4.00	10.00
AFPM Patrick Marleau	3.00	8.00
AFPR Patrick Roy	15.00	40.00
AFPU Keith Primeau	3.00	8.00
AFRB Ray Bourque	6.00	15.00
AFRC Roman Cechmanek	3.00	8.00
AFRO Jeremy Roenick	6.00	15.00
AFRW Ray Whitney	3.00	8.00
AFRY Patrick Roy	15.00	40.00
AFSA Miroslav Satan	3.00	8.00
AFSC Joe Sakic	10.00	25.00
AFSD Shane Doan	3.00	8.00
AFSF Sergei Fedorov	8.00	20.00
AFSH Steve Shields	3.00	8.00
AFSK Saku Koivu	4.00	10.00
AFSN Brendan Shanahan	4.00	10.00
AFSS Sergei Samsonov	3.00	8.00
AFSU Steve Sullivan	3.00	8.00
AFSV Sergei Samsonov	3.00	8.00
AFSY Steve Yzerman	15.00	40.00
AFTA Alex Tanguay	3.00	8.00
AFTH Jose Theodore	8.00	20.00
AFTT Jocelyn Thibault	3.00	8.00
AFWG Wayne Gretzky	25.00	60.00
AFZP Zigmund Palffy	4.00	10.00
CFCS T.Connolly/M.Satan	6.00	15.00
CFDT P.Demitra/K.Tkachuk	6.00	15.00
CFFO Peter Forsberg Dual	20.00	50.00
CFFP Felix Potvin Dual	6.00	15.00
CFGR Wayne Gretzky Dual	30.00	80.00
CFJB J.Jagr/P.Bondra	6.00	15.00
CFJJ Jaromir Jagr Dual	10.00	25.00
CFJS Joe Sakic Dual	12.50	30.00
CFLK M.Lemieux/P.Kariya	15.00	40.00
CFMO Mike Modano Dual	8.00	20.00
CFNB J.Nieuwendyk/M.Brodeur	10.00	25.00
CFSH B.Shanahan/B.Hull	6.00	15.00
CFTB J.Thibault/M.Brodeur	10.00	25.00
CFTK J.Theodore/S.Koivu	12.50	30.00
CFTL K.Tkachuk/J.LeClair	6.00	15.00
CFTS J.Thornton/S.Samsonov	6.00	15.00
CFWD D.Weight/P.Demitra	6.00	15.00
CFWG Wayne Gretzky Dual	50.00	125.00
CFYR S.Yzerman/L.Robitaille	10.00	25.00

2002-03 SP Game Used Authentic Fabrics Gold

This 83-card set paralleled the basic insert set but each card was serial-numbered in gold foil to just 99 copies.

*GOLD: .5X TO 1.25X BASIC JERSEYS
GOLD PRINT RUN 99 SER.#'d SETS

2002-03 SP Game Used Authentic Fabrics Rainbow

This 83-card set paralleled the basic insert set but each card was serial-numbered in rainbow foil to just ten copies.

NOT PRICED DUE TO SCARCITY

2002-03 SP Game Used First Rounder Patches

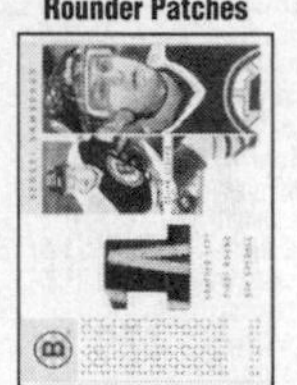

Randomly inserted, this 58-card set featured swatches of game-worn jersey patches from the featured player. Each card was serial-numbered out of 30 on the card front and carried a "PC" prefix on the card back.

Card	Low	High
AD Adam Deadmarsh	15.00	40.00
AK Alexei Kovalev	15.00	40.00
AL Jason Allison	15.00	40.00
AT Alex Tanguay	15.00	40.00
AY Alexei Yashin	15.00	40.00
BB Brian Boucher	15.00	40.00
BG Bill Guerin	15.00	40.00
BI Martin Biron	15.00	40.00
BS Brendan Shanahan	25.00	60.00
CP Chris Pronger	15.00	40.00
DB Daniel Briere	15.00	40.00
DL David Legwand	15.00	40.00
EL Eric Lindros	25.00	60.00
GO Sergei Gonchar	15.00	40.00
IK Ilya Kovalchuk	30.00	80.00
JA Jason Arnott	15.00	40.00
JD J-P Dumont	15.00	40.00
JG Jean-Sebastien Giguere	15.00	40.00
JI Jarome Iginla	30.00	80.00
JJ Jaromir Jagr	30.00	80.00
JR Jeremy Roenick	30.00	80.00
JS Joe Sakic	40.00	100.00
JT Joe Thornton	30.00	80.00
JW Justin Williams	15.00	40.00
KK Krys Kolanos	15.00	40.00
KP Keith Primeau	15.00	40.00
KT Keith Tkachuk	25.00	60.00
MA Manny Malhotra	15.00	40.00
MB Martin Brodeur	40.00	100.00
MD Marc Denis	15.00	40.00
ML Mario Lemieux	60.00	150.00
MM Mike Modano	30.00	80.00
MN Markus Naslund	25.00	60.00
MS Mats Sundin	25.00	60.00
NO Mika Noronen	15.00	40.00
OK Olaf Kolzig	15.00	40.00
ON Owen Nolan	15.00	40.00
PF Peter Forsberg	30.00	80.00
PK Paul Kariya	25.00	60.00
PM Patrick Marleau	15.00	40.00
PS Patrik Stefan	15.00	40.00
RB Ray Bourque	40.00	100.00
RK Rostislav Klesla	15.00	40.00
RL Roberto Luongo	30.00	80.00
RT Raffi Torres	15.00	40.00
SD Shane Doan	15.00	40.00
SG Simon Gagne	15.00	40.00
SH Scott Hartnell	15.00	40.00
SK Saku Koivu	25.00	60.00
SS Sergei Samsonov	15.00	40.00
SY Steve Yzerman	75.00	150.00
TC Tim Connolly	15.00	40.00
TL Trevor Linden	15.00	40.00
TP Taylor Pyatt	15.00	40.00
TS Teemu Selanne	25.00	60.00
VL Vincent Lecavalier	25.00	60.00
BLA Dan Blackburn	15.00	40.00
BLE Brian Leetch	25.00	60.00

2002-03 SP Game Used Future Fabrics

Randomly inserted, this 31-card set featured swatches of game-worn jerseys on the card fronts. Each card was serial-numbered in silver foil out of 225.

Card	Low	High
FFAE David Aebischer	3.00	8.00
FFAT Alex Tanguay	3.00	8.00
FFBJ Brent Johnson	3.00	8.00
FFBM Brenden Morrow	3.00	8.00
FFCA Kyle Calder	3.00	8.00
FFDA Denis Arkhipov	3.00	8.00
FFDB Daniel Briere	3.00	8.00
FFEB Eric Belanger	3.00	8.00
FFHA Jeff Halpern	3.00	8.00
FFIB Ilja Bryzgalov	4.00	10.00
FFIK Ilya Kovalchuk	8.00	20.00
FFJG Jean-Sebastien Giguere	3.00	8.00
FFJH Jeff Halpern	3.00	8.00
FFKC Kyle Calder	3.00	8.00
FFKO Ilya Kovalchuk	8.00	20.00
FFMA Maxim Afinogenov	3.00	8.00
FFMB Mark Bell	3.00	8.00
FFME Martin Erat	3.00	8.00
FFMM Manny Malhotra	3.00	8.00
FFMP Matt Pettinger	3.00	8.00
FFMR Mike Ribeiro	3.00	8.00
FFMT Marty Turco	3.00	8.00
FFPB Pavel Brendl	3.00	8.00
FFRI Mike Ribeiro	3.00	8.00
FFRK Rostislav Klesla	3.00	8.00
FFSG Simon Gagne	3.00	8.00
FFSH Scott Hartnell	3.00	8.00
FFSR Steven Reinprecht	3.00	8.00
FFTC Tim Connolly	3.00	8.00
FFTP Taylor Pyatt	3.00	8.00
FFVN Ville Nieminen	3.00	8.00

2002-03 SP Game Used Future Fabrics Gold

This 31-card set paralleled the basic insert set but each card was serial-numbered in gold foil to just 99 copies.

*GOLD: .5X TO 1.25X BASIC JERSEY

2002-03 SP Game Used Future Fabrics Rainbow

This 31-card set paralleled the basic insert set but each card was serial-numbered in holographic rainbow foil to just 10 copies.

NOT PRICED DUE TO SCARCITY

2002-03 SP Game Used Piece of History

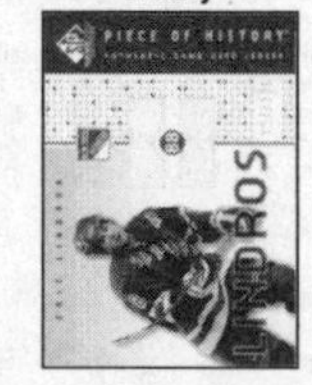

Randomly inserted, this 87-card set featured swatches of game-worn jerseys on the card fronts. Each card was serial-numbered in silver foil out of 225.

Card	Low	High
PHAD Adam Deadmarsh	6.00	15.00
PHAL Jason Allison	6.00	15.00
PHAM Tony Amonte	6.00	15.00
PHAT Alex Tanguay	6.00	15.00
PHAY Alexei Yashin	6.00	15.00
PHAZ Alexei Zhamnov	6.00	15.00
PHBD Peter Bondra	6.00	15.00
PHBH Brett Hull	8.00	20.00
PHBI Martin Biron	6.00	15.00
PHBL Brian Leetch	6.00	15.00
PHBO Peter Bondra	6.00	15.00
PHBQ Ray Bourque	8.00	20.00
PHBS Brendan Shanahan	6.00	15.00
PHCC Chris Chelios	6.00	15.00
PHCD Chris Drury	6.00	15.00
PHCJ Curtis Joseph	6.00	15.00
PHCK Roman Cechmanek	6.00	15.00
PHCL Claude Lemieux	6.00	15.00
PHDL David Legwand	6.00	15.00
PHDR Chris Drury	6.00	15.00
PHDU Mike Dunham	6.00	15.00
PHED Eric Daze	6.00	15.00
PHEK Espen Knutsen	6.00	15.00
PHEL Eric Lindros	6.00	15.00
PHFO Peter Forsberg	10.00	25.00
PHFP Felix Potvin	6.00	15.00
PHFV Sergei Fedorov	8.00	20.00
PHGO Sergei Gonchar	6.00	15.00
PHGU Bill Guerin	6.00	15.00
PHGY Wayne Gretzky	30.00	80.00
PHJA Jason Allison	6.00	15.00
PHJD J.P. Dumont	6.00	15.00
PHJG Jaromir Jagr	8.00	20.00
PHJI Jarome Iginla	8.00	20.00
PHJJ Jaromir Jagr	8.00	20.00
PHJL John LeClair	6.00	15.00
PHJN Joe Nieuwendyk	6.00	15.00
PHJO Jocelyn Thibault	6.00	15.00
PHJR Jeremy Roenick	8.00	20.00
PHJS Joe Sakic	10.00	25.00
PHJT Joe Thornton	8.00	20.00
PHKA Paul Kariya	8.00	20.00
PHKK Ilya Kovalchuk	8.00	20.00
PHKO Steve Konowalchuk	6.00	15.00
PHKP Keith Primeau	6.00	15.00
PHKU Saku Koivu	6.00	15.00
PHLM Nicklas Lidstrom	6.00	15.00
PHMB Martin Brodeur	12.50	30.00
PHMD Marc Denis	6.00	15.00
PHMH Milan Hejduk	6.00	15.00
PHML Mario Lemieux	15.00	40.00
PHMM Mike Modano	8.00	20.00
PHMN Markus Naslund	6.00	15.00
PHMO Mike Modano	10.00	25.00
PHMR Mark Recchi	6.00	15.00
PHMS Mats Sundin	6.00	15.00
PHMY Mike York	6.00	15.00
PHNA Markus Naslund	6.00	15.00
PHNL Nicklas Lidstrom	6.00	15.00
PHPB Pavel Bure	6.00	15.00
PHPF Peter Forsberg	10.00	25.00
PHPK Paul Kariya	6.00	15.00
PHPM Patrick Marleau	6.00	15.00
PHPR Patrick Roy	15.00	40.00
PHRB Ray Bourque	8.00	20.00
PHRC Roman Cechmanek	6.00	15.00
PHRK Jeremy Roenick	8.00	20.00
PHRO Rob Blake	6.00	15.00
PHRT Roman Turek	6.00	15.00
PHRY Patrick Roy	15.00	40.00
PHSA Marc Savard	6.00	15.00
PHSB Sean Burke	6.00	15.00
PHSC Joe Sakic	10.00	25.00
PHSF Sergei Fedorov	8.00	20.00
PHSG Simon Gagne	6.00	15.00
PHSH Brendan Shanahan	6.00	15.00
PHSK Saku Koivu	6.00	15.00
PHSS Sergei Samsonov	6.00	15.00
PHSU Mats Sundin	6.00	15.00
PHSV Sergei Samsonov	6.00	15.00
PHSY Steve Yzerman	15.00	40.00
PHTA Alex Tanguay	6.00	15.00
PHTC Tim Connolly	6.00	15.00
PHTH Jose Theodore	8.00	20.00
PHTS Teemu Selanne	6.00	15.00
PHTT Jocelyn Thibault	6.00	15.00
PHZP Zigmund Palffy	6.00	15.00

2002-03 SP Game Used Piece of History Gold

This 87-card set paralleled the basic insert set but each card was serial-numbered in gold foil to just 99 copies.

*GOLD: ..5X TO 1.25X BASIC JERSEYS

2002-03 SP Game Used Piece of History Rainbow

This 87-card set paralleled the basic insert set but each card was serial-numbered in a rainbow foil to just ten copies.

NOT PRICED DUE TO SCARCITY

2002-03 SP Game Used Signature Style

Inserted at 1:12, this 32-card set featured authentic player autographs. Each card carried a "SS" prefix on the card backs.

Card	Low	High
AF Alexander Frolov	10.00	25.00
BO Bobby Orr	125.00	250.00
BR Pavel Brendl	6.00	15.00
CJ Curtis Joseph	12.00	30.00
DH Dany Heatley	10.00	25.00
EB Ed Belfour	15.00	40.00
EC Erik Cole	6.00	15.00
GH Gordie Howe	50.00	125.00
IK Ilya Kovalchuk	12.00	30.00
JI Jarome Iginla	10.00	25.00
JL John LeClair	6.00	15.00
JT Joe Thornton	12.00	30.00
JW Justin Williams	6.00	15.00
KH Kristian Huselius	6.00	15.00
MA Maxim Afinogenov	6.00	15.00
MB Martin Brodeur	40.00	100.00
MC Mike Comrie	6.00	15.00
MFO Manny Fernandez	6.00	15.00
MH Martin Havlat	6.00	15.00
MK Milan Kraft	6.00	15.00
NK Nikolai Khabibulin	10.00	25.00
PB Pavel Bure	8.00	20.00
PR Patrick Roy	60.00	150.00
RB Ray Bourque	20.00	50.00
SC Stanislav Chistov	10.00	25.00
SG Simon Gagne	6.00	15.00
SH Scott Hartnell	6.00	15.00
SP Jason Spezza	20.00	50.00
SS Sergei Samsonov	6.00	15.00
SY Steve Yzerman	30.00	80.00
TS Teemu Selanne	6.00	15.00
WG Wayne Gretzky	150.00	300.00

2002-03 SP Game Used Tools of the Game

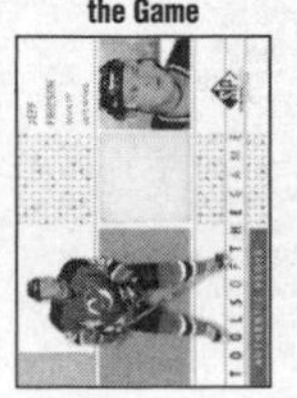

Randomly inserted, this 30-card set featured swatches of game-worn gloves or goalie leg pads on the card fronts. Each card was serial-numbered in silver foil out of 99. Cards carried a "TG" prefix on the card backs.

Card	Low	High
AK Alexei Kovalev G	10.00	25.00
AM Alexander Mogilny G	10.00	25.00
BB Brian Boucher P	10.00	25.00
BD Byron Dafoe P	10.00	25.00
BE Ed Belfour P	12.50	30.00
BH Brett Hull G	15.00	40.00
BS Brendan Shanahan G	12.50	30.00
DH Dominik Hasek P	15.00	40.00
EB Ed Belfour G	12.50	30.00
JF Jeff Friesen G	10.00	25.00
JJ Jaromir Jagr G	15.00	40.00
JL John LeClair G	12.50	30.00
JR Jeremy Roenick G	15.00	40.00
JT Joe Thornton G	15.00	40.00
KP Keith Primeau G	10.00	25.00
KT Keith Tkachuk G	12.50	30.00
MD Marc Denis P	10.00	25.00
MS Mats Sundin G	12.50	30.00
OK Olaf Kolzig P	10.00	25.00
PB Peter Bondra G	10.00	25.00
PR Patrick Roy P	20.00	50.00
RC Roman Cechmanek P	10.00	25.00
RD Rick DiPietro P	10.00	25.00
RF Ron Francis G	10.00	25.00
RL Roberto Luongo P	15.00	40.00
SF Sergei Fedorov G	12.50	30.00
SH Steve Shields P	10.00	25.00
SS Sergei Samsonov G	10.00	25.00
TH Jose Theodore P	12.00	30.00
TS Teemu Selanne G	12.50	30.00

2003-04 SP Game Used

This 130-card set consisted of 50 veteran cards; Tier 1 rookie cards (51-82 and 123-130) serial-numbered to 600; Tier 2 rookies (83-92) serial-numbered to 99 and veteran jersey cards (93-122). Cards 123-130 were only available in packs of UD Rookie Update and were serial-numbered out of 600.

Card	Low	High
COMP.SET w/o SP's (50)	25.00	60.00
1 Jean-Sebastien Giguere	.50	1.25
2 Sergei Fedorov	1.25	3.00
3 Dany Heatley	1.25	3.00
4 Ilya Kovalchuk	1.25	3.00
5 Joe Thornton	1.50	4.00
6 Sergei Samsonov	.50	1.25
7 Chris Drury	.50	1.25
8 Jarome Iginla	1.00	2.50
9 Ron Francis	.50	1.25
10 Jocelyn Thibault	.50	1.25
11 Joe Sakic	2.00	5.00
12 Peter Forsberg	2.50	6.00
13 Paul Kariya	.75	2.00
14 Rick Nash	1.00	2.50
15 Marty Turco	.50	1.25
16 Mike Modano	1.50	4.00
17 Steve Yzerman	5.00	12.00
18 Dominik Hasek	2.00	5.00
19 Ales Hemsky	.50	1.25
20 Mike Comrie	.50	1.25
21 Roberto Luongo	1.00	2.50
22 Zigmund Palffy	.50	1.25
23 Marian Gaborik	2.00	5.00
24 Jose Theodore	1.00	2.50
25 Saku Koivu	.75	2.00
26 Tomas Vokoun	.50	1.25
27 Martin Brodeur	2.50	6.00
28 Alexei Yashin	.40	1.00
29 Eric Lindros	.75	2.00
30 Pavel Bure	.75	2.00
31 Patrick Lalime	.50	1.25
32 Marian Hossa	.75	2.00
33 Jason Spezza	.75	2.00
34 Simon Gagne	.75	2.00
35 Jeremy Roenick	1.25	3.00
36 Sean Burke	.50	1.25
37 Mario Lemieux	6.00	15.00
38 Niko Dimitrakos	.40	1.00
39 Evgeni Nabokov	.50	1.25
40 Al MacInnis	.50	1.25
41 Keith Tkachuk	.75	2.00
42 Chris Pronger	.50	1.25
43 Nikolai Khabibulin	.75	2.00
44 Vincent Lecavalier	.75	2.00
45 Owen Nolan	.50	1.25
46 Ed Belfour	.75	2.00
47 Mats Sundin	.75	2.00
48 Markus Naslund	.75	2.00
49 Todd Bertuzzi	.75	2.00
50 Jaromir Jagr	1.50	4.00
51 Jiri Hudler RC	4.00	10.00
52 Patrice Bergeron RC	8.00	20.00
53 Milan Bartovic RC	2.00	5.00
54 Matthew Lombardi RC	3.00	8.00
55 Lasse Kukkonen RC	2.00	5.00
56 Travis Moen RC	3.00	8.00
57 Marek Svatos RC	6.00	15.00
58 John-Michael Liles RC	3.00	8.00
59 Cody McCormick RC	2.00	5.00
60 Dan Fritsche RC	2.00	5.00
61 Antti Miettinen RC	2.00	5.00
62 Esa Pirnes RC	2.00	5.00
63 Tim Gleason RC	2.00	5.00
64 Brent Burns RC	3.00	8.00
65 Christoph Brandner RC	2.00	5.00
66 Chris Higgins RC	10.00	25.00
67 Dan Hamhuis RC	3.00	8.00
68 Marek Zidlicky RC	2.00	5.00
69 Wade Brookbank RC	2.00	5.00
70 David Hale RC	2.00	5.00
71 Paul Martin RC	2.00	5.00
72 Sean Bergenheim RC	2.00	5.00
73 Antoine Vermette RC	3.00	8.00
74 Matthew Spiller RC	2.00	5.00
75 Matt Murley RC	2.00	5.00
76 Christian Ehrhoff RC	2.00	5.00
77 Alexander Semin RC	12.00	30.00

78 Tom Preissing RC 2.00 5.00
79 Peter Sejna RC 2.00 5.00
80 Maxim Kondratiev RC 2.00 5.00
81 Matt Stajan RC 8.00 20.00
82 Boyd Gordon RC 3.00 8.00
83 Joffrey Lupul RC 15.00 40.00
84 Eric Staal RC 50.00 125.00
85 Tuomo Ruutu RC 25.00 50.00
86 Pavel Vorobiev RC 10.00 25.00
87 Nathan Horton RC 25.00 60.00
88 Dustin Brown RC 10.00 25.00
89 Jordin Tootoo RC 20.00 50.00
90 Joni Pitkanen RC 12.00 30.00
91 Marc-Andre Fleury RC 60.00 150.00
92 Milan Michalek RC 25.00 60.00
93 Joe Thornton 10.00 25.00
94 Jason Blake 4.00 10.00
95 Pavol Demitra 4.00 10.00
96 Martin St. Louis 4.00 10.00
97 Zigmund Palffy 4.00 10.00
98 Sean Burke 4.00 10.00
99 Todd Marchant 4.00 10.00
100 Jarome Iginla 8.00 20.00
101 Doug Weight 4.00 10.00
102 Henrik Zetterberg 10.00 25.00
103 Ilya Kovalchuk 10.00 25.00
104 Alexei Yashin 4.00 10.00
105 Mario Lemieux 12.50 30.00
106 Milan Hejduk 6.00 15.00
107 Martin Biron 4.00 10.00
108 Tomas Vokoun 4.00 10.00
109 Tommy Salo 4.00 10.00
110 Anson Carter 4.00 10.00
111 Nikolai Khabibulin 5.00 12.00
112 Keith Tkachuk 5.00 12.00
113 Martin Brodeur 15.00 40.00
114 Steve Yzerman 12.50 30.00
115 Jeremy Roenick 6.00 15.00
116 Mike Modano 10.00 25.00
117 Marian Hossa 5.00 12.00
118 Paul Kariya 5.00 12.00
119 Marty Turco 4.00 10.00
120 Peter Forsberg 8.00 20.00
121 Todd Bertuzzi 5.00 12.00
122 David Aebischer 4.00 10.00
123 Fedor Tyutin RC 2.00 5.00
124 John Pohl RC 2.00 5.00
125 Ryan Kesler RC 2.00 5.00
126 Fredrik Sjostrom RC 2.00 5.00
127 Aaron Johnson RC 2.00 5.00
128 Brad Boyes RC 4.00 10.00
129 Nikolai Zherdev RC 6.00 15.00
130 Tomas Plekanec RC 3.00 8.00

2003-04 SP Game Used Gold

*STARS: 4X TO 10X BASE HI
*TIER 1 ROOKIES: .75X TO 2X
1-82 PRINT RUN 40 SER.#'d SETS
*TIER 2 ROOKIES: .5X TO 1.25X
TIER 2 PRINT RUN 25 SER.#'d SETS
*JERSEYS: 1X TO 2.5X
JERSEY PRINT RUN 30 SER.#'d SETS

2003-04 SP Game Used Authentic Fabrics

This 72-card set featured single, dual or quad jersey swatches. Single and dual swatch cards were serial-numbered to 99 while quad swatch cards were serial-numbered out of 55.

AFAF Alexander Frolov 5.00 12.00
AFEL Eric Lindros 6.00 15.00
AFIIA Marcel Hossa 3.00 8.00
AFJG Jean-Sebastien Giguere 5.00 12.00
AFJI Jarome Iginla 10.00 25.00
AFJJ Jaromir Jagr 10.00 25.00
AFJR Jeremy Roenick 10.00 25.00
AFJS Jason Spezza 8.00 20.00
AFJT Joe Thornton 10.00 25.00
AFMH Marian Hossa 6.00 15.00
AFML Mario Lemieux 15.00 40.00
AFON Owen Nolan 5.00 12.00
AFPR Patrick Roy 15.00 40.00
AFPS Peter Sejna 3.00 8.00
AFRL Roberto Luongo 8.00 20.00
AFRN Rick Nash 12.50 30.00
AFSF Sergei Fedorov 10.00 25.00
AFSG Simon Gagne 6.00 15.00
AFSK Saku Koivu 6.00 15.00
AFTB Todd Bertuzzi 6.00 15.00
AFWG Wayne Gretzky 40.00 100.00
AFZP Zigmund Palffy 5.00 12.00
DFBJ R.Blake/E.Jovanovski 8.00 20.00
DFBL J.Bouwmeester/R.Luongo 15.00 40.00
DFBP M.Brodeur/P.Leclaire 15.00 40.00
DFBR M.Brodeur/P.Roy 25.00 60.00
DFBT Z.Palffy/A.Frolov 8.00 20.00
DFCM C.Drury/M.Satan 6.00 15.00
DFDS T.Domi/J.Shelley 8.00 20.00
DFFS P.Forsberg/J.Sakic 15.00 40.00
DFGR J.Giguere/P.Roy 20.00 50.00
DFGS W.Gretzky/J.Spezza 50.00 100.00
DFHC A.Hemsky/M.Comrie 8.00 20.00
DFHG G.Howe/W.Gretzky 50.00 125.00
DFHH M.Hossa/M.Hossa 10.00 25.00
DFHK D.Heatley/I.Kovalchuk 15.00 40.00
DFHL D.Hasek/N.Lidstrom 10.00 25.00
DFHY B.Hull/S.Yzerman 15.00 40.00
DFJR J.Jagr/P.Bondra 8.00 20.00
DFKF P.Kariya/P.Forsberg 12.00 30.00
DFKH S.Koivu/M.Hossa 8.00 20.00
DFKS P.Kariya/T.Selanne 8.00 20.00
DFLG M.Lemieux/W.Gretzky 50.00 125.00
DFLK G.Lafleur/S.Koivu 8.00 20.00
DFLP B.Leetch/T.Poti 8.00 20.00
DFMT M.Modano/M.Turco 15.00 40.00
DFNB M.Naslund/T.Bertuzzi 12.00 30.00
DFND R.Nash/M.Denis 8.00 20.00
DFNM R.Nash/T.Marchant 8.00 20.00
DFPC Z.Palffy/R.Cechmanek 6.00 15.00
DFRG J.Roenick/S.Gagne 8.00 20.00
DFSG S.Bowman/G.Lafleur 15.00 40.00
DFSH J.Spezza/M.Hossa 15.00 40.00
DFTK J.Theodore/S.Koivu 12.50 30.00
DFTM J.Thornton/G.Murray 8.00 20.00
DFVN V.Lecavalier/N.Khabibulin 8.00 20.00
DFWT D.Weight/K.Tkachuk 6.00 15.00
DFYH S.Yzerman/G.Howe 30.00 80.00
DFYP A.Yashin/M.Peca 6.00 15.00
DFZH H.Zetterberg/B.Hull 15.00 40.00
DFZT A.Zhamnov/J.Thibault 6.00 15.00
QARGL Amonte/Roen/Gags/LeC 25.00 60.00
QFSKS Frsbrg/Selne/Karya/Sakic 40.00 100.00
QKTHK Koivu/Thedre/Hossa/Kmisrek 50.00 125.00
QLGHL Lem/Gretz/Howe/Lafleur 150.00 350.00
QMGTM Mike Modano 25.00 60.00
Bill Guerin
Marty Turco
Brenden Morrow
QNBJM Naslund/Bert/Jov/Morr 30.00 80.00
QRGBT Roy/Giggy/Brodeur/Turco 60.00 150.00
QSAHL Spza/Alfrdson/Hossa/Lalime 25.00 60.00
QSNBM Sndin/Nolan/Bllour/Mogilny 25.00 60.00
QSNZH Spza/Nash/Zettrbrg/Hemsky 60.00 150.00
QYBHH Yzrmn/Bowmn/Hull/Hasek 75.00 200.00

2003-04 SP Game Used Authentic Fabrics Gold

This 72-card set paralleled the basic inserts set but with gold foil highlights and serial-numbering to 21 copies each. Some cards were autographed by the player(s) featured. Please note that there have been some inconsistencies in this checklist regarding the autographs, any additional info can be sent to hockey-mag@beckett.com.

PRINT RUN 21 SER.#'d SETS
NOT PRICED DUE TO SCARCITY

2003-04 SP Game Used Authentic Patches

PRINT RUN 15 SERIAL #'d SETS
NOT PRICED DUE TO SCARCITY
APG1 Wayne Gretzky
APJSG Jean-Sebastien Giguere
APJTH Jose Theodore
APAH Ales Hemsky
APAY Alexei Yashin
APBG Bill Guerin
APCD Chris Drury
APDH Dominik Hasek
APEB Ed Belfour
APEL Eric Lindros
APHZ Henrik Zetterberg
APIK Ilya Kovalchuk
APJI Jarome Iginla
APJR Jeremy Roenick
APJT Joe Thornton
APMB Martin Brodeur
APMH Marcel Hossa
APML Mario Lemieux
APMM Mike Modano
APMN Markus Naslund
APMS Miroslav Satan
APON Owen Nolan
APPF Peter Forsberg
APPL Patrick Lalime
APPR Patrick Roy
APRN Rick Nash
APSF Sergei Fedorov
APTA Tony Amonte
APVL Vincent Lecavalier
APWG Wayne Gretzky

2003-04 SP Game Used Double Threads

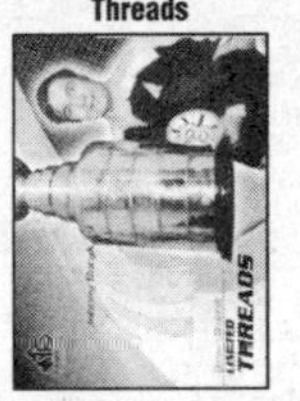

This 27-card set featured dual-patch swatches of the featured players. Each card was serial-numbered out of 60.

DTAR D.Aebischer/P.Roy 60.00 150.00
DTBL J.Bouwmeester/R.Luongo 30.00 80.00
DTBR M.Brodeur/P.Roy 60.00 150.00
DTDS C.Drury/M.Satan 20.00 50.00
DTFS P.Forsberg/J.Sakic 30.00 80.00
DTKH S.Koivu/M.Hossa 20.00 50.00
DTKS P.Kariya/T.Selanne 20.00 50.00
DTLG M.Lemieux/W.Gretzky 75.00 200.00
DTLK V.Lecavalier/N.Khabibulin 30.00 80.00
DTLS V.Lecavalier/M.St. Louis 20.00 50.00
DTMG M.Modano/B.Guerin 25.00 60.00
DTMT M.Modano/M.Turco 30.00 80.00
DTNB M.Naslund/T.Bertuzzi 30.00 80.00
DTND R.Nash/M.Denis 30.00 80.00
DTNN R.Niedermayer/S.Niedermayer 25.00 60.00
DTPF Zigmund Palffy 20.00 50.00
Alexander Frolov
DTPK P.Kariya/P.Kariya 20.00 50.00
DTRA J.Roenick/T.Amonte 20.00 50.00
DTSB M.Sundin/E.Belfour 25.00 60.00
DTSF S.Fedorov/S.Fedorov 40.00 100.00
DTSH J.Spezza/M.Hossa 30.00 80.00
DTSN M.Sundin/O.Nolan 25.00 60.00
DTTM J.Thornton/G.Murray 20.00 50.00
DTTS J.Thornton/S.Samsonov 20.00 50.00
DTWG W.Gretzky/W.Gretzky 150.00 400.00
DTYZ S.Yzerman/H.Zetterberg 30.00 80.00
DTZT A.Zhamnov/J.Thibault 20.00 50.00

2003-04 SP Game Used Game Gear

PRINT RUN 99 SERIAL #'d SETS
GGBB Brian Boucher 6.00 15.00
GGBD Byron Dafoe 6.00 15.00
GGCJ Curtis Joseph 8.00 20.00
GGCO Chris Osgood 6.00 15.00
GGDH Dominik Hasek 12.50 30.00
GGGF Grant Fuhr 15.00 40.00
GGJF Jeff Friesen 6.00 15.00
GGJGR Jaromir Jagr 12.50 30.00
GGJH Johan Hedberg/36 6.00 15.00
GGJJ Jaromir Jagr 12.50 30.00
GGJT Jose Theodore 12.50 30.00
GGMB Martin Brodeur 15.00 40.00
GGMD Marc Denis 6.00 15.00
GGMS Mats Sundin 8.00 20.00
GGMT Marty Turco 6.00 15.00
GGOK Olaf Kolzig 6.00 15.00
GGPL Patrick Lalime 6.00 15.00
GGPR Patrick Roy 15.00 40.00
GGRC Roman Cechmanek 6.00 15.00
GGRD Rick DiPietro 6.00 15.00
GGRL Roberto Luongo 12.50 30.00
GGSAM Sergei Samsonov 6.00 15.00
GGSS Steve Shields 6.00 15.00
GGTS Teemu Selanne 8.00 20.00
GGTSA Tommy Salo 6.00 15.00

2003-04 SP Game Used Game Gear Combo

*COMBO: .5X TO 1.5X BASIC GEAR
PRINT RUN 85 SERIAL #'d SETS

2003-04 SP Game Used Limited Threads

PRINT RUN 75 SERIAL #'d SETS
GOLD PRINT RUN 21 SER.#'d SETS
GOLD NOT PRICED DUE TO SCARCITY
LTG1 Wayne Gretzky 50.00 100.00
LTWGR Wayne Gretzky 50.00 100.00
LTJBU Johnny Bucyk 6.00 15.00
LTMHO Marian Hossa 8.00 20.00
LTJTH Jocelyn Thibault 6.00 15.00
LTJSG Jean-Sebastien Giguere 6.00 15.00
LTDHA Dominik Hasek 12.50 30.00
LTAH Ales Hemsky 6.00 15.00
LTAK Ales Kotalik 6.00 15.00
LTAY Alexei Yashin 6.00 15.00
LTBG Bill Guerin 6.00 15.00
LTBL Brian Leetch 6.00 15.00
LTCD Chris Drury 6.00 15.00
LTDH Dany Heatley 10.00 25.00
LTGL Guy Lafleur 12.50 30.00
LTIK Ilya Kovalchuk 10.00 25.00
LTJB Jay Bouwmeester 6.00 15.00
LTJJ Jaromir Jagr 10.00 25.00
LTJS Jason Spezza 10.00 25.00
LTJT Joe Thornton 12.50 30.00
LTLM Lanny McDonald 6.00 15.00
LTMB Mike Bossy 6.00 15.00
LTMH Gordie Howe 25.00 60.00
LTMM Mike Modano 10.00 25.00
LTMN Markus Naslund 8.00 20.00
LTMS Mats Sundin 8.00 20.00
LTMT Marty Turco 6.00 15.00
LTPD Pavel Datsyuk 15.00 40.00
LTPF Peter Forsberg 15.00 40.00
LTPK Paul Kariya 8.00 20.00
LTPR Patrick Roy 30.00 80.00
LTRL Roberto Luongo 10.00 25.00
LTRN Rick Nash 10.00 25.00
LTSB Scotty Bowman 20.00 50.00
LTSF Sergei Fedorov 10.00 25.00
LTSU Scottie Upshall 6.00 15.00
LTSY Steve Yzerman 15.00 40.00
LTTA Tony Amonte 6.00 15.00
LTTB Todd Bertuzzi 8.00 20.00
LTTS Teemu Selanne 8.00 20.00
LTVL Vincent Lecavalier 8.00 20.00
LTWG Wayne Gretzky 50.00 100.00

2003-04 SP Game Used Premium Patches

PRINT RUN 6 SER.#'d SETS
NOT PRICED DUE TO SCARCITY
PPJSG Jean-Sebastien Giguere
PPJSA Joe Sakic
PPDH Dany Heatley
PPGL Guy Lafleur
PPJJ Jaromir Jagr
PPJR Jeremy Roenick
PPJS Jason Spezza
PPJT Jocelyn Thibault
PPMB Martin Brodeur
PPMC Mike Comrie
PPMH Marian Hossa
PPML Mario Lemieux
PPMS Mats Sundin
PPMT Marty Turco
PPPB Pavel Bure
PPPK Paul Kariya
PPPR Patrick Roy
PPRL Roberto Luongo
PPRN Rick Nash
PPSF Sergei Fedorov
PPSY Steve Yzerman
PPTB Todd Bertuzzi
PPTH Joe Thornton
PPTS Teemu Selanne
PPWG Wayne Gretzky

2003-04 SP Game Used Rookie Exclusives

PRINT RUN 100 SERIAL #'d SETS
RE1 Patrice Bergeron 20.00 50.00
RE2 Dustin Brown 10.00 25.00
RE3 Marc-Andre Fleury 30.00 80.00
RE4 Nathan Horton 15.00 40.00
RE5 Jiri Hudler 10.00 25.00
RE6 Joffrey Lupul 10.00 25.00
RE7 Joni Pitkanen 10.00 25.00
RE8 Tuomo Ruutu 15.00 40.00
RE9 Eric Staal 30.00 80.00
RE10 Jordin Tootoo 15.00 40.00

2003-04 SP Game Used Signers

STATED ODDS 1:7
SPSBO Bobby Orr 100.00 200.00
SPSCJ Curtis Joseph 6.00 15.00
SPSDA David Aebischer 6.00 15.00
SPSEL Eric Lindros 12.50 30.00
SPSGH Gordie Howe 30.00 80.00
SPSHA Marian Hossa 6.00 15.00
SPSHV Martin Havlat 6.00 15.00
SPSHZ Henrik Zetterberg 10.00 25.00
SPSJB Jaromir Jagr SP 25.00 50.00
SPSJI Jarome Iginla 10.00 25.00
SPSJR Jeremy Roenick 8.00 20.00
SPSJS Jason Spezza 8.00 20.00
SPSJT Joe Thornton 10.00 25.00
SPSMG Marian Gaborik 12.50 30.00
SPSMH Marcel Hossa 6.00 15.00
SPSMT Marty Turco 6.00 15.00
SPSPB Pavel Bure 6.00 15.00
SPSPR Patrick Roy SP 60.00 150.00
SPSRB Ray Bourque 15.00 40.00
SPSRL Roberto Luongo 12.50 30.00
SPSRN Rick Nash 12.50 30.00
SPSSF Sergei Fedorov 12.50 30.00
SPSTB Todd Bertuzzi 6.00 15.00
SPSWG Wayne Gretzky SP 75.00 200.00
SSJSG Jean-Sebastien Giguere 6.00 15.00

2003-04 SP Game Used Team Threads

This 17-card set featured patch swatches from three teammates. Each card was serial-numbered out of 10.

NOT PRICED DUE TO SCARCITY
TTARL Amonte/Roenick/LeClair
TTBLK Bure/Lindros/Kovalev
TTBSG Brodeur/Stevens/Gomez
TTDSS Domi/Shelley/Brashear
TTFGC Fedorov/Giguere/Chistov
TTFSK Forsberg/Selanne/Kariya
TTHSC Hemsky/Salo/Comrie
TTKHK Kovalchuk/Heatley/Kozlov
TTKTH Koivu/Theodore/Hossa
TTLBF Lemieux/Bowman/Francis
TTLGH Lemieux/Gretzky/Howe
TTMGT Modano/Guerin/Turco
TTNBJ Naslund/Bertuzzi/Jovanovski
TTSHL Spezza/Hossa/Lalime
TTSNB Sundin/Nolan/Belfour
TTTMS Thornton/Murray/Samsonov
TTYZH Yzerman/Zetterberg/Hasek

2003-04 SP Game Used Top Threads

This 6-card set featured patch swatches from four star players. Each card was serial-numbered out of 6 and cards carried a "TP" prefix on the card back.

NOT PRICED DUE TO SCARCITY
ARGL Amnte/Rnick/Gagne/LeClair
FSKS Forsbrg/Selne/Krya/Sakic
LGHL Lemux/Gretz/Howe/Lafleur
NBJM Nslnd/Bertzi/Jovo/Morrson
SAHL Spezz/Alfrdsn/Hossa/Lalime
YZHH Yzerman/Zettbrg/Hull/Hasek

2004 SP Game Used Hawaii Trade Conference Patches *

These eight cards were part of a larger set of multi-sport cards given away as promotional items during the 2004 Kit Young Hawaii Trade Conference. The cards are unpriced to due to scarcity, though sales of unsigned versions have been reported in the $300-400 range.

COMPLETE SET (8)
PP11 Joe Thornton/10
PP19 Mario Lemieux/10
PP22 Mike Modano/10
PP24 Peter Forsberg/10
PP30 Steve Yzerman/10
PP33 Wayne Gretzky/10
PPA6 Gordie Howe AU/10
PPA8 Wayne Gretzky AU/10

2005-06 SP Game Used

This 240-card set was issued in both product-specific unopened and as inserts in Rookie Update. Cards numbered 1-190 were issued in three-card packs with an $29.99 SRP, which came six to a box and six boxes to a case. Cards numbered 1-100 are veterans while cards 101-240 are all Rookie Cards and all of those cards were issued to a stated print run of 999 serial numbered copies.

COMP.SET w/o SP's (100) 40.00 100.00
RC PRINT RUN 999 SER.#'d SETS
1 Jean-Sebastien Giguere .75 2.00
2 Teemu Selanne 1.00 2.50
3 Scott Niedermayer .60 1.50
4 Ilya Kovalchuk 1.25 3.00
5 Kari Lehtonen 1.00 2.50
6 Marian Hossa .75 2.00
7 Peter Bondra .75 2.00
8 Glen Murray .60 1.50
9 Brian Leetch 1.00 2.50
10 Andrew Raycroft .75 2.00
11 Patrice Bergeron 1.00 2.50
12 Chris Drury .75 2.00
13 Martin Biron .75 2.00
14 Maxim Afinogenov .60 1.50
15 Jarome Iginla .75 2.00
16 Miikka Kiprusoff 1.00 2.50
17 Tony Amonte .75 2.00
18 Erik Cole .60 1.50
19 Eric Staal .75 2.00
20 Nikolai Khabibulin 1.00 2.50
21 Tuomo Ruutu .60 1.50
22 Tyler Arnason .60 1.50
23 Joe Sakic 2.00 5.00
24 Milan Hejduk 1.00 2.50
25 Alex Tanguay .75 2.00
26 David Aebischer .75 2.00
27 Rob Blake .75 2.00
28 Rick Nash 1.25 3.00
29 Nikolai Zherdev .75 2.00
30 Sergei Fedorov 1.00 2.50
31 Mike Modano 1.00 2.50
32 Bill Guerin .60 1.50
33 Marty Turco .75 2.00
34 Brendan Shanahan 1.00 2.50
35 Steve Yzerman 2.50 6.00
36 Pavel Datsyuk 1.00 2.50
37 Henrik Zetterberg 1.00 2.50
38 Manny Legace 1.00 2.50
39 Ryan Smyth .75 2.00
40 Chris Pronger .75 2.00
41 Ty Conklin .75 2.00
42 Stephen Weiss .60 1.50
43 Joe Nieuwendyk .75 2.00
44 Roberto Luongo 1.50 4.00
45 Jeremy Roenick 1.00 2.50
46 Luc Robitaille .75 2.00
47 Pavol Demitra .75 2.00
48 Alexander Frolov .75 2.00
49 Marian Gaborik 1.25 3.00
50 Dwayne Roloson .75 2.00
51 Mike Ribeiro .60 1.50
52 Jose Theodore 1.00 2.50
53 Michael Ryder .75 2.00
54 Saku Koivu 1.00 2.50
55 Paul Kariya 1.00 2.50
56 Steve Sullivan .60 1.50
57 Tomas Vokoun .75 2.00
58 Martin Brodeur 2.00 5.00
59 Patrik Elias .75 2.00
60 Scott Gomez .75 2.00
61 Alexander Mogilny .75 2.00
62 Alexei Yashin .60 1.50
63 Miroslav Satan .60 1.50
64 Rick DiPietro .75 2.00
65 Mark Parrish .60 1.50
66 Kevin Weekes .75 2.00
67 Jaromir Jagr 1.50 4.00
68 Dany Heatley 1.00 2.50
69 Dominik Hasek 1.25 3.00
70 Jason Spezza 1.00 2.50
71 Martin Havlat .75 2.00
72 Peter Forsberg 1.50 4.00
73 Keith Primeau .60 1.50
74 Simon Gagne 1.00 2.50
75 Robert Esche .75 2.00
76 Shane Doan .60 1.50
77 Curtis Joseph 1.00 2.50
78 John LeClair 1.00 2.50
79 Mario Lemieux 4.00 10.00
80 Zigmund Palffy .75 2.00
81 Joe Thornton 1.50 4.00
82 Jonathan Cheechoo 1.00 2.50
83 Evgeni Nabokov .75 2.00
84 Patrick Marleau .75 2.00
85 Keith Tkachuk 1.00 2.50
86 Doug Weight .75 2.00
87 Martin St. Louis .75 2.00
88 Vincent Lecavalier 1.00 2.50
89 Brad Richards .75 2.00
90 Sean Burke .75 2.00
91 Mats Sundin 1.00 2.50
92 Ed Belfour 1.00 2.50
93 Eric Lindros 1.00 2.50
94 Jason Allison .60 1.50
95 Nik Antropov .60 1.50
96 Markus Naslund 1.00 2.50
97 Brendan Morrison .60 1.50
98 Todd Bertuzzi 1.25 3.00
99 Olaf Kolzig .75 2.00
100 Brendan Witt .60 1.50
101 Sidney Crosby RC 125.00 250.00
102 Brandon Bochenski RC 4.00 10.00
103 Rostislav Olesz RC 5.00 12.00
104 Jeff Hoggan RC 4.00 10.00
105 Brett Lebda RC 4.00 10.00
106 Brad Winchester RC 4.00 10.00
107 Wojtek Wolski RC 8.00 20.00
108 Patrick Eaves RC 6.00 15.00
109 Braydon Coburn RC 5.00 12.00
110 Yann Danis RC 6.00 12.00
111 Alexander Ovechkin RC 60.00 120.00
112 Peter Budaj RC 3.00 8.00
113 Jeff Carter RC 10.00 25.00
114 Duncan Keith RC 4.00 10.00
115 Mike Richards RC 12.00 30.00
116 Rene Bourque RC 4.00 10.00
117 Keith Ballard RC 4.00 10.00
118 Thomas Vanek RC 8.00 20.00
119 Robert Nilsson RC 5.00 12.00
120 Kevin Nastiuk RC 5.00 12.00
121 Jaroslav Balastik RC 4.00 10.00
122 Brent Seabrook RC 8.00 20.00
123 Maxime Talbot RC 4.00 10.00
124 Niklas Nordgren RC 4.00 10.00
125 David Leneveu RC 5.00 12.00
126 Eric Nystrom RC 5.00 12.00
127 Timo Helbling RC 4.00 10.00
128 George Parros RC 4.00 10.00
129 Lee Stempniak RC 3.00 8.00
130 Dion Phaneuf RC 12.00 30.00
131 Henrik Lundqvist RC 12.00 30.00
132 Cam Ward RC 5.00 12.00
133 Ryan Hollweg RC 4.00 10.00
134 Corey Perry RC 10.00 25.00
135 Matt Foy RC 4.00 10.00
136 Alexander Steen RC 6.00 15.00
137 Jim Slater RC 3.00 8.00
138 Ryan Suter RC 5.00 12.00
139 Gilbert Brule RC 5.00 12.00
140 Andrej Meszaros RC 4.00 10.00
141 Andrew Alberts RC 4.00 10.00
142 Zach Parise RC 12.00 30.00
143 Kevin Dallman RC 4.00 10.00
144 Chris Campoli RC 4.00 10.00
145 Johan Franzen RC 12.00 30.00
146 Jay McClement RC 4.00 10.00
147 Ryan Getzlaf RC 25.00 60.00
148 Alexander Perezhogin RC 3.00 8.00
149 Andrew Wozniewski RC 4.00 10.00
150 Jim Howard RC 10.00 25.00
151 Jeff Woywitka RC 4.00 10.00
152 Hannu Toivonen RC 6.00 15.00
153 Petteri Nokelainen RC 4.00 10.00
154 Jussi Jokinen RC 6.00 15.00
155 Ryane Clowe RC 4.00 10.00
156 Milan Jurcina RC 4.00 10.00
157 Mark Streit RC 4.00 10.00
158 Raitis Ivanans RC 4.00 10.00
159 Petr Prucha RC 4.00 10.00
160 Josh Gorges RC 4.00 10.00
161 Anthony Stewart RC 2.00 5.00
162 Alvaro Montoya RC 4.00 10.00
163 Paul Ranger RC 2.00 5.00
164 Chris Hull RC 2.00 5.00
165 Wade Skolney RC 2.00 5.00
166 Cam Barker RC 6.00 15.00
167 Adam Berkhoel RC 2.00 5.00
168 Kyle Brodziak RC 4.00 10.00
169 Brian McGrattan RC 4.00 10.00
170 Mikko Koivu RC 3.00 8.00
171 Derek Boogaard RC 5.00 12.00
172 Nick Tarnasky RC 2.00 5.00
173 Evgeny Artyukhin RC 2.00 5.00
174 Colin Hemingway RC 2.00 5.00
175 Michael Wall RC 2.00 5.00
176 Steve Goertzen RC 2.00 5.00
177 Junior Lessard RC 2.00 5.00
178 Vojtech Polak RC 2.00 5.00
179 Jakub Klepis RC 2.00 5.00
180 Jordan Sigalet RC 3.00 6.00
181 Steve Bernier RC 4.00 10.00
182 Dimitri Patzold RC 3.00 8.00
183 R.J. Umberger RC 3.00 5.00
184 Christoph Schubert RC 2.00 5.00
185 Staffan Kronwall RC 2.00 5.00
186 Ryan Whitney RC 3.00 8.00
187 Erik Christensen RC 3.00 8.00
188 Brian Eklund RC 2.00 5.00
189 Rob McVicar RC 2.00 5.00
190 Tomas Fleischmann RC 2.00 5.00
191 Zenon Konopka RC 2.00 5.00
192 Dustin Penner RC 3.00 8.00
193 Ben Walter RC 2.00 5.00
194 Daniel Paille RC 2.00 5.00
195 Chris Thorburn RC 2.00 5.00
196 Richie Regehr RC 2.00 5.00
197 Andrew Ladd RC 3.00 8.00
198 Chad Larose RC 2.00 5.00
199 Danny Richmond RC 2.00 5.00
200 Martin St. Pierre RC 2.00 5.00
201 Corey Crawford RC 2.00 5.00
202 Brad Richardson RC 2.00 5.00
203 Vitaly Kolesnik RC 2.00 5.00
204 Alexandre Picard RC 2.00 5.00
205 Ole-Kristian Tollefsen RC 2.00 5.00
206 Joakim Lindstrom RC 2.00 5.00
207 Kyle Quincey RC 2.00 5.00
208 Valtteri Filppula RC 2.00 5.00
209 Danny Syvret RC 2.00 5.00
210 Matt Greene RC 2.00 5.00
211 J-F Jacques RC 2.00 5.00
212 Greg Jacina RC 2.00 5.00
213 Rob Globke RC 2.00 5.00
214 Yanick Lehoux RC 2.00 5.00
215 Jeff Tambellini RC 2.00 5.00
216 Petr Kanko RC 2.00 5.00
217 Maxim Lapierre RC 2.00 5.00
218 J-P Cote RC 2.00 5.00
219 Andrei Kostitsyn RC 4.00 10.00
220 Kevin Klein RC 2.00 5.00
221 Pekka Rinne RC 3.00 8.00
222 Barry Tallackson RC 2.00 5.00
223 Jason Ryznar RC 2.00 5.00
224 Jeremy Colliton RC 2.00 5.00
225 Bruno Gervais RC 2.00 5.00
226 Stefan Ruzicka RC 2.00 5.00
227 Ben Eager RC 2.00 5.00
228 Alexandre Picard RC 2.00 5.00
229 Matt Jones RC 2.00 5.00
230 Colby Armstrong RC 4.00 10.00
231 Doug Murray RC 2.00 5.00
232 Grant Stevenson RC 2.00 5.00
233 Dennis Wideman RC 2.00 5.00
234 Doug O'Brien RC 2.00 5.00
235 Darren Reid RC 2.00 5.00
236 Ryan Craig RC 3.00 5.00
237 Jay Harrison RC 2.00 5.00
238 Tomas Mojzis RC 2.00 5.00
239 Kevin Bieksa RC 2.00 5.00
240 Mike Green RC 3.00 8.00

2005-06 SP Game Used Autographs

PRINT RUN 5 SER.#'d SETS
NOT PRICED DUE TO SCARCITY

2005-06 SP Game Used Gold

COMMON CARD (1-100) 2.50 6.00
*STARS: 4X TO 10X BASE HI
1-100 PRINT RUN 100 SER.#'d SETS
*ROOKIES: 1X TO 2.5X
ROOKIE PRINT RUN 25 SER.#'d SETS
35 Steve Yzerman 10.00 25.00
58 Martin Brodeur 10.00 25.00
72 Peter Forsberg 6.00 15.00
79 Mario Lemieux 15.00 40.00
101 Sidney Crosby 300.00 500.00
111 Alexander Ovechkin 150.00 300.00

2005-06 SP Game Used Authentic Fabrics

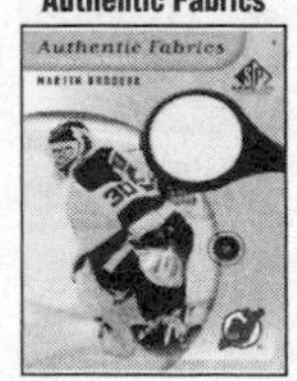

OVERALL MEM. ODDS 1:1
AFAE David Aebischer 5.00 12.00
AFAF Alexander Frolov 5.00 12.00
AFAR Andrew Raycroft 5.00 12.00
AFAT Alex Tanguay 5.00 12.00
AFAY Alexei Yashin 5.00 12.00
AFBE Daniel Briere 6.00 15.00
AFBG Bill Guerin 4.00 10.00
AFBL Rob Blake 5.00 12.00
AFBM Brendan Morrison 4.00 10.00

AFBO Mike Bossy 6.00 15.00
AFBR Martin Brodeur 8.00 20.00
AFBS Brendan Shanahan 6.00 15.00
AFCD Chris Drury 5.00 12.00
AFCJ Curtis Joseph 6.00 15.00
AFCN Cam Neely 5.00 12.00
AFCP Chris Pronger 5.00 12.00
AFDA Daniel Alfredsson 5.00 12.00
AFDB Dustin Brown 5.00 12.00
AFDC Dan Cloutier 5.00 12.00
AFDE Pavol Demitra 5.00 12.00
AFDH Dany Heatley 6.00 15.00
AFDW Doug Weight 5.00 12.00
AFEB Ed Belfour 6.00 15.00
AFGM Glen Murray 5.00 12.00
AFGO Scott Gomez 6.00 15.00
AFHA Dominik Hasek 6.00 15.00
AFHJ Milan Hejduk 6.00 15.00
AFHO Marian Hossa 5.00 12.00
AFHU Trent Hunter 4.00 10.00
AFHV Martin Havlat 5.00 12.00
AFHZ Henrik Zetterberg 6.00 15.00
AFIK Ilya Kovalchuk 8.00 20.00
AFJB Jay Bouwmeester 5.00 12.00
AFJC Jonathan Cheechoo 6.00 15.00
AFJF Jeff Friesen 5.00 12.00
AFJG Jean-Sebastien Giguere 5.00 12.00
AFJI Jarome Iginla 5.00 12.00
AFJJ Jaromir Jagr 6.00 15.00
AFJR Jeremy Roenick 6.00 15.00
AFJS Joe Sakic 6.00 15.00
AFJT Joe Thornton 5.00 12.00
AFKD Kris Draper 2.00 5.00
AFKL Kari Lehtonen 6.00 15.00
AFKP Keith Primeau 4.00 10.00
AFKT Keith Tkachuk 6.00 15.00
AFLE Manny Legace 6.00 15.00
AFMB Martin Biron 5.00 12.00
AFMD Marcel Dionne SP 6.00 15.00
AFMG Marian Gaborik 5.00 12.00
AFMI Mike Ribeiro 4.00 10.00
AFML Mario Lemieux 10.00 25.00
AFMM Mike Modano 5.00 12.00
AFMN Markus Naslund 6.00 15.00
AFMP Mark Parrish 5.00 12.00
AFMR Mark Recchi 5.00 12.00
AFMT Marty Turco 5.00 12.00
AFMW Brenden Morrow 5.00 12.00
AFNH Nathan Horton 5.00 12.00
AFNK Nikolai Khabibulin 6.00 15.00
AFNL Nicklas Lidstrom 6.00 15.00
AFNZ Nikolai Zherdev 5.00 12.00
AFOK Olaf Kolzig 5.00 12.00
AFPB Patrice Bergeron 6.00 15.00
AFPD Pavel Datsyuk 6.00 15.00
AFPE Patrik Elias 5.00 12.00
AFPF Peter Forsberg 5.00 12.00
AFPK Paul Kariya 6.00 15.00
AFPM Patrick Marleau 5.00 12.00
AFPR Patrick Roy 10.00 25.00
AFRB Ray Bourque 5.00 12.00
AFRD Rick DiPietro 5.00 12.00
AFRE Robert Esche 5.00 12.00
AFRI Brad Richards 5.00 12.00
AFRL Roberto Luongo 10.00 25.00
AFRN Rick Nash 8.00 20.00
AFRS Ryan Smyth 5.00 12.00
AFRY Michael Ryder 5.00 12.00
AFSA Miroslav Satan 4.00 10.00
AFSD Shane Doan 5.00 12.00
AFSF Sergei Fedorov 6.00 15.00
AFSG Simon Gagne 6.00 15.00
AFSK Saku Koivu 6.00 15.00
AFSP Jason Spezza 6.00 15.00
AFST Matt Stajan 5.00 12.00
AFSU Mats Sundin 6.00 15.00
AFSW Stephen Weiss 4.00 10.00
AFSY Steve Yzerman 8.00 20.00
AFTB Todd Bertuzzi 8.00 20.00
AFTC Ty Conklin 5.00 12.00
AFTH Jose Theodore 6.00 15.00
AFTP Tom Poti 4.00 10.00
AFTR Tuomo Ruutu 5.00 12.00
AFTV Tomas Vokoun 5.00 12.00
AFVL Vincent Lecavalier 6.00 15.00
AFZC Zdeno Chara 6.00 15.00
AFZP Zigmund Palffy 5.00 12.00

2005-06 SP Game Used Authentic Fabrics Autographs

*STARS: 1.5X TO 4X BASIC JERSEY
PRINT RUN 75 SER.#'d SETS
AAFJC Jonathan Cheechoo 25.00 60.00
AAFWG Wayne Gretzky 150.00 300.00

2005-06 SP Game Used Authentic Fabrics Dual

PRINT RUN 100 SER.#'d SETS
AH Daniel Alfredsson 10.00 25.00
Dany Heatley
BB Martin Biron 8.00 20.00
Daniel Briere
BF Dustin Brown 8.00 20.00
Alexander Frolov
BM Ed Belfour 8.00 20.00
Bryan McCabe
BN Martin Biron 8.00 20.00
Mika Noronen
CO Patrick Roy 12.50 30.00
Ray Bourque
DH Shane Doan 8.00 20.00
Brett Hull
DJ Dany Heatley 10.00 25.00
Jason Spezza
EB Patrik Elias 12.50 30.00
Martin Brodeur
ER Robert Esche 8.00 20.00
Peter Forsberg
GH Wayne Gretzky 50.00 100.00
Gordie Howe
GK Wayne Gretzky 50.00 100.00
Jari Kurri
GS Jean-Sebastien Giguere 8.00 20.00
Teemu Selanne
HH Dominik Hasek 10.00 25.00
Martin Havlat
HK Marian Hossa 8.00 20.00
Ilya Kovalchuk
HL Adam Hall 8.00 20.00
David Legwand
HS Trent Hunter 8.00 20.00
Miroslav Satan
IK Jarome Iginla 12.50 30.00
Miikka Kiprusoff
IS Jarome Iginla 8.00 20.00
Martin St.Louis
KK Nikolai Khabibulin 8.00 20.00
Miikka Kiprusoff
KT Saku Koivu 8.00 20.00
Jose Theodore
KV Paul Kariya 10.00 25.00
Tomas Vokoun
LN Kari Lehtonen 8.00 20.00
Mika Noronen
LS Vincent Lecavalier 10.00 25.00
Martin St. Louis
MC Patrick Marleau 8.00 20.00
Jonathan Cheechoo
MO Mats Sundin 8.00 20.00
Owen Nolan
MT Markus Naslund 8.00 20.00
Todd Bertuzzi
NB Cam Neely 10.00 25.00
Ray Bourque
NT Rick Nash 10.00 25.00
Joe Thornton
NY Bryan Trottier 8.00 20.00
Mike Bossy
PB Joe Thornton 8.00 20.00
Patrice Bergeron
PC Chris Pronger 8.00 20.00
Ty Conklin
PE Joni Pitkanen 8.00 20.00
Robert Esche
PG Keith Primeau 8.00 20.00
Simon Gagne
RA Raffi Torres 8.00 20.00
Ales Hemsky
RB Mike Ribeiro 6.00 15.00
Patrice Bergeron
RF Dwayne Roloson 8.00 20.00
Manny Fernandez
RR Michael Ryder 8.00 20.00
Mike Ribeiro
SA Jason Spezza 10.00 25.00
Daniel Alfredsson
SB Joe Sakic 8.00 20.00
Rob Blake
SC Ryan Smyth 8.00 20.00
Ty Conklin
SP Darryl Sittler 10.00 25.00
Gilbert Perreault
SR Philippe Sauve 8.00 20.00
Andrew Raycroft
SS Matt Stajan 8.00 20.00
Eric Staal
TH Alex Tanguay 8.00 20.00
Milan Hejduk
TM Marty Turco 8.00 20.00
Mike Modano
WB Peter Worrell 8.00 20.00
Donald Brashear
WH Stephen Weiss 8.00 20.00
Nathan Horton
WT Doug Weight 8.00 20.00
Keith Tkachuk
YS Steve Yzerman 12.50 30.00
Brendan Shanahan
ZD Henrik Zetterberg 8.00 20.00
Kris Draper

2005-06 SP Game Used Authentic Fabrics Dual Autographs

PRINT RUN 25 SER.#'d SETS
AH Daniel Alfredsson
Dany Heatley
BB Martin Biron 20.00 50.00
Daniel Briere
CO Patrick Roy 125.00 200.00
Ray Bourque
DJ Dany Heatley 40.00 100.00
Jason Spezza
DT Marcel Dionne 20.00 50.00
Bryan Trottier
GH Wayne Gretzky 300.00 500.00
Gordie Howe
HH Dominik Hasek 30.00 80.00
Martin Havlat
HK Marian Hossa 30.00 80.00
Ilya Kovalchuk
HS Trent Hunter 15.00 40.00
Miroslav Satan
IS Jarome Iginla 25.00 60.00
Martin St.Louis
KT Saku Koivu 30.00 80.00
Jose Theodore
LD Guy Lafleur EXCH 60.00 125.00
Marcel Dionne
LN Kari Lehtonen 20.00 50.00
Mika Noronen
LS Vincent Lecavalier 40.00 100.00
Martin St. Louis
MO Mats Sundin 30.00 80.00
Owen Nolan
MT Markus Naslund 20.00 50.00
Todd Bertuzzi
NB Cam Neely 75.00 150.00
Ray Bourque
NT Rick Nash EXCH 50.00 125.00
Joe Thornton
PB Joe Thornton 30.00 80.00
Patrice Bergeron
PC Chris Pronger 20.00 50.00
Ty Conklin
PE Joni Pitkanen 15.00 40.00
Robert Esche
PG Keith Primeau 15.00 40.00
Simon Gagne
RB Mike Ribeiro 20.00 50.00
Patrice Bergeron
RR Michael Ryder 20.00 50.00
Mike Ribeiro
SA Jason Spezza
Daniel Alfredsson
SR Philippe Sauve 15.00 40.00
Andrew Raycroft
SS Matt Stajan 25.00 60.00
Eric Staal
TH Alex Tanguay 25.00 60.00
Milan Hejduk
TM Marty Turco 30.00 80.00
Mike Modano
WH Stephen Weiss 15.00 40.00
Nathan Horton

2005-06 SP Game Used Authentic Fabrics Gold

*STARS: .75X TO 2X
PRINT RUN 100 SER.#'d SETS
AFWG Wayne Gretzky 40.00 100.00

2005-06 SP Game Used Authentic Fabrics Quad

PRINT RUN 10 SER.#'d SETS
NOT PRICED DUE TO SCARCITY
BADS Martin Biron
Maxim Afinogenov
Chris Drury
Daniel Briere
BEGK Martin Brodeur
Patrick Elias
Scott Gomez
Viktor Kozlov
BLSR Sean Burke
Vincent Lecavalier
Martin St.Louis
Brad Richards
DLBN Tie Domi
Eric Lindros
Ed Belfour
Owen Nolan
EMMR Patrik Elias
Paul Martin
Alexander Mogilny
Brian Rafalski
FRRG Alexander Frolov
Jeremy Roenick
Luc Robitaille
Matheiu Garon
GFEP Simon Gagne
Peter Forsberg
Robert Esche
Keith Primeau
GFRB Marian Gaborik
Manny Fernandez
Dwayne Roloson
Pierre-Marc Bouchard
GMCF Wayne Gretzky
Mark Messier
Jari Kurri
Grant Fuhr
HLBJ Nathan Horton
Roberto Luongo
Jay Bouwmeester
Olli Jokinen
IAKL Jarome Iginla
Tony Amonte
Miikka Kiprusoff
Matthew Lombardi
KBJL Ryan Kesler
Todd Bertuzzi
Ed Jovanovski
Trevor Linden
KHLS Ilya Kovalchuk
Marian Hossa
Kari Lehtonen
Patrik Stefan
KLHV Paul Kariya
David Legwand
Adam Hall
Tomas Vokoun
LZDC Nicklas Lidstrom
Henrik Zetterberg
Pavel Datsyuk
Chris Chelios
MLYS Mark Messier
Mario Lemieux
Steve Yzerman
Joe Sakic
MNDB Ryan Miller
Mika Noronen
J.P Dumont
Daniel Briere
MTGA Mike Modano
Marty Turco
Bill Guerin
Jason Arnott
NSZB Rick Nash
Jason Spezza
Henrik Zetterberg
Jay Bouwmeester
NZDF Rick Nash
Nikolai Zherdev
Marc Denis
Sergei Fedorov
RBBF Patrick Roy
Rob Blake
Ray Bourque
Adam Foote
RBLT Patrick Roy
Martin Brodeur
Roberto Luongo
Jose Theodore
SAHH Jason Spezza
Daniel Alfredsson
Martin Havlat
Dany Heatley
SATH Joe Sakic
David Aebischer
Alex Tanguay
Milan Hejduk
SDYH Miroslav Satan
Rick Dipietro
Alexei Yashin
Trent Hunter
SGLC Teemu Selanne
Jean-Sebastien Giguere
Joffrey Lupul
Stanislav Chistov
SNSA Matt Stajan
Owen Nolan
Mats Sundin
Nikolai Antropov
TBYS Bryan Trottier
Mike Bossy
Alexei Yashin
Miroslav Satan
TRGL Keith Tkachuk
Jeremy Roenick
Bill Guerin
John LeClair
TRRK Jose Theodore
Michael Ryder
Mike Ribeiro
Saku Koivu
TRSB Joe Thornton
Andrew Raycroft
Sergei Samsonov
Patrice Bergeron
YDSL Steve Yzerman
Kris Draper
Brendan Shanahan
Manny Legace
SCPTB Ryan Smyth
Ty Conklin
Chris Pronger
Eric Brewer

2005-06 SP Game Used Authentic Patches Quad

PRINT RUN 5 SER.#'d SETS
NOT PRICED DUE TO SCARCITY

2005-06 SP Game Used Authentic Fabrics Triple

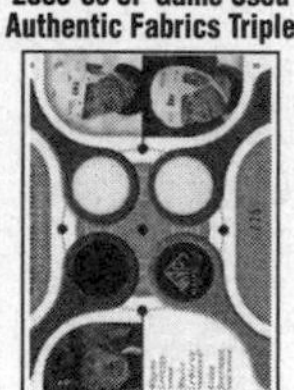

PRINT RUN 25 SER.#'d SETS
ARS Daniel Alfredsson 40.00 80.00
Brad Richards
Martin St.Louis
BBP Ray Bourque 20.00 50.00
Rob Blake
Chris Pronger
BBT Martin Brodeur 50.00 100.00
Ed Belfour
Marty Turco
BIS Martin Brodeur 60.00 125.00
Jarome Iginla
Martin St.Louis
BTR Martin Brodeur 100.00 200.00
Jose Theodore
Patrick Roy
CEA Ty Conklin 30.00 60.00
Robert Esche
David Aebischer
CNP Zdeno Chara 30.00 60.00
Scott Niedermeyar
Chris Pronger
CRH Zdeno Chara 30.00 60.00
Wade Redden
Dominik Hasek
DBS Tie Domi 20.00 50.00
Donald Brashear
Chris Simon
DKF Pavel Datsyuk 75.00 150.00
Ilya Kovalchuk
Sergei Fedorov
DLP Kris Draper 30.00 60.00
Jere Lehtinen
Michael Peca
GLY Wayne Gretzky 200.00 350.00
Mario Lemieux
Steve Yzerman
GNP Sergei Gonchar 20.00 50.00
Scott Niedermayer
Chris Pronger
HJH Dominik Hasek 50.00 100.00
Jaromir Jagr
Martin Havlat
HND Brett Hull 20.00 50.00
Ladislav Nagy
Shane Doan
INK Jarome Iginla 40.00 80.00
Rick Nash
Ilya Kovalchuk
ISL Jarome Iginla 40.00 80.00
Brendan Shanahan
Trevor Linden
KNS Ilya Kovalchuk 30.00 60.00
Markus Naslund
Cory Stillman
KRT Miikka Kiprusoff 40.00 80.00
Dwayne Roloson
Marty Turco
KSK Jari Kurri 60.00 125.00
Teemu Selanne
Saku Koivu
MLR Mike Modano 30.00 80.00
Trevor Linden
Jeremy Roenick
NKL Mika Noronen 40.00 80.00
Miikka Kiprusoff
Kari Lehtonen
NPJ Owen Nolan 30.00 60.00
Keith Primeau
Jaromir Jagr
NSL Owen Nolan 20.00 50.00
Mats Sundin
Eric Lindros
PCS Chris Pronger 20.00 50.00
Ty Conklin
Ryan Smyth
RLA Andrew Raycroft 50.00 100.00
Kari Lehtonen
David Aebischer
SEL Joe Sakic 30.00 60.00
Patrik Elias
Robert Lang
SFI Martin St.Louis 30.00 60.00
Peter Forsberg
Jarome Iginla
SFN Mats Sundin 40.00 80.00
Peter Forsberg
Markus Naslund
SHA Martin St. Louis
Marian Hossa
Daniel Alfredsson
SNI Martin St.Louis 40.00 80.00
Markus Naslund
Jarome Iginla
TBM Joe Thornton 30.00 60.00
Patrice Bergeron
Glen Murray
TSY Joe Thornton 50.00 100.00
Joe Sakic
Steve Yzerman
VKL Tomas Vokoun 20.00 50.00
Paul Kariya
David Legwand
YSP Alexei Yashin 40.00 80.00
Miroslav Satan
Mark Parrish

2005-06 SP Game Used Authentic Patches

*SINGLE COLORS: 2X TO .5X HI
*3+ COLORS: 1X TO 2X HI
PRINT RUN 75 SER.#'d SETS
APAE David Aebischer 15.00 40.00
APAF Alexander Frolov 15.00 40.00
APAR Andrew Raycroft 15.00 40.00
APAT Alex Tanguay 15.00 40.00
APAY Alexei Yashin 12.00 30.00
APBE Daniel Briere 10.00 25.00
APBG Bill Guerin 12.00 30.00
APBL Rob Blake 15.00 40.00
APBM Brendan Morrison 12.00 30.00
APBO Mike Bossy 12.00 30.00
APBR Martin Brodeur 30.00 80.00
APBS Brendan Shanahan 20.00 50.00
APCD Chris Drury 15.00 40.00
APCJ Curtis Joseph 20.00 50.00
APCN Cam Neely 12.00 30.00
APCP Chris Pronger 15.00 40.00
APDA Daniel Alfredsson 15.00 40.00
APDB Dustin Brown 12.00 30.00
APDC Dan Cloutier 15.00 40.00
APDE Pavol Demitra 15.00 40.00
APDH Dany Heatley 20.00 50.00
APDW Doug Weight 15.00 40.00
APEB Ed Belfour 20.00 50.00
APGM Glen Murray 12.00 30.00
APGO Scott Gomez 15.00 40.00
APHA Dominik Hasek 20.00 50.00
APHJ Milan Hejduk 20.00 50.00
APHO Marian Hossa 15.00 40.00
APHU Trent Hunter 12.00 30.00
APHV Martin Havlat 15.00 40.00
APHZ Henrik Zetterberg 20.00 50.00
APIK Ilya Kovalchuk 20.00 50.00
APJB Jay Bouwmeester 12.00 30.00
APJC Jonathan Cheechoo 15.00 40.00
APJF Jeff Friesen 12.00 30.00
APJG Jean-Sebastien Giguere 15.00 40.00
APJI Jarome Iginla 20.00 50.00
APJJ Jaromir Jagr 20.00 50.00
APJR Jeremy Roenick 20.00 50.00
APJS Joe Sakic 25.00 60.00
APJT Joe Thornton 20.00 50.00
APKD Kris Draper 6.00 15.00
APKL Kari Lehtonen 15.00 40.00
APKP Keith Primeau 10.00 25.00
APKT Keith Tkachuk 20.00 50.00
APLE Manny Legace 20.00 50.00
APMB Martin Biron 15.00 40.00
APMD Marcel Dionne 12.00 30.00
APMG Marian Gaborik 20.00 50.00
APMI Mike Ribeiro 12.00 30.00
APML Mario Lemieux 40.00 100.00
APMM Mike Modano 15.00 40.00
APMN Markus Naslund 20.00 50.00
APMP Mark Parrish 12.00 30.00
APMR Mark Recchi 15.00 40.00
APMS Martin St. Louis 15.00 40.00
APMT Marty Turco 12.00 30.00
APMW Brenden Morrow 15.00 40.00
APNH Nathan Horton 12.00 30.00
APNK Nikolai Khabibulin 20.00 50.00
APNL Nicklas Lidstrom 20.00 50.00
APNZ Nikolai Zherdev 15.00 40.00
APOK Olaf Kolzig 15.00 40.00
APPB Patrice Bergeron 20.00 50.00
APPD Pavel Datsyuk 20.00 50.00
APPE Patrik Elias 15.00 40.00
APPF Peter Forsberg 20.00 50.00
APPK Paul Kariya 20.00 50.00
APPM Patrick Marleau 15.00 40.00
APPR Patrick Roy 40.00 100.00
APRB Ray Bourque 20.00 50.00
APRD Rick DiPietro 15.00 40.00
APRE Robert Esche 15.00 40.00
APRI Brad Richards 15.00 40.00
APRL Roberto Luongo 40.00 100.00
APRN Rick Nash 25.00 60.00
APRS Ryan Smyth 12.00 30.00
APRY Michael Ryder 15.00 40.00
APSA Miroslav Satan 12.00 30.00
APSD Shane Doan 12.00 30.00
APSF Sergei Fedorov 20.00 50.00
APSG Simon Gagne 20.00 50.00
APSK Saku Koivu 20.00 50.00
APSP Jason Spezza 15.00 40.00
APST Matt Stajan 12.00 30.00
APSU Mats Sundin 20.00 50.00
APSW Stephen Weiss 12.00 30.00
APSY Steve Yzerman 30.00 80.00
APTB Todd Bertuzzi 25.00 60.00
APTC Ty Conklin 15.00 40.00
APTH Jose Theodore 20.00 50.00
APTP Tom Poti 12.00 30.00
APTR Tuomo Ruutu 12.00 30.00
APTV Tomas Vokoun 15.00 40.00
APVL Vincent Lecavalier 20.00 50.00
APWG Wayne Gretzky 60.00 150.00
APZC Zdeno Chara 15.00 40.00
APZP Zigmund Palffy 15.00 40.00

2005-06 SP Game Used Authentic Patches Autographs

*STARS: .75X TO 2X BASE PATCH
PRINT RUN 50 SER.#'d SETS

2005-06 SP Game Used Authentic Patches Dual

*DUAL PATCH: 1X TO 2.5X DUAL JSY
PRINT RUN 35 SER.#'d SETS
CO Patrick Roy 60.00 150.00
Ray Bourque
GH Wayne Gretzky 200.00 350.00
Gordie Howe
GK Wayne Gretzky 100.00 250.00
Jari Kurri
GL Wayne Gretzky 150.00 300.00
Mario Lemieux
LD Guy Lafleur 30.00 80.00
Marcel Dionne
MC Patrick Marleau 40.00 100.00
Jonathan Cheechoo
NT Rick Nash 75.00 200.00
Joe Thornton

2005-06 SP Game Used Authentic Patches Dual Autographs

PRINT RUN 10 SER.#'d SETS
NOT PRICED DUE TO SCARCITY

2005-06 SP Game Used Authentic Patches Triple

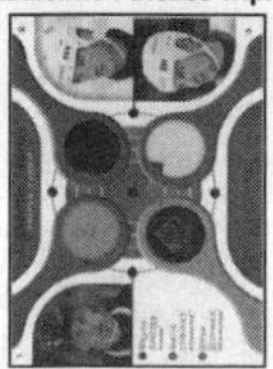

PRINT RUN 10 SER.#'d SETS
NOT PRICED DUE TO SCARCITY

2005-06 SP Game Used Auto Draft

PRINT RUNS LISTED BELOW
UNDER 24 NOT PRICED DUE TO SCARCITY
ADAF Alexander Frolov/20
ADAL Daniel Alfredsson/133 6.00 15.00
ADAM Alvaro Montoya/29 30.00 60.00
ADAO Alexander Ovechkin/1
ADAP Alexander Perezhogin/25 25.00 50.00
ADAS Alexander Steen/24 25.00 50.00
ADBL Brian Leetch/9
ADBO Ray Bourque/8
ADBR Brad Richards/64 10.00 25.00
ADBU Peter Budaj/63 15.00 40.00
ADBW Brad Winchester/35 8.00 20.00
ADBY Matthew Barnaby/83 6.00 15.00
ADCA Michael Cammalleri/49 10.00 25.00
ADCC Craig Conroy/123 6.00 15.00
ADCD Chris Drury/72 10.00 25.00
ADCN Cam Neely/9
ADCP Corey Perry/28 25.00 60.00
ADCW Cam Ward/25 30.00 75.00
ADDA David Aebischer/161 6.00 15.00
ADDB Daniel Briere/24 25.00 60.00
ADDC Dan Cloutier/26 12.00 30.00
ADDF Dan Fritsche/46 6.00 15.00
ADDK Duncan Keith/54 10.00 25.00
ADDL David Leneveu/46 12.00 30.00
ADDM Darren McCarty/46 10.00 25.00
ADDP Dion Phaneuf/9
ADEC Erik Cole/71 8.00 20.00
ADED Eric Daze/90 6.00 15.00
ADFT Fedor Tjutin/40 12.50 30.00
ADGB Gilbert Brule/6
ADGL Georges Laraque/31 15.00 40.00
ADGU Guy Lafleur/1
ADHE Jochen Hecht/49 10.00 25.00
ADHT Hannu Toivonen/29 20.00 50.00
ADHV Martin Havlat/26 25.00 60.00
ADJA Jason Arnott/7
ADJC Jonathan Cheechoo/29 25.00 60.00
ADJE Jeff Carter/11
ADJF Johan Franzen/97 8.00 20.00
ADJH Jim Howard/64 15.00 40.00
ADJI Jarome Iginla/11
ADJJ Jussi Jokinen/192 8.00 20.00
ADJK Jari Kurri/69 20.00 50.00
ADJO Joe Thornton/1
ADJS Jim Slater/30 10.00 25.00
ADJT Jose Theodore/44 15.00 40.00
ADJV Josef Vasicek/91 6.00 15.00
ADJW Justin Williams/28 15.00 40.00
ADKD Kris Draper/62 10.00 25.00
ADKH Kristian Huselius/47 6.00 15.00
ADKW Kevin Weekes/41 8.00 20.00
ADLR Luc Robitaille/171 50.00 100.00
ADMA Maxim Afinogenov/69 8.00 20.00
ADMB Martin Brodeur/20 60.00 150.00
ADMC Jay McClement/57 8.00 20.00
ADMF Matt Foy/175 6.00 15.00
ADMG Marian Gaborik/3
ADMH Milan Hejduk/87 8.00 20.00
ADMI Milan Bartovic/35 8.00 20.00
ADMJ Milan Jurcina/241
ADMM Mike Modano/1
ADMN Markus Naslund/16 15.00 40.00
ADMR Mike Ribeiro/45 6.00 15.00
ADMS Matt Stajan/57 15.00 40.00
ADMW Brenden Morrow/25 12.00 30.00
ADNK Nikolai Khabibulin/204 6.00 15.00
ADNO Mika Noronen/21
ADNY Michael Nylander/59 8.00 20.00
ADPB Patrice Bergeron/45 20.00 50.00
ADPE Patrick Eaves/29 15.00 40.00
ADPR Patrick Roy/51 100.00 175.00
ADPS Philippe Sauve/38 8.00 20.00
ADRB Rob Blake/70 8.00 20.00
ADRC Mark Recchi/67
ADRE Robert Esche/139 6.00 15.00
ADRG Ryan Getzlaf/19 60.00 150.00
ADRI Mike Richards/24 50.00 100.00
ADRK Ryan Kesler/23 10.00 25.00
ADRN Rick Nash/1
ADSB Sean Burke/24 10.00 25.00
ADSC Sidney Crosby/1
ADSG Simon Gagne/22 30.00 60.00
ADSH Sheldon Souray/71 6.00 15.00
ADSK Saku Koivu/21 30.00 60.00
ADSN Scott Niedermayer/3
ADSP Jason Spezza/2
ADSS Steve Sullivan/233 6.00 15.00
ADSU Mats Sundin/1
ADSV Marc Savard/91
ADSZ Sergei Zubov/85 6.00 15.00
ADTA Tyler Arnason/183 6.00 15.00
ADTB Todd Bertuzzi/23
ADTG Tim Gleason/23 10.00 25.00
ADTH Trent Hunter/150 6.00 15.00
ADTP Tom Poti/59 6.00 15.00
ADTS Timofei Shishkanov/33 8.00 20.00
ADTV Thomas Vanek/5
ADVL Vincent Lecavalier/1
ADVP Vaclav Prospal/71 6.00 15.00
ADZC Zdeno Chara/56 8.00 20.00

2005-06 SP Game Used Awesome Authentics

PRINT RUN 100 SER.#'d SETS
AAAF Alexander Frolov
AAAH Ales Hemsky 10.00 25.00
AAAR Andrew Raycroft 10.00 25.00
AAAT Alex Tanguay 10.00 25.00
AAAY Alexei Yashin 10.00 25.00
AABG Bill Guerin 8.00 20.00

AABI Martin Biron 10.00 25.00
AABM Bryan McCabe 10.00 25.00
AABR Brad Richards 10.00 25.00
AABS Brendan Shanahan 12.00 30.00
AACD Chris Drury 10.00 25.00
AACJ Curtis Joseph 12.00 30.00
AACP Chris Pronger 10.00 25.00
AADA Daniel Alfredsson 10.00 25.00
AADB Daniel Briere 15.00 40.00
AADC Dan Cloutier 10.00 25.00
AADH Dany Heatley 10.00 25.00
AADL David Legwand 10.00 25.00
AADU Dustin Brown 10.00 25.00
AADW Doug Weight 10.00 25.00
AAEB Ed Belfour 12.00 30.00
AAEL Eric Lindros 12.00 30.00
AAES Eric Staal 8.00 20.00
AAGM Glen Murray 10.00 25.00
AAHJ Milan Hejduk 12.00 30.00
AAHK Dominik Hasek/75 15.00 40.00
AAHV Martin Havlat 10.00 25.00
AAHZ Henrik Zetterberg 12.00 30.00
AAIK Ilya Kovalchuk 10.00 25.00
AAJB Jay Bouwmeester 6.00 15.00
AAJG Jean-Sebastien Giguere 10.00 25.00
AAJI Jarome Iginla 10.00 25.00
AAJJ Jaromir Jagr 15.00 40.00
AAJL John LeClair 8.00 20.00
AAJO Joe Thornton 12.00 30.00
AAJR Jeremy Roenick 10.00 25.00
AAJS Jason Spezza 10.00 25.00
AAJT Jocelyn Thibault 10.00 25.00
AAJW Justin Williams 10.00 25.00
AAKP Keith Primeau 8.00 20.00
AAKT Keith Tkachuk 12.00 30.00
AALN Ladislav Nagy 10.00 25.00
AALU Joffrey Lupul 10.00 25.00
AALX Mario Lemieux 40.00 100.00
AAMB Martin Brodeur 25.00 60.00
AAMF Manny Fernandez 10.00 25.00
AAMG Marian Gaborik 12.00 30.00
AAMK Miikka Kiprusoff 12.00 30.00
AAML Manny Legace 12.00 30.00
AAMM Mike Modano 10.00 25.00
AAMN Markus Naslund 12.00 30.00
AAMO Brendan Morrison 8.00 20.00
AAMP Mark Parrish 10.00 25.00
AAMS Matt Stajan 10.00 25.00
AAMT Marty Turco 10.00 25.00
AAMW Brenden Morrow 10.00 25.00
AANH Nathan Horton 10.00 25.00
AANK Nikolai Khabibulin 12.00 30.00
AANL Nicklas Lidstrom 12.00 30.00
AANZ Nikolai Zherdev 10.00 25.00
AAOK Olaf Kolzig 10.00 25.00
AAPB Patrice Bergeron 12.00 30.00
AAPE Patrik Elias 10.00 25.00
AAPF Peter Forsberg 12.00 30.00
AAPK Paul Kariya 12.00 30.00
AARA Brian Rafalski 10.00 25.00
AARB Rob Blake 10.00 25.00
AARD Rick DiPietro 10.00 25.00
AARE Mark Recchi 10.00 25.00
AARF Ruslan Fedotenko 10.00 25.00
AARL Roberto Luongo 12.00 30.00
AARN Rick Nash 10.00 25.00
AARO Robert Esche 10.00 25.00
AARS Ryan Smyth 15.00 40.00
AARY Michael Ryder 10.00 25.00
AARZ Richard Zednik 6.00 15.00
AASA Joe Sakic 15.00 40.00
AASD Shane Doan 10.00 25.00
AASF Sergei Fedorov/75 12.00 30.00
AASG Simon Gagne 12.00 30.00
AASK Saku Koivu 12.00 30.00
AASL Martin St. Louis 10.00 25.00
AASU Mats Sundin 12.00 30.00
AASY Steve Yzerman 25.00 60.00
AATC Ty Conklin 10.00 25.00
AATH Jose Theodore 10.00 25.00
AATR Tuomo Ruutu 10.00 25.00
AATS Teemu Selanne 12.00 30.00
AATV Tomas Vokoun 10.00 25.00
AAVL Vincent Lecavalier 12.00 30.00
AAWR Wade Redden 6.00 15.00
AAZP Zigmund Palffy 10.00 25.00

2005-06 SP Game Used Awesome Authentics Gold

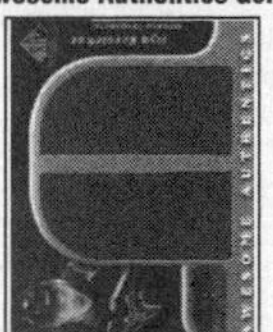

*GOLD: .6X TO 1.5X BASE JSY
PRINT RUN 25 SER.#'d SETS

2005-06 SP Game Used By the Letter

PRINT RUNS VARY
NOT PRICED DUE TO SCARCITY
LMAK Alexei Kovalev/7
LMBS Brendan Shanahan/8
LMEB Ed Belfour /7
LMEJ Ed Jovanovski/10
LMHZ Henrik Zetterberg/10
LMIK Ilya Kovalchuk/9
LMJI Jarome Iginla/6
LMML Mario Lemieux/7
LMMT Marty Turco/5
LMPB Patrice Bergeron/8
LMPR Patrick Roy/3
LMRB Ray Bourque/7
LMSF Sergei Fedorov/7
LMSP Jason Spezza/6
LMSY Steve Yzerman/7

2005-06 SP Game Used Endorsed Equipment

PRINT RUN 5 SER.#'d SETS
NOT PRICED DUE TO SCARCITY
EEEB Ed Belfour
EEGF Grant Fuhr
EEJT Jose Theodore
EEMF Marc-Andre Fleury
EEMT Marty Turco
EEOK Olaf Kolzig
EEPR Patrick Roy
EETE Tony Esposito

2005-06 SP Game Used Game Gear

PRINT RUN 100 SER.#'d SETS
UNLESS OTHERWISE NOTED
GGAF Maxim Afinogenov 4.00 10.00
GGAK Alexei Kovalev 5.00 12.00
GGAM Alexander Mogilny 8.00 20.00
GGAO Alexander Ovechkin 30.00 80.00
GGAP Alexander Perezhogin 4.00 10.00
GGAR Andrew Raycroft 8.00 20.00
GGAS Alexander Steen 6.00 15.00
GGAT Alex Tanguay/45 10.00 25.00
GGBA Rod Brind'Amour 8.00 20.00
GGBE Patrice Bergeron 10.00 25.00
GGBG Bill Guerin 4.00 10.00
GGBL Rob Blake 8.00 20.00
GGBO Ray Bourque 10.00 25.00
GGBR Martin Brodeur 12.00 30.00
GGBS Billy Smith 5.00 12.00
GGBT Bryan Trottier 5.00 12.00
GGCB Cam Barker 8.00 20.00
GGCD Chris Drury 8.00 20.00
GGCE Christian Ehrhoff 4.00 10.00
GGCH Jonathan Cheechoo 10.00 25.00
GGCN Cam Neely 6.00 15.00
GGCP Chris Pronger 8.00 20.00
GGDB Daniel Briere 4.00 10.00
GGDH Dany Heatley 10.00 25.00
GGDL David Legwand 8.00 20.00
GGDP Dion Phaneuf 12.00 30.00
GGEN Eric Nystrom 4.00 10.00
GGES Eric Staal 8.00 20.00
GGGB Gilbert Brule 8.00 20.00
GGGL Guy Lafleur 10.00 25.00
GGHA Dominik Hasek 12.00 30.00
GGHL Henrik Lundqvist 12.00 30.00
GGHT Hannu Toivonen 6.00 15.00
GGHZ Henrik Zetterberg 10.00 25.00
GGIK Ilya Kovalchuk 12.00 30.00
GGJB Jean Beliveau 10.00 25.00
GGJC Jeff Carter 8.00 20.00
GGJF Jeff Friesen 4.00 10.00
GGJG Jean-Sebastien Giguere 4.00 10.00
GGJH Jim Howard 8.00 20.00
GGJI Jarome Iginla 8.00 20.00
GGJJ Jaromir Jagr 15.00 40.00
GGJO Joe Thornton 15.00 40.00
GGJP Joni Pitkanen 4.00 10.00
GGJR Jeremy Roenick
GGJS Jason Spezza 10.00 25.00
GGKP Keith Primeau 6.00 15.00
GGKT Keith Tkachuk 10.00 25.00
GGMA Paul Martin 4.00 10.00
GGMB Mike Bossy 6.00 15.00
GGML Mario Lemieux 20.00 50.00
GGMM Mike Modano 8.00 20.00
GGMR Mike Ribeiro 4.00 10.00
GGMT Marty Turco 8.00 20.00
GGOK Olaf Kolzig 8.00 20.00
GGOR Brooks Orpik 4.00 10.00
GGPB Peter Bondra 8.00 20.00
GGPC Corey Perry 6.00 15.00
GGPF Peter Forsberg 10.00 25.00
GGPK Paul Kariya 10.00 25.00
GGPM Pierre-Marc Bouchard 4.00 10.00
GGPS Philippe Sauve 8.00 20.00
GGRB Ray Bourque 10.00 25.00
GGRF Ruslan Fedotenko 4.00 10.00
GGRG Ryan Getzlaf 8.00 20.00
GGRI Mike Richards 6.00 15.00
GGRK Steve Klesla 4.00 10.00
GGRM Ryan Malone 4.00 10.00
GGRN Rick Nash 12.00 30.00
GGRT Raffi Torres 4.00 10.00
GGRY Michael Ryder 8.00 20.00
GGSA Joe Sakic 15.00 40.00
GGSC Sidney Crosby 50.00 125.00
GGSG Simon Gagne 10.00 25.00
GGSH Brendan Shanahan 10.00 25.00
GGSK Saku Koivu 10.00 25.00
GGST Anthony Stewart 4.00 10.00
GGSU Mats Sundin 12.00 30.00
GGSY Steve Yzerman 15.00 40.00
GGTH Trent Hunter 4.00 10.00
GGTV Thomas Vanek 8.00 20.00
GGWW Wojtek Wolski 8.00 20.00
GGYD Yann Danis 4.00 10.00
GGZP Zach Parise 8.00 20.00
GGBH2 Bobby Hull 12.00 30.00
GGGH1 Gordie Howe 12.00 30.00
GGGH2 Gordie Howe 12.00 30.00
GGPR1 Patrick Roy 20.00 50.00
GGPR2 Patrick Roy 20.00 50.00

2005-06 SP Game Used Game Gear Autographs

PRINT RUN 10 SER.#'d SETS
NOT PRICED DUE TO SCARCITY

2005-06 SP Game Used Heritage Classic

PRINT RUN 100 SER.#'d SETS
HCBR Bill Ranford 8.00 20.00
HCBS Borje Salming 6.00 15.00
HCDG Doug Gilmour 8.00 20.00
HCDS Darryl Sittler 6.00 15.00
HCDW Tiger Williams 6.00 15.00
HCGF Grant Fuhr 6.00 15.00
HCKM Kirk Muller 6.00 15.00
HCLM Larry Murphy 6.00 15.00
HCMC Lanny McDonald 6.00 15.00
HCMK Mike Krushelnyski 6.00 15.00
HCPS Peter Stastny 6.00 15.00
HCRB Ray Bourque 8.00 20.00
HCRE Ron Ellis 6.00 15.00
HCRL Rod Langway 6.00 15.00
HCRV Rick Vaive 6.00 15.00
HCSS Steve Shutt 6.00 15.00
HCWC Wendel Clark 8.00 20.00

2005-06 SP Game Used Heritage Classic Autographs

*AUTO: 1X TO 2.5X BASE JSY
PRINT RUN 100 SER.#'d SETS

2005-06 SP Game Used Heritage Classic Patches

*PATCH: .75X TO 2X BASE JSY
PRINT RUN 25 SER.#'d SETS

2005-06 SP Game Used Heritage Classic Patches Autographed

PRINT RUN 10 SER.#'d SETS
NOT PRICED DUE TO SCARCITY

2005-06 SP Game Used Oldtimer's Challenge

PRINT RUN 100 SER.#'d SETS
OCBB Bob Bourne 4.00 10.00
OCBO Ray Bourque 10.00 25.00
OCBP Bob Probert 4.00 10.00
OCDB Doug Bodger 4.00 10.00
OCDG Doug Gilmour 10.00 25.00
OCDS Darryl Sittler 6.00 15.00
OCDW Tiger Williams 4.00 10.00
OCGA Glenn Anderson 4.00 10.00
OCGF Grant Fuhr 6.00 15.00
OCGL Guy Lafleur 5.00 12.00
OCGP Gilbert Perreault 4.00 10.00
OCKM Kirk Muller 4.00 10.00
OCMC Lanny McDonald 6.00 15.00
OCRB Richard Brodeur 4.00 10.00
OCSS Steve Shutt 4.00 10.00

2005-06 SP Game Used Oldtimer's Challenge Autographs

PRINT RUN 100 SER.#'d SETS
OCABB Bob Bourne 10.00 25.00
OCABO Ray Bourque 20.00 50.00
OCABP Bob Probert 12.00 30.00
OCADB Doug Bodger 10.00 25.00
OCADG Doug Gilmour 20.00 50.00
OCADS Darryl Sittler 15.00 40.00
OCADW Tiger Williams 10.00 25.00
OCAGA Glenn Anderson 10.00 25.00
OCAGF Grant Fuhr 15.00 40.00
OCAGL Guy Lafleur 20.00 50.00
OCAGP Gilbert Perreault 10.00 25.00
OCAKM Kirk Muller 10.00 25.00
OCAMC Lanny McDonald 15.00 40.00
OCARB Richard Brodeur 10.00 25.00
OCASS Steve Shutt 10.00 25.00

2005-06 SP Game Used Oldtimer's Challenge Patches Autographed

PRINT RUN 10 SER.#'d SETS
NOT PRICED DUE TO SCARCITY

2005-06 SP Game Used Rookie Exclusives

PRINT RUN 100 SER.#'d SETS
AA Andrew Alberts 4.00 10.00
AL Al Montoya 6.00 15.00
AM Andrej Meszaros 4.00 10.00
AO Alexander Ovechkin 175.00 300.00
AP Alexander Perezhogin 6.00 15.00
AS Alexander Steen 10.00 25.00
AW Andrew Wozniewski 4.00 10.00
BB Brandon Bochenski 4.00 10.00
BC Braydon Coburn 4.00 10.00
BL Brett Lebda 4.00 10.00
BS Brent Seabrook 4.00 10.00
BW Brad Winchester 4.00 10.00
CB Cam Barker 6.00 15.00
Error-G.Brule autograph
CC Chris Campoli 4.00 10.00
CP Corey Perry 15.00 40.00
CW Cam Ward 20.00 50.00
DK Duncan Keith 8.00 20.00
DL David Leneveu 4.00 10.00
DP Dion Phaneuf 40.00 80.00
EN Eric Nystrom 4.00 10.00
GB Gilbert Brule 10.00 25.00
GP George Parros 4.00 10.00
HL Henrik Lundqvist 40.00 80.00
HT Hannu Toivonen 6.00 15.00
JB Jaroslav Balastik 4.00 10.00
JC Jeff Carter 15.00 40.00
JF Johan Franzen 20.00 40.00
JG Josh Gorges 4.00 10.00
JH Jim Howard 12.00 30.00
JJ Jussi Jokinen 6.00 15.00
JM Jay McClement 4.00 10.00
JS Jim Slater 4.00 10.00
JW Jeff Woywitka 4.00 10.00
KB Keith Ballard 4.00 10.00
KD Kevin Dallman 4.00 10.00
KN Kevin Nastiuk 4.00 10.00
LS Lee Stempniak 4.00 10.00
MF Matt Foy 4.00 10.00
MJ Milan Jurcina 4.00 10.00
MR Mike Richards 15.00 40.00
MT Maxime Talbot 4.00 10.00
NN Niklas Nordgren 4.00 10.00
PB Peter Budaj 6.00 15.00
PE Patrick Eaves 6.00 15.00
PN Petteri Nokelainen 4.00 10.00
PP Petr Prucha 6.00 15.00
RB Rene Bourque 4.00 10.00
RC Ryane Clowe 4.00 10.00
RG Ryan Getzlaf 25.00 60.00
RH Ryan Hollweg 4.00 10.00
RI Raitis Ivanans 4.00 10.00
RN Robert Nilsson 4.00 10.00
RO Rostislav Olesz 6.00 15.00
RS Ryan Suter 6.00 15.00
SC Sidney Crosby 300.00 500.00
ST Anthony Stewart 4.00 10.00
TV Thomas Vanek 20.00 50.00
WW Wojtek Wolski 15.00 40.00
YD Yann Danis 6.00 15.00
ZP Zach Parise 15.00 40.00

2005-06 SP Game Used Rookie Exclusives Silver

PRINT RUN 5 SER.#'d SETS
NOT PRICED DUE TO SCARCITY

2005-06 SP Game Used Signature Sticks

PRINT RUN 5 SER.#'d SETS
NOT PRICED DUE TO SCARCITY
SSAR Andrew Raycroft
SSAT Alex Tanguay
SSBT Bryan Trottier
SSCD Chris Drury
SSES Eric Staal
SSJB Jean Beliveau
SSJC Jonathan Cheechoo
SSJP Joni Pitkanen
SSKP Keith Primeau
SSMA Maxim Afinogenov
SSMB Mike Bossy
SSOK Olaf Kolzig
SSPB Patrice Bergeron
SSPS Philippe Sauve
SSRB Rob Blake
SSRF Ruslan Fedotenko
SSTE Tony Esposito
SSTH Trent Hunter
SSBH1 Bobby Hull
SSBH2 Bobby Hull
SSGH1 Gordie Howe
SSGH2 Gordie Howe

2005-06 SP Game Used SIGnificance

PRINT RUN 100 SER.#'d SETS
AF Alexander Frolov 6.00 15.00
AL Daniel Alfredsson 6.00 15.00
AY Alexei Yashin 6.00 15.00
BM Brendan Morrison 6.00 15.00
BR Brad Richards 10.00 25.00
CD Chris Drury 6.00 15.00
CO Chris Osgood 6.00 15.00
CP Chris Pronger 6.00 15.00
CS Cory Stillman 6.00 15.00
DA David Aebischer 6.00 15.00
DB Dustin Brown 6.00 15.00
DC Dan Cloutier 6.00 15.00
DH Dany Heatley 12.50 30.00
DL David Legwand 6.00 15.00
DM Darren McCarty 6.00 15.00
DR Dwayne Roloson 6.00 15.00
EC Erik Cole 6.00 15.00
ED Eric Daze 6.00 15.00
EJ Ed Jovanovski 6.00 15.00
EN Evgeni Nabokov 6.00 15.00
ES Eric Staal 12.00 30.00
GH Gordie Howe 40.00 80.00
GM Glen Murray 6.00 15.00
HO Marian Hossa 6.00 15.00
HZ Henrik Zetterberg 10.00 25.00
IK Ilya Kovalchuk 20.00 50.00
JA Jason Arnott 6.00 15.00
JB Jay Bouwmeester 6.00 15.00
JC Jonathan Cheechoo 10.00 25.00
JI Jarome Iginla 15.00 40.00
JL Joffrey Lupul 6.00 15.00
JN Jocelyn Thibault 6.00 15.00
JO Jeff O'Neill 6.00 15.00
JP Joni Pitkanen 6.00 15.00
JR Jeremy Roenick 10.00 25.00
JS Jason Spezza 12.00 30.00
JT Joe Thornton 20.00 50.00
KD Kris Draper 6.00 15.00
KP Keith Primeau 6.00 15.00
MB Martin Brodeur 30.00 80.00
MC Mike Cammalleri 6.00 15.00
MH Martin Havlat 6.00 15.00
ML Manny Legace 6.00 15.00
MN Markus Naslund 6.00 15.00
MP Mark Parrish 6.00 15.00
MR Michael Ryder 6.00 15.00
MS Miroslav Satan 6.00 15.00
MT Marty Turco 6.00 15.00
MW Brenden Morrow 6.00 15.00
NY Michael Nylander 6.00 15.00
NZ Nikolai Zherdev 5.00 12.00
OK Olaf Kolzig 10.00 25.00
PB Patrice Bergeron 10.00 25.00
PM Pierre-Marc Bouchard 6.00 15.00
PR Patrick Roy 60.00 125.00
PS Philippe Sauve 6.00 15.00
RA Brian Rafalski 6.00 15.00
RB Rob Blake 6.00 15.00
RE Robert Esche 6.00 15.00
RF Ruslan Fedotenko 6.00 15.00
RL Roberto Luongo 10.00 25.00
RM Ryan Miller 10.00 25.00
RN Rick Nash 12.50 30.00
RO Rob Niedermayer 6.00 15.00
RS Ryan Smyth 6.00 15.00
SB Sean Burke 6.00 15.00
SD Shane Doan 6.00 15.00
SL Martin St. Louis 6.00 15.00
SN Scott Niedermayer 6.00 15.00
SS Sheldon Souray 6.00 15.00
SU Mats Sundin 12.00 30.00
SW Stephen Weiss 6.00 15.00
SZ Sergei Zubov 6.00 15.00
TA Tyler Arnason 6.00 15.00
TH Trent Hunter 6.00 15.00
TL Trevor Linden 10.00 25.00
VL Vincent Lecavalier 10.00 25.00
VP Vaclav Prospal 6.00 15.00
ZC Zdeno Chara 6.00 15.00

2005-06 SP Game Used SIGnificance Gold

PRINT RUN 25 SER.#'d SETS

2005-06 SP Game Used SIGnificance Extra

PRINT RUN 25 SER.#'d SETS
BL Martin Brodeur 100.00 200.00
Roberto Luongo
CR Jonathan Cheechoo 20.00 50.00
Michael Ryder
FB Alex Frolov 12.50 30.00
Dustin Brown
GH Gordie Howe 300.00 500.00
Wayne Gretzky
HH Dany Heatley 25.00 60.00
Martin Havlat
HK Marian Hossa 25.00 60.00
Ilya Kovalchuk
HP Trent Hunter
Mark Parrish
IH Jarome Iginla 20.00 50.00
Milan Hejduk
MS Ryan Miller 12.50 30.00
Philippe Sauve
MT Brenden Morrow 12.50 30.00
Marty Turco
NM Markus Naslund 20.00 50.00
Brendan Morrison
PE Keith Primeau 12.50 30.00
Robert Esche
RR Michael Ryder 15.00 40.00
Mike Ribeiro
SA Mats Sundin 20.00 50.00
Nik Antropov
SC Ryan Smyth 15.00 40.00
Ty Conklin
SF Martin St. Louis 15.00 40.00
Ruslan Fedotenko
TA Marty Turco 20.00 50.00
David Aebischer
TB Joe Thornton
Patrice Bergeron
WH Stephen Weiss 20.00 50.00
Nathan Horton
ZN Nikolai Zherdev 20.00 50.00
Rick Nash

2005-06 SP Game Used SIGnificance Extra Gold

PRINT RUN 10 SER.#'d SETS
NOT PRICED DUE TO SCARCITY

2005-06 SP Game Used Significant Numbers

PRINT RUNS LISTED BELOW
UNDER 24 NOT PRICED DUE TO SCARCITY
SNAF Alexander Frolov/24 15.00 30.00
SNAL Daniel Alfredsson/11
SNAM Alvaro Montoya/29 25.00 60.00
SNAO Alexander Ovechkin/8
SNAP Alexander Perezhogin/42 15.00 40.00
SNAS Alexander Steen/10
SNAY Alexei Yashin/79 8.00 20.00
SNBL Rob Blake/4
SNBM Brendan Morrison/7
SNBR Brian Rafalski/28 15.00 40.00
SNBS Brent Seabrook/7
SNBU Peter Budaj/31 30.00 60.00
SNBY Mike Bossy/22
SNCB Cam Barker/25 25.00 60.00
Error-G.Brule autograph
SNCO Corey Perry/61 15.00 40.00
SNCP Chris Pronger/44 10.00 25.00
SNCW Cam Ward/30 40.00 80.00
SNDB Dustin Brown/23
SNDC Dan Cloutier/39 12.00 30.00
SNDH Dany Heatley/15
SNDL David Leneveu/30 20.00 50.00
SNDP Dion Phaneuf/3
SNDW Doug Weight/39 10.00 25.00
SNEA Patrick Eaves/44 15.00 40.00
SNEB Ed Belfour/20 50.00 100.00
SNED Eric Daze/55 8.00 20.00
SNEJ Ed Jovanovski/55 8.00 20.00
SNEN Eric Nystrom/23
SNGB Gilbert Brule/17
SNGH Gordie Howe/9
SNGM Glen Murray/27 20.00 50.00
SNGP George Parros/57 8.00 20.00
SNHK Dominik Hasek/39 50.00 125.00
SNHL Henrik Lundqvist/30 75.00 150.00
SNHO Marian Hossa/18
SNHT Hannu Toivonen/33 20.00 50.00
SNHV Martin Havlat/9
SNHZ Henrik Zetterberg/40 25.00 60.00
SNIK Ilya Kovalchuk/17
SNJC Jeff Carter/17
SNJF Johan Franzen/39 12.00 30.00
SNJH Jim Howard/35 25.00 60.00
SNJI Jarome Iginla/12
SNJJ Jussi Jokinen/36 15.00 40.00
SNJK Jari Kurri/17
SNJO Joe Thornton/19
SNJP Joni Pitkanen/44 10.00 25.00
SNJR Jeremy Roenick/97 10.00 25.00
SNJS Jason Spezza/19
SNJT Jose Theodore/61 20.00 50.00
SNJW Jeff Woywitka/29
SNKD Kris Draper/33 10.00 25.00
SNKL Kari Lehtonen/32 30.00 80.00
SNKP Keith Primeau/25 10.00 25.00
SNLR Luc Robitaille/20
SNMB Martin Brodeur/30 75.00 200.00
SNMG Marian Gaborik/10
SNMH Milan Hejduk/23
SNMJ Milan Jurcina/62 8.00 20.00
SNMM Mike Modano/9
SNMN Markus Naslund/19
SNMP Michael Peca/37 10.00 25.00
SNMR Mike Richards/18
SNMS Miroslav Satan/81 8.00 20.00
SNMT Marty Turco/35 15.00 40.00
SNMW Brenden Morrow/10
SNNA Nik Antropov/80 8.00 20.00
SNNH Nathan Horton/16
SNNI Robert Nilsson/21
SNNK Nikolai Khabibulin/53 15.00 40.00
SNNZ Nikolai Zherdev/13
SNON Jeff O'Neill/92 8.00 20.00
SNPB Patrice Bergeron/37 25.00 50.00
SNPE Phil Esposito/77 30.00 80.00
SNPM Pierre-Marc Bouchard/96 8.00 20.00
SNPR Patrick Roy/33 125.00 250.00
SNRB Ray Bourque/77 25.00 60.00
SNRF Ruslan Fedotenko/17
SNRG Ryan Getzlaf/51 15.00 40.00
SNRL Roberto Luongo/1
SNRN Rick Nash/61 20.00 50.00
SNRO Rostislav Olesz/85 6.00 15.00
SNRS Ryan Smyth/94 8.00 20.00
SNRT Raffi Torres/14
SNRY Michael Ryder/73 10.00 25.00
SNSC Sidney Crosby/87 300.00 450.00
SNSD Shane Doan/19
SNSG Simon Gagne/12
SNSL Martin St. Louis/26 15.00 40.00
SNSM Ryan Suter/20
SNSN Scott Niedermayer/27 12.50 30.00
SNST Anthony Stewart/57 8.00 20.00
SNSU Mats Sundin/13
SNTB Todd Bertuzzi/44 15.00 40.00
SNTV Thomas Vanek/26 40.00 100.00
SNVL Vincent Lecavalier/4
SNYD Yann Danis/75 10.00 25.00
SNZP Zach Parise/9

2005-06 SP Game Used Statscriptions

PRINT RUNS LISTED BELOW
UNDER 24 NOT PRICED DUE TO SCARCITY
STAF Alexander Frolov/79 10.00 25.00
STAH Ales Hemsky/64 10.00 25.00
STAR Andrew Raycroft/29 15.00 40.00
STAY Alexei Yashin/44 10.00 25.00
STBA Matthew Barnaby/43 8.00 20.00
STBG Bernie Geoffrion/50 30.00 80.00
STBH Bobby Hull/58 20.00 50.00
STBM Bryan McCabe/63 10.00 25.00
STBP Brad Park/57 8.00 20.00
STBR Brendan Morrison/71 6.00 15.00
STBT Bryan Trottier/50 6.00 15.00
STCB Christian Backman/18
STCC Craig Conroy/69 6.00 15.00
STCD Chris Drury/50 8.00 20.00
STCO Chris Osgood/45 8.00 20.00
STDA Daniel Alfredsson/37 15.00 40.00
STDB Dustin Brown/31 8.00 20.00
STDC Dan Cloutier/33 10.00 25.00
STDH Dany Heatley/41 15.00 40.00
STDL David Legwand/48 8.00 20.00
STDT Dave Taylor/47 6.00 15.00
STDW Doug Weight/79 10.00 25.00
STED Eric Daze/38 8.00 20.00
STES Eric Staal/81 12.00 30.00
STFT Fedor Tjutin/25 10.00 25.00
STGL Guy Lafleur/60 15.00 40.00
STGM Glen Murray/44 8.00 20.00
STHO Marcel Hossa/59 10.00 25.00
STHV Martin Havlat/31 15.00 40.00
STHZ Henrik Zetterberg/44 20.00 50.00
STIL Ian Laperriere/78 10.00 25.00
STJA Jason Arnott/68 6.00 15.00
STJB Jay Bouwmeester/82 6.00 15.00
STJC Jonathan Cheechoo/63 12.00 30.00
STJH Jochen Hecht/52 10.00 25.00
STJI Jarome Iginla/52 20.00 50.00
STJL Jamie Lundmark/29 6.00 15.00
STJM John-Michael Liles/79 6.00 15.00
STJO Jeff O'Neill/41 8.00 20.00
STJP Joni Pitkanen/71 8.00 20.00
STJS Jason Spezza/55 15.00 40.00
STJT Jocelyn Thibault/36 10.00 25.00
STJV Josef Vasicek/45 8.00 20.00
STKD Kris Draper/40 8.00 20.00
STKH Kristian Huselius/45 6.00 15.00
STKL Kari Lehtonen/30 20.00 50.00
STKP Keith Primeau/57 8.00 20.00
STKT Kimmo Timonen/55 8.00 20.00
STKW Kevin Weekes/66 8.00 20.00
STLM Larry Murphy/63 6.00 15.00
STLU Roberto Luongo/25 30.00 80.00
STLU Joffrey Lupul/34 10.00 25.00
STMA Marc-Andre Fleury/46 30.00 60.00
STMB Mike Bossy/69 10.00 25.00
STMD Marcel Dionne/59 12.00 30.00
STMG Martin Gerber/54 12.00 30.00
STMN Michael Nylander/64 8.00 20.00
STMR Mike Ribeiro/65 6.00 15.00
STMS Matt Stajan/27 15.00 40.00
STMT Marty Turco/37 15.00 40.00
STMW Brenden Morrow/48 6.00 15.00
STNA Nik Antropov/45 6.00 15.00
STNH Nathan Horton/55 6.00 15.00
STNZ Nikolai Zherdev/34 10.00 25.00
STOK Olaf Kolzig/41 25.00 60.00
STPB Patrice Bergeron/39 20.00 40.00
STPC Grant Fuhr/40 25.00 60.00
STPL Pascal Leclaire/62 8.00 20.00
STPM Pierre-Marc Bouchard/42 8.00 20.00
STPS Peter Stastny/47 10.00 25.00
STRA Brian Rafalski/52 10.00 25.00
STRB Rob Blake/68 8.00 20.00
STRE Robert Esche/11
STRF Ruslan Fedotenko/41 8.00 20.00
STRK Ryan Kesler/28 10.00 25.00
STRL Reggie Leach/61 8.00 20.00
STRM Ryan Miller/18
STRN Rob Niedermayer/61 8.00 20.00
STRS Ryan Smyth/39 12.00 30.00
STRV Rogie Vachon/33 15.00 40.00
STRY Michael Ryder/63 10.00 25.00
STRZ Richard Zednik/50 6.00 15.00
STSA Philippe Sauve/27 8.00 20.00
STSB Sean Burke/35 8.00 20.00
STSD Shane Doan/68 6.00 15.00
STSG Simon Gagne/66 10.00 25.00
STSL Martin St. Louis/38 12.00 30.00
STSN Scott Niedermayer/57 8.00 20.00
STST Marco Sturm/48 10.00 25.00
STSZ Sergei Zubov/79 6.00 15.00
STTA Tyler Arnason/55 8.00 20.00
STTE Tony Esposito/35 15.00 40.00
STTH Trent Hunter/51 8.00 20.00
STTL Trevor Linden/25 40.00 100.00
STTP Tom Poti/48 6.00 15.00
STTR Tuomo Ruutu/44 12.00 30.00
STVL Vincent Lecavalier/33 30.00 80.00
STVR Mike Van Ryn/37 10.00 25.00
STWC Wayne Cashman/30 8.00 20.00
STWG Wayne Gretzky/9

2006-07 SP Game Used

COMPLETE SET w/o SPs (100) 50.00 100.00
RC PRINT RUN 999 #'d SETS
1 Chris Pronger .75 2.00
2 Teemu Selanne 1.00 2.50
3 Jean-Sebastien Giguere 1.00 2.50
4 Ilya Kovalchuk 1.25 3.00
5 Kari Lehtonen 1.00 2.50
6 Marian Hossa .75 2.00
7 Patrice Bergeron .75 2.00
8 Brad Boyes .60 1.50
9 Hannu Toivonen 1.00 2.50
10 Bobby Orr 2.00 5.00
11 Ryan Miller 1.00 2.50
12 Chris Drury .75 2.00
13 Jarome Iginla 1.50 4.00
14 Miikka Kiprusoff 1.00 2.50
15 Alex Tanguay .75 2.00
16 Dion Phaneuf 1.25 3.00

17 Eric Staal .75 2.00
18 Cam Ward 1.50 4.00
19 Erik Cole .60 1.50
20 Rod Brind'Amour .75 2.00
21 Nikolai Khabibulin 1.00 2.50
22 Martin Havlat .75 2.00
23 Tuomo Ruutu .60 1.50
24 Joe Sakic 2.00 5.00
25 Jose Theodore 1.00 2.50
26 Milan Hejduk .75 2.00
27 Marek Svatos .60 1.50
28 Rick Nash 1.00 2.50
29 Sergei Fedorov 1.00 2.50
30 Pascal LeClaire 1.00 2.50
31 Mike Modano 1.00 2.50
32 Marty Turco .75 2.00
33 Eric Lindros 1.00 2.50
34 Gordie Howe 1.50 4.00
35 Henrik Zetterberg 1.00 2.50
36 Pavel Datsyuk 1.00 2.50
37 Dominik Hasek 1.25 3.00
38 Nicklas Lidstrom 1.00 2.50
39 Ales Hemsky .60 1.50
40 Ryan Smyth .75 2.00
41 Joffrey Lupul .60 1.50
42 Ed Belfour 2.50 6.00
43 Jay Bouwmeester .60 1.50
44 Todd Bertuzzi .75 2.00
45 Olli Jokinen .60 1.50
46 Wayne Gretzky 3.00 8.00
47 Alexander Frolov .60 1.50
48 Rob Blake .75 2.00
49 Marian Gaborik 1.50 4.00
50 Manny Fernandez 1.00 2.50
51 Pavol Demitra .60 1.50
52 Cristobal Huet 1.00 2.50
53 Patrick Roy 2.00 5.00
54 Michael Ryder .75 2.00
55 Saku Koivu 1.00 2.50
56 Alexei Kovalev .60 1.50
57 Paul Kariya 1.00 2.50
58 Tomas Vokoun .75 2.00
59 Jason Arnott .60 1.50
60 Martin Brodeur 2.50 6.00
61 Brian Gionta .60 1.50
62 Patrik Elias .60 1.50
63 Alexei Yashin .60 1.50
64 Miroslav Satan .60 1.50
65 Brendan Shanahan 1.00 2.50
66 Jaromir Jagr 1.50 4.00
67 Henrik Lundqvist 1.50 4.00
68 Dany Heatley 1.00 2.50
69 Martin Gerber 1.00 2.50
70 Daniel Alfredsson .75 2.00
71 Jason Spezza 1.00 2.50
72 Simon Gagne 1.00 2.50
73 Peter Forsberg 1.50 4.00
74 Jeff Carter 1.00 2.50
75 Joni Pitkanen .60 1.50
76 Shane Doan .75 2.00
77 Jeremy Roenick 1.00 2.50
78 Owen Nolan .75 2.00
79 Curtis Joseph 1.00 2.50
80 Sidney Crosby 4.00 10.00
81 Mario Lemieux 2.00 5.00
82 Marc-Andre Fleury 1.00 2.50
83 Mark Recchi .60 1.50
84 Joe Thornton 1.50 4.00
85 Patrick Marleau .75 2.00
86 Jonathan Cheechoo 1.00 2.50
87 Doug Weight .60 1.50
88 Keith Tkachuk .75 2.00
89 Vincent Lecavalier 1.00 2.50
90 Martin St. Louis 1.00 2.50
91 Brad Richards 1.00 2.50
92 Alexander Steen .75 2.00
93 Mats Sundin 1.00 2.50
94 Andrew Raycroft .75 2.00
95 Michael Peca .60 1.50
96 Markus Naslund 1.00 2.50
97 Roberto Luongo 2.00 5.00
98 Brendan Morrison .60 1.50
99 Alexander Ovechkin 3.00 8.00
100 Olaf Kolzig 1.25 3.00
101 Shane O'Brien RC 4.00 10.00
102 Ryan Shannon RC 4.00 10.00
103 Yan Stastny RC 4.00 10.00
104 Mark Stuart RC 4.00 10.00
105 Nate Thompson RC 2.00 5.00
106 Phil Kessel RC 10.00 25.00
107 Matt Lashoff RC 4.00 10.00
108 Dave Bolland RC 8.00 20.00
109 Michael Blunden RC 4.00 10.00
110 Dustin Byfuglien RC 8.00 20.00
111 Paul Stastny RC 12.00 30.00
112 Fredrik Norrena RC 4.00 10.00
113 Loui Eriksson RC 4.00 10.00
114 Tomas Kopecky RC 5.00 12.00
115 Alexei Mikhnov RC 4.00 10.00
116 Marc-Antoine Pouliot RC 5.00 12.00
117 Patrick Thoresen RC 4.00 10.00
118 Ladislav Smid RC 4.00 10.00
119 Janis Sprukts RC 4.00 10.00
120 Konstantin Pushkaryov RC 4.00 10.00
121 Patrick O'Sullivan RC 5.00 12.00
122 Anze Kopitar RC 8.00 20.00
123 Benoit Pouliot RC 5.00 12.00
124 Miroslav Kopriva RC 4.00 10.00
125 Niklas Backstrom RC 3.00 8.00
126 Guillaume Latendresse RC 8.00 20.00
127 Alexander Radulov RC 8.00 20.00
128 Shea Weber RC 5.00 12.00
129 Mikko Lehtonen RC 2.00 5.00
130 Alex Brooks RC 2.00 5.00
131 John Oduya RC 4.00 10.00
132 Travis Zajac RC 5.00 12.00
133 Drew Stafford RC 3.00 8.00
134 Masi Marjamaki RC 4.00 10.00
135 Jarkko Immonen RC 4.00 10.00
136 Nigel Dawes RC 4.00 10.00
137 Alexei Kaigorodov RC 4.00 10.00
138 Lars Jonsson RC 2.00 5.00
139 Ryan Potulny RC 5.00 12.00
140 Triston Grant RC 2.00 5.00
141 Enver Lisin RC 4.00 10.00
142 Brandon Prust RC 4.00 10.00
143 Keith Yandle RC 4.00 10.00
144 Patrick Fischer RC 2.00 5.00
145 Noah Welch RC 4.00 10.00
146 Michel Ouellet RC 5.00 12.00
147 Jordan Staal RC 10.00 25.00
148 Kristopher Letang RC 6.00 15.00
149 Evgeni Malkin RC 20.00 50.00
150 Matt Carle RC 5.00 12.00
151 Marc-Edouard Vlasic RC 4.00 10.00
152 D.J. King RC 2.00 5.00
153 Roman Polak RC 2.00 5.00
154 Ben Ondrus RC 4.00 10.00
155 Brendan Bell RC 4.00 10.00
156 Ian White RC 4.00 10.00
157 Dustin Boyd RC 5.00 12.00
158 Luc Bourdon RC 5.00 12.00
159 Eric Fehr RC 5.00 12.00
160 Jonas Johansson RC 2.00 5.00

2006-07 SP Game Used Gold

GOLD: 2X to 5X BASE HI
RCs: .5 to 1.5X BASE HI
PRINT RUN 100 #'d SETS
1 Chris Pronger 4.00 10.00
2 Teemu Selanne 5.00 12.00
3 Jean-Sebastien Giguere 5.00 12.00
4 Ilya Kovalchuk 6.00 15.00
5 Kari Lehtonen 5.00 12.00
6 Marian Hossa 4.00 10.00
7 Patrice Bergeron 4.00 10.00
8 Brad Boyes 3.00 8.00
9 Hannu Toivonen 5.00 12.00
10 Bobby Orr 12.00 30.00
11 Ryan Miller 5.00 12.00
12 Chris Drury 4.00 10.00
13 Jarome Iginla 8.00 20.00
14 Miikka Kiprusoff 5.00 12.00
15 Alex Tanguay 4.00 10.00
16 Dion Phaneuf 6.00 15.00
17 Eric Staal 5.00 12.00
18 Cam Ward 8.00 20.00
19 Erik Cole 3.00 8.00
20 Rod Brind'Amour 4.00 10.00
21 Nikolai Khabibulin 5.00 12.00
22 Martin Havlat 4.00 10.00
23 Tuomo Ruutu 3.00 8.00
24 Joe Sakic 8.00 20.00
25 Jose Theodore 5.00 12.00
26 Milan Hejduk 4.00 10.00
27 Marek Svatos 3.00 8.00
28 Rick Nash 5.00 12.00
29 Sergei Fedorov 5.00 12.00
30 Pascal LeClaire 5.00 12.00
31 Mike Modano 5.00 12.00
32 Marty Turco 4.00 10.00
33 Eric Lindros 5.00 12.00
34 Gordie Howe 6.00 15.00
35 Henrik Zetterberg 5.00 12.00
36 Pavel Datsyuk 5.00 12.00
37 Dominik Hasek 5.00 12.00
38 Nicklas Lidstrom 5.00 12.00
39 Ales Hemsky 3.00 8.00
40 Ryan Smyth 4.00 10.00
41 Joffrey Lupul 3.00 8.00
42 Ed Belfour 12.00 30.00
43 Jay Bouwmeester 3.00 8.00
44 Todd Bertuzzi 4.00 10.00
45 Olli Jokinen 3.00 8.00
46 Wayne Gretzky 15.00 40.00
47 Alexander Frolov 3.00 8.00
48 Rob Blake 4.00 10.00
49 Marian Gaborik 8.00 20.00
50 Manny Fernandez 5.00 12.00
51 Pavol Demitra 3.00 8.00
52 Cristobal Huet 5.00 12.00
53 Patrick Roy 12.00 30.00
54 Michael Ryder 4.00 10.00
55 Saku Koivu 5.00 12.00
56 Alexei Kovalev 3.00 8.00
57 Paul Kariya 5.00 12.00
58 Tomas Vokoun 4.00 10.00
59 Jason Arnott 3.00 8.00
60 Martin Brodeur 10.00 25.00
61 Brian Gionta 3.00 8.00
62 Patrik Elias 3.00 8.00
63 Alexei Yashin 3.00 8.00
64 Miroslav Satan 3.00 8.00
65 Brendan Shanahan 5.00 12.00
66 Jaromir Jagr 8.00 20.00
67 Henrik Lundqvist 8.00 20.00
68 Dany Heatley 5.00 12.00
69 Martin Gerber 5.00 12.00
70 Daniel Alfredsson 4.00 10.00
71 Jason Spezza 5.00 12.00
72 Simon Gagne 5.00 12.00
73 Peter Forsberg 8.00 20.00
74 Jeff Carter 5.00 12.00
75 Joni Pitkanen 3.00 8.00
76 Shane Doan 4.00 10.00
77 Jeremy Roenick 5.00 12.00
78 Owen Nolan 4.00 10.00
79 Curtis Joseph 5.00 12.00
80 Sidney Crosby 25.00 60.00
81 Mario Lemieux 12.00 30.00
82 Marc-Andre Fleury 5.00 12.00
83 Mark Recchi 3.00 8.00
84 Joe Thornton 8.00 20.00
85 Patrick Marleau 4.00 10.00
86 Jonathan Cheechoo 5.00 12.00
87 Doug Weight 3.00 8.00
88 Keith Tkachuk 4.00 10.00
89 Vincent Lecavalier 5.00 12.00
90 Martin St. Louis 5.00 12.00
91 Brad Richards 5.00 12.00
92 Alexander Steen 4.00 10.00
93 Mats Sundin 5.00 12.00
94 Andrew Raycroft 4.00 10.00
95 Michael Peca 3.00 8.00
96 Markus Naslund 5.00 12.00
97 Roberto Luongo 10.00 25.00
98 Brendan Morrison 3.00 8.00
99 Alexander Ovechkin 12.00 30.00
100 Olaf Kolzig 6.00 15.00
101 Shane O'Brien 8.00 20.00
102 Ryan Shannon 8.00 20.00
103 Yan Stastny 8.00 20.00
104 Mark Stuart 8.00 20.00
105 Nate Thompson 4.00 10.00
106 Phil Kessel 10.00 25.00
107 Matt Lashoff 8.00 20.00
108 Dave Bolland 15.00 40.00
109 Michael Blunden 8.00 20.00
110 Dustin Byfuglien 15.00 40.00
111 Paul Stastny 15.00 40.00
112 Fredrik Norrena 8.00 20.00
113 Loui Eriksson 8.00 20.00
114 Tomas Kopecky 10.00 25.00
115 Alexei Mikhnov 8.00 20.00
116 Marc-Antoine Pouliot 10.00 25.00
117 Patrick Thoresen 8.00 20.00
118 Ladislav Smid 8.00 20.00
119 Janis Sprukts 8.00 20.00
120 Konstantin Pushkaryov 8.00 20.00
121 Patrick O'Sullivan 10.00 25.00
122 Anze Kopitar 12.00 30.00
123 Benoit Pouliot 10.00 25.00
124 Miroslav Kopriva 8.00 20.00
125 Niklas Backstrom 8.00 20.00
126 Guillaume Latendresse 10.00 25.00
127 Alexander Radulov 10.00 25.00
128 Shea Weber 10.00 25.00
129 Mikko Lehtonen 4.00 10.00
130 Alex Brooks 4.00 10.00
131 John Oduya 8.00 20.00
132 Travis Zajac 12.00 30.00
133 Drew Stafford 10.00 25.00
134 Masi Marjamaki 8.00 20.00
135 Jarkko Immonen 8.00 20.00
136 Nigel Dawes 8.00 20.00
137 Alexei Kaigorodov 8.00 20.00
138 Lars Jonsson 4.00 10.00
139 Ryan Potulny 10.00 25.00
140 Triston Grant 4.00 10.00
141 Enver Lisin 8.00 20.00
142 Brandon Prust 8.00 20.00
143 Keith Yandle 8.00 20.00
144 Patrick Fischer 4.00 10.00
145 Noah Welch 8.00 20.00
146 Michel Ouellet 12.00 30.00
147 Jordan Staal 15.00 40.00
148 Kristopher Letang 12.00 30.00
149 Evgeni Malkin 25.00 60.00
150 Matt Carle 10.00 25.00
151 Marc-Edouard Vlasic 8.00 20.00
152 D.J. King 4.00 10.00
153 Roman Polak 4.00 10.00
154 Ben Ondrus 8.00 20.00
155 Brendan Bell 8.00 20.00
156 Ian White 8.00 20.00
157 Dustin Boyd 10.00 25.00
158 Luc Bourdon 10.00 25.00
159 Eric Fehr 10.00 25.00
160 Jonas Johansson 4.00 10.00

2006-07 SP Game Used Rainbow

PRINT RUN 25 #'d SETS
NOT PRICED DUE TO SCARCITY

2006-07 SP Game Used Authentic Fabrics

OVERALL MEM. ODDS 1:1
AFAF Alexander Frolov 4.00 10.00
AFAH Ales Hemsky 4.00 10.00
AFAL Daniel Alfredsson 5.00 12.00
AFAO Alexander Ovechkin SP 15.00 40.00
AFAS Alexander Steen 5.00 12.00
AFAT Alex Tanguay 5.00 12.00
AFAY Alexei Yashin 4.00 10.00
AFBB Brad Boyes 4.00 10.00
AFBG Brian Gionta 4.00 10.00
AFBL Brian Leetch 4.00 10.00
AFBM Brenden Morrow 5.00 12.00
AFBO Pierre-Marc Bouchard 4.00 10.00
AFBR Brad Richards 6.00 15.00
AFBS Brendan Shanahan 6.00 15.00
AFCD Chris Drury 5.00 12.00
AFCJ Curtis Joseph 6.00 15.00
AFCS Curtis Sanford 5.00 12.00
AFCW Cam Ward 10.00 25.00
AFDA David Aebischer 5.00 12.00
AFDE Pavol Demitra 4.00 10.00
AFDH Dominik Hasek 6.00 15.00
AFDP Dion Phaneuf 6.00 15.00
AFDR Dwayne Roloson 5.00 12.00
AFDS Daniel Sedin 4.00 10.00
AFDW Doug Weight 4.00 10.00
AFEB Ed Belfour 15.00 40.00
AFEJ Ed Jovanovski 4.00 10.00
AFES Eric Staal 5.00 12.00
AFGA Simon Gagne 6.00 15.00
AFGR Gary Roberts 2.00 5.00
AFHE Dany Heatley 6.00 15.00
AFHL Henrik Lundqvist 10.00 25.00
AFHS Henrik Sedin 4.00 10.00
AFHT Hannu Toivonen 6.00 15.00
AFHZ Henrik Zetterberg 6.00 15.00
AFIK Ilya Kovalchuk SP 10.00 25.00
AFJB Jay Bouwmeester 4.00 10.00
AFJC Jeff Carter 6.00 15.00
AFJD J.P. Dumont 4.00 10.00
AFJI Jarome Iginla 10.00 25.00
AFJJ Jaromir Jagr SP 10.00 25.00
AFJL Jere Lehtinen 4.00 10.00
AFJN Joe Nieuwendyk 5.00 12.00
AFJP Joni Pitkanen 4.00 10.00
AFJS Joe Sakic 10.00 25.00
AFJT Joe Thornton 8.00 20.00
AFJW Jason Williams 2.00 5.00
AFLU Joffrey Lupul 4.00 10.00
AFMA Mark Recchi 4.00 10.00
AFMB Martin Brodeur SP 20.00 50.00
AFMC Mike Cammalleri 4.00 10.00
AFME Martin Erat 2.00 5.00
AFMF Manny Fernandez 6.00 15.00
AFMG Marian Gaborik 10.00 25.00
AFMH Milan Hejduk 5.00 12.00
AFMI Miroslav Satan 4.00 10.00
AFMM Mike Modano 5.00 12.00
AFMN Markus Naslund 6.00 15.00
AFMO Brendan Morrison 4.00 10.00
AFMP Michael Peca 4.00 10.00
AFMR Michael Ryder 5.00 12.00
AFMS Mats Sundin 6.00 15.00
AFNH Nathan Horton 4.00 10.00
AFNL Nicklas Lidstrom 6.00 15.00
AFOK Olaf Kolzig 8.00 20.00
AFPB Patrice Bergeron 6.00 15.00
AFPD Pavel Datsyuk 6.00 15.00
AFPE Patrik Elias 4.00 10.00
AFPF Peter Forsberg 6.00 15.00
AFPK Paul Kariya 6.00 15.00
AFPL Pascal LeClaire 6.00 15.00
AFPM Patrick Marleau 5.00 12.00
AFPS Patrik Stefan 2.00 5.00
AFPT Pierre Turgeon 4.00 10.00
AFRB Rob Blake 5.00 12.00
AFRD Rick DiPietro 6.00 15.00
AFRE Robert Esche 5.00 12.00
AFRF Ruslan Fedotenko 4.00 10.00
AFRG Ryan Getzlaf 5.00 12.00
AFRL Roberto Luongo 12.00 30.00
AFRM Ryan Malone 4.00 10.00
AFRN Rick Nash 6.00 15.00
AFRS Ryan Smyth 5.00 12.00
AFSC Sidney Crosby SP 40.00 80.00
AFSF Sergei Fedorov 6.00 15.00
AFSG Scott Gomez 4.00 10.00
AFSJ Matt Stajan 4.00 10.00
AFSK Saku Koivu 6.00 15.00
AFSM Martin St. Louis 6.00 15.00
AFSN Scott Niedermayer 4.00 10.00
AFSP Jason Spezza 6.00 15.00
AFSS Sergei Samsonov 5.00 12.00
AFST Jarret Stoll 4.00 10.00
AFSU Steve Sullivan 4.00 10.00
AFTA Tony Amonte 2.00 5.00
AFTH Tomas Holmstrom 4.00 10.00
AFTS Teemu Selanne 6.00 15.00
AFTT Tim Thomas 6.00 15.00
AFTV Tomas Vokoun 5.00 12.00
AFVL Vincent Lecavalier 6.00 15.00

2006-07 SP Game Used Authentic Fabrics Parallel

*PARALLEL 1X to 1.25X
STATED PRINT RUN 100 SER.#'d SETS
AFAF Alexander Frolov 6.00 15.00
AFAH Ales Hemsky 6.00 15.00
AFAL Daniel Alfredsson 6.00 15.00
AFAO Alexander Ovechkin 25.00 60.00
AFAS Alexander Steen 6.00 15.00
AFAT Alex Tanguay 6.00 15.00
AFAY Alexei Yashin 6.00 15.00
AFBB Brad Boyes 6.00 15.00
AFBG Brian Gionta 6.00 15.00
AFBL Brian Leetch 5.00 12.00
AFBM Brenden Morrow 6.00 15.00
AFBO Pierre-Marc Bouchard 6.00 15.00
AFBR Brad Richards 8.00 20.00
AFBS Brendan Shanahan 8.00 20.00
AFCD Chris Drury 8.00 20.00
AFCJ Curtis Joseph 8.00 20.00
AFCS Curtis Sanford 6.00 15.00
AFCW Cam Ward 12.00 30.00
AFDA David Aebischer 6.00 15.00
AFDE Pavol Demitra 6.00 15.00
AFDH Dominik Hasek 10.00 25.00
AFDP Dion Phaneuf 10.00 25.00
AFDR Dwayne Roloson 6.00 15.00
AFDS Daniel Sedin 6.00 15.00
AFDW Doug Weight 6.00 15.00
AFEB Ed Belfour 20.00 50.00
AFEJ Ed Jovanovski 6.00 15.00
AFES Eric Staal 6.00 15.00
AFGA Simon Gagne 8.00 20.00
AFGR Gary Roberts 3.00 8.00
AFHE Dany Heatley 8.00 20.00
AFHL Henrik Lundqvist 12.00 30.00
AFHS Henrik Sedin 6.00 15.00
AFHT Hannu Toivonen 8.00 20.00
AFHZ Henrik Zetterberg 8.00 20.00
AFIK Ilya Kovalchuk 10.00 25.00
AFJB Jay Bouwmeester 6.00 15.00
AFJC Jeff Carter 8.00 20.00
AFJD J.P. Dumont 6.00 15.00
AFJI Jarome Iginla 12.00 30.00
AFJJ Jaromir Jagr 12.00 30.00
AFJL Jere Lehtinen 6.00 15.00
AFJN Joe Nieuwendyk 6.00 15.00
AFJP Joni Pitkanen 6.00 15.00
AFJS Joe Sakic 15.00 40.00
AFJT Joe Thornton 12.00 30.00
AFJW Jason Williams 3.00 8.00
AFLU Joffrey Lupul 6.00 15.00
AFMA Mark Recchi 6.00 15.00
AFMB Martin Brodeur 20.00 50.00
AFMC Mike Cammalleri 6.00 15.00
AFME Martin Erat 3.00 8.00
AFMF Manny Fernandez 8.00 20.00
AFMG Marian Gaborik 12.00 30.00
AFMH Milan Hejduk 6.00 15.00
AFMI Miroslav Satan 6.00 15.00
AFMM Mike Modano 8.00 20.00
AFMN Markus Naslund 8.00 20.00
AFMO Brendan Morrison 6.00 15.00
AFMP Michael Peca 6.00 15.00
AFMR Michael Ryder 6.00 15.00
AFMS Mats Sundin 8.00 20.00
AFNH Nathan Horton 6.00 15.00
AFNL Nicklas Lidstrom 8.00 20.00
AFOK Olaf Kolzig 10.00 25.00
AFPB Patrice Bergeron 8.00 20.00
AFPD Pavel Datsyuk 8.00 20.00
AFPE Patrik Elias 6.00 15.00
AFPF Peter Forsberg 12.00 30.00
AFPK Paul Kariya 8.00 20.00
AFPL Pascal LeClaire 8.00 20.00
AFPM Patrick Marleau 6.00 15.00
AFPS Patrik Stefan 3.00 8.00
AFPT Pierre Turgeon 6.00 15.00
AFRB Rob Blake 6.00 15.00
AFRD Rick DiPietro 6.00 15.00
AFRE Robert Esche 6.00 15.00
AFRF Ruslan Fedotenko 6.00 15.00
AFRG Ryan Getzlaf 6.00 15.00
AFRL Roberto Luongo 15.00 40.00
AFRM Ryan Malone 6.00 15.00
AFRN Rick Nash 8.00 20.00
AFRS Ryan Smyth 6.00 15.00
AFSC Sidney Crosby 30.00 80.00
AFSF Sergei Fedorov 8.00 20.00
AFSG Scott Gomez 6.00 15.00
AFSJ Matt Stajan 6.00 15.00
AFSK Saku Koivu 8.00 20.00
AFSM Martin St. Louis 8.00 20.00
AFSN Scott Niedermayer 6.00 15.00
AFSP Jason Spezza 8.00 20.00
AFSS Sergei Samsonov 6.00 15.00
AFST Jarret Stoll 6.00 15.00
AFSU Steve Sullivan 6.00 15.00
AFTA Tony Amonte 3.00 8.00
AFTH Tomas Holmstrom 6.00 15.00
AFTS Teemu Selanne 8.00 20.00
AFTT Tim Thomas 8.00 20.00
AFTV Tomas Vokoun 6.00 15.00
AFVL Vincent Lecavalier 8.00 20.00

2006-07 SP Game Used Authentic Fabrics Patches

PATCHES: 2X to 4X HI BASE JERSEYS
PRINT RUN 50 SER. #'d SETS
AFAF Alexander Frolov 15.00 40.00
AFAH Ales Hemsky 15.00 40.00
AFAL Daniel Alfredsson 20.00 50.00
AFAO Alexander Ovechkin 60.00 150.00
AFAS Alexander Steen 20.00 50.00
AFAT Alex Tanguay 20.00 50.00
AFAY Alexei Yashin 15.00 40.00
AFBB Brad Boyes 15.00 40.00
AFBG Brian Gionta 15.00 40.00
AFBL Brian Leetch 15.00 40.00
AFBM Brenden Morrow 20.00 50.00
AFBO Pierre-Marc Bouchard 15.00 40.00
AFBR Brad Richards 25.00 60.00
AFBS Brendan Shanahan 25.00 60.00
AFCD Chris Drury 20.00 50.00
AFCJ Curtis Joseph 25.00 60.00
AFCS Curtis Sanford 20.00 50.00
AFCW Cam Ward 40.00 100.00
AFDA David Aebischer 20.00 50.00
AFDE Pavol Demitra 15.00 40.00
AFDH Dominik Hasek 25.00 60.00
AFDP Dion Phaneuf 25.00 60.00
AFDR Dwayne Roloson 20.00 50.00
AFDS Daniel Sedin 15.00 40.00
AFDW Doug Weight 15.00 40.00
AFEB Ed Belfour 60.00 150.00
AFEJ Ed Jovanovski 15.00 40.00
AFES Eric Staal 20.00 50.00
AFGA Simon Gagne 25.00 60.00
AFGR Gary Roberts 8.00 20.00
AFHE Dany Heatley 25.00 60.00
AFHL Henrik Lundqvist 40.00 100.00
AFHS Henrik Sedin 15.00 40.00
AFHT Hannu Toivonen 25.00 60.00
AFHZ Henrik Zetterberg 25.00 60.00
AFIK Ilya Kovalchuk 25.00 60.00
AFJB Jay Bouwmeester 15.00 40.00
AFJC Jeff Carter 25.00 60.00
AFJD J.P. Dumont 15.00 40.00
AFJI Jarome Iginla 40.00 100.00
AFJJ Jaromir Jagr 30.00 80.00
AFJL Jere Lehtinen 15.00 40.00
AFJN Joe Nieuwendyk 20.00 50.00
AFJP Joni Pitkanen 15.00 40.00
AFJS Joe Sakic 40.00 100.00
AFJT Joe Thornton 30.00 80.00
AFJW Jason Williams 8.00 20.00
AFLU Joffrey Lupul 15.00 40.00
AFMA Mark Recchi 15.00 40.00
AFMB Martin Brodeur 40.00 100.00
AFMC Mike Cammalleri 15.00 40.00
AFME Martin Erat 8.00 20.00
AFMF Manny Fernandez 25.00 60.00
AFMG Marian Gaborik 40.00 100.00
AFMH Milan Hejduk 20.00 50.00
AFMI Miroslav Satan 15.00 40.00
AFMM Mike Modano 20.00 50.00
AFMN Markus Naslund 25.00 60.00
AFMO Brendan Morrison 15.00 40.00
AFMP Michael Peca 15.00 40.00
AFMR Michael Ryder 20.00 50.00
AFMS Mats Sundin 25.00 60.00
AFNH Nathan Horton 15.00 40.00
AFNL Nicklas Lidstrom 25.00 60.00
AFOK Olaf Kolzig 30.00 80.00
AFPB Patrice Bergeron 20.00 50.00
AFPD Pavel Datsyuk 25.00 60.00
AFPE Patrik Elias 15.00 40.00
AFPF Peter Forsberg 30.00 80.00
AFPK Paul Kariya 25.00 60.00
AFPL Pascal LeClaire 25.00 60.00
AFPM Patrick Marleau 20.00 50.00
AFPS Patrik Stefan 8.00 20.00
AFPT Pierre Turgeon 15.00 40.00
AFRB Rob Blake 20.00 50.00
AFRD Rick DiPietro 25.00 60.00
AFRE Robert Esche 20.00 50.00
AFRF Ruslan Fedotenko 15.00 40.00
AFRG Ryan Getzlaf 20.00 50.00
AFRL Roberto Luongo 50.00 125.00
AFRM Ryan Malone 15.00 40.00
AFRN Rick Nash 25.00 60.00
AFRS Ryan Smyth 20.00 50.00
AFSC Sidney Crosby 60.00 150.00
AFSF Sergei Fedorov 25.00 60.00
AFSG Scott Gomez 15.00 40.00
AFSJ Matt Stajan 15.00 40.00
AFSK Saku Koivu 25.00 60.00
AFSM Martin St. Louis 25.00 60.00
AFSN Scott Niedermayer 15.00 40.00
AFSP Jason Spezza 25.00 60.00
AFSS Sergei Samsonov 20.00 50.00
AFST Jarret Stoll 15.00 40.00
AFSU Steve Sullivan 15.00 40.00
AFTA Tony Amonte 8.00 20.00
AFTH Tomas Holmstrom 15.00 40.00
AFTS Teemu Selanne 25.00 60.00
AFTT Tim Thomas 25.00 60.00
AFTV Tomas Vokoun 20.00 50.00
AFVL Vincent Lecavalier 25.00 60.00

2006-07 SP Game Used Authentic Fabrics Dual

COMMONS 3.00 8.00
STATED PRINT RUN 100 #'d SETS
AF2AB Maxim Afinogenov 6.00 15.00
Daniel Briere
AF2AH David Aebischer 8.00 20.00
Cristobal Huet
AF2AS Jason Arnott 3.00 8.00
Steve Sullivan
AF2BF Rob Blake 4.00 10.00
Alexander Frolov
AF2BG Martin Brodeur 10.00 25.00
Brian Gionta
AF2BH Jay Bouwmeester 3.00 8.00
Nathan Horton
AF2DG Pavol Demitra 6.00 15.00
Marian Gaborik
AF2DM Chris Drury 6.00 15.00
Ryan Miller
AF2FC Peter Forsberg 6.00 15.00
Jeff Carter
AF2HK Martin Havlat 6.00 15.00
Nikolai Khabibulin
AF2HL Ales Hemsky 3.00 8.00
Joffrey Lupul
AF2HO Dominik Hasek 10.00 25.00
Chris Osgood
AF2HS Milan Hejduk 3.00 8.00
Marek Svatos
AF2HZ Tomas Holmstrom 8.00 20.00
Henrik Zetterberg
AF2IK Jarome Iginla 10.00 25.00
Miikka Kiprusoff
AF2JL Jaromir Jagr 10.00 25.00
Henrik Lundqvist
AF2KG Sami Kapanen 3.00 8.00
Simon Gagne
AF2KH Marian Hossa 6.00 15.00
Ilya Kovalchuk
AF2KO Olaf Kolzig 12.00 30.00
Alexander Ovechkin
AF2KR Saku Koivu 4.00 10.00
Michael Ryder
AF2KV Paul Kariya 6.00 15.00
Tomas Vokoun
AF2LC Pascal LeClaire 3.00 8.00
Ty Conklin
AF2LJ Jere Lehtinen 3.00 8.00
Jussi Jokinen
AF2LR Vincent Lecavalier 8.00 20.00
Brad Richards
AF2ML Mike Modano 6.00 15.00
Eric Lindros
AF2MT Patrick Marleau 8.00 20.00
Joe Thornton
AF2ND Owen Nolan 4.00 10.00
Shane Doan
AF2NF Rick Nash 8.00 20.00
Sergei Fedorov
AF2NL Markus Naslund 6.00 15.00
Roberto Luongo
AF2PB Mark Parrish 3.00 8.00
Pierre-Marc Bouchard
AF2PT Michael Peca 4.00 10.00
Darcy Tucker
AF2RC Mark Recchi 20.00 50.00
Sidney Crosby
AF2RL Guy Lapointe 4.00 15.00
Larry Robinson
AF2SB Marc Savard 6.00 15.00
Patrice Bergeron
AF2SC Brad Stuart 3.00 8.00
Zdeno Chara
AF2SD Miroslav Satan 4.00 10.00
Rick DiPietro
AF2SH Jason Spezza 8.00 20.00
Dany Heatley
AF2SJ Brendan Shanahan 10.00 25.00
Jaromir Jagr
AF2SP Teemu Selanne 6.00 15.00
Corey Perry
AF2SS Mats Sundin 6.00 15.00
Alexander Steen
AF2SW Eric Staal 6.00 15.00
Cam Ward
AF2TK Alex Tanguay 4.00 10.00
Chuck Kobasew
AF2TM Marty Turco 4.00 10.00
Brenden Morrow
AF2TP Raffi Torres 3.00 8.00
Fernando Pisani
AF2TS Pierre Turgeon 8.00 20.00
Joe Sakic
AF2TT Hannu Toivonen 4.00 10.00
Tim Thomas
AF2WB Justin Williams 3.00 8.00
Rod Brind'Amour
AF2WG Doug Weight 3.00 8.00
Bill Guerin

2006-07 SP Game Used Authentic Fabrics Dual Patches

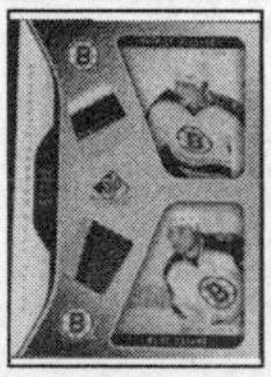

PATCHES: 2X to 4X DUAL JSY HI
PRINT RUN 25 #'d SETS
AF2AB Maxim Afinogenov 25.00 60.00
Daniel Briere
AF2AH David Aebischer 40.00 100.00
Cristobal Huet
AF2AS Jason Arnott 20.00 40.00
Steve Sullivan
AF2BF Rob Blake 25.00 60.00
Alexander Frolov
AF2BG Martin Brodeur 50.00 125.00
Brian Gionta
AF2BH Jay Bouwmeester 20.00 40.00
Nathan Horton
AF2DG Pavol Demitra 25.00 60.00
Marian Gaborik
AF2DM Chris Drury 25.00 60.00
Ryan Miller
AF2FC Peter Forsberg 30.00 80.00
Jeff Carter
AF2HK Martin Havlat 25.00 60.00
Nikolai Khabibulin
AF2HL Ales Hemsky 20.00 40.00
Joffrey Lupul
AF2HO Dominik Hasek 50.00 125.00
Chris Osgood
AF2HS Milan Hejduk 20.00 40.00
Marek Svatos
AF2HZ Tomas Holmstrom 30.00 80.00
Henrik Zetterberg
AF2IK Jarome Iginla 40.00 100.00
Miikka Kiprusoff
AF2JL Jaromir Jagr 50.00 125.00
Henrik Lundqvist
AF2KG Sami Kapanen 20.00 40.00
Simon Gagne
AF2KH Marian Hossa 30.00 80.00
Ilya Kovalchuk
AF2KO Olaf Kolzig 40.00 100.00
Alexander Ovechkin
AF2KR Saku Koivu 25.00 60.00
Michael Ryder
AF2KV Paul Kariya 25.00 60.00
Tomas Vokoun
AF2LC Pascal LeClaire 20.00 40.00
Ty Conklin
AF2LJ Jere Lehtinen 20.00 40.00
Jussi Jokinen
AF2LR Vincent Lecavalier 30.00 80.00
Brad Richards
AF2ML Mike Modano 25.00 60.00
Eric Lindros
AF2MT Patrick Marleau 30.00 80.00
Joe Thornton
AF2ND Owen Nolan 20.00 40.00
Shane Doan
AF2NF Rick Nash 30.00 80.00
Sergei Fedorov
AF2NL Markus Naslund 25.00 60.00
Roberto Luongo
AF2PB Mark Parrish 20.00 40.00
Pierre-Marc Bouchard
AF2PT Michael Peca 20.00 40.00
Darcy Tucker
AF2RC Mark Recchi 100.00 200.00
Sidney Crosby
AF2RL Guy Lapointe 25.00 60.00

Larry Robinson
AF2SB Marc Savard 25.00 60.00
Patrice Bergeron
AF2SC Brad Stuart 20.00 40.00
Zdeno Chara
AF2SD Miroslav Satan 20.00 40.00
Rick DiPietro
AF2SH Jason Spezza 30.00 80.00
Dany Heatley
AF2SJ Brendan Shanahan 40.00 100.00
Jaromir Jagr
AF2SP Teemu Selanne 25.00 60.00
Corey Perry
AF2SS Mats Sundin 30.00 80.00
Alexander Steen
AF2SW Eric Staal 25.00 60.00
Cam Ward
AF2TK Alex Tanguay 20.00 40.00
Chuck Kobasew
AF2TM Marty Turco 20.00 40.00
Brenden Morrow
AF2TP Raffi Torres 20.00 40.00
Fernando Pisani
AF2TS Pierre Turgeon 30.00 80.00
Joe Sakic
AF2TT Hannu Toivonen 20.00 40.00
Tim Thomas
AF2WB Justin Williams 20.00 40.00
Rod Brind'Amour
AF2WG Doug Weight 20.00 40.00
Bill Guerin

2006-07 SP Game Used Authentic Fabrics Triple

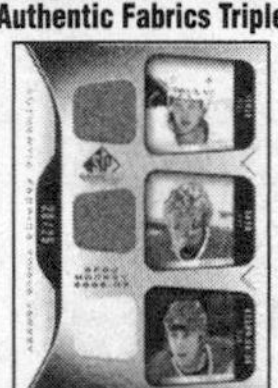

PRINT RUN 25 #'d SETS
AF3ANA Teemu Selanne 20.00 50.00
Chris Pronger
Scott Niedermayer
AF3ATL Marian Hossa 25.00 60.00
Ilya Kovalchuk
Kari Lehtonen
AF3BOS Brad Boyes 20.00 50.00
Zdeno Chara
Patrice Bergeron
AF3BUF Chris Drury 25.00 60.00
Daniel Briere
Ryan Miller
AF3CAR Rod Brind'Amour 20.00 50.00
Eric Staal
Cam Ward
AF3CGY Jarome Iginla 30.00 80.00
Alex Tanguay
Miikka Kiprusoff
AF3CHI Martin Havlat 20.00 50.00
Tuomo Ruutu
Nikolai Khabibulin
AF3CLB Pascal LeClaire 25.00 60.00
Rick Nash
Sergei Federov
AF3COL Joe Sakic 40.00 100.00
Milan Hejduk
Jose Theodore
AF3DAL Mike Modano 25.00 60.00
Eric Lindros
Marty Turco
AF3DET Dominik Hasek 40.00 100.00
Nicklas Lidstrom
Henrik Zetterberg
AF3EDM Ryan Smyth 15.00 40.00
Dwayne Roloson
Ales Hemsky
AF3FLA Ed Belfour 20.00 50.00
Todd Bertuzzi
Jay Bouwmeester
AF3LAK Rob Blake 15.00 40.00
Alexander Frolov
Mike Cammalleri
AF3MIN Pavol Demitra 20.00 50.00
Marian Gaborik
Pierre-Marc Bouchard
AF3MTL Sergei Samsonov 30.00 80.00
Saku Koivu
Michael Ryder
AF3NAS Paul Kariya 20.00 50.00
Tomas Vokoun
Jason Arnott
AF3NJD Martin Brodeur 30.00 80.00
Patrik Elias
Brian Gionta
AF3NYI Miroslav Satan 20.00 50.00
Alexei Yashin
Rick DiPietro
AF3NYR Brendan Shanahan 50.00 100.00
Jaromir Jagr
Henrik Lundqvist
AF3OTT Daniel Alfredsson 25.00 60.00
Jason Spezza
Dany Heatley
AF3PHI Peter Forsberg 20.00 50.00
Robert Esche
Simon Gagne
AF3PHX Curtis Joseph 15.00 40.00
Jeremy Roenick
Shane Doan
AF3PIT Mark Recchi 50.00 125.00
Ryan Malone
Sidney Crosby
AF3SJS Patrick Marleau 30.00 80.00
Joe Thornton
Jonathan Cheechoo
AF3STL Doug Weight 15.00 40.00
Keith Tkachuk
Manny Legace
AF3TBL Vincent Lecavalier 30.00 80.00
Brad Richards
Martin St. Louis
AF3TOR Mats Sundin 25.00 60.00
Andrew Raycroft
Alexander Steen
AF3VAN Markus Naslund 25.00 60.00
Henrik Sedin
Daniel Sedin
AF3WAS Alexander Ovechkin 30.00 80.00
Olaf Kolzig
Richard Zednik

2006-07 SP Game Used Authentic Fabrics Triple Patches

PRINT RUN 10 #'d SETS
NOT PRICED DUE TO SCARCITY
AF3ANA Teemu Selanne
Chris Pronger
Scott Niedermayer
AF3ATL Marian Hossa
Ilya Kovalchuk
Kari Lehtonen
AF3BOS Brad Boyes
Zdeno Chara
Patrice Bergeron
AF3BUF Chris Drury
Daniel Briere
Ryan Miller
AF3CAR Rod Brind'Amour
Eric Staal
Cam Ward
AF3CGY Jarome Iginla
Alex Tanguay
Miikka Kiprusoff
AF3CHI Martin Havlat
Tuomo Ruutu
Nikolai Khabibulin
AF3CLB Pascal LeClaire
Rick Nash
Sergei Federov
AF3COL Joe Sakic
Milan Hejduk
Jose Theodore
AF3DAL Mike Modano
Eric Lindros
Marty Turco
AF3DET Dominik Hasek
Nicklas Lidstrom
Henrik Zetterberg
AF3EDM Ryan Smyth
Dwayne Roloson
Ales Hemsky
AF3FLA Ed Belfour
Todd Bertuzzi
Jay Bouwmeester
AF3LAK Rob Blake
Alexander Frolov
Mike Cammalleri
AF3MIN Pavol Demitra
Marian Gaborik
Pierre-Marc Bouchard
AF3MTL Sergei Samsonov
Saku Koivu
Michael Ryder
AF3NAS Paul Kariya
Tomas Vokoun
Jason Arnott
AF3NJD Martin Brodeur
Patrik Elias
Brian Gionta
AF3NYI Miroslav Satan
Alexei Yashin
Rick DiPietro
AF3NYR Brendan Shanahan
Jaromir Jagr
Henrik Lundqvist
AF3OTT Daniel Alfredsson
Jason Spezza
Dany Heatley
AF3PHI Peter Forsberg
Robert Esche
Simon Gagne
AF3PHX Curtis Joseph
Jeremy Roenick
Shane Doan
AF3PIT Mark Recchi
Ryan Malone
Sidney Crosby
AF3SJS Patrick Marleau
Joe Thornton
Jonathan Cheechoo
AF3STL Doug Weight
Keith Tkachuk
Manny Legace
AF3TBL Vincent Lecavalier
Brad Richards
Martin St. Louis
AF3TOR Mats Sundin
Andrew Raycroft
Alexander Steen
AF3VAN Markus Naslund
Henrik Sedin
Daniel Sedin
AF3WAS Olaf Kolzig
Richard Zednik
Alexander Ovechkin

2006-07 SP Game Used Authentic Fabrics Quads

PRINT RUN 10 #'d SETS
NOT PRICED DUE TO SCARCITY
AF4BJTW Ed Belfour
Curtis Joseph
Marty Turco
Cam Ward
AF4BPJM Rob Blake
Chris Pronger
Ed Jovanovski
Bryan McCabe
AF4FCSW Tony Esposito
Rogie Vachon
Billy Smith
Gump Worsley
AF4IDCH Jarome Iginla
Shane Doan
Jonathan Cheechoo
Dany Heatley
AF4JHEG Jaromir Jagr
Marian Hossa
Patrik Elias
Marian Gaborik
AF4LMSB Vincent Lecavalier
Patrick Marleau
Jason Spezza
Patrice Bergeron
AF4MWGD Mike Modano
Doug Weight
Scott Gomez
Chris Drury
AF4NMBT Cam Neely
Mike Bossy
Dave Taylor
Darryl Sittler
AF4RBTL Jose Theodore
Roberto Luongo
Patrick Roy
Martin Brodeur
AF4SFSZ Mats Sundin
Peter Forsberg
Henrik Sedin
Henrik Zetterberg
AF4SKGN Brendan Shanahan
Paul Kariya
Simon Gagne
Rick Nash
AF4STSC Joe Sakic
Joe Thornton
Eric Staal
Sidney Crosby

2006-07 SP Game Used Authentic Fabrics Quads Patches

PRINT RUN 5 #'d SETS
NOT PRICED DUE TO SCARCITY
AF4BJTW Ed Belfour
Curtis Joseph
Marty Turco
Cam Ward
AF4BPJM Rob Blake
Chris Pronger
Ed Jovanovski
Bryan McCabe
AF4FCSW Tony Esposito
Rogie Vachon
Billy Smith
Gump Worsley
AF4IDCH Jarome Iginla
Shane Doan
Jonathan Cheechoo
Dany Heatley
AF4JHEG Jaromir Jagr
Marian Hossa
Patrik Elias
Marian Gaborik
AF4LMSB Vincent Lecavalier
Patrick Marleau
Jason Spezza
Patrice Bergeron
AF4MWGD Mike Modano
Doug Weight
Scott Gomez
Chris Drury
AF4NMBT Cam Neely
Mike Bossy
Dave Taylor
Darryl Sittler
AF4RBTL Patrick Roy
Martin Brodeur
Jose Theodore
Roberto Luongo
AF4SFSZ Mats Sundin
Peter Forsberg
Henrik Sedin
Henrik Zetterberg
AF4SKGN Brendan Shanahan
Paul Kariya
Simon Gagne
Rick Nash
AF4STSC Joe Sakic
Joe Thornton
Eric Staal
Sidney Crosby

2006-07 SP Game Used Authentic Fabrics Fives

PRINT RUN 10 #'d SETS
NOT PRICED DUE TO SCARCITY
AF51ST Rick DiPietro
Ilya Kovalchuk
Rick Nash
Sidney Crosby
Alexander Ovechkin
AF550G Jaromir Jagr
Ilya Kovalchuk
Jonathan Cheechoo
Dany Heatley
Alexander Ovechkin
AF5ASG Joe Sakic
Teemu Selanne
Bill Guerin
Mark Recchi
Dany Heatley
AF5AST Jaromir Jagr
Brad Richards
Joe Thornton
Marc Savard
Jason Spezza
AF5DPT Sergei Zubov
Chris Pronger
Nicklas Lidstrom
Scott Niedermayer
Bryan McCabe
AF5GAA Dominik Hasek
Manny Legace
Henrik Lundqvist
Cristobal Huet
Miikka Kiprusoff
AF5GWG Olli Jokinen
Brian Gionta
Jonathan Cheechoo
Henrik Zetterberg
Marek Svatos
AP5PTS Jaromir Jagr
Joe Thornton
Daniel Alfredsson
Dany Heatley
Alexander Ovechkin
AP5RPT Brad Boyes
Marek Svatos
Sidney Crosby
Alexander Ovechkin
Jussi Jokinen
AP5SCP Chris Pronger
Cory Stillman
Daniel Briere
Shawn Horcoff
Eric Staal

2006-07 SP Game Used Authentic Fabrics Fives Patches

PRINT RUN 5 #'d SETS
NOT PRICED DUE TO SCARCITY
AF51ST Rick DiPietro
Ilya Kovalchuk
Rick Nash
Sidney Crosby
Alexander Ovechkin
AF550G Jaromir Jagr
Ilya Kovalchuk
Jonathan Cheechoo
Dany Heatley
Alexander Ovechkin
AF5ASG Joe Sakic
Teemu Selanne
Bill Guerin
Mark Recchi
Dany Heatley
AF5AST Jaromir Jagr
Brad Richards
Joe Thornton
Marc Savard
Jason Spezza
AF5DPT Sergei Zubov
Chris Pronger
Nicklas Lidstrom
Scott Niedermayer
Bryan McCabe
AF5GAA Dominik Hasek
Manny Legace
Henrik Lundqvist
Cristobal Huet
Miikka Kiprusoff
AF5GWG Olli Jokinen
Brian Gionta
Jonathan Cheechoo
Henrik Zetterberg
Marek Svatos
AP5PTS Jaromir Jagr
Joe Thornton
Daniel Alfredsson
Dany Heatley
Alexander Ovechkin
AP5RPT Brad Boyes
Marek Svatos
Sidney Crosby
Alexander Ovechkin
Jussi Jokinen
AP5SCP Chris Pronger
Cory Stillman
Daniel Briere
Shawn Horcoff
Eric Staal

2006-07 SP Game Used Authentic Fabrics Sixes

PRINT RUN 7 #'d SETS
NOT PRICED DUE TO SCARCITY
AF6500 Pierre Turgeon
Joe Sakic
Brendan Shanahan
Jaromir Jagr
Mats Sundin
Joe Nieuwendyk
AF6BYN Joe Sakic
Paul Kariya
Pavol Demitra
Brad Richards
Pavel Datsyuk
Wayne Gretzky
AF6JEN Patrick Roy
Ed Belfour
Martin Brodeur
Dominik Hasek
Robert Esche
Miikka Kiprusoff
AF6MAS Mario Lemieux
Teemu Selanne
Saku Koivu
Bryan Berard
Cam Neely
Gary Roberts
AF6MRT Teemu Selanne
Milan Hejduk
Jonathan Cheechoo
Rick Nash
Jarome Iginla
Ilya Kovalchuk
AF6NOR Chris Chelios
Rob Blake
Chris Pronger
Nicklas Lidstrom
Scott Niedermayer
Ray Bourque
AF6SEL Jere Lehtinen
Michael Peca
Kris Draper
Rod Brind'Amour
Sergei Federov
Doug Gilmour
AF6WIN Patrick Roy
Ed Belfour
Curtis Joseph
Martin Brodeur
Dominik Hasek
Grant Fuhr

2006-07 SP Game Used Authentic Fabrics Sixes Patches

PRINT RUN 3 #'d SETS
NOT PRICED DUE TO SCARCITY
AF6500 Pierre Turgeon
Joe Sakic
Mats Sundin
Joe Nieuwendyk
Brendan Shanahan
Jaromir Jagr
AF6BYN Joe Sakic
Paul Kariya
Pavol Demitra
Brad Richards
Pavel Datsyuk
Wayne Gretzky
AF6JEN Patrick Roy
Ed Belfour
Martin Brodeur
Dominik Hasek
Robert Esche
Miikka Kiprusoff
AF6MAS Mario Lemieux
Teemu Selanne
Saku Koivu
Bryan Berard
Cam Neely
Gary Roberts
AF6MRT Teemu Selanne
Milan Hejduk
Jarome Iginla
Ilya Kovalchuk
Jonathan Cheechoo
Rick Nash
AF6NOR Chris Chelios
Rob Blake
Chris Pronger
Nicklas Lidstrom
Scott Niedermayer
Ray Bourque
AF6SEL Jere Lehtinen
Michael Peca
Kris Draper
Rod Brind'Amour
Sergei Federov
Doug Gilmour
AF6WIN Patrick Roy
Ed Belfour
Curtis Joseph
Martin Brodeur
Dominik Hasek
Grant Fuhr

2006-07 SP Game Used Authentic Fabrics Sevens

PRINT RUN 5 #'d SETS
NOT PRICED DUE TO SCARCITY
AF7ART Mario Lemieux
Jaromir Jagr
Joe Thornton
Peter Forsberg
Jarome Iginla
Martin St. Louis
Wayne Gretzky
AF7CAL Scott Gomez
Chris Drury
Barret Jackman
Evgeni Nabokov
Andrew Raycroft
Dany Heatley
Alexander Ovechkin
AF7CON Patrick Roy
Mario Lemieux
Joe Sakic
Brad Richards
Nicklas Lidstrom
Jean-Sebastien Giguere
Cam Ward
AF7LBP Mario Lemieux
Joe Sakic
Jaromir Jagr
Dominik Hasek
Markus Naslund
Jarome Iginla
Martin St. Louis
AF7MVP Joe Thornton
Peter Forsberg
Jose Theodore
Martin St. Louis
Joe Sakic
Jaromir Jagr
Chris Pronger
AF7VEZ Patrick Roy
Ed Belfour
Olaf Kolzig
Martin Brodeur
Dominik Hasek
Jose Theodore
Miikka Kiprusoff

2006-07 SP Game Used Authentic Fabrics Sevens Patches

PRINT RUN 2 #'d SETS
NOT PRICED DUE TO SCARCITY
AF7ART Mario Lemieux
Jaromir Jagr
Joe Thornton
Peter Forsberg
Jarome Iginla
Martin St. Louis
Wayne Gretzky
AF7CAL Scott Gomez
Chris Drury
Barret Jackman
Evgeni Nabokov
Andrew Raycroft
Dany Heatley
Alexander Ovechkin
AF7CON Patrick Roy
Mario Lemieux
Joe Sakic
Brad Richards
Nicklas Lidstrom
Jean-Sebastien Giguere
Cam Ward
AF7LBP Mario Lemieux
Joe Sakic
Jaromir Jagr
Dominik Hasek
Markus Naslund
Jarome Iginla
Martin St. Louis
AF7MVP Joe Sakic
Jaromir Jagr
Chris Pronger
Joe Thornton
Peter Forsberg
Jose Theodore
Martin St. Louis
AF7VEZ Patrick Roy
Ed Belfour
Olaf Kolzig
Martin Brodeur
Dominik Hasek
Jose Theodore
Miikka Kiprusoff

2006-07 SP Game Used Authentic Fabrics Eights

PRINT RUN 3 #'d SETS
NOT PRICED DUE TO SCARCITY
AF8CAN Joe Sakic
Brendan Shanahan
Paul Kariya
Vincent Lecavalier
Martin Brodeur
Joe Thornton
Roberto Luongo
Jarome Iginla
AF8CEN Jason Spezza
Patrice Bergeron
Mike Ribeiro
Jarret Stoll
Eric Staal
Sidney Crosby
Alexander Steen
Jeff Carter
AF8FIN Teemu Selanne
Jere Lehtinen
Saku Koivu
Olli Jokinen
Miikka Kiprusoff
Joni Pitkanen
Kari Lehtonen
Jussi Jokinen
AF8HOF Patrick Roy
Mario Lemieux
Phil Esposito
Mike Bossy
Guy Lafleur
Wayne Gretzky
Gordie Howe
Ray Bourque
AF8RUS Sergei Zubov
Evgeni Nabokov
Pavel Datsyuk
Ilya Kovalchuk
Alexei Kovalev
Nikolai Khabibulin
Sergei Federov
Alexander Ovechkin
AF8SWE Mats Sundin
Markus Naslund
Nicklas Lidstrom
Peter Forsberg
Daniel Alfredsson
Tomas Holmstrom
Henrik Zetterberg
Henrik Lundqvist

2006-07 SP Game Used Authentic Fabrics Eights Patches

PRINT RUN 1/1
NOT PRICED DUE TO SCARCITY
AF8CAN Joe Sakic
Brendan Shanahan
Martin Brodeur
Joe Thornton
Roberto Luongo
Jarome Iginla
Paul Kariya
Vincent Lecavalier
AF8CEN Mike Ribeiro
Jarret Stoll
Jason Spezza
Patrice Bergeron
Eric Staal
Sidney Crosby
Alexander Steen
Jeff Carter
AF8FIN Teemu Selanne
Jere Lehtinen
Saku Koivu
Olli Jokinen
Miikka Kiprusoff
Joni Pitkanen
Kari Lehtonen
Jussi Jokinen
AF8HOF Patrick Roy
Mario Lemieux
Phil Esposito
Mike Bossy
Guy Lafleur
Wayne Gretzky
Gordie Howe
Ray Bourque
AF8RUS Sergei Zubov
Evgeni Nabokov
Pavel Datsyuk
Ilya Kovalchuk
Alexei Kovalev
Nikolai Khabibulin
Sergei Federov
Alexander Ovechkin
AF8SWE Mats Sundin
Markus Naslund
Nicklas Lidstrom
Peter Forsberg
Daniel Alfredsson
Tomas Holmstrom
Henrik Zetterberg
Henrik Lundqvist

2006-07 SP Game Used Autographs

PRINT RUN 10 #'d SETS
NOT PRICED DUE TO SCARCITY
4 Ilya Kovalchuk
5 Kari Lehtonen
8 Brad Boyes
9 Hannu Toivonen
10 Bobby Orr
11 Ryan Miller
13 Jarome Iginla
16 Dion Phaneuf
17 Eric Staal
19 Erik Cole
21 Nikolai Khabibulin
22 Martin Havlat
23 Tuomo Ruutu
25 Jose Theodore
26 Milan Hejduk
27 Marek Svatos
28 Rick Nash
31 Mike Modano
32 Marty Turco
34 Gordie Howe
35 Henrik Zetterberg
37 Dominik Hasek
38 Nicklas Lidstrom
39 Ales Hemsky
40 Ryan Smyth
43 Jay Bouwmeester
44 Todd Bertuzzi
46 Wayne Gretzky
47 Alexander Frolov
49 Marian Gaborik
52 Cristobal Huet
54 Michael Ryder
55 Saku Koivu
58 Tomas Vokoun
59 Jason Arnott
60 Martin Brodeur
61 Brian Gionta
62 Patrik Elias
63 Alexei Yashin
64 Miroslav Satan
68 Dany Heatley
69 Martin Gerber
74 Jeff Carter
75 Joni Pitkanen
76 Shane Doan
77 Jeremy Roenick
80 Sidney Crosby
82 Marc-Andre Fleury
85 Patrick Marleau
86 Jonathan Cheechoo
90 Martin St. Louis
94 Andrew Raycroft
95 Michael Peca
97 Roberto Luongo
101 Shane O'Brien
102 Ryan Shannon
103 Yan Stastny
104 Mark Stuart
106 Phil Kessel
107 Matt Lashoff
109 Michael Blunden
110 Dustin Byfuglien
111 Paul Stastny
112 Fredrik Norrena
113 Loui Eriksson
116 Marc-Antoine Pouliot
117 Patrick Thoresen
118 Ladislav Smid
119 Janis Sprukts
120 Konstantin Pushkaryov
121 Patrick O'Sullivan
122 Anze Kopitar
126 Guillaume Latendresse
127 Alexander Radulov
128 Shea Weber
130 Alex Brooks
132 Travis Zajac
133 Drew Stafford
135 Jarkko Immonen
136 Nigel Dawes
139 Ryan Potulny
143 Keith Yandle
145 Noah Welch
146 Michel Ouellet
147 Jordan Staal
149 Evgeni Malkin
150 Matt Carle
151 Marc-Edouard Vlasic
154 Ben Ondrus
155 Brendan Bell
156 Ian White
157 Dustin Boyd
159 Eric Fehr

2006-07 SP Game Used By The Letter

PRINT RUNS VARY FROM 3 - 10
NOT PRICED DUE TO SCARCITY
BLAM Maxim Afinogenov/10
BLAO Alexander Ovechkin/8
BLBO Mike Bossy/5
BLDH Dany Heatley/7
BLES Eric Staal/5
BLHA Dominik Hasek/5
BLHE Milan Hejduk/6
BLJJ Jaromir Jagr/4
BLJO Joe Sakic/5
BLJP Joni Pitkanen/8
BLJT Joe Thornton/8
BLKD Kris Draper/6
BLKL Kari Lehtonen/8
BLKT Keith Tkachuk/7
BLLC John LeClair/7
BLLE Jordan Leopold/7

BLLR Luc Robitaille/10
BLMA Mats Sundin/6
BLMB Martin Brodeur/7
BLMF Manny Fernandez/5
BLMH Martin Havlat/6
BLMI Miroslav Satan/5
BLMK Miikka Kiprusoff/8
BLML Mario Lemieux/7
BLMM Mike Modano/6
BLMN Markus Naslund/7
BLMP Michael Peca/4
BLMR Mark Recchi/6
BLMS Martin St. Louis/7
BLMT Marty Turco/5
BLNL Nicklas Lidstrom/8
BLOK Olaf Kolzig/6
BLPB Patrice Bergeron/8
BLPD Pavel Datsyuk/7
BLPE Patrik Elias/5
BLPF Peter Forsberg/8
BLPK Paul Kariya/6
BLPM Patrick Marleau/7
BLPR Patrick Roy/3
BLPS Peter Stastny/7
BLRB Ray Bourque/7
BLRD Rick DiPietro/8
BLRH Ron Hextall/7
BLRI Mike Ribeiro/7
BLRL Roberto Luongo/6
BLRM Ryan Miller/6
BLRN Rick Nash/4
BLRS Ryan Smyth/5
BLRY Michael Ryder/5
BLSC Sidney Crosby/6
BLSD Shane Doan/4
BLSF Sergei Fedorov/7
BLSK Saku Koivu/5
BLTB Todd Bertuzzi/8
BLTH Jose Theodore/8
BLTS Teemu Selanne/7
BLTV Tomas Vokoun/6
BLVL Vincent Lecavalier/10
BLWG Wayne Gretzky/7

2006-07 SP Game Used Inked Sweaters

PRINT RUN 100 #'d SETS
SP PRINT RUN 25 #'d SETS
ISAF Alexander Frolov 6.00 15.00
ISAH Ales Hemsky 8.00 20.00
ISAN Antero Niittymaki 10.00 25.00
ISAO Alexander Ovechkin SP 75.00 150.00
ISAR Andrew Raycroft 10.00 25.00
ISAY Alexei Yashin 6.00 15.00
ISBB Brad Boyes 6.00 15.00
ISBG Brian Gionta 6.00 15.00
ISBM Bryan McCabe 6.00 15.00
ISBS Borje Salming SP
ISCA Matt Carle 10.00 25.00
ISCH Chris Higgins 10.00 25.00
ISCN Cam Neely SP 25.00 60.00
ISCP Chris Pronger SP 15.00 40.00
ISCW Cam Ward 8.00 20.00
ISDA Dany Heatley 12.00 30.00
ISDB Daniel Briere 12.00 30.00
ISDH Dominik Hasek SP 40.00 80.00
ISDI Dion Phaneuf SP 25.00 60.00
ISDR Dwayne Roloson 10.00 25.00
ISDS Denis Savard SP 15.00 40.00
ISDT Darcy Tucker 10.00 25.00
ISEF Eric Fehr 6.00 15.00
ISEL Patrik Elias 8.00 20.00
ISES Eric Staal 12.00 30.00
ISFP Fernando Pisani 6.00 15.00
ISGE Martin Gerber 8.00 20.00
ISGH Gordie Howe SP
ISHA Martin Havlat 10.00 25.00
ISHE Milan Hejduk 8.00 20.00
ISHO Tomas Holmstrom 8.00 20.00
ISHT Hannu Toivonen 10.00 25.00
ISHU Cristobal Huet 12.00 30.00
ISIK Ilya Kovalchuk SP 25.00 60.00
ISIM Jarkko Immonen 8.00 20.00
ISJA Jason Arnott 6.00 15.00
ISJI Jarome Iginla SP 25.00 60.00
ISJL Joffrey Lupul 6.00 15.00
ISJP Joni Pitkanen 6.00 15.00
ISJS Jarret Stoll 6.00 15.00
ISJT Joe Thornton SP 25.00 60.00
ISJW Justin Williams 6.00 15.00
ISKD Kris Draper 6.00 15.00
ISKL Kari Lehtonen 10.00 25.00
ISKO Mikko Koivu 8.00 20.00
ISLN Ladislav Nagy 6.00 15.00
ISLR Luc Robitaille SP
ISMA Al MacInnis SP 20.00 50.00
ISMB Martin Brodeur SP 60.00 150.00
ISMC Mike Cammalleri 8.00 20.00
ISMG Marian Gaborik 15.00 40.00
ISMI Ryan Miller 12.00 30.00
ISML Mario Lemieux SP 100.00 200.00
ISMM Milan Michalek 6.00 15.00
ISMO Mike Modano SP 20.00 50.00
ISMP Mark Parrish 6.00 15.00
ISMR Mike Ribeiro 6.00 15.00
ISMT Marty Turco 10.00 25.00
ISNL Nicklas Lidstrom SP 25.00 60.00
ISNZ Nikolai Zherdev 6.00 15.00
ISPB Pierre-Marc Bouchard 6.00 15.00
ISPE Michael Peca 6.00 15.00
ISPM Patrick Marleau 8.00 20.00
ISPO Marc-Antoine Pouliot 8.00 20.00
ISPP Petr Prucha 8.00 20.00
ISPR Patrick Roy SP 125.00 250.00
ISRG Ryan Getzlaf 10.00 25.00
ISRH Ron Hextall SP
ISRI Mike Richards 8.00 20.00
ISRN Rick Nash SP 25.00 60.00
ISRS Ryan Smyth 10.00 25.00
ISSA Marc Savard 8.00 20.00
ISSB Steve Bernier 8.00 20.00
ISSC Sidney Crosby 125.00 250.00
ISSG Scott Gomez 8.00 20.00
ISSK Saku Koivu SP 20.00 50.00
ISSV Marek Svatos 8.00 20.00
ISSW Shea Weber 10.00 25.00
ISTV Tomas Vokoun 10.00 25.00
ISVL Vincent Lecavalier SP 25.00 60.00
ISVT Vesa Toskala 10.00 25.00
ISWG Wayne Gretzky SP 200.00 300.00
ISWR Wade Redden 6.00 15.00
ISZC Zdeno Chara 6.00 15.00

2006-07 SP Game Used Inked Sweaters Patches

PATCHES: 1.25X to 2X JSY HI
PRINT RUN 25 #'d SETS
SPs PRINT RUN 10 #'d SETS
SPs NOT PRICED DUE TO SCARCITY
ISAF Alexander Frolov 12.00 30.00
ISAH Ales Hemsky 15.00 40.00
ISAN Antero Niittymaki 25.00 60.00
ISAO Alexander Ovechkin SP 200.00 350.00
ISAR Andrew Raycroft 30.00 80.00
ISAY Alexei Yashin 12.00 30.00
ISBB Brad Boyes 12.00 30.00
ISBG Brian Gionta 12.00 30.00
ISBM Bryan McCabe 12.00 30.00
ISBS Borje Salming SP
ISCA Matt Carle 20.00 50.00
ISCH Chris Higgins 20.00 50.00
ISCN Cam Neely SP
ISCP Chris Pronger SP
ISCW Cam Ward 20.00 50.00
ISDA Dany Heatley 40.00 100.00
ISDB Daniel Briere 25.00 60.00
ISDH Dominik Hasek SP
ISDI Dion Phaneuf SP
ISDR Dwayne Roloson 20.00 50.00
ISDS Denis Savard SP
ISDT Darcy Tucker 20.00 50.00
ISEF Eric Fehr 12.00 30.00
ISEL Patrik Elias 15.00 40.00
ISES Eric Staal 20.00 50.00
ISFP Fernando Pisani 12.00 30.00
ISGE Martin Gerber 15.00 40.00
ISHA Martin Havlat 25.00 60.00
ISHE Milan Hejduk 15.00 40.00
ISHO Tomas Holmstrom 15.00 40.00
ISHT Hannu Toivonen 20.00 50.00
ISHU Cristobal Huet 30.00 80.00
ISIK Ilya Kovalchuk SP 60.00 100.00
ISIM Jarkko Immonen 15.00 40.00
ISJA Jason Arnott 12.00 30.00
ISJI Jarome Iginla SP 125.00 200.00
ISJL Joffrey Lupul 12.00 30.00
ISJP Joni Pitkanen 12.00 30.00
ISJS Jarret Stoll 12.00 30.00
ISJT Joe Thornton SP 125.00 200.00
ISJW Justin Williams 12.00 30.00
ISKD Kris Draper 15.00 40.00
ISKL Kari Lehtonen 20.00 50.00
ISKO Mikko Koivu 20.00 50.00
ISLN Ladislav Nagy 12.00 30.00
ISLR Luc Robitaille SP
ISMA Al MacInnis SP
ISMB Martin Brodeur SP
ISMC Mike Cammalleri 15.00 40.00
ISMG Marian Gaborik 30.00 80.00
ISMI Ryan Miller 25.00 60.00
ISML Mario Lemieux SP
ISMM Milan Michalek 12.00 30.00
ISMO Mike Modano SP
ISMP Mark Parrish 12.00 30.00
ISMR Mike Ribeiro 12.00 30.00
ISMT Marty Turco 20.00 50.00
ISNL Nicklas Lidstrom SP
ISNZ Nikolai Zherdev 12.00 30.00
ISPB Pierre-Marc Bouchard 12.00 30.00
ISPE Michael Peca
ISPM Patrick Marleau 15.00 40.00
ISPO Marc-Antoine Pouliot 15.00 40.00
ISPP Petr Prucha 20.00 50.00
ISPR Patrick Roy SP
ISRG Ryan Getzlaf 20.00 50.00
ISRH Ron Hextall SP
ISRI Mike Richards 15.00 40.00
ISRN Rick Nash SP
ISRS Ryan Smyth 20.00 50.00
ISSA Marc Savard 15.00 40.00
ISSB Steve Bernier 15.00 40.00
ISSC Sidney Crosby 250.00 400.00
ISSG Scott Gomez 15.00 40.00
ISSK Saku Koivu SP
ISSV Marek Svatos 15.00 40.00
ISSW Shea Weber 20.00 50.00
ISTH Jose Theodore SP
ISTV Tomas Vokoun 15.00 40.00
ISVL Vincent Lecavalier SP 75.00 150.00
ISVT Vesa Toskala 25.00 60.00
ISWG Wayne Gretzky SP
ISWR Wade Redden 12.00 30.00
ISZC Zdeno Chara 12.00 30.00

2006-07 SP Game Used Inked Sweaters Dual

PRINT RUN 50 #'d SETS
SP PRINT RUN 10 #'d SETS
IS2AS Jason Arnott 8.00 20.00
Steve Sullivan
IS2BB Brad Boyes 12.00 30.00
Patrice Bergeron
IS2BL Martin Brodeur 200.00 300.00
Roberto Luongo SP
IS2BP Denis Potvin 100.00 175.00
Ray Bourque SP
IS2CL Bobby Clarke
Guy Lafleur SP
IS2CP Gerry Cheevers 15.00 40.00
Brad Park
IS2DM Chris Drury 15.00 40.00
Ryan Miller
IS2EG Patrik Elias 10.00 25.00
Brian Gionta
IS2EP Robert Esche 8.00 20.00
Joni Pitkanen
IS2FC Alexander Frolov 10.00 25.00
Mike Cammalleri
IS2FR Grant Fuhr 20.00 50.00
Bill Ranford
IS2GB Marian Gaborik 20.00 50.00
Pierre-Marc Bouchard
IS2GC Simon Gagne
Jeff Carter
IS2GL Mario Lemieux
Wayne Gretzky SP
IS2HA David Aebischer 15.00 40.00
Cristobal Huet
IS2HH Michal Handzus 8.00 20.00
Martin Havlat
IS2HO Dominik Hasek 20.00 50.00
Chris Osgood
IS2HS Jarret Stoll 8.00 20.00
Ales Hemsky
IS2HT Milan Hejduk 10.00 25.00
Jose Theodore
IS2HV Tomas Vokoun 75.00 125.00
Dominik Hasek SP
IS2IT Jarome Iginla 15.00 40.00
Alex Tanguay
IS2KL Ilya Kovalchuk 25.00 60.00
Kari Lehtonen
IS2KR Saku Koivu 12.00 30.00
Michael Ryder
IS2LP Henrik Lundqvist 25.00 60.00
Petr Prucha
IS2LS Nicklas Lidstrom 20.00 50.00
Borje Salming
IS2MC Patrick Marleau 15.00 40.00
Jonathan Cheechoo
IS2MM Joe Mullen 12.00 30.00
Al MacInnis
IS2MS Marc Savard 10.00 25.00
Glen Murray
IS2MT Mike Modano 12.00 30.00
Marty Turco
IS2NH Dany Heatley 20.00 50.00
Rick Nash
IS2NM Markus Naslund 15.00 40.00
Brendan Morrison
IS2OJ Olli Jokinen 8.00 20.00
Jay Bouwmeester
IS2OK Ilya Kovalchuk 125.00 200.00
Alexander Ovechkin SP
IS2PT Michael Peca 15.00 40.00
Darcy Tucker
IS2RB Patrick Roy 200.00 300.00
Ray Bourque SP
IS2RD Jeremy Roenick 10.00 25.00
Shane Doan
IS2RG Wade Redden 10.00 25.00
Martin Gerber
IS2RS Andrew Raycroft 15.00 40.00
Alexander Steen
IS2RT Luc Robitaille 25.00 60.00
Dave Taylor
IS2SD Martin St. Louis 12.00 30.00
Marc Denis
IS2SR Ryan Smyth 12.00 30.00
Dwayne Roloson
IS2SS Jason Spezza 50.00 125.00
Eric Staal SP
IS2SW Justin Williams 10.00 25.00
Eric Staal
IS2SY Miroslav Satan 8.00 20.00
Alexei Yashin
IS2VW Tomas Vokoun 12.00 30.00
Shea Weber
IS2WP Dave Williams 12.00 30.00
Bob Probert
IS2WR Dwayne Roloson 12.00 30.00
Cam Ward
IS2ZH Tomas Holmstrom 20.00 50.00
Henrik Zetterberg
IS2HH2 Bobby Hull 150.00 225.00
Gordie Howe SP

2006-07 SP Game Used Inked Sweaters Dual Patches

PRINT RUN 15 #'d SETS
SP PRINT RUN 5 #'d SETS
NOT PRICED DUE TO SCARCITY
IS2AS Jason Arnott
Steve Sullivan
IS2BB Brad Boyes
Patrice Bergeron
IS2BL Martin Brodeur
Roberto Luongo SP
IS2BP Denis Potvin
Ray Bourque SP
IS2CL Bobby Clarke
Guy Lafleur SP
IS2CP Gerry Cheevers
Brad Park
IS2DM Chris Drury
Ryan Miller
IS2EG Patrik Elias
Brian Gionta
IS2EP Robert Esche
Joni Pitkanen
IS2FC Alexander Frolov
Mike Cammalleri
IS2GB Marian Gaborik
Pierre-Marc Bouchard
IS2GC Simon Gagne
Jeff Carter
IS2GL Mario Lemieux
Wayne Gretzky SP
IS2HA David Aebischer
Cristobal Huet
IS2HO Dominik Hasek
Chris Osgood
IS2HS Jarret Stoll
Ales Hemsky
IS2HT Milan Hejduk
Jose Theodore
IS2HV Tomas Vokoun
Dominik Hasek SP
IS2IT Jarome Iginla
Alex Tanguay
IS2KL Ilya Kovalchuk
Kari Lehtonen
IS2KR Saku Koivu
Michael Ryder
IS2LP Henrik Lundqvist
Petr Prucha
IS2LS Nicklas Lidstrom
Borje Salming
IS2MC Patrick Marleau
Jonathan Cheechoo
IS2MM Joe Mullen
Al MacInnis
IS2MS Marc Savard
Glen Murray
IS2MT Mike Modano
Marty Turco
IS2NH Dany Heatley
Rick Nash
IS2NM Markus Naslund
Brendan Morrison
IS2OJ Olli Jokinen
Jay Bouwmeester
IS2OK Ilya Kovalchuk
Alexander Ovechkin SP
IS2PT Michael Peca
Darcy Tucker
IS2RB Patrick Roy
Ray Bourque SP
IS2RD Jeremy Roenick
Shane Doan
IS2RG Wade Redden
Martin Gerber
IS2RS Andrew Raycroft
Alexander Steen
IS2RT Luc Robitaille
Dave Taylor
IS2SD Martin St. Louis
Marc Denis
IS2SR Ryan Smyth
Dwayne Roloson
IS2SS Jason Spezza
Eric Staal SP
IS2SW Justin Williams
Eric Staal
IS2SY Miroslav Satan
Alexei Yashin
IS2VW Tomas Vokoun
Shea Weber
IS2WP Dave Williams
Bob Probert
IS2WR Dwayne Roloson
Cam Ward
IS2ZH Tomas Holmstrom
Henrik Zetterberg
IS2HH2 Bobby Hull
Gordie Howe SP

2006-07 SP Game Used Legendary Fabrics

LFBC Bobby Clarke/100 6.00 15.00
LFGH Gordie Howe/25 20.00 50.00
LFGL Guy Lafleur/100 10.00 25.00
LFJB Jean Beliveau/100 12.00 30.00
LFMB Mike Bossy/100 6.00 15.00
LFML Mario Lemieux/25 30.00 80.00
LFPE Phil Esposito/25 12.00 30.00
LFPR Patrick Roy/25 40.00 100.00
LFRB Ray Bourque/25 20.00 50.00
LFWG Wayne Gretzky/25 75.00 150.00

2006-07 SP Game Used Legendary Fabrics Autographs

PRINT RUN 100 #'d SETS
LFBC Bobby Clarke 15.00 40.00
LFGH Gordie Howe 60.00 125.00
LFGL Guy Lafleur 20.00 50.00
LFJB Jean Beliveau 25.00 60.00
LFMB Mike Bossy 15.00 40.00
LFML Mario Lemieux SP 50.00 125.00
LFPE Phil Esposito SP 25.00 60.00
LFPR Patrick Roy SP
LFRB Ray Bourque SP 50.00 100.00
LFWG Wayne Gretzky SP 250.00 400.00

2006-07 SP Game Used Letter Marks

PRINT RUN 50 #'d SETS
LMAF Alexander Frolov 40.00 100.00
LMAK Andrei Kostitsyn 30.00 80.00
LMAL Andrew Ladd 25.00 60.00
LMAN Antero Niittymaki 30.00 60.00
LMBB Brad Boyes 30.00 60.00
LMBG Brian Gionta 40.00 80.00
LMBM Brenden Morrow 40.00 100.00
LMBP Bernie Parent 30.00 60.00
LMBQ Ray Bourque 75.00 150.00
LMBR Bill Ranford 40.00 80.00
LMCG Clark Gillies 30.00 80.00
LMCH Cristobal Huet 30.00 80.00
LMCK Chuck Kobasew 25.00 60.00
LMCN Cam Neely 60.00 125.00
LMCW Cam Ward 30.00 80.00
LMDC Dino Ciccarelli 25.00 60.00
LMDP Denis Potvin 30.00 80.00
LMDR Dwayne Roloson 25.00 60.00
LMDS Denis Savard 50.00 125.00
LMDW Dave Williams 25.00 60.00
LMEC Erik Cole 25.00 60.00
LMEL Patrik Elias 40.00 100.00
LMEM Evgeni Malkin
LMES Eric Staal 40.00 100.00
LMFP Fernando Pisani 25.00 60.00
LMGC Gerry Cheevers 40.00 80.00
LMGL Guillaume Latendresse 60.00 100.00
LMHA Dominik Hasek 60.00 100.00
LMHE Milan Hejduk 40.00 80.00
LMHO Gordie Howe 100.00 225.00
LMIK Ilya Kovalchuk 60.00 100.00
LMJA Jason Arnott 25.00 60.00
LMJC Jeff Carter 30.00 80.00
LMJI Jarome Iginla 75.00 175.00
LMJJ Jussi Jokinen 40.00 80.00
LMJL Joffrey Lupul 25.00 60.00
LMJP Joni Pitkanen 25.00 60.00
LMJT Jose Theodore 30.00 80.00
LMKD Kris Draper 30.00 80.00
LMLR Luc Robitaille 40.00 100.00
LMLU Roberto Luongo 100.00 225.00
LMMA Matt Carle 30.00 60.00
LMMB Martin Brodeur 200.00 350.00
LMMF Marc-Andre Fleury 75.00 200.00
LMMG Marian Gaborik 60.00 150.00
LMMI Mike Cammalleri 30.00 80.00
LMMM Mike Modano 75.00 200.00
LMMN Markus Naslund 50.00 125.00
LMMR Michael Ryder 30.00 80.00
LMMT Marty Turco 40.00 80.00
LMNL Nicklas Lidstrom 40.00 100.00
LMOJ Olli Jokinen 25.00 60.00
LMOR Bobby Orr 250.00 500.00
LMPE Michael Peca 30.00 80.00
LMPI Pierre-Marc Bouchard 25.00 60.00
LMPK Phil Kessel 40.00 80.00
LMPM Patrick Marleau 30.00 80.00
LMPO Ryan Potulny 25.00 60.00
LMPP Petr Prucha 75.00 150.00
LMRH Ron Hextall 60.00 150.00
LMRI Mike Ribeiro 25.00 60.00
LMRL Reggie Leach 25.00 60.00
LMRM Mike Richards 30.00 80.00
LMRV Rogie Vachon 30.00 80.00
LMRY Ryan Miller 75.00 175.00
LMSB Steve Bernier 50.00 100.00
LMSC Sidney Crosby 300.00 600.00
LMSK Saku Koivu 40.00 150.00
LMSM Ryan Smyth 50.00 125.00
LMSV Marek Svatos 30.00 80.00
LMTH Tomas Holmstrom 30.00 60.00
LMTL Ted Lindsay 30.00 80.00
LMTO Terry O'Reilly 30.00 80.00
LMVA Thomas Vanek 60.00 150.00
LMWG Wayne Gretzky 400.00 600.00
LMZC Zdeno Chara 25.00 60.00

2006-07 SP Game Used Rookie Exclusives Autographs

PRINT RUN 100 #'d SETS
REAB Adam Burish 3.00 8.00
REAE Alexander Edler 6.00 15.00
REAK Anze Kopitar 30.00 80.00
REAL Alex Brooks 3.00 8.00
REAR Alexander Radulov 30.00 80.00
REBB Brendan Bell 6.00 15.00
REBO Ben Ondrus 6.00 15.00
REBR Mike Brown 5.00 12.00
RECA Mike Card 3.00 8.00
REDB Dustin Byfuglien 12.00 30.00
REDL Drew Larman 3.00 8.00
REDS Drew Stafford 15.00 40.00
REDU Dustin Boyd 12.00 30.00
REEF Eric Fehr 8.00 20.00
REEM Evgeni Malkin 60.00 150.00
REGL Guillaume Latendresse 40.00 100.00
REIW Ian White 6.00 15.00
REJF Jean-Francois Racine 8.00 20.00
REJI Jarkko Immonen 6.00 15.00
REJS Jordan Staal 50.00 100.00
REJW Jeremy Williams 6.00 15.00
REKP Konstantin Pushkaryov 6.00 15.00
REKY Keith Yandle 6.00 15.00
RELE Loui Eriksson 6.00 15.00
RELS Ladislav Smid 6.00 15.00
REMB Michael Blunden 6.00 15.00
REMC Matt Carle 8.00 20.00
REMM Masi Marjamaki 6.00 15.00
REMO Michel Ouellet 12.00 30.00
REMP Marc-Antoine Pouliot 12.00 30.00
REMS Mark Stuart 6.00 15.00
REMV Marc-Edouard Vlasic 12.00 30.00
REND Nigel Dawes 6.00 15.00
RENM Nathan McIver 3.00 8.00
RENO Fredrik Norrena 6.00 15.00
RENW Noah Welch 6.00 15.00
REPO Patrick O'Sullivan 8.00 20.00
REPK Phil Kessel 40.00 100.00
REPO Ryan Potulny 8.00 20.00
REPS Paul Stastny 30.00 80.00
REPT Patrick Thoresen 10.00 25.00
RERS Ryan Shannon 6.00 15.00
RESO Shane O'Brien 6.00 15.00
RESP Janis Sprukts 6.00 15.00
RESW Shea Weber 8.00 20.00
RETK Tomas Kopecky 8.00 20.00
RETZ Travis Zajac 12.00 30.00
REYS Yan Stastny 6.00 15.00

2006-07 SP Game Used SIGnificance

PRINT RUN 50 #'d SETS
SAF Alexander Frolov 8.00 20.00
SAH Ales Hemsky 8.00 20.00
SAK Andrei Kostitsyn 6.00 15.00
SAL Andrew Ladd 8.00 20.00
SAM Al Montoya 10.00 25.00
SAN Antero Niittymaki 8.00 20.00
SBG Brian Gionta 8.00 20.00
SBM Bryan McCabe 8.00 20.00
SBN Bob Nystrom 6.00 15.00
SBR Daniel Briere 12.00 30.00
SCB Cam Barker 8.00 20.00
SCH Cristobal Huet 20.00 50.00
SCK Chuck Kobasew 6.00 15.00
SCN Cam Neely 12.00 30.00
SCW Cam Ward 10.00 25.00
SDB Dustin Brown 8.00 20.00
SDC Don Cherry 20.00 50.00
SDE Denis Savard 10.00 25.00
SDK Duncan Keith 6.00 15.00
SDP Denis Potvin 6.00 15.00
SDR Dwayne Roloson 6.00 15.00
SDS Derek Sanderson 12.00 30.00
SDT Dave Taylor 8.00 20.00
SEC Erik Cole 6.00 15.00
SEM Evgeni Malkin 75.00 150.00
SEN Eric Nystrom 6.00 15.00
SES Eric Staal 10.00 25.00
SFP Fernando Pisani 6.00 15.00
SGA Marian Gaborik 12.00 30.00
SGH Gordie Howe 30.00 80.00
SGL Guillaume Latendresse 30.00 60.00
SHI Chris Higgins 10.00 25.00
SHO Marcel Hossa 5.00 12.00
SHT Hannu Toivonen 8.00 20.00
SHZ Henrik Zetterberg 12.00 30.00
SIK Ilya Kovalchuk 15.00 40.00
SJA Jason Arnott 8.00 20.00
SJB Jay Bouwmeester 6.00 15.00
SJC Jeff Carter 8.00 20.00
SJP Joni Pitkanen 6.00 15.00
SJS Jarret Stoll 8.00 20.00
SKB Keith Ballard 6.00 15.00
SKD Kris Draper 8.00 20.00
SKL Kari Lehtonen 10.00 25.00
SKO Mikko Koivu 8.00 20.00
SLE Reggie Leach 8.00 20.00
SLN Ladislav Nagy 5.00 12.00
SMA Ryan Malone 8.00 20.00
SMB Martin Brodeur 60.00 100.00
SMC Mike Cammalleri 10.00 25.00
SMD Andy McDonald 6.00 15.00
SMG Martin Gerber 12.00 30.00
SMH Michal Handzus 5.00 12.00
SMM Milan Michalek 6.00 15.00
SMP Michael Peca 8.00 20.00
SMR Mike Richards 12.00 30.00
SMT Marty Turco 8.00 20.00
SNH Nathan Horton 8.00 20.00
SNZ Nikolai Zherdev 5.00 12.00
SPA Mark Parrish 5.00 12.00
SPB Pierre-Marc Bouchard 6.00 15.00
SPH Chris Phillips 5.00 12.00
SPP Petr Prucha 6.00 15.00
SRB Richard Brodeur 8.00 20.00
SRE Robert Esche 8.00 20.00
SRF Ruslan Fedotenko 5.00 12.00
SRH Ron Hextall 15.00 40.00
SRI Mike Ribeiro 5.00 12.00
SRK Rostislav Klesla 5.00 12.00
SRM Ryan Miller 20.00 50.00
SRN Rick Nash 10.00 25.00
SRS Ryan Smyth 6.00 15.00
SRV Rogie Vachon 15.00 40.00
SRW Ryan Whitney 5.00 12.00
SRY Michael Ryder 8.00 20.00
SSA Marc Savard 6.00 15.00
SSB Steve Bernier 6.00 15.00
SSC Sidney Crosby 150.00 250.00
SSV Marek Svatos 6.00 15.00
SSW Stephen Weiss 6.00 15.00
STH Tomas Holmstrom 6.00 15.00
STL Ted Lindsay 8.00 20.00
STO Terry O'Reilly 10.00 25.00
STU Darcy Tucker 10.00 25.00
STV Tomas Vokoun 8.00 20.00
SVA Thomas Vanek 12.00 30.00
SVF Valtteri Filppula 8.00 20.00
SVT Vesa Toskala 10.00 25.00
SWR Wade Redden 5.00 12.00
SZC Zdeno Chara 6.00 15.00

2007-08 SP Game Used

This set was issued into the hobby in three-card packs, with a $29.99 SRP, which came six packs to a box and 12 boxes to a case. Cards numbered 1-100 are veterans while cards 101-200 are Rookie Cards. Within the Rookie Card subset: Cards numbered 101-190 were issued to a stated print run of 999 serial numbered sets and cards 191-200 were issued to a stated print run of 99 serial numbered sets.

COMP.SET w/o SPs (100) 25.00 60.00
(101-190) PRINT RUN 999 SER.#'d SETS
(191-200) PRINT RUN 99 SER.#'d SETS
1 Alexander Ovechkin 2.50 6.00
2 Olaf Kolzig .75 2.00
3 Alexander Semin .75 2.00
4 Roberto Luongo 1.25 3.00
5 Markus Naslund .75 2.00
6 Henrik Sedin .50 1.25
7 Daniel Sedin .50 1.25
8 Mats Sundin .75 2.00
9 Vesa Toskala .60 1.50
10 Darcy Tucker .60 1.50
11 Alexander Steen .50 1.25
12 Martin St. Louis .60 1.50
13 Vincent Lecavalier .75 2.00
14 Brad Richards .60 1.50
15 Doug Weight .50 1.25
16 Keith Tkachuk .60 1.50
17 Paul Kariya .75 2.00
18 Joe Thornton 1.00 2.50
19 Jonathan Cheechoo .60 1.50
20 Evgeni Nabokov .60 1.50
21 Patrick Marleau .60 1.50
22 Jordan Staal 1.00 2.50
23 Sidney Crosby 4.00 10.00
24 Marc-Andre Fleury .75 2.00
25 Evgeni Malkin 2.00 5.00
26 Shane Doan .50 1.25
27 Ed Jovanovski .50 1.25
28 Simon Gagne .75 2.00
29 Daniel Briere .75 2.00
30 Jeff Carter .50 1.25
31 Jason Spezza .75 2.00
32 Daniel Alfredsson .60 1.50
33 Ray Emery .60 1.50
34 Dany Heatley 1.00 2.50
35 Jaromir Jagr 1.25 3.00
36 Henrik Lundqvist 1.00 2.50
37 Chris Drury .60 1.50
38 Bill Guerin .50 1.25
39 Rick DiPietro .60 1.50
40 Miroslav Satan .50 1.25
41 Martin Brodeur 2.00 5.00
42 Patrik Elias .50 1.25
43 Zach Parise .60 1.50
44 Chris Mason .60 1.50
45 Alexander Radulov .75 2.00
46 Jason Arnott .50 1.25
47 Saku Koivu .60 1.50
48 Cristobal Huet .60 1.50
49 Michael Ryder .50 1.25
50 Guillaume Latendresse .60 1.50
51 Marian Gaborik 1.00 2.50
52 Pierre-Marc Bouchard .50 1.25
53 Mikko Koivu .50 1.25
54 Anze Kopitar .75 2.00
55 Rob Blake .60 1.50
56 Alexander Frolov .50 1.25
57 Tomas Vokoun .75 2.00
58 Nathan Horton .50 1.25
59 Olli Jokinen .50 1.25
60 Dwayne Roloson .60 1.50
61 Ales Hemsky .50 1.25
62 Jarret Stoll .50 1.25
63 Pavel Datsyuk .75 2.00
64 Henrik Zetterberg .75 2.00
65 Nicklas Lidstrom .75 2.00
66 Dominik Hasek 1.00 2.50
67 Mike Modano .75 2.00
68 Marty Turco .75 2.00
69 Mike Ribeiro .50 1.25
70 Rick Nash .75 2.00
71 Sergei Fedorov .75 2.00
72 David Vyborny .50 1.25
73 Joe Sakic 1.50 4.00
74 Ryan Smyth .60 1.50
75 Milan Hejduk .60 1.50
76 Paul Stastny .75 2.00
77 Nikolai Khabibulin .75 2.00
78 Martin Havlat .60 1.50
79 Tuomo Ruutu .50 1.25
80 Eric Staal .75 2.00
81 Cam Ward .75 2.00
82 Justin Williams .50 1.25
83 Jarome Iginla 1.25 3.00
84 Alex Tanguay .60 1.50
85 Miikka Kiprusoff 1.00 2.50
86 Dion Phaneuf .75 2.00
87 Thomas Vanek .60 1.50
88 Ryan Miller .75 2.00
89 Jason Pominville .50 1.25
90 Drew Stafford .60 1.50
91 Patrice Bergeron .75 2.00
92 Manny Fernandez .60 1.50
93 Phil Kessel .75 2.00
94 Ilya Kovalchuk 1.00 2.50
95 Marian Hossa .75 2.00
96 Kari Lehtonen .75 2.00
97 Chris Pronger .75 2.00
98 Ryan Getzlaf .60 1.50
99 Jean-Sebastien Giguere .75 2.00
100 Scott Niedermayer .50 1.25
101 Jeff Schultz RC 4.00 10.00
102 Jamie Hunt RC 4.00 10.00
103 Mason Raymond RC 10.00 25.00
104 Jannik Hansen RC 4.00 10.00
105 Matt Smaby RC 4.00 10.00
106 Mike Lundin RC 4.00 10.00
107 Erik Johnson RC 8.00 20.00
108 David Perron RC 6.00 15.00
109 Steve Wagner RC 4.00 10.00
110 Torrey Mitchell RC 5.00 12.00
111 Tomas Plihal RC 5.00 12.00
112 Martin Hanzal RC 5.00 12.00
113 Craig Weller RC 4.00 10.00
114 Daniel Winnik RC 4.00 10.00
115 Daniel Carcillo RC 5.00 12.00
116 Ryan Parent RC 5.00 12.00
117 Stefan Meyer RC 4.00 10.00
118 Denis Tolpeko RC 4.00 10.00
119 Nathan Guenin RC 4.00 10.00
120 Riley Cote RC 5.00 12.00
121 Danny Bois RC 4.00 10.00
122 Nick Foligno RC 6.00 15.00

123 Brian Elliott RC 5.00 12.00
124 Marc Staal RC 10.00 25.00
125 Brandon Dubinsky RC 6.00 15.00
126 Ryan Callahan RC 6.00 15.00
127 Daniel Girardi RC 4.00 10.00
128 Frans Nielsen RC 4.00 10.00
129 Drew Fata RC 4.00 10.00
130 Nicklas Bergfors RC 5.00 12.00
131 Andy Greene RC 4.00 10.00
132 Mark Fraser RC 4.00 10.00
133 David Clarkson RC 4.00 10.00
134 Rod Pelley RC 4.00 10.00
135 Ville Koistinen RC 4.00 10.00
136 Rich Peverley RC 4.00 10.00
137 Kyle Chipchura RC 6.00 15.00
138 Jaroslav Halak RC 12.00 30.00
139 Duncan Milroy RC 4.00 10.00
140 Petr Kalus RC 4.00 10.00
141 Lauri Tukonen RC 4.00 10.00
142 Jonathan Bernier RC 10.00 25.00
143 Jack Johnson RC 6.00 15.00
144 Brady Murray RC 4.00 10.00
145 John Zeiler RC 4.00 10.00
146 Shay Stephenson RC 4.00 10.00
147 Joe Piskula RC 4.00 10.00
148 Gabe Gauthier RC 4.00 10.00
149 Martin Lojek RC 4.00 10.00
150 Cory Murphy RC 4.00 10.00
151 Rob Schremp RC 5.00 12.00
152 Andrew Cogliano RC 10.00 25.00
153 Tom Gilbert RC 5.00 12.00
154 Bryan Young RC 4.00 10.00
155 Zach Stortini RC 4.00 10.00
156 Sebastien Bisaillon RC 4.00 10.00
157 Matt Ellis RC 4.00 10.00
158 Matt Niskanen RC 4.00 10.00
159 Tobias Stephan RC 5.00 12.00
160 Joel Lundqvist RC 4.00 10.00
161 Chris Conner RC 4.00 10.00
162 Kris Russell RC 6.00 15.00
163 Tomas Popperle RC 5.00 12.00
164 Marc Methot RC 4.00 10.00
165 Jared Boll RC 4.00 10.00
166 Curtis Glencross RC 4.00 10.00
167 Tyler Weiman RC 5.00 12.00
168 Jaroslav Hlinka RC 5.00 12.00
169 Jeff Finger RC 4.00 10.00
170 Colin Fraser RC 4.00 10.00
171 Bryan Bickell RC 4.00 10.00
172 Magnus Johansson RC 4.00 10.00
173 Jonas Nordqvist RC 4.00 10.00
174 David Koci RC 4.00 10.00
175 Curtis McElhinney RC 5.00 12.00
176 Matt Keetley RC 5.00 12.00
177 David Moss RC 6.00 15.00
178 Tomi Maki RC 4.00 10.00
179 Mark Mancari RC 5.00 12.00
180 Patrick Kaleta RC 4.00 10.00
181 David Krejci RC 8.00 20.00
182 Milan Lucic RC 10.00 25.00
183 Jonathan Sigalet RC 4.00 10.00
184 Brett Sterling RC 4.00 10.00
185 Tobias Enstrom RC 6.00 15.00
186 Ondrej Pavelec RC 6.00 15.00
187 Drew Miller RC 4.00 10.00
188 Ryan Carter RC 5.00 12.00
189 Jonas Hiller RC 10.00 25.00
190 Kent Huskins RC 4.00 10.00
191 Nicklas Backstrom/99 RC 40.00 100.00
192 Paul Mueller/99 RC 30.00 80.00
193 Jiri Tlusty/99 RC 25.00 60.00
194 Carey Price/99 RC 75.00 150.00
195 James Sheppard/99 RC 10.00 25.00
196 Devin Setoguchi/99 RC 20.00 50.00
197 Sam Gagner/99 RC 20.00 50.00
198 Jonathan Toews/99 RC 75.00 150.00
199 Patrick Kane/99 RC 60.00 120.00
200 Bryan Little/99 RC 15.00 40.00

2007-08 SP Game Used Gold

*GOLD (1-100): 2.5X TO 6X
(1-100) PRINT RUN 100 SER.#'d SETS
*GOLD RCs (101-190): 1X TO 2.5X
*GOLD RCs (191-200): .5X TO 1.2X
(101-200) PRINT RUN 50 SER.#'d SETS
194 Carey Price 60.00 120.00
198 Jonathan Toews 60.00 120.00
199 Patrick Kane 50.00 100.00

2007-08 SP Game Used Gold Spectrum

STATED PRINT RUN 1 SER.#'d SET
NOT PRICED DUE TO SCARCITY

2007-08 SP Game Used Spectrum

*SPEC (1-100): 3X TO 8X
*SPEC RCs (101-190): 1.2X TO 3X
*SPEC RCs (191-200): .6X TO 1.5X
STATED PRINT RUN 25 SER.#'d SETS
194 Carey Price 75.00 150.00
198 Jonathan Toews 75.00 150.00
199 Patrick Kane 60.00 120.00

2007-08 SP Game Used Authentic Fabrics

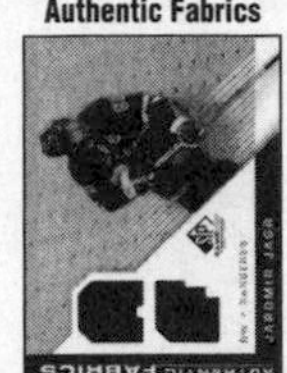

AFAK Alex Kovalev 4.00 10.00
AFAO Adam Oates 4.00 10.00
AFAR Alexander Radulov 6.00 15.00
AFAS Anton Stastny 4.00 10.00
AFAY Alexei Yashin 4.00 10.00
AFBB Bob Bourne 4.00 10.00
AFBG Bill Guerin 4.00 10.00
AFBI Bill Ranford 5.00 12.00
AFBM Brendan Morrison 4.00 10.00
AFBO Brad Boyes 5.00 12.00
AFBP Bob Probert 5.00 12.00
AFBR Brandon Bochenski 4.00 10.00
AFBS Billy Smith 6.00 15.00
AFBW Brendan Witt 4.00 10.00
AFCA Colby Armstrong 4.00 10.00
AFCC Chris Chelios 4.00 10.00
AFCD Chris Drury 5.00 12.00
AFCH Chris Higgins 5.00 12.00
AFCN Cam Neely 6.00 15.00
AFCO Mike Commodore 4.00 10.00
AFCW Cam Ward 6.00 15.00
AFDA Daniel Alfredsson 5.00 12.00
AFDG Doug Gilmour 5.00 12.00
AFDH Dale Hawerchuk 5.00 12.00
AFDL David Legwand 4.00 10.00
AFDR Dwayne Roloson 5.00 12.00
AFDW Doug Weight 4.00 10.00
AFEB Ed Belfour 6.00 15.00
AFEN Evgeni Nabokov 5.00 12.00
AFES Eric Staal 6.00 15.00
AFEV Evgeni Malkin 15.00 40.00
AFFM Frank Mahovlich 10.00 25.00
AFGF Grant Fuhr 10.00 25.00
AFGI Brian Gionta 4.00 10.00
AFGM Glen Murray 4.00 10.00
AFGR Gary Roberts 4.00 10.00
AFHE Dany Heatley 8.00 20.00
AFHL Henrik Lundqvist 8.00 20.00
AFHT Hannu Toivonen 5.00 12.00
AFIK Ilya Kovalchuk 8.00 20.00
AFJB Jay Bouwmeester 4.00 10.00
AFJC Jonathan Cheechoo 5.00 12.00
AFJG Jean-Sebastien Giguere 6.00 15.00
AFJI Jarome Iginla 10.00 25.00
AFJJ Jaromir Jagr 10.00 25.00
AFJL Joffrey Lupul 4.00 10.00
AFJO Joe Sakic 12.00 30.00
AFJP Joni Pitkanen 4.00 10.00
AFJS Jarret Stoll 4.00 10.00
AFJT Joe Thornton 8.00 20.00
AFJU Jussi Jokinen 4.00 10.00
AFJW Justin Williams 4.00 10.00
AFKL Kari Lehtonen 6.00 15.00
AFKO Anze Kopitar 6.00 15.00
AFKT Keith Tkachuk 5.00 12.00
AFLN Ladislav Nagy 4.00 10.00
AFLR Larry Robinson 8.00 20.00
AFMA Marc Savard 4.00 10.00
AFMB Martin Brodeur 15.00 40.00
AFMC Bryan McCabe 4.00 10.00
AFMF Manny Fernandez 5.00 12.00
AFMG Marian Gaborik 8.00 20.00
AFMH Marian Hossa 6.00 15.00
AFMK Mikko Koivu 4.00 10.00
AFML Manny Legace 6.00 15.00
AFMM Mike Modano 6.00 15.00
AFMN Markus Naslund 6.00 15.00
AFMO Brenden Morrow 5.00 12.00
AFMR Mike Ribeiro 4.00 10.00
AFMS Miroslav Satan 4.00 10.00
AFMT Marty Turco 6.00 15.00
AFON Owen Nolan 5.00 12.00
AFOV Alexander Ovechkin 20.00 50.00
AFPB Patrice Bergeron 6.00 15.00
AFPD Pavel Datsyuk 6.00 15.00
AFPE Patrik Elias 4.00 10.00
AFPR Patrick Roy 20.00 50.00
AFRA Andrew Raycroft 5.00 12.00
AFRB Brian Rafalski 4.00 10.00
AFRE Mark Recchi 4.00 10.00
AFRI Brad Richards 5.00 12.00
AFRL Roberto Luongo 10.00 25.00
AFRN Rick Nash 6.00 15.00
AFRS Ryan Smyth 5.00 12.00
AFRY Michael Ryder 4.00 10.00
AFSA Borje Salming 5.00 12.00
AFSC Sidney Crosby 25.00 60.00
AFSG Simon Gagne 4.00 10.00
AFSH Brendan Shanahan 6.00 15.00
AFSK Saku Koivu 5.00 12.00
AFSM Martin St. Louis 5.00 12.00
AFSN Scott Niedermayer 5.00 12.00
AFSP Jason Spezza 6.00 15.00
AFST Brad Stuart 4.00 10.00
AFSU Mats Sundin 6.00 15.00
AFSV Marek Svatos 4.00 10.00
AFTH Jose Theodore 6.00 15.00
AFTW Tiger Williams 5.00 12.00
AFVL Vincent Lecavalier 6.00 15.00

2007-08 SP Game Used Authentic Fabrics Rainbow

*RAINBOW: 1X TO 2X JSY HI
STATED PRINT RUN 100 #'d SETS

2007-08 SP Game Used Authentic Fabrics Duals

STATED PRINT RUN 100 SER.#'d SETS
AF2AD Alex Tanguay 4.00 10.00
Dion Phaneuf
AF2AH Daniel Alfredsson 4.00 10.00
Dany Heatley
AF2AM Maxim Afinogenov 4.00 10.00
Ryan Miller
AF2BB Ed Belfour 8.00 20.00
Martin Brodeur
AF2BG Martin Brodeur 8.00 20.00
Brian Gionta
AF2BH Jay Bouwmeester 3.00 8.00
Nathan Horton
AF2BK Patrice Bergeron 4.00 10.00
Phil Kessel
AF2BL Martin Brodeur 10.00 25.00
Roberto Luongo
AF2BW Rod Brind'Amour 4.00 10.00
Cam Ward
AF2CB Jonathan Cheechoo 4.00 10.00
Steve Bernier
AF2CM Sidney Crosby 40.00 100.00
Evgeni Malkin
AF2CO Sidney Crosby 40.00 100.00
Alexander Ovechkin
AF2CR Chris Chelios 3.00 8.00
Brian Rafalski
AF2CS Mike Commodore 3.00 8.00
Eric Staal
AF2DD Kris Draper 4.00 10.00
Pavel Datsyuk
AF2DG Pavol Demitra 4.00 10.00
Marian Gaborik
AF2DS Rick DiPietro 4.00 10.00
Billy Smith
AF2EJ Eric Staal 6.00 15.00
Jordan Staal
AF2FB Manny Fernandez 4.00 10.00
Patrice Bergeron
AF2FR Grant Fuhr 6.00 20.00
Bill Ranford
AF2FS Peter Forsberg 6.00 15.00
Borje Salming
AF2FT Manny Fernandez 4.00 10.00
Hannu Toivonen
AF2GB Marian Gaborik 4.00 12.00
Pierre-Marc Bouchard
AF2GC Simon Gagne 4.00 10.00
Jeff Carter
AF2GJ Mike Green 3.00 8.00
Milan Jurcina
AF2GK Marian Gaborik 5.00 12.00
Mikko Koivu
AF2GL Simon Gagne 4.00 10.00
Joffrey Lupul
AF2GS Bill Guerin 3.00 8.00
Miroslav Satan
AF2HD Dominik Hasek 8.00 20.00
Pavel Datsyuk
AF2HK Marian Hossa 5.00 12.00
Ilya Kovalchuk
AF2HL Dominik Hasek 8.00 20.00
Nicklas Lidstrom
AF2IK Jarome Iginla 8.00 20.00
Miikka Kiprusoff
AF2JC Jaromir Jagr 5.00 12.00
Chris Drury
AF2JD Jason Spezza 4.00 10.00
Dany Heatley
AF2JH Olli Jokinen 3.00 8.00
Nathan Horton
AF2JJ Joe Sakic 6.00 15.00
Joe Thornton
AF2JL Jaromir Jagr 5.00 12.00
Henrik Lundqvist
AF2JP Jaromir Jagr 5.00 12.00
Petr Prucha
AF2JR Joe Sakic 5.00 12.00
Ryan Smyth
AF2KB Paul Kariya 4.00 10.00
Brad Boyes
AF2KK Saku Koivu 4.00 10.00
Mikko Koivu
AF2KT Paul Kariya 4.00 10.00
Keith Tkachuk
AF2LA David Legwand 3.00 8.00
Jason Arnott
AF2LB Pascal Leclaire 3.00 8.00
Gilbert Brule
AF2LC Mario Lemieux 25.00 60.00
Sidney Crosby
AF2LH Michael Ryder 4.00 10.00
Cristobal Huet
AF2LJ Jere Lehtinen 4.00 10.00
Jussi Jokinen
AF2LM Mario Lemieux 12.00 30.00
Mark Messier
AF2LR David Legwand 3.00 8.00
Alexander Radulov
AF2LZ Nicklas Lidstrom 5.00 12.00
Henrik Zetterberg
AF2MA Mats Sundin 4.00 10.00
Andrew Raycroft
AF2MB Mats Sundin 4.00 10.00
Borje Salming
AF2MC Michael Ryder 3.00 8.00
Chris Higgins
AF2MJ Mike Modano 4.00 10.00
Joe Mullen
AF2ML Mats Sundin 5.00 12.00
Alexander Steen
AF2MM Lanny McDonald 4.00 10.00
Joe Mullen
AF2MR Mike Modano 4.00 10.00
Mike Ribeiro
AF2MT Patrick Marleau 5.00 12.00
Joe Thornton
AF2NB Cam Neely 6.00 15.00
Ray Bourque
AF2NG Scott Niedermayer 3.00 8.00
Jean-Sebastien Giguere
AF2NI Owen Nolan 4.00 10.00
Jarome Iginla
AF2NK Ladislav Nagy 3.00 8.00
Anze Kopitar
AF2NL Markus Naslund 6.00 15.00
Roberto Luongo
AF2NM Martin Havlat 4.00 10.00
Nikolai Khabibulin
AF2NO Cam Neely 5.00 12.00
Adam Oates
AF2OM Alexander Ovechkin 8.00 20.00
Evgeni Malkin
AF2PB Mark Parrish 3.00 8.00
Pierre-Marc Bouchard
AF2PM Dion Phaneuf 4.00 10.00
Al MacInnis
AF2PV Gilbert Perreault 4.00 10.00
Thomas Vanek
AF2RB Patrick Roy 12.00 30.00
Martin Brodeur
AF2RH Dwayne Roloson 3.00 8.00
Ales Hemsky
AF2RR Gary Roberts 3.00 8.00
Mark Recchi
AF2SA Saku Koivu 4.00 10.00
Alex Kovalev
AF2SB Billy Smith 4.00 10.00
Bob Bourne
AF2SC Mike Comrie 3.00 8.00
Miroslav Satan
AF2SE Henrik Sedin 3.00 8.00
Daniel Sedin
AF2SF Mats Sundin 5.00 12.00
Peter Forsberg
AF2SH Sergei Samsonov 3.00 8.00
Martin Havlat
AF2SL Manny Legace 3.00 8.00
Brad Boyes
AF2SM Marc Savard 3.00 8.00
Glen Murray
AF2SN Teemu Selanne 4.00 10.00
Scott Niedermayer
AF2SP Jarret Stoll 3.00 8.00
Fernando Pisani
AF2SR Steve Shutt 4.00 10.00
Larry Robinson
AF2SS Joe Sakic 6.00 15.00
Peter Stastny
AF2ST Joe Sakic 5.00 12.00
Jose Theodore
AF2SW Marek Svatos 3.00 8.00
Wojtek Wolski
AF2TC Joe Thornton 5.00 12.00
Jonathan Cheechoo
AF2TM Marty Turco 4.00 10.00
Brenden Morrow
AF2TO Matt Stajan 4.00 10.00
Alexander Steen
AF2TP Raffi Torres 3.00 8.00
Fernando Pisani
AF2VB Vincent Lecavalier 5.00 12.00
Brad Richards
AF2VC Markus Naslund 4.00 10.00
Mattias Ohlund
AF2VJ Tomas Vokoun 3.00 8.00
Olli Jokinen
AF2WK Doug Wilson 3.00 8.00
Duncan Keith
AF2WS Justin Williams 4.00 10.00
Eric Staal
AF2WT Doug Weight 3.00 8.00
Keith Tkachuk
AF2ZF Nikolai Zherdev 4.00 10.00
Sergei Fedorov

2007-08 SP Game Used Authentic Fabrics Duals Patches

*PATCHES: 2X TO 4X HI
STATED PRINT RUN 25 #'d SETS
AF2CM Sidney Crosby 125.00 300.00
Evgeni Malkin
AF2LC Mario Lemieux 200.00 400.00
Sidney Crosby
AF2OM Alexander Ovechkin 125.00 300.00
Evgeni Malkin

2007-08 SP Game Used Authentic Fabrics Triples

STATED PRINT RUN 25 #'d SETS
AF3AMV Maxim Afinogenov 25.00 50.00
Ryan Miller
Thomas Vanek
AF3ASH Daniel Alfredsson 25.00 50.00
Jason Spezza
Dany Heatley
AF3BCC Rob Blake 15.00 30.00
Kyle Calder
Mike Cammalleri
AF3BEG Martin Brodeur 30.00 60.00
Patrik Elias
Brian Gionta
AF3BLK Martin Brodeur 30.00 80.00
Roberto Luongo
Miikka Kiprusoff
AF3BPG Todd Bertuzzi 20.00 40.00
Corey Perry
Ryan Getzlaf
AF3BSW Rod Brind'Amour 20.00 40.00
Eric Staal
Cam Ward
AF3CCW Mike Commodore 15.00 30.00
Erik Cole
Justin Williams
AF3CVP Tim Connolly 15.00 30.00
Thomas Vanek
Daniel Paille
AF3DGK Pavol Demitra 15.00 30.00
Marian Gaborik
Mikko Koivu
AF3FBK Manny Fernandez 25.00 50.00
Patrice Bergeron
Phil Kessel
AF3FCM Marc-Andre Fleury
Sidney Crosby
Evgeni Malkin
AF3GBB Simon Gagne 25.00 50.00
Daniel Briere
Martin Biron
AF3GDH Scott Gomez 25.00 50.00
Chris Drury
Ryan Hollweg
AF3GSD Bill Guerin 15.00 30.00
Miroslav Satan
Rick DiPietro
AF3HDD Dominik Hasek 30.00 60.00
Kris Draper
Pavel Datsyuk
AF3HKL Marian Hossa
Ilya Kovalchuk
Kari Lehtonen
AF3HSB Milan Hejduk 20.00 40.00
Marek Svatos
Peter Budaj
AF3ITK Jarome Iginla 20.00 40.00
Alex Tanguay
Miikka Kiprusoff
AF3JSP Jaromir Jagr 25.00 50.00
Martin Straka
Petr Prucha
AF3KGO Olaf Kolzig 40.00 80.00
Mike Green
Alexander Ovechkin
AF3KPK Alex Kovalev 15.00 30.00
Alexander Perezhogin
Andrei Kostitsyn
AF3KRK Saku Koivu 30.00 60.00
Michael Ryder
Alex Kovalev
AF3KWT Paul Kariya 20.00 40.00
Doug Weight
Keith Tkachuk
AF3LAR David Legwand 20.00 40.00
Jason Arnott
Alexander Radulov
AF3LBS Manny Legace 10.00 25.00
Brad Boyes
Lee Stempniak
AF3LGM Mario Lemieux
Wayne Gretzky
Mark Messier
AF3LHZ Nicklas Lidstrom 20.00 50.00
Tomas Holmstrom
Henrik Zetterberg
AF3LNF Sergei Fedorov 15.00 30.00
Pascal Leclaire
Rick Nash
AF3LRC Joffrey Lupul 20.00 40.00
Mike Richards
Jeff Carter
AF3LRS Vincent Lecavalier 20.00 40.00
Brad Richards
Martin St. Louis
AF3LSS Roberto Luongo
Henrik Sedin
Daniel Sedin
AF3MBC Milan Michalek 10.00 25.00
Steve Bernier
Matt Carle
AF3MMM Lanny McDonald
Joe Mullen
Al MacInnis
AF3MRT Mike Modano
Mike Ribeiro
Marty Turco
AF3NFK Ladislav Nagy
Alexander Frolov
Anze Kopitar
AF3NMK Markus Naslund 25.00 50.00
Brendan Morrison
Ryan Kesler
AF3NRL Owen Nolan 10.00 25.00
Robyn Regehr
Matthew Lombardi
AF3PBM Mark Parrish 10.00 25.00
Pierre-Marc Bouchard
Dominic Moore
AF3REM Wade Redden 15.00 30.00
Ray Emery
Andrej Meszaros
AF3RMA Mark Recchi
Ryan Malone
Colby Armstrong
AF3SFA Mats Sundin 30.00 60.00
Peter Forsberg
Daniel Alfredsson
AF3SHR Sergei Samsonov 15.00 30.00
Martin Havlat
Tuomo Ruutu
AF3SKK Brent Seabrook 10.00 25.00
Duncan Keith
Nikolai Khabibulin
AF3SLT Joe Sakic 25.00 50.00
Vincent Lecavalier
Joe Thornton
AF3SMC Marc Savard 20.00 40.00
Glen Murray
Zdeno Chara
AF3SMT Mats Sundin 20.00 40.00
Bryan McCabe
Vesa Toskala
AF3SNG Teemu Selanne 15.00 30.00
Scott Niedermayer
Jean-Sebastien Giguere
AF3SRH Jarret Stoll 15.00 30.00
Dwayne Roloson
Ales Hemsky
AF3SSJ Joe Sakic 20.00 40.00
Brendan Shanahan
Jaromir Jagr
AF3SSW Matt Stajan 10.00 25.00
Alexander Steen
Ian White
AF3STS Joe Sakic 20.00 40.00
Jose Theodore
Ryan Smyth
AF3SWV Denis Savard 10.00 25.00
Doug Wilson
Rick Vaive
AF3THP Raffi Torres 10.00 25.00
Shawn Horcoff
Fernando Pisani
AF3TNC Joe Thornton
Evgeni Nabokov
Jonathan Cheechoo
AF3VJB Tomas Vokoun 15.00 30.00
Olli Jokinen
Jay Bouwmeester
AF3VSB David Vyborny 10.00 25.00
Jody Shelley
Gilbert Brule
AF3ZLM Sergei Zubov 20.00 40.00
Jere Lehtinen
Brenden Morrow

2007-08 SP Game Used Authentic Fabrics Triples Patches

STATED PRINT RUN 10 #'d SETS
NOT PRICED DUE TO SCARCITY
AF3AMV Maxim Afinogenov
Ryan Miller
Thomas Vanek
AF3ASH Daniel Alfredsson
Jason Spezza
Dany Heatley
AF3BCC Rob Blake
Kyle Calder
Mike Cammalleri
AF3BEG Martin Brodeur
Patrik Elias
Brian Gionta
AF3BLK Martin Brodeur
Roberto Luongo
Miikka Kiprusoff
AF3BPG Todd Bertuzzi
Corey Perry
Ryan Getzlaf
AF3BSW Rod Brind'Amour
Eric Staal
Cam Ward
AF3CCW Mike Commodore
Erik Cole
Justin Williams
AF3CVP Tim Connolly
Thomas Vanek
Daniel Paille
AF3DGK Pavol Demitra
Marian Gaborik
Mikko Koivu
AF3FBK Manny Fernandez
Patrice Bergeron
Phil Kessel
AF3FCM Marc-Andre Fleury
Sidney Crosby
Evgeni Malkin
AF3GBB Simon Gagne
Daniel Briere
Martin Biron
AF3GDH Scott Gomez
Chris Drury
Ryan Hollweg
AF3GSD Bill Guerin
Miroslav Satan
Rick DiPietro
AF3HDD Dominik Hasek
Kris Draper
Pavel Datsyuk
AF3HKL Marian Hossa
Ilya Kovalchuk
Kari Lehtonen
AF3HSB Milan Hejduk
Marek Svatos
Peter Budaj
AF3ITK Jarome Iginla
Alex Tanguay
Miikka Kiprusoff
AF3JSP Jaromir Jagr
Martin Straka
Petr Prucha
AF3KGO Olaf Kolzig
Mike Green
Alexander Ovechkin
AF3KPK Alex Kovalev
Alexander Perezhogin
Andrei Kostitsyn
AF3KRK Saku Koivu
Michael Ryder
Alex Kovalev
AF3KWT Paul Kariya
Doug Weight
Keith Tkachuk
AF3LAR David Legwand
Jason Arnott
Alexander Radulov
AF3LBS Manny Legace
Brad Boyes
Lee Stempniak
AF3LGM Mario Lemieux
Wayne Gretzky
Mark Messier
AF3LHZ Nicklas Lidstrom
Tomas Holmstrom
Henrik Zetterberg
AF3LNF Pascal Leclaire
Rick Nash
Sergei Fedorov
AF3LRC Joffrey Lupul
Mike Richards
Jeff Carter
AF3LRS Vincent Lecavalier
Brad Richards
Martin St. Louis
AF3LSS Roberto Luongo
Henrik Sedin
Daniel Sedin
AF3MBC Milan Michalek
Steve Bernier
Matt Carle
AF3MMM Lanny McDonald
Joe Mullen
Al MacInnis
AF3MRT Mike Modano
Mike Ribeiro
Marty Turco
AF3NFK Ladislav Nagy
Alexander Frolov
Anze Kopitar
AF3NMK Markus Naslund
Brendan Morrison
Ryan Kesler
AF3NRL Owen Nolan
Robyn Regehr
Matthew Lombardi
AF3PBM Mark Parrish
Pierre-Marc Bouchard
Dominic Moore
AF3REM Wade Redden
Ray Emery
Andrej Meszaros
AF3RMA Mark Recchi
Ryan Malone
Colby Armstrong
AF3SFA Mats Sundin
Peter Forsberg
Daniel Alfredsson
AF3SHR Sergei Samsonov
Martin Havlat
Tuomo Ruutu
AF3SKK Brent Seabrook
Duncan Keith
Nikolai Khabibulin
AF3SLT Joe Sakic
Vincent Lecavalier
Joe Thornton
AF3SMC Marc Savard
Glen Murray
Zdeno Chara
AF3SMT Mats Sundin
Bryan McCabe
Vesa Toskala
AF3SNG Teemu Selanne
Scott Niedermayer
Jean-Sebastien Giguere
AF3SRH Jarret Stoll
Dwayne Roloson
Ales Hemsky
AF3SSJ Joe Sakic
Brendan Shanahan
Jaromir Jagr
AF3SSW Matt Stajan
Alexander Steen
Ian White
AF3STS Joe Sakic
Jose Theodore
Ryan Smyth
AF3SWV Denis Savard
Doug Wilson
Rick Vaive
AF3THP Raffi Torres
Shawn Horcoff
Fernando Pisani
AF3TNC Joe Thornton
Evgeni Nabokov
Jonathan Cheechoo
AF3VJB Tomas Vokoun
Olli Jokinen
Jay Bouwmeester
AF3VSB David Vyborny
Jody Shelley
Gilbert Brule
AF3ZLM Sergei Zubov
Jere Lehtinen
Brenden Morrow

2007-08 SP Game Used Authentic Fabrics Quads

STATED PRINT RUN 10 SER.#'d SETS
NOT PRICED DUE TO SCARCITY
AF4ANA Jean-Sebastien Giguere
Todd Bertuzzi
Corey Perry
Ryan Getzlaf
AF4AST Joe Thornton
Marc Savard
Henrik Sedin
Sidney Crosby
AF4AWD Martin Brodeur
Nicklas Lidstrom
Sidney Crosby
Evgeni Malkin
AF4BOS Marc Savard
Glen Murray
Patrice Bergeron
Phil Kessel
AF4BUF Tim Connolly
Maxim Afinogenov
Ryan Miller
Thomas Vanek
AF4CAN Joe Sakic
Paul Kariya
Martin Brodeur
Jarome Iginla
AF4CAR Erik Cole
Justin Williams
Rod Brind'Amour
Eric Staal
AF4CGY Owen Nolan
Jarome Iginla
Alex Tanguay
Matthew Lombardi
AF4CHI Sergei Samsonov
Robert Lang
Martin Havlat
Tuomo Ruutu
AF4CLB David Vyborny
Rick Nash
Nikolai Zherdev
Sergei Fedorov
AF4COL Joe Sakic
Milan Hejduk
Ryan Smyth
Wojtek Wolski
AF4CZE Jaromir Jagr
Dominik Hasek
Milan Hejduk
Patrik Elias
AF4DAL Mike Modano
Jere Lehtinen
Mike Ribeiro
Jussi Jokinen
AF4DET Dominik Hasek
Nicklas Lidstrom
Pavel Datsyuk
Henrik Zetterberg
AF4EDM Jarret Stoll
Dwayne Roloson
Ales Hemsky
Joni Pitkanen
AF4FIN Teemu Selanne
Saku Koivu
Olli Jokinen
Miikka Kiprusoff
AF4FLA Tomas Vokoun
Olli Jokinen
Jay Bouwmeester
Nathan Horton
AF4GOL Teemu Selanne

Vincent Lecavalier
Dany Heatley
Alexander Ovechkin
AF4LAK Rob Blake
Alexander Frolov
Mike Cammalleri
Anze Kopitar
AF4LDR Vincent Lecavalier
Martin Brodeur
Scott Niedermayer
Sidney Crosby
AF4MIN Pavol Demitra
Marian Gaborik
Pierre-Marc Bouchard
Mikko Koivu
AF4MTL Saku Koivu
Michael Ryder
Cristobal Huet
Chris Higgins
AF4NJD Martin Brodeur
Patrik Elias
Brian Gionta
Zach Parise
AF4NYI Bill Guerin
Miroslav Satan
Rick DiPietro
Trent Hunter
AF4NYR Jaromir Jagr
Martin Straka
Chris Drury
Henrik Lundqvist
AF4OTT Wade Redden
Jason Spezza
Dany Heatley
Ray Emery
AF4PHI Simon Gagne
Daniel Briere
Martin Biron
Jeff Carter
AF4PIT Mark Recchi
Marc-Andre Fleury
Sidney Crosby
Evgeni Malkin
AF4PTS Vincent Lecavalier
Joe Thornton
Dany Heatley
Sidney Crosby
AF4RUS Ilya Kovalchuk
Alexander Ovechkin
Evgeni Malkin
Alexander Radulov
AF4SHO Martin Brodeur
Dominik Hasek
Evgeni Nabokov
Miikka Kiprusoff
AF4SJS Patrick Marleau
Joe Thornton
Jonathan Cheechoo
Steve Bernier
AF4SLO Marian Hossa
Pavol Demitra
Miroslav Satan
Marian Gaborik
AF4STL Paul Kariya
Doug Weight
Keith Tkachuk
Manny Legace
AF4SWE Mats Sundin
Markus Naslund
Nicklas Lidstrom
Peter Forsberg
AF4TBL Vincent Lecavalier
Brad Richards
Martin St. Louis
Ryan Craig
AF4TOR Mats Sundin
Bryan McCabe
Vesa Toskala
Alexander Steen
AF4UDC Mario Lemieux
Wayne Gretzky
Gordie Howe
Mark Messier
AF4USA Mike Modano
Keith Tkachuk
Ryan Miller
Zach Parise
AF4VAN Markus Naslund
Roberto Luongo
Henrik Sedin
Daniel Sedin

2007-08 SP Game Used Authentic Fabrics Quads Patches

STATED PRINT RUN 7 #'d SETS
NOT PRICED DUE TO SCARCITY
AF4ANA Jean-Sebastien Giguere
Todd Bertuzzi
Corey Perry
Ryan Getzlaf
AF4AST Joe Thornton
Marc Savard
Henrik Sedin
Sidney Crosby
AF4AWD Martin Brodeur
Nicklas Lidstrom
Sidney Crosby
Evgeni Malkin
AF4BOS Marc Savard
Glen Murray
Patrice Bergeron
Phil Kessel
AF4BUF Tim Connolly
Maxim Afinogenov
Ryan Miller
Thomas Vanek
AF4CAN Joe Sakic
Paul Kariya
Martin Brodeur
Jarome Iginla
AF4CAR Erik Cole
Justin Williams
Rod Brind'Amour
Eric Staal
AF4CGY Owen Nolan
Jarome Iginla
Alex Tanguay
Matthew Lombardi
AF4CHI Sergei Samsonov
Robert Lang
Martin Havlat
Tuomo Ruutu
AF4CLB David Vyborny
Rick Nash
Nikolai Zherdev
Sergei Fedorov
AF4COL Joe Sakic
Milan Hejduk
Ryan Smyth
Wojtek Wolski
AF4CZE Jaromir Jagr
Dominik Hasek
Milan Hejduk
Patrik Elias
AF4DAL Mike Modano
Jere Lehtinen
Mike Ribeiro
Jussi Jokinen
AF4DET Dominik Hasek
Nicklas Lidstrom
Pavel Datsyuk
Henrik Zetterberg
AF4EDM Jarret Stoll
Dwayne Roloson
Ales Hemsky
Joni Pitkanen
AF4FIN Teemu Selanne
Saku Koivu
Olli Jokinen
Miikka Kiprusoff
AF4FLA Tomas Vokoun
Olli Jokinen
Jay Bouwmeester
Nathan Horton
AF4GOL Teemu Selanne
Vincent Lecavalier
Dany Heatley
Alexander Ovechkin
AF4LAK Rob Blake
Alexander Frolov
Mike Cammalleri
Anze Kopitar
AF4LDR Vincent Lecavalier
Martin Brodeur
Scott Niedermayer
Sidney Crosby
AF4MIN Pavol Demitra
Marian Gaborik
Pierre-Marc Bouchard
Mikko Koivu
AF4MTL Saku Koivu
Michael Ryder
Cristobal Huet
Chris Higgins
AF4NJD Martin Brodeur
Patrik Elias
Brian Gionta
Zach Parise
AF4NYI Bill Guerin
Miroslav Satan
Rick DiPietro
Trent Hunter
AF4NYR Jaromir Jagr
Martin Straka
Chris Drury
Henrik Lundqvist
AF4OTT Wade Redden
Jason Spezza
Dany Heatley
Ray Emery
AF4PHI Simon Gagne
Daniel Briere
Martin Biron
Jeff Carter
AF4PIT Mark Recchi
Marc-Andre Fleury
Sidney Crosby
Evgeni Malkin
AF4PTS Vincent Lecavalier
Joe Thornton
Dany Heatley
Sidney Crosby
AF4RUS Ilya Kovalchuk
Alexander Ovechkin
Evgeni Malkin
Alexander Radulov
AF4SHO Martin Brodeur
Dominik Hasek
Evgeni Nabokov
Miikka Kiprusoff
AF4SJS Patrick Marleau
Joe Thornton
Jonathan Cheechoo
Steve Bernier
AF4SLO Marian Hossa
Pavol Demitra
Miroslav Satan
Marian Gaborik
AF4STL Paul Kariya
Doug Weight
Keith Tkachuk
Manny Legace
AF4SWE Mats Sundin
Markus Naslund
Nicklas Lidstrom
Peter Forsberg
AF4TBL Vincent Lecavalier
Brad Richards
Martin St. Louis
Ryan Craig
AF4TOR Mats Sundin
Bryan McCabe
Vesa Toskala
Alexander Steen
AF4UDC Mario Lemieux
Wayne Gretzky
Gordie Howe
Mark Messier
AF4USA Mike Modano
Keith Tkachuk
Ryan Miller
Zach Parise
AF4VAN Markus Naslund
Roberto Luongo
Henrik Sedin
Daniel Sedin

2007-08 SP Game Used Authentic Fabrics Fives

STATED PRINT RUN 8 #'d SETS
NOT PRICED DUE TO SCARCITY
AF5NEC Mats Sundin
Tim Connolly
Saku Koivu
Jason Spezza
Patrice Bergeron
AF5NEG Manny Fernandez
Vesa Toskala
Ryan Miller
Ray Emery
Cristobal Huet
AF5NER Maxim Afinogenov
Daniel Alfredsson
Darcy Tucker
Glen Murray
Michael Ryder
AF5NWC Joe Sakic
Henrik Sedin
Shawn Horcoff
Pierre-Marc Bouchard
Matthew Lombardi
AF5NWG Jose Theodore
Roberto Luongo
Dwayne Roloson
Miikka Kiprusoff
Peter Budaj
AF5NWL Brian Rolston
Daniel Sedin
Ryan Smyth
Raffi Torres
Alex Tanguay
AF5NWR Markus Naslund
Milan Hejduk
Jarome Iginla
Marian Gaborik
Ales Hemsky
AF5SEC Vincent Lecavalier
Viktor Kozlov
Bobby Holik
Stephen Weiss
Eric Staal
AF5SEG Tomas Vokoun
Olaf Kolzig
Marc Denis
Kari Lehtonen
Cam Ward
AF5SEL Vaclav Prospal
Richard Zednik
Ilya Kovalchuk
Erik Cole
Alexander Ovechkin
AF5ATLC Mike Comrie
Patrik Elias
Chris Drury
Sidney Crosby
Jeff Carter
AF5ATLG Martin Brodeur
Martin Biron
Rick DiPietro
Henrik Lundqvist
Marc-Andre Fleury
AF5ATLL Simon Gagne
Ruslan Fedotenko
Marcel Hossa
Zach Parise
Evgeni Malkin
AF5ATLR Jaromir Jagr
Bill Guerin
Mark Recchi
Brian Gionta
Joffrey Lupul
AF5CENC Doug Weight
Jason Arnott
Robert Lang
Pavel Datsyuk
Sergei Fedorov
AF5CEND Nicklas Lidstrom
Barret Jackman
Rostislav Klesla
Brent Seabrook
Shea Weber
AF5CENG Dominik Hasek
Chris Osgood
Manny Legace
Pascal Leclaire
Nikolai Khabibulin
AF5CENL Paul Kariya
Sergei Samsonov
Martin Erat
Henrik Zetterberg
Rick Nash
AF5CENR Martin Havlat
Lee Stempniak
Alexander Radulov
David Vyborny
Tomas Holmstrom
AF5NHL1 Nicklas Lidstrom
Scott Niedermayer
Dany Heatley
Sidney Crosby
Alexander Ovechkin
AF5NHL2 Vincent Lecavalier
Chris Pronger
Roberto Luongo
Martin St. Louis
Thomas Vanek
AF5PACC Mike Modano
Joe Thornton
Steven Reinprecht
Mike Cammalleri
Ryan Getzlaf
AF5PACD Sergei Zubov
Rob Blake
Scott Niedermayer
Ed Jovanovski
Matt Carle
AF5PACG Curtis Joseph
Dan Cloutier
Jean-Sebastien Giguere
Evgeni Nabokov
Marty Turco
AF5PACR Jere Lehtinen
Todd Bertuzzi
Shane Doan
Jonathan Cheechoo
Dustin Brown

2007-08 SP Game Used Authentic Fabrics Fives Patches

STATED PRINT RUN 7 #'d SETS
NOT PRICED DUE TO SCARCITY
AF5NEC Saku Koivu
Jason Spezza
Patrice Bergeron
Mats Sundin
Tim Connolly
AF5NEG Manny Fernandez
Vesa Toskala
Ryan Miller
Ray Emery
Cristobal Huet
AF5NER Maxim Afinogenov
Daniel Alfredsson
Darcy Tucker
Glen Murray
Michael Ryder
AF5NWC Joe Sakic
Henrik Sedin
Shawn Horcoff
Pierre-Marc Bouchard
Matthew Lombardi
AF5NWG Jose Theodore
Roberto Luongo
Dwayne Roloson
Miikka Kiprusoff
Peter Budaj
AF5NWL Brian Rolston
Daniel Sedin
Ryan Smyth
Raffi Torres
Alex Tanguay
AF5NWR Markus Naslund
Milan Hejduk
Jarome Iginla
Marian Gaborik
Ales Hemsky
AF5SEC Vincent Lecavalier
Viktor Kozlov
Bobby Holik
Stephen Weiss
Eric Staal
AF5SEG Tomas Vokoun
Olaf Kolzig
Marc Denis
Kari Lehtonen
Cam Ward
AF5SEL Vaclav Prospal
Richard Zednik
Ilya Kovalchuk
Erik Cole
Alexander Ovechkin
AF5ATLC Mike Comrie
Patrik Elias
Chris Drury
Sidney Crosby
Jeff Carter
AF5ATLG Martin Brodeur
Martin Biron
Rick DiPietro
Henrik Lundqvist
Marc-Andre Fleury
AF5ATLL Simon Gagne
Ruslan Fedotenko
Marcel Hossa
Zach Parise
Evgeni Malkin
AF5ATLR Jaromir Jagr
Bill Guerin
Mark Recchi
Brian Gionta
Joffrey Lupul
AF5CENC Doug Weight
Jason Arnott
Robert Lang
Pavel Datsyuk
Sergei Fedorov
AF5CEND Nicklas Lidstrom
Barret Jackman
Rostislav Klesla
Brent Seabrook
Shea Weber
AF5CENG Dominik Hasek
Chris Osgood
Manny Legace
Pascal Leclaire
Nikolai Khabibulin
AF5CENL Paul Kariya
Sergei Samsonov
Martin Erat
Henrik Zetterberg
Rick Nash
AF5CENR David Vyborny
Tomas Holmstrom
Martin Havlat
Lee Stempniak
Alexander Radulov
AF5NHL1 Nicklas Lidstrom
Scott Niedermayer
Dany Heatley
Sidney Crosby
Alexander Ovechkin
AF5NHL2 Vincent Lecavalier
Chris Pronger
Roberto Luongo
Martin St. Louis
Thomas Vanek
AF5PACC Mike Modano
Joe Thornton
Steven Reinprecht
Mike Cammalleri
Ryan Getzlaf
AF5PACD Sergei Zubov
Rob Blake
Scott Niedermayer
Ed Jovanovski
Matt Carle
AF5PACG Curtis Joseph
Dan Cloutier
Jean-Sebastien Giguere
Evgeni Nabokov
Marty Turco
AF5PACR Jere Lehtinen
Todd Bertuzzi
Shane Doan
Jonathan Cheechoo
Dustin Brown

2007-08 SP Game Used Authentic Fabrics Sixes

STATED PRINT RUN 7 #'d SETS
NOT PRICED DUE TO SCARCITY
AF6SC00 Ed Belfour
Mike Modano
Sergei Zubov
Martin Brodeur
Patrik Elias
Scott Stevens
AF6SC01 Patrick Roy
Ed Belfour
Joe Sakic
Mike Modano
Sergei Zubov
Ray Bourque
AF6SC02 Brendan Shanahan
Nicklas Lidstrom
Chris Osgood
Sami Kapanen
Erik Cole
Rod Brind'Amour
AF6SC03 Paul Kariya
Scott Gomez
Martin Brodeur
Petr Sykora
Jean-Sebastien Giguere
Scott Stevens
AF6SC04 Vincent Lecavalier
Jarome Iginla
Martin St. Louis
Jordan Leopold
Miikka Kiprusoff
Nikolai Khabibulin
AF6SC06 Dwayne Roloson
Ales Hemsky
Fernando Pisani
Rod Brind'Amour
Eric Staal
Cam Ward
AF6SC07 Teemu Selanne
Daniel Alfredsson
Scott Niedermayer
Jean-Sebastien Giguere
Dany Heatley
Ray Emery
AF6SC83 Grant Fuhr
Jari Kurri
Mike Bossy
Bryan Trottier
Denis Potvin
Glenn Anderson
AF6SC84 Grant Fuhr
Mike Bossy
Denis Potvin
Billy Smith
Wayne Gretzky
Mark Messier
AF6SC89 Patrick Roy
Chris Chelios
Lanny McDonald
Joe Mullen
Al MacInnis
Larry Robinson
AF6SC92 Ed Belfour
Chris Chelios
Mario Lemieux
Jaromir Jagr
Jeremy Roenick
Joe Mullen
AF6SC93 Patrick Roy
Luc Robitaille
Rob Blake
Denis Savard
Wayne Gretzky
Kirk Muller
AF6SC98 Brendan Shanahan
Olaf Kolzig
Peter Bondra
Nicklas Lidstrom
Sergei Fedorov
Adam Oates
AF6SC99 Ed Belfour
Mike Modano
Jere Lehtinen
Dominik Hasek
Michael Peca
Miroslav Satan

2007-08 SP Game Used Authentic Fabrics Sixes Patches

STATED PRINT RUN 5 #'d SETS
NOT PRICED DUE TO SCARCITY
AF6SC00 Ed Belfour
Mike Modano
Sergei Zubov
Martin Brodeur
Patrik Elias
Scott Stevens
AF6SC01 Patrick Roy
Ed Belfour
Joe Sakic
Mike Modano
Sergei Zubov
Ray Bourque
AF6SC02 Brendan Shanahan
Nicklas Lidstrom
Chris Osgood
Sami Kapanen
Erik Cole
Rod Brind'Amour
AF6SC03 Paul Kariya
Scott Gomez
Martin Brodeur
Petr Sykora
Jean-Sebastien Giguere
Scott Stevens
AF6SC04 Vincent Lecavalier
Jarome Iginla
Martin St. Louis
Jordan Leopold
Miikka Kiprusoff
Nikolai Khabibulin
AF6SC06 Dwayne Roloson
Ales Hemsky
Fernando Pisani
Rod Brind'Amour
Eric Staal
Cam Ward
AF6SC07 Teemu Selanne
Daniel Alfredsson
Scott Niedermayer
Jean-Sebastien Giguere
Dany Heatley
Ray Emery
AF6SC83 Grant Fuhr
Jari Kurri
Mike Bossy
Bryan Trottier
Denis Potvin
Glenn Anderson
AF6SC84 Grant Fuhr
Mike Bossy
Denis Potvin
Billy Smith
Wayne Gretzky
Mark Messier
AF6SC89 Patrick Roy
Chris Chelios
Lanny McDonald
Joe Mullen
Al MacInnis
Larry Robinson
AF6SC92 Ed Belfour
Chris Chelios
Mario Lemieux
Jaromir Jagr
Jeremy Roenick
Joe Mullen
AF6SC93 Patrick Roy
Luc Robitaille
Rob Blake
Denis Savard
Wayne Gretzky
Kirk Muller
AF6SC98 Brendan Shanahan
Olaf Kolzig
Peter Bondra
Nicklas Lidstrom
Sergei Fedorov
Adam Oates
AF6SC99 Ed Belfour
Mike Modano
Jere Lehtinen
Dominik Hasek
Michael Peca
Miroslav Satan

2007-08 SP Game Used Authentic Fabrics Sevens

STATED PRINT RUN 6 #'d SETS
NOT PRICED DUE TO SCARCITY
AF7D Denis Potvin
Larry Murphy
Borje Salming
Ray Bourque
Al MacInnis
Brad Park
Larry Robinson
AF7G Patrick Roy
Grant Fuhr
Gerry Cheevers
Rogie Vachon
Billy Smith
Ron Hextall
Richard Brodeur
AF7CE Mario Lemieux
Stan Mikita
Peter Stastny
Bryan Trottier
Wayne Gretzky
Dale Hawerchuk
Mark Messier
AF7LW Brendan Shanahan
Wendel Clark
Luc Robitaille
Bobby Hull
Glenn Anderson
Frank Mahovlich
Steve Shutt
AF7RW Cam Neely
Lanny McDonald
Mike Bossy
Dino Ciccarelli
Guy Lafleur
Gordie Howe
Joe Mullen
AF7500 Joe Sakic
Teemu Selanne
Mike Modano
Brendan Shanahan
Jaromir Jagr
Mats Sundin
Mark Recchi
AF7ASG Joe Sakic
Teemu Selanne
Bill Guerin
Mark Recchi
Daniel Briere
Dany Heatley
Wayne Gretzky
AF7AST Jaromir Jagr
Scott Gomez
Joe Thornton
Peter Forsberg
Mark Recchi
Martin St. Louis
Adam Oates
AF7MRT Teemu Selanne
Vincent Lecavalier
Milan Hejduk
Jarome Iginla
Ilya Kovalchuk
Jonathan Cheechoo
Rick Nash
AF7NO1 Vincent Lecavalier
Rick DiPietro
Ilya Kovalchuk
Rick Nash
Marc-Andre Fleury
Sidney Crosby
Alexander Ovechkin
AF7PTS Mario Lemieux
Jaromir Jagr
Joe Thornton
Peter Forsberg
Jarome Iginla
Martin St. Louis
Sidney Crosby

2007-08 SP Game Used Authentic Fabrics Sevens Patches

STATED PRINT RUN 3 #'d SETS
NOT PRICED DUE TO SCARCITY
AF7D Denis Potvin
Larry Murphy
Borje Salming
Ray Bourque
Al MacInnis
Brad Park
Larry Robinson
AF7CE Mario Lemieux
Stan Mikita
Peter Stastny
Bryan Trottier
Wayne Gretzky
Dale Hawerchuk
Mark Messier
AF7LW Brendan Shanahan
Wendel Clark
Luc Robitaille
Bobby Hull
Glenn Anderson
Frank Mahovlich
Steve Shutt
AF7RW Cam Neely
Lanny McDonald
Mike Bossy
Dino Ciccarelli
Guy Lafleur
Gordie Howe
Joe Mullen
AF7500 Joe Sakic
Teemu Selanne
Mike Modano
Brendan Shanahan
Jaromir Jagr
Mats Sundin
Mark Recchi
AF7ASG Joe Sakic
Teemu Selanne
Bill Guerin
Mark Recchi
Daniel Briere
Dany Heatley
Wayne Gretzky
AF7AST Jaromir Jagr
Scott Gomez
Joe Thornton
Peter Forsberg
Mark Recchi
Martin St. Louis
Adam Oates
AF7MRT Teemu Selanne
Vincent Lecavalier
Milan Hejduk
Jarome Iginla
Ilya Kovalchuk
Jonathan Cheechoo
Rick Nash
AF7NO1 Vincent Lecavalier
Rick DiPietro
Ilya Kovalchuk
Rick Nash
Marc-Andre Fleury
Sidney Crosby
Alexander Ovechkin
AF7PTS Mario Lemieux
Jaromir Jagr
Joe Thornton
Peter Forsberg
Jarome Iginla
Martin St. Louis
Sidney Crosby

2007-08 SP Game Used Authentic Fabrics Eights

STATED PRINT RUN 5 #'d SETS
NOT PRICED DUE TO SCARCITY
AF8CAN Joe Sakic
Vincent Lecavalier
Martin Brodeur
Joe Thornton
Roberto Luongo
Jarome Iginla
Dany Heatley
Sidney Crosby
AF8CZE Tomas Vokoun
Jaromir Jagr
Martin Straka
Dominik Hasek
Milan Hejduk
Patrik Elias
Petr Sykora
Ales Hemsky
AF8FIN Teemu Selanne
Jere Lehtinen
Saku Koivu
Olli Jokinen
Vesa Toskala
Miikka Kiprusoff
Mikko Koivu
Jussi Jokinen
AF8RUS Evgeni Nabokov
Pavel Datsyuk
Ilya Kovalchuk
Alexander Frolov
Sergei Fedorov
Alexander Ovechkin

Evgeni Malkin
Alexander Radulov
AF8SLO Marian Hossa
Pavol Demitra
Ladislav Nagy
Miroslav Satan
Marian Gaborik
Zdeno Chara
Marek Svatos
Peter Budaj
AF8SWE Mats Sundin
Markus Naslund
Nicklas Lidstrom
Peter Forsberg
Daniel Alfredsson
Daniel Sedin
Tomas Holmstrom
Henrik Lundqvist
AF8USA Chris Chelios
Mike Modano
Doug Weight
Keith Tkachuk
Bill Guerin
Chris Drury
Ryan Miller
Zach Parise

2007-08 SP Game Used Authentic Fabrics Eights Patches

STATED PRINT RUN 1 SER.#'d SET
NOT PRICED DUE TO SCARCITY
AF8CAN Joe Sakic
Vincent Lecavalier
Martin Brodeur
Joe Thornton
Roberto Luongo
Jarome Iginla
Dany Heatley
Sidney Crosby
AF8CZE Tomas Vokoun
Jaromir Jagr
Martin Straka
Dominik Hasek
Milan Hejduk
Patrik Elias
Petr Sykora
Ales Hemsky
AF8FIN Teemu Selanne
Jere Lehtinen
Saku Koivu
Olli Jokinen
Vesa Toskala
Miikka Kiprusoff
Mikko Koivu
Jussi Jokinen
AF8RUS Evgeni Nabokov
Pavel Datsyuk
Ilya Kovalchuk
Alexander Frolov
Sergei Fedorov
Alexander Ovechkin
Evgeni Malkin
Alexander Radulov
AF8SLO Marian Hossa
Pavol Demitra
Ladislav Nagy
Miroslav Satan
Marian Gaborik
Zdeno Chara
Marek Svatos
Peter Budaj
AF8SWE Mats Sundin
Markus Naslund
Nicklas Lidstrom
Peter Forsberg
Daniel Alfredsson
Daniel Sedin
Tomas Holmstrom
Henrik Lundqvist
AF8USA Chris Chelios
Mike Modano
Doug Weight
Keith Tkachuk
Bill Guerin
Chris Drury
Ryan Miller
Zach Parise

2007-08 SP Game Used Autographs

STATED PRINT RUN 10 SER.#'d SETS
NOT PRICED DUE TO SCARCITY
1 Alexander Ovechkin
5 Markus Naslund
10 Darcy Tucker
12 Martin St. Louis
13 Vincent Lecavalier
18 Joe Thornton
19 Jonathan Cheechoo
20 Evgeni Nabokov
21 Patrick Marleau
22 Jordan Staal
23 Sidney Crosby
24 Marc-Andre Fleury
25 Evgeni Malkin
26 Shane Doan
28 Simon Gagne
29 Daniel Briere
30 Jeff Carter
34 Dany Heatley
36 Henrik Lundqvist
40 Miroslav Satan
41 Martin Brodeur
42 Patrik Elias
43 Zach Parise
45 Alexander Radulov
47 Saku Koivu
48 Cristobal Huet
49 Michael Ryder
50 Guillaume Latendresse
51 Marian Gaborik
52 Pierre-Marc Bouchard
54 Anze Kopitar
56 Alexander Frolov
57 Tomas Vokoun
58 Nathan Horton
60 Dwayne Roloson
61 Ales Hemsky
62 Jarret Stoll
64 Henrik Zetterberg
65 Nicklas Lidstrom
66 Dominik Hasek
67 Mike Modano
68 Marty Turco
69 Mike Ribeiro
70 Rick Nash
75 Milan Hejduk
76 Paul Stastny
77 Nikolai Khabibulin
78 Martin Havlat
80 Eric Staal
81 Cam Ward
82 Justin Williams
83 Jarome Iginla
84 Alex Tanguay
86 Dion Phaneuf
87 Thomas Vanek
88 Ryan Miller
90 Drew Stafford
91 Patrice Bergeron
93 Phil Kessel
94 Ilya Kovalchuk
96 Kari Lehtonen
98 Ryan Getzlaf
99 Jean-Sebastien Giguere

2007-08 SP Game Used By The Letter

PRINT RUNS VARY
NOT PRICED DUE TO SCARCITY
BLAH Ales Hemsky/6
BLAK Anze Kopitar/7
BLAM Al MacInnis/8
BLAO Alexander Ovechkin/8
BLAT Alex Tanguay/7
BLBC Bobby Clarke/6
BLBO Mike Bossy/5
BLBS Billy Smith/5
BLCD Chris Drury/5
BLCN Cam Neely/5
BLCW Cam Ward/4
BLDA Daniel Alfredsson/10
BLDB Daniel Briere/5
BLDH Dale Hawerchuk/9
BLDR Dwayne Roloson/7
BLEM Evgeni Malkin/6
BLES Eric Staal/5
BLGF Grant Fuhr/4
BLGP Gilbert Perreault/9
BLHA Dominik Hasek/5
BLHE Dany Heatley/7
BLHL Henrik Lundqvist/9
BLHZ Henrik Zetterberg/10
BLIK Ilya Kovalchuk/9
BLJC Jonathan Cheechoo/8
BLJG Jean-Sebastien Giguere/7
BLJI Jarome Iginla/6
BLJJ Jaromir Jagr/4
BLJO Joe Sakic/5
BLJS Jason Spezza/6
BLJT Joe Thornton/8
BLKL Kari Lehtonen/8
BLLR Larry Robinson/8
BLMB Martin Brodeur/7
BLMG Marian Gaborik/7
BLMH Marian Hossa/5
BLMK Miikka Kiprusoff/9
BLML Mario Lemieux/7
BLMM Mark Messier/7
BLMN Markus Naslund/7
BLMO Mike Modano/6
BLMR Mark Recchi/6
BLMS Martin St. Louis/8
BLMT Marty Turco/5
BLNL Nicklas Lidstrom/8
BLPB Patrice Bergeron/8
BLPF Peter Forsberg/8
BLPK Paul Kariya/6
BLPR Patrick Roy/3
BLRB Ray Bourque/7
BLRL Roberto Luongo/6
BLRN Rick Nash/4
BLRY Michael Ryder/5
BLSA Borje Salming/7
BLSC Sidney Crosby/6
BLSH Brendan Shanahan/8
BLSK Saku Koivu/5
BLSU Mats Sundin/6
BLVL Vincent Lecavalier/10

2007-08 SP Game Used Extra SIGnificance

PRINT RUN EITHER 25 or 10
MOST NOT PRICED DUE TO LACK OF MARKET INFORMATION
XSAM Anton Stastny 25.00 50.00
Marian Stastny
XSBB Kevin Bieksa 25.00 50.00
Luc Bourdon
XSBO Sergei Samsonov 10.00 25.00
Rene Bourque
XSDB Brent Sutter 12.00 30.00
Darryl Sutter
XSGD Scott Gomez 12.00 30.00
Nigel Dawes
XSGH Wayne Gretzky 250.00 350.00
Gordie Howe
XSJP Jack Johnson 12.00 30.00
Ryan Parent
XSMA Ryan Malone 20.00 40.00
Colby Armstrong
XSMT Mike Modano 12.00 30.00
Marty Turco
XSMW Marek Svatos 12.00 30.00
Wojtek Wolski
XSPD Petr Prucha 12.00 30.00
Nigel Dawes
XSRH Michael Ryder 12.00 30.00
Cristobal Huet
XSSR Steve Bernier 12.00 30.00
Ryane Clowe
XSWL Ryan Whitney 12.00 30.00
Kristopher Letang

2007-08 SP Game Used Inked Sweaters

STATED PRINT RUN 50#'d SETS
ISAF Alexander Frolov 12.00 30.00
ISAH Ales Hemsky 6.00 15.00
ISAK Andrei Kostitsyn 12.00 30.00
ISAR Alexander Radulov 20.00 50.00
ISAT Alex Tanguay 15.00 40.00
ISBB Brad Boyes 15.00 40.00
ISBF Bernie Federko 12.00 30.00
ISBG Brian Gionta 12.00 30.00
ISBM Brendan Morrison 12.00 30.00
ISBO Pierre-Marc Bouchard 12.00 30.00
ISBR Daniel Briere 20.00 50.00
ISCH Cristobal Huet 15.00 40.00
ISCK Chuck Kobasew 12.00 30.00
ISCP Corey Perry 10.00 25.00
ISCW Cam Ward 20.00 50.00
ISDB Dustin Brown 12.00 30.00
ISDH Dany Heatley 25.00 60.00
ISDP Dion Phaneuf 20.00 50.00
ISDR Dwayne Roloson 15.00 40.00
ISDW Doug Wilson 25.00 60.00
ISEM Evgeni Malkin 50.00 100.00
ISES Eric Staal 20.00 50.00
ISFP Fernando Pisani 12.00 30.00
ISGA Simon Gagne 12.00 30.00
ISGB Gilbert Brule 12.00 30.00
ISGE Martin Gerber 15.00 40.00
ISGL Guy Lafleur 30.00 80.00
ISGM Glen Murray 12.00 30.00
ISHE Milan Hejduk 15.00 40.00
ISHL Henrik Lundqvist 25.00 60.00
ISHT Hannu Toivonen 15.00 40.00
ISHU Trent Hunter 12.00 30.00
ISIW Ian White 12.00 30.00
ISJA Jason Arnott 12.00 30.00
ISJB Jay Bouwmeester 12.00 30.00
ISJC Jeff Carter 12.00 30.00
ISJG Jean-Sebastien Giguere 20.00 50.00
ISJI Jarome Iginla 30.00 80.00
ISJO Jonathan Cheechoo 15.00 40.00
ISJS Jarret Stoll 12.00 30.00
ISJT Jose Theodore 20.00 50.00
ISJW Justin Williams 12.00 30.00
ISKB Kevin Bieksa 12.00 30.00
ISKC Kyle Calder 12.00 30.00
ISKD Kris Draper 15.00 40.00
ISKL Kari Lehtonen 20.00 50.00
ISKO Anze Kopitar 20.00 50.00
ISLI John-Michael Liles 12.00 30.00
ISLN Ladislav Nagy 12.00 30.00
ISLS Ladislav Smid 12.00 30.00
ISMA Martin St. Louis 15.00 40.00
ISMB Martin Biron 15.00 40.00
ISMC Matt Carle 12.00 30.00
ISMF Marc-Andre Fleury 20.00 50.00
ISMG Marian Gaborik 25.00 60.00
ISMH Martin Havlat 15.00 40.00
ISMI Mike Richards 25.00 60.00
ISMJ Milan Jurcina 12.00 30.00
ISMM Mike Modano 20.00 50.00
ISMN Markus Naslund 20.00 50.00
ISMO Brenden Morrow 15.00 40.00
ISMP Marc-Antoine Pouliot 12.00 30.00
ISMR Michael Ryder 12.00 30.00
ISMS Marc Savard 12.00 30.00
ISMT Marty Turco 20.00 50.00
ISNH Nathan Horton 12.00 30.00
ISNL Nicklas Lidstrom 20.00 50.00
ISNZ Nikolai Zherdev 12.00 30.00
ISPB Patrice Bergeron 20.00 50.00
ISPE Patrik Elias 12.00 30.00
ISPK Phil Kessel 20.00 50.00
ISPL Pascal Leclaire 15.00 40.00
ISPP Petr Prucha 12.00 30.00
ISRA Andrew Raycroft 15.00 40.00
ISRE Robert Esche 15.00 40.00
ISRG Ryan Getzlaf 15.00 40.00
ISRI Mike Ribeiro 15.00 40.00
ISRK Ryan Kesler 12.00 30.00
ISRM Ryan Malone 12.00 30.00
ISRN Rick Nash 20.00 50.00
ISRY Ryan Miller 20.00 50.00
ISSA Miroslav Satan 12.00 30.00
ISSB Steve Bernier 12.00 30.00
ISSC Sidney Crosby 100.00 200.00
ISSD Shane Doan 12.00 30.00
ISSG Scott Gomez 12.00 30.00
ISSV Marek Svatos 12.00 30.00
ISSW Shea Weber 12.00 30.00
ISTF Tomas Fleischmann 6.00 15.00
ISTH Tomas Holmstrom 15.00 40.00
ISTV Tomas Vokoun 20.00 50.00
ISVL Vincent Lecavalier 20.00 50.00
ISWE Stephen Weiss 12.00 30.00
ISWW Wojtek Wolski 12.00 30.00
ISZP Zach Parise 15.00 40.00

2007-08 SP Game Used Inked Sweaters Patches

*PATCHES: 1.25X TO 2X JSY HI
STATED PRINT RUN 25 #'d SETS
ISAF Alexander Frolov 20.00 50.00
ISAH Ales Hemsky 20.00 50.00
ISAK Andrei Kostitsyn 25.00 60.00
ISAR Alexander Radulov 30.00 80.00
ISAT Alex Tanguay 25.00 60.00
ISBB Brad Boyes 25.00 60.00
ISBF Bernie Federko 20.00 50.00
ISBG Brian Gionta 20.00 50.00
ISBM Brendan Morrison 20.00 50.00
ISBO Pierre-Marc Bouchard 20.00 50.00
ISBR Daniel Briere 30.00 80.00
ISCH Cristobal Huet 25.00 60.00
ISCK Chuck Kobasew 20.00 50.00
ISCP Corey Perry 25.00 60.00
ISCW Cam Ward 30.00 80.00
ISDB Dustin Brown 20.00 50.00
ISDH Dany Heatley 40.00 100.00
ISDP Dion Phaneuf 30.00 80.00
ISDR Dwayne Roloson 25.00 60.00
ISDW Doug Wilson 40.00 100.00
ISEM Evgeni Malkin 60.00 120.00
ISES Eric Staal 30.00 80.00
ISFP Fernando Pisani 20.00 50.00
ISGA Simon Gagne 30.00 80.00
ISGB Gilbert Brule 20.00 50.00
ISGE Martin Gerber 25.00 60.00
ISGL Guy Lafleur 50.00 120.00
ISGM Glen Murray 20.00 50.00
ISHE Milan Hejduk 25.00 60.00
ISHL Henrik Lundqvist 40.00 100.00
ISHT Hannu Toivonen 25.00 60.00
ISHU Trent Hunter 20.00 50.00
ISIW Ian White 20.00 50.00
ISJA Jason Arnott 20.00 50.00
ISJB Jay Bouwmeester 20.00 50.00
ISJC Jeff Carter 20.00 50.00
ISJG Jean-Sebastien Giguere 30.00 80.00
ISJI Jarome Iginla 50.00 120.00
ISJO Jonathan Cheechoo 25.00 60.00
ISJS Jarret Stoll 20.00 50.00
ISJT Jose Theodore 30.00 80.00
ISJW Justin Williams 20.00 50.00
ISKB Kevin Bieksa 20.00 50.00
ISKC Kyle Calder 20.00 50.00
ISKD Kris Draper 25.00 60.00
ISKL Kari Lehtonen 30.00 80.00
ISKO Anze Kopitar 30.00 80.00
ISLI John-Michael Liles 20.00 50.00
ISLN Ladislav Nagy 20.00 50.00
ISLS Ladislav Smid 20.00 50.00
ISMA Martin St. Louis 25.00 60.00
ISMB Martin Biron 25.00 60.00
ISMC Matt Carle 20.00 50.00
ISMF Marc-Andre Fleury 30.00 80.00
ISMG Marian Gaborik 50.00 120.00
ISMH Martin Havlat 25.00 60.00
ISMI Mike Richards 60.00 150.00
ISMJ Milan Jurcina 20.00 50.00
ISMM Mike Modano 30.00 80.00
ISMN Markus Naslund 30.00 80.00
ISMO Brenden Morrow 25.00 60.00
ISMP Marc-Antoine Pouliot 20.00 50.00
ISMR Michael Ryder 20.00 50.00
ISMS Marc Savard 20.00 50.00
ISMT Marty Turco 30.00 80.00
ISNH Nathan Horton 20.00 50.00
ISNL Nicklas Lidstrom 30.00 80.00
ISNZ Nikolai Zherdev 20.00 50.00
ISPB Patrice Bergeron 30.00 80.00
ISPE Patrik Elias 20.00 50.00
ISPK Phil Kessel 30.00 80.00
ISPL Pascal Leclaire 25.00 60.00
ISPP Petr Prucha 20.00 50.00
ISRA Andrew Raycroft 25.00 60.00
ISRE Robert Esche 25.00 60.00
ISRG Ryan Getzlaf 25.00 60.00
ISRI Mike Ribeiro 20.00 50.00
ISRK Ryan Kesler 20.00 50.00
ISRM Ryan Malone 20.00 50.00
ISRN Rick Nash 30.00 80.00
ISRY Ryan Miller 30.00 80.00
ISSA Miroslav Satan 20.00 50.00
ISSB Steve Bernier 20.00 50.00
ISSC Sidney Crosby 200.00 350.00
ISSD Shane Doan 20.00 50.00
ISSG Scott Gomez 20.00 50.00
ISSV Marek Svatos 20.00 50.00
ISSW Shea Weber 20.00 50.00
ISTF Tomas Fleischmann 10.00 25.00
ISTH Tomas Holmstrom 26.00 60.00
ISTV Tomas Vokoun 30.00 80.00
ISVL Vincent Lecavalier 30.00 80.00
ISWE Stephen Weiss 20.00 50.00
ISWW Wojtek Wolski 20.00 50.00
ISZP Zach Parise 25.00 60.00

2007-08 SP Game Used Inked Sweaters Dual

STATED PRINT RUN 25 #'d SETS
IS2CB Jonathan Cheechoo 15.00 30.00
Steve Bernier
IS2DA Dwayne Roloson 10.00 25.00
Ales Hemsky
IS2EG Patrik Elias 10.00 25.00
Brian Gionta
IS2FK Alexander Frolov 20.00 40.00
Anze Kopitar
IS2FM Marc-Andre Fleury 40.00 80.00
Evgeni Malkin
IS2GB Marian Gaborik 15.00 40.00
Pierre-Marc Bouchard
IS2GC Simon Gagne 20.00 40.00
Jeff Carter
IS2GH Jean-Sebastien Giguere 15.00 30.00
Dan Cloutier
IS2GP Scott Gomez 20.00 50.00
Petr Prucha
IS2HL Dominik Hasek 30.00 60.00
Nicklas Lidstrom
IS2HS Milan Hejduk
Marek Svatos
IS2IP Jarome Iginla 40.00 80.00
Dion Phaneuf
IS2LT Vincent Lecavalier 20.00 50.00
Joe Thornton
IS2MR Mike Modano 20.00 40.00
Mike Ribeiro
IS2MW Ryan Miller 20.00 40.00
Cam Ward
IS2NM Markus Naslund 15.00 30.00
Brendan Morrison
IS2OR Alexander Ovechkin
Alexander Radulov
IS2PG Corey Perry 20.00 50.00
Ryan Getzlaf
IS2RB Patrick Roy 75.00 150.00
Ray Bourque
IS2RH Michael Ryder 20.00 40.00
Cristobal Huet
IS2SB Marc Savard 12.00 30.00
Patrice Bergeron
IS2SN Martin St. Louis 15.00 40.00
Rick Nash
IS2VH Tomas Vokoun 15.00 30.00
Nathan Horton
IS2WS Justin Williams 12.00 30.00
Eric Staal

2007-08 SP Game Used Legendary Fabrics

STATED PRINT RUN 100 SER.#'d SETS
LFAM Al MacInnis 8.00 20.00
LFAO Adam Oates 6.00 15.00
LFBB Bob Bourne 6.00 15.00
LFBC Bobby Clarke 10.00 25.00
LFBN Bernie Nicholls 6.00 15.00
LFBP Bob Probert 8.00 20.00
LFBR Bill Ranford 8.00 20.00
LFBS Billy Smith 10.00 25.00
LFBU Johnny Bucyk 6.00 15.00
LFCN Cam Neely 10.00 25.00
LFDC Dino Ciccarelli 8.00 20.00
LFDE Denis Savard 8.00 20.00
LFDG Doug Gilmour 8.00 20.00
LFDH Dale Hawerchuk 8.00 20.00
LFDW Doug Wilson 12.00 30.00
LFFM Frank Mahovlich 15.00 40.00
LFGA Glenn Anderson 8.00 20.00
LFGF Grant Fuhr 15.00 40.00
LFGL Guy Lafleur 10.00 25.00
LFGP Gilbert Perreault 8.00 20.00
LFJM Joe Mullen 6.00 15.00
LFLM Lanny McDonald 8.00 20.00
LFLR Larry Robinson 12.00 30.00
LFML Mario Lemieux 20.00 40.00
LFMM Mark Messier 12.00 30.00
LFMU Larry Murphy 3.00 8.00
LFNY Bob Nystrom 6.00 15.00
LFPR Patrick Roy 20.00 40.00
LFPS Peter Stastny 8.00 20.00
LFRB Ray Bourque 12.00 30.00
LFRH Ron Hextall 8.00 20.00
LFRI Richard Brodeur 8.00 20.00
LFRO Luc Robitaille 8.00 20.00
LFRV Rogie Vachon 10.00 25.00
LFSA Borje Salming 8.00 20.00
LFSH Steve Shutt 8.00 20.00
LFSS Scott Stevens 8.00 20.00
LFTW Tiger Williams 8.00 20.00
LFWG Wayne Gretzky 30.00 60.00
LFZP Zigmund Palffy 5.00 12.00

2007-08 SP Game Used Legendary Fabrics Autographs

STATED PRINT RUN 25 #'d SETS
NOT PRICED DUE TO LACK OF MARKET INFO
LAFAM Al MacInnis
LAFAO Adam Oates
LAFBB Bob Bourne
LAFBC Bobby Clarke
LAFBN Bernie Nicholls
LAFBP Bob Probert
LAFBR Bill Ranford
LAFBS Billy Smith
LAFBU Johnny Bucyk
LAFCN Cam Neely
LAFDC Dino Ciccarelli
LAFDE Denis Savard
LAFDG Doug Gilmour
LAFDH Dale Hawerchuk
LAFDW Doug Wilson
LAFFM Frank Mahovlich
LAFGA Glenn Anderson
LAFGF Grant Fuhr
LAFGL Guy Lafleur
LAFGP Gilbert Perreault
LAFJM Joe Mullen
LAFLM Lanny McDonald
LAFLR Larry Robinson
LAFML Mario Lemieux
LAFMM Mark Messier
LAFMU Larry Murphy
LAFNY Bob Nystrom
LAFPR Patrick Roy
LAFPS Peter Stastny
LAFRB Ray Bourque
LAFRH Ron Hextall
LAFRI Richard Brodeur
LAFRO Luc Robitaille
LAFSA Borje Salming
LAFSH Steve Shutt
LAFSS Scott Stevens
LAFTW Tiger Williams
LAFWG Wayne Gretzky
LAFZP Zigmund Palffy

2007-08 SP Game Used Legends Classic Jerseys

STATED PRINT RUN 100 SER.#'d SETS
HGJAS Anton Stastny 6.00 15.00
HGJBB Bob Bourne 6.00 15.00
HGJBG Butch Goring
HGJBN Bernie Nicholls 6.00 15.00
HGJBR Bill Ranford 8.00 20.00
HGJBS Billy Smith 10.00 25.00
HGJBT Bryan Trottier 5.00 12.00
HGJDG Doug Gilmour 8.00 20.00
HGJDH Dale Hawerchuk 8.00 20.00
HGJDS Darryl Sittler 8.00 20.00
HGJGA Glenn Anderson 8.00 20.00
HGJGF Grant Fuhr 15.00 40.00
HGJHA Dale Hawerchuk 8.00 20.00
HGJJM Joe Mullen 6.00 15.00
HGJLM Lanny McDonald 8.00 20.00
HGJLR Larry Robinson 12.00 30.00
HGJMU Larry Murphy 3.00 8.00
HGJPS Peter Stastny 8.00 20.00
HGJRB Richard Brodeur 8.00 20.00
HGJRE Ron Ellis 6.00 15.00
HGJRV Rick Vaive 8.00 20.00
HGJSA Borje Salming 8.00 20.00
HGJSS Steve Shutt 8.00 20.00
HGJTW Tiger Williams 8.00 20.00
HGJWC Wendel Clark 0.00 20.00

2007-08 SP Game Used Legends Classic Jerseys Patches

*PATCHES: 1X TO 2.5X JSY HI
STATED PRINT RUN 50 #'d SETS
HGJAS Anton Stastny 15.00 40.00
HGJBB Bob Bourne 15.00 40.00
HGJBN Bernie Nicholls 15.00 40.00
HGJBR Bill Ranford 25.00 60.00
HGJBS Billy Smith 25.00 60.00
HGJBT Bryan Trottier 12.00 30.00
HGJDG Doug Gilmour 20.00 50.00
HGJDH Dale Hawerchuk 20.00 50.00
HGJGA Glenn Anderson 20.00 50.00
HGJGF Grant Fuhr 40.00 100.00
HGJHA Dale Hawerchuk 20.00 50.00
HGJJM Joe Mullen 15.00 40.00
HGJLM Lanny McDonald 20.00 50.00
HGJLR Larry Robinson 30.00 80.00
HGJMU Larry Murphy 8.00 20.00
HGJPS Peter Stastny 20.00 50.00
HGJRB Richard Brodeur 20.00 50.00
HGJSA Borje Salming 20.00 50.00
HGJSS Steve Shutt 20.00 50.00
HGJTW Tiger Williams 20.00 50.00
HGJWC Wendel Clark 20.00 50.00

2007-08 SP Game Used Legends Classic Jerseys Autographs

*AUTOs: 1X to 2.5X JSY HI
STATED PRINT RUN 50 #'d SETS
HGJAS Anton Stastny 15.00 40.00
HGJBB Bob Bourne 15.00 40.00
HGJBN Bernie Nicholls 15.00 40.00
HGJBR Bill Ranford 20.00 50.00
HGJBS Billy Smith 25.00 60.00
HGJBT Bryan Trottier 12.00 30.00
HGJDG Doug Gilmour 20.00 50.00
HGJDH Dale Hawerchuk 20.00 50.00
HGJDS Darryl Sittler 20.00 50.00
HGJGA Glenn Anderson 20.00 50.00
HGJGF Grant Fuhr 40.00 100.00
HGJHA Dale Hawerchuk 20.00 50.00
HGJJM Joe Mullen 15.00 40.00
HGJLM Lanny McDonald 20.00 50.00
HGJLR Larry Robinson 30.00 80.00
HGJMU Larry Murphy 8.00 20.00
HGJPS Peter Stastny 20.00 50.00
HGJRB Richard Brodeur 20.00 50.00
HGJRE Ron Ellis 15.00 40.00
HGJRV Rick Vaive 20.00 50.00
HGJSA Borje Salming 15.00 40.00
HGJSS Steve Shutt 20.00 50.00
HGJTW Tiger Williams 20.00 50.00
HGJWC Wendel Clark 20.00 50.00

2007-08 SP Game Used Legends Classic Jerseys Autographs Patches

* PATCH AU: 1.5X TO 4X JSY HI
STATED PRINT RUN 25 #'d SETS
HGJAS Anton Stastny 25.00 60.00
HGJBB Bob Bourne 25.00 60.00
HGJBN Bernie Nicholls 25.00 60.00
HGJBR Bill Ranford 40.00 100.00
HGJBS Billy Smith 40.00 100.00
HGJBT Bryan Trottier 20.00 50.00
HGJDG Doug Gilmour 30.00 80.00
HGJDH Dale Hawerchuk 30.00 80.00
HGJGA Glenn Anderson 30.00 80.00
HGJGF Grant Fuhr 60.00 150.00
HGJHA Dale Hawerchuk 30.00 80.00
HGJJM Joe Mullen 25.00 60.00
HGJLM Lanny McDonald 30.00 80.00
HGJLR Larry Robinson 50.00 120.00
HGJMU Larry Murphy 12.00 30.00
HGJPS Peter Stastny 30.00 80.00
HGJRB Richard Brodeur 30.00 80.00
HGJRV Rick Vaive 30.00 80.00
HGJSA Borje Salming 30.00 80.00
HGJSS Steve Shutt 30.00 80.00
HGJTW Tiger Williams 30.00 80.00
HGJWC Wendel Clark 30.00 80.00

2007-08 SP Game Used Letter Marks

STATED PRINT RUN 50#'d SETS
LMAC Andrew Cogliano 40.00 80.00
LMAF Alexander Frolov 30.00 60.00
LMAH Ales Hemsky 75.00 125.00
LMAK Anze Kopitar 100.00 175.00
LMAM Al MacInnis 30.00 60.00
LMAT Alex Tanguay
LMBC Bobby Clarke 75.00 125.00
LMBF Bernie Federko 30.00 60.00
LMBG Brian Gionta
LMBN Bob Nystrom
LMBP Bernie Parent 50.00 100.00
LMBU Johnny Bucyk 50.00 100.00
LMCA Mike Cammalleri 40.00 80.00
LMCG Clark Gillies 40.00 80.00
LMCN Cam Neely 60.00 100.00
LMCP Corey Perry
LMCW Cam Ward 50.00 100.00
LMDM Dickie Moore
LMDP Denis Potvin 40.00 80.00
LMDT Darcy Tucker
LMDW Doug Wilson 30.00 60.00
LMEM Evgeni Malkin 125.00 225.00
LMES Eric Staal 40.00 80.00
LMGC Gerry Cheevers
LMGH Gordie Howe 75.00 150.00
LMHE Milan Hejduk 40.00 80.00
LMJB Jean Beliveau
LMJG Jean-Sebastien Giguere 75.00 125.00
LMJJ Jack Johnson 40.00 80.00
LMJK Jari Kurri 75.00 150.00
LMJS Jordan Staal 40.00 80.00
LMJT Jonathan Toews 125.00 200.00
LMKD Kris Draper 40.00 80.00
LMKE Phil Kessel 40.00 80.00
LMLA Guy Lafleur 100.00 200.00
LMMB Mike Bossy 60.00 120.00
LMMC Andy McDonald
LMMD Marcel Dionne 30.00 60.00
LMMF Marc-Andre Fleury 50.00 100.00
LMMR Mike Ribeiro
LMMS Milt Schmidt 40.00 80.00
LMMU Peter Mueller 60.00 100.00
LMPA Paul Henderson
LMPE Phil Esposito 40.00 80.00
LMPK Patrick Kane 125.00 250.00
LMPR Carey Price 250.00 400.00
LMPS Paul Stastny
LMRA Andrew Raycroft 30.00 60.00
LMRH Ron Hextall 50.00 100.00
LMRM Ryan Miller 40.00 80.00
LMRS Rob Schremp 40.00 80.00
LMSK Jack Skille
LMSM Stan Mikita 30.00 60.00
LMTE Tony Esposito 100.00 200.00
LMTL Ted Lindsay 50.00 100.00
LMTO Terry O'Reilly 40.00 80.00
LMTV Tomas Vokoun 50.00 100.00
LMVL Vincent Lecavalier/25 75.00 150.00
LMWG Wayne Gretzky 250.00 400.00

2007-08 SP Game Used Number Marks

STATED PRINT RUN 25 #'d SETS
NMAH Ales Hemsky 75.00 150.00
NMAK Anze Kopitar 75.00 150.00
NMAO Alexander Ovechkin 200.00 350.00
NMAR Andrew Raycroft 40.00 80.00
NMBC Bobby Clarke 75.00 150.00
NMBF Bernie Federko
NMBH Bobby Hull
NMBO Bobby Orr 400.00 700.00
NMBR Martin Brodeur 175.00 300.00
NMCA Jeff Carter 60.00 125.00
NMCP Corey Perry
NMCW Cam Ward 50.00 100.00
NMDH Dany Heatley
NMDP Dion Phaneuf
NMDR Dwayne Roloson
NMDT Darcy Tucker
NMEM Evgeni Malkin 100.00 200.00
NMES Eric Staal 40.00 80.00
NMGH Gordie Howe 125.00 250.00
NMGP Gilbert Perreault
NMHA Dominik Hasek 75.00 150.00
NMHL Henrik Lundqvist 75.00 150.00
NMIK Ilya Kovalchuk
NMJC Jonathan Cheechoo 40.00 80.00
NMJI Jarome Iginla 75.00 150.00
NMJJ Jack Johnson 50.00 100.00
NMJK Jari Kurri 100.00 175.00
NMJS Jordan Staal 50.00 100.00
NMJT Jose Theodore 60.00 125.00
NMMB Mike Bossy 75.00 150.00
NMMC Mike Cammalleri 40.00 80.00
NMMG Marian Gaborik
NMMN Markus Naslund
NMMO Mike Modano 75.00 150.00
NMMR Michael Ryder 40.00 80.00
NMMS Martin St. Louis 50.00 100.00
NMMT Marty Turco
NMNL Nicklas Lidstrom 75.00 125.00
NMPE Patrik Elias
NMPK Phil Kessel 40.00 80.00
NMPR Pat LaFontaine
NMPS Paul Stastny 100.00 250.00
NMRA Alexander Radulov 100.00 200.00
NMRB Ray Bourque 75.00 150.00
NMRG Ryan Getzlaf
NMRM Ryan Miller 75.00 150.00
NMRN Rick Nash 75.00 150.00
NMRS Rob Schremp
NMSA Miroslav Satan
NMSC Sidney Crosby 350.00 600.00
NMSD Shane Doan 75.00 150.00
NMSG Simon Gagne
NMSK Saku Koivu
NMSV Marek Svatos 40.00 80.00
NMTE Tony Esposito 100.00 175.00
NMTH Joe Thornton 60.00 120.00
NMTV Tomas Vokoun 40.00 60.00
NMVL Vincent Lecavalier 75.00 150.00
NMWG Wayne Gretzky 400.00 700.00
NMZP Zach Parise

2007-08 SP Game Used Rookie Exclusives Autographs

STATED PRINT RUN 100 SER.#'d SETS
REAC Andrew Cogliano 15.00 40.00
REAG Andy Greene 6.00 15.00
REAS Anton Stralman 8.00 20.00
REBA Nicklas Backstrom 25.00 60.00
REBD Brandon Dubinsky 15.00 40.00
REBE Jonathan Bernier 12.00 30.00
REBL Bryan Little 8.00 20.00
REBR Bobby Ryan 25.00 60.00
REBS Brett Sterling 6.00 15.00
RECA Ryan Callahan 10.00 25.00
RECM Curtis McElhinney 8.00 20.00
RECP Carey Price 100.00 200.00
REDC Daniel Carcillo 8.00 20.00
REDG Daniel Girardi 6.00 15.00
REDK David Krejci 12.00 30.00
REDM Drew Miller 6.00 15.00
REDP David Perron 10.00 25.00
REDS Devin Setoguchi 15.00 40.00
REEJ Erik Johnson 25.00 60.00
REEL Brian Elliott 8.00 20.00
REFN Frans Nielsen 6.00 15.00
REHA Jaroslav Halak 12.00 30.00
REHL Jaroslav Hlinka 8.00 20.00
REJA Jannik Hansen 6.00 15.00
REJB Jared Boll 6.00 15.00
REJH Jonas Hiller 15.00 40.00
REJJ Jack Johnson 10.00 25.00
REJS Jonathan Sigalet 6.00 15.00
REJT Jonathan Toews 60.00 120.00
REKR Kris Russell 8.00 20.00
RELT Lauri Tukonen 6.00 15.00
REMA Matt Smaby 6.00 15.00
REME Matt Ellis 6.00 15.00
REMH Martin Hanzal 8.00 20.00
REML Milan Lucic 15.00 40.00
REMM Marc Methot 6.00 15.00
REMN Matt Niskanen 6.00 15.00
REMR Mason Raymond 15.00 40.00
REMS Marc Staal 15.00 40.00
REMU Cory Murphy 6.00 15.00
RENB Nicklas Bergfors 8.00 20.00

RENF Nick Foligno 10.00 25.00
REOP Ondrej Pavelec 10.00 25.00
REPA Ryan Parent 8.00 20.00
REPK Patrick Kane 60.00 120.00
REPM Peter Mueller 15.00 40.00
RERC Ryan Carter 8.00 20.00
RERP Rod Pelley 6.00 15.00
RERS Rob Schremp 8.00 20.00
RESG Sam Gagner 15.00 40.00
RESH James Sheppard 6.00 15.00
RESM Stefan Meyer 6.00 15.00
RETE Tobias Enstrom 10.00 25.00
RETG Tom Gilbert 8.00 20.00
RETL Jiri Tlusty 15.00 40.00
RETM Torrey Mitchell 8.00 20.00
RETP Tomas Plihal 8.00 20.00
RETS Tobias Stephan 8.00 20.00
RETW Tyler Weiman 8.00 20.00

2007-08 SP Game Used SIGnificance

STATED PRINT RUN 50 #'d SETS
SAA Andrew Alberts 12.00 30.00
SAF Alexander Frolov 12.00 30.00
SAK Andrei Kostitsyn 12.00 30.00
SAM Al Montoya 15.00 40.00
SAO Adam Oates 12.00 30.00
SAR Alexander Radulov 15.00 40.00
SBB Brad Boyes 15.00 40.00
SBC Blake Comeau 8.00 20.00
SBG Brian Gionta 12.00 30.00
SBI Kevin Bieksa 8.00 20.00
SBM Barry Melrose 10.00 25.00
SBO David Booth 8.00 20.00
SBP Benoit Pouliot 8.00 20.00
SBW Ben Walter 8.00 20.00
SCA Colby Armstrong 8.00 20.00
SCB Christian Backman 8.00 20.00
SCH Chuck Kobasew 8.00 20.00
SCK Chris Kunitz 8.00 20.00
SCM Matt Carle 8.00 20.00
SCP Chris Phillips 8.00 20.00
SCR Craig MacTavish 4.00 10.00
SDA Daniel Briere 20.00 50.00
SDB Dustin Brown 12.00 30.00
SDK Duncan Keith 12.00 30.00
SDS Drew Stafford 15.00 40.00
SDW Doug Wilson 25.00 60.00
SEC Erik Christensen 12.00 30.00
SEF Eric Fehr 8.00 20.00
SFN Fredrik Norrena 15.00 40.00
SGH Gordie Howe 40.00 100.00
SHA Michal Handzus 8.00 20.00
SHL Hakan Loob 20.00 50.00
SIW Ian White 8.00 20.00
SJA Jason Arnott 12.00 30.00
SJG Josh Gorges 8.00 20.00
SJI Jarkko Immonen
SJM Jay McClement 8.00 20.00
SJP Joe Pavelski 12.00 30.00
SKB Keith Ballard 8.00 20.00
SKC Kyle Calder 8.00 20.00
SKD Kris Draper 15.00 40.00
SKH Kristian Huselius 8.00 20.00
SKL Rostislav Klesla 8.00 20.00
SKO Anze Kopitar 15.00 40.00
SKQ Kyle Quincey 8.00 20.00
SLA Pat LaFontaine 10.00 25.00
SLE Loui Eriksson 8.00 20.00
SLI John-Michael Liles 8.00 20.00
SLN Ladislav Nagy 8.00 20.00
SMA Maxim Afinogenov 12.00 30.00
SMB Martin Biron 15.00 40.00
SMC Andy McDonald 8.00 20.00
SMG Martin Gerber 15.00 40.00
SMH Marcel Hossa 8.00 20.00
SMI Mike Cammalleri 15.00 40.00
SMJ Milan Jurcina 8.00 20.00
SML Maxim Lapierre 8.00 20.00
SMN Markus Naslund 20.00 50.00
SMR Mike Richards 25.00 60.00
SMS Marek Svatos 12.00 30.00
SMT Maxime Talbot 8.00 20.00
SMV Marc-Edouard Vlasic 8.00 20.00
SNZ Nikolai Zherdev 12.00 30.00
SON Ben Ondrus 8.00 20.00
SPB Brandon Prust 8.00 20.00
SPE Corey Perry 15.00 40.00
SPI Pierre-Marc Bouchard 12.00 30.00
SPL Pascal Leclaire 15.00 40.00
SPO Patrick O'Sullivan 15.00 40.00
SPP Petr Prucha 12.00 30.00
SPR Bob Probert 15.00 40.00
SRB Rene Bourque 8.00 20.00
SRC Ryane Clowe 8.00 20.00
SRD Ron Duguay 25.00 60.00
SRG Ryan Getzlaf 15.00 40.00
SRK Red Kelly 10.00 25.00
SRL Rejean Lemelin 10.00 25.00
SRM Ryan Malone 8.00 20.00
SRP Ryan Potulny 8.00 20.00
SRW Ryan Whitney 10.00 25.00
SSB Steve Bernier 12.00 30.00
SSC Milt Schmidt 10.00 25.00
SSD Shane Doan 12.00 30.00
SSG Scott Gomez 12.00 30.00
SSI Sidney Crosby 100.00 200.00
SSS Sergei Samsonov 12.00 30.00
SST Mark Stuart 8.00 20.00
SSW Shea Weber 8.00 20.00
STH Tomas Holmstrom 15.00 40.00
STV Thomas Vanek 15.00 40.00
SVF Valtteri Filppula 12.00 30.00
SVO Tomas Vokoun 20.00 50.00
SWE Stephen Weiss 8.00 20.00
SWG Wayne Gretzky 100.00 200.00
SWW Wojtek Wolski 12.00 30.00
SYS Yan Stastny 8.00 20.00
SZP Zach Parise 15.00 40.00

2007-08 SP Game Used SIGnificant Numbers

PRINT RUNS UNDER 19 NOT PRICED
SNAF Alexander Frolov/24 12.00 30.00
SNAK Anze Kopitar/11
SNAM Al MacInnis/2
SNAO Adam Oates/12
SNAR Alexander Radulov/47 10.00 25.00
SNAT Alex Tanguay/40 8.00 20.00
SNBB Brad Boyes/38 8.00 20.00
SNBC Bobby Clarke/16
SNBG Brian Gionta/14
SNBM Brenden Morrow/10
SNBN Bob Nystrom/23
SNBR Bill Ranford/30 15.00 40.00
SNBS Borje Salming/21
SNCA Colby Armstrong/20
SNCN Cam Neely/8
SNCP Corey Perry/10
SNCW Cam Ward/30 8.00 20.00
SNDC Dino Ciccarelli/22 10.00 25.00
SNDG Doug Gilmour/93 6.00 15.00
SNDH Dany Heatley/15
SNDP Dion Phaneuf/3
SNDS Darryl Sittler/27 10.00 25.00
SNEM Evgeni Malkin/71 15.00 40.00
SNES Eric Staal/12
SNFM Frank Mahovlich/27 15.00 40.00
SNGB Gilbert Brule/17
SNGF Grant Fuhr/31 20.00 40.00
SNGL Guy Lafleur/10
SNGP Gilbert Perreault/11
SNHA Dominik Hasek/39 12.00 30.00
SNHL Henrik Lundqvist/30
SNIK Ilya Kovalchuk/17
SNJA Jason Arnott/19
SNJC Jonathan Cheechoo/14
SNJE Jeff Carter/17
SNJG Jean-Sebastien Giguere/35 15.00 40.00
SNJI Jarome Iginla/12
SNJK Jari Kurri/17
SNJM Joe Mullen/7
SNJO Jordan Staal/11
SNJS Jarret Stoll/16
SNJT Joe Thornton/19 20.00 50.00
SNKD Kris Draper/33
SNKL Kari Lehtonen/32
SNLM Lanny McDonald/9
SNMB Martin Brodeur/30 20.00 50.00
SNMC Mike Cammalleri/13
SNMF Marc-Andre Fleury/29
SNMG Marian Gaborik/10
SNMH Milan Hejduk/23 10.00 25.00
SNMM Mark Messier/11
SNMN Markus Naslund/19 15.00 40.00
SNMO Mike Modano/9
SNMR Michael Ryder/73 4.00 10.00
SNMS Marc Savard/71 8.00 20.00
SNMT Marty Turco/35
SNNL Nicklas Lidstrom/5
SNOV Alexander Ovechkin/8
SNPB Patrice Bergeron/37 12.00 30.00
SNRA Andrew Raycroft/1
SNRG Ryan Getzlaf/15
SNRH Ron Hextall/27 15.00 40.00
SNRI Mike Ribeiro/71 4.00 10.00
SNRM Ryan Miller/30 15.00 40.00
SNRN Rick Nash/61 8.00 20.00
SNSC Sidney Crosby/87 30.00 80.00
SNSD Shane Doan/19 12.00 30.00
SNSG Simon Gagne/12
SNSS Steve Shutt/22
SNST Martin St. Louis/26 6.00 15.00
SNTH Tomas Holmstrom/96 10.00 25.00
SNTJ Jose Theodore/60 5.00 12.00
SNTV Tomas Vokoun/29 15.00 40.00
SNVL Vincent Lecavalier/4

2007-08 SP Game Used Triple SIGnificance

STATED PRINT RUN 10 SER.#'d SETS
NOT PRICED DUE TO SCARCITY
TSBCO Johnny Bucyk
Gerry Cheevers
Terry O'Reilly
TSCBP Jonathan Cheechoo
Steve Bernier
Joe Pavelski
TSEGZ Patrik Elias
Brian Gionta
Travis Zajac
TSEHM Tony Esposito
Bobby Hull
Stan Mikita/5
TSFKT Alexander Frolov
Anze Kopitar
Lauri Tukonen
TSFMS Marc-Andre Fleury
Evgeni Malkin
Jordan Staal
TSGLP Scott Gomez
Henrik Lundqvist
Petr Prucha
TSHDF Tomas Holmstrom
Kris Draper
Valtteri Filppula
TSHLH Dominik Hasek
Nicklas Lidstrom
Tomas Holmstrom
TSIHN Jarome Iginla
Dany Heatley
Rick Nash
TSITP Jarome Iginla
Alex Tanguay
Dion Phaneuf
TSKGM Jari Kurri
Wayne Gretzky
Mark Messier/5
TSLGH Mario Lemieux
Wayne Gretzky
Gordie Howe/5
TSLMM Hakan Loob
Joe Mullen
Al MacInnis
TSLSR Guy Lafleur
Steve Shutt
Larry Robinson
TSMPG Andy McDonald
Corey Perry
Ryan Getzlaf
TSNOB Cam Neely
Bobby Orr
Ray Bourque/5
TSNZB Rick Nash
Nikolai Zherdev
Gilbert Brule
TSPAM Peter Stastny
Anton Stastny
Marian Stastny
TSRBF Patrick Roy
Martin Brodeur
Grant Fuhr/5
TSSSS Brian Sutter
Brent Sutter
Darryl Sutter
TSSWS Marek Svatos
Wojtek Wolski
Paul Stastny
TSWSW Justin Williams
Eric Staal
Cam Ward

2008-09 SP Game Used

This set was released on January 28, 2009. The base set consists of 200 cards. Cards 1-100 feature veterans, and cards 101-200 are all rookies. Cards 101-190 are serial numbered of 999, and cards 191-200 are serial numbered of 99.

COMP.SET w/o SPs (100) 40.00 80.00
(101-190) STATED PRINT RUN 999 SERIAL #'d SETS
(191-200) STATED PRINT RUN 99 SERIAL #'d SETS
1 Scott Niedermayer .60 1.50
2 Corey Perry 1.00 2.50
3 Chris Pronger .75 2.00
4 Ryan Getzlaf 1.25 3.00
5 Jean-Sebastien Giguere 1.00 2.50
6 Ilya Kovalchuk 1.25 3.00
7 Kari Lehtonen .60 1.50
8 Marc Savard .60 1.50
9 Bobby Orr 3.00 8.00
10 Michael Ryder .75 2.00
11 Phil Kessel 1.00 2.50
12 Thomas Vanek 1.00 2.50
13 Ryan Miller 1.00 2.50
14 Jason Pominville .75 2.00
15 Derek Roy .60 1.50
16 Jarome Iginla 2.00 5.00
17 Miikka Kiprusoff 1.00 2.50
18 Dion Phaneuf 1.00 2.50
19 Eric Staal 1.50 4.00
20 Cam Ward 1.00 2.50
21 Brian Campbell 1.50 4.00
22 Patrick Sharp .60 1.50
23 Jonathan Toews 3.00 8.00
24 Patrick Kane 2.50 6.00
25 Cristobal Huet 1.00 2.50
26 Patrick Roy 3.00 8.00
27 Joe Sakic 1.50 4.00
28 Milan Hejduk .75 2.00
29 Paul Stastny 1.00 2.50
30 Rick Nash 1.00 2.50
31 Pascal Leclaire .75 2.00
32 Brad Richards .75 2.00
33 Mike Modano 1.00 2.50
34 Marty Turco .75 2.00
35 Mike Ribeiro .60 1.50
36 Chris Osgood .60 1.50
37 Johan Franzen .60 1.50
38 Pavel Datsyuk 1.00 2.50
39 Henrik Zetterberg 2.00 5.00
40 Nicklas Lidstrom 1.00 2.50
41 Marian Hossa 1.50 4.00
42 Shawn Horcoff .60 1.50
43 Ales Hemsky .60 1.50
44 Tomas Vokoun 1.00 2.50
45 Nathan Horton .60 1.50
46 Gordie Howe 4.00 10.00
47 Wayne Gretzky 5.00 12.00
48 Anze Kopitar 1.00 2.50
49 Alexander Frolov .60 1.50
50 Brent Burns .60 1.50
51 Marian Gaborik 1.50 4.00
52 Pierre-Marc Bouchard .60 1.50
53 Niklas Backstrom 1.00 2.50
54 Alex Tanguay .75 2.00
55 Carey Price 3.00 8.00
56 Saku Koivu 1.00 2.50
57 Alex Kovalev 1.00 2.50
58 J.P. Dumont .60 1.50
59 Dan Ellis .60 1.50
60 Jason Arnott .60 1.50
61 Martin Brodeur 2.00 5.00
62 Patrik Elias .60 1.50
63 Zach Parise 1.00 2.50
64 Rick DiPietro 1.00 2.50
65 Nikolai Zherdev .60 1.50
66 Mark Messier 2.00 5.00
67 Brian Leetch 1.25 3.00
68 Henrik Lundqvist 2.00 5.00
69 Chris Drury 1.00 2.50
70 Jason Spezza 1.25 3.00
71 Daniel Alfredsson .75 2.00
72 Dany Heatley 1.25 3.00
73 Mike Richards 1.50 4.00
74 Martin Biron .75 2.00
75 Simon Gagne .75 2.00
76 Daniel Briere 1.00 2.50
77 Olli Jokinen .60 1.50
78 Shane Doan .60 1.50
79 Peter Mueller 1.25 3.00
80 Miroslav Satan .60 1.50
81 Mario Lemieux 2.50 6.00
82 Jordan Staal 1.50 4.00
83 Sidney Crosby 5.00 12.00
84 Marc-Andre Fleury 1.00 2.50
85 Evgeni Malkin 2.50 6.00
86 Rob Blake 1.00 2.50
87 Joe Thornton 1.50 4.00
88 Jonathan Cheechoo 1.00 2.50
89 Evgeni Nabokov 1.00 2.50
90 Brad Boyes .75 2.00
91 Paul Kariya 1.00 2.50
92 Martin St. Louis 1.00 2.50
93 Vincent Lecavalier 1.00 2.50
94 Mats Sundin 1.00 2.50
95 Vesa Toskala 1.00 2.50
96 Roberto Luongo 1.50 4.00
97 Henrik Sedin 1.00 2.50
98 Daniel Sedin 1.00 2.50
99 Nicklas Backstrom 2.00 5.00
100 Alexander Ovechkin 4.00 10.00
101 Adam Pineault RC 4.00 10.00
102 Alex Foster RC 3.00 8.00
103 Alex Goligoski RC 8.00 20.00
104 Andrew Ebbett RC 4.00 10.00
105 Andrew Murray RC 3.00 8.00
106 B.J. Crombeen RC 3.00 8.00
107 Boris Valabik RC 5.00 12.00
108 Brandon Nolan RC 5.00 12.00
109 Brian Boyle RC 4.00 10.00
110 Brian Lee RC 4.00 10.00
111 Chris Minard RC 4.00 10.00
112 Claude Giroux RC 8.00 20.00
113 Nikita Filatov RC 15.00 40.00
114 Cody McLeod RC 3.00 8.00
115 Colin Stuart RC 3.00 8.00
116 Corey Locke RC 4.00 10.00
117 Dan LaCosta RC 5.00 12.00
118 Danny Taylor RC 4.00 10.00
119 Darren Helm RC 6.00 15.00
120 Darryl Boyce RC 3.00 8.00
121 David Brine RC 3.00 8.00
122 Derick Brassard RC 8.00 20.00
123 Erik Ersberg RC 4.00 10.00
124 Garrett Stafford RC 5.00 12.00
125 Ilya Zubov RC 4.00 10.00
126 Jack Hillen RC 3.00 8.00
127 Jesse Winchester RC 4.00 10.00
128 Joe Jensen RC 4.00 10.00
129 Joey Mormina RC 3.00 8.00
130 Jon Filewich RC 3.00 8.00
131 Jonathan Ericsson RC 6.00 15.00
132 Jordan Hendry RC 3.00 8.00
133 Jordan LaVallee RC 4.00 10.00
134 Justin Abdelkader RC 8.00 20.00
135 Brandon Sutter RC 5.00 12.00
136 Kyle Greentree RC 5.00 12.00
137 Kyle Okposo RC 8.00 20.00
138 James Neal RC 6.00 15.00
139 Lauri Korpikoski RC 4.00 10.00
140 Marc-Andre Gragnani RC 3.00 8.00
141 Mark Fistric RC 3.00 8.00
142 Matt D'Agostini RC 6.00 15.00
143 Mattias Ritola RC 5.00 12.00
144 Mike Brown RC 5.00 12.00
145 Mike Iggulden RC 3.00 8.00
146 Mike Mole RC 3.00 8.00
147 Niklas Hjalmarsson RC 6.00 15.00
148 Pascal Pelletier RC 3.00 8.00
149 Luca Sbisa RC 6.00 15.00
150 Robbie Earl RC 3.00 8.00
151 Ryan Stone RC 4.00 10.00
152 Sami Lepisto RC 4.00 10.00
153 Shawn Matthias RC 4.00 10.00
154 Steve Mason RC 10.00 25.00
155 Colton Gillies RC 4.00 10.00
156 Michael Frolik RC 8.00 20.00
157 Nikolai Kulemin RC 6.00 15.00
158 T.J. Oshie RC 10.00 25.00
159 Patrik Berglund RC 10.00 25.00
160 Patric Hornqvist RC 4.00 10.00
161 Ryan Jones RC 5.00 12.00
162 Chris Porter RC 4.00 10.00
163 Viktor Tikhonov RC 4.00 10.00
164 Kevin Porter RC 3.00 8.00
165 Jonas Frogren RC 5.00 12.00
166 John Mitchell RC 4.00 10.00
167 Paul Bissonnette RC 5.00 12.00
168 Derek Dorsett RC 5.00 12.00
169 Janne Niskala RC 4.00 10.00
170 Vladimir Mihalik RC 4.00 10.00
171 Jared Ross RC 5.00 12.00
172 Wayne Simmonds RC 4.00 10.00
173 Andrew Pardy RC 4.00 10.00
174 Dane Byers RC 3.00 8.00
175 Mitch Fritz RC 3.00 8.00
176 Zach Fitzgerald RC 4.00 10.00
177 Ben Bishop RC 6.00 15.00
178 Anssi Salmela RC 5.00 12.00
179 Andreas Nodl RC 4.00 10.00
180 Petr Vrana RC 4.00 10.00
181 Zach Boychuk RC 6.00 15.00
182 Nathan Oystrick RC 4.00 10.00
183 Oscar Moller RC 4.00 10.00
184 Teddy Purcell RC 4.00 10.00
185 Theo Peckham RC 4.00 10.00
186 Tim Conboy RC 3.00 8.00
187 Tim Ramholt RC 3.00 8.00
188 Tom Cavanagh RC 3.00 8.00
189 Tom Sestito RC 3.00 8.00
190 Tyler Plante RC 4.00 10.00
191 Mikkel Boedker RC 15.00 40.00
192 Kyle Turris RC 30.00 60.00
193 Fabian Brunnstrom RC 50.00 100.00
194 Jakub Voracek RC 25.00 60.00
195 Blake Wheeler RC 75.00 150.00
196 Luke Schenn RC 60.00 120.00
197 Zach Bogosian RC 25.00 60.00
198 Alex Pietrangelo RC 25.00 60.00
199 Drew Doughty RC 40.00 80.00
200 Steven Stamkos RC 75.00 150.00

2008-09 SP Game Used Gold

*GOLD (1-100): .6X TO 1.5X BASE
STATED PRINT RUN 100 SERIAL #'d SETS
*GOLD (101-190): .5X TO 1.2X BASE
STATED PRINT RUN 100 SERIAL #'d SETS
*GOLD (191-200): .2X TO .5X BASE
STATED PRINT RUN 50 SERIAL #'d SETS
192 Kyle Turris 15.00 40.00
195 Blake Wheeler 40.00 100.00
196 Luke Schenn 40.00 80.00
200 Steven Stamkos 40.00 100.00

2008-09 SP Game Used Gold Spectrum

STATED PRINT RUN 10 SERIAL #'d SETS
NOT PRICED DUE TO SCARCITY

2008-09 SP Game Used Platinum

Although this set is called SP Game Used Platinum, it is highlighted with red foil markings and it is serial numbered to 25.

192 Kyle Turris 30.00 60.00
195 Blake Wheeler 60.00 120.00
196 Luke Schenn 40.00 100.00
200 Steven Stamkos 60.00 120.00

2008-09 SP Game Used Platinum Spectrum

STATED PRINT RUN 1 SERIAL #'d SET
NOT PRICED DUE TO SCARCITY

2008-09 SP Game Used Authentic Fabrics Duos

STATED PRINT RUN 100 SERIAL #'d SETS
AF2AN Vesa Toskala 5.00 12.00
Nik Antropov
AF2BG Martin Brodeur 10.00 25.00
Doug Gilmour
AF2BJ Anze Kopitar 5.00 12.00
Jack Johnson
AF2BL Martin Brodeur 10.00 25.00
Roberto Luongo
AF2BM Martin Brodeur 10.00 25.00
Ryan Miller
AF2BP Martin Brodeur 15.00 40.00
Carey Price
AF2BR Mike Richards 8.00 20.00
Daniel Briere
AF2CM Sidney Crosby 25.00 60.00
Evgeni Malkin
AF2CR Chris Chelios 6.00 15.00
Brian Rafalski
AF2CT Erik Cole 5.00 12.00
Tim Thomas
AF2CW Erik Cole 5.00 12.00
Gilbert Brule
AF2DB Pavol Demitra 3.00 8.00
Steve Bernier
AF2DK Sergei Fedorov 8.00 20.00
Ilya Kovalchuk
AF2DM Evgeni Malkin 12.00 30.00
Ruslan Fedotenko
AF2DW J.P. Dumont 3.00 8.00
Shea Weber
AF2ED J.P. Dumont 4.00 10.00
David Legwand
AF2EE Phil Esposito 8.00 20.00
Tony Esposito
AF2EJ Eric Staal 8.00 20.00
Jordan Staal
AF2EP Zach Parise 5.00 12.00
Patrik Elias
AF2FM Evgeni Malkin 12.00 30.00
Sergei Fedorov
AF2FN Marc-Andre Fleury
Antero Niittymaki
AF2FO Marc-Andre Fleury 5.00 12.00
Chris Osgood
AF2FP Theoren Fleury 6.00 15.00
Dion Phaneuf
AF2GB Marian Gaborik 8.00 20.00
Pierre-Marc Bouchard
AF2GC Simon Gagne 5.00 12.00
Jeff Carter
AF2GD Scott Gomez 5.00 12.00
Chris Drury
AF2GK Marian Gaborik 8.00 20.00
Mikko Koivu
AF2GP Zach Parise 5.00 12.00
Brian Gionta
AF2GW Sergei Gonchar
Ryan Whitney
AF2HF Peter Forsberg 8.00 20.00
Milan Hejduk
AF2HG Shawn Horcoff 8.00 20.00
Sam Gagner
AF2HH Marian Hossa 8.00 20.00
Marcel Hossa
AF2IK Alex Kovalev
Ilya Kovalchuk
AF2JH Shane Doan 3.00 8.00
Olli Jokinen
AF2JJ Jack Johnson 6.00 15.00
Erik Johnson
AF2JM Jordan Staal
Marc-Andre Fleury
AF2JP Joe Sakic 8.00 20.00
Paul Stastny
AF2JR Jason Spezza
Rick Nash
AF2KK Saku Koivu 5.00 12.00
Alex Kovalev
AF2KM Ilya Kovalchuk 12.00 30.00
Evgeni Malkin
AF2KO Alexander Ovechkin 20.00 50.00
Ilya Kovalchuk
AF2KP Paul Kariya 5.00 12.00
David Perron
AF2KV Saku Koivu 5.00 12.00
Mikko Koivu
AF2LA Lanny McDonald
Al MacInnis
AF2LB Roberto Luongo
Steve Bernier
AF2LC Mario Lemieux 25.00 60.00
Sidney Crosby
AF2LH Nicklas Lidstrom 5.00 12.00
Tomas Holmstrom
AF2LI Vincent Lecavalier 5.00 12.00
Mike Lundin
AF2LN Henrik Lundqvist 10.00 25.00
Markus Naslund
AF2LS Vincent Lecavalier 5.00 12.00
Martin St. Louis
AF2LT Roberto Luongo 8.00 20.00
Marty Turco
AF2MG Mike Modano 5.00 12.00
Bill Guerin
AF2MJ Joe Sakic 8.00 20.00
Marek Svatos
AF2MM Marian Gaborik 8.00 20.00
Marian Hossa
AF2MP Al MacInnis
Dion Phaneuf
AF2MS Borje Salming 5.00 12.00
Lanny McDonald
AF2NH Markus Naslund 5.00 12.00
Tomas Holmstrom
AF2NK Evgeni Nabokov 5.00 12.00
Miikka Kiprusoff
AF2NL Vincent Lecavalier 5.00 12.00
Rick Nash
AF2NS Rick Nash
Martin St. Louis
AF2OB Alexander Ovechkin 20.00 50.00
Nicklas Backstrom
AF2OF Alexander Ovechkin 20.00 50.00
Sergei Fedorov
AF2PB Phil Kessel
Patrice Bergeron
AF2PC Dion Phaneuf 5.00 12.00
Zdeno Chara
AF2PG Ryan Getzlaf 6.00 15.00
Corey Perry
AF2PS Patrick Sharp 4.00 10.00
Brent Seabrook
AF2PZ Markus Naslund 5.00 12.00
Nikolai Zherdev
AF2RB Pierre-Marc Bouchard
Mikko Koivu
AF2RD Luc Robitaille 5.00 12.00
Marcel Dionne
AF2RF Patrick Roy 15.00 40.00
Peter Forsberg
AF2RJ Ryan Smyth 6.00 15.00
Jason Spezza
AF2RN Luc Robitaille 4.00 10.00
Bernie Nicholls
AF2SD Marc Staal 5.00 12.00
Chris Drury
AF2SF Mats Sundin 8.00 20.00
Peter Forsberg
AF2SG Teemu Selanne 6.00 15.00
Ryan Getzlaf
AF2SL Marc Savard 10.00 25.00
Milan Lucic
AF2SM Shane Doan
Peter Mueller
AF2SN Mats Sundin 5.00 12.00
Markus Naslund
AF2SS Joe Sakic 8.00 20.00
Ryan Smyth
AF2TB Marty Turco 4.00 10.00
Peter Budaj
AF2TC Joe Thornton 8.00 20.00
Jonathan Cheechoo
AF2TL Kari Lehtonen 5.00 12.00
Vesa Toskala
AF2TM Vincent Lecavalier 5.00 12.00
Ryan Malone
AF2TN Joe Thornton 8.00 20.00
Rick Nash
AF2TP Jonathan Toews 15.00 40.00
Carey Price
AF2TR Tuukka Rask 5.00 12.00
Vesa Toskala
AF2TT Tim Thomas 5.00 12.00
Tuukka Rask
AF2VH Dominik Hasek 8.00 20.00
Tomas Vokoun
AF2WL Wade Redden 10.00 25.00
Henrik Lundqvist
AF2ZC Evgeni Malkin 12.00 30.00
Henrik Zetterberg
AF2ZD Nikolai Zherdev
Chris Drury
AF2ZF Sergei Fedorov 8.00 20.00
Maxim Afinogenov
AF2ZM Zach Parise 5.00 12.00
Mike Modano

2008-09 SP Game Used Authentic Fabrics Duos Patches

STATED PRINT RUN 25 SERIAL #'d SETS
AF2AN Vesa Toskala
Nik Antropov
AF2BB Daniel Briere 10.00 25.00
Patrice Bergeron
AF2BG Martin Brodeur 20.00 50.00
Doug Gilmour
AF2BJ Jack Johnson 10.00 25.00
Anze Kopitar
AF2BK Nicklas Backstrom
Patrick Kane
AF2BL Martin Brodeur
Roberto Luongo
AF2BM Ryan Miller 20.00 50.00
Martin Brodeur
AF2BP Martin Brodeur
Carey Price
AF2BR Daniel Briere
Mike Richards
AF2CM Sidney Crosby 50.00 120.00
Evgeni Malkin
AF2CR Chris Chelios 12.00 30.00
Brian Rafalski
AF2CT Erik Cole 10.00 25.00
Tim Thomas
AF2CW Erik Cole
Gilbert Brule
AF2DB Pavol Demitra
Steve Bernier
AF2DK Ilya Kovalchuk
Sergei Fedorov
AF2DM Evgeni Malkin
Ruslan Fedotenko
AF2DW J.P. Dumont
Shea Weber
AF2ED J.P. Dumont 8.00 20.00
David Legwand
AF2EE Phil Esposito 15.00 40.00
Tony Esposito
AF2EJ Eric Staal
Jordan Staal
AF2EP Patrik Elias 10.00 25.00
Zach Parise
AF2FM Sergei Fedorov 25.00 60.00
Evgeni Malkin
AF2FN Antero Niittymaki 10.00 25.00
Marc-Andre Fleury
AF2FO Chris Osgood 10.00 25.00
Marc-Andre Fleury
AF2FP Dion Phaneuf
Theoren Fleury
AF2GB Marian Gaborik 15.00 40.00
Pierre-Marc Bouchard
AF2GC Simon Gagne
Jeff Carter
AF2GD Scott Gomez 10.00 25.00
Chris Drury
AF2GK Marian Gaborik 10.00 25.00
Mikko Koivu
AF2GP Brian Gionta
Zach Parise
AF2GW Sergei Gonchar
Ryan Whitney
AF2HF Milan Hejduk
Peter Forsberg
AF2HG Shawn Horcoff
Sam Gagner
AF2HH Marcel Hossa
Marian Hossa
AF2IK Alex Kovalev
Ilya Kovalchuk
AF2JH Olli Jokinen
Shane Doan
AF2JJ Jack Johnson 12.00 30.00
Erik Johnson
AF2JM Marc-Andre Fleury
Jordan Staal
AF2JP Joe Sakic
Paul Stastny
AF2JR Jason Spezza
Rick Nash
AF2KK Saku Koivu
Alex Kovalev
AF2KM Ilya Kovalchuk 25.00 60.00
Evgeni Malkin
AF2KO Ilya Kovalchuk
Alexander Ovechkin
AF2KP Paul Kariya 10.00 25.00
David Perron
AF2KV Saku Koivu 10.00 25.00
Mikko Koivu
AF2LA Lanny McDonald 10.00 25.00
Al MacInnis
AF2LB Roberto Luongo 15.00 40.00
Steve Bernier
AF2LC Mario Lemieux 50.00 120.00
Sidney Crosby
AF2LE Kari Lehtonen 10.00 25.00
Tobias Enstrom
AF2LH Nicklas Lidstrom
Tomas Holmstrom
AF2LI Vincent Lecavalier
Mike Lundin
AF2LN Henrik Lundqvist
Markus Naslund
AF2LR Jere Lehtinen 6.00 15.00
Mike Ribeiro
AF2LS Vincent Lecavalier 10.00 25.00
Martin St. Louis
AF2LT Marty Turco
Roberto Luongo
AF2MG Mike Modano
Bill Guerin
AF2MJ Joe Sakic 15.00 40.00
Marek Svatos
AF2MM Marian Hossa
Marian Gaborik
AF2MP Dion Phaneuf 12.00 30.00
Al MacInnis
AF2MS Lanny McDonald 10.00 25.00
Borje Salming
AF2NH Tomas Holmstrom 10.00 25.00
Markus Naslund
AF2NK Evgeni Nabokov
Miikka Kiprusoff
AF2NL Vincent Lecavalier 10.00 25.00
Rick Nash
AF2NS Martin St. Louis 10.00 25.00
Rick Nash
AF2OB Alexander Ovechkin 40.00 100.00
Nicklas Backstrom
AF2OF Sergei Fedorov 40.00 100.00
Alexander Ovechkin
AF2PA Gilbert Perreault
Maxim Afinogenov
AF2PB Patrice Bergeron 10.00 25.00
Phil Kessel
AF2PC Zdeno Chara 10.00 25.00
Dion Phaneuf
AF2PG Corey Perry
Ryan Getzlaf
AF2PS Patrick Sharp
Brent Seabrook
AF2PZ Markus Naslund 10.00 25.00
Nikolai Zherdev
AF2RB Pierre-Marc Bouchard 10.00 25.00
Mikko Koivu
AF2RD Luc Robitaille
Marcel Dionne
AF2RF Patrick Roy 30.00 80.00
Peter Forsberg
AF2RJ Jason Spezza 12.00 30.00
Ryan Smyth
AF2RN Luc Robitaille
Bernie Nicholls
AF2SA Drew Stafford 10.00 25.00
Maxim Afinogenov
AF2SD Chris Drury
Marc Staal
AF2SF Mats Sundin 15.00 40.00
Peter Forsberg
AF2SG Teemu Selanne 12.00 30.00
Ryan Getzlaf
AF2SL Marc Savard
Milan Lucic
AF2SM Shane Doan 12.00 30.00
Peter Mueller
AF2SN Mats Sundin 10.00 25.00
Markus Naslund

AF2SS Joe Sakic 15.00 40.00
Ryan Smyth
AF2TB Marty Turco
Peter Budaj
AF2TC Joe Thornton 15.00 40.00
Jonathan Cheechoo
AF2TK Jonathan Toews 30.00 80.00
Patrick Kane
AF2TL Vesa Toskala 10.00 25.00
Kari Lehtonen
AF2TM Vincent Lecavalier 10.00 25.00
Ryan Malone
AF2TN Joe Thornton
Rick Nash
AF2TP Jonathan Toews 30.00 80.00
Carey Price
AF2TR Vesa Toskala 10.00 25.00
Tuukka Rask
AF2TT Tim Thomas
Tuukka Rask
AF2VH Tomas Vokoun 15.00 40.00
Dominik Hasek
AF2WL Wade Redden 20.00 50.00
Henrik Lundqvist
AF2ZC Henrik Zetterberg
Evgeni Malkin
AF2ZD Chris Drury
Nikolai Zherdev
AF2ZF Sergei Fedorov
Maxim Afinogenov
AF2ZM Mike Modano
Zach Parise

2008-09 SP Game Used Authentic Fabrics Trios

STATED PRINT RUN 25 SERIAL #'d SETS
AF3BEP Martin Brodeur 15.00 40.00
Patrik Elias
Zach Parise
AF3BKJ Anze Kopitar
Jack Johnson
Dustin Brown
AF3BLF Martin Brodeur
Roberto Luongo
Marc-Andre Fleury
AF3BLM Martin Brodeur 15.00 40.00
Henrik Lundqvist
Ryan Miller
AF3BMG Nicklas Backstrom
Sam Gagner
Peter Mueller
AF3BSS Rod Brind'Amour 12.00 30.00
Eric Staal
Sergei Samsonov
AF3CHO Dominik Hasek 12.00 30.00
Chris Osgood
Chris Chelios
AF3CTN Sidney Crosby 25.00 60.00
Jonathan Toews
Rick Nash
AF3DKO Alexander Ovechkin 30.00 80.00
Ilya Kovalchuk
Nikolai Zherdev
AF3DWS J.P. Dumont 5.00 12.00
Shea Weber
Steve Sullivan
AF3GBR Mike Richards 12.00 30.00
Daniel Briere
Simon Gagne
AF3GGP Marian Gaborik 12.00 30.00
Ryan Getzlaf
Zach Parise
AF3GHC Wayne Gretzky 40.00 100.00
Gordie Howe
Sidney Crosby
AF3GND Scott Gomez 8.00 20.00
Chris Drury
Markus Naslund
AF3HCG Shawn Horcoff 12.00 30.00
Erik Cole
Sam Gagner
AF3HEG Marian Gaborik 12.00 30.00
Marian Hossa
Patrik Elias
AF3HEW Bobby Hull
Tony Esposito
Doug Wilson
AF3HSW Ryan Smyth 6.00 15.00
Wojtek Wolski
Milan Hejduk
AF3JDM Shane Doan
Peter Mueller
Olli Jokinen
AF3KBJ Paul Kariya 10.00 25.00
Erik Johnson
David Perron
AF3KOM Alexander Ovechkin
Evgeni Malkin
Ilya Kovalchuk
AF3LBD Roberto Luongo 12.00 30.00
Steve Bernier
Pavol Demitra
AF3LCM Mario Lemieux 40.00 100.00
Sidney Crosby
Evgeni Malkin
AF3LNZ Henrik Lundqvist 15.00 40.00
Markus Naslund
Nikolai Zherdev
AF3LPG Nicklas Lidstrom
Dion Phaneuf
Sergei Gonchar
AF3LSM Vincent Lecavalier
Martin St. Louis
Ryan Malone
AF3LTS Vincent Lecavalier
Martin St. Louis
Joe Thornton
AF3MFM Lanny McDonald 8.00 20.00
Theoren Fleury
Al MacInnis
AF3MGP Marc Staal
Sam Gagner
David Perron
AF3MPG Ryan Getzlaf
Corey Perry
Brendan Morrison
AF3MRL Mike Modano
Mike Ribeiro
Jere Lehtinen
AF3MSS Mike Modano
Mats Sundin
Brendan Shanahan
AF3NGB Marian Gaborik 12.00 30.00
Pierre-Marc Bouchard
Owen Nolan
AF3OGB Alexander Ovechkin
Nicklas Backstrom
Mike Green
AF3RBP Patrick Roy 25.00 60.00
Martin Brodeur
Carey Price
AF3RSF Patrick Roy
Joe Sakic
Peter Forsberg
AF3RTL Marty Turco 6.00 15.00
Jere Lehtinen
Mike Ribeiro
AF3SAA Saku Koivu
Andrei Kostitsyn
Alex Kovalev
AF3SAS Mats Sundin
Nik Antropov
Matt Stajan
AF3SFW Marc-Andre Fleury 8.00 20.00
Petr Sykora
Ryan Whitney
AF3SHF Joe Sakic 12.00 30.00
Peter Forsberg
Milan Hejduk
AF3SKF Teemu Selanne
Paul Kariya
Sergei Fedorov
AF3SKJ Teemu Selanne
Saku Koivu
Olli Jokinen
AF3SKK Teemu Selanne 8.00 20.00
Saku Koivu
Mikko Koivu
AF3SNF Mats Sundin
Markus Naslund
Peter Forsberg
AF3SNH Markus Naslund 8.00 20.00
Mats Sundin
Tomas Holmstrom
AF3SPG Teemu Selanne 10.00 25.00
Ryan Getzlaf
Corey Perry
AF3SSS Eric Staal
Jordan Staal
Marc Staal
AF3SSW Joe Sakic 12.00 30.00
Ryan Smyth
Wojtek Wolski
AF3TKL Miikka Kiprusoff
Kari Lehtonen
Vesa Toskala
AF3TLM Henrik Lundqvist
Ryan Miller
Vesa Toskala
AF3TNC Joe Thornton 12.00 30.00
Jonathan Cheechoo
Evgeni Nabokov
AF3VKL Olaf Kolzig 8.00 20.00
Kari Lehtonen
Tomas Vokoun
AF3WSS Eric Staal
Sergei Samsonov
Justin Williams
AF3ZGF Sergei Fedorov
Sergei Zubov
Sergei Gonchar
AF3ZLC Henrik Zetterberg
Nicklas Lidstrom
Chris Chelios

2008-09 SP Game Used Authentic Fabrics Trios Patches

STATED PRINT RUN 15 SERIAL #'d SETS
NOT PRICED DUE TO SCARCITY

2008-09 SP Game Used Authentic Fabrics Quads

STATED PRINT RUN 10 SERIAL #'d SETS
NOT PRICED DUE TO SCARCITY
AF4ADSK Ilya Kovalchuk
Alex Kovalev
Sergei Samsonov
Maxim Afinogenov
AF4BBSS Martin Brodeur
Richard Brodeur
Peter Stastny
Paul Stastny
AF4BEGP Martin Brodeur
Zach Parise
Patrik Elias
Brian Gionta
AF4BGJJ Erik Johnson
Jack Johnson
Mike Green
Jay Bouwmeester
AF4BLMT Martin Brodeur
Henrik Lundqvist
Ryan Miller
Vesa Toskala
AF4BOLN Martin Brodeur
Roberto Luongo
Evgeni Nabokov
Chris Osgood
AF4BPLN Ray Bourque
Dion Phaneuf
Nicklas Lidstrom
Scott Niedermayer
AF4CAPS Alexander Ovechkin
Nicklas Backstrom
Sergei Fedorov
Mike Green
AF4COMK Sidney Crosby
Alexander Ovechkin
Evgeni Malkin
Ilya Kovalchuk
AF4DBKM Shane Doan
Peter Mueller
Anze Kopitar
Dustin Brown
AF4FCMS Sidney Crosby
Evgeni Malkin
Marc-Andre Fleury
Jordan Staal
AF4FRAM Mark Messier
Glenn Anderson
Grant Fuhr
Bill Ranford
AF4GNDL Henrik Lundqvist
Markus Naslund
Scott Gomez
Chris Drury
AF4GSHC Marian Gaborik
Marek Svatos
Dominik Hasek
Zdeno Chara
AF4GSNP Ryan Getzlaf
Teemu Selanne
Rob Niedermayer
Corey Perry
AF4HDHC Dominik Hasek
Kris Draper
Tomas Holmstrom
Chris Chelios
AF4KKSR Saku Koivu
Alex Kovalev
Steve Shutt
Larry Robinson
AF4KTPW Paul Kariya
Keith Tkachuk
David Perron
Andy Wozniewski
AF4LBOD Roberto Luongo
Steve Bernier
Mattias Ohlund
Pavol Demitra
AF4LHWD Nicklas Lidstrom
Tomas Holmstrom
Shea Weber
J.P. Dumont
AF4LKRT Roberto Luongo
Miikka Kiprusoff
Andrew Raycroft
Marty Turco
AF4MLRM Mike Modano
Marty Turco
Mike Ribeiro
Jere Lehtinen
AF4MTNC Joe Thornton
Jonathan Cheechoo
Evgeni Nabokov
Patrick Marleau
AF4NGBK Marian Gaborik
Mikko Koivu
Pierre-Marc Bouchard
Owen Nolan
AF4PBHC Dion Phaneuf
Todd Bertuzzi
Shawn Horcoff
Erik Cole
AF4RGCN Mike Richards
Simon Gagne
Jeff Carter
Antero Niittymaki
AF4RLHM Gordie Howe
Mario Lemieux
Patrick Roy
Mark Messier
AF4SBTK Patrice Bergeron
Phil Kessel
Marc Savard
Tim Thomas
AF4SCUP Henrik Zetterberg
Nicklas Lidstrom
Sidney Crosby
Sergei Gonchar
AF4SHTS Joe Sakic
Ryan Smyth
Darcy Tucker
Milan Hejduk
AF4SMTA Mats Sundin
Vesa Toskala
Nik Antropov
Dominic Moore
AF4SNTL Jason Spezza
Rick Nash
Joe Thornton
Vincent Lecavalier
AF4SSHS Joe Sakic
Paul Stastny
Milan Hejduk
Marek Svatos
AF4SSSF Joe Sakic
Mats Sundin
Brendan Shanahan
Peter Forsberg
AF4TKKS Jonathan Toews
Patrick Kane
Nikolai Khabibulin
Brent Seabrook
AF4TMOS Mats Sundin
Vesa Toskala
Jason Spezza
Martin Gerber
AF4VLSH Vincent Lecavalier
Martin St. Louis
Nathan Horton
Tomas Vokoun
AF4WBSW Eric Staal
Cam Ward
Justin Williams
Rod Brind'Amour

2008-09 SP Game Used Authentic Fabrics Quads Patches

STATED PRINT RUN 9 SERIAL #'d SETS
NOT PRICED DUE TO SCARCITY

2008-09 SP Game Used Authentic Fabrics Fives

STATED PRINT RUN 5 SERIAL #'d SETS
NOT PRICED DUE TO SCARCITY
AF5BROS Phil Esposito
Tony Esposito
Eric Staal
Jordan Staal
Marc Staal
AF5BSTN Patrice Bergeron
Phil Kessel
Tim Thomas
Zdeno Chara
Michael Ryder
AF5CALG Dion Phaneuf
Miikka Kiprusoff
Mike Cammalleri
Todd Bertuzzi
Matthew Lombardi
AF5COLO Joe Sakic
Peter Forsberg
Paul Stastny
Wojtek Wolski
Milan Hejduk
AF5DALL Marty Turco
Mike Modano
Brad Richards
Mike Ribeiro
Sergei Zubov
AF5DVLS Martin Brodeur
Zach Parise
Patrik Elias
Brian Gionta
Brian Rolston
AF5FNLD Miikka Kiprusoff
Vesa Toskala
Kari Lehtonen
Antero Niittymaki
Tuukka Rask
AF5GR85 Gordie Howe
Wayne Gretzky
Mario Lemieux
Patrick Roy
Mark Messier
AF5HABS Carey Price
Saku Koivu
Alex Kovalev
Andrei Kostitsyn
Alex Tanguay
AF5HALL Wayne Gretzky
Gordie Howe
Mark Messier
Mario Lemieux
Bobby Hull
AF5HITS Nicklas Lidstrom
Dion Phaneuf
Scott Niedermayer
Chris Chelios
Zdeno Chara
AF5MWVC Roberto Luongo
Pavol Demitra
Marian Gaborik
Mikko Koivu
Pierre-Marc Bouchard
AF5NETS Patrick Roy
Martin Brodeur
Tony Esposito
Grant Fuhr
Dominik Hasek
AF5NEXT Sidney Crosby
Alexander Ovechkin
Evgeni Malkin
Ilya Kovalchuk
Eric Staal
AF5PENS Sidney Crosby
Evgeni Malkin
Marc-Andre Fleury
Jordan Staal
Kristopher Letang
AF5QBCF Mario Lemieux
Luc Robitaille
Gilbert Perreault
J.P. Dumont
Patrice Bergeron
AF5RNGR Markus Naslund
Henrik Lundqvist
Scott Gomez
Chris Drury
Nikolai Zherdev
AF5RSSN Alexander Ovechkin
Evgeni Malkin
Ilya Kovalchuk
Sergei Fedorov
Nikolai Zherdev
AF5RVLS Mats Sundin
Vesa Toskala
Jason Spezza
Martin Gerber
Chris Phillips
AF5SCNC Ryan Getzlaf
Teemu Selanne
Joe Thornton
Evgeni Nabokov
Jonathan Cheechoo
AF5STOP Martin Brodeur
Roberto Luongo
Marc-Andre Fleury
Ryan Miller
Henrik Lundqvist
AF5VANC Roberto Luongo
Pavol Demitra
Steve Bernier
Ryan Kesler
Mattias Ohlund
AF5WNGS Henrik Zetterberg
Nicklas Lidstrom
Chris Osgood
Dominik Hasek
Tomas Holmstrom
AF5YNGS Jonathan Toews
Carey Price
Patrick Kane
Nicklas Backstrom
Peter Mueller

2008-09 SP Game Used Authentic Fabrics Fives Patches

STATED PRINT RUN 4 SERIAL #'d SETS
NOT PRICED DUE TO SCARCITY

2008-09 SP Game Used Authentic Fabrics Sixes

STATED PRINT RUN 6 SERIAL #'d SETS
NOT PRICED DUE TO SCARCITY
AF62004 Alexander Ovechkin
Evgeni Malkin
Drew Stafford
Wojtek Wolski
Mike Green
Mike Lundin
AF62005 Sidney Crosby
Carey Price
Anze Kopitar
Paul Stastny
Jack Johnson
Tuukka Rask
AF6500G Joe Sakic
Mats Sundin
Brendan Shanahan
Mike Modano
Keith Tkachuk
Mark Recchi
AF6AMZG Wayne Gretzky
Gordie Howe
Mark Messier
Patrick Roy
Mario Lemieux
Sidney Crosby
AF6BSMC Patrick Roy
Carey Price
Alex Kovalev
Gilbert Perreault
Ryan Miller
Maxim Afinogenov
AF6CNHL Roberto Luongo
Carey Price
Miikka Kiprusoff
Vesa Toskala
Dwayne Roloson
Martin Gerber
AF6EDCG Mark Messier
Grant Fuhr
Glenn Anderson
Lanny McDonald
Al MacInnis
Theoren Fleury
AF6FLOR Vincent Lecavalier
Martin St. Louis
Ryan Malone
Nathan Horton
Tomas Vokoun
Cory Stillman
AF6GSCR Alexander Ovechkin
Ilya Kovalchuk
Rick Nash
Ryan Getzlaf
Marian Gaborik
Marian Hossa
AF6MONT Patrick Roy
Carey Price
Saku Koivu
Alex Kovalev
Andrei Kostitsyn
Mike Komisarek
AF6NETS Marty Turco
Chris Osgood
Evgeni Nabokov
Tim Thomas
Rick DiPietro
Tomas Vokoun
AF6QUEB Martin Brodeur
Patrick Roy
Roberto Luongo
Mike Bossy
Luc Robitaille
Gilbert Perreault
AF6RIVL Mike Modano
Brad Richards
Mike Ribeiro
Joe Sakic
Peter Forsberg
Milan Hejduk
AF6SAVE Tony Esposito
Ron Hextall
Grant Fuhr
Dominik Hasek
Martin Brodeur
Roberto Luongo
AF6SWED Henrik Zetterberg
Mats Sundin
Peter Forsberg
Markus Naslund
Nicklas Lidstrom
Henrik Lundqvist
AF6YNGG Jonathan Toews
Patrick Kane
Nicklas Backstrom
Peter Mueller
Jordan Staal
Sam Gagner

2008-09 SP Game Used Authentic Fabrics Sixes Patches

STATED PRINT RUN 3 SERIAL #'d SETS
NOT PRICED DUE TO SCARCITY

2008-09 SP Game Used Authentic Fabrics Sevens

STATED PRINT RUN 7 SERIAL #'d SETS
NOT PRICED DUE TO SCARCITY
AF7ABTA Jay Bouwmeester
Mark Messier
Shane Doan
Ryan Smyth
Scott Niedermayer
Chris Osgood
Mike Green
AF7AMZG Mario Lemieux
Wayne Gretzky
Gordie Howe
Mark Messier
Bobby Hull
Luc Robitaille
Marcel Dionne
AF7CLDR Evgeni Nabokov
Evgeni Malkin
Alexander Ovechkin
Patrick Kane
Teemu Selanne
Scott Gomez
Chris Drury
AF7CNDA Martin Brodeur
Sidney Crosby
Vincent Lecavalier
Martin St. Louis
Joe Thornton
Rick Nash
Jonathan Toews
AF7CONN Patrick Roy
Mario Lemieux
Joe Sakic
Cam Ward
Nicklas Lidstrom
Brad Richards
Scott Niedermayer
AF7FNLD Teemu Selanne
Joni Pitkanen
Saku Koivu
Olli Jokinen
Mikko Koivu
Miikka Kiprusoff
Kari Lehtonen
AF7HART Alexander Ovechkin
Wayne Gretzky
Sidney Crosby
Joe Thornton
Martin St. Louis
Peter Forsberg
Jose Theodore
AF7PICK Patrick Kane
Erik Johnson
Marc-Andre Fleury
Ilya Kovalchuk
Rick Nash
Rick DiPietro
Vincent Lecavalier
AF7QBEC Patrick Roy
Mario Lemieux
Mike Bossy
Gilbert Perreault
Martin Brodeur
Roberto Luongo
Marc-Andre Fleury
AF7RUSA Sergei Zubov
Sergei Gonchar
Alexander Ovechkin
Evgeni Malkin
Ilya Kovalchuk
Sergei Fedorov
Nikolai Zherdev
AF7SAVE Martin Brodeur
Patrick Roy
Grant Fuhr
Ron Hextall
Dominik Hasek
Henrik Lundqvist
Marc-Andre Fleury
AF7SWDN Peter Forsberg
Tomas Holmstrom
Mats Sundin
Henrik Zetterberg
Henrik Lundqvist
Markus Naslund
Nicklas Backstrom

2008-09 SP Game Used Authentic Fabrics Sevens Patches

STATED PRINT RUN 2 SERIAL #'d SETS
NOT PRICED DUE TO SCARCITY

2008-09 SP Game Used Authentic Fabrics Eights

STATED PRINT RUN 8 SERIAL #'d SETS
NOT PRICED DUE TO SCARCITY
AF8ASTR Mats Sundin
Joe Sakic
Peter Forsberg
Brendan Shanahan
Teemu Selanne
Paul Kariya
Mike Modano
Saku Koivu
AF8LGND Bryan Trottier
Luc Robitaille
Marcel Dionne
Dale Hawerchuk
Lanny McDonald
Borje Salming
Darryl Sittler
Al MacInnis
AF8NETM Patrick Roy
Ron Hextall
Martin Brodeur
Roberto Luongo
Grant Fuhr
Dominik Hasek
Henrik Lundqvist
Ryan Miller
AF8SCUP Sidney Crosby
Evgeni Malkin
Jordan Staal
Marc-Andre Fleury
Henrik Zetterberg
Nicklas Lidstrom
Chris Chelios
Chris Osgood
AF8SSTR Marian Gaborik
Sidney Crosby
Alexander Ovechkin
Ilya Kovalchuk
Evgeni Malkin
Eric Staal
Vincent Lecavalier
Jason Spezza
AF8STAR Wayne Gretzky
Gordie Howe
Mario Lemieux
Mark Messier
Sidney Crosby
Alexander Ovechkin
Evgeni Malkin
Ilya Kovalchuk
AF8YSTR Carey Price
Jonathan Toews
Patrick Kane
Nicklas Backstrom
Peter Mueller
Sam Gagner
Erik Johnson
Marc Staal

2008-09 SP Game Used Authentic Fabrics Eights Patches

STATED PRINT RUN 1 SERIAL #'d SET
NOT PRICED DUE TO SCARCITY

2008-09 SP Game Used By The Letter

STATED PRINT RUN 3-11 SERIAL #'d SETS
NOT PRICED DUE TO SCARCITY
BTLAF Alexander Frolov/6
BTLAH Ales Hemsky/6
BTLAK Anze Kopitar/7
BTLAM Maxim Afinogenov/10
BTLAO Alexander Ovechkin/8
BTLBB Brad Boyes/5
BTLBD Martin Brodeur/7
BTLBM Brenden Morrow/6
BTLBR Brendan Morrison/6
BTLBS Brendan Shanahan/8
BTLCA Carey Price/5
BTLCH Jonathan Cheechoo/8
BTLCP Chris Pronger/7
BTLDH Dominik Hasek/5
BTLDP Dion Phaneuf/7
BTLEM Evgeni Malkin/6
BTLES Eric Staal/5
BTLHO Marian Hossa/5
BTLHZ Henrik Zetterberg/10
BTLIK Ilya Kovalchuk/9
BTLJB Jay Bouwmeester/11
BTLJC Jeff Carter/6
BTLJI Jarome Iginla/6
BTLJL Jere Lehtinen/6
BTLJM Joe Mullen/5
BTLJS Jason Spezza/6
BTLJT Jonathan Toews/8
BTLJW Justin Williams/7
BTLKV Alex Kovalev/7
BTLLE Mario Lemieux/7
BTLMA Adam Oates/5
BTLMB Martin Biron/5
BTLMG Marian Gaborik/7
BTLMH Milan Hejduk/6
BTLMI Miroslav Satan/5
BTLMK Mikko Koivu/5
BTLML Manny Legace/6
BTLMN Markus Naslund/7
BTLMR Mike Richards/8
BTLMS Mats Sundin/6
BTLNA Nik Antropov/8
BTLOZ Chris Osgood/6
BTLPD Pavel Datsyuk/7
BTLPE Patrik Elias/5
BTLPF Peter Forsberg/8
BTLPK Patrick Kane/4
BTLPL Pascal Leclaire/8
BTLPR Patrick Roy/3
BTLPS Paul Stastny/7
BTLRM Ryan Miller/6
BTLSA Joe Sakic/5
BTLSC Sidney Crosby/6
BTLSK Saku Koivu/5
BTLSV Marek Svatos/6
BTLTH Jose Theodore/8
BTLTW Tiger Williams/8
BTLVL Vincent Lecavalier/10
BTLZP Zach Parise/6

2008-09 SP Game Used Dual Authentic Fabrics

AFAM Andrei Markov 5.00 12.00
AFAN Antero Niittymaki 6.00 15.00
AFAO Alexander Ovechkin 25.00 60.00
AFAS Anton Stastny 4.00 10.00
AFBB Bob Bourne 4.00 10.00
AFBG Patrice Bergeron 6.00 15.00
AFBL Rob Blake 6.00 15.00
AFBN Bernie Nicholls 4.00 10.00
AFBQ Ray Bourque 12.00 30.00
AFBR Steve Bernier 4.00 10.00
AFBS Billy Smith 5.00 12.00
AFBZ Todd Bertuzzi 6.00 15.00
AFCC Chris Chelios 0.00 20.00
AFCH Jonathan Cheechoo 6.00 15.00
AFDB Doug Gilmour 8.00 20.00
AFDC Dino Ciccarelli 4.00 10.00
AFDE Pavol Demitra 4.00 10.00
AFDH Dominik Hasek 10.00 25.00
AFDL Darryl Sittler 6.00 15.00
AFDP Dion Phaneuf 6.00 15.00
AFDS Denis Savard 6.00 15.00
AFDW Doug Weight 4.00 10.00
AFEL Patrik Elias 4.00 10.00
AFEM Evgeni Malkin 15.00 40.00
AFES Eric Staal 10.00 25.00
AFGA Glenn Anderson 5.00 12.00
AFGN Simon Gagne 5.00 12.00
AFGP Gilbert Perreault 6.00 15.00
AFHK Roman Hamrlik 4.00 10.00
AFHL Henrik Lundqvist 12.00 30.00
AFHM Marian Hossa 10.00 25.00
AFHO Tomas Holmstrom 5.00 12.00
AFHW Dale Hawerchuk 6.00 15.00
AFIK Ilya Kovalchuk 8.00 20.00
AFJL Jere Lehtinen 4.00 10.00
AFJM Joe Mullen 6.00 15.00
AFJS Jordan Staal 10.00 25.00
AFJW Justin Williams 4.00 10.00
AFKL Kari Lehtonen 4.00 10.00
AFKM Mike Komisarek 5.00 12.00
AFKO Mikko Koivu 6.00 15.00
AFKV Saku Koivu 8.00 15.00
AFLG Roberto Luongo 10.00 25.00
AFLM Lanny McDonald 6.00 15.00
AFLR Larry Robinson 6.00 15.00
AFMA Maxim Afinogenov
AFMB Martin Brodeur 12.00 30.00
AFMF Ryan Malone 4.00 10.00
AFMF Marc-Andre Fleury 6.00 15.00
AFMG Marian Gaborik 10.00 25.00
AFMH Milan Hejduk 5.00 12.00
AFMK Miikka Kiprusoff 6.00 15.00
AFMM Mike Modano 6.00 15.00
AFMN Manny Fernandez 6.00 15.00

AFMP Michael Peca 5.00 12.00
AFMR Mike Ribeiro 4.00 10.00
AFMS Marek Svatos 4.00 10.00
AFMT Marty Turco 5.00 12.00
AFNL Nicklas Lidstrom 6.00 15.00
AFNS Markus Naslund 6.00 15.00
AFNZ Nikolai Zherdev 4.00 10.00
AFOJ Olli Jokinen 4.00 10.00
AFPA Paul Kariya 6.00 15.00
AFPB Pierre-Marc Bouchard 4.00 10.00
AFPF Peter Forsberg 10.00 25.00
AFPK Phil Kessel 6.00 15.00
AFRB Richard Brodeur 5.00 12.00
AFRD Rod Brind'Amour 5.00 12.00
AFRE Ron Ellis 4.00 10.00
AFRF Ruslan Fedotenko 4.00 10.00
AFRG Ryan Getzlaf 8.00 20.00
AFRH Ron Hextall 6.00 15.00
AFRK Ryan Kesler 4.00 10.00
AFRL Rod Langway 8.00 20.00
AFRM Ryan Miller 6.00 15.00
AFRN Rick Nash 6.00 15.00
AFRO Patrick Roy 20.00 50.00
AFRS Ryan Smyth 5.00 12.00
AFRY Michael Ryder 5.00 12.00
AFSC Sidney Crosby 30.00 80.00
AFSD Shane Doan 4.00 10.00
AFSF Sergei Fedorov 10.00 25.00
AFSH Shawn Horcoff 4.00 10.00
AFSK Joe Sakic 10.00 25.00
AFSP Jason Spezza 8.00 20.00
AFSS Steve Shutt 6.00 15.00
AFST Miroslav Satan 4.00 10.00
AFSU Mats Sundin 6.00 15.00
AFSV Marc Savard 4.00 10.00
AFSY Peter Stastny 6.00 15.00
AFSZ Sergei Zubov 4.00 10.00
AFTH Tim Thomas 6.00 15.00
AFTR Tuukka Rask 6.00 15.00
AFTS Teemu Selanne 6.00 15.00
AFTW Tiger Williams 4.00 10.00
AFVL Vincent Lecavalier 6.00 15.00
AFVO Tomas Vokoun 6.00 15.00
AFVT Vesa Toskala 6.00 15.00
AFWB Shea Weber 4.00 10.00
AFZP Zach Parise 6.00 15.00

2008-09 SP Game Used Dual Authentic Fabrics Gold

*GOLD: .5X TO 1.2X BASE
STATED PRINT RUN 50 SERIAL #'d SETS

2008-09 SP Game Used Dual Authentic Fabrics Platinum

*PLATINUM: .6X TO 1.5X BASE
STATED PRINT RUN 25 SERIAL #'d SETS

2008-09 SP Game Used Extra SIGnificance

STATED PRINT RUN 25 SERIAL #'d SETS
XSGBC Daniel Carcillo 10.00 25.00
Adam Burish
XSGBE Martin Brodeur 25.00 60.00
Patrik Elias
XSGBK Patrick Kane 30.00 80.00
Nicklas Backstrom
XSGBM Brandon Dubinsky 15.00 40.00
Marc Staal
XSGCG Sam Gagner
Andrew Cogliano
XSGCH Ron Hextall 12.00 30.00
Bobby Clarke
XSGCM Peter Mueller 15.00 40.00
Daniel Carcillo
XSGDB Darryl Sittler 12.00 30.00
Borje Salming
XSGDD Brandon Dubinsky
Chris Drury
XSGDK Devin Setoguchi 12.00 30.00
Kristopher Letang
XSGDT Marcel Dionne
Dave Taylor
XSGDV Dan Cleary
Valtteri Filppula
XSGEE Tony Esposito 20.00 50.00
Phil Esposito
XSGEJ Eric Staal
Jordan Staal
XSGEM Elmer Lach 20.00 50.00
Milt Schmidt
XSGES Phil Esposito
Derek Sanderson
XSGGB Nicklas Backstrom
Mike Green
XSGGS Billy Smith
Clark Gillies
XSGHD Kris Draper
Tomas Holmstrom
XSGHG Dany Heatley
Martin Gerber
XSGHM Henrik Zetterberg 25.00 60.00
Marian Hossa
XSGHP Carey Price 40.00 100.00
Jaroslav Halak
XSGHS Josh Harding
James Sheppard
XSGIC Jarome Iginla
Mike Cammalleri
XSGIK Ilya Kovalchuk
Kari Lehtonen
XSGIP Jarome Iginla
Dion Phaneuf
XSGJP Jason Pominville
Daniel Paille
XSGKN Kyle Chipchura
Nick Foligno
XSGKT Kari Lehtonen
Tobias Enstrom
XSGLE Nicklas Lidstrom 12.00 30.00
Tobias Enstrom
XSGLS Vincent Lecavalier
Martin St. Louis
XSGMD Mark Mancari 10.00 25.00
Daniel Paille
XSGMF Theoren Fleury 15.00 40.00
Joe Mullen
XSGMG Brian Gionta
Mike Modano
XSGMH Ryan Miller 12.00 30.00
Josh Harding
XSGMJ Marc Staal
Jordan Staal
XSGMM Mike Modano 12.00 30.00
Brenden Morrow
XSGMP Milan Hejduk 12.00 30.00
Paul Stastny
XSGMS Ryan Miller 12.00 30.00
Drew Stafford
XSGNP Evgeni Nabokov
Dimitri Patzold
XSGNT Nathan Horton
Tomas Vokoun
XSGOB Alexander Ovechkin 50.00 120.00
Nicklas Backstrom
XSGOM Evgeni Malkin 50.00 120.00
Alexander Ovechkin
XSGPP Patrice Bergeron
Phil Kessel
XSGPT Paul Stastny 12.00 30.00
T.J. Hensick
XSGPV Thomas Vanek
Jason Pominville
XSGRC Mike Richards 20.00 50.00
Jeff Carter
XSGRK Mason Raymond 8.00 20.00
Ryan Kesler
XSGRM Brenden Morrow
Mike Ribeiro
XSGRT Ryane Clowe
Torrey Mitchell
XSGS2 Paul Stastny 12.00 30.00
Peter Stastny
XSGSH Ryan Smyth 10.00 25.00
Milan Hejduk
XSGSS Daniel Sedin
Henrik Sedin
XSGST Jiri Tlusty
Matt Stajan
XSGSW Eric Staal
Cam Ward
XSGTF Marc-Andre Fleury 10.00 25.00
Maxime Talbot
XSGTH Chris Higgins
Alex Tanguay
XSGTK Jonathan Toews 40.00 100.00
Patrick Kane
XSGTM Joe Thornton 20.00 50.00
Milan Michalek
XSGTP Carey Price 40.00 100.00
Jonathan Toews
XSGVP Thomas Vanek
Daniel Paille
XSGVW Cam Ward 12.00 30.00
Tomas Vokoun
XSGZK Sam Gagner 20.00 50.00
Sergei Kostitsyn

2008-09 SP Game Used Famous Fight Straps

STATED PRINT RUN 3 SERIAL #'d SETS
NOT PRICED DUE TO SCARCITY
FSAO Alexander Ovechkin
FSCN Cam Neely
FSCP Carey Price
FSDC Dino Ciccarelli
FSEM Evgeni Malkin
FSGL Brendan Shanahan
FSHZ Henrik Zetterberg
FSIK Ilya Kovalchuk
FSJI Jarome Iginla
FSJS Joe Sakic
FSJT Jonathan Toews
FSMB Martin Brodeur
FSML Mario Lemieux
FSMM Mark Messier
FSMS Mats Sundin
FSPF Peter Forsberg
FSPR Patrick Roy
FSRH Ron Hextall
FSSC Sidney Crosby
FSVL Vincent Lecavalier

2008-09 SP Game Used Famous Fight Straps Combos

STATED PRINT RUN 1 SERIAL #'d SETS
NOT PRICED DUE TO SCARCITY
FSCBC Donald Brashear
Zdeno Chara
FSCCM Bobby Clarke
Stan Mikita
FSCCR Sidney Crosby
Mike Richards
FSCDP Dion Phaneuf
Shane Doan
FSCFC Theoren Fleury
Chris Chelios
FSCFJ Jarome Iginla
Ed Jovanovski
FSCFP Adam Foote
Bob Probert
FSCGA Doug Gilmour
Daniel Alfredsson
FSCGC Brian Gionta
Mike Comrie
FSCIK Jarome Iginla
Ryan Kesler
FSCLI Vincent Lecavalier
Jarome Iginla
FSCOM Alexander Ovechkin
Evgeni Malkin
FSCPG Dion Phaneuf
Ryan Getzlaf
FSCPH Ron Hextall
Denis Potvin
FSCRD Mike Richards
Chris Drury
FSCRH Patrick Roy
Dominik Hasek
FSCRO Patrick Roy
Chris Osgood
FSCSG Joe Sakic
Doug Gilmour
FSCSM Jason Spezza
Andrei Markov
FSCTP Dion Phaneuf
Keith Tkachuk

2008-09 SP Game Used Inked Sweaters Dual

STATED PRINT RUN 25 SERIAL #'d SETS
INKAL Lanny McDonald
Al MacInnis
INKBM Martin Brodeur
Ryan Miller
INKBP Martin Brodeur
Carey Price
INKBV Peter Budaj
Tomas Vokoun
INKFS Marc-Andre Fleury 25.00 60.00
Jordan Staal
INKKM Evgeni Malkin
Ilya Kovalchuk
INKLG Wayne Gretzky
Mario Lemieux
INKLS Vincent Lecavalier 15.00 40.00
Martin St. Louis
INKLZ Nicklas Lidstrom 30.00 80.00
Henrik Zetterberg
INKMM Mike Modano 15.00 40.00
Mike Ribeiro
INKMT Mike Modano
Marty Turco
INKNZ Markus Naslund
Nikolai Zherdev
INKOB Alexander Ovechkin
Nicklas Backstrom
INKSC Scott Gomez 15.00 40.00
Chris Drury
INKSH Ryan Smyth
Milan Hejduk
INKSW Cam Ward 25.00 60.00
Eric Staal
INKTK Patrick Kane 50.00 120.00
Jonathan Toews
INKZH Henrik Zetterberg 30.00 80.00
Marian Hossa

2008-09 SP Game Used Letter Marks

STATED PRINT RUN 50 SERIAL #'d SETS
LMBP Bob Probert 40.00 100.00
LMCA Daniel Carcillo 15.00 40.00
LMDS Denis Savard 25.00 60.00
LMEJ Erik Johnson 30.00 80.00
LMGC Guy Carbonneau 30.00 80.00
LMHS Henrik Sedin 25.00 60.00
LMJI Jarome Iginla 50.00 125.00
LMKT Kyle Turris 50.00 120.00
LMMH Marian Hossa 40.00 100.00
LMMK Mike Knuble 25.00 60.00
LMNH Nathan Horton 15.00 40.00
LMPK Phil Kessel
LMPS Paul Stastny 25.00 60.00
LMRG Ryan Getzlaf 30.00 80.00
LMRK Red Kelly 30.00 80.00
LMSC Sidney Crosby 150.00 300.00
LMSE Daniel Sedin 25.00 60.00
LMTV Thomas Vanek 25.00 60.00

2008-09 SP Game Used Nickname Edition

STATED PRINT RUN 50 SERIAL #'d SETS
NEBH Bobby Hull 40.00 100.00
NEBN Bob Nystrom 15.00 40.00
NEDC Don Cherry 50.00 120.00
NEDG Doug Gilmour 25.00 60.00
NEDS Dave Schultz 15.00 40.00
NEEM Evgeni Malkin 50.00 120.00
NEEN Evgeni Nabokov 20.00 50.00
NEES Eddie Shack 20.00 50.00
NEGH Gordie Howe 100.00 175.00
NEJB Johnny Bucyk 20.00 50.00
NEJI Jarome Iginla
NELR Luc Robitaille 15.00 40.00
NEMF Marc-Andre Fleury 40.00 80.00
NEML Mario Lemieux 50.00 120.00
NEMM Mark Messier 100.00 175.00
NEMN Markus Naslund 20.00 50.00
NEMT Marty Turco 15.00 40.00
NERS Ryan Smyth
NETE Tony Esposito 50.00 100.00
NETO Terry O'Reilly

2008-09 SP Game Used Number Marks

STATED PRINT RUN 25 SERIAL#'d SETS
NMAD Alex Delvecchio
NMBB Bob Baun 25.00 60.00
NMBC Bobby Clarke
NMBD Brandon Dubinsky 20.00 50.00
NMBN Bernie Nicholls 15.00 40.00
NMBO Pierre-Marc Bouchard
NMBR Bobby Ryan 40.00 100.00
NMBS Borje Salming
NMCB Cam Barker 15.00 40.00
NMCG Clark Gillies 20.00 50.00
NMCP Carey Price
NMDB Dan Boyle
NMDP Dustin Penner 15.00 40.00
NMDS Drew Stafford 25.00 60.00
NMES Eric Staal
NMGF Grant Fuhr 25.00 60.00
NMGL Guillaume Latendresse 20.00 50.00
NMJB Jonathan Bernier
NMJM Joe Mullen
NMJT Jonathan Toews 80.00 200.00
NMLM Lanny McDonald 25.00 60.00
NMMC Marty McSorley
NMMH Martin Havlat 20.00 50.00
NMMM Milan Michalek 15.00 40.00
NMMR Mike Ribeiro
NMMS Marco Sturm
NMPB Peter Budaj
NMPE Patrik Elias 15.00 40.00
NMPK Patrick Kane 60.00 150.00
NMPS Peter Stastny
NMRA Bill Ranford
NMRV Rogie Vachon
NMSB Steve Bernier 15.00 40.00
NMSE Devin Setoguchi/30 25.00 60.00
NMSS Steve Shutt 25.00 60.00
NMST Martin St. Louis 25.00 60.00
NMTF Theoren Fleury 30.00 80.00
NMTH Tomas Holmstrom
NMWG Wayne Gretzky/9

2008-09 SP Game Used Rookie Exclusive Autographs

STATED PRINT RUN 100 SERIAL #'d SETS
REAE Andrew Ebbett 8.00 20.00
REAG Alex Goligoski 15.00 40.00
REAP Adam Pineault 8.00 20.00
REBB Brian Boyle 8.00 20.00
REBL Brian Lee 8.00 20.00
REBO Zach Boychuk 12.00 30.00
REBS Brandon Sutter 10.00 25.00
REBV Boris Valabik 10.00 25.00
REBW Blake Wheeler 60.00 120.00
RECG Claude Giroux 15.00 40.00
REDB Derick Brassard 15.00 40.00
REDD Drew Doughty 25.00 60.00
REDH Darren Helm 12.00 30.00
REDL Dan LaCosta 10.00 25.00
REEE Erik Ersberg 8.00 20.00
REFB Fabian Brunnstrom
REFR Jonas Frogren 10.00 25.00
REGI Colton Gillies 8.00 20.00
REIG Mike Iggulden 6.00 15.00
REIZ Ilya Zubov 8.00 20.00
REJA Justin Abdelkader 15.00 40.00
REJE Jonathan Ericsson 12.00 30.00
REJF Jon Filewich 6.00 15.00
REJM John Mitchell 8.00 20.00
REJN James Neal 12.00 30.00
REJV Jakub Voracek 15.00 40.00
REKO Kyle Okposo 15.00 40.00
REKP Kevin Porter 6.00 15.00
REKT Kyle Turris 15.00 40.00
RELK Lauri Korpikoski 8.00 20.00
RELS Luca Sbisa 12.00 30.00
REMA Steve Mason 60.00 120.00
REMB Mikkel Boedker 12.00 30.00
REMD Matt D'Agostini 12.00 30.00
REMF Mark Fistric 6.00 15.00
REMG Marc-Andre Gragnani 6.00 15.00
REMI Michael Frolik 15.00 40.00
REMR Mattias Ritola 10.00 25.00
RENF Nikita Filatov 30.00 80.00
RENK Nikolai Kulemin 8.00 20.00
RENO Nathan Oystrick
REOM Oscar Moller 8.00 20.00
REPB Patrik Berglund 20.00 50.00
REPH Patric Hornqvist 8.00 20.00
REPI Alex Pietrangelo 12.00 30.00
REPV Petr Vrana 10.00 25.00
RERE Robbie Earl 6.00 15.00
RERJ Ryan Jones 10.00 25.00
RERS Ryan Stone 8.00 20.00
RESC Luke Schenn 25.00 60.00
RESM Shawn Matthias 8.00 20.00
RESS Steven Stamkos 75.00 150.00
RETO T.J. Oshie 20.00 50.00
RETS Tom Sestito 6.00 15.00
REVM Vladimir Mihalik 8.00 20.00
REVT Viktor Tikhonov
REZB Zach Bogosian 15.00 40.00

2008-09 SP Game Used SIGnificance

STATED PRINT RUN 50 SERIAL #'d SETS
SIGAC Andrew Cogliano 12.00 30.00
SIGAE Alexander Edler 6.00 15.00
SIGAM Al MacInnis
SIGAO Alexander Ovechkin 50.00 100.00
SIGAT Alex Tanguay 6.00 15.00
SIGBB Bob Baun 8.00 20.00
SIGBD Brandon Dubinsky 6.00 15.00
SIGBE Jonathan Bernier
SIGBG Brian Gionta
SIGBM Brenden Morrow 6.00 15.00
SIGBO Brad Boyes
SIGCA Daniel Carcillo
SIGCB Cam Barker 5.00 12.00
SIGCD Chris Drury 8.00 20.00
SIGCI Dino Ciccarelli 5.00 12.00
SIGCK Chris Kunitz 5.00 12.00
SIGCP Carey Price
SIGCS Cory Stillman 5.00 12.00
SIGCW Cam Ward 8.00 20.00
SIGDA David Perron
SIGDB David Booth
SIGDC Dan Cleary 8.00 20.00
SIGDJ David Jones 5.00 12.00
SIGDP Daniel Paille 6.00 15.00
SIGDR Dwayne Roloson 6.00 15.00
SIGDS Daniel Sedin 8.00 20.00
SIGEJ Erik Johnson 10.00 25.00
SIGEL Patrik Elias
SIGEM Evgeni Malkin 30.00 60.00
SIGES Eric Staal 12.00 30.00
SIGFN Fredrik Norrena 8.00 20.00
SIGGZ Scott Gomez 6.00 15.00
SIGHA Michal Handzus
SIGHE Milan Hejduk 6.00 15.00
SIGHI Jonas Hiller 8.00 20.00
SIGHO Tomas Holmstrom 6.00 15.00
SIGJC Jeff Carter 8.00 20.00
SIGJH Jaroslav Halak 8.00 20.00
SIGJI Jarome Iginla 15.00 40.00
SIGJJ Jack Johnson 6.00 15.00
SIGJL Joffrey Lupul 5.00 12.00
SIGJP Jason Pominville 6.00 15.00
SIGJS Jordan Staal 12.00 30.00
SIGJT Jiri Tlusty 8.00 20.00
SIGKA Petr Kalus
SIGKC Kyle Chipchura
SIGKE Phil Kessel 8.00 20.00
SIGKL Kari Lehtonen 5.00 12.00
SIGKO Chuck Kobasew 5.00 12.00
SIGLE Kristopher Letang
SIGMA Matt Stajan
SIGMC Bryan McCabe 6.00 15.00
SIGMF Marc-Andre Fleury
SIGMH Martin Havlat 6.00 15.00
SIGMI Ryan Miller 8.00 20.00
SIGMK Mike Knuble 8.00 20.00
SIGMM Milan Michalek
SIGMR Mason Raymond 5.00 12.00
SIGMS Marco Sturm
SIGMT Maxime Talbot 6.00 15.00
SIGNB Nicklas Backstrom 15.00 40.00
SIGNH Nathan Horton
SIGNZ Nikolai Zherdev 5.00 12.00
SIGPA Paul Stastny
SIGPB Pierre-Marc Bouchard 5.00 12.00
SIGPE Corey Perry
SIGPH Dion Phaneuf
SIGPK Patrick Kane
SIGPM Peter Mueller
SIGPS Peter Stastny 8.00 20.00
SIGRI Mike Ribeiro
SIGRM Ryan Malone
SIGRS Ryan Smyth 6.00 15.00
SIGSB Steve Bernier
SIGSE Devin Setoguchi 8.00 20.00
SIGSG Sam Gagner 12.00 30.00
SIGSK Sergei Kostitsyn 8.00 20.00
SIGST Martin St. Louis 8.00 20.00
SIGTE Tobias Enstrom 8.00 20.00
SIGTH T.J. Hensick 6.00 15.00
SIGTM Torrey Mitchell
SIGTO Jonathan Toews 25.00 60.00
SIGTR Tuukka Rask 8.00 20.00
SIGTV Thomas Vanek 8.00 20.00
SIGTY Tyler Kennedy
SIGTZ Travis Zajac 5.00 12.00
SIGVO Tomas Vokoun 8.00 20.00

2008-09 SP Game Used SIGnificant Numbers Dual Swatches

STATED PRINT RUN 2-96 SERIAL #'d SETS
SOME NOT PRICED DUE TO SCARCITY
SNAO Alexander Ovechkin/8
SNBB Bob Bourne/14
SNBE Patrice Bergeron/37
SNBH Bobby Hull/9
SNBL Brian Lee/55
SNBS Borje Salming/21
SNBY Mike Bossy/22
SNCD Chris Drury/23
SNCN Cam Neely/8
SNCP Carey Price/31
SNCW Cam Ward/30
SNDB Derick Brassard/16
SNDC Dino Ciccarelli/20
SNDP David Perron/57 10.00 25.00
SNDR Dwayne Roloson/35
SNEL Patrik Elias/26
SNES Eric Staal/12
SNFT Mark Fistric/28
SNGF Grant Fuhr/31
SNGH Gordie Howe/9
SNGP Gilbert Perreault/11
SNGX Claude Giroux/56 15.00 40.00
SNHE Milan Hejduk/23
SNHZ Henrik Zetterberg/40
SNIK Ilya Kovalchuk/17
SNJC Jeff Carter/17
SNJJ Jack Johnson/3
SNJS Jordan Staal/11
SNJT Joe Thornton/19
SNKT Kyle Turris/91 20.00 50.00
SNKY Kyle Okposo/21
SNLH Brian Leetch/2
SNLY Lanny McDonald/9
SNMB Martin Brodeur/30 50.00 100.00
SNMF Marc-Andre Fleury/29 40.00 80.00
SNMH Marian Hossa/81 12.00 30.00
SNMI Ryan Miller/30 15.00 40.00
SNML Milan Lucic/17
SNMM Mark Messier/11
SNMN Markus Naslund/91
SNMO Mike Modano/9
SNMR Michael Ryder/73 10.00 25.00
SNMS Steve Mason/30 60.00 120.00
SNMT Marty Turco/35
SNNB Nicklas Backstrom/19
SNNH Nathan Horton/16
SNNL Nicklas Lidstrom/5
SNNZ Nikolai Zherdev/13
SNPB Pierre-Marc Bouchard/96 8.00 20.00
SNPE Corey Perry/10
SNPH Phil Esposito/7
SNPK Phil Kessel/81 15.00 40.00
SNPM Peter Mueller/88 10.00 25.00
SNPO Denis Potvin/5
SNPS Paul Stastny/26 15.00 40.00
SNRC Mike Richards/18
SNRG Ryan Getzlaf/15
SNRI Mike Ribeiro/63 8.00 20.00
SNRM Ryan Malone/12
SNRS Ryan Smyth/94 8.00 20.00
SNSB Steve Bernier/56
SNSC Sidney Crosby/87 60.00 120.00
SNSL Martin St. Louis/26 15.00 40.00
SNSS Steve Shutt/22
SNST Matt Stajan/14
SNSW Shea Weber/6
SNTH Tomas Holmstrom/96 10.00 25.00
SNTO Jonathan Toews/19
SNTR Tuukka Rask/40 15.00 40.00
SNVL Vincent Lecavalier/4
SNVO Tomas Vokoun/29 15.00 40.00
SNWG Wayne Gretzky/9

2008-09 SP Game Used SIGnificant Swatches

STATED PRINT RUN 50 SERIAL #'d SETS
SSAG Alex Goligoski
SSAL Al MacInnis 15.00 40.00
SSAO Adam Oates 12.00 30.00
SSAP Adam Pineault 12.00 30.00
SSBB Bob Bourne 8.00 20.00
SSBL Brian Lee
SSBO Pierre-Marc Bouchard 8.00 20.00
SSBS Mike Bossy 12.00 30.00
SSBT Mark Fistric
SSBU Peter Budaj 10.00 25.00
SSBY Brian Boyle
SSCC Dino Ciccarelli
SSCD Chris Drury 12.00 30.00
SSCO Chris Osgood
SSCP Corey Perry
SSCS Cory Stillman
SSDA David Perron
SSDB Derick Brassard 25.00 60.00
SSDC Dino Ciccarelli 8.00 20.00
SSDG Doug Gilmour 15.00 40.00
SSDP Daniel Paille
SSDS Drew Stafford 12.00 30.00
SSDT Darcy Tucker 10.00 25.00
SSEJ Erik Johnson
SSEM Evgeni Malkin 40.00 100.00
SSES Eric Staal 20.00 50.00
SSGB Gilbert Brule
SSGC Guy Carbonneau 15.00 40.00
SSGH Gordie Howe 40.00 100.00
SSGP Gilbert Perreault 12.00 30.00
SSGX Claude Giroux
SSGZ Scott Gomez
SSIK Ilya Kovalchuk 15.00 40.00
SSIZ Ilya Zubov
SSJB Johnny Bucyk 12.00 30.00
SSJC Jeff Carter 12.00 30.00
SSJJ Jack Johnson 10.00 25.00
SSJK Jari Kurri 12.00 30.00
SSJO Joe Thornton
SSJS Jordan Staal 20.00 50.00
SSJT Jonathan Toews 40.00 100.00
SSKA Patrick Kane 30.00 80.00
SSKT Kyle Turris 25.00 60.00
SSLE Kristopher Letang
SSLM Lanny McDonald 12.00 30.00
SSLU Joffrey Lupul 8.00 20.00
SSMA Ryan Malone 8.00 20.00
SSMD Marcel Dionne
SSMG Marc-Andre Gragnani 10.00 25.00
SSMH Milan Hejduk 10.00 25.00
SSMI Mike Lundin 8.00 20.00
SSML Milan Lucic 25.00 60.00
SSMN Matt Niskanen 8.00 20.00
SSMO Brendan Morrison 8.00 20.00
SSMP Michael Peca
SSMR Mike Ribeiro
SSMT Marty Turco
SSNB Nicklas Backstrom 25.00 60.00
SSNH Nathan Horton 8.00 20.00
SSNZ Nikolai Zherdev 8.00 20.00
SSOK Kyle Okposo
SSOV Alexander Ovechkin 50.00 120.00
SSPB Patrice Bergeron 12.00 30.00
SSPE Patrik Elias
SSPH Chris Phillips 8.00 20.00
SSPK Phil Kessel 12.00 30.00
SSPM Peter Mueller 15.00 40.00
SSPO Denis Potvin 10.00 25.00
SSPR Carey Price 40.00 100.00
SSPS Paul Stastny
SSPT Peter Stastny 12.00 30.00
SSRB Richard Brodeur 10.00 25.00
SSRE Robbie Earl 10.00 25.00
SSRH Ron Hextall 12.00 30.00
SSRI Mike Richards 20.00 50.00
SSRK Ryan Kesler 8.00 20.00
SSRL Rod Langway 15.00 40.00
SSRM Ryan Miller
SSRN Ryan Stone 12.00 30.00
SSRV Rick Vaive
SSSB Steve Bernier 8.00 20.00
SSSG Sam Gagner 20.00 50.00
SSSH Shawn Matthias 12.00 30.00
SSST Matt Stajan 10.00 25.00
SSSV Steve Mason 30.00 80.00
SSSW Stephen Weiss 8.00 20.00
SSTF Theoren Fleury 15.00 40.00
SSTH Tomas Holmstrom 10.00 25.00
SSTR Tuukka Rask
SSVO Tomas Vokoun 12.00 30.00

2008-09 SP Game Used SIGnificant Swatches Patches

STATED PRINT RUN 10 SERIAL #'d SETS
NOT PRICED DUE TO SCARCITY

2008-09 SP Game Used Team Marks

STATED PRINT RUN 50 SERIAL #'d SETS
TMAM Al MacInnis 25.00 60.00
TMAO Alexander Ovechkin/25
TMBC Bobby Clarke 20.00 50.00
TMBF Bernie Federko 15.00 40.00
TMBO Bobby Orr 75.00 150.00
TMCN Cam Neely
TMCP Carey Price 75.00 150.00
TMCW Cam Ward
TMEL Patrik Elias
TMEM Evgeni Malkin
TMEN Evgeni Nabokov 20.00 50.00
TMES Eric Staal 30.00 80.00
TMGA Sam Gagner
TMGF Grant Fuhr 20.00 50.00
TMGH Gordie Howe 75.00 150.00
TMGP Gilbert Perreault 20.00 50.00
TMHE Dany Heatley 25.00 60.00
TMHS Henrik Sedin 20.00 50.00
TMJC Jeff Carter 20.00 50.00
TMJI Jarome Iginla 40.00 100.00
TMJK Jari Kurri
TMJM Joe Mullen
TMJT Jonathan Toews 60.00 150.00
TMLR Luc Robitaille 15.00 40.00
TMMB Martin Brodeur/25
TMME Mark Messier 75.00 150.00
TMMF Marc-Andre Fleury
TMMI Mike Bossy 20.00 50.00
TMMM Mike Modano 20.00 50.00
TMMN Markus Naslund
TMMS Martin St. Louis
TMNL Nicklas Lidstrom
TMPK Patrick Kane 50.00 120.00
TMPS Paul Stastny 20.00 50.00
TMRB Ray Bourque/25 40.00 100.00
TMRG Ryan Getzlaf 25.00 60.00
TMRL Rod Langway 25.00 60.00
TMRM Ryan Miller 20.00 50.00
TMRO Larry Robinson 20.00 50.00
TMSC Sidney Crosby 100.00 175.00
TMST Peter Stastny 20.00 50.00
TMTF Tony Esposito
TMTV Thomas Vanek 20.00 50.00

2008-09 SP Game Used Triple Authentic Fabrics

3AFAM Andrei Markov 6.00 15.00
3AFAO Adam Oates 8.00 20.00
3AFAS Anton Stastny 5.00 12.00
3AFBB Bob Bourne
3AFBL Rob Blake 8.00 20.00
3AFBN Brendan Morrison
3AFBO Pierre-Marc Bouchard
3AFBQ Ray Bourque 15.00 40.00
3AFBU Peter Budaj
3AFBY Billy Smith 6.00 15.00
3AFCA Carey Price
3AFCC Dino Ciccarelli
3AFCH Jonathan Cheechoo
3AFCJ Curtis Joseph 8.00 20.00
3AFCL David Clarkson
3AFCM Mike Commodore
3AFDC Dino Ciccarelli
3AFDG Doug Gilmour 10.00 25.00
3AFDH Dominik Hasek
3AFDP Dion Phaneuf
3AFDT Darcy Tucker 6.00 15.00
3AFEM Evgeni Malkin
3AFES Eric Staal
3AFFM Frank Mahovlich 8.00 20.00
3AFGA Simon Gagne 6.00 15.00
3AFGN Glenn Anderson 6.00 15.00
3AFHA Dale Hawerchuk 8.00 20.00
3AFHL Henrik Lundqvist
3AFHO Marian Hossa
3AFHR Trent Hunter 5.00 12.00
3AFJM Joe Mullen
3AFJT Jonathan Toews
3AFJW Justin Williams
3AFKA Paul Kariya
3AFKK Mike Komisarek 6.00 15.00
3AFKL Kari Lehtonen
3AFKO Mikko Koivu 8.00 20.00
3AFLA Rod Langway 10.00 25.00
3AFLG Robert Lang
3AFLM Lanny McDonald 8.00 20.00
3AFLT Brian Leetch
3AFLW Rod Langway 10.00 25.00
3AFMB Martin Brodeur
3AFMC Bryan McCabe
3AFMD Lanny McDonald 8.00 20.00
3AFME Ryan Malone
3AFMF Marc-Andre Fleury
3AFMG Marian Gaborik 12.00 30.00
3AFMH Milan Hejduk
3AFMK Miikka Kiprusoff
3AFMM Mike Modano 8.00 20.00
3AFMN Markus Naslund
3AFMR Michael Ryder
3AFMT Matt Carle 5.00 12.00
3AFMY Marty Turco
3AFNC Bernie Nicholls 5.00 12.00
3AFNL Nicklas Lidstrom 8.00 20.00
3AFNY Cam Neely
3AFNZ Nikolai Zherdev
3AFOK Olaf Kolzig 8.00 20.00
3AFOV Alexander Ovechkin 30.00 80.00
3AFPB Patrice Bergeron
3AFPE Gilbert Perreault 8.00 20.00
3AFPF Peter Forsberg 12.00 30.00
3AFPK Patrick Roy 25.00 60.00
3AFPM Patrick Marleau 6.00 15.00
3AFPT Peter Stastny 8.00 20.00
3AFRB Rod Brind'Amour
3AFRD Richard Brodeur
3AFRL Roberto Luongo
3AFRM Ryan Miller
3AFRN Rick Nash
3AFRV Rick Vaive 5.00 12.00
3AFRW Ryan Whitney
3AFRY Ryan Smyth
3AFSA Borje Salming 8.00 20.00
3AFSB Steve Bernier
3AFSC Sidney Crosby 40.00 100.00
3AFSF Sergei Fedorov 12.00 30.00
3AFSI Darryl Sittler 8.00 20.00
3AFSK Saku Koivu 8.00 20.00
3AFSL Steve Sullivan
3AFSS Sergei Samsonov 5.00 12.00
3AFST Jordan Staal 12.00 30.00
3AFSU Mats Sundin
3AFSV Steve Shutt
3AFSW Shea Weber 5.00 12.00
3AFTH Tomas Holmstrom
3AFTL Trevor Linden
3AFTP Tomas Plekanec 5.00 12.00
3AFTS Teemu Selanne
3AFTT Tim Thomas
3AFTU Tuomo Ruutu
3AFTW Tiger Williams
3AFVL Vincent Lecavalier
3AFVT Vesa Toskala 8.00 20.00
3AFWR Wade Redden
3AFWW Wojtek Wolski 5.00 12.00
3AFZP Zach Parise
3AFZV Sergei Zubov

2008-09 SP Game Used Triple Authentic Fabrics Gold

*GOLD: .6X TO 1.5X BASE
STATED PRINT RUN 25 SERIAL #'d SETS

2008-09 SP Game Used Triple Authentic Fabrics Platinum

STATED PRINT RUN 10 SERIAL #'d SETS
NOT PRICED DUE TO SCARCITY

2008-09 SP Game Used Triple SIGnificance

STATED PRINT RUN 10 SERIAL #'d SETS
NOT PRICED DUE TO SCARCITY
3SGBFP Martin Brodeur
Marc-Andre Fleury
Carey Price
3SGHSS Paul Stastny
Milan Hejduk
Ryan Smyth
3SGHTK Bobby Hull
Patrick Kane
Jonathan Toews
3SGITP Jarome Iginla
Dion Phaneuf
Mike Cammalleri
3SGKGM Wayne Gretzky
Mark Messier
Jari Kurri
3SGKOM Evgeni Malkin

Alexander Ovechkin
Ilya Kovalchuk
3SGKZK Ilya Kovalchuk
Nikolai Zherdev
Sergei Kostitsyn
3SGLHZ Henrik Zetterberg
Nicklas Lidstrom
Tomas Holmstrom
3SGLRC Mike Richards
Jeff Carter
Joffrey Lupul
3SGLSM Vincent Lecavalier
Martin St. Louis
Ryan Malone
3SGMSS Lanny McDonald
Borje Salming
Darryl Sittler
3SGMTM Marty Turco
Brenden Morrow
Mike Modano
3SGNSS Daniel Sedin
Henrik Sedin
Steve Bernier
3SGPMV Thomas Vanek
Ryan Miller
Jason Pominville
3SGRKL Patrick Roy
Guy Lafleur
Saku Koivu
3SGWSW Cam Ward
Eric Staal
Justin Williams

2009-10 SP Game Used

COMP.SET w/o SPS (100) 30.00 60.00
(101-190) PRINT RUN 999 SER.#'d SETS
(191-200) PRINT RUN 99 SER.#'d SETS
1 Ryan Getzlaf 1.25 3.00
2 Teemu Selanne .75 2.00
3 Saku Koivu .75 2.00
4 Ilya Kovalchuk 1.00 2.50
5 Nik Antropov .60 1.50
6 Bryan Little .75 2.00
7 Zdeno Chara .50 1.25
8 Tim Thomas .75 2.00
9 Marc Savard .50 1.25
10 Milan Lucic .75 2.00
11 Thomas Vanek .75 2.00
12 Ryan Miller .75 2.00
13 Derek Roy .75 2.00
14 Jason Pominville .75 2.00
15 Jarome Iginla 1.50 4.00
16 Olli Jokinen .50 1.25
17 Dion Phaneuf 1.25 3.00
18 Miikka Kiprusoff .75 2.00
19 Eric Staal 1.00 2.50
20 Cam Ward .75 2.00
21 Rod Brind'Amour .60 1.50
22 Jonathan Toews 2.00 5.00
23 Patrick Kane 1.50 4.00
24 Marian Hossa 1.25 3.00
25 Brian Campbell .60 1.50
26 Milan Hejduk .60 1.50
27 Paul Stastny .75 2.00
28 Craig Anderson .60 1.50
29 Rick Nash .75 2.00
30 Steve Mason 1.25 3.00
31 Derick Brassard .75 2.00
32 Mike Modano .75 2.00
33 Mike Ribeiro .50 1.25
34 Marty Turco .60 1.50
35 Henrik Zetterberg 1.50 4.00
36 Pavel Datsyuk .75 2.00
37 Johan Franzen .50 1.25
38 Nicklas Lidstrom 1.00 2.50
39 Ales Hemsky .60 1.50
40 Nikolai Khabibulin .75 2.00
41 Sam Gagner 1.00 2.50
42 Andrew Cogliano 1.00 2.50
43 Tomas Vokoun .50 1.25
44 David Booth .60 1.50
45 Michael Frolik .60 1.50
46 Drew Doughty 1.50 4.00
47 Ryan Smyth .75 2.00
48 Anze Kopitar .75 2.00
49 Mikko Koivu .75 2.00
50 Niklas Backstrom .75 2.00
51 Martin Havlat .60 1.50
52 Carey Price 2.00 5.00
53 Scott Gomez .75 2.00
54 Mike Cammalleri .60 1.50
55 Andrei Markov .60 1.50
56 Pekka Rinne .60 1.50
57 Jason Arnott .50 1.25
58 Shea Weber .60 1.50
59 Martin Brodeur 2.00 5.00
60 Patrik Elias .60 1.50
61 Zach Parise .75 2.00
62 Kyle Okposo .75 2.00
63 Doug Weight .50 1.25
64 Josh Bailey .60 1.50
65 Henrik Lundqvist 1.50 4.00
66 Marian Gaborik 1.25 3.00
67 Chris Drury .60 1.50
68 Jason Spezza 1.00 2.50
69 Daniel Alfredsson .75 2.00
70 Jonathan Cheechoo .75 2.00
71 Mike Richards 1.50 4.00
72 Jeff Carter .75 2.00
73 Simon Gagne .75 2.00
74 Shane Doan .60 1.50
75 Peter Mueller 1.00 2.50
76 Ilya Bryzgalov .60 1.50
77 Sidney Crosby 4.00 10.00
78 Evgeni Malkin 2.00 5.00
79 Marc-Andre Fleury .75 2.00
80 Jordan Staal 1.00 2.50
81 Joe Thornton 1.50 4.00
82 Dany Heatley 1.50 4.00
83 Patrick Marleau .75 2.00
84 Devin Setoguchi .60 1.50
85 David Perron .60 1.50
86 Paul Kariya .75 2.00
87 Patrik Berglund 1.50 4.00
88 Steven Stamkos 2.00 5.00
89 Vincent Lecavalier 1.00 2.50
90 Martin St. Louis .75 2.00
91 Phil Kessel .75 2.00
92 Luke Schenn 1.25 3.00
93 Tomas Kaberle .50 1.25
94 Roberto Luongo 2.00 5.00
95 Daniel Sedin 1.00 2.50
96 Henrik Sedin 1.25 3.00
97 Ryan Kesler .60 1.50
98 Alexander Ovechkin 3.00 8.00
99 Nicklas Backstrom 1.50 4.00
100 Mike Green 1.50 4.00
101 Yannick Weber RC 5.00 12.00
102 Wes O'Neill RC 4.00 10.00
103 Ville Leino RC 5.00 12.00
104 Viktor Stalberg RC 6.00 15.00
105 Tyson Strachan RC 2.50 6.00
106 Tyler Myers RC 15.00 40.00
107 Troy Bodie RC 3.00 8.00
108 Tom Wandell RC 12.00 30.00
109 Tim Wallace RC 2.50 6.00
110 Teemu Laakso RC 2.50 6.00
111 Taylor Chorney RC 4.00 10.00
112 T.J. Galiardi RC 5.00 12.00
113 Spencer Machacek RC 3.00 8.00
114 Sergei Shirokov RC 6.00 15.00
115 Sean Collins RC 3.00 8.00
116 Sean Bentivoglio RC 3.00 8.00
117 Tyler Ennis RC 10.00 25.00
118 Ryan Wilson RC 4.00 10.00
119 Ryan Vesce RC 3.00 8.00
120 Ryan O'Reilly RC 8.00 20.00
121 Riley Armstrong RC 3.00 8.00
122 Riku Helenius RC 4.00 10.00
123 Ray Macias RC 4.00 10.00
124 Peter Regin RC 5.00 12.00
125 Perttu Lindgren RC 4.00 10.00
126 Daniel Larsson RC 5.00 12.00
127 Mike Santorelli RC 2.50 6.00
128 Mike McKenna RC 3.00 8.00
129 Mikael Backlund RC 6.00 15.00
130 Mika Pyorala RC 4.00 10.00
131 Michal Neuvirth RC 10.00 25.00
132 John Carlson RC 8.00 20.00
133 Michael Sauer RC 3.00 8.00
134 Michael Del Zotto RC 8.00 20.00
135 Matt Pelech RC 4.00 10.00
136 Matt Hendricks RC 3.00 8.00
137 Matt Gilroy RC 5.00 12.00
138 Matt Climie RC 3.00 8.00
139 Matt Beleskey RC 4.00 10.00
140 Luca Caputi RC 5.00 12.00
141 Logan Couture RC 8.00 20.00
142 Lars Eller RC 6.00 15.00
143 Kris Chucko RC 3.00 8.00
144 Kevin Westgarth RC 3.00 8.00
145 Kevin Quick RC 2.50 6.00
146 John Scott RC 4.00 10.00
147 John Negrin RC 3.00 8.00
148 Johan Backlund RC 4.00 10.00
149 Joel Rechlicz RC 4.00 10.00
150 Jhonas Enroth RC 5.00 12.00
151 Jesse Joensuu RC 5.00 12.00
152 Jay Rosehill RC 2.50 6.00
153 Jay Beagle RC 4.00 10.00
154 Jason Demers RC 3.00 8.00
155 Matthew Corrente RC 4.00 10.00
156 Jamie Fraser RC 3.00 8.00
157 James Reimer RC 4.00 10.00
158 Devan Dubnyk RC 5.00 12.00
159 Jamie Sifers RC 3.00 8.00
160 Ivan Vishnevskiy RC 5.00 12.00
161 Ilkka Pikkarainen RC 4.00 10.00
162 Geoff Kinrade RC 4.00 10.00
163 Frazer McLaren RC 2.50 6.00
164 Bobby Sanguinetti RC 3.00 8.00
165 Erik Karlsson RC 12.00 30.00
166 Dmitry Kulikov RC 4.00 10.00
167 Derek Peltier RC 2.50 6.00
168 Davis Drewiske RC 4.00 10.00
169 David Van Der Gulik RC 3.00 8.00
170 David Sloane RC 5.00 12.00
171 David Schlemko RC 3.00 8.00
172 Jakub Kindl RC 5.00 12.00
173 Colin Wilson RC 8.00 20.00
174 Cody Franson RC 4.00 10.00
175 Christian Hanson RC 5.00 12.00
176 Chris Durno RC 3.00 8.00
177 Cal O'Reilly RC 4.00 10.00
178 Byron Bitz RC 3.00 8.00
179 Bryan Rodney RC 3.00 8.00
180 Brian Salcido RC 3.00 8.00
181 Brandon Segal RC 3.00 8.00
182 Brad Marchand RC 5.00 12.00
183 Benn Ferriero RC 4.00 10.00
184 Ben Lovejoy RC 6.00 15.00
185 Artem Anisimov RC 5.00 12.00
186 Andrew MacDonald RC 3.00 8.00
187 Alexander Sulzer RC 2.50 6.00
188 Alec Martinez RC 2.50 6.00
189 Aaron MacKenzie RC 5.00 12.00
190 Aaron Gagnon RC 2.50 6.00
191 Jamie Benn RC/99 15.00 40.00
192 Victor Hedman RC/99 20.00 50.00
193 Tyler Bozak RC/99 25.00 60.00
194 Antti Niemi RC/99 30.00 80.00
195 Michael Grabner RC/99 12.00 30.00
196 Evander Kane RC/99 25.00 60.00
197 Jonas Gustavsson RC/99 25.00 60.00
198 James van Riemsdyk RC/99 25.00 60.00
199 Matt Duchene RC/99 60.00 120.00
200 John Tavares RC/99 60.00 120.00

2009-10 SP Game Used Gold

*GOLD 1-100: 1.2X TO 3X BASE
1-100 PRINT RUN 100 SER.#'d SETS
*GOLD ROOKIES 101-190: .5X TO 1.2X BASE
*GOLD ROOKIES 191-200: .25X TO .6X BASE
101-200 PRINT RUN 50 SER.#'d SETS
199 Matt Duchene 30.00 80.00
200 John Tavares 60.00 120.00

2009-10 SP Game Used Gold Spectrum

STATED PRINT RUN 1 SER.#'d SET
NOT PRICED DUE TO SCARCITY

2009-10 SP Game Used Silver Spectrum

STATED PRINT RUN 10 SER.#'d SETS
NOT PRICED DUE TO SCARCITY

2009-10 SP Game Used Authentic Fabrics

OVERALL G-U/AU ODDS 1 PER PACK
AFAC Andrew Cogliano 6.00 15.00
AFAF Alexander Frolov 4.00 10.00
AFAM Andrei Markov 4.00 10.00
AFAO Adam Oates 5.00 12.00
AFAS Alexander Semin 5.00 12.00
AFBC Brian Campbell 4.00 10.00
AFBL Brian Leetch 5.00 12.00
AFBO David Booth 3.00 8.00
AFBW Blake Wheeler 6.00 15.00
AFCN Cam Neely 8.00 20.00
AFCP Carey Price 12.00 30.00
AFDD Drew Doughty 10.00 25.00
AFDE Derick Brassard 5.00 12.00
AFDG Doug Gilmour 5.00 12.00
AFDP Dion Phaneuf 8.00 20.00
AFDR Derek Roy 5.00 12.00
AFDS Daniel Sedin 6.00 15.00
AFDY Darcy Tucker 4.00 10.00
AFEM Evgeni Malkin 12.00 30.00
AFGF Grant Fuhr 6.00 15.00
AFGH Gordie Howe 15.00 40.00
AFGI Claude Giroux 10.00 25.00
AFGR Mike Green 10.00 25.00
AFGW Gump Worsley 8.00 20.00
AFHL Henrik Lundqvist 10.00 25.00
AFHS Henrik Sedin 8.00 20.00
AFHZ Henrik Zetterberg 10.00 25.00
AFIK Ilya Kovalchuk 6.00 15.00
AFJA Jason Arnott 3.00 8.00
AFJB Jay Bouwmeester 5.00 12.00
AFJC Jeff Carter 5.00 12.00
AFJD J.P. Dumont 3.00 8.00
AFJF Johan Franzen 3.00 8.00
AFJP Jason Pominville 5.00 12.00
AFJS Jason Spezza 6.00 15.00
AFJT Joe Thornton 10.00 25.00
AFJV Jakub Voracek 5.00 12.00
AFKE Phil Kessel 5.00 12.00
AFKM Mike Komisarek 4.00 10.00
AFLS Luke Schenn 8.00 20.00
AFMB Martin Brodeur 12.00 30.00
AFMC Mike Cammalleri 4.00 10.00
AFME Ryan Malone
AFMF Marc-Andre Fleury 5.00 12.00
AFMG Marian Gaborik 8.00 20.00
AFMK Miikka Kiprusoff 5.00 12.00
AFML Milan Lucic 5.00 12.00
AFMM Mike Modano 6.00 15.00
AFMR Mike Richards 10.00 25.00
AFMS Martin St. Louis
AFMT Marty Turco 4.00 10.00
AFNB Nicklas Backstrom 10.00 25.00
AFNF Nick Foligno 5.00 12.00
AFNH Nathan Horton 3.00 8.00
AFNL Nicklas Lidstrom 6.00 15.00
AFOV Alexander Ovechkin 15.00 40.00
AFPA Paul Stastny 5.00 12.00
AFPB Patrik Berglund 10.00 25.00
AFPD Pavel Datsyuk 5.00 12.00
AFPK Patrick Kane 10.00 25.00
AFPO Patrick O'Sullivan 4.00 10.00
AFPR Patrick Roy 15.00 40.00
AFRH Roman Hamrlik 3.00 8.00
AFRK Ryan Kesler 4.00 10.00
AFRL Roberto Luongo 12.00 30.00
AFRM Ryan Miller 5.00 12.00
AFRN Rick Nash 5.00 12.00
AFRS Ryan Smyth 5.00 12.00
AFSC Sidney Crosby 15.00 40.00
AFSG Sam Gagner 6.00 15.00
AFSK Saku Koivu 5.00 12.00
AFSM Steve Mason 8.00 20.00
AFSS Steven Stamkos 12.00 30.00
AFST Jordan Staal 6.00 15.00
AFSW Shea Weber 4.00 10.00
AFSY Steve Yzerman 15.00 40.00
AFTK Tomas Kaberle 3.00 8.00
AFTT Tim Thomas 5.00 12.00
AFTU Tuukka Rask 6.00 15.00
AFTV Thomas Vanek
AFVL Vincent Lecavalier 6.00 15.00
AFVO Tomas Vokoun 5.00 12.00
AFWG Wayne Gretzky 20.00 50.00
AFZP Zach Parise 5.00 12.00

2009-10 SP Game Used Authentic Fabrics Gold

*SINGLES: .5X TO 1.2X BASIC INSERTS
STATED PRINT RUN 100 SER.#'d SETS

2009-10 SP Game Used Authentic Fabrics Patches

*SINGLES: 1X TO 2.5X BASIC INSERTS
STATED PRINT RUN 35 SER.#'d SETS

2009-10 SP Game Used Authentic Fabrics Dual

STATED PRINT RUN 100 SER.#'d SETS
AF2AA Alexander Frolov 6.00 15.00
Anze Kopitar
AF2AD Jason Arnott 4.00 10.00
J.P. Dumont
AF2AG Andrew Cogliano 8.00 20.00
Sam Gagner
AF2AW Jason Arnott 5.00 12.00
Shea Weber
AF2BO Dustin Brown 5.00 12.00
Patrick O'Sullivan
AF2BP Martin Brodeur 15.00 40.00
Zach Parise
AF2BS Rod Brind'Amour 8.00 20.00
Eric Staal
AF2BV Derick Brassard
Jakub Voracek
AF2CG Wendel Clark 10.00 25.00
Doug Gilmour
AF2CM Sidney Crosby 20.00 50.00
Evgeni Malkin
AF2CO Sidney Crosby 40.00 80.00
Alexander Ovechkin
AF2CT Brian Campbell
Jonathan Toews
AF2DB Drew Doughty 12.00 30.00
Zach Bogosian
AF2DH Henrik Sedin 10.00 25.00
Daniel Sedin
AF2DL Shane Doan 5.00 12.00
Matthew Lombardi
AF2DR Ryan Smyth 6.00 15.00
Dustin Brown
AF2DW J.P. Dumont 5.00 12.00
Shea Weber
AF2DZ Pavel Datsyuk 12.00 30.00
Henrik Zetterberg
AF2EC Eric Staal 8.00 20.00
Cam Ward
AF2EF Ray Emery 6.00 15.00
Marc-Andre Fleury
AF2FC Marc-Andre Fleury 20.00 50.00
Sidney Crosby
AF2FK Grant Fuhr 8.00 20.00
Jari Kurri
AF2FS Marc-Andre Fleury 8.00 20.00
Jordan Staal
AF2GC Scott Gomez 6.00 15.00
Mike Cammalleri
AF2GD Mike Green 12.00 30.00
Drew Doughty
AF2GK Marian Gaborik 10.00 25.00
Phil Kessel
AF2GM Doug Gilmour 6.00 15.00
Al MacInnis
AF2HB Nathan Horton 4.00 10.00
David Booth
AF2HD Tomas Holmstrom 6.00 15.00
Pavel Datsyuk
AF2HF Tomas Holmstrom 5.00 12.00
Johan Franzen
AF2HH Marian Hossa 10.00 25.00
Cristobal Huet
AF2HM Roman Hamrlik 5.00 12.00
Andrei Markov
AF2HW Wade Redden 12.00 30.00
Henrik Lundqvist
AF2IK Jarome Iginla 12.00 30.00
Miikka Kiprusoff
AF2JC Jeff Carter 12.00 30.00
Claude Giroux
AF2JD Jay Bouwmeester 10.00 25.00
Dion Phaneuf
AF2JI Olli Jokinen 12.00 30.00
Jarome Iginla
AF2KL Ilya Kovalchuk 8.00 20.00
Kari Lehtonen
AF2KP Paul Kariya 6.00 15.00
David Perron
AF2KR Roberto Luongo 15.00 40.00
Miikka Kiprusoff
AF2KS Patrick Kane 15.00 40.00
Steven Stamkos
AF2LI Vincent Lecavalier 12.00 30.00
Jarome Iginla
AF2LN Cam Neely 10.00 25.00
Milan Lucic
AF2LR Roberto Luongo 15.00 40.00
Mason Raymond
AF2LS Nicklas Lidstrom
Borje Salming
AF2LZ Nicklas Lidstrom 12.00 30.00
Henrik Zetterberg
AF2MM Mike Modano 6.00 15.00
Marty Turco
AF2MR Mike Modano 6.00 15.00
Brad Richards
AF2MS Lanny McDonald
Darryl Sittler
AF2MW Marek Svatos 4.00 10.00
Wojtek Wolski
AF2NB Cam Neely 10.00 25.00
Ray Bourque
AF2NM Rick Nash 10.00 25.00
Steve Mason
AF2NV Rick Nash 6.00 15.00
Jakub Voracek
AF2OB Alexander Ovechkin 20.00 50.00
Nicklas Backstrom
AF2OM Alexander Ovechkin 20.00 50.00
Evgeni Malkin
AF2PK Zach Parise 12.00 30.00
Patrick Kane
AF2PM Carey Price 15.00 40.00
Steve Mason
AF2PP Peter Stastny 6.00 15.00
Paul Stastny
AF2PR Jason Pominville
Derek Roy
AF2RC Mike Richards 12.00 30.00
Jeff Carter
AF2RD Daniel Sedin 8.00 20.00
Ryan Kesler
AF2RJ Jason Pominville 6.00 15.00
Ryan Miller
AF2RL Patrick Roy 20.00 50.00
Roberto Luongo
AF2RR Roberto Luongo 15.00 40.00
Ryan Kesler
AF2RS Ryan Miller
Drew Stafford
AF2RV Derek Roy 6.00 15.00
Thomas Vanek
AF2SB Jarret Stoll 5.00 12.00
Dustin Brown
AF2SD Ryan Smyth 12.00 30.00
Drew Doughty
AF2SR Steve Shutt
Larry Robinson
AF2SS Eric Staal 8.00 20.00
Jordan Staal
AF2SW Marek Svatos 6.00 15.00
Paul Stastny
AF2TD Thomas Vanek
Drew Stafford
AF2TL Tomas Kaberle 10.00 25.00
Luke Schenn
AF2TM Tim Thomas 6.00 15.00
Milan Lucic
AF2TR Michael Ryder 6.00 15.00
Tim Thomas
AF2VH Tomas Vokoun 6.00 15.00
Nathan Horton
AF2VS Vincent Lecavalier 15.00 40.00
Steven Stamkos
AF2WH Stephen Weiss
Nathan Horton
AF2YB Steve Yzerman 20.00 50.00
Scotty Bowman
AF2YG Steve Yzerman 25.00 60.00
Wayne Gretzky
AF2ZL Luke Schenn 10.00 25.00
Zach Bogosian

2009-10 SP Game Used Authentic Fabrics Dual Patches

*SINGLES: .8X TO 2X BASIC INSERTS
STATED PRINT RUN 25 SER.#'d SETS
AF2DZ Pavel Datsyuk 30.00 80.00
Henrik Zetterberg
AF2KP Paul Kariya 15.00 40.00
David Perron
AF2KS Patrick Kane 40.00 100.00
Steven Stamkos
AF2NV Rick Nash 15.00 40.00
Jakub Voracek
AF2OB Alexander Ovechkin 40.00 100.00
Nicklas Backstrom
AF2OM Alexander Ovechkin 40.00 100.00
Evgeni Malkin

2009-10 SP Game Used Authentic Fabrics Eights

STATED PRINT RUN 5 SER.#'d SETS
NOT PRICED DUE TO SCARCITY

2009-10 SP Game Used Authentic Fabrics Eights Patches

STATED PRINT RUN 1 SER.#'d SET
NOT PRICED DUE TO SCARCITY

2009-10 SP Game Used Authentic Fabrics Fives

STATED PRINT RUN 8 SER.#'d SETS
NOT PRICED DUE TO SCARCITY

2009-10 SP Game Used Authentic Fabrics Fives Patches

STATED PRINT RUN 7 SER.#'d SETS
NOT PRICED DUE TO SCARCITY

2009-10 SP Game Used Authentic Fabrics Quads

STATED PRINT RUN 10 SER.#'d SETS
NOT PRICED DUE TO SCARCITY

2009-10 SP Game Used Authentic Fabrics Quads Patches

STATED PRINT RUN 8 SER.#'d SETS
NOT PRICED DUE TO SCARCITY

2009-10 SP Game Used Authentic Fabrics Sevens

STATED PRINT RUN 6 SER.#'d SETS
NOT PRICED DUE TO SCARCITY

2009-10 SP Game Used Authentic Fabrics Sevens Patches

STATED PRINT RUN 3 SER.#'d SETS
NOT PRICED DUE TO SCARCITY

2009-10 SP Game Used Authentic Fabrics Sixes

STATED PRINT RUN 7 SER.#'d SETS
NOT PRICED DUE TO SCARCITY

2009-10 SP Game Used Authentic Fabrics Sixes Patches

STATED PRINT RUN 5 SER.#'d SETS
NOT PRICED DUE TO SCARCITY

2009-10 SP Game Used Authentic Fabrics Triples

STATED PRINT RUN 25 SER.#'d SETS
AF3ADW Jason Arnott
J.P. Dumont
Shea Weber
AF3ASF Daniel Alfredsson 10.00 25.00
Jason Spezza
Nick Foligno
AF3BLM Martin Brodeur 20.00 50.00
Henrik Lundqvist
Ryan Miller
AF3BSO Dustin Brown 8.00 20.00
Drew Stafford
Kyle Okposo
AF3BSW Rod Brind'Amour
Eric Staal
Cam Ward
AF3BVM Derick Brassard 12.00 30.00
Jakub Voracek
Steve Mason
AF3CBP Martin Brodeur 20.00 50.00
Zach Parise
David Clarkson
AF3CMS Sidney Crosby 40.00 100.00
Evgeni Malkin
Jordan Staal
AF3COM Sidney Crosby 40.00 100.00
Alexander Ovechkin
Evgeni Malkin
AF3DSB Drew Doughty 15.00 40.00
Luke Schenn
Zach Bogosian
AF3DSS Pavol Demitra
Henrik Sedin
Daniel Sedin
AF3ERC Ray Emery 15.00 40.00
Mike Richards
Jeff Carter
AF3FBK Alexander Frolov 8.00 20.00
Dustin Brown
Anze Kopitar
AF3FCM Marc-Andre Fleury 40.00 100.00
Sidney Crosby
Evgeni Malkin
AF3FGT Georges Laraque 8.00 20.00
Donald Brashear
Milan Lucic
AF3GMP Scott Gomez 20.00 50.00
Andrei Markov
Carey Price
AF3HTK Marian Hossa 20.00 50.00
Jonathan Toews
Patrick Kane
AF3IKP Jarome Iginla 12.00 30.00
Miikka Kiprusoff
Dion Phaneuf
AF3KKS Tomas Kaberle 12.00 30.00
Mike Komisarek
Luke Schenn
AF3KOG Nikolai Khabibulin
Patrick O'Sullivan
Sam Gagner
AF3KSM Ilya Kovalchuk 20.00 50.00
Alexander Semin
Evgeni Malkin
AF3LHN Vincent Lecavalier 15.00 40.00
Dany Heatley
Rick Nash
AF3LHZ Nicklas Lidstrom 15.00 40.00
Tomas Holmstrom
Henrik Zetterberg
AF3LKR Roberto Luongo
Ryan Kesler
Mason Raymond
AF3LMS Vincent Lecavalier 20.00 50.00
Ryan Malone
Steven Stamkos
AF3LOD Nicklas Lidstrom 10.00 25.00
Chris Osgood
Pavel Datsyuk
AF3LSS Vincent Lecavalier 20.00 50.00
Martin St. Louis
Steven Stamkos
AF3MAH Lanny McDonald 8.00 20.00
Glenn Anderson
Dale Hawerchuk
AF3MMM Lanny McDonald
Joe Mullen
Al MacInnis
AF3MRT Mike Modano
Mike Ribeiro
Marty Turco
AF3MSH Lanny McDonald
Steve Shutt
Dale Hawerchuk
AF3MVS Ryan Miller 8.00 20.00
Thomas Vanek
Drew Stafford
AF3NBV Rick Nash 8.00 20.00
Derick Brassard
Jakub Voracek
AF3OCG Patrick O'Sullivan 10.00 25.00
Andrew Cogliano
Sam Gagner
AF3OGB Alexander Ovechkin 30.00 80.00
Mike Green
Nicklas Backstrom
AF3PHM Roman Hamrlik 15.00 40.00
Andrei Markov
Tomas Plekanec
AF3PMC Andrei Markov 15.00 40.00
Mike Cammalleri
Tomas Plekanec
AF3PMV Jason Pominville 8.00 20.00
Ryan Miller
Thomas Vanek
AF3PVS Jason Pominville 8.00 20.00
Thomas Vanek
Drew Stafford
AF3RBM Patrick Roy 25.00 60.00
Martin Brodeur
Steve Mason
AF3RCG Mike Richards 15.00 40.00
Jeff Carter
Claude Giroux
AF3RGL Wade Redden 15.00 40.00
Marian Gaborik
Henrik Lundqvist
AF3RHD Roberto Luongo 20.00 50.00
Henrik Sedin
Daniel Sedin
AF3SBS Sergei Samsonov 10.00 25.00
Rod Brind'Amour
Eric Staal
AF3SGB Alexander Semin
Mike Green
Nicklas Backstrom
AF3SNT Jason Spezza 20.00 50.00
Rick Nash
Jonathan Toews
AF3SOB Alexander Semin
Alexander Ovechkin
Nicklas Backstrom
AF3SSK Henrik Sedin 30.00 80.00
Daniel Sedin
Ryan Kesler
AF3SSS Eric Staal 10.00 25.00
Jordan Staal
Marc Staal
AF3VHB Tomas Vokoun 8.00 20.00
Nathan Horton
David Booth
AF3YGM Steve Yzerman 40.00 100.00
Wayne Gretzky
Mark Messier
AF3DROP Georges Laraque 8.00 20.00
Mike Komisarek
Milan Lucic

2009-10 SP Game Used Authentic Fabrics Triples Patches

STATED PRINT RUN 15 SER.#'d SETS
NOT PRICED DUE TO SCARCITY

2009-10 SP Game Used By The Letter

SEE CHECKLIST FOR PRINT RUNS
NOT PRICED DUE TO SCARCITY
AFWG Ales Hemsky/6
BLAK Anze Kopitar/7
BLAO Alexander Ovechkin/8
BLBC Brian Campbell/8
BLBD Brandon Dubinsky/8
BLBM Brenden Morrow/6
BLBW Blake Wheeler/7
BLCO Chris Osgood/6
BLCP Carey Price/5
BLCW Cam Ward/4
BLDA Daniel Alfredsson/10
BLDD Drew Doughty/7
BLDH Dale Hawerchuk/9
BLDP Dion Phaneuf/7
BLDS Daniel Sedin/5
BLEM Evgeni Malkin/6
BLJI Jarome Iginla/6
BLJS Jason Spezza/6
BLJT Jonathan Toews/5
BLKT Keith Tkachuk/7
BLLR Luc Robitaille/10
BLMB Martin Brodeur/7
BLMK Miikka Kiprusoff/9
BLMR Mike Richards/8
BLMS Mats Sundin/6
BLPE Corey Perry/5
BLSA Joe Sakic/5
BLSC Sidney Crosby/6
BLSM Steve Mason/5
BLSY Steve Yzerman/7
BLTH Tomas Holmstrom/9
BLTS Teemu Selanne/7
BLTT Tim Thomas/6
BLTV Thomas Vanek/5
BLWG Wayne Gretzky/7
BLZP Zach Parise/6

2009-10 SP Game Used Extra SIGnificance

STATED PRINT RUN 25 SER.#'d SETS
SIGTV Jean Beliveau 30.00 60.00
Butch Bouchard
XSGBO T.J. Oshie 20.00 50.00
Patrik Berglund
XSGBP David Backes
Alex Pietrangelo
XSGCG Andrew Cogliano 12.00 30.00
Sam Gagner
XSGCS Carey Price 25.00 60.00
Steve Mason
XSGDZ Pavel Datsyuk 20.00 50.00
Henrik Zetterberg
XSGEE Phil Esposito 20.00 50.00
Tony Esposito
XSGEJ Eric Staal 12.00 30.00
Jordan Staal
XSGFH Grant Fuhr 12.00 30.00
Dale Hawerchuk
XSGGB Mike Green 20.00 50.00
Nicklas Backstrom
XSGGK Jari Kurri 125.00 200.00
Wayne Gretzky
XSGGL Marian Gaborik 20.00 50.00
Henrik Lundqvist
XSGGS Luke Schenn 25.00 60.00
Jonas Gustavsson
XSGGW Mike Green 20.00 50.00
Shea Weber
XSGHD Henrik Sedin 25.00 50.00
Daniel Sedin
XSGHR Bobby Ryan 20.00 50.00
Jonas Hiller
XSGIP Jarome Iginla 20.00 50.00
Dion Phaneuf
XSGJB Jack Johnson 10.00 25.00
Jonathan Bernier
XSGJM John Tavares 75.00 150.00
Matt Duchene
XSGKJ Phil Kessel 25.00 60.00
Jonas Gustavsson
XSGKO Terry O'Reilly 10.00 25.00
Daniel Carcillo
XSGLD Ted Lindsay
Alex Delvecchio
XSGLM Mario Lemieux 75.00 150.00
Evgeni Malkin
XSGLS Vincent Lecavalier
Steven Stamkos
XSGML Brian Leetch
Mark Messier
XSGMV Ryan Miller
Thomas Vanek
XSGOB Kyle Okposo 10.00 25.00
Josh Bailey
XSGOE Erik Ersberg
Oscar Moller
XSGOH Bobby Orr 125.00 200.00
Bobby Hull
XSGOK Ilya Kovalchuk 40.00 100.00
Alexander Ovechkin
XSGOM Alexander Ovechkin 60.00 120.00
Evgeni Malkin
XSGRB Patrick Roy 75.00 150.00
Martin Brodeur
XSGRM Andrei Markov 12.00 30.00
Larry Robinson
XSGTK Jonathan Toews 40.00 80.00
Patrick Kane
XSGYG Steve Yzerman 125.00 200.00
Gordie Howe
XSGZM Henrik Zetterberg 25.00 60.00
Evgeni Malkin

2009-10 SP Game Used Fight Straps

STATED PRINT RUN 10 SER.#'d SETS
NOT PRICED DUE TO SCARCITY
BLTS Ales Hemsky
FSAM Al MacInnis
FSAO Alexander Ovechkin
FSBB Bob Bourne
FSBC Bobby Clarke
FSBH Bobby Hull
FSBL Brian Leetch
FSBR Brad Richards
FSBS Brendan Shanahan
FSBW Blake Wheeler
FSCN Cam Neely
FSCP Carey Price
FSDA Daniel Alfredsson
FSDC Dino Ciccarelli
FSDG Doug Gilmour
FSDH Dany Heatley
FSDP Dion Phaneuf
FSEM Evgeni Malkin
FSES Eric Staal
FSFM Frank Mahovlich

FSGF Grant Fuhr
FSGP Gilbert Perreault
FSHL Henrik Lundqvist
FSHZ Henrik Zetterberg
FSIK Ilya Kovalchuk
FSJC Jeff Carter
FSJI Jarome Iginla
FSJK Jari Kurri
FSJS Jason Spezza
FSJT Joe Thornton
FSKO Kyle Okposo
FSKS Phil Kessel
FSLA Guy Lafleur
FSLM Lanny McDonald
FSLR Larry Robinson
FSLU Milan Lucic
FSMB Martin Brodeur
FSMD Marcel Dionne
FSMH Marian Hossa
FSMK Miikka Kiprusoff
FSML Mario Lemieux
FSMM Mark Messier
FSMR Mike Richards
FSMS Mats Sundin
FSPK Patrick Kane
FSPM Patrick Marleau
FSPR Patrick Roy
FSRB Ray Bourque
FSRG Ryan Getzlaf
FSRL Roberto Luongo
FSRN Rick Nash
FSSA Joe Sakic
FSSC Sidney Crosby
FSSM Stan Mikita
FSSN Scott Niedermayer
FSSY Steve Yzerman
FSTO Jonathan Toews
FSVL Vincent Lecavalier
FSWG Wayne Gretzky
FSZC Zdeno Chara

2009-10 SP Game Used Fight Straps Combos

STATED PRINT RUN 2 SER.#'d SETS
NOT PRICED DUE TO SCARCITY
DISST Derick Brassard
James Neal
FSCCB Brian Rafalski
Corey Perry
FSCCF Chris Chelios
Theoren Fleury
FSCCG Sergei Gonchar
Guy Carbonneau
FSCCO Sidney Crosby
Alexander Ovechkin
FSCGA Daniel Alfredsson
Doug Gilmour
FSCGC Bill Guerin
David Clarkson
FSCGJ Jack Johnson
Sam Gagner
FSCHC Bobby Hull
Bobby Clarke
FSCKL Mike Komisarek
Milan Lucic
FSCKW Ilya Kovalchuk
Ian White
FSCLB Georges Laraque
Donald Brashear
FSCLH Marian Hossa
Vincent Lecavalier
FSCLI Vincent Lecavalier
Jarome Iginla
FSCLS Georges Laraque
Jody Shelley
FSCMA Jason Arnott
Mark Messier
FSCMM Stan Mikita
Frank Mahovlich
FSCMZ Henrik Zetterberg
Evgeni Malkin
FSCNB Cam Neely
Donald Brashear
FSCND Scott Niedermayer
Pavel Datsyuk
FSCOM Alexander Ovechkin
Evgeni Malkin
FSCOR Mike Richards
Alexander Ovechkin
FSCPB Dion Phaneuf
Steve Bernier
FSCPC Chris Chelios
Chris Pronger
FSCPG Dion Phaneuf
Ryan Getzlaf
FSCPS Jody Shelley
George Parros
FSCRD Mike Richards
Brandon Dubinsky
FSCRJ Brad Richards
Olli Jokinen
FSCRO Patrick Roy
Chris Osgood
FSCRR Brad Richards
Mike Ribeiro
FSCSC Chris Chelios
Teemu Selanne
FSCSG Joe Sakic
Doug Gilmour
FSCSP Georges Laraque
George Parros
FSCSS Alexander Semin
Marc Staal
FSCTG Joe Thornton
Ryan Getzlaf
FSCVK Tomas Vokoun
Miikka Kiprusoff
FSCWC Jeff Carter
Ryan Whitney
FSCYC Chris Chelios
Steve Yzerman
FSCYS Steve Yzerman
Peter Stastny

2009-10 SP Game Used Game Gear

STATED PRINT RUN 3 SER.#'d SETS
NOT PRICED DUE TO SCARCITY
FSSY Alexander Frolov
GGAH Ales Hemsky
GGAK Andrei Kostitsyn
GGAM Al MacInnis
GGAO Alexander Ovechkin
GGDB David Booth
GGDD Drew Doughty
GGDE Derick Brassard
GGDG Doug Gilmour
GGDP Dion Phaneuf
GGDR Derek Roy
GGDU Dustin Brown
GGEM Evgeni Malkin
GGES Eric Staal
GGFM Frank Mahovlich
GGGP Gilbert Perreault
GGHL Henrik Lundqvist
GGHZ Henrik Zetterberg
GGIK Ilya Kovalchuk
GGJB Josh Bailey
GGJC Jeff Carter
GGJI Jarome Iginla
GGJS Jason Spezza
GGJT Joe Thornton
GGJV Jakub Voracek
GGKE Phil Kessel
GGKO Anze Kopitar
GGLM Lanny McDonald
GGLR Luc Robitaille
GGLS Luke Schenn
GGLU Milan Lucic
GGMB Martin Brodeur
GGMK Miikka Kiprusoff
GGML Mario Lemieux
GGMM Mark Messier
GGMR Mike Richards
GGNL Nicklas Lidstrom
GGOJ Olli Jokinen
GGOK Kyle Okposo
GGPD Pavel Datsyuk
GGPK Patrick Kane
GGPR Patrick Roy
GGPS Patrick Sharp
GGRB Ray Bourque
GGRG Ryan Getzlaf
GGRL Roberto Luongo
GGRM Ryan Miller
GGRN Rick Nash
GGRS Ryan Smyth
GGSA Joe Sakic
GGSC Sidney Crosby
GGSG Sam Gagner
GGSS Steven Stamkos
GGST Paul Stastny
GGTO Jonathan Toews
GGWG Wayne Gretzky
GGYZ Steve Yzerman
GGZP Zach Parise

2009-10 SP Game Used Inked Sweaters

STATED PRINT RUN 50 SER.#'d SETS
CARDS #'d TO 15 NOT PRICED DUE TO SCARCITY
ISAC Andrew Cogliano 10.00 25.00
ISBW Blake Wheeler 10.00 25.00
ISCW Cam Ward 8.00 20.00
ISDC Matt Duchene 40.00 80.00
ISDD Drew Doughty 15.00 40.00
ISDP Dion Phaneuf 12.00 30.00
ISDS Daniel Sedin 10.00 25.00
ISDZ Michael Del Zotto 15.00 40.00
ISEK Evander Kane 20.00 50.00
ISEM Evgeni Malkin/15
ISGB Michael Grabner 10.00 25.00
ISGH Gordie Howe/15
ISGO Scott Gomez 8.00 20.00
ISGR Mike Green 15.00 40.00
ISGV Jonas Gustavsson 30.00 60.00
ISGX Claude Giroux 15.00 40.00
ISHL Henrik Lundqvist 25.00 50.00
ISHS Henrik Sedin 12.00 30.00
ISJA Jason Arnott 5.00 12.00
ISJC Jeff Carter 8.00 20.00
ISJD J.P. Dumont 5.00 12.00
ISJI Jarome Iginla/15
ISJS Jordan Staal 10.00 25.00
ISJV Jakub Voracek 8.00 20.00
ISLS Luke Schenn 12.00 30.00
ISMB Martin Brodeur/15
ISMF Marc-Andre Fleury 20.00 50.00
ISMG Marian Gaborik 12.00 30.00
ISML Mario Lemieux/15
ISNF Nick Foligno 8.00 20.00
ISNH Nathan Horton
ISNK Nikolai Khabibulin 8.00 20.00
ISNL Nicklas Lidstrom 10.00 25.00
ISOV Alexander Ovechkin/15
ISPM Peter Mueller 10.00 25.00
ISPR Patrick Roy/15
ISPS Paul Stastny 8.00 20.00
ISSC Sidney Crosby/15
ISSD Shane Doan 6.00 15.00
ISSG Sam Gagner 10.00 25.00
ISSM Steve Mason 12.00 30.00
ISST Steven Stamkos 20.00 50.00
ISSW Shea Weber 6.00 15.00
ISSY Steve Yzerman/15
ISTA John Tavares 60.00 120.00
ISVO Tomas Vokoun 8.00 20.00
ISVR James van Riemsdyk 20.00 50.00
ISWG Wayne Gretzky/15

2009-10 SP Game Used Inked Sweaters Dual

STATED PRINT RUN 15 SER.#'d SETS
NOT PRICED DUE TO SCARCITY
AF6LA Jason Arnott
J.P. Dumont
DISBL Martin Brodeur
Henrik Lundqvist
DISBW Johnny Bucyk
Blake Wheeler
DISCG Andrew Cogliano
Sam Gagner
DISDH Henrik Sedin
Daniel Sedin
DISFS Marc-Andre Fleury
Jordan Staal
DISGM Scott Gomez
Andrei Markov
DISGY Steve Yzerman
Wayne Gretzky
DISHH Bobby Hull
Gordie Howe
DISHL Nicklas Lidstrom
Tomas Holmstrom
DISIP Jarome Iginla
Dion Phaneuf
DISIT Joe Thornton
Jarome Iginla
DISLM Mario Lemieux
Evgeni Malkin
DISLZ Nicklas Lidstrom
Henrik Zetterberg
DISML Brian Leetch
Mark Messier
DISNO Cam Neely
Adam Oates
DISOB Kyle Okposo
Josh Bailey
DISOR Luc Robitaille
Alexander Ovechkin
DISPM Carey Price
Steve Mason
DISPP Peter Stastny
Paul Stastny
DISRB Patrick Roy
Ray Bourque
DISRK Evander Kane
James van Riemsdyk
DISSM Steve Mason
Steven Stamkos
DISST John Tavares
Steven Stamkos
DISTD John Tavares
Matt Duchene
DISVH Tomas Vokoun
Nathan Horton
DISYL Steve Yzerman
Nicklas Lidstrom
DISZH Tomas Holmstrom
Henrik Zetterberg

2009-10 SP Game Used Legends Classic

STATED PRINT RUN 100 SER.#'d SETS
LCBB Bob Bourne 4.00 10.00
LCBS Billy Smith 8.00 20.00
LCDH Dale Hawerchuk 5.00 12.00
LCGA Glenn Anderson 5.00 12.00
LCLM Lanny McDonald 5.00 12.00
LCPS Peter Stastny 5.00 12.00
LCRL Rod Langway 4.00 10.00
LCSA Borje Salming 5.00 12.00
LCSS Steve Shutt 5.00 12.00
LCTW Tiger Williams 4.00 10.00

2009-10 SP Game Used Legends Classic Patches

*SINGLES: .6X TO 1.5X BASIC INSERTS
STATED PRINT RUN 25 SER.#'d SETS

2009-10 SP Game Used Letter Marks

STATED PRINT RUN 50 SER.#'d SETS
LMAA Artem Anisimov 20.00 50.00
LMAL Andrew Ladd 15.00 40.00
LMBO Mikkel Boedker 12.00 30.00
LMBR Bobby Ryan 20.00 50.00
LMBW Blake Wheeler 20.00 50.00
LMCG Claude Giroux 30.00 80.00
LMCH Christian Hanson 20.00 50.00
LMDB David Backes 40.00 80.00
LMDC Daniel Carcillo 25.00 60.00
LMDP Dion Phaneuf 25.00 60.00
LMGH Gordie Howe 60.00 150.00
LMIV Ivan Vishnevskiy
LMJA Justin Abdelkader 15.00 40.00
LMJC Jeff Carter 15.00 40.00
LMJE Jhonas Enroth 20.00 50.00
LMJI Jarome Iginla 30.00 80.00
LMJK Jari Kurri 15.00 40.00
LMJT Jonathan Toews 40.00 100.00
LMJV Jakub Voracek 15.00 40.00
LMKE Phil Kessel 15.00 40.00
LMLS Luke Schenn 25.00 60.00
LMMB Mikael Backlund 25.00 60.00
LMMG Mike Green 30.00 80.00
LMMP Max Pacioretty 15.00 40.00
LMMR Mike Richards 30.00 80.00
LMNB Nicklas Backstrom 30.00 80.00
LMNG Nathan Gerbe 20.00 50.00
LMPD Pavel Datsyuk 40.00 80.00
LMPK Patrick Kane 30.00 80.00
LMRM Ryan Miller 15.00 40.00
LMSM Steve Mason 25.00 60.00
LMSS Steven Stamkos 40.00 100.00
LMSY Steve Yzerman 75.00 150.00
LMTK Tyler Kennedy 20.00 50.00
LMTV Thomas Vanek 15.00 40.00
LMVL Ville Leino 20.00 50.00

2009-10 SP Game Used Letters of Distinction

STATED PRINT RUN 1 SER.#'d SET
NOT PRICED DUE TO SCARCITY
LDCA Alexander Ovechkin
LDIK Ilya Kovalchuk
LDJI Jarome Iginla
LDJS Joe Sakic
LDJT Jonathan Toews
LDML Mario Lemieux
LDMR Mike Richards
LDNL Nicklas Lidstrom
LDRB Ray Bourque
LDRN Rick Nash
LDSC Sidney Crosby
LDSN Scott Niedermayer
LDSY Steve Yzerman
LDTH Joe Thornton
LDVL Vincent Lecavalier
LDWG Wayne Gretzky

2009-10 SP Game Used Marks of a Nation

STATED PRINT RUN 50 SER.#'d SETS
MNAA Artem Anisimov 20.00 50.00
MNAF Marc-Andre Fleury 40.00 80.00
MNAK Anze Kopitar 15.00 40.00
MNBA Mikael Backlund 25.00 60.00
MNBH Bobby Hull 40.00 100.00
MNBL Brian Leetch 15.00 40.00
MNBO Bobby Orr 200.00 350.00
MNCP Carey Price 40.00 100.00
MNCW Cam Ward 15.00 40.00
MNDB David Backes 25.00 60.00
MNDP Dion Phaneuf 25.00 60.00
MNEM Evgeni Malkin 40.00 100.00
MNGH Gordie Howe 60.00 150.00
MNHZ Henrik Zetterberg 30.00 80.00
MNIV Ivan Vishnevskiy 20.00 50.00
MNJA Justin Abdelkader 15.00 40.00
MNJC Jeff Carter 15.00 40.00
MNJD J.P. Dumont 10.00 25.00
MNJI Jarome Iginla 30.00 80.00
MNJK Jari Kurri 15.00 40.00
MNJT Jonathan Toews 40.00 100.00
MNKE Phil Kessel 15.00 40.00
MNLC Luca Caputi 20.00 50.00
MNLS Luke Schenn 40.00 80.00
MNLV Vincent Lecavalier 20.00 50.00
MNMB Martin Brodeur 40.00 100.00
MNMG Mike Green 30.00 80.00
MNMH Marian Hossa 25.00 60.00
MNML Mario Lemieux 40.00 100.00
MNMM Mark Messier 30.00 80.00
MNMN Markus Naslund 15.00 40.00
MNMR Mike Richards 30.00 80.00
MNNB Nicklas Backstrom 30.00 80.00
MNNL Nicklas Lidstrom 40.00 80.00
MNPB Patrik Berglund 25.00 60.00
MNPD Pavel Datsyuk 40.00 80.00
MNPE Phil Esposito 30.00 80.00
MNPK Patrick Kane 30.00 80.00
MNPR Patrick Roy 50.00 120.00
MNRG Ryan Getzlaf 50.00 100.00
MNRH Riku Helenius
MNRM Ryan Miller 40.00 100.00
MNRN Rick Nash 25.00 60.00
MNSC Sidney Crosby 150.00 250.00
MNSD Shane Doan 12.00 30.00
MNSG Scott Gomez 15.00 40.00
MNSK Saku Koivu 40.00 80.00
MNSM Steve Mason 25.00 60.00
MNSS Steven Stamkos 40.00 100.00
MNSW Shea Weber 25.00 50.00
MNSY Steve Yzerman 125.00 200.00
MNTO T.J. Oshie 25.00 60.00
MNTV Thomas Vanek 20.00 50.00
MNVL Ville Leino 20.00 50.00
MNWG Wayne Gretzky 150.00 300.00
MNYW Yannick Weber 20.00 50.00

2009-10 SP Game Used Marks of a Nation Black Gold

SEE CHECKLIST FOR PRINT RUNS
NOT PRICED DUE TO SCARCITY

2009-10 SP Game Used Rookie Exclusives Autographs

STATED PRINT RUN X SER.#'d SETS
REAA Artem Anisimov 8.00 20.00
REAM Alec Martinez 4.00 10.00
REAN Antti Niemi 20.00 50.00
REBA Mikael Backlund 10.00 25.00
REBB Byron Bitz 5.00 12.00
REBF Benn Ferriero 6.00 15.00
REBM Brad Marchand 8.00 20.00
REBS Brian Salcido 5.00 12.00
RECB Chris Butler 6.00 15.00
RECF Cody Franson 6.00 15.00
RECH Christian Hanson 8.00 20.00
RECO Cal O'Reilly 6.00 15.00
RECW Colin Wilson 12.00 30.00
REDE Michael Del Zotto 12.00 30.00
REDK Dmitry Kulikov 6.00 15.00
REEK Erik Karlsson 20.00 50.00
REFM Frazer McLaren 4.00 10.00
REGR Michael Grabner 8.00 20.00
REIV Ivan Vishnevskiy 8.00 20.00
REJB Jamie Benn 10.00 25.00
REJD Jason Demers 5.00 12.00
REJE Jhonas Enroth 8.00 20.00
REJG Jonas Gustavsson 40.00 80.00
REJJ Jesse Joensuu 8.00 20.00
REJR Jay Rosehill 4.00 10.00
REJS John Scott 6.00 15.00
REJT John Tavares 60.00 120.00
REJV James van Riemsdyk 15.00 40.00
REKA Evander Kane 15.00 40.00
REKC Kris Chucko 5.00 12.00
RELC Luca Caputi 8.00 20.00
RELG Logan Couture 12.00 30.00
REMA Andrew MacDonald 5.00 12.00
REMB Matt Beleskey 6.00 15.00
REMD Matt Duchene 40.00 80.00
REMG Matt Gilroy 8.00 20.00
REMH Matt Hendricks 5.00 12.00
REMN Michal Neuvirth 15.00 40.00
REMP Matt Pelech 6.00 15.00
REMS Michael Sauer 5.00 12.00
REPL Perttu Lindgren 6.00 15.00
REPR Peter Regin 8.00 20.00
RERE Joel Rechlicz 6.00 15.00
RERH Riku Helenius 6.00 15.00
RERM Ray Macias 6.00 15.00
RERO Ryan O'Reilly 12.00 30.00
RESA Mike Santorelli 4.00 10.00
RESM Spencer Machacek 5.00 12.00
RESS Sergei Shirokov 10.00 25.00
RETB Tyler Bozak 15.00 40.00
RETC Taylor Chorney 6.00 15.00
RETG T.J. Galiardi 8.00 20.00
RETM Tyler Myers 25.00 60.00
RETW Tom Wandell 20.00 50.00
REVH Victor Hedman 12.00 30.00
REVL Ville Leino 8.00 20.00
RFVS Viktor Stalberg 10.00 25.00
REYW Yannick Weber 8.00 20.00

2009-10 SP Game Used SIGnificance

STATED PRINT RUN 50 SER.#'d SETS
FSCTG Artem Anisimov
SIGAC Andrew Cogliano 10.00 25.00
SIGAG Alex Goligoski
SIGAK Anze Kopitar 8.00 20.00
SIGAO Alexander Ovechkin/25 50.00 120.00
SIGAP Alex Pietrangelo 6.00 15.00
SIGBA Josh Bailey 6.00 15.00
SIGBK Mikael Backlund 12.00 30.00
SIGBL Brian Leetch 8.00 20.00
SIGBO Bobby Orr/25 100.00 200.00
SIGBR Mikkel Boedker 6.00 15.00
SIGBW Blake Wheeler 10.00 25.00
SIGBZ Todd Bertuzzi 10.00 25.00
SIGCN Cam Neely 12.00 30.00
SIGCO Colton Gillies 10.00 25.00
SIGCP Carey Price 20.00 50.00
SIGDA Darren Helm 10.00 25.00
SIGDC Daniel Carcillo 8.00 20.00
SIGDD Drew Doughty 15.00 40.00
SIGDH Dale Hawerchuk 8.00 20.00
SIGDP Daniel Paille
SIGDS Daniel Sedin
SIGDZ Michael Del Zotto 15.00 40.00
SIGEE Erik Ersberg 6.00 15.00
SIGEM Evgeni Malkin 15.00 40.00
SIGEN Evgeni Nabokov 8.00 20.00
SIGES Eric Staal 10.00 25.00
SIGGA Sam Gagner 10.00 25.00
SIGGB Gilbert Brule 10.00 25.00
SIGGH Gordie Howe/25 50.00 120.00
SIGGI Claude Giroux 15.00 40.00
SIGGP Gilbert Perreault 8.00 20.00
SIGGR Mike Green 15.00 40.00
SIGGV Jonas Gustavsson 20.00 50.00
SIGHK Jaroslav Halak 25.00 50.00
SIGHL Henrik Lundqvist 15.00 40.00
SIGHS Henrik Sedin 12.00 30.00
SIGHZ Henrik Zetterberg 15.00 40.00
SIGIV Ivan Vishnevskiy 10.00 25.00
SIGJA Justin Abdelkader 8.00 20.00
SIGJC Jeff Carter 8.00 20.00
SIGJD J.P. Dumont 5.00 12.00
SIGJE Jonathan Ericsson 8.00 20.00
SIGJM John-Michael Liles 6.00 15.00
SIGJN James Neal 8.00 20.00
SIGJS Jordan Staal 10.00 25.00
SIGJV Jakub Voracek 8.00 20.00
SIGKO Kyle Okposo
SIGKP Kevin Porter 5.00 12.00
SIGLC Luca Caputi 10.00 25.00
SIGLS Luke Schenn 12.00 30.00
SIGMA Steve Mason 12.00 30.00
SIGMB Martin Brodeur/25 30.00 80.00
SIGMD Matt Duchene 30.00 80.00
SIGMG Marian Gaborik 12.00 30.00
SIGMK Mike Knuble 20.00 50.00
SIGML Mario Lemieux/25 30.00 80.00
SIGMM Mark Messier/25 25.00 60.00
SIGNB Nicklas Backstrom 15.00 40.00
SIGNL Nicklas Lidstrom 10.00 25.00
SIGNV Michal Neuvirth 20.00 50.00
SIGOM Oscar Moller 6.00 15.00
SIGOR Terry O'Reilly
SIGPH Dion Phaneuf 12.00 30.00
SIGPN Dustin Penner 5.00 12.00
SIGPR Patrick Roy/25 40.00 100.00
SIGRA Mason Raymond 15.00 40.00
SIGRM Ryan Miller 15.00 40.00
SIGRN Rick Nash 8.00 20.00
SIGSC Sidney Crosby/25 100.00 200.00
SIGSE Devin Setoguchi 6.00 15.00
SIGSK Jack Skille 5.00 12.00
SIGST Steven Stamkos 20.00 50.00
SIGSW Shea Weber 6.00 15.00
SIGSY Steve Yzerman/25 75.00 150.00
SIGTA John Tavares 60.00 120.00
SIGTO Jonathan Toews 20.00 50.00
SIGTV Thomas Vanek 8.00 20.00
SIGTW Ty Wishart 8.00 20.00
SIGVR James van Riemsdyk 25.00 50.00
SIGWG Wayne Gretzky/25 100.00 200.00
SIGZB Zach Bogosian

2009-10 SP Game Used SIGnificant Numbers

SEE CHECKLIST FOR PRINT RUNS
SOME NOT PRICED DUE TO SCARCITY
SNAA Artem Anisimov/42 12.00 30.00
SNAC Andrew Cogliano/13
SNAK Anze Kopitar/11
SNAO Adam Oates/12
SNBA Mikael Backlund/60 15.00 40.00
SNBB Bob Bourne/14
SNBL Brian Leetch/2
SNBW Blake Wheeler/26 12.00 30.00
SNCB Sidney Crosby/1
SNCN Cam Neely/8
SNCP Carey Price/31 25.00 60.00
SNCW Cam Ward/30 10.00 25.00
SNDD Drew Doughty/8
SNDH Dale Hawerchuk/10
SNDS Daniel Sedin/22 12.00 30.00
SNEK Evander Kane/9
SNEM Evgeni Malkin/71 25.00 60.00
SNGB Michael Grabner/20
SNGF Grant Fuhr/31 12.00 30.00
SNGR Mike Green/52 20.00 50.00
SNGV Jonas Gustavsson/9
SNHL Henrik Lundqvist/30 20.00 50.00
SNHS Henrik Sedin/33 15.00 40.00
SNHZ Henrik Zetterberg/40 20.00 50.00
SNIK Ilya Kovalchuk/17
SNIV Ivan Vishnevskiy/59 12.00 30.00
SNJA Jason Arnott/19
SNJB Josh Bailey/12
SNJC Jeff Carter/17
SNJD J.P. Dumont/71 6.00 15.00
SNJE Jhonas Enroth/1
SNJI Jarome Iginla/12
SNJK Jari Kurri/17
SNJO Jonathan Toews/19
SNJP Jason Pominville/29 10.00 25.00
SNJT Joe Thornton/19
SNKE Phil Kessel/81 10.00 25.00
SNKO Kyle Okposo/21
SNLM Lanny McDonald/7
SNLR Larry Robinson/19
SNLS Luke Schenn/2
SNMB Martin Brodeur/30 40.00 80.00
SNMD Matt Duchene/9
SNMF Marc-Andre Fleury/29 30.00 60.00
SNMG Marian Gaborik/10
SNML Mario Lemieux/6
SNMM Mark Messier/11
SNMO Mike Modano/9
SNMR Mason Raymond/21
SNMT Marty Turco/35 8.00 20.00
SNNB Nicklas Backstrom/19
SNNF Nick Foligno/71 10.00 25.00
SNNH Nathan Horton/10
SNNL Nicklas Lidstrom/5
SNOV Alexander Ovechkin/8
SNPD Pavel Datsyuk/13
SNPH Dion Phaneuf/3
SNPK Patrick Kane/88 20.00 50.00
SNPR Patrick Roy/33 60.00 120.00
SNPS Paul Stastny/26 10.00 25.00
SNPT Peter Stastny/26 10.00 25.00
SNRB Ray Bourque/77 15.00 40.00
SNRI Mike Richards/18
SNRM Ryan Miller/30 10.00 25.00
SNRN Rick Nash/61 10.00 25.00
SNSC Sidney Crosby/87 75.00 150.00
SNSD Shane Doan/19
SNSG Sam Gagner/89 12.00 30.00
SNSK Saku Koivu/11
SNSM Steve Mason/1
SNSS Steve Shutt/22
SNST Steven Stamkos/91 25.00 60.00
SNSW Shea Weber/6
SNSY Steve Yzerman/19
SNTA John Tavares/10
SNTV Thomas Vanek/26 10.00 25.00
SNVL Vincent Lecavalier/4
SNVO Tomas Vokoun/29 10.00 25.00
SNVR James van Riemsdyk/51
SNWG Wayne Gretzky/9
SNYW Yannick Weber/68 12.00 30.00

2009-10 SP Game Used Triple SIGnificance

STATED PRINT RUN 10 SER.#'d SETS
NOT PRICED DUE TO SCARCITY
AF8FIN Kris Chucko
Mikael Backlund
Matt Pelech
TSGCPT Steve Yzerman
Nicklas Lidstrom
Gordie Howe
TSGDEF Drew Doughty
Luke Schenn
Zach Bogosian
TSGDET Nicklas Lidstrom
Pavel Datsyuk
Henrik Zetterberg
TSGDGD Chris Drury
Marian Gaborik
Brandon Dubinsky
TSGGR8 Bobby Orr
Bobby Hull
Gordie Howe
TSGLAK Luc Robitaille
Jari Kurri
Wayne Gretzky
TSGLER Jonathan Ericsson
Mattias Ritola
Ville Leino
TSGLSS Vincent Lecavalier
Martin St. Louis
Steven Stamkos
TSGNSH Jason Arnott
J.P. Dumont
Shea Weber
TSGOGB Alexander Ovechkin
Mike Green
Nicklas Backstrom
TSGOMK Ilya Kovalchuk
Alexander Ovechkin
Evgeni Malkin
TSGWOW Mario Lemieux
Steve Yzerman
Wayne Gretzky

1933 Sport Kings

The cards in this 48-card set measure 2 3/8" by 2 7/8". The 1933 Sport Kings set, issued by the Goudey Gum Company, contains cards for the most famous athletic heroes of the times. No less than 18 different sports are represented in the set. The baseball cards of Cobb, Hubbell, and Ruth, and the football cards of Rockne, Grange and Thorpe command premium prices. The cards were issued in one-card penny packs which came 100 packs to a box along with a piece of gum. The catalog designation for this set is R338.

COMPLETE SET 10000.00 16000.00
19 Eddie Shore 400.00 800.00
(hockey)
24 Howie Morenz 600.00 1000.00
(hockey)
29 Ace Bailey 250.00 400.00
(hockey)
30 Ching Johnson 250.00 400.00
(hockey)

1935 Sporting Events and Stars

Cards measure approximately 2" x 3". Cards feature black and white fronts, along with informative backs. Set features 96 cards and was issued by various cigarette makers including Senior Service, Junior Member, and Illingworth's.

31 Ice Hockey 20.00 40.00

2007 Sportkings

COMPLETE SET (48) 600.00 900.00
THREE PER PACK
5 Martin Brodeur 5.00 12.00
19 Mario Lemieux 6.00 15.00
26 Maurice Richard 5.00 12.00
29 Patrick Roy 6.00 15.00
32 Terry Sawchuk 5.00 12.00
33 Milt Schmidt 4.00 10.00

2007 Sportkings Mini

*MINIS: 1X TO 2X BASIC
ONE PER PACK
ANNOUNCED PRINT RUN 93 SETS

2007 Sportkings Admit One Redemptions

RANDOM INSERTS IN PACKS
ANNOUNCED PRINT RUN 1 SET
NO PRICING DUE TO SCARCITY

2007 Sportkings Autograph Silver

RANDOM INSERTS IN PACKS
ANNOUNCED PRINT RUN B/WN 95-99 PER
AMB Martin Brodeur 25.00 50.00
AML Mario Lemieux 50.00 80.00
AMS Milt Schmidt 15.00 30.00
APR Patrick Roy 50.00 80.00

2007 Sportkings Autograph Gold

*GOLD: 1.2X TO 2X BASIC
RANDOM INSERTS IN PACKS
ANNOUNCED PRINT RUN 10 SETS

2007 Sportkings Autograph Memorabilia Silver

RANDOM INSERTS IN PACKS
ANNOUNCED PRINT RUN 40 SETS
AMMB Martin Brodeur Jsy 40.00 70.00
AMML Mario Lemieux Jsy 70.00 120.00
AMMS Milt Schmidt Jsy 20.00 40.00
AMPR Patrick Roy Jsy 60.00 100.00

2007 Sportkings Autograph Memorabilia Gold

*GOLD: 1.2X TO 2X BASIC
RANDOM INSERTS IN PACKS
ANNOUNCED PRINT RUN 10 SETS
AMML Mario Lemieux Jsy 125.00 200.00
AMPR Patrick Roy Jsy 125.00 200.00

2007 Sportkings Cityscapes Silver

ANNOUNCED PRINT RUN 20 SETS
*GOLD: .5X TO 1.2X BASIC
GOLD ANNOUNCED PRINT RUN 10 SETS
RANDOM INSERTS IN PACKS
CS02 Pete Rose Jsy 100.00 175.00
Patrick Roy Jsy
Montreal
CS03 Roger Clemens Jsy 20.00 40.00
Milt Schmidt Jsy
Boston
CS07 Roberto Clemente Pants 40.00 80.00
Mario Lemieux Jsy
Pittsburgh
CS08 Magic Johnson Jsy 20.00 40.00
Terry Sawchuk Jsy
Los Angeles

2007 Sportkings Decades Silver

ANNOUNCED PRINT RUN 20 SETS
*GOLD: .5X TO 1.2X BASIC
GOLD ANNOUNCED PRINT RUN 10 SETS
RANDOM INSERTS IN PACKS
D01 Ted Williams Jsy 100.00 175.00
Maurice Richard Glove
Stan Musial Jsy
1940s
D02 Terry Sawchuk Jsy 40.00 80.00
Willie Shoemaker Silks
Milt Schmidt Jsy
1950s
D06 Troy Aikman Jsy 40.00 80.00
Patrick Roy Jsy
Roger Clemens Jsy
1990s

2007 Sportkings Double Memorabilia Silver

RANDOM INSERTS IN PACKS
ANNOUNCED PRINT RUN 4-40 SETS
DM15, DM16 ANNOUNCED PRINT RUN 4 PER
NO DM15, DM16 PRICING DUE TO SCARCITY
DM4 Mario Lemieux Glove-Jsy 20.00 50.00
DM5 Martin Brodeur Glove-Jsy 12.50 30.00
DM7 Patrick Roy Glove-Jsy 20.00 50.00
DM15 Maurice Richard Glove-Jsy/4 *
DM16 Terry Sawchuk Glove-Jsy/4 *

2007 Sportkings Double Memorabilia Gold

*GOLD: .6X TO 1.5X BASIC
RANDOM INSERTS IN PACKS
ANNOUNCED PRINT RUN 10 SETS
DM15, DM16 ANNOUNCED PRINT RUN 1 PER
NO DM15, DM16 PRICING DUE TO SCARCITY

2007 Sportkings Fall Expo Memorabilia Silver

FE7 Mario Lemieux
FE8 Martin Brodeur
FE9 Maurice Richard
FE10 Milt Schmidt
FE13 Patrick Roy
FE18 Terry Sawchuk

2007 Sportkings Fall Expo Memorabilia Gold

FE7 Mario Lemieux
FE8 Martin Brodeur
FE9 Maurice Richard
FE10 Milt Schmidt
FE13 Patrick Roy
FE18 Terry Sawchuk

2007 Sportkings King-Sized Memorabilia

RANDOM INSERTS IN PACKS
ANNOUNCED PRINT RUN 1 SET
NO PRICING DUE TO SCARCITY

2007 Sportkings Logo Card

RANDOM INSERTS IN PACKS
ANNOUNCED PRINT RUN 1 SET
NO PRICING DUE TO SCARCITY

2007 Sportkings Lumber Silver

RANDOM INSERTS IN PACKS
ANNOUNCED PRINT RUN 30 SETS
WORDED SWATCHES COMMAND PREMIUMS
L1 Martin Brodeur Stick 20.00 40.00
L2 Mario Lemieux Stick 25.00 50.00
L3 Patrick Roy Stick 30.00 60.00
L4 Terry Sawchuk Stick 25.00 50.00
L5 Maurice Richard Stick 30.00 60.00

2007 Sportkings Lumber Gold

*GOLD: .75X TO 1.5 BASIC
RANDOM INSERTS IN PACKS
ANNOUNCED PRINT RUN 10 SETS
WORDED SWATCHES COMMAND PREMIUMS

2007 Sportkings National Convention Preview

8 Maurice Richard
11 Martin Brodeur

2007 Sportkings Papercuts

RANDOM INSERTS IN PACKS
ANNOUNCED PRINT RUNS B/WN 1-10 PER
NO PRICING DUE TO SCARCITY
PCMR Maurice Richard/9 *
PCTS Terry Sawchuk/1 *

2007 Sportkings Patch Silver

ANNOUNCED PRINT RUN 20 SETS
P28-P30 ANNOUNCED PRINT RUN 4 PER
NO P28-P30 PRICING DUE TO SCARCITY
*GOLD: .6X TO 1.2X BASIC
GOLD ANNOUNCED PRINT RUN 10 SETS
GOLD P28-P30 ANCD. PRINT RUN 1 PER
GOLD P28-P30 NO PRICING AVAILABLE
RANDOM INSERTS IN PACKS
P11 Mario Lemieux Jsy 20.00 50.00
P12 Martin Brodeur Jsy 15.00 40.00
P14 Milt Schmidt Jsy 12.50 30.00
P17 Patrick Roy Jsy 30.00 60.00
P28 Terry Sawchuk Jsy/4 *
P29 Maurice Richard Jsy/4 *

2007 Sportkings Quad Memorabilia Silver

ANNOUNCED PRINT RUN 10 SETS
GOLD ANNOUNCED PRINT RUN 1 SET
RANDOM INSERTS IN PACKS
NO PRICING DUE TO SCARCITY
QM03 Ted Williams Jsy
Milt Schmidt Jsy
Carl Yastrzemski Jsy
Larry Bird Jsy
QM05 Mario Lemieux Jsy
Patrick Roy Jsy
Maurice Richard Glove
Martin Brodeur Jsy

2007 Sportkings Single Memorabilia Silver

RANDOM INSERTS IN PACKS
ANNOUNCED PRINT RUN 90 SETS
SM3, SM13 ANNOUNCED PRINT RUN 4 PER
NO SM3, SM13 PRICING DUE TO SCARCITY
SM03 Terry Sawchuk Jsy
SM11 Mario Lemieux Jsy 10.00 25.00
SM12 Martin Brodeur Jsy 6.00 15.00
SM13 Maurice Richard Jsy
SM14 Milt Schmidt Jsy 8.00 20.00
SM42 Patrick Roy Jsy 10.00 25.00

2007 Sportkings Triple Memorabilia Silver

ANNOUNCED PRINT RUN 10 SETS
TM7, TM8 ANNOUNCED PRINT RUN 4 PER
NO TM7, TM8 PRICING DUE TO SCARCITY
GOLD ANNOUNCED PRINT RUN 1 SET
NO GOLD PRICING DUE TO SCARCITY
RANDOM INSERTS IN PACKS
TM04 Mario Lemieux 50.00 100.00
Glove-Jsy-Skate
TM05 Martin Brodeur 30.00 60.00
Glove-Jsy-Stick
TM07 Terry Sawchuk
Glove-Jsy-Pad/4 *
TM08 Maurice Richard
Glove-Jsy-Stick/4 *
TM12 Terry Sawchuk Jsy 50.00 100.00
Patrick Roy Jsy
Martin Brodeur Jsy

2007 Sportkings Vintage Papercuts

RANDOM INSERTS IN PACKS
ANNOUNCED PRINT RUN 1 SET
NO PRICING DUE TO SCARCITY
VPCAB Ace Bailey

2008 Sportkings

FIVE CARDS PER BOX
78 Mark Messier 5.00 10.00
84 Jean Beliveau 6.00 12.00
87 Georges Vezina 6.00 12.00
88 Jacques Plante 7.50 15.00
97 Bobby Hull 6.00 12.00
103 Brett Hull 5.00 10.00

2008 Sportkings Mini

*MINI: 1X TO 2X BASIC
ONE PER BOX

2008 Sportkings 1933 The Year

RANDOM INSERTS IN PACKS
STATED PRINT RUN 1 SERIAL #'d SET
NO PRICING DUE TO SCARCITY
BC Bill Cook

2008 Sportkings Autograph Silver

ANNOUNCED PRINT RUN B/WN 20-90 PER
UNPRICED GOLD PRINT RUN 10
RANDOM INSERTS IN PACKS
MM Mark Messier/80 * 35.00 70.00
BH1 Brett Hull/40 * 20.00 40.00
BH2 Brett Hull/40 * 20.00 40.00
JB1 Jean Beliveau/50 * 20.00 40.00
JB2 Jean Beliveau/50 * 20.00 40.00
BHU1 Bobby Hull/40 * 20.00 40.00
BHU2 Bobby Hull/40 * 20.00 40.00

2008 Sportkings Autograph Memorabilia Silver

ANNOUNCED PRINT RUN B/WN 15-50 PER
GOLD PRINT RUN 10 SETS
NO GOLD PRICING DUE TO SCARCITY
RANDOM INSERTS IN PACKS
BH1 Brett Hull/40 * 25.00 50.00
BH2 Brett Hull/40 * 25.00 50.00
BHU1 Bobby Hull/40 * 25.00 50.00
BHU2 Bobby Hull/40 * 25.00 50.00
JBE Jean Beliveau/50 * 25.00 50.00
JBE2 Jean Beliveau/50 * 25.00 50.00
MM Mark Messier/40 * 40.00 80.00

2008 Sportkings Cityscapes Double Silver

ANNOUNCED PRINT RUN 20 SETS
*GOLD: .5X TO 1.2X BASIC
GOLD PRINT RUN 10 SETS
RANDOM INSERTS IN PACKS
1 Patrick Roy 30.00 60.00
John Elway
Denver
3 Gary Carter 15.00 40.00
Jean Beliveau
Montreal
4 Brett Hull 15.00 40.00
Michael Irvin
Dallas
5 Ernie Banks 20.00 50.00
Bobby Hull
Chicago
6 Bob Gibson 15.00 40.00
Brett Hull
St. Louis
8 Pelé 75.00 125.00
Mark Messier
New York
10 Barry Sanders 20.00 50.00
Brett Hull
Detroit

2008 Sportkings Cityscapes Triple Silver

ANNOUNCED PRINT RUN 20 SETS
*GOLD: .5X TO 1.2X BASIC
GOLD PRINT RUN 10 SETS
RANDOM INSERTS IN PACKS
2 Michael Irvin 20.00 50.00
Troy Aikman
Brett Hull
Dallas
5 Gary Carter 30.00 60.00
Pete Rose
Jean Beliveau
Montreal
6 Mark Messier 75.00 125.00
Don Mattingly
Pelé
New York
7 Lou Brock 20.00 50.00
Ozzie Smith
Brett Hull
St. Louis

2008 Sportkings Decades Silver

ANNOUNCED PRINT RUN 20 SETS
*GOLD: .5X TO 1.2X BASIC
GOLD PRINT RUN 10 SETS
RANDOM INSERTS IN PACKS
1 Ernie Banks 40.00 80.00
Jean Beliveau
Ben Hogan
2 Jim Brown 20.00 50.00
Jacque Plante
Juan Marichal
4 Dan Marino 30.00 60.00
Mark Messier
Robert Parish
5 Brett Hull 20.00 50.00
Michael Irvin
Hakeem Olajuwon

2008 Sportkings Double Memorabilia Silver

ANNOUNCED PRINT RUN 30 SETS
*GOLD: .6X TO 1.5X BASIC
GOLD PRINT RUN 10 SETS
RANDOM INSERTS IN PACKS
3 Jacques Plante 30.00 60.00
Patrick Roy
8 Jacques Plante
Georges Vezina SP/4 *

2008 Sportkings King-Sized Memorabilia

RANDOM INSERTS IN PACKS
STATED PRINT RUN 1 SERIAL #'d SET
NO PRICING DUE TO SCARCITY

2008 Sportkings Logo Card

RANDOM INSERTS IN PACKS
ANNOUNCED PRINT RUN 1 SET
NO PRICING DUE TO SCARCITY

2008 Sportkings Lumber Silver

STATED PRINT RUN 9 SERIAL #'d SETS
GOLD PRINT RUN 1 SERIAL #'d SET
RANDOM INSERTS IN PACKS
NO PRICING DUE TO SCARCITY
1 Mark Messier Stick
2 Georges Vezina Stick
3 Jacques Plante Stick
4 Jean Beliveau Stick
5 Bobby Hull Stick
6 Brett Hull Stick

2008 Sportkings National Convention Memorabilia Silver

UNPRICED PRINT RUN 9 SER.#'d SETS

2008 Sportkings National Convention VIP Promo

11 Patrick Roy 5.00 12.00
Ching Johnson
16 Mark Messier 3.00 8.00
Eddie Shore

2008 Sportkings Numerology Silver

STATED PRINT RUN 9 SERIAL #'d SETS
GOLD PRINT RUN 1 SERIAL #'d SET
RANDOM INSERTS IN PACKS
NO PRICING DUE TO SCARCITY
16 Mario Lemieux
17 Mark Messier
18 Martin Brodeur
22 Patrick Roy

2008 Sportkings Papercuts

RANDOM INSERTS IN PACKS
ANNOUNCED PRINT RUN B/WN 1-10 PER
NO PRICING DUE TO SCARCITY
JP Jacques Plante/1 *

2008 Sportkings Passing the Torch Silver

PRINT RUNS B/WN 4-20 COPIES PER
NO PRICING ON QTY OF 4
*GOLD: .5X TO 1.2X BASIC
GOLD PRINT RUNS B/WN 1-10 PER
RANDOM INSERTS IN PACKS
5 Jean Beliveau 20.00 50.00
Mark Messier
6 Jacques Plante 40.00 80.00
Patrick Roy
11 Georges Vezina
Patrick Roy SP/4 *

2008 Sportkings Patch Silver

ANNOUNCED PRINT RUNS B/WN 4-20 PER
NO PRICING ON QTY OF 4
GOLD PRINT RUNS B/WN 1-10 PER
NO GOLD PRICING DUE TO SCARCITY
RANDOM INSERTS IN PACKS
10 Jacques Plante SP/4 *
12 Jean Beliveau SP/4 *
17 Mark Messier Edmonton 20.00 50.00
18 Mark Messier NY 20.00 50.00
19 Mark Messier Vancouver 20.00 50.00

2008 Sportkings Post Card Redemption Dual Memorabilia

ANNOUNCED PRINT RUN 1 SET
NO PRICING DUE TO SCARCITY
8 Mark Messier
Mario Lemieux

2008 Sportkings Quad Memorabilia Silver

ANNOUNCED PRINT RUN 9 SETS
GOLD PRINT RUN 1 SET
RANDOM INSERTS IN PACKS
NO PRICING DUE TO SCARCITY
3 Mark Messier
Mario Lemieux
Jean Beliveau
Maurice Richard
5 Terry Sawchuk
Patrick Roy
Martin Brodeur
Georges Vezina SP/4 *
6 Pelé
Mark Messier
Joe Frazier
Don Mattingly

2008 Sportkings Single Memorabilia Silver

ANNOUNCED PRINT RUNS B/WN 4-30 PER
NO PRICING ON QTY OF 4
GOLD PRINT RUNS B/WN 1-10 PER
NO GOLD PRICING DUE TO SCARCITY
RANDOM INSERTS IN PACKS
15 Georges Vezina SP/4 *
17 Jacques Plante 10.00 25.00
19 Jean Beliveau 12.50 30.00
28 Mark Messier 8.00 20.00
45 Bobby Hull 10.00 25.00

2008 Sportkings Triple Memorabilia Silver

ANNOUNCED PRINT RUNS B/WN 4-20 PER
NO PRICING ON QTY OF 4
*GOLD: X TO X BASIC
GOLD PRINT RUN 10 SETS
NO GOLD PRICING ON QTY OF 1
RANDOM INSERTS IN PACKS
6 Jean Beliveau 30.00 60.00
Mario Lemieux
Maurice Richard
7 Georges Vezina
Jacque Plante
Patrick Roy SP/4 *
8 Mark Messier 30.00 60.00
Mario Lemieux
Bobby Hull
9 Mark Messier 30.00 60.00
New York-Vancouver-Edmonton
15 Terry Sawchuk 50.00 100.00
Patrick Roy
Martin Brodeur

2008 Sportkings Vintage Memorabilia

RANDOM INSERTS IN PACKS
STATED PRINT RUN 1 SERIAL #'d SET
NO PRICING DUE TO SCARCITY
1 Howie Morenz
3 Eddie Shore
6 Ace Bailey

2008 Sportkings Vintage Papercuts

RANDOM INSERTS IN PACKS
STATED PRINT RUN 1 SERIAL #'d SET
NO PRICING DUE TO SCARCITY
CJ Ching Johnson
ES Eddie Shore

2009 Sportkings

COMPLETE SET (52) 250.00 450.00
COMMON CARD (109-160) 5.00 12.00
SEMISTARS 6.00 15.00
UNLISTED STARS 8.00 20.00
142 Hobey Baker 5.00 12.00
143 Vladislav Tretiak 10.00 25.00
144 Phil Esposito 6.00 15.00
149 Howie Morenz 6.00 15.00

2009 Sportkings Mini

*MINI: .6X TO 1.5X BASIC CARDS
STATED ODDS ONE PER BOX
UNPRICED SILVER PRINT RUN 7 SETS
UNPRICED GOLD PRINT RUN 3 SETS

2009 Sportkings 1933 Redemption

ANNOUNCED PRINT RUN 1 SET
NO PRICING DUE TO SCARCITY
3 Howie Morenz

2009 Sportkings Admit One Redemptions

ANNOUNCED PRINT RUN 1 SET
NO PRICING DUE TO SCARCITY
8 Game Four Summit Series
9/8/72

2009 Sportkings Autograph Silver

ANNOUNCED PRINT RUN B/WN 15-70 PER
GOLD PRINT RUN 10 SETS
NO GOLD PRICING DUE TO SCARCITY
PE1 Phil Esposito/40* 20.00 40.00
PE2 Phil Esposito/40* 20.00 40.00
VT1 Vladislav Tretiak/40* 40.00 80.00
VT2 Vladislav Tretiak/40* 40.00 80.00

2009 Sportkings Autograph Memorabilia Silver

ANNOUNCED PRINT RUN B/WN 15-40 PER
GOLD PRINT RUN 10 SETS
NO GOLD PRICING DUE TO SCARCITY
RANDOM INSERTS IN PACKS
PE1 Phil Esposito Jsy/40* 15.00 30.00
PE2 Phil Esposito Jsy/40* 15.00 30.00
VT1 Vladislav Tretiak Jsy/40* 40.00 80.00
VT2 Vladislav Tretiak Jsy/40* 40.00 80.00

2009 Sportkings AutoThread Silver

ANNOUNCED PRINT RUN 9 SETS
GOLD PRINT RUN 1 SET
NO PRICING DUE TO SCARCITY
RANDOM INSERTS IN PACKS
PE Phil Esposito Jsy

2009 Sportkings Cityscapes Double Silver

ANNOUNCED PRINT RUN 19 SETS
GOLD PRINT RUN 1 SET
NO GOLD PRICING DUE TO SCARCITY
RANDOM INSERTS IN PACKS
4 Mike Schmidt Jsy 25.00 50.00
Bernie Parent Jsy
5 Phil Esposito Jsy 25.00 50.00
Pele Jsy
7 Doug Flutie Jsy 20.00 40.00
Bobby Hull Jsy

2009 Sportkings Cityscapes Triple Silver

ANNOUNCED PRINT RUN 19 SETS
GOLD PRINT RUN 1 SET
NO GOLD PRICING DUE TO SCARCITY
RANDOM INSERTS IN PACKS
3 Lawrence Taylor Jsy 25.00 50.00
Reggie Jackson Jsy
Phil Esposito Jsy
4 Doug Flutie Jsy 20.00 40.00
Bobby Hull Jsy
Tony Esposito Jsy

2009 Sportkings Decades Silver

ANNOUNCED PRINT RUN 19 SETS
GOLD PRINT RUN 1 SET
NO GOLD PRICING DUE TO SCARCITY
RANDOM INSERTS IN PACKS
2 Vladislav Tretiak Jsy 50.00 100.00
Reggie Jackson Jsy
Bela Karolyi Shirt

2009 Sportkings Double Memorabilia Silver

ANNOUNCED PRINT RUN B/WN 1-19 PER
UNPRICED GOLD PRINT RUN 1
RANDOM INSERTS IN PACKS
12 Phil Esposito Jsy/19* 40.00 80.00
Vladislav Tretiak Jsy
15 Howie Morenz Jsy/1*
Maurice Richard Jsy

2009 Sportkings King-Sized Memorabilia

RANDOM INSERTS IN PACKS
PRINT RUN 1 SER. #'d SET
NO PRICING DUE TO SCARCITY
20 Phil Esposito Jsy
21 Phil Esposito Jsy
29 Vladislav Tretiak Jsy

2009 Sportkings Logos

RANDOM INSERTS IN PACKS
PRINT RUN 1 SER. #'d SET
NO PRICING DUE TO SCARCITY
34 Hobey Baker
35 Vladislav Tretiak
36 Phil Esposito
41 Howie Morenz

2009 Sportkings Lumber Silver

ANNOUNCE PRINT RUN 9 SETS
CARDS 3 AND 6 WERE NEVER ISSUED
GOLD PRINT RUN 1 SET
NO PRICING DUE TO SCARCITY
RANDOM INSERTS IN PACKS
1 Phil Esposito Stick
5 Vladislav Tretiak Stick

2009 Sportkings National Convention Memorabilia Silver

STATED PRINT RUN 9 SER. #'d SETS
GOLD PRINT RUN 1 SER. #'d SET
2009 NAT'L CONVENTION EXCLUSIVE
UNPRICED DUE TO SCARCITY
SK16 Alexander Ovechkin
Mark Messier
Steve Yzerman
Gordie Howe
Bobby Orr
Wayne Gretzky
SK17 Martin Brodeur
Patrick Roy
Jacques Plante
Terry Sawchuk
Ken Dryden
Georges Vezina
SK18 Mario Lemieux
Joe Sakic
Mark Messier
Maurice Richard
Gordie Howe
Wayne Gretzky
SK35 Alexander Ovechkin
Mark Messier
Steve Yzerman
Gordie Howe
Bobby Orr
SK36 Martin Brodeur
Patrick Roy
Jacques Plante
Terry Sawchuk
Ken Dryden
SK37 Mario Lemieux
Joe Sakic
Mark Messier
Maurice Richard
Gordie Howe
SK54 Alexander Ovechkin
Mark Messier
Steve Yzerman
Gordie Howe
SK55 Martin Brodeur
Patrick Roy
Jacques Plante
Terry Sawchuk
SK56 Mario Lemieux
Joe Sakic
Mark Messier
Maurice Richard
SK74 Alexander Ovechkin
Mark Messier
Steve Yzerman
SK75 Martin Brodeur
Patrick Roy
Jacques Plante
SK76 Mario Lemieux
Joe Sakic
Mark Messier

2009 Sportkings National Convention Memorabilia Gold

STATED PRINT RUN 1 SER. #'d SET
2009 NAT'L CONVENTION EXCLUSIVE
UNPRICED DUE TO SCARCITY

2009 Sportkings National Convention VIP Promo

COMPLETE SET (7)
1 Ivan Lendl 4.00 10.00
Phil Esposito
Rusty Wallace
Ken Shamrock
Rick Barry
Mike Tyson
2 Lisa Leslie 5.00 12.00
Joe Namath
Doug Flutie
Vladislav Tretiak
Tony Oliva
Akebono Taro
7 Howie Morenz 5.00 12.00
Red Pollard
Rafer Johnson
Bronko Nagurski
Stan Smith
Pele

2009 Sportkings Numerology Silver

ANNOUNCED PRINT RUN B/WN 4-9 PER
GOLD PRINT RUN 1 SET
NO PRICING DUE TO SCARCITY
RANDOM INSERTS IN PACKS
5 Jean Beliveau Jsy/9*
13 Phil Esposito Jsy/9*
14 Phil Esposito Jsy/9*
15 Terry Sawchuk Jsy/9*
19 Vladislav Tretiak Jsy/9*

2009 Sportkings Owner's Box Cut Autographs

RANDOM INSERTS IN PACKS
ANNOUNCED PRINT RUN 1 SET
NO PRICING DUE TO SCARCITY
AW Arthur Wirtz
ES Ed Snider
ML Mario Lemieux

2009 Sportkings Papercuts

RANDOM INSERTS IN PACKS
ANNOUNCED PRINT RUN 1 SET
NO PRICING DUE TO SCARCITY
HM Howie Morenz

2009 Sportkings Patch Silver

ANNOUNCED PRINT RUN B/WN 4-19 PER
UNPRICED GOLD PRINT RUN 1 SET
RANDOM INSERTS IN PACKS
1 Phil Esposito/19* 20.00 40.00
2 Phil Esposito/19* 20.00 40.00
11 Vladislav Tretiak/19* 50.00 100.00

2009 Sportkings Quad Memorabilia Silver

ANNOUNCED PRINT RUN B/WN 3-9 PER
GOLD PRINT RUN 1 SET
NO PRICING DUE TO SCARCITY
RANDOM INSERTS IN PACKS
7 Jean Beliveau Jsy/3
Jacques Plante Jsy
Maurice Richard Jsy
Howie Morenz Jsy

2009 Sportkings Single Memorabilia Silver

ANNOUNCED PRINT RUN B/WN 4-29 PER
UNPRICED GOLD PRINT RUN B/WN 1-4 PER
RANDOM INSERTS IN PACKS
12 Phil Esposito Jsy/29* 10.00 15.00
16 Vladislav Tretiak Jsy/29* 30.00 60.00
25 Howie Morenz Jsy/4*

2009 Sportkings Triple Memorabilia Silver

ANNOUNCED PRINT RUN B/WN 3-19 PER
UNPRICED GOLD PRINT RUN 1 SET
RANDOM INSERTS IN PACKS
9 Howie Morenz Jsy/3*
Maurice Richard Jsy
Jean Beliveau Jsy

2006-07 Springfield Falcons

COMPLETE SET (28) 8.00 15.00
1 Sean Burke .40 1.00
2 Doug O'Brien .20 .50
3 Dan Cavanaugh .20 .50
4 Andy Delmore .20 .50
5 Eric Healey .20 .50
6 Blair Jones .20 .50
7 Sylvain Dufresne .20 .50
8 Mitch Fritz .30 .75
9 Jay Rosehill .20 .50
10 Karri Ramo .40 1.00
11 Zdenek Blatny .20 .50
12 Justin Keller .20 .50
13 Mike Egener .30 .75
14 Darren Reid .20 .50
15 David Spina .20 .50
16 Marek Kvapil .20 .50
17 Norm Milley .20 .50
18 Andy Rogers .20 .50
19 Matt Smaby .40 1.00
20 Jonathan Boutin .40 1.00
21 Zbynek Hrdel .20 .50
22 Steve Stirling HC .10 .25
23 Darren Rumble CO .10 .25
24 Jared Aulin .20 .50
25 Andre Deveaux .20 .50
26 Adam Henrich .20 .50
27 Geoff Waugh .20 .50
28 Screech MASCOT .02 .10

1996-97 SPx

The 1996-97 SPx set was issued in one series totaling 50 cards. The one-card packs retailed for $3.49 each. Each die-cut card features a full-motion hologram. Two special cards of Wayne Gretzky were randomly inserted, including a tribute (found 1:95), and an autographed tribute (found just one in 1297 packs). An additional special insert is the Great Futures card, which includes holoview images of four young stars (Eric Daze, Daniel Alfredsson, Vitali Yachmenev, and Saku Koivu) and was randomly inserted at a rate of 1:75 packs.

COMPLETE SET (50) 25.00 60.00
1 Paul Kariya .60 1.50
2 Teemu Selanne .60 1.50
3 Ray Bourque 1.00 2.50
4 Cam Neely .60 1.50
5 Theo Fleury .40 1.00
6 Chris Chelios .60 1.50
7 Jeremy Roenick .75 2.00
8 Peter Forsberg 1.00 2.50
9 Joe Sakic 1.25 3.00
10 Patrick Roy 2.50 6.00
11 Mike Modano .75 2.00
12 Joe Nieuwendyk .50 1.25
13 Sergei Fedorov .75 2.00
14 Steve Yzerman 2.50 6.00
15 Paul Coffey .60 1.50
16 Chris Osgood .50 1.25
17 Doug Weight .50 1.25
18 Pat LaFontaine .60 1.50
19 Brendan Shanahan .60 1.50
20 Vitali Yachmenev .40 1.00
21 Saku Koivu .60 1.50
22 Pierre Turgeon .50 1.25
23 Petr Sykora .40 1.00
24 Scott Stevens .50 1.25
25 Martin Brodeur 1.50 4.00
26 Brian Leetch .60 1.50
27 Mark Messier .60 1.50
28 Mike Richter .60 1.50
29 Zigmund Palffy .50 1.25
30 Todd Bertuzzi .60 1.50
31 Alexei Yashin .40 1.00
32 Daniel Alfredsson .50 1.25
33 Eric Lindros .60 1.50
34 John LeClair .60 1.50
35 Keith Tkachuk .60 1.50
36 Alexei Zhamnov .50 1.25
37 Mario Lemieux 2.50 6.00
38 Jaromir Jagr 1.00 2.50
39 Wayne Gretzky 4.00 10.00
40 Brett Hull .75 2.00
41 Owen Nolan .50 1.25
42 Roman Hamrlik .50 1.25
43 Mats Sundin .60 1.50
44 Felix Potvin .60 1.50
45 Doug Gilmour .50 1.25
46 Pavel Bure .60 1.50
47 Alexander Mogilny .50 1.25
48 Jim Carey .60 1.50
49 Peter Bondra .50 1.25
50 Eric Daze .50 1.25
P39 Wayne Gretzky PROMO .40 1.00
GF1 Wayne Gretzky 5.00 12.00
Daniel Alfredsson
Eric Daze
Saku Koivu
Vitali Yachmenev
GS1 W.Gretzky Tribute AU 75.00 200.00
GT1 Wayne Gretzky Tribute 8.00 20.00

1996-97 SPx Gold

A parallel to SPx, these cards feature gold foil stock and were inserted 1:7 packs.

*GOLD: 1.2X TO 3X BASIC CARDS

1996-97 SPx Holoview Heroes

Randomly inserted in packs at a rate of 1:24, this 10-card set also was die-cut with a full-motion hologram.

COMPLETE SET (10) 40.00 100.00
HH1 Ray Bourque 4.00 10.00
HH2 Patrick Roy 10.00 25.00
HH3 Steve Yzerman 10.00 25.00
HH4 Paul Coffey 2.00 5.00
HH5 Mark Messier 2.50 6.00
HH6 Mario Lemieux 10.00 25.00
HH7 Wayne Gretzky 15.00 40.00
HH8 Brett Hull 3.00 8.00
HH9 Doug Gilmour 2.00 5.00
HH10 Grant Fuhr 2.00 5.00

1997-98 SPx

The 1997-98 SPx set was issued in one series totaling 50 cards and was distributed in three-card packs with a suggested retail price of $5.99. The fronts features color action player photos printed on 32-point card stock utilizing decorative foil on the exclusive Light F/X/Holoview cards.

COMPLETE SET (50) 25.00 50.00
1 Paul Kariya .40 1.00
2 Teemu Selanne .40 1.00
3 Ray Bourque .60 1.50
4 Dominik Hasek .75 2.00
5 Pat LaFontaine .40 1.00
6 Theo Fleury .20 .50
7 Jarome Iginla .50 1.25
8 Tony Amonte .30 .75
9 Chris Chelios .40 1.00
10 Patrick Roy 2.00 5.00
11 Peter Forsberg 1.00 2.50
12 Joe Sakic .75 2.00
13 Mike Modano .60 1.50
14 Steve Yzerman 2.00 5.00
15 Sergei Fedorov .60 1.50
16 Brendan Shanahan .40 1.00
17 Doug Weight .30 .75
18 Jason Arnott .20 .50
19 Curtis Joseph .40 1.00
20 John Vanbiesbrouck .30 .75
21 Ed Jovanovski .30 .75
22 Geoff Sanderson .30 .75
23 Rob Blake .30 .75
24 Saku Koivu .40 1.00
25 Doug Gilmour .30 .75
26 Scott Stevens .30 .75
27 Martin Brodeur 1.50 4.00
28 Zigmund Palffy .30 .75
29 Bryan Berard .30 .75
30 Wayne Gretzky 2.50 6.00
30S Wayne Gretzky SAMPLE .40 1.00
31 Mike Richter .40 1.00
32 Mark Messier .40 1.00
33 Brian Leetch .40 1.00
34 Daniel Alfredsson .30 .75
35 Alexei Yashin .20 .50
36 Eric Lindros .40 1.00
37 Janne Niinimaa .30 .75
38 John LeClair .40 1.00
39 Jeremy Roenick .50 1.25
40 Keith Tkachuk .40 1.00
41 Ron Francis .30 .75
42 Jaromir Jagr .60 1.50
43 Brett Hull .50 1.25
44 Owen Nolan .30 .75
45 Chris Gratton .30 .75
46 Mats Sundin .40 1.00
47 Pavel Bure .40 1.00
48 Adam Oates .30 .75
49 Joe Juneau .30 .75
50 Peter Bondra .30 .75

1997-98 SPx Bronze

Randomly inserted in packs at the rate of 1:3, this 50-card set is parallel to the base set and is similar in design. The difference is found in the bronze foil enhancements of the cards.

*BRONZE: 1.2X TO 3X BASIC CARDS

1997-98 SPx Gold

Randomly inserted in packs at the rate of 1:17, this 50-card set is parallel to the base set and is similar in design. The difference is found in the gold foil enhancements of the cards.

*GOLD: 4X TO 10X BASIC CARDS

1997-98 SPx Silver

Randomly inserted in packs at the rate of 1:6, this 50-card set is parallel to the base set and is similar in design. The difference is found in the silver foil enhancements of the cards.

*SILVER: 1.5X TO 4X BASIC CARDS

1997-98 SPx Steel

Inserted one in every pack, this 50-card set is parallel to the base set and is similar in design. The difference is found in the gray foil enhancements of the cards.

*STEEL: .8X TO 2X BASIC CARDS
STEEL ODDS 1:1 HOB/RET

1997-98 SPx Dimension

Randomly inserted in packs at the rate of 1:54, this 20-card set features color action player photos printed with a rainbow Light F/X and Litho combination.

COMPLETE SET (20) 150.00 300.00
SPX1 Wayne Gretzky 30.00 80.00
SPX2 Jeremy Roenick 8.00 20.00
SPX3 Mark Messier 6.00 15.00
SPX4 Eric Lindros 6.00 15.00
SPX5 Doug Gilmour 4.00 10.00
SPX6 Pavel Bure 6.00 15.00
SPX7 Brendan Shanahan 6.00 15.00
SPX8 Bryan Berard 2.00 5.00
SPX9 Curtis Joseph 6.00 15.00
SPX10 Chris Chelios 4.00 10.00
SPX11 Sergei Fedorov 8.00 20.00
SPX12 Adam Oates 2.00 5.00
SPX13 Zigmund Palffy 4.00 10.00
SPX14 Theo Fleury 2.00 5.00
SPX15 Keith Tkachuk 2.00 5.00
SPX16 Peter Forsberg 15.00 40.00
SPX17 Mats Sundin 6.00 15.00
SPX18 Teemu Selanne 6.00 15.00
SPX19 Paul Kariya 6.00 15.00
SPX20 Brett Hull 8.00 20.00

1997-98 SPx DuoView

Randomly inserted in packs at the rate of 1:252, this 10-card set features two different holoview images of the player depicted on the card front in a unique silver and gold combination printed on Light F/X holoview cards.

COMPLETE SET (10)	125.00	250.00
1 Wayne Gretzky	30.00	80.00
2 Jaromir Jagr	8.00	20.00
3 Martin Brodeur	20.00	50.00
4 Jarome Iginla	6.00	15.00
5 Steve Yzerman	25.00	60.00
6 Patrick Roy	25.00	60.00
7 Doug Weight	4.00	10.00
8 John Vanbiesbrouck	4.00	10.00
9 Dominik Hasek	10.00	25.00
10 Joe Sakic	10.00	25.00

1997-98 SPx DuoView Autographs

Randomly inserted in packs, this six-card set is a partial parallel version of the DuoView insert set featuring gold foil enhancements and the pictured player's autograph. Only 100 of each card was produced and are sequentially hand numbered.

1 Wayne Gretzky	150.00	300.00
2 Jaromir Jagr	25.00	60.00
3 Martin Brodeur	50.00	125.00
4 Jarome Iginla	15.00	40.00
5 Patrick Roy	75.00	200.00
6 Doug Weight	12.50	30.00

1997-98 SPx Grand Finale

Randomly inserted in packs, this 50-card set is parallel to the base set and is similar in design. The difference is found in the gold foil enhancements and gold Holoview/Hologram on the cards. Only 50 of each card of this set was produced.

*GRAND FINALE: 20X TO 50X BASIC CARDS

1999-00 SPx

The 1999-00 Upper Deck SPx set was released as a 180-card set consisting of both veteran cards and prospect cards. Card numbers 162-180 are short printed, and the majority of them are autographed. The base card is printed on a rainbow holofoil card stock and enhanced with gold foil. Packaged in 18-pack boxes with three card packs, SPx carried a suggested retail price of $5.99. Each box also contained a 4-card pack of Wayne Gretzky exclusive cards.

COMPLETE SET (180)	125.00	250.00
COMP.SET w/o SP's (162)	40.00	80.00
1 Damian Rhodes	.25	.60
2 Nelson Emerson	.10	.30
3 Ray Ferraro	.10	.30
4 Paul Kariya	.30	.75
5 Steve Rucchin	.25	.60
6 Guy Hebert	.25	.60
7 Oleg Tverdovsky	.10	.30
8 Ted Donato	.10	.30
9 Ray Bourque	.50	1.25
10 Sergei Samsonov	.25	.60
11 Joe Thornton	.50	1.25
12 Jason Allison	.10	.30
13 Byron Dafoe	.25	.60
14 Jonathan Girard	.10	.30
15 Dominik Hasek	.60	1.50
16 Alexei Zhitnik	.10	.30
17 Michael Peca	.25	.60
18 Cory Sarich	.25	.60
19 Martin Biron	.25	.60
20 Miroslav Satan	.25	.60
21 Valeri Bure	.10	.30
22 Derek Morris	.10	.30
23 Phil Housley	.25	.60
24 Jarome Iginla	.40	1.00
25 Rico Fata	.10	.30
26 Jean-Sebastien Giguere	.25	.60
27 Marc Savard	.10	.30
28 Arturs Irbe	.25	.60
29 Keith Primeau	.10	.30
30 Sami Kapanen	.10	.30
31 Ron Francis	.10	.30
32 Wendel Clark	.25	.60
33 J-P Dumont	.25	.60
34 Ty Jones	.10	.30
35 Tony Amonte	.25	.60
36 Jocelyn Thibault	.25	.60
37 Doug Gilmour	.25	.60
38 Bryan McCabe	.10	.30
39 Joe Sakic	.60	1.50
40 Peter Forsberg	.75	2.00
41 Alex Tanguay	.25	.60
42 Chris Drury	.25	.60
43 Patrick Roy	1.50	4.00
44 Sandis Ozolinsh	.10	.30
45 Adam Deadmarsh	.10	.30
46 Milan Hejduk	.30	.75
47 Mike Modano	.50	1.25
48 Brett Hull	.40	1.00
49 Darryl Sydor	.25	.60
50 Ed Belfour	.30	.75
51 Jere Lehtinen	.25	.60
52 Jamie Langenbrunner	.10	.30
53 Joe Nieuwendyk	.25	.60
54 Sergei Fedorov	.50	1.25
55 Steve Yzerman	1.50	4.00
56 Brendan Shanahan	.30	.75
57 Chris Osgood	.25	.60
58 Nicklas Lidstrom	.30	.75
59 Igor Larionov	.10	.30
60 Chris Chelios	.30	.75
61 Bill Guerin	.10	.30
62 Doug Weight	.25	.60
63 Mike Grier	.10	.30
64 Tommy Salo	.25	.60
65 Bill Ranford	.25	.60
66 Tom Poti	.10	.30
67 Daniel Cleary	.10	.30
68 Mark Parrish	.10	.30
69 Pavel Bure	.30	.75
70 Oleg Kvasha	.10	.30
71 Viktor Kozlov	.25	.60
72 Trevor Kidd	.25	.60
73 Rob Blake	.25	.60
74 Pavel Rosa	.10	.30
75 Luc Robitaille	.25	.60
76 Zigmund Palffy	.25	.60
77 Aki Berg	.10	.30
78 Saku Koivu	.30	.75
79 Jeff Hackett	.25	.60
80 Trevor Linden	.25	.60
81 Cliff Ronning	.25	.60
82 David Legwand	.25	.60
83 Mike Dunham	.25	.60
84 Scott Stevens	.25	.60
85 Martin Brodeur	.75	2.00
86 Patrik Elias	.25	.60
87 Brendan Morrison	.25	.60
88 Scott Niedermayer	.10	.30
89 Vadim Sharifijanov	.10	.30
90 Mike Watt	.10	.30
91 Felix Potvin	.30	.75
92 Eric Brewer	.10	.30
93 Jorgen Jonsson RC	.25	.60
94 Kenny Jonsson	.10	.30
95 Olli Jokinen	.25	.60
96 Theo Fleury	.10	.30
97 Brian Leetch	.25	.60
98 Mike Richter	.30	.75
99 Petr Nedved	.25	.60
100 Adam Graves	.10	.30
101 Manny Malhotra	.25	.60
102 Alexei Yashin	.10	.30
103 Daniel Alfredsson	.25	.60
104 Ron Tugnutt	.25	.60
105 Magnus Arvedson	.10	.30
106 Sami Salo	.10	.30
107 Marian Hossa	.30	.75
108 Eric Lindros	.30	.75
109 John Vanbiesbrouck	.25	.60
110 John LeClair	.30	.75
111 Rod Brind'Amour	.25	.60
112 Mark Recchi	.25	.60
113 Eric Desjardins	.25	.60
114 Jeremy Roenick	.40	1.00
115 Keith Tkachuk	.30	.75
116 Rick Tocchet	.25	.60
117 Robert Esche RC	1.00	2.50
118 Nikolai Khabibulin	.25	.60
119 Teppo Numminen	.10	.30
120 Jaromir Jagr	.50	1.25
121 Martin Straka	.10	.30
122 Jan Hrdina	.10	.30
123 German Titov	.10	.30
124 Alexei Kovalev	.25	.60
125 Matthew Barnaby	.25	.60
126 Vincent Damphousse	.10	.30
127 Owen Nolan	.25	.60
128 Jeff Friesen	.10	.30
129 Patrick Marleau	.25	.60
130 Marco Sturm	.25	.60
131 Mike Vernon	.25	.60
132 Pavol Demitra	.25	.60
133 Al MacInnis	.25	.60
134 Pierre Turgeon	.25	.60
135 Chris Pronger	.25	.60
136 Jochen Hecht RC	1.00	2.50
137 Vincent Lecavalier	.30	.75
138 Paul Mara	.25	.60
139 Dan Cloutier	.25	.60
140 Andrei Zyuzin	.10	.30
141 Pavel Kubina	.10	.30
142 Kevin Hodson	.25	.60
143 Mats Sundin	.30	.75
144 Curtis Joseph	.30	.75
145 Sergei Berezin	.25	.60
146 Bryan Berard	.10	.30
147 Tomas Kaberle	.10	.30
148 Daniil Markov	.10	.30
149 Mark Messier	.30	.75
150 Bill Muckalt	.25	.60
151 Markus Naslund	.30	.75
152 Mattias Ohlund	.25	.60
153 Ed Jovanovski	.10	.30
154 Steve Kariya RC	1.00	2.50
155 Josh Holden	.10	.30
156 Richard Zednik	.10	.30
157 Jaroslav Svejkovsky	.10	.30
158 Adam Oates	.25	.60
159 Peter Bondra	.25	.60
160 Sergei Gonchar	.10	.30
161 Olaf Kolzig	.25	.60
162 Jan Bulis	.10	.30
163 Patrik Stefan AU RC	8.00	20.00
164 Daniel Sedin AU	6.00	15.00
165 Henrik Sedin AU	6.00	15.00
166 Pavel Brendl AU RC	10.00	25.00
167 Brian Finley AU	6.00	15.00
168 Taylor Pyatt AU	8.00	20.00
169 Jamie Lundmark AU	6.00	15.00
170 Denis Shvidki	2.50	6.00
171 Jani Rita	2.50	6.00
172 Oleg Saprykin RC	6.00	15.00
173 Nick Boynton	2.50	6.00
174 Tim Connolly AU	6.00	15.00
175 Kris Beech AU	6.00	15.00
176 Roberto Luongo	4.00	10.00
177 David Legwand	3.00	8.00
178 Dave Tanabe	2.50	6.00
179 Barret Jackman	2.50	6.00
180 Maxime Ouellet	4.00	10.00

1999-00 SPx Radiance

Randomly inserted in packs, this 135-card set parallels the base SPx set. Cards are enhanced with green foil, and each card is serial numbered out of 100.

*RADIANCE 1-162: 20X TO 50X BASIC CARDS
*RADIANCE 163-180: 1X TO 3X BASIC SP
*RADIANCE 163-180: .5X TO 1.2X BASIC SP AU

164 Daniel Sedin	30.00	60.00
165 Henrik Sedin	25.00	50.00
166 Pavel Brendl	40.00	100.00

1999-00 SPx Spectrum

Randomly inserted in packs, this 135-card set parallels the base SPx set. Cards are enhanced with red foil, and each is numbered one of one.

UNPRICED SPECTRUM PRINT RUN 1

1999-00 SPx 99 Cheers

Randomly inserted in packs at 1:17, this 15-card set pays tribute to Wayne Gretzky by capturing some of his most magical moments. Card backs carry a "CH" prefix.

COMPLETE SET (15)	30.00	60.00
COMMON GRETZKY (CH1-15)	2.50	6.00

1999-00 SPx Highlight Heroes

Randomly seeded in packs at 1:9, this 10-card set focuses on 10 of the NHL's top superstars. Action photos are set against a rainbow holo-foil checkered background. Card backs carry an "HH" prefix.

COMPLETE SET (10)	15.00	30.00
HH1 Wayne Gretzky	4.00	10.00
HH2 Sergei Samsonov	.60	1.50
HH3 Dominik Hasek	1.25	3.00
HH4 Jaromir Jagr	1.00	2.50
HH5 Patrick Roy	3.00	8.00
HH6 Paul Kariya	1.00	2.50
HH7 Pavel Bure	.75	2.00
HH8 Peter Forsberg	1.50	4.00
HH9 Eric Lindros	1.50	4.00
HH10 Teemu Selanne	1.00	2.50

1999-00 SPx Prolifics

Randomly seeded in packs at 1:17, this 15-card set highlights the 15 most collectible defensive players in the NHL. Card backs carry a "P" prefix.

COMPLETE SET (15)	25.00	50.00
P1 Paul Kariya	1.00	2.50
P2 Jaromir Jagr	1.50	4.00
P3 Brett Hull	1.25	3.00
P4 Joe Sakic	2.00	5.00
P5 Sergei Samsonov	1.00	2.50
P6 Keith Tkachuk	1.00	2.50
P7 Brendan Shanahan	1.50	4.00
P8 Vincent Lecavalier	1.00	2.50
P9 Steve Yzerman	5.00	12.00
P10 Jeremy Roenick	1.25	3.00
P11 Mike Modano	1.50	4.00
P12 John LeClair	1.25	3.00
P13 Peter Forsberg	2.50	6.00
P14 Ray Bourque	1.50	4.00
P15 David Legwand	1.00	2.50

1999-00 SPx SPXcitement

Randomly seeded in packs at 1:3, this 20-card set features the most exciting NHL players on a holographic Light F/X background. Card backs carry an "X" prefix.

COMPLETE SET (20)	20.00	40.00
X1 Wayne Gretzky	3.00	8.00
X2 Patrick Roy	2.50	6.00
X3 Pavel Bure	.60	1.50
X4 Steve Yzerman	2.50	6.00
X5 David Legwand	.50	1.25
X6 Dominik Hasek	1.00	2.50
X7 Sergei Samsonov	.50	1.25
X8 Patrik Stefan	1.00	2.50
X9 Eric Lindros	.75	2.00
X10 Brett Hull	.60	1.50
X11 Steve Kariya	.50	1.25
X12 Keith Tkachuk	.50	1.25
X13 Alex Tanguay	.50	1.25
X14 Peter Forsberg	1.25	3.00
X15 Jaromir Jagr	.75	2.00
X16 Paul Kariya	.50	1.25
X17 Brendan Shanahan	.75	2.00
X18 Mike Modano	.75	2.00
X19 John LeClair	.60	1.50
X20 Teemu Selanne	.50	1.25

1999-00 SPx SPXtreme

Randomly inserted in packs at 1:6, this 20-card set showcases some of the most popular players in the NHL. Action shots are set against a holographic Light F/X background. Card backs carry an "XT" prefix.

COMPLETE SET (20)	20.00	40.00
XT1 Al MacInnis	.50	1.25
XT2 Keith Tkachuk	.50	1.25
XT3 Peter Forsberg	1.50	4.00
XT4 Teemu Selanne	.60	1.50
XT5 Patrick Roy	3.00	8.00
XT6 Sergei Samsonov	.50	1.25
XT7 Brendan Shanahan	1.00	2.50
XT8 Mike Modano	1.00	2.50
XT9 Eric Lindros	1.00	2.50
XT10 Paul Kariya	.60	1.50
XT11 Jaromir Jagr	1.00	2.50
XT12 Brett Hull	.75	2.00
XT13 Mats Sundin	.60	1.50
XT14 Dominik Hasek	1.25	3.00
XT15 Ray Bourque	1.00	2.50
XT16 Curtis Joseph	.60	1.50
XT17 John LeClair	.75	2.00
XT18 Ed Belfour	.60	1.50
XT19 David Legwand	.60	1.50
XT20 Wayne Gretzky	4.00	10.00

1999-00 SPx Starscape

Randomly inserted in packs at 1:9, this 10-card set places NHL's hottest in action over a holographic foil backdrop. Card backs carry an "S" prefix.

COMPLETE SET (10)	12.00	25.00
S1 Brett Hull	.75	2.00
S2 Jaromir Jagr	1.00	2.50
S3 Pavel Bure	.75	2.00
S4 Dominik Hasek	1.25	3.00
S5 Eric Lindros	1.00	2.50
S6 Paul Kariya	.60	1.50
S7 Peter Forsberg	1.50	4.00
S8 Teemu Selanne	.60	1.50
S9 Patrick Roy	3.00	8.00
S10 Keith Tkachuk	.60	1.50

1999-00 SPx Winning Materials

Randomly inserted in packs at 1:252, this 12-card set features a swatch of a game-used jersey and puck. Also released with the set were autographed versions of Brett Hull and Wayne Gretzky.

WM1 Mike Modano	15.00	40.00
WM2 Martin Brodeur	25.00	60.00
WM3 Steve Yzerman	25.00	60.00
WM4 Jaromir Jagr	20.00	50.00
WM5 Dominik Hasek	25.00	60.00
WM6 Brett Hull	15.00	40.00
WM7 Patrick Roy	25.00	60.00
WM8 Ray Bourque	20.00	50.00
WM9 Eric Lindros	10.00	25.00
WM10 Wayne Gretzky	50.00	125.00
WMA1 W.Gretzky AU/25	500.00	800.00
WMA2 B.Hull AU/25	125.00	300.00

2000-01 SPx

SPx originally issued the set of 130 cards with 30 short-printed rookies, and 10 short-printed jersey cards. SPx later released an update set of 57 cards, which included 35 short-printed rookies. The card front design used silver-foil and added rainbow-holofoil for the SPx logo. The jersey cards were available in packs of 2000-01 SPx at a rate of 1:13.

COMPLETE SET (130)	250.00	500.00
COMP.SET w/o SP's (90)	20.00	40.00
1 Paul Kariya	.30	.75
2 Teemu Selanne	.30	.75
3 Patrik Stefan	.10	.30
4 Jason Allison	.10	.30
5 Sergei Samsonov	.25	.60
6 Dominik Hasek	.60	1.50
7 Miroslav Satan	.25	.60
8 Fred Brathwaite	.25	.60
9 Valeri Bure	.10	.30
10 Ron Francis	.25	.60
11 Arturs Irbe	.25	.60
12 Tony Amonte	.25	.60
13 Joe Sakic	.60	1.50
14 Milan Hejduk	.30	.75
15 Patrick Roy	1.50	4.00
16 Peter Forsberg	.75	2.00
17 Ray Bourque	.60	1.50
18 Ron Tugnutt	.25	.60
19 Brett Hull	.40	1.00
20 Ed Belfour	.30	.75
21 Mike Modano	.50	1.25
22 Sergei Fedorov	.50	1.25
23 Brendan Shanahan	.30	.75
24 Chris Osgood	.25	.60
25 Steve Yzerman	1.50	4.00
26 Doug Weight	.25	.60
27 Tommy Salo	.25	.60
28 Pavel Bure	.30	.75
29 Trevor Kidd	.25	.60
30 Viktor Kozlov	.25	.60
31 Rob Blake	.25	.60
32 Zigmund Palffy	.25	.60
33 Luc Robitaille	.25	.60
34 Manny Fernandez	.25	.60
35 Saku Koivu	.30	.75
36 David Legwand	.25	.60
37 Martin Brodeur	.75	2.00
38 Patrik Elias	.25	.60
39 Scott Gomez	.10	.30
40 Scott Stevens	.25	.60
41 Mariusz Czerkawski	.25	.60
42 Tim Connolly	.10	.30
43 Mark Messier	.30	.75
44 Mike York	.10	.30
45 Theo Fleury	.10	.30
46 Marian Hossa	.30	.75
47 Radek Bonk	.10	.30
48 Simon Gagne	.30	.75
49 Brian Boucher	.25	.60
50 Rick Tocchet	.25	.60
51 John LeClair	.30	.75
52 Jeremy Roenick	.40	1.00
53 Keith Tkachuk	.30	.75
54 Jaromir Jagr	.50	1.25
55 Jean-Sebastien Aubin	.25	.60
56 Jeff Friesen	.10	.30
57 Steve Shields	.25	.60
58 Brad Stuart	.25	.60
59 Chris Pronger	.25	.60
60 Pavol Demitra	.25	.60
61 Roman Turek	.25	.60
62 Dan Cloutier	.25	.60
63 Vincent Lecavalier	.30	.75
64 Nikolai Antropov	.10	.30
65 Curtis Joseph	.30	.75
66 Mats Sundin	.30	.75
67 Felix Potvin	.30	.75
68 Markus Naslund	.30	.75
69 Adam Oates	.25	.60
70 Olaf Kolzig	.25	.60
71 Peter Forsberg XE	1.00	2.50
72 Brendan Shanahan XE	.60	1.50
73 Scott Stevens XE	.30	.75
74 Mark Messier XE	.50	1.25
75 John LeClair XE	.50	1.25
76 Keith Primeau XE	.40	1.00
77 Keith Tkachuk XE	.40	1.00
78 Jeremy Roenick XE	.50	1.25
79 Owen Nolan XE	.40	1.00
80 Chris Pronger XE	.40	1.00
81 Paul Kariya PRO	.30	.75
82 Dominik Hasek PRO	.75	2.00
83 Patrick Roy PRO	2.00	5.00
84 Ray Bourque PRO	.75	2.00
85 Mike Modano PRO	.60	1.50
86 Steve Yzerman PRO	2.00	5.00
87 Pavel Bure PRO	.50	1.25
88 Martin Brodeur PRO	1.00	2.50
89 John LeClair PRO	.50	1.25
90 Jaromir Jagr PRO	.60	1.50
91 Herbert Vasilijevs RC	2.00	5.00
92 Eric Nickulas RC	2.00	5.00
93 Brandon Smith RC	2.00	5.00
94 Jeff Cowan RC	2.00	5.00
95 Serge Aubin RC	2.00	5.00
96 Mike Minard RC	2.00	5.00
97 Steven Reinprecht RC	2.00	5.00
98 David Gosselin RC	2.00	5.00
99 Colin White RC	2.00	5.00
100 Willie Mitchell RC	2.00	5.00
101 Steve Brule RC	2.00	5.00
102 Steve Valiquette RC	2.00	5.00
103 Petr Mika RC	2.00	5.00
104 Chris Kenady RC	2.00	5.00
105 Johan Witehall RC	2.00	5.00
106 Jani Hurme RC	2.50	6.00
107 Jean-Guy Trudel RC	2.00	5.00
108 Dale Rominski RC	2.00	5.00
109 Greg Andrusak RC	2.00	5.00
110 Martin Havlat RC	6.00	15.00
111 Jeremy Stevenson RC	2.00	5.00
112 Sergei Vyshedkevich RC	2.00	5.00
113 Johnathan Aitken RC	2.00	5.00
114 Keith Aldridge RC	2.00	5.00
115 Rich Parent RC	2.00	5.00
116 Kaspars Astashenko RC	2.00	5.00
117 Matt Elich RC	2.00	5.00
118 Dieter Kochan RC	2.00	5.00
119 Kyle Freadrich RC	2.00	5.00
120 Justin Williams RC	4.00	10.00
121 Andrew Raycroft RC	5.00	12.00
122 Zdenek Blatny RC	3.00	8.00
123 Pavel Brendl	3.00	8.00
124 Jason Jaspers RC	3.00	8.00
125 Fedor Fedorov RC	3.00	8.00
126 Jordan Krestanovich RC	3.00	8.00
127 Marc-Andre Thinel RC	3.00	8.00
128 Damian Surma RC	3.00	8.00
129 Jeff Bateman RC	3.00	8.00
130 Sheldon Keefe	3.00	8.00
131 Ray Ferraro	.10	.30
132 Bill Guerin	.25	.60
133 Ronald Petrovicky RC	.75	2.00
134 Shane Willis	.10	.30
135 Chris Nielsen RC	.75	2.00
136 Petteri Nummelin RC	.75	2.00
137 Igor Larionov	.10	.30
138 Shawn Horcoff RC	3.00	8.00
139 Lance Ward RC	.75	2.00
140 Manny Fernandez	.25	.60
141 Scott Niedermayer	.10	.30
142 Alexei Yashin	.10	.30
143 Claude Lemieux	.10	.30
144 Mario Lemieux	2.00	5.00
145 Milan Kraft	.10	.30
146 Evgeni Nabokov	.25	.60
147 Keith Tkachuk	.30	.75
148 Gary Roberts	.10	.30
149 Daniel Sedin	.10	.30
150 Henrik Sedin	.10	.30
151 Kris Beech	.10	.30
152 Lee Goren RC	2.00	5.00
153 Pavel Kolarik RC	2.00	5.00
154 Greg Kuznik RC	2.00	5.00
155 Josef Vasicek RC	2.00	5.00
156 Rick Berry RC	2.00	5.00
157 David Aebischer RC	5.00	12.00
158 Rostislav Klesla RC	3.00	8.00
159 Marty Turco RC	6.00	15.00
160 Tyler Bouck RC	3.00	8.00
161 Mike Comrie RC	3.00	8.00
162 Eric Belanger RC	2.00	5.00
163 Marian Gaborik RC	15.00	40.00
164 Scott Hartnell RC	3.00	8.00
165 Jason Labarbera RC	3.00	8.00
166 Rick DiPietro RC	8.00	20.00
167 Ruslan Fedotenko RC	2.00	5.00
168 Petr Hubacek RC	2.00	5.00
169 Roman Cechmanek RC	2.50	6.00
170 Roman Simicek RC	2.00	5.00
171 Mark Smith RC	2.00	5.00
172 Jakub Cutta RC	2.00	5.00
173 Marc Chouinard RC	2.00	5.00
174 Darcy Hordichuk RC	2.00	5.00
175 Bryan Adams RC	2.00	5.00
176 Jarno Kultanen RC	2.00	5.00
177 Eric Boulton RC	2.00	5.00
178 Brian Swanson RC	2.00	5.00
179 Lubomir Sekeras RC	2.00	5.00
180 Eric Landry RC	2.00	5.00
181 Mike Commodore RC	2.00	5.00
182 Johan Holmqvist RC	2.00	5.00
183 Jeff Ulmer RC	2.00	5.00
184 Ossi Vaananen RC	2.00	5.00
185 Alexander Khavanov RC	2.00	5.00
186 Bryce Salvador RC	2.00	5.00
187 Reed Low RC	2.00	5.00

2000-01 SPx Spectrum

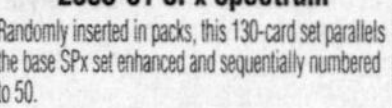

Randomly inserted in packs, this 130-card set parallels the base SPx set enhanced and sequentially numbered to 50.

*STARS: 25X TO 60X BASIC CARDS
*SP's: 1X TO 1.5X BASIC CARDS
*JERSEYS: 1X TO 1.5X BASIC CARDS

2000-01 SPx Highlight Heroes

Randomly inserted in packs at the rate of 1:7, this 14-card set features full color action photography with the words highlight heroes appearing as part of the background. Along the bottom of the card, the player's name and the words Highlight Heroes appear in silver foil.

COMPLETE SET (14)	10.00	20.00
HH1 Paul Kariya	.60	1.50
HH2 Patrik Stefan	.50	1.25
HH3 Joe Thornton	1.00	2.50
HH4 Valeri Bure	.50	1.25
HH5 Milan Hejduk	.60	1.50
HH6 Brett Hull	.75	2.00
HH7 Brendan Shanahan	1.00	2.50
HH8 Pavel Bure	.75	2.00
HH9 Marian Hossa	.60	1.50
HH10 Brian Boucher	.60	1.50
HH11 Jeremy Roenick	.60	1.50
HH12 Jaromir Jagr	1.00	2.50
HH13 Chris Pronger	.50	1.25
HH14 Curtis Joseph	.60	1.50

2000-01 SPx Prolifics

Randomly inserted in packs at the rate of 1:14, this seven card set features an action photograph on the left side of the card front and a portrait style photo on the right. These two photos are separated by a silver foil line and the word Prolifics.

COMPLETE SET (7)	8.00	15.00
P1 Dominik Hasek	1.25	3.00
P2 Ray Bourque	1.25	3.00
P3 Brett Hull	.75	2.00
P4 Steve Yzerman	3.00	8.00
P5 Mark Messier	.75	2.00
P6 John LeClair	.75	2.00
P7 Jaromir Jagr	1.00	2.50

2000-01 SPx Rookie Redemption

Randomly inserted in packs, this 30-card set was issued as team specific redemption cards that were redeemable for rookies who made their NHL debut in the 2001-02 season. Exchange cards expired 5/2002.

RR1 Ilja Bryzgalov	3.00	8.00
RR2 Ilya Kovalchuk	10.00	25.00
RR3 Ivan Huml	2.00	5.00
RR4 Ales Kotalik	3.00	8.00
RR5 Scott Nichol	2.00	5.00
RR6 Erik Cole	3.00	8.00
RR7 Casey Hankinson	2.00	5.00
RR8 Vaclav Nedorost	2.00	5.00
RR9 Martin Spanhel	2.00	5.00
RR10 Niko Kapanen	2.00	5.00
RR11 Pavel Datsyuk	8.00	20.00
RR12 Ty Conklin	3.00	8.00
RR13 Kristian Huselius	3.00	8.00
RR14 Jaroslav Bednar	2.00	5.00
RR15 Nick Schultz	2.00	5.00
RR16 Martti Jarventie	2.00	5.00
RR17 Martin Erat	3.00	8.00
RR18 Andreas Salomonsson	2.00	5.00
RR19 Raffi Torres	3.00	8.00
RR20 Dan Blackburn	3.00	8.00
RR21 Ivan Ciernik	2.00	5.00
RR22 Jiri Dopita	2.00	5.00
RR23 Krys Kolanos	2.00	5.00
RR24 Billy Tibbetts	2.00	5.00
RR25 Jeff Jillson	2.00	5.00
RR26 Mark Rycroft	2.00	5.00
RR27 Nikita Alexeev	2.00	5.00
RR28 Bob Wren	2.00	5.00
RR29 Pat Kavanagh	2.00	5.00
RR30 Brian Sutherby	3.00	5.00

2000-01 SPx SPXcitement

COMPLETE SET (14)	10.00	20.00
STATED ODDS 1:7		
X1 Teemu Selanne	.60	1.50
X2 Sergei Samsonov	.50	1.25
X3 Tony Amonte	.50	1.25
X4 Joe Sakic	1.25	3.00
X5 Mike Modano	1.00	2.50
X6 Sergei Fedorov	1.25	3.00
X7 Pavel Bure	.75	2.00
X8 Martin Brodeur	1.50	4.00
X9 Simon Gagne	.50	1.25
X10 Jaromir Jagr	1.00	2.50
X11 Jeff Friesen	.50	1.25
X12 Roman Turek	.50	1.25
X13 Vincent Lecavalier	.60	1.50
X14 Mats Sundin	.60	1.50

2000-01 SPx SPXtreme

COMPLETE SET (7)	8.00	15.00
STATED ODDS 1:14		
S1 Paul Kariya	.75	2.00
S2 Peter Forsberg	1.50	4.00
S3 Mike Modano	1.00	2.50
S4 Martin Brodeur	1.50	4.00
S5 Mark Messier	.75	2.00
S6 John LeClair	.75	2.00
S7 Jaromir Jagr	1.00	2.50

2000-01 SPx Winning Materials

Randomly seeded in SPx packs at the rate of 1:14 and UD Update packs at 1:60, this 48-card set features a player action photo and a swatch of a game worn jersey as well as a game used stick. Update cards are marked below.

*MULT.COLOR SWATCH/STICK: 1X TO 2X

AC Anson Carter SP	15.00	40.00
BH Brett Hull SP	12.50	30.00
BS Brendan Shanahan	6.00	15.00
CJ Curtis Joseph	8.00	20.00
CO Chris Osgood	5.00	12.00
DH Dominik Hasek	10.00	25.00
FP Felix Potvin	6.00	15.00
JJ Jaromir Jagr	8.00	20.00
JL John LeClair	6.00	15.00
JR Jeremy Roenick	8.00	20.00
JS Joe Sakic	12.50	30.00

KJ Kenny Jonsson 4.00 10.00
KT Keith Tkachuk 6.00 15.00
MB Martin Brodeur SP 20.00 50.00
ML Mario Lemieux 20.00 50.00
MM Mike Modano SP 20.00 50.00
NL Nicklas Lidstrom 6.00 15.00
PD Pavol Demitra SP 5.00 12.00
PF Peter Forsberg 12.50 30.00
PK Paul Kariya SP 12.50 30.00
PR Patrick Roy 15.00 40.00
RB Ray Bourque 12.50 30.00
SF Sergei Fedorov 10.00 25.00
SY Steve Yzerman 20.00 50.00
TO Tony Amonte 5.00 12.00
TS Teemu Selanne 6.00 15.00
WG Wayne Gretzky 40.00 80.00
PBO Peter Bondra SP 8.00 20.00
WBC Brian Boucher Upd 5.00 12.00
WBE Ed Belfour Upd 6.00 15.00
WBI Martin Biron Upd 5.00 12.00
WBO Ray Bourque Upd 15.00 40.00
WBU Valeri Bure Upd 4.00 10.00
WFE Sergei Fedorov Upd 10.00 25.00
WGR Wayne Gretzky Upd 40.00 80.00
WJJ Jaromir Jagr Upd 8.00 20.00
WKA Paul Kariya Upd 6.00 15.00
WLE John LeClair Upd 6.00 15.00
WLU Roberto Luongo Upd 8.00 20.00
WRE Jeremy Roenick Upd 8.00 20.00
WRO Patrick Roy Upd 20.00 50.00
WSA Miroslav Satan Upd 5.00 12.00
WSE Teemu Selanne Upd 6.00 15.00
WSU Mats Sundin Upd 6.00 15.00
WTB Jocelyn Thibault Upd 5.00 12.00
WTH Joe Thornton Upd 12.50 30.00
WTK Keith Tkachuk Upd 6.00 15.00
WYZ Steve Yzerman Upd 20.00 50.00

2000-01 SPx Winning Materials Autographs

Randomly inserted in packs, this 10-card set parallels the SPx Winning Materials set but adds an authentic player autograph. These cards were limited to 25 serial-numbered sets and are not priced due to scarcity and volatility.

NOT PRICED DUE TO SCARCITY
SBH Brett Hull
SCJ Curtis Joseph
SFP Felix Potvin
SJL John LeClair
SKT Keith Tkachuk
SMB Martin Brodeur
SML Mario Lemieux
SRB Ray Bourque
SSY Steve Yzerman
SWG Wayne Gretzky

2001-02 SPx

Released in mid-December 2001, this set originally consisted of 170 cards including 70 base cards, 42 rookie cards (91-132) short printed to 999, and 38 rookie threads cards (133-151) short printed to either 800 or 1500. The rookie threads subset had two versions, home and away, for each player. Cards 197-216 were available in random packs of UD Rookie Update and were serial-numbered to 999.

COMP.SET w/o SP's (155) 40.00 80.00
1 Paul Kariya .30 .75
2 Patrik Stefan .10 .30
3 Sergei Samsonov .25 .60
4 Joe Thornton .50 1.25
5 Bill Guerin .25 .60
6 Martin Biron .25 .60
7 Miroslav Satan .25 .60
8 Jarome Iginla .40 1.00
9 Marc Savard .10 .30
10 Arturs Irbe .25 .60
11 Tony Amonte .25 .60
12 Steve Sullivan .10 .30
13 Joe Sakic .60 1.50
14 Peter Forsberg .75 2.00
15 Ray Bourque .60 1.50
16 Milan Hejduk .30 .75
17 Patrick Roy 1.50 4.00
18 Ron Tugnutt .25 .60
19 Mike Modano .50 1.25
20 Ed Belfour .30 .75
21 Pierre Turgeon .25 .60
22 Steve Yzerman 1.00 2.50
23 Brendan Shanahan .30 .75
24 Sergei Fedorov .50 1.25
25 Luc Robitaille .25 .60
26 Dominik Hasek .60 1.50
27 Tommy Salo .25 .60
28 Mike Comrie .25 .60
29 Pavel Bure .30 .75
30 Zigmund Palffy .25 .60
31 Felix Potvin .30 .75
32 Adam Deadmarsh .10 .30
33 Marian Gaborik .60 1.50
34 Saku Koivu .30 .75
35 David Legwand .25 .60
36 Mike Dunham .25 .60
37 Martin Brodeur .75 2.00
38 Patrik Elias .25 .60
39 Jason Arnott .10 .30
40 Michael Peca .10 .30
41 Rick DiPietro .25 .60
42 Mark Messier .30 .75
43 Theo Fleury .10 .30
44 Marian Hossa .30 .75
45 Radek Bonk .10 .30
46 Jeremy Roenick .40 1.00
47 Roman Cechmanek .25 .60
48 Keith Primeau .10 .30
49 John LeClair .40 1.00
50 Sean Burke .25 .60
51 Alexei Kovalev .25 .60
52 Mario Lemieux 2.00 5.00
53 Johan Hedberg .25 .60
54 Robert Lang .10 .30
55 Evgeni Nabokov .25 .60
56 Teemu Selanne .30 .75
57 Owen Nolan .25 .60
58 Chris Pronger .25 .60
59 Keith Tkachuk .30 .75
60 Doug Weight .25 .60
61 Pavol Demitra .25 .60
62 Brad Richards .25 .60
63 Vincent Lecavalier .30 .75
64 Curtis Joseph .30 .75
65 Mats Sundin .30 .75
66 Markus Naslund .30 .75
67 Daniel Sedin .10 .30
68 Jaromir Jagr .50 1.25
69 Peter Bondra .30 .75
70 Olaf Kolzig .25 .60
71 Paul Kariya .30 .75
72 Peter Forsberg .75 2.00
73 Mike Modano .60 1.50
74 Sergei Fedorov .75 2.00
75 Steve Yzerman 2.00 5.00
76 Pavel Bure .50 1.25
77 Zigmund Palffy .25 .60
78 Mario Lemieux 2.00 5.00
79 Vincent Lecavalier .30 .75
80 Markus Naslund .30 .75
81 Joe Sakic .75 2.00
82 Chris Drury .25 .60
83 Patrick Roy 2.00 5.00
84 Mike Modano .60 1.50
85 Steve Yzerman 2.00 5.00
86 Pavel Bure .50 1.25
87 Martin Brodeur 1.00 2.50
88 John LeClair .40 1.00
89 Mario Lemieux 2.00 5.00
90 Chris Pronger .25 .60
91 Timo Parssinen RC 2.00 5.00
92 Ilja Bryzgalov RC 4.00 10.00
93 Kevin Sawyer RC 2.00 5.00
94 Dany Heatley SP 6.00 15.00
95 Zdenek Kutlak RC 2.00 5.00
96 Greg Crozier RC 2.00 5.00
97 Mika Noronen SP 4.00 10.00
98 Scott Nichol RC 2.00 5.00
99 Erik Cole RC 6.00 15.00
100 Casey Hankinson RC 2.00 5.00
101 Vaclav Nedorost RC 2.00 5.00
102 Jaroslav Obsut RC 2.00 5.00
103 Niko Kapanen RC 4.00 10.00
104 Pavel Datsyuk RC 12.00 30.00
105 Niklas Hagman RC 2.00 5.00
106 Kristian Huselius RC 6.00 15.00
107 Andrej Podkonicky RC 2.00 5.00
108 Francis Belanger RC 2.00 5.00
109 Martin Erat RC 2.00 5.00
110 Bill Bowler RC 2.00 5.00
111 Scott Clemmensen RC 2.00 5.00
112 Josef Boumedienne RC 2.00 5.00
113 Andreas Salomonsson RC 2.00 5.00
114 Mike Jefferson RC 2.00 5.00
115 Stanislav Gron RC 2.00 5.00
116 Radek Martinek RC 2.00 5.00
117 Dan Blackburn RC 3.00 8.00
118 Chris Neil RC 2.00 5.00
119 Ivan Ciernik RC 2.00 5.00
120 Pavel Brendl SP 2.00 5.00
121 David Cullen RC 2.00 5.00
122 Billy Tibbetts RC 2.00 5.00
123 Miikka Kiprusoff SP 6.00 15.00
124 Jeff Jillson RC 2.00 5.00
125 Michel Larocque RC 2.00 5.00
126 Mark Rycroft RC 2.00 5.00
127 Thomas Ziegler RC 2.00 5.00
128 Nikita Alexeev RC 2.00 5.00
129 Bob Wren RC 2.00 5.00
130 Mike Brown SP 2.00 5.00
131 Pat Kavanagh RC 2.00 5.00
132 Brian Sutherby RC 2.00 5.00
133 Brian Pothier AW RC/800 3.00 8.00
133 Brian Pothier HM RC/800 3.00 8.00
134 Dan Snyder HM RC/1500 4.00 10.00
134 Dan Snyder AW RC/1500 4.00 10.00
135 Jody Shelley HM RC/1500 4.00 10.00
135 Jody Shelley AW RC/1500 4.00 10.00
136 Martin Spanhel AW RC/1500 3.00 8.00
136 Martin Spanhel HM RC/1500 3.00 8.00
137 Mathieu Darche AW RC/1500 3.00 8.00
137 Mathieu Darche HM RC/1500 3.00 8.00
138 Matt Davidson AW RC/1500 3.00 8.00
138 Matt Davidson HM RC/1500 3.00 8.00
139 Sean Selmser AW RC/1500 3.00 8.00
139 Sean Selmser HM RC/1500 3.00 8.00
140 Jason Chimera HM RC/800 3.00 8.00
140 Jason Chimera AW RC/800 3.00 8.00
141 Mike Matteucci HM RC/1500 3.00 8.00
141 Mike Matteucci AW RC/1500 3.00 8.00
142 Pascal Dupuis AW RC/800 3.00 8.00
142 Pascal Dupuis HM RC/800 3.00 8.00
143 Peter Smrek AW RC/800 3.00 8.00
143 Peter Smrek HM RC/800 3.00 8.00
144 M.Samuelsson HM RC/1500 4.00 10.00
144 M.Samuelsson AW RC/1500 4.00 10.00
145 J.Kwiatkowski AW RC/1500 3.00 8.00
145 J.Kwiatkowski HM RC/1500 3.00 8.00
146 Kirby Law HM RC/1500 3.00 8.00
146 Kirby Law AW RC/1500 3.00 8.00
147 Tomas Divisek HM RC/1500 3.00 8.00
147 Tomas Divisek AW RC/1500 3.00 8.00
148 Ilya Kovalchuk HM RC 20.00 40.00
148 Ilya Kovalchuk AW RC 20.00 40.00
149 Jaroslav Bednar AW RC/800 3.00 8.00
149 Jaroslav Bednar HM RC/800 3.00 8.00
150 Jiri Dopita HM RC/800 3.00 8.00
150 Jiri Dopita AW RC/800 3.00 8.00
151 Krys Kolanos AW RC/800 3.00 8.00
151 Krys Kolanos HM RC/800 3.00 8.00
152 Jeff Friesen .10 .30
153 Jean-Sebastien Giguere .25 .60
154 Dany Heatley .40 1.00
155 Pascal Rheaume .10 .30
156 Andy Hilbert .10 .30
157 Jozef Stumpel .10 .30
158 Glen Murray .10 .30
159 Maxim Afinogenov .10 .30
160 Roman Turek .25 .60
161 Craig Conroy .10 .30
162 Jeff O'Neill .10 .30
163 Sami Kapanen .10 .30
164 Jocelyn Thibault .25 .60
165 Mark Bell .10 .30
166 Kyle Calder .10 .30
167 Alex Tanguay .25 .60
168 Darius Kasparaitis .10 .30
169 Chris Drury .25 .60
170 Radim Vrbata .10 .30
171 Rostislav Klesla .10 .30
172 Brett Hull .40 1.00
173 Jani Rita .10 .30
174 Mike York .10 .30
175 Roberto Luongo .40 1.00
176 Jason Allison .10 .30
177 Andrew Brunette .10 .30
178 Sergei Berezin .25 .60
179 Donald Audette .10 .30
180 Brian Gionta .10 .30
181 Alexei Yashin .10 .30
182 Chris Osgood .25 .60
183 Pavel Bure .30 .75
184 Tom Poti .10 .30
185 Eric Lindros .30 .75
186 Patrick Lalime .25 .60
187 Martin Havlat .25 .60
188 Brian Boucher .25 .60
189 Simon Gagne .30 .75
190 Brian Savage .10 .30
191 Brent Johnson .25 .60
192 Gordie Dwyer .10 .30
193 Nikolai Khabibulin .30 .75
194 Alexander Mogilny .25 .60
195 Brendan Morrison .25 .60
196 Trevor Linden .10 .30
197 Pasi Nurminen RC 2.00 5.00
198 Ivan Huml RC 2.00 5.00
199 Ales Kotalik RC 3.00 8.00
200 Mike Peluso RC 2.00 5.00
201 Riku Hahl RC 2.00 5.00
202 Kelly Fairchild RC 2.00 5.00
203 Blake Bellefeuille RC 2.00 5.00
204 Sean Avery RC 4.00 10.00
205 Brad Norton RC 2.00 5.00
206 Marcel Hossa RC 4.00 10.00
207 Olivier Michaud RC 2.00 5.00
208 Robert Schnabel RC 2.00 5.00
209 Christian Berglund RC 2.00 5.00
210 Raffi Torres RC 4.00 10.00
211 Toni Dahlman RC 2.00 5.00
212 Branko Radivojevic RC 3.00 8.00
213 Shane Endicott RC 2.00 5.00
214 Tom Kostopoulos RC 2.00 5.00
215 Sebastien Centomo RC 2.00 5.00
216 Karel Pilar RC 2.00 5.00
NNO Steve Yzerman SAMPLE 2.00 5.00

2001-02 SPx Hidden Treasures

Available in random packs of UD Rookie Update, this 22-card set featured swatches of game-used jerseys from two or three different NHL players. Dual jerseys were inserted at a rate of 1:45 while triple jerseys were inserted at 1:90.

DTAD Maxim Afinogenov 8.00 20.00
J-P Dumont
DTBJ Peter Bondra 10.00 25.00
Jaromir Jagr
DTBN Rob Blake 8.00 20.00
Ville Nieminen
DTFC Ruslan Fedotenko 8.00 20.00
Tim Connolly
DTGW Simon Gagne 8.00 20.00
Justin Williams
DTHB Milan Hejduk 8.00 20.00
Rob Blake
DTJD Jason Allison 8.00 20.00
Adam Deadmarsh
DTPS Zigmund Palffy 8.00 20.00
Miroslav Satan
DTSF Mats Sundin 10.00 25.00
Peter Forsberg
DTSG Steve Sullivan 8.00 20.00
Simon Gagne
DTTD Tony Amonte 8.00 20.00
Chris Drury
DTTP Jocelyn Thibault 10.00 25.00
Felix Potvin
DTTT Jocelyn Thibault 8.00 20.00
Jose Theodore
DTYL Mike York 8.00 20.00
Brian Leetch
TTBSS Peter Bondra 12.50 30.00
Teemu Selanne
Mats Sundin
TTBTT Martin Brodeur 25.00 60.00
Jocelyn Thibault
Jose Theodore
TTDBA J-P Dumont 12.50 30.00
Martin Biron
Maxim Afinogenov
TTDSA Eric Daze 12.50 30.00
Steve Sullivan
Tony Amonte
TTFSD Peter Forsberg 15.00 40.00
Brendan Shanahan
Adam Deadmarsh
TTKBL Rostislav Klesla 12.50 30.00
Rob Blake
Nicklas Lidstrom
TTTHN Alex Tanguay 12.50 30.00
Dan Hinote
Ville Nieminen
TTYLS Yzerman/Lemieux/Sakic 100.00 200.00

2001-02 SPx Hockey Treasures

Inserted at a rate of 1:19, this 19-card set featured swatches of game-used jerseys and sticks of the featured players. Cards were silver in color and the swatches were aligned parallel to one another with a color photo of the given player on the right side of the card front.

HTBH Brett Hull 6.00 15.00
HTCJ Curtis Joseph 5.00 12.00
HTDH Dominik Hasek 8.00 20.00
HTHU Brett Hull 6.00 15.00
HTJI Jarome Iginla 6.00 15.00
HTJL John LeClair 5.00 12.00
HTJN Joe Nieuwendyk 6.00 15.00
HTKP Keith Primeau 5.00 12.00
HTLE John LeClair 5.00 12.00
HTMB Martin Brodeur 10.00 25.00
HTML Mario Lemieux 15.00 40.00
HTMM Mike Modano 8.00 20.00
HTMO Mike Modano 6.00 15.00
HTPR Patrick Roy 12.50 30.00
HTRC Roman Cechmanek 5.00 12.00
HTSF Sergei Fedorov 6.00 15.00
HTSS Sergei Samsonov 5.00 12.00
HTSY Steve Yzerman 12.50 30.00
HTTS Teemu Selanne 5.00 12.00

2001-02 SPx Hockey Treasures Autographed

This set partially paralleled the base hockey treasures set but also carried authentic player autographs. Each card was serial-numbered out of 50. Please not that not all cards listed below have a parent card in the base hockey treasures set.

STBO Ray Bourque 75.00 200.00
STCJ Curtis Joseph 25.00 60.00
STJI Jarome Iginla 30.00 80.00
STJL John LeClair 25.00 60.00
STKE Keith Primeau 25.00 60.00
STKP Keith Primeau 25.00 60.00
STLE John LeClair 25.00 60.00
STRB Ray Bourque 75.00 200.00
STSY Steve Yzerman 75.00 200.00
STTU Marty Turco 30.00 80.00

2001-02 SPx Rookie Redemption

Randomly inserted into packs of UD Rookie Update, this 30-card set of redemption cards represented each team in the NHL. Redemption cards were redeemable for rookies who make their debut in the 2002/03 season. Cards were serial-numbered out of 1250. Redemption cards expire 4/30/2005.

R1 Stanislav Chistov 2.00 5.00
R2 Mark Hartigan 2.00 5.00
R3 Tim Thomas 5.00 12.00
R4 Henrik Tallinder 2.00 5.00
R5 Chuck Kobasew 4.00 10.00
R6 Jaroslav Svoboda 2.00 5.00
R7 Shawn Thornton 2.00 5.00
R8 Jeff Paul 2.00 5.00
R9 Rick Nash 10.00 25.00
R10 John Erskine 2.00 5.00
R11 Henrik Zetterberg 10.00 25.00
R12 Ales Hemsky 6.00 15.00
R13 Jay Bouwmeester 4.00 10.00
R14 Alexander Frolov 5.00 12.00
R15 P-M Bouchard 4.00 10.00
R16 Ron Hainsey 2.00 5.00
R17 Scottie Upshall 5.00 12.00
R18 Steve Ott 4.00 10.00
R19 Eric Godard 2.00 5.00
R20 Jamie Lundmark 2.00 5.00
R21 Jason Spezza 8.00 20.00
R22 Radovan Somik 2.00 5.00
R23 Jeff Taffe 2.00 5.00
R24 Shane Endicott 2.00 5.00
R25 Lynn Loyns 2.00 5.00
R26 Curtis Sanford 2.00 5.00
R27 Alexander Svitov 2.00 5.00
R28 Carlo Colaiacovo 2.00 5.00
R29 Fedor Fedorov 2.00 5.00
R30 Steve Eminger 2.00 5.00

2001-02 SPx Rookie Treasures

Available in random packs of UD Rookie Update at a rate of 1:20, this 20-card set resembled the hockey treasures design but focused on rookies and prospects. Each card carried a swatch of game-worn jersey as well as game used stick.

RTDP Brian Pothier 3.00 8.00
RTDA Mathieu Darche 3.00 8.00
RTDS Dan Snyder 6.00 15.00
RTIK Ilya Kovalchuk 12.00 30.00
RTJB Jaroslav Bednar 3.00 8.00
RTJC Jason Chimera 3.00 8.00

RTJD Jiri Dopita 3.00 8.00
RTJK Joel Kwiatkowski 3.00 8.00
RTJS Jody Shelley 6.00 15.00
RTKK Krys Kolanos 3.00 8.00
RTKL Kirby Law 3.00 8.00
RTMD Matt Davidson 3.00 8.00
RTMM Mike Matteucci 3.00 8.00
RTMS Martin Spanhel 3.00 8.00
RTMS Mikael Samuelsson 3.00 8.00
RTPD Pascal Dupuis 3.00 8.00
RTPS Peter Smrek 3.00 8.00
RTRT Raffi Torres 4.00 10.00
RTSS Sean Selmser 3.00 8.00
RTTD Tomas Divisek 3.00 8.00

2001-02 SPx Signs of Xcellence

Inserted at 1:279, this 9-card set featured authentic player autographs. Card fronts were gold toned and displayed a large signing area with a smaller player photo off to the side of the card and a silhouette of the player in the background.

BO Bobby Orr 200.00 300.00
DW Doug Weight 10.00 25.00
GH Gordie Howe 125.00 250.00
JL John LeClair 10.00 25.00
MC Mike Comrie 5.00 12.00
MM Mark Messier 150.00 250.00
SG Simon Gagne 10.00 25.00
TL Trevor Letowski 5.00 12.00
WG Wayne Gretzky 200.00 300.00

2001-02 SPx Yzerman Tribute

This 26-card set paid homage to the long-time captain of the Detroit Red Wings, Steve Yzerman. Cards 1-19 carried authentic autographs and were serial-numbered out of 19 each. Autograph cards were gold toned on the card fronts and each card carried a different small photo of Yzerman. Cards 20-26 were inserted at 1:140 and carried either one or two large pieces of game-used jersey and/or equipment. Cards 20-26 were blue toned in color and each carried a different small photo of Yzerman.

COMMON AUTO (1-19) 200.00 300.00
COMMON SINGLE MEM. (25-26) 10.00 25.00
COMMON DBL.MEM. (20-24) 15.00 40.00

2002-03 SPx

Released in December 2002, this 193-card set consisted of 60 base veteran cards (1-60), 40 "Spxitement" subset cards (#61-100), 25 "SPx Prospects" cards numbered to 999 (#101-125), 20 "Career Achievement" cards (#126-145), 15 rookie jersey/autograph cards (#146-159 and #175), 15 rookie jersey cards numbered to 999 (#160-174) and 17 shortprinted rookie cards numbered to 999 (#176-193). Cards 176-193 were available only in packs of UD Rookie Update. Individual print runs for cards 126-159 and card 175 are listed below.

COMP.SET w/o SP's (100) 50.00 100.00
*MULT.COLOR JSY: .75X TO 2X
1 Paul Kariya .30 .75
2 Jean-Sebastien Giguere .25 .60
3 Ilya Kovalchuk .40 1.00
4 Dany Heatley .40 1.00
5 Joe Thornton .50 1.25
6 Sergei Samsonov .25 .60
7 Miroslav Satan .25 .60
8 Martin Biron .25 .60
9 Roman Turek .25 .60
10 Jarome Iginla .40 1.00
11 Jeff O'Neill .10 .30
12 Ron Francis .25 .60
13 Arturs Irbe .25 .60
14 Eric Daze .25 .60
15 Jocelyn Thibault .25 .60
16 Patrick Roy 1.50 4.00
17 Chris Drury .25 .60
18 Joe Sakic .60 1.50
19 Peter Forsberg .75 2.00
20 Rob Blake .25 .60
21 Rostislav Klesla .10 .30
22 Marc Denis .25 .60
23 Mike Modano .50 1.25
24 Marty Turco .25 .60
25 Bill Guerin .25 .60
26 Steve Yzerman 1.50 4.00
27 Sergei Fedorov .50 1.25
28 Nicklas Lidstrom .30 .75
29 Brett Hull .40 1.00
30 Curtis Joseph .30 .75
31 Brendan Shanahan .30 .75
32 Mike Comrie .25 .60
33 Tommy Salo .25 .60
34 Roberto Luongo .40 1.00
35 Kristian Huselius .10 .30
36 Felix Potvin .30 .75
37 Zigmund Palffy .25 .60
38 Marian Gaborik .60 1.50
39 Manny Fernandez .25 .60
40 Jose Theodore .40 1.00
41 Saku Koivu .30 .75
42 Patrik Elias .25 .60
43 Martin Brodeur .75 2.00
44 Scott Hartnell .10 .30
45 Mike Dunham .25 .60
46 Alexei Yashin .10 .30
47 Chris Osgood .25 .60
48 Michael Peca .10 .30
49 Eric Lindros .30 .75
50 Mike Richter .25 .60
51 Pavel Bure .30 .75
52 Patrick Lalime .25 .60
53 Marian Hossa .30 .75
54 Daniel Alfredsson .25 .60
55 Jeremy Roenick .40 1.00
56 Simon Gagne .30 .75
57 Roman Cechmanek .25 .60
58 Sean Burke .25 .60
59 Tony Amonte .25 .60
60 Alexei Kovalev .25 .60
61 Mario Lemieux 2.00 5.00
62 Owen Nolan .25 .60
63 Evgeni Nabokov .25 .60
64 Keith Tkachuk .30 .75
65 Chris Pronger .25 .60
66 Brent Johnson .25 .60
67 Nikolai Khabibulin .30 .75
68 Vincent Lecavalier .30 .75
69 Alexander Mogilny .25 .60
70 Mats Sundin .30 .75
71 Ed Belfour .30 .75
72 Todd Bertuzzi .30 .75
73 Markus Naslund .30 .75
74 Olaf Kolzig .25 .60
75 Jaromir Jagr .50 1.25
76 Paul Kariya .30 .75
77 Adam Oates .25 .60
78 Sergei Samsonov .25 .60
79 Bobby Orr 2.00 5.00
80 Joe Thornton .50 1.25
81 Jeff O'Neill .10 .30
82 Ron Francis .25 .60
83 Joe Sakic .60 1.50
84 Patrick Roy 1.50 4.00
85 Peter Forsberg .75 2.00
86 Bill Guerin .25 .60
87 Mike Modano .50 1.25
88 Curtis Joseph .30 .75
89 Gordie Howe 1.50 4.00
90 Steve Yzerman 1.50 4.00
91 Mike Comrie .25 .60
92 Jose Theodore .40 1.00
93 Martin Brodeur .75 2.00
94 Pavel Bure .40 1.00
95 Wayne Gretzky 2.00 5.00
96 John LeClair .40 1.00
97 Mario Lemieux 2.00 5.00
98 Evgeni Nabokov .25 .60
99 Mats Sundin .30 .75
100 Jaromir Jagr .50 1.25
101 Pasi Nurminen SP 2.50 5.00
102 Mark Hartigan SP 2.50 5.00
103 Andy Hilbert SP 2.50 5.00
104 Henrik Tallinder SP 2.50 5.00
105 Jaroslav Svoboda SP 2.50 5.00
106 Riku Hahl SP 2.50 5.00
107 Jordan Krestanovich SP 2.50 5.00
108 Andrej Nedorost SP 2.50 5.00
109 Sean Avery SP 4.00 10.00
110 Jani Rita SP 2.50 5.00
111 Stephen Weiss SP 2.50 6.00
112 Lukas Krajicek SP 2.50 5.00
113 Tony Virta SP 2.50 5.00
114 Marcel Hossa SP 2.00 5.00
115 Jan Lasak SP 2.50 5.00
116 Jonas Andersson SP 2.50 5.00
117 Trent Hunter SP 2.50 5.00
118 Martin Prusek SP 2.50 5.00
119 Bruno St. Jacques SP 2.50 5.00
120 Branko Radivojevic SP 2.50 5.00
121 Shane Endicott SP 2.50 5.00
122 Justin Papineau SP 2.50 5.00
123 Sebastien Centomo SP 2.50 5.00
124 Karel Pilar SP 2.50 5.00
125 Sebastien Charpentier SP 2.50 5.00
126 Mark Messier/1804 1.50 4.00
127 Ron Francis/1701 1.50 4.00
128 Steve Yzerman/1662 3.00 8.00
129 Mario Lemieux/1601 4.00 10.00
130 Luc Robitaille/1288 1.50 4.00
131 Joe Sakic/1257 2.00 5.00
132 Brett Hull/1246 2.00 5.00
133 Al MacInnis/1204 1.50 4.00
134 Pierre Turgeon/1192 1.50 4.00
135 Jaromir Jagr/1158 2.00 5.00
136 Mark Recchi/1074 1.50 4.00
137 Brendan Shanahan/1030 1.50 4.00
138 Jeremy Roenick/1014 1.50 4.00
139 Mike Modano/977 2.00 5.00
140 Mats Sundin/942 1.50 4.00
141 Sergei Fedorov/871 2.00 5.00
142 Teemu Selanne/855 1.50 4.00
143 Pavel Bure/749 1.50 4.00
144 Peter Bondra/734 1.50 4.00
145 Eric Lindros/732 1.50 4.00
146 Alexei Smirnov 6.00 15.00
JSY AU/1250 RC
147 Kurt Sauer 6.00 15.00
JSY AU/1250 RC
148 Chuck Kobasew 8.00 20.00
JSY AU/1250 RC
149 R.Nash JSY AU/500 RC 75.00 150.00
150 Jay Bouwmeester 20.00 50.00
JSY AU/500 RC
151 Henrik Zetterberg 60.00 120.00
JSY AU/1250 RC
152 Pierre-Marc Bouchard 8.00 20.00
JSY AU/1250 RC
153 R.Hainsey JSY AU/1250 RC 6.00 15.00
154 Adam Hall 6.00 15.00
JSY AU/1250 RC
155 S.Upshall JSY AU/1250 RC 8.00 20.00
156 S.Chistov JSY AU/500 RC 6.00 15.00
157 Jeff Taffe 6.00 15.00
JSY AU/1250 RC
158 Mikael Tellqvist 10.00 25.00
JSY AU/1250 RC
159 Alexander Svitov 6.00 15.00
JSY AU/1250 RC
160 Ales Hemsky JSY RC 8.00 20.00
161 Alexander Frolov JSY RC 8.00 20.00
162 Steve Eminger JSY RC 6.00 15.00
163 Anton Volchenkov JSY RC 6.00 15.00
164 Sylvain Blouin JSY RC 6.00 15.00
165 Greg Koehler JSY RC 6.00 15.00
166 Martin Gerber JSY RC 8.00 20.00
167 Micki Dupont JSY RC 6.00 15.00
168 Jordan Leopold JSY RC 6.00 15.00
169 Tomi Pettinen JSY RC 6.00 15.00
170 Lynn Loyns JSY RC 6.00 15.00
171 Matt Henderson JSY RC 6.00 15.00
172 Radovan Somik JSY RC 6.00 15.00
173 Patrick Sharp RC 6.00 15.00
174 Jeff Paul JSY RC 6.00 15.00
175 Jason Spezza 100.00 200.00
JSY AU/500 RC
176 Pascal LeClaire RC 4.00 10.00
177 Steve Ott RC 4.00 10.00
178 Brooks Orpik RC 3.00 5.00
179 Jared Aulin RC 3.00 5.00
180 Brandon Reid RC 3.00 5.00
181 Ray Emery RC 6.00 15.00
182 Ari Ahonen RC 2.00 5.00
183 Niko Dimitrakos RC 3.00 5.00
184 Jarret Stoll RC 5.00 12.00
185 Cristobal Huet RC 10.00 25.00
186 Mike Komisarek RC 4.00 10.00
187 Ryan Miller RC 15.00 30.00
188 Jason Bacashihua RC 4.00 10.00
189 Carlo Colaiacovo RC 3.00 5.00
190 Mike Cammalleri RC 4.00 10.00
191 Fernando Pisani RC 4.00 10.00
192 Alexei Semenov RC 3.00 5.00
193 Konstantin Koltsov RC 3.00 5.00

2002-03 SPx Spectrum Gold

STATED PRINT RUN 10 SER.#'d SETS
NOT PRICED DUE TO SCARCITY

2002-03 SPx Spectrum Silver

*STARS: 2X TO 5X BASIC CARDS
STATED PRINT RUN 199 SER.#'d SETS

2002-03 SPx Milestones

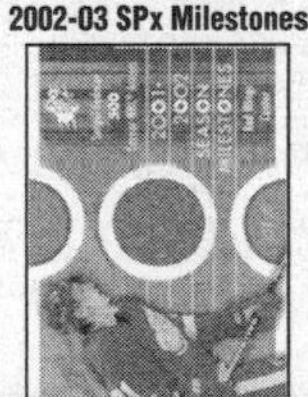

This 15-card set featured game jersey swatches. Cards were serial-numbered out of 99.

*MULT.COLOR SWATCH: .5X TO 1.25X HI
MBL Brian Leetch 6.00 15.00
MBO Peter Bondra 6.00 15.00
MBS Brendan Shanahan 6.00 15.00
MJR Jeremy Roenick 8.00 20.00
MJS Joe Sakic 10.00 25.00
MMB Martin Brodeur 12.50 30.00
MML Mario Lemieux 15.00 40.00
MMM Mike Modano 8.00 20.00
MMR Mark Recchi 6.00 15.00
MPB Pavel Bure 6.00 15.00
MPR Patrick Roy 15.00 40.00
MSF Sergei Fedorov 8.00 20.00
MSH Brendan Shanahan 6.00 15.00
MSY Steve Yzerman 15.00 40.00
MTS Teemu Selanne 6.00 15.00

2002-03 SPx Milestones Gold

This 15 card set paralleled the base insert set but each card was serial-numbered out of 15 in gold foil on the card front. All cards carried a "M" prefix on the card backs. This set is not priced due to scarcity.

NOT PRICED DUE TO SCARCITY

2002-03 SPx Milestones Silver

This 15-card set paralleled the base insert set but each card was serial-numbered out of 30 in silver foil on the card front. All cards carried a "M" prefix on the card backs.

*STARS: .75X TO 2X BASIC CARDS

2002-03 SPx Rookie Redemption

These 30 redemption cards were randomly inserted into packs and were redeemable for players making their debut in 2003-04. Cards R194-R214 were serial-numbered to 1500 and cards R215-223 were serial-numbered to 500.

R194 Matthew Lombardi	3.00	8.00
R195 Pavel Vorobiev	3.00	8.00
R196 Marek Svatos	4.00	10.00
R197 Cody McCormick	3.00	8.00
R198 John-Michael Liles	3.00	8.00
R199 Antti Miettinen	3.00	8.00
R200 Brent Burns	3.00	8.00
R201 Christoph Brandner	3.00	8.00
R202 Chris Higgins	4.00	10.00
R203 Dan Hamhuis	3.00	8.00
R204 Marek Zidlicky	3.00	8.00
R205 Paul Martin	3.00	8.00
R206 Sean Bergenheim	3.00	8.00
R207 Antoine Vermette	4.00	10.00
R208 Matthew Spiller	3.00	8.00
R209 Christian Ehrhoff	3.00	8.00
R210 Peter Sejna	3.00	8.00
R211 Maxim Kondratiev	3.00	8.00
R212 Matt Stajan	4.00	10.00
R213 Boyd Gordon	3.00	8.00
R214 Joffrey Lupul	4.00	10.00
R215 Patrice Bergeron	10.00	25.00
R216 Eric Staal	12.00	30.00
R217 Tuomo Ruutu	5.00	12.00
R218 Nathan Horton	6.00	15.00
R219 Dustin Brown	4.00	10.00
R220 Jordin Tootoo	4.00	10.00
R221 Joni Pitkanen	4.00	10.00
R222 Marc-Andre Fleury	15.00	40.00
R223 Milan Michalek	6.00	15.00

2002-03 SPx Smooth Skaters

This 17-card set featured game jersey swatches. Cards were serial-numbered out of 99.

*MULT.COLOR SWATCH: .5X TO 1.25X HI
ALL CARDS CARRY SS PREFIX

ED Eric Daze	6.00	15.00
JI Jarome Iginla	8.00	20.00
JJ Jaromir Jagr	8.00	20.00
JS Joe Sakic	10.00	25.00
JT Joe Thornton	10.00	25.00
ML Mario Lemieux	15.00	40.00
MM Mike Modano	8.00	20.00
MN Markus Naslund	6.00	15.00
MS Mats Sundin	6.00	15.00
PB Peter Bondra	6.00	15.00
PK Paul Kariya	6.00	15.00
SA Miroslav Satan	6.00	15.00
SG Simon Gagne	6.00	15.00
SS Sergei Samsonov	6.00	15.00
SU Steve Sullivan	6.00	15.00
SY Steve Yzerman	12.50	30.00
WG Wayne Gretzky	20.00	50.00

2002-03 SPx Smooth Skaters Gold

This 17-card set paralleled the base insert set but each card was serial-numbered out of 15 in gold foil on the card front. All cards carried a "SS" prefix on the card backs. This set is not priced due to scarcity.

NOT PRICED DUE TO SCARCITY

2002-03 SPx Smooth Skaters Silver

This 17-card set paralleled the base insert set but each card was serial-numbered out of 50 in silver foil on the card front. All cards carried a "SS" prefix on the card backs.

*STARS: .75X TO 2 X BASIC CARDS

2002-03 SPx Winning Materials

This 35-card memorabilia set had a stated print run of 99 serial-numbered copies each.

*MULT.COLOR SWATCH: .5X TO 1.25X HI

2002-03 SPx Winning Materials Gold

This 35-card set paralleled the base insert set but each card was serial-numbered out of 15 in gold foil on the card front. All cards carried a "WM" prefix on the card backs. This set is not priced due to scarcity.

NOT PRICED DUE TO SCARCITY

2002-03 SPx Winning Materials Silver

This 35-card set paralleled the base insert set but each card was serial-numbered out of 50 in silver foil on the card front. All cards carried a "WM" prefix on the card backs.

*STARS: .75X TO 2X BASIC CARDS

2002-03 SPx Xtreme Talents

This 28-card set featured game jersey swatches. Cards were serial-numbered out of 99.

*MULT.COLOR: .75X TO 1.5X BASE HI
ALL CARDS CARRY X PREFIX

2002-03 SPx Xtreme Talents Gold

This 28-card set paralleled the base insert set but each card was serial-numbered out of 15 in gold foil on the card front. All cards carried a "X" prefix on the card backs. This set is not priced due to scarcity.

NOT PRICED DUE TO SCARCITY

2002-03 SPx Xtreme Talents Silver

This 28-card set paralleled the base insert set but each card was serial-numbered out of 50 in silver foil on the card front. All cards carried an "x" prefix on the card backs.

*STARS: .75X TO 2X BASIC CARDS

2003-04 SPx

This 240-card set consisted of several different subsets. Cards 1-100 were base veteran cards; cards 101-130 made up the Lasting Impressions subset and each card was serial-numbered out of 750; cards 131-155 made up the Xcite subset and each was serial-numbered out of 750; cards 156-175 made up the Next Generation subset and each was serial-numbered out of 500; cards 176-190 made up the Profiles subset and each was serial-numbered out of 250. Cards 191-207 and 230-240 were rookie cards that carried jersey swatches and were serial-numbered out of 999. Cards 208-229 were also rookie jersey cards but they also carried certified "cut" autographs; print runs for these can be found below. Cards 231-240 were only available in packs of UD Rookie Update.

COMP.SET w/o SP's (100)	25.00	50.00
*MULT.COLOR RC JSY: 1X TO 2.5X HI		
1 Jean-Sebastien Giguere	.20	.50
2 Stanislav Chistov	.10	.25
3 Sergei Fedorov	.30	.75
4 Dany Heatley	.30	.75
5 Ilya Kovalchuk	.30	.75
6 Joe Thornton	.40	1.00
7 Sergei Samsonov	.20	.50
8 Glen Murray	.10	.25
9 Felix Potvin	.20	.50
10 Miroslav Satan	.20	.50
11 Maxim Afinogenov	.20	.50
12 Chris Drury	.20	.50
13 Jarome Iginla	.30	.75
14 Roman Turek	.20	.50
15 Steve Reinprecht	.10	.25
16 Ron Francis	.20	.50
17 Jeff O'Neill	.10	.25
18 Alexei Zhamnov	.10	.25
19 Jocelyn Thibault	.20	.50
20 Kyle Calder	.10	.25
21 Joe Sakic	.50	1.25
22 Teemu Selanne	.25	.60
23 Peter Forsberg	.60	1.50
24 David Aebischer	.20	.50
25 Paul Kariya	.25	.60
26 Marc Denis	.20	.50
27 Rick Nash	.30	.75
28 Todd Marchant	.10	.25
29 Bill Guerin	.20	.50
30 Marty Turco	.20	.50
31 Mike Modano	.40	1.00
32 Henrik Zetterberg	.25	.60
33 Brendan Shanahan	.25	.60
34 Steve Yzerman	1.25	3.00
35 Dominik Hasek	.50	1.25
36 Ryan Smyth	.10	.25
37 Ales Hemsky	.20	.50
38 Tommy Salo	.20	.50
39 Mike Comrie	.20	.50
40 Stephen Weiss	.10	.25
41 Roberto Luongo	.30	.75
42 Jay Bouwmeester	.10	.25
43 Olli Jokinen	.20	.50
44 Zigmund Palffy	.20	.50
45 Alexander Frolov	.10	.25
46 Roman Cechmanek	.20	.50
47 Marian Gaborik	.50	1.25
48 Manny Fernandez	.20	.50
49 Pierre-Marc Bouchard	.10	.25
50 Jose Theodore	.30	.75
51 Saku Koivu	.25	.60
52 Mike Komisarek	.10	.25
53 Marcel Hossa	.10	.25
54 Tomas Vokoun	.20	.50
55 David Legwand	.20	.50
56 Scott Stevens	.20	.50
57 Martin Brodeur	.60	1.50
58 Patrik Elias	.20	.50
59 Jamie Langenbrunner	.10	.25
60 Alexei Yashin	.10	.25
61 Rick DiPietro	.20	.50
62 Michael Peca	.10	.25
63 Mike Dunham	.20	.50
64 Eric Lindros	.25	.60
65 Alex Kovalev	.20	.50
66 Patrick Lalime	.20	.50
67 Marian Hossa	.25	.60
68 Daniel Alfredsson	.20	.50
69 Jason Spezza	.25	.60
70 John LeClair	.25	.60
71 Tony Amonte	.20	.50
72 Simon Gagne	.25	.60
73 Jeremy Roenick	.30	.75
74 Chris Gratton	.10	.25
75 Sean Burke	.20	.50
76 Mike Johnson	.10	.25
77 Martin Straka	.10	.25
78 Mario Lemieux	1.50	4.00
79 Sebastien Caron	.20	.50
80 Niko Dimitrakos	.10	.25
81 Evgeni Nabokov	.20	.50
82 Mike Ricci	.10	.25
83 Chris Osgood	.20	.50
84 Al MacInnis	.20	.50
85 Keith Tkachuk	.25	.60
86 Chris Pronger	.20	.50
87 Nikolai Khabibulin	.25	.60
88 Martin St. Louis	.20	.50
89 Vincent Lecavalier	.25	.60
90 Owen Nolan	.20	.50
91 Alexander Mogilny	.20	.50
92 Ed Belfour	.25	.60
93 Mats Sundin	.25	.60
94 Markus Naslund	.25	.60
95 Johan Hedberg	.20	.50
96 Todd Bertuzzi	.25	.60
97 Ed Jovanovski	.20	.50
98 Jaromir Jagr	.40	1.00
99 Olaf Kolzig	.20	.50
100 Peter Bondra	.20	.50
101 Wayne Gretzky LI	15.00	40.00
102 Gordie Howe LI	6.00	15.00
103 Bobby Orr LI	15.00	40.00
104 Bobby Clarke LI	4.00	10.00
105 Scotty Bowman LI	4.00	10.00
106 Lanny McDonald LI	4.00	10.00
107 Stan Mikita LI	4.00	10.00
108 Ted Lindsay LI	4.00	10.00
109 Marcel Dionne LI	4.00	10.00
110 Johnny Bucyk LI	4.00	10.00
111 Jean Beliveau LI	4.00	10.00
112 Mike Bossy LI	4.00	10.00
113 Guy Lafleur LI	4.00	10.00
114 Mario Lemieux LI	8.00	20.00
115 Mark Messier LI	4.00	10.00
116 Patrick Roy LI	6.00	15.00
117 Martin Brodeur LI	5.00	12.00
118 Jarome Iginla LI	4.00	10.00
119 Mike Modano LI	4.00	10.00
120 Steve Yzerman LI	6.00	15.00
121 Peter Forsberg LI	5.00	12.00
122 Marian Gaborik LI	4.00	10.00
123 Scott Stevens LI	4.00	10.00
124 Paul Kariya LI	4.00	10.00
125 Tie Domi LI	4.00	10.00
126 Joe Sakic LI	4.00	10.00
127 Brendan Shanahan LI	4.00	10.00
128 Jeremy Roenick LI	5.00	12.00
129 Joe Thornton LI	4.00	10.00
130 Mats Sundin LI	4.00	10.00
131 Jean-Sebastien Giguere Xcite	4.00	10.00
132 Marian Gaborik Xcite	4.00	10.00
133 Joe Thornton Xcite	4.00	10.00
134 Saku Koivu Xcite	4.00	10.00
135 Dany Heatley Xcite	4.00	10.00
136 Vincent Lecavalier Xcite	4.00	10.00
137 Todd Bertuzzi Xcite	4.00	10.00
138 Sergei Fedorov Xcite	4.00	10.00
139 Marty Turco Xcite	4.00	10.00
140 Paul Kariya Xcite	4.00	10.00
141 Marian Hossa Xcite	4.00	10.00
142 Alexei Yashin Xcite	4.00	10.00
143 Zigmund Palffy Xcite	4.00	10.00
144 Mario Lemieux Xcite	8.00	20.00
145 Ilya Kovalchuk Xcite	4.00	10.00
146 Henrik Zetterberg Xcite	4.00	10.00
147 Mike Modano Xcite	4.00	10.00
148 Tony Amonte Xcite	4.00	10.00
149 Jason Spezza Xcite	4.00	10.00
150 Owen Nolan Xcite	4.00	10.00
151 Ales Hemsky Xcite	4.00	10.00
152 Markus Naslund Xcite	4.00	10.00
153 Teemu Selanne Xcite	4.00	10.00
154 Sergei Samsonov Xcite	4.00	10.00
155 Martin Brodeur Xcite	5.00	12.00
156 Dany Heatley NG	6.00	15.00
157 Marian Hossa NG	5.00	12.00
158 Jean-Sebastien Giguere NG	5.00	12.00
159 Joe Thornton NG	8.00	20.00
160 Henrik Zetterberg NG	5.00	12.00
161 Rick Nash NG	6.00	15.00
162 Jay Bouwmeester NG	5.00	12.00
163 Jason Spezza NG	6.00	15.00
164 Pavel Datsyuk NG	5.00	12.00
165 Mike Komisarek NG	5.00	12.00
166 Ales Hemsky NG	5.00	12.00
167 Marian Gaborik NG	8.00	20.00
168 Alexander Frolov NG	5.00	12.00
169 Steve Ott NG	5.00	12.00
170 Justin Williams NG	5.00	12.00
171 Pierre-Marc Bouchard NG	5.00	12.00
172 Ryan Miller NG	5.00	12.00
173 Ilya Kovalchuk NG	6.00	15.00
174 Kyle Calder NG	5.00	12.00
175 David Aebischer NG	5.00	12.00
176 Mario Lemieux PRO	20.00	50.00
177 Joe Thornton PRO	12.50	30.00
178 Martin Brodeur PRO	15.00	40.00
179 Steve Yzerman PRO	15.00	40.00
180 Joe Sakic PRO	12.50	30.00
181 Mats Sundin PRO	10.00	25.00
182 Saku Koivu PRO	10.00	25.00
183 Sergei Fedorov PRO	12.50	30.00
184 Jeremy Roenick PRO	12.50	30.00
185 Roberto Luongo PRO	12.50	30.00
186 Mike Modano PRO	12.50	30.00
187 Todd Bertuzzi PRO	12.50	30.00
188 Zigmund Palffy PRO	12.50	30.00
189 Jean-Sebastien Giguere PRO	10.00	25.00
190 Markus Naslund PRO	12.50	30.00
191 Dan Fritsche JSY RC	6.00	15.00
192 Tim Gleason JSY RC	6.00	15.00
193 Lasse Kukkonen JSY RC	6.00	15.00
194 John-Michael Liles JSY RC	6.00	15.00
195 Paul Martin JSY RC	6.00	15.00
196 Esa Pirnes JSY RC	6.00	15.00
197 Tom Preissing JSY RC	6.00	15.00
198 David Hale JSY RC	6.00	15.00
199 Marek Svatos JSY RC	10.00	25.00
200 Boyd Kane JSY RC	6.00	15.00
201 Matthew Lombardi JSY RC	6.00	15.00
202 Marek Zidlicky JSY RC	6.00	15.00
203 Matthew Spiller JSY RC	6.00	15.00
204 Andrew Peters JSY RC	6.00	15.00
205 Greg Campbell JSY RC	6.00	15.00
206 Sean Bergenheim JSY RC	6.00	15.00
207 Boyd Gordon JSY RC	6.00	15.00
208 P.Sejna JSY AU/925 RC	6.00	15.00
209 M.Stajan JSY AU/925 RC	12.00	30.00
210 M.Michalek JSY AU/925 RC	12.00	40.00
211 P.Vorobiev JSY AU/925 RC	8.00	20.00
212 D.Hamhuis JSY AU/925 RC	8.00	20.00
213 C.Higgins JSY AU/925 RC	12.00	40.00
214 A.Miettinen JSY AU/925 RC	6.00	15.00
215 C.Ehrhoff JSY AU/925 RC	8.00	20.00
216 A.Semin JSY AU/925 RC	25.00	60.00
217 A.Vermette JSY AU/925 RC	6.00	15.00
218 T.Moen JSY AU/925 RC	6.00	15.00
219 J.Pitkanen JSY AU/925 RC	8.00	20.00
220 P.Bergeron JSY AU/925 RC	15.00	40.00
221 J.Hudler JSY AU/925 RC	8.00	20.00
222 M.Fleury JSY AU/500 RC	50.00	100.00
223 D.Brown JSY AU/500 RC	8.00	20.00
224 J.Lupul JSY AU/925 RC	12.00	30.00
225 T.Ruutu JSY AU/500 RC	15.00	40.00
226 J.Tootoo JSY AU/500 RC	15.00	40.00
227 E.Staal JSY AU/500 RC	40.00	80.00
228 N.Horton JSY AU/500 RC	15.00	40.00
229 T.Salmalainen JSY AU/925 RC	8.00	20.00
230 John Pohl JSY RC	6.00	15.00
231 Sergei Zinovjev JSY RC	6.00	15.00
232 Ryan Kesler JSY RC	6.00	15.00
233 Dominic Moore JSY RC	6.00	15.00
234 Peter Sarno JSY RC	6.00	15.00
235 Ryan Malone JSY RC	8.00	20.00
236 Nikolai Zherdev JSY RC	12.00	30.00
237 Fredrik Sjostrom JSY RC	6.00	15.00
238 Derek Roy JSY RC	8.00	20.00
239 Mikko Luoma JSY RC	6.00	15.00
240 Trevor Daley JSY RC	6.00	15.00

2003-04 SPx Radiance

*STARS: 10X TO 25X
*LAST.IMP/XCITE: 1X TO 2.5X
*NEXT GEN.: .75X TO 2X
*PROFILES: .5X TO 1.2X
*ROOKIE JSY: .5X TO 1.25X
*ROOKIE JSY/AU: .5X TO 1.2X
STATED PRINT RUN 50 SER.#'d SETS

2003-04 SPx Spectrum

STATED PRINT RUN 10 SER.#'d SETS
NOT PRICED DUE TO SCARCITY

2003-04 SPx Big Futures

*MULT.COLOR SWATCH: .75X TO 1.5X
PRINT RUN 99 SER.#'d SETS
*LIMITED: .75X TO 2X
LIMITED PRINT RUN 25 SER.#'d SETS

BFAA Ari Ahonen	8.00	20.00
BFAF Alexander Frolov	8.00	20.00
BFAH Ales Hemsky	10.00	25.00
BFAK Ales Kotalik	8.00	20.00
BFAS Alexander Svitov	8.00	20.00
BFBJ Barret Jackman	8.00	20.00
BFBO Brooks Orpik	8.00	20.00
BFCN Sebastien Caron	8.00	20.00
BFDB Dan Blackburn	8.00	20.00
BFDH Dany Heatley	10.00	25.00
BFHZ Henrik Zetterberg	12.50	30.00
BFIK Ilya Kovalchuk	12.50	30.00
BFIR Igor Radulov	8.00	20.00
BFJB Jay Bouwmeester	8.00	20.00
BFJB Jason Bacashihua	8.00	20.00
BFJL Jordan Leopold	8.00	20.00
BFJS Jason Spezza	12.50	30.00
BFJT Joe Thornton	15.00	40.00
BFMC Mike Cammalleri	8.00	20.00
BFMD Marc Denis	8.00	20.00
BFMG Mathieu Garon	8.00	20.00
BFMH Marcel Hossa	8.00	20.00
BFMP Mark Parrish	8.00	20.00
BFMT Marty Turco	10.00	25.00
BFOJ Olli Jokinen	8.00	20.00
BFPD Pavel Datsyuk	10.00	25.00
BFPL Pascal Leclaire	8.00	20.00
BFPMB Pierre-Marc Bouchard	8.00	20.00
BFRE Robert Esche	10.00	25.00
BFRN Rick Nash	12.50	30.00
BFSC Stanislav Chistov	8.00	20.00
BFSG Simon Gagne	10.00	25.00
BFSO Steve Ott	8.00	20.00
BFSW Stephen Weiss	8.00	20.00

2003-04 SPx Fantasy Franchise

PRINT RUN 75 SER.#'d SETS
*LIMITED: .6X TO 1.5X
LTD PRINT RUN 25 SER.#'d SETS

FFBLK Bure/Lindros/Kovalev	10.00	25.00
FFDSA Drury/Satan/Afinogenov	12.00	30.00
FFEHJ Elias/Hossa/Jagr	12.00	30.00
FFFGC Fedorov/Giguere/Chistov	10.00	25.00
FFGRB Giguere/Roy/Brodeur	30.00	80.00
FFHSL Hossa/Spezza/Lalime	12.00	30.00
FFHYS Hull/Yzerman/Shanahan	40.00	100.00
FFHYZ Howe/Yzerman/Zettrbrg	60.00	150.00
FFKFB Kovalchuk/Fedorov/Bure	20.00	50.00
FFKSF Kariya/Selanne/Forsberg	25.00	60.00
FFKTH Kariya/Thornton/Heatley	15.00	40.00
FFLGH Lemieux/Gretzky/Howe	125.00	250.00
FFLRA LeClair/Roenick/Amonte	15.00	40.00
FFMGT Modano/Guerin/Turco	20.00	50.00
FFNBM Naslund/Bertzzi/Mrrison	15.00	40.00
FFNSM Nolan/Sundin/Mogilny	10.00	25.00
FFNSZ Nash/Spezza/Zetterberg	40.00	100.00
FFSBJ Stevens/Brodeur/Jovnski	20.00	50.00
FFTMS Joe Thornton	15.00	40.00
Glen Murray		
Sergei Samsonov		
FFTWM Tkachuk/Weight/MacInnis	10.00	25.00

2003-04 SPx Hall Pass

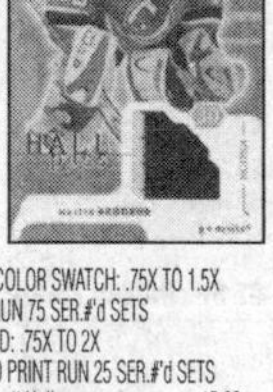

*MULT.COLOR SWATCH: .75X TO 1.5X
PRINT RUN 75 SER.#'d SETS
*LIMITED: .75X TO 2X
LIMITED PRINT RUN 25 SER.#'d SETS

HPBH Brett Hull	15.00	40.00
HPCC Chris Chelios	10.00	25.00
HPDG Doug Gilmour	10.00	25.00
HPDH Dominik Hasek	12.50	30.00
HPMB Martin Brodeur	25.00	60.00
HPML Mario Lemieux	25.00	60.00
HPMM Mark Messier	12.50	30.00
HPPR Patrick Roy	20.00	50.00
HPRB Ray Bourque	12.50	30.00
HPRF Ron Francis	10.00	25.00

2003-04 SPx Origins

*MULT.COLOR SWATCH: .75X TO 1.5X
PRINT RUN 75 SER.#'d SETS

OAY Alexei Yashin	8.00	20.00
OBL Brian Leetch	8.00	20.00
OBS Brendan Shanahan	8.00	20.00
ODH Dany Heatley	15.00	40.00
ODW Doug Weight	8.00	20.00
OEB Ed Belfour	12.50	30.00
OHZ Henrik Zetterberg	15.00	40.00
OJI Jarome Iginla	12.50	30.00
OJJ Jaromir Jagr	15.00	40.00
OJR Jeremy Roenick	15.00	40.00
OJS Jason Spezza	10.00	25.00
OJSG Jean-Sebastien Giguere	8.00	20.00
OJT Joe Thornton	12.50	30.00
OMB Martin Brodeur	20.00	50.00
OMH Marian Hossa	10.00	25.00
OML Mario Lemieux	25.00	60.00
OMN Markus Naslund	10.00	25.00
OMS Mats Sundin	10.00	25.00
OON Owen Nolan	8.00	20.00
OPB Pavel Bure	8.00	20.00
OPE Patrik Elias	8.00	20.00
OPF Peter Forsberg	15.00	40.00
OPR Patrick Roy	25.00	60.00
OSF Sergei Fedorov	15.00	40.00
OSS Sergei Samsonov	8.00	20.00
OTS Teemu Selanne	10.00	25.00
OZP Zigmund Palffy	8.00	20.00

2003-04 SPx Signature Threads

This 26-card set featured over-sized jersey swatches and certified autographs. Each card was limited to 50 serial-numbered copies.

*MULT.COLOR SWATCH: .75X TO 1.5X

STAF Alexander Frolov	20.00	50.00
STAH Ales Hemsky	15.00	40.00
STEL Eric Lindros	30.00	80.00
STHZ Henrik Zetterberg	30.00	80.00
STIK Ilya Kovalchuk	40.00	100.00
STJI Jarome Iginla	25.00	60.00
STJL John LeClair	15.00	40.00
STJR Jeremy Roenick	30.00	80.00
STJS Jason Spezza	50.00	125.00
STJT Jose Theodore	25.00	60.00
STJT Joe Thornton	50.00	125.00
STJSG Jean-Sebastien Giguere	15.00	40.00
STMC Mike Comrie	15.00	40.00
STMG Marian Gaborik		
STMH Marian Hossa	20.00	50.00
STMN Markus Naslund	20.00	50.00
STMT Marty Turco	15.00	40.00
STPB Pavel Bure	15.00	40.00
STRN Rick Nash	60.00	150.00
STSF Sergei Fedorov	25.00	60.00
STSK Saku Koivu	20.00	50.00
STSS Sergei Samsonov	15.00	40.00
STSY Steve Yzerman	75.00	150.00
STTB Todd Bertuzzi	20.00	50.00
STWG Wayne Gretzky	150.00	350.00
STZP Zigmund Palffy	15.00	40.00

2003-04 SPx Style

This 12-card set featured triple jersey swatches from some of the league's elite players. Cards were serial-numbered out of 99. A Limited parallel was also created and serial-numbered out of 25

*MULT.COLOR SWATCH: .75X TO 1.5X
*LIMITED: .5X TO 1.25X

SPXBG Brodeur/Giguere/Luongo	25.00	60.00
SPXBS Bertuzzi/Shanny/Tkachuk	12.50	30.00
SPXBT Belfour/Turco/Esche	12.50	30.00
SPXDS Domi/Stock/Shelley	12.50	30.00
SPXGS Gretzky/Spezza/Thornton	75.00	200.00
SPXHH Hejduk/Hossa/Jagr	20.00	50.00
SPXHN Howe/Nash/Bertuzzi	30.00	80.00
SPXHT Howe/Thornton/Bertuzzi	25.00	60.00
SPXJB Jovanovksi/Blake/Chara	12.50	30.00
SPXLH Lemieux/Heatley/Fedorov	25.00	60.00
SPXNZ Naslund/Zettrbrg/Sundin	25.00	60.00
SPXRB Roy/Brodeur/Giguere	25.00	60.00

2003-04 SPx VIP

*MULT.COLOR SWATCH: .75X TO 1.5X
PRINT RUN 50 SER.#'d SETS
*LIMITED: .6X TO 1.5X
LTD PRINT RUN 25 SER.#'d SETS

VIPDA Chris Drury	12.50	30.00
Maxim Afinogenov		
VIPFG S.Fedorov/J.Giguere	15.00	40.00
VIPFS P.Forsberg/J.Sakic	20.00	50.00
VIPKH S.Koivu/Marcel Hossa	12.50	30.00
VIPLS V.Lecavalier/M.St. Louis	15.00	40.00
VIPMG M.Modano/B.Guerin	12.50	30.00
VIPNB M.Naslund/T.Bertuzzi	12.50	30.00
VIPPF Z.Palffy/A.Frolov	12.50	30.00
VIPSB S.Stevens/M.Brodeur	25.00	60.00
VIPSK T.Selanne/P.Kariya	12.50	30.00
VIPTM J.Thornton/G.Murray	12.50	30.00
VIPYS S.Yzerman/B.Shanahan	25.00	60.00

2003-04 SPx Winning Materials

PRINT RUN 99 SER.#'d SETS
*LIMITED: .6X TO 1.5X
LTD PRINT RUN 25 SER.#'d SETS

WMAD Adam Deadmarsh	6.00	15.00
WMBE Ed Belfour	8.00	20.00
WMBL Rob Blake	6.00	15.00
WMBO Peter Bondra	6.00	15.00
WMCD Chris Drury	6.00	15.00
WMDB Dan Blackburn	6.00	15.00
WMDH Dominik Hasek	12.50	30.00
WMEB Ed Belfour	8.00	20.00
WMFO Peter Forsberg	12.50	30.00
WMGR Wayne Gretzky	40.00	100.00
WMGY Wayne Gretzky	40.00	100.00
WMJB Jay Bouwmeester	6.00	15.00
WMJF Jeff Friesen	6.00	15.00
WMJG Jaromir Jagr	12.50	30.00
WMJI Jarome Iginla	10.00	25.00
WMJJ Jaromir Jagr	12.50	30.00
WMJR Jeremy Roenick	12.50	30.00
WMJS Joe Sakic	15.00	40.00
WMJZ Jason Spezza	12.50	30.00
WMMD Mike Dunham	6.00	15.00
WMMH Marian Hossa	8.00	20.00
WMMM Mark Messier	15.00	40.00
WMMN Markus Naslund	8.00	20.00
WMMO Mike Modano	12.50	30.00
WMMS Mats Sundin	8.00	20.00
WMMT Marty Turco	6.00	15.00
WMPB Pavel Bure	8.00	20.00
WMPF Peter Forsberg	12.50	30.00
WMPK Paul Kariya	8.00	20.00
WMPR Patrick Roy	20.00	50.00
WMRB Ray Bourque	10.00	25.00
WMRN Rick Nash	15.00	40.00
WMRY Patrick Roy	20.00	50.00
WMSA Jason Spezza	12.50	30.00
WMSB Sean Burke	6.00	15.00
WMSF Sergei Fedorov	12.50	30.00
WMSW Stephen Weiss	6.00	15.00
WMTA Tony Amonte	6.00	15.00
WMTB Todd Bertuzzi	8.00	20.00
WMTH Jose Theodore	12.50	30.00
WMTS Teemu Selanne	8.00	20.00
WMWG Wayne Gretzky	40.00	100.00

2005-06 SPx

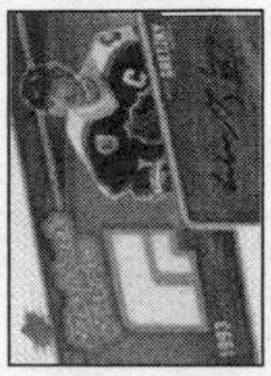

COMP.SET w/o SP's (90)	12.50	25.00
133-153 PRINT RUN 1999 SER.#'d SETS		
154-188 PRINT RUN 1499 SER.#'d SETS		
189-191 PRINT RUN 499 SER.#'d SETS		
192-221/244-293 999 SER.#'d SETS		
*MULTI.COLOR JSY: 1X TO 2.5X HI		
1 Jean-Sebastien Giguere	.30	.75
2 Sergei Fedorov	.40	1.00
3 Ilya Kovalchuk	.50	1.25
4 Kari Lehtonen	.40	1.00
5 Marian Hossa	.30	.75
6 Patrice Bergeron	.40	1.00
7 Joe Thornton	.60	1.50
8 Andrew Raycroft	.30	.75
9 Glen Murray	.25	.60
10 Maxim Afinogenov	.25	.60
11 Chris Drury	.30	.75
12 Jarome Iginla	.30	.75
13 Miikka Kiprusoff	.40	1.00
14 Tony Amonte	.30	.75
15 Erik Cole	.25	.60
16 Eric Staal	.30	.75
17 Tuomo Ruutu	.25	.60
18 Nikolai Khabibulin	.40	1.00
19 Joe Sakic	.75	2.00
20 David Aebischer	.30	.75
21 Milan Hejduk	.40	1.00
22 Alex Tanguay	.30	.75
23 Rick Nash	.50	1.25
24 Nikolai Zherdev	.30	.75
25 Mike Modano	.40	1.00
26 Bill Guerin	.25	.60
27 Marty Turco	.30	.75
28 Steve Yzerman	1.00	2.50
29 Brendan Shanahan	.40	1.00
30 Henrik Zetterberg	.40	1.00
31 Nicklas Lidstrom	.40	1.00
32 Ty Conklin	.30	.75
33 Chris Pronger	.30	.75
34 Ryan Smyth	.30	.75
35 Roberto Luongo	.60	1.50
36 Stephen Weiss	.25	.60
37 Joe Nieuwendyk	.30	.75
38 Jeremy Roenick	.40	1.00
39 Luc Robitaille	.30	.75
40 Alexander Frolov	.30	.75
41 Marian Gaborik	.50	1.25
42 Manny Fernandez	.30	.75
43 Saku Koivu	.40	1.00
44 Jose Theodore	.40	1.00
45 Michael Ryder	.30	.75
46 Mike Ribeiro	.25	.60
47 Paul Kariya	.40	1.00
48 Tomas Vokoun	.30	.75
49 David Legwand	.30	.75
50 Martin Brodeur	1.00	2.50
51 Patrik Elias	.30	.75
52 Alexander Mogilny	.30	.75
53 Scott Gomez	.30	.75
54 Alexei Yashin	.25	.60
55 Rick DiPietro	.30	.75
56 Miroslav Satan	.25	.60
57 Jaromir Jagr	.60	1.50
58 Tom Poti	.25	.60
59 Kevin Weekes	.30	.75
60 Dany Heatley	.40	1.00
61 Daniel Alfredsson	.30	.75
62 Martin Havlat	.30	.75
63 Dominik Hasek	.50	1.25
64 Jason Spezza	.40	1.00
65 Peter Forsberg	.60	1.50
66 Keith Primeau	.25	.60
67 Simon Gagne	.40	1.00
68 Robert Esche		
69 Shane Doan	.25	.60
70 Brett Hull	.30	.75
71 Curtis Joseph	.40	1.00
72 Mario Lemieux	1.50	4.00
73 Zigmund Palffy	.30	.75
74 Mark Recchi	.30	.75
75 Evgeni Nabokov	.30	.75
76 Patrick Marleau	.30	.75
77 Jonathan Cheechoo	.40	1.00
78 Keith Tkachuk	.40	1.00
79 Doug Weight	.30	.75
80 Vincent Lecavalier	.40	1.00
81 Sean Burke	.30	.75
82 Brad Richards	.30	.75
83 Martin St. Louis	.30	.75
84 Mats Sundin	.40	1.00
85 Ed Belfour	.40	1.00

86 Jason Allison .25 .60
87 Eric Lindros .40 1.00
88 Markus Naslund .40 1.00
89 Brendan Morrison .25 .60
90 Olaf Kolzig .30 .75
91 Bernie Geoffrion 75.00 150.00
92 Bobby Hull 40.00 100.00
93 Bobby Clarke 60.00 125.00
94 Borje Salming 30.00 60.00
95 Brian Leetch 125.00 250.00
96 Bryan Trottier 350.00 600.00
97 Cam Neely 75.00 200.00
98 Dominik Hasek 350.00 600.00
99 Doug Weight 150.00 300.00
100 Ed Jovanovski 25.00 60.00
101 Gerry Cheevers 75.00 150.00
102 Gilbert Perreault 250.00 400.00
103 Gordie Howe 500.00 700.00
104 Grant Fuhr 50.00 125.00
105 Guy Lafleur 60.00 150.00
106 Jari Kurri 30.00 60.00
107 Jeremy Roenick 100.00 200.00
108 Johnny Bucyk 50.00 100.00
109 Luc Robitaille 60.00 150.00
110 Marcel Dionne 30.00 80.00
111 Martin Brodeur SP 600.00 800.00
112 Mats Sundin SP 600.00 800.00
113 Mike Bossy 30.00 80.00
114 Mike Modano SP 300.00 500.00
115 Michael Peca 25.00 60.00
116 Miroslav Satan SP 250.00 400.00
117 Owen Nolan FF SSP /10 800.00 1000.00
118 Peter Stastny 50.00 100.00
119 Phil Esposito SP 150.00 400.00
120 Ray Bourque SP 500.00 1000.00
121 Roberto Luongo 60.00 150.00
122 Rogie Vachon 40.00 80.00
123 Ron Hextall 100.00 200.00
124 S Bowman FF SSP /10 800.00 1100.00
125 W Gretzky FF SSP /25 800.00 1200.00
126 Clark Gillies SP 250.00 500.00
127 Lanny McDonald 60.00 150.00
128 Tiger Williams 30.00 75.00
129 J Beliveau FF SSP /25 300.00 500.00
130 W Gretzky FF SSP 15 2000.00 3000.00
131 Butch Goring FF 25.00 60.00
132 Guy Lapointe FF 60.00 125.00
133 Duncan Keith JSY RC 10.00 25.00
134 Jaroslav Balastik JSY RC 3.00 8.00
135 Jay McClement JSY RC 3.00 8.00
136 Jeff Hoggan JSY RC 3.00 8.00
137 Andrew Alberts JSY RC 3.00 8.00
138 Kevin Dallman JSY RC 3.00 8.00
139 Maxime Talbot JSY RC 3.00 8.00
140 Raitis Ivanans JSY RC 3.00 8.00
141 Niklas Nordgren JSY RC 3.00 8.00
142 Kevin Nastiuk JSY RC 3.00 8.00
143 Jim Slater JSY RC 3.00 8.00
144 George Parros JSY RC 4.00 10.00
145 David Leneveu JSY RC 3.00 8.00
146 Andrew Wozniewski JSY RC 3.00 8.00
147 Ryan Hollweg JSY RC 3.00 8.00
148 Brett Lebda JSY RC 3.00 8.00
149 Patrick Eaves JSY RC 5.00 12.00
150 Ryane Clowe JSY RC 3.00 8.00
151 Josh Gorges JSY RC 3.00 8.00
152 Brad Winchester JSY RC 3.00 8.00
153 Matt Foy JSY RC 3.00 8.00
154 Wojtek Wolski JSY AU RC 15.00 40.00
155 Rene Bourque JSY AU RC 6.00 15.00
156 Gilbert Brule JSY AU RC 12.00 30.00
157 Jeff Woywitka JSY AU RC 6.00 15.00
158 H.Toivonen JSY AU RC 8.00 20.00
159 Al Montoya JSY AU RC 10.00 25.00
160 Yann Danis JSY AU RC 6.00 15.00
161 Alexander Perezhogin JSY AU RC 8.00 20.00
162 Cam Barker JSY AU RC 6.00 15.00
163 Zach Parise JSY AU RC 25.00 60.00
164 Dion Phaneuf JSY AU RC 25.00 60.00
165 Mike Richards JSY AU RC 15.00 40.00
166 Cam Ward JSY AU RC 20.00 50.00
167 Robert Nilsson JSY AU RC 6.00 15.00
168 Petteri Nokelainen JSY AU RC 6.00 15.00
169 A.Steen JSY AU RC 12.00 30.00
170 Ryan Getzlaf JSY AU RC 25.00 60.00
171 Corey Perry JSY AU RC 15.00 40.00
172 Rostislav Olesz JSY AU RC 8.00 20.00
173 H.Lundqvist JSY AU RC 40.00 80.00
174 Petr Prucha JSY AU RC 12.00 30.00
175 Jim Howard JSY AU RC 15.00 40.00
176 Johan Franzen JSY AU RC 15.00 40.00
177 Thomas Vanek JSY AU RC 20.00 50.00
178 Andrej Meszaros JSY AU RC 6.00 15.00
179 Brandon Bochenski JSY AU RC 6.00 15.00
180 Jussi Jokinen JSY AU RC 10.00 25.00
181 Braydon Coburn JSY AU RC 6.00 15.00
182 Ryan Suter JSY AU RC 6.00 15.00
183 Peter Budaj JSY AU RC 12.00 30.00
184 Brent Seabrook JSY AU RC 12.00 30.00
185 Keith Ballard JSY AU RC 6.00 15.00
186 Milan Jurcina JSY AU RC 6.00 15.00
187 Anthony Stewart JSY AU RC 6.00 15.00
188 Eric Nystrom JSY AU RC 6.00 15.00
189 Jeff Carter JSY AU RC 40.00 80.00
190 A.Ovechkin JSY AU RC 400.00 650.00
191 Sidney Crosby JSY AU RC 400.00 700.00
192 Lee Stempniak RC 5.00 12.00
193 Andy Roach RC 2.00 5.00
194 Colin Hemingway RC 2.00 5.00
195 Mark Streit RC 2.00 5.00
196 Wade Skolney RC 2.00 5.00
197 Chris Campoli RC 2.00 5.00
198 Paul Ranger RC 2.00 5.00
199 Kyle Brodziak RC 2.00 5.00
200 Chris Holt RC 2.00 5.00
201 Brian McGrattan RC 2.00 5.00
202 Adam Berkhoel RC 5.00 12.00
203 Nick Tarnasky RC 2.00 5.00
204 Evgeny Artyukhin RC 2.00 5.00
205 Timo Helbling RC 2.00 5.00
206 Derek Boogaard RC 2.00 5.00
207 Michael Wall RC 5.00 12.00
208 Steve Goertzen RC 2.00 5.00
209 Junior Lessard RC 2.00 5.00
210 Vojtech Polak RC 2.00 5.00
211 Andrew Penner RC 2.00 5.00
212 Jordan Sigalet RC 4.00 10.00
213 Kevin Colley RC 2.00 5.00
214 Dimitri Patzold RC 2.00 5.00
215 Christoph Schubert RC 2.00 5.00
216 Zenon Konopka RC 2.00 5.00
217 Staffan Kronwall RC 2.00 5.00
218 Erik Christensen RC 2.00 5.00
219 Brian Eklund RC 3.00 8.00
220 Rob McVicar RC 5.00 12.00
221 Tomas Fleischmann RC 3.00 8.00
222 Chris Thorburn JSY AU RC 8.00 20.00
223 Daniel Paille JSY AU RC 8.00 20.00
224 Andrew Ladd JSY AU RC 8.00 20.00
225 Danny Richmond JSY AU RC 8.00 20.00
226 Brad Richardson JSY AU RC 8.00 20.00
227 Ole-Kristian Tollefsen JSY AU RC 8.00 20.00
228 Alexandre Picard JSY AU RC 8.00 20.00
229 Kyle Quincey JSY AU RC 8.00 20.00
230 Valtteri Filppula JSY AU RC 10.00 25.00
231 Jeff Tambellini JSY AU RC 8.00 20.00
232 Mikko Koivu JSY AU RC 10.00 25.00
233 Maxim Lapierre JSY AU RC 8.00 20.00
234 Andrei Kostitsyn JSY AU RC 15.00 40.00
235 Barry Tallackson JSY AU RC 8.00 20.00
236 Jeremy Colliton JSY AU RC 8.00 20.00
237 R.J. Umberger JSY AU RC 12.50 30.00
238 Ben Eager JSY AU RC 10.00 25.00
239 Ryan Whitney JSY AU RC 8.00 20.00
240 Steve Bernier JSY AU RC 8.00 20.00
241 Ryan Craig JSY AU RC 8.00 20.00
242 Kevin Bieksa JSY AU RC 8.00 20.00
243 Jakub Klepis JSY AU RC 6.00 15.00
244 Dustin Penner RC 4.00 10.00
245 Ben Walter RC 2.00 5.00
246 Eric Healey RC 2.00 5.00
247 Nathan Paetsch RC 2.00 5.00
248 Jiri Novotny RC 2.00 5.00
249 Richie Regehr RC 2.00 5.00
250 Chad Larose RC 2.00 5.00
251 Martin St. Pierre RC 2.00 5.00
252 Corey Crawford RC 3.00 8.00
253 James Wisniewski RC 2.00 5.00
254 Vitaly Kolesnik RC 5.00 12.00
255 Geoff Platt RC 2.00 5.00
256 Joakim Lindstrom RC 2.00 5.00
257 Danny Syvret RC 2.00 5.00
258 Kyle Brodziak RC 2.00 5.00
259 J-F Jacques RC 2.00 5.00
260 Matt Greene RC 2.00 5.00
261 Greg Jacina RC 2.00 5.00
262 Rob Globke RC 2.00 5.00
263 Yanick Lehoux RC 2.00 5.00
264 Connor James RC 2.00 5.00
265 Richard Petiot RC 2.00 5.00
266 Petr Kanko RC 2.00 5.00
267 Matt Ryan RC 2.00 5.00
268 J-P Cote RC 2.00 5.00
269 Jonathan Ferland 2.00 5.00
270 Greg Zanon 2.00 5.00
271 Kevin Klein RC 2.00 5.00
272 Pekka Rinne RC 5.00 10.00
273 Cam Janssen RC 2.00 5.00
274 Jason Ryznar RC 2.00 5.00
275 Bruno Gervais RC 2.00 5.00
276 Stefan Ruzicka RC 2.00 5.00
277 Alexandre Picard RC 2.00 5.00
278 Matt Jones RC 2.00 5.00
279 Colby Armstrong RC 5.00 12.00
280 Doug Murray RC 2.00 5.00
281 Grant Stevenson RC 2.00 5.00
282 Dennis Wideman RC 2.00 5.00
283 Chris Beckford-Tseu RC 5.00 12.00
284 Gerald Coleman RC 2.00 5.00
285 Darren Reid RC 2.00 5.00
286 Doug O'Brien RC 2.00 5.00
287 Jay Harrison RC 2.00 5.00
288 Rick Rypien RC 2.00 5.00
289 Alexandre Burrows RC 2.00 5.00
290 Tomas Mojzis RC 2.00 5.00
291 David Steckel RC 2.00 5.00
292 Mike Green RC 5.00 12.00
293 Joey Tenute RC 2.00 5.00

2005-06 SPx Spectrum

COMMON CARD (1-90) 8.00 20.00
*STARS: 15X TO 40X BASE HI
1-90 PRINT RUN 25 SER.#'d SETS
91-132 PRINT RUN 1 SER.#'d SET
91-132 NOT PRICED DUE TO SCARCITY
*ROOKIE JSY: .75X TO 2X
*ROOKIE JSY/AU: 1X TO 2.5X
*ROOKIE: .6X TO 1.5X
133-221 PRINT RUN 25 SER.#'d SETS
28 Steve Yzerman 25.00 60.00
50 Martin Brodeur 25.00 60.00
72 Mario Lemieux 25.00 60.00
156 Gilbert Brule 50.00 100.00
164 Dion Phaneuf 100.00 250.00
166 Cam Ward 75.00 150.00
170 Ryan Getzlaf 60.00 120.00
173 Henrik Lundqvist 100.00 250.00
189 Jeff Carter 100.00 200.00
190 Alexander Ovechkin 600.00 800.00
191 Sidney Crosby 1000.00 1500.00

2005-06 SPx Winning Combos

PRINT RUN 350 SER.#'d SETS
WCAB David Aebischer 4.00 10.00
Rob Blake
WCAN Sergei Fedorov 6.00 15.00
Teemu Selanne
WCBA Martin Biron 4.00 10.00
Maxim Afinogenov
WCBB Raymond Bourque 8.00 20.00
Rob Blake
WCBE Martin Brodeur 10.00 25.00
Patrik Elias
WCBF Dustin Brown 4.00 10.00
Alexander Frolov
WCBH Jay Bouwmeester 4.00 10.00
Nathan Horton
WCBK Mike Bossy 6.00 15.00
Jari Kurri
WCBL Ray Bourque 8.00 20.00
Brian Leetch
WCBM Todd Bertuzzi 4.00 10.00
Brendan Morrison
WCBN Martin Biron 4.00 10.00
Mikka Noronen
WCBO Glenn Murray 6.00 15.00
Joe Thornton
WCBP Rob Blake 4.00 10.00
Chris Pronger
WCBT Martin Brodeur 10.00 25.00
Jose Theodore
WCCH Zdeno Chara 4.00 10.00
Martin Havlat
WCCN Dan Cloutier 4.00 10.00
Markus Naslund
WCCP Ty Conklin 4.00 10.00
Chris Pronger
WCDA Bill Guerin 6.00 15.00
Mike Modano
WCDB Chris Drury 4.00 10.00
Daniel Briere
WCDN Marc Denis 6.00 15.00
Rick Nash
WCDR Marcel Dionne 8.00 20.00
Luc Robitaille
WCED Ryan Smyth 4.00 10.00
Ales Hemsky
WCEJ Eric Staal 4.00 10.00
Justin Williams
WCEM Ed Belfour 8.00 20.00
Marty Turco
WCFG Sergei Fedorov 6.00 15.00
Jean-Sebastian Giguere
WCFL Jay Bouwmeester 6.00 15.00
Roberto Luongo
WCFP Peter Forsberg 6.00 15.00
Keith Primeau
WCFR Sergei Fedorov 6.00 15.00
Jeremy Roenick
WCFS Peter Forsberg 10.00 25.00
Joe Sakic
WCGC Wayne Gretzky 100.00 200.00
Sidney Crosby
WCGF Marian Gaborik 6.00 15.00
Manny Fernandez
WCGM Wayne Gretzky 20.00 50.00
Mark Messier
WCGR Simon Gagne 4.00 10.00
Brad Richards
WCHA Dany Heatley 8.00 20.00
Daniel Alfredsson
WCHD Brett Hull 6.00 15.00
Shane Doan
WCHH Marcel Hossa 6.00 15.00
Marian Hossa
WCHJ Brett Hull 6.00 15.00
Curtis Joseph
WCHK Marcel Hossa 6.00 15.00
Saku Koivu
WCJM Jaromir Jagr 10.00 25.00
Mark Messier
WCJP Joe Thornton 6.00 15.00
Patrice Bergeron
WCJY Jaromir Jagr 6.00 15.00
Alexei Yashin
WCKI Mikka Kiprusoff 8.00 20.00
Jarome Iginla
WCKN Miikka Kiprusoff 6.00 15.00
Evgeni Nabokov
WCKR Nikolai Khabibulin 4.00 10.00
Tuomo Ruutu
WCLA Luc Robitaille 8.00 20.00
Jeremy Roenick
WCLF Mario Lemieux 10.00 25.00
John LeClair
WCLJ Mario Lemieux 12.00 30.00
Jaromir Jagr
WCLK Guy Lafleur 6.00 15.00
Saku Koivu
WCMI Marian Hossa 6.00 15.00
Ilya Kovalchuk
WCMM Mike Modano 6.00 15.00
Brenden Morrow
WCMN Brendan Morrison 4.00 10.00
Markus Naslund
WCMP Mike Ribeiro 6.00 15.00
Patrice Bergeron
WCMT Mark Messier 6.00 15.00
Bryan Trottier
WCNA Owen Nolan 4.00 10.00
Nik Antropov
WCND Ladislav Nagy 4.00 10.00
Shane Doan
WCNY Mike Bossy 6.00 15.00
Bryan Trottier
WCNZ Rick Nash 6.00 15.00
Nikolai Zherdev
WCOT Dany Heatley 6.00 15.00
Martin Havlat
WCPE Keith Primeau 4.00 10.00
Robert Esche
WCPG Keith Primeau 4.00 10.00
Simon Gagne
WCPH Michael Peca 4.00 10.00
Ales Hemsky
WCPR Zigmund Palffy 4.00 10.00
Mark Recchi
WCPS Mark Parrish 4.00 10.00
Miroslav Satan
WCRB Andrew Raycroft 6.00 15.00
Patrice Bergeron
WCRC Wade Redden 4.00 10.00
Zdeno Chara
WCRK Michael Ryder 4.00 10.00
Saku Koivu
WCRL Andrew Raycroft 6.00 15.00
Kari Lehtonen
WCRR Michael Ryder 4.00 10.00
Mike Ribeiro
WCRT Mike Ribeiro 6.00 15.00
Jose Theodore
WCRW Henrik Zetterberg 6.00 15.00
Niklas Lidstrom
WCSA Jason Spezza 6.00 15.00
Daniel Alfredsson
WCSB Jason Spezza 6.00 15.00
Patrice Bergeron
WCSC Ryan Smyth 4.00 10.00
Ty Conklin
WCSF Martin St. Louis 6.00 15.00
Ruslan Fedotenko
WCSH Joe Sakic 6.00 15.00
Milan Hejduk
WCSL Martin St.Louis 6.00 15.00
Vincent Lecavalier
WCSN Mats Sundin 6.00 15.00
Owen Nolan
WCSR Scott Stevens 4.00 10.00
Brian Rafalski
WCST Marty Turco 4.00 10.00
Brenden Morrow
WCSW Matt Stajan 4.00 10.00
Justin Williams
WCSY Brendan Shanahan 10.00 25.00
Steve Yzerman
WCTB Brad Richards 6.00 15.00
Vincent Lecavalier
WCTH Alex Tanguay 4.00 10.00
Milan Hejduk
WCTM Marty Turco 8.00 20.00
Mike Modano
WCTO Mats Sundin 6.00 15.00
Ed Belfour
WCVA Ed Jovanovski 4.00 10.00
Brendan Morrison
WCVH Tomas Vokoun 6.00 15.00
Dominik Hasek
WCWH Stephen Weiss 4.00 10.00
Nathan Horton
WCWL Peter Worrell 4.00 10.00
Georges Laraque
WCWM Doug Weight 4.00 10.00
Al MacInnis
WCWT Doug Weight 4.00 10.00
Keith Tkachuk
WCZD Henrik Zetterberg 4.00 10.00
Kris Draper
WCZL Henrik Zetterberg 6.00 15.00
Manny Legace

2005-06 SPx Winning Combos Autographs

*AUTO: 2XTO 5X BASIC WC
PRINT RUN 25 SER.#'d SETS
AWCBT Martin Brodeur/Jose Theodore 100.00 250.00
AWCGC W.Gretzky/S.Crosby 1500.00 2500.00
AWCHK Marian Hossa/Ilya Kovalchuk 60.00 120.00

2005-06 SPx Winning Combos Gold

*GOLD: .6X TO 1.5X BASIC WC
PRINT RUN 99 SER.#'d SETS

2005-06 SPx Winning Combos Spectrum

PRINT RUN 10 SER.#'d SETS
NOT PRICED DUE TO SCARCITY

2005-06 SPx Winning Materials

PRINT RUN 350 SER.#'d SETS
WMAE David Aebischer 3.00 8.00
WMAF Alexander Frolov 3.00 8.00
WMAH Ales Hemsky 4.00 10.00
WMAR Andrew Raycroft 4.00 10.00
WMAT Alex Tanguay 4.00 10.00
WMBG Bill Guerin 4.00 10.00
WMBH Brett Hull 5.00 12.00
WMBL Brian Leetch 4.00 10.00
WMBM Brendan Morrison 3.00 8.00
WMBR Brad Richards 4.00 10.00
WMBS Brendan Shanahan 4.00 10.00
WMBT Bryan Trottier 4.00 10.00
WMBY Mike Bossy 4.00 10.00
WMCD Chris Drury 4.00 10.00
WMCJ Curtis Joseph 4.00 10.00
WMCP Chris Pronger 4.00 10.00
WMDA Daniel Alfredsson 4.00 10.00
WMDB Daniel Briere 4.00 10.00
WMDH Dany Heatley 6.00 15.00
WMDW Doug Weight 3.00 8.00
WMEB Ed Belfour 4.00 10.00
WMED Eric Daze 3.00 8.00
WMEJ Ed Jovanovski 3.00 8.00
WMGL Guy Lafleur 5.00 12.00
WMHA Dominik Hasek 10.00 25.00
WMHO Marian Hossa 4.00 10.00
WMHV Martin Havlat 3.00 8.00
WMHZ Henrik Zetterberg 5.00 12.00
WMIK Ilya Kovalchuk 6.00 15.00
WMJG Jean Sebastian Giguere 4.00 10.00
WMJI Jarome Iginla 6.00 15.00
WMJJ Jaromir Jagr 6.00 15.00
WMJL John LeClair 4.00 10.00
WMJO Jose Theodore 5.00 12.00
WMJR Jeremy Roenick 5.00 12.00
WMJS Joe Sakic 10.00 25.00
WMJT Joe Thornton 8.00 20.00
WMJW Justin Williams 3.00 8.00
WMKD Kris Draper 3.00 8.00
WMKF Miikka Kiprusoff 5.00 12.00
WMKL Kari Lehtonen 4.00 10.00
WMKP Keith Primeau 3.00 8.00
WMKT Keith Tkachuk 4.00 10.00
WMLN Ladislav Nagy 3.00 8.00
WMLR Luc Robitaille 4.00 10.00
WMLX Mario Lemieux 15.00 40.00
WMMB Martin Brodeur 12.00 30.00
WMMC Bryan McCabe 4.00 10.00
WMMD Marcel Dionne 4.00 10.00
WMMG Marian Gaborik 8.00 20.00
WMMH Milan Hejduk 4.00 10.00
WMML Manny Legace 3.00 8.00
WMMM Mike Modano 5.00 12.00
WMMN Markus Naslund 4.00 10.00
WMMP Mark Parrish 3.00 8.00
WMMR Mike Ribeiro 3.00 8.00
WMMS Mark Messier 5.00 12.00
WMMW Brenden Morrow 3.00 8.00
WMNA Nik Antropov 3.00 8.00
WMNH Nathan Horton 3.00 8.00
WMNK Nikolai Khabibulin 4.00 10.00
WMNZ Nikolai Zherdev 3.00 8.00
WMOK Olaf Kolzig 4.00 10.00
WMON Owen Nolan 4.00 10.00
WMPB Patrice Bergeron 4.00 10.00
WMPE Michael Peca 3.00 8.00
WMPF Peter Forsberg 6.00 15.00
WMPM Patrick Marleau 4.00 10.00
WMRE Robert Esche 3.00 8.00
WMRF Ruslan Fedotenko 3.00 8.00
WMRL Roberto Luongo 6.00 15.00
WMRN Rick Nash 5.00 12.00
WMRS Ryan Smyth 4.00 10.00
WMRY Michael Ryder 4.00 10.00
WMRZ Richard Zednik 3.00 8.00
WMSA Miroslav Satan 4.00 10.00
WMSC Sidney Crosby 40.00 80.00
WMSD Shane Doan 4.00 10.00
WMSF Sergei Fedorov 5.00 12.00
WMSG Simon Gagne 4.00 10.00
WMSK Saku Koivu 4.00 10.00
WMSL Martin St. Louis 4.00 10.00
WMSP Jason Spezza 5.00 12.00
WMST Matt Stajan 3.00 8.00
WMSU Mats Sundin 4.00 10.00
WMSW Stephen Weiss 3.00 8.00
WMSY Steve Yzerman 12.00 30.00
WMTC Ty Conklin 3.00 8.00
WMTR Tuomo Ruutu 4.00 10.00
WMTS Teemu Selanne 4.00 10.00
WMTU Marty Turco 4.00 10.00
WMVL Vincent Lecavalier 4.00 10.00
WMWG Wayne Gretzky 25.00 50.00
WMZC Zdeno Chara 4.00 10.00
WMZP Zigmund Palffy 4.00 10.00

2005-06 SPx Winning Materials Autographs

*AUTO: 1.5X TO 4X BASIC WM
PRINT RUN 50 SER.#'d SETS
AWMHA Dominik Hasek 40.00 100.00
AWMIK Ilya Kovalchuk 30.00 80.00
AWMJI Jarome Iginla 30.00 80.00
AWMJO Joe Thornton 30.00 80.00
AWMKP Keith Primeau 20.00 50.00
AWMMB Martin Brodeur 60.00 150.00
AWMMO Mike Modano 30.00 60.00
AWMPR Patrick Roy 100.00 200.00
AWMRN Rick Nash 30.00 80.00
AWMVL Vincent Lecavalier 30.00 80.00
AWMWG Wayne Gretzky 200.00 350.00

2005-06 SPx Winning Materials Gold

*GOLD: .6X TO 1.5X BASIC WM
PRINT RUN 99 SER.#'d SETS
WMES Eric Staal 12.50 30.00
WMMB Martin Brodeur 20.00 50.00
WMPK Paul Kariya 8.00 20.00
WMSC Sidney Crosby 125.00 250.00

2005-06 SPx Winning Materials Spectrum

PRINT RUN 10 SER.#'d SETS
NOT PRICED DUE TO SCARCITY

2005-06 SPx Xcitement Legends

PRINT RUN 499 SER.#'d SETS
XLBB Bill Barber 2.00 5.00
XLBC Bobby Clarke 3.00 8.00
XLBG Bernie Geoffrion 3.00 8.00
XLBH Bobby Hull 4.00 10.00
XLBN Bob Nystrom 2.00 5.00
XLBO Johnny Bower 3.00 8.00
XLBP Brad Park 2.00 5.00
XLBT Bryan Trottier 2.00 5.00
XLBU Johnny Bucyk 3.00 8.00
XLCG Clark Gillies 2.00 5.00
XLCN Cam Neely 4.00 10.00
XLDC Don Cherry 3.00 8.00
XLDM Dickie Moore 3.00 8.00
XLDS Denis Savard 2.00 5.00
XLDT Dave Taylor 2.00 5.00
XLFM Frank Mahovlich 3.00 8.00
XLGA Glenn Anderson 2.00 5.00
XLGC Gerry Cheevers 4.00 10.00
XLGF Grant Fuhr 4.00 10.00
XLGH Gordie Howe 6.00 15.00
XLGL Guy Lafleur 4.00 10.00
XLGO Butch Goring 2.00 5.00
XLGP Gilbert Perreault 3.00 8.00
XLHL Hakan Loob 2.00 5.00
XLJB Jean Beliveau 4.00 10.00
XLJK Jari Kurri 3.00 8.00
XLKH Ken Hodge 2.00 5.00
XLKM Ken Morrow 2.00 5.00
XLLA Guy Lapointe 2.00 5.00
XLLM Lanny McDonald 2.00 5.00
XLMB Mike Bossy 3.00 8.00
XLMD Marcel Dionne 3.00 8.00
XLMN Mats Naslund 2.00 5.00
XLPE Phil Esposito 4.00 10.00
XLPR Patrick Roy 8.00 20.00
XLPS Peter Stastny 2.00 5.00
XLRH Ron Hextall 3.00 8.00
XLRK Red Kelly 2.00 5.00
XLRL Reggie Leach 2.00 5.00
XLRM Rick Martin 2.00 5.00
XLRR Rene Robert 2.00 5.00
XLRV Rogie Vachon 3.00 8.00
XLSA Derek Sanderson 3.00 8.00
XLSB Scotty Bowman 3.00 8.00
XLSM Stan Mikita 3.00 8.00
XLTE Tony Esposito 4.00 10.00
XLTO Terry O'Reilly 2.00 5.00
XLTW Dave Tiger Williams 2.00 5.00
XLWC Wayne Cashman 2.00 5.00
XLWG Wayne Gretzky 10.00 25.00

2005-06 SPx Xcitement Legends Gold

*GOLD: .75X TO 2X
PRINT RUN 99 SER.#'d SETS

2005-06 SPx Xcitement Legends Spectrum

PRINT RUN 5 SER.#'d SETS
NOT PRICED DUE TO SCARCITY

2005-06 SPx Xcitement Rookies

PRINT RUN 999 SER.#'d SETS
XRAA Andrew Alberts 2.00 5.00
XRAM Andrej Meszaros 2.00 5.00
XRAO Alexander Ovechkin 15.00 40.00
XRAP Alexander Perezhogin 2.00 5.00
XRAS Alexander Steen 3.00 8.00
XRAW Andrew Wozniewski 2.00 5.00
XRBB Brandon Bochenski 2.00 5.00
XRBC Braydon Coburn 2.00 5.00
XRBS Brent Seabrook 2.00 5.00
XRCB Cam Barker 2.00 5.00
XRCC Chris Campoli 2.00 5.00
XRCP Corey Perry 4.00 10.00
XRCW Cam Ward 4.00 10.00
XRDK Duncan Keith 2.50 6.00
XRDL David Leneveu 2.00 5.00
XRDP Dion Phaneuf 8.00 20.00
XREN Eric Nystrom 2.00 5.00
XRGB Gilbert Brule 4.00 10.00
XRHL Henrik Lundqvist 8.00 20.00
XRHT Hannu Toivonen 3.00 8.00
XRJC Jeff Carter 5.00 12.00
XRJF Johan Franzen 4.00 10.00
XRJH Jim Howard 3.00 8.00
XRJJ Jussi Jokinen 3.00 8.00
XRJM Jay McClement 2.00 5.00
XRJS Jim Slater 2.00 5.00
XRJW Jeff Woywitka 2.00 5.00
XRKB Keith Ballard 2.00 5.00
XRKD Kevin Dallman 2.00 5.00
XRKN Kevin Nastiuk 2.00 5.00
XRMF Matt Foy 2.00 5.00
XRMJ Milan Jurcina 2.00 5.00
XRMO Alvaro Montoya 3.00 8.00
XRMR Mike Richards 3.00 8.00
XRMT Maxime Talbot 2.00 5.00
XRPB Peter Budaj 2.00 5.00
XRPN Petteri Nokelainen 2.00 5.00
XRPP Petr Prucha 3.00 8.00
XRRB Rene Bourque 2.00 5.00
XRRC Ryane Clowe 2.00 5.00
XRRG Ryan Getzlaf 5.00 12.00
XRRN Robert Nilsson 2.00 5.00
XRRO Rostislav Olesz 2.00 5.00
XRRS Ryan Suter 2.00 5.00
XRSC Sidney Crosby 40.00 100.00
XRST Anthony Stewart 2.00 5.00
XRTV Thomas Vanek 5.00 12.00
XRWW Wojtek Wolski 3.00 8.00
XRYD Yann Danis 2.00 5.00
XRZP Zach Parise 4.00 10.00

2005-06 SPx Xcitement Rookies Gold

PRINT RUN 99 SER.#'d SETS

2005-06 SPx Xcitement Rookies Spectrum

PRINT RUN 5 SER.#'d SETS
NOT PRICED DUE TO SCARCITY

2005-06 SPx Xcitement Superstars

PRINT RUN 499 SER.#'d SETS
XSAT Alex Tanguay 2.50 6.00
XSBG Bill Guerin 1.50 4.00
XSBH Brett Hull 3.00 8.00
XSBL Brian Leetch 1.50 4.00
XSBR Brad Richards 2.50 6.00
XSBS Brendan Shanahan 2.50 6.00
XSCP Chris Pronger 2.50 6.00
XSDA Daniel Alfredsson 2.50 6.00
XSDH Dany Heatley 4.00 10.00
XSEB Ed Belfour 2.50 6.00
XSED Eric Daze 1.50 4.00
XSEJ Ed Jovanovski 1.50 4.00
XSEN Evgeni Nabokov 2.50 6.00
XSHA Dominik Hasek 5.00 12.00
XSHK Milan Hejduk 1.50 4.00
XSHV Martin Havlat 2.50 6.00
XSHZ Henrik Zetterberg 2.50 6.00
XSIK Ilya Kovalchuk 4.00 10.00
XSJI Jarome Iginla 4.00 10.00
XSJJ Jaromir Jagr 4.00 10.00
XSJO Joe Thornton 4.00 10.00
XSJR Jeremy Roenick 2.50 6.00
XSJS Joe Sakic 5.00 12.00
XSJT Jose Theodore 3.00 8.00
XSKD Kris Draper 1.50 4.00
XSKP Keith Primeau 1.50 4.00
XSKT Keith Tkachuk 1.50 4.00
XSLR Luc Robitaille 2.50 6.00
XSMB Martin Brodeur 6.00 15.00
XSMG Marian Gaborik 4.00 10.00
XSMH Marian Hossa 2.50 6.00
XSML Mario Lemieux 8.00 20.00
XSMM Mark Messier 2.50 6.00
XSMN Markus Naslund 2.50 6.00
XSMO Mike Modano 3.00 8.00
XSMP Mark Parrish 1.50 4.00
XSMS Mats Sundin 2.50 6.00
XSMT Marty Turco 2.50 6.00
XSOK Olaf Kolzig 2.50 6.00
XSON Owen Nolan 1.50 4.00
XSRB Rob Blake 1.50 4.00
XSRL Roberto Luongo 4.00 10.00
XSRN Rick Nash 4.00 10.00
XSSD Shane Doan 1.50 4.00
XSSF Sergei Fedorov 3.00 8.00
XSSG Simon Gagne 2.50 6.00
XSSK Saku Koivu 2.50 6.00
XSSL Martin St. Louis 2.50 6.00
XSSY Steve Yzerman 8.00 20.00
XSVL Vincent Lecavalier 2.50 6.00

2005-06 SPx Xcitement Superstars Gold

*GOLD: .5X TO 1.25X
PRINT RUN 99 SER.#'d SETS

2005-06 SPx Xcitement Superstars Spectrum

PRINT RUN 5 SER.#'d SETS
NOT PRICED DUE TO SCARCITY

2006-07 SPx

This 213-card set was issued in four-card packs, with a $6.99 SRP, which came 18 packs to a box and 14 boxes to a case. Cards numbered 1-100 feature veterans while cards 101-121 have a player-worn jersey swatch and cards numbered 122-142 have both a player-worn swatch and and an autograph. Cards numbered 143-163 are Rookie Cards with a player worn swatch while cards numbered 164-195 are Rookie Cards with both a player-worn swatch and an autograph. The set concludes with Rookie Cards from 196-213 which were issued to a stated print run of 1999 serial numbered sets.

1 Chris Pronger .30 .75
2 Teemu Selanne .40 1.00
3 Jean-Sebastien Giguere .40 1.00
4 Kari Lehtonen .40 1.00
5 Marian Hossa .30 .75
6 Ilya Kovalchuk .50 1.25
7 Patrice Bergeron .30 .75
8 Zdeno Chara .25 .60
9 Brad Boyes .25 .60
10 Ryan Miller .40 1.00
11 Chris Drury .30 .75
12 Alex Tanguay .30 .75
13 Dion Phaneuf .50 1.25
14 Jarome Iginla .60 1.50

15 Miikka Kiprusoff .40 1.00
16 Eric Staal .30 .75
17 Cam Ward .60 1.50
18 Rod Brind'Amour .30 .75
19 Nikolai Khabibulin .40 1.00
20 Martin Havlat .30 .75
21 Tuomo Ruutu .25 .60
22 Joe Sakic .75 2.00
23 Marek Svatos .25 .60
24 Jose Theodore .25 .60
25 Milan Hejduk .30 .75
26 Rick Nash .40 1.00
27 Sergei Fedorov .40 1.00
28 Fredrik Modin .25 .60
29 Eric Lindros .40 1.00
30 Mike Modano .40 1.00
31 Brenden Morrow .30 .75
32 Marty Turco .30 .75
33 Pavel Datsyuk .40 1.00
34 Gordie Howe 1.25 3.00
35 Nicklas Lidstrom .40 1.00
36 Henrik Zetterberg .40 1.00
37 Dominik Hasek .50 1.25
38 Ryan Smyth .30 .75
39 Ales Hemsky .25 .60
40 Joffrey Lupul .25 .60
41 Wayne Gretzky 2.50 6.00
42 Olli Jokinen .25 .60
43 Todd Bertuzzi .30 .75
44 Ed Belfour 1.00 2.50
45 Jay Bouwmeester .25 .60
46 Alexander Frolov .25 .60
47 Rob Blake .30 .75
48 Marian Gaborik .60 1.50
49 Manny Fernandez .40 1.00
50 Pavol Demitra .25 .60
51 Alexei Kovalev .25 .60
52 Cristobal Huet .40 1.00
53 Saku Koivu .40 1.00
54 Michael Ryder .30 .75
55 Mike Ribeiro .25 .60
56 Paul Kariya .40 1.00
57 Tomas Vokoun .30 .75
58 Jason Arnott .25 .60
59 Martin Brodeur 1.25 3.00
60 Brian Gionta .25 .60
61 Patrik Elias .25 .60
62 Scott Gomez .25 .60
63 Rick DiPietro .40 1.00
64 Miroslav Satan .25 .60
65 Alexei Yashin .25 .60
66 Brendan Shanahan .40 1.00
67 Henrik Lundqvist .60 1.50
68 Jaromir Jagr .60 1.50
69 Petr Prucha .25 .60
70 Daniel Alfredsson .30 .75
71 Jason Spezza .40 1.00
72 Dany Heatley .40 1.00
73 Martin Gerber .40 1.00
74 Jeff Carter .40 1.00
75 Peter Forsberg .60 1.50
76 Simon Gagne .40 1.00
77 Shane Doan .30 .75
78 Jeremy Roenick .40 1.00
79 Curtis Joseph .40 1.00
80 Mark Recchi .25 .60
81 Sidney Crosby 3.00 8.00
82 Marc-Andre Fleury .40 1.00
83 Mario Lemieux 1.50 4.00
84 Patrick Marleau .30 .75
85 Joe Thornton .60 1.50
86 Jonathan Cheechoo .40 1.00
87 Keith Tkachuk .30 .75
88 Doug Weight .25 .60
89 Brad Richards .40 1.00
90 Vincent Lecavalier .40 1.00
91 Martin St. Louis .40 1.00
92 Mats Sundin .40 1.00
93 Andrew Raycroft .30 .75
94 Michael Peca .25 .60
95 Alexander Steen .30 .75
96 Roberto Luongo .75 2.00
97 Markus Naslund .40 1.00
98 Brendan Morrison .25 .60
99 Olaf Kolzig .50 1.25
100 Alexander Ovechkin 2.00 5.00
101 Teemu Selanne JSY 6.00 15.00
102 Ilya Kovalchuk JSY 8.00 20.00
103 Jarome Iginla JSY 8.00 20.00
104 Mark Recchi JSY 4.00 10.00
105 Eric Staal JSY 6.00 15.00
106 Joe Sakic JSY 12.00 30.00
107 Sergei Fedorov JSY 6.00 15.00
108 Mike Modano JSY 6.00 15.00
109 Brendan Shanahan JSY 6.00 15.00
110 Mats Sundin JSY 6.00 15.00
111 Bill Ranford JSY 8.00 20.00
112 Roberto Luongo JSY 8.00 20.00
113 Alexei Kovalev JSY 4.00 10.00
114 Paul Kariya JSY 6.00 15.00
115 Jaromir Jagr JSY 8.00 20.00
116 Peter Forsberg JSY 8.00 20.00
117 Richard Brodeur JSY 6.00 15.00
118 Peter Stastny JSY 6.00 15.00
119 Ron Hextall JSY 8.00 20.00
120 Eric Lindros JSY 6.00 15.00
121 Dave Williams JSY 6.00 15.00
122 Cam Neely JSY AU 15.00 40.00
123 Ray Bourque JSY AU 40.00 100.00
124 Gilbert Perreault JSY AU 20.00 50.00
125 Lanny McDonald JSY AU 15.00 40.00
126 Gordie Howe JSY AU 125.00 200.00
127 Grant Fuhr JSY AU 15.00 40.00
128 Wayne Gretzky JSY AU 200.00 350.00
129 Guy Lafleur JSY AU 40.00 100.00
130 Patrick Roy JSY AU 125.00 250.00
131 Martin Brodeur JSY AU 75.00 150.00
132 Mike Bossy JSY AU 15.00 40.00
133 Dominik Hasek JSY AU 25.00 60.00
134 Sidney Crosby JSY AU 125.00 250.00
135 Mario Lemieux SP JSY AU 125.00 250.00
136 Al MacInnis JSY AU 12.00 30.00
137 Borje Salming JSY AU 15.00 40.00
138 Darryl Sittler SP JSY AU 150.00 300.00
139 Steve Shutt JSY AU 15.00 40.00
140 Ed Belfour JSY AU 20.00 50.00
141 Bobby Clarke JSY AU 15.00 40.00
142 Billy Smith JSY AU 15.00 40.00
143 Dustin Byfuglien JSY RC 8.00 20.00
144 Drew Stafford JSY AU RC 12.00 30.00
145 Frank Doyle JSY RC 2.00 5.00
146 Carsen Germyn JSY RC 2.00 5.00
147 David Printz JSY RC 2.00 5.00
148 Masi Marjamaki JSY RC 2.00 5.00
149 Konstantin Pushkaryov JSY RC 2.00 5.00
150 Michel Ouellet JSY RC 6.00 15.00
151 Billy Thompson JSY RC 2.00 5.00
152 Filip Novak JSY RC 2.00 5.00
153 Miroslav Kopriva JSY RC 2.00 5.00
154 Jonas Johansson JSY RC 2.00 5.00
155 Shane O'Brien JSY RC 2.00 5.00
156 John Oduya JSY RC 2.00 5.00
157 Fredrik Norrena JSY RC 4.00 10.00
158 Niklas Backstrom JSY RC 5.00 12.00
159 D.J. King JSY RC 2.00 5.00
160 Patrick Thoresen JSY RC 4.00 10.00
161 Dustin Boyd JSY AU RC 6.00 15.00
162 Mikko Lehtonen JSY RC 2.00 5.00
163 Roman Polak JSY RC 2.00 5.00
164 Yan Stastny JSY AU RC 6.00 15.00
165 Mark Stuart JSY AU RC 6.00 15.00
166 Eric Fehr JSY AU RC 6.00 15.00
167 Ryan Potulny JSY AU RC 6.00 15.00
168 Ben Ondrus JSY AU RC 6.00 15.00
169 Brendan Bell JSY AU RC 6.00 15.00
170 Ian White JSY AU RC 6.00 15.00
171 Jeremy Williams JSY AU RC 6.00 15.00
172 Marc-Antoine Pouliot JSY AU RC 6.00 15.00
173 Noah Welch JSY AU RC 6.00 15.00
174 Shea Weber JSY AU RC 6.00 15.00
175 Jarkko Immonen JSY AU RC 6.00 15.00
176 Tomas Kopecky JSY AU RC 6.00 15.00
177 Matt Carle JSY AU RC 6.00 15.00
178 Ryan Shannon JSY AU RC 6.00 15.00
179 Anze Kopitar JSY AU RC 20.00 50.00
180 Travis Zajac JSY AU RC 6.00 15.00
181 Nigel Dawes JSY AU RC 6.00 15.00
182 Kristopher Letang JSY AU RC 6.00 15.00
183 Marc-Edouard Vlasic JSY AU RC 6.00 15.00
184 Ladislav Smid JSY AU RC 6.00 15.00
185 Loui Eriksson JSY AU RC 6.00 15.00
186 Paul Stastny JSY AU RC 25.00 60.00
187 Alexei Kaigorodov RC 2.00 5.00
188 Patrick O'Sullivan JSY AU RC 10.00 25.00
189 Phil Kessel JSY AU RC 20.00 50.00
190 Guillaume Latendresse JSY AU RC 20.00 50.00
191 Jordan Staal JSY AU RC 30.00 60.00
192 Luc Bourdon JSY AU RC 10.00 25.00
193 Evgeni Malkin JSY AU RC 75.00 150.00
194 Keith Yandle JSY AU RC 4.00 10.00
195 Alexander Radulov JSY AU RC 12.00 30.00
196 Rob Collins RC 2.00 5.00
197 Steve Regier RC 2.00 5.00
198 Matt Koalska RC 2.00 5.00
199 Ryan Caldwell RC 2.00 5.00
200 David Liffiton RC 2.00 5.00
201 Erik Reitz RC 2.00 5.00
202 Adam Burish RC 2.00 5.00
203 Alex Brooks RC 2.00 5.00
204 Joel Perrault RC 2.00 5.00
205 Nate Thompson RC 2.00 5.00
206 Janis Sprukts RC 2.00 5.00
207 Alexei Mikhnov RC 2.00 5.00
208 Dave Bolland RC 2.50 6.00
209 Michael Blunden RC 2.00 5.00
210 Lars Jonsson RC 2.00 5.00
211 Triston Grant RC 2.00 5.00
212 Matt Lashoff RC 2.00 5.00

2006-07 SPx Spectrum

COMMONS 4.00 10.00
*STARS: 12X TO 30X BASE HI
*FLASHBACK FABS: .75X TO 1.5X
PRINT RUN 25 #'d SETS
*BASE RCs: 1.5X TO 3X
*JSY RCs: .75X TO 2X
81 Sidney Crosby 120.00 300.00
128 Wayne Gretzky JSY AU 350.00 600.00
134 Sidney Crosby JSY AU 250.00 500.00
193 Evgeni Malkin JSY AU 350.00 500.00

2006-07 SPx SPxcitement

PRINT RUN 999 #'d SETS
X1 Chris Pronger 2.00 5.00
X2 Teemu Selanne 2.50 6.00
X3 Ilya Kovalchuk 3.00 8.00
X4 Kari Lehtonen 2.50 6.00
X5 Marian Hossa 2.00 5.00
X6 Ray Bourque 2.50 6.00
X7 Cam Neely 2.00 5.00
X8 Patrice Bergeron 1.50 4.00
X9 Brad Boyes 2.00 5.00
X10 Phil Esposito 1.50 4.00
X11 Gilbert Perreault 1.25 3.00
X12 Ryan Miller 2.50 6.00
X13 Chris Drury 2.50 6.00
X14 Lanny McDonald 2.00 5.00
X15 Jarome Iginla 4.00 10.00
X16 Miikka Kiprusoff 2.50 6.00
X17 Alex Tanguay 2.00 5.00
X18 Dion Phaneuf 3.00 8.00
X19 Nikolai Khabibulin 2.00 5.00
X20 Martin Havlat 2.00 5.00
X21 Tuomo Ruutu 2.00 5.00
X22 Joe Sakic 5.00 12.00
X23 Jose Theodore 2.50 6.00
X24 Milan Hejduk 2.50 6.00
X25 Marek Svatos 2.00 5.00
X26 Rick Nash 2.50 6.00
X27 Sergei Fedorov 2.50 6.00
X28 Gilbert Brule 1.00 2.50
X29 Mike Modano 2.50 6.00
X30 Marty Turco 2.00 5.00
X31 Eric Lindros 2.00 5.00
X32 Brenden Morrow 2.00 5.00
X33 Gordie Howe 2.00 5.00
X34 Henrik Zetterberg 2.50 6.00
X35 Pavel Datsyuk 2.50 6.00
X36 Nicklas Lidstrom 2.50 6.00
X37 Ted Lindsay 1.00 2.50
X38 Grant Fuhr 3.00 8.00
X39 Wayne Gretzky 6.00 15.00
X40 Ales Hemsky 2.00 5.00
X41 Ryan Smyth 2.00 5.00
X42 Jay Bouwmeester 2.00 5.00
X43 Nathan Horton 2.00 5.00
X44 Olli Jokinen 2.00 5.00
X45 Todd Bertuzzi 2.00 5.00
X46 Ed Belfour 6.00 15.00
X47 Alexander Frolov 2.00 5.00
X48 Rob Blake 2.00 5.00
X49 Rogie Vachon 3.00 8.00
X50 Marian Gaborik 4.00 10.00
X51 Manny Fernandez 2.50 6.00
X52 Pavol Demitra 2.00 5.00
X53 Patrick Roy 5.00 12.00
X54 Guy Lafleur 2.50 6.00
X55 Saku Koivu 2.50 6.00
X56 Cristobal Huet 2.50 6.00
X57 Michael Ryder 2.00 5.00
X58 Paul Kariya 2.50 6.00
X59 Tomas Vokoun 2.00 5.00
X60 Martin Brodeur 5.00 12.00
X61 Patrik Elias 2.00 5.00
X62 Brian Gionta 2.00 5.00
X63 Mike Bossy 2.00 5.00
X64 Miroslav Satan 2.00 5.00
X65 Alexei Yashin 2.00 5.00
X66 Jaromir Jagr 4.00 10.00
X67 Henrik Lundqvist 4.00 10.00
X68 Brendan Shanahan 2.50 6.00
X69 Dany Heatley 2.50 6.00
X70 Jason Spezza 2.50 6.00
X71 Daniel Alfredsson 2.00 5.00
X72 Martin Gerber 2.00 5.00
X73 Peter Forsberg 4.00 10.00
X74 Simon Gagne 2.00 5.00
X75 Jeff Carter 2.00 5.00
X76 Shane Doan 2.50 6.00
X77 Jeremy Roenick 2.00 5.00
X78 Owen Nolan 2.00 5.00
X79 Mario Lemieux 5.00 12.00
X80 Sidney Crosby 8.00 20.00
X81 Marc-Andre Fleury 2.50 6.00
X82 Joe Thornton 4.00 10.00
X83 Jonathan Cheechoo 2.00 5.00
X84 Patrick Marleau 2.00 5.00
X85 Doug Weight 2.00 5.00
X86 Keith Tkachuk 2.00 5.00
X87 Joe Mullen 1.00 2.50
X88 Vincent Lecavalier 2.50 6.00
X89 Martin St. Louis 2.50 6.00
X90 Brad Richards 2.50 6.00
X91 Borje Salming 1.25 3.00
X92 Darryl Sittler 1.25 3.00
X93 Mats Sundin 2.00 5.00
X94 Andrew Raycroft 2.00 5.00
X95 Alexander Steen 2.00 5.00
X96 Markus Naslund 2.00 5.00
X97 Roberto Luongo 5.00 12.00
X98 Richard Brodeur 3.00
X99 Alexander Ovechkin 6.00 15.00
X100 Olaf Kolzig 2.50 6.00

2006-07 SPx SPxcitement Spectrum

*STARS: 1.5X TO 4X BASE HI
PRINT RUN 99 #'d SETS
X39 Wayne Gretzky 25.00 60.00
X80 Sidney Crosby 40.00 100.00

2006-07 SPx SPxcitement Autographs

PRINT RUN 10 #'d SETS
NOT PRICED DUE TO SCARCITY
X1 Chris Pronger
X3 Ilya Kovalchuk
X4 Kari Lehtonen
X5 Marian Hossa
X6 Ray Bourque
X7 Cam Neely
X8 Patrice Bergeron
X11 Gilbert Perreault
X15 Jarome Iginla
X17 Alex Tanguay
X18 Dion Phaneuf
X19 Nikolai Khabibulin
X20 Martin Havlat
X23 Jose Theodore
X24 Milan Hejduk
X25 Marek Svatos
X26 Rick Nash
X30 Marty Turco
X33 Gordie Howe
X34 Henrik Zetterberg
X36 Nicklas Lidstrom
X38 Grant Fuhr
X39 Wayne Gretzky
X40 Ales Hemsky
X41 Ryan Smyth
X42 Jay Bouwmeester
X43 Nathan Horton
X47 Alexander Frolov
X48 Rob Blake
X50 Marian Gaborik
X53 Patrick Roy
X54 Guy Lafleur
X55 Saku Koivu
X56 Cristobal Huet
X57 Michael Ryder
X60 Martin Brodeur
X61 Patrik Elias
X63 Mike Bossy
X64 Miroslav Satan
X69 Dany Heatley
X76 Shane Doan
X77 Jeremy Roenick
X79 Mario Lemieux
X80 Sidney Crosby
X81 Marc-Andre Fleury
X82 Joe Thornton
X83 Jonathan Cheechoo
X85 Doug Weight
X88 Vincent Lecavalier
X91 Borje Salming
X92 Darryl Sittler
X96 Markus Naslund
X97 Roberto Luongo

2006-07 SPx Winning Materials

WMAF Alexander Frolov 4.00 10.00
WMAH Ales Hemsky 4.00 10.00
WMAM Al MacInnis 4.00 10.00
WMAN Glenn Anderson 6.00 15.00
WMAO Alexander Ovechkin 12.00 30.00
WMAS Alexander Steen 4.00 10.00
WMAT Alex Tanguay 4.00 10.00
WMAY Alexei Yashin 4.00 10.00
WMBB Brad Boyes 4.00 10.00
WMBC Bobby Clarke 5.00 12.00
WMBG Bill Guerin 4.00 10.00
WMBL Brian Leetch 3.00 8.00
WMBM Bryan McCabe 4.00 10.00
WMBO Pierre-Marc Bouchard 4.00 10.00
WMBR Brad Richards 5.00 12.00
WMBS Billy Smith 6.00 15.00
WMBT Bryan Trottier 2.50 6.00
WMCA Jeff Carter 5.00 12.00
WMCC Chris Chelios 2.50 6.00
WMCD Chris Drury 5.00 12.00
WMCH Cristobal Huet 4.00 10.00
WMCJ Curtis Joseph 5.00 12.00
WMCN Cam Neely 3.00 8.00
WMCP Chris Pronger 4.00 10.00
WMCW Cam Ward 8.00 20.00
WMDA Daniel Alfredsson 4.00 10.00
WMDH Dany Heatley 5.00 12.00
WMDP Dion Phaneuf 6.00 15.00
WMDW Doug Weight 4.00 10.00
WMEB Ed Belfour 12.00 30.00
WMES Eric Staal 4.00 10.00
WMGA Simon Gagne 5.00 12.00
WMGF Grant Fuhr 6.00 15.00
WMGI Brian Gionta 4.00 10.00
WMHA Martin Havlat 4.00 10.00
WMHE Milan Hejduk 5.00 12.00
WMHK Dominik Hasek 5.00 12.00
WMHL Henrik Lundqvist 8.00 20.00
WMHO Tomas Holmstrom 4.00 10.00
WMHZ Henrik Zetterberg 5.00 12.00
WMIK Ilya Kovalchuk 6.00 15.00
WMJB Jay Bouwmeester 4.00 10.00
WMJC Jonathan Cheechoo 5.00 12.00
WMJG Jean-Sebastien Giguere 5.00 12.00
WMJI Jarome Iginla 8.00 20.00
WMJJ Jaromir Jagr 6.00 15.00
WMJL Jeffrey Lupul 4.00 10.00
WMJS Joe Sakic 8.00 20.00
WMJT Jose Theodore 5.00 12.00
WMJW Justin Williams 5.00 12.00
WMKC Kyle Calder 4.00 10.00
WMKD Kris Draper 4.00 10.00
WMKL Kari Lehtonen 5.00 12.00
WMKT Keith Tkachuk 4.00 10.00
WMLM Lanny McDonald 4.00 10.00
WMMA Maxim Afinogenov 4.00 10.00
WMMB Martin Brodeur 10.00 25.00
WMMC Mike Cammalleri 4.00 10.00
WMMF Manny Fernandez 5.00 12.00
WMMG Marian Gaborik 8.00 20.00
WMMH Marian Hossa 4.00 10.00
WMMM Mike Modano 4.00 10.00
WMMN Markus Naslund 5.00 12.00
WMMO Brendan Morrison 4.00 10.00
WMMR Michael Ryder 4.00 10.00
WMMS Miroslav Satan 4.00 10.00
WMMT Marty Turco 4.00 10.00
WMMW Brenden Morrow 4.00 10.00
WMNL Nicklas Lidstrom 5.00 12.00
WMOJ Olli Jokinen 4.00 10.00
WMOK Olaf Kolzig 6.00 15.00
WMPB Patrice Bergeron 4.00 10.00
WMPD Pavel Datsyuk 5.00 12.00
WMPE Patrik Elias 4.00 10.00
WMPF Peter Forsberg 6.00 15.00
WMPK Paul Kariya 5.00 12.00
WMPM Patrick Marleau 4.00 10.00
WMPP Petr Prucha 4.00 10.00
WMPT Pierre Turgeon 4.00 10.00
WMRD Rick DiPietro 5.00 12.00
WMRE Robert Esche 4.00 10.00
WMRE Mark Recchi 4.00 10.00
WMRL Roberto Luongo 10.00 25.00
WMRN Rick Nash 5.00 12.00
WMRO Rob Blake 4.00 10.00
WMRS Ryan Smyth 4.00 10.00
WMSA Borje Salming 2.50 6.00
WMSC Sidney Crosby 20.00 50.00
WMSD Shane Doan 5.00 12.00
WMSF Sergei Fedorov 5.00 12.00
WMSG Scott Gomez 4.00 10.00
WMSK Saku Koivu 5.00 12.00
WMSP Jason Spezza 5.00 12.00
WMSS Sergei Samsonov 4.00 10.00
WMST Martin St. Louis 5.00 12.00
WMTH Joe Thornton 6.00 15.00
WMTR Tuomo Ruutu 4.00 10.00
WMTS Teemu Selanne 5.00 12.00
WMTV Tomas Vokoun 4.00 10.00
WMVL Vincent Lecavalier 5.00 12.00

2006-07 SPx Winning Materials Spectrum

PRINT RUN 99 #'d SETS

2006-07 SPx Winning Materials Autographs

PRINT RUN 10 #'d SETS
NOT PRICED DUE TO SCARCITY
WMAF Alexander Frolov
WMAH Ales Hemsky
WMAM Al MacInnis
WMAN Glenn Anderson
WMAT Alex Tanguay
WMAY Alexei Yashin
WMBB Brad Boyes
WMBC Bobby Clarke
WMBM Bryan McCabe
WMBO PierreMarc Bouchard
WMBS Billy Smith
WMCA Jeff Carter
WMCD Chris Drury
WMCH Cristobal Huet
WMCN Cam Neely
WMCP Chris Pronger
WMDH Dany Heatley
WMDP Dion Phaneuf
WMDW Doug Weight
WMEB Ed Belfour
WMES Eric Staal
WMGF Grant Fuhr
WMHA Martin Havlat
WMHE Milan Hejduk
WMHK Dominik Hasek
WMHZ Henrik Zetterberg
WMIK Ilya Kovalchuk
WMJB Jay Bouwmeester
WMJC Jonathan Cheechoo
WMJI Jarome Iginla
WMJT Jose Theodore
WMKC Kyle Calder
WMKD Kris Draper
WMKL Kari Lehtonen
WMMA Maxim Afinogenov
WMMB Martin Brodeur
WMMC Mike Cammalleri
WMMG Marian Gaborik
WMMH Marian Hossa
WMMN Markus Naslund
WMMR Michael Ryder
WMMS Miroslav Satan
WMMT Marty Turco
WMNL Nicklas Lidstrom
WMPB Patrice Bergeron
WMPE Patrik Elias
WMPM Patrick Marleau
WMRE Robert Esche
WMRL Roberto Luongo
WMRN Rick Nash
WMRO Rob Blake
WMRS Ryan Smyth
WMSA Borje Salming
WMSC Sidney Crosby
WMSD Shane Doan
WMSG Scott Gomez
WMSK Saku Koivu
WMSS Sergei Samsonov
WMTH Joe Thornton
WMTR Tuomo Ruutu
WMTV Tomas Vokoun
WMVL Vincent Lecavalier

2007-08 SPx

This 235-card set was released in January, 2008. The set was issued into the hobby in four-card packs, with a $6.99 SRP, which came 18 packs to a box and 14 boxes to a case. Cards numbered 1-100 feature active veterans while cards 101-125 feature a mix of active and retired players with a game-worn jersey swatch. Cards numbered 126-150 feature both game-worn jersey swatches as well as an autograph. Rookie Cards are 151-236 with cards 182-200 having a game-worn jersey swatch and cards 201-236 having both a player-worn jersey swatch and an autograph. A few players did not return their signatures in time for pack out and those cards could be redeemed until December 17,2009.

COMP.SET w/o SPs (100) 12.00 30.00
(151-180) PRINT RUN 999 SER.#'d SETS
(181-200) PRINT RUN 1599 SER.#'d SETS
(201-230) PRINT RUN 999 SER.#'d SETS
(231-235) PRINT RUN 499 SER.#'d SETS
1 Jean-Sebastien Giguere .40 1.00
2 Ryan Getzlaf .30 .75
3 Scott Niedermayer .25 .60
4 Chris Pronger .40 1.00
5 Mike Modano .40 1.00
6 Mike Ribeiro .25 .60
7 Marty Turco .40 1.00
8 Anze Kopitar .40 1.00
9 Alexander Frolov .25 .60
10 Rob Blake .25 .60
11 Shane Doan .25 .60
12 Ed Jovanovski .25 .60
13 David Aebischer .30 .75
14 Joe Thornton .50 1.25
15 Evgeni Nabokov .30 .75
16 Jonathan Cheechoo .30 .75
17 Patrick Marleau .30 .75
18 Jarome Iginla .60 1.50
19 Miikka Kiprusoff .50 1.25
20 Alex Tanguay .30 .75
21 Dion Phaneuf .40 1.00
22 Joe Sakic .75 2.00
23 Paul Stastny .40 1.00
24 Milan Hejduk .30 .75
25 Ales Hemsky .25 .60
26 Dwayne Roloson .30 .75
27 Wayne Gretzky 2.00 5.00
28 Shawn Horcoff .25 .60
29 Marian Gaborik .50 1.25
30 Niklas Backstrom .30 .75
31 Pierre-Marc Bouchard .25 .60
32 Markus Naslund .40 1.00
33 Roberto Luongo .60 1.50
34 Henrik Sedin .25 .60
35 Daniel Sedin .25 .60
36 Martin Havlat .30 .75
37 Nikolai Khabibulin .40 1.00
38 Duncan Keith .40 1.00
39 Rick Nash .40 1.00
40 Fredrik Norrena .30 .75
41 Sergei Fedorov .40 1.00
42 Henrik Zetterberg .40 1.00
43 Gordie Howe 1.00 2.50
44 Pavel Datsyuk .40 1.00
45 Nicklas Lidstrom .40 1.00
46 Chris Mason .30 .75
47 Steve Sullivan .25 .60
48 Alexander Radulov .40 1.00
49 Doug Weight .25 .60
50 Manny Legace .30 .75
51 Paul Kariya .40 1.00
52 Ilya Kovalchuk .50 1.25
53 Kari Lehtonen .40 1.00
54 Marian Hossa .40 1.00
55 Eric Staal .40 1.00
56 Cam Ward .40 1.00
57 Justin Williams .25 .60
58 Nathan Horton .25 .60
59 Tomas Vokoun .40 1.00
60 Olli Jokinen .25 .60
61 Martin St. Louis .30 .75
62 Vincent Lecavalier .40 1.00
63 Brad Richards .30 .75
64 Alexander Ovechkin 1.25 3.00
65 Olaf Kolzig .40 1.00
66 Alexander Semin .40 1.00
67 Patrice Bergeron .40 1.00
68 Bobby Orr 1.50 4.00
69 Phil Kessel .40 1.00
70 Jason Pominville .25 .60
71 Ryan Miller .40 1.00
72 Thomas Vanek .30 .75
73 Saku Koivu .30 .75
74 Cristobal Huet .30 .75
75 Michael Ryder .25 .60
76 Guillaume Latendresse .30 .75
77 Daniel Alfredsson .30 .75
78 Jason Spezza .40 1.00
79 Ray Emery .30 .75
80 Dany Heatley .50 1.25
81 Mats Sundin .40 1.00
82 Vesa Toskala .30 .75
83 Alexander Steen .25 .60
84 Darcy Tucker .25 .60
85 Martin Brodeur 1.00 2.50
86 Patrik Elias .25 .60
87 Zach Parise .30 .75
88 Rick DiPietro .30 .75
89 Miroslav Satan .25 .60
90 Bill Guerin .25 .60
91 Henrik Lundqvist .50 1.25
92 Jaromir Jagr .60 1.50
93 Mark Messier .75 2.00
94 Simon Gagne .40 1.00
95 Daniel Briere .40 1.00
96 Jeff Carter .25 .60
97 Marc-Andre Fleury .40 1.00
98 Evgeni Malkin 1.00 2.50
99 Sidney Crosby 2.00 5.00
100 Mario Lemieux 1.25 3.00
101 Billy Smith JSY 8.00 20.00
102 Bob Nystrom JSY 5.00 12.00
103 Bobby Clarke JSY 8.00 20.00
104 Brendan Shanahan JSY 8.00 20.00
105 Brian Leetch JSY 8.00 20.00
106 Denis Savard JSY 6.00 15.00
107 Dino Ciccarelli JSY 6.00 15.00
108 Doug Gilmour JSY 6.00 15.00
109 Ed Belfour JSY 8.00 20.00
110 Frank Mahovlich JSY 12.00 30.00
111 Guy Lafleur JSY 20.00 50.00
112 Joe Sakic JSY 15.00 40.00
113 Keith Tkachuk JSY 6.00 15.00
114 Lanny McDonald JSY 6.00 15.00
115 Mark Recchi JSY 5.00 12.00
116 Mats Sundin JSY 8.00 20.00
117 Mike Modano JSY 8.00 20.00
118 Nicklas Lidstrom JSY 8.00 20.00
119 Paul Kariya JSY 8.00 20.00
120 Peter Forsberg JSY 10.00 25.00
121 Roberto Luongo JSY 12.00 30.00
122 Saku Koivu JSY 6.00 15.00
123 Sergei Fedorov JSY 8.00 20.00
124 Steve Shutt JSY 6.00 15.00
125 Teemu Selanne JSY 8.00 20.00
126 Al MacInnis JSY AU 15.00 40.00
127 Alexander Ovechkin JSY AU 100.00 200.00
128 Borje Salming JSY AU 15.00 40.00
129 Cam Neely JSY AU 20.00 50.00
130 Dale Hawerchuk SP JSY AU 100.00 200.00
131 Dany Heatley JSY AU 25.00 60.00
132 Darryl Sittler JSY AU 15.00 40.00
133 Dominik Hasek JSY AU 25.00 60.00
134 Doug Wilson JSY AU 25.00 60.00
135 Evgeni Malkin JSY AU 100.00 175.00
136 Gordie Howe SP JSY AU 250.00 400.00
137 Grant Fuhr JSY AU 30.00 80.00
138 Jarome Iginla JSY AU 30.00 80.00
139 Jean Beliveau SP JSY AU 150.00 250.00
140 Joe Thornton JSY AU 25.00 60.00
141 Larry Robinson JSY AU 25.00 60.00
142 Mario Lemieux SP JSY AU 150.00 300.00
143 Mark Messier SP JSY AU 150.00 250.00
144 Martin Brodeur JSY AU 50.00 100.00
145 Ray Bourque JSY AU 25.00 60.00
146 Patrick Roy SP JSY AU 125.00 250.00
147 Peter Stastny JSY AU 15.00 40.00
149 Sidney Crosby JSY AU 125.00 250.00
150 Wayne Gretzky SP JSY AU 500.00 800.00
151 Ryan Carter RC 2.00 5.00
152 Mark Mancari RC 2.00 5.00
153 Patrick Kaleta RC 1.50 4.00
154 David Moss RC 2.50 6.00
155 Colin Fraser RC 1.50 4.00
156 Bryan Bickell RC 1.50 4.00
157 Magnus Johansson RC 1.50 4.00
158 Jonas Nordqvist RC 1.50 4.00
159 Jeff Finger RC 1.50 4.00
160 Tomas Popperle RC 2.00 5.00
161 Chris Conner RC 1.50 4.00
162 Bryan Young RC 1.50 4.00
163 Sebastien Bisaillon RC 1.50 4.00
164 Zach Stortini RC 1.50 4.00
165 Martin Lojek RC 1.50 4.00
166 Joe Piskula RC 1.50 4.00
167 John Zeiler RC 1.50 4.00
168 Brady Murray RC 1.50 4.00
169 Rich Peverley RC 1.50 4.00
170 Mark Fraser RC 1.50 4.00
171 David Clarkson RC 1.50 4.00
172 Denis Tolpeko RC 1.50 4.00
173 Daniel Carcillo RC 2.00 5.00
174 Craig Weller RC 1.50 4.00
175 Daniel Winnik RC 1.50 4.00
176 Thomas Pihal RC 2.00 5.00
177 Steve Wagner RC 1.50 4.00
178 Mike Lundin RC 1.50 4.00
179 Jannik Hansen RC 1.50 4.00
180 Mason Raymond RC 4.00 10.00
181 Jonas Hiller JSY RC 8.00 20.00
182 Tobias Enstrom JSY RC 5.00 12.00
183 Jonathan Sigalet JSY RC 3.00 8.00
184 Jaroslav Hlinka JSY RC 4.00 10.00
185 Tyler Weiman JSY RC 4.00 10.00
186 Jared Boll JSY RC 3.00 8.00
187 Marc Methot JSY RC 3.00 8.00
188 Tobias Stephan JSY RC 4.00 10.00
189 Matt Niskanen JSY RC 3.00 8.00
190 Devin Setoguchi JSY RC 6.00 15.00
191 Matt Ellis JSY RC 3.00 8.00
192 Tom Gilbert JSY RC 4.00 10.00
193 T.Rask JSY AU RC EXCH 12.00 30.00
194 Ville Koistinen JSY RC 3.00 8.00
195 Rod Pelley JSY RC 3.00 8.00
196 Brandon Dubinsky JSY RC 5.00 12.00
197 Daniel Girardi JSY RC 3.00 8.00
198 Ryan Parent JSY RC 4.00 10.00
199 Torrey Mitchell JSY RC 4.00 10.00
200 Matt Smaby JSY RC 3.00 8.00
201 Bobby Ryan JSY AU RC 20.00 50.00
202 Drew Miller JSY AU RC 5.00 12.00
203 Bryan Little JSY AU RC 8.00 20.00
204 Brett Sterling JSY AU RC 5.00 12.00
205 David Krejci JSY AU RC 10.00 25.00
206 Milan Lucic JSY AU RC 12.00 30.00
207 Curtis McElhinney JSY AU RC 6.00 15.00
208 K.Russell JSY AU RC EXCH 8.00 20.00
209 S.Gagner JSY AU RC EXCH 10.00 25.00
210 Andrew Cogliano JSY AU RC 12.00 30.00
211 Rob Schremp JSY AU RC 6.00 15.00
212 S.Downie JSY AU RC EXCH 6.00 15.00
213 Jack Johnson JSY AU RC 8.00 20.00
214 Jonathan Bernier JSY AU RC 12.00 30.00
215 Lauri Tukonen JSY AU RC 5.00 12.00
216 Petr Kalus JSY AU RC 6.00 15.00
217 James Sheppard JSY AU RC 5.00 12.00
218 Kyle Chipchura JSY AU RC 8.00 20.00
219 Jaroslav Halak JSY AU RC 15.00 40.00
220 Nicklas Bergfors JSY AU RC 6.00 15.00
221 Andy Greene JSY AU RC 5.00 12.00
222 Frans Nielsen JSY AU RC 5.00 12.00
223 Ryan Callahan JSY AU RC 8.00 20.00
224 M.Staal JSY AU RC EXCH 12.00 30.00
225 Nick Foligno JSY AU RC 8.00 20.00
226 Brian Elliott JSY AU RC 6.00 15.00
227 Martin Hanzal JSY AU RC 6.00 15.00
228 David Perron JSY AU RC 8.00 20.00
229 Erik Johnson JSY AU RC 10.00 25.00
230 Anton Stralman JSY AU RC 6.00 15.00
231 Jonathan Toews JSY AU RC 60.00 120.00
232 Patrick Kane JSY AU RC 60.00 120.00
233 Carey Price JSY AU RC 60.00 120.00
234 Jiri Tlusty JSY AU RC 20.00 50.00
235 Peter Mueller JSY AU RC 20.00 50.00
236 Nicklas Backstrom JSY AU RC 30.00 80.00

2007-08 SPx Spectrum

*SPEC JSY (1-100): 6X TO 15X
*SPEC JSY (101-125): .5X TO 1.2X
*SPEC JSY AU (126-150): .4X TO 1X
*SPEC (151-180): .8X TO 2X

*SPEC JSY (181-200): .5X TO 1.2X
*SPEC JSY AU (201-230): .5X TO 1.2X
*SPEC JSY AU (231-236): .4X TO 1X
STATED PRINT RUN 25 SER.#'d SETS
143 Mark Messier JSY AU 150.00 250.00
146 Patrick Roy JSY AU 125.00 250.00
149 Sidney Crosby JSY AU 200.00 400.00
150 Wayne Gretzky JSY AU
231 Jonathan Toews JSY AU 300.00 600.00
232 Patrick Kane JSY AU 300.00 600.00
233 Carey Price JSY AU 600.00 900.00
236 Nicklas Backstrom JSY AU 100.00 200.00

2007-08 SPx Force Quad Holograms

STATED ODDS 1:126
F1 Mario Lemieux 30.00 80.00
Sidney Crosby
Wayne Gretzky
Mark Messier
F2 Patrick Roy 20.00 50.00
Martin Brodeur
Roberto Luongo
Jean-Sebastien Giguere
F3 Joe Sakic 12.00 30.00
Vincent Lecavalier
Joe Thornton
Jason Spezza
F4 Jarome Iginla 15.00 40.00
Martin St. Louis
Dany Heatley
Gordie Howe
F5 Nicklas Lidstrom 25.00 60.00
Scott Niedermayer
Bobby Orr
Dion Phaneuf

2007-08 SPx Radiance Autographed Jerseys

STATED PRINT RUN 10 SER.#'d SETS
NOT PRICED DUE TO SCARCITY

2007-08 SPx SPXtreme

COMPLETE SET (70) 75.00 150.00
STATED ODDS 1:18
STATED PRINT RUN 999 #'d SETS
X1 Wayne Gretzky 5.00 12.00
X2 Mario Lemieux 3.00 8.00
X3 Bobby Orr 4.00 10.00
X4 Mark Messier 2.00 5.00
X5 Gordie Howe 2.50 6.00
X6 Patrick Roy 3.00 8.00
X7 Phil Esposito 1.50 4.00
X8 Tony Esposito 1.50 4.00
X9 Stan Mikita .75 2.00
X10 Grant Fuhr 1.50 4.00
X11 Luc Robitaille .75 2.00
X12 Guy Lafleur 2.50 6.00
X13 Mike Bossy .75 2.00
X14 Denis Potvin .75 2.00
X15 Bobby Clarke 1.00 2.50
X16 Bernie Parent 1.25 3.00
X17 Darryl Sittler .75 2.00
X18 Lanny McDonald .75 2.00
X19 Peter Stastny .75 2.00
X20 Dale Hawerchuk .75 2.00
X21 Jean-Sebastien Giguere 1.00 2.50
X22 Ilya Kovalchuk 1.25 3.00
X23 Patrice Bergeron 1.00 2.50
X24 Ryan Miller 1.00 2.50
X25 Jarome Iginla 1.50 4.00
X26 Eric Staal 1.00 2.50
X27 Joe Sakic 2.00 5.00
X28 Rick Nash 1.00 2.50
X29 Mike Modano 1.00 2.50
X30 Henrik Zetterberg 1.00 2.50
X31 Marian Gaborik 1.25 3.00
X32 Saku Koivu .75 2.00
X33 Tomas Vokoun 1.00 2.50
X34 Martin Brodeur 2.50 6.00
X35 Jaromir Jagr 1.50 4.00
X36 Dany Heatley 1.25 3.00
X37 Simon Gagne 1.00 2.50
X38 Sidney Crosby 5.00 12.00
X39 Evgeni Malkin 2.50 6.00
X40 Joe Thornton 1.25 3.00
X41 Vincent Lecavalier 1.00 2.50
X42 Mats Sundin 1.00 2.50
X43 Roberto Luongo 1.50 4.00
X44 Alexander Ovechkin 3.00 8.00
X45 Miikka Kiprusoff 1.25 3.00
X46 Thomas Vanek .75 2.00
X47 Teemu Selanne 1.00 2.50
X48 Anze Kopitar 1.00 2.50
X49 Miroslav Satan .60 1.50
X50 Daniel Alfredsson .75 2.00
X51 Rob Schremp .75 2.00
X52 Jack Johnson 1.00 2.50
X53 Petr Kalus .60 1.50
X54 Carey Price 20.00 50.00
X55 Patrick Kane 15.00 40.00
X56 Nicklas Backstrom 2.50 6.00
X57 Marc Staal 1.50 4.00
X58 Peter Mueller 2.00 5.00
X59 Jonathan Toews 20.00 40.00
X60 Bobby Ryan 2.50 6.00
X61 Nicklas Bergfors .75 2.00
X62 Erik Johnson 1.25 3.00
X63 Sam Gagner 1.25 3.00
X64 Kyle Chipchura 1.00 2.50
X65 Bryan Little .75 2.00
X66 Jonathan Bernier 1.50 4.00
X67 Andrew Cogliano 1.50 4.00
X68 Nick Foligno 1.00 2.50
X69 Brett Sterling .60 1.50
X70 James Sheppard .60 1.50

2007-08 SPx SPXtreme Spectrum

*SPECTRUM 4X TO 10X HI
STATED PRINT RUN 25 SER.#'d SETS
X1 Wayne Gretzky 50.00 120.00
X54 Carey Price 60.00 120.00
X55 Patrick Kane 50.00 100.00
X59 Jonathan Toews 60.00 120.00

2007-08 SPx SPXtreme Radiance Autographs

STATED PRINT RUN 5 SER.#'d SETS
NOT PRICED DUE TO SCARCITY

2007-08 SPx Winning Combos

STATED ODDS 1:18
WCAR Jason Arnott 5.00 12.00
Alexander Radulov
WCBE Martin Brodeur 12.00 30.00
Patrik Elias
WCBH Ed Belfour 6.00 15.00
Dominik Hasek
WCBK Patrice Bergeron 5.00 12.00
Phil Kessel
WCBL Martin Brodeur 12.00 30.00
Roberto Luongo
WCBM Mats Sundin 5.00 12.00
Borje Salming
WCCM Sidney Crosby 25.00 60.00
Evgeni Malkin
WCCO Sidney Crosby 25.00 60.00
Alexander Ovechkin
WCDA Darryl Sittler 4.00 10.00
Alexander Steen
WCDB Pavel Datsyuk 5.00 12.00
Rod Brind`Amour
WCDG Pavol Demitra 6.00 15.00
Marian Gaborik
WCDM Dino Ciccarelli 6.00 15.00
Marian Gaborik
WCDS Rick DiPietro 5.00 12.00
Billy Smith
WCDZ Pavel Datsyuk 5.00 12.00
Henrik Zetterberg
WCFK Alexander Frolov 5.00 12.00
Anze Kopitar
WCFR Grant Fuhr 8.00 20.00
Dwayne Roloson
WCGB Simon Gagne 5.00 12.00
Martin Biron
WCHE Dany Heatley 6.00 15.00
Ray Emery
WCHK Martin Havlat 5.00 12.00
Nikolai Khabibulin
WCIM Marian Hossa 6.00 15.00
Ilya Kovalchuk
WCIT Jarome Iginla 8.00 20.00
Alex Tanguay
WCJD Ed Jovanovski 3.00 8.00
Shane Doan
WCJL Jaromir Jagr 8.00 20.00
Henrik Lundqvist
WCJM Joe Sakic 10.00 25.00
Milan Hejduk
WCJS Jaromir Jagr 8.00 20.00
Peter Stastny
WCKO Olaf Kolzig 15.00 40.00
Alexander Ovechkin
WCKR Saku Koivu 4.00 10.00
Michael Ryder
WCLB Nicklas Lidstrom 6.00 15.00
Ray Bourque
WCLC Mario Lemieux 25.00 60.00
Sidney Crosby
WCLH Guy Lafleur 12.00 30.00
Chris Higgins
WCLS Vincent Lecavalier 5.00 12.00
Martin St. Louis
WCMM Mike Modano 5.00 12.00
Marty Turco
WCMT Lanny McDonald 4.00 10.00
Alex Tanguay
WCMV Ryan Miller 5.00 12.00
Thomas Vanek
WCNF Rick Nash 5.00 12.00
Sergei Fedorov
WCNG Scott Niedermayer 5.00 12.00
Jean-Sebastien Giguere
WCNK Cam Neely 5.00 12.00
Phil Kessel
WCNL Markus Naslund 8.00 20.00
Roberto Luongo
WCOM Alexander Ovechkin 15.00 40.00
Evgeni Malkin
WCPM Dion Phaneuf 5.00 12.00
Al MacInnis
WCRB Patrick Roy 15.00 40.00
Martin Brodeur
WCRH Dwayne Roloson 4.00 10.00
Ales Hemsky
WCSD Miroslav Satan 4.00 10.00
Rick DiPietro
WCSH Denis Savard 4.00 10.00
Martin Havlat
WCSS Joe Sakic 10.00 25.00
Brendan Shanahan
WCST Mats Sundin 5.00 12.00
Darcy Tucker
WCSW Eric Staal 5.00 12.00
Cam Ward
WCTN Joe Thornton 6.00 15.00
Evgeni Nabokov
WCVJ Tomas Vokoun 5.00 12.00
Olli Jokinen
WCWK Paul Kariya 5.00 12.00
Doug Weight

2007-08 SPx Winning Combos Spectrum

*SPEC: .5X TO 1.2X
STATED PRINT RUN 99 SER.#'d SETS

2007-08 SPx Winning Combos Radiance Autographs

STATED PRINT RUN 10 SER.#'d SETS
NOT PRICED DUE TO SCARCITY

2007-08 SPx Winning Materials

STATED ODDS 1:18
WMAH Ales Hemsky 2.50 6.00
WMAM Al MacInnis 3.00 8.00
WMAO Alexander Ovechkin 12.00 30.00
WMAT Alex Tanguay 3.00 8.00
WMBR Brad Richards 3.00 8.00
WMCN Cam Neely 4.00 10.00
WMCW Cam Ward 4.00 10.00
WMDA Daniel Alfredsson 3.00 8.00
WMDB Daniel Briere 4.00 10.00
WMDH Dany Heatley 5.00 12.00
WMDP Dion Phaneuf 4.00 10.00
WMDR Dwayne Roloson 3.00 8.00
WMES Eric Staal 4.00 10.00
WMHA Dominik Hasek 5.00 12.00
WMHL Henrik Lundqvist 5.00 12.00
WMHZ Henrik Zetterberg 4.00 10.00
WMIK Ilya Kovalchuk 5.00 12.00
WMJC Jonathan Cheechoo 3.00 8.00
WMJG Jean-Sebastien Giguere 4.00 10.00
WMJI Jarome Iginla 6.00 15.00
WMJJ Jaromir Jagr 6.00 15.00
WMJS Joe Sakic 8.00 20.00
WMJT Joe Thornton 5.00 12.00
WMKL Kari Lehtonen 4.00 10.00
WMMB Martin Brodeur 10.00 25.00
WMMG Marian Gaborik 5.00 12.00
WMMH Marian Hossa 4.00 10.00
WMMM Mike Modano 4.00 10.00
WMMN Markus Naslund 4.00 10.00
WMMR Michael Ryder 2.50 6.00
WMMS Mats Sundin 4.00 10.00
WMMT Marty Turco 4.00 10.00
WMNL Nicklas Lidstrom 4.00 10.00
WMPB Patrice Bergeron 4.00 10.00
WMPD Pavel Datsyuk 4.00 10.00
WMPF Peter Forsberg 5.00 12.00
WMPK Paul Kariya 4.00 10.00
WMPO Denis Potvin 3.00 8.00
WMRL Roberto Luongo 6.00 15.00
WMRN Rick Nash 4.00 10.00
WMSA Borje Salming 3.00 8.00
WMSC Sidney Crosby 20.00 50.00
WMSG Simon Gagne 4.00 10.00
WMSK Saku Koivu 3.00 8.00
WMTS Teemu Selanne 4.00 10.00
WMTV Tomas Vokoun 4.00 10.00
WMVA Thomas Vanek 3.00 8.00
WMVL Vincent Lecavalier 4.00 10.00
WMVT Vesa Toskala 3.00 8.00
WMZP Zach Parise 3.00 8.00

2007-08 SPx Winning Materials Spectrum

*SPECTRUM: .5X TO 1.2X
STATED PRINT RUN 99 SER.#'d SETS

2007-08 SPx Winning Materials Radiance Autographs

STATED PRINT RUN 25 SER.#'d SETS
SOME NOT PRICED DUE TO SCARCITY
WMAH Ales Hemsky
WMAM Al MacInnis
WMAO Alexander Ovechkin
WMAT Alex Tanguay
WMCN Cam Neely
WMCW Cam Ward
WMDB Daniel Briere
WMDH Dany Heatley
WMDP Dion Phaneuf 40.00 80.00
WMDR Dwayne Roloson
WMES Eric Staal
WMHA Dominik Hasek 40.00 80.00
WMHL Henrik Lundqvist
WMHZ Henrik Zetterberg
WMIK Ilya Kovalchuk
WMJC Jonathan Cheechoo
WMJI Jarome Iginla
WMJT Joe Thornton
WMKL Kari Lehtonen
WMMB Martin Brodeur
WMMG Marian Gaborik 40.00 80.00
WMMH Marian Hossa
WMMM Mike Modano
WMMN Markus Naslund
WMMR Michael Ryder
WMMT Marty Turco
WMNL Nicklas Lidstrom
WMPB Patrice Bergeron
WMPO Denis Potvin
WMRN Rick Nash
WMSA Borje Salming
WMSC Sidney Crosby 200.00 300.00
WMSG Simon Gagne
WMSK Saku Koivu
WMTV Tomas Vokoun
WMVA Thomas Vanek
WMVL Vincent Lecavalier
WMVT Vesa Toskala
WMZP Zach Parise

2008-09 SPx

This set was released on January 14, 2009. The base set consists of 249 cards.

COMP.SET w/o SPs (100) 15.00 40.00
101-130 STATED PRINT RUN 499
131-148, 150-155 STATED PRINT RUN 1299
149, 156-184 STATED PRINT RUN 999
185-190 STATED PRINT RUN 499
191-220 STATED ODDS 1:126
221-250 STATED ODDS 1:252
1 Nicklas Backstrom 1.00 2.50
2 Alexander Ovechkin 2.00 5.00
3 Pavol Demitra .30 .75
4 Roberto Luongo .75 2.00
5 Steve Bernier .30 .75
6 Mats Sundin .50 1.25
7 Vesa Toskala .50 1.25
8 Ryan Malone .30 .75
9 Vincent Lecavalier .50 1.25
10 Olaf Kolzig .50 1.25
11 David Perron .40 1.00
12 Paul Kariya .50 1.25
13 Joe Thornton .75 2.00
14 Jonathan Cheechoo .50 1.25
15 Patrick Marleau .40 1.00
16 Rob Blake .50 1.25
17 Jordan Staal .75 2.00
18 Sidney Crosby 2.50 6.00
19 Marc-Andre Fleury .50 1.25
20 Evgeni Malkin 1.25 3.00
21 Miroslav Satan .30 .75
22 Shane Doan .30 .75
23 Peter Mueller .60 1.50
24 Olli Jokinen .30 .75
25 Mike Richards .75 2.00
26 Martin Biron .40 1.00
27 Simon Gagne .40 1.00
28 Daniel Briere .50 1.25
29 Jason Spezza .60 1.50
30 Martin Gerber .40 1.00
31 Chris Phillips .30 .75
32 Markus Naslund .50 1.25
33 Scott Gomez .40 1.00
34 Wade Redden .30 .75
35 Henrik Lundqvist 1.00 2.50
36 Chris Drury .50 1.25
37 Nikolai Zherdev .30 .75
38 Doug Weight .30 .75
39 Rick DiPietro .50 1.25
40 Martin Brodeur 1.00 2.50
41 Patrik Elias .30 .75
42 Zach Parise .50 1.25
43 Brian Gionta .50 1.25
44 Shea Weber .30 .75
45 Jason Arnott .30 .75
46 Carey Price 1.50 4.00
47 Saku Koivu .50 1.25
48 Alex Kovalev .50 1.25
49 Alex Tanguay .40 1.00
50 Marian Gaborik .75 2.00
51 Pierre-Marc Bouchard .30 .75
52 Anze Kopitar .50 1.25
53 Tomas Vokoun .50 1.25
54 Stephen Weiss .30 .75
55 Shawn Horcoff .30 .75
56 Dwayne Roloson .40 1.00
57 Sam Gagner .75 2.00
58 Marian Hossa .75 2.00
59 Tomas Holmstrom .40 1.00
60 Brian Rafalski .30 .75
61 Henrik Zetterberg 1.00 2.50
62 Nicklas Lidstrom .50 1.25
63 Brad Richards .40 1.00
64 Mike Modano .50 1.25
65 Marty Turco .40 1.00
66 Mike Ribeiro .30 .75
67 Jere Lehtinen .30 .75
68 Pascal Leclaire .40 1.00
69 Rick Nash .50 1.25
70 Joe Sakic .75 2.00
71 Milan Hejduk .40 1.00
72 Paul Stastny .50 1.25
73 Peter Forsberg .75 2.00
74 Marek Svatos .30 .75
75 Darcy Tucker .40 1.00
76 Patrick Sharp .30 .75
77 Jonathan Toews 1.50 4.00
78 Patrick Kane 1.25 3.00
79 Eric Staal .75 2.00
80 Cam Ward .50 1.25
81 Justin Williams .30 .75
82 Mike Cammalleri .50 1.25
83 Jarome Iginla 1.00 2.50
84 Todd Bertuzzi .50 1.25
85 Dion Phaneuf .50 1.25
86 Tuukka Rask .50 1.25
87 Ryan Miller .50 1.25
88 Maxim Afinogenov .30 .75
89 Marc Savard .30 .75
90 Patrice Bergeron .50 1.25
91 Phil Kessel .50 1.25
92 Tim Thomas .50 1.25
93 Zdeno Chara .30 .75
94 Michael Ryder .40 1.00
95 Ilya Kovalchuk .60 1.50
96 Kari Lehtonen .30 .75
97 Tobias Enstrom .50 1.25
98 Corey Perry .50 1.25
99 Ryan Getzlaf .60 1.50
100 Teemu Selanne .50 1.25
101 Adam Pardy RC 4.00 10.00
102 Wayne Simmonds RC 4.00 10.00
103 Nathan Oystrick RC 4.00 10.00
104 Anssi Salmela RC 5.00 12.00
105 Jared Ross RC 5.00 12.00
106 Chris Porter RC 4.00 10.00
107 Janne Niskala RC 4.00 10.00
108 John Mitchell RC 4.00 10.00
109 Mike Brown RC 5.00 12.00
110 Kyle Greentree RC 5.00 12.00
111 Sami Lepisto RC 4.00 10.00
112 Zach Fitzgerald RC 4.00 10.00
113 Darryl Boyce RC 3.00 8.00
114 Jesse Winchester RC 4.00 10.00
115 Corey Locke RC 4.00 10.00
116 Brandon Nolan RC 5.00 12.00
117 Jordan Hendry RC 3.00 8.00
118 Pascal Pelletier RC 3.00 8.00
119 Tom Cavanagh RC 3.00 8.00
120 Theo Peckham RC 4.00 10.00
121 B.J. Crombeen RC 3.00 8.00
122 Joe Jensen RC 4.00 10.00
123 Josh Bailey RC 6.00 15.00
124 Garrett Stafford RC 5.00 12.00
125 Jonas Frogren RC 5.00 12.00
126 Alex Foster RC 3.00 8.00
127 David Brine RC 3.00 8.00
128 Colin Stuart RC 3.00 8.00
129 Andrew Murray RC 3.00 8.00
130 Niklas Hjalmarsson RC 6.00 15.00
131 Jonathan Ericsson JSY RC 10.00 25.00
132 Darren Helm JSY RC 10.00 25.00
133 Erik Ersberg JSY RC 6.00 15.00
134 Matthew Halischuk JSY RC 8.00 20.00
135 Mark Fistric JSY RC 5.00 12.00
136 Adam Pineault JSY RC 6.00 15.00
137 Oscar Moller JSY RC 6.00 15.00
138 Matt D'Agostini JSY RC 10.00 25.00
139 Mattias Ritola JSY RC 8.00 20.00
140 Ryan Stone JSY RC 6.00 15.00
141 Mike Iggulden JSY RC 5.00 12.00
142 Andrew Ebbett JSY RC 6.00 15.00
143 Dan LaCosta JSY RC 8.00 20.00
144 Teddy Purcell JSY RC 6.00 15.00
145 Jamie McGinn JSY RC 6.00 15.00
146 Tim Ramholt JSY RC 5.00 12.00
147 Jon Filewich JSY RC 5.00 12.00
148 Boris Valabik JSY RC 8.00 20.00
149 Cory Schneider JSY AU RC 15.00 40.00
150 Tyler Plante JSY RC 6.00 15.00
151 Petr Vrana JSY RC 8.00 20.00
152 Brian Boyle JSY RC 6.00 15.00
153 Tom Sestito JSY RC 5.00 12.00
154 Ryan Jones JSY RC 8.00 20.00
155 Andreas Nodl JSY RC 6.00 15.00
156 James Neal JSY AU RC 12.00 30.00
157 Jakub Voracek JSY AU RC 15.00 40.00
158 T.J. Oshie JSY AU RC 20.00 50.00
159 Nikita Filatov JSY AU RC 30.00 80.00
160 Brandon Sutter JSY AU RC 10.00 25.00
161 Steve Mason JSY AU RC 20.00 50.00
162 Derick Brassard JSY AU RC 15.00 40.00
163 Kevin Porter JSY AU RC 6.00 15.00
164 Viktor Tikhonov JSY AU RC 8.00 20.00
165 Justin Abdelkader JSY AU RC 15.00 40.00
166 Michael Frolik JSY AU RC 15.00 40.00
167 Zach Boychuk JSY AU RC 12.00 30.00
168 Shawn Matthias JSY AU RC 8.00 20.00
169 Fabian Brunnstrom JSY AU RC 12.00 30.00
170 Patric Hornqvist JSY AU RC 8.00 20.00
171 Nikolai Kulemin JSY AU RC 8.00 20.00
172 Colton Gillies JSY AU RC 8.00 20.00
173 Kyle Okposo JSY AU RC 15.00 40.00
174 Patrik Berglund JSY AU RC 20.00 50.00
175 Lauri Korpikoski JSY AU RC 8.00 20.00
176 Brian Lee JSY AU RC 8.00 20.00
177 Ilya Zubov JSY AU RC 8.00 20.00
178 Robbie Earl JSY AU RC 6.00 15.00
179 Claude Giroux JSY AU RC 15.00 40.00
180 Alex Pietrangelo JSY AU RC 12.00 30.00
181 Alex Goligoski JSY AU RC 15.00 40.00
182 Vladimir Mihalik JSY AU RC 8.00 20.00
183 Luca Sbisa JSY AU RC 12.00 30.00
184 Mikkel Boedker JSY AU RC 12.00 30.00
185 Kyle Turris JSY AU RC 20.00 50.00
186 Blake Wheeler JSY AU RC 25.00 60.00
187 Luke Schenn JSY AU RC 30.00 80.00
188 Zach Bogosian JSY AU RC 20.00 50.00
189 Drew Doughty JSY AU RC 30.00 80.00
190 Steven Stamkos JSY AU RC 75.00 150.00
191 Theoren Fleury FF JSY 10.00 25.00
192 Adam Oates FF JSY 8.00 20.00
193 Grant Fuhr FF JSY 8.00 20.00
194 Zach Parise FF JSY 8.00 20.00
195 Lanny McDonald FF JSY 8.00 20.00
196 Nicklas Lidstrom FF JSY 8.00 20.00
197 Martin Brodeur FF JSY 15.00 40.00
198 Paul Kariya FF JSY 8.00 20.00
199 Teemu Selanne FF JSY 8.00 20.00
200 Peter Forsberg FF JSY 12.00 30.00
201 Mike Bossy FF JSY 8.00 20.00
202 Jeremy Roenick FF JSY 8.00 20.00
203 Joe Sakic FF JSY 12.00 30.00
204 Brendan Shanahan FF JSY 8.00 20.00
205 Chris Chelios FF JSY 10.00 25.00
206 Dominik Hasek FF JSY 12.00 30.00
207 Borje Salming FF JSY 8.00 20.00
208 Frank Mahovlich FF JSY 8.00 20.00
209 Gerry Cheevers FF JSY 12.00 30.00
210 Olli Jokinen FF JSY 5.00 12.00
211 Mats Sundin FF JSY 8.00 20.00
212 Marian Hossa FF JSY 12.00 30.00
213 Guy Carbonneau FF JSY 10.00 25.00
214 Marian Gaborik FF JSY 12.00 30.00
215 Marcel Dionne FF JSY 8.00 20.00
217 Al MacInnis FF JSY 10.00 25.00
218 Rod Langway FF JSY 10.00 25.00
219 Chris Drury FF JSY 8.00 20.00
220 Dale Hawerchuk FF JSY 8.00 20.00
221 Sidney Crosby FF JSY AU 100.00 200.00
222 Brian Leetch FF JSY AU 20.00 50.00
223 Bryan Trottier FF JSY AU 12.00 30.00
224 Borje Salming FF JSY AU 15.00 40.00
225 Ryan Smyth FF JSY AU 12.00 30.00
226 Mario Lemieux FF JSY AU 40.00 100.00
227 Bob Bourne FF JSY AU 10.00 25.00
228 Ron Hextall FF JSY AU 15.00 40.00
229 Steve Shutt FF JSY AU 15.00 40.00
230 Lanny McDonald FF JSY AU 15.00 40.00
231 Mike Modano FF JSY AU 15.00 40.00
232 Simon Gagne FF JSY AU 12.00 30.00
233 Bernie Nicholls FF JSY AU 10.00 25.00
234 Johnny Bucyk FF JSY AU 15.00 40.00
235 Joe Thornton FF JSY AU 25.00 60.00
236 Dominik Hasek FF JSY AU 25.00 60.00
237 Rick Vaive FF JSY AU 10.00 25.00
238 Bobby Hull FF JSY AU 30.00 80.00
239 Alexander Ovechkin FF JSY AU 60.00 150.00
240 Mark Messier FF JSY AU 30.00 80.00
241 Rod Langway FF JSY AU 20.00 50.00
242 Dino Ciccarelli FF JSY AU 10.00 25.00
243 Jari Kurri FF JSY AU 15.00 40.00
244 Luc Robitaille FF JSY AU 12.00 30.00
245 Ray Bourque FF JSY AU 30.00 80.00
246 Vincent Lecavalier FF JSY AU 15.00 40.00
247 Tony Esposito FF JSY AU 15.00 40.00
248 Henrik Zetterberg FF JSY AU 30.00 80.00
249 Patrick Roy FF JSY AU 75.00 150.00
250 Wayne Gretzky FF JSY AU 100.00 200.00

2008-09 SPx Spectrum

*SPECTRUM JSY (1-100): 4X TO 10X BASE
*SPEC (101-130): .6X TO 1.5X BASE
*SPEC JSY RC (131-148, 150-155): .8X TO 2X BASE
*SPEC JSY AU (149, 156-184): 1.2X TO 3X BASE
*SPEC JSY AU RC (185-190): 1.2X TO 3X BASE
*SPEC FF JSY (191-220): .6X TO 1.5X BASE
*SPEC FF JSY AU (191-220): .6X TO 1.5X BASE
STATED PRINT RUN 25 SERIAL #'d SETS
190 Steven Stamkos JSY AU 250.00 400.00

2008-09 SPx Memorable Moments

STATED ODDS 1:126
MMAM Al MacInnis 12.00 30.00
MMBH Bobby Hull
MMBO Bobby Orr
MMBS Billy Smith
MMBT Bryan Trottier
MMCJ Curtis Joseph 10.00 25.00
MMCP Chris Pronger 8.00 20.00
MMDA Dave Andreychuk
MMDC Dino Ciccarelli 6.00 15.00
MMDS Dave Schultz 8.00 20.00
MMGF Grant Fuhr
MMGH Gordie Howe
MMGL Guy Lafleur
MMGR Wayne Gretzky
MMHO Gordie Howe
MMHZ Henrik Zetterberg
MMJK Jari Kurri 10.00 25.00
MMJS Joe Sakic
MMJT Joe Thornton
MMLE Mario Lemieux
MMLR Larry Robinson 10.00 25.00
MMMB Martin Brodeur 20.00 50.00
MMMD Marcel Dionne 10.00 25.00
MMMI Mike Bossy
MMML Mario Lemieux
MMMM Mark Messier
MMMS Martin St. Louis 10.00 25.00
MMPE Phil Esposito 15.00 40.00
MMPF Peter Forsberg
MMPR Patrick Roy 30.00 80.00
MMRH Ron Hextall 10.00 25.00
MMRO Luc Robitaille 8.00 20.00
MMRV Rogie Vachon
MMSB Scotty Bowman 10.00 25.00
MMSC Sidney Crosby 50.00 120.00
MMSF Sergei Fedorov 15.00 40.00
MMSM Stan Mikita
MMTH Jose Theodore 10.00 25.00
MMTS Teemu Selanne
MMTW Tiger Williams
MMWA Wayne Gretzky 50.00 120.00
MMWG Wayne Gretzky 50.00 120.00

2008-09 SPx SPxcitement

COMPLETE SET (70) 150.00 300.00
STATED PRINT RUN 999 SERIAL #'d SETS
X1 Alexander Ovechkin 6.00 15.00
X2 Andrew Cogliano 2.50 6.00
X3 Anze Kopitar 1.50 4.00
X4 Bobby Clarke 1.50 4.00
X5 Bobby Hull 3.00 8.00
X6 Bobby Orr 5.00 12.00
X7 Cam Neely 2.00 5.00
X8 Carey Price 5.00 12.00
X9 Dale Hawerchuk 1.50 4.00
X10 Daniel Alfredsson 1.25 3.00
X11 Dany Heatley 2.00 5.00
X12 Darryl Sittler 1.50 4.00
X13 Denis Potvin 1.25 3.00
X14 Dino Ciccarelli 1.00 2.50
X15 Eric Staal 2.50 6.00
X16 Evgeni Malkin 4.00 10.00
X17 Frank Mahovlich 1.50 4.00
X18 Guy Lafleur 3.00 8.00
X19 Gordie Howe 6.00 15.00
X20 Grant Fuhr 1.50 4.00
X21 Gilbert Perreault 1.50 4.00
X22 Henrik Lundqvist 3.00 8.00
X23 Henrik Zetterberg 3.00 8.00
X24 Ilya Kovalchuk 2.00 5.00
X25 Jari Kurri 1.50 4.00
X26 Jarome Iginla 3.00 8.00
X27 Dion Phaneuf 1.50 4.00
X28 Jean-Sebastien Giguere 1.50 4.00
X29 Joe Sakic 2.50 6.00
X30 Joe Thornton 2.50 6.00
X31 Jonathan Toews 5.00 12.00
X32 Jordan Staal 2.50 6.00
X33 Kyle Okposo 3.00 8.00
X34 Kyle Turris 3.00 8.00
X35 Lanny McDonald 1.50 4.00
X36 Luc Robitaille 1.25 3.00
X37 Marian Gaborik 2.50 6.00
X38 Mario Lemieux 4.00 10.00
X39 Mark Messier 3.00 8.00
X40 Martin Brodeur 3.00 8.00
X41 Martin St. Louis 1.50 4.00
X42 Mats Sundin 1.50 4.00
X43 Miikka Kiprusoff 1.50 4.00
X44 Mike Bossy 1.50 4.00
X45 Mike Modano 1.50 4.00
X46 Nicklas Backstrom 3.00 8.00
X47 Patrick Kane 4.00 10.00
X48 Patrick Roy 5.00 12.00
X49 Paul Stastny 1.50 4.00
X50 Peter Mueller 2.00 5.00
X51 Peter Stastny 1.50 4.00
X52 Phil Esposito 2.50 6.00
X53 Rick Nash 1.50 4.00
X54 Roberto Luongo 2.50 6.00
X55 Ron Hextall 1.50 4.00
X56 Ryan Getzlaf 2.00 5.00
X57 Ryan Miller 1.50 4.00
X58 Saku Koivu 1.50 4.00
X59 Sam Gagner 2.50 6.00
X60 Sidney Crosby 8.00 20.00
X61 Stan Mikita 1.50 4.00
X62 Steve Mason 4.00 10.00
X63 Teemu Selanne 1.50 4.00
X64 Nikita Filatov 6.00 15.00
X65 Tony Esposito 1.50 4.00
X66 Vincent Lecavalier 1.50 4.00
X67 Wayne Gretzky 8.00 20.00
X68 Blake Wheeler 4.00 10.00
X69 Fabian Brunnstrom 2.50 6.00
X70 Steven Stamkos 12.00 30.00

2008-09 SPx Spxcitement Spectrum

*SPECTRUM: 1X TO 2.5X BASE
STATED PRINT RUN 99 SERIAL #'d SETS

2008-09 SPx Winning Combos

STATED ODDS 1:18
WCBG Marian Gaborik 10.00 25.00
Pierre-Marc Bouchard
WCBM Nicklas Backstrom 12.00 30.00
Peter Mueller
WCBO Ray Bourque 12.00 30.00
Adam Oates
WCBP Martin Brodeur 20.00 50.00
Carey Price
WCCB Erik Cole 6.00 15.00
Gilbert Brule
WCCH Ron Hextall 6.00 15.00
Bobby Clarke
WCCP Jonathan Cheechoo 6.00 15.00
Corey Perry
WCDL Darryl Sittler 6.00 15.00
Lanny McDonald
WCEE Tony Esposito 10.00 25.00
Phil Esposito
WCEI Evgeni Malkin 15.00 40.00
Ilya Kovalchuk
WCEM Eric Staal 10.00 25.00
Marc Staal
WCFA Grant Fuhr 6.00 15.00
Glenn Anderson
WCFB Peter Forsberg 12.00 30.00
Nicklas Backstrom
WCGB Sam Gagner 12.00 30.00
Nicklas Backstrom
WCGR Sam Gagner 10.00 25.00
Dwayne Roloson
WCGZ Scott Gomez 5.00 12.00
Nikolai Zherdev
WCHB Milan Hejduk 5.00 12.00
Peter Budaj
WCHE Marian Hossa 10.00 25.00
Patrik Elias
WCHH Bobby Hull 12.00 30.00
Dale Hawerchuk
WCHL Dominik Hasek 10.00 25.00
Nicklas Lidstrom
WCHM Dominik Hasek 10.00 25.00
Ryan Miller
WCKC Patrick Kane 15.00 40.00
Erik Cole
WCKH Saku Koivu 6.00 15.00
Chris Higgins
WCKK Jari Kurri 6.00 15.00
Saku Koivu
WCKS Saku Koivu 6.00 15.00
Steve Shutt
WCLC Vincent Lecavalier 6.00 15.00
Jonathan Cheechoo
WCLH Nicklas Lidstrom 6.00 15.00
Tomas Holmstrom
WCMG Evgeni Malkin 15.00 40.00
Simon Gagne
WCMK Mike Modano 15.00 40.00
Patrick Kane
WCML Mario Lemieux 15.00 40.00

Mark Messier
WCMM Lanny McDonald 8.00 20.00
Al MacInnis
WCMV Lanny McDonald 6.00 15.00
Rick Vaive
WCNE Markus Naslund 6.00 15.00
Patrik Elias
WCNG Markus Naslund 5.00 12.00
Scott Gomez
WCNL Rick Nash 6.00 15.00
Vincent Lecavalier
WCOK Alexander Ovechkin 25.00 60.00
Ilya Kovalchuk
WCOM Alexander Ovechkin 25.00 60.00
Evgeni Malkin
WCPS Ryan Malone 4.00 10.00
Stephen Weiss
WCPZ Rick Nash 5.00 12.00
Michael Peca
WCRK Michael Ryder 6.00 15.00
Phil Kessel
WCRL Larry Robinson 8.00 20.00
Rod Langway
WCRM Mike Ribeiro 5.00 12.00
Marty Turco
WCSD Shane Doan 5.00 12.00
Ryan Smyth
WCSH Steve Shutt 6.00 15.00
Chris Higgins
WCSM Eric Staal 10.00 25.00
Ryan Malone
WCSS Eric Staal 10.00 25.00
Jordan Staal
WCTK Patrick Kane 20.00 50.00
Jonathan Toews
WCVH Dominik Hasek 10.00 25.00
Tomas Vokoun
WCZH Henrik Zetterberg 12.00 30.00
Tomas Holmstrom

2008-09 SPx Winning Combos Spectrum

*SPECTRUM: .5X TO 1.2X BASE
STATED PRINT RUN 99 SERIAL #'d SETS

2008-09 SPx Winning Combos Radiance Autographs

STATED PRINT RUN 25 SERIAL #'d SETS
SOME NOT PRICED DUE TO LACK OF MARKET INFORMATION
WCGB Sam Gagner 40.00 100.00
Nicklas Backstrom
WCHE Patrik Elias 20.00 50.00
Marian Hossa
WCLH Tomas Holmstrom 20.00 50.00
Nicklas Lidstrom
WCMK Mike Modano 40.00 100.00
Patrick Kane
WCMM Lanny McDonald 20.00 50.00
Al MacInnis
WCMV Lanny McDonald 15.00 40.00
Rick Vaive
WCNG Scott Gomez 20.00 50.00
Markus Naslund
WCNL Rick Nash 30.00 80.00
Vincent Lecavalier
WCSM Ryan Malone 20.00 50.00
Eric Staal

2008-09 SPx Winning Materials

STATED ODDS 1:18
WMAM Andrei Markov 4.00 10.00
WMAO Adam Oates 5.00 12.00
WMBH Bobby Hull 10.00 25.00
WMCC Bobby Clarke 5.00 12.00
WMCH Jonathan Cheechoo 5.00 12.00
WMCN Cam Neely 6.00 15.00
WMCP Carey Price 15.00 40.00
WMDG Doug Gilmour 6.00 15.00
WMDH Dominik Hasek 8.00 20.00
WMES Eric Staal 8.00 20.00
WMGF Grant Fuhr 5.00 12.00
WMGG Sam Gagner 8.00 20.00
WMGZ Scott Gomez 4.00 10.00
WMHD Milan Hejduk 4.00 10.00
WMHG Chris Higgins 3.00 8.00
WMHZ Henrik Zetterberg 10.00 25.00
WMIK Ilya Kovalchuk 6.00 15.00
WMJM Joe Mullen 5.00 12.00
WMJS Jordan Staal 8.00 20.00
WMJT Jonathan Toews 15.00 40.00
WMKN Patrick Kane 12.00 30.00
WMLM Lanny McDonald 5.00 12.00
WMMB Martin Brodeur 10.00 25.00
WMMG Marian Gaborik 8.00 20.00
WMMH Marian Hossa 8.00 20.00
WMMM Mark Messier 10.00 25.00
WMMO Mike Modano 5.00 12.00
WMMP Michael Peca 4.00 10.00
WMMR Mike Ribeiro 3.00 8.00
WMNL Nicklas Lidstrom 5.00 12.00
WMOV Alexander Ovechkin 20.00 50.00
WMPE Patrik Elias 3.00 8.00
WMPK Phil Kessel 5.00 12.00
WMPM Peter Mueller 6.00 15.00
WMPS Peter Stastny 5.00 12.00
WMRL Rod Langway 6.00 15.00
WMRM Ryan Malone 3.00 8.00
WMRN Rick Nash 5.00 12.00
WMRV Rick Vaive 3.00 8.00
WMRY Michael Ryder 4.00 10.00
WMSB Steve Bernier 3.00 8.00
WMSC Sidney Crosby 25.00 60.00
WMSG Simon Gagne 4.00 10.00
WMSK Saku Koivu 5.00 12.00
WMSS Steve Shutt 5.00 12.00
WMST Matt Stajan 4.00 10.00
WMSW Shea Weber 3.00 8.00
WMTH Tomas Holmstrom 4.00 10.00
WMVL Vincent Lecavalier 5.00 12.00
WMWC Wendel Clark 4.00 10.00

2008-09 SPx Winning Materials Spectrum

*SPECTRUM: .5X TO 1.2X BASE
STATED PRINT RUN 99 SERIAL #'d SETS

2008-09 SPx Winning Materials Radiance Autographs

STATED PRINT RUN 25 SERIAL #'d SETS
SOME NOT PRICED DUE TO LACK OF MARKET INFORMATION
WMHG Chris Higgins 40.00 100.00
WMIK Ilya Kovalchuk 40.00 100.00
WMJS Jordan Staal 20.00 50.00
WMRM Ryan Malone 20.00 50.00
WMSC Sidney Crosby 100.00 200.00
WMSG Simon Gagne 20.00 50.00
WMSS Steve Shutt 12.00 30.00

2008-09 SPx Winning Trios

STATED PRINT RUN 99 SERIAL #'d SETS
WTAKF Alex Kovalev 15.00 40.00
Maxim Afinogenov
Sergei Fedorov
WTAWL Jason Arnott 8.00 20.00
Shea Weber
David Legwand
WTBMG Nicklas Backstrom 12.00 30.00
Sam Gagner
Peter Mueller
WTBTK Nicklas Backstrom 30.00 80.00
Jonathan Toews
Patrick Kane
WTBTS Bryan Trottier
Mike Bossy
Billy Smith
WTCGY Lanny McDonald 10.00 25.00
Al MacInnis
Theoren Fleury
WTCOM Sidney Crosby 30.00 80.00
Alexander Ovechkin
Evgeni Malkin
WTDMJ Shane Doan 12.00 30.00
Peter Mueller
Olli Jokinen
WTFCM Sidney Crosby 30.00 80.00
Evgeni Malkin
Marc-Andre Fleury
WTFSH Joe Sakic
Peter Forsberg
Milan Hejduk
WTGBN Marian Gaborik
Pierre-Marc Bouchard
Owen Nolan
WTGLM Wayne Gretzky 40.00 100.00
Mario Lemieux
Mark Messier
WTGRC Mike Richards 15.00 40.00
Jeff Carter
Simon Gagne
WTHGA Gordie Howe
Wayne Gretzky
Jean Beliveau
WTHLH Dominik Hasek
Nicklas Lidstrom
Tomas Holmstrom
WTHPN Ron Hextall 10.00 25.00
Bernie Parent
Antero Niittymaki
WTHSF Peter Forsberg
Ryan Smyth
Milan Hejduk
WTKKS Jari Kurri
Saku Koivu
Teemu Selanne
WTKLS Ilya Kovalchuk
Vincent Lecavalier
Eric Staal
WTKTP Paul Kariya
Keith Tkachuk
David Perron
WTLCN Vincent Lecavalier 10.00 25.00
Jonathan Cheechoo
Rick Nash
WTMLT Marty Turco 10.00 25.00
Mike Modano
Jere Lehtinen
WTMSS Borje Salming 10.00 25.00
Lanny McDonald
Darryl Sittler
WTNBO Cam Neely
Ray Bourque
Adam Oates
WTNLP Rick Nash
Pascal Leclaire
Michael Peca
WTNLS Roberto Luongo
Pavol Demitra
Steve Bernier
WTNPR Martin Brodeur 10.00 25.00
Zach Parise
Patrik Elias
WTOKK Alexander Ovechkin 40.00 100.00
Ilya Kovalchuk
Alex Kovalev
WTOMK Alexander Ovechkin 40.00 100.00
Evgeni Malkin
Ilya Kovalchuk
WTPKK Carey Price 30.00 80.00
Alex Kovalev
Saku Koivu
WTPLG Dion Phaneuf 10.00 25.00
Nicklas Lidstrom
Sergei Gonchar
WTRBP Patrick Roy
Martin Brodeur
Carey Price
WTRDV Luc Robitaille 10.00 25.00
Marcel Dionne
Rogie Vachon
WTRSB Patrick Roy
Joe Sakic
Ray Bourque
WTSBT Patrice Bergeron 10.00 25.00
Marc Savard
Tim Thomas
WTSFB Mats Sundin 20.00 50.00
Peter Forsberg
Nicklas Backstrom
WTSKK Teemu Selanne 10.00 25.00
Saku Koivu
Mikko Koivu
WTSNL Mats Sundin 20.00 50.00
Markus Naslund
Henrik Lundqvist
WTSSS Eric Staal
Jordan Staal
Marc Staal
WTSTS Mats Sundin 10.00 25.00
Vesa Toskala
Matt Stajan
WTVHG Marian Gaborik 15.00 40.00
Marian Hossa
Tomas Vokoun

2009-10 SPx

COMP.SET w/o SPs (100) 20.00 50.00
(101-130) PRINT RUN 499 SER.#'d SETS
(131-152) PRINT RUN 799 SER.#'d SETS
(153-174) PRINT RUN 799 SER.#'d SETS
(175-180) PRINT RUN 499 SER.#'d SETS
(189-218) STATED ODDS 1:126
(219-248) STATED ODDS 1:252
1 Sidney Crosby 2.50 6.00
2 Phil Kessel .50 1.25
3 Mike Green 1.00 2.50
4 Henrik Lundqvist 1.00 2.50
5 Mark Messier 1.00 2.50
6 Devin Setoguchi .40 1.00
7 Jeff Carter .50 1.25
8 Henrik Zetterberg 1.00 2.50
9 Martin Brodeur 1.25 3.00
10 Jonathan Toews 1.25 3.00
11 Ryan Kesler .40 1.00
12 Bobby Orr 2.00 5.00
13 Eric Staal .60 1.50
14 David Perron .40 1.00
15 Steven Stamkos 1.25 3.00
16 Steve Mason .75 2.00
17 Marc-Andre Fleury .75 2.00
18 Ilya Kovalchuk .60 1.50
19 Marian Gaborik .75 2.00
20 Miikka Kiprusoff .50 1.25
21 Ryan Getzlaf .75 2.00
22 Alexander Ovechkin 2.00 5.00
23 Tim Thomas .50 1.25
24 Dany Heatley 1.00 2.50
25 Andrew Cogliano .60 1.50
26 David Booth .30 .75
27 Pekka Rinne .40 1.00
28 Mike Ribeiro .30 .75
29 Carey Price 1.25 3.00
30 Shane Doan .40 1.00
31 Brian Campbell .40 1.00
32 Ryan Miller .50 1.25
33 Mike Richards 1.00 2.50
34 Patrick Marleau .50 1.25
35 Nicklas Lidstrom .60 1.50
36 Luke Schenn .75 2.00
37 Anze Kopitar .50 1.25
38 Chris Drury .40 1.00
39 Tomas Vokoun .50 1.25
40 Rick DiPietro .50 1.25
41 Paul Stastny .50 1.25
42 Mario Lemieux 1.25 3.00
43 Sam Gagner .60 1.50
44 Jason Spezza .60 1.50
45 Martin St. Louis .50 1.25
46 Alexander Semin .50 1.25
47 Rick Nash .50 1.25
48 Cam Ward .50 1.25
49 Bobby Ryan .60 1.50
50 Tomas Kaberle .30 .75
51 Patrick Berglund 1.00 2.50
52 Thomas Vanek .50 1.25
53 Andrei Markov .40 1.00
54 Pavel Datsyuk .50 1.25
55 Patrick Roy 1.50 4.00
56 Dion Phaneuf .75 2.00
57 Shea Weber .40 1.00
58 Patrik Elias .50 1.25
59 Bryan Little .50 1.25
60 Marty Turco .40 1.00
61 Jussi Jokinen .50 1.25
62 Patrick Kane 1.00 2.50
63 Nicklas Backstrom .50 1.25
64 Simon Gagne .50 1.25
65 Joe Thornton 1.00 2.50
66 Scottie Upshall .30 .75
67 Marian Hossa .75 2.00
68 Milan Hejduk .30 .75
69 Marc Savard .30 .75
70 Kyle Okposo .50 1.25
71 Jason Blake .30 .75
72 Mike Modano .50 1.25
73 Jordan Staal .60 1.50
74 Ales Hemsky .50 1.25
75 Chris Osgood .60 1.50
76 Derek Roy .50 1.25
77 Daniel Alfredsson .50 1.25
78 Drew Doughty 1.00 2.50
79 Steve Yzerman 1.50 4.00
80 Roberto Luongo 1.25 3.00
81 Michael Frolik .40 1.00
82 Teemu Selanne .50 1.25
83 Ryan Smyth .50 1.25
84 Nicklas Backstrom 1.00 2.50
85 Mike Cammalleri .40 1.00
86 Peter Mueller .60 1.50
87 Kari Lehtonen .50 1.25
88 Gordie Howe 2.00 5.00
89 Scott Gomez .50 1.25
90 Jarome Iginla 1.00 2.50
91 David Backes .40 1.00
92 Zdeno Chara .30 .75
93 Vincent Lecavalier .60 1.50
94 Mikko Koivu .50 1.25
95 Daniel Briere .50 1.25
96 Jason Arnott .30 .75
97 Henrik Sedin .75 2.00
98 Derick Brassard .40 1.00
99 Wayne Gretzky 2.50 6.00
100 Zach Parise .50 1.25
101 Guillaume Desbiens RC 4.00 10.00
102 Davis Drewiske RC 4.00 10.00
103 Ryan Vesce RC 3.00 8.00
104 Alec Martinez RC 2.50 6.00
105 David Schlemko RC 3.00 8.00
106 Jay Beagle RC 4.00 10.00
107 Steven Zalewski RC 3.00 8.00
108 Tim Wallace RC 2.50 6.00
109 Geoff Kinrade RC 4.00 10.00
110 Teemu Laakso RC 2.50 6.00
111 Jakub Petruzalek RC 4.00 10.00
112 Matt Gilroy RC 5.00 12.00
113 Tyson Strachan RC 2.50 6.00
114 James Reimer RC 4.00 10.00
115 Sean Collins RC 3.00 8.00
116 Frazer McLaren RC 2.50 6.00
117 Johan Backlund RC 4.00 10.00
118 Mathieu Perreault RC 5.00 12.00
119 Kevin Quick RC 2.50 6.00
120 Mika Pyorala RC 4.00 10.00
121 Tim Stapleton RC 4.00 10.00
122 Chris Durno RC 3.00 8.00
123 Jaime Sifers RC 3.00 8.00
124 Troy Bodie RC 3.00 8.00
125 Braden Holtby RC 5.00 12.00
126 Sean Bentivoglio RC 3.00 8.00
127 Phil Oreskovic RC 4.00 10.00
128 James Wright RC 3.00 8.00
129 Bryan Rodney RC 3.00 8.00
130 Alexander Sulzer RC 2.50 6.00
131 Matt Beleskey JSY RC 5.00 12.00
132 Jason Demers JSY RC 4.00 10.00
133 Dmitry Kulikov JSY RC 5.00 12.00
134 Cal O'Reilly JSY RC 5.00 12.00
135 Jay Rosehill JSY RC 3.00 8.00
136 T.J. Galiardi JSY RC 6.00 15.00
137 Michael Sauer JSY RC 4.00 10.00
138 Ryan O'Marra JSY RC 4.00 10.00
139 Benn Ferriero JSY RC 5.00 12.00
140 Chris Butler JSY RC 3.00 8.00
141 Mike Santorelli JSY RC 3.00 8.00
142 Andrew MacDonald JSY RC 4.00 10.00
143 John Scott JSY RC 5.00 12.00
144 Matt Pelech JSY RC 5.00 12.00
145 Ray Macias JSY RC 5.00 12.00
146 Cody Franson JSY RC 5.00 12.00
147 Kris Chucko JSY RC 4.00 10.00
148 Joel Rechlicz JSY RC 5.00 12.00
149 Perttu Lindgren JSY RC 5.00 12.00
150 Sergei Shirokov JSY RC 8.00 20.00
151 Spencer Machacek JSY RC 4.00 10.00
152 Yannick Weber JSY RC 6.00 15.00
153 Artem Anisimov JSY AU RC 10.00 25.00
154 Brian Salcido JSY AU RC 6.00 15.00
155 Christian Hanson JSY AU RC 10.00 25.00
156 Ivan Vishnevskiy JSY AU RC 10.00 25.00
157 Jhonas Enroth JSY AU RC 10.00 25.00
158 Michael Grabner JSY AU RC 10.00 25.00
159 Luca Caputi JSY AU RC 10.00 25.00
160 Brad Marchand JSY AU RC 10.00 25.00
161 Mikael Backlund JSY AU RC 12.00 30.00
162 Riku Helenius JSY AU RC 8.00 20.00
163 Ville Leino JSY AU RC 10.00 25.00
164 Lars Eller JSY AU RC 12.00 30.00
165 Erik Karlsson JSY AU RC 25.00 60.00
166 Tyler Myers JSY AU RC 25.00 60.00
167 Ryan O'Reilly JSY AU RC 15.00 40.00
168 Jamie Benn JSY AU RC 12.00 30.00
169 Logan Couture JSY AU RC 15.00 40.00
170 Michael Del Zotto JSY AU RC 15.00 40.00
171 Viktor Stalberg JSY AU RC 12.00 30.00
172 Antti Niemi JSY AU RC 25.00 60.00
173 Tyler Bozak JSY AU RC 20.00 50.00
174 Colin Wilson JSY AU RC 12.00 30.00
175 Matt Duchene JSY AU RC/499 60.00 120.00
176 Jonas Gustavsson JSY AU RC/499 40.00 80.00
177 Victor Hedman JSY AU RC/499 20.00 50.00
178 Evander Kane JSY AU RC/499 25.00 60.00
179 James van Riemsdyk JSY AU RC/499 25.00 60.00
180 John Tavares JSY AU RC/499 100.00 200.00
189 Doug Gilmour FF JSY 6.00 15.00
190 Alexander Ovechkin FF JSY 25.00 60.00
191 Tony Esposito FF JSY 10.00 25.00
192 Steve Shutt FF JSY 6.00 15.00
193 Jay Bouwmeester FF JSY 6.00 15.00
194 Adam Oates FF JSY 6.00 15.00
195 Joe Mullen FF JSY 6.00 15.00
196 Jari Kurri FF JSY 6.00 15.00
197 Patrick Kane FF JSY 12.00 30.00
198 Scott Gomez FF JSY 6.00 15.00
199 Paul Kariya FF JSY 6.00 15.00
200 Mike Modano FF JSY 6.00 15.00
201 Larry Murphy FF JSY 4.00 10.00
202 Luc Robitaille FF JSY 6.00 15.00
203 Nicklas Lidstrom FF JSY 8.00 20.00
204 Vincent Lecavalier FF JSY 8.00 20.00
205 Zach Parise FF JSY 6.00 15.00
206 Ray Bourque FF JSY 10.00 25.00
207 Bernie Federko FF JSY 5.00 12.00
208 Cam Neely FF JSY 10.00 25.00
209 Wade Redden FF JSY 4.00 10.00
210 Bob Bourne FF JSY 5.00 12.00
211 Larry Robinson FF JSY 8.00 20.00
212 Dale Hawerchuk FF JSY 6.00 15.00
213 Teemu Selanne FF JSY 6.00 15.00
214 Johnny Bucyk FF JSY 10.00 25.00
215 Brent Sutter FF JSY 6.00 15.00
216 Grant Fuhr FF JSY 8.00 20.00
217 Alex Tanguay FF JSY 5.00 12.00
218 Gilbert Perreault FF JSY 6.00 15.00
219 Steve Yzerman FF JSY AU 150.00 250.00
220 Martin Brodeur FF JSY AU 60.00 120.00
221 Evgeni Malkin FF JSY AU 40.00 80.00
222 Denis Savard FF JSY AU 15.00 40.00
223 Scotty Bowman FF JSY AU 30.00 60.00
224 Darryl Sittler FF JSY AU 20.00 50.00
225 Patrick Roy FF JSY AU 60.00 120.00
226 Wendel Clark FF JSY AU 25.00 60.00
227 Phil Esposito FF JSY AU 30.00 80.00
228 Patrick Marleau FF JSY AU 15.00 40.00
229 Scott Niedermayer FF JSY AU 20.00 50.00
230 Marian Hossa FF JSY AU 25.00 60.00
231 Mark Messier FF JSY AU 60.00 120.00
232 Marcel Dionne FF JSY AU 20.00 50.00
233 Peter Stastny FF JSY AU 15.00 40.00
234 Mario Lemieux FF JSY AU 60.00 120.00
235 Carey Price FF JSY AU 40.00 100.00
236 Pavel Datsyuk FF JSY AU 15.00 40.00
237 Saku Koivu FF JSY AU 15.00 40.00
238 Nikolai Khabibulin FF JSY AU 15.00 40.00
239 Gordie Howe FF JSY AU 75.00 150.00
240 Frank Mahovlich FF JSY AU 20.00 50.00
241 Guy Lafleur FF JSY AU 25.00 60.00
242 Dino Ciccarelli FF JSY AU EXCH 10.00 25.00
243 Guy Carbonneau FF JSY AU 25.00 60.00
244 Dany Heatley FF JSY AU 30.00 80.00
245 Sidney Crosby FF JSY AU 125.00 200.00
246 Glenn Anderson FF JSY AU 15.00 40.00
247 Dave Taylor FF JSY AU 20.00 50.00
248 Wayne Gretzky FF JSY AU 100.00 200.00

2009-10 SPx Spectrum

STATED PRINT RUN 25 SER.#'d SETS
1 Sidney Crosby JSY 25.00 60.00
2 Phil Kessel JSY 8.00 20.00
4 Henrik Lundqvist JSY 15.00 40.00
5 Mark Messier JSY 15.00 40.00
7 Jeff Carter JSY 8.00 20.00
8 Henrik Zetterberg JSY 15.00 40.00
9 Martin Brodeur JSY 20.00 50.00
10 Jonathan Toews JSY 20.00 50.00
11 Ryan Kesler JSY 6.00 15.00
13 Eric Staal JSY 10.00 25.00
17 Marc-Andre Fleury JSY 15.00 40.00
18 Ilya Kovalchuk JSY 10.00 25.00
19 Marian Gaborik JSY 12.00 30.00
20 Miikka Kiprusoff JSY 8.00 20.00
21 Ryan Getzlaf JSY 12.00 30.00
22 Alexander Ovechkin JSY 25.00 60.00
23 Tim Thomas JSY 8.00 20.00
24 Dany Heatley JSY
25 Andrew Cogliano JSY 10.00 25.00
26 David Booth JSY
27 Pekka Rinne JSY 6.00 15.00
28 Mike Ribeiro JSY 5.00 12.00
29 Carey Price JSY 20.00 50.00
30 Shane Doan JSY 6.00 15.00
31 Brian Campbell JSY
32 Ryan Miller JSY 8.00 20.00
33 Mike Richards JSY 15.00 40.00
34 Patrick Marleau JSY 8.00 20.00
35 Nicklas Lidstrom JSY 10.00 25.00
36 Luke Schenn JSY 12.00 30.00
37 Anze Kopitar JSY 8.00 20.00
38 Chris Drury JSY 6.00 15.00
39 Tomas Vokoun JSY 8.00 20.00
40 Rick DiPietro JSY 8.00 20.00
41 Paul Stastny JSY 8.00 20.00
42 Mario Lemieux JSY 20.00 50.00
43 Sam Gagner JSY 10.00 25.00
44 Jason Spezza JSY 10.00 25.00
45 Martin St. Louis JSY 8.00 20.00
46 Alexander Semin JSY 8.00 20.00
47 Rick Nash JSY 8.00 20.00
48 Cam Ward JSY 8.00 20.00
50 Tomas Kaberle JSY 5.00 12.00
51 Patrik Berglund JSY 15.00 40.00
52 Thomas Vanek JSY 8.00 20.00
53 Andrei Markov JSY 6.00 15.00
54 Pavel Datsyuk JSY 8.00 20.00
55 Patrick Roy JSY 25.00 60.00
56 Dion Phaneuf JSY 12.00 30.00
57 Shea Weber JSY 6.00 15.00
58 Patrik Elias JSY 6.00 15.00
60 Marty Turco JSY 6.00 15.00
61 Jussi Jokinen JSY 8.00 20.00
62 Patrick Kane JSY 15.00 40.00
64 Simon Gagne JSY 8.00 20.00
65 Joe Thornton JSY 15.00 40.00
67 Marian Hossa JSY 12.00 30.00
68 Milan Hejduk JSY 8.00 20.00
69 Marc Savard JSY 5.00 12.00
70 Kyle Okposo JSY 8.00 20.00
72 Mike Modano JSY 8.00 20.00
73 Jordan Staal JSY 10.00 25.00
74 Ales Hemsky JSY 6.00 15.00
75 Chris Osgood JSY 10.00 25.00
76 Derek Roy JSY 8.00 20.00
77 Daniel Alfredsson JSY 8.00 20.00
78 Drew Doughty JSY 15.00 40.00
79 Steve Yzerman JSY 25.00 60.00
80 Roberto Luongo JSY 20.00 50.00
81 Michael Frolik JSY
82 Teemu Selanne JSY 8.00 20.00
83 Ryan Smyth JSY 8.00 20.00
84 Nicklas Backstrom JSY 15.00 40.00
85 Mike Cammalleri JSY 15.00 40.00
86 Peter Mueller JSY 10.00 25.00
87 Kari Lehtonen JSY 8.00 20.00
88 Gordie Howe JSY 25.00 60.00
89 Scott Gomez JSY 8.00 20.00
90 Jarome Iginla JSY 15.00 40.00
93 Vincent Lecavalier JSY 15.00 40.00
94 Mikko Koivu JSY 8.00 20.00
96 Jason Arnott JSY 5.00 12.00
98 Derick Brassard JSY 8.00 20.00
99 Wayne Gretzky JSY 25.00 60.00
100 Zach Parise JSY 8.00 20.00
101 Guillaume Desbiens 5.00 12.00
102 Davis Drewiske 5.00 12.00
103 Ryan Vesce 4.00 10.00
104 Alec Martinez 3.00 8.00
105 David Schlemko 4.00 10.00
106 Jay Beagle 5.00 12.00
107 Steven Zalewski 4.00 10.00
108 Tim Wallace 3.00 8.00
109 Geoff Kinrade 5.00 12.00
110 Teemu Laakso 3.00 8.00
111 Jakub Petruzalek 5.00 12.00
112 Matt Gilroy 6.00 15.00
113 Tyson Strachan 3.00 8.00
114 James Reimer 5.00 12.00
115 Sean Collins 4.00 10.00
116 Frazer McLaren 3.00 8.00
117 Johan Backlund 5.00 12.00
118 Mathieu Perreault 6.00 15.00
119 Kevin Quick 3.00 8.00
120 Mika Pyorala 5.00 12.00
121 Tim Stapleton 5.00 12.00
122 Chris Durno 4.00 10.00
123 Jaime Sifers 4.00 10.00
124 Troy Bodie 4.00 10.00
125 Braden Holtby 6.00 15.00
126 Sean Bentivoglio 4.00 10.00
127 Phil Oreskovic 5.00 12.00
128 James Wright 6.00 15.00
129 Bryan Rodney
130 Alexander Sulzer 3.00 8.00
131 Matt Beleskey PATCH 12.00 30.00
132 Jason Demers PATCH 10.00 25.00
133 Dmitry Kulikov PATCH 12.00 30.00
134 Cal O'Reilly PATCH 12.00 30.00
135 Jay Rosehill PATCH 8.00 20.00
136 T.J. Galiardi PATCH 15.00 40.00
137 Michael Sauer PATCH 10.00 25.00
138 Ryan O'Marra PATCH 10.00 25.00
139 Benn Ferriero PATCH
140 Chris Butler PATCH 12.00 30.00
141 Mike Santorelli PATCH 8.00 20.00
142 Andrew MacDonald PATCH 10.00 25.00
143 John Scott PATCH
144 Matt Pelech PATCH 12.00 30.00
145 Ray Macias PATCH 12.00 30.00
146 Cody Franson PATCH 12.00 30.00
147 Kris Chucko PATCH 10.00 25.00
148 Joel Rechlicz PATCH
149 Perttu Lindgren PATCH 12.00 30.00
150 Sergei Shirokov PATCH 20.00 50.00
151 Spencer Machacek PATCH 10.00 25.00
152 Yannick Weber PATCH 15.00 40.00
153 Artem Anisimov PATCH AU 20.00 50.00
154 Brian Salcido PATCH AU 12.00 30.00
155 Christian Hanson PATCH AU 20.00 50.00
156 Ivan Vishnevskiy PATCH AU 20.00 50.00
157 Jhonas Enroth PATCH AU 20.00 50.00
158 Michael Grabner PATCH AU 20.00 50.00
159 Luca Caputi PATCH AU 20.00 50.00
160 Brad Marchand PATCH AU 20.00 50.00
161 Mikael Backlund PATCH AU 25.00 60.00
162 Riku Helenius PATCH AU 15.00 40.00
163 Ville Leino PATCH AU 20.00 50.00
164 Lars Eller PATCH AU 75.00 150.00
165 Erik Karlsson PATCH AU 100.00 200.00
166 Tyler Myers PATCH AU 300.00 450.00
168 Jamie Benn PATCH AU 25.00 60.00
169 Logan Couture PATCH AU 30.00 80.00
170 Michael Del Zotto PATCH AU 30.00 80.00
171 Viktor Stalberg PATCH AU 60.00 120.00
172 Antti Niemi PATCH AU 50.00 120.00
173 Tyler Bozak PATCH AU 60.00 120.00
174 Colin Wilson PATCH AU 25.00 60.00
183 Matt Duchene PATCH AU 200.00 350.00
184 Jonas Gustavsson PATCH AU 100.00 200.00
185 Victor Hedman PATCH AU 60.00 120.00
186 Evander Kane PATCH AU 60.00 120.00
187 James Van Riemsdyk PATCH AU 100.00 200.00
188 John Tavares PATCH AU 300.00 600.00

2009-10 SPx Shadowbox

STATED ODDS 1:252
SH1 Wayne Gretzky 125.00 200.00
SH2 Evgeni Malkin 25.00 60.00
SH3 Henrik Zetterberg 60.00 120.00
SH4 Jeff Carter 30.00 60.00
SH5 Rick Nash 12.00 30.00
SH6 Zach Parise 25.00 50.00
SH7 Joe Thornton 40.00 80.00
SH8 Patrick Kane 60.00 120.00
SH9 Bobby Orr 75.00 150.00
SH10 Jarome Iginla 30.00 60.00
SH11 Martin St. Louis 25.00 50.00
SH12 Dany Heatley 15.00 40.00
SH13 Ryan Getzlaf 25.00 50.00
SH14 Jason Spezza 25.00 50.00
SH15 Steve Yzerman 60.00 120.00
SH16 Alexander Ovechkin 75.00 150.00
SH17 Mario Lemieux 50.00 100.00
SH18 Dion Phaneuf 10.00 25.00
SH19 Cam Neely 15.00 40.00
SH20 Ilya Kovalchuk 15.00 40.00
SH21 Mike Richards
SH22 Jonathan Toews 60.00 120.00
SH23 Nicklas Backstrom 25.00 50.00
SH24 Mark Messier 75.00 150.00
SH25 Pavel Datsyuk 30.00 60.00
SH26 Eric Staal 25.00 50.00
SH27 Mike Green 25.00 50.00
SH28 Vincent Lecavalier 30.00 60.00
SH29 Gordie Howe 75.00 150.00
SH30 Sidney Crosby 100.00 175.00

2009-10 SPx Shadowbox Stoppers

STATED ODDS 1:252
ST1 Martin Brodeur
ST2 Patrick Roy 60.00 120.00
ST3 Marc-Andre Fleury 30.00 60.00
ST4 Roberto Luongo
ST5 Tony Esposito 30.00 60.00
ST6 Miikka Kiprusoff 30.00 60.00
ST7 Carey Price 50.00 100.00
ST8 Henrik Lundqvist
ST9 Grant Fuhr 25.00 50.00
ST10 Steve Mason 30.00 60.00
ST11 Ron Hextall 25.00 50.00
ST12 Ryan Miller

2009-10 SPx SPXcitement

COMPLETE SET (70) 200.00 400.00
STATED PRINT RUN 999 SER.#'d SETS
X1 Wayne Gretzky 8.00 20.00
X2 Luke Schenn 2.50 6.00
X3 Carey Price 4.00 10.00
X4 Bobby Orr 6.00 15.00
X5 Henrik Zetterberg 3.00 8.00
X6 Marc-Andre Fleury 1.50 4.00
X7 Thomas Vanek 1.50 4.00
X8 Cam Neely 2.50 6.00
X9 Gordie Howe 6.00 15.00
X10 Patrick Marleau 1.50 4.00
X11 Mark Messier 3.00 8.00
X12 Miikka Kiprusoff 1.50 4.00
X13 John Tavares 12.00 30.00
X14 Jonathan Toews 4.00 10.00
X15 Dany Heatley 3.00 8.00
X16 Bobby Clarke 2.50 6.00
X17 Steven Stamkos 4.00 10.00
X18 Alexander Ovechkin 6.00 15.00
X19 Steve Yzerman 5.00 12.00
X20 Phil Kessel 1.50 4.00
X21 Steve Mason 2.50 6.00
X22 Mike Bossy 1.50 4.00
X23 Sam Gagner 2.00 5.00
X24 Eric Staal 2.00 5.00
X25 Matt Duchene 6.00 15.00
X26 Ryan Getzlaf 2.50 6.00
X27 Evgeni Malkin 4.00 10.00
X28 Scott Gomez 1.50 4.00
X29 Joe Thornton 3.00 8.00
X30 Martin Brodeur 4.00 10.00
X31 Mike Ribeiro 1.00 2.50
X32 Pavel Datsyuk 1.50 4.00
X33 Patrick Roy 5.00 12.00
X34 Drew Doughty 3.00 8.00
X35 Vincent Lecavalier 2.00 5.00
X36 Mikko Koivu 1.50 4.00
X37 Zach Parise 1.50 4.00
X38 Marian Hossa 2.50 6.00
X39 Tomas Vokoun 1.50 4.00
X40 Jarome Iginla 3.00 8.00
X41 Ville Leino 2.00 5.00
X42 Henrik Lundqvist 3.00 8.00
X43 Jordan Staal 2.00 5.00
X44 Bobby Ryan 2.00 5.00
X45 Mike Green 3.00 8.00
X46 Ilya Kovalchuk 2.00 5.00
X47 Cam Ward 1.50 4.00
X48 Jonas Gustavsson 8.00 20.00
X49 Ryan Kesler 1.25 3.00
X50 Mikael Backlund 2.50 6.00
X51 Patrick Kane 3.00 8.00
X52 Jason Spezza 2.00 5.00
X53 Jeff Carter 1.50 4.00
X54 David Perron 1.25 3.00
X55 Shea Weber 1.25 3.00
X56 James Van Riemsdyk 4.00 10.00
X57 Devin Setoguchi 1.25 3.00
X58 Tim Thomas 1.50 4.00
X59 Rick DiPietro 1.50 4.00
X60 Nicklas Lidstrom 2.00 5.00
X61 Rick Nash 1.50 4.00
X62 Artem Anisimov 2.00 5.00
X63 James Neal 1.50 4.00
X64 Ryan Miller 1.50 4.00
X65 Brian Campbell 1.25 3.00
X66 Mario Lemieux 4.00 10.00
X67 Paul Stastny 1.50 4.00
X68 Peter Mueller 2.00 5.00
X69 Roberto Luongo 4.00 10.00
X70 Sidney Crosby 8.00 20.00

2009-10 SPx SPXcitement Spectrum

*SINGLES: 1.5X TO 4X BASIC INSERTS
STATED PRINT RUN 25 SER.#'d SETS
X13 John Tavares 60.00 120.00
X48 Jonas Gustavsson 25.00 60.00

2009-10 SPx Winning Combos

STATED ODDS 1:18
WCBK Mikko Koivu 5.00 12.00
Pierre-Marc Bouchard
WCCB Zdeno Chara 5.00 12.00
Patrice Bergeron
WCCG Doug Gilmour 8.00 20.00
Wendel Clark
WCCM Sidney Crosby 25.00 60.00
Evgeni Malkin
WCCO Sidney Crosby 25.00 60.00
Alexander Ovechkin
WCCT Brian Campbell 12.00 30.00
Jonathan Toews
WCCW Brian Campbell 4.00 10.00
Doug Wilson
WCDL Shane Doan 4.00 10.00
Matthew Lombardi
WCEH Tony Esposito 8.00 20.00
Cristobal Huet
WCER Rod Brind'Amour 6.00 15.00
Eric Staal
WCFK Alexander Frolov 5.00 12.00
Anze Kopitar
WCGD Marian Gaborik 8.00 20.00
Chris Drury
WCGF Theoren Fleury 8.00 20.00
Doug Gilmour
WCGG Jean-Sebastien Giguere 8.00 20.00
Ryan Getzlaf
WCGL Kristopher Letang 5.00 12.00
Sergei Gonchar
WCHB David Booth 3.00 8.00
Nathan Horton
WCHD Pavel Datsyuk 5.00 12.00
Tomas Holmstrom
WCHS Patrick Sharp 8.00 20.00
Marian Hossa
WCHW Wade Redden 10.00 25.00
Henrik Lundqvist
WCKF Jari Kurri 6.00 15.00
Grant Fuhr
WCKK Mikko Koivu 5.00 12.00
Saku Koivu
WCKS Jari Kurri 5.00 12.00
Teemu Selanne
WCLD Pavel Datsyuk 6.00 15.00
Nicklas Lidstrom
WCLR Mason Raymond 12.00 30.00
Roberto Luongo
WCLS Borje Salming 6.00 15.00
Nicklas Lidstrom
WCMC Dino Ciccarelli 5.00 12.00
Mike Modano

WCMR Brad Richards 5.00 12.00
Mike Modano
WCNB Ray Bourque 8.00 20.00
Cam Neely
WCNV Jakub Voracek 5.00 12.00
Rick Nash
WCOB Alexander Ovechkin 20.00 50.00
Nicklas Backstrom
WCOM Alexander Ovechkin 20.00 50.00
Evgeni Malkin
WCPP Tomas Plekanec 12.00 30.00
Carey Price
WCPR Jason Pominville 5.00 12.00
Derek Roy
WCRD Drew Stafford 5.00 12.00
Ryan Miller
WCRL Patrick Roy 15.00 40.00
Roberto Luongo
WCRT Dave Taylor 6.00 15.00
Luc Robitaille
WCSB Jarret Stoll 4.00 10.00
Dustin Brown
WCSH Dale Hawerchuk 5.00 12.00
Teemu Selanne
WCSK Patrick Sharp 10.00 25.00
Patrick Kane
WCSM Darryl Sittler 6.00 15.00
Lanny McDonald
WCSR Steve Shutt 6.00 15.00
Larry Robinson
WCSS Eric Staal 6.00 15.00
Jordan Staal
WCSW Marek Svatos 3.00 8.00
Wojtek Wolski
WCYB Scotty Bowman 15.00 40.00
Steve Yzerman

2009-10 SPx Winning Combos Autographs

STATED PRINT RUN 10 SER.#'d SETS
NOT PRICED DUE TO SCARCITY

2009-10 SPx Winning Combos Spectrum

*SINGLES: .5X TO 1.2X BASIC INSERTS
STATED PRINT RUN 25 SER.#'d SETS
WCBP Zach Parise 15.00 40.00
Martin Brodeur
WCFC Marc-Andre Fleury 30.00 80.00
Sidney Crosby
WCHS Patrick Sharp 10.00 25.00
Marian Hossa
WCIK Jarome Iginla 12.00 30.00
Miikka Kiprusoff

2009-10 SPx Winning Materials

STATED ODDS 1:18
WMAC Andrew Cogliano 6.00 15.00
WMAF Alexander Frolov 4.00 10.00
WMBC Brian Campbell 4.00 10.00
WMBS Brent Seabrook 4.00 10.00
WMCH Cristobal Huet 5.00 12.00
WMCO Chris Osgood 6.00 15.00
WMCW Cam Ward 5.00 12.00
WMDB Dustin Brown 4.00 10.00
WMDC Dino Ciccarelli 3.00 8.00
WMDG Doug Gilmour 5.00 12.00
WMDH Dale Hawerchuk 5.00 12.00
WMDR Derek Roy 5.00 12.00
WMDS Darryl Sittler 6.00 15.00
WMDT Dave Taylor 6.00 15.00
WMFM Frank Mahovlich 6.00 15.00
WMGA Glenn Anderson 5.00 12.00
WMGP Gilbert Perreault 5.00 12.00
WMJB Josh Bailey 4.00 10.00
WMJC Jonathan Cheechoo 5.00 12.00
WMJG Jean-Sebastien Giguere 5.00 12.00
WMJI Jarome Iginla 10.00 25.00
WMJK Jari Kurri 5.00 12.00
WMJS Jason Spezza 6.00 15.00
WMJT Jonathan Toews 12.00 30.00
WMKL Kari Lehtonen 5.00 12.00
WMLM Lanny McDonald 5.00 12.00
WMLR Larry Robinson 6.00 15.00
WMLU Luc Robitaille 5.00 12.00
WMMD Marcel Dionne 6.00 15.00
WMMG Marian Gaborik 8.00 20.00
WMMI Milan Lucic 5.00 12.00
WMMK Mikko Koivu 5.00 12.00
WMMM Mark Messier 10.00 25.00
WMMT Marty Turco 4.00 10.00
WMNL Nicklas Lidstrom 6.00 15.00
WMPB Patrice Bergeron 5.00 12.00
WMPM Peter Mueller 6.00 15.00
WMPR Patrick Roy 15.00 40.00
WMPS Patrick Sharp 4.00 10.00
WMRD Rick DiPietro 5.00 12.00
WMRG Ryan Getzlaf 8.00 20.00
WMRL Roberto Luongo 12.00 30.00
WMSD Shane Doan 4.00 10.00
WMSG Simon Gagne 5.00 12.00
WMSK Saku Koivu 5.00 12.00
WMST Drew Stafford 5.00 12.00
WMWG Wayne Gretzky 25.00 60.00

2009-10 SPx Winning Materials Autographs

STATED PRINT RUN 50 SER.#'d SETS
AWMAK Anze Kopitar
AWMAO Adam Oates 12.00 30.00
AWMBC Bobby Clarke 20.00 50.00
AWMBH Bobby Hull 30.00 80.00
AWMBS Brent Sutter
AWMCN Cam Neely 20.00 50.00
AWMCP Carey Price 30.00 80.00
AWMDD Drew Doughty 25.00 60.00
AWMEM Evgeni Malkin 30.00 80.00
AWMES Eric Staal 15.00 40.00
AWMFR Michael Frolik 10.00 25.00
AWMHL Henrik Lundqvist 40.00 80.00
AWMIK Ilya Kovalchuk 15.00 40.00
AWMJK Jari Kurri
AWMJP Jason Pominville 12.00 30.00
AWMJT Joe Thornton 25.00 60.00
AWMJV Jakub Voracek 12.00 30.00
AWMLS Luke Schenn 20.00 50.00
AWMMB Martin Brodeur 50.00 100.00
AWMMF Marc-Andre Fleury 15.00 40.00
AWMMR Mason Raymond 20.00 50.00
AWMNB Nicklas Backstrom 25.00 60.00
AWMNH Nathan Horton 8.00 20.00
AWMPB Patrik Berglund
AWMPD Pavel Datsyuk 15.00 40.00
AWMPE Patrik Elias 10.00 25.00
AWMPH Dion Phaneuf
AWMPK Patrick Kane 25.00 60.00
AWMPL Pascal Leclaire 12.00 30.00
AWMPM Peter Mueller 15.00 40.00
AWMPR Pekka Rinne 10.00 25.00
AWMRH Ron Hextall 25.00 60.00
AWMRI Mike Richards 25.00 60.00
AWMRM Ryan Miller 20.00 50.00
AWMRN Rick Nash 12.00 30.00
AWMRY Michael Ryder
AWMSC Sidney Crosby 150.00 250.00
AWMSH Steve Shutt 12.00 30.00
AWMSW Shea Weber
AWMTE Tony Esposito 20.00 50.00
AWMTO Jonathan Toews 30.00 80.00
AWMTV Tomas Vokoun
AWMVA Thomas Vanek 12.00 30.00

2009-10 SPx Winning Materials Spectrum Patches

*SINGLES: 1X TO 2.5X BASIC INSERTS
STATED PRINT RUN 50 SER.#'d SETS

2009-10 SPx Winning Trios

STATED PRINT RUN 50 SER.#'d SETS
WTALB Dion Phaneuf
Jarome Iginla
Scott Niedermayer
WTAVS Milan Hejduk 8.00 20.00
Wojtek Wolski
Marek Svatos
WTBBR Carey Price 20.00 50.00
Scott Gomez
Tomas Plekanec
WTBCO Carey Price 20.00 50.00
Milan Lucic
Paul Kariya
WTBEL David Clarkson
Jonathan Cheechoo
Jason Spezza
WTBOS Tim Thomas 12.00 30.00
Patrice Bergeron
Michael Ryder
WTBRU Adam Oates
Ray Bourque
Cam Neely
WTBUF Derek Roy 8.00 20.00
Thomas Vanek
Drew Stafford
WTBWK Ron Hextall 15.00 40.00
Chris Osgood
Wade Redden
WTCAR Jussi Jokinen
Tuomo Ruutu
Sergei Samsonov
WTCBH Patrick Kane
Jonathan Toews
Brian Campbell
WTCBJ Jakub Voracek 8.00 20.00
Derick Brassard
Rick Nash
WTCGY Lanny McDonald 8.00 20.00
Al MacInnis
Doug Gilmour
WTCHF Stan Mikita
Bobby Hull
Tony Esposito
WTCHI Brian Campbell 10.00 25.00
Patrick Sharp
Cristobal Huet
WTCOL Paul Stastny 8.00 20.00
Milan Hejduk
Darcy Tucker
WTCON Henrik Zetterberg 20.00 50.00
Evgeni Malkin
Scott Niedermayer
WTCPT Mario Lemieux 40.00 100.00
Mark Messier
Wayne Gretzky
WTCZE Patrik Elias 8.00 20.00
Milan Hejduk
Tomas Plekanec
WTDEF Jay Bouwmeester 12.00 30.00
Dion Phaneuf
Shea Weber
WTDET Kris Draper 10.00 25.00
Tomas Holmstrom
Nicklas Lidstrom
WTDRW Chris Osgood 15.00 40.00
Henrik Zetterberg
Pavel Datsyuk
WTEDM Nikolai Khabibulin 10.00 25.00
Patrick O'Sullivan
Andrew Cogliano
WTEHF Mark Messier 15.00 40.00
Grant Fuhr
Jari Kurri
WTFIN Teemu Selanne
Jari Kurri
Saku Koivu
WTFLD Kari Lehtonen 8.00 20.00
Pekka Rinne
Miikka Kiprusoff
WTFLM Miikka Kiprusoff
Jarome Iginla
Olli Jokinen
WTFND Miikka Kiprusoff 12.00 30.00
Mikko Koivu
Teemu Selanne
WTHAB Frank Mahovlich 10.00 25.00
Steve Shutt
Larry Robinson
WTHAR Alexander Ovechkin 40.00 100.00
Jarome Iginla
Sidney Crosby
WTHOF Mario Lemieux 40.00 100.00
Steve Yzerman
Mark Messier
WTHRT Pavel Datsyuk
Alexander Ovechkin
Evgeni Malkin
WTHUR Eric Staal 10.00 25.00
Rod Brind'Amour
Cam Ward
WTKAM Jarome Iginla 15.00 40.00
Shane Doan
Scott Niedermayer
WTKIN Marcel Dionne 15.00 40.00
Dave Taylor
Larry Murphy
WTKIT Derek Roy 15.00 40.00
Mike Richards
Larry Robinson
WTLAK Justin Williams 6.00 15.00
Jarret Stoll
Dustin Brown
WTLAV Roberto Luongo 20.00 50.00
Mike Bossy
Mario Lemieux
WTLND Joe Thornton 15.00 40.00
Sam Gagner
Jeff Carter
WTLON Dino Ciccarelli 10.00 25.00
Sam Gagner
Rick Nash
WTLOS Anze Kopitar
Drew Doughty
Alexander Frolov
WTMHF Larry Robinson
Jean Beliveau
Patrick Roy
WTMTL Steve Shutt 12.00 30.00
Guy Carbonneau
Larry Robinson
WTNYI Doug Weight 8.00 20.00
Josh Bailey
Rick DiPietro
WTNYR Mark Messier 15.00 40.00
Glenn Anderson
Brian Leetch
WTOIL Mark Messier
Jari Kurri
Glenn Anderson
WTOTT Jason Spezza 10.00 25.00
Pascal Leclaire
Nick Foligno
WTOTW Marc Savard
Derek Roy
Rod Brind'Amour
WTPEN Sidney Crosby 40.00 100.00
Jordan Staal
Evgeni Malkin
WTPET Jordan Staal 25.00 60.00
Eric Staal
Steve Yzerman
WTPHI Jeff Carter 15.00 40.00
Mike Richards
Simon Gagne
WTPHX Peter Mueller 10.00 25.00
Mikkel Boedker
Shane Doan
WTPIT Marc-Andre Fleury 8.00 20.00
Kristopher Letang
Sergei Gonchar
WTPOR Cam Neely 12.00 30.00
Marian Hossa
Mark Messier
WTQMJ Roberto Luongo
Mike Ribeiro
Martin St. Louis
WTQUE Simon Gagne
Guy Lafleur
Mike Ribeiro
WTRIM Vincent Lecavalier 40.00 100.00
Brad Richards
Sidney Crosby
WTRNG Marc Staal
Marian Gaborik
Chris Drury
WTRRT Vincent Lecavalier
Alexander Ovechkin
Jonathan Cheechoo
WTRUS Alexander Ovechkin 30.00 80.00
Ilya Kovalchuk
Evgeni Malkin
WTSAB Thomas Vanek 12.00 30.00
Jason Pominville
Ryan Miller
WTSAS Cam Ward 12.00 30.00
Luke Schenn
Ryan Getzlaf
WTSCC Ryan Getzlaf 40.00 100.00
Sidney Crosby
Pavel Datsyuk
WTSEA Chris Osgood
Glenn Anderson
Patrick Marleau
WTSHF Dale Hawerchuk 12.00 30.00
Al MacInnis
Bernie Federko
WTSHO Martin Brodeur 20.00 50.00
Roberto Luongo
Miikka Kiprusoff
WTSSM Tony Esposito 15.00 40.00
Wayne Gretzky
Joe Thornton
WTSTR Brad Richards 8.00 20.00
Mike Ribeiro
Mike Modano
WTSWE Henrik Lundqvist 15.00 40.00
Nicklas Lidstrom
Henrik Zetterberg
WTTHF Frank Mahovlich 10.00 25.00
Darryl Sittler
Lanny McDonald
WTTML Wendel Clark
Glenn Anderson
Doug Gilmour
WTTOR Borje Salming 10.00 25.00
Frank Mahovlich
Lanny McDonald
WTUDC Wayne Gretzky 100.00 200.00
Steve Yzerman
Sidney Crosby
WTUSA Mike Modano
Zach Parise
Ryan Miller
WTUSP Joe Mullen
Zach Parise
Mike Modano
WTVAN Roberto Luongo
Mason Raymond
Steve Bernier
WTVIC Ron Hextall 25.00 60.00
Grant Fuhr
Patrick Roy
WTWNG Steve Yzerman 30.00 80.00
Henrik Zetterberg
Gordie Howe

1998-99 SPx Finite

The 1998-99 SPx Finite hobby-only Series One was issued with a total of 180 cards. The three-card packs retail for $5.99 each. The 90 regular player cards (1-90) are sequentially numbered to 9,500 and feature color action player photos with a unique bronze foil emblem embedded in the center of the cards. The set contains the subsets: Global Impact (91-120) sequentially numbered to 6,950, NHL Sure Shots, (121-150) numbered to 3,900, Marquee Performers (151-170) numbered to 2,625, and Living Legends (171-180) numbered to 1,620.

COMP.BASE SET (90) 30.00 80.00
1 Teemu Selanne .60 1.50
2 Guy Hebert .50 1.25
3 Josef Marha .20 .50
4 Travis Green .20 .50
5 Sergei Samsonov .50 1.25
6 Jason Allison .20 .50
7 Byron Dafoe .50 1.25
8 Dominik Hasek 1.25 3.00
9 Michael Peca .20 .50
10 Erik Rasmussen .20 .50
11 Matthew Barnaby .20 .50
12 Theo Fleury .20 .50
13 Derek Morris .20 .50
14 Valeri Bure .20 .50
15 Trevor Kidd .50 1.25
16 Sami Kapanen .20 .50
17 Bates Battaglia .20 .50
18 Tony Amonte .50 1.25
19 Dmitri Nabokov .20 .50
20 Daniel Cleary .20 .50
21 Jeff Hackett .50 1.25
22 Joe Sakic 1.25 3.00
23 Valeri Kamensky .50 1.25
24 Patrick Roy 3.00 8.00
25 Wade Belak .20 .50
26 Joe Nieuwendyk .50 1.25
27 Mike Keane .20 .50
28 Jere Lehtinen .20 .50
29 Ed Belfour .60 1.50
30 Steve Yzerman 3.00 8.00
31 Dmitri Mironov .20 .50
32 Brendan Shanahan .60 1.50
33 Nicklas Lidstrom .60 1.50
34 Doug Weight .50 1.25
35 Janne Niinimaa .20 .50
36 Bill Guerin .50 1.25
37 Ray Whitney .20 .50
38 Robert Svehla .20 .50
39 Ed Jovanovski .20 .50
40 Vladimir Tsyplakov .20 .50
41 Jozef Stumpel .50 1.25
42 Rob Blake .50 1.25
43 Mark Recchi .50 1.25
44 Andy Moog .50 1.25
45 Matt Higgins RC .50 1.25
46 Martin Brodeur 1.50 4.00
47 Doug Gilmour .50 1.25
48 Brendan Morrison .50 1.25
49 Patrik Elias .50 1.25
50 Trevor Linden .50 1.25
51 Bryan Berard .20 .50
52 Zdeno Chara .20 .50
53 Wayne Gretzky 4.00 10.00
54 Marc Savard .20 .50
55 Daniel Goneau .20 .50
56 Pat Lafontaine .60 1.50
57 Alexei Yashin .20 .50
58 Marian Hossa .60 1.50
59 Wade Redden .20 .50
60 John LeClair .60 1.50
61 Alexandre Daigle .20 .50
62 Rod Brind'Amour .50 1.25
63 Chris Therien .20 .50
64 Keith Tkachuk .60 1.50
65 Brad Isbister .20 .50
66 Nikolai Khabibulin .60 1.50
67 Robert Dome .20 .50
68 Alexei Morozov .20 .50
69 Stu Barnes .20 .50
70 Tom Barrasso .50 1.25
71 Owen Nolan .50 1.25
72 Marco Sturm .50 1.25
73 Patrick Marleau .20 .50
74 Pierre Turgeon .50 1.25
75 Chris Pronger .50 1.25
76 Pavol Demitra .50 1.25
77 Grant Fuhr .50 1.25
78 Stephane Richer .50 1.25
79 Zac Bierk RC .50 1.25
80 Alexander Selivanov .20 .50
81 Mike Johnson .50 1.25
82 Mats Sundin .60 1.50
83 Alyn McCauley .20 .50
84 Pavel Bure .60 1.50
85 Todd Bertuzzi .60 1.50
86 Garth Snow .50 1.25
87 Peter Bondra .50 1.25
88 Olaf Kolzig .50 1.25
89 Jan Bulis .20 .50
90 Sergei Gonchar .20 .50
91 Pavel Bure GI .75 2.00
92 Joe Sakic GI 2.00 5.00
93 Steve Yzerman GI 5.00 12.00
94 Jaromir Jagr GI 1.50 4.00
95 Peter Forsberg GI 2.50 6.00
96 Brendan Shanahan GI 1.00 2.50
97 Brett Hull GI 1.25 3.00
98 Alexei Yashin GI .75 2.00
99 Wayne Gretzky GI 6.00 15.00
100 Eric Lindros GI 1.00 2.50
101 Sergei Samsonov GI .75 2.00
102 John LeClair GI 1.00 2.50
103 Dominik Hasek GI 2.00 5.00
104 Teemu Selanne GI 1.00 2.50
105 Martin Brodeur GI 2.50 6.00
106 Tony Amonte GI .75 2.00
107 Theo Fleury GI .75 2.00
108 Rob Blake GI .75 2.00
109 Mike Modano GI 1.50 4.00
110 Peter Bondra GI .75 2.00
111 Brian Leetch GI 1.00 2.50
112 Nicklas Lidstrom GI 1.00 2.50
113 Doug Weight GI .75 2.00
114 Zigmund Palffy GI .75 2.00
115 Saku Koivu GI 1.00 2.50
116 Paul Kariya GI 1.00 2.50
117 Ray Bourque GI 1.50 4.00
118 Mats Sundin GI 1.00 2.50
119 Patrick Roy GI 5.00 12.00
120 Chris Chelios GI 1.00 2.50
121 Sergei Samsonov SS 1.50 4.00
122 Mike Johnson SS .60 1.50
123 Patrik Elias SS 1.50 4.00
124 Josef Marha SS .60 1.50
125 Dan Cloutier SS .60 1.50
126 Cameron Mann SS .60 1.50
127 Mattias Ohlund SS .60 1.50
128 Daniel Cleary SS .60 1.50
129 Anders Eriksson SS .60 1.50
130 Patrick Marleau SS .60 1.50
131 Jan Bulis SS .60 1.50
132 Alyn McAuley SS .60 1.50
133 Joe Thornton SS 3.00 8.00
134 Andrei Zyuzin SS .60 1.50
135 Richard Zednik SS .60 1.50
136 Derek Morris SS .60 1.50
137 Bates Battaglia SS .60 1.50
138 Mike Watt SS .60 1.50
139 Olli Jokinen SS 1.50 4.00
140 Marian Hossa SS 2.00 5.00
141 Daniel Goneau SS .60 1.50
142 Erik Rasmussen SS .60 1.50
143 Daniel Briere SS .60 1.50
144 Norm Maracle SS RC 3.00 8.00
145 Brendan Morrison SS 1.50 4.00
146 Brad Isbister SS .60 1.50
147 Robert Dome SS .60 1.50
148 Zac Bierk SS .60 1.50
149 Alexei Morozov SS .60 1.50
150 Marco Sturm SS .60 1.50
151 Wayne Gretzky MP 12.00 30.00
152 Eric Lindros MP 2.00 5.00
153 Paul Kariya MP 2.00 5.00
154 Patrick Roy MP 8.00 20.00
155 Sergei Samsonov MP 2.00 5.00
156 Steve Yzerman MP 8.00 20.00
157 Teemu Selanne MP 2.00 5.00
158 Brendan Shanahan MP 2.00 5.00
159 Dominik Hasek MP 4.00 10.00
160 Mark Messier MP 2.00 5.00
161 Martin Brodeur MP 6.00 15.00
162 Mats Sundin MP 2.00 5.00
163 Joe Sakic MP 4.00 10.00
164 John LeClair MP 2.00 5.00
165 Jaromir Jagr MP 4.00 10.00
166 Peter Forsberg MP 4.00 10.00
167 Theo Fleury MP 1.50 4.00
168 Peter Bondra MP 1.50 4.00
169 Mike Modano MP 3.00 8.00
170 Pavel Bure MP 2.00 5.00
171 Patrick Roy LL 15.00 40.00
172 Eric Lindros LL 6.00 15.00
173 Dominik Hasek LL 10.00 20.00
174 Jaromir Jagr LL 6.00 15.00
175 Steve Yzerman LL 15.00 40.00
176 Martin Brodeur LL 15.00 40.00
177 Ray Bourque LL 6.00 15.00
178 Peter Forsberg LL 10.00 25.00
179 Paul Kariya LL 6.00 15.00
180 Wayne Gretzky LL 20.00 50.00
S99 Wayne Gretzky SAMPLE .60 1.50

1998-99 SPx Finite Radiance

This 180-card silver foil parallel features the same players as in the SPx Finite base set, but with an extra added altered technology. Base radiance cards (#1-90) were serial numbered to 4750. Global impact radiance parallels (#91-120) were serial numbered to 3475, sure shots radiance parallels (#121-150) were numbered to 1300, and marquee performers radiance parallels (#151-170) were numbered to 875. Living legends radiance parallels (#171-180) were also serial numbered to 540.

*RADIANCE 1-90: .8X TO 2X BASIC CARDS
*RADIANCE GI 91-120: .8X TO 2X BASIC CARDS
*RADIANCE SS 121-150: .8X TO 2X BASIC CARDS
*RADIANCE MP 151-170: 1X TO 2.5X BASIC CARDS
*RADIANCE LL 171-180: .8X TO 2X BASIC CARDS

1998-99 SPx Finite Spectrum

Sequentially numbered to 5500, this 180-card rainbow foil parallel again offers the same players as in the SPx Finite base set, but with an even further modified technology. Base spectrum parallels (#1-90) were serial numbered to 300. Global impact spectrum parallels (#91-120) were serial numbered to 225, sure shots spectrum parallels (#121-150) were numbered to 75, and marquee performers spectrum parallels (#151-170) were numbered to 25. Living legends spectrum parallels (#171-180) were also serial numbered to 1/1 and are not priced due to scarcity.

*SPECTRUM 1-90: 10X TO 25X BASIC CARDS
*SPECTRUM GI 91-120: 8X TO 20X BASIC CARDS
*SPECTRUM SS 121-150: 6X TO 15X BASIC CARDS
*SPECTRUM MP 151-170: 10X TO 25X BASIC CARDS

UNPRICED LIVING LEGEND PRINT RUN 1

1998-99 SPx Top Prospects

The 1998-99 SPx Top Prospects set was issued in one series totaling 90 cards and features action color player photos with player information on the backs. Only 1,999 of cards 61-90 were printed. Cards 79 and 80 were only available signed.

COMPLETE SET (90) 60.00 150.00
COMP.SET w/o SP's (60) 20.00 50.00
1 Paul Kariya .60 1.50
2 Teemu Selanne .60 1.50
3 Ray Bourque 1.00 2.50
4 Sergei Samsonov .40 1.00
5 Joe Thornton 1.00 2.50
6 Dominik Hasek 1.25 3.00
7 Theo Fleury .40 1.00
8 Keith Primeau .20 .50
9 Tony Amonte .40 1.00
10 Doug Gilmour .40 1.00
11 J-P Dumont .20 .50
12 Chris Chelios .60 1.50
13 Peter Forsberg 1.50 4.00
14 Patrick Roy 3.00 8.00
15 Joe Sakic 1.25 3.00
16 Milan Hejduk RC 3.00 8.00
17 Chris Drury .40 1.00
18 Mike Modano 1.00 2.50
19 Brett Hull .75 2.00
20 Ed Belfour .60 1.50
21 Steve Yzerman 3.00 8.00
22 Brendan Shanahan .60 1.50
23 Sergei Fedorov 1.00 2.50
24 Chris Osgood .40 1.00
25 Nicklas Lidstrom .60 1.50
26 Bill Guerin .20 .50
27 Doug Weight .40 1.00
28 Tom Poti .20 .50
29 Mark Parrish RC 1.00 2.50
30 Rob Blake .40 1.00
31 Pavel Rosa RC .40 1.00
32 Vincent Damphousse .20 .50
33 Saku Koivu .60 1.50
34 Mike Dunham .20 .50
35 Martin Brodeur 1.50 4.00
36 Zigmund Palffy .40 1.00
37 Eric Brewer .20 .50
38 Wayne Gretzky 4.00 10.00
39 Brian Leetch .60 1.50
40 Manny Malhotra .20 .50
41 Petr Nedved .20 .50
42 Alexei Yashin .20 .50
43 Eric Lindros .60 1.50
44 John LeClair .40 1.00
45 John Vanbiesbrouck .40 1.00
46 Keith Tkachuk .40 1.00
47 Jeremy Roenick .75 2.00
48 Daniel Briere .20 .50
49 Jaromir Jagr 1.00 2.50
50 Patrick Marleau .40 1.00
51 Al MacInnis .20 .50
52 Chris Pronger .40 1.00
53 Vincent Lecavalier .60 1.50
54 Curtis Joseph .60 1.50
55 Mats Sundin .60 1.50
56 Tomas Kaberle RC 1.00 2.50
57 Mark Messier .60 1.50
58 Pavel Bure .60 1.50
59 Bill Muckalt RC .40 1.00
60 Peter Bondra .40 1.00
61 Brian Finley RC 1.50 4.00
62 Roberto Luongo 2.00 5.00
63 Mike Van Ryn 1.50 4.00
64 Harold Druken 1.50 4.00
65 Daniel Tkaczuk 1.50 4.00
66 Brenden Morrow RC 5.00 12.00
67 Jani Rita RC 1.50 4.00
68 Tommi Santala RC 1.50 4.00
69 Teemu Virkkunen RC 1.50 4.00
70 Arto Laaktikainen RC 1.50 4.00
71 Ilkka Mikkola RC 1.50 4.00
72 Miko Jokela RC 1.50 4.00
73 Kirill Safronov RC 1.50 4.00
74 Denis Shvidki 1.50 4.00
75 Denis Arkhipov RC 1.50 4.00
76 Maxim Afinogenov 2.00 5.00
77 Alexander Zevakhin RC 1.50 4.00
78 Alexei Volkov RC 1.50 4.00
79 Daniel Sedin AU 6.00 15.00
80 Henrik Sedin AU 6.00 15.00
81 Jimmie Olvestad RC 1.50 4.00
82 Mattias Weinhandl RC 1.50 4.00
83 Mathias Tjarnqvist RC 1.50 4.00
84 Jakob Johansson RC 1.50 4.00
85 Barrett Heisten RC 1.50 4.00
86 Tim Connolly RC 2.00 5.00
87 Andy Hilbert RC 1.50 4.00
88 David Legwand 1.50 4.00
89 Joe Blackburn RC 1.50 4.00
90 Dave Tanabe RC 1.50 4.00

1998-99 SPx Top Prospects Radiance

Randomly inserted in Finite Radiance hot packs only, this 90-card set is parallel to the base SPx Top Prospects set and is crash numbered to 100. A crash numbered 1 of 1 Spectrum parallel was also available and found only in Finite Spectrum hot packs. Spectrum parallels not priced due to scarcity.

*RADIANCE 1-60: 10X TO 25X BASIC CARDS
*RADIANCE 61-90: 1.2X TO 3X BASIC CARDS
*ROOKIES: 2X TO 5X BASIC CARDS
UNPRICED SPECTRUM PRINT RUN 1

1998-99 SPx Top Prospects Highlight Heroes

Randomly inserted in packs at the rate of 1:8, this 30-card set features action color photos of top NHL players.

COMPLETE SET (30) 75.00 150.00
H1 Paul Kariya 1.50 4.00
H2 Teemu Selanne 1.50 4.00
H3 Ray Bourque 2.50 6.00
H4 Sergei Samsonov 1.25 3.00
H5 Dominik Hasek 3.00 8.00
H6 Theo Fleury 1.25 3.00
H7 Doug Gilmour 1.25 3.00
H8 Joe Sakic 3.00 8.00
H9 Patrick Roy 8.00 20.00
H10 Peter Forsberg 4.00 10.00
H11 Mike Modano 2.50 6.00
H12 Brett Hull 2.00 5.00
H13 Brendan Shanahan 1.50 4.00
H14 Steve Yzerman 8.00 20.00
H15 Sergei Fedorov 2.50 6.00
H16 Saku Koivu 1.50 4.00
H17 Martin Brodeur 4.00 10.00
H18 Wayne Gretzky 10.00 25.00
H19 Zigmund Palffy 1.25 3.00
H20 John Vanbiesbrouck 1.25 3.00
H21 Eric Lindros 1.50 4.00
H22 John LeClair 1.50 4.00
H23 Keith Tkachuk 1.50 4.00
H24 Jeremy Roenick 2.00 5.00
H25 Jaromir Jagr 2.50 6.00
H26 Vincent Lecavalier 1.50 4.00
H27 Mats Sundin 1.50 4.00
H28 Curtis Joseph 1.50 4.00
H29 Pavel Bure 1.50 4.00
H30 Peter Bondra 1.25 3.00

1998-99 SPx Top Prospects Lasting Impressions

COMPLETE SET (30) 40.00 80.00
STATED ODDS 1:3
L1 Vincent Lecavalier .75 2.00
L2 John Vanbiesbrouck .60 1.50
L3 Paul Kariya .75 2.00
L4 Keith Tkachuk .75 2.00
L5 Mike Modano 1.25 3.00
L6 Dominik Hasek 1.50 4.00
L7 Teemu Selanne .75 2.00
L8 Mats Sundin .75 2.00
L9 Brendan Shanahan .75 2.00
L10 Pavel Bure .75 2.00
L11 Theo Fleury .75 2.00
L12 Curtis Joseph .75 2.00
L13 Joe Sakic 1.50 4.00
L14 Eric Lindros .75 2.00
L15 Peter Bondra .60 1.50
L16 Brett Hull 1.00 2.50
L17 Ray Bourque 1.25 3.00
L18 Jaromir Jagr 1.25 3.00
L19 Steve Yzerman 4.00 10.00
L20 Jeremy Roenick 1.00 2.50
L21 Martin Brodeur 2.00 5.00
L22 Saku Koivu .75 2.00
L23 Patrick Roy 4.00 10.00
L24 John LeClair .75 2.00
L25 Doug Gilmour .60 1.50
L26 Sergei Fedorov 1.25 3.00
L27 Wayne Gretzky 5.00 12.00
L28 Peter Forsberg 2.00 5.00
L29 Zigmund Palffy .60 1.50
L30 Sergei Samsonov .60 1.50

1998-99 SPx Top Prospects Premier Stars

COMPLETE SET (30) 100.00 200.00
STATED ODDS 1:17

PS1 Wayne Gretzky 15.00 40.00
PS2 Sergei Samsonov 2.00 5.00
PS3 Ray Bourque 4.00 10.00
PS4 Dominik Hasek 5.00 12.00
PS5 Martin Brodeur 6.00 15.00
PS6 Brian Leetch 2.50 6.00
PS7 Mike Richter 2.50 6.00
PS8 Eric Lindros 2.50 6.00
PS9 John LeClair 2.50 6.00
PS10 John Vanbiesbrouck 2.00 5.00
PS11 Jaromir Jagr 4.00 10.00
PS12 Vincent Lecavalier 2.50 6.00
PS13 Mats Sundin 2.50 6.00
PS14 Curtis Joseph 2.50 6.00
PS15 Peter Bondra 2.00 5.00
PS16 Wayne Gretzky 15.00 40.00
PS17 Teemu Selanne 2.50 6.00
PS18 Paul Kariya 2.50 6.00
PS19 Theo Fleury 2.50 6.00
PS20 Tony Amonte 2.00 5.00
PS21 Patrick Roy 12.50 30.00
PS22 Joe Sakic 5.00 12.00
PS23 Peter Forsberg 6.00 15.00
PS24 Mike Modano 4.00 10.00
PS25 Brett Hull 3.00 8.00
PS26 Steve Yzerman 12.50 30.00
PS27 Brendan Shanahan 2.50 6.00
PS28 Doug Weight 2.00 5.00
PS29 Keith Tkachuk 2.50 6.00
PS30 Mark Messier 2.50 6.00

1998-99 SPx Top Prospects Winning Materials

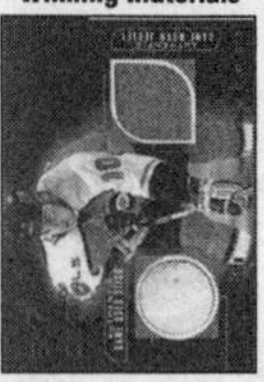

Randomly inserted into packs at the rate of 1:251, this 12-card set features color player photos with pieces of the pictured player's game-used jersey and stick cut and affixed to the card.

CJ Curtis Joseph 8.00 20.00
CO Chris Osgood 8.00 20.00
EL Eric Lindros 8.00 20.00
FP Felix Potvin 8.00 20.00
JJ Jaromir Jagr 12.50 30.00
JL John LeClair 8.00 20.00
JS Joe Sakic 15.00 40.00
JV John Vanbiesbrouck 8.00 20.00
MR Mike Richter 8.00 20.00
MS Mats Sundin 8.00 20.00
PR Patrick Roy 30.00 80.00
RB Ray Bourque 15.00 40.00

1998-99 SPx Top Prospects Year of the Great One

Randomly inserted into packs at the rate of 1:17, this 30-card set features unique photos of Wayne Gretzky with notable quotes about his career from his father, various coaches, NHL greats and former teammates.

COMPLETE SET (30) 150.00 300.00
COMMON GRETZKY (WG1-WG30) 5.00 12.00

1992 Sport-Flash

This 15-card standard-size set was produced by Sport-Flash as the first series of "Hockey Stars since 1940". The accompanying certification of limited edition claims that the production run was 200,000 sets. Each set contained one autographed hockey card signed by the player. On a bright yellow card face, the fronts display close-up color photos enclosed by blue and black border stripes. The player's name appears in the bottom yellow border. The backs are bilingual and present biography, player profile, and career statistics. The cards are numbered on both sides.

COMPLETE SET (15) 4.00 10.00
1 Jacques Laperriere .25 .60
2 Larry Carriere .20 .50
3 Chuck Rayner .30 .75
4 Jean Beliveau .75 2.00
5 BoomBoom Geoffrion .60 1.50
6 Gilles Gilbert .30 .75
7 Marcel Bonin .20 .50
8 Leon Rochefort .20 .50
9 Maurice Richard 2.00 5.00
10 Rejean Houle .20 .50
11 Pierre Mondou .20 .50
12 Yvan Cournoyer .30 .75
13 Henri Richard .40 1.00
14 Checklist Card .02 .10
15 Certification of .02 .10
Limited Edition

1992 Sport-Flash Autographs

Random inserts in the Sport-Flash sets. Each card is signed in blue Sharpie on the card front.

COMPLETE SET (15) 80.00 200.00
1 Jacques Laperriere 4.00 10.00
2 Larry Carriere 4.00 10.00
3 Chuck Rayner 4.00 10.00
4 Jean Beliveau 12.00 30.00
5 BoomBoom Geoffrion 12.00 30.00
6 Gilles Gilbert 4.00 10.00
7 Marcel Bonin 4.00 10.00
8 Leon Rochefort 4.00 10.00
9 Maurice Richard 20.00 50.00
10 Rejean Houle 4.00 10.00
11 Pierre Mondou 4.00 10.00
12 Yvan Cournoyer 8.00 20.00
13 Henri Richard 8.00 20.00
14 Checklist Card .20 .50
NNO Certification of .02 .10
Limited Edition

1989 Sports Illustrated for Kids I

Since its debut issue in January 1989, SI for Kids has included a perforated sheet of nine standard-size cards bound into each magazine. The cards were consecutively numbered 1-324 through December 1991. The athletes featured represent an extremely wide spectrum of sports. Each card features color photos with variously colored borders. The borders are as follows: aqua (1-108), green (109-207), woodgrain (208-216), red (217-315), marble (316-324). The player's name is printed in a white bar at the top, while his or her sport appears at the bottom. The backs carry biographical information, career highlights, and a trivia question with answer. The cards' magazine issue date appears on the back in very small type. Although originally distributed in sheet form, the cards are frequently traded as singles. Thus, they are priced individually. The value of an intact sheet is equal to the sum of the nine cards plus a premium of up to 20%.

1 Mario Lemieux HK 4.00 10.00
15 Joe Nieuwendyk HK .30 .75
19 Wayne Gretzky HK 5.00 12.00
25 Steve Yzerman HK 2.00 5.00
30 Sean Burke HK .20 .50
82 Al MacInnis .30 .75
Hockey
96 Pat LaFontaine HK .75 2.00
100 Mark Messier HK 2.00 5.00

1990 Sports Illustrated for Kids I

116 Brian Leetch HK 1.00 2.50
118 Denis Savard HK .30 .75
126 Dale Hawerchuk HK .30 .75
134 Ray Bourque HK 1.00 2.50
143 Grant Fuhr HK .50 1.25
193 Brett Hull HK 1.25 3.00
214 Gordie Howe HK 1.25 3.00

1991 Sports Illustrated for Kids I

224 Ron Hextall HK .30 .75
228 Bernie Nicholls HK .20 .50
238 Chris Chelios HK .50 1.25
250 Mike Liut .10 .30
Hockey
252 Joe Mullen HK .20 .50
254 Steve Larmer HK .20 .50
300 Paul Coffey HK .50 1.25
317 Bobby Orr HK 4.00 10.00

1992 Sports Illustrated for Kids II

Since its debut issue in January 1989, SI for Kids has included a perforated sheet of nine standard-size cards bound into each magazine. In January 1992, the card numbers started over again at 1. This listing comprises the cards contained from that magazine through the last 2000 issue. The athletes featured represent an extremely wide spectrum of sports. Each card features color photos with borders of various designs and colors. The borders are as follows: navy (1-9, 19-99), clouds (10-18, 55-63, 226-234), marble (100-108, 208-216, 316-324), pink (109-207), purple (217-225), blue (235-315), gold/silver (325-486), clouds (487-495) and gold/silver (496-621). The athlete's name is printed at the top while his or her sport appears at the bottom. The backs carry biographical information, career highlights, and a trivia question with answer. The cards' magazine issue date appears on the back in very small type. Although originally distributed in sheet form, the cards are frequently traded as singles. Thus, they are priced individually. The value of an intact sheet is equal to the sum of the nine cards plus a premium of up to 20 percent. The cards labeled as "MC" were issued in SI for Kids as part of a milk promotion.

9 Tom Barrasso HK .20 .50
10 Mike Eruzione HK .40 1.00
20 Brian Bellows HK .20 .50
33 Ed Belfour HK .25 .60
42 Mark Messier HK .40 1.00
93 Patrick Roy 3.00 8.00
Hockey

2001 Sports Illustrated for Kids

Since its debut issue in January 1989, SI for Kids has included a perforated sheet of nine standard-size cards bound into each magazine. In December 2000, for the second time, the card numbers started over again at 1. The athletes featured represent an extremely wide spectrum of sports. The athlete's name is printed at the top while his or her sport appears at the bottom. The backs carry biographical information, career highlights, and a trivia question with answer. The cards' magazine issue date appears on the back in very small type. Although originally distributed in sheet form, the cards are frequently traded as singles. Thus, they are priced individually. The value of an intact sheet is equal to the sum of the nine cards plus a premium of up to 20 percent.

COMPLETE SET (108) 25.00 50.00
9 Chris Pronger HK .20 .50
11 Mark Messier HK .25 .60
20 Tony Amonte HK .20 .50
31 Nadine Muzerall HK .20 .50
36 Zigmund Palffy HK .20 .50
37 Brian Leetch HK .20 .50
49 Joe Sakic HK .60 1.50
60 Sean Burke HK .20 .50
66 Alexei Kovalev HK .20 .50
76 Adam Oates HK .20 .50
82 Patrick Elias HK .20 .50
96 Nicklas Lidstrom HK .25 .60
106 Patrick Roy HK 2.50 6.00
108 Keith Tkachuk HK .25 .60

2004 Sports Illustrated for Kids

ONE NINE-CARD SHEET PER MAGAZINE
340 Wayne Gretzky HK .75 2.00
343 Marian Hossa HK .20 .50
358 Alex Tanguay HK .10 .30
367 Martin Brodeur HK .40 1.00
371 Robert Lang HK .10 .30
384 Ilya Kovalchuk HK .20 .50
395 Dwayne Roloson HK .10 .30
403 Martin St. Louis HK .20 .50
413 Evgeni Nabokov HK .20 .50

2005 Sports Illustrated for Kids

450 Natalie Darwitz Women's HK .07 .20
469 Marty Sertich College HK .07 .20
534 Rick Nash HK .10 .30

2006 Sports Illustrated for Kids

1 Sidney Crosby HK .60 1.50
11 Roberto Luongo HK .20 .50
24 Jaromir Jagr HK .30 .75
33 Alex Ovechkin HK .40 1.00
41 Dominik Hasek HK .20 .50
47 Simon Gagne HK .10 .30
62 Eric Staal HK .20 .50
67 Nicklas Lidstrom HK .20 .50
81 Teemu Selanne HK .20 .50
90 Chris Pronger HK .20 .50
96 Joe Thornton HK .25 .60
106 Pavel Datsyuk HK .20 .50

2007 Sports Illustrated for Kids

ONE NINE-CARD SHEET PER MAGAZINE
133 Kari Lehtonen HK .08 .25
136 Evgeni Malkin HK .40 1.00
150 Daniel Briere HK .08 .25
159 Dany Heatley HK .20 .50
166 Vincent LeCavalier HK .08 .25
178 Jason Spezza HK .08 .25
189 Scott Niedermayer HK .08 .25
193 Ryan Miller HK .20 .50
200 Alexander Ovechkin HK .40 1.00
215 Henrik Zetterberg HK .20 .50

2008 Sports Illustrated for Kids

233 Patrick Kane HK .30 .75
241 Marian Gaborik HK .20 .50

1977-79 Sportscaster Series 1

COMPLETE SET (24) 17.50 35.00
102 Bobby Orr 2.50 5.00
Ice Hockey

1977-79 Sportscaster Series 2

COMPLETE SET (24) 30.00 60.00
206 Gordie Howe 5.00 10.00
Ice Hockey
213 The Stanley Cup 1.00 2.00
Yvan Cournoyer
Serge Savard
Ice Hockey

1977-79 Sportscaster Series 5

COMPLETE SET (24) 12.50 25.00
520 Bobby Hull HK 2.50 5.00

1977-79 Sportscaster Series 7

COMPLETE SET (24) 15.00 30.00
708 USSR 1.00 2.00
1976 USSR Team
Ice Hockey
717 Brad Park HK 1.00 2.00

1977-79 Sportscaster Series 12

COMPLETE SET (24) 12.50 25.00
1222 Stan Mikita HK 1.25 2.50

1977-79 Sportscaster Series 15

COMPLETE SET (24) 12.50 25.00
1513 Yvan Cournoyer HK 1.25 2.50

1977-79 Sportscaster Series 17

COMPLETE SET (24) 10.00 20.00
1709 Denis Potvin HK 2.00 4.00

1977-79 Sportscaster Series 18

COMPLETE SET (24) 12.50 25.00
1823 Garry Unger .50 1.00
Ice Hockey

1977-79 Sportscaster Series 27

COMPLETE SET (24) 12.50 25.00
2724 National Hockey 1.50 3.00
League: Black Hawks/Caps
(Dennis Hull)
Ice Hockey

1977-79 Sportscaster Series 38

COMPLETE SET (24) 20.00 40.00
3807 The Seven 1.50 3.00
Professional Trophies
Guy Lafleur
Ice Hockey

1977-79 Sportscaster Series 43

COMPLETE SET (24) 12.50 25.00
4304 Major and Minor .75 1.50
Penalties
Maple Leafs/Caps
Ice Hockey
4306 Rogie Vachon HK 1.00 2.00

1977-79 Sportscaster Series 46

COMPLETE SET (24) 12.50 25.00
4614 In the Corners .75 1.50
Leafs/Capitals
Ice Hockey
4621 Bryan Trottier HK 1.50 3.00

1977-79 Sportscaster Series 51

COMPLETE SET (24) 20.00 40.00
5101 Czechoslovakia 1977 .75 1.50
Czechs vs Soviet
Ice Hockey
5118 Guy Lafleur HK 1.50 3.00

1977-79 Sportscaster Series 55

COMPLETE SET (24) 12.50 25.00
5514 Jiri Holik 1.00 2.00
Jaroslav Holik
Two Czech Stars
Ice Hockey
5523 World Hockey Assoc. 4.00 8.00
Bobby Hull
Ice Hockey

1977-79 Sportscaster Series 56

COMPLETE SET (24) 37.50 75.00
5605 Montreal Forum 2.50 5.00
Toronto/Montreal
Ice Hockey

1977-79 Sportscaster Series 60

COMPLETE SET (24) 37.50 75.00
6012 Bobby Clarke HK 4.00 8.00

1977-79 Sportscaster Series 61

COMPLETE SET (24) 50.00 100.00
6103 Lingo 2.50 5.00
Eddie Giacomin
Ice Hockey

1977-79 Sportscaster Series 64

COMPLETE SET (24) 25.00 50.00
6416 Sudden Death 2.50 5.00
Pete Stemkowski
Ice Hockey

1977-79 Sportscaster Series 71

COMPLETE SET (24) 40.00 80.00
7104 Tommy Abrahamsson 2.00 4.00
Christian Abrhamsson
Two Whaler Stars
Ice Hockey
7112 Anders Hedberg 2.50 5.00
Ulf Nilsson
Islanders/Rangers
Ice Hockey

1977-79 Sportscaster Series 73

COMPLETE SET (24) 40.00 80.00
7301 USSR vs. NHL 4.00 8.00
Game Action
(Larry Robinson)
Ice Hockey
7311 Czechoslavakia 1976 Championship 2.50 5.00
Ice Hockey

1977-79 Sportscaster Series 76

COMPLETE SET (24) 30.00 60.00
7603 NCAA Hockey 2.50 5.00
Champions
Minnesota/N. Dakota
(Bill Baker)
Ice Hockey

1977-79 Sportscaster Series 77

COMPLETE SET (24) 150.00 300.00
7710 Wayne Gretzky HK 125.00 250.00

1977-79 Sportscaster Series 81

COMPLETE SET (24) 62.50 125.00
8119 Jacques Lemaire 5.00 10.00
Canadiens/Rangers
Ice Hockey

1977-79 Sportscaster Series 82

COMPLETE SET (24) 50.00 100.00
8205 Scotty Bowman 7.50 15.00
Ice Hockey

1991-92 Stadium Club

The 1991-92 Topps Stadium Club hockey set contains 400 standard-size cards. The fronts feature full-bleed glossy color player photos. At the bottom, the player's name appears in an aqua stripe that is bordered in gold. In the lower left or right corner the Stadium Club logo overlays the stripe. Against the background of a colorful drawing of a hockey rink, the horizontally oriented backs have a biography, The Sporting News Hockey Scouting Report (which consists of strengths and evaluative comments), statistics (last season and career totals), and a miniature photo of the player's first Topps card. There are many cards in the set that can be found with or without "The Sporting News" on the card back; these variations (no added premium) are 13, 16, 22, 46, 50, 60, 68, 149, 190, 204, 230, 249, 264, 276, 297, 298, 307, 320, 332, 339, 341, 342, 348, 351, and 362. There are no key Rookie Cards in this set.

COMPLETE SET (400) 10.00 25.00
1 Wayne Gretzky 1.00 2.50
2 Randy Moller .02 .10
3 Ray Ferraro .02 .10
4 Craig Wolanin .02 .10
5 Shayne Corson .02 .10
6 Chris Chelios .15 .40
7 Joe Mullen .08 .25
8 Ken Wregget .08 .25
9 Rob Cimetta .02 .10
10 Mike Liut .08 .25
11 Martin Gelinas .02 .10
12 Mario Marois .02 .10
13 Rick Vaive .02 .10
14 Brad McCrimmon .02 .10
15 Mark Hunter .02 .10
16 Jim Wiemer .02 .10
17 Sergio Momesso .02 .10
18 Claude Lemieux .02 .10
19 Brian Hayward .08 .25
20 Pat Flatley .02 .10
21 Mark Osborne .02 .10
22 Mike Hudson .02 .10
23 Rejean Lemelin .08 .25
24 Slava Fetisov .02 .10
25 Bobby Smith .08 .25
26 Kris King .02 .10
27 Randy Velischek .02 .10
28 Steve Bozek .02 .10
29 Mike Foligno .02 .10
30 Scott Arniel .02 .10
31 Sergei Makarov .02 .10
32 Rick Zombo .02 .10
33 Christian Ruuttu .02 .10
34 Gino Cavallini .02 .10
35 Rick Tocchet .08 .25
36 Jiri Hrdina .02 .10
37 Peter Bondra .08 .25
38 Craig Ludwig .02 .10
39 Mikael Andersson .02 .10
40 Bob Kudelski .02 .10
41 Guy Carbonneau .08 .25
42 Geoff Smith .02 .10
43 Russ Courtnall .02 .10
44 Michal Pivonka .02 .10
45 Todd Krygier .02 .10
46 Jeremy Roenick .20 .50
47 Doug Brown .02 .10
48 Paul Cavallini .02 .10
49 Ron Sutter .02 .10
50 Paul Ranheim .02 .10
51 Mike Gartner .08 .25
52 Greg Adams .02 .10
53 Dave Capuano .02 .10
54 Mike Krushelnyski .02 .10
55 Ulf Dahlen .02 .10
56 Steven Finn .02 .10
57 Ed Olczyk .02 .10
58 Steve Duchesne .02 .10
59 Bob Probert .08 .25
60 Joe Nieuwendyk .08 .25
61 Petr Klima .02 .10
62 Uwe Krupp .02 .10
63 Jay Miller .02 .10
64 Cam Neely .15 .40
65 Phil Housley .08 .25
66 Michel Goulet .08 .25
67 Brett Hull .25 .60
68 Mike Ridley .02 .10
69 Esa Tikkanen .02 .10
70 Kjell Samuelsson .02 .10
71 Corey Millen RC .02 .10
72 Doug Lidster .02 .10
73 Ron Francis .08 .25
74 Scott Young .02 .10
75 Bob Sweeney .02 .10
76 Sean Burke .08 .25
77 Pierre Turgeon .08 .25
78 David Reid .02 .10
79 Al MacInnis .08 .25
80 Mike Hough .02 .10
81 Steve Yzerman .60 1.50
82 Derek King .02 .10
83 Brad Shaw .02 .10
84 Trevor Linden .08 .25
85 Rick Meagher .02 .10
86 Stephane Richer .08 .25
87 Brian Bellows .02 .10
88 Pete Peeters .08 .25
89 Adam Creighton .02 .10
90 Brent Ashton .02 .10
91 Bryan Trottier .15 .40
92 Mike Richter .15 .40
93 Dave Andreychuk .08 .25
94 Randy Carlyle .02 .10
95 Dave Christian .02 .10
96 Doug Gilmour .08 .25
97 Tony Granato .02 .10
98 Jeff Norton .02 .10
99 Neal Broten .08 .25
100 Jody Hull .02 .10
101 Shawn Burr .02 .10
102 Pat Verbeek .02 .10
103 Ken Daneyko .02 .10
104 Peter Zezel .02 .10
105 Kirk McLean .08 .25
106 Kelly Miller .02 .10
107 Patrick Roy .75 2.00
108 Adam Oates .08 .25
109 Steve Thomas .02 .10
110 Scott Mellanby .02 .10
111 Mark Messier .15 .40
112 Larry Murphy .08 .25
113 Mark Janssens .02 .10
114 Doug Bodger .02 .10
115 Ron Tugnutt .08 .25
116 Glenn Anderson .08 .25
117 Dave Gagner .02 .10
118 Dino Ciccarelli .08 .25
119 Randy Burridge .02 .10
120 Kelly Hrudey .08 .25
121 Jimmy Carson .02 .10
122 Bruce Driver .02 .10
123 Pat LaFontaine .15 .40
124 Wendel Clark .08 .25
125 Peter Sidorkiewicz .08 .25
126 Gary Roberts .08 .25
127 Petr Svoboda .02 .10
128 Vincent Riendeau .08 .25
129 Brian Skrudland .02 .10
130 Tim Kerr .02 .10
131 Doug Wilson .08 .25
132 Pat Elynuik .02 .10
133 Craig MacTavish .02 .10
134 Troy Mallette .02 .10
135 Mike Ramsey .02 .10
136 Tony Hrkac .02 .10
137 Craig Simpson .02 .10
138 Jon Casey .08 .25
139 Steve Kasper .02 .10
140 Kevin Hatcher .08 .25
141 Dave Barr .02 .10
142 Brad Lauer .02 .10
143 Gary Suter .02 .10
144 John MacLean .08 .25
145 Dean Evason .02 .10
146 Vincent Damphousse .02 .10
147 Craig Janney .08 .25
148 Jeff Brown .02 .10
149 Geoff Courtnall .08 .25
150 Igor Larionov .02 .10
151 Jan Erixon .02 .10
152 Bob Essensa .08 .25
153 Gaetan Duchesne .02 .10
154 Jyrki Lumme .02 .10
155 Tom Barrasso .08 .25
156 Curtis Leschyshyn .02 .10
157 Benoit Hogue .02 .10
158 Gary Leeman .02 .10
159 Luc Robitaille .08 .25
160 Jamie Macoun .02 .10
161 Bob Carpenter .02 .10
162 Kevin Dineen .02 .10
163 Gary Nylund .02 .10
164 Dale Hunter .02 .10
165 Gerard Gallant .02 .10
166 Jacques Cloutier .08 .25
167 Troy Murray .02 .10
168 Phil Bourque .02 .10
169 Grant Ledyard .02 .10
170 Joel Otto .02 .10
171 Paul Ysebaert UER .02 .10
(Photo actually
Mike Sillinger)
172 Luke Richardson .02 .10
173 Ron Hextall .08 .25
174 Mario Lemieux .75 2.00
175 Garry Galley .08 .25
176 Murray Craven .02 .10
177 Walt Poddubny .02 .10
178 Scott Pearson .02 .10
179 Kevin Lowe .08 .25
180 Brent Sutter .02 .10
181 Dirk Graham .02 .10
182 Pelle Eklund .02 .10
183 Sylvain Cote .02 .10
184 Rod Brind'Amour .15 .40
185 Fredrik Olausson .02 .10
186 Kelly Kisio .02 .10
187 Mike Modano .30 .75
188 Calle Johansson .02 .10
189 John Tonelli .02 .10
190 Glen Wesley .02 .10
191 Bob Errey .02 .10
192 Rich Sutter .02 .10
193 Kirk Muller .02 .10
194 Rob Zettler .02 .10
195 Alexander Mogilny .15 .40
196 Adrien Plavsic .02 .10
197 Daniel Marois .02 .10
198 Yves Racine .02 .10
199 Brendan Shanahan .15 .40
200 Rob Brown .02 .10
201 Brian Leetch .15 .40
202 Dave McLlwain .02 .10
203 Charlie Huddy .02 .10
204 David Volek .02 .10
205 Trent Yawney .02 .10
206 Brian MacLellan .02 .10
207 Thomas Steen .02 .10
208 Sylvain Lefebvre .02 .10
209 Tomas Sandstrom .02 .10
210 Mike McPhee .02 .10
211 Andy Moog .15 .40
212 Paul Coffey .15 .40
213 Denis Savard .08 .25
214 Eric Desjardins .08 .25
215 Wayne Presley .02 .10
216 Stephane Morin UER .02 .10
(Photo actually
Jeff Jackson)
217 Ric Nattress .02 .10
218 Troy Gamble .08 .25
219 Terry Carkner .02 .10
220 Dave Hannan .02 .10
221 Randy Wood .02 .10
222 Brian Mullen .02 .10
223 Garth Butcher .02 .10
224 Tim Cheveldae .08 .25
225 Rod Langway .02 .10
226 Stephen Leach .02 .10
227 Perry Berezan .02 .10
228 Zarley Zalapski .02 .10
229 Patrik Sundstrom .02 .10
230 Steve Smith .02 .10
231 Daren Puppa .08 .25
232 Dave Taylor .08 .25
233 Ray Bourque .25 .60
234 Kevin Stevens .02 .10
235 Frank Musil .02 .10
236 Mike Keane .02 .10
237 Brian Propp .02 .10
238 Brent Fedyk .02 .10
239 Rob Ramage .02 .10
240 Robert Kron .02 .10
241 Mike McNeil .02 .10
242 Greg Gilbert .02 .10
243 Dan Quinn .02 .10
244 Chris Nilan .02 .10
245 Bernie Nicholls .08 .25
246 Don Beaupre .08 .25
247 Keith Acton .02 .10
248 Gord Murphy .02 .10
249 Bill Ranford .08 .25
250 Dave Chyzowski .02 .10
251 Clint Malarchuk .08 .25
252 Larry Robinson .08 .25
253 Dave Poulin .02 .10
254 Paul MacDermid .02 .10
255 Doug Smail .02 .10
256 Mark Recchi .15 .40
257 Brian Bradley .02 .10
258 Grant Fuhr .15 .40
259 Owen Nolan .15 .40
260 Hubie McDonough .02 .10
261 Mikko Makela .02 .10
262 Mathieu Schneider .02 .10
263 Peter Stastny .08 .25
264 Jim Hrivnak .08 .25
265 Scott Stevens .08 .25
266 Mike Tomlak .02 .10
267 Marty McSorley .02 .10
268 Johan Garpenlov .02 .10
269 Mike Vernon .08 .25
270 Steve Larmer .08 .25
271 Phil Sykes .02 .10
272 Jay Mazur .02 .10
273 John Ogrodnick .02 .10
274 Dave Ellett .02 .10
275 Randy Gilhen .02 .10
276 Tom Chorske .02 .10
277 James Patrick .02 .10
278 Darin Kimble .02 .10
279 Paul Cyr .02 .10
280 Petr Nedved .08 .25
281 Tony McKegney .02 .10
282 Alexei Kasatonov .02 .10
283 Stephen Lebeau .02 .10
284 Everett Sanipass .02 .10
285 Tony Tanti .02 .10
286 Kevin Miller .02 .10
287 Moe Mantha .02 .10
288 Alan May .02 .10
289 John Cullen .02 .10
290 Daniel Berthiaume .08 .25
291 Mark Pederson .02 .10
292 Laurie Boschman .02 .10
293 Neil Wilkinson .02 .10
294 Rick Wamsley .08 .25
295 Ken Linseman .02 .10
296 Jamie Leach .02 .10
297 Chris Terreri .08 .25
298 Cliff Ronning .02 .10
299 Bobby Holik .08 .25
300 Mats Sundin .15 .40
301 Carey Wilson .02 .10
302 Teppo Numminen .02 .10
303 Dave Lowry .02 .10
304 Joe Reekie .02 .10
305 Keith Primeau .02 .10
306 David Shaw .02 .10
307 Nick Kypreos .02 .10
308 Dave Manson .02 .10
309 Mick Vukota .02 .10
310 Todd Elik .02 .10
311 Michel Petit .02 .10
312 Dale Hawerchuk .08 .25
313 Joe Murphy .02 .10
314 Chris Dahlquist .02 .10
315 Petri Skriko .02 .10
316 Sergei Fedorov .25 .60
317 Lee Norwood .02 .10
318 Garry Valk .02 .10
319 Glen Featherstone .02 .10
320 Dave Snuggerud .02 .10
321 Doug Evans .02 .10
322 Marc Bureau .02 .10
323 John Vanbiesbrouck .08 .25
324 John McIntyre .02 .10
325 Wes Walz .02 .10
326 Daryl Reaugh .08 .25
327 Paul Fenton .02 .10
328 Ulf Samuelsson .02 .10
329 Andrew Cassels .02 .10
330 Alexei Gusarov RC .08 .25
331 John Druce .02 .10
332 Adam Graves .08 .25
333 Ed Belfour .15 .40
334 Murray Baron .02 .10
335 John Tucker .02 .10
336 Todd Gill .02 .10
337 Martin Hostak .02 .10
338 Gino Odjick .02 .10
339 Eric Weinrich .02 .10
340 Todd Ewen .02 .10
341 Mike Hartman .02 .10
342 Danton Cole .02 .10
343 Jaromir Jagr .30 .75
344 Mike Craig .02 .10
345 Mark Fitzpatrick .08 .25
346 Darren Turcotte .02 .10
347 Ron Wilson .02 .10
348 Rob Blake .08 .25
349 Dale Kushner .02 .10
350 Jeff Beukeboom .02 .10
351 Tim Bergland .02 .10
352 Peter Ing .08 .25
353 Wayne McBean .02 .10
354 Jim McKenzie .02 .10
355 Theo Fleury .02 .10
356 Jocelyn Lemieux .02 .10
357 Ken Hodge Jr. .02 .10
358 Shawn Anderson .02 .10
359 Dimitri Khristich .02 .10
360 Jon Morris .02 .10
361 Darrin Shannon .02 .10
362 Chris Joseph .02 .10
363 Normand Lacombe .02 .10
364 Frank Pietrangelo .02 .10
365 Joey Kocur .08 .25
366 Anatoli Semenov .02 .10
367 Bob Bassen .02 .10
368 Brad Jones .02 .10
369 Glenn Healy .08 .25
370 Don Sweeney .02 .10
371 Brad Dalgarno .02 .10
372 Al Iafrate .08 .25
373 Patrick Lebeau UER RC .02 .10
374 Terry Yake .02 .10
375 Roger Johansson .02 .10
376 Paul Broten .02 .10
377 Andre Racicot RC .08 .25
378 Scott Thornton .02 .10
379 Zdeno Ciger .02 .10
380 Paul Stanton .02 .10
381 Ray Sheppard .02 .10
382 Kevin Haller RC .02 .10
383 Vladimir Ruzicka .02 .10
384 Bryan Marchment RC .08 .25
385 Bill Berg .02 .10
386 Mike Ricci .15 .40
387 Pat Conacher .02 .10
388 Brian Glynn .02 .10
389 Joe Sakic .30 .75
390 Mikhail Tatarinov .02 .10
391 Stephane Matteau .02 .10
392 Mark Tinordi .02 .10
393 Robert Reichel .02 .10
394 Tim Sweeney .02 .10
395 Rick Tabaracci .08 .25
396 Ken Sabourin .02 .10
397 Jeff Lazaro .02 .10
398 Checklist 1-133 .02 .10
399 Checklist 134-266 .02 .10
400 Checklist 267-400 .02 .10

1992-93 Stadium Club

This 501-card standard-size set features full-bleed color action player photos. The Stadium Club logo appears at the bottom and intersects a gold foil double stripe carrying the team name. The horizontal backs show an artist's rendering of a hockey rink as the background. A mini-reproduction of the player's first Topps card is shown as well as biography, statistics, and The Sporting News Skills Rating System. The Members Choice (241-250 and 251-260) subsets, showing full-bleed color photos, closes the first series and opens the second series. These backs have the same art work background with 1991-92 season statistics. The only notable Rookie Card is Guy Hebert.

COMPLETE SET (501) 8.00 20.00
COMP.SERIES 1 (250) 4.00 10.00
COMP.SERIES 2 (251) 4.00 10.00
1 Brett Hull .20 .50
2 Theo Fleury .02 .10
3 Joe Sakic .25 .60
4 Mike Modano .20 .50
5 Dmitri Mironov .02 .10
6 Yves Racine .02 .10
7 Igor Kravchuk .02 .10
8 Philippe Bozon .02 .10
9 Stephane Richer .07 .20
10 Dave Lowry .02 .10
11 Dean Evason .02 .10
12 Mark Fitzpatrick .07 .20
13 Dave Poulin .02 .10
14 Phil Housley .07 .20
15 Adrien Plavsic .02 .10
16 Claude Boivin .02 .10
17 Bill Guerin RC .50 1.25
18 Wayne Gretzky .75 2.00
19 Steve Yzerman .60 1.50
20 Joe Mullen .07 .20
21 Brad McCrimmon .02 .10
22 Dan Quinn .02 .10
23 Rob Blake .07 .20
24 Wayne Presley .02 .10
25 Zarley Zalapski .02 .10
26 Bryan Trottier .07 .20
27 Peter Sidorkiewicz .07 .20
28 John MacLean .07 .20
29 Brad Schlegel .02 .10
30 Marc Bureau .02 .10
31 Troy Murray .02 .10
32 Tony Amonte .07 .20
33 Rob DiMaio .02 .10
34 Joe Murphy .02 .10
35 Jim Waite .07 .20
36 Ron Sutter .02 .10
37 Joe Nieuwendyk .07 .20
38 Kevin Haller .02 .10
39 Andrew Cassels .02 .10
40 Dale Hunter .07 .20
41 Craig Janney .07 .20
42 Sergio Momesso .02 .10
43 Nicklas Lidstrom .10 .30
44 Luc Robitaille .07 .20
45 Adam Creighton .02 .10
46 Norm Maciver .02 .10
47 Mikhail Tatarinov .02 .10
48 Gary Roberts .02 .10
49 Gord Hynes .02 .10
50 Claude Lemieux .02 .10
51 Brad May .02 .10
52 Paul Stanton .02 .10
53 Rick Wamsley .07 .20
54 Steve Larmer .07 .20
55 Darrin Shannon .02 .10
56 Pat Falloon .02 .10
57 Chris Dahlquist .02 .10
58 John Vanbiesbrouck .07 .20
59 Sylvain Turgeon .02 .10
60 Jay More .02 .10
61 Randy Burridge .02 .10
62 Slava Kozlov UER .07 .20
63 Daniel Marois .02 .10
64 Curt Giles .02 .10
65 Brad Shaw .02 .10
66 Bill Ranford .07 .20
67 Frank Musil .02 .10
68 Steve Leach .02 .10
69 Michel Goulet .07 .20
70 Mathieu Schneider .02 .10
71 Steve Kasper .02 .10
72 Darryl Sydor .02 .10
73 Brian Leetch .10 .30
74 Chris Terreri .07 .20
75 Jim Johnson .02 .10
76 Rick Tocchet .07 .20
77 Teppo Numminen .02 .10
78 Owen Nolan .07 .20
79 Grant Ledyard .02 .10
80 Trevor Linden .07 .20
81 Luciano Borsato .02 .10
82 Derek King .02 .10
83 Robert Cimetta .02 .10
84 Geoff Smith .02 .10
85 Ray Sheppard .02 .10
86 Dimitri Khristich .02 .10
87 Chris Chelios .10 .30
88 Alexander Godynyuk .02 .10
89 Perry Anderson .02 .10
90 Neal Broten .07 .20
91 Brian Benning .02 .10
92 Brent Thompson .02 .10
93 Claude LaPointe .02 .10
94 Mario Lemieux .60 1.50
95 Pat LaFontaine .10 .30
96 Frank Pietrangelo .07 .20
97 Gerald Diduck .02 .10
98 Paul DiPietro .02 .10
99 Valeri Zelepukin .02 .10
100 Rick Zombo .02 .10
101 Daniel Berthiaume .07 .20
102 Tom Fitzgerald .02 .10
103 Ken Baumgartner .02 .10
104 Esa Tikkanen .02 .10
105 Steve Chiasson .02 .10
106 Bobby Holik .07 .20
107 Dominik Hasek .40 1.00
108 Jeff Hackett .07 .20
109 Paul Broten .02 .10
110 Kevin Stevens .02 .10
111 Geoff Sanderson .07 .20
112 Donald Audette .02 .10
113 Jarmo Myllys .02 .10
114 Brian Skrudland .02 .10
115 Andrei Lomakin .02 .10
116 Keith Tkachuk .10 .30
117 John McIntyre .02 .10
118 Jacques Cloutier .07 .20
119 Michel Picard .02 .10
120 Dave Babych .02 .10
121 Dave Gagner .07 .20
122 Bob Carpenter .02 .10
123 Ray Ferraro .02 .10
124 Glenn Anderson .07 .20
125 Craig MacTavish .02 .10
126 Shawn Burr .02 .10
127 Tim Bergland .02 .10
128 Al MacInnis .07 .20
129 Jeff Beukeboom .02 .10
130 Ken Wregget .07 .20
131 Arturs Irbe .10 .30
132 Dave Andreychuk .07 .20
133 Patrick Roy .60 1.50
134 Benoit Brunet .02 .10
135 Rick Tabaracci .07 .20
136 Jamie Baker .02 .10
137 Yanic Dupre .02 .10
138 Jari Kurri .10 .30
139 Adam Burt .02 .10
140 Peter Stastny .07 .20
141 Brad Jones .02 .10
142 Jeff Odgers .02 .10
143 Anatoli Semenov UER .02 .10
144 Paul Ranheim .02 .10
145 Sylvain Cote .02 .10
146 Brent Ashton .02 .10
147 Doug Bodger .02 .10
148 Bryan Marchment .02 .10
149 Bob Kudelski .02 .10
150 Adam Graves .02 .10
151 Scott Stevens .07 .20
152 Russ Courtnall .02 .10
153 Darcy Wakaluk .07 .20
154 Pelle Eklund .02 .10
155 Robert Kron .02 .10
156 Randy Ladouceur .02 .10
157 Ed Olczyk .02 .10
158 Jiri Hrdina .02 .10
159 John Tonelli .02 .10
160 John Cullen .02 .10
161 Jan Erixon .02 .10
162 David Shaw .02 .10
163 Brian Bradley .02 .10
164 Russ Romaniuk .02 .10
165 Eric Weinrich .02 .10
166 Steve Heinze .02 .10
167 Jeremy Roenick .15 .40
168 Mark Pederson .02 .10
169 Paul Coffey .10 .30
170 Bob Errey .02 .10
171 Brian Lawton .02 .10
172 Vincent Riendeau .07 .20
173 Marc Fortier .02 .10
174 Marc Bergevin .02 .10
175 Jim Sandlak .02 .10
176 Bob Bassen .02 .10
177 Uwe Krupp .02 .10
178 Paul MacDermid .02 .10
179 Bob Corkum .02 .10
180 Robert Reichel .02 .10
181 John LeClair .25 .60
182 Mike Hudson .02 .10
183 Mark Recchi .07 .20
184 Rollie Melanson .07 .20
185 Gordie Roberts .02 .10
186 Clint Malarchuk .07 .20
187 Kris King .02 .10
188 Adam Oates .07 .20
189 Jarrod Skalde .02 .10
190 Mike Lalor .02 .10
191 Vincent Damphousse .02 .10
192 Peter Ahola .02 .10
193 Kirk McLean .07 .20
194 Murray Baron .02 .10
195 Michel Petit .02 .10
196 Stephane Fiset .07 .20
197 Pat Verbeek .02 .10
198 Jon Casey .07 .20
199 Tim Cheveldae .07 .20
200 Mike Ridley .02 .10
201 Scott Lachance .02 .10
202 Rod Brind'Amour .07 .20
203 Bret Hedican UER RC .07 .20
204 Wendel Clark .07 .20
205 Shawn McEachern .02 .10
206 Randy Wood .02 .10
207 Ulf Dahlen .02 .10
208 Andy Brickley .02 .10
209 Scott Niedermayer UER .07 .20
210 Bob Essensa .07 .20
211 Patrick Poulin .02 .10
212 Johan Garpenlov .02 .10
213 Marty McInnis .02 .10
214 Josef Beranek .02 .10
215 Rod Langway .02 .10
216 Dave Christian .02 .10
217 Sergei Makarov .02 .10
218 Gerard Gallant .02 .10
219 Neil Wilkinson UER .02 .10
220 Tomas Sandstrom .07 .20
221 Shayne Corson .02 .10
222 John Ogrodnick .02 .10
223 Keith Acton .02 .10
224 Paul Fenton .02 .10
225 Rob Zettler .02 .10
226 Todd Elik .02 .10
227 Petr Svoboda .02 .10
228 Zdeno Ciger .02 .10
229 Kevin Miller .02 .10
230 Rich Pilon .02 .10
231 Pat Jablonski .07 .20
232 Greg Adams .02 .10
233 Martin Brodeur .50 1.25
234 Dave Taylor .07 .20
235 Kelly Buchberger .02 .10
236 Steve Konroyd .02 .10
237 Guy Larose .02 .10
238 Patrice Brisebois .02 .10
239 Checklist 1-125 .02 .10
240 Checklist 126-250 .02 .10
241 Mark Messier MC .08 .25
242 Mike Richter MC .05 .15
243 Ed Belfour MC .07 .20
244 Sergei Fedorov MC .10 .30
245 Adam Oates MC .07 .20
246 Pavel Bure MC .07 .20
247 Luc Robitaille MC .07 .20
248 Brian Leetch MC .07 .20
249 Ray Bourque MC .10 .30
250 Tony Amonte MC .05 .15
251 Mario Lemieux MC .30 .75
252 Patrick Roy MC .30 .75
253 Nicklas Lidstrom MC .07 .20
254 Steve Yzerman MC .30 .75
255 Jeremy Roenick MC .07 .20
256 Wayne Gretzky MC .40 1.00
257 Kevin Stevens MC .02 .10
258 Brett Hull MC .10 .30
259 Pat Falloon MC .02 .10
260 Guy Carbonneau MC .07 .20
261 Todd Gill .02 .10
262 Mike Sullivan .02 .10
263 Jeff Brown .02 .10
264 Joe Reekie .02 .10
265 Geoff Courtnall .02 .10
266 Mike Richter .10 .30
267 Ray Bourque .25 .60
268 Mike Craig .02 .10
269 Scott King .02 .10
270 Don Beaupre .07 .20
271 Ted Donato .02 .10
272 Gary Leeman .02 .10
273 Steve Weeks .07 .20
274 Keith Brown .02 .10
275 Greg Paslawski .02 .10
276 Pierre Turgeon .07 .20
277 Jimmy Carson .02 .10
278 Tom Fergus .02 .10
279 Glen Wesley .02 .10
280 Tomas Forslund .02 .10
281 Tony Granato .02 .10
282 Phil Bourque .02 .10
283 Dave Ellett .02 .10
284 David Bruce .02 .10
285 Stu Barnes .02 .10
286 Peter Bondra .07 .20
287 Garth Butcher .02 .10
288 Ron Hextall .07 .20
289 Guy Carbonneau .02 .10
290 Louie DeBrusk .02 .10
291 Dave Barr .02 .10
292 Ken Sutton .02 .10
293 Brian Bellows .02 .10
294 Mike McNeill .02 .10
295 Rob Brown .02 .10
296 Corey Millen .02 .10
297 Joe Juneau UER .07 .20
298 Jeff Chychrun UER .02 .10
299 Igor Larionov .02 .10
300 Sergei Fedorov .20 .50
301 Kevin Hatcher .02 .10
302 Al Iafrate .07 .20
303 James Black .02 .10
304 Steph Beauregard .07 .20
305 Joel Otto .02 .10
306 Nelson Emerson .02 .10
307 Gaetan Duchesne .02 .10
308 J.J. Daigneault .02 .10
309 Jamie Macoun .02 .10
310 Laurie Boschman .02 .10
311 Mike Gartner .07 .20
312 Tony Tanti .02 .10
313 Steve Duchesne .02 .10
314 Martin Gelinas .02 .10
315 Dominic Roussel .07 .20
316 Cam Neely .10 .30
317 Craig Wolanin .02 .10
318 Randy Gilhen .02 .10
319 David Volek .02 .10
320 Alexander Mogilny .07 .20
321 Jyrki Lumme .02 .10
322 Jeff Reese .02 .10
323 Greg Gilbert .02 .10
324 Jeff Norton .02 .10
325 Jim Hrivnak .07 .20
326 Eric Desjardins .07 .20
327 Curtis Joseph .10 .30
328 Ric Nattress .02 .10
329 Jamie Leach .02 .10
330 Christian Ruuttu .02 .10
331 Doug Brown .02 .10
332 Randy Carlyle .02 .10
333 Brian Propp .02 .10
334 Doug Smail .02 .10
335 Hubie McDonough .02 .10
336 Pat MacLeod .02 .10
337 Don Sweeney .02 .10
338 Felix Potvin .10 .30
339 Kent Manderville .02 .10
340 Sergei Nemchinov .02 .10
341 Calle Johansson .02 .10
342 Dirk Graham .02 .10
343 Craig Billington .07 .20
344 Valeri Kamensky .02 .10
345 Mike Vernon .07 .20
346 Fredrik Olausson .02 .10
347 Peter Ing .07 .20
348 Mikael Andersson .02 .10
349 Mike Keane .02 .10
350 Stephane Quintal .02 .10
351 Tom Chorske .02 .10
352 Ron Francis .07 .20
353 Dana Murzyn .02 .10
354 Craig Ludwig .02 .10
355 Bob Probert .07 .20
356 Glenn Healy .07 .20
357 Troy Loney .02 .10
358 Vladimir Ruzicka .02 .10
359 Doug Gilmour .07 .20
360 Darren Turcotte .02 .10
361 Kelly Miller .02 .10
362 Dennis Vaske .02 .10
363 Stephane Matteau .02 .10
364 Brian Hayward .07 .20
365 Kevin Dineen .02 .10
366 Igor Ulanov .02 .10
367 Sylvain Lefebvre .02 .10
368 Petr Klima .02 .10
369 Steve Thomas .07 .20
370 Daren Puppa .07 .20
371 Brendan Shanahan .10 .30
372 Charlie Huddy .02 .10
373 Cliff Ronning .02 .10
374 Brian Propp .02 .10
375 Larry Murphy .07 .20
376 Bruce Driver .02 .10
377 Rob Pearson .02 .10
378 Paul Ysebaert .02 .10
379 Mark Osborne .02 .10
380 Doug Weight .10 .30
381 Kerry Huffman UER .02 .10
382 Michal Pivonka .02 .10
383 Steve Smith .02 .10
384 Steven Finn .02 .10
385 Kevin Lowe .07 .20
386 Mike Ramsey .02 .10
387 Kirk Muller .02 .10
388 John LeBlanc RC .02 .10
389 Rich Sutter .02 .10
390 Brent Fedyk .02 .10
391 Kelly Hrudey .07 .20
392 Slava Fetisov .02 .10
393 Glen Murray UER .02 .10
394 James Patrick .02 .10
395 Tom Draper .02 .10
396 Mark Hunter .02 .10
397 Wayne McBean .02 .10
398 Joe Sacco .02 .10
399 Dino Ciccarelli .07 .20
400 Brian Noonan .02 .10
401 Guy Hebert RC .40 1.00
402 Peter Douris .02 .10
403 Gilbert Dionne .02 .10
404 Doug Lidster .02 .10
405 John Druce .02 .10
406 Alexei Kasatonov .02 .10
407 Chris Lindberg .02 .10
408 Mike Ricci .07 .20
409 Tom Kurvers .02 .10
410 Pat Elynuik .02 .10
411 Mike Donnelly .02 .10
412 Grant Fuhr .10 .30
413 Curtis Leschyshyn .02 .10
414 Derian Hatcher .07 .20
415 Michel Mongeau .02 .10
416 Tom Barrasso .07 .20
417 Joey Kocur .07 .20
418 Vladimir Konstantinov .10 .30
419 Dale Hawerchuk .07 .20
420 Brian Mullen .02 .10
421 Mark Greig .02 .10
422 Claude Vilgrain .02 .10
423 Gary Suter .07 .20
424 Garry Galley .02 .10
425 Benoit Hogue .02 .10
426 Jeff Finley RC .02 .10
427 Bobby Smith .07 .20
428 Brent Sutter .02 .10
429 Ron Wilson .02 .10
430 Andy Moog .10 .30
431 Stephan Lebeau .02 .10
432 Troy Mallette .02 .10
433 Peter Zezel .02 .10
434 Mike Hough .02 .10
435 Mark Tinordi .02 .10
436 Dave Manson .02 .10
437 Jim Paek .02 .10
438 Frantisek Kucera .02 .10
439 Rob Zamuner RC .07 .20
440 Ulf Samuelsson .02 .10
441 Perry Berezan .02 .10
442 Murray Craven .02 .10
443 Mark Messier .10 .30
444 Alexander Semak .02 .10
445 Gord Murphy .02 .10
446 Jocelyn Lemieux .02 .10
447 Paul Cavallini .02 .10
448 Bernie Nicholls .02 .10
449 Brent Gilchrist .02 .10
450 Randy McKay .02 .10
451 Alexei Gusarov .02 .10
452 Mike McPhee .02 .10
453 Kimbi Daniels .02 .10
454 Kelly Kisio .02 .10
455 Bob Sweeney .02 .10
456 Luke Richardson .02 .10
457 Petr Nedved .07 .20
458 Craig Berube .02 .10
459 Kay Whitmore .10 .30
460 Randy Velischek .02 .10
461 David Williams RC .02 .10
462 Scott Mellanby .02 .10
463 Terry Carkner .02 .10
464 Dale Craigwell .02 .10
465 Kevin Todd .02 .10
466 Kjell Samuelsson .02 .10
467 Denis Savard .02 .10
468 Adam Foote .07 .20
469 Stephane Morin .02 .10
470 Doug Wilson .07 .20
471 Shawn Cronin .02 .10
472 Brian Glynn UER .02 .10
473 Craig Simpson .07 .20
474 Todd Krygier .02 .10
475 Brad Miller .02 .10
476 Yvon Corriveau .02 .10
477 Patrick Flatley .02 .10
478 Mats Sundin .07 .20
479 Joe Cirella .02 .10
480 Gino Cavallini .02 .10
481 Marty McSorley .07 .20
482 Brad Marsh .02 .10
483 Bob McGill .02 .10
484 Randy Moller .02 .10
485 Keith Primeau .07 .20
486 Darin Kimble .02 .10
487 Mike Krushelnyski .02 .10
488 Sutter Brothers .02 .10
489 Pavel Bure .10 .30
490 Ray Whitney RC .20 .50
491 Dave McLlwain .02 .10
492 Per Djoos .02 .10
493 Garry Valk .02 .10
494 Mike Bullard .02 .10
495 Greg Hawgood .02 .10
496 Terry Yake .02 .10
497 Mike Hartman .02 .10
498 Jaromir Jagr .20 .50
499 Checklist 251-384 .02 .10
500 Checklist 385-500 .02 .10
501 Eric Lindros .10 .30

1993-94 Stadium Club

This 500-card standard-size set features borderless color player action shots on the card fronts. The set was issued in two series of 250 cards each. Cards were printed for both the Canadian and U.S. markets. The O-Pee-Chee version has a U.S.A. copyright on back for series one cards only. The player's name appears in gold foil at the bottom, atop blue and gold foil stripes. Included is a ten-card Award Winners subset (141-150) that features the 1992-93 NHL Trophy winners. Rookie Cards include Jason Arnott, Chris Osgood, Jocelyn Thibault and German Titov.

COMPLETE SET (500) 12.00 30.00
COMP.SERIES 1 (250) 6.00 15.00
COMP.SERIES 2 (250) 6.00 15.00
1 Guy Carbonneau .01 .05
2 Joe Cirella .01 .05
3 Laurie Boschman .01 .05
4 Arturs Irbe .02 .10
5 Adam Creighton .01 .05
6 Mike McPhee .01 .05
7 Jeff Beukeboom .01 .05
8 Kevin Todd .01 .05
9 Yvon Corriveau .01 .05
10 Eric Lindros .08 .25
11 Martin Rucinsky .01 .05
12 Michel Goulet .02 .10
13 Scott Pellerin RC .01 .05
14 Mike Eagles .01 .05
15 Steve Heinze .01 .05
16 Gerard Gallant .01 .05
17 Kelly Miller .01 .05
18 Petr Nedved .01 .05
19 Joe Mullen .02 .10
20 Pat LaFontaine .08 .25
21 Garth Butcher .01 .05
22 Jeff Reese .02 .10
23 Dave Andreychuk .02 .10
24 Patrick Flatley .01 .05
25 Tomas Sandstrom .01 .05
26 Andre Racicot .02 .10
27 Patrice Brisebois .01 .05
28 Neal Broten .02 .10
29 Mark Freer .01 .05
30 Kelly Kisio .01 .05
31 Scott Mellanby .01 .05
32 Joe Sakic .20 .50
33 Kerry Huffman .01 .05
34 Evgeny Davydov .01 .05
35 Mark Messier .08 .25
36 Pat Verbeek .01 .05
37 Greg Gilbert .01 .05
38 John Tucker .01 .05
39 Claude Lemieux .01 .05
40 Shayne Corson .01 .05
41 Gordie Roberts .01 .05
42 Jiri Slegr .01 .05
43 Kevin Dineen .01 .05
44 Johan Garpenlov .01 .05
45 Sergei Fedorov .15 .40
46 Rich Sutter .01 .05
47 Dave Hannan .01 .05
48 Sylvain Lefebvre .01 .05
49 Pat Elynuik .01 .05
50 Ray Ferraro .01 .05
51 Brent Ashton .01 .05
52 Paul Stanton .01 .05
53 Kevin Haller .01 .05
54 Kelly Hrudey .02 .10
55 Russ Courtnall .01 .05
56 Alexei Zhamnov .02 .10
57 Andrei Lomakin .01 .05
58 Keith Brown .01 .05
59 Glen Murray .01 .05
60 Kay Whitmore .02 .10
61 Stephane Richer .02 .10
62 Todd Gill .01 .05
63 Bob Sweeney .01 .05
64 Mike Richter .08 .25
65 Brett Hull .10 .30
66 Sylvain Cote .01 .05
67 Kirk Muller .01 .05
68 Ronnie Stern .01 .05
69 Josef Beranek .01 .05
70 Steve Yzerman .50 1.25
71 Don Beaupre .02 .10
72 Ed Courtenay .01 .05
73 Zdeno Ciger .01 .05
74 Andrew Cassels .01 .05
75 Roman Hamrlik .10 .30
76 Benoit Hogue .01 .05
77 Andrei Kovalenko .01 .05
78 Rod Brind'Amour .02 .10
79 Tom Barrasso .02 .10
80 Al Iafrate .01 .05
81 Brett Hedican .01 .05
82 Peter Bondra .02 .10
83 Ted Donato .01 .05
84 Chris Lindberg .01 .05
85 John Vanbiesbrouck .02 .10
86 Ron Sutter .01 .05
87 Luc Robitaille .02 .10
88 Brian Leetch .08 .25
89 Randy Wood .01 .05
90 Dirk Graham .01 .05
91 Alexander Mogilny .02 .10
92 Mike Keane .01 .05
93 Adam Oates .02 .10
94 Viacheslav Butsayev .01 .05
95 John LeClair .08 .25
96 Joe Nieuwendyk .02 .10
97 Mikael Andersson .01 .05
98 Jaromir Jagr .15 .40
99 Ed Belfour .08 .25
100 David Reid .01 .05
101 Darius Kasparaitis .01 .05
102 Zarley Zalapski .01 .05
103 Christian Ruuttu .01 .05
104 Phil Housley .02 .10
105 Al MacInnis .02 .10
106 Tommy Sjodin .01 .05
107 Richard Smehlik .01 .05
108 Jyrki Lumme .01 .05
109 Dominic Roussel .02 .10
110 Mike Gartner .02 .10
111 Bernie Nicholls .01 .05
112 Mark Howe .01 .05
113 Rich Pilon .01 .05
114 Jeff Odgers .01 .05
115 Gilbert Dionne .01 .05
116 Peter Zezel .01 .05
117 Don Sweeney .01 .05
118 Jimmy Carson .01 .05
119 Igor Korolev .01 .05
120 Bob Kudelski .01 .05
121 Dave Lowry .01 .05
122 Steve Kasper .01 .05
123 Mike Ridley .01 .05
124 Dave Tippett .01 .05
125 Cliff Ronning .01 .05
126 Bruce Driver .01 .05
127 Stephane Matteau .01 .05
128 Joel Otto .01 .05
129 Alexei Kovalev .02 .10
130 Mike Modano .15 .40
131 Bill Ranford .02 .10
132 Petr Svoboda .01 .05
133 Roger Johansson .01 .05
134 Marc Bureau .01 .05
135 Keith Tkachuk .08 .25
136 Mark Recchi .02 .10
137 Bob Probert .02 .10
138 Uwe Krupp .01 .05
139 Mike Sullivan .01 .05
140 Doug Gilmour .02 .10
141 Teemu Selanne .08 .25
142 Dave Poulin .01 .05
143 Mario Lemieux TW .08 .25
144 Ed Belfour .08 .25
145 Pierre Turgeon .02 .10
146 Mario Lemieux TW .08 .25
147 Chris Chelios .08 .25
148 Mario Lemieux TW .08 .25
149 Doug Gilmour .02 .10
150 Ed Belfour .08 .25
151 Paul Ranheim .01 .05
152 Gino Cavallini .01 .05
153 Kevin Hatcher .01 .05
154 Marc Bergevin .01 .05
155 Marty McSorley .01 .05
156 Brian Bellows .01 .05
157 Patrick Poulin .01 .05
158 Kevin Stevens .01 .05
159 Bobby Holik .01 .05
160 Ray Bourque .15 .40
161 Bryan Marchment .01 .05
162 Curtis Joseph .08 .25
163 Kirk McLean .02 .10
164 Teppo Numminen .02 .10
165 Kevin Lowe .01 .05
166 Tim Cheveldae .02 .10
167 Brad Dalgarno .01 .05
168 Glenn Anderson .02 .10
169 Frank Musil .01 .05
170 Eric Desjardins .02 .10
171 Doug Zmolek .01 .05
172 Mark Lamb .01 .05
173 Craig Ludwig .01 .05
174 Rob Gaudreau RC .01 .05
175 Bob Carpenter .01 .05
176 Mike Ricci .01 .05
177 Brian Skrudland .01 .05
178 Dominik Hasek .30 .75
179 Pat Conacher .01 .05
180 Mark Janssens .01 .05
181 Brent Fedyk .01 .05
182 Rob DiMaio .01 .05
183 Dave Manson .01 .05
184 Janne Ojanen .01 .05
185 Ryan Walter .01 .05
186 Michael Nylander .01 .05
187 Steve Leach .01 .05
188 Jeff Brown .01 .05
189 Shawn McEachern .01 .05
190 Jeremy Roenick .10 .30
191 Darrin Shannon .01 .05
192 Wendel Clark .02 .10
193 Kevin Miller .01 .05
194 Paul DiPietro .01 .05
195 Steve Thomas .01 .05
196 Nicklas Lidstrom .08 .25
197 Ed Olczyk .01 .05
198 Robert Reichel .01 .05
199 Neil Brady .01 .05
200 Wayne Gretzky .60 1.50
201 Adrien Plavsic .01 .05
202 Joe Juneau .02 .10
203 Brad May .01 .05
204 Igor Kravchuk .01 .05
205 Keith Acton .01 .05
206 Ken Daneyko .01 .05
207 Sean Burke .02 .10
208 Jay More .01 .05
209 John Cullen .01 .05
210 Teemu Selanne .08 .25
211 Brent Sutter .01 .05
212 Brian Bradley .01 .05
213 Donald Audette .01 .05
214 Philippe Bozon .01 .05
215 Derek King .01 .05
216 Cam Neely .08 .25
217 Keith Primeau .01 .05
218 Steve Smith .01 .05
219 Ken Sutton .01 .05
220 Dale Hawerchuk .02 .10
221 Alexei Zhitnik .01 .05
222 Glen Wesley .01 .05
223 Nelson Emerson .01 .05
224 Pat Falloon .01 .05
225 Darryl Sydor .01 .05
226 Tony Amonte .02 .10
227 Brian Mullen .01 .05
228 Gary Suter .01 .05
229 David Shaw .01 .05
230 Troy Murray .01 .05
231 Patrick Roy .50 1.25
232 Mitchel Petit .01 .05
233 Wayne Presley .01 .05
234 Keith Jones .01 .05
235 Gary Roberts .01 .05
236 Steve Larmer .02 .10
237 Valeri Kamensky .02 .10
238 Ulf Dahlen .01 .05
239 Danton Cole .01 .05
240 Vincent Damphousse .01 .05
241 Yuri Khmylev .01 .05
242 Stephane Quintal .01 .05
243 Peter Taglianetti .01 .05
244 Gary Leeman .01 .05
245 Sergei Nemchinov .01 .05
246 Rob Blake .02 .10
247 Steve Chiasson .01 .05
248 Vladimir Malakhov .01 .05
249 Checklist 1-125 .01 .05
250 Checklist 126-250 .01 .05
251 Kjell Samuelsson .01 .05
252 Terry Carkner .01 .05
253 Bill Lindsay .01 .05
254 Bob Essensa .02 .10
255 Jocelyn Lemieux .01 .05
256 Joe Sacco .01 .05
257 Marty McInnis .01 .05
258 Warren Rychel .01 .05
259 Dave Maley .01 .05
260 Grant Fuhr .02 .10
261 Scott Young .01 .05
262 Ed Ronan .01 .05
263 Micah Aivazoff RC .01 .05
264 Murray Craven .01 .05
265 Slava Fetisov .01 .05
266 Chris Dahlquist .01 .05
267 Norm Maciver .01 .05
268 Alexander Godynyuk .01 .05
269 Mikael Renberg .08 .25
270 Adam Graves .01 .05
271 Randy Ladouceur .01 .05
272 Frank Pietrangelo .01 .05
273 Basil McRae .01 .05
274 Bryan Smolinski .01 .05
275 Daren Puppa .02 .10
276 Darcy Wakaluk .02 .10
277 Dimitri Khristich .01 .05
278 Vladimir Vujtek .01 .05
279 Tom Kurvers .01 .05
280 Felix Potvin .08 .25
281 Keith Brown .01 .05
282 Thomas Steen .01 .05
283 Larry Murphy .01 .05
284 Bob Corkum .01 .05
285 Tony Granato .01 .05
286 Cam Russell .01 .05
287 John MacLean .02 .10
288 Shawn Antoski .01 .05
289 Pelle Eklund .01 .05
290 Chris Pronger .10 .30
291 Alexander Karpovtsev .01 .05
292 Paul Laus RC .01 .05
293 Jaroslav Otevrel .01 .05
294 Dino Ciccarelli .02 .10
295 Guy Hebert .02 .10
296 Dave Karpa .01 .05
297 Denis Savard .02 .10
298 Jim Johnson .01 .05
299 Kirk Maltby RC .01 .05
300 Alexandre Daigle .01 .05
301 Dave Poulin .01 .05
302 James Patrick .01 .05
303 Jon Casey .02 .10
304 Yves Racine .01 .05
305 Craig Simpson .01 .05
306 Mike Krushelnyski .01 .05
307 Mark Fitzpatrick .02 .10
308 Charlie Huddy .01 .05
309 Todd Ewen .01 .05
310 Mario Lemieux .50 1.25
311 Dan Keczmer RC .01 .05
312 Sergei Zubov .01 .05
313 Shawn Burr .01 .05
314 Valeri Zelepukin .01 .05
315 Stephane Fiset .02 .10
316 C.J. Young .01 .05
317 Luciano Borsato .01 .05
318 Darcy Loewen .01 .05
319 Mike Vernon .02 .10
320 Chris Gratton .02 .10
321 Matthew Barnaby .02 .10
322 Mike Rathje .01 .05
323 Sergio Momesso .01 .05
324 David Volek .01 .05
325 Ron Tugnutt .02 .10
326 Jeff Hackett .02 .10
327 Robb Stauber .02 .10
328 Chris Terreri .02 .10
329 Rick Tocchet .02 .10
330 John Vanbiesbrouck .02 .10
331 Drake Berehowsky .01 .05
332 Alexei Kasatonov .01 .05
333 Vladimir Konstantinov .02 .10
334 John Blue .02 .10
335 Craig Janney .02 .10
336 Curtis Leschyshyn .01 .05
337 Todd Krygier .01 .05

338 Boris Mironov .01 .05
339 Joby Messier RC .01 .05
340 Tommy Soderstrom .02 .10
341 Randy Cunneyworth .01 .05
342 Mark Ferner RC .01 .05
343 Stephan Lebeau .01 .05
344 Jody Hull .01 .05
345 Jason Arnott RC .50 1.25
346 Gerard Gallant .01 .05
347 Stephane Richer .02 .10
348 Jeff Shantz RC .01 .05
349 Brian Skrudland .01 .05
350 Chris Osgood RC .75 2.00
351 Gary Shuchuk .01 .05
352 Martin Brodeur .30 .75
353 Bob Rouse .01 .05
354 Doug Bodger .01 .05
355 Mike Craig .01 .05
356 Ulf Samuelsson .01 .05
357 Trevor Linden .02 .10
358 Dennis Vaske .01 .05
359 Alexei Yashin .01 .05
360 Paul Ysebaert .01 .05
361 Shaun Van Allen .01 .05
362 Sandis Ozolinsh .01 .05
363 Todd Elik .01 .05
364 German Titov RC .01 .05
365 Alexander Semak .01 .05
366 Allen Pedersen .01 .05
367 Greg Johnson .01 .05
368 Anatoli Semenov .01 .05
369 Scott Mellanby .02 .10
370 Mats Sundin .08 .25
371 Mattias Norstrom RC .01 .05
372 Glen Featherstone .01 .05
373 Sergei Petrenko .01 .05
374 Mike Donnelly .01 .05
375 Nikolai Borschevsky .01 .05
376 Rob Zamuner .01 .05
377 Steven King .01 .05
378 Rick Tabaracci .02 .10
379 Dave Lowry .01 .05
380 Pierre Turgeon .02 .10
381 Garry Galley .01 .05
382 Doug Weight .02 .10
383 Scott Stevens .02 .10
384 Mark Tinordi .01 .05
385 Ron Francis .02 .10
386 Mark Greig .01 .05
387 Sean Hill .01 .05
388 Slava Kozlov .02 .10
389 Brendan Shanahan .08 .25
390 Theo Fleury .01 .05
391 Mathieu Schneider .01 .05
392 Tom Fitzgerald .01 .05
393 Markus Naslund .08 .25
394 Travis Green .02 .10
395 Troy Loney .01 .05
396 Gord Donnelly .01 .05
397 Owen Nolan .02 .10
398 Steve Larmer .02 .10
399 Dave Archibald .01 .05
400 Jari Kurri .08 .25
401 Jim Paek .01 .05
402 Andrei Lomakin .01 .05
403 Scott Niedermayer .01 .05
404 Bob Errey .01 .05
405 Michal Pivonka .01 .05
406 Doug Lidster .01 .05
407 Garry Valk .01 .05
408 Geoff Sanderson .02 .10
409 Stewart Malgunas RC .01 .05
410 Craig MacTavish .01 .05
411 Jaroslav Modry RC .01 .05
412 Shawn Chambers .01 .05
413 Geoff Courtnall .01 .05
414 Mark Hardy .01 .05
415 Martin Straka .01 .05
416 Randy Burridge .01 .05
417 Kent Manderville .01 .05
418 Darren Rumble .01 .05
419 Bill Houlder .01 .05
420 Chris Chelios .08 .25
421 Jim Hrivnak .02 .10
422 Benoit Brunet .01 .05
423 Aaron Ward RC .01 .05
424 Alexei Gusarov .01 .05
425 Mats Sundin .02 .10
426 Kjell Samuelsson .01 .05
427 Mikael Andersson .01 .05
428 Ulf Dahlen .01 .05
429 Nicklas Lidstrom .08 .25
430 Tommy Soderstrom .02 .10
431 Darrin Madeley RC .01 .05
432 Kevin Dahl .01 .05
433 Ron Hextall .02 .10
434 Patrick Carnback RC .01 .05
435 Randy Moller .01 .05
436 Dave Gagner .02 .10
437 Corey Millen .01 .05
438 Olaf Kolzig .02 .10
439 Gord Murphy .01 .05
440 Cam Stewart RC .01 .05
441 Darren McCarty RC .20 .50
442 Frantisek Kucera .01 .05
443 Ted Drury .01 .05
444 Troy Mallette .01 .05
445 Robin Bawa RC .01 .05
446 Steven Rice .01 .05
447 Pat Elynuik .01 .05
448 Jim Cummins RC .01 .05
449 Rob Niedermayer .02 .10
450 Paul Coffey .08 .25
451 Calle Johansson .01 .05
452 Mike Needham .01 .05
453 Glenn Healy .02 .10
454 Dixon Ward .01 .05
455 Al Iafrate .01 .05
456 Jon Casey .02 .10
457 Kevin Stevens .01 .05
458 Tony Amonte .02 .10
459 Chris Chelios .08 .25
460 Pat LaFontaine .02 .10
461 Jamie Baker .01 .05
462 Andre Faust .01 .05
463 Bobby Dollas .01 .05
464 Steven Finn .01 .05
465 Scott Lachance .01 .05
466 Mike Hough .01 .05
467 Bill Guerin .01 .05
468 Dimitri Filimonov .01 .05
469 Dave Ellett .01 .05
470 Andy Moog .02 .10
471 Scott Thomas RC .01 .05
472 Trent Yawney .01 .05
473 Tim Sweeney .01 .05
474 Shjon Podein RC .01 .05
475 J.J. Daigneault .01 .05
476 Darren Turcotte .01 .05
477 Esa Tikkanen .01 .05
478 Vitali Karamnov .01 .05
479 Jocelyn Thibault RC .30 .75
480 Pavel Bure .08 .25
481 Steve Konowalchuk .01 .05
482 Sylvain Turgeon .01 .05
483 Jeff Daniels .01 .05
484 Dallas Drake RC .01 .05
485 Iain Fraser RC .01 .05
486 Joe Reekie .01 .05
487 Evgeny Davydov .01 .05
488 Jozef Stumpel .01 .05
489 Brent Thompson .01 .05
490 Terry Yake .01 .05
491 Derek Plante RC .01 .05
492 Dimitri Yushkevich .01 .05
493 Wayne McBean .01 .05
494 Derian Hatcher .01 .05
495 Jeff Norton .01 .05
496 Adam Foote .01 .05
497 Mike Peluso .01 .05
498 Rob Pearson .01 .05
499 Checklist 251-375 .01 .05
500 Checklist 376-500 .01 .05

1993-94 Stadium Club OPC

COMPLETE SET (250) 12.00 30.00
COMP.SERIES 1 (250) 6.00 15.00
COMP.SERIES 2 (250) 6.00 15.00
*O-PEE-CHEE: .4X TO 1X BASIC CARDS

1993-94 Stadium Club First Day Issue

Randomly inserted at a rate of 1:24 packs, the 500-cards parallel the basic Stadium Club set. The O-Pee-Chee version has a U.S.A. copyright on back for series one cards only. The cards of Wayne Gretzky, Vincent Damphousse, Luc Robitaille and Wayne Presley can be found with the logo in either upper corner.

*VETS: 12X TO 30X BASIC CARDS
*ROOKIES: 5X TO 12X BASIC CARDS

1993-94 Stadium Club All-Stars

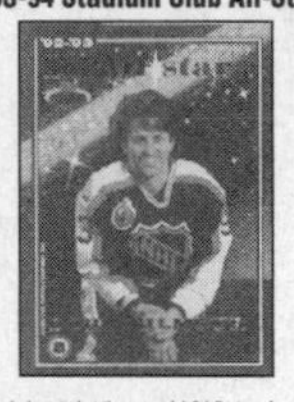

Randomly inserted at the rate of 1:24 first-series packs, each of these 23 standard-size cards features two 1992-93 All-Stars, one from each conference. Both sides carry a posed color player photo superimposed over a stellar background. The cards are unnumbered.

COMPLETE SET (23) 40.00 80.00
*O-PEE-CHEE: .4X TO 1X BASIC INSERTS
1 Patrick Roy 6.00 15.00
Ed Belfour
2 Ray Bourque 2.00 5.00
Paul Coffey
3 Al Iafrate 1.50 4.00
Chris Chelios
4 Jaromir Jagr 2.00 5.00
Brett Hull
5 Pat LaFontaine 4.00 10.00
Steve Yzerman
6 Kevin Stevens 2.00 5.00
Pavel Bure
7 Craig Billington .75 2.00
Jon Casey
8 Steve Duchesne .75 2.00
Steve Chiasson
9 Scott Stevens .75 2.00
Phil Housley
10 Peter Bondra 1.50 4.00
Kelly Kisio
11 Adam Oates 1.50 4.00
Brian Bradley
12 Alexander Mogilny 1.50 4.00
Jari Kurri
13 Peter Sidorkiewicz .75 2.00
Mike Vernon
14 Zarley Zalapski .75 2.00
Dave Manson
15 Brad Marsh .75 2.00
Randy Carlyle
16 Kirk Muller .75 2.00
Gary Roberts
17 Joe Sakic 3.00 8.00
Doug Gilmour
18 Mark Recchi 1.50 4.00
Luc Robitaille
19 Kevin Lowe .75 2.00
Garth Butcher
20 Rick Tocchet 2.00 5.00
Jeremy Roenick
21 Pierre Turgeon 2.00 5.00
Mike Modano
22 Mike Gartner 2.00 5.00
Teemu Selanne
23 Mario Lemieux 10.00 25.00
Wayne Gretzky

1993-94 Stadium Club Finest

Randomly inserted at the rate of 1:24 second-series packs, these 12 standard-size cards feature color player action cutouts on their multicolored metallic fronts. The player's name in gold lettering appears on a silver bar at the lower left. The horizontal back carries a color player photo on the left. The player's name and position appear at the top, with biography, career highlights, and statistics following below on a background that resembles blue ruffled silk. The cards are numbered on the back as "X of 12."

COMPLETE SET (12) 15.00 40.00
1 Wayne Gretzky 6.00 15.00
2 Jeff Brown .20 .50
3 Brett Hull 1.25 3.00
4 Paul Coffey .75 2.00
5 Felix Potvin .75 2.00
6 Mike Gartner .40 1.00
7 Luc Robitaille .40 1.00
8 Marty McSorley .20 .50
9 Gary Roberts .20 .50
10 Mario Lemieux 5.00 12.00
11 Patrick Roy 5.00 12.00
12 Ray Bourque 1.50 4.00

1993-94 Stadium Club Master Photos

Inserted one per U.S. box, and issued in two 12-card series, these 24 oversized cards measure 5" by 7". The fronts feature color player action shots framed by prismatic foil lines and set on a white card face. The cards are numbered on the back for both series as "X of 12," but are listed below as 1-24 to avoid confusion. Winner cards, which could be redeemed for one 5" X 7" card of each of the three players listed on the reverse, were inserted 1:24 packs of '93-94 Stadium Club

COMPLETE SET (24) 12.00 30.00
COMP.SERIES 1 (12) 8.00 20.00
COMP.SERIES 2 (12) 4.00 10.00
*WINNER EXCH: .5X TO 1.2X JUMBOS
1 Pat LaFontaine .30 .75
2 Doug Gilmour .15 .40
3 Ray Bourque .60 1.50
4 Teemu Selanne .30 .75
5 Eric Lindros .30 .75
6 Ray Ferraro .07 .20
7 Patrick Roy 2.00 5.00
8 Wayne Gretzky 2.50 6.00
9 Brett Hull .50 1.25
10 John Vanbiesbrouck .15 .40
11 Adam Oates .15 .40
12 Tom Barrasso .15 .40
13 Esa Tikkanen .07 .20
14 Jari Kurri .30 .75
15 Grant Fuhr .15 .40
16 Scott Lachance .07 .20
17 Theo Fleury .07 .20
18 Adam Graves .07 .20
19 Rick Tabaracci .15 .40
20 Pierre Turgeon .15 .40
21 Steven Finn .07 .20
22 Craig Janney .15 .40
23 Mathieu Schneider .07 .20
24 Felix Potvin .30 .75

1993-94 Stadium Club Team USA

Randomly inserted at the rate of 1:12 second-series packs, these 23 standard-size cards feature color player action shots on their borderless fronts. The player's name appears in gold-foil lettering over a blue stripe near the bottom. The gold foil USA Hockey logo appears in an upper corner. The cards are numbered on the back as "X of 23."

COMPLETE SET (23) 8.00 20.00
1 Mark Beaufait .40 1.00
2 Jim Campbell .60 1.50
3 Ted Crowley .40 1.00
4 Mike Dunham .60 1.50
5 Chris Ferraro .40 1.00
6 Peter Ferraro .40 1.00
7 Brett Hauer .40 1.00
8 Darby Hendrickson .40 1.00
9 Jon Hillebrandt .40 1.00
10 Chris Imes .40 1.00
11 Craig Johnson .40 1.00
12 Peter Laviolette .40 1.00
13 Jeff Lazaro .40 1.00
14 John Lilley .40 1.00
15 Todd Marchant .60 1.50
16 Matt Martin .40 1.00
17 Ian Moran .40 1.00
18 Travis Richards .40 1.00
19 Barry Richter .40 1.00
20 David Roberts .40 1.00
21 Brian Rolston .60 1.50
22 David Sacco .40 1.00
23 Jim Storm .40 1.00

1994 Stadium Club Members Only

Issued to Stadium Club members, this 50-card standard-size set features 45 players who were involved with the 1994 All-Star game, Western Conference All-Stars (1-22), Eastern Conference All-Stars (23-45), and five Stadium Club Finest cards. The fronts have full-bleed color action player photos. The player's name is printed in the bottom left corner, the words "Topps Stadium Club Members Only" in gold foil appear in one of the top corners. On a black background, the horizontal backs carry a color player close-up shot, along with a player profile.

COMP.FACT SET (50) 8.00 20.00
1 Felix Potvin .30 .75
2 Chris Chelios .20 .50
3 Paul Coffey .20 .50
4 Pavel Bure .60 1.50
5 Wayne Gretzky 1.50 4.00
6 Brett Hull .30 .75
7 Al MacInnis .08 .25
8 Rob Blake .08 .25
9 Alexei Kasatonov .02 .10
10 Teemu Selanne .50 1.25
11 Sandis Ozolinsh .08 .25
12 Shayne Corson .02 .10
13 Dave Andreychuk .05 .15
14 Dave Taylor .02 .10
15 Sergei Fedorov .50 1.25
16 Brendan Shanahan .40 1.00
17 Arturs Irbe .20 .50
18 Joe Nieuwendyk .08 .25
19 Russ Courtnall .02 .10
20 Jeremy Roenick .30 .75
21 Doug Gilmour .20 .50
22 Curtis Joseph .30 .75
23 Patrick Roy 1.25 3.00
24 Brian Leetch .20 .50
25 Ray Bourque .40 1.00
26 Alexander Mogilny .20 .50
27 Mark Messier .30 .75
28 Eric Lindros .60 1.50
29 Garry Galley .02 .10
30 Scott Stevens .05 .15
31 Al Iafrate .02 .10
32 Larry Murphy .02 .10
33 Joe Mullen .02 .10
34 Mark Recchi .20 .50
35 Adam Graves .05 .15
36 Geoff Sanderson .20 .50
37 Adam Oates .20 .50
38 Pierre Turgeon .20 .50
39 Joe Sakic .50 1.25
40 John Vanbiesbrouck .20 .50
41 Brian Bradley .02 .10
42 Alexei Yashin .08 .25
43 Bob Kudelski .02 .10
44 Jaromir Jagr .75 2.00
45 Mike Richter .30 .75
46 Martin Brodeur .60 1.50
47 Mikael Renberg .08 .25
48 Derek Plante .02 .10
49 Jason Arnott .08 .25
50 Alexandre Daigle .02 .10

1994-95 Stadium Club

This 270-card standard-size set was issued in one series. Due to the NHL lock-out, series two was replaced on the production schedule by Finest; therefore, this set does not have a comprehensive player selection. There are 12 cards per pack and 24 packs per box. The card fronts feature a full-bleed photo with the player's name and set name printed in gold foil along the bottom. The backs feature two player photos and previous year stats. Subsets include Power Players (55-60), Great Expectations (110-119), Shutouts (178-190), Rink Report (201-204), and Trophy Winners (264-270). There are no key Rookie Cards in this set.

COMPLETE SET (270) 15.00 30.00
1 Mark Messier .10 .30
2 Brad May .02 .10
3 Mike Ricci .02 .10
4 Scott Stevens .05 .15
5 Keith Tkachuk .10 .30
6 Guy Hebert .05 .15
7 Jason Arnott .02 .10
8 Cam Neely .10 .30
9 Adam Graves .02 .10
10 Pavel Bure .10 .30
11 Jeff Odgers .02 .10
12 Dimitri Khristich .02 .10
13 Patrick Poulin .02 .10
14 Mike Donnelly .02 .10
15 Felix Potvin .10 .30
16 Keith Primeau .02 .10
17 Fred Knipscheer .02 .10
18 Mike Keane .02 .10
19 Vitali Prokhorov .02 .10
20 Ray Ferraro .02 .10
21 Shane Churla .02 .10
22 Rob Niedermayer .05 .15
23 Adam Creighton .02 .10
24 Tommy Soderstrom .05 .15
25 Theo Fleury .02 .10
26 Jim Storm .02 .10
27 Bret Hedican .02 .10
28 Sean Hill .02 .10
29 Bill Ranford .05 .15
30 Derek Plante .02 .10
31 Dave McLlwain .02 .10
32 Iain Fraser .02 .10
33 Patrick Roy .60 1.50
34 Martin Straka .02 .10
35 Bruce Driver .02 .10
36 Brian Skrudland .02 .10
37 Bob Errey .02 .10
38 Randy Cunneyworth .02 .10
39 John Slaney .02 .10
40 Ray Sheppard .05 .15
41 Sergei Nemchinov .02 .10
42 Dave Ellett .02 .10
43 Vincent Riendeau .05 .15
44 Trent Yawney .02 .10
45 Dave Gagner .05 .15
46 Igor Korolev .02 .10
47 Gary Shuchuk .02 .10
48 Rob Zamuner .02 .10
49 Frantisek Kucera .02 .10
50 Joe Mullen .05 .15
51 Ron Hextall .05 .15
52 J.J. Daigneault .02 .10
53 Patrick Carnback .02 .10
54 Steven Rice .02 .10
55 Brian Leetch PP .10 .30
56 Al MacInnis PP .05 .15
57 Luc Robitaille PP .05 .15
58 Dave Andreychuk PP .05 .15
59 Jeremy Roenick PP .15 .40
60 Mario Lemieux PP .60 1.50
61 Dave Manson .02 .10
62 Pat Falloon .02 .10
63 Jesse Belanger .02 .10
64 Philippe Boucher .02 .10
65 Sergio Momesso .02 .10
66 Evgeny Davydov .02 .10
67 Alexei Gusarov .02 .10
68 Jaromir Jagr .20 .50
69 Randy Ladouceur .02 .10
70 Chris Chelios .10 .30
71 John Druce .02 .10
72 Kris Draper .02 .10
73 Joey Kocur .02 .10
74 Rich Tabaracci .05 .15
75 Mikael Andersson .02 .10
76 Mark Osborne .02 .10
77 Ray Bourque .20 .50
78 Dimitri Yushkevich .02 .10
79 Mike Vernon .05 .15
80 Steve Thomas .02 .10
81 Steve Duchesne .02 .10
82 Dean Evason .02 .10
83 Jason Smith .02 .10
84 Bryan Marchment .02 .10
85 Boris Mironov .02 .10
86 Jeff Norton .02 .10
87 Donald Audette .02 .10
88 Eric Lindros .10 .30
89 Garry Valk .02 .10
90 Mats Sundin .10 .30
91 Gerald Diduck .02 .10
92 Jeff Shantz .02 .10
93 Scott Niedermayer .02 .10
94 Troy Mallette .02 .10
95 John Vanbiesbrouck .05 .15
96 Ron Francis .05 .15
97 Slava Kozlov .05 .15
98 Ken Baumgartner .02 .10
99 Wayne Gretzky .75 2.00
100 Brett Hull .15 .40
101 Marc Bergevin .02 .10
102 Owen Nolan .05 .15
103 Bryan Smolinski .02 .10
104 Lyle Odelein .02 .10
105 Mike Ridley .02 .10
106 Trevor Kidd .05 .15
107 Derian Hatcher .02 .10
108 Derek King .02 .10
109 Rob Zettler .02 .10
110 Alexandre Daigle GE .02 .10
111 Chris Pronger GE .05 .15
112 Chris Gratton GE .02 .10
113 John Slaney GE .02 .10
114 Jocelyn Thibault GE .10 .30
115 Jason Arnott GE .02 .10
116 Alexei Yashin GE .02 .10
117 Rob Niedermayer GE .05 .15
118 Jason Allison GE .02 .10
119 Martin Brodeur GE .30 .75
120 Pat Verbeek .02 .10
121 Kelly Buchberger .02 .10
122 Doug Lidster .02 .10
123 Sergei Makarov .02 .10
124 Kris King .02 .10
125 Dominik Hasek .25 .60
126 Martin Rucinsky .02 .10
127 Kerry Huffman .02 .10
128 Gord Murphy .02 .10
129 Bobby Holik .02 .10
130 Kirk Muller .02 .10
131 Christian Ruuttu .02 .10
132 Jyrki Lumme .02 .10
133 Ken Wregget .02 .10
134 Dale Hunter .02 .10
135 Rob Blake .02 .10
136 Petr Klima .02 .10
137 Steve Heinze .02 .10
138 Chris Osgood .20 .50
139 John Lilley .02 .10
140 Dave Andreychuk .05 .15
141 Zarley Zalapski .02 .10
142 Curtis Joseph .10 .30
143 Brent Gilchrist .02 .10
144 Vladimir Malakhov .02 .10
145 Mikael Renberg .05 .15
146 Robert Kron .02 .10
147 Dean McAmmond .02 .10
148 Doug Bodger .02 .10
149 Ray Whitney .02 .10
150 Brian Leetch .10 .30
151 Martin Lapointe .02 .10
152 Teppo Numminen .02 .10
153 Scott Young .02 .10
154 Nick Kypreos .02 .10
155 Ed Belfour .10 .30
156 Greg Adams .02 .10
157 Brian Benning .02 .10
158 Bob Carpenter .02 .10
159 Vladimir Konstantinov .05 .15
160 Rick Tocchet .05 .15
161 Joe Sacco .02 .10
162 Darren Puppa .05 .15
163 Randy Burridge .02 .10
164 Darryl Sydor .02 .10
165 Jay More .02 .10
166 Joe Nieuwendyk .05 .15
167 Mike Eastwood .02 .10
168 Murray Baron .02 .10
169 Brent Fedyk .02 .10
170 Russ Courtnall .02 .10
171 Sean Burke .05 .15
172 Uwe Krupp .02 .10
173 Kevin Lowe .02 .10
174 Guy Carbonneau .02 .10
175 Alexei Yashin .02 .10
176 Thomas Steen .02 .10
177 Sandis Ozolinsh .05 .15
178 Patrick Roy SO .40 1.00
179 Dominik Hasek SO .15 .40
180 Ed Belfour SO .10 .30
181 Mike Richter SO .10 .30
182 Ron Hextall SO .05 .15
183 Daren Puppa SO .05 .15
184 Jon Casey SO .05 .15
185 Felix Potvin SO .15 .40
186 Martin Brodeur SO .30 .75
187 Darcy Wakaluk SO .05 .15
188 Kirk McLean SO .05 .15
189 Mike Vernon SO .05 .15
190 Arturs Irbe SO .05 .15
191 Dino Ciccarelli .05 .15
192 Steven Finn .02 .10
193 Pierre Sevigny .02 .10
194 Jim Dowd .02 .10
195 Chris Gratton .02 .10
196 Wayne Presley .02 .10
197 Joel Otto .02 .10
198 Fredrik Olausson .02 .10
199 Jody Hull .02 .10
200 Cliff Ronning .02 .10
201 Darren Turcotte RR .02 .10
202 Al Iafrate RR .02 .10
203 Eric Lindros RR .10 .30
204 Sandis Ozolinsh RR .02 .10
205 Petr Nedved .05 .15
206 Mark Lamb .02 .10
207 Shaun Van Allen .02 .10
208 Kelly Hrudey .05 .15
209 Nikolai Borschevsky .02 .10
210 Glen Wesley .02 .10
211 Shawn McEachern .02 .10
212 Mark Janssens .02 .10
213 Brian Mullen .02 .10
214 Craig Ludwig .02 .10
215 Mike Rathje .02 .10
216 Stephane Matteau .02 .10
217 Tim Cheveldae .05 .15
218 Brent Sutter .02 .10
219 Gord Dineen .02 .10
220 Kevin Hatcher .02 .10
221 Todd Simon RC .02 .10
222 Bill Lindsay .02 .10
223 Kirk McLean .05 .15
224 Chris Joseph .02 .10
225 Valeri Zelepukin .02 .10
226 Terry Yake .02 .10
227 Benoit Brunet .02 .10
228 Nicklas Lidstrom .10 .30
229 Zdeno Ciger .02 .10
230 Gary Roberts .02 .10
231 Andy Moog .10 .30
232 Ed Patterson .02 .10
233 Philippe Bozon .02 .10
234 Brent Hughes .02 .10
235 Chris Pronger .10 .30
236 Travis Green .05 .15
237 Pat Conacher .02 .10
238 Bob Rouse .02 .10
239 Yves Racine .02 .10
240 Nelson Emerson .02 .10
241 Oleg Petrov .02 .10
242 Steve Larmer .05 .15
243 Dan Laperriere .02 .10
244 John McIntyre .02 .10
245 Alexander Semak .02 .10
246 Stephane Fiset .05 .15
247 Peter Bondra .05 .15
248 Dale Hawerchuk .05 .15
249 Jamie Baker .02 .10
250 Sergei Fedorov .20 .50
251 Derek Mayer .02 .10
252 Ivan Droppa .02 .10
253 Kent Manderville .02 .10
254 Sergei Zholtok .02 .10
255 Murray Craven .02 .10
256 Todd Krygier .02 .10
257 Brent Grieve RC .02 .10
258 Esa Tikkanen .02 .10
259 Brad Dalgarno .02 .10
260 Russ Romaniuk .02 .10
261 Stu Barnes .02 .10
262 Dan Keczmer .02 .10
263 Eric Desjardins .05 .15
264 Martin Brodeur TW .30 .75
265 Adam Graves TW .02 .10
266 Cam Neely TW .05 .15
267 Ray Bourque TW .10 .30
268 Sergei Fedorov TW .10 .30
269 Dominik Hasek TW .15 .40
270 Wayne Gretzky TW .60 1.50

1994-95 Stadium Club Members Only Master Set

Issued to Stadium Club members only, this set parallels the basic cards with the exception of the words "Topp's Stadium Club Members Only" printed on the card front.

*STARS: 3X TO 6X BASIC CARD

1994-95 Stadium Club First Day Issue

This is a parallel to the 270 card basic set, inserted at a rate of 1:24 packs. The only difference is the silver foil "First Day Issue" logo on the card front.

*VETS: 25X TO 60X BASIC CARDS
*ROOKIES: 10X TO 25X BASIC CARDS

1994-95 Stadium Club Dynasty and Destiny

According to published odds, the five cards in this set were randomly inserted at the rate of 1:24 packs. Collector and dealer reports suggest they are available at a much easier rate than listed. Each card features two players; one veteran and an up and coming player with the same type of skills. Photos and stats for each player are on the backs. Each card is numbered out of ten, signifying that five more cards were to be included in the never-produced second series.

COMPLETE SET (5) 5.00 12.00
1 Tom Barrasso 1.25 3.00
Arturs Irbe
2 Mark Messier 1.50 4.00
Eric Lindros
3 Brett Hull 2.00 5.00
Pavel Bure
4 Luc Robitaille 1.25 3.00
Mikael Renberg
5 Chris Chelios 1.50 4.00
Chris Pronger

1994-95 Stadium Club Dynasty and Destiny Members Only

Issued to Stadium Club members only, this set parallels the basic cards with the exception of the words "Topp's Stadium Club Members Only" printed on the card front.

*STARS: .75X TO 2X BASIC CARD

1994-95 Stadium Club Finest Inserts

The nine cards in this set were inserted at the rate of 1:12 packs. The cards offer a completely different design from those of the basic Finest set which was released later in the season. These cards feature a cut-out player photo on a blue textured background. The player name is printed on a multi-color bar on the bottom of the card. Backs feature a small photo on the left with text information and limited stats. Cards are numbered out of nine.

COMPLETE SET (9) 15.00 40.00
1 Mario Lemieux 5.00 12.00
2 Brett Hull 1.25 3.00
3 Mark Messier 1.00 2.50
4 Wayne Gretzky 6.00 15.00
5 Pavel Bure 1.00 2.50
6 Sergei Fedorov 1.50 4.00
7 Brian Leetch 1.00 2.50
8 Ray Bourque 1.50 4.00
9 Patrick Roy 5.00 12.00

1994-95 Stadium Club Finest Inserts Members Only

Issued to Stadium Club members only, this set parallels the basic cards with the exception of the words "Topp's Stadium Club Members Only" printed on the card front.

*STARS: .75X TO 2X BASIC CARD

1994-95 Stadium Club Super Teams

The 26 cards in this set were inserted at the rate of 1:24 packs. The card fronts feature a photo of multiple players, or team action shot. The team name and set name are printed in speckled silver foil. Unlike most other inserts, these cards were part of an interactive game which allowed the holder to redeem the card for prizes if the pictured team won a division, conference or Stanley Cup championship. The backs have contest information and the teams record from the 1993-94 season. Holders of the New Jersey Devils card were able to redeem it for complete, specially stamped sets of Stadium Club and Finest. Winning division (Calgary, Detroit, Philadelphia, Quebec) and conference (Detroit, New Jersey) team cards were redeemable for packages of special stamped cards featuring members of that team.

COMPLETE SET (26) 25.00 60.00
1 Anaheim Mighty Ducks 1.00 2.50
(Bob Corkum et al.)
2 Boston Bruins 1.00 2.50
(Adam Oates/Ray Bourque)
3 Buffalo Sabres 1.00 2.50
(Dominik Hasek et al.)
4 Calgary Flames 1.00 2.50
(Andrei Trefilov/Theoren Fleury)
5 Chicago Blackhawks 1.00 2.50
(Ed Belfour et al.)
6 Dallas Stars 1.00 2.50
(Mike Modano/Trent Klatt/
Paul Broten)
7 Detroit Red Wings 2.00 5.00
(Bench)
8 Edmonton Oilers 1.00 2.50
(Bill Ranford/Bob Beers)
9 Florida Panthers 1.00 2.50
(Line change)
10 Hartford Whalers 1.00 2.50
(Sean Burke/Jim Storm/
Ted Crowley)
11 Los Angeles Kings 1.00 2.50
(Lined up for anthem)
12 Montreal Canadiens 2.50 6.00
(Patrick Roy)
13 New Jersey Devils WIN 4.00 10.00
(Martin Brodeur)
14 New York Islanders 1.00 2.50
(Darius Kasparaitis/Yan Kaminsky)
15 New York Rangers 2.00 5.00
(Stanley Cup parade with
Mark Messier raising cup)
16 Ottawa Senators 1.00 2.50
(Practice session)
17 Philadelphia Flyers 1.00 2.50
(Eric Lindros/Mark Recchi/Jason Bowen)
18 Pittsburgh Penguins 2.00 5.00
(Ron Francis/Joe Mullen)
19 Quebec Nordiques 2.00 5.00
(Joe Sakic et al.)

20 St. Louis Blues 1.00 2.50
(Curtis Joseph)
21 San Jose Sharks 1.00 2.50
(Tom Pederson/Sergei Makarov)
22 Tampa Bay Lightning 1.00 2.50
(Denis Savard/Petr Klima)
23 Toronto Maple Leafs 1.00 2.50
(Doug Gilmour/Dave Andreychuk)
24 Vancouver Canucks 2.00 5.00
(Pavel Bure et al.)
25 Washington Capitals 1.00 2.50
(Byron Dafoe/Dave Poulin/
Kevin Hatcher/Calle Johansson)
26 Winnipeg Jets 2.00 5.00
(Teemu Selanne/Alexei Zhamnov)

1994-95 Stadium Club Super Team Winner

These cards were the prizes of the interactive game which allowed the holder to redeem the card if the pictured team won a division, conference or Stanley Cup championship. Holders of the New Jersey Devils card were able to redeem it for complete, specially stamped sets of Stadium Club and Finest. Winning division (Calgary, Detroit, Philadelphia, Quebec) and conference (Detroit, New Jersey) team cards were redeemable for packages of special stamped cards featuring members of that team.

COMPLETE SET (270) 50.00 100.00
*ST WINNERS: 2X TO 5X BASIC CARDS

1995 Stadium Club Members Only

Topps produced a 50-card boxed set for each of the four major sports. With their club membership, members received one set of their choice and had the option of purchasing additional sets for $10.00 each. The five Finest cards (46-50) represent Topps' selection of the top 1994-95 rookies. The color action photos on the fronts have brightly-colored backgrounds and carry the distinctive Topps Stadium Club Members Only gold foil seal. The backs present a second color photo and player profile.

COMP. FACT SET (50) 10.00 25.00
1 Patrick Roy 1.00 2.50
2 Ray Bourque .20 .50
3 Brian Leetch .20 .50
4 Cam Neely .15 .40
5 Jaromir Jagr .60 1.50
6 Alexander Mogilny .15 .40
7 John Vanbiesbrouck .40 1.00
8 Geoff Sanderson .05 .15
9 Mark Recchi .08 .25
10 Scott Stevens .02 .10
11 Roman Hamrlik .05 .15
12 Dominik Hasek .40 1.00
13 Joe Sakic .40 1.00
14 Alexei Yashin .20 .50
15 Eric Lindros .60 1.50
16 Adam Oates .08 .25
17 Ulf Samuelsson .02 .10
18 Wendel Clark .05 .15
19 Mark Messier .30 .75
20 Pierre Turgeon .08 .25
21 Mark Tinordi .02 .10
22 Ron Francis .08 .25
23 Jeff Brown .02 .10
24 Tom Kurvers .02 .10
25 Mike Modano .30 .75
26 Mats Sundin .20 .50
27 Jeremy Roenick .20 .50
28 Kevin Hatcher .02 .10
29 Curtis Joseph .20 .50
30 Paul Coffey .20 .50
31 Jason Arnott .08 .25
32 Wayne Gretzky 1.25 3.00
33 Theo Fleury .20 .50
34 Al MacInnis .07 .20
35 Ed Belfour .20 .50
36 Sergei Fedorov .40 1.00
37 Brett Hull .30 .75
38 Chris Chelios .20 .50
39 Keith Tkachuk .30 .75
40 Felix Potvin .20 .50
41 Pavel Bure .40 1.00
42 Ulf Dahlen .02 .10
43 Teemu Selanne .40 1.00
44 Doug Gilmour .20 .50
45 Phil Housley .05 .15
46 Paul Kariya FIN 2.50 6.00
47 Peter Forsberg FIN 2.00 5.00
48 Jim Carey FIN .60 1.50
49 Todd Marchant FIN .20 .50
50 Blaine Lacher FIN .30 .75

1995-96 Stadium Club

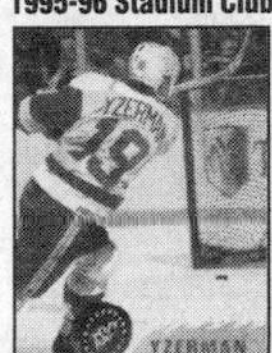

The 1995-96 Stadium Club set was issued in one series totaling 225 cards. The 10-card packs retail for $2.50. The set features two subsets: Extreme Corps (163-189) and Extreme Rookies (190-207). One EC or ER subset card was included per hobby or retail pack (1:2 Canadian packs), making them somewhat more difficult to obtain than regular singles. Of note is the Stadium Club logo on the card fronts, which features the brand name translated into the primary language of the player featured. Rookie Cards in this set include Daniel Alfredsson.

COMPLETE SET (225) 25.00 50.00
1 Alexander Mogilny .05 .15
2 Ray Bourque .20 .50
3 Garry Galley .02 .10
4 Glen Wesley .02 .10
5 Dave Andreychuk .05 .15
6 Daren Puppa .05 .15
7 Shayne Corson .02 .10
8 Kelly Hrudey .05 .15
9 Russ Courtnall .02 .10
10 Chris Chelios .08 .25
11 Ulf Samuelsson .02 .10
12 Mike Vernon .05 .15
13 Al MacInnis .05 .15
14 Joel Otto .02 .10
15 Patrick Roy .60 1.50
16 Steve Thomas .05 .15
17 Pat Verbeek .02 .10
18 Joe Nieuwendyk .05 .15
19 Todd Krygier .02 .10
20 Steve Yzerman .60 1.50
21 Bill Ranford UER .05 .15
22 Ron Francis .05 .15
23 Sylvain Cote .02 .10
24 Grant Fuhr .08 .25
25 Brendan Shanahan .08 .25
26 John MacLean .05 .15
27 Darren Turcotte .02 .10
28 Bernie Nicholls .02 .10
29 Sean Burke .05 .15
30 Brian Leetch .05 .15
31 Dave Gagner .02 .10
32 Rick Tocchet .05 .15
33 Ron Hextall .05 .15
34 Paul Coffey .08 .25
35 John Vanbiesbrouck .05 .15
36 Rod Brind'Amour .05 .15
37 Brian Savage .02 .10
38 Nelson Emerson .02 .10
39 Brian Bradley .02 .10
40 Adam Oates .05 .15
41 Kirk McLean .05 .15
42 Kevin Hatcher .02 .10
43 Mike Keane .02 .10
44 Don Beaupre .05 .15
45 Scott Stevens .05 .15
46 Dale Hawerchuk .08 .25
47 Scott Young .02 .10
48 Mark Recchi .05 .15
49 Mike Richter .08 .25
50 Kevin Stevens .02 .10
51 Mike Ridley .02 .10
52 Joe Murphy .02 .10
53 Stephane Fiset .05 .15
54 Donald Audette .02 .10
55 Ed Belfour .08 .25
56 Rob Blake .05 .15
57 Adam Graves .05 .15
58 Arturs Irbe .05 .15
59 Mathieu Schneider .02 .10
60 Dominik Hasek .25 .60
61 Andrew Cassels .02 .10
62 Johan Garpenlov .02 .10
63 Kyle McLaren RC .02 .10
64 Petr Nedved .05 .15
65 Owen Nolan .05 .15
66 Keith Primeau .02 .10
67 Mark Tinordi .02 .10
68 Dimitri Khristich .02 .10
69 Chris Pronger .08 .25
70 Jaromir Jagr .20 .50
71 Mike Ricci .05 .15
72 Trevor Kidd .05 .15
73 Stu Barnes .02 .10
74 Doug Weight .05 .15
75 Mats Sundin .08 .25
76 Scott Niedermayer .02 .10
77 John LeClair .08 .25
78 Derian Hatcher .02 .10
79 Brad May .02 .10
80 Felix Potvin .08 .25
81 Derek King .02 .10
82 Guy Hebert .05 .15
83 Shawn McEachern .02 .10
84 Slava Kozlov .05 .15
85 Martin Brodeur .30 .75
86 Ray Whitney .05 .15
87 Martin Straka .02 .10
88 Keith Jones .05 .15
89 Roman Hamrlik .05 .15
90 Keith Tkachuk .08 .25
91 Jim Dowd .02 .10
92 Sergei Zubov .02 .10
93 Bryan McCabe .02 .10
94 Rob Niedermayer .05 .15
95 Alexei Zhamnov .05 .15
96 Zarley Zalapski .02 .10
97 Alexandre Daigle .02 .10
98 Jocelyn Thibault .08 .25
99 Zigmund Palffy .05 .15
100 Luc Robitaille .05 .15
101 Radek Bonk .02 .10
102 Todd Marchant .02 .10
103 Todd Harvey .05 .15
104 Blaine Lacher .05 .15
105 Peter Forsberg .30 .75
106 Jeff Friesen .02 .10
107 Kenny Jonsson .02 .10
108 Brett Lindros .02 .10
109 David Oliver .02 .10
110 Mikael Renberg .05 .15
111 Alexander Selivanov .02 .10
112 Stanislav Neckar .02 .10
113 Oleg Tverdovsky .05 .15
114 Shean Donovan .02 .10
115 Jim Carey .05 .15
116 Tony Granato .02 .10
117 Tony Amonte .05 .15
118 Tomas Sandstrom .02 .10
119 Rick Tabaracci .05 .15
120 Ray Ferraro .02 .10
121 Brian Noonan .02 .10
122 Miroslav Satan RC .60 1.50
123 Sergio Momesso .02 .10
124 Gary Suter .02 .10
125 Eric Desjardins .05 .15
126 Steve Duchesne .02 .10
127 Zdeno Ciger .02 .10
128 Cliff Ronning .02 .10
129 Nicklas Lidstrom .08 .25
130 Bill Guerin .05 .15
131 Igor Korolev .02 .10
132 Roman Oksiuta .02 .10
133 Jesse Belanger .02 .10
134 Chris Gratton .05 .15
135 Chris Osgood .05 .15
136 Pat Peake .02 .10
137 Viktor Kozlov .05 .15
138 Aaron Gavey .02 .10
139 Zdenek Nedved .02 .10
140 Rhett Warrener .02 .10
141 Marko Kiprusoff .02 .10
142 Dan Quinn .02 .10
143 Alexei Zhitnik .02 .10
144 Larry Murphy .05 .15
145 Phil Housley .05 .15
146 Don Sweeney .02 .10
147 Jason Dawe .02 .10
148 Marcus Ragnarsson RC .05 .15
149 Andrei Nikolishin .02 .10
150 Dino Ciccarelli .05 .15
151 Jari Kurri .08 .25
152 Bob Probert .05 .15
153 Randy McKay .02 .10
154 Michael Nylander .02 .10
155 Wendel Clark .05 .15
156 Antti Tormanen RC .02 .10
157 Nikolai Khabibulin .05 .15
158 Tom Barrasso .05 .15
159 Vincent Damphousse .02 .10
160 Trevor Linden .05 .15
161 Valeri Kamensky .05 .15
162 Mike Gartner .05 .15
163 Cam Neely EC .20 .50
164 Pat LaFontaine EC .20 .50
165 Theo Fleury EC .20 .50
166 Jeremy Roenick EC .30 .75
167 Joe Sakic EC 1.00 2.50
168 Mike Modano EC .60 1.50
169 Sergei Fedorov EC .60 1.50
170 Scott Mellanby EC .20 .50
171 Jason Arnott EC .25 .60
172 Geoff Sanderson EC .20 .50
173 Wayne Gretzky EC 4.00 8.00
174 Paul Kariya EC 1.25 3.00
175 Pierre Turgeon EC .20 .50
176 Stephane Richer EC .20 .50
177 Kirk Muller EC .20 .50
178 Mark Messier EC .20 .50
179 Craig Janney EC .20 .50
180 Mario Lemieux EC 3.00 6.00
181 Eric Lindros EC .20 .50
182 Alexei Yashin EC .20 .50
183 Brett Hull EC .50 1.25
184 Doug Gilmour EC .30 .75
185 Petr Klima EC .20 .50
186 Pavel Bure EC .20 .50
187 Joe Juneau EC .20 .50
188 Teemu Selanne EC .20 .50
189 Claude Lemieux EC .20 .50
190 Vitali Yachmenev ER .20 .50
191 Jason Bonsignore ER .20 .50
192 Jeff O'Neill ER .20 .50
193 Brendan Witt ER .20 .50
194 Brian Holzinger ER RC .20 .50
195 Eric Daze ER .20 .50
196 Ed Jovanovski ER .20 .50
197 Deron Quint ER .20 .50
198 Marty Murray ER .20 .50
199 Jere Lehtinen ER .20 .50
200 Radek Dvorak ER RC .30 .75
201 Aki Berg ER RC .20 .50
202 Chad Kilger ER RC .20 .50
203 Saku Koivu ER .30 .75
204 Todd Bertuzzi ER RC 1.50 4.00
205 Niklas Sundstrom ER .20 .50
206 Daniel Alfredsson ER RC 1.25 3.00
207 Shane Doan ER RC 1.25 3.00
208 Richard Park .02 .10
209 Peter Bondra .05 .15
210 Bryan Smolinski .02 .10
211 Tommy Salo .05 .15
212 Patrick Poulin .02 .10
213 Mathieu Dandenault RC .02 .10
214 Steve Rucchin .05 .15
215 Ray Sheppard .02 .10
216 Robert Svehla RC .02 .10
217 Olaf Kolzig .05 .15
218 Alexei Kovalev .02 .10
219 Ian Moran .02 .10
220 Valeri Bure .02 .10
221 Dean Malkoc .02 .10
222 Jason Doig .02 .10
223 David Nemirovsky RC .02 .10
224 Jamie Pushor .02 .10
225 Ricard Persson .02 .10

1995-96 Stadium Club Members Only Master Set

Parallel to base set that was only available to members of Topps Stadium Club. Cards are distinguishable by an embossed Members only logo.

*STARS: 10X TO 20X BASIC CARDS
*RC's:2X TO 5X BASIC CARDS

1995-96 Stadium Club Extreme North

Randomly inserted in packs at a rate of 1:48, this 9-card set focuses on some of the best players on Canadian teams. The cards are printed on diffraction foil.

COMPLETE SET (9) 20.00 40.00
EN1 Pavel Bure 2.00 5.00
EN2 Teemu Selanne 2.00 5.00
EN3 Felix Potvin 2.00 5.00
EN4 Patrick Roy 8.00 20.00
EN5 Theo Fleury 1.25 3.00
EN6 Bill Ranford 1.25 3.00
EN7 Pierre Turgeon 1.25 3.00
EN8 Doug Gilmour 1.25 3.00
EN9 Alexander Mogilny 1.25 3.00

1995-96 Stadium Club Extreme North Members Only Master Set

Issued to Stadium Club members only, this set parallels the basic cards with the exception of the words "Topp's Stadium Club Members Only" printed on the card front.

*STARS: .75X TO 2X BASIC INSERTS

1995-96 Stadium Club Fearless

Randomly inserted at a rate of 1:24 retail, and 1:48 hobby and Canadian packs, this 9-card set features hockey's toughest players on double diffraction foil-stamped cards.

COMPLETE SET (9) 8.00 15.00
F1 Brendan Shanahan 1.50 4.00
F2 Chris Chelios 1.50 4.00
F3 Keith Primeau .75 2.00
F4 Scott Stevens 1.25 3.00
F5 Rick Tocchet 1.25 3.00
F6 Kevin Stevens .75 2.00
F7 Ulf Samuelsson .75 2.00
F8 Wendel Clark 1.25 3.00
F9 Keith Tkachuk 1.50 4.00

1995-96 Stadium Club Fearless Members Only Master Set

Issued to Stadium Club members only, this set parallels the basic cards with the exception of the words "Topp's Stadium Club Members Only" printed on the card front.

*STARS: .75X TO 2X BASIC INSERTS

1995-96 Stadium Club Generation TSC

COMPLETE SET (9) 15.00 30.00
GT1 Paul Kariya 1.50 4.00
GT2 Teemu Selanne 1.50 4.00
GT3 Jaromir Jagr 2.00 5.00
GT4 Peter Forsberg 3.00 8.00
GT5 Martin Brodeur 4.00 10.00
GT6 Jim Carey .75 2.00
GT7 Mikael Renberg .75 2.00
GT8 Scott Niedermayer .75 2.00
GT9 Ed Jovanovski .75 2.00

1995-96 Stadium Club Generation TSC Members Only Master Set

Issued to Stadium Club members only, this set parallels the basic cards with the exception of the words "Topp's Stadium Club Members Only" printed on the card front.

*STARS: 2.5X TO 5X BASIC INSERTS

1995-96 Stadium Club Metalists

Randomly inserted at a rate of 1:48 hobby, 1:96 retail, and 1:192 Canadian packs, this 12-card set showcases players who have won two or more major awards during their career on the first ever laser-cut foil hockey cards.

COMPLETE SET (12) 25.00 60.00
M1 Wayne Gretzky 10.00 25.00
M2 Mario Lemieux 6.00 15.00
M3 Patrick Roy 6.00 15.00
M4 Ray Bourque 1.50 4.00
M5 Ed Belfour 1.50 4.00
M6 Tom Barrasso 1.00 2.50
M7 Joe Mullen 1.00 2.50
M8 Brian Leetch 1.00 2.50
M9 Mark Messier 1.50 4.00
M10 Dominik Hasek 3.00 8.00
M11 Paul Coffey 1.00 2.50
M12 Guy Carbonneau 1.00 2.50

1995-96 Stadium Club Metalists Members Only Master Set

Issued to Stadium Club members only, this set parallels the basic cards with the exception of the words "Topp's Stadium Club Members Only" printed on the card front.

*STARS: .75X TO 2X BASIC INSERTS

1995-96 Stadium Club Nemeses

Randomly inserted at a rate of 1:24 hobby, 1:48 retail, and 1:96 Canadian packs, this 9-card set highlights two rival players together on one card. The cards use etched foil on each side.

COMPLETE SET (9) 25.00 60.00
N1 Eric Lindros 1.50 4.00
Scott Stevens
N2 W.Gretzky/M.Lemieux 10.00 25.00
N3 Claude Lemieux 1.50 4.00
Cam Neely
N4 Pavel Bure 1.50 4.00
Mike Richter
N5 Brian Leetch 2.50 6.00
Ray Bourque
N6 Martin Brodeur 4.00 10.00
Dominik Hasek
N7 Doug Gilmour 2.50 6.00
Sergei Fedorov
N8 Mark Messier 1.50 4.00
Joel Otto
N9 Paul Kariya 4.00 10.00
Peter Forsberg

1995-96 Stadium Club Nemeses Members Only Master Set

Issued to Stadium Club members only, this set parallels the basic cards with the exception of the words "Topp's Stadium Club Members Only" printed on the card front.

*STARS: .75X TO 2X BASIC INSERTS

1995-96 Stadium Club Power Streak

Randomly inserted at a rate of 1:12 retail, and 1:24 hobby and Canadian packs, this set features 10 players who have sustained prolonged goal scoring streaks. The cards are printed using Power Matrix technology.

COMPLETE SET (10) 5.00 12.00
PS1 Pierre Turgeon .40 1.00
PS2 Eric Lindros 1.25 3.00
PS3 Ron Francis .75 2.00
PS4 Paul Coffey .75 2.00
PS5 Mikael Renberg .40 1.00
PS6 John LeClair .40 1.00
PS7 Dino Ciccarelli .40 1.00
PS8 Wendel Clark .75 2.00
PS9 Brett Hull 1.25 3.00
PS10 Stephane Richer .40 1.00

1995-96 Stadium Club Power Streak Members Only Master Set

Issued to Stadium Club members only, this set parallels the basic cards with the exception of the words "Topp's Stadium Club Members Only" printed on the card front.

*STARS: 2.5X TO 5X BASIC INSERTS

1995-96 Stadium Club Master Photo Test

This nine-card set measures approximately 3" by 5" and features color action player photos from the 1995-96 Stadium Club set inside a black border bearing the words Master Photo. The backs carry the TSC, NHL, and NHLPA logos. No further information on origin or distribution is available. The cards are unnumbered and checklisted below in alphabetical order. This may be an incomplete checklist; additional information would be appreciated.

COMPLETE SET (9) 25.00 60.00
1 Jason Arnott 2.00 5.00
2 Theo Fleury 4.00 10.00
3 Doug Gilmour 4.00 10.00
4 Trevor Linden 4.00 10.00
5 Kirk McLean 2.00 5.00
6 Alexander Mogilny 2.00 5.00
7 Felix Potvin 4.00 10.00
8 Mats Sundin 6.00 15.00
9 Alexei Yashin 2.00 5.00

1996 Stadium Club Members Only

This 50-card set was available through the direct marketing arm of the Topps Stadium Club. The first 45 cards feature the competitors in the 1996 NHL All-Star Game. The players are pictured in their AS sweaters over a stylized background. the back includes a portrait and player profile. The final five cards in the set picture some of the year's top rookies on Finest-style technology.

COMPLETE SET (50) 8.00 20.00
1 Wayne Gretzky 1.50 4.00
2 Paul Kariya 1.00 2.50
3 Brett Hull .30 .75
4 Chris Chelios .25 .60
5 Paul Coffey .25 .60
6 Ed Belfour .25 .60
7 Theo Fleury .25 .60
8 Owen Nolan .08 .25
9 Al MacInnis .08 .25
10 Alexander Mogilny .20 .50
11 Kevin Hatcher .02 .10
12 Doug Weight .15 .40
13 Felix Potvin .20 .50
14 Teemu Selanne .50 1.25
15 Sergei Fedorov .50 1.25
16 Larry Murphy .02 .10
17 Joe Sakic .50 1.25
18 Mats Sundin .25 .60
19 Nicklas Lidstrom .08 .25
20 Peter Forsberg .60 1.50
21 Chris Osgood .25 .60
22 Mike Gartner .05 .15
23 Denis Savard .05 .15
Craig MacTavish
24 Mario Lemieux 1.25 3.00
25 Jaromir Jagr .75 2.00
26 Brendan Shanahan .50 1.25
27 Scott Stevens .05 .15
28 Ray Bourque .30 .75
29 Martin Brodeur .60 1.50
30 Eric Lindros .75 2.00
31 Peter Bondra .25 .60
32 Scott Mellanby .02 .10
33 Brian Leetch .25 .60
34 John Vanbiesbrouck .25 .60
35 Pat Verbeek .07 .20
36 Cam Neely .20 .50
37 Roman Hamrlik .15 .40
38 Daniel Alfredsson .20 .50
39 Pierre Turgeon .20 .50
40 Mark Messier .30 .75
41 Eric Desjardins .02 .10
42 Dominik Hasek .50 1.25
43 John LeClair .40 1.00
44 Mathieu Schneider .02 .10
45 Ron Francis .20 .50
46 Saku Koivu 1.25 3.00
47 Ed Jovanovski .20 .50
48 Vitali Yachmenev .40 1.00
49 Petr Sykora .75 2.00
50 Eric Daze .75 2.00

1999-00 Stadium Club Promos

Sent out to dealers with the press release for Stadium Club, this 6-card set debuts the new card design for the 1999-2000 brand.

COMPLETE SET (6) .75 2.00
PP1 Chris Osgood .20 .50
PP2 Steve Konowalchuk .08 .25
PP3 Jeremy Roenick .40 1.00
PP4 Rod Brind'Amour .20 .50
PP5 Mattias Norstrom .08 .25
PP6 Clarke Wilm .08 .25

1999-00 Stadium Club

Released as a 200-card set, Stadium Club featured flawless player action shots and blue foil highlights on every base card. Stadium Club was packaged in 24-pack boxes with packs containing six cards and one checklist. Packs carried a suggested retail price of $2.00.

COMPLETE SET (200) 30.00 60.00
1 Jaromir Jagr .30 .75
2 Mats Sundin .20 .50
3 Mark Messier .20 .50
4 Paul Kariya .20 .50
5 Ray Bourque .30 .75
6 Tony Amonte .15 .40
7 Dominik Hasek .40 1.00
8 Peter Forsberg .50 1.25
9 Pavel Bure .20 .50
10 Nicklas Lidstrom .20 .50
11 Kenny Jonsson .05 .15
12 Brian Leetch .20 .50
13 Eric Lindros .20 .50
14 Al MacInnis .15 .40
15 Keith Tkachuk .20 .50
16 Martin Brodeur .50 1.25
17 Saku Koivu .20 .50
18 Jeff Friesen .05 .15
19 Olaf Kolzig .15 .40
20 Mike Modano .30 .75
21 Jarome Iginla .25 .60
22 Alexei Kovalev .05 .15
23 Vincent Lecavalier .20 .50
24 Greg Johnson .05 .15
25 Ron Francis .15 .40
26 Steve Konowalchuk .05 .15
27 Luc Robitaille .15 .40
28 Alexei Yashin .15 .40
29 Mark Parrish .05 .15
30 Todd Warriner .05 .15
31 Brett Hull .25 .60
32 Steve Dubinsky .05 .15
33 Rod Brind'Amour .15 .40
34 Bill Muckalt .05 .15
35 Bryan Berard .05 .15
36 Manny Malhotra .15 .40
37 Jozef Stumpel .15 .40
38 Sergei Fedorov .30 .75
39 Roman Vopat .15 .40
40 Teemu Selanne .20 .50
41 Teppo Numminen .05 .15
42 Mats Lindgren .05 .15
43 Chris Gratton .05 .15
44 Owen Nolan .15 .40
45 Scott Niedermayer .05 .15
46 Sergei Krivokrasov .05 .15
47 Joe Sakic .40 1.00
48 Bill Guerin .05 .15
49 Shayne Corson .05 .15
50 Eric Daze .15 .40
51 Clarke Wilm .05 .15
52 Magnus Arvedson .05 .15
53 Sergei Berezin .05 .15
54 Derian Hatcher .05 .15
55 Jeremy Roenick .25 .60
56 Adam Oates .15 .40
57 Dixon Ward .05 .15
58 Petr Nedved .15 .40
59 Joe Reekie .05 .15
60 Milan Hejduk .20 .50
61 Mike Grier .05 .15
62 Martin Straka .05 .15
63 Petr Sykora .05 .15
64 Harry York .05 .15
65 John LeClair .20 .50
66 Patrick Roy 1.00 2.50
67 Arturs Irbe .05 .15
68 Murray Baron .05 .15
69 Felix Potvin .15 .40
70 Pavol Demitra .15 .40
71 Ray Whitney .05 .15
72 Patrick Marleau .20 .50
73 Tom Fitzgerald .05 .15
74 Jamal Mayers .05 .15
75 Joe Thornton .30 .75
76 Craig Rivet .05 .15
77 Ed Belfour .20 .50
78 Stephane Fiset .15 .40
79 Alexander Karpovtsev .05 .15
80 Miroslav Satan .05 .15
81 Doug Weight .15 .40
82 Marian Hossa .20 .50
83 Markus Naslund .20 .50
84 Derek Morris .05 .15
85 Mike Richter .20 .50
86 Scott Young .05 .15
87 Darcy Tucker .05 .15
88 Jason Allison .05 .15
89 Chris Osgood .20 .50
90 Doug Gilmour .15 .40
91 Ron Tugnutt .15 .40
92 Adam Deadmarsh .05 .15
93 Byron Dafoe .15 .40
94 Rick Tocchet .15 .40
95 Mike Johnson .05 .15
96 Guy Hebert .15 .40
97 Cory Stillman .15 .40
98 Daniel Alfredsson .15 .40
99 Tom Barrasso .15 .40
100 Peter Bondra .15 .40
101 Rob Blake .15 .40
102 Gary Roberts .05 .15
103 Cliff Ronning .05 .15
104 Jason Woolley .05 .15
105 Keith Primeau .05 .15
106 Brendan Shanahan .20 .50
107 Alexei Zhamnov .15 .40
108 Bobby Holik .05 .15
109 Mark Recchi .15 .40
110 Eric Brewer .05 .15
111 Mike Ricci .15 .40
112 Pierre Turgeon .15 .40
113 Martin Rucinsky .05 .15
114 Chris McAllister RC .05 .15
115 Patrik Elias .15 .40
116 Alexander Selivanov .05 .15
117 Fredrik Olausson .05 .15
118 Curtis Joseph .20 .50
119 Wade Redden .05 .15
120 Nikolai Khabibulin .15 .40
121 Chris Drury .15 .40
122 Chris Chelios .20 .50
123 Vincent Damphousse .05 .15
124 Mattias Ohlund .15 .40
125 Mike Dunham .15 .40
126 John Vanbiesbrouck .15 .40
127 John MacLean .15 .40
128 Jocelyn Thibault .15 .40
129 Jan Hrdina .05 .15
130 Mariusz Czerkawski .05 .15
131 Pavel Kubina .05 .15
132 Scott Stevens .15 .40
133 Mattias Norstrom .05 .15
134 Sami Kapanen .05 .15
135 Sergei Samsonov .15 .40
136 Tom Poti .05 .15
137 Steve Shields .15 .40
138 Anson Carter .15 .40
139 Chris McAlpine .05 .15
140 Rob Niedermayer .05 .15
141 Michael Peca .05 .15
142 Valeri Bure .05 .15
143 Joe Nieuwendyk .15 .40
144 Jose Theodore .25 .60
145 Steve Yzerman 1.00 2.50
146 Chris Pronger .15 .40
147 Marty McInnis .05 .15
148 Jere Lehtinen .05 .15
149 Adam Graves .05 .15
150 Deron Quint .05 .15
151 Ray Ferraro .05 .15
152 Niklas Sundstrom .05 .15
153 Damian Rhodes .15 .40
154 Zigmund Palffy .15 .40
155 Valeri Kamensky .05 .15
156 Oleg Tverdovsky .15 .40
157 Bill Ranford .15 .40
158 Kelly Buchberger .05 .15
159 Trevor Linden .05 .15
160 Bryan McCabe .05 .15
161 Dan Cloutier .05 .15
162 Olli Jokinen .15 .40
163 Theo Fleury .05 .15
164 Dave Andreychuk .05 .15
165 Gord Murphy .05 .15
166 Steve Duchesne .15 .40
167 Marc Savard .05 .15
168 Maxim Afinogenov .05 .15
169 Mark Eaton RC .15 .40
170 Pavel Patera RC .05 .15
171 Nikolai Antropov RC .75 2.00
172 Ivan Novoseltsev RC .50 1.25
173 Jochen Hecht RC 1.00 2.50
174 Mike Ribeiro .05 .15
175 Yuri Butsayev RC .05 .15
176 Jorgen Jonsson RC .05 .15
177 Dan Hinote RC .05 .15
178 Dave Tanabe .05 .15
179 John Grahame RC .50 1.25
180 Mika Alatalo RC .15 .40
181 Patrik Stefan RC .50 1.25
182 Mike Fisher RC .40 1.00
183 Niclas Havelid RC .15 .40
184 Paul Comrie RC .05 .15
185 Michal Rozsival RC .05 .15
186 Oleg Saprykin RC .50 1.25
187 Martin Skoula RC .20 .50
188 Simon Gagne .20 .50
189 Brian Rafalski RC .50 1.25
190 J-P Dumont .15 .40
191 Martin Biron .15 .40
192 Rico Fata .05 .15
193 Jan Hlavac .05 .15
194 Alex Tanguay .15 .40
195 Brad Stuart .15 .40
196 Brian Boucher .20 .50
197 Steve Kariya RC .40 1.00
198 Scott Gomez .05 .15
199 Tim Connolly .25 .60
200 David Legwand .15 .40

1999-00 Stadium Club First Day Issue

Randomly inserted in Retail packs at the rate of one in 12, this 200-card set parallels the base Stadium Club set. Each card is enhanced with a foil "First Day Issue" stamp and is sequentially numbered to 150.

*VETS: 12.5X TO 30X BASIC CARDS
*ROOKIES: 3X TO 8X BASIC CARDS

1999-00 Stadium Club One of a Kind

Randomly inserted in Hobby packs, this 200-card set parallels the base Stadium Club set. Each card is sequentially numbered to 150.

*VETS: 12.5X TO 30X BASIC CARDS
*ROOKIES: 3X TO 8X BASIC CARDS

1999-00 Stadium Club Printing Plates Black

Randomly inserted in Hobby packs, one version of each color proof exists for the 200 different cards in the set. These are the proofs that were used in the printing process of Stadium Club.

NOT PRICED DUE TO SCARCITY

1999-00 Stadium Club Printing Plates Cyan

Randomly inserted in Hobby packs, one version of each color proof exists for the 200 different cards in the set. These are the proofs that were used in the printing process of Stadium Club.

NOT PRICED DUE TO SCARCITY

1999-00 Stadium Club Printing Plates Magenta

Randomly inserted in Hobby packs, one version of each color proof exists for the 200 different cards in the set. These are the proofs that were used in the printing process of Stadium Club.

NOT PRICED DUE TO SCARCITY

1999-00 Stadium Club Printing Plates Yellow

Randomly inserted in Hobby packs, one version of each color proof exists for the 200 different cards in the set. These are the proofs that were used in the printing process of Stadium Club.

NOT PRICED DUE TO SCARCITY

1999-00 Stadium Club Capture the Action

Randomly inserted in packs at the rate of 1:12, this 30-card set features blue borders on the top and bottom framing full color close up "in the game" action photographs. Game view parallels were also created and inserted at 1:118. The parallels were serial numbered to just 100.

COMPLETE SET (30) 40.00 80.00
*GAME VIEW/100: 6X TO 15X BASIC INSERTS
CA1 Bill Muckalt .60 1.50
CA2 Chris Drury .75 2.00
CA3 Milan Hejduk 1.25 3.00
CA4 Mark Parrish .60 1.50
CA5 Marian Hossa 1.00 2.50
CA6 Manny Malhotra .75 2.00
CA7 J-P Dumont .75 2.00
CA8 Eric Brewer .60 1.50
CA9 Vincent Lecavalier 1.00 2.50
CA10 Jan Hrdina .60 1.50
CA11 Paul Kariya 1.00 2.50
CA12 Peter Forsberg 2.50 6.00
CA13 Eric Lindros 1.00 2.50
CA14 Martin Brodeur 2.50 6.00
CA15 Teemu Selanne 1.00 2.50
CA16 Keith Tkachuk 1.00 2.50
CA17 Mats Sundin 1.00 2.50
CA18 Pavel Bure 1.00 2.50
CA19 Mike Modano 1.50 4.00
CA20 Nicklas Lidstrom 1.00 2.50
CA21 Ray Bourque 1.50 4.00
CA22 Dominik Hasek 2.00 5.00
CA23 Patrick Roy 5.00 12.00
CA24 Mark Messier 1.00 2.50
CA25 Steve Yzerman 5.00 12.00
CA26 Jaromir Jagr 1.50 4.00
CA27 Paul Coffey 1.00 2.50
CA28 Brett Hull 1.25 3.00
CA29 Al MacInnis .75 2.00
CA30 Larry Murphy .75 2.00

1999-00 Stadium Club Chrome

Randomly inserted in packs at the rate of 1:4, this 50-card set utilizes the base card style, but issues this set on an all foil card stock. Chrome refractor parallels were also created and inserted at a rate of 1:8.

COMPLETE SET (50) 30.00 60.00
*REFRACTORS: .8X TO 2X BASIC INSERTS
1 Jaromir Jagr 1.00 2.50
2 Mats Sundin .60 1.50
3 Mark Messier .60 1.50
4 Paul Kariya .60 1.50
5 Ray Bourque 1.00 2.50
6 Tony Amonte .50 1.25
7 Dominik Hasek 1.25 3.00
8 Peter Forsberg 1.50 4.00
9 Pavel Bure .60 1.50
10 Nicklas Lidstrom .60 1.50
11 Brian Leetch .50 1.25
12 Eric Lindros .60 1.50
13 Al MacInnis .50 1.25
14 Keith Tkachuk .60 1.50
15 Martin Brodeur 1.50 4.00
16 Saku Koivu .60 1.50
17 Jeff Friesen .50 1.25
18 Mike Modano 1.00 2.50
19 Vincent Lecavalier .60 1.50
20 Luc Robitaille .50 1.25
21 Brett Hull .75 2.00
22 Teemu Selanne .60 1.50
23 Joe Sakic 1.25 3.00
24 Jeremy Roenick .75 2.00
25 John LeClair .60 1.50
26 Patrick Roy 3.00 8.00
27 Joe Thornton 1.00 2.50
28 Ed Belfour .60 1.50
29 Doug Weight .50 1.25
30 Marian Hossa .60 1.50
31 Chris Osgood .50 1.25
32 Daniel Alfredsson .50 1.25
33 Peter Bondra .50 1.25
34 Brendan Shanahan .60 1.50
35 Curtis Joseph .60 1.50
36 Chris Drury .50 1.25
37 Sergei Samsonov .50 1.25
38 Anson Carter .50 1.25
39 Joe Nieuwendyk .50 1.25
40 Steve Yzerman 3.00 8.00
41 Zigmund Palffy .50 1.25
42 Theo Fleury .50 1.25
43 Patrik Stefan 1.00 2.50
44 Simon Gagne .60 1.50
45 J-P Dumont .50 1.25
46 Alex Tanguay .50 1.25
47 Steve Kariya .50 1.25
48 Scott Gomez .50 1.25
49 Tim Connolly .75 2.00
50 David Legwand .50 1.25

1999-00 Stadium Club Chrome Oversized

Inserted one per hobby box, this 20-card set utilizes the same design as the base set on oversized cards. Refractor parallels were also created and inserted randomly.

COMPLETE SET (20) 50.00 100.00
*REFRACTORS: .8X TO 2X BASIC INSERTS
1 Jaromir Jagr 1.50 4.00
2 Mats Sundin 1.00 2.50
3 Paul Kariya 1.00 2.50
4 Ray Bourque 1.50 4.00
5 Dominik Hasek 2.00 5.00
6 Peter Forsberg 2.50 6.00
7 Pavel Bure 1.00 2.50
8 Eric Lindros 1.00 2.50
9 Martin Brodeur 2.50 6.00
10 Mike Modano 1.50 4.00
11 Teemu Selanne 1.00 2.50
12 Joe Sakic 2.00 5.00
13 Patrick Roy 5.00 12.00
14 Marian Hossa 1.00 2.50
15 Curtis Joseph 1.00 2.50
16 Steve Yzerman 5.00 12.00
17 Theo Fleury .75 2.00
18 Patrik Stefan 1.50 4.00
19 Steve Kariya .75 2.00
20 David Legwand .75 2.00

1999-00 Stadium Club Co-Signers

Randomly inserted in Hobby packs at the rate of 1:237, this 15-card set features two autographs on each card. Some cards were issued in exchange form.

CS1 Chris Drury / Brendan Morrison 10.00 25.00
CS2 Brendan Morrison / Marian Hossa 10.00 25.00
CS3 Marian Hossa / Chris Drury 10.00 25.00
CS4 Jaromir Jagr / Mats Sundin 30.00 80.00
CS5 Jaromir Jagr / Alexei Yashin 25.00 60.00
CS6 John LeClair / Jaromir Jagr 40.00 100.00
CS7 Alexei Yashin / Mats Sundin 12.00 30.00
CS8 Mats Sundin / John LeClair 12.00 30.00
CS9 Alexei Yashin / John LeClair 10.00 25.00
CS10 Chris Osgood / Ed Belfour 30.00 80.00
CS11 Chris Osgood / Curtis Joseph 25.00 60.00
CS12 Ed Belfour / Curtis Joseph 30.00 80.00
CS13 Ray Bourque / Al MacInnis 50.00 100.00
CS14 Al MacInnis / Wade Redden 10.00 25.00
CS15 Wade Redden / Ray Bourque 25.00 60.00

1999-00 Stadium Club Eyes of the Game

Randomly seeded in packs at the rate of 1:15, this 10-card set features colored borders on the top and bottom and close up portrait photography of each respective player. Refractor parallels were also created and inserted at a rate of 1:75.

COMPLETE SET (10) 8.00 15.00
*REFRACTORS: 1.5X TO 4X BASIC INSERTS
EG1 Jaromir Jagr 1.00 2.50
EG2 Peter Forsberg 1.50 4.00
EG3 Paul Kariya .60 1.50
EG4 Teemu Selanne .60 1.50
EG5 Joe Sakic 1.25 3.00
EG6 Eric Lindros .60 1.50
EG7 Jason Allison .50 1.25
EG8 Mats Sundin .60 1.50
EG9 Pavol Demitra .50 1.25
EG10 Rod Brind'Amour .50 1.25

1999-00 Stadium Club Goalie Cam

Randomly seeded in packs at the rate of 1:24, this 7-card set puts collectors on the ice with photography taken from goalie cams.

COMPLETE SET (7) 8.00 15.00
GC1 Dominik Hasek 2.00 5.00
GC2 Martin Brodeur 2.50 6.00
GC3 Byron Dafoe .75 2.00
GC4 Olaf Kolzig .75 2.00
GC5 Mike Richter 1.00 2.50
GC6 Ron Tugnutt .75 2.00
GC7 Tom Barrasso .75 2.00

1999-00 Stadium Club Lone Star Signatures

Released as a tier insert program, cards LS1-LS3 are seeded at 1:1675, cards LS4-LS9 are seeded at 1:558, card LS10 is seeded at 1:2233, and cards LS11-13 are seeded at 1:419. Each card features an authentic player autograph. Some players were released in exchange card form.

LS1 Jaromir Jagr 40.00 100.00
LS2 Alexei Yashin 5.00 12.00
LS3 Mats Sundin 25.00 60.00
LS4 Ray Bourque 25.00 60.00
LS5 Al MacInnis 6.00 15.00
LS6 Wade Redden 5.00 12.00
LS7 Chris Osgood 6.00 15.00
LS8 Ed Belfour 8.00 20.00
LS9 Curtis Joseph 20.00 50.00
LS10 John LeClair 8.00 20.00
LS11 Chris Drury 6.00 15.00
LS12 Brendan Morrison 6.00 15.00
LS13 Marian Hossa 8.00 20.00

1999-00 Stadium Club Onyx Extreme

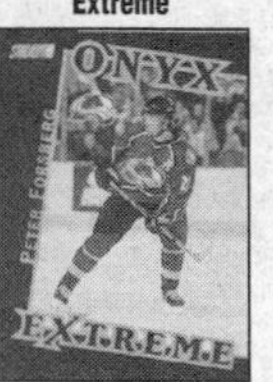

Randomly inserted in packs at the rate of 1:15, this 10-card set features black textured borders around full color action player photos. Each card is enhanced with silver foil highlights. A die-cut parallel was also created and inserted at a rate of 1:75.

COMPLETE SET (10) 8.00 15.00
*DIE-CUT: 1.5X TO 4X BASIC INSERTS
OE1 Jaromir Jagr 1.00 2.50
OE2 Peter Forsberg 1.50 4.00
OE3 Dominik Hasek 1.25 3.00
OE4 Eric Lindros .50 1.25
OE5 Paul Kariya .50 1.25
OE6 Joe Sakic 1.25 3.00
OE7 Nicklas Lidstrom .50 1.25
OE8 Teemu Selanne .50 1.25
OE9 John LeClair .50 1.25
OE10 Pavel Bure .50 1.25

1999-00 Stadium Club Souvenirs

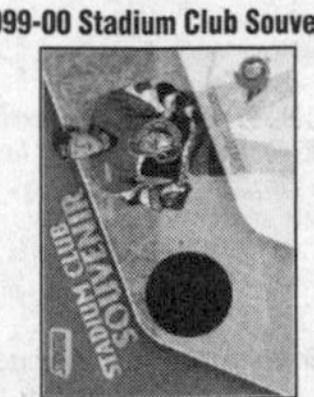

Randomly inserted in Hobby packs at 1:118 for jerseys and 1:197 for stick cards, this 6-card set features swatches of game used memorabilia. Stick cards were issued in redemption form. The MacInnis card appears to be short printed.

SAM Al MacInnis S 5.00 12.00
SCO Chris Osgood J 5.00 12.00
SEB Ed Belfour S 5.00 12.00
SJL John LeClair S 10.00 25.00
SMH Marian Hossa J 5.00 12.00
SMS Mats Sundin J 5.00 12.00

2000-01 Stadium Club

Released in mid December 2000, Stadium Club consists of a 260-card base set divided up into 227 regular player cards and 33 Draft Pick cards. Base set features a full bleed color photo on the top and a name box along the bottom enhanced with silver holofoil and textured like ice. Stadium Club was packaged in 24-pack boxes with packs containing seven cards and carried a suggested retail price of $2.45.

COMPLETE SET (260) 40.00 80.00
1 Pavel Bure .20 .50
2 Brendan Shanahan .20 .50
3 Chris Pronger .15 .40
4 Doug Weight .15 .40
5 Peter Forsberg .50 1.25
6 Jaromir Jagr .30 .75
7 Ed Belfour .20 .50
8 Rod Brind'Amour .15 .40
9 Mike Richter .20 .50
10 Mike Ricci .15 .40
11 Dimitri Yushkevich .05 .15
12 Dominik Hasek .40 1.00
13 Teemu Selanne .20 .50
14 Ed Jovanovski .05 .15
15 Damian Rhodes .05 .15
16 Martin Brodeur .50 1.25
17 Keith Primeau .05 .15
18 Byron Dafoe .15 .40
19 Jeff Hackett .15 .40
20 Brad Isbister .05 .15
21 Jeremy Roenick .25 .60
22 Jocelyn Thibault .15 .40
23 Ray Bourque .40 1.00
24 Steve Yzerman 1.00 2.50
25 Mike Dunham .15 .40
26 Bill Guerin .15 .40
27 Dan Cloutier .15 .40
28 Pavol Demitra .15 .40
29 Richard Smehlik .05 .15
30 Ron Francis .15 .40
31 Zigmund Palffy .15 .40
32 David Legwand .15 .40
33 Scott Stevens .15 .40
34 Daniel Alfredsson .15 .40
35 Michal Rozsival .05 .15
36 John LeClair .20 .50
37 Vincent Lecavalier .20 .50
38 Jason Allison .05 .15
39 Kenny Jonsson .05 .15
40 Patrick Roy 1.00 2.50
41 Derian Hatcher .05 .15
42 Chris Osgood .15 .40
43 Owen Nolan .15 .40
44 Mike York .05 .15
45 Ryan Smyth .15 .40
46 Alexei Kovalev .05 .15
47 Roman Turek .15 .40
48 Mark Recchi .15 .40
49 Ray Ferraro .05 .15
50 Sergei Samsonov .15 .40
51 Paul Kariya .20 .50
52 Jarome Iginla .25 .60
53 Martin Biron .15 .40
54 Tom Poti .05 .15
55 Trevor Linden .15 .40
56 Pierre Turgeon .15 .40
57 Scott Gomez .05 .15
58 Mattias Ohlund .05 .15
59 Tony Amonte .15 .40
60 Yannick Tremblay .05 .15
61 Cliff Ronning .05 .15
62 Marc Savard .15 .40
63 Viktor Kozlov .15 .40
64 Pavel Kubina .05 .15
65 Arturs Irbe .15 .40
66 Stephane Fiset .15 .40
67 John Madden .15 .40
68 Steve Shields .15 .40
69 Theo Fleury .05 .15
70 Chris Simon .05 .15
71 Andy Delmore .05 .15
72 Radek Bonk .05 .15
73 Michal Handzus .05 .15
74 Tommy Salo .15 .40
75 Felix Potvin .20 .50
76 Teppo Numminen .05 .15
77 Bobby Holik .05 .15
78 Phil Housley .15 .40
79 Sergei Gonchar .05 .15
80 Shawn McEachern .05 .15
81 Simon Gagne .20 .50
82 Mike Sillinger .05 .15
83 Tim Connolly .05 .15
84 Eric Daze .15 .40
85 Andrew Brunette .15 .40
86 Mike Modano .30 .75
87 Chris Drury .15 .40
88 Nicklas Lidstrom .20 .50
89 Joe Thornton .30 .75
90 Michael Peca .15 .40
91 Matt Cullen .05 .15
92 Robyn Regehr .05 .15
93 Todd Marchant .05 .15
94 Brett Hull .25 .60
95 Rob Blake .15 .40
96 Sergei Zholtok .05 .15
97 Eric Lindros .20 .50
98 Jean-Sebastien Aubin .15 .40
99 Jason Arnott .15 .40
100 Keith Tkachuk .20 .50
101 Wade Redden .15 .40
102 Sean Burke .15 .40
103 Marian Hossa .20 .50
104 Robert Lang .05 .15
105 Curtis Joseph .20 .50
106 Jeff Friesen .05 .15
107 Dennis Bonvie .05 .15
108 Alexander Korolyuk .05 .15
109 Eric Lacroix .05 .15
110 Todd Bertuzzi .20 .50
111 Bates Battaglia .05 .15
112 Jozef Stumpel .05 .15
113 Alexei Zhamnov .05 .15
114 Milan Hejduk .20 .50
115 Chris Chelios .20 .50
116 Adam Graves .05 .15
117 Patrik Stefan .05 .15
118 Guy Hebert .15 .40
119 Anson Carter .15 .40
120 Fred Brathwaite .15 .40
121 Maxim Afinogenov .05 .15
122 Eric Messier .05 .15
123 Ray Whitney .15 .40
124 Bob Bassen .05 .15
125 Patrick Lalime .15 .40
126 Jonas Hoglund .05 .15
127 Mike Johnson .05 .15
128 Peter Schaefer .05 .15
129 Olaf Kolzig .15 .40
130 Jamie Langenbrunner .05 .15
131 Scott Niedermayer .05 .15
132 Mariusz Czerkawski .05 .15
133 Petr Buzek .05 .15
134 Michal Grosek .05 .15
135 Valeri Bure .05 .15
136 Igor Korolev .05 .15
137 Oleg Tverdovsky .05 .15
138 Fredrik Modin .05 .15
139 Kyle McLaren .05 .15
140 Todd Gill .05 .15
141 Miroslav Satan .15 .40
142 Jeff O'Neill .05 .15
143 Steve Sullivan .05 .15
144 Jon Klemm .05 .15
145 Joe Nieuwendyk .15 .40
146 Luc Robitaille .15 .40
147 Patrice Brisebois .05 .15
148 Travis Green .05 .15
149 Patric Kjellberg .05 .15
150 Mats Sundin .20 .50
151 Brian Rolston .05 .15
152 Patrik Elias .15 .40
153 Markus Naslund .20 .50
154 Trevor Letowski .05 .15
155 Brad Stuart .15 .40
156 Doug Gilmour .15 .40
157 Alexander Mogilny .15 .40
158 Glen Wesley .05 .15
159 Petr Nedved .15 .40
160 Peter Bondra .20 .50
161 Alex Tanguay .15 .40
162 Steve Rucchin .05 .15
163 Nikolai Antropov .05 .15
164 Anders Eriksson .05 .15
165 Martin Rucinsky .05 .15
166 Trevor Kidd .05 .15
167 Zdeno Chara .05 .15
168 Adam Oates .15 .40
169 Eric Desjardins .15 .40
170 Petr Sykora .05 .15
171 Brenden Morrow .15 .40
172 Al MacInnis .15 .40
173 Ethan Moreau .05 .15
174 Chris Tamer .05 .15
175 Jaroslav Spacek .05 .15
176 Paul Mara .05 .15
177 Bryan Smolinski .05 .15
178 Yanic Perreault .05 .15
179 Vaclav Prospal .05 .15
180 Vitali Yachmenev .05 .15
181 Pavel Trnka .05 .15
182 Joe Sakic .40 1.00
183 Vincent Damphousse .05 .15
184 Sergei Fedorov .30 .75
185 Brian Rafalski .15 .40
186 Jochen Hecht .05 .15
187 Shane Doan .15 .40
188 Saku Koivu .20 .50
189 Richard Zednik .05 .15
190 Brian Boucher .20 .50
191 Jeff Halpern .15 .40
192 Matt Cooke .05 .15
193 Darcy Tucker .05 .15
194 Brian Leetch .15 .40
195 Glen Murray .05 .15
196 Robert Svehla .05 .15
197 Kimmo Timonen .05 .15
198 Claude Lapointe .05 .15
199 Brian Savage .05 .15
200 Sami Kapanen .05 .15
201 Scott Pellerin .05 .15
202 Cam Stewart .05 .15
203 Sergei Krivokrasov .05 .15
204 Manny Fernandez .15 .40
205 Darby Hendrickson .05 .15
206 Jamie McLennan .15 .40
207 Kevyn Adams .15 .40
208 Lyle Odelein .05 .15
209 Marc Denis .15 .40
210 Ron Tugnutt .15 .40
211 Tyler Wright .40 1.00
212 Geoff Sanderson .05 .15
213 Mark Messier .20 .50
214 Mike Vernon .15 .40
215 Dave Andreychuk .15 .40
216 Chris Murray .05 .15
217 Joe Juneau .05 .15
218 Vladimir Malakhov .05 .15
219 Paul Coffey .20 .50
220 Roberto Luongo .25 .60
221 Roman Hamrlik .15 .40
222 Sandis Ozolinsh .05 .15
223 Gary Roberts .05 .15
224 Boyd Devereaux .05 .15
225 Scott Thornton .05 .15
226 Igor Larionov .05 .15
227 John Vanbiesbrouck .15 .40
228 Milan Kraft 1.00 2.50
229 Steven McCarthy .40 1.00
230 Kris Beech .05 .15
231 Henrik Sedin .40 1.00
232 Daniel Sedin .40 1.00
233 Oleg Saprykin .40 1.00
234 Maxime Ouellet .40 1.00
235 Taylor Pyatt .40 1.00
236 Brent Johnson .40 1.00
237 Shawn Heins .40 1.00
238 Mika Noronen .40 1.00
239 Samuel Pahlsson .40 1.00
240 Dimitri Kalinin .40 1.00
241 Marian Gaborik RC 2.50 6.00
242 Petr Svoboda RC .40 1.00
243 Niclas Wallin RC .40 1.00
244 Dale Purinton RC .40 1.00
245 Justin Williams RC .75 2.00
246 Roman Simicek RC .40 1.00
247 Brad Tapper RC .40 1.00
248 Rostislav Klesla RC .75 2.00
249 Martin Havlat RC 1.50 4.00
250 Scott Hartnell RC .75 2.00
251 Andrew Raycroft RC 1.50 4.00
252 Ossi Vaananen RC .40 1.00
253 Steven Reinprecht RC .40 1.00
254 Josef Vasicek RC .40 1.00
255 Petr Hubacek RC .40 1.00
256 Lubomir Sekeras RC .40 1.00
257 David Aebischer RC 1.25 3.00
258 Jani Hurme RC .75 2.00
259 Marty Turco RC 1.50 4.00
260 Jarno Kultanen RC .40 1.00

2000-01 Stadium Club Beam Team

Randomly inserted in packs at the rate of 1:53, this luminescent card features player photos on an ice rink background with laser cut accents and die cut borders. Each card is sequentially numbered to 500.

COMPLETE SET (30) 150.00 300.00
BT1 Paul Kariya 4.00 10.00
BT2 Peter Forsberg 10.00 25.00
BT3 Mike Modano 6.00 15.00
BT4 Steve Yzerman 20.00 50.00
BT5 Pavel Bure 5.00 12.00
BT6 Jaromir Jagr 6.00 15.00
BT7 Brett Hull 5.00 12.00
BT8 Joe Sakic 8.00 20.00
BT9 Scott Gomez 3.00 8.00
BT10 Teemu Selanne 4.00 10.00
BT11 Vincent Lecavalier 4.00 10.00
BT12 Patrick Roy 20.00 50.00
BT13 Martin Brodeur 10.00 25.00
BT14 Dominik Hasek 8.00 20.00
BT15 Joe Thornton 6.00 15.00
BT16 Valeri Bure 3.00 8.00
BT17 Ed Belfour 4.00 10.00
BT18 Ray Bourque 8.00 20.00
BT19 Mark Messier 5.00 12.00
BT20 Curtis Joseph 4.00 10.00
BT21 Jason Arnott 3.00 8.00
BT22 Brian Boucher 4.00 10.00
BT23 Tony Amonte 3.00 8.00
BT24 Milan Hejduk 4.00 10.00
BT25 Mark Recchi 3.00 8.00
BT26 Patrik Elias 3.00 8.00
BT27 Zigmund Palffy 3.00 8.00
BT28 Jeremy Roenick 5.00 12.00
BT29 Eric Lindros 6.00 15.00
BT30 Chris Pronger 3.00 8.00

2000-01 Stadium Club Capture the Action

Randomly inserted in packs at the rate of 1:12, this 15-card set features a base card design with borders along the top and bottom and places color action photography against a maroon and purple background. A game view parallel was also created, these cards had a stated print run of 100 sets.

COMPLETE SET (15) 10.00 20.00
*GAME VIEW: 4X TO 10X HI COL.
CA1 Jaromir Jagr 1.00 2.50
CA2 Martin Brodeur 1.50 4.00
CA3 Scott Gomez .50 1.25
CA4 Ed Belfour .60 1.50
CA5 Dominik Hasek 1.25 3.00
CA6 Olaf Kolzig .50 1.25
CA7 Pavel Bure .60 1.50
CA8 John LeClair .60 1.50
CA9 Curtis Joseph .60 1.50
CA10 Chris Pronger .50 1.25
CA11 Peter Forsberg 1.50 4.00
CA12 Teemu Selanne .60 1.50
CA13 Patrik Stefan .50 1.25
CA14 Vincent Lecavalier .60 1.50
CA15 Tim Connolly .50 1.25

2000-01 Stadium Club Co-Signers

Randomly inserted in Hobby packs at the rate of 1:644, this four card set features a split card design with two players and their authentic autographs along the bottom in a whited out box.

CO1 Pavel Bure / Pavol Demitra 15.00 40.00
CO2 Scott Gomez / Martin Brodeur 60.00 150.00
CO3 Nikolai Antropov / Daniel Alfredsson 12.00 30.00
CO4 Anson Carter / Mike York 15.00 40.00

2000-01 Stadium Club Glove Save

Randomly inserted in packs at the rate of 1:10, this 10-card set features an all die cut embossed card in the shape of a goalie glove.

COMPLETE SET (10) 20.00 40.00
GS1 Martin Brodeur 4.00 10.00
GS2 Ed Belfour 1.50 4.00
GS3 Patrick Roy 8.00 20.00
GS4 Curtis Joseph 1.50 4.00
GS5 Brian Boucher 1.25 3.00
GS6 Roman Turek 1.25 3.00
GS7 Olaf Kolzig 1.25 3.00
GS8 Dominik Hasek 3.00 8.00
GS9 Chris Osgood 1.25 3.00
GS10 Fred Brathwaite 1.25 3.00

2000-01 Stadium Club Lone Star Signatures

Randomly inserted in packs at the rate of 1:118 overall, this 10-card set features a base design with the player framed in the middle of an "ice rink" with a whited out portion centered along the bottom for an authentic player autograph.

LS1 Pavel Bure 6.00 15.00
LS2 Martin Brodeur 30.00 80.00
LS3 Scott Gomez 6.00 15.00
LS4 Daniel Alfredsson 6.00 15.00
LS5 Nikolai Antropov 6.00 15.00
LS6 Jose Theodore 15.00 40.00
LS7 Anson Carter 6.00 15.00
LS8 Pavol Demitra 6.00 15.00
LS9 Mike York 6.00 15.00
LS10 Brad Stuart 6.00 15.00

2000-01 Stadium Club Promos

COMPLETE SET (6) 2.00 4.00
PP1 Bill Guerin .30 .75
PP2 Alexei Kovalev .30 .75
PP3 Keith Primeau .30 .75
PP4 Jocelyn Thibault .30 .75
PP5 Brad Isbister .30 .75
PP6 Adam Graves .30 .75

2000-01 Stadium Club Souvenirs

Randomly inserted in packs at the rate of 1:88 overall, this eight card set features full color player photos coupled with a circular swatch of a game worn jersey.

SCS1 Wade Redden 6.00 15.00
SCS2 Joe Sakic 12.50 30.00
SCS3 Derian Hatcher 6.00 15.00
SCS4 Jeff Hackett 6.00 15.00
SCS5 Kenny Jonsson 6.00 15.00
SCS6 Sergei Samsonov 6.00 15.00

SCS7 Darren McCarty 10.00 25.00
SCS8 Tie Domi 6.00 15.00

2000-01 Stadium Club Special Forces

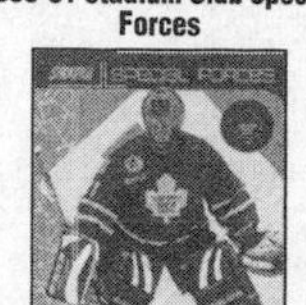

Randomly inserted in packs at the rate of 1:8, this 20-card set features a base design with purple borders along the top and bottom and full color player photography set against a holofoil background in the shape of an ice rink.

COMPLETE SET (20) 15.00 30.00
SF1 Scott Stevens .40 1.00
SF2 Chris Pronger .40 1.00
SF3 Paul Kariya .50 1.25
SF4 Peter Forsberg 1.25 3.00
SF5 Mike Modano .75 2.00
SF6 Steve Yzerman 2.50 6.00
SF7 Pavel Bure .60 1.50
SF8 Jaromir Jagr .75 2.00
SF9 John LeClair .60 1.50
SF10 Mats Sundin .50 1.25
SF11 Owen Nolan .40 1.00
SF12 Brendan Shanahan .75 2.00
SF13 Pavol Demitra .40 1.00
SF14 Nicklas Lidstrom .50 1.25
SF15 Ron Francis .40 1.00
SF16 Patrick Roy 2.50 6.00
SF17 Martin Brodeur 1.25 3.00
SF18 Dominik Hasek 1.00 2.50
SF19 Keith Tkachuk .50 1.25
SF20 Curtis Joseph .50 1.25

2001-02 Stadium Club

Released in November 2001, this 140-card set carried an SRP of $3.00 for a 6-card pack. The base set consisted of 100 veteran cards, 10 transaction cards (inserted 1:4), 10 Premium Prospects cards (inserted 1:4) and 20 rookies (inserted 1:8).

COMPLETE SET (140) 60.00 120.00
1 Martin Brodeur .50 1.25
2 Peter Forsberg .50 1.25
3 Chris Pronger .15 .40
4 Paul Kariya .20 .50
5 Mike Modano .30 .75
6 Curtis Joseph .20 .50
7 Jason Allison .08 .20
8 Brendan Shanahan .20 .50
9 Peter Bondra .20 .50
10 Mark Messier .20 .50
11 Owen Nolan .15 .40
12 Saku Koivu .20 .50
13 Tony Amonte .15 .40
14 Vincent Lecavalier .20 .50
15 Marian Hossa .20 .50
16 Pavel Bure .20 .50
17 Daniel Sedin .08 .20
18 Mario Lemieux 1.25 3.00
19 Rick DiPietro .15 .40
20 Zigmund Palffy .15 .40
21 Ron Tugnutt .15 .40
22 Ron Francis .15 .40
23 Maxim Afinogenov .08 .20
24 Steve Yzerman 1.00 2.50
25 Ray Ferraro .08 .20
26 Tommy Salo .15 .40
27 Marian Gaborik .40 1.00
28 Claude Lemieux .08 .20
29 David Legwand .15 .40
30 Roman Cechmanek .15 .40
31 Jarome Iginla .25 .60
32 Sergei Fedorov .30 .75
33 Bill Guerin .15 .40
34 Brian Leetch .15 .40
35 Alexei Kovalev .15 .40
36 Pavol Demitra .15 .40
37 Olaf Kolzig .15 .40
38 Jose Theodore .25 .60
39 Johan Hedberg .15 .40
40 Teemu Selanne .20 .50
41 Adam Deadmarsh .08 .20
42 Miroslav Satan .15 .40
43 Henrik Sedin .08 .20
44 Ed Belfour .20 .50
45 Sean Burke .15 .40
46 Patrik Elias .15 .40
47 Daniel Alfredsson .15 .40
48 Evgeni Nabokov .15 .40
49 Markus Naslund .20 .50
50 Mats Sundin .20 .50
51 Milan Hejduk .20 .50
52 Eric Belanger .08 .20
53 Darren McCarty .08 .20
54 Keith Tkachuk .20 .50
55 Steve Sullivan .08 .20
56 Mark Recchi .15 .40
57 Rob Blake .15 .40
58 Manny Fernandez .15 .40
59 Patrick Lalime .15 .40
60 Adam Oates .15 .40
61 Joe Sakic .40 1.00
62 Lubomir Visnovsky .08 .20
63 Jeff Halpern .08 .20
64 Shane Willis .08 .20
65 Todd Bertuzzi .20 .50
66 Jeff Friesen .08 .20
67 Mike Dunham .15 .40
68 Alex Tanguay .15 .40
69 J-P Dumont .08 .20
70 Patrick Marleau .15 .40
71 Martin Straka .08 .20
72 Petr Sykora .08 .20
73 Arturs Irbe .15 .40
74 Patrik Stefan .08 .20
75 Brad Richards .15 .40
76 Mike Comrie .15 .40
77 Jason Arnott .08 .20
78 Tie Domi .15 .40
79 Martin Havlat .15 .40
80 Roberto Luongo .25 .60
81 Nicklas Lidstrom .20 .50
82 Simon Gagne .20 .50
83 Marc Savard .08 .20
84 John LeClair .20 .50
85 Gary Roberts .08 .20
86 Ryan Smyth .08 .20
87 Patrick Roy 1.00 2.50
88 Petr Nedved .08 .20
89 Brent Johnson .15 .40
90 Scott Gomez .08 .20
91 Joe Thornton .30 .75
92 Felix Potvin .20 .50
93 Chris Drury .15 .40
94 Keith Primeau .08 .20
95 Rod Brind'Amour .15 .40
96 Joe Nieuwendyk .15 .40
97 Espen Knutsen .08 .20
98 Adam Foote .15 .40
99 Brad Isbister .08 .20
100 Marc Denis .15 .40
101 Eric Lindros .20 .50
102 Alexei Yashin .08 .20
103 Dominik Hasek .40 1.00
104 Michael Peca .08 .20
105 Brett Hull .25 .60
106 Pierre Turgeon .15 .40
107 Doug Weight .15 .40
108 Alexander Mogilny .15 .40
109 Jaromir Jagr .30 .75
110 Jeremy Roenick .25 .60
111 Dany Heatley PP 2.00 5.00
112 Rostislav Klesla PP 1.50 4.00
113 Pavel Brendl PP 1.25 3.00
114 Barrett Heisten PP 1.25 3.00
115 Miikka Kiprusoff PP 1.25 3.00
116 Kris Beech PP 1.25 3.00
117 Pierre Dagenais PP 1.25 3.00
118 Bryan Allen PP 1.25 3.00
119 Jason Williams PP 1.25 3.00
120 Milan Kraft PP 1.25 3.00
121 Ilya Kovalchuk RC 6.00 15.00
122 Peter Smrek RC 1.25 3.00
123 Jiri Dopita RC 1.00 2.50
124 Jeff Jillson RC 1.00 2.50
125 Jukka Hentunen RC 1.00 2.50
126 Vaclav Nedorost RC 1.00 2.50
127 Timo Parssinen RC 1.25 3.00
128 Niklas Hagman RC 1.00 2.50
129 Andreas Salomonsson RC 1.00 2.50
130 Scott Nichol RC 1.25 3.00
131 Dan Blackburn RC 1.50 4.00
132 Kristian Huselius RC 1.25 3.00
133 Ivan Ciernik RC 1.25 3.00
134 Scott Clemmensen RC 1.00 2.50
135 Pascal Dupuis RC 1.00 2.50
136 Jason Chimera RC 1.00 2.50
137 Erik Cole RC 1.00 2.50
138 Brian Sutherby RC 1.00 2.50
139 Pavel Datsyuk RC 5.00 12.00
140 Niko Kapanen RC 1.25 3.00

2001-02 Stadium Club Award Winners

This 140-card set paralleled the base set but each card was serial-numbered out of 100 and carried an "Award Winner" stamp. Collectors could redeem cards from this set for special NHL Award Winners sets if the card they held was of a player who won an NHL award during the 2001/02 season.

*STARS: 8X TO 20X BASIC CARDS
*ROOKIES: .5X TO 1.25X BASIC CARDS
31 Jarome Iginla 10.00 25.00
38 Jose Theodore 40.00 100.00
81 Nicklas Lidstrom 10.00 25.00
111 Dany Heatley 20.00 50.00

2001-02 Stadium Club Master Photos

This 140-card set paralleled the base set but each card was serial-numbered out of 100 and carried a silver "Master Photo" stamp. Stated odds for this set was 1:45.

*STARS: 8X TO 20X BASIC CARDS
*ROOKIES: 1.25X TO 3X BASIC CARDS

2001-02 Stadium Club Gallery

This 40-card set was inserted at 1:5 and featured color artist renditions of some of the top players in the league. Cards were printed on glossy stock and had white borders that resembled a picture frame.

COMPLETE SET (40) 30.00 60.00
G1 Curtis Joseph .60 1.50
G2 Brendan Shanahan .60 1.50
G3 Mats Sundin .60 1.50
G4 Patrik Elias .50 1.25
G5 Martin Havlat .50 1.25
G6 Joe Sakic 1.25 3.00
G7 Mike Modano 1.00 2.50
G8 Chris Drury .50 1.25
G9 Scott Stevens .50 1.25
G10 Olaf Kolzig .50 1.25
G11 Roberto Luongo .75 2.00
G12 Roman Cechmanek .50 1.25
G13 Ed Belfour .60 1.50
G14 Teemu Selanne .60 1.50
G15 Henrik Sedin .40 1.00
G16 Jaromir Jagr 1.00 2.50
G17 Marian Gaborik 1.25 3.00
G18 John LeClair .60 1.50
G19 Keith Tkachuk .60 1.50
G20 Paul Kariya .60 1.50
G21 Mario Lemieux 4.00 10.00
G22 Sergei Fedorov 1.00 2.50
G23 Martin Brodeur 1.50 4.00
G24 Pavel Bure .60 1.50
G25 Mike Comrie .50 1.25
G26 Zigmund Palffy .50 1.25
G27 Milan Hejduk .60 1.50
G28 Nicklas Lidstrom .60 1.50
G29 Patrick Roy 3.00 8.00
G30 Bill Guerin .50 1.25
G31 Evgeni Nabokov .50 1.25
G32 Tony Amonte .50 1.25
G33 Peter Forsberg 1.50 4.00
G34 Rick DiPietro .50 1.25
G35 Saku Koivu .60 1.50
G36 Chris Pronger .50 1.25
G37 Steve Yzerman 3.00 8.00
G38 Daniel Sedin .40 1.00
G39 Vincent Lecavalier .60 1.50
G40 Mark Messier .60 1.50

2001-02 Stadium Club Gallery Gold

This set paralleled the base gallery set but was serial-numbered out of 50 and inserted at a rate of 1:319. The words "Gold Edition" were printed under the player's name on the card fronts.

*GOLD: 10X TO 25X BASIC INSERTS

2001-02 Stadium Club Heart and Soul

This 10-card set was inserted at a rate of 1:20 and featured full color action photos on white card fronts. The words "Heart and Soul" were printed in dark blue across the card top.

COMPLETE SET (10) 15.00 30.00
HS1 Mark Messier 1.00 2.50
HS2 Patrick Roy 4.00 10.00
HS3 Steve Yzerman 4.00 10.00
HS4 Mario Lemieux 5.00 12.00
HS5 Chris Pronger .60 1.50
HS6 Scott Stevens .60 1.50
HS7 Peter Forsberg 2.00 5.00
HS8 Curtis Joseph .60 1.50
HS9 Mike Modano 1.25 3.00
HS10 Brendan Shanahan 1.25 3.00

2001-02 Stadium Club Lone Star Signatures

Inserted at a rate of 1:120, this 7-card set featured authentic player autographs. Color player photos were printed on the top two-thirds of the card front, and a white autograph area was at the card bottom.

LS1 Milan Hejduk 8.00 20.00
LS2 Olaf Kolzig 8.00 20.00
LS3 Marian Gaborik 12.50 30.00
LS4 Martin Havlat 8.00 20.00
LS5 Patrik Elias 8.00 20.00
LS6 Adam Oates 8.00 20.00
LS7 Ilya Kovalchuk 12.50 30.00

2001-02 Stadium Club New Regime

Consisting of 11 regular insert cards and 9 autograph cards, this set featured goalie prospects from around the league. Regular cards were inserted at 1:9. Autographed cards carried a white autograph space at the bottom of each card and a Topps certified stamp on the card backs. The Turco, Hedberg and Aebiscer auto cards were inserted at 1:210, all other autos were inserted at 1:140.

NR1 Marty Turco 2.00 5.00
NR2 David Aebischer 2.00 5.00
NR3 Brent Johnson 2.00 5.00
NR4 Evgeni Nabokov 2.00 5.00
NR5 Marc Denis 2.00 5.00
NR6 Roberto Luongo 2.50 6.00
NR7 Manny Fernandez 2.00 5.00
NR8 Roman Cechmanek 2.00 5.00
NR9 Jani Hurme 2.00 5.00
NR10 Johan Hedberg 2.00 5.00
NR11 Rick DiPietro 2.00 5.00
NRABJ Brent Johnson AU 8.00 20.00
NRADA David Aebischer AU 10.00 25.00
NRAEN Evgeni Nabokov AU 8.00 20.00
NRAJHE Johan Hedberg AU 8.00 20.00
NRAMD Marc Denis AU 8.00 20.00
NRAMF Manny Fernandez AU 8.00 20.00
NRAMT Marty Turco AU 10.00 25.00
NRARC Roman Cechmanek AU 8.00 20.00
NRARL Roberto Luongo AU 10.00 25.00

2001-02 Stadium Club NHL Passport

This 20-card set was inserted at 1:10 and featured international stars who also represent their homelands during world competitions. Cards carried color player photos and a small replica of the player's homeland flag.

COMPLETE SET (20) 20.00 40.00
NHLP1 Peter Forsberg 1.50 4.00
NHLP2 Nicklas Lidstrom .60 1.50
NHLP3 Mats Sundin .60 1.50
NHLP4 Pavel Bure .75 2.00
NHLP5 Sergei Fedorov 1.25 3.00
NHLP6 Alexei Kovalev .50 1.25
NHLP7 Saku Koivu .60 1.50
NHLP8 Teemu Selanne .60 1.50
NHLP9 Roman Cechmanek .50 1.25
NHLP10 Patrik Elias .60 1.50
NHLP11 Milan Hejduk .60 1.50
NHLP12 Petr Sykora .50 1.25
NHLP13 Chris Drury .50 1.25
NHLP14 Bill Guerin .50 1.25
NHLP15 John LeClair .75 2.00
NHLP16 Mike Modano 1.00 2.50
NHLP17 Paul Kariya .60 1.50
NHLP18 Mario Lemieux 4.00 10.00
NHLP19 Joe Sakic 1.25 3.00
NHLP20 Steve Yzerman 3.00 8.00

2001-02 Stadium Club Perennials

This 15-card set was inserted at 1:7 and highlighted players who make the all-star team on a consistent basis.

COMPLETE SET (15) 20.00 40.00
P1 Pavel Bure .75 2.00
P2 Joe Sakic 1.25 3.00
P3 Martin Brodeur 1.50 4.00
P4 Peter Forsberg 1.50 4.00
P5 Patrick Roy 3.00 8.00
P6 John LeClair .75 2.00
P7 Paul Kariya .60 1.50
P8 Steve Yzerman 3.00 8.00
P9 Mario Lemieux 4.00 10.00
P10 Ed Belfour .60 1.50
P11 Keith Tkachuk .60 1.50
P12 Sergei Fedorov 1.25 3.00
P13 Curtis Joseph .60 1.50
P14 Zigmund Palffy .60 1.50
P15 Tony Amonte .60 1.50

2001-02 Stadium Club Souvenirs

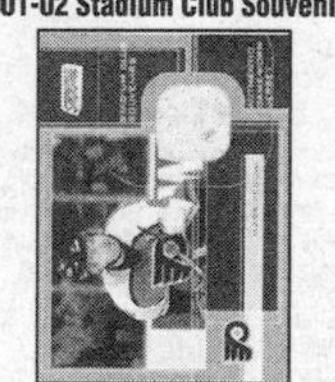
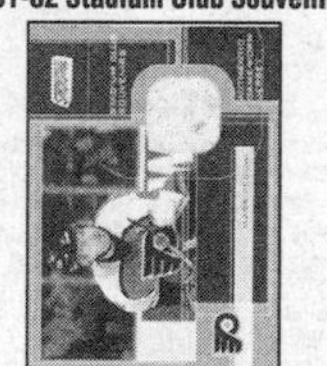

This 35-card hobby only set featured one, two or three swatches of game-worn jerseys from the pictured player(s). Single player cards were inserted at 1:16, dual player cards were inserted at 1:986 and serial-numbered to 25 each. Triple player cards were inserted at 1:3616 and were serial-numbered to 25.

AZ Alexei Zhamnov 4.00 10.00
CO Chris Osgood 6.00 15.00
JI Jarome Iginla 15.00 40.00
JT Joe Thornton 8.00 20.00
MB Martin Brodeur 15.00 40.00
MP Matt Pettinger 4.00 10.00
MR Mark Recchi 6.00 15.00
MT Marty Turco 6.00 15.00
PB Pavel Bure 4.00 10.00
PF Peter Forsberg 15.00 40.00
PK Paul Kariya 8.00 20.00
PM Patrick Marleau 6.00 15.00
SB Sean Burke 6.00 15.00
SF Sergei Fedorov 10.00 25.00
SK Saku Koivu 4.00 10.00
TD Tie Domi 6.00 15.00
TK Tomas Kloucek 4.00 10.00
JHA Jeff Hackett 4.00 10.00
JHL Jan Hlavac 4.00 10.00
MAS Marc Savard 4.00 10.00
MIS Miroslav Satan 6.00 15.00
EBMB Ed Belfour 60.00 120.00
Martin Brodeur
JHSK Jeff Hackett 20.00 50.00
Saku Koivu
JSCD Joe Sakic 30.00 80.00
Chris Drury
MTEB Marty Turco 30.00 80.00
Ed Belfour
PFCD Peter Forsberg 30.00 80.00
Chris Drury
PFJS Peter Forsberg 60.00 120.00
Joe Sakic
PRMB Patrick Roy 60.00 120.00
Martin Brodeur
SFPB Sergei Fedorov 30.00 80.00
Pavel Bure
SSPB Sergei Samsonov 20.00 50.00
Pavel Bure
TDDM Tie Domi 20.00 50.00
Darren McCarty
TKMM Tomas Kloucek 20.00 50.00
Mike Mottau
EBMBPR Ed Belfour 100.00 250.00
Martin Brodeur
Patrick Roy
JSCDPF Joe Sakic 150.00 300.00
Chris Drury
Peter Forsberg
JTJASS Joe Thornton 75.00 150.00
Jason Allison
Sergei Samsonov

2001-02 Stadium Club Toronto Fall Expo

This 6-card set was available only by wrapper redemption from the Topps booth at the 2001 Toronto Fall expo. The cards paralleled the base set, but carry a expo logo on the card fronts and were numbered "# of 6" on the card backs.

COMPLETE SET (6) 1.60 4.00
1 Marian Hossa .40 1.00
2 Peter Forsberg .80 2.00
3 Daniel Alfredsson .20 .50
4 Nicklas Lidstrom .20 .50
5 Brendan Shanahan .30 .75
6 Pavel Bure .40 1.00

2002-03 Stadium Club

Released in mid-November, this 140-card set featured full-color action photos on the card fronts and player stats on the card backs. SP's were inserted at a rate of 1:8.

COMPLETE SET (140) 75.00 150.00
COMP.SET w/o SP's (120) 25.00 50.00
1 Jose Theodore .25 .60
2 Jarome Iginla .25 .60
3 Nicklas Lidstrom .20 .50
4 Ron Francis .15 .40
5 Jaromir Jagr .30 .75
6 Mario Lemieux 1.25 3.00
7 Owen Nolan .15 .40
8 Martin Brodeur .50 1.25
9 Joe Sakic .40 1.00
10 Ilya Kovalchuk .25 .60
11 Mike Modano .30 .75
12 Jason Allison .08 .20
13 Sean Burke .15 .40
14 Mats Sundin .20 .50
15 Markus Naslund .20 .50
16 Jeremy Roenick .25 .60
17 Eric Lindros .20 .50
18 Brent Johnson .15 .40
19 Sergei Fedorov .30 .75
20 Sergei Samsonov .15 .40
21 Chris Drury .15 .40
22 Ryan Smyth .08 .20
23 Scott Hartnell .08 .20
24 Simon Gagne .20 .50
25 Dan Cloutier .15 .40
26 Vincent Lecavalier .20 .50
27 Martin Havlat .15 .40
28 Patrik Elias .15 .40
29 Roberto Luongo .25 .60
30 Rob Blake .15 .40
31 J-P Dumont .08 .20
32 Jeff O'Neill .08 .20
33 Pavel Datsyuk .20 .50
34 Dan Blackburn .15 .40
35 Alexei Kovalev .15 .40
36 Olaf Kolzig .15 .40
37 Milan Hejduk .20 .50
38 Steve Yzerman 1.00 2.50
39 Marc Denis .15 .40
40 Michael Peca .08 .20
41 Saku Koivu .20 .50
42 Marian Gaborik .40 1.00
43 Brad Richards .15 .40
44 Alexander Mogilny .15 .40
45 Mike Comrie .15 .40
46 Peter Forsberg .50 1.25
47 Dany Heatley .25 .60
48 Steve Sullivan .08 .20
49 Keith Tkachuk .20 .50
50 Todd Bertuzzi .20 .50
51 Evgeni Nabokov .15 .40
52 David Legwand .15 .40
53 Scott Stevens .15 .40
54 Eric Daze .08 .20
55 Martin Biron .15 .40
56 Zigmund Palffy .15 .40
57 Paul Kariya .20 .50
58 Krys Kolanos .08 .20
59 Pavel Bure .20 .50
60 Darcy Tucker .08 .20
61 Marian Hossa .20 .50
62 Roman Cechmanek .15 .40
63 Mark Parrish .08 .20
64 Arturs Irbe .15 .40
65 Brian Rolston .08 .20
66 Marty Turco .15 .40
67 Peter Bondra .20 .50
68 Johan Hedberg .15 .40
69 Chris Pronger .15 .40
70 Patrick Lalime .15 .40
71 Mike Dunham .15 .40
72 Kristian Huselius .08 .20
73 Patrick Roy 1.00 2.50
74 Joe Thornton .30 .75
75 Andrew Brunette .08 .20
76 Alexei Yashin .08 .20
77 John LeClair .20 .50
78 Miroslav Satan .15 .40
79 Doug Weight .15 .40
80 Gary Roberts .08 .20
81 Tommy Salo .15 .40
82 Daniel Alfredsson .15 .40
83 Marco Sturm .08 .20
84 Rostislav Klesla .08 .20
85 Richard Zednik .08 .20
86 Roman Turek .15 .40
87 Brian Leetch .15 .40
88 Chris Osgood .15 .40
89 Brendan Morrison .15 .40
90 Jocelyn Thibault .15 .40
91 Teemu Selanne .20 .50
92 Jean-Sebastien Giguere .15 .40
93 Nikolai Khabibulin .20 .50
94 Pavol Demitra .15 .40
95 Brendan Shanahan .20 .50
96 Mark Recchi .15 .40
97 Felix Potvin .20 .50
98 Shane Doan .08 .20
99 Erik Cole .08 .20
100 Brett Hull .25 .60
101 Curtis Joseph .20 .50
102 Bobby Holik .08 .20
103 Ed Belfour .20 .50
104 Bill Guerin .15 .40
105 Petr Sykora .08 .20
106 Scott Young .08 .20
107 Adam Oates .15 .40
108 Jeff Friesen .08 .20
109 Darius Kasparaitis .08 .20
110 Tony Amonte .15 .40
111 Marcel Hossa .20 .50
112 Jamie Lundmark .08 .20
113 Pavel Brendl .08 .20
114 Jaroslav Svoboda .08 .20
115 Stephen Weiss .08 .20
116 Martin Prusek RC .15 .40
117 Jani Rita .08 .20
118 Petr Cajanek .08 .20
119 Trent Hunter .08 .20
120 Jonathan Cheechoo .10 .25
121 Stanislav Chistov RC 2.50 6.00
122 Alexander Svitov RC 4.00 10.00
123 Alexander Frolov RC 4.00 10.00
124 Alexei Smirnov RC 2.00 5.00
125 Chuck Kobasew RC 2.50 6.00
126 Rick Nash RC 6.00 15.00
127 Henrik Zetterberg RC 6.00 15.00
128 Jay Bouwmeester RC 4.00 10.00
129 Ales Hemsky RC 5.00 12.00
130 Martin Gerber RC 2.00 5.00
131 Ron Hainsey RC 2.00 5.00
132 P-M Bouchard RC 4.00 10.00
133 Jason Spezza RC 6.00 15.00
134 Kurt Sauer RC 2.00 5.00
135 Lasse Pirjeta RC 2.00 5.00
136 Adam Hall RC 2.00 5.00
137 Dennis Seidenberg RC 3.00 8.00
138 Patrick Sharp RC 2.00 5.00
139 Steve Eminger RC 2.00 5.00
140 Dmitri Bykov RC 2.00 5.00

2002-03 Stadium Club Silver Decoy Cards

This 140-card set paralleled the base set but was printed on thicker card stock and carried a silver finish on the card fronts. They were inserted at one-per pack to discourage pack searching.

*DECOYS: .5X TO 1.25X BASIC CARDS

2002-03 Stadium Club Proofs

This 140-card proof set paralleled the base set but carried a "Proof" stamp and seria-numbering. Base cards were serial-numbered to 250 and rookies were serial-numbered to 100.

*STARS: 1.5X TO 4X BASIC CARDS
*ROOKIES: .75X TO 2X

2002-03 Stadium Club Beam Team

This 15-card set was inserted at a rate of 1:18.

COMPLETE SET (15) 20.00 40.00
BT1 Steve Yzerman 3.00 8.00
BT2 Mario Lemieux 4.00 10.00
BT3 Patrick Roy 3.00 8.00
BT4 Jarome Iginla .75 2.00
BT5 Jose Theodore .75 2.00
BT6 Brendan Shanahan 1.00 2.50
BT7 Chris Pronger .50 1.25
BT8 Dany Heatley .75 2.00
BT9 Joe Thornton 1.00 2.50
BT10 Peter Forsberg 1.50 4.00
BT11 Ron Francis .50 1.25
BT12 Owen Nolan .50 1.25
BT13 Todd Bertuzzi .60 1.50
BT14 Rob Blake .50 1.25
BT15 Paul Kariya .60 1.50

2002-03 Stadium Club Champions Fabric

Inserted at 1:68, this 10-card set featured swatches of game jerseys.

*MULT.COLOR SWATCH: .5X TO 1.25X HI
FC1 Rob Blake 4.00 10.00
FC2 Derian Hatcher 4.00 10.00
FC3 Alex Tanguay 4.00 10.00
FC4 Martin Brodeur 10.00 25.00
FC5 Milan Hejduk 4.00 10.00
FC6 Mike Modano 6.00 15.00
FC7 Scott Niedermayer 4.00 10.00
FC8 Brian Leetch 4.00 10.00
FC9 Sergei Zubov 4.00 10.00
FC10 Chris Drury 4.00 10.00

2002-03 Stadium Club Champions Patches

A parallel to the basic Champions Fabrics jerseys, this 9 card set featured swatches of game worn jersey patches. Each card was serial-numberde to 25 copies each. Please note that Topps did not produce a patch variation of the Chris Drury card.

*PATCHES: 2X TO 5X BASIC JERSEY

2002-03 Stadium Club Lone Star Signatures Blue

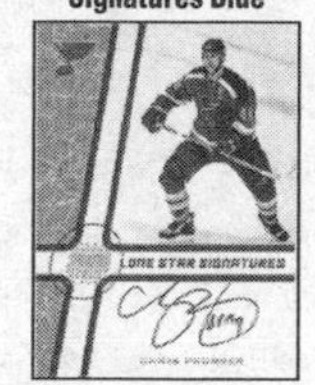

Inserted at 1:56 packs, this 14-card set featured authentic player autographs in blue ink.

LSBG Brian Gionta 8.00 20.00
LSBR Brad Richards 8.00 20.00
LSCP Chris Pronger SP 12.50 30.00
LSDB Daniel Briere 8.00 20.00
LSEC Erik Cole 8.00 20.00
LSED Eric Daze 8.00 20.00
LSIL Ilya Kovalchuk 15.00 40.00
LSJI Jarome Iginla 15.00 40.00
LSJT Jose Theodore 15.00 40.00
LSPL Patrick Lalime 8.00 20.00
LSRK Rostislav Klesla 8.00 20.00
LSSG Simon Gagne 12.50 30.00
LSSW Stephen Weiss 8.00 20.00
LSTB Todd Bertuzzi 12.50 30.00

2002-03 Stadium Club Lone Star Signatures Red

Inserted at 1:144, this set paralleled the basic autograph set but player autographs were signed in red ink.

*RED SIGS: .5X TO 1.25X BLUE

2002-03 Stadium Club Passport

Inserted at 1:40; this 14-card set featured swatches of game-worn jerseys affixed to a passport style card

front. All cards carried a NHLP prefix.

*MULT.COLOR SWATCH: .5X TO 1.25X HI
1 Saku Koivu 6.00 15.00
2 Daniel Alfredsson 4.00 10.00
3 Eric Lindros 6.00 15.00
4 Mats Sundin 6.00 15.00
5 Todd Bertuzzi 6.00 15.00
6 Simon Gagne 6.00 15.00
7 Marian Hossa 6.00 15.00
8 Paul Kariya 6.00 15.00
9 Vincent Lecavalier 6.00 15.00
10 Miroslav Satan 4.00 10.00
11 Markus Naslund 6.00 15.00
12 Zigmund Palffy 4.00 10.00
13 Tony Amonte 4.00 10.00
14 Brian Rolston 4.00 10.00
15 Maxim Afinogenov 4.00 10.00
16 Sergei Samsonov 4.00 10.00
17 Marco Sturm 4.00 10.00

2002-03 Stadium Club Puck Stops Here

COMPLETE SET (15) 10.00 20.00
STATED ODDS 1:6
PSH1 Brent Johnson .50 1.25
PSH2 Roman Cechmanek .50 1.25
PSH3 Evgeni Nabokov .50 1.25
PSH4 Jose Theodore .75 2.00
PSH5 Martin Biron .50 1.25
PSH6 Chris Osgood .50 1.25
PSH7 Marty Turco .50 1.25
PSH8 Nikolai Khabibulin .60 1.50
PSH9 Roberto Luongo .75 2.00
PSH10 Martin Brodeur 1.25 3.00
PSH11 Sean Burke .50 1.25
PSH12 Tommy Salo .50 1.25
PSH13 Mike Richter .60 1.50
PSH14 Patrick Roy 1.50 4.00
PSH15 Jean-Sebastien Giguere .50 1.25

2002-03 Stadium Club St. Patrick Relics

This 16-card set honored the career of Patrick Roy. Single swatch jersey only odds were 1:237 and single swatch stick only cards were inserted at 1:3160. All other print runs are listed below. Print runs of 25 or less not priced due to scarcity.

ALL CARDS CARRY SP PREFIX
*MULT.COLOR SWATCH: .75X TO 1.5X
SAS Patrick Roy 100.00 250.00
Stick Auto/50
CAJ Patrick Roy 12.50 30.00
Colorado Jersey
MCJ Patrick Roy 12.50 30.00
Montreal Jersey
CAJA Patrick Roy 60.00 150.00
Colorado Jersey Auto/250
MCJA Patrick Roy 60.00 150.00
Montreal Jersey Auto/250
SPS Patrick Roy 12.50 30.00
Stick
CAJP Patrick Roy 30.00 80.00
Colorado Patch/100
MCJP Patrick Roy 30.00 80.00
Montreal Patch/100
CAMCJ P.Roy DUAL JSY/500 30.00 80.00
CAMCJA Patrick Roy 200.00 500.00
Dual Jersey Auto/50
CAMCJS Patrick Roy 100.00 250.00
Jersey/Stick/50
CAMCJSA Patrick Roy 200.00 500.00
Jersey/Stick Auto/25
CAJPA Patrick Roy
Colorado Patch Auto/10
MCJPA Patrick Roy
Montreal Patch Auto/10
CAMCJP Patrick Roy
Dual Patch/25
CAMCJPA Patrick Roy
Dual Patch Auto/5

2002-03 Stadium Club World Stage

COMPLETE SET (20) 15.00 30.00
STATED ODDS 1:7
WS1 Sergei Fedorov 1.25 3.00
WS2 Chris Drury .50 1.25
WS3 Martin Brodeur 1.50 4.00
WS4 Joe Sakic 1.25 3.00
WS5 Mike Modano 1.00 2.50
WS6 Jeremy Roenick .75 2.00
WS7 Brett Hull .75 2.00
WS8 Ilya Kovalchuk .75 2.00
WS9 Nicklas Lidstrom .60 1.50
WS10 Jaromir Jagr 1.00 2.50
WS11 Alexei Yashin .50 1.25
WS12 Zigmund Palffy .50 1.25
WS13 Marian Gaborik .75 2.00
WS14 Teemu Selanne .60 1.50
WS15 Alexei Kovalev .50 1.25
WS16 Patrik Elias .50 1.25
WS17 Peter Bondra .50 1.25
WS18 Pavel Bure .75 2.00
WS19 Mats Sundin .60 1.50
WS20 Daniel Alfredsson .50 1.25

2002-03 Stadium Club YoungStars Relics

This 29-card set featured memorabilia worn during the NHL/Topps YoungStars game played in 2002. Single jersey swatch cards (S1-S23) were inserted at 1:28. Double swatch cards (DS1-DS6) were serial-numbered to 100. Odds for the MVP autographed puck were stated at 1:936 and there were only 200 copies available.

*MULT.COLOR SWATCH: .5X TO 1.25X HI
ALL CARDS CARRY YS PREFIX
S1 Ilya Kovalchuk 12.50 30.00
S2 Pavel Datsyuk 8.00 20.00
S3 Mike Comrie 4.00 10.00
S4 Dan Blackburn 4.00 10.00
S5 Dany Heatley 6.00 15.00
S6 Marian Gaborik 8.00 20.00
S7 Kristian Huselius 5.00 12.00
S8 David Legwand 5.00 12.00
S9 Roberto Luongo 8.00 20.00
S10 Brad Richards 5.00 12.00
S11 Justin Williams 5.00 12.00
S12 Kyle Calder 4.00 10.00
S13 Dave Tanabe 4.00 10.00
S14 Brenden Morrow 5.00 12.00
S15 Scott Hartnell 4.00 10.00
S16 Mike Fisher 5.00 12.00
S17 Tim Connolly 5.00 12.00
S18 Nick Boynton 4.00 10.00
S19 Paul Mara 4.00 10.00
S20 Mike Ribeiro 5.00 12.00
S21 Robyn Regehr 4.00 10.00
S22 Andrew Ference 4.00 10.00
S23 Karel Rachunek 4.00 10.00
DS1 Dany Heatley 25.00 60.00
Ilya Kovalchuk
DS2 David Legwand 10.00 25.00
Scott Hartnell
DS3 Kristian Huselius 20.00 50.00
Roberto Luongo
DS4 M.Gaborik/P.Datsyuk 25.00 60.00
DS5 Justin Williams 10.00 25.00
Mike Comrie
DS6 Brad Richards 10.00 25.00
Dan Blackburn
APIK Ilya Kovalchuk 25.00 60.00
Puck Auto/200

1994-95 Stars HockeyKaps

Measuring approximately 1 3/4" in diameter, this set of 25 caps features the Dallas Stars. The caps were given away at Stars games on February 6, 9, 16 and 18. Additional caps could be obtained through a mail-in offer by sending a SASE along with proof-of-purchase from one 46 oz. or one six-pack of 10 oz. Tropicana Twister. A HockeyKap collector game board was also available through a mail-in offer for two proofs-of-purchase of the above-mentioned products. The fronts feature color head shots with a white border. The player's last name is printed in the white border. The backs are blank. The caps are unnumbered and checklisted below in alphabetical order.

COMPLETE SET (25) 3.00 8.00
1 Dave Barr .08 .25
2 Brad Berry .08 .25
3 Neal Broten .20 .50
4 Paul Broten .08 .25
5 Paul Cavallini .08 .25
6 Shane Churla .20 .50
7 Russ Courtnall .15 .40
8 Mike Craig .08 .25
9 Ulf Dahlen .15 .40
10 Dean Evason .08 .25
11 Dave Gagner .15 .40
12 Bob Gainey CO .15 .40
13 Brent Gilchrist .08 .25
14 Derian Hatcher .15 .40
15 Doug Jarvis ACO .02 .10
16 Jim Johnson .08 .25
17 Trent Klatt .08 .25
18 Grant Ledyard .08 .25
19 Craig Ludwig .08 .25
20 Mike McPhee .08 .25
21 Mike Modano .60 1.50
22 Andy Moog .40 1.00
23 Mark Tinordi .08 .25
24 Darcy Wakaluk .15 .40
25 Rick Wilson ACO .02 .10

1994-95 Stars Pinnacle Sheet

Produced by Pinnacle, this promo sheet was given out at Reunion Arena for the Dallas Stars game vs. the Red Wings on April 1, 1995. The sheet measures approximately 12 1/2" by 10 1/2". The left, perforated portion displays nine standard-size player cards, while the right portion consists of an advertisement to purchase 12-packs of Coke products at participating Texaco retailers. The design is the same as the 1994-95 Pinnacle hockey series, with the same numbering. The cards are listed below, beginning at the upper left of the sheet and moving toward the lower right corner.

COMPLETE SHEET (9) 2.00 5.00
3 Mike Modano .60 1.50
55 Derian Hatcher .20 .50
133 Russ Courtnall .20 .50
157 Darcy Wakaluk .20 .50
185 Brent Gilchrist .08 .25
262 Todd Harvey .20 .50
315 Andy Moog .40 1.00
334 Dave Gagner .20 .50
433 Paul Broten .08 .25

1994-95 Stars Postcards

This 23-postcard set of the Dallas Stars was produced by the club for promotional giveaways and autograph signings. The cards feature full-bleed action photos on the fronts, while the backs contain biographical and statistical information. As the cards are unnumbered, they are listed below in alphabetical order.

COMPLETE SET (23) 6.00 15.00
1 Paul Broten .20 .50
2 Paul Cavallini .20 .50
3 Shane Churla .30 .75
4 Gord Donnelly .20 .50
5 Mike Donnelly .20 .50
6 Dean Evason .20 .50
7 Dave Gagner .30 .75
8 Brent Gilchrist .20 .50
9 Todd Harvey .30 .75
10 Derian Hatcher .30 .75
11 Kevin Hatcher .20 .50
12 Mike Kennedy .20 .50
13 Trent Klatt .20 .50
14 Mike Lalor .20 .50
15 Grant Ledyard .20 .50
16 Craig Ludwig .20 .50
17 Richard Matvichuk .30 .75
18 Corey Millen .20 .50
19 Mike Modano 1.25 3.00
20 Andy Moog .75 2.00
21 Darcy Wakaluk .30 .75
22 Peter Zezel .20 .50
23 Doug Zmolek .20 .50

1994-95 Stars Score Sheet

This perforated sheet was given away February 2, 1995, at the Dallas Stars' home game against the San Jose Sharks. The sheet measures approximately 12 1/2" by 10 1/2"; the larger left portion consists of nine standard-size cards, while the smaller right portion presents an advertisement for 1994-95 Score hockey first series. The back of the ad portion mentions Tom Thumb grocery stores as a place to buy Score cards. The cards have the same design as the regular issue cards. Note, however, that Shane Churla does not have a card in the regular series; this is his only appearance on a 1994-95 Score card. The cards are listed below beginning in the upper left and moving across and down toward the lower right.

COMPLETE SHEET (9) 2.00 5.00
17 Mike McPhee .08 .25
43 Russ Courtnall .08 .25
68 Mark Tinordi .08 .25
94 Paul Cavallini .08 .25
113 Neal Broten .20 .50
148 Derian Hatcher .20 .50
173 Andy Moog .40 1.00
188 Mike Modano .60 1.50
NNO Shane Churla .40 1.00

1995-96 Stars Score Sheet

This perforated sheet was given away at a Dallas Stars game at Reunion Arena and measures approximately 12 1/2" by 10 1/2". The left portion displays nine cards with color action player photos while the right consists of sponsor logos and an advertisement to purchase six packs of Coke products at participating Texaco retailers. The cards are listed below beginning at the upper left of the sheet and moving toward the lower right corner.

COMPLETE SHEET (1) 2.00 5.00
12 Kevin Hatcher .08 .25
38 Todd Harvey .20 .50
64 Andy Moog .40 1.00
89 Greg Adams .20 .50
120 Mike Modano .75 2.00
197 Darcy Wakaluk .20 .50
225 Derian Hatcher .20 .50
229 Joe Nieuwendyk .40 1.00
261 Brent Gilchrist .08 .25

1996-97 Stars Postcards

This 27-postcard set was produced by the club for promotional giveaways and autograph signings. The cards feature full color action photos on the front; the backs have biographical information and complete career stats. As the cards are unnumbered, they are listed below alphabetically.

COMPLETE SET 6.00 15.00
1 Greg Adams .20 .50
2 Bob Bassen .20 .50
3 Neal Broten .30 .75
4 Guy Carbonneau .20 .50
5 Bob Gainey .20 .50
6 Brent Gilchrist .20 .50
7 Todd Harvey .30 .75
8 Derian Hatcher .30 .75
9 Ken Hitchcock CO .20 .50
10 Benoit Hogue .20 .50
11 Bill Huard .20 .50
12 Arturs Irbe .30 .75
13 Mike Kennedy .20 .50
14 Mike Lalor .20 .50
15 Jamie Langenbrunner .30 .75
16 Grant Ledyard .20 .50
17 Jere Lehtinen .30 .75
18 Craig Ludwig .20 .50
19 Grant Marshall .20 .50
20 Richard Matvichuk .20 .50
21 Mike Modano 1.00 2.50
22 Joe Nieuwendyk .30 .75
23 Andy Moog .60 1.50
24 Dave Reid .20 .50
25 Darryl Sydor .20 .50
26 Pat Verbeek .30 .75
27 Sergei Zubov .20 .50

1996-97 Stars Score Sheet

For the third straight season, Score and the Stars teamed up to distribute a special, perforated card sheet, this time at a match against the Edmonton Oilers on Sunday, February 23, as well as at a local card show the weekend following. The majority of the cards mirror those found in the 1996-97 Score set. Of note are the cards of Pat Verbeek and Sergei Zubov, which were updated to show them as members of the Stars; Jere Lehtinen, which features green ink on the back instead of red; and Derian Hatcher, who is not included in the regular Score set. Although it typically is sold in sheet form, it is listed below as singles because the unique cards have led to many dealers breaking it up.

COMPLETE SHEET 2.00 5.00
39 Greg Adams .20 .50
72 Mike Modano .75 2.00
86 Todd Harvey .20 .50
94 Pat Verbeek .20 .50
104 Andy Moog .40 1.00
152 Joe Nieuwendyk .30 .75
171 Sergei Zubov .20 .50
246 Jere Lehtinen .20 .50
NNO Derian Hatcher .20 .50

1999-00 Stars Postcards

This 27-card set pictures the 1999-00 Dallas Stars and was sponsored by Southwest Airlines. Each card measures 4 1/4" by 6 1/4".

COMPLETE SET (27) 8.00 20.00
1 Keith Aldridge .20 .50
2 Ed Belfour .75 2.00
3 Guy Carbonneau .30 .75
4 Shawn Chambers .20 .50
5 Manny Fernandez .40 1.00
6 Aaron Gavey .20 .50
7 Derian Hatcher .30 .75
8 Brett Hull .75 2.00
9 Mike Keane .20 .50
10 Jamie Langenbrunner .30 .75
11 Jere Lehtinen .40 1.00
12 Alan Letang .20 .50
13 Juha Lind .20 .50
14 Warren Luhning .20 .50
15 Brad Lukowich .20 .50
16 Grant Marshall .20 .50
17 Richard Matvichuk .20 .50
18 Mike Modano 1.25 3.00
19 Chris Murray .20 .50
20 Joe Nieuwendyk .40 1.00
21 Pavel Patera .20 .50
22 Derek Plante .20 .50
23 Jamie Pushor .20 .50
24 Brian Skrudland .20 .50
25 Blake Sloan .20 .50
26 Darryl Sydor .20 .50
27 Sergei Zubov .20 .50

2000-01 Stars Postcards

This 26-card set was sponsored by Southwest Airlines. The front of each card features an on-ice photo of each player and is bordered on the left hand side in gold with the players name in green letters. The team logo is at the bottom left of each card front. The backs carry individual career stats as well as transactional history for each player.

COMPLETE SET (26) 8.00 20.00
1 Ed Belfour .80 2.00
2 Tyler Bouck .30 .75
3 Gerald Diduck .20 .50
4 Ted Donato .20 .50
5 Derian Hatcher .30 .75
6 Sami Helenius .20 .50
7 Ken Hitchcock HCO .20 .50
8 Brett Hull .80 2.00
9 Richard Jackman .20 .50
10 Mike Keane .20 .50
11 Jamie Langenbrunner .20 .50
12 Jere Lehtinen .60 1.50
13 Brad Lukowich .20 .50
14 Roman Lyashenko .30 .75
15 Grant Marshall .20 .50
16 Richard Matvichuk .20 .50
17 Mike Modano .80 2.00
18 Brenden Morrow .60 1.50
19 Kirk Muller .20 .50
20 Joe Nieuwendyk .30 .75
21 Jon Sim .20 .50
22 Blake Sloan .20 .50
23 Darryl Sydor .20 .50
24 Marty Turco .80 2.00
25 Shaun Van Allen .20 .50
26 Sergei Zubov .20 .50

2001-02 Stars Postcards

This set features the Dallas Stars. Singles were often handed out at player appearances. Sets could be obtained from the club with a donation to the Stars Foundation charity. The cards measures 4 X 6. The cards are listed in alphabetical order.

COMPLETE SET (26) 8.00 20.00
COMMON CARD (1-26)
1 Ed Belfour .80 2.00
2 Benoit Brunet .20 .50
3 Rob DiMaio .20 .50
4 John Erskine .20 .50
5 Derian Hatcher .31 .78
6 Sami Helenius .31 .78
7 Ken Hitchcock CO .20 .50
8 Benoit Hogue .20 .50
9 Valeri Kamensky .20 .50
10 Niko Kapanen .40 1.00
11 Jamie Langenbrunner .40 1.00
12 Jere Lehtinen .40 1.00
13 Brad Lukowich .20 .50
14 Roman Lyashenko .20 .50
15 Dave Manson .20 .50
16 Richard Matvichuk .20 .50
17 Mike Modano 1.20 3.00
18 Brenden Morrow .40 1.00
19 Kirk Muller .20 .50
20 Joe Nieuwendyk .40 1.00
21 Martin Rucinsky .20 .50
22 Darryl Sydor .20 .50
23 Marty Turco .60 1.50
24 Pierre Turgeon .31 .78
25 Pat Verbeek .20 .50
26 Sergei Zubov .20 .50

2001-02 Stars Team Issue

Little is known about this team issued set, but the cards below are known to exist. Please forward any additional info to hockeymag@beckett.com.

1 Brenden Morrow .75 2.00
2 Derian Hatcher .75 2.00
3 John Erskine .40 1.00
4 Niko Kapanen .40 1.00

2002-03 Stars Postcards

Issued by the team, this 24-card set measured 4" X 8". Card backs carried career stats for each player.

COMPLETE SET (24) 10.00 20.00
1 Scott Pellerin .20 .50
2 Sami Helenius .20 .50
3 John Erskine .40 1.00
4 Stephane Robidas .20 .50
5 Jere Lehtinen .60 1.50
6 Sergei Zubov .20 .50
7 Kirk Muller .20 .50
8 Brenden Morrow .40 1.00
9 Mike Modano 1.25 3.00
10 Richard Matvichuk .20 .50
11 Manny Malhotra .20 .50
12 Derian Hatcher .20 .50
13 Scott Young .20 .50
14 Niko Kapanen .40 1.00
15 Bill Guerin .60 1.50
16 Aaron Downey .75 2.00
17 Rob Dimaio .20 .50
18 Pierre Turgeon .30 .75
19 Marty Turco 1.25 3.00
20 Ron Tugnutt .40 1.00
21 Darryl Sydor .20 .50
22 Ulf Dahlen .20 .50
23 Philippe Boucher .20 .50
24 Jason Arnott .30 .75

2003-04 Stars Postcards

These cards were issued by the Stars for use at team events. Complete sets could also be purchased through the team. Although the majority of the cards are in colour, several late-season call-ups were issued in black and white.

COMPLETE SET (31) 10.00 20.00
1 Jason Arnott .20 .50
2 Stu Barnes .20 .50
3 Philippe Boucher .20 .50
4 Trevor Daley .20 .50
5 Rob DiMaio .20 .50
6 Aaron Downey .40 1.00
7 John Erskine .20 .50
8 Steve Gainey .20 .50
9 Bill Guerin .40 1.00
10 Niko Kapanen .30 .75
11 Jon Klemm .20 .50
12 Jere Lehtinen .40 1.00
13 Jeff MacMillan .20 .50
14 Richard Matvichuk .20 .50
15 Antti Miettinen .20 .50
16 Mike Modano .75 2.00
17 Gavin Morgan .20 .50
18 Brenden Morrow .60 1.50
19 Teppo Numminen .20 .50
20 David Oliver .20 .50
21 Steve Ott .75 2.00
22 Blake Sloan .20 .50
23 Mike Smith .40 1.00
24 Don Sweeney .20 .50
25 Mathias Tjarnqvist .20 .50
26 Ron Tugnutt .30 .75
27 Marty Turco .75 2.00
28 Pierre Turgeon .20 .50
29 Rob Valicevic .20 .50
30 Scott Young .20 .50
31 Sergei Zubov .20 .50

2006-07 Stars Team Postcards

Set includes a card of American Idol finalist Celena Rae, who sang the national anthems and was an intermission host for the Stars this season.

COMPLETE SET (28) 15.00 30.00
1 Krys Barch .75 2.00
2 Matthew Barnaby .75 2.00
3 Stu Barnes .40 1.00
4 Philippe Boucher .40 1.00
5 Trevor Daley .40 1.00
6 Loui Eriksson .75 2.00
7 Niklas Hagman .40 1.00
8 Jeff Halpern .40 1.00
9 Jussi Jokinen .40 1.00
10 Jon Klemm .40 1.00
11 Jere Lehtinen .75 2.00
12 Eric Lindros .75 2.00
13 Joel Lundqvist .75 2.00
14 Antti Miettinen .40 1.00
15 Mike Modano 1.25 3.00
16 Brenden Morrow .75 2.00
17 Steve Ott .75 2.00
18 Mike Ribeiro .40 1.00
19 Stephane Robidas .40 1.00
20 Mike Smith .75 2.00
21 Patrik Stefan .40 1.00
22 Darryl Sydor .40 1.00
23 Marty Turco .75 2.00
24 Sergei Zubov .40 1.00
25 Dave Tippett CO .10 .25
26 Celena Rae .40 1.00
27 Brett Hull 1.25 3.00
28 Craig Ludwig .40 1.00

2007-08 Stars Team Issue

COMPLETE SET (25) 15.00 30.00
1 Krys Barch .75 2.00
2 Stu Barnes .40 1.00
3 Philippe Boucher .40 1.00
4 Trevor Daley .40 1.00
5 Loui Eriksson .75 2.00
6 Todd Fedoruk .75 2.00
7 Niklas Grossman .40 1.00
8 Niklas Hagman .40 1.00
9 Jeff Halpern .40 1.00
10 Jussi Jokinen .40 1.00
11 Jere Lehtinen .75 2.00
12 Joel Lundqvist .40 1.00
13 Antti Miettinen .40 1.00
14 Mike Modano 1.25 3.00
15 Brenden Morrow 1.25 3.00
16 Matt Niskanen .75 2.00
17 Mattias Norstrom .40 1.00
18 Steve Ott .75 2.00
19 Mike Ribeiro .40 1.00
20 Stephane Robidas .40 1.00
21 Mike Smith .75 2.00
22 Marty Turco .75 2.00
23 Brad Winchester .40 1.00
24 Sergei Zubov .40 1.00
25 Dave Tippett HC .40 1.00

1975-76 Stingers Kahn's

This set of 14 photos was issued on wrappers of Kahn's Wieners and Beef Franks and features players of the Cincinnati Stingers of the WHA. The wrappers are approximately 2 11/16" wide and 11 5/8" long. The wiener wrappers are predominantly yellow and carry a 2" by 1 1/4" black-and-white posed photo of the player with a facsimile autograph inscribed across the picture. The beef frank wrappers are identical in design but predominantly red in color. The wrappers are unnumbered and checklisted below in alphabetical order.

COMPLETE SET (14) 62.50 125.00
1 Serge Aubry 5.00 10.00
2 Bryan Campbell 5.00 10.00
3 Rick Dudley 7.50 15.00
4 Pierre Guite 5.00 10.00
5 John Hughes 5.00 10.00
6 Claude Larose 6.00 12.00
7 Jacques Locas UER 5.00 10.00
(Misspelled Jacque)
8 Bernie MacNeil 5.00 10.00
9 Mike Pelyk 5.00 10.00
10 Ron Plumb 5.00 10.00
11 Dave Smedsmo 5.00 10.00
12 Dennis Sobchuk 5.00 10.00
13 Gene Sobchuk 5.00 10.00
14 Gary Veneruzzo 5.00 10.00

1976-77 Stingers Kahn's

This set of six photos was issued on wrappers of Kahn's Wieners and features players of the Cincinnati Stingers of the WHA. The wrappers are approximately 2 11/16" wide and 11 5/8" long. On a predominantly yellow wrapper with red lettering, a 2" by 1 1/4" black and white player action photo appears, with a facsimile autograph inscribed across the picture. The wrappers are unnumbered and checklisted below in alphabetical order. This set is distinguished from the previous year by the fact that these card photo poses (for the players in both sets) appear to be taken in an action sequence compared to the posed photographs taken the previous year.

COMPLETE SET (6) 62.50 125.00
1 Rick Dudley 15.00 30.00
2 Dave Inkpen 12.50 25.00
3 John Hughes 10.00 20.00
4 Claude Larose 12.50 25.00
5 Jacques Locas 10.00 20.00
6 Ron Plumb 10.00 20.00
7 Dennis Sobchuk 10.00 20.00

1997-98 Studio

The 1997-98 Studio set was issued in one series totaling 110 cards and was distributed in five-card packs with an 8x10 Studio Portrait enclosed. The fronts feature color player portraits, while the backs carry an action player photos and player information.

COMPLETE SET (110) 15.00 30.00
1 Wayne Gretzky 1.00 2.50
2 Dominik Hasek .30 .75
3 Eric Lindros .15 .40
4 Paul Kariya .15 .40
5 Jaromir Jagr .25 .60
6 Brendan Shanahan .15 .40
7 Patrick Roy .75 2.00
8 Keith Tkachuk .15 .40
9 Mark Messier .15 .40
10 Steve Yzerman .75 2.00
11 Brett Hull .20 .50
12 Jarome Iginla .20 .50
13 Mike Modano .25 .60
14 Pavel Bure .15 .40
15 Peter Forsberg .40 1.00
16 Ryan Smyth .10 .30
17 John Vanbiesbrouck .10 .30
18 Teemu Selanne .15 .40
19 Saku Koivu .15 .40
20 Martin Brodeur .40 1.00
21 Sergei Fedorov .25 .60
22 John LeClair .15 .40
23 Joe Sakic .30 .75
24 Jose Theodore .20 .50
25 Marc Denis .10 .30
26 Dainius Zubrus .15 .40
27 Bryan Berard .10 .30
28 Ray Bourque .25 .60
29 Curtis Joseph .15 .40
30 Chris Chelios .15 .40
31 Alexei Yashin .02 .10
32 Adam Oates .10 .30
33 Anson Carter .10 .30
34 Jim Campbell .02 .10
35 Jason Arnott .02 .10
36 Derek Plante .02 .10
37 Guy Hebert .10 .30
38 Oleg Tverdovsky .02 .10
39 Ed Jovanovski .10 .30
40 Jeremy Roenick .20 .50
41 Scott Mellanby .02 .10
42 Keith Primeau .02 .10
43 Ron Hextall .10 .30
44 Daren Puppa .10 .30
45 Jim Carey .10 .30
46 Zigmund Palffy .10 .30
47 Jaroslav Svejkovsky .10 .30
48 Daymond Langkow .10 .30
49 Mikael Renberg .10 .30
50 Pat LaFontaine .15 .40
51 Mike Grier .02 .10
52 Stephane Fiset .10 .30
53 Luc Robitaille .10 .30
54 Joe Thornton .40 1.00
55 Joe Nieuwendyk .10 .30
56 Mike Dunham .10 .30
57 Mark Recchi .10 .30
58 Ed Belfour .15 .40
59 Mike Richter .15 .40
60 Peter Bondra .10 .30
61 Trevor Kidd .10 .30
62 Sean Burke .10 .30
63 Nikolai Khabibulin .10 .30
64 Pierre Turgeon .10 .30
65 Dino Ciccarelli .02 .10
66 Felix Potvin .15 .40
67 Mats Sundin .15 .40
68 Joe Juneau .10 .30
69 Mike Vernon .10 .30
70 Adam Deadmarsh .02 .10
71 Damian Rhodes .10 .30
72 Mike Peca .02 .10
73 Jean-Sebastien Giguere .10 .30
74 Ron Francis .10 .30
75 Roman Hamrlik .10 .30
76 Vincent Damphousse .10 .30
77 Jocelyn Thibault .10 .30
78 Claude Lemieux .02 .10
79 Steve Shields RC .25 .60
80 Dimitri Khristich .02 .10
81 Theo Fleury .02 .10
82 Sandis Ozolinsh .02 .10
83 Ethan Moreau .02 .10
84 Geoff Sanderson .10 .30
85 Paul Coffey .15 .40
86 Brian Leetch .15 .40
87 Chris Osgood .10 .30
88 Kirk McLean .10 .30
89 Mike Gartner .10 .30
90 Chris Gratton .10 .30
91 Eric Fichaud .10 .30
92 Alexandre Daigle .02 .10
93 Doug Gilmour .10 .30
94 Daniel Alfredsson .10 .30
95 Doug Weight .10 .30
96 Derian Hatcher .02 .10
97 Wade Redden .02 .10
98 Jeff Friesen .02 .10
99 Tony Amonte .10 .30
100 Janne Niinimaa .10 .30
101 Trevor Linden .10 .30
102 Grant Fuhr .10 .30
103 Chris Phillips .10 .30
104 Sergei Berezin .02 .10
105 Brendan Shanahan CL .10 .30
106 Steve Yzerman CL .15 .40
107 Teemu Selanne CL .15 .40
108 Eric Lindros CL .15 .40
109 Wayne Gretzky CL .15 .40
110 Patrick Roy CL .15 .40
P3 Eric Lindros PROMO 1.00 2.50

1997-98 Studio Press Proofs Silver

Randomly inserted in packs, this 110-card set is parallel to the base set. The difference is found in the silver holographic foil and micro-etched borders. Each card is numbered 1 of 1000.

*PP SILVER: 15X TO 40X BASIC CARDS

1997-98 Studio Press Proofs Gold

Randomly inserted in packs, this 110-card set is parallel to the regular Studio set. The difference is found in the special gold holographic foil and micro-etched borders. Each card is numbered as 1 of 250.

*PP GOLD: 25X TO 60X BASIC CARDS

1997-98 Studio Hard Hats

Randomly inserted in packs, this 24-card set displays color portraits of young and veteran stars printed on plastic card stock and featuring a die-cut helmet in the background. The cards are individually numbered to 3000.

COMPLETE SET (24) 75.00 150.00
1 Wayne Gretzky 15.00 40.00
2 Eric Lindros 3.00 8.00
3 Paul Kariya 3.00 8.00
4 Bryan Berard .75 2.00
5 Dainius Zubrus .75 2.00
6 Daymond Langkow .75 2.00
7 Keith Tkachuk 1.50 4.00
8 Ryan Smyth 1.50 4.00
9 Brendan Shanahan 3.00 8.00
10 Steve Yzerman 12.00 30.00
11 Teemu Selanne 3.00 8.00
12 Jarome Iginla 4.00 10.00
13 Zigmund Palffy 1.50 4.00
14 Sergei Berezin .75 2.00
15 Saku Koivu 3.00 8.00
16 Peter Forsberg 8.00 20.00
17 Joe Sakic 6.00 15.00
18 Pavel Bure 3.00 8.00
19 Jaromir Jagr 5.00 12.00
20 Brett Hull 4.00 10.00
21 Sergei Fedorov 4.00 10.00
22 Mike Grier .75 2.00
23 Ethan Moreau .75 2.00
24 Mats Sundin 3.00 8.00

1997-98 Studio Portraits

Inserted one per pack, this 36-card set is a partial parallel 8" by 10" version of the base set and features portraits of the top stars printed on large cards with a signable UV coating.

COMPLETE SET (36) 30.00 60.00
1 Wayne Gretzky 2.00 5.00
2 Dominik Hasek .60 1.50
3 Eric Lindros .30 .75
4 Paul Kariya .30 .75
5 Jaromir Jagr .50 1.25
6 Brendan Shanahan .30 .75
7 Patrick Roy 1.50 4.00
8 Keith Tkachuk .30 .75
9 Mark Messier .30 .75
10 Steve Yzerman 1.50 4.00
11 Brett Hull .40 1.00
12 Jarome Iginla .40 1.00
13 Mike Modano .50 1.25
14 Pavel Bure .30 .75
15 Peter Forsberg .75 2.00
16 Ryan Smyth .25 .60
17 John Vanbiesbrouck .25 .60
18 Teemu Selanne .30 .75
19 Saku Koivu .30 .75
20 Martin Brodeur .75 2.00
21 Sergei Fedorov .50 1.25
22 Joe Thornton .75 2.00
23 Joe Sakic .60 1.50
24 Bryan Berard .25 .60
25 John LeClair .30 .75
26 Marc Denis .25 .60
27 Dainius Zubrus .30 .75
28 Chris Chelios .30 .75
29 Jason Arnott .25 .60
30 Jeremy Roenick .40 1.00
31 Zigmund Palffy .25 .60
32 Jaroslav Svejkovsky .25 .60
33 Mike Richter .30 .75
34 Felix Potvin .30 .75
35 Brian Leetch .30 .75
36 Chris Osgood .25 .60
NNOA Martin Brodeur AU/700 40.00 100.00
NNOB Jarome Iginla AU/1000 15.00 40.00
NNOC Ryan Smyth AU/1000 6.00 15.00

1997-98 Studio Silhouettes

Randomly inserted in packs, this 24-card set features laser die-cutting of star players' facial features. The cards are sequentially numbered to 1,500. An 8"x10" parallel was also created and inserted into packs. These parallels were numbered to 3000.

COMPLETE SET (24) 100.00 200.00
*8x10's: .3X TO .5X BASIC INSERTS
1 Wayne Gretzky 15.00 40.00
2 Eric Lindros 3.00 8.00
3 Patrick Roy 12.00 30.00
4 Martin Brodeur 8.00 20.00
5 Paul Kariya 2.00 5.00
6 Mark Messier 3.00 8.00
7 Dominik Hasek 6.00 15.00
8 Brett Hull 3.00 8.00
9 Pavel Bure 3.00 8.00
10 Steve Yzerman 10.00 25.00
11 Brendan Shanahan 3.00 8.00
12 Joe Sakic 6.00 15.00
13 Peter Forsberg 5.00 12.00
14 Sergei Fedorov 4.00 10.00
15 John LeClair 2.00 5.00
16 John Vanbiesbrouck 2.00 5.00
17 Teemu Selanne 3.00 8.00
18 Keith Tkachuk 2.00 5.00
19 Mike Modano 4.00 10.00
20 Felix Potvin 3.00 8.00
21 Ryan Smyth 2.00 5.00
22 Jaromir Jagr 6.00 15.00
23 Brian Leetch 2.00 5.00
24 Jarome Iginla 5.00 12.00

1995-96 Summit

The 1995-96 Summit set was issued in one series totaling 200 cards. The 7-card packs had a suggested retail of $1.99 each. The set was highlighted by a double thick 24-point card stock. The Cool Trade redemption card was randomly inserted in 1:72 packs, and was redeemable for NHL Cool Trade Upgrade cards of Patrick Roy, Chris Chelios, Ray Bourque and Cam Neely. Rookie Cards include Daniel Alfredsson, Radek Dvorak, Chad Kilger, and Kyle McLaren.

COMPLETE SET (200) 8.00 20.00
1 Mark Messier .10 .30
2 Paul Kariya .10 .30
3 Alexei Zhamnov .05 .15
4 Adam Oates .05 .15
5 Dale Hunter .05 .15
6 Valeri Kamensky .05 .15
7 Pavel Bure .10 .30
8 Theo Fleury .02 .10
9 Mats Sundin .10 .30
10 Joe Murphy .02 .10
11 Brian Bellows .02 .10
12 Owen Nolan .05 .15
13 Brett Hull .15 .40
14 Mike Modano .20 .50
15 Ulf Dahlen .02 .10
16 Paul Coffey .10 .30
17 Jaromir Jagr .20 .50
18 Jason Arnott .02 .10
19 Eric Lindros .10 .30
20 Jesse Belanger .02 .10
21 Alexandre Daigle .02 .10
22 Darren Turcotte .02 .10
23 Brian Leetch .05 .15
24 Wayne Gretzky .75 2.00
25 Mathieu Schneider .02 .10
26 Mark Recchi .05 .15
27 Martin Brodeur .30 .75
28 Igor Korolev .02 .10
29 Jocelyn Thibault .10 .30
30 Chris Pronger .10 .30
31 Sergei Fedorov .15 .40
32 Jari Kurri .10 .30
33 Ray Bourque .20 .50
34 Pat LaFontaine .10 .30
35 Don Beaupre .05 .15
36 Dave Andreychuk .05 .15
37 Oleg Tverdovsky .02 .10
38 Geoff Sanderson .02 .10
39 Chris Chelios .10 .30
40 Phil Housley .05 .15
41 Kevin Hatcher .02 .10
42 Ron Francis .05 .15
43 Pierre Turgeon .05 .15
44 Mikael Renberg .05 .15
45 Chris Gratton .02 .10
46 Tommy Soderstrom .05 .15
47 Stu Barnes .02 .10
48 Alexander Mogilny .05 .15
49 Craig Janney .02 .10
50 Scott Niedermayer .02 .10
51 Jim Carey .05 .15
52 Stephane Richer .05 .15
53 Dave Gagner .02 .10
54 Teemu Selanne .10 .30
55 Kelly Hrudey .05 .15
56 Roman Hamrlik .05 .15
57 Scott Mellanby .02 .10
58 Guy Hebert .05 .15
59 Gary Suter .02 .10
60 Travis Green .02 .10
61 Joe Sakic .25 .60
62 Doug Gilmour .05 .15
63 Peter Bondra .05 .15
64 Vincent Damphousse .02 .10
65 Dino Ciccarelli .05 .15
66 Adam Graves .02 .10
67 Kevin Stevens .02 .10
68 Jeff Friesen .02 .10
69 Kirk McLean .05 .15
70 Brad May .02 .10
71 Bill Ranford .05 .15
72 Derian Hatcher .02 .10
73 Glen Wesley .02 .10
74 Sergei Zubov .02 .10
75 John LeClair .10 .30
76 Igor Larionov .02 .10
77 Ray Sheppard .02 .10
78 Ulf Samuelsson .02 .10
79 Rod Brind'Amour .05 .15
80 Felix Potvin .10 .30
81 Cam Neely .10 .30
82 Jeremy Roenick .15 .40
83 Slava Kozlov .05 .15
84 Arturs Irbe .05 .15
85 Daren Puppa .05 .15
86 Rob Blake .05 .15
87 Steve Heinze .02 .10
88 Tom Barrasso .05 .15
89 Luc Robitaille .05 .15
90 Al MacInnis .05 .15
91 Petr Nedved .05 .15
92 Joe Mullen .05 .15
93 Mark Tinordi .02 .10
94 Tomas Sandstrom .02 .10
95 Dale Hawerchuk .10 .30
96 Andy Moog .10 .30
97 Alexei Kovalev .02 .10
98 David Oliver .02 .10
99 Patrick Poulin .02 .10
100 Tony Granato .02 .10
101 Alexei Yashin .02 .10
102 Trevor Linden .05 .15
103 Rick Tocchet .05 .15
104 Brett Lindros .02 .10
105 Rob Niedermayer .05 .15
106 John MacLean .05 .15
107 Pat Verbeek .02 .10
108 Ray Ferraro .02 .10
109 Mike Ricci .05 .15
110 Doug Weight .05 .15
111 Bill Guerin .05 .15
112 Ken Wregget .05 .15
113 Teppo Numminen .02 .10
114 Mike Vernon .05 .15
115 Mike Richter .10 .30
116 Dan Quinn .02 .10
117 Peter Forsberg .30 .75
118 Mario Lemieux .60 1.50
119 Geoff Courtnall .02 .10
120 Ed Belfour .10 .30
121 Kirk Muller .02 .10
122 Chris Osgood .05 .15
123 Radek Bonk .02 .10
124 Brendan Shanahan .10 .30
125 Sean Burke .05 .15
126 Larry Murphy .05 .15
127 Blaine Lacher .05 .15
128 Russ Courtnall .02 .10
129 Claude Lemieux .02 .10
130 John Vanbiesbrouck .05 .15
131 Wendel Clark .05 .15
132 Nelson Emerson .02 .10
133 Ron Hextall .05 .15
134 Scott Stevens .05 .15
135 Bernie Nicholls .02 .10
136 Brian Skrudland .02 .10
137 Sandis Ozolinsh .02 .10
138 Trevor Kidd .05 .15
139 Joe Juneau .02 .10
140 Keith Primeau .02 .10
141 Petr Klima .02 .10
142 Viktor Kozlov .05 .15
143 Mike Gartner .05 .15
144 Zigmund Palffy .05 .15
145 Steve Duchesne .02 .10
146 Brian Bradley .02 .10
147 Michal Pivonka .02 .10
148 Todd Harvey .05 .15
149 Patrick Roy .60 1.50
150 Gary Roberts .02 .10
151 Shayne Corson .02 .10
152 Keith Tkachuk .10 .30
153 Dimitri Khristich .02 .10
154 Steve Yzerman .60 1.50
155 Shawn McEachern .02 .10
156 Bryan Smolinski .02 .10
157 Vladimir Malakhov .02 .10
158 Andrew Cassels .02 .10
159 Dominik Hasek .25 .60
160 Stephane Fiset .05 .15
161 Steve Thomas .05 .15
162 Joe Nieuwendyk .05 .15
163 Sergio Momesso .02 .10
164 Jyrki Lumme .02 .10
165 Tony Amonte .05 .15
166 Yanic Perreault .02 .10
167 Brian Savage .02 .10
168 Brian Holzinger RC .10 .30
169 Radek Dvorak RC .20 .50
170 Jamie Langenbrunner .02 .10
171 Ed Jovanovski .10 .30
172 Bryan McCabe .02 .10
173 Jere Lehtinen .05 .15
174 Antti Tormanen .02 .10
175 Aki Berg RC .05 .15
176 Ryan Smyth .05 .15
177 Shean Donovan .02 .10
178 Darby Hendrickson .02 .10
179 Chad Kilger RC .05 .15
180 Vitali Yachmenev .02 .10
181 Deron Quint .02 .10
182 Daniel Alfredsson RC .25 .60
183 Jeff O'Neill .25 .60
184 Corey Hirsch .05 .15
185 Sandy Moger RC .02 .10
186 Saku Koivu .10 .30
187 Niklas Sundstrom .05 .15
188 Shane Doan RC .30 .75
189 Brendan Witt .02 .10
190 Eric Daze .05 .15
191 Marty Murray .02 .10
192 Byron Dafoe .05 .15
193 Todd Bertuzzi RC .40 1.00
194 Kyle McLaren RC .05 .15
195 Marcus Ragnarsson RC .05 .15
196 Robert Svehla RC .02 .10
197 Valeri Bure .02 .10
198 Paul Coffey .10 .30
199 Checklist (1-198) .02 .10
200 Checklist (inserts) .02 .10

1995-96 Summit Artist's Proofs

This set is a parallel version of the regular Summit issue. The card fronts use a gold prismatic foil background, while the words "Artist's Proof" are stamped on the back. The cards were randomly inserted 1:36 packs.

*VETS: 20X TO 50X BASIC CARDS
*ROOKIES: 12X TO 30X

1995-96 Summit Ice

This lower end parallel set of the basic Summit issue features silver prismatic foil print technology on the front, and the words "Summit Ice" on the back. The cards were randomly inserted at a rate of 1:7 packs.

*VETS: 5X TO 12X BASIC CARDS
*ROOKIES: 3X TO 8X

1995-96 Summit GM's Choice

Randomly inserted at a rate of 1:37 packs, this 21-card set features Pinnacle consultant Mike McPhee selecting his top choices for an all-star "dream team". The appearance of the cards is boosted by the use of a holographic gold-foil background.

COMPLETE SET (21) 25.00 50.00
1 Patrick Roy 4.00 10.00
2 Martin Brodeur 2.00 5.00
3 Chris Chelios 1.00 2.50
4 Brian Leetch .50 1.25
5 Eric Lindros 1.00 2.50
6 Keith Tkachuk 1.00 2.50
7 Pavel Bure 1.00 2.50
8 Scott Stevens .50 1.25
9 Paul Coffey 1.00 2.50
10 Mario Lemieux 4.00 10.00
11 Jaromir Jagr 1.50 4.00
12 Cam Neely 1.00 2.50
13 Ray Bourque 1.00 2.50
14 Al MacInnis .50 1.25
15 Sergei Fedorov 1.25 3.00
16 Mark Messier 1.00 2.50
17 Brett Hull 1.25 3.00
18 Wayne Gretzky 6.00 15.00
19 Paul Kariya 1.00 2.50
20 Brendan Shanahan 1.00 2.50
21 Mike McPhee .30 .75

1995-96 Summit In The Crease

Randomly inserted at a rate of 1:91 packs, this 15-card set showcases some of the hottest goaltenders in the league on cards utilizing Spectroetch technology.

COMPLETE SET (15) 25.00 60.00
1 Martin Brodeur 6.00 15.00
2 Dominik Hasek 4.00 10.00
3 Patrick Roy 10.00 25.00
4 Ed Belfour 2.00 5.00
5 Felix Potvin 2.00 5.00
6 Jim Carey 1.25 3.00
7 Jocelyn Thibault 1.25 3.00
8 Stephane Fiset 1.25 3.00
9 Chris Osgood 2.00 5.00
10 Ron Hextall 2.00 5.00
11 Mike Richter 2.00 5.00
12 Andy Moog 1.25 3.00
13 Sean Burke 1.25 3.00
14 Kirk McLean 1.25 3.00
15 John Vanbiesbrouck 2.00 5.00

1995-96 Summit Mad Hatters

Randomly inserted at a rate of 1:23 packs, this 15-card set pays tribute -- not surprisingly -- to some of the top hat trick artists of the 1994-95 season on Spectroetched cards.

COMPLETE SET (15) 15.00 30.00
1 Eric Lindros 1.50 4.00
Owen Nolan
Bernie Nicholls
2 Brett Hull 2.00 5.00
3 John LeClair .75 2.00
4 Cam Neely 1.50 4.00
5 Alexei Zhamnov .60 1.50
6 Jason Arnott .60 1.50
7 Pavel Bure 1.50 4.00
8 Wendel Clark .75 2.00
9 Sergei Fedorov 2.00 5.00
10 Jaromir Jagr 2.50 6.00
11 Peter Bondra .75 2.00
12 Alexei Yashin .60 1.50
13 Joe Nieuwendyk .75 2.00
14 Luc Robitaille .75 2.00
15 Todd Harvey .60 1.50

1996-97 Summit

This 200-card set was distributed in seven-card packs with a suggested retail price of $2.99. The fronts featured color action player photos while the backs carried player information. A 25-card "Rookies" subset and three checklists were included in this set. Key rookies include Kevin Hodson and Ethan Moreau.

COMPLETE SET (200) 15.00 30.00
1 Joe Sakic .30 .75
2 Dominik Hasek .30 .75
3 Paul Coffey .15 .40
4 Todd Gill .02 .10
5 Pat Verbeek .02 .10
6 John LeClair .15 .40
7 Joe Juneau .02 .10
8 Scott Mellanby .08 .25
9 Scott Stevens .08 .25
10 Ron Francis .08 .25
11 Larry Murphy .08 .25
12 Sandis Ozolinsh .02 .10
13 Luc Robitaille .08 .25
14 Grant Fuhr .08 .25
15 Adam Oates .08 .25
16 Keith Primeau .02 .10
17 Mark Recchi .08 .25
18 Brian Bradley .02 .10
19 Zdeno Ciger .02 .10
20 Zigmund Palffy .02 .10
21 Damian Rhodes .08 .25
22 Russ Courtnall .02 .10
23 Mike Modano .25 .60
24 Geoff Sanderson .08 .25
25 Michal Pivonka .02 .10
26 Randy Burridge .02 .10
27 Dimitri Khristich .02 .10
28 Mike Gartner .08 .25
29 Cam Neely .15 .40
30 Mathieu Schneider .02 .10
31 Steve Thomas .02 .10
32 Mario Lemieux .75 2.00
33 Darryl Sydor .02 .10
34 Alexei Yashin .02 .10
35 Brett Hull .20 .50
36 Trevor Kidd .08 .25
37 Alexei Zhamnov .08 .25
38 Uwe Krupp .02 .10
39 Brian Skrudland .02 .10
40 Igor Larionov .02 .10
41 Nikolai Khabibulin .08 .25
42 Pavel Bure .15 .40
43 Chris Chelios .15 .40
44 Andrew Cassels .02 .10
45 Owen Nolan .08 .25
46 Todd Harvey .02 .10
47 Jari Kurri .08 .25
48 Olaf Kolzig .08 .25
49 Greg Johnson .02 .10
50 Dominic Roussel .08 .25
51 Mats Sundin .15 .40
52 Robert Svehla .02 .10
53 Sandy Moger .02 .10
54 Darren Turcotte .02 .10
55 Teppo Numminen .02 .10
56 Benoit Hogue .02 .10
57 Scott Niedermayer .02 .10
58 Alexander Selivanov .02 .10
59 Valeri Kamensky .08 .25
60 Ken Wregget .08 .25
61 Travis Green .08 .25
62 Peter Bondra .08 .25
63 Vladimir Konstantinov .08 .25
64 Craig Janney .08 .25
65 Joe Nieuwendyk .08 .25
66 John Vanbiesbrouck .08 .25
67 Wayne Gretzky 1.00 2.50
68 Kirk McLean .08 .25
69 Alexei Zhitnik .02 .10
70 Mike Ricci .02 .10
71 Jeff Beukeboom .02 .10
72 Felix Potvin .15 .40
73 Mikael Renberg .08 .25
74 Jamie Baker .02 .10
75 Guy Hebert .08 .25
76 Steve Yzerman .75 2.00
77 Daren Puppa .08 .25
78 Scott Young .02 .10
79 Martin Gelinas .02 .10
80 Dave Gagner .02 .10
81 Tomas Sandstrom .02 .10
82 Alexei Kovalev .02 .10
83 Ray Whitney .02 .10
84 Vyacheslav Kozlov .02 .10
85 Jaromir Jagr .25 .60
86 Joe Murphy .02 .10
87 Patrick Roy .75 2.00
88 Ray Sheppard .08 .25
89 Chris Terreri .08 .25
90 Pierre Turgeon .02 .10
91 Theo Fleury .02 .10
92 Doug Weight .08 .25
93 Tom Barrasso .08 .25
94 Jim Carey .15 .40
95 Greg Adams .02 .10
96 Brian Leetch .15 .40
97 Ed Belfour .15 .40
98 Stephane Fiset .08 .25
99 Stephane Richer .08 .25
100 Ron Hextall .08 .25
101 Mike Vernon .08 .25
102 Jocelyn Thibault .15 .40
103 Jason Arnott .02 .10
104 Keith Tkachuk .15 .40
105 Sergei Fedorov .20 .50
106 Alexandre Daigle .02 .10
107 Alexander Mogilny .08 .25
108 German Titov .02 .10
109 Sean Burke .08 .25
110 Arturs Irbe .08 .25
111 Mark Messier .15 .40
112 Nicklas Lidstrom .15 .40
113 Claude Lemieux .02 .10
114 Martin Brodeur .40 1.00
115 Bernie Nicholls .02 .10
116 Paul Kariya .15 .40
117 Eric Lindros .15 .40
118 Doug Gilmour .08 .25
119 Sergei Zubov .02 .10
120 Adam Graves .02 .10
121 Phil Housley .08 .25
122 Bob Bassen .02 .10
123 Rod Brind'Amour .08 .25
124 Dave Andreychuk .08 .25
125 Corey Hirsch .08 .25
126 Kelly Hrudey .08 .25
127 Pat LaFontaine .15 .40
128 Slava Fetisov .02 .10
129 Oleg Tverdovsky .08 .25
130 Andy Moog .08 .25
131 Stu Barnes .02 .10
132 Roman Hamrlik .08 .25
133 Teemu Selanne .15 .40
134 Trevor Linden .08 .25
135 Chris Osgood .08 .25
136 Vincent Damphousse .02 .10
137 Shayne Corson .02 .10
138 Jeremy Roenick .20 .50
139 Brendan Shanahan .15 .40
140 Wendel Clark .08 .25
141 Ray Bourque .25 .60
142 Peter Forsberg .40 1.00
143 John MacLean .08 .25
144 Jeff Friesen .02 .10
145 Mike Richter .15 .40
146 Dave Reid .02 .10
147 Rob Niedermayer .08 .25
148 Petr Nedved .08 .25
149 Sylvain Lefebvre .02 .10
150 Curtis Joseph .15 .40
151 Eric Daze .08 .25
152 Saku Koivu .15 .40
153 Jere Lehtinen .02 .10
154 Todd Bertuzzi .15 .40
155 Chad Kilger .02 .10
156 Stephane Yelle .02 .10
157 Bryan McCabe .02 .10
158 Aaron Gavey .02 .10
159 Kyle McLaren .02 .10
160 Valeri Bure .02 .10
161 Antti Tormanen .02 .10
162 Brendan Witt .02 .10
163 Ed Jovanovski .08 .25
164 Aki Berg .02 .10
165 Marcus Ragnarsson .02 .10
166 Miroslav Satan .02 .10
167 Daniel Alfredsson .08 .25
168 Jeff O'Neill .02 .10
169 Radek Dvorak .02 .10
170 Petr Sykora .02 .10
171 Vitali Yachmenev .02 .10
172 Niklas Andersson .02 .10
173 Nolan Baumgartner .02 .10
174 Brandon Convery .02 .10
175 Ralph Intranuovo .02 .10
176 Niklas Sundblad .02 .10
177 Patrick Labrecque .08 .25
178 Eric Fichaud .08 .25
179 Martin Biron RC .75 2.00
180 Steve Sullivan RC .20 .50
181 Peter Ferraro .02 .10
182 Jose Theodore .20 .50
183 Kevin Hodson RC .15 .40
184 Ethan Moreau RC .15 .40
185 Curtis Brown .02 .10
186 Daymond Langkow .08 .25
187 Jan Caloun RC .02 .10
188 Landon Wilson .02 .10
189 Tommy Salo .08 .25
190 Anders Eriksson .02 .10
191 David Nemirovsky .02 .10
192 Jamie Langenbrunner .02 .10
193 Zdenek Nedved .02 .10
194 Todd Hlushko .02 .10
195 Alexei Yegorov RC .02 .10
196 Jamie Pushor .02 .10
197 Anders Myrvold .02 .10
198 Mark Messier CL .15 .40
199 Brett Hull CL .15 .40
200 Pavel Bure CL .15 .40

1996-97 Summit Artist's Proofs

Randomly inserted in packs at a rate of 1:35, this 200-card parallel set to the regular 1996-97 Summit set was distinguished in design by a holographic foil stamped Artist's Proof logo on the front.

*VETS: 20X TO 50X BASIC CARDS
*ROOKIES: 8X TO 20X

1996-97 Summit Ice

Randomly inserted in packs at the rate of 1:6, this 200-card parallel set featured prismatic foil printing which distinguished it from the regular Summit set. Values for all singles can be determined by using the multipliers below on the corresponding card from the base set.

*VETS: 6X TO 15X BASIC CARDS
*ROOKIES: 2.5X TO 6X

1996-97 Summit Metal

COMPLETE SET (200) 20.00 50.00
*METAL: 1.5X TO 4X BASIC CARDS

1996-97 Summit Premium Stock

A parallel to the standard Summit set, Premium Stock was distributed only to hobby outlets, and featured enhanced card stock with mirrored-foil backgrounds. Many of the Premium Stock cards came damaged out of the packs as the cards were highly condition sensitive.

COMPLETE SET (200) 20.00 50.00
*VETS: 1.5X TO 4X BASIC CARDS
*ROOKIES: .6X TO 1.5X BASIC CARDS

1996-97 Summit High Voltage

This 16-card Spectroetch insert set spotlighted the high-energy play of the NHL's superstar elite. The fronts featured a color player image on a silver and black lightning displayed background. The backs carried another player photo with player information. Just 1,500 copies of each card in this set were produced and sequentially numbered. A parallel "Mirage" version of these cards was randomly inserted into packs and sequentially numbered to 600.

COMPLETE SET (16) 60.00 150.00
*MIRAGE: .8X TO 2X BASIC INSERTS
1 Mark Messier 4.00 10.00
2 Joe Sakic 8.00 20.00
3 Paul Kariya 4.00 10.00
4 Daniel Alfredsson 2.00 5.00
5 Wayne Gretzky 15.00 40.00
6 Peter Forsberg 6.00 15.00
7 Eric Daze 2.00 5.00
8 Mario Lemieux 12.00 30.00
9 Eric Lindros 4.00 10.00
10 Jeremy Roenick 4.00 10.00
11 Alexander Mogilny 2.00 5.00
12 Teemu Selanne 4.00 10.00
13 Sergei Fedorov 4.00 10.00
14 Saku Koivu 4.00 10.00
15 Jaromir Jagr 6.00 15.00
16 Brett Hull 4.00 10.00
P16 Eric Lindros PROMO 2.00 5.00

1996-97 Summit In The Crease

This 16-card insert set featured the NHL's top goalies. A gold-foil stamped print technology was utilized which gave the cards a distinctive feel and look, and created a sense of depth in the cards. 6,000 copies of each of the cards in this set were produced and sequentially numbered. A premium stock parallel was also created. The premium stock version had an enhanced foil background and was numbered with the prefix PSITC.

COMPLETE SET (16) 30.00 80.00
*PREM.STOCK: .8X TO 2X BASIC INSERTS
1 Patrick Roy 10.00 25.00
2 Mike Richter 3.00 8.00
3 Ed Belfour 3.00 8.00
4 Daren Puppa 2.00 5.00
5 Curtis Joseph 3.00 8.00
6 Jim Carey 2.00 5.00
7 Damian Rhodes 2.00 5.00
8 Martin Brodeur 6.00 15.00
9 Felix Potvin 3.00 8.00
10 John Vanbiesbrouck 2.00 5.00
11 Jocelyn Thibault 2.00 5.00
12 Nikolai Khabibulin 2.00 5.00
13 Chris Osgood 2.00 5.00
14 Dominik Hasek 4.00 10.00
15 Corey Hirsch 2.00 5.00
16 Ron Hextall 2.00 5.00

1996-97 Summit Untouchables

This 18-card insert set was an all-foil version of the regular series which honored 12 skaters who amassed 100 or more points and six goaltenders who notched 30 wins during the 1995-96 season. Although the cards were intended to mention this fact, all the goalie cards read 100 points along the bottom front, the same as the skaters. No corrected versions were produced. Just 1,000 copies of this set were produced and each card was sequentially numbered.

COMPLETE SET (18) 75.00 150.00
1 Mario Lemieux 12.00 30.00
2 Jaromir Jagr 4.00 10.00
3 Joe Sakic 6.00 15.00
4 Ron Francis 2.00 5.00
5 Peter Forsberg 3.00 8.00
6 Eric Lindros 3.00 8.00
7 Paul Kariya 3.00 8.00
8 Teemu Selanne 3.00 8.00
9 Alexander Mogilny 2.00 5.00
10 Sergei Fedorov 4.00 10.00
11 Doug Weight 2.00 5.00
12 Wayne Gretzky 20.00 50.00
13 Chris Osgood 2.00 5.00
14 Jim Carey 2.00 5.00
15 Patrick Roy 12.00 30.00
16 Martin Brodeur 8.00 20.00
17 Felix Potvin 3.00 8.00
18 Ron Hextall 3.00 8.00

2006-07 Sunkist

COMPLETE SET (10) 10.00 20.00
1 Alex Kovalev .40 1.00
2 Jason Spezza .75 2.00
3 Mats Sundin 1.25 3.00
4 Jarome Iginla 1.25 3.00
5 Ryan Smyth .75 2.00
6 Markus Naslund .75 2.00

7 Alexander Ovechkin 2.00 5.00
8 Vincent Lecavalier 1.25 3.00
9 Joe Thornton 1.50 4.00
10 Miikka Kiprusoff 1.25 3.00

2007-08 Sunkist

COMPLET SET (10) 10.00 25.00
1 Saku Koivu 1.25 3.00
2 Mats Sundin 1.25 3.00
3 Dany Heatley 1.25 3.00
4 Ales Hemsky 1.25 3.00
5 Jarome Iginla 1.50 4.00
6 Roberto Luongo 1.50 4.00
7 Joe Thornton 1.25 3.00
8 Vincent LeCavalier 1.50 4.00
9 Chris Pronger 1.25 3.00
10 Eric Staal 1.25 3.00

1910-11 Sweet Caporal Postcards

These black-and-white photo postcards apparently were used by the artists working on the C55 cards of the next year, 1911-12. Printed by the British American Tobacco Co. in England, these cards were distributed by Imperial Tobacco of Canada. One card was reportedly packed in each 50-cigarette tin of Sweet Caporal cigarettes. The backs show the postcard design. The cards are checklisted below according to teams as follows: Quebec Bulldogs (1-8), Ottawa Senators (10-17), Renfrew Millionaires (18-26), Montreal Wanderers (27-36), and Montreal Canadiens (37-45).

COMPLETE SET (45) 9000.00 18000.00
1 Paddy Moran 250.00 500.00
2 Joe Hall 175.00 350.00
3 Barney Holden 100.00 200.00
4 Joe Malone 500.00 1000.00
5 Ed Oatman 100.00 200.00
6 Tom Dunderdale 175.00 350.00
7 Ken Mallen 100.00 200.00
8 Jack MacDonald 100.00 200.00
9 Fred Lake 100.00 200.00
10 Albert Kerr 100.00 200.00
11 Marty Walsh 175.00 350.00
12 Hamby Shore 100.00 200.00
13 Alex Currie 100.00 200.00
14 Bruce Ridpath 100.00 200.00
15 Bruce Stuart 175.00 350.00
16 Percy Lesueur 175.00 350.00
17 Jack Darragh 175.00 350.00
18 Steve Vair 100.00 200.00
19 Don Smith 100.00 200.00
20 Cyclone Taylor 600.00 1200.00
21 Bert Lindsay 125.00 250.00
22 H.L.(Larry) Gilmour 175.00 350.00
23 Bobby Rowe 100.00 200.00
24 Sprague Cleghorn 300.00 600.00
25 Odie Cleghorn 125.00 250.00
26 Skein Ronan 100.00 200.00
27 Walter Smaill 125.00 250.00
28 Ernest(Moose) Johnson 200.00 400.00
29 Jack Marshall 175.00 350.00
30 Harry Hyland 175.00 350.00
31 Art Ross 600.00 1200.00
32 Riley Hern 175.00 350.00
33 Gordon Roberts 175.00 350.00
34 Frank Glass 100.00 200.00
35 Ernest Russell 200.00 400.00
36 James Gardner 175.00 350.00
37 Art Bernier 100.00 200.00
38 Georges Vezina 2000.00 4000.00
39 G.(Henri) Dallaire 100.00 200.00
40 R.(Rocket) Power 100.00 200.00
41 Didier(Pit) Pitre 175.00 350.00
42 Newsy Lalonde 600.00 1200.00
43 Eugene Payan 100.00 200.00
44 George Poulin 100.00 200.00
45 Jack Laviolette 200.00 400.00

1934-35 Sweet Caporal

This colorful set of 48 large (approximately 6 3/4" by 10 1/2") pictures were actually inserts in Montreal Forum programs during Canadiens and Maroons home games during the 1934-35 season. Apparently a different photo was inserted each game. Players in the checklist below are identified as part of the following teams, Montreal Canadiens (MC), Montreal Maroons (MM), Boston Bruins (BB), Chicago Blackhawks (CBH), Detroit Red Wings (DRW), New York Rangers (NYR), and Toronto Maple Leafs (TML). Card backs contain player biography and an ad for Sweet Caporal Cigarettes, both in French. The cards are unnumbered.

COMPLETE SET (48) 2500.00 5000.00
1 Gerald Carson MC 25.00 50.00
2 Nels Crutchfield MC 25.00 50.00
3 Wilfrid Cude MC 30.00 60.00
4 Roger Jenkins MC 25.00 50.00
5 Aurel Joliat MC 175.00 350.00
6 Joe Lamb MC 25.00 50.00
7 Wildor Larochelle MC 25.00 50.00
8 Pete Lepine MC 25.00 50.00
9 Georges Mantha MC 25.00 50.00
10 Sylvio Mantha MC 50.00 100.00
11 Jack McGill MC 25.00 50.00
12 Armand Mondou MC 25.00 50.00
13 Paul Marcel Raymond MC 25.00 50.00
14 Jack Riley MC 25.00 50.00
15 Russ Blinco MM 25.00 50.00
16 Herb Cain MM 40.00 80.00
17 Lionel Conacher MM 125.00 250.00
18 Alex Connell MM 62.50 125.00
19 Stewart Evans MM 25.00 50.00
20 Norman Gainor MM 25.00 50.00
21 Paul Haynes MM 25.00 50.00
22 Gus Marker MM 25.00 50.00
23 Baldy Northcott MM 30.00 60.00
24 Earl Robinson MM 25.00 50.00
25 Hooley Smith MM 50.00 100.00
26 Dave Trottier MM 25.00 50.00
27 Jimmy Ward MM 25.00 50.00
28 Cy Wentworth MM 30.00 60.00
29 Eddie Shore BB 250.00 500.00
30 Babe Siebert BB 62.50 125.00
31 Nels Stewart BB 75.00 150.00
32 Cecil(Tiny) Thompson BB 75.00 150.00
33 Lorne Chabot CBH 50.00 100.00
34 Harold March CBH 25.00 50.00
35 Howie Morenz CBH 400.00 800.00
36 Larry Aurie DRW 25.00 50.00
37 Ebbie Goodfellow DRW 50.00 100.00
38 Herbie Lewis DRW 25.00 50.00
39 Cooney Weiland DRW 50.00 100.00
40 Bill Cook NYR 50.00 100.00
41 Fred(Bun) Cook NYR 50.00 100.00
42 Ivan(Ching) Johnson NYR 67.50 135.00
43 Dave Kerr NYR 40.00 80.00
44 Frank(King) Clancy TML 200.00 400.00
45 Charlie Conacher TML 200.00 400.00
46 Red Horner TML 62.50 125.00
47 Busher Jackson TML 75.00 150.00
48 Joe Primeau TML 100.00 200.00

2006-07 Sweet Shot

This 160-card set was released in May, 2007. The set was issued into the hobby in four-card packs (tins) with an $85 SRP which came 20 packs (tins) to a case. Cards numbered 1-100 feature a mix of veterans and retired greats while cards 101-160 are all Rookie Cards which also have a player-worn jersey swatch. Those Rookie Cards were all issued to a stated print run of 499 serial numbered sets.

JSY RCs #'d TO 499
1 Teemu Selanne 1.50 4.00
2 Chris Pronger 1.25 3.00
3 Jean-Sebastien Giguere 1.50 4.00
4 Ilya Kovalchuk 2.00 5.00
5 Marian Hossa 1.25 3.00
6 Kari Lehtonen 1.50 4.00
7 Patrice Bergeron 1.25 3.00
8 Zdeno Chara 1.00 2.50
9 Cam Neely 1.25 3.00
10 Bobby Orr 8.00 20.00
11 Phil Esposito 1.50 4.00
12 Ray Bourque 2.00 5.00
13 Ryan Miller 1.50 4.00
14 Maxim Afinogenov 1.00 2.50
15 Chris Drury 1.25 3.00
16 Gilbert Perreault 1.00 2.50
17 Alex Tanguay 1.25 3.00
18 Dion Phaneuf 2.00 5.00
19 Jarome Iginla 2.50 6.00
20 Miikka Kiprusoff 1.50 4.00
21 Cam Ward 2.50 6.00
22 Eric Staal 1.25 3.00
23 Nikolai Khabibulin 1.50 4.00
24 Martin Havlat 1.25 3.00
25 Bobby Hull 1.50 4.00
26 Tony Esposito 2.50 6.00
27 Joe Sakic 4.00 10.00
28 Jose Theodore 1.50 4.00
29 Milan Hejduk 1.25 3.00
30 Patrick Roy 6.00 15.00
31 Rick Nash 1.50 4.00
32 Sergei Fedorov 1.50 4.00
33 Pascal LeClaire 1.50 4.00
34 Mike Modano 1.50 4.00
35 Eric Lindros 1.50 4.00
36 Marty Turco 1.25 3.00
37 Henrik Zetterberg 1.50 4.00
38 Nicklas Lidstrom 1.50 4.00
39 Pavel Datsyuk 1.50 4.00
40 Dominik Hasek 2.00 5.00
41 Gordie Howe 6.00 15.00
42 Ted Lindsay 1.00 2.50
43 Ales Hemsky 1.00 2.50
44 Dwayne Roloson 1.25 3.00
45 Wayne Gretzky 10.00 25.00
46 Jari Kurri 1.00 2.50
47 Grant Fuhr 2.50 6.00
48 Ed Belfour 4.00 10.00
49 Olli Jokinen 1.00 2.50
50 Rob Blake 1.25 3.00
51 Alexander Frolov 1.00 2.50
52 Manny Fernandez 1.50 4.00
53 Pavol Demitra 1.00 2.50
54 Marian Gaborik 2.50 6.00
55 Saku Koivu 1.50 4.00
56 Cristobal Huet 1.50 4.00
57 Michael Ryder 1.25 3.00
58 Guy Lafleur 1.50 4.00
59 Larry Robinson .75 2.00
60 Paul Kariya 1.50 4.00
61 Tomas Vokoun 1.25 3.00
62 Brian Gionta 1.25 3.00
63 Martin Brodeur 5.00 12.00
64 Patrik Elias 1.00 2.50
65 Rick DiPietro 1.50 4.00
66 Alexei Yashin 1.00 2.50
67 Mike Bossy 1.25 3.00
68 Billy Smith 2.00 5.00
69 Denis Potvin 1.25 3.00
70 Jaromir Jagr 2.50 6.00
71 Henrik Lundqvist 2.50 6.00
72 Brendan Shanahan 1.50 4.00
73 Dany Heatley 1.50 4.00
74 Jason Spezza 1.50 4.00
75 Daniel Alfredsson 1.25 3.00
76 Peter Forsberg 2.50 6.00
77 Simon Gagne 1.50 4.00
78 Bobby Clarke 1.50 4.00
79 Jeremy Roenick 1.50 4.00
80 Shane Doan 1.25 3.00
81 Curtis Joseph 1.50 4.00
82 Sidney Crosby 15.00 40.00
83 Marc-Andre Fleury 1.50 4.00
84 Mario Lemieux 6.00 15.00
85 Peter Stastny 1.00 2.50
86 Joe Thornton 2.50 6.00
87 Patrick Marleau 1.25 3.00
88 Jonathan Cheechoo 1.50 4.00
89 Doug Weight 1.00 2.50
90 Brad Richards 1.50 4.00
91 Vincent Lecavalier 1.50 4.00
92 Martin St. Louis 1.50 4.00
93 Mats Sundin 1.50 4.00
94 Andrew Raycroft 1.25 3.00
95 Darcy Tucker 1.00 2.50
96 Johnny Bower 2.50 6.00
97 Darryl Sittler 1.00 2.50
98 Roberto Luongo 3.00 8.00
99 Markus Naslund 1.50 4.00
100 Alexander Ovechkin 6.00 15.00
101 Shane O'Brien JSY RC 4.00 10.00
102 Ryan Shannon JSY RC 4.00 10.00
103 David McKee JSY RC 5.00 12.00
104 Phil Kessel JSY RC 15.00 40.00
105 Yan Stastny JSY RC 4.00 10.00
106 Mark Stuart JSY RC 4.00 10.00
107 Matt Lashoff JSY RC 4.00 10.00
108 Clarke MacArthur JSY RC 4.00 10.00
109 Drew Stafford JSY RC 6.00 15.00
110 Masi Marjamaki JSY RC 4.00 10.00
111 Michael Funk JSY RC 2.00 5.00
112 Brandon Prust JSY RC 4.00 10.00
113 Dustin Boyd JSY RC 6.00 15.00
114 Dustin Byfuglien JSY RC 8.00 20.00
115 Dave Bolland JSY RC 8.00 20.00
116 Michael Blunden JSY RC 4.00 10.00
117 Paul Stastny JSY RC 15.00 40.00
118 Fredrik Norrena JSY RC 5.00 12.00
119 Niklas Grossman JSY RC 5.00 12.00
120 Loui Eriksson JSY RC 4.00 10.00
121 Tomas Kopecky JSY RC 6.00 15.00
122 Stefan Liv JSY RC 6.00 15.00
123 Patrick Thoresen JSY RC 6.00 15.00
124 Marc-Antoine Pouliot JSY RC 6.00 15.00
125 Ladislav Smid JSY RC 4.00 10.00
126 Janis Sprukts JSY RC 4.00 10.00
127 Jeff Deslauriers JSY RC 5.00 12.00
128 David Booth JSY RC 4.00 10.00
129 Konstantin Pushkaryov JSY RC 4.00 10.00
130 Anze Kopitar JSY RC 10.00 25.00
131 Patrick O'Sullivan JSY RC 6.00 15.00
132 Benoit Pouliot JSY RC 6.00 15.00
133 Niklas Backstrom JSY RC 6.00 15.00
134 Guillaume Latendresse JSY RC 15.00 40.00
135 Shea Weber JSY RC 6.00 15.00
136 Alexander Radulov JSY RC 10.00 25.00
137 Travis Zajac JSY RC 6.00 15.00
138 Nigel Dawes JSY RC 4.00 10.00
139 Jarkko Immonen JSY RC 4.00 10.00
140 Josh Hennessy JSY RC 4.00 10.00
141 Jussi Timonen JSY RC 2.00 5.00
142 Ryan Potulny JSY RC 6.00 15.00
143 Keith Yandle JSY RC 4.00 10.00
144 Michel Ouellet JSY RC 6.00 15.00
145 Jordan Staal JSY RC 12.00 30.00
146 Evgeni Malkin JSY RC 25.00 60.00
147 Noah Welch JSY RC 4.00 10.00
148 Kristopher Letang JSY RC 6.00 15.00
149 Matt Carle JSY RC 5.00 12.00
150 Marc-Edouard Vlasic JSY RC 4.00 10.00
151 Joe Pavelski JSY RC 12.00 30.00
152 Marek Schwarz JSY RC 8.00 20.00
153 Karri Ramo JSY RC 4.00 10.00
154 Blair Jones JSY RC 4.00 10.00
155 Ian White JSY RC 4.00 10.00
156 Jeremy Williams JSY RC 4.00 10.00
157 Luc Bourdon JSY RC 5.00 12.00
158 Jesse Schultz JSY RC 4.00 10.00
159 Alexander Edler JSY RC 4.00 10.00
160 Eric Fehr JSY RC 5.00 12.00

2006-07 Sweet Shot Endorsed Equipment

STATED PRINT RUN 25 SER.#'d SETS
EEAR Andrew Raycroft 50.00 100.00
EEBR Bill Ranford 50.00 100.00
EEEB Ed Belfour 50.00 100.00
EEGC Gerry Cheevers 60.00 125.00
EEGF Grant Fuhr 50.00 100.00
EEJT Jose Theodore 30.00 80.00
EEMF Marc-Andre Fleury 100.00 150.00
EEMT Marty Turco 50.00 100.00
EEPR Patrick Roy 200.00 350.00
EETE Tony Esposito 60.00 125.00

2006-07 Sweet Shot Rookie Jerseys Autographs

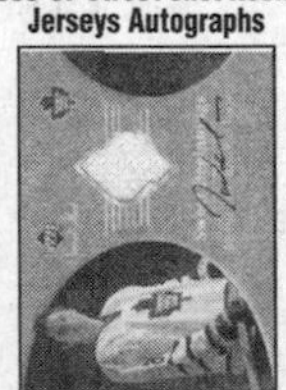

*AUs: 3X to 7X RC HI
STATED PRINT RUN 25 #'d SETS
101 Shane O'Brien 25.00 60.00
102 Ryan Shannon 25.00 60.00
103 David McKee 30.00 80.00
104 Phil Kessel 40.00 100.00
105 Yan Stastny 25.00 60.00
106 Mark Stuart 25.00 60.00
107 Matt Lashoff 25.00 60.00
108 Clarke MacArthur 25.00 60.00
109 Drew Stafford 50.00 125.00
110 Masi Marjamaki 25.00 60.00
111 Michael Funk 12.00 30.00
112 Brandon Prust 25.00 60.00
113 Dustin Boyd 30.00 80.00
114 Dustin Byfuglien 50.00 120.00
115 Dave Bolland 50.00 120.00
116 Michael Blunden 25.00 60.00
117 Paul Stastny 75.00 175.00
118 Fredrik Norrena 25.00 60.00
119 Niklas Grossman 25.00 60.00
120 Loui Eriksson 25.00 60.00
121 Tomas Kopecky 30.00 80.00
122 Stefan Liv 30.00 80.00
123 Patrick Thoresen 25.00 60.00
124 Marc-Antoine Pouliot 30.00 80.00
125 Ladislav Smid 25.00 60.00
126 Janis Sprukts 25.00 60.00
127 Jeff Deslauriers 30.00 80.00
128 David Booth 25.00 60.00
129 Konstantin Pushkaryov 25.00 60.00
130 Anze Kopitar 60.00 150.00
131 Patrick O'Sullivan 30.00 80.00
132 Benoit Pouliot 30.00 80.00
133 Niklas Backstrom 25.00 60.00
134 Guillaume Latendresse 40.00 100.00
135 Shea Weber 30.00 80.00
136 Alexander Radulov 30.00 80.00
137 Travis Zajac 40.00 100.00
138 Nigel Dawes 25.00 60.00
139 Jarkko Immonen 25.00 60.00
140 Josh Hennessy 25.00 60.00
141 Jussi Timonen 12.00 30.00
142 Ryan Potulny 30.00 80.00
143 Keith Yandle 25.00 60.00
144 Michel Ouellet 40.00 100.00
145 Jordan Staal 75.00 150.00
146 Evgeni Malkin 125.00 250.00
147 Noah Welch 25.00 60.00
148 Kristopher Letang 40.00 100.00
149 Matt Carle 30.00 80.00
150 Marc-Edouard Vlasic 25.00 60.00
151 Joe Pavelski 80.00 200.00
152 Marek Schwarz 50.00 120.00
153 Karri Ramo 25.00 60.00
154 Blair Jones 25.00 60.00
155 Ian White 25.00 60.00
156 Jeremy Williams 25.00 60.00
157 Luc Bourdon 30.00 80.00
158 Jesse Schultz 25.00 60.00
159 Alexander Edler 25.00 60.00
160 Eric Fehr 30.00 80.00

2006-07 Sweet Shot Signature Shots/Saves

SSAF Alexander Frolov 3.00 8.00
SSAH Ales Hemsky 3.00 8.00
SSAK Anze Kopitar 15.00 40.00
SSAO Adam Oates 3.00 8.00
SSAR Andrew Raycroft 5.00 12.00
SSAT Alex Tanguay SP 5.00 12.00
SSBB Brad Boyes 3.00 8.00
SSBE Jean Beliveau SP 50.00 100.00
SSBF Bernie Federko 3.00 8.00
SSBG Brian Gionta 8.00 20.00
SSBH Bobby Hull SP 25.00 60.00
SSBI Martin Biron 5.00 12.00
SSBM Brenden Morrow 5.00 12.00
SSBO Pierre-Marc Bouchard 3.00 8.00
SSBR Martin Brodeur SP 40.00 80.00
SSCA Colby Armstrong 3.00 8.00
SSCH Jonathan Cheechoo 6.00 15.00
SSCI Dino Ciccarelli 3.00 8.00
SSCN Cam Neely SP 15.00 30.00
SSCP Corey Perry 5.00 12.00
SSCW Cam Ward 6.00 15.00
SSDC Don Cherry SP 30.00 80.00
SSDH Dominik Hasek 8.00 20.00
SSDI Dick Irvin 8.00 20.00
SSDP Denis Potvin SP 10.00 25.00
SSDR Dwayne Roloson 5.00 12.00
SSDS Drew Stafford 6.00 15.00
SSEM Evgeni Malkin 40.00 100.00
SSES Eric Staal 20.00 50.00
SSGB Gilbert Brule 6.00 15.00
SSGE Martin Gerber 6.00 15.00
SSGF Grant Fuhr SP 15.00 30.00
SSGH Gordie Howe 30.00 80.00
SSGL Guillaume Latendresse 12.00 30.00
SSGO Scott Gomez 6.00 15.00
SSHA Dale Hawerchuk 5.00 12.00
SSHE Dany Heatley SP 12.00 30.00
SSHI Chris Higgins 5.00 12.00
SSHU Cristobal Huet 10.00 25.00
SSHZ Henrik Zetterberg SP 20.00 50.00
SSIK Ilya Kovalchuk 8.00 20.00
SSJB Johnny Bucyk SP 8.00 20.00
SSJC Jeff Carter 6.00 15.00
SSJG Jean-Sebastien Giguere 5.00 12.00
SSJI Jarome Iginla 8.00 20.00
SSJP Joni Pitkanen 3.00 8.00
SSJS Jarret Stoll 8.00 20.00
SSJT Joe Thornton SP 20.00 50.00
SSKD Kris Draper 20.00 50.00
SSKL Kari Lehtonen 6.00 15.00
SSMA Matt Carle SP 5.00 12.00
SSMB Mike Bossy SP 6.00 15.00
SSMC Mike Cammalleri 3.00 8.00
SSME Barry Melrose 10.00 25.00
SSMF Marc-Andre Fleury 10.00 25.00
SSMG Marian Gaborik 10.00 25.00
SSMH Martin Havlat 5.00 12.00
SSMI Milan Hejduk 10.00 25.00
SSMK Miikka Kiprusoff 6.00 15.00
SSML Mario Lemieux SP 90.00 150.00
SSMM Marty McSorley 3.00 8.00
SSMO Mike Modano SP 12.00 30.00
SSMP Michael Peca 3.00 8.00
SSMR Michael Ryder 5.00 12.00
SSMS Marc Savard 8.00 20.00
SSMT Marty Turco 5.00 12.00
SSND Nigel Dawes 3.00 8.00
SSNL Nicklas Lidstrom SP 20.00 40.00
SSNZ Nikolai Zherdev 3.00 8.00
SSOR Bobby Orr 100.00 175.00
SSPB Patrice Bergeron 6.00 15.00
SSPE Patrik Elias 8.00 20.00
SSPK Phil Kessel 6.00 15.00
SSPM Patrick Marleau SP 5.00 12.00
SSPO Patrick O'Sullivan 5.00 12.00
SSPP Petr Prucha 12.00 30.00
SSPS Paul Stastny 12.00 30.00
SSRA Alexander Radulov 10.00 25.00
SSRB Ray Bourque SP 25.00 60.00
SSRH Ron Hextall 8.00 20.00
SSRM Ryan Miller 8.00 20.00
SSRN Rick Nash 6.00 15.00
SSRS Ryan Smyth 10.00 25.00
SSSC Sidney Crosby 75.00 150.00
SSSG Simon Gagne 10.00 25.00
SSST Jordan Staal 30.00 60.00
SSSV Marek Svatos 3.00 8.00
SSTH Jose Theodore SP 12.00 30.00
SSTO Terry O'Reilly 5.00 12.00
SSTV Tomas Vokoun 6.00 15.00
SSVL Vincent Lecavalier SP 25.00 60.00
SSVT Vesa Toskala 5.00 12.00
SSWG Wayne Gretzky SP 150.00 250.00
SSWO Willie O'Ree 8.00 20.00
SSZC Zdeno Chara 3.00 8.00

2006-07 Sweet Shot Signature Shots/Saves Ice Signings

STATED PRINT RUN 100 SER.#'d SETS
SSIAH Ales Hemsky 6.00 15.00
SSIAR Alexander Radulov 25.00 60.00
SSIBB Brad Boyes 6.00 15.00
SSIBO Bobby Orr 100.00 200.00
SSICA Colby Armstrong 12.00 30.00
SSICW Cam Ward 10.00 25.00
SSIDH Dominik Hasek 25.00 60.00
SSIEM Evgeni Malkin 100.00 150.00
SSIES Eric Staal 10.00 25.00
SSIGH Gordie Howe 40.00 80.00
SSIHE Dany Heatley 15.00 40.00
SSIHZ Henrik Zetterberg 15.00 40.00
SSIIK Ilya Kovalchuk 15.00 40.00
SSIJG Jean-Sebastien Giguere 15.00 40.00
SSIJI Jarome Iginla 20.00 50.00
SSIJK Jari Kurri 20.00 50.00
SSIJS Jarret Stoll 6.00 15.00
SSIJT Joe Thornton 30.00 80.00
SSIKL Kari Lehtonen 12.00 30.00
SSILR Larry Robinson 10.00 25.00
SSIMB Martin Brodeur 50.00 100.00
SSIMD Marcel Dionne 10.00 25.00
SSIMG Marian Gaborik 20.00 50.00
SSIMH Martin Havlat 12.00 30.00
SSIMK Miikka Kiprusoff 15.00 40.00
SSIMM Mike Modano 12.00 30.00
SSIMR Michael Ryder 10.00 25.00
SSIMS Marek Svatos 6.00 15.00
SSIMT Marty Turco 12.00 30.00
SSINL Nicklas Lidstrom 20.00 50.00
SSIPE Patrik Elias 6.00 15.00
SSIPK Phil Kessel 25.00 60.00
SSIRB Ray Bourque 30.00 80.00
SSIRK Red Kelly 12.00 30.00
SSIRM Ryan Miller 20.00 50.00
SSIRN Rick Nash 15.00 40.00
SSISC Sidney Crosby 150.00 300.00
SSISG Simon Gagne 10.00 25.00
SSIST Jordan Staal 30.00 80.00
SSITV Tomas Vokoun 10.00 25.00
SSIWG Wayne Gretzky 150.00 300.00

2006-07 Sweet Shot Signature Shots/Saves Sticks

STATED PRINT RUN 25 SER.#'d SETS
SSSAB Andy Bathgate 15.00 40.00
SSSAF Alexander Frolov 15.00 40.00
SSSAH Ales Hemsky 25.00 60.00
SSSAK Anze Kopitar 75.00 150.00
SSSAR Andrew Raycroft 25.00 60.00
SSSBB Brad Boyes 40.00
SSSBC Bobby Clarke 25.00 60.00
SSSBG Brian Gionta 20.00 50.00
SSSBH Bobby Hull 40.00 100.00
SSSBM Brenden Morrow 25.00 60.00
SSSBO Mike Bossy 30.00 80.00
SSSBP Bernie Parent 50.00 125.00
SSSBR Brent Sutter 15.00 40.00
SSSBS Borje Salming
SSSBU Johnny Bucyk 20.00 50.00
SSSCA Colby Armstrong
SSSCD Chris Drury 25.00 60.00
SSSCH Cristobal Huet 40.00 80.00
SSSCN Cam Neely 30.00 80.00
SSSDC Don Cherry 75.00 150.00
SSSDE Denis Potvin 20.00 50.00
SSSDH Dominik Hasek 40.00 80.00
SSSDP Dion Phaneuf 40.00 80.00
SSSDR Dwayne Roloson 25.00 60.00
SSSDS Denis Savard 15.00 40.00
SSSDT Dave Taylor 20.00 50.00
SSSDW Doug Wilson 15.00 40.00
SSSEM Evgeni Malkin 150.00 250.00
SSSES Eric Staal 25.00 60.00
SSSGB Gilbert Brule 25.00 60.00
SSSGE Martin Gerber
SSSGF Grant Fuhr 30.00 80.00
SSSGH Gordie Howe 75.00 150.00
SSSGL Guillaume Latendresse 60.00 150.00
SSSGP Gilbert Perreault
SSSHE Dany Heatley 30.00 60.00
SSSHZ Henrik Zetterberg 60.00 120.00
SSSIK Ilya Kovalchuk 30.00 80.00
SSSJA Jason Arnott
SSSJB Jean Beliveau 50.00 125.00
SSSJC Jonathan Cheechoo 30.00 60.00
SSSJE Jeff Carter 25.00 60.00
SSSJI Jarome Iginla 40.00 80.00
SSSJK Jari Kurri 30.00 80.00
SSSJO Johnny Bower
SSSJR Jeremy Roenick 30.00 80.00
SSSJS Jordan Staal 100.00 200.00
SSSJT Jose Theodore
SSSKL Kari Lehtonen
SSSLA Guy Lafleur 50.00 100.00
SSSLR Luc Robitaille
SSSMA Matt Carle 15.00 40.00
SSSMB Martin Brodeur 100.00 200.00
SSSMC Mike Cammalleri 25.00 60.00
SSSMD Marcel Dionne 30.00 60.00
SSSMF Marc-Andre Fleury 50.00 100.00
SSSMG Marian Gaborik 50.00 125.00
SSSMH Martin Havlat 30.00 60.00
SSSMI Milan Hejduk
SSSMK Miikka Kiprusoff 30.00 80.00
SSSML Mario Lemieux 100.00 250.00
SSSMM Mike Modano 40.00 80.00
SSSMP Michael Peca
SSSMR Michael Ryder 25.00 60.00
SSSMS Marek Svatos 20.00 50.00
SSSMT Marty Turco 25.00 60.00
SSSNL Nicklas Lidstrom 25.00 60.00
SSSNZ Nikolai Zherdev 20.00 50.00
SSSOR Bobby Orr 300.00 450.00
SSSPA Patrice Bergeron 25.00 60.00
SSSPB Pierre-Marc Bouchard
SSSPE Patrik Elias 20.00 50.00
SSSPH Phil Esposito 50.00 125.00
SSSPK Phil Kessel 50.00 125.00
SSSPM Patrick Marleau 30.00 60.00
SSSPO Patrick O'Sullivan 15.00 40.00
SSSPS Paul Stastny 75.00 150.00
SSSRA Alexander Radulov 50.00 125.00
SSSRB Ray Bourque 40.00 100.00
SSSRH Ron Hextall 40.00 100.00
SSSRM Ryan Miller 25.00 60.00
SSSRN Rick Nash 25.00 60.00
SSSRO Larry Robinson 20.00 50.00
SSSRS Ryan Smyth 30.00 60.00
SSSRV Rick Vaive 25.00 60.00
SSSSC Sidney Crosby 300.00 450.00
SSSSG Scott Gomez 20.00 50.00
SSSSI Darryl Sittler 25.00 60.00
SSSSJ Jarret Stoll 15.00 40.00
SSSSK Saku Koivu 25.00 60.00
SSSST Peter Stastny 30.00 80.00
SSSSU Brian Sutter 15.00 40.00
SSSTE Tony Esposito 25.00 60.00
SSSTH Joe Thornton 40.00 100.00
SSSTL Ted Lindsay
SSSTV Tomas Vokoun 30.00 60.00
SSSVL Vincent Lecavalier 25.00 60.00
SSSWG Wayne Gretzky 350.00 500.00

2006-07 Sweet Shot Signature Sticks

STATED PRINT RUN 15 SER.#'d SETS
STAM Al MacInnis 30.00 80.00
STAO Adam Oates
STAR Andrew Raycroft 25.00 60.00
STBB Bob Bourne 25.00 60.00
STBC Bobby Clarke 60.00 125.00
STBH Bobby Hull 75.00 150.00
STBL Rob Blake 30.00 80.00
STBO Bobby Orr 400.00 600.00
STBP Bernie Parent 75.00 150.00
STBS Billy Smith 30.00 80.00
STCD Chris Drury 30.00 80.00
STCG Clark Gillies
STCH Cristobal Huet 40.00 100.00
STCW Cam Ward 30.00 80.00
STDA David Aebischer 30.00 80.00
STDB Daniel Briere 40.00 100.00
STDG Doug Gilmour 100.00 175.00
STDH Dominik Hasek 60.00 125.00
STDP Dion Phaneuf 75.00 150.00
STDR Dwayne Roloson 30.00 80.00
STEM Evgeni Malkin 100.00 200.00
STES Eric Staal 40.00 100.00
STFM Frank Mahovlich 60.00 150.00
STGH Gordie Howe 175.00 300.00
STGL Guy Lafleur 60.00 125.00
STGP Gilbert Perreault 40.00 100.00
STHA Dale Hawerchuk 40.00 80.00
STHE Dany Heatley 60.00 125.00
STHZ Henrik Zetterberg 60.00 125.00
STIK Ilya Kovalchuk 60.00 125.00
STJB Jean Beliveau 75.00 150.00
STJC Jonathan Cheechoo 60.00 125.00
STJG Jean-Sebastien Giguere 40.00 100.00
STJI Jarome Iginla 125.00 250.00
STJK Jari Kurri 60.00 125.00
STJL Joffrey Lupul 25.00 60.00
STJM Joe Mullen 25.00 60.00
STJP Joni Pitkanen 25.00 60.00
STJR Jeremy Roenick 75.00 150.00
STJT Joe Thornton 75.00 175.00
STKL Kari Lehtonen 40.00 100.00
STLE Manny Legace 25.00 60.00
STLM Larry Murphy 25.00 60.00
STLR Luc Robitaille 40.00 100.00
STMB Martin Brodeur 150.00 250.00
STMG Marian Gaborik 75.00 150.00
STMH Milan Hejduk 25.00 60.00
STMI Mike Bossy 75.00 125.00
STMK Miikka Kiprusoff 60.00 125.00
STML Mario Lemieux 225.00 400.00
STMM Mike Modano 60.00 125.00
STMN Markus Naslund 40.00 80.00
STMP Michael Peca 40.00 100.00
STMR Michael Ryder 40.00 100.00
STMS Martin St. Louis 40.00 100.00
STMT Marty Turco 40.00 100.00
STNL Nicklas Lidstrom 40.00 100.00
STNZ Nikolai Zherdev 30.00 80.00
STPB Patrice Bergeron 30.00 80.00
STPE Patrik Elias 25.00 60.00
STPI Pierre-Marc Bouchard 30.00 60.00
STPK Phil Kessel 60.00 125.00
STPM Patrick Marleau 30.00 80.00
STPO Denis Potvin 30.00 80.00
STPR Patrick Roy 300.00 500.00
STRB Ray Bourque 75.00 150.00
STRH Ron Hextall 50.00 100.00
STRM Ryan Malone 25.00 60.00
STRN Rick Nash 60.00 125.00
STRO Larry Robinson 25.00 60.00
STRY Ryan Miller 40.00 100.00
STSA Denis Savard 25.00 60.00
STSK Saku Koivu 40.00 100.00
STST Jordan Staal 125.00 250.00
STSV Marek Svatos 25.00 60.00
STTE Tony Esposito 30.00 80.00
STTR Tuomo Ruutu 25.00 60.00
STTV Tomas Vokoun 40.00 100.00
STWG Wayne Gretzky 500.00 800.00

2006-07 Sweet Shot Sweet Stitches

STATED PRINT RUN 200 SER.#'d SETS
SSAF Alexander Frolov 2.50 6.00
SSAH Ales Hemsky 2.50 6.00
SSAL Daniel Alfredsson 3.00 8.00
SSAN Antero Niittymaki 3.00 8.00
SSAO Alexander Ovechkin 8.00 20.00
SSAR Andrew Raycroft 3.00 8.00
SSAS Alexander Steen 3.00 8.00
SSAT Alex Tanguay 3.00 8.00
SSBG Brian Gionta 2.50 6.00
SSBL Rob Blake 3.00 8.00
SSBO Pierre-Marc Bouchard 2.50 6.00
SSBR Brendan Shanahan 3.00 8.00
SSBS Billy Smith 3.00 8.00
SSBT Bryan Trottier 3.00 8.00
SSCD Chris Drury 2.50 6.00
SSCH Cristobal Huet 4.00 10.00
SSCN Cam Neely 4.00 10.00
SSCP Chris Pronger 3.00 8.00
SSCW Cam Ward 3.00 8.00
SSDA Dany Heatley 5.00 12.00
SSDH Dominik Hasek 5.00 12.00
SSDP Dion Phaneuf 4.00 10.00
SSDS Darryl Sittler 3.00 8.00
SSDW Doug Weight 2.50 6.00
SSEL Eric Lindros 3.00 8.00
SSES Eric Staal 3.00 8.00
SSFM Frank Mahovlich 3.00 8.00
SSGF Grant Fuhr 4.00 10.00
SSGL Guy Lafleur 4.00 10.00
SSGP Gilbert Perreault 3.00 8.00
SSHA Dale Hawerchuk 2.50 6.00
SSHE Milan Hejduk 2.50 6.00
SSHL Henrik Lundqvist 4.00 10.00
SSHO Marian Hossa 3.00 8.00
SSHZ Henrik Zetterberg 3.00 8.00
SSIK Ilya Kovalchuk 4.00 10.00
SSJC Jonathan Cheechoo 3.00 8.00
SSJG Jean-Sebastien Giguere 3.00 8.00
SSJI Jarome Iginla 5.00 12.00
SSJJ Jaromir Jagr 5.00 12.00
SSJL Joffrey Lupul 2.50 6.00
SSJM Joe Mullen 2.50 6.00
SSJS Joe Sakic 6.00 15.00
SSJT Jose Theodore 3.00 8.00
SSKL Kari Lehtonen 4.00 10.00
SSLR Luc Robitaille 3.00 8.00
SSMA Maxim Afinogenov 2.50 6.00
SSMB Martin Brodeur 8.00 20.00
SSMF Manny Fernandez 3.00 8.00
SSMG Marian Gaborik 5.00 12.00
SSMH Martin Havlat 3.00 8.00
SSMI Mike Bossy 3.00 8.00
SSMK Miikka Kiprusoff 3.00 8.00
SSML Mario Lemieux 12.00 30.00
SSMM Mike Modano 4.00 10.00
SSMN Markus Naslund 3.00 8.00
SSMR Michael Ryder 3.00 8.00
SSMS Marek Svatos 2.50 6.00
SSMT Marty Turco 3.00 8.00
SSNL Nicklas Lidstrom 3.00 8.00
SSOJ Olli Jokinen 2.50 6.00
SSOK Olaf Kolzig 3.00 8.00
SSPB Patrice Bergeron 3.00 8.00
SSPD Pavel Datsyuk 3.00 8.00
SSPE Patrik Elias 2.50 6.00
SSPF Peter Forsberg 5.00 12.00
SSPK Paul Kariya 3.00 8.00
SSPL Pascal LeClaire 3.00 8.00
SSPM Patrick Marleau 3.00 8.00
SSPO Denis Potvin 3.00 8.00
SSPR Patrick Roy 12.00 30.00
SSPS Peter Stastny 2.50 6.00
SSRB Ray Bourque 5.00 12.00
SSRE Mark Recchi 2.50 6.00
SSRH Ron Hextall 4.00 10.00
SSRI Brad Richards 3.00 8.00
SSRL Roberto Luongo 5.00 12.00
SSRM Ryan Miller 3.00 8.00
SSRN Rick Nash 3.00 8.00
SSRO Larry Robinson 3.00 8.00
SSRS Ryan Smyth 3.00 8.00
SSRV Rogie Vachon 3.00 8.00
SSSA Miroslav Satan 2.50 6.00
SSSB Borje Salming 3.00 8.00
SSSC Sidney Crosby 25.00 60.00
SSSD Shane Doan 2.50 6.00
SSSF Sergei Fedorov 3.00 8.00
SSSH Steve Shutt 2.50 6.00
SSSK Saku Koivu 3.00 8.00
SSSP Jason Spezza 3.00 8.00
SSSS Sergei Samsonov 3.00 8.00

SSST Martin St. Louis 3.00 8.00
SSSU Mats Sundin 3.00 8.00
SSSZ Sergei Zubov 2.50 6.00
SSTH Joe Thornton 5.00 12.00
SSTS Teemu Selanne 3.00 8.00
SSTV Tomas Vokoun 3.00 8.00
SSVL Vincent Lecavalier 3.00 8.00
SSWG Wayne Gretzky 20.00 50.00
SSZC Zdeno Chara 2.50 6.00

2006-07 Sweet Shot Sweet Stitches Duals

*DUALS: .75X to 2X SINGLE SWATCH
STATED PRINT RUN 50 SER.#'d SETS
SSAF Alexander Frolov 4.00 10.00
SSAH Ales Hemsky 4.00 10.00
SSAL Daniel Alfredsson 6.00 15.00
SSAN Antero Niittymaki 6.00 15.00
SSAO Alexander Ovechkin 15.00 40.00
SSAR Andrew Raycroft 6.00 15.00
SSAS Alexander Steen 6.00 15.00
SSAT Alex Tanguay 6.00 15.00
SSBG Brian Gionta 4.00 10.00
SSBL Rob Blake 6.00 15.00
SSBO Pierre-Marc Bouchard 4.00 10.00
SSBR Brendan Shanahan 6.00 15.00
SSBS Billy Smith 6.00 15.00
SSBT Bryan Trottier 6.00 15.00
SSCD Chris Drury 5.00 12.00
SSCH Cristobal Huet 8.00 20.00
SSCN Cam Neely 6.00 15.00
SSCP Chris Pronger 6.00 15.00
SSCW Cam Ward 6.00 15.00
SSDA Dany Heatley 6.00 15.00
SSDH Dominik Hasek 10.00 25.00
SSDP Dion Phaneuf 6.00 15.00
SSDS Darryl Sittler 6.00 15.00
SSDW Doug Weight 4.00 10.00
SSEL Eric Lindros 6.00 15.00
SSES Eric Staal 6.00 15.00
SSFM Frank Mahovlich 5.00 12.00
SSGF Grant Fuhr 6.00 15.00
SSGL Guy Lafleur 8.00 20.00
SSGP Gilbert Perreault 6.00 15.00
SSHA Dale Hawerchuk 4.00 10.00
SSHE Milan Hejduk 4.00 10.00
SSHL Henrik Lundqvist 6.00 15.00
SSHO Marian Hossa 6.00 15.00
SSHZ Henrik Zetterberg 6.00 15.00
SSIK Ilya Kovalchuk 6.00 15.00
SSJC Jonathan Cheechoo 6.00 15.00
SSJG Jean-Sebastien Giguere 6.00 15.00
SSJI Jarome Iginla 6.00 15.00
SSJJ Jaromir Jagr 8.00 20.00
SSJL Joffrey Lupul 4.00 10.00
SSJM Joe Mullen 4.00 10.00
SSJS Joe Sakic 10.00 25.00
SSJT Jose Theodore 6.00 15.00
SSKL Kari Lehtonen 6.00 15.00
SSLR Luc Robitaille 6.00 15.00
SSMA Maxim Afinogenov 6.00 15.00
SSMB Martin Brodeur 15.00 40.00
SSMF Manny Fernandez 5.00 12.00
SSMG Marian Gaborik 6.00 15.00
SSMH Martin Havlat 6.00 15.00
SSMI Mike Bossy 6.00 15.00
SSMK Miikka Kiprusoff 8.00 20.00
SSML Mario Lemieux 25.00 60.00
SSMM Mike Modano 6.00 15.00
SSMN Markus Naslund 6.00 15.00
SSMR Michael Ryder 6.00 15.00
SSMS Marek Svatos 4.00 10.00
SSMT Marty Turco 6.00 15.00
SSNL Nicklas Lidstrom 6.00 15.00
SSOJ Olli Jokinen 4.00 10.00
SSOK Olaf Kolzig 6.00 15.00
SSPB Patrice Bergeron 6.00 15.00
SSPD Pavel Datsyuk 6.00 15.00
SSPE Patrik Elias 4.00 10.00
SSPF Peter Forsberg 8.00 20.00
SSPK Paul Kariya 6.00 15.00
SSPL Pascal LeClaire 6.00 15.00
SSPM Patrick Marleau 6.00 15.00
SSPO Dennis Potvin 6.00 15.00
SSPR Patrick Roy 25.00 60.00
SSPS Peter Stastny 4.00 10.00
SSRB Ray Bourque 8.00 20.00
SSRE Mark Recchi 4.00 10.00
SSRH Ron Hextall 8.00 20.00
SSRI Brad Richards 6.00 15.00
SSRL Roberto Luongo 6.00 15.00
SSRM Ryan Miller 6.00 15.00
SSRN Rick Nash 6.00 15.00
SSRO Larry Robinson 6.00 15.00
SSRS Ryan Smyth 6.00 15.00
SSRV Rogie Vachon 6.00 15.00
SSSA Miroslav Satan 4.00 10.00
SSSB Borje Salming 6.00 15.00
SSSC Sidney Crosby 40.00 80.00
SSSD Shane Doan 4.00 10.00
SSSF Sergei Fedorov 6.00 15.00
SSSH Steve Shutt 5.00 12.00
SSSK Saku Koivu 6.00 15.00
SSSP Jason Spezza 6.00 15.00
SSSS Sergei Samsonov 6.00 15.00
SSST Martin St. Louis 6.00 15.00
SSSU Mats Sundin 6.00 15.00
SSSZ Sergei Zubov 4.00 10.00
SSTH Joe Thornton 8.00 20.00
SSTS Teemu Selanne 6.00 15.00
SSTV Tomas Vokoun 6.00 15.00
SSVL Vincent Lecavalier 6.00 15.00
SSWG Wayne Gretzky 40.00 80.00
SSZC Zdeno Chara 4.00 10.00

2006-07 Sweet Shot Sweet Stitches Triples

STATED PRINT RUN 25 SER.#'d SETS
NOT PRICED THIS MONTH DUE TO SCARCITY
SSSC Sidney Crosby 60.00 150.00
SSWG Wayne Gretzky 75.00 175.00

2007-08 Sweet Shot

This set was released on May 14, 2008. The base set consists of 160 cards. Cards 1-100 feature veterans, and cards 101-160 are jersey rookie cards.

COMP.SET w/o SPs (100) 20.00 50.00

STATED PRINT RUN 599 SER.#'d SETS
1 Ales Hemsky .60 1.50
2 Al MacInnis .75 2.00
3 Alexander Ovechkin 3.00 8.00
4 Bobby Orr 4.00 10.00
5 Alexander Semin 1.00 2.50
6 Anze Kopitar 1.00 2.50
7 Bernie Federko .60 1.50
8 Cam Neely 1.00 2.50
9 Gordie Howe 2.50 6.00
10 Alexander Radulov 1.00 2.50
11 Mark Messier 2.00 5.00
12 Borje Salming .75 2.00
13 Brad Richards .75 2.00
14 Brendan Morrison .60 1.50
15 Brendan Shanahan 1.00 2.50
16 Brian Leetch 1.00 2.50
17 Billy Smith 1.00 2.50
18 Cam Ward 1.00 2.50
19 Daniel Alfredsson .75 2.00
20 Daniel Briere 1.00 2.50
21 Dany Heatley 1.25 3.00
22 Darryl Sittler .75 2.00
23 Denis Potvin .75 2.00
24 Dino Ciccarelli .75 2.00
25 Dion Phaneuf 1.00 2.50
26 Dominik Hasek 1.25 3.00
27 Manny Legace .75 2.00
28 Drew Stafford .75 2.00
29 Eric Staal 1.00 2.50
30 Patrice Bergeron 1.00 2.50
31 Frank Mahovlich 1.50 4.00
32 Gilbert Perreault .75 2.00
33 Patrick Roy 3.00 8.00
34 Grant Fuhr 1.50 4.00
35 Guy Lafleur 2.50 6.00
36 Henrik Lundqvist 1.25 3.00
37 Henrik Zetterberg 1.00 2.50
38 Ilya Kovalchuk 1.25 3.00
39 Jari Kurri 1.00 2.50
40 Jarome Iginla 1.50 4.00
41 Jaromir Jagr 1.50 4.00
42 Jason Spezza 1.00 2.50
43 Jean Beliveau 1.50 4.00
44 Jean-Sebastien Giguere 1.00 2.50
45 Joe Mullen .60 1.50
46 Joe Sakic 2.00 5.00
47 Joe Thornton 1.25 3.00
48 Johnny Bucyk .60 1.50
49 Jonathan Cheechoo .60 1.50
50 Jordan Staal 1.25 3.00
51 Kari Lehtonen 1.00 2.50
52 Larry Robinson 1.25 3.00
53 Luc Robitaille .75 2.00
54 Marc-Andre Fleury 1.00 2.50
55 Marian Gaborik 1.25 3.00
56 Marian Hossa 1.00 2.50
57 Miikka Kiprusoff 1.25 3.00
58 Bobby Hull 1.50 4.00
59 Mark Recchi .60 1.50
60 Markus Naslund .60 1.50
61 Martin Brodeur 2.50 6.00
62 Martin St. Louis 1.00 2.50
63 Marty Turco 1.00 2.50
64 Mats Sundin 1.00 2.50
65 Michael Ryder .60 1.50
66 Mario Lemieux 3.00 8.00
67 Mike Bossy .75 2.00
68 Mike Modano 1.00 2.50
69 Nathan Horton .60 1.50
70 Nicklas Lidstrom 1.00 2.50
71 Evgeni Malkin 2.50 6.00
72 Patrick Marleau .75 2.00
73 Bobby Clarke 1.00 2.50
74 Paul Kariya 1.00 2.50
75 Pavel Datsyuk 1.00 2.50
76 Peter Stastny .75 2.00
77 Ray Bourque 1.25 3.00
78 Phil Esposito 1.50 4.00
79 Phil Kessel 1.00 2.50
80 Paul Stastny 1.00 2.50
81 Rick DiPietro .75 2.00
82 Rick Nash 1.00 2.50
83 Roberto Luongo 1.50 4.00
84 Ron Hextall 1.50 4.00
85 Ryan Miller 1.00 2.50
86 Ryan Smyth .75 2.00
87 Sidney Crosby 5.00 12.00
88 Scott Niedermayer .60 1.50
89 Patrik Elias .60 1.50
90 Shane Doan .60 1.50
91 Saku Koivu .75 2.00
92 Simon Gagne 1.00 2.50
93 Stan Mikita .75 2.00
94 Teemu Selanne 1.00 2.50
95 Thomas Vanek .75 2.00
96 Tomas Vokoun .60 1.50
97 Tony Esposito 1.50 4.00
98 Vincent Lecavalier 1.00 2.50
99 Wayne Gretzky 5.00 12.00
100 Zach Parise .75 2.00
101 Bobby Ryan JSY RC 15.00 40.00
102 Jonathan Toews JSY RC 25.00 60.00
103 Sam Gagner JSY RC 8.00 20.00
104 Carey Price JSY RC 25.00 60.00
105 Nicklas Bergfors JSY RC 5.00 12.00
106 Erik Johnson JSY RC 8.00 20.00
107 Nicklas Backstrom JSY RC 15.00 40.00
108 Jack Johnson JSY RC 6.00 15.00
109 Jonathan Bernier JSY RC 10.00 25.00
110 Bryan Little JSY RC 6.00 15.00
111 Patrick Kane JSY RC 20.00 50.00
112 Kris Russell JSY RC 6.00 15.00
113 Matt Niskanen JSY RC 4.00 10.00
114 Andrew Cogliano JSY RC 10.00 25.00
115 Marc Staal JSY RC 10.00 25.00
116 Nick Foligno JSY RC 6.00 15.00
117 Peter Mueller JSY RC 12.00 30.00
118 Ondrej Pavelec JSY RC 6.00 15.00
119 Martin Hanzal JSY RC 5.00 12.00
120 Matt Smaby JSY RC 4.00 10.00
121 Petr Kalus JSY RC 4.00 10.00
122 Andy Greene JSY RC 4.00 10.00
123 Frans Nielsen JSY RC 4.00 10.00
124 Rob Schremp JSY RC 5.00 12.00
125 James Sheppard JSY RC 4.00 10.00
126 Kyle Chipchura JSY RC 6.00 15.00
127 Ryan Parent JSY RC 5.00 12.00
128 David Krejci JSY RC 8.00 20.00
129 Lauri Tukonen JSY RC 4.00 10.00
130 Tobias Enstrom JSY RC 6.00 15.00
131 Mason Raymond JSY RC 10.00 25.00
132 Brandon Dubinsky JSY RC 6.00 15.00
133 Curtis McElhinney JSY RC 5.00 12.00
134 Brian Elliott JSY RC 5.00 12.00
135 Drew Miller JSY RC 4.00 10.00
136 Ryan Callahan JSY RC 6.00 15.00
137 Ville Koistinen JSY RC 4.00 10.00
138 Torrey Mitchell JSY RC 5.00 12.00
139 David Perron JSY RC 6.00 15.00
140 Jannik Hansen JSY RC 4.00 10.00
141 Jaroslav Halak JSY RC 12.00 30.00
142 Sergei Kostitsyn JSY RC 12.00 30.00
143 Milan Lucic JSY RC 10.00 25.00
144 Tyler Weiman JSY RC 5.00 12.00
145 Jaroslav Hlinka JSY RC 5.00 12.00
146 Tobias Stephan JSY RC 5.00 12.00
147 Tuukka Rask JSY RC 10.00 25.00
148 Ryan Carter JSY RC 5.00 12.00
149 Jared Boll JSY RC 4.00 10.00
150 Casey Borer JSY RC 4.00 10.00
151 Steve Downie JSY RC 5.00 12.00
152 Lukas Kaspar JSY RC 4.00 10.00
153 Matt Ellis JSY RC 4.00 10.00
154 Jiri Tlusty JSY RC 10.00 25.00
155 Daniel Carcillo JSY RC 5.00 12.00
156 Devin Setoguchi JSY RC 8.00 20.00
157 T.J. Hensick JSY RC 5.00 12.00
158 Anton Stralman JSY RC 5.00 12.00
159 David Jones JSY RC 4.00 10.00
160 Jack Skille JSY RC 5.00 12.00

2007-08 Sweet Shot Endorsed Equipment

STATED PRINT RUN 15 SER.#'d SETS
NOT PRICED DUE TO SCARCITY
EEAR Andrew Raycroft
EEBP Bernie Parent
EEBR Bill Ranford
EEBS Billy Smith
EECH Cristobal Huet
EECW Cam Ward
EEDA David Aebischer
EEDH Dominik Hasek
EEDR Dwayne Roloson
EEGC Gerry Cheevers
EEGF Grant Fuhr
EEHL Henrik Lundqvist
EEJG Jean-Sebastien Giguere
EEJT Jose Theodore
EEMB Martin Brodeur
EEMF Marc-Andre Fleury
EEML Manny Legace
EEMT Marty Turco
EEPR Patrick Roy
EERB Richard Brodeur
EERH Ron Hextall
EERM Ryan Miller
EERV Rogie Vachon
EETE Tony Esposito
EETV Tomas Vokoun

2007-08 Sweet Shot Rookie Jerseys Autographs

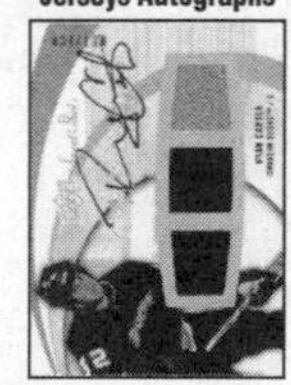

*JSY AU: .8X TO 2X BASE
STATED PRINT RUN 100 SERIAL #'d SETS
102 Jonathan Toews 60.00 120.00
104 Carey Price 60.00 120.00
111 Patrick Kane 50.00 100.00

2007-08 Sweet Shot Signature Saves Ice Signings

STATED PRINT RUN 100 SER.#'d SETS
SSRBP Bernie Parent 15.00 40.00
SSRBR Bill Ranford 10.00 25.00
SSRGF Grant Fuhr 20.00 50.00
SSRJG Jean-Sebastien Giguere 12.00 30.00
SSRMB Martin Brodeur 30.00 80.00
SSRMF Marc-Andre Fleury 12.00 30.00
SSRMT Marty Turco 12.00 30.00
SSRPR Patrick Roy/50 60.00 150.00
SSRRM Ryan Miller 12.00 30.00
SSRTE Tony Esposito 20.00 50.00

2007-08 Sweet Shot Signature Saves Puck Signings

STATED ODDS 1:2
SSPBI Bill Ranford 8.00 20.00
SSPBP Bernie Parent 12.00 30.00
SSPCP Carey Price 30.00 80.00
SSPGF Grant Fuhr 15.00 40.00
SSPHA Dominik Hasek
SSPJG Jean-Sebastien Giguere 10.00 25.00
SSPMT Marty Turco 10.00 25.00
SSPRA Andrew Raycroft 8.00 20.00
SSPRB Richard Brodeur 8.00 20.00
SSPRM Ryan Miller 10.00 25.00
SSPTE Tony Esposito 15.00 40.00

2007-08 Sweet Shot Signature Saves Stick Signings

STATED PRINT RUN 25 SERIAL #'d SETS
SSSBP Bernie Parent 30.00 80.00
SSSBR Bill Ranford 20.00 50.00
SSSCP Carey Price 80.00 200.00
SSSDH Dominik Hasek 30.00 60.00
SSSDR Dwayne Roloson 20.00 50.00
SSSGF Grant Fuhr 40.00 100.00
SSSJG Jean-Sebastien Giguere 25.00 60.00
SSSMB Martin Brodeur 60.00 150.00
SSSMT Marty Turco
SSSPR Patrick Roy/10
SSSRH Ron Hextall 40.00 100.00
SSSRI Richard Brodeur 20.00 50.00
SSSRM Ryan Miller 25.00 60.00
SSSTE Tony Esposito 40.00 100.00
SSSVO Tomas Vokoun 25.00 60.00

2007-08 Sweet Shot Signature Shots Ice Signings

STATED PRINT RUN 100 SERIAL #'d SETS
SSRAK Anze Kopitar 12.00 30.00
SSRAT Alex Tanguay 10.00 25.00
SSRBO Mike Bossy 10.00 25.00
SSRDH Dany Heatley 15.00 40.00
SSRDP Denis Potvin 10.00 25.00
SSREM Evgeni Malkin 50.00 100.00
SSRGH Gordie Howe/50 50.00 100.00
SSRGL Guy Lafleur 30.00 60.00
SSRGP Gilbert Perreault 10.00 25.00
SSRHZ Henrik Zetterberg EXCH 12.00 30.00
SSRIK Ilya Kovalchuk 15.00 40.00
SSRJI Jarome Iginla 20.00 50.00
SSRJK Jari Kurri 12.00 30.00
SSRJT Joe Thornton 15.00 40.00
SSRLR Larry Robinson 15.00 40.00
SSRMG Marian Gaborik 15.00 40.00
SSRMM Mike Modano EXCH 12.00 30.00
SSRMN Markus Naslund 12.00 30.00
SSRMR Michael Ryder 8.00 20.00
SSRMS Martin St. Louis 10.00 25.00
SSRNL Nicklas Lidstrom 12.00 30.00
SSRPB Patrice Bergeron 12.00 30.00
SSRRB Ray Bourque 25.00 50.00
SSRRN Rick Nash 12.00 30.00
SSRSC Sidney Crosby 75.00 150.00
SSRSG Simon Gagne 12.00 30.00
SSRVL Vincent Lecavalier 12.00 30.00

2007-08 Sweet Shot Signature Shots Puck Signings

STATED ODDS 1:2
SSPAK Anze Kopitar 6.00 15.00
SSPAM Andy McDonald 4.00 10.00
SSPAR Alexander Radulov 6.00 15.00
SSPAT Alex Tanguay 5.00 12.00
SSPBB Brad Boyes 5.00 12.00
SSPBC Bobby Clarke 6.00 15.00
SSPBE1 Jean Beliveau
SSPBG Brian Gionta 4.00 10.00
SSPBH Bobby Hull
SSPBL Bryan Little 5.00 12.00
SSPBM Brendan Morrison 4.00 10.00
SSPBO Bobby Orr 75.00 150.00
SSPBR Bobby Ryan 15.00 40.00
SSPCA Mike Cammalleri 5.00 12.00
SSPDB Dan Boyle 4.00 10.00
SSPDM Dickie Moore
SSPDP David Perron 6.00 15.00
SSPDS Darryl Sutter 5.00 12.00
SSPDT Darcy Tucker 5.00 12.00
SSPDU Duane Sutter 4.00 10.00
SSPEJ Erik Johnson 8.00 20.00
SSPEM Evgeni Malkin 40.00 80.00
SSPGA Simon Gagne 6.00 15.00
SSPGH Gordie Howe 30.00 60.00
SSPGL Guy Lafleur 25.00 50.00
SSPGO Scott Gomez 4.00 10.00
SSPGP Gilbert Perreault 5.00 12.00
SSPIK Ilya Kovalchuk 8.00 20.00
SSPJC Jonathan Cheechoo 5.00 12.00
SSPJI Jarome Iginla 10.00 25.00
SSPJJ Jack Johnson 6.00 15.00
SSPJK Jari Kurri 6.00 15.00
SSPJP Joni Pitkanen 4.00 10.00
SSPJT Jonathan Toews 30.00 60.00
SSPKD Kris Draper 5.00 12.00
SSPKE Phil Kessel 6.00 15.00
SSPLR Larry Robinson 8.00 20.00
SSPMC Matt Carle 4.00 10.00
SSPMG Marian Gaborik 8.00 20.00
SSPMH Milan Hejduk 5.00 12.00
SSPMN Markus Naslund 6.00 15.00
SSPMO Brenden Morrow 5.00 12.00
SSPMP Michael Peca 4.00 10.00
SSPMR Michael Ryder 4.00 10.00
SSPMS Marc Staal 10.00 25.00
SSPMU Peter Mueller 12.00 30.00
SSPNB Nicklas Backstrom 15.00 40.00
SSPNF Nick Foligno 6.00 15.00
SSPNL Nicklas Lidstrom 6.00 15.00
SSPOS Patrick O'Sullivan 5.00 12.00
SSPPB Patrice Bergeron 6.00 15.00
SSPPE Corey Perry 6.00 15.00
SSPPK Patrick Kane 25.00 60.00
SSPPO Denis Potvin 5.00 12.00
SSPPS Paul Stastny 6.00 15.00
SSPRI Mike Richards 8.00 20.00
SSPRN Rick Nash 6.00 15.00
SSPRR Ryan Potulny 4.00 10.00
SSPRS Rob Schremp 5.00 12.00
SSPRV Rick Vaive 5.00 12.00
SSPSB Scotty Bowman 5.00 12.00
SSPSC Sidney Crosby 75.00 150.00
SSPSG Sam Gagner 8.00 20.00
SSPSH Steve Shutt 5.00 12.00
SSPSM Ryan Smyth 5.00 12.00
SSPST Martin St. Louis 5.00 12.00
SSPSU Brent Sutter 4.00 10.00
SSPSV Marek Svatos 4.00 10.00
SSPSW Stephen Weiss 4.00 10.00
SSPTH Tomas Holmstrom 5.00 12.00
SSPTS Tomas Steen 4.00 10.00
SSPTV Thomas Vanek 5.00 12.00
SSPVL Vincent Lecavalier 6.00 15.00
SSPWG Wayne Gretzky 150.00 250.00

2007-08 Sweet Shot Signature Shots Stick Signings

STATED PRINT RUN 25 SERIAL #'d SETS
SSSAK Anze Kopitar
SSSAM Al MacInnis 12.00 30.00
SSSAO Alexander Ovechkin 100.00 175.00
SSSAR Alexander Radulov
SSSAT Alex Tanguay 12.00 30.00
SSSBC Bobby Clarke 15.00 40.00
SSSBE Jean Beliveau
SSSBH Bobby Hull
SSSBL Brian Leetch 15.00 40.00
SSSBM Brendan Morrison 10.00 25.00
SSSBO Bobby Orr 175.00 300.00
SSSCH Jonathan Cheechoo 12.00 30.00
SSSCN Cam Neely 15.00 40.00
SSSCR Sidney Crosby 150.00 250.00
SSSDA Dany Heatley EXCH 20.00 50.00
SSSDC Dino Ciccarelli 12.00 30.00
SSSDS Darryl Sittler
SSSDT Darcy Tucker 12.00 30.00
SSSEM Evgeni Malkin 50.00 100.00
SSSGH Gordie Howe 60.00 120.00
SSSGL Guillaume Latendresse 12.00 30.00
SSSGP Gilbert Perreault
SSSHA Dale Hawerchuk EXCH 12.00 30.00
SSSHE Milan Hejduk 12.00 30.00
SSSHZ Henrik Zetterberg EXCH 15.00 40.00
SSSIK Ilya Kovalchuk 20.00 50.00
SSSJB Johnny Bucyk 10.00 25.00
SSSJC Jeff Carter 10.00 25.00
SSSJI Jarome Iginla 25.00 60.00
SSSJJ Jack Johnson 15.00 40.00
SSSJK Jari Kurri 15.00 40.00
SSSJM Joe Mullen
SSSJS Jordan Staal
SSSJT Jonathan Toews 150.00 300.00
SSSKA Patrick Kane 150.00 300.00
SSSLA Guy Lafleur 40.00 100.00
SSSLM Lanny McDonald 12.00 30.00
SSSLR Luc Robitaille 12.00 30.00
SSSMD Marcel Dionne 10.00 25.00
SSSME Mark Messier/10
SSSMG Marian Gaborik 20.00 50.00
SSSMH Marian Hossa 15.00 40.00
SSSMI Mike Bossy
SSSML Mario Lemieux/10
SSSMM Mike Modano 15.00 40.00
SSSMN Markus Naslund 15.00 40.00
SSSMR Michael Ryder 10.00 25.00
SSSMS Martin St. Louis 12.00 30.00
SSSNH Nathan Horton
SSSNL Nicklas Lidstrom
SSSPB Patrice Bergeron 15.00 40.00
SSSPK Phil Kessel
SSSPM Peter Mueller 30.00 80.00
SSSPO Denis Potvin
SSSPS Paul Stastny 15.00 40.00
SSSRB Ray Bourque
SSSRE Ron Ellis 10.00 25.00
SSSRN Rick Nash
SSSRO Larry Robinson
SSSRS Ryan Smyth 12.00 30.00
SSSSA Borje Salming 12.00 30.00
SSSSG Sam Gagner 20.00 50.00
SSSSI Simon Gagne
SSSSK Saku Koivu 12.00 30.00
SSSSM Stan Mikita 12.00 30.00
SSSSP Peter Stastny
SSSSS Steve Shutt
SSSSV Marek Svatos
SSSTH Joe Thornton 20.00 50.00
SSSTV Thomas Vanek 12.00 30.00
SSSVL Vincent Lecavalier
SSSWG Wayne Gretzky/10

2007-08 Sweet Shot Signature Sticks

STATED PRINT RUN 15 SER.#'d SETS
NOT PRICED DUE TO SCARCITY
SSGAK Anze Kopitar
SSGAM Al MacInnis
SSGAO Adam Oates
SSGAR Alexander Radulov
SSGBC Bobby Clarke
SSGBH Bobby Hull
SSGBL Brian Leetch
SSGBO Mike Bossy
SSGBP Bernie Parent
SSGCD Chris Drury
SSGCG Clark Gillies
SSGDC Dino Ciccarelli
SSGDG Doug Gilmour
SSGDH Dale Hawerchuk
SSGDP Denis Potvin
SSGDR Dwayne Roloson
SSGDS Denis Savard
SSGEM Evgeni Malkin
SSGES Eric Staal
SSGGH Gordie Howe
SSGGL Guy Lafleur
SSGGP Gilbert Perreault
SSGHA Dominik Hasek
SSGHZ Henrik Zetterberg
SSGIK Ilya Kovalchuk EXCH
SSGJB Jean Beliveau
SSGJC Jonathan Cheechoo
SSGJG Jean-Sebastien Giguere
SSGJI Jarome Iginla
SSGJK Jari Kurri
SSGJM Joe Mullen
SSGJS Jordan Staal
SSGJT Joe Thornton
SSGLR Larry Robinson
SSGMB Martin Brodeur
SSGMD Marcel Dionne
SSGMG Marian Gaborik
SSGMH Milan Hejduk
SSGML Mario Lemieux/5
SSGMM Mark Messier/5
SSGMN Markus Naslund
SSGMO Mike Modano
SSGMR Michael Ryder
SSGPB Pierre-Marc Bouchard
SSGPE Patrik Elias
SSGPK Phil Kessel
SSGPR Patrick Roy/5
SSGPS Peter Stastny
SSGRB Ray Bourque
SSGRG Ryan Getzlaf
SSGRH Ron Hextall
SSGRM Ryan Miller
SSGRN Rick Nash
SSGRO Luc Robitaille
SSGSK Saku Koivu
SSGST Martin St. Louis
SSGTE Tony Esposito
SSGTV Thomas Vanek
SSGWG Wayne Gretzky/5

2007-08 Sweet Shot Sweet Spot Signatures Baseball Skins

NOT PRICED DUE TO SCARCITY

2007-08 Sweet Shot Sweet Stitches Triples

STATED PRINT RUN 299 SERIAL #'d SETS
SSTAH Ales Hemsky 4.00 10.00
SSTAK Alex Kovalev 4.00 10.00
SSTAM Al MacInnis 5.00 12.00
SSTAO Alexander Ovechkin 20.00 50.00
SSTAR Alexander Radulov 6.00 15.00
SSTAS Alexander Steen 4.00 10.00
SSTAT Alex Tanguay 5.00 12.00
SSTBC Bobby Clarke 6.00 15.00
SSTBL Brian Leetch 6.00 15.00
SSTBN Bernie Nicholls 4.00 10.00
SSTBO Mike Bossy 5.00 12.00
SSTBS Brendan Shanahan 6.00 15.00
SSTCN Cam Neely 6.00 15.00
SSTCP Chris Pronger 6.00 15.00
SSTDA Daniel Alfredsson 5.00 12.00
SSTDE Denis Savard 5.00 12.00
SSTDG Doug Gilmour 5.00 12.00
SSTDH Dale Hawerchuk 5.00 12.00
SSTDP Denis Potvin 5.00 12.00
SSTDR Dwayne Roloson 5.00 12.00
SSTDS Daniel Sedin 4.00 10.00
SSTDW Doug Weight 4.00 10.00
SSTEM Evgeni Malkin 15.00 40.00
SSTEN Evgeni Nabokov 5.00 12.00
SSTES Eric Staal 6.00 15.00
SSTFM Frank Mahovlich 10.00 25.00
SSTGF Grant Fuhr 10.00 25.00
SSTGL Guy Lafleur 15.00 40.00
SSTGP Gilbert Perreault 5.00 12.00
SSTHA Dominik Hasek 8.00 20.00
SSTHE Dany Heatley 8.00 20.00
SSTHL Henrik Lundqvist 8.00 20.00
SSTHM Milan Hejduk 5.00 12.00
SSTHS Henrik Sedin 4.00 10.00
SSTHZ Henrik Zetterberg 6.00 15.00
SSTIK Ilya Kovalchuk 6.00 15.00
SSTJI Jarome Iginla 10.00 25.00
SSTJJ Jaromir Jagr 10.00 25.00
SSTJO Joe Sakic 12.00 30.00
SSTJS Jason Spezza 6.00 15.00
SSTJT Joe Thornton 8.00 20.00
SSTKL Kari Lehtonen 6.00 15.00
SSTKO Anze Kopitar 6.00 15.00
SSTKP Miikka Kiprusoff 8.00 20.00
SSTLM Lanny McDonald 5.00 12.00
SSTLR Larry Robinson 8.00 20.00
SSTMA Martin Havlat 5.00 12.00
SSTMB Martin Brodeur 15.00 40.00
SSTMF Marc-Andre Fleury 6.00 15.00
SSTMG Marian Gaborik 8.00 20.00
SSTMH Marian Hossa 6.00 15.00
SSTMI Stan Mikita 5.00 12.00
SSTMK Mikko Koivu 4.00 10.00
SSTML Mario Lemieux 20.00 50.00
SSTMM Mark Messier 12.00 30.00
SSTMN Markus Naslund 6.00 15.00
SSTMO Mike Modano 6.00 15.00
SSTMR Mark Recchi 4.00 10.00
SSTMS Martin St. Louis 5.00 12.00
SSTMT Marty Turco 6.00 15.00
SSTMV Miroslav Satan 4.00 10.00
SSTNL Nicklas Lidstrom 6.00 15.00
SSTPB Patrice Bergeron 6.00 15.00
SSTPD Pavel Datsyuk 6.00 15.00
SSTPF Peter Forsberg 8.00 20.00
SSTPH Dion Phaneuf 6.00 15.00
SSTPK Paul Kariya 6.00 15.00
SSTPM Patrick Marleau 5.00 12.00
SSTPR Patrick Roy 20.00 50.00
SSTPS Peter Stastny 5.00 12.00
SSTRB Ray Bourque 8.00 20.00
SSTRE Ray Emery 5.00 12.00
SSTRG Ryan Getzlaf 5.00 12.00
SSTRH Ron Hextall 10.00 25.00
SSTRL Roberto Luongo 10.00 25.00
SSTRM Ryan Miller 6.00 15.00
SSTRN Rick Nash 6.00 15.00
SSTRO Luc Robitaille 5.00 12.00
SSTRS Ryan Smyth 5.00 12.00
SSTRV Rogie Vachon 6.00 15.00
SSTRY Michael Ryder 4.00 10.00
SSTSA Borje Salming 5.00 12.00
SSTSC Sidney Crosby 30.00 80.00
SSTSD Shane Doan 4.00 10.00
SSTSF Sergei Fedorov 6.00 15.00
SSTSG Simon Gagne 6.00 15.00
SSTSH Steve Shutt 5.00 12.00
SSTSI Darryl Sittler 5.00 12.00
SSTSK Saku Koivu 5.00 12.00
SSTSM Billy Smith 6.00 15.00
SSTSN Scott Niedermayer 4.00 10.00
SSTSS Scott Stevens 5.00 12.00
SSTST Jordan Staal 8.00 20.00
SSTSU Mats Sundin 6.00 15.00
SSTTS Teemu Selanne 6.00 15.00
SSTTV Tomas Vokoun 5.00 12.00
SSTTW Tiger Williams 5.00 12.00
SSTVL Vincent Lecavalier 6.00 15.00
SSTWG Wayne Gretzky 30.00 80.00
SSTZP Zach Parise 5.00 12.00

1981-82 TCMA

This 13-card set measures the standard size. The front features a color posed photo, with a thin black border on white card stock. The cards are numbered on the back and have biographical information as well as career highlights between two hockey sticks drawn on the sides of the card backs. Supposedly there were only 3000 sets produced. Eleven Hockey Hall of Famers are included in the set.

COMPLETE SET (13) 24.00 60.00
1 Norm Ullman 1.25 3.00
2 Gump Worsley 2.00 5.00
3 J.C. Tremblay .60 1.50
4 Lou Fontinato .60 1.50
5 Johnny Bucyk 1.25 3.00
6 Harry Howell .75 2.00
7 Henri Richard 2.00 5.00
8 Andy Bathgate 1.25 3.00
9 Bobby Orr 10.00 25.00
10 Frank Mahovlich 2.00 5.00
11 Jean Beliveau 4.00 10.00
12 Jacques Plante 4.00 10.00
13 Stan Mikita 3.00 8.00

1935 TCTA

Card measures approximately 3 1/2" x 5 1/2" and is in black and white.

NNO Maple Leaf Arena 25.00 50.00

1974 Team Canada L'Equipe WHA

This 24-photo set measures approximately 4 1/8" by 7 1/2" and features posed, glossy, black-and-white player photos on thin stock. The pictures are attached to red poster board. The player's name and two Team Canada L'Equipe logos appear in the white margin at the bottom. The backs are blank. The cards are unnumbered and checklisted below in alphabetical order.

COMPLETE SET (24) 25.00 50.00
1 Ralph Backstrom 1.00 2.00
2 Serge Bernier .75 1.50
3 Gerry Cheevers 5.00 10.00
4 Al Hamilton 1.00 2.00
5 Billy Harris CO .50 1.00
6 Jim Harrison .75 1.50
7 Ben Hatskin OWN .75 1.50
8 Paul Henderson 2.00 4.00
9 Rejean Houle 1.00 2.00
10 Mark Howe 4.00 8.00
11 Marty Howe 1.00 2.00
12 Bill Hunter .50 1.00
13 Gordon W. Juckes .50 1.00
14 Rick Ley 1.00 2.00
15 Frank Mahovlich 4.00 8.00
16 John McKenzie 1.00 2.00
17 Don McLeod .75 1.50
18 Rick Noonan .75 1.50
19 Brad Selwood .75 1.50
20 Rick Smith .75 1.50
21 Pat Stapleton 1.00 2.00
22 Marc Tardif 1.00 2.00
23 Mike Walton 1.00 2.00
24 Tom Webster 1.00 2.00

2002 Team Canada Coca Cola Coins

1 Mario Lemieux 4.00 10.00
2 Steve Yzerman 4.00 10.00
3 Joe Sakic 1.50 4.00
4 Chris Pronger 1.00 2.50
5 Owen Nolan 1.00 2.50
6 Scott Niedermayer 1.00 2.50
7 Rob Blake 1.00 2.50
8 Paul Kariya 1.50 4.00

1996-97 Team Out

The 1996-97 Team Out set was issued in one series totaling 89 cards. The cards were intended for use in a game, which is explained in the instructions included with the set. While the game itself never quite took off, the cards were quite popular with superstar and team collectors, which led to a fairly wide break of the product.

COMPLETE SET (89) 10.00 25.00
1 Paul Kariya .60 1.50
2 Luc Robitaille .08 .25
3 John LeClair .20 .50
4 Theo Fleury .20 .50
5 Scott Mellanby .08 .25
6 Adam Graves .08 .25
7 Esa Tikkanen .02 .10
8 Slava Kozlov .08 .25
9 Eric Daze .08 .25
10 Ryan Smyth .08 .25
11 Shayne Corson .08 .25
12 Kevin Stevens .08 .25
13 Murray Craven .02 .10
14 Keith Tkachuk .20 .50
15 Zigmund Palffy .20 .50
16 Eric Lindros .40 1.00
17 Mario Lemieux 1.00 2.50
18 Joe Sakic .40 1.00
19 Wayne Gretzky 1.25 3.00
20 Mark Messier .20 .50
21 Sergei Fedorov .40 1.00
22 Jason Arnott .08 .25
23 Chris Gratton .08 .25
24 Pierre Turgeon .08 .25

Card	Low	High
25 Mike Modano	.20	.50
26 Saku Koivu	.20	.50
27 Alexei Yashin	.08	.25
28 Steve Yzerman	.75	2.00
29 Peter Forsberg	.40	1.00
30 Adam Oates	.08	.25
31 Brett Hull	.20	.50
32 Jaromir Jagr	.40	1.00
33 Pavel Bure	.40	1.00
34 Teemu Selanne	.30	.75
35 Stephane Richer	.02	.10
36 Mike Gartner	.08	.25
37 Claude Lemieux	.08	.25
38 Rick Tocchet	.08	.25
39 Alexander Mogilny	.08	.25
40 Peter Bondra	.08	.25
41 Mats Sundin	.08	.25
42 Daniel Alfredsson	.08	.25
43 Owen Nolan	.02	.10
44 Joe Juneau	.08	.25
45 Mikael Renberg	.08	.25
46 Chris Chelios	.20	.50
47 Ray Bourque	.30	.75
48 Scott Stevens	.08	.25
49 Paul Coffey	.20	.50
50 Glen Wesley	.02	.10
51 Nicklas Lidstrom	.20	.50
52 Scott Niedermayer	.08	.25
53 Larry Murphy	.02	.10
54 Sandis Ozolinsh	.08	.25
55 Vladimir Malakhov	.02	.10
56 Robert Svehla	.02	.10
57 Steve Duchesne	.02	.10
58 Sergei Gonchar	.02	.10
59 Darius Kasparaitis	.08	.25
60 Patrick Roy	1.00	2.50
61 Martin Brodeur	.40	1.00
62 Mike Richter	.20	.50
63 John Vanbiesbrouck	.20	.50
64 Ron Hextall	.08	.25
65 Nikolai Khabibulin	.08	.25
66 Grant Fuhr	.08	.25
67 Kirk McLean	.08	.25
68 Jim Carey	.20	.50
69 Dominik Hasek	.30	.75
70 Ed Belfour	.20	.50
71 Chris Osgood	.20	.50
72 Guy Hebert	.08	.25
73 Trevor Kidd	.08	.25
74 Felix Potvin	.20	.50
75 Roman Hamrlik	.08	.25
76 Alexei Zhitnik	.08	.25
77 Al MacInnis	.02	.10
78 Brian Leetch	.20	.50
79 Rob Blake	.08	.25
80 Derian Hatcher	.02	.10
81 Mathieu Schneider	.02	.10
82 Gary Suter	.02	.10
83 Jeff Brown	.02	.10
84 Jyrki Lumme	.02	.10
85 Ed Jovanovski	.08	.25
86 Eric Desjardins	.08	.25
87 Stephane Quintal	.02	.10
88 Marcus Ragnarsson	.02	.10
89 Zarley Zalapski	.02	.10

2005-06 The Cup

1-100 PRINT RUN 249 SER. #'d SETS
PATCH AU PRINT RUN SER. 199 #'d SETS
AU RC PRINT RUN SER. 249 #'d SETS

Card	Low	High
1 Jean-Sebastien Giguere	4.00	10.00
2 Teemu Selanne	8.00	20.00
3 Ilya Kovalchuk	10.00	25.00
4 Marian Hossa	6.00	15.00
5 Kari Lehtonen	6.00	15.00
6 Cam Neely	8.00	20.00
7 Patrice Bergeron	5.00	12.00
8 Ray Bourque	8.00	20.00
9 Johnny Bucyk	6.00	15.00
10 Phil Esposito	8.00	20.00
11 Don Cherry	8.00	20.00
12 Brian Leetch	8.00	20.00
13 Gerry Cheevers	5.00	12.00
14 Gilbert Perreault	5.00	12.00
15 Chris Drury	4.00	10.00
16 Ryan Miller	8.00	20.00
17 Jarome Iginla	10.00	25.00
18 Lanny McDonald	4.00	10.00
19 Miikka Kiprusoff	12.00	30.00
20 Joe Mullen	4.00	10.00
21 Eric Staal	12.50	30.00
22 Doug Weight	4.00	10.00
23 Martin Gerber	4.00	10.00
24 Nikolai Khabibulin	8.00	20.00
25 Denis Savard	8.00	20.00
26 Bobby Hull	8.00	20.00
27 Tony Esposito	6.00	15.00
28 Joe Sakic	15.00	40.00
29 Alex Tanguay	6.00	15.00
30 Milan Hejduk	6.00	15.00
31 Jose Theodore	8.00	20.00
32 Marek Svatos	8.00	20.00
33 Rick Nash	12.00	30.00
34 Sergei Fedorov	8.00	20.00
35 Mike Modano	8.00	20.00
36 Marty Turco	8.00	20.00
37 Brenden Morrow	6.00	15.00
38 Steve Yzerman	20.00	50.00
39 Gordie Howe	15.00	40.00
40 Brendan Shanahan	6.00	15.00
41 Scotty Bowman	4.00	10.00
42 Pavel Datsyuk	6.00	15.00
43 Henrik Zetterberg	6.00	15.00
44 Chris Pronger	4.00	10.00
45 Wayne Gretzky	40.00	100.00
46 Grant Fuhr	8.00	20.00
47 Roberto Luongo	10.00	25.00
48 Olli Jokinen	4.00	10.00
49 Jeremy Roenick	6.00	15.00
50 Luc Robitaille	10.00	25.00
51 Rogie Vachon	4.00	10.00
52 Marian Gaborik	10.00	25.00
53 Saku Koivu	5.00	12.00
54 Jean Beliveau	10.00	25.00
55 Steve Shutt	5.00	12.00
56 Patrick Roy	20.00	50.00
57 Guy Lafleur	8.00	20.00
58 Guy Lapointe	4.00	10.00
59 Michael Ryder	8.00	20.00
60 Tomas Vokoun	10.00	25.00
61 Paul Kariya	6.00	15.00
62 Martin Brodeur	15.00	40.00
63 Patrik Elias	4.00	10.00
64 Alexei Yashin	6.00	15.00
65 Mike Bossy	5.00	12.00
66 Denis Potvin	4.00	10.00
67 Bryan Trottier	8.00	20.00
68 Clark Gillies	8.00	20.00
69 Jaromir Jagr	15.00	40.00
70 Dominik Hasek	15.00	40.00
71 Dany Heatley	15.00	40.00
72 Jason Spezza	10.00	25.00
73 Daniel Alfredsson	4.00	10.00
74 Peter Forsberg	15.00	40.00
75 Ron Hextall	4.00	10.00
76 Simon Gagne	5.00	12.00
77 Bobby Clarke	5.00	12.00
78 Keith Primeau	4.00	10.00
79 Bernie Parent	6.00	15.00
80 Shane Doan	4.00	10.00
81 Curtis Joseph	8.00	20.00
82 Mario Lemieux	20.00	50.00
83 Marc-Andre Fleury	12.00	30.00
84 Jonathan Cheechoo	10.00	25.00
85 Evgeni Nabokov	6.00	15.00
86 Joe Thornton	12.00	30.00
87 Patrick Marleau	5.00	12.00
88 Keith Tkachuk	5.00	12.00
89 Martin St. Louis	5.00	12.00
90 Vincent Lecavalier	6.00	15.00
91 Brad Richards	8.00	20.00
92 Ed Belfour	6.00	15.00
93 Darryl Sittler	6.00	15.00
94 Mats Sundin	10.00	25.00
95 Eric Lindros	8.00	20.00
96 Doug Gilmour	5.00	12.00
97 Markus Naslund	6.00	15.00
98 Todd Bertuzzi	6.00	15.00
99 Ed Jovanovski	4.00	10.00
100 Olaf Kolzig	6.00	15.00
101 Ryan Getzlaf JSY AU RC	175.00	300.00
102 Ryan Whitney JSY AU RC	60.00	100.00
103 R.J. Umberger JSY AU RC	60.00	120.00
104 Cam Ward JSY AU RC	75.00	150.00
105 Brent Seabrook JSY AU RC	50.00	100.00
106 Eric Nystrom JSY AU RC	40.00	80.00
107 Gilbert Brule JSY AU RC	125.00	250.00
108 Hannu Toivonen JSY AU RC	50.00	100.00
109 Robert Nilsson JSY AU RC	50.00	100.00
110 Rostislav Olesz JSY AU RC	60.00	120.00
111 Ryan Suter JSY AU RC	40.00	80.00
112 Jussi Jokinen JSY AU RC	60.00	120.00
113 Zach Parise JSY AU RC	200.00	350.00
114 Wojtek Wolski JSY AU RC	125.00	250.00
115 Andrej Meszaros JSY AU RC	40.00	80.00
116 Johan Franzen JSY AU RC	100.00	200.00
117 Peter Budaj JSY AU RC	75.00	150.00
118 David Leneveu JSY AU RC	30.00	60.00
119 Andrew Alberts JSY AU RC	40.00	80.00
120 Steve Bernier JSY AU RC	75.00	150.00
121 Mikko Koivu JSY AU RC	75.00	150.00
122 Chris Campoli JSY AU RC	30.00	60.00
123 Evgeny Artyukhin JSY AU RC	30.00	60.00
124 Christoph Schubert JSY AU RC	40.00	80.00
125 Tomas Fleischmann JSY AU RC	50.00	100.00
126 Maxime Talbot JSY AU RC	50.00	100.00
127 Jordan Sigalet JSY AU RC	40.00	80.00
128 Danny Richmond JSY AU RC	30.00	60.00
129 Maxim Lapierre JSY AU RC	75.00	150.00
130 Dimitri Patzold JSY AU RC	40.00	80.00
131 Rene Bourque JSY AU RC	50.00	100.00
132 Yann Danis JSY AU RC	30.00	60.00
133 Brad Winchester JSY AU RC	40.00	80.00
134 Jim Slater JSY AU RC	40.00	80.00
135 Petr Prucha JSY AU RC	50.00	100.00
136 Jim Howard JSY AU RC	75.00	150.00
137 Patrick Eaves JSY AU RC	40.00	100.00
138 Ryane Clowe JSY AU RC	50.00	100.00
139 Braydon Coburn JSY AU RC	40.00	80.00
140 Brad Richardson JSY AU RC	40.00	80.00
141 Milan Jurcina JSY AU RC	30.00	60.00
142 Jeff Woywitka JSY AU RC	25.00	50.00
143 Andrei Kostitsyn JSY AU RC	125.00	250.00
144 Derek Boogaard AU RC	12.00	30.00
145 Barry Tallackson JSY AU RC	30.00	60.00
146 Jakub Klepis JSY AU RC	40.00	80.00
147 Alvaro Montoya JSY AU RC	60.00	120.00
148 Andrew Ladd JSY AU RC	50.00	100.00
149 Brandon Bochenski JSY AU RC	40.00	80.00
150 Jeff Tambellini JSY AU RC	30.00	60.00
151 Jaroslav Balastik JSY AU RC	30.00	60.00
152 Lee Stempniak JSY AU RC	50.00	100.00
153 Kevin Dallman JSY AU RC	25.00	50.00
154 Niklas Nordgren JSY AU RC	25.00	50.00
155 Kevin Nastiuk JSY AU RC	30.00	60.00
156 Ryan Craig JSY AU RC	30.00	60.00
157 Erik Christensen JSY AU RC	125.00	200.00
158 Chris Thorburn JSY AU RC	30.00	60.00
159 Josh Gorges JSY AU RC	40.00	80.00
160 Matt Foy JSY AU RC	25.00	60.00
161 O.Tollefsen JSY AU RC	25.00	50.00
162 Kevin Bieksa JSY AU RC	50.00	100.00
163 Kyle Quincey JSY AU RC	50.00	100.00
164 A.Wozniewski JSY AU RC	30.00	60.00
165 Jeff Hoggan JSY AU RC	25.00	50.00
166 Jeremy Colliton JSY AU RC	30.00	60.00
167 Alexandre Picard JSY AU RC	40.00	80.00
168 Ben Eager JSY AU RC	25.00	50.00
169 Daniel Paille JSY AU RC	40.00	80.00
170 Valtteri Filppula JSY AU RC	75.00	150.00
171 A.Perezhogin JSY AU RC	40.00	80.00
172 Mike Richards JSY AU RC	300.00	450.00
173 Corey Perry JSY AU RC	100.00	200.00
174 Alexander Steen JSY AU RC	50.00	100.00
175 Thomas Vanek JSY AU RC	175.00	350.00
176 Jeff Carter JSY AU RC	150.00	300.00
177 Henrik Lundqvist JSY AU RC	300.00	500.00
178 Dion Phaneuf JSY AU/99 RC	600.00	1000.00
179 A.Ovechkin JSY AU/99 RC	3000.00	4500.00
180 Sidney Crosby JSY AU/99 RC	8000.00	10000.00
181 Brett Lebda AU RC	15.00	30.00
182 Jay McClement AU RC	15.00	40.00
183 Cam Barker JSY AU RC	40.00	80.00
184 P.Nokelainen AU RC	10.00	25.00
185 Keith Ballard AU RC	10.00	25.00
186 Duncan Keith AU RC	50.00	100.00
187 George Parros AU RC	15.00	40.00
188 Adam Berkhoel AU RC	15.00	30.00
189 Anthony Stewart AU RC	12.00	30.00
190 Ryan Hollweg AU RC	12.00	30.00
191 Ben Walter AU RC	10.00	25.00

2005-06 The Cup Gold

*1-100 GOLD: 1X TO 2.5X BASE HI
PRINT RUN 25 SER. #'d SETS

Card	Low	High
2 Teemu Selanne	30.00	80.00
3 Ilya Kovalchuk	25.00	60.00
8 Ray Bourque	25.00	60.00
11 Don Cherry	25.00	60.00
17 Jarome Iginla	25.00	60.00
21 Eric Staal	25.00	60.00
26 Bobby Hull	25.00	60.00
28 Joe Sakic	40.00	80.00
33 Rick Nash	40.00	80.00
35 Mike Modano	25.00	60.00
38 Steve Yzerman	60.00	125.00
39 Gordie Howe	30.00	80.00
43 Henrik Zetterberg	25.00	60.00
45 Wayne Gretzky	250.00	400.00
47 Roberto Luongo	25.00	60.00
50 Luc Robitaille	25.00	60.00
52 Marian Gaborik	25.00	60.00
53 Saku Koivu	25.00	60.00
56 Patrick Roy	75.00	150.00
57 Guy Lafleur	25.00	60.00
62 Martin Brodeur	30.00	80.00
69 Jaromir Jagr	25.00	60.00
70 Dominik Hasek	25.00	60.00
71 Dany Heatley	25.00	60.00
72 Jason Spezza	25.00	60.00
74 Peter Forsberg	25.00	60.00
82 Mario Lemieux	60.00	150.00
83 Marc-Andre Fleury	25.00	60.00
86 Joe Thornton	25.00	60.00
90 Vincent Lecavalier	25.00	60.00

2005-06 The Cup Printing Plates Black

101 Ryan Getzlaf AUTO
102 Ryan Whitney AUTO
103 R.J. Umberger AUTO
104 Cam Ward AUTO
105 Brent Seabrook AUTO
106 Eric Nystrom AUTO
107 Gilbert Brule AUTO
108 Hannu Toivonen AUTO
109 Robert Nilsson AUTO
110 Rostislav Olesz AUTO
111 Ryan Suter AUTO
112 Jussi Jokinen AUTO
113 Zach Parise AUTO
114 Wojtek Wolski AUTO
115 Andrej Meszaros AUTO
116 Johan Franzen AUTO
117 Peter Budaj AUTO
118 David Leneveu AUTO
119 Andrew Alberts AUTO
120 Steve Bernier AUTO
121 Mikko Koivu AUTO
122 Chris Campoli AUTO
123 Evgeny Artyukhin AUTO
124 Christoph Schubert AUTO
125 Tomas Fleischmann AUTO
126 Maxime Talbot AUTO
127 Jordan Sigalet AUTO
128 Danny Richmond AUTO
129 Maxim Lapierre AUTO
130 Dimitri Patzold AUTO
131 Rene Bourque AUTO
132 Yann Danis AUTO
133 Brad Winchester AUTO
134 Jim Slater AUTO
135 Petr Prucha AUTO
136 Jim Howard AUTO
137 Patrick Eaves AUTO
138 Ryane Clowe AUTO
139 Braydon Coburn AUTO
140 Brad Richardson AUTO
141 Milan Jurcina AUTO
142 Jeff Woywitka AUTO
143 Andrei Kostitsyn AUTO
144 Derek Boogaard AUTO
145 Barry Tallackson AUTO
146 Jakub Klepis AUTO
147 Alvaro Montoya AUTO
148 Andrew Ladd AUTO
149 Brandon Bochenski AUTO
150 Jeff Tambellini AUTO
151 Jaroslav Balastik AUTO
152 Lee Stempniak AUTO
153 Kevin Dallman AUTO
154 Niklas Nordgren AUTO
155 Kevin Nastiuk AUTO
156 Ryan Craig AUTO
157 Erik Christensen AUTO
158 Chris Thorburn AUTO
159 Josh Gorges AUTO
160 Matt Foy AUTO
161 Ole-Kristian Tollefsen AUTO
162 Kevin Bieksa AUTO
163 Kyle Quincey AUTO
164 Andrew Wozniewski AUTO
165 Jeff Hoggan AUTO
166 Jeremy Colliton AUTO
167 Alexandre Picard AUTO
168 Ben Eager AUTO
169 Daniel Paille AUTO
170 Valtteri Filppula AUTO
171 Alexander Perezhogin AUTO
172 Mike Richards AUTO
173 Corey Perry AUTO
174 Alexander Steen AUTO
175 Thomas Vanek AUTO
176 Jeff Carter AUTO
177 Henrik Lundqvist AUTO
178 Dion Phaneuf AUTO
179 Alexander Ovechkin AUTO
180 Sidney Crosby AUTO
181 Brett Lebda AUTO
182 Jay McClement AUTO
183 Cam Barker AUTO
184 Petteri Nokelainen AUTO
185 Keith Ballard AUTO
186 Duncan Keith AUTO
187 George Parros AUTO
188 Adam Berkhoel AUTO
189 Anthony Stewart AUTO
190 Ryan Hollweg AUTO
191 Ben Walter AUTO

2005-06 The Cup Printing Plates Rookie Update Black

256 Ryan Getzlaf/Jason Spezza AUTO
257 Corey Perry/Alex Tanguay AUTO
258 Hannu Toivonen/Miikka Kiprusoff AUTO
259 Thomas Vanek/Jarome Iginla AUTO
260 Alexander Steen/Mats Sundin AUTO
261 Andrew Ladd/Todd Bertuzzi AUTO
262 Cam Ward/Marty Turco AUTO
263 Wojtek Wolski/Ryan Smyth AUTO
264 Gilbert Brule/Simon Gagne AUTO
265 Valtteri Filppula/Tuomo Ruutu AUTO
266 Rostislav Olesz/Martin Havlat AUTO
267 Mikko Koivu/Saku Koivu AUTO
268 Alexander Perezhogin/Alexei Yashin AUTO
269 Andrei Kostitsyn/Alexander Frolov AUTO
270 Henrik Lundqvist/Dominik Hasek AUTO
271 Andrej Meszaros/Wade Redden AUTO
272 Jeff Carter/Joe Thornton AUTO
273 Mike Richards/Mike Modano AUTO
274 Dion Phaneuf/Chris Pronger AUTO
275 Alexander Ovechkin/Ilya Kovalchuk AUTO
276 Sidney Crosby AUTO

2005-06 The Cup Printing Plates SP Authentic Black

131 Ryan Getzlaf AUTO
132 Corey Perry AUTO
133 Braydon Coburn AUTO
134 Jim Slater AUTO
135 Hannu Toivonen AUTO
136 Andrew Alberts AUTO
137 Milan Jurcina AUTO
138 Kevin Dallman AUTO
139 Thomas Vanek AUTO
140 Dion Phaneuf AUTO
141 Eric Nystrom AUTO
142 Cam Ward AUTO
143 Kevin Nastiuk AUTO
144 Niklas Nordgren AUTO
145 Brent Seabrook AUTO
146 Cam Barker AUTO
147 Duncan Keith AUTO
148 Rene Bourque AUTO
149 Wojtek Wolski AUTO
150 Peter Budaj AUTO
151 Gilbert Brule AUTO
152 Jaroslav Balastik AUTO
153 Jussi Jokinen AUTO
154 Johan Franzen AUTO
155 Jim Howard AUTO
156 Brett Lebda AUTO
157 Brad Winchester AUTO
158 Rostislav Olesz AUTO
159 Anthony Stewart AUTO
160 George Parros AUTO
161 Matt Foy AUTO
162 Derek Boogaard AUTO
163 Alexander Perezhogin AUTO
164 Yann Danis AUTO
165 Raitis Ivanans AUTO
166 Ryan Suter AUTO
167 Zach Parise AUTO
168 Robert Nilsson AUTO
169 Petteri Nokelainen AUTO
170 Alvaro Montoya AUTO
171 Henrik Lundqvist AUTO
172 Petr Prucha AUTO
173 Ryan Hollweg AUTO
174 Patrick Eaves AUTO
175 Brandon Bochenski AUTO
176 Andrej Meszaros AUTO
177 Jeff Carter AUTO
178 Mike Richards AUTO
179 David Leneveu AUTO
180 Keith Ballard AUTO
181 Sidney Crosby AUTO
182 Maxime Talbot AUTO
183 Josh Gorges AUTO
184 Ryane Clowe AUTO
185 Jay McClement AUTO
186 Jeff Hoggan AUTO
187 Jeff Woywitka AUTO
188 Alexander Steen AUTO
189 Andy Wozniewski AUTO
190 Alexander Ovechkin AUTO
191 Ryan Whitney AUTO
192 R.J. Umberger AUTO
193 Mikko Koivu AUTO
194 Steve Bernier AUTO
196 Ryan Craig AUTO
197 Valtteri Filppula AUTO
198 Daniel Paille AUTO
199 Danny Richmond AUTO
200 Maxim Lapierre AUTO
201 Barry Tallackson AUTO
202 Chris Campoli AUTO
203 Jeremy Colliton AUTO
204 Christoph Schubert AUTO
205 Kevin Bieksa AUTO
206 Jordan Sigalet AUTO
207 Adam Berkhoel AUTO
208 Erik Christensen AUTO
209 Ole-Kristian Tollefsen AUTO
210 Dimitri Patzold AUTO
211 Brad Richardson AUTO
212 Lee Stempniak AUTO
213 Andrei Kostitsyn AUTO
214 Evgeny Artyukhin AUTO
215 Ben Eager AUTO
216 Andrew Ladd AUTO
217 Jeff Tambellini AUTO
218 Kyle Quincey AUTO
219 Tomas Fleischmann AUTO
220 Jakub Klepis AUTO

2005-06 The Cup Printing Plates SPx Black

154 Wojtek Wolski AUTO
155 Rene Bourque AUTO
156 Gilbert Brule AUTO
157 Jeff Woywitka AUTO
158 Hannu Toivonen AUTO
159 Alvaro Montoya AUTO
160 Yann Danis AUTO
161 Alexander Perezhogin AUTO
162 Cam Barker AUTO
163 Zach Parise AUTO
164 Dion Phaneuf AUTO
165 Mike Richards AUTO
166 Cam Ward AUTO
167 Robert Nilsson AUTO
168 Petteri Nokelainen AUTO
169 Alexander Steen AUTO
170 Ryan Getzlaf AUTO
171 Corey Perry AUTO
172 Rostislav Olesz AUTO
173 Henrik Lundqvist AUTO
174 Petr Prucha AUTO
175 Jim Howard AUTO
176 Johan Franzen AUTO
177 Thomas Vanek AUTO
178 Andrej Meszaros AUTO
179 Brandon Bochenski AUTO
180 Jussi Jokinen AUTO
181 Braydon Coburn AUTO
182 Ryan Suter AUTO
183 Peter Budaj AUTO
184 Brent Seabrook AUTO
185 Keith Ballard AUTO
186 Milan Jurcina AUTO
187 Anthony Stewart AUTO
188 Eric Nystrom AUTO
189 Jeff Carter AUTO
190 Alexander Ovechkin AUTO
191 Sidney Crosby AUTO
222 Chris Thorburn AUTO
223 Daniel Paille AUTO
224 Andrew Ladd AUTO
225 Danny Richmond AUTO
226 Brad Richardson AUTO
227 Ole-Kristian Tollefsen AUTO
228 Alexandre Picard AUTO
229 Kyle Quincey AUTO
230 Valtteri Filppula AUTO
231 Jeff Tambellini AUTO
232 Mikko Koivu AUTO
233 Maxim Lapierre AUTO
234 Andrei Kostitsyn AUTO
235 Barry Tallackson AUTO
236 Jeremy Colliton AUTO
237 R.J. Umberger AUTO
238 Ben Eager AUTO
239 Ryan Whitney AUTO
240 Steve Bernier AUTO
241 Ryan Craig AUTO
242 Kevin Bieksa AUTO
243 Jakub Klepis AUTO

2005-06 The Cup Printing Plates Ultimate Collection Black

91 Sidney Crosby AUTO
92 Alexander Ovechkin AUTO
93 Gilbert Brule AUTO
94 Corey Perry AUTO
95 Jeff Carter AUTO
96 Alexander Steen AUTO
97 Henrik Lundqvist AUTO
98 Hannu Toivonen AUTO
99 Alexander Perezhogin AUTO
100 Thomas Vanek AUTO
101 Ryan Getzlaf AUTO
102 Braydon Coburn AUTO
103 Milan Jurcina AUTO
104 Andrew Alberts AUTO
105 Dion Phaneuf AUTO
106 Eric Nystrom AUTO
107 Cam Ward AUTO
108 Cam Barker AUTO
109 Brent Seabrook AUTO
110 Rene Bourque AUTO
111 Peter Budaj AUTO
112 Wojtek Wolski AUTO
113 Jussi Jokinen AUTO
114 Jim Howard AUTO
115 Johan Franzen AUTO
116 Brad Winchester AUTO
117 Rostislav Olesz AUTO
118 Anthony Stewart AUTO
119 Matt Foy AUTO
120 Yann Danis AUTO
121 Ryan Suter AUTO
122 Zach Parise AUTO
123 Robert Nilsson AUTO
124 Al Montoya AUTO
125 Petr Prucha AUTO
126 Brandon Bochenski AUTO
127 Andrej Meszaros AUTO
128 Patrick Eaves AUTO
129 Mike Richards AUTO
130 Keith Ballard AUTO
131 Ryane Clowe AUTO
132 Jeff Woywitka AUTO

2005-06 The Cup Autographed Rookie Patches Gold Rainbow

#'d TO PLAYER'S JERSEY NUMBER
LOW PRINT RUNS NOT PRICED DUE TO SCARCITY
UNIQUE SWATCHES MAY EARN SUBSTANTIAL PREMIUM

Card	Low	High
101 Ryan Getzlaf/51	200.00	400.00
102 Ryan Whitney/19		
103 R.J. Umberger/20	75.00	150.00
104 Cam Ward/30	200.00	350.00
105 Brent Seabrook/7		
106 Eric Nystrom/23	60.00	200.00
107 Gilbert Brule/17	200.00	350.00
108 Hannu Toivonen/33	100.00	250.00
109 Robert Nilsson/21	125.00	200.00
110 Rostislav Olesz/85	40.00	100.00
111 Ryan Suter/20	60.00	150.00
112 Jussi Jokinen/36	75.00	200.00
113 Zach Parise/9		
114 Wojtek Wolski/8		
115 Andrej Meszaros/14		
116 Johan Franzen/39	125.00	250.00
117 Peter Budaj/31	125.00	250.00
118 David Leneveu/30	60.00	150.00
119 Andrew Alberts/41	40.00	100.00
120 Steve Bernier/26	200.00	400.00
121 Mikko Koivu/21	150.00	300.00
123 Evgeny Artyukhin/76	20.00	60.00
124 Christoph Schubert/5		
125 Tomas Fleischmann/43	60.00	125.00
126 Maxime Talbot/25	60.00	120.00
127 Jordan Sigalet/57	40.00	100.00
128 Danny Richmond/51	30.00	60.00
129 Maxim Lapierre/40	30.00	60.00
130 Dimitri Patzold/30	40.00	80.00
131 Rene Bourque/14		
132 Yann Danis/75	40.00	100.00
133 Brad Winchester/26	40.00	100.00
134 Jim Slater/23	30.00	80.00
135 Petr Prucha/25	100.00	200.00
136 Jim Howard/35	100.00	200.00
137 Patrick Eaves/44	60.00	150.00
138 Ryane Clowe/29	75.00	150.00
139 Braydon Coburn/4		
140 Brad Richardson/12		
141 Milan Jurcina/68	25.00	60.00
142 Jeff Woywitka/29	30.00	60.00
143 Andrei Kostitsyn/46	75.00	200.00
145 Barry Tallackson/27	40.00	80.00
146 Jakub Klepis/38	50.00	125.00
147 Alvaro Montoya/29	75.00	150.00
148 Andrew Ladd/16		
149 Brandon Bochenski/10		
151 Jaroslav Balastik/40		
152 Lee Stempniak/12		
153 Kevin Dallman/38	30.00	60.00
154 Niklas Nordgren/44	30.00	60.00
155 Kevin Nastiuk/35	30.00	80.00
156 Ryan Craig/34	40.00	100.00
157 Erik Christensen/16		
159 Josh Gorges/6		
160 Matt Foy/83	30.00	60.00
161 Ole-Kristian Tollefsen/55	30.00	60.00
162 Kevin Bieksa/25	50.00	100.00
164 Andrew Wozniewski/56	30.00	60.00
165 Jeff Hoggan/22	40.00	100.00
166 Jeremy Colliton/27	40.00	80.00
167 Alexandre Picard/19	30.00	60.00
168 Ben Eager/55	30.00	60.00
169 Daniel Paille/20	75.00	150.00
171 Alexander Perezhogin/42	30.00	80.00
172 Mike Richards/18		
173 Corey Perry/61	100.00	200.00
174 Alexander Steen/10		
175 Thomas Vanek/26	300.00	600.00
176 Jeff Carter/17	175.00	350.00
177 Henrik Lundqvist/30	250.00	500.00
178 Dion Phaneuf/3		
179 Alexander Ovechkin/8		
180 Sidney Crosby/87	2500.00	4000.00
183 Cam Barker/25	60.00	150.00

2005-06 The Cup Black Rainbow

PRINT RUN 1 SER. #'d SET
NOT PRICED DUE TO SCARCITY

1 Jean-Sebastien Giguere
2 Teemu Selanne
3 Ilya Kovalchuk
4 Marian Hossa
5 Kari Lehtonen
6 Cam Neely
7 Patrice Bergeron
8 Ray Bourque
9 Johnny Bucyk
10 Phil Esposito
11 Don Cherry
12 Brian Leetch
13 Gerry Cheevers
14 Gilbert Perreault
15 Chris Drury
16 Ryan Miller
17 Jarome Iginla
18 Lanny McDonald
19 Miikka Kiprusoff
20 Joe Mullen
21 Eric Staal
22 Doug Weight
23 Martin Gerber
24 Nikolai Khabibulin
25 Denis Savard
26 Bobby Hull
27 Tony Esposito
28 Joe Sakic
29 Alex Tanguay
30 Milan Hejduk
31 Jose Theodore
32 Marek Svatos
33 Rick Nash
34 Sergei Fedorov
35 Mike Modano
36 Marty Turco
37 Brenden Morrow
38 Steve Yzerman
39 Gordie Howe
40 Brendan Shanahan
41 Scotty Bowman
42 Pavel Datsyuk
43 Henrik Zetterberg
44 Chris Pronger
45 Wayne Gretzky
46 Grant Fuhr
47 Roberto Luongo
48 Olli Jokinen
49 Jeremy Roenick
50 Luc Robitaille
51 Rogie Vachon
52 Marian Gaborik
53 Saku Koivu
54 Jean Beliveau
55 Steve Shutt
56 Patrick Roy
57 Guy Lafleur
58 Guy Lapointe
59 Michael Ryder
60 Tomas Vokoun
61 Paul Kariya
62 Martin Brodeur
63 Patrik Elias
64 Alexei Yashin
65 Mike Bossy
66 Denis Potvin
67 Bryan Trottier
68 Clark Gillies
69 Jaromir Jagr
70 Dominik Hasek
71 Dany Heatley
72 Jason Spezza
73 Daniel Alfredsson
74 Peter Forsberg
75 Ron Hextall
76 Simon Gagne
77 Bobby Clarke
78 Keith Primeau
79 Bernie Parent
80 Shane Doan
81 Curtis Joseph
82 Mario Lemieux
83 Marc-Andre Fleury
84 Jonathan Cheechoo
85 Evgeni Nabokov
86 Joe Thornton
87 Patrick Marleau
88 Keith Tkachuk
89 Martin St. Louis
90 Vincent Lecavalier
91 Brad Richards
92 Ed Belfour
93 Darryl Sittler
94 Mats Sundin
95 Eric Lindros
96 Doug Gilmour
97 Markus Naslund
98 Todd Bertuzzi
99 Ed Jovanovski
100 Olaf Kolzig

2005-06 The Cup Black Rainbow Rookies

PRINT RUN 1 SER. #'d SET
NOT PRICED DUE TO SCARCITY

101 Ryan Getzlaf
102 Ryan Whitney
103 R.J. Umberger
104 Cam Ward
105 Brent Seabrook
106 Eric Nystrom
107 Gilbert Brule
108 Hannu Toivonen
109 Robert Nilsson
110 Rostislav Olesz
111 Ryan Suter
112 Jussi Jokinen
113 Zach Parise
114 Wojtek Wolski
115 Andrej Meszaros
116 Johan Franzen
117 Peter Budaj
118 David Leneveu
119 Andrew Alberts
120 Steve Bernier
121 Mikko Koivu
122 Chris Campoli
123 Evgeny Artyukhin
124 Christoph Schubert
125 Tomas Fleischmann
126 Maxime Talbot
127 Jordan Sigalet
128 Danny Richmond
129 Maxim Lapierre
130 Dimitri Patzold
131 Rene Bourque
132 Yann Danis
133 Brad Winchester
134 Jim Slater
135 Petr Prucha
136 Jim Howard
137 Patrick Eaves
138 Ryane Clowe
139 Braydon Coburn
140 Brad Richardson
141 Milan Jurcina
142 Jeff Woywitka
143 Andrei Kostitsyn
144 Derek Boogaard
145 Barry Tallackson
146 Jakub Klepis
147 Alvaro Montoya
148 Andrew Ladd
149 Brandon Bochenski
150 Jeff Tambellini
151 Jaroslav Balastik
152 Lee Stempniak
153 Kevin Dallman
154 Niklas Nordgren
155 Kevin Nastiuk
156 Ryan Craig
157 Erik Christensen
158 Chris Thorburn
159 Josh Gorges
160 Matt Foy
161 Ole-Kristian Tollefsen
162 Kevin Bieksa
163 Kyle Quincey
164 Andrew Wozniewski
165 Jeff Hoggan
166 Jeremy Colliton
167 Alexandre Picard
168 Ben Eager
169 Daniel Paille
170 Valtteri Filppula
171 Alexander Perezhogin
172 Mike Richards

173 Corey Perry
174 Alexander Steen
175 Thomas Vanek
176 Jeff Carter
177 Henrik Lundqvist
178 Dion Phaneuf
179 Alexander Ovechkin
180 Sidney Crosby
181 Brett Lebda
182 Jay McClement
183 Cam Barker
184 Petteri Nokelainen
185 Keith Ballard
186 Duncan Keith
187 George Parros
188 Adam Berkhoel
189 Anthony Stewart
190 Ryan Hollweg
191 Ben Walter

2005-06 The Cup Dual NHL Shields

PRINT RUN 1 SER. #'d SET
NOT PRICED DUE TO SCARCITY
DSAM Alexei Yashin
Miroslav Satan
DSBE Martin Brodeur
Patrik Elias
DSBG Martin Brodeur
Scott Gomez
DSBS Patrice Bergeron
Sergei Samsonov
DSCO Sidney Crosby
Alexander Ovechkin
DSDZ Pavel Datsyuk
Henrik Zetterberg
DSFG Peter Forsberg
Simon Gagne
DSGK Marian Gaborik
Mikko Koivu
DSGL Wayne Gretzky
Mario Lemieux
DSGS Jean-Sebastien Giguere
Teemu Selanne
DSHA Martin Havlat
Daniel Alfredsson
DSHB Marian Hossa
Peter Bondra
DSHS Dany Heatley
Jason Spezza
DSIK Jarome Iginla
Miikka Kiprusoff
DSIL Jarome Iginla
Martin St. Louis
DSIN Jarome Iginla
Rick Nash
DSJC Joffrey Lupul
Corey Perry
DSJD Curtis Joseph
Shane Doan
DSJL Jaromir Jagr
Henrik Lundqvist
DSJM Jeff Carter
Mike Richards
DSKD Ilya Kovalchuk
Pavel Datsyuk
DSKG Keith Primeau
Simon Gagne
DSKJ Miikka Kiprusoff
Olli Jokinen
DSKO Ilya Kovalchuk
Alexander Ovechkin
DSKS Paul Kariya
Teemu Selanne
DSKT Saku Koivu
Jose Theodore
DSKV Paul Kariya
Tomas Vokoun
DSLB Roberto Luongo
Jay Bouwmeester
DSLC Mario Lemieux
Sidney Crosby
DSLJ Mario Lemieux
Jaromir Jagr
DSMA Mats Sundin
Alexander Steen
DSMG Glen Murray
Patrice Bergeron
DSME Mats Sundin
Eric Lindros
DSMG Mike Modano
Bill Guerin
DSMN Brendan Morrison
Markus Naslund
DSMT Mike Modano
Marty Turco
DSNB Markus Naslund
Todd Bertuzzi
DSNZ Markus Naslund
Henrik Zetterberg
DSPC Chris Pronger
Ty Conklin
DSPK Alexander Perezhogin
Saku Koivu
DSPM Peter Forsberg
Mats Sundin
DSRD Luc Robitaille
Pavol Demitra
DSRM Ryan Smyth
Michael Peca
DSRO Roberto Luongo
Olli Jokinen
DSRR Mike Ribeiro
Michael Ryder
DSRT Andrew Raycroft
Hannu Toivonen
DSSA Mats Sundin
Daniel Alfredsson
DSSB Mats Sundin
Ed Belfour
DSSF Joe Sakic
Peter Forsberg
DSST Joe Sakic
Alex Tanguay
DSWT Doug Weight
Keith Tkachuk
DSYP Alexei Yashin
Mark Parrish

2005-06 The Cup Dual NHL Shields Autographs

PRINT RUN 1 SER. #'d SET
NOT PRICED DUE TO SCARCITY
ADSAM Alexei Yashin
Miroslav Satan
ADSAR Ales Hemsky
Ryan Smyth
ADSBL Ray Bourque
Brian Leetch
ADSGK Marian Gaborik
Mikko Koivu
ADSJM Jeff Carter
Mike Richards
ADSKG Keith Primeau
Simon Gagne
ADSKH Ilya Kovalchuk
Marian Hossa
ADSKJ Miikka Kiprusoff
Olli Jokinen
ADSKO Ilya Kovalchuk
Alexander Ovechkin
ADSKT Saku Koivu
Jose Theodore
ADSLA Jeremy Roenick
Luc Robitaille
ADSLK Kari Lehtonen
Ilya Kovalchuk
ADSLL Martin St. Louis
Vincent Lecavalier
ADSLP Henrik Lundqvist
Petr Prucha
ADSMB Glen Murray
Patrice Bergeron
ADSMT Mike Modano
Marty Turco
ADSNB Markus Naslund
Todd Bertuzzi
ADSNZ Markus Naslund
Henrik Zetterberg
ADSPB Chris Pronger
Rob Blake
ADSPC Chris Pronger
Ty Conklin
ADSPK Alexander Perezhogin
Saku Koivu
ADSRB Patrick Roy
Martin Brodeur
ADSRG Rick Nash
Gilbert Brule
ADSRM Ryan Smyth
Michael Peca
ADSRT Andrew Raycroft
Hannu Toivonen
ADSSG Eric Staal
Martin Gerber
ADSTC Joe Thornton
Jonathan Cheechoo
ADSTL Jose Theodore
Roberto Luongo
ADSYP Alexei Yashin
Mark Parrish

2005-06 The Cup Emblems of Endorsement

PRINT RUN 15 SER. #'d SETS
NOT PRICED DUE TO SCARCITY
EEAF Alexander Frolov
EEAO Alexander Ovechkin
EEAR Andrew Raycroft
EEAT Alex Tanguay
EEAY Alexei Yashin
EEBH Bobby Hull
EEBL Brian Leetch
EEBO Jay Bouwmeester
EEBQ Ray Bourque
EEBS Billy Smith
EEBY Mike Bossy
EECD Chris Drury
EECN Cam Neely
EECP Chris Pronger
EEDG Doug Gilmour
EEDH Dany Heatley
EEDS Darryl Sittler
EEDW Doug Weight
EEEB Ed Belfour
EEEN Evgeni Nabokov
EEES Eric Staal
EEFM Frank Mahovlich
EEGC Gerry Cheevers
EEGE Martin Gerber
EEGF Grant Fuhr/12
EEGL Guy Lafleur
EEGM Glen Murray
EEHK Dominik Hasek
EEHO Marian Hossa
EEHV Martin Havlat
EEHZ Henrik Zetterberg
EEIK Ilya Kovalchuk
EEJB Jean Beliveau
EEJC Jonathan Cheechoo
EEJG Jean-Sebastien Giguere
EEJI Jarome Iginla
EEJM Joe Mullen
EEJO Joe Thornton
EEJP Joni Pitkanen
EEJT Jose Theodore
EEKD Kris Draper
EEKL Kari Lehtonen
EEKP Keith Primeau
EELM Larry Murphy
EELR Luc Robitaille
EELU Joffrey Lupul
EEMB Martin Brodeur
EEMC Bryan McCabe
EEMG Marian Gaborik
EEMH Milan Hejduk
EEMK Miikka Kiprusoff
EEML Manny Legace
EEMM Mike Modano
EEMN Markus Naslund
EEMS Miroslav Satan
EEMT Marty Turco
EEMU Lanny McDonald
EEMW Brenden Morrow
EEOJ Olli Jokinen
EEOK Olaf Kolzig
EEPB Patrice Bergeron
EEPH Dion Phaneuf
EEPM Patrick Marleau
EEPR Patrick Roy
EERB Rob Blake
EERH Ron Hextall
EERL Roberto Luongo/10
EERM Ryan Miller
EERN Rick Nash
EERS Ryan Smyth
EERV Rogie Vachon
EERY Michael Ryder
EESC Sidney Crosby
EESG Simon Gagne
EESK Saku Koivu
EESL Martin St. Louis
EESN Scott Niedermayer
EESS Steve Shutt
EESV Marek Svatos
EETB Todd Bertuzzi
EETE Tony Esposito
EETI Dave Williams
EETV Tomas Vokoun
EEVL Vincent Lecavalier
EEWR Wade Redden
EEZC Zdeno Chara

2005-06 The Cup Hardware Heroes

PRINT RUNS VARY
NOT PRICED DUE TO SCARCITY
HHAR Andrew Raycroft/1
HHBH Bobby Hull/3
HHBS Billy Smith/1
HHBT Bryan Trottier/1
HHCD Chris Drury/1
HHCN Cam Neely/1
HHCP Chris Pronger/1
HHDG Doug Gilmour/1
HHDH Dany Heatley/1
HHDT Dave Taylor/1
HHEN Evgeni Nabokov/1
HHFM Frank Mahovlich/1
HHGF Grant Fuhr/1
HHIK Ilya Kovalchuk/1
HHJB John Bucyk/2
HHJM Joe Mullen/2
HHJS Jean-Sebastien Giguere/1
HHJT Jose Theodore/1
HHKD Kris Draper/1
HHLU Luc Robitaille/1
HHMD Marcel Dionne/1
HHMH Milan Hejduk/1
HHMN Markus Naslund/1
HHRH Ron Hextall/1
HHRN Rick Nash/1
HHRO Rob Blake/1
HHSK Saku Koivu/1
HHSN Scott Niedermayer/1
HHBL1 Brian Leetch/1
HHBL2 Brian Leetch/2
HHBL3 Brian Leetch/1
HHBO1 Mike Bossy/1
HHBO2 Mike Bossy/3
HHBO3 Mike Bossy/1
HHBP1 Bernie Parent/2
HHBP2 Bernie Parent/2
HHDO1 Dominik Hasek/2
HHDO2 Dominik Hasek/6
HHDO3 Dominik Hasek/2
HHDP1 Denis Potvin/1
HHDP2 Denis Potvin/3
HHEB2 Ed Belfour/2
HHGH1 Gordie Howe/6
HHGH2 Gordie Howe/6
HHGL1 Guy Lafleur/3
HHGL2 Guy Lafleur/2
HHGL3 Guy Lafleur/3
HHGP1 Gilbert Perreault/1
HHGP2 Gilbert Perreault/1
HHJB1 Jean Beliveau/1
HHJB2 Jean Beliveau/1
HHJI1 Jarome Iginla/1
HHJI2 Jarome Iginla/1
HHJI3 Jarome Iginla/1
HHJI4 Jarome Iginla/2
HHLM1 Lanny McDonald/1
HHLM2 Lanny McDonald/1
HHMB1 Martin Brodeur/1
HHMB2 Martin Brodeur/1
HHMP1 Michael Peca/1
HHMP2 Michael Peca/1
HHPE1 Phil Esposito/5
HHPE2 Phil Esposito/2
HHPE3 Phil Esposito/2
HHPR1 Patrick Roy/2
HHPR2 Patrick Roy/3
HHPR3 Patrick Roy/1
HHRB1 Ray Bourque/1
HHRB2 Ray Bourque/5
HHRB3 Ray Bourque/1
HHSB1 Scotty Bowman/1
HHSB2 Scotty Bowman/1
HHSL1 Martin St. Louis/1
HHSL2 Martin St. Louis/1
HHSL3 Martin St. Louis/1
HHTE1 Tony Esposito/1
HHTE2 Tony Esposito/3
HHWG1 Wayne Gretzky/7
HHWG2 Wayne Gretzky/7
HHWG3 Wayne Gretzky/8
HHWG4 Wayne Gretzky/5
HHWG5 Wayne Gretzky/1
HHWG6 Wayne Gretzky/3
HHWG7 Wayne Gretzky/1
HHWG8 Wayne Gretzky/1

2005-06 The Cup Honorable Numbers

PRINT RUNS VARY
HNAH Ales Hemsky/83 25.00 60.00
HNAO Alexander Ovechkin/8
HNAR Andrew Raycroft/1
HNAT Alex Tanguay/18
HNAY Alexei Yashin/79 40.00 80.00
HNBH Bobby Hull/9
HNBI Martin Biron/43 25.00 50.00
HNBK Rob Blake/4
HNBL Brian Leetch/22 75.00 150.00
HNBM Bryan McCabe/24 40.00 80.00
HNBT Bryan Trottier/19 50.00 100.00
HNBY Mike Bossy/22
HNCD Chris Drury/23 50.00 100.00
HNCH Jonathan Cheechoo/14
HNCN Cam Neely/8
HNCP Chris Pronger/44 30.00 60.00
HNDA David Aebischer/1
HNDG Doug Gilmour/93 40.00 80.00
HNDH Dany Heatley/15
HNDP Dion Phaneuf/3
HNDR Dwayne Roloson/30 25.00 50.00
HNDS Darryl Sittler/27 40.00 80.00
HNDW Doug Weight/39 25.00 50.00
HNED Eric Daze/55 15.00 40.00
HNER Eric Staal/12
HNGC Gerry Cheevers/30 50.00 100.00
HNGE Martin Gerber/29 40.00 80.00
HNGF Grant Fuhr/31 60.00 100.00
HNGL Guy Lafleur/10
HNGM Glen Murray/27 75.00 150.00
HNGP Gilbert Perreault/11
HNHK Dominik Hasek/39 75.00 125.00
HNHO Marian Hossa/18
HNHV Martin Havlat/9
HNIK Ilya Kovalchuk/17 75.00 150.00
HNJB Jean Beliveau/4
HNJC Jeff Carter/17
HNJI Jarome Iginla/12
HNJO Joe Thornton/19
HNJS Jean-Sebastien Giguere/35 75.00 150.00
HNJT Jose Theodore/60 40.00 80.00
HNKL Kari Lehtonen/32 100.00 175.00
HNKP Keith Primeau/25 25.00 50.00
HNLR Luc Robitaille/20 75.00 150.00
HNLU Joffrey Lupul/15
HNMB Martin Brodeur/30 200.00 350.00
HNMC Lanny McDonald/9
HNMG Marian Gaborik/10
HNMH Milan Hejduk/23
HNMK Miikka Kiprusoff/34 75.00 150.00
HNMN Markus Naslund/19
HNMO Brendan Morrison/7
HNMP Mark Parrish/37 20.00 50.00
HNMS Marek Svatos/40 40.00 80.00
HNMT Marty Turco/35 30.00 60.00
HNMW Brenden Morrow/10
HNOK Olaf Kolzig/37 75.00 150.00
HNPB Patrice Bergeron/37 40.00 80.00
HNPE Michael Peca/37 30.00 60.00
HNPM Patrick Marleau/12
HNPO Denis Potvin/5
HNPR Patrick Roy/33 300.00 500.00
HNRB Ray Bourque/77 60.00 120.00
HNRE Robert Esche/42 25.00 50.00
HNRH Ron Hextall/27 75.00 150.00
HNRL Roberto Luongo/1
HNRN Rick Nash/61 75.00 150.00
HNSA Miroslav Satan/81 40.00 80.00
HNSC Sidney Crosby/87 400.00 700.00
HNSG Simon Gagne/12
HNSK Saku Koivu/11
HNSL Martin St. Louis/26 30.00 60.00
HNST Matt Stajan/14
HNTB Todd Bertuzzi/44 30.00 60.00
HNTE Tony Esposito/35 75.00 150.00
HNTV Tomas Vokoun/29 50.00 100.00
HNVL Vincent Lecavalier/4
HNWG Wayne Gretzky/9
HNZP Zigmund Palffy/33 40.00 80.00
HNDS2 Denis Savard/18

2005-06 The Cup Legendary Cuts

PRINT RUNS VARY
NOT PRICED DUE TO SCARCITY
LCBC Bun Cook/2
LCBH Bryan Hextall Sr./1
LCBM Bert McInenly/1
LCCO Bill Cook/3
LCCW Bill Cowley/1
LCDC Dit Clapper/1
LCDH Doug Harvey/5
LCES Eddie Shore/1
LCFS Frank Selke/2
LCHD Hap Day/6
LCHS Harold Starr/1
LCJP Jacques Plante/3
LCKC King Clancy/5
LCMO Bill Mosienko/3
LCSA Sid Abel/2
LCSH Syd Howe/1
LCSY Syl Apps/1
LCTB Toe Blake/2

2005-06 The Cup Limited Logos

PRINT RUNS VARY
LLAO Alexander Ovechkin 300.00 500.00
LLAT Alex Tanguay 60.00 125.00
LLAY Alexei Yashin 40.00 80.00
LLBH Bobby Hull/25
LLBI Martin Biron 60.00 125.00
LLBL Rob Blake 40.00 80.00
LLBS Billy Smith 40.00 80.00
LLBY Mike Bossy 75.00 150.00
LLCD Chris Drury 50.00 100.00
LLCN Cam Neely
LLCP Chris Pronger 60.00 125.00
LLDA David Aebischer 25.00 60.00
LLDG Doug Gilmour/15 150.00 250.00
LLDH Dany Heatley/14 125.00 250.00
LLDP Denis Potvin 60.00 125.00
LLDS Darryl Sittler/5
LLDW Doug Weight/35 40.00 80.00
LLED Eric Daze 40.00 80.00
LLEN Evgeni Nabokov/20 100.00 200.00
LLES Eric Staal 60.00 125.00
LLFM Frank Mahovlich/20 75.00 150.00
LLGE Martin Gerber 50.00 100.00
LLGF Grant Fuhr/45 50.00 100.00
LLGM Glen Murray 60.00 125.00
LLGP Gilbert Perreault 60.00 120.00
LLHA Dominik Hasek 60.00 100.00
LLHJ Milan Hejduk 40.00 80.00
LLHV Martin Havlat 40.00 80.00
LLIK Ilya Kovalchuk 60.00 120.00
LLJC Jonathan Cheechoo/25 50.00 100.00
LLJI Jarome Iginla 175.00 300.00
LLJO Joe Thornton 100.00 175.00
LLJS Jean-Sebastien Giguere 40.00 80.00
LLJT Jose Theodore 40.00 80.00
LLKD Kris Draper 25.00 60.00
LLKP Keith Primeau 20.00 50.00
LLLF Guy Lafleur/10
LLLM Lanny McDonald/25 50.00 100.00
LLLU Luc Robitaille 60.00 125.00
LLMB Martin Brodeur 125.00 250.00
LLMC Bryan McCabe 25.00 60.00
LLMG Marian Gaborik 60.00 125.00
LLMH Marian Hossa 75.00 125.00
LLMK Miikka Kiprusoff 75.00 150.00
LLML Manny Legace/10
LLMM Mike Modano 60.00 120.00
LLMN Markus Naslund 60.00 120.00
LLMO Brendan Morrison 25.00 60.00
LLMP Michael Peca/30 40.00 80.00
LLMT Marty Turco 50.00 100.00
LLMW Brenden Morrow 40.00 80.00
LLOJ Olli Jokinen 25.00 60.00
LLOK Olaf Kolzig 60.00 125.00
LLPB Patrice Bergeron/25 100.00 175.00
LLPM Patrick Marleau/30 50.00 100.00
LLPR Patrick Roy/21 250.00 500.00
LLRB Ray Bourque/45 60.00 120.00
LLRE Robert Esche 20.00 50.00
LLRL Roberto Luongo/40 75.00 150.00
LLRM Ryan Miller 75.00 150.00
LLRN Rick Nash/20 100.00 200.00
LLRS Ryan Smyth 60.00 125.00
LLRV Rogie Vachon/20
LLRY Michael Ryder 50.00 100.00
LLSA Miroslav Satan 25.00 60.00
LLSC Sidney Crosby 500.00 850.00
LLSD Shane Doan 50.00 100.00
LLSG Simon Gagne 25.00 60.00
LLSK Saku Koivu 50.00 100.00
LLSL Martin St. Louis/25 75.00 150.00
LLSN Scott Niedermayer 25.00 60.00
LLSS Steve Shutt 50.00 100.00
LLSW Stephen Weiss 25.00 60.00
LLTB Todd Bertuzzi 40.00 80.00
LLTC Ty Conklin 25.00 60.00
LLTE Tony Esposito/15 300.00 600.00
LLTV Tomas Vokoun 50.00 100.00
LLVL Vincent Lecavalier 75.00 150.00
LLZP Zigmund Palffy 40.00 80.00

2005-06 The Cup Noble Numbers

PRINT RUNS VARY
UNDER 24 NOT PRICED DUE TO SCARCITY
NNBB Rob Blake
Jay Bouwmeester/4
NNBC Martin Brodeur 60.00 100.00
Gerry Cheevers/30
NNBE Ray Bourque
Phil Esposito/7
NNBL Jean Beliveau
Vincent Lecavalier/4
NNBS Mike Bossy 30.00 60.00
Steve Shutt/22
NNDZ Pavel Datsyuk
Nikolai Zherdev/13
NNFJ Grant Fuhr 40.00 100.00
Curtis Joseph/31
NNFS Peter Forsberg 50.00 100.00
Borje Salming/21
NNGM Simon Gagne
Patrick Marleau/12
NNGT Jean-Sebastien Giguere 25.00 60.00
Marty Turco/35
NNGV Martin Gerber 30.00 80.00
Tomas Vokoun/29
NNHD Milan Hejduk 25.00 60.00
Chris Drury/23
NNHM Bobby Hull
Lanny McDonald/9
NNHR Dany Heatley
Tuomo Ruutu/15
NNIG Jarome Iginla
Simon Gagne/12
NNJJ Jaromir Jagr 40.00 100.00
Milan Jurcina/68
NNJS Jason Spezza
Shane Doan/19
NNKA Saku Koivu
Daniel Alfredsson/11
NNKC Ilya Kovalchuk 60.00 125.00
Jeff Carter/17
NNKL Miikka Kiprusoff 30.00 60.00
Manny Legace/34
NNLA Roberto Luongo
David Aebischer/1
NNLM Henrik Lundqvist 60.00 120.00
Ryan Miller/30
NNLR Roberto Luongo
Andrew Raycroft/1
NNMJ Larry Murphy 25.00 50.00
Ed Jovanovski/55
NNMK Mike Modano
Paul Kariya/9
NNMM Lanny McDonald
Joe Mullen/7
NNMS Frank Mahovlich 40.00 80.00
Darryl Sittler/27
NNMT Joe Mullen
Keith Tkachuk/7
NNNP Rick Nash 30.00 80.00
Corey Perry/61
NNPB Chris Pronger 25.00 60.00
Todd Bertuzzi/44
NNPK Gilbert Perreault
Saku Koivu/11
NNPM Denis Potvin
Larry Murphy/5
NNSC Brendan Shanahan
Jonathan Cheechoo/14
NNSD Mats Sundin
Pavel Datsyuk/13
NNSE Peter Stastny 40.00 80.00
Patrik Elias/26
NNSI Eric Staal
Jarome Iginla/12
NNSL Peter Stastny 30.00 60.00
Martin St. Louis/26
NNSM Eric Staal
Patrick Marleau/12
NNSR Jason Spezza
Brad Richards/19
NNSS Mats Sundin
Teemu Selanne/13
NNST Denis Savard
Alex Tanguay/18
NNTN Joe Thornton
Markus Naslund/19
NNTS Joe Thornton
Jason Spezza/19
NNYS Steve Yzerman 125.00 250.00
Joe Sakic/19
NNYT Steve Yzerman 100.00 200.00
Joe Thornton/19
NNZS Henrik Zetterberg 50.00 100.00
Marek Svatos/40

2005-06 The Cup Noble Numbers Dual

PRINT RUN 10 SER. #'d SETS
NOT PRICED DUE TO SCARCITY
DNNBE Martin Brodeur
Patrik Elias
DNNBJ Todd Bertuzzi
Ed Jovanovski
DNNCL Sidney Crosby
Mario Lemieux
DNNCO Sidney Crosby
Alexander Ovechkin
DNNCV Gerry Cheevers
Rogie Vachon
DNNDV Marcel Dionne
Rogie Vachon
DNNDZ Pavel Datsyuk
Henrik Zetterberg
DNNEH Patrik Elias
Martin Havlat
DNNFD Sergei Fedorov
Pavel Datsyuk
DNNFG Peter Forsberg
Simon Gagne
DNNFI Saku Koivu
Teemu Selanne
DNNFN Sergei Fedorov
Rick Nash
DNNFR Grant Fuhr
Bill Ranford
DNNFS Peter Forsberg
Mats Sundin
DNNGH Marian Gaborik
Marian Hossa
DNNGL Wayne Gretzky
Mario Lemieux
DNNGS Jean-Sebastien Giguere
Teemu Selanne
DNNHI Dany Heatley
Jarome Iginla
DNNHS Bobby Hull
Denis Savard
DNNJA Joe Sakic
Alex Tanguay
DNNJH Jaromir Jagr
Dominik Hasek
DNNJJ Joe Sakic
Joe Thornton
DNNKS Paul Kariya
Teemu Selanne
DNNKT Saku Koivu
Jose Theodore
DNNKV Paul Kariya
Tomas Vokoun
DNNLB Guy Lafleur
Mike Bossy
DNNLG Martin St. Louis
Simon Gagne
DNNLJ Mario Lemieux
Jaromir Jagr
DNNLL Martin St. Louis
Vincent Lecavalier
DNNLR Vincent Lecavalier
Brad Richards
DNNMG Mike Modano
Bill Guerin
DNNMM Lanny McDonald
Joe Mullen
DNNMR Mike Modano
Jeremy Roenick
DNNMS Lanny McDonald
Darryl Sittler
DNNNK Evgeni Nabokov
Nikolai Khabibulin
DNNPJ Peter Forsberg
Joe Sakic
DNNPR Patrick Roy
Ray Bourque
DNNRB Patrick Roy
Martin Brodeur
DNNSL Mats Sundin
Eric Lindros
DNNSP Billy Smith
Denis Potvin
DNNSR Brendan Shanahan
Luc Robitaille
DNNSS Darryl Sittler
Borje Salming
DNNST Eric Staal
Joe Thornton
DNNTB Bryan Trottier
Mike Bossy
DNNTG Keith Tkachuk
Bill Guerin
DNNYL Steve Yzerman
Mario Lemieux
DNNYS Steve Yzerman
Brendan Shanahan

2005-06 The Cup Patch Variation

PRINT RUN 10 SER. #'d SETS
NOT PRICED DUE TO SCARCITY

2005-06 The Cup Patch Variation Autographs

PRINT RUN 1 SER. #'d SET
NOT PRICED DUE TO SCARCITY

2005-06 The Cup Platinum Rookies

COMMON CARD 12.00 30.00
SEMISTARS/GOALIES 15.00 40.00
PRINT RUN 25 SER. #'d SETS
101 Ryan Getzlaf 60.00 120.00
102 Ryan Whitney 20.00 50.00
103 R.J. Umberger 15.00 40.00
104 Cam Ward 60.00 125.00
105 Brent Seabrook 20.00 50.00
106 Eric Nystrom 12.00 30.00
107 Gilbert Brule 30.00 80.00
108 Hannu Toivonen 20.00 50.00
109 Robert Nilsson 15.00 40.00
110 Rostislav Olesz 20.00 50.00
111 Ryan Suter 12.00 30.00
112 Jussi Jokinen 25.00 60.00
113 Zach Parise 60.00 120.00
114 Wojtek Wolski 40.00 100.00
115 Andrej Meszaros 25.00 60.00
116 Johan Franzen 15.00 40.00
117 Peter Budaj 40.00 80.00
118 David Leneveu 15.00 40.00
119 Andrew Alberts 12.00 30.00
120 Steve Bernier 30.00 80.00
121 Mikko Koivu 40.00 80.00
122 Chris Campoli 15.00 40.00
123 Evgeny Artyukhin 12.00 30.00
124 Christoph Schubert 15.00 40.00
125 Tomas Fleischmann 15.00 40.00
126 Maxime Talbot 15.00 40.00
127 Jordan Sigalet 20.00 50.00
128 Danny Richmond 12.00 30.00
129 Maxim Lapierre 12.00 30.00
130 Dimitri Patzold 12.00 30.00
131 Rene Bourque 12.00 30.00
132 Yann Danis 20.00 50.00
133 Brad Winchester 12.00 30.00
134 Jim Slater 12.00 30.00
135 Petr Prucha 40.00 100.00
136 Jim Howard 30.00 80.00
137 Patrick Eaves 15.00 40.00
138 Ryane Clowe 20.00 50.00
139 Braydon Coburn 12.00 30.00
140 Brad Richardson 12.00 30.00
141 Milan Jurcina 12.00 30.00
142 Jeff Woywitka 12.00 30.00
143 Andrei Kostitsyn 50.00 100.00
144 Derek Boogaard 15.00 40.00
145 Barry Tallackson 12.00 30.00
146 Jakub Klepis 12.00 30.00
147 Alvaro Montoya 25.00 60.00
148 Andrew Ladd 15.00 40.00
149 Brandon Bochenski 20.00 50.00
150 Jeff Tambellini 12.00 30.00
151 Jaroslav Balastik 12.00 30.00
152 Lee Stempniak 15.00 40.00
153 Kevin Dallman 12.00 30.00
154 Niklas Nordgren 12.00 30.00
155 Kevin Nastiuk 12.00 30.00
156 Ryan Craig 15.00 40.00
157 Erik Christensen 20.00 50.00
158 Chris Thorburn 12.00 30.00
159 Josh Gorges 12.00 30.00
160 Matt Foy 15.00 40.00
161 Ole-Kristian Tollefsen 12.00 30.00
162 Kevin Bieksa 20.00 50.00
163 Kyle Quincey 15.00 40.00
164 Andrew Wozniewski 12.00 30.00
165 Jeff Hoggan 12.00 30.00
166 Jeremy Colliton 12.00 30.00
167 Alexandre Picard 20.00 50.00
168 Ben Eager 12.00 30.00
169 Daniel Paille 15.00 40.00

170 Valtteri Filppula 20.00 50.00
171 Alexander Perezhogin 25.00 60.00
172 Mike Richards 50.00 125.00
173 Corey Perry 40.00 100.00
174 Alexander Steen 25.00 60.00
175 Thomas Vanek 50.00 100.00
176 Jeff Carter 60.00 120.00
177 Henrik Lundqvist 100.00 200.00
178 Dion Phaneuf 100.00 200.00
179 Alexander Ovechkin 300.00 450.00
180 Sidney Crosby 900.00 1200.00
181 Brett Lebda 12.00 30.00
182 Jay McClement 12.00 30.00
183 Cam Barker 15.00 40.00
184 Petteri Nokelainen 12.00 30.00
185 Keith Ballard 12.00 30.00
186 Duncan Keith 30.00 60.00
187 George Parros 12.00 30.00
188 Adam Berkhoel 15.00 40.00
189 Anthony Stewart 12.00 30.00
190 Ryan Hollweg 12.00 30.00
191 Ben Walter 15.00 40.00

2005-06 The Cup Property of

PRINT RUN 1 SER. #'d SET
NOT PRICED DUE TO SCARCITY
POAT Alex Tanguay
POBH Bobby Hull
POBL Rob Blake
POCP Chris Pronger
PODG Doug Gilmour
PODH Dany Heatley
PODP Denis Potvin
POES Eric Staal
POFM Frank Mahovlich
POGH Gordie Howe
POHA Dominik Hasek
POHJ Milan Hejduk
POHZ Henrik Zetterberg
POIK Ilya Kovalchuk
POJI Jarome Iginla
POJJ Jaromir Jagr
POJK Jari Kurri
POJO Joe Thornton
POJR Jeremy Roenick
POJS Joe Sakic
POJT Jose Theodore
POLR Larry Robinson
POLU Luc Robitaille
POMG Marian Gaborik
POMH Marian Hossa
POMN Markus Naslund
PONK Nikolai Khabibulin
POPD Pavel Datsyuk
POPE Patrik Elias
POPK Paul Kariya
PORB Ray Bourque
PORN Rick Nash
POSK Saku Koivu
POSL Martin St. Louis
POSP Jason Spezza
POSU Mats Sundin
POSY Steve Yzerman
POWG Wayne Gretzky

2005-06 The Cup Scripted Numbers

PRINT RUNS VARY
UNDER 24 NOT PRICED DUE TO SCARCITY
SNBC Martin Brodeur 100.00 200.00
Gerry Cheevers/30
SNBE Ray Bourque
Phil Esposito/7
SNBL Mike Bossy
Brian Leetch/22
SNBN Ed Belfour
Evgeni Nabokov/20
SNBP Patrice Bergeron 30.00 60.00
Michael Peca/37
SNBR Ed Belfour
Luc Robitaille/20
SNBS Mike Bossy
Steve Shutt/22
SNET Marty Turco 40.00 80.00
Tony Esposito/35
SNGM Simon Gagne
Patrick Marleau/12
SNGT Jean-Sebastien Giguere 30.00 60.00
Marty Turco/35
SNGV Martin Gerber 40.00 80.00
Tomas Vokoun/29
SNHD Milan Hejduk 30.00 60.00
Chris Drury/23
SNHH Bobby Hull
Gordie Howe/9
SNHM Bobby Hull
Lanny McDonald/9
SNJV Jean Beliveau
Vincent Lecavalier/4
SNKC Ilya Kovalchuk
Jeff Carter/17
SNKL Miikka Kiprusoff 40.00 100.00
Manny Legace/34
SNLA Roberto Luongo
David Aebischer/1
SNLB Vincent Lecavalier
Rob Blake/4
SNLM Henrik Lundqvist 75.00 200.00
Ryan Miller/30
SNLR Roberto Luongo
Andrew Raycroft/1
SNMH Mike Modano
Martin Havlat/9
SNMM Lanny McDonald
Joe Mullen/7
SNMN Glen Murray 25.00 60.00
Scott Niedermayer/27
SNMS Frank Mahovlich 60.00 125.00
Darryl Sittler/27
SNND Markus Naslund
Shane Doan/19
SNNO Cam Neely
Alexander Ovechkin/8
SNNP Rick Nash 40.00 100.00
Corey Perry/61
SNPB Chris Pronger 25.00 60.00
Todd Bertuzzi/44
SNPC Dion Phaneuf
Zdeno Chara/3
SNSI Eric Staal
Jarome Iginla/12
SNSM Eric Staal
Patrick Marleau/12
SNTH Alex Tanguay
Marian Hossa/18
SNTN Joe Thornton
Markus Naslund/19
SNZS Henrik Zetterberg 30.00 80.00
Marek Svatos/40

2005-06 The Cup Scripted Numbers Dual

PRINT RUN 10 SER. #'d SETS
NOT PRICED DUE TO SCARCITY
DSNBB Martin Brodeur
Ed Belfour
DSNBN Todd Bertuzzi
Markus Naslund
DSNBR Patrice Bergeron
Michael Ryder
DSNCA Lanny McDonald
Joe Mullen
DSNCO Alex Tanguay
Milan Hejduk
DSNCZ Milan Hejduk
Marek Svatos
DSNDA Mike Modano
Brenden Morrow
DSNDM Chris Drury
Ryan Miller
DSNGA Martin Gerber
David Aebischer
DSNGC Doug Gilmour
Wendel Clark
DSNGN Jean-Sebastien Giguere
Scott Niedermayer
DSNHV Dominik Hasek
Tomas Vokoun
DSNIK Jarome Iginla
Miikka Kiprusoff
DSNIN Jarome Iginla
Rick Nash
DSNKH Ilya Kovalchuk
Marian Hossa
DSNKJ Saku Koivu
Olli Jokinen
DSNKL Miikka Kiprusoff
Kari Lehtonen
DSNKO Ilya Kovalchuk
Alexander Ovechkin
DSNLS Guy Lafleur
Steve Shutt
DSNMM Mike Modano
Joe Mullen
DSNNB Cam Neely
Ray Bourque
DSNNS Rick Nash
Eric Staal
DSNPB Chris Pronger
Rob Blake
DSNPL Keith Primeau
Vincent Lecavalier
DSNRB Patrick Roy
Martin Brodeur
DSNRC Luc Robitaille
Wendel Clark
DSNRF Patrick Roy
Grant Fuhr
DSNSM Darryl Sittler
Frank Mahovlich
DSNSV Marian Hossa
Miroslav Satan
DSNSW Eric Staal
Doug Weight
DSNTH Alex Tanguay
Dany Heatley
DSNTL Jose Theodore
Roberto Luongo
DSNTM Joe Thornton
Patrick Marleau
DSNZN Henrik Zetterberg
Markus Naslund

2005-06 The Cup Scripted Swatches

PRINT RUNS VARY
UNDER 24 NOT PRICED DUE TO SCARCITY
SSAF Alexander Frolov 40.00 80.00
SSAH Ales Hemsky 50.00 125.00
SSAO Alexander Ovechkin/15
SSAR Andrew Raycroft 50.00 100.00
SSAS Alexander Steen 50.00 100.00
SSAT Alex Tanguay 60.00 150.00
SSAY Alexei Yashin 40.00 80.00
SSBH Bobby Hull/15 100.00 200.00
SSBL Rob Blake 50.00 100.00
SSBY Mike Bossy 75.00 150.00
SSCD Chris Drury 40.00 80.00
SSCH Jonathan Cheechoo/10
SSCN Cam Neely/18
SSCP Chris Pronger/10
SSDG Doug Gilmour 40.00 100.00
SSDH Dany Heatley 60.00 120.00
SSDP Dion Phaneuf 100.00 175.00
SSDT Dave Taylor 40.00 100.00
SSDW Doug Weight 30.00 80.00
SSEN Evgeni Nabokov 75.00 125.00
SSER Eric Staal 60.00 125.00
SSGC Gerry Cheevers 75.00 150.00
SSGE Martin Gerber 60.00 100.00
SSGF Grant Fuhr 50.00 125.00
SSGL Guy Lafleur/20 150.00 250.00
SSGM Glen Murray 50.00 125.00
SSGP Gilbert Perreault/9
SSHK Dominik Hasek 75.00 150.00
SSHL Henrik Lundqvist 125.00 250.00
SSHO Marian Hossa 40.00 80.00
SSHV Martin Havlat 30.00 60.00
SSIK Ilya Kovalchuk 100.00 200.00
SSJB Jean Beliveau 150.00 250.00
SSJC Jeff Carter 60.00 120.00
SSJI Jarome Iginla 100.00 175.00
SSJO Joe Thornton 100.00 200.00
SSJS Jean-Sebastien Giguere 40.00 100.00
SSJT Jose Theodore 60.00 125.00
SSKL Kari Lehtonen 75.00 150.00
SSKP Keith Primeau 60.00 100.00
SSLR Luc Robitaille 75.00 150.00
SSLU Joffrey Lupul 40.00 80.00
SSMB Martin Brodeur 200.00 300.00
SSMC Lanny McDonald/10
SSMG Marian Gaborik 90.00 150.00
SSMH Milan Hejduk 50.00 125.00
SSMK Miikka Kiprusoff 75.00 150.00
SSMM Mike Modano 75.00 150.00
SSMN Markus Naslund 60.00 100.00
SSMO Brendan Morrison 30.00 60.00
SSMP Mark Parrish 40.00 80.00
SSMT Marty Turco 40.00 80.00
SSMW Brenden Morrow 30.00 80.00
SSOJ Olli Jokinen 40.00 80.00
SSOK Olaf Kolzig 50.00 125.00
SSPB Patrice Bergeron/10
SSPE Michael Peca 40.00 80.00
SSPM Patrick Marleau/15
SSPO Denis Potvin/15
SSRE Robert Esche 40.00 80.00
SSRH Ron Hextall/4
SSRL Roberto Luongo/5
SSRM Ryan Miller 60.00 100.00
SSRY Michael Ryder 50.00 100.00
SSSA Miroslav Satan 50.00 100.00
SSSC Sidney Crosby/10 1250.00 2500.00
SSSD Shane Doan 40.00 80.00
SSSG Simon Gagne 50.00 100.00
SSSK Saku Koivu 50.00 100.00
SSSL Martin St. Louis
SSSN Scott Niedermayer/15
SSST Matt Stajan 40.00 100.00
SSTB Todd Bertuzzi 60.00 125.00
SSTE Tony Esposito 60.00 100.00
SSTV Thomas Vanek 100.00 175.00
SSVL Vincent Lecavalier 60.00 120.00
SSZP Zigmund Palffy 40.00 80.00
SSPR1 Patrick Roy 200.00 400.00
SSPR2 Patrick Roy 200.00 400.00
SSRB1 Ray Bourque 100.00 200.00
SSRB2 Ray Bourque 75.00 150.00

2005-06 The Cup Signature Patches

PRINT RUN 75 SER. #'d SETS
UNIQUE SWATCHES MAY EARN SIGNIFICANT PRE-MIUM
SPAF Alexander Frolov 25.00 60.00
SPAH Ales Hemsky 25.00 60.00
SPAO Alexander Ovechkin 350.00 550.00
SPAR Andrew Raycroft 25.00 60.00
SPAT Alex Tanguay 25.00 60.00
SPAY Alexei Yashin 25.00 60.00
SPBK Rob Blake 20.00 50.00
SPBL Brian Leetch 25.00 60.00
SPBS Billy Smith 30.00 80.00
SPBY Mike Bossy 40.00 100.00
SPCD Chris Drury 20.00 50.00
SPCN Cam Neely/25 60.00 100.00
SPCP Chris Pronger 25.00 60.00
SPDA David Aebischer 20.00 50.00
SPDG Doug Gilmour 25.00 60.00
SPDH Dany Heatley 40.00 80.00
SPDO Dominik Hasek EXCH 50.00 80.00
SPDP Dion Phaneuf 100.00 175.00
SPDW Doug Weight 25.00 60.00
SPES Eric Staal 30.00 80.00
SPFM Frank Mahovlich 25.00 60.00
SPGA Glenn Anderson 20.00 50.00
SPGC Gerry Cheevers/65 40.00 80.00
SPGE Martin Gerber 25.00 60.00
SPGL Guy Lafleur 40.00 100.00
SPGM Glen Murray 30.00 80.00
SPGO Scott Gomez 25.00 60.00
SPGP Gilbert Perreault/40 50.00 125.00
SPHJ Milan Hejduk 25.00 60.00
SPHL Henrik Lundqvist 50.00 100.00
SPHV Martin Havlat 20.00 50.00
SPIK Ilya Kovalchuk 60.00 120.00
SPJC Jeff Carter 60.00 120.00
SPJI Jarome Iginla 60.00 120.00
SPJM Joe Mullen 20.00 50.00
SPJO Joe Thornton 40.00 100.00
SPJP Joni Pitkanen 15.00 40.00
SPJS Jean-Sebastien Giguere 25.00 60.00
SPJT Jose Theodore 25.00 60.00
SPKD Kris Draper 15.00 40.00
SPKP Keith Primeau 15.00 40.00
SPLM Lanny McDonald 20.00 50.00
SPLR Luc Robitaille 30.00 80.00
SPLU Joffrey Lupul 25.00 60.00
SPMB Martin Brodeur 75.00 150.00
SPMG Marian Gaborik 60.00 125.00
SPMH Marian Hossa 25.00 60.00
SPMK Miikka Kiprusoff 50.00 100.00
SPMM Mike Modano 50.00 100.00
SPMN Markus Naslund 25.00 60.00
SPMP Mark Parrish 15.00 40.00
SPMR Mike Richards 30.00 80.00
SPMS Miroslav Satan 15.00 40.00
SPMT Marty Turco 25.00 60.00
SPOJ Olli Jokinen 20.00 50.00
SPOK Olaf Kolzig 30.00 80.00
SPPB Patrice Bergeron 25.00 60.00
SPPE Corey Perry/60 30.00 80.00
SPPO Denis Potvin 30.00 80.00
SPPR Patrick Roy 100.00 250.00
SPRB Ray Bourque 50.00 100.00
SPRE Robert Esche 25.00 60.00
SPRH Ron Hextall/40 50.00 100.00
SPRL Roberto Luongo 50.00 100.00
SPRM Ryan Miller 30.00 80.00
SPRN Rick Nash/40 40.00 100.00
SPRY Michael Ryder 30.00 80.00
SPSC Sidney Crosby 350.00 600.00
SPSD Shane Doan/25 25.00 60.00
SPSG Simon Gagne 25.00 60.00
SPSH Steve Shutt 25.00 60.00
SPSK Saku Koivu 30.00 80.00
SPSL Martin St. Louis/65 20.00 50.00
SPSN Scott Niedermayer 20.00 50.00
SPSV Marek Svatos 25.00 60.00
SPTB Todd Bertuzzi 20.00 50.00
SPTI Dave Williams 20.00 50.00
SPTV Thomas Vanek 100.00 200.00
SPVL Vincent Lecavalier 30.00 80.00
SPVO Tomas Vokoun 25.00 60.00
SPWG Wayne Gretzky/25 400.00 700.00
SPWR Wade Redden 20.00 50.00
SPZC Zdeno Chara 20.00 50.00

2005-06 The Cup Stanley Cup Titlists

PRINT RUNS VARY
NOT PRICED DUE TO SCARCITY
TAT Alex Tanguay/1
TBC Bobby Clarke/2
TBH Bobby Hull/1
TBL Rob Blake/1
TBS Billy Smith/4
TBY Mike Bossy/4
TCD Chris Drury/1
TCO Chris Osgood/2
TDA David Aebischer/1
TDG Doug Gilmour/1
TDH Dominik Hasek/1
TGC Gerry Cheevers/2
TGF Grant Fuhr/5
TGH Gordie Howe/4
TGL Guy Lafleur/5
THJ Milan Hejduk/1
TJA Jason Arnott/1
TJB Jean Beliveau/10
TKD Kris Draper/3
TKM Kirk Muller/1
TLE Brian Leetch/1
TLU Luc Robitaille/1
TMB Martin Brodeur/3
TMC Lanny McDonald/1
TRF Ruslan Fedotenko/1
TSB Scotty Bowman/9
TSG Scott Gomez/2
TSN Scott Niedermayer/3
TTL Ted Lindsay/4
TVL Vincent Lecavalier/1
TWC Wayne Cashman/2
TWG Wayne Gretzky/4 EXCH
TBT1 Bryan Trottier/4
TBT2 Bryan Trottier/2
TFM1 Frank Mahovlich/4
TFM2 Frank Mahovlich/2
TGA1 Glenn Anderson/5
TGA2 Glenn Anderson/1
TJM1 Joe Mullen/2
TJM2 Joe Mullen/1
TLM1 Larry Murphy/2
TLM2 Larry Murphy/2
TPR1 Patrick Roy/2
TPR2 Patrick Roy/2

2006-07 The Cup

This 174-card set was released in July, 2007. The set was issued into the hobby in four-card packs (boxes) that come six to a case. The set is broken down into a mix of Veterans/Retired Greats which are cards numbered 1-90 and are all issued to a stated print run of 249 serial numbered copies. Cards numbered 91-174 are Rookie Cards with cards 91-168 issued to a stated print run of 249 serial numbered sets and cards 169-174 issued to a stated print run of 99 serial numbered sets.

1 Teemu Selanne 5.00 12.00
2 Jean-Sebastian Giguere 4.00 10.00
3 Kari Lehtonen 5.00 12.00
4 Ilya Kovalchuk 6.00 15.00
5 Phil Esposito 5.00 12.00
6 Don Cherry 5.00 12.00
7 Ray Bourque 6.00 15.00
8 Bobby Orr 15.00 40.00
9 Cam Neely 5.00 12.00
10 Patrice Bergeron 5.00 12.00
11 Johnny Bucyk 4.00 10.00
12 Ryan Miller 5.00 12.00
13 Gilbert Perreault 5.00 12.00
14 Jarome Iginla 6.00 15.00
15 Miikka Kiprusoff 5.00 12.00
16 Al MacInnis 3.00 8.00
17 Eric Staal 5.00 12.00
18 Cam Ward 5.00 12.00
19 Bobby Hull 5.00 12.00
20 Tony Esposito 5.00 12.00
21 Stan Mikita 5.00 12.00
22 Joe Sakic 8.00 20.00
23 Patrick Roy 15.00 40.00
24 Rick Nash 5.00 12.00
25 Sergei Fedorov 5.00 12.00
26 Mike Modano 5.00 12.00
27 Dominik Hasek 6.00 15.00
28 Henrik Zetterberg 5.00 12.00
29 Gordie Howe 8.00 20.00
30 Scotty Bowman 4.00 10.00
31 Ted Lindsay 3.00 8.00
32 Red Kelly 4.00 10.00
33 Ales Hemsky 3.00 8.00
34 Grant Fuhr 5.00 12.00
35 Jari Kurri 5.00 12.00
36 Ed Belfour 5.00 12.00
37 Wayne Gretzky 20.00 50.00
38 Rob Blake 4.00 10.00
39 Marcel Dionne 5.00 12.00
40 Luc Robitaille 4.00 10.00
41 Rogie Vachon 5.00 12.00
42 Dino Ciccarelli 4.00 10.00
43 Marian Gaborik 6.00 15.00
44 Saku Koivu 5.00 12.00
45 Michael Ryder 4.00 10.00
46 Guy Lafleur 6.00 15.00
47 Larry Robinson 4.00 10.00
48 Jean Beliveau 5.00 12.00
49 Jacques Lemaire 3.00 8.00
50 Paul Kariya 5.00 12.00
51 Tomas Vokoun 4.00 10.00
52 Martin Brodeur 10.00 25.00
53 Scott Stevens 3.00 8.00
54 Alexei Yashin 3.00 8.00
55 Al Arbour 4.00 10.00
56 Mike Bossy 4.00 10.00
57 Billy Smith 5.00 12.00
58 Denis Potvin 4.00 10.00
59 Jaromir Jagr 6.00 15.00
60 Brendan Shanahan 5.00 12.00
61 Henrik Lundqvist 6.00 15.00
62 Gump Worsley 5.00 12.00
63 Andy Bathgate 3.00 8.00
64 Jason Spezza 5.00 12.00
65 Dany Heatley 5.00 12.00
66 Peter Forsberg 6.00 15.00
67 Simon Gagne 5.00 12.00
68 Bernie Parent 5.00 12.00
69 Bobby Clarke 5.00 12.00
70 Ron Hextall 5.00 12.00
71 Jeremy Roenick 5.00 12.00
72 Shane Doan 3.00 8.00
73 Sidney Crosby 50.00 100.00
74 Marc-Andre Fleury 5.00 12.00
75 Mario Lemieux 15.00 40.00
76 Peter Stastny 3.00 8.00
77 Joe Thornton 6.00 15.00
78 Jonathan Cheechoo 5.00 12.00
79 Patrick Marleau 4.00 10.00
80 Bernie Federko 4.00 10.00
81 Vincent Lecavalier 5.00 12.00
82 Mats Sundin 5.00 12.00
83 Frank Mahovlich 5.00 12.00
84 Darryl Sittler 5.00 12.00
85 Johnny Bower 4.00 10.00
86 Borje Salming 4.00 10.00
87 Roberto Luongo 6.00 15.00
88 Markus Naslund 5.00 12.00
89 Alexander Ovechkin 12.50 30.00
90 Dale Hawerchuk 3.00 8.00
91 Nate Thompson AU RC 6.00 15.00
92 Mike Brown AU RC 6.00 15.00
93 Mike Card AU RC 6.00 15.00
94 Adam Dennis AU RC 8.00 20.00
95 Carsen Germyn AU RC 6.00 15.00
96 Adam Burish AU RC 12.00 30.00
97 Drew Larman AU RC 6.00 15.00
98 Jonas Johansson AU RC 6.00 15.00
99 Joel Perrault AU RC 10.00 25.00
100 Mikko Lehtonen AU RC 6.00 15.00
101 Alex Brooks AU RC 6.00 15.00
102 Frank Doyle AU RC 6.00 15.00
103 Billy Thompson AU RC 6.00 15.00
104 Kelly Guard AU RC 6.00 15.00
105 David Printz AU RC 6.00 15.00
106 D.J. King AU RC 6.00 15.00
107 Jean-Francois Racine AU RC 6.00 15.00
108 Nathan McIver AU RC 6.00 15.00
109 Shane O'Brien JSY AU/50 RC 250.00 550.00
110 Ryan Shannon JSY AU/125 RC 30.00 60.00
111 David McKee JSY AU RC 15.00 40.00
112 Mark Stuart JSY AU RC 20.00 50.00
113 Matt Lashoff JSY AU RC 20.00 50.00
114 Drew Stafford JSY AU RC 50.00 100.00
115 Clarke MacArthur JSY AU RC 20.00 50.00
116 Michael Funk JSY AU RC 15.00 40.00
117 Brandon Prust JSY AU RC 15.00 40.00
118 Dustin Boyd JSY AU RC 30.00 60.00
119 Dustin Byfuglien JSY AU RC 40.00 100.00
120 Dave Bolland JSY AU RC 40.00 80.00
121 Michael Blunden JSY AU RC 30.00 60.00
122 Filip Novak JSY AU RC 15.00 40.00
123 Fredrik Norrena JSY AU RC 20.00 50.00
124 Niklas Grossman JSY AU RC 15.00 40.00
125 Loui Eriksson JSY AU RC 20.00 50.00
126 Tomas Kopecky JSY AU RC 20.00 50.00
127 Stefan Liv JSY AU RC 20.00 50.00
128 Patrick Thoresen JSY AU RC 20.00 50.00
129 Marc-Antoine Pouliot JSY AU RC 20.00 50.00
130 Ladislav Smid JSY AU RC 20.00 50.00
131 Janis Sprukts JSY AU RC 30.00 60.00
132 Jeff Drouin-Deslauriers JSY AU RC 20.00 50.00
133 David Booth JSY AU RC 30.00 60.00
134 Konstantin Pushkaryov JSY AU RC 30.00 60.00
135 Patrick O'Sullivan JSY AU RC 50.00 100.00
136 Benoit Pouliot JSY AU RC 40.00 80.00
137 Niklas Backstrom JSY AU RC 60.00 120.00
138 Guillaume Latendresse JSY AU RC 75.00 150.00
139 Shea Weber JSY AU RC 30.00 60.00
140 Johnny Oduya JSY AU RC 15.00 40.00
141 Travis Zajac JSY AU RC 30.00 60.00
142 Masi Marjamaki JSY AU RC 15.00 40.00
143 Nigel Dawes JSY AU RC 30.00 60.00
144 Jarkko Immonen JSY AU RC 15.00 40.00
145 Josh Hennessy JSY AU RC 15.00 40.00
146 Ryan Potulny JSY AU RC 20.00 50.00
147 Jussi Timonen JSY AU RC 20.00 50.00
148 Keith Yandle JSY AU RC 15.00 40.00
149 Michel Ouellet JSY AU RC 15.00 40.00
150 Noah Welch JSY AU RC 15.00 40.00
151 Kristopher Letang JSY AU RC 50.00 100.00
152 Joe Pavelski JSY AU RC 75.00 150.00
153 Matt Carle JSY AU RC 30.00 60.00
154 Marc-Edouard Vlasic JSY AU RC 30.00 60.00
155 Yan Stastny JSY AU RC 20.00 50.00
156 Marek Schwarz JSY AU RC 30.00 60.00
157 Roman Polak JSY AU RC 30.00 60.00
158 Karri Ramo JSY AU RC 20.00 50.00
159 Blair Jones JSY AU RC 20.00 50.00
160 Brendan Bell JSY AU RC 20.00 50.00
161 Ian White JSY AU RC 20.00 50.00
162 Ben Ondrus JSY AU RC 20.00 50.00
163 Jeremy Williams JSY AU RC 20.00 50.00
164 Miroslav Kopriva JSY AU RC 20.00 50.00
165 Luc Bourdon JSY AU RC 40.00 80.00
166 Jesse Schultz JSY AU RC 20.00 50.00
167 Alexander Edler JSY AU RC 40.00 100.00
168 Eric Fehr JSY AU RC 30.00 60.00
169 Jordan Staal JSY AU/99 RC 250.00 500.00
170 Phil Kessel JSY AU/99 RC 250.00 500.00
171 Evgeni Malkin JSY AU/99 RC 1500.00 2500.00
172 Paul Stastny JSY AU/99 RC 300.00 600.00
173 Anze Kopitar JSY AU/99 RC 350.00 600.00
174 Alexander Radulov JSY AU/99 RC 150.00 300.00

2006-07 The Cup Printing Plates Artifacts Black

STATED PRINT RUN 1 SER.#'d SET
FOUR COLORS OF EACH PLATE
NOT PRICED DUE TO SCARCITY
201 Dustin Byfuglien
202 Yan Stastny
203 Mark Stuart
204 Eric Fehr
205 Bill Thomas
206 Joel Perrault
207 Carsen Germyn
208 Ryan Potulny
209 David Printz
210 Rob Collins
211 Steve Regier
212 Matt Koalska
213 Masi Marjamaki
214 Konstantin Pushkaryov
215 Ben Ondrus
216 Brendan Bell
217 Ian White
218 Jeremy Williams
219 Marc-Antoine Pouliot
220 Noah Welch
221 Michel Ouellet
222 Shea Weber
223 Jarkko Immonen
224 David Liffiton
225 Tomas Kopecky
226 Billy Thompson
227 Filip Novak
228 Matt Carle
229 Erik Reitz
230 Miroslav Kopriva
272 Clarke MacArthur

2006-07 The Cup Printing Plates Be A Player Portraits Black

STATED PRINT RUN 1 SER.#'d SET
NOT PRICED DUE TO SCARCITY
101 Yan Stastny
102 Mark Stuart
103 Evgeni Malkin
104 Patrick Thoresen
105 Patrick O'Sullivan
106 Tomas Kopecky
107 Marc-Antoine Pouliot
108 Konstantin Pushkaryov
109 Phil Kessel
110 Luc Bourdon
111 Shea Weber
112 Guillaume Latendresse
113 Jordan Staal
114 Paul Stastny
115 Anze Kopitar
116 Jarkko Immonen
117 Travis Zajac
118 Nigel Dawes
119 Kristopher Letang
120 Ryan Potulny
121 Ryan Shannon
122 Marc-Edouard Vlasic
123 Noah Welch
124 Ladislav Smid
125 Matt Carle
126 Loui Eriksson
127 Brendan Bell
128 Ian White
129 Jeremy Williams
130 Eric Fehr

2006-07 The Cup Printing Plates Bee Hive Black

STATED PRINT RUN 1 SER.#'d SET
FOUR COLORS OF EACH PLATE
NOT PRICED DUE TO SCARCITY
101 David McKee
102 Ryan Shannon
103 Shane O'Brien
104 Matt Lashoff
105 Phil Kessel
106 Mark Stuart
107 Yan Stastny
108 Clarke MacArthur
109 Drew Stafford
110 Brandon Prust
111 Dustin Boyd
112 Michael Blunden
113 Dave Bolland
114 Paul Stastny
115 Fredrik Norrena
116 Loui Eriksson
117 Tomas Kopecky
118 Stefan Liv
119 Jeff Drouin-Deslauriers
120 Alexei Mikhnov
121 Ladislav Smid
122 Patrick Thoresen
123 Marc-Antoine Pouliot
124 David Booth
125 Anze Kopitar
126 Patrick O'Sullivan
127 Konstantin Pushkaryov
128 Benoit Pouliot
129 Mikhail Grabovski
130 Guillaume Latendresse
131 Alexander Radulov
132 Shea Weber
133 Travis Zajac
134 Johnny Oduya
135 Blake Comeau
136 Nigel Dawes
137 Jarkko Immonen
138 Josh Hennessy
139 Kelly Guard
140 Martin Houle
141 Ryan Potulny
142 Enver Lisin
143 Keith Yandle
144 Evgeni Malkin
145 Kristopher Letang
146 Jordan Staal
147 Michel Ouellet
148 Noah Welch
149 Joe Pavelski
150 Marc-Edouard Vlasic
151 Matt Carle
152 Marek Schwarz
153 Blair Jones
154 Ian White
155 Brendan Bell
156 Kris Newbury
157 Jesse Schultz
158 Alexander Edler
159 Luc Bourdon
160 Eric Fehr

2006-07 The Cup Printing Plates Black

STATED PRINT RUN 1/1
FOUR COLORS FOR EACH PLATE
NOT PRICED DUE TO SCARCITY
1 Teemu Selanne
2 Jean-Sebastian Giguere
3 Kari Lehtonen
4 Ilya Kovalchuk
5 Phil Esposito
6 Don Cherry
7 Ray Bourque
8 Bobby Orr
9 Cam Neely
10 Patrice Bergeron
11 Johnny Bucyk
12 Ryan Miller
13 Gilbert Perreault
14 Jarome Iginla
15 Miikka Kiprusoff
16 Al MacInnis
17 Eric Staal
18 Cam Ward
19 Bobby Hull
20 Tony Esposito
21 Stan Mikita
22 Joe Sakic
23 Patrick Roy
24 Rick Nash
25 Sergei Fedorov
26 Mike Modano
27 Dominik Hasek
28 Henrik Zetterberg
29 Gordie Howe
30 Scotty Bowman
31 Ted Lindsay
32 Red Kelly
33 Ales Hemsky
34 Grant Fuhr
35 Jari Kurri
36 Ed Belfour
37 Wayne Gretzky
38 Rob Blake
39 Marcel Dionne
40 Luc Robitaille
41 Rogie Vachon
42 Dino Ciccarelli
43 Marian Gaborik
44 Saku Koivu
45 Michael Ryder
46 Guy Lafleur
47 Larry Robinson
48 Jean Beliveau
49 Jacques Lemaire
50 Paul Kariya
51 Tomas Vokoun
52 Martin Brodeur
53 Scott Stevens
54 Alexei Yashin
55 Al Arbour
56 Mike Bossy
57 Billy Smith
58 Denis Potvin
59 Jaromir Jagr
60 Brendan Shanahan
61 Henrik Lundqvist
62 Gump Worsley
63 Andy Bathgate
64 Jason Spezza
65 Dany Heatley
66 Peter Forsberg
67 Simon Gagne
68 Bernie Parent
69 Bobby Clarke
70 Ron Hextall
71 Jeremy Roenick
72 Shane Doan
73 Sidney Crosby

74 Marc-Andre Fleury
75 Mario Lemieux
76 Peter Stastny
77 Joe Thornton
78 Jonathan Cheechoo
79 Patrick Marleau
80 Bernie Federko
81 Vincent Lecavalier
82 Mats Sundin
83 Frank Mahovlich
84 Darryl Sittler
85 Johnny Bower
86 Borje Salming
87 Roberto Luongo
88 Markus Naslund
89 Alexander Ovechkin
90 Dale Hawerchuk
91 Nate Thompson AUTO
92 Mike Brown AUTO
93 Mike Card AUTO
94 Adam Dennis AUTO
95 Carsen Germyn AUTO
96 Adam Burish AUTO
97 Drew Larman AUTO
98 Jonas Johansson AUTO
99 Joel Perrault AUTO
100 Mikko Lehtonen AUTO
101 Alex Brooks AUTO
102 Frank Doyle AUTO
103 Billy Thompson AUTO
104 Kelly Guard AUTO
105 David Printz AUTO
106 D.J. King AUTO
107 Jean-Francois Racine AUTO
108 Nathan McIver AUTO
109 Shane O'Brien AUTO
110 Ryan Shannon AUTO
111 David McKee AUTO
112 Mark Stuart AUTO
113 Matt Lashoff AUTO
114 Drew Stafford AUTO
115 Clarke MacArthur AUTO
116 Michael Funk AUTO
117 Brandon Prust AUTO
118 Dustin Boyd AUTO
119 Dustin Byfuglien AUTO
120 Dave Bolland AUTO
121 Michael Blunden AUTO
122 Filip Novak AUTO
123 Fredrik Norrena AUTO
124 Niklas Grossman AUTO
125 Loui Eriksson AUTO
126 Tomas Kopecky AUTO
127 Stefan Liv AUTO
128 Patrick Thoresen AUTO
129 Marc-Antoine Pouliot AUTO
130 Ladislav Smid AUTO
131 Janis Sprukts AUTO
132 Jeff Drouin-Deslauriers AUTO
133 David Booth AUTO
134 Konstantin Pushkaryov AUTO
135 Patrick O'Sullivan AUTO
136 Benoit Pouliot AUTO
137 Niklas Backstrom AUTO
138 Guillaume Latendresse AUTO
139 Shea Weber AUTO
140 Johnny Oduya AUTO
141 Travis Zajac AUTO
142 Masi Marjamaki AUTO
143 Nigel Dawes AUTO
144 Jarkko Immonen AUTO
145 Josh Hennessy AUTO
146 Ryan Potulny AUTO
147 Jussi Timonen AUTO
148 Keith Yandle AUTO
149 Michel Ouellet AUTO
150 Noah Welch AUTO
151 Kristopher Letang AUTO
152 Joe Pavelski AUTO
153 Matt Carle AUTO
154 Marc-Edouard Vlasic AUTO
155 Yan Stastny AUTO
156 Marek Schwarz AUTO
157 Roman Polak AUTO
158 Karri Ramo AUTO
159 Blair Jones AUTO
160 Brendan Bell AUTO
161 Ian White AUTO
162 Ben Ondrus AUTO
163 Jeremy Williams AUTO
164 Miroslav Kopriva AUTO
165 Luc Bourdon AUTO
166 Jesse Schultz AUTO
167 Alexander Edler AUTO
168 Eric Fehr AUTO
169 Jordan Staal AUTO
170 Phil Kessel AUTO
171 Evgeni Malkin AUTO
172 Paul Stastny AUTO
173 Anze Kopitar AUTO
174 Alexander Radulov AUTO

2006-07 The Cup Printing Plates Cyan

1 Teemu Selanne
2 Jean-Sebastian Giguere
3 Kari Lehtonen
4 Ilya Kovalchuk
5 Phil Esposito
6 Don Cherry
7 Ray Bourque
8 Bobby Orr
9 Cam Neely
10 Patrice Bergeron
11 Johnny Bucyk
12 Ryan Miller
13 Gilbert Perreault
14 Jarome Iginla
15 Miikka Kiprusoff
16 Al MacInnis
17 Eric Staal
18 Cam Ward
19 Bobby Hull
20 Tony Esposito
21 Stan Mikita
22 Joe Sakic
23 Patrick Roy
24 Rick Nash
25 Sergei Fedorov
26 Mike Modano
27 Dominik Hasek
28 Henrik Zetterberg
29 Gordie Howe
30 Scotty Bowman
31 Ted Lindsay
32 Red Kelly
33 Ales Hemsky
34 Grant Fuhr
35 Jari Kurri
36 Ed Belfour
37 Wayne Gretzky
38 Rob Blake
39 Marcel Dionne
40 Luc Robitaille
41 Rogie Vachon
42 Dino Ciccarelli
43 Marian Gaborik
44 Saku Koivu
45 Michael Ryder
46 Guy Lafleur
47 Larry Robinson
48 Jean Beliveau
49 Jacques Lemaire
50 Paul Kariya
51 Tomas Vokoun
52 Martin Brodeur
53 Scott Stevens
54 Alexei Yashin
55 Al Arbour
56 Mike Bossy
57 Billy Smith
58 Denis Potvin
59 Jaromir Jagr
60 Brendan Shanahan
61 Henrik Lundqvist
62 Gump Worsley
63 Andy Bathgate
64 Jason Spezza
65 Dany Heatley
66 Peter Forsberg
67 Simon Gagne
68 Bernie Parent
69 Bobby Clarke
70 Ron Hextall
71 Jeremy Roenick
72 Shane Doan
73 Sidney Crosby
74 Marc-Andre Fleury
75 Mario Lemieux
76 Peter Stastny
77 Joe Thornton
78 Jonathan Cheechoo
79 Patrick Marleau
80 Bernie Federko
81 Vincent Lecavalier
82 Mats Sundin
83 Frank Mahovlich
84 Darryl Sittler
85 Johnny Bower
86 Borje Salming
87 Roberto Luongo
88 Markus Naslund
89 Alexander Ovechkin
90 Dale Hawerchuk
91 Nate Thompson AUTO
92 Mike Brown AUTO
93 Mike Card AUTO
94 Adam Dennis AUTO
95 Carsen Germyn AUTO
96 Adam Burish AUTO
97 Drew Larman AUTO
98 Jonas Johansson AUTO
99 Joel Perrault AUTO
100 Mikko Lehtonen AUTO
101 Alex Brooks AUTO
102 Frank Doyle AUTO
103 Billy Thompson AUTO
104 Kelly Guard AUTO
105 David Printz AUTO
106 D.J. King AUTO
107 Jean-Francois Racine AUTO
108 Nathan McIver AUTO
109 Shane O'Brien AUTO
110 Ryan Shannon AUTO
111 David McKee AUTO
112 Mark Stuart AUTO
113 Matt Lashoff AUTO
114 Drew Stafford AUTO
115 Clarke MacArthur AUTO
116 Michael Funk AUTO
117 Brandon Prust AUTO
118 Dustin Boyd AUTO
119 Dustin Byfuglien AUTO
120 Dave Bolland AUTO
121 Michael Blunden AUTO
122 Filip Novak AUTO
123 Fredrik Norrena AUTO
124 Niklas Grossman AUTO
125 Loui Eriksson AUTO
126 Tomas Kopecky AUTO
127 Stefan Liv AUTO
128 Patrick Thoresen AUTO
129 Marc-Antoine Pouliot AUTO
130 Ladislav Smid AUTO
131 Janis Sprukts AUTO
132 Jeff Drouin-Deslauriers AUTO
133 David Booth AUTO
134 Konstantin Pushkaryov AUTO
135 Patrick O'Sullivan AUTO
136 Benoit Pouliot AUTO
137 Niklas Backstrom AUTO
138 Guillaume Latendresse AUTO
139 Shea Weber AUTO
140 Johnny Oduya AUTO
141 Travis Zajac AUTO
142 Masi Marjamaki AUTO
143 Nigel Dawes AUTO
144 Jarkko Immonen AUTO
145 Josh Hennessy AUTO
146 Ryan Potulny AUTO
147 Jussi Timonen AUTO
148 Keith Yandle AUTO
149 Michel Ouellet AUTO
150 Noah Welch AUTO
151 Kristopher Letang AUTO
152 Joe Pavelski AUTO
153 Matt Carle AUTO
154 Marc-Edouard Vlasic AUTO
155 Yan Stastny AUTO
156 Marek Schwarz AUTO
157 Roman Polak AUTO
158 Karri Ramo AUTO
159 Blair Jones AUTO
160 Brendan Bell AUTO
161 Ian White AUTO
162 Ben Ondrus AUTO
163 Jeremy Williams AUTO
164 Miroslav Kopriva AUTO
165 Luc Bourdon AUTO
166 Jesse Schultz AUTO
167 Alexander Edler AUTO
168 Eric Fehr AUTO
169 Jordan Staal AUTO
170 Phil Kessel AUTO
171 Evgeni Malkin AUTO
172 Paul Stastny AUTO
173 Anze Kopitar AUTO
174 Alexander Radulov AUTO

2006-07 The Cup Printing Plates Magenta

1 Teemu Selanne
2 Jean-Sebastian Giguere
3 Kari Lehtonen
4 Ilya Kovalchuk
5 Phil Esposito
6 Don Cherry
7 Ray Bourque
8 Bobby Orr
9 Cam Neely
10 Patrice Bergeron
11 Johnny Bucyk
12 Ryan Miller
13 Gilbert Perreault
14 Jarome Iginla
15 Miikka Kiprusoff
16 Al MacInnis
17 Eric Staal
18 Cam Ward
19 Bobby Hull
20 Tony Esposito
21 Stan Mikita
22 Joe Sakic
23 Patrick Roy
24 Rick Nash
25 Sergei Fedorov
26 Mike Modano
27 Dominik Hasek
28 Henrik Zetterberg
29 Gordie Howe
30 Scotty Bowman
31 Ted Lindsay
32 Red Kelly
33 Ales Hemsky
34 Grant Fuhr
35 Jari Kurri
36 Ed Belfour
37 Wayne Gretzky
38 Rob Blake
39 Marcel Dionne
40 Luc Robitaille
41 Rogie Vachon
42 Dino Ciccarelli
43 Marian Gaborik
44 Saku Koivu
45 Michael Ryder
46 Guy Lafleur
47 Larry Robinson
48 Jean Beliveau
49 Jacques Lemaire
50 Paul Kariya
51 Tomas Vokoun
52 Martin Brodeur
53 Scott Stevens
54 Alexei Yashin
55 Al Arbour
56 Mike Bossy
57 Billy Smith
58 Denis Potvin
59 Jaromir Jagr
60 Brendan Shanahan
61 Henrik Lundqvist
62 Gump Worsley
63 Andy Bathgate
64 Jason Spezza
65 Dany Heatley
66 Peter Forsberg
67 Simon Gagne
68 Bernie Parent
69 Bobby Clarke
70 Ron Hextall
71 Jeremy Roenick
72 Shane Doan
73 Sidney Crosby
74 Marc-Andre Fleury
75 Mario Lemieux
76 Peter Stastny
77 Joe Thornton
78 Jonathan Cheechoo
79 Patrick Marleau
80 Bernie Federko
81 Vincent Lecavalier
82 Mats Sundin
83 Frank Mahovlich
84 Darryl Sittler
85 Johnny Bower
86 Borje Salming
87 Roberto Luongo
88 Markus Naslund
89 Alexander Ovechkin
90 Dale Hawerchuk
91 Nate Thompson AUTO
92 Mike Brown AUTO
93 Mike Card AUTO
94 Adam Dennis AUTO
95 Carsen Germyn AUTO
96 Adam Burish AUTO
97 Drew Larman AUTO
98 Jonas Johansson AUTO
99 Joel Perrault AUTO
100 Mikko Lehtonen AUTO
101 Alex Brooks AUTO
102 Frank Doyle AUTO
103 Billy Thompson AUTO
104 Kelly Guard AUTO
105 David Printz AUTO
106 D.J. King AUTO
107 Jean-Francois Racine AUTO
108 Nathan McIver AUTO
109 Shane O'Brien AUTO
110 Ryan Shannon AUTO
111 David McKee AUTO
112 Mark Stuart AUTO
113 Matt Lashoff AUTO
114 Drew Stafford AUTO
115 Clarke MacArthur AUTO
116 Michael Funk AUTO
117 Brandon Prust AUTO
118 Dustin Boyd AUTO
119 Dustin Byfuglien AUTO
120 Dave Bolland AUTO
121 Michael Blunden AUTO
122 Filip Novak AUTO
123 Fredrik Norrena AUTO
124 Niklas Grossman AUTO
125 Loui Eriksson AUTO
126 Tomas Kopecky AUTO
127 Stefan Liv AUTO
128 Patrick Thoresen AUTO
129 Marc-Antoine Pouliot AUTO
130 Ladislav Smid AUTO
131 Janis Sprukts AUTO
132 Jeff Drouin-Deslauriers AUTO
133 David Booth AUTO
134 Konstantin Pushkaryov AUTO
135 Patrick O'Sullivan AUTO
136 Benoit Pouliot AUTO
137 Niklas Backstrom AUTO
138 Guillaume Latendresse AUTO
139 Shea Weber AUTO
140 Johnny Oduya AUTO
141 Travis Zajac AUTO
142 Masi Marjamaki AUTO
143 Nigel Dawes AUTO
144 Jarkko Immonen AUTO
145 Josh Hennessy AUTO
146 Ryan Potulny AUTO
147 Jussi Timonen AUTO
148 Keith Yandle AUTO
149 Michel Ouellet AUTO
150 Noah Welch AUTO
151 Kristopher Letang AUTO
152 Joe Pavelski AUTO
153 Matt Carle AUTO
154 Marc-Edouard Vlasic AUTO
155 Yan Stastny AUTO
156 Marek Schwarz AUTO
157 Roman Polak AUTO
158 Karri Ramo AUTO
159 Blair Jones AUTO
160 Brendan Bell AUTO
161 Ian White AUTO
162 Ben Ondrus AUTO
163 Jeremy Williams AUTO
164 Miroslav Kopriva AUTO
165 Luc Bourdon AUTO
166 Jesse Schultz AUTO
167 Alexander Edler AUTO
168 Eric Fehr AUTO
169 Jordan Staal AUTO
170 Phil Kessel AUTO
171 Evgeni Malkin AUTO
172 Paul Stastny AUTO
173 Anze Kopitar AUTO
174 Alexander Radulov AUTO

2006-07 The Cup Printing Plates Yellow

1 Teemu Selanne
2 Jean-Sebastian Giguere
3 Kari Lehtonen
4 Ilya Kovalchuk
5 Phil Esposito
6 Don Cherry
7 Ray Bourque
8 Bobby Orr
9 Cam Neely
10 Patrice Bergeron
11 Johnny Bucyk
12 Ryan Miller
13 Gilbert Perreault
14 Jarome Iginla
15 Miikka Kiprusoff
16 Al MacInnis
17 Eric Staal
18 Cam Ward
19 Bobby Hull
20 Tony Esposito
21 Stan Mikita
22 Joe Sakic
23 Patrick Roy
24 Rick Nash
25 Sergei Fedorov
26 Mike Modano
27 Dominik Hasek
28 Henrik Zetterberg
29 Gordie Howe
30 Scotty Bowman
31 Ted Lindsay
32 Red Kelly
33 Ales Hemsky
34 Grant Fuhr
35 Jari Kurri
36 Ed Belfour
37 Wayne Gretzky
38 Rob Blake
39 Marcel Dionne
40 Luc Robitaille
41 Rogie Vachon
42 Dino Ciccarelli
43 Marian Gaborik
44 Saku Koivu
45 Michael Ryder
46 Guy Lafleur
47 Larry Robinson
48 Jean Beliveau
49 Jacques Lemaire
50 Paul Kariya
51 Tomas Vokoun
52 Martin Brodeur
53 Scott Stevens
54 Alexei Yashin
55 Al Arbour
56 Mike Bossy
57 Billy Smith
58 Denis Potvin
59 Jaromir Jagr
60 Brendan Shanahan
61 Henrik Lundqvist
62 Gump Worsley
63 Andy Bathgate
64 Jason Spezza
65 Dany Heatley
66 Peter Forsberg
67 Simon Gagne
68 Bernie Parent
69 Bobby Clarke
70 Ron Hextall
71 Jeremy Roenick
72 Shane Doan
73 Sidney Crosby
74 Marc-Andre Fleury
75 Mario Lemieux
76 Peter Stastny
77 Joe Thornton
78 Jonathan Cheechoo
79 Patrick Marleau
80 Bernie Federko
81 Vincent Lecavalier
82 Mats Sundin
83 Frank Mahovlich
84 Darryl Sittler
85 Johnny Bower
86 Borje Salming
87 Roberto Luongo
88 Markus Naslund
89 Alexander Ovechkin
90 Dale Hawerchuk
91 Nate Thompson AUTO
92 Mike Brown AUTO
93 Mike Card AUTO
94 Adam Dennis AUTO
95 Carsen Germyn AUTO
96 Adam Burish AUTO
97 Drew Larman AUTO
98 Jonas Johansson AUTO
99 Joel Perrault AUTO
100 Mikko Lehtonen AUTO
101 Alex Brooks AUTO
102 Frank Doyle AUTO
103 Billy Thompson AUTO
104 Kelly Guard AUTO
105 David Printz AUTO
106 D.J. King AUTO
107 Jean-Francois Racine AUTO
108 Nathan McIver AUTO
109 Shane O'Brien AUTO
110 Ryan Shannon AUTO
111 David McKee AUTO
112 Mark Stuart AUTO
113 Matt Lashoff AUTO
114 Drew Stafford AUTO
115 Clarke MacArthur AUTO
116 Michael Funk AUTO
117 Brandon Prust AUTO
118 Dustin Boyd AUTO
119 Dustin Byfuglien AUTO
120 Dave Bolland AUTO
121 Michael Blunden AUTO
122 Filip Novak AUTO
123 Fredrik Norrena AUTO
124 Niklas Grossman AUTO
125 Loui Eriksson AUTO
126 Tomas Kopecky AUTO
127 Stefan Liv AUTO
128 Patrick Thoresen AUTO
129 Marc-Antoine Pouliot AUTO
130 Ladislav Smid AUTO
131 Janis Sprukts AUTO
132 Jeff Drouin-Deslauriers AUTO
133 David Booth AUTO
134 Konstantin Pushkaryov AUTO
135 Patrick O'Sullivan AUTO
136 Benoit Pouliot AUTO
137 Niklas Backstrom AUTO
138 Guillaume Latendresse AUTO
139 Shea Weber AUTO
140 Johnny Oduya AUTO
141 Travis Zajac AUTO
142 Masi Marjamaki AUTO
143 Nigel Dawes AUTO
144 Jarkko Immonen AUTO
145 Josh Hennessy AUTO
146 Ryan Potulny AUTO
147 Jussi Timonen AUTO
148 Keith Yandle AUTO
149 Michel Ouellet AUTO
150 Noah Welch AUTO
151 Kristopher Letang AUTO
152 Joe Pavelski AUTO
153 Matt Carle AUTO
154 Marc-Edouard Vlasic AUTO
155 Yan Stastny AUTO
156 Marek Schwarz AUTO
157 Roman Polak AUTO
158 Karri Ramo AUTO
159 Blair Jones AUTO
160 Brendan Bell AUTO
161 Ian White AUTO
162 Ben Ondrus AUTO
163 Jeremy Williams AUTO
164 Miroslav Kopriva AUTO
165 Luc Bourdon AUTO
166 Jesse Schultz AUTO
167 Alexander Edler AUTO
168 Eric Fehr AUTO
169 Jordan Staal AUTO
170 Phil Kessel AUTO
171 Evgeni Malkin AUTO
172 Paul Stastny AUTO
173 Anze Kopitar AUTO
174 Alexander Radulov AUTO

2006-07 The Cup Printing Plates Black Diamond Black

STATED PRINT RUN 1 SER.#'d SET
FOUR COLORS OF EACH PLATE
NOT PRICED DUE TO SCARCITY
148 Roman Polak
149 Joel Perrault
150 Yan Stastny
151 Konstantin Pushkaryov
152 Jarkko Immonen
153 Marc-Antoine Pouliot
154 Jeremy Williams
155 Michel Ouellet
156 Tomas Kopecky
157 Keith Yandle
158 Marc-Edouard Vlasic
159 Shane O'Brien
160 Ryan Shannon
161 John Oduya
162 Fredrik Norrena
163 Kristopher Letang
164 Niklas Backstrom
165 D.J. King
166 Patrick Thoresen
167 Patrick Fischer
168 Mikko Lehtonen

2006-07 The Cup Printing Plates O-Pee-Chee Black

STATED PRINT RUN 1 SER.#'d SET
FOUR COLORS OF EACH PLATE
NOT PRICED DUE TO SCARCITY
501 Dustin Byfuglien
502 Yan Stastny
503 Mark Stuart
504 Eric Fehr
505 Bill Thomas
506 Joel Perrault
507 Frank Doyle
508 Carsen Germyn
509 Ryan Potulny
510 David Printz
511 Rob Collins
512 Steve Regier
513 Matt Koalska
514 Ryan Caldwell
515 Masi Marjamaki
516 Cole Jarrett
517 Konstantin Pushkaryov
518 Ben Ondrus
519 Brendan Bell
520 Ian White
521 Jeremy Williams
522 Marc-Antoine Pouliot
523 Noah Welch
524 Michel Ouellet
525 Shea Weber
526 Jarkko Immonen
527 David Liffiton
528 Tomas Kopecky
529 Billy Thompson
530 Filip Novak
531 Matt Carle
532 Dan Jancevski
533 Erik Reitz
534 Miroslav Kopriva
535 Jonas Johansson
536 Shane O'Brien
537 Ryan Shannon
538 Patrick O'Sullivan
539 Anze Kopitar
540 John Oduya
541 Travis Zajac
542 Fredrik Norrena
543 Phil Kessel
544 Guillaume Latendresse
545 Nigel Dawes
546 Jordan Staal
547 Kristopher Letang
548 Paul Stastny
549 Niklas Backstrom
550 D.J. King
551 Marc-Edouard Vlasic
552 Patrick Thoresen
553 Ladislav Smid
554 Loui Eriksson
555 Patrick Fischer
556 Mikko Lehtonen
557 Roman Polak
558 Luc Bourdon
559 Keith Yandle
560 Enver Lisin
561 Adam Burish
562 Alexei Kaigorodov
563 Alex Brooks
564 Evgeni Malkin
565 Nate Thompson
566 Janis Sprukts
567 Alexander Radulov
568 Alexei Mikhnov
569 Dave Bolland
570 Michael Blunden
571 Lars Jonsson
572 Triston Grant
573 Matt Lashoff
574 Dustin Boyd
575 Brandon Prust
576 Alexander Edler
577 Jan Hejda
578 Drew Stafford
579 Kelly Guard
580 Patrick Coulombe
581 Nathan McIver
582 Mike Brown
583 Jean-Francois Racine
584 Adam Dennis
585 Drew Larman
586 Mike Card
587 Michael Funk
588 Stefan Liv
589 David Booth
590 Blair Jones
591 Jussi Timonen
592 David McKee
593 Michael Ryan
594 Peter Harrold
595 Joe Pavelski
596 Karl Goehring
597 Benoit Pouliot
598 Jesse Schultz
599 Jeff Drouin-Deslauriers
600 Martin Houle

2006-07 The Cup Printing Plates SP Authentic Black

STATED PRINT RUN 1 SER.#'d SET
FOUR COLORS OF EACH PLATE
NOT PRICED DUE TO SCARCITY
161 Ryan Shannon AUTO
162 Shane O'Brien AUTO
163 Phil Kessel AUTO
164 Mark Stuart AUTO
165 Matt Lashoff AUTO
166 Yan Stastny AUTO
167 Nate Thompson AUTO
168 Drew Stafford AUTO
169 Dustin Boyd AUTO
170 Brandon Prust AUTO
171 Dave Bolland AUTO
172 Michael Blunden AUTO
173 Dustin Byfuglien AUTO
174 Paul Stastny AUTO
175 Karri Ramo AUTO
176 Loui Eriksson AUTO
177 Tomas Kopecky AUTO
178 Ladislav Smid AUTO
179 Marc-Antoine Pouliot AUTO
181 Patrick Thoresen AUTO
182 Janis Sprukts AUTO
183 Patrick O'Sullivan AUTO
184 Anze Kopitar AUTO
185 Konstantin Pushkaryov AUTO
186 Guillaume Latendresse AUTO
187 Shea Weber AUTO
188 Alexander Radulov AUTO
189 Travis Zajac AUTO
190 Jarkko Immonen AUTO
191 Nigel Dawes AUTO
192 Kelly Guard AUTO
193 Ryan Potulny AUTO
194 Benoit Pouliot AUTO
195 Keith Yandle AUTO
196 Evgeni Malkin AUTO
197 Noah Welch AUTO
198 Jordan Staal AUTO
199 Michel Ouellet AUTO
200 Kristopher Letang AUTO
201 Matt Carle AUTO
202 Marc-Edouard Vlasic AUTO
204 Jeremy Williams AUTO
205 Ian White AUTO
206 Jesse Schultz AUTO
207 Brendan Bell AUTO
208 Luc Bourdon AUTO
210 Eric Fehr AUTO
211 Daren Machesney
212 Nathan McIver
213 Patrick Coulombe
214 Jesse Schultz
215 Kris Newbury
216 Blair Jones
217 Marek Schwarz
218 David Backes
219 Joe Pavelski
220 Patrick Fischer
221 Bill Thomas
222 Triston Grant
223 Lars Jonsson
224 David Printz
225 Jussi Timonen
226 Martin Houle
227 Josh Hennessy
228 Blake Comeau
229 Masi Marjamaki
230 Ben Ondrus
231 Fredrik Norrena
232 Johnny Oduya
233 Enver Lisin
234 Mikhail Grabovski
235 Mikko Lehtonen
236 Niklas Backstrom
237 Miroslav Kopriva
238 Benoit Pouliot
239 Peter Harrold
240 David Booth
241 Drew Larman
242 Jan Hejda
243 Jeff Drouin-Deslauriers
244 Stefan Liv
245 Adam Burish
246 Michael Funk
247 Mike Card
248 Adam Dennis
249 Clarke MacArthur
250 David McKee

2006-07 The Cup Printing Plates SP Game Used Black

STATED PRINT RUN 1 SER.#'d SET
FOUR COLORS OF EACH PLATE
NOT PRICED DUE TO SCARCITY
101 Shane O'Brien
102 Ryan Shannon
103 Yan Stastny
104 Mark Stuart
105 Nate Thompson
106 Phil Kessel
107 Matt Lashoff
108 Dave Bolland
109 Michael Blunden
110 Dustin Byfuglien
111 Paul Stastny
112 Fredrik Norrena
113 Loui Eriksson
114 Tomas Kopecky
115 Alexei Mikhnov
116 Marc-Antoine Pouliot
117 Patrick Thoresen
118 Ladislav Smid
119 Janis Sprukts
120 Konstantin Pushkaryov
121 Patrick O'Sullivan
122 Anze Kopitar

123 Benoit Pouliot
124 Miroslav Kopriva
125 Niklas Backstrom
126 Guillaume Latendresse
127 Alexander Radulov
128 Shea Weber
129 Mikko Lehtonen
130 Alex Brooks
131 John Oduya
132 Travis Zajac
133 Drew Stafford
134 Masi Marjamaki
135 Jarkko Immonen
136 Nigel Dawes
137 Alexei Kaigorodov
138 Lars Jonsson
139 Ryan Potulny
140 Triston Grant
141 Enver Lisin
142 Brandon Prust
143 Keith Yandle
144 Patrick Fischer
145 Noah Welch
146 Michel Ouellet
147 Jordan Staal
148 Kristopher Letang
149 Evgeni Malkin
150 Matt Carle
151 Marc-Edouard Vlasic
152 D.J. King
153 Roman Polak
154 Ben Ondrus
155 Brendan Bell
156 Ian White
157 Dustin Boyd
158 Luc Bourdon
159 Eric Fehr
160 Jonas Johansson

2006-07 The Cup Printing Plates SPx Black

STATED PRINT RUN 1 SER.#'d SET
FOUR COLORS OF EACH PLATE
NOT PRICED DUE TO SCARCITY
143 Dustin Byfuglien
144 Drew Stafford AUTO
145 Frank Doyle
146 Carsen Germyn
147 David Printz
148 Masi Marjamaki
149 Konstantin Pushkaryov
150 Michel Ouellet
151 Billy Thompson
152 Filip Novak
153 Miroslav Kopriva
154 Jonas Johansson
155 Shane O'Brien
156 John Oduya
157 Fredrik Norrena
158 Niklas Backstrom
159 D.J. King
160 Patrick Thoresen
161 Dustin Boyd AUTO
162 Mikko Lehtonen
163 Roman Polak
164 Yan Stastny AUTO
165 Mark Stuart AUTO
166 Eric Fehr AUTO
167 Ryan Potulny AUTO
168 Ben Ondrus AUTO
169 Brendan Bell AUTO
170 Ian White AUTO
171 Jeremy Williams AUTO
172 Marc-Antoine Pouliot AUTO
173 Noah Welch AUTO
174 Shea Weber AUTO
175 Jarkko Immonen AUTO
176 Tomas Kopecky AUTO
177 Matt Carle AUTO
178 Ryan Shannon AUTO
179 Anze Kopitar AUTO
180 Travis Zajac AUTO
181 Nigel Dawes AUTO
182 Kristopher Letang AUTO
183 Marc-Edouard Vlasic AUTO
184 Ladislav Smid AUTO
185 Loui Eriksson AUTO
186 Paul Stastny AUTO
188 Patrick O'Sullivan AUTO
189 Phil Kessel AUTO
190 Guillaume Latendresse AUTO
191 Jordan Staal AUTO
192 Luc Bourdon AUTO
193 Evgeni Malkin AUTO
194 Keith Yandle AUTO
195 Alexander Radulov AUTO

2006-07 The Cup Printing Plates Sweet Shot Black

STATED PRINT RUN 1 SER.#'d SET
FOUR COLORS OF EACH PLATE
NOT PRICED DUE TO SCARCITY
101 Shane O'Brien
102 Ryan Shannon
103 David McKee
104 Phil Kessel
105 Yan Stastny
106 Mark Stuart
107 Matt Lashoff
108 Clarke MacArthur
109 Drew Stafford
110 Masi Marjamaki
111 Michael Funk
112 Brandon Prust
113 Dustin Boyd
114 Dustin Byfuglien
115 Dave Bolland
116 Michael Blunden
117 Paul Stastny
118 Fredrik Norrena
119 Niklas Grossman
120 Loui Eriksson
121 Tomas Kopecky
122 Stefan Liv
123 Patrick Thoresen
124 Marc-Antoine Pouliot
125 Ladislav Smid
126 Janis Sprukts
127 Jeff Drouin-Deslauriers
128 David Booth
129 Konstantin Pushkaryov
130 Anze Kopitar
131 Patrick O'Sullivan
132 Benoit Pouliot
133 Guillaume Latendresse
134 Mikhail Grabovski
135 Shea Weber
136 Alexander Radulov
137 Travis Zajac
138 Nigel Dawes
139 Jarkko Immonen
140 Josh Hennessy
141 Jussi Timonen
142 Ryan Potulny
143 Keith Yandle
144 Michel Ouellet
145 Jordan Staal
146 Evgeni Malkin
147 Noah Welch
148 Kristopher Letang
149 Matt Carle
150 Marc-Edouard Vlasic
151 Joe Pavelski
152 Marek Schwarz
153 Karri Ramo
154 Blair Jones
155 Ian White
156 Jeremy Williams
157 Luc Bourdon
158 Jesse Schultz
159 Alexander Edler
160 Eric Fehr

2006-07 The Cup Printing Plates UD Powerplay Black

STATED PRINT RUN 1 SER.#'d SET
FOUR COLORS FOR EACH PLATE
NOT PRICED DUE TO SCARCITY
101 Yan Stastny
102 Mark Stuart
103 Carsen Germyn
104 Dustin Byfuglien
105 Tomas Kopecky
106 Marc-Antoine Pouliot
107 Konstantin Pushkaryov
108 Erik Reitz
109 Miroslav Kopriva
110 Shea Weber
111 David Printz
112 Steve Regier
113 Ryan Caldwell
114 Masi Marjamaki
115 Matt Koalska
116 Jarkko Immonen
117 Cole Jarrett
118 Rob Collins
119 Filip Novak
120 Ryan Potulny
121 Bill Thomas
122 Joel Perrault
123 Noah Welch
124 Michel Ouellet
125 Matt Carle
126 Ben Ondrus
127 Brendan Bell
128 Ian White
129 Jeremy Williams
130 Eric Fehr

2006-07 The Cup Printing Plates Ultimate Collection Black

STATED PRINT RUN 1 SER.#'d SET
FOUR COLORS OF EACH PLATE
NOT PRICED DUE TO SCARCITY
61 David McKee
62 Ryan Shannon
63 Clarke MacArthur
64 Andrej Sekera
65 Michael Funk
66 Adam Dennis
67 Mike Card
68 Brandon Prust
69 Troy Brouwer
70 Adam Burish
71 Fredrik Norrena
72 Stefan Liv
73 Tomas Kopecky
74 Jeff Drouin-Deslauriers
75 David Booth
76 Janis Sprukts
77 Barry Brust
78 Konstantin Pushkaryov
79 Shawn Belle
80 Niklas Backstrom
81 Mikhail Grabovski
82 Johnny Oduya
83 Blake Comeau
84 Jarkko Immonen
85 Josh Hennessy
86 Kelly Guard
87 Jussi Timonen
88 Martin Houle
89 Michel Ouellet
90 Yan Stastny
91 Roman Polak
92 Marek Schwarz
93 David Backes
94 Blair Jones
95 Karri Ramo
96 Ian White
97 Brendan Bell
98 Kris Newbury
99 Jean-Francois Racine
100 Jesse Schultz
101 Alexander Edler
102 Daren Machesney
103 Matt Lashoff AUTO
104 Phil Kessel AUTO
105 Mark Stuart AUTO
106 Michael Blunden AUTO
107 Dave Bolland AUTO
108 Paul Stastny AUTO
109 Loui Eriksson AUTO
111 Ladislav Smid AUTO
112 Patrick Thoresen AUTO
113 Marc-Antoine Pouliot AUTO
114 Anze Kopitar AUTO
115 Patrick O'Sullivan AUTO
116 Guillaume Latendresse AUTO
117 Alexander Radulov AUTO
118 Shea Weber AUTO
119 Travis Zajac AUTO
120 Nigel Dawes AUTO
121 Dustin Boyd AUTO
122 Ryan Potulny AUTO
123 Benoit Pouliot AUTO
124 Keith Yandle AUTO
125 Evgeni Malkin AUTO
126 Kristopher Letang AUTO
127 Jordan Staal AUTO
128 Noah Welch AUTO
129 Marc-Edouard Vlasic AUTO
130 Matt Carle AUTO
131 Drew Stafford AUTO
132 Eric Fehr AUTO

2006-07 The Cup Printing Plates Upper Deck MVP Black

STATED PRINT RUN 1 SER.#'d SET
FOUR COLORS OF EACH PLATE
NOT PRICED DUE TO SCARCITY
298 Patrick O'Sullivan
299 Phil Kessel
300 Guillaume Latendresse
301 Jordan Staal
302 Paul Stastny
303 Evgeni Malkin
304 Luc Bourdon
305 Alexei Kaigorodov
306 Anze Kopitar
307 Travis Zajac
308 Nigel Dawes
309 Kristopher Letang
310 Marc-Edouard Vlasic
311 Patrick Thoresen
312 Ladislav Smid
313 Loui Eriksson
314 Shane O'Brien
315 Ryan Shannon
316 John Oduya
317 Fredrik Norrena
318 Niklas Backstrom
319 D.J. King
320 Patrick Fischer
321 Mikko Lehtonen
322 Roman Polak
323 Ben Ondrus
324 Bill Thomas
325 Billy Thompson
326 Brendan Bell
327 Carsen Germyn
328 Keith Yandle
329 Dan Jancevski
330 David Liffiton
331 David Printz
332 Dustin Byfuglien
333 Eric Fehr
334 Erik Reitz
335 Filip Novak
336 Frank Doyle
337 Ian White
338 Jarkko Immonen
339 Jeremy Williams
340 Joel Perrault
341 Jonas Johansson
342 Konstantin Pushkaryov
343 Marc-Antoine Pouliot
344 Mark Stuart
345 Masi Marjamaki
346 Matt Carle
347 Matt Koalska
348 Michel Ouellet
349 Miroslav Kopriva
350 Noah Welch
351 Rob Collins
352 Ryan Caldwell
353 Ryan Potulny
354 Shea Weber
355 Enver Lisin
356 Tomas Kopecky
357 Yan Stastny

2006-07 The Cup Printing Plates Upper Deck Trilogy Black

STATED PRINT RUN 1 SER.#'d SET
FOUR COLORS OF EACH PLATE
NOT PRICED DUE TO SCARCITY
101 Shane O'Brien
102 Ryan Shannon
103 Yan Stastny
104 Mark Stuart
105 Phil Kessel
106 Carsen Germyn
107 Dustin Byfuglien
108 Paul Stastny
109 Filip Novak
110 Fredrik Norrena
111 Loui Eriksson
112 Tomas Kopecky
113 Marc-Antoine Pouliot
114 Patrick Thoresen
115 Ladislav Smid
116 Konstantin Pushkaryov
117 Patrick O'Sullivan
118 Anze Kopitar
119 Erik Reitz
120 Miroslav Kopriva
121 Niklas Backstrom
122 Dan Jancevski
123 Guillaume Latendresse
124 Shea Weber
125 Mikko Lehtonen
126 Frank Doyle
127 John Oduya
128 Travis Zajac
129 Rob Collins
130 Steve Regier
131 Matt Koalska
132 Ryan Caldwell
133 Masi Marjamaki
134 Keith Yandle
135 Enver Lisin
136 Jarkko Immonen
137 David Liffiton
138 Nigel Dawes
139 Alexei Kaigorodov
140 Ryan Potulny
141 David Printz
142 Bill Thomas
143 Joel Perrault
144 Patrick Fischer
145 Noah Welch
146 Michel Ouellet
147 Jordan Staal
148 Kristopher Letang
149 Evgeni Malkin
150 Matt Carle
151 Marc-Edouard Vlasic
152 D.J. King
153 Roman Polak
154 Ben Ondrus
155 Brendan Bell
156 Ian White
157 Jeremy Williams
158 Luc Bourdon
159 Eric Fehr
160 Jonas Johansson

2006-07 The Cup Printing Plates Upper Deck Victory Black

STATED PRINT RUN 1 SER.#'d SET
FOUR COLORS OF EACH PLATE
NOT PRICED DUE TO SCARCITY
201 Tomas Kopecky
202 Billy Thompson
203 Dustin Byfuglien
204 Yan Stastny
205 Eric Fehr
206 Ben Ondrus
207 Rob Collins
208 Brendan Bell
209 Frank Doyle
210 Noah Welch
211 Filip Novak
212 Ian White
213 Konstantin Pushkaryov
214 Dan Jancevski
215 Shea Weber
216 Michel Ouellet
217 Marc-Antoine Pouliot
218 Carsen Germyn
219 Matt Carle
220 Steve Regier
221 Mark Stuart
222 Bill Thomas
223 Jarkko Immonen
224 Erik Reitz
225 Joel Perrault
226 Ryan Potulny
227 Jeremy Williams
228 Masi Marjamaki
229 Miroslav Kopriva
230 Matt Koalska
281 Shane O'Brien
282 Jonas Johansson
283 Ryan Shannon
284 Patrick O'Sullivan
285 Anze Kopitar
286 John Oduya
287 Travis Zajac
288 Fredrik Norrena
289 Phil Kessel
290 Guillaume Latendresse
291 Nigel Dawes
292 Jordan Staal
293 Kristopher Letang
294 Paul Stastny
295 Niklas Backstrom
296 D.J. King
297 Marc-Edouard Vlasic
298 Patrick Thoresen
299 Ladislav Smid
300 Loui Eriksson
301 Patrick Fischer
302 Mikko Lehtonen
303 Roman Polak
304 Evgeni Malkin
305 Luc Bourdon
306 Alexei Kaigorodov
307 Alex Brooks
308 Nate Thompson
309 Janis Sprukts
310 Alexander Radulov
311 Keith Yandle
312 Enver Lisin
313 Cole Jarrett
314 Ryan Caldwell
315 David Printz
316 David Liffiton
317 Adam Burish
318 Dave Bolland
319 Michael Blunden
320 Matt Lashoff
321 Alexei Mikhnov
322 Jan Hejda
323 Lars Jonsson
324 Triston Grant
325 Alexander Edler
326 Brandon Prust
327 Dustin Boyd
328 Drew Stafford
329 Kelly Guard
330 Nathan McIver

2006-07 The Cup Autographed Foundations

STATED PRINT RUN 10 SER.#'d SETS
NOT PRICED DUE TO SCARCITY
CQAH Ales Hemsky
CQAK Anze Kopitar
CQAM Al MacInnis
CQAO Adam Oates
CQAR Andrew Raycroft
CQAY Alexei Yashin
CQBB Brad Boyes
CQBL Rob Blake
CQBS Billy Smith
CQCN Cam Neely
CQCP Chris Pronger
CQCW Cam Ward
CQDG Doug Gilmour SP
CQDH Dale Hawerchuk
CQDS Denis Savard
CQEB Ed Belfour
CQEM Evgeni Malkin
CQEN Evgeni Nabokov
CQES Eric Staal
CQFM Frank Mahovlich
CQGC Gerry Cheevers
CQGF Grant Fuhr
CQGH Gordie Howe
CQGL Guy Lafleur
CQGP Gilbert Perreault
CQHA Dominik Hasek
CQHE Dany Heatley
CQHL Henrik Lundqvist
CQHM Milan Hejduk
CQHZ Henrik Zetterberg
CQIK Ilya Kovalchuk
CQJB Jean Beliveau
CQJC Jonathan Cheechoo
CQJI Jarome Iginla
CQJK Jari Kurri
CQJR Jeremy Roenick
CQJS Jordan Staal
CQJT Joe Thornton
CQKE Phil Kessel
CQKL Kari Lehtonen
CQLM Lanny McDonald
CQLR Larry Robinson
CQMA Stan Mikita
CQMB Martin Brodeur
CQMD Marcel Dionne
CQMG Marian Gaborik
CQMI Mike Bossy
CQML Mario Lemieux
CQMM Mike Modano
CQMN Markus Naslund
CQMR Michael Ryder
CQMS Martin St. Louis
CQMT Marty Turco
CQNL Nicklas Lidstrom
CQOV Alexander Ovechkin
CQPB Patrice Bergeron
CQPE Patrik Elias
CQPH Dion Phaneuf
CQPM Patrick Marleau
CQPR Patrick Roy
CQPS Peter Stastny
CQRB Ray Bourque
CQRE Ron Ellis
CQRH Ron Hextall
CQRM Ryan Miller
CQRN Rick Nash
CQRO Luc Robitaille
CQRS Ryan Smyth
CQRV Rogie Vachon
CQSA Borje Salming
CQSC Sidney Crosby
CQSG Simon Gagne
CQSK Saku Koivu
CQSM Miroslav Satan
CQSP Jason Spezza
CQSS Scott Stevens
CQST Steve Shutt
CQTE Tony Esposito
CQTH Jose Theodore
CQTV Tomas Vokoun
CQVL Vincent Lecavalier
CQWG Wayne Gretzky

2006-07 The Cup Autographed Foundations Patches

STATED PRINT RUN 5 SER.#'d SETS
NOT PRICED DUE TO SCARCITY

2006-07 The Cup Autographed NHL Shields Duals

STATED PRINT RUN 1 SER.#'d SET
NOT PRICED DUE TO SCARCITY
DASAD Dwayne Roloson
Ales Hemsky
DASAN Jean-Sebastien Giguere
Chris Pronger
Teemu Selanne
Joe Sakic
Paul Stastny
Marek Svatos
DASBB Ed Belfour
Todd Bertuzzi
DASBD Chris Drury
Daniel Briere
DASBH Martin Brodeur
Dominik Hasek
DASBK Rob Blake
Anze Kopitar
DASBM Ray Bourque
Al MacInnis
DASBO Glen Murray
Brad Boyes
DASBP Dustin Boyd
Brandon Prust
DASBR Mike Modano
Brenden Morrow
DASBS Ray Bourque
Scott Stevens
DASCO Milan Hejduk
Marek Svatos
DASCT Zdeno Chara
Hannu Toivonen
DASDA Adam Oates
Dale Hawerchuk
DASDJ Jason Spezza
Dany Heatley
DASDM Dany Heatley
Martin Gerber
DASDP Michael Peca
Kris Draper
DASDS Chris Drury
Drew Stafford
DASEC Eric Staal
Cam Ward
DASEO Ryan Smyth
Ales Hemsky
DASEZ Patrik Elias
Travis Zajac
DASFK Alexander Frolov
Anze Kopitar
DASGB Marian Gaborik
Pierre-Marc Bouchard
DASGC Wendel Clark
Doug Gilmour
DASGG Scott Gomez
Brian Gionta
DASGK Jari Kurri
Wayne Gretzky
DASGL Mario Lemieux
Wayne Gretzky
DASGP Simon Gagne
Joni Pitkanen
DASGS Simon Gagne
Martin St. Louis
DASHA David Aebischer
Cristobal Huet
DASHG Simon Gagne
Dany Heatley
DASHH Michal Handzus
Martin Havlat
DASHL Dominik Hasek
Nicklas Lidstrom
DASHN Dany Heatley
Rick Nash
DASHO Dominik Hasek
Chris Osgood
DASHR Wade Redden
Dany Heatley
DASHS Milan Hejduk
Marek Svatos
DASHT Milan Hejduk
Jose Theodore
DASHV Tomas Vokoun
Dominik Hasek
DASHZ Dominik Hasek
Henrik Zetterberg
DASIA Ilya Kovalchuk
Alexander Radulov
DASIK Ilya Kovalchuk
Kari Lehtonen
DASIL Vincent Lecavalier
Jarome Iginla
DASIP Jarome Iginla
Dion Phaneuf
DASIT Jarome Iginla
Alex Tanguay
DASKB Patrice Bergeron
Phil Kessel
DASKL Phil Kessel
Guillaume Latendresse
DASKO Patrick O'Sullivan
Anze Kopitar
DASKR Saku Koivu
Michael Ryder
DASLB Martin Brodeur
Roberto Luongo
DASLD Henrik Lundqvist
Nigel Dawes
DASLH Nicklas Lidstrom
Tomas Holmstrom
DASLN Markus Naslund
Roberto Luongo
DASLP Guillaume Latendresse
Benoit Pouliot
DASLR Patrick Roy
Mario Lemieux
DASLS Jarret Stoll
Joffrey Lupul
DASLT Vesa Toskala
Kari Lehtonen
DASMB Martin Biron
Ryan Miller
DASMC Chris Higgins
Guillaume Latendresse
DASMD Chris Drury
Ryan Miller
DASMI Mike Modano
Mike Ribeiro
DASMK Evgeni Malkin
Phil Kessel
DASMM Patrick Marleau
Milan Michalek
DASMN Marian Gaborik
Benoit Pouliot
DASMO Alexander Ovechkin
Evgeni Malkin
DASMR Evgeni Malkin
Alexander Radulov
DASMS Evgeni Malkin
Jordan Staal
DASMT Mike Modano
Marty Turco
DASNB Cam Neely
Ray Bourque
DASNJ Martin Brodeur
Scott Stevens
DASNM Markus Naslund
Brendan Morrison
DASNZ Rick Nash
Nikolai Zherdev
DASPC Matt Carle
Joe Pavelski
DASPG Glen Murray
Patrice Bergeron
DASRA Jason Arnott
Alexander Radulov
DASRB Patrick Roy
Martin Brodeur
DASRL Michael Ryder
Guillaume Latendresse
DASRP Michael Peca
Andrew Raycroft
DASRT Luc Robitaille
Dave Taylor
DASSC Erik Cole
Eric Staal
DASSK Phil Kessel
Jordan Staal
DASSL Vincent Lecavalier
Martin St. Louis
DASSM Drew Stafford
Clarke MacArthur
DASSS Yan Stastny
Paul Stastny
DASST Eric Staal
Jordan Staal
DASSV Marek Svatos
Paul Stastny
DASSW Justin Williams
Eric Staal
DASTB Joe Thornton
Steve Bernier
DASTC Joe Thornton
Jonathan Cheechoo
DASTM Patrick Marleau
Joe Thornton
DASVS Tomas Vokoun
Steve Sullivan
DASWW Ian White
Jeremy Williams
DASYS Miroslav Satan
Alexei Yashin
DASZN Markus Naslund
Henrik Zetterberg

2006-07 The Cup Autographed Patches

STATED PRINT RUN 1 SER.#'d SET
NOT PRICED DUE TO SCARCITY
2 Jean-Sebastian Giguere
3 Kari Lehtonen
4 Ilya Kovalchuk
7 Ray Bourque
9 Cam Neely
10 Patrice Bergeron
12 Ryan Miller
13 Gilbert Perreault
14 Jarome Iginla
16 Al MacInnis
17 Eric Staal
18 Cam Ward
19 Bobby Hull
20 Tony Esposito
21 Stan Mikita
23 Patrick Roy
24 Rick Nash
26 Mike Modano
27 Dominik Hasek
28 Henrik Zetterberg
29 Gordie Howe
33 Ales Hemsky
34 Grant Fuhr
35 Jari Kurri
36 Ed Belfour
37 Wayne Gretzky
38 Rob Blake
39 Marcel Dionne
40 Luc Robitaille
42 Dino Ciccarelli
43 Marian Gaborik
44 Saku Koivu
45 Michael Ryder
46 Guy Lafleur
47 Larry Robinson
51 Tomas Vokoun
52 Martin Brodeur
53 Scott Stevens
54 Alexei Yashin
56 Mike Bossy
57 Billy Smith
61 Henrik Lundqvist
62 Gump Worsley
64 Jason Spezza
65 Dany Heatley
67 Simon Gagne
69 Bobby Clarke
70 Ron Hextall
71 Jeremy Roenick
73 Sidney Crosby
74 Marc-Andre Fleury
75 Mario Lemieux
76 Peter Stastny
77 Joe Thornton
78 Jonathan Cheechoo
79 Patrick Marleau
80 Bernie Federko
81 Vincent Lecavalier
84 Darryl Sittler
86 Borje Salming
87 Roberto Luongo
88 Markus Naslund
89 Alexander Ovechkin
90 Dale Hawerchuk

2006-07 The Cup Autographed Rookie Masterpiece Pressplates

STATED PRINT RUN 1 SER.#'d SET
NOT PRICED DUE TO SCARCITY
91 Nate Thompson
92 Mike Brown
93 Mike Card
94 Adam Dennis
95 Carsen Germyn
96 Adam Burish
97 Drew Larman
98 Jonas Johansson
99 Joel Perrault
100 Mikko Lehtonen
101 Alex Brooks
102 Frank Doyle
103 Billy Thompson
104 Kelly Guard
105 David Printz
106 D.J. King
107 Jean-Francois Racine
108 Nathan McIver
109 Shane O'Brien
110 Ryan Shannon
111 David McKee
112 Mark Stuart
113 Matt Lashoff

114 Drew Stafford
115 Clarke MacArthur
116 Michael Funk
117 Brandon Prust
118 Dustin Boyd
119 Dustin Byfuglien
120 Dave Bolland
121 Michael Blunden
122 Filip Novak
123 Fredrik Norrena
124 Niklas Grossman
125 Loui Eriksson
126 Tomas Kopecky
127 Stefan Liv
128 Patrick Thoresen
129 Marc-Antoine Pouliot
130 Ladislav Smid
131 Janis Sprukts
132 Jeff Drouin-Deslauriers
133 David Booth
134 Konstantin Pushkaryov
135 Patrick O'Sullivan
136 Benoit Pouliot
137 Niklas Backstrom
138 Guillaume Latendresse
139 Shea Weber
140 Johnny Oduya
141 Travis Zajac
142 Masi Marjamaki
143 Nigel Dawes
144 Jarkko Immonen
145 Josh Hennessy
146 Ryan Potulny
147 Jussi Timonen
148 Keith Yandle
149 Michel Ouellet
150 Noah Welch
151 Kristopher Letang
152 Joe Pavelski
153 Matt Carle
154 Marc-Edouard Vlasic
155 Yan Stastny
156 Marek Schwarz
157 Roman Polak
158 Karri Ramo
159 Blair Jones
160 Brendan Bell
161 Ian White
162 Ben Ondrus
163 Jeremy Williams
164 Miroslav Kopriva
165 Luc Bourdon
166 Jesse Schultz
167 Alexander Edler
168 Eric Fehr
169 Jordan Staal
170 Phil Kessel
171 Evgeni Malkin
172 Paul Stastny
173 Anze Kopitar
174 Alexander Radulov

2006-07 The Cup Black Rainbow

STATED PRINT RUN 1/1
NOT PRICED DUE TO SCARCITY
1 Teemu Selanne
2 Jean-Sebastian Giguere
3 Kari Lehtonen
4 Ilya Kovalchuk
5 Phil Esposito
6 Don Cherry
7 Ray Bourque
8 Bobby Orr
9 Cam Neely
10 Patrice Bergeron
11 Johnny Bucyk
12 Ryan Miller
13 Gilbert Perreault
14 Jarome Iginla
15 Miikka Kiprusoff
16 Al MacInnis
17 Eric Staal
18 Cam Ward
19 Bobby Hull
20 Tony Esposito
21 Stan Mikita
22 Joe Sakic
23 Patrick Roy
24 Rick Nash
25 Sergei Fedorov
26 Mike Modano
27 Dominik Hasek
28 Henrik Zetterberg
29 Gordie Howe
30 Scotty Bowman
31 Ted Lindsay
32 Red Kelly
33 Ales Hemsky
34 Grant Fuhr
35 Jari Kurri
36 Ed Belfour
37 Wayne Gretzky
38 Rob Blake
39 Marcel Dionne
40 Luc Robitaille
41 Rogie Vachon
42 Dino Ciccarelli
43 Marian Gaborik
44 Saku Koivu
45 Michael Ryder
46 Guy Lafleur
47 Larry Robinson
48 Jean Beliveau
49 Jacques Lemaire
50 Paul Kariya
51 Tomas Vokoun
52 Martin Brodeur
53 Scott Stevens
54 Alexei Yashin
55 Al Arbour
56 Mike Bossy
57 Billy Smith
58 Denis Potvin
59 Jaromir Jagr
60 Brendan Shanahan
61 Henrik Lundqvist
62 Gump Worsley
63 Andy Bathgate
64 Jason Spezza
65 Dany Heatley
66 Peter Forsberg
67 Simon Gagne
68 Bernie Parent
69 Bobby Clarke
70 Ron Hextall
71 Jeremy Roenick
72 Shane Doan
73 Sidney Crosby
74 Marc-Andre Fleury
75 Mario Lemieux
76 Peter Stastny
77 Joe Thornton
78 Jonathan Cheechoo
79 Patrick Marleau
80 Bernie Federko
81 Vincent Lecavalier
82 Mats Sundin
83 Frank Mahovlich
84 Darryl Sittler
85 Johnny Bower
86 Borje Salming
87 Roberto Luongo
88 Markus Naslund
89 Alexander Ovechkin
90 Dale Hawerchuk

2006-07 The Cup Foundations

STATED PRINT RUN 25 SER.#'d SETS

CQAH Ales Hemsky	15.00	40.00
CQAK Anze Kopitar	25.00	60.00
CQAM Al MacInnis	15.00	40.00
CQAO Adam Oates	10.00	25.00
CQAR Andrew Raycroft	12.00	30.00
CQAY Alexei Yashin	10.00	25.00
CQBB Brad Boyes	10.00	25.00
CQBL Rob Blake	15.00	40.00
CQBS Billy Smith	15.00	40.00
CQCJ Curtis Joseph	15.00	40.00
CQCN Cam Neely	20.00	50.00
CQCP Chris Pronger	20.00	50.00
CQCW Cam Ward	20.00	50.00
CQDA Daniel Alfredsson	15.00	40.00
CQDC Dino Ciccarelli	10.00	25.00
CQDG Doug Gilmour SP	15.00	40.00
CQDH Dale Hawerchuk	15.00	40.00
CQDS Denis Savard	20.00	50.00
CQEB Ed Belfour	15.00	40.00
CQEL Eric Lindros	20.00	50.00
CQEM Evgeni Malkin	30.00	80.00
CQEN Evgeni Nabokov	15.00	40.00
CQES Eric Staal	10.00	25.00
CQFM Frank Mahovlich	20.00	50.00
CQGC Gerry Cheevers	15.00	40.00
CQGF Grant Fuhr	15.00	40.00
CQGH Gordie Howe	30.00	80.00
CQGL Guy Lafleur	15.00	40.00
CQGP Gilbert Perreault	20.00	50.00
CQHA Dominik Hasek	30.00	80.00
CQHE Dany Heatley	20.00	50.00
CQHL Henrik Lundqvist	20.00	50.00
CQHM Milan Hejduk	10.00	25.00
CQHZ Henrik Zetterberg	20.00	50.00
CQIK Ilya Kovalchuk	20.00	50.00
CQJB Jean Beliveau	20.00	50.00
CQJC Jonathan Cheechoo	20.00	50.00
CQJI Jarome Iginla	20.00	50.00
CQJJ Jaromir Jagr	30.00	80.00
CQJK Jari Kurri	20.00	50.00
CQJO Joe Sakic	30.00	80.00
CQJR Jeremy Roenick	20.00	50.00
CQJS Jordan Staal	25.00	60.00
CQJT Joe Thornton	30.00	80.00
CQKE Phil Kessel	20.00	50.00
CQKL Kari Lehtonen	20.00	50.00
CQLM Lanny McDonald	20.00	50.00
CQLR Larry Robinson	20.00	50.00
CQMA Stan Mikita	20.00	50.00
CQMB Martin Brodeur	40.00	100.00
CQMD Marcel Dionne	20.00	50.00
CQMG Marian Gaborik	25.00	60.00
CQMH Marian Hossa	20.00	50.00
CQMI Mike Bossy	20.00	50.00
CQML Mario Lemieux	50.00	125.00
CQMM Mike Modano	20.00	50.00
CQMN Markus Naslund	20.00	50.00
CQMR Michael Ryder	20.00	50.00
CQMS Martin St. Louis	20.00	50.00
CQMT Marty Turco	20.00	50.00
CQNL Nicklas Lidstrom	20.00	50.00
CQOK Olaf Kolzig	20.00	50.00
CQOV Alexander Ovechkin	40.00	100.00
CQPB Patrice Bergeron	20.00	50.00
CQPD Pavel Datsyuk	20.00	50.00
CQPE Patrik Elias	10.00	25.00
CQPF Peter Forsberg	30.00	80.00
CQPH Dion Phaneuf	20.00	50.00
CQPK Paul Kariya	25.00	60.00
CQPM Patrick Marleau	20.00	50.00
CQPR Patrick Roy	60.00	150.00
CQPS Peter Stastny	15.00	40.00
CQRB Ray Bourque	25.00	60.00
CQRD Rick DiPietro	20.00	50.00
CQRE Ron Ellis	10.00	25.00
CQRH Ron Hextall	20.00	50.00
CQRL Roberto Luongo	25.00	60.00
CQRM Ryan Miller	20.00	50.00
CQRN Rick Nash	20.00	50.00
CQRO Luc Robitaille	20.00	50.00
CQRS Ryan Smyth	15.00	40.00
CQRV Rogie Vachon	20.00	50.00
CQSA Borje Salming	10.00	25.00
CQSC Sidney Crosby	100.00	200.00
CQSF Sergei Fedorov	20.00	50.00
CQSG Simon Gagne	20.00	50.00
CQSH Brendan Shanahan	20.00	50.00
CQSK Saku Koivu	20.00	50.00
CQSM Miroslav Satan	20.00	50.00
CQSP Jason Spezza	25.00	60.00
CQSS Scott Stevens	15.00	40.00
CQST Steve Shutt	10.00	25.00
CQSU Mats Sundin	20.00	50.00
CQTE Tony Esposito	20.00	50.00
CQTH Jose Theodore	20.00	50.00
CQTS Teemu Selanne	20.00	50.00
CQTV Tomas Vokoun	20.00	50.00
CQVL Vincent Lecavalier	20.00	50.00
CQWG Wayne Gretzky	75.00	150.00

2006-07 The Cup Foundations Patches

STATED PRINT RUN 10 SER.#'d SETS
NOT PRICED DUE TO SCARCITY
CQAH Ales Hemsky
CQAK Anze Kopitar
CQAM Al MacInnis
CQAO Adam Oates
CQAR Andrew Raycroft
CQAY Alexei Yashin
CQBB Brad Boyes
CQBL Rob Blake
CQBS Billy Smith
CQCJ Curtis Joseph
CQCN Cam Neely
CQCP Chris Pronger
CQCW Cam Ward
CQDA Daniel Alfredsson
CQDC Dino Ciccarelli
CQDG Doug Gilmour SP
CQDH Dale Hawerchuk
CQDS Denis Savard
CQEB Ed Belfour
CQEL Eric Lindros
CQEM Evgeni Malkin
CQEN Evgeni Nabokov
CQES Eric Staal
CQGC Gerry Cheevers
CQGF Grant Fuhr
CQGH Gordie Howe
CQGL Guy Lafleur
CQGP Gilbert Perreault
CQHA Dominik Hasek
CQHE Dany Heatley
CQHL Henrik Lundqvist
CQHM Milan Hejduk
CQHZ Henrik Zetterberg
CQIK Ilya Kovalchuk
CQJC Jonathan Cheechoo
CQJI Jarome Iginla
CQJJ Jaromir Jagr
CQJK Jari Kurri
CQJO Joe Sakic
CQJR Jeremy Roenick
CQJS Jordan Staal
CQJT Joe Thornton
CQKE Phil Kessel
CQKL Kari Lehtonen
CQLR Larry Robinson
CQMA Stan Mikita
CQMB Martin Brodeur
CQMD Marcel Dionne
CQMG Marian Gaborik
CQMH Marian Hossa
CQMI Mike Bossy
CQML Mario Lemieux
CQMM Mike Modano
CQMN Markus Naslund
CQMR Michael Ryder
CQMS Martin St. Louis
CQMT Marty Turco
CQNL Nicklas Lidstrom
CQOK Olaf Kolzig
CQOV Alexander Ovechkin
CQPB Patrice Bergeron
CQPD Pavel Datsyuk
CQPE Patrik Elias
CQPF Peter Forsberg
CQPH Dion Phaneuf
CQPK Paul Kariya
CQPM Patrick Marleau
CQPR Patrick Roy
CQPS Peter Stastny
CQRB Ray Bourque
CQRD Rick DiPietro
CQRH Ron Hextall
CQRL Roberto Luongo
CQRM Ryan Miller
CQRN Rick Nash
CQRO Luc Robitaille
CQRS Ryan Smyth
CQSA Borje Salming
CQSC Sidney Crosby
CQSF Sergei Federov
CQSG Simon Gagne
CQSH Brendan Shanahan
CQSK Saku Koivu
CQSM Miroslav Satan
CQSP Jason Spezza
CQSS Scott Stevens
CQST Steve Shutt
CQSU Mats Sundin
CQTE Tony Esposito
CQTH Jose Theodore
CQTS Teemu Selanne
CQTV Tomas Vokoun
CQVL Vincent Lecavalier
CQWG Wayne Gretzky

2006-07 The Cup Enshrinements

STATED PRINT RUN 50 SER.#'d SETS

EAK Anze Kopitar	25.00	60.00
EAR Andrew Raycroft	15.00	40.00
EBO Bobby Orr	125.00	250.00
EBP Benoit Pouliot	15.00	40.00
ECD Chris Drury	10.00	25.00
ECN Cam Neely	20.00	50.00
ECW Cam Ward	15.00	40.00
EDB Dustin Boyd	10.00	25.00
EDH Dominik Hasek	25.00	60.00
EDP Dion Phaneuf	20.00	50.00
EDS Drew Stafford	15.00	40.00
EEM Evgeni Malkin	60.00	120.00
EES Eric Staal	15.00	40.00
EFM Frank Mahovlich	15.00	40.00
EGH Gordie Howe	40.00	100.00
EGL Guillaume Latendresse	20.00	50.00
EGR Wayne Gretzky	150.00	250.00
EHE Dany Heatley		
EHZ Henrik Zetterberg	30.00	60.00
EIK Ilya Kovalchuk	25.00	60.00
EJB Johnny Bucyk	10.00	25.00
EJC Jonathan Cheechoo	15.00	40.00
EJG Jean-Sebastian Giguere	20.00	50.00
EJI Jarome Iginla	20.00	50.00
EJK Jari Kurri		
EJM Joe Mullen	10.00	25.00
EJS Jordan Staal	30.00	80.00
EJT Joe Thornton	25.00	60.00
EKL Kari Lehtonen	15.00	40.00
ELR Larry Robinson	10.00	25.00
EMB Martin Brodeur	40.00	100.00
EMD Marcel Dionne	15.00	40.00
EMF Marc-Andre Fleury	20.00	50.00
EMG Marian Gaborik	20.00	50.00
EML Mario Lemieux	75.00	150.00
EMR Michael Ryder	10.00	25.00
EMS Marek Svatos	10.00	25.00
EMT Marty Turco	15.00	40.00
ENL Nicklas Lidstrom	20.00	50.00
EPK Phil Kessel	20.00	50.00
EPL Pat LaFontaine	20.00	50.00
EPR Patrick Roy	75.00	150.00
EPS Paul Stastny	25.00	60.00
ERA Alexander Radulov	30.00	60.00
ERB Ray Bourque	30.00	80.00
ERH Ron Hextall	15.00	40.00
ERL Roberto Luongo		
ERM Ryan Miller	20.00	50.00
ERN Rick Nash	20.00	50.00
ERS Ryan Smyth	15.00	40.00
ESC Sidney Crosby	150.00	300.00
ESS Steve Shutt	10.00	25.00
EST Scott Stevens	15.00	40.00
ETE Tony Esposito	20.00	50.00
ETV Tomas Vokoun	15.00	40.00
ETZ Travis Zajac	15.00	40.00
EVA Thomas Vanek	15.00	40.00
EVL Vincent Lecavalier	20.00	50.00
EVT Vesa Toskala	15.00	40.00
EWG Wayne Gretzky	150.00	250.00

2006-07 The Cup Gold

*GOLD: 1X TO 2.5X HI COLUMN
STATED PRINT RUN 25 #'d SETS

1 Teemu Selanne	15.00	40.00
2 Jean-Sebastian Giguere	12.00	30.00
3 Kari Lehtonen	15.00	40.00
4 Ilya Kovalchuk	20.00	50.00
5 Phil Esposito	20.00	50.00
6 Don Cherry		
7 Ray Bourque	25.00	60.00
8 Bobby Orr	50.00	100.00
9 Cam Neely	20.00	50.00
10 Patrice Bergeron	15.00	40.00
11 Johnny Bucyk		25.00
12 Ryan Miller	15.00	40.00
13 Gilbert Perreault	15.00	40.00
14 Jarome Iginla	20.00	50.00
15 Miikka Kiprusoff	15.00	40.00
16 Al MacInnis	8.00	20.00
17 Eric Staal	15.00	40.00
18 Cam Ward	15.00	40.00
19 Bobby Hull	25.00	60.00
20 Tony Esposito	15.00	40.00
21 Stan Mikita	15.00	40.00
22 Joe Sakic	30.00	80.00
23 Patrick Roy	40.00	100.00
24 Rick Nash	15.00	40.00
25 Sergei Fedorov	15.00	40.00
26 Mike Modano	15.00	40.00
27 Dominik Hasek	25.00	60.00
28 Henrik Zetterberg	15.00	40.00
29 Gordie Howe	30.00	80.00
30 Scotty Bowman		25.00
31 Ted Lindsay	8.00	20.00
32 Red Kelly	8.00	20.00
33 Ales Hemsky	8.00	20.00
34 Grant Fuhr	20.00	50.00
35 Jari Kurri	20.00	50.00
36 Ed Belfour	15.00	40.00
37 Wayne Gretzky	50.00	150.00
38 Rob Blake	12.00	30.00
39 Marcel Dionne	15.00	40.00
40 Luc Robitaille	12.00	30.00
41 Rogie Vachon	15.00	40.00
42 Dino Ciccarelli		20.00
43 Marian Gaborik	20.00	50.00
44 Saku Koivu	15.00	40.00
45 Michael Ryder	12.00	30.00
46 Guy Lafleur	25.00	60.00
47 Larry Robinson	12.00	30.00
48 Jean Beliveau	20.00	50.00
49 Jacques Lemaire		20.00
50 Paul Kariya	15.00	40.00
51 Tomas Vokoun	12.00	30.00
52 Martin Brodeur	40.00	100.00
53 Scott Stevens	10.00	25.00
54 Alexei Yashin	8.00	20.00
55 Al Arbour	8.00	20.00
56 Mike Bossy	12.00	30.00
57 Billy Smith	15.00	40.00
58 Denis Potvin	12.00	30.00
59 Jaromir Jagr	25.00	60.00
60 Brendan Shanahan	15.00	40.00
61 Henrik Lundqvist	20.00	50.00
62 Gump Worsley	12.00	30.00
63 Andy Bathgate	8.00	20.00
64 Jason Spezza	15.00	40.00
65 Dany Heatley	20.00	50.00
66 Peter Forsberg	25.00	60.00
67 Simon Gagne	15.00	40.00
68 Bernie Parent		30.00
69 Bobby Clarke	15.00	40.00
70 Ron Hextall	12.00	30.00
71 Jeremy Roenick	20.00	50.00
72 Shane Doan	8.00	20.00
73 Sidney Crosby	100.00	200.00
74 Marc-Andre Fleury	20.00	50.00
75 Mario Lemieux	40.00	100.00
76 Peter Stastny	8.00	20.00
77 Joe Thornton	25.00	60.00
78 Jonathan Cheechoo	15.00	40.00
79 Patrick Marleau	12.00	30.00
80 Bernie Federko		20.00
81 Vincent Lecavalier	15.00	40.00
82 Mats Sundin	15.00	40.00
83 Frank Mahovlich	15.00	40.00
84 Darryl Sittler	15.00	40.00
85 Johnny Bower	12.00	30.00
86 Borje Salming	12.00	30.00
87 Roberto Luongo	20.00	50.00
88 Markus Naslund	15.00	40.00
89 Alexander Ovechkin	40.00	100.00
90 Dale Hawerchuk	8.00	20.00

2006-07 The Cup Gold Patches

STATED PRINT RUN 10 SER.#'d SETS
NOT PRICED DUE TO SCARCITY
1 Teemu Selanne
2 Jean-Sebastian Giguere
3 Kari Lehtonen
4 Ilya Kovalchuk
5 Phil Esposito
7 Ray Bourque
9 Cam Neely
10 Patrice Bergeron
12 Ryan Miller
13 Gilbert Perreault
14 Jarome Iginla
15 Miikka Kiprusoff
16 Al MacInnis
17 Eric Staal
18 Cam Ward
19 Bobby Hull
20 Tony Esposito
21 Stan Mikita
22 Joe Sakic
23 Patrick Roy
24 Rick Nash
25 Sergei Fedorov
26 Mike Modano
27 Dominik Hasek
28 Henrik Zetterberg
29 Gordie Howe
33 Ales Hemsky
34 Grant Fuhr
35 Jari Kurri
36 Ed Belfour
37 Wayne Gretzky
38 Rob Blake
39 Marcel Dionne
40 Luc Robitaille
42 Dino Ciccarelli
43 Marian Gaborik
44 Saku Koivu
45 Michael Ryder
46 Guy Lafleur
47 Larry Robinson
50 Paul Kariya
51 Tomas Vokoun
52 Martin Brodeur
53 Scott Stevens
54 Alexei Yashin
56 Mike Bossy
57 Billy Smith
58 Denis Potvin
59 Jaromir Jagr
60 Brendan Shanahan
61 Henrik Lundqvist
62 Gump Worsley
64 Jason Spezza
65 Dany Heatley
66 Peter Forsberg
67 Simon Gagne
69 Bobby Clarke
70 Ron Hextall
71 Jeremy Roenick
72 Shane Doan
73 Sidney Crosby
74 Marc-Andre Fleury
75 Mario Lemieux
76 Peter Stastny
77 Joe Thornton
78 Jonathan Cheechoo
79 Patrick Marleau
80 Bernie Federko
81 Vincent Lecavalier
82 Mats Sundin
84 Darryl Sittler
85 Johnny Bower
86 Borje Salming
87 Roberto Luongo
88 Markus Naslund
89 Alexander Ovechkin
90 Dale Hawerchuk

2006-07 The Cup Gold Rainbow Autographed Rookie Patches

109 Shane O'Brien/37	30.00	80.00
110 Ryan Shannon/38	30.00	80.00
111 David McKee/41	30.00	80.00
112 Mark Stuart/45	25.00	60.00
113 Matt Lashoff/49	25.00	60.00
114 Drew Stafford/32	60.00	150.00
115 Clarke MacArthur/41		
116 Michael Funk/3		
117 Brandon Prust/37	20.00	60.00
118 Dustin Boyd/41	30.00	80.00
119 Dustin Byfuglien/52	100.00	175.00
120 Dave Bolland/36	50.00	100.00
121 Michael Blunden/28	30.00	80.00
122 Filip Novak/17	25.00	60.00
123 Fredrik Norrena/30	30.00	100.00
124 Niklas Grossman/2		
125 Loui Eriksson/21		
126 Tomas Kopecky/32	30.00	100.00
127 Stefan Liv/32	25.00	60.00
128 Patrick Thoresen/28	30.00	80.00
129 Marc-Antoine Pouliot/36	30.00	80.00
130 Ladislav Smid/5		
131 Janis Sprukts/38	30.00	80.00
132 Jeff Drouin-Deslauriers/39	25.00	60.00
133 David Booth/46	25.00	60.00
134 Konstantin Pushkaryov/5		
135 Patrick O'Sullivan/12		
136 Benoit Pouliot/67	25.00	60.00
137 Niklas Backstrom/32	50.00	150.00
138 Guillaume Latendresse/84	60.00	120.00
139 Shea Weber/6		
140 Johnny Oduya/29	30.00	80.00
141 Travis Zajac/19		
142 Masi Marjamaki/58	30.00	80.00
143 Nigel Dawes/10		
144 Jarkko Immonen/38	25.00	60.00
145 Josh Hennessy/36	30.00	80.00
146 Ryan Potulny/11		
147 Jussi Timonen/46	25.00	60.00
148 Keith Yandle/3		
149 Michel Ouellet/7		
150 Noah Welch/4		
151 Kristopher Letang/58	75.00	150.00
152 Joe Pavelski/53	100.00	200.00
153 Matt Carle/18		
154 Marc-Edouard Vlasic/44	20.00	80.00
155 Yan Stastny/43	25.00	60.00
156 Marek Schwarz/40		
157 Roman Polak/46	25.00	60.00
158 Karri Ramo/31	30.00	80.00
159 Blair Jones/49	20.00	50.00
160 Brendan Bell/36	25.00	60.00
161 Ian White/7		
162 Ben Ondrus/46	30.00	80.00
163 Jeremy Williams/48	30.00	80.00
164 Miroslav Kopriva/31	25.00	60.00
165 Luc Bourdon/4		
166 Jesse Schultz/20	30.00	80.00
167 Alexander Edler/23	50.00	100.00
168 Eric Fehr/3		
169 Jordan Staal/11	800.00	1200.00
170 Phil Kessel/81	125.00	300.00
171 Evgeni Malkin/71	600.00	1200.00
172 Paul Stastny/26	300.00	600.00
173 Anze Kopitar/11	500.00	750.00
174 Alexander Radulov/47	150.00	300.00

2006-07 The Cup Gold Rainbow Autographed Rookies

PRINT RUNS VARY

91 Nate Thompson/52	10.00	25.00
92 Mike Brown/70	10.00	25.00
93 Mike Card/33	10.00	25.00
94 Adam Dennis/35		
95 Carsen Germyn/39	10.00	25.00
96 Adam Burish/37	8.00	20.00
97 Drew Larman/50	10.00	25.00
98 Jonas Johansson/45	8.00	20.00
99 Joel Perrault/26	10.00	25.00
100 Mikko Lehtonen/42	8.00	20.00
101 Alex Brooks/8		
102 Frank Doyle/1		
103 Billy Thompson/31		
104 Kelly Guard/32	12.00	30.00
105 David Printz/28	12.00	30.00
106 D.J. King/19	15.00	40.00
107 Jean-Francois Racine/35	12.00	30.00
108 Nathan McIver/45	10.00	25.00

2006-07 The Cup Hardware Heroes

PRINT RUNS VARY
NOT PRICED DUE TO SCARCITY
HHAB Andy Bathgate/1
HHEL Elmer Lach/1
HHJL Jacques Lemaire/2
HHMS Milt Schmidt/1
HHPP Pierre Pilote/3
HHBO1 Bobby Orr/8
HHBO2 Bobby Orr/1
HHBO3 Bobby Orr/2
HHBO4 Bobby Orr/3
HHBO5 Bobby Orr/2

2006-07 The Cup Hardware Heroes Patches

PRINT RUNS VARY
NOT PRICED DUE TO SCARCITY
HHCW Cam Ward/1
HHJC Jonathan Cheechoo/1
HHJK Jari Kurri/1
HHJT Joe Thornton/1
HHLR Larry Robinson/2
HHNL Nicklas Lidstrom/4
HHSM Stan Mikita/2
HHML1 Mario Lemieux/1
HHML2 Mario Lemieux/2
HHML3 Mario Lemieux/6
HHML4 Mario Lemieux/2

2006-07 The Cup Honorable Numbers

PRINT RUNS VARY
LOWER PRINT RUNS NOT PRICED DUE TO SCARCITY

HNAH Ales Hemsky/83	25.00	60.00
HNAK Anze Kopitar/11		
HNAM Al MacInnis/2		
HNAO Adam Oates/12		
HNAR Andrew Raycroft/1		
HNBC Bobby Clarke/16		
HNBL Rob Blake/4		
HNBS Billy Smith/31	50.00	100.00
HNCH Jonathan Cheechoo/14		
HNCN Cam Neely/8		
HNCW Cam Ward/30	40.00	80.00
HNDC Dino Ciccarelli/20	40.00	80.00
HNDE Denis Savard/18	60.00	125.00
HNDH Dale Hawerchuk/10		
HNDS Darryl Sittler/27	40.00	80.00
HNDW Doug Wilson/24	40.00	80.00
HNEM Evgeni Malkin/71	150.00	300.00
HNEN Evgeni Nabokov/20	50.00	100.00
HNES Eric Staal/12		
HNGF Grant Fuhr/31	50.00	100.00
HNGH Gordie Howe/9		
HNGL Guillaume Latendresse/84	40.00	80.00
HNGO Scott Gomez/23	50.00	100.00
HNGP Gilbert Perreault/11		
HNHA Dominik Hasek/39	50.00	100.00
HNHE Dany Heatley/15		
HNHL Henrik Lundqvist/30	100.00	200.00
HNHM Milan Hejduk/23	50.00	100.00
HNHZ Henrik Zetterberg/40	75.00	150.00
HNIK Ilya Kovalchuk/17	75.00	150.00
HNJC Jeff Carter/17	60.00	125.00
HNJG Jean-Sebastien Giguere/35	40.00	80.00
HNJI Jarome Iginla/12		
HNJK Jari Kurri/17	125.00	250.00
HNJM Joe Mullen/7		
HNJR Jordan Staal/11		
HNJS Jason Spezza/19		
HNJT Joe Thornton/19	125.00	250.00
HNKL Kari Lehtonen/32	50.00	100.00
HNLA Guy Lafleur/10		
HNLE Loui Eriksson/21	25.00	60.00
HNLM Lanny McDonald/9		
HNLR Larry Robinson/19	40.00	80.00
HNMA Stan Mikita/21	60.00	125.00
HNMB Martin Brodeur/30	150.00	300.00
HNMC Matt Carle/18	60.00	125.00
HNMD Marcel Dionne/16	60.00	125.00
HNMG Marian Gaborik/10		
HNMH Martin Havlat/24	25.00	60.00
HNMI Mike Bossy/22	50.00	100.00
HNML Mario Lemieux/66	125.00	250.00
HNMM Mike Modano/9		
HNMN Markus Naslund/19	75.00	150.00
HNMR Michael Ryder/73	25.00	60.00
HNMS Martin St. Louis/26	50.00	100.00
HNMT Marty Turco/35	25.00	60.00
HNMU Larry Murphy/55	15.00	40.00
HNNL Nicklas Lidstrom/5		
HNNZ Nikolai Zherdev/13		
HNOV Alexander Ovechkin/8		
HNPA Paul Henderson/19	50.00	100.00
HNPB Patrice Bergeron/37	40.00	80.00
HNPE Patrik Elias/26	25.00	60.00
HNPH Dion Phaneuf/3		
HNPK Phil Kessel/81	40.00	80.00
HNPL Pat LaFontaine/16		
HNPM Patrick Marleau/12	50.00	100.00
HNPO Patrick O'Sullivan/12	100.00	175.00
HNPR Patrick Roy/33	175.00	350.00
HNPS Paul Stastny/26	100.00	200.00
HNRA Alexander Radulov/47	60.00	125.00
HNRE Ron Ellis/6		
HNRH Ron Hextall/27	50.00	100.00
HNRL Roberto Luongo/1		
HNRM Ryan Miller/30	75.00	150.00
HNRN Rick Nash/61	50.00	100.00
HNRO Luc Robitaille/20		
HNRS Ryan Smyth/94	40.00	80.00
HNSA Borje Salming/21	40.00	80.00
HNSC Sidney Crosby/87	250.00	400.00
HNSG Simon Gagne/12		
HNSH Steve Shutt/22	25.00	60.00
HNSK Saku Koivu/11		
HNSM Miroslav Satan/81	25.00	60.00
HNSS Scott Stevens/4		
HNST Peter Stastny/26	40.00	80.00
HNSV Marek Svatos/40	25.00	60.00
HNSW Shea Weber/6		
HNTE Tony Esposito/35	60.00	125.00
HNTH Jose Theodore/60	12.00	30.00
HNTV Tomas Vokoun/29	40.00	80.00
HNTW Tiger Williams/22	40.00	80.00

HNVL Vincent Lecavalier/4
HNWG Wayne Gretzky/99 250.00 500.00
HNZC Zdeno Chara/33 25.00 60.00

2006-07 The Cup Jerseys

STATED PRINT RUN 25 SER.#'d SETS
1 Teemu Selanne 20.00 50.00
2 Jean-Sebastian Giguere 12.00 30.00
3 Kari Lehtonen 10.00 25.00
4 Ilya Kovalchuk 10.00 25.00
7 Ray Bourque 20.00 50.00
9 Cam Neely 10.00 25.00
10 Patrice Bergeron 10.00 25.00
12 Ryan Miller 10.00 25.00
13 Gilbert Perreault
14 Jarome Iginla 10.00 25.00
15 Miikka Kiprusoff 20.00 50.00
16 Al MacInnis 10.00 25.00
17 Eric Staal 10.00 25.00
18 Cam Ward 10.00 25.00
19 Bobby Hull 20.00 50.00
20 Tony Esposito 10.00 25.00
21 Stan Mikita 10.00 25.00
22 Joe Sakic 25.00 60.00
23 Patrick Roy 40.00 100.00
24 Rick Nash 12.00 30.00
25 Sergei Fedorov 12.00 30.00
26 Mike Modano 10.00 25.00
27 Dominik Hasek 15.00 40.00
28 Henrik Zetterberg 15.00 40.00
29 Gordie Howe 30.00 60.00
33 Ales Hemsky 10.00 25.00
34 Grant Fuhr 12.00 30.00
35 Jari Kurri 20.00 50.00
36 Ed Belfour 12.00 30.00
37 Wayne Gretzky 100.00 225.00
38 Rob Blake 10.00 25.00
39 Marcel Dionne 12.00 30.00
40 Luc Robitaille 15.00 40.00
41 Rogie Vachon 15.00 40.00
42 Dino Ciccarelli 6.00 15.00
43 Marian Gaborik 20.00 50.00
44 Saku Koivu 20.00 50.00
45 Michael Ryder 10.00 25.00
46 Guy Lafleur 20.00 50.00
47 Larry Robinson 6.00 15.00
48 Jean Beliveau 25.00 60.00
50 Paul Kariya 15.00 40.00
51 Tomas Vokoun 15.00 40.00
52 Martin Brodeur 30.00 80.00
53 Scott Stevens 10.00 25.00
54 Alexei Yashin 6.00 15.00
56 Mike Bossy 15.00 40.00
57 Billy Smith 10.00 25.00
59 Jaromir Jagr 20.00 50.00
60 Brendan Shanahan 15.00 40.00
61 Henrik Lundqvist 25.00 50.00
62 Gump Worsley 12.00 30.00
64 Jason Spezza 10.00 25.00
65 Dany Heatley 12.00 30.00
66 Peter Forsberg 20.00 50.00
67 Simon Gagne 15.00 40.00
69 Bobby Clarke 12.00 30.00
70 Ron Hextall 15.00 40.00
71 Jeremy Roenick
72 Shane Doan 6.00 15.00
73 Sidney Crosby 100.00 200.00
74 Marc-Andre Fleury 20.00 40.00
75 Mario Lemieux 40.00 100.00
76 Peter Stastny 6.00 15.00
77 Joe Thornton 15.00 40.00
78 Jonathan Cheechoo 10.00 25.00
79 Patrick Marleau 15.00 40.00
80 Bernie Federko
81 Vincent Lecavalier 20.00 50.00
82 Mats Sundin 10.00 25.00
83 Frank Mahovlich 10.00 25.00
84 Darryl Sittler 10.00 25.00
86 Borje Salming 10.00 25.00
87 Roberto Luongo 25.00 60.00
88 Markus Naslund 10.00 25.00
89 Alexander Ovechkin 30.00 80.00
90 Dale Hawerchuk 15.00 40.00

2006-07 The Cup Legendary Cuts

PRINT RUNS VARY
NOT PRICED DUE TO SCARCITY
LCAB Sid Abel
LCFS Frank Selke
LCHD Hap Day/5
LCTH Tim Horton

2006-07 The Cup Limited Logos

STATED PRINT RUN 50 SER.#'d SETS
UNIQUE SWATCHES MAY EARN SUBSTANTIAL PREMIUM
SINGLE COLOR SWATCH: .5X TO 1X LO
LLAF Alexander Frolov 75.00 150.00
LLAH Ales Hemsky 40.00 80.00
LLAK Anze Kopitar 175.00 350.00
LLAM Al MacInnis 60.00 125.00
LLAO Adam Oates 40.00 80.00
LLAR Andrew Raycroft 40.00 80.00
LLAT Alex Tanguay 50.00 100.00
LLAY Alexei Yashin 40.00 80.00
LLBB Brad Boyes 25.00 60.00
LLBC Bobby Clarke 50.00 100.00
LLBF Bernie Federko 50.00 100.00
LLBG Brian Gionta 40.00 80.00
LLBL Bill Ranford 50.00 100.00
LLBO Mike Bossy 75.00 150.00
LLBS Billy Smith 40.00 80.00
LLCA Jeff Carter 75.00 150.00
LLCN Cam Neely 100.00 200.00
LLCW Cam Ward 40.00 80.00
LLDA David Aebischer 40.00 80.00
LLDB Daniel Briere 60.00 125.00
LLDC Dino Ciccarelli 40.00 80.00
LLDE Denis Savard 60.00 125.00
LLDG Doug Gilmour 75.00 150.00
LLDH Dale Hawerchuk 50.00 100.00
LLDO Dominik Hasek 60.00 125.00
LLDR Dwayne Roloson 40.00 80.00
LLDS Darryl Sittler 40.00 80.00
LLDW Doug Wilson 25.00 60.00
LLEM Evgeni Malkin 200.00 400.00
LLES Eric Staal 25.00 60.00
LLGA Glenn Anderson 25.00 60.00
LLGE Martin Gerber
LLGH Gordie Howe/25 800.00 1500.00
LLGL Guy Lafleur 60.00 125.00
LLGP Gilbert Perreault 50.00 100.00
LLHE Dany Heatley
LLHL Henrik Lundqvist 100.00 200.00
LLHZ Henrik Zetterberg 40.00 80.00
LLIK Ilya Kovalchuk 75.00 150.00
LLJC Jonathan Cheechoo 40.00 80.00
LLJG Jean-Sebastien Giguere 60.00 120.00
LLJI Jarome Iginla 75.00 150.00
LLJK Jari Kurri 60.00 125.00
LLJM Joe Mullen 25.00 60.00
LLJR Jeremy Roenick 50.00 100.00
LLJS Jordan Staal 175.00 300.00
LLJT Joe Thornton 60.00 120.00
LLKL Kari Lehtonen 40.00 80.00
LLLM Lanny McDonald 40.00 80.00
LLLR Larry Robinson 40.00 80.00
LLMB Martin Brodeur 125.00 250.00
LLMG Marian Gaborik 40.00 80.00
LLMH Martin Havlat 25.00 60.00
LLMI Milan Hejduk 25.00 60.00
LLML Mario Lemieux 200.00 350.00
LLMM Mike Modano 50.00 100.00
LLMR Michael Ryder 25.00 60.00
LLMS Marek Svatos 25.00 60.00
LLMT Marty Turco 25.00 60.00
LLMU Larry Murphy
LLNK Nikolai Khabibulin 40.00 80.00
LLNL Nicklas Lidstrom 60.00 125.00
LLNZ Nikolai Zherdev
LLON Owen Nolan 40.00 80.00
LLOV Alexander Ovechkin 150.00 250.00
LLPA Paul Henderson 75.00 150.00
LLPB Patrice Bergeron 40.00 80.00
LLPE Patrik Elias 25.00 60.00
LLPH Dion Phaneuf 125.00 250.00
LLPK Phil Kessel/25 100.00 175.00
LLPL Pat LaFontaine 60.00 125.00
LLPM Patrick Marleau 40.00 80.00
LLPR Patrick Roy 200.00 400.00
LLPS Peter Stastny 40.00 80.00
LLRL Roberto Luongo 60.00 125.00
LLRM Ryan Miller 100.00 200.00
LLRN Rick Nash 100.00 200.00
LLRS Ryan Smyth 40.00 80.00
LLRV Rogie Vachon 50.00 100.00
LLSA Borje Salming 50.00 100.00
LLSC Sidney Crosby 400.00 700.00
LLSG Simon Gagne 40.00 80.00
LLSH Steve Shutt 40.00 80.00
LLSK Saku Koivu 40.00 80.00
LLSM Miroslav Satan 40.00 80.00
LLSS Scott Stevens 40.00 80.00
LLST Martin St. Louis 50.00 100.00
LLTB Todd Bertuzzi 40.00 80.00
LLTH Jose Theodore 25.00 50.00
LLTU Darcy Tucker 50.00 100.00
LLTV Tomas Vokoun 50.00 100.00
LLVL Vincent Lecavalier 100.00 200.00
LLVT Vesa Toskala 40.00 80.00
LLWC Wendel Clark 75.00 150.00
LLWG Wayne Gretzky 300.00 600.00
LLZC Zdeno Chara 25.00 60.00

2006-07 The Cup NHL Shields Duals

STATED PRINT RUN 1 SER.#'d SET
NOT PRICED DUE TO SCARCITY
DSHAM Alexander Radulov
Mikko Lehtonen
DSHAS Daniel Alfredsson
Jason Spezza
DSHBE Luc Bourdon
Alexander Edler
DSHBN Joe Nieuwendyk
Jay Bouwmeester
DSHBW Noah Welch
Luc Bourdon
DSHCO Sidney Crosby
Alexander Ovechkin
DSHCV Matt Carle
Marc-Edouard Vlasic
DSHCW Shea Weber
Matt Carle
DSHDA Maxim Afinogenov
Chris Drury
DSHDB Dustin Boyd
Brandon Prust
DSHDG Pavol Demitra
Marian Gaborik
DSHDJ Curtis Joseph
Shane Doan
DSHDL Nicklas Lidstrom
Pavel Datsyuk
DSHDS Miroslav Satan
Rick DiPietro
DSHDY Alexei Yashin
Rick DiPietro
DSHEC Ed Belfour
Curtis Joseph
DSHEM Eric Lindros
Mike Ribeiro
DSHEO Ed Belfour
Olli Jokinen
DSHFC Peter Forsberg
Jeff Carter
DSHFD Pavel Datsyuk
Sergei Fedorov
DSHFG Peter Forsberg
Simon Gagne
DSHFL Nicklas Lidstrom
Peter Forsberg
DSHFP Eric Fehr
Ryan Potulny
DSHFZ Nikolai Zherdev
Sergei Fedorov
DSHGF Manny Fernandez
Marian Gaborik
DSHHD Henrik Sedin
Daniel Sedin
DSHHR Martin Havlat
Tuomo Ruutu
DSHIB Jarome Iginla
Dustin Boyd
DSHJA Jordan Staal
Anze Kopitar
DSHJB Brendan Shanahan
Jaromir Jagr
DSHJD Jason Spezza
Dany Heatley
DSHJJ Curtis Joseph
Ed Jovanovski
DSHJK Jordan Staal
Kristopher Letang
DSHJN Curtis Joseph
Ladislav Nagy
DSHJO Joe Sakic
Joe Thornton
DSHJS Jaromir Jagr
Martin Straka
DSHKC Mike Cammalleri
Anze Kopitar
DSHKH Marian Hossa
Ilya Kovalchuk
DSHKK Saku Koivu
Alexei Kovalev
DSHKO Phil Kessel
Patrick O'Sullivan
DSHKR Paul Kariya
Alexander Radulov
DSHKS Paul Kariya
Steve Sullivan
DSHKZ Olaf Kolzig
Richard Zednik
DSHLC Chris Chelios
Nicklas Lidstrom
DSHLE Martin Brodeur
Zach Parise
DSHLL Roberto Luongo
Trevor Linden
DSHLP Guillaume Latendresse
Benoit Pouliot
DSHLR Vincent Lecavalier
Brad Richards
DSHLS Manny Legace
Curtis Sanford
DSHLY Chris Drury
Drew Stafford
DSHLZ Sergei Zubov
Jere Lehtinen
DSHML Mike Modano
Eric Lindros
DSHNL Pascal LeClaire
Rick Nash
DSHNR Joe Nieuwendyk
Gary Roberts
DSHOS Shane O'Brien
Ryan Shannon
DSHOW Michel Ouellet
Noah Welch
DSHPA Phil Kessel
Anze Kopitar
DSHPH Derian Hatcher
Joni Pitkanen
DSHPJ Paul Stastny
Jordan Staal
DSHPL Ladislav Smid
Patrick Thoresen
DSHPN Chris Pronger
Scott Niedermayer
DSHPT Raffi Torres
Fernando Pisani
DSHPY Yan Stastny
Phil Kessel
DSHRE Martin Erat
Alexander Radulov
DSHRL John LeClair
Mark Recchi
DSHRP Ryan Smyth
Patrick Thoresen
DSHRW Robert Lang
Kris Draper
DSHSA Mats Sundin
Daniel Alfredsson
DSHSD Brendan Shanahan
Nigel Dawes
DSHSF Joe Sakic
Peter Forsberg
DSHSG Teemu Selanne
Jean-Sebastien Giguere
DSHSH Joe Sakic
Milan Hejduk
DSHSK Teemu Selanne
Paul Kariya
DSHSL Mark Stuart
Matt Lashoff
DSHSP Teemu Selanne
Chris Pronger
DSHSR Brian Rafalski
Scott Stevens
DSHSS Mats Sundin
Alexander Steen
DSHST Joe Sakic
Jose Theodore
DSHTO Mats Sundin
Andrew Raycroft
DSHTP Michael Peca
Darcy Tucker
DSHTS Jose Theodore
Paul Stastny
DSHTT Hannu Toivonen
Tim Thomas
DSHTW Doug Weight
Keith Tkachuk
DSHVK Paul Kariya
Tomas Vokoun
DSHWB Rod Brind'Amour
Cam Ward
DSHWG Doug Weight
Bill Guerin
DSHZD Travis Zajac
Nigel Dawes
DSHZG Sergei Zubov
Sergei Gonchar

2006-07 The Cup Property of

Confirmed sales include: Larry Robinson, $272.
STATED PRINT RUN 1 SER.#'d SET
NOT PRICED DUE TO SCARCITY
POAK Anze Kopitar
POAM Al MacInnis
POBO Bobby Orr
POBU Peter Budaj
POCG Clark Gillies
PODC Dino Ciccarelli
PODH Dale Hawerchuk
PODT Dave Taylor
POEL Eric Lindros
POEM Evgeni Malkin
POES Eric Staal
POGH Gordie Howe
POHA Dominik Hasek
POHE Dany Heatley
POKE Phil Kessel
POKL Kari Lehtonen
POLR Larry Robinson
POMB Martin Brodeur
POMD Marcel Dionne
POML Mario Lemieux
POMM Mike Modano
POMT Marty Turco
PONL Nicklas Lidstrom
POPR Patrick Roy
POPT Pierre Turgeon
PORB Rob Blake
PORG Ryan Getzlaf
POSD Bobby Clarke
POST Jordan Staal
POTV Thomas Vanek
POWG Wayne Gretzky
POWW Wojtek Wolski

2006-07 The Cup Rookies Black

STATED PRINT RUN 1 SER.#'d SET
NOT PRICED DUE TO SCARCITY
91 Nate Thompson
92 Mike Brown
93 Mike Card
94 Adam Dennis
95 Carsen Germyn
96 Adam Burish
97 Drew Larman
98 Jonas Johansson
99 Joel Perrault
100 Mikko Lehtonen
101 Alex Brooks
102 Frank Doyle
103 Billy Thompson
104 Kelly Guard
105 David Printz
106 D.J. King
107 Jean-Francois Racine
108 Nathan McIver
109 Shane O'Brien
110 Ryan Shannon
111 David McKee
112 Mark Stuart
113 Matt Lashoff
114 Drew Stafford
115 Clarke MacArthur
116 Michael Funk
117 Brandon Prust
118 Dustin Boyd
119 Dustin Byfuglien
120 Dave Bolland
121 Michael Blunden
122 Filip Novak
123 Fredrik Norrena
124 Niklas Grossman
125 Loui Eriksson
126 Tomas Kopecky
127 Stefan Liv
128 Patrick Thoresen
129 Marc-Antoine Pouliot
130 Ladislav Smid
131 Janis Sprukts
132 Jeff Drouin-Deslauriers
133 David Booth
134 Konstantin Pushkaryov
135 Patrick O'Sullivan
136 Benoit Pouliot
137 Niklas Backstrom
138 Guillaume Latendresse
139 Shea Weber
140 Johnny Oduya
141 Travis Zajac
142 Masi Marjamaki
143 Nigel Dawes
144 Jarkko Immonen
145 Josh Hennessy
146 Ryan Potulny
147 Jussi Timonen
148 Keith Yandle
149 Michel Ouellet
150 Noah Welch
151 Kristopher Letang
152 Joe Pavelski
153 Matt Carle
154 Marc-Edouard Vlasic
155 Yan Stastny
156 Marek Schwarz
157 Roman Polak
158 Karri Ramo
159 Blair Jones
160 Brendan Bell
161 Ian White
162 Ben Ondrus
163 Jeremy Williams
164 Miroslav Kopriva
165 Luc Bourdon
166 Jesse Schultz
167 Alexander Edler
168 Eric Fehr
169 Jordan Staal
170 Phil Kessel
171 Evgeni Malkin
172 Paul Stastny
173 Anze Kopitar
174 Alexander Radulov

2006-07 The Cup Rookies Platinum

STATED PRINT RUN 25 SER.#'d SETS
91 Nate Thompson 8.00 20.00
92 Mike Brown 10.00 25.00
93 Mike Card 8.00 20.00
94 Adam Dennis 10.00 25.00
95 Carsen Germyn 8.00 20.00
96 Adam Burish 8.00 20.00
97 Drew Larman 8.00 20.00
98 Jonas Johansson 8.00 20.00
99 Joel Perrault 8.00 20.00
100 Mikko Lehtonen 8.00 20.00
101 Alex Brooks 8.00 20.00
102 Frank Doyle 10.00 25.00
103 Billy Thompson 10.00 25.00
104 Kelly Guard 10.00 25.00
105 David Printz 8.00 20.00
106 D.J. King 8.00 20.00
107 Jean-Francois Racine 10.00 25.00
108 Nathan McIver 8.00 20.00
109 Shane O'Brien 8.00 20.00
110 Ryan Shannon 8.00 20.00
111 David McKee 15.00 40.00
112 Mark Stuart 8.00 20.00
113 Matt Lashoff 10.00 25.00
114 Drew Stafford 30.00 80.00
115 Clarke MacArthur 8.00 20.00
116 Michael Funk 8.00 20.00
117 Brandon Prust 8.00 20.00
118 Dustin Boyd 15.00 40.00
119 Dustin Byfuglien 50.00 100.00
120 Dave Bolland 12.00 30.00
121 Michael Blunden 8.00 20.00
122 Filip Novak 8.00 20.00
123 Fredrik Norrena 15.00 40.00
124 Niklas Grossman 8.00 20.00
125 Loui Eriksson 10.00 25.00
126 Tomas Kopecky 15.00 40.00
127 Stefan Liv 15.00 40.00
128 Patrick Thoresen 15.00 40.00
129 Marc-Antoine Pouliot 15.00 40.00
130 Ladislav Smid 8.00 20.00
131 Janis Sprukts 8.00 20.00
132 Jeff Drouin-Deslauriers 10.00 25.00
133 David Booth 8.00 20.00
134 Konstantin Pushkaryov 8.00 20.00
135 Patrick O'Sullivan 15.00 40.00
136 Benoit Pouliot 15.00 40.00
137 Niklas Backstrom 30.00 60.00
138 Guillaume Latendresse 30.00 80.00
139 Shea Weber 15.00 40.00
140 Johnny Oduya 8.00 20.00
141 Travis Zajac 20.00 50.00
142 Masi Marjamaki 10.00 25.00
143 Nigel Dawes 8.00 20.00
144 Jarkko Immonen 8.00 20.00
145 Josh Hennessy 8.00 20.00
146 Ryan Potulny 15.00 40.00
147 Jussi Timonen 8.00 20.00
148 Keith Yandle 8.00 20.00
149 Michel Ouellet 15.00 40.00
150 Noah Welch 8.00 20.00
151 Kristopher Letang 15.00 40.00
152 Joe Pavelski 50.00 100.00
153 Matt Carle 15.00 40.00
154 Marc-Edouard Vlasic 15.00 40.00
155 Yan Stastny 8.00 20.00
156 Marek Schwarz 15.00 40.00
157 Roman Polak 8.00 20.00
158 Karri Ramo 10.00 25.00
159 Blair Jones 10.00 25.00
160 Brendan Bell 8.00 20.00
161 Ian White 8.00 20.00
162 Ben Ondrus 8.00 20.00
163 Jeremy Williams 8.00 20.00
164 Miroslav Kopriva 10.00 25.00
165 Luc Bourdon 15.00 40.00
166 Jesse Schultz 8.00 20.00
167 Alexander Edler 8.00 20.00
168 Eric Fehr 15.00 40.00
169 Jordan Staal 50.00 125.00
170 Phil Kessel 30.00 80.00
171 Evgeni Malkin 150.00 250.00
172 Paul Stastny 50.00 125.00
173 Anze Kopitar 50.00 125.00
174 Alexander Radulov 30.00 80.00

2006-07 The Cup Scripted Swatches

STATED PRINT RUN 25 SER.#'d SETS
SSAO Alexander Ovechkin 125.00 250.00
SSAR Andrew Raycroft 25.00 60.00
SSAT Alex Tanguay 40.00 80.00
SSBO Mike Bossy 50.00 100.00
SSBR Bill Ranford 40.00 80.00
SSBS Borje Salming 40.00 80.00
SSCD Chris Drury 30.00 60.00
SSCN Cam Neely 50.00 100.00
SSCW Cam Ward 40.00 80.00
SSDB Daniel Briere 40.00 80.00
SSDC Dino Ciccarelli 40.00 80.00
SSDH Dale Hawerchuk 40.00 80.00
SSDS Denis Savard 40.00 80.00
SSDT Dave Taylor/10 125.00 250.00
SSDW Dave Williams 20.00 50.00
SSEM Evgeni Malkin 150.00 250.00
SSES Eric Staal 30.00 60.00
SSGA Glenn Anderson 30.00 60.00
SSGC Gerry Cheevers 40.00 80.00
SSGF Grant Fuhr 40.00 80.00
SSGL Guy Lafleur 50.00 100.00
SSGP Gilbert Perreault 40.00 80.00
SSHA Dominik Hasek 50.00 100.00
SSHE Dany Heatley
SSHL Henrik Lundqvist 125.00 225.00
SSHZ Henrik Zetterberg 100.00 200.00
SSIK Ilya Kovalchuk 50.00 100.00
SSJC Jonathan Cheechoo 40.00 80.00
SSJG Jean-Sebastien Giguere 40.00 80.00
SSJI Jarome Iginla 60.00 125.00
SSJK Jari Kurri 50.00 100.00
SSJM Joe Mullen 20.00 50.00
SSJS Jason Spezza
SSJT Joe Thornton 60.00 125.00
SSLR Larry Robinson 40.00 80.00
SSMB Martin Brodeur 200.00 300.00
SSMD Marcel Dionne 40.00 80.00
SSMG Marian Gaborik
SSMH Martin Havlat 20.00 50.00
SSMI Milan Hejduk 40.00 80.00
SSML Mario Lemieux 150.00 300.00
SSMM Mike Modano 40.00 80.00
SSMN Markus Naslund 40.00 80.00
SSMR Michael Ryder 30.00 60.00
SSMS Martin St. Louis 30.00 60.00
SSMT Marty Turco 30.00 60.00
SSNL Nicklas Lidstrom 40.00 80.00
SSPB Patrice Bergeron 40.00 80.00
SSPH Dion Phaneuf 40.00 80.00
SSPK Phil Kessel 50.00 100.00
SSPL Pat LaFontaine 40.00 80.00
SSPM Patrick Marleau 25.00 60.00
SSPR Patrick Roy 175.00 350.00
SSRA Alexander Radulov 75.00 150.00
SSRB Ray Bourque 75.00 150.00
SSRE Ron Ellis 25.00 60.00
SSRH Ron Hextall 40.00 80.00
SSRL Roberto Luongo
SSRM Ryan Miller 50.00 100.00
SSRN Rick Nash 50.00 100.00
SSRO Luc Robitaille 50.00 100.00
SSRS Ryan Smyth 40.00 80.00
SSSC Sidney Crosby 250.00 400.00
SSSG Simon Gagne 40.00 80.00
SSSH Steve Shutt 20.00 50.00
SSSK Saku Koivu 50.00 100.00
SSSS Scott Stevens 60.00 125.00
SSST Jordan Staal 100.00 200.00
SSTE Tony Esposito 50.00 100.00
SSTH Jose Theodore 30.00 60.00
SSTV Tomas Vokoun 30.00 60.00
SSVL Vincent Lecavalier 60.00 125.00

2006-07 The Cup Scripted Swatches Duals

STATED PRINT RUN 5 SER.#'d SETS
NOT PRICED DUE TO SCARCITY
DSAR Ryan Smyth
Ales Hemsky
DSDB Darryl Sittler
Borje Salming
DSDR Luc Robitaille
Marcel Dionne
DSGC Simon Gagne
Jeff Carter
DSGH Wayne Gretzky
Gordie Howe
DSGL Mario Lemieux
Wayne Gretzky
DSHS Jason Spezza
Dany Heatley
DSKF Grant Fuhr
Jari Kurri
DSKL Ilya Kovalchuk
Kari Lehtonen
DSLM Mario Lemieux
Evgeni Malkin
DSLN Markus Naslund
Roberto Luongo
DSLR Guy Lafleur
Larry Robinson
DSLS Vincent Lecavalier
Martin St. Louis
DSMM Lanny McDonald
Al MacInnis
DSNB Cam Neely
Ray Bourque
DSOM Alexander Ovechkin
Evgeni Malkin
DSPP Peter Stastny
Paul Stastny
DSPR Patrick Roy
Ray Bourque
DSRB Patrick Roy
Martin Brodeur
DSSS Eric Staal
Jordan Staal
DSTC Joe Thornton
Jonathan Cheechoo
DSTI Jarome Iginla
Alex Tanguay
DSZL Nicklas Lidstrom
Henrik Zetterberg

2006-07 The Cup Signature Patches

STATED PRINT RUN 75 SER.#'d SETS
UNIQUE SWATCHES MAY EARN SUBSTANTIAL PREMIUM
WHITE SWATCHES: .5X TO 1X LO
SPAF Alexander Frolov 20.00 50.00
SPAH Ales Hemsky 20.00 50.00
SPAK Anze Kopitar 50.00 100.00
SPAM Al MacInnis 25.00 60.00
SPAO Alexander Ovechkin 125.00 250.00
SPAR Alexander Radulov 50.00 100.00
SPAT Alex Tanguay 25.00 60.00
SPBC Bobby Clarke 40.00 80.00
SPBR Martin Brodeur 100.00 175.00
SPBS Billy Smith 25.00 60.00
SPCH Cristobal Huet 25.00 60.00
SPCN Cam Neely 25.00 60.00
SPCW Cam Ward 25.00 60.00
SPDA David Aebischer 20.00 50.00
SPDB Daniel Briere 25.00 60.00
SPDC Dino Ciccarelli 25.00 60.00
SPDH Dale Hawerchuk 25.00 60.00
SPDI Dion Phaneuf 50.00 100.00
SPDS Denis Savard 25.00 60.00
SPDT Dave Taylor 40.00 80.00
SPDW Doug Wilson 15.00 40.00
SPEL Patrik Elias 15.00 40.00
SPEM Evgeni Malkin 150.00 250.00
SPES Eric Staal 20.00 50.00
SPGC Gerry Cheevers 40.00 80.00
SPGF Grant Fuhr 40.00 80.00
SPGH Gordie Howe/25 175.00 300.00
SPGL Guy Lafleur 25.00 60.00
SPGO Scott Gomez/25 20.00 50.00
SPGP Gilbert Perreault 25.00 60.00
SPHA Dominik Hasek 40.00 80.00
SPHE Dany Heatley
SPHZ Henrik Zetterberg 50.00 100.00
SPIK Ilya Kovalchuk 50.00 100.00
SPJC Jonathan Cheechoo 25.00 60.00
SPJG Jean-Sebastien Giguere 25.00 60.00
SPJI Jarome Iginla 40.00 80.00
SPJK Jari Kurri 20.00 50.00
SPJO Jordan Staal 75.00 150.00
SPJR Jeremy Roenick 25.00 60.00
SPJS Jason Spezza 40.00 80.00
SPJT Joe Thornton 40.00 80.00
SPKL Kari Lehtonen 25.00 60.00
SPLA Guillaume Latendresse 40.00 80.00
SPLB Luc Bourdon 30.00 60.00
SPLM Lanny McDonald 15.00 40.00
SPLR Larry Robinson 25.00 60.00
SPLX Mario Lemieux/25 250.00 400.00
SPMB Mike Bossy 40.00 80.00
SPMC Matt Carle 25.00 60.00
SPMD Marcel Dionne/25 75.00 150.00
SPMG Marian Gaborik 50.00 100.00
SPMI Milan Hejduk 25.00 60.00
SPMM Mike Modano 25.00 60.00
SPMR Michael Ryder 25.00 60.00
SPMS Martin St. Louis 20.00 50.00
SPMT Marty Turco 15.00 40.00
SPNL Nicklas Lidstrom 25.00 60.00
SPPA Brad Park 15.00 40.00
SPPB Patrice Bergeron 20.00 50.00
SPPH Paul Henderson 20.00 50.00
SPPK Phil Kessel 40.00 80.00
SPPM Patrick Marleau 20.00 50.00
SPPO Patrick O'Sullivan 30.00 60.00
SPPS Paul Stastny 75.00 150.00
SPRA Andrew Raycroft 12.00 30.00
SPRE Ron Ellis 15.00 40.00
SPRH Ron Hextall 25.00 60.00
SPRI Richard Brodeur 20.00 50.00
SPRL Roberto Luongo
SPRM Ryan Miller 25.00 60.00
SPRN Rick Nash 25.00 60.00
SPRO Luc Robitaille 40.00 80.00
SPRS Ryan Smyth 25.00 60.00
SPRV Rogie Vachon 25.00 60.00
SPSA Borje Salming 20.00 50.00
SPSC Sidney Crosby 250.00 500.00
SPSE Scott Stevens 25.00 60.00
SPSG Simon Gagne 20.00 50.00
SPSK Saku Koivu 20.00 50.00
SPSM Stan Mikita 25.00 60.00
SPSS Steve Shutt 20.00 50.00
SPST Peter Stastny 25.00 60.00
SPSU Brent Sutter 15.00 40.00
SPSV Marek Svatos 20.00 50.00
SPTB Todd Bertuzzi 20.00 50.00
SPTE Tony Esposito 25.00 60.00
SPTH Jose Theodore 15.00 40.00
SPTV Tomas Vokoun 25.00 60.00
SPVL Vincent Lecavalier 25.00 60.00
SPWG Wayne Gretzky/25 250.00 500.00

SPBO1 Ray Bourque 40.00 80.00
SPBO2 Ray Bourque 40.00 80.00
SPPR1 Patrick Roy 100.00 200.00
SPPR2 Patrick Roy 100.00 200.00

2006-07 The Cup Stanley Cup Signatures

STATED PRINT RUN 25 SER.#'d SETS
CSAA Al Arbour 30.00 60.00
CSAM Al MacInnis 40.00 80.00
CSAT Alex Tanguay 25.00 50.00
CSBA Bob Baun 30.00 60.00
CSBC Bobby Clarke 30.00 60.00
CSBD Butch Bouchard 40.00 80.00
CSBH Bobby Hull 50.00 100.00
CSBI Bill Ranford 40.00 100.00
CSBO Bobby Orr 300.00 400.00
CSBP Bernie Parent 40.00 80.00
CSBR Martin Brodeur 100.00 200.00
CSBS Billy Smith 40.00 80.00
CSBU Johnny Bucyk 40.00 80.00
CSCG Clark Gillies
CSCM Craig MacTavish 25.00 50.00
CSCS Clint Smith 60.00 125.00
CSCW Cam Ward 30.00 80.00
CSDG Doug Gilmour 30.00 60.00
CSDH Dominik Hasek 50.00 100.00
CSDP Denis Potvin 25.00 50.00
CSES Eric Staal 30.00 60.00
CSFM Frank Mahovlich 40.00 80.00
CSFR Frank Mahovlich 30.00 60.00
CSGA Glenn Anderson 40.00 80.00
CSGC Gerry Cheevers 30.00 60.00
CSGF Grant Fuhr 40.00 80.00
CSGH Gordie Howe 75.00 175.00
CSGL Guy Lafleur 60.00 125.00
CSHE Milan Hejduk 25.00 50.00
CSJB Jean Beliveau 50.00 100.00
CSJK Jari Kurri 40.00 100.00
CSJL Jacques Lemaire 30.00 60.00
CSJM Joe Mullen 30.00 60.00
CSJO Johnny Bower 25.00 60.00
CSKE Red Kelly 30.00 60.00
CSLA Larry Murphy
CSLE Elmer Lach 40.00 80.00
CSLR Larry Robinson 20.00 50.00
CSMB Mike Bossy 40.00 80.00
CSML Mario Lemieux 150.00 300.00
CSMM Mike Modano 50.00 100.00
CSMS Milt Schmidt 40.00 80.00
CSMU Joe Mullen 30.00 60.00
CSNL Nicklas Lidstrom 40.00 80.00
CSPE Phil Esposito 30.00 60.00
CSPR Patrick Roy 150.00 250.00
CSRB Ray Bourque 50.00 100.00
CSRK Red Kelly 30.00 60.00
CSRL Reggie Leach
CSRO Patrick Roy 125.00 200.00
CSRV Rogie Vachon 30.00 60.00
CSSB Scotty Bowman 40.00 80.00
CSSH Steve Shutt 25.00 50.00
CSSM Stan Mikita 30.00 60.00
CSSS Scott Stevens
CSST Martin St. Louis 25.00 50.00
CSTL Ted Lindsay 30.00 60.00
CSVL Vincent Lecavalier 30.00 60.00
CSWG Wayne Gretzky 350.00 550.00

2006-07 The Cup Stanley Cup Titlists

PRINT RUNS VARY
NOT PRICED DUE TO SCARCITY
TAA Al Arbour/4
TBB Bob Baun/4
TBO Bobby Orr/2
TBU Johnny Bucyk/2
TCG Clark Gillies/4
TEL Elmer Lach/3
TJB Johnny Bower/4
TJL Jacques Lemaire/8
TMS Milt Schmidt/2
TRK Red Kelly/8

2006-07 The Cup Stanley Cup Titlists Patches

PRINT RUNS VARY
NOT PRICED DUE TO SCARCITY
TAM Al MacInnis/1
TCW Cam Ward/1
TES Eric Staal/1
TJK Jari Kurri/5
TLR Larry Robinson/6
TML Mario Lemieux/2
TRB Ray Bourque/1
TRE Ron Ellis/1
TSS Scott Stevens/3

2007-08 The Cup

(1-100) PRINT RUN 249 SER.#'d SETS
(101-118) PRINT RUN 199 SER.#'d SETS
(119-184) PRINT RUN 249 SER.#'d SETS
(185-190) PRINT RUN 99 SER.#'d SETS
1 Dale Hawerchuk 4.00 10.00
2 Bobby Hull 8.00 20.00
3 Alexander Ovechkin 15.00 40.00
4 Dino Ciccarelli 4.00 10.00
5 Markus Naslund 5.00 12.00
6 Roberto Luongo 8.00 20.00
7 Richard Brodeur 4.00 10.00
8 Mats Sundin 6.00 12.00
9 Frank Mahovlich 8.00 20.00
10 Darryl Sittler 4.00 10.00
11 Borje Salming 4.00 10.00
12 Vincent Lecavalier 5.00 12.00
13 Martin St. Louis 4.00 10.00
14 Brad Richards 4.00 10.00
15 Paul Kariya 5.00 12.00
16 Bernie Federko 3.00 8.00
17 Joe Mullen 3.00 8.00
18 Joe Thornton 6.00 15.00
19 Jonathan Cheechoo 4.00 10.00
20 Patrick Marleau 4.00 10.00
21 Sidney Crosby 25.00 60.00
22 Evgeni Malkin 12.00 30.00
23 Mario Lemieux 15.00 40.00
24 Marc-Andre Fleury 5.00 12.00
25 Jordan Staal 6.00 15.00
26 Shane Doan 3.00 8.00
27 Simon Gagne 5.00 12.00
28 Bobby Clarke 5.00 12.00
29 Ron Hextall 8.00 20.00
30 Bernie Parent 6.00 15.00
31 Dany Heatley 6.00 15.00
32 Jason Spezza 5.00 12.00
33 Daniel Alfredsson 4.00 10.00
34 Mark Messier 10.00 25.00
35 Jaromir Jagr 8.00 20.00
36 Brendan Shanahan 5.00 12.00
37 Brian Leetch 5.00 12.00
38 Andy Bathgate 4.00 10.00
39 Mike Bossy 5.00 12.00
40 Clark Gillies 4.00 10.00
41 Denis Potvin 4.00 10.00
42 Billy Smith 5.00 12.00
43 Martin Brodeur 12.00 30.00
44 Zach Parise 5.00 12.00
45 Alexander Radulov 5.00 12.00
46 Peter Forsberg 6.00 15.00
47 Saku Koivu 4.00 10.00
48 Michael Ryder 3.00 8.00
49 Larry Robinson 6.00 15.00
50 Guy Lafleur 12.00 30.00
51 Patrick Roy 15.00 40.00
52 Jean Beliveau 8.00 20.00
53 Marian Gaborik 6.00 15.00
54 Mikko Koivu 3.00 8.00
55 Marcel Dionne 3.00 8.00
56 Anze Kopitar 5.00 12.00
57 Rob Blake 4.00 10.00
58 Gordie Howe 12.00 30.00
59 Tomas Vokoun 5.00 12.00
60 Jari Kurri 5.00 12.00
61 Grant Fuhr 8.00 20.00
62 Wayne Gretzky 25.00 60.00
63 Ales Hemsky 3.00 8.00
64 Dwayne Roloson 4.00 10.00
65 Dominik Hasek 6.00 15.00
66 Henrik Zetterberg 5.00 12.00
67 Nicklas Lidstrom 5.00 12.00
68 Pavel Datsyuk 5.00 12.00
69 Marty Turco 5.00 12.00
70 Mike Modano 5.00 12.00
71 Rick Nash 5.00 12.00
72 Sergei Fedorov 5.00 12.00
73 Joe Sakic 10.00 25.00
74 Paul Stastny 5.00 12.00
75 Milan Hejduk 4.00 10.00
76 Stan Mikita 4.00 10.00
77 Tony Esposito 8.00 20.00
78 Nikolai Khabibulin 5.00 12.00
79 Denis Savard 4.00 10.00
80 Eric Staal 5.00 12.00
81 Cam Ward 5.00 12.00
82 Jarome Iginla 8.00 20.00
83 Miikka Kiprusoff 6.00 15.00
84 Lanny McDonald 4.00 10.00
85 Al MacInnis 4.00 10.00
86 Ryan Miller 5.00 12.00
87 Gilbert Perreault 4.00 10.00
88 Thomas Vanek 4.00 10.00
89 Patrice Bergeron 5.00 12.00
90 Ray Bourque 6.00 15.00
91 Cam Neely 5.00 12.00
92 Bobby Orr 20.00 50.00
93 Johnny Bucyk 3.00 8.00
94 Phil Kessel 5.00 12.00
95 Ilya Kovalchuk 6.00 15.00
96 Marian Hossa 5.00 12.00
97 Kari Lehtonen 5.00 12.00
98 Jean-Sebastien Giguere 5.00 12.00
99 Ryan Getzlaf 4.00 10.00
100 Teemu Selanne 5.00 12.00
101 Matt Keetley AU RC 8.00 20.00
102 Tyler Kennedy AU RC 10.00 25.00
103 Petteri Wirtanen AU RC 6.00 15.00
104 Matt Hunwick AU RC 8.00 20.00
105 Tomas Popperle AU RC 8.00 20.00
106 Johnny Boychuk AU RC 6.00 15.00
107 Alexander Nikulin AU RC 8.00 20.00
108 Mark Mancari AU RC 8.00 20.00
109 Craig Weller AU RC 6.00 15.00
110 Jake Dowell AU RC 6.00 15.00
111 David Clarkson AU RC 6.00 15.00
112 Drew MacIntyre AU RC 8.00 20.00
113 Kris Versteeg AU RC 100.00 200.00
114 Greg Moore AU RC 6.00 15.00
115 Tomas Plihal AU RC 8.00 20.00
116 Mike Lundin AU RC 6.00 15.00
117 Rich Peverley AU RC 6.00 15.00
118 Cody Bass AU RC 8.00 20.00
119 Bobby Ryan JSY AU RC 60.00 120.00
120 Ondrej Pavelec JSY AU RC 30.00 80.00
121 Jack Johnson JSY AU RC 30.00 80.00
122 Nicklas Bergfors JSY AU RC 25.00 60.00
123 Erik Johnson JSY AU RC 40.00 100.00
124 Bryan Little JSY AU RC 30.00 80.00
125 Kris Russell JSY AU RC 30.00 80.00
126 Matt Niskanen JSY AU RC 20.00 50.00
127 Andrew Cogliano JSY AU RC 50.00 120.00
128 Jonathan Bernier JSY AU RC 50.00 120.00
129 Marc Staal JSY AU RC 20.00 50.00
130 Nick Foligno JSY AU RC 30.00 80.00
131 Peter Mueller JSY AU RC 60.00 150.00
132 Brett Sterling JSY AU RC 20.00 50.00
133 Petr Kalus JSY AU RC 20.00 50.00
134 Rob Schremp JSY AU RC 25.00 60.00
135 Andy Greene JSY AU RC 20.00 50.00
136 Frans Nielsen JSY AU RC 20.00 50.00
137 Martin Hanzal JSY AU RC 25.00 60.00
138 Devin Setoguchi JSY AU RC 40.00 100.00
139 Matt Smaby JSY AU RC 20.00 50.00
140 James Sheppard JSY AU RC 20.00 50.00
141 Kyle Chipchura JSY AU RC 30.00 80.00
142 Ryan Parent JSY AU RC 25.00 60.00
143 David Krejci JSY AU RC 40.00 100.00
144 Lauri Tukonen JSY AU RC 20.00 50.00
145 Anton Stralman JSY AU RC 25.00 60.00
146 Tobias Enstrom JSY AU RC 30.00 80.00
147 Brandon Dubinsky JSY AU RC 30.00 80.00
148 Mason Raymond JSY AU RC 50.00 120.00
149 Drew Miller JSY AU RC 20.00 50.00
150 Curtis McElhinney JSY AU RC 25.00 60.00
151 Ryan Callahan JSY AU RC 30.00 80.00
152 Brian Elliott JSY AU RC 25.00 60.00
153 Jonathan Sigalet JSY AU RC 20.00 50.00
154 Ville Koistinen JSY AU RC 20.00 50.00
155 Torrey Mitchell JSY AU RC 25.00 60.00
156 David Perron JSY AU RC 30.00 80.00
157 Jannik Hansen JSY AU RC 20.00 50.00
158 Jaroslav Halak JSY AU RC 100.00 200.00
159 Milan Lucic JSY AU RC 50.00 120.00
160 Lukas Kaspar JSY AU RC 20.00 50.00
161 Marc Methot JSY AU RC 20.00 50.00
162 Tyler Weiman JSY AU RC 25.00 60.00
163 Ryan Carter JSY AU RC 25.00 60.00
164 Jared Boll JSY AU RC 20.00 50.00
165 Jonas Hiller JSY AU RC 50.00 120.00
166 Jaroslav Hlinka JSY AU RC 20.00 50.00
167 Matt Ellis JSY AU RC 20.00 50.00
168 Cory Murphy JSY AU RC 20.00 50.00
169 Steve Wagner JSY AU RC 20.00 50.00
170 Stefan Meyer JSY AU RC 20.00 50.00
171 Daniel Carcillo JSY AU RC 25.00 60.00
172 Tuukka Rask JSY AU RC 100.00 200.00
173 David Jones JSY AU RC 20.00 50.00
174 Tobias Stephan JSY AU RC 25.00 60.00
175 Tom Gilbert JSY AU RC 25.00 60.00
176 Cal Clutterbuck JSY AU RC 20.00 50.00
177 Rod Pelley JSY AU RC 20.00 50.00
178 Daniel Girardi JSY AU RC 20.00 50.00
179 Chris Bourque JSY AU RC 25.00 60.00
180 T.J. Hensick JSY AU RC 25.00 60.00
181 Steve Downie JSY AU RC 25.00 60.00
182 Jack Skille JSY AU RC 30.00 80.00
183 Casey Borer JSY AU RC 20.00 50.00
184 Sergei Kostitsyn JSY AU RC 60.00 120.00
185 Patrick Kane JSY AU/99 RC 500.00 1000.00
186 Sam Gagner JSY AU/99 RC 200.00 400.00
187 Nicklas Backstrom JSY AU/99 RC 300.00 600.00
188 Jiri Tlusty JSY AU/99 RC 75.00 150.00
189 Carey Price JSY AU/99 RC 1000.00 1600.00
190 Jonathan Toews JSY AU/99 RC 600.00 1200.00

2007-08 The Cup Black

STATED PRINT RUN 1 SER.#'d SET
NOT PRICED DUE TO SCARCITY

2007-08 The Cup Gold

*GOLD (1-100): .8X TO 2X
STATED PRINT RUN 25 SER.#'d SETS

2007-08 The Cup All-Star Royalty

STATED PRINT RUNS RANGE FROM 1 TO 23 SERIAL #'d CARDS
NOT PRICED DUE TO SCARCITY
ASRAM1 Al MacInnis/3
ASRAM2 Al MacInnis Blues/15
ASRAO Alexander Ovechkin/1
ASRAT Alex Tanguay/1
ASRBC Bobby Clarke/8
ASRBH Bobby Hull/12
ASRBL Brian Leetch/11
ASRBO Mike Bossy/8
ASRCN Cam Neely/5
ASRDC Dino Ciccarelli/4
ASRDG Doug Gilmour/9
ASRDH Dany Heatley/2
ASREM Evgeni Malkin/1
ASREN Evgeni Nabokov/1
ASRES Eric Staal/1
ASRFM Frank Mahovlich/15
ASRGF Grant Fuhr/1
ASRGH Gordie Howe/23
ASRGL Guy Lafleur/6
ASRGP Gilbert Perreault/9
ASRHO Marian Hossa/4
ASRIK Ilya Kovalchuk/1
ASRJB Jean Beliveau/14
ASRJC Jonathan Cheechoo/1
ASRJI Jarome Iginla/3
ASRJK1 Jari Kurri Oilers/8
ASRJK2 Jari Kurri Kings/2
ASRJR1 Jeremy Roenick/5
ASRJR2 Jeremy Roenick/3
ASRJS Jordan Staal/1
ASRJT Joe Thornton/4
ASRLR Luc Robitaille/8
ASRMB Martin Brodeur/9
ASRMG Marian Gaborik/1
ASRML Mario Lemieux/12
ASRMM1 Mark Messier/1
ASRMM2 Mark Messier Rangers/15
ASRMN Markus Naslund/5
ASRMO Mike Modano Stars/6
ASRMO1 Mike Modano N.Stars/8
ASRMS Martin St. Louis/3
ASRMT Marty Turco/3
ASRNL Nicklas Lidstrom/9
ASROA1 Adam Oates Blues/4
ASROA2 Adam Oates Bruins/5
ASROA3 Adam Oates Capitals/4
ASROR Bobby Orr/7
ASRPB Patrice Bergeron/1
ASRPE1 Phil Esposito Bruins/10
ASRPE2 Phil Esposito/2
ASRPK Phil Kessel/1
ASRPR1 Patrick Roy Canadiens/11
ASRPR2 Patrick Roy Avalanche/3
ASRRB1 Ray Bourque Bruins/19
ASRRB2 Ray Bourque Avalanche/4
ASRRH Ron Hextall/1
ASRRM Ryan Miller/1
ASRRN Rick Nash/2
ASRRO1 Larry Robinson Canadiens/10
ASRRO2 Larry Robinson/6
ASRRS Ryan Smyth/1
ASRSC Sidney Crosby/1
ASRSD Shane Doan/1
ASRSG Simon Gagne/2
ASRSK Saku Koivu/2
ASRSM Stan Mikita/9
ASRTE Tony Esposito/6
ASRTV Thomas Vanek/1
ASRVL Vincent Lecavalier/2
ASRVO Tomas Vokoun/1
ASRWG1 Wayne Gretzky/9
ASRWG2 Wayne Gretzky/6
ASRWG3 Wayne Gretzky/3

2007-08 The Cup Autographed NHL Shields Duals

STATED PRINT RUN 1 SERIAL #'d SET
NOT PRICED DUE TO SCARCITY

2007-08 The Cup Black Patches

STATED PRINT RUN 1 SER.#'d SET
NOT PRICED DUE TO SCARCITY

2007-08 The Cup Chirography

STATED PRINT RUN 50 SERIAL #'d SETS
CCAM Al MacInnis 10.00 25.00
CCAO Alexander Ovechkin 75.00 150.00
CCBC Bobby Clarke 12.00 30.00
CCBF Bernie Federko 8.00 20.00
CCBH Bobby Hull 20.00 50.00
CCBL Brian Leetch 12.00 30.00
CCBO Bobby Orr 100.00 200.00
CCBP Bernie Parent 15.00 40.00
CCBR Martin Brodeur 50.00 100.00
CCCG Clark Gillies 10.00 25.00
CCCN Cam Neely 12.00 30.00
CCDC Dino Ciccarelli 10.00 25.00
CCDH Dany Heatley 15.00 40.00
CCDP Denis Potvin 10.00 25.00
CCDS Darryl Sittler 10.00 25.00
CCEM Evgeni Malkin 40.00 80.00
CCES Eric Staal 12.00 30.00
CCFM Frank Mahovlich 20.00 50.00
CCGF Grant Fuhr 20.00 50.00
CCGH Gordie Howe 60.00 120.00
CCGL Guy Lafleur 25.00 60.00
CCGP Gilbert Perreault 10.00 25.00
CCHA Dale Hawerchuk 15.00 40.00
CCIK Ilya Kovalchuk 15.00 40.00
CCJB Jean Beliveau 20.00 50.00
CCJC Jonathan Cheechoo 12.00 30.00
CCJI Jarome Iginla 30.00 60.00
CCJK Jari Kurri 15.00 40.00
CCJM Joe Mullen 8.00 20.00
CCJT Joe Thornton 15.00 40.00
CCLM Lanny McDonald 15.00 40.00
CCLR Luc Robitaille 25.00 60.00
CCMB Mike Bossy 20.00 50.00
CCMD Marcel Dionne 15.00 40.00
CCMG Marian Gaborik 20.00 50.00
CCML Mario Lemieux 75.00 150.00
CCMM Mark Messier 60.00 120.00
CCMN Markus Naslund 12.00 30.00
CCMO Mike Modano 15.00 40.00
CCMS Martin St. Louis 15.00 40.00
CCMT Marty Turco 12.00 30.00
CCPE Phil Esposito 20.00 50.00
CCPR Patrick Roy 75.00 150.00
CCRB Ray Bourque 30.00 60.00
CCRH Ron Hextall 20.00 50.00
CCRO Larry Robinson 15.00 40.00
CCSA Borje Salming 10.00 25.00
CCSC Sidney Crosby 175.00 300.00
CCSD Shane Doan 8.00 20.00
CCSG Simon Gagne 20.00 50.00
CCSK Saku Koivu 20.00 50.00
CCSM Stan Mikita 20.00 50.00
CCTE Tony Esposito 20.00 50.00
CCVL Vincent Lecavalier
CCWG Wayne Gretzky 150.00 300.00

2007-08 The Cup Emblems of Endorsement

STATED PRINT RUN 15 SERIAL #'d SETS
NOT PRICED DUE TO SCARCITY

2007-08 The Cup Enshrinements

STATED PRINT RUN 50 SERIAL #'d SETS
EAM Al MacInnis 12.00 30.00
EAO Alexander Ovechkin 50.00 120.00
EBC Bobby Clarke 15.00 40.00
EBF Bernie Federko 10.00 25.00
EBH Bobby Hull 25.00 60.00
EBL Brian Leetch 15.00 40.00
EBO Bobby Orr 125.00 250.00
EBP Bernie Parent 20.00 50.00
ECG Clark Gillies 12.00 30.00
ECN Cam Neely 15.00 40.00
EDC Dino Ciccarelli 12.00 30.00
EDH Dany Heatley 20.00 50.00
EDP Denis Potvin 12.00 30.00
EDS Darryl Sittler 12.00 30.00
EEM Evgeni Malkin 60.00 120.00
EES Eric Staal 15.00 40.00
EFM Frank Mahovlich 25.00 60.00
EGF Grant Fuhr 25.00 60.00
EGH Gordie Howe 40.00 100.00
EGL Guy Lafleur 40.00 100.00
EGP Gilbert Perreault 12.00 30.00
EHA Dale Hawerchuk 12.00 30.00
EIK Ilya Kovalchuk 20.00 50.00
EJB Jean Beliveau 25.00 60.00
EJC Jonathan Cheechoo 12.00 30.00
EJI Jarome Iginla 40.00 80.00
EJK Jari Kurri 15.00 40.00
EJM Joe Mullen 10.00 25.00
EJT Joe Thornton 20.00 50.00
ELM Lanny McDonald 12.00 30.00
ELR Luc Robitaille 12.00 30.00
EMB Martin Brodeur 40.00 100.00
EMD Marcel Dionne 10.00 25.00
EMG Marian Gaborik 20.00 50.00
EMI Mike Bossy 12.00 30.00
EML Mario Lemieux 100.00 200.00
EMM Mark Messier 60.00 120.00
EMN Markus Naslund 15.00 40.00
EMO Mike Modano 15.00 40.00
EMS Martin St. Louis 12.00 30.00
EMT Marty Turco 15.00 40.00
EPE Phil Esposito 25.00 60.00
EPR Patrick Roy 75.00 150.00
ERB Ray Bourque 20.00 50.00
ERH Ron Hextall 25.00 60.00
ERO Larry Robinson 20.00 50.00
ESA Borje Salming 12.00 30.00
ESC Sidney Crosby 125.00 250.00
ESD Shane Doan 10.00 25.00
ESG Simon Gagne 15.00 40.00
ESK Saku Koivu 12.00 30.00
ESM Stan Mikita 12.00 30.00
ETE Tony Esposito 25.00 60.00
EVL Vincent Lecavalier 15.00 40.00
EWG Wayne Gretzky 150.00 250.00

2007-08 The Cup Enshrinements Duals

STATED PRINT RUN 25 SERIAL #'d SETS
NOT PRICED DUE TO LACK OF MARKET ACTIVITY

2007-08 The Cup Enshrinements Trios

STATED PRINT RUN 10 SERIAL #'d SETS
NOT PRICED DUE TO SCARCITY

2007-08 The Cup Foundations

STATED PRINT RUN 25 SERIAL #'d SETS
CFAK Anze Kopitar 8.00 20.00
CFAM Al MacInnis
CFAO Adam Oates 5.00 12.00
CFAR Alexander Radulov 8.00 20.00
CFAS Alexander Steen 5.00 12.00
CFAT Alex Tanguay 6.00 15.00
CFBC Bobby Clarke 8.00 20.00
CFBH Bobby Hull 12.00 30.00
CFBL Brian Leetch 6.00 15.00
CFBO Mike Bossy 6.00 15.00
CFBR Bill Ranford 6.00 15.00
CFBS Billy Smith 8.00 20.00
CFBU Johnny Bucyk 5.00 12.00
CFCN Cam Neely 8.00 20.00
CFCP Chris Pronger 8.00 20.00
CFDA Daniel Alfredsson 6.00 15.00
CFDC Dino Ciccarelli 6.00 15.00
CFDE Denis Savard 6.00 15.00
CFDH Dale Hawerchuk 6.00 15.00
CFDP Denis Potvin 6.00 15.00
CFDR Dwayne Roloson
CFDS Darryl Sittler 6.00 15.00
CFEM Evgeni Malkin 15.00 40.00
CFEN Evgeni Nabokov 6.00 15.00
CFEP Phil Esposito 12.00 30.00
CFES Eric Staal 8.00 20.00
CFFM Frank Mahovlich 12.00 30.00
CFGF Grant Fuhr 12.00 30.00
CFGH Gordie Howe 40.00 80.00
CFGL Guy Lafleur
CFGP Gilbert Perreault
CFHA Dominik Hasek 10.00 25.00
CFHE Dany Heatley 10.00 25.00
CFHL Henrik Lundqvist 10.00 25.00
CFHO Marian Hossa 8.00 20.00
CFHZ Henrik Zetterberg 8.00 20.00
CFIK Ilya Kovalchuk 10.00 25.00
CFJB Jean Beliveau 12.00 30.00
CFJI Jarome Iginla 12.00 30.00
CFJJ Jaromir Jagr
CFJK Jari Kurri 8.00 20.00
CFJO Joe Sakic 15.00 40.00
CFJS Jason Spezza 8.00 20.00
CFJT Joe Thornton 10.00 25.00
CFKI Miikka Kiprusoff 10.00 25.00
CFKL Kari Lehtonen 8.00 20.00
CFLM Lanny McDonald 6.00 15.00
CFLR Larry Robinson
CFMB Martin Brodeur 20.00 50.00
CFMF Marc-Andre Fleury 8.00 20.00
CFMG Marian Gaborik 10.00 25.00
CFMH Milan Hejduk 6.00 15.00
CFMK Mikko Koivu
CFML Mario Lemieux 25.00 60.00
CFMM Mark Messier 20.00 50.00
CFMN Markus Naslund 8.00 20.00
CFMO Mike Modano 8.00 20.00
CFMR Mark Recchi 5.00 12.00
CFMS Martin St. Louis 6.00 15.00
CFNL Nicklas Lidstrom 8.00 20.00
CFOV Alexander Ovechkin 25.00 60.00
CFPB Patrice Bergeron 8.00 20.00
CFPD Pavel Datsyuk 8.00 20.00
CFPE Corey Perry 6.00 15.00
CFPF Peter Forsberg 10.00 25.00
CFPH Dion Phaneuf 8.00 20.00
CFPK Paul Kariya 8.00 20.00
CFPM Patrick Marleau 6.00 15.00
CFPR Patrick Roy 25.00 60.00
CFPS Peter Stastny 6.00 15.00
CFRB Ray Bourque 10.00 25.00
CFRE Ron Ellis
CFRH Ron Hextall 12.00 30.00
CFRI Brad Richards
CFRL Roberto Luongo 12.00 30.00
CFRN Rick Nash 12.00 30.00
CFRO Luc Robitaille 12.00 30.00
CFRS Ryan Smyth 6.00 15.00
CFRV Rogie Vachon 8.00 20.00
CFRY Michael Ryder 5.00 12.00
CFSA Borje Salming 6.00 15.00
CFSC Sidney Crosby 60.00 120.00
CFSD Shane Doan 5.00 12.00
CFSF Sergei Fedorov 8.00 20.00
CFSG Simon Gagne 8.00 20.00
CFSH Brendan Shanahan 8.00 20.00
CFSK Saku Koivu 6.00 15.00
CFSL Steve Sullivan 5.00 12.00
CFSM Stan Mikita 6.00 15.00
CFSN Scott Niedermayer
CFSS Steve Shutt
CFST Scott Stevens 6.00 15.00
CFSU Mats Sundin 8.00 20.00
CFTS Teemu Selanne 8.00 20.00
CFTV Tomas Vokoun 8.00 20.00
CFTW Tiger Williams 6.00 15.00
CFVL Vincent Lecavalier 8.00 20.00
CFVT Vesa Toskala 6.00 15.00
CFWG Wayne Gretzky 100.00 200.00
CFZP Zach Parise 6.00 15.00

2007-08 The Cup Foundations Autographs

STATED PRINT RUN 10 SERIAL #'d SETS
NOT PRICED DUE TO SCARCITY

2007-08 The Cup Foundations Patches

STATED PRINT RUN 10 SERIAL #'d SETS
NOT PRICED DUE TO SCARCITY

2007-08 The Cup Foundations Patches Autographs

STATED PRINT RUN 5 SERIAL #'d SETS
NOT PRICED DUE TO SCARCITY

2007-08 The Cup Gold Jerseys

*GOLD JSY: 1X TO 2.5X
STATED PRINT RUN 25 SERIAL #'d SETS

2007-08 The Cup Gold Patches

STATED PRINT RUN 10 SER.#'d SETS
NOT PRICED DUE TO SCARCITY

2007-08 The Cup Gold Rainbow Autographed Rookies

STATED PRINT RUN FROM 59 TO 1 SER.#'d CARDS
SOME NOT PRICED DUE TO SCARCITY
101 Matt Keetley/36 15.00 40.00
102 Tyler Kennedy/34 25.00 60.00
103 Petteri Wirtanen/56 6.00 15.00
104 Matt Hunwick/48 8.00 20.00
105 Tomas Popperle/1
106 Johnny Boychuk/28 15.00 40.00
107 Alexander Nikulin/8
108 Mark Mancari/25
109 Craig Weller/12
110 Jake Dowell/49 8.00 20.00
111 David Clarkson/27 10.00 25.00
112 Drew MacIntyre/34 15.00 40.00
113 Kris Versteeg/32 175.00 300.00
114 Greg Moore/47 15.00 40.00
115 Tomas Plihal/59 10.00 25.00
116 Mike Lundin/39 10.00 25.00
117 Rich Peverley/37 8.00 20.00
118 Cody Bass/21

2007-08 The Cup Gold Rainbow Autographed Rookie Patches

STATED PRINT RUN FROM 1 TO 89 SER.#'d CARDS
SOME NOT PRICED DUE TO SCARCITY
119 Bobby Ryan/9 100.00 200.00
120 Ondrej Pavelec/33 30.00 60.00
121 Jack Johnson/33 50.00 100.00
122 Nicklas Bergfors/12
123 Erik Johnson/6
124 Bryan Little/10
125 Kris Russell/2
126 Matt Niskanen/5
127 Andrew Cogliano/13
128 Jonathan Bernier/45 40.00 100.00
129 Marc Staal/18
130 Nick Foligno/71 15.00 40.00
131 Peter Mueller/88 50.00 120.00
132 Brett Sterling/21
133 Petr Kalus/23
134 Rob Schremp/44 15.00 40.00
135 Andy Greene/6
136 Frans Nielsen/51 20.00 50.00
137 Martin Hanzal/11
138 Devin Setoguchi/16
139 Matt Smaby/32 30.00 80.00
140 James Sheppard/15
141 Kyle Chipchura/28 40.00 80.00
142 Ryan Parent/77 25.00 60.00
143 David Krejci/46 30.00 60.00
144 Lauri Tukonen/28 30.00 60.00
145 Anton Stralman/36 20.00 50.00
146 Tobias Enstrom/35 20.00 50.00
147 Brandon Dubinsky/54 40.00 100.00
148 Mason Raymond/21
149 Drew Miller/18
150 Curtis McElhinney/31 40.00 80.00
151 Ryan Callahan/43 40.00 80.00
152 Brian Elliott/30 20.00 50.00
153 Jonathan Sigalet/50 15.00 40.00
154 Ville Koistinen/4
155 Torrey Mitchell/17
156 David Perron/57 50.00 100.00
157 Jannik Hansen/59 15.00 40.00
158 Jaroslav Halak/41 100.00 200.00
159 Milan Lucic/17
160 Lukas Kaspar/43 15.00 40.00
161 Marc Methot/48 25.00 60.00
162 Tyler Weiman/35 20.00 50.00
163 Ryan Carter/52 15.00 40.00
164 Jared Boll/40 25.00 60.00
165 Jonas Hiller/1
166 Jaroslav Hlinka/17
167 Matt Ellis/8
168 Cory Murphy/21
169 Steve Wagner/49 12.00 30.00
170 Stefan Meyer/64 20.00 50.00
171 Daniel Carcillo/13
172 Tuukka Rask/40 125.00 200.00
173 David Jones/36 25.00 60.00
174 Tobias Stephan/31 15.00 40.00
175 Tom Gilbert/77 25.00 60.00
176 Cal Clutterbuck/22
177 Rod Pelley/22
178 Daniel Girardi/46 12.00 30.00
179 Chris Bourque/56 20.00 50.00
180 T.J. Hensick/34 25.00 60.00
181 Steve Downie/25 12.00 30.00
182 Jack Skille/48 40.00 80.00
183 Casey Borer/25 15.00 40.00
184 Sergei Kostitsyn/25
185 Patrick Kane/88 250.00 500.00
186 Sam Gagner/89 75.00 150.00
187 Nicklas Backstrom/19
188 Jiri Tlusty/41 75.00 150.00
189 Carey Price/31 1500.00 2000.00
190 Jonathan Toews/19

2007-08 The Cup Hardware Heroes

STATED PRINT RUNS 1 TO 5 SERIAL #'d SETS
NOT PRICED DUE TO SCARCITY

2007-08 The Cup Honorable Numbers

STATED PRINT RUN 2 TO 94 SERIAL #'d SETS
SOME NOT PRICED DUE TO SCARCITY
HNAC Andrew Cogliano/13
HNAM Al MacInnis/2
HNAO Alexander Ovechkin/8
HNBC Bobby Clarke/16
HNBL Brian Leetch/2
HNBN Bernie Nicholls/9
HNBR Martin Brodeur/30 150.00 300.00
HNBS Borje Salming/21
HNCN Cam Neely/8
HNCP Carey Price/31 400.00 800.00
HNDC Dino Ciccarelli/22 40.00 100.00
HNDH Dale Hawerchuk/10
HNDS Darryl Sittler/27 20.00 50.00
HNEM Evgeni Malkin/71 75.00 150.00
HNES Eric Staal/12
HNGA Sam Gagner/89 60.00 120.00
HNGF Grant Fuhr/31 40.00 80.00
HNGH Gordie Howe/9
HNGP Gilbert Perreault/11
HNHA Dominik Hasek/39 40.00 100.00
HNHE Dany Heatley/15
HNHZ Henrik Zetterberg/40 60.00 120.00
HNIK Ilya Kovalchuk/17
HNJB Jonathan Bernier/45 50.00 100.00
HNJC Jonathan Cheechoo/14
HNJG Jean-Sebastien Giguere/35 25.00 60.00
HNJI Jarome Iginla/12
HNJK Jari Kurri/17
HNJM Joe Mullen/7
HNJO Jonathan Toews/19 300.00 600.00
HNJS Jordan Staal/11
HNJT Joe Thornton/19 100.00 200.00
HNLM Lanny McDonald/9
HNLR Larry Robinson/19 40.00 80.00
HNMD Marcel Dionne/16
HNMF Marc-Andre Fleury/29 75.00 150.00
HNMG Marian Gaborik/10
HNML Mario Lemieux/66 175.00 350.00
HNMM Mark Messier/11
HNMN Markus Naslund/19 20.00 50.00
HNMO Mike Modano/9
HNMS Martin St. Louis/26 20.00 50.00
HNMT Marty Turco/35 20.00 50.00
HNNB Nicklas Backstrom/19
HNNL Nicklas Lidstrom/5
HNPE Phil Esposito/7
HNPK Patrick Kane/88 125.00 250.00
HNPM Peter Mueller/88 60.00 120.00
HNPR Patrick Roy/33 150.00 300.00
HNPS Paul Stastny/26 40.00 80.00
HNRB Ray Bourque/77 40.00 80.00
HNRG Ryan Getzlaf/15
HNRM Ryan Miller/30 50.00 100.00
HNRN Rick Nash/61 40.00 100.00
HNRO Luc Robitaille/20 25.00 60.00
HNRS Ryan Smyth/94 15.00 40.00
HNSC Sidney Crosby/87 150.00 300.00
HNSD Shane Doan/19 25.00 60.00
HNSG Simon Gagne/12
HNSH Steve Shutt/22
HNSK Saku Koivu/11
HNST Peter Stastny/26 50.00 100.00
HNTE Tony Esposito/35 40.00 80.00
HNTL Jiri Tlusty/41 25.00 60.00
HNTV Thomas Vanek/26 25.00 60.00
HNVL Vincent Lecavalier/4

2007-08 The Cup Honorable Numbers Dual

STATED PRINT RUN 2 TO 81 SERIAL #'d SETS
SOME NOT PRICED DUE TO SCARCITY
HN2AB Brian Leetch
Al MacInnis/2
HN2BS Mike Bossy 75.00 150.00
Steve Shutt/22
HN2DC Marcel Dionne 100.00
Bobby Clarke/16
HN2EM Phil Esposito
Joe Mullen/7
HN2GT Jean-Sebastien Giguere 50.00 100.00
Marty Turco/35
HN2HG Dany Heatley
Ryan Getzlaf/15
HN2HH Bobby Hull
Gordie Howe/9
HN2IG Jarome Iginla
Simon Gagne/12
HN2KK Jari Kurri
Ilya Kovalchuk/17
HN2KS Saku Koivu
Jordan Staal/11
HN2LH Guy Lafleur
Dale Hawerchuk/10
HN2NM Bernie Nicholls
Lanny McDonald/9
HN2NO Cam Neely
Alexander Ovechkin/8
HN2PH Corey Perry
Dale Hawerchuk/10
HN2PM Gilbert Perreault
Mark Messier/11
HN2RC Luc Robitaille
Dino Ciccarelli/20
HN2SK Miroslav Satan 40.00 80.00
Phil Kessel/81
HN2SM Jordan Staal
Mark Messier/11
HN2SS Peter Stastny 75.00 150.00
Paul Stastny/26
HN2TD Joe Thornton
Shane Doan/19

2007-08 The Cup Jerseys Trios

STATED PRINT RUN 15 SERIAL #'d SETS
NOT PRICED DUE TO SCARCITY

2007-08 The Cup Jerseys Trios Patches

STATED PRINT RUN 10 SERIAL #'d SETS
NOT PRICED DUE TO SCARCITY

2007-08 The Cup Jerseys Quads

STATED PRINT RUN 10 SERIAL #'d SETS
NOT PRICED DUE TO SCARCITY

2007-08 The Cup Jerseys Quads Patches

STATED PRINT RUN 5 SERIAL #'d SETS
NOT PRICED DUE TO SCARCITY

2007-08 The Cup Limited Logos

STATED PRINT RUN 50 SERIAL #'d SETS
UNLESS NOTED IN CHECKLIST BELOW
SOME NOT PRICED DUE TO SCARCITY
LLAC Andrew Cogliano/25 60.00 120.00
LLAH Ales Hemsky
LLAK Anze Kopitar/31 100.00 200.00
LLAM Al MacInnis/30 25.00 60.00
LLAO Adam Oates 20.00 50.00
LLAR Alexander Radulov 30.00 80.00
LLAT Alex Tanguay 25.00 60.00
LLBG Brian Gionta 20.00 50.00
LLBL Brian Leetch 30.00 80.00
LLBN Bernie Nicholls 40.00 80.00
LLBR Bill Ranford 25.00 60.00
LLCA Jeff Carter 30.00 80.00
LLCD Chris Drury 25.00 60.00
LLCN Cam Neely/25 60.00 120.00
LLCP Corey Perry
LLCW Cam Ward
LLCY Carey Price 250.00 400.00
LLDC Dino Ciccarelli 30.00 80.00
LLDG Doug Gilmour 25.00 60.00
LLDH Dale Hawerchuk 25.00 60.00
LLDR Dwayne Roloson 25.00 60.00
LLEL Patrik Elias 20.00 50.00
LLEM Evgeni Malkin/25 125.00 250.00
LLEN Evgeni Nabokov/25 30.00 80.00
LLES Eric Staal 30.00 80.00
LLGA Sam Gagner/25 125.00 250.00
LLGF Grant Fuhr/25 50.00 100.00
LLGL Guy Lafleur/3
LLGP Gilbert Perreault/25 30.00 80.00
LLHA Dominik Hasek 40.00 100.00
LLHE Dany Heatley 25.00 60.00
LLHZ Henrik Zetterberg 100.00 150.00
LLIK Ilya Kovalchuk 60.00 120.00
LLJA Jason Arnott 20.00 50.00
LLJB Jonathan Bernier 60.00 120.00
LLJC Jonathan Cheechoo 25.00 60.00
LLJG Jean-Sebastien Giguere 40.00 100.00
LLJI Jarome Iginla 40.00 100.00
LLJK Jari Kurri/25 40.00 100.00
LLJM Joe Mullen 20.00 50.00
LLJO Jonathan Toews 200.00 400.00
LLJS Jordan Staal 40.00 100.00
LLJT Joe Thornton 40.00 100.00
LLJW Justin Williams 20.00 50.00
LLLM Lanny McDonald 25.00 60.00
LLLR Larry Robinson/28 40.00 80.00
LLMA Martin Brodeur 150.00 250.00
LLMD Marcel Dionne/22 125.00 200.00
LLMF Marc-Andre Fleury 40.00 100.00
LLMG Marian Gaborik 75.00 150.00
LLMH Marian Hossa 30.00 80.00
LLMI Milan Hejduk 25.00 60.00
LLML Mario Lemieux 150.00 250.00
LLMM Mark Messier 100.00 200.00
LLMN Markus Naslund 30.00 80.00
LLMO Mike Modano 30.00 80.00
LLMS Martin St. Louis 25.00 60.00
LLMT Marty Turco 30.00 80.00
LLNB Nicklas Backstrom 100.00 200.00
LLNL Nicklas Lidstrom 60.00 120.00
LLOV Alexander Ovechkin 100.00 200.00
LLPB Patrice Bergeron 30.00 80.00
LLPK Patrick Kane 200.00 400.00
LLPM Peter Mueller 50.00 100.00
LLPR Patrick Roy 150.00 250.00
LLPS Paul Stastny 30.00 80.00
LLRB Ray Bourque 40.00 100.00
LLRG Ryan Getzlaf 25.00 60.00
LLRI Richard Brodeur 25.00 60.00
LLRM Ryan Miller 30.00 80.00
LLRN Rick Nash 40.00 100.00
LLRO Luc Robitaille 25.00 60.00
LLRS Ryan Smyth 25.00 60.00
LLSA Borje Salming 25.00 60.00
LLSC Sidney Crosby 300.00 500.00
LLSD Shane Doan 20.00 50.00
LLSG Simon Gagne 30.00 80.00
LLSH Steve Shutt 25.00 60.00
LLSK Saku Koivu 25.00 60.00
LLSM Stan Mikita/25 100.00 200.00
LLST Peter Stastny/32 75.00 150.00
LLSV Marek Svatos 40.00 100.00
LLTL Jiri Tlusty 40.00 100.00
LLTR Tuomo Ruutu 20.00 50.00
LLTV Thomas Vanek 25.00 60.00
LLVL Vincent Lecavalier 60.00 120.00
LLVO Tomas Vokoun 30.00 80.00
LLWG Wayne Gretzky/5

2007-08 The Cup NHL Shields Duals

STATED PRINT RUN 1 SERIAL #'d SET
NOT PRICED DUE TO SCARCITY

2007-08 The Cup Property of

STATED PRINT RUN 1 SERIAL #'d SET
NOT PRICED DUE TO SCARCITY

2007-08 The Cup Rookies Platinum

STATED PRINT RUN 25 SER.#'d SETS
101 Matt Keetley 8.00 20.00
102 Tyler Kennedy 10.00 25.00
103 Petteri Wirtanen 6.00 15.00
104 Matt Hunwick 8.00 20.00
105 Tomas Popperle 8.00 20.00
106 Johnny Boychuk 6.00 15.00
107 Alexander Nikulin 8.00 20.00
108 Mark Mancari 8.00 20.00
109 Craig Weller 6.00 15.00
110 Jake Dowell 6.00 15.00
111 David Clarkson 6.00 15.00
112 Drew MacIntyre 8.00 20.00
113 Kris Versteeg 75.00 150.00
114 Greg Moore 6.00 15.00
115 Tomas Plihal 8.00 20.00
116 Mike Lundin 6.00 15.00
117 Rich Peverley 6.00 15.00
118 Cody Bass 8.00 20.00
119 Bobby Ryan 25.00 60.00
120 Ondrej Pavelec 10.00 25.00
121 Jack Johnson 10.00 25.00
122 Nicklas Bergfors 8.00 20.00
123 Erik Johnson 12.00 30.00
124 Bryan Little 8.00 20.00
125 Kris Russell 8.00 20.00
126 Matt Niskanen 6.00 15.00
127 Andrew Cogliano 40.00 80.00
128 Jonathan Bernier 15.00 40.00
129 Marc Staal 15.00 40.00
130 Nick Foligno 10.00 25.00
131 Peter Mueller 20.00 50.00
132 Brett Sterling 6.00 15.00
133 Petr Kalus 6.00 15.00
134 Rob Schremp 8.00 20.00
135 Andy Greene 6.00 15.00
136 Frans Nielsen 6.00 15.00
137 Martin Hanzal 8.00 20.00
138 Devin Setoguchi 12.00 30.00
139 Matt Smaby 6.00 15.00
140 James Sheppard 6.00 15.00
141 Kyle Chipchura 10.00 25.00
142 Ryan Parent 8.00 20.00
143 David Krejci 12.00 30.00
144 Lauri Tukonen 6.00 15.00
145 Anton Stralman 8.00 20.00
146 Tobias Enstrom 10.00 25.00
147 Brandon Dubinsky 10.00 25.00
148 Mason Raymond 15.00 40.00
149 Drew Miller 6.00 15.00
150 Curtis McElhinney 8.00 20.00
151 Ryan Callahan 10.00 25.00
152 Brian Elliott 8.00 20.00
153 Jonathan Sigalet 6.00 15.00
154 Ville Koistinen 6.00 15.00
155 Torrey Mitchell 8.00 20.00
156 David Perron 10.00 25.00
157 Jannik Hansen 6.00 15.00
158 Jaroslav Halak 60.00 120.00
159 Milan Lucic 15.00 40.00
160 Lukas Kaspar 6.00 15.00
161 Marc Methot 6.00 15.00
162 Tyler Weiman 8.00 20.00
163 Ryan Carter 8.00 20.00
164 Jared Boll 6.00 15.00
165 Jonas Hiller 15.00 40.00
166 Jaroslav Hlinka 8.00 20.00
167 Matt Ellis 6.00 15.00
168 Cory Murphy 6.00 15.00
169 Steve Wagner 6.00 15.00
170 Stefan Meyer 6.00 15.00
171 Daniel Carcillo 8.00 20.00
172 Tuukka Rask 15.00 40.00
173 David Jones 6.00 15.00
174 Tobias Stephan 8.00 20.00
175 Tom Gilbert 8.00 20.00
176 Cal Clutterbuck 6.00 15.00
177 Rod Pelley 6.00 15.00
178 Daniel Girardi 6.00 15.00
179 Chris Bourque 8.00 20.00
180 T.J. Hensick 8.00 20.00
181 Steve Downie 8.00 20.00
182 Jack Skille 10.00 25.00
183 Casey Borer 6.00 15.00
184 Sergei Kostitsyn 40.00 80.00
185 Patrick Kane 100.00 200.00
186 Sam Gagner 40.00 80.00
187 Nicklas Backstrom 100.00 200.00
188 Jiri Tlusty 15.00 40.00
189 Carey Price 250.00 400.00
190 Jonathan Toews 50.00 120.00

2007-08 The Cup Scripted Swatches

STATED PRINT RUN 25 SERIAL #'d SETS
SSAC Andrew Cogliano 50.00 120.00
SSAO Alexander Ovechkin 100.00 200.00
SSAR Alexander Radulov 25.00 60.00
SSAT Alex Tanguay 25.00 60.00
SSBC Bobby Clarke 30.00 80.00
SSBL Brian Leetch 30.00 80.00
SSBR Martin Brodeur 100.00 200.00
SSCN Cam Neely/10
SSCP Carey Price 200.00 300.00
SSCW Cam Ward 30.00 80.00
SSDC Dino Ciccarelli 25.00 60.00
SSDG Doug Gilmour 25.00 60.00
SSDH Dale Hawerchuk 25.00 60.00
SSDS Darryl Sittler/10
SSEL Patrik Elias 20.00 50.00
SSEM Evgeni Malkin 80.00 200.00
SSES Eric Staal 30.00 80.00
SSGA Sam Gagner 100.00 200.00
SSGP Gilbert Perreault/10
SSHA Dominik Hasek 30.00 80.00
SSHE Dany Heatley 30.00 80.00
SSHZ Henrik Zetterberg 60.00 120.00
SSIK Ilya Kovalchuk 40.00 100.00
SSJB Jonathan Bernier 50.00 100.00
SSJG Jean-Sebastien Giguere 30.00 80.00
SSJI Jarome Iginla 50.00 120.00
SSJM Joe Mullen 20.00 50.00
SSJO Jonathan Toews 200.00 350.00
SSJS Jordan Staal 40.00 100.00
SSJT Joe Thornton 40.00 100.00
SSLM Lanny McDonald 25.00 60.00
SSLR Larry Robinson 40.00 100.00
SSMB Mike Bossy/10
SSMD Marcel Dionne 20.00 50.00
SSMF Marc-Andre Fleury 30.00 80.00
SSMG Marian Gaborik 40.00 100.00
SSMH Marian Hossa 30.00 80.00
SSMI Milan Hejduk 25.00 60.00
SSML Mario Lemieux 125.00 250.00
SSMM Mark Messier 125.00 250.00
SSMN Markus Naslund 30.00 80.00
SSMO Mike Modano 30.00 80.00
SSMS Martin St. Louis 25.00 60.00
SSMT Marty Turco 30.00 80.00
SSNB Nicklas Backstrom 150.00 250.00
SSNL Nicklas Lidstrom 30.00 80.00
SSPB Patrice Bergeron 30.00 80.00
SSPK Patrick Kane 250.00 400.00
SSPM Peter Mueller 50.00 100.00
SSPR Patrick Roy 150.00 250.00
SSPS Paul Stastny 30.00 80.00
SSRB Ray Bourque 40.00 100.00
SSRG Ryan Getzlaf 25.00 60.00
SSRH Ron Hextall/9
SSRM Ryan Miller 30.00 80.00
SSRN Rick Nash 30.00 80.00
SSRO Luc Robitaille 25.00 60.00
SSRS Ryan Smyth 25.00 60.00
SSSA Borje Salming 25.00 60.00
SSSC Sidney Crosby 250.00 350.00
SSSD Shane Doan 20.00 50.00
SSSG Simon Gagne 30.00 80.00
SSSH Steve Shutt 25.00 60.00
SSSK Saku Koivu 25.00 60.00
SSST Peter Stastny 25.00 60.00
SSTL Jiri Tlusty 50.00 100.00
SSVL Vincent Lecavalier 30.00 80.00
SSWG Wayne Gretzky 350.00 500.00

2007-08 The Cup Scripted Swatches Dual

STATED PRINT RUN 5 SERIAL #'d SETS
NOT PRICED DUE TO SCARCITY

2007-08 The Cup Signature Patches

STATED PRINT RUN 75 SERIAL #'d SETS
SPAK Anze Kopitar 20.00 50.00
SPAO Alexander Ovechkin 100.00 200.00
SPAT Alex Tanguay 15.00 40.00
SPBL Brian Leetch 20.00 50.00
SPBR Martin Brodeur/25 100.00 200.00
SPBS Borje Salming 15.00 40.00
SPCD Chris Drury 15.00 40.00
SPCH Jonathan Cheechoo 15.00 40.00
SPCN Cam Neely/10
SPCP Carey Price 150.00 300.00
SPCW Cam Ward 20.00 50.00
SPDC Dino Ciccarelli 15.00 40.00
SPDH Dominik Hasek/25 75.00 150.00
SPEM Evgeni Malkin 75.00 150.00
SPES Eric Staal 20.00 50.00
SPGA Sam Gagner 60.00 120.00
SPGF Grant Fuhr/10
SPGP Gilbert Perreault/10
SPHA Dale Hawerchuk 15.00 40.00
SPHE Dany Heatley 25.00 60.00
SPIK Ilya Kovalchuk 25.00 60.00
SPJA Jason Arnott 12.00 30.00
SPJB Jonathan Bernier 25.00 60.00
SPJG Jean-Sebastien Giguere 20.00 50.00
SPJI Jarome Iginla 30.00 80.00
SPJM Joe Mullen 12.00 30.00
SPJS Jordan Staal 30.00 80.00
SPJT Joe Thornton/25 40.00 100.00
SPKE Patrick Kane 125.00 250.00
SPLM Lanny McDonald 15.00 40.00
SPLR Luc Robitaille 15.00 40.00
SPMB Mike Bossy/10
SPMG Marian Gaborik 30.00 80.00
SPMH Milan Hejduk 15.00 40.00
SPML Mario Lemieux/25 100.00 200.00
SPMM Mike Modano 20.00 50.00
SPMN Markus Naslund 20.00 50.00
SPMS Martin St. Louis 15.00 40.00
SPMT Marty Turco 20.00 50.00
SPNB Nicklas Backstrom 60.00 120.00
SPNL Nicklas Lidstrom 20.00 50.00
SPPB Patrice Bergeron 25.00 60.00
SPPE Patrik Elias 15.00 40.00
SPPK Phil Kessel 20.00 50.00
SPPM Peter Mueller 30.00 80.00
SPPR Patrick Roy/25 150.00 300.00
SPPS Peter Stastny 20.00 50.00
SPRB Ray Bourque/25 25.00 60.00
SPRM Ryan Miller 20.00 50.00
SPRN Rick Nash 20.00 50.00
SPSC Sidney Crosby 175.00 350.00
SPSD Shane Doan 12.00 30.00
SPSG Simon Gagne 30.00 80.00
SPSK Saku Koivu 25.00 60.00
SPST Paul Stastny 25.00 60.00
SPTL Jiri Tlusty 30.00 80.00
SPTO Jonathan Toews 125.00 250.00
SPTV Tomas Vokoun 20.00 50.00
SPVL Vincent Lecavalier 20.00 50.00

2007-08 The Cup Stanley Cup Signatures

STATED PRINT RUN 25 SERIAL #'d SETS
SCAM Andy McDonald 20.00 50.00
SCBC Bobby Clarke 30.00 80.00
SCBD Bill Dineen 25.00 60.00
SCBG Brian Gionta 20.00 50.00
SCBH Bobby Hull 40.00 100.00
SCBL Brian Leetch 30.00 80.00
SCBN Bob Nystrom 20.00 50.00
SCBO Mike Bossy 25.00 60.00
SCBP Bernie Parent 40.00 100.00
SCBS Brent Sutter 20.00 50.00
SCCD Chris Drury 25.00 60.00
SCCP Corey Perry
SCDB Dan Boyle 20.00 50.00
SCDP Denis Potvin 25.00 60.00
SCEL Patrik Elias 20.00 50.00
SCFM1 Frank Mahovlich 25.00 60.00
SCFM2 Frank Mahovlich 25.00 60.00
SCGF Grant Fuhr 25.00 60.00
SCGH Gordie Howe 100.00 200.00
SCGL Guy Lafleur 60.00 120.00
SCHL Hakan Loob 30.00 80.00
SCJA Jason Arnott 20.00 50.00
SCJB Johnny Bucyk 20.00 50.00
SCJG Jean-Sebastien Giguere 30.00 80.00
SCJK Jari Kurri 30.00 80.00
SCJW Justin Williams 20.00 50.00
SCKD Kris Draper 25.00 60.00
SCLM Lanny McDonald 25.00 60.00
SCLR Larry Robinson 25.00 60.00
SCLU Luc Robitaille
SCMB Martin Brodeur 125.00 250.00
SCME Mark Messier 100.00 200.00
SCML Mario Lemieux 100.00 200.00
SCMM Mark Messier 100.00 200.00
SCMO Mike Modano 30.00 80.00
SCNB Neal Broten 20.00 50.00
SCOR Bobby Orr 300.00 500.00
SCPE Phil Esposito 40.00 100.00
SCPR1 Patrick Roy 125.00 250.00
SCPR2 Patrick Roy 125.00 250.00
SCRE Ron Ellis 20.00 50.00
SCRG Ryan Getzlaf 25.00 60.00
SCSA Denis Savard 25.00 60.00
SCSB Scotty Bowman 25.00 60.00
SCSC Scotty Bowman 25.00 60.00
SCST Scott Gomez
SCSM Stan Mikita 25.00 60.00
SCSU Duane Sutter 20.00 50.00
SCWG Wayne Gretzky 300.00 500.00

2007-08 The Cup Stanley Cup Titlists

STATED PRINT RUN 1 TO 5 SERIAL #'d SETS
NOT PRICED DUE TO SCARCITY

2008-09 The Cup

COMP.SET w/o SPs (60)
STATED PRINT RUN 249 SER.#'d SETS
AU RC STATED PRINT RUN 199
JSY AU RC (79-144) STATED PRINT RUN 249
JSY AU RC (145-150) STATED PRINT RUN 99
1 Wayne Gretzky 20.00 50.00
2 Vincent Lecavalier 4.00 10.00
3 Tony Esposito 4.00 10.00
4 Thomas Vanek 4.00 10.00
5 Teemu Selanne 4.00 10.00
6 Brian Leetch 5.00 12.00
7 Sidney Crosby 20.00 50.00
8 Saku Koivu 4.00 10.00
9 Ryan Miller 4.00 10.00
10 Ryan Getzlaf 5.00 12.00
11 Ron Hextall 4.00 10.00
12 Roberto Luongo 6.00 15.00
13 Rick Nash 4.00 10.00
14 Ray Bourque 8.00 20.00
15 Phil Esposito 6.00 15.00
16 Brendan Shanahan 4.00 10.00
17 Pavel Datsyuk 4.00 10.00
18 Paul Stastny 4.00 10.00
19 Paul Kariya 4.00 10.00
20 Mats Sundin 4.00 10.00
21 Patrick Roy 12.00 30.00
22 Patrick Kane 10.00 25.00
23 Nicklas Lidstrom 4.00 10.00
24 Mike Richards 6.00 15.00
25 Marty Turco 3.00 8.00
26 Martin St. Louis 4.00 10.00
27 Martin Brodeur 8.00 20.00
28 Markus Naslund 4.00 10.00
29 Mark Messier 8.00 20.00
30 Mario Lemieux 10.00 25.00
31 Marian Gaborik 6.00 15.00
32 Marc-Andre Fleury 4.00 10.00
33 Luc Robitaille 3.00 8.00
34 Lanny McDonald 4.00 10.00
35 Jonathan Toews 12.00 30.00
36 Joe Thornton 6.00 15.00
37 Joe Sakic 6.00 15.00
38 Joe Mullen 4.00 10.00
39 Jean Beliveau 6.00 15.00
40 Jason Spezza 5.00 12.00
41 Jarome Iginla 8.00 20.00
42 Jari Kurri 4.00 10.00
43 Ilya Kovalchuk 5.00 12.00
44 Henrik Zetterberg 8.00 20.00
45 Guy Lafleur 8.00 20.00
46 Grant Fuhr 4.00 10.00
47 Gordie Howe 15.00 40.00
48 Frank Mahovlich 4.00 10.00
49 Evgeni Malkin 10.00 25.00
50 Eric Staal 6.00 15.00
51 Dominik Hasek 6.00 15.00
52 Dino Ciccarelli 2.50 6.00
53 Dany Heatley 5.00 12.00
54 Dale Hawerchuk 4.00 10.00
55 Carey Price 12.00 30.00
56 Cam Neely 5.00 12.00
57 Bobby Orr 12.00 30.00
58 Bobby Hull 8.00 20.00
59 Alexander Ovechkin 15.00 40.00
60 Al MacInnis 5.00 12.00
61 Nathan Oystrick AU RC 8.00 20.00
62 Marc-Andre Gragnani AU RC 6.00 15.00
63 Derek Dorsett AU RC 10.00 25.00
64 Maxsim Mayorov AU RC 15.00 40.00
65 Wayne Simmonds AU RC 8.00 20.00
66 Danny Taylor AU RC 8.00 20.00
67 Tim Ramholt AU RC 6.00 15.00
68 Mike Iggulden AU RC 6.00 15.00
69 Trevor Smith AU RC 6.00 15.00
70 Dane Byers AU RC 6.00 15.00
71 Dustin Jeffrey AU RC 12.00 30.00
72 Tom Cavanagh AU RC 6.00 15.00
73 Derek Joslin AU RC 6.00 15.00
74 Paul Szczechura AU RC 10.00 25.00
75 Jonas Frogren AU RC 10.00 25.00
76 John Mitchell AU RC 8.00 20.00
77 Simeon Varlamov AU RC 75.00 150.00
78 Oskar Osala AU RC 20.00 50.00
79 Andrew Ebbett JSY AU RC 15.00 40.00
80 Brendan Mikkelson JSY AU RC 10.00 25.00
81 Zach Bogosian JSY AU RC 30.00 80.00
82 Boris Valabik JSY AU RC 20.00 50.00
83 Nathan Gerbe JSY AU RC 30.00 80.00
84 Tim Kennedy JSY AU RC 25.00 60.00
85 Zach Boychuk JSY AU RC 25.00 60.00
86 Brandon Sutter JSY AU RC 20.00 50.00
87 Chris Stewart JSY AU RC 20.00 50.00
88 Dan LaCosta JSY AU RC 20.00 50.00
89 Steve Mason JSY AU RC 150.00 300.00
90 Tom Sestito JSY AU RC 12.00 30.00
91 Nikita Filatov JSY AU RC 50.00 100.00
92 Jakub Voracek JSY AU RC 30.00 80.00
93 Adam Pineault JSY AU RC 15.00 40.00
94 Derick Brassard JSY AU RC 30.00 80.00
95 Mark Fistric JSY AU RC 20.00 50.00
96 Fabian Brunnstrom JSY AU RC 25.00 60.00
97 James Neal JSY AU RC 25.00 60.00
98 Justin Abdelkader JSY AU RC 30.00 80.00
99 Jonathan Ericsson JSY AU RC 25.00 60.00
100 Mattias Ritola JSY AU RC 20.00 50.00
101 Darren Helm JSY AU RC 25.00 60.00
102 Michael Frolik JSY AU RC 30.00 80.00
103 Shawn Matthias JSY AU RC 15.00 40.00
104 Tyler Plante JSY AU RC 15.00 40.00
105 Michal Repik JSY AU RC 15.00 40.00
106 Kenndal McArdle JSY AU RC 15.00 40.00
107 Brian Boyle JSY AU RC 15.00 40.00
108 Oscar Moller JSY AU RC 15.00 40.00
109 Erik Ersberg JSY AU RC 15.00 40.00
110 Teddy Purcell JSY AU RC 15.00 40.00
111 Colton Gillies JSY AU RC 15.00 40.00
112 Max Pacioretty JSY AU RC 40.00 100.00
113 Matt D'Agostini JSY AU RC 25.00 60.00
114 Ben Maxwell JSY AU RC 25.00 60.00
115 Patric Hornqvist JSY AU RC 25.00 60.00
116 Ryan Jones JSY AU RC 20.00 50.00
117 Matthew Halischuk JSY AU RC 20.00 50.00
118 Petr Vrana JSY AU RC 20.00 50.00
119 Josh Bailey JSY AU RC 30.00 80.00
120 Kyle Okposo JSY AU RC 30.00 80.00
121 Trevor Lewis JSY AU RC 15.00 40.00
122 Lauri Korpikoski JSY AU RC 15.00 40.00
123 Brian Lee JSY AU RC 15.00 40.00
124 Ilya Zubov JSY AU RC 15.00 40.00
125 Claude Giroux JSY AU RC 75.00 150.00
126 Luca Sbisa JSY AU RC 25.00 60.00
127 Andreas Nodl JSY AU RC 15.00 40.00
128 Viktor Tikhonov JSY AU RC 15.00 40.00
129 Kevin Porter JSY AU RC 12.00 30.00
130 Mikkel Boedker JSY AU RC 25.00 60.00
131 Alex Goligoski JSY AU RC 30.00 80.00
132 Jonathan Filewich JSY AU RC 12.00 30.00
133 Ryan Stone JSY AU RC 15.00 40.00
134 Jamie McGinn JSY AU RC 15.00 40.00
135 Alex Pietrangelo JSY AU RC 25.00 60.00
136 Patrik Berglund JSY AU RC 40.00 100.00
137 Ben Bishop JSY AU RC 25.00 60.00
138 T.J. Oshie JSY AU RC 40.00 100.00
139 Vladimir Mihalik JSY AU RC 15.00 40.00
140 Ty Wishart JSY AU RC 15.00 40.00
141 Robbie Earl JSY AU RC 12.00 30.00
142 Nikolai Kulemin JSY AU RC 15.00 40.00
143 Cory Schneider JSY AU RC 30.00 80.00
144 Karl Alzner JSY AU RC 25.00 60.00
145 Justin Pogge JSY AU RC/99 75.00 150.00
146 Drew Doughty JSY AU RC/99 200.00 350.00
147 Blake Wheeler JSY AU RC/99 125.00 250.00
148 Luke Schenn JSY AU RC/99 150.00 300.00
149 Kyle Turris JSY AU RC/99 125.00 250.00
150 Steven Stamkos JSY AU RC/99 800.00 1200.00

2008-09 The Cup Black

STATED PRINT RUN 1 SER.#'d SET
NOT PRICED DUE TO SCARCITY

2008-09 The Cup Black Patches

This 58-card partial parallel set features 1 of 1 patch cards with a portion of the cards also featuring an on-card autograph. See checklist below for those cards with an autograph.

NOT PRICED DUE TO SCARCITY
STATED PRINT RUN 1 SER.#'d SET

2008-09 The Cup Gold

*SINGLES (1-60): .8X TO 2X BASIC CARDS
*SINGLES (61-78): .5X TO 1.2X BASIC CARDS
*SINGLES (79-144): .3X TO .8X BASIC CARDS
STATED PRINT RUN 25 SER.#'d SETS
77 Simeon Varlamov 125.00 250.00
89 Steve Mason 100.00 200.00
91 Nikita Filatov 50.00 100.00
145 Justin Pogge 20.00 50.00
146 Drew Doughty 40.00 80.00
147 Blake Wheeler 50.00 100.00
148 Luke Schenn 40.00 100.00
149 Kyle Turris 30.00 80.00
150 Steven Stamkos 100.00 200.00

2008-09 The Cup Gold Rainbow

(1-60) STATED PRINT RUN 10
ROOKIES #'d TO JERSEY NUMBER
SOME NOT PRICED DUE TO SCARCITY
1 Wayne Gretzky JSY
2 Vincent Lecavalier JSY
3 Tony Esposito JSY
4 Thomas Vanek JSY
5 Teemu Selanne JSY
6 Brian Leetch JSY
7 Sidney Crosby JSY
8 Saku Koivu JSY
9 Ryan Miller JSY
10 Ryan Getzlaf JSY
11 Ron Hextall JSY
12 Roberto Luongo JSY
13 Rick Nash JSY
14 Ray Bourque JSY
15 Phil Esposito JSY
16 Brendan Shanahan JSY
17 Pavel Datsyuk JSY
18 Paul Stastny JSY
19 Paul Kariya JSY
20 Mats Sundin JSY
21 Patrick Roy JSY
22 Patrick Kane JSY
23 Nicklas Lidstrom JSY
24 Mike Richards JSY
25 Marty Turco JSY
26 Martin St. Louis JSY
27 Martin Brodeur JSY
28 Markus Naslund JSY
29 Mark Messier JSY
30 Mario Lemieux JSY
31 Marian Gaborik JSY
32 Marc-Andre Fleury JSY
33 Luc Robitaille JSY
34 Lanny McDonald JSY
35 Jonathan Toews JSY
36 Joe Thornton JSY
37 Joe Sakic JSY
38 Joe Mullen JSY
39 Jean Beliveau JSY
40 Jason Spezza JSY
41 Jarome Iginla JSY
42 Jari Kurri JSY
43 Ilya Kovalchuk JSY
44 Henrik Zetterberg JSY
45 Guy Lafleur JSY
46 Grant Fuhr JSY
47 Gordie Howe JSY
48 Frank Mahovlich JSY
49 Evgeni Malkin JSY
50 Eric Staal JSY
51 Dominik Hasek JSY
52 Dino Ciccarelli JSY
53 Dany Heatley JSY
54 Dale Hawerchuk JSY
55 Carey Price JSY
56 Cam Neely JSY
57 Bobby Orr JSY
58 Bobby Hull JSY
59 Alexander Ovechkin JSY
60 Al MacInnis JSY
61 Nathan Oystrick AU/47 12.00 30.00
62 Marc-Andre Gragnani AU/17
63 Derek Dorsett AU/15
64 Maxsim Mayorov AU/43 15.00 40.00
65 Wayne Simmonds AU/57 10.00 25.00
66 Danny Taylor AU/46 8.00 20.00
67 Tim Ramholt AU/47 12.00 30.00
68 Mike Iggulden AU/46 8.00 20.00
69 Trevor Smith AU/77 8.00 20.00
70 Dane Byers AU/54 8.00 20.00
71 Dustin Jeffrey AU/42 8.00 20.00
72 Tom Cavanagh AU/47 8.00 20.00
73 Derek Joslin AU/65 8.00 20.00
74 Paul Szczechura AU/38 8.00 20.00
75 Jonas Frogren AU/24
76 John Mitchell AU/39 10.00 25.00
77 Simeon Varlamov AU/40 125.00 250.00
78 Oskar Osala AU/48 25.00 60.00
79 Andrew Ebbett PATCH AU/48 15.00 40.00
80 Brendan Mikkelson PATCH AU/60 15.00 40.00
81 Zach Bogosian PATCH AU/4
82 Boris Valabik PATCH AU/48 30.00 80.00
83 Nathan Gerbe PATCH AU/42 25.00 60.00
84 Tim Kennedy PATCH AU/58 25.00 60.00
85 Zach Boychuk PATCH AU/23
86 Brandon Sutter PATCH AU/16
87 Chris Stewart PATCH AU/42 15.00 40.00
88 Dan LaCosta PATCH AU/29 20.00 50.00
89 Steve Mason PATCH AU/30 150.00 300.00
90 Tom Sestito PATCH AU/43 25.00 60.00
91 Nikita Filatov PATCH AU/28 75.00 150.00
92 Jakub Voracek PATCH AU/93 40.00 100.00
93 Adam Pineault PATCH AU/41 20.00 50.00
94 Derick Brassard PATCH AU/16
95 Mark Fistric PATCH AU/28 25.00 60.00
96 Fabian Brunnstrom PATCH AU/96 40.00 100.00
97 James Neal PATCH AU/18
98 Justin Abdelkader PATCH AU/8
99 Jonathan Ericsson PATCH AU/52 30.00 80.00
100 Mattias Ritola PATCH AU/42 25.00 60.00
101 Darren Helm PATCH AU/43 60.00 120.00
102 Michael Frolik PATCH AU/67 40.00 100.00
103 Shawn Matthias PATCH AU/41 15.00 40.00
104 Tyler Plante PATCH AU/35 25.00 60.00
105 Michal Repik PATCH AU/32 25.00 60.00
106 Kenndal McArdle PATCH AU/71 15.00 40.00
107 Brian Boyle PATCH AU/22
108 Oscar Moller PATCH AU/51 30.00 80.00
109 Erik Ersberg PATCH AU/31 25.00 60.00
110 Teddy Purcell PATCH AU/54 25.00 60.00
111 Colton Gillies PATCH AU/18
112 Max Pacioretty PATCH AU/67 30.00 80.00
113 Matt D'Agostini PATCH AU/36 25.00 60.00
114 Ben Maxwell PATCH AU/80 25.00 60.00
115 Patric Hornqvist PATCH AU/27 25.00 60.00
116 Ryan Jones PATCH AU/28 20.00 50.00
117 Matthew Halischuk PATCH AU/63 20.00 50.00
118 Petr Vrana PATCH AU/22
119 Josh Bailey PATCH AU/12
120 Kyle Okposo PATCH AU/21
121 Trevor Lewis PATCH AU/61 15.00 40.00
122 Lauri Korpikoski PATCH AU/60 20.00 50.00
123 Brian Lee PATCH AU/55 15.00 40.00
124 Ilya Zubov PATCH AU/53 15.00 40.00
125 Claude Giroux PATCH AU/28 150.00 300.00
126 Luca Sbisa PATCH AU/47 20.00 50.00
127 Andreas Nodl PATCH AU/41 15.00 40.00
128 Viktor Tikhonov PATCH AU/41 20.00 50.00
129 Kevin Porter PATCH AU/23 20.00 50.00
130 Mikkel Boedker PATCH AU/89 20.00 50.00
131 Alex Goligoski PATCH AU/67 30.00 80.00
132 Jonathan Filewich PATCH AU/34 20.00 50.00
133 Ryan Stone PATCH AU/33 12.00 30.00
134 Jamie McGinn PATCH AU/64 20.00 50.00
135 Alex Pietrangelo PATCH AU/52 30.00 80.00
136 Patrik Berglund PATCH AU/58 30.00 80.00
137 Ben Bishop PATCH AU/30 30.00 80.00
138 T.J. Oshie PATCH AU/74 75.00 150.00
139 Vladimir Mihalik PATCH AU/56
140 Ty Wishart PATCH AU/3
141 Robbie Earl PATCH AU/52 12.00 30.00
142 Nikolai Kulemin PATCH AU/41 20.00 50.00
143 Cory Schneider PATCH AU/35 40.00 100.00
144 Karl Alzner PATCH AU/27
145 Justin Pogge PATCH AU/29 75.00 150.00
146 Drew Doughty PATCH AU/13
147 Blake Wheeler PATCH AU/26 100.00 200.00
148 Luke Schenn PATCH AU/2
149 Kyle Turris PATCH AU/91 60.00 120.00
150 Steven Stamkos PATCH AU/91 400.00 600.00

2008-09 The Cup Platinum Jerseys

*SINGLES: 1.2X TO 3X BASE SET
STATED PRINT RUN 25 SER.#'d SETS
1 Wayne Gretzky 60.00 150.00
2 Vincent Lecavalier 12.00 30.00
3 Tony Esposito 12.00 30.00
4 Thomas Vanek 12.00 30.00
5 Teemu Selanne 12.00 30.00
6 Brian Leetch 15.00 40.00
7 Sidney Crosby 60.00 150.00
8 Saku Koivu 12.00 30.00
9 Ryan Miller 12.00 30.00
10 Ryan Getzlaf 15.00 40.00
11 Ron Hextall 12.00 30.00
12 Roberto Luongo 20.00 50.00
13 Rick Nash 12.00 30.00
14 Ray Bourque 25.00 60.00
15 Phil Esposito 20.00 50.00
16 Brendan Shanahan 12.00 30.00
17 Pavel Datsyuk 12.00 30.00
18 Paul Stastny 12.00 30.00
19 Paul Kariya 12.00 30.00
20 Mats Sundin 12.00 30.00
21 Patrick Roy 40.00 100.00
22 Patrick Kane 30.00 80.00
23 Nicklas Lidstrom 12.00 30.00
24 Mike Richards 20.00 50.00
25 Marty Turco 10.00 25.00
26 Martin St. Louis 12.00 30.00
27 Martin Brodeur 25.00 60.00
28 Markus Naslund 12.00 30.00
29 Mark Messier 25.00 60.00
30 Mario Lemieux 30.00 80.00
31 Marian Gaborik 20.00 50.00
32 Marc-Andre Fleury 12.00 30.00
33 Luc Robitaille 10.00 25.00

34 Lanny McDonald 12.00 30.00
35 Jonathan Toews 40.00 100.00
36 Joe Thornton 20.00 50.00
37 Joe Sakic 20.00 50.00
38 Joe Mullen 12.00 30.00
39 Jean Beliveau 20.00 50.00
40 Jason Spezza 15.00 40.00
41 Jarome Iginla 25.00 60.00
42 Jari Kurri 12.00 30.00
43 Ilya Kovalchuk 15.00 40.00
44 Henrik Zetterberg 25.00 60.00
45 Guy Lafleur 25.00 60.00
46 Grant Fuhr 12.00 30.00
47 Gordie Howe 50.00 120.00
48 Frank Mahovlich 12.00 30.00
49 Evgeni Malkin 30.00 80.00
50 Eric Staal 20.00 50.00
51 Dominik Hasek 20.00 50.00
52 Dino Ciccarelli 8.00 20.00
53 Dany Heatley 15.00 40.00
54 Dale Hawerchuk 12.00 30.00
55 Carey Price 40.00 100.00
56 Cam Neely 15.00 40.00
58 Bobby Hull 25.00 60.00
59 Alexander Ovechkin 50.00 120.00
60 Al MacInnis 15.00 40.00

2008-09 The Cup 20 Years of Greatness

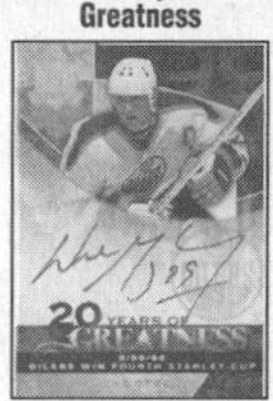

COMMON GRETZKY 600.00 900.00
STATED PRINT RUN 5 SER.#'d SETS
20YG1 Wayne Gretzky 600.00 900.00
20YG2 Wayne Gretzky 600.00 900.00
20YG3 Wayne Gretzky 600.00 900.00
20YG4 Wayne Gretzky 600.00 900.00
20YG5 Wayne Gretzky 600.00 900.00
20YG6 Wayne Gretzky 600.00 900.00
20YG7 Wayne Gretzky 600.00 900.00
20YG8 Wayne Gretzky 600.00 900.00
20YG9 Wayne Gretzky 600.00 900.00
20YG10 Wayne Gretzky 600.00 900.00
20YG11 Wayne Gretzky 600.00 900.00
20YG12 Wayne Gretzky 600.00 900.00
20YG13 Wayne Gretzky 600.00 900.00
20YG14 Wayne Gretzky 600.00 900.00
20YG15 Wayne Gretzky 600.00 900.00
20YG16 Wayne Gretzky 600.00 900.00
20YG17 Wayne Gretzky 600.00 900.00
20YG18 Wayne Gretzky 600.00 900.00
20YG19 Wayne Gretzky 600.00 900.00
20YG20 Wayne Gretzky 600.00 900.00

2008-09 The Cup 500 Goal Club Swatches

STATED PRINT RUN 5 SER.#'d SETS
NOT PRICED DUE TO SCARCITY
500GCBH Bobby Hull
500GCBU Johnny Bucyk
500GCDC Dino Ciccarelli
500GCDH Dale Hawerchuk
500GCFM Frank Mahovlich
500GCGH Gordie Howe
500GCGP Gilbert Perreault
500GCJB Jean Beliveau
500GCJK Jari Kurri
500GCJM Joe Mullen
500GCLM Lanny McDonald
500GCLR Luc Robitaille
500GCMB Mike Bossy
500GCMD Marcel Dionne
500GCML Mario Lemieux
500GCMM Mark Messier
500GCPE Phil Esposito
500GCWG Wayne Gretzky

2008-09 The Cup Auto Draft Boards

STATED PRINT RUN 50 SER.#'d SETS
DBAC Andrew Cogliano 40.00 100.00
DBAK Anze Kopitar 25.00 60.00
DBAP Alex Pietrangelo 40.00 100.00
DBBE Jonathan Bernier 30.00 80.00
DBBO Zach Boychuk 40.00 100.00
DBBR Bobby Ryan 40.00 100.00
DBBS Brandon Sutter 30.00 80.00
DBCG Colton Gillies 25.00 60.00
DBCP Carey Price 150.00 300.00
DBCS Chris Stewart 30.00 80.00
DBDB Derick Brassard 75.00 150.00
DBDD Drew Doughty 125.00 250.00
DBDS Devin Setoguchi 75.00 150.00
DBFO Nick Foligno 25.00 60.00
DBGI Claude Giroux 100.00 200.00
DBJB Josh Bailey 60.00 120.00
DBJS Jordan Staal 40.00 100.00
DBJT Jonathan Toews 125.00 250.00
DBJV Jakub Voracek 75.00 150.00
DBKA Karl Alzner 40.00 100.00
DBKE Phil Kessel 60.00 120.00
DBKM Kenndal McArdle 25.00 60.00
DBKO Kyle Okposo 75.00 150.00
DBKT Kyle Turris 100.00 200.00
DBLE Brian Lee 25.00 60.00
DBLS Luke Schenn 125.00 250.00
DBLW Trevor Lewis 25.00 60.00
DBMB Mikkel Boedker 40.00 100.00
DBMF Michael Frolik
DBMH Martin Hanzal
DBMN Matt Niskanen
DBMP Max Pacioretty 75.00 150.00
DBMS Marc Staal 30.00 80.00
DBNB Nicklas Backstrom 100.00 200.00
DBNF Nikita Filatov 100.00 200.00
DBNI Nicklas Bergfors 40.00 100.00
DBPB Patrik Berglund
DBPK Patrick Kane 100.00 200.00
DBPM Peter Mueller 30.00 80.00
DBSB Luca Sbisa 40.00 100.00
DBSC Sidney Crosby 600.00 800.00
DBSD Steve Downie 25.00 60.00
DBSG Sam Gagner 75.00 150.00
DBSH James Sheppard 25.00 60.00
DBSS Steven Stamkos 175.00 300.00
DBSV Simeon Varlamov 100.00 200.00
DBTO T.J. Oshie 125.00 250.00
DBTR Tuukka Rask 50.00 100.00
DBTW Ty Wishart 25.00 60.00
DBVT Viktor Tikhonov 25.00 60.00
DBZB Zach Bogosian 60.00 120.00

2008-09 The Cup Chirography

STATED PRINT RUN 50 SER.#'d SETS
CCAO Alexander Ovechkin 75.00 150.00
CCBH Bobby Hull 25.00 60.00
CCBO Bobby Orr 100.00 200.00
CCBR Martin Brodeur 50.00 100.00
CCEM Evgeni Malkin 30.00 80.00
CCFM Frank Mahovlich 15.00 40.00
CCGH Gordie Howe 60.00
CCGP Gilbert Perreault 12.00 30.00
CCIK Ilya Kovalchuk 15.00 40.00
CCJB Jean Beliveau 20.00 50.00
CCJI Jarome Iginla 25.00 60.00
CCJT Joe Thornton 20.00 50.00
CCMB Mike Bossy 12.00 30.00
CCML Mario Lemieux 50.00 100.00
CCMM Mark Messier 50.00 100.00
CCPE Phil Esposito 20.00 50.00
CCPR Patrick Roy 75.00 150.00
CCRB Ray Bourque 25.00 60.00
CCRH Ron Hextall 12.00 30.00
CCRO Larry Robinson 12.00 30.00
CCSC Sidney Crosby 125.00 250.00
CCVL Vincent Lecavalier 12.00 30.00
CCWG Wayne Gretzky 150.00 250.00

2008-09 The Cup Emblems of Endorsement

STATED PRINT RUN 15 SER.#'d SETS
NOT PRICED DUE TO SCARCITY
EEJC Jeff Carter
EEJS Jordan Staal
EEPB Patrice Bergeron
EEAK Anze Kopitar
EEAO Adam Oates
EEAP Alex Pietrangelo
EEBE Patrik Berglund
EEBL Brian Leetch
EEBO Mikkel Boedker
EEBS Brandon Sutter
EECG Colton Gillies
EECN Cam Neely
EECP Carey Price
EECS Cory Schneider
EECW Cam Ward
EEDB Derick Brassard
EEDC Dino Ciccarelli
EEDD Drew Doughty
EEDG Doug Gilmour
EEDH Dale Hawerchuk
EEEM Evgeni Malkin
EEES Eric Staal
EEFB Fabian Brunnstrom
EEFR Michael Frolik
EEGA Simon Gagne
EEGH Gordie Howe
EEGK Marian Gaborik
EEHA Dominik Hasek
EEHE Dany Heatley
EEHL Henrik Lundqvist
EEHZ Henrik Zetterberg
EEIK Ilya Kovalchuk
EEJI Jarome Iginla
EEJP Jean-Pierre Dumont
EEJT Joe Thornton
EEKT Kyle Turris
EELE Mario Lemieux
EELM Lanny McDonald
EELS Luke Schenn
EEMB Martin Brodeur
EEMF Marc-Andre Fleury
EEMG Mike Green
EEMI Milan Hejduk
EEMM Mark Messier
EEMN Markus Naslund
EEMO Mike Modano
EEMS Martin St. Louis
EEMT Marty Turco
EENB Nicklas Backstrom
EENK Nikolai Kulemin
EENL Nicklas Lidstrom
EEOS T.J. Oshie
EEPE Corey Perry
EEPK Patrick Kane
EEPM Peter Mueller
EEPR Patrick Roy
EERB Ray Bourque
EERG Ryan Getzlaf
EERM Ryan Miller
EERN Rick Nash
EERO Luc Robitaille
EESC Sidney Crosby
EESG Sam Gagner
EESP Peter Stastny
EESS Steven Stamkos
EETO Jonathan Toews
EEVL Vincent Lecavalier
EEVO Tomas Vokoun
EEWG Wayne Gretzky
EEZA Zach Boychuk
EEZB Zach Bogosian

2008-09 The Cup Enshrinements

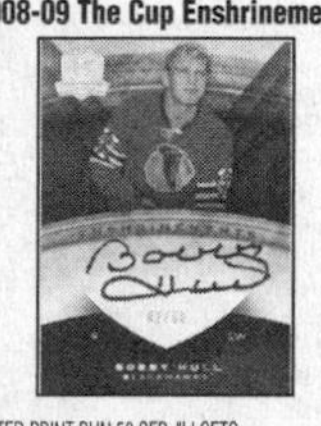

STATED PRINT RUN 50 SER.#'d SETS
CEAB Andy Bathgate 12.00 30.00
CEAO Alexander Ovechkin 60.00 120.00
CEBB Butch Bouchard 15.00 40.00
CEBC Bobby Clarke 12.00 30.00
CEBH Bobby Hull 25.00 60.00
CEBL Brian Leetch 15.00 40.00
CEBO Bobby Orr 60.00 120.00
CEBS Borje Salming 12.00 30.00
CEBU Johnny Bucyk 12.00 30.00
CECN Cam Neely 15.00 40.00
CEDH Dany Heatley 15.00 40.00
CEEM Evgeni Malkin 30.00 80.00
CEES Eric Staal 20.00 50.00
CEFM Frank Mahovlich 12.00 30.00
CEGF Grant Fuhr 12.00 30.00
CEGH Gordie Howe 60.00 120.00
CEGP Gilbert Perreault 12.00 30.00
CEHA Dominik Hasek 20.00 50.00
CEHZ Henrik Zetterberg 25.00 60.00
CEJB Jean Beliveau 20.00 50.00
CEJI Jarome Iginla 25.00 60.00
CEJK Jari Kurri 12.00 30.00
CEJO Johnny Bower 15.00 40.00
CEJT Joe Thornton 20.00 50.00
CELR Larry Robinson 12.00 30.00
CEMB Martin Brodeur 50.00 100.00
CEML Mario Lemieux 60.00 120.00
CEMM Mark Messier 50.00 100.00
CEMO Mike Modano 12.00 30.00
CENL Nicklas Lidstrom 12.00 30.00
CEPE Phil Esposito 20.00 50.00
CEPH Dion Phaneuf 12.00 30.00
CEPR Patrick Roy 50.00 100.00
CERB Ray Bourque 25.00 60.00
CERL Rod Langway 15.00 40.00
CERN Rick Nash 12.00 30.00
CESC Sidney Crosby 100.00 200.00
CETE Tony Esposito 12.00 30.00
CEWG Wayne Gretzky 150.00 250.00

2008-09 The Cup Enshrinements Dual

STATED PRINT RUN 25 SER.#'d SETS
CE2BH Jean Beliveau 80.00 200.00
Gordie Howe
CE2BL Ted Lindsay 25.00 60.00
Butch Bouchard
CE2BM Johnny Bucyk
Frank Mahovlich
CE2BT Marty Turco 40.00 100.00
Martin Brodeur
CE2HM Bobby Hull 40.00 100.00
Stan Mikita
CE2HN Rick Nash 25.00 60.00
Dany Heatley
CE2IS Jarome Iginla 40.00 100.00
Eric Staal
CE2KH Jari Kurri 20.00 50.00
Dale Hawerchuk
CE2KM Ilya Kovalchuk 50.00 120.00
Evgeni Malkin
CE2LG Rod Langway 25.00 60.00
Clark Gillies
CE2NB Nicklas Lidstrom 20.00 50.00
Borje Salming
CE2PB Scotty Bowman
Denis Potvin
CE2RD Patrick Roy 60.00 150.00
Dick Duff
CE2SM Denis Savard 20.00 50.00
Joe Mullen

2008-09 The Cup Enshrinements Triple

STATED PRINT RUN 10 SER.#'d SETS
NOT PRICED DUE TO SCARCITY
CE3BBD Dick Duff
Butch Bouchard
Jean Beliveau
CE3COB Cam Neely
Bobby Orr
Ray Bourque
CE3EBO Bobby Orr
Johnny Bucyk
Phil Esposito
CE3EHM Bobby Hull
Tony Esposito
Stan Mikita
CE3KGM Jari Kurri
Wayne Gretzky
Mark Messier
CE3LHD Ted Lindsay
Gordie Howe
Alex Delvecchio
CE3LSP Denis Savard
Gilbert Perreault
Mario Lemieux
CE3LZS Henrik Zetterberg
Nicklas Lidstrom
Borje Salming
CE3RBV Rogie Vachon
Patrick Roy
Martin Brodeur

2008-09 The Cup Foundations Jerseys

STATED PRINT RUN 25 SER.#'d SETS
CFBT Bryan Trottier 6.00 15.00
CFKA Karl Alzner 12.00 30.00
CFAK Anze Kopitar 8.00 20.00
CFAO Adam Oates 8.00 20.00
CFBC Bobby Clarke
CFBH Bobby Hull 15.00 40.00
CFBK Mikkel Boedker 12.00 30.00
CFBL Brian Leetch 10.00 25.00
CFBM Ben Maxwell
CFBS Brandon Sutter 10.00 25.00
CFBU Johnny Bucyk 8.00 20.00
CFBW Blake Wheeler 20.00 50.00
CFCG Colton Gillies 8.00 20.00
CFCS Cory Schneider 15.00 40.00
CFDB Derick Brassard 15.00 40.00
CFDD Drew Doughty 25.00 60.00
CFDE Denis Savard 8.00 20.00
CFEM Evgeni Malkin 20.00 50.00
CFEP Phil Esposito 12.00 30.00
CFES Eric Staal 12.00 30.00
CFFB Fabian Brunnstrom 12.00 30.00
CFGF Grant Fuhr 8.00 20.00
CFGH Gordie Howe 30.00 80.00
CFHA Dominik Hasek 12.00 30.00
CFHE Dany Heatley 10.00 25.00
CFHL Henrik Lundqvist 15.00 40.00
CFHO Marian Hossa 12.00 30.00
CFHZ Henrik Zetterberg
CFIK Ilya Kovalchuk 10.00 25.00
CFJI Jarome Iginla 15.00 40.00
CFJK Carey Price 25.00 60.00
CFJN James Neal 12.00 30.00
CFJO Joe Sakic 12.00 30.00
CFJP Jean-Pierre Dumont 5.00 12.00
CFJS Jason Spezza 10.00 25.00
CFJT Joe Thornton 12.00 30.00
CFJV Jakub Voracek 15.00 40.00
CFKL Kari Lehtonen 5.00 12.00
CFKO Kyle Okposo 15.00 40.00
CFKT Kyle Turris 15.00 40.00
CFKV Alex Kovalev 8.00 20.00
CFLS Luke Schenn 25.00 60.00
CFMB Martin Brodeur 15.00 40.00
CFMF Marc-Andre Fleury 15.00 40.00
CFMG Sam Gagner 12.00 30.00
CFMH Milan Hejduk 6.00 15.00
CFMK Nicklas Backstrom 15.00 40.00
CFML Mario Lemieux 20.00 50.00
CFMM Mark Messier 15.00 40.00
CFMO Mike Modano 8.00 20.00
CFMR Mike Richards 12.00 30.00
CFMS Martin St. Louis 8.00 20.00
CFMT Marty Turco 6.00 15.00
CFNF Nikita Filatov 30.00 80.00
CFNL Nicklas Lidstrom 8.00 20.00
CFOV Alexander Ovechkin 30.00 80.00
CFPB Patrice Bergeron 8.00 20.00
CFPD Pavel Datsyuk 8.00 20.00
CFPH Dion Phaneuf 8.00 20.00
CFPK Paul Kariya 8.00 20.00
CFPR Patrick Roy 25.00 60.00
CFPS Paul Stastny 8.00 20.00
CFRB Ray Bourque 15.00 40.00
CFRL Roberto Luongo 12.00 30.00
CFRN Rick Nash 8.00 20.00
CFRS Ryan Smyth 6.00 15.00
CFRV Rogie Vachon 8.00 20.00
CFSC Sidney Crosby 60.00 120.00
CFSD Shane Doan 5.00 12.00
CFSF Sergei Fedorov 12.00 30.00
CFSG Simon Gagne 6.00 15.00
CFSK Saku Koivu 8.00 20.00
CFSL Jordan Staal 12.00 30.00
CFSS Steven Stamkos 30.00 80.00
CFST Chris Stewart 10.00 25.00
CFSU Mats Sundin 8.00 20.00
CFSV Simeon Varlamov
CFSY Peter Stastny 8.00 20.00
CFTH Tomas Holmstrom
CFTS Teemu Selanne 8.00 20.00
CFTV Thomas Vanek 8.00 20.00
CFTW Peter Mueller 10.00 25.00
CFVL Vincent Lecavalier 8.00 20.00
CFWG Wayne Gretzky 60.00 120.00
CFWR Wade Redden 5.00 12.00
CFZB Zach Bogosian 15.00 40.00
CFZP Zach Parise 8.00 20.00

2008-09 The Cup Foundations Jerseys Autographs

STATED PRINT RUN 10 SER.#'d SETS
NOT PRICED DUE TO SCARCITY
CFJS Jordan Staal
CFAK Anze Kopitar
CFAO Adam Oates
CFBC Bobby Clarke
CFBH Bobby Hull
CFBK Mikkel Boedker

CFBL Brian Leetch
CFBM Ben Maxwell
CFBS Brandon Sutter
CFBU Johnny Bucyk
CFBW Blake Wheeler
CFCG Colton Gillies
CFCS Cory Schneider
CFDB Derick Brassard
CFDC Jonathan Toews
CFDD Drew Doughty
CFDE Denis Savard
CFDH Patrick Kane
CFEM Evgeni Malkin
CFEP Phil Esposito
CFES Eric Staal
CFFB Fabian Brunnstrom
CFGF Grant Fuhr
CFGH Gordie Howe
CFHA Dominik Hasek
CFHE Dany Heatley
CFHL Henrik Lundqvist
CFHZ Henrik Zetterberg
CFIK Ilya Kovalchuk
CFJI Jarome Iginla
CFJK Carey Price
CFJN James Neal
CFJP Jean-Pierre Dumont
CFJT Joe Thornton
CFJV Jakub Voracek
CFKA Karl Alzner
CFKO Kyle Okposo
CFKT Kyle Turris
CFLS Luke Schenn
CFMB Martin Brodeur
CFMF Marc-Andre Fleury
CFMG Sam Gagner
CFMH Milan Hejduk
CFMK Nicklas Backstrom
CFML Mario Lemieux
CFMM Mark Messier
CFMO Mike Modano
CFMR Mike Richards
CFMS Martin St. Louis
CFMT Marty Turco
CFNF Nikita Filatov
CFNL Nicklas Lidstrom
CFPB Patrice Bergeron
CFPD Pavel Datsyuk
CFPR Patrick Roy
CFRB Ray Bourque
CFRN Rick Nash
CFRV Rogie Vachon
CFSC Sidney Crosby
CFSG Simon Gagne
CFSS Steven Stamkos
CFST Chris Stewart
CFSY Peter Stastny
CFTW Peter Mueller
CFVL Vincent Lecavalier
CFWG Wayne Gretzky
CFZB Zach Bogosian

2008-09 The Cup Foundations Patches

STATED PRINT RUN 10 SER.#'d SETS
NOT PRICED DUE TO SCARCITY
CFAK Alex Kovalev
CFTS Teemu Selanne
CFZP Zach Parise
CFAK Anze Kopitar
CFAO Adam Oates
CFBC Bobby Clarke
CFBH Bobby Hull
CFBK Mikkel Boedker
CFBL Brian Leetch
CFBM Ben Maxwell
CFBS Brandon Sutter
CFBU Johnny Bucyk
CFBW Blake Wheeler
CFCG Colton Gillies
CFCS Cory Schneider
CFDB Derick Brassard
CFDC Jonathan Toews
CFDD Drew Doughty
CFDH Patrick Kane
CFEM Evgeni Malkin
CFES Eric Staal
CFFB Fabian Brunnstrom
CFGF Grant Fuhr
CFGH Gordie Howe
CFHA Dominik Hasek
CFHE Dany Heatley
CFHL Henrik Lundqvist
CFHO Marian Hossa
CFHZ Henrik Zetterberg
CFIK Ilya Kovalchuk
CFJI Jarome Iginla
CFJK Carey Price
CFJN James Neal
CFJO Joe Sakic
CFJP Jean-Pierre Dumont
CFJS Jason Spezza
CFJT Joe Thornton
CFJV Jakub Voracek
CFKL Kari Lehtonen
CFKO Kyle Okposo
CFKT Kyle Turris
CFLS Luke Schenn
CFMB Martin Brodeur
CFMF Marc-Andre Fleury
CFMG Sam Gagner
CFMH Milan Hejduk
CFMK Nicklas Backstrom
CFML Mario Lemieux
CFMM Mark Messier
CFMO Mike Modano
CFMR Mike Richards
CFMS Martin St. Louis
CFMT Marty Turco
CFNF Nikita Filatov
CFNL Nicklas Lidstrom
CFOV Alexander Ovechkin
CFPB Patrice Bergeron
CFPD Pavel Datsyuk
CFPH Dion Phaneuf
CFPK Paul Kariya
CFPR Patrick Roy
CFPS Paul Stastny
CFRB Ray Bourque
CFRL Roberto Luongo
CFRN Rick Nash
CFRS Ryan Smyth
CFSC Sidney Crosby
CFSD Shane Doan
CFSF Sergei Fedorov
CFSG Simon Gagne
CFSK Saku Koivu
CFSL Jordan Staal
CFSS Steven Stamkos
CFST Chris Stewart
CFSU Mats Sundin
CFSY Peter Stastny
CFTH Tomas Holmstrom
CFTV Thomas Vanek
CFTW Peter Mueller
CFVL Vincent Lecavalier
CFWR Wade Redden
CFZB Zach Bogosian

2008-09 The Cup Foundations Patches Autographs

STATED PRINT RUN 5 SER.#'d SETS
NOT PRICED DUE TO SCARCITY
CFAK Anze Kopitar
CFAO Adam Oates
CFBC Bobby Clarke
CFBH Bobby Hull
CFBK Mikkel Boedker
CFBL Brian Leetch
CFBM Ben Maxwell
CFBS Brandon Sutter
CFBU Johnny Bucyk
CFBW Blake Wheeler
CFCG Colton Gillies
CFCS Cory Schneider
CFDB Derick Brassard
CFDC Jonathan Toews
CFDD Drew Doughty
CFDH Patrick Kane
CFEM Evgeni Malkin
CFES Eric Staal
CFFB Fabian Brunnstrom
CFGF Grant Fuhr
CFGH Gordie Howe
CFHA Dominik Hasek
CFHE Dany Heatley
CFHL Henrik Lundqvist
CFHZ Henrik Zetterberg
CFIK Ilya Kovalchuk
CFJI Jarome Iginla
CFJK Carey Price
CFJN James Neal
CFJP Jean-Pierre Dumont
CFJT Joe Thornton
CFJV Jakub Voracek
CFKO Kyle Okposo
CFKT Kyle Turris
CFLS Luke Schenn
CFMB Martin Brodeur
CFMF Marc-Andre Fleury
CFMG Sam Gagner
CFMH Milan Hejduk
CFMK Nicklas Backstrom
CFML Mario Lemieux
CFMM Mark Messier
CFMO Mike Modano
CFMR Mike Richards
CFMS Martin St. Louis
CFMT Marty Turco
CFNF Nikita Filatov
CFNL Nicklas Lidstrom
CFPB Patrice Bergeron
CFPD Pavel Datsyuk
CFPR Patrick Roy
CFPS Paul Stastny
CFRB Ray Bourque
CFRN Rick Nash
CFSC Sidney Crosby
CFSD Shane Doan
CFSG Simon Gagne
CFSS Steven Stamkos
CFST Chris Stewart
CFSY Peter Stastny
CFTW Peter Mueller
CFVL Vincent Lecavalier
CFWG Wayne Gretzky
CFZB Zach Bogosian

2008-09 The Cup Honorable Numbers

SER.#'d TO JERSEY NUMBER
SOME NOT PRICED DUE TO SCARCITY
HNAP Alex Pietrangelo/27 15.00 40.00
HNBK Mikkel Boedker/89 20.00 50.00
HNBL Brian Leetch/2
HNBS Brandon Sutter/16
HNBW Blake Wheeler/26 75.00 150.00
HNCG Colton Gillies/18
HNCN Cam Neely/8
HNCP Carey Price/31 100.00 200.00
HNDB Derick Brassard/16
HNDC Dino Ciccarelli/22
HNDD Drew Doughty/8
HNEM Evgeni Malkin/71 100.00 200.00
HNES Eric Staal/12
HNFB Fabian Brunnstrom/96 25.00 60.00
HNGA Sam Gagner/89 40.00 100.00
HNGF Grant Fuhr/31 30.00 80.00
HNGL Guy Lafleur/10
HNHL Henrik Lundqvist/30 100.00 200.00
HNIK Ilya Kovalchuk/17
HNJI Jarome Iginla/12
HNJS Jordan Staal/11
HNJT Jonathan Toews/19
HNJV Jakub Voracek/93 25.00 60.00
HNKO Kyle Okposo/21
HNKT Kyle Turris/91 40.00 100.00
HNLS Luke Schenn/2
HNMB Martin Brodeur/30 100.00 200.00
HNMF Michael Frolik/67 25.00 60.00
HNML Mario Lemieux/66 100.00 200.00
HNMM Mark Messier/11
HNMT Marty Turco/35 50.00 100.00
HNNB Nicklas Backstrom/19
HNNF Nikita Filatov/28 60.00 120.00
HNNL Nicklas Lidstrom/5
HNPK Patrick Kane/88 40.00 100.00
HNPM Peter Mueller/88 25.00 60.00
HNPR Patrick Roy/33 125.00 250.00
HNRB Ray Bourque/77 40.00 100.00
HNRM Ryan Miller/30 25.00 60.00
HNRN Rick Nash/61 30.00 80.00
HNSC Sidney Crosby/87 200.00 350.00
HNSG Simon Gagne/12
HNSS Steven Stamkos/91 75.00 150.00
HNTH Joe Thornton/19
HNTV Thomas Vanek/26
HNVL Vincent Lecavalier/4
HNWG Wayne Gretzky/1
HNZB Zach Bogosian/4

2008-09 The Cup Honorable Numbers Dual

SER.#'d TO JERSEY NUMBER
SOME NOT PRICED DUE TO SCARCITY
HN2AG Glenn Anderson
Marian Gaborik/10
HN2BM Martin Brodeur 125.00 250.00
Ryan Miller/30
HN2BS Brandon Sutter
Derick Brassard/16
HN2DB Shane Doan
Nicklas Backstrom/19
HN2FG Claude Giroux 150.00 300.00
Nikita Filatov/28
HN2FP Carey Price
Grant Fuhr/31
HN2GS Chris Stewart
Nathan Gerbe/42
HN2HG Ryan Getzlaf
Dany Heatley/15
HN2IS Eric Staal
Jarome Iginla/12
HN2KK Jari Kurri
Ilya Kovalchuk/17
HN2KM Patrick Kane
Peter Mueller/88
HN2KS Jordan Staal
Saku Koivu/11
HN2LG Guy Lafleur
Marian Gaborik/10
HN2LP Denis Potvin
Nicklas Lidstrom/5
HN2NG Colton Gillies
James Neal/18
HN2NR Mike Richards
James Neal/18
HN2SB Eric Staal
Josh Bailey/12
HN2SG Jean-Sebastien Giguere
Cory Schneider/35
HN2SS Peter Stastny 60.00 120.00
Paul Stastny/26
HN2SW Blake Wheeler
Paul Stastny/26
HN2TB Joe Thornton
Nicklas Backstrom/19
HN2TK Nikolai Kulemin 30.00 80.00
Viktor Tikhonov/41
HN2TS Kyle Turris 100.00 200.00
Steven Stamkos/91
HN2TT Jonathan Toews
Joe Thornton/19

2008-09 The Cup Legendary Cuts

LCAJ Aurel Joliat/3
LCAR Art Ross/1
LCBC Bill Cook/1
LCBG Bernie Geoffrion/1
LCBM Bill Mosienko/2
LCBP Babe Pratt/4
LCCA Clarence Campbell/6
LCCC Charlie Conacher/1
LCCO Bun Cook/2
LCCR Chuck Rayner/3
LCCS Conn Smythe/1
LCDC Dit Clapper/1

LCDH Doug Harvey/1
LCFB Frank Boucher/3
LCFS Frank Selke/3
LCGD Gordie Drillon/3
LCGW Gump Worsley/1
LCHB Herb Brooks/2
LCHD Hap Day/1
LCHM Howie Morenz/3
LCHO Harry Oliver/4
LCHW Harry Watson/1
LCJP Jacques Plante/4
LCKC King Clancy/1
LCLP Lester Patrick/1
LCLS Lord Stanley/1
LCMB Max Bentley/3
LCMM Murray Murdoch/5
LCMR Maurice Richard/6
LCPA Lynn Patrick/3
LCPI Punch Imlach/5
LCPK Pep Kelly/1
LCPL Pit Lepine/2
LCRC Roger Crozier/1
LCSA Syl Apps/1
LCSH Syd Howe/1
LCSM Sylvio Mantha/1
LCTB Turk Broda/2
LCTH Tim Horton/6
LCTS Terry Sawchuk/1

2008-09 The Cup Limited Logos

STATED PRINT RUN 50 SER.#'d SETS
LLJC Jeff Carter 40.00 100.00
LLJS Jordan Staal 30.00 80.00
LLPB Patrice Bergeron 20.00 50.00
LLAP Alex Pietrangelo 30.00 80.00
LLBL Brian Leetch 25.00 60.00
LLBO Mikkel Boedker 30.00 80.00
LLBS Brandon Sutter 25.00 60.00
LLBW Blake Wheeler 75.00 150.00
LLCD Chris Drury 20.00 50.00
LLCG Colton Gillies 20.00 50.00
LLCP Carey Price 100.00 200.00
LLCS Cory Schneider 40.00 100.00
LLCW Cam Ward 20.00 50.00
LLDB Derick Brassard 60.00 120.00
LLDD Drew Doughty 60.00 120.00
LLDG Doug Gilmour 25.00 60.00
LLDH Dany Heatley 25.00 60.00
LLDS Daniel Sedin 20.00 50.00
LLEM Evgeni Malkin 100.00 175.00
LLES Eric Staal 30.00 80.00
LLFR Michael Frolik 40.00 100.00
LLGA Glenn Anderson 15.00 40.00
LLHA Dominik Hasek 30.00 80.00
LLHE Milan Hejduk 15.00 40.00
LLHL Henrik Lundqvist 100.00 175.00
LLHS Henrik Sedin 20.00 50.00
LLHZ Henrik Zetterberg 40.00 100.00
LLIK Ilya Kovalchuk 25.00 60.00
LLJI Jarome Iginla 40.00 100.00
LLJN James Neal 30.00 80.00
LLJT Joe Thornton 30.00 80.00
LLJV Jakub Voracek 40.00 100.00
LLKA Karl Alzner
LLKE Phil Kessel 20.00 50.00
LLKO Anze Kopitar 20.00 50.00
LLKT Kyle Turris 40.00 100.00
LLLK Lauri Korpikoski 20.00 50.00
LLLR Luc Robitaille 25.00 60.00
LLLS Luke Schenn 40.00 100.00
LLMB Martin Brodeur 100.00 200.00
LLMC Mike Cammalleri 20.00 50.00
LLMF Marc-Andre Fleury 50.00 100.00
LLMG Marian Gaborik 30.00 80.00
LLMH Marian Hossa
LLML Mario Lemieux 125.00 200.00
LLMM Mark Messier 75.00 150.00
LLMN Markus Naslund 20.00 50.00
LLMO Mike Modano 20.00 50.00
LLMS Martin St. Louis 20.00 50.00
LLMT Marty Turco 15.00 40.00
LLNB Nicklas Backstrom 40.00 100.00
LLNF Nikita Filatov 100.00 200.00
LLNK Nikolai Kulemin 20.00 50.00
LLNL Nicklas Lidstrom 20.00 50.00
LLOS T.J. Oshie 60.00 120.00
LLPD Pavel Datsyuk 40.00 100.00
LLPH Patric Hornqvist 20.00 50.00
LLPK Patrick Kane 60.00 120.00
LLPM Peter Mueller 25.00 60.00
LLPR Patrick Roy 100.00 200.00
LLPV Petr Vrana 25.00 60.00
LLRB Ray Bourque 40.00 100.00
LLRI Mike Richards 30.00 80.00
LLRM Ryan Miller 60.00 120.00
LLRN Rick Nash 25.00 60.00
LLSC Sidney Crosby 300.00 600.00
LLSG Sam Gagner 30.00 80.00
LLSH Steve Shutt 20.00 50.00
LLSI Simon Gagne 15.00 40.00
LLSP Peter Stastny 20.00 50.00
LLSS Steven Stamkos 125.00 250.00
LLTO Jonathan Toews 60.00 120.00
LLVL Vincent Lecavalier 30.00 80.00
LLVO Tomas Vokoun 20.00 50.00
LLZB Zach Bogosian 40.00 100.00

2008-09 The Cup NHL Shields Dual

STATED PRINT RUN 1 SER.#'d SET
NOT PRICED DUE TO SCARCITY

2008-09 The Cup NHL Shields Dual Autographs

STATED PRINT RUN 1 SER.#'d SET
NOT PRICED DUE TO SCARCITY
ADSBD Brad Boyes
David Perron
ADSTS Darcy Tucker
Paul Stastny
ADSBB Fabian Brunnstrom
Patrik Berglund
ADSBE Andrew Ebbett
Brian Boyle
ADSBP Carey Price
Martin Brodeur
ADSBW Blake Wheeler
Patrice Bergeron
ADSDZ Pavel Datsyuk
Henrik Zetterberg
ADSEB Ray Bourque
Phil Esposito
ADSEJ Eric Staal
Jordan Staal
ADSES Luke Schenn
Robbie Earl
ADSFT Viktor Tikhonov
Nikita Filatov
ADSGD Scott Gomez
Chris Drury
ADSHM Ryan Miller
Dominik Hasek
ADSHZ Henrik Zetterberg
Marian Hossa
ADSIH Dany Heatley
Jarome Iginla
ADSJH Patric Hornqvist
Ryan Jones
ADSKB Zach Bogosian
Ilya Kovalchuk
ADSKD Derick Brassard
Kyle Okposo
ADSKG Sam Gagner
Phil Kessel
ADSKM Mark Messier
Jari Kurri
ADSKO Phil Kessel
Kyle Okposo
ADSLM Evgeni Malkin
Mario Lemieux
ADSLN Luke Schenn
Nikolai Kulemin
ADSML Mario Lemieux
Mark Messier
ADSNF Mark Fistric
James Neal
ADSPM Steve Mason
Adam Pineault
ADSPO T.J. Oshie
Alex Pietrangelo
ADSRK Luc Robitaille
Jari Kurri
ADSRP Patrick Roy
Carey Price
ADSSL Luca Sbisa
Simon Gagne
ADSSM Cory Schneider
Steve Mason
ADSSK3 Steven Stamkos
Kyle Turris

2008-09 The Cup Programme of Excellence

STATED PRINT RUN 10 SER.#'d SETS
NOT PRICED DUE TO SCARCITY
PEAP Alex Pietrangelo
PEBC Bobby Clarke
PEBH Bobby Hull
PEBO Bobby Orr
PEBS Brandon Sutter
PECG Colton Gillies
PECW Cam Ward
PEDD Drew Doughty
PEDG Doug Gilmour
PEDH Dale Hawerchuk
PEDP Denis Potvin
PEES Eric Staal
PEGA Glenn Anderson
PEGF Grant Fuhr
PEGL Guy Lafleur
PEGP Gilbert Perreault
PEHE Dany Heatley
PEJI Jarome Iginla
PEJT Joe Thornton
PEKT Kyle Turris
PELM Lanny McDonald
PELR Luc Robitaille
PELS Luke Schenn
PEMB Martin Brodeur
PEML Mario Lemieux
PEMM Mark Messier
PEMS Martin St. Louis
PEPE Phil Esposito
PEPS Peter Stastny
PERB Ray Bourque
PERH Ron Hextall
PERN Rick Nash
PERV Rogie Vachon
PESC Sidney Crosby
PESG Simon Gagne
PESM Steve Mason
PESS Steve Shutt
PEST Steven Stamkos
PETO Jonathan Toews
PEVL Vincent Lecavalier
PEWG Wayne Gretzky
PEZB Zach Boychuk

2008-09 The Cup Property Of

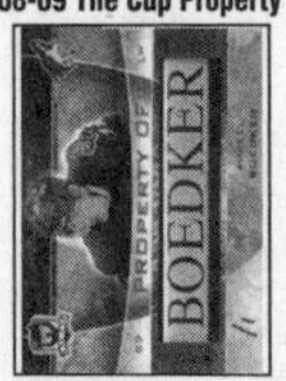

STATED PRINT RUN 1 SER.#'d SET
NOT PRICED DUE TO SCARCITY
POAC Andrew Cogliano
POAS Alexander Steen
POBD Brandon Dubinsky
POBL Bryan Little
POBO Mikkel Boedker
POBS Brendan Shanahan
POBW Blake Wheeler
POCN Cam Neely
PODA Dave Bolland
PODB Daniel Briere
PODD Drew Doughty
PODL David Legwand
PODP David Perron
PODS Devin Setoguchi
POGH Gordie Howe
POJB Jean Beliveau
POJG Jean-Sebastien Giguere
POJM Joe Mullen
POJN James Neal
POKL Kristopher Letang
POLE Manny Legace
POLS Luke Schenn
POMB Mike Bossy
POMF Michael Frolik
POML Mario Lemieux
POMR Mason Raymond
POMS Marc Staal
POPB Patrik Berglund
POPE Phil Esposito
POPR Pekka Rinne
PORB Ray Bourque
PORH Ron Hextall
POSS Steven Stamkos
POTV Tomas Vokoun

2008-09 The Cup Quads

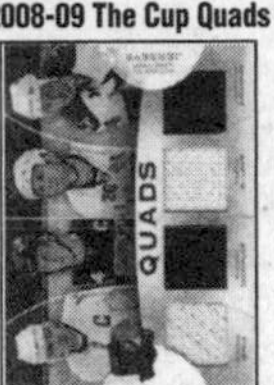

STATED PRINT RUN 10 SER.#'d SETS
NOT PRICED DUE TO SCARCITY
CJ4CMFS Marc-Andre Fleury
Jordan Staal
Evgeni Malkin
Sidney Crosby
CJ4EBLB Phil Esposito
Johnny Bucyk
Jean Beliveau
Guy Lafleur
CJ4EESS Tony Esposito
Phil Esposito
Jordan Staal
Eric Staal
CJ4GBFW Zach Boychuk
Blake Wheeler
Colton Gillies
Michael Frolik
CJ4GRDK Marcel Dionne
Wayne Gretzky
Luc Robitaille
Jari Kurri
CJ4HSNT Jonathan Toews
Rick Nash
Dany Heatley
Jason Spezza
CJ4LSC Vincent Lecavalier
Martin St. Louis
Jarome Iginla
Jonathan Cheechoo
CJ4KSKK Teemu Selanne
Mikko Koivu
Jari Kurri
Saku Koivu
CJ4KTBM Jonathan Toews
Patrick Kane
Nicklas Backstrom
Peter Mueller
CJ4LSGS Eric Staal
Ryan Getzlaf
Jason Spezza
Vincent Lecavalier
CJ4MAKF Jari Kurri
Glenn Anderson
Mark Messier
Grant Fuhr
CJ4MMMG Lanny McDonald
Al MacInnis
Joe Mullen
Doug Gilmour
CJ4OCNF Rick Nash
Marc-Andre Fleury
Sidney Crosby
Alexander Ovechkin
CJ4OMKF Alexander Ovechkin
Sergei Fedorov
Ilya Kovalchuk
Evgeni Malkin
CJ4RBHP Martin Brodeur
Ron Hextall
Carey Price
Patrick Roy
CJ4STBV Fabian Brunnstrom
Steven Stamkos
Kyle Turris
Jakub Voracek
CJ4ZLDH Nicklas Lidstrom
Marian Hossa
Henrik Zetterberg
Pavel Datsyuk

2008-09 The Cup Quads Patches

STATED PRINT RUN 5 SER.#'d SETS
NOT PRICED DUE TO SCARCITY

2008-09 The Cup Scripted Swatches

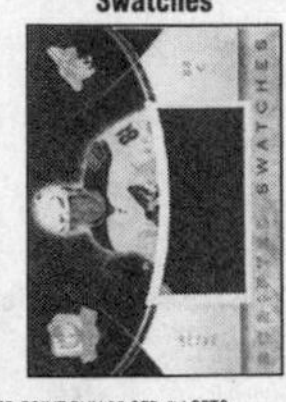

STATED PRINT RUN 25 SER.#'d SETS
SSBO Mikkel Boedker 25.00 60.00
SSBS Brandon Sutter 20.00 50.00
SSBW Blake Wheeler 50.00 100.00
SSCG Claude Giroux 60.00 120.00
SSCP Carey Price 60.00 120.00
SSCW Cam Ward 15.00 40.00
SSDB Derick Brassard 30.00 80.00
SSDC Dino Ciccarelli
SSDD Drew Doughty 50.00 120.00
SSDG Doug Gilmour 20.00 50.00
SSDH Dany Heatley 20.00 50.00
SSEM Evgeni Malkin 40.00 100.00
SSES Eric Staal 25.00 60.00
SSFB Fabian Brunnstrom 30.00 80.00
SSFR Michael Frolik 30.00 80.00
SSGA Simon Gagne 12.00 30.00
SSGI Colton Gillies 15.00 40.00
SSHA Dominik Hasek 25.00 60.00
SSHL Henrik Lundqvist 60.00 120.00
SSHZ Henrik Zetterberg 30.00 60.00
SSIK Ilya Kovalchuk 20.00 50.00
SSJI Jarome Iginla 30.00 80.00
SSJN James Neal 25.00 60.00
SSJT Joe Thornton 25.00 60.00
SSJV Jakub Voracek 30.00 80.00
SSKO Kyle Okposo 30.00 80.00
SSKT Kyle Turris 30.00 80.00
SSLS Luke Schenn 40.00 100.00
SSMB Martin Brodeur 60.00 120.00
SSMC Mike Cammalleri 15.00 40.00
SSMF Marc-Andre Fleury 30.00 80.00
SSML Mario Lemieux 75.00 150.00
SSMM Mark Messier 75.00 150.00
SSMN Markus Naslund 15.00 40.00
SSMS Martin St. Louis 15.00 40.00
SSMT Marty Turco 12.00 30.00
SSNB Nicklas Backstrom 30.00 80.00
SSNF Nikita Filatov 50.00 100.00
SSNL Nicklas Lidstrom 40.00 100.00
SSOS T.J. Oshie 50.00 100.00
SSPB Patrik Berglund 40.00 100.00
SSPH Patric Hornqvist 15.00 40.00
SSPK Patrick Kane 40.00 100.00
SSPM Peter Mueller 20.00 50.00
SSPR Patrick Roy 100.00 200.00
SSRN Rick Nash 25.00 60.00
SSSC Sidney Crosby 175.00 300.00
SSSD Shane Doan
SSSG Sam Gagner 25.00 60.00
SSSS Steven Stamkos 75.00 150.00
SSST Peter Stastny 15.00 40.00
SSTO Jonathan Toews 50.00 120.00
SSTV Thomas Vanek
SSVL Vincent Lecavalier 15.00 40.00
SSZB Zach Bogosian 30.00 80.00

2008-09 The Cup Scripted Swatches Dual

STATED PRINT RUN 5 SER.#'d SETS
NOT PRICED DUE TO SCARCITY
DSSBF Derick Brassard
Nikita Filatov
DSSBP Martin Brodeur
Carey Price
DSSDM Shane Doan
Peter Mueller
DSSDS Luke Schenn
Drew Doughty
DSSGS Colton Gillies
Brandon Sutter
DSSHH Gordie Howe
Bobby Hull
DSSHL Nicklas Lidstrom
Marian Hossa
DSSHM Ryan Miller
Dominik Hasek
DSSIO Jarome Iginla
Kyle Okposo
DSSLM Evgeni Malkin
Mario Lemieux
DSSNL Markus Naslund
Henrik Lundqvist
DSSNZ Markus Naslund
Henrik Zetterberg
DSSOB Patrik Berglund
T.J. Oshie
DSSPB Alex Pietrangelo
Zach Bogosian
DSSPJ Jonathan Toews
Patrick Kane
DSSRB Patrick Roy
Martin Brodeur
DSSSM Steve Mason
Cory Schneider
DSSSS Eric Staal
Jordan Staal
DSSTB Kyle Turris
Mikkel Boedker

2008-09 The Cup Signature Patches

STATED PRINT RUN 75 SER.#'d SETS
SPPS Paul Stastny 15.00 40.00
SPAK Anze Kopitar 15.00 40.00
SPBH Bobby Hull/25 40.00 100.00
SPBK Mikkel Boedker 25.00 60.00
SPBS Brandon Sutter 20.00 50.00
SPBW Blake Wheeler 40.00 100.00
SPCG Colton Gillies 15.00 40.00
SPCP Carey Price 50.00 120.00
SPDB Derick Brassard 30.00 80.00
SPDD Drew Doughty 50.00 120.00
SPDH Dany Heatley 20.00 50.00
SPEM Evgeni Malkin 40.00 100.00
SPES Eric Staal 25.00 60.00
SPFB Fabian Brunnstrom 25.00 60.00
SPFL Marc-Andre Fleury 30.00 80.00
SPGH Gordie Howe/25 100.00 200.00
SPHA Dale Hawerchuk 15.00 40.00
SPHK Dominik Hasek 25.00 60.00
SPIK Ilya Kovalchuk 20.00 50.00
SPJI Jarome Iginla 30.00 80.00
SPJN James Neal 25.00 60.00
SPJT Jonathan Toews 50.00 120.00
SPJV Jakub Voracek 30.00 80.00
SPKA Patrick Kane 40.00 100.00
SPKT Kyle Turris 25.00 60.00
SPLS Luke Schenn 40.00 100.00
SPMB Martin Brodeur/25 75.00 150.00
SPME Mark Messier/25 60.00 120.00
SPMF Michael Frolik 30.00 80.00
SPML Mario Lemieux/25 175.00 300.00
SPMR Mike Richards 25.00 60.00
SPMS Martin St. Louis 15.00 40.00
SPMT Marty Turco 12.00 30.00
SPNB Nicklas Backstrom 30.00 80.00
SPNF Nikita Filatov 40.00 100.00
SPNL Nicklas Lidstrom 25.00 60.00
SPPK Phil Kessel 15.00 40.00
SPPM Peter Mueller 20.00 50.00
SPPR Patrick Roy/25 125.00 250.00
SPRB Ray Bourque 30.00 80.00
SPRN Rick Nash 15.00 40.00
SPSC Sidney Crosby/25 175.00 300.00
SPSG Simon Gagne 12.00 30.00
SPSS Steven Stamkos 75.00 150.00
SPTH Joe Thornton 25.00 60.00
SPVL Vincent Lecavalier 15.00 40.00
SPWG Wayne Gretzky/25 200.00 400.00
SPZB Zach Boychuk 25.00 60.00

2008-09 The Cup Stanley Cup Signatures

STATED PRINT RUN 50 SER.#'d SETS
SCSBH Bobby Hull 25.00 60.00
SCSBO Bobby Orr 125.00 250.00
SCSES Eric Staal 20.00 50.00
SCSFM Frank Mahovlich 12.00 30.00
SCSGF Grant Fuhr 25.00 60.00
SCSGH Gordie Howe 75.00 150.00
SCSHZ Henrik Zetterberg 30.00 60.00
SCSJB Jean Beliveau 20.00 50.00
SCSJM Joe Mullen 12.00 30.00
SCSLM Lanny McDonald 12.00 30.00
SCSMB Martin Brodeur 50.00 100.00
SCSMI Mike Bossy 25.00 60.00
SCSML Mario Lemieux 60.00 120.00
SCSMM Mark Messier 60.00 120.00
SCSMS Martin St. Louis 12.00 30.00
SCSNL Nicklas Lidstrom 20.00 50.00
SCSPD Pavel Datsyuk 25.00 60.00
SCSPR Patrick Roy 75.00 150.00
SCSRB Ray Bourque 25.00 60.00
SCSVL Vincent Lecavalier 25.00 60.00
SCSWG Wayne Gretzky 175.00 350.00

2008-09 The Cup Trios

STATED PRINT RUN 15 SER.#'d SETS
NOT PRICED DUE TO SCARCITY
CJ3BHH Ron Hextall
Dominik Hasek
Martin Brodeur
CJ3BMP Al MacInnis
Dion Phaneuf
Ray Bourque
CJ3BNC Blake Wheeler
Colton Gillies
Michael Frolik
CJ3BNO Ray Bourque
Adam Oates
Cam Neely
CJ3CMF Marc-Andre Fleury
Sidney Crosby
Evgeni Malkin
CJ3COS Sidney Crosby
Alexander Ovechkin
Steven Stamkos
CJ3DMP Marcel Dionne
Lanny McDonald
Gilbert Perreault
CJ3ELT Bryan Trottier
Phil Esposito
Guy Lafleur
CJ3FSZ Mats Sundin
Henrik Zetterberg
Peter Forsberg
CJ3GLC Sidney Crosby
Mario Lemieux
Wayne Gretzky
CJ3GMH Gordie Howe
Wayne Gretzky
Mark Messier
CJ3GMK Anze Kopitar
Ryan Getzlaf
Peter Mueller
CJ3GPC Jonathan Cheechoo
Dion Phaneuf
Ryan Getzlaf
CJ3HNT Dany Heatley
Rick Nash
Jonathan Toews
CJ3HTK Bobby Hull
Patrick Kane
Jonathan Toews
CJ3KKM Alex Kovalev
Saku Koivu
Andrei Markov
CJ3KMC Patrick Kane
Chris Chelios
Mike Modano
CJ3LRM Mark Recchi
Mario Lemieux
Joe Mullen
CJ3LSS Jason Spezza
Vincent Lecavalier
Martin St. Louis
CJ3LTI Vincent Lecavalier
Jarome Iginla
Joe Thornton
CJ3MAJ Glenn Anderson
Jari Kurri
Mark Messier
CJ3MLK Alex Kovalev
Brian Leetch
Mark Messier
CJ3MMM Lanny McDonald
Al MacInnis
Joe Mullen
CJ3OCI Jarome Iginla
Sidney Crosby
Alexander Ovechkin
CJ3OMK Alexander Ovechkin
Ilya Kovalchuk
Evgeni Malkin
CJ3PMV Gilbert Perreault
Thomas Vanek
Ryan Miller
CJ3PTK Jonathan Toews
Carey Price
Patrick Kane
CJ3QGF Patrick Roy
Roberto Luongo
Marc-Andre Fleury
CJ3RBP Martin Brodeur
Patrick Roy
Carey Price
CJ3RSB Patrick Roy
Ray Bourque
Joe Sakic
CJ3SBK Marc Savard
Patrice Bergeron
Phil Kessel
CJ3SBP Patrice Bergeron
Zach Parise
Jordan Staal
CJ3SEB Joe Sakic
Phil Esposito
Ray Bourque
CJ3SSF Mats Sundin
Joe Sakic
Peter Forsberg
CJ3STB Kyle Turris
Steven Stamkos
Fabian Brunnstrom
CJ3VFB Derick Brassard
Jakub Voracek
Nikita Filatov

2008-09 The Cup Trios Patches

STATED PRINT RUN 10 SER.#'d SETS
NOT PRICED DUE TO SCARCITY

2002-03 Thrashers Postcards

This 20-card set was issued by the team.
COMPLETE SET (20) 10.00 25.00
1 Lubos Bartecko .40 1.00
2 Yuri Butsayev .40 1.00
3 Jeff Cowan .40 1.00
4 Dany Heatley 2.00 5.00
5 Milan Hnilicka .40 1.00
6 Tony Hrkac .40 1.00
7 Frantisek Kaberle .40 1.00
8 Ilya Kovalchuk 2.00 5.00
9 Slava Kozlov .40 1.00
10 Francis Lessard .40 1.00
11 Pasi Nurminen .60 1.50
12 Jeff Odgers .60 1.50
13 Kamil Piros .40 1.00
14 Dan Snyder .75 2.00
15 Patrik Stefan .40 1.00
16 Andy Sutton .40 1.00
16 Per Svartvadet .40 1.00
17 Chris Tamer .40 1.00
18 Brad Tapper .40 1.00
20 J.P. Vigier .40 1.00

2003-04 Thrashers Postcards

Issued by the team at public events or in response to fan requests, these are standard postcard size. The checklist may not be complete.

COMPLETE SET (23) 10.00 25.00
1 Serge Aubin .40 1.00
2 Jeff Cowan .40 1.00
3 Byron Dafoe .60 1.50
4 Garnet Exelby .60 1.50
5 Bob Hartley CO .20 .50
6 Frank Kaberle .40 1.00
7 Tomas Kloucek .40 1.00
8 Slava Kozlov .40 1.00
9 Ilya Kovalchuk 2.00 5.00
10 Brad Larsen .40 1.00
11 Francis Lessard .40 1.00
12 Ivan Majesky .40 1.00
13 Shawn McEachern .40 1.00
14 Pasi Nurminen .40 1.00
15 Ronald Petrovicky .40 1.00
16 Randy Robitaille .40 1.00
17 Marc Savard .60 1.50
18 Ben Simon .40 1.00
19 Patrik Stefan .40 1.00
20 Andy Sutton .40 1.00
21 Chris Tamer .40 1.00
22 Daniel Tjarnqvist .40 1.00
23 J.P. Vigier .40 1.00

1994-95 Thunder Bay Flyers

We have no pricing information on this set.

1 Jeremy Adduono
2 Teddy Belisle
3 Curtis Bois
4 Christian Bragnalo
5 Ryan Brindley
6 Jason Cupp
7 Bob Depiero ACO
8 Rob Douglas
9 Brad Duce
10 Russell George
11 David Hoogsteen
12 Dustin Koss
13 Simon Lacroix
14 Marc Lafleur
15 Kurtis Mintenko
16 Darren Nicholas ACO
17 Gary Ricciardi
18 Dan Sims
19 Shawn Sobush
20 Doug Teskey
21 Brad Williamson
22 Larry Wintoneak CO
23 Gregg Zaporzan
24 Captain Flyer MASCOT

2000-01 Titanium

Released in April 2001, this 150-card set had a hobby SRP of $14.99 for a 5-card pack and a retail SRP of $3.99 for a 3-card pack. Hobby packs featured a memorabilia card in every pack. The set also boasted 50 randomly inserted Short Prints of rookies and prospects, serial numbered to just 99 in hobby packs and 199 in retail. The base cards were printed on a premium holographic foil base containing a color action player photo on a team logo background.

COMPLETE SET w/o SP's (100) 25.00 50.00
1 Paul Kariya .30 .75
2 Teemu Selanne .30 .75
3 Donald Audette .10 .25
4 Jason Allison .10 .25
5 Byron Dafoe .25 .60
6 Bill Guerin .25 .60
7 Joe Thornton .50 1.25
8 J-P Dumont .10 .25
9 Doug Gilmour .25 .60
10 Dominik Hasek .60 1.50
11 Jarome Iginla .40 1.00
12 Marc Savard .10 .25
13 Mike Vernon .25 .60
14 Ron Francis .25 .60
15 Arturs Irbe .25 .60
16 Tony Amonte .25 .60
17 Steve Sullivan .10 .25
18 Jocelyn Thibault .25 .60
19 Ray Bourque .50 1.25
20 Peter Forsberg .75 2.00
21 Milan Hejduk .30 .75
22 Patrick Roy 1.50 4.00
23 Joe Sakic .60 1.50
24 Alex Tanguay .25 .60
25 Geoff Sanderson .10 .25
26 Ron Tugnutt .25 .60
27 Ed Belfour .30 .75
28 Brett Hull .40 1.00
29 Mike Modano .50 1.25

30 Joe Nieuwendyk .25 .60
31 Sergei Fedorov .50 1.25
32 Manny Legace .25 .60
33 Nicklas Lidstrom .30 .75
34 Brendan Shanahan .30 .75
35 Steve Yzerman 1.50 4.00
36 Tommy Salo .25 .60
37 Ryan Smyth .10 .25
38 Doug Weight .25 .60
39 Pavel Bure .30 .75
40 Trevor Kidd .25 .60
41 Rob Blake .25 .60
42 Ziggy Palffy .25 .60
43 Luc Robitaille .25 .60
44 Jamie Storr .25 .60
45 Manny Fernandez .25 .60
46 Scott Pellerin .10 .25
47 Saku Koivu .30 .75
48 Trevor Linden .25 .60
49 Martin Rucinsky .10 .25
50 Jose Theodore .40 1.00
51 David Legwand .25 .60
52 Cliff Ronning .10 .25
53 Jason Arnott .10 .25
54 Martin Brodeur .75 2.00
55 Patrik Elias .25 .60
56 Alexander Mogilny .25 .60
57 Tim Connolly .10 .25
58 Mariusz Czerkawski .10 .25
59 John Vanbiesbrouck .25 .60
60 Theo Fleury .10 .25
61 Brian Leetch .25 .60
62 Mark Messier .30 .75
63 Mike Richter .30 .75
64 Radek Bonk .10 .25
65 Marian Hossa .30 .75
66 Patrick Lalime .25 .60
67 Alexei Yashin .10 .25
68 Brian Boucher .25 .60
69 Simon Gagne .30 .75
70 John LeClair .30 .75
71 Eric Lindros .30 .75
72 Sean Burke .25 .60
73 Jeremy Roenick .40 1.00
74 Keith Tkachuk .30 .75
75 Jaromir Jagr .50 1.25
76 Alexei Kovalev .25 .60
77 Mario Lemieux 2.00 5.00
78 Garth Snow .25 .60
79 Martin Straka .10 .25
80 Pavol Demitra .25 .60
81 Chris Pronger .25 .60
82 Roman Turek .25 .60
83 Pierre Turgeon .25 .60
84 Vincent Damphousse .10 .25
85 Patrick Marleau .25 .60
86 Owen Nolan .25 .60
87 Steve Shields .25 .60
88 Mike Johnson .10 .25
89 Vincent Lecavalier .30 .75
90 Sergei Berezin .10 .25
91 Curtis Joseph .30 .75
92 Gary Roberts .10 .25
93 Mats Sundin .30 .75
94 Andrew Cassels .10 .25
95 Brendan Morrison .25 .60
96 Markus Naslund .30 .75
97 Felix Potvin .30 .75
98 Peter Bondra .30 .75
99 Olaf Kolzig .25 .60
100 Adam Oates .25 .60
101 Samuel Pahlsson SP 6.00 15.00
102 Scott Fankhouser SP 6.00 15.00
103 Tomi Kallio SP 6.00 15.00
104 Brad Tapper RC 8.00 20.00
105 Andrew Raycroft RC 30.00 80.00
106 Denis Hamel SP 6.00 15.00
107 Jeff Cowan RC 15.00 40.00
108 Oleg Saprykin SP 6.00 15.00
109 Josef Vasicek RC 8.00 20.00
110 Shane Willis SP 6.00 15.00
111 David Aebischer RC 30.00 80.00
112 Serge Aubin RC 8.00 20.00
113 Marc Denis SP 6.00 15.00
114 Chris Nielsen RC 8.00 20.00
115 David Vyborny SP 6.00 15.00
116 Marty Turco RC 50.00 100.00
117 Mike Comrie RC 30.00 80.00
118 Shawn Horcoff RC 25.00 60.00
119 Dominic Pittis SP 6.00 15.00
120 Roberto Luongo SP 8.00 20.00
121 Ivan Novoseltsev SP 6.00 15.00
122 Serge Payer SP 6.00 15.00
123 Denis Shvidki SP 6.00 15.00
124 Steven Reinprecht RC 15.00 40.00
125 Lubomir Visnovsky RC 15.00 40.00
126 Marian Gaborik RC 100.00 200.00
127 Filip Kuba SP 6.00 15.00
128 Mathieu Garon SP 6.00 15.00
129 Eric Landry RC 8.00 20.00
130 Andrei Markov SP 6.00 15.00
131 Marian Cisar SP 6.00 15.00
132 Scott Hartnell RC 15.00 40.00
133 Rick DiPietro RC 60.00 150.00
134 Martin Havlat RC 50.00 125.00
135 Jani Hurme RC 15.00 40.00
136 Petr Schastlivy SP 6.00 15.00
137 Ruslan Fedotenko RC 15.00 40.00
138 Justin Williams RC 30.00 80.00
139 Robert Esche SP 6.00 15.00
140 Milan Kraft SP 6.00 15.00
141 Brent Johnson SP 6.00 15.00
142 Reed Low RC 8.00 20.00
143 Evgeni Nabokov SP 6.00 15.00
144 Alexander Kharitonov RC 8.00 20.00
145 Dieter Kochan RC 12.00 30.00
146 Brad Richards SP 12.00 30.00
147 Adam Mair SP 6.00 15.00
148 Daniel Sedin SP 6.00 15.00
149 Henrik Sedin SP 6.00 15.00
150 Trent Whitfield SP 6.00 15.00

2000-01 Titanium Blue

This 100-card set paralleled the Pacific Private Stock Titanium base set. The cards had a blue tone and were serial numbered to the depicted player's jersey number. This set is not priced due to scarcity of many of the cards.

NOT PRICED DUE TO SCARCITY

2000-01 Titanium Gold

This 100-card set paralleled the Pacific Private Stock Titanium base set. The cards had a gold tone and were serial numbered to 99. They were available in random hobby packs only.

*STARS: 5X TO 12X BASIC CARDS

2000-01 Titanium Premiere Date

Inserted at a rate of 1 per hobby box, this 100-card set paralleled the Pacific Private Stock Titanium base set. The cards were serial numbered to 185.

*STARS: 5X TO 10X BASIC CARDS

2000-01 Titanium Red

This 100-card set paralleled the Pacific Private Stock Titanium base set. The cards had a red tone and were serial numbered to 299. They were available in random retail packs only.

*STARS: 4X TO 8X BASIC CARDS

2000-01 Titanium Retail

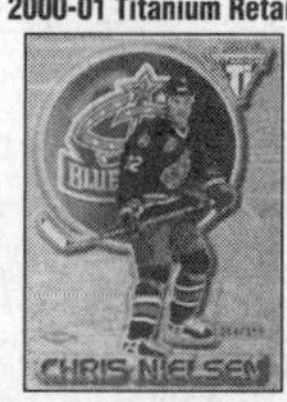

Released through retail channels, this 150-card set is the same as the hobby set in most ways. The base cards were printed on a premium holographic foil base containing a color action player photo on a team logo background. SP's were serial numbered out of 199.

*RETAIL SINGLES SAME VALUE AS HOBBY
*RETAIL RC's: .2X TO .5X HOBBY CARDS

2000-01 Titanium All-Stars

Randomly inserted and serial-numbered to 1000, this die-cut set actually represents two different sets of all-star players. All-stars from the North American team and from the World team are featured. Card numbers do not carry a NA or W prefix, but it is added below for checklisting purposes.

COMPLETE SET (20) 50.00 100.00
1W Dominik Hasek 2.50 6.00
1NA Paul Kariya 1.25 3.00
2W Peter Forsberg 3.00 8.00
2NA Bill Guerin 1.00 2.50
3W Sergei Fedorov 2.50 6.00
3NA Ray Bourque 2.50 6.00
4W Nicklas Lidstrom 1.25 3.00
4NA Patrick Roy 6.00 15.00
5W Pavel Bure 1.50 4.00
5NA Joe Sakic 2.50 6.00
6W Ziggy Palffy 1.00 2.50
6NA Brett Hull 1.50 4.00
7W Marian Hossa 1.25 3.00
7NA Martin Brodeur 4.00 10.00
8W Evgeni Nabokov 2.50 6.00
8NA Theo Fleury 1.00 2.50
9W Mats Sundin 1.25 3.00
9NA Mario Lemieux 6.00 15.00
10A North-American Team/100 8.00 20.00
10W World Team/100 8.00 20.00

2000-01 Titanium Game Gear

Inserted at a rate of 1:1 hobby and 1:49 retail, these cards feature game-used swatches of jerseys or sticks. Cards 1-50 were stick cards and 51-150 were jersey cards. Each stick card is serial numbered and the total is listed beside the player's name below. Cards 152-155 are dual player cards and carry two swatches of jersey. Dual player cards are serial numbered out of 100.

1 Phil Housley/212 6.00 15.00
2 Martin Gelinas/255 6.00 15.00
3 Sami Kapanen/246 6.00 15.00
4 Sandis Ozolinsh/244 6.00 15.00
5 Tony Amonte/251 6.00 15.00
6 Alexei Zhamnov/206 6.00 15.00
7 Peter Forsberg/235 12.00 30.00
8 Patrick Roy/255 15.00 40.00
9 Joe Sakic/224 12.00 30.00
10 Stephane Yelle/253 6.00 15.00
11 Marc Denis/253 6.00 15.00
12 Kevin Dineen/248 2.50 6.00
13 Ron Tugnutt/253 6.00 15.00
14 Ted Donato/247 6.00 15.00
15 Brett Hull/224 10.00 25.00
16 Chris Chelios/252 8.00 20.00
17 Steve Yzerman/212 20.00 50.00
18 Olli Jokinen/249 6.00 15.00
19 Rob Blake/253 6.00 15.00
20 Rob Blake/251 6.00 15.00
21 Nelson Emerson/193 6.00 15.00
22 Ziggy Palffy/252 6.00 15.00
23 Zigmund Palffy 6.00 15.00
24 Bryan Smolinski/213 6.00 15.00
25 Jozef Stumpel/252 6.00 15.00
26 Jeff Hackett/245 6.00 15.00
27 Trevor Linden/246 8.00 20.00
28 Trevor Linden/247 6.00 15.00
29 Eric Weinrich/252 6.00 15.00
30 Alexander Mogilny/251 6.00 15.00
31 Mariusz Czerkawski/251 6.00 15.00
32 Radek Dvorak/205 6.00 15.00
33 Theo Fleury/203 6.00 15.00
34 Adam Graves/242 6.00 15.00
35 Valeri Kamensky/237 6.00 15.00
36 Brian Leetch/206 6.00 15.00
37 Sandy McCarthy/214 6.00 15.00
38 Kirk McLean/254 6.00 15.00
39 Kirk McLean/251 6.00 15.00
40 Petr Nedved/253 6.00 15.00
41 Daniel Alfredsson/251 6.00 15.00
42 John LeClair/248 8.00 20.00
43 Teppo Numminen/254 6.00 15.00
44 Mario Lemieux/254 20.00 50.00
45 Roman Turek/255 6.00 15.00
46 Yanic Perreault/245 6.00 15.00
47 Gary Roberts/211 6.00 15.00
48 Andrew Cassels/254 6.00 15.00
49 Felix Potvin/254 8.00 20.00
50 Steve Konowalchuk/243 6.00 15.00
51 Guy Hebert 2.50 6.00
52 Guy Hebert 2.50 6.00
53 Mike Leclerc 2.50 6.00
54 Teemu Selanne 8.00 20.00
55 Per Johan Axelsson 2.50 6.00
56 Byron Dafoe 2.50 6.00
57 Andre Savage 2.50 6.00
58 Stu Barnes 2.50 6.00
59 Dominik Hasek 8.00 20.00
60 Erik Rasmussen 2.50 6.00
61 Rob Ray 2.50 6.00
62 Richard Smehlik 2.50 6.00
63 Alexei Zhitnik 2.50 6.00
64 Fred Brathwaite 2.50 6.00
65 Valeri Bure 2.50 6.00
66 Rico Fata 2.50 6.00
67 Phil Housley 2.50 6.00
68 Jarome Iginla 5.00 12.00
69 Marc Savard 2.50 6.00
70 Jeff Shantz 2.50 6.00
71 Cory Stillman 2.50 6.00
72 Boris Mironov 2.50 6.00
73 Alexei Zhamnov 2.50 6.00
74 Peter Forsberg 8.00 20.00
75 Jon Klemm 2.50 6.00
76 Aaron Miller 2.50 6.00
77 Dave Reid 2.50 6.00
78 Patrick Roy 15.00 40.00
79 Joe Sakic 10.00 25.00
80 Lyle Odelein 2.50 6.00
81 Ed Belfour 4.00 10.00
82 Derian Hatcher 2.50 6.00
83 Benoit Hogue 2.50 6.00
84 Brett Hull 6.00 15.00
85 Mike Keane 2.50 6.00
86 Jamie Langenbrunner 2.50 6.00
87 Jere Lehtinen 2.50 6.00
88 Grant Marshall 2.50 6.00
89 Mike Modano 6.00 15.00
90 Joe Nieuwendyk 2.50 6.00
91 Blake Sloan 2.50 6.00
92 Darryl Sydor 2.50 6.00
93 Sergei Zubov 2.50 6.00
94 Chris Chelios 4.00 10.00
95 Mathieu Dandenault 4.00 10.00
96 Chris Osgood 2.50 6.00
97 Brendan Shanahan 4.00 10.00
98 Steve Yzerman 12.00 30.00
99 Robert Svehla 2.50 6.00
100 Benoit Brunet 2.50 6.00
101 Eric Weinrich 2.50 6.00
102 Sergei Zholtok 2.50 6.00
103 Patric Kjellberg 2.50 6.00
104 David Legwand 2.50 6.00
105 Martin Brodeur 10.00 25.00
106 Scott Niedermayer 2.50 6.00
107 Chris Terreri 2.50 6.00
108 Mariusz Czerkawski 2.50 6.00
109 Wade Flaherty 2.50 6.00
110 Kenny Jonsson 2.50 6.00
111 Theo Fleury 2.50 6.00
112 Theo Fleury 2.50 6.00
113 Adam Graves 2.50 6.00
114 Brian Leetch 2.50 6.00
115 Sylvain Lefebvre 2.50 6.00
116 Manny Malhotra 2.50 6.00
117 Petr Nedved 2.50 6.00
118 Mike Richter 4.00 10.00
119 Daniel Alfredsson 2.50 6.00
120 Alexei Yashin 2.50 6.00
121 Eric Desjardins 2.50 6.00
122 John LeClair 4.00 10.00
123 Mika Alatalo 2.50 6.00
124 Sean Burke 2.50 6.00
125 Shane Doan 2.50 6.00
126 Nikolai Khabibulin 4.00 10.00
127 Jyrki Lumme 2.50 6.00
128 Teppo Numminen 2.50 6.00
129 Jeremy Roenick 6.00 15.00
130 Jean-Sebastien Aubin 2.50 6.00
131 Rene Corbet 2.50 6.00
132 Jan Hrdina 2.50 6.00
133 Jaromir Jagr 8.00 20.00
134 Darius Kasparaitis 2.50 6.00
135 Alexei Kovalev 2.50 6.00
136 Robert Lang 2.50 6.00
137 Alexei Morozov 2.50 6.00
138 Rich Parent 2.50 6.00
139 Wayne Primeau 2.50 6.00
140 Michal Rozsival 2.50 6.00
141 Kevin Stevens 2.50 6.00
142 Martin Straka 2.50 6.00
143 Matthew Barnaby 2.50 6.00
144 Tie Domi 2.50 6.00
145 Glenn Healy 2.50 6.00
146 Curtis Joseph 4.00 10.00
147 Dimitri Yushkevich 2.50 6.00
148 Dan Cloutier 2.50 6.00
149 Felix Potvin 2.50 6.00
150 Olaf Kolzig 2.50 6.00
151 Mario Lemieux/100 60.00 150.00
152 Mario Lemieux 60.00 150.00
Jaromir Jagr/100
153 Peter Forsberg 50.00 100.00
Joe Sakic/100
154 B.Hull/M.Modano/100 50.00 100.00
155 Alexei Kovalev 15.00 40.00
Martin Straka/100

2000-01 Titanium Game Gear Patches

Randomly inserted in packs, these cards parallel cards 51-150 of the base game gear set. Each card features a premium swatch of jersey patch. Cards were serial numbered and the total number is listed beside the player's name below.

*PATCHES: 1.25X TO 3X JSY HI

2000-01 Titanium Three-Star Selections

Randomly inserted in packs, these cards highlight some of the top rookies, stars and goalies in the league. Cards 1-10 feature goalies and were numbered out of 1400. Cards 11-20 feature veteran stars and were numbered out of 1100. Cards 21-30 feature star rookies and are numbered to just 750.

COMPLETE SET (30) 40.00 80.00
1 Dominik Hasek 1.25 3.00
2 Patrick Roy 3.00 8.00
3 Ed Belfour .75 2.00
4 Martin Brodeur 1.50 4.00
5 Mike Richter .75 2.00
6 Brian Boucher .60 1.50
7 Roman Turek .60 1.50
8 Curtis Joseph .75 2.00
9 Felix Potvin .75 2.00
10 Olaf Kolzig .60 1.50
11 Paul Kariya .75 2.00
12 Joe Sakic 1.50 4.00
13 Mike Modano 1.25 3.00
14 Sergei Fedorov 1.25 3.00
15 Ziggy Palffy .60 1.50
16 Theo Fleury .60 1.50
17 Jaromir Jagr 1.25 3.00
18 Mario Lemieux 5.00 12.00
19 Vincent Lecavalier .75 2.00
20 Mats Sundin .75 2.00
21 Shane Willis 1.50 4.00
22 Steven Reinprecht 2.00 5.00
23 Marian Gaborik 6.00 15.00
24 Rick DiPietro 5.00 12.00
25 Martin Havlat 6.00 15.00
26 Brent Johnson 1.00 2.50
27 Evgeni Nabokov 4.00 10.00
28 Brad Richards 2.00 5.00
29 Daniel Sedin .60 1.50
30 Henrik Sedin .60 1.50

2001-02 Titanium

Released in early April 2002, this set consisted of 144 base cards and 40 rookies short printed to the particular player's jersey number. Each card featured a full color action photo on a mirrored card front with a hologram image of the player in the background. Card backs carry individual stats and a short bio. Please note that not all shortprints have been verified and cards with print runs under 25 are not priced due to scarcity.

COMP.SET w/o SP's (144) 40.00 80.00
1 Jeff Friesen .10 .25
2 Jean-Sebastien Giguere .25 .60
3 Paul Kariya .30 .75
4 Dany Heatley .40 1.00
5 Milan Hnilicka .25 .60
6 Patrik Stefan .10 .25
7 Byron Dafoe .25 .60
8 Bill Guerin .25 .60
9 Brian Rolston .10 .25
10 Sergei Samsonov .25 .60
11 Joe Thornton .50 1.25
12 Stu Barnes .10 .25
13 Martin Biron .25 .60
14 Tim Connolly .10 .25
15 J-P Dumont .10 .25
16 Miroslav Satan .25 .60
17 Craig Conroy .10 .25
18 Jarome Iginla .40 1.00
19 Dean McAmmond .10 .25
20 Derek Morris .10 .25
21 Marc Savard .10 .25
22 Roman Turek .25 .60
23 Tom Barrasso .25 .60
24 Ron Francis .25 .60
25 Arturs Irbe .25 .60
26 Sami Kapanen .10 .25
27 Jeff O'Neill .10 .25
28 Tony Amonte .25 .60
29 Mark Bell .10 .25
30 Kyle Calder .10 .25
31 Eric Daze .10 .25
32 Jocelyn Thibault .25 .60
33 Alexei Zhamnov .10 .25
34 Rob Blake .25 .60
35 Milan Hejduk .30 .75
36 Patrick Roy 1.50 4.00
37 Joe Sakic .60 1.50
38 Radim Vrbata .40 1.00
39 Marc Denis .25 .60
40 Rostislav Klesla .10 .25
41 Ron Tugnutt .25 .60
42 Ray Whitney .10 .25
43 Ed Belfour .30 .75
44 Jere Lehtinen .25 .60
45 Mike Modano .50 1.25
46 Joe Nieuwendyk .25 .60
47 Pierre Turgeon .25 .60
48 Sergei Fedorov .50 1.25
49 Dominik Hasek .60 1.50
50 Brett Hull .40 1.00
51 Nicklas Lidstrom .30 .75
52 Luc Robitaille .25 .60
53 Brendan Shanahan .30 .75
54 Steve Yzerman 1.50 4.00
55 Anson Carter .25 .60
56 Mike Comrie .25 .60
57 Tommy Salo .25 .60
58 Ryan Smyth .10 .25
59 Pavel Bure .30 .75
60 Viktor Kozlov .10 .25
61 Roberto Luongo .40 1.00
62 Marcus Nilsson .10 .25
63 Jason Allison .10 .25
64 Adam Deadmarsh .10 .25
65 Steve Heinze .10 .25
66 Zigmund Palffy .25 .60
67 Felix Potvin .30 .75
68 Andrew Brunette .10 .25
69 Jim Dowd .10 .25
70 Marian Gaborik .60 1.50
71 Dwayne Roloson .25 .60
72 Doug Gilmour .25 .60
73 Yanic Perreault .10 .25
74 Mike Ribeiro .10 .25
75 Brian Savage .10 .25
76 Jose Theodore .40 1.00
77 Mike Dunham .25 .60
78 Scott Hartnell .10 .25
79 David Legwand .25 .60
80 Cliff Ronning .10 .25
81 Jason Arnott .10 .25
82 Martin Brodeur .75 2.00
83 J-F Damphousse .25 .60
84 Patrik Elias .25 .60
85 Scott Stevens .25 .60
86 Mariusz Czerkawski .10 .25
87 Rick DiPietro .25 .60
88 Chris Osgood .25 .60
89 Mark Parrish .10 .25
90 Michael Peca .10 .25
91 Alexei Yashin .10 .25
92 Theo Fleury .10 .25
93 Brian Leetch .25 .60
94 Eric Lindros .30 .75
95 Mark Messier .30 .75
96 Mike Richter .30 .75
97 Mike York .10 .25
98 Daniel Alfredsson .25 .60
99 Martin Havlat .25 .60
100 Marian Hossa .30 .75
101 Patrick Lalime .25 .60
102 Todd White .10 .25
103 Roman Cechmanek .25 .60
104 Simon Gagne .30 .75
105 John LeClair .30 .75
106 Mark Recchi .25 .60
107 Jeremy Roenick .40 1.00
108 Sean Burke .25 .60
109 Daymond Langkow .25 .60
110 Claude Lemieux .10 .25
111 Johan Hedberg .25 .60
112 Alexei Kovalev .25 .60
113 Robert Lang .10 .25
114 Mario Lemieux 2.00 5.00
115 Pavol Demitra .25 .60
116 Brent Johnson .25 .60
117 Al MacInnis .25 .60
118 Chris Pronger .25 .60
119 Keith Tkachuk .30 .75
120 Doug Weight .25 .60
121 Vincent Damphousse .10 .25
122 Evgeni Nabokov .25 .60
123 Owen Nolan .25 .60
124 Teemu Selanne .30 .75
125 Nikolai Khabibulin .30 .75
126 Vincent Lecavalier .30 .75
127 Brad Richards .25 .60
128 Martin St. Louis .25 .60
129 Curtis Joseph .30 .75
130 Alexander Mogilny .25 .60
131 Gary Roberts .10 .25
132 Mats Sundin .30 .75
133 Darcy Tucker .10 .25
134 Todd Bertuzzi .30 .75
135 Dan Cloutier .25 .60
136 Brendan Morrison .25 .60
137 Markus Naslund .30 .75
138 Daniel Sedin .10 .25
139 Henrik Sedin .10 .25
140 Peter Bondra .30 .75
141 Sergei Gonchar .10 .25
142 Jaromir Jagr .50 1.25
143 Olaf Kolzig .25 .60
144 Adam Oates .25 .60
145 Ilja Bryzgalov/30 60.00 125.00
146 Timo Parssinen/29 30.00 80.00
147 Ilya Kovalchuk/17
148 Kamil Piros/25 25.00 60.00
149 Brian Pothier/3
150 Andy Hilbert/29 25.00 60.00
151 Jukka Hentunen/24
152 Erik Cole/26 75.00 200.00
153 Vaclav Nedorost/22
154 John Erskine/3
155 Niko Kapanen/39 30.00 80.00
156 Pavel Datsyuk/13
157 Jason Chimera/28 40.00 100.00
158 Ty Conklin/1
159 Jussi Markkanen/30 30.00 80.00
160 Niklas Hagman/14
161 Kristian Huselius/22
162 Jaroslav Bednar/7
163 David Cullen/24
164 Pascal Dupuis/11
165 Nick Schultz/55 25.00 60.00
166 Martin Erat/19
167 Brian Gionta/14
168 Andreas Salomonsson/15
169 Radek Martinek/24
170 Raffi Torres/16
171 Dan Blackburn/31 25.00 60.00
172 Mikael Samuelsson/37 30.00 80.00
173 Chris Neil/25 50.00 125.00
174 Jiri Dopita/20
175 Bruno St. Jacques/42
176 Krystofer Kolanos/36 25.00 60.00
177 Josef Melichar/2
178 Billy Tibbetts/12
179 Mark Rycroft/42 20.00 50.00
180 Jeff Jillson/5
181 Nikita Alexeev/15
182 Brad Leeb/38 12.50 30.00
183 Chris Corrinet/48 20.00 50.00
184 Brian Sutherby/41 30.00 80.00

2001-02 Titanium Hobby Parallel

This 144-card set directly paralleled the base hobby set with red foil highlights. Each card was also serial numbered out of 94 on the card front.

*STARS: 5X TO 12X BASIC CARD

2001-02 Titanium Premiere Date

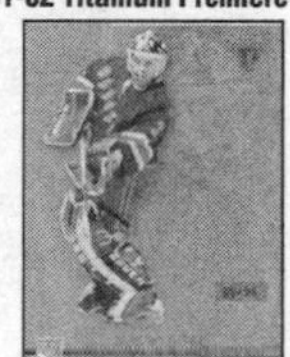

This 144-card set was a parallel to the base set but carried a premiere date stamp on the card fronts. Each card was serial numbered out of 94, and these cards were available in hobby packs only at a rate of 1:7.

*STARS: 5X TO 12X BASIC CARD

2001-02 Titanium Retail

This 184-card set resembles the hobby version, but the card stock was slightly thicker and the mirrored effect on the hobby card fronts was removed for this version. Rookies in the retail version were serial-numbered out of 534.

COMPLETE SET (184) 300.00 600.00
*STARS:SAME VALUE AS HOBBY
145 Ilja Bryzgalov RC 4.00 10.00
146 Timo Parssinen RC 3.00 8.00
147 Ilya Kovalchuk RC 20.00 50.00
148 Kamil Piros RC 3.00 8.00
149 Brian Pothier RC 3.00 8.00
150 Andy Hilbert SP 3.00 8.00
151 Jukka Hentunen RC 3.00 8.00
152 Erik Cole RC 4.00 12.00
153 Vaclav Nedorost RC 3.00 8.00
154 John Erskine RC 3.00 8.00
155 Niko Kapanen RC 3.00 8.00
156 Pavel Datsyuk RC 15.00 40.00
157 Jason Chimera RC 3.00 8.00
158 Ty Conklin RC 3.00 8.00
159 Jussi Markkanen SP 3.00 8.00
160 Niklas Hagman RC 3.00 8.00
161 Kristian Huselius RC 5.00 12.00
162 Jaroslav Bednar RC 3.00 8.00
163 David Cullen RC 3.00 8.00
164 Pascal Dupuis RC 3.00 8.00
165 Nick Schultz RC 3.00 8.00
166 Martin Erat RC 3.00 8.00
167 Brian Gionta SP 3.00 8.00
168 Andreas Salomonsson RC 3.00 8.00
169 Radek Martinek RC 3.00 8.00
170 Raffi Torres RC 4.00 10.00
171 Dan Blackburn RC 4.00 10.00
172 Mikael Samuelsson RC 3.00 8.00
173 Chris Neil RC 3.00 8.00
174 Jiri Dopita RC 3.00 8.00
175 Bruno St. Jacques RC 3.00 8.00
176 Krystofer Kolanos RC 3.00 8.00
177 Josef Melichar SP 3.00 8.00
178 Billy Tibbetts RC 3.00 8.00
179 Mark Rycroft RC 3.00 8.00
180 Jeff Jillson RC 3.00 8.00
181 Nikita Alexeev RC 3.00 8.00
182 Brad Leeb SP 3.00 8.00
183 Chris Corrinet RC 3.00 8.00
184 Brian Sutherby RC 3.00 8.00

2001-02 Titanium Retail Parallel

This 144-card set directly paralleled the base retail set with red foil highlights. Each card was also serial numbered out of 131 on the card front.

*RETAIL PARALLEL: 4X TO 10X BASIC CARD

2001-02 Titanium All-Stars

Inserted at a rate of 1:7 hobby and 1:25 retail packs, this 20 card set featured players chosen for the 2002 NHL All-Star Game. The cards carried a photo of the given player on the front alongside a bronze foil logo from the game.

COMPLETE SET (20) 20.00 40.00
1 Joe Thornton 1.00 2.50
2 Jarome Iginla .75 2.00
3 Sami Kapanen .50 1.25
4 Eric Daze .50 1.25
5 Rob Blake .50 1.25
6 Patrick Roy 3.00 8.00
7 Dominik Hasek 1.25 3.00
8 Sergei Fedorov 1.25 3.00
9 Nicklas Lidstrom .60 1.50
10 Brendan Shanahan 1.00 2.50
11 Zigmund Palffy .50 1.25
12 Jose Theodore .75 2.00
13 Patrik Elias .50 1.25
14 Alexei Yashin .50 1.25
15 Chris Pronger .50 1.25
16 Owen Nolan .50 1.25
17 Teemu Selanne .60 1.50
18 Nikolai Khabibulin .60 1.50
19 Mats Sundin .60 1.50
20 Jaromir Jagr 1.00 2.50

2001-02 Titanium Double-Sided Patches

This 55-card set partially paralleled the jersey set but featured game-worn jersey patch swatches. Individual print runs are listed below.

1 Steve Rucchin 10.00 25.00
Paul Kariya/56
2 Jeff Friesen 10.00 25.00
Oleg Tverdovsky/213
3 Sergei Samsonov 10.00 25.00
Bill Guerin/215
4 J-P Dumont 10.00 25.00
Alexei Zhitnik/181
9 Kyle Calder 10.00 25.00
Michael Nylander/46
11 Milan Hejduk 10.00 25.00
Chris Drury/219
12 J.Sakic/A.Tanguay/259 20.00 50.00
13 Patrick Roy 30.00 80.00
Rob Blake/39
14 Alex Tanguay 10.00 25.00
Vaclav Nedorost/117
16 Mike Modano 10.00 25.00
Jamie Langenbrunner/19
17 Felix Potvin 10.00 25.00
Zigmund Palffy/174
18 Adam Deadmarsh 10.00 25.00
Bryan Smolinski/163
20 Jose Theodore 10.00 25.00
Felix Potvin/94
21 J-P Dumont 10.00 25.00
Scott Stevens/255
24 Eric Daze 10.00 25.00
Mark Bell/116
25 Eric Lindros 10.00 25.00
Theo Fleury/288
26 Brian Leetch 10.00 25.00

Rico Fata/198
27 Eric Lindros 12.50 30.00
Mark Messier/166
29 Mike Richter 12.50 30.00
Brian Leetch/104
30 Daniel Alfredsson 10.00 25.00
Mats Sundin/63
33 Pavel Brendl 10.00 25.00
Josef Beranek/39
34 Martin Straka 10.00 25.00
Michal Rozsival/302
35 Jan Hrdina 10.00 25.00
Ian Moran/88
38 Scott Young 10.00 25.00
Jochen Hecht/62
40 Vincent Lecavalier 10.00 25.00
Petr Svoboda/45
41 Curtis Joseph 10.00 25.00
Glenn Healy/140
42 Mats Sundin 20.00 50.00
JoeSakic/53
43 Jaromir Jagr 15.00 40.00
Dainius Zubrus/56
44 Tom Barrasso 10.00 25.00
Arturs Irbe/199
45 Ron Francis 10.00 25.00
Jeff O'Neill/194
46 Rod Brind'mour 10.00 25.00
Erik Cole/215
47 Martin Havlat 12.50 30.00
Marian Hossa/118
48 Daniel Alfredsson 10.00 25.00
Patrick Lalime/114
49 Jiri Dopita 10.00 25.00
Roman Cechmanek/202
50 Jeremy Roenick 10.00 25.00
John LeClair/216
51 Simon Gagne 10.00 25.00
John LeClair/169
52 M.Modano/P.Turgeon/216 15.00 40.00
53 Marty Turco 10.00 25.00
Ed Belfour/212
54 Henrik Sedin 15.00 40.00
Daniel Sedin/218
55 Todd Bertuzzi 10.00 25.00
Brendan Morrison/215
56 Markus Naslund 10.00 25.00
Dan Cloutier/164
57 Brendan Morrison 10.00 25.00
Marty Turco/119
58 Markus Naslund 10.00 25.00
Daniel Alfredsson/164
59 Jeremy Roenick 10.00 25.00
Tom Barrasso/113
60 Martin Havlat 10.00 25.00
Roman Cechmanek/109
61 Ron Francis 12.50 30.00
Arturs Irbe/154
62 Jeff O'Neill 10.00 25.00
Erik Cole/163
63 Marian Hossa 10.00 25.00
Jiri Dopita/166
64 Patrick Lalime 10.00 25.00
Simon Gagne/163
65 Ed Belfour 10.00 25.00
Pierre Turgeon/165
66 Martin Biron 10.00 25.00
Miroslav Satan/256
67 M.Gaborik/M.Fernandez/104 15.00 40.00
69 Patrik Elias 10.00 25.00
Scott Gomez/260
70 Jamie McLennan 10.00 25.00
Filip Kuba/569
71 Krystofer Kolanos 10.00 25.00
Daymond Langkow/116
72 Michal Handzus 10.00 25.00
Sergei Berezin/260
73 Steve Sullivan 10.00 25.00
Mark Bell/264
75 Jason Allison 10.00 25.00
Zigmund Palffy/106

2001-02 Titanium Rookie Team

This ten card set was inserted in hobby packs at 1:121 and each card was serial-numbered out of 70. Each card featured a player from the year's rookie class with both an action photo and a head shot.

1 Dany Heatley 10.00 25.00
2 Ilya Kovalchuk 10.00 25.00
3 Erik Cole 6.00 15.00
4 Mark Bell 4.00 10.00
5 Radim Vrbata 2.00 5.00
6 Kristian Huselius 2.00 5.00
7 Mike Ribeiro 2.00 5.00
8 Rick DiPietro 6.00 15.00
9 Raffi Torres 4.00 10.00
10 Krystofer Kolanos 2.00 5.00

2001-02 Titanium Saturday Knights

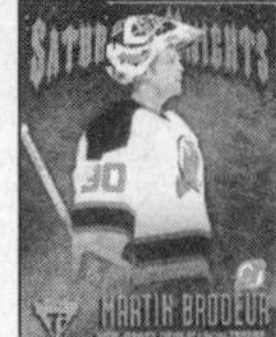

COMPLETE SET (20) 40.00 80.00
STATED ODDS 1:25 HOBBY/1:97 RETAIL
1 Paul Kariya 1.00 2.50
2 Joe Thornton 1.50 4.00
3 Jarome Iginla 1.25 3.00
4 Ed Belfour 1.00 2.50
5 Dominik Hasek 2.00 5.00
6 Brendan Shanahan 1.50 4.00
7 Steve Yzerman 5.00 12.00
8 Mike Comrie .75 2.00
9 Pavel Bure 1.25 3.00
10 Marian Gaborik 2.00 5.00
11 Jose Theodore 1.25 3.00
12 Martin Brodeur 2.50 6.00
13 Mike Peca .75 2.00
14 Eric Lindros 1.50 4.00
15 Daniel Alfredsson .75 2.00
16 Martin Havlat .75 2.00
17 Jeremy Roenick 1.25 3.00
18 Mario Lemieux 6.00 15.00
19 Curtis Joseph 1.00 2.50
20 Mats Sundin 1.00 2.50

2001-02 Titanium Three-Star Selections

This 30-card set featured top goalies, veterans and rookies with full color action photos on the card front surrounded by gold foil highlights. Cards 1-10 were seeded at 1:7 hobby packs/1:25 retail, cards 11-20 were seeded at 1:13 hobby/1:49 retail, and cards 21-30 were seeded at 1:25 hobby/1:97 retail.

COMPLETE SET (30) 50.00 100.00
1 Roman Turek .50 1.25
2 Tom Barrasso .50 1.25
3 Patrick Roy 3.00 8.00
4 Dominik Hasek 1.25 3.00
5 Martin Brodeur 1.50 4.00
6 Chris Osgood .50 1.25
7 Mike Richter .60 1.50
8 Evgeni Nabokov .50 1.25
9 Nikolai Khabibulin .60 1.50
10 Curtis Joseph .60 1.50
11 Paul Kariya .60 1.50
12 Jarome Iginla 1.00 2.50
13 Joe Sakic 1.50 4.00
14 Brendan Shanahan .60 1.50
15 Steve Yzerman 4.00 10.00
16 Eric Lindros .60 1.50
17 Mike York .50 1.25
18 Mario Lemieux 5.00 12.00
19 Mats Sundin .75 2.00
20 Jaromir Jagr 1.00 2.50
21 Dany Heatley 4.00 10.00
22 Ilya Kovalchuk 6.00 15.00
23 Erik Cole 1.50 4.00
24 Mark Bell 1.50 4.00
25 Radim Vrbata 1.50 4.00
26 Kristian Huselius 1.50 4.00
27 Mike Ribeiro 1.50 4.00
28 Rick DiPietro 1.50 4.00
29 Raffi Torres 1.50 4.00
30 Krystofer Kolanos 1.50 4.00

2002-03 Titanium

This 140-card set consisted of 100 base veteran cards and 40 rookie cards shortprinted to 99 copies each. Cards were highlighted by gold foil.

COMP.SET w/o SP's (100) 40.00 80.00
1 Jean-Sebastien Giguere .25 .60
2 Paul Kariya .30 .75
3 Petr Sykora .10 .25
4 Dany Heatley .40 1.00
5 Ilya Kovalchuk .40 1.00
6 Pasi Nurminen .10 .25
7 Glen Murray .10 .25
8 Brian Rolston .10 .25
9 Steve Shields .25 .60
10 Joe Thornton .50 1.25
11 Martin Biron .25 .60
12 Chris Gratton .10 .25
13 Miroslav Satan .25 .60
14 Chris Drury .30 .75
15 Jarome Iginla .40 1.00
16 Roman Turek .25 .60
17 Rod Brind'Amour .25 .60
18 Ron Francis .25 .60
19 Jeff O'Neill .10 .25
20 Kevin Weekes .25 .60
21 Tyler Arnason .25 .60
22 Theo Fleury .10 .25
23 Jocelyn Thibault .25 .60
24 Peter Forsberg .75 2.00
25 Milan Hejduk .30 .75
26 Patrick Roy 1.50 4.00
27 Joe Sakic .60 1.50
28 Andrew Cassels .10 .25
29 Marc Denis .25 .60
30 Geoff Sanderson .10 .25
31 Bill Guerin .25 .60
32 Mike Modano .50 1.25
33 Marty Turco .25 .60
34 Pierre Turgeon .25 .60
35 Sergei Fedorov .50 1.25
36 Brett Hull .40 1.00
37 Curtis Joseph .30 .75
38 Nicklas Lidstrom .30 .75
39 Brendan Shanahan .30 .75
40 Steve Yzerman 1.50 4.00
41 Anson Carter .25 .60
42 Mike Comrie .25 .60
43 Tommy Salo .25 .60
44 Ryan Smyth .10 .25
45 Kristian Huselius .10 .25
46 Olli Jokinen .25 .60
47 Roberto Luongo .40 1.00
48 Jason Allison .10 .25
49 Eric Belanger .10 .25
50 Ziggy Palffy .30 .75
51 Felix Potvin .30 .75
52 Manny Fernandez .25 .60
53 Marian Gaborik .60 1.50
54 Cliff Ronning .10 .25
55 Saku Koivu .30 .75
56 Yanic Perreault .10 .25
57 Jose Theodore .40 1.00
58 Richard Zednik .10 .25
59 Andreas Johansson .10 .25
60 David Legwand .25 .60
61 Tomas Vokoun .25 .60
62 Martin Brodeur .75 2.00
63 Scott Gomez .10 .25
64 John Madden .10 .25
65 Rick DiPietro .25 .60
66 Michael Peca .10 .25
67 Alexei Yashin .10 .25
68 Pavel Bure .30 .75
69 Eric Lindros .30 .75
70 Tom Poti .10 .25
71 Daniel Alfredsson .25 .60
72 Marian Hossa .30 .75
73 Patrick Lalime .25 .60
74 Roman Cechmanek .25 .60
75 Simon Gagne .30 .75
76 Jeremy Roenick .40 1.00
77 Tony Amonte .25 .60
78 Brian Boucher .25 .60
79 Shane Doan .10 .25
80 Johan Hedberg .25 .60
81 Alex Kovalev .25 .60
82 Mario Lemieux 2.00 5.00
83 Brent Johnson .25 .60
84 Cory Stillman .10 .25
85 Doug Weight .25 .60
86 Patrick Marleau .25 .60
87 Evgeni Nabokov .25 .60
88 Teemu Selanne .30 .75
89 Nikolai Khabibulin .30 .75
90 Vincent Lecavalier .30 .75
91 Martin St. Louis .30 .75
92 Ed Belfour .30 .75
93 Alexander Mogilny .25 .60
94 Mats Sundin .30 .75
95 Todd Bertuzzi .30 .75
96 Dan Cloutier .25 .60
97 Brendan Morrison .25 .60
98 Markus Naslund .30 .75
99 Jaromir Jagr .50 1.25
100 Michael Nylander .10 .25
101 Stanislav Chistov RC 8.00 20.00
102 Martin Gerber RC 12.00 40.00
103 Kurt Sauer RC 8.00 20.00
104 Alexei Smirnov RC 8.00 20.00
105 Shaone Morrisonn RC 8.00 20.00
106 Tim Thomas RC 15.00 40.00
107 Ryan Miller RC 50.00 100.00
108 Chuck Kobasew RC 12.00 40.00
109 Jordan Leopold RC 8.00 20.00
110 Pascal Leclaire RC 15.00 40.00
111 Rick Nash RC 125.00 250.00
112 Steve Ott RC 12.00 30.00
113 Dmitri Bykov RC 8.00 20.00
114 Henrik Zetterberg RC 75.00 150.00
115 Ales Hemsky RC 40.00 80.00
116 Jay Bouwmeester RC 15.00 40.00
117 Michael Cammalleri RC 15.00 40.00
118 Alexander Frolov RC 25.00 60.00
119 P-M Bouchard RC 12.00 40.00
120 Stephane Veilleux RC 8.00 20.00
121 Kyle Wanvig SP 8.00 20.00
122 Ron Hainsey RC 8.00 20.00
123 Vernon Fiddler RC 8.00 20.00
124 Adam Hall RC 8.00 20.00
125 Scottie Upshall RC 12.00 30.00
126 Jason Spezza RC 125.00 250.00
127 Anton Volchenkov RC 8.00 20.00
128 Dennis Seidenberg RC 8.00 20.00
129 Radovan Somik RC 8.00 20.00
130 Jeff Taffe RC 8.00 20.00
131 Sebastien Caron SP 8.00 20.00
132 Brooks Orpik RC 8.00 20.00
133 Dick Tarnstrom RC 8.00 20.00
134 Tom Koivisto RC 8.00 20.00
135 Curtis Sanford RC 8.00 20.00
136 Lynn Loyns RC 8.00 20.00
137 Alexander Svitov RC 8.00 20.00
138 Carlo Colaiacovo RC 8.00 20.00
139 Mikael Tellqvist RC 12.00 40.00
140 Steve Eminger RC 8.00 20.00

2002-03 Titanium Blue

*STARS: .5X TO 1.25X BASIC CARDS
*SP's: .05X TO .15X
STATED PRINT RUN 450 SER.#'d SETS

2002-03 Titanium Red

*STARS: 1X TO 2.5X BASE HI
*SP's: .10X TO .25X
STATED PRINT RUN 299 SER.#'d SETS

2002-03 Titanium Retail

These cards mirrored the hobby set but carried silver foil highlights.

*BASE CARDS SAME VALUE HOBBY
*SP's: .05X TO .15X HOBBY VERSION
SP PRINT RUN 1475 SER.#'d SETS

2002-03 Titanium Jerseys

Inserted one per hobby pack, this 75-card set featured swatches of game worn jerseys. Each card was individually serial-numbered. A retail variation was also created that carried silver foil in place of the gold foil on the hobby version.

*MULT.COLOR SWATCH: .5X TO 1.25X
1 Mike Leclerc/376 3.00 8.00
2 Dany Heatley/715 6.00 15.00
3 Ilya Kovalchuk/606 6.00 15.00
4 Patrik Stefan/1183 3.00 8.00
5 Joe Thornton/160 10.00 25.00
6 Martin Biron/1019 3.00 8.00
7 J-P Dumont/948 3.00 8.00
8 Rod BrindAmour/1231 3.00 8.00
9 Arturs Irbe/829 3.00 8.00
10 Jeff O'Neill/283 3.00 8.00
11 Chris Drury/514 3.00 8.00
12 Roman Turek/1160 3.00 8.00
13 Mark Bell/957 3.00 8.00
14 Sergei Berezin/304 3.00 8.00
15 Steve Sullivan/641 3.00 8.00
16 Rob Blake/1020 3.00 8.00
17 Milan Hejduk/1160 4.00 10.00
18 Patrick Roy/150 25.00 60.00
19 Rostislav Klesla/1099 3.00 8.00
20 Geoff Sanderson/1307 3.00 8.00
21 Ron Tugnutt/1338 3.00 8.00
22 Marty Turco/552 3.00 8.00
23 Sergei Fedorov/561 8.00 20.00
24 Dominik Hasek/253 8.00 20.00
25 Brett Hull/899 6.00 15.00
26 Luc Robitaille/717 3.00 8.00
27 Jason Williams/1270 3.00 8.00
28 Mike Comrie/503 3.00 8.00
29 Tommy Salo/801 3.00 8.00
30 Ryan Smyth/1052 3.00 8.00
31 Valeri Bure/1352 3.00 8.00
32 Kristian Huselius/1305 3.00 8.00
33 Roberto Luongo/1403 5.00 12.00
34 Marian Gaborik 8.00 20.00
35 Yanic Perreault/1285 3.00 8.00
36 Jose Theodore/316 5.00 12.00
37 David Legwand/857 3.00 8.00
38 Scott Walker/1307 3.00 8.00
39 Scott Gomez/872 3.00 8.00
40 Scott Stevens/1273 3.00 8.00
41 Michael Peca/553 3.00 8.00
42 Alexei Yashin/743 3.00 8.00
43 Pavel Bure/908 4.00 10.00
44 Eric Lindros/583 4.00 10.00
45 Mark Messier/809 4.00 10.00
46 Daniel Alfredsson/532 3.00 8.00
47 Martin Havlat/545 3.00 8.00
48 Patrick Lalime/826 3.00 8.00
49 Simon Gagne/1028 4.00 10.00
50 Michal Handzus/636 3.00 8.00
51 Tomi Kallio/1301 3.00 8.00
52 John LeClair/942 4.00 10.00
53 Johan Hedberg/1004 3.00 8.00
54 Mario Lemieux 15.00 40.00
55 Toby Petersen 3.00 8.00
56 Pavol Demitra/1256 3.00 8.00
57 Ray Ferraro/1288 3.00 8.00
58 Chris Pronger/1249 3.00 8.00
59 Keith Tkachuk/914 4.00 10.00
60 Sergei Varlamov/1152 3.00 8.00
61 Miikka Kiprusoff/1203 3.00 8.00
62 Patrick Marleau/730 3.00 8.00
63 Owen Nolan/439 3.00 8.00
64 Nikolai Khabibulin/1002 4.00 10.00
65 Fredrik Modin/1260 3.00 8.00
66 Alexander Mogilny/710 3.00 8.00
67 Gary Roberts/1260 3.00 8.00
68 Darcy Tucker/1260 3.00 8.00
69 Dan Cloutier/867 3.00 8.00
70 Brendan Morrison/638 3.00 8.00
71 Daniel Sedin/1105 3.00 8.00
72 Henrik Sedin/1100 3.00 8.00
73 Peter Bondra/1289 3.00 8.00
74 Jaromir Jagr/171 6.00 15.00
75 Olaf Kolzig/1303 3.00 8.00

2002-03 Titanium Jerseys Retail

*RETAIL: .6X TO 1.5X HOBBY

2002-03 Titanium Patches

This hobby-only set paralleled the basic jerseys but carried patch variations. Individual print runs are listed below. Print runs of 25 or less were not priced due to scarcity.

1 Mike Leclerc/10
2 Dany Heatley/20
3 Ilya Kovalchuk/25 20.00 50.00
4 Patrik Stefan/250 8.00 20.00
5 Joe Thornton/225 15.00 40.00
6 Martin Biron/65 8.00 20.00
8 Rod Brind'Amour/125 8.00 20.00
9 Arturs Irbe/21
10 Jeff O'Neill/250 8.00 20.00
11 Chris Drury/250 8.00 20.00
13 Mark Bell/225 8.00 20.00
14 Sergei Berezin/260 8.00 20.00
15 Steve Sullivan/100 8.00 20.00
16 Rob Blake/250 8.00 20.00
17 Milan Hejduk/250 10.00 25.00
19 Rostislav Klesla/50 8.00 20.00
20 Geoff Sanderson/25
21 Ron Tugnutt/250 8.00 20.00
22 Marty Turco/195 8.00 20.00
23 Sergei Fedorov/45 20.00 50.00
24 Dominik Hasek/35 20.00 50.00
25 Brett Hull/85 15.00 40.00
27 Jason Williams/250 8.00 20.00
28 Mike Comrie/150 8.00 20.00
30 Ryan Smyth/65 8.00 20.00
31 Valeri Bure/210 8.00 20.00
32 Kristian Huselius/250 8.00 20.00
33 Roberto Luongo/250 12.50 30.00
35 Yanic Perreault/200 8.00 20.00
36 Jose Theodore/65 12.50 30.00
37 David Legwand/180 8.00 20.00
38 Scott Walker/250 8.00 20.00
39 Scott Gomez/250 8.00 20.00
40 Scott Stevens/185 8.00 20.00
42 Alexei Yashin/30 8.00 20.00
43 Pavel Bure/20
44 Mark Messier/140 10.00 25.00
45 Eric Lindros/75 10.00 25.00
46 Daniel Alfredsson/100 8.00 20.00
47 Martin Havlat/250 8.00 20.00
48 Patrick Lalime/250 8.00 20.00
49 Simon Gagne/100 10.00 25.00
50 Michal Handzus/250 8.00 20.00
53 Johan Hedberg/250 8.00 20.00
54 Mario Lemieux/60 40.00 100.00
55 Toby Petersen/250 8.00 20.00
56 Pavol Demitra/165 8.00 20.00
57 Ray Ferraro/165 8.00 20.00
58 Chris Pronger/15
59 Keith Tkachuk/145 10.00 25.00
60 Sergei Varlamov/250 8.00 20.00
61 Miikka Kiprusoff/250 8.00 20.00
62 Patrick Marleau/175 8.00 20.00
63 Owen Nolan/15
64 Nikolai Khabibulin/35 15.00 40.00
65 Fredrik Modin/250 8.00 20.00
66 Alexander Mogilny/70 8.00 20.00
67 Gary Roberts/140 8.00 20.00
69 Dan Cloutier/250 8.00 20.00
70 Brendan Morrison/40 8.00 20.00
72 Henrik Sedin/25 10.00 25.00
74 Jaromir Jagr/110 15.00 40.00
75 Olaf Kolzig/175 8.00 20.00

2002-03 Titanium Saturday Knights

COMPLETE SET (10) 15.00 30.00
STATED ODDS 1:17
1 Jarome Iginla 1.00 2.50
2 Patrick Roy 4.00 10.00
3 Joe Sakic 1.50 4.00
4 Steve Yzerman 4.00 10.00
5 Jose Theodore 1.00 2.50
6 Marian Hossa .75 2.00
7 Mario Lemieux 5.00 12.00
8 Ed Belfour .75 2.00
9 Mats Sundin .75 2.00
10 Todd Bertuzzi .75 2.00

2002-03 Titanium Masked Marauders

COMPLETE SET (8) 10.00 25.00
STATED ODDS 1:25
1 Patrick Roy 4.00 10.00
2 Marty Turco 1.25 3.00
3 Curtis Joseph 1.25 3.00
4 Jose Theodore 1.50 4.00
5 Martin Brodeur 2.50 6.00
6 Nikolai Khabibulin 1.25 3.00
7 Ed Belfour 1.25 3.00
8 Dan Cloutier 1.25 3.00

2002-03 Titanium Right on Target

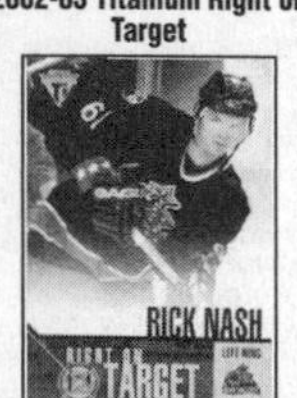

COMPLETE SET (20) 20.00 50.00
STATED ODDS 1:9
1 Stanislav Chistov 1.25 3.00
2 Ivan Huml .75 2.00
3 Chuck Kobasew 1.25 3.00
4 Jordan Leopold .75 2.00
5 Tyler Arnason .75 2.00
6 Rick Nash 3.00 8.00
7 Henrik Zetterberg 2.50 6.00
8 Ales Hemsky 2.00 5.00
9 Jay Bouwmeester 1.25 3.00
10 Stephen Weiss 1.25 3.00
11 Michael Cammalleri 1.25 3.00
12 Alexander Frolov 1.25 3.00
13 P-M Bouchard 1.25 3.00
14 Scottie Upshall 1.25 3.00
15 Rick DiPietro 1.50 4.00
16 Jamie Lundmark .75 2.00
17 Jason Spezza 2.50 6.00
18 Barret Jackman .75 2.00
19 Jonathan Cheechoo 2.00 5.00
20 Fedor Fedorov .75 2.00

2002-03 Titanium Shadows

COMPLETE SET (6) 30.00 60.00
STATED ODDS 1:49
1 Ilya Kovalchuk 1.50 4.00
2 Joe Thornton 2.00 5.00
3 Patrick Roy 6.00 15.00
4 Joe Sakic 2.50 6.00
5 Steve Yzerman 6.00 15.00
6 Marian Gaborik 2.50 6.00

2003-04 Titanium

This 215-card set consisted of 100 veteran cards (1-100); 40 short-printed rookie cards (101-140) serial-numbered to 99; 50 veteran jersey cards (141-190) serial-numbered out of 875 (unless noted otherwise); 15 short-printed veteran jersey cards (191-205) serial-numbered to 99 (unless otherwise noted) and 10 short-printed rookie jersey cards (individual numbers are listed below). Titanium Hobby carried gold foil highlights which distinguished it from the Retail brand.

COMP.SET w/o SP's (100) 15.00 30.00
PRINT RUNS UNDER 25
NOT PRICED DUE TO SCARCITY
1 Martin Gerber .25 .60
2 Steve Rucchin .10 .25
3 Petr Sykora .10 .25
4 Frantisek Kaberle .10 .25
5 Slava Kozlov .10 .25
6 Pasi Nurminen .25 .60
7 Marc Savard .10 .25
8 Mike Knuble .10 .25
9 Glen Murray .10 .25
10 Felix Potvin .25 .60
11 Andrew Raycroft .25 .60
12 Martin Biron .25 .60
13 Daniel Briere .10 .25
14 J-P Dumont .10 .25
15 Miroslav Satan .25 .60
16 Shean Donovan .10 .25
17 Miikka Kiprusoff .25 .60
18 Jordan Leopold .10 .25
19 Erik Cole .10 .25
20 Ron Francis .25 .60
21 Jeff O'Neill .10 .25
22 Josef Vasicek .10 .25
23 Kevin Weekes .25 .60
24 Mark Bell .10 .25
25 Kyle Calder .10 .25
26 Jocelyn Thibault .25 .60
27 Alexei Zhamnov .10 .25
28 Rob Blake .25 .60
29 Alex Tanguay .25 .60
30 Marc Denis .25 .60
31 Rick Nash .40 1.00
32 David Vyborny .10 .25
33 Jason Arnott .10 .25
34 Jere Lehtinen .25 .60
35 Pavel Datsyuk .30 .75
36 Dominik Hasek .60 1.50
37 Curtis Joseph .30 .75
38 Henrik Zetterberg .30 .75
39 Tommy Salo .25 .60
40 Raffi Torres .10 .25
41 Mike York .10 .25
42 Valeri Bure .10 .25
43 Viktor Kozlov .10 .25
44 Stephen Weiss .10 .25
45 Roman Cechmanek .25 .60
46 Alexander Frolov .10 .25
47 Cristobal Huet .25 .60
48 Luc Robitaille .25 .60
49 Andrew Brunette .10 .25
50 Alexandre Daigle .10 .25
51 Manny Fernandez .25 .60
52 Marian Gaborik .60 1.50
53 Dwayne Roloson .25 .60
54 Marcel Hossa .10 .25
55 Mike Ribeiro .10 .25
56 Michael Ryder .10 .25
57 Sheldon Souray .10 .25
58 David Legwand .25 .60
59 Tomas Vokoun .25 .60
60 Jeff Friesen .10 .25
61 Scott Gomez .10 .25
62 Scott Niedermayer .10 .25
63 Jason Blake .10 .25
64 Mariusz Czerkawski .10 .25
65 Trent Hunter .10 .25
66 Garth Snow .25 .60
67 Mike Dunham .25 .60
68 Brian Leetch .25 .60
69 Mark Messier .30 .75
70 Radek Bonk
71 Zdeno Chara .10 .25
72 Peter Schaefer .10 .25
73 Tony Amonte .25 .60
74 Robert Esche .25 .60
75 Michal Handzus .10 .25
76 Mark Recchi .10 .25
77 Sean Burke .25 .60
78 Shane Doan .10 .25
79 Ladislav Nagy .10 .25
80 Sebastien Caron .25 .60
81 Rico Fata .10 .25
82 Dick Tarnstrom .10 .25
83 Pavol Demitra .25 .60
84 Chris Pronger .25 .60
85 Keith Tkachuk .30 .75
86 Jonathan Cheechoo .12 .30
87 Vincent Damphousse .10 .25
88 Patrick Marleau .25 .60
89 Evgeni Nabokov .25 .60
90 Marco Sturm .10 .25
91 John Grahame .25 .60
92 Cory Stillman .10 .25
93 Joe Nieuwendyk .25 .60
94 Darcy Tucker .10 .25
95 Jason King .10 .25
96 Daniel Sedin .10 .25
97 Henrik Sedin .10 .25
98 Peter Bondra .25 .60
99 Sergei Gonchar .10 .25
100 Robert Lang .10 .25
101 Garrett Burnett RC 6.00 15.00
102 Tony Martensson RC 6.00 15.00
103 Sergei Zinovjev RC 6.00 15.00
104 Andrew Peters RC 6.00 15.00
105 Brent Krahn RC 8.00 20.00
106 Eric Staal RC 60.00 150.00
107 Travis Moen RC 8.00 20.00
108 Tuomo Ruutu RC 20.00 50.00
109 Pavel Vorobiev RC 10.00 25.00
110 Mikhail Yakubov RC 6.00 15.00
111 Cody McCormick RC 6.00 15.00
112 Dan Fritsche RC 8.00 20.00
113 Kent McDonell RC 6.00 15.00
114 Nikolai Zherdev RC 30.00 60.00
115 Trevor Daley RC 8.00 20.00
116 Antti Miettinen RC 8.00 20.00
117 Jiri Hudler RC 15.00 40.00
118 Niklas Kronwall RC 12.00 30.00
119 Nathan Robinson RC 6.00 15.00
120 Peter Sarno RC 6.00 15.00
121 Tim Gleason RC 6.00 15.00
122 Esa Pirnes RC 6.00 15.00
123 Brent Burns RC 10.00 25.00
124 Dan Hamhuis RC 10.00 25.00
125 Marek Zidlicky RC 8.00 20.00
126 David Hale RC 6.00 15.00
127 Paul Martin RC 6.00 15.00
128 Sean Bergenheim RC 6.00 15.00
129 Dominic Moore RC 6.00 15.00
130 Joni Pitkanen RC 10.00 25.00
131 Fredrik Sjostrom RC 6.00 15.00
132 Marc-Andre Fleury RC 60.00 150.00
133 Matt Murley RC 6.00 15.00
134 John Pohl RC 6.00 15.00
135 Peter Sejna RC 6.00 15.00
136 Milan Michalek RC 30.00 60.00
137 Maxim Kondratiev RC 6.00 15.00
138 Ryan Kesler RC 10.00 25.00
139 Alexander Semin RC 60.00 120.00
140 Rastislav Stana RC 6.00 15.00
141 Martin Gerber 6.00 15.00
142 Sergei Fedorov JSY 8.00 20.00
143 Jean-Sebastien Giguere JSY 6.00 15.00
144 Sergei Samsonov JSY 6.00 15.00
145 Ryan Miller/785 JSY 6.00 15.00
146 Jarome Iginla JSY 10.00 25.00
147 David Aebischer JSY 6.00 15.00
148 Milan Hejduk JSY 8.00 20.00
149 Joe Sakic JSY 12.50 30.00
150 Teemu Selanne JSY 8.00 20.00
151 Mike Modano JSY 8.00 20.00
152 Marty Turco JSY 8.00 20.00
153 Brendan Shanahan JSY 8.00 20.00
154 Ales Hemsky JSY 6.00 15.00
155 Ryan Smyth JSY 6.00 15.00
156 Jay Bouwmeester JSY 6.00 15.00
157 Olli Jokinen JSY 6.00 15.00
158 Roberto Luongo JSY 10.00 25.00
159 Jason Allison JSY 6.00 15.00
160 Ziggy Palffy JSY 6.00 15.00
161 Saku Koivu JSY 8.00 20.00
162 Jose Theodore JSY 8.00 20.00
163 Richard Zednik JSY 6.00 15.00
164 Martin Erat JSY 6.00 15.00
165 Scott Walker JSY 6.00 15.00
166 Patrik Elias JSY 6.00 15.00
167 Rick DiPietro JSY 6.00 15.00
168 Michael Peca JSY 6.00 15.00
169 Alexei Yashin JSY 6.00 15.00
170 Jaromir Jagr JSY 10.00 25.00
171 Eric Lindros JSY 8.00 20.00
172 Daniel Alfredsson JSY 6.00 15.00
173 Marian Hossa JSY 8.00 20.00
174 Patrick Lalime JSY 6.00 15.00
175 Jason Spezza JSY 8.00 20.00
176 Jeff Hackett JSY 6.00 15.00
177 Jeremy Roenick JSY 10.00 25.00
178 Barret Jackman JSY 6.00 15.00
179 Chris Osgood JSY 6.00 15.00
180 Doug Weight JSY 6.00 15.00
181 Nikolai Khabibulin JSY 6.00 15.00
182 Vincent Lecavalier JSY 8.00 20.00
183 Martin St. Louis/640 JSY 8.00 20.00
184 Owen Nolan JSY 6.00 15.00
185 Gary Roberts/835 JSY 6.00 15.00
186 Mats Sundin JSY 8.00 20.00
187 Dan Cloutier JSY 6.00 15.00
188 Brendan Morrison JSY 6.00 15.00
189 Markus Naslund JSY 8.00 20.00
190 Olaf Kolzig JSY 6.00 15.00
191 Ilya Kovalchuk JSY 12.50 30.00
192 Dany Heatley/39 JSY 20.00 50.00
193 Joe Thornton JSY 12.50 30.00
194 Peter Forsberg JSY 12.00 30.00

195 Paul Kariya JSY .30 .75
196 Bill Guerin JSY 8.00 20.00
197 Brett Hull JSY 12.50 30.00
198 Nicklas Lidstrom JSY 8.00 20.00
199 Steve Yzerman JSY 15.00 40.00
200 Martin Brodeur JSY 15.00 40.00
201 Pavel Bure JSY 8.00 20.00
202 John LeClair JSY 8.00 20.00
203 Mario Lemieux JSY 20.00 50.00
204 Ed Belfour JSY 8.00 20.00
205 Todd Bertuzzi JSY 8.00 20.00
206 Joffrey Lupul/15
207 Patrice Bergeron/37 125.00 200.00
208 Matthew Lombardi/18
209 Nathan Horton/16
210 Dustin Brown/23
211 Christopher Higgins/88 20.00 50.00
212 Jordin Tootoo/55 30.00 80.00
213 Antoine Vermette/20
214 Matt Stajan/14
215 Boyd Gordon/15

2003-04 Titanium Hobby Jersey Number Parallels

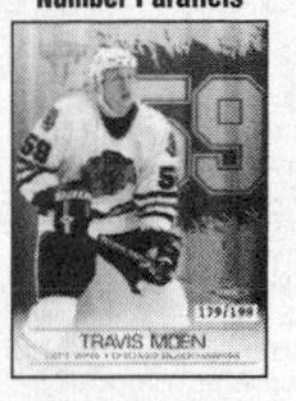

This 190-card partial parallel set differed from the base set in that the player's jersey number was on the card front in place of the team logo. Cards 1-100 were serial-numbered to 150 sets; cards 101-140 were serial-numbered to 199 sets and cards 141-190 were serial-numbered to 50 sets.

*STARS: 5X TO 12X
1-100 PRINT RUN 150 SER.#'d SETS
*ROOKIES 101-140: .06X TO .15X
101-140 PRINT RUN 199 SER.#'d SETS
*JSYS: 1.25X TO 3X
JSY PRINT RUN 50 SER.#'d SETS

2003-04 Titanium Patches

*PATCH: 1 X TO 2.5X BASIC JERSEYS
PRINT RUNS OF 25 OR LESS NOT PRICED
DUE TO SCARCITY

2003-04 Titanium Retail

The Retail set carried silver foil highlights that distinguished it form the Hobby set.

*STARS: SAME VALUE AS HOBBY
*JSYS: 1X TO 2.5X
JSY PRINT RUN 170 SER.#'d SETS
COMMON RC (101-140) 2.50 6.00
RC PRINT RUN 750 SER.#'d SETS
101 Garrett Burnett RC 2.50 6.00
102 Tony Martensson RC 2.50 6.00
103 Sergei Zinovjev RC 2.50 6.00
104 Andrew Peters RC 2.50 6.00
105 Brent Krahn RC 2.50 6.00
106 Eric Staal RC 10.00 25.00
107 Travis Moen RC 2.50 6.00
108 Tuomo Ruutu RC 4.00 10.00
109 Pavel Vorobiev RC 2.50 6.00
110 Mikhail Yakubov RC 2.50 6.00
111 Cody McCormick RC 2.50 6.00
112 Dan Fritsche RC 2.50 6.00
113 Kent McDonell RC 2.50 6.00
114 Nikolai Zherdev RC 6.00 15.00
115 Trevor Daley RC 2.50 6.00
116 Antti Miettinen RC 2.50 6.00
117 Jiri Hudler RC 3.00 8.00
118 Niklas Kronwall RC 2.50 6.00
119 Nathan Robinson RC 2.50 6.00
120 Peter Sarno RC 2.50 6.00
121 Tim Gleason RC 2.50 6.00
122 Esa Pirnes RC 2.50 6.00
123 Brent Burns RC 2.50 6.00
124 Dan Hamhuis RC 2.50 6.00
125 Marek Zidlicky RC 2.50 6.00
126 David Hale RC 2.50 6.00
127 Paul Martin RC 2.50 6.00
128 Sean Bergenheim RC 2.50 6.00
129 Dominic Moore RC 2.50 6.00
130 Joni Pitkanen RC 3.00 8.00
131 Fredrik Sjostrom RC 2.50 6.00
132 Marc-Andre Fleury RC 12.00 30.00
133 Matt Murley RC 2.50 6.00
134 John Pohl RC 2.50 6.00
135 Peter Sejna RC 2.50 6.00
136 Milan Michalek RC 4.00 10.00
137 Maxim Kondratiev RC 2.50 6.00
138 Ryan Kesler RC 2.50 6.00
139 Alexander Semin RC 5.00 12.00
140 Rastislav Stana RC 2.50 6.00

2003-04 Titanium Retail Jersey Number Parallels

This 140-card partial parallel set differed from the base set in that the player's jersey number was on the card front in place of the team logo. Cards 1-100 were serial-numbered to 250 sets and cards 101-140 were serial-numbered to 225 sets.

*STARS: 4X TO 10X BASE HI
*ROOKIES 101-140: .5X TO 1.25X RETAIL HI

2003-04 Titanium Highlight Reels

COMPLETE SET (8) 12.50 25.00
STATED ODDS 1:17 HOBBY
1 Ilya Kovalchuk 1.00 2.50
2 Joe Thornton 1.25 3.00
3 Peter Forsberg 2.00 5.00
4 Joe Sakic 1.50 4.00
5 Dominik Hasek 1.50 4.00
6 Steve Yzerman 2.50 6.00
7 Martin Brodeur 2.00 5.00
8 Mario Lemieux 3.00 8.00

2003-04 Titanium Masked Marauders

COMPLETE SET (10) 10.00 20.00
STATED ODDS 1:9
1 Jean-Sebastien Giguere .60 1.50
2 David Aebischer .60 1.50
3 Marty Turco .60 1.50
4 Dominik Hasek 1.50 4.00
5 Jose Theodore 1.00 2.50
6 Martin Brodeur 2.00 5.00
7 Rick DiPietro .60 1.50
8 Patrick Lalime .60 1.50
9 Nikolai Khabibulin .75 2.00
10 Ed Belfour .75 2.00

2003-04 Titanium Right on Target

COMPLETE SET (16) 10.00 20.00
STATED ODDS 1:5
1 Joffrey Lupul .30 .75
2 Patrice Bergeron 1.50 4.00
3 Eric Staal .75 2.00
4 Rick Nash .50 1.25
5 Henrik Zetterberg .40 1.00
6 Ales Hemsky .30 .75
7 Jay Bouwmeester .30 .75
8 Nathan Horton .75 2.00
9 Michael Ryder .30 .75
10 Jordin Tootoo .60 1.50
11 Jason Spezza .40 1.00
12 Joni Pitkanen .30 .75
13 Marc-Andre Fleury 2.00 5.00
14 Barret Jackman .30 .75
15 Matt Stajan .75 2.00
16 Jason King .30 .75

2003-04 Titanium Stat Masters

COMPLETE SET (10) 8.00 15.00
STATED ODDS 1:9
1 Sergei Fedorov .75 2.00
2 Ilya Kovalchuk .75 2.00
3 Peter Forsberg 1.50 4.00
4 Rick Nash .75 2.00
5 Pavel Datsyuk .60 1.50
6 Brett Hull .75 2.00
7 Marian Hossa .60 1.50
8 Mario Lemieux 2.50 6.00
9 Todd Bertuzzi .60 1.50
10 Markus Naslund .60 1.50

2000-01 Titanium Draft Day Edition

This 176-card set was released at the 2001 NHL Draft in 2-card packs containing one jersey card and one short-printed first year player per pack. Cards 1-100 were jersey cards while cards 101-176 were short-printed prospect cards. The set introduced 25 new players not included in Titanium. The short prints were serial numbered to 1000. Jersey card print runs are listed below. Cards with print runs less than 20 are nt priced due to scarcity.

COMP.SET w/o JSYs (76) 150.00 350.00
1 Jean-Sebastien Giguere/1010 3.00 8.00
2 Mike Leclerc/520 3.00 8.00
3 P.J. Axelsson/520 3.00 8.00
4 Byron Dafoe/520 3.00 8.00
5 Kyle McLaren/520 3.00 8.00
6 Sergei Samsonov/520 6.00 15.00
7 Don Sweeney/535 3.00 8.00
8 Joe Thornton/535 8.00 20.00
9 Eric Weinrich/1020 3.00 8.00
10 Stu Barnes/535 3.00 8.00
11 Dominik Hasek/535 8.00 20.00
12 Erik Rasmussen/1020 3.00 8.00
13 Fred Brathwaite/1010 3.00 8.00
14 Valeri Bure/1020 3.00 8.00
15 Marc Savard/1020 3.00 8.00
16 Tony Amonte/1020 3.00 8.00
17 Eric Daze/1020 3.00 8.00
18 Boris Mironov/1020 3.00 8.00
19 Michael Nylander/1020 3.00 8.00
20 Steve Sullivan/1020 3.00 8.00
21 Jocelyn Thibault/1020 3.00 8.00
22 Alexei Zhamnov/1020 3.00 8.00
23 Chris Dingman/520 3.00 8.00
24 Peter Forsberg/520 8.00 20.00
25 Patrick Roy/58 75.00 200.00
26 Joe Sakic/535 8.00 20.00
27 Lyle Odelein/535 3.00 8.00
28 Ed Belfour/110 10.00 25.00
29 Derian Hatcher/990 3.00 8.00
30 Brett Hull/115 12.00 30.00
31 Jamie Langenbrunner/985 3.00 8.00
32 Jere Lehtinen/520 3.00 8.00
33 Mike Modano/1015 6.00 15.00
34 Joe Nieuwendyk/1015 3.00 8.00
35 Darryl Sydor/835 3.00 8.00
36 Chris Chelios/520 4.00 10.00
37 Matthieu Dandenault/520 3.00 8.00
38 Nicklas Lidstrom/110 6.00 15.00
39 Darren McCarty/520 3.00 8.00
40 Chris Osgood/1020 3.00 8.00
41 Brendan Shanahan/520 6.00 15.00
42 Steve Yzerman/105 25.00 60.00
43 Anson Carter/55 12.50 30.00
44 Ryan Smyth/1015 3.00 8.00
45 Doug Weight/520 3.00 8.00
46 Pavel Bure/55 15.00 40.00
47 Robert Svehla/1015 3.00 8.00
48 Felix Potvin/100 10.00 25.00
49 Benoit Brunet/1015 3.00 8.00
50 Jeff Hackett/520 3.00 8.00
51 Sergei Zholtok/1010 3.00 8.00
52 Mike Dunham/1020 3.00 8.00
53 Tom Fitzgerald/520 3.00 8.00
54 Patric Kjellberg/520 3.00 8.00
55 David Legwand/520 3.00 8.00
56 Cliff Ronning/520 3.00 8.00
57 Kimmo Timonen/520 3.00 8.00
58 Scott Walker/520 3.00 8.00
59 Bobby Holik/520 3.00 8.00
60 Scott Niedermayer/995 3.00 8.00
61 Mariusz Czerkawski/1020 3.00 8.00
62 Kenny Jonsson/520 3.00 8.00
63 Claude Lapointe/1015 3.00 8.00
64 Chris Terreri/1020 3.00 8.00
65 Theo Fleury/870 3.00 8.00
66 Brian Leetch/520 3.00 8.00
67 Petr Nedved/1015 3.00 8.00
68 Mike Richter/1010 4.00 10.00
69 Mike York/1015 3.00 8.00
70 Daniel Alfredsson/520 3.00 8.00
71 Alexei Yashin/285 3.00 8.00
72 Eric Desjardins/520 3.00 8.00
73 John LeClair/520 4.00 10.00
74 Mika Alatalo/520 3.00 8.00
75 Sean Burke/1010 3.00 8.00
76 Shane Doan/535 3.00 8.00
77 Jyrki Lumme/520 3.00 8.00
78 Jeremy Roenick/520 6.00 15.00
79 Radoslav Suchy/1015 3.00 8.00
80 Jean-Sebastien Aubin/1015 3.00 8.00
81 Jan Hrdina/1020 3.00 8.00
82 Jaromir Jagr/520 8.00 20.00
83 Darius Kasparaitis/1010 3.00 8.00
84 Alexei Kovalev/1015 3.00 8.00
85 Milan Kraft/1015 3.00 8.00
86 Mario Lemieux/115 25.00 60.00
87 Kevin Stevens/1020 3.00 8.00
88 Martin Straka/1010 3.00 8.00
89 Dallas Drake/535 3.00 8.00
90 Cory Stillman/1010 3.00 8.00
91 Vincent Damphousse/1015 3.00 8.00
92 Teemu Selanne/1020 4.00 10.00
93 Vincent Lecavalier/535 6.00 15.00
94 Shayne Corson/1010 3.00 8.00
95 Tie Domi/535 3.00 8.00
96 Curtis Joseph/535 6.00 15.00
97 Mats Sundin/535 6.00 15.00
98 Peter Bondra/15
99 Ulf Dahlen/535 3.00 8.00
100 Dainius Zubrus/520 3.00 8.00
101 Samuel Pahlsson 1.50 4.00
102 Scott Fankhouser 1.50 4.00
103 Tomi Kallio 1.50 4.00
104 Brad Tapper RC 2.00 5.00
105 Andrew Raycroft RC 6.00 15.00
106 Denis Hamel 1.50 4.00
107 Jeff Cowan RC 2.00 5.00
108 Oleg Saprykin 1.50 4.00
109 Josef Vasicek RC 2.00 5.00
110 Shane Willis 1.50 4.00
111 David Aebischer RC 6.00 15.00
112 Serge Aubin RC 2.00 5.00
113 Marc Denis 1.50 4.00
114 Chris Nielsen RC 2.00 5.00
115 David Vyborny 1.50 4.00
116 Marty Turco RC 8.00 20.00
117 Mike Comrie RC 3.00 8.00
118 Shawn Horcoff RC 3.00 8.00
119 Dominic Pittis 1.50 4.00
120 Roberto Luongo 2.00 5.00
121 Ivan Novoseltsev 1.50 4.00
122 Serge Payer 1.50 4.00
123 Denis Shvidki 1.50 4.00
124 Steven Reinprecht RC 3.00 8.00
125 Lubomir Visnovsky RC 2.00 5.00
126 Marian Gaborik RC 8.00 20.00
127 Filip Kuba 1.50 4.00
128 Mathieu Garon 1.50 4.00
129 Eric Landry RC 2.00 5.00
130 Andrei Markov 1.50 4.00
131 Marian Cisar 1.50 4.00
132 Scott Hartnell RC 2.50 6.00
133 Rick DiPietro RC 6.00 15.00
134 Martin Havlat RC 8.00 20.00
135 Jani Hurme RC 3.00 8.00
136 Petr Schastlivy 1.50 4.00
137 Ruslan Fedotenko RC 1.50 4.00
138 Justin Williams RC 3.00 8.00
139 Robert Esche 1.50 4.00
140 Milan Kraft 1.50 4.00
141 Brent Johnson 1.50 4.00
142 Reed Low RC 2.00 5.00
143 Evgeni Nabokov 6.00 15.00
144 Alexander Kharitonov RC 2.00 5.00
145 Dieter Kochan RC 2.00 5.00
146 Brad Richards 1.50 4.00
147 Adam Mair 1.50 4.00
148 Daniel Sedin 1.50 4.00
149 Henrik Sedin 1.50 4.00
150 Trent Whitfield 1.50 4.00
151 Marc Chouinard RC 2.00 5.00
152 Jonas Ronnqvist RC 2.00 5.00
153 Petr Tenkrat RC 2.00 5.00
154 Ronald Petrovicky RC 2.00 5.00
155 Craig Adams RC 2.00 5.00
156 Niclas Wallin RC 2.00 5.00
157 Rostislav Klesla RC 3.00 8.00
158 Petteri Nummelin RC 2.00 5.00
159 Tyler Bouck RC 2.00 5.00
160 Michel Riesen RC 2.00 5.00
161 Eric Belanger RC 2.00 5.00
162 Roman Simicek RC 2.00 5.00
163 Xavier Delisle 1.50 4.00
164 Greg Classen RC 2.00 5.00
165 Mike Commodore RC 2.00 5.00
166 Sascha Goc RC 2.00 5.00
167 Jeff Ulmer RC 2.00 5.00
168 Shane Hnidy RC 2.00 5.00
169 Roman Cechmanek RC 2.00 5.00
170 Todd Fedoruk RC 2.00 5.00
171 Ossi Vaananen RC 2.00 5.00
172 Bryce Salvador RC 2.00 5.00
173 Mark Smith RC 2.00 5.00
174 Mike Brown RC 2.00 5.00
175 Jakub Cutta RC 2.00 5.00
176 Johan Hedberg RC 3.00 8.00

2000-01 Titanium Draft Day Edition Patches

This 74-card set was the parallel set to the jersey cards in the base set (cards 1-100). Please note that the cards have different print runs which are player specific, and the set did not include patch cards for all of the players that had jersey cards. Cards with print runs less than 25 are not priced due to scarcity.

1 Jean-Sebastien Giguere/115 10.00 25.00
2 Mike Leclerc/114 10.00 25.00
3 P.J. Axelsson/114 10.00 25.00
4 Byron Dafoe/70 10.00 25.00
6 Sergei Samsonov/43 20.00 50.00
8 Joe Thornton/24 40.00 100.00
9 Eric Weinrich/116 10.00 25.00
10 Stu Barnes/57 10.00 25.00
12 Erik Rasmussen/113 10.00 25.00
13 Fred Brathwaite/106 10.00 25.00
14 Valeri Bure/110 10.00 25.00
15 Marc Savard/106 10.00 25.00
16 Tony Amonte/110 10.00 25.00
17 Eric Daze/114 10.00 25.00
18 Boris Mironov/116 10.00 25.00
19 Michael Nylander/113 10.00 25.00
20 Steve Sullivan/113 10.00 25.00
21 Jocelyn Thibault/113 10.00 25.00
22 Alexei Zhamnov/116 10.00 25.00
23 Chris Dingman/120 10.00 25.00
24 Peter Forsberg/112 20.00 50.00
27 Lyle Odelein/113 10.00 25.00
29 Derian Hatcher/114 10.00 25.00
31 Jamie Langenbrunner/109 10.00 25.00
33 Mike Modano/112 20.00 50.00
34 Joe Nieuwendyk/106 10.00 25.00
35 Darryl Sydor/107 10.00 25.00
36 Chris Chelios/112 20.00 50.00
37 Matthieu Dandenault/115 10.00 25.00
40 Chris Osgood/106 10.00 25.00
41 Brendan Shanahan/117 20.00 50.00
44 Ryan Smyth/24
45 Doug Weight/110 10.00 25.00
46 Pavel Bure/116 20.00 50.00
47 Robert Svehla/105 10.00 25.00
49 Benoit Brunet/111 10.00 25.00
51 Sergei Zholtok/103 10.00 25.00
52 Mike Dunham/113 10.00 25.00
54 Patric Kjellberg/118 10.00 25.00
55 David Legwand/116 10.00 25.00
56 Cliff Ronning/56 10.00 25.00
58 Scott Walker/94 10.00 25.00
59 Bobby Holik/49 10.00 25.00
60 Scott Niedermayer/102 10.00 25.00
61 Mariusz Czerkawski/79 10.00 25.00
62 Kenny Jonsson/92 10.00 25.00
63 Claude Lapointe/40 10.00 25.00
64 Chris Terreri/72 10.00 25.00
65 Theo Fleury/38 10.00 25.00
66 Brian Leetch/117 10.00 25.00
67 Petr Nedved/34 10.00 25.00
68 Mike Richter/114 25.00 60.00
69 Mike York/109 10.00 25.00
70 Daniel Alfredsson/56 10.00 25.00
71 Alexei Yashin/46 10.00 25.00
73 John LeClair/89 20.00 50.00
74 Mika Alatalo/117 10.00 25.00
75 Sean Burke/111 10.00 25.00
77 Jyrki Lumme/108 10.00 25.00
78 Jeremy Roenick/42 30.00 80.00
79 Radoslav Suchy/107 10.00 25.00
80 Jean-Sebastien Aubin/112 10.00 25.00
81 Jan Hrdina/112 10.00 25.00
83 Darius Kasparaitis/114 10.00 25.00
84 Alexei Kovalev/114 10.00 25.00
85 Milan Kraft/112 10.00 25.00
87 Kevin Stevens/115 10.00 25.00
88 Martin Straka/108 10.00 25.00
89 Dallas Drake/36 10.00 25.00
90 Cory Stillman/114 10.00 25.00
91 Vincent Damphousse/114 10.00 25.00
92 Teemu Selanne/118 15.00 40.00
94 Shayne Corson/38 10.00 25.00
95 Tie Domi/110 10.00 25.00

2000-01 Titanium Draft Day Promos

Produced as promotional give-aways, this 76-card set resembles the base set in every way except that they are numbered XXXX/1000 and have the word "sample" printed across the back. According to reports, approximately 150 sets were produced. A few of these cards have found their way to the secondary market, but not enough market information is available to price them at this time.

NOT PRICED DUE TO SCARCITY

2001-02 Titanium Draft Day Edition

Released in conjunction with the 2002 NHL Entry Draft, this 172-card set featured jersey cards and short printed prospects. Cards 1-100 carried game-worn jersey swatches of the given player, while cards 101-172 were short printed to just 780. An autographed version of the Ilya Kovalchuk card was also randomly seeded in packs and numbered to just 500 copies.

1 Jeff Friesen 3.00 6.00
2 Paul Kariya 5.00 12.00
3 Oleg Tverdovsky 3.00 6.00
4 Dany Heatley 5.00 12.00
5 Milan Hnilicka 4.00 10.00
6 Tomi Kallio 3.00 6.00
7 Ilya Kovalchuk 6.00 15.00
8 Patrik Stefan 3.00 6.00
9 Bill Guerin 4.00 10.00
10 Kyle McLaren 3.00 6.00
11 Joe Thornton 6.00 15.00
12 Martin Biron 4.00 10.00
13 J-P Dumont 3.00 6.00
14 Erik Rasmussen 3.00 6.00
15 Jarome Iginla 6.00 15.00
16 Marc Savard 3.00 6.00
17 Roman Turek 4.00 10.00
18 Erik Cole 3.00 6.00
19 Jeff O'Neill 3.00 6.00
20 Tony Amonte 4.00 10.00
21 Kyle Calder 3.00 6.00
22 Tom Fitzgerald 3.00 6.00
23 Phil Housley 3.00 6.00
24 Steve Sullivan 3.00 6.00
25 Rob Blake 4.00 10.00
26 Vaclav Nedorost 2.00 5.00
27 Joe Sakic 8.00 20.00
28 Alex Tanguay 4.00 10.00
29 Marc Denis 4.00 10.00
30 Rostislav Klesla 3.00 6.00
31 Ron Tugnutt 4.00 10.00
32 Jason Arnott 3.00 6.00
33 Derian Hatcher 3.00 6.00
34 Mike Modano 6.00 15.00
35 Pierre Turgeon 4.00 10.00
36 Sergei Zubov 3.00 6.00
37 Dominik Hasek 8.00 20.00
38 Brett Hull 5.00 12.00
39 Mike Comrie 4.00 10.00
40 Jochen Hecht 2.00 5.00
41 Jason Allison 2.00 5.00
42 Adam Deadmarsh 2.00 5.00
43 Felix Potvin 5.00 12.00
44 Manny Fernandez 4.00 10.00
45 Marian Gaborik 6.00 15.00
46 Filip Kuba 2.00 5.00
47 Jamie McLennan 2.00 5.00
48 Sergei Berezin 2.00 5.00
49 Jeff Hackett 4.00 10.00
50 Jukka Hentunen 2.00 5.00
51 Martin Brodeur 10.00 25.00
52 Scott Gomez 2.00 5.00
53 Bobby Holik 2.00 5.00
54 Jamie Langenbrunner 2.00 5.00
55 Scott Stevens 4.00 10.00
56 Mats Lindgren 2.00 5.00
57 Kip Miller 2.00 5.00
58 Chris Osgood 4.00 10.00
59 Theo Fleury 3.00 8.00
60 Brian Leetch 4.00 10.00
61 Eric Lindros 5.00 12.00
62 Mark Messier 5.00 12.00
63 Mike Richter 5.00 12.00
64 Daniel Alfredsson 4.00 10.00
65 Martin Havlat 4.00 10.00
66 Marian Hossa 5.00 12.00
67 Patrick Lalime 4.00 10.00
68 Roman Cechmanek 3.00 8.00
69 Jiri Dopita 2.00 5.00
70 Simon Gagne 5.00 12.00
71 John LeClair 5.00 12.00
72 Jeremy Roenick 6.00 15.00
73 Michal Handzus 2.00 5.00
74 Krystofer Kolanos 2.00 5.00
75 Daymond Langkow 2.00 5.00
76 Teppo Numminen 2.00 5.00
77 Kris Beech 2.00 5.00
78 Johan Hedberg 3.00 8.00
79 Robert Lang 2.00 5.00
80 Mario Lemieux 15.00 40.00
81 Rich Parent 2.00 5.00
82 Toby Petersen 2.00 5.00
83 Mike Eastwood 2.00 5.00
84 Ray Ferraro 2.00 5.00
85 Patrick Marleau 4.00 10.00
86 Evgeni Nabokov 4.00 10.00
87 Owen Nolan 4.00 10.00
88 Vincent Lecavalier 5.00 12.00
89 Tom Barrasso 4.00 10.00
90 Mats Sundin 5.00 12.00
91 Dimitri Yushkevich 2.00 5.00
92 Todd Bertuzzi 5.00 12.00
93 Andrew Cassels 2.00 5.00
94 Dan Cloutier 4.00 10.00
95 Brendan Morrison 4.00 10.00
96 Markus Naslund 5.00 12.00
97 Daniel Sedin 2.00 5.00
98 Henrik Sedin 3.00 6.00
99 Peter Bondra 5.00 12.00
100 Jaromir Jagr 8.00 20.00
101 Ilja Bryzgalov RC 3.00 8.00
102 Andy McDonald SP 2.00 5.00
103 Timo Parssinen RC 2.00 5.00
104 Dany Heatley SP 4.00 10.00
105 Ilya Kovalchuk RC 12.00 30.00
106 Pasi Nurminen RC 2.50 6.00
107 Kamil Piros RC 2.00 5.00
108 Brian Pothier RC 2.00 5.00
109 Daniel Tjarnqvist SP 2.00 5.00
110 Andy Hilbert SP 2.00 5.00
111 Ales Kotalik RC 2.50 6.00
112 Mika Noronen SP 2.00 5.00
113 Erik Cole RC 3.00 8.00
114 Tyler Arnason RC 2.50 6.00
115 Mark Bell SP 2.00 5.00
116 Vaclav Nedorost RC 2.00 5.00
117 Radim Vrbata SP 2.00 5.00
118 Brian Willsie SP 2.00 5.00
119 Mathieu Darche RC 2.00 5.00
120 Rostislav Klesla SP 4.00 10.00
121 Jody Shelley RC 2.50 6.00
122 Martin Spanhel RC 2.00 5.00
123 John Erskine RC 2.00 5.00
124 Niko Kapanen RC 2.50 6.00
125 Sean Avery RC 2.00 5.00
126 Pavel Datsyuk RC 8.00 20.00
127 Maxim Kuznetsov SP 2.00 5.00
128 Jason Chimera RC 2.00 5.00
129 Ty Conklin RC 2.00 5.00
130 Jussi Markkanen SP 2.00 5.00
131 Niklas Hagman RC 2.00 5.00
132 Kristian Huselius RC 2.50 6.00
133 Stephen Weiss RC 4.00 10.00
134 Jaroslav Bednar RC 2.00 5.00
135 David Cullen RC 2.00 5.00
136 Pascal Dupuis RC 2.00 5.00
137 Nick Schultz RC 2.00 5.00
138 Mathieu Garon SP 2.00 5.00
139 Marcel Hossa RC 2.00 5.00
140 Mike Ribeiro SP 2.00 5.00
141 Bubba Berenzweig SP 2.00 5.00
142 Martin Erat RC 2.00 5.00
143 Jukka Hentunen RC 2.00 5.00
144 Nathan Perrott RC 2.00 5.00
145 Christian Berglund RC 2.00 5.00
146 Scott Clemmensen RC 2.00 5.00
147 J-F Damphousse SP 2.00 5.00
148 Brian Gionta SP 2.00 5.00
149 Andreas Salomonsson RC 2.00 5.00
150 Radek Martinek RC 2.00 5.00
151 Raffi Torres RC 2.50 6.00
152 Dan Blackburn RC 3.00 8.00
153 Mikael Samuelsson RC 2.00 5.00
154 Chris Neil RC 2.00 5.00
155 Pavel Brendl SP 2.00 5.00
156 Jiri Dopita RC 2.00 5.00
157 Bruno St. Jacques RC 2.00 5.00
158 Billy Tibbetts RC 2.00 5.00
159 Darcy Hordichuk SP 2.00 5.00
160 Krystofer Kolanos RC 2.00 5.00
161 Josef Melichar RC 2.00 5.00
162 Mark Rycroft RC 2.00 5.00
163 Sergei Varlamov SP 2.00 5.00
164 Matt Bradley SP 2.00 5.00
165 Jeff Jillson RC 2.00 5.00
166 Vesa Toskala SP 2.00 5.00
167 Nikita Alexeev RC 2.00 5.00
168 Alexei Ponikarovsky SP 2.00 5.00
169 Chris Corrinet RC 2.00 5.00
170 Stephen Peat SP 2.00 5.00
171 Matt Pettinger SP 2.00 5.00
172 Brian Sutherby RC 2.00 5.00
1AU Ilya Kovalchuk/500 AU 20.00 50.00

1993 Titrex Guy Lafleur Insert

This standard-size card was inserted in Canadian packages of Power Bar, made by Titrex International, a firm specializing in dietary products. Also included in the package was an order form in French for ordering the 24-card Guy Lafleur Collection set. The card features on its front and back a horizontal borderless shot of Guy Lafleur on ice wearing a Titrex jersey, with the Guy Lafleur Collection logo appearing at the bottom. The front has a glossy finish, and Lafleur's name is highlighted in gold foil. The unglossy back carries the Titrex logo at the upper left, and also has the years Lafleur played for each hockey team within a gray stripe down the left edge. The card is unnumbered.

1 Guy Lafleur 1.25 3.00
(Wearing Titrex jersey)

1994 Titrex Guy Lafleur

This 24-card standard size set presents the progression of Guy Lafleur's career. The cards were printed on heavier card stock and came with a card storage album measuring approximately 6 1/4" by 8" and a certificate of authenticity. The borderless fronts feature both horizontal and vertical black-and-white photos. The Guy Lafleur Collection emblem appears inside a red rectangle at the bottom. On a white background with a fading red stripe to the left, the backs carry horizontal and vertical black-and-white photos with the date and a brief photo description (in French and English) below. The cards are unnumbered and checklisted below in chronological order. The set could be obtained by mailing in the order form (plus 24.95 Canadian) that accompanied the 1993 Titrex Guy Lafleur Power Bar Insert in packages of Titrex's Power Bar.

COMPLETE SET (24) 12.00 30.00
COMMON LAFLEUR (1-24) .75 2.00

1954-55 Topps

Topps introduced its first hockey set in 1954-55. The issue includes 60 cards of players on the four American (Boston, Chicago, Detroit and New York) teams. Cards measure approximately 2 5/8" by 3 3/4". Color fronts feature the player on a white background with facsimile autograph and team logo. The player's name, team name and position appear in bottom borders that are in team colors. The backs, printed in red and blue, contain player biographies, 1953-54 statistics and a hockey fact section. The cards were printed in the USA. Rookie Cards include Camille Henry and Doug Mohns. An early and very popular card of Gordie Howe is the main attraction in this set.

COMPLETE SET (60) 3000.00 4500.00
1 Dick Gamble 75.00 150.00
2 Bob Chrystal RC 20.00 40.00
3 Harry Howell 50.00 100.00
4 Johnny Wilson 20.00 40.00
5 Red Kelly 75.00 150.00
6 Real Chevrefils 20.00 40.00
7 Bob Armstrong 20.00 40.00
8 Gordie Howe 1200.00 1800.00
9 Benny Woit 20.00 40.00
10 Gump Worsley 125.00 200.00
11 Andy Bathgate 50.00 100.00
12 Bucky Hollingworth RC 20.00 40.00
13 Ray Timgren 20.00 40.00
14 Jack Evans 20.00 40.00
15 Paul Ronty 20.00 40.00
16 Glen Skov 20.00 40.00
17 Gus Mortson 20.00 40.00
18 Doug Mohns RC 75.00 125.00
19 Leo Labine 25.00 60.00
20 Bill Gadsby 50.00 80.00
21 Jerry Toppazzini 25.00 60.00
22 Wally Hergesheimer 20.00 40.00
23 Danny Lewicki 20.00 40.00
24 Metro Prystai 20.00 40.00
25 Fern Flaman 25.00 60.00
26 Al Rollins 40.00 80.00
27 Marcel Pronovost 40.00 80.00
28 Lou Jankowski 20.00 40.00
29 Nick Mickoski 20.00 40.00
30 Frank Martin 20.00 40.00
31 Lorne Ferguson 20.00 40.00
32 Camille Henry RC 40.00 80.00
33 Pete Conacher 25.00 60.00
34 Marty Pavelich 20.00 40.00
35 Don McKenney RC 40.00 80.00
36 Fleming Mackell 25.00 60.00
37 Jim Henry 40.00 80.00
38 Hal Laycoe 20.00 40.00
39 Alex Delvecchio 75.00 150.00
40 Larry Wilson 20.00 40.00
41 Allan Stanley 50.00 100.00
42 George Sullivan 20.00 40.00
43 Jack McIntyre 20.00 40.00
44 Ivan Irwin RC 20.00 40.00
45 Tony Leswick 20.00 40.00
46 Bob Goldham 20.00 40.00
47 Cal Gardner 25.00 60.00
48 Ed Sandford 20.00 40.00
49 Bill Quackenbush 50.00 80.00
50 Warren Godfrey 20.00 40.00
51 Ted Lindsay 75.00 150.00
52 Earl Reibel 25.00 60.00
53 Don Raleigh 20.00 40.00
54 Bill Mosienko 50.00 80.00
55 Larry Popein RC 25.00 60.00
56 Edgar Laprade 25.00 60.00
57 Bill Dineen 25.00 60.00
58 Terry Sawchuk 400.00 700.00
59 Marcel Bonin RC 20.00 40.00
60 Milt Schmidt 150.00 250.00

1957-58 Topps

After a two year hiatus, Topps returned to producing hockey cards for 1957-58. Reportedly, Topps spent the interim evaluating the hockey card market. Cards in this 66-card set were reduced to measure the standard 2 1/2" by 3 1/2". The players in this set are from the four U.S. based teams. The cards are in team order: Boston 1-18, Chicago 19-33, Detroit 34-50 and New York 51-66. Bilingual backs feature 1956-57 statistics, a short player biography and a cartoon question and answer section. Rookie Cards in this include Johnny Bucyk, Glenn Hall, Pierre Pilote, and Norm Ullman.

COMPLETE SET (66) 1500.00 3000.00
1 Real Chevrefils 30.00 50.00
2 Jack Bionda RC 12.00 20.00
3 Bob Armstrong 12.00 20.00
4 Fern Flaman 15.00 25.00
5 Jerry Toppazzini 12.00 20.00

6 Larry Regan RC	12.00	20.00
7 Bronco Horvath RC	18.00	30.00
8 Jack Caffery	12.00	20.00
9 Leo Labine	15.00	25.00
10 Johnny Bucyk RC	150.00	250.00
11 Vic Stasiuk	12.00	20.00
12 Doug Mohns	15.00	25.00
13 Don McKenney	12.00	20.00
14 Don Simmons RC	15.00	25.00
15 Allan Stanley	18.00	30.00
16 Fleming Mackell	15.00	25.00
17 Larry Hillman RC	15.00	25.00
18 Leo Boivin	15.00	25.00
19 Bob Bailey	12.00	20.00
20 Glenn Hall RC	250.00	400.00
21 Ted Lindsay	40.00	80.00
22 Pierre Pilote RC	60.00	100.00
23 Jim Thomson	12.00	20.00
24 Eric Nesterenko	15.00	25.00
25 Gus Mortson	12.00	20.00
26 Ed Litzenberger RC	18.00	30.00
27 Elmer Vasko RC	18.00	30.00
28 Jack McIntyre	12.00	20.00
29 Ron Murphy	12.00	20.00
30 Glen Skov	12.00	20.00
31 Hec Lalande RC	12.00	20.00
32 Nick Mickoski	12.00	20.00
33 Wally Hergesheimer	12.00	20.00
34 Alex Delvecchio	30.00	50.00
35 Terry Sawchuk UER (Misspelled Sawchuck on card front)	150.00	250.00
36 Guyle Fielder RC	15.00	25.00
37 Tom McCarthy	12.00	20.00
38 Al Arbour	25.00	40.00
39 Billy Dea RC	12.00	20.00
40 Lorne Ferguson	12.00	20.00
41 Warren Godfrey	12.00	20.00
42 Gordie Howe	300.00	500.00
43 Marcel Pronovost	15.00	25.00
44 Bill McNeil RC	12.00	20.00
45 Earl Reibel	12.00	20.00
46 Norm Ullman RC	150.00	250.00
47 Johnny Wilson	12.00	20.00
48 Red Kelly	30.00	50.00
49 Bill Dineen	15.00	25.00
50 Forbes Kennedy RC	15.00	25.00
51 Harry Howell	25.00	40.00
52 Jean-Guy Gendron RC	15.00	25.00
53 Gump Worsley	60.00	100.00
54 Larry Popein	12.00	20.00
55 Jack Evans	12.00	20.00
56 George Sullivan	12.00	20.00
57 Gerry Foley RC	12.00	20.00
58 Andy Hebenton RC	15.00	25.00
59 Larry Cahan	12.00	20.00
60 Andy Bathgate	25.00	40.00
61 Danny Lewicki	12.00	20.00
62 Dean Prentice	15.00	25.00
63 Camille Henry	15.00	25.00
64 Lou Fontinato RC	25.00	40.00
65 Bill Gadsby	18.00	30.00
66 Dave Creighton	30.00	50.00

1958-59 Topps

The 1958-59 Topps set contains 66 color standard-size cards of players from the four U.S. based teams. Bilingual backs feature 1957-58 statistics, player biographies and a cartoon information section on the player. The set features the Rookie Card of Bobby Hull. Due to being the last card and subject to wear as well as being chronically off-center, the Hull card is quite scarce in top grades. Other Rookie Cards include Eddie Shack and Ken Wharram.

COMPLETE SET (66)	3000.00	4500.00
1 Bob Armstrong	25.00	40.00
2 Terry Sawchuk	100.00	175.00
3 Glen Skov	10.00	20.00
4 Leo Labine	12.50	25.00
5 Dollard St.Laurent	10.00	20.00
6 Danny Lewicki	10.00	20.00
7 John Hanna RC	10.00	20.00
8 Gordie Howe UER (Misspelled Gordy on card front)	300.00	500.00
9 Vic Stasiuk	10.00	20.00
10 Larry Regan	10.00	20.00
11 Forbes Kennedy	10.00	20.00
12 Elmer Vasko	12.50	25.00
13 Glenn Hall	90.00	150.00
14 Ken Wharram RC	12.50	25.00
15 Len Lunde RC	10.00	20.00
16 Ed Litzenberger	12.50	25.00
17 Norm Johnson RC	10.00	20.00
18 Earl Ingarfield RC	10.00	20.00
19 Les Colwill RC	10.00	20.00
20 Leo Boivin	12.50	25.00
21 Andy Bathgate	25.00	40.00
22 Johnny Wilson	10.00	20.00
23 Larry Cahan	10.00	20.00
24 Marcel Pronovost	12.50	25.00
25 Larry Hillman	12.50	25.00
26 Jim Bartlett RC	10.00	20.00
27 Nick Mickoski	10.00	20.00
28 Larry Popein	10.00	20.00
29 Fleming Mackell	12.50	25.00
30 Eddie Shack RC	150.00	250.00
31 Jack Evans	10.00	20.00
32 Dean Prentice	12.50	25.00
33 Claude Laforge RC	10.00	20.00
34 Bill Gadsby	18.00	30.00
35 Bronco Horvath	12.50	25.00
36 Pierre Pilote	30.00	50.00
37 Earl Balfour	10.00	20.00
38 Gus Mortson	10.00	20.00
39 Gump Worsley	50.00	80.00
40 Johnny Bucyk	75.00	125.00
41 Lou Fontinato	12.50	25.00
42 Tod Sloan	10.00	20.00
43 Charlie Burns RC	10.00	20.00
44 Don Simmons	12.50	25.00
45 Jerry Toppazzini	10.00	20.00
46 Andy Hebenton	10.00	20.00
47 Pete Goegan RC	10.00	20.00
48 George Sullivan	10.00	20.00
49 Hank Ciesla RC	10.00	20.00
50 Doug Mohns	10.00	20.00
51 Jean-Guy Gendron	10.00	20.00
52 Alex Delvecchio	25.00	40.00
53 Eric Nesterenko	12.50	25.00
54 Camille Henry	12.50	25.00
55 Lorne Ferguson	10.00	20.00
56 Fern Flaman	12.50	25.00
57 Earl Reibel	10.00	20.00
58 Warren Godfrey	10.00	20.00
59 Ron Murphy	10.00	20.00
60 Harry Howell	18.00	30.00
61 Red Kelly	25.00	40.00
62 Don McKenney	10.00	20.00
63 Ted Lindsay	25.00	40.00
64 Al Arbour	12.50	25.00
65 Norm Ullman	60.00	100.00
66 Bobby Hull RC	2200.00	3000.00

1959-60 Topps

The 1959-60 Topps set contains 66 color standard-size cards of players from the four U.S. based teams. The fronts have the player's name and position at the bottom with team name and logo at the top. Bilingual backs feature 1958-59 statistics, a short biography and a cartoon question section.

COMPLETE SET (66)	1200.00	2000.00
1 Eric Nesterenko	30.00	50.00
2 Pierre Pilote	25.00	40.00
3 Elmer Vasko	15.00	25.00
4 Peter Goegan	10.00	20.00
5 Lou Fontinato	15.00	25.00
6 Ted Lindsay	25.00	40.00
7 Leo Labine	15.00	25.00
8 Alex Delvecchio	25.00	40.00
9 Don McKenney UER (Misspelled McKenny on card front)	10.00	20.00
10 Earl Ingarfield	10.00	20.00
11 Don Simmons	15.00	25.00
12 Glen Skov	10.00	20.00
13 Tod Sloan	10.00	20.00
14 Vic Stasiuk	10.00	20.00
15 Gump Worsley	35.00	60.00
16 Andy Hebenton	15.00	25.00
17 Dean Prentice	15.00	25.00
18 Action picture	10.00	20.00
19 Fleming Mackell	15.00	25.00
20 Harry Howell	15.00	25.00
21 Larry Popein	10.00	20.00
22 Len Lunde	10.00	20.00
23 Johnny Bucyk	35.00	60.00
24 Jean-Guy Gendron	10.00	20.00
25 Barry Cullen	10.00	20.00
26 Leo Boivin	15.00	25.00
27 Warren Godfrey	10.00	20.00
28 Action Picture (Glenn Hall and Camille Henry)	25.00	40.00
29 Fern Flaman	15.00	25.00
30 Jack Evans	10.00	20.00
31 John Hanna	10.00	20.00
32 Glenn Hall	60.00	100.00
33 Murray Balfour RC	15.00	25.00
34 Andy Bathgate	25.00	40.00
35 Al Arbour	15.00	25.00
36 Jim Morrison	10.00	20.00
37 Nick Mickoski	10.00	20.00
38 Jerry Toppazzini	10.00	20.00
39 Bob Armstrong	10.00	20.00
40 Charlie Burns UER (Misspelled Charley on card front)	10.00	20.00
41 Bill McNeil	10.00	20.00
42 Terry Sawchuk	90.00	150.00
43 Dollard St.Laurent	10.00	20.00
44 Marcel Pronovost	15.00	25.00
45 Norm Ullman	35.00	60.00
46 Camille Henry	15.00	25.00
47 Bobby Hull	400.00	600.00
48 Action Picture (Gordie Howe and Jack Evans)	50.00	80.00
49 Lou Marcon RC	10.00	20.00
50 Earl Balfour	10.00	20.00
51 Jim Bartlett	10.00	20.00
52 Forbes Kennedy	10.00	20.00
53 Action Picture (Nick Mickoski and Johnny Hanna)	10.00	20.00
54 Action Picture (Norm Johnson, Gump Worsley and Harry Howell)	25.00	40.00
55 Brian Cullen	10.00	20.00
56 Bronco Horvath	15.00	25.00
57 Eddie Shack	60.00	100.00
58 Doug Mohns	15.00	25.00
59 George Sullivan	10.00	20.00
60 Pierre Pilote/Flem Mackell IA	10.00	20.00
61 Ed Litzenberger	10.00	20.00
62 Bill Gadsby	18.00	30.00
63 Gordie Howe	250.00	400.00
64 Claude Laforge	10.00	20.00
65 Red Kelly	25.00	40.00
66 Ron Murphy	30.00	50.00

1960-61 Topps

The 1960-61 Topps set contains 66 color standard-size cards featuring players from Boston (1-20), Chicago (23-42) and New York (45-63). In addition to player and team names, the typical card front features color patterns according to the player's team. The backs are bilingual and have 1959-60 statistics and a cartoon trivia quiz. Cards titled "All-Time Greats" are an attractive feature to this set and include the likes of Georges Vezina and Eddie Shore. The All-Time Great players are indicated by ATG in the checklist below. Stan Mikita's Rookie Card is part of this set. The existence of an album issued by Topps to store this set has recently been confirmed. It is valued at approximately $150.

COMPLETE SET (66)	1100.00	1800.00
1 Lester Patrick ATG	45.00	80.00
2 Paddy Moran ATG	12.00	20.00
3 Joe Malone ATG	18.00	30.00
4 Ernest (Moose) Johnson ATG	9.00	15.00
5 Nels Stewart ATG	18.00	30.00
6 Bill Hay RC	9.00	15.00
7 Eddie Shack	50.00	80.00
8 Cy Denneny ATG	9.00	15.00
9 Jim Morrison	7.00	12.00
10 Bill Cook ATG	9.00	15.00
11 Johnny Bucyk	30.00	50.00
12 Murray Balfour	7.00	12.00
13 Leo Labine	7.00	12.00
14 Stan Mikita RC	300.00	400.00
15 George Hay ATG RC	9.00	15.00
16 Mervyn(Red) Dutton ATG	9.00	15.00
17 Dickie Boon ATG RC	7.00	12.00
18 George Sullivan	7.00	12.00
19 Georges Vezina ATG	40.00	60.00
20 Eddie Shore ATG	35.00	60.00
21 Ed Litzenberger	7.00	12.00
22 Bill Gadsby	12.00	20.00
23 Elmer Vasko	7.00	12.00
24 Charlie Burns	7.00	12.00
25 Glenn Hall	50.00	80.00
26 Dit Clapper ATG	18.00	30.00
27 Art Ross ATG	30.00	50.00
28 Jerry Toppazzini	7.00	12.00
29 Frank Boucher ATG	9.00	15.00
30 Jack Evans	7.00	12.00
31 Jean-Guy Gendron	7.00	12.00
32 Chuck Gardiner ATG	15.00	25.00
33 Ab McDonald	7.00	12.00
34 Frank Frederickson ATG RC	9.00	15.00
35 Frank Nighbor ATG	15.00	25.00
36 Gump Worsley	30.00	50.00
37 Dean Prentice	9.00	15.00
38 Hugh Lehman ATG RC	9.00	15.00
39 Jack McCartan RC	18.00	30.00
40 Don McKenney UER (Misspelled McKenny on card front)	7.00	12.00
41 Ron Murphy	7.00	12.00
42 Andy Hebenton	7.00	12.00
43 Don Simmons	9.00	15.00
44 Herb Gardiner ATG	9.00	15.00
45 Andy Bathgate	15.00	25.00
46 Cyclone Taylor ATG	18.00	30.00
47 King Clancy ATG	30.00	50.00
48 Newsy Lalonde ATG	18.00	30.00
49 Harry Howell	9.00	15.00
50 Ken Schinkel RC	7.00	12.00
51 Tod Sloan	7.00	12.00
52 Doug Mohns	9.00	15.00
53 Camille Henry	9.00	15.00
54 Bronco Horvath	9.00	15.00
55 Tiny Thompson ATG	25.00	40.00
56 Bob Armstrong	7.00	12.00
57 Fern Flaman	9.00	15.00
58 Bobby Hull	300.00	500.00
59 Howie Morenz ATG	40.00	60.00
60 Dick Irvin ATG RC	18.00	30.00
61 Lou Fontinato	7.00	12.00
62 Leo Boivin	9.00	15.00
63 Moose Goheen ATG RC	9.00	15.00
64 Al Arbour	9.00	15.00
65 Pierre Pilote	18.00	30.00
66 Vic Stasiuk	18.00	30.00

1960-61 Topps Stamps

There are 52 stamps in this scarce set. They were issued as pairs as an insert in with the 1960-61 Topps Hockey regular issue cards. The players in the set are either members of the Boston Bruins (BB), Chicago Blackhawks (CBH), New York Rangers (NYR), or All-Time Greats (ATG). The stamps are unnumbered, so they are listed below alphabetically. Stan Mikita's stamp is notable in that it appears in Stan's Rookie Card year. Dallas Smith's stamp precedes his RC by one year. Intact pairs of stamps with tabs are more difficult to find and would be valued 50 percent higher than the sum of the two players.

COMPLETE SET (52)	900.00	1500.00
1 Murray Balfour	15.00	30.00
2 Andy Bathgate	15.00	30.00
3 Leo Boivin	12.50	25.00
4 Dickie Boon	15.00	30.00
5 Frank Boucher	20.00	40.00
6 Johnny Bucyk	20.00	40.00
7 Charlie Burns	15.00	30.00
8 King Clancy	20.00	50.00
9 Dit Clapper	15.00	30.00
10 Sprague Cleghorn	20.00	40.00
11 Alex Connell	15.00	30.00
12 Bill Cook	15.00	30.00
13 Cy Denneny	15.00	30.00
14 Jack Evans	10.00	20.00
15 Frank Frederickson	15.00	30.00
16 Chuck Gardiner	15.00	30.00
17 Herb Gardiner	15.00	30.00
18 Eddie Gerard	15.00	30.00
19 Moose Goheen	15.00	30.00
20 Glenn Hall	25.00	50.00
21 Doug Harvey	20.00	40.00
22 Bill(Red) Hay	15.00	30.00
23 George Hay	15.00	30.00
24 Andy Hebenton	10.00	20.00
25 Camille Henry	12.50	25.00
26 Bronco Horvath	15.00	30.00
27 Harry Howell	12.50	25.00
28 Bobby Hull	75.00	150.00
29 Dick Irvin	15.00	30.00
30 Ernest(Moose) Johnson	15.00	30.00
31 Newsy Lalonde	20.00	40.00
32 Albert Langlois	15.00	30.00
33 Hugh Lehman	15.00	30.00
34 Joe Malone	20.00	40.00
35 Don McKenney	10.00	20.00
36 Stan Mikita	50.00	100.00
37 Doug Mohns	10.00	20.00
38 Paddy Moran	15.00	30.00
39 Howie Morenz	30.00	60.00
40 Ron Murphy	15.00	30.00
41 Frank Nighbor	25.00	50.00
42 Murray Oliver	10.00	20.00
43 Pierre Pilote	15.00	30.00
44 Dean Prentice	10.00	20.00
45 Andre Pronovost	10.00	20.00
46 Art Ross	25.00	50.00
47 Dallas Smith	10.00	20.00
48 Nels Stewart	15.00	30.00
49 Cyclone Taylor	15.00	30.00
50 Elmer Vasko	10.00	20.00
51 Georges Vezina	40.00	80.00
52 Gump Worsley	20.00	40.00

1961-62 Topps

The 1961-62 Topps set contains 66 color standard-size cards featuring players from Boston, Chicago and New York. The card numbering in this set is basically by team order, e.g., Boston Bruins (1-22), Chicago Blackhawks (23-44), and New York Rangers (45-65). Bilingual backs contain 1960-61 statistics and brief career highlights. For the first time, Topps cards were printed in Canada. Rookie Cards include New York Ranger stars Rod Gilbert and Jean Ratelle. The set marks the debut of team and checklist cards within Topps hockey card sets.

COMPLETE SET (66)	750.00	1500.00
1 Phil Watson CO	15.00	25.00
2 Ted Green RC	25.00	40.00
3 Earl Balfour	7.00	12.00
4 Dallas Smith RC	15.00	25.00
5 Andre Pronovost UER (Misspelled Provonost on card back)	7.00	12.00
6 Dick Meissner RC	7.00	12.00
7 Leo Boivin	9.00	15.00
8 Johnny Bucyk	25.00	40.00
9 Jerry Toppazzini	7.00	12.00
10 Doug Mohns	9.00	15.00
11 Charlie Burns	7.00	12.00
12 Don McKenney	7.00	12.00
13 Bob Armstrong	7.00	12.00
14 Murray Oliver	7.00	12.00
15 Orland Kurtenbach RC	15.00	25.00
16 Terry Gray RC	7.00	12.00
17 Don Head RC	9.00	15.00
18 Pat Stapleton RC	15.00	25.00
19 Cliff Pennington RC	7.00	12.00
20 Team Picture	25.00	40.00
21 Action Picture (Earl Balfour and Fern Flaman)	8.00	14.00
22 Action Picture (Andy Bathgate and Glenn Hall)	15.00	25.00
23 Rudy Pilous CO RC	9.00	15.00
24 Pierre Pilote	15.00	25.00
25 Elmer Vasko	7.00	12.00
26 Reg Fleming RC	9.00	15.00
27 Ab McDonald	7.00	12.00
28 Eric Nesterenko	9.00	15.00
29 Bobby Hull	200.00	350.00
30 Ken Wharram	9.00	15.00
31 Dollard St.Laurent	7.00	12.00
32 Glenn Hall	40.00	60.00
33 Murray Balfour	7.00	12.00
34 Ron Murphy	7.00	12.00
35 Bill(Red) Hay	7.00	12.00
36 Stan Mikita	125.00	200.00
37 Denis DeJordy RC	25.00	40.00
38 Wayne Hillman RC	9.00	15.00
39 Rino Robazzo RC	7.00	12.00
40 Bronco Horvath	7.00	12.00
41 Bob Turner	7.00	12.00
42 Blackhawks Team	25.00	40.00
43 Action Picture (Ken Wharram)	8.00	14.00
44 Action Picture (Dollard St.Laurent helps Glenn Hall)	15.00	25.00
45 Doug Harvey CO	25.00	40.00
46 Junior Langlois	7.00	12.00
47 Irv Spencer RC	7.00	12.00
48 George Sullivan	7.00	12.00
49 Earl Ingarfield	7.00	12.00
50 Gump Worsley	25.00	40.00
51 Harry Howell	9.00	15.00
52 Larry Cahan	7.00	12.00
53 Andy Bathgate	12.00	20.00
54 Dean Prentice	9.00	15.00
55 Andy Hebenton	7.00	12.00
56 Camille Henry	9.00	15.00
57 Jean-Guy Gendron	7.00	12.00
58 Pat Hannigan RC	7.00	12.00
59 Ted Hampson	7.00	12.00
60 Jean Ratelle RC	75.00	150.00
61 Al Lebrun RC	7.00	12.00
62 Rod Gilbert RC	75.00	150.00
63 Team Picture	25.00	40.00
64 Action Picture (Dick Meissner and Camille Henry)	12.00	20.00
65 Action Picture (Gump Worsley)	12.00	20.00
66 Checklist Card	175.00	300.00

1962-63 Topps

The 1962-63 Topps set contains 66 color standard-size cards featuring players from Boston, Chicago, and New York. The card numbering in this set is by team order, e.g., Boston Bruins (1-22), Chicago Blackhawks (23-44), and New York Rangers (45-65). Included within the numbering sequence are team cards. Bilingual backs feature 1961-62 statistics and career highlights. The cards were printed in Canada. Rookie Cards include Vic Hadfield, Chico Maki, and Jim "The Chief" Neilson.

COMPLETE SET (66)	800.00	1300.00
1 Phil Watson CO	15.00	25.00
2 Bob Perreault RC	9.00	15.00
3 Bruce Gamble RC	20.00	40.00
4 Warren Godfrey	6.00	12.00
5 Leo Boivin	9.00	15.00
6 Doug Mohns	9.00	15.00
7 Ted Green	9.00	15.00
8 Pat Stapleton	9.00	15.00
9 Dallas Smith	9.00	15.00
10 Don McKenney	7.00	12.00
11 Johnny Bucyk	18.00	30.00
12 Murray Oliver	7.00	12.00
13 Jerry Toppazzini	7.00	12.00
14 Cliff Pennington	7.00	12.00
15 Charlie Burns	7.00	12.00
16 Jean-Guy Gendron	7.00	12.00
17 Irv Spencer	7.00	12.00
18 Wayne Connelly	7.00	12.00
19 Andre Pronovost	7.00	12.00
20 Terry Gray	7.00	12.00
21 Tom Williams RC	9.00	15.00
22 Bruins Team	25.00	40.00
23 Rudy Pilous CO	7.00	12.00
24 Glenn Hall	35.00	50.00
25 Denis DeJordy	9.00	15.00
26 Jack Evans	7.00	12.00
27 Elmer Vasko	7.00	12.00
28 Pierre Pilote	12.00	20.00
29 Bob Turner	7.00	12.00
30 Dollard St.Laurent	7.00	12.00
31 Wayne Hillman	9.00	15.00
32 Al McNeil	6.00	12.00
33 Bobby Hull	200.00	350.00
34 Stan Mikita	60.00	125.00
35 Bill(Red) Hay	7.00	12.00
36 Murray Balfour	7.00	12.00
37 Chico Maki RC	12.00	20.00
38 Ab McDonald	7.00	12.00
39 Ken Wharram	9.00	15.00
40 Ron Murphy	6.00	12.00
41 Eric Nesterenko	8.00	15.00
42 Reg Fleming	8.00	15.00
43 Murray Hall RC	7.00	12.00
44 Blackhawks Team	25.00	40.00
45 Gump Worsley	25.00	40.00
46 Harry Howell	7.00	12.00
47 Albert Langlois	7.00	12.00
48 Larry Cahan	7.00	12.00
49 Jim Neilson RC	12.00	20.00
50 Al Lebrun	7.00	12.00
51 Earl Ingarfield	7.00	12.00
52 Andy Bathgate	12.00	20.00
53 Dean Prentice	9.00	15.00
54 Andy Hebenton	7.00	12.00
55 Ted Hampson	7.00	12.00
56 Dave Balon RC	7.00	12.00
57 Bert Olmstead	9.00	15.00
58 Jean Ratelle	30.00	50.00
59 Rod Gilbert	30.00	50.00
60 Vic Hadfield RC	35.00	60.00
61 Frank Paice TR RC	7.00	12.00
62 Camille Henry	9.00	15.00
63 Bronco Horvath	7.00	12.00
64 Pat Hannigan	7.00	12.00
65 Rangers Team	25.00	40.00
66 Checklist Card	150.00	250.00

1962-63 Topps Hockey Bucks

These "bucks" are actually inserts printed to look like Canadian currency on thin paper stock. They were distributed as an inserted folded in one buck per wax pack. Since these bucks are unnumbered, they are ordered below in alphabetical order by player's name. The bucks are approximately 4 1/16" by 1 11/16"; there is no information on the backs, just a green-patterned design.

COMPLETE SET (24)	600.00	1000.00
1 Dave Balon	20.00	40.00
2 Andy Bathgate	20.00	40.00
3 Leo Boivin	20.00	40.00
4 Johnny Bucyk	25.00	50.00
5 Reg Fleming	20.00	40.00
6 Warren Godfrey	20.00	40.00
7 Ted Green	20.00	40.00
8 Glenn Hall	40.00	80.00
9 Bill(Red) Hay	25.00	50.00
10 Andy Hebenton	20.00	40.00
11 Harry Howell	20.00	40.00
12 Bobby Hull	100.00	200.00
13 Earl Ingarfield	20.00	40.00
14 Albert Langlois	20.00	40.00
15 Ab McDonald	20.00	40.00
16 Don McKenney	20.00	40.00
17 Stan Mikita	50.00	100.00
18 Doug Mohns	20.00	40.00
19 Murray Oliver	20.00	40.00
20 Pierre Pilote	25.00	50.00
21 Dean Prentice	20.00	40.00
22 Jerry Toppazzini	20.00	40.00
23 Elmer Vasko	20.00	40.00
24 Gump Worsley	40.00	80.00

1963-64 Topps

The 1963-64 Topps standard-size set contains 66 color cards featuring players and team cards from Boston (1-21), Chicago (22-43) and New York (44-65). Bilingual backs contain 1962-63 statistics and a short player biography. A question section, the answer for which could be obtained by rubbing the edge of a coin over a blank space under the question, also appears on the card backs. The cards were printed in Canada. The notable Rookie Cards in this set are Ed Johnston, Gilles Villemure, and Ed Westfall. Jacques Plante makes his first appearance in a Topps set.

COMPLETE SET (66)	700.00	1000.00
1 Milt Schmidt CO	15.00	25.00
2 Ed Johnston RC	25.00	50.00
3 Doug Mohns	8.00	12.00
4 Tom Johnson	8.00	12.00
5 Leo Boivin	8.00	12.00
6 Bob McCord RC	6.00	10.00
7 Ted Green	8.00	12.00
8 Ed Westfall RC	18.00	30.00
9 Charlie Burns	6.00	10.00
10 Murray Oliver	8.00	12.00
11 Johnny Bucyk	15.00	25.00
12 Tom Williams	8.00	12.00
13 Dean Prentice	8.00	12.00
14 Bob Leiter RC	6.00	10.00
15 Andy Hebenton	6.00	10.00
16 Jean-Guy Gendron	6.00	10.00
17 Wayne Rivers RC	6.00	10.00
18 Jerry Toppazzini	6.00	10.00
19 Forbes Kennedy	6.00	10.00
20 Orland Kurtenbach	8.00	12.00
21 Bruins Team	25.00	40.00
22 Billy Reay CO	6.00	10.00
23 Glenn Hall	25.00	40.00
24 Denis DeJordy	8.00	12.00
25 Pierre Pilote	10.00	15.00
26 Elmer Vasko	6.00	10.00
27 Wayne Hillman	8.00	12.00
28 Al McNeil	6.00	10.00
29 Howie Young RC	6.00	10.00
30 Ed Van Impe RC	9.00	15.00
31 Reg Fleming (Gordie Howe also shown)	10.00	15.00
32 Bob Turner	6.00	10.00
33 Bobby Hull	150.00	250.00
34 Bill(Red) Hay	6.00	10.00
35 Murray Balfour	6.00	10.00
36 Stan Mikita	60.00	100.00
37 Ab McDonald	6.00	10.00
38 Ken Wharram	8.00	12.00
39 Eric Nesterenko	8.00	12.00
40 Ron Murphy	6.00	10.00
41 Chico Maki	6.00	10.00
42 John McKenzie	10.00	15.00
43 Blackhawks Team	25.00	40.00
44 George Sullivan	6.00	10.00
45 Jacques Plante	75.00	125.00
46 Gilles Villemure RC	18.00	30.00
47 Doug Harvey	18.00	30.00
48 Harry Howell	8.00	12.00
49 Albert Langlois	6.00	10.00
50 Jim Neilson	8.00	12.00
51 Larry Cahan	6.00	10.00
52 Andy Bathgate	10.00	15.00
53 Don McKenney	6.00	10.00
54 Vic Hadfield	9.00	15.00
55 Earl Ingarfield	6.00	10.00
56 Camille Henry	6.00	10.00
57 Rod Gilbert	18.00	30.00
58 Phil Goyette (Gordie Howe also shown in background)	10.00	15.00
59 Don Marshall	8.00	12.00
60 Dick Meissner	6.00	10.00
61 Val Fonteyne	6.00	10.00
62 Ken Schinkel	6.00	10.00
63 Jean Ratelle	18.00	30.00
64 Don Johns RC	6.00	10.00
65 Rangers Team	25.00	40.00
66 Checklist Card	125.00	200.00

1964-65 Topps

The 1964-65 Topps hockey set features 110 color cards of players from all six NHL teams. The size of the card is larger than in previous years at 2 1/2" by 4 11/16". Colorful fronts contain a solid player background with team name at the top and player name and position at the bottom. Bilingual backs have 1963-64 statistics, a brief player bio and a cartoon section featuring a fact about the player. The cards were printed in Canada. Eleven of the cards in each series appear to have been short printed based upon configurations found on uncut sheets. They are designated SP below. Rookie Cards include single prints of Gary Dornhoefer and Marcel Paille found in the last series. Other Rookie Cards include Roger Crozier, Jim Pappin, Pit Martin, Rod Seiling and Lou Angotti.

COMPLETE SET (110)	4000.00	6000.00
1 Pit Martin RC	60.00	125.00
2 Gilles Tremblay	12.00	20.00
3 Terry Harper	15.00	25.00
4 John Ferguson	25.00	40.00
5 Elmer Vasko	12.00	20.00
6 Terry Sawchuk UER (Misspelled Sawchuck on card back)	65.00	100.00
7 Bill(Red) Hay	12.00	20.00
8 Gary Bergman SP RC	15.00	25.00
9 Doug Barkley	12.00	20.00
10 Bob McCord	12.00	20.00
11 Parker MacDonald	12.00	20.00
12 Glenn Hall	35.00	60.00
13 Albert Langlois	12.00	20.00
14 Camille Henry SP	12.00	20.00
15 Norm Ullman	18.00	30.00
16 Ab McDonald	12.00	20.00
17 Charlie Hodge	12.00	20.00
18 Orland Kurtenbach	12.00	20.00
19 Dean Prentice	12.00	20.00
20 Bobby Hull SP	200.00	350.00
21 Ed Johnston	15.00	25.00
22 Denis DeJordy	12.00	20.00
23 Claude Provost	12.00	20.00
24 Rod Gilbert	25.00	40.00
25 Doug Mohns	12.00	20.00
26 Al McNeil	12.00	20.00
27 Billy Harris SP	12.00	20.00
28 Ken Wharram SP	12.00	20.00
29 George Sullivan	12.00	20.00
30 John McKenzie	12.00	20.00
31 Stan Mikita	65.00	100.00
32 Ted Green SP	12.00	20.00
33 Jean Beliveau SP	50.00	100.00
34 Arnie Brown RC	12.00	20.00
35 Reg Fleming	12.00	20.00
36 Jim Mikol RC	12.00	20.00
37 Dave Balon	12.00	20.00
38 Billy Reay CO	12.00	20.00
39 Marcel Pronovost SP	15.00	25.00
40 Johnny Bower	35.00	60.00
41 Wayne Hillman	12.00	20.00
42 Floyd Smith	12.00	20.00
43 Toe Blake CO	18.00	30.00
44 Red Kelly	18.00	30.00
45 Punch Imlach CO	15.00	25.00
46 Dick Duff	15.00	25.00
47 Roger Crozier RC	35.00	60.00
48 Henri Richard SP	60.00	100.00
49 Larry Jeffrey	12.00	20.00
50 Leo Boivin	12.00	20.00
51 Ed Westfall SP	15.00	25.00
52 Jean-Guy Talbot	12.00	20.00
53 Jacques Laperriere	15.00	25.00
54 1st Series Checklist	175.00	300.00
55 2nd Series Checklist SP	300.00	450.00
56 Ron Murphy	25.00	60.00
57 Bob Baun	25.00	50.00
58 Tom Williams SP	75.00	150.00
59 Pierre Pilote SP	150.00	250.00
60 Bob Pulford	25.00	50.00
61 Red Berenson	25.00	50.00
62 Vic Hadfield	25.00	50.00
63 Bob Leiter	25.00	60.00
64 Jim Pappin RC	35.00	60.00
65 Earl Ingarfield	25.00	60.00
66 Lou Angotti RC	30.00	50.00
67 Rod Seiling RC	30.00	50.00
68 Jacques Plante	100.00	175.00
69 George Armstrong UER	40.00	100.00
70 Milt Schmidt CO	30.00	50.00
71 Eddie Shack	65.00	100.00
72 Gary Dornhoefer SP RC	100.00	200.00
73 Chico Maki SP	100.00	200.00
74 Gilles Villemure SP	75.00	200.00
75 Carl Brewer	25.00	50.00
76 Bruce MacGregor	25.00	60.00
77 Bob Nevin	25.00	50.00
78 Ralph Backstrom	30.00	80.00
79 Murray Oliver	25.00	60.00
80 Bobby Rousseau SP	75.00	150.00
81 Don McKenney	25.00	60.00
82 Ted Lindsay	45.00	75.00
83 Harry Howell	35.00	60.00
84 Doug Robinson RC	25.00	60.00
85 Frank Mahovlich	75.00	125.00
86 Andy Bathgate	35.00	60.00
87 Phil Goyette	25.00	60.00
88 J.C. Tremblay	35.00	60.00
89 Gordie Howe	300.00	500.00
90 Murray Balfour	25.00	60.00
91 Eric Nesterenko SP	75.00	150.00
92 Marcel Paille SP RC	150.00	250.00
93 Sid Abel CO	25.00	60.00
94 Dave Keon	60.00	125.00
95 Alex Delvecchio	45.00	75.00
96 Bill Gadsby	25.00	50.00
97 Don Marshall	25.00	50.00
98 Bill Hicke SP	75.00	150.00
99 Ron Stewart	25.00	60.00
100 Johnny Bucyk	45.00	75.00
101 Tom Johnson	25.00	50.00
102 Tim Horton	80.00	150.00
103 Jim Neilson	25.00	50.00
104 Allan Stanley	25.00	50.00
105 Tim Horton AS SP	200.00	400.00
106 Stan Mikita AS SP	175.00	300.00
107 Bobby Hull AS	125.00	200.00
108 Ken Wharram AS	25.00	60.00
109 Pierre Pilote AS	35.00	60.00
110 Glenn Hall AS	90.00	150.00

1965-66 Topps

The 1965-66 Topps set contains 128 standard-size cards. Bilingual backs contain 1964-65 statistics, a short biography and a scratch-off question section. The cards were printed in Canada. The cards are grouped by team: Montreal (1-10, 67-76), Toronto (11-20, 77-86), New York (21-30, 87-95), Boston (31-40, 96-105), Detroit (41-53, 106-112) and Chicago (54-65, 113-120). Cards 122-128 are quite scarce and considered single prints. The seven cards were not included on checklist card 121. Rookie Cards include Gerry Cheevers, Yvan Cournoyer, Phil Esposito, Ed Giacomin, Paul Henderson, Ken Hodge and Dennis Hull. Eleven cards in the set were double printed including Cournoyer's Rookie Card.

COMPLETE SET (128) 1700.00 2700.00
1 Toe Blake CO 35.00 60.00
2 Gump Worsley 18.00 30.00
3 Jacques Laperriere 6.00 10.00
4 Jean-Guy Talbot 5.00 8.00
5 Ted Harris RC 5.00 8.00
6 Jean Beliveau 35.00 60.00
7 Dick Duff 6.00 10.00
8 Claude Provost DP 4.00 6.00
9 Red Berenson 6.00 10.00
10 John Ferguson 6.00 10.00
11 Punch Imlach CO 6.00 10.00
12 Terry Sawchuk 45.00 75.00
13 Bob Baun 6.00 10.00
14 Kent Douglas 5.00 8.00
15 Red Kelly 12.00 20.00
16 Jim Pappin 6.00 10.00
17 Dave Keon 30.00 50.00
18 Bob Pulford 6.00 10.00
19 George Armstrong 9.00 15.00
20 Orland Kurtenbach 5.00 8.00
21 Ed Giacomin RC 90.00 150.00
22 Harry Howell 6.00 10.00
23 Rod Seiling 5.00 8.00
24 Mike McMahon RC 5.00 8.00
25 Jean Ratelle 15.00 25.00
26 Doug Robinson 5.00 8.00
27 Vic Hadfield 6.00 10.00
28 Garry Peters UER RC 5.00 8.00
29 Don Marshall 6.00 10.00
30 Bill Hicke 5.00 8.00
31 Gerry Cheevers RC 125.00 200.00
32 Leo Boivin 6.00 10.00
33 Albert Langlois 5.00 8.00
34 Murray Oliver DP 4.00 6.00
35 Tom Williams 5.00 8.00
36 Ron Schock RC 5.00 8.00
37 Ed Westfall 6.00 10.00
38 Gary Dornhoefer 6.00 10.00
39 Bob Dillabough 5.00 8.00
40 Paul Popiel RC 5.00 8.00
41 Sid Abel CO 6.00 10.00
42 Roger Crozier 6.00 10.00
43 Doug Barkley 5.00 8.00
44 Bill Gadsby 5.00 8.00
45 Bryan Watson RC 9.00 15.00
46 Bob McCord 5.00 8.00
47 Alex Delvecchio 12.00 15.00
48 Andy Bathgate 9.00 15.00
49 Norm Ullman 9.00 15.00
50 Ab McDonald 5.00 8.00
51 Paul Henderson RC 30.00 50.00
52 Pit Martin 6.00 10.00
53 Billy Harris DP 4.00 6.00
54 Billy Reay CO 6.00 10.00
55 Glenn Hall 18.00 30.00
56 Pierre Pilote 9.00 15.00
57 Al McNeil 5.00 8.00
58 Camille Henry 5.00 8.00
59 Bobby Hull 125.00 200.00
60 Stan Mikita 40.00 60.00
61 Ken Wharram 6.00 10.00
62 Bill(Red) Hay 5.00 8.00
63 Fred Stanfield RC 6.00 10.00
64 Dennis Hull DP RC 18.00 30.00
65 Ken Hodge RC 20.00 40.00
66 Checklist Card 125.00 200.00
67 Charlie Hodge 6.00 10.00
68 Terry Harper 5.00 8.00
69 J.C. Tremblay 6.00 10.00
70 Bobby Rousseau DP 4.00 6.00
71 Henri Richard 30.00 50.00
72 Dave Balon 5.00 8.00
73 Ralph Backstrom 6.00 10.00
74 Jim Roberts RC 6.00 10.00
75 Claude Larose RC 6.00 10.00
76 Yvan Cournoyer DP RC 70.00 100.00
77 Johnny Bower DP 15.00 25.00
78 Carl Brewer 6.00 10.00
79 Tim Horton 30.00 50.00
80 Marcel Pronovost 6.00 10.00
81 Frank Mahovlich 25.00 40.00
82 Ron Ellis RC 18.00 30.00
83 Larry Jeffrey 5.00 8.00
84 Pete Stemkowski RC 6.00 10.00
85 Eddie Joyal RC 5.00 8.00
86 Mike Walton RC 6.00 10.00
87 George Sullivan 5.00 8.00
88 Don Simmons 6.00 10.00
89 Jim Neilson 6.00 10.00
90 Arnie Brown 5.00 8.00
91 Rod Gilbert 15.00 25.00
92 Phil Goyette 5.00 8.00
93 Bob Nevin 6.00 10.00
94 John McKenzie 6.00 10.00
95 Ted Taylor RC 5.00 8.00
96 Milt Schmidt CO DP 6.00 10.00
97 Ed Johnston 6.00 10.00
98 Ted Green 6.00 10.00
99 Don Awrey RC 6.00 10.00
100 Bob Woytowich DP RC 4.00 6.00
101 Johnny Bucyk 12.00 20.00
102 Dean Prentice 6.00 10.00
103 Ron Stewart 5.00 8.00
104 Reg Fleming 5.00 8.00
105 Parker MacDonald 5.00 8.00
106 Hank Bassen RC 6.00 10.00
107 Gary Bergman 5.00 8.00
108 Gordie Howe DP 90.00 150.00
109 Floyd Smith 5.00 8.00
110 Bruce MacGregor 5.00 8.00
111 Ron Murphy 5.00 8.00
112 Don McKenney 5.00 8.00
113 Denis DeJordy DP 4.00 6.00
114 Elmer Vasko 5.00 8.00
115 Matt Ravlich RC 5.00 8.00
116 Phil Esposito RC 200.00 400.00
117 Chico Maki 5.00 8.00
118 Doug Mohns 6.00 10.00
119 Eric Nesterenko 6.00 10.00
120 Pat Stapleton 6.00 10.00
121 Checklist Card 125.00 200.00
122 Gordie Howe SP 250.00 400.00
(600 Goals)
123 Toronto Maple Leafs 50.00 80.00
Team Card SP
124 Chicago Blackhawks 50.00 80.00
Team Card SP
125 Detroit Red Wings 50.00 80.00
Team Card SP
126 Montreal Canadiens 50.00 80.00
Team Card SP
127 New York Rangers 50.00 80.00
Team Card SP
128 Boston Bruins 125.00 200.00
Team Card SP

1966-67 Topps

At 132 standard-size cards, the 1966-67 issue was the largest Topps set to date. The front features a distinctive wood grain border with a television screen look. Bilingual backs feature a short biography, 1965-66 and career statistics. The cards are grouped by team: Montreal (1-10/67-75), Toronto (11-20/76-84), New York (21-30/85-93), Boston (31-41/94-101), Detroit (42-52/102-109) and Chicago (53-64/110-117). The cards were printed in Canada. The key card in the set is Bobby Orr's Rookie Card. Other Rookie Cards include Emile Francis, Harry Sinden and Peter Mahovlich. The backs of card numbers 127-132 form a puzzle of Bobby Orr.

COMPLETE SET (132) 2800.00 4500.00
1 Toe Blake CO 30.00 80.00
2 Gump Worsley 12.00 20.00
3 Jean-Guy Talbot 6.00 10.00
4 Gilles Tremblay 6.00 10.00
5 J.C. Tremblay 7.00 12.00
6 Jim Roberts 7.00 12.00
7 Bobby Rousseau 6.00 10.00
8 Henri Richard 20.00 35.00
9 Claude Provost 6.00 10.00
10 Claude Larose 7.00 12.00
11 Punch Imlach CO 7.00 12.00
12 Johnny Bower 15.00 25.00
13 Terry Sawchuk 40.00 65.00
14 Mike Walton 7.00 12.00
15 Pete Stemkowski 6.00 10.00
16 Allan Stanley 7.00 12.00
17 Eddie Shack 18.00 30.00
18 Brit Selby RC 7.00 12.00
19 Bob Pulford 7.00 12.00
20 Marcel Pronovost 7.00 12.00
21 Emile Francis RC 12.00 20.00
22 Rod Seiling 6.00 10.00
23 Ed Giacomin 30.00 50.00
24 Don Marshall 7.00 12.00
25 Orland Kurtenbach 6.00 10.00
26 Rod Gilbert 12.00 20.00
27 Bob Nevin 7.00 12.00
28 Phil Goyette 6.00 10.00
29 Jean Ratelle 12.00 20.00
30 Earl Ingarfield 6.00 10.00
31 Harry Sinden CO RC 25.00 40.00
32 Ed Westfall 7.00 12.00
33 Joe Watson RC 7.00 12.00
34 Bob Woytowich 6.00 10.00
35 Bobby Orr RC 2000.00 3000.00
36 Gilles Marotte RC 7.00 12.00
37 Ted Green 7.00 12.00
38 Tom Williams 6.00 10.00
39 Johnny Bucyk 12.00 20.00
40 Wayne Connelly 6.00 10.00
41 Pit Martin 7.00 12.00
42 Sid Abel CO 6.00 10.00
43 Roger Crozier 7.00 12.00
44 Andy Bathgate 7.00 12.00
45 Dean Prentice 6.00 10.00
46 Paul Henderson 9.00 15.00
47 Gary Bergman 6.00 10.00
48 Bryan Watson 7.00 12.00
49 Bob Wall RC 6.00 10.00
50 Leo Boivin 7.00 12.00
51 Bert Marshall RC 6.00 10.00
52 Norm Ullman 9.00 15.00
53 Billy Reay CO 7.00 12.00
54 Glenn Hall 15.00 25.00
55 Wally Boyer RC 6.00 10.00
56 Fred Stanfield 6.00 10.00
57 Pat Stapleton 7.00 12.00
58 Matt Ravlich 6.00 10.00
59 Pierre Pilote 7.00 12.00
60 Eric Nesterenko 7.00 12.00
61 Doug Mohns 7.00 12.00
62 Stan Mikita 30.00 50.00
63 Phil Esposito 75.00 125.00
64 Leading Scorer 50.00 75.00
(Bobby Hull)
65 Vezina Trophy 15.00 25.00
(Charlie Hodge/
Gump Worsley)
66 Checklist Card 200.00 400.00
67 Jacques Laperriere 7.00 12.00
68 Terry Harper 6.00 10.00
69 Ted Harris 6.00 10.00
70 John Ferguson 7.00 12.00
71 Dick Duff 7.00 12.00
72 Yvan Cournoyer 30.00 50.00
73 Jean Beliveau 30.00 50.00
74 Dave Balon 6.00 10.00
75 Ralph Backstrom 6.00 10.00
76 Jim Pappin 6.00 10.00
77 Frank Mahovlich 18.00 30.00
78 Dave Keon 18.00 30.00
79 Red Kelly 12.00 20.00
80 Tim Horton 25.00 40.00
81 Ron Ellis 7.00 12.00
82 Kent Douglas 6.00 10.00
83 Bob Baun 6.00 10.00
84 George Armstrong 9.00 15.00
85 Bernie Geoffrion 15.00 25.00
86 Vic Hadfield 7.00 12.00
87 Wayne Hillman 6.00 10.00
88 Jim Neilson 6.00 10.00
89 Al McNeil 6.00 10.00
90 Arnie Brown 6.00 10.00
91 Harry Howell 7.00 12.00
92 Red Berenson 7.00 12.00
93 Reg Fleming 6.00 10.00
94 Ron Stewart 6.00 10.00
95 Murray Oliver 6.00 10.00
96 Ron Murphy 6.00 10.00
97 John McKenzie 7.00 12.00
98 Bob Dillabough 6.00 10.00
99 Ed Johnston 7.00 12.00
100 Ron Schock 6.00 10.00
101 Dallas Smith 6.00 10.00
102 Alex Delvecchio 12.00 20.00
103 Peter Mahovlich RC 18.00 30.00
104 Bruce MacGregor 6.00 10.00
105 Murray Hall 6.00 10.00
106 Floyd Smith 6.00 10.00
107 Hank Bassen 7.00 12.00
108 Val Fonteyne 6.00 10.00
109 Gordie Howe 125.00 200.00
110 Chico Maki 6.00 10.00
111 Doug Jarrett RC 6.00 10.00
112 Bobby Hull 90.00 150.00
113 Dennis Hull 7.00 12.00
114 Ken Hodge 9.00 15.00
115 Denis DeJordy 7.00 12.00
116 Lou Angotti 6.00 10.00
117 Ken Wharram 6.00 10.00
118 Montreal Canadiens 15.00 25.00
Team Card
119 Detroit Red Wings 15.00 25.00
Team Card
120 Checklist Card 200.00 400.00
121 Gordie Howe AS 60.00 100.00
122 Jacques Laperriere AS 7.00 12.00
123 Pierre Pilote AS 7.00 12.00
124 Stan Mikita AS 20.00 40.00
125 Bobby Hull AS 50.00 80.00
126 Glenn Hall AS 15.00 30.00
127 Jean Beliveau AS 15.00 30.00
128 Allan Stanley AS 7.00 12.00
129 Pat Stapleton AS 7.00 12.00
130 Gump Worsley AS 15.00 30.00
131 Frank Mahovlich AS 15.00 30.00
132 Bobby Rousseau AS 15.00 30.00

1966-67 Topps USA Test

This 66-card standard-size set was apparently a test issue with limited distribution solely in America as it is quite scarce. The cards feature the same format as the 1966-67 Topps regular hockey cards. The primary difference is that the card backs in this scarce issue are only printed in English, i.e., no French. The card numbering has some similarities to the regular issue, e.g., Bobby Orr is number 35 in both sets, however there are also many differences from the regular Topps Canadian version which was mass produced. The wood grain border on the front of the cards is slightly lighter than that of the regular issue.

COMPLETE SET (66) 8000.00 12000.00
1 Dennis Hull 50.00 80.00
2 Gump Worsley 70.00 120.00
3 Dallas Smith 25.00 50.00
4 Gilles Tremblay 25.00 50.00
5 J.C. Tremblay 25.00 50.00
6 Ralph Backstrom 25.00 50.00
7 Bobby Rousseau 25.00 50.00
8 Henri Richard 125.00 200.00
9 Claude Provost 25.00 50.00
10 Red Berenson 25.00 50.00
11 Punch Imlach CO 25.00 50.00
12 Johnny Bower 70.00 120.00
13 Yvan Cournoyer 90.00 150.00
14 Mike Walton 25.00 50.00
15 Pete Stemkowski 25.00 50.00
16 Allan Stanley 40.00 70.00
17 George Armstrong 40.00 70.00
18 Harry Howell 35.00 60.00
19 Vic Hadfield 35.00 60.00
20 Marcel Pronovost 35.00 60.00
21 Pete Mahovlich 35.00 60.00
22 Rod Seiling 25.00 50.00
23 Gordie Howe 500.00 800.00
24 Don Marshall 25.00 50.00
25 Orland Kurtenbach 25.00 50.00
26 Rod Gilbert 50.00 80.00
27 Bob Nevin 25.00 50.00
28 Phil Goyette 25.00 50.00
29 Jean Ratelle 60.00 100.00
30 Dave Keon 90.00 150.00
31 Jean Beliveau 175.00 300.00
32 Ed Westfall 25.00 50.00
33 Ron Murphy 25.00 50.00
34 Wayne Hillman 25.00 50.00
35 Bobby Orr 5000.00 8000.00
36 Boom Boom Geoffrion 90.00 150.00
37 Ted Green 25.00 50.00
38 Tom Williams 25.00 50.00
39 Johnny Bucyk 50.00 80.00
40 Bobby Hull 350.00 600.00
41 Ted Harris 25.00 50.00
42 Red Kelly 50.00 80.00
43 Roger Crozier 35.00 60.00
44 Ken Wharram 25.00 50.00
45 Dean Prentice 25.00 50.00
46 Paul Henderson 50.00 80.00
47 Gary Bergman 25.00 50.00
48 Arnie Brown 25.00 50.00
49 Jim Pappin 25.00 50.00
50 Denis DeJordy 35.00 60.00
51 Frank Mahovlich 75.00 125.00
52 Norm Ullman 50.00 80.00
53 Chico Maki 25.00 50.00
54 Reg Fleming 25.00 50.00
55 Jim Neilson 25.00 50.00
56 Bruce MacGregor 25.00 50.00
57 Pat Stapleton 25.00 50.00
58 Matt Ravlich 25.00 50.00
59 Pierre Pilote 40.00 70.00
60 Eric Nesterenko 25.00 50.00
61 Doug Mohns 25.00 50.00
62 Stan Mikita 175.00 300.00
63 Alex Delvecchio 60.00 100.00
64 Ed Johnston 35.00 60.00
65 John Ferguson 35.00 60.00
66 John McKenzie 50.00 80.00

1967-68 Topps

The 1967-68 Topps set features 132 standard-size cards. Players on the six expansion teams (Los Angeles, Minnesota, Oakland, Philadelphia, Pittsburgh, and St. Louis) were not included until 1968-69. Bilingual backs feature a short biography, 1966-67 and career records. The backs are identical in format to the 1966-67 cards. The cards are grouped by team: Montreal (1-10/67-75), Toronto (11-20/76-83), New York (21-31/84-91), Boston (32-42/92-100), Detroit (43-52/101-108) and Chicago (53-63/109-117). The cards were printed in Canada. Rookie Cards include Jacques Lemaire, Derek Sanderson, Glen Sather, and Rogatien Vachon.

COMPLETE SET (132) 2000.00 3000.00
1 Gump Worsley 25.00 40.00
2 Dick Duff 6.00 10.00
3 Jacques Lemaire RC 40.00 60.00
4 Claude Larose 6.00 10.00
5 Gilles Tremblay 5.00 8.00
6 Terry Harper 5.00 8.00
7 Jacques Laperriere 6.00 10.00
8 Garry Monahan RC 5.00 8.00
9 Carol Vadnais RC 6.00 10.00
10 Ted Harris 5.00 8.00
11 Dave Keon 12.00 20.00
12 Pete Stemkowski 5.00 8.00
13 Allan Stanley 6.00 10.00
14 Ron Ellis 6.00 10.00
15 Mike Walton 6.00 10.00
16 Tim Horton 20.00 35.00
17 Brian Conacher RC 5.00 8.00
18 Bruce Gamble 6.00 10.00
19 Bob Pulford 6.00 10.00
20 Duane Rupp RC 5.00 8.00
21 Larry Jeffrey 5.00 8.00
22 Wayne Hillman 5.00 8.00
23 Don Marshall 6.00 10.00
24 Red Berenson 6.00 10.00
25 Phil Goyette 5.00 8.00
26 Camille Henry 5.00 8.00
27 Rod Seiling 5.00 8.00
28 Bob Nevin 6.00 10.00
29 Bernie Geoffrion 15.00 30.00
30 Reg Fleming 5.00 8.00
31 Jean Ratelle 9.00 15.00
32 Phil Esposito 45.00 75.00
33 Derek Sanderson RC 75.00 125.00
34 Eddie Shack 15.00 25.00
35 Ross Lonsberry RC 6.00 10.00
36 Fred Stanfield 5.00 8.00
37 Don Awrey UER 5.00 8.00
(Photo actually
Skip Krake)
38 Glen Sather RC 18.00 30.00
39 John McKenzie 6.00 10.00
40 Tom Williams 5.00 8.00
41 Dallas Smith 5.00 8.00
42 Johnny Bucyk 12.00 20.00
43 Gordie Howe 90.00 150.00
44 Gary Jarrett RC 5.00 8.00
45 Dean Prentice 5.00 8.00
46 Bert Marshall 5.00 8.00
47 Gary Bergman 5.00 8.00
48 Roger Crozier 6.00 10.00
49 Howie Young 5.00 8.00
50 Doug Roberts RC 5.00 8.00
51 Alex Delvecchio 12.00 20.00
52 Floyd Smith 5.00 8.00
53 Doug Shelton RC 5.00 8.00
54 Gerry Goyer RC 5.00 8.00
55 Wayne Maki RC 5.00 8.00
56 Dennis Hull 6.00 10.00
57 Dave Dryden RC 9.00 15.00
58 Paul Terbenche RC 5.00 8.00
59 Gilles Marotte 5.00 8.00
60 Eric Nesterenko 6.00 10.00
61 Pat Stapleton 6.00 10.00
62 Pierre Pilote 6.00 10.00
63 Doug Mohns 5.00 8.00
64 Triple Winner 18.00 30.00
(Stan Mikita)
65 Vezina Trophy 12.00 20.00
(Glenn Hall/
Denis DeJordy)
66 Checklist Card 150.00 250.00
67 Ralph Backstrom 6.00 10.00
68 Bobby Rousseau 5.00 8.00
69 John Ferguson 5.00 8.00
70 Yvan Cournoyer 18.00 30.00
71 Claude Provost 5.00 8.00
72 Henri Richard 15.00 25.00
73 J.C. Tremblay 6.00 10.00
74 Jean Beliveau 25.00 40.00
75 Rogatien Vachon RC 50.00 80.00
76 Johnny Bower 12.00 20.00
77 Wayne Carleton RC 5.00 8.00
78 Jim Pappin 5.00 8.00
79 Frank Mahovlich 15.00 25.00
80 Larry Hillman 5.00 8.00
81 Marcel Pronovost 6.00 10.00
82 Murray Oliver 5.00 8.00
83 George Armstrong 9.00 15.00
84 Harry Howell 5.00 8.00
85 Ed Giacomin 18.00 30.00
86 Gilles Villemure 6.00 10.00
87 Orland Kurtenbach 5.00 8.00
88 Vic Hadfield 6.00 10.00
89 Arnie Brown 5.00 8.00
90 Rod Gilbert 9.00 15.00
91 Jim Neilson 5.00 8.00
92 Bobby Orr 400.00 700.00
93 Skip Krake UER RC 5.00 8.00
94 Ted Green 6.00 10.00
95 Ed Westfall 6.00 10.00
96 Ed Johnston 6.00 10.00
97 Gary Doak RC 6.00 10.00
98 Ken Hodge 6.00 10.00
99 Gerry Cheevers 30.00 50.00
100 Ron Murphy 5.00 8.00
101 Norm Ullman 9.00 15.00
102 Bruce MacGregor 5.00 8.00
103 Paul Henderson 6.00 10.00
104 Jean-Guy Talbot 5.00 8.00
105 Bart Crashley RC 5.00 8.00
106 Roy Edwards RC 6.00 10.00
107 Jim Watson RC 5.00 8.00
108 Ted Hampson 5.00 8.00
109 Bill Orban RC 5.00 8.00
110 Geoffrey Powis RC 5.00 8.00
111 Chico Maki 5.00 8.00
112 Doug Jarrett 5.00 8.00
113 Bobby Hull 75.00 125.00
114 Stan Mikita 25.00 40.00
115 Denis DeJordy 6.00 10.00
116 Pit Martin 6.00 10.00
117 Ken Wharram 5.00 8.00
118 Calder Trophy 150.00 300.00
(Bobby Orr)
119 Norris Trophy 5.00 8.00
(Harry Howell)
120 Checklist Card 150.00 250.00
121 Harry Howell AS 5.00 8.00
122 Pierre Pilote AS 5.00 8.00
123 Ed Giacomin AS 9.00 15.00
124 Bobby Hull AS 50.00 80.00
125 Ken Wharram AS 5.00 8.00
126 Stan Mikita AS 15.00 25.00
127 Tim Horton AS 12.00 20.00
128 Bobby Orr AS 200.00 400.00
129 Glenn Hall AS 12.00 20.00
130 Don Marshall AS 5.00 8.00
131 Gordie Howe AS 60.00 100.00
132 Norm Ullman AS 12.00 20.00

1968-69 Topps

The 1968-69 Topps set consists of 132 standard-size cards featuring all 12 teams including the first cards of players from the six expansion teams. The fronts feature a horizontal format with the player in the foreground and an artistically rendered hockey scene in the background. The backs include a short biography, 1967-68 and career statistics as well as a cartoon-illustrated fact about the player. The cards are grouped by team: Boston (1-11), Chicago (12-22), Detroit (23-33), Los Angeles (34-44), Minnesota (45-55), Montreal (56-66), New York (67-77), Oakland (78-88), Philadelphia (89-99), Pittsburgh (100-110), St. Louis (111-120) and Toronto (122-132). With O-Pee-Chee printing cards for the Canadian market, text on back is English only. For the first time since 1960-61, Topps cards were printed in the U.S. The only Rookie Card of consequence is Bernie Parent.

COMPLETE SET (132) 450.00 750.00
1 Gerry Cheevers 12.00 20.00
2 Bobby Orr 150.00 250.00
3 Don Awrey UER 2.00 4.00
(Photo actually
Skip Krake)
4 Ted Green 2.50 5.00
5 Johnny Bucyk 3.50 7.00
6 Derek Sanderson 15.00 25.00
7 Phil Esposito 18.00 30.00
8 Ken Hodge 2.50 5.00
9 John McKenzie 2.50 5.00
10 Fred Stanfield 2.00 4.00
11 Tom Williams 2.00 4.00
12 Denis DeJordy 2.50 5.00
13 Doug Jarrett 2.00 4.00
14 Gilles Marotte 2.00 4.00
15 Pat Stapleton 2.50 5.00
16 Bobby Hull 35.00 50.00
17 Chico Maki 2.00 4.00
18 Pit Martin 2.50 5.00
19 Doug Mohns 2.00 4.00
20 Stan Mikita 12.00 20.00
21 Jim Pappin 2.00 4.00
22 Ken Wharram 2.00 4.00
23 Roger Crozier 2.50 5.00
24 Bob Baun 2.50 5.00
25 Gary Bergman 2.00 4.00
26 Kent Douglas 2.00 4.00
27 Ron Harris 2.00 4.00
28 Alex Delvecchio 3.50 7.00
29 Gordie Howe 45.00 70.00
30 Bruce MacGregor 2.00 4.00
31 Frank Mahovlich 7.00 12.00
32 Dean Prentice 2.00 4.00
33 Pete Stemkowski 2.00 4.00
34 Terry Sawchuk 25.00 40.00
35 Larry Cahan 2.00 4.00
36 Real Lemieux RC 2.00 4.00
37 Bill White RC 3.00 6.00
38 Gord Labossiere 2.00 4.00
39 Ted Irvine 2.00 4.00
40 Eddie Joyal 2.00 4.00
41 Dale Rolfe RC 2.00 4.00
42 Lowell MacDonald RC 3.00 6.00
43 Skip Krake UER 2.00 4.00
(Photo actually
Don Awrey)
44 Terry Gray 2.00 4.00
45 Cesare Maniago 2.50 5.00
46 Mike McMahon 2.00 4.00
47 Wayne Hillman 2.00 4.00
48 Larry Hillman 2.00 4.00
49 Bob Woytowich 2.00 4.00
50 Wayne Connelly 2.00 4.00
51 Claude Larose 2.00 4.00
52 Danny Grant RC 5.00 10.00
53 Andre Boudrias 2.00 4.00
54 Ray Cullen RC 2.00 4.00
55 Parker MacDonald 2.00 4.00
56 Gump Worsley 6.00 10.00
57 Terry Harper 2.00 4.00
58 Jacques Laperriere 2.50 5.00
59 J.C. Tremblay 2.50 5.00
60 Ralph Backstrom 2.50 5.00
61 Jean Beliveau 9.00 15.00
62 Yvan Cournoyer 7.00 12.00
63 Jacques Lemaire 9.00 15.00
64 Henri Richard 7.00 12.00
65 Bobby Rousseau 2.00 4.00
66 Gilles Tremblay 2.00 4.00
67 Ed Giacomin 7.00 12.00
68 Arnie Brown 2.00 4.00
69 Harry Howell 2.50 5.00
70 Jim Neilson 2.00 4.00
71 Rod Seiling 2.00 4.00
72 Rod Gilbert 3.50 7.00
73 Phil Goyette 2.00 4.00
74 Vic Hadfield 2.50 5.00
75 Don Marshall 2.50 5.00
76 Bob Nevin 2.50 5.00
77 Jean Ratelle 3.50 7.00
78 Charlie Hodge 2.50 5.00
79 Bert Marshall 2.00 4.00
80 Billy Harris 2.00 4.00
81 Carol Vadnais 2.50 5.00
82 Howie Young 2.00 4.00
83 John Brenneman RC 2.00 4.00
84 Gerry Ehman 2.00 4.00
85 Ted Hampson 2.00 4.00
86 Bill Hicke 2.00 4.00
87 Gary Jarrett 2.00 4.00
88 Doug Roberts 2.00 4.00
89 Bernie Parent RC 40.00 60.00
90 Joe Watson 2.00 4.00
91 Ed Van Impe 2.00 4.00
92 Larry Zeidel 2.00 4.00
93 John Miszuk RC 2.00 4.00
94 Gary Dornhoefer 2.00 4.00
95 Leon Rochefort RC 2.00 4.00
96 Brit Selby 2.00 4.00
97 Forbes Kennedy 2.00 4.00
98 Ed Hoekstra 2.00 4.00
99 Garry Peters 2.00 4.00
100 Les Binkley RC 5.00 10.00
101 Leo Boivin 2.50 5.00
102 Earl Ingarfield 2.00 4.00
103 Lou Angotti 2.00 4.00
104 Andy Bathgate 3.00 6.00
105 Wally Boyer 2.00 4.00
106 Ken Schinkel 2.00 4.00
107 Ab McDonald 2.00 4.00
108 Charlie Burns 2.00 4.00
109 Val Fonteyne 2.00 4.00
110 Noel Price 2.00 4.00
111 Glenn Hall 6.00 10.00
112 Bob Plager RC 6.00 12.00
113 Jim Roberts 2.50 5.00
114 Red Berenson 2.00 4.00
115 Larry Keenan 2.00 4.00
116 Camille Henry 2.00 4.00
117 Gary Sabourin RC 2.00 4.00
118 Ron Schock 2.00 4.00
119 Gary Veneruzzo RC 2.00 4.00
120 Gerry Melnyk 2.00 4.00
121 Checklist Card 60.00 100.00
122 Johnny Bower 6.00 10.00
123 Tim Horton 8.00 15.00
124 Pierre Pilote 3.00 6.00
125 Marcel Pronovost 2.50 5.00
126 Ron Ellis 2.50 5.00
127 Paul Henderson 2.50 5.00
128 Dave Keon 4.00 7.00
129 Bob Pulford 2.50 5.00
130 Floyd Smith 2.00 4.00
131 Norm Ullman 3.00 6.00
132 Mike Walton 3.00 6.00

1969-70 Topps

The 1969-70 Topps set consists of 132 standard-size cards. The backs contain 1968-69 and career statistics, a short biography and a cartoon-illustrated fact about the player. Those players in this set who were also included in the insert set of stamps have a place on the card back for placing that player's stamp. This is not recommended as it would be considered a means of defacing the card and lowering its grade. The cards are grouped by team: Montreal (1-11), St. Louis (12-21), Boston (22-32), New York (33-43), Toronto (44-54),

Detroit (55-65), Chicago (66-76), Oakland (77-87), Philadelphia (88-98), Los Angeles (99-109), Pittsburgh (110-120) and Minnesota (121-131). The only notable Rookie Card in the set is Serge Savard.

COMPLETE SET (132) 400.00 600.00
1 Gump Worsley 8.00 15.00
2 Ted Harris 1.50 3.00
3 Jacques Laperriere 2.00 4.00
4 Serge Savard RC 10.00 20.00
5 J.C. Tremblay 2.00 4.00
6 Yvan Cournoyer 2.50 5.00
7 John Ferguson 2.00 4.00
8 Jacques Lemaire 2.50 5.00
9 Bobby Rousseau 1.50 3.00
10 Jean Beliveau 7.00 12.00
11 Henri Richard 5.00 8.00
12 Glenn Hall 5.00 8.00
13 Bob Plager 1.50 3.00
14 Jim Roberts 1.50 3.00
15 Jean-Guy Talbot 2.00 4.00
16 Andre Boudrias 1.50 3.00
17 Camille Henry 1.50 3.00
18 Ab McDonald 1.50 3.00
19 Gary Sabourin 1.50 3.00
20 Red Berenson 1.50 3.00
21 Phil Goyette 1.50 3.00
22 Gerry Cheevers 6.00 10.00
23 Ted Green 1.50 3.00
24 Bobby Orr 75.00 125.00
25 Dallas Smith 1.50 3.00
26 Johnny Bucyk 3.00 6.00
27 Ken Hodge 2.00 4.00
28 John McKenzie 2.00 4.00
29 Ed Westfall 2.00 4.00
30 Phil Esposito 12.00 20.00
31 Derek Sanderson 9.00 15.00
32 Fred Stanfield 1.50 3.00
33 Ed Giacomin 6.00 10.00
34 Arnie Brown 1.50 3.00
35 Jim Neilson 1.50 3.00
36 Rod Seiling 1.50 3.00
37 Rod Gilbert 2.50 5.00
38 Vic Hadfield 2.00 4.00
39 Don Marshall 1.50 3.00
40 Bob Nevin 1.50 3.00
41 Ron Stewart 1.50 3.00
42 Jean Ratelle 2.50 5.00
43 Walt Tkaczuk RC 2.50 5.00
44 Bruce Gamble 2.00 4.00
45 Tim Horton 7.00 12.00
46 Ron Ellis 2.00 4.00
47 Paul Henderson 2.00 4.00
48 Brit Selby 1.50 3.00
49 Floyd Smith 1.50 3.00
50 Mike Walton 2.00 4.00
51 Dave Keon 2.50 5.00
52 Murray Oliver 1.50 3.00
53 Bob Pulford 2.00 4.00
54 Norm Ullman 2.50 5.00
55 Roger Crozier 2.00 4.00
56 Roy Edwards 2.00 4.00
57 Bob Baun 2.00 4.00
58 Gary Bergman 1.50 3.00
59 Carl Brewer 2.00 4.00
60 Wayne Connelly 1.50 3.00
61 Gordie Howe 30.00 50.00
62 Frank Mahovlich 5.00 8.00
63 Bruce MacGregor 1.50 3.00
64 Alex Delvecchio 3.00 6.00
65 Pete Stemkowski 1.50 3.00
66 Denis DeJordy 2.00 4.00
67 Doug Jarrett 1.50 3.00
68 Gilles Marotte 1.50 3.00
69 Pat Stapleton 2.00 4.00
70 Bobby Hull 25.00 40.00
71 Dennis Hull 2.00 4.00
72 Doug Mohns 1.50 3.00
73 Jim Pappin 1.50 3.00
74 Ken Wharram 1.50 3.00
75 Pit Martin 2.00 4.00
76 Stan Mikita 7.00 12.00
77 Charlie Hodge 2.00 4.00
78 Gary Smith 2.00 4.00
79 Harry Howell 2.00 4.00
80 Bert Marshall 1.50 3.00
81 Doug Roberts 1.50 3.00
82 Carol Vadnais 2.00 4.00
83 Gerry Ehman 1.50 3.00
84 Bill Hicke 1.50 3.00
85 Gary Jarrett 1.50 3.00
86 Ted Hampson 1.50 3.00
87 Earl Ingarfield 1.50 3.00
88 Doug Favell RC 5.00 10.00
89 Bernie Parent 15.00 25.00
90 Larry Hillman 1.50 3.00
91 Wayne Hillman 1.50 3.00
92 Ed Van Impe 1.50 3.00
93 Joe Watson 1.50 3.00
94 Gary Dornhoefer 2.00 4.00
95 Reg Fleming 1.50 3.00
96 Jean-Guy Gendron 1.50 3.00
97 Jim Johnson 1.50 3.00
98 Andre Lacroix 2.00 4.00
99 Gerry Desjardins RC 5.00 8.00
100 Dale Rolfe 1.50 3.00
101 Bill White 1.50 3.00
102 Bill Flett 1.50 3.00
103 Ted Irvine 1.50 3.00
104 Ross Lonsberry 1.50 3.00
105 Leon Rochefort 1.50 3.00
106 Eddie Shack 2.50 5.00

107 Dennis Hextall RC 2.50 5.00
108 Eddie Joyal 1.50 3.00
109 Gord Labossiere 1.50 3.00
110 Les Binkley 2.00 4.00
111 Tracy Pratt 1.50 3.00
112 Bryan Watson 1.50 3.00
113 Bob Woytowich 1.50 3.00
114 Keith McCreary 1.50 3.00
115 Dean Prentice 1.50 3.00
116 Glen Sather 2.00 4.00
117 Ken Schinkel 1.50 3.00
118 Wally Boyer 1.50 3.00
119 Val Fonteyne 1.50 3.00
120 Ron Schock 1.50 3.00
121 Cesare Maniago 2.00 4.00
122 Leo Boivin 1.50 3.00
123 Bob McCord 1.50 3.00
124 John Miszuk 1.50 3.00
125 Danny Grant 2.00 4.00
126 Claude Larose 1.50 3.00
127 Jean-Paul Parise 2.00 4.00
128 Tom Williams 1.50 3.00
129 Charlie Burns 1.50 3.00
130 Ray Cullen 1.50 3.00
131 Danny O'Shea RC 1.50 3.00
132 Checklist Card 35.00 60.00

1970-71 Topps

The 1970-71 Topps set consists of 132 standard-size cards. Card fronts have solid player backgrounds that differ in color according to team. The player's name, team and position are at the bottom. The backs feature the player's 1969-70 and career statistics as well as a short biography. Players from the expansion Buffalo Sabres and Vancouver Canucks are included. For the most part, cards are grouped by team. However, team names on front are updated on some cards to reflect transactions that occurred late in the off-season. Rookie Cards include Wayne Cashman, Brad Park and Gilbert Perreault.

COMPLETE SET (132) 300.00 400.00
1 Gerry Cheevers 8.00 15.00
2 Johnny Bucyk 2.00 5.00
3 Bobby Orr 50.00 75.00
4 Don Awrey .75 1.50
5 Fred Stanfield .75 1.50
6 John McKenzie 1.00 2.50
7 Wayne Cashman RC 5.00 8.00
8 Ken Hodge 1.00 2.50
9 Wayne Carleton .75 1.50
10 Garnet Bailey RC 1.00 2.00
11 Phil Esposito 10.00 20.00
12 Lou Angotti .75 1.50
13 Jim Pappin .75 1.50
14 Dennis Hull 1.00 2.50
15 Bobby Hull 20.00 40.00
16 Doug Mohns .75 1.50
17 Pat Stapleton 1.00 2.50
18 Pit Martin 1.00 2.50
19 Eric Nesterenko 1.00 2.50
20 Stan Mikita 7.00 12.00
21 Roy Edwards 1.00 2.50
22 Frank Mahovlich 1.50 4.00
23 Ron Harris .75 1.50
24 Bob Baun 1.00 2.50
25 Pete Stemkowski .75 1.50
26 Garry Unger 1.00 2.50
27 Bruce MacGregor .75 1.50
28 Larry Jeffrey .75 1.50
29 Gordie Howe 35.00 50.00
30 Billy Dea .75 1.50
31 Denis DeJordy 1.00 2.50
32 Matt Ravlich .75 1.50
33 Dave Amadio .75 1.50
34 Gilles Marotte .75 1.50
35 Eddie Shack 1.50 4.00
36 Bob Pulford 1.00 2.50
37 Ross Lonsberry 1.00 2.50
38 Gord Labossiere .75 1.50
39 Eddie Joyal .75 1.50
40 Gump Worsley 1.50 4.00
41 Bob McCord .75 1.50
42 Leo Boivin 1.00 2.50
43 Tom Reid RC .75 1.50
44 Charlie Burns .75 1.50
45 Bob Barlow .75 1.50
46 Bill Goldsworthy 1.00 2.50
47 Danny Grant 1.00 2.50
48 Norm Beaudin RC .75 1.50
49 Rogatien Vachon 3.00 6.00
50 Yvan Cournoyer 1.50 4.00
51 Serge Savard 1.50 4.00
52 Jacques Laperriere 1.00 2.50
53 Terry Harper .75 1.50
54 Ralph Backstrom 1.00 2.50
55 Jean Beliveau 6.00 10.00
56 Claude Larose UER .75 1.50
57 Jacques Lemaire 1.50 4.00
58 Peter Mahovlich 1.00 2.50
59 Tim Horton 6.00 10.00
60 Bob Nevin .75 1.50
61 Dave Balon .75 1.50
62 Vic Hadfield 1.00 2.50
63 Rod Gilbert 1.50 4.00
64 Ron Stewart .75 1.50
65 Ted Irvine .75 1.50
66 Arnie Brown .75 1.50
67 Brad Park RC 18.00 25.00
68 Ed Giacomin 1.50 4.00
69 Gary Smith 1.00 2.50
70 Carol Vadnais 1.00 2.50
71 Doug Roberts .75 1.50
72 Harry Howell 1.00 2.50
73 Joe Szura .75 1.50
74 Mike Laughton .75 1.50
75 Gary Jarrett .75 1.50
76 Bill Hicke .75 1.50
77 Paul Andrea RC .75 1.50
78 Bernie Parent 9.00 15.00
79 Joe Watson .75 1.50
80 Ed Van Impe .75 1.50
81 Larry Hillman .75 1.50
82 George Swarbrick .75 1.50
83 Bill Sutherland .75 1.50
84 Andre Lacroix 1.00 2.50
85 Gary Dornhoefer 1.00 2.50
86 Jean-Guy Gendron .75 1.50
87 Al Smith RC 1.00 2.50
88 Bob Woytowich .75 1.50
89 Duane Rupp .75 1.50
90 Jim Morrison .75 1.50
91 Ron Schock .75 1.50
92 Ken Schinkel .75 1.50
93 Keith McCreary .75 1.50
94 Bryan Hextall 1.00 2.50
95 Wayne Hicks RC .75 1.50
96 Gary Sabourin .75 1.50
97 Ernie Wakely RC 1.00 2.50
98 Bob Wall .75 1.50
99 Barclay Plager 1.00 2.50
100 Jean-Guy Talbot .75 1.50
101 Gary Veneruzzo .75 1.50
102 Tim Ecclestone .75 1.50
103 Red Berenson 1.00 2.50
104 Larry Keenan .75 1.50
105 Bruce Gamble 1.00 2.50
106 Jim Dorey .75 1.50
107 Mike Pelyk RC .75 1.50
108 Rick Ley .75 1.50
109 Mike Walton .75 1.50
110 Norm Ullman 1.50 4.00
111 Brit Selby .75 1.50
112 Garry Monahan .75 1.50
113 George Armstrong 1.50 4.00
114 Gary Doak .75 1.50
115 Darryl Sly RC .75 1.50
116 Wayne Maki .75 1.50
117 Orland Kurtenbach .75 1.50
118 Murray Hall .75 1.50
119 Marc Reaume .75 1.50
120 Pat Quinn 3.00 5.00
121 Andre Boudrias .75 1.50
122 Paul Popiel .75 1.50
123 Paul Terbenche .75 1.50
124 Howie Menard .75 1.50
125 Gerry Meehan RC 1.50 4.00
126 Skip Krake .75 1.50
127 Phil Goyette .75 1.50
128 Reg Fleming .75 1.50
129 Don Marshall 1.00 2.50
130 Bill Inglis RC .75 1.50
131 Gilbert Perreault RC 20.00 40.00
132 Checklist Card 35.00 60.00

1970-71 Topps/OPC Sticker Stamps

This set consists of 33 unnumbered, full-color sticker stamps measuring 2 1/2" by 3 1/2". The backs are blank. The checklist below is ordered alphabetically for convenience. The sticker cards were issued as an insert in the regular issue wax packs of the 1970-71 Topps hockey as well as in first series wax packs of 1970-71 O-Pee-Chee.

COMPLETE SET (33) 300.00 450.00
1 Jean Beliveau 15.00 30.00
2 Red Berenson 6.00 12.00
3 Wayne Carleton 6.00 12.00
4 Tim Ecclestone 6.00 12.00
5 Ron Ellis 6.00 12.00
6 Phil Esposito 15.00 30.00
7 Tony Esposito 15.00 40.00
8 Bill Flett 6.00 12.00
9 Ed Giacomin 10.00 20.00
10 Rod Gilbert 10.00 20.00
11 Danny Grant 6.00 12.00
12 Bill Hicke 6.00 12.00
13 Gordie Howe 20.00 50.00
14 Bobby Hull 15.00 40.00
15 Earl Ingarfield 6.00 12.00
16 Eddie Joyal 6.00 12.00
17 Dave Keon 15.00 30.00
18 Andre Lacroix 6.00 12.00
19 Jacques Laperriere 6.00 12.00
20 Jacques Lemaire 10.00 20.00
21 Frank Mahovlich 10.00 20.00
22 Keith McCreary 6.00 12.00
23 Stan Mikita 10.00 20.00
24 Bobby Orr 40.00 100.00
25 Jean-Paul Parise 6.00 12.00
26 Jean Ratelle 7.50 20.00
27 Derek Sanderson 12.50 25.00
28 Frank St.Marseille 6.00 12.00
29 Ron Schock 6.00 12.00
30 Garry Unger 6.00 12.00
31 Carol Vadnais 6.00 12.00
32 Ed Van Impe 6.00 12.00
33 Bob Woytowich 6.00 12.00

1971-72 Topps

The 1971-72 Topps set consists of 132 standard-size cards. For the first time, Topps included the player's NHL year-by-year career record on back. A short player biography and a cartoon-illustrated fact about the player also appear on back. A League Leaders (1-6) subset is exclusive to the Topps set of this year. The only noteworthy Rookie Card is of Ken Dryden. An additional key card in the set is Gordie Howe (70). Howe does not have a basic card in the 1971-72 O-Pee-Chee set.

COMPLETE SET (132) 200.00 350.00
1 Goal Leaders 12.50 30.00
Phil Esposito
Johnny Bucyk
Bobby Hull
2 Assists Leaders 12.50 30.00
Bobby Orr
Phil Esposito
Johnny Bucyk
3 Scoring Leaders 9.00 15.00
Phil Esposito
Bobby Orr
Johnny Bucyk
4 Goalies Win Leaders 6.00 10.00
Tony Esposito
Ed Johnston
Gerry Cheevers
Ed Giacomin
5 Shutouts Leaders 3.00 6.00
Ed Giacomin
Tony Esposito
Cesare Maniago
6 Goals Against 7.00 12.00
Average Leaders
Jacques Plante
Ed Giacomin
Tony Esposito
7 Fred Stanfield .60 1.50
8 Mike Robitaille RC .60 1.50
9 Vic Hadfield 1.00 2.00
10 Jacques Plante 9.00 15.00
11 Bill White .60 1.50
12 Andre Boudrias .60 1.50
13 Jim Lorentz .60 1.50
14 Arnie Brown .60 1.50
15 Yvan Cournoyer 1.50 3.00
16 Bryan Hextall 1.00 2.00
17 Gary Croteau .60 1.50
18 Gilles Villemure 1.00 2.00
19 Serge Bernier RC 1.00 2.00
20 Phil Esposito 7.00 12.00
21 Charlie Burns .60 1.50
22 Doug Barrie RC .60 1.50
23 Eddie Joyal .60 1.50
24 Rosaire Paiement .60 1.50
25 Pat Stapleton 1.00 2.00
26 Garry Unger 1.00 2.00
27 Al Smith 1.00 2.00
28 Bob Woytowich .60 1.50
29 Marc Tardif 1.00 2.00
30 Norm Ullman 1.50 3.00
31 Tom Williams .60 1.50
32 Ted Harris .60 1.50
33 Andre Lacroix .60 1.50
34 Mike Byers .60 1.50
35 Johnny Bucyk 2.00 4.00
36 Roger Crozier 1.00 2.00
37 Alex Delvecchio 1.50 3.00
38 Frank St.Marseille .60 1.50
39 Pit Martin 1.00 2.00
40 Brad Park 6.00 10.00
41 Greg Polis RC .60 1.50
42 Orland Kurtenbach .60 1.50
43 Jim McKenny RC .60 1.50
44 Bob Nevin .60 1.50
45 Ken Dryden RC 75.00 125.00
46 Carol Vadnais 1.00 2.00
47 Bill Flett .60 1.50
48 Jim Johnson .60 1.50
49 Al Hamilton .60 1.50
50 Bobby Hull 25.00 50.00
51 Chris Bordeleau RC .60 1.50
52 Tim Ecclestone .60 1.50
53 Rod Seiling .60 1.50
54 Gerry Cheevers 3.00 6.00
55 Bill Goldsworthy 1.00 2.00
56 Ron Schock .60 1.50
57 Jim Dorey .60 1.50
58 Wayne Maki .60 1.50
59 Terry Harper .60 1.50
60 Gilbert Perreault 9.00 15.00
61 Ernie Hicke RC .60 1.50
62 Wayne Hillman .60 1.50
63 Denis DeJordy 1.00 2.00
64 Ken Schinkel .60 1.50
65 Derek Sanderson 3.00 6.00
66 Barclay Plager 1.00 2.00
67 Paul Henderson 1.00 2.00
68 Jude Drouin .60 1.50
69 Keith Magnuson 1.00 2.00
70 Gordie Howe 30.00 60.00
71 Jacques Lemaire 1.50 3.00
72 Doug Favell 1.00 2.00
73 Bert Marshall .60 1.50
74 Gerry Meehan 1.00 2.00
75 Walt Tkaczuk 1.00 2.00
76 Bob Berry RC 1.00 2.00
77 Syl Apps RC 1.50 3.00
78 Tom Webster 1.00 2.00
79 Danny Grant 1.00 2.00
80 Dave Keon 1.50 3.00
81 Ernie Wakely 1.00 2.00
82 John McKenzie 1.00 2.00
83 Doug Roberts .60 1.50
84 Peter Mahovlich 1.00 2.00
85 Dennis Hull 1.00 2.00
86 Juha Widing RC .60 1.50
87 Gary Doak .60 1.50
88 Phil Goyette .60 1.50
89 Gary Dornhoefer 1.00 2.00
90 Ed Giacomin 1.50 3.00
91 Red Berenson 1.00 2.00
92 Mike Pelyk .60 1.50
93 Gary Jarrett .60 1.50
94 Bob Pulford 1.00 2.00
95 Dale Tallon 1.00 2.00
96 Eddie Shack 1.50 3.00
97 Jean Ratelle 1.50 3.00
98 Jim Pappin .60 1.50
99 Roy Edwards 1.00 2.00
100 Bobby Orr 30.00 50.00
101 Ted Hampson .60 1.50
102 Mickey Redmond 1.50 3.00
103 Bob Plager 1.00 2.00
104 Bruce Gamble 1.00 2.00
105 Frank Mahovlich 1.50 3.00
106 Tony Featherstone RC .60 1.50
107 Tracy Pratt .60 1.50
108 Ralph Backstrom 1.00 2.00
109 Murray Hall .60 1.50
110 Tony Esposito 12.00 20.00
111 Checklist Card 35.00 60.00
112 Jim Neilson .60 1.50
113 Ron Ellis 1.00 2.00
114 Bobby Clarke 18.00 30.00
115 Ken Hodge 1.00 2.00
116 Jim Roberts 1.00 2.00
117 Cesare Maniago 1.00 2.00
118 Jean Pronovost 1.00 2.00
119 Gary Bergman .60 1.50
120 Henri Richard 1.50 3.00
121 Ross Lonsberry .60 1.50
122 Pat Quinn 1.00 2.00
123 Rod Gilbert 1.50 3.00
124 Gary Smith 1.00 2.00
125 Stan Mikita 6.00 10.00
126 Ed Van Impe .60 1.50
127 Wayne Connelly .60 1.50
128 Dennis Hextall 1.00 2.00
129 Wayne Cashman 1.50 3.00
130 J.C. Tremblay 1.00 2.00
131 Bernie Parent 1.50 3.00
132 Dunc McCallum RC 3.00 6.00

1972-73 Topps

The 1972-73 production marked Topps' largest set to date at 176 standard-size cards. Expansion plays a part in the increase as the Atlanta Flames and New York Islanders join the league. Tan borders include team name down the left side. A tan colored bar that crosses the bottom portion of the player photo includes the player's name and team logo. The back contains the year-by-year NHL career record of the player, a short biography and a cartoon illustrated fact about the player. The key cards in the set are the first Topps cards of Marcel Dionne and Guy Lafleur. The set was printed on two sheets of 132 cards creating 88 double-printed cards. The double prints are noted in the checklist below by DP. Topps gives collectors a look at the various NHL hardware in the Trophy subset (170-176).

COMPLETE SET (176) 200.00 400.00
1 World Champions DP 3.00 6.00
Boston Bruins Team
2 Playoff Game 1 .40 1.00
Bruins 6
Rangers 5
3 Playoff Game 2 .40 1.00
Bruins 2
Rangers 1
4 Playoff Game 3 .40 1.00
Rangers 5
Bruins 2
5 Playoff Game 4 DP .25 .50
Bruins 3
Rangers 2
6 Playoff Game 5 DP .40 1.00
Rangers 3
Bruins 2
7 Playoff Game 6 DP .25 .50
Bruins 3
Rangers 0
8 Stanley Cup Trophy 2.50 5.00
9 Ed Van Impe DP .25 .50
10 Yvan Cournoyer DP .60 1.50
11 Syl Apps DP .60 1.50
12 Bill Plager RC .60 1.50
13 Ed Johnston DP .60 1.50
14 Walt Tkaczuk .50 1.25
15 Dale Tallon DP .25 .50
16 Gerry Meehan .50 1.25
17 Reggie Leach 1.50 3.00
18 Marcel Dionne DP 6.00 12.00
19 Andre Dupont RC .60 1.50
20 Tony Esposito 7.00 12.00
21 Bob Berry DP .25 .50
22 Craig Cameron .40 1.00
23 Ted Harris .40 1.00
24 Jacques Plante 7.00 12.00
25 Jacques Lemaire DP .60 1.50
26 Simon Nolet DP .25 .50
27 Keith McCreary DP .25 .50
28 Duane Rupp .40 1.00
29 Wayne Cashman .60 1.50
30 Brad Park 3.00 6.00
31 Roger Crozier .40 1.00
32 Wayne Maki .40 1.00
33 Tim Ecclestone .40 1.00
34 Rick Smith .40 1.00
35 Garry Unger DP .25 .50
36 Serge Bernier DP .25 .50
37 Brian Glennie .40 1.00
38 Gerry Desjardins DP .50 1.25
39 Danny Grant .50 1.25
40 Bill White DP .25 .50
41 Gary Dornhoefer DP .25 .50
42 Peter Mahovlich .50 1.25
43 Greg Polis DP .25 .50
44 Larry Hale DP RC .25 .50
45 Dallas Smith .40 1.00
46 Orland Kurtenbach DP .25 .50
47 Steve Atkinson .40 1.00
48 Joey Johnston DP .25 .50
49 Gary Bergman .40 1.00
50 Jean Ratelle .60 1.50
51 Rogatien Vachon DP .60 1.50
52 Phil Roberto DP .25 .50
53 Brian Spencer DP .25 .50
54 Jim McKenny DP .25 .50
55 Gump Worsley .60 1.50
56 Stan Mikita DP 2.50 5.00
57 Guy Lapointe .50 1.25
58 Lew Morrison DP .25 .50
59 Ron Schock DP .25 .50
60 Johnny Bucyk 1.25 2.50
61 Goals Leaders 6.00 10.00
Phil Esposito
Vic Hadfield
Bobby Hull
62 Assists Leaders DP 6.00 12.00
Bobby Orr
Phil Esposito
Jean Ratelle
63 Scoring Leaders DP 6.00 12.00
Phil Esposito
Bobby Orr
Jean Ratelle
64 Goals Against 3.00 6.00
Average Leaders
Tony Esposito
Gilles Villemure
Gump Worsley
65 Penalty Minutes .40 1.00
Leaders DP
Bryan Watson
Keith Magnuson
Gary Dornhoefer
66 Jim Neilson .40 1.00
67 Nick Libett DP .25 .50
68 Jim Lorentz .40 1.00
69 Gilles Meloche RC 3.00 5.00
70 Pat Stapleton .50 1.25
71 Frank St.Marseille DP .25 .50
72 Butch Goring .50 1.25
73 Paul Henderson DP .25 .50
74 Doug Favell .50 1.25
75 Jocelyn Guevremont DP .25 .50
76 Tom Miller RC .40 1.00
77 Bill MacMillan RC .40 1.00
78 Doug Mohns .40 1.00
79 Guy Lafleur DP 10.00 20.00
80 Rod Gilbert DP .60 1.50
81 Gary Doak .40 1.00
82 Dave Burrows DP RC .25 .50
83 Gary Croteau .40 1.00
84 Tracy Pratt DP .25 .50
85 Carol Vadnais DP .25 .50
86 Jacques Caron DP RC .25 .50
87 Keith Magnuson .60 1.50
88 Dave Keon .60 1.50
89 Mike Corrigan .40 1.00
90 Bobby Clarke 8.00 15.00
91 Dunc Wilson DP .25 .50
92 Gerry Hart RC .40 1.00
93 Lou Nanne .50 1.25
94 Checklist 1-176 DP 15.00 25.00
95 Red Berenson DP .25 .50
96 Bob Plager .50 1.25
97 Jim Rutherford RC 3.00 6.00
98 Rick Foley DP RC .25 .50
99 Pit Martin DP .25 .50
100 Bobby Orr DP 25.00 50.00
101 Stan Gilbertson .40 1.00
102 Barry Wilkins .40 1.00
103 Terry Crisp DP .25 .50
104 Cesare Maniago DP .25 .50
105 Marc Tardif .40 1.00
106 Don Luce DP .25 .50
107 Mike Pelyk .40 1.00
108 Juha Widing DP .25 .50
109 Phil Myre DP RC 1.50 3.00
110 Vic Hadfield .25 .50
111 Arnie Brown DP .25 .50
112 Ross Lonsberry DP .25 .50
113 Dick Redmond .40 1.00
114 Gary Smith .50 1.25
115 Bill Goldsworthy .50 1.25
116 Bryan Watson .40 1.00
117 Dave Balon DP .25 .50
118 Bill Mikkelson DP RC .25 .50
119 Terry Harper DP .25 .50
120 Gilbert Perreault DP 3.00 6.00
121 Tony Esposito AS1 3.00 6.00
122 Bobby Orr AS1 12.00 20.00
123 Brad Park AS1 1.50 3.00
124 Phil Esposito AS1 2.50 5.00
(Brother Tony pic-
tured in background)
125 Rod Gilbert AS1 .40 1.00
126 Bobby Hull AS1 9.00 15.00
127 Ken Dryden AS2 DP 8.00 20.00
128 Bill White AS2 DP .25 .50
129 Pat Stapleton AS2 DP .25 .50
130 Jean Ratelle AS2 DP .60 1.50
131 Yvan Cournoyer AS2 DP .60 1.50
132 Vic Hadfield AS2 DP .25 .50
133 Ralph Backstrom DP .25 .50
134 Bob Baun DP .25 .50
135 Fred Stanfield DP .25 .50
136 Barclay Plager DP .25 .50
137 Gilles Villemure .50 1.25
138 Ron Harris DP .25 .50
139 Bill Flett DP .25 .50
140 Frank Mahovlich 2.00 4.00
141 Alex Delvecchio DP .60 1.50
142 Paul Popiel .40 1.00
143 Jean Pronovost DP .25 .50
144 Denis DeJordy DP .25 .50
145 Richard Martin DP 1.50 3.00
146 Ivan Boldirev RC .60 1.50
147 Jack Egers RC .40 1.00
148 Jim Pappin .40 1.00
149 Rod Seiling .40 1.00
150 Phil Esposito 5.00 10.00
151 Gary Edwards .50 1.25
152 Ron Ellis DP .25 .50
153 Jude Drouin .40 1.00
154 Ernie Hicke DP .25 .50
155 Mickey Redmond .60 1.50
156 Joe Watson DP .25 .50
157 Bryan Hextall .40 1.00
158 Andre Boudrias .40 1.00
159 Ed Westfall .50 1.25
160 Ken Dryden 18.00 30.00
161 Rene Robert DP RC 1.00 2.50
162 Bert Marshall DP .25 .50
163 Gary Sabourin .40 1.00
164 Dennis Hull .50 1.25
165 Ed Giacomin DP .60 1.50
166 Ken Hodge .50 1.25
167 Gilles Marotte DP .25 .50
168 Norm Ullman DP .60 1.50
169 Barry Gibbs RC .40 1.00
170 Art Ross Trophy .75 1.50
171 Hart Memorial Trophy .75 1.50
172 James Norris Trophy .75 1.50
173 Vezina Trophy DP .75 1.50
174 Calder Trophy DP .75 1.50
175 Lady Byng Trophy DP .75 1.50
176 Conn Smythe Trophy DP .75 1.50

1973-74 Topps

Once again increasing in size, the 1973-74 Topps set consists of 198 standard-size cards. The fronts of the cards have distinct colored borders including blue and green. This differs from O-Pee-Chee which used red borders for cards 1-198. The backs contain the player's 1972-73 season record, career numbers, a short biography and a cartoon-illustrated fact about the player. Team cards (92-107) give team and player records on the back. Since the set was printed on two 132-card sheets, there are 66 double-printed cards. These double prints are noted in the checklist below by DP. Rookie Cards include Bill Barber, Billy Smith and Dave Schultz. Ken Dryden (10) is only in the Topps set.

COMPLETE SET (198) 125.00 200.00
1 Goal Leaders 1.25 3.00
Phil Esposito
Rick MacLeish
2 Assists Leaders 1.25 3.00
Phil Esposito
Bobby Clarke
3 Scoring Leaders 1.25 3.00
Phil Esposito
Bobby Clarke
4 Goals Against 2.50 6.00
Average Leaders
Ken Dryden
Tony Esposito
5 Penalty Min. Leaders 1.25 3.00
Jim Schoenfeld
Dave Schultz
6 Power Play Goals 1.25 3.00
Leaders
Phil Esposito
Rick MacLeish
7 Paul Henderson DP .20 .40
8 Gregg Sheppard DP UER .20 .40
(Misspelled Greg
on card front)
9 Rod Seiling DP .20 .40
10 Ken Dryden 25.00 40.00
11 Jean Pronovost DP .20 .40
12 Dick Redmond .20 .40
13 Keith McCreary DP .20 .40
14 Ted Harris DP .20 .40
15 Garry Unger .40 1.00
16 Neil Komadoski RC .30 .75
17 Marcel Dionne 6.00 10.00
18 Ernie Hicke DP .20 .40
19 Andre Boudrias .30 .75
20 Bill Flett .30 .75
21 Marshall Johnston .30 .75
22 Gerry Meehan .30 .75
23 Ed Johnston DP .20 .40
24 Serge Savard .50 1.25
25 Walt Tkaczuk .40 1.00
26 Johnny Bucyk .75 2.00
27 Dave Burrows .30 .75
28 Cliff Koroll .30 .75
29 Rey Comeau DP .20 .40
30 Barry Gibbs .30 .75
31 Wayne Stephenson .40 1.00
32 Dan Maloney DP .20 .40
33 Henry Boucha DP .20 .40
34 Gerry Hart .30 .75
35 Bobby Schmautz .30 .75
36 Ross Lonsberry DP .20 .40
37 Ted McAneeley .30 .75
38 Don Luce DP .20 .40
39 Jim McKenny DP .20 .40
40 Frank Mahovlich .50 1.25
41 Bill Fairbairn .30 .75
42 Dallas Smith .30 .75
43 Bryan Hextall .30 .75
44 Keith Magnuson .40 1.00
45 Dan Bouchard .40 1.00
46 Jean-Paul Parise DP .20 .40
47 Barclay Plager .30 .75
48 Mike Corrigan .30 .75
49 Nick Libett DP .20 .40
50 Bobby Clarke 7.00 12.00
51 Bert Marshall DP .20 .40
52 Craig Patrick .40 1.00
53 Richard Lemieux .30 .75
54 Tracy Pratt DP .20 .40
55 Ron Ellis DP .20 .40
56 Jacques Lemaire .50 1.25
57 Steve Vickers DP .20 .40
58 Carol Vadnais .30 .75
59 Jim Rutherford DP .20 .40
60 Dennis Hull .40 1.00
61 Pat Quinn DP .20 .40
62 Bill Goldsworthy DP .20 .40
63 Fran Huck RC .30 .75
64 Rogatien Vachon DP .20 .40
65 Gary Bergman DP .20 .40
66 Bernie Parent .50 1.25
67 Ed Westfall .40 1.00
68 Ivan Boldirev .40 1.00
69 Don Tannahill DP .20 .40
70 Gilbert Perreault DP 3.00 6.00
71 Mike Pelyk DP .20 .40
72 Guy Lafleur DP 7.50 15.00
73 Jean Ratelle .50 1.25
74 Gilles Gilbert DP RC 2.00 4.00
75 Greg Polis .30 .75
76 Doug Jarrett DP .20 .40
77 Phil Myre DP .20 .40
78 Fred Harvey DP .20 .40
79 Jack Egers .30 .75
80 Terry Harper .30 .75
81 Bill Barber RC 6.00 10.00
82 Roy Edwards DP .20 .40
83 Brian Spencer .40 1.00
84 Reggie Leach DP .20 .40
85 Dave Keon .50 1.25
86 Jim Schoenfeld .75 2.00
87 Henri Richard DP .20 .40
88 Rod Gilbert DP .20 .40
89 Don Marcotte DP .20 .40
90 Tony Esposito 3.00 6.00
91 Joe Watson .30 .75
92 Flames Team .75 1.50
93 Bruins Team .75 1.50
94 Sabres Team DP .75 1.50
95 Golden Seals Team DP .75 1.50
96 Blackhawks Team .75 1.50
97 Red Wings Team DP .75 1.50
98 Kings Team DP .75 1.50
99 North Stars Team .75 1.50
100 Canadiens Team .75 1.50
101 Islanders Team .75 1.50
102 Rangers Team DP .75 1.50
103 Flyers Team DP .75 1.50
104 Penguins Team .75 1.50
105 Blues Team .75 1.50
106 Maple Leafs Team .75 1.50
107 Canucks Team .75 1.50
108 Roger Crozier DP .20 .40
109 Tom Reid .30 .75
110 Hilliard Graves RC .30 .75
111 Don Lever .40 1.00
112 Jim Pappin .30 .75
113 Ron Schock DP .20 .40
114 Gerry Desjardins .40 1.00
115 Yvan Cournoyer DP .20 .40
116 Checklist Card 12.00 20.00
117 Bob Leiter .30 .75
118 Ab DeMarco .30 .75
119 Doug Favell .40 1.00
120 Phil Esposito 3.00 6.00
121 Mike Robitaille .30 .75
122 Real Lemieux .30 .75
123 Jim Neilson .30 .75
124 Tim Ecclestone DP .20 .40
125 Jude Drouin .30 .75
126 Gary Smith DP .20 .40
127 Walt McKechnie .30 .75
128 Lowell MacDonald .30 .75
129 Dale Tallon DP .20 .40
130 Billy Harris RC .40 1.00
131 Randy Manery DP .20 .40
132 Darryl Sittler DP 3.00 6.00
133 Ken Hodge .40 1.00
134 Bob Plager .40 1.00
135 Rick MacLeish .75 2.00
136 Dennis Hextall .30 .75
137 Jacques Laperriere DP .20 .40
138 Butch Goring .40 1.00
139 Rene Robert .40 1.00
140 Ed Giacomin .50 1.25
141 Alex Delvecchio DP .20 .40
142 Jocelyn Guevremont .30 .75
143 Joey Johnston .30 .75
144 Bryan Watson DP .20 .40
145 Stan Mikita 3.00 5.00
146 Cesare Maniago .40 1.00
147 Craig Cameron .30 .75
148 Norm Ullman DP .20 .40
149 Dave Schultz RC 6.00 12.00
150 Bobby Orr 18.00 30.00
151 Phil Roberto .30 .75
152 Curt Bennett RC .30 .75
153 Gilles Villemure DP .20 .40
154 Chuck Lefley RC .30 .75
155 Richard Martin 1.00 2.50
156 Juha Widing .30 .75
157 Orland Kurtenbach .30 .75
158 Bill Collins DP .20 .40
159 Bob Stewart RC .30 .75
160 Syl Apps .40 1.00
161 Danny Grant .30 .75
162 Billy Smith RC 15.00 25.00
163 Brian Glennie .30 .75
164 Pit Martin DP .20 .40
165 Brad Park 2.00 4.00
166 Wayne Cashman DP .20 .40
167 Gary Dornhoefer .30 .75
168 Steve Durbano RC .30 .75
169 Jacques Richard .30 .75
170 Guy Lapointe .40 1.00
171 Jim Lorentz .30 .75
172 Bob Berry DP .20 .40
173 Dennis Kearns .30 .75
174 Red Berenson .40 1.00
175 Gilles Meloche DP .20 .40
176 Al McDonough .30 .75
177 Dennis O'Brien RC .30 .75
178 Germaine Gagnon UER DP .20 .40
179 Rick Kehoe DP .20 .40

180 Bill White .30 .75
181 Vic Hadfield DP .20 .40
182 Derek Sanderson 1.50 3.00
183 Andre Dupont DP .20 .40
184 Gary Sabourin .30 .75
185 Larry Romanchych RC .30 .75
186 Peter Mahovlich .40 1.00
187 Dave Dryden .40 1.00
188 Gilles Marotte .30 .75
189 Bobby Lalonde .30 .75
190 Mickey Redmond .40 1.00
191 Series A .30 .75
Canadiens 4
Sabres 2
192 Series B .30 .75
Flyers 4
North Stars 2
193 Series C .30 .75
Blackhawks 4
Blues 1
194 Series D .30 .75
Rangers 4
Bruins
195 Series E .30 .75
Canadiens 4
Flyers 1
196 Series F .30 .75
Blackhawks 4
Rangers 1
197 Series G .30 .75
Canadiens 4
Blackhawks 2
198 Stanley Cup Champs 1.00 2.50

1974-75 Topps

Topps produced a set of 264 standard-size cards for 1974-75. Design of card fronts offers a hockey stick down the left side. The team name, player name and team logo appear at the bottom in a border that features one of the team colors. The backs feature the player's 1973-74 and career statistics, a short biography and a cartoon-illustrated fact about the player. Players from the 1974-75 expansion Washington Capitals and Kansas City Scouts (presently New Jersey Devils) appear in this set. The set marks the return of coach cards, including Don Cherry and Scotty Bowman.

COMPLETE SET (264) 125.00 200.00
1 Goal Leaders 1.50 3.00
Phil Esposito
Bill Goldsworthy
2 Assists Leaders 3.00 5.00
Bobby Orr
Dennis Hextall
3 Scoring Leaders 2.00 4.00
Phil Esposito
Bobby Clarke
4 Goals Against Average .60 1.50
Leaders
Doug Favell
Bernie Parent
5 Penalty Min. Leaders .25 .50
Bryan Watson
Dave Schultz
6 Power Play Goal .25 .50
Leaders
Mickey Redmond
Rick MacLeish
7 Gary Bromley RC .30 .75
8 Bill Barber 2.00 4.00
9 Emile Francis CO .25 .60
10 Gilles Gilbert .60 1.50
11 John Davidson RC 4.00 8.00
12 Ron Ellis .30 .75
13 Syl Apps .25 .60
14 Flames Leaders .25 .50
Jacques Richard
Tom Lysiak
Keith McCreary
15 Dan Bouchard .30 .75
16 Ivan Boldirev .30 .75
17 Gary Coalter RC .25 .60
18 Bob Berry .25 .60
19 Red Berenson .30 .75
20 Stan Mikita 2.00 4.00
21 Fred Shero CO RC 1.25 2.50
22 Gary Smith .30 .75
23 Bill Mikkelson .25 .60
24 Jacques Lemaire UER .60 1.50
(Shown in Sabres
sweater)
25 Gilbert Perreault 2.00 4.00
26 Cesare Maniago .30 .75
27 Bobby Schmautz .25 .60
28 Bruins Leaders 4.00 8.00
Phil Esposito
Bobby Orr
Johnny Bucyk
29 Steve Vickers .30 .75
30 Lowell MacDonald .25 .60
31 Fred Stanfield .25 .60
32 Ed Westfall .30 .75
33 Curt Bennett .25 .60
34 Bep Guidolin CO .25 .60
35 Cliff Koroll .25 .60
36 Gary Croteau .25 .60
37 Mike Corrigan .25 .60
38 Henry Boucha .25 .60
39 Ron Low .30 .75
40 Darryl Sittler 2.50 5.00
41 Tracy Pratt .25 .60
42 Sabres Leaders .25 .50
Richard Martin
Rene Robert
43 Larry Carriere .25 .60
44 Gary Dornhoefer .30 .75
45 Denis Herron RC 1.25 2.50
46 Doug Favell .30 .75
47 Dave Gardner RC .25 .60
48 Morris Mott RC .25 .60
49 Marc Boileau CO .25 .60
50 Brad Park 1.50 3.00
51 Bob Leiter .25 .60
52 Tom Reid .25 .60
53 Serge Savard .60 1.50
54 Checklist 1-132 7.00 12.00
55 Terry Harper .25 .60
56 Golden Seals .25 .50
Leaders
Joey Johnston
Walt McKechnie
57 Guy Charron .25 .60
58 Pit Martin .25 .60
59 Chris Evans .25 .60
60 Bernie Parent .60 1.50
61 Jim Lorentz .25 .60
62 Dave Kryskow RC .25 .60
63 Lou Angotti CO .25 .60
64 Bill Flett .25 .60
65 Vic Hadfield .30 .75
66 Wayne Merrick RC .25 .60
67 Andre Dupont .25 .60
68 Tom Lysiak RC .60 1.50
69 Blackhawks Leaders .25 .50
Jim Pappin
Stan Mikita
J.P. Bordeleau
70 Guy Lapointe .30 .75
71 Gerry O'Flaherty .25 .60
72 Marcel Dionne 3.00 6.00
73 Brent Hughes .25 .60
74 Butch Goring .30 .75
75 Keith Magnuson .25 .60
76 Red Kelly CO .25 .60
77 Pete Stemkowski .25 .60
78 Jim Roberts .25 .60
79 Don Luce .25 .60
80 Don Awrey .25 .60
81 Rick Kehoe .30 .75
82 Billy Smith 3.00 6.00
83 Jean-Paul Parise .25 .60
84 Red Wings Leaders .25 .50
Mickey Redmond
Marcel Dionne
Bill Hogaboam
85 Ed Van Impe .25 .60
86 Randy Manery .25 .60
87 Barclay Plager .30 .75
88 Inge Hammarstrom RC .25 .60
89 Ab DeMarco .25 .60
90 Bill White .25 .60
91 Al Arbour CO .60 1.50
92 Bob Stewart .25 .60
93 Jack Egers .25 .60
94 Don Lever .25 .60
95 Reggie Leach .30 .75
96 Dennis O'Brien .25 .60
97 Peter Mahovlich .30 .75
98 Kings Leaders .25 .50
Butch Goring
Frank St.Marseille
Don Kozak
99 Gerry Meehan .25 .60
100 Bobby Orr 15.00 30.00
101 Jean Potvin RC .25 .60
102 Rod Seiling .25 .60
103 Keith McCreary .25 .60
104 Phil Maloney CO RC .25 .60
105 Denis Dupere .25 .60
106 Steve Durbano .25 .60
107 Bob Plager UER .30 .75
(Photo actually
Barclay Plager)
108 Chris Oddleifson RC .25 .60
109 Jim Neilson .25 .60
110 Jean Pronovost .30 .75
111 Don Kozak RC .25 .60
112 North Stars .30 .75
Leaders
Bill Goldsworthy
Dennis Hextall
Danny Grant
113 Jim Pappin .25 .60
114 Richard Lemieux .25 .60
115 Dennis Hextall .25 .60
116 Bill Hogaboam .25 .60
117 Canucks Leaders .25 .50
Dennis Ververgaert
Bob Schmautz
Andre Boudrias
Don Tannahill
118 Jimmy Anderson CO .25 .60
119 Walt Tkaczuk .30 .75
120 Mickey Redmond .30 .75
121 Jim Schoenfeld .60 1.50
122 Jocelyn Guevremont .25 .60
123 Bob Nystrom .60 1.50
124 Canadiens Leaders 1.00 2.00
Yvan Cournoyer
Frank Mahovlich
Claude Larose
125 Lew Morrison .25 .60
126 Terry Murray .30 .75
127 Richard Martin AS .30 .75
128 Ken Hodge AS .25 .50
129 Phil Esposito AS 1.25 2.50
130 Bobby Orr AS 7.00 12.00
131 Brad Park AS .60 1.50
132 Gilles Gilbert AS .25 .50
133 Lowell MacDonald AS .25 .50
134 Bill Goldsworthy AS .25 .50
135 Bobby Clarke AS 2.00 4.00
136 Bill White AS .25 .50
137 Dave Burrows AS .25 .50
138 Bernie Parent AS .60 1.50
139 Jacques Richard .25 .60
140 Yvan Cournoyer .60 1.50
141 Rangers Leaders .60 1.50
Rod Gilbert
Brad Park
142 Rene Robert .30 .75
143 J. Bob Kelly RC .25 .60
144 Ross Lonsberry .25 .60
145 Jean Ratelle .60 1.50
146 Dallas Smith .25 .60
147 Bernie Geoffrion CO 1.25 2.50
148 Ted McAneeley .25 .60
149 Pierre Plante .25 .60
150 Dennis Hull .30 .75
151 Dave Keon .60 1.50
152 Dave Dunn RC .25 .60
153 Michel Belhumeur .30 .75
154 Flyers Leaders 1.00 2.00
Bobby Clarke
Dave Schultz
155 Ken Dryden 7.50 15.00
156 John Wright RC .25 .60
157 Larry Romanchych .25 .60
158 Ralph Stewart .25 .60
159 Mike Robitaille .25 .60
160 Ed Giacomin 1.00 2.00
161 Don Cherry CO RC 15.00 25.00
162 Checklist 133-264 7.00 12.00
163 Rick MacLeish .60 1.50
164 Greg Polis .25 .60
165 Carol Vadnais .25 .60
166 Pete Laframboise .25 .60
167 Ron Schock .25 .60
168 Lanny McDonald RC 7.00 12.00
169 Scouts Emblem .40 1.00
Draft Selections
on back
170 Tony Esposito 2.50 5.00
171 Pierre Jarry .25 .60
172 Dan Maloney .30 .75
173 Peter McDuffe .30 .75
174 Danny Grant .30 .75
175 John Stewart .25 .60
176 Floyd Smith CO .25 .60
177 Bert Marshall .25 .60
178 Chuck Lefley UER .25 .60
(Photo actually
Pierre Bouchard)
179 Gilles Villemure .30 .75
180 Borje Salming RC 7.00 12.00
181 Doug Mohns .25 .60
182 Barry Wilkins .25 .60
183 Penguins Leaders .30 .75
Lowell MacDonald
Syl Apps
184 Gregg Sheppard .25 .60
185 Joey Johnston .25 .60
186 Dick Redmond .25 .60
187 Simon Nolet .25 .60
188 Ron Stackhouse .25 .60
189 Marshall Johnston .25 .60
190 Richard Martin .60 1.50
191 Andre Boudrias .25 .60
192 Steve Atkinson .25 .60
193 Nick Libett .25 .60
194 Bob Murdoch RC .25 .60
195 Denis Potvin RC 15.00 25.00
196 Dave Schultz 1.00 2.00
197 Blues Leaders .25 .50
Garry Unger
Pierre Plante
198 Jim McKenny .25 .60
199 Gerry Hart .25 .60
200 Phil Esposito 2.00 4.00
201 Rod Gilbert .60 1.50
202 Jacques Laperriere .30 .75
203 Barry Gibbs .25 .60
204 Billy Reay CO .30 .75
205 Gilles Meloche .30 .75
206 Wayne Cashman .30 .75
207 Dennis Ververgaert RC .25 .60
208 Phil Roberto .25 .60
209 Quarter Finals .35 .75
Flyers sweep
Flames
210 Quarter Finals .35 .75
Rangers over
Canadiens
211 Quarter Finals .35 .75
Bruins sweep
Maple Leafs
212 Quarter Finals .35 .75
Blackhawks over
L.A. Kings
213 Stanley Cup Semifinals .35 .75
Flyers over Rangers
214 Stanley Cup Semifinals .35 .75
Bruins over
Blackhawks
215 Stanley Cup Finals .35 .75
Flyers over Bruins
216 Stanley Cup Champions .60 1.50
217 Joe Watson .25 .60
218 Wayne Stephenson .30 .75
219 Maple Leaf Leaders .60 1.50
Darryl Sittler
Norm Ullman
Paul Henderson
Denis Dupere
220 Bill Goldsworthy .30 .75
221 Don Marcotte .25 .60
222 Alex Delvecchio CO .30 .75
223 Stan Gilbertson .25 .60
224 Mike Murphy .25 .60
225 Jim Rutherford .30 .75
226 Phil Russell .25 .60
227 Lynn Powis .25 .60
228 Billy Harris .25 .60
229 Bob Pulford CO .30 .75
230 Ken Hodge .30 .75
231 Bill Fairbairn .25 .60
232 Guy Lafleur 7.00 12.00
233 Islanders Leaders 1.25 2.50
Billy Harris
Ralph Stewart
Denis Potvin
234 Fred Barrett .25 .60
235 Rogatien Vachon .60 1.50
236 Norm Ullman .60 1.50
237 Garry Unger .30 .75
238 Jack Gordon CO RC .25 .60
239 Johnny Bucyk .60 1.50
240 Bob Dailey RC .25 .60
241 Dave Burrows .25 .60
242 Len Frig RC .25 .60
243 Masterson Trophy .60 1.50
Henri Richard
244 Hart Trophy 1.25 2.50
Phil Esposito
245 Johnny Bucyk Byng .40 1.00
246 Ross Trophy 1.25 2.50
Phil Esposito
247 Prince of Wales .30 .75
Trophy
248 Norris Trophy 7.00 12.00
Bobby Orr
249 Bernie Parent Vezina .60 1.50
250 Stanley Cup .30 .75
251 Smythe Trophy .60 1.50
Bernie Parent
252 Calder Trophy 3.00 6.00
Denis Potvin
253 Campbell Trophy .30 .75
254 Pierre Bouchard .25 .60
255 Jude Drouin .25 .60
256 Capitals Emblem .40 1.00
(Draft Selections
on back)
257 Michel Plasse .30 .75
258 Juha Widing .25 .60
259 Bryan Watson .25 .60
260 Bobby Clarke 4.00 8.00
261 Scotty Bowman CO RC 15.00 30.00
262 Craig Patrick .30 .75
263 Craig Cameron .25 .60
264 Ted Irvine .60 1.50

1975-76 Topps

At 330 standard-size cards, the 1975-76 Topps set stands as the company's largest until 1990-91. Fronts feature team name at top and player name at the bottom. The player's position appears in a puck at the bottom. The backs contain year-by-year and NHL career records, a short biography and a cartoon-illustrated hockey fact or referee's signal with interpretation. For the first time, team cards (81-98) with team checklist on back appear in a Topps set.

COMPLETE SET (330) 75.00 150.00
1 Stanley Cup Finals .60 1.50
Philadelphia 4
Buffalo 2
2 Semi-Finals .20 .50
Philadelphia 4
N.Y. Islanders 3
3 Semi-Finals .20 .50
Buffalo 4
Montreal 2
4 Quarter Finals .20 .50
N.Y. Islanders 4
Pittsburgh 2
5 Quarter Finals .20 .50
Montreal 4
Vancouver 1
6 Quarter Finals .20 .50
Buffalo 4
Chicago 1
7 Quarter Finals .20 .50
Philadelphia 4
Toronto 0
8 Curt Bennett .20 .50
9 Johnny Bucyk .50 1.25
10 Gilbert Perreault 1.25 3.00
11 Darryl Edestrand .20 .50
12 Ivan Boldirev .20 .50
13 Nick Libett .20 .50
14 Jim McElmury RC .20 .50
15 Frank St.Marseille .20 .50
16 Blake Dunlop .20 .50
17 Yvon Lambert .25 .60
18 Gerry Hart .20 .50
19 Steve Vickers .20 .50
20 Rick MacLeish .25 .60
21 Bob Paradise .20 .50
22 Red Berenson .25 .60
23 Lanny McDonald 1.50 4.00
24 Mike Robitaille .20 .50
25 Ron Low .25 .60
26 Bryan Hextall .20 .50
27 Carol Vadnais .20 .50
28 Jim Lorentz .20 .50
29 Gary Simmons .25 .60
30 Stan Mikita 1.25 3.00
31 Bryan Watson .20 .50
32 Guy Charron .20 .50
33 Bob Murdoch .20 .50
34 Norm Gratton .20 .50
35 Ken Dryden 9.00 15.00
36 Jean Potvin .20 .50
37 Rick Middleton 1.50 3.00
38 Ed Van Impe .20 .50
39 Rick Kehoe .25 .60
40 Garry Unger .25 .60
41 Ian Turnbull .25 .60
42 Dennis Ververgaert .20 .50
43 Mike Marson .20 .50
44 Randy Manery .20 .50
45 Gilles Gilbert .25 .60
46 Rene Robert .25 .60
47 Bob Stewart .20 .50
48 Pit Martin .20 .50
49 Danny Grant .25 .60
50 Peter Mahovlich .25 .60
51 Dennis Patterson RC .20 .50
52 Mike Murphy .20 .50
53 Dennis O'Brien .20 .50
54 Garry Howatt .20 .50
55 Ed Giacomin .60 1.50
56 Andre Dupont .20 .50
57 Chuck Arnason .20 .50
58 Bob Gassoff RC .20 .50
59 Ron Ellis .25 .60
60 Andre Boudrias .20 .50
61 Yvon Labre .20 .50
62 Hilliard Graves .20 .50
63 Wayne Cashman .25 .60
64 Danny Gare RC 1.00 2.00
65 Rick Hampton .20 .50
66 Darcy Rota .20 .50
67 Bill Hogaboam .20 .50
68 Denis Herron .25 .60
69 Sheldon Kannegiesser .20 .50
70 Yvan Cournoyer UER .50 1.25
71 Ernie Hicke .20 .50
72 Bert Marshall .20 .50
73 Derek Sanderson .75 2.00
74 Tom Bladon .25 .60
75 Ron Schock .20 .50
76 Larry Sacharuk RC .20 .50
77 George Ferguson .20 .50
78 Ab DeMarco .20 .50
79 Tom Williams .20 .50
80 Phil Roberto .20 .50
81 Bruins Team 1.00 2.50
82 Seals Team 1.00 2.50
83 Sabres Team UER 1.00 2.50
84 Blackhawks Team UER 1.00 2.50
85 Flames Team 1.00 2.50
86 Kings Team 1.00 2.50
87 Red Wings Team 1.00 2.50
88 Scouts Team UER 1.00 2.50
89 North Stars Team 1.00 2.50
90 Canadiens Team 1.00 2.50
91 Maple Leafs Team 1.00 2.50
92 Islanders Team 1.00 2.50
93 Penguins Team 1.00 2.50
94 Rangers Team 1.00 2.50
95 Flyers Team UER 1.00 2.50
96 Blues Team 1.00 2.50
97 Canucks Team 1.00 2.50
98 Capitals Team 1.00 2.50
99 Checklist 1-110 6.00 10.00
100 Bobby Orr 12.00 20.00
101 Germaine Gagnon UER .20 .50
102 Phil Russell .20 .50
103 Billy Lochead .20 .50
104 Robin Burns .20 .50
105 Gary Edwards .25 .60
106 Dwight Bialowas .20 .50
107 Doug Risebrough UER RC 1.00 2.00
108 Dave Lewis .20 .50
109 Bill Fairbairn .20 .50
110 Ross Lonsberry .20 .50
111 Ron Stackhouse .20 .50
112 Claude Larose .20 .50
113 Don Luce .20 .50
114 Errol Thompson RC .20 .50
115 Gary Smith .25 .60
116 Jack Lynch .20 .50
117 Jacques Richard .20 .50
118 Dallas Smith .20 .50
119 Dave Gardner .20 .50
120 Mickey Redmond .25 .60
121 John Marks .20 .50
122 Dave Hudson .20 .50
123 Bob Nevin .20 .50
124 Fred Barrett .20 .50
125 Gerry Desjardins .25 .60
126 Guy Lafleur UER 4.00 10.00
(Listed as Defense
on card front)
127 Jean-Paul Parise .20 .50
128 Walt Tkaczuk .25 .60
129 Gary Dornhoefer .25 .60
130 Syl Apps .20 .50
131 Bob Plager .25 .60
132 Stan Weir .20 .50
133 Tracy Pratt .20 .50
134 Jack Egers .20 .50
135 Eric Vail .20 .50
136 Al Sims .20 .50
137 Larry Patey .20 .50
138 Jim Schoenfeld .25 .60
139 Cliff Koroll .20 .50
140 Marcel Dionne 1.50 4.00
141 Jean-Guy Lagace .20 .50
142 Juha Widing .20 .50
143 Lou Nanne .25 .60
144 Serge Savard .50 1.25
145 Glenn Resch 1.25 3.00
146 Ron Greschner RC 1.00 2.00
147 Dave Schultz .25 .60
148 Barry Wilkins .20 .50
149 Floyd Thomson .20 .50
150 Darryl Sittler .50 1.25
151 Paulin Bordeleau .20 .50
152 Ron Lalonde RC .20 .50
153 Larry Romanchych .20 .50
154 Larry Carriere .20 .50
155 Andre Savard .20 .50
156 Dave Hrechkosy RC .20 .50
157 Bill White .20 .50
158 Dave Kryskow .20 .50
159 Denis Dupere .20 .50
160 Rogatien Vachon .60 1.50
161 Doug Rombough .20 .50
162 Murray Wilson .25 .60
163 Bob Bourne RC 1.00 2.00
164 Gilles Marotte .20 .50
165 Vic Hadfield .25 .60
166 Reggie Leach .25 .60
167 Jerry Butler .20 .50
168 Inge Hammarstrom .20 .50
169 Chris Oddleifson .20 .50
170 Greg Joly .20 .50
171 Checklist 111-220 6.00 10.00
172 Pat Quinn .25 .60
173 Dave Forbes .20 .50
174 Len Frig .20 .50
175 Richard Martin .25 .60
176 Keith Magnuson .20 .50
177 Dan Maloney .20 .50
178 Craig Patrick .25 .60
179 Tom Williams .20 .50
180 Bill Goldsworthy .25 .60
181 Steve Shutt .50 1.25
182 Ralph Stewart .20 .50
183 John Davidson 1.25 3.00
184 Bob Kelly .20 .50
185 Ed Johnston .25 .60
186 Dave Burrows .20 .50
187 Dave Dunn .20 .50
188 Dennis Kearns .20 .50
189 Bill Clement 1.25 3.00
190 Gilles Meloche .25 .60
191 Bob Leiter .20 .50
192 Jerry Korab .20 .50
193 Joey Johnston .20 .50
194 Walt McKechnie .20 .50
195 Wilf Paiement .20 .50
196 Bob Berry .20 .50
197 Dean Talafous RC .20 .50
198 Guy Lapointe .25 .60
199 Clark Gillies RC 2.00 4.00
200 Phil Esposito 1.25 3.00
201 Greg Polis .20 .50
202 Jimmy Watson .25 .60
203 Gord McRae RC .25 .60
204 Lowell MacDonald .20 .50
205 Barclay Plager .25 .60
206 Don Lever .20 .50
207 Bill Mikkelson .20 .50
208 Goals Leaders 1.25 3.00
Phil Esposito
Guy Lafleur
Richard Martin
209 Assists Leaders 1.50 4.00
Bobby Clarke
Bobby Orr
Pete Mahovlich
210 Scoring Leaders 2.00 5.00
Bobby Orr
Phil Esposito
Marcel Dionne
211 Penalty Min. Leaders .20 .50
Dave Schultz
Andre Dupont
Phil Russell
212 Power Play .60 1.50
Goal Leaders
Phil Esposito
Richard Martin
Danny Grant
213 Goals Against 2.00 5.00
Average Leaders
Bernie Parent
Rogatien Vachon
Ken Dryden
214 Barry Gibbs .20 .50
215 Ken Hodge .25 .60
216 Jocelyn Guevremont .20 .50
217 Warren Williams RC .20 .50
218 Dick Redmond .20 .50
219 Jim Rutherford .25 .60
220 Simon Nolet .20 .50
221 Butch Goring .25 .60
222 Glen Sather .25 .60
223 Mario Tremblay RC 1.50 3.00
224 Jude Drouin .20 .50
225 Rod Gilbert .50 1.25
226 Bill Barber .50 1.25
227 Gary Inness RC .25 .60
228 Wayne Merrick .20 .50
229 Rod Seiling .20 .50
230 Tom Lysiak .25 .60
231 Bob Dailey .20 .50
232 Michel Belhumeur .25 .60
233 Bill Hajt RC .20 .50
234 Jim Pappin .20 .50
235 Gregg Sheppard .20 .50
236 Gary Bergman .20 .50
237 Randy Rota .20 .50
238 Neil Komadoski .20 .50
239 Craig Cameron .20 .50
240 Tony Esposito 1.25 3.00
241 Larry Robinson 2.50 6.00
242 Billy Harris .20 .50
243 Jean Ratelle .50 1.25
244 Ted Irvine UER .20 .50
(Photo actually
Ted Harris)
245 Bob Neely .20 .50
246 Bobby Lalonde .20 .50
247 Ron Jones RC .20 .50
248 Rey Comeau .20 .50
249 Michel Plasse .25 .60
250 Bobby Clarke 2.50 6.00
251 Bobby Schmautz .20 .50
252 Peter McNab RC 1.25 2.50
253 Al MacAdam .20 .50
254 Dennis Hull .20 .50
255 Terry Harper .20 .50
256 Peter McDuffe .25 .60
257 Jean Hamel .20 .50
258 Jacques Lemaire .50 1.25
259 Bob Nystrom .25 .60
260 Brad Park .75 2.00
261 Cesare Maniago .25 .60
262 Don Saleski .20 .50
263 J. Bob Kelly .20 .50
264 Bob Hess RC .20 .50
265 Blaine Stoughton .20 .50
266 John Gould .20 .50
267 Checklist 221-330 6.00 10.00
268 Dan Bouchard .25 .60
269 Don Marcotte .20 .50
270 Jim Neilson .20 .50
271 Craig Ramsay .20 .50
272 Grant Mulvey RC .25 .60
273 Larry Giroux RC .20 .50
274 Real Lemieux .20 .50
275 Denis Potvin 2.50 6.00
276 Don Kozak .20 .50
277 Tom Reid .20 .50
278 Bob Gainey 1.50 4.00
279 Nick Beverley .20 .50
280 Jean Pronovost .25 .60
281 Joe Watson .20 .50
282 Chuck Lefley .20 .50
283 Borje Salming 2.00 5.00
284 Garnet Bailey .20 .50
285 Gregg Boddy .20 .50
286 Bobby Clarke AS1 1.25 3.00
287 Denis Potvin AS1 1.25 3.00
288 Bobby Orr AS1 6.00 10.00
289 Richard Martin AS1 .20 .50
290 Guy Lafleur AS1 1.50 4.00
291 Bernie Parent AS1 .50 1.25
292 Phil Esposito AS2 .75 2.00
293 Guy Lapointe AS2 .20 .50
294 Borje Salming AS2 1.00 2.50
295 Steve Vickers AS2 .20 .50
296 Rene Robert AS2 .20 .50
297 Rogatien Vachon AS2 .50 1.25
298 Buster Harvey RC .20 .50
299 Gary Sabourin .20 .50
300 Bernie Parent .50 1.25
301 Terry O'Reilly .25 .60
302 Ed Westfall .25 .60
303 Pete Stemkowski .20 .50
304 Pierre Bouchard .20 .50
305 Pierre Larouche RC 2.00 4.00
306 Lee Fogolin RC .20 .50
307 Gerry O'Flaherty .20 .50
308 Phil Myre .25 .60
309 Pierre Plante .20 .50
310 Dennis Hextall .20 .50
311 Jim McKenny .20 .50
312 Vic Venasky .20 .50
313 Flames Leaders .20 .50
Eric Vail
Tom Lysiak
Tom Lysiak
Tom Lysiak
314 Bruins Leaders 2.00 5.00
Phil Esposito
Bobby Orr
Phil Esposito
Johnny Bucyk
315 Sabres Leaders .20 .50
Richard Martin
Rene Robert
Rene Robert
Richard Martin
316 Seals Leaders .20 .50
Dave Hrechkosy
Larry Patey
Stan Weir
Stan Weir
Larry Patey
Dave Hrechkosy
317 Blackhawks Leaders .20 .50
Stan Mikita
Jim Pappin
Stan Mikita
Stan Mikita
318 Red Wings Leaders .20 .50
Danny Grant
Marcel Dionne
Marcel Dionne
Danny Grant
319 Scouts Leaders .20 .50
Simon Nolet
Wilf Paiement
Simon Nolet
Guy Charron
Simon Nolet
320 Kings Leaders .20 .50
Bob Nevin
Bob Nevin
Bob Nevin
Bob Nevin
Juha Widing
Bob Berry
321 North Stars Leaders .20 .50
Bill Goldsworthy
Dennis Hextall
Dennis Hextall
Bill Goldsworthy
322 Canadiens Leaders .60 1.50
Guy Lafleur
Pete Mahovlich
Guy Lafleur
Guy Lafleur
323 Islanders Leaders .60 1.50
Bob Nystrom
Denis Potvin
Denis Potvin
Clark Gillies
324 Rangers Leaders .20 .50
Steve Vickers
Steve Vickers
Rod Gilbert
Rod Gilbert
Jean Ratelle
325 Flyers Leaders .20 .50
Reggie Leach
Bobby Clarke
Bobby Clarke
Reggie Leach
326 Penguins Leaders .20 .50
Jean Pronovost
Ron Schock
Ron Schock
Jean Pronovost
327 Blues Leaders .20 .50
Garry Unger
Garry Unger
Garry Unger
Garry Unger

Larry Sacharuk
328 Maple Leafs Leaders .60 1.50
Darryl Sittler
Darryl Sittler
Darryl Sittler
Darryl Sittler
329 Canucks Leaders .20 .50
Don Lever
Don Lever
Andre Boudrias
Andre Boudrias
330 Capitals Leaders .20 .50
Tommy Williams
Garnet Bailey
Tommy Williams
Garnet Bailey
Tommy Williams

1976-77 Topps

The 1976-77 Topps set contains 264 color standard-size cards. The fronts contain team name and logo at the top with player name and position at the bottom. The backs feature 1975-76 and career statistics, career highlights and a cartoon-illustrated fact. The first cards of Colorado Rockies (formerly Kansas City) players appear this year. Rookie Cards in this set include Bryan Trottier and Dennis Maruk.

COMPLETE SET (264) 100.00 200.00
1 Goals Leaders .75 2.00
Reggie Leach
Guy Lafleur
Pierre Larouche
2 Assists Leaders .75 2.00
Bobby Clarke
Peter Mahovlich
Guy Lafleur
Gilbert Perrault
Jean Ratelle
3 Scoring Leaders .75 2.00
Guy Lafleur
Bobby Clarke
Gilbert Perrault
4 Penalty Min. Leaders .20 .50
Steve Durbano
Bryan Watson
Dave Schultz
5 Power Play Goals .75 2.00
Leaders
Phil Esposito
Guy Lafleur
Richard Martin
Pierre Larouche
Denis Potvin
6 Goals Against 1.25 3.00
Average Leaders
Ken Dryden
Glenn Resch
Michel Larocque
7 Gary Doak .20 .50
8 Jacques Richard .20 .50
9 Wayne Dillon .20 .50
10 Bernie Parent .75 2.00
11 Ed Westfall .25 .60
12 Dick Redmond .20 .50
13 Bryan Hextall .20 .50
14 Jean Pronovost .25 .60
15 Peter Mahovlich .25 .60
16 Danny Grant .25 .60
17 Phil Myre .25 .60
18 Wayne Merrick .20 .50
19 Steve Durbano .20 .50
20 Derek Sanderson .60 1.50
21 Mike Murphy .20 .50
22 Borje Salming 1.00 2.50
23 Mike Walton .20 .50
24 Randy Manery .20 .50
25 Ken Hodge .25 .60
26 Mel Bridgman RC .40 1.00
27 Jerry Korab .20 .50
28 Gilles Gratton .25 .60
29 Andre St.Laurent .20 .50
30 Yvan Cournoyer .40 1.00
31 Phil Russell .20 .50
32 Dennis Hextall .20 .50
33 Lowell MacDonald .20 .50
34 Dennis O'Brien .20 .50
35 Gerry Meehan .20 .50
36 Gilles Meloche .25 .60
37 Wilf Paiement .25 .60
38 Bob MacMillan RC .40 1.00
39 Ian Turnbull .25 .60
40 Rogatien Vachon .40 1.00
41 Nick Beverley .20 .50
42 Rene Robert .25 .60
43 Andre Savard .20 .50
44 Bob Gainey 1.00 2.50
45 Joe Watson .20 .50
46 Billy Smith 1.00 2.50
47 Darcy Rota .20 .50
48 Rick Lapointe RC .20 .50
49 Pierre Jarry .20 .50
50 Syl Apps .20 .50
51 Eric Vail .20 .50
52 Greg Joly .20 .50
53 Don Lever .20 .50
54 Bob Murdoch .20 .50
55 Denis Herron .25 .60
56 Mike Bloom .20 .50
57 Bill Fairbairn .20 .50
58 Fred Stanfield .20 .50
59 Steve Shutt .75 2.00
60 Brad Park .60 1.50
61 Gilles Villemure .25 .60
62 Bert Marshall .20 .50
63 Chuck Lefley .20 .50
64 Simon Nolet .20 .50
65 Reggie Leach RB .25 .60
66 Darryl Sittler RB .40 1.00
67 Bryan Trottier RB 3.00 8.00
68 Garry Unger RB .25 .60
69 Ron Low .25 .60
70 Bobby Clarke 1.50 4.00
71 Michel Bergeron RC .20 .50
72 Ron Stackhouse .20 .50
73 Bill Hogaboam .20 .50
74 Bob Murdoch .20 .50
75 Steve Vickers .20 .50
76 Pit Martin .20 .50
77 Gerry Hart .20 .50
78 Craig Ramsay .20 .50
79 Michel Larocque .25 .60
80 Jean Ratelle .40 1.00
81 Don Saleski .20 .50
82 Bill Clement .40 1.00
83 Dave Burrows .20 .50
84 Wayne Thomas .25 .60
85 John Gould .20 .50
86 Dennis Maruk RC 1.00 2.00
87 Ernie Hicke .20 .50
88 Jim Rutherford .25 .60
89 Dale Tallon .20 .50
90 Rod Gilbert .40 1.00
91 Marcel Dionne 1.25 3.00
92 Chuck Arnason .20 .50
93 Jean Potvin .20 .50
94 Don Luce .20 .50
95 Johnny Bucyk .40 1.00
96 Larry Goodenough .20 .50
97 Mario Tremblay .25 .60
98 Nelson Pyatt RC .20 .50
99 Brian Glennie .20 .50
100 Tony Esposito .75 2.00
101 Dan Maloney .20 .50
102 Barry Wilkins .20 .50
103 Dean Talafous .20 .50
104 Ed Staniowski RC .20 .50
105 Dallas Smith .20 .50
106 Jude Drouin .20 .50
107 Pat Hickey .20 .50
108 Jocelyn Guevremont .20 .50
109 Doug Risebrough .40 1.00
110 Reggie Leach .25 .60
111 Dan Bouchard .25 .60
112 Chris Oddleifson .20 .50
113 Rick Hampton .20 .50
114 John Marks .20 .50
115 Bryan Trottier RC 20.00 35.00
116 Checklist 1-132 3.00 6.00
117 Greg Polis .20 .50
118 Peter McNab .40 1.00
119 Jim Roberts .20 .50
120 Gerry Cheevers .75 2.00
121 Rick MacLeish .25 .60
122 Billy Lochead .20 .50
123 Tom Reid .20 .50
124 Rick Kehoe .25 .60
125 Keith Magnuson .20 .50
126 Clark Gillies .40 1.00
127 Rick Middleton .75 2.00
128 Bill Hajt .20 .50
129 Jacques Lemaire .40 1.00
130 Terry O'Reilly .40 1.00
131 Andre Dupont .20 .50
132 Flames Team .75 2.00
133 Bruins Team .75 2.00
134 Sabres Team .75 2.00
135 Seals Team .75 2.00
136 Blackhawks Team .75 2.00
137 Red Wings Team .75 2.00
138 Scouts Team .75 2.00
139 Kings Team .75 2.00
140 North Stars Team .75 2.00
141 Canadiens Team .75 2.00
142 Islanders Team .75 2.00
143 Rangers Team .75 2.00
144 Flyers Team .75 2.00
145 Penguins Team .75 2.00
146 Blues Team .75 2.00
147 Maple Leafs Team .75 2.00
148 Canucks Team .75 2.00
149 Capitals Team .75 2.00
150 Dave Schultz .40 1.00
151 Larry Robinson 1.50 4.00
152 Al Smith .25 .60
153 Bob Nystrom .25 .60
154 Ron Greschner UER .20 .50
155 Gregg Sheppard .20 .50
156 Alain Daigle .20 .50
157 Ed Van Impe .20 .50
158 Tim Young RC .25 .60
159 Gary Bergman .20 .50
160 Ed Giacomin .60 1.50
161 Yvon Labre .20 .50
162 Jim Lorentz .20 .50
163 Guy Lafleur 2.50 6.00
164 Tom Bladon .20 .50
165 Wayne Cashman .25 .60
166 Pete Stemkowski .25 .60
167 Grant Mulvey .20 .50
168 Yves Belanger RC .25 .60
169 Bill Goldsworthy .25 .60
170 Denis Potvin 1.50 4.00
171 Nick Libett .20 .50
172 Michel Plasse .25 .60
173 Lou Nanne .25 .60
174 Tom Lysiak .25 .60
175 Dennis Ververgaert .20 .50
176 Gary Simmons .25 .60
177 Pierre Bouchard .20 .50
178 Bill Barber .60 1.50
179 Darryl Edestrand .20 .50
180 Gilbert Perreault .75 2.00
181 Dave Maloney RC .40 1.00
182 Jean-Paul Parise .20 .50
183 Bobby Sheehan .20 .50
184 Pete Lopresti RC .25 .60
185 Don Kozak .20 .50
186 Guy Charron .20 .50
187 Stan Gilbertson .20 .50
188 Bill Nyrop RC .20 .50
189 Bobby Schmautz .20 .50
190 Wayne Stephenson .25 .60
191 Brian Spencer .20 .50
192 Gilles Marotte .20 .50
193 Lorne Henning .20 .50
194 Bob Neely .20 .50
195 Dennis Hull .25 .60
196 Walt McKechnie .20 .50
197 Curt Ridley RC .20 .50
198 Dwight Bialowas .20 .50
199 Pierre Larouche .40 1.00
200 Ken Dryden 6.00 12.00
201 Ross Lonsberry .20 .50
202 Curt Bennett .20 .50
203 Hartland Monahan RC .20 .50
204 John Davidson .75 2.00
205 Serge Savard .40 1.00
206 Garry Howatt .20 .50
207 Darryl Sittler 1.25 3.00
208 J.P. Bordeleau .20 .50
209 Henry Boucha .20 .50
210 Richard Martin .25 .60
211 Vic Venasky .20 .50
212 Buster Harvey .20 .50
213 Bobby Orr 10.00 20.00
214 French Connection .75 2.00
Richard Martin
Gilbert Perreault
Rene Robert
215 LCB Line 1.00 2.50
Reggie Leach
Bobby Clarke
Bill Barber
216 Long Island Lightning 1.25 3.00
Clark Gillies
Bryan Trottier
Billy Harris
217 Checking Line .40 1.00
Bob Gainey
Doug Jarvis
Jim Roberts
218 Bicentennial Line .25 .60
Lowell MacDonald
Syl Apps
Jean Pronovost
219 Bob Kelly .20 .50
220 Walt Tkaczuk .25 .60
221 Dave Lewis .20 .50
222 Danny Gare .40 1.00
223 Guy Lapointe .25 .60
224 Hank Nowak RC .20 .50
225 Stan Mikita 1.00 2.50
226 Vic Hadfield .25 .60
227 Bernie Wolfe RC .25 .60
228 Bryan Watson .20 .50
229 Ralph Stewart .20 .50
230 Gerry Desjardins .25 .60
231 John Bednarski RC .20 .50
232 Yvon Lambert .20 .50
233 Orest Kindrachuk .20 .50
234 Don Marcotte .20 .50
235 Bill White .20 .50
236 Red Berenson .25 .60
237 Al MacAdam .20 .50
238 Rick Blight RC .20 .50
239 Butch Goring .25 .60
240 Cesare Maniago .25 .60
241 Jim Schoenfeld .25 .60
242 Cliff Koroll .20 .50
243 Mickey Redmond .25 .60
244 Rick Chartraw .20 .50
245 Phil Esposito 1.00 2.50
246 Dave Forbes .20 .50
247 Joe Watson .20 .50
248 Ron Schock .20 .50
249 Fred Barrett .20 .50
250 Glenn Resch .75 2.00
251 Ivan Boldirev .20 .50
252 Billy Harris .20 .50
253 Lee Fogolin .20 .50
254 Murray Wilson .20 .50
255 Gilles Gilbert .25 .60
256 Gary Dornhoefer .25 .60
257 Carol Vadnais .25 .60
258 Checklist 133-264 3.00 6.00
259 Errol Thompson .20 .50
260 Garry Unger .25 .60
261 J. Bob Kelly .20 .50
262 Terry Harper .20 .50
263 Blake Dunlop .20 .50
264 Stanley Cup Champs .60 1.50

1976-77 Topps Glossy Inserts

This 22-card insert set was issued with the 1976-77 Topps hockey card set but not with the O-Pee-Chee hockey cards unlike the glossy insert produced "jointly" by Topps and O-Pee-Chee the next year. This set is very similar to (but much more difficult to find than) the glossy insert set of the following year. The cards were printed in the United States. These rounded-corner cards are approximately 2 1/4" by 3 1/4".

COMPLETE SET (22) 40.00 80.00
1 Bobby Clarke 2.00 4.00
2 Brad Park 1.25 2.50
3 Tony Esposito 1.50 3.00
4 Marcel Dionne 2.00 4.00
5 Ken Dryden 7.50 15.00
6 Glenn Resch 1.00 2.00
7 Phil Esposito 2.50 5.00
8 Darryl Sittler 1.50 3.00
9 Gilbert Perreault 1.00 2.00
10 Denis Potvin 2.00 4.00
11 Guy Lafleur 4.00 8.00
12 Bill Barber 1.00 2.00
13 Syl Apps .50 1.00
14 Johnny Bucyk 1.00 2.00
15 Bryan Trottier 7.50 15.00
16 Dennis Hull .50 1.00
17 Guy Lapointe .75 1.50
18 Rod Gilbert 1.25 2.50
19 Richard Martin .75 1.50
20 Bobby Orr 12.50 25.00
21 Reggie Leach .75 1.50
22 Jean Ratelle 1.25 2.50

1977-78 Topps

The 1977-78 Topps set consists of 264 standard-size cards. Cards 203 (Stan Gilbertson) and 255 (Bill Fairbairn) differ from those of O-Pee-Chee. Card fronts have team name and logo, player name and position at the bottom. Yearly statistics including minor league numbers are featured on the back along with a short biography and a cartoon-illustrated fact about the player. After the initial print run, Topps changed the photos on card numbers 131, 138, 149 and 152. Two of the changes (138 and 149) were necessary corrections. Rookie Cards include Mike Milbury and Mike Palmateer.

COMPLETE SET (264) 45.00 90.00
1 Goals Leaders 1.00 2.50
Steve Shutt
Guy Lafleur
Marcel Dionne
2 Assists Leaders .60 1.50
Guy Lafleur
Marcel Dionne
Larry Robinson
Borje Salming
Tim Young
3 Scoring Leaders .75 2.00
Guy Lafleur
Marcel Dionne
Steve Shutt
4 Penalty Min. Leaders .15 .40
Dave(Tiger) Williams
Dennis Polonich
Bob Gassoff
5 Power Play Goals .30 .75
Leaders
Lanny McDonald
Phil Esposito
Tom Williams
6 Goals Against 1.00 2.50
Average Leaders
Michel Larocque
Ken Dryden
Glenn Resch
7 Game Winning .60 1.50
Goals Leaders
Gilbert Perreault
Steve Shutt
Guy Lafleur
Rick MacLeish
Peter McNab
8 Shutouts Leaders 1.25 3.00
Ken Dryden
Rogatien Vachon
Bernie Parent
Dunc Wilson
9 Brian Spencer .10 .25
10 Denis Potvin AS2 .30 .75
11 Nick Fotiu .30 .75
12 Bob Murray .10 .25
13 Pete Lopresti .15 .40
14 J. Bob Kelly .10 .25
15 Rick MacLeish .30 .75
16 Terry Harper .10 .25
17 Willi Plett RC .30 .75
18 Peter McNab .15 .40
19 Wayne Thomas .15 .40
20 Pierre Bouchard .10 .25
21 Dennis Maruk .30 .75
22 Mike Murphy .10 .25
23 Cesare Maniago .15 .40
24 Paul Gardner RC .10 .25
25 Rod Gilbert .30 .75
26 Orest Kindrachuk .10 .25
27 Bill Hajt .10 .25
28 John Davidson .30 .75
29 Jean-Paul Parise .10 .25
30 Larry Robinson AS1 1.25 3.00
31 Yvon Labre .10 .25
32 Walt McKechnie .10 .25
33 Rick Kehoe .15 .40
34 Randy Holt RC .10 .25
35 Garry Unger .15 .40
36 Lou Nanne .10 .25
37 Dan Bouchard .15 .40
38 Darryl Sittler .75 2.00
39 Bob Murdoch .10 .25
40 Jean Ratelle .30 .75
41 Dave Maloney .10 .25
42 Danny Gare .30 .75
43 Jimmy Watson .10 .25
44 Tom Williams .10 .25
45 Serge Savard .30 .75
46 Derek Sanderson .30 .75
47 John Marks .10 .25
48 Al Cameron RC .10 .25
49 Dean Talafous .10 .25
50 Glenn Resch .30 .75
51 Ron Schock .10 .25
52 Gary Croteau .10 .25
53 Gerry Meehan .10 .25
54 Ed Staniowski .10 .25
55 Phil Esposito .75 2.00
56 Dennis Ververgaert .10 .25
57 Rick Wilson .10 .25
58 Jim Lorentz .10 .25
59 Bobby Schmautz .10 .25
60 Guy Lapointe AS2 .15 .40
61 Ivan Boldirev .10 .25
62 Bob Nystrom .10 .25
63 Rick Hampton .10 .25
64 Jack Valiquette .10 .25
65 Bernie Parent .60 1.50
66 Dave Burrows .10 .25
67 Butch Goring .15 .40
68 Checklist 1-132 2.00 4.00
69 Murray Wilson .10 .25
70 Ed Giacomin .30 .75
71 Flames Team .50 1.25
72 Bruins Team .50 1.25
73 Sabres Team .50 1.25
74 Blackhawks Team .50 1.25
75 Barons Team .50 1.25
76 Rockies Team .50 1.25
77 Red Wings Team .50 1.25
78 Kings Team .50 1.25
79 North Stars Team .50 1.25
80 Canadiens Team .50 1.25
81 Islanders Team .50 1.25
82 Rangers Team .50 1.25
83 Flyers Team .50 1.25
84 Penguins Team .50 1.25
85 Blues Team .50 1.25
86 Maple Leafs Team .50 1.25
87 Canucks Team .50 1.25
88 Capitals Team .50 1.25
89 Keith Magnuson .10 .25
90 Walt Tkaczuk .15 .40
91 Bill Nyrop .10 .25
92 Michel Plasse .15 .40
93 Bob Bourne .15 .40
94 Lee Fogolin .10 .25
95 Gregg Sheppard .10 .25
96 Hartland Monahan .10 .25
97 Curt Bennett .10 .25
98 Bob Dailey .10 .25
99 Bill Goldsworthy .15 .40
100 Ken Dryden AS1 3.00 8.00
101 Grant Mulvey .10 .25
102 Pierre Larouche .30 .75
103 Nick Libett .10 .25
104 Rick Smith .10 .25
105 Bryan Trottier 4.00 10.00
106 Pierre Jarry .10 .25
107 Red Berenson .15 .40
108 Jim Schoenfeld .15 .40
109 Gilles Meloche .15 .40
110 Lanny McDonald AS2 .60 1.50
111 Don Lever .10 .25
112 Greg Polis .10 .25
113 Gary Sargent RC .10 .25
114 Earl Anderson RC .10 .25
115 Bobby Clarke 1.25 3.00
116 Dave Lewis .10 .25
117 Darcy Rota .10 .25
118 Andre Savard .10 .25
119 Denis Herron .15 .40
120 Steve Shutt AS1 .30 .75
121 Mel Bridgman .10 .25
122 Buster Harvey .10 .25
123 Roland Eriksson RC .10 .25
124 Dale Tallon .10 .25
125 Gilles Gilbert .15 .40
126 Billy Harris .10 .25
127 Tom Lysiak .15 .40
128 Jerry Korab .10 .25
129 Bob Gainey .60 1.50
130 Wilf Paiement .15 .40
131A Tom Bladon Standing 1.00 2.00
131B Tom Bladon Skating .10 .25
132 Ernie Hicke .10 .25
133 J.P. LeBlanc .10 .25
134 Mike Milbury RC 2.50 5.00
135 Pit Martin .10 .25
136 Steve Vickers .10 .25
137 Don Awrey .10 .25
138A Bernie Wolfe MacAdam 1.00 2.00
138B Bernie Wolfe COR .10 .25
139 Doug Jarvis .30 .75
140 Borje Salming AS1 .60 1.50
141 Bob MacMillan .10 .25
142 Wayne Stephenson .15 .40
143 Dave Forbes .10 .25
144 Jean Potvin .10 .25
145 Guy Charron .10 .25
146 Cliff Koroll .10 .25
147 Danny Grant .10 .25
148 Bill Hogaboam UER .10 .25
(Photo actually
Michel Bergeron)
149A Al MacAdam ERR Wolfe 1.00 2.00
149B Al MacAdam COR .10 .25
150 Gerry Desjardins .15 .40
151 Yvon Lambert .10 .25
152A Rick Lapointe ERR 1.00 2.00
152B Rick Lapointe COR .10 .25
153 Ed Westfall .15 .40
154 Carol Vadnais .10 .25
155 Johnny Bucyk .30 .75
156 J.P. Bordeleau .10 .25
157 Ron Stackhouse .10 .25
158 Glen Sharpley RC .10 .25
159 Michel Bergeron .10 .25
160 Rogatien Vachon AS2 .30 .75
161 Fred Stanfield .10 .25
162 Gerry Hart .10 .25
163 Mario Tremblay .15 .40
164 Andre Dupont .10 .25
165 Don Marcotte .10 .25
166 Wayne Dillon .10 .25
167 Claude Larose .10 .25
168 Eric Vail .10 .25
169 Tom Edur .10 .25
170 Tony Esposito .60 1.50
171 Andre St.Laurent .10 .25
172 Dan Maloney .10 .25
173 Dennis O'Brien .10 .25
174 Blair Chapman RC .10 .25
175 Dennis Kearns .10 .25
176 Wayne Merrick .10 .25
177 Michel Larocque .15 .40
178 Bob Kelly .10 .25
179 Dave Farrish RC .10 .25
180 Richard Martin AS2 .30 .75
181 Gary Doak .10 .25
182 Jude Drouin .10 .25
183 Barry Dean RC .10 .25
184 Gary Smith .15 .40
185 Reggie Leach .30 .75
186 Ian Turnbull .15 .40
187 Vic Venasky .10 .25
188 Wayne Bianchin RC .10 .25
189 Doug Risebrough .15 .40
190 Brad Park .30 .75
191 Craig Ramsay .15 .40
192 Ken Hodge .15 .40
193 Phil Myre .15 .40
194 Garry Howatt .10 .25
195 Stan Mikita .75 2.00
196 Garnet Bailey .10 .25
197 Dennis Hextall .10 .25
198 Nick Beverley .10 .25
199 Larry Patey .10 .25
200 Guy Lafleur AS1 2.00 5.00
201 Don Edwards RC 2.50 2.50
202 Gary Dornhoefer .15 .40
203 Stan Gilbertson .10 .25
204 Alex Pirus RC .10 .25
205 Peter Mahovlich .15 .40
206 Bert Marshall .10 .25
207 Gilles Gratton .15 .40
208 Alain Daigle .10 .25
209 Chris Oddleifson .10 .25
210 Gilbert Perreault AS2 .60 1.50
211 Mike Palmateer RC 2.50 5.00
212 Billy Lochead .10 .25
213 Dick Redmond .10 .25
214 Guy Lafleur RB .60 1.50
215 Ian Turnbull RB .10 .25
216 Guy Lafleur RB .60 1.50
217 Steve Shutt RB .30 .75
218 Guy Lafleur RB .60 1.50
219 Lorne Henning .10 .25
220 Terry O'Reilly .30 .75
221 Pat Hickey .10 .25
222 Rene Robert .15 .40
223 Tim Young .10 .25
224 Dunc Wilson .15 .40
225 Dennis Hull .15 .40
226 Rod Seiling .10 .25
227 Bill Barber .30 .75
228 Dennis Polonich RC .10 .25
229 Billy Smith .60 1.50
230 Yvan Cournoyer .30 .75
231 Don Luce .10 .25
232 Mike McEwen RC .10 .25
233 Don Saleski .10 .25
234 Wayne Cashman .30 .75
235 Phil Russell .10 .25
236 Mike Corrigan .10 .25
237 Guy Chouinard .15 .40
238 Steve Jensen RC .10 .25
239 Jim Rutherford .15 .40
240 Marcel Dionne AS1 1.25 2.50
241 Rejean Houle .10 .25
242 Jocelyn Guevremont .10 .25
243 Jim Harrison .10 .25
244 Don Murdoch RC .10 .25
245 Rick Green RC .30 .75
246 Rick Middleton .30 .75
247 Joe Watson .10 .25
248 Syl Apps .10 .25
249 Checklist 133-264 2.00 4.00
250 Clark Gillies .30 .75
251 Bobby Orr 9.00 15.00
252 Nelson Pyatt .10 .25
253 Gary McAdam RC .10 .25
254 Jacques Lemaire .30 .75
255 Bill Fairbairn .10 .25
256 Ron Greschner .15 .40
257 Ross Lonsberry .10 .25
258 Dave Gardner .10 .25
259 Rick Blight .10 .25
260 Gerry Cheevers .30 .75
261 Jean Pronovost .15 .40
262 Semi-Finals .15 .40
Canadiens Skate
Past Islanders
263 Semi-Finals .15 .40
Bruins Advance
to Finals
264 Canadiens Champs .30 .75

1977-78 Topps/O-Pee-Chee Glossy

This set of 22 numbered cards was issued with either square or round corners as an insert with both the Topps and O-Pee-Chee hockey cards of 1977-78. Cards were numbered on the back and measure 2 1/4" by 3 1/4". They are essentially the same as the O-Pee-Chee insert issue of the same year. The O-Pee-Chee inserts have the same card numbers and pictures, same values, but different copyright lines on the reverses. The cards are priced below for the round cornered version; the square cornered cards are worth approximately 10 percent more than the prices below.

COMPLETE SET (22) 7.50 15.00
1 Wayne Cashman .20 .40
2 Gerry Cheevers .75 1.50
3 Bobby Clarke .75 1.50
4 Marcel Dionne .75 1.50
5 Ken Dryden 2.00 4.00
6 Clark Gillies .20 .40
7 Guy Lafleur 1.25 2.50
8 Reggie Leach .18 .35
9 Rick MacLeish .25 .50
10 Dave Maloney .13 .25
11 Richard Martin .20 .40
12 Don Murdoch .13 .25
13 Brad Park .38 .75
14 Gilbert Perreault .50 1.00
15 Denis Potvin .75 1.50
16 Jean Ratelle .38 .75
17 Glenn Resch .38 .75
18 Larry Robinson .75 1.50
19 Steve Shutt .38 .75
20 Darryl Sittler .63 1.25
21 Rogatien Vachon .38 .75
22 Tim Young .13 .25

1978-79 Topps

The 1978-79 Topps set consists of 264 standard-size cards. Card fronts have team name, logo and player position in the top left corner. The player's name is within the top border. A short biography, yearly statistics including minor leagues and a facsimile autograph are included on the back.

COMPLETE SET (264) 40.00 80.00
1 Mike Bossy HL ! 4.00 8.00
2 Phil Esposito HL .40 1.00
3 Guy Lafleur HL .40 1.00
4 Darryl Sittler HL .25 .60
5 Garry Unger HL .05 .15
6 Gary Edwards .08 .25
7 Rick Blight .05 .15
8 Larry Patey .05 .15
9 Craig Ramsay .05 .15
10 Bryan Trottier AS1 2.00 5.00
11 Don Murdoch .05 .15
12 Phil Russell .05 .15
13 Doug Jarvis .08 .25
14 Gene Carr .05 .15
15 Bernie Parent .40 1.00
16 Perry Miller .05 .15
17 Kent-Erik Andersson RC .05 .15
18 Gregg Sheppard .05 .15
19 Dennis Owchar .05 .15
20 Rogatien Vachon .25 .60
21 Dan Maloney .05 .15
22 Guy Charron .05 .15
23 Dick Redmond .05 .15
24 Checklist 1-132 1.00 2.50
25 Anders Hedberg .08 .25
26 Mel Bridgman .08 .25
27 Lee Fogolin .05 .15
28 Gilles Meloche .08 .25
29 Garry Howatt .05 .15
30 Darryl Sittler AS2 .60 1.50
31 Curt Bennett .05 .15
32 Andre St.Laurent .05 .15
33 Blair Chapman .05 .15
34 Keith Magnuson .05 .15
35 Pierre Larouche .25 .60
36 Michel Plasse .08 .25
37 Gary Sargent .05 .15
38 Mike Walton .05 .15
39 Robert Picard RC .05 .15
40 Terry O'Reilly AS2 .08 .25
41 Dave Farrish .05 .15
42 Gary McAdam .05 .15
43 Joe Watson .05 .15
44 Yves Belanger .08 .25
45 Steve Jensen .05 .15
46 Bob Stewart .05 .15
47 Darcy Rota .05 .15
48 Dennis Hextall .05 .15
49 Bert Marshall .05 .15
50 Ken Dryden AS1 2.50 6.00
51 Peter Mahovlich .08 .25
52 Dennis Ververgaert .05 .15
53 Inge Hammarstrom .05 .15
54 Doug Favell .08 .25
55 Steve Vickers .05 .15
56 Syl Apps .05 .15
57 Errol Thompson .05 .15
58 Don Luce .05 .15
59 Mike Milbury .25 .60
60 Yvan Cournoyer .25 .60
61 Kirk Bowman .05 .15
62 Billy Smith .25 .60
63 Goal Leaders 1.50 4.00
Guy Lafleur
Mike Bossy
Steve Shutt
64 Assist Leaders .60 1.50
Bryan Trottier
Guy Lafleur
Darryl Sittler
65 Scoring Leaders .60 1.50
Guy Lafleur
Bryan Trottier
Darryl Sittler
66 Penalty Minutes .10 .30

Leaders
Dave Schultz
Dave(Tiger) Williams
Dennis Polonich
67 Power Play Goal 1.00 2.50
Leaders
Mike Bossy
Phil Esposito
Steve Shutt
68 Goals Against 1.00 2.50
Average Leaders
Ken Dryden
Bernie Parent
Gilles Gilbert
69 Game Winning .50 1.25
Goal Leaders
Guy Lafleur
Bill Barber
Darryl Sittler
Bob Bourne
70 Shutout Leaders 1.00 2.50
Bernie Parent
Ken Dryden
Don Edwards
Tony Esposito
Mike Palmateer
71 Bob Kelly .05 .15
72 Ron Stackhouse .05 .15
73 Wayne Dillon .05 .15
74 Jim Rutherford .08 .25
75 Stan Mikita .60 1.50
76 Bob Gainey .40 1.00
77 Gerry Hart .05 .15
78 Lanny McDonald .40 1.00
79 Brad Park .40 1.00
80 Richard Martin .25 .60
81 Bernie Wolfe .08 .25
82 Bob MacMillan .05 .15
83 Brad Maxwell RC .05 .15
84 Mike Fidler .05 .15
85 Carol Vadnais .05 .15
86 Don Lever .05 .15
87 Phil Myre .08 .25
88 Paul Gardner .05 .15
89 Bob Murray .05 .15
90 Guy Lafleur AS1 1.50 4.00
91 Bob Murdoch .05 .15
92 Ron Ellis .08 .25
93 Jude Drouin .05 .15
94 Jocelyn Guevremont .05 .15
95 Gilles Gilbert .08 .25
96 Bob Sirois .05 .15
97 Tom Lysiak .08 .25
98 Andre Dupont .05 .15
99 Per-Olov Brasar RC .05 .15
100 Phil Esposito .75 2.00
101 J.P. Bordeleau .05 .15
102 Pierre Mondou RC .25 .60
103 Wayne Bianchin .05 .15
104 Dennis O'Brien .05 .15
105 Glenn Resch .25 .60
106 Dennis Polonich .05 .15
107 Kris Manery RC .05 .15
108 Bill Hajt .05 .15
109 Jere Gillis RC .05 .15
110 Garry Unger .08 .25
111 Nick Beverley .05 .15
112 Pat Hickey .05 .15
113 Rick Middleton .25 .60
114 Orest Kindrachuk .05 .15
115 Mike Bossy RC 25.00 50.00
116 Pierre Bouchard .05 .15
117 Alain Daigle .05 .15
118 Terry Martin .05 .15
119 Tom Edur .05 .15
120 Marcel Dionne .75 2.00
121 Barry Beck RC .40 1.00
122 Billy Lochead .05 .15
123 Paul Harrison .08 .25
124 Wayne Cashman .25 .60
125 Rick MacLeish .25 .60
126 Bob Bourne .08 .25
127 Ian Turnbull .05 .15
128 Gerry Meehan .05 .15
129 Eric Vail .05 .15
130 Gilbert Perreault .25 .60
131 Bob Dailey .05 .15
132 Dale McCourt RC .25 .60
133 John Wensink RC .25 .60
134 Bill Nyrop .05 .15
135 Ivan Boldirev .05 .15
136 Lucien DeBlois RC .25 .60
137 Brian Spencer .05 .15
138 Tim Young .05 .15
139 Ron Sedlbauer .05 .15
140 Gerry Cheevers .40 1.00
141 Dennis Maruk .08 .25
142 Barry Dean .05 .15
143 Bernie Federko RC 3.00 6.00
144 Stefan Persson RC .05 .15
145 Wilf Paiement .08 .25
146 Dale Tallon .05 .15
147 Yvon Lambert .05 .15
148 Greg Joly .05 .15
149 Dean Talafous .05 .15
150 Don Edwards AS2 .05 .15
151 Butch Goring .08 .25
152 Tom Bladon .05 .15
153 Bob Nystrom .05 .15
154 Ron Greschner .08 .25
155 Jean Ratelle .25 .60
156 Russ Anderson RC .05 .15
157 John Marks .05 .15
158 Michel Larocque .08 .25
159 Paul Woods RC .05 .15
160 Mike Palmateer .08 .25
161 Jim Lorentz .05 .15
162 Dave Lewis .05 .15
163 Harvey Bennett .05 .15
164 Rick Smith .05 .15
165 Reggie Leach .25 .60
166 Wayne Thomas .08 .25
167 Dave Forbes .05 .15
168 Doug Wilson RC 3.00 6.00
169 Dan Bouchard .08 .25
170 Steve Shutt AS2 .25 .60
171 Mike Kaszycki RC .05 .15
172 Dennis Herron .08 .25
173 Rick Bowness .08 .25
174 Rick Hampton .05 .15
175 Glen Sharpley .05 .15
176 Bill Barber .25 .60
177 Ron Duguay RC .75 2.00
178 Jim Schoenfeld .08 .25
179 Pierre Plante .05 .15
180 Jacques Lemaire .25 .60
181 Stan Jonathan .05 .15
182 Billy Harris .05 .15
183 Chris Oddleifson .05 .15
184 Jean Pronovost .08 .25
185 Fred Barrett .05 .15
186 Ross Lonsberry .05 .15
187 Mike McEwen .05 .15
188 Rene Robert .08 .25
189 J. Bob Kelly .05 .15
190 Serge Savard AS2 .08 .25
191 Dennis Kearns .05 .15
192 Flames Team .20 .50
(checklist back)
193 Bruins Team .20 .50
(checklist back)
194 Sabres Team .20 .50
(checklist back)
195 Blackhawks Team .20 .50
(checklist back)
196 Rockies Team .20 .50
(checklist back)
197 Red Wings Team .20 .50
(checklist back)
198 Kings Team .20 .50
(checklist back)
199 North Stars Team .20 .50
(checklist back)
200 Canadiens Team .20 .50
(checklist back)
201 Islanders Team .20 .50
(checklist back)
202 Rangers Team .20 .50
(checklist back)
203 Flyers Team .20 .50
(checklist back)
204 Penguins Team .20 .50
(checklist back)
205 Blues Team .20 .50
(checklist back)
206 Maple Leafs Team .20 .50
(checklist back)
207 Canucks Team .20 .50
(checklist back)
208 Capitals Team .20 .50
(checklist back)
209 Danny Gare .08 .25
210 Larry Robinson AS1 .60 1.50
211 John Davidson .25 .60
212 Peter McNab .08 .25
213 Rick Kehoe .08 .25
214 Terry Harper .05 .15
215 Bobby Clarke .75 2.00
216 Bryan Maxwell UER .05 .15
217 Ted Bulley .05 .15
218 Red Berenson .08 .25
219 Ron Grahame .08 .25
220 Clark Gillies AS1 .08 .25
221 Dave Maloney .05 .15
222 Derek Smith RC .05 .15
223 Wayne Stephenson .08 .25
224 John Van Boxmeer .05 .15
225 Dave Schultz .08 .25
226 Reed Larson RC .25 .60
227 Rejean Houle .05 .15
228 Doug Hicks .05 .15
229 Mike Murphy .08 .25
230 Pete Lopresti .08 .25
231 Jerry Korab .05 .15
232 Ed Westfall .08 .25
233 Greg Malone RC .08 .25
234 Paul Holmgren .25 .60
235 Walt Tkaczuk .08 .25
236 Don Marcotte .05 .15
237 Ron Low .08 .25
238 Rick Chartraw .05 .15
239 Cliff Koroll .05 .15
240 Borje Salming AS1 .40 1.00
241 Roland Eriksson .05 .15
242 Ric Seiling RC .05 .15
243 Jim Bedard RC .08 .25
244 Peter Lee RC .08 .25
245 Denis Potvin AS2 .60 1.50
246 Greg Polis .05 .15
247 Jimmy Watson .05 .15
248 Bobby Schmautz .05 .15
249 Doug Risebrough .08 .25
250 Tony Esposito .50 1.25
251 Nick Libett .05 .15
252 Ron Zanussi RC .05 .15
253 Andre Savard .05 .15
254 Dave Burrows .05 .15
255 Ulf Nilsson .25 .60
256 Richard Mulhern .05 .15
257 Don Saleski .05 .15
258 Wayne Merrick .05 .15
259 Checklist 133-264 1.00 2.50
260 Guy Lapointe .08 .25
261 Grant Mulvey .05 .15
262 Stanley Cup: Semis .10 .30
Canadiens sweep
Maple Leafs
263 Stanley Cup: Semis .10 .30
Bruins skate
past Flyers
264 Stanley Cup: Finals .40 1.00
Canadiens win 3rd
Straight Cup

1978-79 Topps Team Inserts

This set of 17 team inserts measures the standard size. Each team insert consists of two decals: a team logo and a second decal consisting of three mini-decals. The mini-decals picture hockey equipment (mask, stick(s), or puck), a hockey word (center, defense, goal!, goalie, score! or wing), and a number between zero and nine. The backs are blank. Several different combinations of the stickers are known to exist.

COMPLETE SET (17) 7.50 15.00
1 Atlanta Flames .75 1.50
2 Boston Bruins .75 1.50
3 Buffalo Sabres .50 1.00
4 Chicago Blackhawks .75 1.50
5 Colorado Rockies .75 1.50
6 Detroit Red Wings .75 1.50
7 Los Angeles Kings .50 1.00
8 Minnesota North Stars .50 1.00
9 Montreal Canadiens .75 1.50
10 New York Islanders .50 1.00
11 New York Rangers .75 1.50
12 Philadelphia Flyers .50 1.00
13 Pittsburgh Penguins .50 1.00
14 St. Louis Blues .50 1.00
15 Toronto Maple Leafs .75 1.50
16 Vancouver Canucks .50 1.00
17 Washington Capitals .50 1.00

1979-80 Topps

The 1979-80 Topps set consists of 264 standard-size cards. Card numbers 81 and 82 (Stanley Cup Playoffs), 163 (Ulf Nilsson RB) and 261 (NHL Entries) differ from those of O-Pee-Chee. Unopened packs consist of ten cards plus a piece of bubble gum. The fronts contain a blue border that is prone to chipping. The player's name, team and position are at the top with team logo at the bottom. Career and 1978-79 statistics, short biography and a cartoon-illustrated fact about the player appear on the back. Included in this set are players from the four remaining WHA franchises that were absorbed by the NHL. The franchises are the Edmonton Oilers, Hartford Whalers, Quebec Nordiques and Winnipeg Jets. The set features the Rookie Card of Wayne Gretzky and the last cards of a Hall of Fame crop including Gordie Howe, Bobby Hull, Ken Dryden and Stan Mikita.

COMPLETE SET (264) 400.00 600.00
1 Goal Leaders 1.25 3.00
Mike Bossy
Marcel Dionne
Guy Lafleur
2 Assist Leaders .60 1.50
Bryan Trottier
Guy Lafleur
Marcel Dionne
Bob MacMillan
3 Scoring Leaders .60 1.50
Bryan Trottier
Marcel Dionne
Guy Lafleur
4 Penalty Minutes .15 .40
Leaders
Dave(Tiger) Williams
Randy Holt
Dave Schultz
5 Power Play .75 2.00
Goal Leaders
Mike Bossy
Marcel Dionne
Paul Gardner
Lanny McDonald
6 Goals Against 1.00 2.50
Average Leaders
Ken Dryden
Glenn Resch
Bernie Parent
7 Game Winning 1.00 2.50
Goals Leaders
Guy Lafleur
Mike Bossy
Bryan Trottier
Jean Pronovost
Ted Bulley
8A Shutout Leaders ERR 3.00 8.00
Ken Dryden
Tony Esposito
Mario Lessard
Mike Palmateer
Bernie Parent
(Palmateer and Lessard
photos switched)
8B Shutout Leaders COR 1.25 3.00
Ken Dryden
Tony Esposito
Mario Lessard
Mike Palmateer
Bernie Parent
9 Greg Malone .15 .40
10 Rick Middleton .25 .60
11 Greg Smith .15 .40
12 Rene Robert .25 .60
13 Doug Risebrough .25 .60
14 Bob Kelly .15 .40
15 Walt Tkaczuk .25 .60
16 John Marks .15 .40
17 Willie Huber RC .15 .40
18 Wayne Gretzky RC ! 250.00 550.00
19 Ron Sedlbauer .15 .40
20 Glenn Resch AS2 .25 .60
21 Blair Chapman .15 .40
22 Ron Zanussi .15 .40
23 Brad Park .25 .60
24 Yvon Lambert .15 .40
25 Andre Savard .15 .40
26 Jimmy Watson .15 .40
27 Hal Philipoff RC .15 .40
28 Dan Bouchard .25 .60
29 Bob Sirois .15 .40
30 Ulf Nilsson .25 .60
31 Mike Murphy .15 .40
32 Stefan Persson .15 .40
33 Garry Unger .25 .60
34 Rejean Houle .15 .40
35 Barry Beck .25 .60
36 Tim Young .15 .40
37 Rick Dudley .15 .40
38 Wayne Stephenson .25 .60
39 Peter McNab .25 .60
40 Borje Salming AS2 .25 .60
41 Tom Lysiak .15 .40
42 Don Maloney RC .40 1.00
43 Mike Rogers .25 .60
44 Dave Lewis .15 .40
45 Peter Lee .15 .40
46 Marty Howe .25 .60
47 Serge Bernier .15 .40
48 Paul Woods .15 .40
49 Bob Sauve .25 .60
50 Larry Robinson AS1 .60 1.50
51 Tom Gorence RC .15 .40
52 Gary Sargent .15 .40
53 Thomas Gradin RC .40 1.00
54 Dean Talafous .15 .40
55 Bob Murray .15 .40
56 Bob Bourne .25 .60
57 Larry Patey .15 .40
58 Ross Lonsberry .15 .40
59 Rick Smith .15 .40
60 Guy Chouinard .25 .60
61 Danny Gare .25 .60
62 Jim Bedard .25 .60
63 Dale McCourt .15 .40
64 Steve Payne RC .15 .40
65 Pat Hughes RC .15 .40
66 Mike McEwen .15 .40
67 Reg Kerr RC .15 .40
68 Walt McKechnie .15 .40
69 Michel Plasse .25 .60
70 Denis Potvin AS1 .40 1.00
71 Dave Dryden .25 .60
72 Gary McAdam .15 .40
73 Andre St.Laurent .15 .40
74 Jerry Korab .15 .40
75 Rick MacLeish .40 1.00
76 Dennis Kearns .15 .40
77 Jean Pronovost .25 .60
78 Ron Greschner .25 .60
79 Wayne Cashman .40 1.00
80 Tony Esposito .40 1.00
81 Cup Semi-Finals .15 .40
Canadiens squeak
past Bruins
82 Cup Semi-Finals .15 .40
Rangers upset
Islanders in Six
83 Stanley Cup Finals .15 .40
84 Brian Sutter .75 2.00
85 Gerry Cheevers .40 1.00
86 Pat Hickey .15 .40
87 Mike Kaszycki .15 .40
88 Grant Mulvey .15 .40
89 Derek Smith .15 .40
90 Steve Shutt .40 1.00
91 Robert Picard .15 .40
92 Dan Labraaten .15 .40
93 Glen Sharpley .15 .40
94 Denis Herron .25 .60
95 Reggie Leach .40 1.00
96 John Van Boxmeer .15 .40
97 Dave(Tiger) Williams .25 .60
98 Butch Goring .25 .60
99 Don Marcotte .15 .40
100 Bryan Trottier AS1 1.00 2.50
101 Serge Savard AS2 .40 1.00
102 Cliff Koroll .15 .40
103 Gary Smith .25 .60
104 Al MacAdam .15 .40
105 Don Edwards .25 .60
106 Errol Thompson .15 .40
107 Andre Lacroix .25 .60
108 Marc Tardif .25 .60
109 Rick Kehoe .25 .60
110 John Davidson .25 .60
111 Behn Wilson RC .25 .60
112 Doug Jarvis .25 .60
113 Tom Rowe RC .15 .40
114 Mike Milbury .25 .60
115 Billy Harris .15 .40
116 Greg Fox RC .15 .40
117 Curt Fraser RC .15 .40
118 Jean-Paul Parise .15 .40
119 Ric Seiling .15 .40
120 Darryl Sittler .40 1.00
121 Rick Lapointe .15 .40
122 Jim Rutherford .25 .60
123 Mario Tremblay .25 .60
124 Randy Carlyle .40 1.00
125 Bobby Clarke .60 1.50
126 Wayne Thomas .25 .60
127 Ivan Boldirev .15 .40
128 Ted Bulley .15 .40
129 Dick Redmond .15 .40
130 Clark Gillies AS1 .25 .60
131 Checklist 1-132 2.00 4.00
132 Vaclav Nedomansky .15 .40
133 Richard Mulhern .15 .40
134 Dave Schultz .25 .60
135 Guy Lapointe .25 .60
136 Gilles Meloche .25 .60
137 Randy Pierce RC .15 .40
138 Cam Connor .15 .40
139 George Ferguson .15 .40
140 Bill Barber .25 .60
141 Mike Walton .15 .40
142 Wayne Babych RC .15 .40
143 Phil Russell .15 .40
144 Bobby Schmautz .15 .40
145 Carol Vadnais .15 .40
146 John Tonelli RC 2.00 4.00
147 Peter Marsh RC .15 .40
148 Thommie Bergman .15 .40
149 Richard Martin .40 1.00
150 Ken Dryden AS1 2.00 5.00
151 Kris Manery .15 .40
152 Guy Charron .15 .40
153 Lanny McDonald .25 .60
154 Ron Stackhouse .15 .40
155 Stan Mikita .60 1.50
156 Paul Holmgren .25 .60
157 Perry Miller .15 .40
158 Gary Croteau .15 .40
159 Dave Maloney .15 .40
160 Marcel Dionne AS2 .75 2.00
161 Mike Bossy RB 1.00 2.50
162 Don Maloney RB .15 .40
163 Ulf Nilsson RB .15 .40
164 Brad Park RB .15 .40
165 Bryan Trottier RB .40 1.00
166 Al Hill RC .15 .40
167 Gary Bromley .25 .60
168 Don Murdoch .15 .40
169 Wayne Merrick .15 .40
170 Bob Gainey .40 1.00
171 Jim Schoenfeld .25 .60
172 Gregg Sheppard .15 .40
173 Dan Bolduc RC .15 .40
174 Blake Dunlop .15 .40
175 Gordie Howe 14.00 20.00
176 Richard Brodeur .25 .60
177 Tom Younghans .15 .40
178 Andre Dupont .15 .40
179 Ed Johnstone RC .15 .40
180 Gilbert Perreault .40 1.00
181 Bob Lorimer RC .15 .40
182 John Wensink .15 .40
183 Lee Fogolin .15 .40
184 Greg Carroll RC .15 .40
185 Bobby Hull 10.00 15.00
186 Harold Snepsts .15 .40
187 Peter Mahovlich .25 .60
188 Eric Vail .15 .40
189 Phil Myre .25 .60
190 Wilf Paiement .25 .60
191 Charlie Simmer RC 2.00 4.00
192 Per-Olov Brasar .15 .40
193 Lorne Henning .15 .40
194 Don Luce .15 .40
195 Steve Vickers .15 .40
196 Bob Miller RC .15 .40
197 Mike Palmateer .25 .60
198 Nick Libett .15 .40
199 Pat Ribble RC .15 .40
200 Guy Lafleur AS1 1.25 3.00
201 Mel Bridgman .25 .60
202 Morris Lukowich RC .15 .40
203 Don Lever .15 .40
204 Tom Bladon .15 .40
205 Garry Howatt .15 .40
206 Bobby Smith RC 2.00 4.00
207 Craig Ramsay .25 .60
208 Ron Duguay .25 .60
209 Gilles Gilbert .25 .60
210 Bob MacMillan .15 .40
211 Pierre Mondou .15 .40
212 J.P. Bordeleau .15 .40
213 Reed Larson .25 .60
214 Dennis Ververgaert .15 .40
215 Bernie Federko .40 1.00
216 Mark Howe .75 2.00
217 Bob Nystrom .15 .40
218 Orest Kindrachuk .15 .40
219 Mike Fidler .15 .40
220 Phil Esposito .40 1.00
221 Bill Hajt .15 .40
222 Mark Napier .25 .60
223 Dennis Maruk .25 .60
224 Dennis Polonich .15 .40
225 Jean Ratelle .25 .60
226 Bob Dailey .15 .40
227 Alain Daigle .15 .40
228 Ian Turnbull .15 .40
229 Jack Valiquette .15 .40
230 Mike Bossy AS2 5.00 10.00
231 Brad Maxwell .15 .40
232 Dave Taylor 2.00 5.00
233 Pierre Larouche .40 1.00
234 Rod Schutt RC .15 .40
235 Rogatien Vachon .25 .60
236 Ryan Walter RC .40 1.00
237 Checklist 133-264 2.00 4.00
238 Terry O'Reilly .25 .60
239 Real Cloutier .25 .60
240 Anders Hedberg .25 .60
241 Ken Linseman RC 1.00 2.50
242 Billy Smith .25 .60
243 Rick Chartraw .15 .40
244 Flames Team .60 1.50
245 Bruins Team .60 1.50
246 Sabres Team .60 1.50
247 Blackhawks Team .60 1.50
248 Rockies Team .60 1.50
249 Red Wings Team .60 1.50
250 Kings Team .60 1.50
251 North Stars Team .60 1.50
252 Canadiens Team .60 1.50
253 Islanders Team .60 1.50
254 Rangers Team .60 1.50
255 Flyers Team .60 1.50
256 Penguins Team .60 1.50
257 Blues Team .60 1.50
258 Maple Leafs Team .60 1.50
259 Canucks Team .60 1.50
260 Capitals Team .60 1.50
261 New NHL Entries CL ! 7.00 12.00
262 Jean Hamel .15 .40
263 Stan Jonathan .15 .40
264 Russ Anderson .40 1.00

1979-80 Topps Team Inserts

This set of 21 team inserts measures the standard size, 2 1/2" by 3 1/2". They were issued one per wax pack. Each team insert consists of two decals: a team logo decal, and a second decal that is subdivided into three mini-decals. The three mini-decals picture a pair of hockey sticks, a hockey word (goal, wing, score, defense), and a one-digit number. The horizontally oriented back has an offer for personalized trading cards which expired 12/31/80.

COMPLETE SET (21) 9.00 18.00
1 Atlanta Flames .75 1.50
2 Boston Bruins .75 1.50
3 Buffalo Sabres .50 1.00
4 Chicago Blackhawks .75 1.50
5 Colorado Rockies .75 1.50
6 Detroit Red Wings .75 1.50
7 Edmonton Oilers .75 1.50
8 Hartford Whalers .50 1.00
9 Los Angeles Kings .50 1.00
10 Minnesota North Stars .50 1.00
11 Montreal Canadiens .75 1.50
12 New York Islanders .50 1.00
13 New York Rangers .75 1.50
14 Philadelphia Flyers .50 1.00
15 Pittsburgh Penguins UER .75 1.50
16 Quebec Nordiques .75 1.50
17 St. Louis Blues .50 1.00
18 Toronto Maple Leafs .75 1.50
19 Vancouver Canucks .50 1.00
20 Washington Capitals .50 1.00
21 Winnipeg Jets .50 1.00

1980-81 Topps

The 1980-81 Topps set features 264 standard-size cards. The fronts contain a puck (black ink) at the bottom right which can be scratched-off to reveal the player's name. Yearly statistics including minor leagues, a short biography and a cartoon-illustrated hockey fact are included on the back. Members of the U.S. Olympic team are designated by USA.

COMPLETE SET (264) 150.00 275.00
*SCRATCHED: 25X to .40X
1 Phila. Flyers RB .30 .75
35 Game Streak& Longest in Sports History
2 Ray Bourque RB 5.00 10.00
65 Pts.: Record for
Rookie Defenseman
3 Wayne Gretzky RB 10.00 20.00
Youngest Ever&
50-goal Scorer
4 Charlie Simmer RB .10 .30
Scores in 13th Straight
Game& NHL Record
5 Billy Smith RB .10 .30
First Goalie to
Score a Goal
6 Jean Ratelle .15 .40
7 Dave Maloney .07 .20
8 Phil Myre .15 .40
9 Ken Morrow OLY RC .40 1.00
10 Guy Lafleur .75 2.00
11 Bill Derlago RC .07 .20
12 Doug Wilson .30 .75
13 Craig Ramsay .07 .20
14 Pat Boutette .07 .20
15 Eric Vail .07 .20
16 Mike Foligno .10 .30
Red Wings Scoring Leaders
(checklist back)
17 Bobby Smith .50 1.25
18 Rick Kehoe .15 .40
19 Joel Quenneville .07 .20
20 Marcel Dionne .40 1.00
21 Kevin McCarthy .07 .20
22 Jim Craig OLY RC 2.50 6.00
23 Steve Vickers .07 .20
24 Ken Linseman .15 .40
25 Mike Bossy 1.50 4.00
26 Serge Savard .30 .75
27 Grant Mulvey .10 .30
Blackhawks Scoring Leaders
(checklist back)
28 Pat Hickey .07 .20
29 Peter Sullivan .07 .20
30 Blaine Stoughton .15 .40
31 Mike Liut RC 1.50 4.00
32 Blair MacDonald .07 .20
33 Rick Green .07 .20
34 Al MacAdam .07 .20
35 Robbie Florek .07 .20
36 Dick Redmond .07 .20
37 Ron Duguay .07 .20
38 Danny Gare .10 .30
Sabres Scoring Leaders
(checklist back)
39 Brian Propp RC 1.25 3.00
40 Bryan Trottier .60 1.50
41 Rich Preston .07 .20
42 Pierre Mondou .07 .20
43 Reed Larson .07 .20
44 George Ferguson .07 .20
45 Guy Chouinard .15 .40
46 Billy Harris .07 .20
47 Gilles Meloche .15 .40
48 Blair Chapman .07 .20
49 Mike Gartner 1.50 4.00
Capitals Scoring Leaders
(checklist back)
50 Darryl Sittler .30 .75
51 Richard Martin .15 .40
52 Ivan Boldirev .07 .20
53 Craig Norwich RC .07 .20
54 Dennis Polonich .07 .20
55 Bobby Clarke .40 1.00
56 Terry O'Reilly .15 .40
57 Carol Vadnais .07 .20
58 Bob Gainey .30 .75
59 Blaine Stoughton .10 .30
Whalers Scoring Leaders
(checklist back)
60 Billy Smith .15 .40
61 Mike O'Connell RC .15 .40
62 Lanny McDonald .15 .40
63 Lee Fogolin .07 .20
64 Rocky Saganiuk RC .07 .20
65 Rolf Edberg RC .07 .20
66 Paul Shmyr .07 .20
67 Michel Goulet RC 5.00 10.00
68 Dan Bouchard .15 .40
69 Mark Johnson OLY RC .15 .40
70 Reggie Leach .15 .40
71 Bernie Federko .10 .30
Blues Scoring Leaders
(checklist back)
72 Peter Mahovlich .15 .40
73 Anders Hedberg .15 .40
74 Brad Park .15 .40
75 Clark Gillies .15 .40
76 Doug Jarvis .07 .20
77 John Garrett .15 .40
78 Dave Hutchinson .07 .20
79 John Anderson RC .07 .20
80 Gilbert Perreault .30 .75
81 Marcel Dionne AS1 .30 .75
82 Guy Lafleur AS1 .40 1.00
83 Charlie Simmer AS1 .10 .30
84 Larry Robinson AS1 .10 .30
85 Borje Salming AS1 .10 .30
86 Tony Esposito AS1 .30 .75
87 Wayne Gretzky AS2 12.50 25.00
88 Danny Gare AS2 .10 .30
89 Steve Shutt AS2 .10 .30
90 Barry Beck AS2 .10 .30
91 Mark Howe AS2 .15 .40
92 Don Edwards AS2 .10 .30
93 Tom McCarthy RC .07 .20
94 Peter McNab/Rick Middleton .15 .40
Bruins Scoring Leaders
(checklist back)
95 Mike Palmateer .15 .40
96 Jim Schoenfeld .15 .40
97 Jordy Douglas .07 .20
98 Keith Brown RC .07 .20
99 Dennis Ververgaert .07 .20
100 Phil Esposito .30 .75
101 Jack Brownschidle .07 .20
102 Bob Nystrom .07 .20
103 Steve Christoff OLY RC .10 .30
104 Rob Palmer .07 .20
105 Dave(Tiger) Williams .15 .40
106 Kent Nilsson .10 .30
Flames Scoring Leaders
checklist back)
107 Morris Lukowich .15 .40
108 Jack Valiquette .07 .20
109 Richie Dunn RC .07 .20
110 Rogatien Vachon .15 .40
111 Mark Napier .07 .20
112 Gordie Roberts .07 .20
113 Stan Jonathan .07 .20
114 Brett Callighen .07 .20
115 Rick MacLeish .15 .40
116 Ulf Nilsson .15 .40
117 Rick Kehoe .10 .30
Penguins Scoring Leaders
(checklist back)
118 Dan Maloney .07 .20
119 Terry Ruskowski .07 .20
120 Denis Potvin .40 1.00
121 Wayne Stephenson .15 .40
122 Rich Leduc .07 .20
123 Checklist 1-132 1.50 4.00
124 Don Lever .07 .20
125 Jim Rutherford .15 .40
126 Ray Allison RC .07 .20
127 Mike Ramsey OLY RC .75 2.00
128 Stan Smyl .10 .30
Canucks Scoring Leaders
(checklist back)
129 Al Secord RC 1.00 2.50
130 Denis Herron .15 .40
131 Bob Dailey .07 .20
132 Dean Talafous .07 .20
133 Ian Turnbull .07 .20
134 Ron Sedlbauer .07 .20
135 Tom Bladon .07 .20
136 Bernie Federko .60 1.50
137 Dave Taylor .75 2.00
138 Bob Lorimer .07 .20
139 Al MacAdam/Steve Payne .10 .30
North Stars Scoring Leaders
(checklist back)
140 Ray Bourque RC 40.00 80.00
141 Glen Hanlon .15 .40
142 Willy Lindstrom .07 .20
143 Mike Rogers .07 .20
144 Tony McKegney RC .07 .20
145 Behn Wilson .07 .20
146 Lucien DeBlois .07 .20
147 Dave Burrows .07 .20
148 Paul Woods .07 .20
149 Phil Esposito .30 .75
Rangers Scoring Leaders
(checklist back)
150 Tony Esposito .40 1.00
151 Pierre Larouche .15 .40
152 Brad Maxwell .07 .20
153 Stan Weir .07 .20
154 Ryan Walter .07 .20
155 Dale Hoganson .07 .20
156 Anders Kallur RC .07 .20
157 Paul Reinhart RC .30 .75
158 Greg Millen .15 .40
159 Ric Seiling .07 .20
160 Mark Howe .40 1.00
161 Goals Leaders .10 .30
Danny Gare (1)
Charlie Simmer (1)
Blaine Stoughton (1)
162 Assists Leaders 5.00 10.00

Wayne Gretzky (1)
Marcel Dionne (2)
Guy Lafleur (3)
163 Scoring Leaders 5.00 10.00
Marcel Dionne (1)
Wayne Gretzky (1)
Guy Lafleur (3)
164 Penalty Minutes .10 .30
Leaders
Jimmy Mann (1)
Dave(Tiger) Williams (2)
Paul Holmgren (3)
165 Power Play Goals .10 .30
Leaders
Charlie Simmer (1)
Marcel Dionne (2)
Danny Gare (2)
Steve Shutt (2)
Darryl Sittler (2)
166 Goals Against Average .10 .30
Leaders
Bob Sauve (1)
Denis Herron (2)
Don Edwards (3)
167 Game-Winning Goals .10 .30
Leaders
Danny Gare (1)
Peter McNab (2)
Blaine Stoughton (2)
168 Shutout Leaders .40 1.00
Tony Esposito (1)
Gerry Cheevers (2)
Bob Sauve (2)
Rogatien Vachon (2)
169 Perry Turnbull RC .07 .20
170 Barry Beck .15 .40
171 Charlie Simmer .10 .30
Kings Scoring Leaders
(checklist back)
172 Paul Holmgren .15 .40
173 Willie Huber .07 .20
174 Tim Young .07 .20
175 Gilles Gilbert .15 .40
176 Dave Christian OLY RC .75 2.00
177 Lars Lindgren RC .07 .20
178 Real Cloutier .07 .20
179 Laurie Boschman RC .07 .20
180 Steve Shutt .07 .20
181 Bob Murray .07 .20
182 Wayne Gretzky 7.50 15.00
Oilers Scoring Leaders
(checklist back)
183 John Van Boxmeer .07 .20
184 Nick Fotiu .15 .40
185 Mike McEwen .07 .20
186 Greg Malone .07 .20
187 Mike Foligno RC 1.00 2.50
188 Dave Langevin RC .07 .20
189 Mel Bridgman .07 .20
190 John Davidson .15 .40
191 Mike Milbury .15 .40
192 Ron Zanussi .07 .20
193 Darryl Sittler .10 .30
Maple Leafs Scoring Leaders
(checklist back)
194 John Marks .07 .20
195 Mike Gartner RC 7.50 20.00
196 Dave Lewis .07 .20
197 Kent Nilsson RC 1.25 3.00
198 Rick Ley .07 .20
199 Derek Smith .07 .20
200 Bill Barber .15 .40
201 Guy Lapointe .15 .40
202 Vaclav Nedomansky .07 .20
203 Don Murdoch .07 .20
204 Mike Bossy .40 1.00
Islanders Scoring Leaders
(checklist back)
205 Pierre Hamel RC .30 .75
206 Mike Eaves RC .07 .20
207 Doug Halward .07 .20
208 Stan Smyl RC .30 .75
209 Mike Zuke RC .07 .20
210 Borje Salming .15 .40
211 Walt Tkaczuk .15 .40
212 Grant Mulvey .07 .20
213 Rob Ramage RC .75 2.00
214 Tom Rowe .07 .20
215 Don Edwards .07 .20
216 Guy Lafleur .30 .75
Pierre Larouche
Canadiens Scoring Leaders
(checklist back)
217 Dan Labraaten .07 .20
218 Glen Sharpley .07 .20
219 Stefan Persson .07 .20
220 Peter McNab .07 .20
221 Doug Hicks .07 .20
222 Bengt Gustafsson RC .07 .20
223 Michel Dion .15 .40
224 Jimmy Watson .07 .20
225 Wilf Paiement .07 .20
226 Phil Russell .07 .20
227 Morris Lukowich .10 .30
Jets Scoring Leaders
(checklist back)
228 Ron Stackhouse .07 .20
229 Ted Bulley .07 .20
230 Larry Robinson .30 .75
231 Don Maloney .07 .20
232 Rob McClanahan OLY RC .10 .30
233 Al Sims .07 .20
234 Errol Thompson .07 .20
235 Glenn Resch .15 .40
236 Bob Miller .07 .20
237 Gary Sargent .07 .20
238 Real Cloutier .10 .30
Nordiques Scoring Leaders
(checklist back)
239 Rene Robert .15 .40
240 Charlie Simmer .50 1.25
241 Thomas Gradin .07 .20
242 Rick Vaive RC .75 2.00
243 Ron Wilson RC .07 .20
244 Brian Sutter .15 .40
245 Dale McCourt .07 .20
246 Yvon Lambert .07 .20
247 Tom Lysiak .07 .20
248 Ron Greschner .07 .20
249 Reggie Leach .10 .30
Flyers Scoring Leaders
(checklist back)
250 Wayne Gretzky UER 25.00 60.00
(1978-79 GP should
be 80& not 60)
251 Rick Middleton .15 .40
252 Al Smith .15 .40
253 Fred Barrett .07 .20
254 Butch Goring .15 .40
255 Robert Picard .07 .20
256 Marc Tardif .07 .20
257 Checklist 133-264 1.50 4.00
258 Barry Long .07 .20
259 Rene Robert .10 .30
Rockies Scoring Leaders
(checklist back)
260 Danny Gare .15 .40
261 Rejean Houle .07 .20
262 Stanley Cup Semifinals .10 .30
Islanders-Sabres
263 Stanley Cup Semifinals .10 .30
Flyers-North Stars
264 Stanley Cup Finals .40 1.00
Islanders win 1st

1980-81 Topps Team Posters

The 1980-81 Topps pin-up posters were issued as folded inserts (approximately 5" by 7" horizontal) to the 1980-81 Topps regular hockey issue. These 16 numbered posters are in full color with a white border on very thin stock. The posters feature posed shots (on ice) of the entire 1979-80 hockey team. The name of the team is indicated in large letters to the left of the hockey puck, which contains the designation 1979-80 Season. Fold lines or creases are natural and do not detract from the condition of the poster. For some reason the Edmonton Oilers, Quebec Nordiques, and Winnipeg Jets were not included in this set.

COMPLETE SET (16) 12.50 25.00
1 New York Islanders .60 1.50
2 New York Rangers .75 2.00
3 Philadelphia Flyers .60 1.50
4 Boston Bruins 1.00 2.50
5 Hartford Whalers 1.50 4.00
(Gordie Howe included)
6 Buffalo Sabres .60 1.50
7 Chicago Blackhawks 1.00 2.50
8 Detroit Red Wings 1.00 2.50
9 Minn. North Stars .75 2.00
10 Toronto Maple Leafs 1.00 2.50
11 Montreal Canadiens 1.00 2.50
12 Colorado Rockies 1.00 2.50
13 Los Angeles Kings 1.25 3.00
(Jack Carlson)
14 Vancouver Canucks .60 1.50
15 St. Louis Blues .60 1.50
16 Washington Capitals .60 1.50

1981 Topps Thirst Break

These small premiums were issued as part of a multi-sport themed gum product that was tested in limited parts of the U.S. They actually are wrappers, about the size of a Bazooka Joe comic, and feature a rendition of the player. They are extremely condition sensitive.

43 Gerry Cheevers 3.00 8.00
44 Dave Schultz 2.00 5.00
50 Bobby Hull 4.00 10.00
51 Bobby Hull 4.00 10.00
52 Bobby Hull 4.00 10.00

1981-82 Topps

Topps regionalized distribution of its 198-card standard-size set for 1981-82, and issued two types of wax boxes, commonly referred to as either "East" boxes or "West" boxes. There is no way to differentiate which type of box you have without opening the packs. While the first 66 cards of the set were distributed nationally in both pack types, cards numbered 67 East through 132 East and 67 West through 132 West were distributed regionally. The card fronts contain the Topps logo at the top, with team logo, player name and position at the bottom. The team name appears in large letters placed over the bottom portion of the photo. The backs feature player biographies and yearly statistics including minor leagues. As for the regionally distributed portions of the set, the card numbering is in order by team starting with Boston.

COMPLETE SET (198) 35.00 70.00
1 Dave Babych RC .20 .50
2 Bill Barber .08 .25
3 Barry Beck .08 .25
4 Mike Bossy .75 2.00
5 Ray Bourque 3.00 6.00
6 Guy Chouinard .02 .10
7 Dave Christian .08 .25
8 Bill Derlago .02 .10
9 Marcel Dionne .20 .50
10 Brian Engblom .02 .10
11 Tony Esposito .20 .50
12 Bernie Federko .20 .50
13 Bob Gainey .20 .50
14 Danny Gare .02 .10
15 Thomas Gradin .08 .25
16 Wayne Gretzky UER 8.00 20.00
(1978-79 GP should
be 80& not 60)
17 Rick Kehoe .02 .10
18 Jari Kurri RC 2.50 6.00
19 Guy Lafleur .40 1.00
20 Mike Liut .20 .50
21 Dale McCourt .02 .10
22 Rick Middleton .02 .10
23 Mark Napier .02 .10
24 Kent Nilsson .08 .25
25 Wilf Paiement .02 .10
26 Willi Plett .02 .10
27 Denis Potvin .20 .50
28 Paul Reinhart .02 .10
29 Jacques Richard .02 .10
30 Pat Riggin RC .08 .25
31 Larry Robinson .08 .25
32 Mike Rogers .02 .10
33 Borje Salming .08 .25
34 Steve Shutt .02 .10
35 Charlie Simmer .20 .50
36 Darryl Sittler .20 .50
37 Bobby Smith .08 .25
38 Stan Smyl .02 .10
39 Peter Stastny RC 1.50 4.00
40 Dave Taylor .20 .50
41 Bryan Trottier .20 .50
42 Ian Turnbull .02 .10
43 Eric Vail .02 .10
44 Rick Vaive .08 .25
45 Behn Wilson .02 .10
46 Rick Middleton .08 .25
Bruins Leaders
47 Danny Gare .02 .10
Sabres Leaders
48 Kent Nilsson .02 .10
Flames Leaders
49 Tom Lysiak .02 .10
Blackhawks Leaders
50 Lanny McDonald .08 .25
Rockies Leaders
51 Dale McCourt .02 .10
Red Wings Leaders
52 Wayne Gretzky 1.25 3.00
Oilers Leaders
53 Mike Rogers .02 .10
Whalers Leaders
54 Marcel Dionne .08 .25
Kings Leaders
55 Bobby Smith .08 .25
North Stars Leaders
56 Steve Shutt .08 .25
Canadiens Leaders
57 Mike Bossy .02 .10
Islanders Leaders
58 Anders Hedberg .02 .10
Rangers Leaders
59 Bill Barber .02 .10
Flyers Leaders
60 Rick Kehoe .02 .10
Penguins Leaders
61 Peter Stastny .02 .10
Nordiques Leaders
62 Bernie Federko .08 .25
Blues Leaders
63 Wilf Paiement .02 .10
Maple Leafs Leaders
64 Thomas Gradin .02 .10
Canucks Leaders
65 Dennis Maruk .02 .10
Capitals Leaders
66 Dave Christian .02 .10
Jets Leaders
E67 Dwight Foster .02 .10
E68 Steve Kasper RC .40 1.00
E69 Peter McNab .02 .10
E70 Mike O'Connell .08 .25
E71 Terry O'Reilly .08 .25
E72 Brad Park .08 .25
E73 Dick Redmond .02 .10
E74 Rogatien Vachon .08 .25
E75 Don Edwards .02 .10
E76 Tony McKegney .02 .10
E77 Bob Sauve .08 .25
E78 Andre Savard .02 .10
E79 Derek Smith .02 .10
E80 John Van Boxmeer .02 .10
E81 Pat Boutette .02 .10
E82 Mark Howe .20 .50
E83 Dave Keon .20 .50
E84 Warren Miller RC .02 .10
E85 Al Sims .02 .10
E86 Blaine Stoughton .08 .25
E87 Bob Bourne .02 .10
E88 Clark Gillies .08 .25
E89 Butch Goring .08 .25
E90 Anders Kallur .02 .10
E91 Ken Morrow .08 .25
E92 Stefan Persson .02 .10
E93 Billy Smith .08 .25
E94 Mike Allison RC .02 .10
E95 John Davidson .08 .25
E96 Ron Duguay .02 .10
E97 Ron Greschner .02 .10
E98 Anders Hedberg .08 .25
E99 Ed Johnstone .02 .10
E100 Dave Maloney .02 .10
E101 Don Maloney .02 .10
E102 Ulf Nilsson .08 .25
E103 Bobby Clarke .20 .50
E104 Bob Dailey .02 .10
E105 Paul Holmgren .02 .10
E106 Reggie Leach .08 .25
E107 Ken Linseman .08 .25
E108 Rick MacLeish .08 .25
E109 Pete Peeters .20 .50
E110 Brian Propp .20 .50
E111 Checklist 1-132 .40 1.00
E112 Randy Carlyle .20 .50
E113 Paul Gardner .02 .10
E114 Peter Lee .02 .10
E115 Greg Millen .08 .25
E116 Rod Schutt .02 .10
E117 Mike Gartner 2.50 5.00
E118 Rick Green .02 .10
E119 Bob Kelly .02 .10
E120 Dennis Maruk .08 .25
E121 Mike Palmateer .08 .25
E122 Ryan Walter .02 .10
E123 Bill Barber SA .08 .25
E124 Barry Beck SA .02 .10
E125 Mike Bossy SA .20 .50
E126 Ray Bourque SA 1.00 2.50
E127 Danny Gare SA .02 .10
E128 Rick Kehoe SA .02 .10
E129 Rick Middleton SA .08 .25
E130 Denis Potvin SA .20 .50
E131 Mike Rogers SA .02 .10
E132 Bryan Trottier SA .20 .50
W67 Keith Brown .05 .15
W68 Ted Bulley .05 .15
W69 Tim Higgins RC .05 .15
W70 Reg Kerr .05 .15
W71 Tom Lysiak .05 .15
W72 Grant Mulvey .05 .15
W73 Bob Murray .05 .15
W74 Terry Ruskowski .05 .15
W75 Denis Savard RC 5.00 10.00
W76 Glen Sharpley .05 .15
W77 Darryl Sutter RC .20 .50
W78 Doug Wilson .20 .50
W79 Lucien DeBlois .05 .15
W80 Paul Gagne RC .05 .15
W81 Merlin Malinowski RC .05 .15
W82 Lanny McDonald .08 .25
W83 Joel Quenneville .05 .15
W84 Rob Ramage .02 .10
W85 Glenn Resch .08 .25
W86 Steve Tambellini .05 .15
W87 Mike Foligno .20 .50
W88 Gilles Gilbert .08 .25
W89 Willie Huber .05 .15
W90 Mark Kirton RC .05 .15
W91 Jim Korn RC .05 .15
W92 Reed Larson .02 .10
W93 Gary McAdam .05 .15
W94 Vaclav Nedomansky .05 .15
W95 John Ogrodnick .20 .50
W96 Billy Harris .05 .15
W97 Jerry Korab .05 .15
W98 Mario Lessard .08 .25
W99 Don Luce .05 .15
W100 Larry Murphy RC 4.00 8.00
W101 Mike Murphy .05 .15
W102 Kent-Erik Andersson .05 .15
W103 Don Beaupre RC 1.25 3.00
W104 Steve Christoff .05 .15
W105 Dino Ciccarelli RC 5.00 10.00
W106 Craig Hartsburg .02 .10
W107 Al MacAdam .05 .15
W108 Tom McCarthy .05 .15
W109 Gilles Meloche .08 .25
W110 Steve Payne .05 .15
W111 Gordie Roberts .02 .10
W112 Greg Smith .05 .15
W113 Tim Young .05 .15
W114 Wayne Babych .05 .15
W115 Blair Chapman .05 .15
W116 Tony Currie .05 .15
W117 Blake Dunlop .05 .15
W118 Ed Kea .05 .15
W119 Rick Lapointe .05 .15
W120 Checklist 1-132 .60 1.50
W121 Jorgen Pettersson RC .05 .15
W122 Brian Sutter .08 .25
W123 Perry Turnbull .05 .15
W124 Mike Zuke .05 .15
W125 Marcel Dionne SA .20 .50
W126 Tony Esposito SA .20 .50
W127 Bernie Federko SA .08 .25
W128 Mike Liut SA .08 .25
W129 Dale McCourt SA .05 .15
W130 Charlie Simmer SA .05 .15
W131 Bobby Smith SA .05 .15
W132 Dave Taylor SA .20 .50

1984-85 Topps

After a two year hiatus, Topps returned to hockey with a set of 165 standard size cards. The set contains 66 single print cards which are noted in the checklist by SP. Teams from the United States have a greater player representation than the Canadian teams. Card fronts (much like 1983 Topps baseball) are color coordinated by team and feature two photos. A small photo at bottom right has player name, position and team name to the left. Card backs contain complete career statistics. Cards are in team order starting with Boston.

COMPLETE SET (165) 25.00 50.00
1 Ray Bourque .75 2.00
2 Keith Crowder SP .07 .20
3 Tom Fergus .02 .10
4 Doug Keans RC .02 .10
5 Gord Kluzak SP .07 .20
6 Mike Krushelnyski SP .07 .20
7 Nevin Markwart RC .02 .10
8 Rick Middleton .05 .15
9 Mike O'Connell .02 .10
10 Terry O'Reilly SP .07 .20
11 Barry Pederson .02 .10
12 Pete Peeters .05 .15
13 Dave Andreychuk SP RC 2.00 5.00
14 Tom Barrasso RC 1.25 3.00
15 Real Cloutier SP .07 .20
16 Mike Foligno .05 .15
17 Bill Hajt SP .07 .20
18 Phil Housley SP RC .40 1.00
19 Gilbert Perreault .05 .15
20 Larry Playfair SP .07 .20
21 Craig Ramsay SP .07 .20
22 Mike Ramsey .05 .15
23 Lindy Ruff SP .07 .20
24 Ed Beers .02 .10
25 Rejean Lemelin SP .05 .15
26 Lanny McDonald .05 .15
27 Murray Bannerman .05 .15
28 Keith Brown SP .07 .20
29 Curt Fraser .02 .10
30 Steve Larmer .60 1.50
31 Tom Lysiak .02 .10
32 Bob Murray .02 .10
33 Jack O'Callahan SP RC .07 .20
34 Rich Preston .02 .10
35 Denis Savard .08 .25
36 Darryl Sutter .02 .10
37 Doug Wilson .05 .15
38 Ivan Boldirev .02 .10
39 Colin Campbell SP .07 .20
40 Ron Duguay SP .07 .20
41 Dwight Foster SP .07 .20
42 Danny Gare SP .07 .20
43 Ed Johnstone .02 .10
44 Reed Larson SP .07 .20
45 Eddie Mio SP .07 .20
46 John Ogrodnick .02 .10
47 Brad Park .05 .15
48 Greg Stefan SP RC .07 .20
49 Steve Yzerman RC 15.00 40.00
50 Paul Coffey .75 2.00
51 Wayne Gretzky 4.00 8.00
52 Jari Kurri .50 1.25
53 Bob Crawford RC .02 .10
54 Ron Francis .60 1.50
55 Marty Howe .02 .10
56 Mark Johnson SP .07 .20
57 Greg Malone SP .07 .20
58 Greg Millen SP .07 .20
59 Ray Neufeld .02 .10
60 Joel Quenneville SP .07 .20
61 Risto Siltanen .02 .10
62 Sylvain Turgeon RC .05 .15
63 Mike Zuke SP .07 .20
64 Marcel Dionne .08 .25
65 Brian Engblom SP .07 .20
66 Jim Fox SP .07 .20
67 Bernie Nicholls .30 .75
68 Terry Ruskowski SP .07 .20
69 Charlie Simmer .05 .15
70 Don Beaupre .05 .15
71 Brian Bellows .20 .50
72 Neal Broten SP .07 .20
73 Dino Ciccarelli .08 .25
74 Paul Holmgren SP .07 .20
75 Al MacAdam SP .07 .20
76 Dennis Maruk .05 .15
77 Brad Maxwell SP .07 .20
78 Tom McCarthy SP .07 .20
79 Gilles Meloche SP .07 .20
80 Steve Payne .02 .10
81 Guy Lafleur .08 .25
82 Larry Robinson .08 .25
83 Bobby Smith .05 .15
84 Mel Bridgman .02 .10
85 Joe Cirella .02 .10
86 Don Lever .02 .10
87 Dave Lewis .02 .10
88 Jan Ludvig RC .02 .10
89 Glenn Resch .05 .15
90 Pat Verbeek RC 2.00 5.00
91 Mike Bossy .20 .50
92 Bob Bourne .02 .10
93 Greg Gilbert RC .02 .10
94 Clark Gillies SP .07 .20
95 Butch Goring SP .07 .20
96 Pat LaFontaine SP RC 3.00 8.00
97 Ken Morrow .02 .10
98 Bob Nystrom SP .07 .20
99 Stefan Persson SP .07 .20
100 Denis Potvin .05 .15
101 Billy Smith SP .08 .25
102 Brent Sutter SP .08 .25
103 John Tonelli .05 .15
104 Bryan Trottier .08 .25
105 Barry Beck .02 .10
106 Glen Hanlon SP .07 .20
107 Anders Hedberg SP .07 .20
108 Pierre Larouche SP .05 .15
109 Don Maloney SP .07 .20
110 Mark Osborne SP .07 .20
111 Larry Patey .02 .10
112 James Patrick RC .08 .25
113 Mark Pavelich SP .07 .20
114 Mike Rogers SP .07 .20
115 Reijo Ruotsalainen SP .07 .20
116 Peter Sundstrom SP RC .07 .20
117 Bob Froese .05 .15
118 Mark Howe .05 .15
119 Tim Kerr SP .05 .15
120 Dave Poulin RC .40 1.00
121 Darryl Sittler SP .08 .25
122 Ron Sutter RC .08 .25
123 Mike Bullard SP .07 .20
124 Ron Flockhart SP .07 .20
125 Rick Kehoe .05 .15
126 Kevin McCarthy SP .07 .20
127 Mark Taylor .02 .10
128 Dan Bouchard SP .07 .20
129 Michel Goulet .08 .25
130 Peter Stastny SP .08 .25
131 Bernie Federko .05 .15
132 Mike Liut .05 .15
133 Joe Mullen SP .40 1.00
134 Rob Ramage .02 .10
135 Brian Sutter .05 .15
136 John Anderson SP .07 .20
137 Dan Daoust .02 .10
138 Rick Vaive .02 .10
139 Darcy Rota SP .07 .20
140 Stan Smyl SP .07 .20
141 Tony Tanti .02 .10
142 Dave Christian SP .07 .20
143 Mike Gartner SP .60 1.50
144 Bengt Gustafsson SP .07 .20
145 Doug Jarvis .02 .10
146 Al Jensen .02 .10
147 Rod Langway .08 .25
148 Pat Riggin .05 .15
149 Scott Stevens SP .75 2.00
150 Dave Babych .02 .10
151 Laurie Boschman .02 .10
152 Dale Hawerchuk .40 1.00
153 Michel Goulet AS .05 .15
154 Wayne Gretzky AS 1.00 2.50
155 Mike Bossy AS .08 .25
156 Rod Langway AS .02 .10
157 Ray Bourque AS .08 .25
158 Tom Barrasso AS .20 .50
159 Mark Messier AS .08 .25
160 Bryan Trottier AS .08 .25
161 Jari Kurri AS .08 .25
162 Denis Potvin AS .05 .15
163 Paul Coffey AS .08 .25
164 Pat Riggin AS .02 .10
165 Checklist 1-165 SP .60 1.50

1985-86 Topps

This set of 165 standard-size cards is very similar to Topps' hockey set of the previous season in that there are 66 single prints. The single prints are noted in the checklist by SP. Unopened packs consist of 12 cards plus one sticker and a piece of bubble gum. The fronts have player name and position at the bottom with the team logo at the top right or left. Backs contain complete career statistics and personal notes. The key Rookie Card is Mario Lemieux.

COMPLETE SET (165) 125.00 225.00
1 Lanny McDonald .40 1.00
2 Mike O'Connell SP .20 .50
3 Curt Fraser SP .20 .50
4 Steve Penney .08 .25
5 Brian Engblom .08 .25
6 Ron Sutter .08 .25
7 Joe Mullen .40 1.00
8 Rod Langway .08 .25
9 Mario Lemieux RC ! 60.00 150.00
10 Dave Babych .08 .25
11 Bob Nystrom .08 .25
12 Andy Moog SP 1.00 2.50
13 Dino Ciccarelli .40 1.00
14 Dwight Foster SP .20 .50
15 James Patrick SP .40 1.00
16 Thomas Gradin SP .20 .50
17 Mike Foligno .20 .50
18 Mario Gosselin RC .20 .50
19 Mike Zuke SP .20 .50
20 John Anderson SP .20 .50
21 Dave Pichette .08 .25
22 Nick Fotiu SP .20 .50
23 Tom Lysiak .08 .25
24 Peter Zezel RC .40 1.00
25 Denis Potvin .20 .50
26 Bob Carpenter .08 .25
27 Murray Bannerman SP .20 .50
28 Gordie Roberts SP .20 .50
29 Steve Yzerman 8.00 20.00
30 Phil Russell .08 .25
31 Peter Stastny .40 1.00
32 Craig Ramsay SP .20 .50
33 Terry Ruskowski SP .20 .50
34 Kevin Dineen SP RC 1.25 3.00
35 Mark Howe .20 .50
36 Glenn Resch .20 .50
37 Danny Gare SP .20 .50
38 Doug Bodger RC .20 .50
39 Mike Rogers .08 .25
40 Ray Bourque 1.50 4.00
41 John Tonelli .20 .50
42 Mel Bridgman .08 .25
43 Sylvain Turgeon SP .20 .50
44 Mark Johnson .08 .25
45 Doug Wilson .20 .50
46 Mike Gartner .40 1.00
47 Brent Peterson .08 .25
48 Paul Reinhart SP .20 .50
49 Mike Krushelnyski .08 .25
50 Brian Bellows .40 1.00
51 Chris Chelios 1.50 4.00
52 Barry Pederson SP .20 .50
53 Murray Craven SP .20 .50
54 Pierre Larouche SP .20 .50
55 Reed Larson .08 .25
56 Pat Verbeek SP .20 .50
57 Randy Carlyle .08 .25
58 Ray Neufeld SP .20 .50
59 Keith Brown SP .20 .50
60 Bryan Trottier .40 1.00
61 Jim Fox SP .20 .50
62 Scott Stevens .40 1.00
63 Phil Housley .40 1.00
64 Rick Middleton .20 .50
65 Steve Payne .08 .25
66 Dave Lewis .08 .25
67 Mike Bullard .08 .25
68 Stan Smyl SP .20 .50
69 Mark Pavelich SP .20 .50
70 John Ogrodnick .08 .25
71 Bill Derlago SP .20 .50
72 Brad Marsh SP .40 1.00
73 Denis Savard .40 1.00
74 Mark Fusco RC .08 .25
75 Pete Peeters .20 .50
76 Doug Gilmour 3.00 6.00
77 Mike Ramsey .08 .25
78 Anton Stastny SP .20 .50
79 Steve Kasper SP .20 .50
80 Bryan Erickson SP RC .20 .50
81 Clark Gillies .20 .50
82 Keith Acton .08 .25
83 Pat Flatley .20 .50
84 Kirk Muller RC ! 1.00 2.50
85 Paul Coffey 1.25 3.00
86 Ed Olczyk RC .30 .75
87 Charlie Simmer SP .40 1.00
88 Mike Liut .08 .25
89 Dave Maloney .20 .50
90 Marcel Dionne .20 .50
91 Tim Kerr .20 .50
92 Ivan Boldirev SP .20 .50
93 Ken Morrow SP .20 .50
94 Don Maloney SP .20 .50
95 Rejean Lemelin .08 .25
96 Curt Giles .08 .25
97 Bob Bourne .08 .25
98 Joe Cirella .08 .25
99 Dave Christian SP .20 .50
100 Darryl Sutter .08 .25
101 Kelly Kisio .20 .50
102 Mats Naslund .20 .50
103 Joel Quenneville SP .20 .50
104 Bernie Federko .20 .50
105 Tom Barrasso .40 1.00
106 Rick Vaive .08 .25
107 Brent Sutter .08 .25
108 Wayne Babych .08 .25
109 Dale Hawerchuk .40 1.00
110 Pelle Lindbergh SP 5.00 10.00
111 Dennis Maruk SP .40 1.00
112 Reijo Ruotsalainen SP .20 .50
113 Tom Fergus SP .20 .50
114 Bob Murray SP .20 .50
115 Patrik Sundstrom .08 .25
116 Ron Duguay SP .40 1.00
117 Alan Haworth SP .20 .50
118 Greg Malone .08 .25
119 Bill Hajt .08 .25
120 Wayne Gretzky 10.00 20.00
121 Craig Redmond .08 .25
122 Kelly Hrudey RC 1.25 3.00
123 Tomas Sandstrom RC 1.25 3.00
124 Neal Broten .20 .50
125 Moe Mantha SP .20 .50
126 Greg Gilbert SP .20 .50
127 Bruce Driver SP RC .40 1.00
128 Dave Poulin .20 .50
129 Morris Lukowich SP .20 .50
130 Mike Bossy .50 1.25
131 Larry Playfair SP .20 .50
132 Steve Larmer .40 1.00
133 Doug Keans SP .20 .50
134 Bob Manno .08 .25
135 Brian Sutter .08 .25
136 Pat Riggin .20 .50
137 Pat LaFontaine 1.25 3.00
138 Barry Beck SP .20 .50
139 Rich Preston SP .20 .50
140 Ron Francis 1.00 2.50
141 Brian Propp SP .40 1.00
142 Don Beaupre .20 .50
143 Dave Andreychuk SP .40 1.00
144 Ed Beers .08 .25
145 Paul MacLean .08 .25
146 Troy Murray SP .20 .50
147 Larry Robinson .20 .50
148 Bernie Nicholls .40 1.00
149 Glen Hanlon SP .40 1.00
150 Michel Goulet .40 1.00
151 Doug Jarvis SP .20 .50
152 Warren Young .08 .25
153 Tony Tanti .08 .25
154 Tomas Jonsson SP .20 .50
155 Jari Kurri .75 2.00
156 Tony McKegney .08 .25
157 Greg Stefan SP .40 1.00
158 Brad McCrimmon SP .40 1.00
159 Keith Crowder SP .20 .50
160 Gilbert Perreault .20 .50
161 Tim Bothwell SP .20 .50
162 Bob Crawford SP .20 .50
163 Paul Gagne SP .20 .50
164 Dan Daoust SP .20 .50
165 Checklist 1-165 SP 1.00 2.50

1985-86 Topps Box Bottoms

This 16-card standard-size set was issued in sets of four on the bottom of the 1985-86 Topps wax pack boxes. Complete box bottom panels are valued at a 25 percent premium above the prices listed below. The back, written in English, includes statistical information. The cards are lettered rather than numbered. The key card in the set is Mario Lemieux, pictured in his Rookie Card year.

COMPLETE SET (16) 26.00 65.00
A Brian Bellows .25 .60
B Ray Bourque 1.00 2.50
C Bob Carpenter .15 .40
D Chris Chelios 1.50 4.00
E Marcel Dionne .50 1.25
F Ron Francis 1.00 2.50
G Wayne Gretzky 10.00 25.00
H Tim Kerr .15 .40
I Mario Lemieux 20.00 50.00
J John Ogrodnick .15 .40
K Gilbert Perreault .30 .75
L Glenn Resch .25 .60
M Reijo Ruotsalainen .15 .40
N Brian Sutter .25 .60
O John Tonelli .15 .40
P Doug Wilson .25 .60

1985-86 Topps Sticker Inserts

This set of 33 "Hockey Helmet Stickers" features stickers of 12 All-Star players (1-12) and 21 stickers of team logos, pucks, and numbers. The stickers were inserted in with the 1985-86 Topps hockey regular issue wax packs and as such are also 2 1/2" by 3 1/2". The card backs are printed in blue and red on white card stock. These stickers were also included in some O-Pee-Chee packs that year, which may explain why this particular year of stickers is relatively plentiful. The last seven team stickers can be found with the team logos on the top or bottom.

COMPLETE SET (33) 8.00 20.00
1 John Ogrodnick .08 .25
2 Wayne Gretzky 4.00 10.00
3 Jari Kurri .40 1.00
4 Paul Coffey .60 1.50
5 Ray Bourque .60 1.50
6 Pelle Lindbergh 1.50 4.00
7 John Tonelli .08 .25
8 Dale Hawerchuk .30 .75
9 Mike Bossy .40 1.00
10 Rod Langway .08 .25
11 Doug Wilson .08 .25
12 Tom Barrasso .15 .40
13 Toronto Maple Leafs .08 .25
14 Buffalo Sabres .05 .15
15 Detroit Red Wings .08 .25
16 Pittsburgh Penguins .05 .15
17 New York Rangers .08 .25
18 Calgary Flames .05 .15
19 Winnipeg Jets .05 .15
20 Quebec Nordiques .08 .25
21 Chicago Blackhawks .08 .25
22 Los Angeles Kings .05 .15
23 Montreal Canadiens .08 .25
24 Vancouver Canucks .05 .15
25 Hartford Whalers .05 .15
26 Philadelphia Flyers .05 .15
27 New Jersey Devils .05 .15
28 St. Louis Blues .05 .15
29 Minnesota North Stars .05 .15
30 Washington Capitals .05 .15
31 Boston Bruins .08 .25
32 New York Islanders .05 .15
33 Edmonton Oilers .05 .15

1986-87 Topps

This set of 198 cards measures the standard size. There are 66 double prints that are noted in the checklist by DP. Card fronts feature player name, team, team logo and position at the bottom with a team colored stripe up the right border. Card backs contain complete career statistics and career highlights. The key Rookie Card in this set is Patrick Roy.

COMPLETE SET (198) 90.00 150.00
1 Ray Bourque 1.00 2.50
2 Pat LaFontaine DP .60 1.50
3 Wayne Gretzky 10.00 20.00
4 Lindy Ruff .05 .15
5 Brad McCrimmon .05 .15
6 Dave(Tiger) Williams .15 .40
7 Denis Savard DP .15 .40
8 Lanny McDonald .05 .15
9 John Vanbiesbrouck DP RC 6.00 12.00
10 Greg Adams RC .40 1.00
11 Steve Yzerman 7.50 15.00
12 Craig Hartsburg .05 .15
13 John Anderson DP .05 .15
14 Bob Bourne DP .05 .15
15 Kjell Dahlin RC .05 .15
16 Dave Andreychuk .40 1.00
17 Rob Ramage DP .05 .15
18 Ron Greschner DP .05 .15
19 Bruce Driver .05 .15
20 Peter Stastny .15 .40
21 Dave Christian .30 .75
22 Doug Keans .05 .15
23 Scott Bjugstad RC .05 .15
24 Doug Bodger DP .05 .15
25 Troy Murray DP .05 .15
26 Al Iafrate .40 1.00
27 Kelly Hrudey .40 1.00
28 Doug Jarvis .05 .15
29 Rich Sutter .05 .15
30 Marcel Dionne .15 .40
31 Curt Fraser .05 .15
32 Doug Lidster .05 .15
33 Brian MacLellan .05 .15
34 Barry Pederson .05 .15
35 Craig Laughlin .05 .15
36 Ilkka Sinisalo DP .05 .15
37 John MacLean RC 1.00 2.50
38 Brian Mullen .05 .15
39 Duane Sutter DP .05 .15
40 Brian Engblom .05 .15
41 Chris Cichocki .05 .15
42 Gordie Roberts .05 .15
43 Ron Francis .60 1.50
44 Joe Mullen .40 1.00
45 Moe Mantha DP .05 .15
46 Pat Verbeek .05 .15
47 Clint Malarchuk RC .40 1.00
48 Bob Brooke DP .05 .15
49 Darryl Sutter DP .05 .15
50 Stan Smyl DP .05 .15
51 Greg Stefan .15 .40
52 Bill Hajt DP .05 .15
53 Patrick Roy RC 40.00 100.00
54 Gord Kluzak .05 .15
55 Bob Froese DP .05 .15
56 Grant Fuhr 1.00 2.50
57 Mark Hunter DP .05 .15
58 Dana Murzyn RC .05 .15
59 Mike Gartner .40 1.00
60 Dennis Maruk .05 .15
61 Rich Preston .05 .15
62 Larry Robinson DP .05 .15
63 Dave Taylor DP .05 .15
64 Bob Murray DP .05 .15
65 Ken Morrow .05 .15
66 Mike Ridley RC .40 1.00
67 John Tucker RC .05 .15
68 Miroslav Frycer .05 .15
69 Danny Gare .15 .40
70 Randy Burridge RC .40 1.00
71 Dave Poulin .05 .15
72 Brian Sutter .15 .40
73 Dave Babych .05 .15
74 Dale Hawerchuk DP .40 1.00
75 Brian Bellows .05 .15
76 Dave Pasin DP RC .05 .15
77 Pete Peeters DP .05 .15
78 Tomas Jonsson DP .05 .15
79 Gilbert Perreault DP .05 .15
80 Glenn Anderson DP .40 1.00
81 Don Maloney .05 .15
82 Ed Olczyk DP .05 .15
83 Mike Bullard DP .05 .15
84 Tom Fergus .05 .15
85 Dave Lewis .05 .15
86 Brian Propp .15 .40
87 John Ogrodnick .05 .15
88 Kevin Dineen DP .40 1.00
89 Don Beaupre .15 .40
90 Mike Bossy DP .50 1.25
91 Tom Barrasso DP .05 .15
92 Michel Goulet DP .05 .15
93 Doug Gilmour 1.25 3.00
94 Kirk Muller .40 1.00
95 Larry Melnyk DP RC .05 .15
96 Bob Gainey DP .40 1.00
97 Steve Kasper .05 .15
98 Petr Klima RC .15 .40
99 Neal Broten DP .05 .15
100 Al Secord DP .05 .15
101 Bryan Erickson DP .05 .15
102 Rejean Lemelin .05 .15
103 Sylvain Turgeon .05 .15
104 Bob Nystrom .05 .15
105 Bernie Federko .15 .40
106 Doug Wilson DP .05 .15
107 Alan Haworth .05 .15
108 Jari Kurri .60 1.50
109 Ron Sutter .05 .15
110 Reed Larson DP .05 .15
111 Terry Ruskowski DP .05 .15
112 Mark Johnson DP .05 .15
113 James Patrick .05 .15
114 Paul MacLean .05 .15
115 Mike Ramsey DP .05 .15
116 Kelly Kisio DP .05 .15
117 Brent Sutter .05 .15
118 Joel Quenneville .05 .15
119 Curt Giles DP .05 .15
120 Tony Tanti DP .05 .15
121 Doug Sulliman DP .05 .15
122 Mario Lemieux 15.00 30.00
123 Mark Howe DP .05 .15
124 Bob Sauve .15 .40
125 Anton Stastny .05 .15
126 Scott Stevens DP .40 1.00
127 Mike Foligno .05 .15
128 Reijo Ruotsalainen DP .05 .15
129 Denis Potvin .15 .40
130 Keith Crowder .05 .15
131 Bob Janecyk DP .05 .15
132 John Tonelli .05 .15
133 Mike Liut DP .05 .15
134 Tim Kerr DP .05 .15
135 Al Jensen .05 .15
136 Mel Bridgman .05 .15
137 Paul Coffey DP .60 1.50
138 Dino Ciccarelli DP .15 .40
139 Steve Larmer .40 1.00
140 Mike O'Connell .05 .15
141 Clark Gillies .15 .40
142 Phil Russell DP .05 .15
143 Dirk Graham DP RC .40 1.00
144 Randy Carlyle .05 .15
145 Charlie Simmer .05 .15
146 Ron Flockhart DP .05 .15
147 Tom Laidlaw .05 .15
148 Dave Tippett RC .05 .15
149 Wendel Clark DP RC 3.00 8.00
150 Bob Carpenter DP .05 .15
151 Bill Watson RC .05 .15
152 Roberto Romano DP RC .05 .15
153 Doug Shedden .05 .15
154 Phil Housley .40 1.00
155 Bryan Trottier .40 1.00
156 Patrik Sundstrom DP .05 .15
157 Rick Middleton DP .05 .15
158 Glenn Resch .15 .40
159 Bernie Nicholls DP .40 1.00
160 Ray Ferraro RC 1.00 2.50
161 Mats Naslund DP .05 .15
162 Pat Flatley DP .05 .15
163 Joe Cirella .05 .15
164 Rod Langway DP .05 .15
165 Checklist 1-99 .40 1.00
166 Carey Wilson .05 .15
167 Murray Craven .05 .15
168 Paul Gillis RC .05 .15
169 Borje Salming .05 .15
170 Perry Turnbull .05 .15
171 Chris Chelios 1.25 3.00
172 Keith Acton .05 .15
173 Al MacInnis 2.00 5.00
174 Russ Courtnall RC 1.00 2.50
175 Brad Marsh .05 .15
176 Guy Carbonneau .15 .40
177 Ray Neufeld .05 .15
178 Craig MacTavish RC .40 1.00
179 Rick Lanz .05 .15
180 Murray Bannerman .05 .15
181 Brent Ashton .05 .15
182 Jim Peplinski .05 .15
183 Mark Napier .05 .15
184 Laurie Boschman .05 .15
185 Larry Murphy .15 .40
186 Mark Messier .40 1.00
187 Risto Siltanen .05 .15
188 Bobby Smith .15 .40
189 Gary Suter RC .75 2.00
190 Peter Zezel .05 .15
191 Rick Vaive .05 .15
192 Dale Hunter .15 .40
193 Mike Krushelnyski .05 .15
194 Scott Arniel .05 .15
195 Larry Playfair .05 .15
196 Doug Risebrough .05 .15
197 Kevin Lowe .05 .15
198 Checklist 100-198 .40 1.00

1986-87 Topps Box Bottoms

This sixteen-card standard-size set was issued in sets of four on the bottom of the 1986-87 Topps wax pack boxes. Complete box bottom panels are valued at a 25 percent premium above the prices listed below. The front presents a color action photo with various color borders, with the team's logo in the lower right hand corner. The back includes statistical information, is written in English, and is printed on blue with black ink. The cards are lettered rather than numbered.

COMPLETE SET (16) 14.00 35.00
A Greg Adams .20 .50
B Mike Bossy .40 1.00
C Dave Christian .08 .25
D Mike Foligno .08 .25
E Michel Goulet .20 .50
F Wayne Gretzky 6.00 15.00
G Tim Kerr .08 .25
H Jari Kurri .60 1.50
I Mario Lemieux 8.00 20.00
J Lanny McDonald .20 .50
K Bernie Nicholls .20 .50
L Mike Ridley .20 .50
M Larry Robinson .20 .50
N Denis Savard .20 .50
O Brian Sutter .08 .25
P Bryan Trottier .30 .75

1986-87 Topps Sticker Inserts

This set of 33 "Hockey Helmet Stickers" features stickers of 12 All-Star players (1-12) and 21 stickers of team logos, pucks, and numbers. The stickers were inserted in with the 1986-87 Topps hockey regular issue wax packs and as such are also 2 1/2" by 3 1/2". The card backs are printed in blue and red on white card stock. The last seven team stickers can be found with the team logos on the top or bottom.

COMPLETE SET (33) 12.00 30.00
1 John Vanbiesbrouck 3.00 8.00
2 Michel Goulet .20 .50
3 Wayne Gretzky 4.00 10.00
4 Mike Bossy .40 1.00
5 Paul Coffey .60 1.50
6 Mark Howe .15 .40
7 Bob Froese .15 .40
8 Mats Naslund .15 .40
9 Mario Lemieux 4.00 10.00
10 Jari Kurri .60 1.50
11 Ray Bourque .75 2.00
12 Larry Robinson .20 .50
13 Toronto Maple Leafs .08 .25
14 Buffalo Sabres .05 .15
15 Detroit Red Wings .08 .25
16 Pittsburgh Penguins .05 .15
17 New York Rangers .08 .25
18 Calgary Flames .05 .15
19 Winnipeg Jets .05 .15
20 Quebec Nordiques .05 .15
21 Chicago Blackhawks .08 .25
22 Los Angeles Kings .05 .15
23 Montreal Canadiens .08 .25
24 Vancouver Canucks .05 .15
25 Hartford Whalers .05 .15
26 Philadelphia Flyers .05 .15
27 New Jersey Devils .05 .15
28 St. Louis Blues .05 .15
29 Minnesota North Stars .05 .15
30 Washington Capitals .05 .15
31 Boston Bruins .08 .25
32 New York Islanders .05 .15
33 Edmonton Oilers .05 .15

1987-88 Topps

The 1987-88 Topps hockey set contains 198 standard size cards. There are 66 double printed cards which are indicated by DP below. Again, unopened packs had 12 cards plus one sticker and a piece of gum. The fronts feature a design that includes a hockey stick at the bottom with which the player's name is located. At bottom right, the team name appears in a large puck. The card backs contain career statistics, game winning goals from 1986-87 and highlights.

COMPLETE SET (198) 60.00 120.00
1 Denis Potvin DP .08 .25
2 Rick Tocchet RC 3.00 6.00
3 Dave Andreychuk .20 .50
4 Stan Smyl .08 .25
5 Dave Babych DP .01 .05
6 Pat Verbeek .02 .10
7 Esa Tikkanen RC 1.50 4.00
8 Mike Ridley .08 .25
9 Randy Carlyle .08 .25
10 Greg Paslawski RC .02 .10
11 Neal Broten .08 .25
12 Wendel Clark DP 1.00 2.50
13 Bill Ranford RC DP 2.00 5.00
14 Doug Wilson .08 .25
15 Mario Lemieux 10.00 20.00
16 Mats Naslund .08 .25
17 Mel Bridgman .02 .10
18 James Patrick DP .01 .05
19 Rollie Melanson .08 .25
20 Lanny McDonald .08 .25
21 Peter Stastny .08 .25
22 Murray Craven .02 .10
23 Ulf Samuelsson DP RC .60 1.50
24 Michel Thelven DP UER .01 .05
(Misspelled Thelvin on card front)
25 Scott Stevens .20 .50
26 Petr Klima .08 .25
27 Brent Sutter DP .01 .05
28 Tomas Sandstrom .20 .50
29 Tim Bothwell .02 .10
30 Bob Carpenter DP .01 .05
31 Brian MacLellan DP .01 .05
32 John Chabot .02 .10
33 Phil Housley DP .08 .25
34 Patrik Sundstrom DP .01 .05
35 Dave Ellett .08 .25
36 John Vanbiesbrouck 4.00 8.00
37 Dave Lewis .02 .10
38 Tom McCarthy DP .01 .05
39 Dave Poulin .08 .25
40 Mike Foligno .08 .25
41 Gordie Roberts .02 .10
42 Luc Robitaille RC 10.00 20.00
43 Duane Sutter .02 .10
44 Pete Peeters .08 .25
45 John Anderson .02 .10
46 Aaron Broten .02 .10
47 Keith Brown .02 .10
48 Bobby Smith .08 .25
49 Don Maloney .02 .10
50 Mark Hunter .02 .10
51 Moe Mantha .02 .10
52 Charlie Simmer .08 .25
53 Wayne Gretzky 7.50 15.00
54 Mark Howe .08 .25
55 Bob Gould .02 .10
56 Steve Yzerman DP 3.00 6.00
57 Larry Playfair .02 .10
58 Alain Chevrier .08 .25
59 Steve Larmer .20 .50
60 Bryan Trottier .20 .50
61 Stewart Gavin DP .01 .05
62 Russ Courtnall DP .20 .50
63 Mike Ramsey DP .01 .05
64 Bob Brooke .02 .10
65 Rick Wamsley DP .01 .05
66 Ken Morrow DP .01 .05
67 Gerard Gallant UER RC .02 .10
68 Kevin Hatcher RC .60 1.50
69 Cam Neely .75 2.00
70 Sylvain Turgeon DP .01 .05
71 Peter Zezel .02 .10
72 Al MacInnis 1.00 2.50
73 Terry Ruskowski DP .01 .05
74 Troy Murray .02 .10
75 Jim Fox DP .01 .05
76 Kelly Kisio .02 .10
77 Michel Goulet DP .08 .25
78 Tom Barrasso DP .08 .25
79 Bruce Driver DP .01 .05
80 Craig Simpson DP RC .08 .25
81 Dino Ciccarelli .08 .25
82 Gary Nylund DP .01 .05
83 Bernie Federko .08 .25
84 John Tonelli DP .01 .05
85 Brad McCrimmon DP .01 .05
86 Dave Tippett DP .01 .05
87 Ray Bourque DP .50 1.25
88 Dave Christian .08 .25
89 Glen Hanlon .08 .25
90 Brian Curran .02 .10
91 Paul MacLean .08 .25
92 Jimmy Carson RC .08 .25
93 Willie Huber .02 .10
94 Brian Bellows .08 .25
95 Doug Jarvis DP .01 .05
96 Clark Gillies .08 .25
97 Tony Tanti .02 .10
98 Pelle Eklund DP RC .08 .25
99 Paul Coffey .60 1.50
100 Brent Ashton DP .01 .05
101 Mark Johnson .02 .10
102 Greg Johnston RC .02 .10
103 Ron Flockhart .02 .10
104 Ed Olczyk .02 .10
105 Mike Bossy .25 .60
106 Chris Chelios .60 1.50
107 Gilles Meloche .08 .25
108 Rod Langway .08 .25
109 Ray Ferraro DP .20 .50
110 Ron Duguay DP .01 .05
111 Al Secord DP .01 .05
112 Mark Messier .20 .50
113 Ron Sutter .02 .10
114 Darren Veitch RC .02 .10
115 Rick Middleton DP .01 .05
116 Doug Sulliman .02 .10
117 Dennis Maruk DP .01 .05
118 Dave Taylor .08 .25
119 Kelly Hrudey .20 .50
120 Tom Fergus .02 .10
121 Christian Ruuttu RC .02 .10
122 Brian Benning RC .02 .10
123 Adam Oates RC 5.00 10.00
124 Kevin Dineen .15 .40
125 Doug Bodger DP .01 .05
126 Joe Mullen .10 .30
127 Denis Savard .08 .25
128 Brad Marsh .02 .10
129 Marcel Dionne DP .08 .25
130 Bryan Erickson DP .02 .10
131 Reed Larson DP .01 .05
132 Don Beaupre .08 .25
133 Larry Murphy DP .08 .25
134 John Ogrodnick DP .01 .05
135 Greg Adams DP .01 .05
136 Pat Flatley .02 .10
137 Scott Arniel DP .01 .05
138 Dana Murzyn .02 .10
139 Greg C. Adams .02 .10
140 Bob Sauve .08 .25
141 Mike O'Connell .02 .10
142 Walt Poddubny DP .01 .05
143 Paul Reinhart .02 .10
144 Tim Kerr DP .08 .25
145 Brian Lawton RC .02 .10
146 Gino Cavallini RC .02 .10
147 Doug Keans DP .01 .05
148 Jari Kurri .20 .50
149 Dale Hawerchuk .20 .50
150 Randy Cunneyworth RC .02 .10
151 Jay Wells .02 .10
152 Mike Liut DP .08 .25
153 Steve Konroyd .02 .10
154 John Tucker .02 .10
155 Rick Vaive DP .01 .05
156 Bob Murray .02 .10
157 Kirk Muller DP .20 .50
158 Brian Propp .02 .10
159 Ron Greschner .02 .10
160 Rob Ramage .02 .10
161 Craig Laughlin .02 .10
162 Steve Kasper DP .01 .05
163 Patrick Roy 10.00 25.00
164 Shawn Burr DP RC .08 .25
165 Craig Hartsburg DP .01 .05
166 Dean Evason RC .08 .25
167 Bob Bourne .02 .10
168 Mike Gartner .20 .50
169 Ron Hextall RC 4.00 10.00
170 Joe Cirella .02 .10
171 Dan Quinn DP .01 .05
172 Tony McKegney .02 .10
173 Pat LaFontaine DP .20 .50
174 Allen Pedersen DP RC .01 .05
175 Doug Gilmour .08 .25
176 Gary Suter DP .02 .10
177 Barry Pederson DP .01 .05
178 Grant Fuhr DP .20 .50
179 Wayne Presley DP RC .08 .25
180 Wilf Paiement .08 .25
181 Doug Smail .02 .10
182 Doug Crossman DP .01 .05
183 Bernie Nicholls UER .08 .25
(Misspelled Nichols on card front)
184 Dirk Graham UER .08 .25
(Misspelled Dick on card front)
185 Anton Stastny .02 .10
186 Greg Stefan .08 .25
187 Ron Francis .20 .50
188 Steve Thomas DP .15 .40
189 Kelly Miller RC .08 .25
190 Tomas Jonsson .02 .10
191 John MacLean .20 .50
192 Larry Robinson DP .08 .25
193 Doug Wickenheiser DP .01 .05
194 Keith Crowder DP .01 .05
195 Bob Froese .08 .25
196 Jim Johnson .02 .10
197 Checklist 1-99 .30 .75
198 Checklist 100-198 .30 .75

1987-88 Topps Box Bottoms

This sixteen-card standard-size set was issued in sets of four on the bottom of the 1987-88 Topps wax pack boxes. The cards feature team scoring leaders. Complete box bottom panels are valued at a 25 percent premium above the prices listed below. The cards are in the same design as the 1987-88 Topps regular issues except they are bordered in yellow. The backs are printed in red and black ink and give statistical information. The cards are lettered rather than numbered.

COMPLETE SET (16) 10.00 25.00
A Wayne Gretzky 4.00 10.00
B Tim Kerr .08 .25
C Steve Yzerman 2.00 5.00
D Luc Robitaille 1.50 4.00
E Doug Gilmour .40 1.00
F Ray Bourque .75 2.00
G Joe Mullen .20 .50
H Larry Murphy .20 .50
I Dale Hawerchuk .25 .60
J Ron Francis .40 1.00
K Walt Poddubny .05 .15
L Mats Naslund .15 .40
M Michel Goulet .20 .50
N Denis Savard .20 .50
O Bryan Trottier .25 .60
P Russ Courtnall .20 .50

1987-88 Topps Sticker Inserts

This set of 33 "Hockey Helmet Stickers" features stickers of 12 All-Star players (1-12) and 21 stickers of team logos, pucks, and numbers. The stickers were inserted in with the 1987-88 Topps hockey regular issue wax packs and as such are also 2 1/2" by 3 1/2". The card backs are printed in blue and red on white card stock. The last seven team stickers can be found with the team logos on the top or bottom.

COMPLETE SET (33) 8.00 20.00
1 Ray Bourque .75 2.00
2 Ron Hextall 1.00 2.50
3 Mark Howe .15 .40
4 Jari Kurri .30 .75
5 Wayne Gretzky 3.00 8.00
6 Michel Goulet .15 .40
7 Larry Murphy .15 .40
8 Mike Liut .15 .40
9 Al MacInnis .20 .50
10 Tim Kerr .08 .25
11 Mario Lemieux 4.00 10.00
12 Luc Robitaille 1.50 4.00
13 Toronto Maple Leafs .08 .25
14 Buffalo Sabres .05 .15
15 Detroit Red Wings .08 .25
16 Pittsburgh Penguins .05 .15
17 New York Rangers .08 .25
18 Calgary Flames .05 .15
19 Winnipeg Jets .05 .15
20 Quebec Nordiques .05 .15
21 Chicago Blackhawks .05 .15
22 Los Angeles Kings .05 .15
23 Montreal Canadiens .08 .25
24 Vancouver Canucks .05 .15
25 Hartford Whalers .05 .15
26 Philadelphia Flyers .05 .15
27 New Jersey Devils .05 .15
28 St. Louis Blues .05 .15
29 Minnesota North Stars .05 .15
30 Washington Capitals .05 .15
31 Boston Bruins .08 .25
32 New York Islanders .05 .15
33 Edmonton Oilers .05 .15

1988-89 Topps

The 1988-89 Topps hockey set contains 198 standard size cards. There are 66 double printed cards that are indicated by DP in the checklist below. The fronts feature colored borders and each player's team logo. The backs contain yearly statistics, playoff statistics, game winning goals from 1987-88 and highlights. Wayne Gretzky (120) appears as a King for the first time. The press conference photo has Gretzky holding his new Kings jersey. Be careful of counterfeit Brett Hull RCs.

COMPLETE SET (198) 30.00 60.00
1 Mario Lemieux DP 2.50 5.00
2 Bob Joyce DP RC .01 .05
3 Joel Quenneville DP .01 .05
4 Tony McKegney .02 .10
5 Stephane Richer DP .20 .50
6 Mark Howe DP .01 .05
7 Brent Sutter DP .01 .05
8 Gilles Meloche DP .01 .05
9 Jimmy Carson DP .01 .05
10 John MacLean .08 .25
11 Gary Leeman .02 .10
12 Gerard Gallant DP .01 .05
13 Marcel Dionne .08 .25
14 Dave Christian DP .01 .05
15 Gary Nylund .02 .10
16 Joe Nieuwendyk RC 1.50 4.00
17 Billy Smith DP .08 .25
18 Christian Ruuttu .02 .10
19 Randy Cunneyworth .02 .10
20 Brian Lawton .02 .10
21 Scott Mellanby DP RC .40 1.00
22 Peter Stastny DP .01 .05
23 Gord Kluzak .02 .10
24 Sylvain Turgeon .02 .10
25 Clint Malarchuk .08 .25
26 Denis Savard .08 .25
27 Craig Simpson .02 .10
28 Petr Klima .02 .10
29 Pat Verbeek .08 .25
30 Moe Mantha .02 .10
31 Chris Nilan .02 .10
32 Barry Pederson .02 .10
33 Randy Burridge .02 .10
34 Ron Hextall .40 1.00
35 Gaston Gingras .02 .10
36 Kevin Dineen DP .01 .05
37 Tom Laidlaw .02 .10
38 Paul MacLean DP .01 .05
39 John Chabot DP .01 .05
40 Lindy Ruff .02 .10
41 Dan Quinn DP .01 .05
42 Don Beaupre .08 .25
43 Gary Suter .02 .10
44 Mikko Makela DP RC .01 .05
45 Mark Johnson DP .01 .05
46 Dave Taylor .08 .25
47 Ulf Dahlen DP RC .20 .50
48 Jeff Sharples RC .02 .10
49 Chris Chelios .40 1.00
50 Mike Gartner DP .08 .25
51 Darren Pang DP RC .20 .50
52 Ron Francis .20 .50
53 Ken Morrow .02 .10
54 Michel Goulet .08 .25
55 Ray Sheppard RC .60 1.50
56 Doug Gilmour .08 .25
57 David Shaw DP .01 .05
58 Cam Neely DP .08 .25
59 Grant Fuhr DP .20 .50
60 Scott Stevens .08 .25
61 Bob Brooke .02 .10
62 Dave Hunter .02 .10
63 Alan Kerr RC .02 .10
64 Brad Marsh .02 .10
65 Dale Hawerchuk DP .08 .25
66 Brett Hull DP RC 10.00 25.00
67 Patrik Sundstrom DP .01 .05
68 Greg Stefan .08 .25
69 James Patrick .02 .10
70 Dale Hunter DP .01 .05
71 Al Iafrate .08 .25
72 Bob Carpenter .02 .10
73 Ray Bourque DP .40 1.00
74 John Tucker DP .01 .05
75 Carey Wilson .02 .10
76 Joe Mullen .08 .25
77 Rick Vaive .02 .10
78 Shawn Burr DP .01 .05
79 Murray Craven DP .01 .05
80 Clark Gillies .08 .25
81 Bernie Federko .08 .25
82 Tony Tanti .02 .10
83 Greg Gilbert .02 .10
84 Kirk Muller .08 .25
85 Dave Tippett .02 .10
86 Kevin Hatcher DP .08 .25
87 Rick Middleton DP .01 .05
88 Bobby Smith .08 .25
89 Doug Wilson DP .01 .05
90 Scott Arniel .02 .10
91 Brian Mullen .02 .10
92 Mike O'Connell DP .01 .05
93 Mark Messier DP .20 .50
94 Sean Burke RC 1.25 3.00
95 Brian Bellows DP .01 .05
96 Doug Bodger .02 .10
97 Bryan Trottier .20 .50
98 Anton Stastny .02 .10
99 Checklist 1-99 .20 .50
100 Dave Poulin DP .01 .05
101 Bob Bourne DP .01 .05
102 John Vanbiesbrouck .08 .25
103 Allen Pedersen .02 .10
104 Mike Ridley .02 .10
105 Andrew McBain .02 .10
106 Troy Murray DP .01 .05
107 Tom Barrasso .08 .25
108 Tomas Jonsson .02 .10
109 Rob Brown RC .02 .10
110 Hakan Loob DP .01 .05
111 Ilkka Sinisalo DP .01 .05
112 Dave Archibald RC .02 .10
113 Doug Halward .02 .10
114 Ray Ferraro .02 .10
115 Doug Brown RC .02 .10
116 Patrick Roy DP 1.50 4.00
117 Greg Millen .08 .25
118 Ken Linseman .02 .10
119 Phil Housley DP .08 .25
120 Wayne Gretzky 8.00 20.00
(Holding up Kings sweater)
121 Tomas Sandstrom .08 .25
122 Brendan Shanahan RC 6.00 15.00
123 Pat LaFontaine .20 .50
124 Luc Robitaille DP .75 2.00
125 Ed Olczyk DP .01 .05
126 Ron Sutter .02 .10
127 Mike Liut .08 .25
128 Brent Ashton DP .01 .05
129 Tony Hrkac RC .02 .10
130 Kelly Miller .02 .10
131 Alan Haworth .02 .10
132 Dave McLlwain RC .02 .10
133 Mike Ramsey .02 .10
134 Bob Sweeney RC .02 .10
135 Dirk Graham DP .01 .05
136 Ulf Samuelsson .20 .50
137 Petri Skriko .02 .10
138 Aaron Broten DP .01 .05
139 Jim Fox .02 .10
140 Randy Wood DP RC .01 .05
141 Larry Murphy .08 .25
142 Daniel Berthiaume DP .01 .05
143 Kelly Kisio .02 .10
144 Neal Broten .02 .10
145 Reed Larson .02 .10
146 Peter Zezel DP .01 .05
147 Jari Kurri .20 .50
148 Jim Johnson .02 .10
149 Gino Cavallini DP .01 .05
150 Glen Hanlon DP .08 .25
151 Bengt Gustafsson .02 .10
152 Mike Bullard DP .01 .05
153 John Ogrodnick .02 .10
154 Steve Larmer .08 .25
155 Kelly Hrudey .08 .25
156 Mats Naslund .02 .10
157 Bruce Driver .02 .10
158 Randy Hillier .02 .10
159 Craig Hartsburg .02 .10
160 Rollie Melanson .08 .25
161 Adam Oates DP .60 1.50
162 Greg Adams DP .01 .05
163 Dave Andreychuk DP .08 .25
164 Dave Babych .02 .10
165 Brian Noonan RC .02 .10
166 Glen Wesley RC .02 .10
167 Dave Ellett .02 .10
168 Brian Propp .02 .10
169 Bernie Nicholls .08 .25
170 Walt Poddubny .02 .10
171 Steve Konroyd .02 .10
172 Doug Sulliman DP .01 .05
173 Mario Gosselin .08 .25
174 Brian Benning .02 .10
175 Dino Ciccarelli .08 .25
176 Steve Kasper .02 .10
177 Rick Tocchet .40 1.00
178 Brad McCrimmon .02 .10
179 Paul Coffey .40 1.00
180 Pete Peeters .08 .25
181 Bob Probert DP RC .60 1.50
182 Steve Duchesne DP RC .40 1.00
183 Russ Courtnall .08 .25
184 Mike Foligno DP .01 .05
185 Wayne Presley DP .01 .05
186 Rejean Lemelin .08 .25
187 Mark Hunter .02 .10
188 Joe Cirella .02 .10
189 Glenn Anderson DP .08 .25
190 John Anderson .02 .10
191 Pat Flatley .02 .10
192 Rod Langway .02 .10
193 Brian MacLellan .02 .10
194 Pierre Turgeon RC 4.00 10.00
195 Brian Hayward .08 .25
196 Steve Yzerman DP 1.25 3.00
197 Doug Crossman .02 .10
198 Checklist 100-198 .20 .50

1988-89 Topps Box Bottoms

This sixteen-card standard-size set was issued in sets of four on the bottom of the 1988-89 Topps wax pack boxes. The cards feature team scoring leaders. Complete box bottom panels are valued at a 25 percent premium above the prices listed below. The cards are in the same design as the 1988-89 Topps regular issues except they are bordered only in gray. The backs are printed in purple on orange background and give statistical information. The cards are lettered rather than numbered.

COMPLETE SET (16) 5.60 14.00
A Ron Francis .30 .75
B Wayne Gretzky 2.50 6.00
C Pat LaFontaine .30 .75

D Bobby Smith .08 .25
E Bernie Federko .08 .25
F Kirk Muller .20 .50
G Ed Olczyk .05 .15
H Denis Savard .20 .50
I Ray Bourque .60 1.50
J Murray Craven and Brian Propp .05 .15
K Dale Hawerchuk .20 .50
L Steve Yzerman 1.25 3.00
M Dave Andreychuk .15 .40
N Mike Gartner .20 .50
O Hakan Loob .08 .25
P Luc Robitaille .40 1.00

1988-89 Topps Sticker Inserts

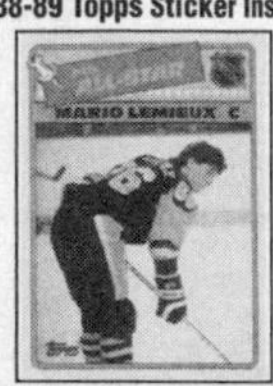

This set of 33 "Hockey Helmet Stickers" features stickers of 12 All-Star players (1-12) and 21 stickers of team logos, pucks, and numbers. The stickers were inserted in with the 1988-89 Topps hockey regular issue wax packs and as such are also 2 1/2" by 3 1/2". The card backs are printed in blue and red on white card stock. The last seven team stickers can be found with the team logos on the top or bottom.

COMPLETE SET (33) 6.00 15.00
1 Luc Robitaille .60 1.50
2 Mario Lemieux 1.50 4.00
3 Hakan Loob .08 .25
4 Scott Stevens .15 .40
5 Ray Bourque .30 .75
6 Grant Fuhr .20 .50
7 Michel Goulet .15 .40
8 Wayne Gretzky 2.00 5.00
9 Cam Neely .30 .75
10 Brad McCrimmon .08 .25
11 Gary Suter .08 .25
12 Patrick Roy 2.00 5.00
13 Toronto Maple Leafs .08 .25
14 Buffalo Sabres .05 .15
15 Detroit Red Wings .08 .25
16 Pittsburgh Penguins .05 .15
17 New York Rangers .08 .25
18 Calgary Flames .05 .15
19 Winnipeg Jets .05 .15
20 Quebec Nordiques .05 .15
21 Chicago Blackhawks .08 .25
22 Los Angeles Kings .05 .15
23 Montreal Canadiens .08 .25
24 Vancouver Canucks .05 .15
25 Hartford Whalers .05 .15
26 Philadelphia Flyers .05 .15
27 New Jersey Devils .05 .15
28 St. Louis Blues .05 .15
29 Minnesota North Stars .05 .15
30 Washington Capitals .05 .15
31 Boston Bruins .08 .25
32 New York Islanders .05 .15
33 Edmonton Oilers .05 .15

1989-90 Topps

The 1989-90 Topps set contains 198 standard-size cards. There are 66 double-printed cards which are marked as DP in the checklist below. The fronts feature blue borders on top and bottom that are prone to chipping. An ice blue border is on either side. A team logo and the player's name are at the bottom. The backs contain yearly statistics, playoff statistics, game-winning goals from 1988-89 and highlights. The key Rookie Card in this set is Joe Sakic.

COMPLETE SET (198) 15.00 30.00
1 Mario Lemieux 1.50 4.00
2 Ulf Dahlen DP .02 .10
3 Terry Carkner RC .02 .10
4 Tony McKegney .02 .10
5 Denis Savard .08 .25
6 Derek King DP RC .20 .50
7 Lanny McDonald .08 .25
8 John Tonelli .02 .10
9 Tom Kurvers DP .02 .10
10 Dave Archibald .02 .10
11 Peter Sidorkiewicz RC .08 .25
12 Esa Tikkanen .08 .25
13 Dave Barr .02 .10
14 Brent Sutter .08 .25
15 Cam Neely .20 .50
16 Calle Johansson RC .02 .10
17 Patrick Roy DP .75 2.00
18 Dale DeGray DP RC .02 .10
19 Phil Bourque RC .02 .10
20 Kevin Dineen .02 .10
21 Mike Bullard DP .02 .10
22 Gary Leeman .02 .10
23 Greg Stefan DP .08 .25
24 Brian Mullen .02 .10
25 Pierre Turgeon DP .30 .75
26 Bob Rouse DP RC .02 .10
27 Peter Zezel .02 .10
28 Jeff Brown DP .20 .50
29 Andy Brickley DP RC .02 .10
30 Mike Gartner .08 .25
31 Darren Pang .08 .25
32 Pat Verbeek .02 .10
33 Petri Skriko DP .02 .10
34 Tom Laidlaw .02 .10
35 Randy Wood .02 .10
36 Tom Barrasso DP .08 .25
37 John Tucker DP .02 .10
38 Andrew McBain .02 .10
39 David Shaw DP .02 .10
40 Rejean Lemelin .08 .25
41 Dino Ciccarelli DP .08 .25
42 Jeff Sharples .02 .10
43 Jari Kurri .20 .50
44 Murray Craven DP .02 .10
45 Cliff Ronning DP RC .50 1.25
46 Dave Babych .02 .10
47 Bernie Nicholls DP .08 .25
48 Jon Casey RC .08 .25
49 Al MacInnis .08 .25
50 Bob Errey DP RC .08 .25
51 Glen Wesley .02 .10
52 Dirk Graham .02 .10
53 Guy Carbonneau DP .08 .25
54 Tomas Sandstrom .08 .25
55 Rod Langway DP .02 .10
56 Patrick Sundstrom .02 .10
57 Michel Goulet .08 .25
58 Dave Taylor .08 .25
59 Phil Housley .08 .25
60 Pat LaFontaine DP .20 .50
61 Kirk McLean DP RC .30 .75
62 Ken Linseman .02 .10
63A Randy Cunneyworth ERR (Pittsburgh Penguins) 2.50 6.00
63B Randy Cunneyworth COR .02 .10
64 Tony Hrkac DP .02 .10
65 Mark Messier DP .20 .50
66 Carey Wilson DP .02 .10
67 Stephen Leach RC .02 .10
68 Christian Ruuttu .02 .10
69 Dave Ellett .02 .10
70 Ray Ferraro .02 .10
71 Colin Patterson RC .02 .10
72 Tim Kerr .08 .25
73 Bob Joyce .02 .10
74 Doug Gilmour DP .08 .25
75 Lee Norwood DP .02 .10
76 Dale Hunter .08 .25
77 Jim Johnson DP .02 .10
78 Mike Foligno DP .02 .10
79 Al Iafrate DP .08 .25
80 Rick Tocchet DP .08 .25
81 Greg Hawgood DP RC .02 .10
82 Steve Thomas .08 .25
83 Steve Yzerman DP .75 2.00
84 Mike McPhee .02 .10
85 David Volek DP RC .02 .10
86 Brian Benning .02 .10
87 Neal Broten .08 .25
88 Luc Robitaille .08 .25
89 Trevor Linden RC .50 1.25
90 James Patrick DP .02 .10
91 Brian Lawton .02 .10
92 Sean Burke DP .08 .25
93 Scott Stevens .08 .25
94 Pat Elynuik DP RC .08 .25
95 Paul Coffey .20 .50
96 Jan Erixon DP .02 .10
97 Mike Liut .08 .25
98 Wayne Presley .02 .10
99 Craig Simpson .08 .25
100 Kjell Samuelsson RC .08 .25
101 Shawn Burr DP .02 .10
102 John MacLean .08 .25
103 Tom Fergus .02 .10
104 Mike Krushelnyski .02 .10
105 Gary Nylund .02 .10
106 Dave Andreychuk .08 .25
107 Bernie Federko .08 .25
108 Gary Suter .08 .25
109 Dave Gagner DP .08 .25
110 Ray Bourque .30 .75
111 Geoff Courtnall RC .40 1.00
112 Doug Wilson .08 .25
113 Joe Sakic RC 6.00 15.00
114 John Vanbiesbrouck .08 .25
115 Dave Poulin .02 .10
116 Rick Meagher .02 .10
117 Kirk Muller DP .08 .25
118 Mats Naslund .08 .25
119 Ray Sheppard .20 .50
120 Jeff Norton RC .02 .10
121 Randy Burridge DP .02 .10
122 Dale Hawerchuk DP .08 .25
123 Steve Duchesne .08 .25
124 John Anderson .02 .10
125 Rick Vaive DP .02 .10
126 Randy Hillier .02 .10
127 Jimmy Carson .02 .10
128 Larry Murphy .08 .25
129 Paul MacLean DP .02 .10
130 Joe Cirella .02 .10
131 Kelly Miller DP .02 .10
132 Alain Chevrier DP .08 .25
133 Ed Olczyk .02 .10
134 Dave Tippett .02 .10
135 Bob Sweeney .02 .10
136 Brian Leetch RC 3.00 6.00
137 Greg Millen .08 .25
138 Joe Nieuwendyk .20 .50
139 Brian Propp .02 .10
140 Mike Ramsey .02 .10
141 Mike Allison .02 .10
142 Shawn Chambers RC .02 .10
143 Peter Stastny DP .08 .25
144 Glen Hanlon .08 .25
145 John Cullen RC .08 .25
146 Kevin Hatcher .02 .10
147 Brendan Shanahan .20 .50
148 Paul Reinhart .02 .10
149 Bryan Trottier .20 .50
150 Dave Manson RC .20 .50
151 Marc Habscheid DP RC .02 .10
152 Dan Quinn .02 .10
153 Stephane Richer DP .08 .25
154 Doug Bodger DP .02 .10
155 Ron Hextall .20 .50
156 Wayne Gretzky 1.50 4.00
157 Steve Tuttle DP RC .02 .10
158 Charlie Huddy DP .02 .10
159 Dave Christian DP .02 .10
160 Andy Moog .08 .25
161 Tony Granato RC .20 .50
162 Sylvain Cote RC .02 .10
163 Mike Vernon .30 .75
164 Steve Chiasson RC .20 .50
165 Mike Ridley .02 .10
166 Kelly Hrudey .08 .25
167 Bob Carpenter DP .02 .10
168 Zarley Zalapski RC .20 .50
169 Derek Laxdal RC .02 .10
170 Clint Malarchuk DP .08 .25
171 Kelly Kisio .02 .10
172 Gerard Gallant .02 .10
173 Ron Sutter .02 .10
174 Chris Chelios .20 .50
175 Ron Francis .20 .50
176 Gino Cavallini .02 .10
177 Brian Bellows DP .02 .10
178 Greg C. Adams DP .02 .10
179 Steve Larmer .08 .25
180 Aaron Broten .02 .10
181 Brent Ashton DP .02 .10
182 Gerald Diduck DP RC .02 .10
183 Paul MacDermid RC .02 .10
184 Walt Poddubny DP .02 .10
185 Adam Oates .20 .50
186 Brett Hull 1.25 3.00
187 Scott Arniel .02 .10
188 Bobby Smith .08 .25
189 Guy Lafleur .08 .25
190 Craig Janney RC .30 .75
191 Mark Howe .08 .25
192 Grant Fuhr DP .20 .50
193 Rob Brown .02 .10
194 Steve Kasper DP .02 .10
195 Pete Peeters .08 .25
196 Joe Mullen .08 .25
197 Checklist 1-99 .02 .10
198 Checklist 100-198 DP .02 .10

1989-90 Topps Box Bottoms

This sixteen-card standard-size set was issued in sets of four on the bottom of the 1989-90 Topps wax pack boxes. The cards feature sixteen NHL star players who were scoring leaders on their teams. Complete box bottom panels are valued at a 25 percent premium above the prices listed below. A color action photo appears on the front and the player's name, team, and team logo at the bottom of the picture. The back is printed in red and black ink and gives the player's position and statistical information. The cards are lettered rather than numbered. The set features such NHL stars as Wayne Gretzky, Brett Hull, and Mario Lemieux.

COMPLETE SET (16) 4.00 10.00
A Mario Lemieux 1.50 4.00
B Mike Ridley .08 .25
C Tomas Sandstrom .08 .25
D Petri Skriko .08 .25
E Wayne Gretzky 1.50 4.00
F Brett Hull .75 2.00
G Tim Kerr .08 .25
H Mats Naslund .08 .25
I Jari Kurri .20 .50
J Steve Larmer .20 .50
K Cam Neely .30 .75
L Steve Yzerman .75 2.00
M Kevin Dineen .08 .25
N Dave Gagner .15 .40
O Joe Mullen .15 .40
P Pierre Turgeon .30 .75

1989-90 Topps Sticker Inserts

This 33-card standard-size set was issued as a one per pack insert in the 1989-90 Topps Hockey packs. This set is divided into the first 12 cards being the 1989-90 NHL all-stars and the next 21 cards being the various team logos along with some number stickers and stickers of hockey pucks. For some reason Topps apparently printed these sticker cards on sheets in such a way that there were three complete sets of 33 and then three more rows of 11 double-printed cards instead of merely printing four complete sets on the printing sheet.

COMPLETE SET (33) 4.00 10.00
1 Chris Chelios .30 .75
2 Gerard Gallant DP .05 .15
3 Mario Lemieux 2.00 5.00
4 Al MacInnis .20 .50
5 Joe Mullen DP .08 .25
6 Patrick Roy 1.50 4.00
7 Ray Bourque .30 .75
8 Rob Brown .08 .25
9 Geoff Courtnall DP .08 .25
10 Steve Duchesne DP .05 .15
11 Wayne Gretzky 2.00 5.00
12 Mike Vernon .15 .40
13 Toronto Maple Leafs .05 .15
14 Buffalo Sabres .05 .15
15 Detroit Red Wings .05 .15
16 Pittsburgh Penguins .05 .15
17 New York Rangers .05 .15
18 Calgary Flames .05 .15
19 Winnipeg Jets .05 .15
20 Quebec Nordiques .05 .15
21 Chicago Blackhawks .05 .15
22 Los Angeles Kings .05 .15
23 Montreal Canadiens .05 .15
24 Vancouver Canucks .05 .15
25 Hartford Whalers .05 .15
26 Philadelphia Flyers .05 .15
27 New Jersey Devils DP .02 .10
28 St. Louis Blues DP .02 .10
29 Minn. North Stars DP .02 .10
30 Washington Capitals DP .02 .10
31 Boston Bruins DP .02 .10
32 New York Islanders DP .02 .10
33 Edmonton Oilers DP .02 .10

1990-91 Topps

The 1990-91 Topps hockey set contains 396 standard-size cards. The fronts feature color action photos with color borders (according to team) on all four sides. A hockey stick is superimposed over the picture at the top border. The backs have yearly statistics, playoff statistics, and game winning goals from 1989-90. Included in the set is a three-card Tribute to Wayne Gretzky (1-3). Team cards have action scenes with the team's previous season standings and power play stats on back.

COMPLETE SET (396) 5.00 15.00
COMP.FACT.SET (396) 10.00 20.00
1 Gretzky Tribute Indianapolis Racers .40 1.00
2 Gretzky Tribute .20 .50
3 Gretzky Tribute .20 .50
4 Brett Hull HL .08 .25
5 Jari Kurri HL .02 .10
6 Bryan Trottier HL .02 .10
7 Jeremy Roenick RC .40 1.00
8 Brian Propp .01 .05
9 Jim Hrivnak RC .02 .10
10 Mick Vukota RC .01 .05
11 Tom Kurvers .01 .05
12 Ulf Dahlen .01 .05
13 Bernie Nicholls .02 .10
14 Peter Sidorkiewicz .02 .10
15 Peter Zezel .01 .05
16 Mike Hartman RC .01 .05
17 Kings Team .01 .05
18 Jim Sandlak .01 .05
19 Rob Brown .01 .05
20 Paul Ranheim RC .01 .05
21 Rick Zombo RC .01 .05
22 Paul Gillis .01 .05
23 Brian Hayward .02 .10
24 Brent Ashton .01 .05
25 Mark Lamb .01 .05
26 Rick Tocchet .02 .10
27 Slava Fetisov RC .02 .10
28 Denis Savard .02 .10
29 Chris Chelios .08 .25
30 Janne Ojanen RC .01 .05
31 Don Maloney .01 .05
32 Allan Bester .02 .10
33 Geoff Smith RC .01 .05
34 Daniel Shank RC .01 .05
35 Mikael Andersson RC .01 .05
36 Gino Cavallini .01 .05
37 Rob Murphy RC .01 .05
38 Flames Team .01 .05
39 Laurie Boschman .01 .05
40 Craig Wolanin RC .01 .05
41 Phil Bourque .01 .05
42 Alexander Mogilny RC .40 1.00
43 Ray Bourque .15 .40
44 Mike Liut .02 .10
45 Ron Sutter .01 .05
46 Bob Kudelski RC .01 .05
47 Larry Murphy .02 .10
48 Darren Turcotte RC .02 .10
49 Paul Ysebaert RC .01 .05
50 Alan Kerr .01 .05
51 Randy Carlyle .01 .05
52 Iiro Jarvi .01 .05
53 Don Barber RC .01 .05
54 Carey Wilson .01 .05
55 Joey Kocur RC .15 .40
56 Steve Larmer .02 .10
57 Paul Cavallini .01 .05
58 Shayne Corson .01 .05
59 Canucks Team .01 .05
60 Sergei Makarov RC .08 .25
61 Kjell Samuelsson .01 .05
62 Tony Granato .01 .05
63 Tom Fergus .01 .05
64 Martin Gelinas RC .15 .40
65 Tom Barrasso .02 .10
66 Pierre Turgeon .02 .10
67 Randy Cunneyworth .01 .05
68 Michal Pivonka RC .01 .05
69 Cam Neely .08 .25
70 Brian Bellows .01 .05
71 Pat Elynuik .01 .05
72 Doug Crossman .01 .05
73 Sylvain Turgeon .01 .05
74 Shawn Burr .01 .05
75 John Vanbiesbrouck .02 .10
76 Steve Bozek .01 .05
77 Brett Hull .20 .50
78 Zarley Zalapski .01 .05
79 Wendel Clark .02 .10
80 Flyers Team .01 .05
81 Kelly Miller .01 .05
82 Mark Pederson RC .01 .05
83 Adam Creighton .01 .05
84 Scott Young .01 .05
85 Petr Klima .01 .05
86 Steve Duchesne .01 .05
87 Joe Nieuwendyk .02 .10
88 Andy Brickley .01 .05
89 Phil Housley .02 .10
90 Neal Broten .02 .10
91 Al Iafrate .02 .10
92 Steve Thomas .01 .05
93 Guy Carbonneau .02 .10
94 Steve Chiasson .01 .05
95 Mike Tomlak RC .01 .05
96 Roger Johansson RC .01 .05
97 Randy Wood .01 .05
98 Jim Johnson .01 .05
99 Bob Sweeney .01 .05
100 Dino Ciccarelli .02 .10
101 Rangers Team .01 .05
102 Mike Ramsey .01 .05
103 Kelly Hrudey .02 .10
104 Dave Ellett .01 .05
105 Bob Brooke .01 .05
106 Greg Adams .01 .05
107 Joe Cirella .01 .05
108 Jari Kurri .02 .10
109 Pete Peeters .02 .10
110 Paul MacLean .01 .05
111 Doug Wilson .02 .10
112 Pat Verbeek .01 .05
113 Bob Beers RC .01 .05
114 Mike O'Connell .01 .05
115 Brian Bradley .01 .05
116 Paul Coffey .08 .25
117 Doug Brown .01 .05
118 Aaron Broten .01 .05
119 Bob Essensa RC .15 .40
120 Wayne Gretzky UER (1302 career assists not 13102) .50 1.25
121 Vincent Damphousse .01 .05
122 Nordiques Team .01 .05
123 Mike Foligno .01 .05
124 Russ Courtnall .01 .05
125 Rick Meagher .01 .05
126 Craig Fisher RC .01 .05
127 Al MacInnis .02 .10
128 Derek King .01 .05
129 Dale Hunter .01 .05
130 Mark Messier UER (Shown as LW& should be C) .08 .25
131 James Patrick UER (Orange border& should be blue) .01 .05
132 Checklist 1-132 UER (54 Cary Wilson should be Carey) .01 .05
133 Red Wings Team .08 .25
134 Barry Pederson .01 .05
135 Gary Leeman .01 .05
136 Doug Gilmour .02 .10
137 Mike McPhee .01 .05
138 Bob Murray .01 .05
139 Bob Carpenter .01 .05
140 Sean Burke .02 .10
141 Dale Hawerchuk .02 .10
142 Guy Lafleur .08 .25
143 Lindy Ruff .01 .05
144 Whalers Team .01 .05
145 Glenn Anderson .02 .10
146 Dave Chyzowski RC .01 .05
147 Kevin Hatcher .01 .05
148 Rick Vaive .01 .05
149 Adam Oates .02 .10
150 Garth Butcher .01 .05
151 Basil McRae .01 .05
152 Ilkka Sinisalo .01 .05
153 Steve Kasper .01 .05
154 Greg Paslawski .01 .05
155 Brad Marsh .01 .05
156 Esa Tikkanen .01 .05
157 Tony Tanti .01 .05
158 Mario Marois (oi in last name line below rest of name) .01 .05
159 Sylvain Lefebvre RC .01 .05
160 Troy Murray .01 .05
161 Gary Roberts .01 .05
162 Randy Ladouceur .01 .05
163 John Chabot .01 .05
164 Calle Johansson .01 .05
165 Bruins Team .01 .05
166 Jeff Norton .01 .05
167 Mike Krushelnyski .01 .05
168 Dave Gagner .02 .10
169 Dave Andreychuk .02 .10
170 Dave Capuano RC .01 .05
171 Curtis Joseph RC .50 1.25
172 Bruce Driver .01 .05
173 Scott Mellanby .02 .10
174 John Ogrodnick .01 .05
175 Mario Lemieux .50 1.25
176 Marc Fortier .01 .05
177 Vincent Riendeau RC .02 .10
178 Mark Johnson .01 .05
179 Dirk Graham .01 .05
180 Jets Team (Keith Acton breaking in on Daniel Berthiaume) .01 .05
181 Robb Stauber RC .02 .10
182 Christian Ruuttu .01 .05
183 Dave Tippett .01 .05
184 Pat LaFontaine .08 .25
185 Mark Howe .01 .05
186 Stephane Richer .01 .05
187 Jan Erixon .01 .05
188 Neil Sheehy .01 .05
189 Craig MacTavish .01 .05
190 Randy Burridge .01 .05
191 Bernie Federko .02 .10
192 Shawn Chambers .01 .05
193 Mark Messier AS1 .08 .25
194 Luc Robitaille AS1 .01 .05
195 Brett Hull AS1 .02 .10
196 Ray Bourque AS1 .02 .10
197 Al MacInnis AS1 .01 .05
198 Patrick Roy AS1 .20 .50
199 Wayne Gretzky AS2 .25 .60
200 Brian Bellows AS2 .01 .05
201 Cam Neely AS2 .02 .10
202 Paul Coffey AS2 .01 .05
203 Doug Wilson AS2 .01 .05
204 Daren Puppa AS2 UER (Misspelled Darren on front and back) .02 .10
205 Gary Suter .01 .05
206 Ed Olczyk .01 .05
207 Doug Lidster .01 .05
208 John Cullen .01 .05
209 Luc Robitaille .02 .10
210 Tim Kerr .01 .05
211 Scott Stevens .02 .10
212 Craig Janney .02 .10
213 Kevin Dineen .01 .05
214 Jim Waite RC .02 .10
215 Benoit Hogue .01 .05
216 Curtis Leschyshyn RC .01 .05
217 Brad Lauer .01 .05
218 Joe Mullen .02 .10
219 Patrick Roy .40 1.00
220 Blues Team .01 .05
221 Brian Leetch .10 .30
222 Steve Yzerman .40 1.00
223 Stephane Beauregard RC .02 .10
224 John MacLean .02 .10
225 Trevor Linden .02 .10
226 Bill Ranford .02 .10
227 Mark Osborne .01 .05
228 Curt Giles .01 .05
229 Mikko Makela .01 .05
230 Bob Errey .01 .05
231 Jimmy Carson .01 .05
232 Kay Whitmore RC .02 .10
233 Gary Nylund .01 .05
234 Jiri Hrdina RC .01 .05
235 Stephen Leach RC .01 .05
236 Greg Hawgood .01 .05
237 Jocelyn Lemieux RC .01 .05
238 Daren Puppa .02 .10
239 Kelly Kisio .01 .05
240 Craig Simpson .01 .05
241 Maple Leafs Team .01 .05
242 Fredrik Olausson .01 .05
243 Ron Hextall .02 .10
244 Sergio Momesso RC .01 .05
245 Kirk Muller .01 .05
246 Petr Svoboda .01 .05
247 Daniel Berthiaume .02 .10
248 Andrew McBain .01 .05
249 Jeff Jackson UER (Game total for '89-90 is 65 not 0) .01 .05
250 Randy Gilhen RC .01 .05
251 Oilers Team .01 .05
252 Rick Bennett RC .01 .05
253 Don Beaupre .02 .10
254 Pelle Eklund .01 .05
255 Greg Gilbert .01 .05
256 Gordie Roberts .01 .05
257 Kirk McLean .02 .10
258 Brent Sutter .01 .05
259 Brendan Shanahan .08 .25
260 Todd Krygier RC .01 .05
261 Larry Robinson UER (No '80-81 stats on card& totals wrong) .02 .10
262 Sabres Team .01 .05
263 Dave Christian .01 .05
264 Checklist 133-264 .01 .05
265 Jamie Macoun .01 .05
266 Glen Hanlon .02 .10
267 Daniel Marois .01 .05
268 Doug Smail .01 .05
269 Jon Casey .02 .10
270 Brian Skrudland .01 .05
271 Michel Petit .01 .05
272 Dan Quinn .01 .05
273 Geoff Courtnall .01 .05
274 Mike Bullard .01 .05
275 Randy Gregg .01 .05
276 Keith Brown .01 .05
277 Troy Mallette RC .01 .05
278 Steve Tuttle .01 .05
279 Brad Shaw RC .01 .05
280 Mark Recchi RC .50 1.25
281 John Tonelli .01 .05
282 Doug Bodger .01 .05
283 Thomas Steen .01 .05
284 Devils Team .01 .05
285 Lee Norwood .01 .05
286 Brian MacLellan .01 .05
287 Bobby Smith .02 .10
288 Rob Cimetta RC .01 .05
289 Rob Zettler RC .01 .05
290 David Reid RC .01 .05
291 Bryan Trottier .02 .10
292 Brian Mullen .01 .05
293 Paul Reinhart .01 .05
294 Andy Moog .02 .10
295 Jeff Brown .01 .05
296 Ryan Walter .01 .05
297 Trent Yawney .01 .05
298 John Druce RC .01 .05
299 Dave McLlwain UER (Card says shoots right, should be left) .01 .05
300 David Volek .01 .05
301 Tomas Sandstrom .01 .05
302 Gord Murphy RC .01 .05
303 Lou Franceschetti RC .01 .05
304 Dana Murzyn .01 .05
305 North Stars Team .01 .05
306 Patrik Sundstrom .01 .05
307 Kevin Lowe .01 .05
308 Dave Barr .01 .05
309 Wendell Young .02 .10
310 Darrin Shannon RC .01 .05
311 Ron Francis .02 .10
312 Stephane Fiset RC .15 .40
313 Paul Fenton .01 .05
314 Dave Taylor .02 .10
315 Islanders Team .01 .05
316 Petri Skriko .01 .05
317 Rob Ramage .01 .05
318 Murray Craven .01 .05
319 Gaetan Duchesne .01 .05
320 Brad McCrimmon .01 .05
321 Grant Fuhr .02 .10
322 Gerard Gallant .01 .05
323 Tommy Albelin .01 .05
324 Scott Arniel .01 .05
325 Mike Keane RC .01 .05
326 Penguins Team .01 .05
327 Mike Ridley .01 .05
328 Dave Babych .01 .05
329 Michel Goulet .02 .10
330 Mike Richter RC .30 .75
331 Garry Galley RC .01 .05
332 Rod Brind'Amour RC .25 .60
333 Tony McKegney .01 .05
334 Peter Stastny .02 .10
335 Greg Millen .02 .10
336 Ray Ferraro .01 .05
337 Miloslav Horava RC .01 .05
338 Paul MacDermid .01 .05
339 Craig Coxe RC .01 .05
340 Dave Snuggerud RC .01 .05
341 Mike Lalor RC .01 .05
342 Marc Habscheid .01 .05
343 Rejean Lemelin .02 .10
344 Charlie Huddy .01 .05
345 Ken Linseman .01 .05
346 Canadiens Team .01 .05
347 Troy Loney RC .01 .05
348 Mike Modano RC .50 1.25
349 Jeff Reese RC .01 .05
350 Pat Flatley .01 .05
351 Mike Vernon .02 .10
352 Todd Elik RC .01 .05
353 Rod Langway .01 .05
354 Moe Mantha .01 .05
355 Keith Acton .01 .05
356 Scott Pearson RC .01 .05
357 Perry Berezan RC .01 .05
358 Alexei Kasatonov RC .01 .05
359 Igor Larionov RC .15 .40
360 Kevin Stevens RC .01 .05
361 Yves Racine RC .01 .05
362 Dave Poulin .01 .05
363 Blackhawks Team .01 .05
364 Yvon Corriveau RC .01 .05
365 Brian Benning .01 .05
366 Hubie McDonough RC .01 .05
367 Ron Tugnutt .02 .10
368 Steve Smith .01 .05
369 Joel Otto .01 .05
370 Dave Lowry RC .01 .05
371 Clint Malarchuk .02 .10
372 Mathieu Schneider RC .01 .05
373 Mike Gartner .02 .10
374 John Tucker .01 .05
375 Chris Terreri RC .02 .10
376 Dean Evason .01 .05
377 Jamie Leach RC .01 .05
378 Jacques Cloutier RC .02 .10
379 Glen Wesley .01 .05
380 Vladimir Krutov RC .02 .10
381 Terry Carkner .01 .05
382 John McIntyre RC .01 .05
383 Ville Siren RC .01 .05
384 Joe Sakic .25 .60
385 Teppo Numminen RC .01 .05
386 Theo Fleury .20 .50
387 Glen Featherstone RC .01 .05
388 Stephan Lebeau RC .01 .05
389 Kevin McClelland .01 .05
390 Uwe Krupp .01 .05
391 Mark Janssens RC .01 .05
392 Marty McSorley .01 .05
393 Vladimir Ruzicka RC .01 .05
394 Capitals Team .01 .05
395 Mark Fitzpatrick RC .01 .05
396 Checklist 265-396 .01 .05

1990-91 Topps Tiffany

Parallel to base set, Topps only produced 3000 sets. Cards can be distinguished by a glossy coating not found on regular issued cards.

COMPLETE SET (396) 60.00 150.00
*VETS: 10X TO 25X BASIC CARDS
*ROOKIES: 5X TO 10X BASIC CARDS

1990-91 Topps Box Bottoms

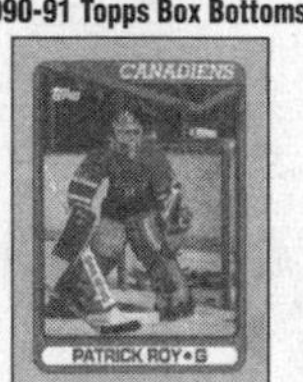

This 16-card standard-size set was issued in sets of four on the bottom of the 1990-91 Topps wax pack boxes. The cards are lettered rather than numbered. Complete box bottom panels are valued at a 25 percent premium above the prices listed below. The front design of these cards is essentially the same as the regular issue cards. The horizontally oriented backs have special statistics in blue lettering on a pale green background. The checklist does not agree with the actual grouping of the players in the four sets.

COMPLETE SET (16) 3.00 8.00
A Alexander Mogilny .50 1.25
B Jon Casey .15 .40
C Paul Coffey .25 .60
D Wayne Gretzky 1.00 2.50
E Patrick Roy .60 1.50
F Mike Modano .30 .75
G Mario Lemieux .60 1.50
H Al MacInnis .15 .40
I Ray Bourque .25 .60
J Steve Yzerman .40 1.00
K Darren Turcotte .08 .25
L Mike Vernon .15 .40
M Pierre Turgeon .20 .50
N Doug Wilson .08 .25
O Don Beaupre .15 .40
P Sergei Makarov .08 .25

1990-91 Topps Team Scoring Leaders

The 21-cards in this standard size set was included as a one per pack insert in the 1990-91 Topps hockey packs. This set has a glossy front with a full color action shot of the team's leading scorer while the back of the card has a list of the ten leading scorers for each team.

COMPLETE SET (21) 3.00 7.50
*TIFFANY: 4X TO 10X BASIC INSERTS
1 Steve Larmer .07 .20
2 Brett Hull .30 .75
3 Cam Neely .20 .50
4 Stephane Richer .08 .25
5 Paul Reinhart .02 .10
6 Dino Ciccarelli .08 .25
7 Kirk Muller .08 .25
8 Joe Nieuwendyk .10 .30
9 Rick Tocchet .08 .25
10 Pat LaFontaine .08 .25
11 Dale Hawerchuk .20 .50
12 Wayne Gretzky .75 2.00
13 Gary Leeman .02 .10
14 Joe Sakic .40 1.00
15 Brian Bellows .07 .20
16 Mark Messier .30 .75
17 Mario Lemieux .60 1.50
18 John Ogrodnick .02 .10
19 Steve Yzerman .40 1.00
20 Pierre Turgeon .20 .50
21 Ron Francis .20 .50

1991-92 Topps

The 1991-92 O-Pee-Chee and Topps hockey sets contain 528 standard-size cards. Both sets feature a Guy Lafleur Tribute (1-3) and a Super Rookie (4-13) subset. Topps hockey cards were sold in 15-card packs that included a bonus team scoring leader card, whereas the O-Pee-Chee cards were sold in nine-card wax packs that included a stick of gum plus one insert card from a special 66-card insert set. The fronts have glossy color action player photos, with two different color border stripes and a white card face. In the lower right corner, the team logo appears as a hockey puck superimposed on a hockey stick. They present full player information, including biography, statistics, 1990-91 game-winning goals, and NHL playoff record (the OPC cards present player information in French as well as English). The card number appears next to a hockey skate in the upper right corner of the back. Rookie Cards in this set include Tony Amonte, Valeri Kamensky and John LeClair.

COMPLETE SET (528) 5.00 12.00
COMP.FACT.SET (528) 5.00 12.00
1 Lafleur Tribute .02 .10
Goodbye Guy
2 Lafleur Tribute .02 .10
Gueeey's Last Hoorah
3 Lafleur Tribute .02 .10
Guy Bids Farewell
4 Ed Belfour SR .02 .10
5 Ken Hodge Jr. SR .01 .05
6 Rob Blake SR UER .01 .05
(Center on back& should say Defense)
7 Bobby Holik SR .01 .05
8 Sergei Fedorov SR UER .07 .20
(Name misspelled on front and in stats)
9 Jaromir Jagr SR .02 .10
10 Eric Weinrich SR .01 .05
11 Mike Richter SR .02 .10
12 Mats Sundin SR .02 .10
13 Mike Ricci SR .01 .05
14 Eric Desjardins .01 .05
15 Paul Ranheim .01 .05
16 Joe Sakic .15 .40
17 Curt Giles .01 .05
18 Mike Foligno .01 .05
19 Brad Marsh .01 .05
20 Ed Belfour .07 .20
21 Steve Smith .01 .05
22 Kirk Muller .01 .05
23 Kelly Chase .01 .05
24 Jim McKenzie .01 .05
25 Mick Vukota .01 .05
26 Tony Amonte RC .50 1.25
27 Danton Cole .01 .05
28 Jay Mazur RC .01 .05
29 Pete Peeters .02 .10
30 Petri Skriko .01 .05
31 Steve Duchesne .01 .05
32 Sabres Team .01 .05
33 Phil Bourque UER .01 .05
(Born Chelmford& should be Chelmsford)
34 Tim Bergland .01 .05
35 Tim Cheveldae .02 .10
36 Bill Armstrong .01 .05
37 John McIntyre .01 .05
38 Dave Andreychuk .02 .10
39 Curtis Leschyshyn .01 .05
40 Jaromir Jagr .10 .30
41 Craig Janney .02 .10
42 Doug Brown .01 .05
43 Ken Sabourin .01 .05
44 North Stars Team .01 .05
45 Fredrik Olausson UER .01 .05
(Misspelled Clausson on card front)
46 Mike Gartner UER .02 .10
(No italics or diamond 81-82 GP)
47 Mark Fitzpatrick .01 .05
48 Joe Murphy .01 .05
49 Doug Wilson .02 .10
50 Brian MacLellan .01 .05
51 Bob Bassen .01 .05
52 Robert Kron .01 .05
53 Roger Johansson .01 .05
54 Guy Carbonneau UER .02 .10
(No italics or diamond 85-86 GP)
55 Rob Ramage .01 .05
56 Bobby Holik .02 .10
57 Alan May .01 .05
58 Rick Meagher .01 .05
59 Cliff Ronning .01 .05
60 Red Wings Team .01 .05
61 Bob Kudelski .01 .05
62 Wayne McBean .01 .05
63 Craig MacTavish .01 .05
64 Owen Nolan .07 .20
65 Dale Hawerchuk .02 .10
66 Ray Bourque .07 .20
67 Sean Burke .02 .10
68 Frank Musil .01 .05
69 Joe Mullen .02 .10
70 Drake Berehowsky .01 .05
71 Darren Turcotte .01 .05
72 Randy Carlyle .01 .05
73 Paul Cyr .01 .05
74 Dave Gagner .01 .05
75 Steve Larmer .02 .10
76 Petr Svoboda .01 .05
77 Keith Acton .01 .05
78 Dimitri Khristich .01 .05
79 Brad McCrimmon .01 .05
80 Pat LaFontaine UER .07 .20
(Should be lower case a in name& not d)
81 Jeff Reese .01 .05
82 Mario Marois .01 .05
83 Rob Brown .01 .05
84 Grant Fuhr .07 .20
85 Carey Wilson .01 .05
86 Garry Galley .01 .05
87 Troy Murray .01 .05
88 Tony Granato .01 .05
89 Gord Murphy UER .01 .05
(No italics or diamond 90-91 GP)
90 Brent Gilchrist .01 .05
91 Mike Richter .07 .20
92 Eric Weinrich .01 .05
93 Marc Bureau .01 .05
94 Bob Errey .01 .05
95 Dave McLlwain .01 .05
96 Nordiques Team .01 .05
97 Clint Malarchuk UER .02 .10
(Center on front)
98 Shawn Antoski UER .01 .05
(Admirals are in IHL& not AHL)
99 Bob Sweeney .01 .05
100 Stephen Leach .01 .05
101 Gary Nylund .01 .05
102 Lucien DeBlois .01 .05
103 Oilers Team .01 .05
104 Jimmy Carson .01 .05
105 Rod Langway .01 .05
106 Jeremy Roenick .08 .25
107 Mike Vernon .02 .10
108 Brian Leetch .02 .10
109 Mark Hunter .01 .05
110 Brian Bellows .01 .05
111 Pelle Eklund .01 .05
112 Rob Blake .02 .10
113 Mike Hough .01 .05
114 Frank Pietrangelo .01 .05
115 Christian Ruuttu .01 .05
116 Bryan Marchment RC .02 .10
117 Garry Valk .01 .05
118 Ken Daneyko UER .01 .05
(No italics or diamond 90-91 GP)
119 Russ Courtnall .01 .05
120 Ron Wilson .01 .05
121 Shayne Stevenson .01 .05
122 Bill Berg .01 .05
123 Maple Leafs Team .01 .05
124 Glenn Anderson .02 .10
125 Kevin Miller .01 .05
126 Calle Johansson .01 .05
127 Jimmy Waite .02 .10
128 Allen Pedersen .01 .05
129 Brian Mullen .01 .05
130 Ron Francis .02 .10
131 Jergus Baca .01 .05
132 Checklist 1-132 .01 .05
133 Tony Tanti .01 .05
134 Wes Walz .01 .05
135 Stephan Lebeau .01 .05
136 Ken Wregget .02 .10
137 Scott Arniel UER .01 .05
(No italics or diamond 85-86 GP)
138 Dave Taylor .02 .10
139 Steven Finn .01 .05
140 Brendan Shanahan .07 .20
141 Petr Nedved .01 .05
142 Chris Dahlquist .01 .05
143 Rich Sutter .01 .05
144 Joe Reekie .01 .05
145 Peter Ing .01 .05
146 Ken Linseman .01 .05
147 Dave Barr .01 .05
148 Al Iafrate .01 .05
149 Greg Gilbert .01 .05
150 Craig Ludwig .01 .05
151 Gary Suter .01 .05
152 Jan Erixon .01 .05
153 Mario Lemieux .50 1.25
154 Mike Liut UER .02 .10
(In stats 84-85 repeats for 85-86 thru 89-90)
155 Uwe Krupp .01 .05
156 Darin Kimble .01 .05
157 Shayne Corson .01 .05
158 Jets Team .01 .05
159 Stephane Morin UER .01 .05
(Photo actually Jeff Jackson)
160 Rick Tocchet .01 .05
161 John Tonelli UER .01 .05
(No italics or diamond 81-82 GP)
162 Adrien Plavsic .01 .05
163 Jason Miller .01 .05
164 Tim Kerr .01 .05
165 Brent Sutter .01 .05
166 Michel Petit .01 .05
167 Adam Graves .01 .05
168 Jamie Macoun .01 .05
169 Terry Yake .01 .05
170 Bruins Team .01 .05
171 Alexander Mogilny .02 .10
172 Kal Dykhuis .01 .05
Top Prospect
173 Tomas Sandstrom .01 .05
174 Bernie Nicholls .01 .05
175 Slava Fetisov .01 .05
176 Andrew Cassels .01 .05
177 Ulf Dahlen .01 .05
178 Brian Hayward .02 .10
179 Doug Lidster .01 .05
180 Dave Lowry .01 .05
181 Ron Tugnutt UER .02 .10
(Birthplace and home should be Ontario& not Quebec)
182 Ed Olczyk .01 .05
183 Paul Coffey .07 .20
184 Shawn Burr UER .01 .05
(No italics or diamond 90-91 GP)
185 Whalers Team .01 .05
186 Mark Janssens .01 .05
187 Mike Craig .01 .05
188 Gary Leeman .01 .05
189 Phil Sykes .01 .05
190 Brett Hull LL .02 .10
191 Devils Team .01 .05
192 Cam Neely .07 .20
193 Petr Klima .01 .05
194 Mike Ricci .01 .05
195 Kelly Hrudey .02 .10
196 Mark Recchi .02 .10
197 Mikael Andersson .01 .05
198 Bob Probert .01 .05
199 Craig Wolanin .01 .05
200 Scott Mellanby .01 .05
201 Wayne Gretzky HL UER .25 .60
(Thomas Sandstrom mentioned on back)
202 Laurie Boschman .01 .05
203 Gino Odjick .01 .05
204 Garth Butcher .01 .05
205 Randy Wood .01 .05
206 John Druce .01 .05
207 Doug Bodger .01 .05
208 Doug Gilmour .02 .10
209 John LeClair RC .40 1.00
210 Steve Thomas .01 .05
211 Kjell Samuelsson .01 .05
212 Daniel Marois .01 .05
213 Jiri Hrdina .01 .05
214 Darrin Shannon .01 .05
215 Rangers Team .01 .05
216 Bob McGill .01 .05
217 Dirk Graham UER .01 .05
(No italics or diamond 85-86 or 90-91 GP)
218 Thomas Steen .01 .05
219 Mats Sundin .07 .20
220 Kevin Lowe UER .02 .10
(No italics or diamond 81-82 GP)
221 Kirk McLean .02 .10
222 Jeff Brown .01 .05
223 Joe Nieuwendyk .02 .10
224 Wayne Gretzky LL .25 .60
225 Marty McSorley .01 .05
226 John Cullen .01 .05
227 Brian Propp UER .01 .05
(No italics or diamond 81-82 GP)
228 Yves Racine .01 .05
229 Dale Hunter .01 .05
230 Dennis Vaske .01 .05
231 Sylvain Turgeon .01 .05
232 Ron Sutter .01 .05
233 Chris Chelios .07 .20
234 Brian Bradley .01 .05
235 Scott Young .01 .05
236 Mike Ramsey UER .01 .05
(No italics or diamond 81-82 GP)
237 Jon Casey .02 .10
238 Nevin Markwart .01 .05
239 John MacLean .02 .10
240 Brent Ashton .01 .05
241 Tony Hrkac .01 .05
242 Canucks Team .01 .05
243 Jeff Norton .01 .05
244 Martin Gelinas .01 .05
245 Mike Ridley .01 .05
246 Pat Jablonski RC .02 .10
247 Flames Team .01 .05
248 Paul Ysebaert .01 .05
249 Sylvain Cote .01 .05
250 Marc Habscheid .01 .05
251 Todd Elik .01 .05
252 Mike McPhee .01 .05
253 James Patrick .01 .05
254 Murray Craven .01 .05
255 Trent Yawney .01 .05
256 Rob Cimetta .01 .05
257 Wayne Gretzky LL .25 .60
258 Wayne Gretzky AS .25 .60
259 Brett Hull AS .02 .10
260 Luc Robitaille AS .02 .10
261 Ray Bourque AS .02 .10
262 Al MacInnis AS .01 .05
263 Ed Belfour AS .02 .10
264 Checklist 133-264 .01 .05
265 Adam Oates AS .01 .05
266 Cam Neely AS .02 .10
267 Kevin Stevens AS .01 .05
268 Chris Chelios AS .02 .10
269 Brian Leetch AS .01 .05
270 Patrick Roy AS .10 .30
271 Ed Belfour LL .02 .10
272 Rob Zettler .01 .05
273 Donald Audette .01 .05
274 Teppo Numminen .01 .05
275 Peter Stastny UER .02 .10
(No italics or diamond 81-82 GP)
276 Dave Christian .01 .05
277 Larry Murphy .02 .10
278 Johan Garpenlov .01 .05
279 Tom Fitzgerald .01 .05
280 Gerald Diduck .01 .05
281 Gino Cavallini .01 .05
282 Theo Fleury .01 .05
283 Kings Team .01 .05
284 Jeff Beukeboom .01 .05
285 Kevin Dineen .01 .05
286 Jacques Cloutier .02 .10
287 Tom Chorske .01 .05
288 Ed Belfour LL .02 .10
289 Ray Sheppard .01 .05
290 Olaf Kolzig .02 .10
291 Terry Carkner .01 .05
292 Benoit Hogue .01 .05
293 Mike Peluso .01 .05
294 Bruce Driver .01 .05
295 Jari Kurri .07 .20
296 Peter Sidorkiewicz .01 .05
297 Scott Pearson .01 .05
298 Canadiens Team .01 .05
299 Vincent Damphousse .01 .05
300 John Carter .01 .05
301 Geoff Smith .01 .05
302 Steve Kasper UER .01 .05
(No italics or diamond 85-86 GP)
303 Brett Hull .08 .25
304 Ray Ferraro .01 .05
305 Geoff Courtnall .01 .05
306 David Shaw .01 .05
307 Bob Essensa .02 .10
308 Mark Tinordi .01 .05
309 Keith Primeau .01 .05
310 Kevin Hatcher .01 .05
311 Chris Nilan .01 .05
312 Trevor Kidd .02 .10
Top Prospect
313 Daniel Berthiaume .02 .10
314 Adam Creighton .01 .05
315 Everett Sanipass .01 .05
316 Ken Baumgartner .01 .05
317 Sheldon Kennedy .01 .05
318 Dave Capuano .01 .05
319 Don Sweeney .01 .05
320 Gary Roberts .01 .05
321 Wayne Gretzky .50 1.25
322 Theo Fleury and .01 .05
Marty McSorley UER
(Name misspelled McSorely on both sides of card)
323 Ulf Samuelsson .01 .05
324 Mike Krushelnyski .01 .05
325 Dean Evason .01 .05
326 Pat Elynuik .01 .05
327 Michal Pivonka .01 .05
328 Paul Cavallini .01 .05
329 Flyers Team .01 .05
330 Denis Savard .02 .10
331 Paul Fenton .01 .05
332 Jon Morris .01 .05
333 Daren Puppa .02 .10
334 Doug Smail .01 .05
335 Kelly Kisio .01 .05
336 Michel Goulet UER .02 .10
(No italics or diamond 81-82 GP)
337 Mike Sillinger .01 .05
338 Andy Moog .02 .10
339 Paul Stanton .01 .05
340 Greg Adams .01 .05
341 Doug Crossman UER .01 .05
(No italics or diamond 85-86 GP)
342 Kelly Miller .01 .05
343 Pat Flatley .01 .05
344 Zarley Zalapski .01 .05
345 Mark Osborne UER .01 .05
(No italics or diamond 81-82 GP)
346 Mark Messier .07 .20
347 Blues Team .01 .05
348 Neil Wilkinson .01 .05
349 Brian Skrudland .01 .05
350 Lyle Odelein .01 .05
351 Luke Richardson .01 .05
352 Zdeno Ciger .01 .05
353 John Vanbiesbrouck .02 .10
354 Lou Franceschetti .01 .05
355 Alexei Gusarov RC .02 .10
356 Bill Ranford .02 .10
357 Normand Lacombe .01 .05
358 Randy Burridge .01 .05
359 Brian Benning .01 .05
360 Dave Hannan .01 .05
361 Todd Gill .01 .05
362 Peter Bondra .02 .10
363 Mike Hartman .01 .05
364 Trevor Linden .02 .10
365 John Ogrodnick .01 .05
366 Steve Konroyd .01 .05
367 Mike Modano .15 .40
368 Glenn Healy .02 .10
369 Stephane Richer .02 .10
370 Vincent Riendeau .01 .05
371 Randy Moller .01 .05
372 Penguins Team .01 .05
373 Murray Baron .01 .05
374 Troy Crowder .01 .05
375 Rick Tabaracci .02 .10
376 Brent Fedyk .01 .05
377 Randy Velischek .01 .05
378 Esa Tikkanen .01 .05
379 Rich Pilon .01 .05
380 Jeff Lazaro RC .01 .05
381 Dave Ellett .01 .05
382 Jeff Hackett .02 .10
383 Stephane Matteau .01 .05
384 Capitals Team .01 .05
385 Wayne Presley .01 .05
386 Grant Ledyard .01 .05
387 Kip Miller .01 .05
388 Dean Kennedy .01 .05
389 Hubie McDonough .01 .05
390 Anatoli Semenov .01 .05
391 Daryl Reaugh .02 .10
392 Mathieu Schneider .01 .05
393 Dan Quinn .01 .05
394 Claude Lemieux .01 .05
395 Phil Housley .01 .05
396 Checklist 265-396 .01 .05
397 Steve Bozek .01 .05
398 Bobby Smith .02 .10
399 Mark Pederson .01 .05
400 Kevin Todd RC .01 .05
401 Sergei Fedorov .15 .40
402 Tom Barrasso .02 .10
403 Brett Hull HL .02 .10
404 Bob Carpenter UER .01 .05
(No italics or diamond 85-86 or 90-91 GP)
405 Luc Robitaille .02 .10
406 Mark Hardy .01 .05
407 Neil Sheehy .01 .05
408 Mike McNeill .01 .05
409 Dave Manson .01 .05
410 Mike Tomlak .01 .05
411 Robert Reichel .01 .05
412 Islanders Team .01 .05
413 Patrick Roy .40 1.00
414 Shaun Van Allen RC .01 .05
415 Dale Kushner .01 .05
416 Pierre Turgeon .02 .10
417 Curtis Joseph .07 .20
418 Randy Gilhen .01 .05
419 Jyrki Lumme .01 .05
420 Neal Broten .01 .05
421 Kevin Stevens .01 .05
422 Chris Terreri .02 .10
423 David Reid .01 .05
424 Steve Yzerman .40 1.00
425 Ed Belfour LL .02 .10
426 Jim Johnson .01 .05
427 Joey Kocur .01 .05
428 Joel Otto .01 .05
429 Dino Ciccarelli .02 .10
430 Blackhawks Team .01 .05
431 Claude Lapointe RC .01 .05
432 Chris Joseph .01 .05
433 Gaetan Duchesne .01 .05
434 Mike Keane .01 .05
435 Dave Chyzowski .01 .05
436 Glen Featherstone .01 .05
437 Jim Paek RC .01 .05
438 Doug Evans .01 .05
439 Alexei Kasatonov UER .01 .05
(Misspelled Alexi on card back)
440 Ken Hodge Jr. .01 .05
441 Dave Snuggerud .01 .05
442 Brad Shaw .01 .05
443 Gerard Gallant .01 .05
444 Jiri Latal .01 .05
445 Peter Zezel .01 .05
446 Troy Gamble .02 .10
447 Craig Coxe .01 .05
448 Adam Oates .01 .05
449 Todd Krygier .01 .05
450 Andre Racicot RC .02 .10
451 Patrik Sundstrom .01 .05
452 Glen Wesley UER .01 .05
(No italics or diamond 90-91 GP)
453 Jocelyn Lemieux .01 .05
454 Rick Zombo .01 .05
455 Derek King .01 .05
456 J.J. Daigneault .01 .05
457 Rick Vaive .01 .05
458 Larry Robinson .01 .05
459 Rick Wamsley .02 .10
460 Craig Simpson .01 .05
461 Corey Millen RC .01 .05
462 Sergio Momesso .01 .05
463 Paul MacDermid .01 .05
464 Wendel Clark .02 .10
465 Mikhail Tatarinov .01 .05
466 Mark Howe .01 .05
467 Jay Miller .01 .05
468 Grant Jennings .01 .05
469 Paul Gillis .01 .05
470 Ron Hextall .02 .10
471 Alexander Godynyuk RC .01 .05
472 Bryan Trottier .07 .20
473 Kevin Haller RC .02 .10
474 Troy Mallette .01 .05
475 Jim Wiemer .01 .05
476 David Maley .01 .05
477 Moe Mantha UER .01 .05
(Photo actually Paul MacDermid)
478 Brad Jones .01 .05
479 Craig Muni .01 .05
480 Igor Larionov .01 .05
481 Scott Stevens .02 .10
482 Sergei Makarov .01 .05
483 Mike Lalor .01 .05
484 Tony McKegney .01 .05
485 Perry Berezan .01 .05
486 Derrick Smith .01 .05
487 Jim Hrivnak .01 .05
488 David Volek .01 .05
489 Sylvain Lefebvre .01 .05
490 Rod Brind'Amour .02 .10
491 Al MacInnis .02 .10
492 Jamie Leach .01 .05
493 Robert Dirk .01 .05
494 Gordie Roberts .01 .05
495 Mike Hudson .01 .05
496 Frank Breault .01 .05
497 Rejean Lemelin .02 .10
498 Kris King .01 .05
499 Pat Verbeek .01 .05
500 Bryan Fogarty .01 .05
501 Perry Anderson .01 .05
502 Joe Cirella .01 .05
503 Mikko Makela .01 .05
504 Paul Coffey HL UER .02 .10
(Misspelled Coffee and Dennis Potvin on card back; date 12/22/90 in English& but 12/23/90 in French)
505 Don Beaupre .02 .10
506 Brian Glynn .01 .05
507 Dave Poulin .01 .05
508 Steve Chiasson .01 .05
509 Myles O'Connor RC .01 .05
510 Ilkka Sinisalo .01 .05
511 Nick Kypreos .01 .05
512 Doug Houda UER .01 .05
(No position after name on back)
513 Valeri Kamensky RC .02 .10
514 Sergei Nemchinov .01 .05
515 Dimitri Mironov .02 .10
516 Brett Hull Hart .02 .10
517 Ray Bourque Norris .02 .10
518 Ed Belfour Calder .02 .10
519 Ed Belfour UER .02 .10
Vezina Trophy
(Georges misspelled as George)
520 Wayne Gretzky Byng .25 .60
521 Dirk Graham Selke .01 .05
522 Wayne Gretzky Ross .25 .60
523 Mario Lemieux Smythe .25 .60
524 Wayne Gretzky HL .25 .60
525 Sharks Logo .01 .05
526 Lightning Logo .01 .05
(Card back states team will play in Orlando for 1992-93 if arena is not complete. The Lightning played at Tampa Expo Hall.)
527 Senators Logo .01 .05
528 Checklist 397-528 .01 .05

1991-92 Topps/Bowman Preview Sheet

This nine-card unperforated sheet of Topps and Bowman hockey cards was sent to dealers to show them the graphic design of the coming year's hockey cards. The fronts of these preview cards are identical to the regular issue. In blue lettering, the backs have the player's name, the words "Pre-Production Sample", "1991 Topps (or as the case may be, Bowman) Card", and a tagline. The cards are unnumbered on the back and hence are listed below beginning with the upper left corner, counting across, and ending with the lower right corner. The cards are arranged so that Topps and Bowman cards alternate with one another.

COMPLETE SET (9) 4.00 10.00
1 Mario Lemieux 1.00 2.50
(Topps)
2 Wayne Gretzky 1.25 3.00
(Bowman)
3 Joe Sakic .50 1.25
(Topps)
4 Ray Bourque .30 .75
(Bowman)
5 Ed Belfour .30 .75
(Topps)
6 Mark Messier .40 1.00
(Bowman)
7 Pat LaFontaine .20 .50
(Topps)
8 Steve Yzerman .60 1.50
(Bowman)
9 Brett Hull .40 1.00
(Topps)

1991-92 Topps Team Scoring Leaders

This 21-card standard-size set was inserted at a rate of one per '91-92 Topps pack and features the top scorer from every team on the front, while the back ranks the top 10 point leaders for that team.

COMPLETE SET (21) 2.50 6.00
1 Pat Verbeek .15 .40
2 Dale Hawerchuk .15 .40
3 Steve Yzerman .60 1.50
4 Brian Leetch .20 .50
5 Mark Recchi .15 .40
6 Esa Tikkanen .02 .10
7 Dave Gagner .02 .10
8 Joe Sakic .40 1.00
9 Vincent Damphousse .15 .40
10 Wayne Gretzky 1.25 3.00
11 Phil Housley .02 .10
12 Pat LaFontaine .15 .40
13 Rick Tocchet .15 .40
14 Theo Fleury UER .15 .40
(Misspelled Fluery on card back)
15 John MacLean .02 .10
16 Kevin Hatcher .02 .10
17 Trevor Linden .15 .40
18 Russ Courtnall .02 .10
19 Ray Bourque .20 .50
20 Brett Hull .25 .60
21 Steve Larmer .02 .10

1992-93 Topps

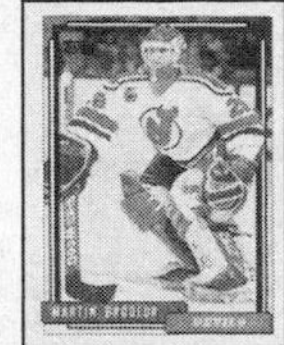

The 1992-93 Topps set contains 529 standard-size cards. Topps switched to white card stock this year allowing for a better looking product. Card fronts have team and player name at the bottom. Colorful backs include yearly statistics, playoff statistics and game-winning goals from 1991-92. The early print-run cards of Randy Moller (407) suffer from a print flaw which appears to be large finger impression on the card face. The only Rookie Card of note is Guy Hebert.

COMPLETE SET (529) 8.00 20.00
COMP.FACT.SET (549) 12.50 30.00
1 Wayne Gretzky .60 1.50
2 Brett Hull .10 .30
3 Felix Potvin .08 .25
4 Mark Tinordi .01 .05
5 Paul Coffey HL .05 .15
6 Tony Amonte .05 .15
7 Pat Falloon .01 .05
8 Pavel Bure .05 .15
9 Nicklas Lidstrom .02 .10
10 Dominic Roussel .01 .05
11 Nelson Emerson .01 .05
12 Donald Audette .01 .05
13 Gilbert Dionne .01 .05
14 Vladimir Konstantinov .08 .25
15 Kevin Todd .01 .05
16 Steve Leach .01 .05
17 Ed Olczyk .01 .05
18 Jim Hrivnak .02 .10
19 Gilbert Dionne .01 .05
20 Mike Vernon .02 .10
21 Dave Christian .01 .05
22 Ed Belfour .08 .25
23 Andrew Cassels .01 .05
24 Jaromir Jagr .10 .30
25 Arturs Irbe .08 .25
26 Petr Klima .01 .05
27 Randy Gilhen .01 .05
28 Ulf Dahlen .01 .05
29 Kelly Hrudey .02 .10
30 Dave Ellett .01 .05
31 Tom Fitzgerald .01 .05
32 Cam Neely .08 .25
33 Greg Paslawski .01 .05
34 Brad May .01 .05
35 Slava Kozlov .02 .10
36 Mark Hunter .01 .05
37 Steve Chiasson .01 .05
38 Joe Murphy .01 .05
39 Darryl Sydor .01 .05
40 Ron Hextall .02 .10
41 Jim Sandlak .01 .05
42 Dave Lowry .01 .05
43 Claude Lemieux .01 .05
44 Gerald Diduck .01 .05
45 Mike McPhee .01 .05
46 Rod Langway .01 .05
47 Guy Larose .01 .05
48 Craig Billington .02 .10
49 Daniel Marois .01 .05
50 Todd Nelson RC .01 .05
51 Jari Kurri .08 .25
52 Keith Brown .01 .05
53 Valeri Kamensky .01 .05
54 Jim Johnson .01 .05
55 Vincent Damphousse .01 .05
56 Pat Elynuik .01 .05
57 Jeff Beukeboom .01 .05
58 Paul Ysebaert .01 .05
59 Ken Sutton .01 .05
60 Dale Craigwell .01 .05
61 Marc Bergevin .01 .05
62 Stephane Beauregard .02 .10
63 Bob Probert .01 .05
64 Jergus Baca .01 .05
65 Brian Propp .01 .05
66 Jacques Cloutier .02 .10
67 Jim Thomson RC .01 .05
68 Anatoli Semenov .01 .05
69 Stephan Lebeau .01 .05
70 Rick Tocchet .02 .10
71 James Patrick .01 .05
72 Rob Brown .01 .05
73 Peter Ahola .01 .05
74 Bob Corkum .01 .05
75 Brent Sutter .01 .05
76 Neil Wilkinson .01 .05
77 Mark Osborne .01 .05
78 Ron Wilson .01 .05
79 Todd Richards .01 .05
80 Robert Kron .01 .05
81 Cliff Ronning .01 .05
82 Zarley Zalapski .01 .05
83 Randy Burridge .01 .05
84 Jarrod Skalde .01 .05
85 Gary Leeman .01 .05
86 Mike Ricci .02 .10
87 Dennis Vaske .01 .05
88 John LeBlanc RC .01 .05

89 Brad Shaw .01 .05
90 Rod Brind'Amour .02 .10
91 Colin Patterson .01 .05
92 Gerard Gallant .01 .05
93 Per Djoos .01 .05
94 Claude Lapointe .01 .05
95 Bob Errey .01 .05
96 Norm Maciver .01 .05
97 Todd Elik .01 .05
98 Chris Chelios .08 .25
99 Keith Primeau .01 .05
100 Jim Waite .02 .10
101 Luc Robitaille .02 .10
102 Keith Tkachuk .08 .25
103 Benoit Hogue .01 .05
104 Brian Mullen .01 .05
105 Joe Nieuwendyk .02 .10
106 Randy McKay .01 .05
107 Michal Pivonka .01 .05
108 Darcy Wakaluk .02 .10
109 Andy Brickley .01 .05
110 Patrick Roy .20 .50
Goals Against
Average Leader
111 Bob Sweeney .01 .05
112 Guy Hebert RC .20 .50
113 Joe Mullen .02 .10
114 Gord Murphy .01 .05
115 Evgeny Davydov .01 .05
116 Gary Roberts .01 .05
117 Pelle Eklund .01 .05
118 Tom Kurvers .01 .05
119 John Tonelli .01 .05
120 Fredrik Olausson .01 .05
121 Mike Donnelly .01 .05
122 Doug Gilmour .02 .10
123 Wayne Gretzky .30 .75
Assists Leader
124 Curtis Leschyshyn .01 .05
125 Guy Carbonneau .02 .10
126 Bill Ranford .02 .10
127 Ulf Samuelsson .01 .05
128 Joey Kocur .02 .10
129 Kevin Miller .01 .05
130 Kirk McLean .02 .10
131 Kevin Dineen .01 .05
132 John Cullen .01 .05
133 Al Iafrate .02 .10
134 Craig Janney .02 .10
135 Patrick Flatley .01 .05
136 Dominik Hasek .30 .75
137 Benoit Brunet .01 .05
138 Dave Babych .01 .05
139 Doug Brown .01 .05
140 Mike Lalor .01 .05
141 Thomas Steen .01 .05
142 Frank Musil .01 .05
143 Dan Quinn .01 .05
144 Dimitri Mironov .01 .05
145 Bob Kudelski .01 .05
146 Mike Bullard .01 .05
147 Randy Carlyle .01 .05
148 Kent Manderville .01 .05
149 Kevin Hatcher .01 .05
150 Steve Kasper .01 .05
151 Mikael Andersson .01 .05
152 Alexei Kasatonov .01 .05
153 Jan Erixon .01 .05
154 Craig Ludwig .01 .05
155 Dave Poulin .01 .05
156 Scott Stevens .02 .10
157 Robert Reichel .01 .05
158 Uwe Krupp .01 .05
159 Brian Noonan .01 .05
160 Stephane Richer .02 .10
161 Brent Thompson .01 .05
162 Glenn Anderson .02 .10
163 Joe Cirella .01 .05
164 Dave Andreychuk .02 .10
165 Vladimir Konstantinov .08 .25
166 Mike McNeill .01 .05
167 Darrin Shannon .01 .05
168 Rob Pearson .01 .05
169 John Vanbiesbrouck .02 .10
170 Randy Wood .01 .05
171 Marty McSorley .01 .05
172 Mike Hudson .01 .05
173 Paul Fenton .01 .05
174 Jeff Brown .01 .05
175 Mark Greig .01 .05
176 Gordie Roberts .01 .05
177 Josef Beranek .01 .05
178 Shawn Burr .01 .05
179 Marc Bureau .01 .05
180 Mikhail Tatarinov .01 .05
181 Robert Cimetta .01 .05
182 Paul Coffey UER .08 .25
(Still pictured
as a Penguin)
183 Bob Essensa .02 .10
184 Joe Reekie .01 .05
185 Jeff Hackett .02 .10
186 Tomas Forslund .01 .05
187 Claude Vilgrain .01 .05
188 John Druce .01 .05
189 Patrice Brisebois .01 .05
190 Peter Douris .01 .05
191 Brent Ashton .01 .05
192 Eric Desjardins .02 .10
193 Nick Kypreos .01 .05
194 Dana Murzyn .01 .05
195 Don Beaupre .02 .10
196 Jeff Chychrun .01 .05
197 Dave Barr .01 .05
198 Brian Glynn .01 .05
199 Keith Acton .01 .05
200 Igor Kravchuk .01 .05
201 Shayne Corson .01 .05
202 Curt Giles .01 .05
203 Darren Turcotte .01 .05
204 David Volek .01 .05
205 Ray Whitney RC .15 .40
206 Donald Audette .01 .05
207 Steve Yzerman .40 1.00
208 Craig Berube .01 .05
209 Bob McGill .01 .05
210 Stu Barnes .01 .05
211 Rob Blake .02 .10
212 Mario Lemieux .40 1.00
213 Dominic Roussel .02 .10
214 Sergio Momesso .01 .05
215 Brad Marsh .01 .05
216 Mark Fitzpatrick .02 .10
217 Ken Baumgartner .01 .05
218 Greg Gilbert .01 .05
219 Ric Nattress .01 .05
220 Theo Fleury .01 .05
221 Ray Bourque .15 .40
222 Steve Thomas .02 .10
223 Scott Niedermayer .01 .05
224 Jeff Lazaro .01 .05
225 Tim Cheveldae .01 .05
Kirk McLean
Wins Leaders
226 Marc Fortier .01 .05
227 Rob Zettler .01 .05
228 Kevin Todd .01 .05
229 Tony Amonte .02 .10
230 Mark Lamb .01 .05
231 Chris Dahlquist .01 .05
232 James Black .01 .05
233 Paul Cavallini .01 .05
234 Gino Cavallini .01 .05
235 Tony Tanti .01 .05
236 Mike Ridley .01 .05
237 Curtis Joseph .08 .25
238 Mike Craig .01 .05
239 Luciano Borsato .01 .05
240 Brian Bellows .01 .05
241 Barry Pederson .01 .05
242 Tony Granato .01 .05
243 Jim Paek .01 .05
244 Tim Bergland .01 .05
245 Jay More .01 .05
246 Laurie Boschman .01 .05
247 Doug Bodger .01 .05
248 Murray Craven .01 .05
249 Kris Draper .02 .10
250 Brian Benning .01 .05
251 Jarmo Myllys .01 .05
252 Sergei Fedorov .10 .30
253 Mathieu Schneider .01 .05
254 Dave Gagner .02 .10
255 Michel Goulet .02 .10
256 Alexander Godynyuk .01 .05
257 Ray Sheppard .01 .05
258 Mark Messier AS .05 .15
259 Kevin Stevens AS .01 .05
260 Brett Hull AS .08 .25
261 Brian Leetch AS .07 .20
262 Ray Bourque AS .07 .20
263 Patrick Roy AS .20 .50
264 Mike Gartner HL .01 .05
265 Mario Lemieux AS .20 .50
266 Luc Robitaille AS .02 .10
267 Mark Recchi AS .01 .05
268 Phil Housley AS .01 .05
269 Scott Stevens AS .01 .05
270 Kirk McLean AS .01 .05
271 Steve Duchesne .01 .05
272 Jiri Hrdina .01 .05
273 John MacLean .02 .10
274 Mark Messier .08 .25
275 Geoff Smith .01 .05
276 Russ Courtnall .01 .05
277 Yves Racine .01 .05
278 Tom Draper .01 .05
279 Charlie Huddy .01 .05
280 Trevor Kidd .02 .10
281 Garth Butcher .01 .05
282 Mike Sullivan .01 .05
283 Adam Burt .01 .05
284 Troy Murray .01 .05
285 Stephane Fiset .02 .10
286 Perry Anderson .01 .05
287 Sergei Nemchinov .01 .05
288 Rick Zombo .01 .05
289 Pierre Turgeon .02 .10
290 Kevin Lowe .02 .10
291 Brian Bradley .01 .05
292 Martin Gelinas UER .01 .05
(Transaction date should
be 8-9-88 not 8-9-89)
293 Brian Leetch .08 .25
294 Peter Bondra .02 .10
295 Brendan Shanahan .08 .25
296 Dale Hawerchuk .02 .10
297 Mike Hough .01 .05
298 Rollie Melanson .02 .10
299 Brad Jones .01 .05
300 Jocelyn Lemieux .01 .05
301 Brad McCrimmon .01 .05
302 Marty McInnis .01 .05
303 Chris Terreri .02 .10
304 Dean Evason .01 .05
305 Glenn Healy .02 .10
306 Ken Hodge Jr. .01 .05
307 Mike Liut .02 .10
308 Gary Suter .01 .05
309 Neal Broten .02 .10
310 Tim Cheveldae .02 .10
311 Tom Fergus .01 .05
312 Petr Svoboda .01 .05
313 Tom Chorske .01 .05
314 Paul Ysebaert .01 .05
Plus/Minus Leader
315 Steve Smith .01 .05
316 Stephane Morin .01 .05
317 Pat MacLeod .01 .05
318 Dino Ciccarelli .02 .10
319 Peter Zezel .01 .05
320 Chris Lindberg .01 .05
321 Grant Ledyard .01 .05
322 Ron Francis .02 .10
323 Adrien Plavsic .01 .05
324 Ray Ferraro .01 .05
325 Wendel Clark .02 .10
326 Corey Millen .01 .05
327 Mark Pederson .01 .05
328 Patrick Poulin .01 .05
329 Adam Graves .01 .05
330 Bobby Holik .02 .10
331 Kelly Kisio .01 .05
332 Peter Sidorkiewicz .02 .10
333 Vladimir Ruzicka .01 .05
334 J.J. Daigneault .01 .05
335 Troy Mallette .01 .05
336 Craig MacTavish .01 .05
337 Michel Petit .01 .05
338 Claude Loiselle .01 .05
339 Teppo Numminen .01 .05
340 Brett Hull .08 .25
Goal Scoring Leader
341 Sylvain Lefebvre .01 .05
342 Perry Berezan .01 .05
343 Kevin Stevens .01 .05
344 Randy Ladouceur .01 .05
345 Pat LaFontaine .08 .25
346 Glen Wesley .01 .05
347 Michel Goulet HL .01 .05
348 Jamie Macoun .01 .05
349 Owen Nolan .02 .10
350 Grant Fuhr .08 .25
351 Tim Kerr .01 .05
352 Kjell Samuelsson .01 .05
353 Pavel Bure .08 .25
354 Murray Baron .01 .05
355 Paul Broten .01 .05
356 Craig Simpson .01 .05
357 Ken Daneyko .01 .05
358 Greg Hawgood .01 .05
359 Johan Garpenlov .01 .05
360 Garry Galley .01 .05
361 Paul DiPietro .01 .05
362 Jamie Leach .01 .05
363 Clint Malarchuk .02 .10
364 Dan Lambert .01 .05
365 Joe Juneau UER .02 .10
(Shoots left not right)
366 Scott Lachance .01 .05
367 Mike Richter .08 .25
368 Sheldon Kennedy .01 .05
369 John McIntyre .01 .05
370 Glen Murray UER .01 .05
(Misspelled Glenn
on both sides)
371 Ron Sutter .01 .05
372 David Williams RC .01 .05
373 Bill Lindsay RC .01 .05
374 Todd Gill .01 .05
375 Sylvain Turgeon .01 .05
376 Dirk Graham .01 .05
377 Brad Schlegel .01 .05
378 Bob Carpenter .01 .05
379 Jon Casey .02 .10
380 Andrei Lomakin .01 .05
381 Kay Whitmore .02 .10
382 Alexander Mogilny .02 .10
383 Garry Valk .01 .05
384 Bruce Driver .01 .05
385 Jeff Reese .01 .05
386 Brent Gilchrist .01 .05
387 Kerry Huffman .01 .05
388 Bobby Smith .02 .10
389 Dave Manson .01 .05
390 Russ Romaniuk .01 .05
391 Paul MacDermid .01 .05
392 Louie DeBrusk .01 .05
393 Dave McLlwain .01 .05
394 Andy Moog .08 .25
395 Tie Domi .08 .25
396 Pat Jablonski .02 .10
397 Troy Loney .01 .05
398 Jimmy Carson .01 .05
399 Eric Weinrich .01 .05
400 Jeremy Roenick .10 .30
401 Brent Fedyk .01 .05
402 Geoff Sanderson .02 .10
403 Doug Lidster .01 .05
404 Mike Gartner .02 .10
405 Derian Hatcher .02 .10
406 Gaetan Duchesne .01 .05
407 Randy Moller .01 .05
408 Brian Skrudland .01 .05
409 Luke Richardson .01 .05
410 Mark Recchi .02 .10
411 Steve Konroyd .01 .05
412 Troy Gamble .02 .10
413 Greg Johnston .01 .05
414 Denis Savard .02 .10
415 Mats Sundin .08 .25
416 Bryan Trottier .02 .10
417 Don Sweeney .01 .05
418 Pat Falloon .01 .05
419 Alexander Semak .01 .05
420 David Shaw .01 .05
421 Tomas Sandstrom .02 .10
422 Petr Nedved .02 .10
423 Peter Ing .02 .10
424 Wayne Presley .01 .05
425 Rick Wamsley .02 .10
426 Rob Zamuner RC .02 .10
427 Claude Boivin .01 .05
428 Sylvain Cote .01 .05
429 Kevin Stevens HL .01 .05
430 Randy Velischek .01 .05
431 Derek King .01 .05
432 Terry Yake .01 .05
433 Philippe Bozon .01 .05
434 Rich Sutter .01 .05
435 Brian Lawton .01 .05
436 Brian Hayward .02 .10
437 Robert Dirk .01 .05
438 Bernie Nicholls .02 .10
439 Michel Picard .01 .05
440 Nicklas Lidstrom .08 .25
441 Mike Modano .15 .40
442 Phil Bourque .01 .05
443 Wayne McBean .01 .05
444 Scott Mellanby .01 .05
445 Kevin Haller .01 .05
446 Dave Taylor UER .02 .10
(Games played total
***& should be 1030)
447 Larry Murphy .02 .10
448 David Bruce .01 .05
449 Steven Finn .01 .05
450 Mike Krushelnyski .01 .05
451 Adam Creighton .01 .05
452 Al MacInnis .02 .10
453 Rick Tabaracci .02 .10
454 Bob Bassen .01 .05
455 Kelly Buchberger .01 .05
456 Phil Housley .02 .10
457 Daren Puppa .02 .10
458 Slava Fetisov .01 .05
459 Doug Smail .01 .05
460 Paul Stanton .01 .05
461 Steve Weeks .02 .10
462 Valeri Zelepukin .01 .05
463 Stephane Matteau .01 .05
464 Dale Hunter .02 .10
465 Terry Carkner .01 .05
466 Vincent Riendeau .02 .10
467 Sergei Makarov .01 .05
468 Igor Ulanov .01 .05
469 Peter Stastny .02 .10
470 Dimitri Khristich .01 .05
471 Joel Otto .01 .05
472 Geoff Courtnall .01 .05
473 Mike Ramsey .01 .05
474 Yvon Corriveau .01 .05
475 Adam Oates .02 .10
476 Esa Tikkanen .01 .05
477 Doug Weight .08 .25
478 Mike Keane .01 .05
479 Kelly Miller .01 .05
480 Nelson Emerson .01 .05
481 Shawn McEachern .01 .05
482 Doug Wilson .02 .10
483 Jeff Odgers .01 .05
484 Stephane Quintal .01 .05
485 Christian Ruuttu .01 .05
486 Paul Ranheim .01 .05
487 Craig Wolanin .01 .05
488 Rob DiMaio .01 .05
489 Shawn Cronin .01 .05
490 Kirk Muller .01 .05
491 Patrick Roy .20 .50
Save Pct. Leader
492 Rich Pilon .01 .05
493 Pat Verbeek .01 .05
494 Ken Wregget .02 .10
495 Joe Sakic .15 .40
496 Zdeno Ciger .01 .05
497 Steve Larmer .02 .10
498 Calle Johansson .01 .05
499 Trevor Linden .02 .10
500 John LeClair .15 .40
501 Bryan Marchment .01 .05
502 Todd Krygier .01 .05
503 Tom Barrasso .02 .10
504 Mario Lemieux LL .20 .50
505 Daniel Berthiaume UER .02 .10
(Headings on back are
for non-goalies)
506 Jamie Baker .01 .05
507 Greg Adams .01 .05
508 Patrick Roy .40 1.00
509 Kris King .01 .05
510 Jyrki Lumme .01 .05
511 Darin Kimble .01 .05
512 Igor Larionov .01 .05
513 Martin Brodeur .30 .75
514 Denny Felsner RC .02 .10
515 Yanic Dupre .01 .05
516 Bill Guerin RC .40 1.00
517 Bret Hedican RC UER .02 .10
(Misspelled Brett
on both sides)
518 Mike Hartman .01 .05
519 Steve Heinze UER .01 .05
(Photo actually
Gord Hynes)
520 Frantisek Kucera .01 .05
521 David Reid .01 .05
522 Frank Pietrangelo .02 .10
523 Martin Rucinsky .01 .05
524 Tony Hrkac .01 .05
525 Checklist 1-132 .01 .05
526 Checklist 133-264 .01 .05
527 Checklist 265-396 .01 .05
528 Checklist 397-528 UER .01 .05
(529 not listed)
529 Eric Lindros UER .08 .25
(Acquired 6-30-92
not 6-20-92)

1992-93 Topps Gold

Gold foil versions of all 529 cards in the 1992-93 Topps Hockey set were produced: one was inserted in each foil pack, three in each jumbo pack, and 20 were included in factory sets as a bonus. Deciding against producing Gold checklists, Topps made cards 525-528 of players not featured in the basic set. On a white card face, the fronts display color action player photos inside a two-color picture frame. The player's name and team name appear in two short colored bars toward the bottom of the picture. The backs carry biography, statistics, and player profile. The following cards were printed in a horizontal format: 90, 164, 195, 225, 272, 307, 324, 337, 350, 366, 413 and 420.

*VETS: 4X TO 10X BASIC CARDS
*ROOKIES: 1.5X TO 4X BASIC CARDS
525G Al Conroy .20 .50
526G Jeff Norton .20 .50
527G Rob Robinson .20 .50
528G Adam Foote .40 1.00

1993-94 Topps Premier Promo Sheet

This nine-card promo sheet measures approximately 7 3/4" by 10 3/4" and features white-bordered color player photos on the front. The player's name and position appear at the bottom of each card within a team color-coded stripe, and the Premier logo is displayed in the lower left. The horizontal backs carry color player action shots on their left sides. At the top, the player's name, uniform number, team, and position appear within a team color-coded stripe. Below this, and to the right of the player photo, appear the player's biography and stats on a background that resembles white ruffled silk. The team, NHL, and NHLPA logos in the lower left round out the back.

COMPLETE SET (9) 1.50 4.00
1 Patrick Roy .60 1.50
15 Mike Vernon .15 .40
22 Jamie Baker .08 .25
100 Theo Fleury .15 .40
156 Geoff Sanderson .15 .40
244 Dave Lowry .08 .25
257 Scott Lachance .08 .25
601 Mark Messier .20 .50
602 Ray Bourque .20 .50

1993-94 Topps Premier

Both series of the 1993-94 Topps (and O-Pee-Chee) Premier hockey set consisted of 264 standard-size cards. The fronts feature white-bordered color player photos. The player's name and position appear at the bottom of each card within a team color-coded stripe, and the Premier logo is displayed in the lower left. The horizontal backs carry color player action shots on their left sides. Topical subsets featured are Super Rookies (121-130), and 1st Team All-Stars, 2nd Team All-Stars, and League Leaders scattered throughout the set. Except for some information in French on the backs, the O-Pee-Chee Premier set is identical to the Topps Premier set.

COMPLETE SET (528) 8.00 20.00
COMP.SERIES 1 (264) 4.00 10.00
COMP.SERIES 2 (264) 4.00 10.00
1 Patrick Roy .40 1.00
2 Alexei Zhitnik .01 .05
3 Uwe Krupp .01 .05
4 Todd Gill .01 .05
5 Paul Stanton .01 .05
6 Petr Nedved .02 .10
7 Dale Hawerchuk .02 .10
8 Kevin Miller .01 .05
9 Nicklas Lidstrom .07 .20
10 Joe Sakic .15 .40
11 Thomas Steen .01 .05
12 Peter Bondra .02 .10
13 Brian Noonan .01 .05
14 Glen Featherstone .01 .05
15 Mike Vernon .02 .10
16 Janne Ojanen .01 .05
17 Neil Brady .01 .05
18 Dimitri Yushkevich .01 .05
19 Rob Zamuner .01 .05
20 Zarley Zalapski .01 .05
21 Mike Sullivan .01 .05
22 Jamie Baker .01 .05
23 Craig MacTavish .01 .05
24 Mark Tinordi .01 .05
25 Brian Leetch .07 .20
26 Brian Skrudland .01 .05
27 Keith Tkachuk .07 .20
28 Patrick Flatley .01 .05
29 Doug Bodger .01 .05
30 Felix Potvin .07 .20
31 Shawn Antoski .01 .05
32 Eric Desjardins .02 .10
33 Mike Donnelly .01 .05
34 Kjell Samuelsson .01 .05
35 Nelson Emerson .01 .05
36 Phil Housley .02 .10
37 Mario Lemieux LL .07 .20
38 Shayne Corson .01 .05
39 Steve Smith .01 .05
40 Bob Kudelski .01 .05
41 Joe Cirella .01 .05
42 Sergei Nemchinov .01 .05
43 Kerry Huffman .01 .05
44 Bob Beers .01 .05
45 Al Iafrate .01 .05
46 Mike Modano .10 .30
47 Pat Verbeek .01 .05
48 Joel Otto .01 .05
49 Dino Ciccarelli .02 .10
50 Adam Oates .02 .10
51 Pat Elynuik .01 .05
52 Bobby Holik .01 .05
53 Johan Garpenlov .01 .05
54 Jeff Beukeboom .01 .05
55 Tommy Soderstrom .02 .10
56 Rob Blake .02 .10
57 Marty McInnis .01 .05
58 Dixon Ward .01 .05
59 Patrice Brisebois .01 .05
60 Ed Belfour .07 .20
61 Donald Audette .01 .05
62 Mike Ricci .01 .05
63 Fredrik Olausson .01 .05
64 Norm Maciver .01 .05
65 Andrew Cassels .01 .05
66 Tim Cheveldae .02 .10
67 David Reid .01 .05
68 Philippe Bozon .01 .05
69 Drake Berehowsky .01 .05
70 Tony Amonte .02 .10
71 Dave Manson .01 .05
72 Rick Tocchet .02 .10
73 Steve Kasper .01 .05
74 Assist Leader .02 .10
Adam Oates
75 Ulf Dahlen .01 .05
76 Chris Lindberg .01 .05
77 Doug Wilson .02 .10
78 Mike Ridley .01 .05
79 Viacheslav Butsayev .01 .05
80 Scott Stevens .02 .10
81 Cliff Ronning .01 .05
82 Andrei Lomakin .01 .05
83 Shawn Burr .01 .05
84 Benoit Brunet .01 .05
85 Valeri Kamensky .02 .10
86 Randy Carlyle .01 .05
87 Chris Joseph .01 .05
88 Dirk Graham .01 .05
89 Ken Sutton .01 .05
90 Luc Robitaille AS .02 .10
91 Mario Lemieux AS .07 .20
92 Teemu Selanne AS .07 .20
93 Ray Bourque AS .07 .20
94 Chris Chelios AS .07 .20
95 Ed Belfour AS .07 .20
96 Keith Jones .01 .05
97 Sylvain Turgeon .01 .05
98 Jim Johnson .01 .05
99 Michael Nylander .01 .05
100 Theo Fleury .01 .05
101 Shawn Chambers .01 .05
102 Alexander Semak .01 .05
103 Ron Sutter .01 .05
104 Glenn Anderson .02 .10
105 Jaromir Jagr .10 .30
106 Adam Graves .01 .05
107 Nikolai Borschevsky .01 .05
108 Vladimir Konstantinov .02 .10
109 Robb Stauber .02 .10
110 Arturs Irbe .02 .10
111 Felix Potvin .02 .10
G.A.A. Leader
112 Darius Kasparaitis .01 .05
113 Kirk McLean .02 .10
114 Glen Wesley .01 .05
115 Rod Brind'Amour .02 .10
116 Mike Eagles .01 .05
117 Brian Bradley .01 .05
118 Dave Christian .01 .05
119 Randy Wood .01 .05
120 Craig Janney .02 .10
121 Eric Lindros SR .07 .20
122 Tommy Soderstrom SR .02 .10
123 Shawn McEachern SR .01 .05
124 Andrei Kovalenko SR .01 .05
125 Joe Juneau SR .02 .10
126 Felix Potvin SR .02 .10
127 Dixon Ward SR .01 .05
128 Alexei Zhamnov SR .02 .10
129 Vladimir Malakhov SR .01 .05
130 Teemu Selanne SR .07 .20
131 Neal Broten .02 .10
132 Ulf Samuelsson .01 .05
133 Mark Janssens .01 .05
134 Claude Lemieux .01 .05
135 Mike Richter .07 .20
136 Doug Weight .02 .10
137 Rob Pearson .01 .05
138 Sylvain Cote .01 .05
139 Mike Keane .01 .05
140 Benoit Hogue .01 .05
141 Michel Petit .01 .05
142 Mark Freer .01 .05
143 Doug Zmolek .01 .05
144 Tony Granato .01 .05
145 Paul Coffey .07 .20
146 Ted Donato .01 .05
147 Brent Sutter .01 .05
148 Alexander Mogilny .08 .25
Teemu Selanne
Goal Scoring Leaders
149 James Patrick .01 .05
150 Mikael Andersson .01 .05
151 Steve Duchesne .01 .05
152 Terry Carkner .01 .05
153 Russ Courtnall .01 .05
154 Brian Mullen .01 .05
155 Martin Straka .01 .05
156 Geoff Sanderson .02 .10
157 Mark Howe .01 .05
158 Stephane Richer .02 .10
159 Doug Crossman .01 .05
160 John Vanbiesbrouck .02 .10
161 Bob Essensa .02 .10
162 Wayne Presley .01 .05
163 Mathieu Schneider .01 .05
164 Jiri Slegr .01 .05
165 Stephane Fiset .02 .10
166 Wendell Young .02 .10
167 Kevin Dineen .01 .05
168 Sandis Ozolinsh .01 .05
169 Mike Krushelnyski .01 .05
170 Kevin Stevens AS .01 .05
171 Pat LaFontaine AS .02 .10
172 Alexander Mogilny AS .02 .10
173 Larry Murphy AS .01 .05
174 Al Iafrate AS .01 .05
175 Tom Barrasso AS .02 .10
176 Derek King .01 .05
177 Bob Probert .01 .05
178 Gary Suter .01 .05
179 David Shaw .01 .05
180 Luc Robitaille .02 .10
181 John LeClair .07 .20
182 Troy Murray .01 .05
183 Dave Gagner .02 .10
184 Darcy Loewen .01 .05
185 Mario Lemieux LL .07 .20
186 Pat Jablonski .01 .05
187 Alexei Kovalev .01 .05
188 Todd Krygier .01 .05
189 Larry Murphy .01 .05
190 Pierre Turgeon .02 .10
191 Craig Ludwig .01 .05
192 Brad May .01 .05
193 John MacLean .01 .05
194 Ron Wilson .01 .05
195 Eric Weinrich .01 .05
196 Steve Chiasson .01 .05
197 Dmitri Kvartalnov .01 .05
198 Andrei Kovalenko .01 .05
199 Rob Gaudreau RC .01 .05
200 Evgeny Davydov .01 .05
201 Adrien Plavsic .01 .05
202 Brian Bellows .01 .05
203 Doug Evans .01 .05
204 Tom Barrasso .02 .10
Wins Leader
205 Joe Nieuwendyk .02 .10
206 Jari Kurri .07 .20
207 Bob Rouse .01 .05
208 Yvon Corriveau .01 .05
209 John Blue .02 .10
210 Dimitri Khristich .01 .05
211 Brent Fedyk .01 .05
212 Jody Hull .01 .05
213 Chris Terreri .02 .10
214 Mike McPhee .01 .05
215 Chris Kontos .01 .05
216 Greg Gilbert .01 .05
217 Sergei Zubov .01 .05
218 Grant Fuhr .02 .10
219 Charlie Huddy .01 .05
220 Mario Lemieux .40 1.00
221 Sheldon Kennedy .01 .05
222 Curtis Joseph .07 .20
Save Pct. Leader
223 Brad Dalgarno .01 .05
224 Bret Hedican .01 .05
225 Trevor Linden .02 .10
226 Darryl Sydor .01 .05
227 Jay More .01 .05
228 Dave Poulin .01 .05
229 Frank Musil .01 .05
230 Mark Recchi .02 .10
231 Craig Simpson .01 .05
232 Gino Cavallini .01 .05
233 Vincent Damphousse .01 .05
234 Luciano Borsato .01 .05
235 Dave Andreychuk .02 .10
236 Ken Daneyko .01 .05
237 Chris Chelios .07 .20
238 Andrew McBain .01 .05
239 Rick Tabaracci .02 .10
240 Steve Larmer .02 .10
241 Sean Burke .02 .10
242 Rob DiMaio .01 .05
243 Jim Paek .01 .05
244 Dave Lowry .01 .05
245 Alexander Mogilny .02 .10
246 Darren Turcotte .01 .05
247 Brendan Shanahan .07 .20
248 Peter Taglianetti .01 .05
249 Scott Mellanby .01 .05
250 Guy Carbonneau .01 .05
251 Claude LaPointe .01 .05
252 Pat Conacher .01 .05
253 Roger Johansson .01 .05
254 Cam Neely .07 .20
255 Garry Galley .01 .05
256 Keith Primeau .02 .10
257 Scott Lachance .01 .05
258 Bill Ranford .02 .10
259 Pat Falloon .01 .05
260 Pavel Bure .07 .20
261 Darrin Shannon .01 .05
262 Mike Foligno .01 .05
263 Checklist 1-132 .01 .05
264 Checklist 133-264 .01 .05
265 Peter Douris .01 .05
266 Warren Rychel .01 .05
267 Owen Nolan .02 .10
268 Mark Osborne .01 .05
269 Teppo Numminen .01 .05
270 Rob Niedermayer .02 .10
271 Mark Lamb .01 .05
272 Curtis Joseph .07 .20
273 Joe Murphy .01 .05
274 Bernie Nicholls .01 .05
275 Gord Roberts .01 .05
276 Al MacInnis .02 .10
277 Ken Wregget .02 .10
278 Calle Johansson .01 .05
279 Tom Kurvers .01 .05
280 Steve Yzerman .40 1.00
281 Roman Hamrlik .02 .10
282 Esa Tikkanen .01 .05
283 Darrin Madeley RC .01 .05
284 Robert Dirk .01 .05
285 Derek Plante RC .01 .05
286 Ron Tugnutt .02 .10
287 Frank Pietrangelo .02 .10
288 Paul DiPietro .01 .05
289 Alexander Godynyuk .01 .05
290 Kirk Maltby RC .01 .05
291 Olaf Kolzig .02 .10
292 Vitali Karamnov .01 .05
293 Alexei Gusarov .01 .05
294 Bryan Erickson .01 .05
295 Jocelyn Lemieux .01 .05
296 Bryan Trottier .02 .10
297 Dave Ellett .01 .05
298 Tim Watters .01 .05
299 Joe Juneau .02 .10
300 Steve Thomas .01 .05
301 Mark Greig .01 .05
302 Jeff Reese .01 .05
303 Steven King .01 .05
304 Don Beaupre .02 .10
305 Denis Savard .02 .10
306 Greg Smyth .01 .05
307 Jaroslav Modry RC .01 .05
308 Petr Svoboda .01 .05
309 Mike Craig .01 .05
310 Eric Lindros .07 .20
311 Dana Murzyn .01 .05
312 Sean Hill .01 .05
313 Andre Racicot .02 .10
314 John Vanbiesbrouck .02 .10
315 Doug Lidster .01 .05
316 Garth Butcher .01 .05
317 Alexei Yashin .01 .05
318 Sergei Fedorov .10 .30

319 Louie DeBrusk .01 .05
320 Dominik Hasek .07 .20
321 Michal Pivonka .01 .05
322 Bobby Holik .01 .05
323 Roman Hamrlik .02 .10
324 Petr Svoboda .01 .05
325 Jaromir Jagr .07 .20
326 Steven Finn .01 .05
327 Stephane Richer .02 .10
328 Claude Loiselle .01 .05
329 Joe Sacco .01 .05
330 Wayne Gretzky .50 1.25
331 Sylvain Lefebvre .01 .05
332 Sergei Bautin .01 .05
333 Craig Simpson .01 .05
334 Don Sweeney .01 .05
335 Dominic Roussel .02 .10
336 Scott Thomas RC .01 .05
337 Geoff Courtnall .01 .05
338 Tom Fitzgerald .01 .05
339 Kevin Haller .01 .05
340 Troy Loney .01 .05
341 Ronnie Stern .01 .05
342 Mark Astley RC .01 .05
343 Jeff Daniels .01 .05
344 Marc Bureau .01 .05
345 Micah Aivazoff RC .01 .05
346 Matthew Barnaby .02 .10
347 C.J. Young .01 .05
348 Dale Craigwell .01 .05
349 Ray Ferraro .01 .05
350 Ray Bourque .10 .30
351 Stu Barnes .01 .05
352 Allan Conroy RC .01 .05
353 Shawn McEachern .01 .05
354 Garry Valk .01 .05
355 Christian Ruuttu .01 .05
356 Darren Rumble .01 .05
357 Stu Grimson .01 .05
358 Alexander Karpovtsev .01 .05
359 Wendel Clark .02 .10
360 Michal Pivonka .01 .05
361 Peter Popovic RC .01 .05
362 Kevin Dahl .01 .05
363 Jeff Brown .01 .05
364 Daren Puppa .02 .10
365 Dallas Drake RC .01 .05
366 Dean McAmmond .01 .05
367 Martin Rucinsky .01 .05
368 Shane Churla .01 .05
369 Todd Ewen .01 .05
370 Kevin Stevens .01 .05
371 David Volek .01 .05
372 J.J. Daigneault .01 .05
373 Marc Bergevin .01 .05
374 Craig Billington .02 .10
375 Mike Gartner .02 .10
376 Jimmy Carson .01 .05
377 Bruce Driver .01 .05
378 Steve Heinze .01 .05
379 Patrick Carnback RC .01 .05
380 Wayne Gretzky CAN .07 .20
381 Jeff Brown CAN .01 .05
382 Gary Roberts CAN .01 .05
383 Ray Bourque CAN .07 .20
384 Mike Gartner CAN .02 .10
385 Felix Potvin CAN .07 .20
386 Michel Goulet .02 .10
387 Dave Tippett .01 .05
388 Jim Waite .02 .10
389 Yuri Khmylev .01 .05
390 Doug Gilmour .02 .10
391 Brad McCrimmon .01 .05
392 Brent Severyn RC .01 .05
393 Jocelyn Thibault RC .25 .60
394 Boris Mironov .01 .05
395 Marty McSorley .01 .05
396 Shaun Van Allen .01 .05
397 Gary Leeman .01 .05
398 Ed Olczyk .01 .05
399 Darcy Wakaluk .02 .10
400 Murray Craven .01 .05
401 Martin Brodeur .20 .50
402 Paul Laus RC .01 .05
403 Bill Houlder .01 .05
404 Robert Reichel .01 .05
405 Alexandre Daigle .01 .05
406 Brent Thompson .01 .05
407 Keith Acton .01 .05
408 Dave Karpa .01 .05
409 Igor Korolev .01 .05
410 Chris Gratton .02 .10
411 Vincent Riendeau .02 .10
412 Darren McCarty RC .15 .40
413 Bob Carpenter .01 .05
414 Joe Cirella .01 .05
415 Stephane Matteau .01 .05
416 Jozef Stumpel .01 .05
417 Rich Pilon .01 .05
418 Mattias Norstrom RC .01 .05
419 Dmitri Moronov .01 .05
420 Alexei Zhamnov .02 .10
421 Bill Guerin .01 .05
422 Greg Hawgood .01 .05
423 Randy Cunneyworth .01 .05
424 Ron Francis .02 .10
425 Brett Hull .08 .25
426 Tim Sweeney .01 .05
427 Mike Rathje .01 .05
428 Dave Babych .01 .05
429 Chris Tancill .01 .05
430 Mark Messier .07 .20
431 Bob Sweeney .01 .05
432 Terry Yake .01 .05
433 Joe Reekie .01 .05
434 Tomas Sandstrom .01 .05
435 Kevin Hatcher .01 .05
436 Bill Lindsay .01 .05
437 Jon Casey .02 .10
438 Dennis Vaske .01 .05
439 Allen Pedersen .01 .05
440 Pavel Bure .07 .20
441 Sergei Fedorov .07 .20
442 Arturs Irbe .02 .10
443 Darius Kasparaitis .01 .05
444 Evgeny Davydov .01 .05
445 Vladimir Malakhov .01 .05
446 Tom Barrasso .02 .10
447 Jeff Norton .01 .05
448 David Emma .01 .05
449 Pelle Eklund .01 .05
450 Jeremy Roenick .08 .25
451 Jesse Belanger .01 .05
452 Vitali Prokhorov .01 .05
453 Arto Blomsten .01 .05
454 Peter Zezel .01 .05
455 Kelly Kisio .01 .05
456 Zdeno Ciger .01 .05
457 Greg Johnson .01 .05
458 Dave Archibald .01 .05
459 Vladimir Vujtek .01 .05
460 Mats Sundin .07 .20
461 Dan Keczmer .01 .05
462 Stephan Lebeau .01 .05
463 Dominik Hasek .20 .50
464 Kevin Lowe .01 .05
465 Gord Murphy .01 .05
466 Bryan Smolinski .01 .05
467 Josef Beranek .01 .05
468 Ron Hextall .02 .10
469 Randy Ladouceur .01 .05
470 Scott Niedermayer .01 .05
471 Kelly Hrudey .02 .10
472 Mike Needham .01 .05
473 John Tucker .01 .05
474 Kelly Miller .01 .05
475 Jyrki Lumme .01 .05
476 Andy Moog .02 .10
477 Glen Murray .01 .05
478 Mark Ferner RC .01 .05
479 John Cullen .01 .05
480 Gilbert Dionne .01 .05
481 Paul Ranheim .01 .05
482 Mike Hough .01 .05
483 Teemu Selanne .07 .20
484 Aaron Ward RC .01 .05
485 Chris Pronger .02 .10
486 Glenn Healy .02 .10
487 Curtis Leschyshyn .01 .05
488 Jim Montgomery RC .01 .05
489 Travis Green .02 .10
490 Pat LaFontaine .07 .20
491 Bobby Dollas RC .01 .05
492 Alexei Kasatonov .01 .05
493 Corey Millen .01 .05
494 Slava Kozlov .02 .10
495 Igor Kravchuk .01 .05
496 Dimitri Filimonov .01 .05
497 Jeff Odgers .01 .05
498 Joe Mullen .02 .10
499 Gary Shuchuk .01 .05
500 Jeremy Roenick USA .08 .25
501 Tom Barrasso USA .02 .10
502 Keith Tkachuk USA .07 .20
503 Phil Housley USA .02 .10
504 Tony Granato USA .01 .05
505 Brian Leetch USA .07 .20
506 Anatoli Semenov .01 .05
507 Steve Leach .01 .05
508 Brian Skrudland .01 .05
509 Kirk Muller .01 .05
510 Gary Roberts .01 .05
511 Gerard Gallant .01 .05
512 Joey Kocur .01 .05
513 Tie Domi .01 .05
514 Kay Whitmore .02 .10
515 Vladimir Malakhov .01 .05
516 Stewart Malgunas RC .01 .05
517 Jamie Macoun .01 .05
518 Alan May .01 .05
519 Guy Hebert .02 .10
520 Derian Hatcher .01 .05
521 Richard Smehlik .01 .05
522 Joby Messier RC .01 .05
523 Trent Klatt .01 .05
524 Tom Chorske .01 .05
525 Iain Fraser RC .01 .05
526 Dan Laperriere .01 .05
527 Checklist 265-396 .01 .05
528 Checklist 397-528 .01 .05

1993-94 Topps Premier Gold

Every regular Premier 12-card pack included 11 regular cards plus one Premier Gold card. Also, one in four packs contained 10 regular cards plus two Premier Gold cards; and four Gold cards were inserted in every Topps jumbo pack. Aside from the gold-foil, the Premier Gold cards are identical to their regular issue counterparts. The four regular issue Premier checklists (263, 264, 527, and 528) were replaced by Gold cards of players not included in the basic set. The cards are numbered on the back. Except for some information in French on the backs, the O-Pee-Chee Premier Gold set is identical to the Topps Premier Gold set.

*GOLD VETS: 2X TO 5X BASIC CARDS
*GOLD ROOKIES: 1.2X TO 3X
263G Martin Lapointe CL REP .40 1.00
264G Kevin Miehm CL REP .40 1.00
527G Myles O'Connor CL REP .40 1.00
528G Jamie Leach CL REP .40 1.00

1993-94 Topps Premier Black Gold

Randomly inserted in Topps packs, these 24 standard-size cards feature on their white-bordered fronts color player action shots set on ghosted and darkened backgrounds. Gold foil inner borders at the top and bottom carry multiple Premier Black Gold logos. The player's name appears in white lettering within a black stripe across the lower gold-foil inner margin. The horizontal back carries a color action cutout set on a bluish background on the left. Career highlights appear within a purple area on the right. The player's name and team name appear within a black bar across the top. The cards are numbered on the back. Collectors could also find in packs a Winner Card A, redeemable for the entire 12-card first-series set; a Winner Card B, redeemable for the 12-card second series; and a Winner Card AB, redeemable for the entire 24 card set. The Winner cards expired May 31, 1994.

1 Teemu Selanne .60 1.50
2 Steve Duchesne .15 .40
3 Felix Potvin .60 1.50
4 Shawn McEachern .15 .40
5 Adam Oates .30 .75
6 Paul Coffey .60 1.50
7 Wayne Gretzky 4.00 10.00
8 Alexei Zhamnov .30 .75
9 Mario Lemieux 3.00 8.00
10 Gary Suter .15 .40
11 Tom Barrasso .30 .75
12 Joe Juneau .30 .75
13 Eric Lindros .60 1.50
14 Ed Belfour .60 1.50
15 Ray Bourque 1.00 2.50
16 Steve Yzerman 3.00 8.00
17 Andrei Kovalenko .15 .40
18 Curtis Joseph .60 1.50
19 Phil Housley .30 .75
20 Pierre Turgeon .30 .75
21 Brett Hull .75 2.00
22 Patrick Roy 3.00 8.00
23 Larry Murphy .30 .75
24 Pat LaFontaine .60 1.50
A Winner 1-12 Expired .75 2.00
B Winner 13-24 Expired .60 1.50
AB Winner 1-24 Expired .60 1.50

1993-94 Topps Premier Finest

Randomly inserted in both Topps and OPC second-series packs, these 12 standard-size cards feature on their metallic fronts color player action shots framed by a gold line and bordered in blue. The player's name and position appear in gold lettering in the lower blue margin. The cards are numbered on the back as "X of 12."

COMPLETE SET (12) 8.00 20.00
1 Alexandre Daigle .20 .50
2 Roman Hamrlik .40 1.00
3 Eric Lindros .75 2.00
4 Owen Nolan .40 1.00
5 Mats Sundin .75 2.00
6 Mike Modano 1.25 3.00
7 Pierre Turgeon .40 1.00
8 Joe Murphy .20 .50
9 Wendel Clark .40 1.00
10 Mario Lemieux 4.00 10.00
11 Dale Hawerchuk .40 1.00
12 Rob Ramage .20 .50

1993-94 Topps Premier Team USA

Randomly inserted at a rate of 1:12 second-series Topps Premier packs, these 23 standard-size cards feature borderless color player photos on their fronts. The player's name and the USA Hockey logo appear at the bottom in gold foil. The red, white, and blue back carries the player's name and position at the top, followed below by biography, player photo, career highlights, and statistics. The cards are numbered on the back as "X of 23."

COMPLETE SET (23) 10.00 20.00
1 Mike Dunham .75 2.00
2 Ian Moran .40 1.00
3 Peter Laviolette .40 1.00
4 Darby Hendrickson .40 1.00
5 Brian Rolston .75 2.00
6 Mark Beaufait .40 1.00
7 Travis Richards .40 1.00
8 John Lilley .40 1.00
9 Chris Ferraro .75 2.00
10 Jon Hillebrandt .40 1.00
11 Chris Imes .40 1.00
12 Ted Crowley .40 1.00
13 David Sacco .40 1.00
14 Todd Marchant .75 2.00
15 Peter Ferraro .40 1.00
16 David Roberts .40 1.00
17 Jim Campbell .75 2.00
18 Barry Richter .40 1.00
19 Craig Johnson .40 1.00
20 Brett Hauer .40 1.00
21 Jeff Lazaro .40 1.00
22 Jim Storm .40 1.00
23 Matt Martin .40 1.00

1994-95 Topps Premier

This 550-card set was issued in two series of 275 cards each. OPC packs contained 14 cards and Topps packs contained 12 cards. Both boxes contained 36 packs. It was announced in press material that no more than 2,000 cases of each series of the OPC version were printed. Because of this shorter quantity, OPC versions earn a slight premium. Card fronts feature a full white border with a color bar enclosing the player's name near the bottom. Position runs vertically down the right side of the name, team name directly below it. All text is printed in silver foil. Backs have a black border with a cutout player photo, full stats including playoffs, and personal information. The OPC back text is in French and English. The Topps version is in English only. Since some of the cards have no written text, such as the All-Star cards, they are impossible to positively identify as being from one set or the other. Both versions have "The Topps Company, Inc." printed on the back. Several subsets appear scattered throughout the set, including All-Stars, Goaltending Duos, League Leaders, Rookie Sensations, Team of the Future, Tools of the Game, The Trade and Power.

COMPLETE SET (550) 15.00 40.00
COMP.SERIES 1 (275) 6.00 15.00
COMP.SERIES 2 (275) 10.00 25.00
1 Mark Messier .08 .25
2 Darren Turcotte .01 .05
3 Mikhail Shtalenkov RC .01 .05
4 Rob Gaudreau .01 .05
5 Tony Amonte .02 .10
6 Stephane Quintal .01 .05
7 Iain Fraser .01 .05
8 Doug Weight .02 .10
9 German Titov .01 .05
10 Larry Murphy .02 .10
11 Danton Cole .01 .05
12 Pat Peake .01 .05
13 Chris Terreri .02 .10
14 Yuri Khmylev .01 .05
15 Paul Coffey .08 .25
16 Brian Savage .01 .05
17 Rod Brind'Amour .02 .10
18 Nathan Lafayette .01 .05
19 Gord Murphy .01 .05
20 Al Iafrate .01 .05
21 Kevin Miller .01 .05
22 Peter Zezel .01 .05
23 Sylvain Turgeon .01 .05
24 Mark Tinordi .01 .05
25 Jari Kurri .02 .10
26 Benoit Hogue .01 .05
27 Jeff Reese .01 .05
28 Brian Noonan .01 .05
29 Denis Tsygurov RC .01 .05
30 James Patrick .01 .05
31 Bob Corkum .01 .05
32 Valeri Kamensky .02 .10
33 Ray Whitney .01 .05
34 Joe Murphy .01 .05
35 Dominik Hasek AS .08 .25
36 Ray Bourque AS .08 .25
37 Brian Leetch AS .08 .25
38 Dave Andreychuk AS .02 .10
39 Pavel Bure AS .08 .25
40 Sergei Fedorov AS .08 .25
41 Bob Beers .01 .05
42 Byron Dafoe RC .15 .40
43 Lyle Odelein .01 .05
44 Markus Naslund .08 .25
45 Dean Chynoweth RC .01 .05
46 Trent Klatt .01 .05
47 Murray Craven .01 .05
48 Dave Mackey .01 .05
49 Norm Maciver .01 .05
50 Alexander Mogilny .02 .10
51 David Reid .01 .05
52 Nicklas Lidstrom .08 .25
53 Tom Fitzgerald .01 .05
54 Roman Hamrlik .02 .10
55 Wendel Clark .02 .10
56 Dominic Roussel .02 .10
57 Alexei Zhitnik .01 .05
58 Valeri Zelepukin .01 .05
59 Calle Johansson .01 .05
60 Craig Janney .02 .10
61 Randy Wood .01 .05
62 Curtis Leschyshyn .01 .05
63 Stephan Lebeau .01 .05
64 Dallas Drake .01 .05
65 Vincent Damphousse .01 .05
66 Scott Lachance .01 .05
67 Dirk Graham .01 .05
68 Kevin Smyth .01 .05
69 Denis Savard .02 .10
70 Mike Richter .08 .25
71 Ronnie Stern .01 .05
72 Kirk Maltby .01 .05
73 Kjell Samuelsson .01 .05
74 Neal Broten .02 .10
75 Trevor Linden .02 .10
76 Todd Elik .01 .05
77 Andrew McBain .01 .05
78 Alexei Kudashov .01 .05
79 Ken Daneyko .01 .05
80 Dominik Hasek .08 .25
Grant Fuhr DUO
81 Andy Moog .08 .25
Darcy Wakaluk DUO
82 John Vanbiesbrouck .02 .10
Mark Fitzpatrick DUO
83 Martin Brodeur .08 .25
Chris Terreri DUO
84 Tom Barrasso .02 .10
Ken Wregget DUO
85 Kirk McLean .02 .10
Kay Whitmore DUO
86 Darryl Sydor .01 .05
87 Chris Osgood .15 .40
88 Ted Donato .01 .05
89 Dave Lowry .01 .05
90 Mark Recchi .02 .10
91 Jim Montgomery .01 .05
92 Bill Houlder .01 .05
93 Richard Smehlik .01 .05
94 Benoit Brunet .01 .05
95 Teemu Selanne .08 .25
96 Paul Ranheim .01 .05
97 Andrei Kovalenko .01 .05
98 Grant Ledyard .01 .05
99 Brent Grieve RC .01 .05
100 Joe Juneau .02 .10
101 Martin Gelinas .01 .05
102 Jamie Macoun .01 .05
103 Craig MacTavish .01 .05
104 Micah Aivazoff .01 .05
105 Stephane Richer .02 .10
106 Eric Weinrich .01 .05
107 Pat Elynuik .01 .05
108 Tomas Sandstrom .01 .05
109 Darrin Madeley .01 .05
110 Al MacInnis .02 .10
111 Cam Stewart .01 .05
112 Dixon Ward .01 .05
113 Vlastimil Kroupa .01 .05
114 Rob DiMaio .01 .05
115 Pierre Turgeon .02 .10
116 Mike Hough .01 .05
117 John LeClair .08 .25
118 Dave Hannan .01 .05
119 Todd Ewen .01 .05
120 Stanley Cup Card .02 .10
121 Dave Manson .01 .05
122 Jocelyn Lemieux .01 .05
123 Jocelyn Thibault .08 .25
124 Scott Pearson .01 .05
125 Patrick Roy AS .20 .50
126 Scott Stevens AS .02 .10
127 Al MacInnis AS .02 .10
128 Adam Graves AS .01 .05
129 Cam Neely AS .02 .10
130 Wayne Gretzky AS .30 .75
131 Tom Chorske .01 .05
132 John Tucker .01 .05
133 Steve Smith .01 .05
134 Kay Whitmore .02 .10
135 Adam Oates .02 .10
136 Bill Berg .01 .05
137 Wes Walz .01 .05
138 Jeff Beukeboom .01 .05
139 Ron Francis .02 .10
140 Alexandre Daigle .01 .05
141 Josef Beranek .01 .05
142 Tom Pederson .01 .05
143 Jamie McLennan .02 .10
144 Scott Mellanby .02 .10
145 Slava Kozlov .02 .10
146 Marty McSorley .01 .05
147 Tim Sweeney .01 .05
148 Luciano Borsato .01 .05
149 Jason Dawe .01 .05
150 Wayne Gretzky LL .30 .75
151 Pavel Bure LL .08 .25
152 Dominik Hasek LL .08 .25
153 Scott Stevens LL .02 .10
154 Wayne Gretzky LL .30 .75
155 Mike Richter LL .08 .25
156 Dominik Hasek LL .08 .25
157 Ted Drury .01 .05
158 Peter Popovic .01 .05
159 Alexei Kasatonov .01 .05
160 Mats Sundin .08 .25
161 Brad Shaw .01 .05
162 Bret Hedican .01 .05
163 Mike McPhee .01 .05
164 Martin Straka .01 .05
165 Dmitri Mironov .01 .05
166 Andrei Trefilov .01 .05
167 Joe Reekie .01 .05
168 Gary Suter .01 .05
169 Greg Gilbert .01 .05
170 Igor Larionov .01 .05
171 Mike Sillinger .01 .05
172 Igor Kravchuk .01 .05
173 Glen Murray .01 .05
174 Shawn Chambers .01 .05
175 John MacLean .02 .10
176 Yves Racine .01 .05
177 Andrei Lomakin .01 .05
178 Patrick Flatley .01 .05
179 Igor Ulanov .01 .05
180 Pat LaFontaine .08 .25
181 Mathieu Schneider .01 .05
182 Petr Stastny .02 .10
183 Tony Granato .01 .05
184 Peter Douris .01 .05
185 Alexei Kovalev .01 .05
186 Geoff Courtnall .01 .05
187 Richard Matvichuk .01 .05
188 Troy Murray .01 .05
189 Todd Gill .01 .05
190 Martin Brodeur RS .08 .25
191 Mikael Renberg RS .02 .10
192 Alexei Yashin RS .02 .10
193 Jason Arnott RS .01 .05
194 Derek Plante RS .01 .05
195 Alexandre Daigle RS .01 .05
196 Bryan Smolinski RS .01 .05
197 Jesse Belanger RS .01 .05
198 Chris Pronger RS .02 .10
199 Chris Osgood RS .02 .10
200 Jeremy Roenick .10 .30
201 Johan Garpenlov .01 .05
202 Dave Karpa .01 .05
203 Darren McCarty .01 .05
204 Claude Lemieux .01 .05
205 Geoff Sanderson .02 .10
206 Tom Barrasso .02 .10
207 Kevin Dineen .01 .05
208 Sylvain Cote .01 .05
209 Brent Gretzky .01 .05
210 Shayne Corson .01 .05
211 Darius Kasparaitis .01 .05
212 Peter Andersson .01 .05
213 Robert Reichel .01 .05
214 Jozef Stumpel .01 .05
215 Brendan Shanahan .08 .25
216 Craig Muni .01 .05
217 Alexei Zhamnov .02 .10
218 Robert Lang .01 .05
219 Brian Bellows .01 .05
220 Steven Smith .01 .05
221 Sergei Zubov .01 .05
222 Kelly Miller .01 .05
223 Ilya Byakin .01 .05
224 Chris Tamer RC .01 .05
225 Doug Gilmour .02 .10
226 Shawn Antoski .01 .05
227 Andrew Cassels .01 .05
228 Craig Wolanin .01 .05
229 Jon Casey .02 .10
230 Mike Modano .15 .40
231 Bill Guerin .01 .05
232 Gaetan Duchesne .01 .05
233 Steve Dubinsky .01 .05
234 Jason Bowen .01 .05
235 Steve Yzerman .50 1.25
236 Dave Poulin .01 .05
237 Michael Nylander .01 .05
238 Felix Potvin FUT .02 .10
239 Sandis Ozolinsh FUT .01 .05
240 Scott Niedermayer FUT .01 .05
241 Eric Lindros FUT .08 .25
242 Keith Tkachuk FUT .08 .25
243 Teemu Selanne FUT .08 .25
244 Marty McInnis .01 .05
245 Bob Kudelski .01 .05
246 Paul Cavallini .01 .05
247 Brian Bradley .01 .05
248 Robb Stauber .02 .10
249 Jay Wells .01 .05
250 Mario Lemieux .50 1.25
251 Tommy Albelin .01 .05
252 Paul DiPietro .01 .05
253 Mike Gartner .02 .10
254 Darrin Shannon .01 .05
255 Alexander Karpovtsev .01 .05
256 Dave Babych .01 .05
257 Greg Johnson .01 .05
258 Frank Musil .01 .05
259 Michal Pivonka .01 .05
260 Arturs Irbe .02 .10
261 Paul Broten .01 .05
262 Don Sweeney .01 .05
263 Doug Brown .01 .05
264 Bobby Dollas .01 .05
265 Brian Skrudland .01 .05
266 Dan Plante RC .01 .05
267 Chad Penney .01 .05
268 Steve Leach .01 .05
269 Damian Rhodes .02 .10
270 Glenn Anderson .02 .10
271 Randy McKay .01 .05
272 Jeff Brown .01 .05
273 Steve Konowalchuk .01 .05
274 Checklist 1-136 .01 .05
275 Checklist 137-275 .01 .05
276 Sergei Fedorov .08 .25
277 Adam Oates .02 .10
278 Mark Messier .08 .25
279 Doug Gilmour .02 .10
280 Wayne Gretzky .30 .75
281 Rick Tocchet .02 .10
282 Guy Carbonneau .01 .05
283 Peter Bondra .02 .10
284 Valeri Karpov RC .01 .05
285 Ed Belfour .08 .25
286 Petr Nedved .02 .10
287 Mikael Andersson .01 .05
288 Boris Mironov .01 .05
289 Donald Audette .01 .05
290 Kevin Stevens .01 .05
291 Cliff Ronning .01 .05
292 Bruce Driver .01 .05
293 Mariusz Czerkawski RC .10 .30
294 Mikael Renberg .02 .10
295 Theo Fleury .01 .05
296 Robert Kron .01 .05
297 Wendel Clark .02 .10
298 Dave Gagner .02 .10
299 Ulf Dahlen .01 .05
300 Keith Tkachuk .08 .25
301 Mike Ridley .01 .05
302 Mike Vernon .02 .10
303 Troy Mallette .01 .05
304 Derek King .01 .05
305 Kirk Muller .01 .05
306 Rob Niedermayer .02 .10
307 Ian Laperriere RC .01 .05
308 Mike Donnelly .01 .05
309 Joe Sacco .01 .05
310 Patrick Roy .20 .50
311 Tom Barrasso .02 .10
312 Dominik Hasek .08 .25
313 Felix Potvin .08 .25
314 Mike Richter .08 .25
315 Bobby Holik .01 .05
316 Patrick Poulin .01 .05
317 Stephane Matteau .01 .05
318 Petr Klima .01 .05
319 Fredrik Olausson .01 .05
320 Dale Hawerchuk .02 .10
321 Jim Dowd .01 .05
322 Chris Therien .01 .05
323 Ravil Gusmanov RC .01 .05
324 Vincent Riendeau .02 .10
325 Pavel Bure .08 .25
326 Jimmy Carson .01 .05
327 Steve Chiasson .01 .05
328 Ken Wregget .02 .10
329 Kenny Jonsson .01 .05
330 Keith Primeau .01 .05
331 Bob Errey .01 .05
332 Derian Hatcher .01 .05
333 Stephane Fiset .02 .10
334 Brent Severyn .01 .05
335 Ray Ferraro .01 .05
336 Pavol Demitra .01 .05
337 Valeri Bure .01 .05
338 Guy Hebert .02 .10
339 Matt Johnson RC .01 .05
340 Curtis Joseph .08 .25
341 Rob Pearson .01 .05
342 Jeff Shantz .01 .05
343 Eric Charron RC .01 .05
344 Jason Smith .01 .05
345 Mats Sundin .02 .10
Wendel Clark
346 Rick Tocchet .02 .10
Luc Robitaille
347 Al MacInnis .02 .10
Phil Housley
348 Mike Vernon .02 .10
Steve Chiasson
349 Craig Simpson .01 .05
350 Adam Graves .01 .05
351 Kevin Haller .01 .05
352 Nelson Emerson .01 .05
353 Phil Housley .02 .10
354 Shawn McEachern .01 .05
355 Felix Potvin .08 .25
356 Sergio Momesso .01 .05
357 Glen Wesley .01 .05
358 David Shaw .01 .05
359 Terry Carkner .01 .05
360 John Vanbiesbrouck .02 .10
361 Dean Evason .01 .05
362 Michal Sykora .01 .05
363 Troy Loney .01 .05
364 Sylvain Lefebvre .01 .05
365 Alexei Yashin .01 .05
366 Gilbert Dionne .01 .05
367 Rick Tabaracci .02 .10
368 Paul Ysebaert .01 .05
369 Craig Johnson .01 .05
370 Scott Stevens .02 .10
371 Philippe Boucher .01 .05
372 Garry Valk .01 .05
373 Jason Muzzatti .02 .10
374 Chris Joseph .01 .05
375 Wayne Gretzky .60 1.50
376 Teppo Numminen .01 .05
377 Oleg Petrov .01 .05
378 Patrik Juhlin RC .01 .05
379 Zarley Zalapski .01 .05
380 Martin Brodeur TOTF .08 .25
381 Chris Pronger .02 .10
382 Sergei Zubov .01 .05
383 Mikael Renberg .02 .10
384 Brett Lindros .01 .05
385 Peter Forsberg .15 .40
386 Brandon Convery .01 .05
387 Steve Heinze .01 .05
388 Glenn Healy .02 .10
389 Brian Benning .01 .05
390 Pat Verbeek .01 .05
391 Ulf Samuelsson .01 .05
392 Turner Stevenson .01 .05
393 Bob Rouse .01 .05
394 Steve Konroyd .01 .05
395 Russ Courtnall .01 .05
396 Sergei Makarov .01 .05
397 Kirk McLean .02 .10
398 Steven Finn .01 .05
399 Yan Kaminsky .01 .05
400 Eric Lindros .08 .25
401 Steve Duchesne .01 .05
402 John Slaney .01 .05
403 Bernie Nicholls .02 .10
404 Kelly Buchberger .01 .05
405 Paul Kariya .08 .25
406 Michel Petit .01 .05
407 Cale Hulse RC .01 .05
408 Sheldon Kennedy .01 .05
409 Brad May .01 .05
410 Daren Puppa .02 .10
411 Janne Laukkanen .01 .05
412 Mats Sundin .08 .25
413 Trevor Kidd .02 .10
414 Greg Adams .01 .05
415 Pavel Bure .08 .25
416 Teemu Selanne .08 .25
417 Brett Hull .08 .25
418 Steve Larmer .02 .10
419 Cam Neely .02 .10
420 Ray Bourque .15 .40
421 Andrei Nikolishin .01 .05
422 Jim Paek .01 .05
423 John Cullen .01 .05
424 Darcy Wakaluk .02 .10
425 Peter Forsberg .30 .75
426 Yves Racine .01 .05
427 Jody Hull .01 .05
428 Ron Sutter .01 .05
429 Ray Sheppard .02 .10
430 Sandis Ozolinsh .02 .10
431 Brent Grieve .01 .05
432 Shaun Van Allen .01 .05
433 Craig Berube .01 .05
434 Vladislav Boulin RC .01 .05
435 Bill Ranford .02 .10
436 Denny Felsner .01 .05
437 Jamie Storr .02 .10
438 Brian Rolston .01 .05
439 Chris Gratton .01 .05
440 Dominik Hasek .20 .50
441 Garth Butcher .01 .05
442 Jyrki Lumme .01 .05
443 Sergei Nemchinov .01 .05
444 Tie Domi .01 .05
445 Gary Roberts .01 .05
446 Dave McLlwain .01 .05
447 John Gruden RC .01 .05
448 Vladimir Konstantinov .02 .10
449 Adam Deadmarsh .01 .05
450 Brian Leetch .08 .25
451 Scott Stevens .02 .10
452 Mark Tinordi .01 .05
453 Al Iafrate .01 .05
454 Ray Bourque .08 .25
455 Patrick Roy .40 1.00
456 Viktor Gordiouk .01 .05
457 Owen Nolan .02 .10
458 Stu Barnes .01 .05
459 Zigmund Palffy .02 .10
460 Jaromir Jagr .15 .40
461 Andrei Nazarov .01 .05
462 Kelly Hrudey .02 .10
463 Jason Wiemer RC .01 .05
464 Oleg Tverdovsky .02 .10
465 Brett Hull .10 .30
466 Luke Richardson .01 .05
467 Jason Allison .01 .05
468 Dimitri Yushkevich .01 .05
469 Todd Simon RC .01 .05
470 Martin Brodeur .25 .60
471 Thomas Steen .01 .05
472 Vesa Viitakoski .01 .05
473 Todd Harvey .01 .05
474 Kent Manderville .01 .05
475 Chris Chelios .08 .25
476 Joby Messier .01 .05
477 Jassen Cullimore .01 .05
478 Jamie Pushor .01 .05
479 Bryan Smolinski .01 .05
480 Joe Sakic .20 .50
481 David Wilkie .01 .05
482 Craig Billington .02 .10
483 Pat Neaton .01 .05
484 Chris Pronger .08 .25

485 Brian Leetch	.08	.25
486 Chris Chelios	.08	.25
487 Jeff Brown	.01	.05
488 Al MacInnis	.02	.10
489 Paul Coffey	.08	.25
490 Ray Bourque	.08	.25
491 Phil Housley	.02	.10
492 Larry Murphy	.02	.10
493 Sergei Zubov	.01	.05
494 Scott Stevens	.02	.10
495 Steve Thomas	.01	.05
496 Jim Waite	.02	.10
497 Mike Keane	.01	.05
498 Rob Blake	.02	.10
499 John Lilley	.01	.05
500 Brian Leetch	.08	.25
501 Derek Plante	.01	.05
502 Tim Cheveldae	.02	.10
503 Vladimir Vujtek	.01	.05
504 Esa Tikkanen	.01	.05
505 Cam Neely	.08	.25
506 Dale Hunter	.01	.05
507 Marc Bergevin	.01	.05
508 Joel Otto	.01	.05
509 Brent Fedyk	.01	.05
510 Dave Andreychuk	.02	.10
511 Andy Moog	.08	.25
512 Jaroslav Modry	.01	.05
513 Sergei Krivokrasov	.01	.05
514 Brett Lindros	.01	.05
515 Cory Stillman RC	.01	.05
516 Jon Rohloff RC	.01	.05
517 Joe Mullen	.02	.10
518 Evgeny Davydov	.01	.05
519 Scott Young	.01	.05
520 Sergei Fedorov	.10	.30
521 Pat Falloon	.01	.05
522 Bill Lindsay	.01	.05
523 Ron Tugnutt	.02	.10
524 Anatoli Semenov	.01	.05
525 Geoff Courtnall	.01	.05
526 Luc Robitaille	.02	.10
527 Geoff Sanderson	.02	.10
528 Esa Tikkanen	.01	.05
529 Brendan Shanahan	.08	.25
530 Jason Arnott	.01	.05
531 Michal Grosek RC	.01	.05
532 Steve Larmer	.02	.10
533 Eric Fichaud RC	.02	.10
534 Dimitri Khristich	.01	.05
535 Garry Galley	.01	.05
536 Aaron Gavey	.01	.05
537 Joe Nieuwendyk	.02	.10
538 Mike Craig	.01	.05
539 Scott Niedermayer	.01	.05
540 Luc Robitaille	.02	.10
541 Dino Ciccarelli	.02	.10
542 Sean Burke	.02	.10
543 Jiri Slegr	.01	.05
544 Jesse Belanger	.01	.05
545 Sean Hill	.01	.05
546 Vladimir Malakhov	.01	.05
547 Jeff Friesen	.01	.05
548 Mike Ricci	.01	.05
549 Checklist 276-414	.01	.05
550 Checklist 415-550	.01	.05

1994-95 Topps Premier Special Effects

One card from this parallel set was issued in every other pack of OPC and Topps Premier. The cards can be differentiated from the basic set by the reflective rainbow foil which appears in the card background when held at an angle to a light source. Card backs are the same. The OPC versions are slightly more desirable because they were printed in smaller quantities than the Topps cards. Cards 274, 275, 549 and 550 replaced the checklists with players not featured in the basic set.

*SER.1 SE VETS: 4X TO 10X BASIC CARDS
*SER.1 SE ROOKIES: 1.5X TO 4X
*SER.2 SE VETS: 6X TO 15X BASIC CARDS
*SER.2 SE ROOKIES: 3X TO 8X

CL REPLACE (274/275/549/55)	.40	1.00

1994-95 Topps Premier Finest Inserts

The 23 cards in this set were randomly inserted at a rate of 1:36 Topps Premier series one packs. The set includes all players who scored at least 40 goals in 1993-94. Cards feature an isolated player photo over a textured rainbow background. A reflective rainbow border is broken up by the player name and his goal scoring mark. Premier Finest is written across the top of the card. Backs have a small player photo with brief personal information, and scoring breakdown by division. Cards are numbered "X" of 23.

COMPLETE SET (23)	15.00	40.00
1 Pavel Bure	1.50	4.00
2 Brett Hull	2.00	5.00
3 Sergei Fedorov	1.50	4.00
4 Dave Andreychuk	.75	2.00
5 Brendan Shanahan	1.50	4.00
6 Ray Sheppard	.40	1.00
7 Adam Graves	.40	1.00
8 Cam Neely	1.50	4.00
9 Mike Modano	2.00	5.00
10 Wendel Clark	.75	2.00
11 Jeremy Roenick	2.00	5.00
12 Eric Lindros	1.50	4.00
13 Luc Robitaille	.75	2.00
14 Steve Thomas	.40	1.00
15 Geoff Sanderson	.40	1.00
16 Gary Roberts	.40	1.00
17 Kevin Stevens	.40	1.00
18 Keith Tkachuk	.75	2.00
19 Theo Fleury	.40	1.00
20 Robert Reichel	.40	1.00
21 Mark Recchi	.75	2.00
22 Vincent Damphousse	.40	1.00
23 Bob Kudelski	.40	1.00

1994-95 Topps Premier The Go To Guy

This 15-card set was issued in both Topps and OPC Premier series two product at the rate of 1:36 packs. There is no difference between the cards inserted in each product.

COMPLETE SET (15)	12.00	30.00
1 Wayne Gretzky	5.00	12.00
2 Joe Sakic	1.50	4.00
3 Brett Hull	1.00	2.50
4 Mike Modano	1.25	3.00
5 Pavel Bure	.75	2.00
6 Pat LaFontaine	.75	2.00
7 Theo Fleury	.15	.40
8 Jeremy Roenick	1.00	2.50
9 Sergei Fedorov	1.00	2.50
10 Eric Lindros	.75	2.00
11 Kirk Muller	.15	.40
12 Steve Yzerman	4.00	10.00
13 Alexander Mogilny	.30	.75
14 Doug Gilmour	.30	.75
15 Mark Messier	.75	2.00

1994-96 Topps Finest Bronze

This trio of sets were made available to collectors exclusively through Topps Stadium Club program. The sets cost approximately $95 each, including shipping, from the club. Each bronze card features embossed color action player images on a metallic background of the team logo in a marbleized black border and thin gold frame. The gold backs carry player information and career statistics. Cards 1-6 were issued as a first series in 1994.

1 Jaromir Jagr	12.00	30.00
2 Eric Lindros	12.00	30.00
3 Patrick Roy	20.00	50.00
4 Pavel Bure	10.00	25.00
5 Teemu Selanne	10.00	25.00
6 Doug Gilmour	8.00	20.00
7 Sergei Fedorov	10.00	25.00
8 Brett Hull	10.00	25.00
9 Paul Kariya	15.00	40.00
10 Cam Neely	8.00	20.00
11 Mats Sundin	8.00	20.00
12 Martin Brodeur	10.00	25.00
13 Jeremy Roenick	8.00	20.00
14 Brian Leetch	6.00	15.00
15 Mark Messier	8.00	20.00
16 Mario Lemieux	20.00	50.00
17 Peter Forsberg	12.00	30.00
18 Felix Potvin	8.00	20.00
19 Alexander Mogilny	4.00	10.00
20 Ray Bourque	12.00	30.00
21 Ed Jovanovski	6.00	15.00
22 Mikael Renberg	4.00	10.00

1995-96 Topps

The 385-card set was issued in two series of 220 and 165 cards, respectively. The 13-card packs had an SRP of $1.29.

COMPLETE SET (385)	10.00	25.00
COMP.SERIES 1 (220)	6.00	15.00
COMP.SERIES 2 (165)	4.00	10.00
1 Eric Lindros MM	.07	.20
2 Dominik Hasek MM	.07	.20
3 Jeremy Roenick MM	.08	.25
4 Paul Coffey MM	.07	.20
5 Mark Messier MM	.07	.20
6 Peter Bondra MM	.02	.10
7 Paul Kariya MM	.07	.20
8 Chris Chelios	.07	.20
9 Martin Brodeur MM	.07	.20
10 Brett Hull MM	.07	.20
11 Mike Vernon MM	.02	.10
12 Trevor Linden MM	.02	.10
13 Pat LaFontaine MM	.02	.10
14 Geoff Sanderson MM	.02	.10
15 Cam Neely MM	.02	.10
16 Brendan Shanahan MM	.07	.20
17 Jason Arnott MM	.01	.05
18 Mikael Renberg MM	.01	.05
19 Mats Sundin MM	.07	.20
20 Pavel Bure MM	.07	.20
21 Pierre Turgeon MM	.02	.10
22 Alexei Zhamnov MM	.01	.05
23 Blaine Lacher	.02	.10
24 Brian Holzinger RC	.07	.20
25 Theo Fleury	.01	.05
26 Eric Daze	.02	.10
27 Mike Kennedy RC	.01	.05
28 Darren McCarty	.01	.05
29 Todd Marchant	.01	.05
30 Andrew Cassels	.01	.05
31 Rob Niedermayer	.02	.10
32 Eric Lacroix RC	.01	.05
33 Steve Rucchin RC	.01	.05
34 Turner Stevenson	.01	.05
35 Sergei Brylin	.01	.05
36 Mathieu Schneider	.01	.05
37 Pat Verbeek	.01	.05
38 Steve Larouche RC	.01	.05
39 Rod Brind'Amour	.02	.10
40 Luc Robitaille	.02	.10
41 Brett Lindros	.01	.05
42 Shean Donovan RC	.01	.05
43 David Roberts	.01	.05
44 Cory Cross	.01	.05
45 Todd Warriner	.01	.05
46 Yevgeny Namestnikov	.01	.05
47 Sergei Gonchar	.01	.05
48 Nikolai Khabibulin	.02	.10
49 Alexei Zhitnik	.01	.05
50 Ray Bourque	.10	.30
51 Paul Kruse	.01	.05
52 Murray Craven	.01	.05
53 Andy Moog	.07	.20
54 Keith Primeau	.01	.05
55 Shayne Corson	.01	.05
56 Johan Garpenlov	.01	.05
57 Marek Malik	.01	.05
58 Tony Granato	.01	.05
59 Bob Corkum	.01	.05
60 Patrick Roy	.40	1.00
61 Chris McAlpine RC	.01	.05
62 Chris Marinucci RC	.01	.05
63 Jeff Beukeboom	.01	.05
64 Radek Bonk	.01	.05
65 John LeClair	.07	.20
66 Len Barrie	.01	.05
67 Teppo Numminen	.01	.05
68 Ray Whitney	.02	.10
69 Jeff Norton	.01	.05
70 Chris Gratton	.01	.05
71 Benoit Hogue	.01	.05
72 Bret Hedican	.01	.05
73 Keith Jones	.02	.10
74 John Cullen	.01	.05
75 Brian Leetch	.02	.10
76 Dave Reid	.01	.05
77 Dino Ciccarelli	.02	.10
78 Gary Roberts	.01	.05
79 Tony Amonte	.02	.10
80 Mike Modano	.10	.30
81 Doug Brown	.01	.05
82 Scott Thornton	.01	.05
83 Bill Lindsay	.01	.05
84 Frantisek Kucera	.01	.05
85 Wayne Gretzky	.50	1.25
86 Joe Sacco	.01	.05
87 Benoit Brunet	.01	.05
88 Bill Guerin	.02	.10
89 Travis Green	.01	.05
90 Alexei Kovalev	.01	.05
91 Stanislav Neckar	.01	.05
92 Rob Dimaio	.01	.05
93 Chris Joseph	.01	.05
94 Craig Martin RC	.01	.05
95 Craig Janney	.02	.10
96 Greg Gilbert	.01	.05
97 Alexander Semak	.01	.05
98 Mike Gartner	.02	.10
99 Cliff Ronning	.01	.05
100 Mario Lemieux	.40	1.00
101 Jassen Cullimore	.01	.05
102 Steve Duchesne	.01	.05
103 Derek Plante	.01	.05
104 John Gruden	.01	.05
105 Michal Sykora	.01	.05
106 Trent Klatt	.01	.05
107 Nicklas Lidstrom	.07	.20
108 Luke Richardson	.01	.05
109 Steven Rice	.01	.05
110 Stu Barnes	.01	.05
111 John Druce	.01	.05
112 Guy Hebert	.02	.10
113 Vladimir Malakhov	.01	.05
114 Claude Lemieux	.01	.05
115 Kirk Muller	.01	.05
116 Darren Langdon RC	.01	.05
117 Rob Gaudreau	.01	.05
118 Karl Dykhuis	.01	.05
119 Richard Park	.01	.05
120 Dave Manson	.01	.05
121 Andrei Nazarov	.01	.05
122 Bernie Nicholls	.01	.05
123 Mikael Andersson	.01	.05
124 Todd Gill	.01	.05
125 Trevor Linden	.02	.10
126 Kelly Miller	.01	.05
127 Don Sweeney	.01	.05
128 Jason Dawe	.01	.05
129 Steve Chiasson	.01	.05
130 Ed Belfour	.07	.20
131 Kerry Huffman	.01	.05
132 Tim Taylor	.01	.05
133 Kirk Maltby	.02	.10
134 Jody Hull	.01	.05
135 Sean Burke	.02	.10
136 Philippe Boucher	.01	.05
137 Valeri Karpov	.01	.05
138 Yves Racine	.01	.05
139 Patrick Flatley	.01	.05
140 John MacLean	.02	.10
141 Sergei Nemchinov	.01	.05
142 Don Beaupre	.02	.10
143 Kevin Dineen	.01	.05
144 Ulf Samuelsson	.01	.05
145 Al MacInnis	.02	.10
146 Igor Korolev	.01	.05
147 Pat Falloon	.01	.05
148 Brian Bradley	.01	.05
149 Josef Beranek	.01	.05
150 Mats Sundin	.07	.20
151 Keith Tkachuk	.07	.20
152 Geoff Courtnall	.01	.05
153 Mariusz Czerkawski	.01	.05
154 Trevor Kidd	.02	.10
155 Garry Galley	.01	.05
156 Gary Suter	.01	.05
157 Grant Ledyard	.01	.05
158 Doug Weight	.02	.10
159 Jesse Belanger	.01	.05
160 Mike Vernon	.02	.10
161 Robert Kron	.01	.05
162 Marty McSorley	.01	.05
163 Todd Krygier	.01	.05
164 Scott Niedermayer	.01	.05
165 Mark Recchi	.02	.10
166 Phil Housley	.02	.10
167 Ron Hextall	.02	.10
168 Richard Smehlik	.01	.05
169 Chris Tamer	.01	.05
170 Alexei Yashin	.01	.05
171 Sergei Makarov	.01	.05
172 Patrice Tardif	.01	.05
173 Milos Holan	.01	.05
174 J.C. Bergeron	.01	.05
175 Dave Andreychuk	.02	.10
176 Martin Gelinas	.01	.05
177 Dale Hunter	.02	.10
178 Kevin Haller	.01	.05
179 Jeff Shantz	.01	.05
180 Adam Oates	.02	.10
181 Ronnie Stern	.01	.05
182 Jamie Langenbrunner	.02	.10
183 Mark Fitzpatrick	.02	.10
184 Adam Burt	.01	.05
185 Sergei Fedorov	.10	.30
186 Robert Lang	.01	.05
187 Craig Conroy RC	.01	.05
188 Ken Daneyko	.01	.05
189 Marko Tuomainen	.01	.05
190 Ken Wregget	.02	.10
191 Mike Rathje	.01	.05
192 Dimitri Yushkevich	.01	.05
193 Roman Hamrlik	.02	.10
194 Russ Courtnall	.01	.05
195 Teemu Selanne	.07	.20
196 Jon Rohloff	.01	.05
197 Derian Hatcher	.01	.05
198 Mark Tinordi	.01	.05
199 Patrice Brisebois	.01	.05
200 Jaromir Jagr	.10	.30
201 Randy McKay	.01	.05
202 Derek King	.01	.05
203 Tony Twist	.02	.10
204 Jyrki Lumme	.01	.05
205 Steve Smith	.01	.05
206 Bob Rouse	.01	.05
207 Dave Ellett	.01	.05
208 Kevin Dean	.01	.05
209 Rusty Fitzgerald RC	.01	.05
210 Jim Carey	.02	.10
211 Kenny Jonsson	.01	.05
212 Mike Richter	.07	.20
213 Glen Wesley	.01	.05
214 Donald Audette	.01	.05
215 Curtis Joseph	.07	.20
216 Joe Juneau	.01	.05
217 Paul Kariya	.07	.20
218 1995 Stanley Cup Champions	.02	.10
219 Checklist 1-110	.01	.05
220 Checklist 111-220	.01	.05
221 Cam Neely	.07	.20
222 Wayne Primeau RC	.01	.05
223 Yanic Perreault	.01	.05
224 Pierre Turgeon	.02	.10
225 Alexander Mogilny	.02	.10
226 Daren Puppa	.02	.10
227 Ulf Dahlen	.01	.05
228 Tomas Sandstrom	.01	.05
229 Shayne Corson	.01	.05
230 Chris Chelios	.07	.20
231 Stephane Richer	.02	.10
232 Paul Ranheim	.01	.05
233 Joe Nieuwendyk	.02	.10
234 Doug Gilmour	.02	.10
235 Jeremy Roenick	.08	.25
236 Joel Otto	.01	.05
237 Steve Yzerman	.40	1.00
238 Petr Klima	.01	.05
239 Jari Kurri	.07	.20
240 Mark Messier	.07	.20
241 Bill Ranford	.02	.10
242 Grant Fuhr	.07	.20
243 Brent Severyn	.01	.05
244 Ron Francis	.02	.10
245 Ray Ferraro	.01	.05
246 Martin Straka	.01	.05
247 Gerald Diduck	.01	.05
248 Dimitri Khristich	.01	.05
249 Wade Flaherty RC	.01	.05
250 Pat LaFontaine	.07	.20
251 Darren Turcotte	.01	.05
252 John Vanbiesbrouck	.02	.10
253 Brian Bellows	.01	.05
254 Dave Gagner	.01	.05
255 Larry Murphy	.02	.10
256 Steve Thomas	.01	.05
257 Robert Svehla RC	.01	.05
258 Deron Quint	.01	.05
259 Kjell Samuelsson	.01	.05
260 Scott Mellanby	.01	.05
261 Dan Quinn	.01	.05
262 Tom Barrasso	.02	.10
263 Zarley Zalapski	.01	.05
264 Rick Tocchet	.02	.10
265 Paul Coffey	.07	.20
266 Joe Sakic	.15	.40
267 Aki Berg RC	.02	.10
268 Jeff Brown	.01	.05
269 Wendel Clark	.02	.10
270 Vincent Damphousse	.01	.05
271 Dale Hawerchuk	.07	.20
272 Rhett Warrener RC	.01	.05
273 Kevin Hatcher	.01	.05
274 Calle Johansson	.01	.05
275 Scott Stevens	.02	.10
276 Geoff Courtnall	.01	.05
277 Kirk McLean	.02	.10
278 Steve Heinze	.01	.05
279 Sylvain Lefebvre	.01	.05
280 Joe Murphy	.01	.05
281 Mike Keane	.01	.05
282 Kevin Stevens	.01	.05
283 Miroslav Satan RC	.25	.60
284 Stephane Fiset	.02	.10
285 Jeff O'Neill	.01	.05
286 Denny Lambert	.01	.05
287 Marcus Ragnarsson RC	.02	.10
288 Adam Deadmarsh	.01	.05
289 Eric Weinrich	.01	.05
290 Eric Desjardins	.02	.10
291 Tim Cheveldae	.02	.10
292 Glenn Healy	.02	.10
293 Byron Dafoe	.02	.10
294 Tom Fitzgerald	.01	.05
295 Adam Graves	.01	.05
296 Arturs Irbe UER front reads Aturs	.02	.10
297 Shaun Van Allen	.01	.05
298 Kelly Buchberger	.01	.05
299 Bob Probert	.02	.10
300 Pavel Bure	.07	.20
301 Chad Kilger RC	.01	.05
302 Dominik Hasek	.15	.40
303 Bobby Holik	.01	.05
304 Petr Nedved	.02	.10
305 Owen Nolan	.02	.10
306 Saku Koivu	.07	.20
307 Rob Blake	.02	.10
308 Chris Pronger	.07	.20
309 Kyle McLaren RC	.01	.05
310 Peter Bondra	.02	.10
311 Nelson Emerson	.01	.05
312 Bryan McCabe	.01	.05
313 Darcy Wakaluk	.02	.10
314 Shane Doan RC	.20	.50
315 Felix Potvin	.07	.20
316 Jim Dowd	.01	.05
317 Roman Oksiuta	.01	.05
318 Geoff Sanderson	.01	.05
319 Radek Dvorak RC	.15	.40
320 Paul Ysebaert	.01	.05
321 Shawn McEachern	.01	.05
322 Vyacheslav Kozlov	.02	.10
323 Marty McInnis	.01	.05
324 Ted Donato	.01	.05
325 Martin Brodeur	.20	.50
326 Patrick Poulin	.01	.05
327 Eric Lindros	.07	.20
328 Dallas Drake	.01	.05
329 Sean Hill	.01	.05
330 Michal Pivonka	.01	.05
331 Alexei Zhamnov	.02	.10
332 Cory Stillman	.01	.05
333 Sergei Zubov	.01	.05
334 Tommy Soderstrom	.02	.10
335 Patrik Carnback	.01	.05
336 Joe Dziedzic	.01	.05
337 Steve Duchesne	.01	.05
338 Marty Murray	.01	.05
339 Todd Bertuzzi RC	.50	1.25
340 Jason Arnott	.01	.05
341 Niklas Sundstrom	.01	.05
342 Alexandre Daigle	.01	.05
343 Jocelyn Thibault	.07	.20
344 Mikhail Shtalenkov	.01	.05
345 Chris Osgood	.02	.10
346 Brendan Witt	.01	.05
347 Ian Laperriere	.01	.05
348 Zigmund Palffy	.02	.10
349 Brian Savage	.01	.05
350 Mike Peca	.02	.10
351 Vitali Yachmenev	.01	.05
352 Luc Robitaille	.02	.10
353 Mikael Renberg	.02	.10
354 Ed Jovanovski	.07	.20
355 Jason Doig	.01	.05
356 Todd Harvey	.02	.10
357 Viktor Kozlov	.02	.10
358 Valeri Bure	.01	.05
359 Peter Forsberg	.20	.50
360 Jeff Friesen	.01	.05
361 Andrei Nikolishin	.01	.05
362 Brian Rolston	.01	.05
363 Jamie Storr	.02	.10
364 Chris Therien	.01	.05
365 Oleg Tverdovsky	.01	.05
366 David Oliver	.01	.05
367 Alexander Selivanov	.01	.05
368 Alex Stojanov	.01	.05
369 Daniel Alfredsson RC	.25	.60
370 Brendan Shanahan	.07	.20
371 Yuri Khmylev	.01	.05
372 Brett Hull	.08	.25
373 Sergei Fedorov MM	.07	.20
374 Jaromir Jagr MM	.07	.20
375 Wayne Gretzky MM	.40	1.00
376 Alexander Mogilny MM	.01	.05
377 Patrick Roy MM	.30	.75
378 Ed Belfour MM	.07	.20
379 Luc Robitaille MM	.01	.05
380 Peter Forsberg MM	.07	.20
381 Adam Oates MM	.02	.10
382 Theo Fleury MM	.01	.05
383 Jim Carey MM	.01	.05
384 Checklist 221-304	.01	.05
385 Checklist 305-385	.01	.05

1995-96 Topps O-Pee-Chee Parallel

The 1995-96 OPC Insert set is a parallel to the 1995-96 Topps set. The set is identical save for the silver foil OPC logo in place of the gold foil Topps. The cards were inserted one per second series Canadian foil pack; cards from both series were included in this manner and were not available in separate packs as in the past. Several of the cards on the D printing sheet were short printed according to Topps Canada.

*VETS: 6X TO 15X BASIC TOPPS
*ROOKIES: 2.5X TO 6X TOPPS
*SP's: 10X TO 25X TOPPS

1995-96 Topps Canadian Gold

These ten cards featured some of the top players to don their whites in Canadian rinks; they were randomly inserted at a rate of 1:36 series 1 Canadian retail packs. These packs, unlike the American ones, contained just five cards each.

COMPLETE SET (10)	30.00	60.00
1CG Patrick Roy	12.50	30.00
2CG Alexei Yashin	2.00	5.00
3CG Jason Arnott	2.00	5.00
4CG Trevor Kidd	2.00	5.00
5CG Pavel Bure	2.50	6.00
6CG Theo Fleury	2.00	5.00
7CG Pierre Turgeon	2.00	5.00
8CG Felix Potvin	2.50	6.00
9CG Teemu Selanne	2.50	6.00
10CG Mats Sundin	2.50	6.00

1995-96 Topps Canadian World Juniors

The cards in this set, featuring the member of the World Champion Canadian junior team, could be found randomly inserted at a rate of 1:18 series one Canadian Topps packs.

COMPLETE SET (22)	10.00	20.00
1CJ Wade Redden	.60	1.50
2CJ Jamie Storr	.60	1.50
3CJ Larry Courville	.40	1.00
4CJ Jason Allison	.60	1.50
5CJ Alexandre Daigle	.40	1.00
6CJ Marty Murray	.40	1.00
7CJ Bryan McCabe	.60	1.50
8CJ Ryan Smyth	.75	2.00
9CJ Lee Sorochan	.40	1.00
10CJ Todd Harvey	.40	1.00
11CJ Nolan Baumgartner	.40	1.00
12CJ Denis Pederson	.40	1.00
13CJ Shean Donovan	.40	1.00
14CJ Jason Botterill	.40	1.00
15CJ Jeff Friesen	.40	1.00
16CJ Darcy Tucker	.60	1.50
17CJ Chad Allan	.40	1.00
18CJ Dan Cloutier	.60	1.50
19CJ Eric Daze	.40	1.00
20CJ Jeff O'Neill	.40	1.00
21CJ Jamie Rivers	.40	1.00
22CJ Ed Jovanovski	.60	1.50

1995-96 Topps Hidden Gems

The cards in this set focus on star players who were mined in the sixth round or later of the NHL entry draft. The cards were randomly inserted in series 1 packs at a rate of 1:24.

COMPLETE SET (15)	8.00	20.00
1HG Theo Fleury	.75	2.00
2HG Luc Robitaille	.75	2.00
3HG Doug Gilmour	.75	2.00
4HG Dominik Hasek	2.00	5.00
5HG Pavel Bure	1.25	3.00
6HG Peter Bondra	.75	2.00
7HG Steve Larmer	.40	1.00
8HG David Oliver	.40	1.00
9HG Gary Suter	.40	1.00
10HG Brett Hull	1.25	3.00
11HG Kevin Stevens	.40	1.00
12HG Ron Hextall	.75	2.00
13HG Kirk McLean	.40	1.00
14HG Andy Moog	.75	2.00
15HG Rick Tocchet	.40	1.00

1995-96 Topps Home Grown Canada

These cards, randomly inserted in Canadian series two retail packs only (HGC1-HGC15) at a rate of 1:36 and randomly inserted in Canadian series 2 hobby packs only (HGC16-HGC30) at a rate of 1:36, feature players born in the Great White North. The hobby-only cards are somewhat harder to find, as Topps announced that an indeterminate number of the 1-15 cards were inserted in their place, resulting in fewer of the 16-30 cards being released.

COMPLETE SET (30)	40.00	80.00
HGC1 Patrick Roy	6.00	15.00
HGC2 Wendel Clark	.60	1.50
HGC3 Pierre Turgeon	.60	1.50
HGC4 Doug Gilmour	.60	1.50
HGC5 Theo Fleury	.30	.75
HGC6 Eric Lindros	1.25	3.00
HGC7 Paul Kariya	1.25	3.00
HGC8 Bill Ranford	.60	1.50
HGC9 Ray Bourque	2.00	5.00
HGC10 Brendan Shanahan	1.25	3.00
HGC11 Paul Coffey	1.25	3.00
HGC12 Trevor Linden	.60	1.50
HGC13 Trevor Kidd	.60	1.50
HGC14 Alexandre Daigle	.60	1.50
HGC15 Chris Pronger	1.25	3.00
HGC16 Steve Yzerman	6.00	15.00
HGC17 Todd Harvey	.60	1.50
HGC18 Felix Potvin	1.25	3.00
HGC19 Luc Robitaille	.60	1.50
HGC20 Wayne Gretzky	8.00	20.00
HGC21 Keith Primeau	.30	.75
HGC22 Al MacInnis	.60	1.50
HGC23 Cam Neely	1.25	3.00
HGC24 Ed Belfour	1.25	3.00
HGC25 Joe Juneau	.30	.75
HGC26 Adam Graves	.30	.75
HGC27 Mark Recchi	.60	1.50
HGC28 Stephane Richer	.60	1.50
HGC29 Mark Messier	1.25	3.00
HGC30 Mario Lemieux	6.00	15.00

1995-96 Topps Home Grown USA

This 10-card set features some of the top US-born players in the NHL. The cards were randomly inserted at a rate of 1:36 series two US packs.

COMPLETE SET (10)	10.00	20.00
HGA1 Brian Leetch	.60	1.50
HGA2 Jeremy Roenick	1.50	4.00
HGA3 Mike Modano	2.00	5.00
HGA4 Pat LaFontaine	1.25	3.00
HGA5 Keith Tkachuk	1.25	3.00
HGA6 Chris Chelios	1.25	3.00
HGA7 Darren Turcotte	.30	.75
HGA8 John Vanbiesbrouck	.60	1.50
HGA9 John LeClair	1.25	3.00
HGA10 Mike Richter	1.25	3.00

1995-96 Topps Marquee Men Power Boosters

This 33-card set is a parallel to the Marquee Men cards found in the base Topps issue, with numbering on the back matching those cards as well. Cards 1-22 were randomly inserted in series 1 packs at a rate of 1:36; cards 373-383 used the same odds in series 2 packs. Because there were more cards distributed throughout the series 1 production run (22 to 11) the series one cards are somewhat more difficult to acquire. These cards can be differentiated from the base issues by the use of much thicker 28-point card stock and the prismatic foil front.

COMPLETE SET (33)	30.00	80.00
1 Eric Lindros	1.25	3.00
2 Dominik Hasek	2.50	6.00
3 Jeremy Roenick	1.50	4.00
4 Paul Coffey	1.25	3.00
5 Mark Messier	1.25	3.00
6 Peter Bondra	.60	1.50
7 Paul Kariya	1.25	3.00
8 Chris Chelios	1.25	3.00
9 Martin Brodeur	3.00	8.00
10 Brett Hull	1.50	4.00
11 Mike Vernon	.60	1.50
12 Trevor Linden	.60	1.50
13 Pat LaFontaine	1.25	3.00
14 Geoff Sanderson	.40	1.00
15 Cam Neely	1.25	3.00
16 Brendan Shanahan	1.25	3.00
17 Jason Arnott	.40	1.00
18 Mikael Renberg	.40	1.00
19 Mats Sundin	1.25	3.00
20 Pavel Bure	1.25	3.00
21 Pierre Turgeon	.40	1.00
22 Alexei Zhamnov	.40	1.00
373 Sergei Fedorov	1.50	4.00
374 Jaromir Jagr	2.00	5.00
375 Wayne Gretzky	6.00	15.00
376 Alexander Mogilny	.60	1.50
377 Patrick Roy	5.00	12.00
378 Ed Belfour	1.25	3.00
379 Luc Robitaille	.60	1.50
380 Peter Forsberg	2.50	6.00
381 Adam Oates	.60	1.50
382 Theo Fleury	.40	1.00
383 Jim Carey	.40	1.00

1995-96 Topps Mystery Finest

These unique chase cards featured three top positional stars on the back and an opaque protective foil covering on the front. When removed, it would reveal a full frontal shot of one of the three players on the back, hence the mystery. The cards, which utilized the Finest technology, were randomly inserted 1:36 series 2 packs. A parallel refractor version of the set also existed. These cards were much more difficult to pull, coming out of 1:216 packs. Multipliers for these cards are included in the headers below.

COMPLETE SET (22)	50.00	100.00
*REFRACTORS: 1.5X TO 4X BASIC INSERTS		
M1 Wayne Gretzky	10.00	25.00
M2 Mario Lemieux	8.00	20.00
M3 Mark Messier	1.50	4.00
M4 Eric Lindros	1.50	4.00
M5 Sergei Fedorov	2.50	6.00
M6 Joe Sakic	3.00	8.00
M7 Brett Hull	2.00	5.00
M8 Jaromir Jagr	2.50	6.00
M9 Teemu Selanne	1.50	4.00
M10 Brendan Shanahan	1.50	4.00
M11 Cam Neely	1.50	4.00
M12 Mikael Renberg	.75	2.00
M13 Paul Kariya	1.50	4.00
M14 Keith Tkachuk	1.50	4.00
M15 Pavel Bure	1.50	4.00
M16 Brian Leetch	.75	2.00
M17 Scott Stevens	.75	2.00
M18 Chris Chelios	1.50	4.00
M19 Dominik Hasek	3.00	8.00
M20 Patrick Roy	8.00	20.00
M21 Martin Brodeur	4.00	10.00
M22 Felix Potvin	1.50	4.00

1995-96 Topps New To The Game

This 22-card set featured some of the top players just beginning to make their marks in the NHL. The cards were inserted one per US series 1 retail packs.

COMPLETE SET (22)	3.00	8.00
1NG Jim Carey	.20	.50
2NG Sergei Brylin	.08	.25
3NG Todd Marchant	.08	.25

4NG Oleg Tverdovsky .08 .25
5NG Paul Kariya .40 1.00
6NG Adam Deadmarsh .08 .25
7NG Mike Kennedy .08 .25
8NG Roman Oksiuta .08 .25
9NG Kenny Jonsson .08 .25
10NG Peter Forsberg 1.00 2.50
11NG Alexander Selivanov .08 .25
12NG Chris Therien .08 .25
13NG Brian Rolston .08 .25
14NG David Oliver .08 .25
15NG Blaine Lacher .20 .50
16NG Sergei Krivokrasov .08 .25
17NG Todd Harvey .20 .50
18NG Jeff Friesen .08 .25
19NG Mariusz Czerkawski .08 .25
20NG Ian Laperriere .08 .25
21NG Brian Savage .08 .25
22NG Andrei Nikolishin .08 .25

1995-96 Topps Power Lines

These ten three player-cards feature the top lines of the 1994-95 NHL season. The cards were randomly inserted in 1:12 series 1 packs.

COMPLETE SET (10) 4.00 10.00
1PL Eric Lindros .40 1.00
John LeClair
Mikael Renberg
2PL Keith Tkachuk .40 1.00
Teemu Selanne
Alexei Zhamnov
3PL Adam Graves .40 1.00
Mark Messier
Pat Verbeek
4PL Pat Poulin .40 1.00
Jeremy Roenick
Tony Amonte
5PL Kevin Stevens .75 2.00
Jaromir Jagr
Ron Francis
6PL Jason Dawe .40 1.00
Pat Lafontaine
Alexander Mogilny
7PL Adam Oates .40 1.00
Cam Neely
Mariusz Czerkawski
8PL Slava Kozlov 1.00 2.50
Sergei Fedorov
Doug Brown
9PL Vin Damphousse .40 1.00
Pierre Turgeon
Mark Recchi
10PL Mike Peluso .40 1.00
Bobby Holik
Randy McKay

1995-96 Topps Profiles

Mark Messier knows a bit about hockey, as he demonstrates here with his choices of and commentary on some of the game's finest. The cards were inserted in both series 1 (1-10) and series 2 (11-20) packs at a rate of 1:12.

COMPLETE SET (20) 12.00 30.00
PF1 Wayne Gretzky 4.00 10.00
PF2 Brian Leetch .30 .75
PF3 Patrick Roy 2.50 6.00
PF4 Jaromir Jagr 1.00 2.50
PF5 Sergei Fedorov 1.00 2.50
PF6 Martin Brodeur 1.50 4.00
PF7 Eric Lindros .60 1.50
PF8 Jeremy Roenick .75 2.00
PF9 John Vanbiesbrouck .30 .75
PF10 Cam Neely .60 1.50
PF11 Pavel Bure .60 1.50
PF12 Paul Coffey .60 1.50
PF13 Scott Stevens .30 .75
PF14 Dominik Hasek 1.25 3.00
PF15 Mario Lemieux 2.50 6.00
PF16 Ed Belfour .60 1.50
PF17 Doug Gilmour .30 .75
PF18 Teemu Selanne .60 1.50
PF19 Brett Hull .75 2.00
PF20 Joe Sakic 1.25 3.00

1995-96 Topps Rink Leaders

Topps selected players who are top guys both on the ice and in the dressing room for this ten-card tribute. The cards were randomly inserted in series 1 hobby packs at a rate of 1:36.

COMPLETE SET (10) 30.00 60.00
1RL Mark Messier 2.00 5.00
2RL Mario Lemieux 8.00 20.00
3RL Ray Bourque 3.00 8.00
4RL Brett Hull 2.50 6.00
5RL Pat LaFontaine 2.00 5.00
6RL Scott Stevens 1.00 2.50
7RL Keith Tkachuk 2.00 5.00
8RL Doug Gilmour 1.00 2.50
9RL Chris Chelios 2.00 5.00
10RL Wayne Gretzky 12.50 30.00

1995-96 Topps Young Stars

Topps honors fifteen of the brightest young stars in the game with this set which utilizes the Power Matrix printing technology. The cards were randomly inserted at 1:24 series 2 packs.

COMPLETE SET (15) 12.00 25.00
YS1 Paul Kariya 1.00 2.50
YS2 Martin Brodeur 2.50 6.00
YS3 Mikael Renberg .50 1.25
YS4 Peter Forsberg 2.50 6.00
YS5 Alexei Yashin UER .25 .60
front reads "Alexi"
YS6 Jeff Friesen .25 .60
YS7 Oleg Tverdovsky .25 .60
YS8 Jim Carey .50 1.25
YS9 Alexei Kovalev .25 .60
YS10 Jason Arnott .25 .60
YS11 Teemu Selanne 1.00 2.50
YS12 Chris Osgood .50 1.25
YS13 Roman Hamrlik .50 1.25
YS14 Scott Niedermayer .25 .60
YS15 Jaromir Jagr 1.50 4.00

1998-99 Topps

The 1998-99 Topps set was issued in one series totaling 242 cards. The 11-card packs retail for $1.29 each. The fronts featured color action photos and the backs carried player information and statistics.

COMPLETE SET (242) 12.50 25.00
1 Peter Forsberg .30 .75
2 Petr Sykora .02 .10
3 Byron Dafoe .08 .25
4 Ron Francis .08 .25
5 Alexei Yashin .02 .10
6 Dave Ellett .02 .10
7 Jamie Langenbrunner .02 .10
8 Doug Weight .08 .25
9 Jason Woolley .02 .10
10 Paul Coffey .10 .30
11 Uwe Krupp .02 .10
12 Tomas Sandstrom .02 .10
13 Scott Mellanby .02 .10
14 Vladimir Tsyplakov .02 .10
15 Martin Rucinsky .02 .10
16 Mikael Renberg .08 .25
17 Marco Sturm .02 .10
18 Eric Lindros .10 .30
19 Sean Burke .02 .10
20 Martin Brodeur .30 .75
21 Boyd Devereaux .02 .10
22 Kelly Buchberger .02 .10
23 Scott Stevens .08 .25
24 Jamie Storr .08 .25
25 Anders Eriksson .02 .10
26 Gary Suter .02 .10
27 Theo Fleury .02 .10
28 Steve Leach .02 .10
29 Felix Potvin .10 .30
30 Brett Hull .15 .40
31 Mike Grier .02 .10
32 Cale Hulse .02 .10
33 Larry Murphy .08 .25
34 Rick Tocchet .08 .25
35 Eric Desjardins .08 .25
36 Igor Kravchuk .02 .10
37 Rob Niedermayer .02 .10
38 Bryan Smolinski .02 .10
39 Valeri Kamensky .08 .25
40 Ryan Smyth .08 .25
41 Bruce Driver .02 .10
42 Mike Johnson .02 .10
43 Rob Zamuner .02 .10
44 Steve Duchesne .02 .10
45 Martin Straka .02 .10
46 Bill Houlder .02 .10
47 Craig Conroy .02 .10
48 Guy Hebert .08 .25
49 Colin Forbes .02 .10
50 Mike Modano .20 .50
51 Jamie Pushor .02 .10
52 Jarome Iginla .15 .40
53 Paul Kariya .10 .30
54 Mattias Ohlund .08 .25
55 Sergei Berezin .08 .25
56 Peter Zezel .02 .10
57 Teppo Numminen .02 .10
58 Dale Hunter .02 .10
59 Sandy Moger .02 .10
60 John LeClair .10 .30
61 Wade Redden .02 .10
62 Patrik Elias .08 .25
63 Rob Blake .08 .25
64 Todd Marchant .02 .10
65 Claude Lemieux .02 .10
66 Trevor Kidd .08 .25
67 Sergei Fedorov .20 .50
68 Joe Sakic .25 .60
69 Derek Morris .02 .10
70 Alexei Morozov .02 .10
71 Mats Sundin .10 .30
72 Daymond Langkow .08 .25
73 Kevin Hatcher .02 .10
74 Damian Rhodes .08 .25
75 Brian Leetch .10 .30
76 Saku Koivu .10 .30
77 Rick Tabaracci .02 .10
78 Bernie Nicholls .02 .10
79 Alyn McCauley .02 .10
80 Patrice Brisebois .02 .10
81 Bret Hedican .02 .10
82 Sandy McCarthy .02 .10
83 Viktor Kozlov .02 .10
84 Derek King .02 .10
85 Alexander Selivanov .02 .10
86 Mike Vernon .08 .25
87 Jeff Beukeboom .02 .10
88 Tommy Salo .08 .25
89 Adam Graves .02 .10
90 Randy McKay .02 .10
91 Rich Pilon .02 .10
92 Richard Zednik .02 .10
93 Jeff Hackett .08 .25
94 Michael Peca .02 .10
95 Brent Gilchrist .02 .10
96 Stu Grimson .02 .10
97 Bob Probert .02 .10
98 Stu Barnes .02 .10
99 Ruslan Salei .02 .10
100 Al MacInnis .08 .25
101 Ken Daneyko .02 .10
102 Paul Ranheim .02 .10
103 Marty McInnis .02 .10
104 Marian Hossa .10 .30
105 Darren McCarty .02 .10
106 Guy Carbonneau .02 .10
107 Dallas Drake .02 .10
108 Sergei Samsonov .08 .25
109 Teemu Selanne .10 .30
110 Checklist .02 .10
111 Jaromir Jagr .20 .50
112 Joe Thornton .20 .50
113 Jon Klemm .02 .10
114 Grant Fuhr .08 .25
115 Nikolai Khabibulin .08 .25
116 Rod Brind'Amour .08 .25
117 Trevor Linden .08 .25
118 Vincent Damphousse .02 .10
119 Dino Ciccarelli .08 .25
120 Pat Verbeek .02 .10
121 Sandis Ozolinsh .02 .10
122 Garth Snow .08 .25
123 Ed Belfour .10 .30
124 Keith Primeau .02 .10
125 Jason Allison .02 .10
126 Peter Bondra .08 .25
127 Ulf Samuelsson .02 .10
128 Jeff Friesen .02 .10
129 Jason Bonsignore .02 .10
130 Daniel Alfredsson .08 .25
131 Bobby Holik .02 .10
132 Jozef Stumpel .08 .25
133 Brian Bellows .02 .10
134 Chris Osgood .08 .25
135 Alexei Zhamnov .02 .10
136 Mattias Norstrom .02 .10
137 Drake Berehowsky .02 .10
138 Mark Messier .10 .30
139 Geoff Courtnall .02 .10
140 Marc Bureau .02 .10
141 Don Sweeney .02 .10
142 Wendel Clark .08 .25
143 Scott Niedermayer .02 .10
144 Chris Therien .02 .10
145 Kirk Muller .02 .10
146 Wayne Primeau .02 .10
147 Tony Granato .02 .10
148 Derian Hatcher .02 .10
149 Daniel Briere .02 .10
150 Fredrik Olausson .02 .10
151 Joe Juneau .08 .25
152 Michal Grosek .02 .10
153 Jamie Laukkanen .02 .10
154 Keith Tkachuk .10 .30
155 Marty McSorley .02 .10
156 Owen Nolan .08 .25
157 Mark Tinordi .02 .10
158 Steve Washburn .02 .10
159 Luke Richardson .02 .10
160 Kris King .02 .10
161 Joe Nieuwendyk .08 .25
162 Travis Green .02 .10
163 Dominik Hasek .25 .60
164 Dimitri Khristich .02 .10
165 Dave Manson .02 .10
166 Chris Chelios .10 .30
167 Claude LaPointe .02 .10
168 Kris Draper .02 .10
169 Brad Isbister .02 .10
170 Patrick Marleau .02 .10
171 Jeremy Roenick .15 .40
172 Darren Langdon .02 .10
173 Kevin Dineen .02 .10
174 Luc Robitaille .08 .25
175 Steve Yzerman .60 1.50
176 Sergei Zubov .02 .10
177 Ed Jovanovski .02 .10
178 Sami Kapanen .02 .10
179 Adam Oates .08 .25
180 Pavel Bure .10 .30
181 Chris Pronger .08 .25
182 Pat Falloon .02 .10
183 Darcy Tucker .02 .10
184 Zigmund Palffy .08 .25
185 Curtis Brown .02 .10
186 Curtis Joseph .10 .30
187 Valeri Zelepukin .02 .10
188 Russ Courtnall .02 .10
189 Adam Foote .02 .10
190 Patrick Roy .60 1.50
191 Cory Stillman .02 .10
192 Alexei Zhitnik .02 .10
193 Olaf Kolzig .08 .25
194 Mark Fitzpatrick .02 .10
195 Eric Daze .08 .25
196 Zarley Zalapski .02 .10
197 Niklas Sundstrom .02 .10
198 Bryan Berard .08 .25
199 Jason Arnott .02 .10
200 Mike Richter .10 .30
201 Ken Baumgartner .02 .10
202 Jason Dawe .02 .10
203 Nicklas Lidstrom .10 .30
204 Tony Amonte .08 .25
205 Kjell Samuelsson .02 .10
206 Ray Bourque .20 .50
207 Alexander Mogilny .08 .25
208 Pierre Turgeon .08 .25
209 Tom Barrasso .08 .25
210 Richard Matvichuk .02 .10
211 Sergei Krivokrasov .02 .10
212 Ted Drury .02 .10
213 Matthew Barnaby .02 .10
214 Denis Pederson .02 .10
215 John Vanbiesbrouck .08 .25
216 Brendan Shanahan .10 .30
217 Jocelyn Thibault .08 .25
218 Nelson Emerson .02 .10
219 Wayne Gretzky .75 2.00
220 Checklist .02 .10
221 Ramzi Abid RC .30 .75
222 Mark Bell RC .30 .75
223 Michael Henrich RC .30 .75
224 Vincent Lecavalier .40 1.00
225 Rico Fata .10 .30
226 Bryan Allen .10 .30
227 Daniel Tkaczuk .20 .50
228 Brad Stuart RC .30 .75
229 Derrick Walser RC .20 .50
230 Jonathan Cheechoo RC 3.00 8.00
231 Sergei Varlamov .10 .30
232 Scott Gomez RC 2.00 5.00
233 Jeff Heerema RC .30 .75
234 David Legwand .20 .50
235 Manny Malhotra .10 .30
236 Michael Rupp RC .30 .75
237 Alex Tanguay .30 .75
238 Mathieu Biron RC .10 .30
239 Bujar Amidovski RC .10 .30
240 Brian Finley RC .30 .75
241 Philippe Sauve RC .75 2.00
242 Jiri Fischer RC .30 .75

1998-99 Topps O-Pee-Chee Parallel

This 242-card parallel set, offered only in Canadian hobby packs, offers the same players as the Topps base set, but was emblazoned with the O-Pee-Chee foil stamp logo.

*1-220 VETS: 5X TO 12X BASIC CARDS
*221-242 ROOKIES: 1.5X TO 4X

1998-99 Topps Autographs

Randomly inserted into packs at the rate of 1:209, this nine-card set features autographed color action player photos with player information on the backs.

A1 Jason Allison 4.00 10.00
A2 Sergei Samsonov 6.00 15.00
A3 John LeClair 8.00 20.00
A4 Mattias Ohlund 4.00 10.00
A5 Jaromir Jagr 20.00 50.00
A6 Keith Tkachuk 6.00 15.00
A7 Patrik Elias 4.00 10.00
A8 Dominik Hasek 25.00 60.00
A9 Brian Leetch 8.00 20.00

1998-99 Topps Blast From The Past

Randomly inserted in packs at a rate of 1:23, this 10-card insert set features early reprint cards of true heroes of the game including Gordie Howe, Phil Esposito and Stan Mikita. These cards resemble the originals in every way except a small note on the back that states "Reprint X of 10".

COMPLETE SET (10) 25.00 50.00
1 Wayne Gretzky 5.00 12.00
2 Mark Messier 2.00 5.00
3 Ray Bourque 3.00 8.00
4 Patrick Roy 4.00 10.00
5 Grant Fuhr 2.00 5.00
6 Brett Hull 2.00 5.00
7 Gordie Howe 5.00 12.00
8 Stan Mikita 2.50 6.00
9 Bobby Hull 3.00 8.00
10 Phil Esposito 2.50 6.00

1998-99 Topps Blast From The Past Autographs

Randomly inserted into packs at the rate of 1:1878, this 4-card set mirrored the basic inserts but included autographs of the retired players. The Mikita card had insertion odds of 1:3756.

7 Gordie Howe 60.00 150.00
8 Stan Mikita 30.00 80.00
9 Bobby Hull 40.00 100.00
10 Phil Esposito 30.00 80.00

1998-99 Topps Board Members

Randomly inserted in packs at a rate of 1:36, this 15-card insert features color action photography of superstar defensemen on vibrant foilboard.

COMPLETE SET (15) 10.00 25.00
B1 Chris Pronger 1.25 3.00
B2 Chris Chelios 1.50 4.00
B3 Brian Leetch 1.50 4.00
B4 Ray Bourque 2.00 5.00
B5 Mattias Ohlund .75 2.00
B6 Nicklas Lidstrom 1.50 4.00
B7 Sergei Zubov .75 2.00
B8 Scott Niedermayer .75 2.00
B9 Larry Murphy .75 2.00
B10 Sandis Ozolinsh .75 2.00
B11 Rob Blake 1.25 3.00
B12 Scott Stevens .75 2.00
B13 Derian Hatcher .75 2.00
B14 Kevin Hatcher .75 2.00
B15 Wade Redden .75 2.00

1998-99 Topps Ice Age 2000

Randomly inserted in packs at a rate of 1:12, this 15-card insert was printed with dot-matrix technology.

COMPLETE SET (15) 8.00 15.00
I1 Paul Kariya .60 1.50
I2 Marco Sturm .20 .50
I3 Jarome Iginla .75 2.00
I4 Denis Pederson .20 .50
I5 Wade Redden .20 .50
I6 Jason Allison .20 .50
I7 Chris Pronger .50 1.25
I8 Peter Forsberg 1.50 4.00
I9 Saku Koivu .60 1.50
I10 Eric Lindros .60 1.50
I11 Sergei Samsonov .50 1.25
I12 Mattias Ohlund .50 1.25
I13 Joe Thornton 1.00 2.50
I14 Mike Johnson .20 .50
I15 Nikolai Khabibulin .50 1.25

1998-99 Topps Local Legends

Randomly inserted in packs at a rate of 1:18, this worldly 15-card insert honors players on foilboard cards that actually depict that player's country of origin.

COMPLETE SET (15) 30.00 60.00
L1 Peter Forsberg 2.50 6.00
L2 Mats Sundin 1.00 2.50
L3 Zigmund Palffy .75 2.00
L4 Jaromir Jagr 1.50 4.00
L5 Dominik Hasek 2.00 5.00
L6 Martin Brodeur 2.50 6.00
L7 Wayne Gretzky 6.00 15.00
L8 Patrick Roy 5.00 12.00
L9 Eric Lindros 1.00 2.50
L10 Joe Sakic 2.00 5.00
L11 Mark Messier 1.00 2.50
L12 Mike Modano 1.50 4.00
L13 Sergei Fedorov 1.50 4.00
L14 Pavel Bure 1.00 2.50
L15 Teemu Selanne 1.00 2.50

1998-99 Topps Mystery Finest Bronze

Sequentially numbered and arranged by jersey (home, away and All-Star), this 20-card insert honors the 20 best players in the NHL today. The set was also grouped and randomly inserted in Bronze 1:36; Silver 1:72; and Gold 1:108 variations. Refractor parallels for each color were also created and inserted at the following rates: bronze at 1:108, silver at 1:216, and gold at 1:324.

COMPLETE SET (20) 40.00 80.00
*BRONZE REF.: .6X TO 2X BASIC INSERTS
*GOLD: .8X TO 2X BASIC INSERTS
*GOLD REF.: 4X TO 10X BASIC INSERTS
*SILVER: .6X TO 1.5X BASIC INSERTS
*SILVER REF.: 1.2X TO 3X BASIC INSERTS
M1 Teemu Selanne 1.50 4.00
M2 Olaf Kolzig 1.25 3.00
M3 Pavel Bure 1.50 4.00
M4 Wayne Gretzky 10.00 25.00
M5 Mike Modano 2.50 6.00
M6 Jaromir Jagr 2.50 6.00
M7 Dominik Hasek 3.00 8.00
M8 Peter Forsberg 4.00 10.00
M9 Eric Lindros 1.50 4.00
M10 John LeClair 1.50 4.00
M11 Zigmund Palffy 1.25 3.00
M12 Martin Brodeur 4.00 10.00
M13 Keith Tkachuk 1.50 4.00
M14 Peter Bondra 1.25 3.00
M15 Nicklas Lidstrom 1.50 4.00
M16 Patrick Roy 8.00 20.00
M17 Chris Chelios 1.25 3.00
M18 Saku Koivu 1.50 4.00
M19 Mark Messier 1.50 4.00
M20 Joe Sakic 3.00 8.00

1998-99 Topps Season's Best

Randomly inserted in packs at a rate of 1:6, this 30-card insert features color action photography in five distinct categories: NetMinders salutes the league's top goalies, Sharpshooters features the top scoring leaders, Puck Providers showcases assist leaders, Performers Plus features those that lead ice time by plus/minus ratio, and Ice Hot introduces the powerful rookies.

COMPLETE SET (30) 15.00 40.00
SB1 Dominik Hasek 1.50 4.00
SB2 Martin Brodeur 2.00 5.00
SB3 Ed Belfour .75 2.00
SB4 Curtis Joseph .75 2.00
SB5 Jeff Hackett .60 1.50
SB6 Tom Barrasso .60 1.50
SB7 Mike Johnson .30 .75
SB8 Sergei Samsonov .60 1.50
SB9 Patrik Elias .60 1.50
SB10 Patrick Marleau .60 1.50
SB11 Mattias Ohlund .60 1.50
SB12 Marco Sturm .30 .75
SB13 Teemu Selanne .75 2.00
SB14 Peter Bondra .60 1.50
SB15 Pavel Bure .75 2.00
SB16 John LeClair 1.00 2.50
SB17 Zigmund Palffy .60 1.50
SB18 Keith Tkachuk .75 2.00
SB19 Jaromir Jagr 1.25 3.00
SB20 Wayne Gretzky 4.00 10.00
SB21 Peter Forsberg 1.25 3.00
SB22 Ron Francis .60 1.50
SB23 Adam Oates .60 1.50
SB24 Jozef Stumpel .60 1.50
SB25 Chris Pronger .60 1.50
SB26 Larry Murphy .60 1.50
SB27 Jason Allison .30 .75
SB28 John LeClair .75 2.00
SB29 Randy McKay .30 .75
SB30 Dainius Zubrus .30 .75

1999-00 Topps Arena Giveaways

These promo cards were issued in various NHL cities as part of a stadium giveaway program that included six cards per team. Manufacturers Topps, Upper Deck, and Pacific were all represented with two cards per team set.

COMPLETE SET 15.00 30.00
ANALK Ladislav Kohn .20 .50
ANAOT Oleg Tverdovsky .20 .50
ATLMJ Matt Johnson .20 .50
ATLPS Patrik Stefan .40 1.00
BOSJG Jonathan Girard .20 .50
BOSJT Joe Thornton 1.50 4.00
BUFMA Maxim Afinogenov .40 1.00
BUFMB Martin Biron .40 1.00
CALDG Denis Gauthier .20 .50
CALRR Robyn Regehr .20 .50
CARBB Bates Battaglia .20 .50
CARDT David Tanabe .20 .50
CHIED Eric Daze .20 .50
CHIJD J-P Dumont .20 .50
COLAT Alex Tanguay .40 1.00
COLMD Marc Denis .40 1.00
DALBM Brenden Morrow .75 2.00
DALJS Jon Sim .20 .50
DETJF Jiri Fischer .20 .50
DETMD Mathieu Dandenault .20 .50
EDMGL Georges Laraque .40 1.00
EDMPC Paul Comrie .20 .50
FLOIN Ivan Novoseltsev .20 .50
FLOOK Oleg Kvasha .20 .50
LAFK Frantisek Kaberle .20 .50
LAJS Jamie Storr .40 1.00
NASDL David Legwand .20 .50
NASTV Tomas Vokoun .40 1.00
NJPE Patrik Elias .20 .50
NJSG Scott Gomez .20 .50
NYIOJ Olli Jokinen .20 .50
NYIRL Roberto Luongo 2.00 5.00
NYRKJ Kim Johnsson .20 .50
NYRMY Mike York .20 .50
OTTMF Mike Fisher .20 .50
OTTMH Marian Hossa .40 1.00
PHORS Radoslav Suchy .20 .50
PHOTL Trevor Letowski .20 .50
PITAF Andrew Ference .20 .50
PITJH Jan Hrdina .20 .50
SJBS Brad Stuart .20 .50
SJMS Marco Sturm .20 .50
STLJH Jochen Hecht .20 .50
STLTN Tyson Nash .20 .50
TBPM Paul Mara .20 .50
TBVL Vincent Lecavalier 1.25 3.00
TORNA Nikolai Antropov .40 1.00
TORTK Tomas Kaberle .20 .50
VANEJ Ed Jovanovski .20 .50
VANSK Steve Kariya .40 1.00
WASJH Jeff Halpern .20 .50
WASRZ Richard Zednik .20 .50

1999-00 Topps

Released as a 286-card set, there are actually a total of 330-cards in this release. Five versions of cards 276-286 were released. The complete set prices below reflect sets with one version of cards 276-286. Base cards feature full color action shots with blue borders and gold foil highlights. The O-Pee-Chee version of this set exactly parallels the base set, but book at a slight premium.

COMPLETE SET (275) 25.00 50.00
COMP.SET w/MMs (330) 60.00 120.00

1 Joe Sakic .25 .60
2 Alexei Yashin .02 .10
3 Paul Kariya .10 .30
4 Keith Tkachuk .10 .30
5 Jaromir Jagr .20 .50
6 Mike Modano .20 .50
7 Eric Lindros .10 .30
8 Zigmund Palffy .08 .25
9 Dominik Hasek .25 .60
10 Pavel Bure .10 .30
11 Ray Bourque .20 .50
12 Peter Forsberg .30 .75
13 Al MacInnis .08 .25
14 Steve Yzerman .60 1.50
15 Mats Sundin .10 .30
16 Patrick Roy .60 1.50
17 Teemu Selanne .10 .30
18 Keith Primeau .02 .10
19 John LeClair .10 .30
20 Martin Brodeur .30 .75
21 Joe Thornton .20 .50
22 Rob Blake .08 .25
23 Ron Francis .08 .25
24 Grant Fuhr .08 .25
25 Nicklas Lidstrom .10 .30
26 Vladimir Orszagh RC .02 .10
27 Glen Wesley .02 .10
28 Adam Deadmarsh .02 .10
29 Zdeno Chara .02 .10
30 Brian Leetch .10 .30
31 Valeri Bure .02 .10
32 Ryan Smyth .02 .10
33 Jean-Sebastien Aubin .08 .25
34 Dave Reid .02 .10
35 Ed Jovanovski .02 .10
36 Anders Eriksson .02 .10
37 Mike Ricci .02 .10
38 Todd Bertuzzi .10 .30
39 Shawn Bates .02 .10
40 Kip Miller .02 .10
41 Jozef Stumpel .08 .25
42 Jeremy Roenick .15 .40
43 Todd Marchant .02 .10
44 Josh Holden .02 .10
45 Rob Niedermayer .02 .10
46 Cory Sarich .02 .10
47 Nikolai Khabibulin .08 .25
48 Marty McInnis .02 .10
49 Marty Reasoner .08 .25
50 Gary Roberts .02 .10
51 Manny Malhotra .08 .25
52 Adam Foote .02 .10
53 Luc Robitaille .08 .25
54 Bryan Marchment .02 .10
55 Mark Janssens .02 .10
56 Steve Heinze .02 .10
57 Cory Stillman .02 .10
58 Guy Hebert .08 .25
59 Mike Richter .10 .30
60 Jamie Langenbrunner .02 .10
61 Wade Redden .02 .10
62 Steve Smith .02 .10
63 Daniil Markov .02 .10
64 Erik Rasmussen .02 .10
65 Glen Murray .02 .10
66 Alexei Kovalev .02 .10
67 Peter Bondra .08 .25
68 Dimitri Khristich .02 .10
69 Sami Kapanen .02 .10
70 Tom Poti .02 .10
71 Trevor Linden .02 .10
72 Tomas Vokoun .08 .25
73 Steve Webb .02 .10
74 Jarome Iginla .15 .40
75 Scott Mellanby .02 .10
76 Mattias Ohlund .02 .10
77 Steve Konowalchuk .02 .10
78 Bryan Berard .08 .25
79 Chris Pronger .08 .25
80 Teppo Numminen .02 .10
81 John MacLean .02 .10
82 Jeff Hackett .08 .25
83 Ray Whitney .02 .10
84 Chris Osgood .08 .25
85 Doug Zmolek .02 .10
86 Curtis Brown .02 .10
87 Reid Simpson .02 .10
88 Milan Hejduk .10 .30
89 Donald Audette .02 .10
90 Saku Koivu .10 .30
91 Martin Straka .02 .10
92 Mark Messier .10 .30
93 Richard Zednik .02 .10
94 Curtis Joseph .10 .30
95 Colin Forbes .02 .10
96 Jeff Friesen .02 .10
97 Eric Brewer .02 .10
98 Darius Kasparaitis .02 .10
99 Marian Hossa .10 .30
100 Petr Sykora .02 .10
101 Vladimir Malakhov .02 .10
102 Jamie Storr .08 .25
103 Doug Gilmour .08 .25
104 Doug Weight .08 .25
105 Derian Hatcher .02 .10
106 Chris Drury .08 .25
107 Arturs Irbe .08 .25
108 Fred Brathwaite .08 .25
109 Jason Allison .02 .10
110 Roman Hamrlik .02 .10
111 Rico Fata .02 .10
112 Janne Niinimaa .02 .10

113 Kenny Jonsson .02 .10
114 Marco Sturm .02 .10
115 Steve Thomas .02 .10
116 Garth Snow .08 .25
117 Rick Tocchet .08 .25
118 Jean-Marc Pelletier .08 .25
119 Bobby Holik .02 .10
120 Sergei Fedorov .20 .50
121 J-P Dumont .08 .25
122 Jason Woolley .02 .10
123 James Patrick .02 .10
124 Blake Sloan .10 .30
125 Marcus Nilsson .02 .10
126 Shayne Corson .02 .10
127 Tom Fitzgerald .02 .10
128 Brian Rolston .02 .10
129 Ron Tugnutt .08 .25
130 Mark Recchi .08 .25
131 Matthew Barnaby .02 .10
132 Olaf Kolzig .08 .25
133 Paul Mara .02 .10
134 Patrick Marleau .10 .30
135 Magnus Arvedson .02 .10
136 Felix Potvin .10 .30
137 Bill Guerin .08 .25
138 Brett Hull .15 .40
139 Vitali Yachmenev .02 .10
140 Ruslan Salei .02 .10
141 Mark Parrish .02 .10
142 Randy Cunneyworth .02 .10
143 Damian Rhodes .08 .25
144 Daniel Briere .02 .10
145 Craig Conroy .02 .10
146 Sergei Gonchar .02 .10
147 Vincent Lecavalier .10 .30
148 Adam Graves .02 .10
149 Doug Bodger .02 .10
150 Jeff O'Neill .02 .10
151 Darby Hendrickson .02 .10
152 Sergei Samsonov .08 .25
153 Ed Belfour .10 .30
154 Robert Svehla .02 .10
155 Cliff Ronning .02 .10
156 Brendan Morrison .08 .25
157 Daniel Alfredsson .08 .25
158 Eric Desjardins .08 .25
159 Mike Vernon .08 .25
160 Vadim Sharifijanov .02 .10
161 Jaroslav Svejkovsky .02 .10
162 Michael Peca .08 .25
163 Shane Willis .02 .10
164 Sandis Ozolinsh .02 .10
165 Mathieu Dandenault .02 .10
166 Martin Rucinsky .02 .10
167 Scott Stevens .02 .10
168 Sami Salo .02 .10
169 Tom Barrasso .08 .25
170 Chris Gratton .02 .10
171 Markus Naslund .10 .30
172 Mike Johnson .02 .10
173 Bob Boughner .02 .10
174 Todd Simpson .02 .10
175 Fredrik Olausson .02 .10
176 Jocelyn Thibault .08 .25
177 Juha Ylonen .02 .10
178 Brad Bombardir .02 .10
179 Jan Hrdina .02 .10
180 Adrian Aucoin .02 .10
181 Mike Eagles .02 .10
182 Petr Nedved .08 .25
183 Rem Murray .02 .10
184 Mikael Renberg .08 .25
185 Mike Eastwood .02 .10
186 Byron Dafoe .08 .25
187 Tony Amonte .08 .25
188 Darren McCarty .02 .10
189 Sergei Krivokrasov .02 .10
190 Dave Lowry .02 .10
191 Michal Handzus .08 .25
192 Tie Domi .08 .25
193 Brian Holzinger .02 .10
194 Jason Arnott .02 .10
195 Jose Theodore .15 .40
196 Brendan Shanahan .10 .30
197 Derek Morris .02 .10
198 Steve Rucchin .02 .10
199 Kevin Hodson .08 .25
200 Oleg Kvasha .02 .10
201 John Vanbiesbrouck .08 .25
202 Adam Oates .08 .25
203 Anson Carter .08 .25
204 Sebastien Bordeleau .02 .10
205 Pavol Demitra .08 .25
206 Owen Nolan .08 .25
207 Pavel Rosa .02 .10
208 Petr Svoboda .02 .10
209 Tomas Kaberle .02 .10
210 Claude Lapointe .02 .10
211 Todd Harvey .02 .10
212 Trent McCleary .02 .10
213 Vyacheslav Kozlov .02 .10
214 Marc Denis .08 .25
215 Joe Nieuwendyk .08 .25
216 Kelly Buchberger .02 .10
217 Tommy Albelin .02 .10
218 Kyle McLaren .02 .10
219 Chris Chelios .10 .30
220 Joel Bouchard .02 .10
221 Mats Lindgren .02 .10
222 Jyrki Lumme .02 .10
223 Pierre Turgeon .08 .25
224 Bill Muckalt .02 .10
225 Antti Aalto .02 .10
226 Jere Lehtinen .08 .25
227 Theo Fleury .02 .10
228 Dmitri Mironov .02 .10
229 Scott Niedermayer .02 .10
230 Sean Burke .08 .25
231 Eric Daze .08 .25
232 Alexei Zhitnik .02 .10
233 Christian Matte .02 .10
234 Patrik Elias .08 .25
235 Alexandre Korolyuk .02 .10
236 Sergei Berezin .02 .10
237 Ray Ferraro .02 .10
238 Rod Brind'Amour .08 .25
239 Darcy Tucker .02 .10
240 Darryl Sydor .02 .10
241 Mike Dunham .08 .25
242 Marc Bergevin .02 .10
243 Ray Sheppard .02 .10
244 Miroslav Satan .08 .25
245 Andreas Dackell .02 .10
246 Mike Grier .02 .10
247 Alexei Zhamnov .02 .10
248 David Legwand .08 .25
249 Daniel Tkaczuk .02 .10
250 Roberto Luongo .15 .40
251 Simon Gagne .10 .30
252 Jamie Lundmark .08 .25
253 Alexandre Giroux RC .02 .10
254 Dusty Jamieson RC .08 .25
255 Jamie Chamberlain RC .08 .25
256 Radim Vrbata RC 2.50 6.00
257 Scott Cameron RC .08 .25
258 Simon Lajeunesse RC .40 1.00
259 Tim Connolly .02 .10
260 Kris Beech .02 .10
261 Brian Finley .08 .25
262 Alex Auld RC .40 1.00
263 Martin Grenier RC .08 .25
264 Sheldon Keefe RC .40 1.00
265 Justin Mapletoft RC .08 .25
266 Edward Hill RC .08 .25
267 Nolan Yonkman RC .15 .40
268 Oleg Saprykin RC .40 1.00
269 Branislav Mezei RC .10 .30
270 Chris Kelly RC .08 .25
271 Pavel Brendl RC 1.50 4.00
272 Brett Lysak RC .10 .30
273 Matt Carkner RC .08 .25
274 Luke Sellars RC .15 .40
275 Brad Ralph RC .08 .25
276A Ray Bourque MM .40 1.00
276B Ray Bourque MM .40 1.00
276C Ray Bourque MM .40 1.00
276D Ray Bourque MM .40 1.00
276E Ray Bourque MM .40 1.00
277A Peter Forsberg MM .60 1.50
277B Peter Forsberg MM .60 1.50
277C Peter Forsberg MM .60 1.50
277D Peter Forsberg MM .60 1.50
277E Peter Forsberg MM .60 1.50
278A Joe Nieuwendyk MM .10 .30
278B Joe Nieuwendyk MM .10 .30
278C Joe Nieuwendyk MM .10 .30
278D Joe Nieuwendyk MM .10 .30
278E Joe Nieuwendyk MM .10 .30
279A Dominik Hasek MM .50 1.25
279B Dominik Hasek MM .50 1.25
279C Dominik Hasek MM .50 1.25
279D Dominik Hasek MM .50 1.25
279E Dominik Hasek MM .50 1.25
280A Jaromir Jagr MM .40 1.00
280B Jaromir Jagr MM .40 1.00
280C Jaromir Jagr MM .40 1.00
280D Jaromir Jagr MM .40 1.00
280E Jaromir Jagr MM .40 1.00
281A Paul Kariya MM .10 .30
281B Paul Kariya MM .10 .30
281C Paul Kariya MM .10 .30
281D Paul Kariya MM .10 .30
281E Paul Kariya MM .10 .30
282A Eric Lindros MM .08 .25
282B Eric Lindros MM .50 1.25
282C Eric Lindros MM .50 1.25
282D Eric Lindros MM .50 1.25
282E Eric Lindros MM .50 1.25
283A Mark Messier MM .10 .30
283B Mark Messier MM .30 .75
283C Mark Messier MM .30 .75
283D Mark Messier MM .30 .75
283E Mark Messier MM .30 .75
284A Patrick Roy MM 1.25 3.00
284B Patrick Roy MM 1.25 3.00
284C Patrick Roy MM 1.25 3.00
284D Patrick Roy MM 1.25 3.00
284E Patrick Roy MM 1.25 3.00
285A Joe Sakic MM .50 1.25
285B Joe Sakic MM .50 1.25
285C Joe Sakic MM .50 1.25
285D Joe Sakic MM .50 1.25
285E Joe Sakic MM .50 1.25
286A Steve Yzerman MM 1.25 3.00
286B Steve Yzerman MM 1.25 3.00
286C Steve Yzerman MM 1.25 3.00
286D Steve Yzerman MM 1.25 3.00
286E Steve Yzerman MM 1.25 3.00

1999-00 Topps All-Topps

Randomly inserted in Topps and OPC packs at the rate of 1:18, this 15-card set features top players on a card with full color action shots and holographic foil highlights. Card backs carry an "AT" prefix.

COMPLETE SET (15) 20.00 40.00
AT1 Dominik Hasek 1.50 4.00
AT2 Martin Brodeur 2.00 5.00
AT3 Ray Bourque 1.25 3.00
AT4 Al MacInnis .75 2.00
AT5 Nicklas Lidstrom .75 2.00
AT6 Brian Leetch .75 2.00
AT7 John LeClair 1.00 2.50
AT8 Paul Kariya .75 2.00
AT9 Keith Tkachuk .75 2.00
AT10 Eric Lindros 1.25 3.00
AT11 Peter Forsberg 2.00 5.00
AT12 Steve Yzerman 4.00 10.00
AT13 Jaromir Jagr 1.25 3.00
AT14 Teemu Selanne .75 2.00
AT15 Pavel Bure 1.00 2.50

1999-00 Topps Autographs

Randomly inserted in Topps packs at the rate of 1:517, this 10-card set features authentic player autographs.

TA1 Joe Sakic 12.00 30.00
TA2 Dominik Hasek 15.00 40.00
TA3 Curtis Joseph 10.00 25.00
TA4 Alexei Yashin 8.00 20.00
TA5 Mats Sundin 15.00 40.00
TA6 Chris Drury 8.00 20.00
TA7 Milan Hejduk 10.00 25.00
TA8 Marian Hossa 10.00 25.00
TA9 Vincent Lecavalier 10.00 25.00
TA10 Joe Thornton 12.00 30.00

1999-00 Topps A-Men

COMPLETE SET (6) 6.00 12.00
STATED ODDS 1:10 TOPPS
AM1 Jaromir Jagr .75 2.00
AM2 Peter Forsberg 1.25 3.00
AM3 Paul Kariya 1.25 3.00
AM4 Teemu Selanne 1.25 3.00
AM5 Joe Sakic 1.00 2.50
AM6 Eric Lindros .75 2.00

1999-00 Topps Fantastic Finishers

COMPLETE SET (6) 3.00 8.00
STATED ODDS 1:10 TOPPS
FF1 Teemu Selanne .50 1.25
FF2 Jaromir Jagr .75 2.00
FF3 Tony Amonte .40 1.00
FF4 Alexei Yashin .40 1.00
FF5 John LeClair .60 1.50
FF6 Joe Sakic 1.00 2.50

1999-00 Topps Ice Futures

COMPLETE SET (6) 1.25 3.00
STATED ODDS 1:10 TOPPS
IF1 Mark Parrish .25 .60
IF2 Chris Drury .50 1.25
IF3 Bill Muckalt .25 .60
IF4 Marian Hossa .25 .60
IF5 Milan Hejduk .50 1.25
IF6 Brendan Morrison .50 1.25

1999-00 Topps Ice Masters

COMPLETE SET (20) 40.00 80.00
STATED ODDS 1:30 TOPPS
IM1 Joe Sakic 2.00 5.00
IM2 Dominik Hasek 2.00 5.00
IM3 Eric Lindros 1.50 4.00
IM4 Jaromir Jagr 1.50 4.00
IM5 John LeClair 1.25 3.00
IM6 Mats Sundin 1.25 3.00
IM7 Ray Bourque 1.50 4.00
IM8 Mike Modano 1.50 4.00
IM9 Peter Forsberg 2.50 6.00
IM10 Brian Leetch 1.25 3.00
IM11 Martin Brodeur 2.50 6.00
IM12 Al MacInnis 1.00 2.50
IM13 Paul Kariya 1.25 3.00
IM14 Alexei Yashin 1.00 2.50
IM15 Steve Yzerman 5.00 12.00
IM16 Ed Belfour 1.25 3.00
IM17 Keith Tkachuk 1.25 3.00
IM18 Patrick Roy 5.00 12.00
IM19 Nicklas Lidstrom 1.25 3.00
IM20 Teemu Selanne 1.25 3.00

1999-00 Topps Now Starring

COMPLETE SET (15) 10.00 20.00
STATED ODDS 1:18
NS1 Anson Carter .75 2.00
NS2 Marian Hossa .75 2.00
NS3 Michael Peca .75 2.00
NS4 Kenny Jonsson .60 1.50
NS5 Petr Sykora .60 1.50
NS6 Chris Drury .75 2.00
NS7 Byron Dafoe .75 2.00
NS8 Wade Redden .60 1.50
NS9 Jeff Friesen .60 1.50
NS10 Jamie Langenbrunner .60 1.50
NS11 Mike Johnson .60 1.50
NS12 Keith Primeau .60 1.50
NS13 Vincent Lecavalier .75 2.00
NS14 Mattias Ohlund .75 2.00
NS15 Pavol Demitra .75 2.00

1999-00 Topps Positive Performers

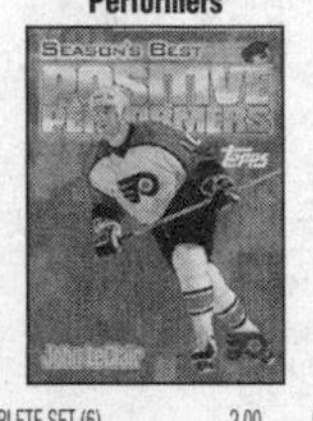

COMPLETE SET (6) 2.00 5.00
STATED ODDS 1:10 TOPPS
PP1 Alexander Karpovtsev .15 .40
PP2 John LeClair .60 1.50
PP3 Eric Lindros .75 2.00
PP4 Magnus Arvedson .15 .40
PP5 Al MacInnis .40 1.00
PP6 Jere Lehtinen .40 1.00

1999-00 Topps Postmasters

COMPLETE SET (6) 5.00 12.00
STATED ODDS 1:10 TOPPS
PM1 Dominik Hasek 1.00 2.50
PM2 Byron Dafoe .40 1.00
PM3 Nikolai Khabibulin .40 1.00
PM4 Ed Belfour .50 1.25
PM5 Patrick Roy 2.50 6.00
PM6 Martin Brodeur 1.25 3.00

1999-00 Topps Stanley Cup Heroes

Randomly inserted in Topps and OPC packs at the rate of 1:23, this 20-card die cut set features full color player shots in the foreground and the Stanley cup in the background. A refractor parallel was also created and inserted at a rate of 1:120.

COMPLETE SET (20) 50.00 100.00
*REFRACTORS: 1.5X TO 4X BASIC INSERTS
SC1 Mario Lemieux 6.00 15.00
SC2 Mike Bossy 2.00 5.00
SC3 Guy Lafleur 2.00 5.00
SC4 Rocket Richard 8.00 20.00
SC5 Lanny McDonald 3.00 8.00
SC6 Frank Mahovlich 1.00 2.50
SC7 Steve Yzerman 6.00 15.00
SC8 Mark Messier 1.50 4.00
SC9 Patrick Roy 6.00 15.00
SC10 Joe Sakic 2.50 6.00
SC11 Jaromir Jagr 3.00 8.00
SC12 Peter Forsberg 3.00 8.00
SC13 Claude Lemieux 1.00 2.50
SC14 Martin Brodeur 3.00 8.00
SC15 Brian Leetch 1.50 4.00
SC16 Mike Richter 1.50 4.00
SC17 Theo Fleury 1.00 2.50
SC18 Chris Osgood 1.25 3.00
SC19 Ed Belfour 1.50 4.00
SC20 Joe Nieuwendyk 1.25 3.00

1999-00 Topps Stanley Cup Heroes Autographs

Randomly inserted in Topps and OPC packs at the rate of 1:697, this 6-card set features a die cut card and authentic player autographs.

COMPLETE SET (6)
SCA1 Mario Lemieux 150.00 250.00
SCA2 Mike Bossy 40.00 80.00
SCA3 Guy Lafleur 50.00 100.00
SCA4 Maurice Richard 250.00 350.00
SCA5 Lanny McDonald 30.00 60.00
SCA6 Frank Mahovlich 30.00 60.00

1999-00 Topps Top of the World

COMPLETE SET (20) 30.00 60.00
STATED ODDS 1:30
TW1 Teemu Selanne 1.00 2.50
TW2 Saku Koivu 1.00 2.50
TW3 Jere Lehtinen .75 2.00
TW4 Peter Forsberg 2.50 6.00
TW5 Mats Sundin 1.00 2.50
TW6 Nicklas Lidstrom 1.00 2.50
TW7 Alexei Yashin 1.00 2.50
TW8 Nikolai Khabibulin .75 2.00
TW9 Pavel Bure 1.25 3.00
TW10 John LeClair 1.25 3.00
TW11 Keith Tkachuk 1.00 2.50
TW12 Mike Modano 1.50 4.00
TW13 Paul Kariya 1.00 2.50
TW14 Joe Sakic 2.00 5.00
TW15 Martin Brodeur 2.50 6.00
TW16 Dominik Hasek 2.00 5.00
TW17 Jaromir Jagr 1.50 4.00
TW18 Peter Bondra .75 2.00
TW19 Olaf Kolzig .75 2.00
TW20 Marco Sturm .75 2.00

2000 Topps AS Sittler

This single was issued as a wrapper redemption at the 2000 NHL All-Star Game by Topps.

1 Darryl Sittler 1.20 3.00

2000-01 Topps

Released as a 330-card set, Topps/OPC features action player photography set on a card with silver borders and gold foil highlights. Topps/OPC was packaged in 36-pack boxes with packs containing 10 cards and carried a suggested retail price of $1.29. Card numbers 251-270 were exclusive to Topps or OPC. "A" version cards are found in Topps, "B" version cards are found in OPC.

COMPLETE SET (330) 15.00 30.00
1 Jaromir Jagr .20 .50
2 Patrick Roy .60 1.50
3 Paul Kariya .10 .30
4 Mats Sundin .10 .30
5 Ron Francis .08 .25
6 Pavel Bure .10 .30
7 John LeClair .10 .30
8 Olaf Kolzig .08 .25
9 Chris Pronger .08 .25
10 Jeremy Roenick .15 .40
11 Owen Nolan .08 .25
12 Theo Fleury .02 .10
13 Zigmund Palffy .08 .25
14 Patrik Stefan .02 .10
15 Jarome Iginla .15 .40
16 Joe Thornton .20 .50
17 Tony Amonte .08 .25
18 Mike Modano .20 .50
19 Alexander Mogilny .08 .25
20 Mark Messier .10 .30
21 Dominik Hasek .25 .60
22 Steve Yzerman .60 1.50
23 Marian Hossa .10 .30
24 David Legwand .08 .25
25 Jose Theodore .15 .40
26 Vincent Lecavalier .10 .30
27 Mike Ricci .02 .10
28 Scott Stevens .08 .25
29 Kevin Weekes .08 .25
30 Sean Burke .08 .25
31 Alexei Kovalev .02 .10
32 Trevor Linden .02 .10
33 Joe Juneau .02 .10
34 Niklas Sundstrom .02 .10
35 Dan Cloutier .08 .25
36 Drake Berehowsky .02 .10
37 Jonas Hoglund .02 .10
38 Sami Kapanen .02 .10
39 Matthew Barnaby .02 .10
40 Anson Carter .08 .25
41 Miroslav Satan .08 .25
42 Mark Recchi .08 .25
43 Pavol Demitra .08 .25
44 Peter Bondra .08 .25
45 Mike Richter .10 .30
46 Guy Hebert .08 .25
47 Robert Svehla .02 .10
48 Martin Skoula .02 .10
49 Ed Belfour .10 .30
50 Alexei Zhamnov .02 .10
51 Fred Brathwaite .08 .25
52 Andrew Brunette .02 .10
53 Byron Dafoe .08 .25
54 Claude Lemieux .02 .10
55 Sergei Berezin .02 .10
56 Felix Potvin .10 .30
57 Rod Brind'Amour .08 .25
58 Doug Gilmour .10 .30
59 Brett Hull .15 .40
60 Nicklas Lidstrom .10 .30
61 Mike York .02 .10
62 Al MacInnis .08 .25
63 Brian Boucher .10 .30
64 Teemu Selanne .10 .30
65 Mike Vernon .08 .25
66 Bill Guerin .08 .25
67 Ray Bourque .25 .60
68 Bryan McCabe .02 .10
69 Ray Ferraro .02 .10
70 Stephane Fiset .02 .10
71 Sergei Gonchar .02 .10
72 Mattias Ohlund .02 .10
73 Todd Marchant .02 .10
74 Derek Morris .02 .10
75 Brian Rolston .02 .10
76 Damian Rhodes .08 .25
77 Chris Drury .08 .25
78 Curtis Joseph .10 .30
79 Teppo Numminen .02 .10
80 Petr Nedved .02 .10
81 Doug Weight .08 .25
82 Arturs Irbe .08 .25
83 Chris Osgood .08 .25
84 Chris Gratton .02 .10
85 Jocelyn Thibault .08 .25
86 Oleg Tverdovsky .02 .10
87 Derian Hatcher .02 .10
88 Ray Whitney .02 .10
89 Saku Koivu .10 .30
90 Cliff Ronning .02 .10
91 Claude Lapointe .02 .10
92 Fredrik Modin .02 .10
93 Chris Simon .02 .10
94 Todd Harvey .02 .10
95 Martin Rucinsky .02 .10
96 Valeri Bure .02 .10
97 Brad Isbister .02 .10
98 Daymond Langkow .08 .25
99 Todd Bertuzzi .10 .30
100 Roman Turek .08 .25
101 Kenny Jonsson .02 .10
102 Mike Dunham .08 .25
103 Rob Blake .08 .25
104 Darius Kasparaitis .02 .10
105 Daniel Alfredsson .08 .25
106 Bobby Holik .02 .10
107 Tommy Salo .08 .25
108 Sergei Samsonov .08 .25
109 Joe Sakic .25 .60
110 Bryan Smolinski .02 .10
111 Luc Robitaille .08 .25
112 Ryan Smyth .02 .10
113 Eric Daze .08 .25
114 Mariusz Czerkawski .02 .10
115 Brendan Shanahan .10 .30
116 Brian Rafalski .02 .10
117 Mark Parrish .02 .10
118 Jamie Langenbrunner .02 .10
119 Peter Forsberg .30 .75
120 Phil Housley .02 .10
121 Jeff O'Neill .02 .10
122 Stu Barnes .02 .10
123 Glen Murray .02 .10
124 Jeff Hackett .08 .25
125 Sergei Fedorov .20 .50
126 Kyle McLaren .02 .10
127 Michael Nylander .02 .10
128 Sergei Zubov .02 .10
129 Steve Rucchin .02 .10
130 Nelson Emerson .02 .10
131 Martin Brodeur .30 .75
132 Mike Grier .02 .10
133 Paul Coffey .10 .30
134 Radek Bonk .02 .10
135 Marc Savard .02 .10
136 Milan Hejduk .10 .30
137 Curtis Brown .02 .10
138 Viktor Kozlov .02 .10
139 Jason Woolley .02 .10
140 Adam Foote .02 .10
141 Radek Dvorak .02 .10
142 Jason Arnott .02 .10
143 German Titov .02 .10
144 Scott Thornton .02 .10
145 Brendan Morrison .02 .10
146 Keith Tkachuk .10 .30
147 Patrik Elias .08 .25
148 Donald Audette .02 .10
149 Jochen Hecht .02 .10
150 Dave Scatchard .02 .10
151 Tom Barrasso .08 .25
152 Adam Deadmarsh .02 .10
153 Brian Leetch .08 .25
154 Sergei Krivokrasov .02 .10
155 Randy Robitaille .02 .10
156 Petr Sykora .02 .10
157 Dave Andreychuk .02 .10
158 Mathieu Biron .08 .25
159 Sergei Zholtok .02 .10
160 Shawn McEachern .02 .10
161 Steve Shields .08 .25
162 Petr Svoboda .02 .10
163 Nikolai Antropov .02 .10
164 Michal Handzus .02 .10
165 Martin Straka .02 .10
166 Shane Doan .02 .10
167 Eric Desjardins .02 .10
168 Peter Schaefer .02 .10
169 Adam Oates .08 .25
170 Scott Niedermayer .02 .10
171 Dallas Drake .02 .10
172 Josh Green .02 .10
173 Mike Sillinger .02 .10
174 Adam Graves .02 .10
175 Lubos Bartecko .02 .10
176 Steve Konowalchuk .02 .10
177 Jozef Stumpel .02 .10
178 Vincent Damphousse .02 .10
179 Tomas Kaberle .02 .10
180 Maxim Afinogenov .02 .10
181 Marty McInnis .02 .10
182 Chris Chelios .10 .30
183 Joe Nieuwendyk .08 .25
184 Petr Buzek .02 .10
185 Calle Johansson .02 .10
186 Jeff Friesen .02 .10
187 Paul Mara .02 .10
188 Markus Naslund .10 .30
189 Scott Young .02 .10
190 Trevor Letowski .02 .10
191 Steve Thomas .02 .10
192 Martin Biron .08 .25
193 Jason Allison .02 .10
194 Bob Probert .02 .10
195 Jere Lehtinen .08 .25
196 Tom Poti .02 .10
197 Eric Lindros .10 .30
198 Rob Niedermayer .02 .10
199 Gary Roberts .02 .10
200 Richard Zednik .02 .10
201 Dainius Zubrus .02 .10
202 Tom Fitzgerald .02 .10
203 Scott Gomez .02 .10
204 Travis Green .02 .10
205 Pierre Turgeon .08 .25
206 Ed Jovanovski .02 .10
207 Trevor Kidd .08 .25
208 Jan Hrdina .02 .10
209 Valeri Zelepukin .02 .10
210 Vaclav Prospal .02 .10
211 Matt Cullen .02 .10
212 Karlis Skrastins .02 .10
213 Robyn Regehr .02 .10
214 Darren McCarty .02 .10
215 John Madden .02 .10
216 Scott Mellanby .02 .10
217 Tim Connolly .02 .10
218 Pat Verbeek .02 .10
219 Richard Matvichuk .02 .10
220 Rick Tocchet .02 .10
221 Jan Hlavac .02 .10
222 Jeff Halpern .02 .10
223 Patrick Marleau .08 .25
224 Robert Lang .02 .10
225 Wade Redden .02 .10
226 Stephane Richer .02 .10
227 Kim Johnsson .02 .10
228 Greg Adams .02 .10
229 Alex Tanguay .08 .25
230 Andre Savage .02 .10
231 Slava Kozlov .02 .10
232 Steve Sullivan .02 .10
233 Alexander Selivanov .02 .10
234 Tommy Westlund .02 .10
235 Darcy Tucker .02 .10
236 Simon Gagne .10 .30
237 Brad Stuart .02 .10
238 Jean-Sebastien Aubin .08 .25
239 Mike Johnson .02 .10
240 Shayne Corson .02 .10
241 Michael Peca .02 .10
242 Keith Primeau .02 .10
243 Martin Lapointe .02 .10
244 Tie Domi .08 .25
245 Janne Niinimaa .02 .10
246 Brenden Morrow .08 .25
247 Sandis Ozolinsh .02 .10
248 Ron Tugnutt .08 .25
249 Andrei Nazarov .02 .10
250 Bates Battaglia .02 .10
251A Dean Sylvester .02 .10
251B Yannick Tremblay .02 .10
252A Hal Gill .02 .10
252B Grant Fuhr .08 .25
253A Vladimir Tsyplakov .02 .10
253B Cory Stillman .02 .10
254A Sean Hill .02 .10
254B Jason Wiemer .02 .10
255A Michal Grosek .02 .10
255B Martin Gelinas .02 .10
256A Darryl Sydor .02 .10
256B Mike Keane .02 .10
257A Igor Larionov .02 .10
257B Ethan Moreau .02 .10
258A Jaroslav Spacek .02 .10
258B Jason Smith .02 .10
259A Mattias Norstrom .02 .10
259B Kelly Buchberger .02 .10
260A Ladislav Kohn .02 .10
260B Benoit Brunet .02 .10
261A Patric Kjellberg .02 .10
261B Brian Savage .02 .10
262A Marty Reasoner .02 .10
262B Sheldon Souray .02 .10
263A Zdeno Chara .02 .10
263B Greg Johnson .02 .10
264A Mathieu Schneider .02 .10
264B Magnus Arvedson .02 .10
265A John Vanbiesbrouck .08 .25
265B Patrick Lalime .08 .25
266A Jyrki Lumme .02 .10
266B Wayne Primeau .02 .10
267A Janne Laukkanen .02 .10

267B Igor Korolev .02 .10
268A Alexander Korolyuk .02 .10
268B Yanic Perreault .02 .10
269A Pavel Kubina .02 .10
269B Adrian Aucoin .02 .10
270A Ulf Dahlen .02 .10
270B Andrew Cassels .02 .10
271 Roberto Luongo .15 .40
272 Harold Druken .02 .10
273 Marc Denis .08 .25
274 Oleg Saprykin .02 .10
275 Glen Metropolit .02 .10
276 Mark Eaton .02 .10
277 Dmitri Yakushin .02 .10
278 Scott Hannan .02 .10
279 Dave Tanabe .02 .10
280 Jiri Fischer .02 .10
281 Dmitri Nabokov .02 .10
282 Ivan Novoseltsev .02 .10
283 Manny Fernandez .08 .25
284 Maxim Balmochnyk .02 .10
285 Brian Campbell .02 .10
286 Sergei Varlamov .02 .10
287 Ville Nieminen RC .02 .10
288 Colin White RC .15 .40
289 Mike Fisher .02 .10
290 Matt Elich RC .08 .25
291 Zenith Komarniski .02 .10
292 Eric Nickulas RC .08 .25
293 Steven McCarthy .02 .10
294 Jason Krog .02 .10
295 Robert Esche .02 .10
296 Adam Mair .02 .10
297 Ladislav Nagy .02 .10
298 Sergei Vyshedkevich .10 .30
299 Steve Begin .02 .10
300 Brad Ference .02 .10
301 Andy Delmore .02 .10
302 Brent Sopel RC .10 .30
303 Evgeni Nabokov .08 .25
304 David Gosselin RC .10 .30
305 Travis Hansen .02 .10
306 Ray Giroux .02 .10
307 Serge Aubin RC .10 .30
308 Shane Willis .02 .10
309 Vitali Vishnevski .02 .10
310 Richard Jackman .02 .10
311 Petr Schastlivy .02 .10
312 Ryan Bonni .02 .10
313 Alexei Tezikov .02 .10
314 Zac Bierk .08 .25
315 Mike Ribeiro .02 .10
316 Darryl Laplante .02 .10
317 Kyle Calder .02 .10
318 Dmitri Kalinin .02 .10
319 Jean-Sebastien Giguere .08 .25
320 Willie Mitchell RC .08 .25
321 Stephen Valiquette RC .10 .30
322 Brian Willsie .02 .10
323 Jarkko Ruutu .02 .10
324 Jon Sim .02 .10
325 Jonathan Girard .02 .10
326 Martin Brodeur HL .50 1.25
327 Ray Bourque HL .40 1.00
328 The Bure Brothers HL .10 .30
329 Steve Yzerman HL 1.00 2.50
330 Brett Hull HL .25 .60

2000-01 Topps Foil Parallel

Randomly inserted in Topps packs at the rate of 1:39 and OPC packs at the rate of 1:31, this 330-card set parallels the base Topps/OPC set on cards enhanced with an all foil card stock. Each card is sequentially numbered to 100. Topps Parallels are found in O-Pee-Chee packs and O-Pee-Chee Parallels are found in Topps packs. Card numbers 251-270 were exclusive to Topps or OPC. "A" version cards are found in Topps, "B" version cards are found in OPC.

*STARS: 25X TO 60X BASIC CARDS
*ROOKIES: 10X TO 25X BASIC CARDS

2000-01 Topps Autographs

Randomly inserted in packs at the rate of 1:502, this 11-card set features authentic player autographs on a card front that has action photography set against a whiteout background.

ACP Chris Pronger 6.00 15.00
AFB Fred Brathwaite 6.00 15.00
AJL John LeClair 10.00 25.00
AJT Jose Theodore 12.50 30.00
AMM Mike Modano 15.00 40.00
AMR Mark Recchi 6.00 15.00
ARB Ray Bourque 30.00 80.00
ART Roman Turek 6.00 15.00
ASG Scott Gomez 6.00 15.00
ATA Tony Amonte EXCH 6.00 15.00
AVB Valeri Bure 6.00 15.00

2000-01 Topps Combos

Randomly inserted in Topps packs at the rate of 1:12 and OPC packs at the rate of 1:24, this 10-card set features original artist rendered pictures that pair up some of the NHL's finest.

COMPLETE SET (10) 15.00 40.00
*JUMBOS: .5X TO 1.25X
JUMBOS: ONE PER BOX
TC1 Pavel Bure 1.50 4.00
Valeri Bure
TC2 Teemu Selanne 1.25 3.00
Paul Kariya
TC3 John LeClair 1.00 2.50
Tony Amonte
TC4 Curtis Joseph 2.00 5.00
Dominik Hasek
TC5 M.Modano/P.Forsberg 2.00 5.00
TC6 Raymond Bourque 2.00 5.00
Chris Pronger
TC7 Vincent Lecavalier 2.00 5.00
Joe Thornton
TC8 Patrick Roy 4.00 10.00
Martin Brodeur
TC9 S.Yzerman/B.Hull 3.00 8.00
TC10 Jaromir Jagr 3.00 8.00
Mario Lemieux

2000-01 Topps Game Worn Sweaters

Randomly inserted in packs at the rate of 1:460, this six card set features swatches of authentic game worn jerseys.

GWAG Adam Graves 8.00 20.00
GWBH Bobby Holik 30.00 80.00
GWDL David Legwand 8.00 20.00
GWDM Darren McCarty 8.00 20.00
GWJJ Jaromir Jagr 12.50 30.00
GWTD Tie Domi 8.00 20.00

2000-01 Topps Hobby Masters

This 10-card set was inserted in Topps Hobby packs at the rate of 1:18 and OPC packs at the rate of 1:20.

COMPLETE SET (10) 12.00 30.00
HM1 Martin Brodeur 2.00 5.00
HM2 Pavel Bure .75 2.00
HM3 Peter Forsberg 1.25 3.00
HM4 Dominik Hasek 1.50 4.00
HM5 Jaromir Jagr 1.25 3.00
HM6 Curtis Joseph .75 2.00
HM7 Paul Kariya .75 2.00
HM8 Mike Modano 1.00 2.50
HM9 Patrick Roy 4.00 10.00
HM10 Steve Yzerman 3.00 8.00

2000-01 Topps Lemieux Reprints

Randomly inserted in packs at the rate of 1:12, this 23-card set pays tribute to Mario Lemieux by reprinting both his base Topps and O-Pee-Chee cards.

COMPLETE SET (23) 50.00 100.00
COMMON CARD (1-23) 3.00 8.00

2000-01 Topps Lemieux Reprints Autographs

Randomly seeded in packs at the rate of 1:5456, this 23-card set parallels the base Lemieux Reprints set on cards enhanced with a Mario Lemieux autograph.

COMMON CARD (1-23) 100.00 200.00

2000-01 Topps NHL Draft

Randomly inserted in packs at the rate of 1:31, this 14-card set features seven number one draft selections and seven of the NHL's standout players.

COMPLETE SET (14) 20.00 40.00
D1 Vincent Lecavalier 1.25 3.00
D2 Eric Lindros 2.00 5.00

D3 Mike Modano 2.00 5.00
D4 Owen Nolan 1.00 2.50
D5 Patrik Stefan 1.00 2.50
D6 Mats Sundin 1.25 3.00
D7 Joe Thornton 2.00 5.00
D8 Pavel Bure 1.50 4.00
D9 Anson Carter 1.00 2.50
D10 Pavol Demitra 1.00 2.50
D11 Doug Gilmour 1.25 3.00
D12 Dominik Hasek 2.50 6.00
D13 Brett Hull 1.50 4.00
D14 Luc Robitaille 1.00 2.50

2000-01 Topps Own the Game

Randomly inserted in packs at the rate of 1:7, this 30-card set spotlights NHL leaders in each of these three categories: Points (OTG1-OTG10), Wins (OTG11-OTG20), and Rookie Points (OTG21-OTG30).

COMPLETE SET (30) 20.00 50.00
OTG1 Jaromir Jagr 1.50 4.00
OTG2 Pavel Bure 1.00 2.50
OTG3 Mark Recchi .75 2.00
OTG4 Paul Kariya 1.00 2.50
OTG5 Teemu Selanne 1.00 2.50
OTG6 Owen Nolan .75 2.00
OTG7 Tony Amonte .75 2.00
OTG8 Mike Modano 1.25 3.00
OTG9 Joe Sakic 2.00 5.00
OTG10 Steve Yzerman 3.00 8.00
OTG11 Martin Brodeur 2.00 5.00
OTG12 Roman Turek .40 1.00
OTG13 Olaf Kolzig .75 2.00
OTG14 Curtis Joseph 1.00 2.50
OTG15 Arturs Irbe .75 2.00
OTG16 Patrick Roy 4.00 10.00
OTG17 Ed Belfour 1.00 2.50
OTG18 Chris Osgood .75 2.00
OTG19 Guy Hebert .75 2.00
OTG20 Steve Shields .75 2.00
OTG21 Scott Gomez .75 2.00
OTG22 Alex Tanguay .75 2.00
OTG23 Mike York .40 1.00
OTG24 Simon Gagne .75 2.00
OTG25 Jan Hlavac .40 1.00
OTG26 Trevor Letowski .40 1.00
OTG27 Brad Stuart .40 1.00
OTG28 Maxim Afinogenov .40 1.00
OTG29 Tim Connolly .40 1.00
OTG30 Jochen Hecht .40 1.00

2000-01 Topps Stanley Cup Heroes

Randomly inserted in packs at the rate of 1:55, this five card set features top NHL stars of the past on an all foil die cut card in the shape of the Stanley Cup.

COMPLETE SET (5) 20.00 40.00
SHBG Bob Gainey 4.00 10.00
SHBP Bernie Parent 5.00 12.00
SHBT Bryan Trottier 5.00 12.00
SHLR Larry Robinson 5.00 12.00
SHTL Ted Lindsay 4.00 10.00

2000-01 Topps Stanley Cup Heroes Autographs

Randomly inserted in packs at the rate of 1:1104, this five card set parallels the base Stanley Cup Heroes insert set but is enhanced with authentic player autographs.

SHBG Bob Gainey 25.00 60.00
SHBP Bernie Parent 15.00 40.00
SHBT Bryan Trottier 15.00 40.00
SHLR Larry Robinson 15.00 40.00
SHTL Ted Lindsay 25.00 60.00

2000-01 Topps 1000 Point Club

Randomly inserted in packs at the rate of 1:27, this 16-card set spotlights players that have accumulated more than 1000 points on an all foil insert card.

COMPLETE SET (16) 25.00 50.00
PC1 Mark Messier 1.50 4.00
PC2 Steve Yzerman 6.00 15.00
PC3 Ron Francis 1.00 2.50
PC4 Paul Coffey 1.25 3.00
PC5 Ray Bourque 2.50 6.00
PC6 Doug Gilmour 1.25 3.00
PC7 Adam Oates 1.00 2.50
PC8 Larry Murphy 1.00 2.50
PC9 Dave Andreychuk 1.00 2.50
PC10 Luc Robitaille 1.00 2.50
PC11 Phil Housley 1.00 2.50
PC12 Brett Hull 1.50 4.00
PC13 Al MacInnis 1.00 2.50
PC14 Pierre Turgeon 1.00 2.50
PC15 Joe Sakic 2.50 6.00
PC16 Pat Verbeek 1.00 2.50

2001-02 Topps

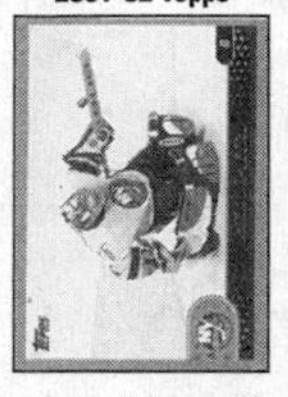

2001 Topps was released in August as a 360-card set with cards #330-360 in packs as redemption cards for to be determined rookies. The list of rookies redeemable for these cards was not made public until November. Pack SRP was $1.49 for a 10-card pack and there were 36 packs per box. Cards carrying a "U" prefix were available in packs of Topps Chrome at 1:4. These cards were inserted as updates for players who had changed teams since the release of the base set. The "U" was added for checklisting purposes only, it was not printed on the cards.

COMPLETE SET (360) 125.00 250.00
COMP.SET w/o ROOK.RED. (330) 25.00 50.00
1 Mario Lemieux .75 2.00
2 Steve Yzerman .60 1.50
3 Martin Brodeur .30 .75
4 Brian Leetch .10 .25
5 Tony Amonte .10 .25
6 Bill Guerin .10 .25
7 Olaf Kolzig .10 .25
8 Pavel Bure .12 .30
9 Patrick Marleau .10 .25
10 Mariusz Czerkawski .02 .10
11 Teemu Selanne .12 .30
12 Alex Tanguay .10 .25
13 Keith Primeau .02 .10
14 Alexei Yashin .02 .10
14U Alexei Yashin .02 .10
15 Markus Naslund .12 .30
16 Chris Pronger .10 .25
17 Sergei Zubov .02 .10
18 Marian Gaborik .25 .60
19 Mats Sundin .12 .30
20 Kevin Weekes .02 .10
21 J.P. Dumont .02 .10
22 Nicklas Lidstrom .12 .30
23 Ron Francis .10 .25
24 Doug Weight .10 .25
24U Doug Weight .12 .30
25 Zigmund Palffy .10 .25
26 Jason Allison .02 .10
27 Joe Sakic .25 .60
28 Paul Kariya .12 .30
29 Marian Hossa .12 .30
30 Owen Nolan .10 .25
31 Jason Arnott .02 .10
32 Jaromir Jagr .20 .50
32U Jaromir Jagr .25 .60
33 Justin Williams .02 .10
34 Peter Bondra .12 .30
35 Chris Drury .10 .25
36 Radek Bonk .02 .10
37 Theo Fleury .02 .10
38 Keith Tkachuk .12 .30
39 Rick DiPietro .10 .25
40 Ed Jovanovski .10 .25
41 Scott Stevens .10 .25
42 John LeClair .12 .30
43 Jochen Hecht .02 .10
44 Vincent Lecavalier .12 .30
45 Henrik Sedin .02 .10
46 David Aebischer .02 .10
47 Patrick Roy .60 1.50
48 Valeri Bure .02 .10
49 Dominik Hasek .25 .60
49U Dominik Hasek .30 .75
50 Ray Ferraro .02 .10
51 Milan Hejduk .12 .30
52 Mike Modano .20 .50
53 Sergei Fedorov .20 .50
54 Luc Robitaille .10 .25
55 Mark Messier .12 .30
56 Sean Burke .10 .25
57 Jeff Friesen .02 .10
58 Alexander Mogilny .10 .25
58U Alexander Mogilny .10 .25
59 Roman Cechmanek .10 .25
60 Martin Straka .02 .10
61 Pavol Demitra .10 .25
62 Curtis Joseph .12 .30
63 Daniel Sedin .02 .10
64 Brad Richards .10 .25
65 Simon Gagne .12 .30
66 Saku Koivu .12 .30
67 Jamie McLennan .02 .10
68 Roberto Luongo .15 .40
69 Brendan Shanahan .12 .30
70 Espen Knutsen .02 .10
71 Rob Blake .10 .25
72 Steve Sullivan .02 .10
73 Arturs Irbe .10 .25
74 Maxim Afinogenov .02 .10
75 Patrik Stefan .02 .10
76 Scott Gomez .02 .10
77 Brad Isbister .02 .10
78 Robert Lang .02 .10
79 Pierre Turgeon .12 .30
79U Pierre Turgeon .10 .25
80 Gary Roberts .02 .10
81 Adam Oates .10 .25
82 Evgeni Nabokov .10 .25
83 Petr Nedved .02 .10
84 Mike Dunham .10 .25
85 Chris Osgood .10 .25
85U Chris Osgood .10 .25
86 Brett Hull .15 .40
86U Brett Hull .15 .40
87 Peter Forsberg .30 .75
88 Joe Thornton .20 .50
89 Ray Bourque .25 .60
90 Ed Belfour .12 .30
91 Patrik Elias .10 .25
92 Michael York .02 .10
93 Martin Havlat .10 .25
94 Jeremy Roenick .15 .40
94U Jeremy Roenick .15 .40
95 Alexei Kovalev .10 .25
96 Al MacInnis .10 .25
97 Marco Sturm .02 .10
98 Jose Theodore .15 .40
99 Joe Nieuwendyk .10 .25
100 Darren McCarty .02 .10
101 Mark Recchi .10 .25
102 Daniel Alfredsson .10 .25
103 Miroslav Satan .10 .25
104 Sergei Samsonov .10 .25
105 Roman Turek .10 .25
105U Roman Turek .10 .25
106 Jarome Iginla .15 .40
107 Jeff O'Neill .02 .10
108 Tommy Salo .10 .25
109 Petr Sykora .02 .10
110 Adam Deadmarsh .02 .10
111 Oleg Tverdovsky .02 .10
112 Damian Rhodes .10 .25
113 Bob Probert .02 .10
114 Jere Lehtinen .10 .25
115 Cale Hulse .02 .10
116 Andy Sutton .02 .10
117 Wade Redden .02 .10
118 Brad Stuart .10 .25
119 Tomas Kaberle .02 .10
120 Sergei Gonchar .02 .10
121 Jean-Sebastien Aubin .10 .25
122 Adam Graves .02 .10
123 Teppo Numminen .02 .10
124 Martin Rucinsky .02 .10
125 Scott Young .02 .10
126 Pat Verbeek .02 .10
127 Michael Nylander .02 .10
128 Marc Savard .02 .10
129 Brian Rolston .02 .10
130 Sandis Ozolinsh .02 .10
131 Mike Grier .02 .10
132 Eric Belanger .02 .10
133 Patrick Lalime .10 .25
134 Steve Thomas .02 .10
135 Viktor Kozlov .02 .10
136 Manny Legace .10 .25
137 Oleg Saprykin .02 .10
138 Sami Kapanen .02 .10
139 Janne Niinimaa .02 .10
140 Scott Hartnell .02 .10
141 Tim Connolly .02 .10
142 Travis Green .02 .10
143 Matthew Barnaby .02 .10
144 Brendan Morrison .10 .25
145 Darcy Tucker .02 .10
146 Gary Suter .02 .10
147 Mattias Ohlund .02 .10
148 Patric Kjellberg .02 .10
149 Lubomir Visnovsky .02 .10
150 Claude Lapointe .10 .25
151 Martin Skoula .02 .10
152 Mike Vernon .10 .25
153 Stu Barnes .02 .10
154 Brenden Morrow .10 .25
155 Jim Dowd .02 .10
156 Shane Doan .02 .10
157 Peter Schaefer .02 .10
158 Jeff Halpern .02 .10
159 Sergei Berezin .02 .10
160 Mike Ricci .02 .10
161 Radek Dvorak .02 .10
162 Brian Savage .02 .10
163 Bryan Smolinski .02 .10
164 Derian Hatcher .02 .10
165 Shane Willis .02 .10
166 Ron Tugnutt .10 .25
167 Peter Worrell .02 .10
168 Richard Zednik .02 .10
169 Todd Marchant .02 .10
170 Andrew Brunette .02 .10
171 Derek Morris .02 .10
172 Kyle Calder .02 .10
173 Felix Potvin .12 .30
174 Bobby Holik .02 .10
175 Manny Fernandez .10 .25
176 Rick Tocchet .10 .25
177 Jonas Hoglund .02 .10
178 Todd Bertuzzi .12 .30
179 Garth Snow .10 .25
180 Cliff Ronning .02 .10
181 Martin Lapointe .02 .10
182 Jason Smith .02 .10
183 Byron Dafoe .10 .25
184 Rob Niedermayer .02 .10
185 Steve Rucchin .02 .10
186 Alexei Zhamnov .02 .10
187 Mike Richter .12 .30
188 Michal Handzus .02 .10
189 Pavel Kubina .02 .10
190 Donald Brashear .02 .10
191 Trevor Letowski .02 .10
192 Randy McKay .02 .10
193 Trevor Linden .02 .10
194 Mike Sillinger .02 .10
195 David Vyborny .02 .10
196 Dave Tanabe .02 .10
197 Scott Niedermayer .02 .10
198 Anson Carter .10 .25
199 Mike Leclerc .02 .10
200 Dave Scatchard .02 .10
201 Jan Hrdina .02 .10
202 Brian Holzinger .02 .10
203 Steve Konowalchuk .02 .10
204 Tie Domi .10 .25
205 Brent Johnson .10 .25
206 Shawn McEachern .02 .10
207 Jozef Stumpel .02 .10
208 Jamie Langenbrunner .02 .10
209 Jocelyn Thibault .10 .25
210 Donald Audette .02 .10
211 Serge Aubin .02 .10
212 Andrew Cassels .02 .10
213 Tyson Nash .02 .10
214 Colin White .02 .10
215 Tom Poti .02 .10
216 Rod Brind'Amour .10 .25
217 Fred Brathwaite .02 .10
218 Marc Denis .10 .25
219 Roman Simicek .02 .10
220 Jan Hlavac .02 .10
221 Darius Kasparaitis .02 .10
222 Vincent Damphousse .02 .10
223 Bob Boughner .02 .10
224 Yanic Perreault .02 .10
225 Chris Simon .02 .10
226 Chris Gratton .02 .10
227 Josef Vasicek .02 .10
228 Slava Kozlov .02 .10
229 Kelly Buchberger .02 .10
230 Jeff Hackett .10 .25
231 Taylor Pyatt .02 .10
232 Niklas Sundstrom .02 .10
233 Dan Cloutier .10 .25
234 Eric Daze .10 .25
235 Ryan Smyth .02 .10
236 Marty McInnis .02 .10
237 John Madden .02 .10
238 Claude Lemieux .02 .10
239 Steve Heinze .02 .10
240 Nikolai Antropov .02 .10
241 Cory Stillman .02 .10
242 Geoff Sanderson .02 .10
243 Trevor Kidd .10 .25
244 David Legwand .10 .25
245 Eric Desjardins .02 .10
246 Fredrik Modin .02 .10
247 Brett Clark .02 .10
248 Bryan Muir .02 .10
249 Ron Sutter .02 .10
250 Ken Klee .02 .10
251 Steve Halko .02 .10
252 Steve McKenna .02 .10
253 Marc Bergevin .02 .10
254 Scott Lachance .02 .10
255 Jamie Rivers .02 .10
256 Dixon Ward .02 .10
257 Gord Murphy .02 .10
258 Bret Hedican .02 .10
259 Bob Corkum .02 .10
260 Brent Sopel .02 .10
261 Todd Simpson .02 .10
262 Reid Simpson .02 .10
263 Chris McAlpine .02 .10
264 Deron Quint .02 .10
265 Josh Holden .02 .10
266 Mike Mottau .02 .10
267 Jakub Cutta .02 .10
268 Maxime Ouellet .10 .25
269 Peter Smrek RC .60 1.50
270 Daniel Corso .02 .10
271 Rostislav Klesla .02 .10
272 Mika Noronen .10 .25
273 Kris Beech .02 .10
274 Sheldon Keefe .10 .25
275 Miikka Kiprusoff .10 .25
276 Mathieu Garon .10 .25
277 Jason Chimera RC .60 1.50
278 Mark Bell .02 .10
279 Chris Nielsen .02 .10
280 Eric Chouinard .02 .10
281 Pierre Dagenais .02 .10
282 Branislav Mezei .02 .10
283 Milan Kraft .02 .10
284 Tomas Kloucek .02 .10
285 Petr Schastlivy .02 .10
286 Lee Goren .02 .10
287 Daniel Tkaczuk .02 .10
288 Andreas Lilja .02 .10
289 Tomas Divisek RC .60 1.50
290 Alexei Ponikarovsky .02 .10
291 Mikael Samuelsson RC .60 1.50
292 Petr Svoboda .02 .10
293 Mike Comrie .10 .25
294 Johan Hedberg .10 .25
295 Tyler Moss .02 .10
296 Martin Spanhel RC .60 1.50
297 Mike Brown .02 .10
298 Derek Gustafson .10 .25
299 Matt Pettinger .02 .10
300 Mike Commodore .02 .10
301 Antti-Jussi Niemi .02 .10
302 Brad Tapper .02 .10
303 Rick Berry .02 .10
304 Andrew Raycroft .02 .10
305 Bryan Allen .02 .10
306 Ivan Novoseltsev .02 .10
307 Jason Williams .02 .10
308 Gregg Naumenko .02 .10
309 Jiri Dicek .02 .10
310 Mathieu Darche RC .60 1.50
311 Brian Campbell .02 .10
312 Jeff Farkas .02 .10
313 Rico Fata .02 .10
314 Kristian Kudroc .02 .10
315 Roman Cechmanek AS .10 .25
316 Nicklas Lidstrom AS .12 .30
317 Ray Bourque AS .25 .60
318 Joe Sakic AS .25 .60
319 Patrik Elias AS .10 .25
320 Jaromir Jagr AS .20 .50
321 John Madden/Randy McKay .02 .10
322 Mark Recchi .10 .25
323 Vincent Damphousse .02 .10
324 Patrick Roy .60 1.50
325 Jaromir Jagr .20 .50
326 Mario Lemieux 2.00 5.00
327 Mario Lemieux 2.00 5.00
328 Mario Lemieux 2.00 5.00
329 Mario Lemieux 2.00 5.00
330 Mario Lemieux 2.00 5.00
331 Ilya Kovalchuk RC 6.00 15.00
332 Dan Blackburn RC 1.00 2.50
333 Vaclav Nedorost RC 1.00 2.50
334 Krys Kolanos RC 1.00 2.50
335 Kristian Huselius RC 2.00 5.00
336 Martin Erat RC 1.00 2.50
337 Timo Parssinen RC 1.00 2.50
338 Scott Nichol RC 1.00 2.50
339 Nick Schultz RC 1.00 2.50
340 Jukka Hentunen RC 1.00 2.50
341 Pascal Dupuis RC 1.00 2.50
342 Radek Martinek RC 1.00 2.50
343 Scott Clemmensen RC 1.00 2.50
344 Jeff Jillson RC 1.00 2.50
345 Brian Sutherby RC 1.00 2.50
346 Nikita Alexeev RC 1.00 2.50
347 Niklas Hagman RC 1.00 2.50
348 Erik Cole RC 2.00 5.00
349 Pavel Datsyuk RC 3.00 8.00
350 Ilja Bryzgalov RC 2.00 5.00
351 Chris Neil RC 2.00 5.00
352 Mark Rycroft RC 1.00 2.50
353 Kamil Piros RC 1.00 2.50
354 Niko Kapanen RC 1.00 2.50
355 Jiri Dopita RC 1.00 2.50
356 Andreas Salomonsson RC 1.00 2.50
357 Ivan Ciernik RC 1.00 2.50
358 Jaroslav Bednar RC 1.00 2.50
359 Ty Conklin RC 1.00 2.50
360 Raffi Torres RC 2.00 5.00

2001-02 Topps Heritage Parallel

Inserted at a rate of 1:1, this 110-card set parallels the first 110 cards of the Topps base set. The card fronts carry the same photo as the base cards, but use the 1971-72 Topps design. Card backs are the same as the base set. A limited parallel to these inserts was also created, these parallels look the same but carry different colored foil and serial numbering out of 50.

*STARS: 1.25X TO 2.5X BASIC CARDS
*LIMITED: 40X TO 80X BASIC CARDS

2001-02 Topps OPC Parallel

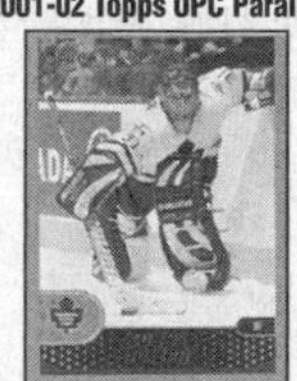

Inserted at a rate of 1:4, this 330-card set parallel the base set except that card fronts carried the O-Pee-Chee stamp in silver. Card backs were the same as the base cards.

*STARS: 1.5X TO 4X BASIC CARDS

2001-02 Topps Autographs

This 10-card set was inserted into hobby packs at a rate of 1:507 and retail packs at 1:390. Card fronts were a blue and white ice design with the white portion being where the players signed. Card backs carried a Topps certified sticker.

ACD Chris Drury 10.00 25.00
AEN Evgeni Nabokov 10.00 25.00
AGR Gary Roberts 8.00 20.00
AJA Jason Arnott 8.00 20.00
AMY Mike York 8.00 20.00
ARF Ron Francis 8.00 20.00
ASG Simon Gagne 12.00 30.00
AVL Vincent Lecavalier 20.00 50.00
AMHA Martin Havlat 8.00 20.00
AMHE Milan Hejduk 12.00 30.00

2001-02 Topps Captain's Cloth

Available only in hobby packs, this 3-card set featured four swatches of game-used jerseys from four different players who were the captains of their respective teams. Each swatch was affixed in the shape of a "C" on the card front. Card backs carried photos and bios of each player along with the Topps certified sticker.

CC1 Jaromir Jagr 150.00 300.00
Joe Sakic
Paul Kariya
Vincent Lecavalier
CC2 Chris Pronger 100.00 200.00
Saku Koivu
Tony Amonte
Jaromir Jagr
CC3 Ron Francis 100.00 200.00
Jason Allison
Paul Kariya
Vincent Lecavalier

2001-02 Topps Game-Worn Jersey

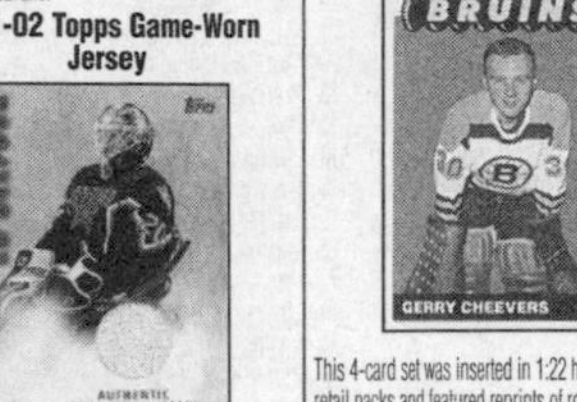

Inserted at 1:253 hobby and 1:195 retail, this 10-card set featured game-worn jersey swatches of the featured players. Card backs carried a Topps certified sticker.

*MULT.COLORS: 1X TO 1.5X BASIC CARDS
JBB Brian Boucher 6.00 15.00
JBH Brett Hull 10.00 25.00
JCD Chris Drury 8.00 20.00
JEB Ed Belfour 8.00 20.00
JJA Jason Arnott 6.00 15.00
JMY Mike York 6.00 15.00
JPK Paul Kariya 8.00 20.00
JRF Ron Francis 6.00 15.00
JSG Simon Gagne 8.00 20.00
JVL Vincent Lecavalier 6.00 15.00

2001-02 Topps Jumbo Jersey Autographs

Inserted at stated odds of 1:16,895 hobby and 1:12,996 retail, this 6-card set featured larger than normal swatches of game-worn jerseys. The jersey swatches were also signed by the featured player. Due to scarcity, we are unable to price or verify all of these cards at this time.

JJACD Chris Drury
JJAJA Jason Arnott
JJAMY Mike York
JJARF Ron Francis
JJASG Simon Gagne
JJAVL Vincent Lecavalier

2001-02 Topps Mario Lemieux Reprints

Inserted at 1:12 hobby and 1:10 retail, this 10-card set featured reprints of past Topps cards of Mario Lemieux.

COMPLETE SET (10) 20.00 50.00
COMMON CARD (1-10) 2.50 6.00

2001-02 Topps Mario Returns Autographs

Numbered to just 66 sets, this 5-card set parallels the Mario Returns base cards, but also feature a certified autograph on the card front. These cards were inserted at 1:7679 hobby and 1:5907 retail.

COMMON CARD (1-5) 100.00 250.00

2001-02 Topps Own The Game

This 30-card set was inserted at 1:6 hobby and 1:5 retail. Cards were produced on foil stock and featured league leaders in points, wins and rookie points.

COMPLETE SET (30) 15.00 30.00
OTG1 Jaromir Jagr .60 1.50
OTG2 Joe Sakic .75 2.00
OTG3 Patrik Elias .30 .75
OTG4 Jason Allison .12 .30
OTG5 Alexei Kovalev .30 .75
OTG6 Martin Straka .12 .30
OTG7 Pavel Bure .50 1.25
OTG8 Doug Weight .30 .75
OTG9 Peter Forsberg .75 2.00
OTG10 Zigmund Palffy .30 .75
OTG11 Brad Richards .30 .75
OTG12 Shane Willis .12 .30
OTG13 Martin Havlat .30 .75
OTG14 Lubomir Visnovsky .12 .30
OTG15 Marian Gaborik .75 2.00
OTG16 Ruslan Fedotenko .30 .75
OTG17 Steven Reinprecht .12 .30
OTG18 Daniel Sedin .12 .30
OTG19 Karel Rachunek .12 .30
OTG20 David Vyborny .12 .30
OTG21 Martin Brodeur 1.00 2.50
OTG22 Patrick Roy 2.00 5.00
OTG23 Dominik Hasek .75 2.00
OTG24 Olaf Kolzig .30 .75
OTG25 Arturs Irbe .30 .75
OTG26 Patrick Lalime .30 .75
OTG27 Tommy Salo .30 .75
OTG28 Roman Cechmanek .30 .75
OTG29 Ed Belfour .40 1.00
OTG30 Curtis Joseph .40 1.00

2001-02 Topps Promos

COMPLETE SET (6) 1.50 4.00

2001-02 Topps Rookie Reprints

This 4-card set was inserted in 1:22 hobby and 1:17 retail packs and featured reprints of rookie cards of four NHL Hall-of-Famers.

COMPLETE SET (4) 10.00 20.00
1 Denis Potvin 2.00 5.00
2 Yvan Cournoyer 2.00 5.00
3 Phil Esposito 2.00 5.00
4 Gerry Cheevers 2.00 5.00

2001-02 Topps Rookie Reprint Autographs

This 4-card set paralleled the regular rookie reprint set but included authentic autographs from the featured players. A Topps certified sticker was placed on the card backs of this set.

1 Denis Potvin 15.00 40.00
2 Yvan Cournoyer 15.00 40.00
3 Phil Esposito 15.00 40.00
4 Gerry Cheevers 15.00 40.00

2001-02 Topps Shot Masters

COMPLETE SET (18) 15.00 30.00
STATED ODDS 1:13 HOBBY/1:10 RETAIL
SM1 Mario Lemieux 2.50 6.00
SM2 Pavel Bure .50 1.25
SM3 Brett Hull .50 1.25
SM4 Joe Sakic .75 2.00
SM5 Jaromir Jagr .60 1.50
SM6 Steve Yzerman 2.00 5.00
SM7 Milan Hejduk .40 1.00
SM8 Tony Amonte .30 .75
SM9 Zigmund Palffy .30 .75
SM10 Paul Kariya .40 1.00
SM11 Bill Guerin .30 .75
SM12 Peter Bondra .40 1.00
SM13 Patrik Elias .30 .75
SM14 Alexei Kovalev .30 .75
SM15 John LeClair .50 1.25
SM16 Alexei Yashin 1.00 2.50
SM17 Teemu Selanne .40 1.00
SM18 Alexander Mogilny .30 .75

2001-02 Topps Stanley Cup Heroes

Inserted at 1:66 hobby and 1:51 retail, this 4-card set features vintage players on a chrome die-cut design.

COMPLETE SET (4) 15.00 30.00
SCHDP Denis Potvin 4.00 10.00
SCHGC Gerry Cheevers 5.00 12.00
SCHPE Phil Esposito 4.00 10.00
SCHYC Yvan Cournoyer 5.00 12.00

2001-02 Topps Stanley Cup Heroes Autographs

This set paralleled the base heroes set but included player autographs and a Topps certified sticker on the card backs. Odds for this set were 1:1584 hobby and 1:1218 retail.

SCHADP Denis Potvin 15.00 40.00
SCHAGC Gerry Cheevers 15.00 40.00
SCHAPE Phil Esposito 20.00 50.00
SCHAYC Yvan Cournoyer 15.00 40.00

2001-02 Topps Stars of the Game

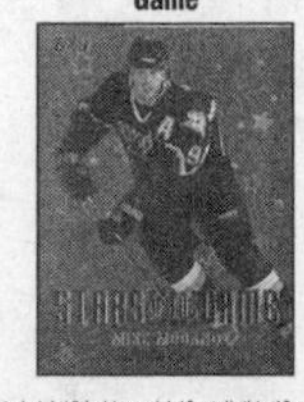

Inserted at 1:12 hobby and 1:10 retail, this 10-card set highlighted players who were recognized most often as one of the "Three Stars of the Game" media voting during the 2000/01 season.

COMPLETE SET (10) 8.00 15.00
SG1 Mario Lemieux 2.50 6.00
SG2 Sean Burke .30 .75
SG3 Pavel Bure .50 1.25
SG4 Joe Sakic .75 2.00
SG5 Patrik Elias .30 .75
SG6 Mike Modano .60 1.50
SG7 Curtis Joseph .40 1.00
SG8 Alexei Kovalev .30 .75
SG9 Sergei Fedorov .75 2.00
SG10 Tommy Salo .30 .75

2002-03 Topps

This 340-card set was released as a 330 card set and an available 10-card rookie update set. The rookie update set was available by mail by sending in special redemption cards found in packs. Cards with a "U" prefix were update cards found in packs of Topps Chrome. The "U" prefix is for checklisting purposes only.

COMPLETE SET (340) 25.00 50.00
COMP.SET w/o ROOK.RED. (330) 20.00 40.00
1 Patrick Roy .60 1.50
2 Mario Lemieux .75 2.00
3 Martin Brodeur .30 .75
4 Steve Yzerman .60 1.50
5 Jaromir Jagr .20 .50
6 Chris Pronger .10 .25
7 John LeClair .12 .30
8 Paul Kariya .12 .30
9 Tony Amonte .10 .25
9U Tony Amonte .10 .25
10 Joe Thornton .20 .50
11 Ilya Kovalchuk .15 .40
12 Jarome Iginla .15 .40
13 Mike Modano .20 .50
14 Vincent Lecavalier .12 .30
15 Michael Peca .02 .10
16 Pavel Bure .12 .30
17 Eric Lindros .12 .30
18 Felix Potvin .12 .30
19 Ron Francis .10 .25
20 Miroslav Satan .10 .25
21 Rostislav Klesla .02 .10
22 Mike Comrie .10 .25
23 Daniel Alfredsson .10 .25
24 Sean Burke .10 .25
25 David Legwand .10 .25
26 Marian Gaborik .25 .60
27 Saku Koivu .12 .30
28 Owen Nolan .10 .25
29 Mats Sundin .12 .30
30 J-P Dumont .02 .10
31 Chris Drury .10 .25
31U Chris Drury .10 .25
32 Markus Naslund .12 .30
33 Anson Carter .10 .25
34 Dwayne Roloson .02 .10
35 Brad Isbister .02 .10
36 Daniel Briere .02 .10
37 Martin St. Louis .10 .25
38 Shayne Corson .02 .10
39 Keith Tkachuk .12 .30
40 Mark Recchi .10 .25
41 Patrice Brisebois .02 .10
42 Niklas Hagman .02 .10
43 Marc Denis .10 .25
44 Robyn Regehr .02 .10
45 Byron Dafoe .10 .25
46 Sergei Fedorov .20 .50
47 Andrew Brunette .02 .10
48 Denis Arkhipov .02 .10
49 Martin Havlat .10 .25
50 Mike Rathje .02 .10
51 Mattias Ohlund .02 .10
52 Ulf Dahlen .02 .10
53 Tim Connolly .02 .10
54 Valeri Bure .02 .10
55 Brian Boucher .10 .25
56 Pascal Dupuis .02 .10
57 Brian Leetch .10 .25
58 Daniel Sedin .02 .10
59 Kenny Jonsson .02 .10
60 Erik Cole .02 .10
61 Patrick Lalime .10 .25
62 Mike Leclerc .02 .10
63 Patrick Marleau .10 .25
64 Tom Poti .02 .10
65 Lubos Bartecko .02 .10
66 Tom Barrasso .10 .25
67 Ryan Smyth .02 .10
68 Sami Kapanen .02 .10
69 Michal Handzus .02 .10
70 Martin Straka .02 .10
71 Peter Forsberg .30 .75
72 Marc Savard .02 .10
73 Jeff Friesen .02 .10
73U Jeff Friesen .02 .10
74 Manny Fernandez .10 .25
75 Jason Smith .02 .10
76 Mike Ribeiro .02 .10
77 Steve Heinze .02 .10
78 Adam Foote .02 .10
79 Sandy McCarthy .02 .10
80 Toni Lydman .02 .10
81 Tie Domi .10 .25
82 Scott Stevens .10 .25
83 Radim Vrbata .02 .10
84 Oleg Petrov .02 .10
85 Marty Turco .10 .25
86 Kristian Huselius .02 .10
87 Jeremy Roenick .15 .40
88 Gary Roberts .02 .10
89 Dean McAmmond .02 .10
90 Chris Chelios .12 .30
91 Andy McDonald .02 .10
92 Brett Hull .15 .40
93 Danny Markov .02 .10
94 Eric Daze .10 .25
95 Alex Tanguay .10 .25
96 Petr Nedved .02 .10
97 Simon Gagne .12 .30
98 Roman Turek .10 .25
99 Milan Hejduk .12 .30
100 Mariusz Czerkawski .02 .10
100U Mariusz Czerkawski .02 .10
101 Jaroslav Modry .02 .10
102 Dan Cloutier .10 .25
103 Mark Bell .02 .10
104 Brendan Witt .02 .10
105 Teemu Selanne .12 .30
106 Johan Hedberg .10 .25
107 Mike Ricci .02 .10
108 Roberto Luongo .15 .40
109 Vaclav Prospal .02 .10
110 Zigmund Palffy .10 .25
111 Ed Jovanovski .10 .25
112 Scott Gomez .02 .10
113 Pierre Turgeon .10 .25
114 Niklas Sundstrom .02 .10
115 Martin Biron .10 .25
116 Keith Primeau .02 .10
117 Jean-Sebastien Giguere .10 .25
118 Filip Kuba .02 .10
119 Dave Tanabe .02 .10
120 Brian Savage .02 .10
121 Alexei Zhamnov .02 .10
122 Brent Johnson .10 .25
123 Dan Blackburn .10 .25
124 Eric Belanger .02 .10
125 Janne Niinimaa .02 .10
126 Jonas Hoglund .02 .10
127 Marian Hossa .12 .30
128 Mike Richter .12 .30
129 Peter Bondra .12 .30
130 Rod Brind'Amour .10 .25
131 Shane Doan .02 .10
132 Viktor Kozlov .02 .10
133 Yanic Perreault .02 .10
134 Sergei Samsonov .10 .25
135 Nikolai Khabibulin .12 .30
136 Rob Ray .02 .10
137 Roman Cechmanek .10 .25
138 Patrik Stefan .02 .10
139 Matt Cullen .02 .10
140 Kim Johnsson .02 .10
141 Jim Dowd .02 .10
142 Glen Murray .02 .10
143 Dominik Hasek .25 .60
144 Brad Richards .10 .25
145 Cory Stillman .02 .10
146 Josef Vasicek .02 .10
147 Alexei Kovalev .10 .25
148 Adam Deadmarsh .02 .10
149 Brendan Morrison .10 .25
150 Eric Brewer .02 .10
151 Jason Arnott .02 .10
152 Brenden Morrow .02 .10
153 Manny Legace .10 .25
154 Michael Nylander .02 .10
155 Pavol Demitra .02 .10
156 Olaf Kolzig .10 .25
157 Sergei Berezin .02 .10
158 Teppo Numminen .02 .10
159 Vladimir Orszagh .02 .10
160 Brian Rafalski .02 .10
161 Doug Gilmour .10 .25
162 Jere Lehtinen .02 .10
163 Mark Parrish .02 .10
164 Petr Sykora .02 .10
164U Petr Sykora .02 .10
165 Sergei Zholtok .02 .10
166 Wade Redden .02 .10
167 Scott Niedermayer .02 .10
168 Olli Jokinen .10 .25
169 Kyle Calder .02 .10
170 Jamie Langenbrunner .02 .10
171 Darcy Tucker .02 .10
172 Alexei Morozov .02 .10
173 Adam Oates .10 .25
173U Adam Oates .10 .25
174 Chris Osgood .10 .25
175 Espen Knutsen .02 .10
176 Jochen Hecht .02 .10
177 Maxim Afinogenov .02 .10
178 Radek Dvorak .02 .10
179 Steve Sullivan .02 .10
180 Trevor Linden .02 .10
181 Tomi Kallio .02 .10
182 Robert Lang .02 .10
182U Robert Lang .02 .10
183 Milan Hnilicka .10 .25
184 Justin Williams .02 .10
185 Greg Johnson .02 .10
186 Craig Conroy .02 .10
187 Alexander Mogilny .10 .25
188 Adrian Aucoin .02 .10
189 Fredrik Modin .02 .10
190 Jose Theodore .15 .40
191 Ray Whitney .02 .10
192 Mikael Renberg .02 .10
193 Mike Sillinger .02 .10
194 Richard Zednik .02 .10
195 Mike Dunham .10 .25
196 Joe Sakic .25 .60
197 Fred Brathwaite .10 .25
198 Chris Simon .02 .10
199 Al MacInnis .10 .25
200 Georges Laraque .02 .10
201 Jozef Stumpel .02 .10
202 Theo Fleury .02 .10
203 Rob Blake .10 .25
204 Todd White .02 .10
205 Dany Heatley .15 .40
206 Scott Hartnell .02 .10
207 Oleg Tverdovsky .02 .10
208 Krys Kolanos .02 .10
209 Ian Laperriere .02 .10
210 Vincent Damphousse .02 .10
211 Nick Boynton .02 .10
212 Curtis Joseph .12 .30
212U Curtis Joseph .12 .30
213 Henrik Sedin .02 .10
214 Kris Beech .02 .10
215 Sandis Ozolinsh .02 .10
216 Ron Tugnutt .10 .25
217 Todd Bertuzzi .12 .30
218 Tommy Salo .10 .25
219 Martin Lapointe .02 .10
220 Derian Hatcher .02 .10
221 David Vyborny .02 .10
222 Jocelyn Thibault .10 .25
223 Nicklas Lidstrom .12 .30
224 Marcus Nilsson .02 .10
225 Sergei Zubov .02 .10
226 Bryan McCabe .02 .10
227 Claude Lemieux .02 .10
228 Jean-Luc Grand-Pierre .02 .10
229 Bill Guerin .10 .25
229U Bill Guerin .10 .25
230 Sergei Brylin .02 .10
231 Bryan Smolinski .02 .10
232 Luc Robitaille .10 .25
233 Alexei Yashin .02 .10
234 Evgeni Nabokov .10 .25
235 Pavel Datsyuk .12 .30
236 Martin Erat .02 .10
237 Stu Barnes .02 .10
238 Derek Morris .02 .10
239 Bates Battaglia .02 .10
240 Jason Allison .02 .10
241 Peter Worrell .02 .10
242 Mark Messier .12 .30
243 Shawn Bates .02 .10
244 Daymond Langkow .10 .25
245 Ed Belfour .12 .30
245U Ed Belfour .12 .30
246 Jan Hrdina .02 .10
247 Pavel Kubina .02 .10
248 Scott Young .02 .10
249 Curtis Brown .02 .10
250 Brian Rolston .02 .10
251 Jiri Dopita .02 .10
252 Kimmo Timonen .02 .10
253 Marco Sturm .02 .10
254 Arturs Irbe .10 .25
255 Joe Nieuwendyk .10 .25
256 Sergei Gonchar .02 .10
257 Doug Weight .10 .25
258 Jeff O'Neill .02 .10
259 Mike York .02 .10
260 Radek Bonk .02 .10
261 Patrik Elias .10 .25
262 Phil Housley .02 .10
263 Brendan Shanahan .12 .30
264 Sheldon Keefe .02 .10
265 Rick DiPietro .10 .25
266 J-F Fortin .02 .10
267 Jason Chimera .02 .10
268 Andy Hilbert .02 .10
269 Brian Gionta .02 .10
270 Sergei Varlamov .02 .10
271 Alex Auld .02 .10
272 Pavel Brendl .02 .10
273 Branko Radivojevic .02 .10
274 Kamil Piros .02 .10
275 Steve Gainey .02 .10
276 Mike Moltau .02 .10
277 Jimmie Olvestad .02 .10
278 Jeff Jillson .02 .10
279 Ilja Bryzgalov .10 .25
280 Taylor Pyatt .02 .10
281 Andrew Raycroft .10 .25
282 Christian Berglund .02 .10
283 Patrick DesRochers .02 .10
284 Lukas Krajicek .02 .10
285 Riku Hahl .02 .10
286 Ivan Huml .02 .10
287 Jani Rita .02 .10
288 Kristian Kudroc .02 .10
289 Juraj Kolnik .02 .10
290 John Erskine .02 .10
291 Brian Sutherby .02 .10
292 Bruno St-Jacques .02 .10
293 Nick Schultz .02 .10
294 Pasi Nurminen .10 .25
295 Norm Milley .02 .10
296 Marcel Hossa .02 .10
297 Ales Kotalik .02 .10
298 Bryan Allen .02 .10
299 Mika Noronen .10 .25
300 Tyler Arnason .10 .25
301 Petr Schastlivy .02 .10
302 Mike Van Ryn .02 .10
303 Steve Montador .02 .10
304 Denis Shvidki .02 .10
305 Stephen Weiss .02 .10
306 Nikita Alexeev .02 .10
307 Vaclav Nedorost .02 .10
308 Raffi Torres .02 .10
309 Guillaume Lefebvre .02 .10
310 Sean Avery .02 .10
311 Shane Endicott .02 .10
312 Ty Conklin .10 .25
313 J-F Damphousse .10 .25
314 Jeremy Roenick .15 .40
315 Ron Francis .10 .25
316 Brendan Shanahan .20 .50
317 Patrick Roy .60 1.50
318 Luc Robitaille .10 .25
319 Jose Theodore .15 .40
320 Patrick Roy .60 1.50
321 Sergei Gonchar .02 .10
322 Bryan McCabe .02 .10
323 Chris Chelios .12 .30
324 Nicklas Lidstrom .12 .30
325 Simon Gagne .12 .30
326 Brendan Shanahan .20 .50
327 Jaromir Jagr .20 .50
328 Jarome Iginla .15 .40
329 Mats Sundin .12 .30
330 Joe Sakic .25 .60
331 Henrik Zetterberg RC 4.00 10.00
332 P-M Bouchard RC 1.25 3.00
333 Alexander Frolov RC 1.25 3.00
334 Alexander Svitov RC 1.00 2.50
335 Jason Spezza RC 2.00 5.00
336 Jay Bouwmeester RC 1.25 3.00
337 Ales Hemsky RC 2.00 5.00
338 Rick Nash RC 2.50 6.00
339 Chuck Kobasew RC 1.00 2.50
340 Stanislav Chistov RC 1.25 3.00

2002-03 Topps OPC Blue Parallel

Inserted at 1:6 for the regular cards and 1:1,813 for the rookie redemption card, this 331-card set paralleled the base Topps set but carried blue borders and blue foil highlights. The O-Pee-Chee logo was printed on the card fronts in place of the Topps logo and each card was serial-numbered out of 500.

*STARS: 3X TO 8X BASIC CARDS
*ROOKIES: 1.25X TO 3X

2002-03 Topps OPC Red Parallel

Inserted at 1:25 for the regular cards and 1:9,869 for the rookie redemption card, this 331-card set paralleled the base Topps set but carried red borders and red foil highlights. The O-Pee-Chee logo was printed on the card fronts in place of the Topps logo and each card was serial-numbered out of 100.

*STARS: 8X TO 20X BASIC CARDS
*ROOKIES: 4X TO 10X

2002-03 Topps Captain's Cloth

This 17-card set fetured swatches of game jersey from team captains around the league. Single swatch cards were serial-numbered to 100 and inserted at 1:939. Multi-swatch cards were serial-numbered to 50 and inserted at 1:2691.

CC1 Lemieux/Sakic/Francis 75.00 200.00
CC2 Keith Primeau 60.00 150.00
John LeClair
Mark Recchi
CC3 Hatcher/Zubov/Modano 75.00 150.00
CC4 Chris Pronger 60.00 125.00
Paul Kariya
Ron Francis
CC5 Saku Koivu 40.00 100.00
Markus Naslund
Mats Sundin
CC6 Lemieux/Sundin/Primeau 75.00 200.00
CC7 Paul Kariya 60.00 150.00
Saku Koivu
Joe Sakic
CC8 Mario Lemieux 20.00 50.00
CC9 Keith Primeau 12.50 30.00
CC10 Markus Naslund 10.00 25.00
CC11 Mats Sundin 10.00 25.00
CC12 Paul Kariya 10.00 25.00
CC13 Joe Sakic 15.00 40.00
CC14 Saku Koivu 12.50 30.00
CC15 Ron Francis 12.50 30.00
CC16 Derian Hatcher 12.50 30.00
CC17 Chris Pronger 12.50 30.00

2002-03 Topps Coast to Coast

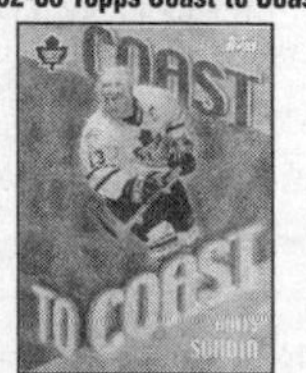

COMPLETE SET (10) 10.00 20.00
STATED ODDS 1:12
CC1 Mario Lemieux 4.00 10.00
CC2 Pavel Bure .75 2.00
CC3 Jarome Iginla .75 2.00
CC4 Mats Sundin .60 1.50
CC5 Peter Bondra .60 1.50
CC6 Ilya Kovalchuk .75 2.00
CC7 Joe Thornton 1.00 2.50
CC8 Paul Kariya .60 1.50
CC9 Joe Sakic 1.25 3.00
CC10 Patrik Elias .75 2.00

2002-03 Topps First Round Fabric

STATED ODDS 1:216
ALL CARDS CARRY FRF PREFIX
DB Dan Blackburn 6.00 15.00
EL Eric Lindros 8.00 20.00
KP Keith Primeau 6.00 15.00
MB Martin Biron 6.00 15.00
MM Mike Modano 10.00 25.00
MN Markus Naslund 10.00 25.00
MS Mats Sundin 10.00 25.00
PM Patrick Marleau 6.00 15.00
RD Radek Dvorak 6.00 15.00
SN Scott Niedermayer 6.00 15.00
JPD J-P Dumont 6.00 15.00

2002-03 Topps First Round Fabric Autographs

This autographed parallel was inserted at 1:1191 packs.

ALL CARDS CARRY FRF PREFIX
KP Keith Primeau 12.50 30.00
MB Martin Biron 12.50 30.00
MM Mike Modano 20.00 50.00
MS Mats Sundin 20.00 50.00
RD Radek Dvorak 12.50 30.00
SN Scott Niedermayer 15.00 40.00

2002-03 Topps/OPC Hometown Heroes

This 40-card set was split into two subsets: Canadian and USA heroes. Cards HHC1-HHC20 were available only in OPC packs and cards HHU1-HHU20 were inserted into Topps packs. Odds were 1:12.

COMP.CANADA SET (20) 10.00 20.00
COMP.USA SET (20) 15.00 30.00
HHC1 Jarome Iginla .60 1.50
HHC2 Ed Jovanovski .40 1.00
HHC3 Ryan Smyth .40 1.00
HHC4 Mike York .40 1.00
HHC5 Mats Sundin .50 1.25
HHC6 Todd Bertuzzi .50 1.25
HHC7 Markus Naslund .50 1.25
HHC8 Saku Koivu .50 1.25
HHC9 Jose Theodore .60 1.50
HHC10 Daniel Alfredsson .40 1.00
HHC11 Patrick Lalime .40 1.00
HHC12 Roman Turek .40 1.00
HHC13 Mike Comrie .40 1.00
HHC14 Tommy Salo .40 1.00
HHC15 Anson Carter .40 1.00
HHC16 Doug Gilmour .40 1.00
HHC17 Yanic Perreault .40 1.00
HHC18 Radek Bonk .40 1.00
HHC19 Darcy Tucker .40 1.00
HHC20 Curtis Joseph .50 1.25
HHU1 Martin Brodeur 1.25 3.00
HHU2 Joe Sakic .75 2.50
HHU3 Mario Lemieux 3.00 8.00
HHU4 Steve Yzerman 2.50 6.00
HHU5 Paul Kariya .50 1.25
HHU6 Mike Modano .75 2.00
HHU7 Brett Hull .60 1.50
HHU8 Bill Guerin .40 1.00
HHU9 Tony Amonte .40 1.00
HHU10 Jeremy Roenick .60 1.50
HHU11 John LeClair .50 1.25
HHU12 Brendan Shanahan .75 2.00
HHU13 Owen Nolan .40 1.00
HHU14 Al MacInnis .40 1.00
HHU15 Chris Pronger .40 1.00
HHU16 Doug Weight .40 1.00
HHU17 Ilya Kovalchuk .60 1.50
HHU18 Joe Thornton .75 2.00
HHU19 Patrick Roy 2.50 6.00
HHU20 Ron Francis .40 1.00

2002-03 Topps Own The Game

COMPLETE SET (20) 5.00 10.00
STATED ODDS 1:6
OTG1 Jarome Iginla .25 .60
OTG2 Markus Naslund .20 .50
OTG3 Todd Bertuzzi .20 .50
OTG4 Mats Sundin .20 .50
OTG5 Jaromir Jagr .30 .75
OTG6 Jarome Iginla .25 .60
OTG7 Mats Sundin .20 .50
OTG8 Bill Guerin .15 .40

OTG9 Glen Murray .15 .40
OTG10 Markus Naslund .20 .50
OTG11 Dany Heatley .25 .60
OTG12 Ilya Kovalchuk .25 .60
OTG13 Kristian Huselius .15 .40
OTG14 Erik Cole .15 .40
OTG15 Pavel Datsyuk .20 .50
OTG16 Dominik Hasek .40 1.00
OTG17 Martin Brodeur .50 1.25
OTG18 Evgeni Nabokov .15 .40
OTG19 Byron Dafoe .15 .40
OTG20 Brent Johnson .15 .40

2002-03 Topps Patrick Roy Reprints

Inserted at odds of 1:18, this 14-card set featured reprints of goalie great Patrick Roy. Each card carried a gold foil Topps logo on the card front.

COMMON CARD (1-14) 2.50 6.00

2002-03 Topps Patrick Roy Reprints Autographs

This 14-card set paralleled the regular reprint set but included a certified autograph on each card. This set was serial-numbered to just 33.

COMMON CARD (1-14) 60.00 150.00

2002-03 Topps Rookie Reprints

STATED ODDS 1:18
1 Pat LaFontaine 2.00 5.00
2 Mike Gartner 2.00 5.00
3 Pete Mahovlich 3.00 8.00
4 Andy Bathgate 3.00 8.00
5 Gump Worsley 3.00 8.00
6 Danny Gare 2.00 5.00
7 Harry Howell 2.00 5.00
8 Andy Moog 2.00 5.00
9 Keith Magnuson 2.00 5.00
10 Milt Schmidt 3.00 8.00
11 Glen Sather 2.00 5.00
12 Dick Duff 2.00 5.00
13 Garry Unger 2.00 5.00
14 Darren Pang 2.00 5.00
15 Chico Resch 3.00 8.00

2002-03 Topps Rookie Reprint Autographs

This autographed parallel was inserted at 1:1191 packs.

1 Pat LaFontaine 15.00 40.00
2 Mike Gartner 15.00 40.00
3 Pete Mahovlich 30.00 60.00
4 Andy Bathgate 25.00 60.00
5 Gump Worsley 25.00 60.00
6 Danny Gare 15.00 40.00
7 Harry Howell 15.00 40.00
8 Andy Moog 20.00 50.00
9 Keith Magnuson 40.00 100.00
10 Milt Schmidt 30.00 80.00
11 Glen Sather 30.00 80.00
12 Dick Duff 20.00 50.00
13 Garry Unger 30.00 80.00
14 Darren Pang 15.00 40.00
15 Chico Resch 25.00 60.00

2002-03 Topps Signs of the Future

Inserted at 1:1191, this 6-card set featured certified player autographs. All cards carried a "SF" prefix on the card back.

DL David Legwand 12.50 30.00
IK Ilya Kovalchuk 15.00 40.00
KK Krys Kolanos 12.50 30.00
MC Mike Comrie 12.50 30.00
MH Martin Havlat 12.50 30.00
RV Radim Vrbata 12.50 30.00

2002-03 Topps Stanley Cup Heroes

COMPLETE SET (5) 25.00 40.00
STATED ODDS 1:36
ALL CARDS CARRY SCH PREFIX
DS Derek Sanderson 4.00 10.00
JF John Ferguson 4.00 10.00
RL Reggie Leach 4.00 10.00
RM Rick MacLeish 4.00 10.00
SS Steve Shutt 4.00 10.00

2002-03 Topps Stanley Cup Heroes Autographs

This autographed parallel was inserted at 1:375 hobby packs.

ALL CARDS CARRY SCHA PREFIX
DS Derek Sanderson 20.00 50.00
JF John Ferguson 15.00 40.00
RL Reggie Leach 12.50 30.00
RM Rick MacLeish 25.00 60.00
SS Steve Shutt 12.50 30.00

2002-03 Topps Promos

This set was released in late-Spring of 2002 to generate early buzz around the release of the 2002-03 Topps set.

COMPLETE SET (6) 1.60 4.00
PP1 Simon Gagne 1.00
PP2 Jason Allison .40 1.00
PP3 Sergei Gonchar .20 .50
PP4 Wade Redden .20 .50
PP5 Byron Dafoe .40 1.00
PP6 Patrik Elias .40 1.00

2003-04 Topps

Released in late-August, this 330-card set featured full-color action photos with blue-green borders on the card fronts. A rookie redemption card redeemable for cards 331-340 was also randomly inserted at 1:36. Cards PP1-PP6 were promos sent out to announce the products release.

COMPLETE SET (340) 40.00 80.00
1 Joe Thornton .20 .50
2 Chris Osgood .10 .25
3 Brian Rafalski .02 .10
4 Chris Chelios .12 .30
5 Marian Gaborik .25 .60
6 Pavel Bure .12 .30
7 Ladislav Nagy .02 .10
8 Stephen Weiss .02 .10
9 Mike Modano .20 .50
10 Paul Kariya .12 .30
11 Daymond Langkow .02 .10
12 Patrick Lalime .10 .25
13 Alyn McCauley .02 .10
14 Steve Rucchin .02 .10
15 Mike Johnson .02 .10
16 Georges Laraque .02 .10
17 Brian Sutherby .02 .10
18 Petr Sykora .02 .10
19 Joe Sakic .25 .60
20 Henrik Sedin .02 .10
21 Nikolai Khabibulin .12 .30
22 Kevin Weekes .10 .25
23 Jan Bulis .02 .10
24 Ales Kotalik .02 .10
25 Niko Kapanen .02 .10
26 Jaroslav Modry .02 .10
27 Dan Cloutier .10 .25
28 Olli Jokinen .02 .10
29 Todd Marchant .02 .10
30 Jaromir Jagr .20 .50
31 Rick Nash .15 .40
32 Sami Kapanen .02 .10
33 Brian Boucher .10 .25
34 P.J. Stock .02 .10
35 Teemu Selanne .12 .30
36 Ossi Vaananen .02 .10
37 Jan Hlavac .02 .10
38 Ville Nieminen .02 .10
39 Jere Lehtinen .10 .25
40 Markus Naslund .12 .30
41 Anson Carter .10 .25
42 Steve Sullivan .02 .10
43 Dwayne Roloson .10 .25
44 Frantisek Kaberle .02 .10
45 Cory Stillman .02 .10
46 Shawn Horcoff .02 .10
47 Robert Lang .02 .10
48 Barret Jackman .10 .25
49 Joe Nieuwendyk .10 .25
50 Alexei Kovalev .10 .25
51 Niclas Wallin .02 .10
52 Cory Sarich .02 .10
53 Brendan Witt .02 .10
54 Mike Fisher .02 .10
55 Ed Belfour .12 .30
56 Sergei Zubov .02 .10
57 Ryan Miller .10 .25
58 Tyler Arnason .10 .25
59 Matt Cooke .02 .10
60 Brian Leetch .10 .25
61 Pavel Datsyuk .12 .30
62 Miikka Kiprusoff .10 .25
63 Michal Handzus .02 .10
64 Steve Shields .10 .25
65 Jason Arnott .02 .10
66 Miroslav Satan .10 .25
67 Nick Schultz .02 .10
68 Daniel Briere .02 .10
69 Alexei Yashin .02 .10
70 Martin Straka .02 .10
71 Martin Biron .10 .25
72 Michael Peca .02 .10
73 Simon Gagne .12 .30
74 Alexei Morozov .02 .10
75 Owen Nolan .10 .25
76 Niklas Hagman .02 .10
77 Kim Johnsson .02 .10
78 David Legwand .10 .25
79 Mark Parrish .02 .10
80 Marcel Hossa .02 .10
81 Mike Rathje .02 .10
82 Ruslan Fedotenko .02 .10
83 Bryan Berard .02 .10
84 Richard Zednik .02 .10
85 Viktor Kozlov .02 .10
86 John Madden .02 .10
87 Roman Hamrlik .02 .10
88 Eric Lindros .12 .30
89 Patrik Elias .10 .25
90 Sergei Fedorov .15 .40
91 Pavel Kubina .02 .10
92 Chris Phillips .02 .10
93 Marc Savard .02 .10
94 Janne Niinimaa .02 .10
95 Michael Nylander .02 .10
96 Radek Bonk .02 .10
97 Dmitri Bykov .02 .10
98 Dave Scatchard .02 .10
99 Marian Hossa .12 .30
100 Mario Lemieux .75 2.00
101 Mark Messier .12 .30
102 Tim Connolly .02 .10
103 Henrik Zetterberg .12 .30
104 Brendan Morrison .10 .25
105 Craig Conroy .02 .10
106 Darcy Tucker .02 .10
107 Steve Konowalchuk .02 .10
108 Valeri Bure .02 .10
109 Rod Brind'Amour .10 .25
110 Jeremy Roenick .15 .40
111 Zdeno Chara .02 .10
112 Mathieu Schneider .02 .10
113 Scott Hartnell .02 .10
114 Vincent Damphousse .02 .10
115 Brian Gionta .02 .10
116 Jeff O'Neill .02 .10
117 Pascal Dupuis .02 .10
118 Patrik Stefan .02 .10
119 Eric Daze .10 .25
120 Jose Theodore .15 .40
121 Yanic Perreault .02 .10
122 Shawn McEachern .02 .10
123 Daniel Alfredsson .10 .25
124 Peter Bondra .10 .25
125 Doug Weight .10 .25
126 Chris Drury .10 .25
127 Ed Jovanovski .10 .25
128 Scott Stevens .10 .25
129 Adam Foote .02 .10
130 Curtis Joseph .12 .30
131 Phil Housley .02 .10
132 Philippe Boucher .02 .10
133 Patrice Brisebois .02 .10
134 Josef Vasicek .02 .10
135 Peter Worrell .02 .10
136 Mike Knuble .02 .10
137 Jocelyn Thibault .10 .25
138 Keith Primeau .10 .25
139 Marc Chouinard .02 .10
140 Mats Sundin .12 .30
141 Martin Skoula .02 .10
142 Sergei Gonchar .02 .10
143 Pavol Demitra .10 .25
144 Tie Domi .10 .25
145 Denis Arkhipov .02 .10
146 Oleg Saprykin .02 .10
147 Tommy Salo .10 .25
148 Andrei Markov .02 .10
149 Brent Johnson .10 .25
150 Jarome Iginla .15 .40
151 Darryl Sydor .02 .10
152 Bryan Smolinski .02 .10
153 Roberto Luongo .15 .40
154 Sandis Ozolinsh .02 .10
155 Alexander Svitov .02 .10
156 J.P. Dumont .02 .10
157 Mike York .02 .10
158 Martin Brodeur .30 .75
159 Scott Gomez .02 .10
160 Peter Forsberg .30 .75
161 Kimmo Timonen .02 .10
162 Derek Morris .02 .10
163 Justin Williams .02 .10
164 Mike Comrie .02 .10
165 Mattias Weinhandl .02 .10
166 Dimitri Kalinin .02 .10
167 John LeClair .12 .30
168 Evgeni Nabokov .10 .25
169 Alexander Mogilny .10 .25
170 Derian Hatcher .02 .10
171 Adam Deadmarsh .02 .10
172 Alexei Smirnov .02 .10
173 Nikolai Antropov .02 .10
174 Radoslav Suchy .02 .10
175 Nick Boynton .02 .10
176 Marc Denis .10 .25
177 Ivan Huml .02 .10
178 Dan Blackburn .10 .25
179 Roman Cechmanek .10 .25
180 Tony Amonte .10 .25
181 Jason Blake .02 .10
182 Erik Cole .02 .10
183 P-M Bouchard .02 .10
184 Reed Low .02 .10
185 Geoff Sanderson .02 .10
186 Andrei Zyuzin .02 .10
187 Jean-Sebastien Giguere .10 .25
188 Patrick Marleau .10 .25
189 Nicklas Lidstrom .12 .30
190 Ilya Kovalchuk .15 .40
191 Petr Nedved .02 .10
192 Vincent Lecavalier .12 .30
193 Andreas Johansson .02 .10
194 Dennis Seidenberg .02 .10
195 Alex Tanguay .10 .25
196 Slava Kozlov .02 .10
197 Eric Brewer .02 .10
198 Adam Hall .02 .10
199 Steve Reinprecht .02 .10
200 Todd Bertuzzi .12 .30
201 Rob Blake .10 .25
202 Olaf Kolzig .10 .25
203 Roman Turek .10 .25
204 Brian Rolston .02 .10
205 Bill Guerin .10 .25
206 Johan Hedberg .10 .25
207 Vladimir Orszagh .02 .10
208 Jordan Leopold .02 .10
209 Donald Brashear .02 .10
210 Saku Koivu .12 .30
211 Dave Andreychuk .02 .10
212 Luc Robitaille .10 .25
213 Shaun Van Allen .02 .10
214 Trevor Linden .02 .10
215 Jason Allison .02 .10
216 Marty Turco .10 .25
217 Kyle McLaren .02 .10
218 Daniel Sedin .02 .10
219 Eric Belanger .02 .10
220 Mattias Ohlund .02 .10
221 Brad Richards .10 .25
222 Kyle Calder .02 .10
223 Alexander Frolov .02 .10
224 Tomas Kaberle .02 .10
225 Martin Havlat .10 .25
226 Patrick Roy .60 1.50
227 Jamie Lundmark .02 .10
228 Wade Redden .02 .10
229 Mark Recchi .02 .10
230 Tomas Vokoun .10 .25
231 Scott Niedermayer .02 .10
232 Bob Boughner .02 .10
233 Rick Dipietro .10 .25
234 Chris Gratton .02 .10
235 Keith Tkachuk .12 .30
236 Rostislav Klesla .02 .10
237 Ruslan Salei .02 .10
238 Jeff Friesen .02 .10
239 Felix Potvin .12 .30
240 Dany Heatley .15 .40
241 Brad Stuart .02 .10
242 Andrew Cassels .02 .10
243 Ray Whitney .02 .10
244 Chris Pronger .02 .10
245 Garth Snow .10 .25
246 Sean Hill .02 .10
247 Kristian Huselius .02 .10
248 Jamie Langenbrunner .02 .10
249 Martin St. Louis .10 .25
250 Ron Francis .10 .25
251 Tyler Wright .02 .10
252 Doug Gilmour .10 .25
253 Mike Dunham .10 .25
254 Jozef Stumpel .02 .10
255 Andrew Brunette .02 .10
256 Bobby Holik .02 .10
257 Brendan Shanahan .12 .30
258 Martin Gelinas .02 .10
259 Sergei Berezin .02 .10
260 Zigmund Palffy .10 .25
261 Yannick Tremblay .02 .10
262 Pasi Nurminen .10 .25
263 Robyn Regehr .02 .10
264 Espen Knutsen .02 .10
265 Al MacInnis .10 .25
266 Adam Oates .10 .25
267 Ryan Smyth .02 .10
268 Marco Sturm .02 .10
269 Tom Poti .02 .10
270 Brett Hull .15 .40
271 David Aebischer .10 .25
272 Milan Hejduk .12 .30
273 Steve McKenna .02 .10
274 Dick Tarnstrom .02 .10
275 Kenny Jonsson .02 .10
276 Glen Murray .02 .10
277 Stu Barnes .02 .10
278 Jay Bouwmeester .02 .10
279 Darius Kasparaitis BM .02 .10
280 Scott Stevens BM .10 .25
281 Zdeno Chara BM .02 .10
282 Donald Brashear BM .02 .10
283 Reed Low BM .02 .10
284 Jody Shelley BM .02 .10
285 Eric Cairns BM .02 .10
286 Brendan Witt BM .02 .10
287 Rob Ray BM .02 .10
288 Georges Laraque BM .02 .10
289 Brett Hull SH .15 .40
290 Martin Brodeur SH .30 .75
291 Jean-Sebastien Giguere SH .10 .25
292 Paul Kariya SH .12 .30
293 New Jersey Devils .12 .30
Stanley Cup Champions
294 Marty Turco AS .10 .25
295 Patrick Lalime AS .10 .25
296 Paul Kariya AS .12 .30
297 Nicklas Lidstrom AS .12 .30
298 Al MacInnis AS .10 .25
299 Scott Stevens AS .10 .25
300 Marian Gaborik AS .25 .60
301 Dany Heatley AS .15 .40
302 Jaromir Jagr AS .20 .50
303 Olli Jokinen AS .02 .10
304 Bill Guerin AS .10 .25
305 Todd Bertuzzi AS .12 .30
306 Bruno St. Jacques .02 .10
307 Mathieu Darche .02 .10
308 Mathias Johansson .02 .10
309 Joe DiPenta RC .12 .30
310 Milan Bartovic RC .12 .30
311 Rick Mrozik RC .02 .10
312 Kent McDonell RC .12 .30
313 Fernando Pisani .02 .10
314 Kip Brennan .02 .10
315 Miroslav Zalesak .02 .10
316 Peter Sejna RC .75 2.00
317 Matt Stajan RC 1.50 4.00
318 Ivan Ciernik .02 .10
319 Shaone Morrisonn .02 .10
320 Garnet Exelby .02 .10
321 Ari Ahonen .02 .10
322 Mike Rupp .02 .10
323 Kris Vernarsky .02 .10
324 Tomas Kurka .02 .10
325 Brandon Reid .02 .10
326 Jim Vandermeer .02 .10
327 Jared Aulin .02 .10
328 Cristobal Huet .10 .25
329 Alexei Ponikarovsky .02 .10
330 Alexei Semenov .02 .10
331 Patrice Bergeron RC 2.50 6.00
332 Jiri Hudler RC 1.50 4.00
333 Antti Miettinen RC .75 2.00
334 Eric Staal RC 2.50 6.00
335 Nathan Horton RC 2.00 5.00
336 Joffrey Lupul RC .75 2.00
337 Tuomo Ruutu RC 2.00 5.00
338 Jordin Tootoo RC 2.00 5.00
339 Dustin Brown RC .75 2.00
340 Marc-Andre Fleury RC 3.00 8.00
PP1 Marian Hossa .12 .30
PP2 Jaromir Jagr .25 .60
PP3 Curtis Joseph .20 .50
PP4 Mike Modano .25 .60
PP5 Markus Naslund .12 .30
PP6 Alexei Yashin .02 .10
NNO Rookie Redemption .20 .50

2003-04 Topps Blue

This 330-card set paralleled the base set but carried blue glitter borders and the O-Pee-Chee logo. These parallels were inserted at 1:4 and each card was serial numbered out of 500. The Rookie Redemption parallel card was inserted at 1:1298.

*STARS: 4X TO 10X BASIC CARDS
*ROOKIES: .75X TO 2X

2003-04 Topps Gold

This 330-card set paralleled the base set but carried gold glitter borders and the O-Pee-Chee logo. These parallels were inserted at 1:28 and each card was serial numbered out of 50. The Rookie Redemption parallel card was inserted at 1:9028. A "Golden Ticket" card redeemable for the entire gold parallel set was also randomly inserted at a rate of 1:97,056, due to scarcity, that card was not priced.

*STARS: 10X TO 25X BASIC CARDS
*ROOKIES: 2.5X TO 6X

2003-04 Topps Red

This 330-card set paralleled the base set but carried red glitter borders and the O-Pee-Chee logo. These parallels were inserted at 1:21and each card was serial numbered out of 100. The Rookie Redemption parallel card was inserted at 1:5468.

*STARS: 8X TO 20X BASIC CARDS
*ROOKIES: 2X TO 4X

2003-04 Topps First Overall Fabrics

SINGLE JSY.ODDS 1:4734
SINGLE PRINT RUN 50 SER.#'D SETS
DUAL JSY.ODDS 1:3769
DUAL PRINT RUN 25 SER.#'d SETS
ALL CARDS CARRY FO PREFIX
EL Eric Lindros 20.00 50.00
IL Ilya Kovalchuk 25.00 60.00
JT Joe Thornton 30.00 80.00
ML Mario Lemieux 50.00 125.00
MM Mike Modano 20.00 50.00
MS Mats Sundin 15.00 40.00
RN Rick Nash 20.00 50.00
VL Vincent Lecavalier 20.00 50.00
JTIK J.Thornton/I.Kovalchuk 50.00 125.00
JTVL J.Thornton/V.Lecavalier 60.00 150.00
MLMM M.Lemieux/M.Modano 75.00 200.00
MLRN M.Lemieux/R.Nash 75.00 200.00
MMMS M.Modano/M.Sundin 75.00 200.00
MSEL M.Sundin/E.Lindros 50.00 125.00
RNIK R.Nash/I.Kovalchuk 60.00 150.00
VLEL V.Lecavalier/E.Lindros 50.00 125.00

2003-04 Topps First Round Fabrics

SINGLE JSY.ODDS 1:238
DUAL JSY.ODDS 1:9706
ALL CARDS CARRY FR PREFIX
AY Alexei Yashin 6.00 15.00
BG Bill Guerin 6.00 15.00
JB Jay Bouwmeester 6.00 15.00
JI Jarome Iginla 12.50 30.00
JJ Jaromir Jagr 10.00 25.00
JL Jamie Lundmark 6.00 15.00
JP Jason Spezza 10.00 25.00
TB Todd Bertuzzi 6.00 15.00
BGJI B.Guerin/J.Iginla 30.00 80.00
JJJL J.Jagr/J.Lundmark
JSJB J.Spezza/J.Bouwmeester 30.00 80.00
TBAY T.Bertuzzi/A.Yashin 50.00 125.00

2003-04 Topps/OPC Idols

Inserted at 1:12, this 60-card insert set consisted of 3 subsets: Canadian Idols; USA Idols and International Idols. USA and International Idols were found in Topps packs while Canadian Idols were found in Canadian packs.

CI1 Dany Heatley .30 .75
CI2 Martin Brodeur .60 1.50
CI3 Todd Bertuzzi .25 .60
CI4 Mario Lemieux 1.50 4.00
CI5 Joe Thornton .40 1.00
CI6 Ed Belfour .25 .60
CI7 Michael Peca .08 .20
CI8 Jarome Iginla .30 .75
CI9 Marty Turco .20 .50
CI10 Steve Yzerman 1.25 3.00
CI11 Patrick Lalime .20 .50
CI12 Jose Theodore .30 .75
CI13 Rick Nash .30 .75
CI14 Joe Sakic .50 1.25
CI15 Vincent Lecavalier .25 .60
CI16 Mark Messier .25 .60
CI17 Brendan Shanahan .25 .60
CI18 Patrick Roy 1.25 3.00
CI19 Paul Kariya .25 .60
CI20 Jocelyn Thibault .20 .50
II1 Marian Gaborik .50 1.25
II2 Alex Kovalev .20 .50
II3 Patrik Elias .20 .50
II4 Daniel Alfredsson .20 .50
II5 Alexei Yashin .08 .20
II6 Peter Bondra .20 .50
II7 Milan Hejduk .25 .60
II8 Sergei Fedorov .30 .75
II9 Alexander Mogilny .20 .50
II10 Olli Jokinen .20 .50
II11 Pavel Bure .25 .60
II12 Jaromir Jagr .40 1.00
II13 Nicklas Lidstrom .25 .60
II14 Ilya Kovalchuk .30 .75
II15 Teemu Selanne .25 .60
II16 Marian Hossa .25 .60
II17 Markus Naslund .25 .60
II18 Peter Forsberg .60 1.50
II19 Saku Koivu .25 .60
II20 Mats Sundin .25 .60
UI1 Bill Guerin .20 .50
UI2 Jeremy Roenick .30 .75
UI3 Doug Weight .20 .50
UI4 Chris Drury .20 .50
UI5 Mike Modano .40 1.00
UI6 Chris Chelios .25 .60
UI7 Scott Gomez .08 .20
UI8 Brian Rolston .08 .20
UI9 Keith Tkachuk .25 .60
UI10 Mark Parrish .08 .20
UI11 John LeClair .25 .60
UI12 Mike Dunham .20 .50
UI13 Tyler Arnason .20 .50
UI14 Tony Amonte .20 .50
UI15 Mike York .08 .20
UI16 David Legwand .20 .50
UI17 Brian Leetch .20 .50
UI18 Brent Johnson .20 .50
UI19 Erik Cole .08 .20
UI20 Jamie Langenbrunner .08 .20

2003-04 Topps Lost Rookies

This 11-card set features "rookie" cards of superstars who didn't have a card issued during their rookie season. Cards from this set were inserted at 1:12.

BH Brett Hull .60 1.50
BS Brendan Shanahan .50 1.25
CJ Curtis Joseph .50 1.25
EB Ed Belfour .50 1.25
JR Jeremy Roenick .60 1.50
JS Joe Sakic 1.00 2.50
ML Mario Lemieux 3.00 8.00
MM Mike Modano .75 2.00
PR Patrick Roy 3.00 8.00
RF Ron Francis .50 1.25
SY Steve Yzerman 2.50 6.00

2003-04 Topps Own the Game

COMPLETE SET (20) 6.00 12.00
STATED ODDS 1:6
OTG1 Peter Forsberg .60 1.50
OTG2 Markus Naslund .20 .50
OTG3 Joe Thornton .30 .75
OTG4 Milan Hejduk .20 .50
OTG5 Todd Bertuzzi .20 .50
OTG6 Henrik Zetterberg .20 .50
OTG7 Tyler Arnason .15 .40
OTG8 Rick Nash .25 .60
OTG9 Ales Kotalik .15 .40
OTG10 Niko Kapanen .15 .40
OTG11 Martin Brodeur .60 1.50
OTG12 Patrick Lalime .15 .40
OTG13 Ed Belfour .20 .50
OTG14 Patrick Roy 1.00 2.50
OTG15 Jean-Sebastien Giguere .15 .40
OTG16 Jody Shelley .15 .40
OTG17 Reed Low .15 .40
OTG18 Matt Johnson .15 .40
OTG19 Wade Belak .15 .40
OTG20 Peter Worrell .15 .40

2003-04 Topps Signs of Toughness

STATED ODDS 1:1277
GL Georges Laraque 15.00 40.00
KS Kevin Sawyer 15.00 40.00
PW Peter Worrell 15.00 40.00
RR Rob Ray 20.00 50.00
SM Sandy McCarthy 15.00 40.00
SP Scott Parker 15.00 40.00
PJS P.J. Stock 15.00 40.00

2003-04 Topps Signs of Youth

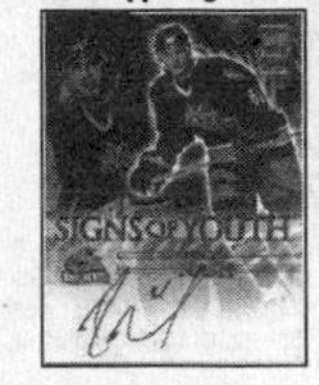

STATED ODDS 1:635
BG Brian Gionta 5.00 12.00
BR Brad Richards 12.50 30.00
IK Ilya Kovalchuk 15.00 40.00
KH Kristian Huselius 10.00 25.00
RN Rick Nash 20.00 50.00
SW Stephen Weiss 10.00 25.00

2003-04 Topps Stanley Cup Heroes

STATED ODDS 1:36
BC Bobby Clarke 4.00 10.00
BN Bobby Nystrom 4.00 10.00
BS Billy Smith 4.00 10.00
DS Dave Schultz 4.00 10.00
GF Grant Fuhr 5.00 12.00
JL Jacques Lemaire 4.00 10.00
SS Serge Savard 4.00 10.00

2003-04 Topps Stanley Cup Heroes Autographs

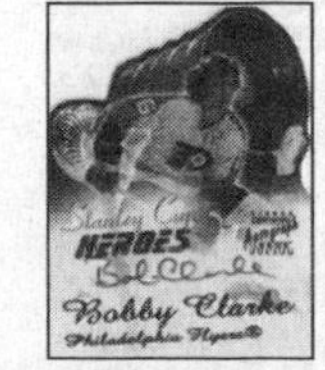

STATED ODDS 1:250
BC Bobby Clarke 15.00 40.00
BN Bobby Nystrom 12.50 30.00
BS Billy Smith 12.50 30.00
DS Dave Schultz 12.50 30.00
GF Grant Fuhr 15.00 40.00
JL Jacques Lemaire 12.50 30.00
SS Serge Savard

2003-04 Topps Tough Materials

SINGLE JSY.ODDS 1:191
DUAL JSY.ODDS 1:1505

DL Darren Langdon 6.00 15.00
EC Eric Cairns 6.00 15.00
GL Georges Laraque 8.00 20.00
KS Kevin Sawyer 6.00 15.00
PW Peter Worrell 8.00 20.00
RL Reed Low 6.00 15.00
RR Rob Ray 8.00 20.00
SM Sandy McCarthy 6.00 15.00
SP Scott Parker 6.00 15.00
PJS P.J. Stock 8.00 20.00
GLSP G.Laraque/S.Parker 20.00 50.00
KSRL K.Sawyer/R.Low 12.50 30.00
PSRR P.Stock/R.Ray 20.00 50.00
PWDL P.Worrell/D.Langdon 20.00 50.00
SMEC S.McCarthy/E.Cairns 15.00 40.00

2003-04 Topps Tough Materials Signed

STATED ODDS 1:1277
GL Georges Laraque 15.00 40.00
KS Kevin Sawyer 15.00 40.00
PW Peter Worrell 15.00 40.00
RR Rob Ray 15.00 40.00
SM Sandy McCarthy 15.00 40.00
SP Scott Parker 15.00 40.00
PJS P.J. Stock 15.00 40.00

2003 Topps All-Star Block Party

Given away exclusively at the Topps booth during the 2003 NHL All-Star block party, this 6-card set resembles the base Topps set but carried different numbering and an All-Star log on the card fronts. Each card was numbered "X of 6".

COMPLETE SET (6) 12.00
1 Patrick Roy 2.00 5.00
2 Jaromir Jagr .80 2.00
3 Jarome Iginla .40 1.00
4 Henrik Zetterberg 1.60 3.00
5 Rick Nash 1.60 4.00
6 Jay Bouwmeester 1.20 2.00

2004 Topps NHL All-Star FANtasy

This 6-card set was given away via a wrapper redemption at the Topps booth during the 2004 NHL All-Star weekend. Cards are numbered "X of 6" on the card backs.

COMPLETE SET (6) 6.00 15.00
1 Marian Gaborik .60 1.50
2 Dwayne Roloson .60 1.50
3 Patrice Bergeron 1.50 5.00
4 Marc-Andre Fleury 2.00 5.00
5 Eric Staal 1.00 2.00
6 Tuomo Ruutu 1.25 3.00

2001-02 Topps Archives

Released in mid-February 2002, this 81-card set had an SRP of $4.00 for a 8-card pack and featured reprints of past Topps/OPC rookie cards. Each card was embossed with a gold Topps Archives stamp in the top right corner and printed on 24-point white card stock.

COMPLETE SET (81) 30.00 60.00
1 Andy Bathgate .50 1.25
2 Bill Gadsby .50 1.25
3 Tony Esposito .75 2.00
4 Harry Howell .40 1.00
5 Larry Robinson .40 1.00
6 Jacques Plante .75 2.00
7 Pierre Pilote .50 1.25
8 Glenn Hall .50 1.25
9 Dale Hunter .25 .60
10 Guy Lapointe .25 .60
11 Norm Ullman .40 1.00
12 Bryan Trottier .60 1.50
13 Alex Delvecchio .50 1.25
14 Stan Mikita .60 1.50
15 Neal Broten .25 .60
16 Bernie Parent .50 1.25
17 Johnny Bucyk .50 1.25
18 Rick Middleton .40 1.00
19 Bobby Clarke .50 1.25
20 Billy Smith .50 1.25
21 Peter Stastny .40 1.00
22 Tim Kerr .25 .60
23 Gerry Cheevers .60 1.50
24 Andy Moog .40 1.00
25 Dennis Hull .40 1.00
26 Nick Fotiu .25 .60
27 Marcel Dionne .40 1.00
28 Guy Lafleur .60 1.50
29 Yvan Cournoyer .50 1.25
30 Brian Mullen .25 .60
31 Wayne Cashman .25 .60
32 Steve Shutt .40 1.00
33 Grant Fuhr .40 1.00
34 Ed Johnston .40 1.00
35 Clark Gillies .25 .60
36 Rick MacLeish .25 .60
37 Denis Potvin .40 1.00
38 Bill Clement .25 .60
39 Darryl Sittler .50 1.25
40 Pierre Larouche .25 .60
41 Vic Hadfield .25 .60
42 Derek Sanderson .40 1.00
43 Reggie Leach .25 .60
44 Brian Propp .25 .60
45 Barry Melrose .40 1.00
46 Danny Gare .25 .60
47 Darren Pang .40 1.00
48 Dick Duff .25 .60
49 Joel Quenneville .25 .60
50 John Ferguson .40 1.00
51 Ed Westfall .25 .60
52 Johnny Bower .50 1.25
53 Serge Savard .50 1.25
54 Keith Magnuson .25 .60
55 Ken Hodge .25 .60
56 Garry Unger .25 .60
57 Lindy Ruff .25 .60
58 Glenn Resch .40 1.00
59 Gump Worsley .50 1.25
60 Bernie Federko .25 .60
61 Mike Foligno .25 .60
62 Milt Schmidt .40 1.00
63 Mike Bossy .40 1.00
64 Ron Low .40 1.00
65 Jacques Lemaire .50 1.25
66 Dave Schultz .40 1.00
67 Glen Sather .40 1.00
68 Doug Wilson .25 .60
69 Terry Sawchuk 1.00 2.50
70 Mike Milbury .25 .60
71 Terry O'Reilly .40 1.00
72 Red Kelly .50 1.25
73 Peter McNab .25 .60
74 Paul Holmgren .25 .60
75 Ken Linseman .25 .60
76 Tim Horton .50 1.25
77 Bobby Smith .25 .60
78 Bobby Hull .75 2.00
79 Pat LaFontaine .40 1.00
80 Pete Mahovlich .25 .60
81 Mike Gartner .40 1.00

2001-02 Topps Archives Arena Seats

This 28-card set was inserted at a rate of 1:10 and featured a piece of an arena seat from either Boston Gardens, Maple Leaf Gardens or the Montreal Forum. Each card carried a reprinted card photo alongside the seat piece.

ASAD Alex Delvecchio 5.00 12.00
ASBF Bernie Federko 5.00 12.00
ASBS Bobby Smith 5.00 12.00
ASBT Bryan Trottier 5.00 12.00
ASDH Dennis Hull 5.00 12.00
ASDS Derek Sanderson 5.00 12.00
ASDSI Darryl Sittler 5.00 12.00
ASDWI Doug Wilson 5.00 12.00
ASGC Gerry Cheevers 6.00 15.00
ASGHA Glenn Hall 6.00 15.00
ASGL Guy Lapointe 5.00 12.00
ASGLA Guy Lafleur 6.00 15.00
ASJB John Bucyk 5.00 12.00
ASJL Jacques Lemaire 5.00 12.00
ASKH Ken Hodge 5.00 12.00
ASLR Larry Robinson 5.00 12.00
ASMD Marcel Dionne 5.00 12.00
ASNB Neal Broten 5.00 12.00
ASNU Norm Ullman 5.00 12.00
ASPL Pierre Larouche 5.00 12.00
ASPP Pierre Pilote 5.00 12.00
ASSM Stan Mikita 6.00 15.00
ASSSA Serge Savard 5.00 12.00
ASSSH Steve Shutt 5.00 12.00
ASTE Tony Esposito 6.00 15.00
ASTO Terry O'Reilly 5.00 12.00
ASWC Wayne Cashman 5.00 12.00
ASYC Yvan Cournoyer 5.00 12.00

2001-02 Topps Archives Autographs

Inserted at an overall rate of 1:17 hobby or retail packs, these cards were reprints of rookie cards of past players adorned with authentic autographs. Card #20, originally checklisted as Billy Smith, has been proven not to exist, and thus has been removed from the listing.

1 Gerry Cheevers 10.00 25.00
2 Yvan Cournoyer 10.00 25.00

3 Denis Potvin 10.00 25.00
4 John Bucyk 10.00 25.00
5 Glenn Hall 10.00 25.00
6 Pierre Pilote 10.00 25.00
7 Norm Ullman 10.00 25.00
8 Jacques Lemaire 10.00 25.00
9 Grant Fuhr 12.00 30.00
10 Stan Mikita 15.00 40.00
11 Guy Lafleur 20.00 50.00
12 Tony Esposito SP 30.00 60.00
13 Alex Delvecchio 10.00 25.00
14 Dennis Hull 10.00 25.00
15 Marcel Dionne 10.00 25.00
16 Bobby Clarke 15.00 40.00
17 Darryl Sittler 10.00 25.00
18 Dave Schultz SP 50.00 100.00
19 Bryan Trottier 10.00 25.00
21 Terry O'Reilly SP 25.00 60.00
22 Serge Savard SP 40.00 80.00
23 Vic Hadfield SP 60.00 150.00
24 Rick Middleton SP 100.00 200.00
25 Peter McNab SP 75.00 200.00
26 Peter Stastny SP 50.00 125.00
27 Ken Linseman SP 25.00 60.00
28 Ed Westfall SP 50.00 125.00
29 Clark Gillies SP 25.00 60.00
30 Bobby Hull SP 100.00 200.00

2001-02 Topps Archives Autoproofs

Inserted at a rate of 1:1696 hobby or retail packs, these cards were actual vintage cards that were bought back by Topps, autographed by the player and then randomly inserted into packs. Each card was serial-numbered out of 50. Due to scarcity and volatility, these cards are not priced.

1 Marcel Dionne
2 Bobby Clarke
3 Denis Potvin
4 Guy Lafleur
Assists Leaders

2001-02 Topps Archives Relics

This 15-card set featured smaller rookie reprint photos alongside swatches of game-used jerseys and sticks. Jersey cards were inserted at 1:8 and stick cards were inserted at 1:264. Jersey swatches were affixed using a rubber seal around the swatch.

*MULT.COLOR SWATCH : .75X TO 1.5X HI
JAD Alex Delvecchio J 5.00 12.00
JAM Andy Moog J 5.00 12.00
JBC Bobby Clarke J 15.00 40.00
JBM Brian Mullen J 5.00 12.00
JEW Ed Westfall J 5.00 12.00
JGF Grant Fuhr J 8.00 20.00
JLR Larry Robinson J 6.00 15.00
JMG Mike Gartner J 5.00 12.00
JPM Pete Mahovlich J 5.00 12.00
JSM Stan Mikita J 6.00 15.00
JBIS Billy Smith J 6.00 15.00
JBOS Bobby Smith J 5.00 12.00
SBC Bobby Clarke S 15.00 40.00
SDH Dale Hawerchuk S 8.00 20.00
STE Tony Esposito S 15.00 40.00

2003-04 Topps C55

This 165-card set was released in late December and pays homage to the original 1911-12 C55 set. Ten different players have two different cards each depicting them in either a cropped head and shoulders shot or a full length body shot, the cards are noted below with a "B" suffix (for checklisting purposes only). The set is considered incomplete without these 10 variation cards. A complete original C55 set was also inserted into packs at a rate of 1:6390. Since the buyback cards were not altered, prices can be found under the original set listing.

COMPLETE SET (165) 30.00 60.00
COMP.SET w/o SP's
1 Peter Forsberg .50 1.25
1B Peter Forsberg Full Length .50 1.25
2 Brian Leetch .15 .40
3 Jarome Iginla .25 .60
4 Scott Stevens .15 .40
5 Nicklas Lidstrom .20 .50
6 Patrick Lalime .15 .40
7 Henrik Zetterberg .20 .50
7B Henrik Zetterberg Full Length .20 .50
8 Patrick Marleau .15 .40
9 Mike Modano .30 .75
10 Marian Hossa .20 .50
11 Owen Nolan .15 .40
12 John Madden .10 .25
13 Mats Sundin .20 .50
14 Adam Hall .10 .25
15 Ron Francis .15 .40
16 Peter Bondra .15 .40
17 Ilya Kovalchuk .25 .60
17B Ilya Kovalchuk Full Length .25 .60
18 Miroslav Satan .15 .40
19 Joe Sakic .40 1.00
20 Vincent Lecavalier .20 .50
21 Rick Nash .25 .60
21B Rick Nash Full Length .25 .60
22 Anson Carter .15 .40
23 Doug Weight .15 .40
24 Rick DiPietro .15 .40
25 Tyler Arnason .15 .40
26 Mike Johnson .10 .25
27 Jeremy Roenick .25 .60
28 Teemu Selanne .20 .50
29 Roberto Luongo .25 .60
30 Martin Brodeur .50 1.25
30B Martin Brodeur Full Length .50 1.25
31 Bill Guerin .15 .40
32 Tim Connolly .10 .25
33 Roman Turek .15 .40
34 Olli Jokinen .15 .40
35 Radek Bonk .10 .25
36 Steve Rucchin .10 .25
37 Barret Jackman .15 .40
38 Dominik Hasek .40 1.00
39 Petr Nedved .10 .25
40 Marian Gaborik .40 1.00
40B Marian Gaborik Full Length .40 1.00
41 Josef Vasicek .10 .25
42 Ladislav Nagy .10 .25
43 Felix Potvin .15 .40
44 Jay Bouwmeester .15 .40
45 Sergei Gonchar .10 .25
46 Niklas Hagman .10 .25
47 Glen Murray .10 .25
48 Kyle Calder .10 .25
49 Ed Belfour .20 .50
50 Milan Hejduk .20 .50
51 Alex Kovalev .15 .40
52 Petr Sykora .10 .25
53 Scott Hartnell .10 .25
54 Tony Amonte .15 .40
55 Ed Jovanovski .15 .40
56 Sergei Zubov .10 .25
57 Mark Recchi .15 .40
58 Markus Naslund .20 .50
59 Zigmund Palffy .15 .40
60 Marty Turco .15 .40
61 Jocelyn Thibault .15 .40
62 Martin Biron .15 .40
63 Roman Hamrlik .10 .25
64 Stanislav Chistov .10 .25
65 Tomas Kaberle .10 .25
66 Mario Lemieux 1.25 3.00
66B Mario Lemieux Full Length 1.25 3.00
67 Rob Blake .15 .40
68 Jaromir Jagr .30 .75
69 Nikolai Khabibulin .20 .50
70 Brett Hull .25 .60
71 Slava Kozlov .10 .25
72 Michael Peca .10 .25
73 Jeff O'Neill .10 .25
74 Joe Nieuwendyk .15 .40
75 Yanic Perreault .10 .25
76 Derian Hatcher .10 .25
77 Chris Gratton .10 .25
78 Olaf Kolzig .15 .40
79 Alexei Yashin .10 .25
80 Martin St. Louis .15 .40
81 Chris Pronger .15 .40
82 Dick Tarnstrom .10 .25
83 Nick Schultz .10 .25
84 Ossi Vaananen .10 .25
85 Tie Domi .10 .25
86 Patrik Elias .15 .40
87 Jim Vandermeer .10 .25
88 Alexei Morozov .10 .25
89 Alexander Mogilny .15 .40
90 Dany Heatley .25 .60
91 Marcel Hossa .10 .25
92 Mike Comrie .15 .40
92B Mike Comrie Full Length .15 .40
93 Niko Kapanen .10 .25
94 David Legwand .15 .40
95 Alex Tanguay .15 .40
96 Alyn McCauley .10 .25
97 Brendan Morrison .15 .40
98 Chris Drury .15 .40
99 Paul Kariya .20 .50
100 Joe Thornton .30 .75
100B Joe Thornton Full Length .30 .75
101 Tomas Vokoun .15 .40
102 Tommy Salo .15 .40
103 Brad Richards .15 .40
104 Geoff Sanderson .10 .25
105 Daniel Briere .10 .25
106 Mike Dunham .15 .40
107 Kyle McLaren .10 .25
108 Zdeno Chara .10 .25
109 Curtis Joseph .20 .50
110 Todd Bertuzzi .20 .50
111 Saku Koivu .20 .50
112 Martin Havlat .15 .40
113 Dave Andreychuk .10 .25
114 Dan Cloutier .15 .40
115 Pavol Demitra .15 .40
116 Dave Scatchard .10 .25
117 Ryan Smyth .10 .25
118 Craig Conroy .10 .25
119 Eric Brewer .10 .25
120 Jean-Sebastien Giguere .15 .40
120B Jean-Sebastien Giguere Full Length .15 .40
121 Alexander Frolov .10 .25
122 Al MacInnis .15 .40
123 Martin Straka .10 .25
124 Brian Rolston .10 .25
125 Jamie Langenbrunner .10 .25
126 Pierre-Marc Bouchard .10 .25
127 Jan Bulis .10 .25
128 Rostislav Klesla .10 .25
129 Pasi Nurminen .15 .40
130 Jose Theodore .25 .60
131 Tuomo Ruutu RC 2.00 5.00
132 Andrew Peters RC 1.00 2.50
133 Jordin Tootoo RC 1.50 4.00
134 Joe DiPenta RC 1.00 2.50
135 Milan Bartovic RC 1.00 2.50
136 Rick Mrozik RC 1.00 2.50
137 Kent McDonell RC 1.00 2.50
138 Antti Miettinen RC 1.00 2.50
139 Alexander Semin RC 2.00 5.00
140 Dustin Brown RC 1.00 2.50
141 Peter Sejna RC 1.00 2.50
142 Matt Stajan RC 1.50 4.00
143 Brent Burns RC 1.00 2.50
144 Paul Martin RC 1.00 2.50
145 Antoine Vermette RC 1.00 2.50
146 Sean Bergenheim RC 1.00 2.50
147 Joni Pitkanen RC 1.00 2.50
148 Patrice Bergeron RC 2.50 6.00
149 Eric Staal RC 3.00 8.00
150 Dan Hamhuis RC 1.00 2.50
151 Marc-Andre Fleury RC 4.00 10.00
152 Jiri Hudler RC 1.25 3.00
153 David Hale RC 1.00 2.50
154 Milan Michalek RC 1.50 4.00
155 John-Michael Liles RC 1.00 2.50

2003-04 Topps C55 Minis

These mini-cards were inserted one per pack and parallel the base set. There were several different parallels of the mini set that carried differing card backs, those sets proceed this set listing.

*STARS: .5X TO 1.25X BASE HI
*ROOKIES: .5X TO 1.25X

2003-04 Topps C55 Minis American Back

*BLACK STARS: .75X TO 2X BASE HI
*BLACK ROOKIES: .6X TO 1.5X
BLACK ODDS 1:9
*RED STARS: 2X TO 5X
*RED ROOKIES: .75X TO 2X
RED ODDS 1:33

2003-04 Topps C55 Minis Bazooka Back

This 165-card parallel set was the toughest pull of the variations. It is believed that only 5 copies of each card exist.

STATED ODDS 1:687
NOT PRICED DUE TO SCARCITY

2003-04 Topps C55 Minis Brooklyn Back

*STARS: .75X TO 2X BASE HI
*ROOKIES: .6X TO 1.5X
STATED ODDS 1:9

2003-04 Topps C55 Minis Hat Trick Back

*STARS: 2X TO 5X BASE HI
*ROOKIES: .75X TO 2X
STATED ODDS 1:38

2003-04 Topps C55 Minis O Canada Back

*BLACK STARS: .75X TO 2X BASE HI
*BLACK ROOKIES: .6X TO 1.5X
BLACK ODDS 1:9
*RED STARS: 2X TO 5X
*RED ROOKIES: .75X TO 2X
RED ODDS 1:33

2003-04 Topps C55 Minis Stanley Cup Back

*STARS: .6X TO 1.5X
*ROOKIES: .6X TO 1.5X
STATED ODDS 1:4

2003-04 Topps C55 Autographs

This 12-card set featured certified autographs on mini-cards. Each card was held in a grey "C55" holder and shrink wrapped in clear plastic.

GROUP A ODDS 1:81
GROUP B ODDS 1:417
GROUP C ODDS 1:71
TACD Chris Drury C 6.00 15.00
TAEC Erik Cole A 6.00 15.00
TAHZ Henrik Zetterberg A 10.00 25.00
TAIK Ilya Kovalchuk B 12.50 30.00
TAJG Jean-Sebastien Giguere A 8.00 20.00
TAKH Kristian Huselius A 6.00 15.00
TAMH Marian Hossa A 8.00 20.00
TAPE Patrik Elias C 6.00 15.00
TARN Rick Nash A 10.00 25.00
TARV Radim Vrbata C 6.00 15.00
TASW Stephen Weiss A 6.00 15.00
TATB Todd Bertuzzi C 8.00 20.00

2003-04 Topps C55 Award Winners

These decoy cards represented trophy winners from the previous campaign. Cards from this set and the Stanley Cup Winners set were inserted one per non-memorabilia pack.

1 Mighty Ducks of Anaheim .20 .50
2 New Jersey Devils .20 .50
3 Ottawa Senators .20 .50
4 Barret Jackman .20 .50

5 Brendan Shanahan .25 .60
6 Peter Forsberg .40 1.00
7 Martin Brodeur .40 1.00
8 Alexander Mogilny .20 .50
9 Steve Yzerman .75 2.00
10 Nicklas Lidstrom .25 .60
11 Markus Naslund .25 .60
12 Milan Hejduk .25 .60
13 Peter Forsberg .40 1.00
14 Jere Lehtinen .20 .50
15 Jean-Sebastien Giguere .20 .50
16 Martin Brodeur .40 1.00

2003-04 Topps C55 Relics

This 45-card set featured jersey swatches on mini-cards. Each card was held in a grey "C55" holder and shrink wrapped in clear plastic.

GROUP A ODDS 1:15788
GROUP B ODDS 1:948
GROUP C ODDS 1:268
GROUP D ODDS 1:56
GROUP E ODDS 1:15
TRAH Adam Hall E 3.00 8.00
TRAS Alexander Svitov E 3.00 8.00
TRAY Alexei Yashin E 3.00 8.00
TRBG Bill Guerin E 3.00 8.00
TRBH Brett Hull D 8.00 20.00
TRBM Brendan Morrison D 3.00 8.00
TRBRA Branko Radivojevic E 3.00 8.00
TRBR Brad Richards D 4.00 10.00
TRDA Daniel Alfredsson D 4.00 10.00
TRDH Dany Heatley C 6.00 15.00
TRDL David Legwand C 4.00 10.00
TREB Ed Belfour D 6.00 15.00
TRGL Georges Laraque E 3.00 8.00
TRIK Ilya Kovalchuk D 8.00 20.00
TRJB Jay Bouwmeester E 3.00 8.00
TRJI Jarome Iginla E 6.00 15.00
TRJJ Jaromir Jagr E 8.00 20.00
TRJL Jordan Leopold E 3.00 8.00
TRJS Jason Spezza E 6.00 15.00
TRJT Jose Theodore E 6.00 15.00
TRJTH Joe Thornton E 8.00 20.00
TRMC Mike Comrie B 8.00 20.00
TRMG Marian Gaborik E 8.00 20.00
TRMHE Milan Hejduk D 5.00 12.00
TRMH Marian Hossa E 5.00 12.00
TRML Mario Lemieux A 250.00 400.00
TRMM Mike Modano B 50.00 125.00
TRMN Markus Naslund D 5.00 12.00
TRMS Mats Sundin D 5.00 12.00
TRMT Marty Turco E 4.00 10.00
TRNK Nikolai Khabibulin E 5.00 12.00
TRNS Nick Schultz E 3.00 8.00
TRPB Pavel Bure E 5.00 12.00
TRPK Paul Kariya B 30.00 80.00
TRPL Patrick Lalime D 4.00 10.00
TRRB Rob Blake E 4.00 10.00
TRRL Roberto Luongo C 6.00 15.00
TRRM Ryan Miller E 5.00 12.00
TRRN Rick Nash E 6.00 15.00
TRSK Saku Koivu E 5.00 12.00
TRSN Scott Niedermayer B 30.00 80.00
TRSP Scott Parker E 3.00 8.00
TRTB Todd Bertuzzi E 5.00 12.00
TRTC Tim Connolly B 20.00 50.00
TRVL Vincent Lecavalier B 50.00 125.00

2003-04 Topps C55 Stanley Cup Winners

These decoy cards represented Cup winners from previous years. Cards from this set and the Award Winners set were inserted one per non-memorabilia pack.

1 Ottawa Senators .30 .75
2 New York Rangers .30 .75
3 Boston Bruins .30 .75
4 Montreal Canadiens .30 .75
5 Montreal Canadiens .30 .75
6 Toronto Maple Leafs .30 .75
7 New York Rangers .30 .75
8 Chicago Blackhawks .30 .75
9 Montreal Maroons .30 .75
10 Detroit Red Wings .30 .75
11 Detroit Red Wings .30 .75
12 Chicago Blackhawks .30 .75
13 Boston Bruins .30 .75
14 New York Rangers .30 .75
15 Boston Bruins .30 .75
16 Toronto Maple Leafs .30 .75
17 Detroit Red Wings .30 .75
18 Montreal Canadiens .30 .75
19 Toronto Maple Leafs .30 .75
20 Montreal Canadiens .30 .75
21 Toronto Maple Leafs .30 .75
22 Toronto Maple Leafs .30 .75
23 Toronto Maple Leafs .30 .75
24 Detroit Red Wings .30 .75
25 Toronto Maple Leafs .30 .75
26 Detroit Red Wings .30 .75
27 Montreal Canadiens .30 .75
28 Detroit Red Wings .30 .75
29 Detroit Red Wings .30 .75
30 Montreal Canadiens .30 .75
31 Montreal Canadiens .30 .75
32 Montreal Canadiens .30 .75
33 Montreal Canadiens .30 .75
34 Montreal Canadiens .30 .75
35 Chicago Blackhawks .30 .75
36 Toronto Maple Leafs .30 .75
37 Toronto Maple Leafs .30 .75
38 Toronto Maple Leafs .30 .75
39 Montreal Canadiens .30 .75
40 Montreal Canadiens .30 .75
41 Toronto Maple Leafs .30 .75
42 Montreal Canadiens .30 .75
43 Montreal Canadiens .30 .75
44 Boston Bruins .30 .75
45 Montreal Canadiens .30 .75
46 Boston Bruins .30 .75
47 Montreal Canadiens .30 .75
48 Philadelphia Flyers .30 .75
49 Philadelphia Flyers .30 .75
50 Montreal Canadiens .30 .75
51 Montreal Canadiens .30 .75
52 Montreal Canadiens .30 .75
53 Montreal Canadiens .30 .75
54 New York Islanders .30 .75
55 New York Islanders .30 .75
56 New York Islanders .30 .75
57 New York Islanders .30 .75
58 Edmonton Oilers .30 .75
59 Edmonton Oilers .30 .75
60 Montreal Canadiens .30 .75
61 Edmonton Oilers .30 .75
62 Edmonton Oilers .30 .75
63 Calgary Flames .30 .75
64 Edmonton Oilers .30 .75
65 Pittsburgh Penguins .30 .75
66 Pittsburgh Penguins .30 .75
67 Montreal Canadiens .30 .75
68 New York Rangers .30 .75
69 New Jersey Devils .30 .75
70 Colorado Avalanche .30 .75
71 Detroit Red Wings .30 .75
72 Detroit Red Wings .30 .75
73 Dallas Stars .30 .75
74 New Jersey Devils .30 .75
75 Colorado Avalanche .30 .75
76 Detroit Red Wings .30 .75
77 New Jersey Devils .30 .75

2002-03 Topps Factory Set

Available only in gift box factory sets, this 340-card set paralleled the regular Topps and OPC sets but featured gold foil highlights instead of the silver highlights found on cards distributed in packs. Each gift box contained 330 veteran cards, a redemption card for a 10-card rookie subset, a 20-card Hometown Heroes set, and a Patrick Roy Reprint card.

COMPLETE FACTORY SET (340) 25.00 50.00
COMP.BASE SET (330) 20.00 40.00
*STARS: .5X TO 1.25X REG.TOPPS
*ROOKIES: .5X TO 1.5X REG.TOPPS

2002-03 Topps Factory Set Hometown Heroes

This 20-card set was inserted into every gift box of Topps and OPC Complete factory set. The cards paralleled the regular Hometown Heroes cards found in packs but did not carry the same glossy finish. Cards HHU1-HHU20 were available in Topps and HHC1-HHC20 were available in OPC.

*SAME VALUE AS REGULAR HOME.HERO

2002-03 Topps Factory Set Patrick Roy Reprints

Available in gift boxes of Topps and OPC Complete factory set, this 14-card set paralleled the reprints available in packs, but carried a silver foil logo.

COMPLETE SET (14) 30.00 60.00
COMMON ROY (1-14) 2.50 6.00

1999-00 Topps Chrome

The 1999-00 Topps/OPC Chrome set released as a 297-card set printed on 16-point foil stock and consisted of 247 regular player cards and 39 subset cards, (24) 1999 NHL Draft Picks, 4-CHL Stars, and 11-

Magic Moments which is comprised of five different versions of each card highlighting five significant moments in each player's career. Packaged in 24-pack boxes and 4-card packs, Topps/OPC Chrome packs carried a suggested retail price of $3.00.

COMPLETE SET (297) 150.00 300.00
COMP.SET w/MMs (341) 200.00 400.00
FIVE VERSIONS OF MM 276-286 EXIST
ALL VERSIONS SAME VALUE
1 Joe Sakic 1.00 2.50
2 Alexei Yashin .25 .60
3 Paul Kariya .50 1.25
4 Keith Tkachuk .50 1.25
5 Jaromir Jagr .75 2.00
6 Mike Modano .75 2.00
7 Eric Lindros .50 1.25
8 Zigmund Palffy .40 1.00
9 Dominik Hasek 1.00 2.50
10 Pavel Bure .50 1.25
11 Ray Bourque .75 2.00
12 Peter Forsberg 1.25 3.00
13 Al MacInnis .40 1.00
14 Steve Yzerman 2.50 6.00
15 Mats Sundin .50 1.25
16 Patrick Roy 2.50 6.00
17 Teemu Selanne .50 1.25
18 Keith Primeau .25 .60
19 John LeClair .50 1.25
20 Martin Brodeur 1.25 3.00
21 Joe Thornton .75 2.00
22 Rob Blake .40 1.00
23 Ron Francis .40 1.00
24 Grant Fuhr .40 1.00
25 Nicklas Lidstrom .50 1.25
26 Vladimir Orszagh RC .25 .60
27 Glen Wesley .25 .60
28 Adam Deadmarsh .25 .60
29 Zdeno Chara .25 .60
30 Brian Leetch .50 1.25
31 Valeri Bure .25 .60
32 Ryan Smyth .25 .60
33 Jean-Sebastien Aubin .40 1.00
34 Dave Reid .25 .60
35 Ed Jovanovski .25 .60
36 Anders Eriksson .25 .60
37 Mike Ricci .25 .60
38 Todd Bertuzzi .50 1.25
39 Shawn Bates .25 .60
40 Kip Miller .25 .60
41 Jozef Stumpel .25 .60
42 Jeremy Roenick .60 1.50
43 Todd Marchant .25 .60
44 Josh Holden .25 .60
45 Rob Niedermayer .25 .60
46 Cory Sarich .25 .60
47 Nikolai Khabibulin .40 1.00
48 Marty McInnis .25 .60
49 Marty Reasoner .40 1.00
50 Gary Roberts .25 .60
51 Manny Malhotra .40 1.00
52 Adam Foote .25 .60
53 Luc Robitaille .40 1.00
54 Bryan Marchment .25 .60
55 Mark Janssens .25 .60
56 Steve Heinze .25 .60
57 Cory Stillman .25 .60
58 Guy Hebert .40 1.00
59 Mike Richter .50 1.25
60 Jamie Langenbrunner .25 .60
61 Wade Redden .25 .60
62 Steve Smith .25 .60
63 Daniil Markov .25 .60
64 Erik Rasmussen .25 .60
65 Glen Murray .25 .60
66 Alexei Kovalev .25 .60
67 Peter Bondra .40 1.00
68 Dimitri Khristich .25 .60
69 Sami Kapanen .25 .60
70 Tom Poti .25 .60
71 Trevor Linden .25 .60
72 Tomas Vokoun .40 1.00
73 Steve Webb .25 .60
74 Jarome Iginla .60 1.50
75 Scott Mellanby .25 .60
76 Mattias Ohlund .25 .60
77 Steve Konowalchuk .25 .60
78 Bryan Berard .40 1.00
79 Chris Pronger .40 1.00
80 Teppo Numminen .25 .60
81 John MacLean .25 .60
82 Jeff Hackett .40 1.00
83 Ray Whitney .25 .60
84 Chris Osgood .40 1.00
85 Doug Zmolek .25 .60
86 Curtis Brown .25 .60
87 Reid Simpson .25 .60
88 Milan Hejduk .50 1.25
89 Donald Audette .25 .60
90 Saku Koivu .50 1.25
91 Martin Straka .25 .60
92 Mark Messier .50 1.25
93 Richard Zednik .25 .60
94 Curtis Joseph .50 1.25
95 Colin Forbes .25 .60
96 Jeff Friesen .25 .60
97 Eric Brewer .25 .60
98 Darius Kasparaitis .25 .60
99 Marian Hossa .50 1.25
100 Petr Sykora .25 .60
101 Vladimir Malakhov .25 .60
102 Jamie Storr .40 1.00
103 Doug Gilmour .40 1.00
104 Doug Weight .40 1.00
105 Derian Hatcher .25 .60
106 Chris Drury .40 1.00
107 Arturs Irbe .40 1.00
108 Fred Brathwaite .40 1.00
109 Jason Allison .25 .60
110 Roman Hamrlik .25 .60
111 Rico Fata .25 .60
112 Janne Niinimaa .25 .60
113 Kenny Jonsson .25 .60
114 Marco Sturm .25 .60
115 Steve Thomas .25 .60
116 Garth Snow .40 1.00
117 Rick Tocchet .40 1.00
118 Jean-Marc Pelletier .40 1.00
119 Bobby Holik .25 .60
120 Sergei Fedorov .75 2.00
121 J-P Dumont .40 1.00
122 Jason Woolley .25 .60
123 James Patrick .25 .60
124 Blake Sloan .50 1.25
125 Marcus Nilsson .25 .60
126 Shayne Corson .25 .60
127 Tom Fitzgerald .25 .60
128 Brian Rolston .25 .60
129 Ron Tugnutt .40 1.00
130 Mark Recchi .40 1.00
131 Matthew Barnaby .25 .60
132 Olaf Kolzig .40 1.00
133 Paul Mara .25 .60
134 Patrick Marleau .50 1.25
135 Magnus Arvedson .25 .60
136 Felix Potvin .50 1.25
137 Bill Guerin .40 1.00
138 Brett Hull .60 1.50
139 Vitali Yachmenev .25 .60
140 Ruslan Salei .25 .60
141 Mark Parrish .25 .60
142 Randy Cunneyworth .25 .60
143 Damian Rhodes .40 1.00
144 Daniel Briere .25 .60
145 Craig Conroy .25 .60
146 Sergei Gonchar .25 .60
147 Vincent Lecavalier .50 1.25
148 Adam Graves .25 .60
149 Doug Bodger .25 .60
150 Jeff O'Neill .25 .60
151 Darby Hendrickson .25 .60
152 Sergei Samsonov .40 1.00
153 Ed Belfour .50 1.25
154 Robert Svehla .25 .60
155 Cliff Ronning .25 .60
156 Brendan Morrison .40 1.00
157 Daniel Alfredsson .40 1.00
158 Eric Desjardins .25 .60
159 Mike Vernon .40 1.00
160 Vadim Sharifijanov .25 .60
161 Jaroslav Svejkovsky .25 .60
162 Michael Peca .40 1.00
163 Shane Willis .25 .60
164 Sandis Ozolinsh .25 .60
165 Mathieu Dandenault .25 .60
166 Martin Rucinsky .25 .60
167 Scott Stevens .25 .60
168 Sami Salo .25 .60
169 Tom Barrasso .40 1.00
170 Chris Gratton .25 .60
171 Markus Naslund .50 1.25
172 Mike Johnson .25 .60
173 Bob Boughner .25 .60
174 Todd Simpson .25 .60
175 Fredrik Olausson .25 .60
176 Jocelyn Thibault .40 1.00
177 Juha Ylonen .25 .60
178 Brad Bombardir .25 .60
179 Jan Hrdina .25 .60
180 Adrian Aucoin .25 .60
181 Mike Eagles .25 .60
182 Petr Nedved .40 1.00
183 Rem Murray .25 .60
184 Mikael Renberg .40 1.00
185 Mike Eastwood .25 .60
186 Byron Dafoe .40 1.00
187 Tony Amonte .40 1.00
188 Darren McCarty .25 .60
189 Sergei Krivokrasov .25 .60
190 Dave Lowry .25 .60
191 Michal Handzus .40 1.00
192 Tie Domi .40 1.00
193 Brian Holzinger .25 .60
194 Jason Arnott .25 .60
195 Jose Theodore .60 1.50
196 Brendan Shanahan .50 1.25
197 Derek Morris .25 .60
198 Steve Rucchin .25 .60
199 Kevin Hodson .40 1.00
200 Oleg Kvasha .25 .60
201 John Vanbiesbrouck .40 1.00
202 Adam Oates .40 1.00
203 Anson Carter .40 1.00
204 Sebastien Bordeleau .25 .60
205 Pavol Demitra .40 1.00
206 Owen Nolan .40 1.00
207 Pavel Rosa .25 .60
208 Petr Svoboda .25 .60
209 Tomas Kaberle .25 .60
210 Claude Lapointe .25 .60
211 Todd Harvey .25 .60
212 Trent McCleary .25 .60
213 Vyacheslav Kozlov .25 .60
214 Marc Denis .40 1.00
215 Joe Nieuwendyk .40 1.00
216 Kelly Buchberger .25 .60
217 Tommy Albelin .25 .60
218 Kyle McLaren .25 .60
219 Chris Chelios .50 1.25
220 Joel Bouchard .25 .60
221 Mats Lindgren .25 .60
222 Jyrki Lumme .25 .60
223 Pierre Turgeon .40 1.00
224 Bill Muckalt .25 .60
225 Antti Aalto .25 .60
226 Jere Lehtinen .40 1.00
227 Theo Fleury .25 .60
228 Dmitri Mironov .25 .60
229 Scott Niedermayer .25 .60
230 Sean Burke .40 1.00
231 Eric Daze .40 1.00
232 Alexei Zhitnik .25 .60
233 Christian Matte .25 .60
234 Patrik Elias .40 1.00
235 Alexandre Korolyuk .25 .60
236 Sergei Berezin .25 .60
237 Ray Ferraro .25 .60
238 Rod Brind'Amour .40 1.00
239 Darcy Tucker .25 .60
240 Darryl Sydor .25 .60
241 Mike Dunham .40 1.00
242 Marc Bergevin .25 .60
243 Ray Sheppard .25 .60
244 Miroslav Satan .40 1.00
245 Andreas Dackell .25 .60
246 Mike Grier .25 .60
247 Alexei Zhamnov .25 .60
248 David Legwand .40 1.00
249 Daniel Tkaczuk .25 .60
250 Roberto Luongo .60 1.50
251 Simon Gagne .50 1.25
252 Jamie Lundmark .40 1.00
253 Alexandre Giroux RC .40 1.00
254 Dusty Jamieson RC .40 1.00
255 Jamie Chamberlain RC .40 1.00
256 Radim Vrbata RC 2.00 5.00
257 Scott Cameron RC .40 1.00
258 Simon Lajeunesse RC .60 1.50
259 Tim Connolly .25 .60
260 Kris Beech .25 .60
261 Brian Finley .40 1.00
262 Alex Auld RC .60 1.50
263 Martin Grenier RC .40 1.00
264 Sheldon Keefe RC 1.25 3.00
265 Justin Mapletoft RC .40 1.00
266 Edward Hill RC .40 1.00
267 Nolan Yonkman RC .50 1.25
268 Oleg Saprykin RC 1.00 2.50
269 Branislav Mezei RC 1.25 3.00
270 Chris Kelly RC .40 1.00
271 Pavel Brendl RC 2.00 5.00
272 Brett Lysak RC .50 1.25
273 Matt Carkner RC .40 1.00
274 Luke Sellars RC .50 1.25
275 Brad Ralph RC .40 1.00
276A Ray Bourque MM 1.25 3.00
277A Peter Forsberg MM 2.00 5.00
278A Joe Nieuwendyk MM .40 1.00
279A Dominik Hasek MM 1.50 4.00
280A Jaromir Jagr MM 1.25 3.00
281A Paul Kariya MM .50 1.25
282A Eric Lindros MM
283A Mark Messier MM .50 1.25
284A Patrick Roy MM 4.00 10.00
285A Joe Sakic MM 1.50 4.00
286A Steve Yzerman MM 5.00 12.00
287 Alex Tanguay .40 1.00
288 Brad Stuart .40 1.00
289 Brian Boucher .50 1.25
290 Steve Kariya RC .60 1.50
291 Scott Gomez .25 .60
292 Mikko Eloranta RC .60 1.50
293 Patrik Stefan RC 1.00 2.50
294 John Madden RC 1.00 2.50
295 Per Svartvadet RC .60 1.50
296 Jiri Fischer .25 .60
297 Nikolai Antropov RC 1.25 3.00

1999-00 Topps Chrome Refractors

Randomly inserted in Topps packs at 1:12, this 297-card set parallels the base set and is enhanced by the rainbow holo-foil refractor effect. Above the card number on the back, the word "REFRACTOR" appears.

*VETERANS: 4X TO 10X BASIC CARDS
*ROOKIES: 1.2X TO 3X
*MM: 2X TO 5X BASIC CARDS

1999-00 Topps Chrome All-Topps

Randomly seeded in Topps and OPC packs at 1:24, this 15-card set features brilliant action photography of the best active players at a particular position, while the card backs contain comparisons with all-time greats at that same position. Refractor parallels of this set were also randomly inserted at 1:120.

COMPLETE SET (15) 15.00 40.00
*REFRACTORS: 1.5X TO 3X BASIC INSERTS
AT1 Dominik Hasek 2.00 5.00
AT2 Martin Brodeur 2.50 6.00
AT3 Ray Bourque 1.50 4.00
AT4 Al MacInnis .75 2.00
AT5 Nicklas Lidstrom 1.00 2.50
AT6 Brian Leetch .75 2.00
AT7 John LeClair .75 2.00
AT8 Paul Kariya 1.00 2.50
AT9 Keith Tkachuk .75 2.00
AT10 Eric Lindros 1.00 2.50
AT11 Peter Forsberg 1.50 4.00
AT12 Steve Yzerman 4.00 10.00
AT13 Jaromir Jagr 1.50 4.00
AT14 Teemu Selanne 1.00 2.50
AT15 Pavel Bure 1.00 2.50

1999-00 Topps Chrome A-Men

Randomly inserted in Topps and OPC packs at 1:24, this 6-card set focuses on the NHL's leading assist men. Action photos are set against a silver foil background. Refractor parallels of this set were also randomly inserted at 1:120.

COMPLETE SET (6) 10.00 20.00
*REFRACTORS: 1.5X TO 3X BASIC INSERTS
AM1 Jaromir Jagr 1.50 4.00
AM2 Peter Forsberg 2.50 6.00
AM3 Paul Kariya 1.50 4.00
AM4 Teemu Selanne 1.50 4.00
AM5 Joe Sakic 2.00 5.00
AM6 Eric Lindros 1.50 4.00

1999-00 Topps Chrome Fantastic Finishers

Randomly inserted in Topps and OPC packs at 1:24, this 6-card set features the NHL's top goal scorers. Action player photos are set against a foil true-life background. Refractor parallels of this set were also randomly inserted at 1:120.

COMPLETE SET (6) 6.00 12.00
*REFRACTORS: 1.5X TO 3X BASIC INSERTS
FF1 Teemu Selanne 1.00 2.50
FF2 Jaromir Jagr 1.50 4.00
FF3 Tony Amonte .75 2.00
FF4 Alexei Yashin .75 2.00
FF5 John LeClair 1.00 2.50
FF6 Joe Sakic 2.00 5.00

1999-00 Topps Chrome Ice Futures

Randomly inserted in Topps and OPC packs at 1:24, this 6-card set focuses on the NHL's hottest prospects. Action photos are set against a blue foil checkerboard background. Refractor parallels of this set were also randomly inserted at 1:120.

COMPLETE SET (6) 4.00 10.00
*REFRACTORS: 1.5X TO 3X BASIC INSERTS
IF1 Mark Parrish .75 2.00
IF2 Chris Drury 1.00 2.50
IF3 Bill Muckalt .75 2.00
IF4 Marian Hossa 1.25 3.00
IF5 Milan Hejduk 1.00 2.50
IF6 Brendan Morrison .75 2.00

1999-00 Topps Chrome Ice Masters

Randomly inserted in Topps and OPC packs at 1:18, this 20-card set showcases some of hockey's elite players on a blue and silver foil card that is textured like ice. Refractor parallels of this set were also randomly inserted at 1:90.

COMPLETE SET (20) 25.00 50.00
*REFRACTORS: 1.5X TO 3X BASIC INSERTS
IM1 Joe Sakic 1.50 4.00
IM2 Dominik Hasek 1.50 4.00
IM3 Eric Lindros .75 2.00
IM4 Jaromir Jagr 1.25 3.00
IM5 John LeClair .75 2.00
IM6 Mats Sundin .75 2.00
IM7 Ray Bourque 1.25 3.00
IM8 Mike Modano 1.25 3.00
IM9 Peter Forsberg 2.00 5.00
IM10 Brian Leetch .75 2.00
IM11 Martin Brodeur 2.00 5.00
IM12 Al MacInnis .60 1.50
IM13 Paul Kariya .75 2.00
IM14 Alexei Yashin .60 1.50
IM15 Steve Yzerman 4.00 10.00
IM16 Ed Belfour .75 2.00
IM17 Keith Tkachuk .75 2.00
IM18 Patrick Roy 4.00 10.00
IM19 Nicklas Lidstrom .75 2.00
IM20 Teemu Selanne .75 2.00

1999-00 Topps Chrome Positive Performers

Randomly inserted in Topps and OPC packs at 1:24, this 6-card set features players with the best plus/minus rating in the game.Refractor parallels of this set were also randomly inserted at 1:120.

COMPLETE SET (6) 3.00 8.00
*REFRACTORS: 1.5X TO 3X BASIC INSERTS
PP1 Alexander Karpovtsev .60 1.50
PP2 John LeClair 1.00 2.50
PP3 Eric Lindros 1.00 2.50
PP4 Magnus Arvedson .60 1.50
PP5 Al MacInnis .75 2.00
PP6 Jere Lehtinen .75 2.00

1999-00 Topps Chrome Postmasters

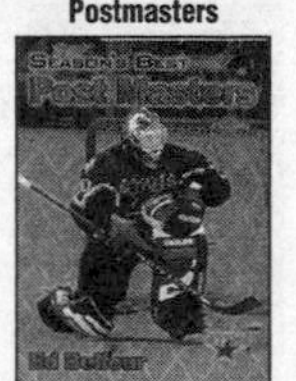

Randomly inserted in Topps and OPC packs at 1:24, this 6-card set focuses on the NHL's toughest goaltenders. Refractor parallels of this set were also randomly inserted at 1:120.

COMPLETE SET (6) 10.00 20.00
*REFRACTORS: 1.5X TO 3X BASIC INSERTS
PM1 Dominik Hasek 2.00 5.00
PM2 Byron Dafoe .75 2.00
PM3 Nikolai Khabibulin .75 2.00
PM4 Ed Belfour 1.00 2.50
PM5 Patrick Roy 5.00 12.00
PM6 Martin Brodeur 2.50 6.00

2000-01 Topps Chrome

Released in late January 2001, this 251-card set is comprised of 160 veteran cards, 5 Season Highlight cards, 55 NHL Prospects, and 30 Chrome Expansion cards. Cards #241-251 were sequentially numbered to 1250. Base cards have silver borders and are printed on an all chrome card stock. Two parallel versions were issued for the Expansion cards, numbers 240-251, and these cards are also sequentially numbered to 1250. Topps Chrome was packaged in 24-pack boxes with packs containing four cards and carried a suggested retail price of $3.00.

COMPLETE SET (250) 100.00 200.00
COMP.SET w/o SP's (240) 30.00 60.00
1 Jaromir Jagr .75 2.00
2 Patrick Roy 2.50 6.00
3 Paul Kariya .50 1.25
4 Mats Sundin .50 1.25
5 Ron Francis .40 1.00
6 Pavel Bure .50 1.25
7 John LeClair .50 1.25
8 Olaf Kolzig .40 1.00
9 Chris Pronger .40 1.00
10 Jeremy Roenick .60 1.50
11 Owen Nolan .40 1.00
12 Theo Fleury .20 .50
13 Zigmund Palffy .40 1.00
14 Patrik Stefan .20 .50
15 Jarome Iginla .60 1.50
16 Joe Thornton .75 2.00
17 Tony Amonte .40 1.00
18 Mike Modano .75 2.00
19 Mark Messier .50 1.25
20 Dominik Hasek 1.00 2.50
21 Steve Yzerman 2.50 6.00
22 Marian Hossa .50 1.25
23 David Legwand .40 1.00
24 Jose Theodore .60 1.50
25 Vincent Lecavalier .50 1.25
26 Scott Stevens .40 1.00
27 Mark Parrish .20 .50
28 Sean Burke .40 1.00
29 Alexei Kovalev .40 1.00
30 Dan Cloutier .20 .50
31 Sami Kapanen .20 .50
32 Anson Carter .40 1.00
33 Miroslav Satan .40 1.00
34 Mark Recchi .40 1.00
35 Pavol Demitra .40 1.00
36 Peter Bondra .50 1.25
37 Mike Richter .50 1.25
38 Guy Hebert .40 1.00
39 Martin Skoula .20 .50
40 Ed Belfour .50 1.25
41 Fred Brathwaite .40 1.00
42 Andrew Brunette .20 .50
43 Byron Dafoe .40 1.00
44 Felix Potvin .50 1.25
45 Rod Brind'Amour .40 1.00
46 Doug Gilmour .40 1.00
47 Brett Hull .60 1.50
48 Nicklas Lidstrom .50 1.25
49 Mike York .20 .50
50 Al MacInnis .40 1.00
51 Brian Boucher .50 1.25
52 Teemu Selanne .50 1.25
53 Bill Guerin .40 1.00
54 Ray Bourque .75 2.00
55 Ray Ferraro .20 .50
56 Sergei Gonchar .20 .50
57 Mattias Ohlund .20 .50
58 Todd Marchant .20 .50
59 Damian Rhodes .40 1.00
60 Chris Drury .40 1.00
61 Curtis Joseph .50 1.25
62 Teppo Numminen .20 .50
63 Petr Nedved .20 .50
64 Doug Weight .40 1.00
65 Arturs Irbe .40 1.00
66 Chris Osgood .40 1.00
67 Jocelyn Thibault .40 1.00
68 Oleg Tverdovsky .20 .50
69 Derian Hatcher .20 .50
70 Ray Whitney .20 .50
71 Saku Koivu .50 1.25
72 Cliff Ronning .20 .50
73 Claude Lapointe .20 .50
74 Chris Simon .20 .50
75 Martin Rucinsky .20 .50
76 Valeri Bure .20 .50
77 Brad Isbister .20 .50
78 Roman Turek .40 1.00
79 Kenny Jonsson .20 .50
80 Mike Dunham .40 1.00
81 Rob Blake .40 1.00
82 Daniel Alfredsson .40 1.00
83 Tommy Salo .40 1.00
84 Sergei Samsonov .40 1.00
85 Joe Sakic 1.00 2.50
86 Bryan Smolinski .20 .50
87 Luc Robitaille .40 1.00
88 Mariusz Czerkawski .20 .50
89 Brendan Shanahan .50 1.25
90 Brian Rafalski .20 .50
91 Jamie Langenbrunner .20 .50
92 Peter Forsberg 1.25 3.00
93 Phil Housley .20 .50
94 Glen Murray .20 .50
95 Jeff Hackett .40 1.00
96 Sergei Fedorov .75 2.00
97 Sergei Zubov .20 .50
98 Martin Brodeur 1.25 3.00
99 Mike Grier .20 .50
100 Paul Coffey .50 1.25
101 Radek Bonk .20 .50
102 Milan Hejduk .50 1.25
103 Viktor Kozlov .40 1.00
104 Jason Arnott .20 .50
105 Brendan Morrison .40 1.00
106 Keith Tkachuk .50 1.25
107 Patrik Elias .40 1.00
108 Jochen Hecht .20 .50
109 Brian Leetch .40 1.00
110 Petr Sykora .20 .50
111 Dave Andreychuk .40 1.00
112 Steve Shields .40 1.00
113 Nikolai Antropov .20 .50
114 Martin Straka .20 .50
115 Eric Desjardins .40 1.00
116 Adam Oates .40 1.00
117 Adam Graves .20 .50
118 Jozef Stumpel .20 .50
119 Vincent Damphousse .20 .50
120 Maxim Afinogenov .20 .50
121 Chris Chelios .50 1.25
122 Joe Nieuwendyk .40 1.00
123 Petr Buzek .20 .50
124 Jeff Friesen .20 .50
125 Markus Naslund .50 1.25
126 Trevor Letowski .20 .50
127 Steve Thomas .20 .50
128 Jason Allison .20 .50
129 Jere Lehtinen .40 1.00
130 Tom Poti .20 .50
131 Eric Lindros .50 1.25
132 Rob Niedermayer .40 1.00
133 Gary Roberts .20 .50
134 Scott Gomez .20 .50
135 Pierre Turgeon .40 1.00
136 Trevor Kidd .40 1.00
137 Jan Hrdina .20 .50
138 John Madden .20 .50
139 Tim Connolly .20 .50
140 Pat Verbeek .20 .50
141 Jeff Halpern .20 .50
142 Patrick Marleau .40 1.00
143 Wade Redden .20 .50
144 Alex Tanguay .40 1.00
145 Darcy Tucker .20 .50
146 Simon Gagne .50 1.25
147 Brad Stuart .40 1.00
148 Jean-Sebastien Aubin .40 1.00
149 Mike Johnson .20 .50
150 Shayne Corson .20 .50
151 Michael Peca .20 .50
152 Keith Primeau .20 .50
153 Tie Domi .40 1.00
154 Brenden Morrow .40 1.00
155 Sandis Ozolinsh .20 .50
156 Mike Keane .20 .50
157 Patric Kjellberg .20 .50
158 Patrick Lalime .40 1.00
159 John Vanbiesbrouck .40 1.00
160 Andrew Cassels .20 .50
161 Scott Stephens HL .20 .50
162 Ed Belfour HL .50 1.25
163 Martin Brodeur HL .60 1.50
164 Mike Modano HL .40 1.00
165 Jason Arnott HL .20 .50
166 Roberto Luongo .60 1.50
167 Harold Druken .20 .50
168 Marc Denis .40 1.00
169 Oleg Saprykin .20 .50
170 Glen Metropolit .20 .50
171 Daniel Sedin .20 .50
172 Dmitri Yakushin .20 .50
173 Scott Hannan .20 .50
174 Dave Tanabe .20 .50
175 Jiri Fischer .20 .50
176 Dmitri Nabokov .20 .50
177 Ivan Novoseltsev .20 .50
178 Manny Fernandez .40 1.00
179 Maxim Balmochnykh .20 .50
180 Brian Campbell .20 .50
181 Sergei Varlamov .20 .50
182 Ville Nieminen RC 2.00 5.00
183 Colin White RC .75 2.00
184 Mike Fisher .20 .50
185 Matt Elich RC .75 2.00
186 Zenith Komarniski .20 .50
187 Eric Nickulas RC .75 2.00
188 Steven McCarthy .20 .50
189 Jason Krog .20 .50
190 Robert Esche .20 .50
191 Adam Mair .20 .50
192 Ladislav Nagy .20 .50
193 Sergei Vyshedkevich RC .75 2.00
194 Steve Begin .20 .50
195 Brad Ference .20 .50
196 Andy Delmore .20 .50
197 Brent Sopel RC .75 2.00
198 Evgeni Nabokov .40 1.00
199 David Gosselin RC .75 2.00
200 Tavis Hansen .20 .50
201 Ray Giroux .20 .50
202 Serge Aubin RC .75 2.00
203 Shane Willis .20 .50
204 Vitali Vishnevsky .20 .50
205 Richard Jackman .20 .50
206 Petr Schastlivy .20 .50
207 Ryan Bonni .20 .50
208 Alexei Tezikov .20 .50
209 Henrik Sedin .20 .50
210 Mike Ribeiro .20 .50
211 Darryl Laplante .20 .50
212 Kyle Calder .20 .50
213 Dimitri Kalinin .20 .50
214 Jean-Sebastien Giguere .20 .50
215 Willie Mitchell RC .75 2.00
216 Steve Valiquette RC .75 2.00
217 Brian Willsie .20 .50
218 Jarkko Ruutu .20 .50
219 Jon Sim .20 .50
220 Jonathan Girard .20 .50
221 Ron Tugnutt .40 1.00
222 Lyle Odelein .20 .50
223 Jean-Luc Grand-Pierre .20 .50
224 Geoff Sanderson .20 .50
225 Robert Kron .20 .50
226 Kevin Dineen .20 .50
227 Kevyn Adams .20 .50
228 Tyler Wright .20 .50
229 Jamie Pushor .20 .50
230 David Vyborny .20 .50
231 Jamie McLennan .20 .50
232 Jeff Nielsen .20 .50
233 Scott Pellerin .20 .50
234 Darby Hendrickson .20 .50
235 Jim Dowd .20 .50
236 Filip Kuba .20 .50
237 Stacy Roest .20 .50
238 Sean O'Donnell .20 .50
239 Aaron Gavey .20 .50
240 Sergei Krivokrasov .20 .50
241 Justin Williams RC 2.00 5.00
242 Marian Gaborik RC 8.00 20.00
243 Marty Turco RC 4.00 10.00
244 David Aebischer RC 3.00 8.00
245 Rostislav Klesla RC 2.50 6.00
246 Petr Hubacek RC 2.00 5.00
247 Scott Hartnell RC 2.00 5.00
248 Martin Havlat RC 3.00 8.00
249 Steven Reinprecht RC 2.00 5.00
250 Andrew Raycroft RC 3.00 8.00
251 Rick DiPietro RC 2.00 5.00

2000-01 Topps Chrome Blue

Randomly inserted in packs, this 11-card set parallels the base rookie cards from the Topps Chrome set, card numbers 241-251. Each card is enhanced with a blue border and is sequentially numbered to 1250.

*BLUE: SAME VALUE AS BASIC CARDS

2000-01 Topps Chrome Red

Randomly inserted in packs, this 11-card set parallels the base rookie cards from the Topps Chrome set, card numbers 241-251. Each card is enhanced with a red border and is sequentially numbered to 1250.

*REDS SAME VALUE AS BASIC CARDS

2000-01 Topps Chrome OPC Refractors

Randomly inserted in packs at the rate of 1:9 for card numbers 1-220, and 1:383 for card numbers 241-251, this 251-card set parallels the base Topps Chrome set enhanced with the O-Pee-Chee logo in the lower right hand corner and the rainbow holofoil refractor effect. Card numbers 241-251 are all sequentially numbered to 35.

*STARS: 1.5X TO 4X BASIC CARDS
*EXPANSION REF.: 1.5X TO 4X BASIC CARDS
*ROOKIE REF: 2X TO 4X BASIC CARDS

2000-01 Topps Chrome OPC Refractors Blue

Randomly inserted in packs at the rate of 1:383, this 11-card set parallels the last 11 cards in the base Topps Chrome set, card numbers 241-251. Each card is enhanced with a blue border, the rainbow holofoil refractor effect, and is sequentially numbered to 35.

*BLUE.OPC.REF.: 2X TO 4X BASIC CARDS

2000-01 Topps Chrome OPC Refractors Red

Randomly inserted in packs at the rate of 1:383, this 11-card set parallels the last 11 cards in the base Topps Chrome set, card numbers 241-251. Each card is enhanced with a red border, the rainbow holofoil refractor effect, and is sequentially numbered to 35.

*RED.OPC.REF.: 2X TO 4X BASIC CARDS

2000-01 Topps Chrome Refractors

Randomly inserted in packs at the rate of 1:9 for card numbers 1-220, and randomly inserted for card numbers 241-250, this 250-card set parallels the base Topps Chrome set enhanced with the Topps Chrome logo in one of the front lower corners and the rainbow holofoil refractor effect. Card numbers 241-251 are all sequentially numbered to 25.

*STARS: 2X TO 5X BASIC CARDS
*EXPANSION REF.: 1.5X TO 4X BASIC CARDS
*ROOKIE REF.: 3X TO 5X BASIC CARDS

2000-01 Topps Chrome Refractors Blue

Randomly inserted in packs, this 11-card set parallels the last 11 cards in the base Topps Chrome set, card numbers 241-251. Each card is enhanced with a blue border, the rainbow holofoil refractor effect, and is sequentially numbered to 25.

*BLUE REF.: 3X TO 5X BASIC CARDS

2000-01 Topps Chrome Refractors Red

Randomly inserted in packs, this 11-card set parallels the last 11 cards in the base Topps Chrome set, card numbers 241-251. Each card is enhanced with a red border, the rainbow holofoil refractor effect, and is sequentially numbered to 25.

*RED REF.: 3X TO 5X BASIC CARDS

2000-01 Topps Chrome Combos

Randomly inserted in packs at the rate of one in 20, this 10-card set features original artwork of two top NHL players. The bottom of the card has their names and a brief explanation why they are paired in a green box. Cards are printed on all chrome card stock. Refractor parallels of this set were also randomly inserted at 1:200.

COMPLETE SET (10) 15.00 40.00
TC1 Pavel Bure 1.00 2.50
Valeri Bure
TC2 Teemu Selanne 1.00 2.50
Paul Kariya
TC3 John LeClair 1.00 2.50
Tony Amonte
TC4 Curtis Joseph 2.00 5.00
Dominik Hasek
TC5 M.Modano/P.Forsberg 3.00 8.00
TC6 Raymond Bourque 2.00 5.00
Chris Pronger
TC7 Vincent Lecavalier 1.00 2.50
Joe Thornton
TC8 Patrick Roy 5.00 12.00
Martin Brodeur
TC9 S.Yzerman/B.Hull 4.00 10.00
TC10 Jaromir Jagr 4.00 10.00
Mario Lemieux

2000-01 Topps Chrome Hobby Masters Refractors

Randomly inserted in Hobby packs at the rate of 1:400, this 10-card set features a player photo with a diagonal line above the lower right hand corner with the player's name and the words "Hobby Master" in yellow. Backgrounds are enhanced with the rainbow holofoil refractor effect.

COMPLETE SET (10) 75.00 150.00
HM1 Martin Brodeur 10.00 25.00
HM2 Pavel Bure 6.00 15.00
HM3 Peter Forsberg 10.00 25.00
HM4 Dominik Hasek 8.00 20.00
HM5 Jaromir Jagr 6.00 15.00
HM6 Curtis Joseph 5.00 12.00
HM7 Paul Kariya 5.00 12.00
HM8 Mike Modano 5.00 12.00
HM9 Patrick Roy 20.00 50.00
HM10 Steve Yzerman 20.00 50.00

2000-01 Topps Chrome Mario Lemieux Reprints

Randomly inserted in packs at the rate of 1:18, this 23-card set features reprinted versions of Mario Lemieux's cards dating back to 85-86 Topps and OPC. Cards are printed on an all chrome card stock. Refractor parallels of this set were also randomly inserted at 1:180.

COMPLETE SET (23) 75.00 150.00

COMMON LEMIEUX (1-23) 4.00 10.00
COMMON LEM.REF. (1-23) 12.50 30.00

2000-01 Topps Chrome Rocket's Flare

Randomly inserted in packs at the rate of 1:14, this 10-card set features top players on a die cut card stock. The bottom of the card is red and the player's name appears in a black name box. A silver die cut "diamond shape" appears behind a full color player action photo. Refractor parallels of this set were also randomly inserted at 1:140.

COMPLETE SET (10) 10.00 20.00
*REFRACTORS: .8X TO 2X BASIC INSERTS
RF1 Pavel Bure 1.00 2.50
RF2 Paul Kariya 1.00 2.50
RF3 John LeClair 1.00 2.50
RF4 Jaromir Jagr 1.50 4.00
RF5 Luc Robitaille .75 2.00
RF6 Milan Hejduk 1.00 2.50
RF7 Tony Amonte .75 2.00
RF8 Patrik Elias .75 2.00
RF9 Miroslav Satan .75 2.00
RF10 Teemu Selanne 1.00 2.50

2000-01 Topps Chrome 1000 Point Club Refractors

Randomly inserted in Retail packs at the rate of 1:250, this 16-card set features 1000 point club members on an all holofoil refractor card. Player photos are in full color, and the words, "1000 Point Club" appear on the top of the card. Card numbers carry a "1000PC" prefix.

1 Mark Messier 5.00 12.00
2 Steve Yzerman 20.00 50.00
3 Ron Francis 3.00 8.00
4 Paul Coffey 4.00 10.00
5 Ray Bourque 8.00 20.00
6 Doug Gilmour 3.00 8.00
7 Adam Oates 3.00 8.00
8 Larry Murphy 3.00 8.00
9 Dave Andreychuk 3.00 8.00
10 Luc Robitaille 3.00 8.00
11 Phil Housley 3.00 8.00
12 Brett Hull 5.00 12.00
13 Al MacInnis 3.00 8.00
14 Pierre Turgeon 3.00 8.00
15 Joe Sakic 10.00 25.00
16 Pat Verbeek 3.00 8.00

2001-02 Topps Chrome

Released in late February 2002, this 182-card set carried an SRP of $3.00 for a 4-card pack. Cards were printed on a chromium card stock. Short printed rookie cards were inserted at 1:3. Update cards for 2001-02 Topps were also randomly seeded in packs at 1:3. Update cards are listed with the base Topps set.

COMPLETE SET (182) 200.00 400.00
1 Mario Lemieux 2.50 6.00
2 Steve Yzerman 2.00 5.00
3 Martin Brodeur 1.25 3.00
4 Brian Leetch .40 1.00
5 Tony Amonte .40 1.00
6 Bill Guerin .40 1.00
7 Olaf Kolzig .40 1.00
8 Pavel Bure .50 1.25
9 Patrick Marleau .40 1.00
10 Mariusz Czerkawski .20 .50
11 Teemu Selanne .50 1.25
12 Alex Tanguay .40 1.00
13 Keith Primeau .20 .50
14 Alexei Yashin .20 .50
15 Markus Naslund .50 1.25
16 Chris Pronger .40 1.00
17 Sergei Zubov .20 .50
18 Marian Gaborik 1.00 2.50
19 Mats Sundin .50 1.25
20 David Legwand .40 1.00
21 J-P Dumont .20 .50
22 Nicklas Lidstrom .50 1.25
23 Ron Francis .40 1.00
24 Doug Weight .40 1.00
25 Zigmund Palffy .40 1.00
26 Jason Allison .20 .50
27 Joe Sakic 1.00 2.50
28 Paul Kariya .50 1.25
29 Marian Hossa .50 1.25
30 Owen Nolan .40 1.00
31 Jason Arnott .20 .50
32 Jaromir Jagr .75 2.00
33 Claude Lemieux .20 .50
34 Peter Bondra .40 1.00
35 Chris Drury .40 1.00
36 Radek Bonk .20 .50
37 Theo Fleury .20 .50
38 Keith Tkachuk .50 1.25
39 Rick DiPietro .40 1.00
40 Ed Jovanovski .40 1.00
41 Scott Stevens .40 1.00
42 John LeClair .50 1.25
43 Ryan Smyth .20 .50
44 Vincent Lecavalier .50 1.25
45 Henrik Sedin .20 .50
46 David Aebischer .40 1.00
47 Patrick Roy 2.50 6.00
48 Valeri Bure .20 .50
49 Dominik Hasek 1.00 2.50
50 Ray Ferraro .20 .50
51 Milan Hejduk .50 1.25
52 Mike Modano .75 2.00
53 Sergei Fedorov .75 2.00
54 Luc Robitaille .40 1.00
55 Mark Messier .50 1.25
56 Sean Burke .40 1.00
57 Jeff Friesen .20 .50
58 Alexander Mogilny .40 1.00
59 Roman Cechmanek .40 1.00
60 Martin Straka .20 .50
61 Pavol Demitra .40 1.00
62 Curtis Joseph .50 1.25
63 Daniel Sedin .20 .50
64 Brad Richards .40 1.00
65 Simon Gagne .50 1.25
66 Saku Koivu .50 1.25
67 Eric Daze .40 1.00
68 Roberto Luongo .60 1.50
69 Brendan Shanahan .50 1.25
70 Espen Knutsen .20 .50
71 Rob Blake .40 1.00
72 Steve Sullivan .20 .50
73 Arturs Irbe .40 1.00
74 Maxim Afinogenov .20 .50
75 Dan Cloutier .40 1.00
76 Josef Vasicek .20 .50
77 Vincent Damphousse .20 .50
78 Robert Lang .20 .50
79 Pierre Turgeon .40 1.00
80 Gary Roberts .20 .50
81 Adam Oates .40 1.00
82 Evgeni Nabokov .40 1.00
83 Petr Nedved .20 .50
84 Mike Dunham .40 1.00
85 Chris Osgood .40 1.00
86 Brett Hull .60 1.50
87 Peter Forsberg 1.25 3.00
88 Joe Thornton .75 2.00
89 Marc Denis .40 1.00
90 Ed Belfour .50 1.25
91 Patrik Elias .40 1.00
92 Michael York .20 .50
93 Martin Havlat .40 1.00
94 Jeremy Roenick .60 1.50
95 Alexei Kovalev .40 1.00
96 Al MacInnis .40 1.00
97 Marco Sturm .20 .50
98 Jose Theodore .60 1.50
99 Joe Nieuwendyk .40 1.00
100 Darren McCarty .20 .50
101 Mark Recchi .40 1.00
102 Daniel Alfredsson .40 1.00
103 Miroslav Satan .40 1.00
104 Sergei Samsonov .40 1.00
105 Roman Turek .40 1.00
106 Jarome Iginla .60 1.50
107 Jeff O'Neill .20 .50
108 Tommy Salo .40 1.00
109 Petr Sykora .20 .50
110 Adam Deadmarsh .20 .50
111 Oleg Tverdovsky .20 .50
112 Sami Kapanen .20 .50
113 Scott Hartnell .20 .50
114 Jere Lehtinen .40 1.00
115 Darcy Tucker .20 .50
116 Stu Barnes .20 .50
117 Jim Dowd .20 .50
118 Derek Morris .20 .50
119 Felix Potvin .50 1.25
120 Manny Fernandez .40 1.00
121 Jason Smith .20 .50
122 Byron Dafoe .20 .50
123 Teppo Numminen .20 .50
124 Mike Richter .50 1.25
125 Anson Carter .40 1.00
126 Jocelyn Thibault .40 1.00
127 Dany Heatley .60 1.50
128 Marc Savard .20 .50
129 Brian Rolston .20 .50
130 Martin Biron .40 1.00
131 Mark Parrish .20 .50
132 Mike Peca .20 .50
133 Patrick Lalime .40 1.00
134 Eric Lindros .50 1.25
135 Brian Boucher .20 .50
136 Nikolai Khabibulin .50 1.25
137 John Madden .20 .50
138 Rostislav Klesla .20 .50
139 Mika Noronen .40 1.00
140 Kris Beech .20 .50
141 Miikka Kiprusoff .40 1.00
142 Mathieu Garon .40 1.00
143 Mark Bell .20 .50
144 Jussi Markkanen .40 1.00
145 Mike Comrie .40 1.00
146 Johan Hedberg .40 1.00
147 Andrew Raycroft .40 1.00
148 Daniel Corso .20 .50
149 Ilya Kovalchuk RC 6.00 15.00
150 Dan Blackburn RC 1.50 4.00
151 Vaclav Nedorost RC 1.50 4.00
152 Krys Kolanos RC 1.50 4.00
153 Kristian Huselius RC 1.50 4.00
154 Martin Erat RC 1.50 4.00
155 Timo Parssinen RC 1.50 4.00
156 Scott Nichol RC 1.50 4.00
157 Nick Schultz RC 1.50 4.00
158 Jukka Hentunen RC 1.50 4.00
159 Pascal Dupuis RC 1.50 4.00
160 Radek Martinek RC 1.50 4.00
161 Scott Clemmensen RC 1.50 4.00
162 Jeff Jillson RC 1.50 4.00
163 Brian Sutherby RC 1.50 4.00
164 Nikita Alexeev RC 1.50 4.00
165 Niklas Hagman RC 1.50 4.00
166 Erik Cole RC 1.50 4.00
167 Pavel Datsyuk RC 4.00 10.00
168 Ilja Bryzgalov RC 2.00 5.00
169 Chris Neil RC 1.50 4.00
170 Mark Rycroft RC 1.50 4.00
171 Kamil Piros RC 1.50 4.00
172 Niko Kapanen RC 1.50 4.00
173 Jiri Dopita RC 1.50 4.00
174 Andreas Salomonsson RC 1.50 4.00
175 Ivan Ciernik RC 1.50 4.00
176 Jaroslav Bednar RC 1.50 4.00
177 Ty Conklin RC 1.50 4.00
178 Richard Scott RC 1.50 4.00
179 Raffi Torres RC 2.00 5.00
180 Vaclav Pletka RC 1.50 4.00
181 Mikael Samuelsson RC 1.50 4.00
182 Mike Farrell RC 1.50 4.00

2001-02 Topps Chrome Refractors

This 182-cards set paralleled the base set with the rainbow holofoil refractor effect. Refractors were inserted at a rate of 1:6 packs.

*STARS: 1.5X TO 4X BASIC CARDS
*SP's: .75X TO 2X BASIC CARDS

2001-02 Topps Chrome Black Border Refractors

Serial-numbered to just 50 copies each, this 182-card set paralleled the base set with a rainbow holofoil refractor effect and black borders.

*STARS: 5X TO 12X BASIC CARD
*SP's: 1.5X TO 4X BASIC CARDS

2001-02 Topps Chrome Mario Lemieux Reprints

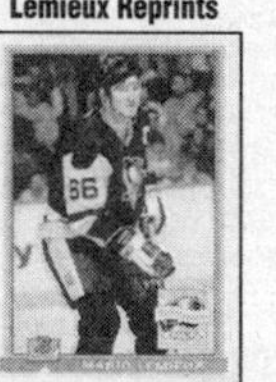

Inserted at 1:12, 10-card set featured reprints of past Topps cards of Mario Lemieux on chrome stock. Refractor parallels of this set were also created and inserted at 1:120.

COMPLETE SET (10) 30.00 60.00
COMMON LEMIEUX 3.00 8.00
*REFRACTORS: 1.25X TO 3X BASIC CARD

2001-02 Topps Chrome Mario Returns

This 5-card set highlighted the return of Mario Lemieux to the NHL. Cards from this set were inserted at odds of 1:24. Refractor parallels of this set were also created and inserted at 1:240.

COMPLETE SET (5) 25.00 50.00
COMMON LEMIEUX (MR1-MR5) 4.00 10.00
REFRACTORS: 1.25X TO 3X BASIC CARD

2001-02 Topps Chrome Reprints

This 10-card set featured rookie card reprints of past greats on chrome stock. Cards from this set were inserted at 1:12 packs. A refractor parallel was also created and inserted at 1:120

COMPLETE SET (10) 15.00 40.00
*REFRACTORS: 1.25X TO 3X BASIC CARD
1 Billy Smith 2.00 5.00
2 Wayne Cashman 2.00 5.00
3 Barry Melrose 2.00 5.00
4 Bernie Federko 2.00 5.00
5 Neal Broten 2.00 5.00
6 Bill Clement 2.00 5.00
7 Guy Lapointe 2.00 5.00
8 Bernie Parent 2.00 5.00
9 Larry Robinson 2.00 5.00
10 Ken Hodge 2.00 5.00

2001-02 Topps Chrome Reprint Autographs

Inserted at 1:247, this 10-card set paralleled the reprints set but was enhanced with authentic autographs of the featured players. Card backs carried a Topps authentic sticker.

1 Billy Smith 12.50 30.00
2 Wayne Cashman 12.50 30.00
3 Barry Melrose 15.00 40.00
4 Bernie Federko 12.50 30.00
5 Neal Broten 12.50 30.00
6 Bill Clement 12.50 30.00
7 Guy Lapointe 12.50 30.00
8 Bernie Parent 20.00 50.00
9 Larry Robinson 15.00 40.00
10 Ken Hodge 12.50 30.00

2002 Topps Chrome All-Star Fantasy

Available as wrapper redemptions from the Topps booth at the NHL All-Star Fantasy in Los Angeles, this 6-card set featured players involved in All-Star events. Each card was numbered "x of 6" on the card back. The card front carried the All-Star logo.

COMPLETE SET (6) 6.00 15.00
1 Paul Kariya 1.20 3.00
2 Zigmund Palffy .40 1.00
3 Joe Sakic 1.20 3.00
4 Jaromir Jagr 1.20 3.00
5 Dominik Hasek .80 2.00
6 Ilya Kovalchuk 2.00 5.00

2002-03 Topps Chrome

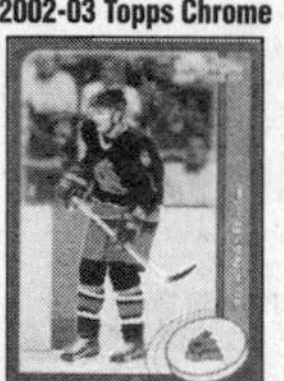

Released in February, this 181-card set consisted of 148 base veteran cards and 33 shortprinted rookie cards. Rookies were inserted at 1:3.

COMPLETE SET (182) 150.00 300.00
COMMON RC (149-182) 2.00 5.00
1 Patrick Roy 2.50 6.00
2 Mario Lemieux 3.00 8.00
3 Martin Brodeur 1.25 3.00
4 Steve Yzerman 2.50 6.00
5 Jaromir Jagr .75 2.00
6 Chris Pronger .40 1.00
7 John LeClair .50 1.25
8 Paul Kariya .50 1.25
9 Tony Amonte .40 1.00
10 Joe Thornton .75 2.00
11 Ilya Kovalchuk .60 1.50
12 Jarome Iginla .60 1.50
13 Mike Modano .75 2.00
14 Vincent Lecavalier .50 1.25
15 Michael Peca .20 .50
16 Pavel Bure .50 1.25
17 Eric Lindros .50 1.25
18 Felix Potvin .50 1.25
19 Ron Francis .40 1.00
20 Miroslav Satan .40 1.00
21 Rostislav Klesla .20 .50
22 Mike Comrie .40 1.00
23 Daniel Alfredsson .40 1.00
24 Sean Burke .40 1.00
25 David Legwand .40 1.00
26 Marian Gaborik 1.00 2.50
27 Saku Koivu .50 1.25
28 Owen Nolan .40 1.00
29 Mats Sundin .50 1.25
30 J-P Dumont .20 .50
31 Chris Drury .40 1.00
32 Markus Naslund .50 1.25
33 Anson Carter .40 1.00
34 Daniel Briere .20 .50
35 Keith Tkachuk .50 1.25
36 Mark Recchi .40 1.00
37 Marc Denis .40 1.00
38 Sergei Fedorov .75 2.00
39 Andrew Brunette .20 .50
40 Martin Havlat .40 1.00
41 Brian Leetch .40 1.00
42 Erik Cole .20 .50
43 Patrick Lalime .40 1.00
44 Patrick Marleau .40 1.00
45 Ryan Smyth .20 .50
46 Sami Kapanen .20 .50
47 Martin Straka .20 .50
48 Peter Forsberg 1.25 3.00
49 Jeff Friesen .20 .50
50 Manny Fernandez .40 1.00
51 Scott Stevens .40 1.00
52 Radim Vrbata .20 .50
53 Marty Turco .40 1.00
54 Kristian Huselius .20 .50
55 Jeremy Roenick .60 1.50
56 Gary Roberts .20 .50
57 Chris Chelios .50 1.25
58 Brett Hull .60 1.50
59 Eric Daze .40 1.00
60 Alex Tanguay .40 1.00
61 Simon Gagne .50 1.25
62 Roman Turek .40 1.00
63 Milan Hejduk .50 1.25
64 Mariusz Czerkawski .20 .50
65 Dan Cloutier .40 1.00
66 Teemu Selanne .50 1.25
67 Johan Hedberg .40 1.00
68 Mike Ricci .20 .50
69 Roberto Luongo .60 1.50
70 Zigmund Palffy .40 1.00
71 Ed Jovanovski .40 1.00
72 Scott Gomez .20 .50
73 Pierre Turgeon .40 1.00
74 Martin Biron .40 1.00
75 Keith Primeau .20 .50
76 Jean-Sebastien Giguere .40 1.00
77 Alexei Zhamnov .20 .50
78 Brent Johnson .40 1.00
79 Dan Blackburn .40 1.00
80 Mike Richter .50 1.25
81 Peter Bondra .40 1.00
82 Rod Brind'Amour .40 1.00
83 Shane Doan .20 .50
84 Sergei Samsonov .40 1.00
85 Nikolai Khabibulin .50 1.25
86 Roman Cechmanek .40 1.00
87 Glen Murray .20 .50
88 Brad Richards .40 1.00
89 Alexei Kovalev .40 1.00
90 Adam Deadmarsh .20 .50
91 Brendan Morrison .40 1.00
92 Jason Arnott .20 .50
93 Brenden Morrow .40 1.00
94 Pavol Demitra .40 1.00
95 Olaf Kolzig .40 1.00
96 Doug Gilmour .40 1.00
97 Jere Lehtinen .40 1.00
98 Petr Sykora .20 .50
99 Wade Redden .20 .50
100 Adam Oates .40 1.00
101 Chris Osgood .40 1.00
102 Espen Knutsen .20 .50
103 Maxim Afinogenov .20 .50
104 Steve Sullivan .20 .50
105 Robert Lang .20 .50
106 Milan Hnilicka .40 1.00
107 Craig Conroy .20 .50
108 Alexander Mogilny .40 1.00
109 Jose Theodore .60 1.50
110 Mike Dunham .40 1.00
111 Joe Sakic 1.00 2.50
112 Al MacInnis .40 1.00
113 Marian Hossa .50 1.25
114 Rob Blake .40 1.00
115 Dany Heatley .60 1.50
116 Scott Hartnell .20 .50
117 Krys Kolanos .20 .50
118 Vincent Damphousse .20 .50
119 Curtis Joseph .50 1.25
120 Todd Bertuzzi .50 1.25
121 Tommy Salo .40 1.00
122 Jocelyn Thibault .40 1.00
123 Nicklas Lidstrom .50 1.25
124 Bryan McCabe .20 .50
125 Bill Guerin .40 1.00
126 Luc Robitaille .40 1.00
127 Alexei Yashin .20 .50
128 Evgeni Nabokov .40 1.00
129 Pavel Datsyuk .50 1.25
130 Stu Barnes .20 .50
131 Derek Morris .20 .50
132 Jason Allison .20 .50
133 Mark Messier .50 1.25
134 Ed Belfour .50 1.25
135 Scott Young .20 .50
136 Marco Sturm .20 .50
137 Arturs Irbe .40 1.00
138 Joe Nieuwendyk .40 1.00
139 Sergei Gonchar .20 .50
140 Doug Weight .40 1.00
141 Jeff O'Neill .20 .50
142 Mike York .20 .50
143 Patrik Elias .40 1.00
144 Brendan Shanahan .50 1.25
145 Rick DiPietro .40 1.00
146 Jani Rita .20 .50
147 Stephen Weiss .20 .50
148 Nikita Alexeev .20 .50
149 Micki DuPont RC 2.00 5.00
150 Ivan Majesky RC 2.00 5.00
151 Jason Spezza RC 6.00 15.00
152 Eric Godard RC 2.00 5.00
153 Shawn Thornton RC 2.00 5.00
154 Jeff Paul RC 2.00 5.00
155 Lasse Pirjeta RC 2.00 5.00
156 Adam Hall RC 2.00 5.00
157 Mikael Tellqvist RC 2.00 5.00
158 Tomi Pettinen RC 2.00 5.00
159 Radovan Somik RC 2.00 5.00
160 Jordan Leopold RC 2.00 5.00
161 Dmitri Bykov RC 2.00 5.00
162 Tim Thomas RC 3.00 8.00
163 Martin Gerber RC 3.00 8.00
164 Tom Koivisto RC 2.00 5.00
165 Patrick Sharp RC 2.00 5.00
166 Steve Eminger RC 2.00 5.00
167 Anton Volchenkov RC 2.00 5.00
168 Scottie Upshall RC 2.00 5.00
169 Ron Hainsey RC 2.00 5.00
170 Kurt Sauer RC 2.00 5.00
171 Jeff Taffe RC 2.00 5.00
172 Dennis Seidenberg RC 2.00 5.00
173 Stanislav Chistov RC 2.00 5.00
174 Chuck Kobasew RC 2.00 5.00
175 Rick Nash RC 6.00 15.00
176 Ales Hemsky RC 4.00 10.00
177 Jay Bouwmeester RC 3.00 8.00
178 Alexei Smirnov RC 2.00 5.00
179 Alexander Svitov RC 2.00 5.00
180 P-M Bouchard RC 3.00 8.00
181 Alexander Frolov RC 4.00 10.00
182 Henrik Zetterberg RC 5.00 12.00

2002-03 Topps Chrome Black Border Refractors

Inserted at 1:20, these refractor parallels mirrored the base set but carried black borders. Cards were serial-numbered to 100 copies each.

*STARS: 2.5X TO 6X BASIC CARD
*SP's: 1.25X TO 3X

2002-03 Topps Chrome Refractors

*STARS: 1.25X TO 3X BASIC CARDS
*SP's: .75X TO 2X

2002-03 Topps Chrome e-Topps Decoy Cards

This 6-card set was inserted into packs of Topps Chrome as decoy cards to discourage pack searching. The cards advertised the upcoming release of 2003 e-Topps and pictured different player's e-Topps cards.

1 Jarome Iginla .30 .75
2 Pavel Bure .30 .75
3 Patrick Roy .30 .75
4 Mats Sundin .30 .75
5 Jaromir Jagr .30 .75
6 Martin Brodeur .30 .75

2002-03 Topps Chrome Chromographs

Inserted at 1:134, this 6-card set carried authentic player autographs.

CGBG Brian Gionta 4.00 10.00
CGBR Brad Richards 6.00 15.00
CGCJ Curtis Joseph 15.00 40.00
CGEC Erik Cole 4.00 10.00
CGRV Radim Vrbata 4.00 10.00
CGSW Stephen Weiss 4.00 10.00

2002-03 Topps Chrome Chromograph Refractors

*REFRACTORS: 1X TO 2.5X BASIC AUTO
STATED ODDS 1:1205

2002-03 Topps Chrome First Round Fabric Patches

This 9-card set featured swatches of game jersey patches. Cards were serial-numbered to 50 copies each.

ALL CARDS CARRY FRFP PREFIX
DB Dan Blackburn 12.50 30.00
EL Eric Lindros 15.00 40.00
JP J-P Dumont 12.50 30.00
KP Keith Primeau 12.50 30.00
MB Martin Biron 12.50 30.00
MM Mike Modano 30.00 80.00
MN Markus Naslund 15.00 40.00
MS Mats Sundin 15.00 40.00
PM Patrick Marleau 12.50 30.00
RD Radek Dvorak 12.50 30.00
SN Scott Niedermayer 12.50 30.00

2002-03 Topps Chrome Patrick Roy Reprints

COMPLETE SET (25) 25.00 50.00
STATED ODDS 1:6
1 1986-87 Topps 1.00 2.50
2 1987-88 Topps 1.00 2.50
3 1988-89 Topps 1.00 2.50
4 1989-90 Topps 1.00 2.50
5 1990-91 Topps 1.00 2.50
6 1991-92 Topps 1.00 2.50
7 1992-93 Topps 1.00 2.50
8 1993-94 Premier 1.00 2.50
9 1994-95 Premier 1.00 2.50
10 1995-96 Topps 1.00 2.50
11 1998-99 Topps 1.00 2.50
12 1999-00 Topps 1.00 2.50
13 2000-01 Topps 1.00 2.50
14 2001-02 Topps 1.00 2.50
15 1986-87 OPC 1.00 2.50
16 1987-88 OPC 1.00 2.50
17 1988-89 OPC 1.00 2.50
18 1989-90 OPC 1.00 2.50
19 1990-91 OPC 1.00 2.50
20 1991-92 OPC 1.00 2.50
21 1992-93 OPC 1.00 2.50

22 1998-99 OPC 1.00 2.50
23 1999-00 OPC 1.00 2.50
24 2000-01 OPC 1.00 2.50
25 2001-02 OPC 1.00 2.50

2002-03 Topps Chrome Patrick Roy Reprints Refractors

*REFRACTOR: 2X TO 5X BASIC CARD

2002-03 Topps Chrome Patrick Roy Reprint Autographs

Inserted at 1:904 and serial-numbered to 400 copies each, this 2-card set carried certified autographs of Patrick Roy on reprints of his rookie cards.

COMMON CARD 40.00 80.00
COA Patrick Roy OPC 40.00 80.00
CTA Patrick Roy TOPPS 40.00 80.00

2002-03 Topps Chrome Patrick Roy Reprint Autograph Refractors

Inserted at 1:11,452, this 2-card set paralleled the basic autograph set on refractor card fronts. Each card was serial-numbered out of 33.

*REFRACTOR: 1.5X TO 4X BASIC AUTOGRAPH
COA Patrick Roy OPC 125.00 300.00
CTA Patrick Roy Topps 125.00 300.00

2002-03 Topps Chrome Patrick Roy Reprint Relics

This 4-card set featured jersey or patch swatches affixed to reprints of Roy's rookie cards. Jersey swatches were inserted at 1:1446 and patch swatches were inserted at 1:19,376. Jersey cards were serial-numbered to 250 and patches to 10. Patch cards are not priced due to scarcity.

PRJO1 Patrick Roy OPC Jersey 25.00 60.00
PRJT1 Patrick Roy Topps Jersey 25.00 60.00
PRP1 Patrick Roy OPC Patch
PRPT1 Patrick Roy Topps Patch

2002-03 Topps Chrome Patrick Roy Reprint Relics Refractors

Inserted at a rate of 1:5812, this 2-card set paralleled the base jersey cards on a refractor card front. Cards were serial-numbered to just 33 copies each.

PRJO1 Patrick Roy OPC Jersey 75.00 200.00
PRJT1 Patrick Roy Topps Jersey 75.00 200.00

1998-99 Topps Gold Label Class 1

This 100-card set features color player photos printed on 35-point spectral-reflective rainbow polycarbonate stock with gold stamping. Each card showcases an NHL player on three different versions of his base card. Displayed in the foreground of the Class 1 set is a photo of the player with an action shot appearing in the background featuring players skating and goalies standing upright. Three parallel versions of the Class 1 set were also produced: The Black Label Parallel with the Black Topps Gold Label logo inserted at 1:18, the Red Label Parallel identified by the Red Topps Gold Label logo and sequentially numbered to 100 (inserted 1:73), and the One of One Parallel printed on special silver foil backs and numbered 1 of 1.

COMPLETE SET (100) 40.00 80.00
*CLASS I BLACK VETS: 2X TO 5X BASIC CARDS
*CLASS I BLACK ROOKIES: 1.2X TO 3X
*CLASS I RED VETS: 10X TO 25X BASIC CARDS
*CLASS 1 RED ROOKIES: 8X TO 20X
UNPRICED ONE-OF-ONE OVERALL ODDS 1:787
1 Brendan Shanahan .50 1.25
2 Mike Modano .75 2.00
3 Chris Chelios .50 1.25
4 Wayne Gretzky 3.00 8.00
5 Jaromir Jagr .75 2.00
6 Mark Messier .50 1.25
7 Teemu Selanne .50 1.25
8 Theo Fleury .10 .30
9 Ray Bourque .75 2.00
10 Martin Brodeur 1.25 3.00
11 Alexei Yashin .10 .30
12 Keith Tkachuk .50 1.25
13 Eric Lindros .50 1.25
14 Owen Nolan .40 1.00
15 Al MacInnis .40 1.00
16 Peter Bondra .40 1.00
17 Saku Koivu .50 1.25
18 Doug Weight .40 1.00
19 Robert Reichel .10 .30
20 Sergei Fedorov .75 2.00
21 Peter Forsberg 1.25 3.00
22 Ron Francis .40 1.00
23 Dimitri Khristich .10 .30
24 Ed Belfour .50 1.25
25 Oleg Kvasha RC .50 1.25
26 Ray Whitney .10 .30
27 Kenny Jonsson .10 .30
28 Randy McKay .10 .30
29 Pavol Demitra .40 1.00
30 Pierre Turgeon .40 1.00
31 Steve Yzerman 2.50 6.00
32 Ryan Smyth .40 1.00
33 Tony Amonte .40 1.00
34 Dominik Hasek 1.00 2.50
35 Jarome Iginla .60 1.50
36 Sami Kapanen .10 .30
37 Patrik Elias .40 1.00
38 Daniel Cleary .10 .30
39 Curtis Joseph .50 1.25
40 Joe Juneau .10 .30
41 Adam Graves .10 .30
42 Trevor Linden .40 1.00
43 Olli Jokinen .40 1.00
44 Joe Nieuwendyk .40 1.00
45 Sergei Samsonov .40 1.00
46 Rico Fata .10 .30
47 Mark Recchi .40 1.00
48 Rick Tocchet .40 1.00
49 Chris Pronger .40 1.00
50 Jason Allison .10 .30
51 Paul Kariya .50 1.25
52 Stu Barnes .10 .30
53 Mats Sundin .50 1.25
54 Mike Richter .50 1.25
55 Cliff Ronning .10 .30
56 Keith Primeau .10 .30
57 Guy Hebert .40 1.00
58 Nicklas Lidstrom .50 1.25
59 John Vanbiesbrouck .40 1.00
60 Jeff Friesen .10 .30
61 Vincent Lecavalier 1.00 2.50
62 Alexander Mogilny .40 1.00
63 Olaf Kolzig .40 1.00
64 Doug Gilmour .40 1.00
65 Joe Sakic 1.00 2.50
66 Mike Johnson .10 .30
67 Vincent Damphousse .10 .30
68 Eric Brewer .10 .30
69 Daniel Alfredsson .40 1.00
70 Nikolai Khabibulin .40 1.00
71 Marco Sturm .10 .30
72 Marty Reasoner .40 1.00
73 Bill Muckalt RC .10 .30
74 Pavel Bure .50 1.25
75 Bill Guerin .10 .30
76 Chris Osgood .40 1.00
77 Patrick Roy 2.50 6.00
78 Tom Barrasso .40 1.00
79 Alyn McCauley .10 .30
80 Adam Oates .40 1.00
81 Joe Thornton .75 2.00
82 Brendan Morrison .40 1.00
83 Mike Dunham .40 1.00
84 Jeremy Roenick .60 1.50
85 Brian Leetch .50 1.25
86 John LeClair .50 1.25
87 Mattias Ohlund .40 1.00
88 Wade Redden .10 .30
89 Mark Parrish RC 1.25 3.00
90 Milan Hejduk RC 1.25 3.00
91 Michael Peca .40 1.00
92 Brett Hull .60 1.50
93 Manny Malhotra .10 .30
94 Patrick Marleau .40 1.00
95 Grant Fuhr .40 1.00
96 Rob Blake .40 1.00
97 Damian Rhodes .40 1.00
98 Eric Daze .40 1.00
99 Rod Brind'Amour .40 1.00
100 Scott Stevens .40 1.00

1998-99 Topps Gold Label Class 2

Randomly inserted into packs at the rate of one in six, this 100-card set features color player photos printed on 35-point spectral-reflective rainbow polycarbonate stock with gold stamping. Each card showcases an NHL player on three different version of his base card. Displayed in the foreground of the Class 2 set is a photo of the player with an action shot appearing in the background featuring players shooting and goalies sprawling. Three parallel versions of this set were also produced: The Black Label Parallel with the Black Topps Gold Label logo inserted at a rate 1:36, the Red Label Parallel identified by the Red Topps Gold Label logo and sequentially numbered to 50 (inserted at 1:146), and the One to One Parallel printed on special silver foil backs and numbered 1 of 1.

COMPLETE SET (100) 100.00 200.00
*CLASS 2: 1X TO 2.5X BASIC CLASS 1
*CLASS 2 BLACK: 1.5X TO 4X BASIC CLASS 1
*CLASS 2 RED: 15X TO 40X BASIC CLASS 1
UNPRICED ONE-OF-ONE OVERALL ODDS 1:787

1998-99 Topps Gold Label Class 3

Randomly inserted into packs at the rate of 1:12, this 100-card set features color player photos printed on 35-point spectral-reflective rainbow polycarbonate stock with gold stamping. Each card showcases an NHL player on three different version of his base card. Displayed in the foreground of the Class 3 set is a photo of the player with an action shot appearing in the background featuring players celebrating and goalies with their masks off. Three parallel versions of this set were also produced: The Black Label Parallel with the Black Topps Gold Label logo, the Red Label Parallel identified by the Red Topps Gold Label logo and sequentially numbered to 25 (inserted at 1:293) and the One to One Parallel printed on special silver foil backs and numbered 1 of 1.

COMPLETE SET (100) 150.00 300.00
*CLASS 3: 1.5X TO 4X BASIC CLASS 1
*CLASS 3 BLACK: 5X TO 12X BASIC CLASS 1
*CLASS 3 RED: 60X TO 150X BASIC CLASS 1
UNPRICED ONE-OF-ONE OVERALL ODDS 1:787

1998-99 Topps Gold Label Goal Race '99

Randomly inserted in packs at the rate of 1:18, this 10-card set features color action photos of the top players who strike fear in the hearts of goalies night after night. Three parallel versions of this set were also produced: Black Label Parallel with the Black Topps Gold Label logo and insertion rate of 1:54; Red Label Parallel with the Red Topps Gold Label logo, insertion rate of 1:795, and sequentially numbered to 92; and One of One parallel version printed on special silver foil backs and sequentially numbered 1 of 1.

*BLACK: 1.25X TO 2.5X BASIC INSERTS
*RED: 3X TO 8X BASIC INSERTS
GR1 Eric Lindros 2.50 6.00
GR2 John LeClair 2.50 6.00
GR3 Teemu Selanne 2.50 6.00
GR4 Paul Kariya 2.50 6.00
GR5 Jaromir Jagr 4.00 10.00
GR6 Keith Tkachuk 2.50 6.00
GR7 Theo Fleury 2.50 6.00
GR8 Brendan Shanahan 2.50 6.00
GR9 Tony Amonte 2.00 5.00
GR10 Joe Sakic 5.00 12.00

1999-00 Topps Gold Label Class 1

This 100-card set features color player photos printed on 35-point spectral-reflective rainbow polycarbonate stock with gold stamping. Each card showcases an NHL player on three different versions of his base card. Displayed in the foreground of the Class 1 set is a photo of the player with an action shot appearing in the background featuring players skating and goalies standing upright. Three parallel versions of this set were also produced: The Black Label Parallel with the Black Topps Gold Label logo (inserted 1:18), the Red Label Parallel identified by the Red Topps Gold Label logo and sequentially numbered to 100 (inserted 1:32), and the One to One Parallel numbered 1 of 1.

COMPLETE SET (100) 30.00 60.00
*CLASS 1 BLACK VETS: 2.5X TO 6X BASIC CARDS
*CLASS 1 BLACK ROOKIES: 1.2X TO 3X
CLASS 1 BLACK STATED ODDS 1:18
*CLASS 1 RED VETS: 15X TO 40X BASIC CARDS
*CLASS 1 RED ROOKIES: 8X TO 20X
CLASS 1 RED/100 STATED ODDS 1:32
NINE UNPRICED 1 OF 1 PARALLELS ISSUED
1 Dominik Hasek .75 2.00
2 Al MacInnis .30 .75
3 Luc Robitaille .30 .75
4 Steve Yzerman 2.00 5.00
5 Michael Peca .30 .75
6 Keith Tkachuk .40 1.00
7 Saku Koivu .40 1.00
8 Tony Amonte .30 .75
9 Peter Bondra .30 .75
10 Pavel Bure .40 1.00
11 Ron Francis .30 .75
12 Eric Lindros .40 1.00
13 Paul Kariya .40 1.00
14 Theo Fleury .08 .25
15 Jaromir Jagr .60 1.50
16 Patrick Roy 2.00 5.00
17 Zigmund Palffy .30 .75
18 Ed Belfour .40 1.00
19 Sergei Samsonov .30 .75
20 Nicklas Lidstrom .40 1.00
21 Pavol Demitra .30 .75
22 Sergei Fedorov .60 1.50
23 Teemu Selanne .40 1.00
24 Martin Brodeur 1.00 2.50
25 John LeClair .40 1.00
26 Ray Bourque .60 1.50
27 Peter Forsberg 1.00 2.50
28 Doug Weight .30 .75
29 Brian Leetch .40 1.00
30 Mark Recchi .30 .75
31 Jason Allison .08 .25
32 Rob Blake .30 .75
33 Scott Niedermayer .08 .25
34 Chris Pronger .30 .75
35 Joe Sakic .75 2.00
36 Mark Messier .40 1.00
37 Daniel Alfredsson .30 .75
38 Guy Hebert .30 .75
39 Bobby Holik .08 .25
40 Joe Thornton .60 1.50
41 Ron Tugnutt .30 .75
42 Jeff Friesen .08 .25
43 Jeremy Roenick .50 1.25
44 Wade Redden .08 .25
45 Chris Osgood .30 .75
46 Arturs Irbe .30 .75
47 Valeri Bure .08 .25
48 Chris Drury .30 .75
49 Owen Nolan .30 .75
50 Kenny Jonsson .08 .25
51 Petr Sykora .08 .25
52 Byron Dafoe .30 .75
53 Brett Hull .50 1.25
54 Mike Richter .40 1.00
55 Brendan Shanahan .40 1.00
56 Mats Sundin .40 1.00
57 Miroslav Satan .30 .75
58 Markus Naslund .40 1.00
59 Rod Brind'Amour .30 .75
60 Joe Nieuwendyk .30 .75
61 Petr Nedved .30 .75
62 Sergei Berezin .30 .75
63 Trevor Linden .30 .75
64 Marian Hossa .40 1.00
65 Pierre Turgeon .30 .75
66 Vincent Lecavalier .40 1.00
67 Sami Kapanen .08 .25
68 Andrew Brunette .08 .25
69 Brian Savage .08 .25
70 Derian Hatcher .08 .25
71 Curtis Joseph .40 1.00
72 Scott Stevens .30 .75
73 Radek Bonk .08 .25
74 Jarome Iginla .50 1.25
75 Adam Graves .08 .25
76 Alexander Selivanov .08 .25
77 Alexander Mogilny .30 .75
78 Cliff Ronning .30 .75
79 Vincent Damphousse .30 .75
80 Alexei Kovalev .08 .25
81 Yanic Perreault .08 .25
82 Alexander Korolyuk .08 .25
83 Jozef Stumpel .08 .25
84 Viktor Kozlov .08 .25
85 Mike Modano .60 1.50
86 David Legwand .30 .75
87 Scott Gomez .08 .25
88 Tim Connolly .08 .25
89 Brad Stuart .30 .75
90 Peter Schaefer .08 .25
91 Alex Tanguay .30 .75
92 Simon Gagne .40 1.00
93 Dave Tanabe .08 .25
94 Roberto Luongo .50 1.25
95 Martin Biron .30 .75
96 Mike Fisher RC .50 1.25
97 Patrik Stefan RC 1.25 3.00
98 Nikolai Antropov RC .75 2.00
99 Jochen Hecht RC 1.00 2.50
100 Steve Kariya RC .50 1.25

1999-00 Topps Gold Label Class 2

Randomly inserted into packs, this 100-card set features color player photos printed on 35-point spectral-reflective rainbow polycarbonate stock with gold stamping. Each card showcases an NHL player on three different version of his base card. Displayed in the foreground of the Class 2 set is a photo of the player with an action shot appearing in the background featuring players shooting and goalies sprawling. Three parallel versions of this set were also produced: The Black Label Parallel with the Black Topps Gold Label logo, the Red Label Parallel identified by the Red Topps Gold Label logo and sequentially numbered to 50, and the One to One Parallel numbered 1 of 1.

COMPLETE SET (100) 75.00 150.00
*CLASS 2: 1X TO 2.5X CLASS 1
*CLASS 2 BLACK VETS: 5X TO 12X CLASS 1
*CLASS 2 BLACK ROOKIES: 3X TO 8X
*CLASS 2 RED VETS: 25X TO 60X CLASS 1
*CLASS 2 RED ROOKIES: 15X TO 40X
CLASS 2 RED/50 STATED ODDS 1:84

1999-00 Topps Gold Label Class 3

Randomly inserted into packs this 100-card set features color player photos printed on 35-point spectral-reflective rainbow polycarbonate stock with gold stamping. Each card showcases an NHL player on three different version of his base card. Displayed in the foreground of the Class 3 set is a photo of the player with an action shot appearing in the background featuring players celebrating and goalies with their masks off. Three parallel versions of this set were also produced: The Black Label Parallel with the Black Topps Gold Label logo (inserted 1:72), the Red Label Parallel identified by the Red Topps Gold Label logo and sequentially numbered to 25 (inserted 1:129) and the One to One Parallel numbered 1 of 1.

COMPLETE SET (100) 150.00 300.00
*CLASS 3: 1.5X TO 4X CLASS 1
*CLASS 3 BLACK VETS: 20X TO 50X CLASS 1
*CLASS 3 BLACK ROOKIES: 5X TO 12X
*CLASS 3 RED VETS: 50X TO 120X CLASS 1
*CLASS 3 RED ROOKISE: 15X TO 40X

1999-00 Topps Gold Label Fresh Gold

Randomly inserted in packs at one in 30, this 20-card set focuses on young stars looking to make their mark on the game. Each card features an action foreground shot and a silhouette background shot. Black and Red Label parallels of this set were also randomly inserted in packs. Black parallels were inserted at 1:150 and were red parallels were inserted at 1:644 and serial numbered to 25. Card backs carry an "FG" prefix.

COMPLETE SET (20) 15.00 30.00
*BLACK: 1.5X TO 4X BASIC INSERTS
*RED: 10X TO 25X BASIC INSERTS
UNPRICED 1/1 GOLD, BLACK, RED ISSUED
FG1 Sergei Samsonov .75 2.00
FG2 Joe Thornton 2.00 5.00
FG3 Wade Redden .75 2.00
FG4 Chris Drury .75 2.00
FG5 Petr Sykora .75 2.00
FG6 Patrik Stefan 2.00 5.00
FG7 Anson Carter .75 2.00
FG8 Martin Biron .75 2.00
FG9 Alex Tanguay .75 2.00
FG10 Milan Hejduk 1.25 3.00
FG11 Mark Parrish .75 2.00
FG12 David Legwand .75 2.00
FG13 Brendan Morrison .75 2.00
FG14 Scott Gomez .75 2.00
FG15 Tim Connolly 1.25 3.00
FG16 Marian Hossa 1.25 3.00
FG17 Jan Hrdina .75 2.00
FG18 Steve Kariya .75 2.00
FG19 Jochen Hecht 1.50 4.00
FG20 Vincent Lecavalier 1.25 3.00

1999-00 Topps Gold Label Prime Gold

Randomly inserted in packs at one in 20, this 15-card set showcases 15 veterans who have set their own standards, and have influenced how future players will be evaluated. The foreground features a full color action shot that is set against a silhouette background shot. Black and Red label parallels were also released of this set. Black parallels were inserted at 1:100 and were red parallels were inserted at 1:859 and serial numbered to 25. Card backs carry a "PG" prefix.

COMPLETE SET (15) 30.00 60.00
*BLACK: 1.5X TO 4X BASIC CARDS
*RED/25: 10X TO 25X BASIC CARDS
UNPRICED 1/1 GOLD, BLACK, RED ISSUED
PG1 Dominik Hasek 3.00 8.00
PG2 Paul Kariya 1.50 4.00
PG3 Theo Fleury 1.25 3.00
PG4 Jaromir Jagr 2.50 6.00
PG5 Zigmund Palffy 1.25 3.00
PG6 Nicklas Lidstrom 1.50 4.00
PG7 Teemu Selanne 1.50 4.00
PG8 John LeClair 1.50 4.00
PG9 Ray Bourque 2.50 6.00
PG10 Peter Forsberg 4.00 10.00
PG11 Joe Sakic 3.00 8.00
PG12 Jeremy Roenick 2.00 5.00
PG13 Mike Modano 2.50 6.00
PG14 Pavel Bure 1.50 4.00
PG15 Curtis Joseph 1.50 4.00

1999-00 Topps Gold Label Quest for the Cup

Randomly seeded in packs at 1:12, this 10-card set celebrates the 10 teams most likely to contend for the 2000 Stanley Cup. Card fronts feature the player that best represents his respective team set against the teams full color logo and the Stanley cup itself. Card backs carry a "QC" prefix. Black, red and gold parallels were also created and seeded randomly. Black parallels were inserted at 1:60. Red parallels were inserted at 1:1289 and were serial numbered to 25. Gold, black and red 1/1's also exist, but are not priced due to scarcity.

COMPLETE SET (10) 15.00 30.00
*BLACK: 1.5X TO 4X BASIC INSERTS
*RED/25: 20X TO 50X BASIC INSERTS
QC1 Steve Yzerman 4.00 10.00
QC2 Keith Tkachuk .75 2.00
QC3 Eric Lindros .75 2.00
QC4 Patrick Roy 4.00 10.00
QC5 Martin Brodeur 2.00 5.00
QC6 Chris Pronger .60 1.50
QC7 Daniel Alfredsson .60 1.50
QC8 Owen Nolan .60 1.50
QC9 Brett Hull 1.00 2.50
QC10 Mats Sundin .75 2.00

2000-01 Topps Gold Label Class 1

This 115-card set features color player photos printed on 35-point spectral-reflective rainbow styrene stock with gold stamping. Each card showcases an NHL player on three different versions of his base card. Displayed in the foreground of the Class 1 set is a photo of the player with an action shot appearing in the background featuring players skating and goalies standing upright. The last 15 cards in the set were sequentially numbered to 999. A gold parallel version of this set was also available in random packs where the same photos were used on gold tinted stock. In that version, cards 1-100 were sequentially numbered to 399 and cards 101-115 were numbered to 99. Topps Gold Label was packaged in 24-pack boxes with packs containing five cards and carried a suggested retail price of $5.00.

COMPLETE SET (115) 75.00 150.00
*GOLD STARS: 1.5X TO 3X BASIC CARDS
*GOLD ROOKIES: 1X TO 1.5X BASIC CARDS
1 Ray Bourque .75 2.00
2 Brendan Shanahan .40 1.00
3 Mark Recchi .30 .75
4 Olaf Kolzig .30 .75
5 Brett Hull .50 1.25
6 Valeri Bure .08 .25
7 Joe Thornton .60 1.50
8 Pavel Bure .40 1.00
9 Jeff Hackett .30 .75
10 Patrik Elias .30 .75
11 Marian Hossa .40 1.00
12 Patrick Marleau .30 .75
13 Markus Naslund .40 1.00
14 Jaromir Jagr .60 1.50
15 Tim Connolly .08 .25
16 Zigmund Palffy .30 .75
17 Peter Forsberg 1.00 2.50
18 Byron Dafoe .30 .75
19 Patrik Stefan .08 .25
20 Arturs Irbe .30 .75
21 Jocelyn Thibault .30 .75
22 Bill Guerin .30 .75
23 Keith Primeau .08 .25
24 Mats Sundin .40 1.00
25 Adam Oates .30 .75
26 Owen Nolan .30 .75
27 Mike Richter .40 1.00
28 Luc Robitaille .30 .75
29 Chris Drury .30 .75
30 Maxim Afinogenov .08 .25
31 Jarome Iginla .50 1.25
32 Joe Nieuwendyk .30 .75
33 Maxim Sushinski .08 .25
34 Daniel Alfredsson .30 .75
35 Pierre Turgeon .30 .75
36 Jason Allison .08 .25
37 Mario Lemieux 2.50 6.00
38 Sergei Fedorov .60 1.50
39 Paul Kariya .40 1.00
40 Scott Stevens .30 .75
41 Keith Tkachuk .40 1.00
42 Curtis Joseph .40 1.00
43 Peter Bondra .40 1.00
44 Roman Turek .40 1.00
45 Alexei Kovalev .30 .75
46 Brian Boucher .40 1.00
47 Mark Messier .40 1.00
48 Saku Koivu .40 1.00
49 Tommy Salo .30 .75
50 Ron Tugnutt .30 .75
51 Patrick Roy 2.00 5.00
52 Fred Brathwaite .30 .75
53 Donald Audette .08 .25
54 Doug Gilmour .30 .75
55 Alexander Mogilny .30 .75
56 John LeClair .40 1.00
57 Scott Young .08 .25
58 Jeff Friesen .08 .25
59 Simon Gagne .40 1.00
60 Theo Fleury .08 .25
61 Scott Gomez .08 .25
62 Guy Hebert .30 .75
63 Roberto Luongo .50 1.25
64 Mike Modano .60 1.50
65 Joe Sakic .75 2.00
66 Dominik Hasek .75 2.00
67 Pavol Demitra .30 .75
68 Daniel Sedin .08 .25
69 Vincent Lecavalier .40 1.00
70 Jeremy Roenick .50 1.25
71 Martin Brodeur 1.00 2.50
72 Rob Blake .30 .75
73 Ed Belfour .40 1.00
74 Tony Amonte .30 .75
75 Miroslav Satan .30 .75
76 Alexei Yashin .08 .25
77 Henrik Sedin .08 .25
78 David Legwand .30 .75
79 Steve Yzerman 2.00 5.00
80 Ron Francis .30 .75
81 Milan Hejduk .40 1.00
82 Teemu Selanne .40 1.00
83 Brad Isbister .30 .75
84 Jean-Sebastien Aubin .30 .75
85 Chris Pronger .30 .75
86 Nicklas Lidstrom .40 1.00
87 Brad Richards .08 .25
88 Brent Johnson .08 .25
89 Oleg Saprykin .08 .25
90 Anson Carter .30 .75
91 Brian Leetch .30 .75
92 Evgeni Nabokov .30 .75
93 Ian Laperriere .08 .25
94 Peter White .08 .25
95 Wes Walz .08 .25
96 Jason Arnott .08 .25
97 Tommy Albelin .08 .25
98 Jeff Toms .08 .25
99 Brad Brown .08 .25
100 Garry Valk .08 .25
101 Andrew Raycroft RC 4.00 10.00
102 Marian Gaborik RC 12.50 30.00
103 David Aebischer RC 5.00 12.00
104 Scott Hartnell RC 2.50 6.00
105 Marty Turco RC 8.00 20.00
106 Justin Williams RC 3.00 8.00
107 Steven Reinprecht RC 1.25 3.00
108 Josef Vasicek RC 1.25 3.00
109 Martin Havlat RC 8.00 20.00
110 Rostislav Klesla RC 3.00 8.00
111 Jani Hurme RC 2.50 6.00
112 Rick DiPietro RC 5.00 12.00
113 Alexander Kharitonov RC 1.25 3.00
114 Matt Pettinger RC 1.25 3.00
115 Roman Cechmanek RC 1.50 4.00

2000-01 Topps Gold Label Class 2

Randomly inserted into packs, this 115-card set features color player photos printed on 35-point spectral-reflective rainbow styrene stock with gold stamping. Each card showcases an NHL player on three different versions of his base card. Displayed in the foreground of the Class 2 set is a photo of the player with an action shot appearing in the background featuring players shooting and goalies defending the net. The last 15 cards in this set were sequentially numbered to 666. A gold parallel version of this set was also available in random packs where the same photos were used on gold tinted stock. In that version, cards 1-100 were sequentially numbered to 299 and cards 101-115 were numbered to 66.

*STARS: 1.5X TO 3X CLASS 1 BASIC CARDS
*ROOKIES: 1X TO 1.5X CLASS 1 BASIC CARDS
*GOLD STARS: 3X TO 5X CLASS 1 BASIC CARDS
*GOLD ROOKIE: 1X TO 2X CLASS 1 BASIC CARDS

2000-01 Topps Gold Label Class 3

Randomly inserted into packs, this 115-card set features color player photos printed on 35-point spectral-reflective rainbow styrene stock with gold stamping. Each card showcases an NHL player on three different version of his base card. Displayed in the foreground of the Class 3 set is a photo of the player with an action shot appearing in the background featuring players defending and goalies playing the puck. The last 15 cards in this set were sequentially numbered to 333. A gold parallel version of this set was also available in random packs where the same photos were used on gold tinted stock. In that version, cards 1-100 were sequentially numbered to 199 and cards 101-115 were numbered to 33.

*STARS: 3X TO 5X CLASS 1 BASIC CARDS
*ROOKIES: X TO X CLASS 1 BASIC CARDS
*GOLD STARS: 4X TO 8X CLASS 1 BASIC CARDS
*GOLD ROOKIE: 2X TO 4X CLASS 1 BASIC CARDS

2000-01 Topps Gold Label Autographs

This 10-card set features authentic autographs of each player accompanied by an action photo and a large team logo on a reflective silver background. Each card also carries the Topps Certified Autograph stamp on front and a Topps Genuine Issue sticker on card back.

These cards were available in random packs at stated odds of 1:57. The Gomez card was originally issued as an exchange card.

GLABB Brian Boucher 4.00 10.00
GLABR Brad Richards 6.00 15.00
GLAJW Justin Williams 4.00 10.00
GLAMG Marian Gaborik 10.00 25.00
GLAMK Milan Kraft 4.00 10.00
GLAMT Marty Turco 8.00 20.00
GLAMY Mike York 4.00 10.00
GLARB Ray Bourque 20.00 50.00
GLASG Scott Gomez 4.00 10.00
GLASH Scott Hartnell 4.00 10.00

2000-01 Topps Gold Label Behind the Mask

This 10-card set was available in random packs at a stated odd of 1:7. The card fronts featured a color action shot of the player in the foreground over a larger player photo in the background. The players name is stamped in gold on the front along with a color team logo. A sparkle-texture treated parallel numbered 1 of 1 was also randomly available.

COMPLETE SET (10) 10.00 20.00
BTM1 Curtis Joseph .75 2.00
BTM2 Ed Belfour .75 2.00
BTM3 Dominik Hasek 1.50 4.00
BTM4 Martin Brodeur 2.00 5.00
BTM5 Brian Boucher .75 2.00
BTM6 Roman Turek .75 2.00
BTM7 Olaf Kolzig .75 2.00
BTM8 Patrick Roy 4.00 10.00
BTM9 Arturs Irbe .75 2.00
BTM10 Mike Richter .75 2.00

2000-01 Topps Gold Label Bullion

This 10-card set features photos of three teammates on a gold team logo background. These cards were available in random packs at stated odds of 1:21. A sparkle-texture treated parallel numbered 1 of 1 was also randomly available.

COMPLETE SET (10) 30.00 60.00
B1 M.Brodeur/S.Gomez/J.Arnott 4.00 10.00
B2 E.Belfour/M.Modano/B.Hull 3.00 8.00
B3 Steve Yzerman 6.00 12.00
Brendan Shanahan
Sergei Fedorov
B4 Patrick Roy 6.00 15.00
Ray Bourque
Peter Forsberg
B5 RomanTurek 2.00 5.00
Chris Pronger
Pavol Demitra
B6 Mats Sundin 4.00 10.00
Curtis Joseph
Tie Domi
B7 Jeremy Roenick 3.00 8.00
Keith Tkachuk
Teppo Numminen
B8 Jeff Friesen 3.00 8.00
Patrick Marleau
Owen Nolan
B9 Mark Messier 2.00 5.00
Brian Leetch
Mike Richter
B10 Daniel Sedin 2.00 5.00
Markus Naslund
Henrik Sedin

2000-01 Topps Gold Label Game-Worn Jerseys

This 6-card set was randomly available in packs at stated odds of 1:37. The card fronts featured a swatch of game-used jersey from the player featured along with an action photo of the player on a sparkle-texture treated foil. The card backs also contained a Topps Genuine Issue sticker.

GLJJL John LeClair 5.00 12.00
GLJKT Keith Tkachuk 5.00 12.00
GLJMB Martin Brodeur 10.00 25.00
GLJPF Peter Forsberg 10.00 25.00
GLJPM Patrick Marleau 5.00 12.00
GLJSF Sergei Fedorov 6.00 15.00

2000-01 Topps Gold Label Golden Greats

This 15-card set highlights players who scored 50-plus goals in a single season. The card fronts carry a gold-bordered action photo of the player. These cards were available in random packs at stated odds of 1:5. A sparkle-texture treated parallel numbered 1 of 1 was also randomly available.

GG1 Pavel Bure 1.25 3.00
GG2 Paul Kariya 1.00 2.50
GG3 Jaromir Jagr 1.50 4.00
GG4 John LeClair 1.00 2.50
GG5 Steve Yzerman 4.00 10.00
GG6 Brett Hull 1.25 3.00
GG7 Alexander Mogilny .75 2.00
GG8 Joe Sakic 2.00 5.00
GG9 Keith Tkachuk 1.00 2.50
GG10 Teemu Selanne 1.00 2.50
GG11 Sergei Fedorov 2.00 5.00
GG12 Luc Robitaille .75 2.00
GG13 Mike Modano 1.50 4.00
GG14 Brendan Shanahan 1.50 4.00
GG15 Jeremy Roenick 1.25 3.00

2000-01 Topps Gold Label New Generation

This 15-card set featured a color action photo of each player in the foreground and a larger photo of the players face in the background all set on a blue-bordered card front which also displayed the players name, position, and team logo. These cards were available in random packs at stated odds of 1:14. A sparkle-texture treated parallel numbered 1 of 1 was also randomly available.

NG1 Scott Gomez .75 2.00
NG2 Vincent Lecavalier 1.50 4.00
NG3 Joe Thornton 2.00 5.00
NG4 Alex Tanguay 1.25 3.00
NG5 Marian Hossa 1.50 4.00
NG6 Brad Stuart .75 2.00
NG7 Henrik Sedin .75 2.00
NG8 Marian Gaborik 3.00 8.00
NG9 Roberto Luongo 2.00 5.00
NG10 David Legwand .75 2.00
NG11 Daniel Sedin .75 2.00
NG12 Patrik Stefan .75 2.00
NG13 Brian Boucher 1.25 3.00
NG14 Chris Drury 1.25 3.00
NG15 Tim Connolly .75 2.00

2000-01 Topps Heritage

Topps Heritage was released in 2000-01 as a 247-card set. The cards had the same design as that of the 1954-55 Topps set. The rookies from the set were short-printed and serial numbered to 1955. They were available in packs at a rate of 1:12.

COMP.SET w/o SP's 25.00 50.00
1 Ray Bourque .75 2.00
2 Martin Brodeur 1.00 2.50
3 Jaromir Jagr .60 1.50
4 Vincent Lecavalier .40 1.00
5 Olaf Kolzig .30 .75
6 Alexei Yashin .10 .30
7 Mark Messier .40 1.00
8 Paul Kariya .40 1.00
9 Pavel Bure .40 1.00
10 Steve Yzerman 2.00 5.00
11 Patrik Stefan .10 .30
12 Joe Thornton .60 1.50
13 Mats Sundin .40 1.00
14 Brett Hull .50 1.25
15 Zigmund Palffy .30 .75
16 Peter Bondra .40 1.00
17 Owen Nolan .30 .75
18 Tony Amonte .30 .75
19 Henrik Sedin .10 .30
20 Keith Tkachuk .40 1.00
21 Tim Connolly .10 .30
22 Doug Weight .30 .75
23 Ed Belfour .40 1.00
24 Patrick Roy 2.00 5.00
25 Brad Richards .10 .30
26 Dominik Hasek .75 2.00
27 Brendan Shanahan .40 1.00
28 Teemu Selanne .40 1.00
29 Scott Gomez .10 .30
30 John LeClair .40 1.00
31 Chris Pronger .30 .75
32 Ron Francis .30 .75
33 Daniel Sedin .10 .30
34 Curtis Joseph .40 1.00
35 Roman Turek .30 .75
36 Jeremy Roenick .50 1.25
37 Mark Recchi .30 .75
38 Patrik Elias .30 .75
39 Saku Koivu .40 1.00
40 Luc Robitaille .30 .75
41 Sergei Fedorov .60 1.50
42 Peter Forsberg 1.00 2.50
43 Milan Kraft .30 .75
44 Jason Allison .10 .30
45 Mike Modano .60 1.50
46 Roberto Luongo .50 1.25
47 David Legwand .30 .75
48 Pierre Turgeon .30 .75
49 Maxime Ouellet .30 .75
50 Oleg Saprykin .10 .30
51 Pavol Demitra .30 .75
52 Adam Oates .30 .75
53 Doug Gilmour .30 .75
54 Joe Sakic .75 2.00
55 Daniel Alfredsson .30 .75
56 Brian Leetch .30 .75
57 Bill Guerin .30 .75
58 Brent Johnson .10 .30
59 Scott Stevens .30 .75
60 Rob Blake .30 .75
61 Nicklas Lidstrom .40 1.00
62 Milan Hejduk .40 1.00
63 Arturs Irbe .30 .75
64 Maxim Afinogenov .10 .30
65 Taylor Pyatt .10 .30
66 Tommy Salo .30 .75
67 Theo Fleury .10 .30
68 Marian Hossa .40 1.00
69 Simon Gagne .40 1.00
70 Jarome Iginla .50 1.25
71 Alexander Mogilny .30 .75
72 Chris Drury .30 .75
73 Mario Lemieux 2.50 6.00
74 Petr Hubacek RC 3.00 10.00
75 Marty Turco RC 8.00 20.00
76 Rostislav Klesla RC 6.00 15.00
77 Martin Havlat RC 10.00 25.00
78 David Aebischer RC 8.00 20.00
79 Reto Von Arx RC 3.00 10.00
80 Mike Comrie RC 6.00 15.00
81 Tomas Kloucek RC 3.00 10.00
82 Steven Reinprecht RC 3.00 10.00
83 Brad Tapper RC 3.00 10.00
84 Petr Svoboda RC 3.00 10.00
85 Marian Gaborik RC 10.00 25.00
86 Josef Vasicek RC 3.00 10.00
87 Lubomir Visnovsky RC 3.00 10.00
88 Roman Cechmanek RC 3.00 8.00
89 Reed Low RC 3.00 10.00
90 Jani Hurme RC 3.00 8.00
91 Petteri Nummelin RC 3.00 10.00
92 Colin White RC 3.00 10.00
93 Andrew Raycroft RC 5.00 12.00
94 Greg Classen RC 3.00 10.00
95 Alexander Kharitonov RC 3.00 10.00
96 Rick DiPietro RC 8.00 20.00
97 Justin Williams RC 6.00 15.00
98 Eric Belanger RC 3.00 10.00
99 Scott Hartnell RC 3.00 10.00
100 Michel Riesen RC 3.00 10.00
101 Brian Boucher .30 .75
102 Mike Richter .40 1.00
103 John Vanbiesbrouck .30 .75
104 Jamie McLennan .10 .30
105 Andrei Markov .10 .30
106 Ron Tugnutt .30 .75
107 Jean-Sebastien Aubin .30 .75
108 Brad Stuart .10 .30
109 Gary Roberts .10 .30
110 Rod Brind'Amour .30 .75
111 Keith Primeau .10 .30
112 Jeff Halpern .10 .30
113 Jochen Hecht .10 .30
114 Valeri Bure .10 .30
115 Donald Audette .10 .30
116 Brenden Morrow .30 .75
117 Mike Mottau .10 .30
118 Kevin Weekes .10 .30
119 Jamie Storr .10 .30
120 Shane Willis .10 .30
121 Matt Cooke .10 .30
122 Martin Lapointe .10 .30
123 Alexei Kovalev .30 .75
124 Felix Potvin .40 1.00
125 Sean Burke .30 .75
126 Jeff Hackett .30 .75
127 Brad Isbister .10 .30
128 Derian Hatcher .10 .30
129 Marc Savard .10 .30
130 Sergei Samsonov .30 .75
131 Maxim Sushinski .10 .30
132 Radek Bonk .10 .30
133 Mika Noronen .10 .30
134 Adam Graves .10 .30
135 Sheldon Keefe .10 .30
136 Markus Naslund .40 1.00
137 Trevor Letowski .10 .30
138 Jeff Friesen .10 .30
139 Alex Tanguay .30 .75
140 Byron Dafoe .30 .75
141 Chris Osgood .30 .75
142 Mike York .10 .30
143 Scott Young .10 .30
144 Sami Kapanen .10 .30
145 Evgeni Nabokov .30 .75
146 Brendan Morrison .30 .75
147 Joe Nieuwendyk .30 .75
148 Tomi Kallio .10 .30
149 Guy Hebert .10 .30
150 Randy McKay .10 .30
151 Mike Johnson .10 .30
152 Miroslav Satan .30 .75
153 Patrick Marleau .30 .75
154 Jocelyn Thibault .30 .75
155 Martin Straka .10 .30
156 Fred Brathwaite .30 .75
157 Cliff Ronning .10 .30
158 Denis Shvidki .10 .30
159 Espen Knutsen .10 .30
160 Alexei Zhamnov .10 .30
161 Georges Laraque .10 .30
162 Jose Theodore .50 1.25
163 Rick Tocchet .10 .30
164 Donald Brashear .10 .30
165 Darren Langdon .10 .30
166 Rob Ray .10 .30
167 Matthew Barnaby .10 .30
168 Chris Simon .10 .30
169 Ken Belanger .10 .30
170 Tie Domi .30 .75
171 Roman Hamrlik .10 .30
172 Olli Jokinen .30 .75
173 Steve Rucchin .10 .30
174 Jim Cummins .10 .30
175 Tyson Nash .10 .30
176 Scott Parker .10 .30
177 Matt Johnson .10 .30
178 Sandy McCarthy .10 .30
179 Daniel Cleary .10 .30
180 Michal Handzus .10 .30
181 Nikolai Antropov .10 .30
182 Scott Thornton .10 .30
183 Shane Doan .10 .30
184 Wade Redden .10 .30
185 Ray Whitney .10 .30
186 Teppo Numminen .10 .30
187 Pat Verbeek .10 .30
188 Bobby Holik .10 .30
189 Mike Dunham .30 .75
190 Rob Niedermayer .10 .30
191 Ray Ferraro .10 .30
192 Steve Sullivan .10 .30
193 Sergei Zubov .10 .30
194 Scott Walker .10 .30
195 Geoff Sanderson .10 .30
196 Bob Probert .10 .30
197 Andrew Brunette .10 .30
198 Marty Murray .10 .30
199 Steve Staios .10 .30
200 Kay Whitmore .10 .30
201 Jonas Hoglund .10 .30
202 Niklas Andersson .10 .30
203 Joaquin Gage .10 .30
204 Mike Ricci .10 .30
205 Bryan Helmer .10 .30
206 Patrick Traverse .10 .30
207 Mike Rucinski .10 .30
208 Brantt Myhres .10 .30
209 Claude Lapointe .10 .30
210 Frank Musil .10 .30
211 Sandis Ozolinsh .10 .30
212 Tomas Vokoun .30 .75
213 Jarrod Skalde .10 .30
214 Sergei Gonchar .10 .30
215 Anson Carter .30 .75
216 Steve Yzerman AS 1.00 2.50
217 Mike Modano AS .30 .75
218 Paul Kariya AS .20 .50
219 Brendan Shanahan AS .30 .75
220 Pavel Bure AS .20 .50
221 Jaromir Jagr AS .30 .75
222 Chris Pronger AS .10 .30
223 Nicklas Lidstrom AS .20 .50
224 Rob Blake AS .10 .30
225 Eric Desjardins AS .10 .30
226 Olaf Kolzig AS .10 .30
227 Roman Turek AS .10 .30
228 S.Stevens/C.Pronger LL .10 .30
229 S.Gomez/A.Tanguay LL .20 .50
230 P.Bure/O.Nolan LL .30 .75
231 M.Brodeur/R.Turek LL .40 1.00
232 M.Czerkawski/O.Nolan LL .10 .30
233 J.Theodore/E.Belfour LL .20 .50
234 J.Madden/T.Amonte LL .20 .50
235 J.Jagr/P.Kariya LL .20 .50
236 E.Desjardins/N.Lidstrom LL .20 .50
237 B.Boucher/R.Turek LL .20 .50
238 Steve Yzerman AW 1.00 2.50
239 Scott Stevens AW .10 .30
240 Scott Gomez AW .15 .40
241 Roman Turek AW .10 .30
242 Pavol Demitra AW .10 .30
243 Pavel Bure AW .40 1.00
244 Olaf Kolzig AW .10 .30
245 Jaromir Jagr AW .30 .75
246 Chris Pronger AW .10 .30
247 New Jersey Devils SC .10 .30

2000-01 Topps Heritage Chrome Parallel

Randomly inserted in packs of Topps Heritage, the 100-card parallel set featured the chrome version of the base set. The cards were serial numbered to 555.

*STARS: 3X TO 6X BASIC CARDS
*ROOKIES: .25X TO .6X

2000-01 Topps Heritage Arena Relics

Randomly inserted in packs of 2000-01 Topps Heritage at a rate of 1:128, this 15-card set featured original pieces from the old arenas. The 2 autographed cards were available in packs at a rate of 1:12345. The multi-piece arena relic was available in packs at a rate of 1:11536.

OSAJT Joe Thornton 10.00 25.00
OSAMM Mark Messier 10.00 25.00

OSAMS Mats Sundin 10.00 25.00
OSASK Saku Koivu 10.00 25.00
OSASY Steve Yzerman 12.50 30.00
OSATA Tony Amonte 10.00 25.00
OSABG Bill Gadsby 10.00 25.00
OSAGH Gordie Howe 12.50 30.00
OSALW Gump Worsley 10.00 25.00
OSAMR Maurice Richard 20.00 50.00
OSAMS Milt Schmidt 10.00 25.00
OSATK Ted Kennedy 10.00 25.00
OSA Multi Arena Relic/55 200.00 400.00
HAAGH Gordie Howe AU/25 250.00 400.00
HAALW Gump Worsley AU/25 150.00 300.00

2000-01 Topps Heritage Autographs

This 12-card set was randomly inserted in packs at a rate of 1:184 for the current players and 1:97 for the reprints of former NHL players. Please note that at the time of its release Topps included Joe Thornton and Tony Amonte as exchange/redemption cards. Tony Amonte did not sign his cards, the exchange card was redeemable for a similar card from other Topps issues.

HAAG Adam Graves 10.00 25.00
HACJ Curtis Joseph 10.00 25.00
HAJH Jeff Hackett 5.00 12.00
HAJT Joe Thornton 20.00 50.00
HASF Sergei Fedorov 20.00 50.00
HATA Exchange Card
HAAB Andy Bathgate 10.00 25.00
HAAD Alex Delvecchio 10.00 25.00
HAGH Gordie Howe 75.00 150.00
HALW Gump Worsley 15.00 40.00
HARK Red Kelly 10.00 25.00
HATL Ted Lindsay 10.00 25.00

2000-01 Topps Heritage Autoproofs

Randomly inserted in 2000-01 Topps Heritage packs, this 6-card set was created by using original 1954-55 Topps Hockey cards and having the featured player autograph the card. The cards were then serial numbered to 10 for each player. Please note that the Gordie Howe and Andy Bathgate cards were issued as exchange/redemption cards. These cards are not priced due to scarcity.

5 Red Kelly
8 Gordie Howe
10 Gump Worsley
11 Andy Bathgate
39 Alex Delvecchio
51 Ted Lindsay

2000-01 Topps Heritage Heroes

COMPLETE SET (20) 25.00 50.00
STATED ODDS: 1:14
HH1 Ray Bourque 1.50 4.00
HH2 Jaromir Jagr 1.25 3.00
HH3 Steve Yzerman 4.00 10.00
HH4 Mike Modano 1.25 3.00
HH5 Patrick Roy 4.00 10.00
HH6 Martin Brodeur 2.00 5.00
HH7 Mark Messier 1.00 2.50
HH8 Peter Forsberg 2.00 5.00
HH9 Scott Stevens .60 1.50
HH10 Teemu Selanne .75 2.00
HH11 Pavel Bure 1.00 2.50
HH12 Curtis Joseph .75 2.00
HH13 John LeClair 1.00 2.50
HH14 Brett Hull 1.00 2.50
HH15 Keith Tkachuk .75 2.00
HH16 Tony Amonte .60 1.50
HH17 Ed Belfour .75 2.00
HH18 Brendan Shanahan 1.25 3.00
HH19 Dominik Hasek 1.50 4.00
HH20 Paul Kariya .75 2.00

2000-01 Topps Heritage New Tradition

COMPLETE SET (10) 6.00 12.00
STATED ODDS: 1:8
NT1 Marian Hossa .50 1.25
NT2 Daniel Sedin .40 1.00
NT3 Milan Hejduk .50 1.25
NT4 Vincent Lecavalier .50 1.25
NT5 Joe Thornton .75 2.00
NT6 Scott Gomez .40 1.00
NT7 Chris Drury .40 1.00
NT8 Brian Boucher .40 1.00

NT9 Henrik Sedin .40 1.00
NT10 Marian Gaborik 2.00 5.00

2000-01 Topps Heritage Original Six Relics

Randomly inserted in packs at a rate of 1:409, this 16-card set featured original pieces from game-used hockey sticks or jerseys. The 2 autographed jersey cards were available in packs at a rate of 1:8240. The multi-piece relics were available in packs at a rate of 1:11,536. The jersey cards were available in packs at a rate of 1:541. Tony Amonte did not sign his autograph cards, the exchange card was redeemed for similar cards from other Topps issues.

*MULT.COLOR STICK/SWATCH: 1X TO 2X
OSJAZ Alexei Zhamnov J 5.00 12.00
OSJCO Chris Osgood J 5.00 12.00
OSJJT Joe Thornton J 8.00 20.00
OSJSK Saku Koivu J 5.00 12.00
OSJTD Tie Domi J 5.00 12.00
OSJTF Theo Fleury J 5.00 12.00
OSSBP Bob Probert S 5.00 12.00
OSSJA Jason Allison S 10.00 25.00
OSSJH Jeff Hackett S 10.00 25.00
OSSMM Mark Messier S 10.00 25.00
OSSMS Mats Sundin S 10.00 25.00
OSSSY Steve Yzerman S 15.00 40.00
OSJ Alexei Zhamnov 125.00 250.00
Theo Fleury
Chris Osgood
Joe Thornton
Saku Koivu
Tie Domi/55
OSJAJH Jeff Hackett 40.00 80.00
JSY AU/25
OSJAJT Joe Thornton 75.00 200.00
JSY AU/25

2001-02 Topps Heritage

Released in early December 2001, this 187-card set borrowed from the 1957-58 Topps design. This set carried an SRP of $3.00 for an 6-card pack, and each pack included a stick of gum. Rookies were seeded at 1:3.

COMPLETE SET (187) 100.00 200.00
1 Mario Lemieux 2.50 6.00
2 Evgeni Nabokov .30 .75
3 Nicklas Lidstrom .40 1.00
4 Patrik Elias .30 .75
5 Olaf Kolzig .30 .75
6 Mats Sundin .40 1.00
7 Jason Allison .10 .30
8 Mike Modano .60 1.50
9 Keith Tkachuk .40 1.00
10 John LeClair .40 1.00
11 Pavel Bure .40 1.00
12 Tony Amonte .30 .75
13 Zigmund Palffy .30 .75
14 Mark Messier .40 1.00
15 Sean Burke .30 .75
16 Markus Naslund .40 1.00
17 Milan Hejduk .40 1.00
18 Teemu Selanne .40 1.00
19 Espen Knutsen .10 .30
20 David Legwand .30 .75
21 Saku Koivu .40 1.00
22 Ron Francis .30 .75
23 Ray Ferraro .10 .30
24 Brendan Shanahan .40 1.00
25 Rick DiPietro .30 .75
26 Brad Richards .30 .75
27 Henrik Sedin .10 .30
28 Marian Hossa .40 1.00
29 Marian Gaborik .75 2.00
30 Ed Belfour .40 1.00
31 Miroslav Satan .30 .75
32 Roberto Luongo .50 1.25
33 Brian Leetch .30 .75
34 Chris Pronger .30 .75
35 Peter Bondra .40 1.00
36 Keith Primeau .10 .30
37 Johan Hedberg .30 .75
38 Steve Yzerman 2.00 5.00
39 Peter Forsberg 1.00 2.50
40 Jarome Iginla .50 1.25
41 Jose Theodore .50 1.25
42 Curtis Joseph .40 1.00
43 Martin Havlat .30 .75
44 Sergei Fedorov .60 1.50
45 Arturs Irbe .30 .75
46 Martin Brodeur 1.00 2.50
47 Owen Nolan .30 .75
48 Daniel Sedin .10 .30
49 Mark Recchi .30 .75
50 Adam Deadmarsh .10 .30
51 Tommy Salo .30 .75
52 Alexei Kovalev .30 .75
53 Steve Sullivan .10 .30
54 Paul Kariya .40 1.00
55 Vincent Lecavalier .40 1.00
56 Alex Tanguay .30 .75
57 Joe Thornton .60 1.50
58 Brent Johnson .30 .75
59 Roman Cechmanek .30 .75
60 Petr Sykora .10 .30
61 J-P Dumont .10 .30
62 Mike Comrie .30 .75
63 Daniel Alfredsson .30 .75
64 Eric Daze .30 .75
65 Felix Potvin .40 1.00
66 Chris Drury .30 .75
67 Manny Fernandez .30 .75
68 Claude Lemieux .10 .30
69 Rob Blake .30 .75
70 Bill Guerin .30 .75
71 Mike Dunham .30 .75
72 Simon Gagne .40 1.00
73 Jeff Friesen .10 .30
74 Joe Sakic .75 2.00
75 Jason Arnott .10 .30
76 Patrick Roy 2.00 5.00
77 Josef Vasicek .30 .75
78 Marty Turco .30 .75
79 Al MacInnis .30 .75
80 Anson Carter .30 .75
81 Tomi Kallio .10 .30
82 Eric Belanger .10 .30
83 Patrick Lalime .30 .75
84 Scott Young .10 .30
85 Scott Gomez .10 .30
86 Marc Denis .30 .75
87 Jeff O'Neill .10 .30
88 Sergei Samsonov .30 .75
89 Robert Lang .10 .30
90 Byron Dafoe .30 .75
91 Scott Stevens .30 .75
92 Adam Oates .30 .75
93 Patrick Marleau .30 .75
94 Petr Nedved .10 .30
95 Ryan Smyth .10 .30
96 Adam Foote .10 .30
97 Marc Savard .10 .30
98 Brad Isbister .10 .30
99 Martin Straka .10 .30
100 Joe Nieuwendyk .30 .75
101 Shane Willis .10 .30
102 Pavol Demitra .30 .75
103 Jeff Halpern .10 .30
104 Sergei Zubov .10 .30
105 David Vyborny .10 .30
106 Gary Roberts .10 .30
107 Martin Biron .30 .75
108 Lubomir Visnovsky .10 .30
109 Fredrik Modin .10 .30
110 Brenden Morrow .30 .75
111 Stanley Cup .40 1.00
112 Nicklas Lidstrom AS .20 .50
113 Jaromir Jagr AS .30 .75
114 Patrik Elias AS .20 .50
115 Joe Sakic AS .40 1.00
116 Dominik Hasek AS .40 1.00
117 Rob Blake AS .15 .40
118 Scott Stevens AS .15 .40
119 Roman Cechmanek AS .15 .40
120 Mario Lemieux AS 1.25 3.00
121 Pavel Bure AS .30 .75
122 Luc Robitaille AS .20 .50
123 Jaromir Jagr .30 .75
Joe Sakic LL
124 Pavel Bure .30 .75
Joe Sakic LL
125 Patrik Elias .40 1.00
Joe Sakic LL
126 Brian Leetch .20 .50
Nicklas Lidstrom LL
127 Arturs Irbe .15 .40
Tommy Salo LL
128 M.Brodeur/P.Roy LL 1.00 2.50
129 Marty Turco .15 .40
Roman Cechmanek LL
130 Joe Sakic AW .40 1.00
131 Patrick Roy AW 1.00 2.50
132 Pavel Bure AW .30 .75
133 Evgeni Nabokov AW .15 .40
134 Nicklas Lidstrom AW .20 .50
135 Dominik Hasek AW .40 1.00
136 John Madden AW .05 .15
137 Jaromir Jagr AW .30 .75
138 Ilya Kovalchuk RC 5.00 12.00
139 Niko Kapanen RC 2.00 5.00
140 Brian Sutherby RC 2.00 5.00
141 Jeff Jillson RC 2.00 5.00
142 Jiri Dopita RC 2.00 5.00
143 Andreas Salomonsson RC 2.00 5.00
144 Timo Parssinen RC 2.00 5.00
145 Vaclav Nedorost RC 2.00 5.00
146 Kristian Huselius RC 2.00 5.00
147 Dan Blackburn RC 1.50 4.00
148 Nikita Alexeev RC 2.00 5.00
149 Peter Smrek RC 2.00 5.00
150 Krys Kolanos RC 2.00 5.00
151 Pavel Datsyuk RC 5.00 12.00
152 Jaroslav Bednar RC 2.00 5.00
153 Chris Neil RC 2.00 5.00
154 Erik Cole RC 2.50 6.00
155 Niklas Hagman RC 2.00 5.00
156 Jason Chimera RC 2.00 5.00
157 Scott Clemmensen RC 2.00 5.00
158 Andrew Brunette .30 .75
159 Dominik Hasek 2.50 6.00
160 Jaromir Jagr .60 1.50
161 Doug Weight 1.00 2.50

162 Brett Hull 1.50 4.00
163 Pierre Turgeon 1.00 2.50
164 Jeremy Roenick 1.50 4.00
165 Alexander Mogilny 1.00 2.50
166 Luc Robitaille 1.00 2.50
167 Michael Peca .30 .75
168 Roman Turek 1.00 2.50
169 Martin Lapointe .30 .75
170 Alexei Yashin .30 .75
171 Adam Graves .30 .75
172 Valeri Bure .30 .75
173 Tim Connolly .30 .75
174 Kris Beech .30 .75
175 Donald Audette .30 .75
176 Jochen Hecht .30 .75
177 Fred Brathwaite 1.00 2.50
178 Rob Niedermayer .30 .75
179 Eric Lindros .40 1.00
180 Bill Muckalt .30 .75
181 Eric Weinrich .30 .75
182 Taylor Pyatt .30 .75
183 Pavel Brendl 1.00 2.50
184 Craig Berube .30 .75
185 Dany Heatley .50 1.25
186 Ken Sutton .30 .75
187 Slava Kozlov .30 .75

2001-02 Topps Heritage Refractors

Printed on chrome reflective stock, this 110-card set paralleled the base set and was serial numbered to just 558 sets.

*REFRACTORS: 3X TO 6X BASIC CARD

2001-02 Topps Heritage Arena Relics

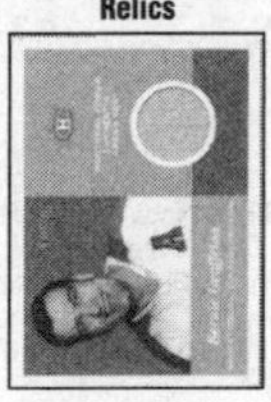

This 13-card hobby only set featured pieces of arena seats from the Montreal Forum and Boston Gardens. Cards featuring single players were inserted at 1:149. Dual player cards were serial-numbered to 100 and inserted at 1:994 Dual payer cards included two pieces of arena seats. Autographed versions of this set were inserted at 1:1401 for single player and 1:3076 for dual player. Autographed cards with dual players were serial-numbered out of 25 and are not priced due to scarcity.

RBG Bernie Geoffrion 6.00 15.00
RHR Henri Richard 6.00 15.00
RJBE Jean Beliveau 10.00 25.00
RJBU John Bucyk 8.00 20.00
RJB/BG J.Bucyk/B.Geoffrion 20.00 50.00
RJB/HR John Bucyk 20.00 50.00
Henri Richard
RJB/JB John Bucyk 30.00 80.00
Jean Beliveau
ARBG Bernie Geoffrion AU 30.00 80.00
ARHR Henri Richard AU 40.00 100.00
ARJBE Jean Beliveau AU 30.00 80.00
ARJBU John Bucyk AU 60.00 150.00
ARJB/BG John Bucyk AU
Bernie Geoffrion AU
ARJB/HR John Bucyk AU
Henri Richard AU
ARJB/JB John Bucyk AU
Jean Beliveau AU

2001-02 Topps Heritage Autographs

This 16-card set featured authentic autographs of current and former players on the classic 1957-58 design. Current player cards were inserted at 1:156, reprints were inserted at 1:91 and cards #ABG, AHR and AJBE were inserted at 1:182. Overall odds of autograph cards were 1:44.

AAA Al Arbour 10.00 25.00
ABG Bernie Geoffrion 20.00 50.00
AGH Glenn Hall 12.00 30.00
AHH Harry Howell 10.00 25.00
AHR Henri Richard 12.00 30.00
AIK Ilya Kovalchuk 20.00 50.00
AJH Johan Hedberg 10.00 25.00
AJW Justin Williams 10.00 25.00
AMG Marian Gaborik 15.00 40.00
AMS Miroslav Satan 10.00 25.00
ANU Norm Ullman 10.00 25.00
AOK Olaf Kolzig 10.00 25.00
APP Pierre Pilote 10.00 25.00
AVL Vincent Lecavalier 10.00 25.00

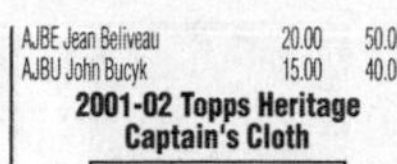

AJBE Jean Beliveau 20.00 50.00
AJBU John Bucyk 15.00 40.00

2001-02 Topps Heritage Captain's Cloth

This 6-card set featured game-worn jersey swatches from team captains from around the league. Cards from this set were randomly inserted at 1:76 hobby packs.

*MULT.COLOR SWATCH: .75X TO 1.5X
CCAO Adam Oates 6.00 15.00
CCDH Derian Hatcher 6.00 15.00
CCED Eric Desjardins 8.00 20.00
CCPK Paul Kariya 8.00 20.00
CCSK Saku Koivu 8.00 20.00
CCVL Vincent Lecavalier 8.00 20.00

2001-02 Topps Heritage Jerseys

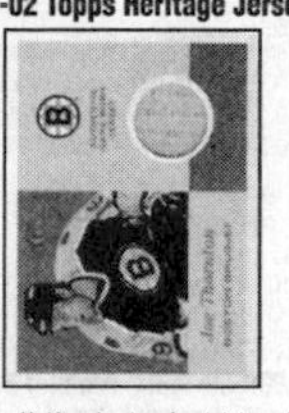

This 10-card hobby only set was inserted at overall odds of 1:17 packs. Cards from this set featured swatches of game-worn jerseys from the featured players.

JRL Brian Leetch 6.00 15.00
JJI Jarome Iginla 8.00 20.00
JJL John LeClair 6.00 15.00
JJT Joe Thornton 8.00 20.00
JMB Martin Brodeur 12.50 30.00
JMS Martin Straka 6.00 15.00
JPF Peter Forsberg 10.00 25.00
JPM Patrick Marleau 6.00 15.00
JRL Robert Lang 6.00 15.00
JSF Sergei Fedorov 8.00 20.00

2001-02 Topps Heritage Salute

This 9-card set featured 6 reprints from the 1957-58 Topps set and 3 "cards that never were" (S7-S9). Cards from this set were inserted at 1:16.

COMPLETE SET (9) 10.00 30.00
S1 John Bucyk 2.50 6.00
S2 Al Arbour 2.00 5.00
S3 Glenn Hall 2.50 6.00
S4 Harry Howell 2.00 5.00
S5 Pierre Pilote 2.00 5.00
S6 Norm Ullman 2.00 5.00
S7 Jean Beliveau 2.50 6.00
S8 Henri Richard 2.00 5.00
S9 Bernie Geoffrion 2.50 6.00

2001 Topps Heritage Avalanche NHL All-Star Game

This six card set was produced by Topps as a wrapper redemption for the 2001 All-Star Fan Fest. Base cards feature full color player action photos set against a white background with the Avalanche logo in the upper left hand corner and a blue and red border along the card bottom. Overlaying the pictures is a facsimile of the featured player's autograph.

COMPLETE SET (6) 12.00 30.00
1 Ray Bourque 3.20 8.00
2 Patrick Roy 4.00 10.00
3 Peter Forsberg 3.20 8.00
4 Joe Sakic 2.40 6.00
5 Milan Hejduk 1.60 4.00
6 Chris Drury 1.60 4.00

2002-03 Topps Heritage

Released in December 2002, this 180-card set borrowed from the classic "woodgrain" design of 1966-67 Topps. Cards 131-180 were inserted at a rate of 1:4. Original 1966-67 cards were also repurchased and randomly inserted into packs at 1:1687.

COMPLETE SET (180) 125.00 250.00
COMP.SET w/o SP's (130) 40.00 80.00
1 Nicklas Lidstrom .40 1.00
2 Jarome Iginla .50 1.25
3 Jose Theodore .50 1.25
4 Ron Francis .30 .75

5 Joe Thornton .60 1.50
6 Jaromir Jagr .60 1.50
7 Mario Lemieux 2.50 6.00
8 Roberto Luongo .50 1.25
9 Dany Heatley .50 1.25
10 Pavel Bure .40 1.00
11 Brett Hull .50 1.25
12 Keith Tkachuk .40 1.00
13 Mats Sundin .40 1.00
14 Pavel Datsyuk .40 1.00
15 Daniel Alfredsson .30 .75
16 Marian Gaborik .75 2.00
17 Peter Forsberg 1.00 2.50
18 Miroslav Satan .30 .75
19 Martin Brodeur 1.00 2.50
20 Jeremy Roenick .50 1.25
21 Teemu Selanne .40 1.00
22 Todd Bertuzzi .40 1.00
23 Erik Cole .10 .30
24 Jason Allison .10 .30
25 Sean Burke .30 .75
26 Eric Daze .30 .75
27 Patrick Roy 2.00 5.00
28 Simon Gagne .40 1.00
29 Nikolai Khabibulin .40 1.00
30 Alexei Yashin .10 .30
31 Dennis Arkhipov .10 .30
32 Steve Yzerman 2.00 5.00
33 Mike Modano .60 1.50
34 Joe Sakic .75 2.00
35 Sergei Samsonov .30 .75
36 Saku Koivu .40 1.00
37 Paul Kariya .40 1.00
38 Doug Weight .30 .75
39 Tie Domi .30 .75
40 Kevin Weekes .30 .75
41 Rostislav Klesla .10 .30
42 Zigmund Palffy .30 .75
43 Chris Osgood .30 .75
44 Owen Nolan .30 .75
45 Markus Naslund .40 1.00
46 Martin Biron .30 .75
47 Ryan Smyth .10 .30
48 Mike Dunham .30 .75
49 Martin Havlat .30 .75
50 Patrik Elias .30 .75
51 Peter Bondra .40 1.00
52 Craig Conroy .10 .30
53 Rob Blake .30 .75
54 Mike Richter .40 1.00
55 Stephen Weiss .10 .30
56 Johan Hedberg .30 .75
57 Brendan Morrison .30 .75
58 Chris Pronger .30 .75
59 Patrick Lalime .30 .75
60 David Legwand .30 .75
61 Jocelyn Thibault .30 .75
62 Chris Drury .30 .75
63 Sergei Fedorov .60 1.50
64 Michael Peca .10 .30
65 Tommy Salo .30 .75
66 Scott Stevens .30 .75
67 Mark Recchi .30 .75
68 Vincent Damphousse .10 .30
69 Vincent Lecavalier .40 1.00
70 Olaf Kolzig .30 .75
71 Shane Doan .10 .30
72 Marty Turco .30 .75
73 Marian Hossa .40 1.00
74 Eric Lindros .40 1.00
75 Brent Johnson .30 .75
76 John LeClair .40 1.00
77 Dan Cloutier .30 .75
78 Radim Vrbata .10 .30
79 Ilya Kovalchuk .50 1.25
80 Brendan Shanahan .40 1.00
81 Stu Barnes .10 .30
82 Alexander Mogilny .30 .75
83 Felix Potvin .40 1.00
84 Jeff O'Neill .10 .30
85 Glen Murray .10 .30
86 Marc Denis .30 .75
87 Brad Richards .30 .75
88 Roman Cechmanek .30 .75
89 Brian Leetch .30 .75
90 Roman Turek .30 .75
91 Andrew Brunette .10 .30
92 Krys Kolanos .10 .30
93 Alyn McCauley .10 .30
94 Jean-Sebastien Giguere .30 .75
95 Alexei Kovalev .30 .75
96 Peter Worrell .10 .30
97 Alexei Zhamnov .10 .30
98 Evgeni Nabokov .30 .75
99 Pavol Demitra .30 .75
100 Chris Drury .30 .75
101 Jarome Iginla .50 1.25
102 Patrick Roy 1.00 2.50
103 Dany Heatley .20 .50
104 Nicklas Lidstrom .20 .50
105 Jose Theodore .25 .60
106 Michael Peca .05 .15
107 Ron Francis .15 .40
108 J.Iginla/M.Sundin .30 .75
109 J.Iginla/M.Sundin .30 .75
110 J.Allison/A.Oates .30 .75
111 P.Datsyuk/D.Heatley .30 .75
112 C.Chelios/J.Roenick .30 .75
113 N.Lidstrom/S.Gonchar .30 .75
114 K.Sawyer/P.Worrell .30 .75
115 R.Turek/M.Brodeur .30 .75
116 P.Roy/J.Theodore .50 1.25
117 P.Roy/R.Cechmanek .40 1.00
118 Joe Sakic .40 1.00
119 Jarome Iginla .50 1.25
120 Markus Naslund .40 1.00
121 Nicklas Lidstrom .40 1.00
122 Chris Chelios .40 1.00
123 Patrick Roy 1.00 2.50
124 Mats Sundin .40 1.00
125 Bill Guerin .30 .75
126 Brendan Shanahan .30 .75
127 Rob Blake .30 .75
128 Sergei Gonchar .10 .30
129 Jose Theodore .50 1.25
130 Stanley Cup Champions UER .40 1.00
Card reads 2002-03 Champions
131 Henrik Zetterberg RC 6.00 15.00
132 Martin Gerber RC 3.00 8.00
133 Alexander Frolov RC 4.00 10.00
134 Alexei Smirnov RC 2.00 5.00
135 Stanislav Chistov RC 2.00 5.00
136 Alexander Svitov RC 2.00 5.00
137 Adam Hall RC 2.00 5.00
138 Jay Bouwmeester RC 3.00 8.00
139 Ales Hemsky RC 5.00 12.00
140 Rick Nash RC 8.00 20.00
141 Chuck Kobasew RC 2.50 6.00
142 Shawn Thornton RC 2.00 5.00
143 Dennis Seidenberg RC 2.00 5.00
144 Ron Hainsey RC 2.00 5.00
145 Kurt Sauer RC 2.00 5.00
146 Lasse Pirjeta RC 2.00 5.00
147 Jason Spezza RC 8.00 20.00
148 Tom Koivisto RC 2.00 5.00
149 P-M Bouchard RC 4.00 10.00
150 Patrick Sharp RC 2.00 5.00
151 Scottie Upshall RC 2.00 5.00
152 Steve Eminger RC 2.00 5.00
153 Radovan Somik RC 2.00 5.00
154 Anton Volchenkov RC 2.00 5.00
155 Dmitri Bykov RC 2.00 5.00
156 Bobby Holik SP .40 1.00
157 Curtis Joseph SP .40 1.00
158 Jeff Friesen SP .40 1.00
159 Petr Sykora SP .40 1.00
160 Ed Belfour SP 1.00 2.50
161 Darius Kasparaitis SP .40 1.00
162 Scott Young SP .40 1.00
163 Bill Guerin SP .75 2.00
164 Adam Oates SP .75 2.00
165 Tony Amonte SP .75 2.00
166 Jochen Hecht SP .40 1.00
167 Randy McKay SP .40 1.00
168 Jamie Lundmark SP .40 1.00
169 Mariusz Czerkawski SP .40 1.00
170 Bryan Berard SP .40 1.00
171 Shawn McEachern SP .40 1.00
172 Brian Boucher SP .75 2.00
173 Jiri Dopita SP .40 1.00
174 Erik Rasmussen SP .40 1.00
175 Robert Lang SP .40 1.00
176 Steve Shields SP .75 2.00
177 Kelly Buchberger SP .40 1.00
178 Andrew Cassels SP .40 1.00
179 Oleg Tverdovsky SP .40 1.00
180 Ron Tugnutt SP .75 2.00
NNO Checklist 4 of 6 .10 .30
NNO Checklist 6 of 6 .10 .30
NNO Checklist 2 of 6 .10 .30
NNO Checklist 1 of 6 .10 .30
NNO Checklist 3 of 6 .10 .30
NNO Checklist 5 of 6 .10 .30

2002-03 Topps Heritage Chrome Parallel

This 100-card set paralleled the base set on chrome card stock. Each card was serial-numbered out of 667 on the cardbacks.

*STARS: 2X TO 5X BASIC CARD

2002-03 Topps Heritage Autographs

Inserted at 1:55, this 9-card set featured certified player autographs in blue ink.

AM Al MacInnis 6.00 15.00
BM Bryan McCabe 6.00 15.00
CD Chris Drury 6.00 15.00
EC Erik Cole 6.00 15.00
KK Krys Kolanos 6.00 15.00
MP Mike Peca 6.00 15.00
PE Patrik Elias 6.00 15.00
SW Stephen Weiss 6.00 15.00
TB Todd Bertuzzi 8.00 20.00

2002-03 Topps Heritage Autographs Black

Inserted at 1:155, this parallel set carried player autographs in black ink.

*BLACK: .75X TO 2X BASIC AUTO

2002-03 Topps Heritage Autographs Red

Inserted at 1:495, this parallel set carried player autographs in red ink.

*RED: 1.5X TO 4X BASIC AUTO

2002-03 Topps Heritage Calder Cloth

This 8-card set featured swatches of game jerseys from past Calder trophy winners. Cards in group "A" were inserted at 1:1160 and cards in group "B" were inserted at 1:217.

ALL CARD CARRY CC PREFIX
BL Brian Leetch B 6.00 15.00
CD Chris Drury A 15.00 40.00
DA Daniel Alfredsson B 6.00 15.00
DH Dany Heatley B 15.00 40.00
MB Martin Brodeur A 20.00 50.00
PF Peter Forsberg A 15.00 40.00
SG Scott Gomez B 6.00 15.00
SS Sergei Samsonov A 10.00 25.00

2002-03 Topps Heritage Calder Cloth Patches

*PATCHES: 1.25X TO 3X BASIC JERSEYS
PATCH ODDS 1:2774

2002-03 Topps Heritage Crease Piece

Inserted at 1:39, this 9-card set carried swatches of goalie game jerseys.

ALL CARDS CARRY CP PREFIX
BB Brian Boucher 4.00 10.00
BD Byron Dafoe 4.00 10.00
DB Dan Blackburn 4.00 10.00
DC Dan Cloutier 4.00 10.00
FP Felix Potvin 6.00 15.00
ML Manny Legace 4.00 10.00
MT Marty Turco 6.00 15.00
PL Patrick Lalime 4.00 10.00
SB Sean Burke 4.00 10.00

2002-03 Topps Heritage Crease Piece Patches

*PATCH: 1X TO 2.5X BASE HI
STATED ODDS 1:775

2002-03 Topps Heritage Great Skates

This 10-card memorabilia set was inserted at 1:50.

ALL CARDS CARRY GS PREFIX
AK Alexei Kovalev 5.00 12.00
AT Alex Tanguay 5.00 12.00
BL Brian Leetch 5.00 12.00
BM Brendan Morrison 5.00 12.00
MH Milan Hejduk 6.00 15.00
MR Mark Recchi 5.00 12.00
MS Marco Sturm 5.00 12.00
SG Simon Gagne 6.00 15.00
TA Tony Amonte 5.00 12.00
MHO Marian Hossa 6.00 15.00

2002-03 Topps Heritage Great Skates Patches

*PATCH: 1.25X TO 3X BASE HI
STATED ODDS 1:1550

2002-03 Topps Heritage Reprint Autographs

Inserted at 1:139, this 5-card set partially paralleled the base reprint set but included certified autographs on the cardfronts. Cards carried a TMLA prefix on the cardbacks.

ES Eddie Shack 15.00 40.00
JB Johnny Bower 15.00 40.00
JP Jim Pappin 10.00 25.00
RK Red Kelly 10.00 25.00
RP Bob Pulford 15.00 40.00

2002-03 Topps Heritage Reprint Relics

Inserted at 1:127, this 7-card set paralleled the base reprint set but also featured a piece of stadium seat from Maple Leaf Gardens. Cards carried a TMLS prefix on the cardbacks.

ES Eddie Shack 10.00 25.00
JB Johnny Bower 10.00 25.00
JP Jim Pappin 8.00 20.00
RK Red Kelly 8.00 20.00
RP Robert Pulford 8.00 20.00
TH Tim Horton 12.50 30.00
TS Terry Sawchuk 25.00 60.00

2002-03 Topps Heritage Reprints

Inserted at 1:8, this 7-card set featured reprinted versions of original 1966-67 cards of members of the Toronto Maple Leafs. Cards carried a TML prefix on the cardbacks.

ES Eddie Shack 1.00 2.50
JB Johnny Bower 1.25 3.00
JP Jim Pappin 1.00 2.50
RK Red Kelly 1.25 3.00
RP Robert Pulford 1.00 2.50
TH Tim Horton 1.25 3.00
TS Terry Sawchuk 1.50 4.00

2002-03 Topps Heritage USA Test Parallel

In keeping with the tradition of the 1966-67 Topps set, this 10-card parallel set featured a sampling of players with a much lighter woodgrain borders. This set was inserted at 1:20.

2 Jarome Iginla 1.50 4.00
3 Jose Theodore 1.50 4.00
6 Jaromir Jagr 2.00 5.00
7 Mario Lemieux 8.00 20.00
10 Pavel Bure 1.25 3.00
13 Mats Sundin 1.25 3.00
17 Peter Forsberg 3.00 8.00
27 Patrick Roy 6.00 15.00
32 Steve Yzerman 6.00 15.00
79 Ilya Kovalchuk 1.50 4.00

1948 Topps Magic Photos

The 1948 Topps Magic Photos set contains 252 small (approximately 7/8" by 1 7/16") individual cards featuring sport and non-sport subjects. They were issued in 19 lettered series with cards numbered within each series. The fronts were developed, much like a photograph, from a "blank" appearance by using moisture and sunlight. Due to varying degrees of photographic sensitivity, the clarity of these cards ranges from fully developed to poorly developed. This set contains Topps' first baseball cards. A premium album holding 126-cards was also issued. The set is sometimes confused with Topps' 1956 Hocus-Focus set, although the cards in this set are slightly smaller than those in the Hocus-Focus set. The checklist below is presented by series. Poorly developed cards are considered in lesser condition and hence have lesser value. The catalog designation for this set is R714-27. Each type of card subject has a letter prefix as follows: Boxing Champions (A), All-American Basketball (B), All-American Football (C), Wrestling Champions (D), Track and Field Champions (E), Stars of Stage and Screen (F), American Dogs (G), General Sports (H), Movie Stars (J), Baseball Hall of Fame (K), Aviation Pioneers (L), Famous Landmarks (M), American Inventors (N), American Military Leaders (O), American Explorers (P), Basketball Thrills (Q), Football Thrills (R), Figures of the Wild West (S), and General Sports (T).

COMPLETE SET (252) 3000.00 5000.00
T3 Ice Hockey 15.00 30.00

1999 Topps Pearson Award

This card was available only by mail for those who voted online for Jaromir Jagr for the 1999 Lester B.Pearson award.

1 Jaromir Jagr 6.00 15.00

1996-97 Topps Picks

This limited production 90-card set was distributed in seven-card packs (five-cards in Canadian packs) with a suggested retail price of $.99. Topps and Fleer card companies joined together to each select a team of 90 hockey players. The cards in Topps set all have odd numbers because Topps had the first pick of players. Each card features color player photos with player career statistics, biographical information, and a "Topps Prediction" section which gave the upcoming season's goals, assists, wins and shutouts totals for each player as predicted by the Topps Sports Department. Each pack contained an official NHL/NHLPA Draft Game registration form which allowed the collectors the chance to draft their own players and create teams in order to win prizes in a fantasy league.

COMPLETE SET (90) 5.00 15.00
1 Jaromir Jagr .20 .50
3 Mario Lemieux .60 1.50
5 Peter Forsberg .30 .75
7 Teemu Selanne .10 .30
9 Alexander Mogilny .05 .15
11 Patrick Roy .60 1.50
13 Jim Carey .10 .30
15 Pavel Bure .10 .30
17 Sergei Fedorov .15 .40
19 Chris Chelios .10 .30
21 Sandis Ozolinsh .01 .05
23 Doug Weight .05 .15
25 Mark Messier .10 .30
27 Martin Brodeur .30 .75
29 Brett Hull .15 .40
31 Steve Yzerman .60 1.50
33 Kevin Hatcher .01 .05
35 Roman Hamrlik .05 .15
37 Petr Nedved .05 .15
39 Valeri Kamensky .05 .15
41 Gary Suter .01 .05
43 Mats Sundin .10 .30
45 Trevor Linden .05 .15
47 Jeremy Roenick .15 .40
49 Al MacInnis .05 .15
51 Mike Modano .20 .50
53 Mathieu Schneider .01 .05
55 Michal Pivonka .01 .05
57 Owen Nolan .05 .15
59 Martin Rucinsky .01 .05
61 Joe Nieuwendyk .05 .15
63 Mark Recchi .05 .15
65 Geoff Sanderson .05 .15
67 Vyacheslav Kozlov .01 .05
69 Pat Verbeek .01 .05
71 Brian Bradley .01 .05
73 Steve Duchesne .01 .05
75 Steve Thomas .01 .05
77 Eric Daze .05 .15
79 Alexei Kovalev .01 .05
81 Kevin Stevens .01 .05
83 Curtis Joseph .10 .30
85 Bill Ranford .05 .15
87 Luc Robitaille .05 .15
89 Claude Lemieux .01 .05
91 Sergei Gonchar .01 .05
93 Eric Desjardins .05 .15
95 Garry Galley .01 .05
97 Oleg Tverdovsky .05 .15
99 Rob Niedermayer .05 .15
101 Scott Mellanby .05 .15
103 Adam Deadmarsh .01 .05
105 Cliff Ronning .01 .05
107 Russ Courtnall .01 .05
109 Keith Primeau .01 .05
111 Rick Tocchet .05 .15
113 Scott Young .01 .05
115 Scott Stevens .05 .15
117 Al Iafrate .05 .15
119 Ray Ferraro .01 .05
121 Todd Bertuzzi .10 .30
123 Alexander Selivanov .01 .05
125 Steve Chiasson .01 .05
127 Dave Andreychuk .05 .15
129 Ray Sheppard .05 .15
131 Bernie Nicholls .01 .05
133 Tony Amonte .05 .15
135 Nelson Emerson .01 .05
137 Cam Neely .10 .30
139 Shayne Corson .01 .05
141 Bill Guerin .01 .05
143 Joe Murphy .01 .05
145 Cory Stillman .01 .05
147 Radek Bonk .01 .05
149 Geoff Courtnall .01 .05
151 Chad Kilger .01 .05
153 Sylvain Cote .01 .05
155 Glen Wesley .01 .05
157 Jeff Norton .01 .05
159 Rob Blake .05 .15
161 Calle Johansson .01 .05
163 Uwe Krupp .01 .05
165 James Patrick .01 .05
167 Dmitri Mironov .01 .05
169 Vladimir Konstantinov .05 .15
171 Mattias Norstrom .01 .05
173 David Wilkie .01 .05
175 Bryan McCabe .01 .05
177 Barry Richter .01 .05
179 Ed Belfour .10 .30

1996-97 Topps Picks 500 Club

Randomly inserted at the rate of 1:36 packs, this eight-card insert set featured the eight active players who had scored their 500th career goal by the end of the 1995-96 season. The set featured color player photos and player information printed on rainbow diffraction foilboard.

COMPLETE SET (8) 12.00 30.00
FC1 Wayne Gretzky 6.00 15.00
FC2 Mike Gartner .75 2.00
FC3 Jari Kurri .75 2.00
FC4 Dino Ciccarelli .75 2.00
FC5 Mario Lemieux 4.00 10.00
FC6 Mark Messier 1.25 3.00
FC7 Steve Yzerman 3.00 8.00
FC8 Dale Hawerchuk .75 2.00

1996-97 Topps Picks Fantasy Team

Randomly inserted at the rate of 1:24 packs, this 22 card set featured a dream team made up of the elite hockey stars which any NHL general manager would want playing for him. Printed with Power Matrix technology, the fronts displayed color player photos while the backs carried player information.

COMPLETE SET (22) 20.00 50.00
FT1 Patrick Roy 3.00 8.00
FT2 Chris Osgood .40 1.00
FT3 Martin Brodeur 2.00 5.00
FT4 Ray Bourque 1.25 3.00
FT5 Brian Leetch .75 2.00
FT6 Chris Chelios .75 2.00
FT7 Paul Coffey .75 2.00
FT8 Ed Jovanovski .40 1.00
FT9 Roman Hamrlik .40 1.00
FT10 Wayne Gretzky 4.00 10.00
FT11 Paul Kariya 1.25 3.00
FT12 Brett Hull 1.25 3.00
FT13 Pavel Bure 1.25 3.00
FT14 Jaromir Jagr 1.50 4.00
FT15 Mario Lemieux 3.00 8.00
FT16 Peter Forsberg 1.50 4.00
FT17 Sergei Fedorov 1.25 3.00
FT18 Jeremy Roenick 1.25 3.00
FT19 Alexander Mogilny .75 2.00
FT20 Joe Sakic 2.00 5.00
FT21 Teemu Selanne 1.25 3.00
FT22 Eric Lindros 1.25 3.00

1996-97 Topps Picks Ice D

Randomly inserted at the rate of 1:24 packs, this 15-card set featured five of the best defensemen and ten top goalies. Color player photos were printed on rainbow prismatic foil with player information on the backs.

COMPLETE SET (15) 20.00 40.00
ID1 Brian Leetch 1.25 3.00
ID2 Ray Bourque 2.00 5.00
ID3 Chris Chelios 1.25 3.00
ID4 Scott Stevens 1.00 2.50
ID5 Ed Jovanovski 1.00 2.50
ID6 Martin Brodeur 3.00 8.00
ID7 Patrick Roy 4.00 10.00
ID8 Chris Osgood 1.00 2.50
ID9 Jim Carey 1.25 3.00
ID10 Dominik Hasek 2.50 6.00
ID11 Ron Hextall 1.00 2.50
ID12 John Vanbiesbrouck 1.00 2.50
ID13 Mike Richter 1.25 3.00
ID14 Felix Potvin 1.25 3.00
ID15 Grant Fuhr 1.00 2.50

1996-97 Topps Picks OPC Inserts

Randomly inserted in Canadian packs only at the rate of 1:4, this 90-card set was parallel to the regular 1996-97 Topps NHL Picks set. These inserts are differentiated in that OPC cards have foil backgrounds and feature the OPC logo on the front. Values for the cards can be determined by using the multipliers below on the base cards.

*OPC: 4X TO 10X BASIC CARDS

1996-97 Topps Picks Rookie Stars

Inserted at the rate of one per pack, this 18-card set showcased hockey's best and brightest young stars. The fronts displayed color player photos while the backs carried player information. OPC parallels were also created and inserted in random Canadian packs.

COMPLETE SET (18) 5.00 10.00
*OPC: 4X TO 10X BASIC INSERTS
RS1 Daniel Alfredsson .20 .50
RS2 Jere Lehtinen .60 1.50
RS3 Vitali Yachmenev .20 .50
RS4 Eric Daze .20 .50
RS5 Saku Koivu .60 1.50
RS6 Petr Sykora .20 .50
RS7 Marcus Ragnarsson .20 .50
RS8 Valeri Bure .20 .50
RS9 Cory Stillman .20 .50
RS10 Todd Bertuzzi .60 1.50
RS11 Ed Jovanovski .40 1.00
RS12 Miroslav Satan .40 1.00
RS13 Kyle McLaren .20 .50
RS14 Byron Dafoe .40 1.00
RS15 Eric Fichaud .20 .50
RS16 Corey Hirsch .20 .50
RS17 Jeff O'Neill .20 .50
RS18 Niklas Sundstrom .20 .50

1996-97 Topps Picks Top Shelf

Randomly inserted at the rate of 1:12 packs, this 15-card set featured red foil-stamped cards of the league's top scorers and award winners of the 1995-96 season. The fronts displayed color player photos while the backs carried player information.

COMPLETE SET (15) 15.00 40.00
TS1 John LeClair .60 1.50
TS2 Wayne Gretzky 4.00 10.00
TS3 Eric Lindros 1.00 2.50
TS4 Paul Kariya 1.00 2.50
TS5 Mark Messier 1.00 2.50
TS6 Jaromir Jagr 1.50 4.00
TS7 Peter Forsberg 1.50 4.00
TS8 Teemu Selanne 1.00 2.50
TS9 Alexander Mogilny .60 1.50
TS10 Brett Hull 1.25 3.00
TS11 Sergei Fedorov 1.25 3.00
TS12 Joe Sakic 2.00 5.00
TS13 Mats Sundin 1.00 2.50
TS14 Theo Fleury .60 1.50
TS15 Steve Yzerman 2.50 6.00

2009-10 Topps Puck Attax

COMPLETE SET (192) 25.00 60.00
1 Ryan Getzlaf .50 1.25
2 Corey Perry .30 .75
3 Teemu Selanne .30 .75
4 Scott Niedermayer .20 .50
5 Ryan Whitney .20 .50
6 Jonas Hiller .40 1.00
7 Bryan Little .30 .75
8 Ilya Kovalchuk .40 1.00
9 Chris Thorburn .20 .50
10 Tobias Enstrom .30 .75
11 Ron Hainsey .20 .50
12 Kari Lehtonen .30 .75
13 Marc Savard .20 .50
14 David Krejci .25 .60
15 Milan Lucic .30 .75
16 Chuck Kobasew .20 .50
17 Zdeno Chara .20 .50
18 Dennis Wideman .20 .50
19 Tim Thomas .30 .75
20 Derek Roy .30 .75
21 Paul Gaustad .25 .60
22 Thomas Vanek .30 .75
23 Craig Rivet .20 .50
24 Toni Lydman .20 .50
25 Ryan Miller .30 .75
26 Olli Jokinen .20 .50
27 Jarome Iginla .60 1.50
28 Curtis Glencross .20 .50
29 Dion Phaneuf .50 1.25
30 Jay Bouwmeester .30 .75
31 Miikka Kiprusoff .30 .75
32 Eric Staal .40 1.00
33 Chad LaRose .20 .50
34 Ray Whitney .20 .50
35 Joe Corvo .20 .50
36 Joni Pitkanen .25 .60
37 Cam Ward .30 .75
38 Jonathan Toews .75 2.00
39 Patrick Kane .60 1.50
40 Patrick Sharp .25 .60
41 Brian Campbell .25 .60
42 Duncan Keith .25 .60
43 Cristobal Huet .30 .75
44 Milan Hejduk .30 .75
45 Paul Stastny .30 .75
46 Cody McLeod .20 .50
47 John-Michael Liles .25 .60
48 Ruslan Salei .20 .50
49 Peter Budaj .30 .75
50 Rick Nash .30 .75
51 Kristian Huselius .30 .75
52 R.J. Umberger .25 .60
53 Fedor Tyutin .20 .50
54 Mike Commodore .20 .50
55 Steve Mason .50 1.25
56 Mike Ribeiro .25 .60
57 Brad Richards .25 .60
58 Mike Modano .30 .75
59 Matt Niskanen .20 .50
60 Stephane Robidas .20 .50
61 Marty Turco .25 .60
62 Dan Cleary .30 .75
63 Johan Franzen .20 .50
64 Pavel Datsyuk .30 .75
65 Henrik Zetterberg .60 1.50
66 Brian Rafalski .20 .50
67 Nicklas Lidstrom .40 1.00
68 Niklas Kronwall .25 .60
69 Chris Osgood .40 1.00
70 Sam Gagner .40 1.00
71 Ethan Moreau .20 .50
72 Ales Hemsky .25 .60
73 Sheldon Souray .20 .50
74 Tom Gilbert .20 .50
75 Denis Grebeshkov .20 .50
76 Nikolai Khabibulin .30 .75
77 Stephen Weiss .20 .50
78 David Booth .20 .50
79 Nathan Horton .20 .50
80 Keith Ballard .20 .50
81 Bryan McCabe .20 .50
82 Tomas Vokoun .30 .75
83 Ryan Smyth .30 .75
84 Anze Kopitar .30 .75
85 Wayne Simmonds .30 .75
86 Drew Doughty .60 1.50
87 Matt Greene .20 .50
88 Jonathan Quick .50 1.25
89 Martin Havlat .25 .60
90 Mikko Koivu .30 .75
91 Cal Clutterbuck .25 .60
92 Marek Zidlicky .20 .50
93 Brent Burns .20 .50
94 Niklas Backstrom .30 .75
95 Mike Cammalleri .25 .60
96 Maxim Lapierre .20 .50
97 Andrei Kostitsyn .25 .60
98 Brian Gionta .30 .75
99 Scott Gomez .30 .75
100 Jaroslav Spacek .20 .50
101 Andrei Markov .25 .60
102 Carey Price .75 2.00
103 David Legwand .25 .60
104 Joel Ward .20 .50
105 Jason Arnott .20 .50
106 Shea Weber .25 .60
107 Ryan Suter .20 .50
108 Pekka Rinne .25 .60
109 Zach Parise .30 .75
110 Patrik Elias .25 .60
111 Jamie Langenbrunner .20 .50
112 Paul Martin .20 .50
113 John Oduya .20 .50
114 Martin Brodeur .75 2.00
115 Doug Weight .20 .50
116 Frans Nielsen .20 .50
117 Kyle Okposo .30 .75
118 Mark Streit .20 .50
119 Bruno Gervais .20 .50
120 Dwayne Roloson .25 .60
121 Rick DiPietro .30 .75
122 Marian Gaborik .50 1.25
123 Brandon Dubinsky .25 .60
124 Chris Drury .25 .60
125 Sean Avery .25 .60
126 Dan Girardi .20 .50
127 Marc Staal .40 1.00
128 Henrik Lundqvist .60 1.50
129 Jason Spezza .40 1.00
130 Chris Kelly .20 .50
131 Daniel Alfredsson .30 .75
132 Filip Kuba .20 .50
133 Chris Campoli .25 .60
134 Pascal Leclaire .30 .75
135 Jeff Carter .30 .75
136 Mike Richards .60 1.50
137 Arron Asham .25 .60
138 Chris Pronger .25 .60
139 Kimmo Timonen .25 .60
140 Braydon Coburn .20 .50
141 Ray Emery .25 .60
142 Matthew Lombardi .20 .50
143 Peter Mueller .40 1.00
144 Shane Doan .25 .60
145 Zbynek Michalek .25 .60
146 Ed Jovanovski .20 .50
147 Ilya Bryzgalov .25 .60
148 Jason LaBarbera .25 .60
149 Maxime Talbot .30 .75
150 Evgeni Malkin .75 2.00
151 Sidney Crosby 1.50 4.00
152 Jordan Staal .40 1.00
153 Kris Letang .30 .75
154 Sergei Gonchar .20 .50
155 Marc-Andre Fleury .30 .75
156 Joe Thornton .60 1.50
157 Ryane Clowe .20 .50
158 Devin Setoguchi .25 .60
159 Dan Boyle .20 .50
160 Rob Blake .30 .75
161 Evgeni Nabokov .30 .75
162 Brad Boyes .25 .60
163 Keith Tkachuk .25 .60
164 Jay McClement .20 .50
165 Barret Jackman .20 .50
166 Carlo Colaiacovo .20 .50
167 Chris Mason .20 .50
168 Vincent Lecavalier .40 1.00
169 Steven Stamkos .75 2.00
170 Martin St. Louis .30 .75
171 Mattias Ohlund .20 .50
172 Andrej Meszaros .20 .50
173 Mike Smith .25 .60
174 Matt Stajan .25 .60
175 Jason Blake .20 .50
176 Alexei Ponikarovsky .20 .50
177 Luke Schenn .50 1.25
178 Mike Komisarek .25 .60
179 Tomas Kaberle .20 .50
180 Vesa Toskala .30 .75
181 Henrik Sedin .50 1.25
182 Alex Burrows .25 .60
183 Daniel Sedin .40 1.00
184 Sami Salo .30 .75
185 Kevin Bieksa .20 .50
186 Roberto Luongo .75 2.00
187 Nicklas Backstrom .60 1.50
188 Alexander Ovechkin 1.25 3.00
189 David Steckel .20 .50
190 Mike Green .60 1.50
191 Shaone Morrisonn .20 .50
192 Simeon Varlamov .60 1.50

2009-10 Topps Puck Attax Black Foil

*SINGLES: .8X TO 2X BASIC CARDS
STATED ODDS 1 PER PACK

2009-10 Topps Puck Attax Gold Foil

*SINGLES: 2X TO 5X BASIC CARDS

2009-10 Topps Puck Attax Platinum Blister

COMPLETE SET (6) 6.00 15.00
STATED ODDS 1 PER BLISTER
1 Mike Modano 1.00 2.50
2 Jarome Iginla 2.00 5.00
3 Ilya Kovalchuk 1.25 3.00
4 Rick Nash 1.00 2.50
5 Vincent Lecavalier 1.25 3.00
6 Henrik Sedin 1.50 4.00

2009-10 Topps Puck Attax Platinum Starter

COMPLETE SET (6) 10.00 25.00
STATED ODDS 1 PER STARTER PACK
1 Sidney Crosby 5.00 12.00
2 Alexander Ovechkin 4.00 10.00
3 Eric Staal 1.25 3.00
4 Nicklas Lidstrom 1.25 3.00
5 Andrei Markov .75 2.00
6 Henrik Lundqvist 2.00 5.00

1999-00 Topps Premier Plus

Topps Premier Plus was released as a 140-card set comprised of 81 veteran cards and 59 prospect cards. Printed on a canvas card-stock, this set features crystal clear player action shots with a blue name box across the bottom for veterans and a red name box across the bottom for the prospects. Packaged at 24-packs per box and eight cards per pack, packs carried a suggested retail price of $2.50.

COMPLETE SET (140) 40.00 80.00
1 Curtis Joseph .20 .50
2 Peter Bondra .15 .40
3 Theo Fleury .05 .15
4 Steve Yzerman 1.00 2.50
5 Peter Forsberg .50 1.25
6 Ray Bourque .30 .75
7 Dominik Hasek .40 1.00
8 Chris Drury .15 .40
9 Brett Hull .25 .60
10 Chris Osgood .15 .40
11 Luc Robitaille .15 .40
12 Bobby Holik .15 .40
13 John LeClair .20 .50
14 Jeremy Roenick .25 .60
15 Owen Nolan .15 .40
16 Wade Redden .05 .15
17 Teemu Selanne .20 .50
18 Doug Weight .15 .40
19 Vincent Lecavalier .20 .50
20 Pierre Turgeon .15 .40
21 Ron Francis .15 .40
22 Sergei Samsonov .15 .40
23 Patrick Roy 1.00 2.50
24 Mark Messier .20 .50
25 Al MacInnis .15 .40
26 Mark Parrish .05 .15
27 Ron Tugnutt .15 .40
28 Joe Nieuwendyk .15 .40
29 Valeri Bure .05 .15
30 Jason Allison .05 .15
31 Tony Amonte .15 .40
32 Scott Niedermayer .05 .15
33 Kenny Jonsson .05 .15
34 Jaromir Jagr .30 .75
35 Sergei Berezin .15 .40
36 Olaf Kolzig .15 .40
37 Byron Dafoe .15 .40
38 Adam Deadmarsh .05 .15
39 Alexei Zhitnik .05 .15
40 Paul Kariya .20 .50
41 Chris Pronger .15 .40
42 Markus Naslund .20 .50
43 Damian Rhodes .15 .40
44 Marian Hossa .20 .50
45 Adam Graves .05 .15
46 Scott Stevens .15 .40
47 Nicklas Lidstrom .20 .50
48 Ed Belfour .20 .50
49 Miroslav Satan .15 .40
50 Rob Blake .15 .40
51 Petr Nedved .15 .40
52 Mark Recchi .15 .40
53 Jeff Friesen .05 .15
54 Mats Sundin .20 .50
55 Arturs Irbe .15 .40
56 Derian Hatcher .05 .15
57 Mike Modano .30 .75
58 Brendan Shanahan .20 .50
59 Zigmund Palffy .15 .40
60 Saku Koivu .20 .50
61 Brian Leetch .20 .50
62 Rod Brind'Amour .15 .40
63 Keith Tkachuk .20 .50
64 Pavol Demitra .15 .40
65 Magnus Arvedson .05 .15
66 Martin Brodeur .50 1.25
67 Chris Chelios .20 .50
68 Joe Sakic .40 1.00
69 Anson Carter .15 .40
70 Sergei Fedorov .30 .75
71 Pavel Bure .20 .50
72 Petr Sykora .05 .15
73 Daniel Alfredsson .15 .40
74 Guy Hebert .15 .40
75 Jere Lehtinen .15 .40
76 Mike Richter .20 .50
77 Michael Peca .15 .40
78 Sandis Ozolinsh .05 .15
79 Joe Thornton .30 .75
80 Eric Lindros .20 .50
81 Milan Hejduk .20 .50
82 Ladislav Nagy RC 1.00 2.50
83 Francis Bouillon RC .15 .40
84 Mark Eaton RC .30 .75
85 Robert Valicevic RC .15 .40
86 Sami Helenius RC .15 .40
87 Travis Brigley RC .15 .40
88 Glen Metropolit RC .60 1.50
89 Alan Letang RC .15 .40
90 Brad Chartrand RC .15 .40
91 Marc Rodgers RC .15 .40
92 Hans Jonsson RC .15 .40
93 Kim Johnsson RC .15 .40
94 Richard Lintner RC .15 .40
95 Andrew Ference .15 .40
96 Jeff Halpern RC .75 2.00
97 Brad Lukowich RC .15 .40
98 Tyson Nash RC .20 .50
99 Oleg Saprykin RC .75 2.00
100 John Grahame RC .75 2.00
101 Patrik Stefan RC .75 2.00
102 Jason Blake RC .15 .40
103 Kyle Calder RC .20 .50
104 John Madden RC .75 2.00
105 Dan Hinote RC .50 1.25
106 Pavel Patera RC .15 .40
107 Yuri Butsayev RC .15 .40
108 Paul Comrie RC .15 .40
109 Ivan Novoseltsev RC .60 1.50
110 Niclas Havelid RC .20 .50
111 Brian Rafalski RC .60 1.50
112 Jorgen Jonsson RC .15 .40
113 Mike Fisher RC .50 1.25
114 Mika Alatalo RC .15 .40
115 Michal Rozsival RC .15 .40
116 Jochen Hecht RC 1.00 2.50
117 Nikolai Antropov RC 1.00 2.50
118 Steve Kariya RC .60 1.50
119 Brian Campbell RC .60 1.50
120 Maxim Afinogenov .05 .15
121 Roberto Luongo .25 .60
122 Petr Buzek .05 .15
123 Per Svartvadet RC .15 .40
124 Dave Tanabe .05 .15
125 Brad Stuart .15 .40
126 Michael York .05 .15
127 Jiri Fischer .05 .15
128 Peter Schaefer .15 .40
129 Martin Biron .15 .40
130 Rico Fata .05 .15
131 J-P Dumont .15 .40
132 Martin Skoula RC .60 1.50
133 Alex Tanguay .15 .40
134 Mike Ribeiro .15 .40
135 David Legwand .15 .40
136 Scott Gomez .05 .15
137 Tim Connolly .05 .15
138 Jan Hlavac .05 .15
139 Simon Gagne .20 .50
140 Brian Boucher .20 .50
CTW1 Chris Drury AU 10.00 20.00

1999-00 Topps Premier Plus Foil Parallel

Randomly inserted in packs at 1:16, this die-cut foil parallel is labeled on the back "Limited Edition of 250." Cards are randomly inserted into packs.

*VETS: 12X TO 30X BASIC CARDS
*ROOKIES: 8X TO 20X BASIC CARDS

1999-00 Topps Premier Plus Calling All Calders

Randomly inserted in packs at 1:16, this 10-card set features Calder Trophy winners spanning from the late 1980's to 1999. This foil insert places player action shots against a background that shows The Calder Trophy.

COMPLETE SET (10) 12.00 25.00
CAC1 Chris Drury .75 2.00
CAC2 Sergei Samsonov 1.00 2.50
CAC3 Daniel Alfredsson .75 2.00
CAC4 Peter Forsberg 2.50 6.00
CAC5 Martin Brodeur 2.50 6.00
CAC6 Teemu Selanne .75 2.00
CAC7 Pavel Bure 1.25 3.00
CAC8 Ed Belfour 1.00 2.50
CAC9 Joe Nieuwendyk .75 2.00
CAC10 Brian Leetch 1.00 2.50

1999-00 Topps Premier Plus Club Signings

Randomly inserted in packs, this 9-card set featured authentic player autographs. Single autographs were inserted at 1:476 and dual autos were inserted at 1:1905.

CS1 Ray Bourque 30.00 80.00
CS2 Cam Neely 20.00 50.00
CS3 Curtis Joseph 12.50 30.00
CS4 Johnny Bower 10.00 25.00
CS5 Jaromir Jagr 25.00 60.00
CS6 Mario Lemieux 40.00 100.00
CSC1 Ray Bourque 60.00 150.00
Cam Neely
CSC2 Curtis Joseph 40.00 100.00
Johnny Bower
CSC3 Jaromir Jagr 200.00 300.00
Mario Lemieux

1999-00 Topps Premier Plus Code Red

COMPLETE SET (8) 20.00 40.00
STATED ODDS 1:40
CR1 Keith Tkachuk 1.50 4.00
CR2 Teemu Selanne 1.50 4.00
CR3 Zigmund Palffy 1.50 4.00
CR4 Steve Yzerman 8.00 20.00
CR5 Theo Fleury 1.50 4.00
CR6 Jaromir Jagr 2.50 6.00
CR7 Peter Bondra 1.25 3.00
CR8 Pavel Bure 2.00 5.00

1999-00 Topps Premier Plus Feature Presentations

COMPLETE SET (8) 8.00 15.00
STATED ODDS 1:10
FP1 Joe Sakic 1.25 3.00
FP2 Mark Messier .75 2.00
FP3 Steve Yzerman 3.00 8.00
FP4 Mike Modano 1.00 2.50
FP5 Paul Kariya .75 2.00
FP6 Pavel Bure .75 2.00

FP7 Jaromir Jagr 1.00 2.50
FP8 Ray Bourque 1.00 2.50

1999-00 Topps Premier Plus Game Pieces

Randomly inserted in packs, this 5-card set consists of a card front displaying a piece of game-used stick (inserted at 1:960) or game-used sweater (inserted at 1:190) from the league's top veterans and prospects.

GPCD Chris Drury S 40.00 100.00
GPDL David Legwand S 7.50 15.00
GPDW Doug Weight J 7.50 15.00
GPMR Mike Richter S 15.00 40.00
GPNL Nicklas Lidstrom J 7.50 15.00
GPSG Scott Gomez J 7.50 15.00

1999-00 Topps Premier Plus Imperial Guard

COMPLETE SET(8) 20.00 40.00
STATED ODDS 1:40
IG1 Ed Belfour 1.50 4.00
IG2 Patrick Roy 8.00 20.00
IG3 Martin Brodeur 4.00 10.00
IG4 Dominik Hasek 3.00 8.00
IG5 Curtis Joseph 1.50 4.00
IG6 John Vanbiesbrouck 1.25 3.00
IG7 Mike Richter 1.50 4.00
IG8 Byron Dafoe 1.25 3.00

1999-00 Topps Premier Plus Premier Rookies

Randomly inserted in packs at 1:12, this 10-card set features some of the NHL's eligible Calder Trophy winners. A parallel variation numbered to just 250 was also created and inserted at 1:229.

COMPLETE SET (10) 10.00 20.00
*FOIL/250: 1.5X TO 4X BASIC INSERTS
PR1 Alex Tanguay 1.50 4.00
PR2 Brad Stuart 1.25 3.00
PR3 Peter Schaefer .75 2.00
PR4 Scott Gomez .75 2.00
PR5 Patrik Stefan .75 2.00
PR6 Jochen Hecht 1.25 3.00
PR7 David Legwand 1.50 4.00
PR8 Steve Kariya 1.50 4.00
PR9 J-P Dumont 1.00 2.50
PR10 Simon Gagne 1.50 4.00

1999-00 Topps Premier Plus Premier Team

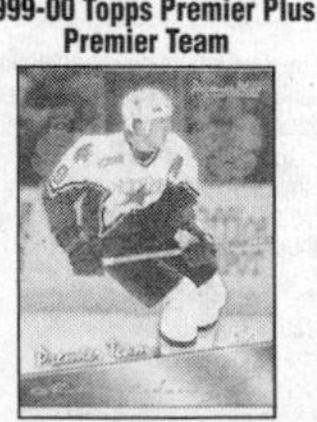

Seeded in packs at 1:12, this 10-card set pictures NHL superstars who have separated themselves from the rest of the league. Card backs carry a "PT" prefix. A parallel variation numbered to just 250 was also created and inserted at 1:299.

COMPLETE SET (10) 15.00 30.00
*FOIL/250: 4X TO 10X BASIC INSERTS
PT1 Paul Kariya .75 2.00
PT2 Jaromir Jagr 1.25 3.00
PT3 Eric Lindros .75 2.00
PT4 Mike Modano 1.25 3.00
PT5 Mats Sundin .75 2.00
PT6 Peter Forsberg 2.00 5.00
PT7 Steve Yzerman 4.00 10.00
PT8 Patrick Roy 4.00 10.00
PT9 Martin Brodeur 2.00 5.00
PT10 Dominik Hasek 1.50 4.00

1999-00 Topps Premier Plus Signing Bonus

Randomly inserted in packs at 1:229, this 5-card set features five of the NHL's top prospects. Each card is autographed and contains the "Topps Certified Autograph" stamp and 3M authentication sticker. Card backs carry an "SB" prefix.

SB1 David Legwand 5.00 12.00
SB2 Scott Gomez 5.00 12.00
SB3 Peter Schaefer 5.00 12.00
SB4 Patrik Stefan 5.00 12.00
SB5 Alex Tanguay 10.00 25.00

1999-00 Topps Premier Plus The Next Ones

COMPLETE SET (8) 6.00 12.00
STATED ODDS 1:10
TN01 Vincent Lecavalier 1.00 2.50
TN02 Marian Hossa 1.00 2.50
TN03 Chris Drury .75 2.00
TN04 Joe Thornton 1.50 4.00
TN05 Steve Kariya .30 .75
TN06 David Legwand .75 2.00
TN07 Patrik Stefan .30 .75
TN08 Milan Hejduk 1.00 2.50

1999-00 Topps Premier Plus Promos

This set of six promo cards was widely distributed prior to the release of the Premier Plus set. The cards feature the same photos as the base cards, but different numbers, including a PP-prefix.

COMPLETE SET (6) 2.00 5.00
PP1 Curtis Joseph .60 1.50
PP2 J.P. Dumont .20 .50
PP3 Marian Hossa .60 1.50
PP4 Saku Koivu .30 .75
PP5 Chris Drury .40 1.00
PP6 Ron Francis .20 .50

2000-01 Topps Premier Plus

Topps Premier Plus was issued as a 140-card set with an additional NNO card of Scott Gomez with the checklist on the back. The card design had an embossed front and looked like the base Topps 2000-01. The card backs had a small photo of the featured player and some of his statistics from his NHL career.

COMPLETE SET (140) 30.00 60.00
1 Scott Gomez .05 .15
2 Brian Boucher .20 .50
3 Patrik Stefan .05 .15
4 David Legwand .15 .40
5 Tim Connolly .05 .15
6 Jaromir Jagr .30 .75
7 Owen Nolan .15 .40
8 Patrick Roy 1.00 2.50
9 Joe Thornton .30 .75
10 Paul Kariya .20 .50
11 Mark Messier .20 .50
12 Jeremy Roenick .25 .60
13 Jeff Friesen .05 .15
14 Al MacInnis .15 .40
15 Curtis Joseph .20 .50
16 Olaf Kolzig .15 .40
17 Dominik Hasek .40 1.00
18 Arturs Irbe .15 .40
19 Joe Sakic .40 1.00
20 Sergei Fedorov .30 .75
21 Zigmund Palffy .15 .40
22 Jason Arnott .05 .15
23 Marian Hossa .20 .50
24 Pierre Turgeon .15 .40
25 Ron Tugnutt .15 .40
26 Valeri Bure .05 .15
27 Tony Amonte .15 .40
28 Jeff Hackett .15 .40
29 Mariusz Czerkawski .05 .15
30 Wade Redden .05 .15
31 Mark Recchi .15 .40
32 Jean-Sebastien Aubin .15 .40
33 Jason Allison .05 .15
34 Michael Peca .15 .40
35 Teemu Selanne .20 .50
36 Martin Brodeur .50 1.25

37 Simon Gagne .20 .50
38 Chris Simon .05 .15
39 Doug Weight .15 .40
40 Jocelyn Thibault .15 .40
41 Ed Belfour .20 .50
42 Ray Bourque .40 1.00
43 Mike Richter .20 .50
44 Curtis Leschyshyn .05 .15
45 Pavol Demitra .15 .40
46 Alexei Kovalev .15 .40
47 Brad Stuart .15 .40
48 Jarome Iginla .25 .60
49 Ron Francis .15 .40
50 Brendan Shanahan .20 .50
51 Rob Blake .15 .40
52 Miroslav Satan .15 .40
53 Theo Fleury .05 .15
54 John LeClair .20 .50
55 Roman Turek .15 .40
56 Brett Hull .25 .60
57 Peter Forsberg .50 1.25
58 Steve Yzerman 1.00 2.50
59 Derian Hatcher .05 .15
60 Pavel Bure .20 .50
61 Patrik Elias .15 .40
62 Daniel Alfredsson .15 .40
63 Adam Oates .15 .40
64 Andrew Brunette .05 .15
65 Chris Pronger .15 .40
66 Mario Lemieux 1.25 3.00
67 Keith Tkachuk .20 .50
68 Markus Naslund .20 .50
69 Mike Modano .30 .75
70 Nicklas Lidstrom .20 .50
71 Scott Stevens .15 .40
72 Vincent Lecavalier .20 .50
73 Luc Robitaille .15 .40
74 Mats Sundin .20 .50
75 Milan Hejduk .20 .50
76 Rod Brind'amour .15 .40
77 Tommy Salo .15 .40
78 Byron Dafoe .15 .40
79 Doug Gilmour .15 .40
80 Guy Hebert .15 .40
81 Keith Primeau .05 .15
82 Chris Drury .15 .40
83 Saku Koivu .20 .50
84 Alexei Yashin .05 .15
85 Martin St. Louis .15 .40
86 Steve McCarthy .05 .15
87 Henrik Sedin .05 .15
88 Kris Beech .05 .15
89 Dimitri Kalinin .05 .15
90 Maxime Ouellet .15 .40
91 Shawn Heins .05 .15
92 Mika Noronen .05 .15
93 Taylor Pyatt .05 .15
94 Brent Johnson .15 .40
95 Oleg Saprykin .05 .15
96 Daniel Tkaczuk .05 .15
97 Daniel Sedin .05 .15
98 Milan Kraft .05 .15
99 Jeff Farkas .05 .15
100 Denis Shvidki .05 .15
101 Mathieu Garon .15 .40
102 Mike Mottau .05 .15
103 Andrei Markov .05 .15
104 Brad Richards .15 .40
105 Brian Swanson RC .20 .50
106 Josef Vasicek RC .20 .50
107 Reto Von Arx RC .20 .50
108 Lubomir Sekeras RC .20 .50
109 Ruslan Fedotenko RC .20 .50
110 Roman Simicek RC .20 .50
111 Michel Riesen RC .05 .15
112 Petteri Nummelin RC .05 .15
113 Brad Tapper RC .20 .50
114 Alexander Kharitonov RC .20 .50
115 Andrew Raycroft RC 1.25 3.00
116 Ossi Vaananen RC .20 .50
117 Tyler Bouck RC .20 .50
118 Steven Reinprecht RC .20 .50
119 Rostislav Klesla RC .75 2.00
120 Martin Havlat RC 1.50 4.00
121 Scott Hartnell RC .50 1.25
122 David Aebischer RC 1.25 3.00
123 Bryce Salvador RC .20 .50
124 Jani Hurme RC .60 1.50
125 Eric Belanger RC .20 .50
126 Marty Turco RC 1.50 4.00
127 Rick DiPietro RC 1.25 3.00
128 Justin Williams RC .75 2.00
129 Dale Purinton RC .20 .50
130 Marian Gaborik RC 2.00 5.00
131 Petr Svoboda RC .20 .50
132 Niclas Wallin RC .20 .50
133 Petr Hubacek RC .20 .50
134 Colin White RC .20 .50
135 Greg Classen RC .20 .50
136 Roman Cechmanek RC .25 .60
137 Eric Boulton RC .20 .50
138 Sascha Goc RC .20 .50
139 Lubomir Visnovsky RC .05 .15
140 Ronald Petrovicky .20 .50
NNO Scott Gomez .05 .15
Oversized CL

2000-01 Topps Premier Plus Blue Ice

Randomly inserted in packs of 2000-01 Topps Premier Plus at a rate of 1:15, this 140-card set is parallel to the base set. The cards were serial numbered to 250.The card design was the same as the base set with the exceptions of a red border instead of blue and the ice in the photo was blue, the cards were die-cut on all 4 sides and the card front used an embossed foilboard design.

*STARS: 4X TO 10X BASIC CARDS
*BLUE RC'S: 1.5X TO 3X BASIC CARDS

2000-01 Topps Premier Plus Aspirations

COMPLETE SET (10) 10.00 20.00
STATED ODDS 1:16
PA1 Scott Gomez .75 2.00
PA2 Vincent Lecavalier 1.25 3.00
PA3 Maxim Afinogenov .75 2.00
PA4 Milan Hejduk 1.25 3.00
PA5 Joe Thornton 2.00 5.00
PA6 Marian Hossa 1.25 3.00
PA7 Oleg Saprykin .75 2.00
PA8 Shane Willis .75 2.00
PA9 David Legwand 1.00 2.50
PA10 Tim Connolly .75 2.00

2000-01 Topps Premier Plus Club Signings

The Signings were randomly inserted in packs of 2000-01 Topps Premier Plus at a rate of 1:219 for the single signed cards and a rate of 1:1751 for the dual signed cards.

CS1 Billy Smith 8.00 20.00
CS2 John Vanbiesbrouck 8.00 20.00
CS3 John LeClair 8.00 20.00
CS4 Bobby Clarke 12.50 30.00
CS5 Luc Robitaille 8.00 20.00
CS6 Marcel Dionne 8.00 20.00
CSC1 J.V'brouck/B.Smith 40.00 100.00
CSC2 John LeClair 30.00 80.00
Bobby Clarke
CSC3 Luc Robitaille 30.00 60.00
Marcel Dionne

2000-01 Topps Premier Plus Game-Used Memorabilia

Randomly inserted in packs of 2000-01 Topps Premier Plus at a rate of 1:66 for the jersey cards, 1:658 for the stick cards, and 1:1752 for the combo relic cards. The 18-card set featured pieces of game-used memorabilia from the NHL.

*MULT.COLOR SWATCH: 1X TO 2X
GPAO Adam Oates S 8.00 20.00
GPEB Ed Belfour S 20.00 50.00
GPJI Jarome Iginla J 12.00 30.00
GPJV John Vanbiesbrouck S 12.00 30.00
GPKB Kris Beech J 4.00 10.00
GPMB Max Balmochnyk J 4.00 10.00
GPMT Marty Turco J 8.00 20.00
GPOS Oleg Saprykin J 4.00 10.00
GPRF Rico Fata J 4.00 10.00
GPTP Taylor Pyatt J 4.00 10.00
GPTS Teemu Selanne S 12.00 30.00
GPVB Valeri Bure J 4.00 10.00
GPAOKB Kris Beech 8.00 20.00
Adam Oates
GPEBMT Marty Turco 30.00 80.00
Ed Belfour
GPJIRF Rico Fata 20.00 50.00
Jarome Iginla
GPJVTP Taylor Pyatt 20.00 50.00
John Vanbiesbrouck
GPTSMB Max Balmochnyk 12.00 30.00
Teemu Selanne
GPVBOS Oleg Saprykin 8.00 20.00
Valeri Bure

2000-01 Topps Premier Plus Masters of the Break

COMPLETE SET (20) 30.00 60.00
STATED ODDS 1:24
MB1 Jaromir Jagr 1.50 4.00
MB2 Teemu Selanne 1.00 2.50
MB3 Pavel Bure 1.25 3.00
MB4 Tony Amonte .75 2.00
MB5 Milan Hejduk 1.00 2.50
MB6 Patrik Elias .75 2.00
MB7 Paul Kariya 1.00 2.50
MB8 Peter Forsberg 2.50 6.00
MB9 Sergei Fedorov 2.00 5.00
MB10 Mike Modano 1.50 4.00
MB11 Martin Brodeur 2.50 6.00
MB12 Patrick Roy 5.00 12.00
MB13 Ed Belfour 1.00 2.50
MB14 Curtis Joseph 1.00 2.50
MB15 Dominik Hasek 2.00 5.00
MB16 Olaf Kolzig .60 1.50
MB17 Roman Turek .60 1.50
MB18 Brian Boucher 1.00 2.50
MB19 Mike Richter 1.00 2.50
MB20 Tommy Salo .60 1.50

2000-01 Topps Premier Plus Private Signings

Randomly inserted in packs of Topps Premier Plus at a rate of 1:175 for the rookies and 1:350 for the veterans and 1:526 for the Gomez. This 13-card set featured autographs from some of the top players in the NHL. The cards carried a 'PS' prefix except for the Gomez which carried a 'CT' prefix for the card number. Exchange expiration was 03/01/02.

CTW1 Scott Gomez Calder 10.00 25.00
PSBR Brad Richards 8.00 20.00
PSBS Brad Stuart 4.00 10.00
PSCP Chris Pronger 8.00 20.00
PSDS Daniel Sedin 8.00 20.00
PSEN Evgeni Nabokov 8.00 20.00
PSHS Henrik Sedin 8.00 20.00
PSJW Justin Williams 4.00 10.00
PSMB Martin Brodeur 30.00 80.00
PSMG Marian Gaborik 20.00 50.00
PSMK Milan Kraft 4.00 10.00
PSMT Marty Turco 12.00 30.00
PSSH Scott Hartnell 4.00 10.00

2000-01 Topps Premier Plus Rookies

Randomly inserted in packs of 2000-01 Topps Premier Plus at a rate of 1:12, the 10-card set highlighted the top newcomers to the NHL. A blue ice parallel variation numbered to just 250 was also created and inserted at 1:213.

COMPLETE SET (10) 10.00 20.00
*BLUE ICE: 1.5X TO 3X BASIC CARDS
PR1 Marian Gaborik 3.00 8.00
PR2 Henrik Sedin .40 1.00
PR3 Rostislav Klesla 1.00 2.50
PR4 Brad Richards 1.50 4.00
PR5 Justin Williams 1.00 2.50
PR6 Josef Vasicek .40 1.00
PR7 Daniel Sedin .40 1.00
PR8 Maxime Ouellet 1.25 3.00
PR9 Andrei Markov .40 1.00
PR10 Oleg Saprykin .75 2.00

2000-01 Topps Premier Plus Team

Randomly inserted in packs of 2000-01 Topps Premier Plus at a rate of 1:12, the 10-card set highlighted the top players in the NHL. A blue ice parallel variation numbered to just 250 was also created and inserted at 1:213.

COMPLETE SET (10) 8.00 15.00
*BLUE ICE: 1X TO 1.5X BASIC CARDS
PT1 Paul Kariya .50 1.25
PT2 Peter Forsberg 1.50 4.00
PT3 John LeClair .50 1.25
PT4 Mike Modano 1.00 2.50
PT5 Martin Brodeur 1.50 4.00
PT6 Pavel Bure .50 1.25
PT7 Curtis Joseph .50 1.25
PT8 Jaromir Jagr 1.00 2.50
PT9 Chris Pronger .50 1.25
PT10 Teemu Selanne .50 1.25

2000-01 Topps Premier Plus Trophy Tribute

COMPLETE SET (15) 15.00 30.00
STATED ODDS 1:16
TT1 Dominik Hasek 1.25 3.00
TT2 Jaromir Jagr 1.00 2.50
TT3 Patrick Roy 3.00 8.00
TT4 Chris Pronger .50 1.25
TT5 Paul Kariya .60 1.50
TT6 Ed Belfour .60 1.50
TT7 Mark Messier .75 2.00
TT8 Ray Bourque 1.25 3.00
TT9 Steve Yzerman 3.00 8.00
TT10 Sergei Fedorov 1.25 3.00
TT11 Brett Hull .75 2.00
TT12 Ron Francis .50 1.25
TT13 Pavel Bure .75 2.00
TT14 Teemu Selanne .60 1.50
TT15 Brian Leetch .50 1.25

2000-01 Topps Premier Plus World Premier

COMPLETE SET (20) 30.00 60.00
STATED ODDS 1:24
WP1 Patrick Roy 5.00 12.00
WP2 Martin Brodeur 2.50 6.00
WP3 Chris Pronger .75 2.00
WP4 Sergei Zubov .60 1.50
WP5 Scott Stevens .75 2.00
WP6 Ray Bourque 2.00 5.00
WP7 Nicklas Lidstrom 1.00 2.50
WP8 Rob Blake .75 2.00
WP9 Paul Kariya 1.00 2.50
WP10 John LeClair 1.25 3.00
WP11 Keith Tkachuk 1.00 2.50
WP12 Brendan Shanahan 1.50 4.00
WP13 Vincent Lecavalier 1.00 2.50
WP14 Steve Yzerman 5.00 12.00
WP15 Mike Modano 1.50 4.00
WP16 Peter Forsberg 2.50 6.00
WP17 Pavel Bure 1.25 3.00
WP18 Teemu Selanne 1.00 2.50
WP19 Brett Hull .75 2.00
WP20 Jaromir Jagr 1.50 4.00

2003-04 Topps Pristine

This 190-card set was released in January and was packaged 5 packs per box with 8 cards per pack. Each pack contained two additional packs with a memorabilia card and a "uncirculated" card in each pack. Uncirculated cards were incased in clear plastic slabs. Rookies in the set each had three different variations; common, uncommon and rare. Unpriced 1/1 Press Plates in 4 different colors also exist for each card below.

COMMON RC PRINT RUN 1199 SER.#'d SETS
UNCOMMON PRINT RUN 699 SER.#'d SETS
RARE PRINT RUN 199 SER.#'d SETS
1 Jean-Sebastien Giguere .75 2.00
2 Slava Kozlov .40 1.00
3 Steve Shields .75 2.00
4 Martin Biron .75 2.00
5 Roman Turek .75 2.00
6 Kevin Weekes .75 2.00
7 Kyle Calder .40 1.00
8 Patrik Elias .75 2.00
9 Rob Blake .75 2.00
10 Marty Turco .75 2.00
11 Bill Guerin .75 2.00
12 Nicklas Lidstrom 1.00 2.50
13 Mike Comrie .75 2.00
14 Roberto Luongo 1.25 3.00
15 Ziggy Palffy .75 2.00
16 Paul Kariya 1.00 2.50
17 Stanislav Chistov .40 1.00
18 Andrew Brunette .40 1.00
19 Richard Zednik .40 1.00
20 Martin Brodeur 2.50 6.00
21 Alexei Yashin .40 1.00
22 Brian Leetch .75 2.00
23 Patrick Lalime .75 2.00
24 Simon Gagne 1.00 2.50
25 Mike Johnson .40 1.00
26 Mario Lemieux 4.00 10.00
27 Alyn McCauley .40 1.00
28 Kyle McLaren .40 1.00
29 Brent Johnson .75 2.00
30 Vincent Lecavalier 1.00 2.50
31 Ed Belfour 1.00 2.50
32 Todd Bertuzzi 1.00 2.50
33 Brendan Morrison .75 2.00
34 Olaf Kolzig .75 2.00
35 Ilya Kovalchuk 1.25 3.00
36 Johan Hedberg .75 2.00
37 Mike Knuble .40 1.00
38 Ales Kotalik .40 1.00
39 Chris Drury .75 2.00
40 Joe Thornton 1.50 4.00
41 Dominik Hasek 2.00 5.00
42 Daniel Alfredsson .75 2.00
43 Marc Denis .75 2.00
44 Mike Modano 1.50 4.00
45 Sergei Fedorov 1.25 3.00
46 Henrik Zetterberg 1.00 2.50
47 Tommy Salo .75 2.00
48 Olli Jokinen .75 2.00
49 Felix Potvin 1.00 2.50
50 Dany Heatley 1.25 3.00
51 Marian Gaborik 2.00 5.00
52 Saku Koivu 1.00 2.50
53 Tomas Vokoun .75 2.00
54 Eric Brewer .40 1.00
55 Rick DiPietro .75 2.00
56 Mike Dunham .75 2.00
57 Marian Hossa 1.00 2.50
58 Jeremy Roenick 1.25 3.00
59 Brian Boucher .75 2.00
60 Milan Hejduk 1.00 2.50
61 Patrick Marleau .75 2.00
62 Pavol Demitra .75 2.00
63 Al MacInnis .75 2.00
64 Nikolai Khabibulin 1.00 2.50
65 Mats Sundin 1.00 2.50
66 Miroslav Satan .75 2.00
67 Sergei Gonchar .40 1.00
68 Pasi Nurminen .75 2.00
69 Glen Murray .40 1.00
70 Brett Hull 1.25 3.00
71 Jarome Iginla 1.25 3.00
72 Ron Francis .75 2.00
73 Tyler Arnason .40 1.00
74 Joe Sakic 2.00 5.00
75 David Aebischer .75 2.00
76 Geoff Sanderson .40 1.00
77 Derian Hatcher .40 1.00
78 Jocelyn Thibault .75 2.00
79 Curtis Joseph 1.00 2.50
80 Markus Naslund 1.00 2.50
81 Kristian Huselius .40 1.00
82 Alexander Frolov .40 1.00
83 Petr Sykora .40 1.00
84 Dwayne Roloson .75 2.00
85 Jose Theodore 1.25 3.00
86 David Legwand .75 2.00
87 Scott Stevens .75 2.00
88 Michael Peca .40 1.00
89 Alex Kovalev .75 2.00
90 Jaromir Jagr 1.50 4.00
91 Tony Amonte .75 2.00
92 Daymond Langkow .40 1.00
93 Martin Straka .40 1.00
94 Evgeni Nabokov .75 2.00
95 Chris Pronger .75 2.00
96 Martin St. Louis .75 2.00
97 Alexander Mogilny .75 2.00
98 Owen Nolan .75 2.00
99 Dan Cloutier .75 2.00
100 Peter Forsberg 2.50 6.00
101 Tuomo Ruutu C RC 4.00 10.00
102 Tuomo Ruutu U 4.00 10.00
103 Tuomo Ruutu R 10.00 25.00
104 Marc-Andre Fleury C RC 10.00 25.00
105 Marc-Andre Fleury U 6.00 15.00
106 Marc-Andre Fleury R 25.00 60.00
107 Patrice Bergeron C RC 6.00 15.00
108 Patrice Bergeron U 5.00 12.00
109 Patrice Bergeron R 20.00 50.00
110 Milan Michalek C RC 3.00 8.00
111 Milan Michalek U 2.00 5.00
112 Milan Michalek R 12.50 30.00
113 Dominic Moore C RC 2.50 6.00
114 Dominic Moore U 2.00 5.00
115 Dominic Moore R 10.00 25.00
116 Dustin Brown C RC 2.50 6.00
117 Dustin Brown U 2.00 5.00
118 Dustin Brown R 10.00 25.00
119 Nathan Horton C RC 4.00 10.00
120 Nathan Horton U 3.00 8.00
121 Nathan Horton R 12.50 30.00
122 Chris Higgins C RC 4.00 10.00
123 Chris Higgins U 3.00 8.00
124 Chris Higgins R 12.50 30.00
125 Antti Miettinen C RC 2.50 6.00
126 Antti Miettinen U 2.00 5.00
127 Antti Miettinen R 10.00 25.00
128 Tom Preissing C RC 2.50 6.00
129 Tom Preissing U 2.00 5.00
130 Tom Preissing R 10.00 25.00
131 Marek Svatos C RC 4.00 10.00
132 Marek Svatos U 3.00 8.00
133 Marek Svatos R 10.00 25.00
134 Peter Sejna C RC 2.50 6.00
135 Peter Sejna U 2.00 5.00
136 Peter Sejna R 10.00 25.00
137 Matt Stajan C RC 4.00 10.00
138 Matt Stajan U 4.00 10.00
139 Matt Stajan R 12.50 30.00
140 Jiri Hudler C RC 3.00 8.00
141 Jiri Hudler U 2.50 6.00
142 Jiri Hudler R 10.00 25.00
143 Joni Pitkanen C RC 3.00 8.00
144 Joni Pitkanen U 2.50 6.00
145 Joni Pitkanen R 10.00 25.00
146 Garnet Exelby C 2.50 6.00
147 Garnet Exelby U 2.00 5.00
148 Garnet Exelby R 10.00 25.00
149 Eric Staal C RC 10.00 25.00
150 Eric Staal U 6.00 15.00
151 Eric Staal R 25.00 60.00
152 Sean Bergenheim C RC 2.50 6.00
153 Sean Bergenheim U 2.00 5.00
154 Sean Bergenheim R 10.00 25.00
155 Gregory Campbell C RC 2.50 6.00
156 Gregory Campbell U 2.00 5.00
157 Gregory Campbell R 10.00 25.00
158 Dan Hamhuis C RC 2.50 6.00
159 Dan Hamhuis U 2.00 5.00
160 Dan Hamhuis R 10.00 25.00
161 Maxim Kondratiev C RC 2.50 6.00
162 Maxim Kondratiev U 2.00 5.00
163 Maxim Kondratiev R 10.00 25.00
164 Matthew Lombardi C RC 2.50 6.00
165 Matthew Lombardi U 2.00 5.00
166 Matthew Lombardi R 10.00 25.00
167 Alexander Semin C RC 8.00 20.00
168 Alexander Semin U 5.00 12.00
169 Alexander Semin R 12.00 30.00
170 John-Michael Liles C RC 2.50 6.00
171 John-Michael Liles U 2.00 5.00
172 John-Michael Liles R 8.00 20.00
173 Andrew Peters C RC 2.50 6.00
174 Andrew Peters U 2.00 5.00
175 Andrew Peters R 10.00 25.00
176 Dan Fritsche C RC 2.50 6.00
177 Dan Fritsche U 2.00 5.00
178 Dan Fritsche R 8.00 20.00
179 Antoine Vermette C RC 2.50 6.00
180 Antoine Vermette U 2.00 5.00
181 Antoine Vermette R 10.00 25.00
182 David Hale C RC 2.50 6.00
183 David Hale U 2.00 5.00
184 David Hale R 10.00 25.00
185 Joffrey Lupul C RC 3.00 8.00
186 Joffrey Lupul U 2.50 6.00
187 Joffrey Lupul R 10.00 25.00
188 Jordin Tootoo C RC 4.00 10.00
189 Jordin Tootoo U 3.00 8.00
190 Jordin Tootoo R 10.00 25.00

2003-04 Topps Pristine Gold Refractor Die Cuts

One per box in boxtopper packs.

*STARS: 3X TO 8X
*COMMON ROOKIE: 2X TO 5X
*UNCOMMON ROOKIE: 3X TO 8X
*RARE ROOKIE: 1X TO 2.5X
PRINT RUN 33 SER.#'d SETS
149 Eric Staal C 40.00 100.00
150 Eric Staal U 50.00 120.00

2003-04 Topps Pristine Refractors

*STARS: 2.5X TO 6X
1-100 PRINT RUN 59 SER.#'d SETS
*COMMON ROOKIE: .6X TO 1.5X
COMMON PRINT RUN 499 SER.#'d SETS
*UNCOMMON ROOKIE: .75X TO 2X
UNCOMMON PRINT RUN 199 SER.#'d SETS
*RARE ROOKIE: 1X TO 2.5X
RARE PRINT RUN 59 SER.#'d SETS

2003-04 Topps Pristine Autographs

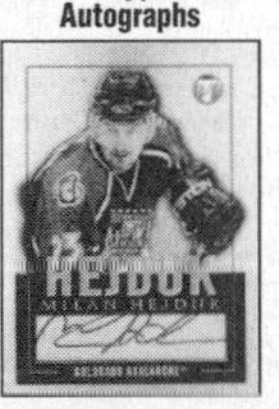

This 7-card set featured certified autographs on silver metallic cards. A Gold metallic parallel was also created.

GROUP A ODDS 1:11
GROUP B ODDS 1:26
GROUP C ODDS 1:8
PEMT Marty Turco C 6.00 15.00
PEJG Jean-Sebastien Giguere A 5.00 12.00
PEMN Markus Naslund B 8.00 20.00
PERN Rick Nash A 12.50 30.00
PEMH Milan Hejduk A 5.00 12.00
PEMS Martin St. Louis C 8.00 20.00
PESC Stanislav Chistov C 5.00 12.00

2003-04 Topps Pristine Autographs Gold

*GOLD: 1.5X TO 4X BASIC INSERTS
STATED PRINT RUN 25 SER.#'d SETS

2003-04 Topps Pristine Jersey Portions

GROUP A ODDS 4:5
GROUP B ODDS: 1:27
PPJPL Patrick Lalime B 2.50 6.00
PPJEL Eric Lindros A 3.00 8.00
PPJML Manny Legace A 4.00 10.00
PPJTB Todd Bertuzzi B 3.00 8.00
PPJMB Martin Biron A 2.50 6.00
PPJRL Roberto Luongo A 3.00 8.00
PPJMHO Marian Hossa A 3.00 8.00
PPJTV Tomas Vokoun A 2.50 6.00
PPJFP Felix Potvin A 3.00 8.00
PPJDA Daniel Alfredsson A 2.50 6.00
PPJDBL Dan Blackburn A 2.50 6.00
PPJDH Dany Heatley A 5.00 12.00
PPJDMN Brendan Morrison A 2.50 6.00
PPJMSA Miroslav Satan A 2.50 6.00
PPJMA Maxim Afinogenov A 2.50 6.00
PPJMHE Milan Hejduk A 3.00 8.00
PPJBRI Brad Richards A 5.00 12.00
PPJDL David Legwand B 2.50 6.00
PPJED Eric Desjardins A 2.50 6.00
PPJMSU Mats Sundin A 3.00 8.00
PPJDC Dan Cloutier A 2.50 6.00
PPJSK Saku Koivu A 3.00 8.00
PPJBMW Brenden Morrow A 2.50 6.00
PPJJD J-P Dumont A 2.50 6.00
PPJRB Rob Blake A 2.50 6.00
PPJPR Patrick Roy B 12.50 30.00
PPJIK Ilya Kovalchuk A 5.00 12.00
PPJKP Keith Primeau A 2.50 6.00
PPJZP Zigmund Palffy A 2.50 6.00
PPJBRO Brian Rolston A 2.50 6.00
PPJMT Marty Turco B 2.50 6.00
PPJPM Patrick Marleau A 2.50 6.00
PPJJW Justin Williams A 2.50 6.00
PPJRF Ron Francis A 2.50 6.00
PPJMG Marian Gaborik B 6.00 15.00

2003-04 Topps Pristine Jersey Portion Refractors

*STARS: 2X TO 5X
PRINT RUN 25 SER.#'d SETS

2003-04 Topps Pristine Mini

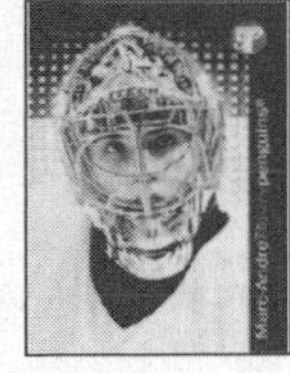

Inserted at just one per box on average, these smaller cards were inserted into a fourth pack.

MINI AUTO ODDS 1:318
PMDR Dwayne Roloson 2.00 5.00
PMMD Mike Dunham 2.00 5.00
PMPN Pasi Nurminen 2.00 5.00
PMJSG Jean-Sebastien Giguere 2.00 5.00
PMMDE Marc Denis 2.00 5.00
PMNH Nathan Horton 4.00 10.00
PMTS Tommy Salo 2.00 5.00
PMRT Roman Turek 2.00 5.00
PMMSO Matt Stajan 3.00 8.00
PMRE Robert Esche 2.00 5.00
PMOK Olaf Kolzig 2.00 5.00
PMES Eric Staal 8.00 20.00
PMDB Dustin Brown 2.00 5.00
PMJTH Jose Theodore 3.00 8.00
PMSC Sebastien Caron 2.00 5.00
PMMB Martin Brodeur 4.00 10.00
PMPL Patrick Lalime 2.00 5.00
PMEN Evgeni Nabokov 2.00 5.00
PMDC Dan Cloutier 2.00 5.00
PMTV Tomas Vokoun 2.00 5.00
PMNK Nikolai Khabibulin 2.50 6.00
PMJHU Jiri Hudler 3.00 8.00
PMRC Roman Cechmanek 2.00 5.00
PMEB Ed Belfour 2.50 6.00
PMJTO Jordin Tootoo 5.00 12.00
PMRD Rick DiPietro 2.00 5.00
PMPS Peter Sejna 2.00 5.00
PMMBI Martin Biron 2.00 5.00
PMMAF Marc-Andre Fleury 8.00 20.00
PMJT Jocelyn Thibault 2.00 5.00
PMCO Chris Osgood 2.00 5.00
PMAM Antti Miettinen 2.00 5.00
PMDA David Aebischer 2.00 5.00
PMRL Roberto Luongo 3.00 8.00
PMSB Sean Burke 2.00 5.00
PMMT Marty Turco 2.00 5.00
PMJL Joffrey Lupul 3.00 8.00
PMFP Felix Potvin 2.50 6.00
PMKW Kevin Weekes 2.00 5.00
PMDH Dominik Hasek 3.00 8.00
PMAJG Jean-Sebastien Giguere AU 15.00 40.00

2003-04 Topps Pristine Patches

*MULT.COLOR SWATCH: .75X TO 2X
STATED ODDS 1:16
STATED PRINT RUN 50 SER.#'d SETS
REFRACTOR PRINT RUN 10 SER.#'d SETS
REF.NOT PRICED DUE TO SCARCITY
PPSG Simon Gagne 12.00 30.00
PPPF Peter Forsberg 15.00 40.00
PPDL David Legwand 8.00 20.00
PPMA Maxim Afinogenov 12.00 30.00
PPMSA Miroslav Satan 12.00 30.00
PPFP Felix Potvin 12.00 30.00
PPML Manny Legace 12.00 30.00
PPMG Marian Gaborik 20.00 50.00
PPEL Eric Lindros 15.00 40.00
PPVL Vincent Lecavalier 15.00 40.00
PPPL Patrick Lalime 8.00 20.00
PPDB Dan Blackburn 8.00 20.00
PPMT Marty Turco 12.00 30.00
PPJI Jarome Iginla 20.00 50.00
PPKH Kristian Huselius 8.00 20.00
PPRL Roberto Luongo 15.00 40.00
PPZP Zigmund Palffy 12.00 30.00
PPMC Mike Comrie 8.00 20.00
PPMST Marco Sturm 8.00 20.00
PPMB Martin Biron 12.00 30.00
PPMM Mike Modano 15.00 40.00
PPBM Brendan Morrison 8.00 20.00
PPRB Rob Blake 8.00 20.00
PPTB Todd Bertuzzi 12.00 30.00
PPDH Dany Heatley 15.00 40.00
PPAT Alex Tanguay 8.00 20.00

PPDA Daniel Alfredsson 12.00 30.00
PPMHO Marian Hossa 12.00 30.00
PPMSU Mats Sundin 12.00 30.00
PPJW Justin Williams 8.00 20.00
PPIK Ilya Kovalchuk 15.00 40.00
PPMN Markus Naslund 12.00 30.00
PPSK Saku Koivu 12.00 30.00
PPBRO Brian Rolston 8.00 20.00
PPPR Patrick Roy 30.00 80.00
PPMHE Milan Hejduk 8.00 20.00
PPJL John LeClair 8.00 20.00
PPKP Keith Primeau 8.00 20.00
PPJD J-P Dumont 8.00 20.00
PPPD Pavel Datsyuk 12.00 30.00
PPJS Joe Sakic 15.00 40.00

2003-04 Topps Pristine Popular Demand Relics

GROUP A ODDS 1:127
GROUP B ODDS 1:12
GROUP C ODDS 1:5
PDMR Mark Recchi B 4.00 10.00
PDBG Bill Guerin C 4.00 10.00
PDSN Scott Niedermayer B 4.00 10.00
PDPK Paul Kariya A 8.00 20.00
PDAZ Alexei Zhamnov B 4.00 10.00
PDSG Simon Gagne A 12.50 30.00
PDJTH Jose Theodore C 6.00 15.00
PDJSP Jason Spezza B 6.00 15.00
PDMM Mike Modano B 6.00 15.00
PDPB Pavel Bure C 5.00 12.00
PDJJ Jaromir Jagr C 8.00 20.00
PDJL John LeClair B 5.00 12.00
PDML Mario Lemieux A 20.00 50.00
PDMN Markus Naslund A 6.00 15.00
PDMSK Martin Straka C 4.00 10.00
PDJI Jarome Iginla B 5.00 12.00
PDTC Tim Connolly A 4.00 10.00
PDJB Jay Bouwmeester C 4.00 10.00
PDMST Marco Sturm B 4.00 10.00
PDNK Nikolai Khabibulin C 4.00 10.00
PDKH Kristian Huselius C 4.00 10.00
PDPD Pavel Datsyuk C 6.00 15.00
PDJT Joe Thornton C 8.00 20.00
PDTD Tie Domi B 4.00 10.00
PDAY Alexei Yashin C 4.00 10.00

2003-04 Topps Pristine Popular Demand Relic Refractors

GRP.A PRINT RUN 10 SER.#'d SETS
GRP.A NOT PRICED DUE TO SCARCITY
*GRP.B/C REFRACTOR: 1.5X TO 4X
GRP.B/C PRINT RUN 25 SER.#'d SETS

2003-04 Topps Pristine Stick Portions

STATED ODDS: 1:27
REFRACTOR PRINT RUN 10 SER.#'d SETS
REF.NOT PRICED DUE TO SCARCITY
PPSMM Mark Messier 8.00 20.00
PPSMS Mats Sundin 5.00 12.00
PPSVB Valeri Bure 4.00 10.00
PPSCJ Curtis Joseph 5.00 12.00
PPSPS Patrik Stefan 4.00 10.00
PPSED Eric Desjardins 4.00 10.00
PPSSY Steve Yzerman 20.00 50.00
PPSJL John LeClair 5.00 12.00
PPSDA Daniel Alfredsson 5.00 12.00
PPSJI Jarome Iginla 6.00 15.00
PPSAO Adam Oates 5.00 12.00
PPSDW Doug Weight 5.00 12.00

2001-02 Topps Reserve

Released in late January 2002, this 121-card hobby only set featured color player photos on gold sparkle card stock. Each 10-pack box contained an autographed team logo puck, a PSA graded serial-numbered rookie card, a non-graded serial-numbered rookie cards and two jersey cards. Rookie cards were serial-numbered to 1599, 1099, or 699. Approximately half of each rookie print run was graded.

COMP.SET w/o SP's (100) 40.00 80.00
1 Joe Sakic 1.00 2.50
2 Patrik Elias .40 1.00
3 Mario Lemieux 3.00 8.00
4 Chris Pronger .40 1.00
5 Simon Gagne .50 1.25
6 Steve Yzerman 2.50 6.00
7 Bill Guerin .40 1.00
8 Pavel Bure .50 1.25
9 Mark Messier .50 1.25
10 Evgeni Nabokov .40 1.00
11 Peter Bondra .50 1.25
12 Martin Havlat .40 1.00
13 Mike Dunham .40 1.00
14 Mike Comrie .40 1.00
15 Ed Belfour .50 1.25
16 Tony Amonte .40 1.00
17 Patrik Stefan .15 .40
18 Paul Kariya .50 1.25
19 Patrick Roy 2.50 6.00
20 Sean Burke .40 1.00
21 Vincent Lecavalier .50 1.25
22 Henrik Sedin .15 .40
23 Petr Sykora .15 .40
24 Marian Gaborik 1.00 2.50
25 Rod Brind'Amour .40 1.00
26 Miroslav Satan .40 1.00
27 Zigmund Palffy .40 1.00
28 Sergei Fedorov .75 2.00
29 Ron Tugnutt .40 1.00
30 Jason Allison .15 .40
31 Marian Hossa .50 1.25
32 John LeClair .50 1.25
33 Keith Tkachuk .50 1.25
34 Adam Oates .50 1.25
35 Johan Hedberg .40 1.00
36 Saku Koivu .50 1.25
37 Peter Forsberg 1.00 2.50
38 Jarome Iginla .60 1.50
39 Nicklas Lidstrom .50 1.25
40 Martin Brodeur 1.25 3.00
41 Daniel Alfredsson .40 1.00
42 Alexei Kovalev .40 1.00
43 Mats Sundin .50 1.25
44 Brian Leetch .40 1.00
45 Owen Nolan .40 1.00
46 Cliff Ronning .15 .40
47 Mike Modano .75 2.00
48 Milan Hejduk .50 1.25
49 Joe Thornton .75 2.00
50 Ray Ferraro .15 .40
51 Geoff Sanderson .15 .40
52 Roberto Luongo .60 1.50
53 Manny Fernandez .40 1.00
54 Mark Recchi .40 1.00
55 Curtis Joseph .50 1.25
56 Philippe Boucher .15 .40
57 Patrick Lalime .40 1.00
58 Rick DiPietro .40 1.00
59 Adam Deadmarsh .15 .40
60 Pierre Turgeon .40 1.00
61 Roman Turek .40 1.00
62 Jeff Friesen .15 .40
63 Eric Lindros .50 1.25
64 Martin Straka .15 .40
65 Markus Naslund .50 1.25
66 J-P Dumont .15 .40
67 Daniel Sedin .15 .40
68 Alexei Yashin .15 .40
69 Felix Potvin .50 1.25
70 Chris Drury .40 1.00
71 Martin Biron .40 1.00
72 Tommy Salo .40 1.00
73 Stanislav Neckar .15 .40
74 Jaromir Jagr .60 1.50
75 Brendan Shanahan .50 1.25
76 Jose Theodore .60 1.50
77 Teemu Selanne .50 1.25
78 Alexander Mogilny .15 .40
79 Niclas Havelid .15 .40
80 Colin Forbes .15 .40
81 Michael Peca .15 .40
82 Jason Arnott .15 .40
83 Arturs Irbe .40 1.00
84 Garry Valk .15 .40
85 Roman Cechmanek .40 1.00
86 Scott Gomez .15 .40
87 Chris McAllister .15 .40
88 Shane Doan .15 .40
89 David Harlock .15 .40
90 Jeff O'Neill .15 .40
91 Rob Blake .40 1.00
92 Dominik Hasek 1.00 2.50
93 Olaf Kolzig .40 1.00
94 Brent Johnson .40 1.00
95 Jeremy Roenick .60 1.50
96 Brad Richards .40 1.00
97 Steve Sullivan .15 .40
98 Alex Tanguay .40 1.00
99 Brett Hull .60 1.50
100 Doug Weight .40 1.00
101 Niklas Hagman/1099 RC 3.00 8.00
102 Scott Clemmensen/1599 RC 3.00 8.00
103 Brian Sutherby/1099 RC 3.00 8.00
104 Erik Cole/1599 RC 3.00 8.00
105 Vaclav Nedorost/1599 RC 3.00 8.00
106 Jaroslav Bednar/1099 RC 3.00 8.00
107 Nick Schultz/699 RC 3.00 8.00
108 Jiri Dopita/699 RC 3.00 8.00
109 Krys Kolanos/1599 RC 3.00 8.00
110 Jukka Hentunen/1099 RC 3.00 8.00
111 Niko Kapanen/699 RC 4.00 10.00
112 Timo Parssinen/1099 RC 3.00 8.00
113 Kristian Huselius/1599 RC 3.00 8.00
114 A.Salomonsson RC/699 3.00 8.00
115 Ilya Kovalchuk/1599 RC 8.00 20.00
116 Dan Blackburn/1599 RC 3.00 8.00
117 Pavel Datsyuk/699 RC 12.50 30.00
118 Peter Smrek/699 RC 3.00 8.00
119 Jeff Jillson/1099 RC 3.00 8.00
120 Nikita Alexeev/1599 RC 3.00 8.00
121 Scott Nichol/699 RC 3.00 8.00

2001-02 Topps Reserve Emblems

This 56-card set paralleled the base jersey set but each card carried a piece of the team logo from the player's jersey. These cards were inserted at 1:32. Each card carried a "TRL" prefix.

*EMBLEMS: 1X TO 2.5X JERSEYS

2001-02 Topps Reserve Jerseys

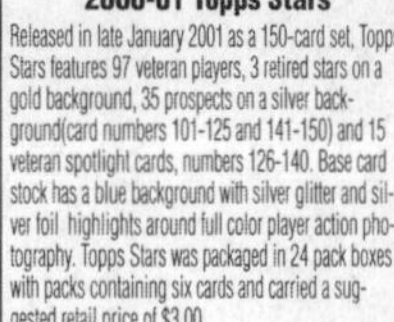

Inserted at 1:4 packs, this 56-card set featured swatches of game-worn jerseys alongside color player photos on team colored card fronts. All cards carried a "TR" prefix that has been left off of the listing below for checklisting purposes.

*MULT.COLOR SWATCH: 1X TO 1.5X
AK Alexei Kovalev 3.00 8.00
AO Adam Oates 3.00 8.00
AZ Alexei Zhamnov 3.00 8.00
BB Brian Boucher 3.00 8.00
BL Brian Leetch 5.00 12.00
CD Chris Drury 4.00 10.00
DH Derian Hatcher 3.00 8.00
DM Darren McCarty 4.00 10.00
DY Dimitri Yushkevich 3.00 8.00
EB Ed Belfour 5.00 12.00
ED Eric Desjardins 3.00 8.00
JH Jeff Hackett 3.00 8.00
JI Jarome Iginla 6.00 15.00
JL John LeClair 4.00 10.00
JS Joe Sakic 6.00 15.00
JT Joe Thornton 8.00 20.00
KJ Kenny Jonsson 3.00 8.00
KO Krzysztof Oliwa 3.00 8.00
MB Martin Brodeur 8.00 20.00
MC Mariusz Czerkawski 3.00 8.00
ML Mario Lemieux 12.50 30.00
MM Mike Mottau 3.00 8.00
MP Matt Pettinger 3.00 8.00
MR Mark Recchi 4.00 10.00
MT Marty Turco 5.00 12.00
MY Mike York 3.00 8.00
OS Oleg Saprykin 3.00 8.00
PB Pavel Bure 5.00 12.00
PF Peter Forsberg 6.00 15.00
PK Paul Kariya 5.00 12.00
PM Patrick Marleau 4.00 10.00
PR Patrick Roy 10.00 25.00
RL Robert Lang 3.00 8.00
SB Sean Burke 3.00 8.00
SF Sergei Fedorov 6.00 15.00
SG Simon Gagne 5.00 12.00
SK Saku Koivu 5.00 12.00
SM Shawn McEachern 3.00 8.00
SS Sergei Samsonov 5.00 12.00
SZ Sergei Zubov 3.00 8.00
TA Tony Amonte 4.00 10.00
TD Tie Domi 4.00 10.00
TF Theo Fleury 3.00 8.00
TK Tomas Kloucek 3.00 8.00
TL Trevor Letowski 3.00 8.00
TV Tomas Vokoun 5.00 12.00
VL Vincent Lecavalier 5.00 12.00
WR Wade Redden 3.00 8.00
DAB Daniel Briere 4.00 10.00
DOB Donald Brashear 4.00 10.00
JAI Jason Allison 4.00 10.00
JAR Jason Arnott 4.00 10.00
MIS Miroslav Satan 4.00 10.00
MSA Marc Savard 4.00 10.00
MST Martin Straka 4.00 10.00
ROF Ron Francis 4.00 10.00

2001-02 Topps Reserve Name Plates

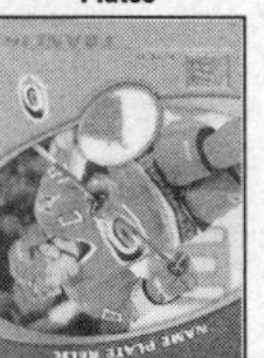

This 56-card set paralleled the base jersey set but each card carried a piece of the name plate from the player's jersey. These cards were inserted at 1:32. Each card carried a "TRN" prefix.

*NAME PLATES: 1X TO 2.5X JERSEYS

2001-02 Topps Reserve Numbers

This 56-card set paralleled the base jersey set but each card carried a piece of the jersey number from the player's jersey. These cards were inserted at 1:29 packs. Each card carried a "TR#" prefix. Please note that card #JAH did not have a parent card in the base jersey set, thus it is priced seperately below.

*NUMBERS: 1X TO 2.5X JERSEYS
JAH Jan Hlavac 12.50 30.00

2001-02 Topps Reserve Patches

This 56-card set paralleled the base jersey set but each card carried jersey patch from the player's jersey. These cards were inserted at 1:257. Each card carried a "TRP" prefix.

*PATCHES: 1.25X TO 3X JERSEYS

2000-01 Topps Stars

Released in late January 2001 as a 150-card set, Topps Stars features 97 veteran players, 3 retired stars on a gold background, 35 prospects on a silver background(card numbers 101-125 and 141-150) and 15 veteran spotlight cards, numbers 126-140. Base card stock has a blue background with silver glitter and silver foil highlights around full color player action photography. Topps Stars was packaged in 24 pack boxes with packs containing six cards and carried a suggested retail price of $3.00.

COMPLETE SET (150) 30.00 60.00
1 Vincent Lecavalier .20 .50
2 Patrick Roy 1.00 2.50
3 Scott Gomez .05 .15
4 Steve Yzerman 1.00 2.50
5 Paul Kariya .20 .50
6 Dominik Hasek .40 1.00
7 Mike Modano .30 .75
8 Zigmund Palffy .15 .40
9 John LeClair .20 .50
10 Mats Sundin .20 .50
11 Owen Nolan .15 .40
12 Tony Amonte .15 .40
13 Patrik Stefan .05 .15
14 Brett Hull .25 .60
15 Chris Pronger .15 .40
16 Jeremy Roenick .25 .60
17 Martin Brodeur .50 1.25
18 Doug Weight .15 .40
19 Ray Bourque .40 1.00
20 Olaf Kolzig .15 .40
21 Jaromir Jagr .30 .75
22 Daniel Alfredsson .15 .40
23 Jeff Hackett .05 .15
24 Jason Allison .15 .40
25 Joe Sakic .40 1.00
26 Brendan Shanahan .20 .50
27 David Legwand .15 .40
28 Tim Connolly .05 .15
29 Mark Recchi .15 .40
30 Brad Stuart .15 .40
31 Pierre Turgeon .15 .40
32 Ed Belfour .20 .50
33 Valeri Bure .05 .15
34 Pavel Bure .20 .50
35 Teemu Selanne .20 .50
36 Patrik Elias .15 .40
37 Mattias Ohlund .05 .15
38 Rod Brind'Amour .15 .40
39 Derian Hatcher .05 .15
40 Peter Forsberg .50 1.25
41 Eric Lindros .20 .50
42 Curtis Joseph .20 .50
43 Keith Tkachuk .20 .50
44 Mike Ricci .05 .15
45 Al MacInnis .15 .40
46 Nicklas Lidstrom .20 .50
47 Rob Blake .15 .40
48 Scott Stevens .15 .40
49 Milan Hejduk .20 .50
50 Theo Fleury .05 .15
51 Joe Thornton .30 .75
52 Tommy Salo .15 .40
53 Eric Desjardins .15 .40
54 Pavol Demitra .15 .40
55 Adam Oates .15 .40
56 Jeff Friesen .05 .15
57 Mariusz Czerkawski .05 .15
58 Luc Robitaille .15 .40
59 Jeff O'Neill .05 .15
60 Andrew Brunette .05 .15
61 Fred Brathwaite .15 .40
62 Robert Svehla .05 .15
63 Kimmo Timonen .05 .15
64 Teppo Numminen .05 .15
65 Nikolai Antropov .05 .15
66 Marian Hossa .20 .50
67 Joe Nieuwendyk .15 .40
68 Michael Peca .05 .15
69 Saku Koivu .20 .50
70 Alexei Kovalev .15 .40
71 Sergei Gonchar .05 .15
72 Brian Leetch .15 .40
73 Ryan Smyth .05 .15
74 Jarome Iginla .25 .60
75 Byron Dafoe .05 .15
76 Ray Whitney .05 .15
77 Wade Redden .05 .15
78 Pavel Kubina .05 .15
79 Markus Naslund .20 .50
80 Brian Boucher .20 .50
81 Martin Rucinsky .05 .15
82 Roman Turek .15 .40
83 Jocelyn Thibault .15 .40
84 Miroslav Satan .15 .40
85 Cliff Ronning .05 .15
86 Mike Richter .20 .50
87 Chris Chelios .20 .50
88 Arturs Irbe .15 .40
89 Steve Thomas .05 .15
90 Felix Potvin .20 .50
91 Jason Arnott .05 .15
92 Mark Messier .20 .50
93 Scott Pellerin .05 .15
94 John Vanbiesbrouck .15 .40
95 Dave Andreychuk .15 .40
96 Paul Coffey .20 .50
97 Ron Tugnutt .15 .40
98 Larry Robinson .15 .40
99 Billy Smith .15 .40
100 Mario Lemieux 2.00 5.00
101 Martin Havlat RC 2.00 5.00
102 Petr Hubacek RC .40 1.00
103 Niclas Wallin RC .40 1.00
104 Alexander Khavanov RC .40 1.00
105 Roman Cechmanek RC .50 1.25
106 Bryce Salvador RC .40 1.00
107 Jonas Ronnqvist RC .40 1.00
108 Rostislav Klesla RC 1.00 2.50
109 Justin Williams RC .40 1.00
110 Sascha Goc RC .40 1.00
111 Andrew Raycroft RC 1.50 4.00
112 Marty Turco RC 2.00 5.00
113 Marian Gaborik RC 2.00 5.00
114 Josef Vasicek RC .40 1.00
115 Steven Reinprecht RC .40 1.00
116 Jani Hurme RC .40 1.00
117 David Aebischer RC 1.50 4.00
118 Dale Purinton RC .40 1.00
119 Jarno Kultanen RC .40 1.00
120 Petr Svoboda RC .40 1.00
121 Eric Belanger RC .40 1.00
122 Petteri Nummelin RC .40 1.00
123 Michel Riesen RC .40 1.00
124 Jason Labarbera RC .40 1.00
125 Tyler Bouck RC .40 1.00
126 Martin Brodeur SL .25 .60
127 Pavel Bure SL .10 .30
128 Peter Forsberg SL .25 .60
129 Scott Gomez SL .10 .25
130 Dominik Hasek SL .20 .50
131 Brett Hull SL .12 .30
132 Jaromir Jagr SL .15 .40
133 Curtis Joseph SL .12 .30
134 Paul Kariya SL .20 .50
135 Chris Pronger SL .10 .25
136 Patrick Roy SL .50 1.25
137 Joe Sakic SL .20 .50
138 Teemu Selanne SL .10 .25
139 Steve Yzerman SL .50 1.25
140 Vincent Lecavalier SL .10 .25
141 Samuel Pahlsson SL .10 .25
142 Maxime Ouellet SL .10 .25
143 Kris Beech SL .10 .25
144 Henrik Sedin SL .10 .25
145 Daniel Sedin SL .10 .25
146 Milan Kraft SL .10 .25
147 Marty Turco SL .10 .25
148 Oleg Saprykin SL .10 .25
149 Brent Johnson SL .10 .25
150 Marian Gaborik SL .10 .25

2000-01 Topps Stars Blue

Randomly inserted in packs at the rate of 1:8, this 150-card set parallels the base set enhanced with blue foil. Card numbers 126-140 are sequentially numbered to 99, and the rest are sequentially numbered to 299.

*BLUE STARS: 4X TO 10X BASIC CARDS
*BLUE YNG.STARS: 3X TO 8X BASIC CARDS
*BLUE RC's: 1.5X TO 3X BASIC CARDS

2000-01 Topps Stars All-Star Authority

COMPLETE SET (11) 8.00 15.00
STATED ODDS 1:9
ASA1 Ray Bourque .60 1.50
ASA2 Brett Hull .40 1.00
ASA3 Mark Messier .40 1.00
ASA4 Patrick Roy 2.00 5.00
ASA5 Jaromir Jagr .60 1.50
ASA6 Dominik Hasek .60 1.50
ASA7 Teemu Selanne .40 1.00
ASA8 Steve Yzerman 2.00 5.00
ASA9 Joe Sakic .60 1.50
ASA10 Pavel Bure .50 1.25
ASA11 John LeClair .40 1.00

2000-01 Topps Stars Autographs

Randomly inserted in packs at the rate of 1:15 (combined odds between Game Gear and Autographs), this 10-card set features a framed player photo on the left side of the card front with a whiteout area extending from the left card border down along the bottom border of the card where the player autograph appears. Each card is enhanced with gold foil highlights.

ABB Brian Boucher 6.00 15.00
ACP Chris Pronger 10.00 25.00
ALR Larry Robinson 10.00 25.00
AML Mario Lemieux 75.00 150.00
AMM Mike Modano 15.00 40.00
AMY Mike York 6.00 15.00
AVL Vincent Lecavalier 12.00 30.00
ABSM Billy Smith 12.00 30.00
ABST Brad Stuart 6.00 15.00

2000-01 Topps Stars Game Gear

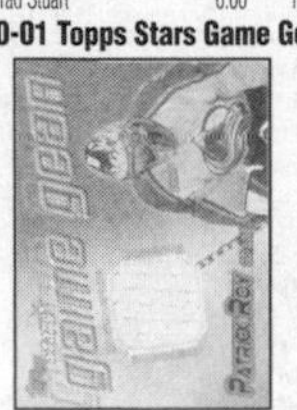

Randomly inserted in packs at the rate of 1:15 (combined odds between Game Gear and Autographs), this 18-card set featured either a swatch of game worn jersey or game used stick. Two different game gear autograph cards were also available, and randomly inserted in packs at the rate of 1:5568 for the jersey cards and 1:12528 for the stick cards. The Don Cherry suit cards were randomly inserted at 1:49 Canadian packs or 1:392 Canadian packs for the autographed version.

*MULT.COLOR SWATCH: .75X TO 1.5X
GGAG Adam Graves J 3.00 8.00
GGCP Chris Pronger J 4.00 10.00
GGDC Don Cherry Suit 10.00 25.00
GGDCA D.Cherry Suit/AU 40.00 100.00
GGDL David Legwand J 3.00 8.00
GGDM Darren McCarty J 3.00 8.00
GGJA Jason Allison J 3.00 8.00
GGKT Keith Tkachuk S 10.00 25.00
GGMC Mariusz Czerkawski J 3.00 8.00
GGML Martin Lapointe J 3.00 8.00
GGMM Mike Modano S 10.00 25.00
GGMR Mike Richter J 4.00 10.00
GGPH Phil Housley J 3.00 8.00
GGPR Patrick Roy J 30.00 60.00
GGRT Ron Tugnutt S 10.00 25.00
GGSZ Sergei Zubov J 3.00 8.00
GGTA Tony Amonte J 3.00 8.00
GGTS Teemu Selanne J 4.00 10.00
GGZP Zigmund Palffy S 10.00 25.00
GGMR Mark Recchi S 10.00 25.00
GGCP Chris Pronger J/AU 100.00 200.00
GGMM Mike Modano S/AU 150.00 300.00

2000-01 Topps Stars Progression

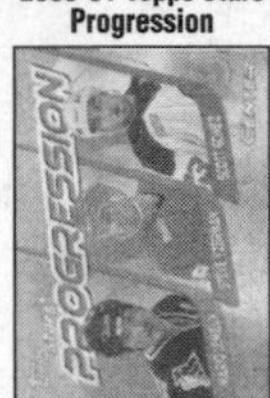

Randomly inserted in packs at the rate of 1:11, this nine-card set features three players of the same position on an all foil card stock. Three portrait style photos are set against a blue background with yellow foil highlights. From left to right, the photos feature an established veteran star, an established star, and a young star.

COMPLETE SET (9) 15.00 40.00
P1 Mario Lemieux 3.00 8.00
Mike Modano
Vincent Lecavalier
P2 Mario Lemieux 3.00 8.00
Peter Forsberg
Patrik Stefan
P3 Mario Lemieux 3.00 8.00
Steve Yzerman
Scott Gomez
P4 Billy Smith 3.00 8.00
Patrick Roy
Roberto Luongo
P5 Billy Smith 2.00 5.00
Martin Brodeur
Marty Turco
P6 Billy Smith 1.25 3.00
Ed Belfour
Brian Boucher
P7 Larry Robinson .75 2.00
Scott Stevens
Rostislav Klesla
P8 Larry Robinson 2.00 5.00
Ray Bourque
Brad Stuart
P9 Larry Robinson .75 2.00
Chris Pronger
Martin Skoula

2000-01 Topps Stars Walk of Fame

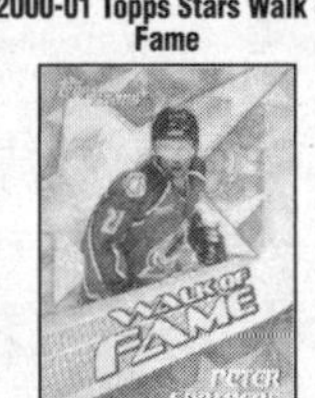

COMPLETE SET (10) 10.00 20.00
STATED ODDS 1:10
WF1 Pavel Bure .60 1.50
WF2 Paul Kariya .60 1.50
WF3 Jaromir Jagr .75 2.00
WF4 Peter Forsberg 1.25 3.00
WF5 Mike Modano .60 1.50
WF6 Patrick Roy 2.50 6.00
WF7 Steve Yzerman 2.50 6.00
WF8 Dominik Hasek 1.00 2.50
WF9 John LeClair .60 1.50
WF10 Martin Brodeur 1.25 3.00

1995-96 Topps SuperSkills

The 1995-96 Topps SuperSkills set was issued in one series totaling 90 cards. The 11-card packs originally retailed for $3.99. The set was a special one-off project designed to capitalize on Topps sponsorship of the SuperSkills program held in conjunction with the 1996 All-Star Game in Boston. The set features the players who were expected to compete in the following categories: Puck Control (1-18), Fastest Skater (19-36), Hardest Shot (37-54), Accuracy Shooting (55-72) and Rapid Fire/Breakaway Relay (73-90). The packs clearly identified which conference and event the cards inside would picture. A one-card-per-pack parallel set, "Platinum", is identical to the basic set save for a platinum trim along the edges of the cards. Multipliers can be found in the header below to determine values for these.

COMPLETE SET (90) 8.00 20.00
1 Mario Lemieux .75 2.00
2 Adam Oates .15 .40
3 Donald Audette .07 .20
4 Andrew Cassels .07 .20
5 Pat LaFontaine .15 .40
6 Mathieu Schneider .07 .20
7 Scott Stevens .07 .20
8 Mikael Renberg .15 .40
9 Pierre Turgeon .15 .40
10 Steve Yzerman .75 2.00
11 Russ Courtnall .07 .20
12 Oleg Tverdovsky .15 .40
13 Craig Janney .07 .20
14 Doug Gilmour .20 .50
15 Wayne Gretzky 1.25 3.00
16 Paul Kariya .60 1.50
17 Joe Sakic .40 1.00
18 Peter Forsberg .40 1.00
19 Brian Leetch .20 .50
20 Jaromir Jagr .40 1.00
21 Geoff Sanderson .07 .20
22 Rob Niedermayer .15 .40
23 Ray Ferraro .07 .20
24 Alexandre Daigle .07 .20
25 Joe Juneau .15 .40
26 Don Sweeney .07 .20
27 Scott Niedermayer .07 .20
28 Mike Gartner .07 .20
29 Paul Coffey .15 .40
30 Pavel Bure .40 1.00
31 Teemu Selanne .30 .75
32 Mats Sundin .20 .50
33 Trevor Linden .15 .40
34 Sergei Fedorov .30 .75
35 Theo Fleury .20 .50
36 Alexander Mogilny .15 .40
37 Garry Galley .07 .20
38 Stu Barnes .07 .20
39 Glen Wesley .07 .20
40 Eric Lindros .40 1.00
41 Stephane Richer .07 .20
42 John LeClair .20 .50
43 Pat Verbeek .15 .40
44 Bill Guerin .07 .20
45 Wendel Clark .15 .40
46 Mike Modano .20 .50
47 Keith Primeau .15 .40
48 Brett Hull .25 .60
49 Al MacInnis .15 .40
50 Chris Chelios .20 .50
51 Keith Tkachuk .20 .50
52 Dave Andreychuk .07 .20
53 Kevin Hatcher .07 .20
54 Chris Pronger .07 .20
55 Brendan Shanahan .20 .50
56 Luc Robitaille .15 .40
57 Ray Bourque .30 .75
58 Mark Recchi .15 .40
59 Brian Bradley .07 .20
60 Mark Messier .25 .60
61 Kevin Stevens .07 .20
62 John MacLean .07 .20
63 Cam Neely .20 .50
64 Rick Tocchet .07 .20
65 Jeremy Roenick .20 .50
66 Phil Housley .07 .20
67 Jason Arnott .15 .40
68 Todd Harvey .07 .20
69 Jeff Friesen .15 .40
70 Alexei Zhamnov .15 .40
71 David Oliver .07 .20
72 Bernie Nicholls .07 .20
73 Jim Carey .15 .40
74 Mike Richter .15 .40
75 Dominik Hasek .30 .75
76 Sean Burke .07 .20
77 Ron Hextall .15 .40
78 John Vanbiesbrouck .20 .50
79 Tom Barrasso .15 .40
80 Martin Brodeur .40 1.00
81 Patrick Roy .75 2.00
82 Trevor Kidd .15 .40
83 Andy Moog .15 .40
84 Mike Vernon .07 .20
85 Felix Potvin .20 .50
86 Bill Ranford .15 .40
87 Kelly Hrudey .15 .40
88 Grant Fuhr .15 .40
89 Kirk McLean .15 .40
90 Ed Belfour .20 .50

1995-96 Topps SuperSkills Platinum

COMPLETE SET (90) 15.00 40.00
*PLATINUM: .6X TO 1.5X BASIC CARDS
ONE PER PACK
1 Mario Lemieux 1.25 3.00
2 Adam Oates .25 .60
3 Donald Audette .10 .30
4 Andrew Cassels .10 .30
5 Pat LaFontaine .25 .60
6 Mathieu Schneider .10 .30
7 Scott Stevens .10 .30
8 Mikael Renberg .25 .60
9 Pierre Turgeon .25 .60
10 Steve Yzerman 1.25 3.00
11 Russ Courtnall .10 .30
12 Oleg Tverdovsky .25 .60
13 Craig Janney .10 .30
14 Doug Gilmour .30 .75
15 Wayne Gretzky 2.50 5.00
16 Paul Kariya 1.00 2.50
17 Joe Sakic .60 1.50
18 Peter Forsberg .60 1.50
19 Brian Leetch .30 .75
20 Jaromir Jagr .60 1.50
21 Geoff Sanderson .10 .30
22 Rob Niedermayer .25 .60
23 Ray Ferraro .10 .30
24 Alexandre Daigle .10 .30
25 Joe Juneau .25 .60
26 Don Sweeney .10 .30
27 Scott Niedermayer .10 .30
28 Mike Gartner .10 .30
29 Paul Coffey .25 .60
30 Pavel Bure .60 1.50

31 Teemu Selanne .50 1.25
32 Mats Sundin .30 .75
33 Trevor Linden .25 .60
34 Sergei Fedorov .50 1.25
35 Theo Fleury .30 .75
36 Alexander Mogilny .25 .60
37 Garry Galley .10 .30
38 Stu Barnes .10 .30
39 Glen Wesley .10 .30
40 Eric Lindros .60 1.50
41 Stephane Richer .10 .30
42 John LeClair .30 .75
43 Pat Verbeek .25 .60
44 Bill Guerin .10 .30
45 Wendel Clark .25 .60
46 Mike Modano .30 .75
47 Keith Primeau .25 .60
48 Brett Hull .40 1.00
49 Al MacInnis .25 .60
50 Chris Chelios .30 .75
51 Keith Tkachuk .30 .75
52 Dave Andreychuk .10 .30
53 Kevin Hatcher .10 .30
54 Chris Pronger .10 .30
55 Brendan Shanahan .30 .75
56 Luc Robitaille .25 .60
57 Ray Bourque .50 1.25
58 Mark Recchi .25 .60
59 Brian Bradley .10 .30
60 Mark Messier .40 1.00
61 Kevin Stevens .10 .30
62 John MacLean .10 .30
63 Cam Neely .30 .75
64 Rick Tocchet .10 .30
65 Jeremy Roenick .30 .75
66 Phil Housley .10 .30
67 Jason Arnott .25 .60
68 Todd Harvey .10 .30
69 Jeff Friesen .25 .60
70 Alexei Zhamnov .25 .60
71 David Oliver .10 .30
72 Bernie Nicholls .10 .30
73 Jim Carey .25 .60
74 Mike Richter .25 .60
75 Dominik Hasek .50 1.25
76 Sean Burke .10 .30
77 Ron Hextall .25 .60
78 John Vanbiesbrouck .30 .75
79 Tom Barrasso .25 .60
80 Martin Brodeur .60 1.50
81 Patrick Roy 1.25 3.00
82 Trevor Kidd .25 .60
83 Andy Moog .25 .60
84 Mike Vernon .10 .30
85 Felix Potvin .30 .75
86 Bill Ranford .25 .60
87 Kelly Hrudey .25 .60
88 Grant Fuhr .25 .60
89 Kirk McLean .25 .60
90 Ed Belfour .30 .75

1995-96 Topps SuperSkills Super Rookies

Inserted one per Topps SuperSkills pack, this 15-card set features the cream of the 1995-96 rookie crop on 20 point all-foil board stock with gild-edge technology.

COMPLETE SET (15) 4.80 12.00
SR1 Ed Jovanovski .20 .50
SR2 Jason Bonsignore .08 .25
SR3 Jeff O'Neill .40 1.00
SR4 Cory Stillman .08 .25
SR5 Chad Kilger .20 .50
SR6 Aki Berg .20 .50
SR7 Todd Bertuzzi 1.25 3.00
SR8 Shane Doan .40 1.00
SR9 Kyle McLaren .20 .50
SR10 Radek Dvorak .20 .50
SR11 Saku Koivu 1.25 3.00
SR12 Daniel Alfredsson .40 1.00
SR13 Antti Tormanen .08 .25
SR14 Niklas Sundstrom .20 .50
SR15 Vitali Yachmenev .08 .25

2002-03 Topps Total

Released in late February, this 440-card set was one of the largest base sets of the year.

COMPLETE SET (440) 15.00 40.00
1 Nicklas Lidstrom .15 .40
2 Mikko Eloranta .05 .15
3 Richard Park .05 .15
4 Eric Lindros .15 .40
5 Vincent Lecavalier .15 .40
6 Dany Heatley .20 .50
7 Roman Turek .12 .30
8 Rostislav Klesla .05 .15
9 Paul Kariya .15 .40
10 Marian Hossa .15 .40
11 Patrick Roy .75 2.00
12 Henrik Sedin .05 .15
13 Adam Graves .05 .15
14 Ian Laperriere .05 .15
15 Jiri Fischer .05 .15
16 Nick Schultz .05 .15
17 Steve Sullivan .05 .15
18 Sandis Ozolinsh .05 .15
19 Evgeni Nabokov .12 .30
20 Dimitri Khristich .05 .15
21 Danny Markov .05 .15
22 Adam Foote .05 .15
23 David Vyborny .05 .15
24 Jocelyn Thibault .12 .30
25 Mike Leclerc .05 .15
26 Pavol Demitra .12 .30
27 Scott Mellanby .05 .15
28 Brent Sopel .05 .15
29 Brad Isbister .05 .15
30 Sami Salo .05 .15
31 Jose Theodore .20 .50
32 Simon Gagne .15 .40
33 Rem Murray .05 .15
34 Mike Ricci .05 .15
35 Kim Johnsson .05 .15
36 Adam Oates .12 .30
37 Taylor Pyatt .05 .15
38 Rod Brind'Amour .12 .30
39 Mike Modano .25 .60
40 Jason Woolley .05 .15
41 Dimitri Yushkevich .05 .15
42 Craig Johnson .05 .15
43 Tony Hrkac .05 .15
44 Scott Young .05 .15
45 Marian Gaborik .30 1.00
46 Patrik Stefan .05 .15
47 Jon Klemm .05 .15
48 Andy McDonald .05 .15
49 Chris Pronger .12 .30
50 Frantisek Kaberle .05 .15
51 Jean-Sebastien Giguere .12 .30
52 Luc Robitaille .05 .15
53 Scott Stevens .12 .30
54 Roberto Luongo .20 .50
55 Teppo Numminen .05 .15
56 Alyn McCauley .05 .15
57 John Grahame .12 .30
58 David Legwand .12 .30
59 Hal Gill .05 .15
60 Mattias Ohlund .05 .15
61 Radim Vrbata .05 .15
62 Doug Gilmour .12 .30
63 Vaclav Prospal .05 .15
64 Brian Leetch .12 .30
65 Sheldon Keefe .05 .15
66 Randy McKay .05 .15
67 Mikael Samuelsson .05 .15
68 Pavel Bure .15 .40
69 Zdeno Chara .05 .15
70 P.J. Stock .05 .15
71 Shawn McEachern .05 .15
72 Radek Martinek .05 .15
73 Mike Rathje .05 .15
74 Kenny Jonsson .05 .15
75 Jamie Langenbrunner .05 .15
76 Chris Phillips .05 .15
77 Zigmund Palffy .12 .30
78 Stu Barnes .05 .15
79 Robert Reichel .05 .15
80 Jason Allison .05 .15
81 Dimitri Kalinin .05 .15
82 Chris Simon .05 .15
83 Arturs Irbe .12 .30
84 Tony Amonte .12 .30
85 Ruslan Salei .05 .15
86 Pascal Rheaume .05 .15
87 Marc Denis .12 .30
88 Marc Chouinard .05 .15
89 Jim Dowd .05 .15
90 Claude Lemieux .05 .15
91 Alexei Zhamnov .05 .15
92 Al MacInnis .12 .30
93 Cory Stillman .05 .15
94 Bob Boughner .05 .15
95 Kris Draper .05 .15
96 Mario Lemieux 1.00 2.50
97 Sean Burke .12 .30
98 Wes Walz .05 .15
99 Brenden Morrow .05 .15
100 Dave Andreychuk .05 .15
101 Jaromir Jagr .25 .60
102 Markus Naslund .15 .40
103 Nick Boynton .05 .15
104 Sean Hill .05 .15
105 Trevor Linden .05 .15
106 Bryan Berard .05 .15
107 Chris Neilson .05 .15
108 Marco Sturm .05 .15
109 Oleg Petrov .05 .15
110 Scott Gomez .05 .15
111 Luke Richardson .05 .15
112 Manny Malhotra .05 .15
113 Valeri Bure .05 .15
114 Marcel Hossa .05 .15
115 Todd Marchant .05 .15
116 Radek Bonk .05 .15
117 Matt Bradley .05 .15
118 Jochen Hecht .05 .15
119 Dan McGillis .05 .15
120 Adrian Aucoin .05 .15
121 Eric Belanger .05 .15
122 Peter Forsberg .40 1.00
123 Alexei Morozov .05 .15
124 Jimmie Olvestad .05 .15
125 Ed Jovanovski .12 .30
126 Chris Drury .12 .30
127 Alexander Mogilny .12 .30
128 Stephen Weiss .05 .15
129 Manny Legace .12 .30
130 Jarome Iginla .20 .50
131 Doug Weight .12 .30
132 Martin St. Louis .12 .30
133 Alexander Khavanov .05 .15
134 Chris Chelios .15 .40
135 Viktor Kozlov .05 .15
136 Bret Hedican .05 .15
137 Denis Arkhipov .05 .15
138 Jere Lehtinen .12 .30
139 Mathieu Schneider .05 .15
140 Tomas Kaberle .05 .15
141 Brian Gionta .05 .15
142 Janne Niinimaa .05 .15
143 Mark Parrish .05 .15
144 Todd White .05 .15
145 Geoff Sanderson .05 .15
146 Yanic Perreault .05 .15
147 Roman Hamrlik .05 .15
148 Mike Fisher .05 .15
149 Jiri Dopita .05 .15
150 Claude Lapointe .05 .15
151 Vaclav Nedorost .05 .15
152 Mikael Renberg .05 .15
153 Jozef Stumpel .05 .15
154 Felix Potvin .15 .40
155 Chris Gratton .05 .15
156 Adam Deadmarsh .05 .15
157 Sergei Fedorov .25 .60
158 Mike Sillinger .05 .15
159 Kris Beech .05 .15
160 Grant Marshall .05 .15
161 Brent Johnson .12 .30
162 Alexei Kovalev .12 .30
163 Darren McCarty .05 .15
164 Marc Savard .05 .15
165 Janne Laukkanen .05 .15
166 Phil Housley .05 .15
167 Tomas Holmstrom .05 .15
168 Bill Guerin .12 .30
169 Darius Kasparaitis .05 .15
170 Jaroslav Modry .05 .15
171 Martin Gelinas .05 .15
172 Peter Bondra .12 .30
173 Steven Reinprecht .05 .15
174 Anson Carter .12 .30
175 Eric Brewer .05 .15
176 Magnus Arvedson .05 .15
177 Patrice Brisebois .05 .15
178 Sergei Brylin .05 .15
179 Vitali Vishnevski .05 .15
180 Marcus Nilsson .05 .15
181 Niklas Sundstrom .05 .15
182 Daymond Langkow .12 .30
183 Craig Conroy .05 .15
184 Gary Roberts .05 .15
185 Justin Williams .05 .15
186 Matt Cooke .05 .15
187 Pierre Turgeon .12 .30
188 Steve Konowalchuk .05 .15
189 Yannick Tremblay .05 .15
190 Tom Poti .05 .15
191 Sergei Zholtok .05 .15
192 Robyn Regehr .05 .15
193 Mike Richter .15 .40
194 Shawn Bates .05 .15
195 Pavel Trnka .05 .15
196 Martin Straka .05 .15
197 Jonas Hoglund .05 .15
198 Filip Kuba .05 .15
199 Chris Osgood .12 .30
200 Brad May .05 .15
201 David Aebischer .12 .30
202 Fred Brathwaite .12 .30
203 Lubos Bartecko .05 .15
204 Marty Turco .12 .30
205 Petr Nedved .05 .15
206 Shayne Corson .05 .15
207 Sergei Samsonov .12 .30
208 Patrik Elias .12 .30
209 Martin Erat .05 .15
210 Krystofer Kolanos .05 .15
211 Joe Thornton .25 .60
212 Ivan Novoseltsev .05 .15
213 Eric Messier .05 .15
214 Daniel Cleary .05 .15
215 Alex Tanguay .12 .30
216 Robert Lang .05 .15
217 Wade Redden .05 .15
218 Scott Walker .05 .15
219 Milan Hejduk .15 .40
220 Ken Daneyko .05 .15
221 J-P Dumont .05 .15
222 Ian Moran .05 .15
223 Christian Berglund .05 .15
224 Alexei Yashin .05 .15
225 Brad Stuart .05 .15
226 Donald Brashear .05 .15
227 Curtis Brown .12 .30
228 John LeClair .15 .40
229 Manny Fernandez .12 .30
230 Maxim Afinogenov .05 .15
231 Roman Cechmanek .12 .30
232 Tyler Wright .05 .15
233 Slava Kozlov .05 .15
234 Tyler Arnason .12 .30
235 Sandy McCarthy .05 .15
236 Pascal Dupuis .05 .15
237 Olaf Kolzig .12 .30
238 Kyle Calder .05 .15
239 Jeremy Roenick .20 .50
240 Mathieu Dandenault .05 .15
241 Jeff O'Neill .05 .15
242 Dave Tanabe .05 .15
243 Calle Johansson .05 .15
244 Greg deVries .05 .15
245 Andrew Brunette .05 .15
246 Dan Hinote .05 .15
247 Jason Smith .05 .15
248 Mark Bell .05 .15
249 Pavel Kubina .05 .15
250 Teemu Selanne .12 .30
251 Vladimir Orszagh .05 .15
252 Brad Ference .05 .15
253 Darryl Sydor .05 .15
254 Vitali Yachmenev .05 .15
255 Scott Hartnell .05 .15
256 Fredrik Modin .05 .15
257 Alexei Zhitnik .05 .15
258 Brett Hull .20 .50
259 Glen Murray .05 .15
260 Michael Peca .05 .15
261 Owen Nolan .12 .30
262 Tie Domi .12 .30
263 Ville Nieminen .05 .15
264 Rob Blake .12 .30
265 Greg Johnson .05 .15
266 Andrei Markov .05 .15
267 Josef Vasicek .05 .15
268 Ryan Smyth .05 .15
269 Vincent Damphousse .05 .15
270 Mark Recchi .12 .30
271 Rob Niedermayer .05 .15
272 Mariusz Czerkawski .05 .15
273 Glen Wesley .05 .15
274 Brian Boucher .12 .30
275 Bryan McCabe .05 .15
276 Ron Tugnutt .12 .30
277 Daniel Briere .05 .15
278 Igor Larionov .05 .15
279 Keith Tkachuk .15 .40
280 Mats Sundin .15 .40
281 Dwayne Roloson .12 .30
282 Andrew Cassels .05 .15
283 Brendan Morrison .12 .30
284 Bryan Smolinski .05 .15
285 Jan Hlavac .05 .15
286 Jamal Mayers .05 .15
287 Kevin Weekes .12 .30
288 Tim Connolly .05 .15
289 Steve Yzerman .75 2.00
290 Derek Morris .05 .15
291 Derian Hatcher .05 .15
292 Steve Shields .12 .30
293 Martin Brodeur .40 1.00
294 Marcus Ragnarsson .05 .15
295 Scott Thornton .05 .15
296 Oleg Kvasha .05 .15
297 Mike York .05 .15
298 Tomi Kallio .05 .15
299 Martin Skoula .05 .15
300 Jeff Halpern .05 .15
301 Ed Belfour .15 .40
302 Andrew Ference .05 .15
303 Nikolai Khabibulin .15 .40
304 Bryce Salvador .05 .15
305 Lubomir Visnovsky .05 .15
306 Dan Cloutier .12 .30
307 Andy Delmore .05 .15
308 Martin Lapointe .05 .15
309 Daniel Sedin .05 .15
310 Kelly Buchberger .05 .15
311 Darcy Tucker .05 .15
312 Sergei Berezin .05 .15
313 Ruslan Fedotenko .05 .15
314 Mark Messier .15 .40
315 Mike Comrie .12 .30
316 Bobby Holik .05 .15
317 Shane Doan .05 .15
318 Michal Handzus .05 .15
319 Joe Sakic .30 .75
320 Kristian Huselius .05 .15
321 Ben Clymer .05 .15
322 Mattias Norstrom .05 .15
323 Pavel Datsyuk .15 .40
324 Richard Matvichuk .05 .15
325 Dainius Zubrus .05 .15
326 Craig Rivet .05 .15
327 Eric Desjardins .05 .15
328 Patrick Marleau .12 .30
329 Mike Grier .05 .15
330 Steve Rucchin .05 .15
331 Kimmo Timonen .05 .15
332 Brendan Witt .05 .15
333 Sami Kapanen .05 .15
334 Todd Bertuzzi .15 .40
335 Ilya Kovalchuk .20 .50
336 Donald Audette .05 .15
337 Georges Laraque .05 .15
338 Jason Arnott .05 .15
339 John Madden .05 .15
340 Petr Sykora .05 .15
341 Tommy Salo .12 .30
342 Daniel Alfredsson .12 .30
343 Eric Weinrich .05 .15
344 Radek Dvorak .05 .15
345 Stephane Yelle .05 .15
346 Sergei Zubov .05 .15
347 Milan Hnilicka .12 .30
348 Lubomir Sekeras .05 .15
349 Espen Knutsen .05 .15
350 Travis Green .05 .15
351 Jan Hrdina .05 .15
352 Paul Laus .05 .15
353 Bates Battaglia .05 .15
354 Miroslav Satan .12 .30
355 Craig Berube .05 .15
356 Sean O'Donnell .05 .15
357 Joe Nieuwendyk .12 .30
358 Patrick Lalime .12 .30
359 Brian Rafalski .05 .15
360 Michael Nylander .05 .15
361 Jean-Luc Grand Pierre .05 .15
362 Ron Francis .12 .30
363 Andrei Nikolishin .05 .15
364 Dallas Drake .05 .15
365 Eric Daze .05 .15
366 Andreas Dackell .05 .15
367 Scott Niedermayer .05 .15
368 Chris Clark .05 .15
369 Brendan Shanahan .15 .40
370 Tomas Vokoun .12 .30
371 Johan Hedberg .12 .30
372 Nikita Alexeev .05 .15
373 Dave Scatchard .05 .15
374 Matt Cullen .05 .15
375 Steve Thomas .05 .15
376 Brian Rolston .05 .15
377 Richard Zednik .05 .15
378 Sergei Gonchar .05 .15
379 Keith Primeau .05 .15
380 Jeff Friesen .05 .15
381 Keith Carney .05 .15
382 Kirk Maltby .05 .15
383 Erik Cole .05 .15
384 Martin Biron .12 .30
385 Jody Shelley .05 .15
386 Brad Richards .12 .30
387 Michal Rozsival .05 .15
388 Martin Havlat .12 .30
389 Igor Korolev .05 .15
390 Ladislav Nagy .05 .15
391 Curtis Joseph .15 .40
392 Toni Lydman .05 .15
393 Antti Laaksonen .05 .15
394 Jeff Jillson .05 .15
395 Saku Koivu .15 .40
396 Trevor Letowski .05 .15
397 Ray Whitney .05 .15
398 Olli Jokinen .12 .30
399 Colin White .05 .15
400 Mike Dunham .12 .30
401 Dan Blackburn .12 .30
402 Ron Hainsey RC .60 1.50
403 Scottie Upshall RC .60 1.50
404 Anton Volchenkov RC .60 1.50
405 Dmitri Bykov RC .60 1.50
406 Steve Eminger RC .60 1.50
407 Lasse Pirjeta RC .60 1.50
408 Tomi Pettinen RC .60 1.50
409 Ales Hemsky RC 2.00 3.00
410 Chuck Kobasew RC 1.00 2.50
411 Jason Spezza RC 2.50 5.00
412 Jeff Paul RC .60 1.50
413 Adam Hall RC .60 1.50
414 Rick Nash RC 2.50 5.00
415 Kurt Sauer RC .60 1.50
416 Alexander Frolov RC 1.25 3.00
417 Patrick Sharp RC .60 1.50
418 Alexei Smirnov RC .60 1.50
419 Tom Koivisto RC .60 1.50
420 Jay Bouwmeester RC 1.25 2.50
421 Mikael Tellqvist RC .60 1.50
422 P-M Bouchard RC 1.25 2.50
423 Radovan Somik RC .60 1.50
424 Ivan Majesky RC .60 1.50
425 Jamie Lundmark .05 .15
426 Henrik Zetterberg RC 2.50 4.00
427 Dennis Seidenberg RC .60 1.50
428 Jeff Taffe RC .60 1.50
429 Martin Gerber RC 1.00 2.50
430 Lynn Loyns RC .60 1.50
431 Micki DuPont RC .60 1.50
432 Jonathan Cheechoo .08 .20
433 Eric Godard RC .60 1.50
434 Stanislav Chistov RC .05 .15
435 Alexander Svitov RC .60 1.50
436 Fedor Fedorov .05 .15
437 Stephane Veilleux RC .60 1.50
438 Curtis Sanford RC .05 .15
439 Jordan Leopold RC .60 1.50
440 Carlo Colaiacovo RC .60 1.50

2002-03 Topps Total Award Winners

COMPLETE SET (10) 8.00 15.00
STATED ODDS 1:36
AW1 Jarome Iginla .75 2.00
AW2 Patrick Roy 2.50 6.00
AW3 Nicklas Lidstrom .60 1.50
AW4 Jose Theodore .75 2.00
AW5 Dany Heatley .75 2.00
AW6 Ron Francis .50 1.25
AW7 Eric Daze .50 1.25
AW8 Chris Chelios .60 1.50
AW9 Saku Koivu .60 1.50
AW10 Michael Peca .50 1.25

2002-03 Topps Total Production

COMPLETE SET (15) 6.00 12.00
STATED ODDS 1:12
TP1 Jarome Iginla .40 1.00
TP2 Joe Sakic .60 1.50
TP3 Mats Sundin .30 .75
TP4 Peter Forsberg .75 2.00
TP5 Bill Guerin .25 .60
TP6 Brendan Shanahan .50 1.25
TP7 Sergei Fedorov .60 1.50
TP8 Pavel Bure .40 1.00
TP9 Jeremy Roenick .40 1.00
TP10 Tony Amonte .25 .60
TP11 Teemu Selanne .30 .75
TP12 Alexander Mogilny .25 .60
TP13 Markus Naslund .30 .75
TP14 Todd Bertuzzi .30 .75
TP15 Jaromir Jagr .50 1.25

2002-03 Topps Total Signatures

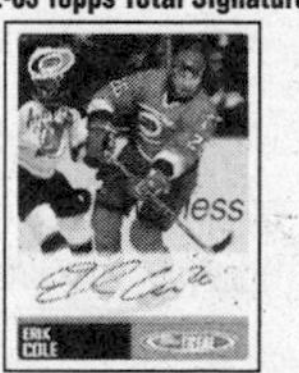

Inserted at a rate of 1:926, this 6-card set looked like the base set but carried certified autographs on the card fronts. As of press time, not all cards have been verified.

BG Brian Gionta 6.00 15.00
EC Erik Cole 6.00 15.00
KK Krystofer Kolanos EXISTS?
RK Rostislav Klesla 12.50 30.00
RV Radim Vrbata 6.00 15.00
SW Stephen Weiss EXISTS? 15.00 40.00

2002-03 Topps Total Team Checklists

COMPLETE SET (30) 6.00 15.00
TTC1 Ilya Kovalchuk .40 1.00
TTC2 Joe Thornton .40 1.00
TTC3 Miroslav Satan .10 .25
TTC4 Jarome Iginla .40 1.00
TTC5 Ron Francis .10 .25
TTC6 Jocelyn Thibault .10 .25
TTC7 Patrick Roy 1.25 3.00
TTC8 Rick Nash .40 1.00
TTC9 Mike Modano .40 1.00
TTC10 Steve Yzerman .75 2.00
TTC11 Tommy Salo .10 .25
TTC12 Roberto Luongo .40 1.00
TTC13 Jason Allison .10 .25
TTC14 Paul Kariya .30 .75
TTC15 Marian Gaborik .40 1.00
TTC16 Jose Theodore .40 1.00
TTC17 Mike Dunham .20 .50
TTC18 Martin Brodeur .75 2.00
TTC19 Michael Peca .10 .25
TTC20 Pavel Bure .30 .75
TTC21 Daniel Alfredsson .20 .50
TTC22 John LeClair .10 .25
TTC23 Tony Amonte .10 .25
TTC24 Mario Lemieux 1.25 3.00
TTC25 Owen Nolan .20 .50
TTC26 Keith Tkachuk .20 .50
TTC27 Nikolai Khabibulin .30 .75
TTC28 Mats Sundin .30 .75
TTC29 Todd Bertuzzi .10 .25
TTC30 Jaromir Jagr .60 1.50

2002-03 Topps Total Topps

COMPLETE SET (20) 8.00 15.00
STATED ODDS 1:6
TT1 Jarome Iginla .25 .60
TT2 Patrick Roy 1.00 2.50
TT3 Nicklas Lidstrom .20 .50
TT4 Jose Theodore .25 .60
TT5 Joe Sakic .40 1.00
TT6 Mats Sundin .20 .50
TT7 Ilya Kovalchuk .25 .60
TT8 Joe Thornton .30 .75
TT9 Mike Modano .30 .75
TT10 Brett Hull .25 .60
TT11 Steve Yzerman 1.00 2.50
TT12 Curtis Joseph .20 .50
TT13 Paul Kariya .20 .50
TT14 Patrik Elias .12 .30
TT15 Martin Brodeur .50 1.25
TT16 Eric Lindros .20 .50
TT17 Daniel Alfredsson .12 .30
TT18 Mario Lemieux 1.25 3.00
TT19 Owen Nolan .12 .30
TT20 Jaromir Jagr .30 .75

2003-04 Topps Traded

Released in late-April, this 165-card set consisted of 84 veterans who were traded earlier in the season and rookies who made their debut late in the season.

COMPLETE SET (165) 25.00 50.00
TT1 Felix Potvin .10 .25
TT2 Chris Drury .10 .25
TT3 Karel Rachunek .02 .10
TT4 Miikka Kiprusoff .10 .25
TT5 Justin Williams .02 .10
TT6 Bryan Berard .02 .10
TT7 Jim Vandermeer .02 .10
TT8 Shayne Corson .02 .10
TT9 Teemu Selanne .12 .30
TT10 Peter Worrell .02 .10
TT11 Darryl Sydor .02 .10
TT12 Todd Marchant .02 .10
TT13 Ray Whitney .02 .10
TT14 Robert Lang .02 .10
TT15 Adam Oates .10 .25
TT16 Jozef Stumpel .02 .10
TT17 Luc Robitaille .10 .25
TT18 Roman Cechmanek .10 .25
TT19 Martin Straka .02 .10
TT20 Sergei Fedorov .15 .40
TT21 Michael Nylander .02 .10
TT22 Steve Sullivan .02 .10
TT23 Steve Konowalchuk .02 .10
TT24 Valeri Bure .02 .10
TT25 Jaromir Jagr .20 .50
TT26 Peter Bondra .10 .25
TT27 Mike Grier .02 .10
TT28 Cory Stillman .02 .10
TT29 Joe Nieuwendyk .10 .25
TT30 Brian Leetch .10 .25
TT31 Johan Hedberg .10 .25
TT32 Andrew Raycroft .10 .25
TT33 Chuck Kobasew .02 .10
TT34 Brett McLean .02 .10
TT35 Craig Andersson .02 .10
TT36 Michael Leighton .10 .25
TT37 Matthew Barnaby .02 .10
TT38 Philippe Sauve .10 .25
TT39 Chris Gratton .02 .10
TT40 Radek Dvorak .02 .10
TT41 Raffi Torres .02 .10
TT42 Ossi Vaananen .02 .10
TT43 Trent Klatt .02 .10
TT44 Alexander Daigle .02 .10
TT45 Sergei Gonchar .02 .10
TT46 Niklas Sundstrom .02 .10
TT47 Michael Ryder .02 .10
TT48 Igor Larionov .02 .10
TT49 Jan Hrdina .02 .10
TT50 Cliff Ronning .02 .10
TT51 Trent Hunter .02 .10
TT52 Alexei Zhamnov .02 .10
TT53 Tommy Salo .10 .25
TT54 Danny Markov .02 .10
TT55 Sean Burke .10 .25
TT56 Shane Doan .02 .10
TT57 Konstantin Koltsov .02 .10
TT58 Mike Danton .02 .10
TT59 John Grahame .10 .25
TT60 Dimitry Afanasenkov .02 .10
TT61 Bryan Marchment .02 .10
TT62 Mikael Tellqvist .10 .25
TT63 Jason King .02 .10
TT64 Anson Carter .10 .25
TT65 Steve Shields .10 .25
TT66 Ron Francis .10 .25
TT67 Petr Nedved .02 .10
TT68 Alexander Svitov .02 .10
TT69 Ville Nieminen .02 .10
TT70 Martin Skoula .02 .10
TT71 Steve Yzerman .60 1.50
TT72 Jason Spezza .12 .30
TT73 Stanislav Chistov .02 .10
TT74 Pascal Leclaire .10 .25
TT75 Mike Comrie .10 .25
TT76 Brent Johnson .10 .25
TT77 Mike Rupp .02 .10
TT78 Derek Morris .02 .10
TT79 Geoff Sanderson .02 .10
TT80 Martin Rucinsky .02 .10
TT81 Shaone Morrisonn .02 .10
TT82 Paul Kariya .12 .30
TT83 Alex Kovalev .10 .25
TT84 Jeff Jillson .02 .10
TT85 Kari Lehtonen RC 3.00 8.00
TT86 Karl Stewart RC .75 2.00
TT87 Sergei Zinovjev RC .75 2.00
TT88 Carl Corazzini RC .75 2.00
TT89 Andrew Peters RC .75 2.00
TT90 Derek Roy RC .75 2.00
TT91 Matthew Lombardi RC .75 2.00
TT92 Alan Rourke RC .75 2.00
TT93 Pavel Vorobiev RC .75 2.00
TT94 Lasse Kukkonen RC .75 2.00
TT95 Travis Moen RC .75 2.00
TT96 Matt Keith RC .75 2.00
TT97 Marek Svatos RC 2.00 5.00
TT98 Cody McCormick RC .75 2.00
TT99 Mike Green RC .75 2.00
TT100 Mikhail Kuleshov RC .75 2.00
TT101 Dan Fritsche RC .75 2.00
TT102 Nikolai Zherdev RC 2.00 5.00
TT103 Aaron Johnson RC .75 2.00
TT104 Tim Jackman RC .75 2.00
TT105 Trevor Daley RC .75 2.00
TT106 Nathan Robinson RC .75 2.00
TT107 Niklas Kronwall RC .75 2.00
TT108 Darryl Bootland RC .75 2.00
TT109 Tony Salmelainen RC .75 2.00
TT110 Mike Bishai RC .75 2.00
TT111 Gregory Campbell RC .75 2.00
TT112 Tim Gleason RC .75 2.00
TT113 Dustin Brown .75 2.00
TT114 Noah Clarke RC .75 2.00
TT115 Chris Kunitz RC .75 2.00
TT116 Tony Martensson RC .75 2.00
TT117 Brent Burns RC .75 2.00
TT118 Chris Higgins RC 1.25 3.00
TT119 Dan Hamhuis RC .75 2.00
TT120 Marek Zidlicky RC .75 2.00
TT121 Andrew Hutchinson RC .75 2.00
TT122 Paul Martin RC .75 2.00
TT123 Aleksandar Suglobov RC .75 2.00
TT124 David Hale RC .75 2.00
TT125 Sean Bergenheim RC .75 2.00
TT126 Jed Ortmeyer RC .75 2.00
TT127 Lawrence Nycholat RC .75 2.00
TT128 Dominic Moore RC .75 2.00
TT129 Fedor Tyutin RC .75 2.00
TT130 Garth Murray RC .75 2.00
TT131 Antoine Vermette RC .75 2.00
TT132 Joni Pitkanen RC .75 2.00
TT133 Antero Niittymaki RC 2.00 5.00
TT134 Matthew Spiller RC .75 2.00
TT135 Fredrik Sjostrom RC .75 2.00
TT136 Ryan Malone RC .75 2.00
TT137 Matt Murley RC .75 2.00
TT138 Andy Chiodo RC .75 2.00
TT139 Tom Preissing RC .75 2.00
TT140 Wade Brookbank RC .75 2.00
TT141 Ryan Kesler RC .75 2.00
TT142 Nathan Smith RC .75 2.00
TT143 Boyd Gordon RC .75 2.00
TT144 Alexander Semin RC 1.00 2.50
TT145 Rastislav Stana RC .75 2.00
TT146 Cory Larose RC .75 2.00
TT147 Rob Scuderi RC .75 2.00
TT148 Ryan Barnes RC .75 2.00
TT149 Matt Ellison RC .75 2.00
TT150 Milan Michalek RC .75 2.00
TT151 Kyle Wellwood RC .75 2.00
TT152 Jame Pollock RC .75 2.00
TT153 Dwayne Zinger RC .75 2.00
TT154 Dan Ellis RC .75 2.00
TT155 Patrick Leahy RC .75 2.00
TT156 Jozef Balej RC .75 2.00
TT157 Colton Orr RC .75 2.00
TT158 Julien Vauclair RC .75 2.00
TT159 Darcy Verot RC .75 2.00
TT160 Christian Ehrhoff RC .75 2.00
TT161 Boyd Kane RC .75 2.00

TT162 Tuomas Pihlman RC .75 2.00
TT163 John-Michael Liles RC .75 2.00
TT164 Anton Babchuk RC .75 2.00
TT165 Owen Fussey RC .75 2.00

2003-04 Topps Traded Blue

*STARS: 5X TO 12X BASE HI
*ROOKIES: .75X TO 2X
PRINT RUN 500 SER.#'d SETS

2003-04 Topps Traded Gold

*STARS: 10X TO 25X BASE HI
*ROOKIES: 1.5X TO 4X
PRINT RUN 50 SER.#'d SETS

2003-04 Topps Traded Red

*STARS: 8X TO 20X BASE HI
*ROOKIES: 1.25X TO 3X
PRINT RUN 100 SER.#'d SETS

2003-04 Topps Traded Franchise Fabrics

Memorabilia in Topps Traded was inserted at an overall rate of 3:24. No further insertion info was made available.

*MULT.COLOR SWATCH: .5X TO 1.25X
FFJTH Jose Theodore 5.00 12.00
FFJS Joe Sakic 5.00 12.00
FFJSG Jean-Sebastien Giguere 3.00 8.00
FFVL Vincent Lecavalier 5.00 12.00
FFZP Zigmund Palffy 3.00 8.00
FFJT Joe Thornton 5.00 12.00
FFML Mario Lemieux 20.00 50.00
FFJI Jarome Iginla 5.00 12.00
FFMB Martin Brodeur 15.00 40.00
FFMG Marian Gaborik 5.00 12.00
FFRN Rick Nash 5.00 12.00
FFIK Ilya Kovalchuk
FFRL Roberto Luongo 5.00 12.00
FFTB Todd Bertuzzi
FFDA Daniel Alfredsson 3.00 8.00
FFTV Tomas Vokoun 3.00 8.00
FFMT Marty Turco 3.00 8.00
FFBG Bill Guerin 3.00 8.00
FFMS Mats Sundin 4.00 10.00
FFPM Patrick Marleau 4.00 10.00
FFMR Mark Recchi 3.00 8.00
FFAY Alexei Yashin 3.00 8.00
FFKP Keith Primeau 3.00 8.00

2003-04 Topps Traded Future Phenoms

Memorabilia in Topps Traded was inserted at an overall rate of 3:24. No further insertion info was made available.

*MULT.COLOR SWATCH: .5X TO 1.25X
FPJL Jordan Leopold 2.00 5.00
FPAT Alex Tanguay 4.00 10.00
FPRM Ryan Miller 5.00 12.00
FPJB Jay Bouwmeester 4.00 10.00
FPPD Pavel Datsyuk 4.00 10.00
FPAH Adam Hall 2.00 5.00
FPPS Peter Sejna 2.00 5.00
FPNH Nathan Horton 4.00 10.00
FPRR Robyn Regehr 2.00 5.00
FPSC Stanislav Chistov 2.00 5.00
FPDA David Aebischer 4.00 10.00
FPAV Antoine Vermette 2.00 5.00
FPMS Matthew Stajan 4.00 10.00
FPAF Alexander Frolov 4.00 10.00
FPAM Antti Miettinen 2.00 5.00
FPSW Stephen Weiss 2.00 5.00
FPSB Sean Bergenheim 2.00 5.00
FPJP Joni Pitkanen 2.00 5.00
FPBJ Barret Jackman 2.00 5.00
FPJOL Joffrey Lupul 4.00 10.00
FPNB Nick Boynton 2.00 5.00
FPBR Brad Richards 5.00 12.00
FPMW Mattias Weinhandl 2.00 5.00
FPMR Mike Ribeiro 2.00 5.00
FPJLU Jamie Lundmark 2.00 5.00
FPDH Dan Hamhuis 2.00 5.00

1963-64 Toronto Star

This set of 42 photos was distributed one per week with the Toronto Star and was also available as a complete set directly. The photos measure approximately 4 3/4" by 6 3/4" and are entitled, "Hockey Stars in Action." There is a short write-up on the back of each photo. The player's team is identified in the checklist below, Boston Bruins (BB), Chicago Blackhawks (CBH), Detroit Red Wings (DRW), Montreal Canadiens (MC), New York Rangers (NYR), and Toronto Maple Leafs (TML). Since the photos are unnumbered, they are listed below in alphabetical order.

COMPLETE SET (42) 150.00 300.00
1 George Armstrong TML 4.00 8.00
2 Andy Bathgate NYR 4.00 8.00
3 Bob Baun TML 2.50 5.00
4 Jean Beliveau MC 7.50 15.00
5 Leo Boivin BB 2.50 5.00
6 Johnny Bower TML 5.00 10.00
7 Carl Brewer TML 2.50 5.00
8 Johnny Bucyk BB 4.00 8.00
9 Alex Delvecchio DRW 5.00 10.00
10 Kent Douglas TML 2.00 4.00
11 Dick Duff TML 2.50 5.00
12 Bill Gadsby DRW 3.00 6.00
13 Jean-Guy Gendron BB 2.00 4.00
14 BoomBoom Geoffrion MC 7.50 15.00
15 Glenn Hall CBH 6.00 12.00
16 Doug Harvey NYR 5.00 10.00
17 Bill(Red) Hay CBH 2.50 5.00
18 Camille Henry NYR 2.50 5.00
19 Tim Horton TML 7.50 15.00
20 Gordie Howe DRW 25.00 50.00
21 Bobby Hull CBH 15.00 30.00
22 Red Kelly TML 5.00 10.00
23 Dave Keon TML 7.50 15.00
24 Parker MacDonald DRW 2.00 4.00
25 Frank Mahovlich TML 7.50 15.00
26 Stan Mikita CBH 7.50 15.00
27 Dickie Moore MC 5.00 10.00
28 Eric Nesterenko CBH 2.50 5.00
29 Marcel Pronovost DRW 2.50 5.00
30 Claude Provost MC 2.50 5.00
31 Bob Pulford TML 3.00 6.00
32 Henri Richard MC 7.50 15.00
33 Terry Sawchuk DRW 10.00 20.00
34 Eddie Shack TML 5.00 10.00
35 Allan Stanley TML 3.00 6.00
36 Ron Stewart TML 2.00 4.00
37 Jean-Guy Talbot MC 2.50 5.00
38 Gilles Tremblay MC 2.00 4.00
39 J.C. Tremblay MC 2.50 5.00
40 Norm Ullman DRW 4.00 8.00
41 Elmer(Moose) Vasko CBH 2.00 4.00
42 Ken Wharram CBH 2.50 5.00

1964-65 Toronto Star

This set of 48 photos was distributed one per week with the Toronto Star and was also available as a complete set directly. The direct complete sets also included a booklet and glossy photo of Dave Keon in the mail-away package. These blank-backed photos measure approximately 4 1/8" by 5 1/8". The player's team is identified in the checklist below, Boston Bruins (BB), Chicago Blackhawks (CBH), Detroit Red Wings (DRW), Montreal Canadiens (MC), New York Rangers (NYR), and Toronto Maple Leafs (TML). Since the photos are unnumbered, they are listed below in alphabetical order. There was an album (actually a folder) available for each team to slot in cards. However when the cards were placed in the album it rendered the card's caption unreadable as only the action photo was visible.

COMPLETE SET (48) 150.00 300.00
1 Dave Balon MC 2.00 4.00
2 Andy Bathgate TML 4.00 8.00
3 Bob Baun TML 3.00 6.00
4 Jean Beliveau MC 7.50 15.00
5 Red Berenson MC 2.50 5.00
6 Leo Boivin BB 3.00 6.00
7 Carl Brewer TML 2.50 5.00
8 Alex Delvecchio DRW 4.00 8.00
9 Rod Gilbert NYR 4.00 8.00
10 Ted Green BB 2.50 5.00
11 Glenn Hall CBH 5.00 10.00
12 Billy Harris TML 2.00 4.00
13 Bill(Red) Hay CBH 2.00 4.00
14 Paul Henderson DRW 3.00 6.00
15 Wayne Hillman CBH 2.00 4.00
16 Charlie Hodge MC 3.00 6.00
17 Tim Horton TML 7.50 15.00
18 Gordie Howe DRW 20.00 40.00
19 Harry Howell NYR 3.00 6.00
20 Bobby Hull CBH 12.50 25.00
21 Larry Jeffrey DRW 2.00 4.00
22 Tom Johnson BB 3.00 6.00
23 Forbes Kennedy BB 2.00 4.00
24 Dave Keon TML 6.00 12.00
25 Orland Kurtenbach BB 2.50 5.00
26 Jacques Laperriere MC 2.50 5.00
27 Parker MacDonald DRW 2.00 4.00
28 Al MacNeil CBH 2.00 4.00
29 Frank Mahovlich TML 6.00 12.00
30 Chico Maki CBH 2.00 4.00
31 Don McKenney TML 2.00 4.00
32 John McKenzie CBH 2.00 4.00
33 Stan Mikita CBH 6.00 12.00
34 Jim Neilson NYR 2.00 4.00
35 Jim Pappin TML 2.00 4.00
36 Pierre Pilote CBH 3.00 6.00
37 Jacques Plante NYR 10.00 20.00
38 Marcel Pronovost DRW 3.00 6.00
39 Claude Provost MC 2.50 5.00
40 Bob Pulford TML 3.00 6.00
41 Henri Richard MC 6.00 12.00
42 Wayne Rivers BB 2.00 4.00
43 Floyd Smith DRW 2.00 4.00
44 Allan Stanley TML 4.00 8.00
45 Ron Stewart TML 2.00 4.00
46 J.C. Tremblay MC 2.50 5.00
47 Norm Ullman DRW 4.00 8.00
48 Elmer Vasko CBH 2.00 4.00
xx Album/Folder 12.50 25.00

1971-72 Toronto Sun

This set of 294 photo cards with two punch holes has never been very popular with collectors. The photos are quite fragile, printed on thin paper, and measure approximately 5" by 7". The checklist below is in team order as follows: Boston Bruins (1-21), Buffalo Sabres (22-41), California Golden Seals (42-61), Chicago Blackhawks (62-82), Detroit Red Wings (83-103), Los Angeles Kings (104-124), Minnesota North Stars (125-145), Montreal Canadiens (146-166), New York Rangers (167-186), Philadelphia Flyers (187-208), Pittsburgh Penguins (209-230), St. Louis Blues (231-252), Toronto Maple Leafs (253-274), and Vancouver Canucks (275-294). The cards were intended to fit in a two-ring binder specially made to hold the cards. Also included was and introduction photo, with text by Scott Young.

COMPLETE SET (294) 300.00 600.00
1 Boston Bruins 1.50 3.00
2 Don Awrey .50 1.00
3 Garnet Bailey .50 1.00
4 Ivan Boldirev .50 1.00
5 Johnny Bucyk 3.00 6.00
6 Wayne Cashman .75 1.50
7 Gerry Cheevers 4.00 8.00
8 Phil Esposito 10.00 20.00
9 Ted Green .75 1.50
10 Ken Hodge .75 1.50
11 Ed Johnston 1.50 3.00
12 Reggie Leach 1.50 3.00
13 Don Marcotte .50 1.00
14 John McKenzie .50 1.00
15 Bobby Orr 30.00 60.00
16 Derek Sanderson 4.00 8.00
17 Dallas Smith .50 1.00
18 Richard Allan Smith .50 1.00
19 Fred Stanfield .50 1.00
20 Mike Walton .75 1.50
21 Ed Westfall .75 1.50
22 Buffalo Sabres 1.00 2.00
23 Doug Barrie .50 1.00
24 Roger Crozier 2.00 4.00
25 Dave Dryden 1.00 2.00
26 Dick Duff .75 1.50
27 Phil Goyette .50 1.00
28 Al Hamilton .50 1.00
29 Larry Keenan .50 1.00
30 Danny Lawson .50 1.00
31 Don Luce .50 1.00
32 Richard Martin 1.00 2.00
33 Ray McKay .50 1.00
34 Gerry Meehan .75 1.50
35 Kevin O'Shea .50 1.00
36 Gilbert Perreault 4.00 8.00
37 Tracy Pratt .50 1.00
38 Mike Robitaille .50 1.00
39 Eddie Shack 2.00 4.00
40 Jim Watson .50 1.00
41 Rod Zaine .50 1.00
42 California Seals 1.50 3.00
43 Wayne Carleton .50 1.00
44 Lyle Carter .50 1.00
45 Gary Croteau .50 1.00
46 Norm Ferguson .50 1.00
47 Stan Gilbertson .50 1.00
48 Ernie Hicke .50 1.00
49 Gary Jarrett 1.00 2.00
50 Joey Johnston .50 1.00
51 Marshall Johnston .50 1.00
52 Bert Marshall .50 1.00
53 Walt McKechnie .50 1.00
54 Don O'Donoghue .50 1.00
55 Gerry Pinder .75 1.50
56 Dick Redmond .50 1.00
57 Robert Sheehan .50 1.00
58 Paul Shmyr .50 1.00
59 Ron Stackhouse SP 6.00 12.00
60 Carol Vadnais .50 1.00
61 Tom Williams .50 1.00
62 Chicago Blackhawks 1.50 3.00
63 Lou Angotti .50 1.00
64 Bryan Campbell .50 1.00
65 Tony Esposito 10.00 20.00
66 Bobby Hull 15.00 30.00
67 Dennis Hull 1.00 2.00
68 Doug Jarrett .50 1.00
69 Jerry Korab .50 1.00
70 Cliff Koroll .50 1.00
71 Darryl Maggs .50 1.00
72 Keith Magnuson .75 1.50
73 Chico Maki .50 1.00
74 Dan Maloney .50 1.00
75 Pit Martin .75 1.50
76 Stan Mikita 6.00 12.00
77 Eric Nesterenko .50 1.00
78 Danny O'Shea .50 1.00
79 Jim Pappin .50 1.00
80 Gary Smith 1.00 2.00
81 Pat Stapleton .50 1.00
82 Bill White .50 1.00
83 Detroit Red Wings 1.50 3.00
84 Red Berenson .75 1.50
85 Gary Bergman .75 1.50
86 Arnie Brown .50 1.00
87 Guy Charron .50 1.00
88 Bill Collins .50 1.00
89 Brian Conacher .50 1.00
90 Joe Daley 1.50 3.00
91 Alex Delvecchio 3.00 6.00
92 Marcel Dionne 7.50 15.00
93 Tim Ecclestone .50 1.00
94 Ron Harris .50 1.00
95 Gerry Hart .50 1.00
96 Gordie Howe 25.00 50.00
97 Al Karlander .50 1.00
98 Nick Libett .75 1.50
99 Ab McDonald .50 1.00
100 James Niekamp .50 1.00
101 Mickey Redmond 2.00 4.00
102 Leon Rochefort .50 1.00
103 Al Smith .75 1.50
104 Los Angeles Kings 1.00 2.00
105 Ralph Backstrom .75 1.50
106 Bob Berry .75 1.50
107 Mike Byers .50 1.00
108 Larry Cahan .50 1.00
109 Paul Curtis .50 1.00
110 Denis DeJordy 1.50 3.00
111 Gary Edwards 1.00 2.00
112 Bill Flett .50 1.00
113 Butch Goring .75 1.50
114 Lucien Grenier .50 1.00
115 Larry Hillman .50 1.00
116 Dale Hoganson .50 1.00
117 Harry Howell 1.50 3.00
118 Eddie Joyal .50 1.00
119 Real Lemieux .50 1.00
120 Ross Lonsberry .50 1.00
121 Al McDonough .50 1.00
122 Jean Potvin .50 1.00
123 Bob Pulford 1.50 3.00
124 Juha Widing .75 1.50
125 Minnesota North Stars 1.00 2.00
126 Fred Barrett .50 1.00
127 Charlie Burns .50 1.00
128 Jude Drouin .50 1.00
129 Barry Gibbs .50 1.00
130 Gilles Gilbert 2.00 4.00
131 Bill Goldsworthy 1.00 2.00
132 Danny Grant .75 1.50
133 Ted Hampson .50 1.00
134 Ted Harris .50 1.00
135 Fred Harvey .50 1.00
136 Cesare Maniago 2.00 4.00
137 Doug Mohns .75 1.50
138 Lou Nanne .75 1.50
139 Bob Nevin .75 1.50
140 Dennis O'Brien .50 1.00
141 Murray Oliver .50 1.00
142 Jean-Paul Parise .75 1.50
143 Dean Prentice .75 1.50
144 Tom Reid .50 1.00
145 Gump Worsley 3.00 6.00
146 Montreal Canadiens 1.50 3.00
147 Pierre Bouchard .50 1.00
148 Yvan Cournoyer 3.00 6.00
149 Ken Dryden 25.00 50.00
150 Terry Harper .75 1.50
151 Rejean Houle .75 1.50
152 Guy Lafleur 15.00 30.00
153 Jacques Laperriere 1.00 2.00
154 Guy Lapointe 1.50 3.00
155 Claude Larose .50 1.00
156 Jacques Lemaire 2.00 4.00
157 Frank Mahovlich 6.00 12.00
158 Pete Mahovlich .75 1.50
159 Phil Myre 1.50 3.00
160 Larry Pleau .75 1.50
161 Henri Richard 6.00 12.00
162 Phil Roberto .50 1.00
163 Serge Savard 1.50 3.00
164 Marc Tardif .50 1.00
165 J.C. Tremblay .75 1.50
166 Rogatien Vachon 3.00 6.00
167 New York Rangers 1.50 3.00
168 Dave Balon .50 1.00
169 Ab DeMarco .50 1.00
170 Jack Egers .50 1.00
171 Bill Fairbairn .50 1.00
172 Ed Giacomin 4.00 8.00
173 Rod Gilbert 2.00 4.00
174 Vic Hadfield .75 1.50
175 Ted Irvine .50 1.00
176 Bruce MacGregor .50 1.00
177 Jim Neilson .50 1.00
178 Brad Park 3.00 6.00
179 Jean Ratelle 2.00 4.00
180 Dale Rolfe .50 1.00
181 Bobby Rousseau .75 1.50
182 Glen Sather 1.50 3.00
183 Rod Seiling .50 1.00
184 Pete Stemkowski .75 1.50
185 Walt Tkaczuk .75 1.50
186 Gilles Villemure 1.50 3.00
187 Philadelphia Flyers 1.50 3.00
188 Barry Ashbee 1.00 2.00
189 Serge Bernier .50 1.00
190 Larry Brown .50 1.00
191 Bobby Clarke 10.00 20.00
192 Gary Dornhoefer .75 1.50
193 Doug Favell 1.50 3.00
194 Bruce Gamble 2.00 4.00
195 Jean-Guy Gendron .50 1.00
196 Larry Hale .50 1.00
197 Wayne Hillman .50 1.00
198 Brent Hughes .50 1.00
199 Jim Johnson .50 1.00
200 Bob Kelly .50 1.00
201 Andre Lacroix .75 1.50
202 Bill Lesuk .50 1.00
203 Rick MacLeish 1.00 2.00
204 Larry Mickey .50 1.00
205 Simon Nolet .50 1.00
206 Pierre Plante .50 1.00
207 Ed Van Impe .50 1.00
208 Joe Watson .50 1.00
209 Pittsburgh Penguins 1.00 2.00
210 Syl Apps .75 1.50
211 Les Binkley 1.50 3.00
212 Wally Boyer .50 1.00
213 Darryl Edestrand .50 1.00
214 Roy Edwards 1.50 3.00
215 Nick Harbaruk .50 1.00
216 Bryan Hextall .75 1.50
217 Bill Hicke .50 1.00
218 Tim Horton 5.00 10.00
219 Sheldon Kannegiesser .50 1.00
220 Bob Leiter .50 1.00
221 Keith McCreary .50 1.00
222 Joe Noris .50 1.00
223 Greg Polis .50 1.00
224 Jean Pronovost .75 1.50
225 Rene Robert .75 1.50
226 Duane Rupp .50 1.00
227 Ken Schinkel .50 1.00
228 Ron Schock .50 1.00
229 Bryan Watson .50 1.00
230 Bob Woytowich .50 1.00
231 St. Louis Blues 1.00 2.00
232 Al Arbour 1.50 3.00
233 John Arbour .50 1.00
234 Chris Bordeleau .50 1.00
235 Carl Brewer .75 1.50
236 Gene Carr .50 1.00
237 Wayne Connelly .50 1.00
238 Terry Crisp .75 1.50
239 Jim Lorentz .50 1.00
240 Peter McDuffe 1.00 2.00
241 George Morrison .50 1.00
242 Michel Parizeau .50 1.00
243 Noel Picard .50 1.00
244 Barclay Plager .75 1.50
245 Bob Plager .75 1.50
246 Jim Roberts .50 1.00
247 Gary Sabourin .50 1.00
248 Jim Shires .50 1.00
249 Frank St.Marseille .50 1.00
250 Bill Sutherland .50 1.00
251 Garry Unger 1.00 2.00
252 Ernie Wakely 1.50 3.00
253 Toronto Maple Leafs 1.50 3.00
254 Bob Baun .75 1.50
255 Jim Dorey .50 1.00
256 Denis Dupere .50 1.00
257 Ron Ellis .75 1.50
258 Brian Glennie .50 1.00
259 Jim Harrison .50 1.00
260 Paul Henderson 1.00 2.00
261 Dave Keon 3.00 6.00
262 Rick Ley .50 1.00
263 Billy MacMillan .50 1.00
264 Don Marshall .50 1.00
265 Jim McKenny .50 1.00
266 Garry Monahan .50 1.00
267 Bernie Parent 6.00 12.00
268 Mike Pelyk .50 1.00
269 Jacques Plante 10.00 20.00
270 Brad Selwood .50 1.00
271 Darryl Sittler 6.00 12.00
272 Brian Spencer 1.00 2.00
273 Guy Trottier .50 1.00
274 Norm Ullman 2.50 5.00
275 Vancouver Canucks 1.00 2.00
276 Andre Boudrias .50 1.00
277 George Gardiner .50 1.00
278 Jocelyn Guevremont .75 1.50
279 Murray Hall .50 1.00
280 Danny Johnson .50 1.00
281 Dennis Kearns .50 1.00
282 Orland Kurtenbach .75 1.50
283 Bobby Lalonde .50 1.00
284 Wayne Maki .50 1.00
285 Rosaire Paiement .50 1.00
286 Paul Popiel .50 1.00
287 Pat Quinn 1.00 2.00
288 John Schella .50 1.00
289 Bobby Schmautz .75 1.50
290 Fred Speck .50 1.00
291 Dale Tallon .75 1.50
292 Ron Ward .50 1.00
293 Barry Wilkins .50 1.00
294 Dunc Wilson 1.50 3.00
xx Binder 12.50 25.00
NNO Introduction Card 2.00 4.00
(Written by Scott Young)

1972 Tower Hockey Instructions Booklets

Sponsored by Towers and Donimart stores, we have very little information about these oddball hockey instruction booklets.

1 Skating Skills 10.00 20.00

1936 Triumph Postcards

This eleven-card set was issued as a supplement to The Triumph (a newspaper). The cards measure approximately 3 1/2" by 5 1/2" and are in the postcard format. The borderless fronts feature full-length black and white posed action shots. The player's name and team name appear in the lower left corner. The back carries the typical postcard design with each player's name and biographical information in the upper corner. Different dates appear on the back of the cards, which represent the date each card was distributed. The cards were issued three the first week with The Triumph, then one per week thereafter. The cards are unnumbered and checklisted below in alphabetical order. The date mentioned below is the issue date as noted on the card back in Canadian style, day/month/year.

COMPLETE SET (11) 650.00 1300.00
1 Lionel Conacher 125.00 250.00
22/2/36
2 Harvey(Busher) Jackson 125.00 250.00
18/1/36
3 Ivan(Ching) Johnson 62.50 125.00
8/2/36
4 Herbie Lewis 40.00 80.00
7/3/36
5 Sylvio Mantha 62.50 125.00
18/1/36
6 Nick Metz 40.00 80.00
15/2/36
7 Baldy Northcott 45.00 90.00
Montreal Maroons
1/2/36
8 Eddie Shore 250.00 500.00
25/1/36
9 Paul Thompson 40.00 80.00
29/2/36
10 Roy Worters 62.50 125.00
New York Americans
18/1/36
11 Charley Conacher 40.00 80.00

2004-05 UD All-World

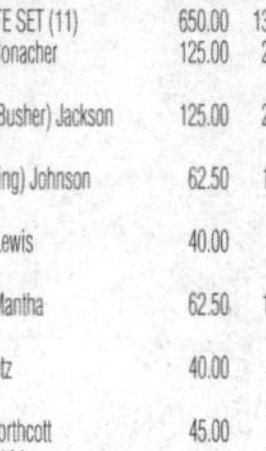

Released in June, this 120-card set featured NHL players who spent the lockout season playing in Europe as well as European legends. Two subsets, "Up Close and Personal" and "Euro-Legends" were inserted at 1:8 odds. Please note that cards #'s 108 and 119 do not exist and that card #110 is used on three different cards. Those cards are noted below with "A,B and C" suffixes.

COMPLETE SET (120)
1 Roman Turek .25 .60
2 Jiri Fischer .20 .50
3 Martin Rucinsky .20 .50
4 Ales Hemsky .25 .60
5 Milan Hejduk .30 .75
6 Zigmund Palffy .25 .60
7 Peter Stastny .20 .50
8 Petr Nedved .20 .50
9 Radek Bonk .20 .50
10 Roman Hamrlik .20 .50
11 Martin Havlat .25 .60
12 Jarkko Ruutu .20 .50
13 Matti Hagman .20 .50
14 Tomas Vokoun .25 .60
15 Mika Noronen .25 .60
16 Jari Kurri .40 1.00
17 Teemu Selanne .30 .75
18 Dwayne Roloson .20 .50
19 Saku Koivu .30 .75
20 Erik Cole .20 .50
21 Marco Sturm .20 .50
22 Mike York .20 .50
23 Ryan Malone .20 .50
24 Alex Kovalev .25 .60
25 Brad Richards .25 .60
26 Ilya Kovalchuk .40 1.00
27 Nikolai Khabibulin .30 .75
28 Vincent Lecavalier .30 .75
29 Jaromir Jagr .50 1.25
30 Alexander Frolov .25 .60
31 Nikolai Zherdev .20 .50
32 Maxim Afinogenov .20 .50
33 Pavel Datsyuk .30 .75
34 Nikolai Antropov .20 .50
35 Evgeni Nabokov .25 .60
36 Patrik Elias .25 .60
37 Petr Sykora .20 .50
38 Sergei Gonchar .20 .50
39 Michael Nylander .20 .50
40 Fedor Fedorov .20 .50
41 Alexei Zhamnov .20 .50
42 Pavol Demitra .25 .60
43 Miroslav Satan .25 .60
44 Borje Salming .40 1.00
45 Ulf Nilsson .20 .50
46 Tyler Arnason .20 .50
47 Mats Naslund .40 1.00
48 Jose Theodore .30 .75
49 Marty Turco .25 .60
50 Kent Nilsson .20 .50
51 Marian Gaborik .60 1.50
52 Mike Comrie .20 .50
53 Sheldon Souray .20 .50
54 Zdeno Chara .20 .50
55 Hakan Loob .20 .50
56 Thomas Steen .20 .50
57 Daniel Alfredsson .25 .60
58 Jonathan Cheechoo .25 .60
59 Michael Ryder .20 .50
60 Brendan Morrison .25 .60
61 Justin Williams .20 .50
62 Tomas Holmstrom .20 .50
63 Adrian Aucoin .20 .50
64 Daniel Sedin .20 .50
65 Henrik Sedin .20 .50
66 Markus Naslund .30 .75
67 Peter Forsberg .75 2.00
68 Anders Hedberg .20 .50
69 Ladislav Nagy .20 .50
70 Marcel Hossa .20 .50
71 Marian Hossa .30 .75
72 Trent Hunter .20 .50
73 Dick Tarnstrom .20 .50
74 Olli Jokinen .25 .60
75 Fredrik Modin .20 .50
76 Henrik Zetterberg .30 .75
77 Miikka Kiprusoff .25 .60
78 Joe Thornton .50 1.25
79 Rick Nash .40 1.00
80 Martin St. Louis .25 .60
81 Alex Tanguay .25 .60
82 David Aebischer .25 .60
83 Martin Gelinas .20 .50
84 Daniel Briere .20 .50
85 Dany Heatley .40 1.00
86 Niko Kapanen .20 .50
87 Igor Larionov .20 .50
88 Richard Zednik .20 .50
89 Jochen Hecht .20 .50
90 Vladislav Tretiak .25 .60
91 Wayne Gretzky UCP 4.00 10.00
92 Gordie Howe UCP 3.00 8.00
93 Patrick Roy UCP 4.00 10.00
94 Joe Thornton UCP 2.50 6.00
95 Rick Nash UCP 2.50 6.00
96 Martin Brodeur UCP 4.00 10.00
97 Marty Turco UCP 2.00 5.00
98 Jarome Iginla UCP 2.50 6.00
99 Joe Sakic UCP 3.00 8.00
100 Peter Forsberg UCP 3.00 8.00
101 Mario Lemieux UCP 4.00 10.00
102 Markus Naslund UCP 2.00 5.00
103 Martin St. Louis UCP 2.00 5.00
104 Mike Bossy UCP 2.00 5.00
105 Jose Theodore UCP 2.50 6.00
106 Matti Hagman EL 2.00 5.00
107 Teemu Selanne EL 2.00 5.00
109 Borje Salming EL 2.50 6.00
110A Ulf Nilsson EL 3.00 8.00
110B Jari Kurri EL 2.50 6.00
110C Igor Larionov EL 3.00 8.00
111 Anders Hedberg EL 2.00 5.00
112 Vladislav Tretiak EL 4.00 10.00
113 Mats Naslund EL 3.00 8.00
114 Peter Stastny EL 2.00 5.00
115 Thomas Steen EL 2.00 5.00
116 Hakan Loob EL 2.50 6.00
117 Kent Nilsson EL 2.00 5.00
118 Saku Koivu EL 2.00 5.00
120 Jaromir Jagr EL 3.00 8.00

2004-05 UD All-World Gold

*GOLD: 8X TO 20X BASE CARD
PRINT RUN 50 SER.#'d SETS

2004-05 UD All-World Autographs

1-90 STATED ODDS 1:24
91-119 PRINT RUN 10 SER.#'d SETS
91-119 NOT PRICED DUE TO SCARCITY
SKIP NUMBERED SET

1 Roman Turek 6.00 10.00
4 Ales Hemsky 8.00 20.00
5 Milan Hejduk 8.00 20.00
6 Zigmund Palffy SP
7 Peter Stastny 8.00 20.00
11 Martin Havlat 10.00 25.00
12 Jarkko Ruutu 4.00 10.00
13 Matti Hagman 6.00 10.00
15 Mika Noronen 6.00 10.00
16 Jari Kurri 8.00 20.00
18 Dwayne Roloson 12.00 30.00
20 Erik Cole 8.00 15.00
26 Ilya Kovalchuk SP
27 Nikolai Khabibulin SP 40.00 80.00
28 Vincent Lecavalier SP
30 Alexander Frolov 6.00 15.00
31 Nikolai Zherdev 8.00 15.00
32 Maxim Afinogenov 6.00 15.00
44 Borje Salming 12.00 30.00
45 Ulf Nilsson 10.00 25.00
46 Tyler Arnason 6.00 10.00
47 Mats Naslund 15.00 40.00
48 Jose Theodore SP
50 Kent Nilsson 6.00 15.00
51 Marian Gaborik 20.00 50.00
52 Mike Comrie 6.00 15.00
53 Sheldon Souray 6.00 15.00
54 Zdeno Chara 6.00 15.00
55 Hakan Loob 12.00 30.00
56 Thomas Steen 6.00 15.00
57 Daniel Alfredsson SP
58 Jonathan Cheechoo 10.00 25.00
59 Michael Ryder SP
60 Brendan Morrison 6.00 15.00
61 Justin Williams 8.00 15.00
66 Markus Naslund SP
68 Anders Hedberg 6.00 15.00
69 Ladislav Nagy 6.00 10.00
70 Marcel Hossa 6.00 10.00
71 Marian Hossa SP
72 Trent Hunter 6.00 15.00
76 Henrik Zetterberg SP 25.00 60.00
78 Joe Thornton 15.00 40.00
79 Rick Nash SP 60.00 150.00
80 Martin St. Louis SP
81 Alex Tanguay SP
82 David Aebischer SP 15.00 40.00
84 Daniel Briere 12.00 30.00
85 Dany Heatley SP
87 Igor Larionov 10.00 25.00
88 Richard Zednik 6.00 15.00
90 Vladislav Tretiak 20.00 50.00
91 Wayne Gretzky
92 Gordie Howe
94 Joe Thornton
95 Rick Nash
97 Marty Turco
102 Markus Naslund
103 Martin St. Louis
104 Mike Bossy
106 Matti Hagman
108 Jari Kurri 10.00 25.00
109 Borje Salming 10.00 25.00
110 Ulf Nilsson
111 Anders Hedberg
112 Vladislav Tretiak 15.00 40.00
113 Mats Naslund
114 Peter Stastny
115 Thomas Steen
116 Hakan Loob
117 Kent Nilsson 6.00 10.00
119 Igor Larionov 6.00 15.00

2004-05 UD All-World Dual Autographs

PRINT RUN 25 SER.#'d SETS
ADPS Ziggy Palffy/Peter Stastny 25.00 60.00
ADHN Matti Hagman/Mika Noronen 25.00 60.00
ADHH Milan Hejduk/Ales Hemsky 30.00 80.00
AD[illegible] Maxim Afinogenov/Alexander Frolov 20.00 50.00
AD[illegible] Alexander Frolov/Nikolai Zherdev 30.00 80.00
ADJA Joe Thornton/Alex Tanguay 75.00 150.00
ADKK Jari Kurri/Saku Koivu 100.00 200.00
ADKL Jari Kurri/Hakan Loob 30.00 80.00
ADLK V.Lecavalier/N.Khabibulin 75.00 150.00
ADLS Hakan Loob/Thomas Steen 30.00 80.00
ADMM Marian Hossa/Marcel Hossa
ADNN Mats Naslund/Markus Naslund
ADNT R.Nash/J.Thornton 125.00 250.00
ADSC Sheldon Souray/Zdeno Chara 25.00 60.00
ADSN Borje Salming/Kent Nilsson 30.00 80.00

2004-05 UD All-World Triple Autographs

PRINT RUN 20 SER.#'d SETS
NOT PRICED DUE TO SCARCITY
ATCWR Cheechoo/J.Williams/J.Ruutu
ATKHK Jari Kurri/Matti Hagman/Saku Koivu
ATKSN Jari Kurri/Peter Stastny/Mats Naslund
ATLTZ Igor Larionov/Vladislav Tretiak/Nikolai Zherdev
ATNLN Mats Naslund/Hakan Loob/Kent Nilsson
ATRCM M.Ryder/Cheechoo/B.Morrison
ATSHH Peter Stastny/Milan Hejduk/Ales Hemsky
ATSLN Thomas Steen/Hakan Loob/Ulf Nilsson
ATTAR Jose Theodore/David Aebischer/Dwayne Roloson
ATZFA Nikolai Zherdev/Alexander Frolov/Maxim Afinogenov

2004-05 UD All-World Quad Autographs

PRINT RUN 15 SER.#'d SETS
NOT PRICED DUE TO SCARCITY
AQGSC Joe Thornton

Rick Nash
Dany Heatley
Daniel Briere
AQALS Jari Kurri/Kent Nilsson/Hakan Loob/Matti Hagman
AQYFW Jonathan Cheechoo
Justin Williams
Alexander Frolov
Trent Hunter
AQGOL Jose Theodore/David Aebischer/Evgeni Nabokov/Dwayne Roloson
AQSWE Thomas Steen/Kent Nilsson/Michael Ryder/Justin Williams
AQOAS Peter Stastny/Mats Naslund/Ulf Nilsson/Hakan Loob
AQRUS Ilya Kovalchuk/Maxim Afinogenov/Vladislav Tretiak/Igor Larionov
AQNAM Mats Naslund/Markus Naslund/Marian Hossa/Marcel Hossa

2004-05 UD All-World Five Autographs

PRINT RUN 10 SER.#'d SETS
NOT PRICED DUE TO SCARCITY
AFGOL Vladislav Tretiak/Nikolai Khabibulin/Evgeni Nabokov/David Aebischer/Marty Turco
AFAST Jari Kurri/Peter Stastny/Igor Larionov/Borje Salming/Vladislav Tretiak
AFYAO Peter Stastny/Ziggy Palffy/Ales Hemsky/Thomas Steen/Martin Havlat
AFYGN Vincent Lecavalier/Ilya Kovalchuk/Alexander Frolov/Nikolai Zherdev/Nikolai Khabibulin

2004-05 UD All-World Six Autographs

PRINT RUN 5 SER.#'d SETS
NOT PRICED DUE TO SCARCITY
ASSWD Markus Naslund
Marian Gaborik
Michael Ryder
Henrik Zetterberg
Justin Williams
Jonathan Cheechoo
ASRUS Ilya Kovalchuk/Brad Richards/Vincent Lecavalier/Alexander Frolov/Nikolai Zherdev/Maxim Afinogenov
ASSWT Joe Thornton
Rick Nash
Martin St. Louis
Dany Heatley
Daniel Briere
Alex Tanguay

2002-03 UD Artistic Impressions

Released in mid-April 2003, this 135-card set featured artist renderings of the featured player's on the card fronts. Rookies in this set were inserted at 1:4.

COMPLETE SET (135) 60.00 125.00
COMP.SET w/o SP's (90) 20.00 40.00
1 Jean-Sebastien Giguere .20 .50
2 Paul Kariya .25 .60
3 Dany Heatley .40 1.00
4 Ilya Kovalchuk .40 1.00
5 Ray Bourque .60 1.50
6 Joe Thornton .50 1.25
7 Bobby Orr 2.00 5.00
8 Sergei Samsonov .20 .50
9 Maxim Afinogenov .10 .25
10 Martin Biron .20 .50
11 Miroslav Satan .20 .50
12 Roman Turek .20 .50
13 Jarome Iginla .30 .75
14 Arturs Irbe .20 .60
15 Ron Francis .20 .50
16 Jeff O'Neill .10 .25
17 Alexei Zhamnov .10 .25
18 Eric Daze .20 .50
19 Jocelyn Thibault .20 .50
20 Rob Blake .20 .50
21 Patrick Roy 1.50 4.00
22 Joe Sakic .60 1.50
23 Peter Forsberg .75 2.00
24 Ray Bourque .60 1.50
25 Marc Denis .20 .50
26 Espen Knutsen .10 .25
27 Rostislav Klesla .10 .25
28 Marty Turco .20 .50
29 Bill Guerin .20 .50
30 Mike Modano .50 1.25
31 Steve Yzerman 1.50 4.00
32 Nicklas Lidstrom .25 .60
33 Sergei Fedorov .50 1.25
34 Curtis Joseph .25 .60
35 Brendan Shanahan .25 .60
36 Gordie Howe 1.50 4.00
37 Mike Comrie .20 .50
38 Tommy Salo .20 .50
39 Wayne Gretzky 2.00 5.00
40 Roberto Luongo .30 .75
41 Kristian Huselius .10 .25
42 Zigmund Palffy .20 .50
43 Felix Potvin .25 .60
44 Jason Allison .10 .25
45 Manny Fernandez .20 .50
46 Marian Gaborik .60 1.50
47 Saku Koivu .25 .60
48 Doug Gilmour .20 .50
49 Jose Theodore .30 .75
50 David Legwand .20 .50
51 Tomas Vokoun .20 .50
52 Martin Brodeur .75 2.00
53 Patrik Elias .20 .50
54 Joe Nieuwendyk .20 .50
55 Alexei Yashin .10 .25
56 Michael Peca .10 .25
57 Chris Osgood .20 .50
58 Eric Lindros .25 .60
59 Pavel Bure .25 .60
60 Brian Leetch .20 .50
61 Martin Havlat .20 .50
62 Marian Hossa .25 .60
63 Daniel Alfredsson .20 .50
64 John LeClair .25 .60
65 Jeremy Roenick .30 .75
66 Simon Gagne .25 .60
67 Tony Amonte .20 .50
68 Sean Burke .20 .50
69 Daniel Briere .10 .25
70 Alex Kovalev .20 .50
71 Johan Hedberg .20 .50
72 Mario Lemieux 2.00 5.00
73 Teemu Selanne .25 .60
74 Evgeni Nabokov .25 .60
75 Owen Nolan .20 .50
76 Chris Pronger .20 .50
77 Doug Weight .20 .50
78 Keith Tkachuk .25 .60
79 Brad Richards .25 .60
80 Nikolai Khabibulin .25 .60
81 Vincent Lecavalier .25 .60
82 Mats Sundin .25 .60
83 Ed Belfour .25 .60
84 Alexander Mogilny .20 .50
85 Todd Bertuzzi .25 .60
86 Dan Cloutier .20 .50
87 Markus Naslund .25 .60
88 Jaromir Jagr .50 1.25
89 Peter Bondra .20 .50
90 Olaf Kolzig .20 .50
91 Jonathan Hedstrom RC .75 2.00
92 Henrik Zetterberg RC 3.00 8.00
93 Steve Ott RC 1.25 3.00
94 Jay Bouwmeester RC 1.50 4.00
95 Rick Nash RC 4.00 10.00
96 Pascal LeClaire RC 1.25 3.00
97 Jason Spezza RC 3.00 8.00
98 Dick Tarnstrom RC .75 2.00
99 Alexei Smirnov RC 1.00 2.50
100 Ron Hainsey RC .75 2.00
101 Michael Leighton RC 2.00 5.00
102 Ian MacNeil RC .75 2.00
103 Anton Volchenkov RC .75 2.00
104 Ales Hemsky RC 1.50 4.00
105 Steve Eminger RC .75 2.00
106 Shaone Morrisonn RC .75 2.00
107 Levente Szuper RC .75 2.00
108 Brooks Orpik RC .75 2.00
109 Curtis Sanford RC 1.00 2.50
110 Jared Aulin RC .75 2.00
111 Eric Godard RC .75 2.00
112 Jim Fahey RC .75 2.00
113 Rickard Wallin RC .75 2.00
114 Mike Cammalleri RC 1.00 2.50
115 Mikael Tellqvist RC .75 2.00
116 Chuck Kobasew RC 1.00 2.50
117 Scottie Upshall RC 1.25 3.00
118 Jerred Smithson RC .75 2.00
119 Jeff Taffe RC .75 2.00
120 Cody Rudkowsky RC .75 2.00
121 Alexander Frolov RC 1.50 4.00
122 Alexander Svitov RC 1.00 2.50
123 Stanislav Chistov RC 1.00 2.50
124 P-M Bouchard RC 1.50 4.00
125 Patrick Sharp RC .75 2.00
126 Ryan Miller RC 2.50 6.00
127 Tomas Malec RC .75 2.00
128 Curtis Murphy RC .75 2.00
129 Jordan Leopold RC .75 2.00
130 Carlo Colaiacovo RC 1.00 2.50
131 Alexei Semenov RC .75 2.00
132 Craig Andersson RC 4.00 10.00
133 Jim Vandermeer RC .75 2.00
134 Ray Emery RC 2.00 5.00
135 Paul Manning RC .75 2.00

2002-03 UD Artistic Impressions Gold

*STARS: 1.5X TO 4X
STATED PRINT RUN 199 SER.#'d SETS
*SP's: .75X TO 2X
SP STATED PRINT RUN 75 SER.#'d SETS

2002-03 UD Artistic Impressions Artist's Touch

Singles in this 25-card memorabilia set were serial-numbered to 499 copies each.

*MULT.COLOR SWATCH: .5X TO 1.25X HI
ATBS Brendan Shanahan 3.00 8.00
ATCJ Curtis Joseph 3.00 8.00
ATDH Dany Heatley 4.00 10.00
ATFP Felix Potvin 3.00 8.00
ATIK Ilya Kovalchuk 5.00 12.00
ATJI Jarome Iginla 4.00 10.00
ATJJ Jaromir Jagr 4.00 10.00
ATJR Jeremy Roenick 4.00 10.00
ATJS Joe Sakic 5.00 12.00
ATJT Joe Thornton 5.00 12.00
ATMB Martin Brodeur 8.00 20.00
ATMD Mike Dunham 3.00 8.00
ATML Mario Lemieux 10.00 25.00
ATMM Mike Modano 5.00 12.00
ATMS Mats Sundin 3.00 8.00
ATOK Olaf Kolzig 3.00 8.00
ATPF Peter Forsberg 5.00 12.00
ATPK Paul Kariya 3.00 8.00
ATPR Patrick Roy 10.00 25.00
ATRB Ray Bourque 5.00 12.00
ATSB Sean Burke 3.00 8.00
ATSF Sergei Fedorov 4.00 10.00
ATSG Simon Gagne 3.00 8.00
ATTH Jose Theodore 4.00 10.00
ATZP Zigmund Palffy 3.00 8.00

2002-03 UD Artistic Impressions Artist's Touch Gold

*STARS: .5X TO 1.25X BASIC INSERTS
STATED PRINT RUN 99 SER.#'d SETS

2002-03 UD Artistic Impressions Artwork Originals

Randomly inserted, these one of one framed prints were the original art used for the set. Several of the pieces were signed by the player though we are unable to verify which ones exactly as only a few have been verified. These pieces are not priced due to scarcity.

AI1 Ray Bourque AU
AI2 Martin Brodeur AU
AI3 Simon Gagne
AI4 Mike Comrie
AI5 Dany Heatley
AI6 Gordie Howe
AI7 Jarome Iginla
AI8 Curtis Joseph
AI9 Ilya Kovalchuk
AI10 John LeClair
AI11 Markus Naslund
AI12 Nikolai Khabibulin
AI13 Patrick Roy
AI14 Sergei Samsonov AU
AI15 Jose Theodore
AI16 Joe Thornton AU
AI17 Steve Yzerman AU
AI18 Martin Havlat
AI19 Marty Turco
AI20 Brad Richards

2002-03 UD Artistic Impressions Artwork Signed

Inserted at one per case, these framed prints of the artwork used for the set carried certified player autographs under the print in the frame.

AI1 Ray Bourque 75.00 150.00
AI2 Martin Brodeur 100.00 200.00
AI3 Pavel Bure 30.00 80.00
AI4 Mike Comrie 25.00 60.00
AI5 Dany Heatley 50.00 100.00
AI6 Gordie Howe 200.00 400.00
AI7 Jarome Iginla 30.00 80.00
AI8 Curtis Joseph 60.00 120.00
AI9 Ilya Kovalchuk 75.00 150.00
AI10 John LeClair 25.00 60.00
AI11 Markus Naslund 25.00 60.00
AI12 Bobby Orr 300.00 600.00
AI13 Patrick Roy 125.00 250.00
AI14 Sergei Samsonov 25.00 60.00
AI15 Jose Theodore 60.00 120.00
AI16 Joe Thornton 75.00 150.00
AI17 Steve Yzerman 100.00 200.00

2002-03 UD Artistic Impressions Common Ground

COMPLETE SET (22) 20.00 40.00
STATED ODDS 1:8
CG1 Patrick Roy 2.00 5.00
Pascal Leclaire
CG2 Ales Hemsky 1.25 3.00
Jaromir Jagr
CG3 Wayne Gretzky 2.50 6.00
Jason Spezza
CG4 Jay Bouwmeester 1.25 3.00
Nicklas Lidstrom
CG5 Roman Cechmanek 1.25 3.00
Levente Szuper
CG6 R.Nash/M.Lemieux 2.00 5.00
CG7 Ray Bourque 1.50 4.00
Jay Bouwmeester
CG8 Pierre-Marc Bouchard 1.25 3.00
Saku Koivu
CG9 G.Howe/R.Nash 1.50 4.00
CG10 Alexander Frolov 1.25 3.00
Pavel Bure
CG11 Rob Blake 1.25 3.00
Brooks Orpik
CG12 Henrik Zetterberg 1.25 3.00
Mats Sundin
CG13 Sergei Samsonov 1.25 3.00
Stanislav Chistov
CG14 Jordan Leopold 1.25 3.00
Ray Bourque
CG15 Bill Guerin 1.25 3.00
Chuck Kobasew
CG16 Alexander Svitov 1.25 3.00
Sergei Fedorov
CG17 Jeremy Roenick 1.50 4.00
Scottie Upshall
CG18 Carlo Colaiacovo 1.25 3.00
Nicklas Lidstrom
CG19 Steve Yzerman 1.25 3.00
Steve Ott
CG20 J.Taffe/M.Modano 1.25 3.00
CG21 Peter Forsberg 2.00 5.00
Henrik Zetterberg
CG22 P.LeClaire/M.Brodeur 1.50 4.00

2002-03 UD Artistic Impressions Common Ground Gold

*STARS: 1.5X TO 4X BASIC INSERTS
STATED PRINT RUN 150 SER.#'d SETS

2002-03 UD Artistic Impressions Flashbacks

STATED ODDS 1:20
UD1 Joe Sakic 2.00 5.00
UD2 Mike Modano 1.50 4.00
UD3 Mario Lemieux 3.00 8.00
UD4 Brian Leetch .75 2.00
UD5 Ron Francis .75 2.00
UD6 Pavel Bure .75 2.00
UD7 Ray Bourque 2.00 5.00
UD8 Sergei Fedorov 1.50 4.00
UD9 Jaromir Jagr 1.50 4.00
UD10 Jeremy Roenick 1.00 2.50
UD11 Gordie Howe 2.50 6.00

2002-03 UD Artistic Impressions Flashbacks Gold

*STARS: .75X TO 2X BASIC INSERTS
STATED PRINT RUN 75 SER.#'d SETS

2002-03 UD Artistic Impressions Great Depictions

COMPLETE SET (12) 20.00 40.00
STATED ODDS 1:20
GD1 Wayne Gretzky 3.00 8.00
GD2 Patrick Roy 2.50 6.00
GD3 Martin Brodeur 2.50 6.00
GD4 Bobby Orr 3.00 8.00
GD5 Ilya Kovalchuk 1.00 2.50
GD6 Mario Lemieux 3.00 8.00
GD7 Ray Bourque 2.00 5.00
GD8 Steve Yzerman 2.50 6.00
GD9 Gordie Howe 2.00 5.00
GD10 Pavel Bure .75 2.00
GD11 Marian Gaborik 1.50 4.00
GD12 Joe Thornton 1.25 3.00

2002-03 UD Artistic Impressions Great Depictions Gold

*STARS: .75X TO 2X BASIC INSERTS
STATED PRINT RUN 75 SER.#'d SETS

2002-03 UD Artistic Impressions Performers

Singles in this 6-card memorabilia set were serial-numbered to 199.

*MULT.COLOR SWATCH: .5X TO 1.25X HI
SSJJ Jaromir Jagr 4.00 10.00
SSJL John LeClair 3.00 8.00
SSMB Martin Brodeur 12.50 30.00
SSMM Mark Messier 3.00 8.00
SSPR Patrick Roy 15.00 40.00
SSSY Steve Yzerman 12.50 30.00

2002-03 UD Artistic Impressions Performers Gold

*STARS: .5X TO 1.25X BASIC INSERTS
STATED PRINT RUN 75 SER.#'d SETS

2002-03 UD Artistic Impressions Retrospectives

This 100-card set was inserted one per pack. These cards were smaller versions of the base card with colorful borders.

COMPLETE SET (100) 30.00 60.00
STATED ODDS 1:1
R1 Jean-Sebastien Giguere .25 .60
R2 Paul Kariya .30 .75
R3 Dany Heatley .40 1.00
R4 Ilya Kovalchuk .40 1.00
R5 Ray Bourque .60 1.50
R6 Joe Thornton .50 1.25
R7 Bobby Orr 2.00 5.00
R8 Sergei Samsonov .25 .60
R9 Maxim Afinogenov .25 .60
R10 Martin Biron .25 .60
R11 Miroslav Satan .25 .60
R12 Roman Turek .25 .60
R13 Jarome Iginla .40 1.00
R14 Arturs Irbe .25 .60
R15 Ron Francis .25 .60
R16 Jeff O'neill .25 .60
R17 Alexei Zhamnov .25 .60
R18 Eric Daze .25 .60
R19 Jocelyn Thibault .25 .60
R20 Rob Blake .25 .60
R21 Patrick Roy 2.00 5.00
R22 Joe Sakic .60 1.50
R23 Peter Forsberg .75 2.00
R24 Ray Bourque .60 1.50
R25 Marc Denis .25 .60
R26 Espen Knutsen .25 .60
R27 Rostislav Klesla .25 .60
R28 Marty Turco .25 .60
R29 Bill Guerin .25 .60
R30 Mike Modano .50 1.25
R31 Steve Yzerman 1.50 4.00
R32 Nicklas Lidstrom .30 .75
R33 Sergei Fedorov .50 1.25
R34 Curtis Joseph .30 .75
R35 Brendan Shanahan .30 .75
R36 Gordie Howe 1.50 4.00
R37 Mike Comrie .25 .60
R38 Tommy Salo .25 .60
R39 Wayne Gretzky 2.00 5.00
R40 Roberto Luongo .40 1.00
R41 Kristian Huselius .25 .60
R42 Zigmund Palffy .25 .60
R43 Felix Potvin .30 .75
R44 Jason Allison .25 .60
R45 Manny Fernandez .25 .60
R46 Marian Gaborik .60 1.50
R47 Saku Koivu .30 .75
R48 Doug Gilmour .25 .60
R49 Jose Theodore .40 1.00
R50 David Legwand .25 .60
R51 Tomas Vokoun .25 .60
R52 Martin Brodeur 1.50 4.00
R53 Patrik Elias .25 .60
R54 Joe Nieuwendyk .25 .60
R55 Alexei Yashin .25 .60
R56 Michael Peca .25 .60
R57 Chris Osgood .25 .60
R58 Eric Lindros .30 .75
R59 Pavel Bure .30 .75
R60 Brian Leetch .25 .60
R61 Martin Havlat .25 .60
R62 Marian Hossa .30 .75
R63 Daniel Alfredsson .25 .60
R64 John LeClair .30 .75
R65 Jeremy Roenick .40 1.00
R66 Simon Gagne .30 .75
R67 Tony Amonte .25 .60
R68 Sean Burke .25 .60
R69 Daniel Briere .25 .60
R70 Alexei Kovalev .25 .60
R71 Johan Hedberg .25 .60
R72 Mario Lemieux 2.00 5.00
R73 Teemu Selanne .30 .75
R74 Evgeni Nabokov .25 .60
R75 Owen Nolan .25 .60
R76 Chris Pronger .25 .60
R77 Doug Weight .25 .60
R78 Keith Tkachuk .30 .75
R79 Brad Richards .25 .60
R80 Nikolai Khabibulin .30 .75
R81 Vincent Lecavalier .30 .75
R82 Mats Sundin .30 .75
R83 Ed Belfour .30 .75
R84 Alexander Mogilny .25 .60
R85 Todd Bertuzzi .30 .75
R86 Dan Cloutier .25 .60
R87 Markus Naslund .30 .75
R88 Jaromir Jagr .50 1.25
R89 Peter Bondra .25 .60
R90 Olaf Kolzig .25 .60
R91 Jason Spezza 2.50 6.00
R92 Rick Nash 3.00 8.00
R93 Jay Bouwmeester 2.00 5.00
R94 Stanislav Chistov 2.00 5.00
R95 P-M Bouchard 2.00 5.00
R96 Pascal LeClaire 2.00 5.00
R97 Brooks Orpik .75 2.00
R98 Steve Ott 1.25 3.00
R99 Alexander Frolov 1.50 4.00
R100 Alexander Svitov 1.00 2.50

2002-03 UD Artistic Impressions Retrospectives Gold

*STARS: 6X TO 15X BASIC INSERTS
STATED PRINT RUN 25 SER.#'d SETS
SKIP NUMBERED SET

2002-03 UD Artistic Impressions Retrospectives Signed

This autographed partial parallel set was serial-numbered to just 25 copies each. Cards are not priced due to scarcity.

STATED PRINT RUN 25 SER.#'d SETS
NOT PRICED DUE TO SCARCITY
SKIP NUMBERED SET
R7 Bobby Orr

2002-03 UD Artistic Impressions Retrospectives Silver

*STARS: 1.5X TO 4X BASIC CARDS
STATED PRINT RUN 99 SER.#'d SETS

2002-03 UD Artistic Impressions Right Track

Singles in this 11-card memorabilia set were serial-numbered to 299.

*MULT.COLOR SWATCH: .5X TO 1.25X HI
RTAF Alexander Frolov 3.00 8.00
RTDB Daniel Briere 3.00 8.00
RTDH Dany Heatley 5.00 12.00
RTJA Jared Aulin 6.00 15.00
RTJL Jamie Lundmark 4.00 10.00
RTJW Justin Williams 3.00 8.00
RTKC Kyle Calder 3.00 8.00
RTMA Maxim Afinogenov 3.00 8.00
RTME Martin Erat 3.00 8.00
RTSC Stanislav Chistov 5.00 12.00
RTSR Steve Reinprecht 3.00 8.00

2002-03 UD Artistic Impressions Right Track Gold

*STARS: .5X TO 1.25X BASIC INSERTS
STATED PRINT RUN 175 SER.#'d SETS

2006-07 UD Biography of a Season

COMPLETE SET (15) 4.00 10.00
BOS1 Eric Staal .40 1.00
BOS2 Brendan Shanahan .40 1.00
BOS3 Mats Sundin .40 1.00
BOS4 Evgeni Malkin .75 2.00
BOS5 Evgeni Malkin .75 2.00
BOS6 Ryan Miller .75 2.00
BOS7 Patrick Roy .75 2.00
BOS8 Chris Pronger .40 1.00
BOS9 Sidney Crosby 1.25 3.00
BOS10 Alexander Ovechkin .75 2.00
BOS11 Daniel Briere .40 1.00
BOS12 Zach Parise .40 1.00
BOS13 Mark Recchi .40 1.00
BOS14 Joe Sakic .75 2.00
BOS15 Sidney Crosby 1.25 3.00

2008-09 UD Black

Cards #103-#124 were Rookie Cards issued as exchange cards. All of these were signed and numbered to 99 copies.

STATED PRINT RUN 99 SERIAL #'d SETS
AU RCs PRINT RUN 399 SERIAL #'d SETS
RCs PRINT RUN 399 SERIAL #'d SETS
1 Alexander Ovechkin 30.00 80.00
2 Cam Neely 10.00 25.00
3 Saku Koivu 8.00 20.00
4 Dany Heatley 10.00 25.00
5 Dino Ciccarelli 5.00 12.00
6 Dominik Hasek 12.00 30.00
7 Eric Staal 12.00 30.00
8 Evgeni Malkin 20.00 50.00
9 Henrik Lundqvist 15.00 40.00
10 Henrik Zetterberg 15.00 40.00
11 Ilya Kovalchuk 10.00 25.00
12 Peter Forsberg 12.00 30.00
13 Jarome Iginla 15.00 40.00
14 Jaromir Jagr 10.00 25.00
15 Sidney Crosby 40.00 100.00
16 Roberto Luongo 12.00 30.00
17 Joe Sakic 12.00 30.00
18 Joe Thornton 12.00 30.00
19 Jonathan Cheechoo 8.00 20.00
20 Jordan Staal 12.00 30.00
21 Lanny McDonald 8.00 20.00
22 Jason Spezza 10.00 25.00
23 Luc Robitaille 6.00 15.00
24 Marian Gaborik 12.00 30.00
25 Ryan Miller 8.00 20.00
26 Mario Lemieux 20.00 50.00
27 Mark Messier 15.00 40.00
28 Markus Naslund 8.00 20.00
29 Martin Brodeur 15.00 40.00
30 Martin St. Louis 8.00 20.00
31 Mats Sundin 8.00 20.00
32 Michael Ryder 6.00 15.00
33 Miikka Kiprusoff 8.00 20.00
34 Mike Modano 8.00 20.00
35 Nicklas Lidstrom 8.00 20.00
36 Patrice Bergeron 8.00 20.00
37 Simon Gagne 6.00 15.00
38 Patrick Roy 25.00 60.00
39 Paul Kariya 8.00 20.00
40 Vincent Lecavalier 8.00 20.00
41 Ray Bourque 15.00 40.00
42 Daniel Alfredsson 6.00 15.00
43 Derick Brassard AU RC 25.00 60.00
44 Mark Fistric AU RC 10.00 25.00
45 Alex Goligoski AU RC 25.00 60.00
46 Claude Giroux AU RC 25.00 60.00
47 Jon Filewich AU RC 10.00 25.00
48 Robbie Earl AU RC 10.00 25.00
49 Ilya Zubov AU RC 12.00 30.00
50 Steve Mason AU RC 30.00 80.00
51 Brian Boyle AU RC 12.00 30.00
52 Shawn Matthias AU RC 12.00 30.00
53 Ryan Stone AU RC 12.00 30.00
54 Teddy Purcell AU RC 12.00 30.00
55 Tom Cavanagh AU RC EXCH 10.00 25.00
56 Kyle Okposo AU RC 25.00 60.00
57 Marc-Andre Gragnani AU RC 10.00 25.00
58 Jonathan Ericsson AU RC 20.00 50.00
59 Kyle Turris AU RC 25.00 60.00
60 Brian Lee RC 10.00 25.00
61 Justin Abdelkader RC 20.00 50.00
62 Theo Peckham RC 10.00 25.00
63 Adam Pineault RC 10.00 25.00
64 Boris Valabik RC 12.00 30.00
65 Darren Helm RC 15.00 40.00
66 Mike Iggulden RC 8.00 20.00
67 Tim Ramholt RC 8.00 20.00
68 Matt D'Agostini RC 15.00 40.00
69 Andrew Ebbett RC 10.00 25.00
70 Sami Lepisto RC 10.00 25.00
71 Tyler Plante RC 10.00 25.00
72 Niklas Hjalmarsson RC 15.00 40.00
73 Alex Foster RC 8.00 20.00
74 Clay Wilson RC 6.00 15.00
75 Zach Fitzgerald RC 10.00 25.00
76 Kyle Greentree RC 12.00 30.00
77 Joe Jensen RC 10.00 25.00
78 David Brine RC 8.00 20.00
79 B.J. Crombeen RC 8.00 20.00
80 Mike Brown RC 12.00 30.00
81 Jordan Hendry RC 8.00 20.00
82 Corey Locke RC 10.00 25.00
83 Cody McLeod RC 8.00 20.00
84 Jesse Winchester RC 10.00 25.00
85 Lauri Korpikoski RC 10.00 25.00
86 Jack Hillen RC 8.00 20.00
87 Mike Mole RC 8.00 20.00
88 Jordan LaVallee RC 10.00 25.00
89 Erik Ersberg RC 10.00 25.00
90 Darryl Boyce RC 8.00 20.00
91 Tom Sestito RC 8.00 20.00
92 Joey Mormina RC 8.00 20.00
93 Chris Minard RC 10.00 25.00
94 Pascal Pelletier RC 8.00 20.00
95 Tim Conboy RC 8.00 20.00
96 Kevin Doell RC 6.00 15.00
97 Andrew Murray RC 8.00 20.00
98 Brandon Nolan RC 12.00 30.00
99 Colin Stuart RC 8.00 20.00
100 Danny Taylor RC 10.00 25.00
101 Dan LaCosta RC 12.00 30.00
102 Mattias Ritola RC 12.00 30.00
103 Steven Stamkos AU RC 150.00 300.00
104 Nikita Filatov AU RC 50.00 120.00
105 Jakub Voracek AU RC 25.00 60.00
106 Fabian Brunnstrom AU RC 100.00 200.00
107 Michael Frolik AU RC 25.00 60.00
108 Drew Doughty AU RC 40.00 100.00
109 Colton Gillies AU RC 12.00 30.00
110 Patric Hornqvist AU RC 12.00 30.00
111 Petr Vrana AU RC 15.00 40.00
112 Luca Sbisa AU RC 20.00 50.00
113 Mikkel Boedker AU RC 20.00 50.00
114 Viktor Tikhonov AU RC 12.00 30.00
115 T.J. Oshie AU RC 30.00 80.00
116 Patrik Berglund AU RC 30.00 80.00
117 Alex Pietrangelo AU RC 20.00 50.00
118 Nikolai Kulemin AU RC 12.00 30.00
119 Luke Schenn AU RC 40.00 80.00
120 Blake Wheeler AU RC 40.00 80.00
121 Brandon Sutter AU RC 15.00 40.00
122 Zach Bogosian AU RC 25.00 60.00
123 James Neal AU RC 20.00 50.00
124 Zach Boychuk AU RC 20.00 50.00

2008-09 UD Black Blue

STATED PRINT RUN 1 SERIAL #'d SET
NOT PRICED DUE TO SCARCITY

2008-09 UD Black Gold

STATED PRINT RUN 15 SERIAL #'d SETS
NOT PRICED DUE TO SCARCITY

2008-09 UD Black Autographs Cuts Duals

STATED PRINT RUN 1 SERIAL #'d SET
NOT PRICED DUE TO SCARCITY
C2AH Syl Apps
Red Horner
C2BD Toe Blake
Hap Day
C2DB Bob Davidson
Max Bentley
C2DS John D'Amico
Red Storey
C2HG Foster Hewitt
Danny Gallivan
C2SB Eddie Shore
Ace Bailey

2008-09 UD Black Autographs Jerseys

STATED PRINT RUN 25 SERIAL #'d SETS
BAJAF Alexander Frolov
BAJAH Ales Hemsky
BAJAK Anze Kopitar
BAJAM Al MacInnis
BAJAO Alexander Ovechkin 100.00 200.00
BAJBL Brian Leetch 25.00 60.00
BAJBS Borje Salming 20.00 50.00
BAJDH Dominik Hasek 30.00 80.00
BAJES Eric Staal 30.00 80.00
BAJHA Dale Hawerchuk 20.00 50.00
BAJHE Dany Heatley
BAJHJ Milan Hejduk 15.00 40.00
BAJHZ Henrik Zetterberg 40.00 100.00
BAJIK Ilya Kovalchuk 25.00 60.00
BAJJG Jean-Sebastien Giguere 20.00 50.00
BAJJI Jarome Iginla 40.00 100.00
BAJJJ Jack Johnson 15.00 40.00
BAJJT Jonathan Toews 60.00 120.00
BAJLR Luc Robitaille 15.00 40.00
BAJMB Martin Brodeur 75.00 150.00
BAJMF Marc-Andre Fleury 40.00 80.00
BAJMG Marian Gaborik
BAJMM Mike Modano 20.00 50.00
BAJMN Markus Naslund 20.00 50.00
BAJMR Michael Ryder 15.00 40.00
BAJMS Martin St. Louis 20.00 50.00
BAJMT Marty Turco 15.00 40.00
BAJMU Peter Mueller 25.00 60.00
BAJPB Patrice Bergeron 20.00 50.00
BAJPK Patrick Kane 60.00 120.00
BAJPR Patrick Roy 100.00 200.00
BAJPS Paul Stastny 20.00 50.00
BAJRB Ray Bourque 40.00 100.00
BAJRG Ryan Getzlaf 25.00 60.00
BAJRL Rod Langway 25.00 60.00
BAJRM Ryan Miller 20.00 50.00
BAJRV Alexander Radulov
BAJSC Sidney Crosby 175.00 300.00
BAJSG Simon Gagne 15.00 40.00
BAJST Peter Stastny 40.00 80.00
BAJTH Joe Thornton 30.00 80.00
BAJVL Vincent Lecavalier 20.00 50.00

2008-09 UD Black Autographs Jerseys Duals

STATED PRINT RUN 15 SERIAL #'d SETS
NOT PRICED DUE TO SCARCITY
BAJ2AR Al MacInnis
Rod Langway
BAJ2BF Martin Brodeur
Marc-Andre Fleury EXCH
BAJ2BK Patrice Bergeron
Phil Kessel EXCH
BAJ2BN Ray Bourque
Cam Neely
BAJ2EJ Eric Staal
Jordan Staal
BAJ2FR Grant Fuhr
Dwayne Roloson
BAJ2GB Marian Gaborik
Pierre-Marc Bouchard
BAJ2GC Simon Gagne
Bobby Clarke EXCH
BAJ2GD Chris Drury
Scott Gomez EXCH
BAJ2GG Jean-Sebastien Giguere
Ryan Getzlaf EXCH
BAJ2GH Gordie Howe
Wayne Gretzky
BAJ2GS Simon Gagne
Martin St. Louis
BAJ2HD Henrik Sedin
Daniel Sedin
BAJ2HE Dany Heatley
Ray Emery
BAJ2HS Paul Stastny
Milan Hejduk EXCH
BAJ2IH Dany Heatley

Jarome Iginla
BAJ2IT Jarome Iginla
Alex Tanguay EXCH
BAJ2KF Anze Kopitar
Alexander Frolov
BAJ2KM Patrick Kane
Peter Mueller EXCH
BAJ2KO Alexander Ovechkin
Ilya Kovalchuk EXCH
BAJ2KR Saku Koivu
Michael Ryder
BAJ2LG Wayne Gretzky
Mario Lemieux EXCH
BAJ2LR Larry Robinson
Rod Langway
BAJ2LS Borje Salming
Nicklas Lidstrom
BAJ2LZ Nicklas Lidstrom
Henrik Zetterberg EXCH
BAJ2MB Mark Messier
Brian Leetch EXCH
BAJ2ML Mario Lemieux
Mark Messier
BAJ2MM Mike Modano
Joe Mullen
BAJ2MT Mike Modano
Marty Turco
BAJ2MV Ryan Miller
Thomas Vanek
BAJ2NB Johnny Bucyk
Cam Neely
BAJ2NY Mark Messier
Brian Leetch
BAJ2NZ Henrik Zetterberg
Markus Naslund
BAJ2OK Alexander Ovechkin
Patrick Kane
BAJ2OM Alexander Ovechkin
Evgeni Malkin
BAJ2RB Patrick Roy
Martin Brodeur
BAJ2RG Wayne Gretzky
Luc Robitaille EXCH
BAJ2RS Luc Robitaille
Steve Shutt
BAJ2SS Peter Stastny
Paul Stastny
BAJ2TC Joe Thornton
Jonathan Cheechoo
BAJ2VH Dominik Hasek
Tomas Vokoun
BAJ2VM Vincent Lecavalier
Martin St. Louis

2008-09 UD Black Autographs Patches

STATED PRINT RUN 5 SERIAL #'d SETS
NOT PRICED DUE TO SCARCITY
BAJAF Alexander Frolov
BAJAH Ales Hemsky
BAJAK Anze Kopitar
BAJAM Al MacInnis
BAJAO Alexander Ovechkin
BAJBL Brian Leetch
BAJBS Borje Salming
BAJDH Dominik Hasek
BAJES Eric Staal
BAJHA Dale Hawerchuk
BAJHE Dany Heatley
BAJHJ Milan Hejduk
BAJHZ Henrik Zetterberg
BAJIK Ilya Kovalchuk
BAJJG Jean-Sebastien Giguere
BAJJI Jarome Iginla
BAJJJ Jack Johnson
BAJJT Jonathan Toews
BAJLR Luc Robitaille
BAJMB Martin Brodeur
BAJMF Marc-Andre Fleury
BAJMG Marian Gaborik
BAJMM Mike Modano
BAJMN Markus Naslund
BAJMR Michael Ryder
BAJMS Martin St. Louis
BAJMT Marty Turco
BAJMU Peter Mueller
BAJPB Patrice Bergeron
BAJPK Patrick Kane
BAJPR Patrick Roy
BAJPS Paul Stastny
BAJRB Ray Bourque
BAJRG Ryan Getzlaf
BAJRL Rod Langway
BAJRM Ryan Miller
BAJRV Alexander Radulov
BAJSC Sidney Crosby
BAJSG Simon Gagne
BAJST Peter Stastny
BAJTH Joe Thornton
BAJVL Vincent Lecavalier

2008-09 UD Black Autographs Patches Duals

STATED PRINT RUN 3 SERIAL #'d SETS
NOT PRICED DUE TO SCARCITY
BAJ2AR Rod Langway
Al MacInnis
BAJ2BF Martin Brodeur
Marc-Andre Fleury
BAJ2BK Phil Kessel
Patrice Bergeron
BAJ2BN Cam Neely
Ray Bourque
BAJ2EJ Eric Staal
Jordan Staal
BAJ2FR Dwayne Roloson
Grant Fuhr
BAJ2GB Marian Gaborik
Pierre-Marc Bouchard
BAJ2GC Bobby Clarke
Simon Gagne
BAJ2GD Scott Gomez
Chris Drury
BAJ2GG Jean-Sebastien Giguere
Ryan Getzlaf
BAJ2GH Wayne Gretzky
Gordie Howe
BAJ2GS Simon Gagne
Martin St. Louis
BAJ2HD Henrik Sedin
Daniel Sedin
BAJ2HE Dany Heatley
Ray Emery
BAJ2HS Milan Hejduk
Paul Stastny
BAJ2IH Jarome Iginla
Dany Heatley
BAJ2IT Jarome Iginla
Alex Tanguay
BAJ2KF Alexander Frolov
Anze Kopitar
BAJ2KM Patrick Kane
Peter Mueller
BAJ2KO Ilya Kovalchuk
Alexander Ovechkin
BAJ2KR Saku Koivu
Michael Ryder
BAJ2LG Mario Lemieux
Wayne Gretzky
BAJ2LR Larry Robinson
Rod Langway
BAJ2LS Nicklas Lidstrom
Borje Salming
BAJ2LZ Nicklas Lidstrom
Henrik Zetterberg
BAJ2MB Brian Leetch
Mark Messier
BAJ2ML Mario Lemieux
Mark Messier
BAJ2MM Mike Modano
Joe Mullen
BAJ2MT Mike Modano
Marty Turco
BAJ2MV Thomas Vanek
Ryan Miller
BAJ2NB Cam Neely
Johnny Bucyk
BAJ2NY Brian Leetch
Mark Messier
BAJ2NZ Markus Naslund
Henrik Zetterberg
BAJ2OK Alexander Ovechkin
Patrick Kane
BAJ2OM Alexander Ovechkin
Evgeni Malkin
BAJ2RB Patrick Roy
Martin Brodeur
BAJ2RG Luc Robitaille
Wayne Gretzky
BAJ2RS Steve Shutt
Luc Robitaille
BAJ2SS Paul Stastny
Peter Stastny
BAJ2TC Joe Thornton
Jonathan Cheechoo
BAJ2VH Tomas Vokoun
Dominik Hasek
BAJ2VM Vincent Lecavalier
Martin St. Louis

2008-09 UD Black Game Night Autographs Tickets

STATED PRINT RUN 25 SERIAL #'d SETS
GNAO Alexander Ovechkin 75.00 150.00
GNBC Bobby Clarke 20.00 50.00
GNBO Bobby Orr
GNCN Cam Neely 25.00 60.00
GNCP Carey Price 100.00 175.00
GNDC Dino Ciccarelli 12.00 30.00
GNDH Dale Hawerchuk EXCH 20.00 50.00
GNDS Devin Setoguchi 20.00 50.00
GNEM Evgeni Malkin 50.00 120.00
GNFM Frank Mahovlich 20.00 50.00
GNGF Grant Fuhr 20.00 50.00
GNGH Gordie Howe 100.00 175.00
GNGL Guy Lafleur 40.00 100.00
GNHA Dominik Hasek 60.00 120.00
GNHE Dany Heatley 50.00 100.00
GNIK Ilya Kovalchuk EXCH 25.00 60.00
GNJB Johnny Bucyk 20.00 50.00
GNJI Jarome Iginla 40.00 80.00
GNJJ Jack Johnson 15.00 40.00
GNJK Jari Kurri 40.00 80.00
GNJS James Sheppard 20.00 50.00
GNJT Jiri Tlusty EXCH 30.00 60.00
GNLM Lanny McDonald 20.00 50.00
GNLR Larry Robinson
GNMB Mike Bossy 20.00 50.00
GNMM Mark Messier 60.00 120.00
GNMN Markus Naslund 20.00 50.00
GNMO Mike Modano 20.00 50.00
GNMS Marc Staal 25.00 60.00
GNMT Marty Turco 15.00 40.00
GNNB Nicklas Backstrom 40.00 100.00
GNNF Nick Foligno 20.00 50.00
GNNL Nicklas Lidstrom 40.00 80.00
GNPK Patrick Kane 75.00 150.00
GNPM Peter Mueller
GNPS Paul Stastny 20.00 50.00
GNRB Ray Bourque 40.00 100.00
GNRL Rod Langway 25.00 60.00
GNRN Rick Nash 30.00 60.00
GNRO Luc Robitaille
GNRS Ryan Smyth 15.00 40.00
GNSC Sidney Crosby 125.00 250.00
GNSG Sam Gagner 50.00 100.00
GNSS Steve Shutt 20.00 50.00
GNST Peter Stastny 30.00 60.00
GNTH Joe Thornton 30.00 80.00
GNTL Ted Lindsay 20.00 50.00
GNTO Jonathan Toews 75.00 150.00
GNVL Vincent Lecavalier 40.00 80.00
GNWG Wayne Gretzky 200.00 300.00

2008-09 UD Black Game Night Autographs Tickets Blue

STATED PRINT RUN 1 SERIAL #'d SET
NOT PRICED DUE TO SCARCITY

2008-09 UD Black Game Night Autographs Tickets Gold

STATED PRINT RUN 10 SERIAL #'d SETS
NOT PRICED DUE TO SCARCITY

2008-09 UD Black Game Night Autographs Tickets Duals

STATED PRINT 10 SERIAL #'d SETS
NOT PRICED DUE TO SCARCITY
GN2AC Jason Arnott
Andrew Cogliano
GN2BC Martin Brodeur
Jeff Carter
GN2BL Henrik Lundqvist
Martin Brodeur
GN2BW Daniel Briere
Cam Ward
GN2GB Brad Boyes
Marian Gaborik
GN2GG Wayne Gretzky
Doug Gilmour
GN2GH Jean-Sebastien Giguere
Dany Heatley
GN2GK Patrick Kane
Marian Gaborik
GN2HK Patrick Kane
Dominik Hasek
GN2HR Dany Heatley
Michael Ryder
GN2IG Simon Gagne
Jarome Iginla
GN2JS Joe Thornton
Sam Gagner
GN2KK Phil Kessel
Anze Kopitar
GN2KM Peter Mueller
Chris Kunitz
GN2KP Carey Price
Phil Kessel
GN2LB Martin Brodeur
Vincent Lecavalier
GN2LM Mario Lemieux
Mark Messier
GN2LS Vincent Lecavalier
Eric Staal
GN2MB Patrice Bergeron
Mike Modano
GN2MD Mike Bossy
Dino Ciccarelli
GN2ME Michael Ryder
Eric Staal
GN2MJ Erik Johnson
Peter Mueller
GN2MS Mike Modano
Paul Stastny
GN2MT Mike Modano
Joe Thornton
GN2NC Jonathan Cheechoo
Markus Naslund
GN2NG Ryan Getzlaf
Rick Nash
GN2NI Markus Naslund
Jarome Iginla
GN2NK Jari Kurri
Cam Neely
GN2NT Rick Nash
Jonathan Toews
GN2RB Patrick Roy
Martin Brodeur
GN2RJ Jack Johnson
Bobby Ryan
GN2RM Ryan Miller
Michael Ryder
GN2RS Paul Stastny
Alexander Radulov
GN2SK Ilya Kovalchuk
Martin St. Louis
GN2SM Miroslav Satan
Ryan Miller
GN2TG Jonathan Toews
Sam Gagner
GN2VL Tomas Vokoun
Henrik Lundqvist
GN2VP Ondrej Pavelec
Tomas Vokoun
GN2ZG Henrik Zetterberg
Ryan Getzlaf
GN2ZH Henrik Zetterberg
Josh Harding

2008-09 UD Black Game Night Autographs Tickets Duals Blue

STATED PRINT RUN 1 SERIAL #'d SET
NOT PRICED DUE TO SCARCITY

2008-09 UD Black Game Night Autographs Tickets Duals Gold

STATED PRINT RUN 5 SERIAL #'d SETS
NOT PRICED DUE TO SCARCITY

2008-09 UD Black Jerseys 3 on 3

STATED PRINT RUN 5 SERIAL #'d SETS
NOT PRICED DUE TO SCARCITY
J302SC Dominik Hasek
Brendan Shanahan
Sergei Fedorov
Luc Robitaille
Pavel Datsyuk
Nicklas Lidstrom
J303SC Martin Brodeur
Scott Niedermayer
Patrik Elias
Brian Gionta
Brian Rafalski
Scott Gomez
J304SC Nikolai Khabibulin
Vincent Lecavalier
Martin St. Louis
Brad Richards
Cory Stillman
Ruslan Fedotenko
J306SC Cam Ward
Eric Staal
Rod Brind'Amour
Justin Williams
Doug Weight
Mark Recchi
J307SC Jean-Sebastien Giguere
Scott Niedermayer
Ryan Getzlaf
Chris Pronger
Corey Perry
Rob Niedermayer
J31AST Sidney Crosby
Alexander Ovechkin
Dany Heatley
Scott Niedermayer
Nicklas Lidstrom
Martin Brodeur
J3ALTA Miikka Kiprusoff
Jarome Iginla
Dion Phaneuf
Dwayne Roloson
Sam Gagner
Ales Hemsky
J3AS08 Jarome Iginla
Pavel Datsyuk
Marian Gaborik
Daniel Alfredsson
Alexander Ovechkin
Ilya Kovalchuk
J3BOMT Patrice Bergeron
Phil Kessel
Marc Savard
Saku Koivu
Michael Ryder
Alex Kovalev
J3CLDD Marc Staal
Erik Johnson
Jack Johnson
Tobias Enstrom
Mike Lundin
Matt Niskanen
J3CLDF Jonathan Toews
Patrick Kane
Sam Gagner
Brandon Dubinsky
Peter Mueller
David Perron
J3CNTR Wayne Gretzky
Gordie Howe
Mario Lemieux
Mark Messier
Sidney Crosby
Joe Sakic
J3GOAL Martin Brodeur
Roberto Luongo
Marc-Andre Fleury
Miikka Kiprusoff
Henrik Lundqvist
Tomas Vokoun
J3HAWK Bobby Hull
Doug Wilson
Tony Esposito
Denis Savard
Jonathan Toews
Patrick Kane
J3HOFS Lanny McDonald
Bobby Clarke
Guy Lafleur
Gilbert Perreault
Phil Esposito
Steve Shutt
J3ONTO Jason Spezza
Daniel Alfredsson
Dany Heatley
Mats Sundin
Alexander Steen
Darcy Tucker
J3PENN Sidney Crosby
Evgeni Malkin
Jordan Staal
Simon Gagne
Daniel Briere
Jeff Carter
J3RWBH Henrik Zetterberg
Pavel Datsyuk
Nicklas Lidstrom
Jonathan Toews
Patrick Kane
Nikolai Khabibulin

2008-09 UD Black Jerseys 3 on 3 Blue

STATED PRINT RUN 1 SERIAL #'d SET
NOT PRICED DUE TO SCARCITY

2008-09 UD Black Jerseys 3 on 3 Gold

STATED PRINT RUN 5 SERIAL #'d SETS
NOT PRICED DUE TO SCARCITY

2008-09 UD Black Jerseys 4 on 4

STATED PRINT RUN 5 SERIAL #'d SETS
NOT PRICED DUE TO SCARCITY
J4500G Brendan Shanahan
Joe Sakic
Jaromir Jagr
Mats Sundin
Teemu Selanne
Mark Recchi
Mike Modano
Jeremy Roenick
J460GS Alexander Ovechkin
Wayne Gretzky
Mario Lemieux
Jaromir Jagr
Teemu Selanne
Jari Kurri
Lanny McDonald
Guy Lafleur
J4CHMP Martin Brodeur
Joe Sakic
Dominik Hasek
Vincent Lecavalier
Brendan Shanahan
Scott Niedermayer
Eric Staal
Mike Modano
J4EAST Ryan Miller
Martin Brodeur
Sidney Crosby
Alexander Ovechkin
Daniel Briere
Simon Gagne
Dany Heatley
Vincent Lecavalier
J4NO1P Patrick Kane
Erik Johnson
Sidney Crosby
Alexander Ovechkin
Marc-Andre Fleury
Rick Nash
Ilya Kovalchuk
Rick DiPietro
J4PTSL Wayne Gretzky
Gordie Howe
Mark Messier
Mario Lemieux
Phil Esposito
Ray Bourque
Joe Sakic
Stan Mikita
J4ROKG Teemu Selanne
Evgeni Malkin
Alexander Ovechkin
Dale Hawerchuk
Luc Robitaille
Mario Lemieux
Peter Stastny
Gilbert Perreault
J4ROSS Wayne Gretzky
Sidney Crosby
Joe Thornton
Martin St. Louis
Jarome Iginla
Jaromir Jagr
Mario Lemieux
Marcel Dionne
J4SHOS Curtis Joseph
Martin Brodeur
Tony Esposito
Dominik Hasek
Patrick Roy
Chris Osgood
Nikolai Khabibulin
Evgeni Nabokov
J4TROP Sidney Crosby
Evgeni Malkin
Martin Brodeur
Nicklas Lidstrom
Pavel Datsyuk
Phil Kessel
Scott Niedermayer
Vincent Lecavalier
J4VEZN Martin Brodeur
Miikka Kiprusoff
Dominik Hasek
Patrick Roy
Grant Fuhr
Ron Hextall
Jose Theodore
Tony Esposito
J4WEST Roberto Luongo
Miikka Kiprusoff
Scott Niedermayer
Nicklas Lidstrom
Joe Thornton
Joe Sakic
Jonathan Cheechoo
Henrik Zetterberg

2008-09 UD Black Jerseys 4 on 4 Blue

STATED PRINT RUN 1 SERIAL #'d SET
NOT PRICED DUE TO SCARCITY

2008-09 UD Black Jerseys 4 on 4 Gold

STATED PRINT RUN 3 SERIAL #'d SETS
NOT PRICED DUE TO SCARCITY

2008-09 UD Black Jerseys Duals

STATED PRINT RUN 50 SERIAL #'d SETS
BDJ2AS Jason Spezza 15.00 40.00
Daniel Alfredsson
BDJ2BJ Brendan Shanahan 20.00 50.00
Joe Sakic
BDJ2BP Martin Brodeur 12.00 30.00
Zach Parise
BDJ2BS Eric Staal 20.00 50.00
Rod Brind'Amour
BDJ2CG Wayne Gretzky 60.00 120.00
Sidney Crosby
BDJ2DD Pavel Datsyuk 12.00 30.00
Kris Draper
BDJ2DZ Henrik Zetterberg 25.00 60.00
Pavel Datsyuk
BDJ2FB Patrice Bergeron 12.00 30.00
Manny Fernandez
BDJ2GD Rick DiPietro 12.00 30.00
Bill Guerin
BDJ2GK Marian Gaborik 12.00 30.00
Mikko Koivu
BDJ2HG Marian Gaborik 20.00 50.00
Marian Hossa
BDJ2IK Miikka Kiprusoff 25.00 60.00
Jarome Iginla
BDJ2JL Jaromir Jagr 25.00 60.00
Henrik Lundqvist
BDJ2JP Joe Sakic 30.00 60.00
Patrick Roy
BDJ2JR Joe Sakic 20.00 50.00
Ryan Smyth
BDJ2KB Paul Kariya 12.00 30.00
Brad Boyes
BDJ2KL Ilya Kovalchuk 15.00 40.00
Kari Lehtonen
BDJ2KP Dion Phaneuf 12.00 30.00
Miikka Kiprusoff
BDJ2LC Sidney Crosby 50.00 100.00
Mario Lemieux
BDJ2LK Roberto Luongo 20.00 50.00
Miikka Kiprusoff
BDJ2LM Mario Lemieux
Larry Murphy
BDJ2LN Roberto Luongo 20.00 50.00
Markus Naslund
BDJ2LS Vincent Lecavalier 15.00 40.00
Jason Spezza
BDJ2MA Mats Sundin 12.00 30.00
Alexander Steen
BDJ2MH Evgeni Malkin 30.00 80.00
Marian Hossa
BDJ2MM Lanny McDonald 12.00 30.00
Joe Mullen
BDJ2MR Mike Modano 12.00 30.00
Jeremy Roenick
BDJ2MT Joe Thornton 20.00 50.00
Patrick Marleau
BDJ2NL Markus Naslund 12.00 30.00
Trevor Linden
BDJ2PG Jean-Sebastien Giguere 12.00 30.00
Cam Ward
Brad Richards
Scott Niedermayer
BDJ2PM Patrick Roy 40.00 80.00
Martin Brodeur
BDJ2PN Scott Niedermayer 10.00 25.00
Chris Pronger
BDJ2RB Luc Robitaille 12.00 30.00
Rob Blake
BDJ2RH Dwayne Roloson 10.00 25.00
Ales Hemsky
BDJ2RP Rick Nash 12.00 30.00
Pascal Leclaire
BDJ2RS Rod Langway 12.00 30.00
Steve Shutt
BDJ2RT Vesa Toskala 12.00 30.00
Andrew Raycroft
BDJ2SN Rick Nash 12.00 30.00
Brendan Shanahan
BDJ2SR Luc Robitaille 12.00 30.00
Brendan Shanahan
BDJ2SS Joe Sakic 20.00 50.00
Paul Stastny
BDJ2VJ Tomas Vokoun 12.00 30.00
Olli Jokinen
BDJ2VM Vincent Lecavalier 12.00 30.00
Martin St. Louis

2008-09 UD Black Jerseys Duals Blue

STATED PRINT RUN 5 SERIAL #'d SETS
NOT PRICED DUE TO SCARCITY

2008-09 UD Black Jerseys Duals Gold

*GOLD: .5X TO 1.2X BASIC
STATED PRINT RUN 25 SERIAL #'d SETS

2008-09 UD Black Jerseys Foursomes

STATED PRINT RUN 25 SERIAL #'d SETS
UBJ4EHMS Bobby Hull 25.00 60.00
Denis Savard
Doug Wilson
Tony Esposito
UBJ4ENBB Phil Esposito 25.00 60.00
Johnny Bucyk
Ray Bourque
Cam Neely
UBJ4FKAM Mark Messier 50.00 100.00
Jari Kurri
Grant Fuhr
Glenn Anderson
UBJ4HMMH Gordie Howe 60.00 120.00
Bobby Hull
Frank Mahovlich
Stan Mikita
UBJ4IGSK Jarome Iginla
Martin St. Louis
Simon Gagne
Patrick Kane
UBJ4KTHN Dany Heatley 15.00 40.00
Rick Nash
Paul Kariya
Alex Tanguay
UBJ4LCGM Wayne Gretzky 100.00 175.00
Mario Lemieux
Mark Messier
Sidney Crosby
UBJ4LDBP Mario Lemieux 30.00 60.00
Marcel Dionne
Gilbert Perreault
Jean Beliveau
UBJ4LZKM Mark Messier 50.00 100.00
Brian Leetch
Alex Kovalev
Sergei Zubov
UBJ4MRTM Mike Modano 12.00 30.00
Jeremy Roenick
Joe Mullen
Keith Tkachuk
UBJ4NBLH Gordie Howe 50.00 120.00
Guy Lafleur
Mike Bossy
Cam Neely
UBJ4PPBR Ray Bourque 25.00 60.00
Larry Robinson
Denis Potvin
Dion Phaneuf
UBJ4PPJJ Chris Pronger 15.00 40.00
Dion Phaneuf
Jack Johnson
Erik Johnson
UBJ4RBFE Patrick Roy 12.00 30.00
Grant Fuhr
Tony Esposito
Martin Brodeur
UBJ4RBLF Patrick Roy 40.00 100.00
Martin Brodeur
Marc-Andre Fleury
Roberto Luongo
UBJ4RNGW Scott Niedermayer 12.00 30.00
Cam Ward
Brad Richards
Jean-Sebastien Giguere
UBJ4SLTS Joe Sakic 20.00 50.00
Joe Thornton
Vincent Lecavalier
Jason Spezza
UBJ4SNAZ Mats Sundin 25.00 60.00
Daniel Alfredsson
Markus Naslund
Henrik Zetterberg
UBJ4SRBH Bobby Hull 25.00 60.00
Johnny Bucyk
Luc Robitaille
Brendan Shanahan
UBJ4TPKG Jonathan Toews
Patrick Kane
Sam Gagner
Carey Price

2008-09 UD Black Jerseys Trios

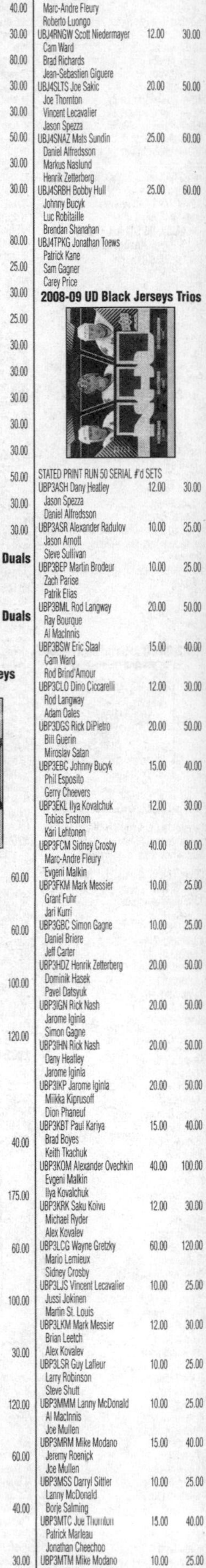

STATED PRINT RUN 50 SERIAL #'d SETS
UBP3ASH Dany Heatley 12.00 30.00
Jason Spezza
Daniel Alfredsson
UBP3ASR Alexander Radulov 10.00 25.00
Jason Arnott
Steve Sullivan
UBP3BEP Martin Brodeur 10.00 25.00
Zach Parise
Patrik Elias
UBP3BML Rod Langway 20.00 50.00
Ray Bourque
Al MacInnis
UBP3BSW Eric Staal 15.00 40.00
Cam Ward
Rod Brind'Amour
UBP3CLO Dino Ciccarelli 12.00 30.00
Rod Langway
Adam Oates
UBP3DGS Rick DiPietro 20.00 50.00
Bill Guerin
Miroslav Satan
UBP3EBC Johnny Bucyk 15.00 40.00
Phil Esposito
Gerry Cheevers
UBP3EKL Ilya Kovalchuk 12.00 30.00
Tobias Enstrom
Kari Lehtonen
UBP3FCM Sidney Crosby 40.00 80.00
Marc-Andre Fleury
Evgeni Malkin
UBP3FKM Mark Messier 10.00 25.00
Grant Fuhr
Jari Kurri
UBP3GBC Simon Gagne 10.00 25.00
Daniel Briere
Jeff Carter
UBP3HDZ Henrik Zetterberg 20.00 50.00
Dominik Hasek
Pavel Datsyuk
UBP3IGN Rick Nash 20.00 50.00
Jarome Iginla
Simon Gagne
UBP3IHN Rick Nash 20.00 50.00
Dany Heatley
Jarome Iginla
UBP3IKP Jarome Iginla 20.00 50.00
Miikka Kiprusoff
Dion Phaneuf
UBP3KBT Paul Kariya 15.00 40.00
Brad Boyes
Keith Tkachuk
UBP3KOM Alexander Ovechkin 40.00 100.00
Evgeni Malkin
Ilya Kovalchuk
UBP3KRK Saku Koivu 12.00 30.00
Michael Ryder
Alex Kovalev
UBP3LCG Wayne Gretzky 60.00 120.00
Mario Lemieux
Sidney Crosby
UBP3LJS Vincent Lecavalier 10.00 25.00
Jussi Jokinen
Martin St. Louis
UBP3LKM Mark Messier 12.00 30.00
Brian Leetch
Alex Kovalev
UBP3LSR Guy Lafleur 10.00 25.00
Larry Robinson
Steve Shutt
UBP3MMM Lanny McDonald 10.00 25.00
Al MacInnis
Joe Mullen
UBP3MRM Mike Modano 15.00 40.00
Jeremy Roenick
Joe Mullen
UBP3MSS Darryl Sittler 10.00 25.00
Lanny McDonald
Borje Salming
UBP3MTC Joe Thornton 15.00 40.00
Patrick Marleau
Jonathan Cheechoo
UBP3MTM Mike Modano 10.00 25.00
Marty Turco
Brenden Morrow
UBP3NBO Ray Bourque 20.00 50.00

2008-09 UD Black Autographs Patches

Cam Neely
Adam Oates
UBP3NGG Jean-Sebastien Giguere 15.00 40.00
Ryan Getzlaf
Scott Niedermayer
UBP3NLM Roberto Luongo 15.00 40.00
Markus Naslund
Brendan Morrison
UBP3RBL Patrick Roy 30.00 80.00
Martin Brodeur
Roberto Luongo
UBP3RSB Joe Sakic 20.00 50.00
Ray Bourque
Patrick Roy
UBP3RVG Wayne Gretzky 50.00 100.00
Luc Robitaille
Rogie Vachon
UBP3RWH Patrick Roy 30.00 80.00
Ron Hextall
Cam Ward
UBP3SBK Patrice Bergeron 10.00 25.00
Phil Kessel
Marc Savard
UBP3SJL Jaromir Jagr 20.00 50.00
Brendan Shanahan
Henrik Lundqvist
UBP3SNA Mats Sundin 15.00 40.00
Markus Naslund
Daniel Alfredsson
UBP3SSS Joe Sakic 15.00 40.00
Paul Stastny
Ryan Smyth
UBP3STS Mats Sundin 15.00 40.00
Darcy Tucker
Alexander Steen

2008-09 UD Black Jerseys Trios Blue

STATED PRINT RUN 1 SERIAL #'d SET
NOT PRICED DUE TO SCARCITY

2008-09 UD Black Lustrous Materials Autographs Jerseys

STATED PRINT RUN 25 SERIAL #'d SETS
LM2AH Ales Hemsky 40.00 80.00
LM2AO Alexander Ovechkin 75.00 150.00
LM2AR Alexander Radulov
LM2BC Bobby Clarke 25.00 60.00
LM2BF Bernie Federko 12.00 30.00
LM2BL Brian Leetch 20.00 50.00
LM2CD Chris Drury 25.00 60.00
LM2CN Cam Neely 25.00 60.00
LM2DH Dany Heatley 20.00 50.00
LM2DR Dwayne Roloson 20.00 50.00
LM2EJ Erik Johnson 20.00 50.00
LM2EM Evgeni Malkin 40.00 80.00
LM2ES Eric Staal 25.00 60.00
LM2GA Simon Gagne 20.00 50.00
LM2HZ Henrik Zetterberg 50.00 100.00
LM2IK Ilya Kovalchuk
LM2JG Jean-Sebastien Giguere 20.00 50.00
LM2JI Jarome Iginla 50.00 100.00
LM2JJ Jack Johnson 20.00 50.00
LM2JT Jonathan Toews 60.00 120.00
LM2KO Anze Kopitar
LM2MB Martin Brodeur 75.00 150.00
LM2MC Mike Cammalleri 15.00 40.00
LM2ME Mark Messier 100.00 200.00
LM2MG Marian Gaborik
LM2MM Mike Modano 25.00 60.00
LM2MN Markus Naslund 15.00 40.00
LM2MR Michael Ryder 12.00 30.00
LM2MS Miroslav Satan 30.00 60.00
LM2PK Patrick Kane 60.00 120.00
LM2PM Peter Mueller 40.00 80.00
LM2PR Patrick Roy 75.00 150.00
LM2PS Paul Stastny 25.00 60.00
LM2RB Ray Bourque 40.00 80.00
LM2RG Ryan Getzlaf 25.00 60.00
LM2RN Rick Nash 20.00 50.00
LM2SC Sidney Crosby 175.00 300.00
LM2SG Sam Gagner 50.00 100.00
LM2TH Joe Thornton 25.00 60.00
LM2TV Thomas Vanek 15.00 40.00
LM2VO Tomas Vokoun 15.00 40.00
LM2WG Wayne Gretzky 175.00 350.00

2008-09 UD Black Lustrous Materials Autographs Jerseys Blue

STATED PRINT RUN 1 SERIAL #'d SET
NOT PRICED DUE TO SCARCITY

2008-09 UD Black Lustrous Materials Autographs Jerseys Gold

STATED PRINT RUN 10 SERIAL #'d SETS
NOT PRICED DUE TO SCARCITY

2008-09 UD Black Marks of Obsidian Autographs Patches

STATED PRINT RUN 35 SERIAL #'d SETS
MOAM Al MacInnis
MOAO Alexander Ovechkin 60.00 120.00
MOAT Alex Tanguay 10.00 25.00
MOBC Bobby Clarke 12.00 30.00
MOBH Bobby Hull 25.00 60.00
MOBL Brian Leetch 15.00 40.00
MOBO Mike Bossy 12.00 30.00
MOBS Borje Salming 12.00 30.00
MOCN Cam Neely 15.00 40.00
MODC Dino Ciccarelli 8.00 20.00
MODH Dany Heatley 15.00 40.00
MODO Dominik Hasek 20.00 50.00
MOEM Evgeni Malkin 30.00 80.00
MOES Eric Staal 20.00 50.00
MOGF Grant Fuhr 20.00 50.00
MOGL Guy Lafleur 25.00 60.00
MOGP Gilbert Perreault 12.00 30.00
MOHA Dale Hawerchuk 12.00 30.00
MOHF Milan Hejduk 10.00 25.00
MOHZ Henrik Zetterberg 30.00 60.00
MOIK Ilya Kovalchuk 15.00 40.00
MOJB Johnny Bucyk 12.00 30.00
MOJC Jonathan Cheechoo 12.00 30.00
MOJG Jean-Sebastien Giguere 15.00 40.00
MOJK Jari Kurri 12.00 30.00
MOJM Joe Mullen 12.00 30.00
MOJT Joe Thornton 20.00 50.00
MOLM Lanny McDonald 12.00 30.00
MOLR Luc Robitaille 10.00 25.00
MOMB Martin Brodeur 50.00 100.00
MOMD Marcel Dionne 12.00 30.00
MOMG Marian Gaborik
MOMH Marian Hossa 25.00 60.00
MOMM Mike Modano 20.00 50.00
MOMN Markus Naslund 12.00 30.00
MOMR Michael Ryder 10.00 25.00
MOMT Marty Turco 10.00 25.00
MONL Nicklas Lidstrom 15.00 40.00
MOOA Adam Oates 12.00 30.00
MOPK Phil Kessel 12.00 30.00
MOPS Peter Stastny 12.00 30.00
MORB Ray Bourque 25.00 60.00
MORH Ron Hextall 20.00 50.00
MORO Larry Robinson 12.00 30.00
MORS Ryan Smyth 10.00 25.00
MOSC Sidney Crosby 100.00 200.00
MOSG Simon Gagne 15.00 40.00
MOSK Saku Koivu 15.00 40.00
MOSM Stan Mikita 20.00 50.00
MOVL Vincent Lecavalier 25.00 60.00

2008-09 UD Black Marks of Obsidian Autographs Patches Blue

STATED PRINT RUN 1 SERIAL #'d SET
NOT PRICED DUE TO SCARCITY

2008-09 UD Black Marks of Obsidian Autographs Patches Gold

GOLD: 4X TO 1X BASIC
STATED PRINT RUN 25 SERIAL #'d SETS
MOAM Al MacInnis 15.00 40.00

2008-09 UD Black Marks of Obsidian Autographs Patches Duals

STATED PRINT RUN 25 SERIAL #'d SETS
MO2BG Mike Bossy 15.00 40.00
Clark Gillies
MO2BP Johnny Bucyk 15.00 40.00
Gilbert Perreault
MO2CG Sam Gagner 25.00 60.00
Andrew Cogliano
MO2DV Marcel Dionne 20.00 50.00
Rogie Vachon
MO2EH Bobby Hull 30.00 80.00
Tony Esposito
MO2EJ Eric Staal
Jordan Staal
MO2EO Bobby Orr 150.00 250.00
Phil Esposito
MO2FJ Frank Mahovlich 20.00 50.00
Johnny Bower
MO2FK Grant Fuhr 50.00 100.00
Jari Kurri
MO2FM Evgeni Malkin 50.00 100.00
Marc-Andre Fleury
MO2FT Jiri Tlusty 15.00 40.00
Nick Foligno
MO2GB Marian Gaborik
Pierre-Marc Bouchard
MO2GG Jean-Sebastien Giguere 25.00 60.00
Ryan Getzlaf
MO2HN Dany Heatley 30.00 80.00
Rick Nash
MO2HS Paul Stastny 15.00 40.00
Milan Hejduk
MO2IT Jarome Iginla 30.00 80.00
Alex Tanguay
MO2JJ Jack Johnson 20.00 50.00
Erik Johnson
MO2JM Jordan Staal 25.00 60.00
Marc Staal
MO2KK Jari Kurri 15.00 40.00
Saku Koivu
MO2LH Gordie Howe 60.00 150.00
Ted Lindsay
MO2LM Mario Lemieux 100.00 200.00
Mark Messier
MO2LS Guy Lafleur 15.00 40.00
Steve Shutt
MO2LZ Henrik Zetterberg 40.00 100.00
Nicklas Lidstrom
MO2ML Mark Messier 100.00 200.00
Brian Leetch
MO2MM Mike Modano 20.00 50.00
Joe Mullen
MO2MS Lanny McDonald 20.00 50.00
Borje Salming
MO2NB Ray Bourque 30.00 80.00
Cam Neely
MO2NO Cam Neely 20.00 50.00
Adam Oates
MO2NZ Henrik Zetterberg 30.00 80.00
Markus Naslund
MO2OM Alexander Ovechkin 100.00 200.00
Evgeni Malkin
MO2PH Carey Price 150.00 300.00
Josh Harding
MO2PP Peter Stastny 50.00 100.00
Paul Stastny
MO2PR Carey Price 125.00 250.00
Tuukka Rask
MO2RB Martin Brodeur 125.00 250.00
Patrick Roy
MO2RC Jeff Carter
Mike Richards
MO2RP Michael Ryder 50.00 120.00
Carey Price
MO2SS Daniel Sedin 15.00 40.00
Henrik Sedin
MO2TB Jonathan Toews 100.00 200.00
Nicklas Backstrom
MO2TC Joe Thornton
Jonathan Cheechoo
MO2TK Patrick Kane 150.00 300.00
Jonathan Toews

2008-09 UD Black Marks of Obsidian Autographs Patches Duals Blue

STATED PRINT RUN 1 SERIAL #'d SET
NOT PRICED DUE TO SCARCITY

2008-09 UD Black Marks of Obsidian Autographs Patches Duals Gold

STATED PRINT RUN 10 SERIAL #'d SETS
NOT PRICED DUE TO SCARCITY

2008-09 UD Black Modern Era Autographs Cuts

STATED PRINT RUN 1 SERIAL #'d SET
NOT PRICED DUE TO SCARCITY
CMEBM Bob Marley
CMEBZ Babe Zaharias
CMECS Charles Schultz
CMEFF F. Scott Fitzgerald
CMEFS Frank Sinatra
CMEGS Gene Sarazen
CMEIG Indira Gandhi
CMEJC Johnny Cash
CMEJD John Diefenbaker
CMEJJ James J. Braddock
CMEMB Max Baer
CMEMD Miles Davis
CMEMG Marvin Gaye
CMENC Nat King Cole
CMEPT Pierre Trudeau
CMESG Sir Alec Guiness
CMESM Steve McQueen

2008-09 UD Black Past and Present Cuts Autographs

STATED PRINT RUN 1 SERIAL #'d SET
NOT PRICED DUE TO SCARCITY
PPCBB Turk Broda
Johnny Bower
PPCBG Danny Gallivan
Jean Beliveau
PPCBS Terry Sawchuk
Martin Brodeur
PPCHH Bryan Hextall Sr.
Ron Hextall
PPCHR George Hainsworth
Patrick Roy
PPCMT Pierre Trudeau
Frank Mahovlich
PPCRH Doug Harvey
Larry Robinson

2008-09 UD Black Patches Foursomes Blue

STATED PRINT RUN 1 SERIAL #'d SET
NOT PRICED DUE TO SCARCITY

2008-09 UD Black Patches Foursomes Gold

STATED PRINT RUN 5 SERIAL #'d SETS
NOT PRICED DUE TO SCARCITY
UBP4BNPB Ray Bourque
Scott Niedermayer
Dion Phaneuf
Rob Blake
UBP4EHMS Tony Esposito
Bobby Hull
Stan Mikita
Denis Savard
UBP4ENBB Phil Esposito
Cam Neely
Johnny Bucyk
Ray Bourque
UBP4FKAM Grant Fuhr
Jari Kurri
Glenn Anderson
Mark Messier
UBP4HMMH Bobby Hull
Stan Mikita
Frank Mahovlich
Gordie Howe
UBP4IGSK Jarome Iginla
Simon Gagne
Martin St. Louis
Patrick Kane
UBP4KTHN Paul Kariya
Alex Tanguay
Dany Heatley
Rick Nash
UBP4LCGM Mario Lemieux
Sidney Crosby
Wayne Gretzky
Mark Messier
UBP4LDBP Mario Lemieux
Marcel Dionne
Jean Beliveau
Gilbert Perreault
UBP4LZKM Brian Leetch
Sergei Zubov
Alex Kovalev
Mark Messier
UBP4MRTM Mike Modano
Jeremy Roenick
Keith Tkachuk
Joe Mullen
UBP4NCLH Cam Neely
Guy Lafleur
Gordie Howe
Dino Ciccarelli
UBP4PPJJ Chris Pronger
Dion Phaneuf
Jack Johnson
Erik Johnson
UBP4RBFE Patrick Roy
Martin Brodeur
Grant Fuhr
Tony Esposito
UBP4RBLF Patrick Roy
Martin Brodeur
Roberto Luongo
Marc-Andre Fleury
UBP4RNGW Jean-Sebastien Giguere
Cam Ward
UBP4SLTS Joe Sakic
Vincent Lecavalier
Joe Thornton
Jason Spezza
UBP4SNAZ Markus Naslund
Daniel Alfredsson
Henrik Zetterberg
Mats Sundin
UBP4SRBH Brendan Shanahan
Luc Robitaille
Johnny Bucyk
Bobby Hull
UBP4TPKG Jonathan Toews
Carey Price
Patrick Kane
Sam Gagner

2008-09 UD Black Patches Trios Gold

STATED PRINT RUN 10 SERIAL #'d SETS
NOT PRICED DUE TO SCARCITY
UBP3ASH Daniel Alfredsson
Jason Spezza
Dany Heatley
UBP3ASR Jason Arnott
Steve Sullivan
Alexander Radulov
UBP3BEP Martin Brodeur
Patrik Elias
Zach Parise
UBP3BML Al MacInnis
Rod Langway
Ray Bourque
UBP3BSW Rod Brind'Amour
Eric Staal
Cam Ward
UBP3CLO Dino Ciccarelli
Rod Langway
Adam Oates
UBP3DGS Bill Guerin
Miroslav Satan
Rick DiPietro
UBP3EBC Phil Esposito
Johnny Bucyk
Gerry Cheevers
UBP3FCM Marc-Andre Fleury
Sidney Crosby
Evgeni Malkin
UBP3FKM Grant Fuhr
Jari Kurri
Mark Messier
UBP3GBC Simon Gagne
Daniel Briere
Jeff Carter
UBP3HDZ Dominik Hasek
Pavel Datsyuk
Henrik Zetterberg
UBP3HKL Kari Lehtonen
Tobias Enstrom
Ilya Kovalchuk
UBP3IGN Jarome Iginla
Simon Gagne
Rick Nash
UBP3IHN Jarome Iginla
Dany Heatley
Rick Nash
UBP3IKP Jarome Iginla
Miikka Kiprusoff
Dion Phaneuf
UBP3KBT Keith Tkachuk
Brad Boyes
Paul Kariya
UBP3KOM Ilya Kovalchuk
Alexander Ovechkin
Evgeni Malkin
UBP3KRK Saku Koivu
Michael Ryder
Alex Kovalev
UBP3LCG Mario Lemieux
Sidney Crosby
Wayne Gretzky
UBP3LJS Vincent Lecavalier
Martin St. Louis
Jussi Jokinen
UBP3LKM Brian Leetch
Alex Kovalev
Mark Messier
UBP3LSR Guy Lafleur
Steve Shutt
Larry Robinson
UBP3MMM Lanny McDonald
Joe Mullen
Al MacInnis
UBP3MRM Mike Modano
Jeremy Roenick
Joe Mullen
UBP3MSS Lanny McDonald
Darryl Sittler
Borje Salming
UBP3MTC Patrick Marleau
Joe Thornton
Jonathan Cheechoo
UBP3MTM Mike Modano
Marty Turco
Brenden Morrow
UBP3NBO Cam Neely
Ray Bourque
Adam Oates
UBP3NGG Scott Niedermayer
Jean-Sebastien Giguere
Ryan Getzlaf
UBP3NLM Markus Naslund
Roberto Luongo
Brendan Morrison
UBP3RBL Patrick Roy
Martin Brodeur
Roberto Luongo
UBP3RSB Patrick Roy
Joe Sakic
Ray Bourque
UBP3RVG Luc Robitaille
Rogie Vachon
Wayne Gretzky
UBP3RWH Patrick Roy
Cam Ward
Ron Hextall
UBP3SBK Marc Savard
Patrice Bergeron
Phil Kessel
UBP3SJL Brendan Shanahan
Jaromir Jagr
Henrik Lundqvist
UBP3SNA Mats Sundin
Markus Naslund
Daniel Alfredsson
UBP3SSS Joe Sakic
Ryan Smyth
Paul Stastny
UBP3STS Mats Sundin
Darcy Tucker
Alexander Steen

2008-09 UD Black Pride of a Nation Autographs Patches

STATED PRINT RUN 25 SERIAL #'d SETS
PNAK Anze Kopitar
PNAO Alexander Ovechkin 150.00 300.00
PNAR Alexander Radulov
PNBC Bobby Clarke 30.00 80.00
PNBL Brian Leetch 40.00 100.00
PNBO Bobby Orr 300.00 450.00
PNCP Carey Price 175.00 300.00
PNDH Dominik Hasek 50.00 120.00
PNDR Dwayne Roloson 25.00 60.00
PNDS Devin Setoguchi 30.00 80.00
PNEM Evgeni Malkin 75.00 150.00
PNES Eric Staal 50.00 120.00
PNGH Gordie Howe 125.00 200.00
PNGL Guy Lafleur 60.00 150.00
PNGP Gilbert Perreault 30.00 80.00
PNHA Dale Hawerchuk 30.00 80.00
PNHE Dany Heatley 40.00 100.00
PNHL Henrik Lundqvist
PNHZ Henrik Zetterberg 60.00 150.00
PNIK Ilya Kovalchuk 40.00 100.00
PNJC Jonathan Cheechoo 30.00 80.00
PNJG Jean-Sebastien Giguere 30.00 80.00
PNJI Jarome Iginla 60.00 150.00
PNJK Jari Kurri 30.00 80.00
PNJM Joe Mullen 30.00 80.00
PNJS Jordan Staal 50.00 120.00
PNJT Joe Thornton 50.00 120.00
PNKE Phil Kessel 30.00 80.00
PNLR Larry Robinson 30.00 80.00
PNMB Martin Brodeur 100.00 200.00
PNMF Marc-Andre Fleury 75.00 150.00
PNMG Marian Gaborik
PNMH Marian Hossa 50.00 120.00
PNMI Milan Hejduk 25.00 60.00
PNMN Markus Naslund
PNMO Mike Modano 30.00 80.00
PNMR Mike Richards 75.00 150.00
PNMS Miroslav Satan 60.00 120.00
PNMT Marty Turco 25.00 60.00
PNNB Nicklas Backstrom 60.00 150.00
PNNL Nicklas Lidstrom 30.00 80.00
PNPE Phil Esposito 40.00 100.00
PNPK Patrick Kane 125.00 250.00
PNPS Paul Stastny 30.00 80.00
PNRG Ryan Getzlaf 40.00 100.00
PNRM Ryan Miller 30.00 80.00
PNRN Rick Nash 30.00 80.00
PNRS Ryan Smyth
PNSC Sidney Crosby 200.00 350.00
PNSG Sam Gagner 60.00 120.00
PNSK Saku Koivu 40.00 80.00
PNST Martin St. Louis 30.00 80.00
PNTE Tony Esposito 30.00 80.00
PNTL Jiri Tlusty 30.00 80.00
PNTO Jonathan Toews 125.00 250.00
PNTR Tuukka Rask 50.00 120.00
PNTV Thomas Vanek 30.00 80.00
PNVL Vincent Lecavalier 30.00 80.00
PNVO Tomas Vokoun 30.00 80.00
PNZP Zach Parise

2008-09 UD Black Pride of a Nation Autographs Patches Blue

STATED PRINT RUN 1 SERIAL #'d SET
NOT PRICED DUE TO SCARCITY

2008-09 UD Black Pride of a Nation Autographs Patches Gold

STATED PRINT RUN 10 SERIAL #'d SETS
NOT PRICED DUE TO SCARCITY

2008-09 UD Black Trophy Cuts Autographs

STATED PRINT RUN 1 SERIAL #'d SET
NOT PRICED DUE TO SCARCITY
TWCBC Clarence Campbell
Ray Bourque
TWCCG Clarence Campbell
Doug Gilmour
TWCCI Clarence Campbell
Jarome Iginla
TWCCL Clarence Campbell
Lanny McDonald
TWCCM Clarence Campbell
Mark Messier
TWCCR Maurice Richard
Jonathan Cheechoo
TWCFC Clarence Campbell
Grant Fuhr
TWCGS Lord Stanley
Wayne Gretzky
TWCHC Clarence Campbell
Dominik Hasek
TWCIC King Clancy
Jarome Iginla
TWCIR Maurice Richard
Jarome Iginla
TWCJG Clarence Campbell
Jean-Sebastien Giguere
TWCKR Maurice Richard
Ilya Kovalchuk
TWCLC Clarence Campbell
Nicklas Lidstrom
TWCLN James Norris
Nicklas Lidstrom
TWCLR Clarence Campbell
Luc Robitaille
TWCMC King Clancy
Lanny McDonald
TWCMH Cecil Hart
Mark Messier
TWCMM Clarence Campbell
Mike Modano
TWCNR Maurice Richard
Rick Nash
TWCOP Lester B. Pearson
Alexander Ovechkin
TWCOR Art Ross
Alexander Ovechkin
TWCOS Lord Stanley
Bobby Orr
TWCRC Clarence Campbell
Patrick Roy
TWCRG Clarence Campbell
Ryan Getzlaf
TWCRL Maurice Richard
Vincent Lecavalier
TWCRO Maurice Richard
Alexander Ovechkin
TWCSC Frank Selke
Guy Carbonneau
TWCSZ Conn Smythe
Henrik Zetterberg
TWCWG Clarence Campbell
Wayne Gretzky

2009-10 UD Black

STATED PRINT RUN 99 SER.#'d SETS
STATED PRINT RUN 499 SER.#'d SETS
STATED PRINT RUN 499 SER.#'d SETS
EXCH EXPIRATION 9/15/2011
1 Ilya Kovalchuk 8.00 20.00
2 Cam Neely 10.00 25.00
3 Phil Esposito 12.00 30.00
4 Ray Bourque 10.00 25.00
5 Jarome Iginla 12.00 30.00
6 Miikka Kiprusoff 6.00 15.00
7 Eric Staal 8.00 20.00
8 Tony Esposito 10.00 25.00
9 Jonathan Toews 15.00 40.00
10 Patrick Kane 12.00 30.00
11 Rick Nash 6.00 15.00
12 Marty Turco 5.00 12.00
13 Mike Modano 6.00 15.00
14 Gordie Howe 25.00 60.00
15 Henrik Zetterberg 12.00 30.00
16 Nicklas Lidstrom 8.00 20.00
17 Pavel Datsyuk 6.00 15.00
18 Grant Fuhr 8.00 20.00
19 Jari Kurri 6.00 15.00
20 Wayne Gretzky 30.00 80.00
21 Marian Gaborik 10.00 25.00
22 Carey Price 15.00 40.00
23 Larry Robinson 8.00 20.00
24 Patrick Roy 20.00 50.00
25 Martin Brodeur 15.00 40.00
26 Mike Bossy 6.00 15.00
27 Henrik Lundqvist 12.00 30.00
28 Mark Messier 12.00 30.00
29 Markus Naslund 6.00 15.00
30 Ron Hextall 12.00 30.00
31 Peter Mueller 8.00 20.00
32 Evgeni Malkin 15.00 40.00
33 Sidney Crosby 30.00 80.00
34 Mario Lemieux 15.00 40.00
35 Marc-Andre Fleury 6.00 15.00
36 Joe Thornton 12.00 30.00
37 Vincent Lecavalier 8.00 20.00
38 Borje Salming 6.00 15.00
39 Mats Sundin 6.00 15.00
40 Roberto Luongo 15.00 40.00
41 Alexander Ovechkin 25.00 60.00
42 Dale Hawerchuk 6.00 15.00
43 John Negrin RC 8.00 15.00
44 Tom Wandell RC 25.00 60.00
45 Ray Macias RC 8.00 20.00
46 Jay Beagle RC 8.00 20.00
47 Jakub Petruzalek RC 8.00 20.00
48 Alexander Sulzer RC 5.00 12.00
49 Taylor Chorney RC 8.00 20.00
50 Yannick Weber RC 10.00 25.00
51 Cal O'Reilly RC 8.00 20.00
52 Tim Wallace RC 5.00 12.00
53 Kevin Quick RC 5.00 12.00
54 Jesse Joensuu RC 10.00 25.00
55 Spencer Machacek RC 6.00 15.00
56 T.J. Galiardi RC 10.00 25.00
57 Michael Sauer RC 6.00 15.00
58 Matt Beleskey RC 8.00 20.00
59 Tim Stapleton RC 8.00 20.00
60 Grant Lewis RC 6.00 15.00
61 Mikael Backlund AU RC 12.00 30.00
62 Riku Helenius AU RC 8.00 20.00
63 Ville Leino AU RC 10.00 25.00
64 Michal Neuvirth AU RC 20.00 50.00
65 Artem Anisimov AU RC 12.00 30.00
66 Jhonas Enroth AU RC 8.00 20.00
67 Kris Chucko AU RC 8.00 20.00
68 Luca Caputi AU RC 12.00 30.00
69 Christian Hanson AU RC 12.00 30.00
70 Matt Pelech AU RC 10.00 25.00
71 Brian Salcido AU RC 8.00 20.00
72 Ivan Vishnevskiy AU RC 12.00 30.00
73 John Tavares AU RC EXCH 200.00 300.00
74 Matt Duchene AU RC EXCH 125.00 200.00
75 Victor Hedman AU RC EXCH 50.00 100.00
76 Evander Kane AU RC EXCH 50.00 100.00
77 James Van Riemsdyk AU RC EXCH 50.00 100.00
78 Jonas Gustavsson AU RC EXCH 75.00 150.00
79 Logan Couture AU RC EXCH 50.00 100.00
80 Brad Marchand AU RC EXCH 25.00 60.00
81 Tyler Myers AU RC EXCH 75.00 150.00
82 Jamie Benn AU RC EXCH 50.00 100.00
83 Colin Wilson AU RC EXCH 30.00 60.00
84 Michael Del Zotto AU RC EXCH 60.00 120.00
85 Viktor Stalberg AU RC EXCH 30.00 60.00
86 Michael Grabner AU RC EXCH 50.00 100.00
87 Tyler Bozak AU RC EXCH 50.00 100.00
88 Erik Karlsson AU RC EXCH 60.00 120.00
89 Matt Gilroy AU RC EXCH 30.00 60.00
90 Ryan O'Reilly AU RC EXCH 60.00 120.00
91 Dmitry Kulikov AU RC EXCH 15.00 40.00
92 Sergei Shirokov AU RC EXCH 30.00 60.00
93 Cody Franson AU RC EXCH 30.00 60.00

2009-10 UD Black Cold War Jerseys

STATED PRINT RUN 10 SER.#'d SETS
NOT PRICED DUE TO SCARCITY
CANRUS Dion Phaneuf
Rick Nash
Evgeni Nabokov
Sidney Crosby
Evgeni Malkin
Wayne Gretzky
Carey Price
Andrei Markov
Jonathan Toews
Ilya Kovalchuk
Sergei Zubov
Shea Weber
Alexander Ovechkin
CANUSA Brian Rafalski
Mike Modano
Martin Brodeur
Bill Guerin
Rick DiPietro
Ryan Whitney
Scott Niedermayer
Joe Thornton
Rob Blake
Shane Doan
Keith Tkachuk
Paul Kariya
USASWE Keith Yandle
Rick DiPietro
Alexander Edler
Daniel Sedin
Jack Johnson
Zach Parise
Nicklas Backstrom
Phil Kessel
Henrik Zetterberg
Patrick Kane
Tobias Enstrom
Henrik Lundqvist

2009-10 UD Black Cut Autographs Duals

STATED PRINT RUN 1 SER.#'d SET
NOT PRICED DUE TO SCARCITY
CUT2BB Ace Bailey
Bill Barilko
CUT2BS Ace Bailey
Eddie Shore
CUT2DB Toe Blake
Hap Day
CUT2DH Bob Davidson
Red Horner
CUT2HS Tim Horton
Terry Sawchuk
CUT2PJ Joe Primeau
Busher Jackson
CUT2PP Lester Patrick
Lynn Patrick
CUT2RM Babe Ruth
Howie Morenz
CUT2SB Turk Broda
Terry Sawchuk
CUT2WL Harry Watson
Harry Lumley

2009-10 UD Black Cut Autographs Wood

STATED PRINT RUN 1 SER.#'d SET
NOT PRICED DUE TO SCARCITY
WCAM Armand Mondou
WCCH Cecil Hart
WCDH Doug Harvey
WCGH George Hainsworth
WCHD Hap Day
WCHM Howie Morenz
WCSA Syl Apps
WCTB Turk Broda
WCTH Tim Horton

2009-10 UD Black Foursomes Jerseys

STATED PRINT RUN 25 SER.#'d SETS
T4JBDLM Martin Brodeur 30.00 60.00
Henrik Lundqvist
Ryan Miller
Rick DiPietro
T4JDKOM Evgeni Malkin
Ilya Kovalchuk
Pavel Datsyuk
Alexander Ovechkin
T4JDSSB Steven Stamkos 20.00 40.00
Luke Schenn
Drew Doughty
Mikkel Boedker
T4JECMP Gilbert Perreault 30.00 60.00
Frank Mahovlich
Bobby Clarke
Phil Esposito
T4JHLDZ Pavel Datsyuk
Henrik Zetterberg
Nicklas Lidstrom
Marian Hossa
T4JISCN Martin St. Louis 30.00 60.00
Jonathan Cheechoo
Jarome Iginla
Rick Nash
T4JKTKP Alex Kovalev 15.00 30.00
Saku Koivu
Alex Tanguay
Carey Price
T4JLGHM Mark Messier 125.00 200.00
Wayne Gretzky
Gordie Howe

Mario Lemieux
T4JRBLF Marc-Andre Fleury 50.00 100.00
Roberto Luongo
Martin Brodeur
Patrick Roy
T4JSKJK Saku Koivu 50.00 80.00
Jari Kurri
Olli Jokinen
Teemu Selanne
T4JSKTK Patrick Sharp 35.00 60.00
Jonathan Toews
Nikolai Khabibulin
Patrick Kane
T4JSLTC Vincent Lecavalier 40.00 80.00
Sidney Crosby
Joe Sakic
Joe Thornton

2009-10 UD Black Foursomes Patches

STATED PRINT RUN 3 SER.#'d SETS
NOT PRICED DUE TO SCARCITY

2009-10 UD Black Game Night Ticket Autographs

STATED PRINT RUN 35 SER.#'d SETS
GNAP Alex Pietrangelo 15.00 30.00
GNBC Bobby Clarke 25.00 50.00
GNBM Brendan Mikkelson 10.00 25.00
GNBO Bobby Orr 150.00 250.00
GNBS Brandon Sutter 20.00 40.00
GNBW Blake Wheeler 25.00 50.00
GNCG Colton Gillies 15.00 30.00
GNCP Carey Price 60.00 120.00
GNCS Cory Schneider 25.00 50.00
GNDD Drew Doughty 30.00 60.00
GNDG Doug Gilmour 30.00 60.00
GNEM Evgeni Malkin 50.00 100.00
GNFB Fabian Brunnstrom 12.50 25.00
GNHL Henrik Lundqvist 30.00 60.00
GNHZ Henrik Zetterberg 40.00 80.00
GNIK Ilya Kovalchuk 25.00 50.00
GNJI Jarome Iginla 40.00 80.00
GNJK Jari Kurri 30.00 60.00
GNJP Justin Pogge 15.00 30.00
GNJS Jordan Staal 25.00 50.00
GNJT Jonathan Toews 30.00 60.00
GNKA Karl Alzner 25.00 50.00
GNLS Luke Schenn 25.00 60.00
GNMB Mike Bossy 25.00 50.00
GNMG Marian Gaborik 25.00 50.00
GNMM Mark Messier 40.00 80.00
GNMP Max Pacioretty
GNMR Mike Richards 30.00 60.00
GNNB Nicklas Backstrom 30.00 60.00
GNRH Ron Hextall 35.00 80.00
GNRN Rick Nash 30.00 60.00
GNSC Sidney Crosby 150.00 250.00
GNSM Steve Mason 40.00 80.00
GNSS Steven Stamkos 40.00 80.00
GNTH Joe Thornton 30.00 60.00
GNTK Tim Kennedy 15.00 40.00
GNTV Thomas Vanek 25.00 50.00
GNZB Zach Bogosian 25.00 50.00

2009-10 UD Black Game Night Ticket Autographs Duals

STATED PRINT RUN 25 SER.#'d SETS
EXCH EXPIRATION 10/1/2011
GN2BH Ron Hextall
Ray Bourque
GN2CP Bobby Clarke 35.00 60.00
Gilbert Perreault
GN2DT Pavel Datsyuk 35.00 60.00
Jonathan Toews
GN2EB Tony Esposito 50.00 80.00
Jean Beliveau EXCH
GN2ES Phil Esposito 30.00 60.00
Borje Salming
GN2GH Dany Heatley 25.00 50.00
Jean-Sebastien Giguere EXCH
GN2KP Phil Kessel
Carey Price
GN2KS Ilya Kovalchuk 25.00 50.00
Eric Staal
GN2LI Jarome Iginla 25.00 50.00
Vincent Lecavalier
GN2LK Vincent Lecavalier 25.00 50.00
Ilya Kovalchuk
GN2LM Nicklas Lidstrom 50.00 100.00
Evgeni Malkin
GN2MB Martin Brodeur 50.00 80.00
Mike Modano EXCH
GN2NK Patrick Kane 30.00 60.00
Rick Nash EXCH
GN2NM Rick Nash 30.00 60.00
Peter Mueller EXCH
GN2NT Evgeni Nabokov 30.00 60.00
Marty Turco
GN2RB Martin Brodeur 100.00 200.00
Patrick Roy EXCH
GN2RM Evgeni Malkin 40.00 80.00
Mike Richards
GN2TM Ryan Miller 50.00 100.00
Joe Thornton
GN2ZF Henrik Zetterberg 50.00 80.00
Marc-Andre Fleury EXCH

2009-10 UD Black Generations Jerseys

STATED PRINT RUN 25 SER.#'d SETS
GLW Markus Naslund 75.00 150.00
Ilya Kovalchuk
Johnny Bucyk
Bobby Hull
Glenn Anderson
Steve Shutt
Alexander Ovechkin
Frank Mahovlich
Luc Robitaille
Dany Heatley
Paul Kariya
Rick Nash
GCEN Mario Lemieux 150.00 250.00
Joe Thornton
Gilbert Perreault
Evgeni Malkin
Sidney Crosby
Jason Spezza
Marcel Dionne
Wayne Gretzky
Pavel Datsyuk
Dale Hawerchuk
Vincent Lecavalier
Mark Messier
GDEF Brian Leetch 100.00 200.00
Andrei Markov
Larry Robinson
Brian Campbell
Nicklas Lidstrom
Mike Green (Wa Capitals)
Ray Bourque
Borje Salming
Denis Potvin
Scott Niedermayer
Al MacInnis
Dion Phaneuf
GEDM Glenn Anderson 250.00 400.00
Jari Kurri
Shawn Horcoff
Wayne Gretzky
Patrick O'Sullivan
Andrew Cogliano
Mark Messier
Sam Gagner
Marc-Antoine Pouliot
Grant Fuhr
Bill Ranford
Ales Hemsky
GGOL Bill Ranford 150.00 250.00
Grant Fuhr
Carey Price
Patrick Roy
Tony Esposito
Henrik Lundqvist
Martin Brodeur
Roberto Luongo
Marty Turco
Ron Hextall
Bernie Parent
Marc-Andre Fleury
GSTR Mario Lemieux 250.00 500.00
Jarome Iginla
Sidney Crosby
Evgeni Malkin
Alexander Ovechkin
Ray Bourque
Nicklas Lidstrom
Gordie Howe
Wayne Gretzky
Martin Brodeur
Mark Messier
Patrick Roy

2009-10 UD Black Jerseys Autographs

STATED PRINT RUN 25 SER.#'d SETS
AJAK Anze Kopitar 20.00 40.00
AJBL Brian Leetch 20.00 40.00
AJBS Borje Salming 20.00 40.00
AJBW Blake Wheeler 25.00 50.00
AJCN Cam Neely 20.00 40.00
AJCP Carey Price 40.00 80.00
AJDD Drew Doughty 25.00 50.00
AJDH Dale Hawerchuk 15.00 30.00
AJDP Dion Phaneuf 20.00 40.00
AJEM Evgeni Malkin 60.00 120.00
AJES Eric Staal 15.00 30.00
AJGP Gilbert Perreault 15.00 30.00
AJHL Henrik Lundqvist 30.00 60.00
AJHZ Henrik Zetterberg 30.00 60.00
AJIK Ilya Kovalchuk 25.00 50.00
AJJI Jarome Iginla 25.00 60.00
AJJN James Neal 25.00 50.00
AJJS Jordan Staal 25.00 50.00
AJJT Jonathan Toews
AJLS Luke Schenn 30.00 60.00
AJMG Marian Gaborik 25.00 50.00
AJMH Marian Hossa 20.00 40.00
AJMN Markus Naslund 15.00 30.00
AJNB Nicklas Backstrom 20.00 40.00
AJPK Patrick Kane 25.00 50.00
AJRB Ray Bourque 40.00 80.00
AJRN Rick Nash 25.00 50.00
AJSC Sidney Crosby 150.00 250.00
AJSS Steven Stamkos 30.00 60.00

2009-10 UD Black Jerseys Autographs Duals

STATED PRINT RUN 5 SER.#'d SETS
NOT PRICED DUE TO SCARCITY
AJ2CR Mike Richards
Bobby Clarke
AJ2DZ Pavel Datsyuk
Henrik Zetterberg
AJ2FM Evgeni Malkin
Marc-Andre Fleury
AJ2IP Jarome Iginla
Dion Phaneuf
AJ2LG Mario Lemieux
Wayne Gretzky
AJ2LS Steven Stamkos
Vincent Lecavalier
AJ2NL Markus Naslund
Henrik Lundqvist
AJ2NW Blake Wheeler
Cam Neely
AJ2RP Carey Price
Patrick Roy
AJ2SS Eric Staal
Jordan Staal
AJ2TK Patrick Kane
Jonathan Toews

2009-10 UD Black Jerseys Black Ice

STATED PRINT RUN X SER.#'d SETS
QJAK Alex Kovalev 8.00 20.00
QJAO Alexander Ovechkin 30.00 80.00
QJBL Brian Leetch 8.00 20.00
QJBS Borje Salming 8.00 20.00
QJCN Cam Neely 12.00 30.00
QJCP Carey Price 20.00 50.00
QJEM Evgeni Malkin 20.00 50.00
QJES Eric Staal 10.00 25.00
QJGH Gordie Howe 30.00 80.00
QJGP Gilbert Perreault 8.00 20.00
QJHZ Henrik Zetterberg 15.00 40.00
QJIK Ilya Kovalchuk 10.00 25.00
QJJK Jari Kurri 8.00 20.00
QJJS Jason Spezza 10.00 25.00
QJJT Jonathan Toews 20.00 50.00
QJKL Kari Lehtonen 8.00 20.00
QJKO Anze Kopitar 8.00 20.00
QJLR Larry Robinson 10.00 25.00
QJMB Martin Brodeur 20.00 50.00
QJMG Marian Gaborik 12.00 30.00
QJML Mario Lemieux 20.00 50.00
QJMM Mark Messier 15.00 40.00
QJMS Mats Sundin 8.00 20.00
QJNL Nicklas Lidstrom 10.00 25.00
QJPD Pavel Datsyuk 6.00 15.00
QJPK Paul Kariya 8.00 20.00
QJPM Patrick Marleau
QJPR Patrick Roy 25.00 60.00
QJPS Paul Stastny 8.00 20.00
QJRB Ray Bourque 12.00 30.00
QJRL Roberto Luongo 20.00 50.00
QJRN Rick Nash 8.00 20.00
QJSA Joe Sakic 15.00 40.00
QJSC Sidney Crosby 30.00 80.00
QJSK Saku Koivu 6.00 15.00
QJSS Steven Stamkos 20.00 50.00
QJST Jordan Staal 10.00 25.00
QJTS Teemu Selanne 8.00 20.00
QJVL Vincent Lecavalier 10.00 25.00
QJWG Wayne Gretzky 40.00 80.00
QJZP Zach Parise 8.00 20.00

2009-10 UD Black Jerseys Black Ice Autographs

STATED PRINT RUN 25 SER.#'d SETS
QJBL Brian Leetch 20.00 40.00
QJBS Borje Salming 20.00 40.00
QJCN Cam Neely 20.00 40.00
QJCP Carey Price 40.00 80.00
QJEM Evgeni Malkin 60.00 120.00
QJES Eric Staal 15.00 30.00
QJGH Gordie Howe
QJGP Gilbert Perreault 15.00 30.00
QJHZ Henrik Zetterberg
QJIK Ilya Kovalchuk 25.00 50.00
QJJK Jari Kurri 20.00 40.00
QJJT Jonathan Toews 60.00 120.00
QJKO Anze Kopitar 20.00 40.00
QJLR Larry Robinson 15.00 30.00
QJMB Martin Brodeur 40.00 80.00
QJMG Marian Gaborik 25.00 50.00
QJML Mario Lemieux 50.00 100.00
QJMM Mark Messier 40.00 80.00
QJNL Nicklas Lidstrom 20.00 40.00
QJPR Patrick Roy
QJPS Paul Stastny 20.00 40.00
QJRB Ray Bourque
QJRN Rick Nash 25.00 50.00
QJSC Sidney Crosby 150.00 300.00
QJSK Saku Koivu 20.00 40.00
QJSS Steven Stamkos 30.00 60.00
QJST Jordan Staal 20.00 40.00
QJVL Vincent Lecavalier 20.00 40.00
QJWG Wayne Gretzky 150.00 300.00

2009-10 UD Black Lustrous Materials Jersey Autographs

STATED PRINT RUN 50 SER.#'d SETS
LMAK Anze Kopitar 15.00 40.00
LMAO Adam Oates
LMBL Brian Leetch 20.00 50.00
LMBS Borje Salming 10.00 25.00
LMCD Chris Drury 15.00 30.00
LMCN Cam Neely 20.00 40.00
LMCP Carey Price 40.00 80.00
LMDC Dino Ciccarelli
LMDD Drew Doughty 15.00 30.00
LMDG Doug Gilmour 20.00 40.00
LMDH Dale Hawerchuk 15.00 30.00
LMDP Dion Phaneuf 20.00 40.00
LMEM Evgeni Malkin 40.00 80.00
LMES Eric Staal 15.00 30.00
LMGF Grant Fuhr 20.00 40.00
LMGP Gilbert Perreault 15.00 30.00
LMHE Dany Heatley 15.00 30.00
LMHL Henrik Lundqvist 25.00 50.00
LMHZ Henrik Zetterberg 25.00 50.00
LMIK Ilya Kovalchuk 20.00 40.00
LMJJ Jack Johnson 15.00 30.00
LMJN James Neal 15.00 30.00
LMJS Jordan Staal 20.00 40.00
LMJT Joe Thornton 25.00 50.00
LMLR Larry Robinson 10.00 25.00
LMMG Marian Gaborik 25.00 50.00
LMMM Mike Modano 15.00 30.00
LMMN Markus Naslund 10.00 25.00
LMMR Mike Richards 20.00 40.00
LMMT Marty Turco 15.00 30.00
LMNB Nicklas Backstrom 30.00 60.00
LMPB Patrick Berglund 15.00 30.00
LMPE Patrik Elias 15.00 30.00
LMPM Peter Mueller 10.00 25.00
LMPS Paul Stastny 15.00 30.00
LMRB Ray Bourque 30.00 60.00
LMRG Ryan Getzlaf 20.00 40.00
LMRN Rick Nash 20.00 40.00
LMTO Jonathan Toews 20.00 40.00
LMWG Wayne Gretzky 125.00 250.00

2009-10 UD Black Lustrous Materials Jersey Patch Autographs

STATED PRINT RUN 10 SER.#'d SETS
NOT PRICED DUE TO SCARCITY

2009-10 UD Black Lustrous Materials Patches Autographs

STATED PRINT RUN 1 SER.#'d SET
NOT PRICED DUE TO SCARCITY

2009-10 UD Black Modern Era Cut Autographs

STATED PRINT RUN 1 SER.#'d SET
NOT PRICED DUE TO SCARCITY
MEBE Max Bentley
MEBM Burgess Meredith
MEBW Billy Wilder
MEDL Dorothy Lamour
MEEM Ethel Merman
MEFG Frank Gorshin
MEGA Cal Gardner
MEHL Harper Lee
MEMX Max Baer Jr.
MERS Red Skelton

2009-10 UD Black Patches Black

STATED PRINT RUN 1 SER.#'d SET
NOT PRICED DUE TO SCARCITY

2009-10 UD Black Patches Gold

STATED PRINT RUN 10 SER.#'d SETS
NOT PRICED DUE TO SCARCITY

2009-10 UD Black Pride of a Nation Patches Autographs

STATED PRINT RUN 35 SER.#'d SETS
PNAK Anze Kopitar 20.00 50.00
PNBL Brian Leetch 25.00 50.00
PNBO Bobby Orr 200.00 300.00
PNBR Martin Brodeur 60.00 120.00
PNCD Chris Drury 25.00 50.00
PNCW Cam Ward 30.00 60.00
PNDD Drew Doughty 40.00 80.00
PNDH Dany Heatley 25.00 50.00
PNDP Dion Phaneuf 40.00 80.00
PNEM Evgeni Malkin 60.00 120.00
PNEN Evgeni Nabokov 30.00 60.00
PNFB Fabian Brunnstrom 25.00 50.00
PNGA Simon Gagne 30.00 60.00
PNGH Gordie Howe 100.00 175.00
PNGP Gilbert Perreault 40.00 80.00
PNHZ Henrik Zetterberg 50.00 100.00
PNIK Ilya Kovalchuk 25.00 50.00
PNJI Jarome Iginla 40.00 80.00
PNJS Jordan Staal 40.00 80.00
PNKO Saku Koivu 25.00 50.00
PNLS Luke Schenn 40.00 80.00
PNMB Mikkel Boedker 25.00 50.00
PNME Mark Messier 75.00 150.00
PNMG Marian Gaborik 40.00 80.00
PNMM Mike Modano 30.00 60.00
PNMR Mike Richards 40.00 80.00
PNMT Marty Turco 25.00 50.00
PNNF Nikita Filatov 40.00 80.00
PNPD Pavel Datsyuk
PNPE Patrik Elias 25.00 50.00
PNPK Patrick Kane 75.00 150.00
PNSC Sidney Crosby 125.00 250.00
PNSG Scott Gomez 30.00 60.00
PNSM Stan Mikita 40.00 80.00
PNSS Steven Stamkos
PNTE Tony Esposito 25.00 50.00
PNTV Thomas Vanek 25.00 50.00

2009-10 UD Black Pride of a Nation Patches Autographs Dual

STATED PRINT RUN 25 SER.#'d SETS
EXCH EXPIRATION 10/1/2011
PN2AD Karl Alzner 60.00 120.00
Drew Doughty
PN2CP Bobby Clarke 30.00 60.00
Gilbert Perreault
PN2DM Evgeni Malkin 60.00 120.00
Pavel Datsyuk
PN2EE Phil Esposito 60.00 120.00
Tony Esposito
PN2EO Bobby Orr 200.00 300.00
Phil Esposito
PN2FH Ron Hextall 60.00 120.00
Grant Fuhr
PN2FT Viktor Tikhonov 30.00 60.00
Nikita Filatov
PN2FV Jakub Voracek
Michael Frolik
PN2HG Marian Gaborik 40.00 80.00
Marian Hossa
PN2JS Saku Koivu 50.00 100.00
Jari Kurri
PN2KK Patrick Kane 30.00 60.00
Phil Kessel
PN2LE Erik Ersberg
Henrik Lundqvist
PN2LI Vincent Lecavalier 60.00 120.00
Jarome Iginla
PN2LS Nicklas Lidstrom 30.00 60.00
Borje Salming
PN2MM Mike Modano 30.00 60.00
Joe Mullen
PN2PM Steve Mason
Carey Price
PN2RB Martin Brodeur 150.00 250.00
Patrick Roy EXCH
PN2SP Justin Pogge
Luke Schenn
PN2ZB Fabian Brunnstrom 30.00 60.00
Henrik Zetterberg

2009-10 UD Black Rivals 6 on 6 Jerseys

STATED PRINT RUN 25 SER.#'d SETS
ANALAK Alexander Frolov 75.00 150.00
Anze Kopitar
Dustin Brown
Jarret Stoll
Justin Williams
Drew Doughty
Ryan Getzlaf
Teemu Selanne
Corey Perry
Chris Pronger
Ryan Whitney
Scott Niedermayer
ANASJS Scott Niedermayer 50.00 100.00
Jean-Sebastien Giguere
Ryan Whitney
Corey Perry
Chris Pronger
Ryan Getzlaf
Evgeni Nabokov
Patrick Marleau
Rob Blake
Joe Thornton
Jonathan Cheechoo
Devin Setoguchi
BOSNYR Chris Drury 50.00 100.00
Markus Naslund
Scott Gomez
Nikolai Zherdev
Brandon Dubinsky
Nik Antropov
Marc Savard
Mark Recchi
Patrice Bergeron
Blake Wheeler
Michael Ryder
Zdeno Chara
CARNJD Erik Cole 75.00 150.00
Eric Staal
Rod Brind'Amour
Joni Pitkanen
Jussi Jokinen
Cam Ward
David Clarkson
Martin Brodeur
Brendan Shanahan
Zach Parise
Patrik Elias
Brian Gionta
CGYEDM Shawn Horcoff 75.00 150.00
Gilbert Brule
Marc-Antoine Pouliot
Sam Gagner
Patrick O'Sullivan
Andrew Cogliano
Miikka Kiprusoff
Mike Cammalleri
Todd Bertuzzi
Olli Jokinen
Jarome Iginla
Dion Phaneuf
CHIDET Kris Draper 75.00 150.00
Pavel Datsyuk
Tomas Holmstrom
Henrik Zetterberg
Chris Osgood
Nicklas Lidstrom
Brian Campbell
Dave Bolland
Jonathan Toews
Patrick Sharp
Cristobal Huet
Patrick Kane
CHISTL Patrick Kane 75.00 150.00
Patrick Sharp
Jonathan Toews
Dave Bolland
Brent Seabrook
Nikolai Khabibulin
Patrik Berglund
Keith Tkachuk
Paul Kariya
Manny Legace
Carlo Colaiacovo
David Perron
CLBDET Derick Brassard 50.00 100.00
R.J. Umberger
Raffi Torres
Rostislav Klesla
Rick Nash
Jakub Voracek
Nicklas Lidstrom
Marian Hossa
Brian Rafalski
Tomas Holmstrom
Henrik Zetterberg
Pavel Datsyuk
COLDET Pavel Datsyuk 125.00 250.00
Kris Draper
Henrik Zetterberg
Tomas Holmstrom
Chris Osgood
Nicklas Lidstrom
Wojtek Wolski
Peter Budaj
Marek Svatos
Ryan Smyth
Milan Hejduk
Joe Sakic
FLATBL Steven Stamkos 60.00 120.00
Vincent Lecavalier
Olaf Kolzig
Martin St. Louis
Ryan Malone
Vaclav Prospal
David Booth
Michael Frolik
Jay Bouwmeester
Nathan Horton
Tomas Vokoun
Stephen Weiss
MTLBUF Saku Koivu 60.00 120.00
Andrei Markov
Tomas Plekanec
Alex Kovalev
Mike Komisarek
Carey Price
Drew Stafford
Thomas Vanek
Daniel Paille
Jason Pominville
Derek Roy
Ryan Miller
NYINYR Rick DiPietro 75.00 150.00
Trent Hunter
Doug Weight
Jeff Tambellini
Kyle Okposo
Josh Bailey
Scott Gomez
Markus Naslund
Chris Drury
Nikolai Zherdev
Wade Redden
Henrik Lundqvist
NYRNJD Henrik Lundqvist 60.00 120.00
Nikolai Zherdev
Chris Drury
Markus Naslund
Scott Gomez
Brandon Dubinsky
Brian Gionta
Patrik Elias
Brendan Shanahan
Martin Brodeur
David Clarkson
Zach Parise
PITPHI Antero Niittymaki 150.00 250.00
Joffrey Lupul
Mike Richards
Jeff Carter
Matt Carle
Simon Gagne
Jordan Staal
Evgeni Malkin
Sidney Crosby
Miroslav Satan
Petr Sykora
Marc-Andre Fleury
PITWAS Marc-Andre Fleury 125.00 250.00
Miroslav Satan
Sidney Crosby
Evgeni Malkin
Jordan Staal
Kristopher Letang
Sergei Fedorov
Alexander Ovechkin
Jose Theodore
Nicklas Backstrom
Mike Green (Wa Capitals)
Milan Jurcina
SJSLAK Jarret Stoll 60.00 120.00
Justin Williams
Drew Doughty
Anze Kopitar
Dustin Brown
Alexander Frolov
Joe Thornton
Rob Blake
Patrick Marleau
Evgeni Nabokov
Jonathan Cheechoo
Devin Setoguchi
VANCGY Mike Cammalleri 75.00 150.00
Miikka Kiprusoff
Todd Bertuzzi
Olli Jokinen
Jarome Iginla
Dion Phaneuf
Daniel Sedin
Roberto Luongo
Alexander Edler
Steve Bernier
Kevin Bieksa
Mats Sundin
WASPHI Mike Green (Wa Capitals) 150.00 250.00
Donald Brashear
Nicklas Backstrom
Alexander Ovechkin
Milan Jurcina
Sergei Fedorov
Simon Gagne
Matt Carle
Kimmo Timonen
Jeff Carter
Mike Richards
Joffrey Lupul
BOSMTL1 Tim Thomas 75.00 150.00
Phil Kessel
Carey Price
Andrei Kostitsyn
Mike Komisarek
Alex Kovalev
Andrei Markov
Saku Koivu
Blake Wheeler
Patrice Bergeron
Zdeno Chara
Marc Savard
BOSMTL2 Cam Neely 100.00 200.00
Johnny Bucyk
Steve Shutt
Jean Beliveau
Guy Lafleur
Patrick Roy
Guy Carbonneau
Larry Robinson
Brad Park
Adam Oates
Ray Bourque
Phil Esposito
TORMTL2 Jean Beliveau 75.00 150.00
Guy Lafleur
Steve Shutt
Patrick Roy
Guy Carbonneau
Larry Robinson
Tiger Williams
Doug Gilmour
Ron Ellis
Borje Salming
Darryl Sittler
Lanny McDonald

2009-10 UD Black Signs of History

STATED PRINT RUN 1 SER.#'d SET
NOT PRICED DUE TO SCARCITY

2009-10 UD Black Signs of History Dual

STATED PRINT RUN 1 SER.#'d SET
NOT PRICED DUE TO SCARCITY

2009-10 UD Black Trios Jerseys

STATED PRINT RUN 50 SER.#'d SETS
T3JBEP Patrik Elias 20.00 40.00
Zach Parise
Martin Brodeur
T3JBGW Jay Bouwmeester 15.00 30.00
Mike Green
Shea Weber
T3JCOM Alexander Ovechkin 40.00 80.00
Evgeni Malkin
Sidney Crosby
T3JDKO Pavel Datsyuk 20.00 40.00
Alexander Ovechkin
Ilya Kovalchuk
T3JFBK Dustin Brown 15.00 30.00
Anze Kopitar
Alexander Frolov
T3JGRC Simon Gagne 15.00 30.00
Mike Richards
Jeff Carter
T3JHDZ Pavel Datsyuk 20.00 40.00
Henrik Zetterberg
Marian Hossa
T3JIKP Dion Phaneuf 20.00 40.00
Miikka Kiprusoff
Jarome Iginla
T3JKJS Erik Johnson 20.00 40.00
Steven Stamkos
Patrick Kane
T3JKKP Carey Price 15.00 30.00
Alex Kovalev
Saku Koivu
T3JLGF Roberto Luongo 20.00 40.00
Marc-Andre Fleury
Jean-Sebastien Giguere
T3JLGM Mario Lemieux 40.00 80.00
Wayne Gretzky
Mark Messier
T3JLSS Steven Stamkos 15.00 30.00
Martin St. Louis
Vincent Lecavalier
T3JMCP Bobby Clarke 15.00 30.00
Lanny McDonald
Gilbert Perreault
T3JMDH Henrik Sedin 15.00 30.00
Mats Sundin
Daniel Sedin
T3JNBO Adam Oates 15.00 30.00
Ray Bourque
Cam Neely
T3JNLZ Nikolai Zherdev 15.00 30.00
Henrik Lundqvist
Markus Naslund
T3JPDS Luke Schenn 15.00 30.00
Drew Doughty
Dion Phaneuf
T3JPKK Zach Parise 10.00 25.00
Phil Kessel
Patrick Kane
T3JPMR Larry Robinson 10.00 25.00
Al MacInnis
Denis Potvin
T3JRBH Martin Brodeur 30.00 60.00
Patrick Roy
Ron Hextall
T3JSBK Phil Kessel 10.00 25.00
Marc Savard
Patrice Bergeron
T3JSGH Denis Savard 20.00 40.00
Dale Hawerchuk
Doug Gilmour
T3JSKN Brendan Shanahan 20.00 40.00
Paul Kariya
Rick Nash
T3JSNG Scott Niedermayer 10.00 25.00
Ryan Getzlaf
Teemu Selanne
T3JSSS Jordan Staal 15.00 30.00
Eric Staal
Marc Staal
T3JSTT Jonathan Toews 15.00 30.00
Joe Sakic
Joe Thornton
T3JTKL Miikka Kiprusoff 15.00 30.00
Kari Lehtonen
Vesa Toskala

2009-10 UD Black Trios Patches

STATED PRINT RUN 5 SER.#'d SET
NOT PRICED DUE TO SCARCITY

2009-10 UD Black Trophy Cuts Autographs Quads

STATED PRINT RUN 1 SER.#'d SET
NOT PRICED DUE TO SCARCITY

2009-10 UD Black Trophy Cuts Autographs Triples

STATED PRINT RUN 1 SER.#'d SET
NOT PRICED DUE TO SCARCITY

2001-02 UD Challenge for the Cup

Released in mid-March 2002, this 135-card set carried an SRP of $4.99 per 5-card pack. Cards 91-135 were short printed to 1000 copies each of which 320 copies of each card were graded by Beckett Grading Services.

COMP.SET w/o SP's (90) 20.00 40.00
1 Paul Kariya .40 1.00
2 Jeff Friesen .10 .30
3 Dany Heatley .50 1.25
4 Milan Hnilicka .30 .75
5 Joe Thornton .60 1.50
6 Bill Guerin .30 .75
7 Miroslav Satan .30 .75
8 Martin Biron .30 .75
9 Jarome Iginla .50 1.25

10 Roman Turek .30 .75
11 Craig Conroy .10 .30
12 Jeff O'Neill .10 .30
13 Arturs Irbe .30 .75
14 Tony Amonte .30 .75
15 Steve Sullivan .10 .30
16 Rob Blake .30 .75
17 Joe Sakic .75 2.00
18 Milan Hejduk .40 1.00
19 Chris Drury .30 .75
20 Patrick Roy 2.00 5.00
21 Espen Knutsen .10 .30
22 Ray Whitney .10 .30
23 Pierre Turgeon .30 .75
24 Ed Belfour .40 1.00
25 Mike Modano .60 1.50
26 Sergei Zubov .10 .30
27 Dominik Hasek .75 2.00
28 Steve Yzerman 2.00 5.00
29 Brendan Shanahan .40 1.00
30 Nicklas Lidstrom .40 1.00
31 Luc Robitaille .30 .75
32 Mike Comrie .30 .75
33 Ryan Smyth .30 .75
34 Tommy Salo .30 .75
35 Roberto Luongo .50 1.25
36 Valeri Bure .10 .30
37 Pavel Bure .40 1.00
38 Felix Potvin .40 1.00
39 Jason Allison .10 .30
40 Zigmund Palffy .30 .75
41 Manny Fernandez .30 .75
42 Marian Gaborik .75 2.00
43 Andrew Brunette .10 .30
44 Brian Savage .10 .30
45 Jeff Hackett .10 .30
46 Oleg Petrov .10 .30
47 Cliff Ronning .10 .30
48 Mike Dunham .30 .75
49 Scott Walker .10 .30
50 Martin Brodeur 1.00 2.50
51 Scott Niedermayer .10 .30
52 Scott Gomez .10 .30
53 Patrik Elias .30 .75
54 Alexei Yashin .10 .30
55 Chris Osgood .30 .75
56 Mike Peca .10 .30
57 Mark Messier .40 1.00
58 Theo Fleury .10 .30
59 Eric Lindros .40 1.00
60 Brian Boucher .30 .75
61 John LeClair .40 1.00
62 Jeremy Roenick .50 1.25
63 Keith Primeau .10 .30
64 Michal Handzus .10 .30
65 Claude Lemieux .10 .30
66 Sean Burke .30 .75
67 Alexei Kovalev .30 .75
68 Mario Lemieux 2.50 6.00
69 Johan Hedberg .30 .75
70 Martin Straka .10 .30
71 Owen Nolan .30 .75
72 Evgeni Nabokov .30 .75
73 Teemu Selanne .40 1.00
74 Doug Weight .30 .75
75 Brent Johnson .30 .75
76 Pavol Demitra .30 .75
77 Chris Pronger .30 .75
78 Keith Tkachuk .40 1.00
79 Vincent Lecavalier .40 1.00
80 Brad Richards .30 .75
81 Nikolai Khabibulin .40 1.00
82 Curtis Joseph .40 1.00
83 Alexander Mogilny .30 .75
84 Mats Sundin .40 1.00
85 Trevor Linden .10 .30
86 Markus Naslund .40 1.00
87 Brendan Morrison .30 .75
88 Jaromir Jagr .60 1.50
89 Olaf Kolzig .30 .75
90 Peter Bondra .40 1.00
91 Ilja Bryzgalov RC 2.00 6.00
92 Timo Parssinen RC 1.25 3.00
93 Kevin Sawyer RC 1.25 3.00
94 Brian Pothier RC 1.25 3.00
95 Ilya Kovalchuk RC 10.00 25.00
96 Kamil Piros RC 1.25 3.00
97 Ivan Huml RC 1.25 3.00
98 Jukka Hentunen RC 1.25 3.00
99 Scott Nichol RC 1.25 3.00
100 Erik Cole RC 2.00 5.00
101 Jaroslav Obsut RC 1.25 3.00
102 Vaclav Nedorost RC 1.25 3.00
103 Martin Spanhel RC 1.25 3.00
104 Niko Kapanen RC 1.25 3.00
105 Pavel Datsyuk RC 6.00 15.00
106 Ty Conklin RC 1.25 3.00
107 Niklas Hagman RC 1.25 3.00
108 Kristian Huselius RC 1.25 3.00
109 Jaroslav Bednar RC 1.25 3.00
110 Pascal Dupuis RC 1.25 3.00
111 Mike Matteucci RC 1.25 3.00
112 Nick Schultz RC 1.25 3.00
113 Travis Roche RC 1.25 3.00
114 Martti Jarventie SP 1.25 3.00
115 Martin Erat RC 1.25 3.00
116 Pavel Skrbek RC 1.25 3.00
117 Josef Boumedienne RC 1.25 3.00
118 Andreas Salomonsson RC 1.25 3.00
119 Scott Clemmensen RC 1.25 3.00
120 Mikael Samuelsson RC 1.25 3.00
121 Dan Blackburn RC 1.25 3.00
122 Richard Scott RC 1.25 3.00
123 Radek Martinek RC 1.25 3.00
124 Raffi Torres RC 2.50 6.00
125 Ivan Ciernik RC 1.25 3.00
126 Jiri Dopita RC 1.25 3.00
127 Vaclav Pletka RC 1.25 3.00
128 Krys Kolanos RC 1.25 3.00
129 David Cullen RC 1.25 3.00
130 Jeff Jillson RC 1.25 3.00
131 Mark Rycroft RC 1.25 3.00
132 Ryan Tobler RC 1.25 3.00
133 Nikita Alexeev RC 1.25 3.00
134 Brian Sutherby RC 1.25 3.00
135 Chris Corrinet RC 1.25 3.00

2001-02 UD Challenge for the Cup 500 Game Winner

This 2-card set highlighted the career wins of Patrick Roy. Each card carried a swatch of game-worn jersey. One card also carried an authentic autograph and was serial-numbered to 25. The jersey only card was serial-numbered out of 300. Please note that both cards are numbered 500PR, the "A" on the autograph card is for checklisting only.

500PR Patrick Roy/300 60.00 150.00
500PRA Patrick Roy AU/25 400.00 800.00

2001-02 UD Challenge for the Cup All-Time Lineup

Serial-numbered out of 6, this 6-card set was not priced due to scarcity.

AT1 Bobby Hull
AT2 Wayne Gretzky
AT3 Gordie Howe
AT4 Bobby Orr
AT5 Ray Bourque
AT6 Patrick Roy

2001-02 UD Challenge for the Cup Backstops

Cards from this 10-card goalie set were serial-numbered out of 35 each.

BB1 Roman Turek 12.00 30.00
BB2 Arturs Irbe 12.00 30.00
BB3 Patrick Roy 40.00 100.00
BB4 Dominik Hasek 25.00 60.00
BB5 Tommy Salo 12.00 30.00
BB6 Martin Brodeur 30.00 80.00
BB7 Roman Cechmanek 12.00 30.00
BB8 Evgeni Nabokov 12.00 30.00
BB9 Curtis Joseph 15.00 40.00
BB10 Olaf Kolzig 15.00 40.00

2001-02 UD Challenge for the Cup Century Men

Cards from this 10-card set were serial-numbered to just 100 copies each.

COMPLETE SET (10) 125.00 250.00
CM1 Jeremy Roenick 8.00 20.00
CM2 Joe Sakic 10.00 25.00
CM3 Steve Yzerman 12.50 30.00
CM4 Sergei Fedorov 8.00 20.00
CM5 Luc Robitaille 6.00 15.00
CM6 Mark Messier 6.00 15.00
CM7 Jaromir Jagr 10.00 25.00
CM8 Mario Lemieux 15.00 40.00
CM9 Brett Hull 8.00 20.00
CM10 Pavel Bure 6.00 15.00

2001-02 UD Challenge for the Cup Cornerstones

Cards from this 10-card set were serial-numbered to just 250.

COMPLETE SET (10) 75.00 150.00
CR1 Paul Kariya 1.50 4.00
CR2 Ilya Kovalchuk 8.00 20.00
CR3 Joe Sakic 3.00 8.00
CR4 Mike Modano 2.50 6.00
CR5 Steve Yzerman 6.00 15.00
CR6 Pavel Bure 2.00 5.00
CR7 Mario Lemieux 10.00 25.00
CR8 Chris Pronger 1.25 3.00
CR9 Mats Sundin 1.50 4.00
CR10 Jaromir Jagr 2.50 6.00

2001-02 UD Challenge for the Cup Future Famers

Cards in this 6-card set were serial-numbered to just 25. This set was not priced due to scarcity.

FF1 Joe Sakic
FF2 Patrick Roy
FF3 Brett Hull
FF4 Luc Robitaille
FF5 Steve Yzerman
FF6 Mark Messier

2001-02 UD Challenge for the Cup Jerseys

Inserted at odds of 1:36, this 23-card set consisted of 4 different subsets: Terrific 200, Franchise Players, Then & Now, and the Unstoppable Combos. The Then & Now and the Unstoppable Combos subsets featured two swatches of game used jerseys while the other subsets featured one swatch.

TCJ Curtis Joseph 4.00 10.00
TCO Chris Osgood 4.00 10.00
TDH Dominik Hasek 8.00 20.00
TEB Ed Belfour 6.00 15.00
TFP Felix Potvin 4.00 10.00
TMB Martin Brodeur 12.00 30.00
TMR Mike Richter 4.00 10.00
TPR Patrick Roy SP 20.00 50.00
TSB Sean Burke 4.00 10.00
TTB Tom Barrasso 4.00 10.00
FPDW Doug Weight 4.00 10.00
FPEL Eric Lindros SP 5.00 12.00
FPJA Jason Allison 5.00 12.00
FPJL John LeClair 5.00 12.00
FPML Mario Lemieux 10.00 25.00
FPNL Nicklas Lidstrom 5.00 12.00
FPPF Peter Forsberg 8.00 20.00
FPRB Ray Bourque 8.00 20.00
FPSY Steve Yzerman 10.00 25.00
FPTA Tony Amonte 4.00 10.00
TNAM Al MacInnis Dual 8.00 20.00
TNBS Brendan Shanahan Dual 8.00 20.00
TNCJ Curtis Joseph Dual 8.00 20.00
TNJS Joe Sakic Dual 10.00 25.00
TNKP Keith Primeau Dual 8.00 20.00
TNPR Patrick Roy Dual 15.00 40.00
TNRB Ray Bourque Dual 10.00 25.00
UCLB John LeClair / Brian Boucher 4.00 10.00
UCLL Eric Lindros / Brian Leetch 4.00 10.00
UCMB Mike Modano / Ed Belfour 4.00 10.00
UCPD Zigmund Palffy / Adam Deadmarsh 4.00 10.00
UCSH Joe Sakic / Milan Hejduk 15.00 40.00
UCSJ Mats Sundin / Curtis Joseph 5.00 12.00
UCSY Brendan Shanahan / Steve Yzerman 12.00 30.00

2001-02 UD Challenge for the Cup Jersey Autographs

This 15-card set partially paralleled the base jersey set but also included authentic autographs from the featured players. Single jersey cards were serial-numbered to 75 while dual jersey cards were serial-numbered to 25.

TBE Ed Belfour 20.00 50.00
TBR Martin Brodeur 50.00 100.00
TJO Curtis Joseph 15.00 40.00
TPO Felix Potvin 15.00 40.00
TPR Patrick Roy 75.00 150.00
TRI Mike Richter 15.00 40.00
FPAL Jason Allison 15.00 40.00
FPBO Ray Bourque 25.00 60.00
FPJI Jarome Iginla 25.00 60.00
FPPB Pavel Bure 60.00 120.00
FPWE Doug Weight 15.00 40.00
FPYZ Steve Yzerman 30.00 80.00
TNBO Ray Bourque Dual 40.00 100.00
TNEB Ed Belfour Dual 40.00 100.00
TNJO Curtis Joseph Dual 30.00 80.00
TNKP Keith Primeau Dual 30.00 80.00
TNMA Al MacInnis Dual 30.00 80.00
UCAP Jason Allison / Zigmund Palffy 60.00 120.00
UCBB Ray Bourque / Rob Blake 125.00 250.00
UCLG John LeClair / Simon Gagne 50.00 100.00
UCST Sergei Samsonov / Joe Thornton 50.00 100.00

2002 UD Chicago National Spokesmen

Given away exclusively at the Upper Deck booth during the 2002 Chicago National Convention, this set highlighted player spokesmen from the four major sports. Please note that only the hockey players are listed below.

COMPLETE HOCKEY SET (3) 40.00
N8 Wayne Gretzky 4.80 20.00
N9 Bobby Orr 4.80 20.00
N10 Gordie Howe 4.80 10.00

1998-99 UD Choice

The 1998-99 Upper Deck UD Choice set was issued with a total of 310 cards. The 12-card packs retail for $1.29 each. The set contains the subsets: GM's Choice (221-242), Crease Lightning (244-252), and Jr. Showcase (253-307). The fronts feature color action photos surrounded by a white border.

COMPLETE SET (310) 15.00 30.00
1 Guy Hebert .08 .25
2 Mikhail Shtalenkov .02 .10
3 Josef Marha .02 .10
4 Paul Kariya .10 .30
5 Travis Green .02 .10
6 Steve Rucchin .02 .10
7 Matt Cullen .02 .10
8 Teemu Selanne .10 .30
9 Antti Aalto .02 .10
10 Byron Dafoe .08 .25
11 Ted Donato .02 .10
12 Dimitri Khristich .02 .10
13 Sergei Samsonov .08 .25
14 Jason Allison .02 .10
15 Ray Bourque .20 .50
16 Kyle McLaren .02 .10
17 Cameron Mann .02 .10
18 Shawn Bates .02 .10
19 Joe Thornton .20 .50
20 Vaclav Varada .02 .10
21 Brian Holzinger .02 .10
22 Miroslav Satan .08 .25
23 Dominik Hasek .25 .60
24 Michael Peca .02 .10
25 Erik Rasmussen .02 .10
26 Alexei Zhitnik .02 .10
27 Geoff Sanderson .08 .25
28 Donald Audette .02 .10
29 Derek Morris .02 .10
30 German Titov .02 .10
31 Valeri Bure .02 .10
32 Michael Nylander .02 .10
33 Cory Stillman .02 .10
34 Theo Fleury .02 .10
35 Jarome Iginla .15 .40
36 Gary Roberts .02 .10
37 Jeff O'Neill .02 .10
38 Bates Battaglia .08 .25
39 Keith Primeau .02 .10
40 Sami Kapanen .02 .10
41 Glen Wesley .02 .10
42 Trevor Kidd .08 .25
43 Nelson Emerson .02 .10
44 Daniel Cleary .02 .10
45 Eric Daze .08 .25
46 Chris Chelios .10 .30
47 Gary Suter .02 .10
48 Alexei Zhamnov .02 .10
49 Jeff Hackett .08 .25
50 Dmitri Nabokov .02 .10
51 Tony Amonte .08 .25
52 Jean-Yves Leroux .02 .10
53 Eric Messier .02 .10
54 Patrick Roy .60 1.50
55 Claude Lemieux .02 .10
56 Peter Forsberg .30 .75
57 Adam Deadmarsh .02 .10
58 Valeri Kamensky .02 .10
59 Joe Sakic .25 .60
60 Sandis Ozolinsh .02 .10
61 Jamie Langenbrunner .02 .10
62 Joe Nieuwendyk .08 .25
63 Ed Belfour .10 .30
64 Juha Lind .02 .10
65 Derian Hatcher .02 .10
66 Sergei Zubov .02 .10
67 Darryl Sydor .02 .10
68 Jere Lehtinen .02 .10
69 Mike Modano .20 .50
70 Larry Murphy .08 .25
71 Igor Larionov .02 .10
72 Darren McCarty .02 .10
73 Steve Yzerman .60 1.50
74 Chris Osgood .08 .25
75 Sergei Fedorov .20 .50
76 Brendan Shanahan .10 .30
77 Nicklas Lidstrom .10 .30
78 Vyacheslav Kozlov .02 .10
79 Dean McAmmond .02 .10
80 Roman Hamrlik .02 .10
81 Curtis Joseph .10 .30
82 Ryan Smyth .08 .25
83 Boris Mironov .02 .10
84 Bill Guerin .08 .25
85 Doug Weight .08 .25
86 Janne Niinimaa .02 .10
87 Ray Whitney .02 .10
88 Robert Svehla .02 .10
89 John Vanbiesbrouck .08 .25
90 Scott Mellanby .02 .10
91 Ed Jovanovski .02 .10
92 Dave Gagner .02 .10
93 Dino Ciccarelli .08 .25
94 Rob Niedermayer .02 .10
95 Rob Blake .08 .25
96 Yanic Perreault .02 .10
97 Stephane Fiset .08 .25
98 Luc Robitaille .08 .25
99 Glen Murray .02 .10
100 Jozef Stumpel .08 .25
101 Vladimir Tsyplakov .02 .10
102 Donald MacLean .02 .10
103 Shayne Corson .02 .10
104 Vladimir Malakhov .02 .10
105 Saku Koivu .10 .30
106 Andy Moog .08 .25
107 Matt Higgins RC .08 .25
108 Dave Manson .02 .10
109 Mark Recchi .08 .25
110 Vincent Damphousse .02 .10
111 Brian Savage .02 .10
112 Petr Sykora .02 .10
113 Scott Stevens .08 .25
114 Patrik Elias .08 .25
115 Bobby Holik .02 .10
116 Martin Brodeur .30 .75
117 Doug Gilmour .08 .25
118 Jason Arnott .02 .10
119 Scott Niedermayer .02 .10
120 Brendan Morrison .08 .25
121 Zigmund Palffy .08 .25
122 Trevor Linden .08 .25
123 Bryan Berard .08 .25
124 Zdeno Chara .02 .10
125 Kenny Jonsson .02 .10
126 Robert Reichel .02 .10
127 Bryan Smolinski .02 .10
128 Wayne Gretzky .75 2.00
129 Brian Leetch .10 .30
130 Pat Lafontaine .10 .30
131 Dan Cloutier .02 .10
132 Niklas Sundstrom .02 .10
133 Marc Savard .08 .25
134 Adam Graves .02 .10
135 Mike Richter .10 .30
136 Jeff Beukeboom .02 .10
137 Daniel Goneau .02 .10
138 Shawn McEachern .02 .10
139 Damian Rhodes .08 .25
140 Wade Redden .02 .10
141 Alexei Yashin .02 .10
142 Marian Hossa .10 .30
143 Chris Phillips .02 .10
144 Daniel Alfredsson .08 .25
145 Vaclav Prospal .02 .10
146 Andreas Dackell .02 .10
147 Sean Burke .02 .10
148 Alexandre Daigle .02 .10
149 Rod Brind'Amour .08 .25
150 Chris Gratton .08 .25
151 Paul Coffey .10 .30
152 Eric Lindros .10 .30
153 John LeClair .10 .30
154 Chris Therien .02 .10
155 Keith Carney .02 .10
156 Craig Janney .02 .10
157 Teppo Numminen .02 .10
158 Jeremy Roenick .15 .40
159 Oleg Tverdovsky .02 .10
160 Keith Tkachuk .10 .30
161 Brad Isbister .02 .10
162 Nikolai Khabibulin .08 .25
163 Daniel Briere .02 .10
164 Juha Ylonen .02 .10
165 Tom Barrasso .08 .25
166 Alexei Morozov .02 .10
167 Stu Barnes .02 .10
168 Jaromir Jagr .20 .50
169 Ron Francis .08 .25
170 Peter Skudra .02 .10
171 Robert Dome .02 .10
172 Kevin Hatcher .02 .10
173 Patrick Marleau .02 .10
174 Jeff Friesen .02 .10
175 Owen Nolan .08 .25
176 John MacLean .02 .10
177 Mike Vernon .08 .25
178 Marcus Ragnarsson .02 .10
179 Andrei Zyuzin .02 .10
180 Mike Ricci .08 .25
181 Marco Sturm .02 .10
182 Steve Duchesne .02 .10
183 Brett Hull .15 .40
184 Pierre Turgeon .08 .25
185 Chris Pronger .08 .25
186 Pavol Demitra .08 .25
187 Jamie McLennan .08 .25
188 Al MacInnis .08 .25
189 Jim Campbell .02 .10
190 Geoff Courtnall .02 .10
191 Daren Puppa .08 .25
192 Daymond Langkow .08 .25
193 Stephane Richer .08 .25
194 Paul Ysebaert .02 .10
195 Alexander Selivanov .02 .10
196 Rob Zamuner .02 .10
197 Mikael Renberg .08 .25
198 Mathieu Schneider .02 .10
199 Mike Johnson .02 .10
200 Alyn McCauley .02 .10
201 Sergei Berezin .08 .25
202 Wendel Clark .08 .25
203 Mats Sundin .10 .30
204 Tie Domi .08 .25
205 Jyrki Lumme .02 .10
206 Mattias Ohlund .08 .25
207 Garth Snow .02 .10
208 Pavel Bure .10 .30
209 Dave Scatchard .02 .10
210 Alexander Mogilny .02 .10
211 Mark Messier .10 .30
212 Todd Bertuzzi .02 .10
213 Peter Bondra .08 .25
214 Joe Juneau .08 .25
215 Olaf Kolzig .08 .25
216 Jan Bulis .02 .10
217 Adam Oates .08 .25
218 Richard Zednik .02 .10
219 Calle Johansson .02 .10
220 Phil Housley .02 .10
221 Dominik Hasek GM .10 .30
222 Ray Bourque GM .10 .30
223 Chris Chelios GM .08 .25
224 Paul Kariya GM .10 .30
225 Wayne Gretzky GM .40 1.00
226 Jaromir Jagr GM .10 .30
227 Rob Blake GM .02 .10
228 Adam Foote GM .02 .10
229 Peter Forsberg GM .10 .30
230 Joe Sakic GM .10 .30
231 Mark Recchi GM .02 .10
232 Patrick Roy GM .10 .30
233 Nicklas Lidstrom GM .08 .25
234 Rob Blake GM .02 .10
235 John LeClair GM .10 .30
236 Wayne Gretzky GM .40 1.00
237 Eric Lindros GM .10 .30
238 Brian Leetch GM .02 .10
239 Scott Stevens GM .08 .25
240 Paul Kariya GM .10 .30
241 Peter Forsberg GM .10 .30
242 Teemu Selanne GM .10 .30
243 Patrick Roy CRL .10 .30
244 Dominik Hasek CRL .10 .30
245 Martin Brodeur CRL .10 .30
246 Mike Richter CRL .08 .25
247 John Vanbiesbrouck CRL .08 .25
248 Chris Osgood CRL .08 .25
249 Ed Belfour CRL .10 .30
250 Tom Barrasso CRL .02 .10
251 Curtis Joseph CRL .10 .30
252 Sean Burke CRL .02 .10
253 Josh Holden .02 .10
254 Daniel Tkaczuk .02 .10
255 Manny Malhotra .02 .10
256 Eric Brewer .02 .10
257 Alex Tanguay .08 .25
258 Roberto Luongo .15 .40
259 Vincent Lecavalier .15 .40
260 Mathieu Garon .08 .25
261 Brad Ference .10 .30
262 Jesse Wallin .02 .10
263 Zenith Komarniski .02 .10
264 Sean Blanchard RC .08 .25
265 Cory Sarich .02 .10
266 Mike Van Ryn .02 .10
267 Steve Begin .02 .10
268 Matt Cooke RC .08 .25
269 Daniel Corso .02 .10
270 Brett McLean .02 .10
271 J-P Dumont .02 .10
272 Jason Ward .02 .10
273 Brian Willsie RC .08 .25
274 Matt Bradley RC .02 .10
275 Olli Jokinen .08 .25
276 Teemu Elomo .02 .10
277 Timo Vertala .02 .10
278 Mika Noronen .08 .25
279 Pasi Petrilainen .02 .10
280 Timo Ahmaoja .02 .10
281 Eero Somervuori .02 .10
282 Maxim Afinogenov .30 .75
283 Maxim Balmochnykh .02 .10
284 Artem Chubarov .02 .10
285 Vitali Vishnevsky .02 .10
286 Denis Shvidki .02 .10
287 Dmitri Vlasenkov .02 .10
288 Magnus Nilsson RC .08 .25
289 Mikael Holmqvist RC .08 .25
290 Mattias Karlin RC .02 .10
291 Pierre Hedin .02 .10
292 Henrik Petre .02 .10
293 Johan Forsander .02 .10
294 Daniel Sedin .02 .10
295 Henrik Sedin .02 .10
296 Marcus Nilsson .02 .10
297 Paul Mara .02 .10
298 Brian Gionta RC 1.25 3.00
299 Chris Hajt RC .08 .25
300 Mike Mottau RC .20 .50
301 Jean-Marc Pelletier RC .20 .50
302 David Legwand .20 .50
303 Ty Jones .02 .10
304 Nikos Tselios .02 .10
305 Jesse Boulerice .02 .10
306 Jeff Farkas .02 .10
307 Toby Petersen .02 .10
308 Wayne Gretzky CL .10 .30
309 Patrick Roy CL .08 .25
310 Steve Yzerman CL .08 .25

1998-99 UD Choice Blow-Ups

Inserted as box-toppers in UD choice, these oversized cards resembled the base set but were approximately 5" x 7". Cards were numbered "X of 5".

COMPLETE SET (5) 6.00 15.00
1 Patrick Roy 2.00 5.00
2 Steve Yzerman 2.00 5.00
3 John LeClair .75 2.00
4 Martin Brodeur 1.25 3.00
5 Peter Forsberg 1.50 4.00

1998-99 UD Choice Draw Your Own Trading Card

Inserted one in every pack, this insert asks collectors to submit an 8.5" x 11" piece of paper, their rendering of a trading card of their favorite NHL star. The selected winners' works were featured in the next season's UD Choice Hockey product.

NNO Wayne Gretzky .20 .50

1998-99 UD Choice Hometeam Heroes

This set of 20-cards features members of the Detroit Red Wings. The cards were inserted one-per-pack of UD Choice throughout Michigan at retail outlets.

COMPLETE SET(20) 6.00 12.00
RW1 Steve Yzerman 2.00 5.00
RW2 Sergei Fedorov 1.25 3.00
RW3 Nicklas Lidstrom .40 1.00
RW4 Vyacheslav Kozlov .40 1.00
RW5 Chris Osgood .75 2.00
RW6 Darren McCarty .40 1.00
RW7 Brendan Shanahan 1.25 3.00
RW8 Igor Larionov .20 .50
RW9 Martin Lapointe .20 .50
RW10 Doug Brown .20 .50
RW11 Kirk Maltby .20 .50
RW12 Kris Draper .20 .50
RW13 Tomas Holmstrom .20 .50
RW14 Larry Murphy .20 .50
RW15 Slave Fetisov .20 .50
RW16 Anders Eriksson .20 .50
RW17 Brent Gilchrist .20 .50
RW18 Joey Kocur .20 .50
RW19 Mike Knuble .20 .50
RW20 Kevin Hodson .20 .50

1998-99 UD Choice Mini Bobbing Head

Randomly inserted in packs at a rate of 1:4, this 30-card insert features specially enhanced miniatures that fold into a stand-up figure with a removable bobbing head.

COMPLETE SET (30) 10.00 25.00
BH1 Wayne Gretzky 2.00 5.00
BH2 Keith Tkachuk .30 .75
BH3 Ray Bourque .50 1.25
BH4 Brett Hull .40 1.00
BH5 Jaromir Jagr .50 1.25
BH6 John Leclair .30 .75
BH7 Martin Brodeur .75 2.00
BH8 Eric Lindros .30 .75
BH9 Mark Messier .30 .75
BH10 John Vanbiesbrouck .25 .60
BH11 Paul Kariya .30 .75
BH12 Luc Robitaille .25 .60
BH13 Zigmund Palffy .25 .60
BH14 Peter Forsberg .75 2.00
BH15 Teemu Selanne .30 .75
BH16 Mike Modano .50 1.25
BH17 Mats Sundin .30 .75
BH18 Dominik Hasek .60 1.50
BH19 Joe Sakic .60 1.50
BH20 Rob Blake .25 .60
BH21 Patrick Roy 1.50 4.00
BH22 Sergei Samsonov .25 .60
BH23 Chris Chelios .30 .75
BH24 Brendan Shanahan .30 .75
BH25 Theo Fleury .25 .60
BH26 Ed Belfour .30 .75
BH27 Steve Yzerman 1.50 4.00
BH28 Saku Koivu .30 .75
BH29 Brian Leetch .30 .75
BH30 Pavel Bure .30 .75

1998-99 UD Choice Preview

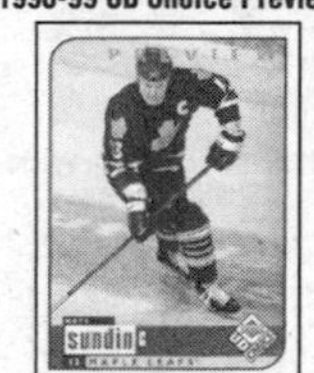

The 1998-99 UD Choice Preview set was issued in one series totaling 60 cards. The 6-card packs retail for $.79 each. Set is skip numbered.

COMPLETE SET (110) 6.00 15.00
219 Calle Johansson .07 .20
1 Guy Hebert .20 .50
3 Josef Marha .07 .20
5 Travis Green .07 .20
7 Matt Cullen .07 .20
9 Antti Aalto .07 .20
11 Ted Donato .07 .20
13 Sergei Samsonov .20 .50
15 Ray Bourque .40 1.00
17 Cameron Mann .07 .20
19 Joe Thornton .40 1.00
21 Brian Holzinger .07 .20
23 Dominik Hasek .50 1.25
25 Erik Rasmussen .07 .20
27 Geoff Sanderson .07 .20
29 Derek Morris .07 .20
31 Valeri Bure .07 .20
33 Cory Stillman .07 .20
35 Jarome Iginla .30 .75
37 Jeff O'Neill .07 .20
39 Keith Primeau .07 .20
41 Glen Wesley .07 .20
43 Nelson Emerson .07 .20
45 Eric Daze .20 .50
47 Gary Suter .07 .20
49 Jeff Hackett .20 .50
51 Tony Amonte .20 .50
53 Eric Messier .07 .20
55 Claude Lemieux .07 .20
57 Adam Deadmarsh .07 .20
59 Joe Sakic .50 1.25
61 Jamie Langenbrunner .07 .20
63 Ed Belfour .25 .60
65 Derian Hatcher .07 .20
67 Daryl Sydor .20 .50
69 Mike Modano .40 1.00

71 Igor Larionov	.07	.20
73 Steve Yzerman	1.25	3.00
75 Sergei Fedorov	.40	1.00
77 Nicklas Lidstrom	.25	.60
78 Slava Kozlov	.20	.50
79 Dean McAmmond	.07	.20
81 Curtis Joseph	.25	.60
83 Boris Mironov	.07	.20
85 Doug Weight	.20	.50
87 Ray Whitney	.07	.20
89 John Vanbiesbrouck	.20	.50
90 Scott Mellanby	.07	.20
91 Ed Jovanovski	.07	.20
93 Dino Ciccarelli	.20	.50
95 Rob Blake	.20	.50
97 Stephane Fiset	.20	.50
99 Glen Murray	.07	.20
101 Vladimir Tsyplakov	.07	.20
103 Shayne Corson	.07	.20
105 Saku Koivu	.25	.60
107 Matt Higgins	.07	.20
109 Mark Recchi	.20	.50
111 Brian Savage	.07	.20
113 Scott Stevens	.20	.50
115 Bobby Holik	.07	.20
117 Doug Gilmour	.20	.50
119 Scott Niedermayer	.07	.20
121 Zigmund Palffy	.20	.50
123 Bryan Berard	.07	.20
125 Kenny Jonsson	.07	.20
127 Bryan Smolinski	.20	.50
129 Brian Leetch	.25	.60
131 Dan Cloutier	.20	.50
133 Marc Savard	.07	.20
135 Mike Richter	.25	.60
137 Daniel Goneau	.07	.20
139 Damian Rhodes	.20	.50
141 Alexei Yashin	.07	.20
143 Chris Phillips	.07	.20
147 Sean Burke	.20	.50
149 Rod Brind'Amour	.20	.50
151 Paul Coffey	.25	.60
153 John LeClair	.25	.60
157 Teppo Numminen	.07	.20
159 Oleg Tverdovsky	.07	.20
161 Brad Isbister	.07	.20
163 Daniel Briere	.07	.20
165 Tom Barrasso	.20	.50
167 Stu Barnes	.07	.20
169 Ron Francis	.20	.50
171 Robert Dome	.07	.20
173 Patrick Marleau	.25	.60
175 Owen Nolan	.20	.50
177 Mike Vernon	.20	.50
179 Andrei Zyuzin	.07	.20
181 Marco Sturm	.20	.50
183 Brett Hull	.30	.75
185 Chris Pronger	.20	.50
187 Jamie McLennan	.20	.50
189 Jim Campbell	.20	.50
190 Geoff Courtnall	.07	.20
191 Daren Puppa	.20	.50
193 Stephane Richer	.20	.50
195 Alexander Selivanov	.07	.20
197 Mikael Renberg	.20	.50
199 Mike Johnson	.07	.20
201 Sergei Berezin	.20	.50
203 Mats Sundin	.25	.60
205 Jyrki Lumme	.07	.20
207 Garth Snow	.20	.50
209 Dave Scatchard	.07	.20
211 Mark Messier	.25	.60
213 Peter Bondra	.25	.60
215 Olaf Kolzig	.07	.20
217 Adam Oates	.20	.50

1998-99 UD Choice Prime Choice Reserve

This hobby-only parallel showcases the same players found in the UD Choice base set, except each card is foil-stamped with the words "Prime Choice Reserve". The set is sequentially numbered to 100.

*VETS: 25X TO 60X BASIC CARDS
*ROOKIES: 25X TO 60X

1998-99 UD Choice Reserve

Randomly inserted in packs at a rate of 1:6, this 310-card parallel showcases the same players found in the UD Choice base set, except each card sports a distinctive foil treatment.

*VETS: 2.5X TO 6X BASIC CARDS
*ROOKIES: 1.5X TO 4X BASIC CARDS
STATED ODDS 1:6

1998-99 UD Choice StarQuest Blue

The 1998-99 UD Choice StarQuest insert set salutes 30 of the NHL's top players with each of four 30-card tiers representing a different insert ratio. The cards feature color action player photos in different colored borders

and with a different number of stars in the left bottom corner according to which tier the card is from. StarQuest Blue has one star and is inserted two per pack; StarQuest Green has two stars with an insertion rate of 1:7; StarQuest Red features three stars and an insertion rate of 1:23; StarQuest Gold is a limited-edition set and displays four stars. Only 100 sequentially numbered Gold sets were made.

COMPLETE SET (30)	8.00	15.00
*GOLD/100: 20X TO 50X BLUE INSERTS		
*GREEN: 1.2X TO 3X BLUE INSERTS		
*RED: 3X TO 8X BLUE INSERTS		
SQ1 Wayne Gretzky	1.25	3.00
SQ2 Pavel Bure	.20	.50
SQ3 Patrick Roy	1.00	2.50
SQ4 Dominik Hasek	.40	1.00
SQ5 Teemu Selanne	.20	.50
SQ6 Sergei Samsonov	.15	.40
SQ7 Brian Leetch	.20	.50
SQ8 Saku Koivu	.20	.50
SQ9 Brendan Shanahan	.20	.50
SQ10 Alexei Yashin	.15	.40
SQ11 Joe Sakic	.40	1.00
SQ12 Patrik Elias	.15	.40
SQ13 Theo Fleury	.15	.40
SQ14 Peter Bondra	.15	.40
SQ15 John LeClair	.20	.50
SQ16 Jaromir Jagr	.30	.75
SQ17 Ed Belfour	.20	.50
SQ18 Steve Yzerman	1.00	2.50
SQ19 Mats Sundin	.20	.50
SQ20 Peter Forsberg	.50	1.25
SQ21 Ray Bourque	.30	.75
SQ22 Brett Hull	.25	.60
SQ23 Martin Brodeur	.50	1.25
SQ24 Mike Modano	.30	.75
SQ25 Paul Kariya	.20	.50
SQ26 Tony Amonte	.15	.40
SQ27 Mike Johnson	.15	.40
SQ28 Eric Lindros	.20	.50
SQ29 Mark Messier	.20	.50
SQ30 Keith Tkachuk	.20	.50

2002 Upper Deck Collectors Club

COMPLETE SET (20)	16.00	40.00
NHL1 Wayne Gretzky	2.00	5.00
NHL2 Gordie Howe	1.20	2.00
NHL3 Bobby Orr	2.00	5.00
NHL4 Ray Bourque	.80	2.00
NHL5 Mario Lemieux	1.60	4.00
NHL6 Patrick Roy	1.60	4.00
NHL7 Steve Yzerman	1.60	4.00
NHL8 Jaromir Jagr	.80	1.50
NHL9 Dominik Hasek	.80	2.00
NHL10 Martin Brodeur	.80	2.00
NHL11 Joe Sakic	.80	2.00
NHL12 Paul Kariya	.80	1.50
NHL13 Teemu Selanne	.40	1.00
NHL14 Chris Pronger	.20	.50
NHL15 Pavel Bure	.40	1.00
NHL16 Peter Forsberg	.80	1.50
NHL17 Nicklas Lidstrom	.40	1.00
NHL18 Ilya Kovalchuk	2.00	3.00
NHL19 Kristian Huselius	.40	.50
NHL20 Dan Blackburn	.80	1.00

2002 Upper Deck Collectors Club Jerseys

One memorabilia card was included in each UD Collector's Club boxed set. The Yzerman features a swatch from a game jersey and appears to be slightly more scarce than the Bourque, which features a practice jersey swatch.

COMPLETE SET (2)	40.00	100.00
RBJ Ray Bourque	16.00	40.00
SYJ Steve Yzerman	30.00	75.00

2002-03 UD Foundations

Released in November 2002, this 167-card set consited of 100 veteran base cards (#1-100), 20 "Speceial Efforts" subset cards (101-121), and 46 "New Foundations" prospect cards (#122-167). All subset cards were serial-numbered out of 1250. Cards 164-167 were available only in packs of UD Rookie Update.

COMP.SET w/o SP's (100)	20.00	40.00
1 Andy Moog	.20	.50
2 Bill Ranford	.20	.50
3 Cam Neely	.25	.60
4 Bobby Orr	1.50	4.00
5 Terry O'Reilly	.12	.30
6 Ray Bourque	.50	1.25
7 Phil Esposito	.60	1.50
8 Clark Gillies	.12	.30
9 Grant Fuhr	.20	.50
10 Dale Hawerchuk	.12	.30
11 Kent Nilsson	.12	.30
12 Willi Plett	.12	.30
13 Al Secord	.12	.30
14 Denis Savard	.20	.50
15 Bob Probert	.12	.30
16 Steve Larmer	.12	.30
17 Patrick Roy	1.25	3.00
18 Ray Bourque	.50	1.25
19 Andy Moog	.20	.50
20 Alex Delvecchio	.25	.60
21 Borje Salming	.20	.50
22 Dino Ciccarelli	.12	.30
23 Gordie Howe	1.25	3.00
24 John Ogrodnick	.12	.30
25 Marcel Dionne	.25	.60
26 Mark Howe	.12	.30
27 Ron Duguay	.12	.30
28 Steve Yzerman	1.25	3.00
29 Andy Moog	.20	.50
30 Bill Ranford	.20	.50
31 Grant Fuhr	.20	.50
32 Mark Messier	.30	.75
33 Marty McSorley	.12	.30
34 Wayne Gretzky	1.50	4.00
35 Glenn Anderson	.12	.30
36 Gordie Howe	1.25	3.00
37 Mark Howe	.12	.30
38 Gordie Howe	1.25	3.00
39 Butch Goring	.20	.50
40 Charlie Simmer	.12	.30
41 Ron Duguay	.12	.30
42 Marcel Dionne	.25	.60
43 Marty McSorley	.12	.30
44 Wayne Gretzky	1.50	4.00
45 Wayne Gretzky	1.50	4.00
46 Brian Bellows	.12	.30
47 Dino Ciccarelli	.12	.30
48 Mike Modano	.40	1.00
49 Brian Bellows	.12	.30
50 Denis Savard	.20	.50
51 Guy Lafleur	.30	.75
52 Mats Naslund	.12	.30
53 Doug Gilmour	.20	.50
54 Patrick Roy	1.25	3.00
55 Rod Langway	.12	.30
56 Ryan Walter	.12	.30
57 Yvan Cournoyer	.25	.60
58 Martin Brodeur	.75	2.00
59 Bob Nystrom	.12	.30
60 Butch Goring	.20	.50
61 Clark Gillies	.12	.30
62 Mike Bossy	.25	.60
63 Glenn Anderson	.12	.30
64 Guy Lafleur	.30	.75
65 Mark Messier	.25	.60
66 Marcel Dionne	.25	.60
67 Phil Esposito	.40	1.00
68 Ron Duguay	.12	.30
69 Steve Larmer	.12	.30
70 Wayne Gretzky	1.50	4.00
71 Brian Propp	.12	.30
72 Jeremy Roenick	.30	.75
73 Mark Howe	.12	.30
74 Ron Hextall	.20	.50
75 Tim Kerr	.12	.30
76 Anton Stastny	.12	.30
77 Dale Hunter	.12	.30
78 Guy Lafleur	.30	.75
79 Ron Hextall	.20	.50
80 Wendel Clark	.20	.50
81 Wilf Paiement	.12	.30
82 Brett Hull	.30	.75
83 Bernie Federko	.12	.30
84 Dale Hawerchuk	.12	.30
85 Grant Fuhr	.20	.50
86 Tony Twist	.12	.30
87 Wayne Gretzky	1.50	4.00
88 Borje Salming	.20	.50
89 Mats Sundin	.25	.60
90 Glenn Anderson	.12	.30
91 Grant Fuhr	.20	.50
92 Wendel Clark	.20	.50
93 Wilf Paiement	.12	.30
94 Harold Snepsts	.12	.30
95 Pavel Bure	.25	.60
96 Tony Tanti	.12	.30
97 Dale Hunter	.12	.30
98 Dino Ciccarelli	.12	.30
99 Rod Langway	.12	.30
100 Dale Hawerchuk	.12	.30
101 Wayne Gretzky SE	3.00	8.00
102 Gordie Howe SE	2.50	6.00
103 Bobby Orr SE	3.00	8.00
104 Gordie Howe SE	2.50	6.00
105 Wayne Gretzky SE	3.00	8.00
106 Wayne Gretzky SE	3.00	8.00
107 Cam Neely SE	.50	1.25
108 Ray Bourque SE	1.00	2.50
109 Phil Esposito SE	1.00	2.50
110 Grant Fuhr SE	.50	1.25
111 Denis Savard SE	.50	1.25
112 Patrick Roy SE	2.50	6.00
113 Steve Yzerman SE	2.50	6.00
114 Marcel Dionne SE	.60	1.50
115 Guy Lafleur SE	.75	2.00
116 Bernie Federko SE	.30	.75
117 Wayne Gretzky SE	3.00	8.00
118 Ray Bourque SE	1.00	2.50
118 Phil Esposito SE	1.00	2.50
119 Mike Bossy SE	.60	1.50
120 Patrick Roy SE	2.50	6.00
121 Bob Nystrom SE	.30	1.25
122 Pasi Nurminen NF	.75	2.00
123 Mark Hartigan NF	.75	2.00
124 Henrik Tallinder NF	.75	2.00
125 Micki Dupont NF RC	1.50	4.00
126 Riku Hahl NF	.75	2.00
127 Andrej Nedorost NF	.75	2.00
128 Ales Pisa NF	.75	2.00
129 Jani Rita NF	.75	2.00
130 Stephen Weiss NF	2.00	5.00
131 Lukas Krajicek NF	.75	2.00
132 Sylvain Blouin NF RC	1.50	4.00
133 Marcel Hossa NF	.75	2.00
134 Adam Hall NF RC	1.50	4.00
135 Jan Lasak NF	.75	2.00
136 Ray Schultz NF RC	1.50	4.00
137 Trent Hunter NF	.75	2.00
138 Martin Prusek NF	.75	2.00
139 Branko Radivojevic NF	.75	2.00
140 Sebastien Centomo NF	.75	2.00
141 Karel Pilar NF	.75	2.00
142 Sebastien Charpentier NF	.75	2.00
143 Stanislav Chistov NF RC	2.00	5.00
144 Alexei Smirnov NF RC	1.50	4.00
145 Joe Thornton SE	1.00	2.50
146 Chuck Kobasew NF RC	1.50	4.00
147 Patrick Roy SE	5.00	12.00
148 Mike Modano SE	2.00	5.00
149 Rick Nash NF RC	6.00	15.00
150 Mike Comrie SE	1.00	2.50
151 Henrik Zetterberg NF RC	6.00	15.00
152 Ales Hemsky NF RC	2.50	6.00
153 Jay Bouwmeester NF RC	2.00	5.00
154 Pavel Bure SE	1.25	3.00
155 Alexander Frolov NF RC	2.50	6.00
156 P-M Bouchard NF RC	2.00	5.00
157 Ron Hainsey NF RC	1.50	4.00
158 Sean Burke SE	1.00	2.50
159 Mario Lemieux SE	3.00	8.00
160 Anton Volchenkov NF RC	1.50	4.00
161 Mats Sundin SE	1.25	3.00
162 Alexander Svitov NF RC	1.50	4.00
163 Steve Eminger NF RC	1.50	4.00
164 Jason Spezza NF RC	6.00	15.00
165 Pascal LeClaire NF RC	2.50	6.00
166 Ari Ahonen NF RC	1.50	4.00
167 Steve Ott NF RC	1.50	4.00

2002-03 UD Foundations 1000 Point Club

This 39-card memorabilia set featured swatches of game jerseys or sticks. Jersey cards were serial-numbered to 110 and stick cards were serial-numbered to 150. Gold jersey parallels numbered to 15 and silver jersey parallels numbered to 85 were also created. Silver prices can be found by using the multipliers below; gold cards are not priced due to scarcity.

*MULT.COLOR SWATCH: .5X TO 1.25X HI		
*SILVER JSY: .5X TO 1.25X BASE HI		
BT Bryan Trottier JSY	5.00	12.00
DC Dino Ciccarelli JSY	4.00	10.00
DE Denis Savard JSY	4.00	10.00
DP Denis Potvin JSY	4.00	10.00
GL Guy Lafleur JSY	4.00	10.00
JB Johnny Bucyk JSY	5.00	12.00
LA Guy Lafleur JSY	4.00	10.00
MB Mike Bossy JSY	6.00	15.00
MG Michel Goulet JSY	4.00	10.00
SY Steve Yzerman JSY	12.50	30.00
WG Wayne Gretzky JSY	25.00	60.00
YZ Steve Yzerman STK	12.50	30.00
AN Glenn Anderson STK	4.00	10.00
AN2 Glenn Anderson STK	4.00	10.00
BE Jean Beliveau STK	8.00	20.00
BO Mike Bossy STK	6.00	15.00
BO1 Ray Bourque STK	8.00	20.00
BO2 Ray Bourque STK	8.00	20.00
BU Johnny Bucyk STK	5.00	12.00
CI Dino Ciccarelli STK	4.00	10.00
DI Marcel Dionne STK	4.00	10.00
DI2 Marcel Dionne STK	4.00	10.00
ES Phil Esposito STK	4.00	10.00
ES2 Phil Esposito STK	4.00	10.00
GA Mike Gartner STK	4.00	10.00
GR Wayne Gretzky STK	20.00	50.00
HA Dale Hawerchuk STK	8.00	20.00
HA2 Dale Hawerchuk STK	8.00	20.00
HO Gordie Howe STK	25.00	60.00
KU Jari Kurri STK	6.00	15.00
KU2 Jari Kurri STK	6.00	15.00
LA1 Guy Lafleur STK	4.00	10.00
LA2 Guy Lafleur STK	4.00	10.00
LA3 Guy Lafleur STK	4.00	10.00
MC Lanny McDonald STK	4.00	10.00
MI Stan Mikita STK	4.00	10.00
PO Denis Potvin STK	4.00	10.00
SA Denis Savard STK	4.00	10.00
TR Bryan Trottier STK	5.00	12.00

2002-03 UD Foundations Calder Winners

Gold parallels of this memorabilia set numbered to 15 and silver parallels numbered to 85 were also created. Silver prices can be found by using the multipliers below; gold cards are not priced due to scarcity.

PRINT RUN 110 SER.#'d SETS		
*SILVER: .5X TO 1.25X BASIC JERSEY		
TBT Bryan Trottier	6.00	15.00
TMB Mike Bossy	8.00	20.00
TPB Pavel Bure	5.00	12.00
TRB Ray Bourque	8.00	20.00
TWP Willi Plett	5.00	12.00

2002-03 UD Foundations Canadian Heroes

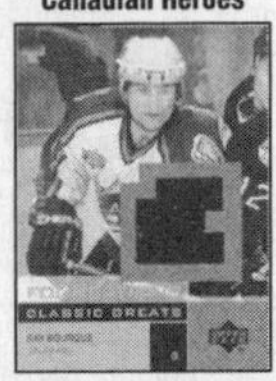

Singles in this 22-card set were serial-numbered to 150. Gold parallels numbered to 50 and silver parallels numbered to 95 were also created. Prices for those parallels can be found by using the multipliers below.

*MULT.COLOR SWATCH: .5X TO 1.25X HI		
*SILVER: .5X TO 1.25X BASIC INSERTS		
*GOLD: .75X TO 2X		
CBO Ray Bourque	8.00	20.00
CBT Bryan Trottier	5.00	12.00
CCN Cam Neely	5.00	12.00
CDC Dino Ciccarelli	5.00	12.00
CGF Grant Fuhr	10.00	25.00
CGL Guy Lafleur	5.00	12.00
CHS Harold Snepsts	5.00	12.00
CJB Johnny Bucyk	5.00	12.00
CMB Mike Bossy	5.00	12.00
CMG Michel Goulet	5.00	12.00
CMH Mark Howe	5.00	12.00
CMM Marty McSorley	5.00	12.00
CPR Patrick Roy	12.50	30.00
CRD Ron Duguay	5.00	12.00
CRO Patrick Roy	12.50	30.00
CRV Rick Vaive	5.00	12.00
CSA Denis Savard	5.00	12.00
CSY Steve Yzerman	12.50	30.00
CTT Tony Twist	5.00	12.00
CWC Wendel Clark	5.00	12.00
CWG Wayne Gretzky	25.00	60.00
CWP Willi Plett	5.00	12.00

2002-03 UD Foundations Classic Greats

Singles in this 17-card memorabilia set were serial-numbered to 150. Gold parallels numbered to 50 and silver parallels numbered to 95 were also created. Prices for those parallels can be found by using the multipliers below.

*SILVER: .5X TO 1.25X BASIC INSERTS		
*GOLD: .75X TO 2X		
GBN Bob Nystrom	5.00	12.00
GBO Ray Bourque	8.00	20.00
GBR Bill Ranford	5.00	12.00
GBS Borje Salming	5.00	12.00
GCN Cam Neely	5.00	12.00
GDC Dino Ciccarelli	5.00	12.00
GDP Denis Potvin	5.00	12.00
GDS Denis Savard	5.00	12.00
GGF Grant Fuhr	10.00	25.00
GGL Guy Lafleur	5.00	12.00
GMB Mike Bossy	5.00	12.00
GMG Michel Goulet	5.00	12.00
GMH Mark Howe	5.00	12.00
GRB Ray Bourque	8.00	20.00
GRD Ron Duguay	5.00	12.00
GWC Wendel Clark	6.00	15.00
GWG Wayne Gretzky	25.00	60.00

2002-03 UD Foundations Defense First

Singles in this 8-card memorabilia set were serial-numbered to 1000. Gold parallels numbered to 15 and silver parallels numbered to 85 were also created. Silver prices can be found by using the multipliers below; gold cards are not priced due to scarcity.

*SILVER: .5X TO 1.25X BASE JSY		
DBO Ray Bourque	8.00	20.00
DBS Borje Salming	5.00	12.00
DDP Denis Potvin	5.00	12.00
DGF Grant Fuhr	10.00	25.00
DHS Harold Snepsts	5.00	12.00
DMH Mark Howe	5.00	12.00
DMM Marty McSorley	5.00	12.00
DRB Ray Bourque	8.00	20.00

2002-03 UD Foundations Lasting Impressions Sticks

STAT.PRINT RUN 150 SER.#'d SETS		
LBN Bob Nystrom	6.00	15.00
LBO Bobby Orr	50.00	125.00
LBR Bill Ranford	6.00	15.00
LCN Cam Neely	6.00	15.00
LJP Jacques Plante	12.50	30.00
LMN Mats Naslund	8.00	20.00
LWC Wendel Clark	6.00	15.00
LYC Yvan Cournoyer	6.00	15.00

2002-03 UD Foundations Milestones

Gold parallels of this memorabilia set numbered to 50 and silver parallels numbered to 95 were also created. Prices for those parallels can be found by using the multipliers below.

PRINT RUN 150 SER.#'d SETS		
*SILVER: .5X TO 1.25X BASE JSY		
*GOLD: .75X TO 2X		
NBO Ray Bourque	8.00	20.00
NBT Bryan Trottier	5.00	12.00
NCN Cam Neely	10.00	25.00
NDP Denis Potvin	5.00	12.00
NGF Grant Fuhr	10.00	25.00
NMB Mike Bossy	5.00	12.00
NPR Patrick Roy	12.50	30.00
NSY Steve Yzerman	12.50	30.00
NWG Wayne Gretzky	25.00	60.00

2002-03 UD Foundations Playoff Performers

Gold parallels of this memorabilia set numbered to 50 and silver parallels numbered to 95 were also created. Prices for those parallels can be found by using the multipliers below.

PRINT RUN 150 SER.#'d SETS		
*SILVER: .5X TO 1.25X BASE JSY		
*GOLD: .75X TO 2X		
PBN Bob Nystrom	5.00	12.00
PBS Borje Salming	5.00	12.00
PBT Bryan Trottier	5.00	12.00
PCN Cam Neely	5.00	12.00
PDC Dino Ciccarelli	5.00	12.00
PGF Grant Fuhr	8.00	20.00
PJB Johnny Bucyk	5.00	12.00
PMB Mike Bossy	5.00	12.00
PMG Michel Goulet	5.00	12.00
PMM Marty McSorley	5.00	12.00
PPB Pavel Bure	5.00	12.00
PPR Patrick Roy	12.50	30.00
PRB Ray Bourque	8.00	20.00
PRO Patrick Roy	12.50	30.00
PSY Steve Yzerman	12.50	30.00
PWG Wayne Gretzky	25.00	60.00

2002-03 UD Foundations Power Stations

Singles in this 11-card set were serial-numbered to 110. Gold parallels onumbered to 15 and silver parallels numbered to 85 were also created. Silver prices can be found by using the multipliers below; gold cards are not priced due to scarcity.

*SILVER: .5X TO 1.25X BASE JSY		
SBN Bob Nystrom	5.00	12.00
SCN Cam Neely	5.00	12.00
SDC Dino Ciccarelli	5.00	12.00
SHS Harold Snepsts	5.00	12.00
SMB Mike Bossy	5.00	12.00
SMH Mark Howe	5.00	12.00
SMM Marty McSorley	5.00	12.00
SRV Rick Vaive	5.00	12.00
STT Tony Twist	5.00	12.00
SWC Wendel Clark	5.00	12.00
SWP Willi Plett	5.00	12.00

2002-03 UD Foundations Signs of Greatness

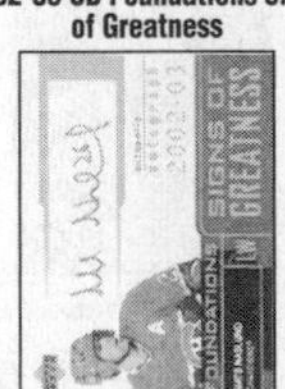

Inserted at 1:53, this 36-card set featured certified player autogrpahs. Known shortprints are listed below.

SGAS Al Secord/26	50.00	100.00
SGBB Brian Bellows/26	25.00	60.00
SGBC Bobby Clarke SP	10.00	25.00
SGBO Bobby Orr/48	200.00	400.00
SGBP Brian Propp/87	12.00	30.00
SGBS Billy Smith	10.00	25.00
SGCG Clark Gillies/26	25.00	60.00
SGCN Cam Neely SP	15.00	40.00
SGCS Charlie Simmer/26	30.00	80.00
SGDC Dino Ciccarelli SP	15.00	40.00
SGDH Dale Hawerchuk	10.00	25.00
SGDP Denis Potvin	10.00	25.00
SGDS Denis Savard SP	20.00	50.00
SGFM Frank Mahovlich SP	10.00	25.00
SGGA Glenn Anderson	10.00	25.00
SGGF Grant Fuhr SP	15.00	40.00
SGGH Gordie Howe/43	75.00	150.00
SGGL Guy Lafleur SP	20.00	50.00
SGGP Gilbert Perreault SP	12.00	30.00
SGJB Jean Beliveau SP	15.00	40.00
SGJBU Johnny Bucyk	10.00	25.00
SGJK Jari Kurri	12.50	30.00
SGLM Lanny McDonald	10.00	25.00
SGMB Mike Bossy	10.00	25.00
SGMD Marcel Dionne SP	10.00	25.00
SGMG Mike Gartner	12.50	30.00
SGMGU Michel Goulet SP	12.00	30.00
SGMN Mats Naslund/87	25.00	60.00
SGPS Peter Stastny	10.00	25.00
SGRA Ray Bourque/23	50.00	100.00
SGRB Ray Bourque/23	50.00	100.00
SGRH Ron Hextall/51	40.00	80.00
SGSL Steve Larmer/26	30.00	80.00
SGSM Stan Mikita SP	10.00	25.00
SGTL Ted Lindsay SP	10.00	25.00
SGWG Wayne Gretzky/46	150.00	400.00

2000-01 UD Heroes

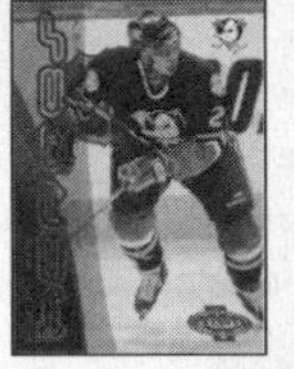

The 2000-01 UD Heroes set consisted of 180 cards. There were 30 rookies and 2 checklist cards. The set design for the card fronts had a photo of the featured player in action and a gold-foil UD Heroes stamp on the bottom of the card by the player name. The card backs used a small photo cut from the card front photo and included the player's vitals and his stats.

COMPLETE SET (180)	30.00	60.00
1 Steve Rucchin	.05	.15
2 Marty McInnis	.05	.15
3 Oleg Tverdovsky	.05	.15
4 Guy Hebert	.15	.40
5 Patrik Stefan	.05	.15
6 Donald Audette	.05	.15
7 Andrew Brunette	.05	.15
8 Jason Allison	.05	.15
9 Sergei Samsonov	.15	.40
10 Joe Thornton	.30	.75
11 Byron Dafoe	.15	.40
12 Dominik Hasek	.40	1.00
13 Miroslav Satan	.15	.40
14 Doug Gilmour	.15	.40
15 J-P Dumont	.05	.15
16 Fred Brathwaite	.15	.40
17 Valeri Bure	.05	.15
18 Marc Savard	.05	.15
19 Cory Stillman	.05	.15
20 Ron Francis	.15	.40
21 Arturs Irbe	.15	.40
22 Jeff O'Neill	.05	.15
23 Sandis Ozolinsh	.05	.15
24 Tony Amonte	.15	.40
25 Jocelyn Thibault	.15	.40
26 Alexei Zhamnov	.05	.15
27 Steve Sullivan	.05	.15
28 Chris Drury	.15	.40
29 Milan Hejduk	.20	.50
30 Alex Tanguay	.15	.40
31 Peter Forsberg	.50	1.25
32 Adam Deadmarsh	.05	.15
33 Marc Denis	.15	.40
34 Ron Tugnutt	.15	.40
35 Tyler Wright	.05	.15
36 David Vyborny	.05	.15
37 Brett Hull	.25	.60
38 Ed Belfour	.20	.50
39 Joe Nieuwendyk	.15	.40
40 Sergei Zubov	.05	.15
41 Jere Lehtinen	.15	.40
42 Sergei Fedorov	.30	.75
43 Martin Lapointe	.05	.15
44 Chris Osgood	.15	.40
45 Pat Verbeek	.05	.15
46 Nicklas Lidstrom	.20	.50
47 Doug Weight	.15	.40
48 Tommy Salo	.15	.40
49 Ryan Smyth	.05	.15
50 Sean Brown	.05	.15
51 Ray Whitney	.05	.15
52 Trevor Kidd	.15	.40
53 Viktor Kozlov	.15	.40
54 Denis Shvidki	.05	.15
55 Rob Blake	.15	.40
56 Zigmund Palffy	.15	.40
57 Luc Robitaille	.15	.40
58 Glen Murray	.05	.15
59 Manny Fernandez	.15	.40
60 Scott Pellerin	.05	.15
61 Maxim Sushinski	.05	.15
62 Saku Koivu	.20	.50
63 Jose Theodore	.25	.60
64 Martin Rucinsky	.05	.15
65 Darryl Shannon	.05	.15
66 Cliff Ronning	.05	.15
67 Randy Robitaille	.05	.15
68 David Legwand	.15	.40
69 Mike Dunham	.05	.15
70 Alexander Mogilny	.15	.40
71 Patrik Elias	.05	.15
72 Bobby Holik	.05	.15
73 Scott Stevens	.15	.40
74 Mariusz Czerkawski	.05	.15
75 Tim Connolly	.05	.15
76 Aris Brimanis	.05	.15
77 John Vanbiesbrouck	.15	.40

78 Brian Leetch .15 .40
79 Mike York .05 .15
80 Theo Fleury .05 .15
81 Mike Richter .20 .50
82 Alexei Yashin .05 .15
83 Ricard Persson .05 .15
84 Radek Bonk .05 .15
85 Patrick Lalime .15 .40
86 Simon Gagne .20 .50
87 Brian Boucher .10 .25
88 Keith Primeau .05 .15
89 Mark Greig .05 .15
90 Teppo Numminen .05 .15
91 Shane Doan .05 .15
92 Keith Tkachuk .10 .25
93 Sean Burke .15 .40
94 Milan Kraft .15 .40
95 Alexei Kovalev .15 .40
96 Jean-Sebastien Aubin .15 .40
97 Martin Straka .05 .15
98 Vincent Damphousse .05 .15
99 Steve Shields .15 .40
100 Brad Stuart .15 .40
101 Owen Nolan .15 .40
102 Chris Pronger .15 .40
103 Pavol Demitra .15 .40
104 Roman Turek .15 .40
105 Pierre Turgeon .15 .40
106 Dan Cloutier .05 .15
107 Brad Richards .15 .40
108 Paul Mara .05 .15
109 Gary Roberts .05 .15
110 Sergei Berezin .05 .15
111 Mats Sundin .20 .50
112 Bryan McCabe .05 .15
113 Henrik Sedin .05 .15
114 Daniel Sedin .05 .15
115 Greg Hawgood .05 .15
116 Adam Oates .05 .15
117 Olaf Kolzig .15 .40
118 Sergei Gonchar .05 .15
119 Bobby Orr 1.25 3.00
120 Cam Neely .20 .50
121 Gilbert Perreault .20 .50
122 Bobby Hull .40 1.00
123 Stan Mikita .30 .75
124 Tony Esposito .30 .75
125 Gordie Howe .40 1.00
126 Wayne Gretzky 1.25 3.00
127 Marcel Dionne .20 .50
128 Maurice Richard .75 2.00
129 Guy Lafleur .30 .75
130 Jean Beliveau .20 .50
131 Bryan Trottier .20 .50
132 Denis Potvin .50
133 Mike Bossy .20 .50
134 Bobby Clarke .30 .75
135 Bernie Parent .20 .50
136 Mario Lemieux 1.25 3.00
137 Michel Goulet .20 .50
138 Frank Mahovlich .20 .50
139 Paul Kariya .20 .50
140 Teemu Selanne .20 .50
141 Patrick Roy 1.00 2.50
142 Joe Sakic .40 1.00
143 Peter Forsberg .50 1.25
144 Ray Bourque .40 1.00
145 Mike Modano .30 .75
146 Steve Yzerman 1.00 2.50
147 Brendan Shanahan .20 .50
148 Pavel Bure .20 .50
149 Martin Brodeur .50 1.25
150 Scott Gomez .05 .15
151 Mark Messier .20 .50
152 Marian Hossa .20 .50
153 John LeClair .10 .25
154 Jeremy Roenick .25 .60
155 Jaromir Jagr .30 .75
156 Jeff Friesen .05 .15
157 Vincent Lecavalier .20 .50
158 Curtis Joseph .20 .50
159 Jonas Ronnqvist RC .20 .50
160 Jeff Cowan RC .20 .50
161 David Aebischer RC 1.25 3.00
162 Rostislav Klesla RC .50 1.25
163 Tyler Bouck RC .20 .50
164 Michel Riesen RC .20 .50
165 Steven Reinprecht RC .20 .50
166 Marian Gaborik RC 2.50 6.00
167 David Gosselin RC .20 .50
168 Scott Hartnell RC .50 1.25
169 Colin White RC .20 .50
170 Rick DiPietro RC 1.25 3.00
171 Johan Holmqvist RC .20 .50
172 Jani Hurme RC .50 1.25
173 Martin Havlat RC 1.50 4.00
174 Justin Williams RC .50 1.25
175 Roman Cechmanek RC .25 .60
176 Roman Simicek RC .20 .50
177 Zdenek Blatny RC .20 .50
178 Jordan Krestanovich RC .20 .50
179 Mark Messier CL .10 .30
180 Wayne Gretzky CL .60 1.50

2000-01 UD Heroes Game-Used Twigs

In 2000-01 UD Heroes inserted the Game-Used Twigs cards in packs at a rate of 1:83. The 20-card set featured a piece of a game-used hockey stick on the card. The card numbering had a 'T' prefix.

*MULT.COLOR STICK: 1X TO 2X
TBH Bobby Hull 12.00 30.00
TBO Bobby Orr 60.00 150.00
TBO Mike Bossy 5.00 12.00
TCJ Curtis Joseph 5.00 12.00
TDH Dominik Hasek 6.00 15.00
TGH Gordie Howe 15.00 40.00
TGP Gilbert Perreault 5.00 12.00
TJJ Jaromir Jagr 6.00 15.00
TJL John LeClair 5.00 12.00
TMB Martin Brodeur 10.00 25.00
TML Mario Lemieux 15.00 40.00
TMM Mark Messier 5.00 12.00
TMS Mats Sundin 5.00 12.00
TPK Paul Kariya 5.00 12.00
TPR Patrick Roy 15.00 40.00
TRB Ray Bourque 6.00 15.00
TSY Steve Yzerman 15.00 40.00
TTF Theo Fleury 5.00 12.00
TTS Teemu Selanne 5.00 12.00
TWG Wayne Gretzky 40.00 100.00

2000-01 UD Heroes Game-Used Twigs Gold

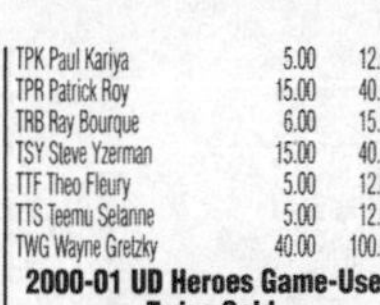

In 2000-01 UD Heroes inserted the Game-Used Twigs Gold cards in packs. The 10-card combo set featured a piece of a game-used hockey stick from both players on the card. The card numbering had a 'C' prefix. The cards were serial numbered to 50.

CBO Ray Bourque 150.00 400.00
Bobby Orr
CFL Theo Fleury 30.00 75.00
John LeClair
CGM Wayne Gretzky 125.00 300.00
Mark Messier
CHB Bobby Hull 60.00 150.00
Mike Bossy
CHP Dominik Hasek 30.00 75.00
Gilbert Perreault
CHY Gordie Howe 150.00 400.00
Steve Yzerman
CJS Curtis Joseph 30.00 75.00
Mats Sundin
CKS Paul Kariya 30.00 75.00
Teemu Selanne
CLJ M.Lemieux/J.Jagr 75.00 200.00
CRB Patrick Roy 60.00 150.00
Martin Brodeur

2000-01 UD Heroes NHL Leaders

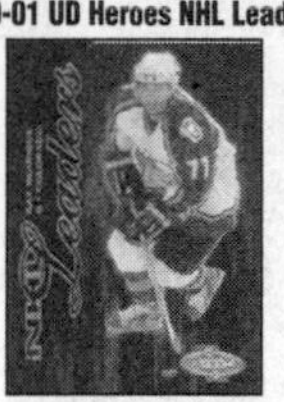

COMPLETE SET (10) 10.00 20.00
STATED ODDS 1:13
L1 Paul Kariya .50 1.25
L2 Ray Bourque 1.25 3.00
L3 Joe Sakic 1.25 3.00
L4 Steve Yzerman 3.00 8.00
L5 Mark Messier .75 2.00
L6 Alexei Yashin .50 1.25
L7 John LeClair .75 2.00
L8 Keith Tkachuk .60 1.50
L9 Jaromir Jagr 1.00 2.50
L10 Al MacInnis .50 1.25

2000-01 UD Heroes Player Idols

Inserted into packs at a rate of 1:23, This 6-card set featured young stars and their idols.

COMPLETE SET (6) 12.00 25.00
PI1 Brendan Shanahan 1.00 2.50
Mark Messier
PI2 M.Brodeur/P.Roy 3.00 8.00
PI3 Maxim Afinogenov 1.00 2.50
Pavel Bure
PI4 Paul Kariya 3.00 8.00
Wayne Gretzky
PI5 Vincent Lecavalier 4.00 10.00
Mario Lemieux
PI6 Roman Turek 1.50 4.00
Dominik Hasek

2000-01 UD Heroes Second Season Heroes

COMPLETE SET (10) 20.00 40.00
STATED ODDS 1:13
SS1 Patrick Roy 4.00 10.00
SS2 Peter Forsberg 2.00 5.00
SS3 Mike Modano 1.00 2.50
SS4 Ed Belfour 1.00 2.50
SS5 Steve Yzerman 4.00 10.00
SS6 Wayne Gretzky 5.00 12.00
SS7 Martin Brodeur 2.00 5.00
SS8 Mark Messier 1.00 2.50
SS9 John LeClair 1.00 2.50
SS10 Jaromir Jagr 1.25 3.00

2000-01 UD Heroes Signs of Greatness

Randomly inserted in 2000-01 UD Heroes packs at a rate of 1:71, this 33-card set featured autograph cards from the top current and former player from the NHL. Please note that at time of release the Orr and Yzerman cards were inserted into packs as redemption cards, also note there are some short prints specified below.

BC Bobby Clarke 10.00 25.00
BH Bobby Hull SP 20.00 50.00
BO Bobby Orr SP 75.00 200.00
BP Bernie Parent 10.00 25.00
BT Bryan Trottier 10.00 25.00
CN Cam Neely 10.00 25.00
DP Denis Potvin 8.00 20.00
FM Frank Mahovlich 10.00 25.00
FP Felix Potvin 12.50 30.00
GH Gordie Howe SP 50.00 100.00
GL Guy Lafleur 15.00 40.00
GP Gilbert Perreault 10.00 25.00
JB Jean Beliveau 10.00 25.00
JL John LeClair 6.00 15.00
JR Jeremy Roenick SP 20.00 50.00
KJ Kenny Jonsson 4.00 10.00
MA Marc Denis 4.00 10.00
MD Marcel Dionne 10.00 25.00
MG Michel Goulet 10.00 25.00
ML Mario Lemieux SP 75.00 150.00
MM Mark Messier SP 50.00 100.00
MS Miroslav Satan 4.00 10.00
MY Mike York 4.00 10.00
PA Pavel Brendl 4.00 10.00
PB Peter Bondra 4.00 10.00
PB Pavel Bure SP 10.00 25.00
RL Roberto Luongo 8.00 20.00
RT Roman Turek 4.00 10.00
SG Scott Gomez 6.00 15.00
SM Stan Mikita 10.00 25.00
SY Steve Yzerman 30.00 80.00
TS Tommy Salo 4.00 10.00
WG Wayne Gretzky SP 100.00 200.00

2000-01 UD Heroes Timeless Moments

COMPLETE SET (10) 10.00 20.00
STATED ODDS 1:13
TM1 Teemu Selanne .60 1.50
TM2 Dominik Hasek 1.25 3.00
TM3 Patrick Roy 3.00 8.00
TM4 Brett Hull .75 2.00
TM5 Pavel Bure .75 2.00
TM6 Martin Brodeur 1.50 4.00
TM7 Mike York .50 1.25
TM8 Brian Boucher .60 1.50
TM9 Jaromir Jagr 1.00 2.50
TM10 Curtis Joseph .60 1.50

2000-01 UD Heroes Today's Snipers

COMPLETE SET (6) 5.00 10.00
STATED ODDS 1:23
TS1 Paul Kariya .60 1.50
TS2 Brendan Shanahan .75 2.00
TS3 Pavel Bure .75 2.00
TS4 John LeClair .75 2.00
TS5 Jaromir Jagr 1.00 2.50
TS6 Mats Sundin .60 1.50

2001-02 Upper Deck Honor Roll

Released in mid-March 2002, this 100-card set carried an SRP of $2.99 fro a 5-card pack. The set consisted of 60 regular cards, 30 shortprinted rookies serial-numbered to 1499 and 10 dual jersey cards serial-numbered to 1000. Dual jersey cards featured one rookie and one veteran player.

COMP.SET w/o SP's (60) 20.00 40.00
1 Bobby Hull .40 1.00
2 Wayne Gretzky .75 2.00
3 Gordie Howe .60 1.50
4 Bobby Orr .60 1.50
5 Ray Bourque .25 .60
6 Patrick Roy .60 1.50
7 Luc Robitaille .10 .25
8 Mario Lemieux .75 2.00
9 Jaromir Jagr .20 .50
10 Chris Pronger .10 .25
11 Rob Blake .10 .25
12 Martin Brodeur .30 .75
13 Paul Kariya .12 .30
14 Joe Sakic .25 .60
15 Pavel Bure .12 .30
16 Nicklas Lidstrom .12 .30
17 Brian Leetch .10 .25
18 Dominik Hasek .25 .60
19 Brendan Shanahan .12 .30
20 Steve Yzerman .60 1.50
21 Teemu Selanne .12 .30
22 Al MacInnis .10 .25
23 Scott Stevens .10 .25
24 Curtis Joseph .12 .30
25 Dany Heatley .15 .40
26 Joe Thornton .20 .50
27 Mark Parrish .10 .25
28 Rostislav Klesla .10 .25
29 Brad Stuart .10 .25
30 Rick DiPietro .10 .25
31 Bobby Hull .40 1.00
32 Wayne Gretzky .75 2.00
33 Gordie Howe .60 1.50
34 Bobby Orr .60 1.50
35 Ray Bourque .25 .60
36 Patrick Roy .60 1.50
37 Luc Robitaille .10 .25
38 Mario Lemieux .75 2.00
39 Jaromir Jagr .20 .50
40 Chris Pronger .10 .25
41 Rob Blake .10 .25
42 Martin Brodeur .30 .75
43 Paul Kariya .12 .30
44 Joe Sakic .25 .60
45 Pavel Bure .15 .40
46 Nicklas Lidstrom .12 .30
47 Brian Leetch .10 .25
48 Dominik Hasek .25 .60
49 Brendan Shanahan .20 .50
50 Steve Yzerman .60 1.50
51 Teemu Selanne .12 .30
52 Al MacInnis .10 .25
53 Scott Stevens .10 .25
54 Curtis Joseph .12 .30
55 Dany Heatley .15 .40
56 Joe Thornton .20 .50
57 Mark Parrish .10 .25
58 Rostislav Klesla .10 .25
59 Brad Stuart .10 .25
60 Rick DiPietro .10 .25
61 Ilja Bryzgalov RC 3.00 8.00
62 Mike Weaver RC 2.00 5.00
63 Kamil Piros RC 2.00 5.00
64 Ron Simon RC 2.00 5.00
65 Ivan Huml RC 2.00 5.00
66 Ales Kotalik RC 2.00 5.00
67 Scott Nichol RC 2.00 5.00
68 Kelly Fairchild RC 2.00 5.00
69 Vaclav Nedorost RC 2.00 5.00
70 Niko Kapanen RC 2.50 6.00
71 Pavel Datsyuk RC 8.00 20.00
72 Sean Avery RC 2.00 5.00
73 Kristian Huselius RC 2.50 6.00
74 Nick Smith RC 2.00 5.00
75 Nick Schultz RC 2.00 5.00
76 Marcel Hossa RC 2.00 5.00
77 Olivier Michaud RC 2.00 5.00
78 Martin Erat RC 2.00 5.00
79 Christian Berglund RC 2.00 5.00
80 Andreas Salomonsson RC 2.00 5.00
81 Radek Martinek RC 2.00 5.00
82 Richard Scott RC 2.00 5.00
83 Ivan Ciernik RC 2.00 5.00
84 Bruno St. Jacques RC 2.00 5.00
85 Dan Focht RC 2.00 5.00
86 Jeff Jillson RC 2.00 5.00
87 Mark Rycroft RC 2.00 5.00
88 Nikita Alexeev RC 2.00 5.00
89 Justin Kurtz RC 2.00 5.00
90 Chris Corrinet RC 2.00 5.00
91 Martin Spanhel 6.00 15.00
Tony Amonte JSY
92 Matt Davidson 8.00 20.00
Chris Drury JSY
93 Jaroslav Bednar 6.00 15.00
Zigmund Palffy JSY
94 Raffi Torres 8.00 20.00
Brendan Shanahan JSY
95 Mikael Samuelsson 6.00 15.00
Sergei Fedorov JSY
96 Dan Blackburn 6.00 15.00
Mike Richter JSY
97 Tomas Divisek 6.00 15.00
John LeClair JSY
98 Jiri Dopita 6.00 15.00
Pavol Demitra JSY
99 Krys Kolanos 6.00 15.00
Mike Modano JSY
100 Ilya Kovalchuk 12.50 30.00
Jaromir Jagr JSY

2001-02 Upper Deck Honor Roll Defense First

Inserted at 1:40, this 6-card set highlights the league's most defensive minded forwards.

COMPLETE SET (6) 10.00 20.00
DF1 Mike Modano 1.25 3.00
DF2 Jere Lehtinen .75 2.00
DF3 Steve Yzerman 4.00 10.00
DF4 Sergei Fedorov 1.25 3.00
DF5 John Madden .75 2.00
DF6 Michael Peca .75 2.00

2001-02 Upper Deck Honor Roll Honor Society

Serial-numbered to just 100 copies each, this 4-card set featured dual game-worn jersey swatches of the featured players. A gold parallel of this set was also created and serial-numbered to just 25 copies each. As of press time, not all cards have been verified.

*GOLD: 1.5X TO 2X BASE HI
HSBB Pavel Bure 20.00 50.00
Valeri Bure
HSCH Roman Cechmanek 20.00 50.00
Dominik Hasek
HSHK Milan Hejduk 20.00 50.00
Paul Kariya
HSRB Patrick Roy 30.00 80.00
Martin Brodeur

2001-02 Upper Deck Honor Roll Jerseys

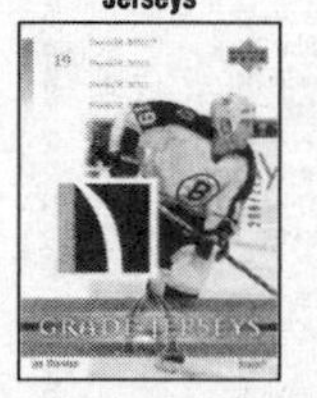

Serial-numbered to 225 copies each, this 31-card set featured game-worn jersey swatches of the featured players. A gold parallel was also created and serial-numbered to just 50 copies each.

*MULT.COLOR SWATCH: 1X TO 1.5X
*GOLD: 1.25X TO 3X BASIC CARD
BB Brian Boucher 4.00 10.00
BH Brett Hull 6.00 15.00
BL Brian Leetch 5.00 12.00
BS Brendan Shanahan 5.00 12.00
CD Chris Drury 4.00 10.00
DL David Legwand 4.00 10.00
DW Doug Weight 4.00 10.00
EB Ed Belfour 5.00 12.00
EL Eric Lindros 5.00 12.00
JH Jochen Hecht 4.00 10.00
JL John LeClair 4.00 10.00
JN Joe Nieuwendyk 4.00 10.00
JS Joe Sakic 8.00 20.00
JT Joe Thornton 6.00 15.00
LI Eric Lindros 5.00 12.00
LR Luc Robitaille 5.00 12.00
MB Martin Brodeur 8.00 20.00
ML Mario Lemieux 12.50 30.00
MM Mike Modano 6.00 15.00
MN Markus Naslund 4.00 10.00
MO Maxime Ouellet 4.00 10.00
MS Miroslav Satan 4.00 10.00
NL Nicklas Lidstrom 4.00 10.00
PB Peter Bondra 4.00 10.00
PD Pavol Demitra 4.00 10.00
PK Paul Kariya 5.00 12.00
RB Ray Bourque 8.00 20.00
RL Roberto Luongo 6.00 15.00
SF Sergei Fedorov 6.00 15.00
SS Sergei Samsonov 5.00 12.00
SU Mats Sundin 5.00 12.00
TC Tim Connolly 4.00 10.00

2001-02 Upper Deck Honor Roll Original Six

This 6-card set was inserted at 1:40 packs.

COMPLETE SET (6) 20.00 40.00
OS1 Bobby Orr 4.00 10.00
OS2 Bobby Hull 2.50 6.00
OS3 Gordie Howe 4.00 10.00
OS4 Patrick Roy 4.00 10.00
OS5 Wayne Gretzky 5.00 12.00
OS6 Curtis Joseph .75 2.00

2001-02 Upper Deck Honor Roll Playoff Matchups

Serial-numbered to 200 copies each, this 6-card set featured dual game-worn jersey swatches of the featured players. A gold parallel was also created and serial-numbered to 25.

*GOLD: 1.5X TO 2X BASE HI
HSHT Brett Hull 12.50 30.00
Keith Tkachuk
HSLH M.Lemieux/D.Hasek 25.00 60.00
HSRB Patrick Roy 30.00 80.00
Martin Brodeur
HSSR Joe Sakic 20.00 50.00
Luc Robitaille
HSSS Mats Sundin 12.50 30.00
Scott Stevens
HSTM Alex Tanguay 12.50 30.00
Al MacInnis

2001-02 Upper Deck Honor Roll Pucks

Serial-numbered to 225 copies each, this 12-card set featured a piece of game-used puck on each card. A gold parallel was also created and serial-numbered to 100 each.

GOLD: 1X TO 2X BASIC CARD
PAK Alexei Kovalev 8.00 20.00
PBL Brian Leetch 8.00 20.00
PJI Jarome Iginla 15.00 40.00
PMH Marian Hossa 10.00 25.00
PMM Mark Messier 10.00 25.00
PMS Mats Sundin 10.00 25.00
PPB Pavel Bure 10.00 25.00
PPE Patrik Elias 8.00 20.00
PPO Peter Bondra 10.00 25.00
PSK Saku Koivu 10.00 25.00
PSS Scott Stevens 8.00 20.00
PVL Vincent Lecavalier 10.00 25.00

2001-02 Upper Deck Honor Roll Sharp Skaters

This 6-card set was inserted at 1:40 packs.

COMPLETE SET (6) 10.00 20.00
SS1 Paul Kariya .75 2.00
SS2 Mike Modano 1.25 3.00
SS3 Sergei Fedorov 1.50 4.00
SS4 Pavel Bure 1.00 2.50
SS5 Marian Hossa .75 2.00
SS6 Simon Gagne .75 2.00

2001-02 Upper Deck Honor Roll Student of the Game

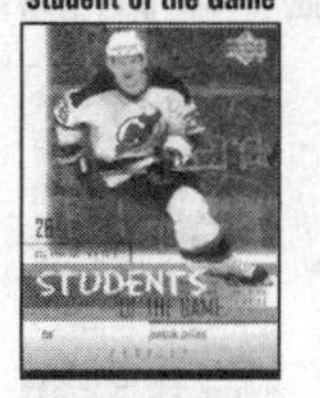

This 6-card set was inserted at 1:40 packs.

COMPLETE SET (6) 10.00 20.00
SG1 Paul Kariya .75 2.00
SG2 Joe Sakic 1.50 4.00
SG3 Mike Modano 1.25 3.00
SG4 Steve Yzerman 4.00 10.00
SG5 Patrik Elias .75 2.00
SG6 Mats Sundin .75 2.00

2001-02 Upper Deck Honor Roll Tough Customers

This 6-card set was inserted at 1:40 packs.

COMPLETE SET (6) 4.00 8.00
TC1 Martin Lapointe .60 1.50
TC2 Rob Blake .60 1.50
TC3 Scott Stevens .60 1.50
TC4 Jeremy Roenick .75 2.00
TC5 Owen Nolan .60 1.50
TC6 Chris Pronger .60 1.50

2001-02 Upper Deck Honor Roll Tribute to 500

This 2-card set featured swatches of game-used jerseys from Patrick Roy. Each card was serial-numbered to 500 copies each.

1 Patrick Roy 40.00 100.00
Montreal
2 Patrick Roy 40.00 100.00
Colorado

2002-03 Upper Deck Honor Roll

This 166-card set consisted of 100 veteran cards, 45 shortprinted rookie cards and 21 Dean's List jersey card rookies. Rookies #101-145 were serial numbered to 1499 each and the jersey cards #146-166 were inserted at 1:48.

COMP.SET w/o SP's (100) 12.50 25.00
*MULT.COLOR JSY: .75X TO 1.5X
1 Paul Kariya .12 .30
2 Jean-Sebastien Giguere .10 .25
3 Ilya Kovalchuk .15 .40
4 Dany Heatley .15 .40
5 Joe Thornton .20 .50
6 Sergei Samsonov .10 .25
7 Miroslav Satan .10 .25
8 Martin Biron .10 .25
9 Chris Drury .10 .25
10 Jarome Iginla .15 .40
11 Ron Francis .10 .25
12 Arturs Irbe .10 .25
13 Tyler Arnason .10 .25
14 Jocelyn Thibault .10 .25
15 Patrick Roy .60 1.50
16 Joe Sakic .25 .60
17 Peter Forsberg .30 .75
18 Rob Blake .10 .25
19 Ray Whitney .08 .20
20 Marc Denis .10 .25
21 Mike Modano .20 .50
22 Marty Turco .10 .25
23 Bill Guerin .10 .25
24 Steve Yzerman .60 1.50
25 Sergei Fedorov .20 .50
26 Nicklas Lidstrom .12 .30
27 Brett Hull .15 .40
28 Curtis Joseph .12 .30
29 Brendan Shanahan .12 .30
30 Mike Comrie .10 .25
31 Tommy Salo .10 .25
32 Roberto Luongo .15 .40
33 Kristian Huselius .08 .20
34 Felix Potvin .12 .30
35 Zigmund Palffy .12 .30
36 Marian Gaborik .25 .60
37 Manny Fernandez .10 .25
38 Jose Theodore .15 .40
39 Saku Koivu .12 .30
40 Patrik Elias .10 .25
41 Martin Brodeur .30 .75
42 David Legwand .10 .25
43 Tomas Vokoun .10 .25
44 Alexei Yashin .08 .20
45 Chris Osgood .10 .25
46 Michael Peca .08 .20
47 Eric Lindros .12 .30
48 Mike Richter .12 .30
49 Pavel Bure .12 .30
50 Marian Hossa .12 .30
51 Daniel Alfredsson .12 .30
52 Jeremy Roenick .15 .40
53 John LeClair .12 .30
54 Roman Cechmanek .10 .25
55 Sean Burke .10 .25
56 Tony Amonte .10 .25
57 Alex Kovalev .10 .25
58 Mario Lemieux .75 2.00
59 Owen Nolan .10 .25
60 Evgeni Nabokov .10 .25
61 Keith Tkachuk .12 .30
62 Brent Johnson .10 .25
63 Nikolai Khabibulin .12 .30
64 Vincent Lecavalier .12 .30
65 Mats Sundin .12 .30
66 Ed Belfour .12 .30
67 Todd Bertuzzi .12 .30
68 Markus Naslund .12 .30
69 Olaf Kolzig .10 .25
70 Jaromir Jagr .20 .50
71 Paul Kariya .12 .30
72 Shawn McEachern .08 .20
73 Joe Thornton .20 .50
74 Stu Barnes .08 .20
75 Craig Conroy .08 .20
76 Ron Francis .10 .25
77 Alexei Zhamnov .08 .20
78 Joe Sakic .25 .60
79 Ray Whitney .08 .20
80 Derian Hatcher .08 .20
81 Steve Yzerman .60 1.50
82 Jason Smith .08 .20
83 Valeri Bure .08 .20
84 Mattias Norstrom .08 .20
85 Andrew Brunette .08 .20
86 Saku Koivu .12 .30
87 Greg Johnson .08 .20
88 Scott Stevens .10 .25
89 Michael Peca .08 .20
90 Brian Leetch .10 .25
91 Daniel Alfredsson .10 .25
92 Keith Primeau .08 .20
93 Teppo Numminen .08 .20
94 Mario Lemieux .75 2.00
95 Owen Nolan .10 .25
96 Chris Pronger .10 .25
97 Vincent Lecavalier .12 .30
98 Mats Sundin .12 .30
99 Markus Naslund .12 .30
100 Steve Konowalchuk .08 .20
101 Alexei Smirnov RC 3.00 8.00
102 Martin Gerber RC 5.00 12.00
103 Kurt Sauer RC 3.00 8.00
104 Tim Thomas RC 5.00 12.00
105 Jordan Leopold RC 3.00 8.00
106 Dany Sabourin RC 3.00 8.00
107 Levente Szuper RC 3.00 8.00
108 Shawn Thornton RC 3.00 8.00
109 Matt Henderson RC 3.00 8.00
110 Lasse Pirjeta RC 3.00 8.00
111 Pascal LeClaire RC 5.00 12.00
112 Dmitri Bykov RC 3.00 8.00
113 Kari Haakana RC 3.00 8.00
114 Craig Andersson RC 6.00 15.00
115 Mike Cammalleri RC 3.00 8.00
116 Stephane Veilleux RC 3.00 8.00
117 Adam Hall RC 3.00 8.00
118 Greg Koehler RC 3.00 8.00
119 Vernon Fiddler RC 3.00 8.00
120 Ray Emery RC 5.00 12.00
121 Eric Godard RC 3.00 8.00
122 Dennis Seidenberg RC 3.00 8.00
123 Jeff Taffe RC 3.00 8.00
124 Dick Tarnstrom RC 3.00 8.00
125 Tom Koivisto RC 3.00 8.00
126 Curtis Sanford RC 3.00 8.00

127 Cody Rudkowsky RC	3.00	8.00
128 Carlo Colaiacovo RC	3.00	8.00
129 Paul Manning RC	3.00	8.00
130 Shaone Morrisonn RC	3.00	8.00
131 Ryan Miller RC	10.00	25.00
132 Jerred Smithson RC	3.00	8.00
133 Alexei Semenov RC	3.00	8.00
134 Michael Leighton RC	10.00	25.00
135 Ian MacNeil RC	3.00	8.00
136 Jared Aulin RC	3.00	8.00
137 Curtis Murphy RC	3.00	8.00
138 Jim Vandermeer RC	3.00	8.00
139 Steve Ott RC	3.00	8.00
140 Brooks Orpik RC	3.00	8.00
141 Jim Fahey RC	3.00	8.00
142 Matt Walker RC	3.00	8.00
143 Rickard Wallin RC	3.00	8.00
144 Tomas Malec RC	3.00	8.00
145 Jonathan Hedstrom RC	3.00	8.00
146 Stanislav Chistov JSY RC	5.00	12.00
147 Chuck Kobasew JSY RC	5.00	12.00
148 Micki Dupont JSY RC	5.00	12.00
149 Jeff Paul JSY RC	5.00	12.00
150 Rick Nash JSY RC	20.00	50.00
151 Henrik Zetterberg JSY RC	15.00	40.00
152 Ales Hemsky JSY RC	10.00	25.00
153 Jay Bouwmeester JSY RC	6.00	15.00
154 Alexander Frolov JSY RC	10.00	25.00
155 P-M Bouchard JSY RC	6.00	15.00
156 Sylvain Blouin JSY RC	5.00	12.00
157 Ron Hainsey JSY RC	5.00	12.00
158 Scottie Upshall JSY RC	5.00	12.00
159 Tomi Pettinen JSY RC	5.00	12.00
160 Jason Spezza JSY RC	15.00	40.00
161 Anton Volchenkov JSY RC	5.00	12.00
162 Radovan Somik JSY RC	5.00	12.00
163 Lynn Loyns JSY RC	5.00	12.00
164 Alexander Svitov JSY RC	5.00	12.00
165 Mikael Tellqvist JSY RC	5.00	12.00
166 Steve Eminger JSY RC	5.00	12.00

2002-03 Upper Deck Honor Roll Grade A Jerseys

*MULT.COLOR SWATCH: .5X TO 1.25X
SINGLE JSY.ODDS 1:26
TRIPLE JSY.ODDS 1:480

GAED Eric Daze	3.00	8.00
GAJJ Jaromir Jagr	5.00	12.00
GAMB Martin Brodeur	8.00	20.00
GAMD Mike Dunham	3.00	8.00
GAMM Mike Modano	4.00	10.00
GAMS Mats Sundin	3.00	8.00
GAOK Olaf Kolzig	3.00	8.00
GAPF Peter Forsberg	5.00	12.00
GAPK Paul Kariya	3.00	8.00
GAPR Patrick Roy	10.00	25.00
GARB Ray Bourque	5.00	12.00
GASA Miroslav Satan	3.00	8.00
GASG Simon Gagne	3.00	8.00
GASK Saku Koivu	3.00	8.00
TJKB Jaromir Jagr	15.00	40.00
Olaf Kolzig		
Peter Bondra		
TPRG Keith Primeau	25.00	60.00
Jeremy Roenick		
Simon Gagne		
TRFS Patrick Roy	50.00	125.00
Peter Forsberg		
Joe Sakic		
TSTM Sergei Samsonov	15.00	40.00
Joe Thornton		
Glen Murray		
TYFS Yzerman/Fedorov/Shanny	30.00	80.00

2002-03 Upper Deck Honor Roll Signature Class

This 19-card autograph set was inserted at 1:480. The Orr and Howe cards were not priced due to scarcity. Printed print runs were provided by Upper Deck.

AS Alexander Svitov	10.00	25.00
BO Bobby Orr/10		
BR Pavel Brendl	6.00	15.00
DH Dany Heatley	10.00	25.00
GH Gordie Howe/9		
HZ Henrik Zetterberg-	75.00	150.00
JB Jay Bouwmeester	12.00	30.00
JL John LeClair	8.00	20.00
JS Jason Spezza	200.00	400.00
MA Maxim Afinogenov	6.00	15.00
MB Martin Brodeur SP	150.00	300.00
MF Manny Fernandez	6.00	15.00
NK Nikolai Khabibulin SP		
PB Pavel Bure	6.00	15.00
PR Patrick Roy	75.00	200.00
SC Stanislav Chistov	12.50	30.00
SY Steve Yzerman	40.00	100.00
TS Teemu Selanne SP		
WG0 Wayne Gretzky/9		

2002-03 Upper Deck Honor Roll Students of the Game

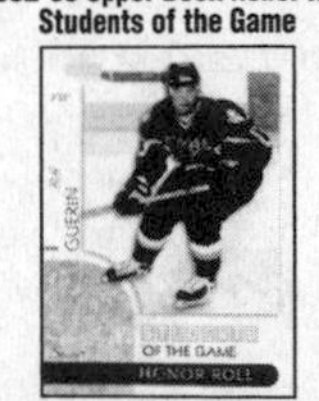

COMPLETE SET (30)	20.00	40.00
STATED ODDS 1:6		
SG1 Paul Kariya	.30	.75
SG2 Dany Heatley	.30	.75
SG3 Joe Thornton	.40	1.00
SG4 Jarome Iginla	.40	1.00
SG5 Chris Drury	.25	.60
SG6 Joe Sakic	.60	1.50
SG7 Patrick Roy	1.50	4.00
SG8 Peter Forsberg	.75	2.00
SG9 Rick Nash	1.25	3.00
SG10 Mike Modano	.50	1.25
SG11 Bill Guerin	.25	.60
SG12 Curtis Joseph	.30	.75
SG13 Steve Yzerman	1.50	4.00
SG14 Sergei Fedorov	.60	1.50
SG15 Mike Comrie	.25	.60
SG16 Marian Gaborik	.30	.75
SG17 Saku Koivu	.30	.75
SG18 Martin Brodeur	.75	2.00
SG19 Alexei Yashin	.25	.60
SG20 Pavel Bure	.50	1.25
SG21 Eric Lindros	.50	1.25
SG22 Jason Spezza	1.00	2.50
SG23 Jeremy Roenick	.40	1.00
SG24 Tony Amonte	.30	.75
SG25 Mario Lemieux	2.00	5.00
SG26 Teemu Selanne	.30	.75
SG27 Keith Tkachuk	.30	.75
SG28 Vincent Lecavalier	.30	.75
SG29 Mats Sundin	.30	.75
SG30 Jaromir Jagr	.75	2.00

2002-03 Upper Deck Honor Roll Team Warriors

COMPLETE SET (15)	10.00	20.00
STATED ODDS 1:12		
TW1 Joe Thornton	.60	1.50
TW2 Jarome Iginla	.50	1.25
TW3 Jeff O'Neill	.30	.75
TW4 Peter Forsberg	1.00	2.50
TW5 Mike Modano	.60	1.50
TW6 Brendan Shanahan	.60	1.50
TW7 Adam Deadmarsh	.30	.75
TW8 Saku Koivu	.40	1.00
TW9 Michael Peca	.30	.75
TW10 Eric Lindros	.40	1.00
TW11 John LeClair	.40	1.00
TW12 Mario Lemieux	2.50	6.00
TW13 Owen Nolan	.30	.75
TW14 Mats Sundin	.40	1.00
TW15 Todd Bertuzzi	.40	1.00

2003-04 Upper Deck Honor Roll

This 191-card set consisted of several subsets: cards 1-90 were base veteran cards; cards 91-110 made up the "Students of the Game" subset and were serial-numbered out of 999; cards 111-125 made up the "Class Reunion" subset and were serial-numbered out of 500; cards 126-132 made up the "Head of the Class" subset and were serial-numbered to 250; cards 133-167 were rookie cards serial-numbered to 800 and cards 133-167 were rookie jersey cards that made up the "Dean's List" subset . The "Dean's List" jerseys were inserted at 1:24. Please note that there is no card #63 and there are two cards numbered #48.

COMPLETE SET (191)		
COMP. SET w/o SP's (90)	8.00	15.00
1 Jean-Sebastien Giguere	.10	.25
2 Sergei Fedorov	.15	.40
3 Dany Heatley	.15	.40
4 Ilya Kovalchuk	.15	.40
5 Felix Potvin	.12	.30
6 Joe Thornton	.20	.50
7 Sergei Samsonov	.10	.25
8 Chris Drury	.10	.25
9 Daniel Briere	.05	.15
10 Jarome Iginla	.15	.40
11 Roman Turek	.10	.25
12 Jamie Storr	.10	.25
13 Ron Francis	.10	.25
14 Kyle Calder	.05	.15
15 Jocelyn Thibault	.10	.25
16 Tyler Arnason	.10	.25
17 David Aebischer	.10	.25
18 Joe Sakic	.25	.60
19 Paul Kariya	.12	.30
20 Peter Forsberg	.30	.75
21 Marc Denis	.10	.25
22 Rick Nash	.15	.40
23 Todd Marchant	.05	.15
24 Bill Guerin	.10	.25
25 Marty Turco	.10	.25
26 Mike Modano	.20	.50
27 Dominik Hasek	.25	.60
28 Henrik Zetterberg	.12	.30
29 Steve Yzerman	.60	1.50
30 Ales Hemsky	.10	.25
31 Mike Comrie	.10	.25
32 Tommy Salo	.10	.25
33 Jay Bouwmeester	.05	.15
34 Olli Jokinen	.10	.25
35 Roberto Luongo	.15	.40
36 Alexander Frolov	.05	.15
37 Jason Allison	.05	.15
38 Roman Cechmanek	.10	.25
39 Zigmund Palffy	.10	.25
40 Manny Fernandez	.10	.25
41 Marian Gaborik	.25	.60
42 Pierre-Marc Bouchard	.05	.15
43 Jose Theodore	.15	.40
44 Marcel Hossa	.05	.15
45 Saku Koivu	.12	.30
46 David Legwand	.10	.25
47 Tomas Vokoun	.10	.25
48 Martin Brodeur	.30	.75
48 Jeff Hackett	.10	.25
49 Scott Gomez	.05	.15
50 Scott Stevens	.10	.25
51 Alexei Yashin	.05	.15
52 Michael Peca	.05	.15
53 Rick DiPietro	.10	.25
54 Alex Kovalev	.10	.25
55 Eric Lindros	.12	.30
56 Mark Messier	.12	.30
57 Mike Dunham	.10	.25
58 Daniel Alfredsson	.10	.25
59 Jason Spezza	.12	.30
60 Marian Hossa	.12	.30
61 Patrick Lalime	.10	.25
62 John LeClair	.12	.30
64 Jeremy Roenick	.15	.40
65 Simon Gagne	.12	.30
66 Mike Johnson	.05	.15
67 Sean Burke	.10	.25
68 Mario Lemieux	.75	2.00
69 Martin Straka	.05	.15
70 Evgeni Nabokov	.10	.25
71 Patrick Marleau	.10	.25
72 Vincent Damphousse	.05	.15
73 Chris Pronger	.10	.25
74 Chris Osgood	.10	.25
75 Doug Weight	.10	.25
76 Keith Tkachuk	.12	.30
77 Pavol Demitra	.10	.25
78 Nikolai Khabibulin	.12	.30
79 Vincent Lecavalier	.12	.30
80 Alexander Mogilny	.10	.25
81 Ed Belfour	.12	.30
82 Mats Sundin	.12	.30
83 Owen Nolan	.10	.25
84 Ed Jovanovski	.10	.25
85 Johan Hedberg	.10	.25
86 Markus Naslund	.12	.30
87 Todd Bertuzzi	.12	.30
88 Jaromir Jagr	.20	.50
89 Olaf Kolzig	.10	.25
90 Peter Bondra	.10	.25
91 Marian Gaborik SOG	1.50	4.00
92 Joe Thornton SOG	1.50	4.00
93 Jean-Sebastien Giguere SOG	.75	2.00
94 Ilya Kovalchuk SOG	1.25	3.00
95 Ales Hemsky SOG	.75	2.00
96 Mike Komisarek SOG	.75	2.00
97 Rick Nash SOG	1.00	2.50
98 Marty Turco SOG	.75	2.00
99 Alexander Frolov SOG	.75	2.00
100 Jay Bouwmeester SOG	.75	2.00
101 Henrik Zetterberg SOG	1.00	2.50
102 Marian Hossa SOG	1.00	2.50
103 Ales Kotalik SOG	.75	2.00
104 Vincent Lecavalier SOG	.75	2.00
105 Pavel Datsyuk SOG	1.00	2.50
106 Andrew Raycroft SOG	.75	2.00
107 Philippe Sauve SOG	.75	2.00
108 Marcel Hossa SOG	.75	2.00
109 Rick DiPietro SOG	.75	2.00
110 Jason Spezza SOG	1.00	2.50
111 Brendan Shanahan CR	1.25	3.00
112 Joe Sakic CR	2.50	6.00
113 Mike Modano CR	2.00	5.00
114 Jeremy Roenick CR	1.50	4.00
115 Teemu Selanne CR	1.25	3.00
116 Mats Sundin CR	1.25	3.00
117 Sergei Fedorov CR	1.50	4.00
118 Owen Nolan CR	1.00	2.50
119 Jaromir Jagr CR	2.00	5.00
120 Peter Forsberg CR	3.00	8.00
121 Markus Naslund CR	1.25	3.00
122 Alexei Yashin CR	.50	1.50
123 Manny Fernandez CR	1.00	2.50
124 Paul Kariya CR	1.25	3.00
125 Saku Koivu CR	1.25	3.00
126 Peter Forsberg HOC	4.00	10.00
127 Steve Yzerman HOC	8.00	20.00
128 Joe Thornton HOC	2.50	6.00
129 Martin Brodeur HOC	6.00	15.00
130 Mario Lemieux HOC	10.00	25.00
131 Ed Belfour HOC	1.50	4.00
132 Mike Modano HOC	2.50	6.00
133 Darryl Bootland RC	2.50	6.00
134 Trevor Daley RC	2.50	6.00
135 John-Michael Liles RC	2.50	6.00
136 Paul Martin RC	2.50	6.00
137 Esa Pirnes RC	2.50	6.00
138 Seamus Kotyk RC	2.50	6.00
139 Pat Rissmiller RC	2.50	6.00
140 Marek Svatos RC	4.00	10.00
141 Maxim Kondratiev RC	2.50	6.00
142 Marek Zidlicky RC	2.50	6.00
143 Matthew Spiller RC	2.50	6.00
144 Nathan Smith RC	2.50	6.00
145 Brent Burns RC	2.50	6.00
146 Boyd Gordon RC	2.50	6.00
147 Andrew Hutchinson RC	2.50	6.00
148 Peter Sarno RC	2.50	6.00
149 Jed Ortmeyer RC	2.50	6.00
150 Cody McCormick RC	2.50	6.00
151 Christoph Brandner RC	2.50	6.00
152 Grant McNeill RC	2.50	6.00
153 Greg Campbell RC	2.50	6.00
154 Tony Salmelainen RC	2.50	6.00
155 Kent McDonell RC	2.50	6.00
156 Martin Strbak RC	2.50	6.00
157 Matt Murley RC	2.50	6.00
158 Rastislav Stana RC	2.50	6.00
159 Karl Stewart RC	2.50	6.00
160 Ryan Malone RC	4.00	10.00
161 Wade Brookbank RC	2.50	6.00
162 Mike Stuart RC	2.50	6.00
163 Sergei Zinovjev RC	2.50	6.00
164 Julien Vauclair RC	2.50	6.00
165 Alan Rourke RC	2.50	6.00
166 John Pohl RC	2.50	6.00
167 Dominic Moore RC	2.50	6.00
168 Peter Sejna JSY RC	3.00	8.00
169 Matt Stajan JSY RC	6.00	15.00
170 Milan Michalek JSY RC	5.00	12.00
171 Pavel Vorobiev JSY RC	4.00	10.00
172 Dan Hamhuis JSY RC	3.00	8.00
173 Chris Higgins JSY RC	8.00	20.00
174 Antti Miettinen JSY RC	3.00	8.00
175 Christian Ehrhoff JSY RC	3.00	8.00
176 Alexander Semin JSY RC	8.00	20.00
177 Antoine Vermette JSY RC	3.00	8.00
178 Travis Moen JSY RC	3.00	8.00
179 Joni Pitkanen JSY RC	3.00	8.00
180 Patrice Bergeron JSY RC	10.00	25.00
181 Jiri Hudler JSY RC	4.00	10.00
182 Marc-Andre Fleury JSY RC	15.00	40.00
183 Dustin Brown JSY RC	3.00	8.00
184 Joffrey Lupul JSY RC	5.00	12.00
185 Tuomo Ruutu JSY RC	4.00	10.00
186 Jordin Tootoo JSY RC	6.00	15.00
187 Eric Staal JSY RC	12.00	30.00
188 Nathan Horton JSY RC	6.00	15.00
189 Tim Gleason JSY RC	3.00	8.00
190 Sean Bergenheim JSY RC	3.00	8.00
191 Matthew Lombardi JSY RC	3.00	8.00

2003-04 Upper Deck Honor Roll Grade A Jerseys

STATED ODDS 1:24		
TRIPLE JSY ODDS 1:480		
GAAY Alexei Yashin	3.00	8.00
GAJI Jarome Iginla	5.00	12.00
GAJT Joe Thornton	5.00	12.00
GAMB Martin Brodeur	8.00	20.00
GAML Mario Lemieux	12.50	30.00
GAMM Mark Messier	8.00	20.00
GAMS Miroslav Satan	4.00	10.00
GASG Simon Gagne	4.00	10.00
GATM Marty Turco	4.00	10.00
GAVL Vincent Lecavalier	4.00	10.00
TBOS Joe Thornton	15.00	40.00
Sergei Samsonov		
Glen Murray		
TCOL Paul Kariya	25.00	60.00
Joe Sakic		
Peter Forsberg		
TDET Dominik Hasek	30.00	80.00
Steve Yzerman		
Henrik Zetterberg		
TNYR Eric Lindros	20.00	50.00
Pavel Bure		
Alex Kovalev		
TTOR Mats Sundin	15.00	40.00
Owen Nolan		
Ed Belfour		
TVAN Markus Naslund	20.00	50.00
Todd Berfuzzi		
Trevor Linden		

2003-04 Upper Deck Honor Roll Signature Class

STATED ODDS 1:480		
PRICED DUE TO SCARCITY		
SC1 David Aebischer/10		
SC2 Todd Bertuzzi/24		
SC3 Martin Brodeur/10		
SC4 Pavel Bure/24		
SC5 Sergei Fedorov/10		
SC6 Marian Gaborik/24		
SC7 Jean-Sebastien Giguere/24		
SC8 Wayne Gretzky/10		
SC9 Scott Hartnell/24		
SC10 Martin Havlat/24		
SC11 Marian Hossa/24		
SC12 Gordie Howe/10		
SC13 Jarome Iginla/24		
SC14 Curtis Joseph/49	20.00	50.00
SC15 Saku Koivu/10		
SC16 Ilya Kovalchuk/10		
SC17 John LeClair/49	12.50	30.00
SC18 Eric Lindros/24		
SC19 Joe Nieuwendyk/24		
SC20 Bobby Orr/10		
SC21 Ziggy Palffy/24		
SC22 Jeremy Roenick/24		
SC23 Patrick Roy/10		
SC24 Sergei Samsonov/49	12.50	30.00
SC25 Jose Theodore/49	20.00	50.00
SC26 Joe Thornton/24		
SC27 Marty Turco/24		
SC28 Adam Hall/24		
SC29 Chuck Kobasew/24		
SC30 Jason Spezza/10		
SC31 Jason Blake/10		
SC32 Mark Parrish/24		

2004-05 UD Legendary Signatures

Released in late-summer 2004, this 100-card set featured some of the more colorful greats of the past.

COMPLETE SET (100)	40.00	80.00
1 Al Iafrate	.30	.75
2 Butch Goring	.30	.75
3 Bernie Federko	.30	.75
4 Bernie Geoffrion	.50	1.25
5 Bill Barber	.30	.75
6 Bill White	.30	.75
7 Bob Nystrom	.30	.75
8 Bobby Clarke	.50	1.25
9 Bobby Hull	1.00	2.50
10 Borje Salming	.40	1.00
11 Brad Marsh	.30	.75
12 Brad Park	.40	1.00
13 Brian Bellows	.30	.75
14 Brian Sutter	.30	.75
15 Bryan Trottier	.40	1.00
16 Cam Neely	.60	1.50
17 Charlie Simmer	.30	.75
18 Clark Gillies	.30	.75
19 Craig Hartsburg	.30	.75
20 Darryl Sittler	.50	1.25
21 Billy Smith	.40	1.00
22 Dave Schultz	.40	1.00
23 Dave Taylor	.30	.75
24 Tiger Williams	.40	1.00
25 Denis Potvin	.40	1.00
26 Dennis Hull	.40	1.00
27 Denis Savard	.50	1.25
28 Dino Ciccarelli	.30	.75
29 Don Cherry	1.00	2.50
30 Don Marcotte	.30	.75
31 Doug Gilmour	.50	1.25
32 Doug Wilson	.30	.75
33 Tony Twist	.30	.75
34 Errol Thompson	.30	.75
35 Frank Mahovlich	.50	1.25
36 Gerry Cheevers	.75	2.00
37 Gilbert Perreault	.50	1.25
38 Glenn Anderson	.30	.75
39 Glenn Hall	.50	1.25
40 Gordie Howe	1.00	2.50
41 Grant Fuhr	.40	1.00
42 Guy Lafleur	1.00	2.50
43 Guy Lapointe	.30	.75
44 Henri Richard	.50	1.25
45 Ian Turnbull	.30	.75
46 Jari Kurri	.50	1.25
47 Jean Beliveau	.60	1.50
48 Brian Propp	.50	1.25
49 Johnny Bower	.50	1.25
50 Johnny Bucyk	.50	1.25
51 Ken Hodge	.30	.75
52 Ken Morrow	.30	.75
53 Lanny McDonald	.40	1.00
54 Gump Worsley	.50	1.25
55 Marcel Dionne	.50	1.25
56 Mark Howe	.30	.75
57 Mike Bossy	.50	1.25
58 Mike Ramsey	.30	.75
59 Neal Broten	.30	.75
60 Pat Stapleton	.30	.75
61 Richard Brodeur	.40	1.00
62 Paul Coffey	.50	1.25
63 Paul Henderson	.40	1.00
64 Peter Mahovlich	.30	.75
65 Phil Esposito	.75	2.00
66 Randy Gregg	.30	.75
67 Red Berenson	.30	.75
68 Reggie Leach	.30	.75
69 Rene Robert	.30	.75
70 Rick Martin	.30	.75
71 Wayne Babych	.30	.75
72 Willi Plett	.30	.75
73 Rod Seiling	.30	.75
74 Ron Ellis	.30	.75
75 Ron Duguay	.30	.75
76 Rogie Vachon	.50	1.25
77 Stan Jonathan	.40	1.00
78 Stan Mikita	.50	1.25
79 Steve Larmer	.40	1.00
80 Steve Shutt	.40	1.00
81 Stu Grimson	.30	.75
82 Ted Lindsay	.50	1.25
83 Terry O'Reilly	.40	1.00
84 Tony Esposito	.50	1.25
85 Tony Tanti	.30	.75
86 Vic Hadfield	.30	.75
87 Wayne Cashman	.30	.75
88 Wayne Gretzky	1.25	3.00
89 Rob McClanahan	.30	.75
90 Yvan Cournoyer	.50	1.25
91 Chris Nilan	.40	1.00
92 Dave Christian	.30	.75
93 Don Awrey	.30	.75
94 J.P. Parise	.30	.75
95 Jim Craig	.40	1.00
96 Keith Brown	.30	.75
97 Ken Linseman	.30	.75
98 Mark Tinordi	.30	.75
99 Harold Snepsts	.30	.75
100 Michel Goulet	.30	.75

2004-05 UD Legendary Signatures AKA Autographs

This 24-card set featured signatures of past greats along with their nicknames. Each card was serial-numbered out of 100.

AKAYC Yvan Cournoyer/Roadrunner	75.00	150.00
AKABN Bob Nystrom/Thor	20.00	50.00
AKASG Stu Grimson/Grim Reaper	20.00	50.00
AKABH Bobby Hull/Golden Jet	75.00	125.00
AKABO Johnny Bower/China Wall	40.00	80.00
AKATW Tony Twist/Twister	20.00	50.00
AKADC Don Cherry/Grapes	40.00	80.00
AKAFM Frank Mahovlich/Big M	25.00	60.00
AKATO Terry O'Reilly/Taz	40.00	80.00
AKAGH Gordie Howe/Mr.Hockey	100.00	175.00
AKAJB John Bucyk/Chief	20.00	50.00
AKADG Doug Gilmour/Killer	25.00	60.00
AKAMJ Mark Johnson/Capt.America	40.00	80.00
AKATE Tony Esposito/Tony O	40.00	80.00
AKAHS Dave Schultz/The Hammer	40.00	80.00
AKAAI Al Iafrate/Wild Thing	20.00	50.00
AKAGL G.Lafleur The Flower	40.00	80.00
AKACN C.Nilan Knuckles	20.00	50.00
AKAJE Jean Beliveau/LeGros Bill	50.00	100.00
AKARD Richard Brodeur/King	20.00	50.00
AKALW Lorne Worsley/Gump	40.00	80.00
AKAHA Glenn Hall/Mr.Goalie	20.00	50.00
AKAGE B.Geoffrion Boom Boom	50.00	100.00
AKAGC Gerry Cheevers/Cheesy	25.00	60.00

2004-05 UD Legendary Signatures Autographs

This 100-card autograph set paralleled the base set with certified player signatures and were inserted one per pack. Known short-print numbers are listed below.

AI Al Iafrate	5.00	12.00
BB Bill Barber	5.00	12.00
BC Bobby Clarke/34	50.00	125.00
BE Brian Bellows	5.00	12.00
BF Bernie Federko	6.00	15.00
BG Butch Goring	6.00	15.00
BH Bobby Hull/81	50.00	125.00
BI Billy Smith	10.00	25.00
BM Brad Marsh	5.00	12.00
BN Bob Nystrom	5.00	12.00
BO Johnny Bower	6.00	15.00
BP Brian Propp	6.00	15.00
BR Brian Sutter	5.00	12.00
BS Borje Salming	15.00	40.00
BT Bryan Trottier	6.00	15.00
BW Bill White	5.00	12.00
CA Cam Neely	15.00	40.00
CG Clark Gillies	5.00	12.00
CH Craig Hartsburg	5.00	12.00
CI Dino Ciccarelli	10.00	25.00
CN Chris Nilan	6.00	15.00
CS Charlie Simmer	5.00	12.00
DC Don Cherry	12.00	30.00
DE Denis Savard	6.00	15.00
DG Doug Gilmour/84	25.00	60.00
DH Dennis Hull	6.00	15.00
DM Don Marcotte	5.00	12.00
DP Denis Potvin	6.00	15.00
DS Darryl Sittler/91	20.00	50.00
DT Dave Taylor	5.00	12.00
DU Ron Duguay	5.00	12.00
DV Dave Christian	5.00	12.00
DW Doug Wilson	5.00	12.00
ET Errol Thompson	5.00	12.00
FM Frank Mahovlich/41	150.00	350.00
GA Glenn Anderson	5.00	12.00
GC Gerry Cheevers	15.00	40.00
GE Bernie Geoffrion	12.00	30.00
GF Grant Fuhr	10.00	25.00
GH Gordie Howe	40.00	100.00
GL Guy Lafleur/25	250.00	400.00
GP Gilbert Perreault/34	100.00	200.00
HA Glenn Hall	12.50	30.00
HR Henri Richard	8.00	20.00
HS Dave Schultz	6.00	15.00
IT Ian Turnbull	5.00	12.00
JB Johnny Bucyk	6.00	15.00
JC Jim Craig	15.00	40.00
JE Jean Beliveau/98	60.00	150.00
JK Jari Kurri	10.00	25.00
JP J.P. Parise	5.00	12.00
KB Keith Brown	5.00	12.00
KH Ken Hodge	5.00	12.00
KL Ken Linseman	5.00	12.00
KM Ken Morrow	5.00	12.00
LA Guy Lapointe	5.00	12.00
LM Lanny McDonald	6.00	15.00
LW Gump Worsley	20.00	50.00
LY Rod Langway	10.00	25.00
MB Mike Bossy	8.00	15.00
MD Marcel Dionne	10.00	25.00
MG Michel Goulet	5.00	12.00
MH Mark Howe	5.00	12.00
MT Mark Tinordi	5.00	12.00
NB Neal Broten	6.00	15.00
PC Paul Coffey	12.50	30.00
PE Phil Esposito/37	100.00	250.00
PH Paul Henderson	10.00	25.00
PM Peter Mahovlich	6.00	15.00
PS Pat Stapleton	5.00	12.00
RA Mike Ramsey	5.00	12.00
RB Red Berenson	5.00	12.00
RD Richard Brodeur	6.00	15.00
RE Ron Ellis	5.00	12.00
RG Randy Gregg	5.00	12.00
RL Reggie Leach	5.00	12.00
RM Rick Martin	5.00	12.00
RR Rene Robert	5.00	12.00
RS Rod Seiling	5.00	12.00
RV Rogie Vachon	10.00	25.00
SC Steve Shutt	6.00	15.00
SG Stu Grimson	5.00	12.00
SJ Stan Jonathan	6.00	15.00
SL Steve Larmer	5.00	12.00
SM Stan Mikita/91	30.00	80.00
SN Harold Snepsts	5.00	12.00
SS Stan Smyl	5.00	12.00
TE Tony Esposito/62	40.00	100.00
TI Tiger Williams	6.00	15.00
TL Ted Lindsay	10.00	25.00
TO Terry O'Reilly/96	25.00	60.00
TT Tony Tanti	5.00	12.00
TW Tony Twist	5.00	12.00
VH Vic Hadfield	5.00	12.00
VP Brad Park	6.00	15.00
WB Wayne Babych	5.00	12.00
WC Wayne Cashman	6.00	15.00
WG Wayne Gretzky	75.00	150.00
WP Willi Plett	5.00	12.00
YC Yvan Cournoyer	6.00	15.00

2004-05 UD Legendary Signatures Buybacks

This 195-card set featured past Upper Deck cards that were "bought back" by UD and autographed by the given player. The original set and print runs are listed below.

PRINT RUNS UNDER 25 NOT PRICED
DUE TO SCARCITY
1 Bernie Federko
UD Legends/2
2 Bernie Federko
UD Legends/2
3 Bernie Geoffrion
UD Retro/2
4 Bernie Geoffrion
UD Legends/1
5 Bill Barber
UD Legends Jerseys/10
6 Bill Barber
UD Legends Milestones/17
7 Billy Smith
UD Legends Sticks/8
8 Billy Smith
UD Vintage Jerseys/38
9 Billy Smith
UD Vintage Jerseys/15
10 Bobby Clarke
UD Century Legends/2
11 Bobby Clarke
UD Retro/4
12 Bobby Clarke
UD Retro Generation/1
13 Bobby Clarke
UD Heroes/2
14 Bobby Clarke
UD Legends/2
15 Bobby Clarke
UD Legends/Enshrined Stars 1
16 Bobby Clarke
UD Legends/4
17 Bobby Clarke
UD Legends Milestones/18
18 Bobby Clarke
UD LegendsSticks/5
19 Bobby Clarke
UD Vintage Jerseys/9
20 Bobby Hull
UD Century Legends/1
21 Bobby Hull
UD Retro/7
22 Bobby Hull
UD Heroes/2
23 Bobby Hull
UD Legends/1
24 Bobby Hull
UD Legends Playoff Heroes/1
25 Bobby Hull
UD Legends/2
26 Bobby Hull
UD Legends/3
27 Bryan Trottier
Upper Deck Locker All-Stars/1
28 Bryan Trottier
Upper Deck/1
29 Bryan Trottier
UD Century Legends/2
30 Bryan Trottier
UD Heroes/3
31 Bryan Trottier
UD Legends/2
32 Bryan Trottier
UD Legends/4
33 Bryan Trottier
UD Legends Milestones/13
34 Bryan Trottier

UD Legends Sticks/6
35 Bryan Trottier
UD Vintage Jerseys/19
36 Cam Neely
Upper Deck/1
37 Cam Neely
Upper Deck/1
38 Cam Neely
Upper Deck SP/1
39 Cam Neely
SP/1
40 Cam Neely
UD Heroes/1
41 Cam Neely
UD Legends/1
42 Cam Neely
UD Legends Jerseys/11
43 Cam Neely
UD Legends Milestones/10
44 Clark Gillies
Upper Deck/1
45 Clark Gillies
UD Legends/1
46 Clark Gillies
UD Legends/5
47 Clark Gillies
UD Legends Jerseys/13
48 Darryl Sittler
Upper Deck AS Sittler/2
49 Darryl Sittler
UD Legends/3
50 Darryl Sittler
UD Legends Sticks/11
51 Denis Potvin
UD Legends Jerseys/8
52 Denis Potvin
UD Legends Milestones/22
53 Denis Potvin
UD Legends Sticks/8
54 Doug Gilmour
Upper Deck/1
55 Doug Gilmour
Upper Deck/1
56 Doug Gilmour
Upper Deck/1
57 Doug Gilmour
Upper Deck/1
58 Doug Gilmour
Upper Deck/1
59 Doug Gilmour
Upper Deck SP/1
60 Doug Gilmour
SP Holoview Collection/1
61 Doug Gilmour
SPx/1
62 Doug Gilmour
SPx Finite/1
63 Doug Gilmour
UD Retro/3
64 Doug Gilmour
UD Heroes/1
65 Doug Gilmour
UD Legends/1
66 Frank Mahovlich
Upper Deck/1
67 Frank Mahovlich
UD Heroes/2
68 Frank Mahovlich
UD Legends/3
69 Frank Mahovlich
UD Legends Sticks/1
70 Gerry Cheevers
UD Retro/4
71 Gerry Cheevers
UD Legends/3
72 Gerry Cheevers
UD Legend/3
73 Gerry Cheevers
UD Legends Jerseys/9
74 Gerry Cheevers
UD Legends Sticks/11
75 Gerry Cheevers
UD Vintage Jerseys/27
76 Gilbert Perreault
UD Heroes/2
77 Gilbert Perreault
UD Heroes Game-Used Twigs/15
78 Gilbert Perreault
UD Legends/1
79 Gilbert Perreault
UD Legends/4
80 Gilbert Perreault
UD Legends Jerseys/10
81 Gilbert Perreault
UD Legends Milestones/21
82 Gilbert Perreault
UD Vintage Jerseys/17
83 Glenn Anderson
Upper Deck/1
84 Glenn Anderson
UD Legends/4
85 Glenn Hall
UD Century Legends/1
86 Glenn Hall
UD Retro/3
87 Gordie Howe
UD All-Star/5
88 Gordie Howe
UD Heroes/1
89 Gordie Howe
UD Legends/2
90 Gordie Howe
UD Legends Enshrined Stars/1
91 Gordie Howe
SP Authentic/1
92 Gordie Howe
UD Legends/3
93 Gordie Howe
UD Legends/3
94 Gordie Howe
UD Legends/3
95 Gordie Howe
UD Legends Fiorentino Collection/1
96 Gordie Howe
UD Legends Jerseys/10
97 Gordie Howe
UD Stanley Cup Champs/1
98 Gordie Howe
UD Vintage Jerseys/1
99 Gordie Howe
SPx/1
100 Gordie Howe
UD Piece of History/1
101 Guy Lafleur
Upper Deck/1
102 Guy Lafleur
UD Heroes/2
103 Guy Lafleur
UD Legends/1
104 Guy Lafleur
UD Legends/2
105 Guy Lafleur
UD Legends/3
106 Guy Lafleur
UD Legends Jerseys/13
107 Guy Lafleur
UD Legends Jerseys/11
108 Guy Lafleur
UD Legends Jerseys/13
109 Guy Lafleur
UD Legends Jerseys/10
110 Guy Lafleur
UD Legends Sticks/13
111 Henri Richard
Upper Deck Locker All-Stars/1
112 Henri Richard
UD Century Legends/1
113 Henri Richard
UD Retro/3
114 Henri Richard
UD Legends/1
115 Jari Kurri
Upper Deck/1
116 Jari Kurri
Upper Deck/1
117 Jari Kurri
Upper Deck/1
118 Jari Kurri
Upper Deck Junior Grade/1
119 Jari Kurri
UD Century Legends/2
120 Jari Kurri
UD Retro/4
121 Jari Kurri
UD Legends/2
122 Jari Kurri
UD Legends/2
123 Jari Kurri
UD Legends/1
124 Jari Kurri
UD Legends Sticks/5
125 Johnny Bucyk
UD Century Legends/1
126 Johnny Bucyk
UD Retro/5
127 Johnny Bucyk
UD Legends/1
128 Johnny Bucyk
UD Legends/2
129 Lanny McDonald
Upper Deck Locker All-Stars/1
130 Lanny McDonald
UD Retro/4
131 Lanny McDonald
UD Legends/1
132 Lanny McDonald
UD Legends/4
133 Lanny McDonald
UD Legends Milestones/18
134 Marcel Dionne
Upper Deck/2
135 Marcel Dionne
UD Century Legends/2
136 Marcel Dionne
UD Retro/3
137 Marcel Dionne
UD Heroes/2
138 Marcel Dionne
UD Legends/1
139 Marcel Dionne
UD Legends/4
140 Marcel Dionne
UD Legends/4
141 Marcel Dionne
UD Legends Sticks/14
142 Michel Goulet
Upper Deck/1
143 Michel Goulet
Upper Deck/1
144 Michel Goulet
UD Heroes/3
145 Michel Goulet
UD Legends/2
146 Michel Goulet
UD Legends/4
147 Mike Bossy
UD Century Legends/1
148 Mike Bossy
UD Retro/3
149 Mike Bossy
UD Heroes/2
150 Mike Bossy
UD Heroes Game-Used/Twigs 3
151 Mike Bossy
UD Legends/2
152 Mike Bossy
UD Legends Legendary Game Jerseys/1
153 Mike Bossy
UD Legends Supreme Milestones/1
154 Mike Bossy
UD Legends/3
155 Mike Bossy
UD Legends/2
156 Mike Bossy
UD Legends Milestones/1
157 Mike Bossy
UD Legends Sticks/18
158 Mike Bossy
UD Foundations/1
159 Neal Broten 30.00 60.00
UD Legends Milestones/37
160 Paul Coffey
Upper Deck Locker All-Stars/1
161 Paul Coffey
Upper Deck/1
162 Paul Coffey
Upper Deck/2
163 Paul Coffey
Upper Deck/1
164 Paul Coffey
Upper Deck/1
165 Paul Coffey
Upper Deck Gretzky's Great Ones/1
166 Paul Coffey
Upper Deck SP/1
167 Paul Coffey
SP/2
168 Paul Coffey
SP Stars/Etoiles/1
169 Paul Coffey
SP Clearcut Winner/1
170 Paul Coffey
UD Century Legends/2
171 Paul Coffey
UD Legends/2
172 Phil Esposito
UD Retro/3
173 Phil Esposito
UD Legends/1
174 Phil Esposito
UD Legends/2
175 Phil Esposito
UD Legends Fiorentino Collection/1
176 Phil Esposito
UD Legends Jerseys/11
177 Phil Esposito
UD Legends Sticks/6
178 Phil Esposito
UD Vintage Jerseys/35
179 Rogie Vachon 40.00 80.00
UD Vintage Jerseys/30
180 Steve Shutt
(UD Legends Milestones/20
181 Steve Shutt
UD Vintage Sweaters of Honor/35
182 Stan Mikita
Upper Deck Locker All-Stars/1
183 Stan Mikita
UD Retro/5
184 Stan Mikita
UD Retro Generation/2
185 Stan Mikita
UD Heroes/1
186 Ted Lindsay
UD Retro/3
187 Ted Lindsay
UD Legends/2
188 Ted Lindsay
UD Legends/4
189 Tony Esposito
UD Retro/4
190 Tony Esposito
UD Heroes/1
191 Tony Esposito
UD Legends/2
192 Tony Esposito
UD Legends Enshrined Stars/1
193 Tony Esposito
UD Legends/2
194 Tony Esposito
UD Legends/2
195 Tony Esposito
UD Legends Sticks/8

2004-05 UD Legendary Signatures HOF Inks

This 14-card set celebrated past great who have been inducted into the Hall of Fame. Each card was serial-numbered to the year in which the star was inducted and those print runs are listed below.

HOFHR Henri Richard/79 20.00 50.00
HOFCG Clarke Gillies/102 15.00 40.00
HOFMB Mike Bossy/91 15.00 40.00
HOFBC Bobby Clarke/87 20.00 50.00
HOFGP Gilbert Perreault/90 15.00 40.00
HOFGF Grant Fuhr/103 25.00 60.00
HOFDS Darryl Sittler/89 20.00 50.00
HOFBO Johnny Bower/76 20.00 50.00
HOFTE Tony Esposito/88 20.00 50.00
HOFJB Johnny Bucyk/81 15.00 40.00
HOFGH Gordie Howe/72 75.00 150.00
HOFHA Glenn Hall/75 30.00 60.00
HOFMD Marcel Dionne/92 20.00 50.00
HOFBI Billy Smith/93 15.00 40.00

2004-05 UD Legendary Signatures Linemates

This 13-card set featured triple autographs of great lines from the past. Each card was serial-numbered to just 50 copies.

BBBCRL Bill Barber/Bobby Clarke
/Reggie Leach 100.00 200.00
BENBCI Bellows/Broten/Ciccarelli 40.00 100.00
BRBFWB Sutter/Federko/Babych 40.00 100.00
CGBTMB Gillies/Trottier/Bossy 75.00 200.00
CSMDDT Charlie Simmer/Marcel Dionne
/Dave Taylor 75.00 175.00
ETDSLM Thompson/Sittler/McDonald 60.00 150.00
GAWGJK Glenn Anderson/Wayne Gretzky
/Jari Kurri 300.00 500.00
RMGPRR Ric Martin/Gilbert Perreault
/Rene Robert 75.00 200.00
SCPMGL Shutt/P.Mahovlich/Lafleur 40.00 100.00
SJDMTO Jonathan/Marcotte/O'Reilly 60.00 120.00
SLDEMG Larmer/Savard/Goulet 40.00 100.00
TISSTT Williams/Smyl/Tanti 40.00 100.00
WCPEKH Wayne Cashman/Phil Esposito
/Ken Hodge 75.00 200.00

2004-05 UD Legendary Signatures Miracle Men

This 18-card set highlighted the 1980 USA Olympic hockey team. Cards were inserted one per US pack.

COMPLETE SET (18) 10.00 20.00
STATED ODDS 1:1 US
USA1 Mike Eruzione 1.50 4.00
USA2 Jim Craig 1.25 3.00
USA3 Rob McClanahan .50 1.25
USA4 Buzz Schneider .50 1.25
USA5 Mark Johnson .60 1.50
USA6 Neal Broten .60 1.50
USA7 Mark Pavelich .50 1.25
USA8 Dave Christian .60 1.50
USA9 Mike Ramsey .50 1.25
USA10 Ken Morrow .50 1.25
USA11 Steve Christoff .50 1.25
USA12 Bill Baker .50 1.25
USA13 Marc Wells .50 1.25
USA14 John Harrington .50 1.25
USA15 Dave Silk .50 1.25
USA16 Steve Janasak .50 1.25
USA17 Eric Strobel .50 1.25
USA18 Bob Suter .50 1.25

2004-05 UD Legendary Signatures Miracle Men Autographs

Inserted at 1:5 packs, this 18-card set featured certified autographs from the 1980 USA Olympic Hockey team. Please note that the Mark Johnson card was issued as a redemption and has yet to be fulfilled though UD states Johnson is committed to signing.

KNOWN PRINT RUNS LISTED BELOW
USASI Dave Silk 12.00 30.00
USAST Steve Christoff 8.00 20.00
USAJC Jim Craig/73 300.00 500.00
USAES Eric Strobel 12.00 30.00
USADV Dave Christian 40.00 80.00
USAJA Steve Janasak 20.00 40.00
USARA Mike Ramsey/97 200.00 300.00
USAKM Ken Morrow 25.00 50.00
USAME Mike Eruzione 40.00 80.00
USABZ Buzz Schneider 8.00 20.00
USAOB Bob Suter 8.00 20.00
USAMP Mark Pavelich 8.00 20.00
USANB Neal Broten/73 500.00 700.00
USAJH John Harrington 8.00 20.00
USARO Rob McClanahan 8.00 20.00
USABI Bill Baker 8.00 20.00
USAMW Marc Wells 8.00 20.00
USAMJ Mark Johnson 20.00 40.00

2004-05 UD Legendary Signatures Rearguard Retrospectives

This 6-card set featured great defensive combinations from the past. Each card carried dual autographs and was limited to 100 copies each.

BMMH Brad Marsh/Mark Howe 12.50 30.00
BSIT Borje Salming/Ian Turnbull 25.00 60.00
CHMT Craig Hartsburg/Mark Tinordi 12.50 30.00
DPKM D.Potvin/K.Morrow 25.00 60.00
DWKB Doug Wilson/Keith Brown 12.50 30.00
PCRG Paul Coffey/Randy Gregg 20.00 50.00

2004-05 UD Legendary Signatures Summit Stars

This 20-card set highlighted the 1972 Canada Cup Canadian team.

COMPLETE SET (20) 10.00 20.00
STATED ODDS 1:1 CANADIAN
CDN1 Phil Esposito 1.00 2.50
CDN2 Paul Henderson .75 2.00
CDN3 Bobby Clarke .60 1.50
CDN4 Yvan Cournoyer .60 1.50
CDN5 Brad Park .50 1.25
CDN6 Dennis Hull .50 1.25
CDN7 J.P. Parise .50 1.25
CDN8 Ron Ellis .50 1.25
CDN9 Gilbert Perreault .60 1.50
CDN10 Frank Mahovlich .60 1.50
CDN11 Peter Mahovlich .50 1.25
CDN12 Bill White .50 1.25
CDN13 Wayne Cashman .50 1.25
CDN14 Stan Mikita .60 1.50
CDN15 Red Berenson .50 1.25
CDN16 Don Awrey .50 1.25
CDN17 Vic Hadfield .50 1.25
CDN18 Rod Seiling .50 1.25
CDN19 Pat Stapleton .50 1.25
CDN20 Tony Esposito .60 1.50

2004-05 UD Legendary Signatures Summit Stars Autographs

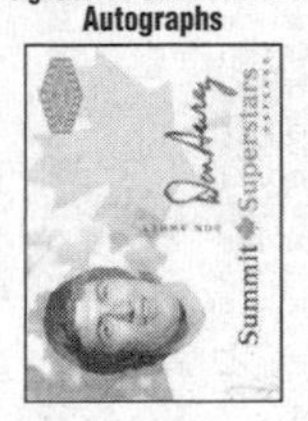

This 20-card set paralleled the basic insert set but carried certified player autographs. Known short-print numbers are listed below.

STATED ODDS 1:5 CANADIAN
KNOWN PRINT RUNS LISTED BELOW
CDNVH Vic Hadfield 6.00 15.00
CDNDH Dennis Hull 6.00 15.00
CDNPH Paul Henderson 12.50 30.00
CDNBW Bill White 6.00 15.00
CDNYC Yvan Cournoyer 12.50 30.00
CDNDA Don Awrey 6.00 15.00
CDNGP Gilbert Perreault/48 60.00 150.00
CDNPE Phil Esposito/48 100.00 250.00
CDNFM Frank Mahovlich/48 100.00 200.00
CDNSM Stan Mikita/97 50.00 125.00
CDNPM Pete Mahovlich 6.00 15.00
CDNRS Rod Seiling 6.00 15.00
CDNPS Pat Stapleton 6.00 15.00
CDNRB Red Berenson 6.00 15.00
CDNBP Brad Park 12.50 30.00
CDNTE Tony Esposito/24 250.00 500.00
CDNRE Ron Ellis 6.00 15.00
CDNWC Wayne Cashman 6.00 15.00
CDNJP J.P. Parise 6.00 15.00
CDNBC Bobby Clarke/73 75.00 150.00

2004-05 UD Legends Classics

Released in late-2004, this 100-card set featured past greats of the NHL.

COMPLETE SET (100) 20.00 40.00
1 Al Iafrate .20 .50
2 Andy Bathgate .30 .75
3 Bernie Geoffrion .30 .75
4 Bill Barber .20 .50
5 Bob Cole .20 .50
6 Bob Nystrom .20 .50
7 Bobby Clarke .40 1.00
8 Bobby Hull .60 1.50
9 Brad Park .25 .60
10 Bryan Trottier .25 .60
11 Butch Goring .20 .50
12 Cam Neely .40 1.00
13 Clark Gillies .25 .60
14 Tiger Williams .25 .60
15 Dave Schultz .25 .60
16 Dave Taylor .20 .50
17 Derek Sanderson .20 .50
18 Dickie Moore .25 .60
19 Don Cherry .60 1.50
20 Doug Wilson .20 .50
21 Frank Mahovlich .30 .75
22 Fred Cusick .20 .50
23 Gerry Cheevers .25 .60
24 Gilbert Perreault .30 .75
25 Glenn Anderson .20 .50
26 Glenn Hall .30 .75
27 Gordie Howe .60 1.50
28 Grant Fuhr .40 1.00
29 Guy Lafleur .50 1.25
30 Jari Kurri .20 .50
31 Jean Beliveau .50 1.25
32 Johnny Bower .30 .75
33 Johnny Bucyk .30 .75
34 Ken Hodge .20 .50
35 Ken Morrow .20 .50
36 Lanny McDonald .25 .60
37 Larry Murphy .20 .50
38 Gump Worsley .30 .75
39 Marcel Dionne .30 .75
40 Mike Bossy .30 .75
41 Patrick Roy .75 2.00
42 Paul Coffey .30 .75
43 Paul Henderson .25 .60
44 Phil Esposito .50 1.25
45 Phil Esposito .50 1.25
46 Red Kelly .20 .50
47 Reggie Leach .20 .50
48 Rene Robert .20 .50
49 Rick Martin .20 .50
50 Stan Mikita .30 .75
51 Ted Lindsay .30 .75
52 Tony Esposito .30 .75
53 Wayne Cashman .20 .50
54 Wayne Gretzky 1.00 2.50
55 Darryl Sittler .30 .75
56 Gordie Howe .60 1.50
57 Gordie Howe .60 1.50
58 Paul Henderson .25 .60
59 Darryl Sittler .30 .75
60 Mike Bossy .30 .75
61 Tiger Williams .25 .60
62 Patrick Roy .75 2.00
63 Paul Coffey .30 .75
64 Marcel Dionne .30 .75
65 Mike Bossy .30 .75
66 Bobby Hull .60 1.50
67 Jari Kurri .30 .75
68 Bryan Trottier .25 .60
69 Phil Esposito .50 1.25
70 Bobby Clarke .40 1.00
71 Jean Beliveau .50 1.25
72 Stan Mikita .30 .75
73 Gilbert Perreault .30 .75
74 Glenn Hall .30 .75
75 Guy Lafleur .50 1.25
76 Ken Morrow .20 .50
77 Tony Esposito .30 .75
78 Johnny Bower .30 .75
79 Wayne Gretzky 1.00 2.50
80 Wayne Gretzky 1.00 2.50
81 Gordie Howe .60 1.50
82 Wayne Gretzky 1.00 2.50
83 Bobby Hull .60 1.50
84 Bobby Clarke .40 1.00
85 Gilbert Perreault .30 .75
86 Darryl Sittler .30 .75
87 Guy Lafleur .50 1.25
88 Glenn Hall .30 .75
89 Andy Bathgate .30 .75
90 Red Kelly .30 .75
91 Tony Esposito .30 .75
92 Jean Beliveau .50 1.25
93 Grant Fuhr .40 1.00
94 Frank Mahovlich .30 .75
95 Gerry Cheevers .25 .60
96 Phil Esposito .50 1.25
97 Bryan Trottier .25 .60
98 Dickie Moore .20 .50
99 Stan Mikita .30 .75
100 Marcel Dionne .30 .75

2004-05 UD Legends Classics Gold

COMMON GRETZKY 40.00 100.00
*GOLD: 10X TO 25X BASE HI
GOLD PRINT RUN 25 SER.'d SETS

2004-05 UD Legends Classics Platinum

PLATINUM PRINT RUN 10 SER.#'d SETS
NOT PRICED DUE TO SCARCITY

2004-05 UD Legends Classics Silver

COMMON GRETZKY 20.00 50.00
*SILVER: 5X TO 12X BASE HI
SILVER PRINT RUN 75 SER.#'d SETS

2004-05 UD Legends Classics Jacket Redemptions

Cards from this set were redeemable for Mitchell & Ness throwback jackets of the teams represented on the card.

STATED ODDS 1:384
JK1 Boston Bruins
JK2 Chicago Blackhawks 150.00 300.00
JK3 Detroit Red Wings
JK4 Montreal Canadiens 125.00 250.00
JK5 Toronto Maple Leafs 150.00 300.00

2004-05 UD Legends Classics Jersey Redemptions

Cards from this set were redeemable for Mitchell & Ness throwback jerseys of the players represented on the card. Please note, some cards have yet to be verified.

STATED ODDS 1:384
JY1 Henri Richard 60.00 150.00
JY2 Jean Beliveau 150.00 300.00
JY3 Maurice Richard 150.00 300.00
JY4 Dickie Moore
JY5 Doug Harvey 60.00 150.00
JY6 Jacques Plante 125.00 250.00
JY7 Bernie Geoffrion 60.00 150.00
JY8 Frank Mahovlich
JY9 T.Sawchuk TOR 175.00 350.00
JY10 Tim Horton 150.00 300.00
JY11 Johnny Bower 60.00 150.00
JY12 Red Kelly 75.00 150.00
JY13 Eddie Shack 60.00 150.00
JY14 Dave Keon 60.00 150.00
JY15 Marcel Pronovost 60.00 150.00
JY16 W.Gretzky EDM 300.00 700.00
JY17 Stan Mikita
JY18 Bobby Orr 250.00 500.00
JY19 Gordie Howe 250.00 500.00
JY20 T.Sawchuk DET 150.00 300.00
JY21 Bobby Clarke 125.00 250.00
JY22 Tony Esposito
JY23 P.Esposito BOS
JY24 P.Esposito NYR
JY25 Guy Lafleur 60.00 150.00
JY26 W.Gretzky AS 350.00 700.00
JY27 Bill Barber
JY28 Dave Williams
JY29 Dave Schultz 60.00 150.00
JY30 Grant Fuhr 60.00 150.00
JY31 Reggie Leach

2004-05 UD Legends Classics Pennants

Inserted one per box, these team pennants were produced by Mitchell & Ness for UD. Numbers P1-P12 were limited to 158 copies and numbers P13-P19 were limited to 88 copies.

P1 The Dynamite Line 20.00 50.00
P2 The Kid Line 12.50 30.00
P3 The Punch Line 10.00 25.00
P4 The Pony Line 12.50 30.00
P5 The Kraut Line 10.00 25.00
P6 The Production Line 20.00 50.00
P7 The Uke Line 15.00 40.00
P8 The LCB Line 10.00 25.00
P9 The Big Three 10.00 25.00
P10 The GAG Line 12.50 30.00
P11 The Triple Crown Line
P12 The French Connection 12.50 30.00
P13 Kansas City Scouts 30.00 80.00
P14 California Golden Seals 20.00 50.00
P15 Colorado Rockies 12.50 30.00
P16 Atlanta Flames 6.00 15.00
P17 Hartford Whalers 15.00 40.00
P18 Quebec Nordiques 10.00 25.00
P19 Winnipeg Jets 15.00 40.00
P20 Boston Bruins 10.00 25.00
P21 NY Rangers 6.00 15.00
P22 Chicago Blackhawks 6.00 15.00
P23 Detroit Red Wings 10.00 25.00
P24 Toronto Maple Leafs 8.00 20.00
P25 Montreal Canadiens 6.00 15.00
P26 Philadelphia Flyers 6.00 15.00
P27 LA Kings 6.00 15.00
P28 St.Louis Blues 8.00 20.00
P29 Minnesota North Stars 10.00 25.00
P30 Pittsburgh Penguins 6.00 15.00
P31 Oakland Seals 6.00 15.00
P32 Detroit Cougars 6.00 15.00
P33 Toronto St.Pats 6.00 15.00

2004-05 UD Legends Classics Signature Moments

PRINT RUN 125 SER.#'d SETS
M1 Wayne Gretzky 125.00 250.00
M2 Gordie Howe 75.00 150.00
M3 Don Cherry 20.00 50.00
M4 Red Kelly 10.00 25.00
M5 Dickie Moore 8.00 20.00
M6 Andy Bathgate 10.00 25.00
M7 Terry O'Reilly 12.50 30.00
M8 Wayne Cashman 8.00 20.00
M9 Tony Esposito 15.00 40.00
M10 Ted Lindsay 15.00 40.00
M11 Stan Mikita 10.00 25.00
M12 Reggie Leach 8.00 20.00
M13 Rene Robert 8.00 20.00
M14 Rick Martin 10.00 25.00
M15 Phil Esposito 20.00 50.00
M16 Paul Henderson 8.00 20.00
M17 Paul Coffey 12.50 30.00
M18 Mike Bossy 10.00 25.00
M19 Lanny McDonald 12.50 30.00
M20 Gump Worsley 10.00 25.00
M21 Marcel Dionne 10.00 25.00
M22 Ken Morrow 8.00 20.00
M23 Ken Hodge 8.00 20.00
M24 Johnny Bucyk 10.00 25.00
M25 Johnny Bower 12.50 30.00
M26 Jari Kurri 12.50 30.00
M27 Cam Neely 15.00 40.00
M28 Jean Beliveau 20.00 50.00
M29 Guy Lafleur 20.00 50.00
M30 Gerry Cheevers 12.50 30.00
M31 Gilbert Perreault 12.50 30.00
M32 Glenn Anderson 8.00 20.00
M33 Glenn Hall 10.00 25.00
M34 Dave Taylor 8.00 20.00
M35 Grant Fuhr 20.00 50.00
M36 Frank Mahovlich 15.00 40.00
M37 Don Cherry 20.00 50.00
M38 Doug Wilson 8.00 20.00
M39 Dave Schultz 8.00 20.00
M40 Tiger Williams 10.00 25.00
M41 Dave Taylor 8.00 20.00
M42 Clark Gillies 10.00 25.00
M43 Bryan Trottier 12.50 30.00
M44 Butch Goring 8.00 20.00
M45 Bernie Geoffrion 12.50 30.00
M46 Al Iafrate 8.00 20.00
M47 Bill Barber 8.00 20.00
M48 Bob Nystrom 8.00 20.00
M49 Bobby Clarke 12.50 30.00
M50 Bobby Hull 25.00 60.00
M51 Brad Park 8.00 20.00
M52 Patrick Roy 60.00 150.00
M53 Ray Bourque 25.00 60.00
M54 Derek Sanderson 15.00 40.00
M55 Reggie Leach 8.00 20.00
M56 Jari Kurri 12.50 30.00
M57 Marcel Dionne 10.00 25.00
M58 Ken Hodge 8.00 20.00
M59 Dave Schultz 8.00 20.00
M60 Brad Park 8.00 20.00
M61 Gilbert Perreault 12.50 30.00
M62 Ken Morrow 8.00 20.00
M63 Gerry Cheevers 15.00 40.00
M64 Ted Lindsay 10.00 25.00
M65 Dave Taylor 8.00 20.00

M66 Cam Neely 20.00 50.00
M67 Johnny Bucyk 10.00 25.00
M68 Larry Murphy 8.00 20.00
M69 Fred Cusick 8.00 20.00
M70 Bob Cole 8.00 20.00

2004-05 UD Legends Classics Signatures

This 98-card set featured 4 different levels including single, dual, triple and quadruple autographs. Overall odds were 1:12 packs. An explanation of noted short-prints is below.

SP PRINT RUN 200 OR FEWER
SSP PRINT RUN 100 OR FEWER
XSP PRINT RUN 55 OR FEWER
DUAL PRINT RUN 75 SER.#'d SETS
TRIPLE PRINT RUN 25 SER.#'d SETS
QUAD PRINT RUN 10 SER.#'d SETS
QUADS NOT PRICED DUE TO SCARCITY
CS1 Wayne Gretzky XSP 200.00 450.00
CS2 Gordie Howe SSP 75.00 150.00
CS3 Don Cherry 15.00 40.00
CS4 Red Kelly 10.00 25.00
CS5 Dickie Moore 10.00 25.00
CS6 Andy Bathgate 10.00 25.00
CS7 Terry O'Reilly 15.00 40.00
CS8 Wayne Cashman 6.00 15.00
CS9 Tony Esposito XSP 40.00 100.00
CS10 Ted Lindsay XSP 20.00 50.00
CS11 Stan Mikita XSP 25.00 60.00
CS12 Reggie Leach 6.00 15.00
CS13 Rene Robert 8.00 20.00
CS14 Rick Martin 8.00 20.00
CS15 Phil Esposito XSP 75.00 125.00
CS16 Paul Henderson 8.00 20.00
CS17 Paul Coffey SSP 20.00 50.00
CS18 Mike Bossy 10.00 25.00
CS19 Lanny McDonald SP 12.50 30.00
CS20 Gump Worsley 20.00 50.00
CS21 Marcel Dionne SSP 25.00 60.00
CS22 Ken Morrow 6.00 15.00
CS23 Ken Hodge 6.00 15.00
CS24 Johnny Bucyk SP 10.00 25.00
CS25 Johnny Bower 10.00 25.00
CS26 Jari Kurri 10.00 25.00
CS27 Cam Neely SP 20.00 50.00
CS28 Jean Beliveau SSP 50.00 100.00
CS29 Guy Lafleur XSP 75.00 150.00
CS30 Gerry Cheevers 12.50 30.00
CS31 Gilbert Perreault XSP 30.00 80.00
CS32 Glenn Anderson 6.00 15.00
CS33 Glenn Hall 10.00 25.00
CS34 Grant Fuhr XSP 30.00 80.00
CS35 Frank Mahovlich XSP 25.00 60.00
CS36 Doug Wilson 6.00 15.00
CS37 Dave Schultz 8.00 20.00
CS38 Tiger Williams 8.00 20.00
CS39 Dave Taylor 6.00 15.00
CS40 Clark Gillies 6.00 15.00
CS41 Bryan Trottier/56 15.00 40.00
CS42 Butch Goring 6.00 15.00
CS43 Bernie Geoffrion SP 25.00 60.00
CS44 Al Iafrate 6.00 15.00
CS45 Bill Barber 6.00 15.00
CS46 Bob Nystrom 6.00 15.00
CS47 Bobby Clarke SP 20.00 50.00
CS48 Bobby Hull XSP 50.00 125.00
CS49 Brad Park 10.00 25.00
CS50 Patrick Roy SSP 75.00 150.00
CS51 Ray Bourque/25 150.00 400.00
CS52 Derek Sanderson 12.00 30.00
CS53 Fred Cusick 6.00 15.00
CS54 Bob Cole 6.00 15.00
CS55 Larry Murphy 8.00 20.00
DC1 T.Esposito/P.Esposito 50.00 100.00
DC2 Jean Beliveau 60.00 120.00
Guy Lafleur
DC3 Stan Mikita 30.00 80.00
Bobby Hull
DC4 Ray Bourque 40.00 100.00
Cam Neely
DC5 Mike Bossy 30.00 80.00
Bryan Trottier
DC6 Derek Sanderson 25.00 60.00
Johnny Bucyk
DC7 Rene Robert 25.00 60.00
Gilbert Perreault
DC8 C.Neely/J.Bucyk 25.00 60.00
DC9 J.Beliveau/D.Moore 30.00 80.00
DC10 B.Park/R.Bourque 40.00 100.00
DC11 Derek Sanderson 25.00 60.00
Phil Esposito
DC12 Tony Esposito 40.00 100.00
Glenn Hall
DC13 Marcel Dionne 30.00 80.00
Guy Lafleur
DC14 Gordie Howe 100.00 250.00
Bobby Hull
DC15 D.Schultz/D.Williams 25.00 60.00
DC16 Larry Murphy 25.00 60.00
Dave Taylor
DC17 Marcel Dionne 25.00 60.00
Dave Taylor
DC18 Bobby Clarke 40.00 100.00
Gilbert Perreault
DC19 Fred Cusick 25.00 60.00
Bob Cole
DC20 Bobby Clarke 30.00 80.00
Bill Barber
DC21 Andy Bathgate 40.00 100.00
Johnny Bower
DC22 Stan Mikita 25.00 60.00
Doug Wilson
TC1 Tony Esposito 200.00 400.00
Gump Worsley
Patrick Roy
TC2 Big M/Henderson/Bower 100.00 250.00
TC3 Gerry Cheevers 75.00 200.00
Phil Esposito
Derek Sanderson
TC4 Glenn Hall 125.00 250.00
Tony Esposito
Gerry Cheevers
TC5 Clark Gillies 60.00 150.00
Bryan Trottier
Mike Bossy
TC6 Barber/Clarke/Leach 75.00 200.00
TC7 Geoffrion/Howe/Beliveau 250.00 500.00
TC8 Ken Hodge
Brad Park
Phil Esposito
TC9 Paul Coffey 60.00 150.00
Larry Murphy
Ray Bourque
TC10 Rick Martin 60.00 150.00
Gilbert Perreault
Rene Robert
TC11 Glenn Anderson 350.00 500.00
Wayne Gretzky
Jari Kurri
TC12 Gump Worsley 60.00 150.00
Jean Beliveau
Dickie Moore
TC13 Gordie Howe 200.00 400.00
Red Kelly
Ted Lindsay
TC14 Wayne Gretzky 300.00 600.00
Marcel Dionne
Guy Lafleur
TC15 Tony Esposito 75.00 200.00
Stan Mikita
Glenn Hall
QC1 Patrick Roy
Tony Esposito
Glenn Hall
Gerry Cheevers
QC2 Gordie Howe
Guy Lafleur
Mike Bossy
Jari Kurri
QC3 Bobby Hull
Frank Mahovlich
Ted Lindsay
Johnny Bucyk
QC4 Wayne Gretzky
Bryan Trottier
Gilbert Perreault
Marcel Dionne
QC5 Phil Esposito
Terry O'Reilly
Cam Neely
Wayne Cashman
QC6 Gordie Howe
Bobby Clarke
Cam Neely
Clark Gillies

2001-02 UD Mask Collection

Released in June, this 190-card had a SRP of $3.99. The set featured 100 regular base cards, 40 Precious Gems rookie cards, 30 Manning the Nets subset cards and 20 Unmasked Warriors subset cards. The Precious Gems cards were serial-numbered out of 1500, the Unmasked Warriors cards were serial-numbered out of 1250, and the Manning the Nets cards were inserted at a rate of 1:3.

COMP.SET w/o SP's (100) 25.00 50.00
1 Paul Kariya .30 .75
2 Jeff Friesen .10 .25
3 Matt Cullen .10 .25
4 Dany Heatley .40 1.00
5 Lubos Bartecko .10 .25
6 Tony Hrkac .10 .25
7 Sergei Samsonov .25 .60
8 Joe Thornton .50 1.25
9 Bill Guerin .25 .60
10 P.J. Stock .10 .25
11 Stu Barnes .10 .25
12 Tim Connolly .10 .25
13 Jarome Iginla .40 1.00
14 Craig Conroy .10 .25
15 Sami Kapanen .10 .25
16 Ron Francis .25 .60
17 Tony Amonte .25 .60
18 Mark Bell .10 .25
19 Steve Sullivan .10 .25
20 Chris Drury .25 .60
21 Milan Hejduk .30 .75
22 Joe Sakic .60 1.50
23 Rob Blake .25 .60
24 Alex Tanguay .25 .60
25 Mike Sillinger .10 .25
26 Ray Whitney .10 .25
27 Rostislav Klesla .10 .25
28 Pierre Turgeon .25 .60
29 Jere Lehtinen .25 .60
30 Mike Modano .50 1.25
31 Sergei Zubov .10 .25
32 Brendan Shanahan .30 .75
33 Steve Yzerman 1.50 4.00
34 Brett Hull .40 1.00
35 Sergei Fedorov .50 1.25
36 Mike Comrie .25 .60
37 Ryan Smyth .10 .25
38 Anson Carter .25 .60
39 Viktor Kozlov .10 .25
40 Marcus Nilsson .10 .25
41 Sandis Ozolinsh .10 .25
42 Adam Deadmarsh .10 .25
43 Jason Allison .10 .25
44 Zigmund Palffy .25 .60
45 Andrew Brunette .10 .25
46 Marian Gaborik .60 1.50
47 Jim Dowd .10 .25
48 Yanic Perreault .10 .25
49 Sergei Berezin .10 .25
50 Donald Audette .10 .25
51 Francois Bouillon .10 .25
52 Karlis Skrastins .10 .25
53 David Legwand .25 .60
54 Scott Hartnell .10 .25
55 Bobby Holik .10 .25
56 Joe Nieuwendyk .25 .60
57 Patrik Elias .25 .60
58 Brian Rafalski .10 .25
59 Mark Parrish .10 .25
60 Michael Peca .10 .25
61 Alexei Yashin .10 .25
62 Petr Nedved .10 .25
63 Theo Fleury .10 .25
64 Pavel Bure .30 .75
65 Eric Lindros .30 .75
66 Martin Havlat .25 .60
67 Daniel Alfredsson .25 .60
68 Marian Hossa .30 .75
69 Radek Bonk .10 .25
70 Simon Gagne .30 .75
71 John LeClair .30 .75
72 Jeremy Roenick .40 1.00
73 Mark Recchi .25 .60
74 Michal Handzus .10 .25
75 Claude Lemieux .10 .25
76 Shane Doan .10 .25
77 Jamie Pushor .10 .25
78 Alexei Kovalev .25 .60
79 Mario Lemieux 2.00 5.00
80 Vincent Damphousse .10 .25
81 Owen Nolan .25 .60
82 Teemu Selanne .30 .75
83 Keith Tkachuk .30 .75
84 Chris Pronger .25 .60
85 Doug Weight .25 .60
86 Pavol Demitra .25 .60
87 Fredrik Modin .10 .25
88 Brad Richards .25 .60
89 Vincent Lecavalier .30 .75
90 Darcy Tucker .10 .25
91 Alexander Mogilny .10 .25
92 Mats Sundin .30 .75
93 Brendan Morrison .25 .60
94 Todd Bertuzzi .30 .75
95 Markus Naslund .30 .75
96 Ed Jovanovski .10 .25
97 Drake Berehowsky .10 .25
98 Ulf Dahlen .10 .25
99 Peter Bondra .30 .75
100 Jaromir Jagr .50 1.25
101 Jean-Sebastien Giguere MTN 1.25 3.00
102 Milan Hnilicka MTN 1.25 3.00
103 Byron Dafoe MTN 1.25 3.00
104 Martin Biron MTN 1.25 3.00
105 Roman Turek MTN 1.25 3.00
106 Arturs Irbe MTN 1.25 3.00
107 Jocelyn Thibault MTN 1.25 3.00
108 Patrick Roy MTN 3.00 8.00
109 Ron Tugnutt MTN 1.25 3.00
110 Ed Belfour MTN 1.50 4.00
111 Dominik Hasek MTN 2.50 6.00
112 Tommy Salo MTN 1.25 3.00
113 Roberto Luongo MTN 2.00 5.00
114 Felix Potvin MTN 1.50 4.00
115 Manny Fernandez MTN 1.25 3.00
116 Jose Theodore MTN 2.00 5.00
117 Mike Dunham MTN 1.25 3.00
118 Martin Brodeur MTN 2.50 6.00
119 Chris Osgood MTN 1.50 4.00
120 Mike Richter MTN 1.50 4.00
121 Patrick Lalime MTN 1.25 3.00
122 Roman Cechmanek MTN 1.25 3.00
123 Sean Burke MTN 1.25 3.00
124 Johan Hedberg MTN 1.25 3.00
125 Evgeni Nabokov MTN 1.25 3.00
126 Brent Johnson MTN 1.25 3.00
127 Nikolai Khabibulin MTN 1.50 4.00
128 Curtis Joseph MTN 1.50 4.00
129 Dan Cloutier MTN 1.25 3.00
130 Olaf Kolzig MTN 1.25 3.00
131 Frederic Cassivi RC 2.00 5.00
132 Ilya Kovalchuk RC 10.00 25.00
133 Pasi Nurminen RC 2.00 5.00
134 Mark Hartigan RC 2.00 5.00
135 Francis Lessard RC 2.00 5.00
136 Ivan Huml RC 2.00 5.00
137 Chris Kelleher RC 2.00 5.00
138 Erik Cole RC 2.50 5.00
139 Mike Peluso RC 2.00 5.00
140 Vaclav Nedorost RC 2.00 5.00
141 Jeff Daw RC 2.00 5.00
142 Andrej Nedorost RC 2.00 5.00
143 Sean Avery RC 2.00 5.00
144 Pavel Datsyuk RC 8.00 20.00
145 Stephen Weiss RC 6.00 10.00
146 Niklas Hagman RC 2.00 5.00
147 Kristian Huselius RC 2.50 6.00
148 Lukas Krajicek RC 2.00 5.00
149 Tony Virta RC 2.00 5.00
150 Olivier Michaud RC 2.00 10.00
151 Marcel Hossa RC 2.00 5.00
152 Martin Erat RC 2.00 5.00
153 Christian Berglund RC 2.00 5.00
154 Raffi Torres RC 2.50 6.00
155 Dan Blackburn RC 2.50 8.00
156 Martin Prusek RC 2.00 5.00
157 Chris Bala RC 2.00 5.00
158 Josh Langfeld RC 2.00 5.00
159 Jiri Dopita RC 2.00 5.00
160 Neil Little RC 2.00 5.00
161 Guillaume Lefebvre RC 2.00 5.00
162 Krys Kolanos RC 2.00 5.00
163 Branko Radivojevic RC 2.00 5.00
164 Shane Endicott RC 2.00 5.00
165 Hannes Hyvonen RC 2.00 5.00
166 Jeff Jillson RC 2.00 5.00
167 Nikita Alexeev RC 2.00 5.00
168 Gaetan Royer RC 2.00 5.00
169 Karel Pilar RC 2.00 5.00
170 Brian Sutherby RC 2.00 5.00
171 Byron Dafoe UW 2.00 5.00
172 Martin Biron UW 2.00 5.00
173 Roman Turek UW 2.00 5.00
174 Arturs Irbe UW 2.00 5.00
175 Patrick Roy UW 6.00 15.00
176 Ed Belfour UW 2.50 6.00
177 Dominik Hasek UW 5.00 12.00
178 Tommy Salo UW 2.00 5.00
179 Felix Potvin UW 2.50 6.00
180 Mike Dunham UW 2.00 5.00
181 Martin Brodeur UW 5.00 12.00
182 Chris Osgood UW 2.00 5.00
183 Mike Richter UW 2.50 6.00
184 Roman Cechmanek UW 2.00 5.00
185 Sean Burke UW 2.00 5.00
186 Johan Hedberg UW 2.00 5.00
187 Evgeni Nabokov UW 2.00 5.00
188 Nikolai Khabibulin UW 2.50 6.00
189 Curtis Joseph UW 2.50 6.00
190 Olaf Kolzig UW 2.00 5.00

2001-02 UD Mask Collection Gold

This 190-card set paralleled the base set. Each card was serial-numbered to just 50 copies each.

GOLD: 5X TO 12X BASIC CARD
GOLD MTN: 4X TO 10X BASIC CARD
GOLD PG: 2X TO 4X BASIC CARD
GOLD UW: 2X TO 5X BASIC CARD

2001-02 UD Mask Collection Double Patches

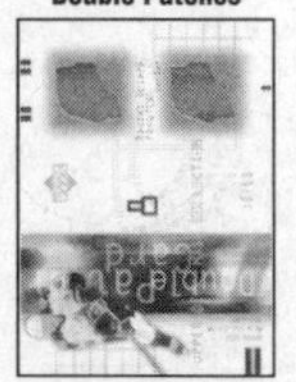

This 60-card set paralleled the jersey card set, but carried two swatches of jersey patches. Cards were serial-numbered out of 100. Swatches were affixed beside a full-color action photo on the card front. Card backs carried a congratulatory message.

*DBL.PATCH: 2X TO 5X JERSEY CARD

2001-02 UD Mask Collection Dual Jerseys

Inserted at a rate of 1:288, this 14-card set featured two game-worn swatches of the players featured. There was two subsets, Premier Matchups and Behind the Mask. Card prefixes denote subset. Swatches were affixed beside a full-color action photo on the card front. Card backs carried a congratulatory message.

*MULT.COLOR SWATCH: .5X TO 1.5X HI
MBBC Brian Boucher 10.00 25.00
Roman Cechmanek
MBBT Martin Brodeur 15.00 40.00
Jose Theodore
MBCJ Curtis Joseph 10.00 25.00
Curtis Joseph
MBFP Felix Potvin 10.00 25.00
Double Jersey
MBPR Patrick Roy 40.00 100.00
Double Jersey
MBRD Mike Richter 10.00 25.00
Mike Dunham
MBTB Jocelyn Thibault 10.00 25.00
Ed Belfour
PMAD Tony Amonte 10.00 25.00
Mike Dunham
PMAJ Jason Arnott 10.00 25.00
Curtis Joseph
PMFT Sergei Fedorov 10.00 25.00
Jocelyn Thibault
PMGB Simon Gagne 10.00 25.00
Martin Biron
PMMJ Mike Modano 10.00 25.00
Brent Johnson
PMSB Joe Sakic 12.50 30.00
Martin Brodeur
PMYR Steve Yzerman 30.00 80.00
Patrick Roy

2001-02 UD Mask Collection Gloves

Inserted at a rate of 1:144, this 13-card set featured game-used glove swatches of the featured player. Swatches were affixed beside a full-color action photo on the card front. Card backs carried a congratulatory message.

*MULT.COLOR SWATCH: .75X TO 2X HI
GGAM Alexander Mogilny 8.00 20.00
GGBD Byron Dafoe 8.00 20.00
GGBH Brett Hull 12.50 30.00
GGBS Brendan Shanahan 10.00 25.00
GGCD Chris Drury 8.00 20.00
GGEB Ed Belfour 10.00 25.00
GGJR Jeremy Roenick 12.50 30.00
GGMM Mark Messier 15.00 40.00
GGRB Ray Bourque 15.00 40.00
GGRD Rick DiPietro 10.00 25.00
GGSF Sergei Fedorov 12.50 30.00
GGSK Sami Kapanen 8.00 20.00
GGTK Keith Tkachuk 10.00 25.00

2001-02 UD Mask Collection Goalie Jerseys

This 39-card set featured game-worn jersey swatches of NHL goalies. There were five different subsets: Masked Marvels (inserted at 1:96), Super Stoppers and Styling Tenders (inserted at 1:168). View from the Cage (inserted at 1:144), and Caged Greats (inserted at 1:288). Card prefixes denote subset. Swatches were affixed beside a full-color action photo on the card front. Card backs carried a congratulatory message.

*MULT.COLOR SWATCH: .75X TO 1.5X HI
MMBB Brian Boucher 4.00 10.00
MMBD Byron Dafoe 4.00 10.00
MMDA David Aebischer 6.00 15.00
MMJT Jocelyn Thibault 4.00 10.00
MMMD Mike Dunham 4.00 10.00
MMMT Marty Turco 6.00 15.00
MMRT Ron Tugnutt 4.00 10.00
MMSB Sean Burke 4.00 10.00
SSBD Byron Dafoe 6.00 15.00
SSBJ Brent Johnson 6.00 15.00
SSFP Felix Potvin 8.00 20.00
SSJT Jocelyn Thibault 6.00 15.00
SSMB Martin Biron 6.00 15.00
SSRL Roberto Luongo 10.00 25.00
SSRT Ron Tugnutt 6.00 15.00
SSTH Jose Theodore 10.00 25.00
SYBB Brian Boucher 6.00 15.00
SYDA David Aebischer 6.00 15.00
SYEB Ed Belfour 8.00 20.00
SYJG Jean-Sebastien Giguere 6.00 15.00
SYMD Mike Dunham 6.00 15.00
SYMN Mika Noronen 6.00 15.00
SYPR Patrick Roy 15.00 40.00
SYRC Roman Cechmanek 6.00 15.00
VCEB Ed Belfour 8.00 20.00
VCFP Felix Potvin 8.00 20.00
VCMB Martin Brodeur 12.50 30.00
VCMD Mike Dunham 6.00 15.00
VCMT Marty Turco 8.00 20.00
VCPR Patrick Roy 15.00 40.00
VCRC Roman Cechmanek 6.00 15.00
VCSB Sean Burke 6.00 15.00
CGCJ Curtis Joseph 8.00 20.00
CGCO Chris Osgood 8.00 20.00
CGDH Dominik Hasek 12.50 30.00
CGMB Martin Brodeur 15.00 40.00
CGMR Mike Richter 8.00 20.00
CGPR Patrick Roy 25.00 60.00
CGSB Sean Burke 8.00 20.00

2001-02 UD Mask Collection Goalie Pads

Inserted at a rate of 1:66, this 8-card set featured game-worn goalie pad swatches of the featured goalie. Swatches were affixed beside a full-color action photo on the card front. Card backs carried a congratulatory message.

*MULT.COLOR SWATCH: .75X TO 1.5X HI
GPBD Byron Dafoe 5.00 12.00
GPDH Dominik Hasek 8.00 20.00
GPJH Johan Hedberg 5.00 12.00
GPJT Jose Theodore 6.00 15.00
GPMB Martin Biron 5.00 12.00
GPMD Marc Denis 5.00 12.00
GPOK Olaf Kolzig 5.00 12.00
GPPR Patrick Roy 12.50 30.00

2001-02 UD Mask Collection Jerseys

This 60-card set featured a game-worn jersey swatch of the featured player. Swatches were affixed beside a full-color action photo on the card front. Card backs carry a congratulatory message.

*MULT.COLOR SWATCH: .75X TO 1.5X HI
JAD Adam Deadmarsh 4.00 10.00
JAT Alex Tanguay 4.00 10.00
JBB Brian Boucher 4.00 10.00
JBE Mark Bell 4.00 10.00

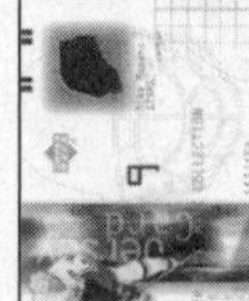

JBJ Brent Johnson 4.00 10.00
JBL Rob Blake 4.00 10.00
JBS Brendan Shanahan 6.00 15.00
JCD Chris Drury 4.00 10.00
JDA David Aebischer 6.00 15.00
JDB Daniel Briere 4.00 10.00
JEB Ed Belfour 6.00 15.00
JEK Espen Knutsen 4.00 10.00
JFP Felix Potvin 6.00 15.00
JGS Geoff Sanderson 4.00 10.00
JJA Jason Allison 4.00 10.00
JJD J-P Dumont 4.00 10.00
JJF Jeff Friesen 4.00 10.00
JJG Jean-Sebastien Giguere 4.00 10.00
JJI Jarome Iginla 8.00 20.00
JJJ Jaromir Jagr 8.00 20.00
JJN Joe Nieuwendyk 4.00 10.00
JJT Jocelyn Thibault 4.00 10.00
JJW Justin Williams 4.00 10.00
JKO Slava Kozlov 4.00 10.00
JKP Keith Primeau 4.00 10.00
JMA Maxim Afinogenov 4.00 10.00
JMB Martin Biron 4.00 10.00
JMD Marc Denis 4.00 10.00
JMH Milan Hejduk 6.00 15.00
JML Mario Lemieux 20.00 50.00
JMM Mike Modano 8.00 20.00
JMR Mike Richter 6.00 15.00
JMS Miroslav Satan 4.00 10.00
JMS Mats Sundin 6.00 15.00
JMT Marty Turco 4.00 10.00
JMY Mike York 4.00 10.00
JNL Nicklas Lidstrom 6.00 15.00
JPD Pavol Demitra 4.00 10.00
JPF Peter Forsberg 10.00 25.00
JPK Paul Kariya 6.00 15.00
JPR Patrick Roy 12.50 30.00
JRB Ray Bourque 10.00 25.00
JRF Ruslan Fedotenko 4.00 10.00
JRK Rostislav Klesla 4.00 10.00
JRT Ron Tugnutt 4.00 10.00
JRW Ray Whitney 4.00 10.00
JSA Marc Savard 4.00 10.00
JSD Shane Doan 4.00 10.00
JSF Sergei Fedorov 8.00 20.00
JSG Simon Gagne 6.00 15.00
JSK Saku Koivu 6.00 15.00
JSS Steve Sullivan 4.00 10.00
JSY Steve Yzerman 15.00 40.00
JTA Tony Amonte 4.00 10.00
JTC Tim Connolly 4.00 10.00
JTH Jose Theodore 8.00 20.00
JTL Trevor Linden 4.00 10.00
JTS Teemu Selanne 6.00 15.00
JVN Ville Nieminen 4.00 10.00
JZP Zigmund Palffy 4.00 10.00

2001-02 UD Mask Collection Jersey and Patch

This 60-card set paralleled the jersey card set, but carried a swatch of jersey patch as well as the jersey swatch. Cards were serial-numbered out of 100. Swatches were affixed beside a full-color action photo on the card front. Card backs carried a congratulatory message.

*JSY/PATCH: 1.25X TO 3X JERSEY CARD

2001-02 UD Mask Collection Mini Masks

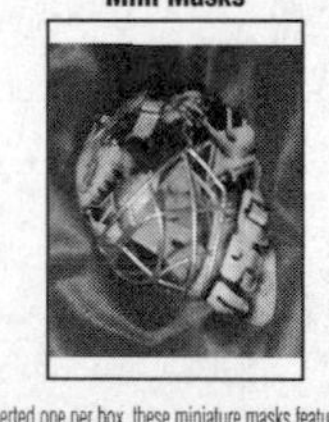

Inserted one per box, these miniature masks feature the artwork sported by some of the league's top goalies. A chrome cage parallel was also created and values can be found by using the multipliers below.

*CHROME MASK: .6X TO 1.5X
CJ Curtis Joseph 12.50 30.00
EN Evgeni Nabokov 15.00 40.00
JH Johan Hedberg 12.50 30.00
JT Jose Theodore 15.00 40.00
MB Martin Brodeur 15.00 40.00
PRA Patrick Roy Col. 20.00 50.00
PRC Patrick Roy Mon. 40.00 100.00
EBGD Ed Belfour Gold 25.00 60.00
EBGN Ed Belfour Green 12.50 30.00

2001-02 UD Mask Collection Signed Patches

This 8-card set featured game-worn jersey swatches that were signed by the featured player. Cards were serial-numbered out of 25. Swatches were affixed below a full-color action photo on the card front.

SPBI Martin Biron 75.00 200.00
SPCJ Curtis Joseph 125.00 300.00
SPEB Ed Belfour 150.00 300.00
SPFP Felix Potvin 125.00 300.00
SPJT Jose Theodore 200.00 500.00
SPMB Martin Brodeur 300.00 500.00
SPMR Mike Richter 200.00 300.00
SPPR Patrick Roy 300.00 600.00

2001-02 UD Mask Collection Signs of History

Little is currently known about this set other than that cards were serial-numbered out of 33 and carried an authentic autograph of Patrick Roy.

PR1 Patrick Roy 125.00 300.00
PR2 Patrick Roy 125.00 300.00
PR3 Patrick Roy 125.00 300.00
PR4 Patrick Roy 125.00 300.00

2001-02 UD Mask Collection Sticks

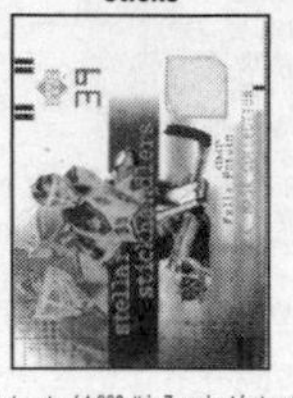

Inserted at a rate of 1:288, this 7-card set featured game-used stick swatches of some of the premier goalies in the league. Swatches were affixed beside a full-color action photo on the card front.

SSBB Brian Boucher 8.00 20.00
SSDH Dominik Hasek 15.00 40.00
SSFP Felix Potvin 12.50 30.00
SSJT Jose Theodore 15.00 40.00
SSMB Martin Brodeur 15.00 40.00
SSOK Olaf Kolzig 8.00 20.00
SSTS Tommy Salo 8.00 20.00

2002-03 UD Mask Collection

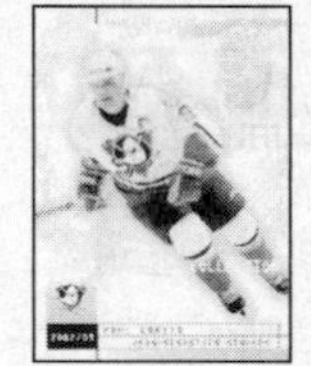

Released in May 2003, this 180-card set featured 90 base cards and two subsets. Cards 1-90 carried a color player photo on the card front with a smaller black and white photo of a teammate in the background. Card backs carried stats of both players. Cards 91-115 were a "Team Saviours" subset and each card was serial-numbered to the featured goalies 2001-02 saves total. Cards 116-180 made up a "Potential Gems" subset. Cards 116-157 were serial-numbered to 1750 and cards 158-180 were serial-numbered to 1250.

COMPLETE SET (180)
COMP.SET w/o SP's (90) 8.00 20.00
1 Jean-Sebastien Giguere .20 .50
Martin Gerber
2 Paul Kariya .25 .60
Jean-Sebastien Giguere
3 Byron Dafoe .20 .50
Milan Hnilicka
4 Milan Hnilicka .20 .50
Byron Dafoe
5 D.Heatley/B.Dafoe .30 .75
6 I.Kovalchuk/B.Dafoe .30 .75
7 Pasi Nurminen .20 .50
Byron Dafoe
8 Jeff Hackett .20 .50
Steve Shields
9 Steve Shields .20 .50
Jeff Hackett
10 J.Thornton/J.Hackett .40 1.00
11 Martin Biron .20 .50
Mika Noronen
12 Mika Noronen .20 .50
Martin Biron
13 Roman Turek .20 .50
Jamie McLennan
14 Jamie McLennan .20 .50
Roman Turek
15 Chris Drury .20 .50
Roman Turek
16 Jarome Iginla .25 .60
Roman Turek
17 Kevin Weekes .20 .50
Arturs Irbe
18 Arturs Irbe .20 .50
Kevin Weekes
19 Jocelyn Thibault .20 .50
Steve Passmore
20 Steve Passmore .20 .50
Jocelyn Thibault
21 P.Roy/D.Aebischer 1.25 3.00
22 David Aebischer .20 .50
Patrick Roy
23 J.Sakic/P.Roy .50 1.25
24 Marc Denis .20 .50
Jean-Francois Labbe
25 Jean-Francois Labbe .20 .50
Marc Denis
26 Marty Turco .20 .50
Ron Tugnutt
27 Ron Tugnutt .20 .50
Marty Turco
28 M.Modano/M.Turco .40 1.00
29 Bill Guerin .20 .50

Marty Turco
30 Curtis Joseph .20 .50
Manny Legace
31 Manny Legace .20 .50
Curtis Joseph
32 S.Yzerman/C.Joseph 1.25 3.00
33 Brendan Shanahan .25 .60
Curtis Joseph
34 Tommy Salo .20 .50
Jussi Markkanen
35 Jussi Markkanen .20 .50
Tommy Salo
36 Mike Comrie .20 .50
Tommy Salo
37 Roberto Luongo .20 .50
Jani Hurme
38 Jani Hurme .20 .50
Roberto Luongo
39 Felix Potvin .25 .60
Jamie Storr
40 Jamie Storr .20 .50
Felix Potvin
41 Zigmund Palffy .20 .50
Felix Potvin
42 Manny Fernandez .20 .50
Dwayne Roloson
43 Dwayne Roloson .20 .50
Manny Fernandez
44 M.Gaborik/M.Fernandez .25 .60
45 Jose Theodore .25 .60
Mathieu Garon
46 Mathieu Garon .20 .50
Jose Theodore
47 Saku Koivu .25 .60
Jose Theodore
48 Jan Lasak .20 .50
Tomas Vokoun
49 Tomas Vokoun .20 .50
Jan Lasak
50 M.Brodeur/C.Schwab .60 1.50
51 Corey Schwab .20 .50
Martin Brodeur
52 Garth Snow .20 .50
Chris Osgood
53 Chris Osgood .20 .50
Garth Snow
54 Mike Dunham .20 .50
Dan Blackburn
55 Dan Blackburn .20 .50
Mike Dunham
56 Jason Labarbera .20 .50
Dan Blackburn
57 Pavel Bure .25 .60
Mike Dunham
58 Patrick Lalime .20 .50
Martin Prusek
59 Martin Prusek .20 .50
Patrick Lalime
60 Roman Cechmanek .20 .50
Robert Esche
61 Robert Esche .20 .50
Roman Cechmanek
62 J.Roenick/R.Cechmanek .25 .60
63 John LeClair .25 .60
Roman Cechmanek
64 Brian Boucher .20 .50
Sean Burke
65 Sean Burke .20 .50
Brian Boucher
66 Jean-Marc Pelletier .20 .50
Brian Boucher
67 Tony Amonte .20 .50
Sean Burke
68 Johan Hedberg .20 .50
Jean-Sebastien Aubin
69 Jean-Sebastien Aubin .20 .50
Johan Hedberg
70 M.Lemieux/J.Hedberg 1.50 4.00
71 Sebastien Caron .20 .50
Johan Hedberg
72 Evgeni Nabokov .20 .50
Miikka Kiprusoff
73 Vesa Toskala .20 .50
Evgeni Nabokov
74 Miikka Kiprusoff .20 .50
Evgeni Nabokov
75 Brent Johnson .20 .50
Fred Brathwaite
76 Tom Barrasso .20 .50
Brent Johnson
77 Fred Brathwaite .20 .50
Brent Johnson
78 Reinhard Divis .20 .50
Brent Johnson
79 Nikolai Khabibulin .25 .60
Kevin Hodson
80 Kevin Hodson .25 .60
Nikolai Khabibulin
81 Evgeny Konstantinov .25 .60
Nikolai Khabibulin
82 Ed Belfour .25 .60
Trevor Kidd
83 Trevor Kidd .20 .50
Ed Belfour
84 M.Sundin/E.Belfour .25 .60
85 Dan Cloutier .20 .50
Peter Skudra
86 Peter Skudra .20 .50
Dan Cloutier
87 J.Jagr/O.Kolzig .40 1.00
88 Olaf Kolzig .20 .50
Craig Billington
89 Craig Billington .20 .50
Olaf Kolzig
90 Sebastien Charpentier .20 .50
Olaf Kolzig
91 Martin Brodeur/1499 3.00 8.00
92 Patrick Roy/1475 4.00 10.00
93 Curtis Joseph/1096 3.00 8.00
94 Roman Cechmanek/1042 3.00 8.00
95 Marty Turco/590 3.00 8.00
96 Jocelyn Thibault/1475 3.00 8.00
97 Jose Theodore/1636 4.00 10.00
98 Jean-Sebastien Giguere/1260 3.00 8.00
99 Ed Belfour/1305 3.00 8.00
100 Steve Shields/771 3.00 8.00
101 Johan Hedberg/1673 3.00 8.00
102 Martin Biron/1630 3.00 8.00
103 Dan Cloutier/1298 3.00 8.00
104 Evgeni Nabokov/1669 3.00 8.00
105 Sean Burke/1574 3.00 8.00
106 Nikolai Khabibulin/1733 3.00 8.00
107 Olaf Kolzig/1785 3.00 8.00
108 Byron Dafoe/1379 3.00 8.00
109 David Aebischer/501 3.00 8.00
110 Manny Fernandez/1032 3.00 8.00
111 Dan Blackburn/840 3.00 8.00
112 Felix Potvin/1529 3.00 8.00
113 Patrick Lalime/1373 3.00 8.00
114 Brent Johnson/1166 3.00 8.00
115 Marc Denis/1046 3.00 8.00
116 Micki Dupont RC 1.50 4.00
117 Cody Rudkowsky RC 1.50 4.00
118 Shawn Thornton RC 1.50 4.00
119 Lasse Pirjeta RC 1.50 4.00
120 Radovan Somik RC 1.50 4.00
121 Tomi Pettinen RC 1.50 4.00
122 Jonathan Hedstrom RC 1.50 4.00
123 Sylvain Blouin RC 1.50 4.00
124 Stephane Veilleux RC 1.50 4.00
125 Curtis Sanford RC 1.50 4.00
126 Kurt Sauer RC 1.50 4.00
127 Vernon Fiddler RC 1.50 4.00
128 Patrick Sharp RC 1.50 4.00
129 Greg Koehler RC 1.50 4.00
130 Dany Sabourin RC 1.50 4.00
131 Dmitri Bykov RC 1.50 4.00
132 Ivan Majesky RC 1.50 4.00
133 Ray Schultz RC 1.50 4.00
134 Matt Henderson RC 1.50 4.00
135 Tom Koivisto RC 1.50 4.00
136 Ian MacNeil RC 1.50 4.00
137 Eric Godard RC 1.50 4.00
138 Dick Tarnstrom RC 1.50 4.00
139 Jeff Paul RC 1.50 4.00
140 Darren Haydar RC 1.50 4.00
141 Levente Szuper RC 1.50 4.00
142 Dennis Seidenberg RC 2.00 5.00
143 Tim Thomas RC 3.00 8.00
144 Fernando Pisani RC 2.00 5.00
145 Alex Henry RC 1.50 4.00
146 Craig Andersson RC 4.00 10.00
147 Kari Haakana RC 1.50 4.00
148 Jared Aulin RC 1.50 4.00
149 Adam Hall RC 1.50 4.00
150 Carlo Colaiacovo RC 1.50 4.00
151 Martin Gerber RC 3.00 8.00
152 Jamie Hodson RC 1.50 4.00
153 Ray Emery RC 3.00 8.00
154 Ari Ahonen RC 1.50 4.00
155 Michael Leighton RC 4.00 10.00
156 Kris Vernarsky RC 1.50 4.00
157 Jim Vandermeer RC 1.50 4.00
158 Chuck Kobasew RC 2.00 5.00
159 Ron Hainsey RC 2.00 5.00
160 P-M Bouchard RC 3.00 8.00
161 Alexander Frolov RC 4.00 10.00
162 Henrik Zetterberg RC 6.00 15.00
163 Alexander Svitov RC 1.50 4.00
164 Mike Cammalleri RC 1.50 4.00
165 Ryan Miller RC 5.00 12.00
166 Anton Volchenkov RC 2.00 5.00
167 Brooks Orpik RC 2.00 5.00
168 Ales Hemsky RC 4.00 10.00
169 Stanislav Chistov RC 2.00 5.00
170 Shaone Morrisonn RC 2.00 5.00
171 Jason Spezza RC 6.00 15.00
172 Jay Bouwmeester RC 2.00 5.00
173 Jordan Leopold RC 2.00 5.00
174 Jeff Taffe RC 2.00 5.00
175 Pascal LeClaire RC 2.50 6.00
176 Scottie Upshall RC 2.00 5.00
177 Alexei Smirnov RC 2.00 5.00
178 Rick Nash RC 8.00 20.00
179 Mikael Tellqvist RC 2.00 5.00
180 Steve Eminger RC 2.00 5.00

2002-03 UD Mask Collection Behind the Mask

Inserted at a rate of 1:60 hobby packs, this 18-card set featured swatches of game-worn jerseys.

*MULT.COLOR SWATCH: .75X TO 1.5X
BMAM Andy Moog SP 10.00 25.00
BMBI Martin Biron 6.00 15.00
BMBJ Brent Johnson 6.00 15.00
BMCJ Curtis Joseph 6.00 15.00
BMDU Mike Dunham 6.00 15.00
BMEB Ed Belfour 8.00 20.00
BMFP Felix Potvin 6.00 15.00
BMJG J-S Giguere 8.00 20.00
BMJH Johan Hedberg 6.00 15.00
BMJT Jose Theodore 6.00 15.00
BMMB Martin Brodeur 8.00 20.00
BMMD Marc Denis 6.00 15.00
BMMN Mika Noronen 6.00 15.00
BMMT Marty Turco 6.00 15.00
BMOK Olaf Kolzig 6.00 15.00
BMPR Patrick Roy 12.50 30.00
BMRC Roman Cechmanek 6.00 15.00
BMRD Rick DiPietro 6.00 15.00

2002-03 UD Mask Collection Career Wins

This 17-card set featured swatches of game-worn jerseys. Each card was serial-numbered to the given goalies career wins total as of press time.

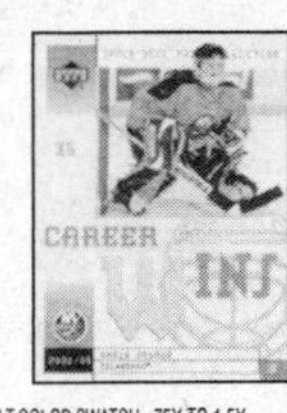

*MULT.COLOR SWATCH: .75X TO 1.5X
CWAM Andy Moog/372 10.00 25.00
CWBD Byron Dafoe/162 10.00 25.00
CWCJ Curtis Joseph/346 10.00 25.00
CWCO Chris Osgood/253 10.00 25.00
CWEB Ed Belfour/364 12.50 30.00
CWFP Felix Potvin/237 10.00 25.00
CWJT Jocelyn Thibault/196 10.00 25.00
CWMB Martin Brodeur/324 12.50 30.00
CWMD Mike Dunham/92 10.00 25.00
CWMR Mike Richter/296 12.50 30.00
CWOK Olaf Kolzig/182 10.00 25.00
CWPR Patrick Roy/289 15.00 40.00
CWRT Ron Tugnutt/168 10.00 25.00
CWRY Patrick Roy/227 15.00 40.00
CWSB Sean Burke/281 10.00 25.00
CWTS Tommy Salo/168 10.00 25.00
CWTU Roman Turek/126 10.00 25.00

2002-03 UD Mask Collection Great Gloves

Inserted at a rate of 1:60 hobby packs, this 18-card set featured swatches of game-worn jerseys.

*MULT.COLOR SWATCH: .75X TO 1.5X
GGBB Brian Boucher 6.00 15.00
GGBR Martin Brodeur 8.00 20.00
GGCJ Curtis Joseph 6.00 15.00
GGDB Dan Blackburn 6.00 15.00
GGDU Mike Dunham 6.00 15.00
GGEB Ed Belfour 8.00 20.00
GGFP Felix Potvin 6.00 15.00
GGJG Jean-Sebastien Giguere 12.50 30.00
GGJT Jose Theodore 8.00 20.00
GGMB Martin Biron 6.00 15.00
GGMD Marc Denis 6.00 15.00
GGMR Mike Richter 6.00 15.00
GGMT Marty Turco 8.00 20.00
GGOK Olaf Kolzig SP 10.00 25.00
GGPR Patrick Roy 12.50 30.00
GGRC Roman Cechmanek 6.00 15.00
GGRL Roberto Luongo 8.00 20.00
GGRT Roman Turek 6.00 15.00

2002-03 UD Mask Collection Instant Offense

Serial-numbered out of 250, this 25-card set featured swatches of game-worn jerseys.

*MULT.COLOR SWATCH: .75X TO 1.5X
IOAY Alexei Yashin 4.00 10.00
IOBS Brendan Shanahan 5.00 12.00
IOCD Chris Drury 4.00 10.00
IOED Eric Daze 4.00 10.00
IOEL Eric Lindros 5.00 12.00
IOJA Jason Allison 4.00 10.00
IOJI Jarome Iginla 6.00 15.00
IOJJ Jaromir Jagr 10.00 25.00
IOJR Jeremy Roenick 6.00 15.00
IOJS Joe Sakic 10.00 25.00
IOJT Joe Thornton 8.00 20.00
IOML Mario Lemieux 12.50 30.00
IOMM Mike Modano 8.00 20.00
IOMN Markus Naslund 5.00 12.00
IOMS Miroslav Satan 4.00 10.00
IOPB Pavel Bure 5.00 12.00
IOPE Patrik Elias 4.00 10.00
IOPF Peter Forsberg 12.50 30.00
IOPK Paul Kariya 5.00 12.00
IOSG Simon Gagne 5.00 12.00
IOSK Saku Koivu 5.00 12.00
IOSS Sergei Samsonov 4.00 10.00
IOSU Mats Sundin 5.00 12.00
IOSY Steve Yzerman 12.50 30.00
IOZP Zigmund Palffy 4.00 10.00

2002-03 UD Mask Collection Masked Marvels

Inserted at a rate of 1:60 hobby packs, this 17-card set featured swatches of game-worn jerseys.

*MULT.COLOR SWATCH: .75X TO 1.5X
MMBI Martin Biron 4.00 10.00
MMCO Chris Osgood 4.00 10.00
MMFP Felix Potvin 5.00 12.00
MMJG Jean-Sebastien Giguere 8.00 20.00
MMJH Johan Hedberg 4.00 10.00
MMJT Jocelyn Thibault 4.00 10.00
MMMB Martin Brodeur 8.00 20.00
MMMD Mike Dunham 4.00 10.00
MMMR Mike Richter 6.00 15.00
MMMT Marty Turco 6.00 15.00
MMOK Olaf Kolzig SP 4.00 10.00
MMPR Patrick Roy 12.50 30.00
MMRC Roman Cechmanek 4.00 10.00
MMRL Roberto Luongo 6.00 15.00
MMRM Ryan Miller 8.00 20.00
MMRT Roman Turek 4.00 10.00
MMTH Jose Theodore SP 6.00 15.00

2002-03 UD Mask Collection Mini Masks

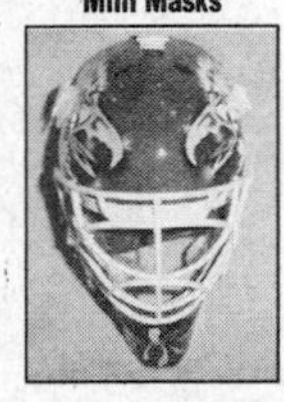

Inserted one per box, these miniature masks feature the artwork sported by some of the league's top goalies. A glitter effect parallel was also created and values can be found by using the multiplier below. Glitter parallels were limited to 25 copies each.

*GLITTER: 1.25X TO 3X
AM Andy Moog 20.00 50.00
CJ Curtis Joseph 15.00 40.00
CR Glenn Resch 12.50 30.00
EB Ed Belfour 20.00 50.00
EN Evgeni Nabokov 12.50 30.00
FP Felix Potvin 15.00 40.00
GC Gerry Cheevers 12.50 30.00
GF1 Grant Fuhr Sabres 12.50 30.00
GF2 Grant Fuhr Blues SP 20.00 50.00
JH Johan Hedberg 12.50 30.00
JP1 Jacque Plante Pretzel 15.00 40.00
JP2 Jacque Plante Alien SP 30.00 80.00
JT Jose Theodore 15.00 40.00
MB Martin Brodeur 20.00 50.00
NK Nikolai Khabibulin 20.00 50.00
PR Patrick Roy 15.00 40.00
TE Tony Esposito 20.00 50.00
TS Terry Sawchuk 15.00 40.00

2002-03 UD Mask Collection Mini Masks Autographs

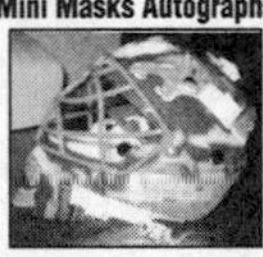

STAT.PRINT RUN 25 SETS
CJ Curtis Joseph 75.00 150.00
EB Ed Belfour 125.00 250.00
EN Evgeni Nabokov 40.00 100.00
GC Gerry Cheevers 30.00 80.00
GF1 Grant Fuhr Sabres 30.00 80.00
GF2 Grant Fuhr Blues SP 50.00 125.00
JT Jose Theodore 60.00 150.00
MB Martin Brodeur 100.00 250.00
NK Nikolai Khabibulin 40.00 100.00
PR Patrick Roy 100.00 250.00
TE Tony Esposito 60.00 150.00

2002-03 UD Mask Collection Nation's Best

Inserted at 1:280, thi 6-card set featured jersey swatches from each of the goalies featured on the card fronts.

NDBJ Brian Boucher 12.50 30.00
Brent Johnson
Rick DiPietro
NJBT Marty Turco 12.00 30.00
Sean Burke
Curtis Joseph
NLBT Jose Theodore 30.00 80.00
Roberto Luongo
Martin Biron
NOBB Chris Osgood 12.50 30.00
Dan Blackburn
Ed Belfour
NRBP Martin Brodeur 30.00 80.00
Patrick Roy
Felix Potvin
NRDM Mike Richter 12.50 30.00
Mike Dunham
Ryan Miller

2002-03 UD Mask Collection Patches

Serial-numbered to the total of goals for forwards and wins for goalies, this 42-card set featured swatches of game-worn jersey patches. Print runs under 25 are not priced due to scarcity.

*SINGLE COLOR PATCH: .25X TO .75X HI
PGBS Brendan Shanahan/37 40.00 100.00
PGDB Daniel Briere/32 25.00 60.00
PGED Eric Daze/37 25.00 60.00
PGEL Eric Lindros/37 30.00 80.00
PGGM Glen Murray/41 25.00 60.00
PGIK Ilya Kovalchuk/29 40.00 100.00
PGJA Jason Allison/19
PGJI Jarome Iginla/52 40.00 100.00
PGJJ Jaromir Jagr/31 40.00 100.00
PGJS Joe Sakic/26 40.00 100.00
PGMM Mike Modano/34 40.00 100.00
PGMN Markus Naslund/40 25.00 60.00
PGMS Mats Sundin/41 25.00 60.00
PGPB Peter Bondra/39 30.00 80.00
PGPE Patrik Elias/29 25.00 60.00
PGPK Paul Kariya/32 50.00 125.00
PGSF Sergei Fedorov/30 30.00 80.00
PGSG Simon Gagne/33 25.00 60.00
PGSY Steve Yzerman/13
PGZP Zigmund Palffy/31 25.00 60.00
PWBJ Brent Johnson/34 30.00 80.00
PWBR Martin Brodeur/38 50.00 125.00
PWCJ Curtis Joseph/29 40.00 100.00
PWCO Chris Osgood/31 25.00 60.00
PWDB Dan Blackburn/12
PWEB Ed Belfour/21
PWFP Felix Potvin/31 25.00 60.00
PWJG Jean-Sebastien Giguere/20
PWJH Johan Hedberg/25 25.00 60.00
PWJT Jocelyn Thibault/32 30.00 80.00
PWMB Martin Biron/31 25.00 60.00
PWMD Mike Dunham/23
PWMR Mike Richter/24 40.00 100.00
PWMT Marty Turco/15
PWOK Olaf Kolzig/31 25.00 60.00
PWPR Patrick Roy/32 200.00 400.00
PWRC Roman Cechmanek/24
PWRL Roberto Luongo/16
PWRT Roman Turek/30 25.00 60.00
PWSB Sean Burke/33 25.00 60.00
PWTH Jose Theodore/31 60.00 150.00
PWTS Tommy Salo/30 30.00 80.00

2002-03 UD Mask Collection Super Stoppers

Inserted at a rate of 1:60 hobby packs, this 8-card set featured swatches of game-worn jerseys.

*MULT.COLOR SWATCH: .75X TO 1.5X
SSCJ Curtis Joseph 5.00 12.00
SSCO Chris Osgood 4.00 10.00
SSJT Jose Theodore 6.00 15.00
SSMB Martin Brodeur 8.00 20.00
SSOK Olaf Kolzig 4.00 10.00
SSPR Patrick Roy 12.50 30.00
SSRC Roman Cechmanek 4.00 10.00
SSRT Roman Turek 4.00 10.00

2002-03 UD Mask Collection View from the Cage

Inserted at a rate of 1:140 hobby packs, this 17-card set featured swatches of game-worn jerseys.

*MULT.COLOR SWATCH: .75X TO 1.5X
VBI Martin Biron 6.00 15.00
VCJ Curtis Joseph 6.00 15.00
VEB Ed Belfour 10.00 25.00
VJG Jean-Sebastien Giguere 6.00 15.00
VJH Johan Hedberg 6.00 15.00
VJT Jocelyn Thibault 6.00 15.00
VMB Martin Brodeur 15.00 40.00
VMR Mike Richter 6.00 15.00
VMT Marty Turco 6.00 15.00
VOK Olaf Kolzig 6.00 15.00
VPR Patrick Roy 12.50 30.00
VRC Roman Cechmanek 6.00 15.00
VRL Roberto Luongo 8.00 20.00
VRT Roman Turek 6.00 15.00
VSB Sean Burke 6.00 15.00
VTH Jose Theodore 8.00 20.00
VTS Tommy Salo 6.00 15.00

2008-09 UD Masterpieces

This set was released on September 9, 2008. The base set consists of 87 cards, which are all veterans and legends.

COMPLETE SET (87) 25.00 60.00
1 Lord Stanley .50 1.25
2 Lester B. Pearson .40 1.00

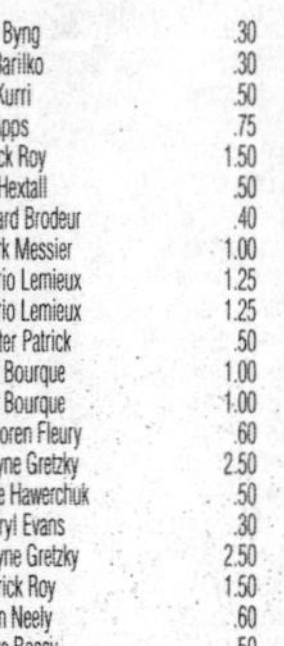

3 Lady Byng .30 .75
4 Bill Barilko .30 .75
5 Jari Kurri .50 1.25
6 Syl Apps .75 2.00
7 Patrick Roy 1.50 4.00
8 Ron Hextall .50 1.25
9 Richard Brodeur .40 1.00
10 Mark Messier 1.00 2.50
11 Mario Lemieux 1.25 3.00
12 Mario Lemieux 1.25 3.00
13 Lester Patrick .50 1.25
14 Ray Bourque 1.00 2.50
15 Ray Bourque 1.00 2.50
16 Theoren Fleury .60 1.50
17 Wayne Gretzky 2.50 6.00
18 Dale Hawerchuk .50 1.25
19 Darryl Evans .30 .75
20 Wayne Gretzky 2.50 6.00
21 Patrick Roy 1.50 4.00
22 Cam Neely .60 1.50
23 Mike Bossy .50 1.25
24 Pat LaFontaine .50 1.25
25 Lanny McDonald .50 1.25
26 Denis Savard .50 1.25
27 Bobby Hull 1.00 2.50
28 Bobby Hull 1.00 2.50
Gordie Howe
29 Georges Vezina 1.00 2.50
30 George Hainsworth .75 2.00
31 Tony Esposito .50 1.25
32 Phil Esposito .75 2.00
33 Bobby Orr 1.50 4.00
34 Bobby Orr 1.50 4.00
35 Jari Kurri .50 1.25
36 Turk Broda .50 1.25
37 Foster Hewitt .30 .75
38 Wayne Gretzky 2.50 6.00
39 Luc Robitaille .40 1.00
40 Rick Vaive .30 .75
41 Borje Salming .50 1.25
42 Darryl Sittler .50 1.25
43 Clark Gillies .40 1.00
44 Scotty Bowman .50 1.25
45 Glenn Anderson .40 1.00
46 Bobby Hull 1.00 2.50
47 Grant Fuhr .50 1.25
48 Ray Bourque 1.00 2.50
49 Brian Leetch .60 1.50
50 Joe Mullen .50 1.25
51 Johnny Bower .60 1.50
52 Bob Baun .50 1.25
53 Guy Lafleur 1.00 2.50
54 Stan Mikita .50 1.25
55 Jean Beliveau .75 2.00
56 Dino Ciccarelli .30 .75
57 Frank Mahovlich .50 1.25
58 Peter Stastny .50 1.25
59 Marcel Dionne .50 1.25
60 Rod Langway .60 1.50
61 Bobby Clarke .50 1.25
62 Darryl Sutter .50 1.25
Duane Sutter
Brent Sutter
Rich Sutter
Ron Sutter
Brian Sutter
63 Steve Shutt .50 1.25
64 Rick McLeish .30 .75
65 Manon Rheaume 1.00 2.50
66 Marty McSorley .30 .75
67 Alex Delvecchio .60 1.50
68 Dale Hawerchuk .50 1.25
69 Gilbert Perreault .50 1.25
70 Rogie Vachon .50 1.25
71 Doug Wilson .30 .75
72 Eddie Shack .50 1.25
73 Willie O'Ree .50 1.25
74 Guy Lafleur 1.00 2.50
75 Bernie Parent .50 1.25
76 Andy Bathgate .50 1.25
77 Craig MacTavish .40 1.00
78 Wayne Gretzky 2.50 6.00
79 Mark Messier 1.00 2.50
80 Gordie Howe 2.00 5.00
81 Mario Lemieux 1.25 3.00
82 Bobby Orr 1.50 4.00
83 Phil Esposito .75 2.00
84 Mark Messier 1.00 2.50
85 Gordie Howe 2.00 5.00
86 Mario Lemieux 1.25 3.00
87 Mark Messier 1.00 2.50

2008-09 UD Masterpieces Black

STATED PRINT RUN 1 SERIAL #'d SET
NOT PRICED DUE TO SCARCITY

2008-09 UD Masterpieces Blue

*BLUE: 3X TO 8X BASE
STATED PRINT RUN 50 SERIAL #'d SETS

2008-09 UD Masterpieces Brown

*BROWN: 1.2X TO 3X
STATED ODDS 1:

2008-09 UD Masterpieces Green

*GREEN: 2.5X TO 6X BASE
STATED PRINT RUN 99 SERIAL #'d SETS

2008-09 UD Masterpieces Red

*RED: 5X TO 12X BASE
STATED PRINT RUN 25 SERIAL #'d SETS

2008-09 UD Masterpieces 5 x 7

COMPLETE SET (24) 40.00 100.00
STATED ODDS 1 PER BOX
XLBH Bobby Hull 4.00 10.00
XLBP Bernie Parent 2.00 5.00
XLBR Richard Brodeur 1.50 4.00
XLBS Borje Salming 2.00 5.00
XLDS Darryl Sittler 2.00 5.00
XLFM Frank Mahovlich 2.00 5.00
XLGF Grant Fuhr 2.00 5.00
XLGH Gordie Howe 8.00 20.00
XLGL Guy Lafleur 4.00 10.00
XLGP Gilbert Perreault 2.00 5.00
XLLM Lanny McDonald 2.00 5.00
XLML Mario Lemieux 5.00 12.00
XLMM Mark Messier 4.00 10.00
XLPE Phil Esposito 3.00 8.00
XLPR Patrick Roy 6.00 15.00
XLRB Ray Bourque 4.00 10.00
XLSB Scotty Bowman 2.00 5.00
XLVT Vladislav Tretiak 1.50 4.00
XLWG Wayne Gretzky 10.00 25.00
XLWO Willie O'Ree 2.00 5.00

2008-09 UD Masterpieces 5 x 7 Autographs

STATED ODDS 1:
XLABB Bob Baun 20.00 50.00
XLABL Brian Leetch 15.00 40.00
XLABO Ray Bourque
XLACN Cam Neely 15.00 40.00
XLAGA Glenn Anderson 10.00 25.00
XLAHH Gordie Howe 100.00 200.00
Bobby Hull
XLAJB Johnny Bower 12.00 30.00
XLAJM Joe Mullen 15.00 40.00
XLALR Luc Robitaille 20.00 50.00
XLAMB Mike Bossy 15.00 40.00
XLAML Mario Lemieux
XLAMM Mark Messier
XLAOR Bobby Orr 125.00 250.00
XLAPL Pat LaFontaine EXCH 15.00 40.00
XLAPR Patrick Roy
XLARH Ron Hextall 15.00 40.00
XLATE Tony Esposito
XLATF Theoren Fleury 15.00 40.00
XLAWG Wayne Gretzky 200.00 350.00

2008-09 UD Masterpieces Brushstrokes Black

STATED PRINT RUN 1 SERIAL #'d SET
NOT PRICED DUE TO SCARCITY

2008-09 UD Masterpieces Brushstrokes Blue

*BLUE: .5X TO 1.2X BROWN
STATED PRINT RUN 10 SERIAL #'d SETS
#'d TO 10 NOT PRICED DUE TO SCARCITY
MBPE Phil Esposito 20.00 50.00

2008-09 UD Masterpieces Brushstrokes Brown

STATED ODDS 1:10
MBAB Andy Bathgate 8.00 20.00
MBAD Alex Delvecchio 10.00 25.00
MBAM Al MacInnis 10.00 25.00
MBAO Adam Oates 8.00 20.00
MBBB Bob Bourne 5.00 12.00
MBBC Bobby Clarke 10.00 25.00
MBBD Bill Dineen 6.00 15.00
MBBF Bernie Federko 6.00 15.00
MBBH Bobby Hull 25.00 60.00
MBBK Johnny Bucyk 8.00 20.00
MBBL Brian Leetch 10.00 25.00
MBBN Bernie Nicholls 5.00 12.00
MBBO Bob Baun 8.00 20.00
MBBR Brian Sutter 8.00 20.00
MBBS Borje Salming 8.00 20.00
MBBU Butch Bouchard 10.00 25.00
MBCA Guy Carbonneau 10.00 25.00
MBCG Clark Gillies 6.00 15.00

MBCH Don Cherry 20.00 50.00
MBCN Cam Neely 20.00 50.00
MBDA Darryl Sutter 5.00 12.00
MBDC Dino Ciccarelli 5.00 12.00
MBDD Dick Duff 8.00 20.00
MBDG Doug Gilmour 10.00 25.00
MBDH Dale Hawerchuk
MBDP Denis Potvin 6.00 15.00
MBDU Duane Sutter 5.00 12.00
MBDW Doug Wilson 5.00 12.00
MBEL Ron Ellis 5.00 12.00
MBES Eddie Shack 8.00 20.00
MBFM Frank Mahovlich 25.00 60.00
MBGA Glenn Anderson 6.00 15.00
MBGF Grant Fuhr 8.00 20.00
MBGH Gordie Howe
MBGL Guy Lafleur 15.00 40.00
MBGP Gilbert Perreault 8.00 20.00
MBHH Harry Howell 8.00 20.00
MBHO Mark Howe 5.00 12.00
MBHX Ron Hextall 15.00 40.00
MBJB Jean Beliveau 25.00 60.00
MBJK Jari Kurri 8.00 20.00
MBJM Joe Mullen 8.00 20.00
MBJO Johnny Bower 10.00 25.00
MBLA Rod Langway 10.00 25.00
MBLM Lanny McDonald 15.00 40.00
MBLR Larry Robinson 8.00 20.00
MBMB Mike Bossy 8.00 20.00
MBMC Craig MacTavish 6.00 15.00
MBMD Marcel Dionne 10.00 25.00
MBMF Mike Foligno 5.00 12.00
MBML Mario Lemieux
MBMM Marty McSorley 5.00 12.00
MBMS Mark Messier 75.00 150.00
MBOR Bobby Orr 100.00 200.00
MBPE Phil Esposito
MBPL Pat LaFontaine
MBPR Patrick Roy
MBPS Peter Stastny 8.00 20.00
MBRB Ray Bourque
MBRD Ron Duguay 8.00 20.00
MBRG Rod Gilbert
MBRH Manon Rheaume 15.00 40.00
MBRI Richard Brodeur 6.00 15.00
MBRK Red Kelly 10.00 25.00
MBRL Rejean Lemelin 5.00 12.00
MBRM Rick McLeish 5.00 12.00
MBRO Luc Robitaille 6.00 15.00
MBRS Rich Sutter 5.00 12.00
MBRV Rogie Vachon 8.00 20.00
MBSA Denis Savard 8.00 20.00
MBSB Scotty Bowman
MBSC Dave Schultz 6.00 15.00
MBSM Stan Mikita 12.00 30.00
MBSR Ron Sutter 6.00 15.00
MBSS Steve Shutt 8.00 20.00
MBSU Brent Sutter 5.00 12.00
MBTE Tony Esposito 8.00 20.00
MBTF Theoren Fleury 10.00 25.00
MBTL Ted Lindsay 8.00 20.00
MBTO Terry O'Reilly 8.00 20.00
MBVT Vladislav Tretiak 25.00 60.00
MBWG Wayne Gretzky 200.00 300.00
MBWO Willie O'Ree 8.00 20.00
MBWT Walt Tkaczuk 5.00 12.00

2008-09 UD Masterpieces Brushstrokes Green

*GREEN: .5X TO 1.2X BROWN
STATED PRINT RUN 35 SERIAL #'d SETS
#'d TO 15 NOT PRICED DUE TO SCARCITY
MBPE Phil Esposito 15.00 40.00

2008-09 UD Masterpieces Brushstrokes Red

STATED PRINT RUN 10 SERIAL #'d SETS
NOT PRICED DUE TO SCARCITY

2008-09 UD Masterpieces Canvas Clippings Black

STATED PRINT RUN 1 SERIAL #'d SET
NOT PRICED DUE TO SCARCITY

2008-09 UD Masterpieces Canvas Clippings Blue

*BLUE: .5X TO 1.2 X BROWN
STATED PRINT RUN 50 SERIAL #'d SETS

2008-09 UD Masterpieces Canvas Clippings Brown

STATED ODDS 1:10
CCAM1 Al MacInnis 6.00 15.00
CCAM2 Al MacInnis 6.00 15.00
CCAO1 Adam Oates 5.00 12.00
CCAO2 Adam Oates 5.00 12.00
CCBC Bobby Clarke 5.00 12.00
CCBF Bernie Federko 4.00 10.00
CCBL Brian Leetch 6.00 15.00
CCBN1 Bernie Nicholls 3.00 8.00
CCBN2 Bernie Nicholls 3.00 8.00
CCBO Bob Bourne 3.00 8.00
CCBR Richard Brodeur 4.00 10.00
CCBS Billy Smith 4.00 10.00
CCBT Bryan Trottier 4.00 10.00
CCBU Johnny Bucyk 5.00 12.00
CCCN Cam Neely 6.00 15.00
CCDC1 Dino Ciccarelli 3.00 8.00
CCDC2 Dino Ciccarelli 3.00 8.00
CCDH Dale Hawerchuk 5.00 12.00
CCDS Darryl Sittler 5.00 12.00
CCFM1 Frank Mahovlich 5.00 12.00
CCFM2 Frank Mahovlich 5.00 12.00
CCGA1 Glenn Anderson 4.00 10.00
CCGA2 Glenn Anderson 4.00 10.00
CCGF Grant Fuhr 5.00 12.00
CCGH Gordie Howe 20.00 50.00
CCGP Gilbert Perreault 5.00 12.00
CCJB Jean Beliveau 10.00 25.00
CCJK Jari Kurri 5.00 12.00
CCJM1 Joe Mullen 5.00 12.00
CCJM2 Joe Mullen 5.00 12.00
CCLM1 Lanny McDonald 5.00 12.00
CCLM2 Lanny McDonald 5.00 12.00
CCLR Larry Robinson 5.00 12.00
CCMD Marcel Dionne 5.00 12.00
CCML Mario Lemieux 12.00 30.00
CCMM1 Mark Messier 10.00 25.00
CCMM2 Mark Messier 10.00 25.00
CCMR Mike Richter 5.00 12.00
CCPE1 Phil Esposito 8.00 20.00
CCPE2 Phil Esposito 8.00 20.00
CCPL Pat LaFontaine 5.00 12.00
CCPR1 Patrick Roy 15.00 40.00
CCPR2 Patrick Roy 15.00 40.00
CCPS Peter Stastny 5.00 12.00
CCRB1 Ray Bourque 10.00 25.00
CCRB2 Ray Bourque 10.00 25.00
CCRE Ron Ellis 3.00 8.00
CCRH Ron Hextall 5.00 12.00
CCRL Rod Langway 6.00 15.00
CCRO Luc Robitaille 4.00 10.00
CCRV1 Rogie Vachon 6.00 15.00
CCRV2 Rogie Vachon 6.00 15.00
CCSA1 Denis Savard 6.00 15.00
CCSA2 Denis Savard 6.00 15.00
CCSB1 Scotty Bowman 5.00 12.00
CCSB2 Scotty Bowman 5.00 12.00
CCSB3 Scotty Bowman 5.00 12.00
CCSG Borje Salming 5.00 12.00
CCSM Stan Mikita 5.00 12.00
CCSS Steve Shutt 5.00 12.00
CCSU Brent Sutter 3.00 8.00
CCTE Tony Esposito 5.00 12.00
CCTF Theoren Fleury 6.00 15.00
CCTW Tiger Williams 3.00 8.00
CCWC1 Wendel Clark 4.00 10.00
CCWC2 Wendel Clark 4.00 10.00
CCWG Wayne Gretzky 40.00 80.00

2008-09 UD Masterpieces Canvas Clippings Green

*GREEN: .4X TO 1X BROWN
STATED PRINT RUN 85 SERIAL #'d SETS

2008-09 UD Masterpieces Canvas Clippings Red

STATED PRINT RUN 10 SERIAL #'d SETS
NOT PRICED DUE TO SCARCITY

2008-09 UD Masterpieces Sketches

STATED PRINT RUN 1 SER.#'d SET
NOT PRICED DUE TO SCARCITY

2006-07 UD Mini Jersey Collection

This 130-card set was issued into the hobby in four-card packs, with an $6.99 SRP, which came 18 to a box. Cards numbered 1-100 feature veterans while cards 101-130 feature 2006-07 NHL rookies.

COMPLETE SET (130) 40.00 100.00
1 Teemu Selanne .40 1.00
2 Jean-Sebastien Giguere .40 1.00
3 Chris Pronger .30 .75
4 Ilya Kovalchuk .50 1.25
5 Kari Lehtonen .40 1.00
6 Marian Hossa .30 .75
7 Patrice Bergeron .30 .75
8 Brad Boyes .25 .60
9 Zdeno Chara .25 .60
10 Thomas Vanek .30 .75
11 Ryan Miller .40 1.00
12 Chris Drury .30 .75
13 Alex Tanguay .30 .75
14 Miikka Kiprusoff .40 1.00
15 Dion Phaneuf .50 1.25
16 Jarome Iginla .60 1.50
17 Eric Staal .40 1.00
18 Cam Ward .60 1.50
19 Erik Cole .25 .60
20 Rod Brind'Amour .30 .75
21 Martin Havlat .30 .75
22 Nikolai Khabibulin .40 1.00
23 Tuomo Ruutu .25 .60
24 Joe Sakic .75 2.00
25 Marek Svatos .25 .60
26 Milan Hejduk .30 .75
27 Jose Theodore .40 1.00
28 Fredrik Modin .25 .60
29 Rick Nash .40 1.00
30 Sergei Fedorov .40 1.00
31 Nikolai Zherdev .25 .60
32 Eric Lindros .40 1.00
33 Mike Modano .40 1.00
34 Marty Turco .30 .75
35 Brenden Morrow .30 .75
36 Henrik Zetterberg .40 1.00
37 Nicklas Lidstrom .40 1.00
38 Dominik Hasek .50 1.25
39 Gordie Howe .75 2.00
40 Pavel Datsyuk .40 1.00
41 Joffrey Lupul .25 .60
42 Fernando Pisani .25 .60
43 Ales Hemsky .25 .60
44 Ryan Smyth .30 .75
45 Dwayne Roloson .30 .75
46 Todd Bertuzzi .30 .75
47 Olli Jokinen .25 .60
48 Ed Belfour 1.00 2.50
49 Rob Blake .30 .75
50 Alexander Frolov .25 .60
51 Marian Gaborik .60 1.50
52 Manny Fernandez .40 1.00
53 Pavol Demitra .25 .60
54 Saku Koivu .40 1.00
55 Michael Ryder .30 .75
56 Patrick Roy 1.25 3.00
57 Sergei Samsonov .30 .75
58 Paul Kariya .40 1.00
59 Tomas Vokoun .30 .75
60 Martin Brodeur 1.25 3.00
61 Patrik Elias .25 .60
62 Alexei Yashin .25 .60
63 Miroslav Satan .25 .60
64 Rick DiPietro .40 1.00
65 Jaromir Jagr .60 1.50
66 Henrik Lundqvist .60 1.50
67 Brendan Shanahan .40 1.00
68 Martin Gerber .40 1.00
69 Jason Spezza .40 1.00
70 Dany Heatley .40 1.00
71 Daniel Alfredsson .30 .75
72 Mike Richards .40 1.00
73 Peter Forsberg .60 1.50
74 Simon Gagne .40 1.00
75 Antero Niittymaki .40 1.00
76 Jeff Carter .40 1.00
77 Shane Doan .30 .75
78 Jeremy Roenick .40 1.00
79 Curtis Joseph .40 1.00
80 Sidney Crosby 2.00 5.00
81 Marc-Andre Fleury .40 1.00
82 Jonathan Cheechoo .40 1.00
83 Vesa Toskala .30 .75
84 Patrick Marleau .30 .75
85 Joe Thornton .60 1.50
86 Keith Tkachuk .30 .75
87 Vincent Lecavalier .40 1.00
88 Martin St. Louis .40 1.00
89 Brad Richards .40 1.00
90 Mats Sundin .40 1.00
91 Alexander Steen .30 .75
92 Bryan McCabe .25 .60
93 Andrew Raycroft .30 .75
94 Darcy Tucker .25 .60
95 Markus Naslund .40 1.00
96 Roberto Luongo .75 2.00
97 Henrik Sedin .25 .60
98 Brendan Morrison .25 .60
99 Olaf Kolzig .50 1.25
100 Alexander Ovechkin 1.50 4.00
101 Yan Stastny RC 2.00 5.00
102 Mark Stuart RC 2.00 5.00
103 Phil Kessel RC 4.00 10.00
104 Ryan Shannon RC 2.00 5.00
105 Tomas Kopecky RC 2.50 6.00
106 Marc-Antoine Pouliot RC 2.50 6.00
107 Konstantin Pushkaryov RC 2.00 5.00
108 Patrick O'Sullivan RC 2.00 5.00
109 Anze Kopitar RC 3.00 8.00
110 Shea Weber RC 2.50 6.00
111 Travis Zajac RC 3.00 8.00
112 Guillaume Latendresse RC 4.00 10.00
113 Marc-Edouard Vlasic RC 2.00 5.00
114 Ladislav Smid RC 2.00 5.00
115 Loui Eriksson RC 1.50 4.00
116 Kristopher Letang RC 3.00 8.00
117 Jarkko Immonen RC 2.00 5.00
118 Nigel Dawes RC 2.00 5.00
119 Luc Bourdon RC 2.50 6.00
120 Ryan Potulny RC 2.50 6.00
121 Keith Yandle RC 2.00 5.00
122 Patrick Thoresen RC 2.00 5.00
123 Noah Welch RC 2.00 5.00
124 Jordan Staal RC 4.00 10.00
125 Matt Carle RC 2.50 6.00
126 Evgeni Malkin RC 8.00 20.00
127 Brendan Bell RC 2.00 5.00
128 Ian White RC 2.00 5.00
129 Jeremy Williams RC 2.00 5.00
130 Eric Fehr RC 2.00 5.00

2006-07 UD Mini Jersey Collection Jerseys

COMPLETE SET (21) 125.00 200.00
ONE PER PACK
AF Alexander Frolov 4.00 10.00
AO Alexander Ovechkin 8.00 20.00
DH Dany Heatley 2.50 6.00
DP Dion Phaneuf 3.00 8.00
EM Evgeni Malkin 8.00 20.00
ES Eric Staal 2.50 6.00
GH Gordie Howe SP 60.00 125.00
HL Henrik Lundqvist 4.00 10.00
IK Ilya Kovalchuk 3.00 8.00
JS Joe Sakic 5.00 12.00
JT Joe Thornton 3.00 8.00
MN Markus Naslund 3.00 8.00
MR Michael Ryder 3.00 8.00
MS Mats Sundin 3.00 8.00
MT Marty Turco 3.00 8.00
PB Patrice Bergeron 2.50 6.00
PF Peter Forsberg 3.00 8.00
PR Patrick Roy 5.00 12.00
RN Rick Nash 3.00 8.00
SC Sidney Crosby 10.00 25.00
TV Thomas Vanek 5.00 12.00

2006-07 UD Mini Jersey Collection Jersey Variations

* VARIATIONS: 1.25X TO 3X HI
AF Alexander Frolov 8.00 20.00
AO Alexander Ovechkin 12.00 30.00
DH Dany Heatley 6.00 15.00
DP Dion Phaneuf 6.00 15.00
EM Evgeni Malkin 20.00 50.00
ES Eric Staal 6.00 15.00
GH Gordie Howe 200.00 350.00
HL Henrik Lundqvist 6.00 15.00
IK Ilya Kovalchuk 6.00 15.00
JS Joe Sakic 8.00 20.00
JT Joe Thornton 8.00 20.00
MN Markus Naslund 6.00 15.00
MR Michael Ryder 6.00 15.00
MS Mats Sundin 6.00 15.00
PB Patrice Bergeron 6.00 15.00
PF Peter Forsberg 6.00 15.00
PR Patrick Roy 12.00 30.00
RN Rick Nash 6.00 15.00
SC Sidney Crosby 25.00 60.00
TV Thomas Vanek 8.00 20.00

2006-07 UD Mini Jersey Collection Jersey Autographs

STATED ODDS 1 PER CASE
AF Alexander Frolov 25.00 60.00
AO Alexander Ovechkin SP 75.00 150.00
DH Dany Heatley SP
DP Dion Phaneuf 50.00 125.00
ES Eric Staal 40.00 80.00
GH Gordie Howe SP 250.00 400.00
IK Ilya Kovalchuk SP 75.00 150.00
JT Joe Thornton SP 75.00 150.00
MN Markus Naslund 25.00 60.00
MR Michael Ryder 25.00 60.00
MT Marty Turco 25.00 60.00
PB Patrice Bergeron SP 50.00 100.00
SC Sidney Crosby SP 300.00 500.00
TV Thomas Vanek 30.00 80.00

2007-08 UD Mini Jersey Collection

This set was released on March 24, 2008. The base set consists of 150 cards. Cards 1-100 feature veterans, and cards 101-150 are rookies.

COMPLETE SET (150) 125.00 250.00
COMP.SET w/o SPs (100) 12.00 30.00
1 Jean-Sebastien Giguere .40 1.00
2 Ryan Getzlaf .30 .75
3 Scott Niedermayer .25 .60
4 Chris Pronger .40 1.00
5 Ilya Kovalchuk .50 1.25
6 Marian Hossa .40 1.00
7 Kari Lehtonen .40 1.00
8 Patrice Bergeron .40 1.00
9 Phil Kessel .40 1.00
10 Zdeno Chara .25 .60
11 Ryan Miller .40 1.00
12 Thomas Vanek .30 .75
13 Jason Pominville .25 .60
14 Derek Roy .25 .60
15 Miikka Kiprusoff .50 1.25
16 Jarome Iginla .60 1.50
17 Alex Tanguay .30 .75
18 Dion Phaneuf .40 1.00
19 Eric Staal .40 1.00
20 Cam Ward .40 1.00
21 Justin Williams .25 .60
22 Martin Havlat .30 .75
23 Nikolai Khabibulin .40 1.00
24 Duncan Keith .40 1.00
25 Joe Sakic .75 2.00
26 Milan Hejduk .30 .75
27 Peter Budaj .30 .75
28 Paul Stastny .40 1.00
29 Marty Turco .40 1.00
30 Mike Modano .40 1.00
31 Mike Ribeiro .25 .60
32 Henrik Zetterberg .40 1.00
33 Nicklas Lidstrom .40 1.00
34 Pavel Datsyuk .40 1.00
35 Dominik Hasek .50 1.25
36 Ales Hemsky .25 .60
37 Dwayne Roloson .30 .75
38 Jarret Stoll .25 .60
39 Shawn Horcoff .25 .60
40 Tomas Vokoun .40 1.00
41 Olli Jokinen .25 .60
42 Nathan Horton .25 .60
43 Anze Kopitar .40 1.00
44 Alexander Frolov .25 .60
45 Rob Blake .30 .75
46 Mike Cammalleri .30 .75
47 Marian Gaborik .50 1.25
48 Niklas Backstrom .30 .75
49 Pierre-Marc Bouchard .25 .60
50 Saku Koivu .30 .75
51 Michael Ryder .25 .60
52 Guillaume Latendresse .30 .75
53 Cristobal Huet .30 .75
54 Alexander Radulov .40 1.00
55 Chris Mason .30 .75
56 Jason Arnott .25 .60
57 Martin Brodeur 1.00 2.50
58 Patrik Elias .25 .60
59 Zach Parise .30 .75
60 Miroslav Satan .25 .60
61 Bill Guerin .25 .60
62 Rick DiPietro .25 .60
63 Jaromir Jagr .60 1.50
64 Henrik Lundqvist .50 1.25
65 Martin Straka .25 .60
66 Dany Heatley .50 1.25
67 Ray Emery .25 .60
68 Daniel Alfredsson .30 .75
69 Jason Spezza .40 1.00
70 Simon Gagne .40 1.00
71 Jeff Carter .25 .60
72 Martin Biron .30 .75
73 Shane Doan .25 .60
74 Ed Jovanovski .25 .60
75 Keith Ballard .25 .60
76 Sidney Crosby 2.00 5.00
77 Evgeni Malkin 1.00 2.50
78 Marc-Andre Fleury .40 1.00
79 Jordan Staal .50 1.25
80 Joe Thornton .50 1.25
81 Patrick Marleau .30 .75
82 Jonathan Cheechoo .30 .75
83 Evgeni Nabokov .30 .75
84 Doug Weight .25 .60
85 Manny Legace .30 .75
86 Brad Boyes .30 .75
87 Vincent Lecavalier .40 1.00
88 Brad Richards .30 .75
89 Martin St. Louis .30 .75
90 Mats Sundin .40 1.00
91 Vesa Toskala .30 .75
92 Alexander Steen .25 .60
93 Darcy Tucker .25 .60
94 Roberto Luongo .60 1.50
95 Markus Naslund .40 1.00
96 Henrik Sedin .25 .60
97 Daniel Sedin .25 .60
98 Alexander Ovechkin 1.25 3.00
99 Olaf Kolzig .40 1.00
100 Alexander Semin .40 1.00
101 Bobby Ryan RC 4.00 10.00
102 Drew Miller RC 1.00 2.50
103 Bryan Little RC 1.50 4.00
104 Ondrej Pavelec RC 1.50 4.00
105 Tuukka Rask RC 2.50 6.00
106 Vladimir Sobotka RC 1.25 3.00
107 Milan Lucic RC 2.50 6.00
108 Curtis McElhinney RC 1.25 3.00
109 Matt Keetley RC 1.25 3.00
110 Jonathan Toews RC 8.00 20.00
111 Patrick Kane RC 6.00 15.00
112 Tyler Weiman RC 1.25 3.00
113 T.J. Hensick RC 1.25 3.00
114 Kris Russell RC 1.50 4.00
115 Jared Boll RC 1.00 2.50
116 Matt Niskanen RC 1.00 2.50
117 Sam Gagner RC 2.00 5.00
118 Andrew Cogliano RC 2.50 6.00
119 Rob Schremp RC 1.25 3.00
120 Stefan Meyer RC 1.00 2.50
121 Jack Johnson RC 1.50 4.00
122 Jonathan Bernier RC 2.50 6.00
123 Petr Kalus RC 1.00 2.50
124 James Sheppard RC 1.00 2.50
125 Cal Clutterbuck RC 1.00 2.50
126 Carey Price RC 8.00 20.00
127 Kyle Chipchura RC 1.50 4.00
128 Nicklas Bergfors RC 1.25 3.00
129 Andy Greene RC 1.00 2.50
130 Frans Nielsen RC 1.00 2.50
131 Marc Staal RC 2.50 6.00
132 Ryan Callahan RC 1.50 4.00
133 Alexander Nikulin RC 1.25 3.00
134 Nick Foligno RC 1.50 4.00
135 Steve Downie RC 1.25 3.00
136 Peter Mueller RC 3.00 8.00
137 Martin Hanzal RC 1.25 3.00
138 Tyler Kennedy RC 1.50 4.00
139 Thomas Greiss RC 1.50 4.00
140 Devin Setoguchi RC 2.00 5.00
141 Torrey Mitchell RC 1.25 3.00
142 Erik Johnson RC 2.00 5.00
143 David Perron RC 1.50 4.00
144 Matt Smaby RC 1.00 2.50
145 Anton Stralman RC 1.25 3.00
146 Jiri Tlusty RC 2.50 6.00
147 Mason Raymond RC 2.50 6.00
148 Jannik Hansen RC 1.00 2.50
149 Chris Bourque RC 1.25 3.00
150 Nicklas Backstrom RC 4.00 10.00

2007-08 UD Mini Jersey Collection Jerseys

COMPLETE SET (30) 50.00 100.00
ONE PER PACK
MINI1 Teemu Selanne 2.00 5.00
MINI2 Kari Lehtonen 2.00 5.00
MINI3 Phil Kessel 2.00 5.00
MINI4 Ryan Miller 2.00 5.00
MINI5 Jarome Iginla 3.00 8.00
MINI6 Cam Ward 2.00 5.00
MINI7 Martin Havlat 1.50 4.00
MINI8 Joe Sakic 4.00 10.00
MINI9 Sergei Fedorov 2.00 5.00
MINI10 Mike Modano 2.00 5.00
MINI11 Henrik Zetterberg 2.00 5.00
MINI12 Dwayne Roloson 1.50 4.00
MINI13 Olli Jokinen 1.25 3.00
MINI14 Anze Kopitar 2.00 5.00
MINI15 Marian Gaborik 2.50 6.00
MINI16 Saku Koivu 1.50 4.00
MINI17 Alexander Radulov 2.00 5.00
MINI18 Martin Brodeur 5.00 12.00
MINI19 Rick DiPietro 1.50 4.00
MINI20 Jaromir Jagr 3.00 8.00
MINI21 Jason Spezza 2.00 5.00
MINI22 Simon Gagne 2.00 5.00
MINI23 Shane Doan 1.25 3.00
MINI24 Sidney Crosby 10.00 25.00
MINI25 Jonathan Cheechoo 1.50 4.00
MINI26 Doug Weight 1.25 3.00
MINI27 Vincent Lecavalier 2.00 5.00
MINI28 Mats Sundin 2.00 5.00
MINI29 Roberto Luongo 3.00 8.00
MINI30 Alexander Ovechkin 6.00 15.00

2007-08 UD Mini Jersey Collection Jerseys Variations

COMPLETE SET (30) 150.00 300.00
*VARIATIONS: .8X TO 2X 4.00 10.00
STATED ODDS 1:9 PACKS

2007-08 UD Mini Jersey Collection Jerseys Autographs

STATED ODDS 1:360
AUTO2 Phil Kessel 30.00 80.00
AUTO3 Ryan Miller 30.00 80.00
AUTO4 Jarome Iginla 50.00 120.00
AUTO5 Cam Ward 30.00 80.00
AUTO6 Martin Havlat
AUTO7 Mike Modano 30.00 80.00
AUTO8 Dwayne Roloson 25.00 60.00
AUTO9 Anze Kopitar 30.00 80.00
AUTO10 Marian Gaborik
AUTO11 Saku Koivu
AUTO12 Alexander Radulov 30.00 80.00
AUTO13 Martin Brodeur 80.00 200.00
AUTO14 Simon Gagne
AUTO15 Sidney Crosby 150.00 400.00
AUTO16 Jonathan Cheechoo 25.00 60.00
AUTO17 Vincent Lecavalier
AUTO18 Alexander Ovechkin 100.00 250.00

2004 Upper Deck National Convention

STATED PRINT RUN 500 SER.#'d SETS
TN13 Wayne Gretzky 3.00 8.00
TN14 Gordie Howe 1.00 2.50
TN15 Joe Thornton .60 1.50
TN17 Jason Spezza .60 1.50

2004 Upper Deck National Convention VIP

VIP5 Wayne Gretzky 4.00 10.00

2007 Upper Deck National Convention

NTL12 Wayne Gretzky 1.25 3.00
NTL13 Rick Nash .75 2.00
NTL14 Sidney Crosby 1.25 3.00
NTL15 Evgeni Malkin 1.00 2.50

2007 Upper Deck National Convention VIP

VIP12 Wayne Gretzky 2.00 5.00
VIP13 Rick Nash 1.25 3.00
VIP14 Sidney Crosby 2.00 5.00
VIP15 Evgeni Malkin 1.50 4.00

2005-06 UD Phenomenal Beginnings

COMPLETE SET (20) 15.00 30.00
COMMON CARD (1-20) .60 1.50
NNO Sidney Crosby AU

2002-03 UD Piece of History

This 150-card set consisted of 90 regular base cards, 18 "Season to Remember subset cards, 12 "Tribute to Greatness" subset cards and 30 shortprinted "History in the Making" rookie cards. Subset cards were serial-numbered to 2999 and rookie cards were serial-numbered to 1500.

COMP.SET w/o SP's (90) 15.00 30.00
1 Paul Kariya .20 .50
2 Jean-Sebastien Giguere .15 .40
3 Ilya Kovalchuk .25 .60
4 Dany Heatley .25 .60
5 Joe Thornton .30 .75
6 Sergei Samsonov .15 .40
7 Glen Murray .08 .20
8 Miroslav Satan .15 .40
9 Tim Connolly .08 .20
10 Martin Biron .15 .40
11 Jeff O'Neill .08 .20
12 Erik Cole .08 .20
13 Ron Francis .15 .40
14 Arturs Irbe .15 .40
15 Roman Turek .15 .40
16 Marc Savard .15 .40
17 Jarome Iginla .25 .60
18 Eric Daze .15 .40
19 Steve Sullivan .08 .20
20 Jocelyn Thibault .15 .40
21 Espen Knutsen .08 .20
22 Rostislav Klesla .08 .20
23 Marc Denis .15 .40
24 Patrick Roy 1.00 2.50
25 Chris Drury .15 .40
26 Joe Sakic .40 1.00
27 Peter Forsberg .50 1.25
28 Alex Tanguay .15 .40
29 Mike Modano .30 .75
30 Marty Turco .15 .40
31 Jason Arnott .08 .20
32 Steve Yzerman 1.00 2.50
33 Sergei Fedorov .30 .75
34 Nicklas Lidstrom .20 .50
35 Brett Hull .25 .60
36 Curtis Joseph .20 .50
37 Brendan Shanahan .20 .50
38 Mike Comrie .15 .40
39 Tommy Salo .15 .40
40 Ryan Smyth .08 .20
41 Roberto Luongo .25 .60
42 Kristian Huselius .08 .20
43 Jason Allison .08 .20
44 Felix Potvin .20 .50
45 Zigmund Palffy .15 .40
46 Marian Gaborik .40 1.00
47 Manny Fernandez .15 .40
48 Jose Theodore .25 .60
49 Saku Koivu .20 .50
50 Patrik Elias .15 .40
51 Martin Brodeur .50 1.25
52 Joe Nieuwendyk .15 .40
53 Scott Hartnell .08 .20
54 Mike Dunham .15 .40
55 Alexei Yashin .08 .20
56 Chris Osgood .15 .40
57 Michael Peca .08 .20
58 Eric Lindros .20 .50
59 Mike Richter .15 .40
60 Pavel Bure .20 .50
61 Brian Leetch .15 .40
62 Patrick Lalime .15 .40
63 Marian Hossa .20 .50
64 Daniel Alfredsson .15 .40
65 Jeremy Roenick .25 .60
66 Simon Gagne .20 .50
67 Roman Cechmanek .15 .40
68 Sean Burke .15 .40
69 Daniel Briere .08 .20
70 Tony Amonte .15 .40
71 Alexei Kovalev .15 .40
72 Mario Lemieux 1.25 3.00
73 Johan Hedberg .20 .50
74 Patrick Marleau .15 .40
75 Owen Nolan .15 .40
76 Evgeni Nabokov .15 .40
77 Keith Tkachuk .20 .50
78 Chris Pronger .15 .40
79 Brent Johnson .15 .40
80 Nikolai Khabibulin .20 .50
81 Vincent Lecavalier .20 .50
82 Alexander Mogilny .15 .40
83 Mats Sundin .20 .50
84 Ed Belfour .20 .50
85 Todd Bertuzzi .20 .50
86 Dan Cloutier .15 .40
87 Markus Naslund .20 .50
88 Olaf Kolzig .15 .40
89 Peter Bondra .15 .40
90 Jaromir Jagr .30 .75
91 Wayne Gretzky SR 2.50 6.00
92 Wayne Gretzky SR 5.00 12.00
93 Mario Lemieux SR 5.00 12.00
94 Patrick Roy SR 4.00 10.00
95 Steve Yzerman SR 4.00 10.00
96 Gordie Howe SR 2.00 5.00
97 Bobby Orr SR 5.00 12.00
98 Ray Bourque SR .75 2.00
99 Brett Hull SR .75 2.00
100 Teemu Selanne SR .20 .50
101 Martin Brodeur SR 2.00 5.00
102 Jaromir Jagr SR 1.25 3.00
103 Eric Lindros SR 1.25 3.00
104 Joe Sakic SR 1.50 4.00
105 Mike Richter SR .60 1.50
106 Sergei Fedorov SR 1.50 4.00
107 Peter Forsberg SR 2.00 5.00
108 Mark Messier SR .20 .50
109 Wayne Gretzky TG 2.50 6.00
110 Wayne Gretzky TG 5.00 12.00
111 Wayne Gretzky TG 5.00 12.00
112 Gordie Howe TG 2.00 5.00
113 Gordie Howe TG 4.00 10.00
114 Gordie Howe TG 4.00 10.00
115 Bobby Orr TG 5.00 12.00
116 Bobby Orr TG 5.00 12.00
117 Bobby Orr TG 5.00 12.00
118 Ray Bourque TG .75 2.00
119 Ray Bourque TG 1.50 4.00
120 Ray Bourque TG 1.50 4.00
121 Stanislav Chistov HM RC 2.00 5.00
122 Alexei Smirnov HM RC 2.00 5.00
123 Henrik Tallinder HM 1.50 4.00
124 Micki Dupont HM RC 1.50 4.00
125 Chuck Kobasew HM RC 1.50 4.00
126 Andrej Nedorost HM 1.50 4.00
127 Rick Nash HM RC 8.00 20.00
128 Henrik Zetterberg HM RC 6.00 15.00
129 Ales Hemsky HM RC 4.00 10.00
130 Jani Rita HM 1.50 4.00
131 Stephen Weiss HM .08 .20
132 Jay Bouwmeester HM RC 3.00 8.00
133 Alexander Frolov HM RC 3.00 8.00
134 P-M Bouchard HM RC 3.00 8.00
135 Sylvain Blouin HM RC 1.50 4.00
136 Ron Hainsey HM RC 1.50 4.00
137 Adam Hall HM RC 1.50 4.00
138 Jan Lasak HM 1.50 4.00
139 Ray Schultz HM RC 1.00 2.50
140 Trent Hunter HM 1.50 4.00
141 Martin Prusek HM 1.50 4.00
142 Anton Volchenkov HM RC 1.50 4.00
143 Patrick Sharp HM RC 1.50 4.00
144 Dennis Seidenberg HM RC 2.00 5.00
145 Branko Radivojevic HM 1.50 4.00
146 Shane Endicott HM 1.50 4.00
147 Alexander Svitov HM RC 2.00 5.00
148 Sebastien Centomo HM 1.50 4.00
149 Karel Pilar HM 1.50 4.00
150 Steve Eminger HM RC 1.50 4.00

2002-03 UD Piece of History Awards Collection

COMPLETE SET (28) 25.00 50.00
STAT.ODDS 1:5 HBBY/1:6 RETAIL
AC1 Paul Kariya .50 1.25
AC2 Ray Bourque 1.00 2.50
AC3 Sergei Samsonov .40 1.00
AC4 Jarome Iginla .60 1.50
AC5 Chris Drury .40 1.00
AC6 Joe Sakic 1.00 2.50
AC7 Rob Blake .40 1.00
AC8 Peter Forsberg 1.25 3.00
AC9 Patrick Roy 2.50 6.00
AC10 Luc Robitaille .40 1.00
AC11 Brett Hull .60 1.50
AC12 Steve Yzerman 2.50 6.00
AC13 Dominik Hasek 1.00 2.50
AC14 Nicklas Lidstrom .50 1.25
AC15 Sergei Fedorov 1.00 2.50
AC16 Wayne Gretzky 3.00 8.00
AC17 Joe Nieuwendyk .40 1.00
AC18 Martin Brodeur 1.25 3.00
AC19 Brian Leetch .40 1.00
AC20 Pavel Bure .60 1.50
AC21 Claude Lemieux .40 1.00
AC22 Mario Lemieux 3.00 8.00
AC23 Evgeni Nabokov .40 1.00

AC24 Teemu Selanne .50 1.25
AC25 Chris Pronger .40 1.00
AC26 Al MacInnis .40 1.00
AC27 Jaromir Jagr .75 2.00
AC28 Olaf Kolzig .40 1.00

2002-03 UD Piece of History Exquisite Combos

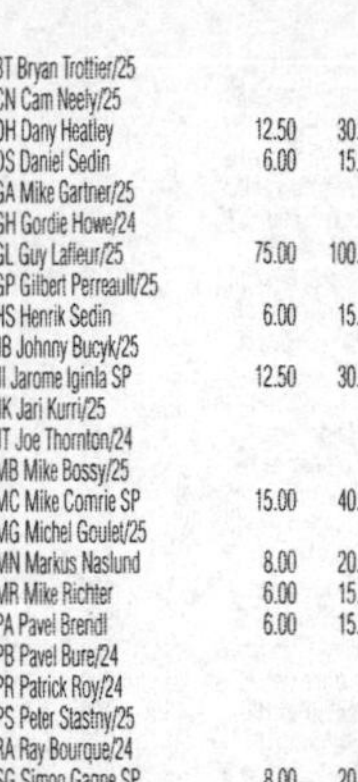

ODDS 1:168 HOBBY ONLY
ECBM Pavel Bure 12.50 30.00
Mark Messier
ECBR Rob Blake 15.00 40.00
Patrick Roy
ECLK M.Lemieux/A.Kovalev 20.00 50.00
ECLM Eric Lindros 12.50 30.00
Mark Messier
ECNB Cam Neely 12.50 30.00
Ray Bourque

2002-03 UD Piece of History Heroes Jerseys

*MULT.COLOR SWATCH: .5X TO 1.25X HI
STATED ODDS 1:48
HHBS Borje Salming 4.00 10.00
HHGP Gilbert Perreault 3.00 8.00
HHJK Jari Kurri 5.00 12.00
HHMG Mike Gartner 3.00 8.00
HHPS Peter Stastny 3.00 8.00

2002-03 UD Piece of History Historical Swatches

*MULT.COLOR SWATCH: .5X TO 1.25X HI
STATED ODDS 1:96
HSBS Borje Salming 6.00 15.00
HSBT Bryan Trottier 5.00 12.00
HSCN Cam Neely 15.00 40.00
HSGL Guy Lafleur 5.00 12.00
HSJB Johnny Bucyk 5.00 12.00
HSMB Mike Bossy 5.00 12.00
HSMG Mike Gartner 5.00 12.00
HSMG Michel Goulet 5.00 12.00
HSRB Ray Bourque 15.00 40.00
HSWG Wayne Gretzky 30.00 80.00

2002-03 UD Piece of History Hockey Beginnings

COMPLETE SET (8) 20.00 40.00
STATED ODDS 1:20
HB1 Bobby Orr 2.50 6.00
HB2 Ray Bourque .75 2.00
HB3 Steve Yzerman 2.00 5.00
HB4 Gordie Howe 2.00 5.00
HB5 Wayne Gretzky 2.50 6.00
HB6 Patrick Roy 2.00 5.00
HB7 Mike Bossy .60 1.50
HB8 Wayne Gretzky 2.50 6.00

2002-03 UD Piece of History Marks of Distinction

This 31-card autograph set was inserted at a rate of 1:168 hobby packs. Print runs listed below were provided by Upper Deck. Print runs of 25 or less not priced due to scarcity.

BO Bobby Orr/24
BR Rod Brind'Amour 6.00 15.00
BT Bryan Trottier/25
CN Cam Neely/25
DH Dany Heatley 12.50 30.00
DS Daniel Sedin 6.00 15.00
GA Mike Gartner/25
GH Gordie Howe/24
GL Guy Lafleur/25 75.00 100.00
GP Gilbert Perreault/25
HS Henrik Sedin 6.00 15.00
JB Johnny Bucyk/25
JI Jarome Iginla SP 12.50 30.00
JK Jari Kurri/25
JT Joe Thornton/24
MB Mike Bossy/25
MC Mike Comrie SP 15.00 40.00
MG Michel Goulet/25
MN Markus Naslund 8.00 20.00
MR Mike Richter 6.00 15.00
PA Pavel Brendl 6.00 15.00
PB Pavel Bure/24
PR Patrick Roy/24
PS Peter Stastny/25
RA Ray Bourque/24
SG Simon Gagne SP 8.00 20.00
SS Sergei Samsonov SP 12.50 30.00
SY Steve Yzerman 40.00 100.00
TS Teemu Selanne 8.00 20.00
VN Vaclav Nedorost 6.00 15.00
WG Wayne Gretzky/24 200.00 500.00

2002-03 UD Piece of History Patches

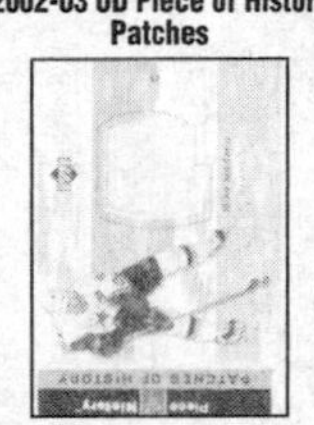

This 28-card memorabilia set had a stated print run of 25 serial-numbered sets.

PHBA Rob Blake 20.00 50.00
PHBL Brian Leetch 20.00 50.00
PHBS Brendan Shanahan 20.00 50.00
PHEL Eric Lindros 20.00 50.00
PHFP Felix Potvin 20.00 50.00
PHJS Joe Sakic 50.00 125.00
PHJT Jose Theodore 25.00 60.00
PHKP Keith Primeau 20.00 50.00
PHMA Maxim Afinogenov 20.00 50.00
PHMD Mike Dunham 20.00 50.00
PHMM Mike Modano 30.00 80.00
PHMN Markus Naslund 20.00 50.00
PHMS Mats Sundin 20.00 50.00
PHMT Marty Turco 20.00 50.00
PHPK Paul Kariya 20.00 50.00
PHPR Patrick Roy 75.00 200.00
PHRB Ray Bourque 50.00 125.00
PHRT Ron Tugnutt 20.00 50.00
PHSA Sergei Samsonov 20.00 50.00
PHSR Sean Burke 20.00 50.00
PHSF Sergei Fedorov 30.00 80.00
PHSG Simon Gagne 20.00 50.00
PHSS Steve Sullivan 20.00 50.00
PHSY Steve Yzerman 75.00 200.00
PHTH Joe Thornton 40.00 100.00
PHTS Teemu Selanne 20.00 50.00
PHWG Wayne Gretzky 125.00 300.00
PHZP Zigmund Palffy 20.00 50.00

2002-03 UD Piece of History Simply the Best

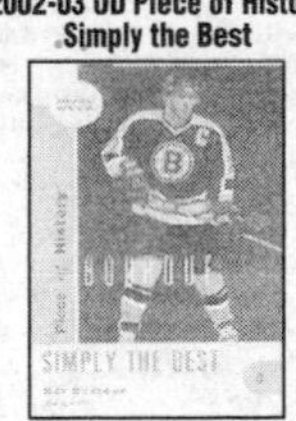

COMPLETE SET (6) 20.00 40.00
STATED ODDS 1:24
SB1 Ray Bourque 1.25 3.00
SB2 Bobby Orr 4.00 10.00
SB3 Patrick Roy 3.00 8.00
SB4 Steve Yzerman 3.00 8.00
SB5 Gordie Howe 3.00 8.00
SB6 Wayne Gretzky 4.00 10.00

2002-03 UD Piece of History Stellar Stitches

*MULT.COLOR SWATCH: .5X TO 1.25X HI
STATED ODDS 1:168 HOBBY PACKS
SSJS Joe Sakic 8.00 20.00
SSJT Joe Thornton 8.00 20.00
SSMM Mike Modano 6.00 15.00
SSMS Mats Sundin 5.00 12.00
SSPK Paul Kariya 5.00 12.00
SSSY Steve Yzerman 12.50 30.00

2002-03 UD Piece of History Threads

*MULT.COLOR SWATCH: .5X TO 1.25X HI
STATED ODDS 1:96 RETAIL PACKS

TTCD Chris Drury 5.00 12.00
TTCL Claude Lemieux 5.00 12.00
TTJT Jose Theodore 6.00 15.00
TTSF Sergei Fedorov 6.00 15.00
TTSG Simon Gagne 5.00 12.00
TTSH Scott Hartnell 5.00 12.00

2001-02 UD Playmakers

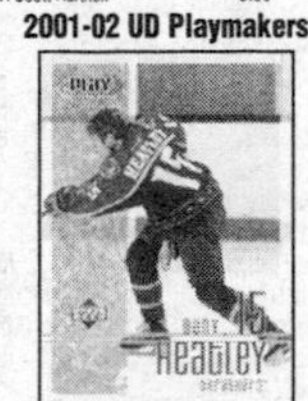

This 145-card set was released in early April and had a SRP of $2.99. The card front featured the a color photo of the player with his name, number and team in team colors in the lower right corner. The left side of the card fronts also were colored the featured team's color. Rookies in this set were short printed out of 1250.

COMP.SET w/o SP's (100) 10.00 20.00
1 Steve Shields .05 .15
2 Jeff Friesen .05 .15
3 Paul Kariya .12 .30
4 Ray Ferraro .05 .15
5 Milan Hnilicka .10 .25
6 Dany Heatley .15 .40
7 Sergei Samsonov .10 .25
8 Joe Thornton .20 .50
9 Byron Dafoe .10 .25
10 Hal Gill .05 .15
11 Miroslav Satan .10 .25
12 Stu Barnes .05 .15
13 Martin Biron .10 .25
14 Marc Savard .05 .15
15 Roman Turek .10 .25
16 Jarome Iginla .15 .40
17 Jeff O'Neill .05 .15
18 Sami Kapanen .05 .15
19 Arturs Irbe .10 .25
20 Steve Sullivan .05 .15
21 Jocelyn Thibault .10 .25
22 Tony Amonte .10 .25
23 Joe Sakic .25 .60
24 Milan Hejduk .12 .30
25 Chris Drury .10 .25
26 Patrick Roy .60 1.50
27 Rob Blake .10 .25
28 Marc Denis .10 .25
29 Ray Whitney .05 .15
30 Rostislav Klesla .05 .15
31 Ed Belfour .12 .30
32 Pierre Turgeon .10 .25
33 Mike Modano .20 .50
34 Brett Hull .15 .40
35 Dominik Hasek .25 .60
36 Brendan Shanahan .12 .30
37 Luc Robitaille .10 .25
38 Steve Yzerman .60 1.50
39 Mike Comrie .10 .25
40 Tommy Salo .10 .25
41 Ryan Smyth .05 .15
42 Anson Carter .05 .15
43 Valeri Bure .05 .15
44 Roberto Luongo .15 .40
45 Pavel Bure .12 .30
46 Felix Potvin .12 .30
47 Jason Allison .05 .15
48 Zigmund Palffy .10 .25
49 Manny Fernandez .10 .25
50 Marian Gaborik .25 .60
51 Andrew Brunette .05 .15
52 Yanic Perreault .05 .15
53 Jose Theodore .15 .40
54 Brian Savage .05 .15
55 David Legwand .10 .25
56 Mike Dunham .10 .25
57 Cliff Ronning .05 .15
58 Martin Brodeur .30 .75
59 Patrik Elias .10 .25
60 Jason Arnott .05 .15
61 Alexei Yashin .05 .15
62 Chris Osgood .10 .25
63 Mark Parrish .05 .15
64 Theo Fleury .05 .15
65 Brian Leetch .10 .25
66 Mark Messier .12 .30
67 Eric Lindros .12 .30
68 Radek Bonk .05 .15
69 Marian Hossa .12 .30
70 Martin Havlat .10 .25
71 John LeClair .12 .30
72 Mark Recchi .10 .25
73 Roman Cechmanek .10 .25
74 Jeremy Roenick .15 .40
75 Michal Handzus .05 .15
76 Shane Doan .05 .15
77 Sean Burke .10 .25
78 Alexei Kovalev .10 .25
79 Mario Lemieux .75 2.00
80 Johan Hedberg .10 .25
81 Owen Nolan .10 .25
82 Teemu Selanne .12 .30
83 Evgeni Nabokov .10 .25
84 Chris Pronger .10 .25
85 Pavol Demitra .10 .25
86 Keith Tkachuk .12 .30
87 Doug Weight .10 .25
88 Vincent Lecavalier .12 .30
89 Brad Richards .10 .25
90 Nikolai Khabibulin .12 .30
91 Wade Belak .05 .15
92 Alexander Mogilny .10 .25
93 Mats Sundin .12 .30
94 Curtis Joseph .12 .30
95 Brendan Morrison .10 .25
96 Trevor Linden .05 .15
97 Markus Naslund .12 .30
98 Peter Bondra .12 .30
99 Olaf Kolzig .10 .25
100 Jaromir Jagr .20 .50
101 Timo Parssinen RC 1.50 4.00
102 Ilja Bryzgalov RC 1.50 4.00
103 Mike Weaver RC 1.50 4.00
104 Ilya Kovalchuk RC 5.00 12.00
105 Ivan Huml RC 1.50 4.00
106 Tony Tuzzolino RC 1.50 4.00
107 Jukka Hentunen RC 1.50 4.00
108 Scott Nichol RC 1.50 4.00
109 Erik Cole RC 1.50 4.00
110 Mike Peluso RC 1.50 4.00
111 Riku Hahl RC 1.50 4.00
112 Vaclav Nedorost RC 1.50 4.00
113 Blake Bellefeuille RC 1.50 4.00
114 Niko Kapanen RC 2.00 5.00
115 John Erskine RC 1.50 4.00
116 Pavel Datsyuk RC 5.00 12.00
117 Ty Conklin RC 1.50 4.00
118 Jason Chimera RC 1.50 4.00
119 Niklas Hagman RC 1.50 4.00
120 Kristian Huselius RC 2.00 5.00
121 Kip Brennan RC 1.50 4.00
122 Pascal Dupuis RC 1.50 4.00
123 Marcel Hossa RC 1.50 4.00
124 Olivier Michaud RC 1.50 4.00
125 Martin Erat RC 1.50 4.00
126 Christian Berglund RC 1.50 4.00
127 Andreas Salomonsson RC 1.50 4.00
128 Raffi Torres RC 2.00 5.00
129 Radek Martinek RC 1.50 4.00
130 Mikael Samuelsson RC 1.50 4.00
131 Dan Blackburn RC 2.00 5.00
132 Toni Dahlman RC 1.50 4.00
133 Bruno St. Jacques RC 1.50 4.00
134 Tomas Divisek RC 1.50 4.00
135 Jiri Dopita RC 1.50 4.00
136 Krys Kolanos RC 1.50 4.00
137 Eric Meloche RC 1.50 4.00
138 Tom Kostopoulos RC 1.50 4.00
139 Jeff Jillson RC 1.50 4.00
140 Mark Rycroft RC 1.50 4.00
141 Josef Boumedienne RC 1.50 4.00
142 Nikita Alexeev RC 1.50 4.00
143 Mike Farrell RC 1.50 4.00
144 Todd Rohloff RC 1.50 4.00
145 Brian Sutherby RC 1.50 4.00

2001-02 UD Playmakers Bobble Heads

Inserted at one per hobby box, this 24-figure set featured 12 players in both home and away jerseys.

CJA Curtis Joseph 5.00 12.00
CJH Curtis Joseph 5.00 12.00
DHA Dominik Hasek 5.00 12.00
DHH Dominik Hasek 5.00 12.00
DWA Doug Weight 5.00 12.00
DWH Doug Weight 5.00 12.00
ELA Eric Lindros 5.00 12.00
ELH Eric Lindros 5.00 12.00
IKA Ilya Kovalchuk 5.00 12.00
IKH Ilya Kovalchuk 10.00 25.00
JJA Jaromir Jagr 5.00 12.00
JJH Jaromir Jagr 5.00 12.00
JSA Joe Sakic 5.00 12.00
JSH Joe Sakic 5.00 12.00
MBA Martin Brodeur 5.00 12.00
MBH Martin Brodeur 5.00 12.00
MMA Mike Modano 5.00 12.00
MMH Mike Modano 5.00 12.00
PBA Pavel Bure 5.00 12.00
PBH Pavel Bure 5.00 12.00
PRA Patrick Roy 10.00 25.00
PRH Patrick Roy 10.00 25.00
SYA Steve Yzerman 10.00 25.00
SYH Steve Yzerman 10.00 25.00

2001-02 UD Playmakers Bobble Heads Autographed

Inserted at one per case, these bobble head figures parallel the regular set but also include authentic player autographs on the base.

CJA Curtis Joseph 30.00 80.00
CJH Curtis Joseph 40.00 100.00
DWA Doug Weight 12.50 30.00
DWH Doug Weight 12.50 30.00
IKA Ilya Kovalchuk 30.00 80.00
IKH Ilya Kovalchuk 30.00 80.00
MBA Martin Brodeur 40.00 100.00
MBH Martin Brodeur 40.00 100.00
PBA Pavel Bure 25.00 60.00
PBH Pavel Bure 25.00 60.00
SYA Steve Yzerman 50.00 125.00
SYH Steve Yzerman 40.00 100.00

2001-02 UD Playmakers Combo Jerseys

Serial-numbered to 100 copies each, this 10-card set featured dual game-worn jersey swatches of the given player. A gold parallel was also created and serial-numbered to 50.

*MULT.COLOR SWATCH: 1X TO 1.5X HI
*GOLD: 1X TO 2X BASIC INSERT
CJJI Jarome Iginla 12.50 30.00
CJJL John LeClair 10.00 25.00
CJMA Maxim Afinogenov 10.00 25.00
CJMD Mike Dunham 10.00 25.00
CJMH Milan Hejduk 10.00 25.00
CJMR Mark Recchi 10.00 25.00
CJPK Paul Kariya 10.00 25.00
CJPR Patrick Roy 25.00 60.00
CJRB Rob Blake 10.00 25.00
CJSG Simon Gagne 12.50 30.00

2001-02 UD Playmakers Jerseys

Inserted at 1:72, this 10-card set featured swatches of game-used jerseys of the featured players. A gold parallel was also created and serial-numbered out of 100.

*GOLD: 1X TO 2X BASIC INSERT
JJI Jarome Iginla 8.00 20.00
JMA Maxim Afinogenov 6.00 15.00
JMB Martin Brodeur 10.00 25.00
JML Mario Lemieux 15.00 40.00
JMR Mark Recchi 6.00 15.00
JPF Peter Forsberg 8.00 20.00
JRT Ron Tugnutt 6.00 15.00
JSG Simon Gagne 6.00 15.00
JTS Teemu Selanne 6.00 15.00
JZP Zigmund Palffy 6.00 15.00

2001-02 UD Playmakers Practice Jerseys

Inserted at 1:48, this 10-card set featured swatches of practice jerseys from the given player. A gold parallel was also created and serial-numbered to 200 copies each.

*GOLD: .75X TO 1.5X BASIC INSERT
PJEB Ed Belfour 6.00 15.00
PJJI Jarome Iginla 8.00 20.00
PJJL John LeClair 6.00 15.00
PJMH Milan Hejduk 6.00 15.00
PJMO Maxime Ouellet 5.00 12.00
PJMS Miroslav Satan 5.00 12.00
PJRB Rod Brind'Amour 5.00 12.00
PJRF Rico Fata 5.00 12.00
PJSG Simon Gagne 6.00 15.00
PJTB Tyler Bouck 5.00 12.00

2005-06 UD PowerPlay

This 172-card set issued into the hobby in six-card packs, with a $2.99 SRP, which came 24 packs to a box. Cards numbered 1-90 feature veterans in team alphabetical order while cards numbered 91-104 is an Impact Photos subset; cards numbered 105-118 are In Action, Cards numbered 119-125 are Cup Celebrations and Cards numbered 126-132 are Goal Robbers. Cards numbered 133-172 are all Rookie Cards. Stated odds for cards 91-118 are one in 12 and 119-132 are one in 24. In addition, four rookie redemptions appear at the end of this checklist and those cards were inserted at a stated rate of one in 12. The letters A, B, C and D refer respectively to cards 133-142, 143-152, 153-162 and 163-172.

COMPLETE SET (1-132) 50.00 100.00
COMPSET w/o SP's (90) 8.00 15.00
IP AND IA ODDS 1:12
GR AND CC ODDS 1:24
1 Jean-Sebastien Giguere .15 .40
2 Joffrey Lupul .10 .25
3 Sergei Fedorov .20 .50
4 Dany Heatley .25 .60
5 Ilya Kovalchuk .25 .60
6 Kari Lehtonen .20 .50
7 Sergei Samsonov .15 .40
8 Joe Thornton .30 .75
9 Andrew Raycroft .15 .40
10 Glen Murray .10 .25
11 Ryan Miller .15 .40
12 Daniel Briere .10 .25
13 Miroslav Satan .10 .25
14 Jarome Iginla .25 .60
15 Jordan Leopold .10 .25
16 Miikka Kiprusoff .20 .50
17 Eric Staal .15 .40
18 Josef Vasicek .10 .25
19 Eric Daze .15 .40
20 Tuomo Ruutu .10 .25
21 Jocelyn Thibault .15 .40
22 Joe Sakic .40 1.00
23 Alex Tanguay .15 .40
24 Milan Hejduk .20 .50
25 Peter Forsberg .30 .75
26 Rick Nash .25 .60
27 Nikolai Zherdev .15 .40
28 Marc Denis .15 .40
29 Mike Modano .20 .50
30 Bill Guerin .10 .25
31 Marty Turco .15 .40
32 Pavel Datsyuk .20 .50
33 Brendan Shanahan .20 .50
34 Steve Yzerman .75 2.00
35 Nicklas Lidstrom .20 .50
36 Ales Hemsky .10 .25
37 Ryan Smyth .15 .40
38 Patrice Bergeron .20 .50
39 Roberto Luongo .25 .60
40 Olli Jokinen .15 .40
41 Luc Robitaille .15 .40
42 Zigmund Palffy .15 .40
43 Lubomir Visnovsky .10 .25
44 Marian Gaborik .40 1.00
45 Dwayne Roloson .15 .40
46 Michael Ryder .15 .40
47 Jose Theodore .25 .60
48 Mike Ribeiro .10 .25
49 Steve Sullivan .10 .25
50 Nathan Horton .10 .25
51 Tomas Vokoun .15 .40
52 Martin Brodeur 1.00 2.50
53 Patrik Elias .15 .40
54 Scott Niedermayer .10 .25
55 Michael Peca .10 .25
56 Mark Messier .20 .50
57 Jaromir Jagr .30 .75
58 Mark Parrish .10 .25
59 Rick DiPietro .15 .40
60 Daniel Alfredsson .15 .40
61 Marian Hossa .15 .40
62 Jason Spezza .20 .50
63 Dominik Hasek .40 1.00
64 Jeremy Roenick .25 .60
65 Keith Primeau .10 .25
66 John LeClair .20 .50
67 Brett Hull .25 .60
68 Ladislav Nagy .10 .25
69 Shane Doan .10 .25
70 Marc-Andre Fleury .15 .40
71 Mario Lemieux 1.25 3.00
72 Mark Recchi .15 .40
73 Jonathan Cheechoo .20 .50
74 Evgeni Nabokov .15 .40
75 Patrick Marleau .15 .40
76 Chris Pronger .15 .40
77 Doug Weight .15 .40
78 Keith Tkachuk .20 .50
79 Brad Richards .15 .40
80 Nikolai Khabibulin .20 .50
81 Martin St. Louis .15 .40
82 Dave Andreychuk .10 .25
83 Joe Nieuwendyk .15 .40
84 Ed Belfour .20 .50
85 Mats Sundin .20 .50
86 Brian Leetch .20 .50
87 Brendan Morrison .10 .25
88 Markus Naslund .20 .50
89 Todd Bertuzzi .20 .50
90 Olaf Kolzig .15 .40
91 Sergei Fedorov IP .40 1.00
92 Dany Heatley IP .50 1.25
93 Joe Thornton IP .60 1.50
94 Daniel Briere IP .20 .50
95 Jarome Iginla IP .50 1.25
96 Joe Sakic IP .75 2.00
97 Steve Yzerman IP 1.50 4.00
98 Martin Havlat IP .30 .75
99 Jeremy Roenick IP .50 1.25
100 Mario Lemieux IP 2.50 6.00
101 Chris Pronger IP .30 .75
102 Dave Andreychuk IP .20 .50
103 Martin St. Louis IP .30 .75
104 Mats Sundin IP .40 1.00
105 Ilya Kovalchuk IA .50 1.25
106 Andrew Raycroft IA .30 .75
107 Peter Forsberg IA .60 1.50
108 Rick Nash IA .50 1.25
109 Jose Theodore IA .50 1.25
110 Tomas Vokoun IA .30 .75
111 Jaromir Jagr IA .60 1.50
112 Mark Messier IA .40 1.00
113 Jason Spezza IA .40 1.00
114 Marc-Andre Fleury IA .30 .75
115 Jonathan Cheechoo IA .40 1.00
116 Patrick Marleau IA .30 .75
117 Nikolai Khabibulin IA .40 1.00
118 Markus Naslund IA .40 1.00
119 Dave Andreychuk CC .25 .60
120 Martin Brodeur CC 2.00 5.00
121 Joe Sakic CC 1.00 2.50
122 Patrick Roy CC 2.50 6.00
123 Wayne Gretzky CC 3.00 8.00
124 Mark Messier CC .50 1.25
125 Steve Yzerman CC 2.00 5.00
126 Andrew Raycroft GR .40 1.00
127 Martin Brodeur GR 2.50 6.00
128 Patrick Roy GR 2.50 6.00
129 Jose Theodore GR .60 1.50
130 Marc-Andre Fleury GR .40 1.00
131 Marty Turco GR .40 1.00
132 Nikolai Khabibulin GR .50 1.25
133 Sidney Crosby RC 12.00 30.00
134 Wojtek Wolski RC 2.50 6.00
135 Hannu Toivonen RC 2.00 5.00
136 Alexander Steen RC 2.00 5.00
137 Jeff Woywitka RC 1.25 3.00
138 Jussi Jokinen RC 2.00 5.00
139 Kevin Nastiuk RC 1.50 4.00
140 Brent Seabrook RC 2.00 5.00
141 Brad Winchester RC 1.50 4.00
142 Brandon Bochenski RC 1.50 4.00
143 Alexander Ovechkin RC 10.00 25.00
144 Thomas Vanek RC 3.00 8.00
145 Yann Danis RC 1.50 4.00
146 Ryan Getzlaf RC 3.00 8.00
147 Ryan Suter RC 1.50 4.00
148 Henrik Lundqvist RC 4.00 10.00
149 Johan Franzen RC 1.50 4.00
150 Rene Bourque RC 1.50 4.00
151 Eric Nystrom RC 1.50 4.00
152 Patrick Eaves RC 1.50 4.00
153 Corey Perry RC 2.50 6.00
154 Alexander Perezhogin RC 2.00 5.00
155 Zach Parise RC 2.50 6.00
156 Mike Richards RC 2.50 6.00
157 Braydon Coburn RC 1.50 4.00
158 Cam Ward RC 2.00 5.00
159 David Leneveu RC 1.50 4.00
160 Andrew Alberts RC 1.50 4.00
161 Petteri Nokelainen RC 1.50 4.00
162 Lee Stempniak RC 1.50 4.00
163 Jeff Carter RC 3.00 8.00
164 Gilbert Brule RC 2.00 5.00
165 Dion Phaneuf RC 4.00 10.00
166 Jim Howard RC 3.00 8.00
167 Rostislav Olesz RC 1.50 4.00
168 Robert Nilsson RC 1.50 4.00
169 Peter Budaj RC 1.50 4.00
170 Andrej Meszaros RC 1.50 4.00
171 Petr Prucha RC 2.00 5.00
172 Matt Foy RC 1.25 3.00
A Rookie Redemption A 10.00 25.00
B Rookie Redemption B 4.00 10.00
C Rookie Redemption C 4.00 10.00
D Rookie Redemption D 4.00 10.00

2005-06 UD PowerPlay Rainbow

PRINT RUNS EQUAL JSY #'s
NOT PRICED DUE TO SCARCITY
1 Jean-Sebastien Giguere
2 Joffrey Lupul
3 Sergei Fedorov
4 Dany Heatley
5 Ilya Kovalchuk
6 Kari Lehtonen
7 Sergei Samsonov
8 Joe Thornton
9 Andrew Raycroft
10 Glen Murray
11 Ryan Miller
12 Daniel Briere
13 Miroslav Satan
14 Jarome Iginla
15 Jordan Leopold
16 Miikka Kiprusoff
17 Eric Staal
18 Josef Vasicek
19 Eric Daze
20 Tuomo Ruutu
21 Jocelyn Thibault
22 Joe Sakic
23 Alex Tanguay
24 Milan Hejduk
25 Peter Forsberg
26 Rick Nash
27 Nikolai Zherdev
28 Marc Denis
29 Mike Modano
30 Bill Guerin
31 Marty Turco
32 Pavel Datsyuk
33 Brendan Shanahan
34 Steve Yzerman
35 Nicklas Lidstrom
36 Ales Hemsky
37 Ryan Smyth
38 Patrice Bergeron
39 Roberto Luongo
40 Olli Jokinen
41 Luc Robitaille
42 Zigmund Palffy
43 Lubomir Visnovsky
44 Marian Gaborik
45 Dwayne Roloson
46 Michael Ryder
47 Jose Theodore
48 Mike Ribeiro
49 Steve Sullivan
50 Nathan Horton
51 Tomas Vokoun
52 Martin Brodeur
53 Patrik Elias
54 Scott Niedermayer
55 Michael Peca
56 Mark Messier
57 Jaromir Jagr
58 Mark Parrish
59 Rick DiPietro
60 Daniel Alfredsson
61 Marian Hossa
62 Jason Spezza
63 Dominik Hasek
64 Jeremy Roenick
65 Keith Primeau
66 John LeClair
67 Brett Hull
68 Ladislav Nagy
69 Shane Doan
70 Marc-Andre Fleury
71 Mario Lemieux
72 Mark Recchi
73 Jonathan Cheechoo
74 Evgeni Nabokov
75 Patrick Marleau
76 Chris Pronger

77 Doug Weight
78 Keith Tkachuk
79 Brad Richards
80 Nikolai Khabibulin
81 Martin St. Louis
82 Dave Andreychuk
83 Joe Nieuwendyk
84 Ed Belfour
85 Mats Sundin
86 Brian Leetch
87 Brendan Morrison
88 Markus Naslund
89 Todd Bertuzzi
90 Olaf Kolzig

2005-06 UD Powerplay Power Marks

STATED ODDS 1:200
PMAC Anson Carter 10.00 25.00
PMBB Brad Boyes 8.00 20.00
PMCK Chuck Kobasew 6.00 15.00
PMDA Daniel Alfredsson SP 20.00 50.00
PMDB Dustin Brown 4.00 10.00
PMEJ Ed Jovanovski 6.00 15.00
PMEN Evgeni Nabokov SP 12.00 30.00
PMFS Fredrik Sjostrom 4.00 10.00
PMGH Gordie Howe SP 125.00 250.00
PMHA Martin Havlat 10.00 25.00
PMHE Milan Hejduk 12.00 30.00
PMHZ Henrik Zetterberg SP 20.00 50.00
PMIK Ilya Kovalchuk SP 50.00 100.00
PMJC Jonathan Cheechoo 12.00 30.00
PMJI Jarome Iginla SP 40.00 80.00
PMJP Joni Pitkanen 4.00 10.00
PMJT Joe Thornton 25.00 60.00
PMJW Justin Williams 10.00 25.00
PMKD Kris Draper 8.00 20.00
PMKP Keith Primeau 4.00 10.00
PMLR Luc Robitaille 30.00 80.00
PMMB Milan Bartovic 4.00 10.00
PMMC Mike Comrie SP 40.00 100.00
PMMG Marian Gaborik SP 20.00 50.00
PMMH Marian Hossa 20.00 50.00
PMMN Markus Naslund 12.00 30.00
PMMP Mark Popovic 4.00 10.00
PMMR Mike Ribeiro 8.00 20.00
PMMS Martin St. Louis SP 25.00 60.00
PMNK Nikolai Khabibulin SP 40.00 80.00
PMNO Mika Noronen 4.00 10.00
PMNS Nathan Smith 4.00 10.00
PMPS Peter Sejna 4.00 10.00
PMRK Ryan Kesler 4.00 10.00
PMRN Rick Nash 20.00 50.00
PMRY Michael Ryder 15.00 40.00
PMSS Sheldon Souray SP 15.00 40.00
PMWG Wayne Gretzky SP 350.00 500.00
PMZP Roman Turek 6.00 15.00
PMZP Zigmund Palffy 12.00 30.00

2005-06 UD Powerplay Specialists

*MULT.COLOR: 1.25X TO 3X HI
STATED ODDS 1:12
TSAB David Aebischer 3.00 8.00
TSAH Ales Hemsky 3.00 8.00
TSAKO Alex Kovalev 4.00 10.00
TSAS Alexei Semenov 3.00 8.00
TSAY Alexei Yashin 3.00 8.00
TSBH Brett Hull 5.00 12.00
TSBK Radek Bonk 3.00 8.00
TSBO Peter Bondra 3.00 8.00
TSBS Brendan Shanahan 4.00 10.00
TSCC Chris Chelios 4.00 10.00
TSCD Chris Drury 3.00 8.00
TSCE Christian Ehrhoff 3.00 8.00
TSDA Daniel Alfredsson 3.00 8.00
TSDH Dany Heatley 5.00 12.00
TSDO Dominik Hasek 6.00 15.00
TSDW Doug Weight 3.00 8.00
TSEB Eric Brewer 3.00 8.00
TSEJ Ed Jovanovski 3.00 8.00
TSGM Glen Murray 3.00 8.00
TSHA Derian Hatcher 3.00 8.00
TSJD J-P Dumont 3.00 8.00
TSJI Jarome Iginla 5.00 12.00
TSJJ Jaromir Jagr 8.00 20.00
TSJL Joffrey Lupul 3.00 8.00
TSJL John LeClair 3.00 8.00
TSJN Joe Nieuwendyk 3.00 8.00
TSJS Jean-Sebastien Giguere 3.00 8.00
TSJT Joe Thornton 6.00 15.00
TSKP Keith Primeau 3.00 8.00
TSLC Pascal Leclaire 3.00 8.00
TSLE Jordan Leopold 3.00 8.00
TSMB Martin Brodeur 10.00 25.00
TSMC Mike Comrie 3.00 8.00
TSMH Milan Hejduk 4.00 10.00
TSML Mario Lemieux 12.00 30.00
TSMM Mike Modano 6.00 15.00
TSMR Mark Recchi 3.00 8.00
TSMT Marty Turco SP 6.00 15.00
TSNA Nikolai Antropov 3.00 8.00
TSOJ Olli Jokinen 3.00 8.00
TSOK Olaf Kolzig 3.00 8.00
TSPB P-M Bouchard 3.00 8.00
TSPB Pavel Bure 4.00 10.00
TSPD Pavol Demitra 3.00 8.00
TSPK Paul Kariya SP 60.00 100.00
TSPL Patrick Lalime 3.00 8.00
TSRB Rob Blake 3.00 8.00
TSRE Robert Esche 3.00 8.00
TSRL Robert Lang 3.00 8.00
TSRT Roman Turek 3.00 8.00
TSSB Sean Burke 3.00 8.00
TSSG Scott Gomez 3.00 8.00
TSSP Jason Spezza 4.00 10.00
TSTA Tony Amonte SP 3.00 8.00
TSTH Jocelyn Thibault 3.00 8.00
TSTL Trevor Linden 8.00 20.00
TSTS Teemu Selanne 4.00 10.00
TSVL Vincent Lecavalier SP 40.00 80.00
TSVN Ville Nieminen 3.00 8.00
TSWG Wayne Gretzky SP 125.00 250.00

2005-06 UD Powerplay Specialists Patches

PRINT RUN 5 SER.#'d SETS
NOT PRICED DUE TO SCARCITY

2006-07 UD Powerplay

This 130-card set was issued into the hobby in six-card packs, with an $2.99 SRP, which came 24 packs to a box and 20 boxes to a case. Cards numbered 1-100 feature veterans in team alphabetical order while cards 101-130 feature Rookie Cards also in team alphabetical order.

COMPLETE SET (130) 40.00 80.00
1 Jean-Sebastien Giguere .30 .75
2 Teemu Selanne .30 .75
3 Chris Pronger .25 .60
4 Ilya Kovalchuk .40 1.00
5 Marian Hossa .25 .60
6 Kari Lehtonen .30 .75
7 Patrice Bergeron .25 .60
8 Brad Boyes .20 .50
9 Hannu Toivonen .30 .75
10 Zdeno Chara .20 .50
11 Chris Drury .25 .60
12 Ryan Miller .30 .75
13 Maxim Afinogenov .20 .50
14 Miikka Kiprusoff .30 .75
15 Jarome Iginla .50 1.25
16 Dion Phaneuf .40 1.00
17 Alex Tanguay .25 .60
18 Eric Staal .25 .60
19 Cam Ward .50 1.25
20 Rod Brind'Amour .25 .60
21 Erik Cole .20 .50
22 Tuomo Ruutu .20 .50
23 Nikolai Khabibulin .30 .75
24 Michal Handzus .10 .25
25 Martin Havlat .25 .60
26 Marek Svatos .20 .50
27 Milan Hejduk .25 .60
28 Joe Sakic .60 1.50
29 Rick Nash .30 .75
30 Sergei Fedorov .30 .75
31 Pascal Leclaire .30 .75
32 Mike Modano .30 .75
33 Brenden Morrow .25 .60
34 Marty Turco .25 .60
35 Eric Lindros .30 .75
36 Henrik Zetterberg .30 .75
37 Nicklas Lidstrom .30 .75
38 Pavel Datsyuk .30 .75
39 Dominik Hasek .40 1.00
40 Joffrey Lupul .20 .50
41 Ales Hemsky .20 .50
42 Ryan Smyth .25 .60
43 Olli Jokinen .20 .50
44 Todd Bertuzzi .25 .60
45 Jay Bouwmeester .20 .50
46 Alexander Frolov .20 .50
47 Rob Blake .25 .60
48 Mike Cammalleri .20 .50
49 Marian Gaborik .50 1.25
50 Manny Fernandez .30 .75
51 Pavol Demitra .20 .50
52 Saku Koivu .30 .75
53 Cristobal Huet .20 .50
54 Alex Kovalev .20 .50
55 Michael Ryder .25 .60
56 Steve Sullivan .20 .50
57 Paul Kariya .30 .75
58 Tomas Vokoun .30 .75
59 Martin Brodeur 1.00 2.50
60 Patrik Elias .20 .50
61 Brian Gionta .20 .50
62 Miroslav Satan .20 .50
63 Alexei Yashin .20 .50
64 Rick DiPietro .30 .75
65 Jaromir Jagr .50 1.25
66 Henrik Lundqvist .50 1.25
67 Brendan Shanahan .30 .75
68 Martin Gerber .30 .75
69 Jason Spezza .30 .75
70 Dany Heatley .30 .75
71 Daniel Alfredsson .25 .60
72 Peter Forsberg .50 1.25
73 Simon Gagne .30 .75
74 Robert Esche .25 .60
75 Jeff Carter .30 .75
76 Shane Doan .25 .60
77 Curtis Joseph .30 .75
78 Jeremy Roenick .30 .75
79 Sergei Gonchar .10 .25
80 Sidney Crosby 1.50 4.00
81 Marc-Andre Fleury .30 .75
82 Joe Thornton .50 1.25
83 Jonathan Cheechoo .30 .75
84 Patrick Marleau .25 .60
85 Doug Weight .20 .50
86 Keith Tkachuk .25 .60
87 Manny Legace .25 .60
88 Brad Richards .30 .75
89 Martin St. Louis .30 .75
90 Vincent Lecavalier .30 .75
91 Mats Sundin .30 .75
92 Alexander Steen .25 .60
93 Bryan McCabe .20 .50
94 Andrew Raycroft .25 .60
95 Markus Naslund .30 .75
96 Roberto Luongo .60 1.50
97 Brendan Morrison .20 .50
98 Henrik Sedin .20 .50
99 Alexander Ovechkin .75 2.00
100 Olaf Kolzig .40 1.00
101 Yan Stastny RC 1.25 3.00
102 Mark Stuart RC 1.25 3.00
103 Carsen Germyn RC 1.25 3.00
104 Dustin Byfuglien RC 2.50 6.00
105 Tomas Kopecky RC 1.25 3.00
106 Marc-Antoine Pouliot RC 1.25 3.00
107 Konstantin Pushkarev RC 1.25 3.00
108 Erik Reitz RC 1.25 3.00
109 Miroslav Kopriva RC 1.25 3.00
110 Shea Weber RC 1.25 3.00
111 David Printz RC 1.25 3.00
112 Steve Regier RC 1.25 3.00
113 Ryan Caldwell RC 1.25 3.00
114 Masi Marjamaki RC 1.25 3.00
115 Matt Koalska RC 1.25 3.00
116 Jarkko Immonen RC 1.25 3.00
117 Cole Jarrett RC .60 1.50
118 Rob Collins RC 1.25 3.00
119 Filip Novak RC 1.25 3.00
120 Ryan Potulny RC 1.50 4.00
121 Bill Thomas RC 1.25 3.00
122 Joel Perrault RC 1.25 3.00
123 Noah Welch RC 1.25 3.00
124 Michel Ouellet RC 1.50 4.00
125 Matt Carle RC 1.25 3.00
126 Ben Ondrus RC 1.25 3.00
127 Brendan Bell RC 1.25 3.00
128 Ian White RC 1.25 3.00
129 Jeremy Williams RC 1.25 3.00
130 Eric Fehr RC 1.25 3.00

2006-07 UD Powerplay Impact Rainbow

*STARS: 15X TO 40X BASE HI
*PROSPECTS 2X TO 5X BASE HI
PRINT RUN 25 SER. #'d SETS
80 Sidney Crosby 80.00 200.00
99 Alexander Ovechkin 50.00 125.00

2006-07 UD Powerplay Cup Celebrations

COMPLETE SET (7) 10.00 25.00
STATED ODDS 1:24
CC1 Eric Staal 1.00 2.50
CC2 Cam Ward 1.00 2.50
CC3 Dominik Hasek 1.50 4.00
CC4 Mike Modano 1.25 3.00
CC5 Martin St. Louis 1.00 2.50
CC6 Mario Lemieux 4.00 10.00
CC7 Patrick Roy 3.00 8.00

2006-07 UD Powerplay Goal Robbers

COMPLETE SET (14) 12.00 30.00
STATED ODDS 1:12
GR1 Jean-Sebastien Giguere 2.00 5.00
GR2 Kari Lehtonen 2.00 5.00
GR3 Ryan Miller 2.00 5.00
GR4 Miikka Kiprusoff 2.00 5.00
GR5 Cam Ward 3.00 8.00
GR6 Jose Theodore 1.25 3.00
GR7 Marty Turco 1.50 4.00
GR8 Marc-Andre Fleury 2.00 5.00
GR9 Roberto Luongo 4.00 10.00
GR10 Manny Fernandez 2.00 5.00
GR11 Tomas Vokoun 1.50 4.00
GR12 Martin Brodeur 3.00 8.00
GR13 Henrik Lundqvist 3.00 8.00
GR14 Cristobal Huet 2.00 5.00

2006-07 UD Powerplay In Action

COMPLETE SET (14) 10.00 25.00
STATED ODDS 1:12
IA1 Jarome Iginla 1.25 3.00
IA2 Joe Sakic 1.50 4.00
IA3 Rick Nash .75 2.00
IA4 Henrik Zetterberg .75 2.00
IA5 Saku Koivu .75 2.00
IA6 Martin Brodeur 2.50 6.00
IA7 Jaromir Jagr 1.25 3.00
IA8 Dany Heatley .75 2.00
IA9 Peter Forsberg 1.25 3.00
IA10 Sidney Crosby 4.00 10.00
IA11 Joe Thornton 1.25 3.00
IA12 Mats Sundin .75 2.00
IA13 Markus Naslund .75 2.00
IA14 Alexander Ovechkin 2.00 5.00

2006-07 UD Powerplay Last Man Standing

COMPLETE SET (7) 6.00 15.00
STATED ODDS 1:24
LM1 Jody Shelley 1.25 3.00
LM2 Derek Boogaard 1.25 3.00
LM3 George Parros 1.25 3.00
LM4 Donald Brashear 1.25 3.00
LM5 Georges Laraque 1.25 3.00
LM6 Chris Simon 1.25 3.00
LM7 Todd Fedoruk 1.25 3.00

2006-07 UD Powerplay Power Marks

STATED ODDS 1:400
PMAA Andrew Alberts 8.00 20.00
PMAM Andrej Meszaros 12.00 30.00
PMAO Alexander Ovechkin
PMAS Anthony Stewart 8.00 20.00
PMAY Alexei Yashin 10.00 25.00
PMBB Brad Boyes 8.00 20.00
PMBE Ben Eager 8.00 20.00
PMCD Chris Drury 10.00 25.00
PMCK Chris Kunitz 10.00 25.00
PMCP Corey Perry
PMDW Doug Weight 8.00 20.00
PMFP Fernando Pisani
PMHZ Henrik Zetterberg 20.00 40.00
PMJH Jeff Hoggan 8.00 20.00
PMJI Jarome Iginla 40.00 80.00
PMJT Joe Thornton
PMMH Marian Hossa
PMMT Maxime Talbot 12.00 30.00
PMMV Mike Van Ryn 8.00 20.00
PMPM Patrick Marleau
PMPR Paul Ranger 8.00 20.00
PMRN Rick Nash
PMRS Ryan Smyth 15.00 40.00
PMSC Sidney Crosby 100.00 200.00
PMSG Scott Gomez 8.00 20.00
PMSH Scott Hartnell 8.00 20.00
PMSK Saku Koivu
PMTH Jose Theodore 30.00 60.00
PMWG Wayne Gretzky
PMZP Zach Parise 10.00 25.00

2006-07 UD Powerplay Specialists

STATED ODDS 1:24
SAF Alexander Frolov 3.00 8.00
SAH Ales Hemsky 3.00 8.00
SAK Alex Kovalev 3.00 8.00
SAL Jason Allison 3.00 8.00
SAO Alexander Ovechkin 20.00 50.00
SAT Alex Tanguay 4.00 10.00
SBG Bill Guerin 3.00 8.00
SBL Brian Leetch 5.00 12.00
SBM Bryan McCabe 3.00 8.00
SBR Brian Rolston 3.00 8.00
SBS Brendan Shanahan 5.00 12.00
SCP Chris Pronger 4.00 10.00
SDB Donald Brashear 3.00 8.00
SDH Dominik Hasek 8.00 20.00
SDP Dion Phaneuf 8.00 20.00
SDW Doug Weight 3.00 8.00
SEB Ed Belfour 5.00 12.00
SEJ Ed Jovanovski 3.00 8.00
SES Eric Staal 5.00 12.00
SGA Simon Gagne 5.00 12.00
SGM Glen Murray 3.00 8.00
SIK Ilya Kovalchuk 8.00 20.00
SJA Jason Arnott 3.00 8.00
SJG Jean-Sebastien Giguere 4.00 10.00
SJI Jarome Iginla 8.00 20.00
SJJ Jaromir Jagr 8.00 20.00
SJL Jere Lehtinen 3.00 8.00
SJS Joe Sakic SP 15.00 40.00
SJT Joe Thornton 8.00 20.00
SKL Kari Lehtonen 5.00 12.00
SKP Keith Primeau 3.00 8.00
SMB Martin Brodeur 12.00 30.00
SMF Manny Fernandez 4.00 10.00
SMG Marian Gaborik 8.00 20.00
SMH Marian Hossa 4.00 10.00
SMK Miikka Kiprusoff 5.00 12.00
SMM Mike Modano 8.00 20.00
SMN Markus Naslund 5.00 12.00
SMO Brendan Morrison 3.00 8.00
SMP Michael Peca 3.00 8.00
SMS Marc Savard 3.00 8.00
SMT Marty Turco 4.00 10.00
SOK Olaf Kolzig 5.00 12.00
SPB Patrice Bergeron 5.00 12.00
SPD Pavel Datsyuk 4.00 10.00
SPF Peter Forsberg 8.00 20.00
SPK Paul Kariya 5.00 12.00
SPM Patrick Marleau 4.00 10.00
SRB Rob Blake 4.00 10.00
SRE Robert Esche 4.00 10.00
SRI Brad Richards 4.00 10.00
SRM Ryan Miller 5.00 12.00
SSC Sidney Crosby SP 30.00 80.00
SSF Sergei Fedorov 5.00 12.00
SSG Scott Gomez 3.00 8.00
SSN Scott Niedermayer 3.00 8.00
SSP Jason Spezza 5.00 12.00
STR Tuomo Ruutu 3.00 8.00
STS Teemu Selanne 5.00 12.00
SZC Zdeno Chara 3.00 8.00

2006-07 UD Powerplay Specialists Patches

PRINT RUN 5 SER. #'d SETS
NOT PRICED DUE TO SCARCITY

2001-02 UD Premier Collection

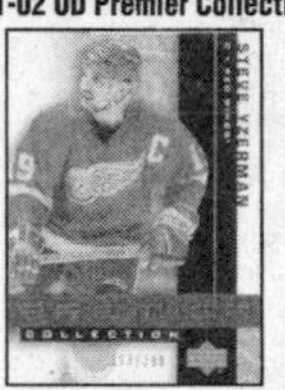

Released in early June, Premier Collection carried a SRP of $100 per pack. Each pack contained a memorabilia card, an autographed card, a serial-numbered rookie card as well as serial-numbered base cards. The base set was made up of 114 cards total, cards 1-87 were serial-numbered to 399, cards 88-108 were serial-numbered to 250 and cards 109-114 were serial-numbered to 199.

1 Paul Kariya 1.00 2.50
2 Dany Heatley 1.25 3.00
3 Joe Thornton 1.50 4.00
4 Ray Bourque 2.00 5.00
5 Bobby Orr 10.00 25.00
6 Sergei Samsonov .75 2.00
7 Tim Connolly .75 2.00
8 Jarome Iginla 1.25 3.00
9 Arturs Irbe .75 2.00
10 Jocelyn Thibault .75 2.00
11 Joe Sakic 2.00 5.00
12 Patrick Roy 5.00 12.00
13 Peter Forsberg 2.00 5.00
14 Chris Drury .75 2.00
15 Milan Hejduk 1.00 2.50
16 Rostislav Klesla .75 2.00
17 Mike Modano 1.50 4.00
18 Ed Belfour 1.00 2.50
19 Gordie Howe 3.00 8.00
20 Brendan Shanahan 1.00 2.50
21 Steve Yzerman 5.00 12.00
22 Brett Hull 1.25 3.00
23 Dominik Hasek 2.00 5.00
24 Sergei Fedorov 1.50 4.00
25 Wayne Gretzky 6.00 15.00
26 Tommy Salo .75 2.00
27 Roberto Luongo 1.25 3.00
28 Felix Potvin 1.00 2.50
29 Marian Gaborik 2.00 5.00
30 Jose Theodore 1.25 3.00
31 Mike Dunham .75 2.00
32 Martin Brodeur 2.50 6.00
33 Alexei Yashin .75 2.00
34 Eric Lindros 1.00 2.50
35 Pavel Bure 1.00 2.50
36 Marian Hossa 1.00 2.50
37 Jeremy Roenick 1.25 3.00
38 John LeClair 1.00 2.50
39 Simon Gagne 1.00 2.50
40 Sean Burke .75 2.00
41 Mario Lemieux 6.00 15.00
42 Evgeni Nabokov .75 2.00
43 Teemu Selanne 1.00 2.50
44 Keith Tkachuk 1.00 2.50
45 Chris Pronger .75 2.00
46 Brad Richards .75 2.00
47 Curtis Joseph 1.00 2.50
48 Mats Sundin 1.00 2.50
49 Markus Naslund 1.00 2.50
50 Jaromir Jagr 1.50 4.00
51 Timo Parssinen RC 3.00 8.00
52 Ben Simon RC 4.00 8.00
53 Frederic Cassivi RC 4.00 8.00
54 Ales Kotalik RC 6.00 15.00
55 Mike Peluso RC 3.00 8.00
56 Steve Moore RC 3.00 8.00
57 Martin Spanhel RC 3.00 8.00
58 Matt Davidson RC 3.00 8.00
59 Mathieu Darche RC 3.00 8.00
60 Duvie Westcott RC 3.00 8.00
61 Blake Bellefeuille RC 3.00 8.00
62 Ty Conklin RC 6.00 15.00
63 Stephen Weiss RC 10.00 25.00
64 Jaroslav Bednar RC 3.00 8.00
65 Pascal Dupuis RC 3.00 8.00
66 Nick Schultz RC 3.00 8.00
67 Travis Roche RC 3.00 8.00
68 Nathan Perrott RC 3.00 8.00
69 Scott Clemmensen RC 3.00 8.00
70 Andreas Salomonsson RC 3.00 8.00
71 Stanislav Gron RC 3.00 8.00
72 Radek Martinek RC 3.00 8.00
73 Mikael Samuelsson RC 6.00 15.00
74 Toni Dahlman RC 3.00 8.00
75 Bruno St. Jacques RC 3.00 8.00
76 Tomas Divisek RC 3.00 8.00
77 Vaclav Pletka RC 3.00 8.00
78 Eric Meloche RC 3.00 8.00
79 Tom Kostopoulos RC 3.00 8.00
80 Mark Rycroft RC 3.00 8.00
81 Martin Cibak RC 3.00 8.00
82 Josef Boumedienne RC 3.00 8.00
83 Karel Pilar RC 3.00 8.00
84 Sebastien Centomo RC 3.00 8.00
85 Justin Kurtz RC 3.00 8.00
86 Ivan Ciernik RC 3.00 8.00
87 Chris Corrinet RC 3.00 8.00
88 Ilja Bryzgalov RC 10.00 25.00
89 Pasi Nurminen RC 4.00 10.00
90 Ivan Huml RC 4.00 10.00
91 Erik Cole RC 8.00 20.00
92 Tyler Arnason RC 4.00 10.00
93 Riku Hahl RC 4.00 10.00
94 Niko Kapanen RC 4.00 10.00
95 Pavel Datsyuk RC 125.00 200.00
96 Sean Avery RC 10.00 25.00
97 Niklas Hagman RC 4.00 10.00
98 Olivier Michaud RC 4.00 10.00
99 Marcel Hossa RC 10.00 25.00
100 Martin Erat RC 8.00 20.00
101 Christian Berglund RC 4.00 10.00
102 Lukas Krajicek RC 4.00 10.00
103 Jiri Dopita RC 4.00 10.00
104 Branko Radivojevic RC 4.00 10.00
105 Shane Endicott RC 4.00 10.00
106 Jeff Jillson RC 4.00 10.00
107 Nikita Alexeev RC 4.00 10.00
108 Brian Sutherby RC 8.00 20.00
109 Ilya Kovalchuk AU RC 300.00 500.00
110 Vaclav Nedorost AU RC 10.00 25.00
111 Kristian Huselius AU RC 25.00 60.00
112 Raffi Torres AU RC 25.00 60.00
113 Dan Blackburn AU RC 12.00 30.00
114 Krys Kolanos AU RC 10.00 25.00

2001-02 UD Premier Collection Dual Jerseys

Serial-numbered to just 100 copies each, this 35-card set featured dual-swatches of game-worn jerseys from the pictured players. A black parallel to this set was also created and serial-numbered to 50 copies each. Black parallels could be identified by both numbering and a small black square in the lower right hand side of each card front.

*MULT.COLOR SWATCH: .75X TO 1.5X HI
*BLACK: .5X TO 1.25X BASE HI
DAT Tony Amonte 8.00 20.00
Jocelyn Thibault
DBA Pavel Bure 8.00 20.00
Maxim Afinogenov
DBB R.Bourque/R.Blake 15.00 40.00
DBP Rob Blake 8.00 20.00
Chris Pronger
DCB Roman Cechmanek 8.00 20.00
Brian Boucher
DDM Chris Drury 12.00 30.00
Mike Modano
DDP Adam Deadmarsh 8.00 20.00
Felix Potvin
DFB Sergei Fedorov 12.00 30.00
Pavel Bure
DFD Peter Forsberg 15.00 40.00
Chris Drury
DGH Wayne Gretzky 30.00 80.00
Brett Hull
DGK W.Gretzky/P.Kariya 25.00 60.00
DGL W.Gretzky/M.Lemieux 50.00 125.00
DGM Wayne Gretzky 50.00 125.00
Mark Messier
DHC Dominik Hasek 12.00 30.00
Roman Cechmanek
DHG Gordie Howe 50.00 125.00
Wayne Gretzky
DHJ Milan Hejduk 12.00 30.00
Jaromir Jagr
DJB Jaromir Jagr 12.00 30.00
Peter Bondra
DJP Curtis Joseph 8.00 20.00
Felix Potvin
DKI Paul Kariya 12.00 30.00
Jarome Iginla
DKS Paul Kariya 15.00 40.00
Joe Sakic
DLH Nicklas Lidstrom 12.00 30.00
Dominik Hasek
DLK M.Lemieux/P.Kariya 20.00 50.00
DLR Brian Leetch 8.00 20.00
Mike Richter
DMB Mike Modano 15.00 40.00
Ed Belfour
DRB P.Roy/M.Brodeur 30.00 80.00
DRJ Mike Richter 8.00 20.00
Curtis Joseph
DSN Teemu Selanne 8.00 20.00
Ville Nieminen
DSP Teemu Selanne 8.00 20.00
Zigmund Palffy
DSR Joe Sakic 20.00 50.00
Patrick Roy
DST Sergei Samsonov 12.00 30.00
Joe Thornton
DSY Brendan Shanahan 20.00 50.00
Steve Yzerman
DTB Jocelyn Thibault 8.00 20.00
Sean Burke
DTN Joe Thornton 12.00 30.00
Joe Nieuwendyk
DBTE Martin Brodeur 15.00 40.00
Jose Theodore
DBTO Ray Bourque 15.00 40.00
Joe Thornton

2001-02 UD Premier Collection Jerseys

This 44-card set featured game-worn jersey swatches of the pictured players. Bronze cards carried a bronze logo and were serial-numbered to 300 copies each. Silver cards carried a silver logo and were serial-numbered to 150 copies each. Gold cards carried a gold logo and were serial-numbered to 50 each.

BBS Brendan Shanahan B 5.00 12.00
BBU Pavel Bure B 5.00 12.00
BCD Chris Drury B 5.00 12.00
BEB Ed Belfour B 5.00 12.00
BEL Eric Lindros B 5.00 12.00
BIK Ilya Kovalchuk B 8.00 20.00
BJA Jaromir Jagr B 8.00 20.00
BJI Jarome Iginla B 6.00 15.00
BJJ Jaromir Jagr B 8.00 20.00
BJL John LeClair B 5.00 12.00
BJS Joe Sakic B 8.00 20.00
BJT Jose Theodore B 6.00 15.00
BMH Milan Hejduk B 5.00 12.00
BMR Mike Richter B 5.00 12.00
BMS Mats Sundin B 5.00 12.00
BOK Olaf Kolzig B 5.00 12.00
BPB Peter Bondra B 5.00 12.00
BPF Peter Forsberg B 8.00 20.00
BPK Paul Kariya B 5.00 12.00
BPR Patrick Roy B 15.00 40.00
BRB Ray Bourque B 10.00 25.00
BSF Sergei Fedorov B 6.00 15.00
BSG Simon Gagne B 5.00 12.00
BSK Saku Koivu B 5.00 12.00
BSS Sergei Samsonov B 5.00 12.00
BTA Tony Amonte B 5.00 12.00
BTF Theo Fleury B 5.00 12.00
BTS Teemu Selanne B 5.00 12.00
BWG Wayne Gretzky B 30.00 80.00
BZP Zigmund Palffy B 5.00 12.00
SCJ Curtis Joseph S 10.00 25.00
SDH Dominik Hasek S 12.00 30.00
SJS Joe Sakic S 15.00 40.00
SJT Joe Thornton S 12.50 30.00
SMB Martin Brodeur S 15.00 40.00
SMM Mike Modano S 12.50 30.00
SPK Paul Kariya S 12.00 30.00
GBH Bobby Hull G 15.00 40.00
GGH Gordie Howe G 30.00 80.00
GML Mario Lemieux G 30.00 80.00
GPR Patrick Roy G 30.00 80.00
GRB Ray Bourque G 25.00 60.00
GSY Steve Yzerman G 30.00 80.00
GWG Wayne Gretzky G 50.00 125.00

2001-02 UD Premier Collection Jerseys Black

This 44-card set paralleled the base jersey set but a black square appeared in the bottom right corner of the card front. Bronze/black cards were serial-numbered to 150, silver/black cards were serial-numbered to 75 and gold/black cards were serial-numbered to 5. Gold/black cards were not priced due to scarcity.

*BRONZE/BLACK: .5X TO 1.25X BASIC INSERTS
*SILVER/BLACK: .5X TO 1.25X BASIC INSERTS

2001-02 UD Premier Collection Signatures

Inserted with overall odds of 1 per pack, this 40 card set featured authentic player autographs under full color action photos. Bronze, silver and gold subsets could be identified by the color of the foil in the Upper Deck logo and a small rectangle at the bottom of each card front. Though not explicitly stated, the silver and gold versions are thought to be more scarce than the bronze.

AI Arturs Irbe B 4.00 10.00

AK Alexei Kovalev B	4.00	10.00
BI Martin Biron B	4.00	10.00
HO Marian Hossa B	6.00	15.00
JH Johan Hedberg B	4.00	10.00
JT Jose Theodore B	10.00	25.00
MC Mike Comrie B	5.00	12.00
MG Marian Gaborik B	10.00	25.00
MH Martin Havlat B	4.00	10.00
MN Markus Naslund B	6.00	15.00
RK Rostislav Klesla B	4.00	10.00
RT Raffi Torres B	5.00	12.00
SA Tommy Salo B	4.00	10.00
TA Tony Amonte B	4.00	10.00
BL Rob Blake S	6.00	15.00
CN Cam Neely S	20.00	50.00
DH Dany Heatley S	10.00	25.00
DW Doug Weight S	8.00	20.00
FP Felix Potvin S	8.00	20.00
HE Milan Hejduk S	8.00	20.00
JI Jarome Iginla S	10.00	25.00
JL John LeClair S	8.00	20.00
MB Mike Bossy S	10.00	25.00
OK Olaf Kolzig S	6.00	15.00
PB Peter Bondra S	8.00	20.00
SG Simon Gagne S	8.00	20.00
ZP Zigmund Palffy S	6.00	15.00
BH Bobby Hull G	20.00	50.00
BO Bobby Orr G	150.00	300.00
BR Dan Blackburn	10.00	25.00
Mike Richter G		
CJ Curtis Joseph G	8.00	20.00
GH Gordie Howe G	50.00	100.00
GR Wayne Gretzky G	150.00	250.00
IK Ilya Kovalchuk G	20.00	50.00
JS Joe Thornton	20.00	50.00
Sergei Samsonov G		
PR Patrick Roy G	75.00	150.00
RB Ray Bourque G	20.00	50.00
SY Steve Yzerman G	30.00	80.00
TS Teemu Selanne G	10.00	25.00
WG Wayne Gretzky G	100.00	250.00

2001-02 UD Premier Collection Signatures Black

This 38-card set paralleled the base autograph set with the addition of black borders and serial numbering. Bronze cards were serial numbered to 100, silver cards were serial numbered to 25, and gold cards were serial numbered to 5. Gold cards are not priced due to scarcity. Black parallels could be identified by both numbering and a small black rectangle under the autograph on each card.

*BRONZE/BLACK: .6X TO 1.5X BASIC AUTO
*SILVER/BLACK: 1X TO 2.5X BASIC AUTO

2001-02 UD Promior Colloction Tribute to 500

Limited to just 50 copies, this single-card set highlighted the career wins of Patrick Roy. Each card carried a swatch of game jersey from both Montreal and Colorado.

1 Patrick Roy Col./Mon.	75.00	200.00

2002-03 UD Premier Collection

Released in April, this 103-card set featured serial-numbered base cards and three different levels of rookie cards. Due to printing errors, several card numbers were duplicated or excluded. Duplicate card numbers are denoted below with a an "A" or "B" suffix, though those letters did not appear on the cards. Cards #1-72 and 88-98 were serial-numbered to 399 sets. Cards #73-77 and 99-103 carried certified player autographs and were serial-numbered to 199. Cards #78-84 carried certified autographs and swatches of jersey patches. Patch/auto cards were serial-numbered to 99 copies each.

*SINGLE COLOR PATCH: .5X TO .75X
CARDS 85,86,87 DO NOT EXIST

1 Paul Kariya	1.25	3.00
2 Ilya Kovalchuk	1.50	4.00
3 Dany Heatley	1.50	4.00
4 Byron Dafoe	.75	2.00
5 Joe Thornton	1.50	4.00
6 Jeff Hackett	.75	2.00
7 Sergei Samsonov	.75	2.00
8 Miroslav Satan	.75	2.00
9 Jarome Iginla	1.50	4.00
10 Ron Francis	.75	2.00
11 Tyler Arnason	.75	2.00
12 Jocelyn Thibault	.75	2.00
13 Peter Forsberg	1.50	4.00
14 Joe Sakic	2.00	5.00
15 Patrick Roy	5.00	12.00
16 Milan Hejduk	1.25	3.00
17 Marc Denis	.75	2.00
18 Mike Modano	1.50	4.00
19 Bill Guerin	.75	2.00
20 Marty Turco	.75	2.00
21 Steve Yzerman	5.00	12.00
22 Curtis Joseph	1.25	3.00
23 Brendan Shanahan	1.25	3.00
24 Nicklas Lidstrom	1.25	3.00
25 Mike Comrie	.75	2.00
26 Stephen Weiss	.75	2.00
27 Roberto Luongo	1.50	4.00
28 Zigmund Palffy	.75	2.00
29 Marian Gaborik	1.50	4.00
30 Saku Koivu	1.25	3.00
31 Jose Theodore	1.50	4.00
32 David Legwand	.75	2.00
33 Martin Brodeur	2.50	6.00
34 Michael Peca	.75	2.00
35 Alexei Kovalev	.75	2.00
36 Eric Lindros	1.25	3.00
37 Pavel Bure	1.25	3.00
38 Mike Dunham	.75	2.00
39 Marian Hossa	1.25	3.00
40 Jeremy Roenick	1.50	4.00
41 John LeClair	1.25	3.00
42 Tony Amonte	.75	2.00
43 Mario Lemieux	6.00	15.00
44A Sebastien Caron	.75	2.00
44B Martin Gerber RC	8.00	20.00
45A Evgeni Nabokov	.75	2.00
45B Tim Thomas RC	10.00	25.00
46A Kyle McLaren	.75	2.00
46B Ryan Miller RC	25.00	50.00
47A Keith Tkachuk	1.25	3.00
47B Jordan Leopold RC	4.00	10.00
48A Vincent Lecavalier	.75	2.00
48B Shaone Morrisonn RC	4.00	10.00
49A Nikolai Khabibulin	1.25	3.00
49B Levente Szuper RC	4.00	10.00
50 Mats Sundin	1.25	3.00
51A Ed Belfour	1.25	3.00
51B Jim Fahey RC	4.00	10.00
52A Todd Bertuzzi	1.25	3.00
52B Dmitri Bykov RC	4.00	10.00
53 Markus Naslund	1.25	3.00
54 Jaromir Jagr	1.50	4.00
55 Olaf Kolzig	.75	2.00
56A Wayne Gretzky/299	8.00	20.00
56B Mike Cammalleri RC	15.00	40.00
57A Bobby Orr/299	10.00	25.00
57B Stephane Veilleux RC	4.00	10.00
58A Gordie Howe/299	3.00	8.00
58B Rickard Wallin RC	4.00	10.00
59A Ray Bourque/299	2.00	5.00
59B Vernon Fiddler RC	4.00	10.00
60A Alexei Semenov RC	4.00	10.00
60B Darren Haydar RC	4.00	10.00
61 Anton Volchenkov RC	4.00	10.00
62 Patrick Sharp RC	5.00	12.00
63 Dennis Seidenberg RC	4.00	10.00
64 Tomas Malec RC	4.00	10.00
65 Craig Andersson RC	20.00	50.00
66 Cody Rudkowsky RC	4.00	10.00
67A Ari Ahonen RC	4.00	10.00
67B Curtis Sanford RC	6.00	15.00
68 Adam Hall RC	4.00	10.00
69 Carlo Colaiacovo RC	8.00	20.00
70A Dick Tarnstrom RC	4.00	10.00
70B Steve Eminger RC	4.00	10.00
71A Jamie Hodson RC	4.00	10.00
71B Alexei Smirnov AU RC	10.00	25.00
72A Jarret Stoll RC	8.00	20.00
72B P-M Bouchard AU RC	15.00	40.00
73 Ron Hainsey AU RC	10.00	25.00
74 Pascal Leclaire AU RC	30.00	60.00
75 Scottie Upshall AU RC	15.00	40.00
76 Jeff Taffe AU RC	10.00	25.00
77 Mikael Tellqvist AU RC	15.00	40.00
78 S.Chistov PATCH AU RC	40.00	100.00
79 C.Kobasew PATCH AU RC	60.00	125.00
80 R.Nash PATCH AU RC	500.00	750.00
81 H.Zetterberg PATCH AU RC	600.00	800.00
82 J.Bouwmeester PATCH AU RC	100.00	350.00
83 Jason Spezza	600.00	1000.00
PATCH AU RC		
84 Alexander Svitov	40.00	100.00
PATCH AU RC		
88 Jerred Smithson RC	4.00	10.00
89 Jim Vandermeer RC	4.00	10.00
90 Michael Leighton RC	12.00	30.00
91 Ray Emery RC	12.00	30.00
92 Tomas Zizka RC	4.00	10.00
93 Bobby Allen RC	4.00	10.00
94 Kris Vernarsky RC	4.00	10.00
95 Cristobal Huet RC	20.00	50.00
96 Fernando Pisani RC	8.00	20.00
97 Jonathan Hedstrom RC	4.00	10.00
98 Konstantin Koltsov RC	4.00	10.00
99 Ales Hemsky AU RC	30.00	80.00
100 Steve Ott AU RC	10.00	25.00
101 Alexander Frolov AU RC	30.00	80.00
102 Brooks Orpik AU RC	12.00	30.00
103 Jared Aulin AU RC	10.00	25.00

2002-03 UD Premier Collection Gold

This 58-card skip-numbered set paralleled the rookie checklist of the base set but carried gold highlights and different serial-numbering. Cards #44-70, 71A, 72A and 88-98 were serial-numbered to 199. Cards #71B, 72B, 73-77 and 99-103 were serial-numbered to 25. Cards 78-84 were serial-numbered to just 15 copies each and are not priced due to scarcity.

*GOLD: .3X TO .75X BASIC CARDS

2002-03 UD Premier Collection Jerseys Bronze

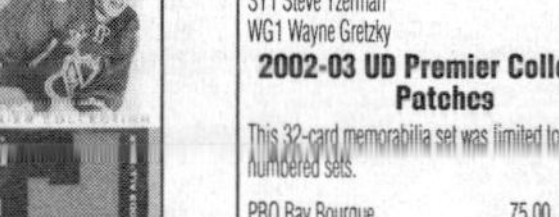

Single swatch jersey cards in this 58-card set were serial-numbered to 299. Dual jersey cards were serial-numbered to 99.

*MULT.COLOR SWATCH: .75X TO 1.5X

AA Ari Ahonen	2.00	5.00
AK Alexei Kovalev	4.00	10.00
AS Alexander Svitov	2.00	5.00
AV Anton Volchenkov	2.00	5.00
AX Alexei Semenov	2.00	5.00
BO Brooks Orpik	2.00	5.00
BS Brendan Shanahan	4.00	10.00
CD Chris Drury	4.00	10.00
CJ Curtis Joseph	4.00	10.00
EL Eric Lindros	4.00	10.00
GM Glen Murray	4.00	10.00
IK Ilya Kovalchuk	6.00	15.00
JG Jaromir Jagr	8.00	20.00
JI Jarome Iginla	6.00	15.00
JJ Jaromir Jagr	8.00	20.00
JK Jeremy Roenick	6.00	15.00
JR Jeremy Roenick	6.00	15.00
JS Joe Sakic	8.00	20.00
JT Jose Theodore	6.00	15.00
MB Martin Brodeur	12.50	30.00
MC Mike Comrie	2.00	5.00
MH Milan Hejduk	4.00	10.00
ML Mario Lemieux	15.00	40.00
MM Mike Modano	6.00	15.00
MO Mike Modano	6.00	15.00
MS Mats Sundin	4.00	10.00
OK Olaf Kolzig	4.00	10.00
PB Pavel Bure	4.00	10.00
PF Peter Forsberg	8.00	20.00
PG Peter Forsberg	8.00	20.00
PK Paul Kariya	8.00	20.00
PL Pascal Leclaire	8.00	20.00
PR Patrick Roy	15.00	40.00
RB Ray Bourque	6.00	15.00
SF Sergei Fedorov	6.00	15.00
SG Simon Gagne	4.00	10.00
SK Saku Koivu	4.00	10.00
SO Steve Ott	2.00	5.00
SS Sergei Samsonov	2.00	5.00
SV Sergei Fedorov	6.00	15.00
SY Steve Yzerman	12.50	30.00
TF Theo Fleury	4.00	10.00
TH Joe Thornton	8.00	20.00
WG Wayne Gretzky	25.00	60.00
BL Pavel Bure	10.00	25.00
Eric Lindros		
BR Rob Blake	12.50	30.00
Patrick Roy		
FH Peter Forsberg	12.00	30.00
Milan Hejduk		
FJ Sergei Fedorov	10.00	25.00
Curtis Joseph		
GL W.Gretzky/M.Lemieux	50.00	125.00
JK Jaromir Jagr	10.00	25.00
Olaf Kolzig		
JR J.Spezza/R.Nash	25.00	60.00
KG Paul Kariya	10.00	25.00
Jean-Sebastien Giguere		
PA Pascal Leclaire	10.00	25.00
Ari Ahonen		
RG Jeremy Roenick	10.00	25.00
Simon Gagne		
SR Joe Sakic	12.50	30.00
Steven Reinprecht		
ST Sergei Samsonov	10.00	25.00
Joe Thornton		
SY Brendan Shanahan	15.00	40.00
Steve Yzerman		
TK Jose Theodore	10.00	25.00
Saku Koivu		

2002-03 UD Premier Collection Jerseys Gold

*SNGL JSY: .6X TO 1.5X BRONZE
SNGL JSY PRINT RUN 50 SER.#'d SETS
*DUAL JSY: .6X TO 1.5X BRONZE
DUAL JSY PRINT RUN 25 SER.#'d SETS

2002-03 UD Premier Collection Jerseys Silver

*SNGL JSY: .5X TO 1.25X BRONZE
SNGL JSY PRINT RUN 99 SER.#'d SETS
*DUAL JSY: .5X TO 1.25X BRONZE
DUAL JSY PRINT RUN 50 SER.#'d SETS

2002-03 UD Premier Collection NHL Patches

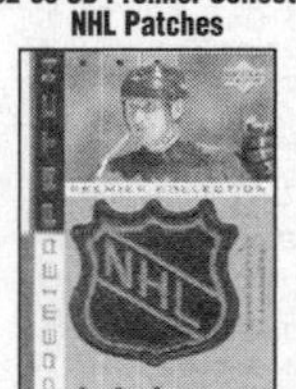

This 10-card set featured the NHL patch from game-worn jerseys on the card fronts. Each card was serial-numbered 1 of 1.

NOT PRICED DUE TO SCARCITY
JJ1 Jaromir Jagr
JS1 Joe Sakic
MB1 Martin Brodeur
ML1 Mario Lemieux
MM1 Mike Modano
MS1 Mats Sundin
PK1 Paul Kariya
PR1 Patrick Roy
SY1 Steve Yzerman
WG1 Wayne Gretzky

2002-03 UD Premier Collection Patches

This 32-card memorabilia set was limited to 25 serial-numbered sets.

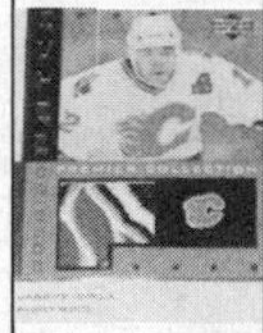

PBO Ray Bourque	75.00	200.00
PBS Brendan Shanahan	50.00	120.00
PCD Chris Drury	50.00	120.00
PCJ Curtis Joseph	50.00	120.00
PEL Eric Lindros	50.00	120.00
PGR Wayne Gretzky	200.00	350.00
PIK Ilya Kovalchuk	60.00	150.00
PJI Jarome Iginla	60.00	150.00
PJJ Jaromir Jagr	75.00	200.00
PJR Jeremy Roenick	100.00	200.00
PJS Joe Sakic	75.00	200.00
PJT Jose Theodore	60.00	150.00
PMB Martin Brodeur	125.00	300.00
PMC Mike Comrie	50.00	120.00
PMH Milan Hejduk	50.00	120.00
PML Mario Lemieux	150.00	400.00
PMM Mike Modano	60.00	150.00
PMS Mats Sundin	50.00	120.00
POK Olaf Kolzig	50.00	120.00
PPB Pavel Bure	50.00	120.00
PPF Peter Forsberg	75.00	200.00
PPK Paul Kariya	50.00	120.00
PPR Patrick Roy	150.00	400.00
PRB Ray Bourque	75.00	200.00
PSF Sergei Fedorov	60.00	150.00
PSG Simon Gagne	50.00	120.00
PSK Saku Koivu	50.00	120.00
PSS Sergei Samsonov	50.00	120.00
PSY Steve Yzerman	125.00	300.00
PTH Joe Thornton	75.00	200.00
PTS Teemu Selanne	40.00	100.00
PWG Wayne Gretzky	200.00	350.00

2002-03 UD Premier Collection Signatures Bronze

This 48-card autograph set was inserted at a rate of 1:2 packs.

SAH Adam Hall SP	5.00	12.00
SAS Alexei Smirnov	5.00	12.00
SBO Bobby Orr	75.00	150.00
SBR Pavel Brendl	5.00	12.00
SBW Jay Bouwmeester	10.00	25.00
SCK Chuck Kobasew	5.00	12.00
SDH Dany Heatley	8.00	20.00
SEB Ed Belfour	10.00	25.00
SEC Erik Cole	5.00	12.00
SGH Gordie Howe	50.00	125.00
SHZ Henrik Zetterberg	10.00	25.00
SIK Ilya Kovalchuk	12.00	30.00
SJB Jay Bouwmeester	10.00	25.00
SJI Jarome Iginla	8.00	20.00
SJL John LeClair	6.00	15.00
SJT Joe Thornton	12.00	30.00
SJW Justin Williams	5.00	12.00
SMA Maxim Afinogenov	5.00	12.00
SMB Martin Brodeur SP	30.00	80.00
SMC Mike Comrie	5.00	12.00
SMF Manny Fernandez	5.00	12.00
SMH Martin Havlat	5.00	12.00
SMN Markus Naslund	6.00	15.00
SMT Mikael Tellqvist SP	10.00	25.00
SNA Rick Nash	15.00	40.00
SNK Nikolai Khabibulin	6.00	15.00
SPB Pavel Bure SP	6.00	15.00
SPM P-M Bouchard	8.00	20.00
SPR Patrick Roy	40.00	100.00
SRA Ray Bourque	15.00	40.00
SRB Ray Bourque	15.00	40.00
SRH Ron Hainsey SP	5.00	12.00
SRN Rick Nash	12.00	30.00
SSC Stanislav Chistov	5.00	12.00
SSG Simon Gagne	6.00	15.00
SSH Scott Hartnell	5.00	12.00
SSP Jason Spezza	12.00	30.00
SSS Sergei Samsonov	5.00	12.00
SSU Scottie Upshall SP	10.00	25.00
SSV Alexander Svitov	5.00	12.00
SSY Steve Yzerman	25.00	60.00
STA Jeff Taffe SP	5.00	12.00
SWG Wayne Gretzky SP	100.00	200.00
ASJT Joe Thornton	12.00	30.00
ASDH Dany Heatley	10.00	25.00
ASJI Jarome Iginla	8.00	20.00
ASMB Martin Brodeur	30.00	80.00
ASPR Patrick Roy SP	40.00	100.00

2002-03 UD Premier Collection Signatures Gold

*GOLD: .6X TO 1.5X BRONZE
GOLD PRINT RUN 50 SER.#'d SETS

2002-03 UD Premier Collection Signatures Silver

*SILVER: .5X TO 1.2X BRONZE
SILVER PRINT RUN 125 SER.#'d SETS

2003-04 UD Premier Collection

This 121-card set featured 59 veteran base cards; 48 short-printed rookie cards (#60-104 and #118-121) serial-numbered out of 399 each and 13 rookie autograph patch cards (#105-117). Cards 105-111 were serial-numbered to 199 and cards 112-117 were serial-numbered to 99 copies each.

COMPLETE SET (121)		
COMPSET w/o SP's (59)	50.00	100.00
*SINGLE COLOR PATCH: .4X TO .75X HI		
1 Jean-Sebastien Giguere	1.00	2.50
2 Sergei Fedorov	1.50	4.00
3 Dany Heatley	1.50	4.00
4 Ilya Kovalchuk	1.50	4.00
5 Sergei Samsonov	1.00	2.50
6 Joe Thornton	1.50	4.00
7 Andrew Raycroft	1.00	2.50
8 Chris Drury	1.00	2.50
9 Jarome Iginla	1.50	4.00
10 Justin Williams	.60	1.50
11 Jocelyn Thibault	1.00	2.50
12 Bryan Berard	.60	1.50
13 David Aebischer	1.00	2.50
14 Joe Sakic	2.50	6.00
15 Paul Kariya	1.25	3.00
16 Peter Forsberg	3.00	8.00
17 Rick Nash	1.50	4.00
18 Marty Turco	1.00	2.50
19 Mike Modano	2.00	5.00
20 Brett Hull	1.50	4.00
21 Pavel Datsyuk	1.25	3.00
22 Steve Yzerman	4.00	10.00
23 Raffi Torres	.60	1.50
24 Ales Hemsky	.60	1.50
25 Roberto Luongo	1.50	4.00
26 Zigmund Palffy	1.00	2.50
27 Marian Gaborik	2.50	6.00
28 Jose Theodore	1.50	4.00
29 Saku Koivu	1.25	3.00
30 Tomas Vokoun	1.00	2.50
31 Scott Stevens	1.00	2.50
32 Martin Brodeur	3.00	8.00
33 Alexei Yashin	.60	1.50
34 Rick DiPietro	1.00	2.50
35 Jaromir Jagr	2.00	5.00
36 Mark Messier	1.25	3.00
37 Eric Lindros	1.25	3.00
38 Jason Spezza	1.25	3.00
39 Marian Hossa	1.25	3.00
40 Patrick Lalime	1.00	2.50
41 Jeremy Roenick	1.50	4.00
42 Tony Amonte	1.00	2.50
43 Mike Comrie	1.00	2.50
44 Brian Boucher	1.00	2.50
45 Mario Lemieux	5.00	12.00
46 Evgeni Nabokov	1.00	2.50
47 Chris Osgood	1.00	2.50
48 Doug Weight	1.00	2.50
49 Keith Tkachuk	1.25	3.00
50 Nikolai Khabibulin	1.25	3.00
51 Mats Sundin	1.25	3.00
52 Owen Nolan	1.00	2.50
53 Ed Belfour	1.25	3.00
54 Ron Francis	1.00	2.50
55 Ed Jovanovski	1.00	2.50
56 Markus Naslund	1.25	3.00
57 Todd Bertuzzi	1.25	3.00
58 Brendan Morrison	1.00	2.50
59 Olaf Kolzig	1.00	2.50
60 Nikolas Kronwall RC	8.00	20.00
61 Derek Roy RC	10.00	25.00
62 Tim Jackman RC	4.00	10.00
63 Timofei Shishkanov RC	4.00	10.00
64 Tomas Plekanec RC	15.00	40.00
65 Aleksander Suglobov RC	5.00	12.00
66 Kyle Wellwood RC	8.00	20.00
67 Mike Smith RC	8.00	20.00
68 Anton Babchuk RC	4.00	10.00
69 Ryan Barnes RC	4.00	10.00
70 Jason Pominville RC	10.00	25.00
71 Pavel Vorobiev RC	5.00	12.00
72 Dustin Brown RC	6.00	15.00
73 Chris Higgins RC	12.00	30.00
74 Dan Hamhuis RC	5.00	12.00
75 Marek Zidlicky RC	5.00	12.00
76 Sean Bergenheim RC	4.00	10.00
77 Antoine Vermette RC	6.00	15.00
78 Milan Michalek RC	8.00	20.00
79 Brad Boyes RC	10.00	25.00
80 Alexander Semin RC	25.00	60.00
81 Carl Corazzini RC	4.00	10.00
82 Sergei Zinovjev RC	4.00	10.00
83 Julien Vauclair RC	4.00	10.00
84 John Pohl RC	4.00	10.00
85 Benoit Dusablon RC	4.00	10.00
86 Tony Salmelainen RC	4.00	10.00
87 Bryce Lampman RC	4.00	10.00
88 Trevor Daley RC	4.00	10.00
89 Dan Ellis RC	10.00	25.00
90 Zbynek Michalek RC	4.00	10.00
91 Goran Bezina RC	4.00	10.00
92 Erik Westrum RC	5.00	12.00
93 Ryan Kesler RC	5.00	12.00
94 Owen Fussey RC	4.00	10.00
95 Josh Olson RC	4.00	10.00
96 Dan Fritsche RC	4.00	10.00
97 Michal Barinka RC	4.00	10.00
98 Kari Lehtonen RC	30.00	60.00
99 Mike Stutzel RC	4.00	10.00
100 Matt Hussey RC	4.00	10.00
101 Roman Tvrdon RC	4.00	10.00
102 Matthew Yeats RC	4.00	10.00
103 Brett Lysak	4.00	10.00
104 Thomas Pock RC	4.00	10.00
105 F.Sjostrom PATCH AU RC	50.00	100.00
106 P.Sejna PATCH AU RC	50.00	100.00
107 M.Stajan PATCH AU RC	100.00	200.00
108 N.Zherdev PATCH AU RC	125.00	250.00
109 P.Bergeron PATCH AU RC	125.00	250.00
110 J.[illegible] PATCH AU RC	[illegible]	120.00
111 J.Lupul PATCH AU RC	75.00	150.00
112 J.Tootoo PATCH AU RC	175.00	350.00
113 N.Horton PATCH AU RC	175.00	300.00
114 E.Staal PATCH AU RC	350.00	600.00
115 J.Hudler PATCH AU RC	150.00	300.00
116 T.Ruutu PATCH AU RC	150.00	300.00
117 M.Fleury PATCH AU RC	500.00	750.00
118 Fedor Tyutin RC	4.00	10.00
119 Denis Grebeshkov RC	4.00	10.00
120 Cory Larose RC	4.00	10.00
121 Andy Chiodo RC	4.00	10.00

2003-04 UD Premier Collection Legends Patches

This set paralleled the basic insert set with authentic patches. This set was serial-numbered out of 10.

NOT PRICED DUE TO SCARCITY

2003-04 UD Premier Collection Matchups

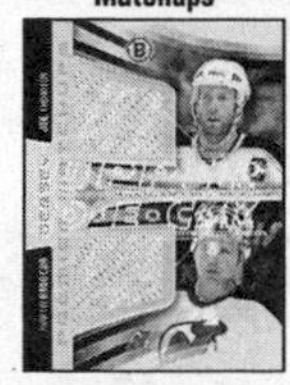

This 6-card set featured dual jersey swatches of two current players. Each card was serial-numbered out of 25.

PMBT Ed Belfour	30.00	80.00
Jose Theodore		
PMGB Marian Gaborik	20.00	50.00
Todd Bertuzzi		
PMHM Ales Hemsky	20.00	50.00
Mike Modano		
PMHR Marian Hossa	20.00	50.00
Jeremy Roenick		
PMRH Patrick Roy	25.00	60.00
Dominik Hasek		
PMTB Joe Thornton	25.00	60.00
Martin Brodeur		

2003-04 UD Premier Collection Matchups Patches

This set paralleled the basic insert set with authentic patches. This set was serial-numbered out of 3.

NOT PRICED DUE TO SCARCITY

2003-04 UD Premier Collection NHL Shields

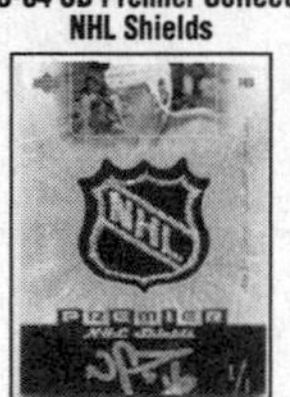

This 35-card set of 1/1's featured the NHL shield patch from the given player's jersey along with a certified autograph.

PRINT RUN 1 SER.#'d SET
NOT PRICED DUE TO SCARCITY
SHAC Todd Bertuzzi
SHAH Ales Hemsky
SHCJ Curtis Joseph
SHDA David Aebischer
SHEL Eric Lindros
SHES Eric Staal
SHGL Martin Brodeur
SHG1 Wayne Gretzky
SHIK Ilya Kovalchuk
SHJH Jiri Hudler
SHJI Jarome Iginla
SHJL Joffrey Lupul
SHJR Jeremy Roenick
SHJS Jason Spezza
SHJT Joe Thornton
SHJR2 Jeremy Roenick
SHJSG Jean-Sebastien Giguere
SHMB Martin Brodeur
SHMG Marian Gaborik
SHMH Marian Hossa
SHMN Markus Naslund
SHMT Marty Turco
SHMAF Marc-Andre Fleury
SHNH Nathan Horton
SHON Owen Nolan
SHPB Patrice Bergeron
SHPR Patrick Roy
SHRL Roberto Luongo
SHRN Rick Nash
SHROY Patrick Roy
SHSK Saku Koivu
SHTB Todd Bertuzzi
SHTH Jose Theodore
SHTR Tuomo Ruutu
SHWG Wayne Gretzky

2003-04 UD Premier Collection Signatures

This 41-card set featured player autographs in silver paint pen on black puck-like backgrounds below a full-color player photo. Cards were inserted one per pack.

PSAC Anson Carter	6.00	15.00
PSAH Ales Hemsky	6.00	15.00
PSBO Pavel Bure SP	10.00	25.00
PSBY Mike Bossy	10.00	25.00
PSCJ Curtis Joseph	8.00	20.00
PSDA David Aebischer	6.00	15.00
PSDC Don Cherry	12.00	30.00
PSEL Eric Lindros	8.00	20.00
PSES Eric Staal	12.00	30.00
PSGL Guy Lafleur SP	25.00	60.00
PSG1 Wayne Gretzky	75.00	150.00
PSHZ Henrik Zetterberg	10.00	25.00
PSIK Ilya Kovalchuk	12.00	30.00
PSJH Jiri Hudler	6.00	15.00
PSJI Jarome Iginla	10.00	25.00
PSJR Jeremy Roenick	8.00	20.00
PSJS Jason Spezza	10.00	25.00
PSJT Joe Thornton	15.00	40.00
PSJSG Jean-Sebastien Giguere	6.00	15.00
PSJTH Jose Theodore	10.00	25.00
PSMB Martin Brodeur	60.00	120.00
PSMG Marian Gaborik	10.00	25.00
PSMH Gordie Howe	40.00	80.00
PSMT Marty Turco	6.00	15.00
PSMAF Marc-Andre Fleury	15.00	30.00
PSMAH Marian Hossa	6.00	15.00
PSMCH Marcel Hossa	6.00	15.00
PSMNH Markus Naslund	6.00	15.00
PSNH Nathan Horton	6.00	15.00
PSON Owen Nolan	6.00	15.00
PSPB Patrice Bergeron SP	15.00	40.00
PSPR Patrick Roy	75.00	150.00
PSRL Roberto Luongo	8.00	20.00
PSRN Rick Nash	12.00	30.00
PSROY Patrick Roy SP	125.00	250.00
PSSK Saku Koivu	10.00	25.00
PSTB Todd Bertuzzi	6.00	15.00
PSTR Tuomo Ruutu	8.00	20.00
PSTOO Jordin Tootoo	10.00	25.00
PSWG Wayne Gretzky	75.00	150.00
PSZP Zigmund Palffy	6.00	15.00

2003-04 UD Premier Collection Signatures Gold

This 38-card set paralleled the basic insert set but utilized gold paint pens. Known print runs are listed below.

NOT PRICED DUE TO SCARCITY
PSAC Anson Carter/2
PSAH Ales Hemsky/1
PSBO Pavel Bure/2
PSBY Mike Bossy/10
PSCJ Curtis Joseph/9
PSDA David Aebischer/10
PSDC Don Cherry/10
PSEL Eric Lindros/10
PSES Eric Staal/1
PSGL Guy Lafleur/10
PSG1 Wayne Gretzky EDM/10
PSHZ Henrik Zetterberg/10
PSIK Ilya Kovalchuk/10
PSJH Jiri Hudler/8
PSJI Jarome Iginla/6
PSJR Jeremy Roenick/4
PSJS Jason Spezza/10
PSJT Joe Thornton/10
PSJSG Jean-Sebastien Giguere/10
PSJTH Jose Theodore/1
PSMB Martin Brodeur/10
PSMG Marian Gaborik/3
PSMH Gordie Howe/7
PSMT Marty Turco/9
PSMAF Marc-Andre Fleury/10
PSMAH Marian Hossa/4
PSNH Nathan Horton/10
PSON Owen Nolan/8
PSPB Patrice Bergeron/10
PSPR Patrick Roy/10
PSRL Roberto Luongo/10
PSRN Rick Nash/10
PSROY Patrick Roy/10
PSSK Saku Koivu/3
PSTB Todd Bertuzzi/10
PSTR Tuomo Ruutu/5
PSWG Wayne Gretzky LA/8
PSZP Zigmund Palffy/8

2003-04 UD Premier Collection Skills

This 6-card set featured dual jersey swatches from two current players. Each card was serial-numbered out of 50.

SKBF Martin Brodeur	25.00	60.00
Marc-Andre Fleury		
SKBT Todd Bertuzzi	12.50	30.00
Keith Tkachuk		
SKFT Peter Forsberg	12.50	30.00
Joe Thornton		
SKLT M.Lemieux/J.Thornton	25.00	60.00
SKRR Jeremy Roenick	12.00	30.00
Tuomo Ruttu		
SKSY J.Sakic/S.Yzerman	25.00	60.00

2003-04 UD Premier Collection Skills Patches

This set paralleled the basic insert set with authentic patches. This set was serial-numbered out of 10.

NOT PRICED DUE TO SCARCITY

2003-04 UD Premier Collection Stars

This 35-card set featured jersey swatches inset in the die-cut letter "e" of the word Premier across the card front. Each card was serial-numbered out of 250.

STAM Alexander Mogilny 4.00 10.00
STBH Brett Hull 5.00 12.00
STDH Dan Hamhuis 4.00 10.00
STDW Doug Weight 4.00 10.00
STES Eric Staal 10.00 25.00
STGM Glenn Murray 4.00 10.00
STIK Ilya Kovalchuk 5.00 12.00
STJH Jiri Hudler 4.00 10.00
STJI Jarome Iginla 5.00 12.00
STJL Joffrey Lupul 4.00 10.00
STJS Joe Sakic 6.00 15.00
STJT Jordin Tootoo 5.00 12.00
STJSG Jean-Sebastien Giguere 4.00 10.00
STLR Luc Robitaille 4.00 10.00
STMD Marc Denis 4.00 10.00
STMF Manny Fernandez 4.00 10.00
STMH Milan Hejduk 4.00 10.00
STMN Markus Naslund 4.00 10.00
STMR Mark Recchi 4.00 10.00
STMR Mike Ribeiro 4.00 10.00
STMS Martin Straka 4.00 10.00
STMAF Marc-Andre Fleury 10.00 25.00
STNH Nathan Horton 4.00 10.00
STNZ Nikolai Zherdev 4.00 10.00
STPB Patrice Bergeron 5.00 12.00
STPD Pavol Demitra 4.00 10.00
STPK Paul Kariya 4.00 10.00
STRC Roman Cechmanek 4.00 10.00
STRL Roberto Luongo 5.00 12.00
STSF Sergei Fedorov 5.00 12.00
STSS Sergei Samsonov 4.00 10.00
STSY Steve Yzerman 8.00 20.00
STTB Todd Bertuzzi 4.00 10.00
STTR Tuomo Ruutu 4.00 10.00
STVL Vincent Lecavalier 4.00 10.00

2003-04 UD Premier Collection Stars Patches

This set paralleled the basic insert set with authentic patches. This set was serial-numbered out of 100.

*PATCHES: 1.25X TO 3X JSY HI

2003-04 UD Premier Collection Super Stars

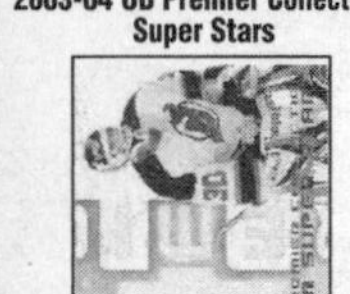

This 6-card set featured jersey swatches of current super stars serial-numbered to 100.

SSJS Jason Spezza 12.50 30.00
SSJT Joe Thornton 12.50 30.00
SSMB Martin Brodeur 25.00 60.00
SSMG Marian Gaborik 12.50 30.00
SSML Mario Lemieux 20.00 50.00
SSPF Peter Forsberg 12.50 30.00

2003-04 UD Premier Collection Super Stars Patches

This set paralleled the basic insert set with authentic patches. This set was serial-numbered out of 25.

SSJS Jason Spezza 40.00 100.00
SSJT Joe Thornton 60.00 150.00
SSMB Martin Brodeur 75.00 200.00
SSMG Marian Gaborik 60.00 150.00
SSML Mario Lemieux 75.00 200.00
SSPF Peter Forsberg 60.00 150.00

2003-04 UD Premier Collection Teammates

Serial-numbered out of 100, this 30-card set featured prominent players on the 30 NHL franchises and swatches of their jerseys.

PTAM Jean-Sebastien Giguere / Sergei Fedorov 8.00 20.00
PTBB1 Joe Thornton / Sergei Samsonov 10.00 25.00
PTBB2 Joe Thornton / Patrice Bergeron 10.00 25.00
PTCB Jocelyn Thibault / Tuomo Ruutu 8.00 20.00
PTCH Ron Francis / Eric Staal 15.00 40.00
PTCA1 Peter Forsberg / Joe Sakic 12.50 30.00
PTCA2 Teemu Selanne / Paul Kariya 8.00 20.00
PTCB1 R.Nash/M.Denis 8.00 20.00
PTCB2 R.Nash/N.Zherdev 8.00 20.00
PTDR1 Steve Yzerman / Dominik Hasek 15.00 40.00
PTDR2 Steve Yzerman / Brett Hull 15.00 40.00
PTDS1 M.Modano/M.Turco 10.00 25.00
PTDS2 Bill Guerin / Mike Modano 8.00 20.00
PTEO1 Wayne Gretzky / Mark Messier 60.00 150.00
PTEO2 Raffi Torres / Ales Hemsky 8.00 20.00
PTFP Roberto Luongo / Olli Jokinen 10.00 25.00
PTLK Zigmund Palffy / Roman Cechmanek 8.00 20.00
PTMC Jose Theodore / Saku Koivu 10.00 25.00
PTMW Marian Gaborik / Manny Fernandez 8.00 20.00
PTND M.Brodeur/S.Stevens 12.50 30.00
PTNR Eric Lindros / Mark Messier 10.00 25.00
PTOS Jason Spezza / Marian Hossa 10.00 25.00
PTPP M.Lemieux/M.Fleury 25.00 60.00
PTPF1 Jeremy Roenick / Tony Amonte 8.00 20.00
PTPF2 Jeremy Roenick / Joni Pitkanen 8.00 20.00
PTSB Keith Tkachuk / Doug Weight 8.00 20.00
PTTL Vincent Lecavalier / Nikolai Khabibulin 10.00 25.00
PTTM1 M.Sundin/O.Nolan 8.00 20.00
PTTM2 Ed Belfour / Mats Sundin 8.00 20.00
PTVC Todd Bertuzzi / Markus Naslund 10.00 25.00

2003-04 UD Premier Collection Teammates Patches

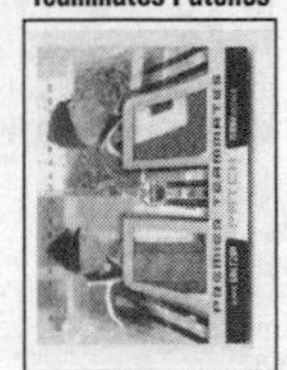

This set paralleled the basic insert set with authentic patches. This set was serial-numbered out of 25.

*PATCHES: 1.5X TO 4X JSY HI
PRINT RUN 25 SERIAL #'d SETS

2000-01 UD Pros and Prospects

Upper Deck Pros and Prospects were released as a 132-card set with 42 short-printed rookie cards. The set design featured a white bordered card with copper-foil lettering, highlights, and logo. The card backs are white and blue with a small photo of the player on the top right corner. SP's are numbered to 1000 sets.

COMPLETE SET (132) 125.00 250.00
COMP.SET w/o SP's 15.00 30.00
1 Paul Kariya .30 .75
2 Teemu Selanne .30 .75
3 Guy Hebert .25 .60
4 Donald Audette .10 .25
5 Adam Burt .10 .25
6 Patrik Stefan .10 .25
7 Joe Thornton .50 1.25
8 Jason Allison .10 .25
9 Sergei Samsonov .25 .60
10 Dominik Hasek .60 1.50
11 Doug Gilmour .25 .60
12 Maxim Afinogenov .10 .25
13 Oleg Saprykin .10 .25
14 Valeri Bure .10 .25
15 Mike Vernon .25 .60
16 Ron Francis .25 .60
17 Jeff O'Neill .10 .25
18 Arturs Irbe .25 .60
19 Steve Sullivan .25 .60
20 Alexei Zhamnov .10 .25
21 Tony Amonte .25 .60
22 Ray Bourque .60 1.50
23 Patrick Roy 1.50 4.00
24 Peter Forsberg .75 2.00
25 Marc Denis .25 .60
26 Tyler Wright .10 .25
27 Mike Modano .50 1.25
28 Brett Hull .40 1.00
29 Ed Belfour .30 .75
30 Brendan Shanahan .30 .75
31 Sergei Fedorov .50 1.25
32 Steve Yzerman 1.50 4.00
33 Ryan Smyth .10 .25
34 Tommy Salo .25 .60
35 Doug Weight .25 .60
36 Pavel Bure .30 .75
37 Ray Whitney .10 .25
38 Viktor Kozlov .10 .25
39 Luc Robitaille .25 .60
40 Rob Blake .25 .60
41 Zigmund Palffy .25 .60
42 Manny Fernandez .25 .60
43 Scott Pellerin .10 .25
44 Jose Theodore .40 1.00
45 Brian Savage .10 .25
46 Martin Rucinsky .10 .25
47 David Legwand .10 .25
48 Mike Dunham .25 .60
49 Cliff Ronning .10 .25
50 Scott Gomez .10 .25
51 Scott Stevens .25 .60
52 Martin Brodeur .75 2.00
53 Tim Connolly .10 .25
54 Brad Isbister .25 .60
55 Roman Hamrlik .10 .25
56 Theo Fleury .10 .25
57 Mike Richter .30 .75
58 Mark Messier .30 .75
59 Marian Hossa .30 .75
60 Alexei Yashin .10 .25
61 Radek Bonk .10 .25
62 John LeClair .30 .75
63 Mark Recchi .25 .60
64 Simon Gagne .30 .75
65 Jeremy Roenick .40 1.00
66 Shane Doan .10 .25
67 Keith Tkachuk .30 .75
68 Jaromir Jagr .50 1.25
69 Mario Lemieux 2.50 6.00
70 Alexei Kovalev .25 .60
71 Owen Nolan .25 .60
72 Jeff Friesen .10 .25
73 Patrick Marleau .25 .60
74 Chris Pronger .25 .60
75 Roman Turek .25 .60
76 Pierre Turgeon .25 .60
77 Kevin Weekes .10 .25
78 Fredrik Modin .10 .25
79 Vincent Lecavalier .30 .75
80 Curtis Joseph .30 .75
81 Mats Sundin .30 .75
82 Gary Roberts .10 .25
83 Markus Naslund .30 .75
84 Daniel Sedin .10 .25
85 Henrik Sedin .10 .25
86 Adam Oates .25 .60
87 Peter Bondra .30 .75
88 Olaf Kolzig .25 .60
89 Mark Messier .30 .75
90 Steve Yzerman 1.50 4.00
91 Jonas Ronnqvist RC 2.00 5.00
92 Andy McDonald RC 2.00 5.00
93 Eric Nickulas RC 2.00 5.00
94 Andrew Raycroft RC 4.00 10.00
95 Jarno Kultanen RC 2.00 5.00
96 Jeff Cowan RC 2.00 5.00
97 Josef Vasicek RC 2.00 5.00
98 Reto Von Arx RC 2.00 5.00
99 David Aebischer RC 5.00 12.00
100 Serge Aubin RC 2.00 5.00
101 Rostislav Klesla RC 3.00 8.00
102 Marty Turco RC 8.00 20.00
103 Tyler Bouck RC 2.00 5.00
104 Brian Swanson RC 2.00 5.00
105 Michel Riesen RC 2.00 5.00
106 Eric Belanger RC 2.00 5.00
107 Steven Reinprecht RC 2.00 5.00
108 Marian Gaborik RC 12.50 30.00
109 Scott Hartnell RC 2.50 6.00
110 Greg Classen RC 2.00 5.00
111 Willie Mitchell RC 2.00 5.00
112 Colin White RC 2.00 5.00
113 Petr Mika RC 2.00 5.00
114 Rick DiPietro RC 5.00 12.00
115 Jason Labarbera RC 3.00 8.00
116 Martin Havlat RC 6.00 15.00
117 Jani Hurme RC 3.00 8.00
118 Petr Hubacek RC 2.00 5.00
119 Justin Williams RC 3.00 8.00
120 Roman Cechmanek RC 2.50 6.00
121 Roman Simicek RC 2.00 5.00
122 Mark Smith RC 2.00 5.00
123 Alexander Kharitonov RC 2.00 5.00
124 Matt Elich RC 2.00 5.00
125 Jakub Cutta RC 2.00 5.00
126 Fedor Fedorov RC 2.00 5.00
127 Marc-Andre Thinel RC 2.00 5.00
128 Zdenek Blatny RC 2.00 5.00
129 Jeff Bateman RC 2.00 5.00
130 Jason Jaspers RC 2.00 5.00
131 Jordan Krestanovich RC 2.00 5.00
132 Damian Surma RC 2.00 5.00

2000-01 UD Pros and Prospects Championship Rings

COMPLETE SET (8) 12.00 25.00
STATED ODDS 1:12
CR1 Patrick Roy 3.00 8.00
CR2 Brendan Shanahan 1.00 2.50
CR3 Steve Yzerman 3.00 8.00
CR4 Wayne Gretzky 4.00 10.00
CR5 Scott Stevens .60 1.50
CR6 Martin Brodeur 1.50 4.00
CR7 Mark Messier .75 2.00
CR8 Jaromir Jagr 1.00 2.50

2000-01 UD Pros and Prospects Game Jerseys

Randomly inserted in Upper Deck Pros and Prospects packs at a rate of 1:30, this 10-card set featured a swatch of game jersey. An exclusives parallel was also created and serial-numbered to 50 and was also created.

*MULT.COLOR SWATCHES: 1X TO 2X
*EXCLUSIVES: 1X TO 2X BASIC INSERTS
BS Brendan Shanahan 3.00 8.00
CP Chris Pronger 3.00 8.00
JJ Jaromir Jagr 5.00 12.00
MM Mike Modano 4.00 10.00
PF Peter Forsberg 6.00 15.00
PK Paul Kariya 3.00 8.00
PR Patrick Roy 8.00 20.00
RB Ray Bourque 8.00 20.00
SF Sergei Fedorov 4.00 10.00
TS Teemu Selanne 3.00 8.00

2000-01 UD Pros and Prospects Game Jersey Autographs

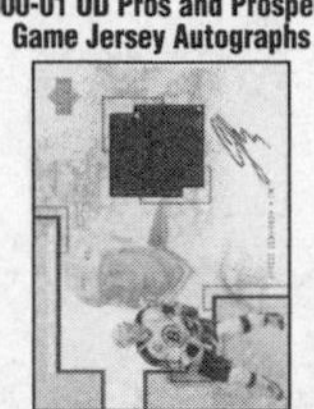

Randomly inserted in Upper Deck Pros and Prospects packs at a rate of 1:96, this 10-card set featured a swatch of game jersey, and an autograph. An exclusives parallel was also created and serial-numbered to 50. Please note at the time of release the Scott Gomez and Wayne Gretzky cards were issued as exchange/redemption cards.

*MULT.COLOR SWATCHES: 1X TO 2X
*EXCLUSIVES: 1X TO 2X BASIC INSERTS
SJL John LeClair 12.50 30.00
SJR Jeremy Roenick 25.00 60.00
SKT Keith Tkachuk 12.50 30.00
SLB Lubos Bartecko 10.00 25.00
SMM Mark Messier 250.00 400.00
SPB Pavel Bure 12.50 30.00
SSG Scott Gomez 10.00 25.00
SSS Sergei Samsonov 12.50 30.00
SSY Steve Yzerman 50.00 125.00
SWG Wayne Gretzky 200.00 300.00

2000-01 UD Pros and Prospects Great Skates

COMPLETE SET (8) 10.00 20.00
STATED ODDS 1:12
GS1 Paul Kariya .60 1.50
GS2 Mario Lemieux 4.00 10.00
GS3 Patrick Roy 3.00 8.00
GS4 Brendan Shanahan 1.00 2.50
GS5 Pavel Bure .75 2.00
GS6 Alexei Yashin .60 1.50
GS7 John LeClair .75 2.00
GS8 Jaromir Jagr 1.00 2.50

2000-01 UD Pros and Prospects NHL Passion

COMPLETE SET (9) 10.00 20.00
STATED ODDS 1:10
NP1 Ray Bourque 1.00 3.00
NP2 Brett Hull .75 2.00
NP3 Steve Yzerman 3.00 8.00
NP4 Mark Messier .75 2.00
NP5 John LeClair .75 2.00
NP6 Jeremy Roenick .75 2.00
NP7 Jaromir Jagr 1.00 2.50
NP8 Mario Lemieux 4.00 10.00
NP9 Curtis Joseph .60 1.50

2000-01 UD Pros and Prospects Now Appearing

COMPLETE SET (8) 10.00 20.00
STATED ODDS 1:12
NA1 Maxim Afinogenov .60 1.50
NA2 Marian Gaborik 3.00 8.00
NA3 Scott Hartnell .75 2.00
NA4 Scott Gomez .60 1.50
NA5 Rick DiPietro 3.00 8.00
NA6 Justin Williams 1.25 3.00
NA7 Daniel Sedin .60 1.50
NA8 Henrik Sedin .60 1.50

2000-01 UD Pros and Prospects ProMotion

COMPLETE SET (9) 10.00 20.00
STATED ODDS 1:10
PM1 Teemu Selanne .75 2.00
PM2 Dominik Hasek 1.50 4.00
PM3 Peter Forsberg 1.50 4.00
PM4 Sergei Fedorov 1.00 3.00
PM5 Mike Modano 1.00 2.50
PM6 Pavel Bure 1.00 2.50
PM7 Martin Brodeur 1.50 4.00
PM8 John LeClair .75 2.00
PM9 Jaromir Jagr 1.00 2.50

2000-01 UD Reserve

The 2000-01 UD Reserve complete set consisted of 120 cards,30 of which were rookies and 2 were checklists. The base set design used silver-foil for the Upper Deck logo and for highlights on the cards, and they had a light-blue border on the left side of the card front. The card backs had a small photo of the player on the top half and statistics below for the past couple seasons and also contained a career statistics line. The card backs also had the UD hologram on the bottom right corner.

COMPLETE SET (120) 40.00 80.00
1 Paul Kariya .25 .60
2 Steve Rucchin .08 .20
3 Teemu Selanne .25 .60
4 Damian Rhodes .08 .20
5 Patrik Stefan .08 .20
6 Byron Dafoe .20 .50
7 Jason Allison .08 .20
8 Joe Thornton .40 1.00
9 Doug Gilmour .20 .50
10 Dominik Hasek .50 1.25
11 Miroslav Satan .20 .50
12 Jarome Iginla .30 .75
13 Oleg Saprykin .08 .20
14 Valeri Bure .08 .20
15 Sandis Ozolinsh .08 .20
16 Ron Francis .20 .50
17 Sami Kapanen .08 .20
18 Steve Sullivan .20 .50
19 Alexei Zhamnov .08 .20
20 Tony Amonte .20 .50
21 Ray Bourque .50 1.25
22 Patrick Roy 1.25 3.00
23 Peter Forsberg .60 1.50
24 Joe Sakic .50 1.25
25 Ron Tugnutt .20 .50
26 Steve Heinze .08 .20
27 Mike Modano .40 1.00
28 Brett Hull .30 .75
29 Ed Belfour .25 .60
30 Brendan Shanahan .25 .60
31 Sergei Fedorov .40 1.00
32 Steve Yzerman 1.25 3.00
33 Ryan Smyth .08 .20
34 Tommy Salo .20 .50
35 Doug Weight .20 .50
36 Pavel Bure .25 .60
37 Ray Whitney .08 .20
38 Roberto Luongo .30 .75
39 Luc Robitaille .20 .50
40 Zigmund Palffy .20 .50
41 Jamie Storr .20 .50
42 Jamie McLennan .08 .20
43 Jim Dowd .08 .20
44 Brian Savage .08 .20
45 Jose Theodore .30 .75
46 Saku Koivu .25 .60
47 David Legwand .20 .50
48 Cliff Ronning .08 .20
49 Tomas Vokoun .20 .50
50 Scott Gomez .08 .20
51 Patrik Elias .20 .50
52 Martin Brodeur .60 1.50
53 Tim Connolly .08 .20
54 Roman Hamrlik .08 .20
55 John Vanbiesbrouck .20 .50
56 Theo Fleury .08 .20
57 Mark Messier .25 .60
58 Brian Leetch .25 .60
59 Marian Hossa .25 .60
60 Patrick Lalime .20 .50
61 Alexei Yashin .08 .20
62 John LeClair .25 .60
63 Mark Recchi .20 .50
64 Keith Primeau .08 .20
65 Jeremy Roenick .30 .75
66 Sean Burke .20 .50
67 Keith Tkachuk .25 .60
68 Jaromir Jagr .40 1.00
69 Milan Kraft .20 .50
70 Mario Lemieux 1.50 4.00
71 Owen Nolan .20 .50
72 Jeff Friesen .08 .20
73 Evgeni Nabokov .20 .50
74 Chris Pronger .20 .50
75 Scott Young .08 .20
76 Roman Turek .20 .50
77 Vincent Lecavalier .25 .60
78 Brad Richards .20 .50
79 Mike Johnson .08 .20
80 Curtis Joseph .25 .60
81 Mats Sundin .25 .60
82 Sergei Berezin .08 .20
83 Markus Naslund .25 .60
84 Daniel Sedin .08 .20
85 Henrik Sedin .08 .20
86 Chris Simon .08 .20
87 Peter Bondra .25 .60
88 Olaf Kolzig .20 .50
89 Andrew Raycroft RC 1.50 4.00
90 Josef Vasicek RC .40 1.00
91 David Aebischer RC 1.50 4.00
92 Rostislav Klesla RC 1.00 2.50
93 Marty Turco RC 2.00 5.00
94 Tyler Bouck RC .60 1.50
95 Shawn Horcoff RC .75 2.00
96 Eric Belanger RC .40 1.00
97 Steven Reinprecht RC .40 1.00
98 Marian Gaborik RC 2.50 6.00
99 Peter Bartos RC .40 1.00
100 Scott Hartnell RC .40 1.00
101 Greg Classen RC .40 1.00
102 Chris Mason RC .40 1.00
103 Willie Mitchell RC .40 1.00
104 Rick DiPietro RC 1.50 4.00
105 Jason Labarbera RC .50 1.25
106 Jani Hurme RC .75 2.00
107 Martin Havlat RC 2.00 5.00
108 Ruslan Fedotenko RC .40 1.00
109 Justin Williams RC 1.00 2.50
110 Petr Hubacek RC .40 1.00
111 Roman Cechmanek RC .50 1.25
112 Mark Smith RC .40 1.00
113 Alexander Khavanov RC .40 1.00
114 Alexander Kharitonov RC .40 1.00
115 Marc-Andre Thinel RC .40 1.00
116 Zdenek Blatny RC .40 1.00
117 Jordan Krestanovich RC .40 1.00
118 Jeff Bateman RC .40 1.00
119 Mark Messier CL .25 .60
120 Curtis Joseph CL .25 .60

2000-01 UD Reserve Buyback Autographs

Randomly inserted in packs at a rate of 1:239, this set features 137 different original Upper Deck cards that Upper Deck bought back and had autographed. Please note these cards have print runs that vary. Cards with print runs of less than 25 are not priced due to scarcity. The Scott Gomez cards were only found in packs as exchange cards and the actual autographed buybacks have yet to be verified. For that reason only the exchange card is priced.

PRINT RUNS OF LESS THAN 20 NOT
PRICED DUE TO SCARCITY
1 Wayne Gretzky 90UD/1
2 Wayne Gretzky 91UD621/1
3 Wayne Gretzky 92UD25/1
4 Wayne Gretzky 92UD33/1
5 Wayne Gretzky 96UD/1
6 Wayne Gretzky 97UD/1
7 Wayne Gretzky 98UD135/1
8 Wayne Gretzky 98UD390/1
9 Wayne Gretzky 99UD9/1
10 Wayne Gretzky 99UD10/1
11 S.Yzerman 90UD303/1
12 S.Yzerman 90UD56/1
13 S.Yzerman 91UD/1
14 S.Yzerman 92UD/1
15 S.Yzerman 93UD/1
16 S.Yzerman 94UD/1
17 S.Yzerman 95UD/1
18 S.Yzerman 96UD/1
19 S.Yzerman 97UD/1
20 S.Yzerman 98UD/1
21 S.Yzerman 99UD304/4
22 S.Yzerman 99UD49/1
23 Sergei Samsonov 99MVPSC/29
24 Scott Gomez EXCH
25 Scott Gomez 99MVPSCSS/27 12.50 25.00
26 Scott Gomez 99UD/9
27 Ray Bourque 90UD204/2
28 Ray Bourque 90UD320/1
29 Ray Bourque 90UD64/1
30 Ray Bourque 91UD/2
31 Ray Bourque 92UD265/2
32 Ray Bourque 92UD626/1
33 Ray Bourque 95UD/3
34 Ray Bourque 96UD/1
35 Ray Bourque 97UD/1
36 Ray Bourque 98UD/1
37 Pavel Brendl 99MVPSC/301 15.00 30.00
38 Pavel Brendl 99UD/9
39 Mike Richter 90UD/6
40 Mike Richter 91UD175/1
41 Mike Richter 91UD34/1
42 Mike Richter 92UD/1
43 Mike Richter 94UD/1
44 Mike Richter 95UD/2
45 Mike Richter 96UD/1
46 Mike Richter 97UD/1
47 Mike Richter 98UD/1
48 Mike Richter 99UD/1
49 Mike Ribeiro 97UD/52
50 Mike Ribeiro 99OVA/1
51 Mike Ribeiro 99UD/25 25.00 60.00
52 M.Modano 90UD346/13
53 M.Modano 90UD46/56 25.00 60.00
54 M.Modano 91UD160/12
55 M.Modano 91UD32/5
56 M.Modano 92UD305/69 25.00 60.00
57 M.Modano 92UD9/10
58 M.Modano 93UD294/2
59 M.Modano 93UD397/5
60 M.Modano 94UD/8
61 M.Modano 95UD/7
62 M.Modano 96UD363/3
63 M.Modano 96UD43/39 40.00 100.00
64 M.Modano 98UD256/8
65 M.Modano 98UD30/1
66 M.Modano 99UD/9
67 M.Brodeur 92UD/2
68 M.Brodeur 94UD/1
69 M.Brodeur 96UD/1
70 M.Brodeur 97UD/7
71 M.Brodeur 99UD/3
72 Mark Messier 90UD321/1
73 Mark Messier 90UD44/1
74 Mark Messier 91UD/1
75 Mark Messier 92UD242/1
76 Mark Messier 92UD34/1
77 Mark Messier 94UD/1
78 Mark Messier 99UD/4
79 Luc Robitaille 90UD/10
80 Luc Robitaille 91UD145/12
81 Luc Robitaille 91UD507/5
82 Luc Robitaille 91UD623/2
83 Luc Robitaille 91UD8/6
84 Luc Robitaille 92UD/13
85 Luc Robitaille 93UD231/12
86 Luc Robitaille 93UD293/5
87 Luc Robitaille 93UD414/13
88 Luc Robitaille 98MVP/2
89 Luc Robitaille 98UD/6
90 Luc Robitaille 99OVA/7
91 Luc Robitaille 99RETRO/3
92 Luc Robitaille 99UD/3
93 Luc Robitaille 99UV/1
94 Keith Tkachuk 92UD364/2
95 Keith Tkachuk 92UD398/2
96 Keith Tkachuk 92UD419/2
97 Keith Tkachuk 94UD/1
98 Keith Tkachuk 95UD/1
99 Keith Tkachuk 97UD/1
100 Keith Tkachuk 99UD/100 75.00 200.00
101 Jose Theodore 95UD/4
102 Jose Theodore 97UD/4
103 Jose Theodore 99MVPSC/356 6.00 15.00
104 John LeClair 91UD/4
105 John LeClair 92UD/2
106 John LeClair 95UD247/1
107 John LeClair 95UD7/2
108 John LeClair 96UD118/3
109 John LeClair 96UD368/2
110 John LeClair 97UD123/7
111 John LeClair 98UD/3
112 John LeClair 99UD/2
113 Henrik Sedin 99UDGR166/3
114 Henrik Sedin 99UDGR308/1
115 Henrik Sedin EXCH
116 Henrik Sedin 99UD166/3
117 Henrik Sedin 99UD308/13
118 Gordie Howe 92UDGH19/1
119 Gordie Howe 92UDGH20/1
120 Gordie Howe 92UDGH21/1
121 Gordie Howe 92UDGH22/1
122 Gordie Howe 92UDGH23/1
123 Gordie Howe 92UDGH24/1
124 Gordie Howe 92UDGH25/1
125 Gordie Howe 92UDGH26/1
126 Gordie Howe 92UDGH27/1
127 Gordie Howe 99OVACS/1
128 Daniel Sedin 99UDGR/2
129 Daniel Sedin 99MVPSC/329 12.50 25.00
130 Daniel Sedin 99UD165/2
131 Daniel Sedin 99UD307/10
132 Curtis Joseph 90UD/10
133 Curtis Joseph 92UD/1
134 Curtis Joseph 94UD/1
135 Curtis Joseph 95UD/1
136 Curtis Joseph 97UD/1
137 Curtis Joseph 98UD/1

2000-01 UD Reserve Gold Strike

COMPLETE SET (10) 12.00 25.00
STATED ODDS 1:14
GS1 Teemu Selanne .75 2.00
GS2 Joe Sakic 1.50 4.00
GS3 Mike Modano 1.25 3.00
GS4 Sergei Fedorov 1.50 4.00
GS5 Pavel Bure 1.00 2.50
GS6 Scott Gomez .60 1.50
GS7 Theo Fleury .60 1.50
GS8 Mario Lemieux 5.00 12.00
GS9 Mats Sundin .75 2.00
GS10 Olaf Kolzig .60 1.50

2000-01 UD Reserve Golden Goalies

COMPLETE SET (10) 10.00 20.00
STATED ODDS 1:14
GG1 Guy Hebert .60 1.50
GG2 Dominik Hasek 1.50 4.00
GG3 Patrick Roy 4.00 10.00
GG4 Tommy Salo .60 1.50
GG5 Jose Theodore .75 2.00
GG6 Mike Dunham .60 1.50
GG7 Martin Brodeur 2.00 5.00
GG8 John Vanbiesbrouck .75 2.00
GG9 Roman Turek .60 1.50
GG10 Curtis Joseph 1.00 2.50

2000-01 UD Reserve On-Ice Success

COMPLETE SET (6) 6.00 12.00
STATED ODDS 1:23
OS1 Paul Kariya .75 2.00
OS2 Tony Amonte .75 2.00
OS3 Joe Sakic 1.50 4.00
OS4 Pavel Bure 1.00 2.50
OS5 Luc Robitaille .75 2.00
OS6 Mark Messier 1.00 2.50

2000-01 UD Reserve Power Portfolios

COMPLETE SET (6) 10.00 20.00
STATED ODDS 1:23
PP1 Patrick Roy 4.00 10.00
PP2 Brett Hull 1.00 2.50
PP3 Steve Yzerman 4.00 10.00
PP4 Martin Brodeur 2.00 5.00
PP5 Mark Messier 1.00 2.50
PP6 Jaromir Jagr 1.25 3.00

2000-01 UD Reserve Practice Session Jerseys

Randomly inserted in packs at a rate of 1:239, this 10-card set featured a swatch of a practice session jersey. The set used player initials for the card numbering. Autographed variations were also created and inserted at 1:479.

*AUTOS: 1.25X TO 3X BASIC INSERTS
CO Chris Osgood 4.00 10.00
JJ Jaromir Jagr 6.00 15.00
JL John LeClair 4.00 10.00
JT Joe Thornton 6.00 15.00
MA Mark Messier 10.00 25.00
MM Mike Modano 6.00 15.00
MR Mark Recchi 4.00 10.00
PF Peter Forsberg 6.00 15.00
TF Theo Fleury 4.00 10.00
TS Teemu Selanne 5.00 12.00

2000-01 UD Reserve The Big Ticket

COMPLETE SET (10) 15.00 30.00
STATED ODDS 1:14
BT1 Paul Kariya .75 2.00
BT2 Dominik Hasek 1.50 4.00
BT3 Ray Bourque 1.50 4.00
BT4 Steve Yzerman 4.00 10.00
BT5 Pavel Bure 1.00 2.50
BT6 Marian Gaborik 3.00 8.00
BT7 Martin Brodeur 2.00 5.00
BT8 John LeClair 1.00 2.50
BT9 Jaromir Jagr 1.25 3.00
BT10 Vincent Lecavalier .75 2.00

2005-06 UD Rookie Class

COMPLETE SET (50) 12.50 30.00
1 Sidney Crosby 2.50 6.00
2 Alexander Ovechkin 1.25 3.00
3 Henrik Lundqvist .75 2.00
4 Marek Svatos .07 .20
5 Thomas Vanek .40 1.00
6 Brad Boyes .07 .20
7 Petr Prucha .25 .60
8 Jussi Jokinen .25 .60
9 Dion Phaneuf .75 2.00
10 Alexander Steen .25 .60
11 Alvaro Montoya .40 1.00
12 Keith Ballard .15 .40
13 Jeff Carter .40 1.00
14 Michel Ouellet .12 .30
15 Andrej Meszaros .15 .40
16 Pavel Vorobiev .07 .20
17 Mike Richards .30 .75
18 Milan Michalek .07 .20
19 Antti Miettinen .07 .20
20 Rene Bourque .15 .40
21 Chris Campoli .15 .40
22 Gilbert Brule .30 .75
23 Andrew Ladd .15 .40
24 R.J. Umberger .12 .30
25 Hannu Toivonen .25 .60
26 Ryan Miller .12 .30
27 Kyle Wellwood .07 .20
28 Fedor Tjutin .07 .20
29 Brent Seabrook
30 Jim Howard .40 1.00
31 Ryan Whitney .07 .20
32 Corey Perry .30 .75
33 Alexander Perezhogin .25 .60
34 Zach Parise .50 1.25
35 Peter Budaj .20 .50
36 Mikko Koivu .15 .40
37 Rostislav Olesz .20 .50
38 Ryan Getzlaf .60 1.50
39 Yann Danis .20 .50
40 Wojtek Wolski .25 .60
41 Ryan Suter .20 .50
42 Patrick Eaves .20 .50
43 Anthony Stewart .20 .50
44 Brandon Bochenski .15 .40
45 Eric Nystrom .20 .50
46 Antero Niittymaki .12 .30
47 Johan Franzen .50 1.25
48 Andrei Kostitsyn .12 .30
49 Carlo Colaiacovo .07 .20
50 Cam Ward .30 .75

2005-06 UD Rookie Class Commemorative Boxtoppers

CC1 Sidney Crosby 6.00 15.00
CC2 Alexander Ovechkin 5.00 12.00
CC3 Henrik Lundqvist 4.00 10.00
CC4 Thomas Vanek 2.00 5.00
CC5 Dion Phaneuf 4.00 10.00
CC6 Alexander Steen 1.00 2.50
CC7 Jeff Carter 2.00 5.00

2004 Upper Deck Sportsfest

These cards were issued in groups of five over the course of three days at the 2004 Sportsfest card show in Chicago. Collectors would receive a group of 5 each day in exchange for 10 Upper Deck card wrappers that carried and SRP valued of $2.99 or higher. A 16th card was issued as an exchange card good for the first pick in the 2004 NBA draft.

STATED PRINT RUN 500 SER.#'d SETS
SF4 Joe Thornton 1.00 2.50
SF5 Wayne Gretzky 4.00 10.00
SF15 Gordie Howe 2.00 5.00

2001-02 UD Stanley Cup Champs

This 86-card set was available in 3-card packs that were inserted one pack per box of various Upper Deck products. The cards featured action photos of past Stanley Cup winners.

1 Phil Esposito 2.00 5.00
2 Bobby Orr 8.00 20.00
3 Glenn Hall 1.00 2.50
4 Bobby Hull 1.50 4.00
5 Ray Bourque 1.50 4.00
6 Gordie Howe 4.00 10.00
7 Ted Lindsay .40 1.00
8 Terry Sawchuk 2.00 5.00
9 Grant Fuhr .60 1.50
10 Wayne Gretzky 5.00 12.00
11 Jari Kurri .75 2.00
12 Bill Ranford .40 1.00
13 Jean Beliveau 1.00 2.50
14 Yvan Cournoyer .75 2.00
15 Guy Lafleur 1.50 4.00
16 Jacques Plante 1.25 3.00
17 Maurice Richard 1.50 4.00
18 Henri Richard .40 1.00
19 Mike Bossy 1.25 3.00
20 Bob Nystrom .40 1.00
21 Ken Morrow .40 1.00
22 Bryan Trottier .60 1.50
23 Bobby Clarke 1.25 3.00
24 Bernie Parent .60 1.50
25 Tim Horton .40 1.00
26 Frank Mahovlich .75 2.00
27 Mike Vernon .60 1.50
28 Theo Fleury .40 1.00
29 Al MacInnis .40 1.00
30 Peter Forsberg 2.00 5.00
31 Dan Hinote .40 1.00
32 Milan Hejduk .75 2.00
33 Alex Tanguay .60 1.50
34 David Aebischer .60 1.50
35 Chris Drury .60 1.50
36 Rob Blake .60 1.50
37 Joe Sakic 1.50 4.00
38 Patrick Roy 4.00 10.00
39 Ville Nieminen .40 1.00
40 Steven Reinprecht .40 1.00
41 Adam Foote .40 1.00
42 Adam Deadmarsh .40 1.00
43 Jon Klemm .40 1.00
44 Sandis Ozolinsh .40 1.00
45 Mike Keane .40 1.00
46 Mike Modano 1.25 3.00
47 Brett Hull 1.00 2.50
48 Joe Nieuwendyk .60 1.50
49 Sergei Zubov .40 1.00
50 Ed Belfour .75 2.00
51 Derian Hatcher .40 1.00
52 Jamie Langenbrunner .40 1.00
53 Grant Marshall .40 1.00
54 Jere Lehtinen .60 1.50
55 Darryl Sydor .40 1.00
56 Sergei Fedorov 1.25 3.00
57 Steve Yzerman 4.00 10.00
58 Nicklas Lidstrom .75 2.00
59 Mathieu Dandenault .40 1.00
60 Slava Kozlov .40 1.00
61 Chris Osgood .60 1.50
62 Darren McCarty .40 1.00
63 Kirk Maltby .40 1.00
64 Brendan Shanahan .75 2.00
65 Tomas Holmstrom .40 1.00
66 John LeClair .75 2.00
67 Patrick Roy 4.00 10.00
68 Eric Desjardins .40 1.00
69 Scott Stevens .60 1.50
70 Patrik Elias .60 1.50
71 Randy McKay .40 1.00
72 Jason Arnott .40 1.00
73 Alexander Mogilny .60 1.50
74 Petr Sykora .40 1.00
75 Scott Gomez .40 1.00
76 Sergei Brylin .40 1.00
77 Bobby Holik .40 1.00
78 Martin Brodeur 2.00 5.00
79 John Madden .40 1.00
80 Scott Niedermayer .40 1.00
81 Claude Lemieux .40 1.00
82 Brian Leetch .60 1.50
83 Mike Richter .75 2.00
84 Mark Messier .75 2.00
85 Jaromir Jagr 1.25 3.00
86 Mario Lemieux 5.00 12.00

2001-02 UD Stanley Cup Champs Champion Signatures

Randomly inserted in box-topper packs, these cards were numbered 1 of 1 and contain a cut signature of the given player. As of press time neither card had been verified, and these cards are not priced due to scarcity.

JP Jacques Plante/1
TS Terry Sawchuk/1

2001-02 UD Stanley Cup Champs Jerseys

Randomly inserted in box topper packs, this 20-card set featured a game-worn jersey swatch of the featured player on the card front and a congratulatory message on the card back. Each card was numbered out of 200.

*MULT.COLOR SWATCH: .5X TO 1.5X HI
TBH Brett Hull 12.50 30.00
TBL Brian Leetch 12.50 30.00
TBS Brendan Shanahan 15.00 40.00
TBT Bryan Trottier 12.50 30.00
TEB Ed Belfour 12.50 30.00
TGL Guy Lafleur 15.00 40.00
TJJ Jaromir Jagr 20.00 50.00
TJS Joe Sakic 20.00 50.00
TKM Ken Morrow 12.50 30.00
TMB Mike Bossy 12.50 30.00
TME Mark Messier 12.50 30.00
TML Mario Lemieux 30.00 80.00
TMM Mike Modano 12.50 30.00
TPF Peter Forsberg 25.00 60.00
TPR Patrick Roy 30.00 80.00
TRB Ray Bourque 25.00 60.00
TRO Patrick Roy 30.00 80.00
TSF Sergei Fedorov 20.00 50.00
TSY Steve Yzerman 30.00 80.00
TTF Theo Fleury 12.50 30.00

2001-02 UD Stanley Cup Champs Pieces of Glory

Randomly inserted in box topper packs, this 30-card set featured pieces of a game-used jersey and stick from the featured player. Each card was serial numbered out of just 50.

GBG Bill Guerin 15.00 40.00
GBH Brett Hull 30.00 80.00
GBL Brian Leetch 15.00 40.00
GBO Mike Bossy 20.00 50.00
GBR Bill Ranford 15.00 40.00
GBS Brendan Shanahan 15.00 40.00
GBT Bryan Trottier 40.00 100.00
GCL Claude Lemieux 15.00 40.00
GCO Chris Osgood 15.00 40.00
GEB Ed Belfour 15.00 40.00
GGL Guy Lafleur 50.00 125.00
GJJ Jaromir Jagr 20.00 50.00
GJN Joe Nieuwendyk 15.00 40.00
GJS Joe Sakic 40.00 100.00
GLM Lanny McDonald 15.00 40.00
GMA Mark Messier 15.00 40.00
GMB Martin Brodeur 50.00 125.00
GML Mario Lemieux 60.00 150.00
GMM Mike Modano 20.00 50.00
GMR Mike Richter 15.00 40.00
GNL Nicklas Lidstrom 15.00 40.00
GPF Peter Forsberg 40.00 100.00
GPR Patrick Roy 60.00 150.00
GRB Ray Bourque 25.00 60.00
GRO Patrick Roy 60.00 150.00
GSF Sergei Fedorov 20.00 50.00
GSY Steve Yzerman 60.00 150.00
GTF Theo Fleury 15.00 40.00
GWG Wayne Gretzky 150.00 300.00

2001-02 UD Stanley Cup Champs Sticks

Randomly inserted into box topper packs, this 29-card set featured pieces of a game-used stick of the featured player on the card front and a congratulatory message on the card back. Each card was numbered out of 150.

SAM Al MacInnis 12.50 30.00
SAT Alex Tanguay 12.50 30.00
SBG Bill Guerin 12.50 30.00
SBH Brett Hull 15.00 40.00
SBK Rob Blake 12.50 30.00
SBL Brian Leetch 12.50 30.00
SBO Mike Bossy 20.00 50.00
SBS Brendan Shanahan 12.50 30.00
SBT Bryan Trottier 15.00 40.00
SCL Claude Lemieux 12.50 30.00
SEB Ed Belfour 12.50 30.00
SGH Gordie Howe 50.00 125.00
SGL Guy Lafleur 20.00 50.00
SJJ Jaromir Jagr 15.00 40.00
SJN Joe Nieuwendyk 12.50 30.00
SJS Joe Sakic 15.00 40.00
SMB Martin Brodeur 20.00 50.00
SML Mario Lemieux 40.00 100.00
SMM Mike Modano 15.00 40.00
SMO Alexander Mogilny 12.50 30.00
SMR Mike Richter 12.50 30.00
SPF Peter Forsberg 15.00 40.00
SPR Patrick Roy 25.00 60.00
SRB Ray Bourque 15.00 40.00
SRO Patrick Roy 25.00 60.00
SSF Sergei Fedorov 15.00 40.00
SSY Steve Yzerman 25.00 60.00
STF Theo Fleury 12.50 30.00
SWG Wayne Gretzky 60.00 150.00

2002-03 UD SuperStars

This 300 card set was released in March, 2003. This set was issued in five card packs with an $3 SRP. The packs were issued in 24 pack boxes which came 12 boxes to a case. The final 50 cards of the set featured two rookies from different sports.

COMPLETE SET (300) 30.00 80.00
6 Paul Kariya .40 1.00
11 Sean Burke .20 .50
22 Ilya Kovalchuk .40 1.00
36 Bobby Orr 1.00 2.50
37 Ray Bourque .40 1.00
41 Jarome Iginla .30 .75
53 Theoren Fleury .25 .60
67 Patrick Roy .75 2.00
68 Joe Sakic .40 1.00
69 Peter Forsberg .50 1.25
75 Mike Modano .40 1.00
81 Gordie Howe .75 2.00
82 Steve Yzerman .75 2.00
83 Curtis Joseph .25 .60
84 Wayne Gretzky 1.25 3.00
123 Zigmund Palffy .20 .50
138 Jose Theodore .30 .75
144 Martin Brodeur .40 1.00
165 Pavel Bure .30 .75
166 Michael Peca .15 .40
190 Jeremy Roenick .40 1.00
197 Mario Lemieux 1.00 2.50
216 Teemu Selanne .40 1.00
235 Keith Tkachuk .20 .50
244 Mats Sundin .15 .40
249 Jaromir Jagr .40 1.00
253 T.J. Duckett / Ilya Kovalchuk .40 1.00
254 Stanislav Chistov / Melvin Ely .40 1.00
255 Dany Heatley / John Ennis .40 1.00
257 Julius Peppers / Eric Cole .75 2.00
261 Andre Davis / Rick Nash 1.50 4.00
268 Henrik Zetterberg / Kalimba Edwards 1.50 4.00
269 Jay Bouwmeester / Caron Butler 1.00 2.50
276 Drew Gooden / Scottie Upshall .75 2.00
283 Pierre-Marc Bouchard / Igor Rakocevic .20 .50

2002-03 UD SuperStars Gold

Randomly inserted in packs, this is a parallel to the UD SuperStars set. These cards were issued to a stated print run of 250 serial numbered sets.

*GOLD 1-250: 2.5X TO 6X BASIC
*GOLD MATSUI: 6X TO 12X BASIC
*GOLD 251-300: 2X TO 5X BASIC

2002-03 UD SuperStars Benchmarks

Inserted at a stated rate of one in 20, these 10 cards feature two athletes from different sports with something in common. It could be being a legendary figure in the sport or playing in the same city.

B1 Joe DiMaggio / Wayne Gretzky 3.00 8.00

2002-03 UD SuperStars City All-Stars Dual Jersey

Inserted at a stated rate of one in 32, these 43 cards featured two jersey swatches from star athletes from the same city. Some cards were issued in smaller quantities and we have notated that information with an SP in our database.

ABZP Adrian Beltre / Zigmund Palffy 4.00 10.00
BGJS Brian Griese / Joe Sakic 6.00 15.00
CDMS Carlos Delgado / Mats Sundin 6.00 15.00
FPPL Felix Potvin / Paul Lo Duca 6.00 15.00
GAPK Garret Anderson / Paul Kariya 6.00 15.00
JLDS John LeClair / Duce Staley 6.00 15.00
KPBA Keith Primeau / Bob Abreu 4.00 10.00
MLBG Mario Lemieux / Brian Giles Pants 15.00 40.00
MMAR Mike Modano / Alex Rodriguez 6.00 15.00
MPEL Mike Piazza / Eric Lindros 6.00 15.00
RCPB Roger Clemens / Pavel Bure 8.00 20.00
SSAW Sergei Samsonov / Antoine Walker 5.00 12.00
THRB Todd Helton / Rob Blake 6.00 15.00
WGJG Wayne Gretzky / Jason Giambi 20.00 50.00

2002-03 UD SuperStars City All-Stars Triple Jersey

Randomly inserted in packs, these cards featured three game-used jersey swatches from all-stars from the same city. These cards were issued to a stated print run of 250 serial numbered sets.

DPE Darin Erstad / Paul Kariya / Elton Brand 10.00 25.00
IMD Ivan Rodriguez / Mike Modano / Dirk Nowitzki 15.00 40.00
JKA Jason Kendall / Kordell Stewart / Alexei Kovalev 15.00 30.00
JLP Jason Giambi / Latrell Sprewell / Pavel Bure 6.00 15.00
JMK J.D. Drew / Marshall Faulk / Keith Tkachuk 10.00 25.00
JSB Joey Harrington / Steve Yzerman / Ben Wallace 25.00 50.00
REA Roger Clemens / Eric Lindros / Allan Houston 15.00 30.00
RSS Randy Johnson / Shawn Marion / Shane Doan 6.00 15.00
SWK Shawn Green / Wayne Gretzky / Kobe Bryant 40.00 80.00

2002-03 UD SuperStars Keys to the City

Inserted at a stated rate of one in six. These 10 cards feature two star athletes from the same city.

COMPLETE SET (10) 10.00 25.00
K6 Patrick Roy / Todd Helton 1.25 3.00
K9 Steve Yzerman / Joey Harrington 1.25 3.00

2002-03 UD SuperStars Legendary Leaders Dual Jersey

Inserted at a stated rate of one in 96, these 20 cards feature game-worn jersey pieces from two star athletes from the same city.

SYJH Steve Yzerman / Joey Harrington 10.00 25.00
ZPSG Zigmund Palffy / Shawn Green 6.00 15.00

2002-03 UD SuperStars Legendary Leaders Triple Jersey

Randomly inserted in packs, these 18 cards feature game-used jersey swatches from three athletes. This set is significant by the usage of game-worn swatches of soccer great David Beckham. Each card was issued to a stated print run of 250 serial numbered sets.

ADJ Allen Iverson / Donovan McNabb / Jeremy Roenick 20.00 50.00
AEM Alex Rodriguez / Emmitt Smith / Mike Modano 20.00 50.00
CJS Cal Ripken / Jaromir Jagr / Stephen Davis 20.00 50.00
JDM Jason Giambi / Drew Bledsoe / Mark Messier 10.00 25.00
JWL Joe DiMaggio / Wayne Gretzky / Larry Bird 100.00 200.00
LBP Larry Walker / Brian Griese / Patrick Roy 15.00 40.00
MCA Mike Piazza / Chad Pennington / Alexei Yashin 10.00 25.00
MPS Mark McGwire / Peyton Manning / Steve Yzerman 30.00 80.00
RJM Roger Clemens / Jerry Rice / Mario Lemieux 30.00 60.00
SEB Sammy Sosa / Eric Daze / Brian Urlacher 10.00 25.00
SWK Shawn Green / Wayne Gretzky / Kobe Bryant 40.00 80.00
TEM Tony Gwynn / Emmitt Smith / Mario Lemieux 30.00 60.00

2002-03 UD SuperStars Magic Moments

Inserted at a stated rate of one in five, this 20 card set featured a mix of active and retired players along with history about key moments in their career.

COMPLETE SET (20) 10.00 25.00
MM17 Bobby Orr 1.50 4.00
MM18 Wayne Gretzky 2.00 5.00
MM19 Patrick Roy 1.25 3.00

2002-03 UD SuperStars Rookie Review

Inserted at a stated rate of one in 20, these 10 cards feature two athletes who made their American professional debut in the same year.

R1 Mark Messier / Ozzie Smith 2.00 5.00

2002-03 UD SuperStars Spokesmen

Issued as a three-card pack topper, these 30 cards feature a mix of players who were also serving as spokesmen for Upper Deck.

*BLACK: 1.25X TO 3X BASIC SPOKESMEN
BLACK/GOLD INSERTS IN SPOKESMEN PACKS
BLACK PRINT RUN 250 SERIAL #'d SETS
*GOLD/25: 3X TO 8X BASIC INSERTS
GOLD PRINT RUN 25 SERIAL #'d SETS
UD12 Bobby Orr 2.00 5.00
UD13 Gordie Howe 1.50 4.00
UD14 Wayne Gretzky 2.50 6.00
UD27 Bobby Orr 2.00 5.00
UD28 Gordie Howe 1.50 4.00
UD29 Wayne Gretzky 2.50 6.00

2001-02 UD Top Shelf

Released in mid-October 2001, this 156-card set carried an SRP of $9.99. The original 97-card base set consisted of 45 veteran cards (1-45), 42 rookie cards (46-66) and 10-exchange rookie cards (67-76). Cards 46-66 were issued in two versions, both versions were serial-numbered to 800 each the only difference between the two versions was that the images on front and back were reversed. Cards 67-76 were redeemable for rookie players who made their debut during the season, and they were serial-numbered to 500 each. Cards 77-135 were available in random packs of UD Rookie Update and cards 122-135 were serial-numbered to 900 each. Cards 136-141 were available by redeeming cards TR1-TR6 of the Rookie Redemption set; they were serial-numbered to just 100 copies each.

COMP.SET w/o SP's (90) 30.00 60.00
1 Paul Kariya .60 1.50
2 Patrik Stefan .20 .50
3 Joe Thornton 1.00 2.50
4 Miroslav Satan .50 1.25
5 Jarome Iginla .75 2.00
6 Jeff O'Neill .20 .50
7 Tony Amonte .50 1.25
8 Joe Sakic 1.25 3.00
9 Peter Forsberg 1.50 4.00
10 Ray Bourque 1.25 3.00
11 Milan Hejduk .60 1.50
12 Patrick Roy 3.00 8.00
13 Rostislav Klesla .20 .50
14 Mike Modano 1.00 2.50
15 Steve Yzerman 3.00 8.00
16 Luc Robitaille .50 1.25
17 Dominik Hasek 1.25 3.00
18 Tommy Salo .50 1.25
19 Pavel Bure .60 1.50
20 Zigmund Palffy .50 1.25
21 Brett Hull .75 2.00
22 Marian Gaborik 1.25 3.00
23 Saku Koivu .60 1.50
24 David Legwand .50 1.25
25 Martin Brodeur 1.50 4.00
26 Patrik Elias .50 1.25
27 Rick DiPietro .50 1.25
28 Eric Lindros .60 1.50
29 Marian Hossa .60 1.50
30 Jeremy Roenick .75 2.00
31 Roman Cechmanek .50 1.25
32 Sean Burke .50 1.25
33 Alexei Kovalev .50 1.25
34 Mario Lemieux 4.00 10.00
35 Johan Hedberg .50 1.25
36 Evgeni Nabokov .50 1.25
37 Teemu Selanne .60 1.50
38 Chris Pronger .50 1.25
39 Keith Tkachuk .60 1.50
40 Vincent Lecavalier .60 1.50
41 Curtis Joseph .60 1.50
42 Mats Sundin .60 1.50
43 Markus Naslund .60 1.50
44 Daniel Sedin .20 .50
45 Jaromir Jagr 1.00 2.50
46 Mikael Samuelsson RC 2.50 6.00
46B Mikael Samuelsson RC 2.50 6.00
47 Dan Snyder RC 4.00 10.00
47B Dan Snyder RC 4.00 10.00
48 Zdenek Kutlak RC 2.50 6.00
48B Zdenek Kutlak RC 2.50 6.00
49 Michel Larocque RC 2.50 6.00
49B Michel Larocque RC 2.50 6.00
50 Casey Hankinson RC 2.50 6.00
50B Casey Hankinson RC 2.50 6.00
51 Bill Bowler RC 2.50 6.00
51B Bill Bowler RC 2.50 6.00
52 Martin Spanhel RC 2.50 6.00
52B Martin Spanhel RC 2.50 6.00
53 Mathieu Darche RC 2.50 6.00
53B Mathieu Darche RC 2.50 6.00
54 Jason Chimera RC 2.50 6.00
54B Jason Chimera RC 2.50 6.00
55 Andrej Podkonicky RC 2.50 6.00
55B Andrej Podkonicky RC 2.50 6.00
56 Pascal Dupuis RC 2.50 6.00
56B Pascal Dupuis RC 2.50 6.00
57 Francis Belanger RC 2.50 6.00
57B Francis Belanger RC 2.50 6.00
58 Mike Jefferson RC 2.50 6.00
58B Mike Jefferson RC 2.50 6.00
59 Stanislav Gron RC 2.50 6.00
59B Stanislav Gron RC 2.50 6.00
60 Joel Kwiatkowski RC 2.50 6.00
60B Joel Kwiatkowski RC 2.50 6.00
61 Kirby Law RC 2.50 6.00
61B Kirby Law RC 2.50 6.00
62 Tomas Divisek RC 2.50 6.00
62B Tomas Divisek RC 2.50 6.00
63 Billy Tibbetts RC 2.50 6.00
63B Billy Tibbetts RC 2.50 6.00
64 Thomas Ziegler RC 2.50 6.00
64B Thomas Ziegler RC 2.50 6.00
65 Mike Brown 2.50 6.00
65B Mike Brown 2.50 6.00
66 Pat Kavanagh RC 2.50 6.00
66B Pat Kavanagh RC 2.50 6.00
67 Ilja Bryzgalov RC 6.00 15.00
68 Ilya Kovalchuk RC 15.00 40.00
69 Vaclav Nedorost RC 4.00 10.00
70 Niko Kapanen RC 4.00 10.00
71 Kristian Huselius RC 4.00 10.00
72 Dan Blackburn RC 4.00 10.00
73 Krystofer Kolanos RC 2.50 6.00
74 Jiri Dopita RC 4.00 10.00
75 Nikita Alexeev RC 4.00 10.00
76 Brian Sutherby RC 4.00 10.00
77 Dany Heatley .75 2.00
78 Sergei Samsonov .50 1.25
79 Bill Guerin .50 1.25
80 Byron Dafoe .50 1.25
81 Martin Biron .50 1.25
82 Roman Turek .50 1.25
83 Arturs Irbe .50 1.25
84 Steve Sullivan .20 .50
85 Mark Bell .20 .50
86 Rob Blake .50 1.25
87 Alex Tanguay .50 1.25
88 Chris Drury .50 1.25
89 Espen Knutsen .20 .50
90 Ed Belfour .60 1.50
91 Brendan Shanahan .60 1.50
92 Nicklas Lidstrom .60 1.50
93 Sergei Fedorov 1.00 2.50
94 Mike Comrie .50 1.25
95 Roberto Luongo .75 2.00
96 Felix Potvin .60 1.50
97 Jason Allison .20 .50
98 Jose Theodore .75 2.00
99 Joe Nieuwendyk .50 1.25
100 Brian Gionta .20 .50
101 Alexei Yashin .20 .50
102 Michael Peca .50 1.25
103 Chris Osgood .50 1.25
104 Mark Parrish .20 .50
105 Juraj Kolnik .20 .50
106 Theo Fleury .20 .50
107 Mike Richter .60 1.50
108 Brian Leetch .60 1.50
109 Pavel Bure .60 1.50
110 Martin Havlat .50 1.25
111 Adam Oates .50 1.25
112 John LeClair .60 1.50
113 Keith Primeau .50 1.25
114 Owen Nolan .50 1.25
115 Pavol Demitra .50 1.25
116 Brent Johnson .50 1.25
117 Doug Weight .50 1.25
118 Nikolai Khabibulin .60 1.50
119 Brad Richards .50 1.25
120 Peter Bondra .60 1.50
121 Olaf Kolzig .50 1.25
122 Pasi Nurminen RC 4.00 10.00
123 Ivan Huml RC 3.00 8.00
124 Erik Cole RC 2.50 6.00
125 Mike Peluso RC 3.00 8.00
126 Riku Hahl RC 3.00 8.00
127 Pavel Datsyuk RC 15.00 30.00
128 Niklas Hagman RC 3.00 8.00
129 Olivier Michaud RC 4.00 10.00
130 Marcel Hossa RC 3.00 8.00
131 Martin Erat RC 3.00 8.00
132 Christian Berglund RC 3.00 8.00
133 Raffi Torres RC 6.00 15.00
134 Branko Radivojevic RC 3.00 8.00
135 Jeff Jillson RC 3.00 8.00
136 Mark Hartigan RC 15.00 40.00
137 Stephen Weiss RC 20.00 50.00
138 Jan Lasak RC 15.00 40.00
139 Trent Hunter RC 20.00 50.00
140 Evgeny Konstantinov RC 15.00 40.00
141 Sebastien Charpentier RC 15.00 40.00

2001-02 UD Top Shelf All-Star Nets

Inserted at 1:287, this 6-card set featured a piece of All-Star game-used netting. Card fronts were team colored and the netting was affixed in an "X" design. Card backs carried a congratulatory message.

NDH Dominik Hasek 25.00 60.00
NEN Evgeni Nabokov 15.00 40.00
NMB Martin Brodeur 25.00 60.00
NPR Patrick Roy 30.00 80.00
NRC Roman Cechmanek 15.00 40.00
NSB Sean Burke 15.00 40.00

2001-02 UD Top Shelf Goalie Gear

This 14-card set featured game-used equipment from some of the top goalies of the NHL, past and present. Cards from this set were inserted at a rate of 1:12. Equipment used on each card is listed below beside the player's name. Card backs carried a congratulatory message.

BJH Johan Hedberg Blocker 5.00 12.00

SCO Chris Osgood Skate 5.00 12.00
GGJH Johan Hedberg Glove 5.00 12.00
LPBB Brian Boucher Pad 5.00 12.00
LPBD Byron Dafoe Pad 5.00 12.00
LPDH Dominik Hasek Pad 10.00 25.00
LPGC Gerry Cheevers Pad 5.00 12.00
LPJH Johan Hedberg Pad 5.00 12.00
LPJT Jose Theodore Pad 6.00 15.00
LPJV John Vanbiesbrouck Pad 5.00 12.00
LPMB Martin Biron Pad 5.00 12.00
LPRC Roman Cechmanek Pad 5.00 12.00
LPRL Roberto Luongo Pad 6.00 15.00
LPSS Steve Shields Pad 5.00 12.00

2001-02 UD Top Shelf Jerseys

This 30-card set featured swatches of game-worn jersey and color player photos on a mostly silver card front. Two subsets made up this set; Stanley Cup Champions jerseys and regular jerseys. Stanley Cup jerseys were inserted at 1:30 and are denoted below with an "SC" beside the player's name. Regular jerseys were inserted at 1:20. Card backs carried a congratulatory message. Cards found in UD Update packs carry a "TJ" prefix.

*MULT.COLOR SWATCH: 1X TO 2X HI
AY Alexei Yashin 4.00 10.00
BH Brett Hull SC 5.00 12.00
BS Brendan Shanahan SC 4.00 10.00
DS Daniel Sedin 4.00 10.00
DW Doug Weight 4.00 10.00
EB Ed Belfour SC 4.00 10.00
HS Henrik Sedin 4.00 10.00
JA Jason Allison 4.00 10.00
JI Jarome Iginla 5.00 12.00
JJ Jaromir Jagr SC 6.00 15.00
JL John LeClair SC 4.00 10.00
JO Jose Theodore 5.00 12.00
JS Joe Sakic SC 8.00 20.00
JT Joe Thornton 5.00 12.00
MH Marian Hossa 4.00 10.00
ML Mario Lemieux SC 20.00 50.00
MM Mike Modano SC 6.00 15.00
MR Mike Richter SC 4.00 10.00
MT Marty Turco 4.00 10.00
PB Peter Bondra 4.00 10.00
PF Peter Forsberg SC 10.00 25.00
PK Paul Kariya 4.00 10.00
PR Patrick Roy SC 12.50 30.00
PS Patrik Stefan 4.00 10.00
RB Ray Bourque SC 10.00 25.00
SF Sergei Fedorov SC 6.00 15.00
SY Steve Yzerman SC 12.50 30.00
TS Teemu Selanne 4.00 10.00
VB Valeri Bure 4.00 10.00
VL Vincent Lecavalier 4.00 10.00
TJBS Brendan Shanahan Upd 4.00 10.00
TJCD Chris Drury Upd 4.00 10.00
TJJI Jarome Iginla Upd 4.00 10.00
TJJW Justin Williams Upd 4.00 10.00
TJMH Milan Hejduk Upd 4.00 10.00
TJMN Markus Naslund Upd 4.00 10.00
TJMS Miroslav Satan Upd 4.00 10.00
TJPD Pavol Demitra Upd 4.00 10.00
TJPK Paul Kariya Upd 8.00 20.00
TJZP Zigmund Palffy Upd 4.00 10.00

2001-02 UD Top Shelf Jersey Autographs

This 18-card set paralleled the basic jersey set, but also incorporates an autograph of the featured player along with the jersey swatch. Each card was serial-numbered out of 100 copies. Card backs carried a congratulatory message.

DS Daniel Sedin 15.00 40.00
DW Doug Weight 15.00 40.00
EB Ed Belfour SC 15.00 40.00
HS Henrik Sedin 15.00 40.00
JA Jason Allison 15.00 40.00
JI Jarome Iginla 20.00 50.00
JL John LeClair SC 15.00 40.00
JO Jose Theodore 20.00 50.00
JT Joe Thornton 20.00 50.00
MH Marian Hossa 15.00 40.00
MM Mike Modano SC 25.00 60.00
MT Marty Turco 15.00 40.00
PS Patrik Stefan 15.00 40.00
RB Ray Bourque SC 40.00 100.00
SY Steve Yzerman SC 50.00 120.00
TS Teemu Selanne 15.00 40.00
VL Vincent Lecavalier 15.00 40.00

2001-02 UD Top Shelf Patches

Inserted at 1:287, this 6-card set partially parallels the base jersey set but each card carried a patch swatch on the card front. Please note that the Brodeur card does not have a parent card in the base jersey set. Card backs carried a congratulatory message.

PJJ Jaromir Jagr 15.00 40.00
PMB Martin Brodeur 30.00 80.00
PMM Mike Modano 15.00 40.00
PPF Peter Forsberg 25.00 60.00
PPR Patrick Roy 30.00 80.00
PSY Steve Yzerman 30.00 80.00

2001-02 UD Top Shelf Rookie Redemption

Available in random packs of UD Rookie Update, this 10-card set of exchange cards were redeemable for a rookie who made his debut late in the 2001/02 season or in the 2002/03 season. Each card was serial-numbered to 100. Shortly after the products release, Upper Deck announced the first six players in the set. Those first six cards can be found at the end of the base set as they were numbered #136-141. The remaining 4 players were not announced until March of 2003 and carry a "TS" prefix.

TS1 Stanislav Chistov 10.00 25.00
TS2 Rick Nash 50.00 100.00
TS3 Henrik Zetterberg 40.00 80.00
TS4 Jason Spezza 40.00 100.00

2001-02 UD Top Shelf Sticks

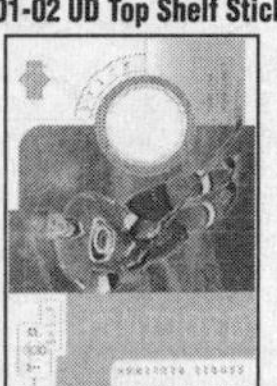

Inserted at overall odds of 1:12, this 29-card set featured dime-sized pieces of game-used sticks from the featured player(s). Card fronts were silver-toned and carried a color picture of the featured player. Card backs carried a congratulatory message.

*SINGLE COLOR SWATCH: .25X TO .75X HI
SBH Brett Hull 8.00 20.00
SBS Brendan Shanahan 6.00 15.00
SCP Chris Pronger 6.00 15.00
SDH Dominik Hasek 8.00 20.00
SJL John LeClair 6.00 15.00
SJR Jeremy Roenick 8.00 20.00
SJS Joe Sakic 10.00 25.00
SKT Keith Tkachuk 6.00 15.00
SMB Martin Brodeur 20.00 50.00
SML Mario Lemieux 20.00 50.00
SMM Mark Messier 6.00 15.00
SNL Nicklas Lidstrom 6.00 15.00
SPB Peter Bondra 6.00 15.00
SPF Peter Forsberg 10.00 25.00
SPK Paul Kariya 6.00 15.00
SPR Patrick Roy 15.00 40.00
SRB Ray Bourque 10.00 25.00
SSF Sergei Fedorov 8.00 20.00
SSO Sandis Ozolinsh 6.00 15.00
SSY Steve Yzerman 12.50 30.00
STF Theo Fleury 6.00 15.00
SWG Wayne Gretzky 40.00 100.00
SZP Zigmund Palffy 6.00 15.00
SPBU Pavel Bure 6.00 15.00
BFJ Bure/Forsberg/Jagr 50.00 125.00
BPR Bourque/Pronger/Roy 60.00 150.00
KSF Kariya/Sakic/Fleury 40.00 100.00
LOH Lidstrom/Ozolinsh/Hasek 30.00 80.00
RSF Roy/Sakic/Forsberg 50.00 125.00

2002-03 UD Top Shelf

Released in August 2002 at an SRP of $4.99, this 165-card set featured 90 regular base cards and 45 rookie redemptions cards. Rookie redemption cards were redeemable for rookies who made their debut in the 2002-03 season. Cards 91-120 were serial-numbered to 1125 and cards 121-135 were serial-numbered to 500.

COMP.SET w/o SP's (90) 60.00 125.00
1 Jean-Sebastien Giguere .50 1.25
2 Jeff Friesen .20 .50
3 Paul Kariya .60 1.50
4 Ilya Kovalchuk .75 2.00
5 Dany Heatley .75 2.00
6 Joe Thornton 1.00 2.50
7 Sergei Samsonov .50 1.25
8 Bill Guerin .50 1.25
9 Martin Biron .50 1.25
10 Miroslav Satan .50 1.25
11 Maxim Afinogenov .20 .50
12 Jarome Iginla .75 2.00
13 Roman Turek .50 1.25
14 Craig Conroy .20 .50
15 Jeff O'Neill .20 .50
16 Arturs Irbe .50 1.25
17 Sami Kapanen .20 .50
18 Jocelyn Thibault .50 1.25
19 Eric Daze .50 1.25
20 Alexei Zhamnov .20 .50
21 Patrick Roy 3.00 8.00
22 Joe Sakic 1.25 3.00
23 Peter Forsberg 1.50 4.00
24 Marc Denis .50 1.25
25 Espen Knutsen .20 .50
26 Mike Modano 1.00 2.50
27 Jason Arnott .20 .50
28 Marty Turco .50 1.25
29 Steve Yzerman 3.00 8.00
30 Sergei Fedorov 1.00 2.50
31 Dominik Hasek 1.25 3.00
32 Brendan Shanahan .60 1.50
33 Ryan Smyth .20 .50
34 Tommy Salo .50 1.25
35 Mike Comrie .50 1.25
36 Roberto Luongo .75 2.00
37 Kristian Huselius .20 .50
38 Sandis Ozolinsh .20 .50
39 Zigmund Palffy .50 1.25
40 Jason Allison .20 .50
41 Felix Potvin .60 1.50
42 Manny Fernandez .50 1.25
43 Marian Gaborik 1.25 3.00
44 Andrew Brunette .20 .50
45 Jose Theodore .75 2.00
46 Saku Koivu .60 1.50
47 Richard Zednik .50 1.25
48 Mike Dunham .50 1.25
49 David Legwand .50 1.25
50 Patrik Elias .50 1.25
51 Joe Nieuwendyk .50 1.25
52 Martin Brodeur 1.50 4.00
53 Scott Niedermayer .20 .50
54 Alexei Yashin .20 .50
55 Michael Peca .20 .50
56 Chris Osgood .50 1.25
57 Mike Richter .60 1.50
58 Pavel Bure .60 1.50
59 Eric Lindros .60 1.50
60 Martin Havlat .50 1.25
61 Patrick Lalime .50 1.25
62 Marian Hossa .60 1.50
63 Jeremy Roenick .75 2.00
64 Roman Cechmanek .50 1.25
65 John LeClair .60 1.50
66 Simon Gagne .60 1.50
67 Ladislav Nagy .20 .50
68 Sean Burke .50 1.25
69 Daniel Briere .20 .50
70 Johan Hedberg .50 1.25
71 Mario Lemieux 4.00 10.00
72 Alexei Kovalev .50 1.25
73 Evgeni Nabokov .50 1.25
74 Owen Nolan .50 1.25
75 Teemu Selanne .60 1.50
76 Brent Johnson .50 1.25
77 Keith Tkachuk .60 1.50
78 Chris Pronger .50 1.25
79 Brad Richards .50 1.25
80 Vincent Lecavalier .60 1.50
81 Nikolai Khabibulin .60 1.50
82 Alexander Mogilny .50 1.25
83 Mats Sundin .60 1.50
84 Curtis Joseph .60 1.50
85 Todd Bertuzzi .60 1.50
86 Brendan Morrison .50 1.25
87 Markus Naslund .60 1.50
88 Jaromir Jagr 1.00 2.50
89 Peter Bondra .60 1.50
90 Olaf Kolzig .50 1.25
91 Tim Thomas RC 6.00 15.00
92 Ivan Majesky RC 2.00 5.00
93 Jay Bouwmeester RC 6.00 15.00
94 Ron Hainsey RC 2.00 5.00
95 Ray Schultz RC 2.00 5.00
96 Tomi Pettinen RC 2.00 5.00
97 Eric Godard RC 2.00 5.00
98 Anton Volchenkov RC 2.00 5.00
99 Dennis Seidenberg RC 2.00 5.00
100 Radovan Somik RC 2.00 5.00
101 Patrick Sharp RC 2.00 5.00
102 Carlo Colaiacovo RC 2.00 5.00
103 Mikael Tellqvist RC 3.00 8.00
104 Steve Eminger RC 2.00 5.00
105 Alex Henry RC 2.00 5.00
106 Kurt Sauer RC 2.00 5.00
107 Micki Dupont RC 2.00 5.00
108 Shawn Thornton RC 2.00 5.00
109 Matt Henderson RC 2.00 5.00
110 Jeff Paul RC 2.00 5.00
111 Lasse Pirjeta RC 2.00 5.00
112 Dmitri Bykov RC 2.00 5.00
113 Kari Haakana RC 2.00 5.00
114 Sylvain Blouin RC 2.00 5.00
115 Stephane Veilleux RC 2.00 5.00
116 Greg Koehler RC 2.00 5.00
117 Lynn Loyns RC 2.00 5.00
118 Tom Koivisto RC 2.00 5.00
119 Curtis Sanford RC 3.00 8.00
120 Cody Rudkowsky RC 2.00 5.00
121 Martin Gerber RC 8.00 20.00
122 Alexei Smirnov RC 4.00 10.00
123 Stanislav Chistov RC 6.00 15.00
124 Jordan Leopold RC 6.00 15.00
125 Chuck Kobasew RC 6.00 15.00
126 Rick Nash RC 30.00 60.00
127 Henrik Zetterberg RC 12.00 30.00
128 Ales Hemsky RC 10.00 25.00
129 Alexander Frolov RC 10.00 25.00
130 P-M Bouchard RC 8.00 20.00
131 Adam Hall RC 6.00 15.00
132 Scottie Upshall RC 6.00 15.00
133 Jason Spezza RC 20.00 50.00
134 Jeff Taffe RC 6.00 15.00
135 Alexander Svitov RC 4.00 10.00

2002-03 UD Top Shelf All-Stars

*MULT.COLOR SWATCH: .75X TO 1.5X HI
PRINT RUN 50 SER.#'d SETS
ASGR Wayne Gretzky 75.00 200.00
ASJJ Jaromir Jagr 15.00 40.00
ASJS Joe Sakic 15.00 40.00
ASKT Keith Tkachuk 10.00 25.00
ASMS Mats Sundin 10.00 25.00
ASPK Paul Kariya 10.00 25.00
ASSF Sergei Fedorov 12.50 30.00
ASSS Scott Stevens 8.00 20.00
ASTA Tony Amonte 8.00 20.00
ASTF Theo Fleury 8.00 20.00
ASTS Teemu Selanne 10.00 25.00
ASWG Wayne Gretzky 75.00 200.00

2002-03 UD Top Shelf Clutch Performers

*MULT.COLOR SWATCH: .75X TO 1.5X HI
PRINT RUN 75 SER.#'d SETS
CPAD Adam Deadmarsh 6.00 15.00
CPAM Al MacInnis 6.00 15.00
CPBG Bill Guerin 6.00 15.00
CPBL Brian Leetch 6.00 15.00
CPBO Peter Bondra 8.00 20.00
CPBS Brendan Shanahan 8.00 20.00
CPCD Chris Drury 6.00 15.00
CPCJ Curtis Joseph 8.00 20.00
CPCL Claude Lemieux 6.00 15.00
CPDW Doug Weight 6.00 15.00
CPEB Ed Belfour 8.00 20.00
CPEL Eric Lindros 8.00 20.00
CPIK Ilya Kovalchuk 15.00 40.00
CPJI Jarome Iginla 10.00 25.00
CPJJ Jaromir Jagr 12.50 30.00
CPJN Joe Nieuwendyk 6.00 15.00
CPJR Jeremy Roenick 10.00 25.00
CPJS Joe Sakic 20.00 50.00
CPJT Joe Thornton 12.50 30.00
CPKT Keith Tkachuk 8.00 20.00
CPLR Luc Robitaille 6.00 15.00
CPMB Martin Brodeur 20.00 50.00
CPMH Milan Hejduk 8.00 20.00
CPML Mario Lemieux 25.00 60.00
CPMM Mike Modano 12.50 30.00
CPMR Mike Richter 8.00 20.00
CPMS Mats Sundin 8.00 20.00
CPNL Nicklas Lidstrom 8.00 20.00
CPPB Pavel Bure 8.00 20.00
CPPK Paul Kariya 8.00 20.00
CPPR Patrick Roy 25.00 60.00
CPRB Ray Bourque 20.00 50.00
CPSB Sean Burke 6.00 15.00
CPSF Sergei Fedorov 12.50 30.00
CPSGA Simon Gagne 8.00 20.00
CPSGO Sergei Gonchar 6.00 15.00
CPSSA Sergei Samsonov 6.00 15.00
CPSSU Steve Sullivan 6.00 15.00
CPSY Steve Yzerman 25.00 60.00
CPTS Teemu Selanne 8.00 20.00
CPWG Wayne Gretzky 50.00 125.00
CPZP Zigmund Palffy 6.00 15.00

2002-03 UD Top Shelf Dual Player Jerseys

Singles in this 42-card memorabilia set were serial-numbered out of 99.

RBD Marc Denis 12.50 30.00
Ed Belfour
RBK Pavel Bure 30.00 80.00
Ilya Kovalchuk
RBP Rob Blake 12.50 30.00
Chris Pronger
RBS Sergei Samsonov 12.50 30.00
Pavel Bure
RBZ Peter Bondra 12.50 30.00
Zigmund Palffy
RFA Sergei Fedorov 12.50 30.00
Maxim Afinogenov
RIW Jarome Iginla 20.00 50.00
Justin Williams
RKG Simon Gagne 12.50 30.00
Paul Kariya
RLK Rostislav Klesla 20.00 50.00
Nickalas Lidstrom
RMC Tim Connolly 12.50 30.00
Mike Modano
RNL David Legwand 12.50 30.00
Joe Nieuwendyk
RPB Felix Potvin 12.50 30.00
Martin Biron
RPT Joe Thornton 12.50 30.00
Keith Primeau
RRT Patrick Roy 40.00 100.00
Jose Theodore
RSF Ruslan Fedotenko 12.50 30.00
Miroslav Satan
RSH Scott Hartnell 12.50 30.00
Brendan Shanahan
RSR Steven Reinprecht 12.50 30.00
Steve Sullivan
RYK K.Kolanos/S.Yzerman 30.00 80.00
STAB Eric Belanger 12.50 30.00
Jason Allison
STBB Ray Bourque 30.00 80.00
Rob Blake
STBD Daniel Briere 12.50 30.00
Shane Doan
STBE Brian Leetch 12.50 30.00
Pavel Bure
STBJ Jaromir Jagr 15.00 40.00
Peter Bondra
STBL Roberto Luongo 12.50 30.00
Valeri Bure
STBN Martin Biron 12.50 30.00
Mika Noronen
STBS M.Brodeur/S.Stevens 20.00 50.00
STBT Joe Thornton 30.00 80.00
Ray Bourque
STDE Martin Erat 12.50 30.00
Mike Dunham
STDT Eric Daze 12.50 30.00
Jocelyn Thibault
STFL Nicklas Lidstrom 12.50 30.00
Sergei Fedorov
STFP Keith Primeau 12.50 30.00
Ruslan Fedotenko
STFR Mike Richter 25.00 60.00
Theo Fleury
STGB Brian Boucher 12.50 30.00
Simon Gagne
STGD Bill Guerin 12.50 30.00
Byron Dafoe
STGK Olaf Kolzig 12.50 30.00
Sergei Gonchar
STGM Mark Messier 75.00 200.00
Wayne Gretzky
STGR Mark Recchi 12.50 30.00
Simon Gagne
STGS Jean-Sebastien Giguere 12.50 30.00
Steve Shields
STHL David Legwand 12.50 30.00
Scott Hartnell
STHR Milan Hejduk 12.50 30.00
Steven Reinprecht
STIS Jarome Iginla 12.50 30.00
Marc Savard
STJK Jaromir Jagr 12.50 30.00
Olaf Kolzig
STKB Krys Kolanos 12.50 30.00
Sean Burke
STKF Jeff Friesen 15.00 40.00
Paul Kariya
STKT Jose Theodore 15.00 40.00
Saku Koivu
STKW Ray Whitney 12.50 30.00
Rostislav Klesla
STLD Claude Lemieux 12.50 30.00
Shane Doan
STMA Jason Arnott 12.50 30.00
Mike Modano
STMM Brenden Morrow 15.00 40.00
Mike Modano
STNL Markus Naslund 12.50 30.00
Trevor Linden
STPD Adam Deadmarsh 12.50 30.00
Zigmund Palffy
STSA Maxim Afinogenov 12.50 30.00
Miroslav Satan
STSH Dan Hinote 15.00 40.00
Joe Sakic
STSM Steve Sullivan 12.50 30.00
Tony Amonte
STSN Owen Nolan 15.00 40.00
Teemu Selanne
STST Joe Thornton 15.00 40.00
Sergei Samsonov
STTD Marc Denis 20.00 50.00
Ron Tugnutt
STTG Bill Guerin 12.50 30.00
Joe Thornton
STYH Jochen Hecht 12.50 30.00
Mike York
STYS Brendan Shanahan 20.00 50.00
Steve Yzerman

2002-03 UD Top Shelf Goal Oriented

*MULT.COLOR SWATCH: .75X TO 1.5X HI
PRINT RUN 75 SER.#'d SETS
GOAD Adam Deadmarsh 10.00 25.00
GOAT Alex Tanguay 10.00 25.00
GOBG Bill Guerin 10.00 25.00
GOBO Peter Bondra 10.00 25.00
GODA Denis Arkhipov 10.00 25.00
GODB Daniel Briere 10.00 25.00
GOED Eric Daze 10.00 25.00
GOGM Glen Murray 10.00 25.00
GOIK Ilya Kovalchuk 15.00 40.00
GOJJ Jaromir Jagr 12.50 30.00
GOJS Joe Sakic 15.00 40.00
GOJT Joe Thornton 12.50 30.00
GOMA Mats Sundin 10.00 25.00
GOMH Milan Hejduk 10.00 25.00
GOMM Mike Modano 12.50 30.00
GOMS Miroslav Satan 10.00 25.00
GOMY Mike York 10.00 25.00
GOPB Pavel Bure 10.00 25.00
GOPK Paul Kariya 10.00 25.00
GORD Radek Dvorak 10.00 25.00
GORL Robert Lang 10.00 25.00
GOSF Sergei Fedorov 15.00 40.00
GOSG Simon Gagne 10.00 25.00
GOSR Steven Reinprecht 10.00 25.00
GOSS Sergei Samsonov 10.00 25.00
GOSU Steve Sullivan 10.00 25.00
GOSY Steve Yzerman 20.00 50.00
GOTA Tony Amonte 10.00 25.00
GOTS Teemu Selanne 10.00 25.00
GOZP Zigmund Palffy 10.00 25.00

2002-03 UD Top Shelf Hardware Heroes

This 10-card memorabilia set featured quad jersey swatches. Each card was limited to 10 copies each. This set is not priced due to scarcity.

HBRBD Ed Belfour
Patrick Roy
Martin Brodeur
Mike Dunham
HFYGC Fedrv./Yze./Glmr./Clrke
HGKSD Wayne Gretzky
Paul Kariya
Joe Sakic
Pavol Demitra
HGSLJ Grtzky/Sak/Lem./Jagr
HHBRK Dominik Hasek
Ed Belfour
Patrick Roy
Olaf Kolzig
HHGLJ Howe/Grtzky/Lem./Jagr
HPMBL Chris Pronger
Al MacInnis
Rob Blake
Nicklas Lidstrom
HSRBF Joe Sakic
Patrick Roy
Rob Blake
Peter Forsberg
HSSBR Sergei Samsonov
Teemu Selanne
Pavel Bure
Luc Robitaille
HYNLR Yze./Nie-dyk/Ltch/Roy

2002-03 UD Top Shelf Milestones Jerseys

This 10-card memorabilia set featured quad jersey swatches. Each card was serial-numbered out of 25.

MBBRR Jeremy Roenick 50.00 125.00
Mark Recchi
Pavel Bure
Peter Bondra
MBMBS Ray Bourque 100.00 250.00
Pavel Bure
Teemu Selanne
Mike Modano
MGBYM Grtz./Brqe/Mess./Yze. 300.00 800.00
MGHLY Grtz./Lem./Hwe/Yze. 500.00 1000.00
MHPBJ Sean Burke 50.00 125.00
Felix Potvin
Tom Barrasso
Dominik Hasek
MLNLA Tony Amonte 50.00 125.00
John LeClair
Eric Lindros
Owen Nolan
MMHYR Mess./Hull/Robit./Yze. 300.00 600.00
MRBRJ Roy/Brodr./Cujo/Richtr 200.00 400.00
MSFRM Theo Fleury 50.00 125.00
Brendan Shanahan
Jeremy Roenick
Mark Messier
MSYVR Shan./Yze./Vbeek/Robit. 150.00 300.00

2002-03 UD Top Shelf Shooting Stars

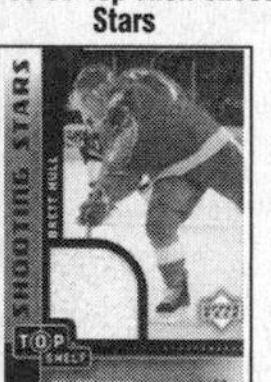

*MULT.COLOR SWATCH: .75X TO 1.5X
SHAR Jason Arnott 8.00 20.00
SHAT Alex Tanguay 8.00 20.00
SHBG Bill Guerin 8.00 20.00
SHBH Brett Hull 12.50 30.00
SHBL Brian Leetch 8.00 20.00
SHBM Brenden Morrow 8.00 20.00
SHBO Peter Bondra 10.00 25.00
SHBS Brendan Shanahan 10.00 25.00
SHDB Daniel Briere 8.00 20.00
SHEK Espen Knutsen 8.00 20.00
SHGM Glen Murray 8.00 20.00
SHJA Jason Allison 8.00 20.00
SHJJ Jaromir Jagr 12.50 30.00
SHJN Joe Nieuwendyk 8.00 20.00
SHKK Krys Kolanos 8.00 20.00
SHLE Rob Blake 8.00 20.00
SHMA Maxim Afinogenov 8.00 20.00
SHMH Milan Hejduk 10.00 25.00
SHML Mario Lemieux 30.00 80.00
SHMM Mike Modano 12.50 30.00
SHMSA Miroslav Satan 8.00 20.00
SHMSU Mats Sundin 10.00 25.00
SHMY Mike York 8.00 20.00
SHNA Nikolai Antropov 6.00 20.00
SHNL Nicklas Lidstrom 10.00 25.00
SHPB Pavel Bure 10.00 25.00
SHPF Peter Forsberg 15.00 40.00
SHPK Paul Kariya 10.00 25.00
SHRB Ray Bourque 15.00 40.00
SHRL Robert Lang 8.00 20.00
SHSD Shane Doan 8.00 20.00
SHSF Sergei Fedorov 12.50 30.00
SHSG Simon Gagne 10.00 25.00
SHSH Scott Hartnell 8.00 20.00
SHSK Saku Koivu 10.00 25.00
SHSR Steven Reinprecht 8.00 20.00
SHSS Steve Sullivan 8.00 20.00
SHSY Steve Yzerman 25.00 60.00
SHTA Tony Amonte 8.00 20.00
SHTF Theo Fleury 8.00 20.00
SHTS Teemu Selanne 10.00 25.00
SHZP Zigmund Palffy 8.00 20.00

2002-03 UD Top Shelf Signatures

Inserted at one per box, this 36-card set featured authentic autographs of the featured players. The Yzerman card was a redemption in pack.

AK Alexei Kovalev 6.00 15.00
BB Brian Boucher SP 8.00 20.00
BG Bill Guerin 6.00 15.00
BL Rob Blake 6.00 15.00
BO Bobby Orr/96 150.00 250.00
DH Dany Heatley 12.50 30.00
DS Daniel Sedin 6.00 15.00
DW Doug Weight/92 12.50 30.00
GH Gordie Howe/27 150.00 400.00
HA Martin Havlat 8.00 20.00
HS Henrik Sedin 6.00 15.00
JA Jason Allison SP 6.00 15.00
JH Johan Hedberg SP 6.00 15.00
JI Jarome Iginla 10.00 25.00
JL John LeClair 8.00 20.00
MB Martin Biron SP 6.00 15.00
MC Mike Comrie 6.00 15.00
MH Milan Hejduk 8.00 20.00
MN Markus Naslund 8.00 20.00
MO Maxime Ouellet 6.00 15.00
PA Pavel Brendl 6.00 15.00
PB Pavel Bure 8.00 20.00
PE Peter Bondra 6.00 15.00
PR Patrick Roy SP 50.00 125.00
RB Ray Bourque SP 25.00 60.00
RD Rick DiPietro 6.00 15.00
RK Rostislav Klesla SP 8.00 20.00
RT Raffi Torres 6.00 15.00
SG Simon Gagne 8.00 20.00
SH Scott Hartnell 6.00 15.00
SS Sergei Samsonov 6.00 15.00
TH Jose Theodore 10.00 25.00
TS Tommy Salo 6.00 15.00
WG Wayne Gretzky/95 150.00 300.00
ZP Zigmund Palffy 6.00 15.00

2002-03 UD Top Shelf Stopper Jerseys

Singles in this 54-card memorabilia set were serial-numbered out of 99.

*MULT.COLOR SWATCH: .75X TO 1.5X
SSBB Brian Boucher 10.00 25.00
SSBD Byron Dafoe 10.00 25.00
SSBI Martin Biron 10.00 25.00
SSBJ Brent Johnson 10.00 25.00
SSCJ Curtis Joseph 10.00 25.00
SSDA David Aebischer 10.00 25.00
SSDB Dan Blackburn 10.00 25.00
SSDH Dominik Hasek 15.00 40.00
SSDU Mike Dunham 10.00 25.00
SSEB Ed Belfour 12.50 30.00
SSFP Felix Potvin 12.50 30.00
SSJGO Jean-Sebastien Giguere 10.00 25.00
SSJTO Jocelyn Thibault 10.00 25.00
SSMB Martin Brodeur 20.00 50.00
SSMD Marc Denis 10.00 25.00
SSMN Mika Noronen 10.00 25.00
SSMR Mike Richter 12.50 30.00
SSOK Olaf Kolzig 10.00 25.00
SSPR Patrick Roy 20.00 50.00
SSRC Roman Cechmanek 10.00 25.00
SSRT Ron Tugnutt 10.00 25.00
SSSB Sean Burke 10.00 25.00
SSSS Steve Shields 10.00 25.00
SSTH Jose Theodore 12.50 30.00

2002-03 UD Top Shelf Sweet Sweaters

*MULT.COLOR SWATCH: .75X TO 1.5X HI
PRINT RUN 50 SER.#'d SETS
SWAD Adam Deadmarsh 10.00 25.00
SWAT Alex Tanguay 10.00 25.00
SWBE Mark Bell 10.00 25.00
SWBG Bill Guerin 10.00 25.00
SWBH Brett Hull 20.00 50.00
SWCD Chris Drury 10.00 25.00
SWCJ Curtis Joseph 10.00 25.00
SWCL Claude Lemieux 10.00 25.00
SWDB Daniel Briere 10.00 25.00
SWDE Marc Denis 10.00 25.00
SWDG Doug Gilmour 10.00 25.00
SWFP Felix Potvin 10.00 25.00
SWJA Jason Allison 10.00 25.00
SWJF Jeff Friesen 10.00 25.00

SWJJ Jaromir Jagr 12.50 30.00
SWJO Joe Thornton 15.00 40.00
SWJS Joe Sakic 25.00 60.00
SWJT Jocelyn Thibault 10.00 25.00
SWKP Keith Primeau 10.00 25.00
SWKT Keith Tkachuk 10.00 25.00
SWMA Maxim Afinogenov 10.00 25.00
SWMB Martin Biron 10.00 25.00
SWMD Mike Dunham 10.00 25.00
SWMM Mike Modano 15.00 40.00
SWMS Mats Sundin 10.00 25.00
SWOK Olaf Kolzig 10.00 25.00
SWPB Pavel Bure 10.00 25.00
SWPK Paul Kariya 10.00 25.00
SWRB Ray Bourque 30.00 80.00
SWRK Rostislav Klesla 10.00 25.00
SWSA Miroslav Satan 10.00 25.00
SWSF Sergei Fedorov 15.00 40.00
SWSK Saku Koivu 10.00 25.00
SWSR Steven Reinprecht 10.00 25.00
SWSS Sergei Samsonov 10.00 25.00
SWSU Steve Sullivan 10.00 25.00
SWSY Steve Yzerman 30.00 80.00
SWTH Jose Theodore 12.50 30.00
SWTS Teemu Selanne 10.00 25.00
SWVN Ville Nieminen 10.00 25.00
SWWG Wayne Gretzky 75.00 200.00
SWZP Zigmund Palffy 10.00 25.00

2002-03 UD Top Shelf Triple Jerseys

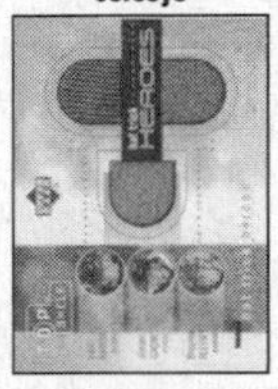

These triple jersey memorabilia cards were randomly inserted into packs. The "Hat Trick" subset cards were serial-numbered out of 25 and the "Three Stars" subset was serial-numbered to just 10 sets and was not priced due to scarcity.

HTAPS Tony Amonte 40.00 100.00
Zigmund Palffy
Teemu Selanne
HTBSB Peter Bondra 40.00 100.00
Pavel Bure
Miroslav Satan
HTGHB Bill Guerin 40.00 100.00
Peter Bondra
Marian Hossa
HTGLB Wayne Gretzky 300.00 600.00
Mario Lemieux
Pavel Bure
HTJHS Milan Hejduk 40.00 100.00
Jaromir Jagr
Teemu Selanne
HTKGF Simon Gagne 40.00 100.00
Paul Kariya
Theo Fleury
HTKYI Iginla/Kariya/Yzerman 150.00 300.00
HTLJT Joe Thornton 125.00 250.00
Jaromir Jagr
Mario Lemieux
HTLRR Jeremy Roenick 100.00 200.00
John LeClair
Mark Recchi
HTNTH Milan Hejduk 40.00 100.00
Joe Thornton
Markus Naslund
HTSHR Brendan Shanahan 100.00 200.00
Brett Hull
Luc Robitaille
HTSIG Joe Sakic 60.00 150.00
Jarome Iginla
Simon Gagne
TSAPP Felix Potvin
Jason Allison
Zigmund Palffy
TSASB Martin Biron
Maxim Afinogenov
Miroslav Satan
TSDPJ Brent Johnson
Chris Pronger
Pavol Demitra
TSGTD Bill Guerin
Byron Dafoe
Joe Thornton
TSJBK Jaromir Jagr
Olaf Kolzig
Peter Bondra
TSLGC John LeClair
Roman Cechmanek
Simon Gagne
TSMMB Brenden Morrow
Ed Belfour
Mike Modano
TSSAT Jocelyn Thibault
Steve Sullivan
Tony Amonte
TSSYH Brendan Shanahan
Dominik Hasek
Steve Yzerman
TSTSR Alex Tanguay
Joe Sakic
Patrick Roy

2003 UD Toronto Fall Expo Priority Signings

This 11-card set was part of a wrapper redemption at the Upper Deck booth during the 2003 Fall Expo. Each card was hand serial-numbered and individual print runs were listed below.

CJ Curtis Joseph/41 20.00 50.00
DH Dany Heatley/25 30.00 80.00
GH Gordie Howe/40 60.00 150.00
IK Ilya Kovalchuk/78 20.00 50.00
JI Jarome Iginla/57 20.00 50.00

JS Jason Spezza/110 15.00 40.00
JT Joe Thornton/107 15.00 40.00
MB Martin Brodeur/70 50.00 125.00
PB Pavel Bure/29 25.00 60.00
PR Patrick Roy/44 75.00 200.00
RB Ray Bourque/75 25.00 60.00

2004 UD Toronto Fall Expo Pride of Canada

This 26-card set was available only at the Upper Deck booth during the 2004 Toronto Fall Expo. Each card was serial-numbered out of 75.

COMPLETE SET (26) 125.00 250.00
1 Martin Brodeur 15.00 40.00
2 Roberto Luongo 6.00 15.00
3 Jose Theodore 8.00 20.00
4 Jay Bouwmeester 4.00 10.00
5 Eric Brewer 4.00 10.00
6 Adam Foote 4.00 10.00
7 Scott Hannan 4.00 10.00
8 Ed Jovanovski 4.00 10.00
9 Scott Niedermayer 4.00 10.00
10 Wade Redden 4.00 10.00
11 Robyn Regehr 4.00 10.00
12 Shane Doan 4.00 10.00
13 Kris Draper 4.00 10.00
14 Simon Gagne 5.00 12.00
15 Dany Heatley 6.00 15.00
16 Jarome Iginla 8.00 20.00
17 Vincent Lecavalier 8.00 20.00
18 Mario Lemieux 15.00 40.00
19 Kirk Maltby 4.00 10.00
20 Patrick Marleau 4.00 10.00
21 Brenden Morrow 4.00 10.00
22 Brad Richards 4.00 10.00
23 Joe Sakic 10.00 25.00
24 Martin St. Louis 4.00 10.00
25 Ryan Smyth 4.00 10.00
26 Joe Thornton 6.00 15.00

2004 UD Toronto Fall Expo Priority Signings

Available only via wrapper redemption during the 2004 Toronto Fall Expo, this 28-card set featured authentic player autographs. Print runs are listed below. Please note, due to a production error, the Tootoo card was pulled from the redemption program though a few copies are known to have been released.

PRINT RUNS UNDER 25
NOT PRICED DUE TO SCARCITY
AH Ales Hemsky/50 10.00 25.00
AY Alexei Yashin/50 10.00 25.00
BU Pavel Bure/10
CK Chuck Kobasew/49 10.00 25.00
GR Wayne Gretzky/25 200.00 300.00
HO Marian Hossa/52 12.50 30.00
JI Jarome Iginla/7
JL John LeClair/50 10.00 25.00
JR Jeremy Roenick/31 40.00 80.00
JS Jason Spezza/39 25.00 60.00
JT Jordin Tootoo ERR
MB Martin Brodeur/14
MG Marian Gaborik/26
MH Martin Havlat/50 12.50 30.00
MN Markus Naslund/50 12.50 30.00
MP Mark Parrish/50 8.00 20.00
MT Marty Turco/35 20.00 50.00
PB Pavel Bure/60 12.50 30.00
PE Mike Peca/27 20.00 50.00
PR Patrick Roy/33 75.00 150.00
RD Rick DiPietro/20
RL Roberto Luongo/50 12.50 30.00
RN Rick Nash/61 30.00 80.00
RO Patrick Roy/10
SF Sergei Fedorov/3
SH Scott Hartnell/78 8.00 20.00
TB Todd Bertuzzi/44 20.00 50.00
WG Wayne Gretzky/9

2005 UD Toronto Fall Expo Priority Signings

PRINT RUNS UNDER 25 NOT
PRICED DUE TO SCARCITY
PSST Matt Stajan/70 10.00 25.00
PSJS Jason Spezza/10
PSRL Roberto Luongo/20
PSRN Rick Nash/20
PSRM Ryan Malone/62 10.00 25.00

PSJG Jean-Sebastien Giguere/5
PSAF Alexander Frolov/40 20.00 50.00
PSTR Tuomo Ruutu/62 10.00 25.00
PSMT Marty Turco/20
PSGR Wayne Gretzky/25 250.00 400.00
PSLU Joffrey Lupul/64 10.00 25.00
PSMB Martin Brodeur/5
PSAR Andrew Raycroft/63 10.00 25.00
PSSY Steve Yzerman/2
PSMM Mike Modano/10
PSAY Alexei Yashin/20
PSDH Dominik Hasek/5
PSGH Gordie Howe/15
PSAH Ales Hemsky/22
PSES Eric Staal/62 25.00 60.00
PSMG Marian Gaborik/10
PSHS Marcel Hossa/16
PSHO Marian Hossa/9
PSMN Markus Naslund/10
PSTH Trent Hunter/61 10.00 25.00
PSJC Jonathan Cheechoo/61 12.00 30.00
PSWG Wayne Gretzky/5
PSPB P-M Bouchard/61 8.00 20.00
PSMH Martin Havlat/24
PSJI Jarome Iginla/10
PSML Matthew Lombardi/61 6.00 15.00
PSJL John LeClair/20
PSRO Patrick Roy/10
PSJT Joe Thornton/5
PSSL Martin St. Louis/10
PSRT Raffi Torres/60 10.00 25.00
PSSM Stan Mikita/1
PSBE Patrice Bergeron/62 12.00 30.00
PSTE Tony Esposito/5
PSMP Mark Parrish/20
PSTB Todd Bertuzzi/10
PSBU Pavel Bure/10
PSRY Michael Ryder/60 20.00 50.00
PSPS Philippe Sauve/63 6.00 15.00
PSPE Michael Peca/20
PSNZ Nikolai Zherdev/61 10.00 25.00
PSBO Brooks Orpik/40 6.00 15.00
PSDA David Aebischer/2
PSPR Patrick Roy/3

2006 UD Toronto Fall Expo Priority Signings

AVAIL. AS REDEMPTION ONLY AT EXPO
PRINT RUNS UNDER 25 NOT PRICED DUE TO SCARCITY
PSAA Aaron Asham/75 4.00 10.00
PSAK Andrei Kostitsyn/10
PSAL Andrew Ladd/10
PSAP Alexandre Picard/10
PSAS Alexander Steen/50 12.00 30.00
PSBB Brad Boyes/50 10.00 25.00
PSBO Jay Bouwmeester/26 12.00 30.00
PSBR Brad Richardson/41 8.00 20.00
PSBS Brent Seabrook/53
PSCH Chris Higgins/82 12.00 30.00
PSDP Dion Phaneuf/15 50.00 80.00
PSFS Fredrik Sjostrom/94 4.00 10.00
PSGB Gilbert Brule/21 20.00 50.00
PSGH Gordie Howe/11
PSHL Henrik Lundqvist/26 30.00 60.00
PSJB Jason Blake/75 6.00 15.00
PSJC Jeff Carter/3
PSJS Jason Spezza/11
PSJT Jeff Tambellini/52 4.00 10.00
PSMB Martin Brodeur/11
PSMG Marian Gaborik/10
PSMP Michael Peca/20
PSMR Mike Richards/4
PSPB Pierre-Marc Bouchard/6
PSRN Robert Nilsson/58 4.00 10.00
PSRU R.J. Umberger/10
PSRW Ryan Whitney/65 8.00 20.00
PSSB Steve Bernier/12
PSSC Sidney Crosby/35 175.00 250.00
PSTV Thomas Vanek/42 20.00 40.00
PSWC Wendel Clark/6
PSWG1 Wayne Gretzky/9
PSWG2 Wayne Gretzky/4
PSZP Zach Parise/12

1998-99 UD3

The 1998-99 UD3 set is comprised of six 30-card subsets each printed with three different technologies and features color action player photos. The Embossed technology subsets include New Era (1-30) inserted 1:1 and Three Star Spotlight (151-180) inserted 1:23. The Light F/X technology subsets include New Era (61-90) inserted 1:1 and Three Star Spotlight (91-120). The Rainbow Foil technology subsets include New Era (121-150) inserted 1:5 and Three Star Spotlight (31-60) inserted 1:1.

COMPLETE SET (180) 300.00 500.00
1 Sergei Samsonov NE .40 1.00
2 Ryan Johnson NE RC .30 .75
3 Josef Marha NE .30 .75
4 Patrick Marleau NE .30 .75
5 Derek Morris NE .30 .75
6 Jamie Storr NE .40 1.00
7 Richard Zednik NE .30 .75
8 Alyn McCauley NE .30 .75
9 Robert Dome NE .30 .75
10 Patrik Elias NE .40 1.00
11 Olli Jokinen NE .40 1.00
12 Warren Luhning NE .30 .75
13 Chris Phillips NE .30 .75
14 Mattias Ohlund NE .40 1.00
15 Joe Thornton NE .75 2.00
16 Matt Cullen NE .30 .75
17 Bates Battaglia NE .30 .75
18 Andrei Zyuzin NE .30 .75
19 Cameron Mann NE .30 .75
20 Zdeno Chara NE .30 .75
21 Marc Savard NE .30 .75
22 Alexei Morozov NE .30 .75
23 Mike Johnson NE .40 1.00
24 Vaclav Varada NE .30 .75
25 Dan Cloutier NE .30 .75
26 Brad Isbister NE .30 .75
27 Marco Sturm NE .30 .75
28 Anders Eriksson NE .30 .75
29 Jan Bulis NE .30 .75
30 Brendan Morrison NE .40 1.00
31 Wayne Gretzky TR 2.50 6.00
32 Jaromir Jagr TR .60 1.50
33 Peter Forsberg TR 1.00 2.50
34 Paul Kariya TR .40 1.00
35 Brett Hull TR .50 1.25
36 Martin Brodeur TR 1.00 2.50
37 Eric Lindros TR .50 1.25
38 Peter Bondra TR .40 1.00
39 Mike Modano TR .60 1.50
40 Theo Fleury TR .40 1.00
41 Curtis Joseph TR .40 1.00
42 Sergei Fedorov TR .60 1.50
43 Saku Koivu TR .40 1.00
44 Zigmund Palffy TR .40 1.00
45 Ed Belfour TR .40 1.00
46 Patrick Roy TR 2.00 5.00
47 Brendan Shanahan TR .40 1.00
48 Mats Sundin TR .40 1.00
49 Alexei Yashin TR .40 1.00
50 Doug Gilmour TR .40 1.00
51 Chris Osgood TR .40 1.00
52 Keith Tkachuk TR .40 1.00
53 Mark Messier TR .50 1.25
54 John Vanbiesbrouck TR .40 1.00
55 Ray Bourque TR .60 1.50
56 John LeClair TR .50 1.25
57 Dominik Hasek TR .75 2.00
58 Teemu Selanne TR .40 1.00
59 Joe Sakic TR .75 2.00
60 Steve Yzerman TR 2.00 5.00
61 Sergei Samsonov NF .40 1.00
62 Ryan Johnson NF .30 .75
63 Josef Marha NF .30 .75
64 Patrick Marleau NF .30 .75
65 Derek Morris NF .30 .75
66 Jamie Storr NF .40 1.00
67 Richard Zednik NF .30 .75
68 Alyn McCauley NF .30 .75
69 Robert Dome NF .30 .75
70 Patrik Elias NF .40 1.00
71 Olli Jokinen NF .40 1.00
72 Warren Luhning NF .30 .75
73 Chris Phillips NF .30 .75
74 Mattias Ohlund NF .40 1.00
75 Joe Thornton NF .75 2.00
76 Matt Cullen NF .30 .75
77 Bates Battaglia NF .30 .75
78 Andrei Zyuzin NF .30 .75
79 Cameron Mann NF .40 1.00
80 Zdeno Chara NF .30 .75
81 Marc Savard NF .30 .75
82 Alexei Morozov NF .40 1.00
83 Mike Johnson NF .40 1.00
84 Vaclav Varada NF .30 .75
85 Dan Cloutier NF .30 .75
86 Brad Isbister NF .30 .75
87 Marco Sturm NF .40 1.00
88 Anders Eriksson NF .30 .75
89 Jan Bulis NF .30 .75
90 Brendan Morrison NF .40 1.00
91 Wayne Gretzky TF 4.00 10.00
92 Jaromir Jagr TF 1.00 2.50
93 Peter Forsberg TF 1.50 4.00
94 Paul Kariya TF .75 2.00
95 Brett Hull TF .75 2.00
96 Martin Brodeur TF 1.50 4.00
97 Eric Lindros TF .75 2.00
98 Peter Bondra TF .75 2.00
99 Mike Modano TF 1.00 2.50
100 Theo Fleury TF .60 1.50
101 Curtis Joseph TF .75 2.00
102 Sergei Fedorov TF 1.00 2.50
103 Saku Koivu TF .75 2.00
104 Zigmund Palffy TF .75 2.00
105 Ed Belfour TF .75 2.00
106 Patrick Roy TF 3.00 8.00
107 Brendan Shanahan TF .75 2.00
108 Mats Sundin TF .75 2.00
109 Alexei Yashin TF .60 1.50
110 Doug Gilmour TF .75 2.00
111 Chris Osgood TF .75 2.00
112 Keith Tkachuk TF .75 2.00
113 Mark Messier TF .75 2.00
114 John Vanbiesbrouck TF .60 1.50
115 Ray Bourque TF 1.00 2.50
116 John LeClair TF .50 1.25
117 Dominik Hasek TF 1.25 3.00
118 Teemu Selanne TF .75 2.00
119 Joe Sakic TF 1.25 3.00
120 Steve Yzerman TF 3.00 8.00
121 Sergei Samsonov NR 1.25 3.00
122 Ryan Johnson NR 1.00 2.50
123 Josef Marha NR 1.00 2.50
124 Patrick Marleau NR 1.00 2.50
125 Derek Morris NR 1.00 2.50
126 Jamie Storr NR 1.25 3.00
127 Richard Zednik NR 1.00 2.50
128 Alyn McCauley NR 1.00 2.50
129 Robert Dome NR 1.00 2.50
130 Patrik Elias NR 1.25 3.00
131 Olli Jokinen NR 1.25 3.00
132 Warren Luhning NR 1.00 2.50
133 Chris Phillips NR 1.00 2.50
134 Mattias Ohlund NR 1.25 3.00
135 Joe Thornton NR 2.50 6.00
136 Matt Cullen NR 1.00 2.50
137 Bates Battglia NR 1.00 2.50
138 Andrei Zyuzin NR 1.00 2.50
139 Cameron Mann NR 1.00 2.50
140 Zdeno Chara NR 1.00 2.50
141 Marc Savard NR 1.00 2.50
142 Alexei Morozov NR 1.25 3.00
143 Mike Johnson NR 1.25 3.00
144 Vaclav Varada NR 1.00 2.50
145 Dan Cloutier NR 1.00 2.50
146 Brad Isbister NR 1.00 2.50
147 Marco Sturm NR 1.25 3.00
148 Anders Eriksson NR 1.00 2.50
149 Jan Bulis NR 1.00 2.50
150 Brendan Morrison NR 1.50 4.00
151 Wayne Gretzky TE 25.00 60.00
152 Jaromir Jagr TE 6.00 15.00
153 Peter Forsberg TE 6.00 15.00
154 Paul Kariya TE 4.00 10.00
155 Brett Hull TE 5.00 12.00
156 Martin Brodeur TE 10.00 25.00
157 Eric Lindros TE 4.00 10.00
158 Peter Bondra TE 4.00 10.00
159 Mike Modano TE 6.00 15.00
160 Theo Fleury TE 3.00 8.00
161 Curtis Joseph TE 4.00 10.00
162 Sergei Fedorov TE 6.00 15.00
163 Saku Koivu TE 4.00 10.00
164 Zigmund Palffy TE 3.00 8.00
165 Ed Belfour TE 4.00 10.00
166 Patrick Roy TE 20.00 50.00
167 Brendan Shanahan TE 4.00 10.00
168 Mats Sundin TE 4.00 10.00
169 Alexei Yashin TE 3.00 8.00
170 Doug Gilmour TE 4.00 10.00
171 Chris Osgood TE 4.00 10.00
172 Keith Tkachuk TE 4.00 10.00
173 Mark Messier TE 4.00 10.00
174 John Vanbiesbrouck TE 4.00 10.00
175 Ray Bourque TE 6.00 15.00
176 John LeClair TE 4.00 10.00
177 Dominik Hasek TE 8.00 20.00
178 Teemu Selanne TE 4.00 10.00
179 Joe Sakic TE 8.00 20.00
180 Steve Yzerman TE 20.00 50.00

1998-99 UD3 Die-Cuts

This 180-card set is a limited edition die-cut parallel version of the base set. The New Era and Three Star Spotlight SE Light F/X card versions (61-120) are sequentially numbered to 1000. The New Era Embossed cards (1-30) are sequentially numbered to 200 with the Three Star Spotlight Embossed (151-180) sequentially numbered to 100. The New Era Rainbow cards (121-150) are sequentially numbered to 50. The Three Star Spotlight Rainbow ones (31-60) are numbered 1 of 1. Cards 31-60 are not priced due to scarcity.

*1-30 EMB.DIE-CUT/200: 6X TO 15X BASIC CARDS
31-60 UNPRICED RAINBOW PRINT RUN 1
*61-90 DIE-CUT/1000: 2X TO 5X
*91-120 DIE-CUT/1000: 2X TO 5X
*121-150 DIE-CUT/50: 10X TO 25X
*151-180 DIE-CUT/100: 2.5X TO 6X

2004-05 Ultimate Collection

Released in early-summer 2005, this 84-card set is was packaged in 4-card packs that contained 1 serial-numbered base card, 1 autograph card, 1 memorabilia card and 1 serial-numbered subset card or extra base card. Cards 1-48 were serial-numbered to 350 and the World Cup subset cards (#59-84) were serial-numbered to 299.

1 Jean-Sebastien Giguere 1.50 4.00
2 Dany Heatley 2.50 6.00
3 Ilya Kovalchuk 2.50 6.00
4 Joe Thornton 2.50 6.00
5 Chris Drury 1.50 4.00
6 Jarome Iginla 2.50 6.00
7 Miikka Kiprusoff 1.50 4.00
8 Eric Staal 1.50 4.00
9 Jocelyn Thibault 1.50 4.00
10 Peter Forsberg 2.50 6.00
11 Joe Sakic 3.00 8.00
12 Rick Nash 2.00 5.00
13 Mike Modano 2.00 5.00
14 Pavel Datsyuk 1.50 4.00
15 Gordie Howe 3.00 8.00
16 Steve Yzerman 5.00 12.00
17 Wayne Gretzky 8.00 20.00
18 Ryan Smyth 1.50 4.00
19 Roberto Luongo 2.50 6.00
20 Luc Robitaille 1.50 4.00
21 Marian Gaborik 2.50 6.00
22 Patrick Roy 6.00 15.00
23 Jose Theodore 2.00 5.00
24 Tomas Vokoun 1.50 4.00
25 Martin Brodeur 4.00 10.00
26 Jaromir Jagr 3.00 8.00
27 Mark Messier 2.00 5.00
28 Michael Peca 1.50 4.00
29 Dominik Hasek 3.00 8.00
30 Jason Spezza 2.00 5.00
31 Jeremy Roenick 2.00 5.00
32 Simon Gagne 2.00 5.00
33 Brett Hull 2.00 5.00
34 Mario Lemieux 6.00 15.00
35 Evgeni Nabokov 1.50 4.00
36 Keith Tkachuk 2.00 5.00
37 Vincent Lecavalier 2.00 5.00
38 Martin St. Louis 1.50 4.00
39 Mats Sundin 2.00 5.00
40 Ed Belfour 2.00 5.00
41 Markus Naslund 2.00 5.00
42 Olaf Kolzig 1.50 4.00
43 Brad Fast RC 1.50 4.00
44 Brennan Evans RC 1.50 4.00
45 Layne Ulmer RC 1.50 4.00
46 Mel Angelstad RC 1.50 4.00
47 Garret Stroshein RC 1.50 4.00
48 Marcel Goc RC 2.50 6.00
49 Alexander Ragulin RC 1.50 4.00
50 Herb Brooks 1.50 4.00
51 Cammie Granato RC 1.50 4.00
52 Foster Hewitt 1.50 4.00
53 Mike Keenan 2.00 5.00
54 Bob Cole 1.50 4.00
55 Lord Stanley 2.00 5.00
56 James Norris 2.00 5.00
57 Ken Hitchcock 1.50 4.00
58 Dave Reece 2.00 5.00
59 Mario Lemieux WC 6.00 15.00
60 Joe Thornton WC 3.00 8.00
61 Dany Heatley WC 2.50 6.00
62 Jarome Iginla WC 2.50 6.00
63 Joe Sakic WC 4.00 10.00
64 Vincent Lecavalier WC 2.00 5.00
65 Martin Brodeur WC 5.00 12.00
66 Jaromir Jagr WC 4.00 10.00
67 Milan Hejduk WC 1.50 4.00
68 Miikka Kiprusoff WC 2.00 5.00
69 Tuomo Ruutu WC 1.50 4.00
70 Teemu Selanne WC 2.00 5.00
71 Marco Sturm WC 1.50 4.00
72 Olaf Kolzig WC 1.50 4.00
73 Ilya Kovalchuk WC 2.50 6.00
74 Sergei Samsonov WC 1.50 4.00
75 Marian Hossa WC 1.50 4.00
76 Marian Gaborik WC 2.50 6.00
77 Nicklas Lidstrom WC 1.50 4.00
78 Mats Sundin WC 1.50 4.00
79 Peter Forsberg WC 2.50 6.00
80 Robert Esche WC 1.50 4.00
81 Mike Modano WC 2.00 5.00
82 Bill Guerin WC 1.50 4.00
83 Tony Amonte WC 1.50 4.00
84 Keith Tkachuk WC 1.50 4.00

2004-05 Ultimate Collection Buybacks

This 96-cards set featured cards that were "bought back" by UD, signed by the players, serial-numbered and then re-inserted into this product. Each card carried a UD hologram and a "Buyback" certificate card.

LOWER PRINT RUNS NOT
PRICED DUE TO SCARCITY
1 Alex Tanguay 15.00 40.00
2002-2003 Upper Deck MVP MVP Souvenirs/28
2 Bobby Clarke
2003-2004 Trilogy Crest of Honor/12
3 Brad Richards
2001-02 Premier Base Card/1
4 Chris Drury 12.50 30.00
2002-2003 Upper Deck MVP Skate Around Jersey/32
5 Dominik Hasek
2000-01 Upper Deck Game Jersey Patches/1
6 Dominik Hasek
2001-2002 UD Mask Collection Goalie Pads/3
7 Dominik Hasek
2001-2002 UD Top Shelf Goalie Gear/7
8 Dominik Hasek
2000-2001 MVP Super Game-Used Souvenirs/5
9 Dominik Hasek
2002-03 SPx Winning Materials/1
10 Eric Staal
2003-2004 Honor Roll Dean's List/12
11 Gordie Howe
2003-2004 UD Trilogy Base Card/1
12 Gordie Howe
2003-2004 UD Trilogy Crest of Honor/12
13 Gordie Howe
2001-2002 Legends Sticks/9
14 Guy Lafleur
2003-2004 UD Trilogy Base Card/1
15 Guy Lafleur
2002-2003 UD Trilogy Crest of Honor/15
16 Ilya Kovalchuk
2003-04 UD Premier Base Card/2
17 Ilya Kovalchuk
2002-2003 Upper Deck Difference Makers/6
18 Ilya Kovalchuk
2003-04 Upper Deck Ice Ice Breakers/1
19 Ilya Kovalchuk
2001-2002 SPx Rookie Treasures/1
20 Jari Kurri
2002-2003 UD Trilogy Crest of Honor/14
21 Jarome Iginla
2001-2002 Upper Deck Next Generation Jerseys/11
22 Jarome Iginla
2002-2003 SP Game-Used Piece of History Gold/5
23 Jarome Iginla
2002-03 UD Premier Jerseys Silver/1
24 Jarome Iginla
2003-04 UD Premier Stars/1
25 Jarome Iginla
2001-2002 UD Top Shelf Jerseys/3
26 Jason Spezza 25.00 60.00
2000-2001 Upper Deck Prospects Game Jerseys/51
27 Jay Bouwmeester
2003-04 UD Trilogy Base Card/1
28 Jay Bouwmeester 15.00 40.00
2000-2001 Upper Deck Prospects Game Jerseys/56
29 Jeremy Roenick
2003-04 UD Premier Base Card/1
30 Jeremy Roenick
2001-2002 UD Mask Collection Great Gloves/8
31 Jeremy Roenick
2000-2001 UD SP Game-Used Tools of the Game/3
32 Jeremy Roenick
2000-2001 SPx Winning Materials Update/9
33 Joe Thornton
2003-04 UD Premier Base Card/1
34 Joe Thornton
2001-2002 UD SP Game-Used Authentic Fabrics/2
35 Joe Thornton
2002-2003 SP Game-Used Authentic Fabrics Gold/3
36 Joe Thornton
2002-2003 Upper Deck Difference Makers/8
37 Joe Thornton 25.00 60.00
2000-2001 UD Ice Game Jerseys Update/22
38 Joe Thornton
2002-2003 SP Game-Used Patches/2
39 Joe Thornton
2002-2003 SP Game-Used Piece of History/2
40 Joe Thornton 25.00 60.00
2002-2003 Upper Deck MVP Skate Around Jersey/24
41 Joe Thornton
2002-2003 SP Game-Used Tools of the Game/1
42 Joe Thornton
2000-2001 SPx Winning Materials Update/6
43 Jose Theodore
2001-2002 Mask Collection Stellar Stickhandlers/3
44 Jose Theodore
2001-2002 Upper Deck MVP Authentic Goalies/8
45 Jose Theodore 40.00 100.00
2001-2002 UD Mask Collection Goalie Pads/23
46 Jose Theodore 40.00 100.00
2001-2002 UD Top Shelf Goalie Gear/18
47 Jose Theodore
2002-2003 SP Game Used Piece of History /3
48 Jose Theodore
2001-2002 UD Mask Collection Super Stoppers/6
49 Jose Theodore
2002-2003 SP Game Used Patches/6
50 Marc-Andre Fleury
2003-2004 UD Honor Roll Dean's List/15
51 Markus Naslund
2001-02 UD Premier Base Card/1
52 Markus Naslund
2003-04 UD Premier Base Card/1
53 Markus Naslund
2003-04 UD Trilogy Base Card/1
54 Markus Naslund
2003-04 Uper Deck Big Playmakers/1
55 Markus Naslund
2002-2003 SP Game Used Patches/3
56 Markus Naslund
2002-2003 SP Game Used Piece of History Gold/2
57 Markus Naslund 15.00 40.00
2001-2002 UD Top Shelf Jerseys/17
58 Martin St. Louis
2003-04 UD Trilogy Base Card/1
59 Martin St. Louis
2003-04 Black Diamond Base Card/1
60 Marty Turco
2003-04 Upper Deck Big Playmakers/1
61 Marty Turco 20.00 50.00
2002 2003 Upper Deck MVP MVP Souvenirs/26
62 Marty Turco
2003-04 UD Rookie Update Superstars Jersey/1
63 Mika Noronen
2001-2002 SP Game Used Authentic Fabrics/21
64 Mika Noronen 12.50 30.00
2001-2002 UD Mask Collection Goalie Jerseys/22
65 Milan Hejduk
2001-2002 Upper Deck Stanley Cup Finals Single Jersey/9
66 Milan Hejduk 12.50 30.00
2001-2002 Upper Deck MVP Morning Skate Jerseys/20
67 Milan Hejduk
2002-03 SP Game Used Pieces of History/1
68 Milan Hejduk
2001-2002 UD Playmakers Player's Club Practice Jersey/8
69 Milan Hejduk 15.00 40.00
2001-2002 UD Top Shelf Jerseys/22
70 Nathan Horton
2003-2004 Honor Roll Dean's List/11
71 Patrick Roy
2000-2001 UD Ice Game Jerseys Update/12
71R Patrick Roy EXCH
72 Patrick Roy
2001-2002 Upper Deck Patch Names/1
73 Patrick Roy
2001-2002 Upper Deck Patch Numbers/2
74 Ray Bourque
2001-2002 UD Challenge for the Cup Franchise Players/7
75 Ray Bourque
2000-2001 Upper Deck MVP Super Game-Used Souvenirs/5
76 Ray Bourque
2000-2001 SPx Winning Materials Update/2
77 R.Nash Trilogy/3
78 Roberto Luongo
2003-04 Upper Deck Big Playmakers/1
79 Roberto Luongo
2002-03 SP Game Used Tools of the Game/2
80 Roberto Luongo
2001-2002 UD Top Shelf Goalie Gear/10
81 Roberto Luongo
2002-03 SP Game Used First Rounder Patches/1
82 Roberto Luongo
2000-2001 MVP Super Game-Used Souvenirs/5
83 Roberto Luongo
2001-2002 UD Mask Collection Super Stoppers/1
84 Roberto Luongo
2000-2001 SPx Winning Materials Update/10
85 Saku Koivu
2003-04 UD Premier Base Card/1

86 Saku Koivu
2001-2002 Upper Deck Pride of a Nation/7
87 Zigmund Palffy
2001-2002 SP Game Used Authentic Fabrics/23
87R Zigmund Palffy EXCH 15.00 40.00
88 Zigmund Palffy
2001-2002 Upper Deck MVP Combo MVP Souvenirs/7
89 Zigmund Palffy
2002-2003 Upper Deck Difference Makers/9-
90 Zigmund Palffy
2001-2002 UD Playmakers Player's Club Jersey/7
91 Zigmund Palffy
2001-2002 UD Mask Collection Jerseys/5
92 Zigmund Palffy 15.00 40.00
2001-2002 Upper Deck Phenomenal Finishers/19
93 Zigmund Palffy
2000-2001 Upper Deck MVP Super Game-Used Souvenirs/5
94 Zigmund Palffy 12.50 30.00
2001-2002 Upper Deck MVP MVP Souvenirs/26
95 Zigmund Palffy
2001-2002 UD Top Shelf Sticks/6
96 Zigmund Palffy 12.50 30.00
2001-2002 UD Top Shelf Jerseys/23

2004-05 Ultimate Collection Dual Logos

This 41-card patch set featured the NHL shields from game-used jerseys of two players. Each card was serial-numbered 1/1.

NOT PRICED DUE TO SCARCITY
UL2AF David Aebischer/Peter Forsberg
UL2BB Ray Bourque/Ray Bourque
UL2BE Martin Brodeur/Patrik Elias
UL2BF Rob Blake/Adam Foote
UL2BG Martin Brodeur/Jean Sebastian Giguere
UL2BS Eddie Belfour/Mats Sundin
UL2FG Sergei Fedorov/Jean-Sebastien Giguere
UL2FS Peter Forsberg/Joe Sakic
UL2GL W.Gretzky/M.Lemieux
UL2GM Wayne Gretzky/Mark Messier
UL2HA Dominik Hasek/Daniel Alfredsson
UL2HF Milan Hejduk/Peter Forsberg
UL2HJ Dominik Hasek/Curtis Joseph
UL2IK Jarome Iginla/Miikka Kiprusoff
UL2IL Jarome Iginla/Vincent LeCavalier
UL2IS Jarome Iginla/Ryan Smith
UL2KL Nikolai Khabibulin/Vincent Lecavalier
UL2KS Paul Kariya/Teemu Selanne
UL2KT Saku Koivu/Jose Theodore
UL2LB Roberto Luongo
Martin Brodeur
UL2LL Martin St. Louis/Vincent Lecavalier
UL2LP John LeClair/Keith Primeau
UL2MD Michael Peca/Rick DiPietro
UL2MP Al MacInnis/Chris Pronger
UL2MT M.Modano/M.Turco
UL2NM Markus Naslund/Brendan Morrison
UL2NR Nicklas Lidstrom/Rob Blake
UL2NT Cam Neely/Joe Thornton
UL2RN R.Nash/N.Zherdev
UL2RB P.Roy/M.Brodeur
UL2RG Jeremy Roenick/Simon Gagne
UL2RL P.Roy/M.Lemieux
UL2SH Jason Spezza/Marian Hossa
UL2SL Brendan Shanahan/Nicklas Lidstrom
UL2SR Mats Sundin/Gary Roberts
UL2ST Joe Sakic/Joe Thornton
UL2SY J.Sakic/S.Yzerman
UL2TL J.Thornton/M.Lemieux
UL2TR Jose Theodore/Patrick Roy
UL2VT Tomas Vokoun/Jordin Tootoo
UL2WT Doug Weight/Keith Tkachuk

2004-05 Ultimate Collection Jerseys

PRINT RUN 250 SER.#'d SETS
UGJAT Alex Tanguay 4.00 10.00
UGJBC Bobby Clarke 5.00 12.00
UGJBH Bobby Hull 8.00 20.00
UGJBO Mike Bossy 4.00 10.00
UGJBT Bryan Trottier 4.00 10.00
UGJCJ Curtis Joseph 4.00 10.00
UGJDH Dany Heatley 6.00 15.00
UGJDO Dominik Hasek 8.00 20.00
UGJGH Gordie Howe 15.00 40.00
UGJGL Guy Lafleur 8.00 20.00
UGJHE Milan Hejduk 4.00 10.00
UGJJB Johnny Bucyk 4.00 10.00
UGJJI Jarome Iginla 8.00 20.00
UGJJJ Jaromir Jagr 10.00 25.00
UGJJK Jari Kurri 5.00 12.00
UGJJO Jose Theodore 5.00 12.00
UGJJR Jeremy Roenick 5.00 12.00
UGJJS Joe Sakic 10.00 25.00
UGJJT Joe Thornton 8.00 20.00
UGJMB Martin Brodeur 10.00 25.00
UGJMH Marian Hossa 4.00 10.00
UGJML Mario Lemieux 15.00 40.00
UGJMM Mark Messier 8.00 20.00
UGJMN Markus Naslund 4.00 10.00
UGJMO Mike Modano 5.00 12.00
UGJMS Martin St.Louis 4.00 10.00
UGJNK Nikolai Khabibulin 4.00 10.00
UGJNZ Nikolai Zherdev 4.00 10.00
UGJPF Peter Forsberg 6.00 15.00
UGJPK Paul Kariya 4.00 10.00
UGJRB Ray Bourque 5.00 12.00
UGJRN Rick Nash 5.00 12.00
UGJSK Saku Koivu 4.00 10.00
UGJSP Jason Spezza 5.00 12.00
UGJSU Mats Sundin 4.00 10.00
UGJSY Steve Yzerman 10.00 25.00
UGJVL Vincent Lecavalier 4.00 10.00
UGJPR1 Patrick Roy 15.00 40.00
UGJPR2 Patrick Roy 15.00 40.00
UGJWG1 Wayne Gretzky AS 30.00 80.00
UGJWG2 Wayne Gretzky EDM 30.00 80.00

2004-05 Ultimate Collection Jerseys Gold

*GOLD: .75X TO 2X JSY HI
PRINT RUN 75 SER.#'d SETS

2004-05 Ultimate Collection Jersey Autographs

PRINT RUN 5 SER.#'d SETS
NOT PRICED DUE TO SCARCITY
UGJARB Ray Bourque
UGJAMN Markus Naslund
UGJASP Jason Spezza
UGJAVL Vincent Lecavalier
UGJAJB Johnny Bucyk
UGJAJR Jeremy Roenick
UGJAJO Jose Theodore
UGJAJI Jarome Iginla
UGJASK Saku Koivu
UGJADH Dany Heatley
UGJANZ Nikolai Zherdev
UGJAJT Joe Thornton
UGJAHE Milan Hejduk
UGJAGH Gordie Howe
UGJANK Nikolai Khabibulin
UGJABT Bryan Trottier
UGJABH Bobby Hull
UGJABO Mike Bossy
UGJAJK Jari Kurri
UGJARN Rick Nash
UGJAGL Guy Lafleur
UGJADO Dominik Hasek
UGJAAT Alex Tanguay
UGJABC Bobby Clarke
UGJAMB Martin Brodeur
UGJAMS Martin St.Louis
UGJAPR1 Patrick Roy COL
UGJAWG1 Wayne Gretzky AS
UGJAWG2 Wayne Gretzky EDM
UGJAPR2 Patrick Roy MTL

2004-05 Ultimate Collection Patches

*SINGLE COLOR SWATCH: .25X TO .5X HI
*4+ COLOR SWATCH: .75X TO 2X
UNIQUENESS OF PATCH MAY EARN UP TO 50% PREMIUM
PRINT RUN 35 SER.#'d SETS
UPMS Martin St.Louis 40.00 80.00
UPHA Dominik Hasek 60.00 120.00
UPPF Peter Forsberg 75.00 150.00
UPJT Joe Thornton 75.00 150.00
UPHE Milan Hejduk 40.00 80.00
UPSU Mats Sundin 50.00 100.00
UPSF Sergei Fedorov 30.00 60.00
UPSK Saku Koivu 50.00 100.00
UPMM Mark Messier 100.00 200.00
UPNK Nikolai Khabibulin 40.00 80.00
UPBT Bryan Trottier 50.00 100.00
UPEB Ed Belfour 60.00 120.00
UPCJ Curtis Joseph 60.00 120.00
UPBL Brian Leetch 75.00 150.00
UPPK Paul Kariya/9
UPBH Brett Hull 50.00 100.00
UPJG Jean-Sebastien Giguere 60.00 120.00
UPBS Brendan Shanahan 60.00 120.00
UPSP Jason Spezza 50.00 100.00
UPMH Marian Hossa 50.00 100.00
UPRN Rick Nash 50.00 100.00
UPMB Martin Brodeur 100.00 200.00
UPML Mario Lemieux 200.00 400.00
UPTK Keith Tkachuk 40.00 80.00
UPMO Mike Modano 50.00 100.00
UPJO Jose Theodore 50.00 100.00
UPSY Steve Yzerman 125.00 250.00
UPVL Vincent Lecavalier 50.00 100.00
UPJR Jeremy Roenick 40.00 80.00
UPIK Ilya Kovalchuk 60.00 120.00
UPJS Joe Sakic 75.00 150.00
UPJJ Jaromir Jagr 75.00 150.00
UPNZ Nikolai Zherdev 50.00 100.00
UPPR1 Patrick Roy COL 175.00 350.00
UPWG1 Wayne Gretzky LA/25 300.00 600.00
UPRB1 Ray Bourque BOS 75.00 150.00
UPPR2 Patrick Roy MTL 200.00 400.00
UPWG2 Wayne Gretzky AS/25 250.00 500.00
UPRB2 Ray Bourque COL 75.00 150.00
UPDHA Dany Heatley JSY 40.00 80.00
UPDHB Dany Heatley PATCH 60.00 120.00
UPMNA Markus Naslund JSY 30.00 60.00
UPMNB Markus Naslund PATCH 40.00 80.00

2004-05 Ultimate Collection Patch Autographs

*SINGLE COLOR SWATCH: .25X TO .5X HI
UNIQUENESS OF PATCH MAY EARN UP TO 50% PREMIUM
SNGL PRINT RUN 50 SER.#'d SETS
DUAL PRINT RUN 10 SER.#'d SETS
DUAL NOT PRICED DUE TO SCARCITY
UPAAT Alex Tanguay 40.00 100.00
UPABR Brad Richards EXCH
UPACD Chris Drury 30.00 80.00
UPADH Dany Heatley 60.00 150.00
UPADO Dominik Hasek 75.00 200.00
UPAEJ Ed Jovanovski 40.00 100.00
UPAJB Jay Bouwmeester 30.00 80.00
UPAJI Jarome Iginla 50.00 125.00
UPAJK Jari Kurri 50.00 125.00
UPAJO Jose Theodore 50.00 125.00
UPAJR Jeremy Roenick 40.00 100.00
UPAJT Joe Thornton 60.00 150.00
UPAMB Martin Brodeur 175.00 350.00
UPAMD Marcel Dionne 40.00 100.00
UPAMH Milan Hejduk 30.00 80.00
UPAMN Markus Naslund 30.00 80.00
UPAMS Martin St.Louis 40.00 100.00
UPAMT Marty Turco 40.00 80.00
UPANK Nikolai Khabibulin 50.00 125.00
UPANZ Nikolai Zherdev 30.00 60.00
UPAPR Patrick Roy 200.00 400.00
UPARB Ray Bourque 60.00 150.00
UPARL Roberto Luongo 60.00 150.00
UPARN Rick Nash 125.00 250.00
UPASK Saku Koivu 40.00 100.00
UPASP Jason Spezza 75.00 150.00
UPAVL Vincent Lecavalier 50.00 125.00
UPAWG1 Wayne Gretzky AS 250.00 500.00
UPAWG2 Wayne Gretzky LA 250.00 500.00
UPAARJT Andrew Raycroft/Joe Thornton
UPAATMH Alex Tanguay/Milan Hejduk
UPABRMS Brad Richards/Martin St. Louis
UPACNRB Cam Neely/Ray Bourque
UPAGHCN Gordie Howe/Cam Neely
UPAIKRN I.Kovalchuk/R.Nash
UPAJIVL Jarome Iginla/Vincent LeCavalier
UPAPRJO Patrick Roy/Jose Theodore
UPAPRMB P.Roy/M.Brodeur
UPARBJB Ray Bourque/Jay Boumeester
UPAWGGH Gordie Howe/Wayne Gretzky
UPAWGJK Wayne Gretzky/Jari Kurri

2004-05 Ultimate Collection Signatures

This 42-card set was seeded at one per pack. Known shortprints are listed below.

USGH Gordie Howe 40.00 80.00
USMN Markus Naslund 6.00 15.00
USJI Jarome Iginla 12.50 30.00
USDH Dany Heatley 10.00 25.00
USMS Martin St. Louis 6.00 15.00
USBC Bobby Clarke 10.00 25.00
USJT Joe Thornton 12.50 30.00
USCD Chris Drury 4.00 10.00
USJK Jari Kurri 6.00 15.00
USBB Brad Boyes 4.00 10.00
USVL Vincent Lecavalier SP 30.00 60.00
USMB Martin Brodeur SP 60.00 150.00
USMR Michael Ryder 8.00 20.00
USJO Jose Theodore SP 30.00 60.00
USSK Saku Koivu SP 12.50 30.00
USNZ Nikolai Zherdev 6.00 15.00
USEJ Ed Jovanovski 4.00 10.00
USRL Roberto Luongo SP 15.00 40.00
USIK Ilya Kovalchuk 12.00 30.00
USRN Rick Nash SP 20.00 50.00
USMT Marty Turco 4.00 10.00
USES Eric Staal 10.00 25.00
USAT Alex Tanguay 4.00 10.00
USKL Kari Lehtonen 8.00 20.00
USBL Brian Leetch 6.00 15.00
USHZ Henrik Zetterberg 8.00 20.00
USBH Bobby Hull SP 50.00 125.00
USBR Brad Richards 6.00 15.00
USSP Jason Spezza 12.50 30.00
USMH Milan Hejduk 4.00 10.00
USNK Nikolai Khabibulin 8.00 20.00
USJB Jay Bouwmeester 6.00 15.00
USKD Kris Draper 4.00 10.00
USMA Marc-Andre Fleury 15.00 30.00
USZP Zigmund Palffy 4.00 10.00
USNH Nathan Horton 4.00 10.00
USAR Andrew Raycroft 6.00 15.00
USBT Bryan Trottier SP 12.50 30.00
USHA Dominik Hasek SP 30.00 80.00
USPR1 Patrick Roy SP 250.00 400.00
USWG1 Wayne Gretzky 100.00 200.00
USRB1 Ray Bourque SP 25.00 60.00

2004-05 Ultimate Collection Signature Logos

This 40-card set featured certified autographs and the NHL shield patch from game-used player jerseys. Each card was serial-numbered 1/1.

PRINT RUN 1 SER.#'d SET
NOT PRICED DUE TO SCARCITY
ULAMT Marty Turco
ULANH Nathan Horton
ULAHA Dominik Hasek
ULABL Brian Leetch
ULAAT Alex Tanguay
ULAJK Jari Kurri
ULAVL Vincent Lecavalier
ULAJR Jeremy Roenick
ULASP Jason Spezza
ULARL Roberto Luongo
ULAEJ Ed Jovanovski
ULANK Nikolai Khabibulin
ULAJO Jose Theodore
ULAJI Jarome Iginla
ULANZ Nikolai Zherdev
ULASK Saku Koivu
ULAMN Markus Naslund
ULAMS Martin St. Louis
ULAMR Michael Ryder
ULAAR Andrew Raycroft
ULAES Eric Staal
ULACD Chris Drury
ULARN Rick Nash
ULAMH Milan Hejduk
ULASG Simon Gagne
ULABT Bryan Trottier
ULABR Brad Richards
ULAKD Kris Draper
ULAZP Zigmund Palffy
ULADH Dany Heatley
ULAJT Joe Thornton
ULAMB Martin Brodeur
ULAKP Keith Primeau
ULAWG1 Wayne Gretzky NYR
ULAPR1 Patrick Roy
ULARB1 Ray Bourque
ULAWG2 Wayne Gretzky LA
ULARB2 Ray Bourque
ULAPR2 Patrick Roy
ULAWG3 Wayne Gretzky AS

2004-05 Ultimate Collection Signature Patches

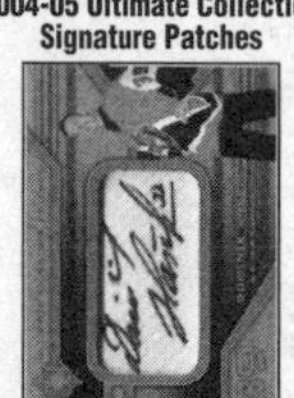

This 41-card set featured certified autographs directly on game-used jersey patches. Cards were serial-numbered out of 10.

NOT PRICED DUE TO SCARCITY
SPBL Brian Leetch
SPNK Nikolai Khabibulin
SPBU Johnny Bucyk
SPJB Jay Bouwmeester
SPAT Alex Tanguay
SPJO Jose Theodore
SPKD Kris Draper
SPHZ Henrik Zetterberg
SPAR Andrew Raycroft
SPHA Dominik Hasek
SPJT Joe Thornton
SPRL Roberto Luongo
SPJI Jarome Iginla
SPPR Patrick Roy
SPDH Dany Heatley
SPMN Markus Naslund
SPJR Jeremy Roenick
SPZP Ziggy Palffy
SPMB Martin Brodeur
SPNH Nathan Horton
SPBR Brad Richards
SPBT Bryan Trottier
SPES Eric Staal
SPMS Martin St. Louis
SPVL Vincent Lecavalier
SPMH Milan Hejduk
SPRN Rick Nash
SPKL Kari Lehtonen
SPRB Ray Bourque
SPCD Chris Drury
SPSP Jason Spezza
SPMR Michael Ryder
SPKP Keith Primeau
SPNZ Nikolai Zherdev
SPMT Marty Turco
SPJK Jari Kurri
SPEJ Ed Jovanovski
SPSK Saku Koivu
SPWG1 Wayne Gretzky EDM/5
SPWG2 Wayne Gretzky LA
SPWG3 Wayne Gretzky NYR

2004-05 Ultimate Collection Ultimate Cuts

This 9-card set featured "cut" signatures of past greats.

PRINT RUN 1 SER.#'d SET
NOT PRICED DUE TO SCARCITY
UCBH Bryan Hextall Sr.
UCPI Punch Imlach
UCBM Bill Mosienko
UCTB Toe Blake
UCDH Doug Harvey
UCHD Hap Day
UCBD Bob Davidson
UCBP Babe Pratt
UCKC King Clancy

2005-06 Ultimate Collection

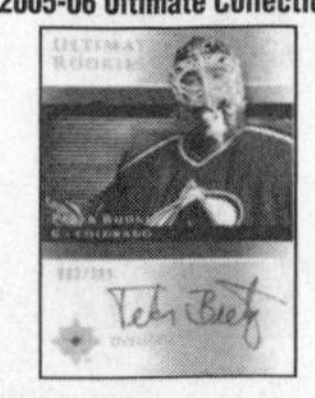

This 232-card set was issued into the hobby in four-card packs, with an $100 SRP, which came four packs to a box and four boxes to a case. Every card in this set is serial numbered. Cards numbered 1-90 feature veterans and those cards were issued to a stated print run of 599 serial numbered sets. The rest of the set features Rookie Cards: Cards numbered 91-118 were signed by the player. Cards numbered 91-100 were issued to a stated print run of 299 serial numbered sets, while cards 101-132 were issued to a stated print run of 399 serial numbered sets and cards numbered 133-232 were issued to a stated print run of 599 serial numbered sets.

1 Teemu Selanne 2.00 5.00
2 Jean-Sebastien Giguere 1.50 4.00
3 Joffrey Lupul 1.25 3.00
4 Ilya Kovalchuk 3.00 8.00
5 Marian Hossa 2.00 5.00
6 Kari Lehtonen 1.50 4.00
7 Andrew Raycroft 1.50 4.00
8 Brad Boyes 1.25 3.00
9 Patrice Bergeron 2.00 5.00
10 Brian Leetch 2.00 5.00
11 Glen Murray 1.25 3.00
12 Chris Drury 1.25 3.00
13 Martin Biron 1.50 4.00
14 Daniel Briere 1.25 3.00
15 Jarome Iginla 2.50 6.00
16 Miikka Kiprusoff 1.50 4.00
17 Doug Weight 1.25 3.00
18 Eric Staal 1.50 4.00
19 Nikolai Khabibulin 2.00 5.00
20 Tuomo Ruutu 1.25 3.00
21 Marek Svatos 1.25 3.00
22 Joe Sakic 4.00 10.00
23 Jose Theodore 2.00 5.00
24 Rob Blake 1.25 3.00
25 Alex Tanguay 1.50 4.00
26 Milan Hejduk 1.50 4.00
27 Rick Nash 3.00 8.00
28 Sergei Fedorov 2.00 5.00
29 Mike Modano 2.50 6.00
30 Bill Guerin 1.25 3.00
31 Marty Turco 2.00 5.00
32 Steve Yzerman 6.00 15.00
33 Nicklas Lidstrom 2.00 5.00
34 Gordie Howe 4.00 10.00
35 Brendan Shanahan 2.00 5.00
36 Pavel Datsyuk 2.00 5.00
37 Henrik Zetterberg 2.00 5.00
38 Ryan Smyth 1.50 4.00
39 Chris Pronger 1.50 4.00
40 Ales Hemsky 1.25 3.00
41 Wayne Gretzky 10.00 25.00
42 Roberto Luongo 2.50 6.00
43 Olli Jokinen 1.25 3.00
44 Jeremy Roenick 2.50 6.00
45 Pavol Demitra 1.25 3.00
46 Luc Robitaille 1.50 4.00
47 Marian Gaborik 2.50 6.00
48 David Aebischer 1.50 4.00
49 Michael Ryder 1.25 3.00
50 Saku Koivu 2.00 5.00
51 Mike Ribeiro 1.25 3.00
52 Tomas Vokoun 1.50 4.00
53 Paul Kariya 2.00 5.00
54 Martin Brodeur 5.00 12.00
55 Patrik Elias 1.25 3.00
56 Rick DiPietro 1.50 4.00
57 Alexei Yashin 1.25 3.00
58 Miroslav Satan 1.25 3.00
59 Jaromir Jagr 3.00 8.00
60 Dominik Hasek 2.50 6.00
61 Dany Heatley 2.50 6.00
62 Jason Spezza 1.50 4.00
63 Martin Havlat 1.25 3.00
64 Daniel Alfredsson 1.50 4.00
65 Peter Forsberg 2.50 6.00
66 Simon Gagne 1.50 4.00
67 Robert Esche 1.50 4.00
68 Keith Primeau 1.25 3.00
69 Curtis Joseph 1.50 4.00
70 Shane Doan 1.25 3.00
71 Mario Lemieux 6.00 15.00
72 Ryan Malone 1.25 3.00
73 Marc-Andre Fleury 1.50 4.00
74 Joe Thornton 3.00 8.00
75 Evgeni Nabokov 1.50 4.00
76 Jonathan Cheechoo 1.50 4.00
77 Patrick Marleau 1.50 4.00
78 Keith Tkachuk 1.50 4.00
79 Brad Richards 1.50 4.00
80 Martin St. Louis 1.50 4.00
81 Vincent Lecavalier 2.00 5.00
82 Bryan McCabe 1.25 3.00
83 Eric Lindros 2.00 5.00
84 Ed Belfour 2.00 5.00
85 Mats Sundin 2.00 5.00
86 Markus Naslund 2.00 5.00
87 Brendan Morrison 1.25 3.00
88 Todd Bertuzzi 2.00 5.00
89 Ed Jovanovski 1.25 3.00
90 Olaf Kolzig 1.25 3.00
91 Sidney Crosby AU RC 600.00 1000.00
92 Alexander Ovechkin AU RC 400.00 600.00
93 Gilbert Brule AU RC 15.00 40.00
94 Corey Perry AU RC 20.00 50.00
95 Jeff Carter AU RC 15.00 40.00
96 Alexander Steen AU RC 20.00 50.00
97 Henrik Lundqvist AU RC 50.00 100.00
98 Hannu Toivonen AU RC 15.00 40.00
99 Alexander Perezhogin AU RC 15.00 40.00
100 Thomas Vanek AU RC 30.00 80.00
101 Ryan Getzlaf AU RC 30.00 80.00
102 Braydon Coburn AU RC 8.00 20.00
103 Milan Jurcina AU RC 8.00 20.00
104 Andrew Alberts AU RC 8.00 20.00
105 Dion Phaneuf AU RC 50.00 100.00
106 Eric Nystrom AU RC 8.00 20.00
107 Cam Ward AU RC 15.00 40.00
108 Cam Barker AU RC 8.00 20.00
109 Brent Seabrook AU RC 10.00 25.00
110 Rene Bourque AU RC 8.00 20.00
111 Peter Budaj AU RC 12.00 30.00
112 Wojtek Wolski AU RC 20.00 50.00
113 Jussi Jokinen AU RC 12.00 30.00
114 Jim Howard AU RC 15.00 40.00
115 Johan Franzen AU RC 25.00 50.00
116 Brad Winchester AU RC 8.00 20.00
117 Rostislav Olesz AU RC 10.00 25.00
118 Anthony Stewart AU RC 8.00 20.00
119 Matt Foy AU RC 6.00 15.00
120 Yann Danis AU RC 8.00 20.00
121 Ryan Suter AU RC 10.00 25.00
122 Zach Parise AU RC 40.00 80.00
123 Robert Nilsson AU RC 8.00 20.00
124 Alvaro Montoya AU RC 12.00 30.00
125 Petr Prucha AU RC 15.00 40.00
126 Brandon Bochenski AU RC 8.00 20.00
127 Andrej Meszaros AU RC 10.00 25.00
128 Patrick Eaves AU RC 10.00 25.00
129 Mike Richards AU RC 30.00 60.00
130 Keith Ballard AU RC 8.00 20.00
131 Ryane Clowe AU RC 8.00 20.00
132 Jeff Woywitka AU RC 6.00 15.00
133 Michael Wall RC 4.00 10.00
134 Zenon Konopka RC 3.00 8.00
135 Jim Slater RC 4.00 10.00
136 Adam Berkhoel RC 4.00 10.00
137 Daniel Paille RC 3.00 8.00
138 Jordan Sigalet RC 4.00 10.00
139 Niklas Nordgren RC 3.00 8.00
140 Kevin Nastiuk RC 4.00 10.00
141 Duncan Keith RC 6.00 15.00
142 Jaroslav Balastik RC 3.00 8.00
143 Steven Goertzen RC 3.00 8.00
144 Alexandre Picard RC 5.00 12.00
145 Junior Lessard RC 3.00 8.00
146 Vojtech Polak RC 3.00 8.00
147 Brett Lebda RC 3.00 8.00
148 Valtteri Filppula RC 3.00 8.00
149 Kyle Brodziak RC 3.00 8.00
150 Matt Greene RC 3.00 8.00
151 Derek Boogaard RC 3.00 8.00
152 Brad Richardson RC 3.00 8.00
153 Mark Streit RC 3.00 8.00
154 Chris Campoli RC 3.00 8.00
155 Petteri Nokelainen RC 3.00 8.00
156 Kevin Colley RC 3.00 8.00
157 Ryan Hollweg RC 3.00 8.00
158 Jeremy Colliton RC 3.00 8.00
159 Brian McGrattan RC 3.00 8.00
160 Christoph Schubert RC 3.00 8.00
161 R.J. Umberger RC 5.00 12.00
162 Ben Eager RC 3.00 8.00
163 David Leneveu RC 4.00 10.00
164 Maxime Talbot RC 3.00 8.00
165 Josh Gorges RC 3.00 8.00
166 Dimitri Patzold RC 4.00 10.00
167 Jay McClement RC 3.00 8.00
168 Jeff Hoggan RC 3.00 8.00
169 Lee Stempniak RC 4.00 10.00
170 Andrei Kostitsyn RC 6.00 15.00
171 Timo Helbling RC 3.00 8.00
172 Paul Ranger RC 3.00 8.00
173 Ryan Craig RC 4.00 10.00
174 Evgeny Artyukhin RC 3.00 8.00
175 Andrew Wozniewski RC 3.00 8.00
176 Staffan Kronwall RC 3.00 8.00
177 Yanick Lehoux RC 3.00 8.00
178 Ryan Whitney RC 4.00 10.00
179 Erik Christensen RC 4.00 10.00
180 Andrew Ladd RC 3.00 8.00
181 Rob McVicar RC 3.00 8.00
182 Tomas Fleischmann RC 3.00 8.00
183 Jakub Klepis RC 3.00 8.00
184 Mike Green RC 10.00 25.00
185 Corey Crawford RC 3.00 8.00
186 Mikko Koivu RC 5.00 12.00
187 Steve Bernier RC 8.00 20.00
188 Cam Janssen RC 3.00 8.00
189 Barry Tallackson RC 3.00 8.00
190 Jeff Tambellini RC 3.00 8.00
191 Maxim Lapierre RC 3.00 8.00
192 Danny Richmond RC 3.00 8.00
193 Dustin Penner RC 5.00 12.00
194 Ben Walter RC 3.00 8.00
195 Chris Thorburn RC 3.00 8.00
196 Jiri Novotny RC 3.00 8.00
197 Richie Regehr RC 3.00 8.00
198 Chad Larose RC 3.00 8.00
199 James Wisniewski RC 3.00 8.00
200 Vitaly Kolesnik RC 4.00 10.00
201 Joakim Lindstrom RC 3.00 8.00
202 Ole-Kristian Tollefsen RC 3.00 8.00
203 Kyle Quincey RC 3.00 8.00
204 Danny Syvret RC 3.00 8.00
205 Jean-Francois Jacques RC 3.00 8.00
206 Greg Jacina RC 3.00 8.00
207 Petr Taticek RC 3.00 8.00
208 Rob Globke RC 3.00 8.00
209 George Parros RC 3.00 8.00
210 Petr Kanko RC 3.00 8.00
211 Richard Petiot RC 3.00 8.00
212 Jean-Philippe Cote RC 3.00 8.00
213 Kevin Klein RC 3.00 8.00
214 Pekka Rinne RC 4.00 10.00
215 Jason Ryznar RC 3.00 8.00
216 Bruno Gervais RC 3.00 8.00
217 Alexandre Picard RC 3.00 8.00
218 Stefan Ruzicka RC 3.00 8.00
219 Matt Jones RC 3.00 8.00
220 Colby Armstrong RC 8.00 20.00
221 Doug Murray RC 3.00 8.00
222 Grant Stevenson RC 3.00 8.00
223 Colin Hemingway RC 3.00 8.00
224 Kevin Dallman RC 3.00 8.00
225 Dennis Wideman RC 3.00 8.00
226 Darren Reid RC 3.00 8.00
227 Doug O'Brien RC 3.00 8.00
228 Gerald Coleman RC 3.00 8.00
229 Nick Tarnasky RC 3.00 8.00
230 Jay Harrison RC 3.00 8.00
231 Kevin Bieksa RC 3.00 8.00
232 Tomas Mojzis RC 3.00 8.00

2005-06 Ultimate Collection Gold

*STARS: 1.5X TO 3X
PRINT RUN 25 #'d SETS
32 Steve Yzerman 20.00 50.00
41 Wayne Gretzky 40.00 100.00
71 Mario Lemieux 25.00 60.00

2005-06 Ultimate Collection Autographed Patches

PRINT RUN 25 SER. #'d SETS
UNIQUE PATCHES MAY EARN SUBSTANTIAL PREMIUMS
91 Sidney Crosby 900.00 1200.00
92 Alexander Ovechkin 400.00 700.00
93 Gilbert Brule 150.00 250.00
94 Corey Perry 75.00 150.00
95 Jeff Carter 60.00 120.00
96 Alexander Steen 60.00 120.00
97 Henrik Lundqvist 125.00 250.00
98 Hannu Toivonen 40.00 80.00
99 Alexander Perezhogin
100 Thomas Vanek 100.00 200.00
101 Ryan Getzlaf 50.00 100.00
102 Braydon Coburn
103 Milan Jurcina 20.00 50.00
104 Andrew Alberts 20.00 50.00
105 Dion Phaneuf 150.00 250.00
106 Eric Nystrom
107 Cam Ward 100.00 200.00
108 Cam Barker 40.00 80.00
109 Brent Seabrook 20.00 50.00
110 Rene Bourque 25.00 60.00
111 Peter Budaj 50.00 100.00
112 Wojtek Wolski
113 Jussi Jokinen 40.00 80.00
114 Jim Howard 60.00 120.00
115 Johan Franzen 25.00 60.00
116 Brad Winchester 25.00 60.00
117 Rostislav Olesz 25.00 60.00
119 Matt Foy 20.00 50.00
120 Yann Danis
121 Ryan Suter 25.00 60.00
122 Zach Parise
123 Robert Nilsson 25.00 60.00
124 Alvaro Montoya 50.00 100.00
126 Brandon Bochenski 25.00 60.00
127 Andrej Meszaros 40.00 80.00
129 Mike Richards 50.00 100.00
130 Keith Ballard 20.00 50.00
131 Ryane Clowe 40.00 80.00
132 Jeff Woywitka 20.00 50.00

2005-06 Ultimate Collection Autographed Shields

PRINT RUN 1/1
NOT PRICED DUE TO SCARCITY
91 Sidney Crosby
92 Alexander Ovechkin
93 Gilbert Brule
94 Corey Perry
95 Jeff Carter
96 Alexander Steen
97 Henrik Lundqvist
98 Hannu Toivonen
99 Alexander Perezhogin
100 Thomas Vanek
101 Ryan Getzlaf
102 Braydon Coburn
103 Milan Jurcina
104 Andrew Alberts
105 Dion Phaneuf
106 Eric Nystrom
107 Cam Ward
108 Cam Barker
109 Brent Seabrook
110 Rene Bourque
111 Peter Budaj
112 Wojtek Wolski
113 Jussi Jokinen
114 Jim Howard
115 Johan Franzen
116 Brad Winchester
117 Rostislav Olesz
119 Matt Foy
120 Yann Danis
121 Ryan Suter
122 Zach Parise
123 Robert Nilsson
124 Alvaro Montoya
127 Andrej Meszaros
128 Patrick Eaves
129 Mike Richards
130 Keith Ballard
131 Ryane Clowe
132 Jeff Woywitka

2005-06 Ultimate Collection Endorsed Emblems

PRINT RUN 35 #'d SETS
EEAT Alex Tanguay
EEAY Alexei Yashin 15.00 30.00
EEBC Bobby Clarke 30.00 80.00
EEBI Martin Biron

EEBK Rob Blake 25.00 60.00
EEBL Brian Leetch 25.00 60.00
EEBM Brendan Morrison 15.00 30.00
EEBU Johnny Bucyk 25.00 60.00
EEBY Mike Bossy 50.00 100.00
EECD Chris Drury 25.00 60.00
EECN Cam Neely 60.00 125.00
EEDA David Aebischer 30.00 80.00
EEDB Dustin Brown 15.00 30.00
EEDG Doug Gilmour EXCH 75.00 125.00
EEDH Dany Heatley 40.00 100.00
EEDL David Legwand 25.00 60.00
EEDP Denis Potvin 50.00 100.00
EEDR Dwayne Roloson 25.00 60.00
EEDS Darryl Sittler 25.00 60.00
EEDW Doug Weight 15.00 30.00
EEEB Ed Belfour 75.00 150.00
EEES Eric Staal EXCH 60.00 100.00
EEGE Martin Gerber 25.00 60.00
EEGF Grant Fuhr 40.00 100.00
EEGL Guy Lafleur 75.00 150.00
EEGM Glen Murray 15.00 30.00
EEHJ Milan Hejduk 25.00 60.00
EEHK Dominik Hasek 75.00 150.00
EEHO Marian Hossa EXCH 40.00 100.00
EEHV Martin Havlat 30.00 80.00
EEHZ Henrik Zetterberg 50.00 125.00
EEIK Ilya Kovalchuk 90.00 150.00
EEJC Jonathan Cheechoo 30.00 80.00
EEJI Jarome Iginla 50.00 100.00
EEJO Joe Thornton 75.00 125.00
EEJP Joni Pitkanen 25.00 60.00
EEJR Jeremy Roenick 25.00 60.00
EEJS Jean-Sebastien Giguere 25.00 60.00
EEJT Jose Theodore 30.00 80.00
EEKL Kari Lehtonen 25.00 60.00
EEKP Keith Primeau 15.00 40.00
EELM Lanny McDonald 75.00 125.00
EELR Luc Robitaille 50.00 100.00
EELU Joffrey Lupul 25.00 60.00
EEMB Martin Brodeur 150.00 300.00
EEMC Bryan McCabe EXCH 15.00 40.00
EEML Manny Legace 15.00 40.00
EEMM Mike Modano 50.00 100.00
EEMN Markus Naslund 40.00 100.00
EEMS Matt Stajan 15.00 30.00
EEMT Marty Turco 25.00 60.00
EEMU Larry Murphy 15.00 30.00
EEMW Brenden Morrow 25.00 60.00
EENZ Nikolai Zherdev
EEOK Olaf Kolzig 30.00 80.00
EEPA Mark Parrish 15.00 30.00
EEPB Patrice Bergeron 30.00 80.00
EEPM Patrick Marleau 25.00 60.00
EEPR Patrick Roy 125.00 250.00
EERB Ray Bourque 75.00 150.00
EERE Robert Esche 15.00 30.00
EERL Roberto Luongo 50.00 100.00
EERM Ryan Miller 75.00 150.00
EERN Rick Nash 75.00 150.00
EERS Ryan Smyth 25.00 60.00
EERY Michael Ryder 30.00 80.00
EERZ Richard Zednik 15.00 30.00
EESG Simon Gagne 30.00 80.00
EESK Saku Koivu 30.00 80.00
EESL Martin St. Louis 25.00 60.00
EESP Jason Spezza 50.00 100.00
EESV Denis Savard 30.00 80.00
EETC Ty Conklin EXCH 15.00 30.00
EEWG Wayne Gretzky 300.00 400.00

2005-06 Ultimate Collection Jerseys

PRINT RUN 250 #'d COPIES, UNLESS NOTED
JAO Alexander Ovechkin 15.00 40.00
JAS Alexander Steen 4.00 10.00
JAY Alexei Yashin 3.00 8.00
JBT Bryan Trottier 4.00 10.00
JCO Corey Perry 4.00 10.00
JCP Chris Pronger 3.00 8.00
JDH Dominik Hasek 6.00 15.00
JDP Dion Phaneuf 10.00 25.00
JDW Doug Weight 3.00 8.00
JEL Eric Lindros 3.00 8.00
JES Eric Staal 4.00 10.00
JGB Gilbert Brule 4.00 10.00
JGH Gordie Howe 15.00 40.00
JHE Dany Heatley 5.00 12.00
JHL Henrik Lundqvist 10.00 25.00
JHT Hannu Toivonen 4.00 10.00
JIK Ilya Kovalchuk 6.00 15.00
JJB Jean Beliveau 8.00 20.00
JJC Jeff Carter 6.00 15.00
JJI Jarome Iginla 5.00 12.00
JJJ Jaromir Jagr/200 6.00 15.00
JJO Joe Thornton 6.00 15.00
JJS Joe Sakic 6.00 15.00
JJT Jose Theodore 5.00 12.00
JKL Kari Lehtonen 3.00 8.00
JLR Luc Robitaille 3.00 8.00
JMA Martin St. Louis 3.00 8.00
JMB Martin Brodeur 8.00 20.00
JMG Marian Gaborik 5.00 12.00
JMH Milan Hejduk 3.00 8.00
JML Mario Lemieux 15.00 40.00
JMM Mike Modano 5.00 12.00
JMN Markus Naslund 3.00 8.00
JMS Mats Sundin 3.00 8.00
JMT Marty Turco 3.00 8.00
JPB Patrice Bergeron 3.00 8.00
JPD Pavel Datsyuk 3.00 8.00
JPE Phil Esposito 5.00 12.00
JPF Peter Forsberg 5.00 12.00
JPK Paul Kariya 3.00 8.00
JPM Patrick Marleau 3.00 8.00
JPR Patrick Roy 12.00 30.00
JRB Ray Bourque 5.00 12.00
JRG Ryan Getzlaf 5.00 12.00
JRL Roberto Luongo 5.00 12.00
JSC Sidney Crosby 30.00 60.00
JSG Simon Gagne [illegible] [illegible]
JSK Saku Koivu/125 8.00 20.00
JSP Jason Spezza 4.00 10.00
JSY Steve Yzerman 10.00 25.00
JTB Todd Bertuzzi 3.00 8.00
JTS Teemu Selanne 3.00 8.00
JTV Tomas Vokoun 3.00 8.00
JVA Thomas Vanek 6.00 15.00
JVL Vincent Lecavalier 3.00 8.00
JWG Wayne Gretzky 30.00 60.00

2005-06 Ultimate Collection Jerseys Dual

PRINT RUN 75 #'d COPIES
DJAL Jason Allison 5.00 12.00
Eric Lindros
DJBR Patrice Bergeron 8.00 20.00
Andrew Raycroft
DJCR Jeff Carter 15.00 40.00
Mike Richards
DJFP Peter Forsberg 10.00 25.00
Keith Primeau
DJFZ Johan Franzen 10.00 25.00
Henrik Zetterberg
DJGC Wayne Gretzky 100.00 200.00
Sidney Crosby
DJHC Dominik Hasek 10.00 25.00
Zdeno Chara
DJHY Gordie Howe 125.00 200.00
Steve Yzerman
DJJD Jason Spezza 12.00 30.00
Dany Heatley
DJJL Curtis Joseph 5.00 12.00
David Leneveu
DJKH Ilya Kovalchuk 10.00 25.00
Marian Hossa
DJKP Saku Koivu 8.00 20.00
Alexander Perezhogin
DJKV Paul Kariya 8.00 20.00
Tomas Vokoun
DJLC Mario Lemieux 90.00 150.00
Sidney Crosby
DJLS Joffrey Lupul 8.00 20.00
Teemu Selanne
DJML Alvaro Montoya 20.00 50.00
Henrik Lundqvist
DJNB Rick Nash 20.00 50.00
Gilbert Brule/30
DJOC Alexander Ovechkin 150.00 250.00
Sidney Crosby
DJPG Corey Perry 10.00 25.00
Ryan Getzlaf
DJPI Dion Phaneuf 20.00 50.00
Jarome Iginla
DJRT Patrick Roy 20.00 50.00
Jose Theodore
DJSB Brent Seabrook 6.00 15.00
Cam Barker
DJSH Joe Sakic 10.00 25.00
Milan Hejduk
DJSL Martin St. Louis 10.00 25.00
Vincent Lecavalier
DJTD Jose Theodore 8.00 20.00
Yann Danis
DJTL Hannu Toivonen 8.00 20.00
Kari Lehtonen
DJWN Cam Ward 12.00 30.00
Kevin Nastiuk

2005-06 Ultimate Collection Jerseys Triple

PRINT RUN 25 SER #'d SETS
TJFGC Peter Forsberg 40.00 80.00
Simon Gagne
Jeff Carter
TJGLC Wayne Gretzky 250.00 400.00
Mario Lemieux
Sidney Crosby
TJHSH Dany Heatley 50.00 100.00
Jason Spezza
Dominik Hasek
TJKTP Saku Koivu 20.00 50.00
Jose Theodore
Alexander Perezhogin
TJLVR Martin St. Louis 30.00 60.00
Vincent Lecavalier
Brad Richards
TJNOC Rick Nash 200.00 350.00
Alexander Ovechkin
Sidney Crosby
TJPGL Corey Perry 20.00 50.00
Ryan Getzlaf
Joffrey Lupul
TJRTB Patrick Roy 40.00 80.00
Jose Theodore
Martin Brodeur
TJSLA Mats Sundin 40.00 80.00
Eric Lindros
Jason Allison

2005-06 Ultimate Collection Marquee Attractions

PRINT RUN 250 #'d SETS
MA1 Corey Perry 3.00 8.00
MA2 Ryan Getzlaf 3.00 8.00
MA3 Jean-Sebastien Giguere 2.50 6.00
MA4 Ilya Kovalchuk 4.00 10.00
MA5 Marian Hossa 2.50 6.00
MA6 Hannu Toivonen 3.00 8.00
MA7 Patrice Bergeron 3.00 8.00
MA8 Andrew Raycroft 1.50 4.00
MA9 Thomas Vanek 3.00 8.00
MA10 Dion Phaneuf 8.00 20.00
MA11 Jarome Iginla 4.00 10.00
MA12 Eric Staal [illegible] [illegible]
MA13 Nikolai Khabibulin 2.50 6.00
MA14 Alex Tanguay 1.50 4.00
MA15 Milan Hejduk 2.50 6.00
MA16 Rick Nash 3.00 8.00
MA17 Mike Modano 3.00 8.00
MA18 Brenden Morrow 2.50 6.00
MA19 Marty Turco 2.50 6.00
MA20 Johan Franzen 1.50 4.00
MA21 Henrik Zetterberg 2.50 6.00
MA22 Chris Pronger 1.50 4.00
MA23 Roberto Luongo 4.00 10.00
MA24 Jeremy Roenick 3.00 8.00
MA25 Mikko Koivu 2.50 6.00
MA26 Alexander Perezhogin 1.50 4.00
MA27 Saku Koivu 3.00 8.00
MA28 Jose Theodore 3.00 8.00
MA29 Martin Brodeur 6.00 15.00
MA30 Miroslav Satan 2.50 6.00
MA31 Henrik Lundqvist 8.00 20.00
MA32 Dominik Hasek 4.00 10.00
MA33 Dany Heatley 4.00 10.00
MA34 Jason Spezza 3.00 8.00
MA35 Jeff Carter 4.00 10.00
MA36 Mike Richards 3.00 8.00
MA37 Keith Primeau 1.50 4.00
MA38 Shane Doan 1.50 4.00
MA39 Sidney Crosby 30.00 80.00
MA40 Mark Recchi 1.50 4.00
MA41 Joe Thornton 5.00 12.00
MA42 Martin St. Louis 1.50 4.00
MA43 Vincent Lecavalier 3.00 8.00
MA44 Alexander Steen 3.00 8.00
MA45 Mats Sundin 2.50 6.00
MA46 Ed Belfour 2.50 6.00
MA47 Markus Naslund 2.50 6.00
MA48 Alexander Ovechkin 12.00 30.00
MA49 Gilbert Brule 3.00 8.00
MA50 Olaf Kolzig 3.00 8.00

2005-06 Ultimate Collection Marquee Attractions Signatures

PRINT RUN 10 #'d SETS
NOT PRICED DUE TO SCARCITY

2005-06 Ultimate Collection National Heroes Jerseys

PRINT RUN 225 #'d COPIES UNLESS NOTED
NHJAF Alexander Frolov 2.50 6.00
NHJAK Alexei Kovalev 2.50 6.00
NHJAL Daniel Alfredsson 3.00 8.00
NHJAO Alexander Ovechkin 20.00 50.00
NHJAY Alexei Yashin 2.50 6.00
NHJBG Bill Guerin 2.50 6.00
NHJBR Brian Rolston 2.50 6.00
NHJCC Chris Chelios 3.00 8.00
NHJCD Chris Drury 2.50 6.00
NHJCP Chris Pronger/200 3.00 8.00
NHJDA David Aebischer 3.00 8.00
NHJDW Doug Weight 2.50 6.00
NHJFO Adam Foote 2.50 6.00
NHJFT Fedor Tyutin 2.50 6.00
NHJGA Marian Gaborik 6.00 15.00
NHJHA Michal Handzus 2.50 6.00
NHJHJ Milan Hejduk 3.00 8.00
NHJHK Dominik Hasek/200 8.00 20.00
NHJHO Marian Hossa 3.00 8.00
NHJHS Marcel Hossa 2.50 6.00
NHJHZ Henrik Zetterberg 3.00 8.00
NHJIK Ilya Kovalchuk 6.00 15.00
NHJJB Jay Bouwmeester 2.50 6.00
NHJJI Jarome Iginla 6.00 15.00
NHJJJ Jaromir Jagr 6.00 15.00
NHJJL Jere Lehtinen 2.50 6.00
NHJJO Joe Thornton 6.00 15.00
NHJJP Joni Pitkanen/200 3.00 8.00
NHJJS Joe Sakic 6.00 15.00
NHJKD Kris Draper 2.50 6.00
NHJKT Keith Tkachuk 3.00 8.00
NHJLE Jordan Leopold 2.50 5.00
NHJMB Martin Brodeur 8.00 20.00
NHJMC Bryan McCabe 2.50 6.00
NHJMG Martin Gerber/200 5.00 12.00
NHJMM Mike Modano 6.00 15.00
NHJMO Mattias Ohlund 2.50 6.00
NHJMP Mark Parrish 2.50 6.00
NHJMS Martin Straka/200 2.50 6.00
NHJMT Marty Turco 3.00 8.00
NHJNA Nik Antropov 2.50 6.00
NHJNL Nicklas Lidstrom 3.00 8.00
NHJOJ Olli Jokinen/200 3.00 8.00
NHJOK Olaf Kolzig 3.00 8.00
NHJPA Pavol Demitra 3.00 8.00
NHJPB Peter Bondra 3.00 8.00
NHJPD Pavel Datsyuk 3.00 8.00
NHJPE Patrik Elias 3.00 8.00
NHJPF Peter Forsberg 6.00 15.00
NHJRA Brian Rafalski/200 2.50 6.00
NHJRB Rob Blake 3.00 8.00
NHJRD Rick DiPietro 5.00 12.00
NHJRE Robert Esche 3.00 8.00
NHJRI Brad Richards 3.00 8.00
NHJRL Roberto Luongo 6.00 15.00
NHJRS Ryan Smyth/200 3.00 8.00
NHJSA Miroslav Satan 2.50 6.00
NHJSG Simon Gagne 3.00 8.00
NHJSO Sandis Ozolinsh 2.50 6.00
NHJSU Mats Sundin 3.00 8.00
NHJSV Marek Svatos/200 2.50 6.00
NHJTB Todd Bertuzzi/200 5.00 12.00
NHJTS Teemu Selanne 3.00 8.00
NHJTV Tomas Vokoun 3.00 8.00
NHJVK Viktor Kozlov 2.50 6.00
NHJVL Vincent Lecavalier 3.00 8.00
NHJWR Wade Redden 2.50 6.00
NHJZC Zdeno Chara 3.00 8.00

2005-06 Ultimate Collection National Heroes Patches

PRINT RUN VARIES 10-25 COPIES
NOT PRICED DUE TO SCARCITY
NHPAF Alexander Frolov/25
NHPAK Alexei Kovalev/25
NHPAL Daniel Alfredsson/25
NHPAO Alexander Ovechkin/10
NHPAY Alexei Yashin/25
NHPBG Bill Guerin/25
NHPBR Brian Rolston/25
NHPCC Chris Chelios/10
NHPCD Chris Drury/25
NHPCP Chris Pronger/10
NHPDA David Aebischer/25
NHPDH Dany Heatley/10
NHPDW Doug Weight/10
NHPFO Adam Foote/25
NHPFT Fedor Tyutin/25
NHPGA Marian Gaborik/25
NHPHA Michal Handzus/25
NHPHJ Milan Hejduk/10
NHPHK Dominik Hasek/10
NHPHO Marian Hossa/10
NHPHS Marcel Hossa/25
NHPHZ Henrik Zetterberg/10
NHPIK Ilya Kovalchuk/10
NHPJB Jay Bouwmeester/10
NHPJI Jarome Iginla/10
NHPJJ Jaromir Jagr/10
NHPJL Jere Lehtinen/25
NHPJO Joe Thornton/10
NHPJP Joni Pitkanen/25
NHPJS Joe Sakic/10
NHPKD Kris Draper/25
NHPKT Keith Tkachuk/25
NHPLE Jordan Leopold/25
NHPMB Martin Brodeur/10
NHPMC Bryan McCabe/25
NHPMG Martin Gerber/25
NHPMM Mike Modano/10
NHPMO Mattias Ohlund/25
NHPMP Mark Parrish/25
NHPMS Martin Straka/25
NHPMT Marty Turco/25
NHPNA Nik Antropov/25
NHPNL Nicklas Lidstrom/25
NHPOJ Olli Jokinen/25
NHPOK Olaf Kolzig/25
NHPPA Pavol Demitra/25
NHPPB Peter Bondra/25
NHPPD Pavel Datsyuk/25
NHPPE Patrik Elias/25
NHPPF Peter Forsberg/10
NHPRA Brian Rafalski/25
NHPRB Rob Blake/25
NHPRD Rick DiPietro/25
NHPRE Robert Esche/25
NHPRI Brad Richards/10
NHPRL Roberto Luongo/25
NHPRN Rick Nash/10
NHPRS Ryan Smyth/25
NHPSA Miroslav Satan/25
NHPSG Simon Gagne/25
NHPSK Saku Koivu/10
NHPSL Martin St. Louis/10
NHPSO Sandis Ozolinsh/25
NHPSU Mats Sundin/10
NHPSV Marek Svatos/25
NHPTB Todd Bertuzzi/25
NHPTS Teemu Selanne/25
NHPTV Tomas Vokoun/25
NHPVK Viktor Kozlov/25
NHPVL Vincent Lecavalier/10
NHPWR Wade Redden/25
NHPZC Zdeno Chara/25

2005-06 Ultimate Collection Premium Patches

PRINT RUN 35 SER. #'d SETS
UNIQUE SWATCHES MAY EARN PREMIUM
PPAO Alexander Ovechkin 150.00 250.00
PPAP Alexander Perezhogin 15.00 40.00
PPAS Alexander Steen 25.00 60.00
PPAY Alexei Yashin 25.00 60.00
PPBS Brendan Shanahan 20.00 50.00
PPCP Chris Pronger 20.00 50.00
PPCW Cam Ward 25.00 60.00
PPDH Dany Heatley/30 25.00 60.00
PPDP Dion Phaneuf 50.00 100.00
PPDW Doug Weight 15.00 40.00
PPEL Eric Lindros
PPES Eric Staal 25.00 60.00
PPGB Gilbert Brule 25.00 60.00
PPHK Dominik Hasek 25.00 60.00
PPHL Henrik Lundqvist 50.00 100.00
PPHT Hannu Toivonen 20.00 50.00
PPIK Ilya Kovalchuk 30.00 80.00
PPJC Jeff Carter 30.00 80.00
PPJF Johan Franzen 20.00 50.00
PPJI Jarome Iginla 30.00 80.00
PPJJ Jaromir Jagr 50.00 125.00
PPJO Joe Thornton 40.00 80.00
PPJR Jeremy Roenick 25.00 60.00
PPJS Joe Sakic 60.00 120.00
PPJT Jose Theodore 25.00 60.00
PPKL Kari Lehtonen 30.00 80.00
PPLR Luc Robitaille 20.00 50.00
PPMB Martin Brodeur 75.00 150.00
PPMG Marian Gaborik 50.00 100.00
PPMH Milan Hejduk 25.00 60.00
PPML Mario Lemieux 100.00 200.00
PPMM Mike Modano 30.00 60.00
PPMN Markus Naslund 20.00 50.00
PPMR Mike Richards 50.00 100.00
PPMS Mats Sundin 40.00 100.00
PPMT Marty Turco 30.00 80.00
PPPB Patrice Bergeron 20.00 50.00
PPPD Pavel Datsyuk 20.00 50.00
PPPE Corey Perry 20.00 50.00
PPPF Peter Forsberg 30.00 80.00
PPPK Paul Kariya 25.00 [illegible]
PPPM Patrick Marleau 20.00 50.00
PPPR Patrick Roy 100.00 200.00
PPPS Jason Spezza 40.00 80.00
PPRB Ray Bourque 30.00 80.00
PPRG Ryan Getzlaf 30.00 80.00
PPRL Roberto Luongo 30.00 80.00
PPRN Rick Nash/15
PPSC Sidney Crosby 250.00 400.00
PPSF Sergei Fedorov 20.00 50.00
PPSG Simon Gagne 20.00 50.00
PPSY Steve Yzerman 75.00 150.00
PPTB Todd Bertuzzi 20.00 50.00
PPTS Teemu Selanne 25.00 60.00
PPTV Thomas Vanek 40.00 100.00
PPVL Vincent Lecavalier 30.00 80.00
PPVO Tomas Vokoun 40.00 100.00
PPWG Wayne Gretzky 75.00 150.00

2005-06 Ultimate Collection Premium Swatches

75 SER. #'d COPIES UNLESS NOTED
PSAO Alexander Ovechkin 30.00 80.00
PSAP Alexander Perezhogin 4.00 10.00
PSAS Alexander Steen 8.00 20.00
PSAY Alexei Yashin 3.00 8.00
PSBS Brendan Shanahan 6.00 15.00
PSCP Chris Pronger 3.00 8.00
PSCW Cam Ward 8.00 20.00
PSDH Dany Heatley/35 12.00 30.00
PSDP Dion Phaneuf 10.00 25.00
PSDW Doug Weight 3.00 8.00
PSEL Eric Lindros 5.00 12.00
PSES Eric Staal 6.00 15.00
PSGB Gilbert Brule 6.00 15.00
PSHL Henrik Lundqvist 10.00 25.00
PSHT Hannu Toivonen 5.00 12.00
PSIK Ilya Kovalchuk 8.00 20.00
PSJC Jeff Carter 8.00 20.00
PSJF Johan Franzen 3.00 8.00
PSJI Jarome Iginla 6.00 15.00
PSJJ Jaromir Jagr/50 15.00 30.00
PSJO Joe Thornton 8.00 20.00
PSJR Jeremy Roenick 4.00 10.00
PSJS Joe Sakic 10.00 25.00
PSJT Jose Theodore 6.00 15.00
PSKL Kari Lehtonen 4.00 10.00
PSLR Luc Robitaille 4.00 10.00
PSMB Martin Brodeur/50 15.00 40.00
PSMG Marian Gaborik 6.00 15.00
PSMH Milan Hejduk 4.00 10.00
PSML Mario Lemieux 20.00 50.00
PSMM Mike Modano 4.00 10.00
PSMN Markus Naslund 4.00 10.00
PSMR Mike Richards 4.00 10.00
PSMS Mats Sundin 4.00 10.00
PSMT Marty Turco 4.00 10.00
PSPB Patrice Bergeron 4.00 10.00
PSPD Pavel Datsyuk 3.00 8.00
PSPE Corey Perry 4.00 10.00
PSPF Peter Forsberg 8.00 20.00
PSPM Patrick Marleau 3.00 8.00
PSPR Patrick Roy 20.00 50.00
PSPS Jason Spezza 5.00 12.00
PSRB Ray Bourque 5.00 12.00
PSRG Ryan Getzlaf 4.00 10.00
PSRL Roberto Luongo 6.00 15.00
PSSC Sidney Crosby 60.00 125.00
PSSK Saku Koivu 4.00 10.00
PSSL Martin St. Louis 4.00 10.00
PSSY Steve Yzerman 15.00 40.00
PSTB Todd Bertuzzi 4.00 10.00
PSTS Teemu Selanne 6.00 15.00
PSTV Thomas Vanek 4.00 10.00
PSVL Vincent Lecavalier 4.00 10.00
PSVO Tomas Vokoun 4.00 10.00
PSWG Wayne Gretzky 75.00 150.00

2005-06 Ultimate Collection Ultimate Achievements

PRINT RUNS VARY
UNDER 20 NOT PRICED DUE TO SCARCITY
UAAR Andrew Raycroft/29 15.00 30.00
UAAT Alex Tanguay/12
UAAY Alexei Yashin/6
UABC Bobby Clarke/3
UABH Bobby Hull/9
UABP Bernie Parent/2
UACN Cam Neely/5
UADH Dany Heatley/26 25.00 60.00
UADW Doug Weight/8
UAEN Evgeni Nabokov/10
UAES Eric Staal/2
UAGH Gordie Howe/6
UAGP Gilbert Perreault/6
UAHK Dominik Hasek/6
UAHO Marian Hossa/12
UAHV Martin Havlat/11
UAHZ Henrik Zetterberg/22 25.00 50.00
UAIK Ilya Kovalchuk/41 20.00 50.00
UAJB Jean Beliveau/2
UAJC Jonathan Cheechoo/28 25.00 50.00
UAJG Jean-Sebastien Giguere/15
UAJI Jarome Iginla/41 20.00 50.00
UAJO Joe Thornton/5
UAJR Jeremy Roenick/9
UAJT Jose Theodore/23
UALA Guy Lafleur/3
UALU Luc Robitaille/6
UAMB Martin Brodeur/4
UAMH Milan Hejduk/4
UAML Manny Legace/10
UAMM Mike Modano/6
UAMN Markus Naslund/9
UAMT Marty Turco/9
UANK Nikolai Khabibulin/16
UAON Jeff O'Neill/5
UAPB Patrice Bergeron/16
UAPE Phil Esposito/5
UAPR Patrick Roy/3
UARB Ray Bourque/5
UARL Roberto Luongo/23 40.00 75.00
UARN Rick Nash/41 15.00 40.00
UARS Ryan Smyth/6
UASG Simon Gagne/17
UASK Saku Koivu/2
UASL Martin St. Louis/24 12.50 30.00
UASN Scott Niedermayer/18
UATB Todd Bertuzzi/4
UATE Tony Esposito/3
UAVL Vincent Lecavalier/9
UAWG Wayne Gretzky/9

2005-06 Ultimate Collection Ultimate Debut Threads Jerseys

PRINT RUN 250 #'d SETS
DTJAA Andrew Alberts 3.00 8.00
DTJAK Andrei Kostitsyn 4.00 10.00
DTJAL Andrew Ladd 4.00 10.00
DTJAM Andrej Meszaros 3.00 8.00
DTJAO Alexander Ovechkin 15.00 40.00
DTJAP Alexander Perezhogin 4.00 10.00
DTJAS Alexander Steen 4.00 10.00
DTJBB Brandon Bochenski 3.00 8.00
DTJBC Braydon Coburn 3.00 8.00
DTJBS Brent Seabrook 3.00 8.00
DTJBT Barry Tallackson 3.00 8.00
DTJBW Brad Winchester 3.00 8.00
DTJCB Cam Barker 3.00 8.00
DTJCC Chris Campoli 3.00 8.00
DTJCP Corey Perry 4.00 10.00
DTJCS Christoph Schubert 3.00 8.00
DTJCW Cam Ward 6.00 15.00
DTJDB Derek Boogaard 3.00 8.00
DTJDL David Leneveu 3.00 8.00
DTJDP Dion Phaneuf 10.00 25.00
DTJEA Evgeny Artyukhin 3.00 8.00
DTJEN Eric Nystrom 3.00 8.00
DTJGB Gilbert Brule 5.00 12.00
DTJHL Henrik Lundqvist 10.00 25.00
DTJHT Hannu Toivonen 4.00 10.00
DTJJC Jeff Carter 6.00 15.00
DTJJF Johan Franzen 3.00 8.00
DTJJH Jim Howard 5.00 12.00
DTJJJ Jussi Jokinen 4.00 10.00
DTJJK Jakub Klepis 3.00 8.00
DTJJM Jay McClement 3.00 8.00
DTJJS Jim Slater 3.00 8.00
DTJJT Jeff Tambellini 3.00 8.00
DTJJW Jeff Woywitka 3.00 8.00
DTJKB Keith Ballard 3.00 8.00
DTJMJ Milan Jurcina 3.00 8.00
DTJMK Mikko Koivu 4.00 10.00
DTJML Maxim Lapierre 3.00 8.00
DTJMO Alvaro Montoya 4.00 10.00
DTJMR Mike Richards 4.00 10.00
DTJMT Maxime Talbot 3.00 8.00
DTJPP Petr Prucha 4.00 10.00
DTJRB Rene Bourque 3.00 8.00
DTJRC Ryane Clowe 3.00 8.00
DTJRG Ryan Getzlaf 5.00 12.00
DTJRJ R.J. Umberger 3.00 8.00
DTJRN Robert Nilsson 3.00 8.00
DTJRO Rostislav Olesz 4.00 10.00
DTJRS Ryan Suter 3.00 8.00
DTJRW Ryan Whitney 3.00 8.00
DTJSB Steve Bernier 4.00 10.00
DTJSC Sidney Crosby 40.00 80.00
DTJSI Jordan Sigalet 4.00 10.00
DTJTF Tomas Fleischmann 3.00 8.00
DTJTV Thomas Vanek 8.00 20.00
DTJWW Wojtek Wolski 4.00 10.00
DTJYD Yann Danis 3.00 8.00
DTJZP Zach Parise 4.00 10.00

2005-06 Ultimate Collection Ultimate Debut Threads Jerseys Autographs

PRINT RUN 25 COPIES
NOT PRICED DUE TO SCARCITY
DAJAO Alexander Ovechkin 300.00 450.00
DAJSC Sidney Crosby 500.00 800.00

2005-06 Ultimate Collection Ultimate Debut Threads Patches

PRINT RUN 60 #'d COPIES UNLESS NOTED
UNIQUE SWATCHES MAY EARN SUBSTANTIAL PREMIUM
DTPAA Andrew Alberts 10.00 25.00
DTPAL Andrew Ladd 20.00 50.00
DTPAO Alexander Ovechkin 100.00 250.00
DTPAP Alexander Perezhogin 20.00 50.00
DTPAS Alexander Steen 20.00 50.00
DTPBB Brandon Bochenski 15.00 40.00
DTPBC Braydon Coburn 15.00 40.00
DTPBS Brent Seabrook 25.00 60.00
DTPBT Barry Tallackson 10.00 25.00
DTPBW Brad Winchester 10.00 25.00
DTPCB Cam Barker 15.00 40.00
DTPCC Chris Campoli/40 15.00 40.00
DTPCP Corey Perry 30.00 80.00
DTPCW Cam Ward 40.00 100.00
DTPDB Derek Boogaard 15.00 40.00
DTPDL David Leneveu 15.00 40.00
DTPDP Dion Phaneuf 50.00 125.00
DTPFA Evgeny Artyukhin/25 25.00 60.00
DTPEN Eric Nystrom 20.00 50.00
DTPGB Gilbert Brule/30 30.00 80.00
DTPHL Henrik Lundqvist 50.00 125.00
DTPHT Hannu Toivonen 25.00 60.00
DTPJC Jeff Carter 40.00 100.00
DTPJF Johan Franzen 10.00 25.00
DTPJH Jim Howard 25.00 60.00
DTPJJ Jussi Jokinen 20.00 50.00
DTPJK Jakub Klepis 10.00 25.00
DTPJM Jay McClement/15
DTPJS Jim Slater 20.00 50.00
DTPJT Jeff Tambellini/30 15.00 40.00
DTPJW Jeff Woywitka 10.00 25.00
DTPKB Keith Ballard 10.00 25.00
DTPMJ Milan Jurcina/30 20.00 50.00
DTPMK Mikko Koivu 20.00 50.00
DTPMO Alvaro Montoya 20.00 50.00
DTPMR Mike Richards 25.00 60.00
DTPMT Maxime Talbot 10.00 25.00
DTPPB Peter Budaj 25.00 60.00
DTPPP Petr Prucha/30 30.00 60.00
DTPRB Rene Bourque 20.00 50.00
DTPRC Ryane Clowe/10
DTPRG Ryan Getzlaf 30.00 80.00
DTPRJ R.J. Umberger/35 15.00 40.00
DTPRN Robert Nilsson 15.00 40.00
DTPRO Rostislav Olesz 15.00 40.00
DTPRS Ryan Suter 15.00 40.00
DTPRW Ryan Whitney 15.00 40.00
DTPSB Steve Bernier/25 30.00 80.00
DTPSC Sidney Crosby/1
DTPSI Jordan Sigalet/35 25.00 50.00
DTPTF Tomas Fleischmann 15.00 40.00
DTPTV Thomas Vanek 40.00 100.00
DTPWW Wojtek Wolski 20.00 50.00
DTPYD Yann Danis 20.00 50.00
DTPZP Zach Parise 30.00 80.00

2005-06 Ultimate Collection Ultimate Debut Threads Patches Autographs

PRINT RUN 10 #'d SETS
NOT PRICED DUE TO SCARCITY

2005-06 Ultimate Collection Ultimate Patches

PRINT RUN 75 SER #'d COPIES
UNIQUE PATCHES MAY EARN SUBSTANTIAL PREMIUM
PAO Alexander Ovechkin 150.00 250.00
PAS Alexander Steen 12.00 30.00
PAY Alexei Yashin 10.00 25.00
PBS Brendan Shanahan 12.00 30.00
PBT Bryan Trottier 15.00 40.00
PCO Corey Perry 10.00 25.00
PCP Chris Pronger 10.00 25.00
PDH Dominik Hasek 15.00 40.00
PDP Dion Phaneuf 20.00 50.00
PDW Doug Weight 8.00 20.00
PEL Eric Lindros 10.00 25.00
PES Eric Staal 12.00 30.00
PGB Gilbert Brule 12.00 30.00
PGH Gordie Howe/10
PHE Dany Heatley 15.00 40.00
PHL Henrik Lundqvist 20.00 50.00
PHT Hannu Toivonen 10.00 25.00
PIK Ilya Kovalchuk 15.00 40.00
PJC Jeff Carter 15.00 40.00
PJI Jarome Iginla 15.00 40.00
PJJ Jaromir Jagr 20.00 50.00
PJO Joe Thornton 20.00 50.00
PJR Jeremy Roenick 15.00 40.00
PJS Joe Sakic 20.00 50.00
PJT Jose Theodore 12.00 30.00
PKL Kari Lehtonen 10.00 25.00
PLR Luc Robitaille 10.00 25.00
PMA Martin St. Louis 8.00 20.00
PMB Martin Brodeur 25.00 60.00
PMG Marian Gaborik 15.00 40.00
PMH Milan Hejduk 10.00 25.00
PML Mario Lemieux 30.00 80.00
PMM Mike Modano 15.00 40.00
PMN Markus Naslund 12.00 30.00
PMS Mats Sundin 12.00 30.00
PMT Marty Turco 10.00 25.00
PPB Patrice Bergeron 12.00 30.00
PPD Pavel Datsyuk 20.00 40.00
PPE Phil Esposito 12.00 30.00
PPF Peter Forsberg/35 20.00 50.00
PPK Paul Kariya 10.00 25.00
PPM Patrick Marleau 8.00 20.00
PPR Patrick Roy 30.00 80.00
PRB Ray Bourque 15.00 40.00
PRG Ryan Getzlaf 15.00 40.00
PRL Roberto Luongo 15.00 40.00
PSC Sidney Crosby 200.00 300.00
PSF Sergei Fedorov 12.00 30.00
PSG Simon Gagne 8.00 20.00
PSK Saku Koivu 10.00 25.00
PSP Jason Spezza 10.00 25.00
PSY Steve Yzerman 25.00 60.00
PTB Todd Bertuzzi 10.00 25.00
PTS Teemu Selanne 10.00 25.00
PTV Tomas Vokoun 12.00 30.00
PVA Thomas Vanek 15.00 40.00
PVL Vincent Lecavalier 12.00 30.00

2005-06 Ultimate Collection Ultimate Patches Dual

PRINT RUN 25 SER #'d SETS
UNIQUE PATCHES MAY EARN SUBSTANTIAL PREMIUMS
DPAL Jason Allison 20.00 50.00
Eric Lindros
DPBR Patrice Bergeron 25.00 60.00
Andrew Raycroft
DPCR Jeff Carter
Mike Richards
DPFP Peter Forsberg
Keith Primeau
DPFZ Johan Franzen 25.00 60.00
Henrik Zetterberg
DPHC Dominik Hasek 30.00 80.00
Zdeno Chara
DPHY Gordie Howe 150.00 300.00
Steve Yzerman
DPJD Jason Spezza 40.00 100.00
Dany Heatley
DPJL Curtis Joseph 15.00 40.00
David Leneveu
DPKH Ilya Kovalchuk 30.00 80.00
Marian Hossa

DPKP Saku Koivu 15.00 40.00
Alexander Perezhogin
DPKV Paul Kariya/Tomas Vokoun 20.00 50.00
DPLC Mario Lemieux 200.00 450.00
Sidney Crosby
DPLS Joffrey Lupul 25.00 60.00
Teemu Selanne
DPML Alvaro Montoya 30.00 80.00
Henrik Lundqvist
DPNB Rick Nash
Gilbert Brule
DPOC Alexander Ovechkin 350.00 600.00
Sidney Crosby
DPPG Corey Perry
Ryan Getzlaf
DPPI Dion Phaneuf 75.00 150.00
Jarome Iginla
DPRT Patrick Roy 150.00 250.00
Jose Theodore
DPSB Brent Seabrook 15.00 40.00
Cam Barker
DPSH Joe Sakic 25.00 60.00
Milan Hejduk
DPSL Martin St. Louis 20.00 50.00
Vincent Lecavalier
DPSY Brendan Shanahan 40.00 80.00
Steve Yzerman
DPTD Jose Theodore 15.00 40.00
Yann Danis
DPTL Hannu Toivonen 40.00 100.00
Kari Lehtonen
DPWN Cam Ward 25.00 50.00
Kevin Nastiuk

2005-06 Ultimate Collection Ultimate Patches Triple

PRINT RUN 5 SER #'d SETS
NOT PRICED DUE TO SCARCITY

2005-06 Ultimate Collection Ultimate Signatures

A Jason Spezza card recently was confirmed to exist.

USAO Alexander Ovechkin 75.00 150.00
USAP Alexander Perezhogin 4.00 10.00
USAR Andrew Raycroft 4.00 10.00
USAT Alex Tanguay SP 15.00 40.00
USAY Alexei Yashin 4.00 10.00
USBC Bobby Clarke 10.00 25.00
USBL Brian Leetch 6.00 15.00
USBM Brenden Morrow 4.00 10.00
USBP Bernie Parent 10.00 25.00
USBR Brad Richards 8.00 20.00
USCH Jonathan Cheechoo 6.00 15.00
USCN Cam Neely 12.00 30.00
USCW Cam Ward 10.00 25.00
USDH Dany Heatley SP 20.00 50.00
USDW Doug Weight 4.00 10.00
USEB Ed Belfour 10.00 25.00
USEC Erik Cole 4.00 10.00
USEN Eric Nystrom 4.00 10.00
USES Eric Staal EXCH 10.00 25.00
USGB Gilbert Brule 8.00 20.00
USGH Gordie Howe 40.00 60.00
USGP Gilbert Perreault 8.00 20.00
USHK Dominik Hasek 15.00 40.00
USHL Henrik Lundqvist 12.00 30.00
USHO Marian Hossa 4.00 10.00
USHT Hannu Toivonen 3.00 8.00
USHV Martin Havlat 3.00 10.00
USHZ Henrik Zetterberg 10.00 25.00
USIK Ilya Kovalchuk 15.00 40.00
USJB Jean Beliveau 12.00 30.00
USJC Jeff Carter 10.00 25.00
USJG Jean-Sebastien Giguere 4.00 10.00
USJH Jim Howard 8.00 20.00
USJI Jarome Iginla 8.00 20.00
USJO Joe Thornton 12.00 30.00
USJS Jason Spezza
USJT Jose Theodore 6.00 15.00
USKL Kari Lehtonen 6.00 15.00
USLR Luc Robitaille 8.00 20.00
USMB Martin Brodeur 40.00 80.00
USMF Marc-Andre Fleury 12.00 30.00
USMH Milan Hejduk 4.00 10.00
USML Manny Legace 4.00 10.00
USMM Mike Modano 10.00 25.00
USMN Markus Naslund 5.00 12.00
USMS Miroslav Satan 6.00 15.00
USMT Marty Turco 4.00 10.00
USNA Evgeni Nabokov 4.00 10.00
USNK Nikolai Khabibulin 6.00 15.00
USNZ Nikolai Zherdev 4.00 10.00
USON Jeff O'Neill 4.00 10.00
USPB Patrice Bergeron 8.00 20.00
USPE Phil Esposito SP 20.00 50.00
USPR Patrick Roy SP 125.00 250.00
USPY Corey Perry 5.00 12.00
USRB Ray Bourque SP 30.00 80.00
USRG Ryan Getzlaf 10.00 25.00
USRL Roberto Luongo 10.00 25.00
USRN Rick Nash 12.00 30.00
USRO Rostislav Olesz 3.00 10.00
USRS Ryan Suter 4.00 10.00
USRW Ryan Whitney 4.00 10.00
USRY Michael Ryder 4.00 10.00
USSC Sidney Crosby 125.00 250.00
USSG Simon Gagne 4.00 10.00
USSK Saku Koivu 8.00 20.00
USSL Martin St. Louis SP 15.00 40.00
USSM Ryan Smyth 8.00 20.00
USSN Scott Niedermayer 4.00 10.00
USST Alexander Steen 6.00 15.00
USSV Marek Svatos 5.00 12.00
USTB Todd Bertuzzi 4.00 10.00
USTE Tony Esposito 20.00 40.00
USTR Tuomo Ruutu 4.00 10.00
USTV Thomas Vanek 10.00 25.00
USVL Vincent Lecavalier 8.00 20.00
USWG Wayne Gretzky SP 200.00 350.00
USWW Wojtek Wolski 6.00 15.00
USYD Yann Danis 6.00 15.00

2005-06 Ultimate Collection Ultimate Signatures Foursomes

PRINT RUN 5 SER #'d SETS
NOT PRICED DUE TO SCARCITY

2005-06 Ultimate Collection Ultimate Signatures Logos

PRINT RUN 1/1
NOT PRICED DUE TO SCARCITY

2005-06 Ultimate Collection Ultimate Signatures Pairings

PRINT RUN 25 SER. #'d SETS
NOT PRICED DUE TO SCARCITY
UPCR Jeff Carter 100.00 200.00
Mike Richards

2005-06 Ultimate Collection Ultimate Signatures Trios

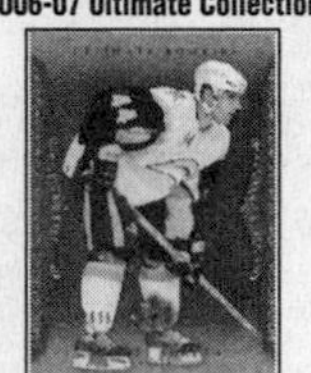

PRINT RUN 10 SER. #'d SETS
NOT PRICED DUE TO SCARCITY

2006-07 Ultimate Collection

1 Teemu Selanne 2.50 6.00
2 Ilya Kovalchuk 3.00 8.00
3 Kari Lehtonen 2.50 6.00
4 Patrice Bergeron 2.00 5.00
5 Bobby Orr 5.00 12.00
6 Ray Bourque 2.50 6.00
7 Phil Esposito 1.50 4.00
8 Ryan Miller 2.50 6.00
9 Gilbert Perreault 1.50 4.00
10 Miikka Kiprusoff 2.50 6.00
11 Jarome Iginla 4.00 10.00
12 Dion Phaneuf 2.50 6.00
13 Eric Staal 2.00 5.00
14 Cam Ward 4.00 10.00
15 Martin Havlat 2.50 6.00
16 Bobby Hull 1.50 4.00
17 Joe Sakic 4.00 10.00
18 Jose Theodore 2.50 6.00
19 Rick Nash 2.50 6.00
20 Mike Modano 2.50 6.00
21 Marty Turco 2.50 6.00
22 Henrik Zetterberg 2.50 6.00
23 Dominik Hasek 2.50 6.00
24 Nicklas Lidstrom 2.50 6.00
25 Gordie Howe 8.00 20.00
26 Ales Hemsky 2.50 6.00
27 Wayne Gretzky 8.00 20.00
28 Jari Kurri 1.00 2.50
29 Ed Belfour 6.00 15.00
30 Rob Blake 2.50 6.00
31 Marian Gaborik 4.00 10.00
32 Saku Koivu 2.50 6.00
33 Michael Ryder 2.50 6.00
34 Patrick Roy 5.00 12.00
35 Tomas Vokoun 2.50 6.00
36 Paul Kariya 2.50 6.00
37 Martin Brodeur 6.00 15.00
38 Alexei Yashin 2.00 5.00
39 Mike Bossy 2.50 6.00
40 Jaromir Jagr 3.00 8.00
41 Brendan Shanahan 2.50 6.00
42 Henrik Lundqvist 3.00 8.00
43 Dany Heatley 2.00 5.00
44 Jason Spezza 2.50 6.00
45 Peter Forsberg 3.00 8.00
46 Shane Doan 2.50 6.00
47 Sidney Crosby 10.00 25.00
48 Marc-Andre Fleury 2.50 6.00
49 Mario Lemieux 5.00 12.00
50 Joe Thornton 3.00 8.00
51 Jonathan Cheechoo 2.50 6.00
52 Patrick Marleau 2.50 6.00
53 Brad Richards 3.00 8.00
54 Vincent Lecavalier 2.50 6.00
55 Martin St. Louis 3.00 8.00
56 Mats Sundin 2.50 6.00
57 Andrew Raycroft 2.50 6.00
58 Markus Naslund 2.50 6.00
59 Roberto Luongo 5.00 12.00
60 Alexander Ovechkin 8.00 20.00
61 David McKee RC 5.00 12.00
62 Ryan Shannon RC 4.00 10.00
63 Clarke MacArthur RC 4.00 10.00
64 Andrej Sekera RC 2.00 5.00
65 Michael Funk RC 2.00 5.00
66 Adam Dennis RC 2.00 5.00
67 Mike Card RC 2.00 5.00
68 Brandon Prust RC 4.00 10.00
69 Troy Brouwer RC 4.00 10.00
70 Adam Burish RC 2.00 5.00
71 Fredrik Norrena RC 4.00 10.00
72 Stefan Liv RC 4.00 10.00
73 Tomas Kopecky RC 5.00 12.00
74 Jeff Drouin-Deslauriers RC 5.00 12.00
75 David Booth RC 4.00 10.00
76 Janis Sprukts RC 4.00 10.00
77 Barry Brust RC 5.00 12.00
78 Konstantin Pushkaryov RC 4.00 10.00
79 Shawn Belle RC 4.00 10.00
80 Niklas Backstrom RC 4.00 10.00
81 Mikhail Grabovski RC 4.00 10.00
82 Johnny Oduya RC 4.00 10.00
83 Blake Comeau RC 4.00 10.00
84 Jarkko Immonen RC 4.00 10.00
85 Josh Hennessy RC 4.00 10.00
86 Kelly Guard RC 5.00 12.00
87 Jussi Timonen RC 2.00 5.00
88 Martin Houle RC 5.00 12.00
89 Michel Ouellet RC 6.00 15.00
90 Yan Stastny RC 4.00 10.00
91 Roman Polak RC 2.00 5.00
92 Marek Schwarz RC 8.00 20.00
93 David Backes RC 3.00 8.00
94 Blair Jones RC 4.00 10.00
95 Karri Ramo RC 4.00 10.00
96 Ian White RC 4.00 10.00
97 Brendan Bell RC 4.00 10.00
98 Kris Newbury RC 4.00 10.00
99 Jean-Francois Racine RC 5.00 12.00
100 Jesse Schultz RC 4.00 10.00
101 Alexander Edler RC 4.00 10.00
102 Daren Machesney RC 4.00 10.00
103 Matt Lashoff AU RC 12.00 30.00
104 Phil Kessel AU/99 RC 60.00 120.00
105 Mark Stuart AU RC 12.00 30.00
106 Michael Blunden AU RC 12.00 30.00
107 Dave Bolland AU RC 25.00 60.00
108 Paul Stastny AU RC 50.00 100.00
109 Loui Eriksson AU RC 12.00 30.00
110 Niklas Grossman AU RC 12.00 30.00
111 Ladislav Smid AU RC 12.00 30.00
112 Patrick Thoresen AU RC 10.00 25.00
113 Marc-Antoine Pouliot AU RC 12.00 30.00
114 Anze Kopitar AU RC 40.00 80.00
115 Patrick O'Sullivan AU RC 12.00 30.00
116 Guillaume Latendresse AU RC 20.00 50.00
117 Alexander Radulov AU RC 25.00 50.00
118 Shea Weber AU RC 12.00 30.00
119 Travis Zajac AU RC 10.00 25.00
120 Nigel Dawes AU RC 12.00 30.00
121 Dustin Boyd AU RC 12.00 30.00
122 Ryan Potulny AU RC 12.00 30.00
123 Benoit Pouliot AU RC 12.00 30.00
124 Keith Yandle AU RC 12.00 30.00
125 Evgeni Malkin AU/99 RC 250.00 500.00
126 Kristopher Letang AU RC 15.00 40.00
127 Jordan Staal AU/99 RC 125.00 250.00
128 Noah Welch AU RC 12.00 30.00
129 Marc-Edouard Vlasic AU RC 12.00 30.00
130 Matt Carle AU RC 12.00 30.00
131 Drew Stafford AU RC 12.00 30.00
132 Eric Fehr AU RC 12.00 30.00

2006-07 Ultimate Collection Autographed Jerseys

STATED PRINT RUN 50 SER.#'d SETS
AJAF Alexander Frolov 12.00 30.00
AJAH Ales Hemsky 12.00 30.00
AJAR Andrew Raycroft 15.00 40.00
AJBB Brad Boyes 12.00 30.00
AJBH Bobby Hull 20.00 50.00
AJBM Brenden Morrow 15.00 40.00
AJBO Mike Bossy 15.00 40.00
AJBP Brad Park 10.00 25.00
AJBS Billy Smith 25.00 60.00
AJCN Cam Neely 15.00 40.00
AJCW Cam Ward 30.00 80.00
AJDH Dany Heatley 20.00 50.00
AJDP Denis Potvin 15.00 40.00
AJDT Dave Taylor 12.00 30.00
AJEL Patrik Elias 12.00 30.00
AJEM Evgeni Malkin 75.00 150.00
AJES Eric Staal 15.00 40.00
AJGC Gerry Cheevers 40.00 100.00
AJGF Grant Fuhr 30.00 80.00
AJGL Guy Lafleur 20.00 50.00
AJGP Gilbert Perreault 20.00 50.00
AJHA Dominik Hasek 25.00 60.00
AJIK Ilya Kovalchuk 25.00 60.00
AJJB Jean Beliveau 15.00 40.00
AJJG Jean-Sebastien Giguere 20.00 50.00
AJJI Jarome Iginla 30.00 80.00
AJJK Jari Kurri 12.00 30.00
AJJR Jeremy Roenick 20.00 50.00
AJJS Jordan Staal 50.00 125.00
AJJT Joe Thornton 30.00 80.00
AJKL Kari Lehtonen 20.00 50.00
AJLM Lanny McDonald 15.00 40.00
AJLR Larry Robinson 10.00 25.00
AJMB Martin Brodeur 50.00 100.00
AJMG Marian Gaborik 30.00 80.00
AJMK Miikka Kiprusoff 20.00 50.00
AJML Mario Lemieux 60.00 150.00
AJMM Mike Modano 25.00 60.00
AJMT Marty Turco 15.00 40.00
AJNL Nicklas Lidstrom 25.00 60.00
AJPE Phil Esposito 20.00 50.00
AJPH Dion Phaneuf 25.00 60.00
AJPK Phil Kessel 40.00 100.00
AJPM Patrick Marleau 15.00 40.00
AJPR Patrick Roy 75.00 175.00
AJRB Ray Bourque 25.00 60.00
AJRM Ryan Miller 20.00 50.00
AJRN Rick Nash 20.00 50.00
AJRV Rogie Vachon 30.00 80.00
AJRY Michael Ryder 15.00 40.00
AJSA Borje Salming 10.00 25.00
AJSC Sidney Crosby 150.00 250.00
AJSG Simon Gagne 20.00 50.00
AJTE Tony Esposito 30.00 80.00
AJTH Jose Theodore 20.00 50.00
AJTV Tomas Vokoun 15.00 40.00
AJVL Vincent Lecavalier 20.00 50.00
AJWG Wayne Gretzky 150.00 250.00

2006-07 Ultimate Collection Autographed Patches

STATED PRINT RUN 15 SER. #'d SETS
NOT PRICED DUE TO SCARCITY
AJAF Alexander Frolov
AJAH Ales Hemsky
AJAR Andrew Raycroft
AJBB Brad Boyes
AJBM Brenden Morrow
AJBO Mike Bossy
AJBP Brad Park
AJBS Billy Smith
AJCN Cam Neely
AJCW Cam Ward
AJDH Dany Heatley
AJDP Denis Potvin
AJDT Dave Taylor
AJEL Patrik Elias
AJEM Evgeni Malkin
AJES Eric Staal
AJGC Gerry Cheevers
AJGF Grant Fuhr
AJGL Guy Lafleur
AJGP Gilbert Perreault
AJHA Dominik Hasek
AJIK Ilya Kovalchuk
AJJB Jean Beliveau
AJJG Jean-Sebastien Giguere
AJJI Jarome Iginla
AJJK Jari Kurri
AJJR Jeremy Roenick
AJJS Jordan Staal
AJJT Joe Thornton
AJKL Kari Lehtonen
AJLM Lanny McDonald
AJLR Larry Robinson
AJMB Martin Brodeur
AJMG Marian Gaborik
AJMK Miikka Kiprusoff
AJML Mario Lemieux
AJMM Mike Modano
AJMT Marty Turco
AJNL Nicklas Lidstrom
AJPE Phil Esposito
AJPH Dion Phaneuf
AJPK Phil Kessel
AJPM Patrick Marleau
AJPR Patrick Roy
AJRB Ray Bourque
AJRM Ryan Miller
AJRN Rick Nash
AJRV Rogie Vachon
AJRY Michael Ryder
AJSA Borje Salming
AJSC Sidney Crosby
AJSG Simon Gagne
AJTH Jose Theodore
AJTV Tomas Vokoun
AJVL Vincent Lecavalier
AJWG Wayne Gretzky

2006-07 Ultimate Collection Jerseys

STATED PRINT RUN 200 SER.#'d SETS
UJAO Alexander Ovechkin 25.00 60.00
UJBC Bobby Clarke 8.00 20.00
UJBI Billy Smith 10.00 25.00
UJBR Martin Brodeur 20.00 50.00
UJBS Brendan Shanahan 6.00 15.00
UJCN Cam Neely 6.00 15.00
UJCW Cam Ward 12.00 30.00
UJDA Daniel Alfredsson 6.00 15.00
UJDH Dominik Hasek 10.00 25.00
UJDP Dion Phaneuf 8.00 20.00
UJDT Dave Taylor 4.00 10.00
UJEL Eric Lindros 8.00 20.00
UJEM Evgeni Malkin 20.00 50.00
UJES Eric Staal 6.00 15.00
UJGC Gerry Cheevers 6.00 15.00
UJGF Grant Fuhr 12.00 30.00
UJGL Guy Lafleur 8.00 20.00
UJGP Gilbert Perreault 5.00 12.00
UJGW Gump Worsley 4.00 10.00
UJHE Dany Heatley 8.00 20.00
UJHL Henrik Lundqvist 15.00 40.00
UJHZ Henrik Zetterberg 8.00 20.00
UJIK Ilya Kovalchuk 10.00 25.00
UJJB Jean Beliveau 6.00 15.00
UJJI Jarome Iginla 12.00 30.00
UJJJ Jaromir Jagr 12.00 30.00
UJJK Jari Kurri 5.00 12.00
UJJS Joe Sakic 15.00 40.00
UJJT Joe Thornton 12.00 30.00
UJKL Kari Lehtonen 8.00 20.00
UJLM Lanny McDonald 6.00 15.00
UJLR Larry Robinson 4.00 10.00
UJMB Mike Bossy 6.00 15.00
UJMD Marcel Dionne 5.00 12.00
UJMG Marian Gaborik 15.00 40.00
UJMH Milan Hejduk 8.00 20.00
UJML Mario Lemieux 15.00 40.00
UJMM Mike Modano 6.00 15.00
UJMN Markus Naslund 8.00 20.00
UJMR Michael Ryder 6.00 15.00
UJMS Mats Sundin 8.00 20.00
UJNL Nicklas Lidstrom 8.00 20.00
UJPB Patrice Bergeron 6.00 15.00
UJPF Peter Forsberg 12.00 30.00
UJPK Paul Kariya 8.00 20.00
UJPO Denis Potvin 6.00 15.00
UJPR Patrick Roy 15.00 40.00
UJPS Peter Stastny 6.00 15.00
UJRB Ray Bourque 10.00 25.00
UJRL Roberto Luongo 20.00 50.00
UJRN Rick Nash 8.00 20.00
UJSA Borje Salming 4.00 10.00
UJSC Sidney Crosby 25.00 60.00
UJSM Stan Mikita 5.00 12.00
UJSP Jason Spezza 8.00 20.00
UJSS Scott Stevens 3.00 8.00
UJST Martin St. Louis 8.00 20.00
UJTS Teemu Selanne 8.00 20.00
UJTV Tomas Vokoun 6.00 15.00
UJVL Vincent Lecavalier 8.00 20.00

2006-07 Ultimate Collection Jerseys Dual

STATED PRINT RUN 50 SER.#'d SETS
UJ2CM Sidney Crosby 40.00 100.00
Evgeni Malkin
UJ2CP Bobby Clarke 15.00 40.00
Gilbert Perreault
UJ2DB Darryl Sittler 8.00 20.00
Borje Salming
UJ2DV Marcel Dionne 8.00 20.00
Rogie Vachon
UJ2EE Phil Esposito 12.00 30.00
Tony Esposito
UJ2FG Peter Forsberg 12.00 30.00
Simon Gagne
UJ2GL Mario Lemieux 50.00 125.00
Wayne Gretzky
UJ2HL Dominik Hasek 10.00 25.00
Nicklas Lidstrom
UJ2HS Ryan Smyth 8.00 20.00
Ales Hemsky
UJ2JL Jaromir Jagr 20.00 50.00
Henrik Lundqvist
UJ2KA Paul Kariya 10.00 25.00
Jason Arnott
UJ2KI Jarome Iginla 15.00 40.00
Miikka Kiprusoff
UJ2KS Teemu Selanne 8.00 20.00
Jari Kurri
UJ2LN Markus Naslund 10.00 25.00
Roberto Luongo
UJ2LS Vincent Lecavalier 10.00 25.00
Martin St. Louis
UJ2ME Lanny McDonald 6.00 15.00
Ron Ellis
UJ2ML Mike Modano 10.00 25.00
Eric Lindros
UJ2MM Joe Mullen 6.00 15.00
Al MacInnis
UJ2NB Cam Neely 12.00 30.00
Patrice Bergeron
UJ2NL Pascal LeClaire 8.00 20.00
Rick Nash
UJ2RB Patrick Roy 15.00 40.00
Ray Bourque
UJ2RD Jeremy Roenick 6.00 15.00
Shane Doan
UJ2RP Denis Potvin 10.00 25.00
Larry Robinson
UJ2SH Jason Spezza 10.00 25.00
Dany Heatley
UJ2SS Joe Sakic 15.00 40.00
Peter Stastny
UJ2SW Eric Staal 8.00 20.00
Cam Ward
UJ2TC Joe Thornton 12.00 30.00
Jonathan Cheechoo
UJ2TH Milan Hejduk 6.00 15.00
Jose Theodore
UJ2ZD Pavel Datsyuk 10.00 25.00
Henrik Zetterberg

2006-07 Ultimate Collection Jerseys Triple

STATED PRINT RUN 25 SER.#'d SETS
UJ3CMS Sidney Crosby 175.00 300.00
Evgeni Malkin
Jordan Staal
UJ3ENK Phil Esposito 50.00 100.00
Cam Neely
Phil Kessel
UJ3GHL Mario Lemieux 125.00 250.00
Wayne Gretzky
Gordie Howe
UJ3LRS Guy Lafleur 25.00 60.00
Steve Shutt
Larry Robinson
UJ3OMK Ilya Kovalchuk 75.00 125.00
Alexander Ovechkin
Evgeni Malkin
UJ3RBL Patrick Roy 75.00 150.00
Martin Brodeur
Roberto Luongo
UJ3SBG Mike Bossy 40.00 80.00
Denis Potvin
Billy Smith
UJ3SFL Nicklas Lidstrom 50.00 100.00
Peter Forsberg
Mats Sundin
UJ3SSH Darryl Sittler 25.00 60.00
Borje Salming
Paul Henderson
UJ3STS Joe Sakic 50.00 100.00
Joe Thornton
Eric Staal

2006-07 Ultimate Collection Patches

STATED PRINT RUN 75 SER.#'d SETS
UNIQUE SWATCHES MAY EARN SUBSTANTIAL PRE-MIUM
UJAO Alexander Ovechkin 25.00 60.00
UJBC Bobby Clarke 15.00 40.00
UJBI Billy Smith 15.00 40.00
UJBR Martin Brodeur 25.00 60.00
UJBS Brendan Shanahan 15.00 40.00
UJCN Cam Neely 15.00 40.00
UJCW Cam Ward 15.00 40.00
UJDA Daniel Alfredsson 10.00 25.00
UJDH Dominik Hasek 20.00 50.00
UJDP Dion Phaneuf 15.00 40.00
UJDT Dave Taylor 10.00 25.00
UJEL Eric Lindros 15.00 40.00
UJEM Evgeni Malkin 40.00 100.00
UJES Eric Staal 15.00 40.00
UJGC Gerry Cheevers 10.00 25.00
UJGF Grant Fuhr 15.00 40.00
UJGL Guy Lafleur 15.00 40.00
UJGP Gilbert Perreault 12.00 30.00
UJGW Gump Worsley 15.00 40.00
UJHE Dany Heatley 20.00 50.00
UJHL Henrik Lundqvist 20.00 50.00
UJHZ Henrik Zetterberg 15.00 40.00
UJIK Ilya Kovalchuk 20.00 50.00
UJJI Jarome Iginla 20.00 50.00
UJJJ Jaromir Jagr 20.00 50.00
UJJK Jari Kurri 20.00 50.00
UJJS Joe Sakic 25.00 60.00
UJJT Joe Thornton 20.00 50.00
UJKL Kari Lehtonen 15.00 40.00
UJLM Lanny McDonald 10.00 25.00
UJLR Larry Robinson 10.00 25.00
UJMB Mike Bossy 10.00 25.00
UJMD Marcel Dionne 15.00 40.00
UJMG Marian Gaborik 20.00 50.00
UJMH Milan Hejduk 8.00 20.00
UJML Mario Lemieux 30.00 80.00
UJMM Mike Modano 15.00 40.00
UJMN Markus Naslund 15.00 40.00
UJMR Michael Ryder 10.00 25.00
UJMS Mats Sundin 15.00 40.00
UJNL Nicklas Lidstrom 15.00 40.00
UJPB Patrice Bergeron 10.00 25.00
UJPF Peter Forsberg 20.00 50.00
UJPK Paul Kariya 15.00 40.00
UJPR Patrick Roy 30.00 80.00
UJPS Peter Stastny 8.00 20.00
UJRB Ray Bourque 15.00 40.00
UJRL Roberto Luongo 20.00 50.00
UJRN Rick Nash 15.00 40.00
UJSA Borje Salming 10.00 25.00
UJSC Sidney Crosby 50.00 125.00
UJSM Stan Mikita 15.00 40.00
UJSP Jason Spezza 15.00 40.00
UJSS Scott Stevens 10.00 25.00
UJST Martin St. Louis 10.00 25.00
UJTS Teemu Selanne 15.00 40.00
UJTV Tomas Vokoun 10.00 25.00
UJVL Vincent Lecavalier 15.00 40.00

2006-07 Ultimate Collection Patches Dual

STATED PRINT RUN 25 SER.#'d SETS
NOT YET PRICED DUE TO LACK OF MARKET DATA
UJ2CM Sidney Crosby 250.00 400.00
Evgeni Malkin
UJ2CP Bobby Clarke 25.00 60.00
Gilbert Perreault
UJ2DB Darryl Sittler 20.00 50.00
Borje Salming
UJ2DV Marcel Dionne 40.00 100.00
Rogie Vachon/15
UJ2EE Phil Esposito 30.00 80.00
Tony Esposito
UJ2FG Peter Forsberg 20.00 50.00
Simon Gagne
UJ2GL Mario Lemieux 250.00 350.00
Wayne Gretzky
UJ2HL Dominik Hasek 25.00 60.00
Nicklas Lidstrom
UJ2HS Ryan Smyth 15.00 40.00
Ales Hemsky
UJ2JL Jaromir Jagr 30.00 80.00
Henrik Lundqvist
UJ2KA Paul Kariya 20.00 50.00
Jason Arnott
UJ2KI Jarome Iginla 25.00 60.00
Miikka Kiprusoff
UJ2KS Teemu Selanne 60.00 150.00
Jari Kurri
UJ2LN Markus Naslund 25.00 60.00
Roberto Luongo
UJ2LS Vincent Lecavalier 30.00 80.00
Martin St. Louis
UJ2ME Lanny McDonald 12.00 30.00
Ron Ellis
UJ2ML Mike Modano 25.00 60.00
Eric Lindros
UJ2MM Joe Mullen 25.00 60.00
Al MacInnis
UJ2NB Cam Neely 25.00 60.00
Patrice Bergeron
UJ2NL Pascal LeClaire 25.00 60.00
Rick Nash
UJ2RB Patrick Roy 60.00 150.00
Ray Bourque
UJ2RD Jeremy Roenick 20.00 50.00
Shane Doan
UJ2SH Jason Spezza 40.00 100.00
Dany Heatley
UJ2SS Joe Sakic 30.00 80.00
Peter Stastny
UJ2SW Eric Staal 15.00 40.00
Cam Ward
UJ2TC Joe Thornton 25.00 60.00
Jonathan Cheechoo
UJ2TH Milan Hejduk 20.00 50.00
Jose Theodore
UJ2ZD Pavel Datsyuk 40.00 100.00
Henrik Zetterberg

2006-07 Ultimate Collection Patches Triple

STATED PRINT RUN 5 SER.#'d SETS
NOT PRICED DUE TO SCARCITY

2006-07 Ultimate Collection Premium Patches

STATED PRINT RUN 25 SER.#'d SETS
UNIQUE SWATCHES MAY EARN PREMIUM
PSAF Alexander Frolov 25.00 60.00
PSAH Ales Hemsky 25.00 60.00
PSAK Alexei Kovalev 20.00 40.00
PSAM Al MacInnis 20.00 40.00
PSAR Andrew Raycroft 25.00 60.00
PSAS Alexander Steen 30.00 60.00
PSAT Alex Tanguay 30.00 60.00
PSAY Alexei Yashin 20.00 40.00
PSBL Rob Blake 30.00 60.00
PSBO Mike Bossy 30.00 60.00
PSBS Borje Salming 30.00 60.00
PSCD Chris Drury 20.00 40.00
PSCJ Curtis Joseph 40.00 80.00
PSCN Cam Neely 40.00 80.00
PSCW Cam Ward 40.00 80.00
PSDB Daniel Briere 30.00 60.00
PSDH Dominik Hasek 50.00 100.00
PSEL Eric Lindros 40.00 80.00
PSES Eric Staal 30.00 60.00
PSGW Gump Worsley 50.00 100.00
PSHA Martin Havlat 30.00 60.00
PSHE Milan Hejduk 25.00 60.00
PSHT Hannu Toivonen 30.00 60.00
PSIK Ilya Kovalchuk 25.00 80.00
PSJB Jay Bouwmeester 20.00 40.00
PSJG Jean-Sebastien Giguere 30.00 60.00
PSJJ Jaromir Jagr 50.00 100.00
PSJL Jere Lehtinen 30.00 80.00
PSJM Joe Mullen 20.00 40.00
PSJP Joni Pitkanen 20.00 40.00
PSJR Jeremy Roenick 40.00 80.00
PSJT Joe Thornton 50.00 100.00
PSKL Kari Lehtonen 30.00 60.00
PSLM Lanny McDonald 30.00 60.00
PSMA Maxim Afinogenov 20.00 40.00
PSMB Martin Brodeur 75.00 150.00
PSMG Marian Gaborik 40.00 80.00
PSMH Marian Hossa 30.00 60.00
PSMK Miikka Kiprusoff 40.00 100.00
PSMM Mike Modano 40.00 80.00
PSMN Markus Naslund 40.00 80.00
PSMP Michael Peca 20.00 40.00
PSMR Mark Recchi 20.00 40.00
PSMS Miroslav Satan 25.00 60.00
PSMT Marty Turco 30.00 60.00
PSOK Olaf Kolzig 40.00 80.00
PSPD Pavel Datsyuk 30.00 60.00
PSPE Patrik Elias 20.00 40.00
PSPL Pascal LeClaire 30.00 60.00
PSPM Patrick Marleau 30.00 60.00
PSRB Ray Bourque 50.00 100.00
PSRE Ron Ellis/20 30.00 60.00
PSRM Ryan Miller 40.00 80.00
PSRS Ryan Smyth 30.00 60.00
PSSF Sergei Fedorov 40.00 80.00
PSSZ Sergei Zubov 20.00 40.00
PSZC Zdeno Chara 20.00 40.00

2006-07 Ultimate Collection Premium Swatches

STATED PRINT RUN 50 SER.#'d SETS
PSAF Alexander Frolov 10.00 25.00
PSAH Ales Hemsky 10.00 25.00
PSAK Alexei Kovalev 10.00 25.00
PSAM Al MacInnis 10.00 25.00
PSAR Andrew Raycroft 12.00 30.00
PSAS Alexander Steen 12.00 30.00
PSAT Alex Tanguay 12.00 30.00
PSAY Alexei Yashin 10.00 25.00
PSBL Rob Blake 12.00 30.00
PSBO Mike Bossy 12.00 30.00
PSBS Borje Salming 8.00 20.00
PSCD Chris Drury 12.00 30.00
PSCJ Curtis Joseph 12.00 30.00
PSCN Cam Neely 10.00 25.00
PSCW Cam Ward 20.00 50.00
PSDB Daniel Briere 12.00 30.00
PSDG Doug Gilmour 10.00 25.00
PSDH Dominik Hasek 15.00 40.00
PSEL Eric Lindros 12.00 30.00
PSES Eric Staal 10.00 25.00
PSGW Gump Worsley 8.00 20.00
PSHA Martin Havlat 12.00 30.00
PSHE Milan Hejduk 12.00 30.00
PSHT Hannu Toivonen 15.00 40.00
PSIK Ilya Kovalchuk 20.00 50.00
PSJB Jay Bouwmeester 10.00 25.00
PSJG Jean-Sebastien Giguere 15.00 40.00
PSJJ Jaromir Jagr 20.00 50.00
PSJL Jere Lehtinen 10.00 25.00
PSJM Joe Mullen 10.00 25.00
PSJP Joni Pitkanen 10.00 25.00
PSJR Jeremy Roenick 12.00 30.00
PSJT Joe Thornton 20.00 50.00
PSKL Kari Lehtonen 15.00 40.00
PSLM Lanny McDonald 12.00 30.00
PSMA Maxim Afinogenov 10.00 25.00
PSMB Martin Brodeur 30.00 80.00
PSMG Marian Gaborik 25.00 60.00
PSMH Marian Hossa 12.00 30.00
PSMK Miikka Kiprusoff 15.00 40.00
PSMM Mike Modano 12.00 30.00
PSMN Markus Naslund 15.00 40.00
PSMP Michael Peca 10.00 25.00
PSMR Mark Recchi 10.00 25.00
PSMS Miroslav Satan 10.00 25.00
PSMT Marty Turco 12.00 30.00
PSMU Larry Murphy 5.00 12.00
PSOK Olaf Kolzig 15.00 40.00
PSPD Pavel Datsyuk 15.00 40.00
PSPE Patrik Elias 10.00 25.00
PSPL Pascal LeClaire 15.00 40.00

PSPM Patrick Marleau 12.00 30.00
PSRB Ray Bourque 10.00 25.00
PSRE Ron Ellis 5.00 12.00
PSRM Ryan Miller 15.00 40.00
PSRS Ryan Smyth 12.00 30.00
PSSF Sergei Fedorov 15.00 40.00
PSSS Scott Stevens 5.00 12.00
PSSZ Sergei Zubov 10.00 25.00
PSZC Zdeno Chara 10.00 25.00

2006-07 Ultimate Collection Rookies Autographed NHL Shields

STATED PRINT RUN 1/1
NOT PRICED DUE TO SCARCITY

2006-07 Ultimate Collection Rookies Autographed Patches

STATED PRINT RUN 25 #'d SETS
UNIQUE SWATCHES MAY EARN SUBSTANTIAL PREMIUM
103 Matt Lashoff 20.00 50.00
104 Phil Kessel 75.00 150.00
105 Mark Stuart 20.00 50.00
106 Michael Blunden 20.00 50.00
107 Dave Bolland 20.00 50.00
108 Paul Stastny 125.00 250.00
109 Loui Eriksson 20.00 50.00
110 Niklas Grossman 20.00 50.00
111 Ladislav Smid 20.00 50.00
112 Patrick Thoresen 25.00 60.00
113 Marc-Antoine Pouliot 25.00 60.00
114 Anze Kopitar 100.00 200.00
115 Patrick O'Sullivan 40.00 80.00
116 Guillaume Latendresse 75.00 150.00
117 Alexander Radulov 75.00 150.00
118 Shea Weber 25.00 60.00
119 Travis Zajac 40.00 80.00
120 Nigel Dawes 20.00 50.00
121 Dustin Boyd 40.00 80.00
122 Ryan Potulny 25.00 60.00
123 Benoit Pouliot 40.00 80.00
124 Keith Yandle 20.00 50.00
125 Evgeni Malkin 250.00 350.00
126 Kristopher Letang 40.00 80.00
127 Jordan Staal 125.00 250.00
128 Noah Welch 20.00 50.00
129 Marc-Edouard Vlasic 20.00 50.00
130 Matt Carle 40.00 80.00
131 Drew Stafford 75.00 150.00
132 Eric Fehr 25.00 60.00

2006-07 Ultimate Collection Signatures

USAF Alexander Frolov
USAH Ales Hemsky 3.00 8.00
USAK Anze Kopitar 12.00 30.00
USAM Al MacInnis 6.00 15.00
USAR Andrew Raycroft 5.00 12.00
USAT Alex Tanguay 5.00 12.00
USBB Brad Boyes 3.00 8.00
USBC Bobby Clarke 6.00 15.00
USBF Bernie Federko 3.00 8.00
USBH Bobby Hull SP 20.00 50.00
USBM Mike Bossy SP 20.00 50.00
USBO Pierre-Marc Bouchard 3.00 8.00
USBP Bernie Parent 8.00 20.00
USBR Richard Brodeur 5.00 12.00
USBU Johnny Bucyk 3.00 8.00
USCA Colby Armstrong 3.00 8.00
USCH Jonathan Cheechoo 6.00 15.00
USCI Dino Ciccarelli 3.00 8.00
USCN Cam Neely 8.00 20.00
USCW Cam Ward 6.00 15.00
USDC Don Cherry 15.00 40.00
USDH Dominik Hasek SP 20.00 50.00
USDR Dwayne Roloson 6.00 15.00
USDS Denis Savard 5.00 12.00
USEM Evgeni Malkin 40.00 80.00
USES Eric Staal 6.00 15.00
USGB Gilbert Brule 6.00 15.00
USGC Gerry Cheevers 10.00 25.00
USGF Grant Fuhr SP 12.00 30.00
USGH Gordie Howe 25.00 60.00
USGL Guillaume Latendresse 8.00 20.00
USGP Gilbert Perreault 6.00 15.00
USHA Dale Hawerchuk 3.00 8.00
USHE Dany Heatley SP 20.00 40.00
USHL Henrik Lundqvist 8.00 20.00
USIK Ilya Kovalchuk 8.00 20.00
USJA Jason Arnott 3.00 8.00
USJB Jean Beliveau SP 50.00 100.00
USJG Jean-Sebastien Giguere 5.00 12.00
USJI Jarome Iginla SP 10.00 25.00
USJK Jari Kurri 6.00 15.00
USJM Joe Mullen 3.00 8.00
USJO Johnny Bower 5.00 12.00
USKL Kari Lehtonen 6.00 15.00
USLR Larry Robinson 5.00 12.00
USMB Martin Brodeur SP 75.00 150.00
USMC Matt Carle 5.00 12.00
USMD Marcel Dionne 6.00 15.00
USMF Marc-Andre Fleury 6.00 15.00
USMG Marian Gaborik 8.00 20.00
USMH Martin Havlat 5.00 12.00
USMI Milan Hejduk 3.00 8.00
USML Mario Lemieux SP 100.00 200.00
USMM Mike Modano 8.00 20.00
USMR Michael Ryder 5.00 12.00
USMS Marek Svatos 3.00 8.00
USMT Marty Turco 5.00 12.00
USNL Nicklas Lidstrom 6.00 15.00
USOR Bobby Orr 75.00 150.00
USPB Patrice Bergeron 6.00 15.00
USPE Patrik Elias 3.00 8.00
USPH Phil Esposito SP 10.00 25.00
USPK Phil Kessel 10.00 25.00
USPM Patrick Marleau SP 8.00 20.00
USPO Denis Potvin 5.00 12.00
USPR Patrick Roy SP 125.00 225.00
USPS Paul Stastny 15.00 40.00
USRA Alexander Radulov 10.00 25.00
USRB Ray Bourque SP 40.00 100.00
USRH Ron Hextall 6.00 15.00
USRM Ryan Miller 8.00 20.00
USRN Rick Nash 6.00 15.00
USRS Ryan Smyth 5.00 12.00
USSB Steve Bernier 3.00 8.00
USSC Sidney Crosby 75.00 150.00
USSG Simon Gagne 6.00 15.00
USSK Saku Koivu SP 25.00 50.00
USSP Peter Stastny 3.00 8.00
USSS Scott Stevens 3.00 8.00
USST Jordan Staal 15.00 40.00
USTE Tony Esposito SP 12.00 30.00
USTH Joe Thornton SP 20.00 50.00
USTL Ted Lindsay 3.00 8.00
USTO Terry O'Reilly 5.00 12.00
USTV Tomas Vokoun 5.00 12.00
USVL Vincent Lecavalier SP 20.00 50.00
USVT Vesa Toskala 5.00 12.00
USWG Wayne Gretzky 100.00 200.00

2006-07 Ultimate Collection Ultimate Achievements

PRINT RUNS VARY
UNDER 10 NOT PRICED DUE TO SCARCITY
UABC Bobby Clarke/89 10.00 25.00
UABH Bobby Hull/58 15.00 40.00
UABO Bobby Orr/6 1000.00 1500.00
UABP Bernie Parent/47 15.00 40.00
UACN Cam Neely/9
UACW Cam Ward/15 50.00 100.00
UADH Dany Heatley/50 15.00 40.00
UAEM Evgeni Malkin/6
UAES Eric Staal/28 15.00 40.00
UAGF Grant Fuhr/23 30.00 60.00
UAGH Gordie Howe/26 60.00 125.00
UAGL Guy Lafleur/60 20.00 50.00
UAGP Gilbert Perreault/72 10.00 25.00
UAHA Dominik Hasek/41 20.00 50.00
UAIK Ilya Kovalchuk/52 12.00 30.00
UAJB Jean Beliveau/10 75.00 150.00
UAJC Jonathan Cheechoo/56 10.00 25.00
UAJI Jarome Iginla/52 15.00 40.00
UAJK Jari Kurri/68 10.00 25.00
UAJT Joe Thornton/96 12.00 30.00
UALR Luc Robitaille/63 20.00 50.00
UAMB Martin Brodeur/43 50.00 100.00
UAMD Marcel Dionne/53 12.00 30.00
UAMF Marc-Andre Fleury/40 20.00 40.00
UAMG Marian Gaborik/38 25.00 50.00
UAMH Milan Hejduk/50 6.00 15.00
UAMI Mike Bossy/9 125.00 200.00
UAMK Miikka Kiprusoff/42 20.00 50.00
UAML Mario Lemieux/8
UAMM Mike Modano/23 25.00 50.00
UANL Nicklas Lidstrom/80 12.00 30.00
UAPE Phil Esposito/76 12.00 30.00
UAPR Patrick Roy/23 125.00 250.00
UAPS Peter Stastny/70 8.00 20.00
UARN Rick Nash/41 15.00 40.00
UASC Sidney Crosby/39 125.00 250.00
UASK Saku Koivu/71 12.00 30.00
UATV Tomas Vokoun/36 12.00 30.00
UAVL Vincent Lecavalier/78 12.00 30.00
UAWG Wayne Gretzky/10 750.00 1000.00

2006-07 Ultimate Collection Ultimate Debut Threads Jerseys

STATED PRINT RUN 150 SER.#'d SETS
DJAK Anze Kopitar 8.00 20.00
DJAR Alexander Radulov 8.00 20.00
DJBB Brendan Bell 3.00 8.00
DJBO Dave Bolland 3.00 8.00
DJBP Benoit Pouliot 4.00 10.00
DJBT Billy Thompson 3.00 8.00
DJCG Carsen Germyn 3.00 8.00
DJDB Dustin Byfuglien 6.00 15.00
DJDK D.J. King 3.00 8.00
DJDP David Printz 3.00 8.00
DJDS Drew Stafford 6.00 15.00
DJDU Dustin Boyd 4.00 10.00
DJEF Eric Fehr 4.00 10.00
DJEM Evgeni Malkin 15.00 40.00
DJFD Frank Doyle 4.00 10.00
DJFN Filip Novak 3.00 8.00
DJGL Guillaume Latendresse 8.00 20.00
DJIW Ian White 3.00 8.00
DJJI Jarkko Immonen 3.00 8.00
DJJJ Jonas Johansson 3.00 8.00
DJJO John Oduya 3.00 8.00
DJJW Jeremy Williams 3.00 8.00
DJKL Kristopher Letang 5.00 12.00
DJKP Konstantin Pushkaryov 3.00 8.00
DJKY Keith Yandle 3.00 8.00
DJLB Luc Bourdon 5.00 12.00
DJLE Loui Eriksson 5.00 12.00
DJLS Ladislav Smid 3.00 8.00
DJMB Michael Blunden 3.00 8.00
DJMC Matt Carle 4.00 10.00
DJMI Mikko Lehtonen 3.00 8.00
DJMK Miroslav Kopriva 4.00 10.00
DJML Matt Lashoff 3.00 8.00
DJMM Masi Marjamaki 3.00 8.00
DJMO Michel Ouellet 4.00 10.00
DJMP Marc-Antoine Pouliot 4.00 10.00
DJMS Mark Stuart 3.00 8.00
DJMV Marc-Edouard Vlasic 3.00 8.00
DJNB Niklas Backstrom 4.00 10.00
DJND Nigel Dawes 5.00 12.00
DJNO Fredrik Norrena 4.00 10.00
DJNW Noah Welch 3.00 8.00
DJON Ben Ondrus 3.00 8.00
DJPK Phil Kessel 8.00 20.00
DJPO Patrick O'Sullivan 4.00 10.00
DJPR Brandon Prust 3.00 8.00
DJPS Paul Stastny 12.00 30.00
DJPT Patrick Thoresen 4.00 10.00
DJRO Roman Polak 3.00 8.00
DJRP Ryan Potulny 4.00 10.00
DJRS Ryan Shannon 3.00 8.00
DJSO Shane O'Brien 3.00 8.00
DJST Jordan Staal 12.00 30.00
DJSW Shea Weber 5.00 12.00
DJTK Tomas Kopecky 4.00 10.00
DJTZ Travis Zajac 4.00 10.00
DJYS Yan Stastny 3.00 8.00

2006-07 Ultimate Collection Ultimate Debut Threads Jerseys Autographs

STATED PRINT RUN 35 SER.#'d SETS
DJAK Anze Kopitar 30.00 80.00
DJAR Alexander Radulov 30.00 80.00
DJBB Brendan Bell 15.00 40.00
DJBO Dave Bolland 30.00 80.00
DJBP Benoit Pouliot 20.00 50.00
DJBT Billy Thompson 15.00 40.00
DJCG Carsen Germyn 15.00 40.00
DJDB Dustin Byfuglien 30.00 80.00
DJDK D.J. King 8.00 20.00
DJDP David Printz 15.00 40.00
DJDS Drew Stafford 15.00 40.00
DJDU Dustin Boyd 20.00 50.00
DJEF Eric Fehr 20.00 50.00
DJEM Evgeni Malkin 80.00 200.00
DJFD Frank Doyle 20.00 50.00
DJFN Filip Novak 15.00 40.00
DJGL Guillaume Latendresse 40.00 100.00
DJIW Ian White 15.00 40.00
DJJI Jarkko Immonen 15.00 40.00
DJJJ Jonas Johansson 8.00 20.00
DJJO John Oduya 15.00 40.00
DJJW Jeremy Williams 15.00 40.00
DJKL Kristopher Letang 25.00 60.00
DJKP Konstantin Pushkaryov 15.00 40.00
DJKY Keith Yandle 15.00 40.00
DJLB Luc Bourdon 20.00 50.00
DJLE Loui Eriksson 15.00 40.00
DJLS Ladislav Smid 15.00 40.00
DJMB Michael Blunden 15.00 40.00
DJMC Matt Carle 20.00 50.00
DJMI Mikko Lehtonen 8.00 20.00
DJMK Miroslav Kopriva 15.00 40.00
DJML Matt Lashoff 15.00 40.00
DJMM Masi Marjamaki 15.00 40.00
DJMO Michel Ouellet 25.00 60.00
DJMP Marc-Antoine Pouliot 20.00 50.00
DJMS Mark Stuart 15.00 40.00
DJMV Marc-Edouard Vlasic 15.00 40.00
DJNB Niklas Backstrom 15.00 40.00
DJND Nigel Dawes 15.00 40.00
DJNO Fredrik Norrena 15.00 40.00
DJNW Noah Welch 15.00 40.00
DJON Ben Ondrus 15.00 40.00
DJPK Phil Kessel 40.00 100.00
DJPO Patrick O'Sullivan 20.00 50.00
DJPR Brandon Prust 15.00 40.00
DJPS Paul Stastny 50.00 120.00
DJPT Patrick Thoresen 15.00 40.00
DJRO Roman Polak 8.00 20.00
DJRP Ryan Potulny 20.00 50.00
DJRS Ryan Shannon 15.00 40.00
DJSO Shane O'Brien 15.00 40.00
DJST Jordan Staal 50.00 125.00
DJSW Shea Weber 20.00 50.00
DJTK Tomas Kopecky 20.00 50.00
DJTZ Travis Zajac 25.00 60.00
DJYS Yan Stastny 15.00 40.00

2006-07 Ultimate Collection Ultimate Debut Threads Patches

STATED PRINT RUN 25 SER.#'d SETS
DJAK Anze Kopitar 50.00 125.00
DJAR Alexander Radulov 60.00 150.00
DJBB Brendan Bell 30.00 80.00
DJBO Dave Bolland 60.00 150.00
DJBP Benoit Pouliot 30.00 80.00
DJBT Billy Thompson 30.00 80.00
DJCG Carsen Germyn 30.00 80.00
DJDB Dustin Byfuglien 60.00 150.00
DJDK D.J. King 15.00 40.00
DJDP David Printz 25.00 60.00
DJDS Drew Stafford 30.00 80.00
DJDU Dustin Boyd 30.00 80.00
DJEF Eric Fehr 30.00 80.00
DJEM Evgeni Malkin 150.00 300.00
DJFD Frank Doyle 30.00 80.00
DJFN Filip Novak 25.00 60.00
DJGL Guillaume Latendresse 40.00 100.00
DJIW Ian White 25.00 60.00
DJJI Jarkko Immonen 30.00 80.00
DJJJ Jonas Johansson 12.00 30.00
DJJO John Oduya 25.00 60.00
DJJW Jeremy Williams 25.00 60.00
DJKL Kristopher Letang 40.00 100.00
DJKP Konstantin Pushkaryov 30.00 80.00
DJKY Keith Yandle 25.00 60.00
DJLB Luc Bourdon 30.00 80.00
DJLE Loui Eriksson 40.00 100.00
DJLS Ladislav Smid 25.00 60.00
DJMB Michael Blunden 25.00 60.00
DJMC Matt Carle 30.00 80.00
DJMI Mikko Lehtonen 12.00 30.00
DJMK Miroslav Kopriva 25.00 60.00
DJML Matt Lashoff 25.00 60.00
DJMM Masi Marjamaki 25.00 60.00
DJMO Michel Ouellet 40.00 100.00
DJMP Marc-Antoine Pouliot 30.00 80.00
DJMS Mark Stuart 30.00 80.00
DJMV Marc-Edouard Vlasic 25.00 60.00
DJNB Niklas Backstrom 25.00 60.00
DJND Nigel Dawes 25.00 60.00
DJNO Fredrik Norrena 25.00 60.00
DJNW Noah Welch 25.00 60.00
DJON Ben Ondrus 25.00 60.00
DJPK Phil Kessel 80.00 200.00
DJPO Patrick O'Sullivan 30.00 80.00
DJPR Brandon Prust 25.00 60.00
DJPS Paul Stastny 100.00 250.00
DJPT Patrick Thoresen 25.00 60.00
DJRO Roman Polak 12.00 30.00
DJRP Ryan Potulny 30.00 80.00
DJRS Ryan Shannon 25.00 60.00
DJSO Shane O'Brien 25.00 60.00
DJST Jordan Staal 100.00 250.00
DJSW Shea Weber 30.00 80.00
DJTK Tomas Kopecky 30.00 80.00
DJTZ Travis Zajac 40.00 100.00
DJYS Yan Stastny 25.00 60.00

2006-07 Ultimate Collection Ultimate Debut Threads Patches Autographs

STATED PRINT RUN 10 SER.#'d SETS
NOT PRICED DUE TO SCARCITY

2006-07 Ultimate Collection Ultimate Signatures Logos

STATED PRINT RUN 1 SER.#'d SET
NOT PRICED DUE TO SCARCITY

2007-08 Ultimate Collection

COMP.SET w/o SP's (60) 100.00 200.00
STATED PRINT RUN 499 SER.#'d SETS
STATED PRINT RUN 499 SER.#'d SETS
STATED PRINT RUN 399 SER.#'d SETS
STATED PRINT RUN 99 SER.#'d SETS
1 Alexander Ovechkin 4.00 10.00
2 Roberto Luongo 2.00 5.00
3 Markus Naslund 1.25 3.00
4 Mats Sundin 1.25 3.00
5 Darcy Tucker 1.00 2.50
6 Darryl Sittler 1.00 2.50
7 Frank Mahovlich 2.00 5.00
8 Vincent Lecavalier 1.25 3.00
9 Martin St. Louis 1.00 2.50
10 Paul Kariya 1.25 3.00
11 Keith Tkachuk 1.00 2.50
12 Joe Thornton 1.50 4.00
13 Jonathan Cheechoo 1.00 2.50
14 Patrick Marleau 1.00 2.50
15 Mario Lemieux 4.00 10.00
16 Sidney Crosby 6.00 15.00
17 Marc-Andre Fleury 1.25 3.00
18 Evgeni Malkin 3.00 8.00
19 Shane Doan .75 2.00
20 Ron Hextall 2.00 5.00
21 Simon Gagne 1.25 3.00
22 Daniel Briere 1.25 3.00
23 Dany Heatley 1.50 4.00
24 Jason Spezza 1.25 3.00
25 Ray Emery 1.00 2.50
26 Jaromir Jagr 2.00 5.00
27 Brendan Shanahan 1.25 3.00
28 Henrik Lundqvist 1.50 4.00
29 Mike Bossy 1.00 2.50
30 Rick DiPietro 1.00 2.50
31 Martin Brodeur 3.00 8.00
32 Zach Parise 1.00 2.50
33 Alexander Radulov 1.25 3.00
34 Saku Koivu 1.00 2.50
35 Michael Ryder .75 2.00
36 Larry Robinson 1.50 4.00
37 Marian Gaborik 1.50 4.00
38 Wayne Gretzky 6.00 15.00
39 Anze Kopitar 1.25 3.00
40 Tomas Vokoun 1.25 3.00
41 Mark Messier 2.50 6.00
42 Dwayne Roloson 1.00 2.50
43 Dominik Hasek 1.50 4.00
44 Henrik Zetterberg 1.25 3.00
45 Gordie Howe 3.00 8.00
46 Mike Modano 1.25 3.00
47 Rick Nash 1.25 3.00
48 Joe Sakic 2.50 6.00
49 Patrick Roy 4.00 10.00
50 Paul Stastny 1.25 3.00
51 Bobby Hull 2.00 5.00
52 Eric Staal 1.25 3.00
53 Jarome Iginla 2.00 5.00
54 Miikka Kiprusoff 1.50 4.00
55 Thomas Vanek 1.00 2.50
56 Ryan Miller 1.25 3.00
57 Patrice Bergeron 1.25 3.00
58 Bobby Orr 5.00 12.00
59 Ilya Kovalchuk 1.50 4.00
60 Jean-Sebastien Giguere 1.25 3.00
61 T.J. Hensick RC 4.00 10.00
62 Jannik Hansen RC 3.00 8.00
63 Jaroslav Halak RC 15.00 40.00
64 Tom Gilbert RC 4.00 10.00
65 Jason Jaffray RC 3.00 8.00
66 Ryan O'Byrne RC 5.00 12.00
67 Steve Downie RC 4.00 10.00
68 David Moss RC 5.00 12.00
69 Mike Weber RC 3.00 8.00
70 Tomas Popperle RC 4.00 10.00
71 Daniel Girardi RC 3.00 8.00
72 Matt Keetley RC 4.00 10.00
73 Cal Clutterbuck RC 3.00 8.00
74 Tobias Stephan RC 4.00 10.00
75 Marc Methot RC 3.00 8.00
76 Matt Hunwick RC 4.00 10.00
77 Mike Lundin RC 3.00 8.00
78 Ryan Carter RC 4.00 10.00
79 Casey Borer RC 3.00 8.00
80 Martin Lojek RC 3.00 8.00
81 Mark Mancari RC 4.00 10.00
82 Jared Boll RC 3.00 8.00
83 Thomas Greiss RC 5.00 12.00
84 Bryan Young RC 3.00 8.00
85 Patrick Kaleta RC 3.00 8.00
86 Rod Pelley RC 3.00 8.00
87 Jonas Hiller RC 8.00 20.00
88 Magnus Johansson RC 3.00 8.00
89 Cory Murphy RC 3.00 8.00
90 Cody Bass RC 4.00 10.00
91 Craig Weller RC 3.00 8.00
92 Steve Wagner RC 3.00 8.00
93 Johnny Boychuk RC 3.00 8.00
94 Matt Ellis RC 3.00 8.00
95 Joel Lundqvist RC 3.00 8.00
96 Jonathan Quick RC 12.00 30.00
97 Daniel Winnik RC 3.00 8.00
98 Drew MacIntyre RC 4.00 10.00
99 Daniel Carcillo RC 4.00 10.00
100 John Zeiler RC 3.00 8.00
101 Brandon Dubinsky RC 5.00 12.00
102 Liam Reddox RC 3.00 8.00
103 Tomas Plihal RC 4.00 10.00
104 Frans Nielsen RC 3.00 8.00
105 Chris Conner RC 3.00 8.00
106 Jack Skille RC 5.00 12.00
107 Tyler Kennedy RC 5.00 12.00
108 Matt Moulson RC 3.00 8.00
109 Sergei Kostitsyn RC 15.00 40.00
110 Tanner Glass RC 3.00 8.00
111 Kent Huskins RC 3.00 8.00
112 Riley Cote RC 4.00 10.00
113 Antti Pihlstrom RC 4.00 10.00
114 Chris Bourque RC 4.00 10.00
115 David Jones RC 3.00 8.00
116 Lukas Kaspar RC 3.00 8.00
117 Nathan Guenin RC 3.00 8.00
118 Kris Russell RC 5.00 12.00
119 Tobias Enstrom RC 5.00 12.00
120 Anton Stralman RC 4.00 10.00
121 Bobby Ryan AU RC 25.00 60.00
122 Sam Gagner AU RC 12.00 30.00
123 Nicklas Bergfors AU RC 8.00 20.00
124 Erik Johnson AU RC 12.00 30.00
125 Jack Johnson AU RC 10.00 25.00
126 Jonathan Bernier AU RC 15.00 40.00
127 Bryan Little AU RC 8.00 20.00
128 Tuukka Rask AU RC 30.00 60.00
129 Matt Niskanen AU RC 6.00 15.00
130 Andrew Cogliano AU RC 15.00 40.00
131 Marc Staal AU RC 15.00 40.00
132 Nick Foligno AU RC 10.00 25.00
133 Brett Sterling AU RC 6.00 15.00
134 Martin Hanzal AU RC 8.00 20.00
135 Matt Smaby AU RC 6.00 15.00
136 Petr Kalus AU RC 6.00 15.00
137 Andy Greene AU RC 6.00 15.00
138 Ondrej Pavelec AU RC 10.00 25.00
139 Rob Schremp AU RC 8.00 20.00
140 Kyle Chipchura AU RC 10.00 25.00
141 Ryan Parent AU RC 8.00 20.00
142 David Krejci AU RC 12.00 30.00
143 Lauri Tukonen AU RC 6.00 15.00
144 James Sheppard AU RC 6.00 15.00
145 Mason Raymond AU RC 15.00 40.00
146 Devin Setoguchi AU RC 12.00 30.00
147 Curtis McElhinney AU RC 8.00 20.00
148 Brian Elliott AU RC 8.00 20.00
149 Drew Miller AU RC 6.00 15.00
150 Ryan Callahan AU RC 10.00 25.00
151 Ville Koistinen AU RC 6.00 15.00
152 Torrey Mitchell AU RC 8.00 20.00
153 David Perron AU RC 10.00 25.00
154 Milan Lucic AU RC 15.00 40.00
155 Jaroslav Hlinka AU RC 8.00 20.00
156 Tyler Weiman AU RC 8.00 20.00
157 Jonathan Toews AU/99 RC 150.00 300.00
158 Carey Price AU/99 RC 150.00 300.00
159 Patrick Kane AU/99 RC 125.00 250.00
160 Nicklas Backstrom AU/99 RC 50.00 120.00
161 Peter Mueller AU/99 RC 40.00 100.00
162 Jiri Tlusty AU/99 RC 30.00 80.00

2007-08 Ultimate Collection Autographed Jerseys

STATED PRINT RUN 25-50 SERIAL #'d SETS
SEE CHECKLIST BELOW
SOME NOT PRICED DUE TO SCARCITY
AJAK Anze Kopitar/50 12.00 30.00
AJAO Alexander Ovechkin/25 100.00 175.00
AJAT Alex Tanguay/50 10.00 25.00
AJBS Borje Salming/50 10.00 25.00
AJCN Cam Neely/25 20.00 50.00
AJCW Cam Ward/50 12.00 30.00
AJEM Evgeni Malkin/25 100.00 175.00
AJES Eric Staal/50 12.00 30.00
AJGF Grant Fuhr/25
AJGL Guy Lafleur/25 30.00 60.00
AJGP Gilbert Perreault/50 10.00 25.00
AJIK Ilya Kovalchuk/50
AJJG Jean-Sebastien Giguere/50 12.00 30.00
AJJI Jarome Iginla/25 20.00 50.00
AJJT Joe Thornton/25 20.00 50.00
AJLR Larry Robinson/50 15.00 40.00
AJMB Martin Brodeur/25 60.00 120.00
AJMF Marc-Andre Fleury/50 30.00 60.00
AJMG Marian Gaborik/25 20.00 50.00
AJMH Milan Hejduk/50 10.00 25.00
AJML Mario Lemieux/25 125.00 200.00
AJMM Mark Messier/25 125.00 200.00
AJMN Markus Naslund/50 12.00 30.00
AJMO Mike Modano/50 12.00 30.00
AJMR Michael Ryder/50 8.00 20.00
AJNL Nicklas Lidstrom/50 20.00 50.00
AJPR Patrick Roy/25 75.00 150.00
AJPS Peter Stastny/50 10.00 25.00
AJSC Sidney Crosby/25 150.00 300.00
AJSM Stan Mikita/50 20.00 50.00
AJTV Tomas Vokoun/50 12.00 30.00
AJVL Vincent Lecavalier/50 12.00 30.00
AJWG Wayne Gretzky/25 175.00 300.00

2007-08 Ultimate Collection Autographed Jerseys Dual

STATED PRINT RUN 10-20 SERIAL #'d SETS
SEE CHECKLIST BELOW
NOT PRICED DUE TO SCARCITY
AJ2BF Marc-Andre Fleury
Martin Brodeur/10
AJ2BP Gilbert Perreault
Johnny Bucyk/20
AJ2LM Mario Lemieux
Mark Messier/10
AJ2MS Stan Mikita
Peter Stastny/20
AJ2OM Evgeni Malkin
Alexander Ovechkin/10 EXCH
AJ2RG Wayne Gretzky
Patrick Roy/10

2007-08 Ultimate Collection Autographed Patches

STATED PRINT RUN 10-25 SERIAL #'d SETS
SOME NOT PRICED DUE TO SCARCITY
AJAK Anze Kopitar/25 40.00 100.00
AJAO Alexander Ovechkin/10
AJAT Alex Tanguay/25 15.00 40.00
AJBS Borje Salming/25 30.00 60.00
AJCN Cam Neely/10
AJCW Cam Ward/25 30.00 60.00
AJEM Evgeni Malkin/10
AJES Eric Staal/25 25.00 50.00
AJGF Grant Fuhr/10
AJGL Guy Lafleur/10
AJGP Gilbert Perreault/25 20.00 40.00
AJIK Ilya Kovalchuk/25 40.00 80.00
AJJG Jean-Sebastien Giguere/25 60.00 120.00
AJJI Jarome Iginla/10
AJJT Joe Thornton/10
AJLR Larry Robinson/25 20.00 50.00
AJMB Martin Brodeur/10
AJMF Marc-Andre Fleury/25 75.00 150.00
AJMG Marian Gaborik/10
AJMH Milan Hejduk/25 20.00 40.00
AJML Mario Lemieux/10
AJMM Mike Modano/25 20.00 50.00
AJMM Mark Messier/10
AJMN Markus Naslund/25 15.00 40.00
AJMR Michael Ryder/25 20.00 50.00
AJMS Martin St. Louis/25
AJNL Nicklas Lidstrom/25 60.00 120.00
AJPR Patrick Roy/10
AJPS Peter Stastny/25 20.00 50.00
AJSC Sidney Crosby/10
AJSM Stan Mikita/25 20.00 50.00
AJTV Tomas Vokoun/25 20.00 50.00
AJVL Vincent Lecavalier/25 50.00 100.00
AJWG Wayne Gretzky/10

2007-08 Ultimate Collection Autographed Patches Dual

STATED PRINT RUN 5-10 SERIAL #'d SETS
NOT PRICED DUE TO SCARCITY
AJ2BF Martin Brodeur
Marc-Andre Fleury/5
AJ2BP Gilbert Perreault
Johnny Bucyk/10
AJ2BR Larry Robinson
Ray Bourque/5
AJ2LM Mario Lemieux
Mark Messier/5
AJ2MS Stan Mikita
Peter Stastny/10

2007-08 Ultimate Collection Jerseys

STATED PRINT RUN 100 SER.#'d SETS
UJAH Ales Hemsky 3.00 8.00
UJAK Anze Kopitar 5.00 12.00

UJAO Alexander Ovechkin 15.00 40.00
UJAT Alex Tanguay 4.00 10.00
UJBC Bobby Clarke 5.00 12.00
UJBL Brian Leetch 5.00 12.00
UJBO Mike Bossy 4.00 10.00
UJBR Brad Richards 4.00 10.00
UJBS Billy Smith 5.00 12.00
UJCN Cam Neely 5.00 12.00
UJCW Cam Ward 5.00 12.00
UJDA Daniel Alfredsson 4.00 10.00
UJDB Daniel Briere 5.00 12.00
UJDH Dale Hawerchuk 4.00 10.00
UJDS Darryl Sittler 4.00 10.00
UJEM Evgeni Malkin 12.00 30.00
UJES Eric Staal 5.00 12.00
UJGP Gilbert Perreault 4.00 10.00
UJHA Dominik Hasek 6.00 15.00
UJHE Dany Heatley 6.00 15.00
UJHL Henrik Lundqvist 6.00 15.00
UJHZ Henrik Zetterberg 5.00 12.00
UJIK Ilya Kovalchuk 6.00 15.00
UJJC Jonathan Cheechoo 4.00 10.00
UJJG Jean-Sebastien Giguere 5.00 12.00
UJJI Jarome Iginla 8.00 20.00
UJJJ Jaromir Jagr 8.00 20.00
UJJO Joe Sakic 10.00 25.00
UJJS Jason Spezza 5.00 12.00
UJJT Joe Thornton 6.00 15.00
UJKL Kari Lehtonen 5.00 12.00
UJMB Martin Brodeur 12.00 30.00
UJMG Marian Gaborik 6.00 15.00
UJMK Miikka Kiprusoff 6.00 15.00
UJML Mario Lemieux 12.00 30.00
UJMM Mike Modano 5.00 12.00
UJMN Markus Naslund 5.00 12.00
UJMR Michael Ryder 3.00 8.00
UJMS Mats Sundin 5.00 12.00
UJPB Patrice Bergeron 5.00 12.00
UJPD Pavel Datsyuk 5.00 12.00
UJPF Peter Forsberg 6.00 15.00
UJPH Dion Phaneuf 5.00 12.00
UJPK Paul Kariya 5.00 12.00
UJPM Patrick Marleau 4.00 10.00
UJPR Patrick Roy 15.00 40.00
UJRB Ray Bourque 6.00 15.00
UJRL Roberto Luongo 8.00 20.00
UJRN Rick Nash 5.00 12.00
UJRS Ryan Smyth 4.00 10.00
UJSA Borje Salming 4.00 10.00
UJSC Sidney Crosby 25.00 50.00
UJSD Shane Doan 3.00 8.00
UJSG Simon Gagne 5.00 12.00
UJSH Brendan Shanahan 5.00 12.00
UJSK Saku Koivu 4.00 10.00
UJSS Scott Stevens 4.00 10.00
UJVL Vincent Lecavalier 5.00 12.00
UJWG Wayne Gretzky 25.00 50.00

2007-08 Ultimate Collection Jerseys Duos

STATED PRINT RUN 50 SERIAL #'d SETS
UJ2BB Johnny Bucyk 6.00 15.00
Patrice Bergeron
UJ2BS Martin Brodeur 15.00 40.00
Scott Stevens
UJ2CG Wayne Gretzky 60.00 120.00
Sidney Crosby
UJ2CS Sidney Crosby 40.00 80.00
Jordan Staal
UJ2DJ Jason Spezza 8.00 20.00
Dany Heatley
UJ2FK Alexander Frolov 6.00 15.00
Anze Kopitar
UJ2FR Grant Fuhr 12.00 30.00
Dwayne Roloson
UJ2GB Simon Gagne 10.00 25.00
Daniel Briere
UJ2GK Marian Gaborik 8.00 20.00
Mikko Koivu
UJ2HD Dominik Hasek 10.00 25.00
Pavel Datsyuk
UJ2HK Marian Hossa 6.00 15.00
Ilya Kovalchuk
UJ2IK Jarome Iginla 12.00 30.00
Miikka Kiprusoff
UJ2JL Jaromir Jagr 12.00 30.00
Henrik Lundqvist
UJ2JP Patrick Marleau 10.00 25.00
Joe Thornton
UJ2KW Paul Kariya 6.00 15.00
Doug Weight
UJ2LM Mario Lemieux 25.00 50.00
Mark Messier
UJ2LR Guy Lafleur
Michael Ryder
UJ2LZ Nicklas Lidstrom 6.00 15.00
Henrik Zetterberg
UJ2ME Mario Lemieux 40.00 80.00
Evgeni Malkin
UJ2MH Stan Mikita 12.00 30.00
Martin Havlat
UJ2MT Mike Modano 6.00 15.00
Marty Turco
UJ2NF Rick Nash 12.00 30.00
Sergei Fedorov
UJ2NK Cam Neely 12.00 30.00
Phil Kessel
UJ2NL Markus Naslund 10.00 25.00
Roberto Luongo
UJ2OM Alexander Ovechkin 20.00 50.00
Evgeni Malkin
UJ2PV Gilbert Perreault 10.00 25.00

Thomas Vanek
UJ2SH Joe Sakic 12.00 30.00
Milan Hejduk
UJ2SS Mats Sundin 5.00 12.00
Borje Salming
UJ2VB Vincent Lecavalier 6.00 15.00
Brad Richards
UJ2VH Tomas Vokoun 6.00 15.00
Nathan Horton

2007-08 Ultimate Collection Jerseys Trios

STATED PRINT RUN 25 SERIAL #'d SETS
UJ3BCP Bobby Clarke 30.00 60.00
Johnny Bucyk
Gilbert Perreault
UJ3BLS Guy Lafleur 25.00 50.00
Mike Bossy
Darryl Sittler
UJ3ISH Martin St. Louis 15.00 40.00
Dany Heatley
Jarome Iginla
UJ3LCG Mario Lemieux 125.00 200.00
Sidney Crosby
Wayne Gretzky
UJ3LPB Nicklas Lidstrom 30.00 60.00
Ray Bourque
Dion Phaneuf
UJ3OMR Evgeni Malkin
Alexander Ovechkin
Alexander Radulov
UJ3RBF Martin Brodeur 50.00 100.00
Marc-Andre Fleury
Patrick Roy
UJ3SKK Teemu Selanne 60.00 120.00
Saku Koivu
Jari Kurri
UJ3SLT Vincent Lecavalier
Joe Sakic
Joe Thornton
UJ3SNZ Mats Sundin 40.00 80.00
Henrik Zetterberg
Markus Naslund

2007-08 Ultimate Collection Patches

STATED PRINT RUN 25 SERIAL #'d SETS
UPAH Ales Hemsky 15.00 40.00
UPAK Anze Kopitar 15.00 40.00
UPAO Alexander Ovechkin 150.00 250.00
UPAR Alexander Radulov 12.00 30.00
UPAS Alexander Steen 15.00 40.00
UPAT Alex Tanguay 15.00 40.00
UPBR Brad Richards 30.00 60.00
UPBS Borje Salming 12.00 30.00
UPCN Cam Neely 10.00 25.00
UPCW Cam Ward 30.00 60.00
UPDA Daniel Alfredsson 20.00 50.00
UPDH Dale Hawerchuk 30.00 60.00
UPDR Dwayne Roloson
UPDW Doug Weight 15.00 40.00
UPES Eric Staal 20.00 50.00
UPHA Dominik Hasek 20.00 50.00
UPHE Dany Heatley 12.00 30.00
UPHL Henrik Lundqvist 30.00 60.00
UPHZ Henrik Zetterberg 15.00 40.00
UPIK Ilya Kovalchuk 20.00 50.00
UPJG Jean-Sebastien Giguere 12.00 30.00
UPJI Jarome Iginla 30.00 50.00
UPJJ Jaromir Jagr 30.00 60.00
UPJS Jason Spezza 15.00 40.00
UPJT Joe Thornton 12.00 30.00
UPKE Phil Kessel 30.00 60.00
UPKL Kari Lehtonen
UPLM Lanny McDonald 10.00 25.00
UPLR Larry Robinson 12.00 30.00
UPMB Martin Brodeur 30.00 60.00
UPMG Marian Gaborik 20.00 50.00
UPMH Marian Hossa 20.00 50.00
UPMI Milan Hejduk 12.00 30.00
UPMK Mikko Koivu 12.00 30.00
UPML Mario Lemieux 50.00 100.00
UPMM Mike Modano
UPMN Markus Naslund 12.00 30.00
UPMR Mark Recchi 10.00 25.00
UPMS Martin St. Louis 10.00 25.00
UPMT Marty Turco 10.00 25.00
UPNL Nicklas Lidstrom 15.00 40.00
UPPB Patrice Bergeron 20.00 50.00
UPPF Peter Forsberg
UPPK Paul Kariya
UPPR Patrick Roy 50.00 100.00
UPPS Peter Stastny
UPRB Ray Bourque 12.00 30.00
UPRG Ryan Getzlaf 15.00 40.00
UPRL Roberto Luongo
UPRN Rick Nash 30.00 60.00
UPRS Ryan Smyth 10.00 25.00
UPSA Joe Sakic
UPSC Sidney Crosby 150.00 300.00
UPSD Shane Doan 10.00 25.00
UPSF Sergei Fedorov 15.00 40.00
UPSG Simon Gagne 10.00 25.00
UPSH Brendan Shanahan 12.00 30.00
UPSK Saku Koivu 15.00 40.00
UPSU Mats Sundin
UPVL Vincent Lecavalier 10.00 25.00

2007-08 Ultimate Collection Patches Duos

STATED PRINT RUN 15 SERIAL #'d SETS
NOT PRICED DUE TO SCARCITY
UP2BL Roberto Luongo
Martin Brodeur
UP2BR Ray Bourque
Larry Robinson
UP2BS Mike Bossy
Billy Smith
UP2DF Sergei Fedorov
Pavel Datsyuk
UP2GG Jean-Sebastien Giguere
Ryan Getzlaf
UP2HK Marian Hossa
Ilya Kovalchuk
UP2HS Jason Spezza
Dany Heatley
UP2IM Jarome Iginla
Lanny McDonald
UP2KG Simon Gagne
Paul Kariya
UP2KK Mikko Koivu
Saku Koivu
UP2LC Jonathan Cheechoo
Vincent Lecavalier
UP2LL Kari Lehtonen
Henrik Lundqvist
UP2LS Nicklas Lidstrom
Borje Salming
UP2LZ Nicklas Lidstrom
Henrik Zetterberg
UP2MB Mats Sundin
Borje Salming
UP2MS Mario Lemieux
Sidney Crosby
UP2MT Mike Modano
Marty Turco
UP2MV Ryan Miller
Thomas Vanek
UP2NA Daniel Alfredsson
Markus Naslund
UP2NK Cam Neely
Phil Kessel
UP2OM Alexander Ovechkin
Evgeni Malkin
UP2RH Dwayne Roloson
Ales Hemsky
UP2RK Alexander Radulov
Anze Kopitar
UP2RS Patrick Roy
Joe Sakic
UP2SH Peter Stastny
Dale Hawerchuk
UP2SJ Brendan Shanahan
Jaromir Jagr
UP2SR Steve Shutt
Michael Ryder
UP2SS Joe Sakic
Ryan Smyth
UP2SW Eric Staal
Cam Ward
UP2VM Vincent Lecavalier
Martin St. Louis

2007-08 Ultimate Collection Patches Trios

STATED PRINT RUN 10 SERIAL #'d SETS
NOT PRICED DUE TO SCARCITY
UP3ISH Martin St. Louis
Dany Heatley
Jarome Iginla
UP3KGN Rick Nash
Paul Kariya
Simon Gagne
UP3LCG Mario Lemieux
Sidney Crosby
Wayne Gretzky
UP3LEK Ray Emery
Miikka Kiprusoff
Roberto Luongo
UP3MDP Mike Modano
Zach Parise
Chris Drury
UP3OMR Evgeni Malkin
Alexander Radulov
Alexander Ovechkin
UP3RBF Martin Brodeur
Marc-Andre Fleury
Patrick Roy
UP3SLT Joe Sakic
Joe Thornton
Vincent Lecavalier
UP3SNZ Henrik Zetterberg
Markus Naslund
Mats Sundin
UP3VJH Dominik Hasek
Tomas Vokoun
Jaromir Jagr

2007-08 Ultimate Collection Premium Patches

STATED PRINT RUN 25 SERIAL #'d SETS
PSAS Alexander Steen
PSBO Borje Salming 75.00 150.00
PSBS Billy Smith 40.00 80.00
PSBU Johnny Bucyk 20.00 50.00
PSCJ Jonathan Cheechoo 20.00 50.00
PSCN Cam Neely 30.00 60.00
PSCP Chris Pronger 30.00 60.00
PSDA Daniel Alfredsson 50.00 100.00
PSDC Dino Ciccarelli 12.00 30.00
PSDG Doug Gilmour 12.00 30.00
PSDH Dale Hawerchuk
PSEL Patrik Elias 10.00 25.00
PSGF Grant Fuhr 40.00 80.00
PSGP Gilbert Perreault 30.00 60.00
PSHE Dany Heatley 30.00 60.00
PSHL Henrik Lundqvist 40.00 80.00
PSHZ Henrik Zetterberg 30.00 60.00
PSIK Ilya Kovalchuk 50.00 100.00
PSJG Jean-Sebastien Giguere 15.00 40.00
PSJI Jarome Iginla 15.00 40.00
PSJJ Jaromir Jagr 75.00 150.00
PSJM Joe Mullen 15.00 40.00
PSJO Joe Sakic 30.00 60.00
PSJS Jason Spezza 30.00 60.00
PSJT Joe Thornton 20.00 50.00
PSLM Lanny McDonald 12.00 30.00
PSMA Al MacInnis 20.00 50.00
PSMB Martin Brodeur 40.00 80.00
PSMG Marian Gaborik 40.00 80.00
PSMH Marian Hossa
PSML Mario Lemieux 60.00 120.00
PSMM Mike Modano 20.00 50.00
PSMN Markus Naslund 15.00 40.00
PSMS Martin St. Louis 15.00 40.00
PSMT Marty Turco 15.00 40.00
PSNL Nicklas Lidstrom 20.00 50.00
PSOV Alexander Ovechkin 75.00 150.00
PSPB Patrice Bergeron 15.00 40.00
PSPD Pavel Datsyuk 75.00 150.00
PSPK Paul Kariya 30.00 60.00
PSPM Patrick Marleau 15.00 40.00
PSPR Patrick Roy 100.00 175.00
PSPS Peter Stastny
PSRB Ray Bourque 25.00 60.00
PSRL Roberto Luongo 30.00 60.00
PSRN Rick Nash 60.00 120.00
PSSC Sidney Crosby 100.00 200.00
PSSG Simon Gagne 20.00 50.00
PSSH Brendan Shanahan 20.00 50.00
PSSI Darryl Sittler 15.00 40.00
PSST Jordan Staal 15.00 40.00
PSSU Mats Sundin 15.00 40.00
PSVL Vincent Lecavalier
PSWG Wayne Gretzky 150.00 250.00

2007-08 Ultimate Collection Premium Swatches

STATED PRINT RUN 50 SERIAL #'d SETS
PSAS Alexander Steen 5.00 12.00
PSBO Borje Salming 6.00 15.00
PSBS Billy Smith 8.00 20.00
PSBU Johnny Bucyk 5.00 12.00
PSCJ Jonathan Cheechoo 6.00 15.00
PSCN Cam Neely 8.00 20.00
PSCP Chris Pronger 8.00 20.00
PSDA Daniel Alfredsson 6.00 15.00
PSDC Dino Ciccarelli 6.00 15.00
PSDG Doug Gilmour 6.00 15.00
PSDH Dale Hawerchuk
PSDS Denis Savard 6.00 15.00
PSEL Patrik Elias 5.00 12.00
PSGF Grant Fuhr 12.00 30.00
PSGP Gilbert Perreault 6.00 15.00
PSHE Dany Heatley 10.00 25.00
PSHL Henrik Lundqvist 10.00 25.00
PSHZ Henrik Zetterberg 8.00 20.00
PSIK Ilya Kovalchuk 10.00 25.00
PSJB Jean Beliveau 12.00 30.00
PSJG Jean-Sebastien Giguere 8.00 20.00
PSJI Jarome Iginla 12.00 30.00
PSJJ Jaromir Jagr 12.00 30.00
PSJM Joe Mullen 5.00 12.00
PSJO Joe Sakic 15.00 40.00
PSJS Jason Spezza 8.00 20.00
PSJT Joe Thornton 12.00 30.00
PSLM Lanny McDonald 5.00 12.00
PSMA Al MacInnis 6.00 15.00
PSMB Martin Brodeur 15.00 40.00
PSMG Marian Gaborik 10.00 25.00
PSMH Marian Hossa 8.00 20.00
PSML Mario Lemieux 15.00 40.00
PSMM Mike Modano 8.00 20.00
PSMN Markus Naslund 8.00 20.00
PSMS Martin St. Louis 6.00 15.00
PSMT Marty Turco 8.00 20.00
PSNL Nicklas Lidstrom 8.00 20.00
PSOV Alexander Ovechkin 30.00 60.00
PSPB Patrice Bergeron 8.00 20.00
PSPD Pavel Datsyuk 8.00 20.00
PSPK Paul Kariya
PSPM Patrick Marleau 6.00 15.00
PSPR Patrick Roy
PSPS Peter Stastny 6.00 15.00
PSRB Ray Bourque 10.00 25.00
PSRH Ron Hextall 12.00 30.00
PSRL Roberto Luongo 12.00 30.00
PSRM Ryan Miller 8.00 20.00
PSRN Rick Nash 8.00 20.00
PSRY Michael Ryder 5.00 12.00
PSSC Sidney Crosby 30.00 60.00
PSSG Simon Gagne
PSSH Brendan Shanahan 8.00 20.00
PSSI Darryl Sittler 6.00 15.00
PSSK Saku Koivu 6.00 15.00
PSST Jordan Staal 10.00 25.00
PSSU Mats Sundin 8.00 20.00
PSVL Vincent Lecavalier 8.00 20.00
PSWG Wayne Gretzky 40.00 80.00

2007-08 Ultimate Collection Rookies Autographed NHL Shields

STATED PRINT RUN 1 SERIAL #'d SET
NOT PRICED DUE TO SCARCITY

2007-08 Ultimate Collection Rookies Autographed Patches

STATED PRINT RUN 25 SERIAL #'d SETS
121 Bobby Ryan 60.00 120.00
122 Sam Gagner 75.00 150.00
123 Nicklas Bergfors 20.00 50.00
124 Erik Johnson 175.00 300.00
125 Jack Johnson
126 Jonathan Bernier 75.00 150.00
127 Bryan Little
128 Tuukka Rask
129 Matt Niskanen
130 Andrew Cogliano 75.00 150.00
131 Marc Staal 40.00 80.00
132 Nick Foligno 30.00 60.00
133 Brett Sterling
134 Martin Hanzal 15.00 40.00
135 Matt Smaby 30.00 60.00
136 Petr Kalus 20.00 50.00
137 Andy Greene 20.00 50.00
138 Ondrej Pavelec
139 Rob Schremp
140 Kyle Chipchura 20.00 50.00
141 Ryan Parent 30.00 60.00
142 David Krejci
143 Lauri Tukonen 15.00 40.00
144 James Sheppard 20.00 50.00
145 Mason Raymond 60.00 120.00
146 Devin Setoguchi 50.00 100.00
147 Curtis McElhinney 15.00 40.00
148 Brian Elliott 15.00 40.00
149 Drew Miller 15.00 40.00
150 Ryan Callahan 40.00 80.00
151 Ville Koistinen 30.00 60.00
152 Torrey Mitchell 15.00 40.00
153 David Perron 40.00 80.00
154 Milan Lucic 100.00 200.00
155 Jaroslav Hlinka 15.00 40.00
156 Tyler Weiman 20.00 50.00
157 Jonathan Toews 200.00 350.00
158 Carey Price 300.00 400.00
159 Patrick Kane 250.00 350.00
160 Nicklas Backstrom 100.00 200.00
161 Peter Mueller 75.00 150.00
162 Jiri Tlusty 60.00 120.00

2007-08 Ultimate Collection Signatures

USAC Andrew Cogliano 10.00 25.00
USAO Alexander Ovechkin 40.00 80.00
USBO Bobby Orr 100.00 200.00
USBP Bernie Parent 8.00 20.00
USCP Carey Price 40.00 80.00
USEM Evgeni Malkin 30.00 60.00
USES Eric Staal 6.00 15.00
USGF Grant Fuhr 10.00 25.00
USGH Gordie Howe 50.00 100.00
USIK Ilya Kovalchuk 8.00 20.00
USJG Jean-Sebastien Giguere 6.00 15.00
USJJ Jack Johnson 6.00 15.00
USJK Jari Kurri 5.00 12.00
USJM Joe Mullen 4.00 10.00
USJS James Sheppard 4.00 10.00
USJT Joe Thornton 8.00 20.00
USLM Lanny McDonald 5.00 12.00
USMA Martin St. Louis 5.00 12.00
USMB Martin Brodeur 30.00 60.00
USMF Marc-Andre Fleury 15.00 40.00
USMG Marian Gaborik 8.00 20.00
USML Mario Lemieux 75.00 150.00
USMM Mark Messier 75.00 150.00
USMN Markus Naslund 6.00 15.00
USMR Michael Ryder 4.00 10.00
USMS Marc Staal 10.00 25.00
USNB Nicklas Backstrom 10.00 25.00
USNF Nick Foligno 6.00 15.00
USNL Nicklas Lidstrom 6.00 15.00
USPE Corey Perry 5.00 12.00
USPK Patrick Kane 30.00 60.00
USPM Peter Mueller 10.00 25.00
USPR Patrick Roy 60.00 120.00
USPS Paul Stastny 6.00 15.00
USRB Ray Bourque 15.00 40.00
USRH Ron Hextall 10.00 25.00
USRM Ryan Miller 6.00 15.00
USSC Sidney Crosby EXCH 100.00 175.00
USSG Sam Gagner 8.00 20.00
USST Jordan Staal 12.00 30.00
USTO Jonathan Toews 30.00 60.00
USTV Tomas Vokoun 6.00 15.00
USVL Vincent Lecavalier 8.00 20.00
USWG Wayne Gretzky 175.00 300.00

2007-08 Ultimate Collection Ultimate Achievements

STATED PRINT RUN 2-31 SERIAL #'d SETS
SOME NOT PRICED DUE TO SCARCITY
UAAF Alexander Frolov/6
UAAK Anze Kopitar/20
UAAO Adam Oates/5
UAAT Alex Tanguay/21
UABC Bobby Clarke/3
UABE Jean Beliveau/10
UABF Bernie Federko/10
UABH Bobby Hull/2
UABO Bobby Orr/3
UABP Bernie Parent/2
UABR Bill Ranford/16
UACH Jonathan Cheechoo/8
UACN Cam Neely/3
UACP Corey Perry/15
UACW Cam Ward/15
UADA Dany Heatley/10
UADC Dino Ciccarelli/4
UADG Doug Gilmour/7
UADH Dominik Hasek/8
UADR Dwayne Roloson/12
UADS Denis Savard/5
UADW Doug Wilson/7
UAEM Evgeni Malkin/6
UAEN Evgeni Nabokov/7
UAES Eric Staal/9
UAGF Grant Fuhr/5
UAGH Gordie Howe/6
UAGL Guy Lafleur/3
UAGP Gilbert Perreault/9
UAHA Dale Hawerchuk/6 EXCH
UAHE Milan Hejduk/23
UAIK Ilya Kovalchuk/3
UAJA Jason Arnott/12
UAJB Johnny Bucyk/2
UAJC Jeff Carter/23
UAJG Jean-Sebastien Giguere/13
UAJI Jarome Iginla/13
UAJK Jari Kurri/7
UAJM Joe Mullen/16
UAJS Jordan Staal/7
UAJT Joe Thornton/2
UAJW Justin Williams/8
UAKD Kris Draper/5
UALM Lanny McDonald/8
UALR Larry Robinson/10
UAMA Martin St. Louis/3
UAMB Martin Brodeur/6
UAMD Marcel Dionne/8
UAME Mark Messier/6
UAMF Marc-Andre Fleury/14
UAMG Marian Gaborik/12
UAMH Marian Hossa/18
UAML Mario Lemieux/6
UAMM Mike Modano/12
UAMR Michael Ryder/17
UAMS Marek Svatos/9
UAMT Marty Turco/3
UANH Nathan Horton/31 EXCH
UANL Nicklas Lidstrom/5
UAOV Alexander Ovechkin/6
UAPE Patrik Elias/6
UAPK Phil Kessel/5
UAPL Pat LaFontaine/7
UAPR Patrick Roy/3
UAPS Paul Stastny/20
UARB Ray Bourque/5
UARG Ryan Getzlaf/25
UARH Ron Hextall/4
UARM Ryan Miller/20
UASA Miroslav Satan/17
UASB Borje Salming/3
UASC Sidney Crosby/6 EXCH
UASD Shane Doan/7
UASG Simon Gagne/13
UASI Darryl Sittler/10
UASK Saku Koivu/22
UASM Stan Mikita/4
UASS Steve Shutt/9
UATH Tomas Holmstrom/5
UAVL Vincent Lecavalier/16
UAVO Tomas Vokoun/5
UAWG Wayne Gretzky/9

2007-08 Ultimate Collection Ultimate Debut Threads Jerseys

STATED PRINT RUN 200 SERIAL #'d SETS
DTAC Andrew Cogliano 10.00 25.00
DTAG Andy Greene 4.00 10.00
DTBA Nicklas Backstrom 8.00 20.00
DTBD Brandon Dubinsky 6.00 15.00
DTBE Brian Elliott 5.00 12.00
DTBL Bryan Little 5.00 12.00
DTBR Bobby Ryan 15.00 40.00
DTBS Brett Sterling 4.00 10.00
DTCM Curtis McElhinney 5.00 12.00
DTCP Carey Price 25.00 50.00
DTDK David Krejci 8.00 20.00
DTDP David Perron 5.00 12.00
DTEJ Erik Johnson 8.00 20.00
DTFN Frans Nielsen 4.00 10.00
DTHA Jannik Hansen 4.00 10.00
DTJB Jonathan Bernier 6.00 15.00
DTJH Jaroslav Hlinka 5.00 12.00
DTJJ Jack Johnson 6.00 15.00
DTJS James Sheppard 4.00 10.00
DTJT Jonathan Toews 15.00 40.00
DTKC Kyle Chipchura 6.00 15.00
DTKR Kris Russell 5.00 12.00
DTMH Martin Hanzal 5.00 12.00
DTML Milan Lucic 10.00 25.00
DTMN Matt Niskanen 4.00 10.00
DTMR Mason Raymond 5.00 12.00
DTMS Marc Staal 10.00 25.00
DTNB Nicklas Bergfors 5.00 12.00
DTNF Nick Foligno 6.00 15.00
DTPK Patrick Kane 15.00 40.00
DTPM Peter Mueller 6.00 15.00
DTRC Ryan Callahan 6.00 15.00
DTRP Ryan Parent 5.00 12.00
DTRS Rob Schremp 6.00 15.00
DTSG Sam Gagner 6.00 15.00
DTSM Matt Smaby 4.00 10.00
DTTM Torrey Mitchell 5.00 12.00
DTTS Tobias Stephan 5.00 12.00
DTTW Tyler Weiman 5.00 12.00

2007-08 Ultimate Collection Ultimate Debut Threads Jerseys Autographs

STATED PRINT RUN 35 SERIAL #'d SETS
DTAC Andrew Cogliano 20.00 50.00
DTAG Andy Greene 8.00 20.00
DTBA Nicklas Backstrom 40.00 80.00
DTBD Brandon Dubinsky 12.00 30.00
DTBE Brian Elliott 10.00 25.00
DTBL Bryan Little 10.00 25.00
DTBR Bobby Ryan 30.00 80.00
DTBS Brett Sterling 8.00 20.00
DTCM Curtis McElhinney 10.00 25.00
DTCP Carey Price 100.00 200.00
DTDK David Krejci 15.00 40.00
DTDP David Perron 12.00 30.00
DTEJ Erik Johnson 15.00 40.00
DTFN Frans Nielsen 8.00 20.00
DTHA Jannik Hansen 8.00 20.00
DTJB Jonathan Bernier
DTJH Jaroslav Hlinka 10.00 25.00
DTJJ Jack Johnson 30.00 60.00
DTJS James Sheppard 8.00 20.00
DTJT Jonathan Toews 75.00 150.00
DTKC Kyle Chipchura 12.00 30.00
DTLT Lauri Tukonen 8.00 20.00
DTMH Martin Hanzal 8.00 20.00
DTML Milan Lucic 20.00 50.00
DTMN Matt Niskanen 8.00 20.00
DTMR Mason Raymond 20.00 50.00
DTMS Marc Staal 20.00 50.00
DTNB Nicklas Bergfors
DTNF Nick Foligno 12.00 30.00
DTPK Patrick Kane 75.00 150.00
DTPM Peter Mueller 20.00 50.00
DTRC Ryan Callahan
DTRP Ryan Parent 10.00 25.00
DTRS Rob Schremp 10.00 25.00
DTSG Sam Gagner 30.00 60.00
DTSM Matt Smaby 8.00 20.00
DTTM Torrey Mitchell
DTTS Tobias Stephan
DTTW Tyler Weiman 10.00 25.00

2007-08 Ultimate Collection Ultimate Debut Threads Patches

STATED PRINT RUN 50 SERIAL #'d SETS
DTAC Andrew Cogliano 30.00 60.00
DTAG Andy Greene 10.00 25.00
DTBA Nicklas Backstrom 40.00 80.00
DTBD Brandon Dubinsky 12.00 30.00
DTBE Brian Elliott 12.00 30.00
DTBL Bryan Little 15.00 40.00
DTBR Bobby Ryan 15.00 40.00
DTBS Brett Sterling 12.00 30.00
DTCM Curtis McElhinney 10.00 25.00
DTCP Carey Price 100.00 200.00
DTDK David Krejci 20.00 50.00
DTDM Drew Miller 10.00 25.00
DTDP David Perron 15.00 40.00
DTEJ Erik Johnson 15.00 40.00
DTFN Frans Nielsen 15.00 40.00
DTHA Jannik Hansen 15.00 40.00
DTJB Jonathan Bernier 12.00 30.00
DTJH Jaroslav Hlinka 12.00 30.00
DTJJ Jack Johnson 15.00 40.00
DTJS James Sheppard 10.00 25.00
DTJT Jonathan Toews 100.00 200.00
DTKA Petr Kalus 12.00 30.00
DTKC Kyle Chipchura 20.00 50.00
DTKR Kris Russell 15.00 40.00
DTLT Lauri Tukonen 10.00 25.00
DTMH Martin Hanzal 10.00 25.00
DTML Milan Lucic 40.00 80.00
DTMN Matt Niskanen 10.00 25.00
DTMR Mason Raymond 10.00 25.00
DTMS Marc Staal 20.00 50.00
DTNB Nicklas Bergfors 12.00 30.00
DTNF Nick Foligno 15.00 40.00
DTPK Patrick Kane 100.00 200.00
DTPM Peter Mueller 30.00 60.00
DTRC Ryan Callahan 15.00 40.00
DTRP Ryan Parent 12.00 30.00
DTRS Rob Schremp 12.00 30.00
DTSG Sam Gagner 25.00 50.00
DTSM Matt Smaby 15.00 40.00
DTTM Torrey Mitchell 40.00 80.00
DTTS Tobias Stephan 15.00 40.00
DTTW Tyler Weiman 40.00 80.00

2007-08 Ultimate Collection Ultimate Debut Threads Patches Autographs

STATED PRINT RUN 10 SERIAL #'d SETS
NOT PRICED DUE TO SCARCITY
DTAC Andrew Cogliano
DTAG Andy Greene
DTBA Nicklas Backstrom
DTBD Brandon Dubinsky
DTBE Brian Elliott
DTBL Bryan Little
DTBR Bobby Ryan
DTBS Brett Sterling
DTCM Curtis McElhinney
DTCP Carey Price
DTDK David Krejci
DTDP David Perron
DTEJ Erik Johnson
DTFN Frans Nielsen
DTHA Jannik Hansen
DTJB Jonathan Bernier
DTJH Jaroslav Hlinka
DTJJ Jack Johnson
DTJS James Sheppard
DTJT Jonathan Toews
DTKC Kyle Chipchura
DTKR Kris Russell
DTLT Lauri Tukonen
DTMH Martin Hanzal
DTML Milan Lucic
DTMN Matt Niskanen
DTMR Mason Raymond
DTMS Marc Staal
DTNB Nicklas Bergfors
DTNF Nick Foligno
DTPK Patrick Kane
DTRC Ryan Callahan
DTRP Ryan Parent
DTRS Rob Schremp
DTSG Sam Gagner
DTSM Matt Smaby
DTTM Torrey Mitchell
DTTS Tobias Stephan
DTTW Tyler Weiman

2007-08 Ultimate Collection Ultimate Signatures Logos

STATED PRINT RUN 1 SERIAL #'d SET
NOT PRICED DUE TO SCARCITY
SLAC Andrew Cogliano
SLAO Alexander Ovechkin
SLCP Carey Price
SLCW Cam Ward
SLDC Dino Ciccarelli
SLEM Evgeni Malkin
SLGF Grant Fuhr
SLHA Dominik Hasek
SLIK Ilya Kovalchuk
SLJG Jean-Sebastien Giguere
SLJI Jarome Iginla
SLJM Joe Mullen
SLJT Joe Thornton
SLMB Martin Brodeur
SLMG Marian Gaborik
SLML Mario Lemieux
SLMM Mike Modano
SLMN Markus Naslund
SLMR Michael Ryder
SLNL Nicklas Lidstrom
SLPB Patrice Bergeron
SLPK Patrick Kane
SLPM Peter Mueller
SLRM Ryan Miller
SLSC Sidney Crosby
SLSG Simon Gagne
SLSK Saku Koivu
SLST Marc Staal
SLTO Jonathan Toews
SLVL Vincent Lecavalier

2008-09 Ultimate Collection

This 102-card set was released in May, 2009. It included 42 veterans and 60 rookies. The veterans were serial numbered to 299 along with 18 of the rookies. The next 36 rookies were serial numbered to 399 and included an on-card autograph. The final six rookies in the set were serial numbered to 99 and also included an on-card autograph. The Fabian Brunnstrom was released with two versions available. The serial numbering on 51 of the cards was set to 399, whil 48 of these cards were serial numbered to 99. Upper Deck can confirm there are only 99 of the cards in these cards in the market. Worthy of note, Brunnstrom signed the first 48 cards without damage in black ink, the remaining 51 were numbered to 399 and were signed in blue ink.

COMP.SET w/o SPs (42) 100.00 200.00

2008-09 Ultimate Collection

(43-60) PRINT RUN 299 SER.#'d SETS
(61-96) PRINT RUN 399 SER.#'d SETS
(97-102) PRINT RUN 99 SER.#'d SETS
BRUNSTROM BLACK INK #'d TO 99
BRUNSTROM BLUE INK #'d TO 399
1 Ilya Kovalchuk 2.00 5.00
2 Bobby Orr 5.00 12.00
3 Thomas Vanek 1.50 4.00
4 Jarome Iginla 3.00 8.00
5 Miikka Kiprusoff 1.50 4.00
6 Eric Staal 2.50 6.00
7 Patrick Kane 4.00 10.00
8 Jonathan Toews 5.00 12.00
9 Joe Sakic 2.50 6.00
10 Paul Stastny 1.50 4.00
11 Rick Nash 1.50 4.00
12 Mike Modano 1.50 4.00
13 Henrik Zetterberg 3.00 8.00
14 Wayne Gretzky 8.00 20.00
15 Mark Messier 3.00 8.00
16 Ray Bourque 3.00 8.00
17 Gordie Howe 6.00 15.00
18 Marian Gaborik 2.50 6.00
19 Carey Price 5.00 12.00
20 Saku Koivu 1.50 4.00
21 Patrick Roy 5.00 12.00
22 Martin Brodeur 3.00 8.00
23 Rick DiPietro 1.50 4.00
24 Markus Naslund 1.50 4.00
25 Henrik Lundqvist 3.00 8.00
26 Dany Heatley 2.00 5.00
27 Jason Spezza 2.00 5.00
28 Mike Richards 2.50 6.00
29 Shane Doan 1.00 2.50
30 Peter Mueller 2.00 5.00
31 Mario Lemieux 4.00 10.00
32 Sidney Crosby 8.00 20.00
33 Marc-Andre Fleury 1.50 4.00
34 Evgeni Malkin 4.00 10.00
35 Joe Thornton 2.50 6.00
36 Paul Kariya 1.50 4.00
37 Vincent Lecavalier 1.50 4.00
38 Martin St. Louis 1.50 4.00
39 Vesa Toskala 1.50 4.00
40 Pavel Datsyuk 1.50 4.00
41 Roberto Luongo 2.50 6.00
42 Alexander Ovechkin 6.00 15.00
43 Max Pacioretty RC 8.00 20.00
44 Justin Pogge RC 6.00 15.00
45 Tim Kennedy RC 5.00 12.00
46 Ben Bishop RC 5.00 12.00
47 Michal Repik RC 4.00 10.00
48 Brian Boyle RC 3.00 8.00
49 Brian Lee RC 3.00 8.00
50 John Curry RC 4.00 10.00
51 Ben Maxwell RC 5.00 12.00
52 Jamie McGinn RC 3.00 8.00
53 Jonas Frogren RC 4.00 10.00
54 Brendan Mikkelson RC 2.00 5.00
55 Ty Wishart RC 3.00 8.00
56 Mark Fistric RC 2.50 6.00
57 Matt D'Agostini RC 5.00 12.00
58 Trevor Lewis RC 3.00 8.00
59 Simeon Varlamov RC 25.00 60.00
60 Wayne Simmonds RC 3.00 8.00
61 Adam Pineault AU RC 6.00 15.00
62 Alex Goligoski AU RC 12.00 30.00
63 Alex Pietrangelo AU RC 10.00 25.00
64 Chris Stewart AU RC 8.00 20.00
65 Brandon Sutter AU RC 8.00 20.00
66 Claude Giroux AU RC 12.00 30.00
67 Colton Gillies AU RC 6.00 15.00
68 Darren Helm AU RC 10.00 25.00
69 Derick Brassard AU RC 12.00 30.00
70 Drew Doughty AU RC 20.00 50.00
71 Kenndal McArdle AU RC 6.00 15.00
72 Josh Bailey AU RC 10.00 25.00
73 James Neal AU RC 10.00 25.00
74 Justin Abdelkader AU RC 12.00 30.00
75 Nathan Gerbe AU RC 12.00 30.00
76 Kyle Okposo AU RC 12.00 30.00
77 Luca Sbisa AU RC 10.00 25.00
78 Luke Schenn AU RC 20.00 50.00
79 Mattias Ritola AU RC 8.00 20.00
80 Michael Frolik AU RC 12.00 30.00
81 Mikkel Boedker AU RC 10.00 25.00
82 Cory Schneider AU RC 12.00 30.00
83 Nikolai Kulemin AU RC 6.00 15.00
84 Oscar Moller AU RC 6.00 15.00
85 Patric Hornqvist AU RC 6.00 15.00
86 Patrik Berglund AU RC 15.00 40.00
87 Petr Vrana AU RC 8.00 20.00
88 Robbie Earl AU RC 5.00 12.00
89 Karl Alzner AU RC 10.00 25.00
90 Shawn Matthias AU RC 6.00 15.00

91 Steve Mason AU RC 40.00 80.00
92 T.J. Oshie AU RC 15.00 40.00
93 Viktor Tikhonov AU RC 6.00 15.00
94 Vladimir Mihalik AU RC 6.00 15.00
95 Zach Bogosian AU RC 12.00 30.00
96 Zach Boychuk AU RC 10.00 25.00
97 Nikita Filatov AU RC/99 50.00 120.00
98 Jakub Voracek AU RC/99 40.00 100.00
99 Fabian Brunnstrom AU RC/51 20.00 50.00
blue ink
99B Fabian Brunnstrom AU RC/48 20.00 50.00
black ink
100 Blake Wheeler AU RC/99 75.00 150.00
101 Kyle Turris AU RC/99 50.00 100.00
102 Steven Stamkos AU RC/99 200.00 400.00

2008-09 Ultimate Collection Debut Threads

STATED PRINT RUN 200 SER.#'d SETS
DT-AG Alex Goligoski 8.00 20.00
DT-AN Andreas Nodl 4.00 10.00
DT-AP Adam Pineault 4.00 10.00
DT-BB Brian Boyle 4.00 10.00
DT-BO Zach Boychuk 6.00 15.00
DT-BP Ben Bishop 6.00 15.00
DT-BS Brandon Sutter 5.00 12.00
DT-BW Blake Wheeler 10.00 25.00
DT-CG Colton Gillies 4.00 10.00
DT-DB Derick Brassard 8.00 20.00
DT-DD Drew Doughty 12.00 30.00
DT-DH Darren Helm 6.00 15.00
DT-EE Erik Ersberg 4.00 10.00
DT-FB Fabian Brunnstrom 6.00 15.00
DT-FR Michael Frolik 8.00 20.00
DT-GI Claude Giroux 8.00 20.00
DT-IZ Ilya Zubov 4.00 10.00
DT-JA Justin Abdelkader 8.00 20.00
DT-JE Jonathan Ericsson 6.00 15.00
DT-JN James Neal 6.00 15.00
DT-JV Jakub Voracek 8.00 20.00
DT-KO Kyle Okposo 8.00 20.00
DT-KP Kevin Porter 3.00 8.00
DT-KT Kyle Turris 8.00 20.00
DT-LK Lauri Korpikoski 4.00 10.00
DT-LS Luca Sbisa 6.00 15.00
DT-MA Shawn Matthias 4.00 10.00
DT-MB Mikkel Boedker 6.00 15.00
DT-MD Matt D'Agostini 6.00 15.00
DT-MF Mark Fistric 3.00 8.00
DT-MR Mattias Ritola 5.00 12.00
DT-NF Nikita Filatov 15.00 40.00
DT-NK Nikolai Kulemin 4.00 10.00
DT-NO Nathan Oystrick 4.00 10.00
DT-OM Oscar Moller 4.00 10.00
DT-PB Patrik Berglund 10.00 25.00
DT-PH Patric Hornqvist 4.00 10.00
DT-PI Alex Pietrangelo 6.00 15.00
DT-PV Petr Vrana 5.00 12.00
DT-RE Robbie Earl 3.00 8.00
DT-RJ Ryan Jones 5.00 12.00
DT-RS Ryan Stone 4.00 10.00
DT-SC Luke Schenn 12.00 30.00
DT-SM Steve Mason 15.00 40.00
DT-SS Steven Stamkos 15.00 40.00
DT-TO T.J. Oshie 10.00 25.00
DT-TS Tom Sestito 3.00 8.00
DT-VM Vladimir Mihalik 4.00 10.00
DT-VT Viktor Tikhonov 4.00 10.00
DT-ZB Zach Bogosian 8.00 20.00

2008-09 Ultimate Collection Debut Threads Autographs

STATED PRINT RUN 35 SER.#'d SETS
SDT-AG Alex Goligoski
SDT-AN Andreas Nodl 10.00 25.00
SDT-AP Adam Pineault 10.00 25.00
SDT-BB Brian Boyle
SDT-BO Zach Boychuk
SDT-BP Ben Bishop 15.00 40.00
SDT-BS Brandon Sutter
SDT-BW Blake Wheeler 20.00 50.00
SDT-CG Colton Gillies 10.00 25.00
SDT-DB Derick Brassard
SDT-DD Drew Doughty 20.00 50.00
SDT-DH Darren Helm 15.00 40.00
SDT-EE Erik Ersberg 10.00 25.00
SDT-FB Fabian Brunnstrom 15.00 40.00
SDT-FR Michael Frolik 20.00 50.00
SDT-GI Claude Giroux 20.00 50.00
SDT-IZ Ilya Zubov 10.00 25.00
SDT-JA Justin Abdelkader 20.00 50.00
SDT-JE Jonathan Ericsson 15.00 40.00
SDT-JN James Neal 15.00 40.00
SDT-JV Jakub Voracek 20.00 50.00
SDT-KO Kyle Okposo
SDT-KP Kevin Porter 8.00 20.00
SDT-KT Kyle Turris 20.00 50.00
SDT-LK Lauri Korpikoski 10.00 25.00
SDT-LS Luca Sbisa 15.00 40.00
SDT-MA Shawn Matthias 10.00 25.00
SDT-MB Mikkel Boedker 15.00 40.00
SDT-MD Matt D'Agostini
SDT-MF Mark Fistric
SDT-MR Mattias Ritola 12.00 30.00
SDT-NF Nikita Filatov 40.00 100.00
SDT-NK Nikolai Kulemin 10.00 25.00
SDT-NO Nathan Oystrick 10.00 25.00
SDT-OM Oscar Moller 10.00 25.00
SDT-PB Patrik Berglund 25.00 60.00
SDT-PH Patric Hornqvist 10.00 25.00
SDT-PI Alex Pietrangelo 15.00 40.00
SDT-PV Petr Vrana 12.00 30.00
SDT-RE Robbie Earl 12.00 30.00
SDT-RJ Ryan Jones 12.00 30.00
SDT-RS Ryan Stone 10.00 25.00
SDT-SC Luke Schenn 30.00 80.00
SDT-SM Steve Mason 60.00 120.00
SDT-SS Steven Stamkos 60.00 120.00
SDT-TO T.J. Oshie 25.00 60.00
SDT-TS Tom Sestito
SDT-VM Vladimir Mihalik 10.00 25.00
SDT-VT Viktor Tikhonov 10.00 25.00
SDT-ZB Zach Bogosian 20.00 50.00

2008-09 Ultimate Collection Debut Threads Patches

*PATCHES: .8X TO 2X DEBUT THREADS
STATED PRINT RUN 50 SER.#'d SETS

2008-09 Ultimate Collection Debut Threads Patches Autographs

STATED PRINT RUN 10 SER.#'d SETS
NOT PRICED DUE TO SCARCITY

2008-09 Ultimate Collection NHL Shields Autographs

STATED PRINT RUN 1 SER.#'d SET
NOT PRICED DUE TO SCARCITY

2008-09 Ultimate Collection NHL Shields Rookie Autographs

STATED PRINT RUN 1 SER.#'d SET
NOT PRICED DUE TO SCARCITY

2008-09 Ultimate Collection Premium Patches

STATED PRINT RUN 25 SER.#'d SETS
PS-AO Alexander Ovechkin
PS-CP Carey Price 60.00 120.00
PS-DH Dale Hawerchuk 12.00 30.00
PS-DP Dion Phaneuf 12.00 30.00
PS-EM Evgeni Malkin
PS-HZ Henrik Zetterberg 25.00 60.00
PS-IK Ilya Kovalchuk 15.00 40.00
PS-JC Jonathan Cheechoo
PS-JI Jarome Iginla 25.00 60.00
PS-JS Joe Sakic 50.00 100.00
PS-JT Joe Thornton 20.00 50.00
PS-KO Anze Kopitar
PS-LM Lanny McDonald
PS-MB Martin Brodeur
PS-MG Marian Gaborik 20.00 50.00
PS-MM Mike Modano 15.00 40.00
PS-MR Mike Richards 20.00 50.00
PS-MS Marc Savard 40.00 80.00
PS-NB Nicklas Backstrom
PS-NL Nicklas Lidstrom 12.00 30.00
PS-OJ Olli Jokinen 8.00 20.00
PS-PB Patrice Bergeron 12.00 30.00
PS-PD Pavel Datsyuk 12.00 30.00
PS-PK Patrick Kane
PS-PM Peter Mueller 15.00 40.00
PS-PS Paul Stastny 12.00 30.00
PS-RB Ray Bourque 25.00 60.00
PS-RG Ryan Getzlaf 15.00 40.00
PS-RM Ryan Miller 25.00 60.00
PS-RN Rick Nash
PS-SC Sidney Crosby 100.00 200.00
PS-SD Shane Doan
PS-SG Simon Gagne 20.00 50.00
PS-SK Saku Koivu 20.00 50.00
PS-SS Steve Shutt 12.00 30.00
PS-SZ Jason Spezza 15.00 40.00
PS-TO Jonathan Toews 50.00 100.00
PS-TS Teemu Selanne 25.00 60.00
PS-TV Thomas Vanek
PS-VL Vincent Lecavalier

2008-09 Ultimate Collection Rookie Patch Autographs

STATED PRINT RUN 25 SER.#'d SETS
121 Adam Pineault 15.00 40.00
122 Alex Goligoski 30.00 80.00
123 Alex Pietrangelo 25.00 60.00
124 Chris Stewart 25.00 60.00
125 Brandon Sutter
126 Claude Giroux 75.00 150.00
127 Colton Gillies 15.00 40.00
128 Darren Helm 25.00 60.00
129 Derick Brassard 30.00 80.00
130 Drew Doughty 50.00 120.00
131 Kenndal McArdle
132 Josh Bailey
133 James Neal 25.00 60.00
134 Justin Abdelkader 30.00 80.00
135 Nathan Gerbe 40.00 100.00
136 Kyle Okposo
137 Luca Sbisa 25.00 60.00
138 Luke Schenn 75.00 150.00
139 Mattias Ritola 20.00 50.00
140 Michael Frolik 30.00 80.00
141 Mikkel Boedker 25.00 60.00
142 Cory Schneider 30.00 80.00
143 Nikolai Kulemin 30.00 80.00
144 Oscar Moller 15.00 40.00
145 Patric Hornqvist 15.00 40.00
146 Patrik Berglund 40.00 100.00
147 Petr Vrana 20.00 50.00
148 Robbie Earl 12.00 30.00
150 Shawn Matthias 15.00 40.00
151 Steve Mason 125.00 250.00
152 T.J. Oshie 40.00 100.00
153 Viktor Tikhonov 15.00 40.00
154 Vladimir Mihalik 15.00 40.00
155 Zach Bogosian 30.00 80.00
156 Zach Boychuk 25.00 60.00
157 Nikita Filatov 75.00 150.00
158 Jakub Voracek 30.00 80.00
159 Fabian Brunnstrom 25.00 60.00
160 Blake Wheeler 125.00 250.00
161 Kyle Turris 30.00 80.00
162 Steven Stamkos 150.00 250.00

2008-09 Ultimate Collection Ultimate Jerseys

STATED PRINT RUN 100 SER.#'d SETS
UJ-AO Alexander Ovechkin 25.00 60.00
UJ-CN Cam Neely 8.00 20.00
UJ-CP Carey Price 20.00 50.00
UJ-EM Evgeni Malkin
UJ-HL Henrik Lundqvist 12.00 30.00
UJ-HZ Henrik Zetterberg 12.00 30.00
UJ-IK Ilya Kovalchuk 8.00 20.00
UJ-JI Jarome Iginla 12.00 30.00
UJ-JS Joe Sakic 10.00 25.00
UJ-MB Martin Brodeur 12.00 30.00
UJ-ME Mark Messier 12.00 30.00
UJ-ML Mario Lemieux 15.00 40.00
UJ-PD Pavel Datsyuk 6.00 15.00
UJ-PR Patrick Roy 20.00 50.00
UJ-RB Ray Bourque 12.00 30.00
UJ-RL Roberto Luongo 10.00 25.00
UJ-RN Rick Nash 6.00 15.00
UJ-SC Sidney Crosby 25.00 60.00
UJ-VL Vincent Lecavalier 6.00 15.00
UJ-WG Wayne Gretzky 25.00 60.00

2008-09 Ultimate Collection Ultimate Jerseys Autographs

STATED PRINT RUN 50 SER.#'d SETS
AJ-AK Anze Kopitar 10.00 25.00
AJ-AO Adam Oates
AJ-BL Brian Leetch 12.00 30.00
AJ-BR Martin Brodeur/25 50.00 100.00
AJ-CN Cam Neely/25
AJ-CP Carey Price 30.00 80.00
AJ-DH Dale Hawerchuk 10.00 25.00
AJ-EM Evgeni Malkin/25
AJ-ES Eric Staal 15.00 40.00
AJ-GF Grant Fuhr/25
AJ-GP Gilbert Perreault 10.00 25.00
AJ-HO Marian Hossa 15.00 40.00
AJ-HZ Henrik Zetterberg/25
AJ-IK Ilya Kovalchuk/25
AJ-JI Jarome Iginla/25
AJ-JS Jordan Staal 15.00 40.00
AJ-JT Joe Thornton/25
AJ-LR Larry Robinson 10.00 25.00
AJ-MF Marc-Andre Fleury 10.00 25.00
AJ-ML Mario Lemieux/25
AJ-MM Mark Messier/25
AJ-MO Mike Modano 10.00 25.00
AJ-MT Marty Turco
AJ-NL Nicklas Lidstrom
AJ-PB Patrice Bergeron 10.00 25.00
AJ-PK Patrick Kane 25.00 60.00
AJ-PR Patrick Roy/25
AJ-RG Ryan Getzlaf
AJ-RN Rick Nash
AJ-SC Sidney Crosby/25 250.00 400.00
AJ-SG Sam Gagner 15.00 40.00
AJ-VL Vincent Lecavalier 10.00 25.00
AJ-WG Wayne Gretzky/25

2008-09 Ultimate Collection Ultimate Jerseys Duos

STATED PRINT RUN 50 SER.#'d SETS
UJ2-HD Pavel Datsyuk 10.00 25.00
Henrik Zetterberg
UJ2-IK Jarome Iginla 10.00 25.00
Miikka Kiprusoff
UJ2-KM Ilya Kovalchuk 12.00 30.00
Evgeni Malkin
UJ2-LM Mario Lemieux 12.00 30.00
Evgeni Malkin
UJ2-LN Henrik Lundqvist 10.00 25.00
Markus Naslund
UJ2-LZ Nicklas Lidstrom 10.00 25.00
Henrik Zetterberg
UJ2-MT Marty Turco
Mike Modano
UJ2-OB Alexander Ovechkin 20.00 50.00
Nicklas Backstrom
UJ2-RB Patrick Roy 15.00 40.00
Martin Brodeur

2008-09 Ultimate Collection Ultimate Jerseys Duos Autographs

STATED PRINT RUN 20 SER.#'d SETS
NOT PRICED DUE TO SCARCITY
2UJ-BN Ray Bourque
Cam Neely
2UJ-DM Shane Doan
Peter Mueller
2UJ-GM Wayne Gretzky
Mark Messier/10
2UJ-HM Dominik Hasek
Ryan Miller
2UJ-LM Mario Lemieux
Evgeni Malkin/10
2UJ-MF Evgeni Malkin
Marc-Andre Fleury
2UJ-MK Evgeni Malkin
Ilya Kovalchuk
2UJ-RB Patrick Roy
Martin Brodeur/10
2UJ-SS Paul Stastny
Peter Stastny
2UJ-TB Jonathan Toews
Nicklas Backstrom
2UJ-ZD Henrik Zetterberg
Pavel Datsyuk

2008-09 Ultimate Collection Ultimate Jerseys Trios

STATED PRINT RUN 25 SER.#'d SETS
UJ3-FWD Vincent Lecavalier 15.00 40.00
Joe Thornton
Jarome Iginla
UJ3-HOF Wayne Gretzky 40.00 100.00
Mark Messier
Mario Lemieux
UJ3-NET Patrick Roy
Martin Brodeur
Carey Price
UJ3-RSN Evgeni Malkin 30.00 80.00
Ilya Kovalchuk
Alexander Ovechkin
UJ3-SWD Henrik Zetterberg 15.00 40.00
Nicklas Lidstrom
Henrik Lundqvist

2008-09 Ultimate Collection Ultimate Patches Autographs

STATED PRINT RUN 25 SER.#'d SETS
PRINT RUN 25 NOT PRICED DUE TO SCARCITY
AJ-AK Anze Kopitar 20.00 50.00
AJ-BL Brian Leetch 40.00 80.00
AJ-BR Martin Brodeur/10
AJ-CN Cam Neely/10
AJ-CP Carey Price 60.00 100.00
AJ-DH Dale Hawerchuk 20.00 50.00
AJ-EM Evgeni Malkin/10
AJ-ES Eric Staal 30.00 80.00
AJ-GF Grant Fuhr 20.00 50.00
AJ-GP Gilbert Perreault
AJ-HO Marian Hossa
AJ-HZ Henrik Zetterberg/10
AJ-IK Ilya Kovalchuk/10
AJ-JI Jarome Iginla/10
AJ-JS Jordan Staal 30.00 80.00
AJ-JT Joe Thornton/10
AJ-LR Larry Robinson
AJ-MF Marc-Andre Fleury 60.00 120.00
AJ-ML Mario Lemieux/10
AJ-MM Mark Messier/10
AJ-MO Mike Modano
AJ-NL Nicklas Lidstrom 20.00 50.00
AJ-PB Patrice Bergeron
AJ-PK Patrick Kane 60.00 120.00
AJ-PR Patrick Roy/10
AJ-SC Sidney Crosby/10
AJ-SG Sam Gagner
AJ-VL Vincent Lecavalier 20.00 50.00
AJ-WG Wayne Gretzky/10

2008-09 Ultimate Collection Ultimate Patches Duos

STATED PRINT RUN 15 SER.#'d SETS
NOT PRICED DUE TO SCARCITY
UJ2-HD Pavel Datsyuk
Henrik Zetterberg
UJ2-IK Jarome Iginla
Miikka Kiprusoff
UJ2-KM Ilya Kovalchuk
Evgeni Malkin
UJ2-LM Mario Lemieux
Evgeni Malkin
UJ2-LN Henrik Lundqvist
Markus Naslund
UJ2-LZ Nicklas Lidstrom
Henrik Zetterberg
UJ2-MT Marty Turco
Mike Modano
UJ2-OB Alexander Ovechkin
Nicklas Backstrom
UJ2-RB Patrick Roy
Martin Brodeur

2008-09 Ultimate Collection Ultimate Patches Duos Autographs

STATED PRINT RUN 10 SER.#'d SETS
NOT PRICED DUE TO SCARCITY
2UJ-BN Ray Bourque
Cam Neely
2UJ-GM Wayne Gretzky
Mark Messier/5
2UJ-HM Dominik Hasek
Ryan Miller
2UJ-KG Patrick Kane
Sam Gagner
2UJ-LM Mario Lemieux
Evgeni Malkin/5
2UJ-MF Evgeni Malkin
Marc-Andre Fleury
2UJ-MK Evgeni Malkin
Ilya Kovalchuk
2UJ-RB Patrick Roy
Martin Brodeur
2UJ-SS Paul Stastny
Peter Stastny
2UJ-TB Jonathan Toews
Nicklas Backstrom
2UJ-ZD Henrik Zetterberg
Pavel Datsyuk

2008-09 Ultimate Collection Ultimate Patches Trios

STATED PRINT RUN 10 SER.#'d SETS
NOT PRICED DUE TO SCARCITY
UJ3-HOF Wayne Gretzky
Mark Messier
Mario Lemieux
UJ3-NET Patrick Roy
Martin Brodeur
Carey Price
UJ3-RSN Evgeni Malkin
Ilya Kovalchuk
Alexander Ovechkin

2008-09 Ultimate Collection Ultimate Signatures

UNLISTED STARS 6.00 15.00
OVERALL AU ODDS 1 PER PACK
US-BK Mikkel Boedker 10.00 25.00
US-BL Brian Leetch 8.00 20.00
US-BO Bobby Orr 60.00 120.00
US-BR Martin Brodeur 50.00 100.00
US-BW Blake Wheeler 15.00 40.00
US-CA Carey Price 20.00 50.00
US-CG Claude Giroux 12.00 30.00
US-DH Dany Heatley 8.00 20.00
US-EM Evgeni Malkin 20.00 50.00
US-ES Eric Staal 8.00 20.00
US-FB Fabian Brunnstrom 10.00 25.00
US-GH Gordie Howe 50.00 100.00
US-JI Jarome Iginla 12.00 30.00
US-JM Joe Mullen 6.00 15.00
US-JS Jordan Staal 10.00 25.00
US-JV Jakub Voracek 12.00 30.00
US-KT Kyle Turris 15.00 40.00
US-LE Brian Lee 6.00 15.00
US-MB Mike Bossy 10.00 25.00
US-MG Marian Gaborik 10.00 25.00
US-ML Mario Lemieux 50.00 100.00
US-MM Mark Messier 40.00 80.00
US-MS Martin St. Louis 6.00 15.00
US-NF Nikita Filatov 10.00 25.00
US-NL Nicklas Lidstrom 10.00 25.00
US-PK Patrick Kane 15.00 40.00
US-PR Patrick Roy 60.00 120.00
US-PS Paul Stastny 6.00 15.00
US-RB Ray Bourque 15.00 40.00
US-RH Ron Hextall 12.00 30.00
US-SC Sidney Crosby 75.00 150.00
US-SS Steven Stamkos 25.00 60.00
US-TH Joe Thornton 10.00 25.00
US-VL Vincent Lecavalier 10.00 25.00
US-WG Wayne Gretzky 100.00 200.00

2009-10 Ultimate Collection

1-60 PRINT RUN 399 SER.#'d SETS
131-170 PRINT RUN 399 SER.#'d SETS
101-136 PRINT RUN 299 SER.#'d SETS
137-142 PRINT RUN 99 SER.#'d SETS
1 Alexander Ovechkin 6.00 15.00
2 Eric Staal 2.00 5.00
3 Marty Turco 1.25 3.00
4 Jarome Iginla 3.00 8.00
5 Martin St. Louis 1.50 4.00
6 Jonathan Toews 4.00 10.00
7 Thomas Vanek 1.50 4.00
8 Gordie Howe 6.00 15.00
9 Jeff Carter 1.50 4.00
10 Rick Nash 1.50 4.00
11 Jason Spezza 2.00 5.00
12 Carey Price 4.00 10.00
13 Devin Setoguchi 1.25 3.00
14 Tim Thomas 1.50 4.00
15 Paul Stastny 1.50 4.00
16 Mario Lemieux 4.00 10.00
17 Shea Weber 1.25 3.00
18 Zach Parise 1.50 4.00
19 Sam Gagner 2.00 5.00
20 Evgeni Malkin 4.00 10.00
21 Marian Gaborik 2.50 6.00
22 Henrik Zetterberg 3.00 8.00
23 Miikka Kiprusoff 1.50 4.00
24 Mark Messier 3.00 8.00
25 Zdeno Chara 1.00 2.50
26 Mike Richards 3.00 8.00
27 Luke Schenn 2.50 6.00
28 Ilya Kovalchuk 2.00 5.00
29 David Perron 1.25 3.00
30 Marc-Andre Fleury 1.50 4.00
31 Nicklas Lidstrom 2.00 5.00
32 Bobby Orr 6.00 15.00
33 Dany Heatley 3.00 8.00
34 Steven Stamkos 4.00 10.00
35 Roberto Luongo 4.00 10.00
36 Mike Modano 1.50 4.00
37 Bobby Ryan 2.00 5.00
38 Patrick Marleau 1.50 4.00
39 Patrick Roy 5.00 12.00
40 Cam Neely 2.50 6.00
41 Steve Mason 2.50 6.00
42 Vincent Lecavalier 2.00 5.00
43 Andrew Cogliano 2.00 5.00
44 Pavel Datsyuk 1.50 4.00
45 Ryan Miller 1.50 4.00
46 Wayne Gretzky 8.00 20.00
47 Saku Koivu 1.50 4.00
48 Patrick Kane 3.00 8.00
49 Henrik Lundqvist 3.00 8.00
50 Joe Thornton 3.00 8.00
51 Doug Gilmour 1.50 4.00
52 Teemu Selanne 3.00 8.00
53 Phil Kessel 1.50 4.00
54 Steve Yzerman 5.00 12.00
55 T.J. Oshie 2.50 6.00
56 Shane Doan 1.25 3.00
57 Martin Brodeur 4.00 10.00
58 Mike Bossy 1.50 4.00
59 Mikko Koivu 1.50 4.00
60 Sidney Crosby 8.00 20.00
101 Matt Beleskey AU RC 5.00 12.00
102 Sergei Shirokov AU RC EXCH 8.00 20.00
103 Logan Couture AU RC 10.00 25.00
104 Matt Gilroy AU RC 6.00 15.00
105 Mikael Backlund AU RC 8.00 20.00
106 Dmitry Kulikov AU RC 6.00 15.00
107 Christian Hanson AU RC 6.00 15.00
108 Kris Chucko AU RC 4.00 10.00
109 Perttu Lindgren AU RC 5.00 12.00
110 Artem Anisimov AU RC 6.00 15.00
111 Tyler Myers AU RC 40.00 80.00
112 Tyler Bozak AU RC 12.00 30.00
113 Yannick Weber AU RC 6.00 15.00
114 Viktor Stalberg AU RC 8.00 20.00
115 Ivan Vishnevskiy AU RC 6.00 15.00
116 Ryan O'Reilly AU RC 10.00 25.00
117 Brad Marchand AU RC 6.00 15.00
118 Cody Franson AU RC 5.00 12.00
119 Michael Del Zotto AU RC 10.00 25.00
120 Ville Leino AU RC 6.00 15.00
121 Jamie Benn AU RC 8.00 20.00
122 Antti Niemi AU RC 15.00 40.00
123 Devan Dubnyk AU RC 6.00 15.00
124 Erik Karlsson AU RC 15.00 40.00
125 Michael Grabner AU RC 6.00 15.00
126 Spencer Machacek AU RC 4.00 10.00
127 Colin Wilson AU RC 10.00 25.00
128 Jakub Kindl AU RC 6.00 15.00
129 Brian Salcido AU RC 4.00 10.00
130 Riku Helenius AU RC EXCH 5.00 12.00
131 Matt Pelech AU RC 5.00 12.00
132 Benn Ferriero AU RC 5.00 12.00
133 Bobby Sanguinetti AU RC 4.00 10.00
134 Matthew Corrente AU RC 5.00 12.00
135 Alec Martinez AU RC 5.00 12.00
136 Lars Eller AU RC 8.00 20.00
137 Matt Duchene AU RC/99 125.00 200.00
138 Victor Hedman AU RC/99 50.00 100.00
139 John Tavares AU RC/99 250.00 400.00
140 James van Riemsdyk AU RC/99 75.00 150.00
141 Evander Kane AU RC/99 60.00 120.00
142 Jonas Gustavsson AU RC/99 EXCH 60.00 120.00
131B Michal Neuvirth RC 8.00 20.00
132B Mikko Lehtonen RC 3.00 8.00
133B Andrei Loktionov RC 4.00 10.00
134B Colin McDonald RC 3.00 8.00
135B John Carlson RC 6.00 15.00
136B MacGregor Sharp RC 3.00 8.00
137B Tyler Eckford RC 2.50 6.00
138B Daniel Larsson RC 4.00 10.00
139B Tyler Ennis RC 8.00 20.00
140B Tom Pyatt RC 4.00 10.00
141B Peter Olvecky RC 3.00 8.00
142B Anton Khudobin RC 3.00 8.00
143 Steven Zalewski RC 2.50 6.00
144 T.J. Galiardi RC 4.00 10.00
145 John Negrin RC 2.50 6.00
146 Oskars Bartulis RC 5.00 12.00
147 Carl Gunnarsson RC 5.00 12.00
148 David Laliberte RC 3.00 8.00
149 Scott Parse RC
150 Andreas Thuresson RC 2.50 6.00
151 Dan Sexton RC 4.00 10.00
152 James Reimer RC 4.00 10.00
153 Ryan Vesce RC 2.50 6.00
154 James Wright RC 4.00 10.00
155 Mathieu Perreault RC 4.00 10.00
156 Phil Oreskovic RC 3.00 8.00
157 Ryan O'Marra RC 2.50 6.00
158 Vladimir Zharkov RC 3.00 8.00
159 Mario Bliznak RC 3.00 8.00
160 Alexander Salak RC 3.00 8.00
161 Chad Johnson RC 2.50 6.00
162 Danny Irmen RC 2.50 6.00
163 Jesse Joensuu RC 4.00 10.00
164 Ryan Wilson RC 3.00 8.00
165 Frazer McLaren RC 2.00 5.00
166 Mathieu Carle RC 4.00 10.00
167 Teemu Laakso RC 2.00 5.00
168 Braden Holtby RC 4.00 10.00
169 Mike Santorelli RC 2.00 5.00
170 Aaron Gagnon RC 2.00 5.00

2009-10 Ultimate Collection Debut Threads

STATED PRINT RUN 200 SER.#'d SETS
UDTAA Artem Anisimov 4.00 10.00
UDTAN Antti Niemi 10.00 25.00
UDTBM Brad Marchand 4.00 10.00
UDTCA Luca Caputi 4.00 10.00
UDTCF Cody Franson 3.00 8.00
UDTCH Christian Hanson 4.00 10.00
UDTCW Colin Wilson 6.00 15.00
UDTDE Michael Del Zotto 6.00 15.00
UDTDK Dmitry Kulikov 3.00 8.00
UDTEK Evander Kane 8.00 20.00
UDTGR Michael Grabner 4.00 10.00
UDTIV Ivan Vishnevskiy 4.00 10.00
UDTJB Jamie Benn 5.00 12.00
UDTJE Jhonas Enroth 4.00 10.00
UDTJG Jonas Gustavsson 8.00 20.00
UDTJT John Tavares 15.00 40.00
UDTJV James van Riemsdyk 8.00 20.00
UDTKA Erik Karlsson 10.00 25.00
UDTLC Logan Couture 6.00 15.00
UDTMB Mikael Backlund 5.00 12.00
UDTMD Matt Duchene 12.00 30.00
UDTMG Matt Gilroy 4.00 10.00
UDTPL Perttu Lindgren 3.00 8.00
UDTSS Sergei Shirokov 5.00 12.00
UDTTB Tyler Bozak 8.00 20.00
UDTTM Tyler Myers 12.00 30.00
UDTVH Victor Hedman 6.00 15.00
UDTVL Ville Leino 4.00 10.00
UDTVS Viktor Stalberg 5.00 12.00
UDTYW Yannick Weber 4.00 10.00

2009-10 Ultimate Collection Debut Threads Autographs

STATED PRINT RUN 50 SER.#'d SETS
SDTAA Artem Anisimov
SDTAN Antti Niemi 25.00 60.00
SDTCA Luca Caputi 10.00 25.00
SDTCF Cody Franson
SDTCH Christian Hanson
SDTCW Colin Wilson 15.00 40.00
SDTDE Michael Del Zotto 15.00 40.00
SDTDK Dmitry Kulikov 8.00 20.00
SDTEK Evander Kane EXCH 20.00 50.00
SDTGR Michael Grabner 10.00 25.00
SDTJB Jamie Benn 12.00 30.00
SDTJE Jhonas Enroth 10.00 25.00
SDTJG Jonas Gustavsson
SDTJT John Tavares 40.00 100.00
SDTJV James van Riemsdyk 20.00 50.00
SDTKA Erik Karlsson 25.00 60.00
SDTLC Logan Couture 15.00 40.00
SDTMB Mikael Backlund 12.00 30.00
SDTMD Matt Duchene 30.00 80.00
SDTMG Matt Gilroy 10.00 25.00
SDTTB Tyler Bozak 20.00 50.00
SDTTM Tyler Myers 30.00 80.00
SDTVL Ville Leino 10.00 25.00
SDTVS Viktor Stalberg 12.00 30.00
SDTYW Yannick Weber 10.00 25.00

2009-10 Ultimate Collection Debut Threads Patches

*SINGLES: 1X TO 2.5X THREADS
STATED PRINT RUN 35 SER.#'d SETS

2009-10 Ultimate Collection Debut Threads Patches Autographs

STATED PRINT RUN 25 SER.#'d SETS
SDTAA Artem Anisimov 25.00 60.00
SDTAN Antti Niemi 40.00 100.00
SDTCA Luca Caputi 40.00 80.00
SDTCF Cody Franson 30.00 60.00
SDTCH Christian Hanson 15.00 40.00
SDTCW Colin Wilson 25.00 60.00
SDTDE Michael Del Zotto 25.00 60.00
SDTDK Dmitry Kulikov 12.00 30.00
SDTEK Evander Kane 30.00 80.00
SDTGR Michael Grabner 40.00 80.00
SDTIV Ivan Vishnevskiy 15.00 40.00
SDTJB Jamie Benn 20.00 50.00
SDTJE Jhonas Enroth 15.00 40.00
SDTJG Jonas Gustavsson
SDTJT John Tavares 200.00 300.00
SDTJV James van Riemsdyk 30.00 80.00
SDTKA Erik Karlsson 40.00 100.00
SDTLC Logan Couture 25.00 60.00
SDTMB Mikael Backlund 25.00 60.00
SDTMD Matt Duchene 50.00 120.00
SDTMG Matt Gilroy 15.00 40.00
SDTTB Tyler Bozak 30.00 80.00
SDTTM Tyler Myers 50.00 120.00
SDTVL Ville Leino 25.00 60.00
SDTVS Viktor Stalberg 20.00 50.00
SDTYW Yannick Weber 15.00 40.00

2009-10 Ultimate Collection Premium Patches

STATED PRINT RUN 25 SER.#'d SETS
PSAC Andrew Cogliano 15.00 40.00
PSAO Alexander Ovechkin 50.00 120.00
PSBC Brian Campbell 10.00 25.00
PSBS Borje Salming 12.00 30.00
PSCN Cam Neely 20.00 50.00
PSDB Derick Brassard 12.00 30.00
PSDD Drew Doughty 25.00 60.00
PSDH Dale Hawerchuk 12.00 30.00
PSDP Dion Phaneuf 20.00 50.00
PSEM Evgeni Malkin 30.00 80.00
PSGA Glenn Anderson 12.00 30.00
PSHZ Henrik Zetterberg 25.00 60.00
PSIK Ilya Kovalchuk 15.00 40.00
PSJB Jay Bouwmeester 12.00 30.00
PSJC Jeff Carter 12.00 30.00
PSJI Jarome Iginla 25.00 60.00
PSJS Jordan Staal 15.00 40.00
PSJT Jonathan Toews 30.00 80.00
PSJV Jakub Voracek 12.00 30.00
PSKA Patrick Kane 25.00 60.00
PSKI Miikka Kiprusoff 12.00 30.00
PSLM Lanny McDonald 12.00 30.00
PSMB Martin Brodeur 30.00 80.00
PSMG Marian Gaborik 20.00 50.00
PSMK Mikko Koivu 12.00 30.00
PSMM Mike Modano 12.00 30.00
PSMR Mike Richards 25.00 60.00
PSNB Nicklas Backstrom 25.00 60.00
PSNL Nicklas Lidstrom 15.00 40.00
PSOJ Olli Jokinen 8.00 20.00
PSPB Patrice Bergeron 12.00 30.00
PSPD Pavel Datsyuk 12.00 30.00
PSPK Phil Kessel 12.00 30.00
PSPS Peter Stastny 12.00 30.00
PSRL Roberto Luongo 30.00 80.00
PSRM Ryan Miller 12.00 30.00
PSRN Rick Nash 12.00 30.00
PSRS Ryan Smyth 12.00 30.00
PSSC Sidney Crosby 60.00 150.00
PSSD Shane Doan 10.00 25.00
PSSG Sam Gagner 15.00 40.00
PSSH Steve Shutt 12.00 30.00
PSSK Saku Koivu 12.00 30.00
PSSP Jason Spezza 15.00 40.00
PSSS Steven Stamkos 30.00 80.00
PSST Paul Stastny 12.00 30.00
PSSY Steve Yzerman 40.00 100.00
PSTH Joe Thornton 25.00 60.00
PSTV Tomas Vokoun 12.00 30.00
PSZP Zach Parise 12.00 30.00

2009-10 Ultimate Collection Premium Swatches

STATED PRINT RUN 35 SER.#'d SETS
PSAO Alexander Ovechkin 20.00 50.00
PSCN Cam Neely 8.00 20.00
PSDB Derick Brassard 5.00 12.00
PSDD Drew Doughty 10.00 25.00
PSDG Doug Gilmour 5.00 12.00
PSDH Dale Hawerchuk 5.00 12.00
PSEM Evgeni Malkin 12.00 30.00
PSES Eric Staal 6.00 15.00
PSIK Ilya Kovalchuk 6.00 15.00
PSJC Jeff Carter 5.00 12.00
PSJV Jakub Voracek 5.00 12.00
PSKA Patrick Kane 10.00 25.00
PSKI Miikka Kiprusoff 5.00 12.00
PSLM Lanny McDonald 5.00 12.00
PSMB Martin Brodeur 12.00 30.00
PSMG Marian Gaborik 8.00 20.00
PSMM Mike Modano 5.00 12.00
PSMR Mike Richards 10.00 25.00
PSNB Nicklas Backstrom 10.00 25.00
PSNL Nicklas Lidstrom 6.00 15.00
PSPD Pavel Datsyuk 5.00 12.00
PSPK Phil Kessel 5.00 12.00
PSPS Peter Stastny 5.00 12.00
PSRL Roberto Luongo 12.00 30.00
PSRM Ryan Miller 5.00 12.00
PSRN Rick Nash 5.00 12.00
PSRS Ryan Smyth 5.00 12.00
PSSD Shane Doan 4.00 10.00
PSSG Sam Gagner 6.00 15.00
PSSH Steve Shutt 5.00 12.00
PSSK Saku Koivu 5.00 12.00
PSST Paul Stastny 5.00 12.00
PSSY Steve Yzerman 15.00 40.00
PSTV Tomas Vokoun 5.00 12.00
PSVL Vincent Lecavalier 6.00 15.00
PSWG Wayne Gretzky 25.00 60.00
PSZP Zach Parise 5.00 12.00

2009-10 Ultimate Collection Rookie NHL Shield Autographs

STATED PRINT RUN 1 SER.#'d SET
NOT PRICED DUE TO SCARCITY
101 Matt Beleskey
103 Logan Couture
104 Matt Gilroy
105 Mikael Backlund
106 Dmitry Kulikov
107 Christian Hanson
108 Kris Chucko
110 Artem Anisimov
111 Tyler Myers
112 Tyler Bozak
113 Yannick Weber
114 Viktor Stalberg
115 Ivan Vishnevskiy
118 Cody Franson
119 Michael Del Zotto
120 Ville Leino
121 Jamie Benn
122 Antti Niemi
123 Devan Dubnyk
124 Erik Karlsson
125 Michael Grabner
126 Spencer Machacek
127 Colin Wilson
128 Jakub Kindl
129 Brian Salcido
131 Matt Pelech
132 Benn Ferriero
133 Bobby Sanguinetti
134 Matthew Corrente
135 Alec Martinez
136 Lars Eller
137 Matt Duchene
139 John Tavares
140 James van Riemsdyk

2009-10 Ultimate Collection Rookie Patch Autographs

STATED PRINT RUN 25 SER.#'d SETS
101 Matt Beleskey 15.00 40.00
103 Logan Couture 40.00 100.00
104 Matt Gilroy 30.00 60.00
105 Mikael Backlund 20.00 50.00
106 Dmitry Kulikov 25.00 50.00
107 Christian Hanson 25.00 60.00
108 Kris Chucko 15.00 40.00
110 Artem Anisimov 15.00 40.00
111 Tyler Myers 100.00 200.00
112 Tyler Bozak 40.00 100.00
113 Yannick Weber 25.00 60.00
114 Viktor Stalberg 25.00 60.00
115 Ivan Vishnevskiy
117 Brad Marchand 40.00 80.00
118 Cody Franson 15.00 40.00
119 Michael Del Zotto 40.00 100.00
120 Ville Leino 25.00 60.00
121 Jamie Benn
122 Antti Niemi 40.00 100.00
123 Devan Dubnyk 20.00 50.00
124 Erik Karlsson 75.00 150.00
125 Michael Grabner 40.00 80.00
126 Spencer Machacek 15.00 40.00
127 Colin Wilson 40.00 80.00
128 Jakub Kindl 25.00 60.00
129 Brian Salcido 20.00 50.00
131 Matt Pelech 15.00 40.00
132 Benn Ferriero 12.00 30.00
133 Bobby Sanguinetti 15.00 40.00
134 Matthew Corrente
135 Alec Martinez 20.00 50.00
136 Lars Eller 25.00 60.00
137 Matt Duchene 125.00 200.00
138 Victor Hedman
139 John Tavares 275.00 400.00
140 James van Riemsdyk 75.00 150.00
141 Evander Kane 60.00 120.00
142 Jonas Gustavsson

2009-10 Ultimate Collection Ultimate Achievements

STATED PRINT RUN 25 SER.#'d SETS
UAAO Alexander Ovechkin 75.00 150.00
UABO Bobby Orr 175.00 300.00
UACN Cam Neely 15.00 40.00
UAEM Evgeni Malkin 40.00 100.00
UAGH Gordie Howe 60.00 120.00
UAJB Jean Beliveau 25.00 60.00
UAJI Jarome Iginla 25.00 60.00
UAJT Jonathan Toews 50.00 100.00
UAMB Martin Brodeur 60.00 120.00
UAMI Mike Bossy 15.00 40.00
UAML Mario Lemieux 60.00 120.00
UAPD Pavel Datsyuk 20.00 50.00
UAPE Phil Esposito 15.00 40.00
UAPR Patrick Roy 60.00 120.00
UARH Ron Hextall 25.00 60.00
UASC Sidney Crosby
UASM Steve Mason 15.00 40.00
UASY Steve Yzerman 75.00 150.00
UAWG Wayne Gretzky 175.00 300.00

2009-10 Ultimate Collection Ultimate Jerseys

STATED PRINT RUN 100 SER.#'d SETS
UJAO Alexander Ovechkin 15.00 40.00
UJBC Bobby Clarke 6.00 15.00
UJBL Brian Leetch 4.00 10.00
UJCN Cam Neely 6.00 15.00
UJCW Cam Ward 4.00 10.00
UJDG Doug Gilmour
UJDH Dany Heatley
UJEM Evgeni Malkin 10.00 25.00
UJES Eric Staal 5.00 12.00
UJGF Grant Fuhr 5.00 12.00
UJGH Gordie Howe 15.00 40.00
UJGP Gilbert Perreault 4.00 10.00
UJHA Dale Hawerchuk 4.00 10.00
UJIK Ilya Kovalchuk 5.00 12.00
UJJB Jean Beliveau 6.00 15.00
UJJC Jeff Carter
UJJK Jari Kurri 4.00 10.00
UJJT Jonathan Toews 10.00 25.00
UJLM Lanny McDonald 4.00 10.00
UJMB Martin Brodeur 10.00 25.00
UJMD Marcel Dionne
UJMG Marian Gaborik 6.00 15.00
UJMK Miikka Kiprusoff 4.00 10.00
UJMM Mike Modano 6.00 15.00
UJMR Mike Richards 8.00 20.00
UJMT Marty Turco 3.00 8.00
UJNB Nicklas Backstrom 8.00 20.00
UJPD Pavel Datsyuk 4.00 10.00
UJPE Phil Esposito 8.00 20.00
UJPK Patrick Kane 8.00 20.00
UJPR Patrick Roy 12.00 30.00
UJPS Peter Stastny 4.00 10.00
UJRB Ray Bourque 6.00 15.00
UJRL Roberto Luongo 10.00 25.00
UJRN Rick Nash 4.00 10.00
UJSA Borje Salming 4.00 10.00
UJSC Sidney Crosby 20.00 50.00
UJST Jordan Staal 5.00 12.00
UJSY Steve Yzerman 12.00 30.00
UJTE Tony Esposito 6.00 15.00
UJVL Vincent Lecavalier 5.00 12.00
UJWG Wayne Gretzky 20.00 50.00
UJZP Zach Parise 4.00 10.00

2009-10 Ultimate Collection Ultimate Jerseys Autographs

STATED PRINT RUN 25 SER.#'d SETS
AJAO Alexander Ovechkin 75.00 150.00
AJBL Brian Leetch 12.00 30.00
AJCN Cam Neely
AJCP Carey Price 30.00 80.00
AJCW Cam Ward 12.00 30.00
AJEM Evgeni Malkin EXCH 30.00 80.00
AJGH Gordie Howe 75.00 150.00
AJGP Gilbert Perreault 12.00 30.00
AJHZ Henrik Zetterberg 25.00 60.00
AJJI Jarome Iginla 25.00 60.00
AJJK Jari Kurri 12.00 30.00
AJMB Martin Brodeur EXCH 60.00 120.00
AJPD Pavel Datsyuk EXCH 30.00 60.00
AJPK Patrick Kane 25.00 60.00
AJPR Patrick Roy EXCH 60.00 120.00
AJRB Ray Bourque 20.00 50.00
AJRN Rick Nash 12.00 30.00
AJSC Sidney Crosby 100.00 200.00
AJSY Steve Yzerman
AJTE Tony Esposito 40.00 80.00
AJTO Jonathan Toews 30.00 80.00
AJWG Wayne Gretzky 150.00 300.00

2009-10 Ultimate Collection Ultimate Jerseys Duos

STATED PRINT RUN 50 SER.#'d SETS
UJ2AS Jason Spezza 10.00 25.00
Daniel Alfredsson
UJ2BL Martin Brodeur 20.00 50.00
Roberto Luongo
UJ2CO Alexander Ovechkin 40.00 100.00
Sidney Crosby
UJ2DP Marcel Dionne 10.00 25.00
Gilbert Perreault
UJ2EE Phil Esposito 15.00 40.00
Tony Esposito
UJ2EH Ray Emery
Ron Hextall
UJ2FC Sidney Crosby 30.00 80.00
Marc-Andre Fleury
UJ2GL Marian Gaborik
Henrik Lundqvist
UJ2HN Rick Nash 15.00 40.00
Dany Heatley
UJ2HT Marian Hossa 20.00 50.00
Jonathan Toews
UJ2KA Glenn Anderson 8.00 20.00
Jari Kurri
UJ2KO Ilya Kovalchuk
Alexander Ovechkin
UJ2LM Mark Messier
Brian Leetch
UJ2LT Vincent Lecavalier
Joe Thornton
UJ2LY Mario Lemieux
Steve Yzerman
UJ2MP Mike Modano
Zach Parise
UJ2PK Zach Parise 15.00 40.00
Patrick Kane
UJ2RB Martin Brodeur 25.00 60.00
Patrick Roy
UJ2RD Larry Robinson
Drew Doughty
UJ2RH Luc Robitaille 20.00 50.00
Bobby Hull
UJ2RP Patrick Roy 25.00 60.00
Carey Price
UJ2SK Teemu Selanne 8.00 20.00
Saku Koivu
UJ2SS Paul Stastny 8.00 20.00
Peter Stastny
UJ2YH Gordie Howe 30.00 80.00
Steve Yzerman
UJ2ZB Nicklas Backstrom
Henrik Zetterberg

2009-10 Ultimate Collection Ultimate Jerseys Duos Autographs

STATED PRINT RUN 10 SER.#'d SETS
NOT PRICED DUE TO SCARCITY
AJ2KO Ilya Kovalchuk
Alexander Ovechkin
AJ2LG Wayne Gretzky
Mario Lemieux
AJ2NB Cam Neely
Ray Bourque
AJ2OM Alexander Ovechkin
Evgeni Malkin
AJ2RB Martin Brodeur
Patrick Roy
AJ2RH Bobby Hull
Luc Robitaille
AJ2TK Jonathan Toews
Patrick Kane
AJ2YH Steve Yzerman
Gordie Howe

2009-10 Ultimate Collection Ultimate Jerseys Trios

STATED PRINT RUN 25 SER.#'d SETS
UJ3CRT Jonathan Toews 30.00 80.00
Mike Richards
Sidney Crosby
UJ3DOM Evgeni Malkin
Pavel Datsyuk
Alexander Ovechkin
UJ3ICO Alexander Ovechkin 40.00 100.00
Sidney Crosby
Jarome Iginla
UJ3LTS Vincent Lecavalier 20.00 50.00
Jason Spezza
Joe Thornton
UJ3MPK Zach Parise 20.00 50.00
Mike Modano
Patrick Kane
UJ3RBL Patrick Roy 30.00 80.00
Martin Brodeur
Roberto Luongo
UJ3YZH Henrik Zetterberg 40.00 100.00
Gordie Howe
Steve Yzerman

2009-10 Ultimate Collection Ultimate Nicknames

STATED PRINT RUN 25 SER.#'d SETS
UNAO Alexander Ovechkin 75.00 150.00
UNBE Jean Beliveau 40.00 80.00
UNBH Bobby Hull 40.00 80.00
UNCN Cam Neely 30.00 60.00
UNDC Don Cherry 50.00 100.00
UNDG Doug Gilmour 40.00 80.00
UNDH Dale Hawerchuk 25.00 50.00
UNEM Evgeni Malkin 40.00 80.00
UNGH Gordie Howe 125.00 250.00
UNJB Johnny Bucyk 15.00 40.00
UNJI Jarome Iginla 25.00 50.00
UNJT Joe Thornton 20.00 50.00
UNLR Luc Robitaille
UNMD Marcel Dionne 15.00 40.00
UNMF Marc-Andre Fleury 20.00 50.00
UNML Mario Lemieux 60.00 120.00
UNPR Patrick Roy 75.00 150.00
UNSC Sidney Crosby EXCH 150.00 250.00
UNSY Steve Yzerman 100.00 175.00
UNTE Tony Esposito 25.00 50.00

2009-10 Ultimate Collection Ultimate Patches

STATED PRINT RUN 35 SER.#'d SETS
UJAO Alexander Ovechkin 40.00 100.00
UJBH Bobby Hull 25.00 60.00
UJBL Brian Leetch 10.00 25.00
UJCW Cam Ward 10.00 25.00
UJDH Dany Heatley 20.00 50.00
UJEM Evgeni Malkin 25.00 60.00
UJHZ Henrik Zetterberg 20.00 50.00
UJIK Ilya Kovalchuk 12.00 30.00
UJJC Jeff Carter 10.00 25.00
UJJI Jarome Iginla 20.00 50.00
UJJK Jari Kurri 10.00 25.00
UJJS Jason Spezza 12.00 30.00
UJJT Jonathan Toews 25.00 60.00
UJKO Mikko Koivu 10.00 25.00
UJMB Martin Brodeur 25.00 60.00
UJME Mark Messier 20.00 50.00
UJMG Marian Gaborik 15.00 40.00
UJMK Miikka Kiprusoff 10.00 25.00
UJML Mario Lemieux 25.00 60.00
UJMM Mike Modano 10.00 25.00
UJMR Mike Richards 20.00 50.00
UJMS Martin St. Louis
UJMT Marty Turco 8.00 20.00
UJNB Nicklas Backstrom 20.00 50.00
UJPD Pavel Datsyuk 10.00 25.00
UJPE Phil Esposito 20.00 50.00
UJPK Patrick Kane 20.00 50.00
UJPR Patrick Roy 30.00 80.00
UJPS Peter Stastny 10.00 25.00
UJRB Ray Bourque
UJRL Roberto Luongo 25.00 60.00
UJRN Rick Nash 10.00 25.00
UJSA Borje Salming 10.00 25.00
UJSC Sidney Crosby 50.00 120.00
UJSN Scott Niedermayer 10.00 25.00
UJST Jordan Staal 12.00 30.00
UJSY Steve Yzerman 30.00 80.00
UJTH Joe Thornton 20.00 50.00
UJTS Teemu Selanne 10.00 25.00
UJWG Wayne Gretzky 50.00 120.00
UJZP Zach Parise 15.00 40.00

2009-10 Ultimate Collection Ultimate Patches Autographs

STATED PRINT RUN 10 SER.#'d SETS
NOT PRICED DUE TO SCARCITY

2009-10 Ultimate Collection Ultimate Patches Duos

STATED PRINT RUN 25 SER.#'d SETS
UJ2AS Jason Spezza 25.00 60.00
Daniel Alfredsson
UJ2BL Martin Brodeur
Roberto Luongo
UJ2CO Alexander Ovechkin 125.00 200.00
Sidney Crosby
UJ2CR Bobby Clarke 75.00 150.00
Mike Richards
UJ2EH Ron Hextall 25.00 60.00
Ray Emery
UJ2FC Sidney Crosby 75.00 150.00
Marc-Andre Fleury
UJ2GL Marian Gaborik 30.00 80.00
Henrik Lundqvist
UJ2HN Rick Nash 30.00 80.00
Dany Heatley
UJ2HT Marian Hossa 40.00 100.00
Jonathan Toews
UJ2IK Jarome Iginla 25.00 60.00
Miikka Kiprusoff
UJ2IS Jarome Iginla
Martin St. Louis
UJ2KA Jari Kurri 15.00 40.00
Glenn Anderson
UJ2KO Ilya Kovalchuk 60.00 150.00
Alexander Ovechkin
UJ2LG Wayne Gretzky 125.00 250.00
Mario Lemieux
UJ2LM Mark Messier
Brian Leetch
UJ2LT Vincent Lecavalier 30.00 80.00
Joe Thornton
UJ2LY Mario Lemieux
Steve Yzerman
UJ2MP Mike Modano 15.00 40.00
Zach Parise
UJ2PK Zach Parise 30.00 80.00
Patrick Kane
UJ2RB Martin Brodeur 50.00 120.00
Patrick Roy
UJ2RD Drew Doughty 30.00 80.00
Larry Robinson
UJ2RH Luc Robitaille 40.00 100.00
Bobby Hull
UJ2SK Teemu Selanne 20.00 50.00
Saku Koivu
UJ2SS Paul Stastny
Peter Stastny
UJ2ZB Nicklas Backstrom
Henrik Zetterberg

2009-10 Ultimate Collection Ultimate Patches Duos Autographs

STATED PRINT RUN 5 SER.#'d SETS
NOT PRICED DUE TO SCARCITY
AJ2KO Ilya Kovalchuk
Alexander Ovechkin
AJ2LG Wayne Gretzky
Mario Lemieux
AJ2NB Cam Neely
Ray Bourque
AJ2OM Alexander Ovechkin
Evgeni Malkin
AJ2RB Martin Brodeur
Patrick Roy
AJ2RH Bobby Hull
Luc Robitaille
AJ2TK Jonathan Toews
Patrick Kane

2009-10 Ultimate Collection Ultimate Patches Trios

STATED PRINT RUN 10 SER.#'d SETS
NOT PRICED DUE TO SCARCITY
UJ3CRT Jonathan Toews
Mike Richards
Sidney Crosby
UJ3DOM Evgeni Malkin
Pavel Datsyuk
Alexander Ovechkin
UJ3ICO Alexander Ovechkin
Sidney Crosby
Jarome Iginla
UJ3LGM Mario Lemieux
Wayne Gretzky
Mark Messier
UJ3LTS Vincent Lecavalier
Jason Spezza
Joe Thornton
UJ3MPK Zach Parise
Mike Modano
Patrick Kane
UJ3RBL Martin Brodeur
Patrick Roy
Roberto Luongo

2009-10 Ultimate Collection Ultimate Signature Logos

STATED PRINT RUN 1 SER.#'d SET
NOT PRICED DUE TO SCARCITY
SLAO Alexander Ovechkin
SLBL Brian Leetch
SLCN Cam Neely
SLCW Cam Ward
SLES Eric Staal
SLGA Simon Gagne
SLHL Henrik Lundqvist
SLHZ Henrik Zetterberg
SLJI Jarome Iginla
SLJS Jordan Staal
SLJT Joe Thornton
SLMF Marc-Andre Fleury
SLMH Milan Hejduk
SLML Mario Lemieux
SLMO Mike Modano
SLMS Martin St. Louis
SLMT Marty Turco
SLNB Nicklas Backstrom
SLNL Nicklas Lidstrom
SLPD Pavel Datsyuk
SLRB Ray Bourque
SLRM Ryan Miller
SLRN Rick Nash
SLSY Steve Yzerman
SLTO Jonathan Toews
SLVL Vincent Lecavalier
SLWG Wayne Gretzky

2009-10 Ultimate Collection Ultimate Signatures

USAA Artem Anisimov 8.00 20.00
USAN Antti Niemi 20.00 50.00
USAO Alexander Ovechkin 40.00 100.00
USBH Bobby Hull 15.00 40.00
USBO Bobby Orr 60.00 120.00
USCF Cody Franson 6.00 15.00
USCP Carey Price 15.00 40.00
USCW Colin Wilson 12.00 30.00
USDE Michael Del Zotto 12.00 30.00
USES Eric Staal 8.00 20.00
USGF Grant Fuhr 8.00 20.00
USGH Gordie Howe 60.00 120.00
USHL Henrik Lundqvist 12.00 30.00
USHZ Henrik Zetterberg 12.00 30.00
USJB Jamie Benn 10.00 25.00
USJC Jeff Carter 6.00 15.00
USJI Jarome Iginla 12.00 30.00
USJK Jari Kurri 6.00 15.00
USJT Jonathan Toews 15.00 40.00
USJV James van Riemsdyk 15.00 40.00
USKA Erik Karlsson 20.00 50.00
USMB Mikael Backlund 10.00 25.00
USMD Matt Duchene 20.00 50.00
USMF Marc-Andre Fleury 12.00 30.00
USMG Michael Grabner 8.00 20.00
USMI Mike Bossy 6.00 15.00
USML Mario Lemieux 50.00 100.00
USMO Mike Modano 6.00 15.00
USPD Pavel Datsyuk
USPE Phil Esposito 15.00 40.00
USPK Phil Kessel 6.00 15.00
USPR Patrick Roy 50.00 100.00
USRM Ryan Miller 10.00 25.00
USRN Rick Nash 6.00 15.00
USRY Bobby Ryan 8.00 20.00
USSC Sidney Crosby 75.00 150.00
USSM Steve Mason 10.00 25.00
USSY Steve Yzerman 60.00 120.00
USTA John Tavares 30.00 80.00
USTB Tyler Bozak 12.00 30.00
USTE Tony Esposito 10.00 25.00
USTH Joe Thornton 12.00 30.00
USTM Tyler Myers 15.00 40.00
USVL Ville Leino 8.00 20.00
USVS Viktor Stalberg 10.00 25.00
USWG Wayne Gretzky

1991-92 Ultimate Original Six

Produced by the Ultimate Trading Card Company, this 100-card standard-size set celebrates the 75th anniversary of the NHL by featuring players from the original six teams in the NHL. The cards were available only in foil packs, with a production run reportedly of 25,000 foil cases. Each foil pack included a sweepstake card; prizes offered included 250 autographed Bobby Hull holograms and 500 sets autographed by those players living at the time. The fronts feature color action photos with white borders, with the player's name in a silver bar at the top and the left lower corner of the picture rolled back to allow space for the producer's logo. The backs have a career summary presented in the format of a newspaper article (with different headlines), with biography and career statistics appearing in a silver box toward the bottom of the card. The cards are numbered on the back and checklisted below as follows: Team Checklists (1-6), Montreal Canadiens (7-17), New York Rangers (18-29), Toronto Maple Leafs (30-46), Boston Bruins (47-56), Chicago Blackhawks (57-65), Detroit Red Wings (66-72), Ultimate Hall of Fame (73-78), All Ultimate Team (79-84), Referees (85-87), Bobby Hull (88-92), and Great Moments (93-97). The cards were produced in both English and French versions. Either version is valued the same.

COMPLETE SET (100) 2.50 6.00
1 Montreal Canadiens Checklist .02 .10
2 New York Rangers Checklist .01 .05
3 Toronto Maple Leafs Checklist .01 .05
4 Boston Bruins Checklist .01 .05
5 Chicago Blackhawks Checklist .01 .05
6 Detroit Red Wings Checklist .01 .05
7 Ralph Backstrom .01 .05
8 Emile(Butch) Bouchard .05 .15
9 John Ferguson .02 .10
10 BoomBoom Geoffrion .25 .60
11 Phil Goyette .01 .05
12 Doug Harvey .15 .40
13 Don Marshall .02 .10
14 Henri Richard .20 .50
15 Dollard St.Laurent .01 .05
16 Jean-Guy Talbot .02 .10
17 Gump Worsley .15 .40
18 Andy Bathgate .07 .20
19 Lou Fontinato .01 .05
20 Ed Giacomin .07 .20
21 Vic Hadfield .02 .10
22 Camille Henry .01 .05
23 Harry Howell .05 .15
24 Orland Kurtenbach .02 .10
25 Jim Neilson .01 .05
26 Bob Nevin .01 .05
27 Dean Prentice .02 .10
28 Leo Reise Jr. .01 .05
29 George Sullivan .01 .05
30 Bob Baun .02 .10
31 Gus Bodnar .01 .05
32 Johnny Bower .07 .20
33 Bob Davidson .01 .05
34 Ron Ellis .02 .10
35 Billy Harris .01 .05
36 Larry Hillman .01 .05
37 Tim Horton .30 .75
38 Red Kelly .10 .30
39 Dave Keon .07 .20
40 Frank Mahovlich .20 .50
41 Eddie Shack .07 .20
42 Tod Sloan .01 .05
43 Sid Smith .02 .10
44 Allan Stanley .07 .20
45 Gaye Stewart .01 .05
46 Harry Watson .05 .15
47 Wayne Carleton .01 .05
48 Fern Flaman .02 .10
49 Ken Hodge UER .02 .10
(Photo actually Ed Westfall)
50 Leo Labine .01 .05
51 Harry Lumley .07 .20
52 John McKenzie .02 .10
53 Doug Mohns .02 .10
54 Fred Stanfield .01 .05
55 Jerry Toppazzini .01 .05
56 Ed Westfall .02 .10
57 Bobby Hull .40 1.00
58 Ed Litzenberger .01 .05
59 Gilles Marotte .01 .05
60 Ab McDonald .01 .05
61 Bill Mosienko .05 .15
62 Jim Pappin .01 .05
63 Pierre Pilote .05 .15
64 Elmer Vasko .01 .05
65 Johnny Wilson .01 .05
66 Sid Abel .07 .20
67 Gary Bergman .01 .05
68 Alex Delvecchio .10 .30
69 Bill Gadsby .07 .20
70 Ted Lindsay .15 .40
71 Marcel Pronovost .05 .15
72 Norm Ullman .07 .20
73 BoomBoom Geoffrion .25 .60
74 Andy Bathgate .07 .20
75 Allan Stanley .07 .20
76 Fern Flaman .05 .15
77 Bobby Hull .40 1.00
78 Norm Ullman .07 .20
79 Red Kelly .10 .30
80 Johnny Bower .10 .30
81 Henri Richard .20 .50
82 Bobby Hull .40 1.00
83 BoomBoom Geoffrion .25 .60
84 Tim Horton .30 .75
85 Bill Friday REF .01 .05
86 Bruce Hood REF .01 .05
87 Ron Wicks REF .01 .05
88 Bobby Hull .20 .50
Electric Slap Shot
89 Bobby Hull .20 .50
The Point Race
90 Bobby Hull .20 .50
1960-61 Stanley Cup
91 Bobby Hull .20 .50
The Curse of Muldoon is lifted
92 Bobby Hull .20 .50
Million Dollar Man
93 Bobby Baun .01 .05
Baun's Heroics
94 Ted Lindsay .05 .15
Lindsay's comeback
95 Henri Richard .05 .15
Richard's 99-year record
96 Bobby Hull .20 .50
Hull breaks 50 goal barrier
97 Tim Horton .08 .25
A Tribute to Horton
98 Keith McCreary .01 .05
99 Checklist 1 .01 .05
100 Checklist 2 .01 .05
NNO Bobby Hull Hologram 10.00 25.00

1991-92 Ultimate Original Six Box Bottoms

This four-card standard-size set was issued on the bottom of foil boxes. The cards feature on the fronts four-color or black and white action photos, with the lower left corner turned upward to allow space for the Ultimate logo. The player's name appears in black in a silver border at the top and the NHL logo is placed toward the end of the silver bar. Bobby Hull's card features red to black screened bars on two sides enclosing an artwork collage. The cards are unnumbered and checklisted below in alphabetical order.

COMPLETE SET (4) .60 1.50
1 Ed Giacomin .20 .50
2 Bobby Hull .40 1.00
The Golden Jet
3 Marcel Pronovost .08 .25
4 Eddie Shack .08 .25

1999-00 Ultimate Victory

The 1999-00 Upper Deck Ultimate Victory set was released as a 120-card set, which features 90 veteran cards, 20 short-printed prospects, and 10 Ultimate Hockey Legacy Wayne Gretzky cards on a front foil card-stock. This product was released in 5-card packs and 24-pack boxes.

COMPLETE SET (120) 60.00 125.00
COMP.SET w/o SP's (90) 10.00 20.00
1 Paul Kariya .25 .60
2 Teemu Selanne .25 .60
3 Jason Marshall .08 .25
4 David Harlock .08 .25
5 Ray Ferraro .08 .25
6 Kelly Buchberger .08 .25
7 Sergei Samsonov .20 .50
8 Ray Bourque .40 1.00
9 Darren Van Impe .08 .25
10 Dominik Hasek .50 1.25
11 Miroslav Satan .20 .50
12 Geoff Sanderson .20 .50
13 Valeri Bure .08 .25
14 Cale Hulse .08 .25
15 Cory Stillman .08 .25
16 Ron Francis .20 .50
17 Andrei Kovalenko .08 .25
18 Sami Kapanen .08 .25
19 Tony Amonte .20 .50
20 Steve Sullivan .08 .25
21 Doug Gilmour .20 .50
22 Milan Hejduk .25 .60
23 Joe Sakic .50 1.25
24 Patrick Roy 1.25 3.00
25 Chris Drury .20 .50
26 Peter Forsberg .60 1.50
27 Mike Modano .40 1.00
28 Brett Hull .30 .75
29 Ed Belfour .25 .60
30 Blake Sloan .08 .25
31 Steve Yzerman 1.25 3.00
32 Chris Osgood .20 .50
33 Brendan Shanahan .25 .60
34 Larry Murphy .20 .50
35 Doug Weight .20 .50
36 Christian Laflamme .08 .25
37 Alexander Selivanov .08 .25
38 Pavel Bure .25 .60
39 Jaroslav Spacek .08 .25
40 Viktor Kozlov .20 .50
41 Luc Robitaille .20 .50
42 Zigmund Palffy .20 .50
43 Rob Blake .20 .50
44 Saku Koivu .25 .60
45 Patrick Poulin .08 .25
46 Brian Savage .08 .25
47 David Legwand .20 .50
48 Sergei Krivokrasov .08 .25
49 Robert Valicevic RC .08 .25
50 Martin Brodeur .60 1.50
51 Scott Stevens .20 .50
52 Krzysztof Oliwa .08 .25
53 Jamie Heward .08 .25
54 Mariusz Czerkawski .08 .25
55 Kenny Jonsson .08 .25
56 Mike Richter .25 .60
57 Theo Fleury .08 .25
58 Tim Taylor .08 .25
59 Brian Leetch .25 .60
60 Andreas Dackell .08 .25
61 Marian Hossa .25 .60
62 Ron Tugnutt .20 .50
63 Craig Berube .08 .25
64 Eric Lindros .25 .60
65 John LeClair .25 .60
66 Dallas Drake .08 .25
67 Keith Tkachuk .25 .60
68 Jeremy Roenick .30 .75
69 Jaromir Jagr .40 1.00
70 Martin Straka .08 .25
71 Rob Brown .08 .25
72 Marcus Ragnarsson .08 .25
73 Steve Shields .20 .50
74 Owen Nolan .20 .50
75 Jeff Friesen .08 .25
76 Pavol Demitra .20 .50
77 Roman Turek .20 .50
78 Mike Eastwood .08 .25
79 Vincent Lecavalier .25 .60
80 Dan Cloutier .20 .50
81 Stan Drulia .08 .25
82 Mats Sundin .25 .60
83 Igor Korolev .08 .25
84 Curtis Joseph .25 .60
85 Mark Messier .25 .60
86 Harry York .20 .50
87 Peter Schaefer .08 .25
88 Olaf Kolzig .20 .50
89 Steve Konowalchuk .08 .25
90 Peter Bondra .25 .60
91 Patrik Stefan SP RC 1.25 3.00
92 Brian Campbell SP RC 1.25 3.00
93 Mikko Eloranta SP RC 1.25 3.00
94 Oleg Saprykin SP RC 1.25 3.00
95 Kyle Calder SP RC 1.50 4.00
96 Jonathan Sim SP RC 1.25 3.00
97 Marc Rodgers SP RC 1.25 3.00
98 Paul Comrie SP RC 1.25 3.00
99 Ivan Novoseltsev SP RC 1.25 3.00
100 Jason Blake SP RC 1.25 3.00
101 Brian Rafalski SP RC 2.00 5.00
102 Jorgen Jonsson SP RC 1.25 3.00
103 Nikolai Antropov SP RC 2.00 5.00
104 Steve Kariya SP RC 1.50 4.00
105 Glen Metropolit RC 1.25 3.00
106 Jochen Hecht SP RC 2.00 5.00
107 Sheldon Keefe SP RC 1.25 3.00
108 Branislav Mezei SP RC 1.25 3.00
109 Pavel Brendl SP RC 1.25 3.00
110 Milan Kraft SP RC 1.25 3.00
111 Wayne Gretzky 1.50 4.00
112 Wayne Gretzky 1.50 4.00
113 Wayne Gretzky 1.50 4.00
114 Wayne Gretzky 1.50 4.00
115 Wayne Gretzky 1.50 4.00
116 Wayne Gretzky 1.50 4.00
117 Wayne Gretzky 1.50 4.00
118 Wayne Gretzky 1.50 4.00
119 Wayne Gretzky 1.50 4.00
120 Wayne Gretzky 1.50 4.00

1999-00 Ultimate Victory Parallel 1/1

Randomly inserted in packs, this 120-card set features the base card in a one of one parallel.

NOT PRICED DUE TO SCARCITY

1999-00 Ultimate Victory Foil Parallel

Randomly inserted in packs, this 120-card parallel set features the base card etched with a vertical rainbow effect.

*VETS 1-90/111-120: 1.2X TO 3X BASIC CARDS
*ROOKIES 91-110: .6X TO 1.5X BASIC SP RC

1999-00 Ultimate Victory Parallel 100

Randomly inserted in packs, this 120-card parallel set is printed on a bronze version of the base card and serial numbered to 100.

*VETS 1-90/111-120: 5X TO 12X BASIC CARDS
*ROOKIES 91-110: 2X TO 5X BASIC SP RC

1999-00 Ultimate Victory Frozen Fury

COMPLETE SET (10) 12.00 25.00
STATED ODDS 1:23
FF1 Eric Lindros 1.25 3.00
FF2 Paul Kariya .75 2.00
FF3 Pavel Bure 1.00 2.50
FF4 Steve Kariya .40 1.00
FF5 Mike Modano 1.25 3.00
FF6 Patrik Stefan .40 1.00
FF7 Martin Brodeur 2.00 5.00
FF8 Jaromir Jagr 1.25 3.00
FF9 Joe Sakic 1.50 4.00
FF10 Steve Yzerman 4.00 10.00

1999-00 Ultimate Victory Legendary Fabrics

Randomly inserted in packs, this five-card set featured single and dual game-worn jersey swatches with the addition of certified autographs on two cards in the set. Lower print runs are not priced due to scarcity.

BOS Bobby Orr/4 AU
LFBO Bobby Orr/99 100.00 250.00
LFWG Wayne Gretzky/99 100.00 250.00
UFS Wayne Gretzky Bobby Orr/10 AU
UF Wayne Gretzky Bobby Orr/99 300.00 600.00

1999-00 Ultimate Victory Net Work

COMPLETE SET (10) 12.00 25.00
STATED ODDS 1:11
NW1 Dominik Hasek 1.50 4.00
NW2 Patrick Roy 5.00 12.00
NW3 Chris Osgood .75 2.00
NW4 Ed Belfour 1.00 2.50
NW5 Mike Richter 1.00 2.50
NW6 Roman Turek .75 2.00
NW7 Steve Shields .75 2.00
NW8 Curtis Joseph .75 2.00
NW9 Guy Hebert .75 2.00
NW10 Martin Brodeur 2.00 5.00

1999-00 Ultimate Victory Smokin Guns

COMPLETE SET (12) 8.00 15.00
STATED ODDS 1:11
SG1 Jaromir Jagr .75 2.00
SG2 Paul Kariya .50 1.25
SG3 Sergei Fedorov 1.00 2.50
SG4 Steve Kariya .30 .75
SG5 Peter Forsberg 1.25 3.00
SG6 Marian Hossa .50 1.25
SG7 Theo Fleury .50 1.25
SG8 Patrik Stefan .75 2.00
SG9 Pavel Bure .60 1.50
SG10 Eric Lindros .75 2.00
SG11 Brett Hull .60 1.50
SG12 Teemu Selanne .50 1.25

1999-00 Ultimate Victory Stature

COMPLETE SET (12) 6.00 12.00
STATED ODDS 1:6
S1 Paul Kariya .30 .75
S2 Joe Sakic .60 1.50
S3 Peter Forsberg .75 2.00
S4 Mike Modano .50 1.25
S5 Brendan Shanahan .50 1.25
S6 Pavel Bure .40 1.00
S7 Martin Brodeur .75 2.00
S8 Theo Fleury .30 .75
S9 Eric Lindros .50 1.25
S10 Keith Tkachuk .30 .75
S11 Jaromir Jagr .50 1.25
S12 Ray Bourque .50 1.25

1999-00 Ultimate Victory The Victors

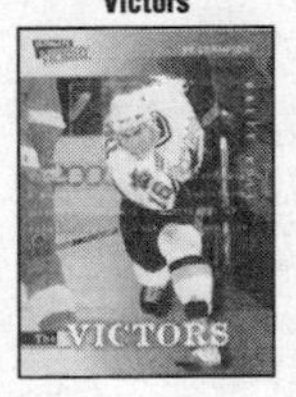

COMPLETE SET (8) 10.00 20.00
STATED ODDS 1:23
V1 Mark Messier .75 2.00
V2 Brett Hull .75 2.00
V3 Steve Yzerman 3.00 8.00
V4 Jaromir Jagr 1.00 2.50
V5 Patrick Roy 3.00 8.00
V6 Martin Brodeur 1.50 4.00
V7 Peter Forsberg 1.50 4.00
V8 Theo Fleury .60 1.50

1999-00 Ultimate Victory UV Extra

COMPLETE SET (8) 12.00 25.00
STATED ODDS 1:23
UV1 Jaromir Jagr 1.00 2.50
UV2 Patrick Roy 3.00 8.00
UV3 Pavel Bure .60 1.50
UV4 Bobby Orr 4.00 10.00
UV5 Paul Kariya 1.25 3.00
UV6 Peter Forsberg 1.50 4.00
UV7 Steve Yzerman 3.00 8.00
UV8 Eric Lindros 1.00 2.50

1992-93 Ultra

The 1992-93 Ultra hockey set consists of 450 standard-size cards. The fronts have glossy color action player photos that are full-bleed except at the bottom where a diagonal gold-foil stripe edges a "blue ice" border. The player's name and team appear on two team color-coded bars that overlay the bottom border. The horizontally oriented backs display action and close-up cut-out player photos against a hockey rink background. The Roenick Harding promo was issued in advance of the series and pictures the two men (the latter, the president of Fleer) in front of the Chicago skyline.

COMPLETE SET (450) 15.00 30.00
COMP.SERIES 1 (250) 10.00 20.00
COMP.SERIES 2 (200) 5.00 10.00
1 Brent Ashton .02 .10
2 Ray Bourque .25 .60
3 Steve Heinze .02 .10
4 Joe Juneau UER .07 .20
(Shoots left not right)
5 Stephen Leach .02 .10
6 Andy Moog .10 .30
7 Cam Neely .10 .30
8 Adam Oates .07 .20
9 Dave Poulin .02 .10
10 Vladimir Ruzicka .02 .10
11 Glen Wesley .02 .10
12 Dave Andreychuk .07 .20
13 Keith Carney RC .08 .25
14 Tom Draper .02 .10
15 Dale Hawerchuk .07 .20
16 Pat LaFontaine .10 .30
17 Brad May .02 .10
18 Alexander Mogilny .07 .20
19 Mike Ramsey .02 .10
20 Ken Sutton .02 .10
21 Theo Fleury .02 .10
22 Gary Leeman .02 .10
23 Al MacInnis .07 .20
24 Sergei Makarov .07 .20
25 Joe Nieuwendyk .07 .20
26 Joel Otto .02 .10
27 Paul Ranheim .02 .10
28 Robert Reichel .02 .10
29 Gary Roberts .02 .10
30 Gary Suter .02 .10
31 Mike Vernon .07 .20
32 Ed Belfour .10 .30
33 Rob Brown .02 .10
34 Chris Chelios .10 .30
35 Michel Goulet .07 .20
36 Dirk Graham .02 .10
37 Mike Hudson .02 .10
38 Igor Kravchuk .02 .10
39 Steve Larmer .07 .20
40 Dean McAmmond RC .02 .10
41 Jeremy Roenick .15 .40
42 Steve Smith .02 .10
43 Brent Sutter .02 .10
44 Shawn Burr .02 .10
45 Jimmy Carson .02 .10
46 Tim Cheveldae .07 .20
47 Dino Ciccarelli .07 .20
48 Sergei Fedorov .10 .30
49 Vladimir Konstantinov .10 .30
50 Slava Kozlov .07 .20
51 Nicklas Lidstrom .10 .30
52 Brad McCrimmon .02 .10
53 Bob Probert .07 .20
54 Paul Ysebaert .02 .10
55 Steve Yzerman .40 1.00
56 Josef Beranek .02 .10
57 Shayne Corson .02 .10
58 Brian Glynn .02 .10
59 Petr Klima .02 .10
60 Kevin Lowe .07 .20
61 Norm Maciver .02 .10
62 Dave Manson .02 .10
63 Joe Murphy .02 .10
64 Bernie Nicholls .07 .20
65 Bill Ranford .07 .20
66 Craig Simpson .02 .10
67 Esa Tikkanen .02 .10
68 Sean Burke .07 .20
69 Adam Burt .02 .10
70 Andrew Cassels .02 .10
71 Murray Craven .02 .10
72 John Cullen .02 .10
73 Randy Cunneyworth .02 .10
74 Tim Kerr .02 .10
75 Geoff Sanderson .07 .20
76 Eric Weinrich .02 .10
77 Zarley Zalapski .02 .10
78 Peter Ahola .02 .10
79 Rob Blake .07 .20
80 Paul Coffey .10 .30
81 Mike Donnelly .02 .10
82 Tony Granato .02 .10
83 Wayne Gretzky .60 1.50
84 Kelly Hrudey .07 .20
85 Jari Kurri .10 .30
86 Corey Millen .02 .10
87 Luc Robitaille .07 .20
88 Tomas Sandstrom .07 .20
89 Neal Broten .07 .20
90 Jon Casey .07 .20
91 Russ Courtnall .02 .10
92 Ulf Dahlen .02 .10
93 Todd Elik .02 .10
94 Dave Gagner .07 .20
95 Jim Johnson .02 .10
96 Mike Modano UER .20 .50
(Born in Livonia, Michigan not Minnesota)
97 Bobby Smith .07 .20
98 Mark Tinordi .02 .10
99 Darcy Wakaluk .07 .20
100 Brian Bellows .07 .20
101 Benoit Brunet .02 .10
102 Guy Carbonneau .07 .20
103 Vincent Damphousse .02 .10
104 Eric Desjardins .07 .20
105 Gilbert Dionne .02 .10
106 Mike Keane .02 .10
107 Kirk Muller .02 .10
108 Patrick Roy .40 1.00
109 Denis Savard .07 .20
110 Mathieu Schneider .02 .10
111 Brian Skrudland .02 .10
112 Tom Chorske .02 .10
113 Zdeno Ciger .02 .10
114 Claude Lemieux .02 .10
115 John MacLean .07 .20
116 Scott Niedermayer .07 .20
117 Stephane Richer .07 .20
118 Peter Stastny .07 .20
119 Scott Stevens .07 .20
120 Chris Terreri .07 .20
121 Kevin Todd .02 .10
122 Valeri Zelepukin .02 .10
123 Ray Ferraro .02 .10
124 Mark Fitzpatrick .07 .20
125 Patrick Flatley .02 .10
126 Glenn Healy .07 .20
127 Benoit Hogue .02 .10
128 Derek King .02 .10
129 Uwe Krupp .02 .10
130 Scott Lachance .02 .10
131 Steve Thomas .07 .20
132 Pierre Turgeon .07 .20
133 Tony Amonte .07 .20
134 Paul Broten .02 .10
135 Mike Gartner .07 .20
136 Adam Graves .07 .20
137 Alexei Kovalev .07 .20
138 Brian Leetch .10 .30
139 Mark Messier .10 .30
140 Sergei Nemchinov .02 .10
141 James Patrick .02 .10
142 Mike Richter .10 .30
143 Darren Turcotte .02 .10
144 John Vanbiesbrouck .07 .20
145 Dominic Lavoie .02 .10
146 Lonnie Loach RC .02 .10
147 Andrew McBain .02 .10
148 Darren Rumble .02 .10
149 Sylvain Turgeon .02 .10
150 Peter Sidorkiewicz .07 .20
151 Brian Benning .02 .10
152 Rod Brind'Amour .07 .20
153 Viacheslav Butsayev RC .02 .10
154 Kevin Dineen .02 .10
155 Pelle Eklund .02 .10
156 Garry Galley .02 .10
157 Eric Lindros .10 .30
158 Mark Recchi .07 .20
159 Dominic Roussel .07 .20
160 Tommy Soderstrom RC .07 .20
161 Dimitri Yushkevich RC .07 .20
162 Tom Barrasso .07 .20
163 Ron Francis .07 .20
164 Jaromir Jagr .20 .50
165 Mario Lemieux .40 1.00
166 Joe Mullen .07 .20
167 Larry Murphy .07 .20
168 Jim Paek .02 .10
169 Kjell Samuelsson .02 .10
170 Ulf Samuelsson .02 .10
171 Kevin Stevens .02 .10
172 Rick Tocchet .07 .20
173 Alexei Gusarov .02 .10
174 Ron Hextall .07 .20
175 Mike Hough .02 .10
176 Claude Lapointe .02 .10
177 Owen Nolan .07 .20
178 Mike Ricci .02 .10
179 Joe Sakic .25 .60
180 Mats Sundin .10 .30
181 Mikhail Tatarinov .02 .10
182 Bob Bassen .02 .10
183 Jeff Brown .02 .10
184 Garth Butcher .02 .10
185 Paul Cavallini .02 .10
186 Brett Hull .20 .50
187 Craig Janney .07 .20
188 Curtis Joseph .10 .30
189 Brendan Shanahan .10 .30
190 Ron Sutter .02 .10
191 David Bruce .02 .10
192 Dale Craigwell .02 .10
193 Dean Evason .02 .10
194 Pat Falloon .02 .10
195 Jeff Hackett .07 .20
196 Kelly Kisio .02 .10
197 Brian Lawton .02 .10
198 Neil Wilkinson .02 .10
199 Doug Wilson .07 .20
200 Marc Bergevin .02 .10
201 Roman Hamrlik RC .08 .25
202 Pat Jablonski .07 .20
203 Michel Mongeau .02 .10
204 Peter Taglianetti .02 .10
205 Steve Tuttle .02 .10
206 Wendell Young .07 .20
207 Glenn Anderson .07 .20
208 Wendel Clark .07 .20
209 Dave Ellett .02 .10
210 Grant Fuhr .10 .30
211 Doug Gilmour .07 .20
212 Jamie Macoun .02 .10
213 Felix Potvin .10 .30
214 Bob Rouse .02 .10
215 Joe Sacco .02 .10
216 Peter Zezel .02 .10
217 Greg Adams .02 .10
218 Dave Babych .02 .10
219 Pavel Bure .10 .30
220 Geoff Courtnall .02 .10
221 Doug Lidster .02 .10
222 Trevor Linden .07 .20
223 Jyrki Lumme .02 .10
224 Kirk McLean .07 .20
225 Sergio Momesso .02 .10
226 Petr Nedved .07 .20
227 Cliff Ronning .02 .10
228 Jim Sandlak .02 .10
229 Don Beaupre .07 .20
230 Peter Bondra .07 .20
231 Kevin Hatcher .02 .10
232 Dale Hunter .07 .20
233 Al Iafrate .07 .20
234 Calle Johansson .02 .10
235 Dimitri Khristich .02 .10
236 Kelly Miller .02 .10
237 Michal Pivonka .02 .10
238 Mike Ridley .02 .10
239 Luciano Borsato .02 .10
240 Bob Essensa .07 .20
241 Phil Housley .07 .20
242 Troy Murray .02 .10
243 Teppo Numminen .02 .10
244 Fredrik Olausson .02 .10
245 Ed Olczyk .02 .10
246 Darrin Shannon .02 .10
247 Thomas Steen .02 .10
248 Checklist 1 .02 .10
249 Checklist 2 .02 .10
250 Checklist 3 .02 .10
251 Ted Donato .02 .10
252 Dmitri Kvartalnov RC .02 .10
253 Gord Murphy .02 .10
254 Gregori Panteleyev RC .02 .10
255 Gordie Roberts .02 .10
256 David Shaw .02 .10
257 Don Sweeney .02 .10
258 Doug Bodger .02 .10
259 Gord Donnelly .02 .10
260 Yuri Khmylev RC .02 .10
261 Daren Puppa .07 .20
262 Richard Smehlik RC .02 .10
263 Petr Svoboda .02 .10
264 Bob Sweeney .02 .10
265 Randy Wood .02 .10
266 Kevin Dahl RC .02 .10
267 Chris Dahlquist .02 .10
268 Roger Johansson .02 .10
269 Chris Lindberg .02 .10
270 Frank Musil .02 .10
271 Ronnie Stern .02 .10
272 Carey Wilson .02 .10
273 Dave Christian .02 .10
274 Karl Dykhuis .02 .10
275 Greg Gilbert .02 .10
276 Sergei Krivokrasov .02 .10
277 Frantisek Kucera .02 .10
278 Bryan Marchment .02 .10
279 Stephane Matteau .02 .10
280 Brian Noonan .02 .10
281 Christian Ruuttu .02 .10
282 Steve Chiasson .02 .10
283 Dino Ciccarelli .07 .20
284 Gerard Gallant .02 .10
285 Mark Howe .02 .10
286 Keith Primeau .02 .10
287 Yves Racine .02 .10
288 Vincent Riendeau .07 .20
289 Ray Sheppard .02 .10
290 Mike Sillinger .02 .10
291 Kelly Buchberger .02 .10
292 Shayne Corson .02 .10
293 Brent Gilchrist .02 .10
294 Craig MacTavish .02 .10
295 Scott Mellanby .02 .10
296 Craig Muni .02 .10
297 Luke Richardson .02 .10
298 Ron Tugnutt .07 .20
299 Shaun Van Allen .02 .10
300 Steve Konroyd .02 .10
301 Nick Kypreos .02 .10
302 Robert Petrovicky RC .02 .10
303 Frank Pietrangelo .07 .20
304 Patrick Poulin .02 .10
305 Pat Verbeek .02 .10
306 Eric Weinrich .02 .10
307 Jim Hiller RC .02 .10
308 Charlie Huddy .02 .10
309 Lonnie Loach .02 .10
310 Marty McSorley .02 .10
311 Robb Stauber .07 .20
312 Darryl Sydor .02 .10
313 Dave Taylor .07 .20
314 Alexei Zhitnik .02 .10
315 Shane Churla .02 .10
316 Russ Courtnall .02 .10
317 Mike Craig .02 .10
318 Gaetan Duchesne .02 .10
319 Derian Hatcher .02 .10
320 Craig Ludwig .02 .10
321 Richard Matvichuk RC .07 .20
322 Mike McPhee .02 .10
323 Tommy Sjodin RC .02 .10
324 Brian Bellows .02 .10
325 Patrice Brisebois .02 .10
326 J.J.Daigneault .02 .10
327 Kevin Haller .02 .10
328 Sean Hill RC .02 .10
329 Stephan Lebeau .02 .10
330 John LeClair .20 .50
331 Lyle Odelein .02 .10
332 Andre Racicot .07 .20
333 Ed Ronan RC .02 .10
334 Craig Billington .07 .20
335 Ken Daneyko .02 .10
336 Bruce Driver .02 .10
337 Slava Fetisov .02 .10
338 Bill Guerin RC .60 1.50
339 Bobby Holik .07 .20
340 Alexei Kasatonov .02 .10
341 Alexander Semak .02 .10
342 Tom Fitzgerald .02 .10
343 Travis Green RC .08 .25
344 Darius Kasparaitis .02 .10
345 Danny Lorenz RC .02 .10
346 Vladimir Malakhov .02 .10
347 Marty McInnis .02 .10
348 Brian Mullen .02 .10
349 Jeff Norton .02 .10
350 David Volek .02 .10
351 Jeff Beukeboom .02 .10
352 Phil Bourque .02 .10
353 Paul Broten .02 .10
354 Mark Hardy .02 .10
355 Steven King RC .02 .10
356 Kevin Lowe .07 .20
357 Ed Olczyk .02 .10
358 Doug Weight .10 .30
359 Sergei Zubov RC .20 .50
360 Jamie Baker .02 .10
361 Daniel Berthiaume .07 .20
362 Chris Luongo RC .02 .10
363 Norm Maciver .02 .10
364 Brad Marsh .02 .10
365 Mike Peluso .02 .10
366 Brad Shaw .02 .10
367 Peter Sidorkiewicz .07 .20
368 Keith Acton .02 .10
369 Stephane Beauregard .07 .20
370 Terry Carkner .02 .10
371 Brent Fedyk .02 .10
372 Andrei Lomakin .02 .10
373 Ryan McGill RC .02 .10
374 Ric Nattress .02 .10
375 Greg Paslawski .02 .10
376 Peter Ahola .02 .10
377 Jeff Daniels .02 .10
378 Troy Loney .02 .10
379 Shawn McEachern .02 .10
380 Mike Needham RC .02 .10
381 Paul Stanton .02 .10
382 Martin Straka RC .20 .50
383 Ken Wregget .07 .20
384 Steve Duchesne .02 .10
385 Ron Hextall .07 .20
386 Kerry Huffman .02 .10
387 Andrei Kovalenko RC .07 .20
388 Bill Lindsay RC .02 .10
389 Mike Ricci .07 .20
390 Martin Rucinsky .02 .10
391 Scott Young .02 .10
392 Philippe Bozon .02 .10
393 Nelson Emerson .02 .10
394 Guy Hebert RC .20 .50
395 Igor Korolev RC .07 .20
396 Kevin Miller .02 .10
397 Vitali Prokhorov RC .02 .10
398 Rich Sutter .02 .10
399 John Carter .02 .10
400 Johan Garpenlov .02 .10
401 Arturs Irbe .08 .25
402 Sandis Ozolinsh .02 .10
403 Tom Pederson RC .02 .10
404 Michel Picard .02 .10
405 Doug Zmolek RC .02 .10
406 Mikael Andersson .02 .10
407 Bob Beers .02 .10
408 Brian Bradley .02 .10
409 Adam Creighton .02 .10
410 Doug Crossman .02 .10
411 Ken Hodge Jr. .02 .10
412 Chris Kontos RC .02 .10
413 Rob Ramage .02 .10
414 John Tucker .02 .10
415 Rob Zamuner RC .07 .20
416 Ken Baumgartner .02 .10
417 Drake Berehowsky .02 .10
418 Nikolai Borschevsky RC .02 .10
419 John Cullen .02 .10
420 Mike Foligno .02 .10
421 Mike Krushelnyski .02 .10
422 Dmitri Mironov .02 .10
423 Rob Pearson .02 .10
424 Gerald Diduck .02 .10
425 Robert Dirk .02 .10
426 Tom Fergus .02 .10
427 Gino Odjick .02 .10
428 Adrien Plavsic .02 .10
429 Anatoli Semenov .02 .10
430 Jiri Slegr .02 .10
431 Dixon Ward RC .07 .20
432 Paul Cavallini .02 .10
433 Sylvain Cote .02 .10
434 Pat Elynuik .02 .10
435 Jim Hrivnak .07 .20
436 Keith Jones RC .08 .25
437 Steve Konowalchuk RC .07 .20
438 Todd Krygier .02 .10
439 Paul MacDermid .02 .10
440 Sergei Bautin RC .02 .10
441 Evgeny Davydov .02 .10
442 John Druce .02 .10
443 Troy Murray .02 .10
444 Teemu Selanne .40 1.00
445 Rick Tabaracci .07 .20
446 Keith Tkachuk .10 .30
447 Alexei Zhamnov .07 .20
448 Checklist 4 .02 .10
449 Checklist 5 .02 .10
450 Checklist 6 .02 .10
NNO Jeremy Roenick/Harding Promo .75 2.00

1992-93 Ultra All-Stars

This 12-card standard-size set was randomly inserted in 1992-93 Ultra first series foil packs. The cards depict First Team All-Stars by conference. The glossy color action player photos on the fronts are full-bleed except at the bottom where a diagonal gold-foil stripe edges a beige marbleized border. A gold-foil insignia with a star is superimposed on the beige border.

COMPLETE SET (12) 8.00 20.00
1 Paul Coffey UER .50 1.25
(Photo on back actually Kevin Stevens)
2 Ray Bourque .75 2.00
3 Patrick Roy 1.50 4.00
4 Mario Lemieux 1.50 4.00
5 Kevin Stevens UER .15 .40
(Photo on back actually Paul Coffey)
6 Jaromir Jagr .75 2.00
7 Chris Chelios .50 1.25
8 Al MacInnis .30 .75
9 Ed Belfour .50 1.25
10 Wayne Gretzky 2.00 5.00
11 Luc Robitaille .30 .75
12 Brett Hull .75 2.00

1992-93 Ultra Award Winners

This ten-card standard-size set was randomly inserted in 1992-93 Ultra first series foil packs. The cards feature 1991-92 award winners. The glossy color action player photos on the fronts are full-bleed except at the bottom where a gold-foil stripe edges into a marbleized border.

COMPLETE SET (10) 6.00 15.00
1 Mark Messier .60 1.50
2 Brian Leetch .50 1.25
3 Guy Carbonneau .30 .75
4 Patrick Roy 1.50 4.00
5 Mario Lemieux 1.50 4.00
6 Wayne Gretzky 2.00 5.00
7 Mark Fitzpatrick .30 .75
8 Ray Bourque .60 1.50
9 Pavel Bure .50 1.25
10 Mark Messier .60 1.50

1992-93 Ultra Imports

Randomly inserted in second series 1992-93 Ultra foil packs, this 25-card set measures the standard size. The cards depict foreign players in the National Hockey League. Fronts feature color action cut out player photos against a purple surreal background showing the player on ice with a globe design in the distance. The player's name is silver foil stamped at the bottom. The horizontal backs carry a close-up of the player, the player's name, and player information. The background is similar to the front.

COMPLETE SET (25) 8.00 20.00
1 Nikolai Borschevsky .20 .50
2 Pavel Bure .75 2.00
3 Sergei Fedorov 1.00 2.50
4 Roman Hamrlik .20 .50
5 Arturs Irbe .40 1.00
6 Jaromir Jagr 1.25 3.00
7 Dimitri Khristich .20 .50
8 Petr Klima .20 .50
9 Andrei Kovalenko .20 .50
10 Alexei Kovalev .40 1.00
11 Jari Kurri .75 2.00
12 Dmitri Kvartalnov .20 .50
13 Nicklas Lidstrom .75 2.00
14 Vladimir Malakhov .20 .50
15 Dmitri Mironov .20 .50
16 Alexander Mogilny .40 1.00
17 Petr Nedved .20 .50
18 Fredrik Olausson .20 .50
19 Sandis Ozolinsh .20 .50
20 Ulf Samuelsson .20 .50
21 Teemu Selanne 2.00 5.00
22 Richard Smehlik .20 .50
23 Tommy Soderstrom .20 .50
24 Peter Stastny .20 .50
25 Mats Sundin .75 2.00

1992-93 Ultra Jeremy Roenick

Randomly inserted in first series 1992-93 Ultra foil packs, this 12-card set measures the standard size. Two of the cards (11, 12) were available through a mail-in offer which was not available in Canada. The set, which features color action photos on front and career highlights on back, spotlights the career of Chicago Blackhawks' Jeremy Roenick. Roenick personally autographed more than 2,000 of his cards. Stated odds suggest the likelihood of pulling an autographed card at 1:8,000 packs.

COMPLETE SET (10) 10.00 20.00
COMMON ROENICK (1-10) .75 2.00
COMMON MAIL-IN (11-12) 1.25 3.00
AU Jeremy Roenick AU 60.00 150.00

1992-93 Ultra Rookies

This eight-card standard-size set was randomly inserted in 1992-93 Ultra series one foil packs. The card fronts feature color, action player photos. A brown marbleized border runs diagonally across the bottom. This border is separated from the photo by a thin gold foil stripe. The player's name and the words "Ultra Rookie" are printed in gold foil on the marbleized border. The backs show a close-up picture with a player profile against a gray marbleized background.

COMPLETE SET (8) 5.00 10.00
1 Tony Amonte .40 1.00
2 Donald Audette .40 1.00
3 Pavel Bure .75 2.00
4 Gilbert Dionne .40 1.00
5 Nelson Emerson .40 1.00
6 Pat Falloon .40 1.00
7 Nicklas Lidstrom .75 2.00
8 Kevin Todd .40 1.00

1993-94 Ultra

The 1993-94 Ultra hockey set consists of 500 standard-size cards. Both the first and second series contained 250 cards. The color action player photos on the fronts are full-bleed except at the bottom where a diagonal gold foil stripe separates the picture from a gray ice border. The player's name, team name, and position are gold foil-stamped on team color-coded bars.

COMPLETE SET (500) 20.00 40.00
COMP.SERIES 1 (250) 10.00 20.00
COMP.SERIES 2 (250) 10.00 20.00
1 Ray Bourque .20 .50
2 Andy Moog .05 .15
3 Brian Benning .02 .10
4 Brian Bellows .02 .10
5 Claude Lemieux .02 .10
6 Jamie Baker .02 .10
7 Steve Duchesne .02 .10
8 Ed Courtenay .02 .10
9 Glenn Anderson .05 .15
10 Sergei Bautin .02 .10
11 Al Iafrate .02 .10
12 Gary Shuchuk .02 .10
13 Matthew Barnaby .05 .15
14 Tim Cheveldae .05 .15
15 Sean Burke .05 .15
16 Ray Ferraro .02 .10
17 Josef Beranek .02 .10
18 Bob Beers .02 .10
19 Greg Adams .02 .10
20 John Cullen .02 .10
21 Kirk Muller .02 .10
22 Ed Belfour .10 .30
23 Kevin Dahl .02 .10
24 Rob Blake .05 .15
25 Mike Gartner .05 .15
26 Tom Barrasso .05 .15
27 Garth Butcher .02 .10
28 Don Beaupre .05 .15
29 Kirk McLean .05 .15
30 Felix Potvin .10 .30
31 Doug Bodger .02 .10
32 Dino Ciccarelli .05 .15
33 Andrew Cassels .02 .10
34 Patrick Flatley .02 .10
35 Jason Bowen RC .02 .10
36 Brian Bradley .02 .10
37 Pavel Bure .10 .30
38 Dave Ellett .02 .10
39 Patrick Roy .60 1.50
40 Chris Chelios .10 .30
41 Theo Fleury .02 .10
42 Jimmy Carson .02 .10
43 Adam Graves .02 .10
44 Ron Francis .05 .15
45 Nelson Emerson .02 .10
46 Peter Bondra .05 .15
47 Sergio Momesso .02 .10
48 Teemu Selanne .10 .30
49 Joe Juneau .05 .15
50 Russ Courtnall .02 .10
51 Shayne Corson .02 .10
52 Patrice Brisebois .02 .10
53 John MacLean .05 .15
54 Daniel Berthiaume .05 .15
55 Stephane Fiset .05 .15
56 Pat Falloon .02 .10
57 Dave Andreychuk .05 .15
58 Evgeny Davydov .02 .10
59 Dimitri Khristich .02 .10
60 Darryl Sydor .02 .10
61 Dirk Graham .02 .10
62 Chris Lindberg .02 .10
63 Tony Granato .02 .10
64 Corey Hirsch .05 .15
65 Jaromir Jagr .20 .50
66 Brett Hodican .02 .10
67 Pat Elynuik .02 .10
68 Petr Nedved .05 .15
69 Thomas Steen .02 .10
70 Philippe Boucher .02 .10
71 Paul Coffey .02 .10

72 Mike Lenarduzzi RC .02 .10
73 Iain Fraser RC .02 .10
74 Rod Brind'Amour .05 .15
75 Shawn Chambers .02 .10
76 Geoff Courtnall .02 .10
77 Todd Gill .02 .10
78 Mathieu Schneider .02 .10
79 Vincent Damphousse .02 .10
80 Igor Kravchuk .02 .10
81 Ulf Dahlen .02 .10
82 Dmitri Kvartalnov .02 .10
83 Johan Garpenlov .02 .10
84 Valeri Kamensky .05 .15
85 Bob Kudelski .02 .10
86 Bernie Nicholls .02 .10
87 Alexei Zhitnik .02 .10
88 Kelly Miller .02 .10
89 Bob Essensa .05 .15
90 Drake Berehowsky .02 .10
91 Jon Casey .05 .15
92 Dave Gagner .05 .15
93 Dave Manson .02 .10
94 Eric Desjardins .05 .15
95 Scott Niedermayer .02 .10
96 Chris Luongo .02 .10
97 Dave Karpa .02 .10
98 Rob Gaudreau RC .02 .10
99 Nikolai Borschevsky .02 .10
100 Phil Housley .05 .15
101 Michal Pivonka .02 .10
102 Dixon Ward .02 .10
103 Grant Fuhr .05 .15
104 Dallas Drake RC .02 .10
105 Michael Nylander .02 .10
106 Glenn Healy .05 .15
107 Kevin Dineen .02 .10
108 Roman Hamrlik .05 .15
109 Trevor Linden .05 .15
110 Doug Gilmour .05 .15
111 Keith Tkachuk .10 .30
112 Sergei Krivokrasov .02 .10
113 Al MacInnis .05 .15
114 Wayne Gretzky .75 2.00
115 Alexei Kovalev .05 .15
116 Mario Lemieux .60 1.50
117 Brett Hull .15 .40
118 Kevin Hatcher .02 .10
119 Cliff Ronning .02 .10
120 Viktor Gordiouk .02 .10
121 Sergei Fedorov .20 .50
122 Patrick Poulin .02 .10
123 Benoit Hogue .02 .10
124 Garry Galley .02 .10
125 Pat Jablonski .05 .15
126 Jyrki Lumme .02 .10
127 Dimitri Mironov .02 .10
128 Alexei Zhamnov .05 .15
129 Steve Larmer .05 .15
130 Joe Nieuwendyk .05 .15
131 Kelly Hrudey .05 .15
132 Brian Leetch .10 .30
133 Shawn McEachern .02 .10
134 Craig Janney .05 .15
135 Dale Hunter .02 .10
136 Jiri Slegr .02 .10
137 Mats Sundin .10 .30
138 Cam Neely .10 .30
139 Derian Hatcher .02 .10
140 Shjon Podein RC .02 .10
141 Gilbert Dionne .02 .10
142 Scott Pellerin RC .02 .10
143 Norm Maciver .02 .10
144 Andrei Kovalenko .02 .10
145 Arturs Irbe .05 .15
146 Wendel Clark .05 .15
147 Fredrik Olausson .02 .10
148 Mike Ridley .02 .10
149 Dale Hawerchuk .05 .15
150 Vladimir Konstantinov .05 .15
151 Geoff Sanderson .02 .10
152 Stephane Richer .05 .15
153 Darren Rumble .02 .10
154 Owen Nolan .05 .15
155 Kelly Kisio .02 .10
156 Adam Oates .05 .15
157 Trent Klatt .02 .10
158 Bill Ranford .05 .15
159 Paul DiPietro .02 .10
160 Darius Kasparaitis .02 .10
161 Eric Lindros .10 .30
162 Chris Kontos .02 .10
163 Joe Murphy .02 .10
164 Robert Reichel .02 .10
165 Jari Kurri .10 .30
166 Alexander Semak .02 .10
167 Brad Shaw .02 .10
168 Mike Ricci .02 .10
169 Sandis Ozolinsh .02 .10
170 Joby Messier RC .02 .10
171 Joe Mullen .05 .15
172 Curtis Joseph .10 .30
173 Yuri Khmylev .02 .10
174 Slava Kozlov .05 .15
175 Pat Verbeek .02 .10
176 Derek King .02 .10
177 Ryan McGill .02 .10
178 Chris LiPuma RC .02 .10
179 Grigori Pantaleyev .02 .10
180 Richard Matvichuk .02 .10
181 Steven Rice .02 .10
182 Sean Hill .02 .10
183 Mark Messier .10 .30
184 Larry Murphy .05 .15
185 Igor Korolev .02 .10
186 Jeremy Roenick .15 .40
187 Gary Roberts .02 .10
188 Robert Lang .02 .10
189 Scott Stevens .05 .15
190 Sylvain Turgeon .02 .10
191 Martin Rucinsky .02 .10
192 J.F. Quintin .02 .10
193 Dave Poulin .02 .10
194 Mike Modano .20 .50
195 Doug Weight .05 .15
196 Mike Keane .02 .10
197 Pierre Turgeon .05 .15
198 Dimitri Yushkevich .05 .15
199 Rob Zamuner .02 .10
200 Richard Smehlik .02 .10
201 Steve Yzerman .60 1.50
202 Tony Amonte .05 .15
203 Sergei Nemchinov .02 .10
204 Ulf Samuelsson .02 .10
205 Kevin Miehm .02 .10
206 Brent Sutter .02 .10
207 Mike Vernon .05 .15
208 Luc Robitaille .05 .15
209 Chris Terreri .05 .15
210 Philippe Bozon .02 .10
211 John Tucker .02 .10
212 Jozef Stumpel .02 .10
213 Mark Tinordi .02 .10
214 Bruce Driver .02 .10
215 John LeClair .10 .30
216 Steve Thomas .02 .10
217 Tommy Soderstrom .05 .15
218 Kevin Miller .02 .10
219 Pat LaFontaine .10 .30
220 Nicklas Lidstrom .10 .30
221 Terry Yake .02 .10
222 Valeri Zelepukin .02 .10
223 Jeff Brown .02 .10
224 Chris Simon RC .30 .75
225 Rick Tocchet .05 .15
226 Gary Suter .02 .10
227 Marty McSorley .05 .15
228 Mike Richter .10 .30
229 Kevin Stevens .02 .10
230 Doug Wilson .05 .15
231 Steve Smith .02 .10
232 Bryan Smolinski .05 .15
233 Tommy Sjodin .02 .10
234 Zarley Zalapski .02 .10
235 Vladimir Malakhov .02 .10
236 Mark Recchi .05 .15
237 David Littman RC .02 .10
238 Alexander Mogilny .05 .15
239 Keith Primeau .02 .10
240 Tyler Wright .02 .10
241 Stephan Lebeau .02 .10
242 Joe Sakic .25 .60
243 Sergei Zubov .02 .10
244 Martin Straka .02 .10
245 Brendan Shanahan .10 .30
246 Tomas Sandstrom .02 .10
247 Milan Tichy RC .02 .10
248 C.J. Young .02 .10
249 Checklist .10 .30
Eric Lindros
250 Checklist .10 .30
Teemu Selanne
251 Patrick Carnback RC .02 .10
252 Todd Ewen .02 .10
253 Stu Grimson .02 .10
254 Guy Hebert .05 .15
255 Sean Hill .02 .10
256 Bill Houlder .02 .10
257 Alexei Kasatonov .02 .10
258 Steven King .02 .10
259 Troy Loney .02 .10
260 Joe Sacco .02 .10
261 Anatoli Semenov .02 .10
262 Tim Sweeney .02 .10
263 Ron Tugnutt .05 .15
264 Shaun Van Allen .02 .10
265 Terry Yake .02 .10
266 Jon Casey .05 .15
267 Ted Donato .02 .10
268 Steve Leach .02 .10
269 David Reid .02 .10
270 Cam Stewart RC .02 .10
271 Don Sweeney .02 .10
272 Glen Wesley .02 .10
273 Donald Audette .02 .10
274 Dominik Hasek .40 1.00
275 Sergei Petrenko .02 .10
276 Derek Plante RC .02 .10
277 Craig Simpson .02 .10
278 Bob Sweeney .02 .10
279 Randy Wood .02 .10
280 Ted Drury .02 .10
281 Trevor Kidd .05 .15
282 Kelly Kisio .02 .10
283 Frank Musil .02 .10
284 Jason Muzzatti RC .05 .15
285 Joel Otto .02 .10
286 Paul Ranheim .02 .10
287 Wes Walz .02 .10
288 Ivan Droppa RC .02 .10
289 Michel Goulet .05 .15
290 Stephane Matteau .02 .10
291 Brian Noonan .02 .10
292 Patrick Poulin .02 .10
293 Rich Sutter .02 .10
294 Kevin Todd .02 .10
295 Eric Weinrich .02 .10
296 Neal Broten .05 .15
297 Mike Craig .02 .10
298 Dean Evason .02 .10
299 Grant Ledyard .02 .10
300 Mike McPhee .02 .10
301 Andy Moog .05 .15
302 Jarkko Varvio .02 .10
303 Micah Aivazoff RC .02 .10
304 Terry Carkner .02 .10
305 Steve Chiasson .02 .10
306 Greg Johnson .02 .10
307 Darren McCarty RC .30 .75
308 Chris Osgood RC 1.00 2.50
309 Bob Probert .05 .15
310 Ray Sheppard .05 .15
311 Mike Sillinger .02 .10
312 Jason Arnott RC .60 1.50
313 Fred Brathwaite RC .25 .60
314 Kelly Buchberger .02 .10
315 Zdeno Ciger .02 .10
316 Craig MacTavish .02 .10
317 Dean McAmmond .02 .10
318 Luke Richardson .02 .10
319 Vladimir Vujtek .02 .10
320 Jesse Belanger .02 .10
321 Brian Benning .02 .10
322 Keith Brown .02 .10
323 Evgeny Davydov .02 .10
324 Tom Fitzgerald .02 .10
325 Alexander Godynyuk .02 .10
326 Scott Levins RC .02 .10
327 Andrei Lomakin .02 .10
328 Scott Mellanby .05 .15
329 Gord Murphy .02 .10
330 Rob Niedermayer .05 .15
331 Brent Severyn RC .02 .10
332 Brian Skrudland .02 .10
333 John Vanbiesbrouck .05 .15
334 Mark Greig .02 .10
335 Bryan Marchment .02 .10
336 James Patrick .02 .10
337 Robert Petrovicky .02 .10
338 Frank Pietrangelo .05 .15
339 Chris Pronger .05 .15
340 Brian Propp .02 .10
341 Darren Turcotte .02 .10
342 Pat Conacher .02 .10
343 Mark Hardy .02 .10
344 Charlie Huddy .02 .10
345 Shawn McEachern .02 .10
346 Warren Rychel .02 .10
347 Robb Stauber .05 .15
348 Dave Taylor .05 .15
349 Benoit Brunet .02 .10
350 Guy Carbonneau .02 .10
351 J.J. Daigneault .02 .10
352 Kevin Haller .02 .10
353 Gary Leeman .02 .10
354 Lyle Odelein .02 .10
355 Andre Racicot .05 .15
356 Ron Wilson .02 .10
357 Martin Brodeur .40 1.00
358 Ken Daneyko .02 .10
359 Bill Guerin .02 .10
360 Bobby Holik .02 .10
361 Corey Millen .02 .10
362 Jaroslav Modry RC .02 .10
363 Jason Smith RC .02 .10
364 Brad Dalgarno .02 .10
365 Travis Green .05 .15
366 Ron Hextall .05 .15
367 Steve Junker .02 .10
368 Tom Kurvers .02 .10
369 Scott Lachance .02 .10
370 Marty McInnis .02 .10
371 Glenn Healy .05 .15
372 Alexander Karpovtsev .02 .10
373 Steve Larmer .05 .15
374 Doug Lidster .02 .10
375 Kevin Lowe .02 .10
376 Mattias Norstrom RC .02 .10
377 Esa Tikkanen .02 .10
378 Craig Billington .05 .15
379 Robert Burakovsky RC .02 .10
380 Alexandre Daigle .02 .10
381 Dmitri Filimonov .02 .10
382 Darrin Madeley RC .02 .10
383 Vladimir Ruzicka .02 .10
384 Alexei Yashin .02 .10
385 Vlacheslav Butsayev .02 .10
386 Pelle Eklund .02 .10
387 Brent Fedyk .02 .10
388 Greg Hawgood .02 .10
389 Milos Holan RC .02 .10
390 Stewart Malgunas RC .02 .10
391 Mikael Renberg .10 .30
392 Dominic Roussel .05 .15
393 Doug Brown .02 .10
394 Marty McSorley .05 .15
395 Markus Naslund .10 .30
396 Mike Ramsey .02 .10
397 Peter Taglianetti .02 .10
398 Bryan Trottier .05 .15
399 Ken Wregget .05 .15
400 Iain Fraser .02 .10
401 Martin Gelinas .02 .10
402 Kerry Huffman .02 .10
403 Claude Lapointe .02 .10
404 Curtis Leschyshyn .02 .10
405 Chris Lindberg .02 .10
406 Jocelyn Thibault RC .40 1.00
407 Murray Baron .02 .10
408 Bob Bassen .02 .10
409 Phil Housley .05 .15
410 Jim Hrivnak .02 .10
411 Tony Hrkac .02 .10
412 Vitali Karamnov .02 .10
413 Jim Montgomery RC .02 .10
414 Vlastimil Kroupa RC .02 .10
415 Igor Larionov .02 .10
416 Sergei Makarov .02 .10
417 Jeff Norton .02 .10
418 Mike Rathje .02 .10
419 Jim Waite .05 .15
420 Ray Whitney .02 .10
421 Mikael Andersson .02 .10
422 Donald Dufresne .02 .10
423 Chris Gratton .05 .15
424 Brent Gretzky RC .02 .10
425 Petr Klima .02 .10
426 Bill McDougall RC .02 .10
427 Daren Puppa .05 .15
428 Denis Savard .05 .15
429 Ken Baumgartner .02 .10
430 Sylvain Lefebvre .02 .10
431 Jamie Macoun .02 .10
432 Matt Martin RC .02 .10
433 Mark Osborne .02 .10
434 Rob Pearson .02 .10
435 Damian Rhodes RC .05 .15
436 Peter Zezel .02 .10
437 Shawn Antoski .02 .10
438 Jose Charbonneau .02 .10
439 Murray Craven .02 .10
440 Gerald Diduck .02 .10
441 Dana Murzyn .02 .10
442 Gino Odjick .02 .10
443 Kay Whitmore .05 .15
444 Randy Burridge .02 .10
445 Sylvain Cote .02 .10
446 Keith Jones .02 .10
447 Olaf Kolzig .05 .15
448 Todd Krygier .02 .10
449 Pat Peake .02 .10
450 Dave Poulin .02 .10
451 Stephane Beauregard .05 .15
452 Luciano Borsato .02 .10
453 Nelson Emerson .02 .10
454 Boris Mironov .02 .10
455 Teppo Numminen .02 .10
456 Stephane Quintal .02 .10
457 Paul Ysebaert .02 .10
458 Adrian Aucoin RC .10 .30
459 Todd Brost RC .02 .10
460 Martin Gendron RC .02 .10
461 David Harlock .02 .10
462 Corey Hirsch .05 .15
463 Todd Hlushko RC .02 .10
464 Fabian Joseph RC .02 .10
465 Paul Kariya 2.00 5.00
466 Brett Lindros RC .02 .10
467 Ken Lovsin RC .02 .10
468 Jason Marshall .02 .10
469 Derek Mayer RC .02 .10
470 Dwayne Norris RC .02 .10
471 Russ Romaniuk .02 .10
472 Brian Savage RC .10 .30
473 Trevor Sim RC .02 .10
474 Chris Therien RC .02 .10
475 Brad Turner RC .02 .10
476 Todd Warriner RC .02 .10
477 Craig Woodcroft RC .02 .10
478 Mark Beaufait RC .02 .10
479 Jim Campbell .02 .10
480 Ted Crowley RC .02 .10
481 Mike Dunham .05 .15
482 Chris Ferraro RC .02 .10
483 Peter Ferraro .02 .10
484 Brett Hauer RC .02 .10
485 Darby Hendrickson RC .02 .10
486 Chris Imes RC .02 .10
487 Craig Johnson RC .02 .10
488 Peter Laviolette RC .02 .10
489 Jeff Lazaro .02 .10
490 John Lilley RC .02 .10
491 Todd Marchant .02 .10
492 Ian Moran RC .02 .10
493 Travis Richards RC .05 .15
494 Barry Richter RC .02 .10
495 David Roberts RC .02 .10
496 Brian Rolston .02 .10
497 David Sacco RC .02 .10
498 Checklist Card .02 .10
499 Checklist Card .02 .10
500 Checklist Card .02 .10
C3C Wayne Gretzky 2/10 6.00 15.00

1993-94 Ultra Adam Oates

As part of Ultra's Signature series, this 12-card standard-size set presents career highlights of Adam Oates. These cards were randomly inserted throughout all packs, and Oates autographed more than 2,000 of his cards. Stated odds suggest the likelihood of pulling an autographed card at 1:10,000 packs. Two additional cards (11, 12) were available only by mail for ten Ultra wrappers plus 1.00.

COMPLETE SET (10) 1.50 4.00
COMMON OATES (1-10) .20 .50
COMMON MAIL-IN (11-12) .75 2.00
NNO Adam Oates/AU 12.00 30.00

1993-94 Ultra All-Rookies

Randomly inserted at a rate of 1:20 19-card first-series jumbo packs, this 10-card standard-size set features on its borderless fronts color player action cutouts "breaking out" of their simulated ice backgrounds. The player's name appears in gold-foil lettering at a lower corner. The blue back carries the player's name at the top in gold-foil lettering, followed below by career highlights and a color player action cutout. The cards are numbered on the back as "X of 10."

COMPLETE SET (10) 3.00 8.00
1 Philippe Boucher .40 1.00
2 Viktor Gordiouk .40 1.00
3 Corey Hirsch .75 2.00
4 Chris LiPuma .40 1.00
5 David Littman .40 1.00
6 Joby Messier .40 1.00
7 Chris Simon .40 1.00
8 Bryan Smolinski .40 1.00
9 Jozef Stumpel .40 1.00
10 Milan Tichy .40 1.00

1993-94 Ultra All-Stars

Randomly inserted into all first series packs, this 18-card standard-size set focuses on 18 of the NHL's best players. The set numbering is by conference All-Stars, Wales (1-9) and Campbell (10-18).

COMPLETE SET (18) 10.00 25.00
1 Patrick Roy 2.50 6.00
2 Ray Bourque .75 2.00
3 Pierre Turgeon .25 .60
4 Pat LaFontaine .50 1.25
5 Alexander Mogilny .25 .60
6 Kevin Stevens .15 .40
7 Adam Oates .25 .60
8 Al Iafrate .15 .40
9 Kirk Muller .15 .40
10 Ed Belfour .50 1.25
11 Teemu Selanne .50 1.25
12 Steve Yzerman 2.50 6.00
13 Luc Robitaille .25 .60
14 Chris Chelios .50 1.25
15 Wayne Gretzky 3.00 8.00
16 Doug Gilmour .25 .60
17 Pavel Bure .50 1.25
18 Phil Housley .25 .60

1993-94 Ultra Award Winners

Randomly inserted into all first series packs, this six-card standard-size set honors NHL award winners of the previous season. Each borderless front features the player with his award. The back has an action photo and career highlights. The cards are numbered "X of 6".

COMPLETE SET (6) 3.00 8.00
1 Ed Belfour .60 1.50
Jennings/Vezina
Trophies
2 Chris Chelios .60 1.50
Norris Trophy
3 Doug Gilmour .30 .75
Selke Trophy
4 Mario Lemieux 2.00 5.00
5 Dave Poulin .20 .50
King Clancy Trophy
6 Teemu Selanne .60 1.50
Calder Trophy

1993-94 Ultra Premier Pivots

Randomly inserted in all series II packs, these ten standard-size cards feature some of the NHL's greatest centers. The borderless fronts have color player action shots on motion-streaked backgrounds. The player's name appears in silver foil at the upper right. The cards are numbered on the back as "X of 10."

COMPLETE SET (10) 8.00 20.00
1 Doug Gilmour .20 .50
2 Wayne Gretzky 2.50 6.00
3 Pat LaFontaine .40 1.00
4 Mario Lemieux 2.00 5.00
5 Eric Lindros .40 1.00
6 Mark Messier .40 1.00
7 Adam Oates .20 .50
8 Jeremy Roenick .50 1.25
9 Pierre Turgeon .20 .50
10 Steve Yzerman 2.00 5.00

1993-94 Ultra Promo Sheet

This (approximately) 11" by 8 1/2" sheet features some of the cards of the 1993-94 Ultra set. It is arranged in three rows with three cards each, the middle card in the middle row is not a player's card but a title card. The backs are also identical to the cards' backs.

NNO Joe Juneau 2.00 5.00
Sergei Fedorov, Mats Sundin, Mark Recchi, Jeremy Roenick, Alexei Kovalev

1993-94 Ultra Prospects

Randomly inserted into first series foil packs, the Ultra Prospects set consists of ten standard-size cards. Borderless fronts feature the player emerging from a solid background. The backs contain a photo and career highlights. The cards are numbered as "X of 10".

COMPLETE SET (10) 3.00 8.00
1 Iain Fraser .40 1.00
2 Rob Gaudreau .40 1.00
3 Dave Karpa .40 1.00
4 Trent Klatt .40 1.00
5 Mike Lenarduzzi .40 1.00
6 Kevin Miehm .40 1.00
7 Michael Nylander .75 2.00
8 J.F. Quintin .40 1.00
9 Gary Shuchuk .40 1.00
10 Tyler Wright .40 1.00

1993-94 Ultra Red Light Specials

Randomly inserted in series 2 packs, this ten-card standard-size set highlights some of the NHL's best goal scorers. The borderless fronts feature two color player action shots, one superimposed upon the other. The player's name appears in red foil at the bottom. The horizontal back carries an on-ice close-up of the player set off to the right. The player's name appears in red foil at the upper left, followed below by the player's goal-scoring highlights, all on the red-screened background from the player close-up. The cards are numbered on the back as "X of 10."

COMPLETE SET (10) 6.00 15.00
1 Dave Andreychuk .40 1.00
2 Pavel Bure .75 2.00
3 Mike Gartner .40 1.00
4 Brett Hull 1.00 2.50
5 Jaromir Jagr 1.25 3.00
6 Mario Lemieux 2.00 5.00
7 Alexander Mogilny .40 1.00
8 Mark Recchi .40 1.00
9 Luc Robitaille .40 1.00
10 Teemu Selanne .75 2.00

1993-94 Ultra Scoring Kings

Randomly inserted into all first series packs, this six-card standard-size set showcases six of the NHL's top scorers. Borderless fronts have action player photos. Backs feature a player photo and career highlights. The player's name appears in gold at the top. The card are numbered "X of 6".

COMPLETE SET (6) 10.00 25.00
1 Pat LaFontaine .60 1.50
2 Wayne Gretzky 4.00 10.00
3 Brett Hull .75 2.00
4 Mario Lemieux 3.00 8.00
5 Pierre Turgeon .30 .75
6 Steve Yzerman 3.00 8.00

1993-94 Ultra Speed Merchants

Randomly inserted in second series jumbo packs, this 10-card standard-size set sports fronts of motion-streaked color player action cutouts set on borderless indigo backgrounds highlighted by ice spray. The cards are numbered on the back as "X of 10."

COMPLETE SET (10) 10.00 25.00
1 Pavel Bure 2.00 5.00
2 Russ Courtnall .75 2.00
3 Sergei Fedorov 2.00 5.00
4 Mike Gartner .75 2.00
5 Al Iafrate .75 2.00
6 Pat LaFontaine 1.50 4.00
7 Alexander Mogilny 1.50 4.00
8 Rob Niedermayer .75 2.00
9 Geoff Sanderson .75 2.00
10 Teemu Selanne 2.00 5.00

1993-94 Ultra Wave of the Future

Randomly inserted in series II packs, these 20 standard-size cards highlight players in their first or second NHL season. The borderless fronts feature color player action shots with "rippled" on-ice backgrounds. The player's name appears in gold foil at a lower corner. The cards are numbered on the back as "X of 20."

COMPLETE SET (20) 6.00 15.00
1 Jason Arnott .40 1.00
2 Martin Brodeur 2.00 5.00
3 Alexandre Daigle .20 .50
4 Ted Drury .20 .50
5 Chris Gratton .20 .50
6 Milos Holan .20 .50
7 Greg Johnson .20 .50
8 Boris Mironov .20 .50
9 Jaroslav Modry .20 .50
10 Markus Naslund .60 1.50
11 Rob Niedermayer .40 1.00
12 Chris Osgood .75 2.00
13 Derek Plante .20 .50
14 Chris Pronger .60 1.50
15 Mike Rathje .20 .50
16 Mikael Renberg .40 1.00
17 Jason Smith .20 .50
18 Jocelyn Thibault .60 1.50
19 Jarkko Varvio .20 .50
20 Alexei Yashin .20 .50

1994-95 Ultra

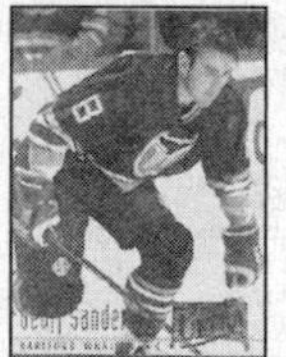

The 1994-95 Ultra hockey set consists of two series of 200 and 150 cards, for a total of 350 standard-size cards. The suggested retail price for 12-card packs was $1.99, and $2.69 for 15-card packs. Every pack included one insert card, and one "Hot Pack" consisting exclusively of insert cards was seeded once every two boxes (or 1:72 packs). Full-bleed card fronts have the player's name, team and Ultra logo in gold foil at the bottom. The backs also have a full-bleed photo with two smaller inset photos. Stats are at the bottom. Each series is arranged alphabetically by team and the player's within each team alphabetized. Rookie Cards include Mariusz Czerkawski and Eric Fichaud.

COMPLETE SET (400) 17.50 35.00
COMP.SERIES 1 (250) 10.00 20.00
COMP.SERIES 2 (150) 7.50 15.00
1 Bob Corkum .02 .10
2 Todd Ewen .02 .10
3 Guy Hebert .05 .15
4 Bill Houlder .02 .10
5 Stephan Lebeau .02 .10
6 Joe Sacco .02 .10
7 Anatoli Semenov .02 .10
8 Tim Sweeney .02 .10
9 Terry Yake .02 .10
10 Ray Bourque .20 .50
11 Mariusz Czerkawski RC .10 .30
12 Ted Donato .02 .10
13 Cam Neely .10 .30
14 Adam Oates .05 .15
15 Vincent Riendeau .05 .15
16 Bryan Smolinski .02 .10
17 Don Sweeney .02 .10
18 Glen Wesley .02 .10
19 Donald Audette .02 .10
20 Doug Bodger .02 .10
21 Jason Dawe .02 .10
22 Dominik Hasek .25 .60
23 Dale Hawerchuk .05 .15
24 Pat LaFontaine .10 .30
25 Brad May .02 .10
26 Alexander Mogilny .05 .15
27 Derek Plante .02 .10
28 Richard Smehlik .02 .10
29 Theo Fleury .02 .10
30 Trevor Kidd .05 .15
31 Frank Musil .02 .10
32 Michael Nylander .02 .10
33 James Patrick .02 .10
34 Robert Reichel .02 .10
35 Gary Roberts .02 .10
36 German Titov .02 .10
37 Wes Walz .02 .10
38 Zarley Zalapski .02 .10
39 Ed Belfour .10 .30
40 Chris Chelios .10 .30
41 Dirk Graham .02 .10
42 Bernie Nicholls .05 .15
43 Patrick Poulin .02 .10
44 Jeremy Roenick .10 .30
45 Steve Smith .02 .10
46 Gary Suter .02 .10
47 Brent Sutter .02 .10
48 Neal Broten .05 .15
49 Paul Cavallini .02 .10
50 Dean Evason .02 .10
51 Dave Gagner .05 .15
52 Derian Hatcher .02 .10
53 Trent Klatt .02 .10
54 Grant Ledyard .02 .10
55 Mike Modano .20 .50
56 Andy Moog .10 .30
57 Mark Tinordi .02 .10
58 Dino Ciccarelli .05 .15
59 Paul Coffey .10 .30
60 Sergei Fedorov .20 .50
61 Vladimir Konstantinov .05 .15
62 Nicklas Lidstrom .10 .30
63 Darren McCarty .02 .10
64 Chris Osgood .20 .50
65 Keith Primeau .02 .10
66 Ray Sheppard .05 .15
67 Steve Yzerman .60 1.50
68 Jason Arnott .02 .10
69 Bob Beers .02 .10
70 Ilya Byakin .02 .10
71 Zdeno Ciger .02 .10
72 Igor Kravchuk .02 .10
73 Boris Mironov .02 .10
74 Fredrik Olausson .02 .10
75 Scott Pearson .02 .10
76 Bill Ranford .05 .15
77 Doug Weight .05 .15
78 Stu Barnes .02 .10
79 Jesse Belanger .02 .10
80 Bob Kudelski .02 .10
81 Andrei Lomakin .02 .10
82 Dave Lowry .02 .10
83 Gord Murphy .02 .10
84 Rob Niedermayer .05 .15
85 Brian Skrudland .02 .10
86 John Vanbiesbrouck .05 .15
87 Sean Burke .05 .15
88 Ted Drury .02 .10
89 Alexander Godynyuk .02 .10
90 Robert Kron .02 .10
91 Chris Pronger .10 .30
92 Brian Propp .02 .10
93 Geoff Sanderson .05 .15
94 Darren Turcotte .02 .10
95 Pat Verbeek .02 .10
96 Rob Blake .05 .15
97 Mike Donnelly .02 .10
98 John Druce .02 .10
99 Kelly Hrudey .05 .15
100 Jari Kurri .05 .15
101 Robert Lang .02 .10
102 Marty McSorley .02 .10
103 Luc Robitaille .05 .15
104 Alexei Zhitnik .02 .10
105 Brian Bellows .02 .10
106 Patrice Brisebois .02 .10
107 Vincent Damphousse .02 .10
108 Eric Desjardins .05 .15
109 Gilbert Dionne .02 .10
110 Mike Keane .02 .10
111 John LeClair .10 .30
112 Lyle Odelein .02 .10
113 Patrick Roy .60 1.50
114 Mathieu Schneider .02 .10
115 Martin Brodeur .30 .75
116 Jim Dowd .02 .10
117 Bill Guerin .05 .15
118 Claude Lemieux .02 .10
119 John MacLean .05 .15
120 Corey Millen .02 .10
121 Scott Niedermayer .02 .10
122 Stephane Richer .05 .15
123 Scott Stevens .05 .15
124 Valeri Zelepukin .02 .10
125 Patrick Flatley .02 .10
126 Travis Green .05 .15
127 Ron Hextall .05 .15
128 Benoit Hogue .02 .10
129 Darius Kasparaitis .02 .10
130 Vladimir Malakhov .02 .10
131 Marty McInnis .02 .10
132 Steve Thomas .02 .10
133 Pierre Turgeon .05 .15
134 Dennis Vaske .02 .10
135 Glenn Anderson .05 .15
136 Jeff Beukeboom .02 .10
137 Adam Graves .02 .10
138 Steve Larmer .05 .15
139 Brian Leetch .10 .30
140 Mark Messier .10 .30
141 Petr Nedved .05 .15
142 Sergei Nemchinov .02 .10
143 Mike Richter .10 .30

144 Sergei Zubov .02 .10
145 Craig Billington .05 .15
146 Alexandre Daigle .02 .10
147 Evgeny Davydov .02 .10
148 Scott Levins .02 .10
149 Norm Maciver .02 .10
150 Troy Mallette .02 .10
151 Brad Shaw .02 .10
152 Alexei Yashin .02 .10
153 Josef Beranek .02 .10
154 Jason Bowen .02 .10
155 Rod Brind'Amour .05 .15
156 Kevin Dineen .02 .10
157 Garry Galley .02 .10
158 Mark Recchi .05 .15
159 Mikael Renberg .05 .15
160 Tommy Soderstrom .05 .15
161 Dimitri Yushkevich .02 .10
162 Tom Barrasso .05 .15
163 Ron Francis .05 .15
164 Jaromir Jagr .20 .50
165 Mario Lemieux .60 1.50
166 Shawn McEachern .02 .10
167 Joe Mullen .05 .15
168 Larry Murphy .05 .15
169 Ulf Samuelsson .02 .10
170 Kevin Stevens .02 .10
171 Martin Straka .02 .10
172 Wendel Clark .05 .15
173 Stephane Fiset .05 .15
174 Iain Fraser .02 .10
175 Andrei Kovalenko .02 .10
176 Sylvain Lefebvre .02 .10
177 Owen Nolan .05 .15
178 Mike Ricci .02 .10
179 Martin Rucinsky .02 .10
180 Joe Sakic .25 .60
181 Scott Young .02 .10
182 Steve Duchesne .02 .10
183 Brett Hull .15 .40
184 Curtis Joseph .10 .30
185 Al MacInnis .05 .15
186 Kevin Miller .02 .10
187 Jim Montgomery .02 .10
188 Vitali Prokhorov .02 .10
189 Brendan Shanahan .10 .30
190 Peter Stastny .05 .15
191 Esa Tikkanen .02 .10
192 Ulf Dahlen .02 .10
193 Todd Elik .02 .10
194 Johan Garpenlov .02 .10
195 Arturs Irbe .05 .15
196 Vlastimil Kroupa .02 .10
197 Igor Larionov .02 .10
198 Sergei Makarov .02 .10
199 Jeff Norton .02 .10
200 Sandis Ozolinsh .02 .10
201 Mike Rathje .02 .10
202 Brian Bradley .02 .10
203 Shawn Chambers .02 .10
204 Danton Cole .02 .10
205 Chris Gratton .02 .10
206 Roman Hamrlik .05 .15
207 Chris Joseph .02 .10
208 Petr Klima .02 .10
209 Daren Puppa .05 .15
210 John Tucker .02 .10
211 Dave Andreychuk .05 .15
212 Ken Baumgartner .02 .10
213 Dave Ellett .02 .10
214 Mike Gartner .05 .15
215 Todd Gill .02 .10
216 Doug Gilmour .05 .15
217 Jamie Macoun .02 .10
218 Dmitri Mironov .02 .10
219 Felix Potvin .10 .30
220 Mats Sundin .10 .30
221 Jeff Brown .02 .10
222 Pavel Bure .10 .30
223 Murray Craven .02 .10
224 Bret Hedican .02 .10
225 Nathan Lafayette .02 .10
226 Trevor Linden .05 .15
227 Jyrki Lumme .02 .10
228 Kirk McLean .05 .15
229 Gino Odjick .02 .10
230 Cliff Ronning .02 .10
231 Peter Bondra .05 .15
232 Sylvain Cote .02 .10
233 Kevin Hatcher .02 .10
234 Dale Hunter .02 .10
235 Calle Johansson .02 .10
236 Dimitri Khristich .02 .10
237 Pat Peake .02 .10
238 Michal Pivonka .02 .10
239 Rick Tabaracci .05 .15
240 Tim Cheveldae .05 .15
241 Dallas Drake .02 .10
242 Nelson Emerson .02 .10
243 Dave Manson .02 .10
244 Teppo Numminen .02 .10
245 Stephane Quintal .02 .10
246 Teemu Selanne .10 .30
247 Keith Tkachuk .10 .30
248 Checklist .02 .10
249 Checklist .02 .10
250 Checklist .02 .10
251 John Lilley .02 .10
252 Mikhail Shtalenkov .02 .10
253 Garry Valk .02 .10
254 John Gruden RC .02 .10
255 Brent Hughes .02 .10
256 Al Iafrate .02 .10
257 Alexei Kasatonov .02 .10
258 Mikko Makela .02 .10
259 Marc Potvin .02 .10
260 Jon Rohloff RC .02 .10
261 Jozef Stumpel .02 .10
262 Grant Fuhr .05 .15
263 Viktor Gordiouk .02 .10
264 Yuri Khmylev .02 .10
265 Craig Muni .02 .10
266 Craig Simpson .02 .10
267 Denis Tsygurov RC .02 .10
268 Steve Chiasson .02 .10
269 Phil Housley .05 .15
270 Joel Otto .02 .10
271 Andrei Trefilov .02 .10
272 Vesa Viitakoski .02 .10
273 Tony Amonte .05 .15
274 Brent Grieve .02 .10
275 Bernie Nicholls .05 .15
276 Christian Soucy RC .05 .15
277 Paul Ysebaert .02 .10
278 Shane Churla .02 .10
279 Russ Courtnall .02 .10
280 Craig Ludwig .02 .10
281 Jarkko Varvio .02 .10
282 Darcy Wakaluk .05 .15
283 Greg Johnson .02 .10
284 Slava Kozlov .05 .15
285 Martin Lapointe .02 .10
286 Tim Taylor RC .02 .10
287 Mike Vernon .05 .15
288 Jason York RC .02 .10
289 Fred Brathwaite .05 .15
290 Kelly Buchberger .02 .10
291 Shayne Corson .02 .10
292 Dean McAmmond .02 .10
293 Vladimir Vujtek .02 .10
294 Doug Barrault .02 .10
295 Keith Brown .02 .10
296 Mark Fitzpatrick .05 .15
297 Mike Hough .02 .10
298 Scott Mellanby .05 .15
299 Jimmy Carson .02 .10
300 Andrew Cassels .02 .10
301 Andrei Nikolishin .02 .10
302 Steven Rice .02 .10
303 Glen Wesley .02 .10
304 Rob Brown .02 .10
305 Tony Granato .02 .10
306 Wayne Gretzky .75 2.00
307 Dan Quinn .02 .10
308 Darryl Sydor .02 .10
309 Rick Tocchet .05 .15
310 Donald Brashear RC .02 .10
311 Valeri Bure .02 .10
312 Jim Montgomery .02 .10
313 Kirk Muller .02 .10
314 Oleg Petrov .02 .10
315 Peter Popovic .02 .10
316 Yves Racine .02 .10
317 Turner Stevenson .02 .10
318 Ken Daneyko .02 .10
319 David Emma .02 .10
320 Brian Rolston .02 .10
321 Alexander Semak .02 .10
322 Jason Smith .02 .10
323 Chris Terreri .05 .15
324 Ray Ferraro .02 .10
325 Derek King .02 .10
326 Scott Lachance .02 .10
327 Brett Lindros .02 .10
328 Jamie McLennan .02 .10
329 Zigmund Palffy .05 .15
330 Corey Hirsch .05 .15
331 Alexei Kovalev .02 .10
332 Stephane Matteau .02 .10
333 Petr Nedved .05 .15
334 Mattias Norstrom .02 .10
335 Mark Osborne .02 .10
336 Randy Cunneyworth .02 .10
337 Pavol Demitra .05 .15
338 Pat Elynuik .02 .10
339 Sean Hill .02 .10
340 Darrin Madeley .02 .10
341 Sylvain Turgeon .02 .10
342 Vladislav Boulin RC .02 .10
343 Ron Hextall .05 .15
344 Patrik Juhlin RC .02 .10
345 Eric Lindros .10 .30
346 Shjon Podein .02 .10
347 Chris Therien .02 .10
348 John Cullen .02 .10
349 Markus Naslund .10 .30
350 Luc Robitaille .05 .15
351 Kjell Samuelsson .02 .10
352 Tomas Sandstrom .02 .10
353 Ken Wregget .05 .15
354 Wendel Clark .05 .15
355 Adam Deadmarsh .05 .15
356 Peter Forsberg .50 1.25
357 Valeri Kamensky .05 .15
358 Uwe Krupp .02 .10
359 Janne Laukkanen .02 .10
360 Sylvain Lefebvre .02 .10
361 Jocelyn Thibault .10 .30
362 Bill Houlder .02 .10
363 Craig Janney .05 .15
364 Pat Falloon .05 .15
365 Jeff Friesen .02 .10
366 Viktor Kozlov .02 .10
367 Andrei Nazarov .02 .10
368 Jeff Odgers .02 .10
369 Michal Sykora .02 .10
370 Mikael Andersson .02 .10
371 Eric Charron RC .02 .10
372 Chris LiPuma .02 .10
373 Denis Savard .05 .15
374 Jason Wiemer RC .02 .10
375 Nikolai Borschevsky .02 .10
376 Eric Fichaud RC .05 .15
377 Kenny Jonsson .02 .10
378 Mike Ridley .02 .10
379 Mats Sundin .10 .30
380 Greg Adams .02 .10
381 Shawn Antoski .02 .10
382 Geoff Courtnall .02 .10
383 Martin Gelinas .02 .10
384 Sergio Momesso .02 .10
385 Jiri Slegr .02 .10
386 Jason Allison .02 .10
387 Don Beaupre .05 .15
388 Joe Juneau .05 .15
389 Steve Konowalchuk .02 .10
390 Kelly Miller .02 .10
391 Dave Poulin .02 .10
392 Tie Domi .05 .15
393 Michal Grosek RC .02 .10
394 Russ Romaniuk .02 .10
395 Darrin Shannon .02 .10
396 Thomas Steen .02 .10
397 Igor Ulanov .02 .10
398 Alexei Zhamnov .05 .15
399 Checklist .02 .10
400 Checklist .02 .10

1994-95 Ultra All-Rookies

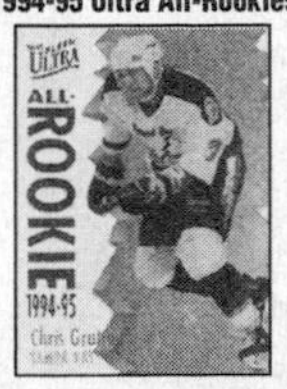

Randomly inserted in first series jumbo packs, this 10-card standard-size set reflects top rookies from the 1993-94 campaign. On acetate stock, the player is on the right superimposed over an ice-like surface. The left side is clear with the set title. The left portion of the back has a brief write-up and photo. Two distinct versions of each card in this set exist; one version carries the words "All-Rookie 1994-95" in a dark, greyish silver tint; the other in a bright, sparkling silver tint.

COMPLETE SET (10) 6.00 15.00
1 Jason Arnott .75 2.00
2 Martin Brodeur 4.00 10.00
3 Alexandre Daigle .75 2.00
4 Chris Gratton .40 1.00
5 Boris Mironov .40 1.00
6 Derek Plante .40 1.00
7 Chris Pronger .75 2.00
8 Mikael Renberg .40 1.00
9 Bryan Smolinski .40 1.00
10 Alexei Yashin .75 2.00

1994-95 Ultra All-Stars

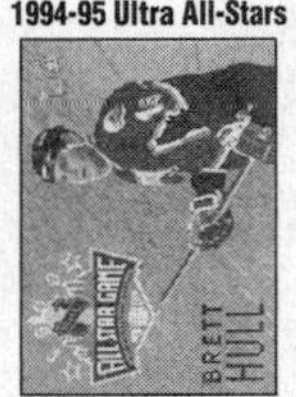

Randomly inserted into first series foil packs at a rate of 1:2, this standard-size set focuses on 12 players who participated in the 1994 NHL All-Star Game in New York. The set is arranged according to Eastern (1-6) and Western Conferences (7-12). Horizontally designed, the front features the player in his All-Star jersey. The background is colorful and flashy. The All-Star logo also appears on front. The backs are much the same with an up-close player photo.

COMPLETE SET (12) 2.50 6.00
1 Ray Bourque .25 .60
2 Brian Leetch .15 .40
3 Eric Lindros .15 .40
4 Mark Messier .15 .40
5 Alexander Mogilny .07 .20
6 Patrick Roy .75 2.00
7 Pavel Bure .15 .40
8 Chris Chelios .15 .40
9 Paul Coffey .15 .40
10 Wayne Gretzky 1.00 2.50
11 Brett Hull .20 .50
12 Felix Potvin .15 .40

1994-95 Ultra Award Winners

Randomly inserted into first series foil packs, this 8-card standard-size set honors NHL award winners of the previous season. Horizontally designed, the fronts have an action photo and, to the left, the player in his tux at the awards ceremony. The backs have a write-up and a player photo.

COMPLETE SET (8) 5.00 12.00
1 Ray Bourque .60 1.50
2 Martin Brodeur 1.00 2.50
3 Sergei Fedorov .60 1.50
4 Adam Graves .10 .30
5 Wayne Gretzky 2.50 6.00
6 Dominik Hasek .75 2.00
7 Brian Leetch .40 1.00
8 Cam Neely .40 1.00

1994-95 Ultra Global Greats

Randomly inserted in second series 15-card jumbo packs at a rate of 1:12, this 10-card standard-size set features superstars who hail from outside North America. On the front, a player photo is superimposed over a background of colorful globes. The back features a write-up and a photo over the same background.

COMPLETE SET (10) 6.00 15.00
1 Sergei Fedorov 1.50 4.00
2 Dominik Hasek 2.00 5.00
3 Arturs Irbe .50 1.25
4 Jaromir Jagr 1.50 4.00
5 Jari Kurri .50 1.25
6 Alexander Mogilny .50 1.25
7 Petr Nedved .50 1.25
8 Mikael Renberg .50 1.25
9 Teemu Selanne 1.00 2.50
10 Alexei Yashin .30 .75

1994-95 Ultra Power

Randomly inserted in first series foil packs and distributed one set per hobby case, this 10-card standard-size set focuses on high scoring forwards. The card fronts contain a player photo superimposed over a glossy and circular background. The backs are horizontal with a player photo, highlights and a similar background.

COMPLETE SET (10) 3.00 8.00
1 Dave Andreychuk .30 .75
2 Jason Arnott .20 .50
3 Chris Gratton .20 .50
4 Adam Graves .20 .50
5 Eric Lindros .60 1.50
6 Cam Neely .60 1.50
7 Mikael Renberg .30 .75
8 Jeremy Roenick .60 1.50
9 Brendan Shanahan .60 1.50
10 Keith Tkachuk .60 1.50

1994-95 Ultra Premier Pad Men

Randomly inserted in first series foil packs at a rate of 1:37, this 6-card standard-size set spotlights leading goaltenders. On front, a gold embossed design serves as background to the player photo. The backs have a solid color background that coordinates with the player's team. A player photo and write-up are in the foreground.

COMPLETE SET (6) 10.00 20.00
1 Dominik Hasek 2.00 5.00
2 Arturs Irbe .50 1.25
3 Curtis Joseph 1.00 2.50
4 Felix Potvin 1.00 2.50
5 Mike Richter 1.00 2.50
6 Patrick Roy 6.00 15.00

1994-95 Ultra Premier Pivots

Randomly inserted in second series foil packs at a rate of 1:4, this 10-card standard-size set spotlights leading NHL centers. The fronts contain a player photo superimposed over a brown checkered background. The backs are similar except for the addition of some player highlights.

COMPLETE SET (10) 6.00 12.00
1 Jason Arnott .10 .30
2 Sergei Fedorov .60 1.50
3 Doug Gilmour .20 .50
4 Wayne Gretzky 2.50 6.00
5 Pat LaFontaine .40 1.00
6 Eric Lindros .40 1.00
7 Mark Messier .40 1.00
8 Mike Modano .60 1.50
9 Adam Oates .20 .50
10 Steve Yzerman 2.00 5.00

1994-95 Ultra Prospects

Randomly inserted in second series 12-card foil packs at a rate of 1:12, this 10-card standard size set focuses on some of the rookie crop from the 1994-95 season. The fronts have an embossed player photo superimposed over a background containing the set name. The backs have a photo and write-up.

COMPLETE SET (10) 15.00 30.00
1 Peter Forsberg 5.00 12.00
2 Todd Harvey .75 2.00
3 Paul Kariya 2.00 5.00
4 Viktor Kozlov .75 2.00
5 Brett Lindros .75 2.00
6 Mike Peca .75 2.00
7 Brian Rolston .75 2.00
8 Jamie Storr 1.50 4.00
9 Oleg Tverdovsky .75 2.00
10 Jason Wiemer .75 2.00

1994-95 Ultra Red Light Specials

Randomly inserted in second series foil packs at a rate of 1:12, this 10-card standard-size set presents top goal scorers. The fronts are horizontally designed with a player photo superimposed over three action strips of the player. The set logo is in red foil at bottom left. The backs offer a photo and highlights.

COMPLETE SET (10) 1.50 4.00
1 Dave Andreychuk .10 .30
2 Pavel Bure .25 .60
3 Mike Gartner .10 .30
4 Adam Graves .07 .20
5 Brett Hull .30 .75
6 Cam Neely .25 .60
7 Gary Roberts .07 .20
8 Teemu Selanne .25 .60
9 Brendan Shanahan .25 .60
10 Kevin Stevens .07 .20

1994-95 Ultra Scoring Kings

Randomly inserted in first series foil packs, this 7-card standard-size set showcases seven of the NHL's top scorers. The fronts provide three player photos with a gold foil set logo at bottom left. The backs have a player photo and write-up.

COMPLETE SET (7) 5.00 10.00
1 Pavel Bure .25 .60
2 Sergei Fedorov .40 1.00
3 Doug Gilmour .10 .30
4 Wayne Gretzky 1.50 4.00
5 Mario Lemieux 1.25 3.00
6 Eric Lindros .25 .60
7 Steve Yzerman 1.25 3.00

1994-95 Ultra Sergei Fedorov

Measuring the standard-size, the first ten cards were randomly inserted in first series foil packs. Card Nos. 11 and 12 were available through a mail-in offer. The set chronicles various stages of Fedorov's career and his abilities. The front offers a photo with a quote from an opposing player, teammate or executive. In addition to providing career information, horizontal backs contain a player photo. An indeterminate number of cards were autographed by Fedorov, and randomly inserted in series one packs.

COMPLETE SET (10) 5.00 10.00
COMMON FEDOROV (1-10) .60 1.50
COMMON FEDOROV AUTO 25.00 60.00
COMMON MAIL-IN (11-12) .75 2.00

1994-95 Ultra Speed Merchants

Randomly inserted in second series foil packs at the rate of 1:2, this 10-card standard-size set salutes the league's fastest and hardest to defend skaters. A player photo is superimposed over an action-oriented background with the player's name and set title in gold foil at the bottom. The backs contain a checkered flag background with a photo and highlights.

COMPLETE SET (10) 1.00 2.50
1 Pavel Bure .20 .50
2 Russ Courtnall .05 .15
3 Sergei Fedorov .30 .75
4 Al Iafrate .05 .15
5 Pat LaFontaine .20 .50
6 Brian Leetch .20 .50
7 Mike Modano .30 .75
8 Alexander Mogilny .08 .25
9 Jeremy Roenick .20 .50
10 Geoff Sanderson .08 .25

1995-96 Ultra

These 400 standard-size cards represent the two series release of the 1995-96 Ultra issue. Issued in 12-card packs, the suggested retail price per pack was $2.49. Each series one pack contains two insert cards. One was a Gold Medallion parallel insert while the other was from one of the five series one Ultra insert sets. Second series packs did not guarantee an insert per pack. The cards are printed on 20-point stock. Key RCs in the set include Daniel Alfredsson, Todd Bertuzzi, Chad Kilger and Kyle McLaren. The Cool Trade Exchange card was randomly inserted 1:360 series two packs, making it the hardest to pull of the five available. The card could be redeemed, until the expiration date of 3/1/97, for special Emotion cards of Jeremy Roenick, Paul Kariya, Saku Koivu and Martin Brodeur.

COMPLETE SET (400) 20.00 50.00
COMP.SERIES 1 (200) 10.00 25.00
COMP.SERIES 2 (200) 10.00 25.00
1 Guy Hebert .05 .15
2 Milos Holan .02 .10
3 Paul Kariya .10 .30
4 Denny Lambert .02 .10
5 Stephan Lebeau .02 .10
6 Oleg Tverdovsky .02 .10
7 Shaun Van Allen .02 .10
8 Ray Bourque .20 .50
9 Mariusz Czerkawski .02 .10
10 Blaine Lacher .05 .15
11 Sandy Moger RC .05 .15
12 Cam Neely .10 .30
13 Adam Oates .05 .15
14 Bryan Smolinski .02 .10
15 Donald Audette .02 .10
16 Jason Dawe .02 .10
17 Garry Galley .02 .10
18 Dominik Hasek .25 .60
19 Brian Holzinger RC .05 .15
20 Pat LaFontaine .10 .30
21 Alexander Mogilny .05 .15
22 Alexei Zhitnik .02 .10
23 Steve Chiasson .02 .10
24 Theo Fleury .02 .10
25 Phil Housley .05 .15
26 Trevor Kidd .05 .15
27 Joel Otto .02 .10
28 Gary Roberts .02 .10
29 Zarley Zalapski .02 .10
30 Ed Belfour .10 .30
31 Chris Chelios .10 .30
32 Eric Daze .05 .15
33 Sergei Krivokrasov .02 .10
34 Bernie Nicholls .02 .10
35 Jeremy Roenick .15 .40
36 Gary Suter .02 .10
37 Todd Harvey .05 .15
38 Derian Hatcher .02 .10
39 Mike Kennedy RC .02 .10
40 Grant Ledyard .02 .10
41 Mike Modano .20 .50
42 Andy Moog .10 .30
43 Mike Torchia RC .05 .15
44 Paul Coffey .10 .30
45 Sergei Fedorov .20 .50
46 Vladimir Konstantinov .05 .15
47 Slava Kozlov .05 .15
48 Keith Primeau .02 .10
49 Ray Sheppard .02 .10
50 Mike Vernon .05 .15
51 Steve Yzerman .60 1.50
52 Jason Arnott .02 .10
53 Shayne Corson .02 .10
54 Igor Kravchuk .02 .10
55 Todd Marchant .02 .10
56 David Oliver .02 .10
57 Bill Ranford .05 .15
58 Doug Weight .05 .15
59 Stu Barnes .02 .10
60 Jesse Belanger .02 .10
61 Gord Murphy .02 .10
62 Rob Niedermayer .05 .15
63 Brian Skrudland .02 .10
64 John Vanbiesbrouck .05 .15
65 Sean Burke .05 .15
66 Andrew Cassels .02 .10
67 Frantisek Kucera .02 .10
68 Andrei Nikolishin .02 .10
69 Chris Pronger .10 .30
70 Geoff Sanderson .02 .10
71 Kevin Smyth .02 .10
72 Darren Turcotte .02 .10
73 Rob Blake .05 .15
74 Wayne Gretzky .75 2.00
75 Kelly Hrudey .05 .15
76 Marty McSorley .02 .10
77 Jamie Storr .05 .15
78 Darryl Sydor .05 .15
79 Rick Tocchet .05 .15
80 Vincent Damphousse .02 .10
81 Vladimir Malakhov .02 .10
82 Mark Recchi .05 .15
83 Patrick Roy .60 1.50
84 Brian Savage .02 .10
85 Pierre Turgeon .05 .15
86 Martin Brodeur .30 .75
87 Neal Broten .05 .15
88 Sergei Brylin .02 .10
89 John MacLean .05 .15
90 Scott Niedermayer .05 .15
91 Stephane Richer .05 .15
92 Scott Stevens .05 .15
93 Ray Ferraro .02 .10
94 Scott Lachance .02 .10
95 Brett Lindros .02 .10
96 Kirk Muller .02 .10
97 Zigmund Palffy .05 .15
98 Tommy Salo RC .20 .50
99 Mathieu Schneider .02 .10
100 Tommy Soderstrom .05 .15
101 Glenn Healy .05 .15
102 Darren Langdon RC .05 .15
103 Steve Larmer .05 .15
104 Brian Leetch .05 .15
105 Mark Messier .10 .30
106 Mattias Norstrom .02 .10
107 Pat Verbeek .02 .10
108 Sergei Zubov .02 .10
109 Don Beaupre .05 .15
110 Radek Bonk .02 .10
111 Alexandre Daigle .02 .10
112 Steve Larouche RC .02 .10
113 Stanislav Neckar .02 .10
114 Alexei Yashin .02 .10
115 Rod Brind'Amour .05 .15
116 Eric Desjardins .05 .15
117 Ron Hextall .05 .15
118 John LeClair .10 .30
119 Eric Lindros .10 .30
120 Mikael Renberg .05 .15
121 Chris Therien .02 .10
122 Ron Francis .05 .15
123 Jaromir Jagr .20 .50
124 Joe Mullen .05 .15
125 Larry Murphy .05 .15
126 Ulf Samuelsson .02 .10
127 Kevin Stevens .02 .10
128 Ken Wregget .05 .15
129 Wendel Clark .05 .15
130 Adam Deadmarsh .02 .10
131 Stephane Fiset .05 .15
132 Peter Forsberg .30 .75
133 Curtis Leschyshyn .02 .10
134 Owen Nolan .05 .15
135 Mike Ricci .05 .15
136 Joe Sakic .25 .60
137 Denis Chasse .02 .10
138 Steve Duchesne .02 .10
139 Brett Hull .15 .40
140 Curtis Joseph .10 .30
141 Ian Laperriere .02 .10
142 Brendan Shanahan .10 .30
143 Esa Tikkanen .02 .10
144 Ulf Dahlen .02 .10
145 Jeff Friesen .02 .10
146 Arturs Irbe .05 .15
147 Craig Janney .02 .10
148 Sergei Makarov .02 .10
149 Sandis Ozolinsh .02 .10
150 Ray Whitney .05 .15
151 Chris Gratton .02 .10
152 Roman Hamrlik .05 .15
153 Petr Klima .02 .10
154 Brantt Myhres RC .02 .10
155 Daren Puppa .05 .15
156 Jason Wiemer .02 .10
157 Paul Ysebaert .02 .10
158 Dave Andreychuk .05 .15
159 Tie Domi .05 .15
160 Doug Gilmour .05 .15
161 Kenny Jonsson .02 .10
162 Felix Potvin .10 .30
163 Mike Ridley .02 .10
164 Mats Sundin .10 .30
165 Jeff Brown .02 .10
166 Pavel Bure .10 .30
167 Geoff Courtnall .02 .10
168 Russ Courtnall .02 .10
169 Trevor Linden .05 .15
170 Kirk McLean .05 .15
171 Roman Oksiuta .02 .10
172 Peter Bondra .05 .15
173 Jim Carey .05 .15
174 Martin Gendron .02 .10
175 Dale Hunter .02 .10
176 Calle Johansson .02 .10
177 Michal Pivonka .02 .10
178 Mark Tinordi .02 .10
179 Nelson Emerson .02 .10
180 Nikolai Khabibulin .05 .15
181 Dave Manson .02 .10
182 Teppo Numminen .02 .10
183 Teemu Selanne .10 .30
184 Keith Tkachuk .10 .30
185 Alexei Zhamnov .05 .15
186 Martin Brodeur SC .30 .75
187 Neal Broten .05 .15
188 Bob Carpenter .02 .10
189 Ken Daneyko .02 .10
190 Bruce Driver .02 .10
191 Bill Guerin .05 .15
192 Claude Lemieux .02 .10
193 John MacLean .05 .15
194 Scott Niedermayer .05 .15
195 Stephane Richer .05 .15
196 Scott Stevens .05 .15
197 Presentation Card .05 .15
Stanley Cup Champions
198 Checklist (1-83) .02 .10
199 Checklist (84-169) .02 .10
200 Checklist (170-200) .02 .10
201 Todd Krygier .02 .10
202 Steve Rucchin .05 .15
203 Mike Sillinger .02 .10
204 Ted Donato .02 .10
205 Shawn McEachern .02 .10
206 Joe Mullen .05 .15
207 Kevin Stevens .02 .10
208 Don Sweeney .02 .10
209 Mark Astley .02 .10
210 Randy Burridge .02 .10
211 Jason Dawe .02 .10
212 Mike Peca .05 .15
213 Michael Nylander .02 .10
214 Cory Stillman .02 .10
215 Pavel Torgajev RC .02 .10
216 Tony Amonte .05 .15
217 Joe Murphy .02 .10
218 Bob Probert .05 .15
219 Denis Savard .05 .15
220 Stephane Fiset .05 .15
221 Valeri Kamensky .05 .15
222 Sylvain Lefebvre .02 .10
223 Claude Lemieux .02 .10
224 Sandis Ozolinsh .02 .10
225 Patrick Roy .60 1.50
226 Scott Young .02 .10
227 Greg Adams .02 .10
228 Guy Carbonneau .10 .30
229 Dave Gagner .02 .10
230 Kevin Hatcher .02 .10
231 Darcy Wakaluk .05 .15
232 Dino Ciccarelli .05 .15
233 Greg Johnson .02 .10
234 Igor Larionov .02 .10
235 Darren McCarty .05 .15
236 Chris Osgood .05 .15
237 Zdeno Ciger .02 .10
238 Bryan Marchment .02 .10
239 Boris Mironov .02 .10
240 Peter White .02 .10
241 Jody Hull .02 .10
242 Scott Mellanby .05 .15
243 Gord Murphy .02 .10
244 Jason Woolley .02 .10
245 Gerald Diduck .02 .10
246 Nelson Emerson .02 .10
247 Brendan Shanahan .10 .30
248 Glen Wesley .02 .10
249 Tony Granato .02 .10
250 Dimitri Khristich .02 .10
251 Jari Kurri .10 .30
252 Eric Lacroix .02 .10
253 Yanic Perreault .02 .10
254 Patrice Brisebois .02 .10
255 Benoit Brunet .02 .10
256 Valeri Bure .02 .10

257 Stephane Quintal .02 .10
258 Jocelyn Thibault .10 .30
259 Shawn Chambers .02 .10
260 Jim Dowd .02 .10
261 Bill Guerin .05 .15
262 Bobby Holik .02 .10
263 Steve Thomas .05 .15
264 Esa Tikkanen .02 .10
265 Wendel Clark .05 .15
266 Travis Green .05 .15
267 Brett Lindros .02 .10
268 Kirk Muller .02 .10
269 Zigmund Palffy .05 .15
270 Mathieu Schneider .02 .10
271 Alexander Semak .02 .10
272 Dennis Vaske .02 .10
273 Ray Ferraro .02 .10
274 Adam Graves .02 .10
275 Alexei Kovalev .02 .10
276 Mike Richter .10 .30
277 Luc Robitaille .05 .15
278 Ulf Samuelsson .02 .10
279 Steve Duchesne .02 .10
280 Trent McCleary RC .02 .10
281 Dan Quinn .02 .10
282 Martin Straka .02 .10
283 Karl Dykhuis .02 .10
284 Pat Falloon .02 .10
285 Joel Otto .02 .10
286 Kjell Samuelsson .02 .10
287 Garth Snow .05 .15
288 Mario Lemieux .60 1.50
289 Norm Maciver .02 .10
290 Dmitri Mironov .02 .10
291 Markus Naslund .10 .30
292 Petr Nedved .05 .15
293 Tomas Sandstrom .02 .10
294 Bryan Smolinski .02 .10
295 Sergei Zubov .02 .10
296 Shayne Corson .02 .10
297 Geoff Courtnall .02 .10
298 Grant Fuhr .10 .30
299 Dale Hawerchuk .10 .30
300 Al MacInnis .05 .15
301 Brian Noonan .02 .10
302 Chris Pronger .10 .30
303 Andrei Nazarov .02 .10
304 Owen Nolan .05 .15
305 Ray Sheppard .02 .10
306 Chris Terreri .05 .15
307 Brian Bellows .02 .10
308 Brian Bradley .02 .10
309 John Cullen .02 .10
310 Alexander Selivanov .02 .10
311 Mike Gartner .05 .15
312 Benoit Hogue .02 .10
313 Sergio Momesso .02 .10
314 Larry Murphy .05 .15
315 Dave Babych .02 .10
316 Bret Hedican .02 .10
317 Alexander Mogilny .05 .15
318 Mike Ridley .02 .10
319 Peter Bondra .05 .15
320 Jim Carey .05 .15
321 Sylvain Cote .02 .10
322 Sergei Gonchar .02 .10
323 Joe Juneau .02 .10
324 Steve Konowalchuk .02 .10
325 Pat Peake .02 .10
326 Dallas Drake .02 .10
327 Igor Korolev .02 .10
328 Darren Turcotte .02 .10
329 Daniel Alfredsson RC .50 1.25
330 Aki Berg RC .05 .15
331 Todd Bertuzzi RC .75 2.00
332 Jason Bonsignore .02 .10
333 Curtis Brown RC .10 .30
334 Byron Dafoe .05 .15
335 Eric Daze .05 .15
336 Shane Doan RC .30 .75
337 Jason Doig .02 .10
338 Radek Dvorak RC .20 .50
339 Joe Dziedzic .02 .10
340 Darby Hendrickson .02 .10
341 Brian Holzinger RC .10 .30
342 Ed Jovanovski .05 .15
343 Chad Kilger RC .02 .10
344 Saku Koivu .10 .30
345 Darren Langdon .02 .10
346 Jamie Langenbrunner .02 .10
347 Jere Lehtinen .05 .15
348 Bryan McCabe .02 .10
349 Kyle McLaren RC .02 .10
350 Marty Murray .02 .10
351 Jeff O'Neill .02 .10
352 Deron Quint .02 .10
353 Marcus Ragnarsson RC .05 .15
354 Tommy Salo .20 .50
355 Miroslav Satan RC .50 1.25
356 Jamie Storr .05 .15
357 Niklas Sundstrom .05 .15
358 Robert Svehla RC .02 .10
359 Denis Pederson .02 .10
360 Antti Tormanen .02 .10
361 Brendan Witt .02 .10
362 Vitali Yachmenev .02 .10
363 Stephane Yelle .02 .10
364 Tom Barrasso NE .05 .15
365 Ed Belfour NE .10 .30
366 Martin Brodeur NE .30 .75
367 Sean Burke NE .05 .15
368 Jim Carey NE .05 .15
369 Stephane Fiset NE .05 .15
370 Dominik Hasek NE .25 .60
371 Ron Hextall NE .05 .15
372 Nikolai Khabibulin NE .05 .15
373 Kirk McLean NE .05 .15
374 Chris Osgood NE .05 .15
375 Felix Potvin NE .05 .15
376 Daren Puppa NE .05 .15
377 Patrick Roy NE .60 1.50
378 John Vanbiesbrouck NE .05 .15
379 Pavel Bure UC .10 .30
380 Chris Chelios UC .10 .30
381 Sergei Fedorov UC .20 .50
382 Theo Fleury UC .02 .10
383 Peter Forsberg UC .30 .75
384 Ron Francis UC .05 .15
385 Wayne Gretzky UC .75 2.00
386 Brett Hull UC .15 .40
387 Jaromir Jagr UC .20 .50
388 Paul Kariya UC .10 .30
389 Pat LaFontaine UC .06 .15
390 Brian Leetch UC .05 .15
391 Mario Lemieux UC .60 1.50
392 Eric Lindros UC .20 .50
393 Mark Messier UC .10 .30
394 Mike Modano UC .10 .30
395 Adam Oates UC .05 .15
396 Jeremy Roenick UC .15 .40
397 Joe Sakic UC .25 .60
398 Alexei Zhamnov UC .05 .15
399 Checklist .02 .10
400 Checklist .02 .10

1995-96 Ultra Gold Medallion

This 200-card standard-size set is a parallel to the basic Ultra series one issue. These cards were issued one per series one pack. No Gold Medallion version exists for series two cards. The fronts have the same photos as the regular cards except the entire background is gold. The Ultra Gold Medallion logo is in the middle of the card and is embossed for effect. The words "Gold Medallion Edition" are located under the player's name. The backs are identical to the regular cards. Gold Medallion version also could be found for series one insert cards. Values for those are included under the appropriate insert header.

*VETS: 2.5X TO 6X BASIC CARDS
*ROOKIES: 1.2X TO 3X

1995-96 Ultra All-Rookie

These ten cards, which were randomly inserted at a rate of 1:4 series one retail packs, focus on the top rookies from the 1994-95 campaign. Gold Medallion parallel versions of these cards also were available, at indeterminate odds.

COMPLETE SET (10) 6.00 15.00
*GOLD MED: .8X TO 2X BASIC INSERTS
1 Jim Carey .40 1.00
2 Mariusz Czerkawski .40 1.00
3 Peter Forsberg 2.00 5.00
4 Jeff Friesen .40 1.00
5 Paul Kariya 1.50 4.00
6 Blaine Lacher .40 1.00
7 Ian Laperriere .40 1.00
8 Todd Marchant .40 1.00
9 Roman Oksiuta .40 1.00
10 David Oliver .40 1.00

1995-96 Ultra Crease Crashers

These twenty cards capture a goalie's worst nightmare - a soft-handed forward with a propensity for invading a netminder's home turf. The cards were randomly inserted in series two retail packs only at a rate of 1:18.

COMPLETE SET (20) 20.00 40.00
1 Jason Arnott .75 2.00
2 Rod Brind'Amour 1.00 2.50
3 Theo Fleury 1.00 2.50
4 Todd Harvey 1.00 2.50
5 John LeClair 1.50 4.00
6 Claude Lemieux 1.00 2.50
7 Trevor Linden 1.00 2.50
8 Eric Lindros 1.50 4.00
9 Darren McCarty 1.00 2.50
10 Scott Mellanby 1.00 2.50
11 Mark Messier 1.50 4.00
12 Cam Neely 1.50 4.00
13 Owen Nolan 1.00 2.50
14 Keith Primeau 1.00 2.50
15 Jeremy Roenick 2.00 5.00
16 Tomas Sandstrom 1.00 2.50
17 Brendan Shanahan 1.50 4.00
18 Kevin Stevens 1.00 2.50
19 Rick Tocchet 1.00 2.50
20 Keith Tkachuk 1.50 4.00

1995-96 Ultra Extra Attackers

When pulling the goalie and down late in the game, these are the guys you'd love to tap on the shoulder. The cards were randomly inserted in series two hobby packs only at a rate of 1:18.

COMPLETE SET (20) 40.00 80.00
1 Peter Bondra .60 1.50
2 Eric Daze .60 1.50
3 Radek Dvorak .60 1.50
4 Sergei Fedorov 2.00 5.00
5 Peter Forsberg 3.00 8.00
6 Ron Francis .60 1.50
7 Wayne Gretzky 8.00 20.00
8 Brett Hull 1.50 4.00
9 Jaromir Jagr 2.00 5.00
10 Ed Jovanovski .60 1.50
11 Paul Kariya 1.25 3.00
12 Saku Koivu 1.25 3.00
13 Mario Lemieux 6.00 15.00
14 Mike Modano 2.00 5.00
15 Alexander Mogilny .60 1.50
16 Adam Oates .60 1.50
17 Joe Sakic 2.50 6.00
18 Niklas Sundstrom .60 1.50
19 Mats Sundin 1.25 3.00
20 Steve Yzerman 6.00 15.00

1995-96 Ultra High Speed

Young stars in a hurry to reach the upper echelon of the NHL pay scale, and some already there trying to prove they're worth it, are featured in this 20-card set. Collectors could find these cards randomly inserted at a rate of 1:5 series two packs.

COMPLETE SET (20) 10.00 20.00
1 Daniel Alfredsson .75 2.00
2 Jason Arnott .20 .50
3 Todd Bertuzzi .75 2.00
4 Radek Bonk .20 .50
5 Martin Brodeur 2.00 5.00
6 Alexandre Daigle .20 .50
7 Shane Doan .40 1.00
8 Peter Forsberg 1.50 4.00
9 Roman Hamrlik .20 .50
10 Todd Harvey .20 .50
11 Paul Kariya .75 2.00
12 Travis Green .20 .50
13 Chris Osgood .40 1.00
14 Zigmund Palffy .40 1.00
15 Marcus Ragnarsson .20 .50
16 Mikael Renberg .20 .50
17 Brian Savage .20 .50
18 Robert Svehla .20 .50
19 Jocelyn Thibault .40 1.00
20 Brendan Witt .20 .50

1995-96 Ultra Premier Pad Men

Cards from this 12-card standard-size set was inserted 1:36 series one packs. This set features leading NHL goaltenders on a special gold foil embossed design. There is also a Gold Medallion parallel version of each card that were inserted at 1:360. Multipliers can be found in the header to determine values for these.

COMPLETE SET (12) 20.00 40.00
*GOLD MED: .8X TO 2X BASIC INSERTS
1 Ed Belfour 1.00 2.50
2 Martin Brodeur 8.00 20.00
3 Sean Burke .50 1.25
4 Jim Carey .50 1.25
5 Dominik Hasek 2.00 5.00
6 Curtis Joseph 1.00 2.50
7 Blaine Lacher .50 1.25
8 Andy Moog 1.00 2.50
9 Felix Potvin 1.00 2.50
10 Patrick Roy 8.00 20.00
11 John Vanbiesbrouck .50 1.25
12 Mike Vernon .50 1.25

1995-96 Ultra Premier Pivots

These 10 standard-size cards were inserted into first series packs at a rate of 1:4. Leading NHL centers are showcased on these cards. There also are Gold Medallion versions of each of these cards which were inserted at 1:40. Multipliers can be found in the header to determine values for these.

COMPLETE SET (10) 6.00 12.00
*GOLD MED: .8X TO 2X BASIC INSERTS
1 Sergei Fedorov .60 1.50
2 Ron Francis .20 .50
3 Wayne Gretzky 2.50 6.00
4 Eric Lindros .40 1.00
5 Mark Messier .40 1.00
6 Adam Oates .20 .50
7 Jeremy Roenick .50 1.25
8 Joe Sakic .75 2.00
9 Mats Sundin .40 1.00
10 Alexei Zhamnov .20 .50

1995-96 Ultra Red Light Specials

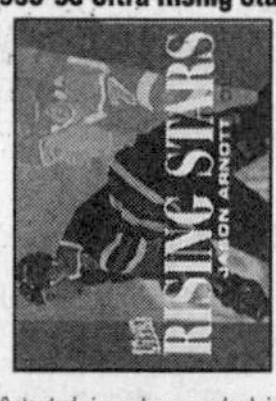

These 10 standard-size cards were inserted into series one packs at a rate of 1:3. These cards feature players who lit the lamp on a regular basis during the '94-95 season. There is also a Gold Medallion parallel version of each card inserted at 1:30. Multipliers can be found in the header to determine values for these.

COMPLETE SET (10) 1.25 3.00
*GOLD MED: .75X TO 2X BASIC INSERTS
1 Peter Bondra .20 .50
2 Theo Fleury .15 .40
3 Brett Hull .30 .75
4 Jaromir Jagr .40 1.00
5 John LeClair .25 .60
6 Eric Lindros .25 .60
7 Cam Neely .25 .60
8 Owen Nolan .20 .50
9 Ray Sheppard .15 .40
10 Alexei Zhamnov .20 .50

1995-96 Ultra Rising Stars

These 10 standard-size cards were randomly inserted 1:4 series one packs. There are also Gold Medallion parallel versions of these cards which were randomly inserted at 1:40. Multipliers can be found in the header below to determine values for these.

COMPLETE SET (10) .75 2.00
*GOLD MED: .8X TO 2X BASIC INSERTS
1 Jason Arnott .15 .40
2 Alexandre Daigle .15 .40
3 Roman Hamrlik .20 .50
4 Trevor Kidd .20 .50
5 Scott Niedermayer .15 .40
6 Keith Primeau .15 .40
7 Mikael Renberg .20 .50
8 Jocelyn Thibault .30 .75
9 Alexei Yashin .15 .40
10 Alexei Zhitnik .15 .40

1995-96 Ultra Ultraview

This 10-card set features the NHL's best on clear acrylic. The cards were randomly inserted at a rate of 1:55 series two packs. A parallel version of these cards could be found in complete set form in randomly inserted Ultraview Hot Packs. These sets, which bore the Hot Pack logo, were found in 1:360 packs. Because they were found in complete set form, dealers tended to discount them slightly at time of sale. Multipliers can be found in the header to determine value for these.

COMPLETE SET (10) 20.00 40.00
*HOT PACK: .2X TO .5X BASIC INSERTS
HOT PACK ODDS 1:360 SERIES 2
1 Sergei Fedorov 1.25 3.00
2 Wayne Gretzky 6.00 15.00
3 Dominik Hasek 2.00 5.00
4 Jaromir Jagr 1.50 4.00
5 Brian Leetch .75 2.00
6 Mario Lemieux 5.00 12.00
7 Eric Lindros 1.00 2.50
8 Jeremy Roenick 1.25 3.00
9 Joe Sakic 2.00 5.00
10 Alexei Zhamnov .75 2.00

1996-97 Ultra

The 1996-97 Ultra set was issued in one series totaling 180 cards. Ten-card packs retailed for $2.49. Key rookies include Dainius Zubrus, Patrick Lalime, and Sergei Berezin. Card fronts feature a color action photo with player information on the back.

COMPLETE SET (180) 15.00 30.00
1 Guy Hebert .05 .15
2 Paul Kariya .10 .30
3 Jari Kurri .05 .15
4 Roman Oksiuta .02 .10
5 Ruslan Salei RC .02 .10
6 Teemu Selanne .10 .30
7 Darren Van Impe .02 .10
8 Ray Bourque .20 .50
9 Kyle McLaren .02 .10
10 Adam Oates .05 .15
11 Bill Ranford .05 .15
12 Rick Tocchet .05 .15
13 Donald Audette .02 .10
14 Curtis Brown .02 .10
15 Jason Dawe .02 .10
16 Dominik Hasek .25 .60
17 Pat LaFontaine .10 .30
18 Jay McKee RC .02 .10
19 Derek Plante .02 .10
20 Wayne Primeau .02 .10
21 Theo Fleury .02 .10
22 Dave Gagner .05 .15
23 Jonas Hoglund .02 .10
24 Jarome Iginla .15 .40
25 Trevor Kidd .05 .15
26 Robert Reichel .02 .10
27 German Titov .02 .10
28 Tony Amonte .05 .15
29 Ed Belfour .10 .30
30 Chris Chelios .10 .30
31 Eric Daze .05 .15
32 Ethan Moreau RC .10 .30
33 Gary Suter .02 .10
34 Adam Deadmarsh .02 .10
35 Peter Forsberg .30 .75
36 Valeri Kamensky .05 .15
37 Claude Lemieux .02 .10
38 Sandis Ozolinsh .02 .10
39 Patrick Roy .60 1.50
40 Joe Sakic .25 .60
41 Landon Wilson .02 .10
42 Derian Hatcher .02 .10
43 Jamie Langenbrunner .02 .10
44 Mike Modano .20 .50
45 Andy Moog .05 .15
46 Joe Nieuwendyk .05 .15
47 Pat Verbeek .02 .10
48 Sergei Zubov .02 .10
49 Anders Eriksson .02 .10
50 Sergei Fedorov .20 .50
51 Vladimir Konstantinov .05 .15
52 Slava Kozlov .05 .15
53 Nicklas Lidstrom .10 .30
54 Chris Osgood .05 .15
55 Brendan Shanahan .10 .30
56 Steve Yzerman .60 1.50
57 Jason Arnott .02 .10
58 Mike Grier RC .30 .75
59 Curtis Joseph .10 .30
60 Rem Murray RC .02 .10
61 Jeff Norton .02 .10
62 Miroslav Satan .02 .10
63 Doug Weight .05 .15
64 Radek Dvorak .02 .10
65 Ed Jovanovski .05 .15
66 Scott Mellanby .05 .15
67 Rob Niedermayer .05 .15
68 Ray Sheppard .05 .15
69 Robert Svehla .02 .10
70 John Vanbiesbrouck .05 .15
71 Steve Washburn RC .05 .15
72 Jeff Brown .02 .10
73 Sean Burke .05 .15
74 Hnat Domenichelli .02 .10
75 Keith Primeau .05 .15
76 Geoff Sanderson .05 .15
77 Rob Blake .05 .15
78 Stephane Fiset .05 .15
79 Dimitri Khristich .02 .10
80 Mattias Norstrom .02 .10
81 Ed Olczyk .02 .10
82 Jamie Storr .05 .15
83 Jan Vopat .02 .10
84 Vitali Yachmenev .02 .10
85 Shayne Corson .02 .10
86 Vincent Damphousse .02 .10
87 Saku Koivu .10 .30
88 Mark Recchi .05 .15
89 Stephane Richer .05 .15
90 Jocelyn Thibault .10 .30
91 David Wilkie .02 .10
92 Dave Andreychuk .05 .15
93 Martin Brodeur .30 .75
94 Scott Niedermayer .02 .10
95 Scott Stevens .05 .15
96 Petr Sykora .02 .10
97 Steve Thomas .02 .10
98 Bryan Berard .10 .30
99 Todd Bertuzzi .10 .30
100 Eric Fichaud .05 .15
101 Travis Green .05 .15
102 Kenny Jonsson .02 .10
103 Zigmund Palffy .05 .15
104 Christian Dube .02 .10
105 Daniel Goneau RC .02 .10
106 Wayne Gretzky .75 2.00
107 Alexei Kovalev .02 .10
108 Brian Leetch .10 .30
109 Mark Messier .10 .30
110 Mike Richter .10 .30
111 Luc Robitaille .05 .15
112 Niklas Sundstrom .02 .10
113 Daniel Alfredsson .05 .15
114 Radek Bonk .02 .10
115 Andreas Dackell RC .02 .10
116 Alexandre Daigle .02 .10
117 Steve Duchesne .02 .10
118 Wade Redden .02 .10
119 Damian Rhodes .05 .15
120 Alexei Yashin .02 .10
121 Rod Brind'Amour .05 .15
122 Paul Coffey .10 .30
123 Eric Desjardins .05 .15
124 Ron Hextall .05 .15
125 John LeClair .10 .30
126 Eric Lindros .10 .30
127 Janne Niinimaa .10 .30
128 Mikael Renberg .02 .10
129 Dainius Zubrus RC .30 .75
130 Mike Gartner .05 .15
131 Craig Janney .05 .15
132 Nikolai Khabibulin .05 .15
133 Dave Manson .02 .10
134 Teppo Numminen .02 .10
135 Jeremy Roenick .15 .40
136 Keith Tkachuk .10 .30
137 Oleg Tverdovsky .05 .15
138 Tom Barrasso .05 .15
139 Ron Francis .05 .15
140 Kevin Hatcher .02 .10
141 Jaromir Jagr .20 .50
142 Patrick Lalime RC .75 2.00
143 Mario Lemieux .60 1.50
144 Jim Campbell .02 .10
145 Grant Fuhr .05 .15
146 Brett Hull .15 .40
147 Al MacInnis .05 .15
148 Pierre Turgeon .05 .15
149 Harry York RC .10 .30
150 Kelly Hrudey .05 .15
151 Al Iafrate .02 .10
152 Bernie Nicholls .02 .10
153 Owen Nolan .05 .15
154 Darren Turcotte .02 .10
155 Brian Bradley .02 .10
156 Dino Ciccarelli .05 .15
157 Roman Hamrlik .05 .15
158 Daymond Langkow .05 .15
159 Daren Puppa .05 .15
160 Alexander Selivanov .02 .10
161 Sergei Berezin RC .40 1.00
162 Wendel Clark .05 .15
163 Doug Gilmour .05 .15
164 Larry Murphy .05 .15
165 Felix Potvin .10 .30
166 Mats Sundin .10 .30
167 Pavel Bure .10 .30
168 Trevor Linden .05 .15
169 Kirk McLean .05 .15
170 Alexander Mogilny .05 .15
171 Esa Tikkanen .02 .10
172 Peter Bondra .05 .15
173 Andrew Brunette RC .25 .60
174 Jim Carey .10 .30
175 Sergei Gonchar .02 .10
176 Phil Housley .05 .15
177 Joe Juneau .02 .10
178 Michal Pivonka .02 .10
179 Checklist (1-143) .02 .10
180 Checklist (143-180/inserts) .02 .10
S125 John LeClair promo .20 .50

1996-97 Ultra Gold Medallion

A one-per-pack parallel, these cards differ from the base cards by the use of gold foil to highlight the player's name on the card front. The words "Gold Medallion" are also included. Values for the cards can be determined by using the multipliers below on the corresponding base card.

*VETS: 2.5X TO 6X BASIC CARDS
*ROOKIES: 1.2X TO 3X

1996-97 Ultra Clear the Ice

Ten players recognized as some of the elite at their position are the subject of this set, which was randomly inserted in packs at the stingy rate of 1:350.

COMPLETE SET (10) 40.00 100.00
1 Jim Carey 4.00 10.00
2 Peter Forsberg 10.00 25.00
3 Dominik Hasek 8.00 20.00
4 Jaromir Jagr 6.00 15.00
5 John LeClair 4.00 10.00
6 Eric Lindros 4.00 10.00
7 Mark Messier 4.00 10.00
8 Patrick Roy 20.00 50.00
9 Brendan Shanahan 4.00 10.00
10 Keith Tkachuk 4.00 10.00

1996-97 Ultra Mr. Momentum

Randomly inserted in retail packs only at a rate of 1:36, these ten cards offer simple fronts and three-photo, text-laden backs.

COMPLETE SET (10) 20.00 40.00
1 Peter Bondra 1.00 2.50
2 Pavel Bure 2.00 5.00
3 Ron Francis 1.00 2.50
4 Brett Hull 2.50 6.00
5 Jaromir Jagr 3.00 8.00
6 Pat LaFontaine 2.00 5.00
7 Eric Lindros 2.00 5.00
8 Mark Messier 2.00 5.00
9 Mats Sundin 2.00 5.00
10 Steve Yzerman 6.00 15.00

1996-97 Ultra Power

The 16 cards in this set were randomly inserted in packs at a rate of 1:16. The cards feature fiery lettering and a glitter-enhanced design. Card fronts also feature a color action photo, with biographical info on the back. The checklist was mirrored in the Red Line and Blue Line sets, although photo choice and card numbering varied slightly.

COMPLETE SET (16) 25.00 60.00
1 Ray Bourque 2.00 5.00
2 Chris Chelios 1.25 3.00
3 Paul Coffey 1.25 3.00
4 Sergei Fedorov 2.00 5.00
5 Wayne Gretzky 8.00 20.00
6 Roman Hamrlik .60 1.50
7 Ed Jovanovski .60 1.50
8 Paul Kariya 1.25 3.00
9 Vladimir Konstantinov .60 1.50
10 Brian Leetch 1.25 3.00
11 Mario Lemieux 6.00 15.00
12 Nicklas Lidstrom 1.25 3.00
13 Alexander Mogilny .60 1.50
14 Adam Oates .60 1.50
15 Joe Sakic 2.50 6.00
16 Teemu Selanne 1.25 3.00

1996-97 Ultra Power Blue Line

Randomly inserted in hobby packs only at a rate of 1:90, this tough insert features eight top defensive players. The cards are sequentially numbered on the back out of 1,082.

COMPLETE SET (8) 10.00 25.00
1 Ray Bourque 4.00 10.00
2 Chris Chelios 2.50 6.00
3 Paul Coffey 2.50 6.00
4 Roman Hamrlik 1.25 3.00
5 Ed Jovanovski 1.25 3.00
6 Vladimir Konstantinov 1.25 3.00
7 Brian Leetch 2.50 6.00
8 Nicklas Lidstrom 2.50 6.00

1996-97 Ultra Power Red Line

Eight of the absolute best offensive weapons grace this tough insert set, randomly seeded only in hobby packs at a rate of 1:90. The cards are sequentially numbered on the back out of 1,082.

COMPLETE SET (8) 30.00 80.00
1 Sergei Fedorov 4.00 10.00
2 Wayne Gretzky 15.00 40.00
3 Paul Kariya 2.50 6.00
4 Mario Lemieux 12.50 30.00
5 Alexander Mogilny 1.25 3.00
6 Adam Oates 1.25 3.00
7 Joe Sakic 5.00 12.00
8 Teemu Selanne 2.50 6.00

1996-97 Ultra Rookies

Randomly inserted in packs at a rate of 1:9, these cards offer a single player photo with the player's name with "Rookie" written on the left-hand side. Flip sides give a smaller photo with several pieces of information about each athlete.

COMPLETE SET (20) 8.00 20.00
1 Bryan Berard .40 1.00
2 Sergei Berezin .40 1.00
3 Curtis Brown .40 1.00
4 Jim Campbell .40 1.00
5 Christian Dube .40 1.00
6 Anders Eriksson .40 1.00
7 Eric Fichaud .75 2.00
8 Daniel Goneau .40 1.00
9 Mike Grier .75 2.00
10 Jarome Iginla 3.00 8.00
11 Jamie Langenbrunner .40 1.00
12 Jay McKee .40 1.00
13 Ethan Moreau .40 1.00
14 Rem Murray .40 1.00
15 Janne Niinimaa .40 1.00
16 Wayne Primeau .40 1.00
17 Wade Redden .75 2.00
18 Jamie Storr .75 2.00
19 David Wilkie .40 1.00
20 Landon Wilson .40 1.00

2005-06 Ultra

This 271-card set was issued into the hobby in eight-card packs, with a $2.99 SRP, which came 24 packs to a box and 12 boxes to a case. Cards numbered 1-200 feature veterans in team alphabetical order while cards 201-271 feature Rookie Cards. Cards numbered 201-250 were issued at a stated rate of one in four and cards 251-271 were inserted at a stated rate of one in 24.

COMPLETE SET (271) 300.00 500.00
COMP.SET w/o SP's (250) 25.00 60.00
1 Jean-Sebastien Giguere .25 .60
2 Teemu Selanne .30 .75
3 Petr Sykora .15 .40
4 Rob Niedermayer .20 .50
5 Scott Niedermayer .20 .50
6 Sandis Ozolinsh .20 .50
7 Joffrey Lupul .20 .50
8 Kari Lehtonen .30 .75
9 Ilya Kovalchuk .40 1.00
10 Peter Bondra .25 .60
11 Marian Hossa .25 .60
12 Patrik Stefan .20 .50
13 Bobby Holik .20 .50
14 Marc Savard .20 .50
15 Andrew Raycroft .25 .60
16 Patrice Bergeron .30 .75
17 Joe Thornton .50 1.25
18 Glen Murray .20 .50

19 Brian Leetch .30 .75
20 Nick Boynton .20 .50
21 Sergei Samsonov .25 .60
22 Shawn McEachern .20 .50
23 Martin Biron .25 .60
24 Chris Drury .25 .60
25 Daniel Briere .25 .60
26 Derek Roy .20 .50
27 Maxim Afinogenov .20 .50
28 J.P. Dumont .20 .50
29 Mika Noronen .20 .50
30 Miikka Kiprusoff .30 .75
31 Jarome Iginla .25 .60
32 Tony Amonte .25 .60
33 Matthew Lombardi .20 .50
34 Robyn Regehr .20 .50
35 Jordan Leopold .20 .50
36 Chuck Kobasew .20 .50
37 Phillippe Sauve .25 .60
38 Darren McCarty .20 .50
39 Martin Gerber .25 .60
40 Eric Staal .25 .60
41 Erik Cole .20 .50
42 Justin Williams .20 .50
43 Glen Wesley .20 .50
44 Oleg Tverdovsky .20 .50
45 Cory Stillman .20 .50
46 Rod Brind'Amour .25 .60
47 Nikolai Khabibulin .30 .75
48 Tuomo Ruutu .20 .50
49 Eric Daze .25 .60
50 Tyler Arnason .20 .50
51 Adrian Aucoin .20 .50
52 Kyle Calder .20 .50
53 Mark Bell .20 .50
54 David Aebischer .25 .60
55 Joe Sakic .60 1.50
56 Milan Hejduk .30 .75
57 Alex Tanguay .25 .60
58 Rob Blake .25 .60
59 John-Michael Liles .20 .50
60 Pierre Turgeon .25 .60
61 Marc Denis .25 .60
62 Rick Nash .40 1.00
63 Nikolai Zherdev .25 .60
64 Rostislav Klesla .20 .50
65 Bryan Berard .20 .50
66 Sergei Fedorov .30 .75
67 Marty Turco .25 .60
68 Mike Modano .30 .75
69 Brenden Morrow .20 .50
70 Bill Guerin .20 .50
71 Sergei Zubov .20 .50
72 Jere Lehtinen .25 .60
73 Manny Legace .30 .75
74 Steve Yzerman .75 2.00
75 Brendan Shanahan .30 .75
76 Pavel Datsyuk .30 .75
77 Nicklas Lidstrom .30 .75
78 Chris Chelios .30 .75
79 Henrik Zetterberg .30 .75
80 Ty Conklin .25 .60
81 Michael Peca .25 .60
82 Ryan Smyth .25 .60
83 Raffi Torres .20 .50
84 Chris Pronger .25 .60
85 Ales Hemsky .20 .50
86 Roberto Luongo .50 1.25
87 Joe Nieuwendyk .25 .60
88 Stephen Weiss .20 .50
89 Olli Jokinen .25 .60
90 Jay Bouwmeester .20 .50
91 Nathan Horton .20 .50
92 Mathieu Garon .25 .60
93 Jeremy Roenick .30 .75
94 Luc Robitaille .25 .60
95 Pavol Demitra .25 .60
96 Dustin Brown .20 .50
97 Alexander Frolov .25 .60
98 Dwayne Roloson .25 .60
99 Marian Gaborik .40 1.00
100 Alexander Daigle .20 .50
101 Pierre-Marc Bouchard .20 .50
102 Filip Kuba .20 .50
103 Manny Fernandez .25 .60
104 Saku Koivu .30 .75
105 Jose Theodore .30 .75
106 Mike Ribeiro .20 .50
107 Michael Ryder .25 .60
108 Sheldon Souray .20 .50
109 Richard Zednik .20 .50
110 Tomas Vokoun .25 .60
111 Paul Kariya .30 .75
112 Steve Sullivan .20 .50
113 David Legwand .25 .60
114 Kimmo Timonen .20 .50
115 Scott Walker .20 .50
116 Martin Brodeur .60 1.50
117 Scott Gomez .25 .60
118 Patrik Elias .25 .60
119 Alexander Mogilny .25 .60
120 Brian Rafalski .20 .50
121 John Madden .20 .50
122 Rick DiPietro .25 .60
123 Alexei Yashin .20 .50
124 Miroslav Satan .20 .50
125 Trent Hunter .20 .50
126 Brent Sopel .20 .50
127 Mark Parrish .20 .50
128 Kevin Weekes .20 .50
129 Jaromir Jagr .50 1.25
130 Marcel Hossa .20 .50
131 Steve Rucchin .20 .50
132 Tom Poti .20 .50
133 Dominik Hasek .40 1.00
134 Jason Spezza .30 .75
135 Dany Heatley .30 .75
136 Martin Havlat .25 .60
137 Wade Redden .20 .50
138 Zdeno Chara .25 .60
139 Daniel Alfredsson .25 .60
140 Robert Esche .25 .60
141 Peter Forsberg .50 1.25
142 Simon Gagne .30 .75
143 Keith Primeau .20 .50
144 Joni Pitkanen .20 .50
145 Kim Johnsson .20 .50
146 Sami Kapanen .20 .50
147 Curtis Joseph .30 .75
148 Shane Doan .20 .50
149 Jamie Lundmark .20 .50
150 Ladislav Nagy .20 .50
151 Mike Ricci .20 .50
152 Petr Nedved .20 .50
153 Jocelyn Thibault .25 .60
154 Mario Lemieux 1.25 3.00
155 Mark Recchi .25 .60
156 Zigmund Palffy .25 .60
157 John LeClair .30 .75
158 Ryan Malone .20 .50
159 Marc-Andre Fleury .25 .60
160 Evgeni Nabokov .25 .60
161 Patrick Marleau .25 .60
162 Jonathan Cheechoo .30 .75
163 Marco Sturm .20 .50
164 Brad Stuart .20 .50
165 Patrick Lalime .25 .60
166 Doug Weight .25 .60
167 Keith Tkachuk .30 .75
168 Mark Rycroft .20 .50
169 Barret Jackman .20 .50
170 Dallas Drake .20 .50
171 Sean Burke .25 .60
172 Martin St. Louis .25 .60
173 Vincent Lecavalier .30 .75
174 Brad Richards .25 .60
175 Ruslan Fedotenko .20 .50
176 Fredrik Modin .20 .50
177 Dave Andreychuk .20 .50
178 Pavel Kubina .20 .50
179 Ed Belfour .30 .75
180 Mats Sundin .30 .75
181 Eric Lindros .30 .75
182 Jeff O'Neill .20 .50
183 Bryan McCabe .20 .50
184 Tie Domi .25 .60
185 Matt Stajan .20 .50
186 Nik Antropov .20 .50
187 Jason Allison .20 .50
188 Dan Cloutier .25 .60
189 Markus Naslund .30 .75
190 Brendan Morrison .20 .50
191 Todd Bertuzzi .40 1.00
192 Ed Jovanovski .25 .60
193 Mattias Ohlund .20 .50
194 Trevor Linden .20 .50
195 Anson Carter .25 .60
196 Ryan Kesler .20 .50
197 Olaf Kolzig .25 .60
198 Jeff Friesen .15 .40
199 Brian Willsie .20 .50
200 Brendan Witt .20 .50
201 Braydon Coburn RC 1.50 4.00
202 Jim Slater RC 1.50 4.00
203 Adam Berkhoel RC 1.50 4.00
204 Andrew Alberts RC 1.25 3.00
205 Kevin Dallman RC 1.25 3.00
206 Milan Jurcina RC 1.25 3.00
207 Niklas Nordgren RC 1.25 3.00
208 Kevin Nastiuk RC 1.50 4.00
209 Brent Seabrook RC 2.50 6.00
210 Rene Bourque RC 1.25 3.00
211 Duncan Keith RC 3.00 8.00
212 Cam Barker RC 1.50 4.00
213 Peter Budaj RC 1.50 4.00
214 Jaroslav Balastik RC 1.25 3.00
215 Jussi Jokinen RC 2.00 5.00
216 Brett Lebda RC 1.25 3.00
217 Johan Franzen RC 4.00 10.00
218 Brad Winchester RC 1.25 3.00
219 Kyle Brodziak RC 1.25 3.00
220 George Parros RC 1.25 3.00
221 Derek Boogaard RC 1.50 4.00
222 Matthew Foy RC 1.25 3.00
223 Yann Danis RC 1.50 4.00
224 Mark Streit RC 1.25 3.00
225 Raitis Ivanans RC 1.25 3.00
226 Ryan Suter RC 1.50 4.00
227 Petteri Nokelainen RC 1.25 3.00
228 Chris Campoli RC 1.25 3.00
229 Ryan Hollweg RC 1.25 3.00
230 Petr Prucha RC 2.00 5.00
231 Al Montoya RC 3.00 8.00
232 Chris Holt RC 1.25 3.00
233 Brandon Bochenski RC 1.25 3.00
234 Andrej Meszaros RC 1.25 3.00
235 Brian McGrattan RC 1.25 3.00
236 Patrick Eaves RC 1.50 4.00
237 Wade Skolney RC 1.25 3.00
238 Keith Ballard RC 1.25 3.00
239 David Leneveu RC 1.50 4.00
240 Maxime Talbot RC 1.25 3.00
241 Ryane Clowe RC 1.25 3.00
242 Josh Gorges RC 1.25 3.00
243 Jay McClement RC 1.25 3.00
244 Jeff Hoggan RC 1.25 3.00
245 Lee Stempniak RC 2.00 5.00
246 Andy Roach RC 1.25 3.00
247 Timo Helbling RC 1.25 3.00
248 Paul Ranger RC 1.25 3.00
249 Andrew Wozniewski RC 1.25 3.00
250 Anthony Stewart RC 1.50 4.00
251 Sidney Crosby RC 50.00 100.00
252 Alexander Ovechkin RC 30.00 60.00
253 Corey Perry RC 3.00 8.00
254 Jeff Carter RC 4.00 10.00
255 Gilbert Brule RC 3.00 8.00
256 Wojtek Wolski RC 2.50 6.00
257 Jeff Woywitka RC 1.50 4.00
258 Hannu Toivonen RC 2.50 6.00
259 Alexander Perezhogin RC 2.50 6.00
260 Zach Parise RC 5.00 12.00
261 Dion Phaneuf RC 8.00 20.00
262 Mike Richards RC 3.00 8.00
263 Cam Ward RC 4.00 10.00
264 Robert Nilsson RC 2.00 5.00
265 Eric Nystrom RC 2.00 5.00
266 Alexander Steen RC 2.50 6.00
267 Ryan Getzlaf RC 6.00 15.00
268 Rostislav Olesz RC 2.00 5.00
269 Henrik Lundqvist RC 8.00 20.00
270 Jim Howard RC 4.00 10.00
271 Thomas Vanek RC 4.00 10.00

2005-06 Ultra Gold

*STARS: 2X TO 5X BASE HI
*ROOKIES: X TO X
*ROOKIES 251-271: .75X TO 2X
ONE PER NON-INSERT PACK
251 Sidney Crosby 200.00 350.00
252 Alexander Ovechkin 75.00 150.00
261 Dion Phaneuf 30.00 60.00
263 Cam Ward 12.00 30.00

2005-06 Ultra Difference Makers

COMPLETE SET (12) 20.00 40.00
STATED ODDS 1:32
DM1 Rick Nash .75 2.00
DM2 Pavel Datsyuk .60 1.50
DM3 Steve Yzerman 1.25 3.00
DM4 Todd Bertuzzi .75 2.00
DM5 Jeff Carter 1.00 2.50
DM6 Sidney Crosby 6.00 15.00
DM7 Tuomo Ruutu .40 1.00
DM8 Patrice Bergeron .40 1.00
DM9 Alexander Ovechkin 3.00 8.00
DM10 Martin St. Louis .40 1.00
DM11 Jarome Iginla .50 1.25
DM12 Andrew Raycroft .40 1.00

2005-06 Ultra Difference Makers Jerseys

STATED ODDS 1:164
DMJAO Alexander Ovechkin 12.00 30.00
DMJAR Andrew Raycroft 4.00 10.00
DMJJC Jeff Carter 6.00 15.00
DMJJI Jarome Iginla 5.00 12.00
DMJPB Patrice Bergeron 4.00 10.00
DMJPD Pavel Datsyuk 4.00 10.00
DMJRN Rick Nash 8.00 20.00
DMJSC Sidney Crosby 30.00 80.00
DMJSL Martin St. Louis 4.00 10.00
DMJSY Steve Yzerman 10.00 25.00
DMJTB Todd Bertuzzi 4.00 10.00
DMJTR Tuomo Ruutu 4.00 10.00

2005-06 Ultra Difference Makers Jersey Autographs

PRINT RUN 10 SER.#'d SETS
NOT PRICED DUE TO SCARCITY
DAJAO Alexander Ovechkin
DAJAR Andrew Raycroft
DAJJC Jeff Carter
DAJJI Jarome Iginla
DAJPB Patrice Bergeron
DAJRN Rick Nash
DAJSC Sidney Crosby
DAJSL Martin St. Louis
DAJTR Tuomo Ruutu

2005-06 Ultra Difference Makers Patches

*PATCHES: 1.5X TO 4X BASE JSY
PRINT RUN 25 SER.#'d SETS

2005-06 Ultra Difference Makers Patch Autographs

PRINT RUN 5 SER.#'d SETS
NOT PRICED DUE TO SCARCITY
DAPAO Alexander Ovechkin
DAPAR Andrew Raycroft
DAPJC Jeff Carter
DAPJI Jarome Iginla
DAPPB Patrice Bergeron
DAPRN Rick Nash
DAPSC Sidney Crosby
DAPSL Martin St. Louis
DAPTR Tuomo Ruutu

2005-06 Ultra Fresh Ink

STATED ODDS 1:360
FIAM Al Montoya 10.00 25.00
FIAO Alexander Ovechkin 75.00 150.00
FIAP Alexander Perezhogin 8.00 20.00
FIAR Andrew Raycroft SP
FIAS Alexander Steen 12.00 30.00
FIAT Alex Tanguay SP 12.50 30.00
FIAW Andrew Wozniewski 4.00 10.00
FIAY Alexei Yashin 8.00 20.00
FIBG Boyd Gordon 4.00 10.00
FIBL Brett Lebda 4.00 10.00
FIBM Brenden Morrow 4.00 10.00
FIBO Derek Boogaard 8.00 20.00
FICA Mike Cammalleri 4.00 10.00
FICB Cam Barker 8.00 20.00
FICD Chris Drury 4.00 10.00
FICE Christian Ehrhoff 4.00 10.00
FICK Chris Kunitz 4.00 10.00
FICP Corey Perry SP 12.00 30.00
FICW Cam Ward 12.00 30.00
FIDB Dustin Brown 4.00 10.00
FIDL David Leneveu 8.00 20.00
FIDP Dion Phaneuf 30.00 60.00
FIDR Dwayne Roloson 4.00 10.00
FIDW Doug Weight 4.00 10.00
FIEJ Ed Jovanovski 8.00 20.00
FIEN Eric Nystrom 4.00 10.00
FIES Eric Staal SP 25.00 60.00
FIGB Gilbert Brule 12.00 30.00
FIGM Glen Murray 6.00 15.00
FIGP George Parros 4.00 10.00
FIHO Jeff Hoggan 4.00 10.00
FIHT Hannu Toivonen 8.00 20.00
FIHV Martin Havlat SP
FIHZ Henrik Zetterberg 10.00 25.00
FIIK Ilya Kovalchuk SP 25.00 60.00
FIIL Ian Laperriere 4.00 10.00
FIJA Jaroslav Balastik 4.00 10.00
FIJB Jay Bouwmeester SP 8.00 20.00
FIJC Jeff Carter 20.00 50.00
FIJG Josh Gorges 4.00 10.00
FIJH Jochen Hecht 4.00 10.00
FIJI Jim Howard 10.00 25.00
FIJI Jarome Iginla 30.00 75.00
FIJL Joffrey Lupul 4.00 10.00
FIJM Jay McClement 4.00 10.00
FIJN Jocelyn Thibault 4.00 10.00
FIJO Jeff O'Neill
FIJR Jeremy Roenick SP 30.00 80.00
FIJS Jason Spezza SP 20.00 50.00
FIJT Joe Thornton SP 25.00 60.00
FIJW Jeff Woywitka 4.00 10.00
FIKD Kevin Dallman 4.00 10.00
FIKP Keith Primeau 4.00 10.00
FIKW Kevin Weekes 6.00 15.00
FILN Ladislav Nagy SP 10.00 25.00
FIMB Martin Brodeur SP 75.00 125.00
FIMC Bryan McCabe 6.00 15.00
FIMO Brendan Morrison 4.00 10.00
FIMP Michael Peca 4.00 10.00
FIMR Mike Richards 15.00 30.00
FIMS Matt Stajan 10.00 25.00
FIMT Marty Turco SP 10.00 25.00
FINI Rob Niedermayer 6.00 15.00
FINN Niklas Nordgren 4.00 10.00
FINS Robert Nilsson 4.00 10.00
FINZ Nikolai Zherdev 8.00 20.00
FION Owen Nolan 6.00 15.00
FIPB Patrice Bergeron SP
FIPE Mark Popovic SP 4.00 10.00
FIRE Robert Esche 4.00 10.00
FIRF Ruslan Fedotenko 4.00 10.00
FIRG Ryan Getzlaf SP 25.00 60.00
FIRH Ryan Hollweg 4.00 10.00
FIRI Raitis Ivanans 4.00 10.00
FIRK Ryan Kesler 4.00 10.00
FIRL Roberto Luongo 10.00 25.00
FIRN Rick Nash SP
FIRO Rostislav Olesz 8.00 20.00
FIRS Ryan Smyth 6.00 15.00
FIRZ Richard Zednik 4.00 10.00
FISA Miroslav Satan 4.00 10.00
FISB Sean Burke 4.00 10.00
FISC Sidney Crosby SP 150.00 250.00
FISD Shane Doan 4.00 10.00
FISG Simon Gagne 12.00 30.00
FISK Saku Koivu SP 25.00 60.00
FISN Scott Niedermayer 6.00 15.00
FISS Sheldon Souray 4.00 10.00
FIST Anthony Stewart 6.00 15.00
FISU Ryan Suter 8.00 20.00
FITH Jose Theodore Sp 20.00 50.00
FITI Timo Helbling 4.00 10.00
FITL Trevor Linden 12.00 30.00
FITR Tuomo Ruutu 6.00 15.00
FITS Timofei Shishkanov 4.00 10.00
FITV Thomas Vanek 12.00 30.00
FIVL Vincent Lecavalier 20.00 50.00
FIWW Wojtek Wolski 10.00 25.00
FIYD Yann Danis
FIZC Zdeno Chara 8.00 20.00
FIZP Zach Parise 15.00 40.00

2005-06 Ultra Fresh Ink Blue

FISC Sidney Crosby 400.00 600.00

2005-06 Ultra Ice

COMMON CARD (1-200) 2.00 5.00
*STARS: 5X TO 12X
*ROOKIES 201-250: 1X TO 2.5X
*ROOKIES 251-271: 1.25X TO 3X
PRINT RUN 25 SER.#'d SETS
209 Brent Seabrook 10.00 25.00
251 Sidney Crosby 400.00 650.00
252 Alexander Ovechkin 150.00 300.00

2005-06 Ultra Rookie Uniformity Jerseys

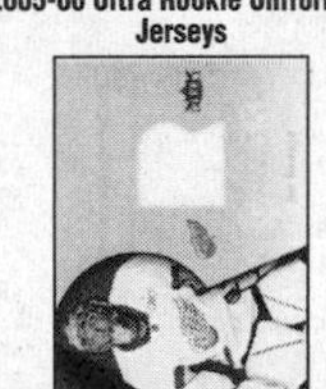

STATED ODDS 1:48
RUAA Andrew Alberts 3.00 8.00
RUAM Andrej Meszaros 3.00 8.00
RUAO Alexander Ovechkin 15.00 40.00
RUAP Alexander Perezhogin 4.00 10.00
RUAS Alexander Steen 4.00 10.00
RUAW Andrew Wozniewski 3.00 8.00
RUBB Brandon Bochenski 3.00 8.00
RUBC Braydon Coburn 4.00 10.00
RUBL Brett Lebda 3.00 8.00
RUBS Brent Seabrook 3.00 8.00
RUBW Brad Winchester 3.00 8.00
RUCB Cam Barker 3.00 8.00
RUCP Corey Perry 6.00 15.00
RUCW Cam Ward 6.00 15.00
RUDK Duncan Keith 4.00 10.00
RUDL David Leneveu 3.00 8.00
RUDP Dion Phaneuf 8.00 20.00
RUEN Eric Nystrom 3.00 8.00
RUGB Gilbert Brule 6.00 15.00
RUGP George Parros 3.00 8.00
RUHL Henrik Lundqvist 8.00 20.00
RUHO Jeff Hoggan 3.00 8.00
RUHT Hannu Toivonen 4.00 10.00
RUJB Jaroslav Balastik 3.00 8.00
RUJC Jeff Carter 6.00 15.00
RUJF Johan Franzen 3.00 8.00
RUJG Josh Gorges 3.00 8.00
RUJH Jim Howard 5.00 12.00
RUJJ Jussi Jokinen 4.00 10.00
RUJM Jay McClement 3.00 8.00
RUJS Jim Slater 3.00 8.00
RUJW Jeff Woywitka 3.00 8.00
RUKB Keith Ballard 3.00 8.00
RUKD Kevin Dallman 3.00 8.00
RUKN Kevin Nastiuk 3.00 8.00
RUMF Matthew Foy 3.00 8.00
RUMJ Milan Jurcina 3.00 8.00
RUMO Al Montoya 4.00 10.00
RUMR Mike Richards 4.00 10.00
RUMT Maxime Talbot 3.00 8.00
RUNN Niklas Nordgren 3.00 8.00
RUPB Peter Budaj 3.00 8.00
RUPE Patrick Eaves 3.00 8.00
RUPN Petteri Nokelainen 3.00 8.00
RUPP Petr Prucha 4.00 10.00
RURB Rene Bourque 3.00 8.00
RURC Ryane Clowe 3.00 8.00
RURG Ryan Getzlaf 5.00 12.00
RURH Ryan Hollweg 3.00 8.00
RURI Raitis Ivanans 3.00 8.00
RURN Robert Nilsson 3.00 8.00
RURO Rostislav Olesz 4.00 10.00
RURS Ryan Suter 4.00 10.00
RUSC Sidney Crosby 40.00 100.00
RUST Anthony Stewart 3.00 8.00
RUTH Timo Helbling 3.00 8.00
RUTV Thomas Vanek 6.00 15.00
RUWW Wojtek Wolski 5.00 12.00
RUYD Yann Danis 3.00 8.00
RUZP Zach Parise 4.00 10.00

2005-06 Ultra Rookie Uniformity Jersey Autographs

*AUTOS: 2X TO 5X BASE JSY
PRINT RUN 25 SER.#'d SETS
ARUAO Alexander Ovechkin 250.00 400.00
ARUDP Dion Phaneuf 75.00 150.00
ARUHL Henrik Lundqvist 75.00 150.00
ARUSC Sidney Crosby 400.00 700.00
ARUTV Thomas Vanek 50.00 100.00

2005-06 Ultra Rookie Uniformity Patches

*PATCHES: 2X TO 4X BASE JSY
PATCH PRINT RUN 35 SER.#'d SETS
RUPSC Sidney Crosby 200.00 350.00

2005-06 Ultra Scoring Kings

COMPLETE SET (40) 25.00 50.00
STATED ODDS 1:12
SK1 Mario Lemieux 2.00 5.00
SK2 Martin St. Louis .40 1.00
SK3 Joe Thornton .50 1.25
SK4 Mats Sundin .50 1.25
SK5 Jarome Iginla .40 1.00
SK6 Mike Modano .50 1.25
SK7 Steve Yzerman 1.25 3.00
SK8 Joe Sakic .60 1.50
SK9 Alex Tanguay .40 1.00
SK10 Dany Heatley .40 1.00
SK11 Sidney Crosby 4.00 10.00
SK12 Jeremy Roenick .40 1.00
SK13 Jason Spezza .50 1.25
SK14 Patrik Elias .40 1.00
SK15 Jaromir Jagr .50 1.25
SK16 Brad Richards .40 1.00
SK17 Markus Naslund .50 1.25
SK18 Alexander Ovechkin 2.00 5.00
SK19 Doug Weight .40 1.00
SK20 Ilya Kovalchuk .40 1.00
SK21 Peter Forsberg .50 1.25
SK22 Sergei Fedorov .50 1.25
SK23 Marian Hossa .40 1.00
SK24 Milan Hejduk .50 1.25
SK25 Bill Guerin .30 .75
SK26 Shane Doan .50 1.25
SK27 Mike Ribeiro .40 1.00
SK28 Martin Havlat .40 1.00
SK29 Corey Perry .40 1.00
SK30 Mike Richards .40 1.00
SK31 Ryan Getzlaf .40 1.00
SK32 Keith Tkachuk .50 1.25
SK33 Glen Murray .50 1.25
SK34 Brendan Shanahan .50 1.25
SK35 Paul Kariya .50 1.25
SK36 Marian Gaborik .50 1.25
SK37 Luc Robitaille .40 1.00
SK38 Daniel Alfredsson .40 1.00
SK39 Vincent Lecavalier .50 1.25
SK40 Eric Daze .40 1.00

2005-06 Ultra Scoring Kings Jerseys

STATED ODDS 1:72
SKJAO Alexander Ovechkin 30.00 60.00
SKJAT Alex Tanguay 3.00 8.00
SKJBG Bill Guerin 3.00 8.00
SKJBR Brad Richards 3.00 8.00
SKJBS Brendan Shanahan 3.00 8.00
SKJCP Corey Perry 3.00 8.00

SKJDA Daniel Alfredsson 3.00 8.00
SKJDH Dany Heatley 4.00 10.00
SKJDW Doug Weight 3.00 8.00
SKJED Eric Daze 3.00 8.00
SKJGM Glen Murray 3.00 8.00
SKJHO Marian Hossa 3.00 8.00
SKJHV Martin Havlat 3.00 8.00
SKJIK Ilya Kovalchuk 4.00 10.00
SKJJI Jarome Iginla 5.00 12.00
SKJJJ Jaromir Jagr 5.00 12.00
SKJJR Jeremy Roenick 4.00 10.00
SKJJS Jason Spezza 4.00 10.00
SKJJS Joe Sakic 6.00 15.00
SKJJT Joe Thornton 5.00 12.00
SKJKT Keith Tkachuk 3.00 8.00
SKJLR Luc Robitaille 3.00 8.00
SKJMG Marian Gaborik 5.00 12.00
SKJMH Milan Hejduk 3.00 8.00
SKJML Mario Lemieux 12.00 30.00
SKJMM Mike Modano 5.00 12.00
SKJMN Markus Naslund 3.00 8.00
SKJMR Mike Ribeiro 3.00 8.00
SKJMS Mats Sundin 3.00 8.00
SKJPE Patrik Elias 3.00 8.00
SKJPF Peter Forsberg 6.00 15.00
SKJPK Paul Kariya 3.00 8.00
SKJRG Ryan Getzlaf 3.00 8.00
SKJRI Mike Richards 3.00 8.00
SKJSC Sidney Crosby 30.00 80.00
SKJSD Shane Doan 3.00 8.00
SKJSF Sergei Fedorov 4.00 10.00
SKJSL Martin St. Louis 3.00 8.00
SKJSY Steve Yzerman 6.00 15.00
SKJVL Vincent Lecavalier 3.00 8.00

2005-06 Ultra Scoring Kings Jersey Autographs

PRINT RUN 20 SER.#'d SETS
NOT PRICED DUE TO SCARCITY
KAJAO Alexander Ovechkin
KAJAT Alex Tanguay
KAJBR Brad Richards
KAJCP Corey Perry
KAJDA Daniel Alfredsson
KAJDH Dany Heatley
KAJDW Doug Weight
KAJED Eric Daze
KAJGM Glen Murray
KAJHO Marian Hossa
KAJHV Martin Havlat
KAJIK Ilya Kovalchuk
KAJJI Jarome Iginla
KAJJR Jeremy Roenick
KAJJS Jason Spezza
KAJJT Joe Thornton
KAJMH Milan Hejduk
KAJMM Mike Modano
KAJMN Markus Naslund
KAJMR Mike Ribeiro
KAJMS Mats Sundin
KAJRG Ryan Getzlaf
KAJRI Mike Richards
KAJSC Sidney Crosby
KAJSD Shane Doan
KAJSL Martin St. Louis
KAJVL Vincent Lecavalier

2005-06 Ultra Scoring Kings Patches

*PATCHES: 1.25X TO 3X BASE JSY
PRINT RUN 50 SER.#'d SETS
SKPAO Alexander Ovechkin 75.00 200.00
SKPCP Corey Perry 20.00 50.00
SKPRG Ryan Getzlaf 20.00 50.00
SKPSC Sidney Crosby 100.00 250.00

2005-06 Ultra Scoring Kings Patch Autographs

PRINT RUN 10 SER.#'d SETS
NOT PRICED DUE TO SCARCITY
KAPAO Alexander Ovechkin
KAPAT Alex Tanguay
KAPBR Brad Richards
KAPCP Corey Perry
KAPDA Daniel Alfredsson
KAPDH Dany Heatley
KAPDW Doug Weight
KAPED Eric Daze
KAPGM Glen Murray
KAPHO Marian Hossa
KAPHV Martin Havlat
KAPIK Ilya Kovalchuk
KAPJI Jarome Iginla
KAPJR Jeremy Roenick
KAPJS Jason Spezza
KAPJT Joe Thornton
KAPMH Milan Hejduk
KAPMM Mike Modano
KAPMN Markus Naslund
KAPMR Mike Ribeiro
KAPRG Ryan Getzlaf
KAPRI Mike Richards
KAPSC Sidney Crosby
KAPSD Shane Doan
KAPSL Martin St. Louis
KAPVL Vincent Lecavalier

2005-06 Ultra Super Six

COMPLETE SET (8) 10.00 25.00
COMMON CARD (1-8)
SS1 Mario Lemieux 2.50 6.00
SS2 Joe Thornton 1.00 2.50
SS3 Martin Brodeur 1.50 4.00
SS4 Ray Bourque .75 2.00
SS5 Joe Sakic 1.25 3.00
SS6 Patrick Roy 2.00 5.00
SS7 Ray Bourque .75 2.00
SS8 Patrick Roy 2.00 5.00

2005-06 Ultra Super Six Jerseys

STATED ODDS 1:288
SSJJS Joe Sakic 12.00 30.00
SSJJT Joe Thornton 10.00 25.00
SSJMB Martin Brodeur 8.00 20.00
SSJML Mario Lemieux 15.00 30.00
SSJPR1 Patrick Roy 15.00 30.00
SSJPR2 Patrick Roy 15.00 30.00
SSJRB1 Ray Bourque 6.00 15.00
SSJRB2 Ray Bourque 6.00 15.00

2005-06 Ultra Super Six Jersey Autographs

PRINT RUN 3 SER.#'d SETS
NOT PRICED DUE TO SCARCITY
SAJJT Joe Thornton
SAJMB Martin Brodeur
SAJPR1 Patrick Roy
SAJPR2 Patrick Roy
SAJRB1 Ray Bourque
SAJRB2 Ray Bourque

2005-06 Ultra Super Six Patches

PATCH PRINT RUN 6 SER.#'d SETS
NOT PRICED DUE TO SCARCITY
UNPRICED PATCH AU 1/1's EXIST

2006-07 Ultra

This 251-card set was issued to the hobby in eight-card packs, with a $2.99 SRP, which came 24 packs to a box and 20 boxes to a case. Cards numbered 1-200 feature players in team alphabetical order while Rookie Cards 201-230 were issued with the product and inserted at a stated rate of one in four. In addition, rookie redemptions were inserted at a stated rate of one in 24 and those turned out to be cards numbered 231-251 in this product.

COMPLETE SET (251) 100.00 250.00
COMP.SET w/o SPs (200) 15.00 40.00
1 Jean-Sebastien Giguere .30 .75
2 Chris Pronger .25 .60
3 Andy McDonald .20 .50
4 Corey Perry .25 .60
5 Teemu Selanne .30 .75
6 Ryan Getzlaf .25 .60
7 Scott Niedermayer .20 .50
8 Kari Lehtonen .30 .75
9 Steve Rucchin .20 .50
10 Marian Hossa .25 .60
11 Ilya Kovalchuk .40 1.00
12 Slava Kozlov .20 .50
13 Bobby Holik .20 .50
14 Patrice Bergeron .25 .60
15 Brad Boyes .20 .50
16 Marc Savard .20 .50
17 Brad Stuart .20 .50
18 Marco Sturm .20 .50
19 Glen Murray .20 .50
20 Zdeno Chara .20 .50
21 Thomas Vanek .25 .60
22 Ryan Miller .30 .75
23 Maxim Afinogenov .20 .50
24 Ales Kotalik .20 .50
25 Chris Drury .25 .60
26 Martin Biron .25 .60
27 Daniel Briere .25 .60
28 Miikka Kiprusoff .30 .75
29 Jarome Iginla .50 1.25
30 Chuck Kobasew .20 .50
31 Kristian Huselius .20 .50
32 Daymond Langkow .20 .50
33 Dion Phaneuf .40 1.00
34 Alex Tanguay .25 .60
35 Cam Ward .50 1.25
36 Andrew Ladd .20 .50
37 Eric Staal .25 .60
38 Justin Williams .20 .50

39 Erik Cole .20 .50
40 Mike Commodore .20 .50
41 Rod Brind'Amour .25 .60
42 Nikolai Khabibulin .30 .75
43 Tuomo Ruutu .20 .50
44 Kyle Calder .20 .50
45 Martin Havlat .25 .60
46 Rene Bourque .20 .50
47 Duncan Keith .40 1.00
48 Jose Theodore .30 .75
49 Joe Sakic .60 1.50
50 Milan Hejduk .25 .60
51 Andrew Brunette .20 .50
52 Marek Svatos .20 .50
53 Pierre Turgeon .30 .75
54 Peter Budaj .25 .60
55 Fredrik Modin .20 .50
56 Nikolai Zherdev .20 .50
57 Rick Nash .30 .75
58 Sergei Fedorov .30 .75
59 Rostislav Klesla .20 .50
60 Bryan Berard .20 .50
61 David Vyborny .20 .50
62 Marty Turco .25 .60
63 Mike Modano .30 .75
64 Sergei Zubov .20 .50
65 Brenden Morrow .25 .60
66 Jussi Jokinen .20 .50
67 Eric Lindros .30 .75
68 Jere Lehtinen .20 .50
69 Tomas Holmstrom .20 .50
70 Henrik Zetterberg .30 .75
71 Nicklas Lidstrom .30 .75
72 Pavel Datsyuk .30 .75
73 Chris Osgood .30 .75
74 Kris Draper .20 .50
75 Steve Yzerman 1.00 2.50
76 Ales Hemsky .20 .50
77 Jarret Stoll .20 .50
78 Joffrey Lupul .20 .50
79 Dwayne Roloson .25 .60
80 Ryan Smyth .25 .60
81 Shawn Horcoff .20 .50
82 Fernando Pisani .20 .50
83 Todd Bertuzzi .25 .60
84 Nathan Horton .20 .50
85 Alex Auld .25 .60
86 Olli Jokinen .20 .50
87 Jay Bouwmeester .20 .50
88 Rostislav Olesz .20 .50
89 Joe Nieuwendyk .25 .60
90 Alexander Frolov .20 .50
91 Mathieu Garon .25 .60
92 Mike Cammalleri .25 .60
93 Rob Blake .25 .60
94 Lubomir Visnovsky .20 .50
95 Dustin Brown .20 .50
96 Marian Gaborik .50 1.25
97 Manny Fernandez .25 .60
98 Mark Parrish .20 .50
99 Pierre-Marc Bouchard .20 .50
100 Brian Rolston .20 .50
101 Pavol Demitra .20 .50
102 Saku Koivu .30 .75
103 Cristobal Huet .30 .75
104 Alex Kovalev .20 .50
105 Michael Ryder .25 .60
106 David Aebischer .25 .60
107 Mike Ribeiro .20 .50
108 Chris Higgins .20 .50
109 Tomas Vokoun .25 .60
110 Steve Sullivan .20 .50
111 David Legwand .20 .50
112 Paul Kariya .30 .75
113 Jason Arnott .20 .50
114 Kimmo Timonen .20 .50
115 Martin Brodeur 1.00 2.50
116 Brian Rafalski .20 .50
117 Patrik Elias .20 .50
118 Brian Gionta .20 .50
119 Scott Gomez .20 .50
120 Zach Parise .25 .60
121 Alexei Yashin .20 .50
122 Rick DiPietro .30 .75
123 Miroslav Satan .20 .50
124 Trent Hunter .20 .50
125 Jason Blake .20 .50
126 Mike Sillinger .20 .50
127 Henrik Lundqvist .50 1.25
128 Martin Straka .20 .50
129 Jaromir Jagr .50 1.25
130 Petr Prucha .20 .50
131 Brendan Shanahan .30 .75
132 Matt Cullen .20 .50
133 Martin Gerber .30 .75
134 Jason Spezza .30 .75
135 Wade Redden .20 .50
136 Dany Heatley .30 .75
137 Daniel Alfredsson .25 .60
138 Patrick Eaves .20 .50
139 Ray Emery .30 .75
140 Peter Forsberg .50 1.25
141 Antero Niittymaki .30 .75
142 Joni Pitkanen .20 .50
143 Simon Gagne .30 .75
144 Keith Primeau .20 .50
145 Jeff Carter .30 .75
146 Robert Esche .25 .60
147 Mike Richards .30 .75
148 Ladislav Nagy .20 .50
149 Curtis Joseph .30 .75
150 Mike Comrie .20 .50
151 Shane Doan .25 .60
152 Ed Jovanovski .25 .60
153 Jeremy Roenick .30 .75
154 Sidney Crosby 1.50 4.00
155 Marc-Andre Fleury .30 .75
156 Ryan Malone .20 .50
157 Colby Armstrong .20 .50
158 Ryan Whitney .20 .50
159 John LeClair .25 .60
160 Evgeni Nabokov .25 .60
161 Joe Thornton .50 1.25
162 Patrick Marleau .25 .60
163 Vesa Toskala .25 .60
164 Jonathan Cheechoo .30 .75
165 Steve Bernier .20 .50
166 Mark Bell .20 .50
167 Keith Tkachuk .25 .60
168 Curtis Sanford .25 .60
169 Doug Weight .20 .50
170 Bill Guerin .20 .50
171 Lee Stempniak .20 .50
172 Petr Cajanek .20 .50
173 Evgeni Artyukhin .20 .50
174 Brad Richards .30 .75
175 Martin St. Louis .30 .75
176 Vincent Lecavalier .30 .75
177 Vaclav Prospal .20 .50
178 Marc Denis .25 .60
179 Ruslan Fedotenko .20 .50
180 Andrew Raycroft .25 .60
181 Mats Sundin .30 .75
182 Bryan McCabe .20 .50
183 Alexander Steen .25 .60
184 Kyle Wellwood .20 .50
185 Darcy Tucker .20 .50
186 Tomas Kaberle .20 .50
187 Michael Peca .20 .50
188 Markus Naslund .30 .75
189 Roberto Luongo .60 1.50
190 Henrik Sedin .20 .50
191 Mattias Ohlund .20 .50
192 Brendan Morrison .20 .50
193 Ryan Kesler .20 .50
194 Daniel Sedin .20 .50
195 Olaf Kolzig .40 1.00
196 Alexander Ovechkin 1.25 3.00
197 Brian Pothier .20 .50
198 Dainius Zubrus .20 .50
199 Chris Clark .20 .50
200 Matt Pettinger .25 .60
201 Yan Stastny RC 1.25 3.00
202 Mark Stuart RC 1.25 3.00
203 Carsen Germyn RC 1.25 3.00
204 Dustin Byfuglien RC 2.50 6.00
205 Dan Jancevski RC 1.25 3.00
206 Tomas Kopecky RC 1.50 4.00
207 Marc-Antoine Pouliot RC 1.50 4.00
208 Konstantin Pushkaryov RC 1.25 3.00
209 Erik Reitz RC 1.25 3.00
210 Miroslav Kopriva RC 1.25 3.00
211 Shea Weber RC 1.50 4.00
212 Frank Doyle RC 1.50 4.00
213 Rob Collins RC 1.25 3.00
214 Steve Regier RC 1.25 3.00
215 Ryan Caldwell RC 1.25 3.00
216 Masi Marjamaki RC 1.25 3.00
217 Jarkko Immonen RC 1.25 3.00
218 Billy Thompson RC 1.25 3.00
219 Filip Novak RC 1.25 3.00
220 Ryan Potulny RC 1.50 4.00
221 Bill Thomas RC 1.25 3.00
222 Joel Perrault RC 1.25 3.00
223 Noah Welch RC 1.25 3.00
224 Michel Ouellet RC 2.00 5.00
225 Matt Carle RC 1.50 4.00
226 Ben Ondrus RC 1.25 3.00
227 Brendan Bell RC 1.25 3.00
228 Ian White RC 1.25 3.00
229 Jeremy Williams RC 1.25 3.00
230 Eric Fehr RC 1.50 4.00
231 Patrick Thoreson RC 1.50 4.00
232 Ryan Shannon RC 1.50 4.00
233 Anze Kopitar RC 8.00 20.00
234 Travis Zajac RC 2.50 6.00
235 Nigel Dawes RC 1.50 4.00
236 Kris Letang RC 2.50 6.00
237 Marc Edouard Vlasic RC 1.50 4.00
238 Keith Yandle RC 1.50 4.00
239 Alexei Mikhnov RC 1.50 4.00
240 Ladislav Smid RC 1.50 4.00
241 Loui Eriksson RC 1.50 4.00
242 Luc Bourdon RC 2.00 5.00
243 Alexander Radulov RC 4.00 10.00
244 Alexei Kaigorodov RC 1.50 4.00
245 Enver Lisin RC 1.50 4.00
246 Patrick O'Sullivan RC 2.00 5.00
247 Jordan Staal RC 6.00 15.00
248 Paul Stastny RC 6.00 15.00
249 Guillaume Latendresse RC 5.00 12.00
250 Phil Kessel RC 5.00 12.00
251 Evgeni Malkin RC 25.00 50.00

2006-07 Ultra Gold Medallion

STARS 2X to 5X BASE HI
ROOKIES .75X to 2X BASE HI
ONE PER PACK
ROOKIE REDEMPTIONS: 1X to 1.5X HI
233 Anze Kopitar 20.00 50.00
242 Luc Bourdon 12.00 30.00
243 Alexander Radulov 20.00 50.00
247 Jordan Staal 30.00 80.00
248 Paul Stastny 25.00 60.00
249 Guillaume Latendresse 20.00 50.00
250 Phil Kessel 25.00 60.00
251 Evgeni Malkin 60.00 125.00

2006-07 Ultra Ice Medallion

STARS: 6X to 15X BASE HI
ROOKIES: 1.5X to 3X BASE HI
STATED PRINT RUN 100 #'d SETS
ROOKIE REDEMPTIONS 1.5X to 3X HI
ROOKIE RED. PRINT RUN 25 #'d SETS
154 Sidney Crosby 30.00 80.00
196 Alexander Ovechkin 20.00 50.00
233 Anze Kopitar 40.00 80.00

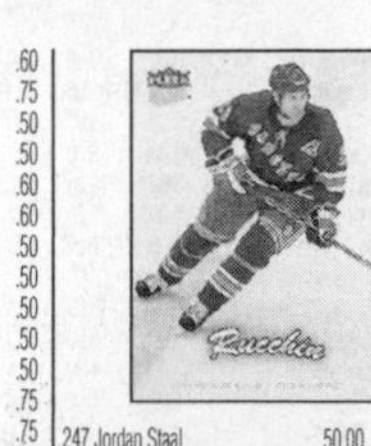

247 Jordan Staal 50.00 125.00
249 Guillaume Latendresse 30.00 80.00
251 Evgeni Malkin 150.00 250.00

2006-07 Ultra Action

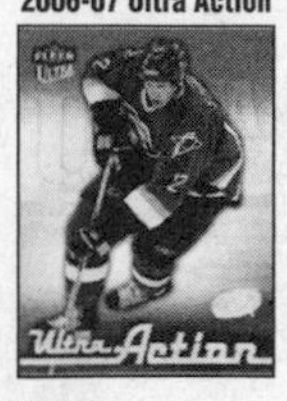

STATED ODDS 1:12
UA1 Kari Lehtonen .75 2.00
UA2 Jarome Iginla 1.25 3.00
UA3 Dion Phaneuf .75 2.00
UA4 Eric Staal .75 2.00
UA5 Joe Sakic 1.25 3.00
UA6 Marek Svatos .40 1.00
UA7 Rick Nash 1.25 3.00
UA8 Mike Modano 1.25 3.00
UA9 Henrik Zetterberg .75 2.00
UA10 Brendan Shanahan .75 2.00
UA11 Chris Pronger .75 2.00
UA12 Roberto Luongo .75 2.00
UA13 Marian Gaborik 1.25 3.00
UA14 Saku Koivu .75 2.00
UA15 Paul Kariya .75 2.00
UA16 Martin Brodeur 2.50 6.00
UA17 Alexei Yashin .40 1.00
UA18 Jaromir Jagr 1.25 3.00
UA19 Dominik Hasek 1.25 3.00
UA20 Dany Heatley 1.25 3.00
UA21 Peter Forsberg 1.25 3.00
UA22 Shane Doan .40 1.00
UA23 Sidney Crosby 4.00 10.00
UA24 Joe Thornton 1.25 3.00
UA25 Evgeni Nabokov .75 2.00
UA26 Martin St. Louis .75 2.00
UA27 Vincent Lecavalier .75 2.00
UA28 Alexander Ovechkin 2.50 6.00
UA29 Mats Sundin .75 2.00
UA30 Markus Naslund .75 2.00

2006-07 Ultra Difference Makers

STATED ODDS 1:12
DM1 Ilya Bryzgalov .75 2.00
DM2 Ilya Kovalchuk 1.25 3.00
DM3 Patrice Bergeron .75 2.00
DM4 Ryan Miller .75 2.00
DM5 Jarome Iginla 1.25 3.00
DM6 Miikka Kiprusoff .75 2.00
DM7 Eric Staal .75 2.00
DM8 Markus Naslund .75 2.00
DM9 Alex Tanguay .75 2.00
DM10 Jose Theodore 1.25 3.00
DM11 Rick Nash 1.25 3.00
DM12 Marty Turco .75 2.00
DM13 Pavel Datsyuk .75 2.00
DM14 Henrik Zetterberg .75 2.00
DM15 Chris Pronger .75 2.00
DM16 Roberto Luongo 1.25 3.00
DM17 Michael Ryder .75 2.00
DM18 Saku Koivu .75 2.00
DM19 Mats Sundin .75 2.00
DM20 Martin Brodeur 2.50 6.00
DM21 Jaromir Jagr 1.25 3.00
DM22 Henrik Lundqvist 1.25 3.00
DM23 Daniel Alfredsson .75 2.00
DM24 Dany Heatley 1.25 3.00
DM25 Jason Spezza .75 2.00
DM26 Peter Forsberg 1.25 3.00
DM27 Alexander Ovechkin 2.50 6.00
DM28 Sidney Crosby 4.00 10.00
DM29 Joe Thornton 1.25 3.00
DM30 Vincent Lecavalier .75 2.00

2006-07 Ultra Fresh Ink

STATED ODDS 1:200
IAL Andrew Ladd SP
IAM Al Montoya 6.00 15.00
IAO Alexander Ovechkin SP 60.00 100.00
IBB Brad Boyes SP 8.00 20.00
IBL Brian Leetch SP 20.00 50.00
IBM Brenden Morrow SP
IBR Martin Brodeur SP
ICD Chris Drury SP 10.00 25.00
ICK Chuck Kobasew 4.00 10.00
ICO Chris Osgood SP 10.00 25.00
IDB Daniel Briere SP 10.00 25.00
IDC Dan Cloutier SP 10.00 25.00
IDL David Leneveu 6.00 15.00
IDR Dwayne Roloson 6.00 15.00
IEN Evgeni Nabokov 6.00 15.00
IGM Glen Murray SP 15.00 40.00
IHE Milan Hejduk SP 12.00 30.00
IJB Jay Bouwmeester SP 10.00 25.00
IJH Jeff Halpern 6.00 15.00
IJI Jarome Iginla SP 25.00 60.00
IJL Jason Labarbera 6.00 15.00
IJO Jeff O'Neill SP 8.00 20.00
IJT Jose Theodore SP 15.00 40.00
IJV Josef Vasicek 8.00 20.00
IMB Martin Biron 6.00 15.00
IMC Mike Cammalleri SP 8.00 20.00
IMG Marian Gaborik SP 15.00 40.00
IMH Michal Handzus 6.00 15.00
IMN Mika Noronen 5.00 12.00
IMR Michael Ryder SP 10.00 25.00
IMS Marc Savard 6.00 15.00
IMT Mikael Tellqvist 8.00 20.00
IMZ Marek Zidlicky SP 8.00 20.00
INA Nikolai Antropov SP 8.00 20.00
IOK Olaf Kolzig SP 12.00 30.00
IPS Philippe Sauve 4.00 10.00
IRF Ruslan Fedotenko SP 8.00 20.00
IRM Ryan Malone SP 10.00 25.00
IRS Ryan Smyth SP 12.00 30.00
ISC Sidney Crosby SP 150.00 250.00
ISG Scott Gomez SP 10.00 25.00
ISH Scott Hartnell SP 8.00 20.00
ISK Saku Koivu SP 12.00 30.00
ISS Sergei Samsonov SP 6.00 15.00
ISU Ryan Suter 8.00 20.00
ITB Todd Bertuzzi SP 15.00 40.00
ITC Ty Conklin SP 8.00 20.00
ITG Tim Gleason 5.00 12.00

2006-07 Ultra Scoring Kings

STATED ODDS 1:12
SK1 Alex Tanguay .75 2.00
SK2 Alexander Ovechkin 2.50 6.00
SK3 Brad Richards .75 2.00
SK4 Brendan Shanahan .75 2.00
SK5 Daniel Alfredsson .75 2.00
SK6 Dany Heatley 1.25 3.00
SK7 Eric Staal .75 2.00
SK8 Henrik Zetterberg .75 2.00
SK9 Ilya Kovalchuk 1.25 3.00
SK10 Jarome Iginla 1.25 3.00
SK11 Jaromir Jagr 1.25 3.00
SK12 Jason Spezza .75 2.00
SK13 Joe Sakic 1.25 3.00
SK14 Joe Thornton 1.25 3.00
SK15 Jonathan Cheechoo .75 2.00
SK16 Ryan Smyth .40 1.00
SK17 Marian Gaborik 1.25 3.00
SK18 Markus Naslund .75 2.00
SK19 Mats Sundin .75 2.00
SK20 Michael Ryder .40 1.00
SK21 Mike Modano 1.25 3.00
SK22 Patrice Bergeron .75 2.00
SK23 Paul Kariya .75 2.00
SK24 Pavel Datsyuk .75 2.00
SK25 Peter Forsberg 1.25 3.00
SK26 Rick Nash 1.25 3.00
SK27 Saku Koivu .75 2.00
SK28 Sidney Crosby 4.00 10.00
SK29 Simon Gagne .75 2.00
SK30 Vincent Lecavalier .75 2.00

2006-07 Ultra Uniformity

STATED ODDS 1:12
UAH Ales Hemsky 3.00 8.00
UAO Alexander Ovechkin 10.00 25.00
UBL Rob Blake 3.00 8.00
UBM Brendan Morrison 3.00 8.00
UBR Martin Brodeur 8.00 20.00
UBS Brad Stuart 3.00 8.00
UCC Carlo Colaiacovo 3.00 8.00
UCD Chris Drury 3.00 8.00
UCP Chris Pronger 4.00 10.00
UDE Pavol Demitra 3.00 8.00
UDH Dan Hamhuis 3.00 8.00
UDL David Legwand 3.00 8.00
UDM Darren McCarty 3.00 8.00
UEB Ed Belfour 4.00 10.00
UED Eric Daze 3.00 8.00
UEJ Ed Jovanovski 3.00 8.00
UEL Eric Lindros 4.00 10.00
UEN Evgeni Nabokov 4.00 10.00
UES Eric Staal 4.00 10.00
UFP Fernando Pisani 3.00 8.00
UGE Martin Gerber 3.00 8.00
UHA Dominik Hasek SP 8.00 20.00
UJA Jason Arnott 3.00 8.00
UJG Jean-Sebastien Giguere 3.00 8.00
UJK Jason King 3.00 8.00
UJL Jere Lehtinen 3.00 8.00
UJS Joe Sakic 8.00 20.00
UJT Joe Thornton 6.00 15.00
UJW Justin Williams 3.00 8.00
UKO Mikko Koivu 3.00 8.00
UKT Keith Tkachuk 3.00 8.00
ULN Ladislav Nagy 3.00 8.00
ULR Luc Robitaille 4.00 10.00
UMB Martin Biron 3.00 8.00
UMC Bryan McCabe 3.00 8.00
UMD Marc Denis 3.00 8.00
UMG Marian Gaborik 6.00 15.00
UMK Miikka Kiprusoff 5.00 12.00
UMM Mike Modano 5.00 12.00
UMN Markus Naslund 4.00 10.00
UMP Mark Parrish 3.00 8.00
UMR Michael Ryder 4.00 10.00
UMS Marek Svatos 3.00 8.00
UNA Nikolai Antropov 3.00 8.00
UPB Pierre-Marc Bouchard 3.00 8.00
UPD Pavel Datsyuk 4.00 10.00
UPE Michael Peca 3.00 8.00
UPF Peter Forsberg 6.00 15.00
UPL Patrick Lalime 3.00 8.00
UPP Petr Prucha 3.00 8.00
URB Radek Bonk 3.00 8.00
URE Robert Esche 3.00 8.00
URR Robyn Regehr 3.00 8.00
URZ Richard Zednik 3.00 8.00
USG Simon Gagne 4.00 10.00
USK Saku Koivu 4.00 10.00
UST Martin Straka 3.00 8.00
USU Mats Sundin 4.00 10.00
USW Stephen Weiss 3.00 8.00
UTS Teemu Selanne 4.00 10.00

2006-07 Ultra Uniformity Patches

NOT PRICED DUE TO SCARCITY
PRINT RUN 25 SER. #'d SETS
UPAH Ales Hemsky 25.00 60.00
UPAO Alexander Ovechkin 80.00 200.00
UPBM Rob Blake 30.00 80.00
UPBO Brendan Morrison 25.00 60.00
UPBO_ Radek Bonk
UPBR Martin Brodeur 40.00 100.00
UPBS Brad Stuart 25.00 60.00
UPCC Carlo Colaiacovo
UPCD Chris Drury 30.00 80.00
UPCP Chris Pronger 30.00 80.00
UPDE Pavol Demitra 25.00 60.00
UPDH Dan Hamhuis 25.00 60.00
UPDL David Legwand 25.00 60.00
UPDM Darren McCarty
UPEB Ed Belfour 100.00 250.00
UPED Eric Daze
UPEJ Ed Jovanovski 25.00 60.00
UPEL Eric Lindros 40.00 100.00
UPEN Evgeni Nabokov 30.00 80.00
UPES Eric Staal 30.00 80.00
UPFP Fernando Pisani 25.00 60.00
UPGA Martin Gerber 40.00 100.00
UPHA Dominik Hasek 40.00 100.00
UPJA Jason Arnott 25.00 60.00
UPJG Jean-Sebastien Giguere 40.00 100.00
UPJK Jason King
UPJL Jere Lehtinen 25.00 60.00
UPJS Joe Sakic 60.00 150.00
UPJT Joe Thornton 50.00 120.00
UPJW Justin Williams 25.00 60.00
UPKO Mikko Koivu 25.00 60.00
UPKT Keith Tkachuk 30.00 80.00
UPLN Ladislav Nagy 25.00 60.00
UPLR Luc Robitaille 30.00 80.00
UPMB Martin Biron 30.00 80.00
UPMD Bryan McCabe 25.00 60.00
UPMG Marc Denis 30.00 80.00
UPMK Marian Gaborik 60.00 150.00
UPMM Miikka Kiprusoff 40.00 100.00
UPMN Mike Modano 40.00 100.00
UPMO Markus Naslund 40.00 100.00
UPMP Mark Parrish 25.00 60.00
UPMR Michael Ryder 30.00 80.00
UPMS Marek Svatos 25.00 60.00
UPNA Nikolai Antropov
UPPA Pierre-Marc Bouchard 25.00 60.00
UPPB_ Peter Forsberg 50.00 120.00
UPPB Pavel Datsyuk 40.00 100.00
UPPD_ Michael Peca 25.00 60.00
UPPL Patrick Lalime
UPPP Petr Prucha 25.00 60.00
UPRE Robert Esche 30.00 80.00
UPRR Robyn Regehr 25.00 60.00
UPRZ Richard Zednik
UPSG Simon Gagne 40.00 100.00
UPSK Saku Koivu 40.00 100.00
UPST Martin Straka 25.00 60.00
UPSU Mats Sundin 40.00 100.00
UPSW Stephen Weiss
UPTS Teemu Selanne 40.00 100.00

2006-07 Ultra Uniformity Autographed Jerseys

AUTOS: 2X to 5X BASE JERSEY
PRINT RUN 35 SER. #'d SETS

2007-08 Ultra

This 271-card set was released in September, 2007. The set was issued into the hobby in eight-card packs which came 24 packs to a box and 12 boxes to a case. Cards numbered 1-200 feature veterans basically in reverse team alphabetical order and cards numbered 201-250 are Rookie Cards which were inserted at a stated rate of one in four. In addition, one rookie redemption card, which becames R251-R271, were inserted into packs at a stated rate of one in 24.

COMP.SET w/o SPs (200) 10.00 25.00
RC (201-250) STATED ODDS 1:4
RC (251-271) STATED ODDS 1:24
1 Alexander Ovechkin 1.00 2.50
2 Alexander Semin .30 .75
3 Chris Clark .20 .50
4 Matt Pettinger .20 .50
5 Olaf Kolzig .30 .75
6 Markus Naslund .30 .75
7 Roberto Luongo .50 1.25
8 Henrik Sedin .20 .50
9 Brendan Morrison .20 .50
10 Kevin Bieksa .20 .50
11 Daniel Sedin .20 .50
12 Andrew Raycroft .25 .60
13 Mats Sundin .30 .75
14 Bryan McCabe .20 .50
15 Alexander Steen .20 .50
16 Kyle Wellwood .20 .50
17 Darcy Tucker .25 .60
18 Tomas Kaberle .20 .50
19 Brad Richards .25 .60
20 Martin St. Louis .25 .60
21 Vincent Lecavalier .30 .75
22 Vaclav Prospal .20 .50
23 Johan Holmqvist .25 .60
24 Ruslan Fedotenko .20 .50
25 Doug Weight .20 .50
26 Brad Boyes .25 .60
27 Manny Legace .25 .60
28 Lee Stempniak .20 .50
29 Evgeni Nabokov .25 .60
30 Joe Thornton .40 1.00
31 Patrick Marleau .25 .60
32 Matt Carle .20 .50
33 Vesa Toskala .25 .60
34 Jonathan Cheechoo .25 .60
35 Steve Bernier .20 .50
36 Bill Guerin .20 .50
37 Sidney Crosby 1.50 4.00
38 Evgeni Malkin .75 2.00
39 Marc-Andre Fleury .30 .75
40 Ryan Malone .20 .50
41 Colby Armstrong .20 .50
42 Ryan Whitney .25 .60
43 Jordan Staal .40 1.00
44 Georges Laraque .20 .50
45 Zbynek Michalek .20 .50
46 Curtis Joseph .25 .60
47 Keith Ballard .20 .50
48 Shane Doan .20 .50
49 Ed Jovanovski .20 .50
50 Mike Richards .40 1.00
51 R.J. Umberger .20 .50
52 Antero Niittymaki .25 .60
53 Joni Pitkanen .20 .50
54 Simon Gagne .30 .75
55 Jeff Carter .20 .50
56 Martin Biron .25 .60
57 Tom Preissing .20 .50
58 Jason Spezza .30 .75
59 Wade Redden .20 .50
60 Dany Heatley .40 1.00
61 Daniel Alfredsson .25 .60
62 Andrej Meszaros .20 .50
63 Ray Emery .25 .60
64 Chris Neil .20 .50
65 Henrik Lundqvist .40 1.00
66 Martin Straka .20 .50
67 Jaromir Jagr .50 1.25
68 Petr Prucha .20 .50
69 Brendan Shanahan .30 .75
70 Michael Nylander .20 .50
71 Sean Avery .20 .50
72 Rick DiPietro .25 .60
73 Miroslav Satan .20 .50
74 Ryan Smyth .25 .60
75 Jason Blake .20 .50
76 Mike Sillinger .20 .50
77 Alexei Yashin .20 .50
78 Jamie Langenbrunner .20 .50
79 Martin Brodeur .75 2.00
80 Brian Rafalski .20 .50
81 Patrik Elias .20 .50
82 Brian Gionta .20 .50
83 Scott Gomez .20 .50
84 Zach Parise .25 .60
85 Peter Forsberg .40 1.00
86 Tomas Vokoun .30 .75
87 Steve Sullivan .20 .50
88 David Legwand .20 .50
89 Paul Kariya .30 .75
90 J.P. Dumont .20 .50
91 Shea Weber .20 .50
92 Radek Bonk .20 .50
93 Saku Koivu .25 .60
94 Cristobal Huet .25 .60
95 Sheldon Souray .20 .50
96 Michael Ryder .20 .50
97 Guillaume Latendresse .25 .60
98 Tomas Plekanec .20 .50
99 Mikko Koivu .20 .50
100 Niklas Backstrom .25 .60
101 Pierre-Marc Bouchard .20 .50
102 Brian Rolston .20 .50
103 Pavol Demitra .20 .50
104 Marian Gaborik .40 1.00
105 Manny Fernandez .25 .60
106 Alexander Frolov .20 .50
107 Mike Cammalleri .25 .60
108 Rob Blake .25 .60
109 Anze Kopitar .30 .75
110 Dustin Brown .20 .50
111 Patrick O'Sullivan .25 .60
112 Nathan Horton .20 .50
113 Ed Belfour .30 .75
114 Olli Jokinen .20 .50
115 Jay Bouwmeester .20 .50
116 Noah Welch .20 .50
117 Ales Hemsky .20 .50
118 Jarret Stoll .20 .50
119 Shawn Horcoff .20 .50
120 Dwayne Roloson .25 .60
121 Petr Sykora .20 .50
122 Joffrey Lupul .20 .50
123 Raffi Torres .20 .50
124 Tomas Holmstrom .25 .60
125 Henrik Zetterberg .30 .75
126 Nicklas Lidstrom .30 .75
127 Pavel Datsyuk .30 .75
128 Dominik Hasek .40 1.00
129 Todd Bertuzzi .25 .60
130 Robert Lang .20 .50
131 Marty Turco .30 .75
132 Mike Modano .30 .75
133 Sergei Zubov .20 .50
134 Brenden Morrow .25 .60
135 Jussi Jokinen .20 .50
136 Eric Lindros .30 .75
137 Jere Lehtinen .20 .50
138 Philippe Boucher .20 .50
139 Fredrik Modin .20 .50
140 Nikolai Zherdev .20 .50
141 Rick Nash .30 .75
142 Sergei Fedorov .30 .75
143 Gilbert Brule .20 .50
144 Fredrik Norrena .25 .60
145 David Vyborny .20 .50
146 Wojtek Wolski .20 .50
147 Jose Theodore .30 .75
148 Joe Sakic .60 1.50
149 Milan Hejduk .25 .60
150 Andrew Brunette .20 .50
151 Marek Svatos .20 .50
152 Paul Stastny .30 .75
153 Peter Budaj .25 .60
154 Nikolai Khabibulin .30 .75
155 Tuomo Ruutu .20 .50
156 Brent Seabrook .20 .50
157 Martin Havlat .25 .60
158 Patrick Sharp .20 .50
159 Duncan Keith .30 .75
160 Cam Ward .30 .75
161 Ray Whitney .20 .50
162 Eric Staal .30 .75
163 Justin Williams .20 .50
164 Erik Cole .20 .50
165 Mike Commodore .20 .50
166 Rod Brind'Amour .25 .60
167 Dustin Boyd .20 .50
168 Miikka Kiprusoff .40 1.00
169 Jarome Iginla .50 1.25
170 Kristian Huselius .20 .50
171 Daymond Langkow .20 .50
172 Dion Phaneuf .30 .75
173 Alex Tanguay .25 .60
174 Thomas Vanek .25 .60
175 Ryan Miller .30 .75
176 Maxim Afinogenov .20 .50
177 Jason Pominville .20 .50
178 Chris Drury .25 .60
179 Drew Stafford .25 .60
180 Daniel Briere .30 .75
181 Patrice Bergeron .30 .75
182 Phil Kessel .30 .75
183 Marc Savard .20 .50
184 Glen Murray .20 .50
185 Zdeno Chara .20 .50
186 Tim Thomas .40 1.00
187 Marco Sturm .20 .50
188 Kari Lehtonen .30 .75
189 Marian Hossa .30 .75
190 Ilya Kovalchuk .40 1.00
191 Slava Kozlov .20 .50
192 Keith Tkachuk .25 .60
193 Jean-Sebastien Giguere .30 .75
194 Chris Pronger .30 .75
195 Andy McDonald .20 .50
196 Corey Perry .25 .60
197 Chris Kunitz .20 .50
198 Teemu Selanne .30 .75
199 Ryan Getzlaf .25 .60
200 Scott Niedermayer .20 .50
201 Aaron Rome RC 1.25 3.00
202 Andy Greene RC 1.25 3.00
203 Brandon Dubinsky RC 2.00 5.00
204 Bryan Bickell RC 1.25 3.00
205 Bryan Young RC 1.25 3.00
206 Colin Fraser RC 1.25 3.00
207 Daniel Girardi RC 1.25 3.00
208 Danny Bois RC 1.25 3.00
209 Curtis Glencross RC 1.25 3.00
210 David Clarkson RC 1.25 3.00
211 David Koci RC 1.25 3.00
212 David Krejci RC 2.50 6.00
213 David Moss RC 2.00 5.00
214 Drew Fata RC 1.25 3.00
215 Drew Miller RC 1.25 3.00
216 Duncan Milroy RC 1.25 3.00
217 Frans Nielsen RC 1.25 3.00
218 Gabe Gauthier RC 1.25 3.00
219 Jack Johnson RC 2.00 5.00
220 Jannik Hansen RC 1.25 3.00
221 Jaroslav Halak RC 4.00 10.00
222 Jeff Finger RC 1.25 3.00
223 Jeff Schultz RC 1.25 3.00
224 Joel Lundqvist RC 1.25 3.00
225 Jonathan Sigalet RC 1.25 3.00
226 Kent Huskins RC 1.25 3.00
227 Krys Barch RC 1.25 3.00
228 Lauri Tukonen RC 1.25 3.00
229 Marc Methot RC 1.25 3.00
230 Mark Fraser RC 1.25 3.00
231 Mark Mancari RC 1.50 4.00
232 Mathieu Roy RC 1.25 3.00
233 Matt Ellis RC 1.25 3.00
234 Nathan Guenin RC 1.25 3.00
235 Patrick Kaleta RC 1.25 3.00
236 Petr Kalus RC 1.25 3.00
237 Rich Peverley RC 1.25 3.00
238 Riley Cote RC 1.50 4.00
239 Rob Schremp RC 1.50 4.00
240 Rod Pelley RC 1.25 3.00
241 Ryan Callahan RC 2.00 5.00
242 Ryan Parent RC 1.50 4.00
243 Scott Munroe RC 1.25 3.00
244 Shay Stephenson RC 1.25 3.00
245 Tobias Stephan RC 1.50 4.00
246 Tom Gilbert RC 1.50 4.00
247 Tomas Popperle RC 1.50 4.00
248 Tomi Maki RC 1.25 3.00
249 Yutaka Fukufuji RC 1.50 4.00
250 Zack Stortini RC 1.25 3.00

251 Carey Price RC 20.00 50.00
252 Jonathan Toews RC 20.00 50.00
253 Sam Gagner RC 3.00 8.00
254 Bobby Ryan RC 6.00 15.00
255 Niklas Bergfors RC 2.00 5.00
256 Erik Johnson RC 3.00 8.00
257 Nicklas Backstrom RC 6.00 15.00
258 Jonathan Bernier RC 4.00 10.00
259 Bryan Little RC 2.50 6.00
260 Patrick Kane RC 15.00 50.00
261 Andrew Cogliano RC 4.00 10.00
262 Marc Staal RC 4.00 10.00
263 Nick Foligno RC 2.50 6.00
264 Peter Mueller RC 5.00 12.00
265 Brett Sterling RC 1.50 4.00
266 Devon Setoguchi RC 3.00 8.00
267 David Perron RC 2.50 6.00
268 James Sheppard RC 1.50 4.00
269 Jiri Tlusty RC 4.00 10.00
270 Mason Raymond RC 4.00 10.00
271 Milan Lucic RC 4.00 10.00

2007-08 Ultra Gold Medallion

*GOLD (1-200): 1.5X TO 4X HI
*GOLD ROOKIES (201-250): .5X TO 1.2X
*GOLD ROOKIES (251-271): .6X TO 1.5X 8.00 20.00

2007-08 Ultra Ice Medallion

*ICE (1-200): 5X TO 12X
*ICE ROOKIES (201-250): 1.5X TO 4X
ICE ROOKIES (251-271): 1.5X TO 4X 10.00 25.00
STATED PRINT RUN 100 SER.#'d SETS

2007-08 Ultra Oversized

1 Alexander Ovechkin 8.00 20.00
6 Markus Naslund 2.50 6.00
7 Roberto Luongo 4.00 10.00
12 Andrew Raycroft 2.00 5.00
13 Mats Sundin 2.50 6.00
20 Martin St. Louis 2.00 5.00
21 Vincent Lecavalier 2.50 6.00
30 Joe Thornton 3.00 8.00
37 Sidney Crosby 12.00 30.00
38 Evgeni Malkin 6.00 15.00
39 Marc-Andre Fleury 2.50 6.00
54 Simon Gagne 2.50 6.00
58 Jason Spezza 2.50 6.00
60 Dany Heatley 3.00 8.00
65 Henrik Lundqvist 3.00 8.00
67 Jaromir Jagr 4.00 10.00
79 Martin Brodeur 6.00 15.00
85 Peter Forsberg 3.00 8.00
93 Saku Koivu 2.00 5.00
96 Michael Ryder 1.50 4.00
104 Marian Gaborik 3.00 8.00
117 Ales Hemsky 1.50 4.00
120 Dwayne Roloson 2.00 5.00
125 Henrik Zetterberg 2.50 6.00
126 Nicklas Lidstrom 2.50 6.00
127 Pavel Datsyuk 2.50 6.00
131 Marty Turco 2.50 6.00
132 Mike Modano 2.50 6.00
141 Rick Nash 2.50 6.00
148 Joe Sakic 5.00 12.00
162 Eric Staal 2.50 6.00
168 Miikka Kiprusoff 3.00 8.00
169 Jarome Iginla 4.00 10.00
172 Dion Phaneuf 2.50 6.00
174 Thomas Vanek 2.00 5.00
175 Ryan Miller 2.50 6.00
181 Patrice Bergeron 2.50 6.00
189 Marian Hossa 2.50 6.00
190 Ilya Kovalchuk 3.00 8.00
194 Chris Pronger 2.50 6.00
198 Teemu Selanne 2.50 6.00
199 Ryan Getzlaf 2.00 5.00

2007-08 Ultra Action

COMPLETE SET (7) 10.00 25.00
STATED ODDS 1:12
UA1 Sidney Crosby 4.00 10.00
UA2 Joe Thornton 1.00 2.50
UA3 Alexander Ovechkin 2.50 6.00
UA4 Martin Brodeur 2.00 5.00
UA5 Roberto Luongo 1.25 3.00
UA6 Jarome Iginla 1.25 3.00
UA7 Daniel Briere .75 2.00

2007-08 Ultra All-Stars

COMPLETE SET (30) 100.00 200.00
RETAIL PACKS ONLY
UAS1 Roberto Luongo 5.00 12.00
UAS2 Nicklas Lidstrom 3.00 8.00
UAS3 Jonathan Cheechoo 2.50 6.00
UAS4 Joe Sakic 6.00 15.00
UAS5 Philippe Boucher 2.00 5.00
UAS6 Joe Thornton 4.00 10.00
UAS7 Teemu Selanne 3.00 8.00
UAS8 Patrick Marleau 2.50 6.00
UAS9 Bill Guerin 2.00 5.00
UAS10 Martin Havlat 2.50 6.00
UAS11 Miikka Kiprusoff 4.00 10.00
UAS12 Marty Turco 3.00 8.00
UAS13 Rick Nash 3.00 8.00
UAS14 Dion Phaneuf 3.00 8.00
UAS15 Yanic Perreault 2.00 5.00
UAS16 Alexander Ovechkin 10.00 25.00
UAS17 Ryan Miller 3.00 8.00
UAS18 Sheldon Souray 2.00 5.00
UAS19 Daniel Briere 3.00 8.00
UAS20 Brian Campbell 2.00 5.00
UAS21 Sidney Crosby 15.00 40.00
UAS22 Vincent Lecavalier 3.00 8.00
UAS23 Simon Gagne 3.00 8.00
UAS24 Brendan Shanahan 3.00 8.00
UAS25 Dany Heatley 4.00 10.00
UAS26 Marian Hossa 3.00 8.00
UAS27 Eric Staal 3.00 8.00
UAS28 Martin St. Louis 2.50 6.00
UAS29 Martin Brodeur 8.00 20.00
UAS30 Cristobal Huet 2.50 6.00

2007-08 Ultra Difference Makers

COMPLETE SET (14) 12.00 30.00
STATED ODDS 1:12
DM1 Ryan Miller .75 2.00
DM2 Jarome Iginla 1.25 3.00
DM3 Rick Nash .75 2.00
DM4 Pavel Datsyuk .75 2.00
DM5 Roberto Luongo 1.25 3.00
DM6 Saku Koivu .60 1.50
DM7 Mats Sundin .75 2.00
DM8 Martin Brodeur 2.00 5.00
DM9 Jaromir Jagr 1.25 3.00
DM10 Dany Heatley 1.00 2.50
DM11 Alexander Ovechkin 2.50 6.00
DM12 Sidney Crosby 4.00 10.00
DM13 Joe Thornton 1.00 2.50
DM14 Teemu Selanne .75 2.00

2007-08 Ultra Flair Showcase

COMPLETE SET (100) 200.00 350.00
1 Alex Tanguay 1.50 4.00
2 Alexander Steen 1.25 3.00
3 Andrej Meszaros 1.25 3.00
4 Andrew Raycroft 1.50 4.00
5 Bill Guerin 1.25 3.00
6 Brad Richards 1.50 4.00
7 Brendan Shanahan 2.00 5.00
8 Chris Drury 1.50 4.00
9 Chris Pronger 2.00 5.00
10 Daniel Alfredsson 1.50 4.00
11 Daniel Briere 2.00 5.00
12 Daniel Sedin 1.25 3.00
13 Dany Heatley 2.50 6.00
14 Dion Phaneuf 2.00 5.00
15 Doug Weight 1.25 3.00
16 Drew Stafford 1.50 4.00
17 Dwayne Roloson 1.50 4.00
18 Ed Belfour 2.00 5.00
19 Ed Jovanovski 1.25 3.00
20 Eric Staal 2.00 5.00
21 Evgeni Nabokov 1.50 4.00
22 Gilbert Brule 1.25 3.00
23 Guillaume Latendresse 1.50 4.00
24 Henrik Sedin 1.25 3.00
25 Ilya Kovalchuk 2.50 6.00
26 Jaroslav Halak 4.00 10.00
27 Jeff Carter 1.25 3.00
28 Jonathan Cheechoo 1.50 4.00
29 Jordan Staal 2.50 6.00
30 Kari Lehtonen 2.00 5.00
31 Lauri Tukonen 1.25 3.00
32 Manny Fernandez 1.50 4.00
33 Manny Legace 1.50 4.00
34 Marc-Andre Fleury 2.00 5.00
35 Michael Ryder 1.25 3.00
36 Miikka Kiprusoff 2.50 6.00
37 Mike Modano 2.00 5.00
38 Mike Ribeiro 1.25 3.00
39 Milan Hejduk 1.50 4.00
40 Miroslav Satan 1.25 3.00
41 Nicklas Lidstrom 2.00 5.00
42 Nikolai Khabibulin 2.00 5.00
43 Patrice Bergeron 2.00 5.00
44 Patrick Marleau 1.50 4.00
45 Patrik Elias 1.25 3.00
46 Pavel Datsyuk 2.00 5.00
47 Peter Forsberg 2.50 6.00
48 Petr Kalus 1.25 3.00
49 Ryan Parent 1.50 4.00
50 Ryan Smyth 1.50 4.00
51 Scott Niedermayer 1.25 3.00
52 Sergei Fedorov 2.00 5.00
53 Shane Doan 1.25 3.00
54 Eric Lindros 2.00 5.00
55 Thomas Vanek 1.50 4.00
56 Tomas Kaberle 1.25 3.00
57 Tomas Vokoun 2.00 5.00
58 Vincent Lecavalier 2.00 5.00
59 Wade Redden 1.25 3.00
60 Zdeno Chara 1.25 3.00
61 Evgeni Malkin 5.00 12.00
62 Henrik Zetterberg 2.50 6.00
63 Jean-Sebastien Giguere 2.00 5.00
64 Jarome Iginla 3.00 8.00
65 Rick Nash 2.00 5.00
66 Jason Spezza 2.00 5.00
67 Simon Gagne 2.00 5.00
68 Henrik Lundqvist 2.50 6.00
69 Jack Johnson 2.00 5.00
70 Rob Schremp 1.50 4.00
71 Anze Kopitar 2.00 5.00
72 Marian Gaborik 2.50 6.00
73 Marty Turco 2.00 5.00
74 Ales Hemsky 1.25 3.00
75 Olli Jokinen 1.25 3.00
76 Paul Kariya 2.00 5.00
77 Mats Sundin 2.00 5.00
78 Markus Naslund 2.00 5.00
79 Olaf Kolzig 2.00 5.00
80 Martin St. Louis 1.50 4.00
81 Joe Thornton 2.50 6.00
82 Phil Kessel 2.00 5.00
83 Marian Hossa 2.00 5.00
84 Ryan Miller 2.00 5.00
85 Martin Havlat 1.50 4.00
86 Cam Ward 2.00 5.00
87 Teemu Selanne 2.00 5.00
88 Rick DiPietro 1.50 4.00
89 Saku Koivu 1.50 4.00
90 Dominik Hasek 2.50 6.00
91 Gordie Howe 5.00 12.00
92 Bobby Orr 8.00 20.00
93 Mark Messier 4.00 10.00
94 Sidney Crosby 10.00 25.00
95 Mario Lemieux 6.00 15.00
96 Alexander Ovechkin 6.00 15.00
97 Roberto Luongo 3.00 8.00
98 Joe Sakic 4.00 10.00
99 Jaromir Jagr 3.00 8.00
100 Martin Brodeur 5.00 12.00

2007-08 Ultra Fresh Ink

FIAA Adrian Aucoin 3.00 8.00
FIAD Adam Dennis 4.00 10.00
FIAF Alexander Frolov 3.00 8.00
FIAK Andrei Kostitsyn 3.00 8.00
FIAL Andrew Ladd 3.00 8.00
FIAO Alexander Ovechkin 75.00 150.00
FIAP Alexandre Picard 3.00 8.00
FIAR Alexander Radulov 5.00 12.00
FIAT Alex Tanguay 4.00 10.00
FIAY Alexei Yashin 3.00 8.00
FIBB Brendan Bell 3.00 8.00
FIBM Brendan Morrison 3.00 8.00
FIBO Dave Bolland
FIBR Brad Richardson 3.00 8.00
FIBW Ben Walter 3.00 8.00
FICC Chris Campoli 3.00 8.00
FICH Chris Higgins 4.00 10.00
FICK Chuck Kobasew
FICO Chris Osgood 4.00 10.00
FIDA David Aebischer 4.00 10.00
FIDB Daniel Briere 5.00 12.00
FIDH Dany Heatley
FIDP Dion Phaneuf 5.00 12.00
FIDS Drew Stafford 4.00 10.00
FIDT Darcy Tucker 4.00 10.00
FIDW Doug Weight 3.00 8.00
FIEC Erik Christensen 3.00 8.00
FIEM Evgeni Malkin 25.00 60.00
FIEN Eric Nystrom 3.00 8.00
FIER Erik Cole 3.00 8.00
FIES Eric Staal 5.00 12.00
FIGL Guillaume Latendresse 4.00 10.00
FIHA Martin Havlat 4.00 10.00
FIHE Milan Hejduk 4.00 10.00
FIHL Henrik Lundqvist
FIHU Cristobal Huet 4.00 10.00
FIHZ Henrik Zetterberg 5.00 12.00
FIJA Jay Bouwmeester 3.00 8.00
FIJB Jaroslav Balastik 3.00 8.00
FIJC Jeff Carter 3.00 8.00
FIJE Jeremy Colliton 3.00 8.00
FIJJ Jussi Jokinen 3.00 8.00
FIJL Joffrey Lupul 3.00 8.00
FIJP Joel Perrault 3.00 8.00
FIJT Joe Thornton 6.00 15.00
FIJW Jeff Woywitka 3.00 8.00
FIKB Kevin Bieksa
FIKC Kyle Calder 3.00 8.00
FIKL Kari Lehtonen
FIKO Anze Kopitar 5.00 12.00
FILA Maxim Lapierre 3.00 8.00
FILN Ladislav Nagy 3.00 8.00
FIMH Marcel Hossa 3.00 8.00
FIMI Michal Handzus 3.00 8.00
FIMK Miikka Kiprusoff 6.00 15.00
FIML Mario Lemieux
FIMN Mika Noronen 3.00 8.00
FIMO Brenden Morrow 4.00 10.00
FIMS Martin St. Louis 4.00 10.00
FINA Evgeni Nabokov 4.00 10.00
FINL Nicklas Lidstrom
FINZ Nikolai Zherdev 3.00 8.00
FIPA Joe Pavelski 3.00 8.00
FIPE Michael Peca 3.00 8.00
FIPK Phil Kessel 5.00 12.00
FIPS Paul Stastny 5.00 12.00
FIPT Patrick Thoresen 3.00 8.00
FIRG Ryan Getzlaf 4.00 10.00
FIRH Ryan Hollweg 3.00 8.00
FIRK Rostislav Klesla 3.00 8.00
FIRN Rick Nash 5.00 12.00
FISG Scott Gomez 3.00 8.00
FITA Maxime Talbot 3.00 8.00
FITR Tuomo Ruutu 3.00 8.00
FIVT Vesa Toskala 4.00 10.00
FIWI Jeremy Williams 3.00 8.00
FIYS Yan Stastny 3.00 8.00
FIZC Zdeno Chara 3.00 8.00

2007-08 Ultra Generations

COMPLETE SET (21) 50.00 100.00
TARGET PACKS ONLY
G1 Mario Lemieux 5.00 12.00
Marc-Andre Fleury
Evgeni Malkin
G2 Patrick Roy 5.00 12.00
Joe Sakic
Paul Stastny
G3 Luc Robitaille 1.50 4.00
Rob Blake
Anze Kopitar
G4 Marcel Dionne 1.25 3.00
Alexander Frolov
Patrick O'Sullivan
G5 Peter Stastny 1.25 3.00
Milan Hejduk
Marek Svatos
G6 Mario Lemieux 8.00 20.00
Sidney Crosby
Jordan Staal
G7 Guy Lafleur 4.00 10.00
Saku Koivu
Guillaume Latendresse
G8 Bobby Orr 6.00 15.00
Patrice Bergeron
Phil Kessel
G9 Gilbert Perreault 1.25 3.00
Thomas Vanek
Drew Stafford
G10 Borje Salming 1.50 4.00
Mats Sundin
Alexander Steen
G11 Gerry Cheevers 2.50 6.00
Tim Thomas
Hannu Toivonen
G12 Bobby Clarke 1.50 4.00
Simon Gagne
Jeff Carter
G13 Jari Kurri 1.50 4.00
Ales Hemsky
Rob Schremp
G14 Guy Lafleur 4.00 10.00
Saku Koivu
Andrei Kostitsyn
G15 Rod Langway 1.00 2.50
Brian Pothier
Mike Green
G16 Gordie Howe 4.00 10.00
Henrik Zetterberg
Jiri Hudler
G17 Gordie Howe 4.00 10.00
Pavel Datsyuk
Valtteri Filppula
G18 Scott Stevens 4.00 10.00
Martin Brodeur
Zach Parise
G19 Patrick Roy 5.00 12.00
Cristobal Huet
Jaroslav Halak
G20 Bobby Hull 2.50 6.00
Martin Havlat
Cam Barker
G21 Lanny McDonald 2.50 6.00
Jarome Iginla
Dustin Boyd

2007-08 Ultra Hot Gloves

COMPLETE SET (15) 75.00 150.00
HG1 Martin Brodeur 12.00 30.00
HG2 Roberto Luongo 8.00 20.00
HG3 Ryan Miller 5.00 12.00
HG4 Cristobal Huet 4.00 10.00
HG5 Miikka Kiprusoff 6.00 15.00
HG6 Marty Turco 5.00 12.00
HG7 Dominik Hasek 6.00 15.00
HG8 Ray Emery 4.00 10.00
HG9 Jean-Sebastien Giguere 5.00 12.00
HG10 Rick DiPietro 4.00 10.00
HG11 Marc-Andre Fleury 5.00 12.00
HG12 Evgeni Nabokov 4.00 10.00
HG13 Peter Budaj 4.00 10.00
HG14 Tomas Vokoun 5.00 12.00
HG15 Henrik Lundqvist 6.00 15.00

2007-08 Ultra Hot Numbers

COMPLETE SET (15) 100.00 200.00
STATED ODDS 1:288
HN1 Jarome Iginla 8.00 20.00
HN2 Mats Sundin 5.00 12.00
HN3 Martin St. Louis 4.00 10.00
HN4 Martin Brodeur 12.00 30.00
HN5 Dominik Hasek 6.00 15.00
HN6 Roberto Luongo 8.00 20.00
HN7 Daniel Briere 5.00 12.00
HN8 Vincent Lecavalier 5.00 12.00
HN9 Dany Heatley 6.00 15.00
HN10 Teemu Selanne 5.00 12.00
HN11 Evgeni Malkin 12.00 30.00
HN12 Alexander Ovechkin 15.00 40.00
HN13 Joe Thornton 6.00 15.00
HN14 Joe Sakic 10.00 25.00
HN15 Sidney Crosby 25.00 60.00

2007-08 Ultra Scoring Kings

COMPLETE SET (14) 12.00 30.00
STATED ODDS 1:12
SK1 Alexander Ovechkin 2.50 6.00
SK2 Dany Heatley 1.00 2.50
SK3 Jarome Iginla 1.25 3.00
SK4 Jaromir Jagr 1.25 3.00
SK5 Jason Spezza .75 2.00
SK6 Joe Sakic 1.50 4.00
SK7 Joe Thornton 1.00 2.50
SK8 Sidney Crosby 4.00 10.00
SK9 Vincent Lecavalier .75 2.00
SK10 Evgeni Malkin 2.00 5.00
SK11 Patrice Bergeron .75 2.00
SK12 Marian Hossa .75 2.00
SK13 Martin St. Louis .60 1.50
SK14 Thomas Vanek .60 1.50

2007-08 Ultra Season Crowns

COMPLETE SET (7) 6.00 15.00
STATED ODDS 1:12
SC1 Niklas Backstrom .60 1.50
SC2 Sidney Crosby 4.00 10.00
SC3 Martin Brodeur 2.00 5.00
SC4 Thomas Vanek .60 1.50
SC5 Ben Eager .50 1.25
SC6 Vincent Lecavalier .75 2.00
SC7 Joe Thornton 1.00 2.50

2007-08 Ultra Team Leaders

COMPLETE SET (30) 50.00 100.00
TL1 Vincent Lecavalier 2.00 5.00
TL2 Teemu Selanne 2.00 5.00
TL3 Simon Gagne 2.00 5.00
TL4 Sidney Crosby 10.00 25.00
TL5 Shane Doan 1.25 3.00
TL6 Saku Koivu 1.50 4.00
TL7 Ray Whitney 1.25 3.00
TL8 Pavel Datsyuk 2.00 5.00
TL9 Paul Kariya 2.00 5.00
TL10 Patrik Elias 1.25 3.00
TL11 Olli Jokinen 1.25 3.00
TL12 Mike Ribeiro 1.25 3.00
TL13 Mike Cammalleri 1.50 4.00
TL14 Mats Sundin 2.00 5.00
TL15 Martin Havlat 1.50 4.00
TL16 Marian Hossa 2.00 5.00
TL17 Marc Savard 1.25 3.00
TL18 Joe Thornton 2.50 6.00
TL19 Joe Sakic 4.00 10.00
TL20 Jason Blake 1.25 3.00
TL21 Jaromir Jagr 3.00 8.00
TL22 Jarome Iginla 3.00 8.00
TL23 Doug Weight 1.25 3.00
TL24 David Vyborny 1.25 3.00
TL25 Dany Heatley 2.50 6.00
TL26 Daniel Sedin 1.25 3.00
TL27 Daniel Briere 2.00 5.00
TL28 Brian Rolston 1.25 3.00
TL29 Alexander Ovechkin 6.00 15.00
TL30 Ales Hemsky 1.25 3.00

2007-08 Ultra Uniformity

UAA Alex Auld 3.00 8.00
UAF Alexander Frolov 2.50 6.00
UAH Ales Hemsky 2.50 6.00
UAK Alex Kovalev 2.50 6.00
UAL Andrew Ladd 2.50 6.00
UAM Andrej Meszaros 2.50 6.00
UAO Alexander Ovechkin 12.00 30.00
UAP Alexander Perezhogin 2.50 6.00
UAR Andrew Raycroft 3.00 8.00
UAS Alexander Steen 2.50 6.00
UAT Alex Tanguay 3.00 8.00
UAY Alexei Yashin 2.50 6.00
UBB Brad Boyes 3.00 8.00
UBG Bill Guerin 2.50 6.00
UBI Brandon Bochenski 2.50 6.00
UBJ Barret Jackman 2.50 6.00
UBM Brendan Morrison 2.50 6.00
UBO Jay Bouwmeester 2.50 6.00
UBR Brad Richards 3.00 8.00
UBS Brendan Shanahan 4.00 10.00
UBT Barry Tallackson 2.50 6.00
UBW Brendan Witt 2.50 6.00
UCH Chris Higgins 3.00 8.00
UCO Chris Osgood 3.00 8.00
UCP Chris Phillips 2.50 6.00
UCS Curtis Sanford 3.00 8.00
UDA Daniel Alfredsson 3.00 8.00
UDB Dustin Brown 2.50 6.00
UDC Dan Cloutier 3.00 8.00
UDH Dany Heatley 5.00 12.00
UDL David Legwand 2.50 6.00
UDM Dominic Moore 2.50 6.00
UDO Dominik Hasek 5.00 12.00
UDP Daniel Paille 2.50 6.00
UDR Dwayne Roloson 3.00 8.00
UDS Daniel Sedin 2.50 6.00
UDW Doug Weight 2.50 6.00
UEB Ed Belfour 4.00 10.00
UEC Erik Cole 2.50 6.00
UEJ Ed Jovanovski 2.50 6.00
UES Eric Staal 4.00 10.00
UFP Fernando Pisani 2.50 6.00
UGL Georges Laraque 2.50 6.00
UGM Glen Murray 2.50 6.00
UGR Gary Roberts 2.50 6.00
UHA Adam Hall 2.50 6.00
UHD Dan Hamhuis 2.50 6.00
UHS Henrik Sedin 2.50 6.00
UHT Hannu Toivonen 3.00 8.00
UIG Jarome Iginla 6.00 15.00
UIK Ilya Kovalchuk 5.00 12.00
UIW Ian White 2.50 6.00
UJA Jason Arnott 2.50 6.00
UJB Jason Blake 2.50 6.00
UJC Jeff Carter 2.50 6.00
UJF Jeff Friesen 2.50 6.00
UJG Jean-Sebastien Giguere 4.00 10.00
UJH Jeff Hoggan 2.50 6.00
UJI Jarkko Immonen 2.50 6.00
UJJ Jaromir Jagr 6.00 15.00
UJK Jakub Klepis 2.50 6.00
UJL Jere Lehtinen 2.50 6.00
UJP Joni Pitkanen 2.50 6.00
UJS Jarret Stoll 2.50 6.00
UJT Joe Thornton 5.00 12.00
UJW Jason Williams 2.50 6.00
UKC Kyle Calder 2.50 6.00
UKL Kari Lehtonen 4.00 10.00
UKO Andrei Kostitsyn 2.50 6.00
ULJ Jamie Lundmark 2.50 6.00
ULU Joffrey Lupul 2.50 6.00
UMB Martin Brodeur 10.00 25.00
UMC Bryan McCabe 2.50 6.00
UMD Marc Denis 3.00 8.00
UMF Manny Fernandez 3.00 8.00
UMG Martin Gerber 3.00 8.00
UMH Marian Hossa 4.00 10.00
UMK Miikka Kiprusoff 5.00 12.00
UMN Markus Naslund 4.00 10.00
UMR Michael Ryder 2.50 6.00
UMS Mats Sundin 4.00 10.00
UMT Marty Turco 4.00 10.00
UON Ben Ondrus 2.50 6.00
UPB Patrice Bergeron 4.00 10.00
UPE Corey Perry 3.00 8.00
UPK Paul Kariya 4.00 10.00
UPR Chris Pronger 4.00 10.00
URA Brian Rafalski 2.50 6.00
URO Brian Rolston 2.50 6.00
USA Joe Sakic 8.00 20.00
USC Sidney Crosby 20.00 50.00
USG Simon Gagne 4.00 10.00
USK Saku Koivu 3.00 8.00
USP Jason Spezza 4.00 10.00
UST Brad Stuart 2.50 6.00
UTH Billy Thompson 2.50 6.00
UTK Keith Tkachuk 3.00 8.00
UTV Tomas Vokoun 4.00 10.00
UWI Justin Williams 2.50 6.00

2007-08 Ultra Uniformity Patches

*PATCHES: 2X TO 5X
STATED PRINT RUN 25 SER.#'d SETS

2008-09 Ultra

This set was released on October 21, 2008. The base set consists of 271 cards. Cards 1-200 feature veterans, and cards 201-271 are rookies. Cards 251-271 were issued as exchange cards and have all been redeemed.

COMP.SET w/o EXCH RC (250) 75.00 150.00
COMP.SET w/o RC's (200) 15.00 40.00
RC (201-250) STATED ODDS 1:4
RC (251-271) STATED ODDS 1:24
1 Ilya Kovalchuk .40 1.00
2 Eric Perrin .20 .50
3 Colby Armstrong .20 .50
4 Kari Lehtonen .20 .50
5 Bryan Little .20 .50
6 Tobias Enstrom .30 .75
7 Patrice Bergeron .30 .75
8 Marc Savard .20 .50
9 Tim Thomas .30 .75
10 Zdeno Chara .20 .50
11 Marco Sturm .20 .50
12 Phil Kessel .30 .75
13 Glen Murray .20 .50
14 Michael Ryder .25 .60
15 Thomas Vanek .30 .75
16 Ryan Miller .30 .75
17 Derek Roy .20 .50
18 Jason Pominville .25 .60
19 Drew Stafford .30 .75
20 Daniel Paille .25 .60
21 Eric Staal .50 1.25
22 Rod Brind'Amour .25 .60
23 Cam Ward .30 .75
24 Justin Williams .20 .50
25 Ray Whitney .20 .50
26 Joni Pitkanen .20 .50
27 Tomas Vokoun .30 .75
28 Nathan Horton .20 .50
29 David Booth .20 .50
30 Stephen Weiss .20 .50
31 Jay Bouwmeester .25 .60
32 Saku Koivu .30 .75
33 Carey Price 1.00 2.50
34 Tomas Plekanec .20 .50
35 Alex Tanguay .25 .60
36 Alex Kovalev .30 .75
37 Chris Higgins .30 .75
38 Andrei Markov .25 .60
39 Guillaume Latendresse .25 .60
40 Martin Brodeur .60 1.50
41 Zach Parise .30 .75
42 Patrik Elias .20 .50
43 Brian Gionta .30 .75
44 John Madden .20 .50
45 Travis Zajac .20 .50
46 Rick DiPietro .30 .75
46 Brian Rolston .20 .50
47 Mike Comrie .20 .50
48 Bill Guerin .20 .50
49 Trent Hunter .20 .50
50 Mark Streit .20 .50
51 Wade Redden .20 .50
52 Michal Rozsival .20 .50
53 Henrik Lundqvist .60 1.50
54 Chris Drury .30 .75
55 Scott Gomez .25 .60
56 Markus Naslund .30 .75
57 Marc Staal .40 1.00
58 Brandon Dubinsky .25 .60
59 Nikolai Zherdev .20 .50
60 Jason Spezza .40 1.00
61 Andrej Meszaros .20 .50
62 Antoine Vermette .20 .50
63 Mike Fisher .20 .50
64 Daniel Alfredsson .25 .60
66 Martin Gerber .25 .60
67 Dany Heatley .40 1.00
68 Martin Biron .25 .60
69 Daniel Briere .30 .75
70 Simon Gagne .25 .60
71 Mike Knuble .30 .75
72 Jeff Carter .30 .75
73 Mike Richards .50 1.25
74 Sidney Crosby 1.50 4.00
75 Marc-Andre Fleury .30 .75
76 Miroslav Satan .20 .50
77 Evgeni Malkin .75 2.00
78 Sergei Gonchar .30 .75
79 Ryan Whitney .20 .50
80 Jordan Staal .50 1.25
81 Ryan Malone .20 .50
82 Vincent Lecavalier .30 .75
83 Mike Smith .25 .60
84 Jussi Jokinen .20 .50
85 Martin St. Louis .30 .75
86 Paul Ranger .20 .50
87 Karri Ramo .25 .60
88 Olaf Kolzig .30 .75
89 Mats Sundin .30 .75
90 Vesa Toskala .30 .75
91 Alexander Steen .30 .75
92 Tomas Kaberle .20 .50
93 Nikolai Antropov .25 .60
94 Matt Stajan .25 .60
95 Jiri Tlusty .30 .75
96 Alexander Ovechkin 1.25 3.00
97 Jose Theodore .30 .75
98 Nicklas Backstrom .60 1.50
99 Sergei Fedorov .50 1.25
100 Mike Green .20 .50
101 Alexander Semin .30 .75
102 Ryan Getzlaf .40 1.00
103 Jean-Sebastien Giguere .30 .75
104 Corey Perry .30 .75
105 Teemu Selanne .30 .75
106 Chris Pronger .25 .60
107 Chris Kunitz .20 .50
108 Scott Niedermayer .20 .50
109 Miikka Kiprusoff .30 .75
110 Jarome Iginla .60 1.50
111 Daymond Langkow .20 .50
112 Dion Phaneuf .30 .75
114 Todd Bertuzzi .30 .75
115 Matthew Lombardi .20 .50
116 Mike Cammalleri .30 .75
117 Patrick Kane .75 2.00
118 Nikolai Khabibulin .30 .75
119 Patrick Sharp .20 .50
120 Brent Seabrook .25 .60
121 Jonathan Toews 1.00 2.50
122 Martin Havlat .25 .60
123 Duncan Keith .25 .60
124 Brian Campbell .50 1.25
125 Darcy Tucker .25 .60
126 Joe Sakic .50 1.25
127 Milan Hejduk .25 .60
128 Marek Svatos .20 .50
129 Paul Stastny .30 .75
130 Wojtek Wolski .20 .50
131 Peter Forsberg .50 1.25
132 Ryan Smyth .25 .60
132 Pascal Leclaire .25 .60
133 R.J. Umberger .20 .50
134 Rostislav Klesla .30 .75
135 Jared Boll .25 .60
136 Rick Nash .30 .75
137 Brad Richards .25 .60
138 Marty Turco .25 .60
139 Mike Ribeiro .20 .50
140 Brenden Morrow .25 .60
141 Jere Lehtinen .20 .50
142 Marian Hossa .50 1.25
142 Mike Modano .30 .75
143 Johan Franzen .20 .50
144 Nicklas Lidstrom .30 .75
145 Pavel Datsyuk .30 .75
146 Chris Osgood .30 .75
147 Henrik Zetterberg .60 1.50
148 Dan Cleary .30 .75
149 Tomas Holmstrom .25 .60
150 Valtteri Filppula .20 .50
151 Sam Gagner .50 1.25
152 Ales Hemsky .20 .50
153 Mathieu Garon .30 .75
154 Shawn Horcoff .20 .50
155 Dustin Penner .20 .50
156 Andrew Cogliano .50 1.25
157 Dwayne Roloson .25 .60
158 Gilbert Brule .30 .75
159 Anze Kopitar .30 .75
160 Alexander Frolov .20 .50
161 Dustin Brown .20 .50
162 Jonathan Bernier .40 1.00
163 Patrick O'Sullivan .25 .60
164 Marian Gaborik .50 1.25
165 Niklas Backstrom .30 .75
166 Pierre-Marc Bouchard .20 .50
168 Josh Harding .25 .60
169 Mikko Koivu .30 .75
170 Alexander Radulov .30 .75
171 Jason Arnott .20 .50
172 Dan Ellis .20 .50
173 Martin Erat .30 .75
174 J.P. Dumont .20 .50
175 David Legwand .25 .60
176 Peter Mueller .40 1.00
177 Shane Doan .20 .50
178 Ilya Bryzgalov .30 .75
179 Ed Jovanovski .20 .50
180 Olli Jokinen .20 .50
181 Martin Hanzal .25 .60
182 Daniel Carcillo .25 .60
183 Evgeni Nabokov .30 .75
184 Jonathan Cheechoo .30 .75
185 Milan Michalek .20 .50
186 Rob Blake .30 .75
187 Patrick Marleau .25 .60
188 Joe Thornton .50 1.25
189 Manny Legace .25 .60
190 Erik Johnson .40 1.00
191 Brad Boyes .25 .60
192 Lee Stempniak .20 .50
193 Keith Tkachuk .30 .75
194 Paul Kariya .30 .75
195 Daniel Sedin .30 .75
196 Steve Bernier .20 .50
197 Ryan Kesler .20 .50
198 Alexander Edler .25 .60
199 Roberto Luongo .50 1.25
200 Henrik Sedin .30 .75
201 Derick Brassard RC 4.00 10.00
202 Mark Fistric RC 1.50 4.00
203 Alex Goligoski RC 4.00 10.00
204 Claude Giroux RC 4.00 10.00
205 Jon Filewich RC 1.50 4.00
206 Robbie Earl RC 1.50 4.00
207 Ilya Zubov RC 2.00 5.00
208 Steve Mason RC 5.00 12.00
209 Brian Boyle RC 2.00 5.00
210 Shawn Matthias RC 2.00 5.00
211 Ryan Stone RC 2.00 5.00
212 Teddy Purcell RC 2.00 5.00
213 Mike Iggulden RC 1.50 4.00
214 Justin Abdelkader RC 4.00 10.00
215 Marc-Andre Gragnani RC 1.50 4.00
216 Jonathan Ericsson RC 3.00 8.00
217 Kyle Okposo RC 4.00 10.00
218 Kyle Turris RC 4.00 10.00
219 Brian Lee RC 2.00 5.00
220 Theo Peckham RC 2.00 5.00
221 Adam Pineault RC 2.00 5.00
222 Boris Valabik RC 2.50 6.00
223 Matt D'Agostini RC 2.50 6.00
224 Andrew Ebbett RC 2.00 5.00
225 Sami Lepisto RC 2.00 5.00
226 Mattias Ritola RC 2.50 6.00
227 Dan LaCosta RC 2.50 6.00
228 Danny Taylor RC 2.00 5.00
229 Cody McLeod RC 1.50 4.00
230 Corey Locke RC 2.00 5.00
231 Jordan Hendry RC 1.50 4.00
232 Mike Brown RC 2.50 6.00
233 B.J. Crombeen RC 1.50 4.00
234 David Brine RC 1.50 4.00
235 Joe Jensen RC 2.00 5.00
236 Kyle Greentree RC 2.50 6.00
237 Zack Fitzgerald RC 2.00 5.00
238 Clay Wilson RC 1.25 3.00
239 Alex Foster RC 1.50 4.00
240 Tom Cavanagh RC 1.50 4.00
241 Erik Ersberg RC 2.00 5.00
242 Tim Conboy RC 1.50 4.00
243 Jordan LaVallee RC 2.00 5.00
244 Mike Mole RC 1.50 4.00
245 Jesse Winchester RC 2.00 5.00
246 Garrett Stafford RC 2.50 6.00
247 Darryl Boyce RC 1.50 4.00

248 Chris Minard RC 2.00 5.00
249 Jack Hillen RC 1.50 4.00
250 Colin Stuart RC 1.50 4.00
251 Steven Stamkos RC 20.00 50.00
252 Fabian Brunnstrom RC 4.00 10.00
253 Jakub Voracek RC 5.00 12.00
254 Blake Wheeler RC 6.00 15.00
255 Brandon Sutter RC 3.00 8.00
256 Zach Boychuk RC 4.00 10.00
257 Alex Pietrangelo RC 4.00 10.00
258 Zach Bogosian RC 5.00 12.00
259 Drew Doughty RC 8.00 20.00
260 Luke Schenn RC 8.00 20.00
261 T.J. Oshie RC 6.00 15.00
262 Mikkel Boedker RC 4.00 10.00
263 Nikita Filatov RC 10.00 25.00
264 James Neal RC 4.00 10.00
265 Colton Gillies RC 2.50 6.00
266 Petr Vrana RC 3.00 8.00
267 Luca Sbisa RC 4.00 10.00
268 Patric Hornqvist RC 2.50 6.00
269 Andreas Nodl RC 2.50 6.00
270 Nikolai Kulemin RC 2.50 6.00
271 Michael Frolik RC 5.00 12.00

2008-09 Ultra Gold Medallion

COMP.SET w/o RC's
*GOLD: 1X TO 2.5X BASE
*GOLD RCs: .6X TO 1.5X BASE RCs
*GOLD EXCH: .6X TO 1.5X BASE
STATED ODDS 1 PER PACK

2008-09 Ultra Ice Medallion

*ICE: 4X TO 10X BASE
*ICE RCs: 1.5X TO 4X BASE
*ICE EXCH: .8X TO 2X BASE
STATED PRINT RUN 100 SERIAL #'d SETS

2008-09 Ultra All-Star Royalty

COMPLETE SET (21) 25.00 60.00
OVERALL NON-AU/MEM ODDS 1:2
ASR1 Alexander Ovechkin 5.00 12.00
ASR2 Roberto Luongo 2.00 5.00
ASR3 Mats Sundin 1.25 3.00
ASR4 Vincent Lecavalier 1.25 3.00
ASR5 Martin St. Louis 1.25 3.00
ASR6 Joe Thornton 2.00 5.00
ASR7 Sidney Crosby 6.00 15.00
ASR8 Evgeni Malkin 3.00 8.00
ASR9 Dany Heatley 1.50 4.00
ASR10 Martin Brodeur 2.50 6.00
ASR11 Saku Koivu 1.25 3.00
ASR12 Marian Gaborik 2.00 5.00
ASR13 Anze Kopitar 1.25 3.00
ASR14 Nicklas Lidstrom 1.25 3.00
ASR15 Rick Nash 1.25 3.00
ASR16 Joe Sakic 2.00 5.00
ASR17 Eric Staal 2.00 5.00
ASR18 Miikka Kiprusoff 1.25 3.00
ASR19 Jarome Iginla 2.50 6.00
ASR20 Ilya Kovalchuk 1.50 4.00
ASR21 Ryan Getzlaf 1.50 4.00

2008-09 Ultra Difference Makers

COMPLETE SET 15.00 40.00
OVERALL NON-AU/MEM ODDS 1:2
DM1 Martin Brodeur 1.25 3.00
DM2 Alexander Ovechkin 2.50 6.00
DM3 Teemu Selanne .60 1.50
DM4 Paul Stastny .60 1.50
DM5 Nicklas Lidstrom .60 1.50
DM6 Ryan Miller .60 1.50
DM7 Joe Thornton 1.00 2.50
DM8 Peter Mueller .75 2.00
DM9 Miikka Kiprusoff .60 1.50
DM10 Martin St. Louis .60 1.50
DM11 Sidney Crosby 3.00 8.00
DM12 Patrick Kane 1.50 4.00
DM13 Jarome Iginla 1.25 3.00
DM14 Pavel Datsyuk .60 1.50
DM15 Peter Forsberg 1.00 2.50
DM16 Carey Price 2.00 5.00
DM17 Patrice Bergeron .60 1.50
DM18 Roberto Luongo 1.00 2.50
DM19 Evgeni Malkin 1.50 4.00
DM20 Mats Sundin .60 1.50

2008-09 Ultra EX Essential Credentials

COMPLETE SET 60.00 120.00
STATED ODDS 1:8
1 Alexander Ovechkin 5.00 12.00
2 Roberto Luongo 2.00 5.00
3 Mats Sundin 1.25 3.00
4 Vincent Lecavalier 1.25 3.00
5 Martin St. Louis 1.25 3.00
6 Paul Kariya 1.25 3.00
7 Joe Thornton 2.00 5.00
8 Sidney Crosby 6.00 15.00
9 Evgeni Malkin 3.00 8.00
10 Peter Mueller 1.50 4.00
11 Simon Gagne 1.00 2.50
12 Dany Heatley 1.50 4.00
13 Daniel Alfredsson 1.00 2.50
14 Jaromir Jagr 1.50 4.00
15 Brendan Shanahan 1.25 3.00
16 Martin Brodeur 2.50 6.00
17 Alexander Radulov 1.25 3.00
18 Carey Price 4.00 10.00
19 Saku Koivu 1.25 3.00
20 Marian Gaborik 2.00 5.00
21 Anze Kopitar 1.25 3.00
22 Tomas Vokoun 1.25 3.00
23 Sam Gagner 2.00 5.00
24 Henrik Zetterberg 2.50 6.00
25 Dominik Hasek 2.00 5.00
26 Nicklas Lidstrom 1.25 3.00
27 Mike Modano 2.00 5.00
28 Marty Turco 1.00 2.50
29 Rick Nash 1.25 3.00
30 Peter Forsberg 2.00 5.00
31 Joe Sakic 2.00 5.00
32 Paul Stastny 1.25 3.00
33 Patrick Kane 3.00 8.00
34 Jonathan Toews 4.00 10.00
35 Eric Staal 2.00 5.00
36 Jarome Iginla 2.50 6.00
37 Miikka Kiprusoff 1.25 3.00
38 Ryan Miller 1.25 3.00
39 Patrice Bergeron 1.25 3.00
40 Ilya Kovalchuk 1.50 4.00
41 Ryan Getzlaf 1.50 4.00
42 Teemu Selanne 1.25 3.00

2008-09 Ultra EX Essential Credentials Green

*GREEN: 1.2X TO 3X
CARDS #'d UNDER 25 NOT PRICED DUE TO SCARCITY

2008-09 Ultra EX Essential Credentials Red

*RED: 1.2X TO 3X BASIC
CARDS #'d UNDER 25 NOT PRICED DUE TO SCARCITY

2008-09 Ultra EX Jambalaya

STATED ODDS 1:864
JAM1 Wayne Gretzky
JAM2 Bobby Orr 60.00 120.00
JAM3 Gordie Howe 60.00 120.00
JAM4 Mark Messier 25.00 60.00
JAM5 Mario Lemieux 25.00 60.00
JAM6 Teemu Selanne 15.00 40.00
JAM7 Joe Sakic 20.00 50.00
JAM8 Mike Modano 10.00 25.00
JAM9 Sidney Crosby 75.00 150.00
JAM10 Alexander Ovechkin 50.00 100.00
JAM11 Evgeni Malkin 25.00 60.00
JAM12 Ilya Kovalchuk
JAM13 Vincent Lecavalier 12.00 30.00
JAM14 Jarome Iginla 15.00 40.00
JAM15 Marian Gaborik 20.00 50.00
JAM16 Dany Heatley
JAM17 Simon Gagne 15.00 40.00
JAM18 Jaromir Jagr 20.00 50.00
JAM19 Mats Sundin 12.00 30.00
JAM20 Jonathan Toews 50.00 100.00

2008-09 Ultra Franchise Players

COMPLETE SET (10) 10.00 25.00
OVERALL NON-AU/MEM ODDS 1:2
FP1 Jarome Iginla 1.25 3.00
FP2 Joe Thornton 1.00 2.50
FP3 Roberto Luongo 1.00 2.50
FP4 Patrick Kane 1.50 4.00
FP5 Joe Sakic 1.00 2.50
FP6 Martin Brodeur 1.25 3.00
FP7 Mats Sundin .60 1.50
FP8 Carey Price 2.00 5.00
FP9 Vincent Lecavalier .60 1.50
FP10 Sidney Crosby 3.00 8.00

2008-09 Ultra Fresh Ink

STATED ODDS 1:288
FIAO Alexander Ovechkin
FIBB Brad Boyes 6.00 15.00
FIBD Brandon Dubinsky 10.00 25.00
FIBE Brendan Bell 3.00 8.00
FIBG Brian Gionta
FIBM Brenden Morrow
FIBR Bobby Ryan 8.00 20.00
FIBW Ben Walter
FICA Colby Armstrong 3.00 8.00
FICB Casey Borer
FICH Cristobal Huet
FICK Chris Kunitz
FICP Carey Price
FICS Cory Stillman 3.00 8.00
FIDA David Perron
FIDB David Booth 8.00 20.00
FIDC David Clarkson
FIDH Dany Heatley
FIDM Drew Miller 6.00 15.00
FIDP Daniel Paille 8.00 20.00
FIEC Erik Christensen 5.00 12.00
FIEM Evgeni Malkin
FIEN Eric Nystrom
FIES Eric Staal
FIFN Fredrik Norrena 8.00 20.00
FIGE Martin Gerber 6.00 15.00
FIGM Greg Moore
FIHA Josh Harding
FIHM Martin Havlat
FIHO Tomas Holmstrom
FIHZ Henrik Zetterberg
FIIK Ilya Kovalchuk
FIJC Jeff Carter
FIJG Jean-Sebastien Giguere
FIJH Jannik Hansen 6.00 15.00
FIJI Jarome Iginla
FIJL John-Michael Liles 6.00 15.00
FIJO Joe Pavelski 5.00 12.00
FIJP Jason Pominville
FIJS Jarret Stoll
FIJT Jiri Tlusty 15.00 40.00
FIJW Justin Williams
FIKC Kyle Calder 6.00 15.00
FIKE Phil Kessel
FIKL Kari Lehtonen
FIKN Mike Knuble
FIKQ Kyle Quincey
FIKY Kyle Chipchura 5.00 12.00
FILE Loui Eriksson
FILK Lukas Kaspar
FILT Lauri Tukonen
FIMA Martin Brodeur
FIMB Martin Biron
FIMG Marian Gaborik
FIMH Marian Hossa
FIMI Michal Handzus 5.00 12.00
FIMK Miikka Kiprusoff
FIML Milan Lucic
FIMM Mike Modano
FIMP Marc-Antoine Pouliot 8.00 20.00
FIMR Mason Raymond 40.00 80.00
FIMS Marek Schwarz 8.00 20.00
FIMT Maxime Talbot 8.00 20.00
FIMV Marc-Edouard Vlasic
FINB Nicklas Backstrom
FIND Nigel Dawes
FINI Niklas Bergfors
FINK Niklas Kronwall
FINL Nicklas Lidstrom
FINW Noah Welch 5.00 12.00
FIOD Johnny Oduya
FIPA Dmitri Patzold
FIPB Peter Budaj
FIPE Corey Perry 8.00 20.00
FIPH Chris Phillips 4.00 10.00
FIPK Patrick Kane
FIPN Petteri Nokelainen
FIPS Paul Stastny
FIRC Ryane Clowe 15.00 40.00
FIRG Ryan Getzlaf
FIRK Rostislav Klesla
FIRN Rick Nash
FIRP Ryan Potulny
FIRS Ryan Smyth
FISC Sidney Crosby 125.00 200.00
FISK Sergei Kostitsyn
FISM Stefan Meyer 8.00 20.00
FISS Steve Sullivan
FIST Martin St. Louis
FISW Shea Weber
FITC Ty Conklin 8.00 20.00
FITE Tobias Enstrom 6.00 15.00
FITG Tom Gilbert 8.00 20.00
FITH Joe Thornton
FITK Tomas Kaberle
FITO Jonathan Toews
FITZ Travis Zajac
FIVF Valtteri Filppula 6.00 15.00
FIWE Stephen Weiss
FIWW Wojtek Wolski

2008-09 Ultra Oversized

COMPLETE SET (42) 40.00 100.00
STATED ODDS
TRU1 Ilya Kovalchuk 1.25 3.00
TRU2 Patrice Bergeron 1.00 2.50
TRU3 Ryan Miller 1.00 2.50
TRU4 Eric Staal 1.50 4.00
TRU5 Saku Koivu 1.00 2.50
TRU6 Carey Price 3.00 8.00
TRU7 Martin Brodeur 2.00 5.00
TRU8 Rick DiPietro 1.00 2.50
TRU9 Henrik Lundqvist 2.00 5.00
TRU10 Jason Spezza 1.25 3.00
TRU11 Dany Heatley 1.25 3.00
TRU12 Mike Richards 1.50 4.00
TRU13 Sidney Crosby 5.00 12.00
TRU14 Marc-Andre Fleury 1.00 2.50
TRU15 Evgeni Malkin 2.50 6.00
TRU16 Vincent Lecavalier 1.00 2.50
TRU17 Vesa Toskala 1.00 2.50
TRU18 Alexander Steen 1.00 2.50
TRU19 Alexander Ovechkin 4.00 10.00
TRU20 Ryan Getzlaf 1.25 3.00
TRU21 Jean-Sebastien Giguere 1.00 2.50
TRU22 Miikka Kiprusoff 1.00 2.50
TRU23 Jarome Iginla 2.00 5.00
TRU24 Patrick Kane 2.50 6.00
TRU25 Jonathan Toews 3.00 8.00
TRU26 Joe Sakic 1.50 4.00
TRU27 Peter Forsberg 1.50 4.00
TRU28 Rick Nash 1.00 2.50
TRU29 Marty Turco .75 2.00
TRU30 Mike Modano 1.00 2.50
TRU31 Nicklas Lidstrom 1.00 2.50
TRU32 Henrik Zetterberg 2.00 5.00
TRU33 Sam Gagner 1.50 4.00
TRU34 Andrew Cogliano 1.50 4.00
TRU35 Anze Kopitar 1.00 2.50
TRU36 Marian Gaborik 1.50 4.00
TRU37 Jason Arnott .60 1.50
TRU38 Peter Mueller 1.25 3.00
TRU39 Jonathan Cheechoo 1.00 2.50
TRU40 Joe Thornton 1.50 4.00
TRU41 Paul Kariya 1.00 2.50
TRU42 Roberto Luongo 1.50 4.00

2008-09 Ultra Rookie Sensations

COMPLETE SET (30) 40.00 100.00
OVERALL NON-AU/MEM ODDS 1:2
RS1 Jon Filewich 1.50 4.00
RS2 Alex Goligoski 4.00 10.00
RS3 Mark Fistric 1.50 4.00
RS4 Jonathan Ericsson 3.00 8.00
RS5 Marc-Andre Gragnani 1.50 4.00
RS6 Brian Lee 2.00 5.00
RS7 Theo Peckham 2.00 5.00
RS8 Ryan Stone 2.00 5.00
RS9 Adam Pineault 2.00 5.00
RS10 Boris Valabik 2.50 6.00
RS11 Darren Helm 3.00 8.00
RS12 Mike Iggulden 1.50 4.00
RS13 Niklas Hjalmarsson 3.00 8.00
RS14 Tom Sestito 1.50 4.00
RS15 Alex Foster 1.50 4.00
RS16 Tom Cavanagh 1.50 4.00
RS17 Jordan Hendry 1.50 4.00
RS18 Cody McLeod 1.50 4.00
RS19 Dan LaCosta 2.50 6.00
RS20 Justin Abdelkader 4.00 10.00
RS21 Steve Mason 5.00 12.00
RS22 Derick Brassard 4.00 10.00
RS23 Claude Giroux 4.00 10.00
RS24 Robbie Earl 1.50 4.00
RS25 Ilya Zubov 2.00 5.00
RS26 Brian Boyle 2.00 5.00
RS27 Shawn Matthias 2.00 5.00
RS28 Kyle Okposo 4.00 10.00
RS29 Kyle Turris 4.00 10.00
RS30 Tyler Plante 2.00 5.00

2008-09 Ultra Scoring Kings

COMPLETE SET (20) 12.00 30.00
OVERALL NON-AU/MEM ODDS 1:2
SK1 Sidney Crosby 3.00 8.00
SK2 Joe Thornton 1.00 2.50
SK3 Vincent Lecavalier .60 1.50
SK4 Jarome Iginla 1.25 3.00
SK5 Joe Sakic 1.00 2.50
SK6 Jaromir Jagr .75 2.00
SK7 Henrik Zetterberg 1.25 3.00
SK8 Daniel Alfredsson .50 1.25
SK9 Marc Savard .40 1.00
SK10 Henrik Sedin .60 1.50
SK11 Evgeni Malkin 1.50 4.00
SK12 Ilya Kovalchuk .75 2.00
SK13 Rick Nash .60 1.50
SK14 Marian Gaborik 1.00 2.50
SK15 Eric Staal 1.00 2.50
SK16 Mike Modano .60 1.50
SK17 Brendan Shanahan .60 1.50
SK18 Dany Heatley .75 2.00
SK19 Peter Forsberg 1.00 2.50
SK20 Alexander Ovechkin 2.50 6.00

2008-09 Ultra Season Crowns

COMPLETE SET (10) 6.00 15.00
OVERALL NON-AU/MEM ODDS 1:2
SC1 Alexander Ovechkin 3.00 8.00
SC2 Joe Thornton 1.25 3.00
SC3 Alexander Ovechkin 3.00 8.00
SC4 Evgeni Nabokov .75 2.00
SC5 Dan Ellis .50 1.25
SC6 Chris Osgood .75 2.00
SC7 Henrik Lundqvist 1.50 4.00
SC8 Pavel Datsyuk .75 2.00
SC9 Daniel Carcillo .50 1.25
SC10 Henrik Zetterberg 1.50 4.00

2008-09 Ultra Team Leaders

COMPLETE SET (30) 40.00 100.00
OVERALL NON-AU/MEM ODDS 1:2
TL1 Mike Richards 2.50 6.00
TL2 Rick DiPietro 1.50 4.00
TL3 Daniel Alfredsson 1.25 3.00
TL4 Carey Price 5.00 12.00
TL5 Marc Savard 1.00 2.50
TL6 Ryan Miller 1.50 4.00
TL7 Eric Staal 2.50 6.00
TL8 Ilya Kovalchuk 2.00 5.00
TL9 Tomas Vokoun 1.50 4.00
TL10 Henrik Zetterberg 3.00 8.00
TL11 J.P. Dumont 1.00 2.50
TL12 Rick Nash 1.50 4.00
TL13 Patrick Kane 4.00 10.00
TL14 Paul Kariya 1.50 4.00
TL15 Marian Gaborik 2.50 6.00
TL16 Ales Hemsky 1.00 2.50
TL17 Marty Turco 1.25 3.00
TL18 Jean-Sebastien Giguere 1.50 4.00
TL19 Shane Doan 1.00 2.50
TL20 Anze Kopitar 1.50 4.00
TL21 Martin Brodeur 3.00 8.00
TL22 Sidney Crosby 8.00 20.00
TL23 Jaromir Jagr 2.00 5.00
TL24 Mats Sundin 1.50 4.00
TL25 Alexander Ovechkin 6.00 15.00
TL26 Vincent Lecavalier 1.50 4.00
TL27 Jarome Iginla 3.00 8.00
TL28 Roberto Luongo 2.50 6.00
TL29 Paul Stastny 1.50 4.00
TL30 Joe Thornton 2.50 6.00

2008-09 Ultra Total D

COMPLETE SET (21) 25.00 60.00
OVERALL NON-AU/MEM ODDS 1:2
TD1 Jean-Sebastien Giguere 2.00 5.00
TD2 Kari Lehtonen 1.25 3.00
TD3 Ryan Miller 2.00 5.00
TD4 Miikka Kiprusoff 2.00 5.00
TD5 Cam Ward 2.00 5.00
TD6 Nikolai Khabibulin 2.00 5.00
TD7 Jose Theodore 2.00 5.00
TD8 Pascal Leclaire 1.50 4.00
TD9 Marty Turco 1.50 4.00
TD10 Vesa Toskala 2.00 5.00
TD11 Chris Osgood 2.00 5.00
TD12 Tomas Vokoun 2.00 5.00
TD13 Josh Harding 1.50 4.00
TD14 Carey Price 6.00 15.00
TD15 Martin Brodeur 4.00 10.00
TD16 Henrik Lundqvist 4.00 10.00
TD17 Martin Biron 1.50 4.00
TD18 Marc-Andre Fleury 2.00 5.00
TD19 Evgeni Nabokov 2.00 5.00
TD20 Manny Legace 1.50 4.00
TD21 Roberto Luongo 3.00 8.00

2008-09 Ultra Uniformity

STATED ODDS 1:12
UAAA Arron Asham 4.00 10.00
UAAE Alexander Edler 4.00 10.00
UAAK Alex Kovalev 5.00 12.00
UAAM Andrej Meszaros 3.00 8.00
UAAO Alexander Ovechkin/250
UAAR Andrew Raycroft 5.00 12.00
UAAS Alexander Semin 5.00 12.00
UABB Brad Boyes 4.00 10.00
UABG Bill Guerin 3.00 8.00
UABJ Barret Jackman 3.00 8.00
UABM Brendan Morrison 3.00 8.00
UABO Brandon Bochenski
UABR Brad Richardson
UACA Colby Armstrong 3.00 8.00
UACC Carlo Colaiacovo
UACH Jonathan Cheechoo 5.00 12.00
UACJ Curtis Joseph 5.00 12.00
UACK Chuck Kobasew 3.00 8.00
UACM Matt Carle 3.00 8.00
UACS Cory Stillman 3.00 8.00
UACW Cam Ward 5.00 12.00
UADB Dustin Brown 3.00 8.00
UADO Donald Brashear 3.00 8.00
UADP Daniel Paille 4.00 10.00
UADS Daniel Sedin 5.00 12.00
UADT Darcy Tucker 4.00 10.00
UADV David Vyborny 3.00 8.00
UAEC Erik Cole 3.00 8.00
UAEJ Ed Jovanovski 3.00 8.00
UAEM Evgeni Malkin/250 12.00 30.00
UAEN Evgeni Nabokov 5.00 12.00
UAES Eric Staal/250 8.00 20.00
UAFP Fernando Pisani 3.00 8.00
UAGB Gilbert Brule 5.00 12.00
UAGE Martin Gerber 4.00 10.00
UAGI Brian Gionta 5.00 12.00
UAGM Glen Murray 3.00 8.00
UAHL Henrik Lundqvist 10.00 25.00
UAHS Henrik Sedin 5.00 12.00
UAHT Hannu Toivonen 4.00 10.00
UAIK Ilya Kovalchuk/250 6.00 15.00
UAIW Ian White 3.00 8.00
UAJA Jason Arnott 3.00 8.00
UAJB Jay Bouwmeester 4.00 10.00
UAJC Jeff Carter
UAJI Jarome Iginla/250 10.00 25.00
UAJJ Jaromir Jagr/250 6.00 15.00
UAJL Jere Lehtinen 3.00 8.00
UAJO Erik Johnson 6.00 15.00
UAJP Joni Pitkanen 3.00 8.00
UAJR Jeremy Roenick 5.00 12.00
UAJS Joe Sakic/250 8.00 20.00
UAJT Joe Thornton/250 8.00 20.00
UAJU Jussi Jokinen 3.00 8.00
UAJW Justin Williams 3.00 8.00
UAKL Kari Lehtonen 3.00 8.00
UAKO Andrei Kostitsyn 4.00 10.00
UAKT Keith Tkachuk 4.00 10.00
UALE Kristopher Letang 3.00 8.00
UALS Lee Stempniak 3.00 8.00
UALU Joffrey Lupul 3.00 8.00
UAMA Martin Straka 3.00 8.00
UAMB Martin Brodeur/250 10.00 25.00
UAMC Bryan McCabe 4.00 10.00
UAMF Manny Fernandez 5.00 12.00
UAMG Marian Gaborik 8.00 20.00
UAMI Milan Michalek 3.00 8.00
UAMK Mikko Koivu 5.00 12.00
UAML Manny Legace 4.00 10.00
UAMM Mike Modano 5.00 12.00
UAMN Markus Naslund 5.00 12.00
UAMO Brenden Morrow 4.00 10.00
UAMP Marc-Antoine Pouliot 5.00 12.00
UAMR Mark Recchi 4.00 10.00
UAMS Martin St. Louis 5.00 12.00
UAMT Marty Turco 4.00 10.00
UAMZ Marek Zidlicky 3.00 8.00
UANA Nikolai Antropov 4.00 10.00
UANL Nicklas Lidstrom 5.00 12.00
UANZ Nikolai Zherdev 3.00 8.00
UAOJ Olli Jokinen 3.00 8.00
UAON Owen Nolan 5.00 12.00
UAPB Patrice Bergeron 5.00 12.00
UAPD Pavol Demitra 3.00 8.00
UAPH Dion Phaneuf 5.00 12.00
UAPK Phil Kessel 5.00 12.00
UAPM Patrick Marleau 4.00 10.00
UARI Mike Richards
UARL Roberto Luongo 8.00 20.00
UARN Rick Nash 5.00 12.00
UARY Michael Ryder 4.00 10.00
UASA Miroslav Satan 3.00 8.00
UASC Sidney Crosby/250 25.00 60.00
UASJ Jordan Staal 8.00 20.00
UASM Matt Stajan 4.00 10.00
UAST Drew Stafford 5.00 12.00
UASU Mats Sundin 5.00 12.00
UATH Jose Theodore 5.00 12.00
UATI Kimmo Timonen 3.00 8.00
UAWR Wade Redden 3.00 8.00

2009-10 Ultra

COMPLETE SET (250) 75.00 150.00
COMP.SET w/o SPs (200) 12.00 30.00
RC STATED ODDS 1:4
EXCH STATED ODDS 1:28
1 Ryan Getzlaf .50 1.25
2 Corey Perry .30 .75
3 Bobby Ryan .40 1.00
4 Jonas Hiller .40 1.00
5 Jean-Sebastien Giguere .30 .75
6 Ilya Kovalchuk .40 1.00
7 Slava Kozlov .20 .50
8 Bryan Little .30 .75
9 Kari Lehtonen .30 .75
10 Marc Savard .20 .50
11 Patrice Bergeron .30 .75
12 Tim Thomas .30 .75
13 David Krejci .25 .60
14 Phil Kessel .30 .75
15 Blake Wheeler .40 1.00
16 Thomas Vanek .30 .75
17 Derek Roy .30 .75
18 Ryan Miller .30 .75
19 Jason Pominville .30 .75
20 Drew Stafford .30 .75
21 Jarome Iginla .60 1.50
22 Robyn Regehr .25 .60
23 Daymond Langkow .20 .50
24 Dion Phaneuf .50 1.25
25 Miikka Kiprusoff .30 .75
26 Olli Jokinen .20 .50
27 Ray Whitney .20 .50
28 Cam Ward .30 .75
29 Eric Staal .40 1.00
30 Rod Brind'Amour .25 .60
31 Patrick Kane .60 1.50
32 Kris Versteeg .40 1.00
33 Jonathan Toews .75 2.00
34 Cristobal Huet .30 .75
35 Brian Campbell .25 .60
36 Patrick Sharp .25 .60
37 Ryan Smyth .30 .75
38 Peter Budaj .30 .75
39 Milan Hejduk .30 .75
40 Paul Stastny .30 .75
41 Wojtek Wolski .20 .50
42 Rick Nash .30 .75
43 Steve Mason .50 1.25
44 Nikita Filatov .60 1.50
45 Derick Brassard .30 .75
46 Jakub Voracek .30 .75
47 Brad Richards .25 .60
48 Loui Eriksson .20 .50
49 Mike Modano .30 .75
50 James Neal .30 .75
51 Marty Turco .25 .60
52 Pavel Datsyuk .30 .75
53 Dan Cleary .30 .75
54 Henrik Zetterberg .60 1.50
55 Nicklas Lidstrom .40 1.00
56 Valtteri Filppula .30 .75
57 Ty Conklin .25 .60
58 Ales Hemsky .25 .60
59 Sheldon Souray .20 .50
60 Andrew Cogliano .40 1.00
61 Ethan Moreau .20 .50
62 Sam Gagner .40 1.00
63 David Booth .20 .50
64 Nathan Horton .20 .50
65 Craig Anderson .25 .60
66 Tomas Vokoun .30 .75
67 Michael Frolik .30 .75
68 Anze Kopitar .30 .75
69 Dustin Brown .30 .75
70 Alexander Frolov .25 .60
71 Drew Doughty .60 1.50
72 Jonathan Quick .50 1.25
73 Mikko Koivu .20 .50
74 Niklas Backstrom .30 .75
75 Antti Miettinen .20 .50
76 Pierre-Marc Bouchard .25 .60
77 Andrew Brunette .20 .50
78 Andrei Markov .25 .60
79 Jaroslav Halak .30 .75
80 Andrei Kostitsyn .25 .60
81 Sergei Kostitsyn .30 .75
82 Carey Price .75 2.00
83 Tomas Plekanec .25 .60
84 J.P. Dumont .20 .50
85 Jason Arnott .20 .50
86 Pekka Rinne .25 .60
87 Shea Weber .25 .60
88 Martin Brodeur .75 2.00
89 Zach Parise .30 .75
90 Patrik Elias .25 .60
91 Travis Zajac .20 .50
92 David Clarkson .20 .50
93 Doug Weight .20 .50
94 Kyle Okposo .30 .75
95 Rick DiPietro .30 .75
96 Josh Bailey .25 .60
97 Henrik Lundqvist .60 1.50
98 Brandon Dubinsky .25 .60
99 Chris Drury .25 .60
100 Nikolai Zherdev .20 .50
101 Scott Gomez .30 .75
102 Daniel Alfredsson .30 .75
103 Dany Heatley .60 1.50
104 Jason Spezza .40 1.00
105 Brian Elliott .25 .60
106 Jeff Carter .30 .75
107 Mike Richards .60 1.50
108 Simon Gagne .30 .75
109 Daniel Carcillo .30 .75
110 Scott Hartnell .20 .50
111 Shane Doan .25 .60
112 Kyle Turris .40 1.00
113 Peter Mueller .40 1.00
114 Mikkel Boedker .25 .60
115 Ilya Bryzgalov .25 .60
116 Evgeni Malkin .75 2.00
117 Sidney Crosby 1.50 4.00
118 Jordan Staal .40 1.00
119 Marc-Andre Fleury .30 .75
120 Rob Scuderi .20 .50
121 Chris Kunitz .30 .75
122 Joe Thornton .60 1.50
123 Patrick Marleau .30 .75
124 Evgeni Nabokov .30 .75
125 Devin Setoguchi .25 .60
126 Dan Boyle .20 .50
127 Brad Boyes .20 .50
128 Patrik Berglund .60 1.50
129 David Perron .25 .60
130 David Backes .25 .60
131 T.J. Oshie .50 1.25
132 Martin St. Louis .30 .75
133 Vincent Lecavalier .40 1.00
134 Vaclav Prospal .20 .50
135 Steven Stamkos .75 2.00
136 Luke Schenn .50 1.25
137 Matt Stajan .20 .50
138 Justin Pogge .60 1.50
139 Alexei Ponikarovsky .20 .50
140 Tomas Kaberle .20 .50
141 Pavol Demitra .25 .60
142 Alexandre Burrows .25 .60
143 Willie Mitchell .20 .50
144 Roberto Luongo .75 2.00
145 Ryan Kesler .25 .60
146 Alexander Ovechkin 1.25 3.00
147 Nicklas Backstrom .60 1.50
148 Mike Green (Wa Capitals) .60 1.50
149 Alexander Semin .30 .75
150 Jose Theodore .30 .75
151 Simeon Varlamov .60 1.50
152 David Steckel .20 .50
153 Steve Bernier .20 .50
154 Kyle Wellwood .20 .50
155 Mikhail Grabovski .25 .60
156 Niklas Hagman .20 .50
157 Ryan Malone .20 .50
158 Chris Mason .25 .60
159 Andy McDonald .20 .50
160 Joe Pavelski .20 .50
161 Brad Lukowich .20 .50
162 Sergei Gonchar .20 .50
163 Eric Godard .20 .50
164 Steven Reinprecht .20 .50
165 Keith Yandle .20 .50
166 Daniel Carcillo .30 .75
167 Riley Cote .20 .50
168 Filip Kuba .20 .50
169 Mike Fisher .25 .60
170 Sean Avery .25 .60
171 Nik Antropov .25 .60
172 Mark Streit .20 .50
173 Joey MacDonald .20 .50
174 Jamie Langenbrunner .20 .50
175 Scott Clemmensen .25 .60
176 Greg Zanon .20 .50
177 Ryan Suter .20 .50
178 Saku Koivu .30 .75
179 Alex Kovalev .30 .75
180 Brent Burns .20 .50
181 Marian Gaborik .50 1.25
182 Jarret Stoll .25 .60
183 Jack Johnson .20 .50
184 Stephen Weiss .20 .50
185 Dustin Penner .20 .50
186 Shawn Horcoff .20 .50
187 Niklas Kronwall .25 .60
188 Tomas Holmstrom .25 .60
189 Brenden Morrow .25 .60
190 Mike Ribeiro .20 .50
191 Antoine Vermette .20 .50
192 Cody McLeod .20 .50
193 Patrick Sharp .20 .50
194 Erik Cole .20 .50
195 Rene Bourque .20 .50
196 Mike Cammalleri .25 .60
197 Tim Connolly .20 .50
198 Milan Lucic .30 .75
199 Todd White .20 .50
200 George Parros .20 .50
201 Alexander Sulzer RC 1.00 2.50
202 Andrew MacDonald RC 1.25 3.00
203 Antti Niemi RC 5.00 12.00
204 Artem Anisimov RC 2.00 5.00
205 Ben Lovejoy RC 2.50 6.00
206 Brandon Segal RC 1.25 3.00

207 Brian Salcido RC 1.25 3.00
208 Bryan Rodney RC 1.25 3.00
209 Byron Bitz RC 1.25 3.00
210 Cal O'Reilly RC 1.50 4.00
211 Chris Durno RC 1.25 3.00
212 David Schlemko RC 1.25 3.00
213 David Van Der Gulik RC 1.25 3.00
214 Davis Drewiske RC 1.50 4.00
215 Derek Peltier RC 1.00 2.50
216 Grant Lewis RC 1.25 3.00
217 Jakub Petruzalek RC 1.50 4.00
218 Jaime Sifers RC 1.25 3.00
219 Jay Beagle RC 1.50 4.00
220 Jesse Joensuu RC 2.00 5.00
221 Jhonas Enroth RC 2.00 5.00
222 Joel Rechlicz RC 1.50 4.00
223 John Scott RC 1.50 4.00
224 Kevin Quick RC 1.00 2.50
225 Kevin Westgarth RC 1.25 3.00
226 Kris Chucko RC 1.25 3.00
227 Kurtis McLean RC 1.25 3.00
228 Luca Caputi RC 2.00 5.00
229 Matt Beleskey RC 1.50 4.00
230 Matt Hendricks RC 1.25 3.00
231 Michael Vernace RC 1.25 3.00
232 Michal Neuvirth RC 4.00 10.00
233 Mikael Backlund RC 2.50 6.00
234 Mike McKenna RC 1.25 3.00
235 Mike Santorelli RC 1.00 2.50
236 Peter Regin RC 2.00 5.00
237 Phil Oreskovic RC 1.50 4.00
238 Riku Helenius RC 1.50 4.00
239 Riley Armstrong RC 1.25 3.00
240 Ryan Vesce RC 1.25 3.00
241 Scott Lehman RC 1.00 2.50
242 Christian Hanson RC 2.00 5.00
243 Spencer Machacek RC 1.25 3.00
244 T.J. Galiardi RC 2.00 5.00
245 Tim Stapleton RC 1.50 4.00
246 Tim Wallace RC 1.00 2.50
247 Tom Wandell RC 5.00 12.00
248 Troy Bodie RC 1.25 3.00
249 Ville Leino RC 2.00 5.00
250 Yannick Weber RC 2.00 5.00
251 John Tavares RC 20.00 50.00
252 Matt Duchene RC 10.00 25.00
253 Victor Hedman RC 5.00 12.00
254 Evander Kane RC 6.00 15.00
255 James van Riemsdyk RC 6.00 15.00
256 Jonas Gustavsson RC 6.00 15.00
257 Jamie Benn RC 4.00 10.00
258 Erik Karlsson RC 8.00 20.00
259 Tyler Myers RC 10.00 25.00
260 Ryan O'Reilly RC 5.00 12.00
261 Matt Gilroy RC 3.00 8.00
262 Michael Del Zotto RC 5.00 12.00
263 Viktor Stalberg RC 4.00 10.00
264 Tyler Bozak RC 6.00 15.00
265 Sergei Shirokov RC 4.00 10.00
266 Colin Wilson RC 5.00 12.00
267 Benn Ferriero RC 2.50 6.00
268 Michael Grabner RC 3.00 8.00
269 Dmitry Kulikov RC 2.50 6.00
270 Cody Franson RC 2.50 6.00

2009-10 Ultra Gold Medallion

COMP.SET w/o SPs (200) 40.00 100.00
*GOLD: 1X TO 2.5X BASIC CARDS
STATED ODDS 1 PER PACK
*GOLD ROOKIE: .6X TO 1.5X BASIC EXCH
ROOKIE STATED ODDS 1:8
COMMON GOLD EXCH 10.00 25.00
EXCH STATED ODDS 1:288

2009-10 Ultra Ice Medallion

*ICE: 3X TO 8X BASIC CARDS
*ICE ROOKIES: 1.5X TO 4X BASIC
STATED PRINT RUN 100 SER.#'d SETS
COMMON ICE EXCH 15.00 40.00
ICE EXCH PRINT RUN 25

2009-10 Ultra Crowning Achievements

COMPLETE SET (10) 10.00 25.00
STATED ODDS 1:4
CA1 Steve Mason 1.25 3.00
CA2 Alexander Ovechkin 3.00 8.00
CA3 Sidney Crosby 4.00 10.00
CA4 Mike Green 1.50 4.00
CA5 Doug Weight .50 1.25
CA6 Keith Tkachuk .60 1.50
CA7 Eric Staal 1.00 2.50
CA8 Martin Brodeur 2.00 5.00
CA9 Jonas Hiller 1.00 2.50
CA10 Tim Thomas .75 2.00

2009-10 Ultra EX Hockey

COMPLETE SET (42) 40.00 100.00
STATED ODDS 1:8
EX1 Ryan Getzlaf 2.00 5.00
EX2 Ilya Kovalchuk 1.50 4.00
EX3 Phil Kessel 1.25 3.00
EX4 Thomas Vanek 1.25 3.00
EX5 Ryan Miller 1.25 3.00
EX6 Jarome Iginla 2.50 6.00
EX7 Miikka Kiprusoff 1.25 3.00
EX8 Eric Staal 1.50 4.00
EX9 Jonathan Toews 3.00 8.00
EX10 Patrick Kane 2.50 6.00
EX11 Joe Sakic 2.50 6.00
EX12 Paul Stastny 1.25 3.00
EX13 Rick Nash 1.25 3.00
EX14 Steve Mason 2.00 5.00
EX15 Mike Modano 1.25 3.00
EX16 Henrik Zetterberg 2.50 6.00
EX17 Pavel Datsyuk 1.25 3.00
EX18 Andrew Cogliano 1.50 4.00
EX19 Tomas Vokoun 1.25 3.00
EX20 Anze Kopitar 1.25 3.00
EX21 Drew Doughty 2.50 6.00
EX22 Marian Gaborik 2.00 5.00
EX23 Carey Price 3.00 8.00
EX24 Saku Koivu 1.25 3.00
EX25 Martin Brodeur 3.00 8.00
EX26 Zach Parise 1.25 3.00
EX27 Henrik Lundqvist 2.50 6.00
EX28 Jason Spezza 1.50 4.00
EX29 Mike Richards 2.50 6.00
EX30 Jeff Carter 1.25 3.00
EX31 Peter Mueller 1.50 4.00
EX32 Sidney Crosby 6.00 15.00
EX33 Evgeni Malkin 3.00 8.00
EX34 Joe Thornton 2.50 6.00
EX35 Patrick Marleau 1.25 3.00
EX36 Paul Kariya 1.25 3.00
EX37 Vincent Lecavalier 1.50 4.00
EX38 Martin St. Louis 1.25 3.00
EX39 Luke Schenn 2.00 5.00
EX40 Roberto Luongo 3.00 8.00
EX41 Alexander Ovechkin 5.00 12.00
EX42 Mike Green 2.50 6.00

2009-10 Ultra EX Hockey Jambalaya

STATED ODDS 1:288
JAM1 Alexander Ovechkin 60.00 150.00
JAM2 Roberto Luongo 40.00 100.00
JAM3 Vincent Lecavalier 20.00 50.00
JAM4 Patrick Marleau 15.00 40.00
JAM5 Evgeni Malkin 40.00 100.00
JAM6 Mario Lemieux 40.00 100.00
JAM7 Sidney Crosby 80.00 200.00
JAM8 Henrik Lundqvist 30.00 80.00
JAM9 Martin Brodeur 40.00 100.00
JAM10 Carey Price 40.00 100.00
JAM11 Patrick Roy 50.00 120.00
JAM12 Mark Messier 30.00 80.00
JAM13 Gordie Howe 60.00 150.00
JAM14 Henrik Zetterberg 30.00 80.00
JAM15 Joe Sakic 30.00 80.00
JAM16 Jonathan Toews 40.00 100.00
JAM17 Patrick Kane 30.00 80.00
JAM18 Jarome Iginla 30.00 80.00
JAM19 Bobby Orr 60.00 150.00
JAM20 Ilya Kovalchuk 20.00 50.00

2009-10 Ultra Fresh Ink

STATED ODDS 1:288
FIAC Andrew Cogliano
FIBA Josh Bailey 5.00 12.00
FIBL Brian Lee 6.00 15.00
FIBM Ben Maxwell 10.00 25.00
FIBS Brandon Sutter
FIBW Blake Wheeler 8.00 20.00
FICB Casey Borer
FICG Colton Gillies 8.00 20.00
FICK Chris Kunitz 6.00 15.00
FICL David Clarkson 4.00 10.00
FICP Carey Price
FICS Chris Stewart 6.00 15.00
FIDC Dan Cleary 6.00 15.00
FIDD Drew Doughty
FIDH Dany Heatley
FIDJ David Jones
FIDP Dion Phaneuf
FIDS Daniel Sedin
FIDU Dustin Penner 4.00 10.00
FIGR Mike Green 25.00 60.00
FIHL Henrik Lundqvist
FIHS Henrik Sedin
FIIK Ilya Kovalchuk
FIJD J.P. Dumont
FIJI Jarome Iginla
FIJN James Neal
FIJP Justin Pogge 12.00 30.00
FIJS Jack Skille 4.00 10.00
FIJT Joe Thornton
FIKA Karl Alzner 6.00 15.00
FIKE Tim Kennedy 6.00 15.00
FIKM Kendal McArdle
FIKV Kris Versteeg 15.00 40.00
FILS Luke Schenn
FIMB Mikkel Boedker
FIMG Marian Gaborik
FIMP Max Pacioretty 6.00 15.00
FINF Nikita Filatov 12.00 30.00
FING Nathan Gerbe 8.00 20.00
FIPB Patrik Berglund
FIPD Pavel Datsyuk
FIPE Patrik Elias
FISB Steve Bernier 4.00 10.00
FISC Cory Schneider 20.00 50.00
FISG Simon Gagne
FISM Steve Mason
FISS Steven Stamkos 15.00 40.00
FISV Simeon Varlamov
FITK Tyler Kennedy
FITL Trevor Lewis 4.00 10.00
FITO T.J. Oshie 10.00 25.00
FITP Tomas Plihal
FITW Ty Wishart 6.00 15.00
FIVT Viktor Tikhonov 6.00 15.00
FIZB Zach Bogosian

2009-10 Ultra Go To Players

COMPLETE SET (5) 10.00 25.00
STATED ODDS 1:4
GT1 Alexander Ovechkin 3.00 8.00
GT2 Henrik Zetterberg 1.50 4.00
GT3 Ilya Kovalchuk 1.00 2.50
GT4 Sidney Crosby 4.00 10.00
GT5 Jonathan Toews 2.00 5.00

2009-10 Ultra Rookie Sensations

COMPLETE SET (30) 40.00 100.00
STATED ODDS 1:4
SPs ANNOUNCED BY UD
RS1 Alex Goligoski .60 1.50
RS2 Alex Pietrangelo .60 1.50
RS3 Blake Wheeler SP 2.00 5.00
RS4 Bobby Ryan SP 2.00 5.00
RS5 Brandon Sutter .75 2.00
RS6 Claude Giroux 1.50 4.00
RS7 Cody McLeod .50 1.25
RS8 Colton Gillies 1.00 2.50
RS9 Derick Brassard SP 1.50 4.00
RS10 Drew Doughty SP 3.00 8.00
RS11 Fabian Brunnstrom .75 2.00
RS12 Jakub Voracek .75 2.00
RS13 James Neal .75 2.00
RS14 Josh Bailey .60 1.50
RS15 Justin Pogge SP 3.00 8.00
RS16 Kris Versteeg SP 2.00 5.00
RS17 Kyle Okposo .75 2.00
RS18 Kyle Turris 1.00 2.50
RS19 Luke Schenn SP 2.50 6.00
RS20 Max Pacioretty .75 2.00
RS21 Michael Frolik .60 1.50
RS22 Mikkel Boedker SP 1.25 3.00
RS23 Nikita Filatov 1.50 4.00
RS24 Nikolai Kulemin .60 1.50
RS25 Patrik Berglund 1.50 4.00
RS26 Shawn Matthias .75 2.00
RS27 Steve Mason SP 2.50 6.00
RS28 Steven Stamkos SP 4.00 10.00
RS29 T.J. Oshie 1.25 3.00
RS30 Zach Bogosian 1.00 2.50

2009-10 Ultra Scoring Kings

COMPLETE SET (10) 12.00 30.00
STATED ODDS 1:4
SK1 Alexander Ovechkin 3.00 8.00
SK2 Martin St. Louis .75 2.00
SK3 Joe Thornton 1.50 4.00
SK4 Sidney Crosby 4.00 10.00
SK5 Evgeni Malkin 2.00 5.00
SK6 Zach Parise .75 2.00
SK7 Pavel Datsyuk .75 2.00
SK8 Jarome Iginla 1.50 4.00
SK9 Ilya Kovalchuk 1.00 2.50
SK10 Ryan Getzlaf 1.25 3.00

2009-10 Ultra Team Leaders

COMPLETE SET (30) 20.00 50.00
STATED ODDS 1:4
SPs PROVIDED BY UD
TL1 Ryan Getzlaf 1.25 3.00
TL2 Ilya Kovalchuk 1.00 2.50
TL3 Tim Thomas SP 1.25 3.00
TL4 Derek Roy .75 2.00
TL5 Jarome Iginla SP 2.50 6.00
TL6 Ray Whitney .50 1.25
TL7 Jonathan Toews SP 3.00 8.00
TL8 Ryan Smyth .75 2.00
TL9 Rick Nash .75 2.00
TL10 Steve Ott .50 1.25
TL11 Pavel Datsyuk SP 1.25 3.00
TL12 Ales Hemsky SP 1.00 2.50
TL13 David Booth .50 1.25
TL14 Anze Kopitar .75 2.00
TL15 Mikko Koivu .75 2.00
TL16 Alex Kovalev SP 1.25 3.00
TL17 J.P. Dumont .50 1.25
TL18 Zach Parise .75 2.00
TL19 Mark Streit .50 1.25
TL20 Henrik Lundqvist SP 2.50 6.00
TL21 Daniel Alfredsson .75 2.00
TL22 Jeff Carter SP 1.25 3.00
TL23 Shane Doan .60 1.50
TL24 Evgeni Malkin SP 3.00 8.00
TL25 Joe Thornton 1.50 4.00
TL26 David Backes .60 1.50
TL27 Martin St. Louis .75 2.00
TL28 Jason Blake .50 1.25
TL29 Roberto Luongo SP 3.00 8.00
TL30 Alexander Ovechkin 3.00 8.00

2009-10 Ultra Total O

COMPLETE SET (5) 6.00 15.00
STATED ODDS 1:4
TO1 Sidney Crosby 4.00 10.00
TO2 Alexander Ovechkin 3.00 8.00
TO3 Evgeni Malkin 2.00 5.00
TO4 Vincent Lecavalier 1.00 2.50
TO5 Pavel Datsyuk .75 2.00

2009-10 Ultra Uniformity

STATED ODDS 1:12
UU-AF Adam Foote 3.00 8.00
UU-AH Adam Hall 3.00 8.00
UU-AK Alex Kovalev 5.00 12.00
UU-AN Anze Kopitar 5.00 12.00
UU-AO Alexander Ovechkin 20.00 50.00
UU-AS Alexander Steen 3.00 8.00
UU-BL Bryan Little 5.00 12.00
UU-BR Dustin Brown 4.00 10.00
UU-CP Carey Price 12.00 30.00
UU-CS Cory Stillman 4.00 10.00
UU-DB David Booth 3.00 8.00
UU-DC David Clarkson 3.00 8.00
UU-DD Drew Doughty 10.00 25.00
UU-DM Dominic Moore 5.00 12.00
UU-DP David Perron 4.00 10.00
UU-DR Derek Roy 5.00 12.00
UU-DS Drew Stafford 5.00 12.00
UU-DT Darcy Tucker 4.00 10.00
UU-EC Erik Cole 3.00 8.00
UU-EM Evgeni Malkin 12.00 30.00
UU-ES Eric Staal 6.00 15.00
UU-FL Marc-Andre Fleury 5.00 12.00
UU-IK Ilya Kovalchuk 6.00 15.00
UU-JB Jay Bouwmeester 5.00 12.00
UU-JC Jonathan Cheechoo 5.00 12.00
UU-JG Jean-Sebastien Giguere 5.00 12.00
UU-JL Joffrey Lupul 5.00 12.00
UU-JN James Neal 5.00 12.00
UU-JP Jason Pominville 5.00 12.00
UU-JS Jason Spezza 6.00 15.00
UU-KL Kari Lehtonen 5.00 12.00
UU-KO Andrei Kostitsyn 4.00 10.00
UU-LE Kristopher Letang 5.00 12.00
UU-MF Manny Fernandez 4.00 10.00
UU-MG Marian Gaborik 8.00 20.00
UU-MI Ryan Miller 5.00 12.00
UU-MM Mike Modano 5.00 12.00
UU-MP Marc-Antoine Pouliot 4.00 10.00
UU-MR Michael Ryder 4.00 10.00
UU-MS Marc Savard 3.00 8.00
UU-MU Peter Mueller 6.00 15.00
UU-NA Nik Antropov 4.00 10.00
UU-NB Nicklas Backstrom 10.00 25.00
UU-NL Nicklas Lidstrom 6.00 15.00
UU-PM Patrick Marleau 5.00 12.00
UU-PO Patrick O'Sullivan 4.00 10.00
UU-PR Chris Pronger 4.00 10.00
UU-RD Rick DiPietro 5.00 12.00
UU-RI Mike Richards 10.00 25.00
UU-RL Roberto Luongo 12.00 30.00
UU-RM Ryan Malone 3.00 8.00
UU-RN Rick Nash 5.00 12.00
UU-SC Sidney Crosby 25.00 60.00
UU-SD Shane Doan 4.00 10.00
UU-SG Sam Gagner 6.00 15.00
UU-SK Saku Koivu 5.00 12.00
UU-ST Marc Staal 6.00 15.00
UU-SV Marek Svatos 3.00 8.00
UU-SW Shea Weber 4.00 10.00

1961-62 Union Oil WHL

This 12-drawing set features players from the Los Angeles Blades (1-8) and the San Francisco Seals (9-12) of the Western Hockey League. The black-and-white drawings by artist Sam Patrick measure approximately 6" by 8" and are printed on textured white paper. The back of each drawing carries the player's career highlights and biographical information. The Union Oil name and logo at the bottom round out the backs. The cards are unnumbered and listed below alphabetically within teams. Reportedly only eight cards were issued to the public, making four of the cards extremely scarce.

COMPLETE SET (12) 50.00 100.00
1 Jack Bownass 3.00 6.00
2 Ed Diachuk 3.00 6.00
3 Leo LaBine 5.00 10.00
4 Willie O'Ree 20.00 40.00
5 Bruce Carmichael 3.00 6.00
6 Gordon Haworth 4.00 8.00
7 Fleming Mackell 5.00 10.00
8 Robert Solinger 3.00 6.00
9 Gary Edmundson 3.00 6.00
10 Al Nicholson 3.00 6.00
11 Orland Kurtenbach 7.50 15.00
12 Tom Thurlby 3.00 6.00

1990-91 Upper Deck

The 1990-91 Upper Deck Hockey set contains 550 standard-size cards. The set was released in two series of 400 and 150 cards, respectively. The card fronts feature color action photos, bordered on the right and bottom in the team's colors with the team logo in the lower right hand corner. The player's name and position in black lettering appear in a pale blue bar at the top of the card front. Two-thirds of back shows another color action photo, while the remaining third presents biographical information and career statistics in pale blue box running the length of the card. The second (or extended) series contains 150 cards and includes newest rookies, traded players, All Stars, Heroes of the NHL, and members of the Canadian National Junior Team. It should also be noted that the Canada's Captains card (473) shows Eric Lindros along with Kris Draper and Steven Rice. The French version of 1990-91 Upper Deck was produced in smaller quantities compared to the English version; multipliers can be found in the header below to determine values for these.

COMPLETE SET (550) 25.00 60.00
COMP.LO SERIES (400) 12.50 30.00
COMP.HI SERIES (150) 12.50 30.00
COMP.HI FACT.SET (150) 15.00 30.00
1 David Volek .02 .10
2 Brian Propp .02 .10
3 Wendel Clark .07 .20
4 Adam Creighton .02 .10
5 Mark Osborne .02 .10
6 Murray Craven .02 .10
7 Doug Crossman .02 .10
8 Mario Marois .02 .10
9 Curt Giles .02 .10
10 Rick Wamsley .07 .20
11 Troy Mallette RC .02 .10
12 John Cullen .02 .10
13 Miloslav Horava RC .02 .10
14 Kevin Stevens RC .02 .10
15 David Shaw .02 .10
16 Randy Wood .02 .10
17 Peter Zezel .02 .10
18 Glenn Healy RC .07 .20
19 Sergio Momesso RC .02 .10
20 Don Maloney .02 .10
21 Craig Muni .02 .10
22 Phil Housley .07 .20
23 Martin Gelinas RC .25 .60
24 Alexander Mogilny RC .60 1.50
25 John Byce RC .02 .10
26 Joe Nieuwendyk .07 .20
27 Ron Tugnutt .07 .20
28 Don Barber .02 .10
29 Gary Roberts .02 .10
30 Basil McRae .02 .10
31 Phil Bourque .02 .10
32 Mike Richter RC .40 1.00
33 Zarley Zalapski .02 .10
34 Bernie Nicholls .07 .20
35 Bob Corkum RC .02 .10
36 Rod Brind'Amour RC .60 1.50
37 Mark Fitzpatrick RC .07 .20
38 Gino Cavallini .02 .10
39 Mick Vukota RC .02 .10
40 Mike Lalor RC .02 .10
41 Dave Andreychuk .07 .20
42 Bill Ranford .07 .20
43 Pierre Turgeon .07 .20
44 Mark Messier .15 .40
45 Rob Blake RC .40 1.00
46 Mike Modano RC 1.00 2.50
47 Theo Fleury .25 .60
48 Neal Broten .07 .20
49 Paul Gillis .02 .10
50 Doug Bodger .02 .10
51 Stephan Lebeau RC .02 .10
52 Larry Robinson .07 .20
53 Dale Hawerchuk .07 .20
54 Wayne Gretzky .75 2.00
55 Ed Belfour RC 1.00 2.50
56 Steve Yzerman .60 1.50
57 Rod Langway .02 .10
58 Bernie Federko .07 .20
59 Mario Lemieux Streak .40 1.00
60 Doug Lidster .02 .10
61 Dave Christian .02 .10
62 Rob Ramage .02 .10
63 Jeremy Roenick RC .60 1.50
64 Ray Bourque .25 .60
65 Jon Morris RC .02 .10
66 Sean Burke .07 .20
67 Ron Francis .07 .20
68 Ron Sutter .02 .10
69 Peter Sidorkiewicz .07 .20
70 Sylvain Turgeon .02 .10
71 Dave Ellett .02 .10
72 Bobby Smith .07 .20
73 Luc Robitaille .07 .20
74 Pat Elynuik .02 .10
75 Jason Soules RC .02 .10
76 Dino Ciccarelli .07 .20
77 Vladimir Krutov RC .07 .20
78 Lee Norwood .02 .10
79 Brian Bradley .02 .10
80 Michal Pivonka RC .02 .10
81 Mark LaForest RC .02 .10
82 Trent Yawney .02 .10
83 Tom Fergus .02 .10
84 Andy Brickley .02 .10
85 Dave Manson .02 .10
86 Gord Murphy RC .02 .10
87 Scott Young .02 .10
88 Tommy Albelin .02 .10
89 Ken Wregget .07 .20
90 Brad Shaw RC .02 .10
91 Mario Gosselin .07 .20
92 Paul Fenton .02 .10
93 Brian Skrudland .02 .10
94 Thomas Steen .02 .10
95 John Tonelli .02 .10
96 Steve Chiasson UER .02 .10
(Back photo actually
Yves Racine)
97 Mike Ridley .02 .10
98 Garth Butcher .02 .10
99 Daniel Shank RC .02 .10
100 Checklist 1-100 .02 .10
101 Jamie Macoun .02 .10
102 Wendell Young .07 .20
103 Laurie Boschman .02 .10
104 Paul Ranheim RC .02 .10
105 Doug Smail .02 .10
106 Shawn Chambers .02 .10
107 Steve Weeks .07 .20
108 Gaetan Duchesne .02 .10
109 Kevin Hatcher .02 .10
110 Paul Reinhart .02 .10
111 Shawn Burr .02 .10
112 Troy Murray .02 .10
113 John Chabot .02 .10
114 Jacques Cloutier RC .07 .20
115 Rick Zombo RC .02 .10
116 Kjell Samuelsson .02 .10
117 Tim Watters .02 .10
118 Pat Flatley .02 .10
119 Tom Laidlaw .02 .10
120 Ilkka Sinisalo .02 .10
121 Tom Barrasso .07 .20
122 Bob Essensa RC .25 .60
123 Sergei Makarov RC .02 .10
124 Paul Coffey .15 .40
125 Bob Beers RC .02 .10
126 Brian Bellows .02 .10
127 Mike Liut .07 .20
128 Igor Larionov RC .40 1.00
129 Craig Simpson .02 .10
130 Kelly Miller .02 .10
131 Dirk Graham .02 .10
132 Jimmy Carson .02 .10
133 Michel Goulet .07 .20
134 Gerard Gallant .02 .10
135 Bruce Hoffort RC .02 .10
136 Steve Duchesne .02 .10
137 Bryan Trottier .07 .20
138 Pelle Eklund .02 .10
139 Gary Nylund .02 .10
140 Steve Kasper .02 .10
141 Joel Otto .02 .10
142 Rob Brown .02 .10
143 Al MacInnis .07 .20
144 Mario Lemieux .75 2.00
145 Peter Eriksson RC .02 .10
146 Jari Kurri .07 .20
147 Petri Skriko .02 .10
148 Steve Smith .02 .10
149 Calle Johansson .02 .10
150 Stewart Gavin .02 .10
151 Randy Ladouceur .02 .10
152 Vincent Riendeau RC .07 .20
153 Patrick Roy UER .60 1.50
(Feet and inches
reversed in stat table)
154 Brett Hull .30 .75
155 Craig Fisher RC .02 .10
156 Cam Neely .15 .40
157 Al Iafrate .07 .20
158 Bob Carpenter .02 .10
159 Doug Brown .02 .10
160 Tom Kurvers .02 .10
161 John MacLean .07 .20
162 Guy Lafleur .15 .40
163 Peter Stastny .07 .20
164 Joe Sakic .40 1.00
165 Robb Stauber RC .07 .20
166 Daren Puppa .07 .20
167 Esa Tikkanen .02 .10
168 Mike Ramsey .02 .10
169 Craig MacTavish .02 .10
170 Christian Ruuttu .02 .10
171 Brian Hayward .07 .20
172 Pat Verbeek .02 .10
173 Adam Oates .07 .20
174 Chris Chelios .15 .40
175 Curtis Joseph RC .75 2.00
176 Slava Fetisov RC .15 .40
177 Dave Poulin .02 .10
178 Mark Recchi RC .60 1.50
179 Daniel Marois .02 .10
180 Mark Johnson .02 .10
181 Michel Petit .02 .10
182 Brian Mullen .02 .10
183 Chris Terreri RC .07 .20
184 Tony Hrkac .02 .10
185 James Patrick .02 .10
186 Craig Ludwig .02 .10
187 Uwe Krupp .02 .10
188 Guy Carbonneau .07 .20
189 Dave Snuggerud RC .02 .10
190 Joe Murphy RC .02 .10
191 Jeff Brown .02 .10
192 Dean Evason .02 .10
193 Petr Svoboda .02 .10
194 Dave Babych .02 .10
195 Steve Tuttle .02 .10
196 Randy Burridge .02 .10
197 Tony Tanti .02 .10
198 Bob Sweeney .02 .10
199 Brad Marsh .02 .10
200 Checklist 101-200 .02 .10
201 Conn Smythe Trophy .07 .20
202 Calder Trophy .02 .10
Sergei Makarov
203 Lady Byng Trophy .15 .40
Brett Hull
204 Norris Trophy .07 .20
Ray Bourque
205 Art Ross Trophy .40 1.00
Wayne Gretzky
206 Hart Trophy .07 .20
Mark Messier
207 Vezina Trophy .30 .75
Patrick Roy
208 Frank Selke Trophy .02 .10
209 William Jennings .02 .10
Trophy
Andy Moog and
Reggie Lemelin
210 Aaron Broten .02 .10
211 John Carter RC .02 .10
212 Marty McSorley .02 .10
213 Greg Millen .07 .20
214 Dave Taylor .07 .20
215 Rejean Lemelin .07 .20
216 Dave McLlwain .02 .10
217 Don Beaupre .07 .20
218 Paul MacDermid .02 .10
219 Dale Hunter .02 .10
220 Brent Ashton .02 .10
221 Steve Thomas .02 .10
222 Ed Olczyk .02 .10
223 Doug Wilson .07 .20
224 Vincent Damphousse .02 .10
225 Rob DiMaio RC .02 .10
226 Hubie McDonough RC .02 .10
227 Ron Hextall .07 .20
228 Dave Chyzowski RC .02 .10
229 Larry Murphy .07 .20
230 Mike Bullard .02 .10
231 Kelly Hrudey .07 .20
232 Andy Moog .07 .20
233 Todd Elik RC .02 .10
234 Craig Janney .07 .20
235 Peter Lappin RC .02 .10
236 Scott Stevens .07 .20
237 Fredrik Olausson .02 .10
238 Geoff Courtnall .02 .10
239 Greg Paslawski .02 .10
240 Allan May RC .02 .10
241 Allan Bester .07 .20
242 Steve Larmer .07 .20
243 Gary Leeman .02 .10
244 Denis Savard .07 .20
245 Eric Weinrich RC .02 .10
246 Pat LaFontaine .15 .40
247 Tim Kerr .02 .10
248 Dave Gagner .07 .20
249 Brent Sutter .02 .10
250 Claude Vilgrain RC .02 .10
251 Tomas Sandstrom .02 .10
252 Joe Mullen .07 .20
253 Brian Leetch .20 .50
254 Mike Vernon .07 .20
255 Daniel Dore RC .02 .10
256 Trevor Linden .07 .20
257 Dave Barr .02 .10
258 John Ogrodnick .02 .10
259 Russ Courtnall .02 .10
260 Dan Quinn .02 .10
261 Mark Howe .02 .10
262 Kevin Lowe .02 .10
263 Rick Tocchet .07 .20
264 Grant Fuhr .07 .20
265 Andrew Cassels RC .07 .20
266 Kevin Dineen .02 .10
267 Kirk Muller .02 .10
268 Randy Cunneyworth .02 .10
269 Brendan Shanahan .15 .40
270 Dave Tippett .02 .10
271 Doug Gilmour .07 .20
272 Tony Granato .02 .10
273 Gary Suter .02 .10
274 Darren Turcotte RC .02 .10
275 Murray Baron RC .02 .10
276 Stephane Richer .07 .20
277 Mike Gartner .07 .20
278 Kirk McLean .07 .20
279 John Vanbiesbrouck .07 .20
280 Shayne Corson .02 .10
281 Paul Cavallini .02 .10
282 Petr Klima .02 .10
283 Ulf Dahlen .02 .10
284 Glenn Anderson .07 .20
285 Rick Meagher .02 .10
286 Alexei Kasatonov RC .02 .10
287 Ulf Samuelsson .02 .10
288 Patrik Sundstrom .02 .10
289 Ray Ferraro .02 .10
290 Janne Ojanen RC .02 .10
291 Jeff Jackson .02 .10
292 Jiri Hrdina RC .02 .10
293 Joe Cirella .02 .10
294 Brad McCrimmon .02 .10
295 Curtis Leschyshyn RC .02 .10
296 Kelly Kisio .02 .10
297 Jyrki Lumme RC .02 .10
298 Mark Janssens RC .02 .10
299 Stan Smyl .02 .10
300 Checklist 201-300 .02 .10
301 Joe Sakic .15 .40
(Quebec Nordiques TC)
302 Petri Skriko .02 .10
303 Steve Yzerman .15 .40
(Detroit Red Wings TC)
304 Tim Kerr .02 .10
305 Mario Lemieux TC .30 .75
306 Pat LaFontaine .07 .20
(New York Islanders TC)
307 Wayne Gretzky .40 1.00
(Los Angeles Kings TC)
308 Brian Bellows TC .02 .10
309 Rod Langway TC .02 .10
310 Gary Leeman TC .02 .10
311 Kirk Muller TC .02 .10
312 Brett Hull .07 .20
(St. Louis Blues TC)
313 Thomas Steen TC .02 .10
314 Ron Francis TC .07 .20
315 Brian Leetch .07 .20
(New York Rangers TC)
316 Jeremy Roenick .15 .40
(Chicago Blackhawks TC)
317 Patrick Roy .30 .75
(Montreal Canadiens TC)
318 Pierre Turgeon .07 .20
(Buffalo Sabres TC)
319 Al MacInnis TC .07 .20
320 Ray Bourque TC .07 .20
321 Mark Messier .07 .20
(Edmonton Oilers TC)
322 Jody Hull RC .02 .10
323 Chris Joseph RC .02 .10
324 Adam Burt RC .02 .10
325 Jason Herter RC .02 .10
326 Geoff Smith ART .02 .10
327 Brad Shaw ART .02 .10
328 Rich Sutter .02 .10
329 Barry Pederson .02 .10
330 Paul MacLean .02 .10
331 Randy Carlyle .02 .10
332 Donald Dufresne RC .02 .10
333 Brent Hughes RC .02 .10
334 Mathieu Schneider RC .02 .10
335 Jason Miller RC .02 .10
336 Sergei Makarov ART .02 .10
337 Bob Essensa ART .07 .20
338 Claude Loiselle RC .02 .10
339 Wayne Presley .02 .10
340 Tony McKegney .02 .10
341 Charlie Huddy .02 .10
342 Greg Adams UER .02 .10
(Front photo actually
Igor Larionov)
343 Mike Tomlak RC .02 .10
344 Adam Graves RC .20 .50
345 Michel Mongeau RC .02 .10
346 Mike Modano UER ART .07 .20
('89 Entry Draft
should say '88)
347 Rod Brind'Amour ART .07 .20
348 Dana Murzyn .02 .10
349 Dave Lowry RC .02 .10
350 Star Rookie CL .02 .10
351 First Four Picks .20 .50
Owen Nolan
Keith Primeau
Petr Nedved
Mike Ricci
Top Ten Draft Pick CL
352 Owen Nolan RC .40 1.00
353 Petr Nedved RC .20 .50
354 Keith Primeau RC .40 1.00
355 Mike Ricci RC .25 .60
356 Jaromir Jagr RC 1.25 3.00
357 Scott Scissons RC .02 .10
358 Darryl Sydor RC .20 .50
359 Derian Hatcher RC .02 .10
360 John Slaney RC .02 .10
361 Drake Berehowsky RC .02 .10
362 Luke Richardson .02 .10
363 Lucien DeBlois .02 .10
364 Dave Reid RC .02 .10
365 Mats Sundin RC .75 2.00
366 Jan Erixon .02 .10
367 Troy Loney RC .02 .10
368 Chris Nilan .02 .10
369 Gord Dineen .02 .10
370 Jeff Bloemberg RC .02 .10
371 John Druce RC .02 .10
372 Brian MacLellan .02 .10
373 Bruce Driver .02 .10
374 Marc Habscheid .02 .10
375 Paul Ysebaert RC .02 .10
376 Rick Vaive .02 .10
377 Glen Wesley .02 .10
378 Mike Foligno .02 .10
379 Garry Galley RC .02 .10
380 Dean Kennedy RC .02 .10
381 Daniel Berthiaume .07 .20
382 Mike Keane RC .07 .20
383 Frank Musil .02 .10
384 Mike McPhee .02 .10
385 Jon Casey .07 .20
386 Jeff Norton .02 .10
387 John Tucker .02 .10
388 Alan Kerr .02 .10
389 Bob Rouse .02 .10
390 Gerald Diduck .02 .10
391 Greg Hawgood .02 .10

392 Randy Velischek .02 .10
393 Tim Cheveldae RC .07 .20
394 Mike Krushelnyski .02 .10
395 Glen Hanlon .07 .20
396 Lou Franceschetti RC .02 .10
397 Scott Arniel .02 .10
398 Terry Carkner .02 .10
399 Clint Malarchuk .07 .20
400 Checklist 301-400 .02 .10
401 Mikhail Tatarinov RC .02 .10
402 Benoit Hogue .02 .10
403 Frank Pietrangelo RC .07 .20
404 Paul Stanton RC .07 .20
405 Anatoli Semenov RC .02 .10
406 Bobby Smith .07 .20
407 Derek King .02 .10
408 Jean-Claude Bergeron RC .02 .10
409 Brian Propp .02 .10
410 Jiri Latal RC .02 .10
411 Joey Kocur RC .25 .60
412 Daniel Berthiaume .07 .20
413 Dave Ellett .02 .10
414 Jay Miller RC .02 .10
415 Steph Beauregard RC .07 .20
416 Mark Hardy .02 .10
417 Todd Krygier RC .02 .10
418 Randy Moller .02 .10
419 Doug Crossman .02 .10
420 Ray Sheppard .07 .20
421 Sylvain Lefebvre RC .02 .10
422 Chris Chelios .15 .40
423 Joe Mullen .07 .20
424 Pete Peeters .07 .20
425 Bryan Trottier .07 .20
426 Denis Savard .07 .20
427 Ken Daneyko .02 .10
428 Eric Desjardins RC .20 .50
429 Zdeno Ciger RC .07 .20
430 Brad McCrimmon .02 .10
431 Ed Olczyk .02 .10
432 Peter Ing RC .07 .20
433 Bob Kudelski RC .02 .10
434 Troy Gamble RC .07 .20
435 Phil Housley .07 .20
436 Scott Stevens .07 .20
437 Normand Rochefort .02 .10
438 Geoff Courtnall .02 .10
439 Ken Baumgartner RC .02 .10
440 Kris King RC .02 .10
441 Troy Crowder RC .02 .10
442 Chris Nilan .02 .10
443 Dale Hawerchuk .07 .20
444 Kevin Miller RC .07 .20
445 Keith Acton .02 .10
446 Jeff Chychrun RC .02 .10
447 Claude Lemieux .02 .10
448 Bob Probert .07 .20
449 Brian Hayward .07 .20
450 Craig Berube RC .02 .10
451 Team Canada .15 .40
452 Mike Sillinger RC .07 .20
453 Jason Marshall RC .02 .10
454 Patrice Brisebois RC .02 .10
455 Brad May RC .07 .20
456 Pierre Sevigny RC .02 .10
457 John Slaney .02 .10
458 Felix Potvin RC .75 2.00
459 Scott Thornton RC .08 .25
460 Greg Johnson RC .02 .10
461 Scott Niedermayer RC .40 1.00
462 Steven Rice RC .02 .10
463 Trevor Kidd RC .40 1.00
464 Dale Craigwell RC .02 .10
465 Kent Manderville RC .02 .10
466 Kris Draper RC .40 1.00
467 Martin Lapointe RC .40 1.00
468 Chris Snell RC .02 .10
469 Pat Falloon RC .02 .10
470 David Harlock RC .02 .10
471 Karl Dykhuis RC .02 .10
472 Mike Craig RC .02 .10
473 Canada's Captains .40 1.00
Kris Draper
Steven Rice
Eric Lindros
474 Brett Hull AS .15 .40
475 Darren Turcotte AS .02 .10
476 Wayne Gretzky AS .40 1.00
477 Steve Yzerman AS .30 .75
478 Theo Fleury AS .02 .10
479 Pat LaFontaine AS .07 .20
480 Trevor Linden AS .07 .20
481 Jeremy Roenick AS .15 .40
482 Scott Stevens AS .07 .20
483 Adam Oates AS .07 .20
484 Vincent Damphousse AS .07 .20
485 Brian Leetch AS .15 .40
486 Kevin Hatcher AS .02 .10
487 Mark Recchi AS .07 .20
488 Rick Tocchet AS .07 .20
489 Ray Bourque AS .07 .20
490 Joe Sakic AS .20 .50
491 Chris Chelios AS .07 .20
492 John Cullen AS .02 .10
493 Cam Neely AS .07 .20
494 Mark Messier AS .15 .40
495 Mike Vernon AS .07 .20
496 Patrick Roy AS .30 .75
497 Al MacInnis AS .07 .20
498 Paul Coffey AS .07 .20
499 Steve Larmer AS .07 .20
500 Checklist 401-500 .02 .10
501 Heroes Checklist .02 .10
502 Red Kelly HERO .02 .10
503 Eric Nesterenko HERO .02 .10
504 Darryl Sittler HERO .02 .10
505 Jim Schoenfeld HERO .02 .10
506 Serge Savard HERO .02 .10
507 Glenn Resch HERO .07 .20
508 Lanny McDonald HERO .02 .10
509 Bobby Clarke HERO .07 .20
510 Phil Esposito HERO .07 .20
511 Harry Howell HERO .02 .10
512 Rod Gilbert HERO .02 .10
513 Pit Martin HERO .02 .10
514 Jimmy Watson HERO .02 .10
515 Denis Potvin HERO .02 .10
516 Robert Ray RC .20 .50
517 Danton Cole RC .02 .10
518 Gino Odjick RC .02 .10
519 Donald Audette RC .20 .50
520 Rick Tabaracci RC .07 .20
521 Sergei Fedorov .30 .75
Johan Garpenlov
(Young Guns Checklist)
522 Kip Miller RC .02 .10
523 Johan Garpenlov RC .02 .10
524 Stephane Morin RC .02 .10
525 Sergei Fedorov RC 1.25 3.00
526 Pavel Bure RC 1.50 4.00
527 Wes Walz RC .02 .10
528 Robert Kron RC .02 .10
529 Ken Hodge Jr. RC .02 .10
530 Gary Valk RC .02 .10
531 Tim Sweeney RC .02 .10
532 Mark Pederson RC .02 .10
533 Robert Reichel RC .15 .40
534 Bobby Holik RC .20 .50
535 Stephane Matteau RC .02 .10
536 Peter Bondra RC .60 1.50
537 Dimitri Khristich RC .02 .10
538 Vladimir Ruzicka RC .02 .10
539 Al Iafrate .07 .20
540 Rick Bennett RC .02 .10
541 Daryl Reaugh RC .02 .10
542 Martin Hostak RC .02 .10
543 Kari Takko RC .07 .20
544 Jocelyn Lemieux RC .02 .10
545 Gretzky's 2000th Point .40 1.00
546 Hull's 50 Goals .15 .40
547 Neil Wilkinson RC .02 .10
548 Bryan Fogarty RC .02 .10
549 Zamboni Machine .07 .20
550 Checklist 501-550 .02 .10

1990-91 Upper Deck French

COMPLETE SET (550) 30.00 60.00
COMP.LO SERIES (400) 15.00 30.00
COMP.HI SERIES (150) 15.00 35.00
COMP.HI FACT.SET (150) 15.00 35.00
*FRENCH: .6X TO 1.5X BASIC UD

1990-91 Upper Deck Holograms

The nine standard-size cards in this set were randomly inserted in 1990-91 Upper Deck foil packs (low and high series). The cards are best described as stereograms because the players show movement when the cards are slowly rotated. On the fronts, the stereograms are enclosed by a frame with rounded corners. The Upper Deck logo and title line "Hockey Superstars" appear in a bar at the top. The backs are blank and can be peeled off to stick the stereogram on a surface. The cards are unnumbered and checklisted below in alphabetical order.

COMPLETE SET (9) 4.00 10.00
1 Wayne Gretzky Stopping .75 2.00
2 Wayne Gretzky Shooting .75 2.00
3 Wayne Gretzky Skating .75 2.00
4 Brett Hull .30 .75
5 Mark Messier .30 .75
6 Mark Messier and Brett Hull .30 .75
7 Mark Messier and Steve Yzerman .40 1.00
8 Steve Yzerman .40 1.00
9 Steve Yzerman .40 1.00

1990-91 Upper Deck Promos

The 1990-91 Upper Deck Promo set is a two-card set featuring Wayne Gretzky and Patrick Roy both numbered as card number 241. The cards were first handed out as samples at the 1990 National Sports Collectors Convention in Arlington. The Arlington National promos were issued as a set in a special screw-down holder commemorating the National; these sets are much more limited and are rarely offered for sale. The photos on the front and back of both of the cards were changed in the regular set, as were the card numbers.

COMPLETE SET (2) 20.00 50.00
241A Wayne Gretzky UER 8.00 20.00
(Wrong height, feet and inches reversed)
241B Patrick Roy UER 6.00 15.00
(Wrong height, feet and inches reversed)

1990-91 Upper Deck Sheets

As an advertising promotion, Upper Deck produced hockey commemorative sheets that were given away during the 1990-91 season at selected games in large arenas. Each sheet measures 8 1/2" by 11" and is printed on card stock. The fronts of the team commemorative sheets feature the team logo and a series of Upper Deck cards of star players on that team. Some of these sheets have a brief history of the team, which is tied in with an Upper Deck advertisement. The All-Star game sheet is distinguished by a hockey stick facsimile autographed by those All-Star players whose cards are displayed. All the sheets have an Upper Deck stamp indicating the production quota; in addition, some of the sheets have the serial number. The backs are blank. The sheets are listed below in chronological order.

COMPLETE SET (11) 64.00 160.00
1 Toronto Maple Leafs 10.00 25.00
vs. Detroit Red Wings
Nov. 17, 1990 (20,000)
Al Iafrate
Ed Olczyk
Vincent Damphousse
Wendel Clark
Gary Leeman
Drake Berehowsky
2 Detroit Red Wings I 6.00 15.00
vs. Boston Bruins
Dec. 4, 1990 (22,000)
Keith Primeau
Shawn Burr
Steve Yzerman
Jimmy Carson
Tim Cheveldae
Steve Chiasson
3 Los Angeles Kings 6.00 15.00
vs. Calgary Flames
Dec. 13, 1990 (19,500)
Steve Duchesne
Luc Robitaille
Rob Blake
Wayne Gretzky
Tony Granato
Tomas Sandstrom
4 New York Rangers I 4.00 10.00
vs. Hartford Whalers
Jan. 13, 1991 (25,700)
Mike Richter
Ray Sheppard
Troy Mallette
Normand Rochefort
Mark Janssens
Dennis Vial
John Ogrodnick
Lindy Ruff
Brian Leetch
5 New York Rangers II 5.00 12.00
vs. Chicago Blackhawks
Jan. 17, 1991 (25,700)
David Shaw
Miloslav Horava
Darren Turcotte
Jan Erixon
Kelly Kisio
Brian Mullen
Bernie Nicholls
John Vanbiesbrouck
James Patrick
6 Campbell All-Stars 12.00 30.00
Chicago Stadium
Jan. 19, 1991 (15,100)
Wayne Gretzky
Chris Chelios
Luc Robitaille
Brett Hull
Al MacInnis
Mike Vernon
7 Wales All-Stars 10.00 25.00
Chicago Stadium
Jan. 19, 1991 (15,100)
Ray Bourque
Rick Tocchet
Joe Sakic
Paul Coffey
Cam Neely
Patrick Roy
8 St. Louis Blues 4.00 10.00
vs. Buffalo Sabres
Jan. 29, 1991 (21,000)
Jeff Brown
Vincent Riendeau
Brent Hull
Paul Cavallini
Curtis Joseph
Gino Cavallini
Adam Oates
Scott Stevens
Rod Brind'Amour
9 Detroit Red Wings II 5.00 12.00
vs. Minnesota North Stars
Feb. 16, 1991 (23,000)
Joey Kocur
Rick Zombo
Sergei Fedorov
Gerard Gallant
Johan Garpenlov
Glen Hanlon
Dave Barr
John Chabot
Bob Probert
10 New York Rangers III 4.00 10.00
vs. New York Islanders
Feb. 18, 1991 (25,700)
Tie Domi
Randy Moller
Mike Gartner
Kevin Miller
Mark Hardy
Jody Hull
Kris King
Bob Froese
Paul Broten
11 All-Rookie Team 8.00 20.00
June 21, 1991 (16,000)
Eric Weinrich
Jaromir Jagr
Ed Belfour
Sergei Fedorov
Rob Blake
Ken Hodge

1991-92 Upper Deck

The 1991-92 UD set was released in two series of 500 and 200 cards, respectively. The front design features action photos with white borders. The player's name and position appear in the top white border, while the team name is given in the bottom white border. Biographical information, statistics, or player profile are displayed on the back alongside a second color photo. The All-Rookie Team and the Star Rookies are marked by the abbreviations ART and SR respectively in the list below. A randomly inserted Glasnost card (SP1) featuring Wayne Gretzky, Brett Hull and Valeri Kamensky and ballots by which fans could vote for their favorite NHL All-Stars were included in foil packs. Special subsets include members of the teams that participated in the IIHF World Junior Championships (650-699).

COMPLETE SET (700) 20.00 40.00
COMP.LO SET (500) 15.00 25.00
COMP.HI SET (200) 5.00 10.00
COMP.HI FACT.SET (200) 6.00 12.00
1 Vladimir Malakhov SS RC .08 .25
2 Alexei Zhamnov SS RC .20 .50
3 Dimitri Filimonov SS RC .01 .05
4 Alexander Semak SS RC .01 .05
5 Slava Kozlov RC .20 .50
6 Sergei Fedorov SS .08 .25
7 Canada Cup Checklist .30 .75
Eric Lindros and
Brett Hull
8 Al MacInnis CC .01 .05
9 Eric Lindros CC .08 .25
10 Bill Ranford CC .02 .10
11 Paul Coffey CC .05 .15
12 Dale Hawerchuk CC .01 .05
13 Wayne Gretzky CC .40 1.00
14 Mark Messier CC .08 .25
15 Steve Larmer CC .01 .05
16 Zigmund Palffy CC RC .75 2.00
17 Josef Beranek CC RC .01 .05
18 Jiri Slegr CC RC .05 .15
19 Martin Rucinsky CC RC .10 .30
20 Jaromir Jagr CC .08 .25
21 Teemu Selanne CC RC 1.25 3.00
22 Janne Laukkanen CC RC .01 .05
23 Markus Ketterer CC RC .01 .05
24 Jari Kurri CC .05 .15
25 Janne Ojanen CC .01 .05
26 Nicklas Lidstrom CC RC 1.00 2.50
27 Tomas Forslund CC RC .01 .05
28 Johan Garpenlov CC .01 .05
29 Niclas Andersson CC RC .01 .05
30 Tomas Sandstrom CC .01 .05
31 Mats Sundin CC .08 .25
32 Mike Modano CC .08 .25
33 Brett Hull CC .08 .25
34 Mike Richter CC .05 .15
35 Brian Leetch CC .05 .15
36 Jeremy Roenick CC .10 .30
37 Chris Chelios CC .05 .15
38 Wayne Gretzky 99 .40 1.00
39 Ed Belfour ART .08 .25
40 Sergei Fedorov ART .08 .25
41 Ken Hodge Jr. ART .01 .05
42 Jaromir Jagr ART .08 .25
43 Rob Blake ART .01 .05
44 Eric Weinrich ART .01 .05
45 The 50/50 Club .40 1.00
Mario Lemieux
Wayne Gretzky
Brett Hull
46 Russ Romaniuk RC .01 .05
47 Mario Lemieux/Geo.Bush .40 1.00
48 Michel Picard RC .01 .05
49 Dennis Vaske .01 .05
50 Eric Murano RC .01 .05
51 Enrico Ciccone .01 .05
52 Shaun Van Allen RC .01 .05
53 Stu Barnes .01 .05
54 Pavel Bure .08 .25
55 Neil Wilkinson .01 .05
56 Tony Hrkac .01 .05
57 Brian Mullen .01 .05
58 Jeff Hackett .05 .15
59 Brian Hayward .05 .15
60 Craig Coxe .01 .05
61 Rob Zettler .01 .05
62 Bob McGill .01 .05
63 Draft Picks Checklist .05 .15
(Martin Lapointe
and Jamie Pushor)
64 Peter Forsberg RC 2.00 5.00
65 Patrick Poulin RC .01 .05
66 Martin Lapointe .05 .15
67 Tyler Wright RC .05 .15
68 Philippe Boucher RC .01 .05
69 Glen Murray RC .40 1.00
70 Martin Rucinsky RC .10 .30
71 Zigmund Palffy RC .75 2.00
72 Jassen Cullimore RC .01 .05
73 Jamie Pushor RC .01 .05
74 Andrew Verner RC .01 .05
75 Jason Dawe RC .01 .05
76 Jamie Matthews RC .01 .05
77 Sandy McCarthy RC .10 .30
78 Cam Neely .05 .15
(Boston Bruins TC)
79 Dale Hawerchuk .01 .05
(Buffalo Sabres TC)
80 Theoren Fleury .01 .05
(Calgary Flames TC)
81 Ed Belfour .08 .25
(Chicago Blackhawks TC)
82 Sergei Fedorov .08 .25
(Detroit Red Wings TC)
83 Esa Tikkanen .01 .05
(Edmonton Oilers TC)
84 John Cullen .01 .05
(Hartford Whalers TC)
85 Tomas Sandstrom .01 .05
(Los Angeles Kings TC)
86 Dave Gagner .01 .05
(Minnesota North Stars TC)
87 Russ Courtnall .01 .05
(Montreal Canadiens TC)
88 John MacLean .01 .05
(New Jersey Devils TC)
89 David Volek .01 .05
(New York Islanders TC)
90 Darren Turcotte .01 .05
(New York Rangers TC)
91 Rick Tocchet .01 .05
(Philadelphia Flyers TC)
92 Mark Recchi .05 .15
(Pittsburgh Penguins TC)
93 Mats Sundin .08 .25
(Quebec Nordiques TC)
94 Adam Oates .01 .05
(St. Louis Blues TC)
95 Neil Wilkinson .01 .05
(San Jose Sharks TC)
96 Dave Ellett .01 .05
(Toronto Maple Leafs TC)
97 Trevor Linden .01 .05
(Vancouver Canucks TC)
98 Kevin Hatcher .01 .05
(Washington Capitals TC)
99 Ed Olczyk .01 .05
(Winnipeg Jets TC)
100 Checklist 1-100 .01 .05
101 Bob Essensa .05 .15
102 Uwe Krupp .01 .05
103 Pelle Eklund .01 .05
104 Christian Ruuttu .01 .05
105 Kevin Dineen .01 .05
106 Phil Housley .05 .15
107 Pat Jablonski RC .05 .15
108 Jarmo Kekalainen RC .05 .15
109 Pat Elynuik .01 .05
110 Corey Millen RC .01 .05
111 Petr Klima .01 .05
112 Mike Ridley .01 .05
113 Peter Stastny .05 .15
114 Jyrki Lumme .01 .05
115 Chris Terreri .05 .15
116 Tom Barrasso .05 .15
117 Bill Ranford .05 .15
118 Peter Ing .05 .15
119 John Tanner .01 .05
120 Troy Gamble .05 .15
121 Stephane Matteau .01 .05
122 Rick Tocchet .05 .15
123 Wes Walz .01 .05
124 Dave Andreychuk .05 .15
125 Mike Craig .01 .05
126 Dale Hawerchuk .05 .15
127 Dean Evason .01 .05
128 Craig Janney .05 .15
129 Tim Cheveldae .05 .15
130 Rick Wamsley .05 .15
131 Peter Bondra .05 .15
132 Scott Stevens .05 .15
133 Kelly Miller .01 .05
134 Mats Sundin .08 .25
135 Mick Vukota .01 .05
136 Vincent Damphousse .01 .05
137 Patrick Roy .50 1.25
138 Hubie McDonough .01 .05
139 Curtis Joseph .08 .25
140 Brent Sutter .01 .05
141 Tomas Sandstrom .01 .05
142 Kevin Miller .01 .05
143 Mike Ricci .08 .25
144 Sergei Fedorov .20 .50
145 Luc Robitaille .05 .15
146 Steve Yzerman .50 1.25
147 Andy Moog .08 .25
148 Rob Blake .05 .15
149 Kirk Muller .01 .05
150 Daniel Berthiaume .05 .15
151 John Druce .01 .05
152 Garry Valk .01 .05
153 Brian Leetch .08 .25
154 Kevin Stevens .01 .05
155 Darren Turcotte .01 .05
156 Mario Lemieux .50 1.25
157 Dimitri Khristich .01 .05
158 Brian Glynn .01 .05
159 Benoit Hogue UER .01 .05
(Back photo actually Dean Kennedy)
160 Mike Modano .25 .60
161 Jimmy Carson .01 .05
162 Steve Thomas .01 .05
163 Mike Vernon .05 .15
164 Ed Belfour .25 .60
165 Joel Otto .01 .05
166 Jeremy Roenick .10 .30
167 Johan Garpenlov .01 .05
168 Russ Courtnall .01 .05
169 John MacLean .05 .15
170 J.J. Daigneault .01 .05
171 Sylvain Lefebvre .01 .05
172 Tony Granato .01 .05
173 David Volek .01 .05
174 Trevor Linden .05 .15
175 Mike Richter .08 .25
176 Pierre Turgeon .05 .15
177 Paul Coffey .08 .25
178 Jan Erixon .01 .05
179 Rick Vaive .01 .05
180 Dave Gagner .01 .05
181 Thomas Steen .01 .05
182 Esa Tikkanen .01 .05
183 Sean Burke .05 .15
184 Paul Cavallini .01 .05
185 Alexei Kasatonov .01 .05
186 Kevin Lowe .05 .15
187 Gino Cavallini .01 .05
188 Doug Gilmour .05 .15
189 Rod Brind'Amour .08 .25
190 Gary Roberts .05 .15
191 Kirk McLean .05 .15
192 Kevin Haller RC .01 .05
193 Pat Verbeek .01 .05
194 Dave Snuggerud .01 .05
195 Gino Odjick .01 .05
196 Dave Ellett .01 .05
197 Don Beaupre .05 .15
198 Rob Brown .01 .05
199 Marty McSorley .01 .05
200 Checklist 101-200 .01 .05
201 Joe Mullen .05 .15
202 Dave Capuano .01 .05
203 Paul Stanton .01 .05
204 Terry Carkner .01 .05
205 Jon Casey .05 .15
206 Ken Wregget .05 .15
207 Gaetan Duchesne .01 .05
208 Cliff Ronning .01 .05
209 Dale Hunter .01 .05
210 Danton Cole .01 .05
211 Jeff Brown .01 .05
212 Mike Foligno .01 .05
213 Michel Mongeau .01 .05
214 Doug Brown .01 .05
215 Todd Krygier .01 .05
216 Jon Morris .01 .05
217 David Reid .01 .05
218 John McIntyre .01 .05
219 Guy Lafleur's Farewell .08 .25
220 Vincent Riendeau .05 .15
221 Tim Hunter .01 .05
222 Dave McLlwain .01 .05
223 Robert Reichel .01 .05
224 Glenn Healy .05 .15
225 Robert Kron .01 .05
226 Patrick Flatley .01 .05
227 Petr Nedved .05 .15
228 Mark Janssens .01 .05
229 Michal Pivonka .01 .05
230 Ulf Samuelsson .01 .05
231 Zarley Zalapski .01 .05
232 Neal Broten .05 .15
233 Bobby Holik .05 .15
234 Cam Neely .08 .25
235 John Cullen .01 .05
236 Brian Bellows .01 .05
237 Chris Nilan .01 .05
238 Mikael Andersson .01 .05
239 Bob Probert .05 .15
240 Teppo Numminen .01 .05
241 Peter Zezel .01 .05
242 Denis Savard .05 .15
243 Al MacInnis .05 .15
244 Stephane Richer .05 .15
245 Theo Fleury .01 .05
246 Mark Messier .08 .25
247 Mike Gartner .05 .15
248 Darren Puppa .05 .15
249 Louie DeBrusk RC .01 .05
250 Glenn Anderson .05 .15
251 Ken Hodge Jr. .01 .05
252 Adam Oates .05 .15
253 Pat LaFontaine .08 .25
254 Adam Creighton .01 .05
255 Ray Bourque .20 .50
256 Jaromir Jagr .20 .50
257 Steve Larmer .05 .15
258 Keith Primeau .01 .05
259 Mike Liut .05 .15
260 Brian Propp .01 .05
261 Stephan Lebeau .01 .05
262 Kelly Hrudey .05 .15
263 Joe Nieuwendyk .05 .15
264 Grant Fuhr .08 .25
265 Guy Carbonneau .05 .15
266 Martin Gelinas .01 .05
267 Alexander Mogilny .08 .25
268 Adam Graves .05 .15
269 Anatoli Semenov .01 .05
270 Dave Taylor .05 .15
271 Dirk Graham .01 .05
272 Gary Leeman .01 .05
273 Valeri Kamensky RC .05 .15
274 Marc Bureau .01 .05
275 James Patrick .01 .05
276 Dino Ciccarelli .05 .15
277 Ron Tugnutt .05 .15
278 Paul Ysebaert .01 .05
279 Laurie Boschman .01 .05
280 Dave Manson .01 .05
281 Dave Chyzowski .01 .05
282 Shayne Corson .01 .05
283 Steve Chiasson .01 .05
284 Craig MacTavish .01 .05
285 Petr Svoboda .01 .05
286 Craig Simpson .01 .05
287 Ron Hoover RC .01 .05
288 Vladimir Ruzicka .01 .05
289 Randy Wood .01 .05
290 Doug Lidster .01 .05
291 Kay Whitmore .05 .15
292 Bruce Driver .01 .05
293 Bobby Smith .05 .15
294 Claude Lemieux .05 .15
295 Mark Tinordi .01 .05
296 Mark Osborne .01 .05
297 Brad Shaw .01 .05
298 Igor Larionov .05 .15
299 Ron Francis .05 .15
300 Checklist 201-300 .01 .05
301 Bob Kudelski .01 .05
302 Larry Murphy .05 .15
303 Brent Ashton .01 .05
304 Brad Jones .01 .05
305 Gord Donnelly .01 .05
306 Murray Craven .01 .05
307 Chris Dahlquist .01 .05
308 Jim Paek RC .01 .05
309 Ron Sutter .01 .05
310 Mike Tomlak .01 .05
311 Ray Ferraro .01 .05
312 Dave Hannan .01 .05
313 Randy McKay .01 .05
314 Rod Langway .01 .05
315 Shawn Burr .01 .05
316 Calle Johansson .01 .05
317 Rich Sutter .01 .05
318 Al Iafrate .05 .15
319 Bob Bassen .01 .05
320 Mike Krushelnyski .01 .05
321 Sergei Makarov .01 .05
322 Darrin Shannon .01 .05
323 Terry Yake .01 .05
324 John Vanbiesbrouck .05 .15
325 Peter Sidorkiewicz .05 .15
326 Troy Mallette .01 .05
327 Ron Hextall .05 .15
328 Mathieu Schneider .01 .05
329 Bryan Trottier .08 .25
330 Kris King .01 .05
331 Daniel Marois .01 .05
332 Shayne Stevenson .01 .05
333 Joe Sakic .25 .60
334 Petri Skriko .01 .05
335 Dominik Hasek RC 1.25 3.00
336 Scott Pearson .01 .05
337 Bryan Fogarty .01 .05
338 Don Sweeney .01 .05
339 Rick Tabaracci .05 .15
340 Steven Finn .01 .05
341 Gary Suter .01 .05
342 Troy Crowder .01 .05
343 Jim Hrivnak .05 .15
344 Eric Weinrich .01 .05
345 John LeClair RC .40 1.00
346 Mark Recchi .08 .25
347 Dan Currie RC .01 .05
348 Ulf Dahlen .01 .05
349 Robert Ray .01 .05
350 Steve Smith .01 .05
351 Shawn Antoski .01 .05
352 Cam Russell .01 .05
353 Scott Thornton .01 .05
354 Chris Chelios .08 .25
355 Sergei Nemchinov .01 .05
356 Bernie Nicholls .05 .15
357 Jeff Norton .01 .05
358 Dan Quinn .01 .05
359 Michel Petit .01 .05
360 Eric Desjardins .05 .15
361 Kevin Hatcher .01 .05
362 Jiri Sejba .01 .05
363 Mark Pederson .01 .05
364 Jeff Lazaro RC .01 .05
365 Alexei Gusarov RC .05 .15
366 Jari Kurri .08 .25
367 Owen Nolan .08 .25
368 Clint Malarchuk .05 .15
369 Patrik Sundstrom .01 .05
370 Glen Wesley .01 .05
371 Wayne Presley .01 .05
372 Craig Muni .01 .05
373 Brent Fedyk .01 .05
374 Michel Goulet .05 .15
375 Tim Sweeney .01 .05
376 Gary Shuchuk .01 .05
377 Andre Racicot RC .05 .15
378 Jay Mazur RC .01 .05
379 Andrew Cassels .01 .05
380 Brian Noonan .01 .05
381 Sergei Kharin .01 .05
382 Derek King .01 .05
383 Fredrik Olausson .01 .05
384 Tom Fergus .01 .05
385 Zdeno Ciger .01 .05
386 Wendel Clark .05 .15
387 Ed Olczyk .01 .05
388 Basil McRae .01 .05
389 Tom Fitzgerald .01 .05
390 Ray Sheppard .01 .05
391 Bob Sweeney .01 .05
392 Gord Murphy .01 .05
393 John Chabot .01 .05
394 Jeff Beukeboom .01 .05
395 Rick Zombo .01 .05
396 Kjell Samuelsson .01 .05
397 Garth Butcher .01 .05
398 Phil Bourque .01 .05
399 Lou Franceschetti .01 .05
400 Checklist 301-400 .01 .05
401 Kevin Todd RC .01 .05
402 Ken Baumgartner .01 .05
403 Peter Douris .01 .05
404 Jiri Latal .01 .05
405 Marc Potvin RC .01 .05
406 Gary Nylund .01 .05
407 Yvon Corriveau .01 .05
408 Sheldon Kennedy .01 .05
409 David Shaw .01 .05
410 Slava Fetisov .01 .05
411 Mario Doyon RC .01 .05
412 Jamie Macoun .01 .05
413 Curtis Leschyshyn .01 .05
414 Mike Peluso RC .01 .05
415 Brian Benning .01 .05
416 Stu Grimson RC .05 .15
417 Ken Sabourin .01 .05
418 Luke Richardson .01 .05
419 Ken Quinney RC .01 .05
420 Mike Donnelly RC .01 .05
421 Darcy Loewen RC .01 .05
422 Brian Skrudland .01 .05
423 Joel Savage RC .01 .05
424 Adrien Plavsic .01 .05
425 Jergus Baca .01 .05
426 Greg Adams .01 .05
427 Tom Chorske .01 .05
428 Scott Scissons .01 .05
429 Dale Kushner .01 .05
430 Todd Richards .01 .05

431 Kip Miller .01 .05
432 Jason Prosofsky RC .01 .05
433 Stephane Morin .01 .05
434 Brian McReynolds .01 .05
435 Ken Daneyko .01 .05
436 Chris Joseph .01 .05
437 Wayne Gretzky .60 1.50
438 Jocelyn Lemieux .01 .05
439 Garry Galley .01 .05
440 Super Rookie Checklist .30 .75
Tony Amonte&
Doug Weight&
and Steven Rice
441 Steven Rice SR .01 .05
442 Patrice Brisebois SR .01 .05
443 Jimmy Waite SR .05 .15
444 Doug Weight SR RC .40 1.00
445 Nelson Emerson SR .01 .05
446 Jarrod Skalde SR RC .01 .05
447 Jamie Leach SR .01 .05
448 Gilbert Dionne SR RC .05 .15
449 Trevor Kidd SR .05 .15
450 Tony Amonte SR RC .40 1.00
451 Pat Murray SR .01 .05
452 Stephane Fiset SR .05 .15
453 Patrick Lebeau RC .01 .05
454 Chris Taylor SR RC .01 .05
455 Chris Tancill SR RC .01 .05
456 Mark Greig SR .01 .05
457 Mike Sillinger SR .01 .05
458 Ken Sutton RC .01 .05
459 Len Barrie SR RC .01 .05
460 Felix Potvin SR .40 1.00
461 Brian Sakic SR RC .01 .05
462 Slava Kozlov RC .20 .50
463 Matt DelGuidice RC .01 .05
464 Brett Hull .20 .50
465 Norm Foster .01 .05
466 Alexander Godynyuk RC .01 .05
467 Geoff Courtnall .05 .15
468 Frantisek Kucera .01 .05
469 Benoit Brunet RC .01 .05
470 Mark Vermette .01 .05
471 Tim Watters .01 .05
472 Paul Ranheim .01 .05
473 Martin Hostak .01 .05
474 Joe Murphy .01 .05
475 Claude Boivin RC .01 .05
476 John Ogrodnick .01 .05
477 Doug Bodger .01 .05
478 Shawn Cronin .01 .05
479 Mark Hunter .01 .05
480 Dave Tippett .01 .05
481 Rob DiMaio .01 .05
482 Lyle Odelein .01 .05
483 Joe Reekie .01 .05
484 Randy Velischek .01 .05
485 Myles O'Connor RC .01 .05
486 Craig Wolanin .01 .05
487 Mike McPhee .01 .05
488 Claude Lapointe RC .01 .05
489 Troy Loney .01 .05
490 Bob Beers .01 .05
491 Sylvain Couturier .01 .05
492 Kimbi Daniels .01 .05
493 Darryl Shannon .01 .05
494 Jim McKenzie .01 .05
495 Don Gibson RC .01 .05
496 Ralph Barahona RC .01 .05
497 Murray Baron .01 .05
498 Yves Racine .01 .05
499 Larry Robinson .05 .15
500 Checklist 401-500 .01 .05
501 Canada Cup Checklist .40 1.00
Paul Coffey and
Wayne Gretzky
502 Dirk Graham CC .01 .05
503 Rick Tocchet CC .01 .05
504 Eric Desjardins CC .01 .05
505 Shayne Corson CC .01 .05
506 Theo Fleury CC .01 .05
507 Luc Robitaille CC .05 .15
508 Tony Granato CC .01 .05
509 Eric Weinrich CC .01 .05
510 Gary Suter CC .01 .05
511 Kevin Hatcher CC .01 .05
512 Craig Janney CC .01 .05
513 Darren Turcotte CC .01 .05
514 Chris Winnes RC .01 .05
515 Kelly Kisio .01 .05
516 Joe Day RC .01 .05
517 Ed Courtenay RC .01 .05
518 Andrei Lomakin .01 .05
519 Kirk Muller .01 .05
520 Rick Lessard RC .01 .05
521 Scott Thornton .01 .05
522 Luke Richardson .01 .05
523 Mike Eagles .01 .05
524 Mike McNeill .01 .05
525 Ken Priestlay .01 .05
526 Louie DeBrusk .01 .05
527 Dave McLlwain .01 .05
528 Gary Leeman .01 .05
529 Adam Foote RC .15 .40
530 Kevin Dineen .01 .05
531 David Reid .01 .05
532 Arturs Irbe .08 .25
533 Mark Osiecki RC .01 .05
534 Steve Thomas .01 .05
535 Vincent Damphousse .01 .05
536 Stephane Richer .05 .15
537 Jarmo Myllys .01 .05
538 Carey Wilson .01 .05
539 Scott Stevens .05 .15
540 Uwe Krupp .01 .05
541 Dave Christian .01 .05
542 Scott Mellanby .01 .05
543 Peter Ahola RC .01 .05
544 Todd Elik .01 .05
545 Mark Messier .15 .40
546 Dwian Hatcher .08 .16
547 Rod Brind'Amour .08 .25
548 Dave Manson .01 .05
549 Darryl Sydor .05 .15
550 Paul Broten .01 .05
551 Andrew Cassels .01 .05
552 Tom Draper RC .05 .15
553 Grant Fuhr .08 .25
554 Pierre Turgeon .05 .15
555 Pavel Bure .08 .25
556 Pat LaFontaine .08 .25
557 Dave Thomlinson .01 .05
558 Doug Gilmour .05 .15
559 Craig Billington RC .05 .15
560 Dean Evason .01 .05
561 Brendan Shanahan .08 .25
562 Mike Hough .01 .05
563 Dan Quinn .01 .05
564 Jeff Daniels .01 .05
565 Troy Murray .01 .05
566 Bernie Nicholls .05 .15
567 Randy Burridge .01 .05
568 Todd Hartje RC .01 .05
569 Charlie Huddy .01 .05
570 Steve Duchesne .01 .05
571 Sergio Momesso .01 .05
572 Brian Lawton .01 .05
573 Ray Sheppard .01 .05
574 Adam Graves .05 .15
575 Rollie Melanson .05 .15
576 Steve Kasper .01 .05
577 Jim Sandlak .01 .05
578 Pat MacLeod RC .01 .05
579 Sylvain Turgeon .01 .05
580 James Black RC .01 .05
581 Darrin Shannon .01 .05
582 Todd Krygier .01 .05
583 Dominic Roussel RC .05 .15
584 Young Guns Checklist .20 .50
Nicklas Lidstrom
585 Donald Audette YG .01 .05
586 Tomas Forslund YG .01 .05
587 Nicklas Lidstrom YG .40 1.00
588 Geoff Sanderson RC .08 .25
589 Valeri Zelepukin YG RC .01 .05
590 Igor Ulanov YG RC .05 .15
591 Corey Foster YG RC .01 .05
592 Dan Lambert YG RC .01 .05
593 Pat Falloon YG .01 .05
594 Vladimir Konstantinov YG RC .40 1.00
595 Josef Beranek YG .01 .05
596 Brad May YG .01 .05
597 Jeff Odgers RC .01 .05
598 Rob Pearson RC .01 .05
599 Luciano Borsato YG RC .01 .05
600 Checklist 501-600 .01 .05
601 Peter Douris .01 .05
602 Mark Fitzpatrick .05 .15
603 Randy Gilhen .01 .05
604 Corey Millen .01 .05
605 Jason Cirone RC .01 .05
606 Kyosti Karjalainen RC .01 .05
607 Garry Galley .01 .05
608 Brent Thompson RC .01 .05
609 Alexander Godynyuk .01 .05
610 All-Star Checklist .08 .25
Mark Messier
Mike Richter
Brian Leetch
611 Mario Lemieux AS .30 .75
612 Brian Leetch AS .05 .15
613 Kevin Stevens AS .01 .05
614 Patrick Roy AS .30 .75
615 Paul Coffey AS .05 .15
616 Joe Sakic AS .08 .25
617 Jaromir Jagr AS .08 .25
618 Alexander Mogilny AS .05 .15
619 Owen Nolan AS .05 .15
620 Mark Messier AS .08 .25
621 Wayne Gretzky AS .40 1.00
622 Brett Hull AS .08 .25
623 Luc Robitaille AS .05 .15
624 Phil Housley AS .01 .05
625 Ed Belfour AS .08 .25
626 Steve Yzerman AS .25 .60
627 Adam Oates AS .01 .05
628 Trevor Linden AS .01 .05
629 Jeremy Roenick AS .10 .30
630 Theo Fleury AS .01 .05
631 Sergei Fedorov AS .08 .25
632 Al MacInnis AS .01 .05
633 Ray Bourque AS .08 .25
634 Mike Richter AS .05 .15
635 Al Secord HERO .05 .15
636 Marcel Dionne HERO .08 .25
637 Ken Morrow HERO .05 .15
638 Guy Lafleur HERO .08 .25
639 Ed Mio HERO .01 .05
640 Clark Gillies HERO .05 .15
641 Bob Nystrom HERO .05 .15
642 Pete Peeters HERO .05 .15
643 Ulf Nilsson HERO .05 .15
644 Stephan Lebeau and .01 .05
Patrick Lebeau
645 The Sutter Brothers .01 .05
Brian Sutter
Duane Sutter
Darryl Sutter
Brent Sutter
Rich Sutter
Ron Sutter
646 Gino Cavallini and .01 .05
Paul Cavallini
647 Valeri Bure .08 .25
and Pavel Bure
648 Chris Ferraro and .05 .15
Peter Ferraro
649 World Jr. Checklist .08 .25
CCCP Team Photo
650 Darius Kasparaitis RC .20 .50
651 Alexei Yashin RC .30 .75
652 Nikolai Khabibulin RC .75 2.00
653 Denis Metlyuk RC .01 .05
654 Konstantin Korotkov RC .01 .05
655 Alexei Kovalev RC .60 1.50
656 Alexander Kuzminsky RC .01 .05
657 Alexander Cherbayev RC .01 .05
658 Sergei Krivokrasov RC .05 .15
659 Sergei Zholtok RC .05 .15
660 Alexei Zhitnik RC .08 .25
661 Sandis Ozolinch RC .20 .50
662 Boris Mironov RC .08 .25
663 Pauli Jaks RC .05 .15
664 Gaetan Voisard RC .01 .05
665 Nicola Celio RC .01 .05
666 Marc Weber RC .01 .05
667 Bernhard Schumperli RC .01 .05
668 Laurent Bucher RC .01 .05
669 Michael Blaha RC .01 .05
670 Tiziano Gianini RC .01 .05
671 Marko Kiprusoff RC .05 .15
672 Janne Gronvall RC .01 .05
673 Juha Ylonen RC .08 .25
674 Sami Kapanen RC .40 1.00
675 Marko Tuomainen RC .05 .15
676 Jarkko Varvio RC .01 .05
677 Tuomas Gronman RC .01 .05
678 Andreas Naumann RC .01 .05
679 Steffen Ziesche RC .01 .05
680 Jens Schwabe RC .01 .05
681 Thomas Schubert RC .01 .05
682 Hans-Jorg Mayer RC .01 .05
683 Marc Seliger RC .08 .25
684 Trevor Kidd RC .05 .15
685 Martin Lapointe RC .08 .25
686 Tyler Wright RC .05 .15
687 Kimbi Daniels RC .01 .05
688 Karl Dykhuis RC .01 .05
689 Jeff Nelson RC .01 .05
690 Jassen Cullimore RC .01 .05
691 Turner Stevenson RC .01 .05
692 Scott Lachance RC .05 .15
693 Mike Dunham RC .40 1.00
694 Brent Bilodeau RC .01 .05
695 Ryan Sittler RC .01 .05
696 Peter Ferraro RC .08 .25
697 Pat Peake RC .01 .05
698 Keith Tkachuk RC .75 2.00
699 Brian Rolston RC .40 1.00
700 Checklist 601-700 .01 .05
SP1 Glasnost On Ice 1.50 4.00
Wayne Gretzky
Valeri Kamensky
Brett Hull

1991-92 Upper Deck French

COMPLETE SET (700) 20.00 40.00
COMPLETE LO SET (500) 15.00 30.00
COMPLETE HI SET (200) 5.00 12.00
COMPLETE HI FACT.SET (200) 5.00 12.00
*FRENCH VERSION: SAME VALUE

1991-92 Upper Deck Award Winner Holograms

This nine-card standard-size hologram set features award-winning hockey players with their respective trophies for most outstanding performance. The name of the award appears in the left border stripe, while the player's name and position are printed in the bottom border stripe. The backs have a color photo of the player with the trophy as well as biographical information. The holograms were randomly inserted into foil packs and subdivided into three groups: AW1-AW3 (low series); AW5-AW7 (late winter, low series); and AW4, AW8, and AW9 (high series).

COMPLETE SET (9) 3.00 8.00
AW1 Wayne Gretzky 1.00 2.50
Art Ross Trophy
AW2 Ed Belfour .40 1.00
William M. Jennings
Trophy
AW3 Brett Hull .30 .75
Hart Trophy
AW4 Ed Belfour .40 1.00
Calder Trophy
AW5A Ray Bourque ERR .30 .75
Norris Trophy
(No best defenseman
notation on back)
AW5B Ray Bourque COR .30 .75
Norris Trophy
(Best defenseman
notation on back)
AW6 Wayne Gretzky 1.00 2.50
Lady Byng Trophy
AW7 Ed Belfour .40 1.00
Vezina Trophy
AW8 Dirk Graham .20 .50
Frank J. Selke Trophy
AW9 Mario Lemieux .75 2.00

1991-92 Upper Deck Box Bottoms

These five box bottoms are printed on glossy cover stock and measure approximately 5 1/2" by 9". Though they were issued with both French and English hockey sets, the New York Rangers' Mark Messier box bottom was available only with the high series. Each bottom features a four-color action photo enclosed by white borders. The Upper Deck logo, player's name, and position appear above the photo while the team name and the 75th NHL Anniversary logo appear beneath the picture superimposed on small black lines. The box bottoms are unnumbered and checklisted below alphabetically.

COMPLETE SET (5) 2.00 5.00
1 Wayne Gretzky .75 2.00
2 Brett Hull .25 .60
3 Mark Messier .25 .60
4 Mark Messier .40 1.00
5 Steve Yzerman .60 1.50

1991-92 Upper Deck Brett Hull Heroes

This ten-card standard-size set was inserted in 1991-92 Upper Deck low series foil packs (French as well as English editions). On a light gray textured background, the fronts have color player photos cut out and superimposed on an emblem. The textured background is enclosed by thin tan border stripes. On the same textured background, the backs summarize various moments in Hull's career. Brett Hull personally signed and numbered 2,500 of the checklist card number 9; these autographed cards were randomly inserted in packs. The signed cards are numbered by hand on the front.

COMPLETE SET (10) 5.00 12.00
COMMON HULL HEROES (1-9) .40 1.00
*FRENCH: 4X TO 1X BASIC INSERTS
9AU Brett Hull AU/2500 25.00 60.00
NNO Hull Header SP 2.00 5.00

1991-92 Upper Deck Euro-Stars

This 18-card standard-size set spotlights NHL players from Finland, the former Soviet Union, Czechoslovakia, and Sweden. One Euro-Star card was inserted in each 1991-92 Upper Deck Hockey jumbo pack in both English and French editions. The front design of the cards is the same as the regular issue except that a Euro-Stars emblem featuring a segment of the player's homeland flag, appears in the lower right corner. On a textured background, the backs present career summary.

COMPLETE SET (18) 3.00 8.00
*FRENCH: 4X TO 1X BASIC INSERTS
1 Jarmo Kekalainen .08 .25
2 Alexander Mogilny .30 .75
3 Bobby Holik .08 .25
4 Anatoli Semenov .08 .25
5 Petr Nedved .20 .50
6 Jaromir Jagr .60 1.50
7 Tomas Sandstrom .20 .50
8 Robert Kron .08 .25
9 Sergei Fedorov .60 1.50
10 Esa Tikkanen .20 .50
11 Christian Ruuttu .08 .25
12 Peter Bondra .30 .75
13 Mats Sundin .50 1.25
14 Dominik Hasek 1.25 3.00
15 Johan Garpenlov .08 .25
16 Alexander Godynyuk .08 .25
17 Ulf Samuelsson .08 .25
18 Igor Larionov .20 .50

1991-92 Upper Deck Sheets

For the second straight year, Upper Deck produced hockey commemorative sheets that were given away during the 1991-92 season at selected games in large arenas. Each sheet measures approximately 8 1/2" by 11" and is printed on card stock. The fronts of the team commemorative sheets feature the team logo and a series of Upper Deck cards of star players on that team. The Alumni sheet features player portraits by sports artist Alan Studt. All the sheets have an Upper Deck stamp indicating the production quota and the serial number. The backs are blank. The sheets are listed below in chronological order.

COMPLETE SET (19) 90.00 225.00
1 Los Angeles Kings 25th 6.00 15.00
vs. Edmonton Oilers
Oct. 8, 1991 (20,000)
Rob Blake
Jari Kurri
Tomas Sandstrom
Wayne Gretzky
Marty McSorley
Kelly Hrudey
2 New York Rangers I 4.00 10.00
vs. Calgary Flames
Nov. 4, 1991 (21,500)
Randy Moller
Paul Broten
Jody Hull
Jan Erixon
Mark Janssens
Brian Leetch
Mike Gartner
Joey Kocur
Mark Hardy
3 St. Louis Blues 4.00 10.00
vs. Philadelphia Flyers
Nov. 5, 1991 (21,500)
Adam Oates
Nelson Emerson
Paul Cavallini
Curtis Joseph
Brett Hull
Jeff Brown
4 New Jersey Devils 10th 4.00 10.00
vs. Chicago Blackhawks
Dec. 21, 1991 (24,000)
New Jersey Devils
Tenth Anniversary
Walt Poddubny
John MacLean
Scott Stevens
Peter Stastny
Claude Lemieux
Stephane Richer
5 Calgary Flames I 5.00 12.00
Tenth Annual Clinic
Dec. 27, 1991 (26,000)
Robert Reichel
Doug Gilmour
Theoren Fleury
Al MacInnis
Joel Otto
Gary Roberts
6 New York Rangers II 4.00 10.00
vs. St. Louis Blues
Jan. 8, 1992 (23,000)
Mike Richter
Kris King
Tie Domi
Tony Amonte
Mark Messier
Joe Cirella
James Patrick
Sergei Nemchinov
7 Philadelphia Flyers I 4.00 10.00
Alumni vs. NHL Heroes
Jan. 17, 1992 (21,000)
Bill Barber
Bill Clement
Keith Allen
Joe Watson
Bobby Clarke
Bernie Parent
8 Campbell All-Stars 10.00 25.00
Philadelphia Spectrum
Jan. 18, 1992 (13,500)
Brett Hull
Al MacInnis
Luc Robitaille
Chris Chelios
Wayne Gretzky
Ed Belfour
9 Wales All-Stars 10.00 25.00
Philadelphia Spectrum
Jan. 18, 1992 (13,500)
Mario Lemieux
Patrick Roy
Kevin Stevens
Paul Coffey
Jaromir Jagr
Ray Bourque
10 Detroit Red Wings I 5.00 12.00
vs. Toronto Maple Leafs
Feb. 7, 1992 (25,000)
Niklas Lidstrom
Steve Yzerman
Tim Cheveldae
Bob Probert
Steve Chiasson
Sergei Fedorov
11 Washington Capitals 4.00 10.00
vs. New York Rangers
Feb. 7, 1992 (20,500)
Kevin Hatcher
Dimitri Khristich
Calle Johansson
Michal Pivonka
Al Iafrate
Dino Ciccarelli
12 Minnesota North Stars 8.00 20.00
Dream Team
Feb.15, 1992 (19,000)
Brian Bellows
Neal Broten
Bill Goldsworthy
Curt Giles
Jon Casey
Craig Hartsburg
13 Pittsburgh Penguins 8.00 20.00
vs. Toronto Maple Leafs
Feb. 18, 1992 (21,000)
Kevin Stevens
Jaromir Jagr
Ulf Samuelsson
Tom Barrasso
Mark Recchi
Joe Mullen
14 New York Rangers III 4.00 10.00
vs. Philadelphia Flyers
Feb. 23, 1992 (23,000)
John Vanbiesbrouck
Kris King
Normand Rochefort
John Ogrodnick
Mark Messier
Jeff Beukeboom
Adam Graves
Darren Turcotte
15 Edmonton Oilers 5.00 12.00
vs. Philadelphia Flyers
Feb. 28, 1992 (22,000)
Kevin Lowe
Craig MacTavish
Esa Tikkanen
Bill Ranford
Craig Simpson
Vincent Damphousse
16 Minnesota North Stars 8.00 20.00
vs. Detroit Red Wings
March 14, 1992 (19,000)
Bobby Smith
Dave Gagner
Mike Modano
Ulf Dahlen
Mark Tinordi
Basil McRae
17 Calgary Flames II 5.00 12.00
vs. Minnesota North Stars
Eighth Fan
Appreciation Night
March 28, 1992 (24,000)
Mike Vernon
Joe Nieuwendyk
Gary Suter
Paul Ranheim
Sergei Makarov
Carey Wilson
18 Detroit Red Wings II 4.00 10.00
vs. Chicago Blackhawks
March 31, 1992 (25,000)
Paul Ysebaert
Yves Racine
Vladimir Konstantinov
Ray Sheppard
Kevin Miller
Jimmy Carson
19 Philadelphia Flyers II 4.00 10.00
April 5, 1992 (21,000)
Mike Ricci
Kevin Dineen
Garry Galley
Steve Duchesne
Rod Brind'Amour
Claude Boivin

1992-93 Upper Deck

The 1992-93 Upper Deck hockey set contains 640 standard-size cards. The set was released in two series of 440 and 200 cards, respectively. Action photos on the fronts are bordered by the player's name and team logo at the bottom. Special subsets featured include Team Checklists (1-24), Bloodlines (35-39), '92 World Juniors (222-236), Russian Stars from Moscow Dynamo (333-353), Rookie Report (354-368), '92 World Championships (369-386), Team USA (392-397), Star Rookies (398-422), and Award Winners (431-440). Pavel Bure is showcased on a special card (SP2) that was randomly inserted in first series foil and jumbo packs. Another special card (SP3) titled "World Champions", honors Canada's 1993 IIHF World Junior Champions team. High series subsets featured are Lethal Lines (453-456), Young Guns (554-583), and World Junior Champions (584-619). The World Junior Champions subset is grouped according to national teams as follows: Canada (585-594), Sweden (595-599), Czechoslovakia (600-604), USA (605-609), Russia (610-614), and Finland (615-619). An Upper Deck Profiles (620-640) subset closes out the set. Card No. 88, Eric Lindros, was short-printed (SP) as it was not included in second series packaging. This was brought about because of a controversy over Lindros' head being superimposed on a teammate's body.

COMPLETE SET (640) 25.00 50.00
COMPLETE LO SET (440) 10.00 20.00
COMPLETE HI SET (200) 15.00 30.00
1 Andy Moog TC .02 .10
2 Donald Audette TC .01 .05
3 Tomas Forslund TC .01 .05
4 Steve Larmer TC .01 .05
5 Tim Cheveldae TC .01 .05
6 Vincent Damphousse TC .01 .05
7 Pat Verbeek TC .01 .05
8 Luc Robitaille TC .02 .10
9 Mike Modano TC .07 .20
10 Denis Savard TC .01 .05
11 Kevin Todd TC .01 .05
12 Ray Ferraro TC .01 .05
13 Tony Amonte TC .05 .15
14 Peter Sidorkiewicz TC .01 .05
15 Rod Brind'Amour TC .01 .05
16 Jaromir Jagr TC .08 .25
17 Owen Nolan TC .01 .05
18 Nelson Emerson TC .01 .05
19 Pat Falloon TC .01 .05
20 Anatoli Semenov TC .01 .05
21 Doug Gilmour TC .02 .10
22 Kirk McLean TC .01 .05
23 Don Beaupre TC .02 .10
24 Phil Housley TC .01 .05
25 Wayne Gretzky .60 1.50
26 Mario Lemieux .40 1.00
27 Valeri Kamensky .01 .05
28 Jaromir Jagr .15 .40
29 Brett Hull .15 .40
30 Neil Wilkinson .01 .05
31 Dominic Roussel .02 .10
32 Kent Manderville .01 .05
33 Gretzky 1500 .40 1.00
34 Presidents' Cup .08 .25
35 Kip Miller BL .01 .05
Kevin Miller
Kelly Miller
36 Brian Sakic BL .08 .25
Joe Sakic
37 Wayne Gretzky BL .30 .75
Keith Gretzky
Brent Gretzky
38 Jamie Linden BL .02 .10
Trevor Linden
39 Geoff Courtnall BL .01 .05
Russ Courtnall
40 Dale Craigwell .01 .05
41 Peter Ahola .01 .05
42 Robert Reichel .01 .05
43 Chris Terreri .02 .10
44 John Vanbiesbrouck .02 .10
45 Alexander Semak .01 .05
46 Mike Sullivan .01 .05
47 Bob Sweeney .01 .05
48 Corey Millen .01 .05
49 Murray Craven .01 .05
50 Dennis Vaske .01 .05
51 David Williams RC .01 .05
52 Tom Fitzgerald .01 .05
53 Corey Foster .01 .05
54 Al Iafrate .02 .10
55 John LeClair .20 .50
56 Stephane Richer .02 .10
57 Claude Boivin .01 .05
58 Rick Tabaracci .02 .10
59 Johan Garpenlov .01 .05
60 Checklist 1-110 .01 .05
61 Steve Leach .01 .05
62 Trent Klatt RC .02 .10
63 Darryl Sydor .01 .05
64 Brian Glynn .01 .05
65 Mike Craig .01 .05
66 Gary Leeman .01 .05
67 Jim Waite .02 .10
68 Jason Marshall .01 .05
69 Robert Kron .01 .05
70 Yanic Perreault RC .20 .50
71 Daniel Marois .01 .05
72 Mark Osborne .01 .05
73 Mark Tinordi .01 .05
74 Brad May .01 .05
75 Kimbi Daniels .01 .05
76 Kay Whitmore .02 .10
77 Luciano Borsato .01 .05
78 Kris King .01 .05
79 Felix Potvin .08 .25
80 Benoit Brunet .01 .05
81 Shawn Antoski .01 .05
82 Randy Gilhen .01 .05
83 Dimitri Mironov .01 .05
84 Dave Manson .01 .05
85 Sergio Momesso .01 .05
86 Cam Neely .08 .25
87 Mike Krushelnyski .01 .05
88 Eric Lindros UER SP .08 .25
(8 games with Canadian
Olympic Team not 7)
89 Wendel Clark .02 .10
90 Enrico Ciccone .01 .05
91 Jarrod Skalde .01 .05
92 Dominik Hasek .30 .75
93 Dave McLlwain .01 .05
94 Russ Courtnall .01 .05
95 Tim Sweeney .01 .05
96 Alexei Kasatonov .01 .05
97 Chris Lindberg .01 .05
98 Steven Rice .01 .05
99 Tie Domi .08 .25
100 Paul Stanton .01 .05
101 Brad Schlegel .01 .05
102 David Bruce .01 .05
103 Mikael Andersson .01 .05
104 Shawn Chambers .01 .05
105 Rob Ramage .01 .05
106 Joe Reekie .01 .05
107 Sylvain Turgeon .01 .05
108 Rob Murphy .01 .05
109 Brad Shaw .01 .05
110 Darren Rumble RC .01 .05
111 Kyosti Karjalainen .01 .05
112 Mike Vernon .02 .10
113 Michel Goulet .02 .10
114 Garry Valk .01 .05
115 Peter Bondra .02 .10
116 Paul Coffey .08 .25
117 Brian Noonan .01 .05
118 John McIntyre .01 .05
119 Scott Mellanby .01 .05
120 Jim Sandlak .01 .05
121 Mats Sundin .08 .25
122 Brendan Shanahan .08 .25
123 Kelly Buchberger .01 .05
124 Doug Smail .01 .05
125 Craig Janney .02 .10
126 Mike Gartner .02 .10
127 Alexei Gusarov .01 .05
128 Joe Nieuwendyk .02 .10
129 Troy Murray .01 .05
130 Jamie Baker .01 .05
131 Dale Hunter .02 .10
132 Darrin Shannon .01 .05
133 Adam Oates .02 .10
134 Trevor Kidd .02 .10
135 Steve Larmer .02 .10
136 Fredrik Olausson .01 .05
137 Jyrki Lumme .01 .05
138 Tony Amonte .02 .10
139 Calle Johansson .01 .05
140 Rob Blake .02 .10
141 Phil Bourque .01 .05
142 Yves Racine .01 .05
143 Rich Sutter .01 .05
144 Joe Mullen .02 .10
145 Mike Richter .08 .25
146 Pat MacLeod .01 .05
147 Claude Lapointe .01 .05
148 Paul Broten .01 .05
149 Patrick Roy .40 1.00
150 Doug Wilson .02 .10
151 Jim Hrivnak .02 .10
152 Joe Murphy .01 .05
153 Randy Burridge .01 .05
154 Thomas Steen .01 .05
155 Steve Yzerman .40 1.00
156 Pavel Bure .08 .25
157 Sergei Fedorov .15 .40
158 Trevor Linden .02 .10
159 Chris Chelios .08 .25
160 Cliff Ronning .01 .05
161 Jeff Beukeboom .01 .05
162 Denis Savard .02 .10
163 Claude Lemieux .01 .05
164 Mike Keane .01 .05
165 Pat LaFontaine .08 .25
166 Nelson Emerson .01 .05
167 Alexander Mogilny .02 .10
168 Jamie Leach .01 .05
169 Darren Turcotte .01 .05
170 Checklist 111-220 .01 .05
171 Steve Thomas .02 .10
172 Brian Bellows .01 .05
173 Mike Ridley .01 .05
174 Dave Gagner .02 .10
175 Pierre Turgeon .02 .10
176 Paul Ysebaert .01 .05
177 Brian Propp .01 .05
178 Nicklas Lidstrom .08 .25
179 Kelly Miller .01 .05
180 Kirk Muller .01 .05
181 Bob Bassen .01 .05
182 Tony Tanti .01 .05
183 Mikhail Tatarinov .01 .05
184 Ron Sutter .01 .05
185 Tony Granato .01 .05

186 Curtis Joseph .08 .25
187 Uwe Krupp .01 .05
188 Esa Tikkanen .01 .05
189 Ulf Samuelsson .01 .05
190 Jon Casey .02 .10
191 Derek King .01 .05
192 Greg Adams .01 .05
193 Ray Ferraro .01 .05
194 Dave Christian .01 .05
195 Eric Weinrich .01 .05
196 Josef Beranek .01 .05
197 Tim Cheveldae .02 .10
198 Kevin Hatcher .01 .05
199 Brent Sutter .01 .05
200 Bruce Driver .01 .05
201 Tom Draper .01 .05
202 Ted Donato .01 .05
203 Ed Belfour .08 .25
204 Pat Verbeek .01 .05
205 John Druce .01 .05
206 Neal Broten .02 .10
207 Doug Bodger .01 .05
208 Troy Loney .01 .05
209 Mark Pederson .01 .05
210 Todd Elik .01 .05
211 Ed Olczyk .01 .05
212 Paul Cavallini .01 .05
213 Stephan Lebeau .01 .05
214 Dave Ellett .01 .05
215 Doug Gilmour .02 .10
216 Luc Robitaille .02 .10
217 Bob Essensa .02 .10
218 Jari Kurri .08 .25
219 Dimitri Khristich .01 .05
220 Joel Otto .01 .05
221 Checklist 221-280 .01 .05
222 Jonas Hoglund RC .08 .25
223 Rolf Wanhainen RC .01 .05
224 Stefan Klockare RC .01 .05
225 Johan Norgren RC .01 .05
226 Roger Kyro RC .01 .05
227 Niklas Sundblad RC .01 .05
228 Calle Carlsson RC .01 .05
229 Jakob Karlsson RC .01 .05
230 Fredrik Jax RC .01 .05
231 Bjorn Nord RC .01 .05
232 Kristian Gahn RC .01 .05
233 Mikael Renberg RC .20 .50
234 Markus Naslund RC 1.00 2.50
235 Peter Forsberg .40 1.00
236 Michael Nylander RC .08 .25
237 Stanley Cup Centennial .01 .05
238 Rick Tocchet .02 .10
239 Igor Kravchuk .01 .05
240 Geoff Courtnall .01 .05
241 Larry Murphy .02 .10
242 Mark Messier .08 .25
243 Tom Barrasso .02 .10
244 Glen Wesley .01 .05
245 Randy Wood .01 .05
246 Gerard Gallant .01 .05
247 Kip Miller .01 .05
248 Bob Probert .02 .10
249 Gary Suter .01 .05
250 Ulf Dahlen .01 .05
251 Dan Lambert .01 .05
252 Bobby Holik .02 .10
253 Jimmy Carson .01 .05
254 Ken Hodge Jr. .01 .05
255 Joe Sakic .20 .50
256 Kevin Dineen .01 .05
257 Al MacInnis .02 .10
258 Vladimir Ruzicka .01 .05
259 Ken Daneyko .01 .05
260 Guy Carbonneau .02 .10
261 Michal Pivonka .01 .05
262 Bill Ranford .02 .10
263 Petr Nedved .02 .10
264 Rod Brind'Amour .02 .10
265 Ray Bourque .20 .50
266 Joe Sacco .01 .05
267 Vladimir Konstantinov .08 .25
268 Eric Desjardins .02 .10
269 Dave Andreychuk .02 .10
270 Kelly Hrudey .02 .10
271 Grant Fuhr .08 .25
272 Dirk Graham .01 .05
273 Frank Pietrangelo .02 .10
274 Jeremy Roenick .10 .30
275 Kevin Stevens .01 .05
276 Phil Housley .02 .10
277 Patrice Brisebois .01 .05
278 Slava Fetisov .01 .05
279 Doug Weight .08 .25
280 Checklist 281-330 .01 .05
281 Dean Evason .01 .05
282 Martin Gelinas .01 .05
283 Philippe Bozon .01 .05
284 Brian Leetch .08 .25
285 Theo Fleury .01 .05
286 Pat Falloon .01 .05
287 Derian Hatcher .01 .05
288 Andrew Cassels .01 .05
289 Gary Roberts .01 .05
290 Bernie Nicholls .02 .10
291 Ron Francis .02 .10
292 Tom Kurvers .01 .05
293 Geoff Sanderson .02 .10
294 Slava Kozlov .02 .10
295 Valeri Zelepukin .01 .05
296 Ray Sheppard .01 .05
297 Scott Stevens .02 .10
298 Sergei Nemchinov .01 .05
299 Kirk McLean .02 .10
300 Igor Ulanov .01 .05
301 Brian Benning .01 .05
302 Dale Hawerchuk .02 .10
303 Kevin Todd .01 .05
304 John Cullen .01 .05
305 Mike Modano .15 .40
306 Donald Audette .01 .05
307 Vincent Damphousse .01 .05
308 Jeff Hackett .02 .10
309 Craig Simpson .01 .05
310 Don Beaupre .02 .10
311 Adam Creighton .01 .05
312 Pat Elynuik .01 .05
313 David Volek .01 .05
314 Sergei Makarov .01 .05
315 Craig Billington .02 .10
316 Zarley Zalapski .01 .05
317 Brian Mullen .01 .05
318 Rob Pearson .01 .05
319 Garry Galley .01 .05
320 James Patrick .01 .05
321 Owen Nolan .02 .10
322 Marty McSorley .01 .05
323 James Black .01 .05
324 Jacques Cloutier .02 .10
325 Benoit Hogue .01 .05
326 Teppo Numminen .01 .05
327 Mark Recchi .02 .10
328 Paul Ranheim .01 .05
329 Andy Moog .08 .25
330 Shayne Corson .01 .05
331 J.J. Daigneault .01 .05
332 Mark Fitzpatrick .02 .10
333 Russian Stars CL .01 .05
Alexander Yudin
Dmitri Yushkevich
Yan Kaminsky
Alexander Andriyevski
334 Alexei Yashin RS .01 .05
335 Darius Kasparaitis RS .01 .05
336 Alexander Yudin RS RC .01 .05
337 Sergei Bautin RS RC .01 .05
338 Igor Korolev RS RC .02 .10
339 Sergei Klimovich RS RC .02 .10
340 Andrei Nikolishin RS RC .01 .05
341 Vitali Karamnov RS RC .01 .05
342 Alex. Andriyevski RS RC .01 .05
343 Sergei Sorokin RS RC .01 .05
344 Yan Kaminsky RS RC .01 .05
345 Andrei Trefilov RS RC .01 .05
346 Sergei Petrenko RS RC .01 .05
347 Ravil Khaidarov RS RC .01 .05
348 Dmitri Frolov RS .01 .05
349 Ravil Yakubov RS RC .01 .05
350 Dmitri Yushkevich RS RC .02 .10
351 Alex Karpovtsev RS RC .02 .10
352 Igor Dorofeyev RS RC .01 .05
353 Alexander Galchenyuk RS RC .01 .05
354 Joe Juneau RR .01 .05
355 Pat Falloon RR .01 .05
356 Gilbert Dionne RR .01 .05
357 Vladimir Konstantinov RR .08 .25
358 Rick Tabaracci RR .01 .05
359 Tony Amonte RR .05 .15
360 Scott Lachance RR .01 .05
361 Tom Draper RR .01 .05
362 Pavel Bure RR .07 .20
363 Nicklas Lidstrom RR .02 .10
364 Keith Tkachuk RR .08 .25
365 Kevin Todd RR .01 .05
366 Dominik Hasek RR .08 .25
367 Igor Kravchuk RR .01 .05
368 Shawn McEachern RR .01 .05
369 '92 World Championships Checklist .20 .50
Arto Blomsten
Peter Forsberg
370 Dieter Hegen RC .01 .05
371 Stefan Ustorf RC .01 .05
372 Ernst Kopf RC .01 .05
373 Raimond Hilger RC .01 .05
374 Mats Sundin .08 .25
375 Peter Forsberg .40 1.00
376 Arto Blomsten RC .02 .10
377 Tommy Soderstom RC .02 .10
378 Michael Nylander RC .02 .10
379 David Jensen RC .01 .05
380 Chris Winnes .01 .05
381 Ray LeBlanc .02 .10
382 Joe Sacco .01 .05
383 Dennis Vaske .01 .05
384 Jorg Eberle RC .01 .05
385 Trevor Kidd .02 .10
386 Pat Falloon .01 .05
387 Rob Brown .01 .05
388 Adam Graves .01 .05
389 Peter Zezel .01 .05
390 Checklist 391-440 .01 .05
391 Don Sweeney .01 .05
392 Sean Hill RC .01 .05
393 Ted Donato .01 .05
394 Marty McInnis .01 .05
395 C.J. Young RC .01 .05
396 Ted Drury RC .01 .05
397 Scott Young .01 .05
398 Star Rookie CL .02 .10
Scott Lachance
Keith Tkachuk
399 Joe Juneau SR UER .01 .05
(Olympic stats should read 8 games, 9 assists 15 points, and 4 PIM)
400 Steve Heinze SR .01 .05
401 Glen Murray SR .01 .05
402 Keith Carney SR RC .08 .25
403 Dean McAmmond SR RC .01 .05
404 Karl Dykhuis SR .01 .05
405 Martin Lapointe SR .02 .10
406 Scott Niedermayer SR .01 .05
407 Ray Whitney SR RC .15 .40
408 Martin Brodeur SR .40 1.00
409 Scott Lachance SR .01 .05
410 Marty McInnis SR .01 .05
411 Bill Guerin SR RC .60 1.50
412 Shawn McEachern SR .01 .05
413 Denny Felsner SR RC .02 .10
414 Bret Hedican SR RC .02 .10
415 Drake Berehowsky SR .01 .05
416 Patrick Poulin SR .01 .05
417 Vladimir Vujtek SR RC .01 .05
418 Steve Konowalchuk SR RC .02 .10
419 Keith Tkachuk SR .08 .25
420 Evgeny Davydov SR .01 .05
421 Yanick Dupre SR .01 .05
422 Jason Woolley RC .01 .05
423 Back-to-Back .30 .75
Brett Hull
Wayne Gretzky
424 Tomas Sandstrom .02 .10
425 Craig MacTavish .01 .05
426 Stu Barnes .01 .05
427 Gilbert Dionne .01 .05
428 Andrei Lomakin .01 .05
429 Tomas Forslund .01 .05
430 Andre Racicot .02 .10
431 Pavel Bure AW .07 .20
Calder Memorial
432 Mark Messier AW .07 .20
Lester B. Pearson
433 Mario Lemieux Ross .25 .60
434 Brian Leetch AW .02 .10
Norris
435 Wayne Gretzky AW .30 .75
Lady Byng
436 Mario Lemieux Smythe .25 .60
437 Mark Messier AW .07 .20
Hart
438 Patrick Roy AW .25 .60
Vezina
439 Guy Carbonneau AW .02 .10
Frank J. Selke
440 Patrick Roy AW .25 .60
William M. Jennings
441 Russ Courtnall .01 .05
442 Jeff Reese .01 .05
443 Brent Fedyk .01 .05
444 Kerry Huffman .01 .05
445 Mark Freer .01 .05
446 Christian Ruuttu .01 .05
447 Nick Kypreos .01 .05
448 Mike Hurlbut RC .01 .05
449 Bob Sweeney .01 .05
450 Checklist 491-540 .01 .05
451 Perry Berezan .01 .05
452 Phil Bourque .01 .05
453 New York Rangers LL .08 .25
Mark Messier
Tony Amonte
Adam Graves
454 Pittsburgh Penguins LL .15 .40
Mario Lemieux
Kevin Stevens
Rick Tocchet
455 Boston Bruins LL .02 .10
Adam Oates
Joe Juneau
Dmitri Kvartalnov
456 Buffalo Sabres LL .02 .10
Pat LaFontaine
Dave Andreychuk
Alexander Mogilny
457 Zdeno Ciger .01 .05
458 Pat Jablonski .02 .10
459 Brent Gilchrist .01 .05
460 Yvon Corriveau .01 .05
461 Dino Ciccarelli .02 .10
462 David Emma .01 .05
463 Corey Hirsch RC .08 .25
464 Jamie Baker .01 .05
465 John Cullen .01 .05
466 Lonnie Loach RC .01 .05
467 Louie DeBrusk .01 .05
468 Brian Mullen .01 .05
469 Gaeten Duchesne .01 .05
470 Eric Lindros .08 .25
471 Brian Bellows .01 .05
472 Bill Lindsay RC .01 .05
473 Dave Archibald .01 .05
474 Reggie Savage .01 .05
475 Tommy Soderstrom .02 .10
476 Vincent Damphousse .01 .05
477 Mike Ricci .02 .10
478 Bob Carpenter .01 .05
479 Kevin Haller .01 .05
480 Peter Sidorkiewicz .02 .10
481 Peter Andersson RC .01 .05
482 Kevin Miller .01 .05
483 Jean-Francois Quintin RC .01 .05
484 Philippe Boucher .01 .05
485 Jozef Stumpel .01 .05
486 Vitali Prokhorov RC .01 .05
487 Stan Drulia RC .01 .05
488 Jay More .01 .05
489 Mike Needham RC .01 .05
490 Glenn Mulvenna RC .01 .05
491 Ed Ronan RC .01 .05
492 Grigori Panteleyev RC .01 .05
493 Kevin Dahl RC .01 .05
494 Ryan McGill RC .01 .05
495 Robb Stauber .02 .10
496 Vladimir Vujtek RC .01 .05
497 Tomas Jelinek RC .01 .05
498 Patrik Kjellberg RC .08 .25
499 Sergei Bautin .01 .05
500 Bobby Holik .02 .10
501 Guy Hebert RC .30 .75
502 Chris Kontos RC .01 .05
503 Vyatcheslav Butsayev RC .01 .05
504 Yuri Khymlev RC .01 .05
505 Richard Matvichuk RC .02 .10
506 Dominik Hasek .20 .50
507 Ed Courtenay .01 .05
508 Jeff Daniels .01 .05
509 Doug Zmolek RC .01 .05
510 Vitali Karamnov .01 .05
511 Norm Maciver .01 .05
512 Terry Yake .01 .05
513 Steve Duchesne .01 .05
514 Andrei Trefilov .01 .05
515 Jiri Slegr .01 .05
516 Sergei Zubov RC .25 .60
517 Dave Karpa RC .01 .05
518 Sean Burke .02 .10
519 Adrien Plavsic .01 .05
520 Michael Nylander .01 .05
521 John MacLean .02 .10
522 Jason Ruff RC .01 .05
523 Sean Hill .01 .05
524 Mike Sillinger .01 .05
525 Dan Laperriere RC .01 .05
526 Peter Ahola .01 .05
527 Guy Larose .01 .05
528 Tommy Sjodin RC .01 .05
529 Rob DiMaio .01 .05
530 Mark Howe .01 .05
531 Greg Paslawski .01 .05
532 Ron Hextall .02 .10
533 Keith Jones RC .08 .25
534 Chris Luongo RC .01 .05
535 Anatoli Semenov .01 .05
536 Stephane Beauregard .02 .10
537 Pat Elynuik .01 .05
538 Mike McPhee .01 .05
539 Jody Hull .01 .05
540 Stephane Matteau .01 .05
541 Shayne Corson .01 .05
542 Mikhail Kravets RC .01 .05
543 Kevin Miehm RC .01 .05
544 Brian Bradley .01 .05
545 Mathieu Schneider .01 .05
546 Steve Chiasson .01 .05
547 Warren Rychel RC .01 .05
548 John Tucker .01 .05
549 Todd Ewen .01 .05
550 Checklist 591-640 .01 .05
551 Petr Klima .01 .05
552 Robert Lang RC .01 .05
553 Eric Weinrich .01 .05
554 Young Guns Checklist .01 .05
555 Roman Hamrlik RC .20 .50
556 Martin Rucinsky YG .01 .05
557 Patrick Poulin YG .01 .05
558 Tyler Wright YG .01 .05
559 Martin Straka YG RC .30 .75
560 Jim Hiller YG RC .01 .05
561 Dmitri Kvartalnov YG RC .01 .05
562 Scott Niedermayer YG .01 .05
563 Darius Kasparaitis YG .01 .05
564 Richard Smehlik RC .01 .05
565 Shawn McEachern YG .01 .05
566 Alexei Zhitnik YG .01 .05
567 Andrei Kovalenko YG RC .02 .10
568 Sandis Ozolinsh YG .01 .05
569 Robert Petrovicky RC .01 .05
570 Dmitri Yushkevich YG .02 .10
571 Scott Lachance YG .01 .05
572 Nikolai Borschevsky YG .01 .05
573 Alexei Kovalev YG .02 .10
574 Teemu Selanne YG .40 1.00
575 Steven King RC .01 .05
576 Guy Leveque YG RC .01 .05
577 Vladimir Malakhov YG .01 .05
578 Alexei Zhamnov YG .02 .10
579 Viktor Gordiouk YG RC .01 .05
580 Dixon Ward YG RC .02 .10
581 Igor Korolev YG .01 .05
582 Sergei Krivokrasov YG .01 .05
583 Rob Zamuner RC .02 .10
584 World Jr. Championship Checklist .01 .05
585 Manny Legace RC .75 2.00
586 Paul Kariya RC 3.00 8.00
587 Alexandre Daigle RC .20 .50
588 Nathan Lafeyette RC .02 .10
589 Mike Rathje RC .01 .05
590 Chris Gratton RC .20 .50
591 Chris Pronger RC 2.50 6.00
592 Brent Tully RC .01 .05
593 Rob Niedermayer RC .30 .75
594 Darcy Werenka RC .01 .05
595 Peter Forsberg .40 1.00
596 Kenny Jonsson RC .08 .25
597 Niklas Sundstrom RC .20 .50
598 Reine Rauhala RC .01 .05
599 Daniel Johansson RC .01 .05
600 David Vyborny RC .20 .50
601 Jan Vopat RC .02 .10
602 Pavol Demitra RC .60 1.50
603 Michal Cerny RC .01 .05
604 Ondrej Steiner RC .01 .05
605 Jim Campbell RC .02 .10
606 Todd Marchant RC .02 .10
607 Mike Pomichter RC .01 .05
608 John Emmons RC .01 .05
609 Adam Deadmarsh RC .20 .50
610 Nikolai Semin RC .01 .05
611 Igor Alexandrov RC .01 .05
612 Vadim Sharifjanov RC .08 .25
613 Viktor Kozlov RC .30 .75
614 Nikolai Tsulygin RC .01 .05
615 Jere Lehtinen RC .60 1.50
616 Ville Peltonen RC .02 .10
617 Saku Koivu RC 1.25 3.00
618 Kimmo Rintanen RC .01 .05
619 Jonni Vauhkonen RC .01 .05
620 Brett Hull .08 .25
621 Wayne Gretzky .30 .75
622 Jaromir Jagr .08 .25
623 Darius Kasparaitis .01 .05
624 Bernie Nicholls .01 .05
625 Gilbert Dionne .01 .05
626 Ray Bourque .08 .25
627 Mike Ricci .02 .10
628 Phil Housley .02 .10
629 Chris Chelios .08 .25
630 Kevin Stevens .01 .05
631 Roman Hamrlik .02 .10
632 Sergei Fedorov .08 .25
633 Alexei Kovalev .02 .10
634 Shawn McEachern .01 .05
635 Tony Amonte .05 .15
636 Brian Bellows .01 .05
637 Adam Oates .02 .10
638 Denis Savard .02 .10
639 Doug Gilmour .02 .10
640 Brian Leetch .02 .10
SP2 Pavel Bure .08 .25
All-Rookie Team
SP3 World Jr. Champs 1.50 4.00
Gold medal winner
Canada

1992-93 Upper Deck All-Rookie Team

This seven-card set was inserted only in low series U.S. foil packs and features six of the NHL's brightest rookies from the 1991-92 season. The fronts show a triple-pose player photo and have a diagonal silver foil stripe in the lower right corner with the words "All-Rookie Team". The backs provide biographical information and a color photo of the player in civilian dress. The checklist card has a group photo of all six players. The cards are numbered on the back with an "AR" prefix.

COMPLETE SET (7) 6.00 15.00
AR1 Tony Amonte .40 1.00
AR2 Gilbert Dionne .40 1.00
AR3 Kevin Todd .40 1.00
AR4 Nicklas Lidstrom 2.00 5.00
AR5 Vladimir Konstantinov 2.00 5.00
AR6 Dominik Hasek 2.00 5.00
AR7 Checklist Card .75 2.00
Tony Amonte
Gilbert Dionne
Kevin Todd
Nicklas Lidstrom
Vladimir Konstantinov
Dominik Hasek

1992-93 Upper Deck All-World Team

This six-card set was randomly inserted only in Canadian low series foil packs. These standard size cards are full bleed with a gold "All-World Team" logo at the bottom of the card. The cards are numbered on the back with a "W" prefix.

COMPLETE SET (6) 8.00 20.00
W1 Wayne Gretzky 4.00 10.00
W2 Brett Hull 1.00 2.50
W3 Jaromir Jagr 1.00 2.50
W4 Nicklas Lidstrom .60 1.50
W5 Vladimir Konstantinov .60 1.50
W6 Patrick Roy 3.00 8.00

1992-93 Upper Deck Ameri/Can Holograms

Randomly inserted in high series foil packs, this six-card hologram standard-size set spotlights the top rookies of either U.S. or Canadian heritage at each position. The cards have the photo superimposed over the hologram.

COMPLETE SET (6) 2.00 5.00
1 Joe Juneau .30 .75
2 Keith Tkachuk .50 1.25
3 Steve Heinze .30 .75
4 Scott Lachance .30 .75
5 Scott Niedermayer .30 .75
6 Dominic Roussel .40 1.00

1992-93 Upper Deck Calder Candidates

Randomly inserted into 1992-93 Upper Deck U.S. high series retail foil packs only, this 20-card standard-size set spotlights top rookies eligible to win the Calder Memorial Trophy for the 1992-93 season. The full-bleed photos on the front are bordered on the top by a gold foil stripe. The team name and player's name appears in bar that shades from black to white. On a background consisting of a stone slab carved with an image of the Calder trophy, the backs present a career summary. The card number appears in a white stripe that cuts across the top of the card. The cards are numbered with a "CC" prefix.

COMPLETE SET (20) 10.00 25.00
CC1 Dixon Ward .40 1.00
CC2 Igor Korolev .40 1.00
CC3 Felix Potvin 1.50 4.00
CC4 Rob Zamuner .40 1.00
CC5 Scott Niedermayer .75 2.00
CC6 Eric Lindros 2.00 5.00
CC7 Alexei Zhitnik .40 1.00
CC8 Roman Hamrlik .40 1.00
CC9 Joe Juneau 1.00 2.50
CC10 Teemu Selanne 2.00 5.00
CC11 Alexei Kovalev .75 2.00
CC12 Vladimir Malakhov .40 1.00
CC13 Darius Kasparaitis .40 1.00
CC14 Shawn McEachern .40 1.00
CC15 Keith Tkachuk 1.50 4.00
CC16 Scott Lachance .40 1.00
CC17 Andrei Kovalenko .40 1.00
CC18 Patrick Poulin .40 1.00
CC19 Evgeny Davydov .40 1.00
CC20 Dimitri Yushkevich .40 1.00

1992-93 Upper Deck Euro-Rookie Team

This six-card standard-size set was randomly inserted in 1992-93 Upper Deck low series packs. The cards feature cut-out color player photos superimposed on a hologram that shows the player in action. The horizontal fronts are bordered on the left and top by gray wood-textured panels. The team logo appears at the top left on a tan wood-textured panel. The horizontal backs feature a player profile on a tan background bordered by gray wood-textured panels. The cards are numbered on the back with an "ERT" prefix.

COMPLETE SET (6) 3.00 8.00
ERT1 Pavel Bure .75 2.00
ERT2 Nicklas Lidstrom .75 2.00
ERT3 Dominik Hasek 2.00 5.00
ERT4 Peter Ahola .20 .50
ERT5 Alexander Semak .20 .50
ERT6 Tomas Forslund .20 .50

1992-93 Upper Deck Euro-Rookies

One per high series jumbo pack, this 20-card standard-size set spotlights European born rookies. The color action player photos on the fronts are full-bleed except on the right side, where a black stripe carries the player's name in bronze foil lettering. At the upper right corner appears a bronze foil "Euro-Rookies" seal, with the flag of the player's country immediately to the right. The cards are numbered on the back with an "ER" prefix.

COMPLETE SET (20) 4.00 10.00
ER1 Richard Smehlik .20 .50
ER2 Michael Nylander .30 .75
ER3 Igor Korolev .20 .50
ER4 Robert Lang .20 .50
ER5 Sergei Krivokrasov .20 .50
ER6 Teemu Selanne .75 2.00
ER7 Darius Kasparaitis .20 .50
ER8 Alexei Zhamnov .30 .75
ER9 Jiri Slegr .20 .50
ER10 Alexei Kovalev .60 1.50
ER11 Roman Hamrlik .40 1.00
ER12 Dimitri Yushkevich .20 .50
ER13 Alexei Zhitnik .20 .50
ER14 Andrei Kovalenko .20 .50
ER15 Vladimir Malakhov .20 .50
ER16 Sandis Ozolinsh .40 1.00
ER17 Evgeny Davydov .20 .50
ER18 Viktor Gordiouk .20 .50
ER19 Martin Straka .30 .75
ER20 Robert Petrovicky .20 .50

1992-93 Upper Deck Euro-Stars

This 20-card standard-size set, issued one per low series jumbo pack, features action color player photos with a silver foil border. The borders are prone to chipping. The pictures are silver-foil stamped with the player's name and with the "Euro Stars" emblem which hangs down from a white, red, and blue ribbon at the upper right corner. The backs display player profile information against a light gray panel with a black, silver, and gold frame design. The cards are numbered on the back with an "E" prefix.

COMPLETE SET (20) 4.00 10.00
E1 Sergei Fedorov .75 2.00
E2 Pavel Bure .40 1.00
E3 Dominik Hasek 1.00 2.50
E4 Vladimir Ruzicka .20 .50
E5 Peter Ahola .20 .50
E6 Kyosti Karjalainen .20 .50
E7 Igor Kravchuk .20 .50
E8 Evgeny Davydov .20 .50
E9 Nicklas Lidstrom .40 1.00
E10 Vlad. Konstantinov .40 1.00
E11 Josef Beranek .20 .50
E12 Valeri Zelepukin .20 .50
E13 Sergei Nemchinov .20 .50
E14 Jaromir Jagr 1.00 2.50
E15 Igor Ulanov .20 .50
E16 Sergei Makarov .20 .50
E17 Andrei Lomakin .20 .50
E18 Mats Sundin .40 1.00
E19 Jarmo Myllys .20 .50
E20 Valeri Kamensky .20 .50

1992-93 Upper Deck Gordie Howe Heroes

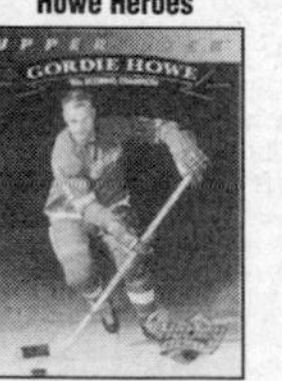

Randomly inserted in high series foil packs, this 10-card "Hockey Heroes" standard-size set showcases Gordie Howe, the NHL's former all-time leader in goals, assists, and points. The backs capture highlights in Howe's career. The cards are numbered on the back and continue from where the Gretzky Heroes left off.

COMPLETE SET (10) 6.00 15.00
COMMON HOWE (19-27) .75 2.00
NNO G.Howe Header SP 1.50 4.00

1992-93 Upper Deck Gordie Howe Selects

Randomly inserted throughout U.S. high series hobby packs only, this 20-card set standard-size features Gordie Howe's selections of ten current NHL superstars and ten rookies who he believes are the NHL's best. The fronts carry full-bleed color player photos. Howe's signature in gold foil sits on top of a black bar (carrying the word "Selects") toward the bottom of the picture, with the player's name and position immediately below. The backs have a color head shot in an oval and a quote of Howe's evaluation of the player's strengths. A small color player cut-out of Howe and the player's statistics complete the back. The cards are numbered on the back with a "G" prefix.

COMPLETE SET (20) 15.00 40.00
G1 Brian Bellows .15 .40
G2 Luc Robitaille .30 .75
G3 Pat LaFontaine .60 1.50
G4 Kevin Stevens .15 .40
G5 Wayne Gretzky 4.00 10.00
G6 Steve Larmer .30 .75
G7 Brett Hull 1.25 3.00
G8 Jeremy Roenick 1.00 2.50
G9 Mario Lemieux 3.00 8.00
G10 Steve Yzerman 3.00 8.00
G11 Joe Juneau .15 .40
G12 Vladimir Malakhov .15 .40
G13 Alexei Kovalev .30 .75
G14 Eric Lindros .75 2.00
G15 Teemu Selanne 1.50 4.00
G16 Patrick Poulin .15 .40
G17 Shawn McEachern .15 .40
G18 Keith Tkachuk .75 2.00
G19 Andrei Kovalenko .15 .40
G20 Ted Donato .15 .40

1992-93 Upper Deck Sheets

For the third straight year, Upper Deck produced hockey commemorative sheets that were given away during the 1992-93 season at selected games in large arenas. Each sheet measures 8 1/2" by 11" and is printed on card stock. The fronts of the team commemorative sheets feature a series of Upper Deck cards of star players on a particular team and the team logo. The 1993 All-Star Game sheets feature a series of Upper Deck cards of players that participated in the All-Star Game. All the sheets have an Upper Deck stamp indicating the production quota and the serial number. Sheets without a production quantity number are listed as NNO. The backs of the sheets are blank. The players are listed as they appear from left to right.

COMPLETE SET (17) 60.00 150.00
1 '91-92 All-Rookie Team 4.00 10.00
June 1992 (17,000)
Gilbert Dionne
Kevin Todd
Vladimir Konstantinov
Tony Amonte
Nicklas Lidstrom
Dominik Hasek
2 New York Rangers 4.00 10.00
Defending Season Champs
Undated (18,000)
Peter Andersson
Phil Bourque
Joe Kocur
Doug Weight
Randy Gilhen
John Vanbiesbrouck
Adam Graves
Mark Messier
3 Gordie Howe Birthday 4.00 10.00
Undated (NNO)
65th Birthday
Celebration Tour
(Nine Howe Hockey Heroes Cards Pictured)
4 Gordie Howe Birthday 4.00 10.00
Undated (NNO)
Hamilton McDonald's
5 Wayne Gretzky Heroes 6.00 15.00
Mail-In (NNO)
6 New York Rangers 2.00 5.00
vs. Quebec Nordiques
Oct. 29, 1992 (18,000)
Paul Broten
Mike Richter
Sergei Nemchinov
Tie Domi
Kris King
Jeff Beukeboom
Brian Leetch Norris
Tony Amonte
7 Los Angeles Kings 4.00 10.00
vs. Vancouver Canucks
Nov. 12, 1992 (18,000)
Luc Robitaille
Paul Coffey
Tony Granato
Rob Blake
Tomas Sandstrom
Kelly Hrudey
8 Minnesota North Stars 6.00 15.00
vs. San Jose Sharks
Nov. 28, 1992 (16,500)
9 Edmonton Oilers 2.00 5.00
vs. Calgary Flames

Dec. 8, 1992 (18,500)
Brian Glynn
Scott Mellanby
Dave Manson
Craig MacTavish
Bernie Nicholls
Bill Ranford
10 Philadelphia Flyers 2.00 5.00
vs. Pittsburgh Penguins
Dec. 17, 1992 (19,000)
Kevin Dineen
Mark Recchi
Garry Galley
Dominic Roussel
Brian Benning
Rod Brind'Amour
11 Minnesota North Stars 6.00 15.00
vs. Tampa Bay Lightning
Jan. 30, 1993 (16,500)
Dave Gagner
Neal Broten
Ulf Dahlen
Todd Elik
Tommy Sjodin
Gaetan Duchesne
12 Campbell All-Stars 4.00 10.00
Montreal Forum
Feb. 6, 1993 (NNO)
Ed Belfour
Paul Coffey
Chris Chelios
Steve Yzerman
Brett Hull
Pavel Bure
13 Wales All-Stars 4.00 10.00
Montreal Forum
Feb. 6, 1993 (NNO)
Patrick Roy
Brian Leetch
Ray Bourque
Kevin Stevens
Mario Lemieux
Jaromir Jagr
14 Washington Capitals 4.00 10.00
vs. St. Louis Blues
Feb. 21, 1993 (17,000)
Jim Hrivnak
Mike Ridley
Peter Bondra
Dale Hunter
Kelly Miller
Don Beaupre
15 Los Angeles Kings 4.00 10.00
vs. Ottawa Senators
Mar.4, 1993 (18,000)
Jari Kurri
Corey Millen
Marty McSorley
Darryl Sydor
Wayne Gretzky
Robb Stauber
16 Quebec Nordiques 6.00 15.00
vs. Hartford Whalers
Mar. 8, 1993 (15,000)
17 St.Louis Blues 2.00 5.00
vs. Vancouver Canucks
Mar. 30, 1993 (17,500)

1992-93 Upper Deck Wayne Gretzky Heroes

Randomly inserted in low series foil packs, this ten-card "Hockey Heroes" standard-size set pays tribute to Wayne Gretzky by chronicling his career. Inside white borders on a gray ice background, the fronts display color photos that are cut out to fit a emblem design. On a gray ice background accented by black, the backs (which continue the numbering from where the Hull Heroes left off) capture highlights in Gretzky's career.

COMPLETE SET (10) 20.00 40.00
COMMON GRETZKY (10-18) 2.00 5.00
NNO W.Gretzky Header SP 5.00 10.00

1992-93 Upper Deck World Junior Grads

Randomly inserted in Canadian high series foil packs, this 20-card standard-size set features top players in the world who have participated in the IIHF Junior Championships. Beneath a black stripe carrying the player's name, the fronts display full-bleed color action player photos. The top portion of a globe and the words "World Junior Grads" are silver foil-stamped at the bottom of the picture. On the backs, a full-size globe serves as a panel for displaying a career summary and a color action player cut-out. The back also includes the year the player participated in the IIHF World Junior Championships. The cards are numbered on the back with a "WG" prefix.

COMPLETE SET (20) 30.00 80.00
WG1 Scott Niedermayer .40 1.00
WG2 Slava Kozlov .40 1.00
WG3 Chris Chelios .75 2.00
WG4 Jari Kurri .75 2.00
WG5 Pavel Bure 1.50 4.00
WG6 Jaromir Jagr 2.00 5.00
WG7 Steve Yzerman 6.00 15.00
WG8 Joe Sakic 2.00 5.00
WG9 Alexei Kovalev .40 1.00
WG10 Wayne Gretzky 8.00 20.00
WG11 Mario Lemieux 6.00 15.00
WG12 Eric Lindros 1.50 4.00
WG13 Pat Falloon .40 1.00
WG14 Trevor Linden .40 1.00
WG15 Brian Leetch .75 2.00
WG16 Sergei Fedorov 3.00 8.00
WG17 Mats Sundin .75 2.00
WG18 Alexander Mogilny .40 1.00
WG19 Jeremy Roenick 1.50 4.00
WG20 Luc Robitaille .75 2.00

1993-94 Upper Deck

The 1993-94 Upper Deck hockey set contains 575 standard-size cards. The set was released in two series of 310 and 265 cards, respectively. The fronts feature a photo with team color-coded inner borders. The player's name, position and team name are at the bottom. The backs have a photo in the upper half with yearly statistics in the bottom portion. The following subsets are included: 100-Point Club (220-235), NHL Star Rookies (236-249), World Jr. Championships - which include Canada (250-260/531-550), Czechoslovakia (261-267/573), Finland (268-271), Russia (272-279/571/574) and USA (551-568) - All-Rookie Team (280-285) and Team Point Leaders (286-309). The set closes with an All-World Junior Team subset (569-574). A special card (SP4) was randomly inserted in Upper Deck series one packs commemorating Teemu Selanne's record-breaking 76 goal rookie season. A Wayne Gretzky card commemorating his 802nd NHL goal was randomly inserted at a rate of 1:36 Parkhurst series two packs. This card is identical to his regular Upper Deck card for '93-94, with the exception of a gold foil stamp that indicates his 802nd goal. The silver version of this card was handed out to Canadian dealers as a promotion for Parkhurst series two, and also given to each of the 16,005 fans attending the next game at the Great Western Forum following the event.

COMPLETE SET (575) 12.00 30.00
COMP.SERIES 1 (310) 6.00 15.00
COMP.SERIES 2 (265) 6.00 15.00
1 Guy Hebert .02 .10
2 Bob Bassen .01 .05
3 Theo Fleury .01 .05
4 Ray Whitney .01 .05
5 Donald Audette .01 .05
6 Martin Rucinsky .01 .05
7 Lyle Odelein .01 .05
8 John Vanbiesbrouck .02 .10
9 Tim Cheveldae .02 .10
10 Jock Callander .01 .05
11 Nick Kypreos .01 .05
12 Jarrod Skalde .01 .05
13 Gary Shuchuk .01 .05
14 Kris King .01 .05
15 Josef Beranek .01 .05
16 Sean Hill .01 .05
17 Bob Kudelski .01 .05
18 Jiri Slegr .01 .05
19 Dmitri Kvartalnov .01 .05
20 Drake Berehowsky .01 .05
21 Jean-Francois Quintin .01 .05
22 Randy Wood .01 .05
23 Jim McKenzie .01 .05
24 Steven King .01 .05
25 Scott Niedermayer .01 .05
26 Alexander Andrijevski .01 .05
27 Alexei Kovalev .02 .10
28 Steve Konowalchuk .01 .05
29 Vladimir Malakhov .01 .05
30 Eric Lindros .08 .25
31 Mathieu Schneider .01 .05
32 Russ Courtnall .01 .05
33 Ron Sutter .01 .05
34 Radek Hamr RC .08 .25
35 Pavel Bure .08 .25
36 Joe Sacco .01 .05
37 Robert Petrovicky .01 .05
38 Anatoli Fedotov RC .08 .25
39 Pat Falloon .01 .05
40 Martin Straka .01 .05
41 Brad Werenka .01 .05
42 Mike Richter .08 .25
43 Mike McPhee .01 .05
44 Sylvain Turgeon .01 .05
45 Tom Barrasso .02 .10
46 Anatoli Semenov .01 .05
47 Joe Murphy .01 .05
48 Rob Pearson .01 .05
49 Patrick Roy .50 1.25
50 Dallas Drake RC .08 .25
51 Mark Messier .08 .25
52 Scott Pellerin RC .08 .25
53 Teppo Numminen .01 .05
54 Chris Kontos .01 .05
55 Richard Matvichuk .01 .05
56 Dale Craigwell .01 .05
57 Mike Eastwood .01 .05
58 Bernie Nicholls .01 .05
59 Travis Green .02 .10
60 Shjon Podein RC .08 .25
61 Darrin Madeley RC .08 .25
62 Dixon Ward .01 .05
63 Andre Faust .01 .05
64 Tony Amonte .02 .10
65 Joe Cirella .01 .05
66 Michel Petit .01 .05
67 David Lowry .01 .05
68 Shawn Chambers .01 .05
69 Joe Sakic .20 .50
70 Michael Nylander .01 .05
71 Peter Andersson .01 .05
72 Sandis Ozolinsh UER .01 .05
(Petri Skriko on back)
73 Joby Messier RC .08 .25
74 John Blue .02 .10
75 Pat Elynuik .01 .05
76 Keith Osborne RC .08 .25
77 Greg Adams .01 .05
78 Chris Gratton .02 .10
79 Louie DeBrusk .01 .05
80 Todd Harkins RC .08 .25
81 Neil Brady .01 .05
82 Philippe Boucher .01 .05
83 Darryl Sydor .01 .05
84 Oleg Petrov .01 .05
85 Andrei Kovalenko .01 .05
86 Dave Andreychuk .02 .10
87 Jeff Daniels .01 .05
88 Kevin Todd .01 .05
89 Mark Tinordi .01 .05
90 Garry Galley .01 .05
91 Shawn Burr .01 .05
92 Tom Pederson .01 .05
93 Warren Rychel .01 .05
94 Stu Barnes .01 .05
95 Peter Bondra .02 .10
96 Brian Skrudland .01 .05
97 Doug MacDonald RC .08 .25
98 Rob Niedermayer .02 .10
99 Wayne Gretzky .60 1.50
100 Peter Taglianetti .01 .05
101 Don Sweeney .01 .05
102 Andrei Lomakin .01 .05
103 Checklist 1-103 .01 .05
104 Sergio Momesso .01 .05
105 Dave Archibald .01 .05
106 Karl Dykhuis .01 .05
107 Scott Mellanby .02 .10
108 Paul DiPietro .01 .05
109 Neal Broten .02 .10
110 Chris Terreri .02 .10
111 Craig MacTavish .01 .05
112 Jody Hull .01 .05
113 Philippe Bozon .01 .05
114 Geoff Courtnall .01 .05
115 Ed Olczyk .01 .05
116 Ray Bourque .15 .40
117 Gilbert Dionne .01 .05
118 Valeri Kamensky .02 .10
119 Scott Stevens .02 .10
120 Pelle Eklund .01 .05
121 Brian Bradley .01 .05
122 Steve Thomas .01 .05
123 Don Beaupre .02 .10
124 Joel Otto .01 .05
125 Arturs Irbe .02 .10
126 Kevin Stevens .01 .05
127 Dimitri Yushkevich .01 .05
128 Adam Graves .01 .05
129 Chris Chelios .08 .25
130 Jeff Brown .01 .05
131 Paul Ranheim .01 .05
132 Shayne Corson .01 .05
133 Curtis Leschyshyn .01 .05
134 John MacLean .02 .10
135 Dimitri Khristich .01 .05
136 Dino Ciccarelli .02 .10
137 Pat LaFontaine .08 .25
138 Patrick Poulin .01 .05
139 Jaromir Jagr .15 .40
140 Kevin Hatcher .01 .05
141 Christian Ruuttu .01 .05
142 Ulf Samuelsson .01 .05
143 Ted Donato .01 .05
144 Bob Essensa .02 .10
145 Dave Gagner .02 .10
146 Tony Granato .01 .05
147 Ed Belfour .08 .25
148 Kirk Muller .01 .05
149 Rob Gaudreau RC .08 .25
150 Nicklas Lidstrom .08 .25
151 Gary Roberts .01 .05
152 Trent Klatt .01 .05
153 Ray Ferraro .01 .05
154 Michal Pivonka .01 .05
155 Mike Foligno .01 .05
156 Kirk McLean .02 .10
157 Curtis Joseph .08 .25
158 Roman Hamrlik .01 .05
159 Felix Potvin .08 .25
160 Brett Hull .10 .30
161 Alexei Zhitnik UER .01 .05
(Listed as being drafted in 1990; should be 1991)
162 Alexei Zhamnov .02 .10
163 Grant Fuhr .02 .10
164 Nikolai Borschevsky .01 .05
165 Tomas Jelinek .01 .05
166 Thomas Steen .01 .05
167 John LeClair .08 .25
168 Vladimir Vujtek .01 .05
169 Richard Smehlik .01 .05
170 Alexandre Daigle .01 .05
171 Sergei Fedorov .15 .40
172 Steve Larmer .02 .10
173 Darius Kasparaitis .01 .05
174 Igor Kravchuk .01 .05
175 Owen Nolan .02 .10
176 Rob DiMaio .01 .05
177 Mike Vernon .02 .10
178 Alexander Semak .01 .05
179 Rick Tocchet .02 .10
180 Bill Ranford .02 .10
181 Sergei Zubov .01 .05
182 Tommy Soderstrom .02 .10
183 Al Iafrate .01 .05
184 Eric Desjardins .01 .05
185 Bret Hedican .01 .05
186 Joe Mullen .02 .10
187 Doug Bodger .01 .05
188 Tomas Sandstrom .01 .05
189 Glen Murray .01 .05
190 Chris Pronger .02 .10
191 Mike Craig .01 .05
192 Jim Paek .01 .05
193 Doug Zmolek .01 .05
194 Yves Racine .01 .05
195 Keith Tkachuk .08 .25
196 Chris Lindberg .01 .05
197 Kelly Buchberger .01 .05
198 Mark Janssens .01 .05
199 Peter Zezel .01 .05
200 Bob Probert .02 .10
201 Brad May .02 .10
202 Rob Zamuner .01 .05
203 Stephane Fiset .02 .10
204 Derian Hatcher .01 .05
205 Mike Gartner .02 .10
206 Checklist 104-206 .01 .05
207 Todd Krygier .01 .05
208 Glen Wesley .01 .05
209 Fredrik Olausson .01 .05
210 Patrick Flatley .01 .05
211 Cliff Ronning .01 .05
212 Kevin Dineen .01 .05
213 Zarley Zalapski .01 .05
214 Stephane Matteau .01 .05
215 Dave Ellett .01 .05
216 Kelly Hrudey .02 .10
217 Steve Duchesne .01 .05
218 Bobby Holik .01 .05
219 Brad Dalgarno .01 .05
220 Mats Sundin 100 CL .02 .10
221 Pat LaFontaine 100 .02 .10
222 Mark Recchi 100 .01 .05
223 Joe Sakic 100 .08 .25
224 Pierre Turgeon 100 .02 .10
225 Craig Janney 100 .02 .10
226 Adam Oates 100 .02 .10
227 Steve Yzerman 100 .25 .60
228 Mats Sundin 100 .02 .10
229 Theo Fleury 100 .01 .05
230 Kevin Stevens 100 .01 .05
231 Luc Robitaille 100 .02 .10
232 Brett Hull 100 .02 .10
233 Rick Tocchet 100 .02 .10
234 Alexander Mogilny 100 .02 .10
235 Jeremy Roenick 100 .05 .15
236 Guy Leveque .01 .05
Turner Stevenson
SR CL
237 Adam Bennett SR RC .08 .25
238 Dody Wood SR RC .08 .25
239 Niclas Andersson SR .01 .05
240 Jason Bowen SR RC .08 .25
241 Steve Junker SR RC .08 .25
242 Bryan Smolinski SR .01 .05
243 Chris Simon SR RC .30 .75
244 Sergei Zholtok SR .01 .05
245 Dan Ratushny SR RC .08 .25
246 Guy Leveque SR .01 .05
247 Scott Thomas RC .08 .25
248 Turner Stevenson SR .01 .05
249 Dan Keczmer SR .01 .05
250 Alexandre Daigle WJC CL .01 .05
251 Adrian Aucoin WJC RC .08 .25
252 Jason Smith WJC .01 .05
253 Ralph Intranuovo WJC RC .08 .25
254 Jason Dawe WJC .01 .05
255 Jeff Bes WJC RC .08 .25
256 Tyler Wright WJC .01 .05
257 Martin Lapointe WJC .01 .05
258 Jeff Shantz WJC RC .08 .25
259 Martin Gendron RC .08 .25
260 Philippe DeRouville WJC RC .08 .25
261 Frantisek Kaberle WJC RC .08 .25
262 Radim Bicanek RC .08 .25
263 Tomas Klimt WJC RC .08 .25
264 Tomas Nemcicky WJC RC .08 .25
265 Richard Kapus RC .08 .25
266 Patrik Krisak RC .08 .25
267 Roman Kadera RC .08 .25
268 Kimmo Timonen RC .30 .75
269 Jukka Ollila WJC RC .08 .25
270 Tuomas Gronman WJC .01 .05
271 Mikko Luovi RC .08 .25
272 Sergei Gonchar RC .30 .75
273 Maxim Galanov RC .08 .25
274 Oleg Belov RC .08 .25
275 Sergei Klimovich RC .08 .25
276 Sergei Brylin RC .08 .25
277 Alexei Yashin WJC .01 .05
278 Vitali Tomilin WJC RC .08 .25
279 Alexander Cherbaev .01 .05
WJC
280 Eric Lindros ART .08 .25
281 Teemu Selanne ART .08 .25
282 Joe Juneau ART .02 .10
283 Vladimir Malakhov ART .01 .05
284 Scott Niedermayer ART .01 .05
285 Felix Potvin ART .02 .10
286 Adam Oates TL .02 .10
287 Pat LaFontaine TL .02 .10
288 Theo Fleury TL .01 .05
289 Jeremy Roenick TL .05 .15
290 Steve Yzerman TL .25 .60
291 Petr Klima TL .01 .05
Doug Weight TL
292 Geoff Sanderson TL .02 .10
293 Luc Robitaille TL .02 .10
294 Mike Modano TL .08 .25
295 Vincent Damphousse TL .01 .05
296 Claude Lemieux TL .01 .05
297 Pierre Turgeon TL .02 .10
298 Mark Messier TL .08 .25
299 Norm Maciver TL .01 .05
300 Mark Recchi TL .01 .05
301 Mario Lemieux TL .25 .60
302 Mats Sundin TL .02 .10
303 Craig Janney TL .02 .10
304 Kelly Kisio TL .01 .05
305 Brian Bradley TL .01 .05
306 Doug Gilmour TL .02 .10
307 Pavel Bure TL .02 .10
308 Peter Bondra TL .02 .10
309 Teemu Selanne TL .08 .25
310 Checklist 207-310 .02 .10
311 Terry Yake .01 .05
312 Bob Sweeney .01 .05
313 Robert Reichel .01 .05
314 Jeremy Roenick .10 .30
315 Paul Coffey .08 .25
316 Geoff Sanderson .02 .10
317 Rob Blake .02 .10
318 Patrice Brisebois .01 .05
319 Jaroslav Modry RC .08 .25
320 Scott Lachance .01 .05
321 Glenn Healy .02 .10
322 Martin Gelinas .01 .05
323 Craig Janney .02 .10
324 Bill McDougall RC .08 .25
325 Shawn Antoski .01 .05
326 Olaf Kolzig .02 .10
327 Adam Oates .02 .10
328 Dirk Graham .01 .05
329 Brent Gilchrist .01 .05
330 Zdeno Ciger .01 .05
331 Pat Verbeek .01 .05
332 Jari Kurri .08 .25
333 Kevin Haller .01 .05
334 Martin Brodeur .30 .75
335 Norm Maciver .01 .05
336 Dominic Roussel .02 .10
337 Ian Fraser RC .08 .25
338 Vitali Karamnov .01 .05
339 Rene Corbet RC .08 .25
340 Wendel Clark .02 .10
341 Mike Ridley .01 .05
342 Nelson Emerson .01 .05
343 Joe Juneau .02 .10
344 Vesa Viitakoski RC .08 .25
345 Steve Chiasson .01 .05
346 Andrew Cassels .01 .05
347 Pierre Turgeon .02 .10
348 Brian Leetch .08 .25
349 Alexei Yashin .01 .05
350 Mark Recchi .02 .10
351 Ron Francis .08 .25
352 Mike Ricci .01 .05
353 Igor Korolev .01 .05
354 Brent Gretzky RC .08 .25
355 Dave Poulin .01 .05
356 Cam Neely .08 .25
357 Gary Suter .01 .05
358 Dave Manson .01 .05
359 Robert Kron .01 .05
360 Ulf Dahlen .01 .05
361 Rod Brind'Amour .02 .10
362 Alexei Gusarov .01 .05
363 Vitali Prokhorov .01 .05
364 Damian Rhodes RC .08 .25
365 Paul Ysebaert .01 .05
366 Vladimir Konstantinov .02 .10
367 Steven Rice .01 .05
368 Brian Propp .01 .05
369 Valeri Zelepukin .01 .05
370 David Volek .01 .05
371 Sergei Nemchinov .01 .05
372 Pavol Demitra .08 .25
373 Brent Fedyk .01 .05
374 Larry Murphy .02 .10
375 Dave Karpa .01 .05
376 Dave Babych .01 .05
377 Keith Jones .01 .05
378 Neil Wilkinson .01 .05
379 Jozef Stumpel .01 .05
380 Vincent Damphousse .01 .05
381 Tom Kurvers .01 .05
382 Doug Gilmour .02 .10
383 Trevor Linden .02 .10
384 Kelly Miller .01 .05
385 Tim Sweeney .01 .05
386 Mikhail Tatarinov .01 .05
387 Dominic Hasek .30 .75
388 Steve Yzerman .50 1.25
389 Scott Pearson .01 .05
390 Brian Bellows .01 .05
391 Claude Lemieux .01 .05
392 Marty McInnis .01 .05
393 Jim Sandlak .01 .05
394 Jocelyn Thibault RC .40 1.00
395 John Cullen .01 .05
396 Joe Nieuwendyk .02 .10
397 Mike Modano .15 .40
398 Ray Sheppard .02 .10
399 Trevor Kidd .02 .10
400 Checklist .01 .05
401 Frank Pietrangelo .02 .10
402 Stephan Lebeau .01 .05
403 Stephane Richer .02 .10
404 Greg Gilbert .01 .05
405 Dmitri Filimonov .01 .05
406 Vyacheslav Butsayev .01 .05
407 Mario Lemieux .50 1.25
408 Kevin Miller .01 .05
409 John Tucker .01 .05
410 Murray Craven .01 .05
411 Dale Hawerchuk .02 .10
412 Al MacInnis .02 .10
413 Keith Primeau .01 .05
414 Luc Robitaille .02 .10
415 Benoit Brunet .01 .05
416 Tom Chorske .01 .05
417 Derek King .01 .05
418 Troy Mallette .01 .05
419 Mats Sundin .08 .25
420 Kent Manderville .01 .05
421 Kip Miller .01 .05
422 Jarkko Varvio .01 .05
423 Jason Arnott RC .40 1.00
424 Craig Billington .02 .10
425 Stewart Malgunas RC .08 .25
426 Ron Tugnutt .02 .10
427 Alexei Kudashov RC .08 .25
428 Harijs Vitolinsh .01 .05
429 Bill Houlder .01 .05
430 Craig Simpson .01 .05
431 Wes Walz .01 .05
432 Micah Aivazoff RC .08 .25
433 Scott Levins RC .08 .25
434 Ron Hextall .02 .10
435 Fred Brathwaite RC .30 .75
436 Chad Penney RC .08 .25
437 Vlastimil Kroupa RC .08 .25
438 Troy Loney .01 .05
439 Matthew Barnaby .02 .10
440 Kevin Todd .01 .05
441 Paul Cavallini .01 .05
442 Doug Weight .02 .10
443 Egeny Davydov .01 .05
444 Dominic Lavoie .01 .05
445 Peter Popovic RC .08 .25
446 Sergei Makarov .01 .05
447 Matt Martin RC .08 .25
448 Teemu Selanne .08 .25
449 Todd Ewen .01 .05
450 Sergei Petrenko .01 .05
451 Jeff Shantz .01 .05
452 Greg Johnson .01 .05
453 Brent Severyn RC .08 .25
454 Shawn McEachern .01 .05
455 Pierre Sevigny .01 .05
456 Benoit Hogue .01 .05
457 Esa Tikkanen .01 .05
458 Brian Glynn .01 .05
459 Doug Brown .01 .05
460 Mike Rathje .01 .05
461 Rudy Poeschek .01 .05
462 Jason Woolley .01 .05
463 Patrick Carnback RC .08 .25
464 Cam Stewart RC .08 .25
465 Petr Svoboda .01 .05
466 Ted Drury .01 .05
467 Ladislav Karabin RC .08 .25
468 Paul Broten .01 .05
469 Alexander Godynyuk .01 .05
470 Bob Jay RC .08 .25
471 Steve Larmer .02 .10
472 Jim Montgomery RC .08 .25
473 Darren Puppa .01 .05
474 Alexei Kasatonov .02 .10
475 Derek Plante RC .08 .25
476 German Titov RC .08 .25
477 Steve Dubinsky RC .08 .25
478 Andy Moog .02 .10
479 Aaron Ward RC .08 .25
480 Dean McAmmond .01 .05
481 Randy Gilhen .01 .05
482 Jason Muzzatti RC .08 .25
483 Corey Millen .01 .05
484 Alexander Karpovtsev .01 .05
485 Bill Huard RC .08 .25
486 Mikael Renberg .08 .25
487 Marty McSorley .01 .05
488 Alexander Mogilny .02 .10
489 Michal Sykora RC .08 .25
490 Checklist .01 .05
491 Tom Tilley .01 .05
492 Boris Mironov .01 .05
493 Sandy McCarthy .01 .05
494 Mark Astley RC .08 .25
495 Slava Kozlov .02 .10
496 Brian Benning .01 .05
497 Eric Weinrich .01 .05
498 Robert Burakovsky RC .08 .25
499 Patrick Lebeau .01 .05
500 Markus Naslund .08 .25
501 Jimmy Waite .02 .10
502 Denis Savard .02 .10
503 Jose Charbonneau RC .08 .25
504 Randy Burridge .01 .05
505 Arto Blomsten .01 .05
506 Shaun Van Allen .01 .05
507 Jon Casey .02 .10
508 Darren McCarty RC .30 .75
509 Roman Oksiuta RC .08 .25
510 Jody Hull .01 .05
511 Scott Scissons .01 .05
512 Jeff Norton .01 .05
513 Dmitri Mironov .01 .05
514 Sergei Bautin .01 .05
515 Garry Valk .01 .05
516 Keith Carney .01 .05
517 James Black .01 .05
518 Pat Peake .01 .05
519 Chris Osgood RC 1.50 4.00
520 Kirk Maltby RC .08 .25
521 Gord Murphy .01 .05
522 Mattias Norstrom RC .08 .25
523 Milos Holan RC .08 .25
524 Dave McLlwain .01 .05
525 Phil Housley .02 .10
526 Petr Klima .01 .05
527 John McIntyre .01 .05
528 Enrico Ciccone .01 .05
529 Stephane Quintal .01 .05
530 World Junior .02 .10
Checklist
531 Anson Carter RC .30 .75
532 Jeff Friesen RC .30 .75
533 Yanick Dube RC .08 .25
534 Jason Botterill RC .08 .25
535 Todd Harvey RC .08 .25
536 Manny Fernandez RC .30 .75
537 Jason Allison RC .30 .75
538 Jamie Storr RC .30 .75
539 Rick Girard RC .08 .25
540 Martin Gendron .01 .05
541 Joel Bouchard RC .08 .25
542 Mike Peca RC .30 .75
543 Nick Stajduhar RC .08 .25
544 Brendan Witt RC .08 .25
545 Aaron Gavey RC .08 .25
546 Chris Armstrong RC .08 .25
547 Curtis Bowen RC .08 .25
548 Brandon Convery RC .08 .25
549 Bryan McCabe RC .08 .25
550 Marty Murray RC .08 .25
551 Ryan Sittler .01 .05
552 Jason McBain RC .08 .25
553 Richard Park RC .08 .25
554 Aaron Ellis RC .08 .25
555 Toby Kvalevog RC .08 .25
556 Jay Pandolfo RC .08 .25
557 John Emmons .01 .05
558 Dave Wilkie RC .08 .25
559 John Varga RC .08 .25
560 Jason Bonsignore WJC RC .08 .25
561 Deron Quint WJC RC .08 .25
562 Adam Deadmarsh WJC .01 .05
563 Jon Coleman RC .08 .25
564 Bob Lachance WJC RC .08 .25
565 Chris O'Sullivan WJC RC .08 .25
566 J.Langenbrunner WJC RC .30 .75
567 Kevin Hilton RC .08 .25
568 Kevyn Adams RC .08 .25
569 Saku Koivu WJC .08 .25
570 Mats Lindgren WJC RC .08 .25
571 Valeri Bure WJC RC .30 .75
572 Edvin Frylen RC .08 .25
573 Jaroslav Miklenda WJC RC .08 .25
574 Vadim Sharifijanov WJC .02 .10
575 Checklist Card .01 .05
99B1 W.Gretzky 802 Silver 6.00 15.00
99B2 W.Gretzky 802 Gold 4.00 10.00
SP4 Teemu Selanne Hologram .08 .25

1993-94 Upper Deck Award Winners

Randomly inserted at a rate of 1:30 Canadian first-series foil packs, this eight-card set measures the standard size. The fronts feature a black-and-white photo of the player and his trophy. The player's name appears at the bottom and in silver-foil letters on the left side.

COMPLETE SET (8) 5.00 12.00
AW1 Mario Lemieux 1.50 4.00
AW2 Teemu Selanne .30 .75
Calder Trophy
AW3 Ed Belfour .30 .75
Jennings Trophy
Vezina Trophy
AW4 Patrick Roy 1.50 4.00
Conn Smythe Trophy
AW5 Chris Chelios .30 .75
Jack Norris Trophy
AW6 Doug Gilmour .15 .40
Frank J. Selke Trophy
AW7 Pierre Turgeon .15 .40
Lady Byng Trophy
AW8 Dave Poulin .08 .25
King Clancy

1993-94 Upper Deck Future Heroes

Randomly inserted at a rate of 1:30 first-series U.S. hobby packs, this 10-card set measures the standard size. The tan-bordered fronts feature sepia-toned action player photos with the player's name in white lettering within a black bar above the photo. The set's title appears below the photo, with the word "Heroes" printed in copper foil. On a gray background, the back carries a player profile. The cards are numbered on the back and continue where the Howe Heroes left off.

COMPLETE SET (10) 4.00 10.00
28 Felix Potvin .30 .75
29 Pat Falloon .08 .25
30 Pavel Bure .30 .75
31 Eric Lindros .30 .75
32 Teemu Selanne .30 .75
33 Jaromir Jagr .50 1.25
34 Alexander Mogilny .08 .25
35 Joe Juneau .08 .25
36 Checklist 2.00 5.00
NNO Header Card .75 2.00

1993-94 Upper Deck Gretzky's Great Ones

Randomly inserted in series one packs and one per series one jumbo, this 10-card set measures the standard size. The fronts feature color player photos with blue and gray bars above, below, and to the left. The player's name and the words "Gretzky's Great Ones" in copper-foil letters appear below and above the photo, respectively. The cards are numbered on the back with a "GG" prefix.

COMPLETE SET (10) 2.00 5.00
GG1 Denis Savard .08 .25
GG2 Chris Chelios .20 .50
GG3 Brett Hull .25 .60
GG4 Mario Lemieux 1.00 2.50
GG5 Mark Messier .20 .50
GG6 Paul Coffey .20 .50
GG7 Theo Fleury .05 .15
GG8 Luc Robitaille .08 .25
GG9 Marty McSorley .05 .15
GG10 Grant Fuhr .08 .25

1993-94 Upper Deck Gretzky Box Bottom

Issued on the bottom of Upper Deck boxes, this card measures approximately 5" by 7" and features Wayne Gretzky on the front. The design is the same as his regular issue card. The back is blank. The card is unnumbered.

1 Wayne Gretzky	.40	1.00

1993-94 Upper Deck Gretzky Sheet

This sheet was mailed to collectors who ordered Wayne Gretzky's 24-Karat Gold Card commemorating his NHL record breaking 802nd goal after Upper Deck had unexpected production difficulties. It could also be ordered through the Upper Deck Authenticated catalog. It measures 8 1/2" by 11". The front features a white border and three color action photos of Wayne Gretzky set against a background with the number "802". A seal on the front carries the serial number and the production figure (30,000). The back is blank.

1 Wayne Gretzky	8.00	20.00

1993-94 Upper Deck Hat Tricks

Inserted one per series one jumbo pack, this 20-card set measures the standard size. The fronts feature color player photos that are borderless, except on the right, where a strip that fades from brown to black carries the player's name. The cards are numbered on the back with an "HT" prefix.

COMPLETE SET (20)	2.00	5.00
HT1 Adam Graves	.08	.25
HT2 Geoff Sanderson	.02	.10
HT3 Gary Roberts	.08	.25
HT4 Robert Reichel	.02	.10
HT5 Adam Oates	.08	.25
HT6 Steve Yzerman	1.00	2.50
HT7 Alexei Kovalev	.08	.25
HT8 Vincent Damphousse	.02	.10
HT9 Rob Gaudreau	.02	.10
HT10 Pat LaFontaine	.08	.25
HT11 Pierre Turgeon	.08	.25
HT12 Rick Tocchet	.08	.25
HT13 Michael Nylander	.02	.10
HT14 Steve Larmer	.08	.25
HT15 Alexander Mogilny	.08	.25
HT16 Owen Nolan	.08	.25
HT17 Luc Robitaille	.20	.50
HT18 Jeremy Roenick	.25	.60
HT19 Kevin Stevens	.02	.10
HT20 Mats Sundin	.20	.50

1993-94 Upper Deck Next In Line

Randomly inserted in all first-series packs, this six-card set measures the standard-size. The horizontal metallic and prismatic fronts feature photos of two NHL players, diagonally divided in the middle. The players' names appear under the photos. The cards are numbered on the back with an "NL" prefix.

COMPLETE SET (6)	7.50	15.00
NL1 Wayne Gretzky Michael Nylander	2.50	6.00
NL2 Brett Hull Patrick Poulin	.75	2.00
NL3 Steve Yzerman Joe Sakic	2.50	6.00
NL4 Ray Bourque Brian Leetch	2.00	5.00
NL5 Doug Gilmour Keith Tkachuk	1.00	2.50
NL6 Patrick Roy Felix Potvin	1.25	3.00

1993-94 Upper Deck NHL's Best

Randomly inserted at a rate of 1:30 first-series U.S. retail packs, this 10-card set measures the standard size. The fronts feature color action player photos that are borderless, except at the bottom, where a black bar carries the player's name. The cards are numbered on the back with an "HB" prefix.

COMPLETE SET (10)	5.00	10.00
HB1 Alexander Mogilny	.10	.30
HB2 Rob Gaudreau	.05	.15
HB3 Brett Hull	.40	1.00
HB4 Dallas Drake	.05	.15
HB5 Pavel Bure	.30	.75
HB6 Alexei Kovalev	.10	.30
HB7 Mario Lemieux	1.50	4.00
HB8 Eric Lindros	.30	.75
HB9 Wayne Gretzky	2.00	5.00
HB10 Joe Juneau	.10	.30

1993-94 Upper Deck NHLPA/Roots

Teamed with the NHL Players Association, Upper Deck issued these clothing tags as a promotion for a new line of clothing produced by the clothing manufacturer, Roots Canada. Called "Hang Out," each article of clothing came with one of ten "hang tag" cards featuring on their fronts a full-bleed photo of the NHL player wearing the clothing. The clothing tags measure the standard size and are punch holed in the upper left corner. Versions of these cards without the punch hole also exist. With a faded and enlarged Upper Deck logo, the backs carry the player's name and an advertisement for the NHLPA apparel. The cards are numbered on the back. The entire set could also be purchased by mail. The first series came out in 1993, while the second series came out in 1994. Reportedly 5,000 sets of the third series were produced. The backs of cards 21-30 also have a NHLPA apparel advertisement but sport a different design than cards 1-20.

COMPLETE SET (30)	16.00	40.00
COMPLETE SERIES 1 (10)	6.00	15.00
COMPLETE SERIES 2 (10)	6.00	15.00
COMPLETE SERIES 3 (10)	6.00	15.00
1 Trevor Linden	.50	1.25
2 Patrick Roy	4.00	10.00
3 Felix Potvin	.60	1.50
4 Steve Yzerman	4.00	10.00
5 Doug Gilmour	.60	1.50
6 Wendel Clark	.50	1.25
7 Kirk McLean	.50	1.25
8 Larry Murphy	.15	.40
9 Guy Carbonneau	.15	.40
10 Mike Ricci	.50	1.25
11 Doug Gilmour	.60	1.50
12 Sergei Fedorov	1.25	3.00
13 Shayne Corson	.15	.40
14 Alexei Yashin	.50	1.25
15 Pavel Bure	1.50	4.00
16 Joe Sakic	1.50	4.00
17 Teemu Selanne	1.25	3.00
18 Dave Andreychuk	.50	1.25
19 Al MacInnis	.50	1.25
20 Rob Blake	.50	1.25
21 Doug Gilmour	.60	1.50
22 Steve Larmer	.15	.40
23 Eric Lindros	1.50	4.00
24 Mike Modano	.75	2.00
25 Vincent Damphousse	.50	1.25
26 Mike Gartner	.50	1.25
27 John Vanbiesbrouck	.60	1.50
28 Theo Fleury	.60	1.50
29 Ken Baumgartner	.15	.40
30 Jeremy Roenick	.60	1.50

1993-94 Upper Deck Program of Excellence

Randomly inserted at a rate of 1:30 Canadian second series packs, this 15-card set measures the standard size. The fronts feature color action player photos that are borderless, except at the right, where the margin carries the player's name in silver-foil letters. The silver-foil "Program of Excellence" logo rests at the lower right. The cards are numbered on the back with an "E" prefix.

COMPLETE SET (15)	8.00	20.00
E1 Adam Smith	.40	1.00
E2 Jason Podollan	.40	1.00
E3 Jason Wiemer	.40	1.00
E4 Jeff O'Neill	.40	1.00
E5 Daniel Goneau	.40	1.00
E6 Christian Laflamme	.40	1.00
E7 Daymond Langkow	.40	1.00
E8 Jeff Friesen	.40	1.00
E9 Wayne Primeau	.40	1.00
E10 Paul Kariya	2.00	5.00
E11 Rob Niedermayer	.40	1.00
E12 Eric Lindros	.75	2.00
E13 Mario Lemieux	2.00	5.00
E14 Steve Yzerman	2.00	5.00
E15 Alexandre Daigle	.40	1.00

1993-94 Upper Deck Silver Skates

The first ten standard-size die-cut cards (H1-H10) listed below were randomly inserted in U.S. second-series hobby packs, while the second ten (R1-R10) were inserted in U.S. retail packs. The fronts feature color player action cutouts set on red and black backgrounds. The trade cards were randomly inserted in both hobby and jumbo packs and could be redeemed for a silver or gold retail set. These cards picture Gretzky, and because the majority were redeemed, they have become highly sought after in their own right.

COMPLETE HOBBY SET (10)	2.50	6.00
COMPLETE RETAIL SET (10)		
*RETAIL GOLD EXCH: .75X TO 1.5X BASIC INSERTS		
H1 Mario Lemieux	1.50	4.00
H2 Pavel Bure	.30	.75
H3 Eric Lindros	.30	.75
H4 Rob Niedermayer	.20	.50
H5 Chris Pronger	.08	.25
H6 Adam Oates	.08	.25
H7 Pierre Turgeon	.20	.50
H8 Alexei Yashin	.08	.25
H9 Joe Sakic	.60	1.50
H10 Alexander Mogilny	.20	.50
R1 Wayne Gretzky	2.00	5.00
R2 Teemu Selanne	.30	.75
R3 Alexandre Daigle	.08	.25
R4 Chris Gratton	.08	.25
R5 Brett Hull	.40	1.00
R6 Steve Yzerman	1.50	4.00
R7 Doug Gilmour	.08	.25
R8 Jaromir Jagr	.50	1.25
R9 Jason Arnott	.60	1.50
R10 Jeremy Roenick	.40	1.00
NNO W.Gretzky Gold Trade	20.00	50.00
NNO W.Gretzky Silver Trade	15.00	40.00

1993-94 Upper Deck SP

Inserted one per second-series pack and two per second-series jumbo, these 180 standard-size cards feature color player action shots on their fronts. The photos are borderless, except at the bottom, where a team color-coded margin carries the player's name and position in white lettering. The player's team name appears in a silver-foil arc above him.

COMPLETE SET (180)	40.00	80.00
1 Sean Hill	.15	.40
2 Troy Loney	.15	.40
3 Joe Sacco	.15	.40
4 Anatoli Semenov	.15	.40
5 Ron Tugnutt	.30	.75
6 Terry Yake	.15	.40
7 Ray Bourque	1.00	2.50
8 Jon Casey	.30	.75
9 Joe Juneau	.30	.75
10 Cam Neely	.60	1.50
11 Adam Oates	.30	.75
12 Bryan Smolinski	.15	.40
13 Matthew Barnaby	.30	.75
14 Philippe Boucher	.15	.40
15 Grant Fuhr	.30	.75
16 Dale Hawerchuk	.30	.75
17 Pat LaFontaine	.60	1.50
18 Alexander Mogilny	.30	.75
19 Craig Simpson	.15	.40
20 Ted Drury	.15	.40
21 Theo Fleury	.15	.40
22 Al MacInnis	.30	.75
23 Joe Nieuwendyk	.30	.75
24 Joel Otto	.15	.40
25 Gary Roberts	.15	.40
26 Vesa Viitakoski	.15	.40
27 Ed Belfour	.60	1.50
28 Chris Chelios	.60	1.50
29 Joe Murphy	.15	.40
30 Patrick Poulin	.15	.40
31 Jeremy Roenick	1.00	2.50
32 Jeff Shantz	.15	.40
33 Kevin Todd	.15	.40
34 Neal Broten	.30	.75
35 Paul Cavallini	.15	.40
36 Russ Courtnall	.15	.40
37 Derian Hatcher	.15	.40
38 Mike Modano	1.00	2.50
39 Andy Moog	.30	.75
40 Jarkko Varvio	.15	.40
41 Dino Ciccarelli	.30	.75
42 Paul Coffey	.60	1.50
43 Dallas Drake	.15	.40
44 Sergei Fedorov	.60	1.50
45 Keith Primeau	.15	.40
46 Bob Probert	.30	.75
47 Steve Yzerman	2.00	5.00
48 Jason Arnott	.30	.75
49 Shayne Corson	.15	.40
50 Dave Manson	.15	.40
51 Dean McAmmond	.15	.40
52 Bill Ranford	.30	.75
53 Doug Weight	.30	.75
54 Brad Werenka	.15	.40
55 Evgeny Davydov	.15	.40
56 Scott Levins	.15	.40
57 Scott Mellanby	.30	.75
58 Rob Niedermayer	.30	.75
59 Brian Skrudland	.15	.40
60 John Vanbiesbrouck	.30	.75
61 Robert Kron	.15	.40
62 Michael Nylander	.15	.40
63 Robert Petrovicky	.15	.40
64 Chris Pronger	.30	.75
65 Geoff Sanderson	.30	.75
66 Darren Turcotte	.15	.40
67 Pat Verbeek	.15	.40
68 Rob Blake	.30	.75
69 Tony Granato	.15	.40
70 Wayne Gretzky	4.00	10.00
71 Kelly Hrudey	.30	.75
72 Shawn McEachern	.15	.40
73 Luc Robitaille	.30	.75
74 Darryl Sydor	.15	.40
75 Alexei Zhitnik	.15	.40
76 Brian Bellows	.15	.40
77 Vincent Damphousse	.15	.40
78 Stephan Lebeau	.15	.40
79 John LeClair	.60	1.50
80 Kirk Muller	.15	.40
81 Patrick Roy	2.50	6.00
82 Pierre Sevigny	.15	.40
83 Claude Lemieux	.15	.40
84 Corey Millen	.15	.40
85 Bernie Nicholls	.15	.40
86 Scott Niedermayer	.15	.40
87 Stephane Richer	.30	.75
88 Alexander Semak	.15	.40
89 Scott Stevens	.30	.75
90 Ray Ferraro	.15	.40
91 Darius Kasparaitis	.15	.40
92 Scott Lachance	.15	.40
93 Vladimir Malakhov	.15	.40
94 Marty McInnis	.15	.40
95 Steve Thomas	.15	.40
96 Pierre Turgeon	.30	.75
97 Tony Amonte	.30	.75
98 Mike Gartner	.30	.75
99 Adam Graves	.15	.40
100 Alexander Karpovtsev	.15	.40
101 Alexei Kovalev	.30	.75
102 Brian Leetch	.60	1.50
103 Mark Messier	.60	1.50
104 Esa Tikkanen	.15	.40
105 Craig Billington	.30	.75
106 Robert Burakovsky	.15	.40
107 Alexandre Daigle	.15	.40
108 Pavol Demitra	.30	.75
109 Dmitri Filimonov	.15	.40
110 Bob Kudelski	.15	.40
111 Norm Maciver	.15	.40
112 Alexei Yashin	.15	.40
113 Josef Beranek	.15	.40
114 Rod Brind'Amour	.30	.75
115 Milos Holan	.15	.40
116 Eric Lindros	.60	1.50
117 Mark Recchi	.30	.75
118 Mikael Renberg	.30	.75
119 Dimitri Yushkevich	.15	.40
120 Tom Barrasso	.30	.75
121 Jaromir Jagr	1.25	3.00
122 Mario Lemieux	2.50	6.00
123 Markus Naslund	.60	1.50
124 Kevin Stevens	.15	.40
125 Martin Straka	.30	.75
126 Rick Tocchet	.30	.75
127 Martin Gelinas	.15	.40
128 Owen Nolan	.30	.75
129 Mike Ricci	.15	.40
130 Joe Sakic	1.25	3.00
131 Chris Simon	.30	.75
132 Mats Sundin	.60	1.50
133 Jocelyn Thibault	.60	1.50
134 Philippe Bozon	.15	.40
135 Jeff Brown	.15	.40
136 Phil Housley	.15	.40
137 Brett Hull	1.00	2.50
138 Craig Janney	.15	.40
139 Curtis Joseph	.60	1.50
140 Brendan Shanahan	.60	1.50
141 Pat Falloon	.15	.40
142 Johan Garpenlov	.15	.40
143 Rob Gaudreau	.15	.40
144 Vlastimil Kroupa	.15	.40
145 Sergei Makarov	.15	.40
146 Sandis Ozolinsh	.15	.40
147 Mike Rathje	.15	.40
148 Brian Bradley	.15	.40
149 Chris Gratton	.30	.75
150 Brent Gretzky	.15	.40
151 Roman Hamrlik	.15	.40
152 Petr Klima	.15	.40
153 Denis Savard	.30	.75
154 Rob Zamuner	.15	.40
155 Dave Andreychuk	.30	.75
156 Nikolai Borschevsky	.15	.40
157 Dave Ellett	.15	.40
158 Doug Gilmour	.30	.75
159 Alexei Kudashov	.15	.40
160 Felix Potvin	.60	1.50
161 Greg Adams	.15	.40
162 Pavel Bure	.60	1.50
163 Geoff Courtnall	.15	.40
164 Trevor Linden	.30	.75
165 Kirk McLean	.30	.75
166 Jiri Slegr	.15	.40
167 Dixon Ward	.15	.40
168 Peter Bondra	.30	.75
169 Kevin Hatcher	.15	.40
170 Al Iafrate	.15	.40
171 Dimitri Khristich	.15	.40
172 Pat Peake	.15	.40
173 Mike Ridley	.15	.40
174 Arto Blomsten	.15	.40
175 Nelson Emerson	.15	.40
176 Boris Mironov	.15	.40
177 Teemu Selanne	.60	1.50
178 Keith Tkachuk	.60	1.50
179 Paul Ysebaert	.15	.40
180 Alexei Zhamnov	.30	.75

1994-95 Upper Deck

The 1994-95 Upper Deck set was issued in two series of 270 and 300 cards for a total of 570 standard-size cards. The product was available in three packaging versions per series: US Hobby, US Retail and Canadian. The fronts have a team color coded bar on the left border. The team name, position and player name are within the bar in gold foil. Due to a printing error, card numbers 22, 65, 85 and 200 each appear with two different numbers. Each variation was printed in the same quantity, so neither version carries a premium. Subsets include Shooter's Edge (227-234), Super Rookies (235-270), World Junior Championship teams including Canada (496-505), Czech Republic (506-509), Finland (510-512), Russia (513-517), Sweden (518-521) and USA (522-525), as well as Calder Candidates (526-540), and 1994 World Tour (541-570).

COMPLETE SET (570)	20.00	50.00
COMP.SERIES 1 (270)	10.00	25.00
COMP.SERIES 2 (300)	10.00	25.00
1 Wayne Gretzky	.75	2.00
2 German Titov	.02	.10
3 Guy Hebert	.05	.15
4 Tony Amonte	.05	.15
5 Dino Ciccarelli	.05	.15
6 Geoff Sanderson	.05	.15
7 Alexei Zhamnov	.05	.15
8 John MacLean	.05	.15
9 Brent Fedyk	.02	.10
10 Adam Graves	.02	.10
11 Adam Oates	.05	.15
12 Ron Francis	.05	.15
13 Bobby Dollas	.02	.10
14 Ray Ferraro	.02	.10
15 Paul Broten	.02	.10
16 Ulf Dahlen	.02	.10
17 Pat LaFontaine	.10	.30
18 Craig Janney	.05	.15
19 Garry Galley	.02	.10
1P Wayne Gretzky JUMBO PROMO	2.00	5.00
20 Gary Roberts	.02	.10
21 Bill Ranford	.05	.15
22 Mario Lemieux	.60	1.50
22B Mike Sillinger ERR	.02	.10
23 Glen Murray	.02	.10
24 Paul Coffey	.10	.30
25 Corey Millen	.02	.10
26 Chris Chelios	.10	.30
27 Ronnie Stern	.02	.10
28 Zdeno Ciger	.02	.10
29 Tony Granato	.02	.10
30 Donald Audette	.02	.10
31 Russ Courtnall	.02	.10
32 Mike Gartner	.05	.15
33 Marty McSorley	.02	.10
34 Jeff Brown	.02	.10
35 Mark Janssens	.02	.10
36 Patrick Poulin	.02	.10
37 Sergei Fedorov	.20	.50
38 Tim Sweeney	.02	.10
39 John Slaney	.02	.10
40 Steve Larmer	.05	.15
41 Dave Karpa	.02	.10
42 Esa Tikkanen	.02	.10
43 Joel Otto	.02	.10
44 Doug Weight	.05	.15
45 Murray Craven	.02	.10
46 John Vanbiesbrouck	.05	.15
47 Nelson Emerson	.02	.10
48 Dean Evason	.02	.10
49 Evgeny Davydov	.02	.10
50 Craig Simpson	.02	.10
51 Mats Sundin	.10	.30
52 Chris Pronger	.10	.30
53 Stephan Lebeau	.02	.10
54 Martin Gelinas	.02	.10
55 Bob Rouse	.02	.10
56 Christian Ruuttu	.02	.10
57 Gilbert Dionne	.02	.10
58 Mike Modano	.20	.50
59 Derek King	.02	.10
60 Peter Stastny	.05	.15
61 Ted Donato	.02	.10
62 Mark Messier	.10	.30
63 Dave Manson	.02	.10
64 Johan Garpenlov	.02	.10
65 Igor Larionov	.02	.10
65B Sergio Momesso ERR	.02	.10
66 Kirk Muller	.02	.10
67 Dave Ellett	.02	.10
68 Dale Hunter	.02	.10
69 Brent Gretzky	.02	.10
70 Tom Barrasso	.05	.15
71 Philippe Boucher	.02	.10
72 Jesse Belanger	.02	.10
73 Scott Stevens	.05	.15
74 Gary Suter	.02	.10
75 Tim Cheveldae	.05	.15
76 Dimitri Khristich	.02	.10
77 Pierre Turgeon	.05	.15
78 Mike Richter	.10	.30
79 Michael Nylander	.02	.10
80 Sergei Krivokrasov	.02	.10
81 Andy Moog UER (Darcy Wakaluk on back)	.10	.30
82 Al Iafrate	.02	.10
83 Bernie Nicholls	.05	.15
84 Darren Turcotte	.02	.10
85 Sergio Momesso	.02	.10
85B Igor Larionov ERR	.02	.10
86 Petr Klima	.02	.10
87 Alexandre Daigle	.02	.10
88 Joe Juneau	.05	.15
89 Glen Wesley	.02	.10
90 Teemu Selanne	.10	.30
91 Curtis Joseph	.10	.30
92 Scott Mellanby	.05	.15
93 Jaromir Jagr	.20	.50
94 Mark Recchi	.05	.15
95 Jiri Slegr	.02	.10
96 Martin Brodeur	.30	.75
97 Scott Pearson	.02	.10
98 Eric Lindros	.10	.30
99 Larry Murphy	.05	.15
100 Sergei Zubov	.02	.10
101 Mathieu Schneider	.02	.10
102 Dale Hawerchuk	.05	.15
103 Owen Nolan	.05	.15
104 Darryl Sydor	.02	.10
105 Anatoli Semenov	.02	.10
106 Marty McInnis	.02	.10
107 Derek Mayer	.02	.10
108 Steve Duchesne	.02	.10
109 Geoff Smith	.02	.10
110 Zarley Zalapski	.02	.10
111 Rod Brind'Amour	.05	.15
112 Nicklas Lidstrom	.10	.30
113 Teppo Numminen	.02	.10
114 Denny Felsner	.02	.10
115 Wendel Clark	.05	.15
116 Arturs Irbe	.05	.15
117 Josef Beranek	.02	.10
118 Brian Bradley	.02	.10
119 Eric Weinrich	.02	.10
120 Kevin Todd	.02	.10
121 Patrick Roy	.60	1.50
122 Guy Carbonneau	.02	.10
123 Tom Kurvers	.02	.10
124 Sergei Makarov	.02	.10
125 Pat Peake	.02	.10
126 Danton Cole	.02	.10
127 Derian Hatcher	.02	.10
128 Kjell Samuelsson	.02	.10
129 Alexei Yashin	.05	.15
130 Chris Osgood	.05	.15
131 Kent Manderville	.02	.10
132 Jim Montgomery	.02	.10
133 Kirk McLean	.05	.15
134 Kelly Buchberger	.02	.10
135 Peter Bondra	.05	.15
136 Stephane Matteau	.02	.10
137 Oleg Petrov	.02	.10
138 Doug Gilmour	.05	.15
139 Vladimir Malakhov	.02	.10
140 Peter Zezel	.02	.10
141 Mike Vernon	.05	.15
142 Derek Plante	.02	.10
143 Valeri Zelepukin	.02	.10
144 Kevin Haller	.02	.10
145 Keith Tkachuk	.10	.30
146 Claude Boivin	.02	.10
147 Jocelyn Thibault	.10	.30
148 Jyrki Lumme	.02	.10
149 Ray Whitney	.02	.10
150 Al MacInnis	.05	.15
151 Kelly Miller	.02	.10
152 Ray Sheppard	.05	.15
153 Aaron Ward	.02	.10
154 Damian Rhodes	.05	.15
155 Jozef Stumpel	.02	.10
156 Sergei Nemchinov	.02	.10
157 Richard Matvichuk	.02	.10
158 Sean Burke	.05	.15
159 Todd Marchant	.02	.10
160 Ryan McGill	.02	.10
161 Sean Hill	.02	.10
162 Iain Fraser	.02	.10
163 Shawn McEachern	.02	.10
164 Petr Nedved	.05	.15
165 John Lilley	.02	.10
166 Joe Sacco	.02	.10
167 Jason Dawe	.02	.10
168 Mike Rathje	.02	.10
169 Phil Housley	.05	.15
170 Ron Hextall	.05	.15
171 Yves Racine	.02	.10
172 Boris Mironov	.02	.10
173 Vitali Prokhorov	.02	.10
174 Roman Hamrlik	.05	.15
175 Robert Lang	.02	.10
176 Jody Hull	.02	.10
177 Mike Ridley	.02	.10
178 Dmitri Filimonov	.02	.10
179 Rene Corbet	.02	.10
180 Rob Pearson	.02	.10
181 Richard Smehlik	.02	.10
182 Rob Gaudreau	.02	.10
183 Bill Houlder	.02	.10
184 Igor Korolev	.02	.10
185 Chris Joseph	.02	.10
186 Shane Churla	.02	.10
187 Rick Tabaracci	.05	.15
188 Alexander Godynyuk	.02	.10
189 Vladimir Konstantinov	.05	.15
190 Markus Naslund	.10	.30
191 Tom Chorske	.02	.10
192 Thomas Steen	.02	.10
193 Patrice Brisebois	.02	.10
194 Luc Robitaille	.05	.15
195 Michal Sykora	.02	.10
196 Troy Mallette	.02	.10
197 Steve Chiasson	.02	.10
198 Jimmy Carson	.02	.10
199 Mike Donnelly	.02	.10
200 Mike Sillinger	.02	.10
200B Mario Lemieux ERR	.60	1.50
201 Martin Rucinsky	.02	.10
202 Adam Bennett	.02	.10
203 Matt Johnson RC	.02	.10
204 Daren Puppa	.05	.15
205 Ted Drury	.02	.10
206 Jon Casey	.05	.15
207 Alexei Kovalev	.05	.15
208 Alexei Kasatonov	.02	.10
209 Ulf Samuelsson	.02	.10
210 Justin Hocking RC	.02	.10
211 Greg Adams	.05	.15
212 Greg Johnson	.02	.10
213 Mike Craig	.02	.10
214 Steve Konowalchuk	.02	.10
215 Luke Richardson	.02	.10
216 Pavol Demitra	.05	.15
217 Brian Benning	.02	.10
218 Corey Hirsch	.05	.15
219 Alexander Semak	.02	.10
220 Travis Green	.05	.15
221 Turner Stevenson	.02	.10
222 Dimitri Mironov	.02	.10
223 Christian Soucy RC	.05	.15
224 Rick Tocchet	.05	.15
225 Craig MacTavish	.02	.10
226 Wayne Gretzky 802 Record Breaker	.75	2.00
227 Pavel Bure	.10	.30
228 Wayne Gretzky	.10	.30
229 Brett Hull	.10	.30
230 Mike Gartner	.05	.15
231 Brian Leetch	.10	.30
232 Al MacInnis	.05	.15
233 Dominik Hasek	.10	.30
234 Mark Messier	.10	.30
235 Paul Kariya	.10	.30
236 Jamie Storr	.05	.15
237 Jeff Friesen	.05	.15
238 Kenny Jonsson	.02	.10
239 Mariusz Czerkawski RC	.15	.40
240 Brett Lindros	.02	.10
241 Andrei Nikolishin	.02	.10
242 Jason Allison	.02	.10
243 Oleg Tverdovsky	.05	.15
244 Brian Savage	.02	.10
245 Peter Forsberg	.50	1.25
246 Patrik Juhlin RC	.02	.10
247 Jassen Cullimore	.02	.10
248 Chris Therien	.02	.10
249 Kevin Brown RC	.02	.10
250 Jeff Nelson	.02	.10
251 Janne Laukkanen	.02	.10
252 Jamie McLennan	.05	.15
253 Craig Johnson	.02	.10
254 Ravil Gusmanov RC	.02	.10
255 Valeri Bure	.02	.10
256 Valeri Karpov RC	.02	.10
257 Mike Peca	.05	.15
258 Brian Rolston	.02	.10
259 Brandon Convery	.02	.10
260 Mark Lawrence RC	.02	.10
261 Adam Deadmarsh	.02	.10
262 Jason Wiemer RC	.02	.10
263 Alexander Cherbayev	.02	.10
264 Sergei Gonchar	.02	.10
265 Viktor Kozlov	.02	.10
266 Vladislav Boulin RC	.02	.10
267 Todd Harvey	.02	.10
268 Cory Stillman RC	.02	.10
269 David Oliver RC	.02	.10
270 Andrei Nazarov	.02	.10
271 Mikael Renberg	.05	.15
272 Andrei Kovalenko	.02	.10
273 Neal Broten	.05	.15
274 Ed Olczyk	.02	.10
275 Steve Thomas	.02	.10
276 Joe Nieuwendyk	.05	.15
277 Rob Gaudreau	.02	.10
278 Pat Verbeek	.02	.10
279 Eric Desjardins	.05	.15
280 Vincent Damphousse	.02	.10
281 John Cullen	.02	.10
282 Garry Valk	.02	.10
283 Daniel Lacroix	.02	.10
284 Mike Ricci	.02	.10
285 Dominik Hasek	.25	.60
286 Geoff Courtnall	.02	.10
287 Rob Niedermayer	.05	.15
288 Alexander Karpovtsev	.02	.10
289 Martin Straka	.02	.10
290 Ed Belfour	.10	.30
291 Dave Lowry	.02	.10
292 Brendan Shanahan	.10	.30
293 Jari Kurri	.05	.15
294 Steven Rice	.02	.10
295 Scott Levins	.02	.10
296 Ray Bourque	.20	.50
297 Mikael Andersson	.02	.10
298 Darius Kasparaitis	.02	.10
299 Chris Simon	.02	.10
300 Steve Yzerman	.60	1.50
301 Don McSween	.02	.10
302 Brian Noonan	.02	.10
303 Claude Lemieux	.02	.10
304 Radek Bonk RC	.20	.50
305 Jason Arnott	.02	.10
306 Ian Laperriere RC	.02	.10
307 Pat Falloon	.02	.10
308 Kris King	.02	.10
309 Brian Bellows	.02	.10
310 Uwe Krupp	.02	.10
311 Paul Cavallini	.02	.10
312 Shaun Van Allen	.02	.10
313 Dave Andreychuk	.05	.15
314 Bobby Holik	.02	.10
315 Theo Fleury	.02	.10
316 Mark Osborne	.02	.10
317 Andrew Cassels	.02	.10
318 Chris Tamer	.02	.10
319 Trevor Linden	.05	.15
320 Tom Fitzgerald	.02	.10
321 Ron Tugnutt	.05	.15
322 Jeremy Roenick	.15	.40
323 Todd Marchant	.02	.10
324 Scott Niedermayer	.02	.10
325 Tim Taylor RC	.02	.10
326 Mike Kennedy RC	.02	.10
327 Steve Heinze	.02	.10
328 David Sacco	.02	.10
329 Sergei Brylin	.02	.10
330 John LeClair	.10	.30
331 Brian Skrudland	.02	.10
332 Kevin Hatcher	.02	.10
333 Brett Hull	.15	.40
334 Alexander Mogilny	.05	.15
335 Sylvain Lefebvre	.02	.10
336 Sylvain Turgeon	.02	.10
337 Keith Primeau	.02	.10
338 Eric Fichaud RC	.05	.15
339 Jeff Beukeboom	.02	.10
340 Cory Cross RC	.02	.10
341 J.J. Daigneault	.02	.10
342 Stephen Leach	.02	.10
343 Zigmund Palffy	.05	.15
344 Igor Korolev	.02	.10
345 Chris Gratton	.02	.10
346 Joe Mullen	.05	.15
347 Brent Gilchrist	.02	.10
348 Adam Creighton	.02	.10
349 Dimitri Yushkevich	.02	.10
350 Wes Walz	.02	.10
351 Shayne Corson	.02	.10
352 Eric Lacroix	.02	.10
353 Maxim Bets	.02	.10
354 Sylvain Cote	.02	.10
355 Valeri Kamensky	.05	.15
356 Shjon Podein	.02	.10
357 Robert Reichel	.02	.10
358 Cliff Ronning	.02	.10
359 Bill Guerin	.05	.15
360 Dallas Drake	.02	.10
361 Robert Petrovicky	.02	.10
362 Ken Wregget	.05	.15
363 Todd Elik	.02	.10
364 Cam Neely	.10	.30
365 Darren McCarty	.02	.10
366 Shean Donovan RC	.02	.10

367 Felix Potvin .10 .30
368 Yuri Khmylev .02 .10
369 Mark Tinordi .02 .10
370 Craig Billington .05 .15
371 Patrick Flatley .02 .10
372 Jocelyn Lemieux .02 .10
373 Slava Kozlov .05 .15
374 Trent Klatt .02 .10
375 Geoff Sarjeant RC .02 .10
376 Bob Kudelski .02 .10
377 Stanislav Neckar RC .02 .10
378 Jon Rohloff RC .02 .10
379 Jeff Shantz .02 .10
380 Dale Craigwell .02 .10
381 Adrien Plavsic .02 .10
382 Dave Gagner .05 .15
383 Dave Archibald .02 .10
384 Gilbert Dionne .02 .10
385 Troy Loney .02 .10
386 Dean McAmmond .02 .10
387 Pauli Jaks .05 .15
388 Stephane Richer .05 .15
389 Don Beaupre .05 .15
390 Kevin Stevens .02 .10
391 Brad May .02 .10
392 Neil Wilkinson .02 .10
393 Kevin Lowe .02 .10
394 Fredrik Olausson .02 .10
395 Trevor Kidd .05 .15
396 Brent Grieve .02 .10
397 Dominic Roussel .05 .15
398 Bret Hedican .02 .10
399 Bryan Smolinski .02 .10
400 Doug Lidster .02 .10
401 Bob Errey .02 .10
402 Pierre Sevigny .02 .10
403 Rob Brown .02 .10
404 Joe Sakic .25 .60
405 Nikolai Borschevsky .02 .10
406 Martin Lapointe .02 .10
407 Jean-Yves Roy RC .02 .10
408 Robert Kron .02 .10
409 Tie Domi .05 .15
410 Jim Dowd .02 .10
411 Keith Jones .02 .10
412 Scott Lachance .02 .10
413 Bob Corkum .02 .10
414 Denis Chasse RC .02 .10
415 Denis Savard .05 .15
416 Joe Murphy .02 .10
417 Vyacheslav Butsayev .02 .10
418 Mattias Norstrom .02 .10
419 Sergei Zholtok .02 .10
420 Nikolai Khabibulin .05 .15
421 Pat Elynuik .02 .10
422 Doug Brown .02 .10
423 Dave McLlwain .02 .10
424 James Patrick .02 .10
425 Alexander Selivanov RC .10 .30
426 Scott Thornton .02 .10
427 Todd Ewen .02 .10
428 Peter Popovic .02 .10
429 Jarkko Varvio .02 .10
430 Paul Ranheim .02 .10
431 Kevin Dineen .02 .10
432 Kelly Hrudey .05 .15
433 Michal Grosek RC .02 .10
434 Slava Fetisov .02 .10
435 Ivan Droppa .02 .10
436 Benoit Hogue .02 .10
437 Sheldon Kennedy .02 .10
438 Gord Murphy .02 .10
439 Jamie Baker .02 .10
440 Todd Gill .02 .10
441 Mark Recchi .05 .15
442 Ted Crowley .02 .10
443 Ryan Smyth RC .75 2.00
444 Brian Leetch .10 .30
445 Bob Sweeney .02 .10
446 Don Sweeney .02 .10
447 Byron Dafoe RC .20 .50
448 Nathan Lafayette .02 .10
449 Keith Carney .02 .10
450 Stephane Fiset .05 .15
451 Kevin Miller .02 .10
452 Craig Darby RC .02 .10
453 Vlastimil Kroupa .02 .10
454 Rob Zettler .02 .10
455 Glenn Healy .05 .15
456 Todd Simon .02 .10
457 Mark Fitzpatrick .05 .15
458 Drake Berehowsky .02 .10
459 Darcy Wakaluk .05 .15
460 Enrico Ciccone .02 .10
461 Tomas Sandstrom .02 .10
462 Mikhail Shtalenkov .02 .10
463 Igor Kravchuk .02 .10
464 Jamie Allison .02 .10
465 Gino Odjick .02 .10
466 Norm Maciver .02 .10
467 Terry Carkner .02 .10
468 Rob Zamuner .02 .10
469 Pavel Bure .10 .30
470 Patrice Tardif RC .02 .10
471 Andrei Lomakin .02 .10
472 Kirk Maltby .02 .10
473 Jaroslav Modry .02 .10
474 Tommy Soderstrom .05 .15
475 Patrik Carnback .02 .10
476 Jeff Reese .02 .10
477 Todd Krygier .02 .10
478 John McIntyre .02 .10
479 Joey Kocur .02 .10
480 Steve Rucchin RC .20 .50
481 Bob Bassen .02 .10
482 Marek Malik RC .02 .10
483 Darrin Shannon .02 .10
484 Shawn Burr .02 .10
485 Louie DeBrusk .02 .10
486 Olaf Kolzig .05 .15
487 Cam Stewart .02 .10
488 Rob Blake .05 .15
489 Eric Charron RC .02 .10
490 Sandis Ozolinsh .02 .10
491 Paul Ysebaert .02 .10
492 Kris Draper .02 .10
493 Stu Barnes .02 .10
494 Doug Bodger .02 .10
495 Blaine Lacher RC .05 .15
496 Ed Jovanovski RC .20 .50
497 Eric Daze RC .20 .50
498 Dan Cloutier RC .30 .75
499 Chad Allen RC .02 .10
500 Todd Harvey .02 .10
501 Jamie Rivers RC .02 .10
502 Bryan McCabe .02 .10
503 Darcy Tucker RC .60 1.50
504 Wade Redden RC .20 .50
505 Nolan Baumgartner RC .02 .10
506 Marek Malik RC .02 .10
507 Petr Cajanek RC .20 .50
508 Jan Hlavac RC .20 .50
509 Ladislav Kohn RC .02 .10
510 Kimmo Timonen .05 .15
511 Antti Aalto RC .05 .15
512 Tommi Rajamaki RC .05 .15
513 Vitali Yachmenev RC .05 .15
514 Vadim Epantchinsev RC .05 .15
515 Dmitri Klevakin RC .05 .15
516 Nikolai Zavarukhin RC .02 .10
517 Alexander Korolyuk RC .15 .40
518 Anders Eriksson .05 .15
519 Jesper Mattsson RC .05 .15
520 Mattias Ohlund RC .20 .50
521 Anders Soderberg RC .05 .15
522 Bryan Berard RC .20 .50
523 Jason Bonsignore .02 .10
524 Deron Quint .02 .10
525 Richard Park .02 .10
526 Jeff Friesen .02 .10
527 Paul Kariya .10 .30
528 Peter Forsberg .30 .75
529 Zigmund Palffy CC .05 .15
530 Kenny Jonsson .02 .10
531 Jamie Storr .05 .15
532 Alexander Selivanov .05 .15
533 Mike Peca CC .05 .15
534 Mariusz Czerkawski .02 .10
535 Jason Allison .02 .10
536 Todd Harvey .02 .10
537 Brett Lindros .02 .10
538 Radek Bonk .02 .10
539 Blaine Lacher .05 .15
540 Oleg Tverdovsky .05 .15
541 Wayne Gretzky .10 .30
542 Radek Bonk .02 .10
543 Mariusz Czerkawski .02 .10
544 Jaromir Jagr .10 .30
545 Dominik Hasek .10 .30
546 Todd Harvey .02 .10
547 Mike Peca WT .02 .10
548 Mats Sundin .05 .15
549 Doug Weight WT .05 .15
550 Steve Yzerman .10 .30
551 Brett Lindros .02 .10
552 Alexander Mogilny .05 .15
553 Patrik Juhlin WT .02 .10
554 Alexei Yashin .02 .10
555 Peter Forsberg .10 .30
556 Michael Nylander WT .02 .10
557 Teemu Selanne .10 .30
558 Marek Malik .02 .10
559 Jari Kurri WT .02 .10
560 Kenny Jonsson .02 .10
561 Mikael Renberg .05 .15
562 Adam Deadmarsh WT .02 .10
563 Mark Messier .10 .30
564 Rob Blake WT .02 .10
565 Janne Laukkanen WT .02 .10
566 Theo Fleury WT .02 .10
567 Alexei Kovalev .02 .10
568 Jamie Storr .05 .15
569 Brett Hull .10 .30
570 Valeri Karpov .02 .10

1994-95 Upper Deck Electric Ice

This is a parallel set to the regular Upper Deck issue and is inserted in packs at the rate of 1:35. The backs are identical to the regular set. The only difference on the front is that the words "Electric Ice" are at the bottom which, along with the player's name and bar enclosing his position, are all in electric foil.

*VETS: 8X TO 20X BASIC CARDS
*ROOKIES: 4X TO 10X BASIC CARDS

1994-95 Upper Deck Ice Gallery

This 15-card set features some of the NHL's top players, along with a few journeymen. The cards were inserted 1:25 packs in Upper Deck series one. The cards feature a close-up headshot with a wide black and gray border. An action photo and text appear on the back. The cards are numbered with an "IG" prefix.

COMPLETE SET (15) 15.00 40.00
IG1 Steve Yzerman 5.00 12.00
IG2 Jason Arnott .30 .75
IG3 Jeremy Roenick 1.25 3.00
IG4 Brendan Shanahan 1.00 2.50
IG5 Scott Stevens .50 1.25
IG6 Scott Niedermayer .30 .75
IG7 Adam Graves .30 .75
IG8 Mike Modano 1.50 4.00
IG9 Kirk Muller .30 .75
IG10 Alexandre Daigle .30 .75
IG11 Martin Brodeur 2.50 6.00
IG12 Garry Valk .30 .75
IG13 Teemu Selanne 1.00 2.50
IG14 Pat LaFontaine 1.00 2.50
IG15 Wayne Gretzky 6.00 15.00

1994-95 Upper Deck Predictor Canadian

The Calder Predictors (C1-C15) were inserted at a rate of 1:20 first series Canadian packs, while the Pearson/Norris cards (C16-C35) were inserted at a rate of 1:20 series two Canadian packs. C1 (Peter Forsberg) was the winning card that could be redeemed for a gold foil Calder set, while C15 (Long Shot) could be redeemed for a silver version. Either C23 (Eric Lindros) or C31 (Paul Coffey) could be redeemed for a 20-card gold foil Pearson/Norris set, while C24 (Jaromir Jagr) netted the collector a silver version of cards C16-C25, and C29 (Chris Chelios) could be redeemed for a silver version of cards C26-C35.

COMPLETE SET (35) 30.00 80.00
*GOLD PRIZE: 2X TO .5X BASIC INSERTS
*SILVER PRIZE: .2X TO .5X BASIC INSERTS
C1 Peter Forsberg WIN 3.00 8.00
C2 Paul Kariya 1.25 3.00
C3 Viktor Kozlov .40 1.00
C4 Jason Allison .40 1.00
C5 Mariusz Czerkawski 1.50 4.00
C6 Valeri Karpov .40 1.00
C7 Brett Lindros .40 1.00
C8 Valeri Bure .40 1.00
C9 Andrei Nikolishin .40 1.00
C10 Mike Peca .40 1.00
C11 Kenny Jonsson .40 1.00
C12 Alexander Cherbayev .40 1.00
C13 Brian Rolston .40 1.00
C14 Oleg Tverdovsky .60 1.50
C15 Calder Long Shot WIN .40 1.00
C16 Wayne Gretzky 5.00 12.00
C17 Brett Hull 1.50 4.00
C18 Doug Gilmour .60 1.50
C19 Jeremy Roenick 1.50 4.00
C20 John Vanbiesbrouck .60 1.50
C21 Sergei Fedorov 2.00 5.00
C22 Mark Messier 1.25 3.00
C23 Eric Lindros WIN 1.25 3.00
C24 Jaromir Jagr WIN 2.00 5.00
C25 Pearson Long Shot .40 1.00
C26 Ray Bourque 2.00 5.00
C27 Sandis Ozolinsh .40 1.00
C28 Brian Leetch 1.25 3.00
C29 Chris Chelios WIN 1.25 3.00
C30 Scott Stevens .60 1.50
C31 Paul Coffey WIN 1.25 3.00
C32 Rob Blake .60 1.50
C33 Al MacInnis .60 1.50
C34 Scott Niedermayer .40 1.00
C35 Norris Long Shot .40 1.00

1994-95 Upper Deck Predictor Hobby

The Hart Predictors (H1-H15) were inserted at a rate of 1:20 first series U.S. hobby packs, while the Art Ross/Vezina cards (H16 H35) were inserted at a rate of 1:20 second series U.S. hobby packs. H8 (Eric Lindros) was redeemable for a gold foil version of the Hart set, while card H15 (Long Shot) was redeemable for a silver version. Either H24 (Jaromir Jagr) or H31 (Dominik Hasek) could be redeemed for a 20-card gold foil version of the Art Ross/Vezina set, while H23 (Eric Lindros) and H27 (Ed Belfour) won gold foil versions of cards H16-H25, and H26-H35, respectively.

COMPLETE SET (35) 40.00 100.00
*GOLD PRIZE: 2X TO .5X BASIC INSERTS
*SILVER PRIZE: .2X TO .5X BASIC INSERTS
H1 Wayne Gretzky 5.00 12.00
H2 Pavel Bure 1.25 3.00
H3 Doug Gilmour .60 1.50
H4 Mark Messier 1.25 3.00
H5 Patrick Roy 4.00 10.00
H6 Sergei Fedorov 2.00 5.00
H7 Chris Chelios 1.25 3.00
H8 Eric Lindros 1.25 3.00
H9 Alexander Mogilny .60 1.50
H10 Peter Forsberg 3.00 8.00
H11 Brian Leetch 1.25 3.00
H12 Martin Brodeur 3.00 8.00
H13 Jeremy Roenick 1.50 4.00
H14 Paul Kariya 1.25 3.00
H15 Hart Long Shot .40 1.00
H16 Wayne Gretzky 5.00 12.00
H17 Joe Sakic 2.50 6.00
H18 Sergei Fedorov 2.00 5.00
H19 Pavel Bure 1.25 3.00
H20 Adam Oates .60 1.50
H21 Doug Gilmour .60 1.50
H22 Steve Yzerman 4.00 10.00
H23 Eric Lindros 1.25 3.00
H24 Jaromir Jagr 2.00 5.00
H25 Art Ross Long Shot .40 1.00
H26 Patrick Roy 4.00 10.00
H27 Ed Belfour 1.25 3.00
H28 Felix Potvin 1.25 3.00
H29 Martin Brodeur 3.00 8.00
H30 Mike Richter 1.25 3.00
H31 Dominik Hasek 2.50 6.00
H32 John Vanbiesbrouck .60 1.50
H33 Curtis Joseph 1.25 3.00
H34 Kirk McLean .60 1.50
H35 Vezina Long Shot .40 1.00

1994-95 Upper Deck Predictor Retail

The Scoring Predictors (R1-R30) were inserted at a rate of 1:20 series one U.S. retail packs, while the Playoff Scoring cards (R31-R60) were inserted at a rate of 1:20 series two U.S. retail packs. Cards R10 (Goals Long Shot), R20 (Assists Long Shot), R28 (Eric Lindros), R29 (Jaromir Jagr), and R30 (Points Long shot) were all redeemable for a 30 card gold foil version of Scoring Predictors. Cards R40 (Goals Long Shot), R50 (Assists Long Shot), and R52 (Sergei Fedorov) were all redeemable for a 30 card gold foil version of the Playoff Scoring Predictors. Cards R39 (Jaromir Jagr), and R60 (Points Long Shot) won gold foil versions of cards R31-40, and R51-60, respectively.

COMPLETE SET (60) 50.00 125.00
*EXCH.CARDS: .2X TO .5X BASIC INSERTS
ONE EXCH.SET VIA MAIL PER PRED.WINNER
R1 Pavel Bure 1.25 3.00
R2 Brett Hull 1.50 4.00
R3 Teemu Selanne 1.25 3.00
R4 Sergei Fedorov 2.00 5.00
R5 Adam Graves .40 1.00
R6 Dave Andreychuk .60 1.50
R7 Brendan Shanahan 1.25 3.00
R8 Jeremy Roenick 1.50 4.00
R9 Eric Lindros 1.25 3.00
R10 Goals Long Shot .40 1.00
R11 Doug Gilmour .60 1.50
R12 Adam Oates .60 1.50
R13 Brian Leetch 1.25 3.00
R14 Ray Bourque 2.00 5.00
R15 Joe Juneau .60 1.50
R16 Craig Janney .60 1.50
R17 Pat LaFontaine 1.25 3.00
R18 Jaromir Jagr 2.00 5.00
R19 Wayne Gretzky 5.00 12.00
R20 Assists Long Shot .40 1.00
R21 Wayne Gretzky 5.00 12.00
R22 Pat LaFontaine 1.25 3.00
R23 Sergei Fedorov 2.00 5.00
R24 Steve Yzerman 4.00 10.00
R25 Pavel Bure 1.25 3.00
R26 Adam Oates .60 1.50
R27 Doug Gilmour .60 1.50
R28 Eric Lindros 1.25 3.00
R29 Jaromir Jagr 2.00 5.00
R30 Points Long Shot .40 1.00
R31 Pavel Bure 1.25 3.00
R32 Brett Hull 1.50 4.00
R33 Cam Neely 1.25 3.00
R34 Mark Messier 1.25 3.00
R35 Dave Andreychuk .60 1.50
R36 Sergei Fedorov 2.00 5.00
R37 Mike Modano 2.00 5.00
R38 Adam Graves .40 1.00
R39 Jaromir Jagr 2.00 5.00
R40 Playoff Goals Long Shot .40 1.00
R41 Theo Fleury .40 1.00
R42 Wayne Gretzky 5.00 12.00
R43 Steve Yzerman 4.00 10.00
R44 Adam Oates .60 1.50
R45 Brian Leetch 1.25 3.00
R46 Al MacInnis .60 1.50
R47 Pat LaFontaine 1.25 3.00
R48 Scott Stevens .60 1.50
R49 Doug Gilmour .60 1.50
R50 Playoff Assists Long Shot .40 1.00
R51 Brian Leetch 1.25 3.00
R52 Sergei Fedorov 2.00 5.00
R53 Pavel Bure 1.25 3.00
R54 Mark Messier 1.25 3.00
R55 Pat LaFontaine 1.25 3.00
R56 Doug Gilmour .60 1.50
R57 Brett Hull 1.50 4.00
R58 Theo Fleury .40 1.00
R59 Wayne Gretzky 5.00 12.00
R60 Playoff Points Long Shot .40 1.00

1994-95 Upper Deck SP Inserts

The 1994-95 Upper Deck SP Insert set was released in two series of 90 cards for a total of 180. One SP Insert was found in each Upper Deck hobby pack, with two per retail pack.

COMPLETE SET (180) 30.00 80.00
*DIE CUT: 1.2X TO 3X BASIC INSERTS
SP1 Maxim Bets .15 .40
SP2 Stephan Lebeau .15 .40
SP3 Garry Valk .15 .40
SP4 Ray Bourque .60 1.50
SP5 Mariusz Czerkawski .25 .60
SP6 Cam Neely .40 1.00
SP7 Adam Oates .25 .60
SP8 Dominik Hasek .75 2.00
SP9 Dale Hawerchuk .25 .60
SP10 Alexander Mogilny .25 .60
SP11 Theo Fleury .25 .60
SP12 Trevor Kidd .25 .60
SP13 Joe Nieuwendyk .25 .60
SP14 Gary Roberts .15 .40
SP15 Ed Belfour .40 1.00
SP16 Chris Chelios .40 1.00
SP17 Jeremy Roenick .60 1.50
SP18 Neal Broten .25 .60
SP19 Russ Courtnall .15 .40
SP20 Derian Hatcher .15 .40
SP21 Mike Modano .60 1.50
SP22 Paul Coffey .40 1.00
SP23 Slava Kozlov .25 .60
SP24 Keith Primeau .15 .40
SP25 Steve Yzerman 2.00 5.00
SP26 Jason Arnott .15 .40
SP27 Bill Ranford .25 .60
SP28 Doug Weight .25 .60
SP29 Bob Kudelski .15 .40
SP30 Rob Niedermayer .25 .60
SP31 John Vanbiesbrouck .25 .60
SP32 Andrew Cassels .15 .40
SP33 Chris Pronger .40 1.00
SP34 Geoff Sanderson .25 .60
SP35 Rob Blake .25 .60
SP36 Wayne Gretzky 3.00 8.00
SP37 Jari Kurri .25 .60
SP38 Alexei Zhitnik .15 .40
SP39 Vincent Damphousse .15 .40
SP40 Kirk Muller .15 .40
SP41 Oleg Petrov .15 .40
SP42 Patrick Roy 2.00 5.00
SP43 Martin Brodeur 1.25 3.00
SP44 Stephane Richer .25 .60
SP45 Scott Stevens .25 .60
SP46 Darius Kasparaitis .15 .40
SP47 Vladimir Malakhov .15 .40
SP48 Pierre Turgeon .25 .60
SP49 Alexei Kovalev .15 .40
SP50 Brian Leetch .40 1.00
SP51 Mark Messier .40 1.00
SP52 Mike Richter .40 1.00
SP53 Craig Billington .25 .60
SP54 Alexandre Daigle .15 .40
SP55 Alexei Yashin .15 .40
SP56 Josef Beranek .15 .40
SP57 Rod Brind'Amour .25 .60
SP58 Mark Recchi .25 .60
SP59 Mikael Renberg .25 .60
SP60 Jaromir Jagr .75 2.00
SP61 Mario Lemieux 2.00 5.00
SP62 Kevin Stevens .15 .40
SP63 Owen Nolan .25 .60
SP64 Mike Ricci .15 .40
SP65 Joe Sakic 1.00 2.50
SP66 Brett Hull .60 1.50
SP67 Craig Janney .25 .60
SP68 Curtis Joseph .40 1.00
SP69 Brendan Shanahan .40 1.00
SP70 Ulf Dahlen .15 .40
SP71 Arturs Irbe .25 .60
SP72 Sergei Makarov .15 .40
SP73 Sandis Ozolinsh .15 .40
SP74 Brian Bradley .15 .40
SP75 Chris Gratton .15 .40
SP76 Denis Savard .25 .60
SP77 Dave Andreychuk .25 .60
SP78 Mike Gartner .25 .60
SP79 Dimitri Mironov .15 .40
SP80 Felix Potvin .40 1.00
SP81 Jeff Brown .15 .40
SP82 Geoff Courtnall .15 .40
SP83 Trevor Linden .25 .60
SP84 Kirk McLean .25 .60
SP85 Peter Bondra .25 .60
SP86 Kevin Hatcher .15 .40
SP87 Dimitri Khristich .15 .40
SP88 Teemu Selanne .40 1.00
SP89 Keith Tkachuk .40 1.00
SP90 Alexei Zhamnov .25 .60
SP91 Paul Kariya .40 1.00
SP92 Valeri Karpov .15 .40
SP93 Oleg Tverdovsky .25 .60
SP94 Al Iafrate .15 .40
SP95 Blaine Lacher .15 .40
SP96 Bryan Smolinski .15 .40
SP97 Donald Audette .15 .40
SP98 Yuri Khmylev .15 .40
SP99 Pat LaFontaine .40 1.00
SP100 Derek Plante .15 .40
SP101 Steve Chiasson .15 .40
SP102 Phil Housley .25 .60
SP103 Michael Nylander .15 .40
SP104 Robert Reichel .15 .40
SP105 Tony Amonte .25 .60
SP106 Bernie Nicholls .25 .60
SP107 Gary Suter .15 .40
SP108 Paul Cavallini .15 .40
SP109 Todd Harvey .15 .40
SP110 Kevin Hatcher .15 .40
SP111 Andy Moog .40 1.00
SP112 Dino Ciccarelli .25 .60
SP113 Sergei Fedorov .60 1.50
SP114 Nicklas Lidstrom .40 1.00
SP115 Mike Vernon .25 .60
SP116 Shayne Corson .15 .40
SP117 David Oliver .15 .40
SP118 Ryan Smyth 1.00 2.50
SP119 Jesse Belanger .15 .40
SP120 Mark Fitzpatrick .25 .60
SP121 Scott Mellanby .25 .60
SP122 Andrei Nikolishin .15 .40
SP123 Darren Turcotte .15 .40
SP124 Pat Verbeek .15 .40
SP125 Glen Wesley .15 .40
SP126 Tony Granato .15 .40
SP127 Marty McSorley .15 .40
SP128 Jamie Storr .25 .60
SP129 Rick Tocchet .25 .60
SP130 Brian Bellows .15 .40
SP131 Valeri Bure .15 .40
SP132 Turner Stevenson .15 .40
SP133 John MacLean .25 .60
SP134 Scott Niedermayer .25 .60
SP135 Brian Rolston .15 .40
SP136 Brett Lindros .15 .40
SP137 Jamie McLennan .25 .60
SP138 Zigmund Palffy .25 .60
SP139 Steve Thomas .15 .40
SP140 Adam Graves .15 .40
SP141 Petr Nedved .25 .60
SP142 Sergei Zubov .15 .40
SP143 Don Beaupre .25 .60
SP144 Radek Bonk .25 .60
SP145 Pavol Demitra .25 .60
SP146 Sylvain Turgeon .15 .40
SP147 Ron Hextall .25 .60
SP148 Patrik Juhlin .15 .40
SP149 Eric Lindros .40 1.00
SP150 Ron Francis .25 .60
SP151 Markus Naslund .40 1.00
SP152 Luc Robitaille .25 .60
SP153 Martin Straka .15 .40
SP154 Wendel Clark .25 .60
SP155 Adam Deadmarsh .15 .40
SP156 Peter Forsberg 1.25 3.00
SP157 Janne Laukkanen .15 .40
SP158 Steve Duchesne .15 .40
SP159 Al MacInnis .25 .60
SP160 Esa Tikkanen .15 .40
SP161 Jeff Friesen .15 .40
SP162 Viktor Kozlov .15 .40
SP163 Ray Whitney .15 .40
SP164 Roman Hamrlik .25 .60
SP165 Alexander Selivanov .25 .60
SP166 Jason Wiemer .15 .40
SP167 Doug Gilmour .25 .60
SP168 Kenny Jonsson .15 .40
SP169 Mike Ridley .15 .40
SP170 Mats Sundin .40 1.00
SP171 Pavel Bure .40 1.00
SP172 Martin Gelinas .15 .40
SP173 Mike Peca .15 .40
SP174 Jason Allison .15 .40
SP175 Joe Juneau .25 .60
SP176 Pat Peake .15 .40
SP177 Mark Tinordi .15 .40
SP178 Tim Cheveldae .25 .60
SP179 Nelson Emerson .15 .40
SP180 Dave Manson .15 .40

1995-96 Upper Deck

The 1995-96 Upper Deck set was issued in two series totaling 570 cards. The set is distinguished primarily through the inclusion of a number of noteworthy rookie cards in the Star Rookie (496-507) and Program of Excellence (508-525) subsets. The Cool Trade Exchange card was randomly inserted in 1:82 series 2 packs. The card could be redeemed for special die-cut cards of Wayne Gretzky, Sergei Fedorov, Peter Forsberg and Doug Gilmour.

COMPLETE SET (570) 30.00 60.00
COMP.SERIES 1 (270) 10.00 20.00
COMP.SERIES 2 (300) 20.00 40.00
1 Cam Neely .10 .30
2 Donald Audette .02 .10
3 Derian Hatcher .02 .10
4 Mike Vernon .05 .15
5 Darryl Sydor .05 .15
6 Patrice Brisebois .02 .10
7 John LeClair .10 .30
8 Luc Robitaille .05 .15
9 Todd Krygier .02 .10
10 Steve Chiasson .02 .10
11 Sergei Krivokrasov .02 .10
12 Marko Tuomainen .02 .10
13 Paul Ranheim .02 .10
14 Brian Rolston .02 .10
15 Alexei Yashin .02 .10
16 Joe Mullen .05 .15
17 Dallas Drake .02 .10
18 Tony Amonte .05 .15
19 Gary Roberts .02 .10
20 Geoff Sanderson .02 .10
21 Gord Murphy .02 .10
22 Dean Evason .02 .10
23 Brantt Myhres RC .02 .10
24 Sergei Makarov .02 .10
25 Joe Juneau .02 .10
26 Greg Adams .02 .10
27 Yuri Khmylev .02 .10
28 Yanic Perreault .02 .10
29 Jason Arnott .02 .10
30 Glenn Healy .05 .15
31 Sergei Brylin .02 .10
32 Ian Laperriere .02 .10
33 Trevor Linden .05 .15
34 Nicklas Lidstrom .10 .30
35 Don Sweeney .02 .10
36 Brian Savage .02 .10
37 Richard Matvichuk .05 .15
38 Dale Hawerchuk .10 .30
39 Patrick Roy .60 1.50
40 Alexander Semak .05 .15
41 Kirk Maltby .05 .15
42 Jiri Slegr .02 .10
43 Joe Sacco .02 .10
44 Claude Lemieux .02 .10
45 Eric Weinrich .05 .15
46 Ron Francis .05 .15
47 Jamie Storr .02 .10
48 Felix Potvin .10 .30
49 Steve Duchesne .02 .10
50 Jody Hull .02 .10
51 Dave Manson .02 .10
52 Marty McInnis .02 .10
53 James Patrick .02 .10
54 Joe Sakic .25 .60
55 Andrei Nikolishin .02 .10
56 Adrian Aucoin .02 .10
57 Wade Flaherty RC .05 .15
58 Marek Malik .02 .10
59 Jason Allison .02 .10
60 Stephane Matteau .02 .10
61 Jason Dawe .02 .10
62 Ray Whitney .05 .15
63 Bill Lindsay .02 .10
64 Alexei Zhamnov .05 .15
65 Adam Deadmarsh .02 .10
66 Vincent Damphousse .02 .10
67 Josef Beranek .02 .10
68 Stanislav Neckar .02 .10
69 Alexei Kasatonov .02 .10
70 Jon Casey .05 .15
71 Todd Marchant .02 .10
72 Mike Sillinger .02 .10
73 Markus Naslund .10 .30
74 John MacLean .05 .15
75 Mike Ridley .02 .10
76 Petr Svoboda .02 .10
77 Milos Holan .02 .10
78 John Tucker .02 .10
79 Doug Brown .02 .10
80 Ted Donato .02 .10
81 Dimitri Yushkevich .02 .10
82 Brett Lindros .02 .10
83 Brian Bradley .02 .10
84 Mario Lemieux .60 1.50
85 Nikolai Khabibulin .05 .15
86 Larry Murphy .05 .15
87 Mike Donnelly .02 .10
88 Brian Holzinger RC .10 .30
89 Steve Larouche RC .02 .10
90 Ray Ferraro .02 .10
91 Mikhail Shtalenkov .02 .10
92 Viktor Kozlov .05 .15
93 Jon Klemm .02 .10
94 Mark Tinordi .02 .10
95 Bret Hedican .02 .10
96 Kevin Stevens .02 .10
97 Bernie Nicholls .02 .10
98 Pat Verbeek .02 .10
99 Wayne Gretzky .75 2.00
100 Rene Corbet .02 .10
101 Shayne Corson .02 .10
102 Cliff Ronning .02 .10
103 Olaf Kolzig .05 .15
104 Dominik Hasek .25 .60
105 Corey Millen .02 .10
106 Patrick Flatley .02 .10
107 Chris Therien .02 .10
108 Ken Wregget .05 .15
109 Paul Ysebaert .02 .10
110 Mike Gartner .05 .15
111 Michal Grosek .02 .10
112 Craig Billington .05 .15
113 Steve Yzerman .60 1.50
114 Neal Broten .05 .15
115 Tom Barrasso .05 .15
116 Brent Fedyk .02 .10
117 Todd Gill .02 .10
118 Petr Klima .02 .10
119 Dave Karpa .02 .10
120 Geoff Courtnall .02 .10
121 Kelly Buchberger .02 .10
122 Eric LaCroix .02 .10
123 Janne Laukkanen .02 .10
124 Radek Bonk .02 .10
125 Sergio Momesso .02 .10
126 Esa Tikkanen .02 .10
127 Jon Rohloff .02 .10
128 Ken Klee RC .02 .10
129 Johan Garpenlov .02 .10
130 Sean Burke .05 .15
131 Shean Donovan .02 .10
132 Alexei Kovalev .02 .10
133 Sylvain Cote .02 .10
134 Jeff Friesen .02 .10
135 Scott Pearson .02 .10
136 Kirk McLean .05 .15
137 Glen Wesley .02 .10
138 Bob Kudelski .02 .10
139 Craig Johnson .02 .10
140 Zigmund Palffy .05 .15
141 Kris King .02 .10
142 Rusty Fitzgerald RC .02 .10
143 Trevor Kidd .05 .15
144 Dave Ellett .02 .10
145 Kelly Hrudey .05 .15
146 Igor Kravchuk .02 .10
147 Mats Sundin .10 .30
148 Shawn Chambers .02 .10
149 Bob Corkum .02 .10
150 Shjon Podein .02 .10
151 Murray Craven .02 .10
152 Roman Hamrlik .05 .15
153 Lyle Odelein .02 .10
154 Vyacheslav Kozlov .05 .15
155 David Emma .02 .10
156 Benoit Brunet .02 .10
157 Jozef Stumpel .02 .10
158 Darrin Madeley .02 .10
159 Keith Primeau .02 .10
160 Jeff Norton .02 .10
161 Mathieu Schneider .02 .10
162 Trent Klatt .02 .10
163 Pat Peake .02 .10
164 Rob Gaudreau .02 .10
165 Doug Bodger .02 .10
166 Sergei Nemchinov .02 .10
167 David Oliver .02 .10
168 Sandis Ozolinsh .02 .10
169 Mark Messier .10 .30
170 Chris Chelios .10 .30
171 Teemu Selanne .10 .30
172 Robert Svehla RC .02 .10
173 Nikolai Borschevsky .02 .10
174 Chris Pronger .10 .30
175 Dave Lowry .02 .10
176 Owen Nolan .05 .15
177 Sylvain Turgeon .02 .10
178 Nelson Emerson .02 .10
179 Theo Fleury .02 .10
180 Patrik Carnback .02 .10
181 Kevin Smyth .02 .10
182 Jeff Shantz .02 .10
183 Bob Carpenter .02 .10
184 Brendan Shanahan .10 .30
185 Tomas Sandstrom .02 .10
186 Eric Desjardins .05 .15
187 Alexei Zhitnik .02 .10
188 Alexander Mogilny .05 .15
189 Mariusz Czerkawski .02 .10
190 Vladimir Konstantinov .05 .15
191 Andy Moog .10 .30
192 Peter Popovic .02 .10
193 Marty McSorley .02 .10
194 Mikael Renberg .05 .15
195 Alek Stojanov RC .02 .10
196 Rick Tabaracci .05 .15

1995-96 Upper Deck

197 Adam Oates .05 .15
198 Garry Galley .02 .10
199 Todd Harvey .05 .15
200 Martin Lapointe .02 .10
201 Tony Granato .02 .10
202 Turner Stevenson .02 .10
203 Jeff Beukeboom .02 .10
204 Adam Foote .05 .15
205 Daren Puppa .05 .15
206 Paul Kariya .10 .30
207 German Titov .02 .10
208 Patrick Poulin .02 .10
209 Jesse Belanger .02 .10
210 Steven Rice .02 .10
211 Martin Brodeur .30 .75
212 Rob Pearson .02 .10
213 Igor Larionov .02 .10
214 Pavel Bure .10 .30
215 Sergei Fedorov .10 .30
216 Ed Belfour .10 .30
217 Mark Messier .10 .30
218 Steve Yzerman .30 .75
219 Mats Sundin .10 .30
220 Mike Modano .20 .50
221 Alexander Mogilny .05 .15
222 Wayne Gretzky .40 1.00
223 Keith Primeau .02 .10
224 Adam Graves .02 .10
225 Owen Nolan .05 .15
226 Paul Coffey .10 .30
227 Jeremy Roenick .15 .40
228 Felix Potvin .10 .30
229 Trevor Kidd .05 .15
230 Ray Bourque .10 .30
231 Mario Lemieux 5 .30 .75
232 Peter Bondra .05 .15
233 Brett Hull .10 .30
234 Alexei Zhamnov .05 .15
235 Theo Fleury .02 .10
236 Brian Leetch .05 .15
237 Cam Neely .05 .15
238 Chris Chelios .10 .30
239 Adam Graves .02 .10
240 Doug Gilmour .05 .15
241 Jeremy Roenick .15 .40
242 Joe Sakic .10 .30
243 Keith Tkachuk .10 .30
244 Luc Robitaille .05 .15
245 Paul Kariya .10 .30
246 Owen Nolan .05 .15
247 John LeClair .10 .30
248 Paul Coffey .10 .30
249 Peter Bondra .05 .15
250 Ray Bourque .10 .30
251 Brett Hull .10 .30
252 Wayne Gretzky .40 1.00
253 Teemu Selanne .10 .30
254 Ray Sheppard .02 .10
255 Ron Francis .05 .15
256 Kevin Hatcher .02 .10
257 Brett Lindros .02 .10
258 Claude Lemieux .02 .10
259 Saku Koivu .10 .30
260 Radek Dvorak RC .20 .50
261 Niklas Sundstrom .05 .15
262 Chad Kilger RC .20 .50
263 Vitali Yachmenev .02 .10
264 Jeff O'Neill .02 .10
265 Brendan Witt .02 .10
266 Jason Bonsignore .02 .10
267 Aki Berg RC .05 .15
268 Eric Daze .05 .15
269 Shane Doan RC .40 1.00
270 Daymond Langkow RC .20 .50
271 Alexandre Daigle .02 .10
272 Brian Noonan .02 .10
273 Guy Carbonneau .10 .30
274 Rick Tocchet .05 .15
275 Teppo Numminen .02 .10
276 Brian Skrudland .02 .10
277 Andrei Trefilov .02 .10
278 Joe Murphy .02 .10
279 Sergei Fedorov .20 .50
280 Doug Weight .05 .15
281 Robert Lang .02 .10
282 Darryl Shannon .02 .10
283 Cory Stillman .02 .10
284 Gary Suter .02 .10
285 Joe Nieuwendyk .05 .15
286 Terry Carkner .02 .10
287 Dimitri Khristich .02 .10
288 Alexander Karpovtsev .02 .10
289 Garth Snow .05 .15
290 Al MacInnis .05 .15
291 Doug Gilmour .05 .15
292 Mike Eastwood .02 .10
293 Steve Heinze .02 .10
294 Phil Housley .05 .15
295 Tim Taylor .02 .10
296 Curtis Joseph .10 .30
297 Patrick Roy .60 1.50
298 Ted Drury .02 .10
299 Igor Korolev .02 .10
300 Ray Bourque .20 .50
301 Darren McCarty .02 .10
302 Miroslav Satan RC .30 .75
303 Adam Burt .02 .10
304 Valeri Bure .02 .10
305 Sergei Gonchar .02 .10
306 Jason York .02 .10
307 Brent Grieve .02 .10
308 Greg Johnson .02 .10
309 Kevin Hatcher .02 .10
310 Rob Niedermayer .05 .15
311 Nelson Emerson .02 .10
312 Mark Janssens .02 .10
313 Tommy Soderstrom .05 .15
314 Joey Kocur .05 .15
315 Craig Janney .02 .10
316 Alexander Selivanov .02 .10
317 Russ Courtnall .02 .10
318 Petr Sykora RC .40 1.00
319 Rick Zombo .02 .10
320 Randy Burridge .02 .10
321 John Vanbiesbrouck .05 .15
322 Dmitri Mironov .02 .10
323 Sean Hill .02 .10
324 Rod Brind'Amour .05 .15
325 Wendel Clark .05 .15
326 Brent Gilchrist .02 .10
327 Tyler Wright .02 .10
328 Scott Daniels RC .02 .10
329 Adam Graves .02 .10
330 Dean Malkoc RC .02 .10
331 Jamie Macoun .02 .10
332 Sandy Moger RC .02 .10
333 Mike Peca .05 .15
334 Greg Johnson .02 .10
335 Jason Woolley .02 .10
336 Rob Dimaio .02 .10
337 Damian Rhodes .05 .15
338 Gino Odjick .02 .10
339 Peter Bondra .05 .15
340 Todd Ewen .02 .10
341 Matthew Barnaby .10 .30
342 Sylvain Lefebvre .02 .10
343 Oleg Petrov .02 .10
344 Jim Carey .05 .15
345 Stu Barnes .02 .10
346 Kelly Miller .02 .10
347 Antti Tormanen RC .02 .10
348 Ray Sheppard .02 .10
349 Igor Larionov .05 .15
350 Kjell Samuelsson .02 .10
351 Benoit Hogue .02 .10
352 Jeff Brown .02 .10
353 Nolan Baumgartner .02 .10
354 Denis Pederson .02 .10
355 Shawn Burr .02 .10
356 Jyrki Lumme .02 .10
357 Kevin Haller .02 .10
358 John Cullen .02 .10
359 Martin Gelinas .02 .10
360 Shawn McEachern .02 .10
361 Sandy McCarthy .02 .10
362 Grant Marshall .02 .10
363 Dean McAmmond .02 .10
364 Kevin Todd .02 .10
365 Bobby Holik .02 .10
366 Joel Otto .02 .10
367 Dave Andreychuk .05 .15
368 Ronnie Stern .02 .10
369 Jocelyn Thibault .10 .30
370 Dave Gagner .02 .10
371 Bryan Marchment .02 .10
372 Jari Kurri .10 .30
373 Bill Guerin .02 .10
374 Eric Lindros .10 .30
375 Adam Creighton .02 .10
376 Dimitri Yushkevich .02 .10
377 Peter Zezel .02 .10
378 Valeri Karpov .02 .10
379 Patrick Labrecque RC .02 .10
380 Mick Vukota .02 .10
381 Ulf Dahlen .02 .10
382 Enrico Ciccone .02 .10
383 Scott Niedermayer .02 .10
384 Ville Peltonen .02 .10
385 Blaine Lacher .02 .10
386 Pat LaFontaine .10 .30
387 Jeff Hackett .05 .15
388 Mike Keane .02 .10
389 Pierre Turgeon .05 .15
390 Scott Lachance .02 .10
391 Jason Wiemer .02 .10
392 Michal Pivonka .02 .10
393 Dennis Bonvie RC .02 .10
394 Glen Murray .02 .10
395 Bobby Dollas .02 .10
396 Paul Coffey .10 .30
397 Stephane Fiset .05 .15
398 Jere Lehtinen .05 .15
399 Scott Mellanby .02 .10
400 Robert Kron .02 .10
401 Doug Lidster .02 .10
402 Don Beaupre .02 .10
403 Arturs Irbe .05 .15
404 Brian Bellows .02 .10
405 Corey Hirsch .05 .15
406 Pavel Bure .10 .30
407 Chris Gratton .02 .10
408 Oleg Tverdovsky .02 .10
409 Derek Plante .02 .10
410 Dan Keczmer .02 .10
411 Donald Brashear .05 .15
412 Andrei Vasilyev RC .02 .10
413 Tommy Salo RC .30 .75
414 Kevin Lowe .05 .15
415 Dody Wood .02 .10
416 Denis Chasse .02 .10
417 Aaron Gavey .02 .10
418 Scott Walker .05 .15
419 Richard Park .02 .10
420 Mike Modano .10 .30
421 Kyle McLaren RC .05 .15
422 Jeremy Roenick .15 .40
423 Mark Fitzpatrick .05 .15
424 Landon Wilson RC .02 .10
425 Steve Rucchin .02 .10
426 Stephane Richer .05 .15
427 Martin Straka .02 .10
428 Ron Hextall .05 .15
429 Joe Dziedzic RC .02 .10
430 Peter Forsberg .30 .75
431 Dino Ciccarelli .05 .15
432 Robert Dirk .02 .10
433 Wayne Primeau RC .02 .10
434 Denis Savard .05 .15
435 Keith Carney .02 .10
436 Tom Fitzgerald .02 .10
437 Cale Hulse .02 .10
438 Mike Richter .10 .30
439 Marcus Ragnarsson RC .05 .15
440 Roman Vopat .02 .10
441 Zdenek Nedved .02 .10
442 Dale Hunter .05 .15
443 Bob Sweeney .02 .10
444 Randy McKay .02 .10
445 Chris Osgood .05 .15
446 Andrei Kovalenko .02 .10
447 Darius Kasparaitis .02 .10
448 Ulf Samuelsson .02 .10
449 Chris Joseph .02 .10
450 Chris Terreri .05 .15
451 Keith Jones .05 .15
452 Tim Cheveldae .05 .15
453 Stephen Leach .02 .10
454 Michael Nylander .02 .10
455 Ed Belfour .10 .30
456 Claude Lemieux .02 .10
457 Mike Ricci .05 .15
458 Shane Churla .02 .10
459 Kris Draper .10 .30
460 Byron Dafoe .05 .15
461 Troy Mallette .02 .10
462 Petr Nedved .05 .15
463 Kenny Jonsson .05 .15
464 Keith Tkachuk .10 .30
465 Jaromir Jagr .20 .50
466 Vladimir Malakhov .02 .10
467 Guy Hebert .05 .15
468 Brad May .02 .10
469 Bob Probert .02 .10
470 Sandis Ozolinsh .02 .10
471 Oleg Mikulchik RC .02 .10
472 Steve Thomas .05 .15
473 Travis Green .05 .15
474 Sergei Zubov .02 .10
475 Bill Houlder .02 .10
476 Roman Oksiuta .02 .10
477 Jamie Rivers .02 .10
478 Rob Blake .05 .15
479 Todd Elik .02 .10
480 Zarley Zalapski .02 .10
481 Darren Turcotte .02 .10
482 Scott Stevens .05 .15
483 Pat Falloon .02 .10
484 Grant Fuhr .10 .30
485 Martin Rucinsky .02 .10
486 Brett Hull .15 .40
487 Brian Leetch .05 .15
488 Shaun Van Allen .02 .10
489 Valeri Kamensky .05 .15
490 Mark Recchi .05 .15
491 Jason Muzzatti .05 .15
492 Andrew Cassels .02 .10
493 Nick Kypreos .02 .10
494 Bryan Smolinski .02 .10
495 Owen Nolan .05 .15
496 Bryan McCabe .02 .10
497 Mathieu Dandenault RC .20 .50
498 Deron Quint .02 .10
499 Jason Doig .02 .10
500 Marty Murray .02 .10
501 Ed Jovanovski .10 .30
502 Stefan Ustorf .02 .10
503 Jamie Langenbrunner .02 .10
504 Daniel Alfredsson RC .50 1.25
505 Darby Hendrickson .02 .10
506 Brett McLean RC .05 .15
507 Daniel Cleary RC .05 .15
508 Todd Robinson .02 .10
509 Arron Asham RC .05 .15
510 Daniel Corso RC .20 .50
511 Darren Van Oene RC .05 .15
512 Trevor Wasyluk RC .10 .30
513 Josh Holden RC .02 .10
514 Etienne Drapeau RC .05 .15
515 Matt Osborne .02 .10
516 Zenith Komarniski RC .05 .15
517 Chris Phillips RC .20 .50
518 Chris Fleury RC .02 .10
519 Cory Sarich RC .05 .15
520 Glenn Crawford RC .02 .10
521 Francois Methot RC .02 .10
522 Geoff Peters RC .02 .10
523 Joey Tetarenko .05 .15
524 Randy Petruk RC .05 .15
525 Mathieu Garon RC 1.00 2.50
526 Daymond Langkow .10 .30
527 Craig Mills RC .02 .10
528 Rhett Warrener .02 .10
529 Marc Denis RC .75 2.00
530 Jose Theodore RC 2.00 5.00
531 Curtis Brown RC .10 .30
532 Chad Allen .02 .10
533 Denis Gauthier RC .02 .10
534 Brad Larsen .02 .10
535 Jamie Wright RC .05 .15
536 Mike Watt RC .05 .15
537 Jason Holland RC .05 .15
538 Robb Gordon RC .05 .15
539 Hnat Domenichelli RC .05 .15
540 Ondrej Kratena RC .05 .15
541 Michal Bros RC .05 .15
542 Marek Posmyk .02 .10
543 Marek Melanovsky RC .05 .15
544 Jan Tomajko .05 .15
545 Ales Pisa RC .05 .15
546 Miika Elomo RC .05 .15
547 Timo Salonen RC .05 .15
548 Teemu Riihijarvi RC .05 .15
549 Antti-Jussi Niemi .05 .15
550 Pasi Petrilainen RC .05 .15
551 Toni Lydman RC .05 .15
552 Dmitri Nabokov .05 .15
553 Alexei Morozov .10 .30
554 Sergei Samsonov .05 .15
555 Alexei Vasilyev RC .05 .15
556 Andrei Petrunin .05 .15
557 Dimitri Riabykin .05 .15
558 Sergei Zimakov RC .05 .15
559 Peter Nylander RC .05 .15
560 Marcus Nilsson UER RC .20 .50
561 Niklas Anger RC .05 .15
562 Per Anton Lundstrom RC .05 .15
563 Patrik Wallenberg RC .05 .15
564 Per Ragnar Bergkvist RC .05 .15
565 Mike Sylvia .05 .15
566 Marty Reasoner .05 .15
567 Reg Berg RC .05 .15
568 Tom Poti RC .20 .50
569 Chris Drury RC 2.00 5.00
570 Michael McBain .02 .10

1995-96 Upper Deck Electric Ice

The Electric Ice cards were inserted one per retail pack, or two per jumbo. These cards featured the Electric Ice logo on a silver foil background.

*VETS: 4X TO 10X BASIC CARDS
*ROOKIES: 1X TO 2.5X

1995-96 Upper Deck Electric Ice Gold

These cards were inserted at the rate of 1:35 retail packs only, and could be differentiated from basic UD cards by the inclusion of the words Electric Ice embossed in gold down the side of the card front. The card J-171 is a recently confirmed jumbo version of the Electric Ice Gold Selanne card. The J prefix was added for checklisting purposes. It is not known whether other jumbo versions exist for Electric Ice Gold cards.

*VETS: 20X TO 50X BASIC CARDS
*ROOKIES: 8X TO 20X

1995-96 Upper Deck All-Star Game Predictors

The thirty cards in this set were handed out one per person at the Upper Deck booth at the All-Star FanFest in Boston. The winning card, no. 21 Ray Bourque, was redeemable for a full thirty card set of All-Star Game Predictors that contained different photos than the original give-aways. Prices below are for the cards handed out at the All-Star game. Separate multipliers to determine values for the redeemed versions can be found in the header below. The redeemed Bourque card is actually worth about 33 percent of the game card; this is due to the mass redemption of the Bourque game card, making it extremely difficult to locate in the secondary market.

*REDEEMED CARDS: 2X TO 3X BASIC PREDICTORS
1 Wayne Gretzky 75.00 200.00
2 Sergei Fedorov 20.00 50.00
3 Brett Hull 15.00 40.00
4 Alexander Mogilny 6.00 15.00
5 Joe Sakic 20.00 50.00
6 Paul Kariya 30.00 75.00
7 Teemu Selanne 20.00 50.00
8 Paul Coffey 10.00 25.00
9 Chris Chelios 15.00 40.00
10 Doug Gilmour 10.00 25.00
11 Peter Forsberg 25.00 60.00
12 Jeremy Roenick 15.00 40.00
13 Theo Fleury 10.00 25.00
14 Mike Modano 15.00 40.00
15 Steve Yzerman 50.00 125.00
16 Mario Lemieux 60.00 150.00
17 Jaromir Jagr 25.00 60.00
18 Eric Lindros 20.00 50.00
19 Mark Messier 15.00 40.00
20 Brendan Shanahan 15.00 40.00
21 Ray Bourque 75.00 200.00
22 Cam Neely 15.00 40.00
23 Ron Francis 6.00 15.00
24 John LeClair 15.00 40.00
25 Brian Leetch 10.00 25.00
26 Peter Bondra 10.00 25.00
27 Scott Stevens 6.00 15.00
28 Adam Oates 6.00 15.00
29 Martin Brodeur 25.00 60.00
30 Longshot 2.00 5.00

1995-96 Upper Deck Freeze Frame

Twenty top stars are featured in this multiple photo insert set which utilizes Upper Deck's Light FX foil printing technology. The cards were randomly inserted at a rate of 1:34 series one packs. Jumbo versions of these cards, measuring 3 1/2" by 6", were inserted one per series one box. Multipliers can be found in the header below to determine values for these.

COMPLETE SET (20) 25.00 60.00
*JUMBOS: .4X TO 1X BASIC INSERTS
F1 Peter Forsberg 2.50 6.00
F2 Wayne Gretzky 6.00 15.00
F3 Eric Lindros 1.25 3.00
F4 Jaromir Jagr 2.00 5.00
F5 Cam Neely 1.25 3.00
F6 Jeremy Roenick 1.25 3.00
F7 Mark Messier 1.25 3.00
F8 Sergei Fedorov 1.25 3.00
F9 Paul Kariya 1.25 3.00
F10 Pavel Bure 1.25 3.00
F11 Dominik Hasek 2.50 6.00
F12 Theo Fleury .40 1.00
F13 Alexei Zhamnov .40 1.00
F14 Martin Brodeur 3.00 8.00
F15 Brett Hull 1.25 3.00
F16 Mario Lemieux 4.00 10.00
F17 Paul Coffey .60 1.50
F18 Brian Leetch .60 1.50
F19 Ray Bourque 1.25 3.00
F20 Jim Carey .40 1.00

1995-96 Upper Deck Gretzky Collection

This 24 card set, which focuses on the many remarkable achievements in the career of Wayne Gretzky, was released through four separate products. Cards G1-G9, along with a header card, could be found in 1995-96 Collector's Choice retail and hobby packs at a rate of 1:11. Cards G10-G13 and a header card were randomly inserted in packs of Upper Deck series 1 at a rate of 1:29. Cards G14-17 along with a header card were randomly inserted in packs of Upper Deck series 2 at a rate of 1:29. Finally, cards G18-G20, along with an NNO header card, were randomly inserted at a rate of 1:45 packs of SP. The cards share a similar design element, but with added foil enhancements for each step up the premium ladder. A jumbo version of cards G1-G9 and the CC header were produced and inserted into some Collector's Choice boxes.

COMPLETE SET (24) 75.00 200.00
COMP.CC SET (10) 15.00 40.00
COMP.SP SET (4) 30.00 80.00
COMP.UD SER.1 (5) 15.00 40.00
COMP.UD SER.2 (4) 15.00 40.00
COMMON CC (G1-G9/HDR) 2.00 5.00
COMMON UD (G10-G17/HUD) 4.00 10.00
COMMON SP (G18-G20/HSP) 12.50 30.00
*JUMBOS: .6X TO 1.5X BASIC INSERTS

1995-96 Upper Deck NHL All-Stars

Randomly inserted in packs at a rate of 1:34 series 2 packs, these twenty two-sided cards highlight the participants in the 1995-96 All-Star Game. The cards utilize the UD Light FX technology. Players from the Western Conference have a teal left border, while players from the Eastern Conference have purple left border. There also were jumbo version of these cards inserted one per series 2 box. Multipliers can be found in the header below to determine value for these.

COMPLETE SET (20) 25.00 50.00
*JUMBOS: .4X TO 1X BASIC INSERTS
AS1 Ray Bourque / Paul Coffey 1.00 2.50
AS2 Scott Stevens / Chris Chelios .75 2.00
AS3 Jaromir Jagr / Brett Hull 1.25 3.00
AS4 Brendan Shanahan / Pavel Bure .75 2.00
AS5 M.Lemieux/W.Gretzky 8.00 20.00
AS6 Martin Brodeur / Ed Belfour 2.00 5.00
AS7 Brian Leetch / Nicklas Lidstrom .75 2.00
AS8 Roman Hamrlik / Gary Suter .75 2.00
AS9 Eric Desjardins / Al MacInnis .75 2.00
AS10 Cam Neely / Alexander Mogilny .75 2.00
AS11 Peter Bondra / Theo Fleury .75 2.00
AS12 Daniel Alfredsson / Teemu Selanne .75 2.00
AS13 Pat Verbeek / Owen Nolan .75 2.00
AS14 John LeClair / Paul Kariya 2.00 5.00
AS15 Pierre Turgeon / Sergei Fedorov 1.00 2.50
AS16 Mark Messier / Doug Weight .75 2.00
AS17 Eric Lindros / Peter Forsberg 2.50 6.00
AS18 Ron Francis / Mats Sundin .75 2.00
AS19 John Vanbiesbrouck / Chris Osgood .75 2.00
AS20 Dominik Hasek / Felix Potvin 2.00 5.00

1995-96 Upper Deck Predictor Hobby

The 40 cards in this set were randomly inserted in series 1 hobby packs (H1-H20) at the rate of 1:30, and series 2 hobby packs (H21-H40) at the rate of 1:23. Each card was a potential winner in an interactive game based on season-end award recipients: if the player pictured on your card came in first or second in the voting for that award, you could redeem your card for a complete set of Predictors from that distribution category. Cards H1-H10 were contestants for the Hart Trophy, cards H11-H20 were goalies competing for the Vezina Trophy, cards H21-H30 were contestants for the Calder Trophy, and cards H31-H40 were vying for the James Norris Trophy. The cards of Mario Lemieux, Mark Messier, Jim Carey, Vezina Long Shot, Daniel Alfredsson, Eric Daze, Chris Chelios and Ray Bourque may be somewhat harder to locate now, because, as winners, many of them were redeemed and destroyed.

COMPLETE SET (40) 30.00 80.00
COMP.HART PRIZE SET (10) 6.00 15.00
COMP.VEZINA PRIZE (10) 5.00 12.00
COMP.CALDER PRIZE (10) 2.50 6.00
COMP.NORRIS PRIZE (10) 2.50 6.00
*PRIZE CARDS: .2X TO .5X BASIC INSERTS
ONE PRIZE SET PER PRED.WINNER
H1 Eric Lindros 1.00 2.50
H2 Jaromir Jagr 1.50 4.00
H3 Paul Coffey 1.00 2.50
H4 Mario Lemieux WIN 4.00 10.00
H5 Martin Brodeur 2.50 6.00
H6 Sergei Fedorov 1.00 2.50
H7 Wayne Gretzky 6.00 15.00
H8 Peter Forsberg 1.50 4.00
H9 Mark Messier WIN 1.25 3.00
H10 Hart Long Shot .40 1.00
H11 Martin Brodeur 2.50 6.00
H12 Mike Richter 1.00 2.50
H13 Dominik Hasek 2.00 5.00
H14 Patrick Roy 4.00 10.00
H15 Blaine Lacher .40 1.00
H16 Jim Carey WIN .40 1.00
H17 Felix Potvin 1.25 3.00
H18 Ed Belfour 1.25 3.00
H19 John Vanbiesbrouck .75 2.00
H20 Vezina Long Shot WIN .40 1.00
H21 Vitali Yachmenev .40 1.00
H22 Saku Koivu 1.00 2.50
H23 Daniel Alfredsson WIN 2.00 5.00
H24 Ed Jovanovski .40 1.00
H25 Aki Berg .40 1.00
H26 Radek Dvorak .40 1.00
H27 Shane Doan .75 2.00
H28 Nicklas Sundstrom .40 1.00
H29 Eric Daze WIN .40 1.00
H30 Calder Long Shot .40 1.00
H31 Paul Coffey .75 2.00
H32 Ray Bourque WIN 1.25 3.00
H33 Brian Leetch .75 2.00
H34 Chris Chelios WIN 1.25 3.00
H35 Scott Stevens .40 1.00
H36 Nicklas Lidstrom 1.00 2.50
H37 Sergei Zubov .40 1.00
H38 Larry Murphy .40 1.00
H39 Roman Hamrlik .40 1.00
H40 Norris Long Shot .40 1.00

1995-96 Upper Deck Predictor Retail

The 60 cards in this interactive set were randomly inserted in retail packs from both series. R1-R30 were inserted at a rate of 1:30 series 1 retail packs, and 1:17 Value Added retail packs, while cards R31-R60 were inserted at a rate of 1:23 retail series 2 packs. A card could be redeemed if the player pictured finished first or second in the race for the scoring category featured. Cards R1-R10 battled for the assists crown, R11-R20 aimed to be the most prolific snipers, R21-R30 aimed to reach the top of the point scoring heap, R31-R40 were shooting for Art Ross, R41-R50 were in search of Lester B. Pearson, and R51-R60 were players looking to be awarded the Conn Smythe. However, a printing error at the printing plant reversed the intended categories on cards R1-R10 and R11-R20. In light of this, Upper Deck decided to honour a card as a winner if the player pictured won in either category. The cards of Mario Lemieux (R32, R42), Jaromir Jagr, Patrick Roy, Ron Francis and the Long Shots in the Assists, Goals, Points, and Smythe categories may be somewhat harder to find, as many were redeemed as winners.

COMPLETE SET (60) 75.00 200.00
COMP.ASSIST PRIZE (10) 4.00 10.00
COMP.GOAL PRIZE (10) 6.00 15.00
COMP.POINT PRIZE (10) 6.00 15.00
COMP.ROSS PRIZE (10) 8.00 20.00
COMP.PEARSON PRIZE (10) 8.00 20.00
COMP.SMYTHE PRIZE (10) 10.00 25.00
*PRIZE CARDS: .2X TO .5X BASIC INSERTS
ONE PRIZE SET PER PRED.WINNER
R1 Cam Neely 1.25 3.00
R2 Eric Lindros 1.25 3.00
R3 Jaromir Jagr WIN 2.00 5.00
R4 Brendan Shanahan 1.25 3.00
R5 Brett Hull 1.50 4.00
R6 Alexander Mogilny .60 1.50
R7 Owen Nolan .60 1.50
R8 Theo Fleury .40 1.00
R9 Pavel Bure 1.25 3.00
R10 Assists Long Shot WIN .40 1.00
R11 Ron Francis WIN .60 1.50
R12 Paul Coffey 1.25 3.00
R13 Wayne Gretzky 6.00 15.00
R14 Joe Sakic 2.50 6.00
R15 Steve Yzerman 4.00 10.00
R16 Adam Oates .60 1.50
R17 Joe Juneau .40 1.00
R18 Brian Leetch .60 1.50
R19 Pat LaFontaine 1.25 3.00
R20 Goals Long Shot WIN .40 1.00
R21 Eric Lindros 1.25 3.00
R22 Jaromir Jagr WIN 2.00 5.00
R23 Wayne Gretzky 6.00 15.00
R24 Sergei Fedorov 1.50 4.00
R25 Peter Forsberg 2.00 5.00
R26 Pavel Bure 1.25 3.00
R27 Joe Sakic 2.50 6.00
R28 Alexei Zhamnov .40 1.00
R29 Pat LaFontaine 1.25 3.00
R30 Points Long Shot WIN .40 1.00
R31 Wayne Gretzky 6.00 15.00
R32 Mario Lemieux WIN 4.00 10.00
R33 Eric Lindros 1.25 3.00
R34 Sergei Fedorov 1.50 4.00
R35 Alexander Mogilny .60 1.50
R36 Joe Sakic 2.50 6.00
R37 Peter Forsberg 2.00 5.00
R38 Jaromir Jagr WIN 2.00 5.00
R39 Mark Messier 1.25 3.00
R40 Ross Long Shot .40 1.00
R41 Wayne Gretzky 6.00 15.00
R42 Mario Lemieux 4.00 10.00
R43 Paul Kariya 1.25 3.00
R44 Sergei Fedorov 1.50 4.00
R45 Joe Sakic 2.50 6.00
R46 Jaromir Jagr WIN 2.00 5.00
R47 Jeremy Roenick 1.50 4.00
R48 Ray Bourque 1.25 3.00
R49 Teemu Selanne 1.25 3.00
R50 Pearson Long Shot .40 1.00
R51 Wayne Gretzky 6.00 15.00
R52 Eric Lindros 1.25 3.00
R53 Mario Lemieux WIN 4.00 10.00
R54 Peter Forsberg 2.00 5.00
R55 Patrick Roy WIN 5.00 12.00
R56 Mark Messier 1.25 3.00
R57 Martin Brodeur 2.50 6.00
R58 Steve Yzerman 4.00 10.00
R59 Mike Modano 1.50 4.00
R60 Smythe Long Shot WIN .40 1.00

1995-96 Upper Deck Special Edition

This 180-card set was inserted one per hobby pack over both series of 1995-96 Upper Deck cards. Cards 1-90 were found in series 1 packs, while 91-180 were in series 2.

COMPLETE SET (180) 20.00 50.00
*GOLDS: 8X TO 20X BASIC INSERTS
SE1 Paul Kariya .25 .60
SE2 Oleg Tverdovsky .07 .20
SE3 Guy Hebert .10 .30
SE4 Ray Bourque .25 .60
SE5 Adam Oates .10 .30
SE6 Mariusz Czerkawski .07 .20
SE7 Blaine Lacher .07 .20
SE8 Garry Galley .07 .20
SE9 Donald Audette .07 .20
SE10 Pat LaFontaine .25 .60
SE11 Alexei Zhitnik .07 .20
SE12 Joe Nieuwendyk .10 .30
SE13 Phil Housley .10 .30
SE14 German Titov .07 .20
SE15 Trevor Kidd .10 .30
SE16 Bernie Nicholls .07 .20
SE17 Chris Chelios .25 .60
SE18 Tony Amonte .10 .30
SE19 Ed Belfour .25 .60
SE20 Jon Klemm .07 .20
SE21 Peter Forsberg .40 1.00
SE22 Adam Deadmarsh .07 .20
SE23 Stephane Fiset .10 .30
SE24 Dave Gagner .07 .20
SE25 Kevin Hatcher .07 .20
SE26 Mike Modano .30 .75
SE27 Keith Primeau .07 .20
SE28 Dino Ciccarelli .10 .30
SE29 Nicklas Lidstrom .25 .60
SE30 Steve Yzerman 1.25 3.00
SE31 Doug Weight .10 .30
SE32 Bill Ranford .10 .30
SE33 Stu Barnes .07 .20
SE34 Bob Kudelski .07 .20
SE35 Rob Niedermayer .10 .30
SE36 Andrew Cassels .07 .20
SE37 Darren Turcotte .07 .20
SE38 Andrei Nikolishin .07 .20
SE39 Sean Burke .10 .30
SE40 Rick Tocchet .10 .30
SE41 Jari Kurri .25 .60
SE42 Rob Blake .10 .30
SE43 Mark Recchi .10 .30
SE44 Pierre Turgeon .10 .30
SE45 Vladimir Malakhov .07 .20
SE46 Valeri Bure .07 .20
SE47 Stephane Richer .10 .30
SE48 Bill Guerin .10 .30
SE49 Scott Stevens .10 .30
SE50 Claude Lemieux .07 .20
SE51 Zigmund Palffy .10 .30
SE52 Kirk Muller .07 .20
SE53 Todd Bertuzzi .10 .30
SE54 Brett Lindros .07 .20
SE55 Brian Leetch .10 .30
SE56 Alexei Kovalev .07 .20
SE57 Adam Graves .07 .20
SE58 Mike Richter .25 .60
SE59 Alexei Yashin .10 .30
SE60 Alexandre Daigle .07 .20
SE61 Don Beaupre .10 .30
SE62 Radek Bonk .07 .20
SE63 John LeClair .25 .60
SE64 Rod Brind'Amour .10 .30
SE65 Ron Hextall .10 .30
SE66 Ron Francis .10 .30
SE67 Markus Naslund .25 .60
SE68 Tom Barrasso .10 .30
SE69 Ian Laperriere .07 .20
SE70 Esa Tikkanen .07 .20
SE71 Al MacInnis .10 .30
SE72 Ulf Dahlen .07 .20
SE73 Craig Janney .07 .20
SE74 Jeff Friesen .07 .20
SE75 Chris Gratton .07 .20
SE76 Roman Hamrlik .10 .30
SE77 Alexander Selivanov .07 .20
SE78 Daren Puppa .10 .30
SE79 Dave Andreychuk .10 .30
SE80 Doug Gilmour .10 .30
SE81 Kenny Jonsson .07 .20
SE82 Trevor Linden .10 .30
SE83 Kirk McLean .10 .30
SE84 Jeff Brown .07 .20
SE85 Keith Jones .07 .20
SE86 Joe Juneau .07 .20
SE87 Jim Carey .10 .30
SE88 Keith Tkachuk .25 .60
SE89 Teemu Selanne .25 .60
SE90 Igor Korolev .07 .20
SE91 Mike Sillinger .07 .20
SE92 Steve Rucchin .10 .30
SE93 Valeri Karpov .07 .20
SE94 Cam Neely .25 .60
SE95 Shawn McEachern .07 .20
SE96 Kevin Stevens .07 .20
SE97 Ted Donato .07 .20
SE98 Dominik Hasek .50 1.25
SE99 Randy Burridge .07 .20
SE100 Jason Dawe .07 .20
SE101 Theo Fleury .07 .20
SE102 Michael Nylander .07 .20
SE103 Rick Tabaracci .10 .30
SE104 Jeremy Roenick .30 .75
SE105 Bob Probert .10 .30
SE106 Patrick Poulin .07 .20
SE107 Gary Suter .07 .20
SE108 Claude Lemieux .07 .20
SE109 Sandis Ozolinsh .07 .20
SE110 Patrick Roy 1.25 3.00
SE111 Joe Sakic .50 1.25
SE112 Derian Hatcher .07 .20
SE113 Greg Adams .07 .20
SE114 Todd Harvey .07 .20
SE115 Sergei Fedorov .40 1.00
SE116 Chris Osgood .10 .30
SE117 Vyacheslav Kozlov .10 .30
SE118 Paul Coffey .25 .60
SE119 Jason Arnott .07 .20
SE120 David Oliver .07 .20
SE121 Todd Marchant .07 .20
SE122 John Vanbiesbrouck .10 .30

SE123 Jody Hull .07 .20
SE124 Jason Woolley .07 .20
SE125 Brendan Shanahan .25 .60
SE126 Nelson Emerson .07 .20
SE127 Geoff Sanderson .07 .20
SE128 Wayne Gretzky 1.50 4.00
SE129 Marty McSorley .07 .20
SE130 Yanic Perreault .07 .20
SE131 Jocelyn Thibault .25 .60
SE132 Brian Savage .07 .20
SE133 Vincent Damphousse .07 .20
SE134 John MacLean .10 .30
SE135 Martin Brodeur .60 1.50
SE136 Steve Thomas .10 .30
SE137 Scott Niedermayer .07 .20
SE138 Travis Green .10 .30
SE139 Wendel Clark .10 .30
SE140 Tommy Soderstrom .10 .30
SE141 Mark Messier .25 .60
SE142 Ulf Samuelsson .07 .20
SE143 Ray Ferraro .07 .20
SE144 Luc Robitaille .10 .30
SE145 Daniel Alfredsson 1.00 2.50
SE146 Martin Straka .07 .20
SE147 Steve Duchesne .07 .20
SE148 Eric Lindros .25 .60
SE149 Mikael Renberg .10 .30
SE150 Eric Desjardins .10 .30
SE151 Joel Otto .07 .20
SE152 Mario Lemieux 1.25 3.00
SE153 Jaromir Jagr .40 1.00
SE154 Petr Nedved .07 .20
SE155 Sergei Zubov .07 .20
SE156 Tomas Sandstrom .07 .20
SE157 Brett Hull .30 .75
SE158 Grant Fuhr .25 .60
SE159 Shayne Corson .07 .20
SE160 Chris Pronger .25 .60
SE161 Ray Sheppard .07 .20
SE162 Arturs Irbe .10 .30
SE163 Owen Nolan .10 .30
SE164 Andrei Nazarov .07 .20
SE165 Paul Ysebaert .07 .20
SE166 Brian Bradley .07 .20
SE167 Petr Klima .07 .20
SE168 Felix Potvin .25 .60
SE169 Mats Sundin .25 .60
SE170 Larry Murphy .10 .30
SE171 Benoit Hogue .07 .20
SE172 Pavel Bure .25 .60
SE173 Alexander Mogilny .10 .30
SE174 Cliff Ronning .07 .20
SE175 Pat Peake .07 .20
SE176 Sylvain Cote .07 .20
SE177 Peter Bondra .10 .30
SE178 Dallas Drake .07 .20
SE179 Tim Cheveldae .10 .30
SE180 Darren Turcotte .07 .20

1996-97 Upper Deck

This two-series, 390-card set was distributed in 12-card packs with the suggested retail price of $2.49. The set was highlighted by the use of actual game dating for much of the photography, the selection of which included some of the most memorable moments of the '96 season. The set is noteworthy for including Wayne Gretzky in his new uniform as a New York Ranger both in the set and on all packaging. The set also contained a 15-card Star Rookie subset (#181-195), a 13-card Through the Glass subset (#196-208), a 10-card On-Ice Insight subset (359-368) and four checklist cards. Several key rookies appeared in this set, including Joe Thornton, Patrick Marleau, Daniel Tkaczuk, and Dainius Zubrus. The "Meet the Stars" promotion was continued in this set, which gave the collector an opportunity to win a chance to meet "The Great One" himself. Trivia cards were inserted one in every four packs and Instant Win cards one in every 56 packs. These cards are not widely traded, but are now worth about ten cents each.

COMPLETE SET (390) 30.00 80.00
COMP.SERIES 1 (210) 10.00 30.00
COMP.SERIES 2 (180) 20.00 50.00
1 Paul Kariya .15 .40
2 Guy Hebert .08 .25
3 J.F. Jomphe RC .02 .10
4 Joe Sacco .02 .10
5 Jason York .02 .10
6 Alex Hicks RC .02 .10
7 Mikhail Shtalenkov .02 .10
8 Bill Ranford .08 .25
9 Kyle McLaren .02 .10
10 Rick Tocchet .08 .25
11 Jon Rohloff .02 .10
12 Jozef Stumpel .02 .10
13 Cam Neely .15 .40
14 Ray Bourque .25 .60
15 Pat LaFontaine .15 .40
16 Brian Holzinger .08 .25
17 Alexei Zhitnik .02 .10
18 Donald Audette .02 .10
19 Jason Dawe .02 .10
20 Wayne Primeau .02 .10
21 Mike Peca .02 .10
22 Theo Fleury .02 .10
23 Sandy McCarthy .02 .10
24 Zarley Zalapski .02 .10
25 Trevor Kidd .08 .25
26 Steve Chiasson .02 .10
27 Michael Nylander .02 .10
28 Ronnie Stern .02 .10
29 Eric Daze .08 .25
30 Jeff Hackett .08 .25
31 Chris Chelios .15 .40
32 Tony Amonte .08 .25
33 Bob Probert .08 .25
34 Eric Weinrich .02 .10
35 Jeremy Roenick .20 .50
36 Mike Ricci .02 .10
37 Sandis Ozolinsh .02 .10
38 Patrick Roy .75 2.00
39 Uwe Krupp .02 .10
40 Stephane Yelle .02 .10
41 Adam Deadmarsh .02 .10
42 Scott Young .02 .10
43 Mike Modano .25 .60
44 Derian Hatcher .02 .10
45 Todd Harvey .02 .10
46 Brent Fedyk .02 .10
47 Grant Marshall .02 .10
48 Jamie Langenbrunner .02 .10
49 Jere Lehtinen .02 .10
50 Steve Yzerman .75 2.00
51 Igor Larionov .02 .10
52 Vladimir Konstantinov .08 .25
53 Chris Osgood .08 .25
54 Jamie Pushor .02 .10
55 Darren McCarty .02 .10
56 Nicklas Lidstrom .15 .40
57 Jason Arnott .02 .10
58 Doug Weight .08 .25
59 Todd Marchant .02 .10
60 David Oliver .02 .10
61 Luke Richardson .02 .10
62 Jason Bonsignore .02 .10
63 John Vanbiesbrouck .08 .25
64 Stu Barnes .02 .10
65 Martin Straka .02 .10
66 Ed Jovanovski .08 .25
67 Robert Svehla .02 .10
68 Gord Murphy .02 .10
69 Tom Fitzgerald .02 .10
70 Jeff O'Neill .02 .10
71 Jason Muzzatti .08 .25
72 Sean Burke .08 .25
73 Jeff Brown .02 .10
74 Andrew Cassels .02 .10
75 Geoff Sanderson .08 .25
76 Dimitri Khristich .02 .10
77 Vitali Yachmenev .02 .10
78 Kevin Stevens .02 .10
79 Yanic Perreault .02 .10
80 Craig Johnson .02 .10
81 John Slaney .02 .10
82 Saku Koivu .15 .40
83 Jocelyn Thibault .15 .40
84 Vladimir Malakhov .02 .10
85 Turner Stevenson .02 .10
86 Vincent Damphousse .02 .10
87 Mark Recchi .08 .25
88 Patrice Brisebois .02 .10
89 Dave Andreychuk .08 .25
90 Bill Guerin .02 .10
91 Martin Brodeur .40 1.00
92 Scott Niedermayer .02 .10
93 Petr Sykora .02 .10
94 Stephane Richer .08 .25
95 John MacLean .08 .25
96 Eric Fichaud .08 .25
97 Zigmund Palffy .08 .25
98 Alexander Semak .02 .10
99 Bryan McCabe .02 .10
100 Darby Hendrickson .02 .10
101 Kenny Jonsson .02 .10
102 Marty McInnis .02 .10
103 Alexei Kovalev .02 .10
104 Ulf Samuelsson .02 .10
105 Jeff Beukeboom .02 .10
106 Marty McSorley .02 .10
107 Niklas Sundstrom .02 .10
108 Wayne Gretzky 1.00 2.50
with Mark Messier
109 Mike Richter .15 .40
110 Alexei Yashin .02 .10
111 Randy Cunneyworth .02 .10
112 Damian Rhodes .08 .25
113 Daniel Alfredsson .08 .25
114 Antti Tormanen .02 .10
115 Ted Drury .02 .10
116 Janne Laukkanen .02 .10
117 Sean Hill .02 .10
118 John LeClair .15 .40
119 Ron Hextall .08 .25
120 Dale Hawerchuk .08 .25
121 Rod Brind'Amour .08 .25
122 Pat Falloon .02 .10
123 Eric Desjardins .08 .25
124 Joel Otto .02 .10
125 Alexei Zhamnov .02 .10
126 Nikolai Khabibulin .08 .25
127 Craig Janney .08 .25
128 Deron Quint .02 .10
129 Oleg Tverdovsky .02 .10
130 Chad Kilger .02 .10
131 Teppo Numminen .02 .10
132 Tom Barrasso .08 .25
133 Ron Francis .08 .25
134 Petr Nedved .08 .25
135 Ken Wregget .08 .25
136 Joe Dziedzic .02 .10
137 Tomas Sandstrom .02 .10
138 Dmitri Mironov .02 .10
139 Shayne Corson .02 .10
140 Grant Fuhr .08 .25
141 Al MacInnis .08 .25
142 Stephen Leach .02 .10
143 Murray Baron .02 .10
144 Chris Pronger .08 .25
145 Jamie Rivers .02 .10
146 Owen Nolan .08 .25
147 Chris Terreri .08 .25
148 Marcus Ragnarsson .02 .10
149 Shean Donovan .02 .10
150 Ray Whitney .02 .10
151 Michal Sykora .02 .10
152 Viktor Kozlov .02 .10
153 Roman Hamrlik .08 .25
154 Bill Houlder .02 .10
155 Mikael Andersson .02 .10
156 Petr Klima .02 .10
157 Jason Wiemer .02 .10
158 Rob Zamuner .02 .10
159 Paul Ysebaert .02 .10
160 Mats Sundin .15 .40
161 Larry Murphy UER .08 .25
(bio info that of Mats Sundin)
162 Doug Gilmour .08 .25
163 Todd Warriner .02 .10
164 Dimitri Yushkevich .02 .10
165 Kirk Muller .02 .10
166 Jamie Macoun .02 .10
167 Alexander Mogilny .08 .25
168 Corey Hirsch .08 .25
169 Trevor Linden .08 .25
170 Markus Naslund .15 .40
171 Martin Gelinas .02 .10
172 Jyrki Lumme .02 .10
173 Bret Hedican .02 .10
174 Jim Carey .15 .40
175 Sergei Gonchar .02 .10
176 Joe Juneau .02 .10
177 Brendan Witt .02 .10
178 Dale Hunter .02 .10
179 Steve Konowalchuk .02 .10
180 Peter Bondra .08 .25
181 Jarome Iginla .20 .50
182 Ralph Intranuovo .02 .10
183 Anders Eriksson .02 .10
184 Andrew Brunette RC .20 .50
185 Steve Sullivan RC .20 .50
186 Brandon Convery .02 .10
187 Ethan Moreau RC .15 .40
188 Marko Kiprusoff .02 .10
189 Jason McBain .02 .10
190 Mark Kolesar RC .02 .10
191 Greg DeVries RC .02 .10
192 Alexei Yegorov RC .02 .10
193 Sebastien Bordeleau RC .02 .10
194 Nick Stajduhar .02 .10
195 Jan Caloun RC .02 .10
196 Dino Ciccarelli TTG .08 .25
197 Ron Hextall TTG .08 .25
198 Murray Baron TTG .02 .10
199 Patrick Roy TTG .15 .40
200 Scott Mellanby TTG .02 .10
201 Tie Domi TTG .08 .25
202 Glenn Healy TTG .08 .25
203 Keith Primeau TTG .02 .10
204 Joe Sakic TTG .15 .40
205 Jeremy Roenick TTG .08 .25
206 Sergei Fedorov TTG .15 .40
207 Claude Lemieux TTG .02 .10
208 Theo Fleury TTG .02 .10
209 Checklist (1-104) .02 .10
210 Checklist (105-210) .02 .10
211 Teemu Selanne .15 .40
212 Jari Kurri .08 .25
213 Darren Van Impe .02 .10
214 Steve Rucchin .02 .10
215 Ruslan Salei RC .02 .10
216 Adam Oates .08 .25
217 Don Sweeney .02 .10
218 Steve Staios RC .02 .10
219 Barry Richter .02 .10
220 Mattias Timander RC .02 .10
221 Ted Donato .02 .10
222 Dominik Hasek .30 .75
223 Derek Plante .02 .10
224 Vaclav Varada RC .02 .10
225 Andrei Trefilov .02 .10
226 Curtis Brown .02 .10
227 German Titov .02 .10
228 Robert Reichel .02 .10
229 Cory Stillman .02 .10
230 Chris O'Sullivan .02 .10
231 Corey Millen .02 .10
232 Jonas Hoglund .02 .10
233 Alexei Zhamnov .08 .25
234 Ed Belfour .15 .40
235 Gary Suter .02 .10
236 Kevin Miller .02 .10
237 Tuomas Gronman .02 .10
238 Enrico Ciccone .02 .10
239 Peter Forsberg .30 .75
240 Joe Sakic .30 .75
241 Valeri Kamensky .08 .25
242 Landon Wilson .02 .10
243 Claude Lemieux .02 .10
244 Eric Lacroix .02 .10
245 Joe Nieuwendyk UER .08 .25
(front Joe Nieuwendky)
246 Sergei Zubov .02 .10
247 Benoit Hogue .02 .10
248 Arturs Irbe .08 .25
249 Pat Verbeek .02 .10
250 Sergei Fedorov .20 .50
251 Vyacheslav Kozlov .02 .10
252 Brendan Shanahan .15 .40
253 Kevin Hodson RC .15 .40
254 Greg Johnson .02 .10
255 Tomas Holmstrom RC .75 2.00
256 Curtis Joseph .15 .40
257 Dean McAmmond .02 .10
258 Ryan Smyth .15 .40
259 Mike Grier RC .20 .50
260 Miroslav Satan .02 .10
261 Rem Murray RC .02 .10
262 Rob Niedermayer .08 .25
263 Ray Sheppard .08 .25
264 Dave Lowry .02 .10
265 Scott Mellanby .08 .25
266 Rhett Warrener .02 .10
267 Per Gustafsson RC .02 .10
268 Paul Coffey .15 .40
269 Nelson Emerson .02 .10
270 Kevin Dineen .02 .10
271 Keith Primeau .02 .10
272 Hnat Domenichelli .02 .10
273 Ray Ferraro .02 .10
274 Stephane Fiset .08 .25
275 Kai Nurminen RC .02 .10
276 Dan Bylsma RC .02 .10
277 Mattias Norstrom .02 .10
278 Rob Blake .08 .25
279 Jose Theodore .20 .50
280 Martin Rucinsky .02 .10
281 Darcy Tucker .02 .10
282 David Wilkie .02 .10
283 Valeri Bure .02 .10
284 Steve Thomas .02 .10
285 Brian Rolston .02 .10
286 Scott Stevens .08 .25
287 Shawn Chambers .02 .10
288 Denis Pederson .02 .10
289 Lyle Odelein .02 .10
290 Travis Green .08 .25
291 Todd Bertuzzi .15 .40
292 Niclas Andersson .02 .10
293 Darius Kasparaitis .02 .10
294 Bryan Berard .15 .40
295 Daniel Goneau RC .02 .10
296 Christian Dube .02 .10
297 Adam Graves .02 .10
298 Sergei Nemchinov .02 .10
299 Mark Messier .15 .40
300 Brian Leetch .15 .40
301 Radek Bonk .02 .10
302 Alexandre Daigle .02 .10
303 Andreas Dackell RC .02 .10
304 Steve Duchesne .02 .10
305 Wade Redden .02 .10
306 Eric Lindros .15 .40
307 Mikael Renberg .08 .25
308 Shjon Podein .02 .10
309 Dainius Zubrus RC .20 .50
310 Janne Niinimaa .15 .40
311 Karl Dykhuis .02 .10
312 Jeremy Roenick .20 .50
313 Keith Tkachuk .15 .40
314 Shane Doan .02 .10
315 Cliff Ronning .02 .10
316 Mike Gartner .08 .25
317 Dave Manson .02 .10
318 Shawn Antoski .02 .10
319 Kevin Hatcher .02 .10
320 Jaromir Jagr .25 .60
321 Mario Lemieux .75 2.00
322 Bryan Smolinski .02 .10
323 Stefan Bergkvist RC .02 .10
324 Brett Hull .20 .50
325 Joe Murphy .02 .10
326 Stephane Matteau .02 .10
327 Geoff Courtnall .02 .10
328 Jim Campbell .02 .10
329 Harry York RC .15 .40
330 Kelly Hrudey .08 .25
331 Al Iafrate .02 .10
332 Jeff Friesen .02 .10
333 Darren Turcotte .02 .10
334 Bernie Nicholls .02 .10
335 Ville Peltonen .02 .10
336 Dino Ciccarelli .08 .25
337 Chris Gratton .08 .25
338 Daren Puppa .08 .25
339 Alexander Selivanov .02 .10
340 Daymond Langkow .08 .25
341 Felix Potvin .15 .40
342 Wendel Clark .08 .25
343 Mathieu Schneider .02 .10
344 Dave Ellett .02 .10
345 Fredrik Modin RC .40 1.00
346 Sergei Berezin RC .30 .75
347 Pavel Bure .15 .40
348 Kirk McLean .08 .25
349 Mike Sillinger .02 .10
350 Russ Courtnall .02 .10
351 Scott Walker .02 .10
352 Esa Tikkanen .02 .10
353 Pat Peake .02 .10
354 Olaf Kolzig .08 .25
355 Michal Pivonka .02 .10
356 Richard Zednik RC .20 .50
357 Phil Housley .08 .25
358 Anson Carter .08 .25
359 Eric Daze OII .08 .25
360 Felix Potvin OII .15 .40
361 Wayne Gretzky OII .60 1.50
362 Ed Jovanovski OII .08 .25
363 Mike Modano OII .08 .25
364 Peter Bondra OII .08 .25
365 Patrick Roy OII .40 1.00
366 Ray Bourque OII .15 .40
367 Roman Hamrlik OII .08 .25
368 John LeClair OII .15 .40
369 Adam Colagiacomo RC .40 1.00
370 Joe Thornton RC 5.00 12.00
371 Patrick DesRochers RC .40 1.00
372 Pierre-Luc Therrien RC .40 1.00
373 Nick Boynton RC .40 1.00
374 Andrew Ference RC .40 1.00
375 Jean-Francois Fortin RC .40 1.00
376 Chad Tetrault RC .40 1.00
377 Luc Theoret RC .40 1.00
378 Mike Van Ryn RC .40 1.00
379 Scott Barney RC .40 1.00
380 Harold Druken RC .40 1.00
381 Dylan Gyori RC .40 1.00
382 Chris Heron RC .40 1.00
383 Chad Hinz RC .40 1.00
384 Patrick Marleau RC 1.25 3.00
385 Serge Payer RC .40 1.00
386 Jeremy Reich RC .40 1.00
387 Daniel Tkaczuk RC .40 1.00
388 Jason Ward RC .40 1.00
389 Checklist (211-298) .02 .10
390 Checklist (299-390) .02 .10

1996-97 Upper Deck Game Jersey

Inserted 1:2500 packs, these highly popular inserts featured swatches of actual game-worn jerseys as part of the card stock. Five cards were inserted in series one packs, while the remaining eight cards were distributed with series two.

*MULTICOLOR SWATCH: .6X TO 1.5X
GJ1 Steve Yzerman 75.00 200.00
GJ2 Brett Hull 40.00 100.00
GJ3 Doug Gilmour 30.00 80.00
GJ4 Jaromir Jagr 75.00 150.00
GJ5 Ray Bourque 40.00 100.00
GJ6 Mario Lemieux 75.00 200.00
GJ7 John Vanbiesbrouck 30.00 80.00
GJ8 Eric Lindros 30.00 80.00
GJ9 Mike Modano 30.00 80.00
GJ10 Pavel Bure 30.00 80.00
GJ11 Mark Messier 60.00 120.00
GJ12 Theo Fleury 30.00 80.00
GJ13 Mats Sundin UER 30.00 80.00

1996-97 Upper Deck Generation Next

Randomly inserted in packs at a rate of 1:4, this double-fronted, series two insert paired up two top players on each card. Both sides were enhanced with silver and gold foil.

COMPLETE SET (40) 30.00 80.00
X1 Paul Kariya 5.00 12.00
Wayne Gretzky
X2 Trevor Linden 1.50 4.00
Peter Forsberg
X3 Joe Sakic 1.25 3.00
Rob Niedermayer
X4 Chris O'Sullivan .40 1.00
Eric Weinrich
X5 Jocelyn Thibault 3.00 8.00
Patrick Roy
X6 Brett Hull 1.25 3.00
Daniel Alfredsson
X7 Chris Osgood .75 2.00
John Vanbiesbrouck
X8 Ray Bourque 1.25 3.00
Roman Hamrlik
X9 Paul Coffey 1.25 3.00
Sandis Ozolinsh
X10 Doug Gilmour 1.25 3.00
Sergei Fedorov
X11 Chris Chelios 1.25 3.00
Ed Jovanovski
X12 Jason Arnott 1.25 3.00
Jeremy Roenick
X13 Doug Weight 3.00 8.00
Steve Yzerman
X14 Brendan Shanahan 1.25 3.00
Todd Bertuzzi
X15 Wendel Clark 1.25 3.00
Keith Tkachuk
X16 Saku Koivu 1.25 3.00
Teemu Selanne
X17 Jaromir Jagr 1.25 3.00
Zigmund Palffy
X18 Ed Belfour 1.50 4.00
Martin Brodeur
X19 Eric Daze .75 2.00
Owen Nolan
X20 Valeri Kamensky .40 1.00
Vitali Yachmenev
X21 Jarome Iginla 1.50 4.00
Mike Modano
X22 Anders Eriksson 1.25 3.00
Niklas Lidstrom
X23 Brian Leetch 1.25 3.00
Bryan Berard
X24 Jari Kurri .40 1.00
Niklas Sundstrom
X25 Adam Deadmarsh .40 1.00
Scott Mellanby
X26 Peter Bondra .40 1.00
Petr Sykora
X27 Curtis Joseph 1.25 3.00
Eric Fichaud
X28 Dominik Hasek 2.00 5.00
Roman Turek
X29 Alexander Mogilny .40 1.00
Valeri Bure
X30 Daymond Langkow .40 1.00
Theo Fleury
X31 Bernie Nicholls .75 2.00
Sergei Berezin
X32 Chris Gratton .75 2.00
Rick Tocchet
X33 Felix Potvin 1.25 3.00
Grant Fuhr
X34 Keith Primeau .40 1.00
Eric Lindros
X35 Rob Blake .40 1.00
Wade Redden
X36 Chris Pronger .75 2.00
Scott Stevens
X37 Gary Suter .40 1.00
Kyle McLaren
X38 Jonas Hoglund .75 2.00
Mats Sundin
X39 Larry Murphy .40 1.00
Sergei Zubov
X40 Adam Oates .75 2.00
Joe Juneau

1996-97 Upper Deck Hart Hopefuls Bronze

Randomly inserted in packs at a rate of 1:30, this series two-only insert consisted of twenty players vying for the title of league MVP and the chance to take home the Hart Trophy. Cards were numbered "One of 5000" on the back. Silver and gold parallels were also created. Silver were inserted at 1:150 and only 1000 were printed. Gold were inserted at 1:1500 and only 100 were produced.

COMPLETE SET (20) 30.00 80.00
*SILVER: 1X TO 2.5X BRONZE
*GOLD: 3X TO 8X BRONZE
HH1 Wayne Gretzky 8.00 20.00
HH2 Mark Messier 1.00 2.50
HH3 Eric Lindros 1.00 2.50
HH4 Sergei Fedorov 1.00 2.50
HH5 Saku Koivu 1.00 2.50
HH6 John Vanbiesbrouck .75 2.00
HH7 Peter Forsberg 1.50 4.00
HH8 Keith Tkachuk .75 2.00
HH9 Paul Kariya 1.00 2.50
HH10 Martin Brodeur 2.50 6.00
HH11 Patrick Roy 5.00 12.00
HH12 Alexander Mogilny .75 2.00
HH13 Brett Hull 1.25 3.00
HH14 Pavel Bure 1.00 2.50
HH15 Teemu Selanne 1.00 2.50
HH16 Mario Lemieux 5.00 12.00
HH17 Jeremy Roenick 1.25 3.00
HH18 Jaromir Jagr 1.50 4.00
HH19 Steve Yzerman 4.00 10.00
HH20 Joe Sakic 2.00 5.00

1996-97 Upper Deck Lord Stanley's Heroes Quarterfinals

Randomly inserted in series one packs at a rate of 1:37, this 20-card set featured numbered inserts (one of 5,000) on cel chrome technology. A player's head photo was displayed on acetate in the middle of the trophy. Semifinals and finals parallel variations were also produced and inserted randomly. Semifinals parallels were inserted at 1:185 and only 1000 sets were produced. Finals parallels were inserted at 1:1850 and only 100 sets were produced.

COMPLETE SET (20) 30.00 80.00
*FINALS: 8X TO 20X QUARTERFINALS
*SEMIFINAL: 1.2X TO 3X QUARTERFINAL
LS1 Wayne Gretzky 8.00 20.00
LS2 Mark Messier 1.50 4.00
LS3 Mario Lemieux 6.00 15.00
LS4 Jaromir Jagr 3.00 8.00
LS5 Martin Brodeur 5.00 12.00
LS6 Patrick Roy 6.00 15.00
LS7 Joe Sakic 4.00 10.00
LS8 Peter Forsberg 3.00 8.00
LS9 Theo Fleury 1.50 4.00
LS10 Paul Coffey 1.50 4.00
LS11 Doug Gilmour 1.50 4.00
LS12 Paul Kariya 1.50 4.00
LS13 Eric Lindros 1.50 4.00
LS14 Sergei Fedorov 2.00 5.00
LS15 Eric Daze 1.50 4.00
LS16 Teemu Selanne 1.50 4.00
LS17 Keith Tkachuk 1.50 4.00
LS18 Pavel Bure 1.50 4.00
LS19 Mats Sundin 1.50 4.00
LS20 Saku Koivu 1.50 4.00

1996-97 Upper Deck Power Performers

Randomly inserted in series two packs at a rate of 1:13, these cards featured a layered design on gold foil. Thirty of the league's toughest physical competitors were highlighted in the set.

COMPLETE SET (30) 15.00 40.00
P1 Brendan Shanahan 1.50 4.00
P2 Mikael Renberg .40 1.00
P3 John LeClair .75 2.00
P4 Keith Primeau .40 1.00
P5 Adam Graves .40 1.00
P6 Jason Arnott .40 1.00
P7 Todd Bertuzzi .75 2.00
P8 Ed Jovanovski .40 1.00
P9 Scott Stevens .40 1.00
P10 Chris Gratton .40 1.00
P11 Bill Guerin .40 1.00
P12 Vladimir Konstantinov .75 2.00
P13 Mike Grier .40 1.00
P14 Theo Fleury .75 2.00
P15 Chris Chelios .75 2.00
P16 Trevor Linden .75 2.00
P17 Claude Lemieux .40 1.00
P18 Owen Nolan .75 2.00
P19 Jarome Iginla 3.00 8.00
P20 Joe Nieuwendyk .40 1.00
P21 Kevin Hatcher .40 1.00
P22 Dino Ciccarelli .40 1.00
P23 Adam Deadmarsh .40 1.00
P24 Chris Pronger .75 2.00
P25 Mike Ricci .40 1.00
P26 Rod Brind'Amour .75 2.00
P27 Derian Hatcher .40 1.00
P28 Mats Sundin 1.50 4.00
P29 Doug Gilmour .75 2.00
P30 Todd Harvey .40 1.00

1996-97 Upper Deck Superstar Showdown

Randomly inserted in first series packs at a rate of 1:4, this 60-card set featured 30 different one-on-one match-ups of the NHL's top stars. Each of the card fronts displayed a single player photo with a die-cut design that enabled the cards to be matched together in pairs.

COMPLETE SET (60) 30.00 80.00
SS1A Pavel Bure .60 1.50
SS1B Paul Kariya .60 1.50
SS2A Patrick Roy 3.00 8.00
SS2B John Vanbiesbrouck .40 1.00
SS3A Eric Lindros .60 1.50
SS3B Ed Jovanovski .40 1.00
SS4A Theo Fleury .40 1.00
SS4B Doug Gilmour .40 1.00
SS5A Wayne Gretzky 4.00 10.00
SS5B Mario Lemieux 3.00 8.00
SS6A Keith Tkachuk .60 1.50
SS6B Brendan Shanahan .60 1.50
SS7A Ray Bourque 1.00 2.50
SS7B Brian Leetch .60 1.50
SS8A Peter Forsberg 1.00 2.50
SS8B Sergei Fedorov .60 1.50
SS9A Mark Messier .60 1.50
SS9B Scott Stevens .40 1.00
SS10A Teemu Selanne .60 1.50
SS10B Alexander Mogilny .40 1.00
SS11A Felix Potvin .60 1.50
SS11B Jocelyn Thibault .60 1.50
SS12A Martin Brodeur 1.50 4.00
SS12B Eric Fichaud .40 1.00
SS13A Roman Hamrlik .40 1.00
SS13B Jaromir Jagr 1.00 2.50
SS14A Jim Carey .60 1.50
SS14B Saku Koivu .60 1.50
SS15A Jeremy Roenick .75 2.00
SS15B Brett Hull .75 2.00
SS16A Joe Sakic 1.25 3.00
SS16B Steve Yzerman 3.00 8.00
SS17A Doug Weight .40 1.00
SS17B Pat LaFontaine .60 1.50
SS18A Daniel Alfredsson .40 1.00
SS18B Eric Daze .40 1.00
SS19A Mike Modano .75 2.00
SS19B Jason Arnott .15 .40
SS20A Paul Coffey .60 1.50
SS20B Sandis Ozolinsh .15 .40
SS21A Zigmund Palffy .40 1.00
SS21B Petr Sykora .15 .40
SS22A Ed Belfour .60 1.50
SS22B Ron Hextall .40 1.00
SS23A Mats Sundin .60 1.50
SS23B Mikael Renberg .40 1.00
SS24A Vitali Yachmenev .15 .40
SS24B Alexei Zhamnov .40 1.00
SS25A Oleg Tverdovsky .40 1.00
SS25B Kyle McLaren .15 .40
SS26A Dominik Hasek 1.25 3.00
SS26B Petr Nedved .40 1.00
SS27A Chris Chelios .60 1.50
SS27B Chris Pronger .40 1.00
SS28A Rob Niedermayer .40 1.00
SS28B Scott Niedermayer .15 .40
SS29A Keith Primeau .15 .40
SS29B Bob Probert .40 1.00
SS30A Bill Ranford .40 1.00
SS30B Chris Osgood .40 1.00

1997-98 Upper Deck

The 1997-98 Upper Deck set was issued in two series totaling 420 cards and was distributed in 12-card packs with a suggested retail price of $2.49. The fronts feature color player photos, while the backs carry player information and career statistics. Series 1 contains the following subsets: Star Rookie (181-195), Fan Favorites (196-208) and two checklists (209-210). Series 2 contains the following subsets: Physical Force (389-398), Program of Excellence (399-418) and two checklists (419-420).

COMPLETE SET (420) 25.00 60.00
COMP.SERIES 1 (210) 10.00 20.00
COMP.SERIES 2 (210) 15.00 40.00
1 Teemu Selanne .15 .40
2 Steve Rucchin .02 .10
3 Kevin Todd .02 .10
4 Darren Van Impe .02 .10
5 Mark Janssens .02 .10
6 Guy Hebert .08 .25
7 Sean Pronger .02 .10
8 Jason Allison .02 .10
9 Ray Bourque .25 .60
10 Landon Wilson .02 .10
11 Anson Carter .08 .25
12 Jean-Yves Roy .02 .10
13 Kyle McLaren .02 .10
14 Don Sweeney .02 .10
15 Brian Holzinger .02 .10
16 Matthew Barnaby .02 .10
17 Wayne Primeau .02 .10
18 Steve Shields RC .40 1.00
19 Jason Dawe .02 .10
20 Donald Audette .02 .10
21 Dixon Ward .02 .10
22 Hnat Domenichelli .02 .10
23 Trevor Kidd .08 .25
24 Jarome Iginla .20 .50
25 Sandy McCarthy .02 .10
26 Marty McInnis .02 .10
27 Jonas Hoglund .02 .10
28 Aaron Gavey .02 .10
29 Keith Primeau .02 .10
30 Geoff Sanderson .08 .25
31 Sean Burke .08 .25
32 Steven Rice .02 .10
33 Stu Grimson .02 .10
34 Jeff O'Neill .02 .10
35 Curtis Leschyshyn .02 .10
36 Chris Chelios .15 .40
37 Sergei Krivokrasov .02 .10
38 Jeff Hackett .08 .25
39 Bob Probert .02 .10
40 Chris Terreri .08 .25
41 Eric Daze .08 .25
42 Alexei Zhamnov .02 .10

1997-98 Upper Deck

43 Patrick Roy .75 2.00
44 Sandis Ozolinsh .02 .10
45 Eric Messier RC .08 .25
46 Adam Deadmarsh .02 .10
47 Claude Lemieux .02 .10
48 Mike Ricci .02 .10
49 Stephane Yelle .02 .10
50 Joe Nieuwendyk .08 .25
51 Derian Hatcher .02 .10
52 Jere Lehtinen .02 .10
53 Roman Turek .08 .25
54 Darryl Sydor .02 .10
55 Todd Harvey .02 .10
56 Mike Modano .25 .60
57 Steve Yzerman .75 2.00
58 Martin Lapointe .02 .10
59 Darren McCarty .02 .10
60 Mike Vernon .08 .25
61 Kirk Maltby .02 .10
62 Kris Draper .02 .10
63 Vladimir Konstantinov .08 .25
64 Todd Marchant .02 .10
65 Doug Weight .08 .25
66 Jason Arnott .02 .10
67 Mike Grier .02 .10
68 Mats Lindgren .02 .10
69 Bryan Marchment .02 .10
70 Rem Murray .02 .10
71 Radek Dvorak .02 .10
72 John Vanbiesbrouck .08 .25
73 Robert Svehla .02 .10
74 Bill Lindsay .02 .10
75 Paul Laus .02 .10
76 Kirk Muller .02 .10
77 Dave Nemirovsky .02 .10
78 Roman Vopat .02 .10
79 Jan Vopat .02 .10
80 Dimitri Khristich .02 .10
81 Glen Murray .02 .10
82 Mattias Norstrom .02 .10
83 Ian Laperriere .02 .10
84 Mark Recchi .08 .25
85 Jose Theodore .20 .50
86 Vincent Damphousse .02 .10
87 Sebastien Bordeleau .02 .10
88 Darcy Tucker .02 .10
89 Martin Rucinsky .02 .10
90 Jocelyn Thibault .08 .25
91 Doug Gilmour .08 .25
92 Brian Rolston .02 .10
93 Jay Pandolfo .02 .10
94 John MacLean .02 .10
95 Scott Stevens .08 .25
96 Dave Andreychuk .02 .10
97 Denis Pederson .02 .10
98 Bryan Berard .08 .25
99 Zigmund Palffy .08 .25
100 Bryan McCabe .02 .10
101 Rich Pilon .02 .10
102 Eric Fichaud .08 .25
103 Todd Bertuzzi .15 .40
104 Robert Reichel .02 .10
105 Christian Dube .02 .10
106 Niklas Sundstrom .02 .10
107 Mike Richter .15 .40
108 Adam Graves .02 .10
109 Wayne Gretzky 1.00 2.50
110 Bruce Driver .02 .10
111 Esa Tikkanen .02 .10
112 Daniel Alfredsson .08 .25
113 Ron Tugnutt .08 .25
114 Steve Duchesne .02 .10
115 Bruce Gardiner RC .02 .10
116 Sergei Zholtok .02 .10
117 Alexandre Daigle .02 .10
118 Wade Redden .02 .10
119 Mikael Renberg .08 .25
120 Trent Klatt .02 .10
121 Rod Brind'Amour .08 .25
122 Dainius Zubrus .15 .40
123 John LeClair .15 .40
124 Janne Niinimaa .08 .25
125 Vaclav Prospal RC .15 .40
126 Keith Tkachuk .15 .40
127 Jeremy Roenick .20 .50
128 Mike Gartner .08 .25
129 Nikolai Khabibulin .08 .25
130 Chad Kilger .02 .10
131 Shane Doan .02 .10
132 Cliff Ronning .02 .10
133 Patrick Lalime .08 .25
134 Greg Johnson .02 .10
135 Ron Francis .08 .25
136 Darius Kasparaitis .02 .10
137 Petr Nedved .08 .25
138 Jason Woolley .02 .10
139 Fredrik Olausson .02 .10
140 Harry York .02 .10
141 Brett Hull .20 .50
142 Chris Pronger .08 .25
143 Jim Campbell .02 .10
144 Libor Zabransky RC .02 .10
145 Grant Fuhr .08 .25
146 Pavol Demitra .08 .25
147 Owen Nolan .08 .25
148 Stephen Guolla RC .02 .10
149 Marcus Ragnarsson .02 .10
150 Bernie Nicholls .02 .10
151 Todd Gill .02 .10
152 Shean Donovan .02 .10
153 Corey Schwab .08 .25
154 Dino Ciccarelli .08 .25
155 Chris Gratton .08 .25
156 Alexander Selivanov .02 .10
157 Roman Hamrlik .08 .25
158 Daymond Langkow .02 .10
159 Paul Ysebaert .02 .10
160 Steve Sullivan .02 .10
161 Sergei Berezin .02 .10
162 Fredrik Modin .02 .10
163 Todd Warriner .02 .10
164 Wendel Clark .08 .25
165 Jason Podollan .02 .10
166 Darby Hendrickson .02 .10
167 Martin Gelinas .02 .10
168 Pavel Bure .15 .40
169 Trevor Linden .08 .25
170 Mike Sillinger .02 .10
171 Corey Hirsch .08 .25
172 Lonny Bohonos .02 .10
173 Markus Naslund .15 .40
174 Steve Konowalchuk .02 .10
175 Dale Hunter .02 .10
176 Joe Juneau .08 .25
177 Adam Oates .08 .25
178 Bill Ranford .08 .25
179 Pat Peake .02 .10
180 Sergei Gonchar .02 .10
181 Mike LeClerc RC .40 1.00
182 Randy Robitaille RC .20 .50
183 Paxton Schafer RC .02 .10
184 Rumun Ndur RC .02 .10
185 Christian Laflamme RC .02 .10
186 Wade Belak RC .08 .25
187 Mike Knuble RC .02 .10
188 Steve Kelly .02 .10
189 Patrik Elias RC 1.00 2.50
190 Ken Belanger RC .02 .10
191 Colin Forbes RC .02 .10
192 Juha Ylonen .02 .10
193 David Cooper RC .02 .10
194 D.J. Smith RC .02 .10
195 Jaroslav Svejkovsky .08 .25
196 Tie Domi .08 .25
197 Bob Probert .02 .10
198 Doug Gilmour .08 .25
199 Dino Ciccarelli .08 .25
200 Martin Gelinas .02 .10
201 Tony Twist .08 .25
202 Claude Lemieux .02 .10
203 Vladimir Konstantinov .08 .25
204 Ulf Samuelsson .02 .10
205 Chris Simon .02 .10
206 Gino Odjick .02 .10
207 Mike Grier .02 .10
208 Tony Amonte .08 .25
209 Wayne Gretzky CL .15 .40
210 Patrick Roy CL .15 .40
211 Paul Kariya .15 .40
212 J.J. Daigneault .02 .10
213 Dmitri Mironov .02 .10
214 Joe Sacco .02 .10
215 Richard Park .02 .10
216 Espen Knutsen RC .50 1.25
217 Dave Karpa .02 .10
218 Joe Thornton .40 1.00
219 Sergei Samsonov .08 .25
220 P.J. Axelsson RC .02 .10
221 Ted Donato .02 .10
222 Dean Chynoweth .02 .10
223 Rob Tallas RC .02 .10
224 Mattias Timander .02 .10
225 Dominik Hasek .30 .75
226 Erik Rasmussen .02 .10
227 Mike Peca .02 .10
228 Rob Ray .02 .10
229 Vaclav Varada .02 .10
230 Curtis Brown .02 .10
231 Jay McKee .02 .10
232 Theo Fleury .02 .10
233 Derek Morris RC .20 .50
234 Chris Dingman RC .02 .10
235 Chris O'Sullivan .02 .10
236 Rick Tabaracci .08 .25
237 Tommy Albelin .02 .10
238 Todd Simpson .02 .10
239 Sami Kapanen .02 .10
UER numbered 229
240 Gary Roberts .02 .10
241 Kevin Dineen .02 .10
242 Kevin Haller .02 .10
243 Nelson Emerson .02 .10
244 Glen Wesley .02 .10
245 Tony Amonte .08 .25
246 Eric Weinrich .02 .10
247 Daniel Cleary .08 .25
248 Jeff Shantz .02 .10
249 Jean-Yves Leroux RC .02 .10
250 Ethan Moreau .02 .10
251 Craig Mills .02 .10
252 Peter Forsberg .40 1.00
253 Joe Sakic .30 .75
254 Valeri Kamensky .08 .25
255 Adam Foote .02 .10
256 Josef Marha .02 .10
257 Christian Matte RC .02 .10
258 Aaron Miller .02 .10
259 Ed Belfour .15 .40
260 Jamie Langenbrunner .02 .10
261 Juha Lind RC .02 .10
262 Pat Verbeek .02 .10
263 Sergei Zubov .02 .10
264 Dave Reid .02 .10
265 Greg Adams .02 .10
266 Sergei Fedorov .25 .60
267 Nicklas Lidstrom .15 .40
268 Brendan Shanahan .15 .40
269 Chris Osgood .08 .25
270 Aaron Ward .02 .10
271 Vyacheslav Kozlov .02 .10
272 Kevin Hodson .08 .25
273 Curtis Joseph .15 .40
274 Ryan Smyth .08 .25
275 Dean McAmmond .02 .10
276 Boris Mironov .02 .10
277 Dennis Bonvie .02 .10
278 Kelly Buchberger .02 .10
279 Kevin Lowe .02 .10
280 Ray Sheppard .02 .10
281 Rob Niedermayer .02 .10
282 Scott Mellanby .02 .10
283 Terry Carkner .02 .10
284 Ed Jovanovski .08 .25
285 Gord Murphy .02 .10
286 Tom Fitzgerald .02 .10
287 Jamie Storr .08 .25
288 Olli Jokinen RC 1.00 2.50
289 Vladimir Tsyplakov .02 .10
290 Luc Robitaille .08 .25
291 Vitali Yachmenev .02 .10
292 Donald MacLean RC .02 .10
293 Saku Koivu .15 .40
294 Andy Moog .08 .25
295 Patrice Brisebois .02 .10
296 Brad Brown RC .02 .10
297 Turner Stevenson .02 .10
298 Shayne Corson .02 .10
299 Brian Savage .02 .10
300 Martin Brodeur .40 1.00
301 Scott Niedermayer .02 .10
302 Krzysztof Oliwa RC .02 .10
303 Valeri Zelepukin .02 .10
304 Bobby Holik .02 .10
305 Ken Daneyko .02 .10
306 Lyle Odelein .02 .10
307 Travis Green .02 .10
308 Steve Webb RC .02 .10
309 Dan Plante .02 .10
310 Bryan Smolinski .02 .10
311 Claude Lapointe .02 .10
312 Kenny Jonsson .02 .10
313 Ulf Samuelsson .02 .10
314 Jeff Beukeboom .02 .10
315 Mike Keane .02 .10
316 Brian Leetch .15 .40
317 Shane Churla .02 .10
318 Pat LaFontaine .15 .40
319 Alexei Kovalev .02 .10
320 Radek Bonk .02 .10
321 Alexei Yashin .02 .10
322 Damian Rhodes .08 .25
323 Andreas Dackell .02 .10
324 Magnus Arvedson RC .02 .10
325 Chris Phillips .02 .10
326 Marian Hossa RC 2.50 6.00
327 Chris Gratton .08 .25
328 Shjon Podein .02 .10
329 Paul Coffey .15 .40
330 Luke Richardson .02 .10
331 Eric Lindros .15 .40
332 Eric Desjardins .08 .25
333 Joel Otto .02 .10
334 Craig Janney .02 .10
335 Oleg Tverdovsky .02 .10
336 Teppo Numminen .02 .10
337 Jim McKenzie .02 .10
338 Dallas Drake .02 .10
339 Rick Tocchet .08 .25
340 Brad Isbister .02 .10
341 Alexei Morozov .08 .25
342 Jaromir Jagr .25 .60
343 Kevin Hatcher .02 .10
344 Ken Wregget .08 .25
345 Chris Tamer .02 .10
346 Robert Dome .02 .10
347 Neil Wilkinson .02 .10
348 Chris McAlpine .02 .10
349 Joe Murphy .02 .10
350 Robert Petrovicky .02 .10
351 Marc Bergevin .02 .10
352 Al MacInnis .08 .25
353 Pierre Turgeon .08 .25
354 Patrick Marleau .25 .60
355 Marco Sturm RC .40 1.00
356 Mike Vernon .08 .25
357 Al Iafrate .02 .10
358 Jeff Friesen .02 .10
359 Viktor Kozlov .02 .10
360 Tony Granato .02 .10
361 Mikael Renberg .08 .25
362 Daren Puppa .08 .25
363 Roman Hamrlik .08 .25
364 Rob Zamuner .02 .10
365 Cory Cross .02 .10
366 Patrick Poulin .02 .10
367 Felix Potvin .15 .40
368 Tie Domi .08 .25
369 Mats Sundin .15 .40
370 Jeff Ware .02 .10
371 Alyn McCauley .08 .25
372 Mathieu Schneider .02 .10
373 Craig Wolanin .02 .10
374 Mark Messier .15 .40
375 Kirk McLean .08 .25
376 Donald Brashear .02 .10
377 Arturs Irbe .08 .25
378 Jyrki Lumme .02 .10
379 Gino Odjick .02 .10
380 Mattias Ohlund .08 .25
381 Jan Bulis RC .08 .25
382 Andrew Brunette .08 .25
383 Calle Johansson .02 .10
384 Brendan Witt .02 .10
385 Mark Tinordi .02 .10
386 Ken Klee .02 .10
387 Chris Simon .02 .10
388 Richard Zednik .02 .10
389 Ed Jovanovski .08 .25
390 Darren McCarty .02 .10
391 Darius Kasparaitis .02 .10
392 Bryan Marchment .02 .10
393 Matthew Barnaby .02 .10
394 Chris Chelios .15 .40
395 Ulf Samuelsson .02 .10
396 Scott Stevens .08 .25
397 Derian Hatcher .02 .10
398 Chris Pronger .08 .25
399 Mathieu Chouinard RC .60 1.50
400 Jake McCracken RC .40 1.00
401 Bryan Allen RC .30 .75
402 Christian Chartier RC .30 .75
403 Jonathan Girard RC .40 1.00
404 Abe Herbst RC .08 .25
405 Stephen Peat RC .08 .25
406 Robyn Regehr RC .30 .75
407 Blair Betts RC .08 .25
408 Eric Chouinard RC .50 1.25
409 Brett DeCecco RC .08 .25
410 Rico Fata RC .40 1.00
411 Simon Gagne RC 2.50 6.00
412 Vincent Lecavalier RC 3.00 8.00
413 Manny Malhotra RC .30 .75
414 Norm Milley RC .40 1.00
415 Justin Papineau RC .40 1.00
416 Garrett Prosofsky RC .02 .10
417 Mike Ribeiro RC .60 1.50
418 Brad Richards RC 2.00 5.00
419 Wayne Gretzky CL .15 .40
420 Patrick Roy CL .15 .40

1997-98 Upper Deck Blow-Ups 3 x 5

Inserted as box-toppers or in special retail packs, these oversized cards resembled the base set but were approximately 3 1/2" x 5". Cards were numbered X of 10. The prefixes below are for checklisting only and designate whether the cards were available in series 1 or series 2 packs.

COMPLETE SET (20) 15.00 40.00
1-1 Wayne Gretzky 4.00 10.00
1-2 Steve Yzerman 3.00 8.00
1-3 Bryan Berard .40 1.00
1-4 Owen Nolan .40 1.00
1-5 Pavel Bure .60 1.50
1-6 Patrick Roy 3.00 8.00
1-7 Teemu Selanne .60 1.50
1-8 Brett Hull .75 2.00
1-9 Keith Tkachuk .60 1.50
1-10 John Vanbiesbrouck .60 1.50
2-1 Paul Kariya .60 1.50
2-2 Joe Thornton 1.50 4.00
2-3 Joe Sakic 1.25 3.00
2-4 Martin Brodeur 1.50 4.00
2-5 Slava Kozlov .40 1.00
2-6 Mark Messier .60 1.50
2-7 Jaromir Jagr 1.00 2.50
2-8 Eric Lindros .60 1.50
2-9 Peter Forsberg 1.50 4.00
2-10 Sergei Samsonov .40 1.00

1997-98 Upper Deck Blow-Ups 5 x 7

Inserted as box-toppers in various distribution forms of Upper Deck, these oversized cards resembled the base set but were approximately 5" x 7". Cards were numbered "X of 5" (the suffixes below are for checklisting only). The checklist below is not complete, please forward any further information to hockeymag@beckett.com.

COMPLETE SET (14) 10.00 25.00
1A Mark Messier .60 1.50
1B Patrick Roy 3.00 8.00
1C Paul Kariya .75 2.00
2A Jaromir Jagr 1.50 4.00
2B Teemu Selanne 1.25 3.00
3A Joe Sakic 1.25 3.00
3B Eric Lindros 1.00 2.50
4A Peter Forsberg 1.50 4.00
4B Martin Brodeur 1.50 4.00
4C Keith Tkachuk .75 2.00
5A Sergei Samsonov .60 1.50
5B Pavel Bure 1.25 3.00
5C Slava Kozlov .60 1.50
5D John Vanbiesbrouck .60 1.50

1997-98 Upper Deck Game Dated Moments Parallel

Randomly inserted in packs at the rate of 1:1500, this 60-card set features color player photos of their top moments of last year and printed on 24 pt. embossed Light F/X cards. The set is skip numbered. It is important to note that these cards are printed on card stock that is approximately 3X thicker than the base set and carry silver foil highlights that distinguish them from the base set cards that also carry the Game Dated stamp.

*GAME DATED: 60X TO 150X BASIC CARDS

1997-98 Upper Deck Game Jerseys

Randomly inserted in packs at the rate of 1:2,500, this 15-card set features color player photos with an actual piece of the player's game-worn jersey embedded in the card. Patrick Roy autographed 33 cards inserted in Series 1 packs, and Wayne Gretzky signed 99 cards containing remnants of his 1997 All-Star Game jersey inserted in Series 2 packs.

GJ1 Patrick Roy HOME 100.00 250.00
GJ2 Patrick Roy AWAY 125.00 300.00
GJ3 Dominik Hasek 50.00 125.00
GJ4 Jarome Iginla 40.00 100.00
GJ5 Sergei Fedorov 40.00 100.00
GJ6 Tony Amonte 20.00 50.00
GJ7 Joe Sakic 60.00 150.00
GJ8 Wayne Gretzky 200.00 500.00
GJ9 Saku Koivu 20.00 50.00
GJ11 Mike Richter 20.00 50.00
GJ12 Doug Weight 20.00 50.00
GJ13 Brendan Shanahan 20.00 50.00
GJ14 Brian Leetch 20.00 50.00
GJ1AU Patrick Roy AU/33 400.00 800.00
GJ8AU Wayne Gretzky AU/99 400.00 800.00

1997-98 Upper Deck Sixth Sense Masters

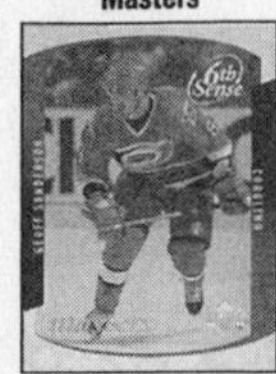

Randomly inserted in Series 2 packs, this 30-card set features color photos of the NHL's brightest stars. Only 2,000 of each card were produced and are sequentially numbered. A holographic die-cut parallel version labeled "Wizards" was alos produced and limited to 100 copies each.

COMPLETE SET (30) 125.00 250.00
*WIZARD/100: 2.5X TO 6X BASIC INSERTS
SS1 Wayne Gretzky 20.00 50.00
SS2 Jaromir Jagr 5.00 12.00
SS3 Sergei Fedorov 4.00 10.00
SS4 Brett Hull 4.00 10.00
SS5 Brian Leetch 2.00 5.00
SS6 Joe Thornton 6.00 15.00
SS7 Ray Bourque 4.00 10.00
SS8 Teemu Selanne 3.00 8.00
SS9 Paul Kariya 3.00 8.00
SS10 Doug Weight 2.00 5.00
SS11 Mark Messier 3.00 8.00
SS12 Adam Oates 2.00 5.00
SS13 Mats Sundin 3.00 8.00
SS14 Brendan Shanahan 3.00 8.00
SS15 Saku Koivu 3.00 8.00
SS16 Doug Gilmour 2.00 5.00
SS17 Eric Lindros 3.00 8.00
SS18 Tony Amonte 2.00 5.00
SS19 Joe Sakic 6.00 15.00
SS20 Steve Yzerman 15.00 40.00
SS21 Peter Forsberg 8.00 20.00
SS22 Geoff Sanderson 2.00 5.00
SS23 Keith Tkachuk 2.00 5.00
SS24 Pavel Bure 4.00 10.00
SS25 Ron Francis 2.00 5.00
SS26 Zigmund Palffy 2.00 5.00
SS27 Daniel Alfredsson 2.00 5.00
SS28 Bryan Berard 2.00 5.00
SS29 Mike Modano 5.00 12.00
SS30 Patrick Roy 15.00 40.00

1997-98 Upper Deck Smooth Grooves

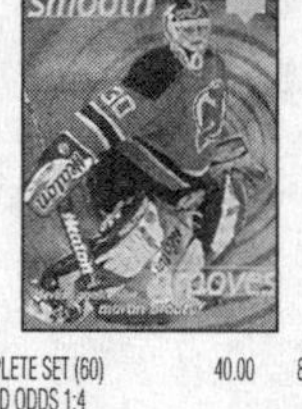

COMPLETE SET (60) 40.00 80.00
STATED ODDS 1:4
SG1 Wayne Gretzky 5.00 12.00
SG2 Patrick Roy 4.00 10.00
SG3 Patrick Marleau 1.25 3.00
SG4 Martin Brodeur 2.00 5.00
SG5 Zigmund Palffy .50 1.25
SG6 Joe Thornton 2.00 5.00
SG7 Chris Chelios .75 2.00
SG8 Teemu Selanne .75 2.00
SG9 Paul Kariya .75 2.00
SG10 Tony Amonte .50 1.25
SG11 Mark Messier .75 2.00
SG12 Jarome Iginla 1.00 2.50
SG13 Mats Sundin .75 2.00
SG14 Brendan Shanahan .75 2.00
SG15 Ed Jovanovski .50 1.25
SG16 Brett Hull 1.00 2.50
SG17 Brian Rolston .20 .50
SG18 Saku Koivu .75 2.00
SG19 Steve Yzerman 4.00 10.00
SG20 Doug Weight .50 1.25
SG21 Peter Forsberg 2.00 5.00
SG22 Brian Leetch .75 2.00
SG23 Alexei Yashin .20 .50
SG24 Owen Nolan .50 1.25
SG25 Mike Grier .20 .50
SG26 Jere Lehtinen .20 .50
SG27 Vaclav Prospal .75 2.00
SG28 Sandis Ozolinsh .20 .50
SG29 Mike Modano 1.25 3.00
SG30 Sergei Samsonov .50 1.25
SG31 Curtis Joseph .75 2.00
SG32 Daymond Langkow .50 1.25
SG33 Doug Gilmour .50 1.25
SG34 Bryan Berard .50 1.25
SG35 Joe Sakic 1.50 4.00
SG36 Wade Redden .20 .50
SG37 Keith Tkachuk .75 2.00
SG38 Jaromir Jagr 1.25 3.00
SG39 Dominik Hasek 1.50 4.00
SG40 Patrick Lalime .50 1.25
SG41 Janne Niinimaa .20 .50
SG42 Oleg Tverdovsky .20 .50
SG43 Vitali Yachmenev .20 .50
SG44 Rob Niedermayer .20 .50
SG45 Nicklas Lidstrom .75 2.00
SG46 Jim Campbell .20 .50
SG47 Roman Hamrlik .50 1.25
SG48 Eric Lindros .75 2.00
SG49 Brian Holzinger .20 .50
SG50 John LeClair .75 2.00
SG51 Sergei Berezin .20 .50
SG52 Jaroslav Svejkovsky .20 .50
SG53 Mike Richter .75 2.00
SG54 John Vanbiesbrouck .50 1.25
SG55 Keith Primeau .20 .50
SG56 Adam Oates .50 1.25
SG57 Jeremy Roenick 1.00 2.50
SG58 Pavel Bure .75 2.00
SG59 Dainius Zubrus .75 2.00
SG60 Jose Theodore 1.00 2.50

1997-98 Upper Deck The Specialists

Randomly inserted in Series 1 packs, this 30-card set features black-and-white action photos of the NHL brightest stars. Only 4,000 of each card were produced and numbered.

COMPLETE SET (30) 50.00 100.00
1 Wayne Gretzky 5.00 12.00
2 Patrick Roy 4.00 10.00
3 Jaromir Jagr 2.00 5.00
4 Joe Sakic 2.50 6.00
5 Mark Messier 1.25 3.00
6 Eric Lindros 1.25 3.00
7 John Vanbiesbrouck 1.00 2.50
8 Teemu Selanne 1.25 3.00
9 Paul Kariya 1.25 3.00
10 Pavel Bure 1.25 3.00
11 Sergei Fedorov 2.00 5.00
12 Peter Bondra 1.00 2.50
13 Mats Sundin 1.25 3.00
14 Brendan Shanahan 1.25 3.00
15 Keith Tkachuk 1.25 3.00
16 Brett Hull 1.50 4.00
17 Jeremy Roenick 1.50 4.00
18 Dominik Hasek 2.50 6.00
19 Steve Yzerman 4.00 10.00
20 John LeClair 1.25 3.00
21 Peter Forsberg 3.00 8.00
22 Zigmund Palffy 1.00 2.50
23 Tony Amonte 1.00 2.50
24 Jarome Iginla 1.25 3.00
25 Curtis Joseph 1.25 3.00
26 Mike Modano 2.00 5.00
27 Ray Bourque 2.00 5.00
28 Brian Leetch 1.25 3.00
29 Bryan Berard 1.00 2.50
30 Martin Brodeur 3.00 8.00

1997-98 Upper Deck Three Star Selects

Randomly inserted in Series 1 packs at the rate of 1:4, this 60-card set features color photos on die-cut cards of three top players that fit together to form 20 different sets.

COMPLETE SET (60) 40.00 80.00
1A Eric Lindros .75 2.00
1B Wayne Gretzky 5.00 12.00
1C Peter Forsberg 2.00 5.00
2A Dominik Hasek 1.50 4.00
2B Patrick Roy 4.00 10.00
2C John Vanbiesbrouck .75 2.00
3A Joe Sakic 1.50 4.00
3B Steve Yzerman 4.00 10.00
3C Paul Kariya .75 2.00
4A Bryan Berard .20 .50
4B Brian Leetch .40 1.00
4C Chris Chelios .40 1.00
5A Teemu Selanne .75 2.00
5B Jaromir Jagr 1.25 3.00
5C Pavel Bure .75 2.00
6A Owen Nolan .40 1.00
6B Brendan Shanahan .75 2.00
6C Keith Tkachuk .40 1.00
7A Sergei Fedorov 1.00 2.50
7B Niklas Sundstrom .20 .50
7C Mike Peca .20 .50
8A Janne Niinimaa .20 .50
8B Saku Koivu .75 2.00
8C Jere Lehtinen .20 .50
9A Tony Amonte .40 1.00
9B John LeClair .40 1.00
9C Brett Hull 1.00 2.50
10A Martin Brodeur 2.00 5.00
10B Curtis Joseph .75 2.00
10C Mike Richter .75 2.00
11A Ray Bourque 1.00 2.50
11B Mark Messier .75 2.00
11C Scott Stevens .20 .50
12A Patrick Lalime .40 1.00
12B Marc Denis .40 1.00
12C Jose Theodore 1.00 2.50
13A Adam Deadmarsh .20 .50
13B Doug Weight .40 1.00
13C Bill Guerin .20 .50
14A Daniel Alfredsson .40 1.00
14B Mats Sundin .75 2.00
14C Nicklas Lidstrom .75 2.00
15A Jim Campbell .20 .50
15B Dainius Zubrus .40 1.00
15C Daymond Langkow .20 .50
16A Mike Grier .20 .50
16B Mike Modano 1.25 3.00
16C Jeremy Roenick 1.00 2.50
17A Jason Arnott .20 .50
17B Trevor Linden .40 1.00
17C Rod Brind'Amour .40 1.00
18A Adam Oates .40 1.00
18B Doug Gilmour .40 1.00
18C Joe Juneau .20 .50
19A Sergei Berezin .20 .50
19B Alexander Mogilny .40 1.00
19C Alexei Zhamnov .20 .50
20A Derian Hatcher .20 .50
20B Wade Redden .20 .50
20C Sandis Ozolinsh .20 .50

1997 Upper Deck Crash the All-Star Game

Distributed one per attendee of the 1997 NHL All-Star Game in San Jose, these one-off Crash the Game cards were redeemable for a special set if the player pictured scored a goal in the contest. The Western Conference cards (1-11) were rumored to be the only ones distributed, although a few copies of each of the Eastern Conference cards have surfaced as well. The complete set price below includes both conferences. The winners are numbered AR1 thru AR20, and feature gold foil and a record of the player's performance in the game.

1 Tony Amonte 8.00 20.00
2 Paul Kariya 50.00 125.00
3 Brett Hull 15.00 40.00
4 Teemu Selanne 25.00 60.00
5 Steve Yzerman 40.00 100.00
6 Owen Nolan 8.00 20.00
7 Mats Sundin 12.00 30.00
8 Pavel Bure 30.00 80.00
9 Brendan Shanahan 25.00 60.00
10 Sandis Ozolinsh 8.00 20.00
11 Keith Tkachuk 12.00 30.00
12 Ray Bourque 15.00 40.00
13 Eric Lindros 30.00 80.00
14 Mark Messier 15.00 40.00
15 John LeClair 20.00 50.00
16 Jaromir Jagr 40.00 100.00
17 Dino Ciccarelli 8.00 20.00
18 Peter Bondra 12.00 30.00
19 Brian Leetch 15.00 40.00
20 Wayne Gretzky 75.00 200.00
AR1 Tony Amonte 4.00 10.00
AR2 Paul Kariya 20.00 50.00
AR3 Brett Hull 6.00 15.00
AR4 Teemu Selanne 10.00 25.00
AR5 Steve Yzerman 15.00 40.00
AR6 Owen Nolan 6.00 15.00
AR7 Mats Sundin 8.00 20.00
AR8 Pavel Bure 10.00 25.00
AR9 Brendan Shanahan 10.00 25.00
AR10 Sandis Ozolinsh 4.00 10.00
AR11 Keith Tkachuk 6.00 15.00
AR12 Ray Bourque 4.00 10.00
AR13 Eric Lindros 20.00 50.00
AR14 Mark Messier 6.00 15.00
AR15 John LeClair 8.00 20.00
AR16 Jaromir Jagr 15.00 40.00
AR17 Dino Ciccarelli 4.00 10.00
AR18 Peter Bondra 5.00 12.00
AR19 Brian Leetch 5.00 12.00
AR20 Wayne Gretzky 30.00 80.00

1998-99 Upper Deck

The 1998-99 Upper Deck set was issued in two series of 210 cards each for a total of 420 cards and was distributed in 10-card packs with a suggested retail price of $2.49. The fronts feature a color action player photo with player information on the backs. Series 1 contains the following subsets: Star Rookies, Rookie Rewind, and three Checklist cards. Series 2 contains the subset Program of Excellence which consists of the top Canadian prospects, eight Calder Candidates, and three Checklist cards.

COMPLETE SET (420) 75.00 150.00
UNPRICED EXCLUSIVES 1/1 ISSUED
1 Antti Aalto SR .40 1.00
2 Cameron Mann SR .40 1.00
3 Norm Maracle SR RC .60 1.50
4 Daniel Cleary SR .40 1.00
5 Brendan Morrison SR .50 1.25
6 Marian Hossa SR .60 1.50
7 Daniel Briere SR .60 1.50
8 Mike Crowley SR RC .40 1.00
9 Darryl Laplante SR RC .40 1.00
10 Sven Butenschon SR .40 1.00
11 Yan Golubovsky SR RC .40 1.00
12 Olli Jokinen SR .40 1.00
13 Jean-Sebastien Giguere SR .60 1.50
14 Mike Watt SR .40 1.00
15 Ryan Johnson SR RC .40 1.00
16 Teemu Selanne RR .60 1.50
17 Paul Kariya RR .60 1.50
18 Pavel Bure RR .60 1.50
19 Joe Thornton RR 1.50 4.00
20 Dominik Hasek RR 1.50 4.00
21 Bryan Berard RR .40 1.00
22 Chris Phillips RR .40 1.00
23 Sergei Fedorov RR 1.25 3.00
24 Sergei Samsonov RR .50 1.25
25 Marc Denis RR .50 1.25
26 Patrick Marleau RR .60 1.50
27 Jaromir Jagr RR 1.25 3.00
28 Saku Koivu RR .60 1.50
29 Peter Forsberg RR 2.00 5.00
30 Mike Modano RR 1.25 3.00
31 Paul Kariya .15 .40
32 Matt Cullen .02 .10
33 Josef Marha .02 .10
34 Teemu Selanne .15 .40
35 Pavel Trnka .02 .10
36 Tom Askey RC .02 .10
37 Tim Taylor .02 .10
38 Ray Bourque .25 .60
39 Sergei Samsonov .08 .25
40 Don Sweeney .02 .10
41 Jason Allison .02 .10
42 Steve Heinze .02 .10
43 Erik Rasmussen .02 .10
44 Dominik Hasek .30 .75
45 Geoff Sanderson .02 .10

46 Michael Peca .02 .10
47 Brian Holzinger .02 .10
48 Vaclav Varada .02 .10
49 Steve Begin .02 .10
50 Denis Gauthier .02 .10
51 Derek Morris .02 .10
52 Valeri Bure .02 .10
53 Hnat Domenichelli .02 .10
54 Cory Stillman .02 .10
55 Jarome Iginla .20 .50
56 Tyler Moss .02 .10
57 Sami Kapanen .02 .10
58 Trevor Kidd .08 .25
59 Glen Wesley .02 .10
60 Nelson Emerson .02 .10
61 Jeff O'Neill .02 .10
62 Bates Battaglia .02 .10
63 Doug Gilmour .08 .25
64 Christian LaFlamme .02 .10
65 Chris Chelios .15 .40
66 Paul Coffey .15 .40
67 Eric Weinrich .02 .10
68 Eric Daze .08 .25
69 Peter Forsberg .40 1.00
70 Eric Messier .02 .10
71 Eric Lacroix .02 .10
72 Adam Deadmarsh .02 .10
73 Claude Lemieux .02 .10
74 Patrick Roy .75 2.00
75 Marc Denis .08 .25
76 Brett Hull .20 .50
77 Mike Keane .02 .10
78 Joe Nieuwendyk .08 .25
79 Darryl Sydor .02 .10
80 Ed Belfour .15 .40
81 Jamie Langenbrunner .02 .10
82 Petr Buzek .02 .10
83 Nicklas Lidstrom .15 .40
84 Mathieu Dandenault .02 .10
85 Steve Yzerman .75 2.00
86 Martin Lapointe .02 .10
87 Brendan Shanahan .15 .40
88 Anders Eriksson .02 .10
89 Tomas Holmstrom .02 .10
90 Doug Weight .08 .25
91 Janne Niinimaa .02 .10
92 Bill Guerin .08 .25
93 Kelly Buchberger .02 .10
94 Mike Grier .02 .10
95 Craig Millar .02 .10
96 Roman Hamrlik .02 .10
97 Ray Whitney .02 .10
98 Viktor Kozlov .02 .10
99 Peter Worrell RC .20 .50
100 Kevin Weekes .08 .25
101 Ed Jovanovski .08 .25
102 Bill Lindsay .02 .10
103 Jozef Stumpel .08 .25
104 Luc Robitaille .08 .25
105 Yanic Perreault .02 .10
106 Donald MacLean .02 .10
107 Jamie Storr .08 .25
108 Ian Laperriere .02 .10
109 Jason Morgan RC .02 .10
110 Vincent Damphousse .02 .10
111 Mark Recchi .08 .25
112 Vladimir Malakhov .02 .10
113 Dave Manson .02 .10
114 Jose Theodore .20 .50
115 Brian Savage .02 .10
116 Jonas Hoglund .02 .10
117 Krzysztof Oliwa .02 .10
118 Martin Brodeur .40 1.00
119 Patrik Elias .08 .25
120 Jason Arnott .02 .10
121 Scott Stevens .08 .25
122 Sheldon Souray RC .40 1.00
123 Brian Rolston .02 .10
124 Trevor Linden .08 .25
125 Warren Luhning .02 .10
126 Zdeno Chara .02 .10
127 Bryan Berard .08 .25
128 Bryan Smolinski .02 .10
129 Jason Dawe .02 .10
130 Kevin Stevens .02 .10
131 P.J. Stock RC .40 1.00
132 Marc Savard .08 .25
133 Pat LaFontaine .15 .40
134 Dan Cloutier .08 .25
135 Wayne Gretzky 1.00 2.50
136 Niklas Sundstrom .02 .10
137 Damian Rhodes .08 .25
138 Magnus Arvedson .02 .10
139 Alexei Yashin .02 .10
140 Chris Phillips .02 .10
141 Janne Laukkanen .02 .10
142 Shawn McEachern .02 .10
143 John LeClair .15 .40
144 Alexandre Daigle .02 .10
145 Dainius Zubrus .02 .10
146 Joel Otto .02 .10
147 Mike Sillinger .02 .10
148 John Vanbiesbrouck .08 .25
149 Chris Gratton .08 .25
150 Eric Desjardins .08 .25
151 Juha Ylonen .02 .10
152 Brad Isbister .02 .10
153 Oleg Tverdovsky .02 .10
154 Keith Tkachuk .15 .40
155 Teppo Numminen .02 .10
156 Cliff Ronning .02 .10
157 Nikolai Khabibulin .08 .25
158 Alexei Morozov .02 .10
159 Kevin Hatcher .02 .10
160 Darius Kasparaitis .02 .10
161 Jaromir Jagr .25 .60
162 Tom Barrasso .08 .25
163 Tuomas Gronman .02 .10
164 Robert Dome .02 .10
165 Peter Skudra .02 .10
166 Marcus Ragnarsson .02 .10
167 Mike Vernon .08 .25
168 Andrei Zyuzin .02 .10
169 Marco Sturm .02 .10
170 Mike Ricci .02 .10
171 Patrick Marleau .02 .10
172 Pierre Turgeon .02 .10
173 Pavol Demitra .08 .25
174 Chris Pronger .08 .25
175 Pascal Rheaume .02 .10
176 Al MacInnis .08 .25
177 Tony Twist .02 .10
178 Jim Campbell .02 .10
179 Mikael Renberg .08 .25
180 Jason Bonsignore .02 .10
181 Zac Bierk RC .40 1.00
182 Alexander Selivanov .02 .10
183 Stephane Richer .02 .10
184 Sandy McCarthy .02 .10
185 Alyn McCauley .02 .10
186 Sergei Berezin .08 .25
187 Mike Johnson .02 .10
188 Wendel Clark .08 .25
189 Tie Domi .08 .25
190 Yannick Tremblay .02 .10
191 Curtis Joseph .15 .40
192 Fredrik Modin .02 .10
193 Pavel Bure .15 .40
194 Todd Bertuzzi .15 .40
195 Mark Messier .15 .40
196 Bret Hedican .02 .10
197 Mattias Ohlund .02 .10
198 Garth Snow .08 .25
199 Adam Oates .08 .25
200 Peter Bondra .08 .25
201 Sergei Gonchar .02 .10
202 Jan Bulis .02 .10
203 Joe Juneau .08 .25
204 Brian Bellows .02 .10
205 Olaf Kolzig .08 .25
206 Richard Zednik .02 .10
207 Wayne Gretzky CL .40 1.00
208 Patrick Roy CL .40 1.00
209 Steve Yzerman CL .40 1.00
210 Mike Dunham .08 .25
211 Johan Davidsson .02 .10
212 Guy Hebert .08 .25
213 Mike Leclerc .02 .10
214 Steve Rucchin .02 .10
215 Travis Green .02 .10
216 Josef Marha .02 .10
217 Ted Donato .02 .10
218 Joe Thornton .25 .60
219 Kyle McLaren .02 .10
220 Peter Nordstrom RC .08 .25
221 Byron Dafoe .08 .25
222 Jonathon Girard .02 .10
223 Antti Laaksonen RC .40 1.00
224 Jason Holland .02 .10
225 Miroslav Satan .08 .25
226 Alexei Zhitnik .02 .10
227 Donald Audette .02 .10
228 Matthew Barnaby .02 .10
229 Rumun Ndur .02 .10
230 Ken Wregget .08 .25
231 Andrew Cassels .02 .10
232 Theo Fleury .02 .10
233 Phil Housley .08 .25
234 Martin St. Louis RC 2.00 5.00
235 Mike Rucinski RC .08 .25
236 Gary Roberts .02 .10
237 Keith Primeau .02 .10
238 Martin Gelinas .02 .10
239 Nolan Pratt RC .02 .10
240 Ray Sheppard .02 .10
241 Ron Francis .08 .25
242 Ty Jones .02 .10
243 Tony Amonte .08 .25
244 Chad Kilger .02 .10
245 Alexei Zhamnov .08 .25
246 Remi Royer RC .02 .10
247 Milan Hejduk RC 1.00 2.50
248 Joe Sakic .30 .75
249 Valeri Kamensky .08 .25
250 Sandis Ozolinsh .02 .10
251 Shean Donovan .02 .10
252 Wade Belak .02 .10
253 Jamie Wright .02 .10
254 Sergei Zubov .02 .10
255 Richard Matvichuk .02 .10
256 Mike Modano .25 .60
257 Pat Verbeek .02 .10
258 Jere Lehtinen .08 .25
259 Derian Hatcher .02 .10
260 Jason Botterill .02 .10
261 Igor Larionov .02 .10
262 Sergei Fedorov .25 .60
263 Chris Osgood .08 .25
264 Vyacheslav Kozlov .08 .25
265 Larry Murphy .08 .25
266 Darren McCarty .02 .10
267 Doug Brown .02 .10
268 Kris Draper .02 .10
269 Uwe Krupp .02 .10
270 Fredrik Lindquist RC .02 .10
271 Dean McAmmond .02 .10
272 Ryan Smyth .08 .25
273 Boris Mironov .02 .10
274 Tom Poti .02 .10
275 Todd Marchant .02 .10
276 Sean Brown .02 .10
277 Rob Niedermayer .02 .10
278 Robert Svehla .02 .10
279 Scott Mellanby .02 .10
280 Radek Dvorak .02 .10
281 Jaroslav Spacek RC .02 .10
282 Mark Parrish RC .40 1.00
283 Ryan Johnson .02 .10
284 Glen Murray .02 .10
285 Rob Blake .08 .25
286 Steve Duchesne .08 .25
287 Vladimir Tsyplakov .02 .10
288 Stephane Fiset .08 .25
289 Mattias Norstrom .02 .10
290 Saku Koivu .15 .40
291 Shayne Corson .08 .25
292 Brad Brown .02 .10
293 Patrice Brisebois .02 .10
294 Terry Ryan .02 .10
295 Jocelyn Thibault .08 .25
296 Miroslav Guren .02 .10
297 Darren Turcotte .08 .25
298 Sebastien Bordeleau .02 .10
299 Jan Vopat .02 .10
300 Blair Atcheynum .02 .10
301 Andrew Brunette .08 .25
302 Sergei Krivokrasov .02 .10
303 Marian Cisar .02 .10
304 Patrick Cote .02 .10
305 J.J. Daigneault .02 .10
306 Greg Johnson .02 .10
307 Chris Terreri .08 .25
308 Scott Niedermayer .02 .10
309 Vadim Sharifijanov .02 .10
310 Petr Sykora .02 .10
311 Sergei Brylin .02 .10
312 Denis Pederson .02 .10
313 Bobby Holik .02 .10
314 Bryan Muir RC .02 .10
315 Zigmund Palffy .08 .25
316 Mike Watt .02 .10
317 Tommy Salo .08 .25
318 Kenny Jonsson .02 .10
319 Dmitri Nabokov .02 .10
320 John MacLean .02 .10
321 Zarley Zalapski .02 .10
322 Brian Leetch .15 .40
323 Todd Harvey .02 .10
324 Mike Richter .15 .40
325 Mike Knuble .02 .10
326 Jeff Beukeboom .02 .10
327 Daniel Alfredsson .08 .25
328 Vaclav Prospal .02 .10
329 Wade Redden .02 .10
330 Igor Kravchuk .02 .10
331 Andreas Dackell .02 .10
332 Mike Maneluk RC .02 .10
333 Eric Lindros .15 .40
334 Rod Brind'Amour .08 .25
335 Colin Forbes .02 .10
336 Dimitri Tertyshny RC .02 .10
337 Shjon Podein .02 .10
338 Chris Therien .02 .10
339 Jeremy Roenick .20 .50
340 Jyrki Lumme .02 .10
341 Rick Tocchet .08 .25
342 Dallas Drake .02 .10
343 Keith Carney .02 .10
344 Greg Adams .02 .10
345 Jan Hrdina RC .40 1.00
346 German Titov .02 .10
347 Stu Barnes .02 .10
348 Kevin Hatcher .02 .10
349 Martin Straka .02 .10
350 Jean-Sebastien Aubin RC .40 1.00
351 Jeff Friesen .02 .10
352 Tony Granato .02 .10
353 Scott Hannan RC .02 .10
354 Owen Nolan .08 .25
355 Stephane Matteau .02 .10
356 Bryan Marchment .02 .10
357 Geoff Courtnall .08 .25
358 Brent Johnson RC .75 2.00
359 Jamie Rivers .02 .10
360 Terry Yake .02 .10
361 Jamie McLennan .08 .25
362 Grant Fuhr .08 .25
363 Michal Handzus RC .40 1.00
364 Bill Ranford .08 .25
365 John Cullen .02 .10
366 Craig Janney .02 .10
367 Daren Puppa .08 .25
368 Pavel Kubina RC .20 .50
369 Wendel Clark .08 .25
370 Mats Sundin .15 .40
371 Felix Potvin .15 .40
372 Daniil Markov RC .02 .10
373 Derek King .02 .10
374 Steve Thomas .02 .10
375 Tomas Kaberle RC .40 1.00
376 Alexander Mogilny .08 .25
377 Bill Muckalt RC .02 .10
378 Brian Noonan .02 .10
379 Markus Naslund .15 .40
380 Brad May .02 .10
381 Matt Cooke RC .02 .10
382 Calle Johansson .02 .10
383 Dale Hunter .02 .10
384 Jaroslav Svejkovsky .02 .10
385 Dmitri Mironov .02 .10
386 Matt Herr RC .02 .10
387 Nolan Baumgartner .02 .10
388 Wayne Gretzky CL .15 .40
389 Steve Yzerman CL .08 .25
390 Wayne Gretzky .15 .40
Steve Yzerman CL
391 Brian Finley PE RC .60 1.50
392 Maxime Ouellet PE RC .75 2.00
393 Kurtis Foster PE RC .60 1.50
394 Barret Jackman PE RC .75 2.00
395 Ross Lupaschuk PE RC .60 1.50
396 Steven McCarthy PE RC .60 1.50
397 Peter Reynolds PE RC .60 1.50
398 Bart Rushmer PE RC .60 1.50
399 Jonathan Zion PE RC .60 1.50
400 Kris Beech PE RC .60 1.50
401 Brandin Cote PE RC .60 1.50
402 Scott Kelman PE RC .60 1.50
403 Jamie Lundmark PE RC .75 2.00
404 Derek MacKenzie PE RC .60 1.50
405 Rory McDade PE RC .60 1.50
406 David Morisset PE RC .60 1.50
407 Mirko Murovic PE RC .60 1.50
408 Taylor Pyatt PE RC .75 2.00
409 Charlie Stephens PE .60 1.50
410 Kyle Wanvig PE RC .60 1.50
411 Krzystof Wieckowski PE RC .60 1.50
412 Michael Zigomanis PE RC .60 1.50
413 Rico Fata CC .60 1.50
414 Vincent Lecavalier CC 1.00 2.50
415 Chris Drury CC .60 1.50
416 Oleg Kvasha CC RC .60 1.50
417 Eric Brewer CC .60 1.50
418 Josh Green CC RC .60 1.50
419 Marty Reasoner CC .60 1.50
420 Manny Malhotra CC .60 1.50

1998-99 Upper Deck Exclusives

Randomly inserted into hobby packs only, this 420-card set is parallel to the base set. Cards are serial numbered to only 100 copies. An exclusive 1 of 1 parallel also exists and randomly inserted into packs.

*1-30 SR/RR: 5X TO 12X BASIC CARDS
*1-30 SR/RR RCs: 4X TO 10X BASIC CARDS
*31-390 VETS: 30X TO 80X BASIC CARDS
*31-390 ROOKIES: 20X TO 50X
*391-412 PE: 4X TO 10X BASIC CARDS
*413-420 CC: 4X TO 10X BASIC CARDS

1998-99 Upper Deck Blow-Ups 5 x 7

Inserted as box-toppers in various distribution forms of Upper Deck, these oversized cards resembled differentr insert sets but were approximately 5" x 7". Cards were numbered the same as the basic insert card.

85 Steve Yzerman Upper Deck 3.00 8.00
P3 Steve Yzerman Profiles 3.00 8.00
FF20 Steve Yzerman Fantastic Finishers 3.00 8.00
FT1 Steve Yzerman Frozen in Time 3.00 8.00
LS14 Steve Yzerman Lord Stanley's Heroes 3.00 8.00

1998-99 Upper Deck Fantastic Finishers

Randomly inserted into Series 1 packs at a rate of 1:12, this 30-card set features color action photos of players considered to be the more prolific and gifted finishers in the NHL. Three Tier Quantum parallel versions of this insert set were also produced and inserted into Series 1 packs. Tier 1 cards were sequentially numbered to 1,500; Tier 2 cards were sequentially numbered to 50, and Tier 3 cards were sequentially numbered to 1.

COMPLETE SET (30) 50.00 100.00
*QUANTUM ONE/1500: .8X TO 2X BASIC INSERTS
*QUANTUM TWO/50: 15X TO 40X BASIC INSERTS
UNPRICED QUANTUM THREE PRINT RUN 1
FF1 Wayne Gretzky 6.00 15.00
FF2 Peter Bondra .75 2.00
FF3 Sergei Samsonov .75 2.00
FF4 Jaromir Jagr 1.50 4.00
FF5 Brendan Shanahan 1.00 2.50
FF6 Joe Sakic 2.00 5.00
FF7 Brett Hull 1.50 4.00
FF8 Paul Kariya 1.00 2.50
FF9 Keith Tkachuk 1.00 2.50
FF10 Zigmund Palffy .75 2.00
FF11 Eric Lindros 1.00 2.50
FF12 Mike Modano 1.50 4.00
FF13 Pavel Bure 1.00 2.50
FF14 Mats Sundin .75 2.00
FF15 Patrik Elias .75 2.00
FF16 Tony Amonte .75 2.00
FF17 Peter Forsberg 2.50 6.00
FF18 Alexei Yashin .75 2.00
FF19 Mark Recchi .75 2.00
FF20 Steve Yzerman 4.00 10.00
FF21 Doug Weight .75 2.00
FF22 Jeremy Roenick 1.25 3.00
FF23 Teemu Selanne 1.00 2.50
FF24 Owen Nolan .75 2.00
FF25 John LeClair 1.00 2.50
FF26 Jason Allison .75 2.00
FF27 Mike Johnson .75 2.00
FF28 Theo Fleury .75 2.00
FF29 Nicklas Lidstrom 1.00 2.50
FF30 Joe Nieuwendyk .75 2.00

1998-99 Upper Deck Frozen In Time

Randomly inserted in Series 1 packs at a rate of 1:23, this 30-card set features color action photos of some of the key moments throughout the careers of the highlighted players. Three Tier Quantum parallel versions of this insert set were also produced and inserted into Series 1 packs. Tier 1 cards were sequentially numbered to 1,000; Tier 2 cards were sequentially numbered to 25; and Tier 3 cards were numbered to 1.

COMPLETE SET (30) 50.00 100.00
*QUANTUM ONE/1000: .8X TO 2X BASIC INSERTS
*QUANTUM TWO/25: 20X TO 50X BASIC INSERTS
FT1 Steve Yzerman 4.00 10.00
FT2 Peter Forsberg 2.50 6.00
FT3 Sergei Samsonov 1.25 3.00
FT4 Martin Brodeur 2.50 6.00
FT5 Theo Fleury .75 2.00
FT6 Paul Kariya 1.50 4.00
FT7 Rob Blake 1.25 3.00
FT8 Jari Kurri .75 2.00
FT9 Eric Lindros 1.50 4.00
FT10 Dominik Hasek 2.00 5.00
FT11 Patrick Roy 4.00 10.00
FT12 Saku Koivu 1.50 4.00
FT13 Mike Modano 1.50 4.00
FT14 Alexei Morozov .75 2.00
FT15 Chris Osgood 1.25 3.00
FT16 Doug Gilmour 1.25 3.00
FT17 Owen Nolan 1.25 3.00
FT18 Mike Johnson 1.25 3.00
FT19 Keith Tkachuk 1.50 4.00
FT20 Adam Oates 1.25 3.00
FT21 Chris Chelios 1.50 4.00
FT22 Brendan Shanahan 1.50 4.00
FT23 Joe Sakic 2.00 5.00
FT24 Pavel Bure 1.50 4.00
FT25 Ray Bourque 2.00 5.00
FT26 Ed Belfour 1.50 4.00
FT27 John LeClair 1.50 4.00
FT28 Teemu Selanne 1.50 4.00
FT29 Jaromir Jagr 1.50 4.00
FT30 Wayne Gretzky 6.00 15.00

1998-99 Upper Deck Game Jerseys

Randomly inserted into Series 1 and Series 2 packs at the rate of one in 2,500 retail and 1:288 hobby, this 24-card set features color action player photos with a piece from an actual game-worn jersey embedded in the cards. Four of the player's autographed some of their cards. The number of cards each player autographed follow the player's name in the checklist below.

GJ1 Wayne Gretzky 75.00 200.00
GJ2 Vincent Lecavalier 25.00 60.00
GJ3 Bobby Hull 25.00 60.00
GJ4 Curtis Joseph 10.00 25.00
GJ5 Roberto Luongo 15.00 40.00
GJ6 Martin Brodeur 25.00 60.00
GJ8 Ed Belfour 10.00 25.00
GJ9 Al MacInnis 6.00 15.00
GJ10 Derian Hatcher 6.00 15.00
GJ11 Daniel Tkaczuk 6.00 15.00
GJ12 Manny Malhotra 6.00 15.00
GJ13 Eric Brewer 6.00 15.00
GJ14 Alex Tanguay 8.00 20.00
GJ15 Brendan Shanahan 10.00 25.00
GJ16 Chris Osgood 8.00 20.00
GJ16 Jaromir Jagr 25.00 60.00
GJ17 Dominik Hasek 25.00 60.00
GJ18 Doug Gilmour 8.00 20.00
GJ19 Mats Sundin 10.00 25.00
GJ20 Darryl Sydor 6.00 15.00
GJ21 Chris Therien 6.00 15.00
GJ22 Darius Kasparaitis 6.00 15.00
GJ23 Alexei Zhamnov 6.00 15.00
GJ24 Joe Nieuwendyk 8.00 20.00
GJA1 Bobby Hull AU/9 900.00 1500.00
GJA2 W.Gretzky AU/99 300.00 500.00
GJA3 V.Lecavalier AU/100 125.00 300.00
GJA4 Gretzky 2Swatch AU/99 400.00 600.00

1998-99 Upper Deck Generation Next

Randomly inserted in Series 2 packs at the rate of 1:23, this 30-card set features color action photos of ten of the top players in the NHL on one side with one of three heir apparent pictured on the other. Quantum parallels of this set were also produced and inserted into Series 2 packs. Three different Quantum parallel sets exist, and each Quantum set was broken into three levels or "tiers". Quantum 1 had tiers that featured ten cards sequentially numbered to 1,000; ten numbered to 500; and ten cards sequentially numbered to 250. Quantum 2 had tiers that contained ten cards sequentially numbered to 75; ten numbered to 25; and ten cards sequentially numbered to 10. Quantum 3 had tiers with ten cards sequentially numbered to 3; ten sequentially numbered to 2; and ten cards numbered to 1. The card numbers in each tier were the same for each set, the card numbers are listed below. Tiers were grouped by serial numbers in descending order. Quantum 2, Tier 3 and Quantum 3 cards are not priced due to their scarcity.

COMPLETE SET (30) 30.00 60.00
*QUANTUM ONE/1000: .6X TO 1.5X BASIC INSERTS
*QUANTUM ONE/500: 1.2X TO 3X BASIC INSERTS
*QUANTUM ONE/250: 2X TO 5X BASIC INSERTS
*QUANTUM TWO/75: 8X TO 20X BASIC INSERTS
*QUANTUM TWO/25: 20X TO 50X BASIC INSERTS
*QUANTUM TWO/10: 25X TO 60X BASIC INSERTS
UNPRICED QUANT.THREE PRINT RUN 1-3
TIER 1 CARDS: 1,4,7,10,13,16,19,22,25,28
TIER 2 CARDS: 2,5,8,11,14,17,20,23,26,29
TIER 3 CARDS: 3,6,9,12,15,18,21,24,27,30
GN1 Wayne Gretzky Sergei Samsonov 2.00 5.00
GN2 Wayne Gretzky Marian Hossa 2.00 5.00
GN3 Wayne Gretzky Vincent Lecavalier 2.00 5.00
GN4 Steve Yzerman Brendan Morrison 1.50 4.00
GN5 Steve Yzerman Marty Reasoner 1.50 4.00
GN6 Steve Yzerman Manny Malhotra 1.50 4.00
GN7 Patrick Roy Jean-Sebastien Giguere 1.50 4.00
GN8 Patrick Roy Jose Theodore 2.00 5.00
GN9 Patrick Roy Marc Denis 1.50 4.00
GN10 Eric Lindros Patrick Marleau .60 1.50
GN11 Eric Lindros Brad Isbister .60 1.50
GN12 Eric Lindros Joe Thornton .60 1.50
GN13 Brendan Shanahan Josh Green .60 1.50
GN14 Brendan Shanahan Ty Jones .60 1.50
GN15 Brendan Shanahan Mike Watt .60 1.50
GN16 Ray Bourque Mattias Ohlund .60 1.50
GN17 Ray Bourque Tom Poti .60 1.50
GN18 Ray Bourque Eric Brewer .75 2.00
GN19 Paul Kariya Daniel Briere .60 1.50
GN20 Paul Kariya Rico Fata .60 1.50
GN21 Paul Kariya Chris Drury .60 1.50
GN22 Jaromir Jagr Robert Dome .60 1.50
GN23 Jaromir Jagr Richard Zednik .60 1.50
GN24 Jaromir Jagr Oleg Kvasha .60 1.50
GN25 Peter Forsberg Olli Jokinen 1.25 3.00
GN26 Peter Forsberg Niklas Sundstrom 1.00 2.50
GN27 Peter Forsberg Brendan Morrison 1.00 2.50
GN28 Pavel Bure Vadim Sharifijanov .60 1.50
GN29 Pavel Bure Dmitri Nabokov .60 1.50
GN30 Pavel Bure Sergei Samsonov .60 1.50

1998-99 Upper Deck Lord Stanley's Heroes

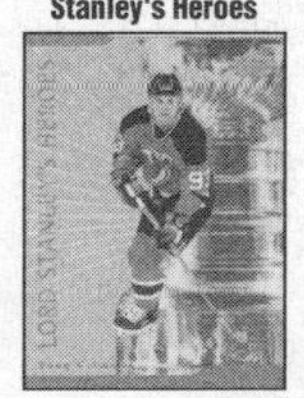

Randomly inserted into Series 1 packs at a rate of one in six, this 30-card set features color action photos of players vying for their chance at claiming the Stanley Cup. Three Tier Quantum parallel versions of this insert set were also produced and inserted into Series 1 packs. Tier 1 cards were sequentially numbered to 2,000; Tier 2 cards were sequentially numbered to 100; and Tier 3 cards were numbered to 1.

COMPLETE SET (30) 30.00 60.00
*QUANTUM 1: .6X TO 1.5X BASIC INSERTS
*QUANTUM 2: 8X TO 20X BASIC INSERTS
UNPRICED LSH PARALLEL #'d OF 1
LS1 Wayne Gretzky 4.00 10.00
LS2 Joe Sakic 1.25 3.00
LS3 Jaromir Jagr 1.00 2.50
LS4 Brendan Shanahan .60 1.50
LS5 Martin Brodeur 1.50 4.00
LS6 Theo Fleury .60 1.50
LS7 Doug Gilmour .40 1.00
LS8 Ron Francis .40 1.00
LS9 Sergei Fedorov 1.00 2.50
LS10 Patrick Roy 3.00 8.00
LS11 Mark Messier .60 1.50
LS12 Peter Forsberg 1.50 4.00
LS13 Brian Leetch .60 1.50
LS14 Steve Yzerman 3.00 8.00
LS15 Sergei Samsonov .40 1.00
LS16 Eric Lindros .60 1.50
LS17 Paul Kariya .60 1.50
LS18 Saku Koivu .60 1.50
LS19 Bryan Berard .40 1.00
LS20 Chris Pronger .40 1.00
LS21 Keith Tkachuk .60 1.50
LS22 Doug Weight .40 1.00
LS23 Ed Belfour .60 1.50
LS24 Mats Sundin .60 1.50
LS25 John LeClair .60 1.50
LS26 Pavel Bure .60 1.50
LS27 Dominik Hasek 1.25 3.00
LS28 Mike Modano 1.00 2.50
LS29 Curtis Joseph .60 1.50
LS30 Teemu Selanne .60 1.50

1998-99 Upper Deck Profiles

Randomly inserted into Series 2 packs at the rate of one in 12, this 30-card set features color action photos of some of the greatest current players in the NHL. Three Tier Quantum parallel versions of this insert set were also produced and inserted into Series 2 packs. Tier 1 cards were sequentially numbered to 1,500; Tier 2 cards were sequentially numbered to 50; and Tier 3 cards were numbered to 1.

COMPLETE SET (30) 30.00 60.00
*QUANTUM ONE/1500: .6X TO 1.5X BASIC INSERTS
*QUANTUM TWO/50: 10X TO 25X BASIC INSERTS
P1 Marty Reasoner .50 1.25
P2 Brett Hull 1.00 2.50
P3 Steve Yzerman 4.00 10.00
P4 Eric Lindros .75 2.00
P5 Eric Brewer .60 1.50
P6 Martin Brodeur 2.00 5.00
P7 John Vanbiesbrouck .50 1.25
P8 Teemu Selanne .75 2.00
P9 Wayne Gretzky 5.00 12.00
P10 Jaromir Jagr 1.25 3.00
P11 Peter Forsberg 2.00 5.00
P12 Manny Malhotra .50 1.25
P13 Sergei Samsonov .50 1.25
P14 Brendan Shanahan .75 2.00
P15 Doug Gilmour .60 1.50
P16 Vincent Lecavalier .75 2.00
P17 Dominik Hasek 1.50 4.00
P18 Mike Modano 1.25 3.00
P19 Saku Koivu .75 2.00
P20 Curtis Joseph .75 2.00
P21 Paul Kariya .75 2.00
P22 Doug Weight .60 1.50
P23 Ray Bourque 1.50 4.00
P24 Patrick Roy 4.00 10.00
P25 John LeClair .75 2.00
P26 Chris Drury .50 1.25
P27 Theo Fleury .60 1.50
P28 Mats Sundin .60 1.50
P29 Sergei Fedorov 1.00 2.50
P30 Rico Fata .60 1.50

1998-99 Upper Deck Wayne Gretzky Game Jersey Autographs

These cards could be found in packs of Black Diamond, Upper Deck MVP, SP Authentic, and SPx Top Prospects. Each product had one version of the card numbered to 40 sets. The cards contain an actual piece of a game worn Wayne Gretzky jersey embedded in the cards and an authentic autograph.

COMMON CARD 200.00 500.00

1998-99 Upper Deck Year of the Great One

Randomly inserted into Series 2 packs at the rate of 1:6, this 30-card set features color photos of Hockey great, Wayne Gretzky. Three Tier Quantum parallel versions of this insert set were also produced and inserted into Series 2 packs. Tier 1 cards were sequentially numbered to 1,999; Tier 2 cards were sequentially numbered to 99; and Tier 3 cards were numbered to 1.

COMPLETE SET (30) 40.00 80.00
COMMON GRETZKY (G01-G030) 1.50 4.00
*QUANTUM ONE/199: 1.5X TO 4X BASIC INSERTS
6.00 15.00
*QUANTUM TWO/99: 6X TO 15X BASIC INSERTS
25.00 60.00

1998 Upper Deck Willie O'Ree Commemorative Card

This card was issued by Upper Deck of the 1998 NHL All-Stars game in Vancouver. It was available at All-Star activities throughout the weekend.

22 Willie O'Ree 5.00 10.00

1999-00 Upper Deck

Upper Deck was released as a 335-card two series set with 270 regular issue cards and 65 short prints. Series one is comprised of 135 regular cards and 35 short prints for a total of 170 cards, and series two was comprised of 135 regular cards and 30 short prints for a total of 165 cards. Base cards have a blue and black border along the bottom edge of the card with enhanced bronze foil stamping. Upper Deck was released in 24-pack boxes with packs containing 10 cards and carried a suggested retail price of $2.99.

COMPLETE SET (335) 40.00 100.00
136-170/306-335 SP ODDS 1:4
1 Wayne Gretzky .60 1.50
2 Wayne Gretzky .60 1.50
3 Wayne Gretzky .60 1.50
4 Wayne Gretzky .60 1.50
5 Wayne Gretzky .60 1.50
6 Wayne Gretzky .60 1.50
7 Wayne Gretzky .60 1.50
8 Wayne Gretzky .60 1.50
9 Wayne Gretzky .60 1.50
10 Wayne Gretzky .60 1.50
11 Paul Kariya .20 .50
12 Matt Cullen .02 .10
13 Steve Rucchin .15 .40
14 Fredrik Olausson .02 .10
15 Damian Rhodes .15 .40
16 Jody Hull .02 .10
17 Ray Bourque .30 .75
18 Joe Thornton .30 .75
19 Jonathan Girard .02 .10
20 Shawn Bates .02 .10
21 Byron Dafoe .15 .40
22 Dominik Hasek .40 1.00
23 Michael Peca .15 .40
24 Miroslav Satan .15 .40
25 Dixon Ward .02 .10
26 Valeri Bure .02 .10
27 Derek Morris .02 .10
28 Jarome Iginla .25 .60
29 Rico Fata .02 .10
30 Jean-Sebastien Giguere .15 .40
31 Arturs Irbe .15 .40
32 Sami Kapanen .02 .10
33 Gary Roberts .02 .10
34 Bates Battaglia .02 .10
35 J-P Dumont .15 .40
36 Ty Jones .02 .10
37 Tony Amonte .15 .40
38 Anders Eriksson .02 .10
39 Peter Forsberg .50 1.25
40 Adam Foote .02 .10
41 Chris Drury .15 .40
42 Milan Hejduk .20 .50
43 Brett Hull .25 .60
44 Ed Belfour .20 .50
45 Jamie Langenbrunner .02 .10
46 Derian Hatcher .02 .10
47 Jon Sim RC .15 .40
48 Joe Nieuwendyk .15 .40
49 Steve Yzerman 1.00 2.50
50 Brendan Shanahan .20 .50
51 Nicklas Lidstrom .20 .50
52 Igor Larionov .02 .10
53 Vyacheslav Kozlov .02 .10
54 Bill Guerin .02 .10
55 Mike Grier .02 .10
56 Tommy Salo .15 .40
57 Tom Poti .02 .10
58 Mark Parrish .15 .40
59 Pavel Bure .20 .50
60 Scott Mellanby .02 .10
61 Chris Allen RC .02 .10
62 Rob Blake .15 .40
63 Pavel Rosa .02 .10
64 Donald Audette .02 .10
65 Vladimir Tsyplakov .02 .10
66 Manny Legace .15 .40
67 Saku Koivu .20 .50
68 Eric Weinrich .02 .10
69 Jeff Hackett .15 .40
70 Arron Asham .02 .10
71 Trevor Linden .15 .40
72 Cliff Ronning .15 .40
73 David Legwand .15 .40
74 Kimmo Timonen .02 .10
75 Sergei Krivokrasov .02 .10
76 Mike Dunham .15 .40
77 Martin Brodeur .50 1.25
78 Patrik Elias .15 .40
79 Petr Sykora .02 .10
80 Vadim Sharifijanov .02 .10
81 John Madden RC .20 .50
82 Eric Brewer .02 .10
83 Dmitri Nabokov .02 .10
84 Kenny Jonsson .02 .10
85 Zdeno Chara .02 .10
86 Wayne Gretzky 1.25 3.00
87 Mike Richter .20 .50
88 Adam Graves .02 .10
89 Manny Malhotra .15 .40
90 Alexei Yashin .02 .10
91 Sami Salo .15 .40
92 Marian Hossa .20 .50
93 Shawn McEachern .02 .10
94 Eric Lindros .20 .50
95 Jean-Marc Pelletier .02 .10
96 Rod Brind'Amour .15 .40
97 Mark Recchi .15 .40
98 Eric Desjardins .15 .40
99 Robert Reichel .02 .10
100 Keith Tkachuk .20 .50
101 Robert Esche RC .60 1.50
102 Oleg Tverdovsky .02 .10
103 Trevor Letowski .02 .10
104 Jaromir Jagr .30 .75
105 Tom Barrasso .15 .40
106 Jan Hrdina .02 .10
107 Matthew Barnaby .15 .40
108 Vincent Damphousse .02 .10
109 Jeff Friesen .02 .10
110 Patrick Marleau .20 .50
111 Mike Ricci .15 .40
112 Scott Hannan .02 .10
113 Pavol Demitra .15 .40
114 Al MacInnis .15 .40
115 Lubos Bartecko .02 .10
116 Jochen Hecht RC .20 .50
117 Vincent Lecavalier .20 .50
118 Paul Mara .02 .10
119 Kevin Hodson .15 .40
120 Dan Cloutier .15 .40
121 Mats Sundin .20 .50
122 Daniil Markov .02 .10
123 Sergei Berezin .02 .10
124 Steve Thomas .02 .10
125 Tomas Kaberle .02 .10
126 Mark Messier .20 .50
127 Bill Muckalt .15 .40
128 Kevin Weekes .02 .10
129 Josh Holden .15 .40
130 Jaroslav Svejkovsky .02 .10
131 Adam Oates .15 .40
132 Peter Bondra .15 .40
133 Jan Bulis .02 .10
134 Wayne Gretzky CL .60 1.50
135 Wayne Gretzky CL .60 1.50
136 Wayne Gretzky SP 1.50 4.00
137 Eric Lindros SP .25 .60
138 Jaromir Jagr SP .40 1.00
139 Paul Kariya SP .25 .60
140 Steve Yzerman SP 1.25 3.00
141 Patrick Roy SP 1.25 3.00
142 Chris Drury SP .20 .50
143 Sergei Samsonov SP .20 .50
144 Brett Hull SP .40 1.00
145 Dominik Hasek SP .50 1.25
146 Keith Tkachuk SP .25 .60
147 Alexei Yashin SP .25 .60
148 Martin Brodeur SP .60 1.50
149 Pavel Bure SP .25 .60
150 Paul Mara SP .20 .50
151 Peter Bondra SP .20 .50
152 Mike Modano SP .40 1.00
153 Teemu Selanne SP .20 .50
154 Peter Forsberg SP .60 1.50
155 Brendan Shanahan SP .20 .50
156 Ray Bourque SP .40 1.00
157 Saku Koivu SP .25 .60
158 John LeClair SP .25 .60
159 Joe Sakic SP .50 1.25
160 David Legwand SP .20 .50
161 Patrik Stefan SP RC .40 1.00
162 Nick Boynton SP .25 .60
163 Roberto Luongo SP .50 1.25
164 Rico Fata SP .20 .50
165 Daniel Sedin SP .20 .50
166 Henrik Sedin SP .20 .50
167 Brad Stuart SP .20 .50
168 Tony Amonte SP .20 .50
169 Oleg Saprykin SP RC .50 1.25
170 Denis Shvidki SP .20 .50
171 Guy Hebert .15 .40
172 Niclas Havelid RC .20 .50
173 Oleg Tverdovsky .02 .10
174 Teemu Selanne .20 .50
175 Damian Rhodes .15 .40
176 Nelson Emerson .02 .10
177 Per Svartvadet RC .02 .10
178 Ray Ferraro .02 .10
179 Kelly Buchberger .02 .10
180 Norm Maracle .15 .40
181 Patrik Stefan .02 .10
182 Dave Andreychuk .15 .40
183 Sergei Samsonov .15 .40
184 John Grahame RC .20 .50
185 Jason Allison .02 .10
186 Kyle McLaren .02 .10
187 Anson Carter .15 .40
188 Martin Biron .15 .40
189 Brian Campbell RC .02 .10
190 Curtis Brown .02 .10
191 Alexei Zhitnik .02 .10
192 David Moravec RC .02 .10
193 Oleg Saprykin .02 .10
194 Grant Fuhr .15 .40
195 Phil Housley .15 .40
196 Marc Savard .02 .10
197 Robyn Regehr .02 .10
198 Martin Gelinas .02 .10
199 Ron Francis .15 .40
200 Jeff O'Neil .02 .10
201 Keith Primeau .02 .10
202 Paul Ranheim .02 .10
203 Kyle Calder RC .02 .10
204 Jocelyn Thibault .15 .40
205 Wendel Clark .15 .40
206 Doug Gilmour .15 .40
207 Josef Marha .02 .10
208 Alexei Zhamnov .02 .10
209 Dan Hinote RC .20 .50
210 Patrick Roy 1.00 2.50
211 Joe Sakic .40 1.00
212 Alex Tanguay .15 .40
213 Sandis Ozolinsh .02 .10
214 Adam Deadmarsh .02 .10
215 Jere Lehtinen .15 .40
216 Mike Modano .30 .75
217 Darryl Sydor .15 .40
218 Sergei Zubov .02 .10
219 Pavel Patera RC .02 .10
220 Jamie Pushor .02 .10
221 Chris Osgood .15 .40
222 Tomas Holmstrom .02 .10
223 Chris Chelios .20 .50
224 Sergei Fedorov .30 .75
225 Jiri Fischer .02 .10
226 Paul Comrie RC .02 .10
227 Frantisek Musil .02 .10
228 Janne Niinimaa .02 .10
229 Doug Weight .15 .40
230 Trevor Kidd .15 .40
231 Oleg Kvasha .15 .40
232 Viktor Kozlov .02 .10
233 Rob Niedermayer .02 .10
234 Luc Robitaille .15 .40
235 Aki Berg .02 .10
236 Bryan Smolinski .15 .40
237 Jozef Stumpel .15 .40
238 Zigmund Palffy .15 .40
239 Stephane Fiset .15 .40
240 Jason Blake RC .15 .40
241 Scott Lachance .02 .10
242 Vladimir Malakhov .02 .10
243 Mike Ribeiro .02 .10
244 Brian Savage .02 .10
245 Tomas Vokoun .02 .10
246 Randy Robitaille .02 .10
247 Sergei Nemchinov .02 .10
248 Brendan Morrison .15 .40
249 Scott Niedermayer .02 .10
250 Scott Stevens .15 .40
251 Scott Gomez .02 .10
252 Mark Lawrence .02 .10
253 Felix Potvin .20 .50
254 Olli Jokinen .15 .40
255 Tim Connolly .02 .10
256 Mariusz Czerkawski .02 .10
257 Valeri Kamensky .02 .10
258 Brian Leetch .20 .50
259 Petr Nedved .15 .40
260 Theo Fleury .02 .10
261 Kevin Hatcher .02 .10
262 Mike York .02 .10
263 Ron Tugnutt .15 .40
264 Chris Phillips .02 .10
265 Daniel Alfredsson .15 .40
266 Radek Bonk .02 .10
267 Wade Redden .02 .10
268 John Vanbiesbrouck .15 .40
269 John LeClair .20 .50
270 Simon Gagne .20 .50
271 Nikolaj Khabibulin .15 .40
272 Daniel Briere .02 .10
273 Jeremy Roenick .25 .60
274 Andrew Ference .02 .10
275 Alexei Kovalev .02 .10
276 Martin Straka .02 .10
277 Alexei Morozov .15 .40
278 Steve Shields .15 .40
279 Marco Sturm .15 .40
280 Niklas Sundstrom .02 .10
281 Brad Stuart .15 .40
282 Owen Nolan .15 .40
283 Roman Turek .15 .40
284 Chris Pronger .15 .40
285 Jim Campbell .02 .10
286 Michal Handzus .15 .40
287 Pierre Turgeon .15 .40
288 Darcy Tucker .02 .10
289 Andrei Zyuzin .02 .10
290 Stephen Guolla .02 .10
291 Curtis Joseph .20 .50
292 Jonas Hoglund .02 .10
293 Bryan Berard .02 .10
294 Mike Johnson .15 .40
295 Garth Snow .15 .40
296 Jason Strudwick .02 .10
297 Steve Kariya RC .20 .50
298 Markus Naslund .20 .50
299 Mattias Ohlund .15 .40
300 Alexander Mogilny .15 .40
301 Olaf Kolzig .15 .40
302 Alexei Tezikov RC .20 .50
303 Alexander Volchkov RC .15 .40
304 Steve Yzerman CL .40 1.00
305 Curtis Joseph CL .15 .40
306 Pavel Brendl SP RC .40 1.00
307 Daniel Sedin SP .20 .50
308 Henrik Sedin SP .20 .50
309 Sheldon Keefe SP RC .40 1.00
310 Ryan Jardine SP RC .40 1.00
311 Maxime Ouellet SP .20 .50
312 Barret Jackman SP .20 .50
313 Kristian Kudroc SP RC .40 1.00
314 Branislav Mezei SP RC .40 1.00
315 Denis Shvidki SP .20 .50
316 Brian Finley SP .20 .50
317 Jonathan Cheechoo SP 2.50 6.00
318 Mark Bell SP .20 .50
319 Taylor Pyatt SP .20 .50
320 Norm Milley SP .20 .50
321 Jamie Lundmark SP .20 .50
322 Alexander Buturlin SP RC .40 1.00
323 Jaroslav Kristek SP RC .40 1.00
324 Kris Beech SP .20 .50
325 Scott Kelman SP .20 .50
326 Milan Kraft SP RC .40 1.00
327 Mattias Weinhandl SP .20 .50
328 Alexei Volkov SP .20 .50
329 Andrei Shefer SP RC .40 1.00
330 Mathieu Chouinard SP .20 .50
331 Justin Papineau SP .20 .50
332 Mike Van Ryn SP .20 .50
333 Jeff Heerema SP .20 .50
334 Michael Zigomanis SP .20 .50
335 Bryan Kazarian SP RC .40 1.00

1999-00 Upper Deck Exclusives

Randomly inserted in packs, this 335-card set parallels the base Upper Deck set with gold foil highlights. Each card is sequentially numbered to 100. Unpriced 1/1 exclusive parallels also exist.

*GRETZKY 1-10: 12X TO 30X BASIC CARDS
*VETS 1-305: 25X TO 60X BASIC CARDS
*ROOKIES 1-305: 12X TO 30X BASIC CARDS
*VETS 136-170/306-335: 10X TO 25X BASIC SP
*YG 136-170/306-335: 2X TO 5X BASIC YG SP

1999-00 Upper Deck Exclusives 1 of 1

Randomly inserted in packs, this 335-card set parallels the base Upper Deck set. Each card is numbered one of one.

UNPRICED EXCLUSIVE 1 of 1 ISSUED

1999-00 Upper Deck 500 Goal Club

Randomly inserted in various Upper Deck products, these cards feature players who attained the 500-goal mark during their career. The front pictures the player and includes a swatch of game-worn jersey or game-used stick. An autographed version of each card, serial-numbered to 25, was also available. Michel Goulet and Stan Mikita were randomly available in Black Diamond with stated odds of 1:1768. Bobby Hull and Brett Hull were randomly available in SP Authentic with stated odds of 1:1339. Gordie Howe was randomly available in Upper Deck Series II packs with stated odds of 1:2989. Bryan Trottier and Mike Bossy were randomly available in Upper Deck MVP SC Edition with stated odds of 1:3995. Luc Robitaille and Marcel Dionne were randomly available in Upper Deck Ovation with stated odds of 1:947. Dino Ciccarelli and Steve Yzerman were randomly available in Upper Deck PowerDeck with stated odds of 1:330. Gilbert Perreault and Maurice Richard were randomly available in Upper Deck Ultimate Victory with stated odds of 1:1113. Guy Lafleur and Jean Beliveau were randomly available in Wayne Gretzky Hockey with stated odds of 1:1259.

500BH Bobby Hull 50.00 125.00
500BHA Bobby Hull AU/25 350.00 550.00
500BTA Bryan Trottier AU/25 200.00 400.00
500BT Bryan Trottier 15.00 40.00
500DC Dino Ciccarelli 30.00 80.00
500DCA Dino Ciccarelli AU/25 150.00 300.00
500GH Gordie Howe 75.00 150.00
500GHA Gordie Howe AU/25 600.00 800.00
500GL Guy Lafleur 125.00 300.00
500GLA Guy Lafleur AU/25 150.00 350.00
500GP Gilbert Perreault 15.00 40.00
500GPA G.Perreault AU/25 400.00 600.00
500JB Jean Beliveau 100.00 200.00
500JBA Jean Beliveau AU/25 300.00 500.00
500LRA Luc Robitaille AU/25 350.00 500.00
500LR Luc Robitaille 20.00 50.00
500MBA Mike Bossy AU/25 400.00 500.00
500MB Mike Bossy 20.00 50.00
500MDAS Marcel Dionne AU/25 125.00 250.00
500MD Marcel Dionne 20.00 50.00
500MGA Michel Goulet AU/25 150.00 300.00
500MG Michel Goulet 15.00 40.00
500MR Maurice Richard 75.00 200.00
500MRA M.Richard AU/25 450.00 700.00
500SMA Stan Mikita AU/25 200.00 400.00
500SM Stan Mikita 50.00 125.00
500SY Steve Yzerman 75.00 150.00
500SYA Steve Yzerman AU/25 500.00 750.00
500BHUA Brett Hull AU/25 250.00 500.00
500BHU Brett Hull 40.00 80.00

1999-00 Upper Deck All-Star Class

Randomly inserted in Series Two packs at the rate of 1:23, this 20-card set features an all blue foil card stock with full color action player photos. Silver and gold parallels were also created and inserted randomly. Silver parallels were limited to 100 serial numbered sets. Gold parallels were numbered 1/1 and are not priced due to scarcity.

COMPLETE SET (20) 30.00 60.00
*SILVER/100: 10X TO 25X BASIC INSERTS
UNPRICED GOLD PRINT RUN 1
AS1 Dominik Hasek 2.00 5.00
AS2 Patrick Roy 5.00 12.00
AS3 Jaromir Jagr 1.50 4.00
AS4 Paul Kariya 1.00 2.50
AS5 Teemu Selanne 1.00 2.50
AS6 Keith Tkachuk 1.00 2.50
AS7 Pavel Bure 1.00 2.50
AS8 John LeClair 1.00 2.50
AS9 Mats Sundin 1.00 2.50
AS10 Steve Yzerman 5.00 12.00
AS11 Peter Forsberg 2.50 6.00
AS12 Eric Lindros 1.00 2.50
AS13 Steve Kariya 1.25 3.00
AS14 Ed Belfour 1.00 2.50
AS15 Nicklas Lidstrom .75 2.00
AS16 Ray Bourque 1.50 4.00
AS17 Sandis Ozolinsh .75 2.00
AS18 Al MacInnis .75 2.00
AS19 Martin Brodeur 2.50 6.00
AS20 Patrik Stefan 1.50 4.00

1999-00 Upper Deck Crunch Time

Randomly inserted in Series One packs at the rate of 1:4, this 30-card set features an all foil card stock with concentric laser rays coming out from behind an action player shot. Background foil color matches the respective player's team colors. Silver and gold parallels were also created and inserted randomly. Silver parallels were limited to 100 serial numbered sets. Unpriced gold parallels were numbered 1/1.

COMPLETE SET (30) 15.00 30.00
*SILVER/100: 25X TO 60X BASIC INSERTS
UNPRICED GOLD PRINT RUN 1
CT1 Vincent Lecavalier .40 1.00
CT2 Steve Yzerman 2.00 5.00
CT3 Peter Bondra .30 .75
CT4 Jean-Marc Pelletier .30 .75
CT5 Brendan Shanahan .40 1.00
CT6 Joe Sakic .75 2.00
CT7 Jean-Sebastien Giguere .30 .75
CT8 Brett Hull .50 1.25
CT9 Jaromir Jagr .60 1.50
CT10 Eric Brewer .30 .75
CT11 Sergei Samsonov .30 .75
CT12 Alexei Yashin .20 .50
CT13 Mats Sundin .40 1.00
CT14 Mike Modano .60 1.50
CT15 Al MacInnis .30 .75
CT16 Paul Mara .20 .50
CT17 David Legwand .30 .75
CT18 Eric Lindros .40 1.00
CT19 Peter Forsberg 1.00 2.50
CT20 Ray Bourque .60 1.50
CT21 Teemu Selanne .40 1.00
CT22 John LeClair .40 1.00
CT23 Dominik Hasek .75 2.00
CT24 Martin Brodeur 1.00 2.50
CT25 Tony Amonte .30 .75
CT26 Keith Tkachuk .40 1.00
CT27 Patrick Roy 2.00 5.00
CT28 Pavel Bure .40 1.00
CT29 Paul Kariya .40 1.00
CT30 Curtis Joseph .40 1.00

1999-00 Upper Deck Fantastic Finishers

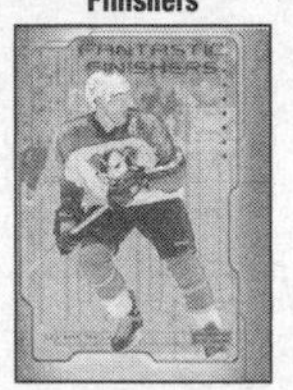

Randomly inserted in Series One packs at the rate of 1:11, this 15-card set features a gray and white border and blue foil stamping. Silver and gold parallels were also created and inserted randomly. Silver parallels were limited to 100 serial numbered sets. Gold parallels were numbered 1/1 and are unpriced due to scarcity.

COMPLETE SET (15) 12.00 25.00
*SILVER/100: 20X TO 50X BASIC INSERTS
UNPRICED GOLD PRINT RUN 1
FF1 Brett Hull .60 1.50
FF2 John LeClair .50 1.25
FF3 Eric Lindros .50 1.25
FF4 Jaromir Jagr .75 2.00
FF5 Sergei Samsonov .40 1.00
FF6 Teemu Selanne .50 1.25
FF7 Alexei Yashin .40 1.00
FF8 Keith Tkachuk .50 1.25
FF9 Pavel Bure .50 1.25
FF10 Peter Forsberg 1.25 3.00
FF11 Brendan Shanahan .50 1.25
FF12 Tony Amonte .40 1.00
FF13 Paul Kariya .50 1.25
FF14 Steve Yzerman 2.50 6.00
FF15 Joe Sakic 1.00 2.50

1999-00 Upper Deck Game Jerseys

Randomly inserted in Series One packs at the rate of 1:287, this 18-card set features player action shots with a swatch of a game worn jersey in the shape of the NHL logo. A special Wayne Gretzky jersey card was released that features a swatch of an NHL jersey and a CHL jersey which are sequentially numbered to 99, and a special Nagano Olympic Gretzky jersey was issued as well. Several players have signed versions that are sequentially numbered to 25.

BH Brett Hull 10.00 25.00
DH Dominik Hasek 12.50 30.00
EL Eric Lindros 8.00 20.00
JJ Jaromir Jagr 12.50 30.00
JL John LeClair 8.00 20.00
JS Joe Sakic 15.00 40.00
MB Martin Brodeur 20.00 50.00
MM Mike Modano 10.00 25.00
PF Peter Forsberg 15.00 40.00
PR Patrick Roy 20.00 50.00
RB Ray Bourque 15.00 40.00
SF Sergei Fedorov 10.00 25.00
SS Sergei Samsonov 8.00 20.00
SY Steve Yzerman 20.00 50.00
TS Teemu Selanne 10.00 25.00
WG1 Wayne Gretzky 30.00 80.00
WG2 W.Gretzky Dual/99 300.00 600.00
WG3 Wayne Gretzky Nagano 125.00 300.00
BHS B.Hull AU/25 150.00 300.00
RBS R.Bourque AU/25 150.00 300.00
SYS S.Yzerman AU/25 250.00 500.00
WGS1 W.Gretzky AU/25 400.00 800.00

1999-00 Upper Deck Game Jerseys Series II

Randomly inserted in Series Two packs at the rate of 1:287, this 16-card set features player action photography coupled with a swatch of a game worn jersey. A special Canadian jersey card was issued for Steve Yzerman, and several players have autographed versions that are sequentially numbered to 25.

AM Al MacInnis 8.00 20.00
CJ Curtis Joseph 8.00 20.00
DH Dominik Hasek 15.00 40.00
EB Ed Belfour 8.00 20.00
JJ Jaromir Jagr 12.00 30.00
JL John LeClair 8.00 20.00
JR Jeremy Roenick 10.00 25.00
JT Joe Thornton 12.00 30.00
MB Martin Brodeur 20.00 50.00
PF Peter Forsberg 12.00 30.00
PK Paul Kariya 10.00 25.00
PR Patrick Roy 20.00 50.00
SF Sergei Fedorov 10.00 25.00
SY Steve Yzerman 20.00 50.00
TS Teemu Selanne 12.00 30.00
WG Wayne Gretzky 30.00 80.00
CJS C.Joseph AU/25 100.00 200.00
EBS E.Belfour AU/25 100.00 200.00
SYC Steve Yzerman CAN 20.00 50.00
SYS S.Yzerman AU/25 250.00 500.00
WGS W.Gretzky AU/25 400.00 800.00

1999-00 Upper Deck Game Jersey Patch

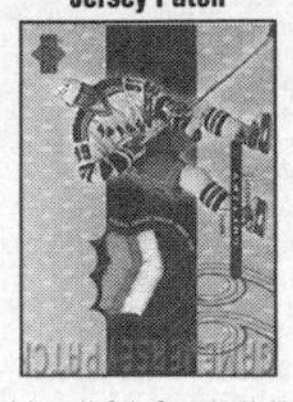

Randomly inserted in Series One packs, this 17-card set features premium swatches of game jersey patches. Unpriced 1/1 parallels also exist.

WG1P Wayne Gretzky 400.00 800.00
WG2P Wayne Gretzky 400.00 800.00
BHP Brett Hull 125.00 300.00
DHP Dominik Hasek 125.00 300.00
ELP Eric Lindros 75.00 200.00
JJP Jaromir Jagr 125.00 300.00
JLP John LeClair 75.00 200.00
JSP Joe Sakic 125.00 300.00
MBP Martin Brodeur 150.00 400.00
MMP Mike Modano 100.00 250.00
PFP Peter Forsberg 125.00 300.00
PRP Patrick Roy 150.00 400.00
RBP Ray Bourque 125.00 300.00
SFP Sergei Fedorov 125.00 300.00
SSP Sergei Samsonov 75.00 200.00
SYP Steve Yzerman 150.00 400.00
TSP Teemu Selanne 75.00 200.00

1999-00 Upper Deck Game Jersey Patch Series II

Randomly inserted in Series Two packs at a rate of 1:7500, this 14-card set features premium swatches of game used jersey patches. Unpriced 1/1 parallels also exist.

CJP Curtis Joseph 100.00 250.00
DHP Dominik Hasek 125.00 300.00
EBP Ed Belfour 100.00 250.00
JJP Jaromir Jagr 125.00 300.00
JLP John LeClair 60.00 150.00
JTP Joe Thornton 100.00 250.00
KTP Keith Tkachuk 60.00 150.00
MBP Martin Brodeur 150.00 350.00
PFP Peter Forsberg 100.00 250.00
PKP Paul Kariya 75.00 200.00
PRP Patrick Roy 150.00 400.00
SFP Sergei Fedorov 75.00 200.00
SYP Steve Yzerman 150.00 400.00
WGP Wayne Gretzky 400.00 800.00

1999-00 Upper Deck Game Pads

Randomly inserted in Series Two packs at the rate of 1:5000, this single card issue features a swatch of Curtis Joseph game used goalie pads.

CJGP Curtis Joseph 20.00 50.00

1999-00 Upper Deck Gretzky Profiles

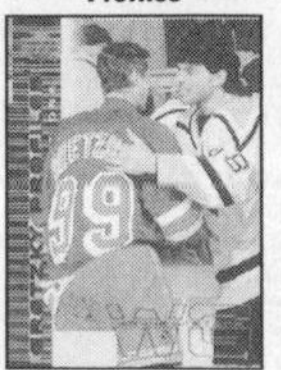

Randomly inserted in Series One Hobby packs at the rate of 1:23, this 10-card set pays tribute to the career of Wayne Gretzky. Both silver and gold parallels were also created. Silver parallels were serial numbered to 100, and gold to 1/1. Gold parallels not priced due to scarcity.

COMPLETE SET (10) 40.00 80.00
COMMON GRETZKY (GP1-GP10) 4.00 10.00
*SILVER/100: 3X TO 8X BASIC INSERTS 30.00 80.00
UNPRICED GOLD PRINT RUN 1

1999-00 Upper Deck Headed for the Hall

Randomly seeded in Series Two pack, this 15-card set features top NHL players on an all silver foil card stock with foil stamp highlights. Silver and gold parallels were also created. Silver parallels were limited to 100 serial numbered sets. Unpriced gold parallels were numbered 1/1.

COMPLETE SET (15) 20.00 40.00
*SILVER STARS: 8X TO 20X BASIC CARDS
UNPRICED GOLD 1/1's EXIST
HOF1 Wayne Gretzky 5.00 12.00
HOF2 Dominik Hasek 1.50 4.00
HOF3 Ray Bourque 1.25 3.00
HOF4 Steve Yzerman 4.00 10.00
HOF5 Jaromir Jagr 1.25 3.00
HOF6 Brett Hull 1.00 2.50
HOF7 Eric Lindros .75 2.00
HOF8 Adam Oates .60 1.50
HOF9 Brian Leetch .75 2.00
HOF10 Patrick Roy 4.00 10.00
HOF11 Mark Messier .75 2.00
HOF12 Luc Robitaille .60 1.50
HOF13 Joe Sakic 1.50 4.00
HOF14 Chris Chelios .75 2.00
HOF15 Curtis Joseph .75 2.00

1999-00 Upper Deck Ice Gallery

Randomly inserted in Series Two packs at the rate of 1:72, this 10-card set features silver foil borders along the top and the two sided of the card with blue foil highlights. Silver and gold parallels were also created and inserted randomly. Silver parallels were limited to 100 serial numbered sets. Unpriced gold parallels were numbered 1/1.

COMPLETE SET (10) 40.00 80.00
*SILVER/100: 4X TO 10X BASIC INSERTS
UNPRICED GOLD PRINT RUN 1
IG1 Jaromir Jagr 4.00 10.00
IG2 Paul Kariya 3.00 8.00
IG3 Peter Forsberg 6.00 15.00
IG4 Dominik Hasek 5.00 12.00
IG5 Patrick Roy 12.50 30.00
IG6 Teemu Selanne 3.00 8.00
IG7 Eric Lindros 3.00 8.00
IG8 Patrik Stefan 4.00 10.00
IG9 Steve Kariya 3.00 8.00
IG10 Pavel Bure 3.00 8.00

1999-00 Upper Deck Marquee Attractions

Randomly seeded in Series One packs, this 15-card set features an all silver foil card stock with color player photography and blue foil highlights. Silver and gold parallels were also created. Silver parallels were limited to 100 serial numbered sets. Gold parallels were numbered 1/1 and are not priced.

COMPLETE SET (15) 12.00 25.00
*SILVER/100: 20X TO 50X BSIC INSERTS
UNPRICED GOLD PRINT RUN 1
MA1 Ray Bourque .75 2.00
MA2 Paul Kariya .50 1.25
MA3 Eric Lindros .50 1.25
MA4 Jaromir Jagr .75 2.00
MA5 Dominik Hasek 1.00 2.50
MA6 Patrick Roy 2.50 6.00
MA7 Alexei Yashin .40 1.00
MA8 Mats Sundin .50 1.25
MA9 Steve Yzerman 2.50 6.00
MA10 Pavel Bure .50 1.25
MA11 Vincent Lecavalier .50 1.25
MA12 Teemu Selanne .50 1.25
MA13 Mike Modano .75 2.00
MA14 Keith Tkachuk .50 1.25
MA15 Peter Forsberg 1.25 3.00

1999-00 Upper Deck New Ice Age

Randomly seeded in Series One packs, this 20-card set features foil card stock with color player photography and highlights several players ready to take the NHL in the 21st Century. Silver and gold parallels were also created. Silver parallels were limited to 100 serial numbered sets. Unpriced gold parallels were numbered 1/1.

COMPLETE SET (20) 20.00 40.00
*SILVER/100: 10X TO 25X BASIC INSERTS
UNPRICED GOLD PRINT RUN 1
N1 Jaromir Jagr 1.50 4.00
N2 Paul Kariya 1.00 2.50
N3 Sergei Samsonov .75 2.00
N4 Vadim Sharifijanov .40 1.00
N5 Ty Jones .40 1.00
N6 Teemu Selanne 1.00 2.50
N7 Martin Brodeur 2.50 6.00
N8 David Legwand .75 2.00
N9 Vincent Lecavalier 1.00 2.50
N10 Paul Mara .75 2.00
N11 Jean-Marc Pelletier .40 1.00
N12 Jean-Sebastien Giguere .75 2.00
N13 Marian Hossa 1.00 2.50
N14 Milan Hejduk 1.00 2.50
N15 Chris Drury .75 2.00
N16 Rico Fata .40 1.00
N17 Patrik Elias .75 2.00
N18 Eric Brewer .75 2.00
N19 Joe Thornton 1.50 4.00
N20 J-P Dumont .75 2.00

1999-00 Upper Deck NHL Scrapbook

Randomly seeded in Series Two packs, this 15-card set features a shadowed background with a full color player photograph and gold foil highlights. Silver and gold parallels were also created. Silver parallels were limited to 100 serial numbered sets. Gold parallels were numbered 1/1 and are not priced due to scarcity.

COMPLETE SET (15) 12.00 25.00
*SILVER/100: 10X TO 25X BASIC CARDS
UNPRICED GOLD PRINT RUN 1
SB1 Patrick Roy 2.50 6.00
SB2 Ray Bourque .75 2.00
SB3 Steve Yzerman 2.50 6.00
SB4 Jaromir Jagr .75 2.00
SB5 Paul Kariya .60 1.50
SB6 Peter Forsberg 1.25 3.00
SB7 Pavel Bure .60 1.50
SB8 Curtis Joseph .60 1.50
SB9 Brett Hull .60 1.50
SB10 Eric Lindros .60 1.50
SB11 Teemu Selanne .60 1.50
SB12 Brendan Shanahan .60 1.50
SB13 John LeClair .60 1.50
SB14 Steve Kariya .60 1.50
SB15 Patrik Stefan .75 2.00

1999-00 Upper Deck PowerDeck Inserts

Randomly inserted in Series 1 Hobby packs at the rate of 1:23 for base cards and one in 288 for Gretzky SP cards, this 9-card set is an actual CD-ROM that contains footage, interviews, and a photo gallery that can be viewed with a PC.

COMPLETE SET (9) 75.00 150.00
PD1 Dominik Hasek 3.00 8.00
PD2 Paul Kariya 2.00 5.00
PD3 Jaromir Jagr 2.50 6.00
PD4 Steve Yzerman 8.00 20.00
PD5 Patrick Roy 8.00 20.00
PD6 Brett Hull 2.00 5.00
PD7 Wayne Gretzky 12.50 25.00
PD8 Wayne Gretzky SP 30.00 80.00
PD9 Wayne Gretzky SP 30.00 80.00

1999-00 Upper Deck Sixth Sense

Randomly inserted in Series Two packs, this 20-card set highlights top players on a "framed" card stock with foil stamp highlights. Silver and gold parallels were also created. Silver parallels were limited to 100 serial numbered sets. Gold parallels were numbered 1/1 and are not priced due to scarcity.

COMPLETE SET (20) 10.00 25.00
*SILVER/100: 25X TO 60X BASIC INSERTS
UNPRICED GOLD PRINT RUN 1

SS1 Paul Kariya .40 1.00
SS2 Patrick Roy 2.00 5.00
SS3 Brett Hull .50 1.25
SS4 Eric Lindros .40 1.00
SS5 Sergei Samsonov .40 1.00
SS6 Peter Forsberg 1.00 2.50
SS7 Patrik Stefan .60 1.50
SS8 Steve Yzerman 2.00 5.00
SS9 Jaromir Jagr .60 1.50
SS10 David Legwand .40 1.00
SS11 Steve Kariya .50 1.25
SS12 Tim Connolly .40 1.00
SS13 Pavel Bure .40 1.00
SS14 Brendan Shanahan .40 1.00
SS15 Martin Brodeur 1.00 2.50
SS16 Dominik Hasek .75 2.00
SS17 Mats Sundin .40 1.00
SS18 Vincent Lecavalier .40 1.00
SS19 Keith Tkachuk .40 1.00
SS20 Mike Modano .60 1.50

1999-00 Upper Deck Ultimate Defense

Randomly inserted in Series Two packs, this 10-card set features top goalies on an all foil card with color borders to match each respective goalie's team colors and blue foil highlights. Silver and gold parallels were also created. Silver parallels were limited to 100 serial numbered sets. Gold parallels were numbered 1/1 and are not priced due to scarcity.

COMPLETE SET (10) 10.00 20.00
*SILVER/100: 12X TO 30X BASIC INSERTS
UNPRICED GOLD PRINT RUN 1
UD1 Byron Dafoe .60 1.50
UD2 Dominik Hasek 1.50 4.00
UD3 Patrick Roy 4.00 10.00
UD4 Chris Osgood .60 1.50
UD5 Ed Belfour .75 2.00
UD6 Roman Turek .60 1.50
UD7 Mike Richter .75 2.00
UD8 Nikolai Khabibulin .60 1.50
UD9 Martin Brodeur 2.00 5.00
UD10 Curtis Joseph .60 1.50

1999-00 Upper Deck Arena Giveaways

These promo cards were issued in various NHL cities and included 6 cards per team. Manufacturers Topps, Upper Deck, and Pacific were all represented with two cards per team set. The cards have the word's Tomorrow's Stars across the top, and are numbered with a team-coded prefix. They are extremely difficult to find in the secondary market, and command strong prices. Only the Upper Deck cards are listed below as the other cards can be found with the manufacturer's listings.

COMPLETE SET (56) 15.00 40.00
AM1 Ladislav Kohn .20 .50
AM2 Mike Leclerc .20 .50
AT1 Patrik Stefan .40 1.00
AT2 Shean Donovan .20 .50
BB1 Jonathan Girard .40 1.00
BB2 Sergei Samsonov 1.25 3.00
BS1 Maxim Afinogenov .75 2.00
BS2 Cory Sarich .20 .50
CA1 Alex Tanguay 1.25 3.00
CA2 Chris Drury 1.25 3.00
CB1 J-P Dumont .40 1.00
CB2 Bryan McCabe .20 .50
CF1 Robyn Regehr .20 .50
CF2 Derek Morris .40 1.00
CH1 Dave Tanabe .20 .50
CH2 Jeff O'Neill .40 1.00
DR1 Jiri Fischer .40 1.00
DR2 Darryl Laplante .20 .50
DS1 Brenden Morrow .75 2.00
DS2 Jamie Langenbrunner .40 1.00
EO1 Paul Comrie .20 .50
EO2 Boyd Devereaux .20 .50
FP1 Ivan Novoseltsev .40 1.00
FP2 Mark Parrish .40 1.00
LK1 Frantisek Kaberle .20 .50
LK2 Aki Berg .20 .50
MC1 Mike Ribeiro .20 .50
MC2 Arron Asham .20 .50
ND1 Scott Gomez .75 2.00
ND2 Sheldon Souray .20 .50
NI1 Roberto Luongo 2.50 6.00
NI2 Tim Connolly .75 2.00
NP1 David Legwand .40 1.00
NP2 Randy Robitaille .20 .50
NR1 Michael York .40 1.00
NR2 Manny Malhotra .20 .50
OS1 Mike Fisher .40 1.00
OS2 Chris Phillips .20 .50
PC1 Trevor Letowski .75 2.00
PC2 Shane Doan .75 2.00
PF1 Simon Gagne 1.25 3.00
PF2 Daymond Langkow .40 1.00
PP1 Andrew Ference .20 .50
PP2 Michal Rozsival .20 .50
SB1 Jochen Hecht .40 1.00
SB2 Michal Handzus .75 2.00
SS1 Brad Stuart .40 1.00
SS2 Jeff Friesen .40 1.00
TL1 Paul Mara .20 .50
TL2 Andrei Zyuzin .20 .50
TM1 Nikolai Antropov .75 2.00
TM2 Danny Markov .20 .50
VC1 Steve Kariya .75 2.00
VC2 Peter Schaefer .20 .50
WC1 Jeff Halpern .40 1.00
WC2 Alexei Tezikov .20 .50

2006-07 Upper Deck Arena Giveaways

ANA1 Corey Perry 2.00 5.00
ANA2 Teemu Selanne 2.50 6.00
ANA3 Andy McDonald 1.50 4.00
ANA4 Scott Niedermayer 1.50 4.00
ANA5 Jean-Sebastien Giguere 2.50 6.00
ANA6 Chris Pronger 2.00 5.00
ATL1 Marian Hossa 2.00 5.00
ATL2 Slava Kozlov 1.50 4.00
ATL3 Bobby Holik 1.50 4.00
ATL4 Ilya Kovalchuk 3.00 8.00
ATL5 Steve Rucchin 1.50 4.00
ATL6 Kari Lehtonen 2.50 6.00
BOS1 Brad Boyes 1.50 4.00
BOS2 Hannu Toivonen 2.50 6.00
BOS3 Patrice Bergeron 2.00 5.00
BOS4 Zdeno Chara 1.50 4.00
BOS5 Marc Savard 1.50 4.00
BOS6 Glen Murray 1.50 4.00
BUF1 Ryan Miller 2.50 6.00
BUF2 Thomas Vanek 2.00 5.00
BUF3 Daniel Briere 2.00 5.00
BUF4 Jason Pominville .75 2.00
BUF5 Maxim Afinogenov 1.50 4.00
BUF6 Chris Drury 2.00 5.00
CAR1 Eric Staal 2.00 5.00
CAR2 Cam Ward 4.00 10.00
CAR3 Justin Williams 1.50 4.00
CAR4 Erik Cole 1.50 4.00
CAR5 Andrew Ladd 1.50 4.00
CAR6 Rod Brind'Amour 2.00 5.00
CGY1 Jarome Iginla 4.00 10.00
CGY2 Dion Phaneuf 3.00 8.00
CGY3 Chuck Kobasew 1.50 4.00
CGY4 Alex Tanguay 2.00 5.00
CGY5 Daymond Langkow 1.50 4.00
CGY6 Miikka Kiprusoff 2.50 6.00
CHI1 Tuomo Ruutu 1.50 4.00
CHI2 Martin Havlat 2.00 5.00
CHI3 Brent Seabrook 1.50 4.00
CHI4 Adrian Aucoin 1.50 4.00
CHI5 Bryan Smolinski .75 2.00
CHI6 Nikolai Khabibulin 2.50 6.00
CLB1 Rick Nash 2.50 6.00
CLB2 Pascal LeClaire 2.50 6.00
CLB3 Adam Foote .75 2.00
CLB4 Fredrik Modin 1.50 4.00
CLB5 Gilbert Brule 1.50 4.00
CLB6 Sergei Fedorov 2.50 6.00
COL1 Jose Theodore 2.50 6.00
COL2 Wojtek Wolski 1.50 4.00
COL3 John-Michael Liles 1.50 4.00
COL4 Joe Sakic 5.00 12.00
COL5 Marek Svatos 1.50 4.00
COL6 Milan Hejduk 2.00 5.00
DAL1 Brenden Morrow 2.00 5.00
DAL2 Jussi Jokinen 1.50 4.00
DAL2 Jussi Jokinen 1.50 4.00
DAL3 Sergei Zubov 1.50 4.00
DAL3 Sergei Zubov 1.50 4.00
DAL4 Mike Modano 2.50 6.00
DAL4 Mike Modano 2.50 6.00
DAL5 Eric Lindros 2.50 6.00
DAL5 Eric Lindros 2.50 6.00
DAL6 Marty Turco 2.00 5.00
DET1 Kris Draper 1.50 4.00
DET2 Dominik Hasek 3.00 8.00
DET3 Chris Chelios 1.25 3.00
DET4 Henrik Zetterberg 2.50 6.00
DET5 Nicklas Lidstrom 2.50 6.00
DET6 Pavel Datsyuk 2.50 6.00
EDM1 Ales Hemsky 1.50 4.00
EDM2 Fernando Pisani 1.50 4.00
EDM3 Jarret Stoll 1.50 4.00
EDM4 Ryan Smyth 2.00 5.00
EDM5 Joffrey Lupul 1.50 4.00
EDM6 Dwayne Roloson 2.00 5.00
FLA1 Jay Bouwmeester 1.50 4.00
FLA2 Nathan Horton 1.50 4.00
FLA3 Stephen Weiss .75 2.00
FLA4 Olli Jokinen 1.50 4.00
FLA5 Ed Belfour 6.00 15.00
FLA6 Todd Bertuzzi 2.00 5.00
LAK1 Alexander Frolov 1.50 4.00
LAK2 Lubomir Visnovsky 1.50 4.00
LAK3 Dustin Brown 1.50 4.00
LAK4 Rob Blake 2.00 5.00
LAK5 Craig Conroy 1.50 4.00
LAK6 Mike Cammalleri 1.50 4.00
MIN1 Marian Gaborik 4.00 10.00
MIN2 Pierre-Marc Bouchard 1.50 4.00
MIN3 Brian Rolston 1.50 4.00
MIN4 Pavol Demitra 1.50 4.00
MIN5 Mark Parrish 1.50 4.00
MIN6 Manny Fernandez 2.50 6.00
NJD1 Martin Brodeur 8.00 20.00
NJD2 Brian Gionta 1.50 4.00
NJD3 Zach Parise 2.00 5.00
NJD4 Brian Rafalski 1.50 4.00
NJD5 Scott Gomez 1.50 4.00
NJD6 Patrik Elias 1.50 4.00
NSH1 Tomas Vokoun 2.00 5.00
NSH2 David Legwand 1.50 4.00
NSH3 Kimmo Timonen 1.50 4.00
NSH4 Paul Kariya 2.50 6.00
NSH5 Jason Arnott 1.50 4.00
NSH6 Steve Sullivan 1.50 4.00
NYI1 Rick DiPietro 2.50 6.00
NYI2 Jeff Tambellini 1.50 4.00
NYI3 Jason Blake 1.50 4.00
NYI4 Trent Hunter 1.50 4.00
NYI5 Alexei Yashin 1.50 4.00
NYI6 Miroslav Satan 1.50 4.00
NYR1 Jaromir Jagr 4.00 10.00
NYR2 Petr Prucha 1.50 4.00
NYR3 Martin Straka 1.50 4.00
NYR4 Henrik Lundqvist 4.00 10.00
NYR5 Michael Nylander 1.50 4.00
NYR6 Brendan Shanahan 2.50 6.00
OTT1 Jason Spezza 2.50 6.00
OTT2 Chris Phillips 1.50 4.00
OTT3 Dany Heatley 2.50 6.00
OTT4 Wade Redden 1.50 4.00
OTT5 Martin Gerber 2.50 6.00
OTT6 Daniel Alfredsson 2.00 5.00
PHI1 Peter Forsberg 4.00 10.00
PHI2 Robert Esche 2.00 5.00
PHI3 Joni Pitkanen 1.50 4.00
PHI4 Simon Gagne 2.50 6.00
PHI5 Antero Niittymaki 2.50 6.00
PHI6 Jeff Carter 2.50 6.00
PHX1 Shane Doan 2.00 5.00
PHX2 Ladislav Nagy 1.50 4.00
PHX3 Ed Jovanovski 1.50 4.00
PHX4 Jeremy Roenick 2.50 6.00
PHX5 Owen Nolan 2.00 5.00
PHX6 Curtis Joseph 2.50 6.00
PIT1 Sidney Crosby 12.00 30.00
PIT2 Colby Armstrong 1.50 4.00
PIT3 Sergei Gonchar .75 2.00
PIT4 Ryan Malone 1.50 4.00
PIT5 Mark Recchi 1.50 4.00
PIT6 Marc-Andre Fleury 2.50 6.00
SJS1 Joe Thornton 4.00 10.00
SJS2 Vesa Toskala 2.00 5.00
SJS3 Steve Bernier 1.50 4.00
SJS4 Patrick Marleau 2.00 5.00
SJS5 Evgeni Nabokov 2.00 5.00
SJS6 Jonathan Cheechoo 2.50 6.00
STL1 Keith Tkachuk 2.00 5.00
STL2 Barret Jackman .75 2.00
STL3 Lee Stempniak 1.50 4.00
STL4 Manny Legace 2.00 5.00
STL5 Bill Guerin 1.50 4.00
STL6 Doug Weight 1.50 4.00
TBL1 Martin St. Louis 2.50 6.00
TBL2 Vaclav Prospal 1.50 4.00
TBL3 Ruslan Fedotenko 1.50 4.00
TBL4 Vincent Lecavalier 2.50 6.00
TBL5 Marc Denis 2.00 5.00
TBL6 Brad Richards 2.50 6.00
TOR1 Mats Sundin 2.50 6.00
TOR2 Darcy Tucker 1.50 4.00
TOR3 Alexander Steen 2.00 5.00
TOR4 Andrew Raycroft 2.00 5.00
TOR5 Michael Peca 1.50 4.00
TOR6 Bryan McCabe 1.50 4.00
VAN1 Markus Naslund 2.50 6.00
VAN2 Henrik Sedin 1.50 4.00
VAN3 Roberto Luongo 5.00 12.00
VAN4 Brendan Morrison 1.50 4.00
VAN5 Trevor Linden .75 2.00
VAN6 Daniel Sedin 1.50 4.00
WSH1 Shaone Morrisonn .75 2.00
WSH2 Alexander Semin 1.25 3.00
WSH3 Alexander Ovechkin 10.00 25.00
WSH4 Richard Zednik .75 2.00
WSH5 Dainius Zubrus 1.50 4.00
WSH6 Olaf Kolzig 3.00 8.00

1999-00 Upper Deck Sobey's Memorial Cup

Released by Upper Deck in conjunction with Sobey's grocery stores and Kraft, this 16-card set features players and designs from the 1999-2000 Upper Deck NHL Prospects set and pays tribute the 2000 Memorial Cup tournament. The cards were available in 4-card cello packs over a four-week period at Sobey's stores in the Halifax area. The cards mirror the UD CHL series issued earlier that year, but feature several small design changes, including the addition of a Sobey's logo.

COMPLETE SET (16) 16.00 25.00
1 Alexei Volkov .75 2.00
2 Justin Papineau .75 2.00
3 Michael Henrich .40 1.00
4 Kris Beech .75 2.00
5 Mark Bell 1.50 4.00
6 Andrei Shefer .40 1.00
7 Pavel Brendl .75 2.00
8 Blake Robson .40 1.00
9 Ben Knopp .40 1.00
10 Maxime Ouellet 1.50 4.00
11 Thatcher Bell .40 1.00
12 Brian Finley .75 2.00
13 Jared Aulin 1.50 4.00
14 Jared Newman .40 1.00
15 Brad Boyes 4.00 10.00
16 Miguel Delisle .40 1.00

2000-01 Upper Deck

Released as a 440-card set, Upper Deck is comprised of 180 veteran cards and 50 short printed prospect cards (181-230) in series one, and 180 veteran cards and 30 short printed prospect cards (411-440) in series two. Base cards have full color action photography and foil highlights. Upper Deck was packaged in 24-pack boxes with packs containing 10 cards and carried a suggested retail price of $2.00.

COMPLETE SET (230) 200.00 400.00
COMP.SER.1 (230) 125.00 250.00
COMP.SER.1 w/o SP's (180) 15.00 30.00
COMP.SER.2 (210) 100.00 200.00
COMP.SER.2 w/o SP's (180) 10.00 25.00
1 Paul Kariya .20 .50
2 Steve Rucchin .02 .10
3 Oleg Tverdovsky .02 .10
4 Mike Leclerc .02 .10
5 Ladislav Kohn .02 .10
6 Guy Hebert .15 .40
7 Dean Sylvester .02 .10
8 Andrew Brunette .15 .40
9 Ray Ferraro .02 .10
10 Donald Audette .02 .10
11 Damian Rhodes .02 .10
12 Patrik Stefan .02 .10
13 Joe Thornton .30 .75
14 Brian Rolston .02 .10
15 John Grahame .15 .40
16 Jason Allison .02 .10
17 Kyle McLaren .02 .10
18 Andre Savage .02 .10
19 Martin Biron .15 .40
20 Doug Gilmour .15 .40
21 Chris Gratton .02 .10
22 Miroslav Satan .15 .40
23 Maxim Afinogenov .02 .10
24 Dimitri Kalinin .02 .10
25 Oleg Saprykin .02 .10
26 Valeri Bure .02 .10
27 Derek Morris .02 .10
28 Marc Savard .02 .10
29 Clarke Wilm .02 .10
30 Fred Brathwaite .15 .40
31 Ron Francis .15 .40
32 Sami Kapanen .02 .10
33 Bates Battaglia .02 .10
34 Arturs Irbe .15 .40
35 Dave Tanabe .02 .10
36 Rod Brind'Amour .15 .40
37 Michal Grosek .02 .10
38 Steve Sullivan .02 .10
39 Eric Daze .15 .40
40 Bryan McCabe .02 .10
41 Michael Nylander .02 .10
42 Alexei Zhamnov .02 .10
43 Milan Hejduk .20 .50
44 Ray Bourque .40 1.00
45 Patrick Roy 1.00 2.50
46 Peter Forsberg .50 1.25
47 Martin Skoula .02 .10
48 Shjon Podein .02 .10
49 Aaron Miller .02 .10
50 Espen Knutsen .02 .10
51 Jamie Pushor .02 .10
52 Kevyn Adams .02 .10
53 Marc Denis .15 .40
54 Ron Tugnutt .15 .40
55 Mike Modano .30 .75
56 Joe Nieuwendyk .15 .40
57 Mike Keane .02 .10
58 Darryl Sydor .02 .10
59 Brenden Morrow .15 .40
60 Jere Lehtinen .15 .40
61 Derian Hatcher .02 .10
62 Brendan Shanahan .20 .50
63 Sergei Fedorov .30 .75
64 Darren McCarty .02 .10
65 Tomas Holmstrom .02 .10
66 Chris Osgood .15 .40
67 Nicklas Lidstrom .20 .50
68 Ryan Smyth .15 .40
69 Igor Ulanov .02 .10
70 Tommy Salo .15 .40
71 Ethan Moreau .02 .10
72 Daniel Cleary .02 .10
73 Bill Guerin .15 .40
74 Pavel Bure .20 .50
75 Ray Whitney .15 .40
76 Lance Pitlick .02 .10
77 Trevor Kidd .15 .40
78 Mike Wilson .02 .10
79 Ivan Novoseltsev .15 .40
80 Luc Robitaille .15 .40
81 Stephane Fiset .15 .40
82 Rob Blake .15 .40
83 Jozef Stumpel .02 .10
84 Craig Johnson .02 .10
85 Glen Murray .02 .10
86 Kelly Buchberger .02 .10
87 Manny Fernandez .15 .40
88 Stacy Roest .02 .10
89 Andy Sutton .02 .10
90 Scott Pellerin .02 .10
91 Jim Dowd .02 .10
92 Dainius Zubrus .02 .10
93 Brian Savage .02 .10
94 Martin Rucinsky .02 .10
95 Craig Darby .02 .10
96 Jose Theodore .25 .60
97 David Legwand .15 .40
98 Rob Valicevic .02 .10
99 Randy Robitaille .02 .10
100 Mike Dunham .15 .40
101 Kimmo Timonen .02 .10
102 Scott Gomez .02 .10
103 Petr Sykora .02 .10
104 Alexander Mogilny .15 .40
105 John Madden .02 .10
106 Jason Arnott .02 .10
107 Sergei Brylin .02 .10
108 Scott Stevens .15 .40
109 Tim Connolly .02 .10
110 Mariusz Czerkawski .02 .10
111 Zdeno Chara .02 .10
112 Kenny Jonsson .02 .10
113 Claude Lapointe .02 .10
114 Theo Fleury .02 .10
115 Mike Richter .20 .50
116 Mike York .02 .10
117 Jan Hlavac .15 .40
118 Adam Graves .02 .10
119 Mark Messier .20 .50
120 Marian Hossa .20 .50
121 Daniel Alfredsson .15 .40
122 Mike Fisher .15 .40
123 Patrick Lalime .15 .40
124 Wade Redden .02 .10
125 Shawn McEachern .02 .10
126 John LeClair .20 .50
127 Mark Recchi .15 .40
128 Brian Boucher .20 .50
129 Simon Gagne .20 .50
130 Eric Desjardins .15 .40
131 Rick Tocchet .15 .40
132 Jeremy Roenick .25 .60
133 Travis Green .02 .10
134 Trevor Letowski .02 .10
135 Teppo Numminen .02 .10
136 Shane Doan .02 .10
137 Mike Sullivan .02 .10
138 Jaromir Jagr .30 .75
139 Robert Lang .02 .10
140 Jan Hrdina .02 .10
141 Matthew Barnaby .02 .10
142 Jean-Sebastien Aubin .15 .40
143 Jiri Slegr .02 .10
144 Owen Nolan .15 .40
145 Jeff Friesen .02 .10
146 Patrick Marleau .15 .40
147 Brad Stuart .15 .40
148 Steve Shields .15 .40
149 Todd Harvey .02 .10
150 Pavol Demitra .15 .40
151 Chris Pronger .15 .40
152 Scott Young .02 .10
153 Todd Reirden .02 .10
154 Roman Turek .15 .40
155 Marty Reasoner .15 .40
156 Mike Johnson .02 .10
157 Todd Warriner .02 .10
158 Paul Mara .02 .10
159 Dan Cloutier .15 .40
160 Fredrik Modin .02 .10
161 Curtis Joseph .20 .50
162 Steve Thomas .02 .10
163 Darcy Tucker .02 .10
164 Yanic Perreault .02 .10
165 Sergei Berezin .02 .10
166 Dimitri Yushkevich .02 .10
167 Markus Naslund .20 .50
168 Andrew Cassels .02 .10
169 Todd Bertuzzi .20 .50
170 Felix Potvin .20 .50
171 Ed Jovanovski .15 .40
172 Trent Klatt .02 .10
173 Adam Oates .15 .40
174 Chris Simon .02 .10
175 Richard Zednik .02 .10
176 Calle Johansson .02 .10
177 Andrei Nikolishin .02 .10
178 Jeff Halpern .02 .10
179 Steve Yzerman CL .20 .50
180 Curtis Joseph CL .15 .40
181 Eric Nickulas RC 2.00 5.00
182 Serge Aubin RC 2.00 5.00
183 Keith Aldridge RC 2.00 5.00
184 Mike Minard RC 2.00 5.00
185 Steven Reinprecht RC 2.00 5.00
186 David Gosselin RC 2.00 5.00
187 Andrew Berenzweig 2.00 5.00
188 Willie Mitchell RC 2.00 5.00
189 Colin White RC 2.00 5.00
190 Petr Mika RC 2.00 5.00
191 Steve Valiquette RC 2.00 5.00
192 Kyle Freadrich RC 2.00 5.00
193 Rich Parent RC 2.00 5.00
194 Greg Andrusak RC 2.00 5.00
195 Brent Sopel RC 2.00 5.00
196 Matt Pettinger RC 2.00 5.00
197 Chris Nielsen RC 2.00 5.00
198 Dany Heatley RC 40.00 80.00
199 Matt Zultek RC 2.00 5.00
200 Dmitri Afanasenkov RC 2.00 5.00
201 Tyler Bouck RC 1.25 3.00
202 Jonas Andersson RC 2.00 5.00
203 Marc-Andre Thinel RC 2.00 5.00
204 Jaroslav Svoboda RC 2.00 5.00
205 Josef Vasicek RC 2.00 5.00
206 Andrew Raycroft RC 5.00 12.00
207 Juraj Kolnik RC 2.00 5.00
208 Zdenek Blatny RC 2.00 5.00
209 Sebastien Caron RC 1.50 4.00
210 Michael Ryder RC 8.00 20.00
211 Jason Jaspers RC 2.00 5.00
212 Pavel Brendl 2.00 5.00
213 Milan Kraft 2.00 5.00
214 Justin Williams RC 3.00 8.00
215 Andreas Karlsson 2.00 5.00
216 Herbert Vasiljevs RC 2.00 5.00
217 Sergei Vyshedkevich RC 2.00 5.00
218 Johnathan Aitken RC 2.00 5.00
219 Brandon Smith RC 2.00 5.00
220 Jeff Cowan RC 2.00 5.00
221 Steve Brule RC 2.00 5.00
222 Johan Witehall RC 2.00 5.00
223 Jani Hurme RC 3.00 8.00
224 Jean-Guy Trudel RC 2.00 5.00
225 Kaspars Astashenko RC 2.00 5.00
226 Scott Hartnell RC 3.00 8.00
227 Dieter Kochan RC 2.00 5.00
228 Rostislav Klesla RC 3.00 8.00
229 Marian Gaborik RC 40.00 80.00
230 Alfie Michaud 2.00 5.00
231 Teemu Selanne .20 .50
232 Matt Cullen .02 .10
233 German Titov .02 .10
234 Vitali Vishnevski .02 .10
235 Pavel Trnka .02 .10
236 Marty McInnis .02 .10
237 Hnat Domenichelli .02 .10
238 Per Svartvadet .02 .10
239 Steve Guolla .02 .10
240 Frantisek Kaberle .02 .10
241 Steve Staios .02 .10
242 Byron Dafoe .15 .40
243 Peter Popovic .02 .10
244 Paul Coffey .20 .50
245 Sergei Samsonov .15 .40
246 Andrei Kovalenko .02 .10
247 Shawn Bates .02 .10
248 Dominik Hasek .40 1.00
249 Stu Barnes .02 .10
250 Curtis Brown .02 .10
251 Alexei Zhitnik .02 .10
252 Jay McKee .02 .10
253 Vaclav Varada .02 .10
254 Jarome Iginla .25 .60
255 Phil Housley .02 .10
256 Cory Stillman .02 .10
257 Mike Vernon .02 .10
258 Jeff Shantz .02 .10
259 Brad Werenka .02 .10
260 Jeff O'Neill .02 .10
261 Martin Gelinas .02 .10
262 Tommy Westlund .02 .10
263 Steve Halko .02 .10
264 Sandis Ozolinsh .02 .10
265 Rob DiMaio .02 .10
266 Tony Amonte .15 .40
267 Jocelyn Thibault .15 .40
268 Boris Mironov .02 .10
269 Dean McAmmond .02 .10
270 Jean-Yves Leroux .02 .10
271 Valeri Zelepukin .02 .10
272 Nolan Pratt .02 .10
273 Joe Sakic .40 1.00
274 Chris Drury .15 .40
275 Alex Tanguay .15 .40
276 Adam Deadmarsh .02 .10
277 Stephane Yelle .02 .10
278 Ron Tugnutt .15 .40
279 Geoff Sanderson .02 .10
280 Steve Heinze .02 .10
281 Jean-Luc Grand-Pierre .02 .10
282 Robert Kron .02 .10
283 Kevin Dineen .02 .10
284 Brett Hull .25 .60
285 Sergei Zubov .02 .10
286 Jamie Langenbrunner .02 .10
287 Ed Belfour .20 .50
288 Roman Lyashenko .02 .10
289 Ted Donato .02 .10
290 Martin LaPointe .02 .10
291 Chris Chelios .20 .50
292 Slava Kozlov .02 .10
293 Steve Yzerman 1.00 2.50
294 Larry Murphy .02 .10
295 Brent Gilchrist .02 .10
296 Doug Weight .15 .40
297 Eric Brewer .02 .10
298 Todd Marchant .02 .10
299 Tom Poti .15 .40
300 Mike Grier .02 .10
301 Georges Laraque .02 .10
302 Igor Larionov .02 .10
303 Roberto Luongo .25 .60
304 Olli Jokinen .02 .10
305 Viktor Kozlov .15 .40
306 Robert Svehla .02 .10
307 Mike Sillinger .02 .10
308 Jere Karalahti .02 .10
309 Zigmund Palffy .15 .40
310 Mattias Norstrom .02 .10
311 Bryan Smolinski .02 .10
312 Jamie Storr .15 .40
313 Ian Laperriere .02 .10
314 Manny Fernandez .15 .40
315 Sergei Krivokrasov .02 .10
316 Darryl Laplante .02 .10
317 Sean O'Donnell .02 .10
318 Scott Pellerin .02 .10
319 Saku Koivu .20 .50
320 Sergei Zholtok .02 .10
321 Jeff Hackett .15 .40
322 Eric Weinrich .02 .10
323 Karl Dykhuis .02 .10
324 Benoit Brunet .02 .10
325 Cliff Ronning .02 .10
326 Patric Kjellberg .02 .10
327 Drake Berehowsky .02 .10
328 Vitali Yachmenev .02 .10
329 Tomas Vokoun .15 .40
330 Greg Johnson .02 .10
331 Patrik Elias .15 .40
332 Bobby Holik .02 .10
333 Randy McKay .02 .10
334 Brian Rafalski .02 .10
335 Martin Brodeur .50 1.25
336 Sergei Brylin .02 .10
337 Brad Isbister .15 .40
338 Roman Hamrlik .02 .10
339 John Vanbiesbrouck .15 .40
340 Dave Scatchard .02 .10
341 Oleg Kvasha .02 .10
342 Mark Parrish .02 .10
343 Petr Nedved .02 .10
344 Brian Leetch .15 .40
345 Radek Dvorak .02 .10
346 Vladimir Malakhov .02 .10
347 Valeri Kamensky .02 .10
348 Rich Pilon .02 .10
349 Radek Bonk .02 .10
350 Vaclav Prospal .02 .10
351 Jason York .02 .10
352 Andreas Dackell .02 .10
353 Magnus Arvedson .02 .10
354 Rob Zamuner .02 .10
355 Daymond Langkow .15 .40
356 Keith Primeau .02 .10
357 Dan McGillis .02 .10
358 Andy Delmore .02 .10
359 Jody Hull .02 .10
360 Luke Richardson .02 .10
361 Joe Juneau .02 .10
362 Mika Alatalo .02 .10
363 Keith Tkachuk .20 .50
364 Radoslav Suchy .02 .10
365 Louie DeBrusk .02 .10
366 Sean Burke .15 .40
367 Martin Straka .02 .10
368 Alexei Kovalev .15 .40
369 Alexei Morozov .02 .10
370 Josef Beranek .02 .10
371 Milan Kraft .02 .10

372 Darius Kasparaitis .02 .10
373 Vincent Damphousse .02 .10
374 Mike Ricci .02 .10
375 Scott Thornton .02 .10
376 Niklas Sundstrom .02 .10
377 Marco Sturm .15 .40
378 Jeff Norton .02 .10
379 Pierre Turgeon .15 .40
380 Al MacInnis .15 .40
381 Jochen Hecht .02 .10
382 Sean Hill .02 .10
383 Pavol Demitra .15 .40
384 Michal Handzus .02 .10
385 Mike Eastwood .02 .10
386 Vincent Lecavalier .20 .50
387 Brian Holzinger .02 .10
388 Pavel Kubina .02 .10
389 Andrei Zyuzin .02 .10
390 Wayne Primeau .02 .10
391 Mats Sundin .20 .50
392 Gary Roberts .02 .10
393 Igor Korolev .02 .10
394 Shayne Corson .02 .10
395 Tomas Kaberle .02 .10
396 Cory Cross .02 .10
397 Peter Schaefer .02 .10
398 Adrian Aucoin .02 .10
399 Brendan Morrison .15 .40
400 Daniel Sedin .02 .10
401 Donald Brashear .02 .10
402 Henrik Sedin .02 .10
403 Joe Murphy .02 .10
404 Steve Konowalchuk .02 .10
405 Joe Reekie .02 .10
406 Sergei Gonchar .02 .10
407 Peter Bondra .20 .50
408 Olaf Kolzig .15 .40
409 Steve Yzerman CL 1.00 2.50
410 Mark Messier CL .20 .50
411 Rick DiPietro RC 8.00 20.00
412 Michel Riesen RC 2.00 5.00
413 Reto Von Arx RC 2.00 5.00
414 Martin Havlat RC 6.00 15.00
415 Matt Elich RC 2.00 5.00
416 Jonas Ronnqvist RC 2.00 5.00
417 Jason Labarbera RC 3.00 8.00
418 Marc Moro RC 2.00 5.00
419 Mark Smith RC 2.00 5.00
420 Petr Hubacek RC 2.00 5.00
421 Niclas Wallin RC 2.00 5.00
422 Brian Swanson RC 2.00 5.00
423 Petteri Nummelin RC 2.50 6.00
424 Alexandre Boikov RC 2.00 5.00
425 Ossi Vaananen RC 2.00 5.00
426 Roman Simicek RC 2.00 5.00
427 Greg Classen RC 2.00 5.00
428 Marty Turco RC 5.00 12.00
429 Shane Hnidy RC 2.00 5.00
430 Lubomir Visnovsky RC 3.00 8.00
431 Bryce Salvador RC 2.00 5.00
432 Lubomir Sekeras RC 2.00 5.00
433 David Aebischer RC 5.00 12.00
434 Peter Ratchuk RC 2.00 5.00
435 Roman Cechmanek RC 2.00 5.00
436 Eric Belanger RC 2.00 5.00
437 Alexander Kharitonov RC 2.00 5.00
438 Jeff Bateman RC 2.00 5.00
439 Damian Surma RC 2.00 5.00
440 Jordan Krestanovich RC 2.00 5.00

2000-01 Upper Deck Exclusives Tier 1

Randomly inserted in Hobby packs, this 440-card set parallels the base set enhanced with silver foil. Each card is sequentially numbered to 100.

*EXC.TIER 1 STARS: 12X TO 30X BASIC CARDS
*EXC.TIER 1 SP's: 1.25X TO 2.5X BASIC CARDS
*EXC.TIER 1 SP RC's: 1X TO 2.5X
198 Dany Heatley 50.00 120.00

2000-01 Upper Deck Exclusives Tier 2

Randomly inserted in Hobby packs, this 440-card set parallels the base set enhanced with gold foil. Each card is sequentially numbered to 25.

*EXC.TIER 2 STARS: 60X TO 150X BASIC CARDS
*EXC.TIER 2 SP's: 2X TO 5X BASIC CARDS
*EXC.TIER 2 SP RC's: 1.5X TO 4X

2000-01 Upper Deck 500 Goal Club

Randomly inserted in various Upper Deck product packs, this set pays tribute to the members of the esteemed 500-goal club. Each card contains a swatch of a game worn jersey or stick in the shape of the NHL logo. Card numbers on the back carry a "500" prefix. Dale Hawerchuk and Mike Gartner were randomly found in Black Diamond and only 650 unsigned versions were produced. Pat Verbeek and Mario Lemieux were randomly available in SPx with a total of 800 unsigned cards produced of each and 25 serial-numbered autographed versions. Phil Esposito was randomly available in Upper Deck Ice with 450 unsigned cards and 25 serial-numbered signed cards produced. Dave Andreychuk and John Bucyk were randomly available in Upper Deck Legends with a total of 900 unsigned cards produced between the two players and 25 serial-numbered autographed versions of each. Frank Mahovlich and Lanny McDonald were randomly available in Upper Deck MVP with 600 unsigned cards produced and 25 serial-numbered autographed versions. Mark Messier was available in Upper Deck Vintage, 300 total cards were issued for the unsigned version, and 25 autographed copies were issued. Jari Kurri, Joe Mullen, Mark Messier, and Wayne Gretzky were all randomly available in Upper Deck Series I packs. A serial-numbered autographed version of each was also produced. Mark Messier was the only player inserted in series 2 packs.

500DA Dave Andreychuk J 12.50 30.00
500DA Dave Andreychuk AU/25 150.00 300.00
500DH Dale Hawerchuk J 15.00 40.00
500DH Dale Hawerchuk AU/25 150.00 300.00
500FM Frank Mahovlich S 50.00 100.00
500FM Frank Mahovlich AU/25 200.00 400.00
500JK Jari Kurri J 40.00 100.00
500JK Jari Kurri AU/25 400.00 600.00
500JM Joe Mullen J 40.00 100.00
500JM Joe Mullen AU/25 100.00 250.00
500LM Lanny McDonald S 30.00 80.00
500LM Lanny McDonald AU/25 350.00 500.00
500MG Michel Goulet AU/25 100.00 250.00
500MG Michel Goulet S 12.50 30.00
500ML Mario Lemieux J 150.00 300.00
500ML M.Lemieux AU/25 800.00 1000.00
500MM Mark Messier J 30.00 80.00
500MM Mark Messier AU/25 400.00 600.00
500PE Phil Esposito/450 S 15.00 40.00
500PE Phil Esposito AU/25 200.00 400.00
500PV Pat Verbeek J 12.50 30.00
500PV Pat Verbeek AU/25 125.00 250.00
500WG Wayne Gretzky J 75.00 200.00
500WG Wayne Gretzky AU/25 1000.00 2000.00
500JBU John Bucyk AU/25 200.00 400.00
500JBU John Bucyk S 12.50 30.00
500MGA Mike Gartner J 12.50 30.00
500MGA Mike Gartner AU/25 300.00 500.00

2000-01 Upper Deck All-Star Class

COMPLETE SET (10) 8.00 15.00
STATED ODDS 1:23 SERIES 2
A1 Teemu Selanne .60 1.50
A2 Valeri Bure .60 1.50
A3 Milan Hejduk .60 1.50
A4 Mike Modano 1.00 2.50
A5 Pavel Bure 1.00 2.50
A6 Marian Hossa .60 1.50
A7 Brian Boucher .60 1.50
A8 Keith Tkachuk .60 1.50
A9 Jaromir Jagr 1.25 3.00
A10 Curtis Joseph .60 1.50

2000-01 Upper Deck Dignitaries

COMPLETE SET (10) 20.00 40.00
STATED ODDS 1:23 SERIES 1
D1 Paul Kariya .75 2.00
D2 Ray Bourque 1.50 4.00
D3 Patrick Roy 4.00 10.00
D4 Brett Hull 1.00 2.50
D5 Steve Yzerman 4.00 10.00
D6 Pavel Bure 1.00 2.50
D7 Luc Robitaille .75 2.00
D8 Brian Leetch .75 2.00
D9 Jaromir Jagr 1.25 3.00
D10 Mark Messier 1.00 2.50

2000-01 Upper Deck e-Cards

Randomly inserted in packs at the rate of 1:12, this twelve card set features an interactive number that can be entered at the Upper Deck website to see if it evolves. Cards can evolve into Game Jersey Cards sequentially numbered to 300, Autographed Cards sequentially numbered to 200, or Autographed Game Jersey Cards sequentially numbered to 50.

EC1 Sergei Samsonov .20 .50
EC2 Brett Hull .30 .75
EC3 Steve Yzerman 1.25 3.00
EC4 Pavel Bure .40 1.00
EC5 John LeClair .30 .75
EC6 Curtis Joseph .25 .60
EC7 Martin Brodeur .60 1.50
EC8 Mark Messier .30 .75
EC9 Chris Osgood .20 .50
EC10 Mike Richter .25 .60
EC11 Ray Bourque .50 1.25
EC12 Jeremy Roenick .30 .75

2000-01 Upper Deck e-Card Prizes

Winning e-Cards may be redeemed for Game Jersey Cards sequentially numbered to 300, Autographed Cards sequentially numbered to 200, or Autographed Game Jersey Cards sequentially numbered to 50. The original checklist contained a Mark Messier jersey card which was later found to be non-existent.

ABH Brett Hull AU 25.00 60.00
ACJ Curtis Joseph AU 25.00 60.00
ACO Chris Osgood AU 12.50 30.00
AJL John LeClair AU 10.00 25.00
AJR Jeremy Roenick AU 15.00 40.00
AMB Martin Brodeur AU 40.00 100.00
AMM Mark Messier AU 75.00 150.00
AMR Mike Richter AU 12.50 30.00
APB Pavel Bure AU 12.50 30.00
ARB Ray Bourque AU 30.00 80.00
ASS Sergei Samsonov AU 12.50 30.00
ASY Steve Yzerman AU 30.00 80.00
EBH Brett Hull Jersey 12.50 30.00
ECJ Curtis Joseph JSY 10.00 25.00
ECO Chris Osgood JSY 10.00 25.00
EJL John LeClair JSY 10.00 25.00
EJR Jeremy Roenick JSY 12.50 30.00
EMB Martin Brodeur JSY 25.00 60.00
EMR Mike Richter JSY 10.00 25.00
EPB Pavel Bure JSY 10.00 25.00
ERB Ray Bourque JSY 20.00 50.00
ESS Sergei Samsonov JSY 10.00 25.00
ESY Steve Yzerman JSY 15.00 40.00
SRB Ray Bourque GJ/AU 75.00 200.00
SEBH B.Hull GJ/AU 60.00 150.00
SECJ C.Joseph GJ/AU 20.00 50.00
SECO Chris Osgood GJ/AU 20.00 50.00
SEJL John LeClair GJ/AU 20.00 50.00
SEJR Jeremy Roenick GJ/AU 20.00 50.00
SEMB Martin Brodeur GJ/AU 100.00 200.00
SEMM Mark Messier GJ/AU 25.00 60.00
SEMR Mike Richter GJ/AU 20.00 50.00
SEPB P.Bure GJ/AU 20.00 50.00
SESS S.Samsonov GJ/AU 20.00 50.00
SESY S.Yzerman GJ/AU 75.00 200.00

2000-01 Upper Deck Fantastic Finishers

COMPLETE SET (11) 15.00 30.00
STATED ODDS 1:23 SERIES 1
FF1 Paul Kariya .75 2.00
FF2 Teemu Selanne .75 2.00
FF3 Peter Forsberg 2.00 5.00
FF4 Brett Hull 1.00 2.50
FF5 Steve Yzerman 4.00 10.00
FF6 Pavel Bure 1.00 2.50
FF7 John LeClair 1.00 2.50
FF8 Keith Tkachuk .75 2.00
FF9 Jaromir Jagr 1.25 3.00
FF10 Owen Nolan .60 1.50
FF11 Mats Sundin .75 2.00

2000-01 Upper Deck Frozen in Time

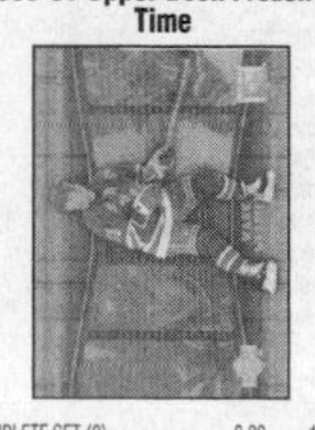

COMPLETE SET (8) 8.00 15.00
STATED ODDS 1:12 SERIES 2
FT1 Doug Gilmour .60 1.50
FT2 Ray Bourque 1.25 3.00
FT3 Brett Hull .75 2.00
FT4 Steve Yzerman 3.00 8.00
FT5 Mark Messier .75 2.00
FT6 Jeremy Roenick .75 2.00
FT7 Jaromir Jagr 1.00 2.50
FT8 Curtis Joseph .60 1.50

2000-01 Upper Deck Fun-Damentals

COMPLETE SET (9) 10.00 20.00
STATED ODDS 1:10 SERIES 2
F1 Paul Kariya .60 1.50
F2 Dominik Hasek 1.25 3.00
F3 Peter Forsberg 1.50 4.00
F4 Mike Modano 1.00 2.50
F5 Sergei Fedorov 1.25 3.00
F6 Pavel Bure .75 2.00
F7 Marian Hossa .60 1.50
F8 Jaromir Jagr 1.00 2.50
F9 Curtis Joseph .60 1.50

2000-01 Upper Deck Game Jerseys

Randomly inserted in packs at the rate of 1:287, this 25-card set features full color player photography and a swatch of a game worn jersey.

BS Brendan Shanahan Ser.1 8.00 20.00
BS Brendan Shanahan Ser.2 8.00 20.00
CP Chris Pronger Ser.1 8.00 20.00
JJ Jaromir Jagr Ser.2 12.50 30.00
JJ Jaromir Jagr Ser.1 12.50 30.00
JL John LeClair Ser.1 8.00 20.00
JN Joe Nieuwendyk Ser.1 8.00 20.00
JS Joe Sakic Ser.2 12.50 30.00
JS Joe Sakic Ser.1 12.50 30.00
JT Joe Thornton Ser.1 10.00 25.00
KT Keith Tkachuk Ser.1 8.00 20.00
MB Martin Brodeur Ser.1 25.00 60.00
MS Mats Sundin Ser.2 8.00 20.00
MS Mats Sundin Ser.1 8.00 20.00
PB Pavel Bure Ser.2 8.00 20.00
PE Peter Bondra Ser.1 8.00 20.00
PF Peter Forsberg Ser.2 15.00 40.00
PK Paul Kariya Ser.1 8.00 20.00
PK Paul Kariya Ser.2 8.00 20.00
SF Sergei Fedorov Ser.2 10.00 25.00
SF Sergei Fedorov Ser.1 10.00 25.00
TS Teemu Selanne Ser.1 8.00 20.00
TS Teemu Selanne Ser.2 8.00 20.00
WG Wayne Gretzky Ser.1 30.00 80.00
WG Wayne Gretzky AS Ser.2 30.00 80.00

2000-01 Upper Deck Game Jersey Autographs

Randomly inserted in Hobby packs at the rate of 1:287, this 18-card set features color action photography coupled with both and authentic player signature and a swatch of a game worn jersey.

HBH Brett Hull Ser.1 40.00 100.00
HCO Chris Osgood Ser.2 10.00 25.00
HJH Jochen Hecht Ser.1 10.00 25.00
HJL John LeClair Ser.2 15.00 40.00
HJR Jeremy Roenick Ser.2 25.00 60.00
HJT Joe Thornton Ser.2 25.00 60.00
HKT Keith Tkachuk Ser.2 15.00 40.00
HMA Martin Biron Ser.1 10.00 25.00
HMR Mike Richter Ser.2 15.00 40.00
HMY Mike York Ser.1 10.00 25.00
HNL Nicklas Lidstrom Ser.1 15.00 40.00
HPB Pavel Bure Ser.1 15.00 40.00
HSG Scott Gomez Ser.1 10.00 25.00
HSS Sergei Samsonov Ser.2 10.00 25.00
HSS Sergei Samsonov Ser.1 10.00 25.00
HSY Steve Yzerman Ser.2 75.00 150.00
HSY Steve Yzerman Ser.1 75.00 150.00
HTC Tim Connolly Ser.1 10.00 25.00

2000-01 Upper Deck Game Jersey Autographs Canadian

Randomly inserted in Canadian Hobby packs at the rate of 1:287, this set features four of Canada's own bright stars. Each card contains both an authentic player signature and a swatch of a game worn jersey.

CCJ Curtis Joseph Ser.1 15.00 40.00
CJT Jose Theodore Ser.2 25.00 60.00
CMM Mark Messier Ser.2 100.00 250.00
CRL Roberto Luongo Ser.1 15.00 40.00

2000-01 Upper Deck Game Jersey Autographs Exclusives

Randomly inserted in packs, this 36-card set partially paralleled the basic jersey set in an autographed version that was hand numbered to 25. The Gretzky, Hecht, and Richter cards were issued as exchanges.

NOT PRICED DUE TO SCARCITY
EBH Brett Hull Ser.1
EBS Brendan Shanahan Ser.1
ECP Chris Pronger Ser.1
EJH Jochen Hecht Ser.1
EJJ Jaromir Jagr Ser.1
EJL John LeClair Ser.1
EJN Joe Nieuwendyk Ser.1
EJS Joe Sakic Ser.1
EJT Joe Thornton Ser.1
EKT Keith Tkachuk Ser.1
EMB Martin Brodeur Ser.1
EMB Martin Biron Ser.1
EMS Mats Sundin Ser.1
EMY Mike York Ser.1
ENL Nicklas Lidstrom Ser.1
EPB Pavel Bure Ser.1
EPE Peter Bondra Ser.1
EPK Paul Kariya Ser.1
ESF Sergei Fedorov Ser.1
ESG Scott Gomez Ser.1
ESY Steve Yzerman Ser.1
ETC Tim Connolly Ser.1
ETS Teemu Selanne Ser.1
EWG Wayne Gretzky Ser.1
ESCO Chris Osgood Ser.2
ESJL John LeClair Ser.2
ESJN Joe Nieuwendyk Ser.2
ESJR Jeremy Roenick Ser.2
ESJT Joe Thornton Ser.2
ESKT Keith Tkachuk Ser.2
ESMR Mike Richter Ser.2
ESPB Pavel Bure Ser.2
ESSF Sergei Fedorov Ser.2
ESSS Sergei Samsonov Ser.2
ESSY Steve Yzerman Ser.2
ESWG Wayne Gretzky AS Ser.2

2000-01 Upper Deck Game Jersey Combos

Randomly inserted in series one packs, this 15-card set features a dual player card design with two swatches of game worn jerseys. Each card is sequentially numbered to 50.

DBF Raymond Bourque 100.00 200.00
Peter Forsberg
DBH Ed Belfour 60.00 150.00
Dominik Hasek
DCL Tim Connolly 20.00 50.00
Roberto Luongo
DFB Sergei Fedorov 30.00 80.00
Pavel Bure
DGB Scott Gomez 75.00 200.00
Martin Brodeur
DGH Wayne Gretzky 175.00 350.00
Brett Hull
DGL W.Gretzky/M.Lemieux 200.00 400.00
DGM Wayne Gretzky 125.00 300.00
Mark Messier
DJL Jaromir Jagr 100.00 250.00
Mario Lemieux
DLC John LeClair 20.00 50.00
Bobby Clarke
DSJ Mats Sundin 20.00 50.00
Curtis Joseph
DSK Teemu Selanne 20.00 50.00
Payl Kariya
DTS Joe Thornton 20.00 50.00
Sergei Samsonov
DYL Mike York 12.00 30.00
Brian Leetch
DYS S.Yzrmn/B.Shnahan 150.00 300.00

2000-01 Upper Deck Game Jersey Doubles

Randomly inserted in series two packs, this 10-card set features top NHL players in action coupled with two swatches of game worn jerseys. Each jersey swatch represents either more than one team played on, or a team and an all-star jersey. Each card is sequentially numbered to 100.

DBH Brett Hull 20.00 50.00
DBS Brendan Shanahan 12.50 30.00
DDH Dominik Hasek 25.00 60.00
DFP Felix Potvin 12.50 30.00
DJJ Jaromir Jagr 30.00 80.00
DJN Joe Nieuwendyk 12.50 30.00
DJS Joe Sakic 30.00 80.00
DPB Pavel Bure 12.50 30.00
DTS Teemu Selanne 12.50 30.00
DWG Wayne Gretzky AS 125.00 300.00

2000-01 Upper Deck Game Jersey Patches

Randomly inserted in series one packs at the rate of 1:2500 and series two packs at the rate of one in 5000, this 36-card set features premium swatches of game worn jersey emblems and patches.

BHP Brett Hull Ser.1 50.00 125.00
BSP Brendan Shanahan Ser.1 40.00 100.00
CJP Curtis Joseph Ser.1 40.00 100.00
DHP Dominik Hasek Ser.1 50.00 125.00
ELP Eric Lindros Ser.1 40.00 100.00
JHP Jochen Hecht Ser.1 30.00 80.00
JJP Jaromir Jagr Ser.1 60.00 150.00
JLP John LeClair Ser.1 40.00 100.00
JSP Joe Sakic Ser.1 75.00 200.00
JTP Joe Thornton Ser.1 75.00 200.00
KTP Keith Tkachuk Ser.1 40.00 100.00
MBP Martin Brodeur Ser.1 125.00 300.00
MMP Mark Messier Ser.1 40.00 100.00
MYP Mike York Ser.1 30.00 80.00
PBP Pavel Bure Ser.1 40.00 100.00
PBS Brendan Shanahan Ser.2 40.00 100.00
PCO Chris Osgood Ser.2 30.00 80.00
PFP Peter Forsberg Ser.1 60.00 150.00
PJJ Jaromir Jagr Ser.2 60.00 150.00
PJL John LeClair Ser.2 40.00 100.00
PKP Paul Kariya Ser.1 40.00 100.00
PKT Keith Tkachuk Ser.2 40.00 100.00
PPF Peter Forsberg Ser.2 75.00 200.00
PPK Paul Kariya Ser.2 40.00 100.00
PRP Patrick Roy Ser.1 125.00 300.00
PSF Sergei Fedorov Ser.2 60.00 150.00
PSY Steve Yzerman Ser.2 75.00 200.00
PTS Teemu Selanne Ser.2 40.00 100.00
PWG W.Gretzky AS Ser.2 250.00 500.00
SFP Sergei Fedorov Ser.1 50.00 125.00
SGP Scott Gomez Ser.1 30.00 80.00
SSP Sergei Samsonov Ser.1 30.00 80.00
SYP Steve Yzerman Ser.1 75.00 200.00
TCP Tim Connolly Ser.1 30.00 80.00
TSP Teemu Selanne Ser.1 40.00 100.00
WGP Wayne Gretzky Ser.1 200.00 500.00

2000-01 Upper Deck Game Jersey Patch Autographs Exclusives

Randomly inserted in packs, this 28-card set parallels the base Game Jersey Patches set enhanced with player autographs. Series 1 cards are numbered one of one, series 2 cards are numbered to the featured player's jersey number. Cards with print runs under 25 are not priced due to scarcity.

BHP Brett Hull Ser.1
BSP Brendan Shanahan Ser.1
CJP Curtis Joseph Ser.1
DHP Dominik Hasek Ser.1
ELP Eric Lindros Ser.1
JHP Jochen Hecht Ser.1
JJP Jaromir Jagr Ser.1
JLP John LeClair Ser.1
JSP Joe Sakic Ser.1
JTP Joe Thornton Ser.1
KTP Keith Tkachuk Ser.1
MBP Martin Brodeur Ser.1
MMP Mark Messier Ser.1
MYP Mike York Ser.1
PBP Pavel Bure Ser.1
PFP Peter Forsberg Ser.1
PKP Paul Kariya Ser.1
PRP Patrick Roy Ser.1
SFP Sergei Fedorov Ser.1
SGP Scott Gomez Ser.1
SSP Sergei Samsonov Ser.1
SYP Steve Yzerman Ser.1
TCP Tim Connolly Ser.1
TSP Teemu Selanne Ser.1
WGP Wayne Gretzky Ser.1
PSJL John LeClair/10
PSSY Steve Yzerman/19
PSWG W.Gretzky AS/99 500.00 1200.00

2000-01 Upper Deck Game Jersey Patch Exclusives Series II

Randomly inserted in series two packs, this 13-card set features premium swatches of game worn player jerseys. Each card is sequentially numbered to 25. These cards are not priced due to scarcity.

EBS Brendan Shanahan
ECO Chris Osgood
EJJ Jaromir Jagr
EJL John LeClair
EKT Keith Tkachuk
EPF Peter Forsberg
EPK Paul Kariya
ESF Sergei Fedorov
ESY Steve Yzerman
ETS Teemu Selanne
EWG Wayne Gretzky AS

2000-01 Upper Deck Gate Attractions

COMPLETE SET (11) 15.00 30.00
STATED ODDS 1:11 SERIES 1
GA1 Paul Kariya .75 2.00
GA2 Dominik Hasek 1.25 3.00
GA3 Ray Bourque 1.25 3.00
GA4 Patrick Roy 3.00 8.00
GA5 Mike Modano .75 2.00
GA6 Steve Yzerman 3.00 8.00
GA7 Pavel Bure .75 2.00
GA8 Martin Brodeur 1.50 4.00
GA9 John LeClair .75 2.00
GA10 Jaromir Jagr 1.00 2.50
GA11 Curtis Joseph .75 2.00

2000-01 Upper Deck Lord Stanley's Heroes

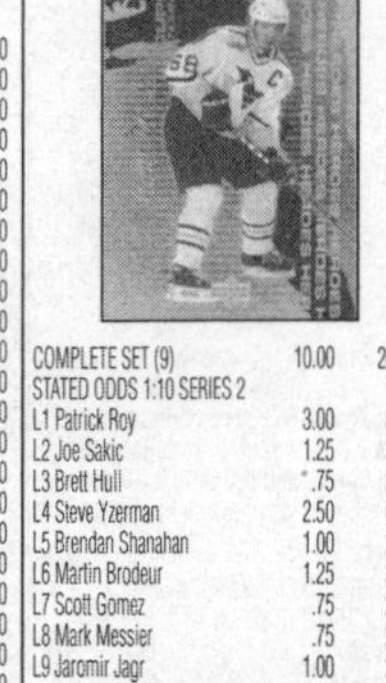

COMPLETE SET (9) 10.00 20.00
STATED ODDS 1:10 SERIES 2
L1 Patrick Roy 3.00 8.00
L2 Joe Sakic 1.25 3.00
L3 Brett Hull .75 2.00
L4 Steve Yzerman 2.50 6.00
L5 Brendan Shanahan 1.00 2.50
L6 Martin Brodeur 1.25 3.00
L7 Scott Gomez .75 2.00
L8 Mark Messier .75 2.00
L9 Jaromir Jagr 1.00 2.50

2000-01 Upper Deck Number Crunchers

COMPLETE SET (10) 10.00 20.00
STATED ODDS 1:9 SERIES 1
NC1 Peter Forsberg 1.50 4.00
NC2 Brendan Shanahan 1.00 2.50
NC3 John LeClair .75 2.00
NC4 Eric Lindros 1.00 2.50
NC5 Keith Tkachuk .60 1.50
NC6 Jeremy Roenick .75 2.00
NC7 Jaromir Jagr 1.00 2.50
NC8 Owen Nolan .60 1.50
NC9 Chris Pronger .60 1.50
NC10 Mark Messier .75 2.00

2000-01 Upper Deck Profiles

COMPLETE SET (10) 12.00 25.00
STATED ODDS 1:23 SERIES 2
P1 Dominik Hasek 1.50 4.00
P2 Joe Sakic 1.50 4.00
P3 Mike Modano 1.25 3.00
P4 Brendan Shanahan 1.25 3.00
P5 Pavel Bure 1.00 2.50
P6 Martin Brodeur 2.00 5.00
P7 John LeClair 1.00 2.50
P8 Jaromir Jagr 1.25 3.00
P9 Mats Sundin .75 2.00
P10 Olaf Kolzig .60 1.50

2000-01 Upper Deck Prospects In Depth

COMPLETE SET (10) 10.00 20.00
STATED ODDS 1:11 SERIES 1
P1 Patrik Stefan 1.00 2.50
P2 Maxim Afinogenov 1.00 2.50
P3 Alex Tanguay 1.00 2.50
P4 Brenden Morrow 1.00 2.50
P5 Scott Gomez 1.00 2.50
P6 Tim Connolly 1.00 2.50
P7 Mike York 1.00 2.50
P8 Simon Gagne 1.25 3.00
P9 Brian Boucher 1.25 3.00
P10 Jochen Hecht 1.00 2.50

2000-01 Upper Deck Rise to Prominence

COMPLETE SET (8) 5.00 12.00
STATED ODDS 1:12 SERIES 2
RP1 Paul Kariya .60 1.50
RP2 Pavel Bure .75 2.00
RP3 Jose Theodore .75 2.00

Card	Low	High
RP4 Scott Gomez	.50	1.25
RP5 Marian Hossa	.60	1.50
RP6 Brian Boucher	.50	1.25
RP7 Roman Turek	.50	1.25
RP8 Vincent Lecavalier	.60	1.50

2000-01 Upper Deck Signs of Greatness

Randomly inserted in series two packs, this nine card set features an all white borderless card stock. The player's name appears along the top of the card in gray tone, and full color action photography is centered on the card. Each card is autographed and numbered out of 250. The Amonte card has yet to be confirmed and it is believed that he never signed.

Card	Low	High
SBO Bobby Orr	100.00	250.00
SCJ Curtis Joseph	20.00	40.00
SKT Keith Tkachuk	20.00	40.00
SMB Martin Brodeur	30.00	80.00
SMY Mike York	12.50	30.00
SPB Pavel Brendl	12.50	30.00
SSS Sergei Samsonov	20.00	40.00
SWG Wayne Gretzky	100.00	250.00

2000-01 Upper Deck Skilled Stars

Card	Low	High
COMPLETE SET (20)	15.00	30.00
STATED ODDS 1:5 SERIES 1		
SS1 Paul Kariya	.50	1.25
SS2 Teemu Selanne	.50	1.25
SS3 Dominik Hasek	1.00	2.50
SS4 Valeri Bure	.40	1.00
SS5 Patrick Roy	2.50	6.00
SS6 Peter Forsberg	1.25	3.00
SS7 Ed Belfour	.50	1.25
SS8 Mike Modano	.75	2.00
SS9 Sergei Fedorov	1.00	2.50
SS10 Brendan Shanahan	.75	2.00
SS11 Pavel Bure	.60	1.50
SS12 Zigmund Palffy	.40	1.00
SS13 Martin Brodeur	1.25	3.00
SS14 Tim Connolly	.40	1.00
SS15 John LeClair	.60	1.50
SS16 Jeremy Roenick	.60	1.50
SS17 Jaromir Jagr	.75	2.00
SS18 Vincent Lecavalier	.50	1.25
SS19 Mats Sundin	.50	1.25
SS20 Olaf Kolzig	.40	1.00

2000-01 Upper Deck Triple Threat

Randomly inserted in series two pack at the rate of 1:72, this 10-card set pairs three players of the same position that dominate year after year. Base cards feature a doctored action shot where three players are present doing what they do best. Cards are all silver foil and are enhanced with light blue foil highlights.

Card	Low	High
COMPLETE SET (10)	30.00	80.00
TT1 Paul Kariya	4.00	10.00
Scott Gomez		
Milan Hejduk		
TT2 Roy/Brodeur/Belfour	10.00	25.00
TT3 Peter Forsberg	6.00	15.00
Mats Sundin		
Henrik Sedin		
TT4 Brett Hull	4.00	10.00
Jeremy Roenick		
John LeClair		
TT5 Yzerman/Sakic/Modano	8.00	20.00
TT6 Brendan Shanahan	4.00	10.00
Keith Tkachuk		
Mark Messier		
TT7 Pavel Bure	3.00	8.00
Sergei Samsonov		
Sergei Fedorov		
TT8 Raymond Bourque	4.00	10.00
Chris Pronger		
Rob Blake		
TT9 Jaromir Jagr	4.00	10.00
Teemu Selanne		
Milan Kraft		
TT10 Roman Turek	4.00	10.00
Dominik Hasek		
Olaf Kolzig		

2000-01 Upper Deck UD Flashback

Randomly inserted in series two packs at the rate of 1:12, this eight card set features players in action on a hololoil version of the 1990-91 Upper Deck card design.

Card	Low	High
COMPLETE SET (8)	3.00	8.00
UD1 Teemu Selanne	.60	1.50
UD2 Tony Amonte	.40	1.00
UD3 Milan Hejduk	.60	1.50
UD4 Scott Gomez	.40	1.00
UD5 Tim Connolly	.40	1.00
UD6 John LeClair	.75	2.00
UD7 Keith Tkachuk	.60	1.50
UD8 Olaf Kolzig	.40	1.00

2001-02 Upper Deck

This 441-card set was released in two different series of 231 cards and 210 cards. Series I was released in late October 2001 and Series II was released in early February 2002. Both series carried an SRP of $2.99 for an 8-card pack. Series I consisted of 180 regular base cards and 51 Young Guns subset shortprints. Series II consisted of 180 regular base cards and 30 Young Guns shortprints. Series II Young Guns had two different versions of each card which were the same value. Shortprints for both series were inserted at 1:4. The Jared Aulin card (#220B) was printed in error and is known to have been inserted into some packs, though only a handful have been verified therefore it is not priced. The "B" suffix on the Aulin card is for checklisting purposes only.

Card	Low	High
COMPLETE SET (441)	300.00	600.00
COMP.SERIES 1 (231)	150.00	300.00
COMP.SER. 1 w/o SP's (180)	15.00	30.00
COMP.SERIES 2 (210)	150.00	300.00
COMP.SER. 2 w/o SP's (180)	15.00	30.00
1 Paul Kariya	.20	.50
2 Jeff Friesen	.02	.10
3 Mike Leclerc	.02	.10
4 Andy McDonald	.02	.10
5 Jean-Sebastien Giguere	.15	.40
6 Steve Rucchin	.02	.10
7 Ray Ferraro	.02	.10
8 Milan Hnilicka	.15	.40
9 Patrik Stefan	.02	.10
10 Jiri Slegr	.02	.10
11 Jeff Odgers	.02	.10
12 Steve Guolla	.02	.10
13 Joe Thornton	.30	.75
14 Sergei Samsonov	.15	.40
15 Kyle McLaren	.02	.10
16 Jonathan Girard	.02	.10
17 Brian Rolston	.02	.10
18 Byron Dafoe	.15	.40
19 Miroslav Satan	.15	.40
20 Curtis Brown	.02	.10
21 Stu Barnes	.02	.10
22 Maxim Afinogenov	.02	.10
23 Vaclav Varada	.02	.10
24 Chris Gratton	.02	.10
25 Jarome Iginla	.25	.60
26 Dave Lowry	.02	.10
27 Derek Morris	.02	.10
28 Marc Savard	.02	.10
29 Oleg Saprykin	.02	.10
30 Craig Conroy	.02	.10
31 Jeff O'Neill	.02	.10
32 Arturs Irbe	.15	.40
33 Shane Willis	.02	.10
34 Dave Tanabe	.02	.10
35 Josef Vasicek	.02	.10
36 Sami Kapanen	.02	.10
37 Steve Sullivan	.02	.10
38 Tony Amonte	.15	.40
39 Michael Nylander	.02	.10
40 Eric Daze	.15	.40
41 Jocelyn Thibault	.15	.40
42 Boris Mironov	.02	.10
43 Ville Nieminen	.02	.10
44 Alex Tanguay	.15	.40
45 Milan Hejduk	.20	.50
46 Chris Drury	.15	.40
47 Peter Forsberg	.50	1.25
48 Steven Reinprecht	.02	.10
49 Ron Tugnutt	.15	.40
50 Ray Whitney	.02	.10
51 Geoff Sanderson	.02	.10
52 Serge Aubin	.02	.10
53 Espen Knutsen	.02	.10
54 Rostislav Klesla	.02	.10
55 Mike Modano	.30	.75
56 Ed Belfour	.20	.50
57 Pierre Turgeon	.15	.40
58 Jamie Langenbrunner	.02	.10
59 Brenden Morrow	.15	.40
60 Donald Audette	.02	.10
61 Steve Yzerman	1.00	2.50
62 Brett Hull	.25	.60
63 Nicklas Lidstrom	.20	.50
64 Darren McCarty	.02	.10
65 Luc Robitaille	.15	.40
66 Dominik Hasek	.40	1.00
67 Mike Comrie	.15	.40
68 Tommy Salo	.15	.40
69 Todd Marchant	.02	.10
70 Mike Grier	.02	.10
71 Ryan Smyth	.02	.10
72 Tom Poti	.02	.10
73 Pavel Bure	.20	.50
74 Marcus Nilsson	.02	.10
75 Roberto Luongo	.25	.60
76 Kevyn Adams	.02	.10
77 Dan Boyle	.02	.10
78 Robert Svehla	.02	.10
79 Zigmund Palffy	.15	.40
80 Eric Belanger	.02	.10
81 Ian Laperriere	.02	.10
82 Bryan Smolinski	.02	.10
83 Jozef Stumpel	.02	.10
84 Adam Deadmarsh	.02	.10
85 Marian Gaborik	.40	1.00
86 Lubomir Sekeras	.02	.10
87 Manny Fernandez	.15	.40
88 Darby Hendrickson	.02	.10
89 Roman Simicek	.02	.10
90 Saku Koivu	.20	.50
91 Richard Zednik	.02	.10
92 Oleg Petrov	.02	.10
93 Patrice Brisebois	.02	.10
94 Brian Savage	.02	.10
95 Jan Bulis	.02	.10
96 David Legwand	.15	.40
97 Cliff Ronning	.02	.10
98 Mike Dunham	.15	.40
99 Greg Johnson	.02	.10
100 Kimmo Timonen	.02	.10
101 Denis Arkhipov	.02	.10
102 Patrik Elias	.15	.40
103 Jason Arnott	.02	.10
104 Scott Niedermayer	.02	.10
105 Scott Gomez	.02	.10
106 Scott Stevens	.15	.40
107 John Madden	.02	.10
108 Rick DiPietro	.15	.40
109 Mark Parrish	.02	.10
110 Brad Isbister	.15	.40
111 Michael Peca	.02	.10
112 Kenny Jonsson	.02	.10
113 Mariusz Czerkawski	.02	.10
114 Mark Messier	.20	.50
115 Theo Fleury	.02	.10
116 Radek Dvorak	.02	.10
117 Brian Leetch	.15	.40
118 Eric Lindros	.20	.50
119 Mike Mottau	.02	.10
120 Radek Bonk	.02	.10
121 Daniel Alfredsson	.15	.40
122 Marian Hossa	.20	.50
123 Magnus Arvedson	.02	.10
124 Patrick Lalime	.15	.40
125 Martin Havlat	.15	.40
126 Eric Desjardins	.15	.40
127 Keith Primeau	.02	.10
128 Mark Recchi	.15	.40
129 Justin Williams	.02	.10
130 Roman Cechmanek	.15	.40
131 Jeremy Roenick	.25	.60
132 Sean Burke	.15	.40
133 Shane Doan	.02	.10
134 Paul Mara	.02	.10
135 Michal Handzus	.02	.10
136 Ladislav Nagy	.02	.10
137 Mike Johnson	.02	.10
138 Mario Lemieux	1.25	3.00
139 Alexei Kovalev	.15	.40
140 Robert Lang	.02	.10
141 Kevin Stevens	.02	.10
142 Andrew Ference	.02	.10
143 Johan Hedberg	.15	.40
144 Owen Nolan	.15	.40
145 Teemu Selanne	.20	.50
146 Scott Thornton	.02	.10
147 Patrick Marleau	.15	.40
148 Alexander Korolyuk	.02	.10
149 Todd Harvey	.02	.10
150 Keith Tkachuk	.20	.50
151 Pavol Demitra	.15	.40
152 Al MacInnis	.15	.40
153 Scott Young	.02	.10
154 Cory Stillman	.02	.10
155 Doug Weight	.15	.40
156 Brad Richards	.15	.40
157 Nikolai Khabibulin	.20	.50
158 Martin St. Louis	.15	.40
159 Fredrik Modin	.02	.10
160 Matthew Barnaby	.02	.10
161 Gary Roberts	.02	.10
162 Jonas Hoglund	.02	.10
163 Curtis Joseph	.20	.50
164 Mats Sundin	.20	.50
165 Darcy Tucker	.02	.10
166 Shayne Corson	.02	.10
167 Markus Naslund	.20	.50
168 Daniel Sedin	.02	.10
169 Henrik Sedin	.02	.10
170 Brendan Morrison	.15	.40
171 Peter Schaefer	.02	.10
172 Harold Druken	.02	.10
173 Peter Bondra	.20	.50
174 Olaf Kolzig	.15	.40
175 Sergei Gonchar	.02	.10
176 Jeff Halpern	.02	.10
177 Andrei Nikolishin	.02	.10
178 Jaromir Jagr	.30	.75
179 Steve Yzerman CL	.20	.50
180 Pavel Bure CL	.20	.50
181 Dan Snyder RC	2.00	5.00
182 Zdenek Kutlak RC	2.00	5.00
183 Michel Larocque RC	2.00	5.00
184 Casey Hankinson RC	2.00	5.00
185 Jody Shelley RC	2.00	5.00
186 Martin Spanhel RC	2.00	5.00
187 Mathieu Darche RC	2.00	5.00
188 Matt Davidson RC	2.00	5.00
189 Sean Selmser RC	2.00	5.00
190 Jason Chimera RC	2.00	5.00
191 Andrej Podkonicky RC	2.00	5.00
192 Mike Matteucci RC	2.00	5.00
193 Pascal Dupuis RC	2.00	5.00
194 Francis Belanger RC	2.00	5.00
195 Bill Bowler RC	2.00	5.00
196 Mike Jefferson RC	2.00	5.00
197 Stanislav Gron RC	2.00	5.00
198 Mikael Samuelsson RC	2.00	5.00
199 Peter Smrek RC	2.00	5.00
200 Joel Kwiatkowski RC	2.00	5.00
201 Tomas Divisek RC	2.00	5.00
202 Kirby Law RC	2.00	5.00
203 David Cullen RC	2.00	5.00
204 Greg Crozier RC	2.00	5.00
205 Billy Tibbetts RC	2.00	5.00
206 Dale Clarke RC	2.00	5.00
207 Jaroslav Obsut RC	2.00	5.00
208 Thomas Ziegler RC	2.00	5.00
209 Pat Kavanagh RC	2.00	5.00
210 Mike Brown	2.00	5.00
211 Ilya Kovalchuk RC	25.00	60.00
212 Ray Bourque	1.50	4.00
213 Brett Hull	1.00	2.50
214 Dominik Hasek	1.50	4.00
215 Vaclav Nedorost RC	2.00	5.00
216 Steve Yzerman	4.00	10.00
217 Mark Messier	.20	.50
218 Mike Modano	1.25	3.00
219 Patrick Roy	4.00	10.00
220 John LeClair	.75	2.00
220B Jared Aulin		
221 Martin Brodeur	2.00	5.00
222 Tony Amonte	.60	1.50
223 Zigmund Palffy	.60	1.50
224 Roman Cechmanek	.60	1.50
225 Jeff Jillson RC	2.00	5.00
226 Jaromir Jagr	1.25	3.00
227 Nikita Alexeev RC	2.00	5.00
228 Krystofer Kolanos RC	2.00	5.00
229 Peter Forsberg	2.00	5.00
230 Pavel Bure	.20	.50
231 Brian Sutherby RC	2.00	5.00
232 Oleg Tverdovsky	.02	.10
233 Steve Shields	.15	.40
234 Matt Cullen	.02	.10
235 Jason York	.02	.10
236 Vitali Vishnevsky	.02	.10
237 Marty McInnis	.02	.10
238 Yannick Tremblay	.02	.10
239 Dany Heatley	.25	.60
240 Lubos Bartecko	.02	.10
241 Damian Rhodes	.15	.40
242 Ilya Kovalchuk	5.00	12.00
243 Hnat Domenichelli	.02	.10
244 Bill Guerin	.15	.40
245 Martin Lapointe	.02	.10
246 Scott Pellerin	.02	.10
247 Rob Zamuner	.02	.10
248 Jozef Stumpel	.02	.10
249 Glen Murray	.02	.10
250 Martin Biron	.15	.40
251 Tim Connolly	.02	.10
252 Slava Kozlov	.02	.10
253 Jay McKee	.02	.10
254 J-P Dumont	.02	.10
255 Alexei Zhitnik	.02	.10
256 Roman Turek	.15	.40
257 Igor Kravchuk	.02	.10
258 Clarke Wilm	.02	.10
259 Robyn Regehr	.02	.10
260 Rob Niedermayer	.02	.10
261 Dean McAmmond	.02	.10
262 Ron Francis	.15	.40
263 Martin Gelinas	.02	.10
264 Rod Brind'Amour	.15	.40
265 Sandis Ozolinsh	.02	.10
266 Bates Battaglia	.02	.10
267 Chris Dingman	.02	.10
268 Igor Korolev	.02	.10
269 Jaroslav Spacek	.02	.10
270 Alexei Zhamnov	.02	.10
271 Steve Thomas	.02	.10
272 Jon Klemm	.02	.10
273 Adam Foote	.02	.10
274 Joe Sakic	.40	1.00
275 Rob Blake	.15	.40
276 Patrick Roy	1.00	2.50
277 Greg deVries	.02	.10
278 Dan Hinote	.02	.10
279 Marc Denis	.15	.40
280 David Vyborny	.02	.10
281 Tyler Wright	.02	.10
282 Mike Sillinger	.02	.10
283 Bruce Gardiner	.02	.10
284 Sergei Zubov	.02	.10
285 Jere Lehtinen	.15	.40
286 Joe Nieuwendyk	.15	.40
287 Darryl Sydor	.02	.10
288 Rob DiMaio	.02	.10
289 Valeri Kamensky	.02	.10
290 Brendan Shanahan	.20	.50
291 Igor Larionov	.02	.10
292 Tomas Holmstrom	.02	.10
293 Mathieu Dandenault	.02	.10
294 Sergei Fedorov	.30	.75
295 Fredrik Olausson	.02	.10
296 Anson Carter	.15	.40
297 Jochen Hecht	.02	.10
298 Daniel Cleary	.02	.10
299 Janne Niinimaa	.02	.10
300 Rem Murray	.02	.10
301 Eric Brewer	.02	.10
302 Valeri Bure	.02	.10
303 Viktor Kozlov	.02	.10
304 Denis Shvidki	.02	.10
305 Olli Jokinen	.15	.40
306 Jason Wiemer	.02	.10
307 Ryan Johnson	.02	.10
308 Felix Potvin	.20	.50
309 Jason Allison	.02	.10
310 Mathieu Schneider	.02	.10
311 Lubomir Visnovsky	.02	.10
312 Mattias Norstrom	.02	.10
313 Steve Heinze	.02	.10
314 Jim Dowd	.02	.10
315 Wes Walz	.02	.10
316 Filip Kuba	.02	.10
317 Andrew Brunette	.02	.10
318 Sergei Zholtok	.02	.10
319 Stacy Roest	.02	.10
320 Jose Theodore	.25	.60
321 Yanic Perreault	.02	.10
322 Doug Gilmour	.02	.10
323 Andreas Dackell	.02	.10
324 Martin Rucinsky	.02	.10
325 Chad Kilger	.02	.10
326 Scott Walker	.02	.10
327 Andy Delmore	.02	.10
328 Patric Kjellberg	.02	.10
329 Tomas Vokoun	.15	.40
330 Vitali Yachmenev	.02	.10
331 Bill Houlder	.02	.10
332 Martin Brodeur	.50	1.25
333 Bobby Holik	.02	.10
334 Petr Sykora	.02	.10
335 Brian Rafalski	.02	.10
336 Sergei Brylin	.02	.10
337 Randy McKay	.02	.10
338 Alexei Yashin	.02	.10
339 Roman Hamrlik	.02	.10
340 Michael Peca	.02	.10
341 Dave Scatchard	.02	.10
342 Claude Lapointe	.02	.10
343 Chris Osgood	.15	.40
344 Mike Richter	.20	.50
345 Mike York	.02	.10
346 Eric Lindros	.20	.50
347 Petr Nedved	.02	.10
348 Barrett Heisten	.02	.10
349 Zdeno Ciger	.02	.10
350 Shawn McEachern	.02	.10
351 Wade Redden	.02	.10
352 Bill Muckalt	.02	.10
353 Andre Roy	.02	.10
354 Sami Salo	.02	.10
355 Todd White	.02	.10
356 John LeClair	.20	.50
357 Brian Boucher	.15	.40
358 Pavel Brendl	.02	.10
359 Jan Hlavac	.02	.10
360 Dan McGillis	.02	.10
361 Simon Gagne	.20	.50
362 Daymond Langkow	.15	.40
363 Sergei Berezin	.02	.10
364 Danny Markov	.02	.10
365 Tyler Bouck	.02	.10
366 Teppo Numminen	.02	.10
367 Trevor Letowski	.02	.10
368 Martin Straka	.02	.10
369 Jan Hrdina	.02	.10
370 Alexei Morozov	.02	.10
371 Darius Kasparaitis	.02	.10
372 Toby Petersen	.02	.10
373 Kris Beech	.02	.10
374 Evgeni Nabokov	.15	.40
375 Mike Ricci	.02	.10
376 Brad Stuart	.02	.10
377 Adam Graves	.02	.10
378 Vincent Damphousse	.02	.10
379 Stephane Matteau	.02	.10
380 Chris Pronger	.15	.40
381 Brent Johnson	.15	.40
382 Fred Brathwaite	.15	.40
383 Dallas Drake	.02	.10
384 Mike Eastwood	.02	.10
385 Daniel Corso	.02	.10
386 Brian Holzinger	.02	.10
387 Vincent Lecavalier	.20	.50
388 Jassen Cullimore	.02	.10
389 Vaclav Prospal	.02	.10
390 Dave Andreychuk	.15	.40
391 Jimmie Olvestad	.02	.10
392 Alexander Mogilny	.15	.40
393 Tomas Kaberle	.02	.10
394 Mikael Renberg	.02	.10
395 Travis Green	.02	.10
396 Robert Reichel	.02	.10
397 Nikolai Antropov	.02	.10
398 Andrew Cassels	.02	.10
399 Dan Cloutier	.15	.40
400 Ed Jovanovski	.15	.40
401 Todd Bertuzzi	.20	.50
402 Trent Klatt	.02	.10
403 Donald Brashear	.02	.10
404 Jaromir Jagr	.30	.75
405 Joe Sacco	.02	.10
406 Steve Konowalchuk	.02	.10
407 Adam Oates	.20	.50
408 Dimitri Khristich	.02	.10
409 Dainius Zubrus	.02	.10
410 John LeClair	.20	.50
411 Martin Brodeur	.50	1.25
412 Timo Parssinen RC	2.00	5.00
413 Ilja Bryzgalov RC	3.00	8.00
414 Kevin Sawyer RC	2.00	5.00
415 Kamil Piros RC	2.50	5.00
416 Ivan Huml RC	2.00	5.00
417 Scott Nichol RC	2.00	5.00
418 Jukka Hentunen RC	2.00	5.00
419 Erik Cole RC	3.00	10.00
420 Ben Simon RC	2.00	5.00
421 Niko Kapanen RC	2.00	5.00
422 Pavel Datsyuk RC	30.00	60.00
423 Ty Conklin RC	2.00	5.00
424 Wayne Gretzky SP	8.00	20.00
425 Niklas Hagman RC	2.00	5.00
426 Kristian Huselius RC	2.00	5.00
427 Jaroslav Bednar RC	2.00	6.00
428 Nick Schultz RC	2.00	5.00
429 Travis Roche RC	2.00	5.00
430 Martin Erat RC	2.00	5.00
431 Andreas Salomonsson RC	2.00	5.00
432 Josef Boumedienne RC	2.00	5.00
433 Scott Clemmensen RC	2.00	5.00
434 Dan Blackburn RC	3.00	8.00
435 Radek Martinek RC	2.00	5.00
436 Raffi Torres RC	3.00	8.00
437 Ivan Ciernik RC	2.00	5.00
438 Jiri Dopita RC	2.00	5.00
439 Mark Rycroft RC	2.00	5.00
440 Ryan Tobler RC	2.00	5.00
441 Chris Corrinet RC	2.00	5.00

2001-02 Upper Deck Exclusives

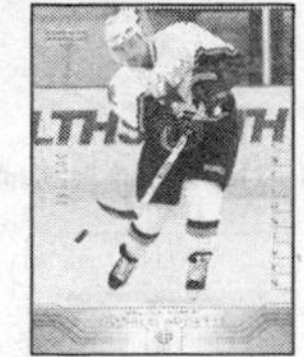

This 441-card set paralleled the base set with serial-numbering added. Regular base cards were serial-numbered to 100 copies each and Young Guns subset cards were serial-numbered to 50 copies each.

*EXCL.: 12X TO 30X BASE CARD
*EXCL.SP's: 4X TO 10X BASE CARD

2001-02 Upper Deck Crunch Timers

Card	Low	High
COMPLETE SET (15)	15.00	30.00
STATED ODDS 1:24 SERIES 2		
CT1 Joe Sakic	1.25	3.00
CT2 Milan Hejduk	.60	1.50
CT3 Chris Drury	.50	1.25
CT4 Mike Modano	1.00	2.50
CT5 Brett Hull	.75	2.00
CT6 Steve Yzerman	3.00	8.00
CT7 Zigmund Palffy	.50	1.25
CT8 Alexei Yashin	.50	1.25
CT9 Jeremy Roenick	.75	2.00
CT10 Mark Recchi	.50	1.25
CT11 Teemu Selanne	.60	1.50
CT12 Keith Tkachuk	.60	1.50
CT13 Markus Naslund	.60	1.50
CT14 Jaromir Jagr	1.00	2.50
CT15 Peter Bondra	.60	1.50

2001-02 Upper Deck Fantastic Finishers

Card	Low	High
COMPLETE SET (10)	10.00	20.00
STATED ODDS 1:36 SERIES 1		
FF1 Pavel Bure	.75	2.00
FF2 Pavol Demitra	.50	1.25
FF3 Markus Naslund	.60	1.50
FF4 Mario Lemieux	4.00	10.00
FF5 John LeClair	.75	2.00
FF6 Keith Tkachuk	.60	1.50
FF7 Marian Hossa	.60	1.50
FF8 Teemu Selanne	.60	1.50
FF9 Joe Sakic	1.25	3.00
FF10 Zigmund Palffy	.50	1.25

2001-02 Upper Deck Franchise Cornerstones

Card	Low	High
COMPLETE SET (15)	25.00	50.00
STATED ODDS 1:24 SERIES 1		
FC1 Paul Kariya	.60	1.50
FC2 Pavel Bure	.75	2.00
FC3 Mario Lemieux	4.00	10.00
FC4 Peter Forsberg	1.50	4.00
FC5 Vincent Lecavalier	.50	1.25
FC6 Joe Sakic	1.25	3.00
FC7 Zigmund Palffy	.50	1.25
FC8 Martin Brodeur	1.50	4.00
FC9 Patrick Roy	3.00	8.00
FC10 Steve Yzerman	3.00	8.00
FC11 Mike Modano	1.00	2.50
FC12 Tony Amonte	.50	1.25
FC13 Teemu Selanne	.60	1.50
FC14 John LeClair	.75	2.00
FC15 Mats Sundin	.60	1.50

2001-02 Upper Deck Game Jerseys

Inserted into random packs of Series I, this 38-card set featured swatches of game-worn jerseys and consisted of 4 subsets: All-Stars, Goalies, Next Generation, and Combos. All-Stars jerseys were denoted with an "A"

prefix and inserted at 1:144. Goalie jerseys were denoted with a "GJ" prefix and inserted at 1:288. Next Generation jerseys were denoted with a "NG" prefix and inserted at 1:144. Combo jerseys were denoted with a "C" prefix fro dual jerseys or numbered using the first letter of the players' last names for triple jerseys. Combo jerseys were inserted at 1:144.

*MULT.COLOR SWATCH: 1X TO 1.5X HI

Card	Low	High
AAM Al MacInnis AS	4.00	10.00
ACC Chris Chelios AS	5.00	12.00
AGL Guy Lafleur AS	4.00	10.00
AJJ Jaromir Jagr AS	8.00	20.00
AJO Joe Sakic AS	10.00	25.00
AMM Mike Modano AS	10.00	20.00
AMS Mats Sundin AS	5.00	12.00
ATF Theo Fleury AS	4.00	10.00
ATS Teemu Selanne AS	5.00	12.00
GJBB Brian Boucher G	10.00	25.00
GJCJ Curtis Joseph G	10.00	25.00
GJDH Dominik Hasek G	12.50	30.00
GJEB Ed Belfour G	10.00	25.00
GJJH Jani Hurme G	10.00	25.00
GJJT Jocelyn Thibault G	10.00	25.00
GJMO Maxime Ouellet G	10.00	25.00
GJMR Mike Richter G	10.00	25.00
GJMT Marty Turco G	10.00	25.00
GJOK Olaf Kolzig G	10.00	25.00
GJPR Patrick Roy G	15.00	40.00
GJRC Roman Cechmanek G	10.00	25.00
GJSB Sean Burke G	10.00	25.00
GJVY Vitali Yeremeyev G	10.00	25.00
NGCB Curtis Brown NG	4.00	10.00
NGDS Daniel Sedin NG	4.00	10.00
NGED Eric Daze NG	4.00	10.00
NGHS Henrik Sedin NG	4.00	10.00
NGJH Jani Hurme NG	4.00	10.00
NGJI Jarome Iginla NG	10.00	25.00
NGJW Justin Williams NG	4.00	10.00
NGMH Marian Hossa NG	5.00	12.00
NGMM Manny Malhotra NG	4.00	10.00
NGMT Marty Turco NG	4.00	10.00
NGMY Mike York NG	4.00	10.00
NGPS Patrik Stefan NG	4.00	10.00
NGRF Ruslan Fedotenko NG	4.00	10.00
NGSD Shane Doan NG	4.00	10.00
NGVL Vincent Lecavalier NG	5.00	12.00
CFR Peter Forsberg	20.00	50.00
Patrick Roy		
CHH Marian Hossa	12.50	30.00
Jani Hurme		
CKS Paul Kariya	12.50	30.00
Teemu Selanne		
CLJ Mario Lemieux	15.00	40.00
Jaromir Jagr		
CMN Mike Modano	15.00	40.00
Joe Nieuwendyk		
CPC Keith Primeau	12.50	30.00
Roman Cechmanek		
CSS Henrik Sedin	12.50	30.00
Daniel Sedin		
FSR Peter Forsberg	25.00	60.00
Joe Sakic		
Patrick Roy		
MNB Mike Modano	20.00	50.00
Joe Nieuwendyk		
Ed Belfour		
YSF Steve Yzerman	25.00	60.00
Brendan Shanahan		
Sergei Fedorov		

2001-02 Upper Deck Game Jerseys Series II

Randomly inserted into Series II packs, this 58-card set featured swatches of game-worn jersey swatches and consisted of 6 subsets: Finals Jerseys, Generation Next, Phenomenal Finishers, Superstar Sweaters, Dual Jerseys and Triple Jerseys. Single swatch jerseys were inserted at 1:144 odds, dual jerseys were inserted at 1:288. Triple swatch jerseys were serial-numbered to just 25 and were not priced due to scarcity.

*MULT.COLOR SWATCH: 1X TO 1.5X HI

Card	Low	High
FJBS Brendan Shanahan	6.00	15.00
FJCD Chris Drury	4.00	10.00
FJCL Claude Lemieux	4.00	10.00
FJCO Chris Osgood	6.00	15.00
FJEB Ed Belfour	6.00	15.00
FJJL John LeClair	4.00	10.00
FJJN Joe Nieuwendyk	4.00	10.00
FJJS Joe Sakic	10.00	25.00
FJMB Martin Brodeur	12.50	30.00
FJMH Milan Hejduk	6.00	15.00
FJMM Mike Modano	8.00	20.00
FJMS Miroslav Satan	4.00	10.00
FJPF Peter Forsberg	10.00	25.00
FJPR Patrick Roy	12.50	30.00
FJSF Sergei Fedorov	8.00	20.00
FJSS Scott Stevens	4.00	10.00
FJSY Steve Yzerman	12.50	30.00
GNJW Justin Williams	4.00	10.00

GNMB Martin Biron	4.00	10.00
GNMM Manny Malhotra	4.00	10.00
GNMO Maxime Ouellet	4.00	10.00
GNMY Mike York	4.00	10.00
GNPM Patrick Marleau	6.00	15.00
GNRB Radek Bonk	4.00	10.00
GNRF Rico Fata	4.00	10.00
GNSA Serge Aubin	4.00	10.00
GNSG Simon Gagne	6.00	15.00
PFAK Alexei Kovalev	4.00	10.00
PFBS Brendan Shanahan	6.00	15.00
PFJJ Jaromir Jagr	8.00	20.00
PFJL John LeClair	6.00	15.00
PFJS Joe Sakic	10.00	25.00
PFKP Keith Primeau	4.00	10.00
PFML Mario Lemieux	15.00	40.00
PFMN Markus Naslund	4.00	10.00
PFPK Paul Kariya	6.00	15.00
PFZP Zigmund Palffy	4.00	10.00
SSAM Al MacInnis	4.00	10.00
SSCD Chris Drury	6.00	15.00
SSMB Martin Brodeur	12.50	30.00
SSMM Mike Modano	8.00	20.00
SSPF Peter Forsberg	10.00	25.00
SSPK Paul Kariya	6.00	15.00
SSPR Patrick Roy	12.50	30.00
SSRB Ray Bourque	8.00	20.00
SSSY Steve Yzerman	12.50	30.00
SSWG Wayne Gretzky	30.00	80.00
DJBR Ray Bourque	20.00	50.00
Patrick Roy		
DJFS Sergei Fedorov	10.00	25.00
Brendan Shanahan		
DJMN Mike Modano	10.00	25.00
Joe Nieuwendyk		
DJSB Scott Stevens	20.00	50.00
Martin Brodeur		
DJSF Joe Sakic	25.00	60.00
Peter Forsberg		
DJSH Miroslav Satan	10.00	25.00
Dominik Hasek		
DJTD Alex Tanguay	10.00	25.00
Chris Drury		
DJYL Steve Yzerman	15.00	40.00
Nicklas Lidstrom		
TJNMB Joe Nieuwendyk	15.00	40.00
Mike Modano		
Ed Belfour		
TJRBH Patrick Roy	60.00	150.00
Joe Sakic		
Milan Hejduk		
TJYFS Steve Yzerman	25.00	60.00
Sergei Fedorov		
Brendan Shanahan		

2001-02 Upper Deck Game Jersey Autographs

Inserted randomly into both Series I and Series II, this 16-card set featured game-worn jersey swatches and authentic player autographs. Series I cards were inserted randomly at 1:288 packs. Series II cards were serial-numbered to 150 copies each.

SDS Daniel Sedin Ser.1	10.00	25.00
SDW Doug Weight Ser.1	15.00	40.00
SHS Henrik Sedin Ser.1	10.00	25.00
SJL John LeClair Ser.1	10.00	25.00
SMM Mike Modano Ser.1	25.00	60.00
SRB Ray Bourque Ser.1	50.00	100.00
SSY Steve Yzerman Ser.1	100.00	200.00
SJBO Ray Bourque Ser.2	40.00	80.00
SJCJ Curtis Joseph Ser.2	15.00	40.00
SJEB Ed Belfour Ser.2	20.00	50.00
SJJL John LeClair Ser.2	10.00	25.00
SJMB Martin Brodeur Ser.2	75.00	150.00
SJMO Maxime Ouellet Ser.2	10.00	25.00
SJRB Ray Bourque Ser.2	40.00	80.00
SJSG Simon Gagne Ser.2	10.00	25.00
SJSY Steve Yzerman Ser.2	100.00	200.00

2001-02 Upper Deck Gate Attractions

COMPLETE SET (15)	20.00	40.00
STATED ODDS 1:24 SERIES 1		
GA1 Mark Messier	.75	2.00
GA2 Theo Fleury	.50	1.25
GA3 Keith Tkachuk	.60	1.50
GA4 John LeClair	.75	2.00
GA5 Mario Lemieux	4.00	10.00
GA6 Alexei Kovalev	.50	1.25
GA7 Chris Drury	.50	1.25
GA8 Joe Sakic	1.25	3.00
GA9 Peter Forsberg	1.50	4.00
GA10 Paul Kariya	.60	1.50
GA11 Teemu Selanne	.60	1.50
GA12 Steve Yzerman	3.00	8.00
GA13 Brendan Shanahan	1.00	2.50
GA14 Mike Modano	1.00	2.50
GA15 Chris Pronger	.50	1.25

2001-02 Upper Deck Goalies in Action

COMPLETE SET (10)	12.50	25.00
STATED ODDS 1:36 SERIES 1		
GL1 Curtis Joseph	.75	2.00
GL2 Ed Belfour	.75	2.00
GL3 Martin Brodeur	2.00	5.00
GL4 Evgeni Nabokov	.60	1.50
GL5 Johan Hedberg	.75	2.00
GL6 Patrick Roy	4.00	10.00
GL7 Tommy Salo	.60	1.50
GL8 Patrick Lalime	.60	1.50
GL9 Olaf Kolzig	.60	1.50
GL10 Roberto Luongo	1.00	2.50

2001-02 Upper Deck Goaltender Threads

Randomly inserted at 1:240 Series II packs, this 10-card set featured swatches game-worn goalie jerseys.

*MULT.COLOR SWATCH: 1X TO 1.5X		
TTBB Brian Boucher	8.00	20.00
TTCJ Curtis Joseph	8.00	20.00
TTCO Chris Osgood	8.00	20.00
TTJO Jose Theodore	10.00	25.00
TTJT Jocelyn Thibault	8.00	20.00
TTMB Martin Brodeur	15.00	40.00
TTMD Mike Dunham	8.00	20.00
TTMR Mike Richter	8.00	20.00
TTPR Patrick Roy	15.00	40.00
TTRC Roman Cechmanek	8.00	20.00

2001-02 Upper Deck Last Line of Defense

COMPLETE SET (10)	12.50	25.00
STATED ODDS 1:36 SERIES 2		
LL1 Patrick Roy	4.00	10.00
LL2 Ed Belfour	.75	2.00
LL3 Dominik Hasek	1.50	4.00
LL4 Felix Potvin	.75	2.00
LL5 Martin Brodeur	2.00	5.00
LL6 Roman Cechmanek	.60	1.50
LL7 Johan Hedberg	.75	2.00
LL8 Evgeni Nabokov	.60	1.50
LL9 Curtis Joseph	.75	2.00
LL10 Olaf Kolzig	.60	1.50

2001-02 Upper Deck Leaders of the Pack

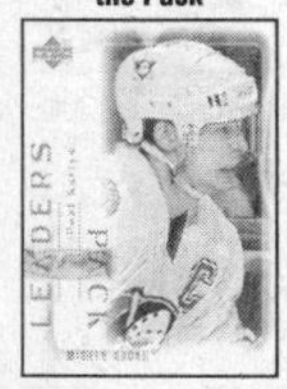

COMPLETE SET (15)	15.00	30.00
STATED ODDS 1:24 SERIES 2		
LP1 Paul Kariya	.60	1.50
LP2 Tony Amonte	.50	1.25
LP3 Joe Sakic	1.25	3.00
LP4 Mike Modano	1.00	2.50
LP5 Steve Yzerman	3.00	8.00
LP6 Pavel Bure	.75	2.00
LP7 Scott Stevens	.50	1.25
LP8 Mark Messier	.75	2.00
LP9 Michael Peca	.50	1.25
LP10 Daniel Alfredsson	.50	1.25
LP11 Mario Lemieux	4.00	10.00
LP12 Owen Nolan	.50	1.25
LP13 Doug Weight	.50	1.25
LP14 Chris Pronger	.50	1.25
LP15 Mats Sundin	.60	1.50

2001-02 Upper Deck Legendary Cut Signatures

Randomly inserted into Series I and Series II packs, this 5-card set featured "cut" signatures from some of the most recognized names in the history of the NHL. Each card was individually serial-numbered and the totals are listed below. These cards were not priced due to scarcity.

LCCC Clarence Campbell/5
Series 2
LCDH Doug Harvey/5
Series 2
LCES Eddie Shore/5
Series1 EXCH
LCJP Jacques Plante/5
Series 1
LCKC King Clancy/5
Series 2
LCLS Lord Stanley/1
Series 2
LCSA Sid Abel/5
Series 2
LCTS Terry Sawchuk/5
Series 1

2001-02 Upper Deck Patches

Inserted at 1:2500 Series I packs, this 19-card set featured swatches of game-used jersey patches.

PBS Brendan Shanahan	25.00	60.00
PDW Doug Weight	25.00	60.00
PEB Ed Belfour	30.00	80.00
PJJ Jaromir Jagr	30.00	80.00
PJL John LeClair	25.00	60.00
PJS Joe Sakic	30.00	80.00
PMH Marian Hossa	15.00	40.00
PML Mario Lemieux	60.00	150.00
PMM Mike Modano	25.00	60.00
PMO Mike Modano	25.00	60.00
PMS Mats Sundin	15.00	40.00
PPF Peter Forsberg	40.00	100.00
PPK Paul Kariya	25.00	60.00
PPR Patrick Roy	50.00	120.00
PRB Ray Bourque	40.00	100.00
PSA Joe Sakic	30.00	80.00
PSF Sergei Fedorov	30.00	80.00
PSY Steve Yzerman	50.00	125.00
PTS Teemu Selanne	15.00	40.00

2001-02 Upper Deck Patches Series II

Randomly inserted into Series II packs, this 24-card set partially paralleled Series II jersey set but featured swatches of jersey logos, name plates or numbers. Number patches were denoted with a "PN" prefix and inserted at 1:2500. Logo patches were denoted with a "PL" prefix and inserted at 1:2500. Name Plate patches were denoted with a "NA" prefix and inserted at 1:7500. Please note that the Modano Name Plate card had a "PL" prefix according to Upper Deck.

PLJJ Jaromir Jagr	30.00	80.00
PLMB Martin Brodeur	40.00	100.00
PLML Mario Lemieux	40.00	100.00
PLPF Peter Forsberg	40.00	100.00
PLPK Paul Kariya	20.00	50.00
PLPR Patrick Roy	40.00	100.00
PLSF Sergei Fedorov	30.00	80.00
PLSY Steve Yzerman	40.00	100.00
PNBS Brendan Shanahan	20.00	50.00
PNJL John LeClair	20.00	50.00
PNJS Joe Sakic	30.00	80.00
PNML Mario Lemieux	40.00	100.00
PNMM Mike Modano	25.00	60.00
PNPK Paul Kariya	20.00	50.00
PNPR Patrick Roy	40.00	100.00
PNSY Steve Yzerman	40.00	100.00
NABS Brendan Shanahan	50.00	120.00
NAJL John LeClair	40.00	100.00
NAJS Joe Sakic	75.00	200.00
NAML Mario Lemieux	100.00	250.00
NAPF Peter Forsberg	75.00	200.00
NAPR Patrick Roy	100.00	250.00
NASY Steve Yzerman	100.00	250.00
PLMM Mike Modano	60.00	150.00

2001-02 Upper Deck Pride of a Nation

Inserted at a rate of 1:240 for single players and 1:576 for double players, this 30-card set highlighted the homelands of players of the NHL. Each card carried game-worn jersey piece(s) of the player(s) featured. Triple player cards were serial-numbered to just twenty and are not priced due to scarcity.

PNBG Bill Guerin	6.00	15.00
PNDH Dominik Hasek	8.00	20.00
PNDW Doug Weight	6.00	15.00
PNJJ Jaromir Jagr	8.00	20.00
PNJS Joe Sakic	10.00	25.00
PNMB Martin Brodeur	12.00	30.00
PNML Mario Lemieux	15.00	40.00
PNPF Peter Forsberg	8.00	20.00
PNPR Patrick Roy	15.00	40.00
PNSF Sergei Fedorov	8.00	20.00
PNSK Saku Koivu	6.00	15.00
PNSY Steve Yzerman	12.00	30.00
PNTA Tony Amonte	6.00	15.00
PNTS Teemu Selanne	6.00	15.00
PNVK Viktor Kozlov	6.00	15.00
DPAG Tony Amonte	12.50	30.00
Bill Guerin		
DPFK Sergei Fedorov	12.50	30.00
Viktor Kozlov		
DPFS Peter Forsberg	15.00	40.00
Mats Sundin		
DPHJ Dominik Hasek	15.00	40.00
Jaromir Jagr		
DPLK M.Lemieux/P.Kariya	15.00	40.00
DPLM J.LeClair/M.Modano	12.50	30.00
DPRS Patrick Roy	30.00	80.00
Joe Sakic		
DPSB Scott Stevens	12.50	30.00
Martin Brodeur		
DPSK Teemu Selanne	12.50	30.00
Saku Koivu		
DPYS Steve Yzerman	25.00	60.00
Brendan Shanahan		
TPAWL Tony Amonte	20.00	50.00
Doug Weight		
Brian Leetch		
TPFKK Sergei Fedorov	20.00	50.00
Alexei Kovalev		
Viktor Kozlov		
TPFSL Peter Forsberg	30.00	80.00
Mats Sundin		
Nicklas Lidstrom		
TPHJL Dominik Hasek	40.00	100.00
Jaromir Jagr		
Robert Lang		
TPYRL Steve Yzerman	60.00	150.00
Patrick Roy		
Mario Lemieux		

2001-02 Upper Deck Pride of the Leafs

Serial-numbered to just 75 sets, this 9 card set featured past and present Toronto Maple Leafs with full color action photos alongside a swatch of game-worn jersey on the card fronts.

MLBJ Borje Salming	40.00	100.00
MLCJ Curtis Joseph	30.00	80.00
MLDG Doug Gilmour	30.00	80.00
MLFP Felix Potvin	40.00	100.00
MLMS Mats Sundin	30.00	80.00
MLNA Nikolai Antropov	25.00	60.00
MLSB Sergei Berezin	20.00	50.00
MLTD Tie Domi	30.00	80.00
MLWC Wendel Clark	50.00	125.00

2001-02 Upper Deck Shooting Stars

COMPLETE SET (20)	15.00	30.00
STATED ODDS 1:9 SERIES 2		
SS1 Paul Kariya	.40	1.00
SS2 Bill Guerin	.30	.75
SS3 Joe Sakic	.75	2.00
SS4 Milan Hejduk	.40	1.00
SS5 Brett Hull	.50	1.25
SS6 Brendan Shanahan	.60	1.50
SS7 Luc Robitaille	.30	.75
SS8 Pavel Bure	.60	1.50
SS9 Zigmund Palffy	.30	.75
SS10 Patrik Elias	.30	.75
SS11 Alexei Yashin	.30	.75
SS12 John LeClair	.50	1.25
SS13 Alexei Kovalev	.30	.75
SS14 Mario Lemieux	2.50	6.00
SS15 Owen Nolan	.30	.75
SS16 Teemu Selanne	.40	1.00
SS17 Alexander Mogilny	.30	.75
SS18 Markus Naslund	.40	1.00
SS19 Jaromir Jagr	.60	1.50
SS20 Peter Bondra	.30	.75

2001-02 Upper Deck Skilled Stars

COMPLETE SET (20)	15.00	30.00
STATED ODDS 1:9 SERIES 1		
SS1 Paul Kariya	.40	1.00
SS2 Mario Lemieux	2.50	6.00
SS3 Chris Pronger	.30	.75
SS4 Teemu Selanne	.40	1.00
SS5 Owen Nolan	.30	.75
SS6 Pavel Bure	.50	1.25
SS7 Keith Tkachuk	.40	1.00
SS8 Mike Modano	.60	1.50
SS9 Peter Forsberg	1.00	2.50
SS10 Zigmund Palffy	.30	.75
SS11 Martin Brodeur	1.00	2.50
SS12 Patrick Roy	2.00	5.00
SS13 Joe Sakic	.75	2.00
SS14 Ray Bourque	.75	2.00
SS15 Steve Yzerman	2.00	5.00
SS16 Roman Cechmanek	.30	.75
SS17 Mark Messier	.50	1.25
SS18 Vincent Lecavalier	.40	1.00
SS19 John LeClair	.50	1.25
SS20 Tony Amonte	.30	.75

2001-02 Upper Deck Tandems

COMPLETE SET (10)	20.00	40.00
STATED ODDS 1:36 SERIES 2		
T1 Sergei Samsonov	2.00	5.00
Joe Thornton		
T2 Joe Sakic	4.00	10.00
Milan Hejduk		
T3 Brendan Shanahan	5.00	12.00
Steve Yzerman		
T4 Valeri Bure	1.25	3.00
Pavel Bure		
T5 Patrik Elias	1.25	3.00
Jason Arnott		
T6 Marian Hossa	1.25	3.00
Radek Bonk		
T7 John LeClair	1.25	3.00
Jeremy Roenick		
T8 Teemu Selanne	1.25	3.00
Owen Nolan		
T9 Keith Tkachuk	1.25	3.00
Pavol Demitra		
T10 Brad Richards	1.25	3.00
Vincent Lecavalier		

2002-03 Upper Deck

This 456-card set was issued in two different series. Series I consisted of 180 base cards; 15 Memorable Season subset cards (181-195) inserted at 1:6; 30 Young Guns subset cards (196-225) inserted at 1:4; 9 more Memorable Seasons subset cards and 12 more Young Guns subset cards (226-246) inserted one per box. Series 2 consisted of 180 base cards and 30 Young Guns subset cards (427-456) inserted at 1:4.

COMP.SER.1 SET (246)	300.00	600.00
COMP.SER.1 SET w/o SP's (225)	60.00	125.00
COMP.SER.2 SET (210)	150.00	300.00
COMP.SER 2 SET w/o SP's (180)	15.00	30.00
1 Vitali Vishnevsky	.02	.10
2 Jean-Sebastien Giguere	.15	.40
3 Steve Rucchin	.02	.10
4 Paul Kariya	.20	.50
5 Andy McDonald	.02	.10
6 Lubos Bartecko	.02	.10
7 Ilya Kovalchuk	.25	.60
8 Tomi Kallio	.02	.10
9 Milan Hnilicka	.15	.40
10 Patrik Stefan	.02	.10
11 Joe Thornton	.30	.75
12 Brian Rolston	.02	.10
13 Martin Lapointe	.02	.10
14 Nick Boynton	.02	.10
15 Andy Hilbert	.02	.10
16 Glen Murray	.02	.10
17 J-P Dumont	.02	.10
18 Tim Connolly	.02	.10
19 Miroslav Satan	.15	.40
20 Maxim Afinogenov	.02	.10
21 Taylor Pyatt	.02	.10
22 Jay McKee	.02	.10
23 Marc Savard	.02	.10
24 Roman Turek	.15	.40
25 Dean McAmmond	.02	.10
26 Craig Conroy	.02	.10
27 Derek Morris	.02	.10
28 Rod Brind'Amour	.15	.40
29 Josef Vasicek	.02	.10
30 Niclas Wallin	.02	.10
31 Jaroslav Svoboda	.02	.10
32 Sami Kapanen	.02	.10
33 Erik Cole	.02	.10
34 Jeff O'Neill	.02	.10
35 Michael Nylander	.02	.10
36 Alexei Zhamnov	.02	.10
37 Jon Klemm	.02	.10
38 Kyle Calder	.02	.10
39 Eric Daze	.02	.10
40 Steve Sullivan	.02	.10
41 Stephane Yelle	.02	.10
42 Rob Blake	.15	.40
43 Patrick Roy	1.00	2.50
44 Radim Vrbata	.02	.10
45 Chris Drury	.15	.40
46 Milan Hejduk	.20	.50
47 Joe Sakic	.40	1.00
48 Peter Forsberg	.50	1.25
49 Rostislav Klesla	.02	.10
50 Marc Denis	.15	.40
51 Grant Marshall	.02	.10
52 Ray Whitney	.02	.10
53 Espen Knutsen	.02	.10
54 Mike Sillinger	.02	.10
55 Bill Guerin	.15	.40
56 Mike Modano	.30	.75
57 Sergei Zubov	.02	.10
58 Marty Turco	.15	.40
59 Jason Arnott	.02	.10
60 Jere Lehtinen	.15	.40
61 Steve Yzerman	1.00	2.50
62 Sergei Fedorov	.30	.75
63 Nicklas Lidstrom	.20	.50
64 Curtis Joseph	.20	.50
65 Igor Larionov	.02	.10
66 Luc Robitaille	.15	.40
67 Tomas Holmstrom	.02	.10
68 Brett Hull	.25	.60
69 Mike Comrie	.15	.40
70 Marty Reasoner	.02	.10
71 Tommy Salo	.15	.40
72 Ryan Smyth	.02	.10
73 Anson Carter	.15	.40
74 Janne Niinimaa	.02	.10
75 Sandis Ozolinsh	.02	.10
76 Roberto Luongo	.25	.60
77 Kristian Huselius	.02	.10
78 Valeri Bure	.02	.10
79 Brad Ference	.02	.10
80 Ian Laperriere	.02	.10
81 Mattias Norstrom	.02	.10
82 Adam Deadmarsh	.02	.10
83 Jason Allison	.02	.10
84 Eric Belanger	.02	.10
85 Felix Potvin	.20	.50
86 Wes Walz	.02	.10
87 Darby Hendrickson	.02	.10
88 Dwayne Roloson	.02	.10
89 Marian Gaborik	.40	1.00
90 Filip Kuba	.02	.10
91 Andrei Markov	.02	.10
92 Jose Theodore	.25	.60
93 Mike Ribeiro	.02	.10
94 Richard Zednik	.02	.10
95 Gino Odjick	.02	.10
96 Saku Koivu	.20	.50
97 Andy Delmore	.02	.10
98 Tomas Vokoun	.15	.40
99 Martin Erat	.02	.10
100 Denis Arkhipov	.02	.10
101 Scott Hartnell	.02	.10
102 Scott Stevens	.15	.40
103 Patrik Elias	.15	.40
104 Jamie Langenbrunner	.02	.10
105 Brian Gionta	.02	.10
106 Joe Nieuwendyk	.15	.40
107 Martin Brodeur	.50	1.25
108 Roman Hamrlik	.02	.10
109 Shawn Bates	.02	.10
110 Steve Webb	.02	.10
111 Alexei Yashin	.02	.10
112 Chris Osgood	.15	.40
113 Mark Parrish	.02	.10
114 Petr Nedved	.02	.10
115 Eric Lindros	.20	.50
116 Dan Blackburn	.15	.40
117 Radek Dvorak	.02	.10
118 Tom Poti	.02	.10
119 Pavel Bure	.20	.50
120 Todd White	.02	.10
121 Patrick Lalime	.15	.40
122 Marian Hossa	.20	.50
123 Daniel Alfredsson	.15	.40
124 Wade Redden	.02	.10
125 Mike Fisher	.02	.10
126 Keith Primeau	.02	.10
127 Jeremy Roenick	.25	.60
128 Eric Weinrich	.02	.10
129 Roman Cechmanek	.15	.40
130 Mark Recchi	.15	.40
131 Justin Williams	.02	.10
132 Brad May	.02	.10
133 Sean Burke	.15	.40
134 Paul Mara	.02	.10
135 Shane Doan	.02	.10
136 Tony Amonte	.15	.40
137 Daniel Briere	.02	.10
138 Kris Beech	.02	.10
139 Martin Straka	.02	.10
140 Alexei Kovalev	.15	.40
141 Mario Lemieux	1.25	3.00
142 Andrew Ference	.02	.10
143 Johan Hedberg	.15	.40
144 Patrick Marleau	.15	.40
145 Owen Nolan	.15	.40
146 Mike Rathje	.02	.10
147 Evgeni Nabokov	.15	.40
148 Marco Sturm	.02	.10
149 Todd Harvey	.02	.10
150 Pavol Demitra	.15	.40
151 Doug Weight	.15	.40
152 Al MacInnis	.15	.40
153 Brent Johnson	.15	.40
154 Keith Tkachuk	.20	.50
155 Cory Stillman	.02	.10
156 Brad Richards	.15	.40
157 Pavel Kubina	.02	.10
158 Nikolai Khabibulin	.20	.50
159 Martin St. Louis	.15	.40
160 Vincent Lecavalier	.20	.50
161 Bryan McCabe	.02	.10
162 Gary Roberts	.02	.10
163 Ed Belfour	.20	.50
164 Mats Sundin	.20	.50
165 Tie Domi	.15	.40
166 Alexander Mogilny	.15	.40
167 Daniel Sedin	.02	.10
168 Todd Bertuzzi	.20	.50
169 Mattias Ohlund	.02	.10
170 Dan Cloutier	.15	.40
171 Markus Naslund	.20	.50
172 Jan Hlavac	.02	.10
173 Olaf Kolzig	.15	.40
174 Peter Bondra	.20	.50
175 Sergei Gonchar	.02	.10
176 Steve Konowalchuk	.02	.10
177 Chris Simon	.02	.10
178 Dainius Zubrus	.02	.10
179 Patrick Roy CL	.75	2.00
180 Steve Yzerman CL	.75	2.00
181 Paul Kariya MS	.50	1.25
182 Bobby Orr MS	3.00	8.00
183 Jarome Iginla MS	.60	1.50
184 Joe Sakic MS	1.00	2.50
185 Patrick Roy MS	2.50	6.00
186 Steve Yzerman MS	2.50	6.00
187 Gordie Howe MS	2.00	5.00
188 Wayne Gretzky MS	4.00	10.00
189 Wayne Gretzky MS	4.00	10.00
190 Martin Brodeur MS	1.25	3.00
191 Mario Lemieux MS	3.00	8.00
192 Brett Hull MS	.60	1.50
193 Jaromir Jagr MS	.75	2.00
194 Pavel Bure MS	.60	1.50
195 Teemu Selanne MS	.60	1.50
196 Mark Hartigan YG	1.25	3.00
197 Pasi Numminen YG	1.25	3.00
198 Henrik Tallinder YG	1.25	3.00
199 Micki Dupont YG RC	1.25	3.00
200 Tyler Arnason YG	2.50	6.00
201 Jordan Krestanovich YG	1.25	3.00
202 Kelly Fairchild YG	1.25	3.00
203 Andrej Nedorost YG	1.25	3.00
204 Sean Avery YG	1.25	3.00
205 Stephen Weiss YG	2.00	5.00
206 Lukas Krajicek YG	1.50	4.00
207 Kyle Rossiter YG	1.25	3.00
208 Eric Beaudoin YG	1.25	3.00
209 Sylvain Blouin YG RC	1.25	3.00
210 Marcel Hossa YG	1.25	3.00
211 Adam Hall YG RC	1.25	3.00
212 Greg Koehler YG RC	1.25	3.00
213 Trent Hunter YG	1.25	3.00
214 Ray Schultz YG RC	1.25	3.00
215 Martin Prusek YG	1.25	3.00
216 Chris Bala YG	1.25	3.00
217 Josh Langfeld YG	1.25	3.00
218 Bruno St. Jacques YG	1.25	3.00
219 Branko Radivojevic YG	1.25	3.00
220 Martin Cibak YG	1.25	3.00
221 Evgeni Konstantinov YG	1.25	3.00
222 Karel Pilar YG	1.25	3.00
223 Sebastien Centomo YG	1.25	3.00
224 Sebastien Charpentier YG	1.25	3.00
225 J-F Fortin YG	1.25	3.00
226 Stanislav Chistov YG RC	6.00	15.00
227 Alexei Smirnov YG RC	5.00	12.00
228 Chuck Kobasew YG RC	6.00	15.00
229 Tony Amonte MS	20.00	50.00
230 Peter Forsberg MS	30.00	80.00
231 Chris Drury MS	25.00	60.00
232 Rick Nash YG RC	50.00	100.00
233 Brendan Shanahan MS	25.00	60.00
234 Henrik Zetterberg YG RC	60.00	120.00
235 Ales Hemsky YG RC	25.00	60.00
236 Jay Bouwmeester YG RC	20.00	50.00
237 Alexei Yashin MS	25.00	60.00
238 Alexander Frolov YG RC	20.00	50.00
239 P-M Bouchard YG RC	12.50	30.00
240 Ron Hainsey YG RC	6.00	15.00
241 Sean Burke MS	20.00	50.00
242 Owen Nolan MS	25.00	60.00
243 Chris Pronger MS	20.00	50.00
244 Mats Sundin MS	25.00	60.00
245 Alexander Svitov YG RC	6.00	15.00
246 Steve Eminger YG RC	6.00	15.00
247 Adam Oates	.15	.40
248 Petr Sykora	.02	.10
249 Fredrik Olausson	.02	.10
250 Matt Cullen	.02	.10
251 Ruslan Salei	.02	.10
252 Slava Kozlov	.02	.10
253 Dany Heatley	.25	.60
254 Frantisek Kaberle	.02	.10
255 Pasi Nurminen	.02	.10
256 Shawn McEachern	.02	.10
257 Sergei Samsonov	.15	.40
258 Steve Shields	.15	.40
259 Jonathan Girard	.02	.10
260 Jozef Stumpel	.02	.10
261 Bryan Berard	.02	.10
262 Marty McInnis	.02	.10
263 Stu Barnes	.02	.10
264 Curtis Brown	.02	.10
265 Chris Gratton	.02	.10
266 Rhett Warrener	.02	.10
267 Jochen Hecht	.02	.10
268 James Patrick	.02	.10
269 Jarome Iginla	.25	.60
270 Martin Gelinas	.02	.10
271 Chris Drury	.15	.40
272 Stephane Yelle	.02	.10
273 Jamie Wright	.02	.10
274 Kevin Weekes	.15	.40
275 Bret Hedican	.02	.10
276 Ron Francis	.15	.40
277 Kevyn Adams	.02	.10
278 Marek Malik	.02	.10
279 Bates Battaglia	.02	.10
280 Theo Fleury	.02	.10
281 Sergei Berezin	.02	.10
282 Mark Bell	.02	.10
283 Alexander Karpovtsev	.02	.10
284 Steve Passmore	.02	.10
285 Bob Probert	.02	.10
286 Alex Tanguay	.15	.40
287 Steven Reinprecht	.02	.10
288 Adam Foote	.02	.10
289 David Aebischer	.15	.40
290 Greg deVries	.02	.10
291 Dan Hinote	.02	.10
292 Derek Morris	.02	.10
293 Scott Parker	.02	.10
294 Geoff Sanderson	.02	.10
295 Andrew Cassels	.02	.10
296 Jean-Luc Grand-Pierre	.02	.10
297 Luke Richardson	.02	.10
298 Tyler Wright	.02	.10
299 Jody Shelley	.02	.10
300 Ron Tugnutt	.15	.40
301 Scott Young	.02	.10
302 Pierre Turgeon	.15	.40
303 Derian Hatcher	.02	.10
304 Richard Matvichuk	.02	.10
305 Kirk Muller	.02	.10
306 Brendan Shanahan	.20	.50
307 Chris Chelios	.20	.50
308 Mathieu Dandenault	.02	.10
309 Pavel Datsyuk	.20	.50
310 Kris Draper	.02	.10
311 Boyd Devereaux	.02	.10
312 Kirk Maltby	.02	.10
313 Manny Legace	.15	.40
314 Jani Rita	.02	.10
315 Todd Marchant	.02	.10
316 Daniel Cleary	.02	.10
317 Georges Laraque	.02	.10
318 Mike York	.02	.10
319 Jason Smith	.02	.10
320 Viktor Kozlov	.02	.10
321 Dimitri Yushkevich	.02	.10
322 Olli Jokinen	.15	40
323 Marcus Nilsson	.02	.10
324 Ivan Novoseltsev	.02	.10
325 Aaron Miller	.02	.10
326 Zigmund Palffy	.15	.40
327 Jamie Storr	.15	.40

328 Bryan Smolinski .02 .10
329 Mathieu Schneider .02 .10
330 Erik Rasmussen .02 .10
331 Andrew Brunette .02 .10
332 Richard Park .02 .10
333 Manny Fernandez .15 .40
334 Matt Johnson .02 .10
335 Ladislav Benysek .02 .10
336 Mariusz Czerkawski .02 .10
337 Sheldon Souray .02 .10
338 Chad Kilger .02 .10
339 Yanic Perreault .02 .10
340 Mathieu Garon .15 .40
341 Craig Rivet .02 .10
342 Mike Dunham .15 .40
343 David Legwand .15 .40
344 Vladimir Orszagh .02 .10
345 Kimmo Timonen .02 .10
346 Cale Hulse .02 .10
347 Oleg Tverdovsky .02 .10
348 Jeff Friesen .02 .10
349 Brian Rafalski .02 .10
350 Sergei Brylin .02 .10
351 John Madden .02 .10
352 Colin White .02 .10
353 Michael Peca .02 .10
354 Eric Cairns .02 .10
355 Dave Scatchard .02 .10
356 Brad Isbister .02 .10
357 Oleg Kvasha .02 .10
358 Mattias Timander .02 .10
359 Matthew Barnaby .02 .10
360 Bobby Holik .02 .10
361 Darius Kasparaitis .02 .10
362 Vladimir Malakhov .02 .10
363 Brian Leetch .15 .40
364 Mark Messier .20 .50
365 Mike Richter .20 .50
366 Martin Havlat .15 .40
367 Radek Bonk .02 .10
368 Petr Schastlivy .02 .10
369 Zdeno Chara .02 .10
370 Chris Neil .02 .10
371 Magnus Arvedson .02 .10
372 Pavel Brendl .02 .10
373 Donald Brashear .02 .10
374 Michal Handzus .02 .10
375 Kim Johnsson .02 .10
376 John LeClair .20 .50
377 Simon Gagne .20 .50
378 Claude Lemieux .02 .10
379 Brian Boucher .15 .40
380 Teppo Numminen .02 .10
381 Daymond Langkow .15 .40
382 Ladislav Nagy .02 .10
383 Brian Savage .02 .10
384 Ville Nieminen .02 .10
385 Randy Robitaille .02 .10
386 Alexei Morozov .02 .10
387 Jan Hrdina .02 .10
388 Michal Rozsival .02 .10
389 Alexandre Daigle .02 .10
390 Mike Ricci .02 .10
391 Vincent Damphousse .02 .10
392 Teemu Selanne .20 .50
393 Adam Graves .02 .10
394 Scott Thornton .02 .10
395 Scott Hannan .02 .10
396 Fred Brathwaite .15 .40
397 Jamal Mayers .02 .10
398 Reed Low .02 .10
399 Chris Pronger .15 .40
400 Scott Mellanby .02 .10
401 Alexander Khavanov .02 .10
402 Ruslan Fedotenko .02 .10
403 Fredrik Modin .02 .10
404 Nikita Alexeev .02 .10
405 Shane Willis .02 .10
406 Dave Andreychuk .02 .10
407 Trevor Kidd .15 .40
408 Robert Reichel .02 .10
409 Robert Svehla .02 .10
410 Alyn McCauley .02 .10
411 Tomas Kaberle .02 .10
412 Travis Green .02 .10
413 Henrik Sedin .02 .10
414 Brendan Morrison .15 .40
415 Matt Cooke .02 .10
416 Ed Jovanovski .15 .40
417 Mattias Ohlund .02 .10
418 Trevor Linden .02 .10
419 Jaromir Jagr .30 .75
420 Robert Lang .02 .10
421 Matt Pettinger .02 .10
422 Ken Klee .02 .10
423 Stephen Peat .02 .10
424 Brian Sutherby .02 .10
425 Joe Thornton .30 .75
426 Wayne Gretzky 1.25 3.00
427 Martin Gerber YG RC 6.00 15.00
428 Kurt Sauer YG RC 3.00 8.00
429 Tim Thomas YG RC 10.00 25.00
430 Jordan Leopold YG RC 3.00 8.00
431 Levente Szuper YG RC 3.00 8.00
432 Shawn Thornton YG RC 3.00 8.00
433 Jeff Paul YG RC 3.00 8.00
434 Lasse Pirjeta YG RC 3.00 8.00
435 Dmitri Bykov YG RC 3.00 8.00
436 Ryan Miller YG RC 15.00 40.00
437 Kari Haakana YG RC 3.00 8.00
438 Ivan Majesky YG RC 3.00 8.00
439 Stephane Veilleux YG RC 3.00 8.00
440 Scottie Upshall YG RC 5.00 12.00
441 Shaone Morrisonn YG RC 3.00 8.00
442 Eric Godard YG RC 3.00 8.00
443 Jason Spezza YG RC 30.00 60.00
444 Anton Volchenkov YG RC 3.00 8.00
445 Dennis Seidenberg YG RC 5.00 12.00
446 Radovan Somik YG RC 3.00 8.00
447 Patrick Sharp YG RC 3.00 8.00
448 Jeff Taffe YG RC 3.00 8.00
449 Lynn Loyns YG RC 3.00 8.00
450 Mike Cammalleri YG RC 8.00 20.00
451 Tom Koivisto YG RC 3.00 8.00
452 Curtis Sanford YG RC 4.00 10.00
453 Cody Rudkowsky YG RC 3.00 8.00
454 Carlo Colaiacovo YG RC 3.00 8.00
455 Mikael Tellqvist YG RC 6.00 15.00
456 Vernon Fiddler YG RC 3.00 8.00

2002-03 Upper Deck Exclusives

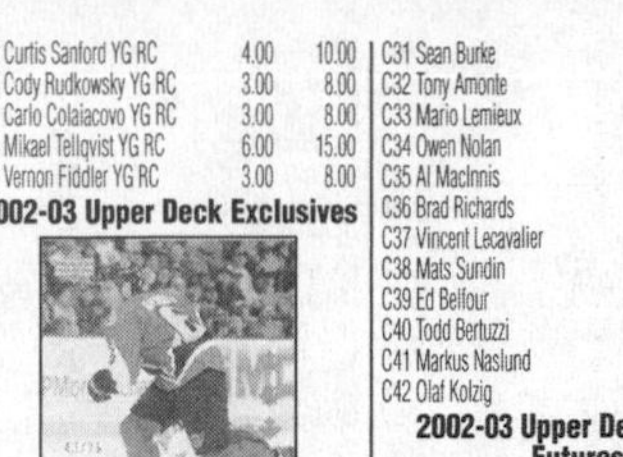
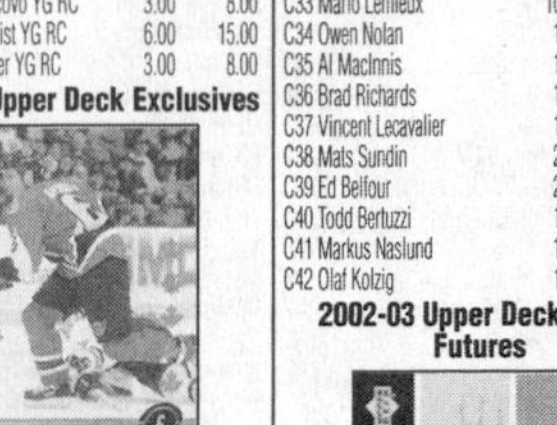

Available only in Canadian hobby packs, this 456-card set paralleled the base set but was enhanced with gold foil maple leafs across the card front and serial-numbered to 75 copies each. Cards 1-180 were available in Series I and cards 181-456 were available in Series II.

*STARS: 3X TO 8X BASE HI
*SER.1 SP's (181-225): 2X TO 5X
*SER.1 SP's (226-
*YG SP's 226-245: .75X TO 2X BASE HI

2002-03 Upper Deck All-Star Jerseys

*MULT.COLOR SWATCH: .75X TO 1.5X
STATED ODDS 1:96 SERIES 1 HOBBY
ASCC Chris Chelios 3.00 8.00
ASEJ Ed Jovanovski 3.00 8.00
ASJS Joe Sakic 6.00 15.00
ASJT Jose Theodore 4.00 10.00
ASMN Markus Naslund 3.00 8.00
ASPK Paul Kariya 3.00 8.00
ASRB Rob Blake 3.00 8.00
ASSB Sean Burke 3.00 8.00
ASSF Sergei Fedorov 5.00 12.00
ASSK Sami Kapanen 3.00 8.00
ASSO Sandis Ozolinsh 3.00 8.00
ASTS Teemu Selanne 3.00 8.00
ASVD Vincent Damphousse 3.00 8.00
ASWG Wayne Gretzky 30.00 80.00

2002-03 Upper Deck All-Star Performers

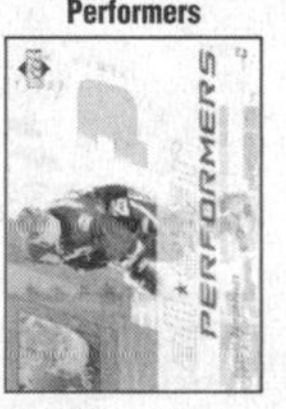

*MULT.COLOR SWATCH: .75X TO 1.5X
STATED ODDS 1:96 SERIES 2
ASEJ Ed Jovanovski 4.00 10.00
ASJT Jose Theodore 5.00 12.00
ASMM Mike Modano 8.00 20.00
ASMN Markus Naslund 3.00 8.00
ASPK Paul Kariya 3.00 8.00
ASPR Patrick Roy 15.00 40.00
ASRB Rob Blake 4.00 10.00
ASSB Sean Burke 4.00 10.00
ASSK Sami Kapanen 4.00 10.00
ASSO Sandis Ozolinsh 3.00 8.00
ASTS Teemu Selanne 3.00 8.00
ASVD Vincent Damphousse 4.00 10.00
ASWG Wayne Gretzky 30.00 80.00

2002-03 Upper Deck Blow-Ups

Found in Canadian retail boxes only, this 42-card set was larger sized parallels of the base set. Cards were serial-numbered out of 299.

COMPLETE SET (42) 150.00
C1 Paul Kariya 6.00 10.00
C2 Ilya Kovalchuk 2.50 6.00
C3 Joe Thornton 2.50 6.00
C4 Roman Turek 1.50 2.00
C5 Jeff O'Neill 1.50 2.00
C6 Rob Blake 1.50 2.00
C7 Patrick Roy 8.00 15.00
C8 Joe Sakic 4.00 10.00
C9 Peter Forsberg 5.00 10.00
C10 Marc Denis 1.50 3.00
C11 Mike Modano 3.00 6.00
C12 Marty Turco 1.50 4.00
C13 Steve Yzerman 8.00 15.00
C14 Curtis Joseph 2.50 6.00
C15 Nicklas Lidstrom 2.00 4.00
C16 Mike Comrie 1.50 4.00
C17 Tommy Salo 1.50 3.00
C18 Roberto Luongo 1.50 3.00
C19 Felix Potvin 2.00 4.00
C20 Marian Gaborik 2.00 6.00
C21 Jose Theodore 2.00 4.00
C22 Saku Koivu 2.00 4.00
C23 Scott Hartnell 3.00
C24 Scott Stevens 1.50 2.00
C25 Martin Brodeur 5.00 10.00
C26 Eric Lindros 2.00 4.00
C27 Pavel Bure 2.50 6.00
C28 Marian Hossa 2.00 4.00
C29 Daniel Alfredsson 1.50 3.00
C30 Keith Primeau 1.50 2.00
C31 Sean Burke 1.50 3.00
C32 Tony Amonte 2.00 4.00
C33 Mario Lemieux 10.00 20.00
C34 Owen Nolan 1.50 3.00
C35 Al MacInnis 1.50 3.00
C36 Brad Richards 1.50 3.00
C37 Vincent Lecavalier 1.50 3.00
C38 Mats Sundin 2.00 4.00
C39 Ed Belfour 2.00 4.00
C40 Todd Bertuzzi 1.50 3.00
C41 Markus Naslund 1.50 3.00
C42 Olaf Kolzig 1.50 3.00

2002-03 Upper Deck Bright Futures

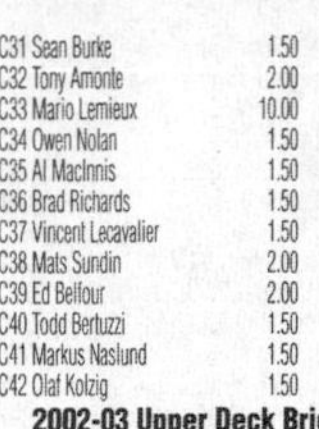

*MULT.COLOR SWATCH: .75X TO 1.5X
STATED ODDS 1:72 SERIES 2
ALL CARDS CARRY BF PREFIX
AM Alexei Morozov 4.00 10.00
BB Brian Boucher 4.00 10.00
DA Denis Arkhipov 4.00 10.00
DL David Legwand 4.00 10.00
IB Ilja Bryzgalov 4.00 10.00
JB Jaroslav Bednar 4.00 10.00
JG Jean-Sebastien Giguere 4.00 10.00
JL Jamie Lundmark 4.00 10.00
ME Martin Erat 4.00 10.00
MM Manny Malhotra 4.00 10.00
MP Matt Pettinger 4.00 10.00
MR Mike Ribeiro 4.00 10.00
MY Mike York 4.00 10.00
PA Timo Parssinen 4.00 10.00
PB Pavel Brendl 4.00 10.00
PS Patrik Stefan 4.00 10.00
RK Rostislav Klesla 4.00 10.00
SG Simon Gagne 4.00 10.00
TC Tim Connolly 4.00 10.00
TP Taylor Pyatt 4.00 10.00
VN Ville Nieminen 4.00 10.00

2002-03 Upper Deck CHL Graduates

*MULT.COLOR SWATCH: .75X TO 1.5X
STATED ODDS 1:96 SERIES 1 HOBBY
CGAT Alex Tanguay 4.00 10.00
CGBL Dan Blackburn 4.00 10.00
CGDB Daniel Briere 4.00 10.00
CGDL David Legwand 4.00 10.00
CGED Eric Daze 4.00 10.00
CGEL Eric Lindros 8.00 20.00
CGGM Glen Murray 4.00 10.00
CGJA Jason Arnott 4.00 10.00
CGJF Jeff Friesen 4.00 10.00
CGJS Joe Sakic 6.00 15.00
CGJT Joe Thornton 8.00 20.00
CGKP Keith Primeau 4.00 10.00
CGMD Marc Denis 4.00 10.00
CGML Mario Lemieux 20.00 50.00
CGMM Mike Modano 8.00 20.00
CGMR Mark Recchi 4.00 10.00
CGRT Ron Tugnutt 4.00 10.00
CGSS Steve Sullivan 4.00 10.00
CGSY Steve Yzerman 12.50 30.00
CGTL Trevor Linden 4.00 10.00

2002-03 Upper Deck CHL Graduates Gold

*GOLD: 2X TO 5X BASIC JERSEY
STATED PRINT RUN 25 SER.#'d SETS

2002-03 Upper Deck Difference Makers

*MULT.COLOR SWATCH: .75X TO 1.5X
STATED ODDS 1:72 SERIES 2
BL Brian Leetch 3.00 8.00
BS Brendan Shanahan 3.00 8.00
ED Eric Daze 3.00 8.00
IK Ilya Kovalchuk 5.00 12.00
JA Jason Allison 3.00 8.00
JI Jarome Iginla 4.00 10.00
JJ Jaromir Jagr 6.00 15.00
JT Joe Thornton 8.00 20.00
JT Jose Theodore 4.00 10.00
MD Mike Dunham 3.00 8.00
ML Mario Lemieux 15.00 40.00
MM Mike Modano 8.00 20.00
MS Mats Sundin 3.00 8.00
PK Paul Kariya 3.00 8.00
PR Patrick Roy 15.00 40.00
RB Rob Blake 3.00 8.00
RT Roman Turek 3.00 8.00
SA Miroslav Satan 3.00 8.00
SS Sergei Samsonov 3.00 8.00
SY Steve Yzerman 10.00 25.00
ZP Zigmund Palffy 3.00 8.00

2002-03 Upper Deck Fan Favorites

STATED ODDS 1:96 SERIES 2 RETAIL
ALL CARDS CARRY FF PREFIX
AD Adam Deadmarsh 3.00 8.00
BL Brian Leetch 3.00 8.00
JI Jarome Iginla 4.00 10.00
JJ Jaromir Jagr 6.00 15.00
KP Keith Primeau 3.00 8.00
MB Martin Brodeur 10.00 25.00
MM Mike Modano 8.00 20.00
MN Markus Naslund 3.00 8.00
NL Nicklas Lidstrom 3.00 8.00
PF Peter Forsberg 10.00 25.00
PK Paul Kariya 3.00 8.00
SD Shane Doan 3.00 8.00
SK Saku Koivu 3.00 8.00
SS Sergei Samsonov 3.00 8.00

2002-03 Upper Deck First Class

*MULT.COLOR SWATCH: .75X TO 1.5X
STATED ODDS 1:288 SERIES 1
UDJJ Jaromir Jagr 8.00 20.00
UDJS Joe Sakic 12.50 30.00
UDJT Jose Theodore 8.00 20.00
UDML Mario Lemieux 15.00 40.00
UDPK Paul Kariya 8.00 20.00
UDPR Patrick Roy 15.00 40.00
UDSY Steve Yzerman 12.50 30.00

2002-03 Upper Deck First Class Gold

This 7-card set paralleled the regular First Class jersey set but was enhanced by gold foil and serial-numbering out of 75.

*GOLD: .75X TO 2X BASIC JERSEY

2002-03 Upper Deck Game Jersey Autographs

*AUTO: 2.5X TO 6X BASIC JERSEY
RANDOM INSERTS IN SERIES 2 PACKS
PRINT RUN 50 SERIAL #'d SETS
ALL CARDS CARRY SGJ PREFIX
PR Patrick Roy 125.00 250.00
SY Steve Yzerman 75.00 150.00
WG Wayne Gretzky 200.00 400.00

2002-03 Upper Deck Game Jersey Series II

*MULT.COLOR SWATCH: .75X TO 1.5X
STATED ODDS 1:96 SERIES 2
GJEB Ed Belfour 4.00 10.00
GJHZ Henrik Zetterberg 12.00 30.00
GJIK Ilya Kovalchuk 5.00 12.00
GJJL John LeClair 3.00 8.00
GJJS Joe Sakic 6.00 15.00
GJJT Joe Thornton 6.00 15.00
GJMB Martin Brodeur 12.50 30.00
GJPB Pavel Bure 3.00 8.00
GJPR Patrick Roy 15.00 40.00
GJSG Simon Gagne 3.00 8.00
GJSH Scott Hartnell 3.00 8.00
GJSS Sergei Samsonov 3.00 8.00
GJSY Steve Yzerman 10.00 25.00
GJWG Wayne Gretzky 30.00 80.00

2002-03 Upper Deck Gifted Greats

COMPLETE SET (14) 15.00 30.00
STATED ODDS 1:12 SERIES 1
GG1 Paul Kariya .40 1.00
GG2 Bobby Orr 2.50 6.00

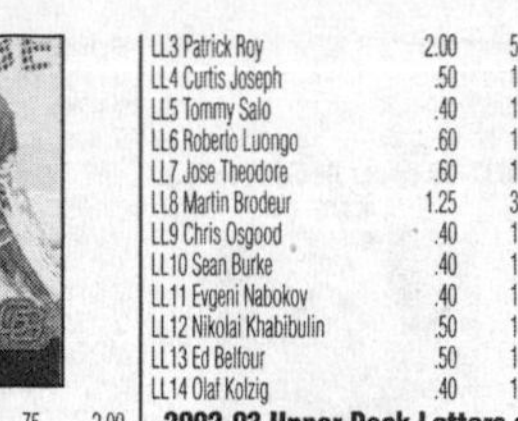

GG3 Joe Sakic .75 2.00
GG4 Patrick Roy 2.00 5.00
GG5 Peter Forsberg 1.00 2.50
GG6 Mike Modano .60 1.50
GG7 Dominik Hasek .75 2.00
GG8 Steve Yzerman 2.00 5.00
GG9 Gordie Howe 2.00 5.00
GG10 Martin Brodeur 1.00 2.50
GG11 Wayne Gretzky 3.00 8.00
GG12 Pavel Bure .40 1.00
GG13 Mario Lemieux 2.50 6.00
GG14 Jaromir Jagr .60 1.50

2002-03 Upper Deck Goaltender Threads

*MULT.COLOR SWATCH: .75X TO 1.5X
STATED ODDS 1:96 SERIES 2
ALL CARDS CARRY GT PREFIX
*GOLD: 2X TO 5X BASE HI
GOLD PRINT RUN 25 SER.#'d SETS
FP Felix Potvin 3.00 8.00
IB Ilja Bryzgalov 3.00 8.00
JG Jean-Sebastien Giguere 3.00 8.00
JT Jose Theodore 4.00 10.00
MB Martin Biron 3.00 8.00
MD Mike Dunham 3.00 8.00
MN Mika Noronen 3.00 8.00
MT Marty Turco 8.00 20.00
OK Olaf Kolzig 3.00 8.00
RC Roman Cechmanek 3.00 8.00
RL Roberto Luongo 4.00 10.00
RT Roman Turek 3.00 8.00
SS Steve Shields 3.00 8.00
TH Jocelyn Thibault 3.00 8.00

2002-03 Upper Deck Good Old Days

This 14-card memorabilia set was inserted at a rate of 1:96 Series 1 packs.

*MULT.COLOR SWATCH: .75X TO 1.5X
GOAM Al MacInnis 3.00 8.00
GOBG Bill Guerin 3.00 8.00
GOBH Brett Hull 6.00 15.00
GOBS Brendan Shanahan 4.00 10.00
GOCJ Curtis Joseph 4.00 10.00
GODM Dominik Hasek 8.00 20.00
GOJN Joe Nieuwendyk 3.00 8.00
GOJS Joe Sakic 8.00 20.00
GOKP Keith Primeau 4.00 10.00
GOKT Keith Tkachuk 4.00 10.00
GOMS Mats Sundin 4.00 10.00
GOPB Pavel Bure 4.00 10.00
GOTF Theo Fleury 4.00 10.00
GOTS Teemu Selanne 4.00 10.00

2002-03 Upper Deck Hot Spots

*MULT.COLOR SWATCH: .75X TO 1.5X
STATED ODDS 1:96 SERIES 1 HOBBY
HSCL Claude Lemieux 3.00 8.00
HSDA Denis Arkhipov 3.00 8.00
HSDB Daniel Briere 3.00 8.00
HSDL David Legwand 4.00 10.00
HSDU Mike Dunham 4.00 10.00
HSIK Ilya Kovalchuk 5.00 12.00
HSMD Marc Denis 4.00 10.00
HSME Martin Erat 3.00 8.00
HSRK Rostislav Klesla 3.00 8.00
HSRW Ray Whitney 3.00 8.00
HSSD Shane Doan 3.00 8.00
HSSH Scott Hartnell 3.00 8.00

2002-03 Upper Deck Last Line of Defense

COMPLETE SET (14) 10.00 20.00
STATED ODDS 1:12 SERIES 2
LL1 Jean-Sebastien Giguere .40 1.00
LL2 Martin Biron .40 1.00
LL3 Patrick Roy 2.00 5.00
LL4 Curtis Joseph .50 1.25
LL5 Tommy Salo .40 1.00
LL6 Roberto Luongo .60 1.50
LL7 Jose Theodore .60 1.50
LL8 Martin Brodeur 1.25 3.00
LL9 Chris Osgood .40 1.00
LL10 Sean Burke .40 1.00
LL11 Evgeni Nabokov .40 1.00
LL12 Nikolai Khabibulin .50 1.25
LL13 Ed Belfour .50 1.25
LL14 Olaf Kolzig .40 1.00

2002-03 Upper Deck Letters of Note

*MULT.COLOR SWATCH: .75X TO 1.5X
STATED ODDS 1:144 SERIES 1
*GOLD: .75X TO 2X BASIC JERSEY
GOLD PRINT RUN 50 SER.#'d SETS
LNCD Chris Drury 6.00 15.00
LNCP Chris Pronger 6.00 15.00
LNJI Jarome Iginla 8.00 20.00
LNJS Joe Sakic 12.50 30.00
LNML Mario Lemieux 20.00 50.00
LNMM Mike Modano 6.00 15.00
LNMN Markus Naslund 6.00 15.00
LNMS Mats Sundin 6.00 15.00
LNON Owen Nolan 6.00 15.00
LNPB Peter Bondra 6.00 15.00
LNPK Paul Kariya 6.00 15.00
LNSK Saku Koivu 6.00 15.00
LNSS Scott Stevens 8.00 20.00
LNSY Steve Yzerman 15.00 40.00

2002-03 Upper Deck Number Crunchers

COMPLETE SET (14) 10.00 20.00
STATED ODDS 1:12 SERIES 2
NC1 Joe Thornton .75 2.00
NC2 Theo Fleury .30 .75
NC3 Brenden Morrow .40 1.00
NC4 Gordie Howe 2.00 5.00
NC5 Brendan Shanahan .50 1.25
NC6 Georges Laraque .30 .75
NC7 Scott Hartnell .30 .75
NC8 Eric Lindros .50 1.25
NC9 Donald Brashear .30 .75
NC10 Keith Primeau .30 .75
NC11 Jeremy Roenick .60 1.50
NC12 Keith Tkachuk .50 1.25
NC13 Ed Jovanovski .40 1.00
NC14 Todd Bertuzzi .50 1.25

2002-03 Upper Deck On the Rise

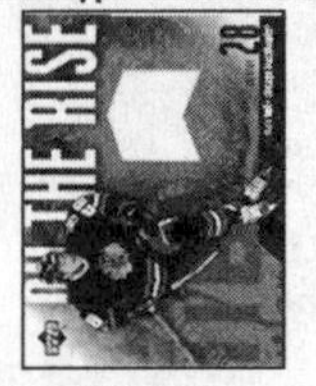

*MULT.COLOR SWATCH: .75X TO 1.5X
STATED ODDS 1:96 SERIES 1 HOBBY
ORBM Brenden Morrow 4.00 10.00
ORDB Dan Blackburn 4.00 10.00
ORIK Ilya Kovalchuk 5.00 12.00
ORKK Krystofer Kolanos 3.00 8.00
ORMB Mark Bell 3.00 8.00
ORRK Rostislav Klesla 3.00 8.00
ORSR Steven Reinprecht 3.00 8.00

2002-03 Upper Deck Patch Card Logo

STATED ODDS 1:7500 SERIES 2
NOT PRICED DUE TO SCARCITY
BS Brendan Shanahan
IK Ilya Kovalchuk
JJ Jaromir Jagr
MH Marian Hossa
ML Mario Lemieux
MN Markus Naslund
MS Mats Sundin
PR Patrick Roy
SG Simon Gagne
SK Saku Koivu
WG Wayne Gretzky

2002-03 Upper Deck Patch Card Name Plate

STATED ODDS 1:7500 SERIES 2
NOT PRICED DUE TO SCARCITY
JJ Jaromir Jagr
JR Jeremy Roenick
MB Martin Brodeur
ML Mario Lemieux
PF Peter Forsberg
PK Paul Kariya
SF Sergei Fedorov
SS Sergei Samsonov
VL Vincent Lecavalier
WG Wayne Gretzky

2002-03 Upper Deck Patch Card Numbers

STATED ODDS 1:7500 SERIES 2
NOT PRICED DUE TO SCARCITY
JS Joe Sakic
JT Jose Theodore
JT Joe Thornton
MB Martin Brodeur
ML Mario Lemieux
MM Mike Modano
OK Olaf Kolzig
PK Paul Kariya
SY Steve Yzerman
WG Wayne Gretzky

2002-03 Upper Deck Patchwork

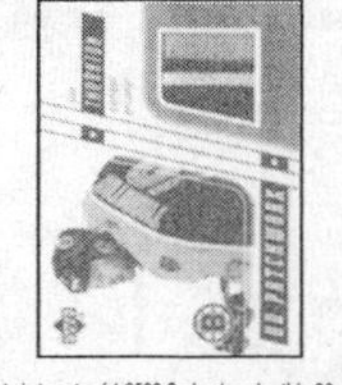

Inserted at a rate of 1:2500 Series 1 packs, this 30-card set featured swatches of game jersey patches. As of press time, not all cards have been verified.

PWAK Alexei Kovalev 40.00 100.00
PWBG Bill Guerin 40.00 100.00
PWBS Brendan Shanahan 40.00 100.00
PWCD Chris Drury 40.00 100.00
PWJJ Jaromir Jagr 100.00 200.00
PWJL John LeClair 40.00 100.00
PWJS Joe Sakic 150.00 300.00
PWJT Joe Thornton 60.00 150.00
PWKP Keith Primeau 40.00 100.00
PWMB Martin Brodeur 125.00 300.00
PWMD Mike Dunham 40.00 100.00
PWMH Milan Hejduk 60.00 150.00
PWML Mario Lemieux 200.00 400.00
PWMM Mike Modano 60.00 150.00
PWMN Markus Naslund 40.00 100.00
PWMS Mats Sundin 40.00 100.00
PWMT Marty Turco 60.00 150.00
PWNL Nicklas Lidstrom 40.00 100.00
PWPF Peter Forsberg 75.00 200.00
PWPK Paul Kariya 125.00 300.00
PWPR Patrick Roy 100.00 250.00
PWSB Sean Burke 40.00 100.00
PWSF Sergei Fedorov 60.00 150.00
PWSG Simon Gagne 40.00 100.00
PWSK Saku Koivu 40.00 100.00
PWSS Sergei Samsonov 40.00 100.00
PWSY Steve Yzerman 125.00 300.00
PWTA Tony Amonte 40.00 100.00
PWTH Jose Theodore 60.00 150.00
PWZP Zigmund Palffy 40.00 100.00

2002-03 Upper Deck Pinpoint Accuracy

*MULT.COLOR SWATCH: .75X TO 1.5X
STATED ODDS 1:96 SERIES 2
PAAT Alex Tanguay 3.00 8.00
PABS Brendan Shanahan 3.00 8.00
PACD Chris Drury 3.00 8.00
PAED Eric Daze 3.00 8.00
PAGS Geoff Sanderson 3.00 8.00
PAJI Jarome Iginla 4.00 10.00
PAJT Joe Thornton 6.00 15.00
PAMH Milan Hejduk 3.00 8.00
PAML Mario Lemieux 12.50 30.00
PAMM Mike Modano 8.00 20.00
PAMR Mark Recchi 3.00 8.00
PAPB Pavel Bure 3.00 8.00
PAPK Paul Kariya 3.00 8.00
PASF Sergei Fedorov 5.00 12.00

2002-03 Upper Deck Playbooks

Extremely limited, this 14-card set featured a "book" style folding card that opened to reveal jersey swatches. Individual print runs are listed below. This set is not priced due to scarcity. Please note that card #PL12 does not exist.

PL1 Paul Kariya/15
PL2 Ray Bourque/10
PL3 Joe Sakic/15
PL4 Patrick Roy/10
PL5 Brendan Shanahan/15
PL6 Sergei Fedorov/15
PL7 Dominik Hasek/10
PL8 Wayne Gretzky/5
PL9 Wayne Gretzky/20

Card	Low	High
PL10 Jose Theodore/15		
PL11 Teemu Selanne/20		
PL13 Curtis Joseph/15		
PL14 Mats Sundin/15		
PL15 Markus Naslund/20		

2002-03 Upper Deck Playbooks Series II

Extremely limited, this 14-card set featured a folding "book" card that opened to reveal dual jersey swatches. Known print runs are listed below. This set is not priced due to scarcity.

FS Peter Forsberg
Joe Sakic
HD Milan Hejduk
Chris Drury
JK Jaromir Jagr
Olaf Kolzig/14
KG Paul Kariya
Jean-Sebastien Giguere/14
KT Saku Koivu
Jose Theodore
LK M.Lemieux/A.Kovalev
LL Brian Leetch
Eric Lindros
LW John LeClair
Justin Williams
MT M.Modano/M.Turco/17
RP Jeremy Roenick
Keith Primeau
RT Patrick Roy
Alex Tanguay
SL Brendan Shanahan
Nicklas Lidstrom
ST Sergei Samsonov
Joe Thornton
YF S.Yzerman/S.Fedorov

2002-03 Upper Deck Reaching Fifty

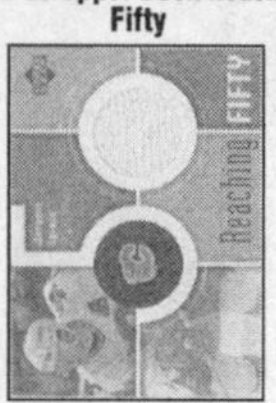

*MULT.COLOR SWATCH: .75X TO 1.5X
STATED ODDS 1:96 SERIES 2

Card	Low	High
50BH Brett Hull	4.00	10.00
50BO Peter Bondra	3.00	8.00
50JI Jarome Iginla	4.00	10.00
50JJ Jaromir Jagr	6.00	15.00
50JL John LeClair	3.00	8.00
50JS Joe Sakic	6.00	15.00
50KT Keith Tkachuk	3.00	8.00
50ML Mario Lemieux	15.00	40.00
50MM Mike Modano	4.00	10.00
50PB Pavel Bure	3.00	8.00
50PK Paul Kariya	3.00	8.00
50SF Sergei Fedorov	4.00	10.00
50SY Steve Yzerman	10.00	25.00
50WG Wayne Gretzky	25.00	60.00

2002-03 Upper Deck Reaching Fifty Gold

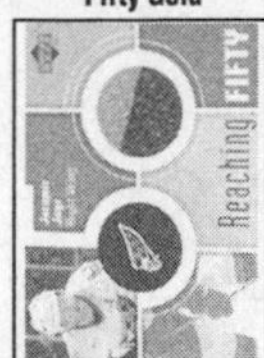

*STARS: 2X TO 5X BASIC JERSEY
PRINT RUN 50 SERIAL #'d SETS

2002-03 Upper Deck Saviors Jerseys

Known print runs and short prints are listed below.

*MULT.COLOR SWATCH: .75X TO 1.5X
STATED ODDS 1:96 SERIES 1

Card	Low	High
SVBB Brian Boucher	3.00	8.00
SVBD Byron Dafoe	3.00	8.00
SVBJ Brent Johnson	3.00	8.00
SVJG Jean-Sebastien Giguere	3.00	8.00
SVJT Jose Theodore SP	5.00	12.00
SVMB Martin Biron	3.00	8.00
SVMD Mike Dunham	3.00	8.00
SVMT Marty Turco	4.00	10.00
SVOK Olaf Kolzig	3.00	8.00
SVPR Patrick Roy SP	25.00	60.00
SVRT Roman Turek	3.00	8.00
SVTH Jocelyn Thibault/100	12.50	30.00
SVTU Ron Tugnutt/100	8.00	20.00

2002-03 Upper Deck Shooting Stars

Card	Low	High
COMPLETE SET (14)	15.00	30.00
STATED ODDS 1:12 SERIES 2		
SS1 Paul Kariya	.40	1.00
SS2 Jarome Iginla	.50	1.25
SS3 Joe Thornton	.60	1.50
SS4 Joe Sakic	.75	2.00
SS5 Mike Modano	.60	1.50
SS6 Gordie Howe	2.00	5.00
SS7 Steve Yzerman	2.00	5.00
SS8 Mike Comrie	.30	.75
SS9 Wayne Gretzky	3.00	8.00
SS10 Pavel Bure	.40	1.00
SS11 Simon Gagne	.40	1.00
SS12 Mario Lemieux	2.50	6.00
SS13 Teemu Selanne	.40	1.00
SS14 Jaromir Jagr	.60	1.50

2002-03 Upper Deck Sizzling Scorers

Card	Low	High
COMPLETE SET (14)	8.00	15.00
STATED ODDS 1:12 SERIES 1		
SS1 Ilya Kovalchuk	.50	1.25
SS2 Joe Thornton	.60	1.50
SS3 Jarome Iginla	.50	1.25
SS4 Ron Francis	.40	1.00
SS5 Joe Sakic	.75	2.00
SS6 Mike Modano	.60	1.50
SS7 Brendan Shanahan	.40	1.00
SS8 Mike Comrie	.40	1.00
SS9 Marian Gaborik	.75	2.00
SS10 Patrik Elias	.40	1.00
SS11 Pavel Bure	.40	1.00
SS12 Jeremy Roenick	.50	1.25
SS13 Mats Sundin	.40	1.00
SS14 Todd Bertuzzi	.40	1.00

2002-03 Upper Deck Specialists

*MULT.COLOR SWATCH: .75X TO 1.5X
STATED ODDS 1:96 SERIES 1 HOBBY

Card	Low	High
SAZ Alexei Zhamnov	3.00	8.00
SBL Brian Leetch	4.00	10.00
SCD Chris Drury	4.00	10.00
SEB Eric Belanger	3.00	8.00
SJL Jere Lehtinen	4.00	10.00
SMM Mike Modano	6.00	15.00
SMR Mark Recchi	4.00	10.00
SMS Miroslav Satan	4.00	10.00
SPB Peter Bondra	4.00	10.00
SRB Jarome Iginla	6.00	15.00
SRL Robert Lang	3.00	8.00
SSF Sergei Fedorov	5.00	12.00
SSS Sergei Samsonov	4.00	10.00
STM Todd Marchant	3.00	8.00

2002-03 Upper Deck Speed Demons

*MULT.COLOR SWATCH: .75X TO 1.5X
STATED ODDS 1:96 SERIES 1 RETAIL

Card	Low	High
SDDB Daniel Briere	3.00	8.00
SDPB Pavel Bure	3.00	8.00
SDSF Sergei Fedorov	5.00	12.00
SDSG Simon Gagne	3.00	8.00
SDSS Steve Sullivan	3.00	8.00
SDTM Todd Marchant	3.00	8.00
SDZP Zigmund Palffy	4.00	10.00

2002-03 Upper Deck Super Saviors

Card	Low	High
COMPLETE SET (14)	12.50	25.00
STATED ODDS 1:12 SERIES 1		
SA1 Martin Biron	.60	1.50
SA2 Roman Turek	.60	1.50
SA3 Arturs Irbe	.60	1.50
SA4 Patrick Roy	2.50	6.00
SA5 Marty Turco	.60	1.50
SA6 Dominik Hasek	1.00	2.50
SA7 Jose Theodore	1.00	2.50
SA8 Martin Brodeur	1.25	3.00
SA9 Chris Osgood	.60	1.50
SA10 Patrick Lalime	.60	1.50
SA11 Sean Burke	.60	1.50
SA12 Evgeni Nabokov	.60	1.50
SA13 Brent Johnson	.60	1.50
SA14 Olaf Kolzig	.60	1.50

2003-04 Upper Deck

This 475-card set was issued in two different sets of 245 cards and 230 cards. The "Young Guns" rookie subset cards were inserted at odds of 1:4.

Card	Low	High
COMPLETE SERIES 1 (245)	200.00	400.00
COMP.SERIES 1 w/o SP's	20.00	40.00
COMPLETE SERIES 2 (230)	125.00	250.00
COMP.SERIES 2 w/o SP's	20.00	40.00
1 Petr Sykora	.02	.10
2 Steve Rucchin	.02	.10
3 Sandis Ozolinsh	.02	.10
4 Jason Krog	.02	.10
5 Sergei Fedorov	.25	.60
6 Rob Niedermayer	.02	.10
7 Jean-Sebastien Giguere	.15	.40
8 Dany Heatley	.25	.60
9 Slava Kozlov	.02	.10
10 Patrik Stefan	.02	.10
11 Yannick Tremblay	.02	.10
12 Shawn McEachern	.02	.10
13 Byron Dafoe	.15	.40
14 Joe Thornton	.30	.75
15 Bryan Berard	.02	.10
16 P-J Axelsson	.02	.10
17 Hal Gill	.02	.10
18 P.J. Stock	.02	.10
19 Mike Knuble	.02	.10
20 Steve Shields	.15	.40
21 Daniel Briere	.02	.10
22 Ales Kotalik	.02	.10
23 Curtis Brown	.02	.10
24 JP Dumont	.02	.10
25 Alexei Zhitnik	.02	.10
26 Maxim Afinogenov	.02	.10
27 Martin Biron	.15	.40
28 Dean McAmmond	.02	.10
29 Jarome Iginla	.25	.60
30 Martin Gelinas	.02	.10
31 Jordan Leopold	.02	.10
32 Chuck Kobasew	.02	.10
33 Roman Turek	.15	.40
34 Jeff O'Neill	.02	.10
35 Ron Francis	.15	.40
36 Sean Hill	.02	.10
37 Erik Cole	.02	.10
38 Pavel Brendl	.02	.10
39 Kevin Weekes	.15	.40
40 Alexei Zhamnov	.02	.10
41 Kyle Calder	.02	.10
42 Tyler Arnason	.15	.40
43 Igor Radulov	.02	.10
44 Jocelyn Thibault	.15	.40
45 Peter Forsberg	.50	1.25
46 Alex Tanguay	.15	.40
47 Derek Morris	.02	.10
48 Rob Blake	.15	.40
49 Paul Kariya	.20	.50
50 Teemu Selanne	.20	.50
51 David Aebischer	.15	.40
52 Patrick Roy	1.00	2.50
53 Pascal Leclaire	.15	.40
54 Geoff Sanderson	.02	.10
55 Rick Nash	.25	.60
56 Rostislav Klesla	.02	.10
57 Jody Shelley	.02	.10
58 Marc Denis	.15	.40
59 Mike Modano	.30	.75
60 Sergei Zubov	.02	.10
61 Jere Lehtinen	.15	.40
62 Steve Ott	.02	.10
63 Niko Kapanen	.02	.10
64 Jason Bacashihua	.15	.40
65 Marty Turco	.15	.40
66 Brett Hull	.25	.60
67 Nicklas Lidstrom	.20	.50
68 Mathieu Schneider	.02	.10
69 Henrik Zetterberg	.20	.50
70 Pavel Datsyuk	.20	.50
71 Derian Hatcher	.02	.10
72 Steve Yzerman	1.00	2.50
73 Manny Legace	.15	.40
74 Ryan Smyth	.02	.10
75 Mike York	.02	.10
76 Ales Hemsky	.15	.40
77 Eric Brewer	.02	.10
78 Fernando Pisani	.02	.10
79 Georges Laraque	.02	.10
80 Tommy Salo	.15	.40
81 Viktor Kozlov	.02	.10
82 Kristian Huselius	.02	.10
83 Stephen Weiss	.02	.10
84 Jay Bouwmeester	.02	.10
85 Roberto Luongo	.25	.60
86 Zigmund Palffy	.15	.40
87 Alexander Frolov	.02	.10
88 Luc Robitaille	.15	.40
89 Ian Laperriere	.02	.10
90 Jared Aulin	.02	.10
91 Roman Cechmanek	.15	.40
92 Marian Gaborik	.40	1.00
93 Pascal Dupuis	.02	.10
94 Andrew Brunette	.02	.10
95 Wes Walz	.02	.10
96 Pierre-Marc Bouchard	.02	.10
97 Willie Mitchell	.02	.10
98 Manny Fernandez	.15	.40
99 Saku Koivu	.20	.50
100 Jan Bulis	.02	.10
101 Marcel Hossa	.02	.10
102 Michael Komisarek	.02	.10
103 Richard Zednik	.02	.10
104 Mathieu Garon	.02	.10
105 Ron Hainsey	.02	.10
106 David Legwand	.15	.40
107 Greg Johnson	.02	.10
108 Scott Hartnell	.02	.10
109 Scottie Upshall	.02	.10
110 Tomas Vokoun	.15	.40
111 Patrik Elias	.15	.40
112 Jeff Friesen	.02	.10
113 Joe Nieuwendyk	.15	.40
114 Scott Niedermayer	.02	.10
115 Grant Marshall	.02	.10
116 Scott Stevens	.15	.40
117 Martin Brodeur	.50	1.25
118 Jason Blake	.02	.10
119 Mark Parrish	.02	.10
120 Michael Peca	.02	.10
121 Adrian Aucoin	.02	.10
122 Rick DiPietro	.15	.40
123 Eric Godard	.02	.10
124 Alex Kovalev	.15	.40
125 Anson Carter	.15	.40
126 Mark Messier	.20	.50
127 Petr Nedved	.02	.10
128 Tom Poti	.02	.10
129 Jamie Lundmark	.02	.10
130 Mike Dunham	.15	.40
131 Marian Hossa	.20	.50
132 Martin Havlat	.15	.40
133 Zdeno Chara	.02	.10
134 Peter Schaefer	.02	.10
135 Ray Emery	.15	.40
136 Jason Spezza	.20	.50
137 Patrick Lalime	.15	.40
138 Mark Recchi	.15	.40
139 Tony Amonte	.15	.40
140 Keith Primeau	.02	.10
141 Simon Gagne	.20	.50
142 Eric Weinrich	.02	.10
143 Jim Vandermeer	.02	.10
144 Robert Esche	.15	.40
145 Shane Doan	.02	.10
146 Chris Gratton	.02	.10
147 Jan Hrdina	.02	.10
148 Daymond Langkow	.02	.10
149 Tyson Nash	.02	.10
150 Brian Boucher	.15	.40
151 Mario Lemieux	1.25	3.00
152 Aleksey Morozov	.02	.10
153 Ramzi Abid	.02	.10
154 Dick Tarnstrom	.02	.10
155 Rico Fata	.02	.10
156 Brooks Orpik	.02	.10
157 Vincent Damphousse	.02	.10
158 Marco Sturm	.02	.10
159 Mike Ricci	.02	.10
160 Jim Fahey	.02	.10
161 Niko Dimitrakos	.02	.10
162 Kyle McLaren	.02	.10
163 Evgeni Nabokov	.15	.40
164 Al MacInnis	.15	.40
165 Scott Mellanby	.02	.10
166 Keith Tkachuk	.20	.50
167 Barret Jackman	.15	.40
168 Reed Low	.02	.10
169 Chris Pronger	.15	.40
170 Chris Osgood	.15	.40
171 Vincent Lecavalier	.20	.50
172 Dave Andreychuk	.15	.40
173 Brad Richards	.15	.40
174 Pavel Kubina	.02	.10
175 Alexander Svitov	.02	.10
176 John Grahame	.15	.40
177 Alexander Mogilny	.15	.40
178 Owen Nolan	.15	.40
179 Darcy Tucker	.02	.10
180 Doug Gilmour	.15	.40
181 Tie Domi	.15	.40
182 Phil Housley	.02	.10
183 Gary Roberts	.02	.10
184 Ed Belfour	.20	.50
185 Markus Naslund	.20	.50
186 Brendan Morrison	.15	.40
187 Ed Jovanovski	.15	.40
188 Matt Cooke	.02	.10
189 Henrik Sedin	.02	.10
190 Brandon Reid	.02	.10
191 Marek Malik	.02	.10
192 Alexander Auld	.02	.10
193 Robert Lang	.02	.10
194 Sergei Gonchar	.02	.10
195 Michael Nylander	.02	.10
196 Mike Grier	.02	.10
197 Steve Konowalchuk	.02	.10
198 Olaf Kolzig	.15	.40
199 Joe Thornton CL	.25	.60
200 Martin Brodeur CL	.40	1.00
201 Garrett Burnett YG RC	2.00	5.00
202 Joffrey Lupul YG RC	4.00	10.00
203 Jiri Hudler YG RC	4.00	10.00
204 Patrice Bergeron YG RC	10.00	25.00
205 Matthew Lombardi YG RC	2.00	5.00
206 Eric Staal YG RC	20.00	40.00
207 Lasse Kukkonen YG RC	2.00	5.00
208 Pavel Vorobiev YG RC	2.00	5.00
209 Travis Moen YG RC	2.00	5.00
210 Tuomo Ruutu YG RC	6.00	15.00
211 Cody McCormick YG RC	2.00	5.00
212 John-Michael Liles YG RC	2.00	5.00
213 Marek Svatos YG RC	6.00	15.00
214 Dan Fritsche YG RC	2.00	5.00
215 Antti Miettinen YG RC	2.00	5.00
216 Nathan Horton YG RC	6.00	15.00
217 Dustin Brown YG RC	3.00	8.00
218 Esa Pirnes YG RC	2.00	5.00
219 Alexander Semin YG RC	15.00	40.00
220 Tim Gleason YG RC	2.00	5.00
221 Brent Burns YG RC	2.00	5.00
222 Christoph Brandner YG RC	2.00	5.00
223 Chris Higgins YG RC	10.00	25.00
224 Dan Hamhuis YG RC	2.00	5.00
225 Jordin Tootoo YG RC	6.00	15.00
226 Marek Zidlicky YG RC	2.00	5.00
227 Wade Brookbank YG RC	2.00	5.00
228 David Hale YG RC	2.00	5.00
229 Paul Martin YG RC	2.00	5.00
230 Sean Bergenheim YG RC	2.00	5.00
231 Antoine Vermette YG RC	2.00	5.00
232 Joni Pitkanen YG RC	4.00	10.00
233 Matthew Spiller YG RC	2.00	5.00
234 Marc-Andre Fleury YG RC	30.00	60.00
235 Matt Murley YG RC	2.00	5.00
236 Ryan Malone YG RC	4.00	10.00
237 Christian Ehrhoff YG RC	2.00	5.00
238 Milan Michalek YG RC	8.00	20.00
239 Andrew Peters YG RC	2.00	5.00
240 Tom Preissing YG RC	2.00	5.00
241 Peter Sejna YG RC	2.00	5.00
242 Matt Stajan YG RC	6.00	15.00
243 Maxim Kondratiev YG RC	2.00	5.00
244 Boyd Gordon YG RC	2.00	5.00
245 Marc-Andre Fleury / Eric Staal / Nathan Horton CL	2.00	5.00
246 Vaclav Prospal	.02	.10
247 Stanislav Chistov	.02	.10
248 Mike Leclerc	.02	.10
249 Keith Carney	.02	.10
250 Martin Gerber	.15	.40
251 Sammy Pahlsson	.02	.10
252 Ruslan Salei	.02	.10
253 Marc Savard	.02	.10
254 Ilya Kovalchuk	.25	.60
255 Kamil Piros	.02	.10
256 Frantisek Kaberle	.02	.10
257 Pasi Nurminen	.15	.40
258 Sergei Samsonov	.15	.40
259 Brian Rolston	.15	.40
260 Travis Green	.02	.10
261 Glen Murray	.02	.10
262 Nick Boynton	.02	.10
263 Jeff Jillson	.02	.10
264 Felix Potvin	.20	.50
265 Andrew Raycroft	.15	.40
266 Jochen Hecht	.02	.10
267 Chris Drury	.15	.40
268 Miroslav Satan	.15	.40
269 Andy Delmore	.02	.10
270 Ryan Miller	.15	.40
271 Tim Connolly	.15	.40
272 Oleg Saprykin	.02	.10
273 Craig Conroy	.02	.10
274 Steve Reinprecht	.02	.10
275 Toni Lydman	.02	.10
276 Robyn Regehr	.02	.10
277 Jamie McLennan	.02	.10
278 Jaroslav Svoboda	.02	.10
279 Rod Brind'Amour	.15	.40
280 Radim Vrbata	.02	.10
281 Bret Hedican	.02	.10
282 Danny Markov	.02	.10
283 Jamie Storr	.15	.40
284 Eric Daze	.15	.40
285 Steve Sullivan	.02	.10
286 Jon Klemm	.02	.10
287 Alexander Karpovtsev	.02	.10
288 Michael Leighton	.15	.40
289 Joe Sakic	.40	1.00
290 Steve Konowalchuk	.02	.10
291 Milan Hejduk	.20	.50
292 Adam Foote	.02	.10
293 Dan Hinote	.02	.10
294 Philippe Sauve	.15	.40
295 Trevor Letowski	.02	.10
296 Andrew Cassels	.02	.10
297 Todd Marchant	.02	.10
298 David Vyborny	.02	.10
299 Darryl Sydor	.02	.10
300 Jaroslav Spacek	.02	.10
301 Espen Knutsen	.02	.10
302 Brenden Morrow	.15	.40
303 Jason Arnott	.02	.10
304 Pierre Turgeon	.15	.40
305 Bill Guerin	.15	.40
306 Teppo Numminen	.02	.10
307 Ron Tugnutt	.15	.40
308 Stu Barnes	.02	.10
309 Brendan Shanahan	.20	.50
310 Ray Whitney	.02	.10
311 Tomas Holmstrom	.02	.10
312 Chris Chelios	.20	.50
313 Jiri Fischer	.02	.10
314 Dominik Hasek	.40	1.00
315 Darren McCarty	.02	.10
316 Brad Isbister	.02	.10
317 Ethan Moreau	.02	.10
318 Raffi Torres	.02	.10
319 Mike Comrie	.15	.40
320 Radek Dvorak	.02	.10
321 Jason Smith	.02	.10
322 Ty Conklin	.15	.40
323 Adam Oates	.20	.50
324 Marcus Nilsson	.02	.10
325 Olli Jokinen	.15	.40
326 Valeri Bure	.02	.10
327 Eric Messier	.02	.10
328 Branislav Mezei	.02	.10
329 Steve Shields	.15	.40
330 Matt Cullen	.02	.10
331 Adam Deadmarsh	.02	.10
332 Jason Allison	.02	.10
333 Jozef Stumpel	.02	.10
334 Eric Belanger	.02	.10
335 Mattias Norstrom	.02	.10
336 Cristobal Huet	.15	.40
337 Martin Straka	.02	.10
338 Antti Laaksonen	.02	.10
339 Sergei Zholtok	.02	.10
340 Alexandre Daigle	.02	.10
341 Filip Kuba	.02	.10
342 Dwayne Roloson	.15	.40
343 Mike Ribeiro	.02	.10
344 Donald Audette	.02	.10
345 Michael Ryder	.02	.10
346 Andrei Markov	.02	.10
347 Jose Theodore	.25	.60
348 Yanic Perreault	.02	.10
349 Andreas Johansson	.02	.10
350 Denis Arkhipov	.02	.10
351 Rem Murray	.02	.10
352 Scott Walker	.02	.10
353 Adam Hall	.02	.10
354 Kimmo Timonen	.02	.10
355 Jason York	.02	.10
356 Sergei Brylin	.02	.10
357 John Madden	.02	.10
358 Scott Gomez	.02	.10
359 Jamie Langenbrunner	.02	.10
360 Brian Gionta	.02	.10
361 Brian Rafalski	.02	.10
362 Corey Schwab	.15	.40
363 Igor Larionov	.02	.10
364 Oleg Kvasha	.02	.10
365 Alexei Yashin	.02	.10
366 Mariusz Czerkawski	.02	.10
367 Roman Hamrlik	.02	.10
368 Janne Niinimaa	.02	.10
369 Arron Asham	.02	.10
370 Garth Snow	.02	.10
371 Jan Hlavac	.02	.10
372 Matthew Barnaby	.02	.10
373 Eric Lindros	.20	.50
374 Brian Leetch	.15	.40
375 Jussi Markkanen	.15	.40
376 Mike Fisher	.02	.10
377 Radek Bonk	.15	.40
378 Bryan Smolinski	.02	.10
379 Daniel Alfredsson	.15	.40
380 Wade Redden	.02	.10
381 Chris Phillips	.02	.10
382 Todd White	.02	.10
383 Jeremy Roenick	.25	.60
384 Michal Handzus	.02	.10
385 Donald Brashear	.02	.10
386 John LeClair	.20	.50
387 Justin Williams	.02	.10
388 Kim Johnsson	.02	.10
389 Eric Desjardins	.02	.10
390 Jeff Hackett	.15	.40
391 Ladislav Nagy	.02	.10
392 Brian Savage	.02	.10
393 Mike Johnson	.02	.10
394 Branko Radivojevic	.02	.10
395 Paul Mara	.02	.10
396 David Tanabe	.02	.10
397 Sean Burke	.15	.40
398 Mike Sillinger	.02	.10
399 Drake Berehowsky	.02	.10
400 Steve McKenna	.02	.10
401 Konstantin Koltsov	.02	.10
402 Michal Rozsival	.02	.10
403 Sebastien Caron	.15	.40
404 Patrick Marleau	.15	.40
405 Wayne Primeau	.02	.10
406 Alexander Korolyuk	.02	.10
407 Jonathan Cheechoo	.05	.12
408 Mike Rathje	.02	.10
409 Brad Stuart	.02	.10
410 Scott Thornton	.02	.10
411 Pavol Demitra	.15	.40
412 Doug Weight	.15	.40
413 Eric Boguniecki	.02	.10
414 Petr Cajanek	.02	.10
415 Brent Johnson	.15	.40
416 Dallas Drake	.02	.10
417 Cory Stillman	.02	.10
418 Fredrik Modin	.02	.10
419 Martin St. Louis	.15	.40
420 Ruslan Fedotenko	.02	.10
421 Dan Boyle	.02	.10
422 Nikolai Khabibulin	.20	.50
423 Mats Sundin	.20	.50
424 Joe Nieuwendyk	.15	.40
425 Nik Antropov	.02	.10
426 Tomas Kaberle	.02	.10
427 Bryan McCabe	.02	.10
428 Mikael Tellqvist	.15	.40
429 Ken Klee	.02	.10
430 Daniel Sedin	.02	.10
431 Magnus Arvedson	.02	.10
432 Trevor Linden	.02	.10
433 Todd Bertuzzi	.20	.50
434 Mattias Ohlund	.02	.10
435 Dan Cloutier	.15	.40
436 Johan Hedberg	.15	.40
437 Jason King	.02	.10
438 Peter Bondra	.15	.40
439 Jeff Halpern	.02	.10
440 Jaromir Jagr	.30	.75
441 Steve Eminger	.02	.10
442 Sebastien Charpentier	.15	.40
443 Dainius Zubrus	.02	.10
444 Mario Lemieux	1.25	3.00
445 Jason Spezza	.20	.50
446 Brent Krahn YG RC	2.00	5.00
447 Boyd Kane YG RC	2.00	5.00
448 Greg Campbell YG RC	2.00	5.00
449 Andrew Hutchinson YG RC	2.00	5.00
450 Mike Stuart YG RC	2.00	5.00
451 Nikolai Zherdev YG RC	4.00	10.00
452 Sergei Zinovjev YG RC	2.00	5.00
453 Julien Vauclair YG RC	2.00	5.00
454 Ryan Kesler YG RC	2.00	5.00
455 Fredrik Sjostrom YG RC	2.00	5.00
456 Mikhail Yakubov YG RC	2.00	5.00
457 Nathan Smith YG RC	2.00	5.00
458 Grant McNeill YG RC	2.00	5.00
459 Seamus Kotyk YG RC	2.00	5.00
460 Alan Rourke YG RC	2.00	5.00
461 John Pohl YG RC	2.00	5.00
462 Dominic Moore YG RC	2.00	5.00
463 Tony Salmelainen YG RC	2.00	5.00
464 Rastislav Stana YG RC	2.00	5.00
465 Karl Stewart YG RC	2.00	5.00
466 Darryl Bootland YG RC	2.00	5.00
467 Trevor Daley YG RC	2.00	5.00
468 Peter Sarno YG RC	2.00	5.00
469 Jed Ortmeyer YG RC	2.00	5.00
470 Nathan Robinson YG RC	2.00	5.00
471 Pat Rissmiller YG RC	2.00	5.00
472 Gretzky/Lafleur/Messier CL	6.00	15.00
473 Jose Theodore HC	3.00	8.00
474 Don Cherry HC	4.00	10.00
475 Salmlinn/Moore/Zinvjev CL	1.00	2.50

2003-04 Upper Deck 500 Goal Club

This 8-card set featured the newest members to the exclusive 500 Goal Club. Cards were inserted at 1:237 for the non-autographed cards and the autographed versions were serial-numbered to 25.

Card	Low	High
500BS Brendan Shanahan	12.50	30.00
500JJ Jaromir Jagr	15.00	40.00
500JN Joe Nieuwendyk	12.50	30.00
500JS Joe Sakic	20.00	50.00
500RF Ron Francis	12.50	30.00
500JJA Jaromir Jagr AU	250.00	400.00
500JNA Joe Nieuwendyk AU	200.00	300.00
500RFA Ron Francis AU	150.00	300.00

2003-04 Upper Deck All-Star Class

Card	Low	High
COMPLETE SET (30)	10.00	20.00
STATED ODDS 1:1 RETAIL		
AS1 Jean-Sebastien Giguere	.25	.60
AS2 Ilya Kovalchuk	.40	1.00
AS3 Joe Thornton	.40	1.00
AS4 Paul Kariya	.30	.75
AS5 Peter Forsberg	.75	2.00
AS6 Teemu Selanne	.30	.75
AS7 Marty Turco	.25	.60
AS8 Mike Modano	.50	1.25
AS9 Steve Yzerman	1.25	3.00
AS10 Dominik Hasek	.60	1.50
AS11 Nicklas Lidstrom	.30	.75
AS12 Jay Bouwmeester	.25	.60
AS13 Zigmund Palffy	.25	.60
AS14 Marian Gaborik	.60	1.50
AS15 Saku Koivu	.30	.75
AS16 Martin Brodeur	.75	2.00
AS17 Alexei Yashin	.25	.60
AS18 Tom Poti	.25	.60
AS19 Jason Spezza	.30	.75
AS20 Marian Hossa	.30	.75
AS21 Jeremy Roenick	.40	1.00
AS22 Sean Burke	.25	.60
AS23 Mario Lemieux	1.50	4.00
AS24 Patrick Marleau	.25	.60
AS25 Chris Pronger	.25	.60
AS26 Vincent Lecavalier	.25	.60
AS27 Mats Sundin	.30	.75
AS28 Ed Belfour	.30	.75
AS29 Todd Bertuzzi	.30	.75
AS30 Jaromir Jagr	.50	1.25

2003-04 Upper Deck All-Star Lineup

Card	Low	High
COMPLETE SET (10)	40.00	80.00
STATED ODDS 1:40		
AS1 Marian Gaborik	3.00	8.00
AS2 Dany Heatley	3.00	8.00
AS3 Joe Thornton	3.00	8.00
AS4 Mario Lemieux	6.00	15.00
AS5 Martin Brodeur	5.00	12.00
AS6 Jason Spezza	2.50	6.00
AS7 Rick Nash	3.00	8.00
AS8 Henrik Zetterberg	2.50	6.00
AS9 Ales Hemsky	2.50	6.00
AS10 Ryan Miller	2.50	6.00

2003-04 Upper Deck Big Playmakers

*MULT.COLOR SWATCH: .5X TO 1.25X
STATED ODDS 1:905
PRINT RUN 50 SERIAL #'d SETS

Card	Low	High
BPDH Dany Heatley	20.00	50.00
BPIK Ilya Kovalchuk	25.00	60.00
BPJB Jason Blake	10.00	25.00

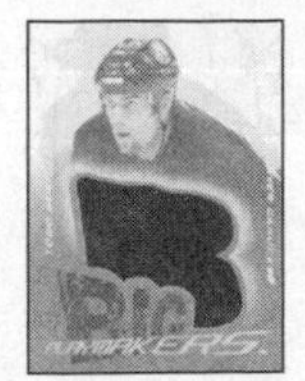

BPJJ Jaromir Jagr 20.00 50.00
BPJL Jamie Langenbrunner 10.00 25.00
BPJR Jeremy Roenick 20.00 50.00
BPJS Jean-Sebastien Giguere 12.50 30.00
BPJT Joe Thornton 25.00 60.00
BPMB Martin Brodeur 40.00 100.00
BPMG Marian Gaborik 25.00 60.00
BPMH Marian Hossa 15.00 40.00
BPML Mario Lemieux 40.00 100.00
BPMM Mike Modano 20.00 50.00
BPMN Markus Naslund 15.00 40.00
BPMS Mats Sundin 15.00 40.00
BPMT Marty Turco 12.50 30.00
BPON Owen Nolan 12.50 30.00
BPPB Pavel Bure 15.00 40.00
BPPF Peter Forsberg 25.00 60.00
BPPL Pavel Brendl 10.00 25.00
BPPR Patrick Roy 40.00 100.00
BPRL Roberto Luongo 20.00 50.00
BPRN Rick Nash 25.00 60.00
BPSF Sergei Fedorov 20.00 50.00
BPSK Saku Koivu 15.00 40.00
BPTB Todd Bertuzzi 15.00 40.00
BPTH Jocelyn Thibault 12.50 30.00
BPTS Teemu Selanne 15.00 40.00
BPWG Wayne Gretzky 100.00 250.00
BPZP Zigmund Palffy 12.50 30.00

2003-04 Upper Deck BuyBacks

This 182-card set featured cards that were "bought back" by UD and then autographed by the player. Print runs and original set ids are listed below.

1 Joe Thornton 96UD/7
2 Joe Thornton 97UD/5
3 Joe Thornton 98UD/9
4 Joe Thornton 99UD/9
5 Joe Thornton 00UD/9
6 Joe Thornton 01UD/2
7 Joe Thornton 02UD/22
8 Markus Naslund 92UD/38 20.00 50.00
9 Markus Naslund 93UD/10
10 Markus Naslund 94 UD/9
11 Markus Naslund 95 UD/10
12 Markus Naslund 96UD/4
13 Markus Naslund 97UD/5
14 Markus Naslund 98UD/10
15 Markus Naslund 99UD/10
16 Markus Naslund 00UD/10
17 Markus Naslund 01UD/9
18 Markus Naslund 02UD/21
19 Todd Bertuzzi 96UD/10
20 Todd Bertuzzi 97UD/10
21 Todd Bertuzzi 98UD/10
22 Todd Bertuzzi 00UD/10
23 Todd Bertuzzi 01 UD/9
24 Todd Bertuzzi 02UD/48 25.00 60.00
25 Jean-Sebastien Giguere 02UD/48 15.00 40.00
26 Bobby Orr 99UD Leg/5
27 Bobby Orr 00 UD Leg/5
28 Bobby Orr 01UD Leg/4
29 Bobby Orr 01UD Leg/5
30 Bobby Orr 02 UD/6
31 Gordie Howe 99UD Leg/9
32 Gordie Howe 00UD Leg/2
33 Gordie Howe 01UD Leg/5
34 Gordie Howe 01UD Leg/7
35 Gordie Howe 01UD Leg/4
36 Gordie Howe 02UD/23
37 Zigmund Palffy 91UD/28 20.00 50.00
38 Zigmund Palffy 94UD/4
39 Zigmund Palffy 95UD/9
40 Zigmund Palffy 96UD/10
41 Zigmund Palffy 97UD/11
42 Zigmund Palffy 98UD/14
43 Zigmund Palffy 99UD/6
44 Zigmund Palffy 00UD/10
45 Zigmund Palffy 01UD/10
46 Zigmund Palffy 01UD/1
47 Zigmund Palffy 02UD/23
48 Jason Spezza 02UD/29 100.00 200.00
49 Jason Spezza 03AS Promo/4
50 Rick Nash 00 UD CHL/2
51 Rick Nash 03 AS Promo/4
52 John LeClair 00UD/5
53 John LeClair 01UD/5
54 John LeClair 02UD/23
55 Pavel Bure 90UD/14
56 Pavel Bure 91UD/5
57 Pavel Bure 91UD/5
58 Pavel Bure 92UD/5
59 Pavel Bure 93UD/5
60 Pavel Bure 95UD/5
61 Pavel Bure 96UD/5
62 Pavel Bure 97UD/5
63 Pavel Bure 98UD/5
64 Pavel Bure 99UD/5
65 Pavel Bure 00UD/5
66 Pavel Bure 01UD/5
67 Pavel Bure 02UD/48 15.00 40.00
68 Pavel Bure MS 02UD/24
69 Mike Comrie 01UD/13
70 Mike Comrie 02UD/30 12.50 30.00
71 Sergei Fedorov 90UD/11
72 Sergei Fedorov ART 91UD/7
73 Sergei Fedorov 91UD/5
74 Sergei Fedorov 92UD/5
75 Sergei Fedorov 93UD/5
76 Sergei Fedorov 94UD/3
77 Sergei Fedorov 95UD/5
78 Sergei Fedorov 96UD/5
79 Sergei Fedorov 97UD/4
80 Sergei Fedorov 98UD/5
81 Sergei Fedorov 99UD/4
82 Sergei Fedorov 00UD/5
83 Sergei Fedorov 01UD/5
84 Sergei Fedorov 02UD/39 30.00 80.00
85 Ron Francis 90-91 UD
86 Ron Francis 91UD/5
87 Ron Francis 92UD/5
88 Ron Francis 93UD/5
89 Ron Francis 94UD/5
90 Ron Francis 95UD/5
91 Ron Francis 96UD/5
92 Ron Francis 97UD/5
93 Ron Francis 99UD/5
94 Ron Francis 00UD/5
95 Ron Francis 01UD/5
96 Ron Francis 02UD/47 20.00 50.00
97 Marian Gaborik 01UD/9
98 Marian Gaborik 02UD/48 20.00 50.00
99 Marian Hossa 97UD/17
100 Marian Hossa 98UD/1
101 Marian Hossa 99UD/10
102 Marian Hossa 00UD/10
103 Marian Hossa 01UD/10
104 Marian Hossa 02UD/48 15.00 40.00
105 Curtis Joseph 90UD/15
106 Curtis Joseph 99UD/5
107 Curtis Joseph 00UD/5
108 Curtis Joseph 01UD/5
109 Curtis Joseph 02UD/48 15.00 40.00
110 Jarome Iginla 97UD/5
111 Jarome Iginla MS 02UD/47 15.00 40.00
112 Jarome Iginla 02UD/48 15.00 40.00
113 Saku Koivu 92UD/14
114 Saku Koivu 93UD/5
115 Saku Koivu 95UD/5
116 Saku Koivu 96UD/3
117 Saku Koivu 97UD/5
118 Saku Koivu 98UD/5
119 Saku Koivu 99UD/5
120 Saku Koivu 00UD/5
121 Saku Koivu 01UD/5
122 Saku Koivu 02UD/48 20.00 50.00
123 Ilya Kovalchuk 01 UD/1
124 Ilya Kovalchuk 01 UD/9
125 Ilya Kovalchuk 02UD/48 25.00 60.00
126 Joe Nieuwendyk 90UD/5
127 Joe Nieuwendyk 91UD/5
128 Joe Nieuwendyk 92UD/5
129 Joe Nieuwendyk 93UD/5
130 Joe Nieuwendyk 94UD/5
131 Joe Nieuwendyk 95UD/5
132 Joe Nieuwendyk 96UD/5
133 Joe Nieuwendyk 97 UD/2
134 Joe Nieuwendyk 98UD/5
135 Joe Nieuwendyk 99UD/5
136 Joe Nieuwendyk 00UD/5
137 Joe Nieuwendyk 01UD/5
138 Joe Nieuwendyk 02UD/48 12.50 30.00
139 Jeremy Roenick 90UD/14
140 Jeremy Roenick 92UD/5
141 Jeremy Roenick 93UD/5
142 Jeremy Roenick 94 UD/5
143 Jeremy Roenick 95UD/5
144 Jeremy Roenick 96UD/5
145 Jeremy Roenick 96UD/5
146 Jeremy Roenick 97UD/5
147 Jeremy Roenick 98UD/5
148 Jeremy Roenick 99UD/5
149 Jeremy Roenick 00UD/5
150 Jeremy Roenick 01UD/5
151 Jeremy Roenick 02UD/48 15.00 40.00
152 Patrick Roy 90UD/5
153 Patrick Roy 91UD/5
154 Patrick Roy 92UD/5
155 Patrick Roy 93UD/5
156 Patrick Roy 94UD/5
157 Patrick Roy 95UD/5
158 Patrick Roy 96UD/5
159 Patrick Roy 97UD/5
160 Patrick Roy 98UD/5
161 Patrick Roy 99UD/5
162 Patrick Roy 00UD/5
163 Patrick Roy 01UD/2
164 Patrick Roy 01UD/5
165 Patrick Roy 02UD/48 50.00 125.00
166 Patrick Roy MS 02UD/48 50.00 125.00
167 Sergei Samsonov 95UD/5
168 Sergei Samsonov 97UD/5
169 Sergei Samsonov 98UD/5
170 Sergei Samsonov 99UD/5
171 Sergei Samsonov 00UD/5
172 Sergei Samsonov 01UD/5
173 Sergei Samsonov 02UD/48 20.00 50.00
174 Jose Theodore 95UD/3
175 Jose Theodore 98 UD/5
176 Jose Theodore 00UD/5
177 Jose Theodore 01UD/5
178 Jose Theodore 02UD/48 15.00 40.00
179 Alexander Frolov 02UD/10
180 Alexander Frolov 03AS Promo/4
181 Stanislav Chistov 02UD/29 25.00 60.00
182 Stanislav Chistov 03AS Promo/5

2003-04 Upper Deck Canadian Exclusives

Inserted exclusively in Canadian hobby boxes, this 475 card parallel set carried distinctive red foil serial-numbering and a red foil maple leaf on the card fronts. Cards 1-445 were numbered out of 50 while cards 446-475 were numbered to 25.

*CARDS 1-200: 6X TO 15X BASE HI
*CARDS 201-245: 1X TO 2.5X
*CARDS 446-475: 1.5X TO 4X

2003-04 Upper Deck Fan Favorites

COMPLETE SET (10) 12.50 25.00
STATED ODDS 1:21
FF1 Jeremy Roenick 1.25 3.00
FF2 Todd Bertuzzi 1.00 2.50
FF3 Roberto Luongo 1.25 3.00
FF4 Georges Laraque .75 2.00
FF5 Tie Domi .75 2.00
FF6 Steve Yzerman 3.00 8.00
FF7 Mike Modano 1.50 4.00
FF8 P.J. Stock .75 2.00
FF9 Mario Lemieux 4.00 10.00
FF10 Jean-Sebastien Giguere .75 2.00

2003-04 Upper Deck Franchise Fabrics

*MULT.COLOR SWATCH: .5X TO 1.25X
STATED ODDS 1:24
FFAY Alexei Yashin 4.00 10.00
FFBL Brian Leetch 4.00 10.00
FFCD Chris Drury 4.00 10.00
FFDH Dany Heatley 5.00 12.00
FFHZ Henrik Zetterberg 4.00 10.00
FFJI Jarome Iginla 6.00 15.00
FFJJ Jaromir Jagr 8.00 20.00
FFJT Joe Thornton 8.00 20.00
FFJT Jose Theodore 6.00 15.00
FFMB Martin Brodeur 10.00 25.00
FFMG Marian Gaborik 8.00 20.00
FFMH Marian Hossa 4.00 10.00
FFML Mario Lemieux 10.00 25.00
FFMN Markus Naslund 4.00 10.00
FFMS Mats Sundin 4.00 10.00
FFMT Marty Turco 4.00 10.00
FFNL Nicklas Lidstrom 4.00 10.00
FFPF Peter Forsberg 6.00 15.00
FFPK Paul Kariya 4.00 10.00
FFRL Roberto Luongo 6.00 15.00
FFRS Ryan Smyth 4.00 10.00
FFSF Sergei Fedorov 6.00 15.00
FFTB Todd Bertuzzi 4.00 10.00
FFVL Vincent Lecavalier 4.00 10.00
FFZP Zigmund Palffy 4.00 10.00

2003-04 Upper Deck Gifted Greats

COMPLETE SET (10) 25.00 60.00
STATED ODDS 1:40
GG1 Wayne Gretzky 6.00 15.00
GG2 Jean-Sebastien Giguere 2.00 5.00
GG3 Joe Thornton 3.00 8.00
GG4 Mario Lemieux 6.00 15.00
GG5 Eric Lindros 2.00 5.00
GG6 Todd Bertuzzi 2.00 5.00
GG7 Marian Gaborik 4.00 10.00
GG8 Dany Heatley 3.00 8.00
GG9 Marian Hossa 2.00 5.00
GG10 Martin Brodeur 5.00 12.00

2003-04 Upper Deck HG

This 475-card parallel set featured a "high-gloss" finish and the letters "HG" embossed on the card fronts. Cards 1-200 and 246-445 were serial-numbered out of 25. Cards 201-245 and 446-475 were serial-numbered out of 10.

*STARS: 10X TO 25X BASE HI
YNG.GUNS NOT PRICED DUE TO SCARCITY

2003-04 Upper Deck Highlight Heroes

COMPLETE SET (10) 15.00 30.00
STATED ODDS 1:40
HHAM Alexander Mogilny 2.00 5.00
HHJJ Jaromir Jagr 3.00 8.00
HHJS Jason Spezza 2.00 5.00
HHJT Jocelyn Thibault 2.00 5.00
HHMG Marian Gaborik 4.00 10.00
HHPB Pavel Bure 2.00 5.00
HHRN Rick Nash 2.50 6.00
HHSS Sergei Samsonov 2.00 5.00
HHTA Tony Amonte 2.00 5.00
HHTS Teemu Selanne 2.00 5.00

2003-04 Upper Deck Highlight Heroes Jerseys

*MULT.COLOR SWATCH: .5X TO 1.25X
STATED ODDS 1:96
HHAM Alexander Mogilny 5.00 12.00
HHJJ Jaromir Jagr 8.00 20.00

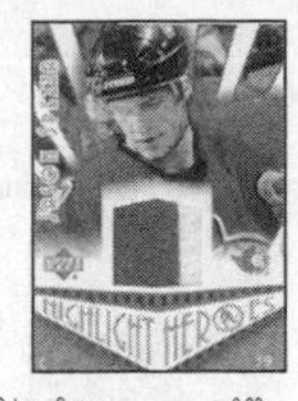

HHJS Jason Spezza 6.00 15.00
HHJT Jocelyn Thibault 5.00 12.00
HHMG Marian Gaborik 10.00 25.00
HHPB Pavel Bure 6.00 15.00
HHRN Rick Nash 8.00 20.00
HHSS Sergei Samsonov 5.00 12.00
HHTA Tony Amonte 5.00 12.00
HHTS Teemu Selanne 6.00 15.00

2003-04 Upper Deck Jerseys

This 27-card memorabilia set was inserted at a rate of 1:96 for Series I and 1:72 for Series 2. Notations are made below distinguishing which cards were available in which series.

*MULT.COLOR SWATCH: .5X TO 1.25X
GJAK Alex Kovalev Ser. 1 6.00 15.00
GJBG Bill Guerin Ser. 1 6.00 15.00
GJEL Eric Lindros Ser. 1 6.00 15.00
GJIK Ilya Kovalchuk Ser. 1 8.00 20.00
GJJB Owen Nolan Ser. 1 6.00 15.00
GJJG Jean-Sebastien Giguere Ser. 1 6.00 15.00
GJJI Jarome Iginla Ser. 1 8.00 20.00
GJMA Maxim Afinogenov Ser. 1 6.00 15.00
GJMB Martin Brodeur Ser. 1 15.00 40.00
GJMC Mike Comrie Ser. 1 6.00 15.00
GJML Mario Lemieux Ser. 1 15.00 40.00
GJMR Mark Recchi Ser. 1 6.00 15.00
GJMS Martin St. Louis Ser. 1 8.00 20.00
GJSK Saku Koivu Ser. 1 6.00 15.00
GJTB Todd Bertuzzi Ser. 1 6.00 15.00
UDAF Alexander Frolov Ser. 2 6.00 15.00
UDAH Ales Hemsky Ser. 2 6.00 15.00
UDBH Brett Hull Ser. 2 8.00 20.00
UDEJ Ed Jovanovski Ser. 2 6.00 15.00
UDIK Ilya Kovalchuk Ser. 2 8.00 20.00
UDJSG Jean-Sebastien Giguere Ser. 2 6.00 15.00
UDMC Mike Comrie Ser. 2 6.00 15.00
UDMH Marian Hossa Ser. 2 6.00 15.00
UDMK Mike Komisarek Ser. 2 6.00 15.00
UDMS Martin St. Louis Ser. 2 6.00 15.00
UDON Owen Nolan Ser. 2 6.00 15.00
UDRB Rob Blake Ser. 2 6.00 15.00

2003-04 Upper Deck Jersey Autographs

STATED ODDS 1:480 SERIES II
SJAH Ales Hemsky 12.00 30.00
SJCJ Curtis Joseph 15.00 40.00
SJDA David Aebischer 15.00 40.00
SJEL Eric Lindros 15.00 40.00
SJJA Jared Aulin 10.00 25.00
SJJI Jarome Iginla 30.00 80.00
SJJR Jeremy Roenick 25.00 60.00
SJJS Jason Spezza 60.00 100.00
SJJT Joe Thornton 20.00 50.00
SJJSG Jean-Sebastien Giguere 12.00 30.00
SJMH Marian Hossa 20.00 50.00
SJPR Patrick Roy 75.00 200.00
SJRN Rick Nash 40.00 100.00
SJSF Sergei Fedorov 20.00 50.00
SJSH Scott Hartnell 10.00 25.00
SJSK Saku Koivu 15.00 40.00
SJSS Sergei Samsonov 12.00 30.00
SJTB Todd Bertuzzi 12.00 30.00
SJWG Wayne Gretzky 225.00 350.00
SJZP Zigmund Palffy 12.00 30.00

2003-04 Upper Deck Magic Moments

COMPLETE SET (15) 30.00 60.00
STATED ODDS 1:14
MM1 Jean-Sebastien Giguere 1.00 2.50
MM2 Scott Stevens 1.00 2.50
MM3 Jason Spezza 1.00 2.50
MM4 Steve Yzerman 3.00 8.00
MM5 Paul Kariya 1.00 2.50
MM6 Patrick Roy 3.00 8.00
MM7 Joe Thornton 1.25 3.00
MM8 Wayne Gretzky 4.00 10.00
MM9 Marc-Andre Fleury 3.00 8.00
MM10 Milan Hejduk 1.00 2.50
MM11 Dominik Hasek 1.50 4.00
MM12 Martin Brodeur 3.00 8.00
MM13 Peter Forsberg 2.00 5.00
MM14 Sergei Fedorov 1.25 3.00
MM15 Jordin Tootoo 2.00 5.00

2003-04 Upper Deck Memorable Matchups

*MULT.COLOR SWATCH: .5X TO 1.25X
STATED ODDS 1:144
MMBG T.Bertuzzi/M.Gaborik 6.00 15.00
MMFK Sergei Fedorov 8.00 20.00
Paul Kariya
MMGB Jean-Sebastien Giguere 12.50 30.00
Martin Brodeur
MMHH Brett Hull 12.50 30.00
Dominik Hasek
MMLS Eric Lindros 6.00 15.00
Scott Stevens
MMNN Rob Niedermayer 5.00 12.00
Scott Niedermayer
MMRR Jeremy Roenick 20.00 50.00
Patrick Roy
MMTH Jose Theodore 5.00 12.00
Ales Hemsky
MMTT Joe Thornton 8.00 20.00
Jose Theodore

2003-04 Upper Deck Mr. Hockey

COMPLETE SET (30) 40.00 80.00
COMMON CARD (GH1-GH30) 2.00 5.00

2003-04 Upper Deck NHL Best

MULT.COLOR SWATCH: .5X TO 1.25X
STATED ODDS 1:48
NBDH Dany Heatley 6.00 15.00
NBGM Glen Murray 5.00 12.00
NBIK Ilya Kovalchuk 6.00 15.00
NBJG Jean-Sebastien Giguere 5.00 12.00
NBJI Jarome Iginla 6.00 15.00
NBJR Jeremy Roenick 6.00 15.00
NBKT Keith Tkachuk 5.00 12.00
NBMB Martin Brodeur 15.00 40.00
NBML Mario Lemieux 15.00 40.00
NBMM Mike Modano 8.00 20.00
NBNL Nicklas Lidstrom 5.00 12.00
NBPR Patrick Roy 15.00 40.00
NBPS Sergei Fedorov 6.00 15.00
NBVL Vincent Lecavalier 5.00 12.00
NBZP Zigmund Palffy 5.00 12.00

2003-04 Upper Deck Patches

This 60-card memorabilia set was inserted at the rate of 1:7500 Series I and Series II packs. Notations are made below distinguishing cards available in each series. As of press time, not all cards have been verified.

LD1 Steve Yzerman Ser.2
LD2 Mike Modano Ser.2
LD3 Mario Lemieux Ser.2 100.00 250.00
LD4 Mats Sundin Ser.2 60.00 150.00
LD5 Joe Thornton Ser.2 75.00 200.00
LD6 Ron Francis Ser.2 60.00 125.00
LD7 Markus Naslund Ser.2 40.00 100.00
LD8 Brian Leetch Ser.2
LD9 Jeremy Roenick Ser.2 60.00 150.00
LD10 Jaromir Jagr Ser.2
SP1 Paul Kariya Ser.
SP2 Marian Gaborik Ser.2
SP3 Jeremy Roenick Ser.2 60.00 150.00
SP4 Brett Hull Ser.2 75.00 200.00
SP5 Dany Heatley Ser.2 75.00 200.00
SP6 Jarome Iginla Ser.2
SP7 Chris Drury Ser.2
SP8 Vincent Lecavalier Ser.2 50.00 125.00
SP9 Bill Guerin Ser.2 30.00 80.00
SP10 Glen Murray Ser.2 50.00 125.00
SV1 Martin Brodeur Ser.2 100.00 200.00
SV2 Roberto Luongo Ser.2 75.00 200.00
SV3 Roman Cechmanek Ser.2 40.00 100.00
SV4 Marty Turco Ser.2
SV5 Tommy Salo Ser.2 40.00 100.00
SV6 Jocelyn Thibault Ser.2
SV7 David Aebischer Ser.2 40.00 100.00
SV8 Patrick Lalime Ser.2 40.00 100.00
SV9 Dominik Hasek Ser.2 50.00 125.00
SV10 Ed Belfour Ser.2 50.00 125.00
PLGJG Jean-Sebastien Giguere Ser.1 40.00 100.00
PLGJS Jason Spezza Ser.1 75.00 200.00
PLGJT Joe Thornton Ser.1 60.00 150.00
PLGMB Martin Brodeur Ser.1 100.00 200.00
PLGMG Marian Gaborik Ser.1
PLGMH Marian Hossa Ser.1 40.00 100.00
PLGML Mario Lemieux Ser.1 100.00 200.00
PLGMN Markus Naslund Ser.1 50.00 125.00
PLGPR Patrick Roy Ser.1 150.00 300.00
PLGRN Rick Nash Ser.1 75.00 200.00
PNMJG Jean-Sebastien Giguere Ser.1 40.00 100.00
PNMJS Jason Spezza Ser.1 75.00 200.00
PNMJT Joe Thornton Ser.1 75.00 200.00
PNMMB Martin Brodeur Ser.1 100.00 200.00
PNMMG Marian Gaborik Ser.1
PNMMH Marian Hossa Ser.1 40.00 100.00
PNMML Mario Lemieux Ser.1 75.00 200.00
PNMMN Markus Naslund Ser.1 50.00 125.00
PNMPR Patrick Roy Ser.1 150.00 300.00
PNMRN Rick Nash Ser.1 75.00 150.00
PNRJG Jean-Sebastien Giguere Ser.1 40.00 100.00
PNRJS Jason Spezza Ser.1 75.00 200.00
PNRJT Joe Thornton Ser.1 75.00 200.00
PNRMB Martin Brodeur Ser.1 100.00 200.00
PNRMG Marian Gaborik Ser.1
PNRMH Marian Hossa Ser.1 40.00 100.00
PNRML Mario Lemieux Ser.1 100.00 250.00
PNRMN Markus Naslund Ser.1 50.00 125.00
PNRPR Patrick Roy Ser.1 150.00 300.00
PNRRN Rick Nash Ser.1 75.00 150.00

2003-04 Upper Deck Performers

COMPLETE SET (15) 20.00 40.00
STATED ODDS 1:14
PS1 Jean-Sebastien Giguere .60 1.50
PS2 Scott Stevens .60 1.50
PS3 Steve Yzerman 2.50 6.00
PS4 Jeremy Roenick .75 2.00
PS5 Peter Forsberg 1.25 3.00
PS6 Jose Theodore .75 2.00
PS7 Marian Gaborik 1.00 2.50
PS8 Martin Brodeur 1.50 4.00
PS9 Ed Belfour .60 1.50
PS10 Mike Modano .75 2.00
PS11 Joe Sakic 1.00 2.50
PS12 Bobby Orr 4.00 10.00
PS13 Mario Lemieux 3.00 8.00
PS14 Wayne Gretzky 4.00 10.00
PS15 Patrick Roy 2.50 6.00

2003-04 Upper Deck Power Zone

COMPLETE SET (10) 10.00 25.00
STATED ODDS 1:21
PZ1 Joe Thornton .75 2.00
PZ2 Keith Tkachuk 1.00 2.50
PZ3 Jeremy Roenick 1.25 3.00
PZ4 Brendan Shanahan 1.00 2.50
PZ5 Todd Bertuzzi 1.00 2.50
PZ6 Rick Nash 1.25 3.00
PZ7 Peter Forsberg 1.50 4.00
PZ8 Owen Nolan 1.00 2.50
PZ9 Mario Lemieux 4.00 10.00
PZ10 Eric Lindros 1.00 2.50

2003-04 Upper Deck Rookie Threads

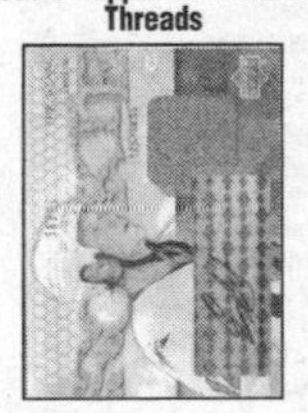

*MULT.COLOR SWATCH: .5X TO 1.25X
PRINT RUN 75 SER.#'d SETS
RT1 Joffrey Lupul 15.00 40.00
RT2 Dustin Brown 15.00 40.00
RT3 Marc-Andre Fleury 40.00 100.00
RT4 Joni Pitkanen 15.00 40.00
RT5 Peter Sejna 12.50 30.00
RT6 Eric Staal 30.00 80.00
RT7 Tuomo Ruutu 15.00 40.00
RT8 Dan Hamhuis 12.50 30.00
RT9 Nathan Horton 25.00 60.00
RT10 Jordin Tootoo 25.00 60.00

2003-04 Upper Deck Shooting Stars

MULT.COLOR SWATCH: .5X TO 1.25X
STATED ODDS 1:48
STAH Ales Hemsky 5.00 12.00
STAS Alexander Svitov 5.00 12.00
STAV Anton Volchenkov 5.00 12.00
STJA Jared Aulin 5.00 12.00
STJB Jay Bouwmeester 5.00 12.00

STJL Jordan Leopold 5.00 12.00
STJS Jason Spezza 8.00 20.00
STJW Justin Williams 5.00 12.00
STMH Marcel Hossa 5.00 12.00
STPM Pierre-Marc Bouchard 5.00 12.00
STRD Rick DiPietro 5.00 12.00
STRM Ryan Miller 5.00 12.00
STRN Rick Nash 20.00 40.00
STSO Steve Ott 5.00 12.00
STSV Alexei Smirnov 5.00 12.00

2003-04 Upper Deck Super Saviors

MULT.COLOR SWATCH: .5X TO 1.25X
STATED ODDS 1:144
SSJG Jean-Sebastien Giguere 8.00 20.00
SSMB Martin Brodeur 12.00 30.00
SSMT Marty Turco 8.00 20.00
SSPL Patrick Lalime 6.00 15.00
SSPR Patrick Roy 15.00 40.00
SSRC Roman Cechmanek 6.00 15.00

2003-04 Upper Deck Superstar Spotlight

This 15-card set featured a holographic mirrored action image on the majority of the card front with a smaller color photo of the featured player along side. This set was inserted at odds of 1:144.

SS1 Jean-Sebastien Giguere 4.00 10.00
SS2 Joe Thornton 6.00 15.00
SS3 Marian Gaborik 6.00 15.00
SS4 Rick Nash 5.00 12.00
SS5 Steve Yzerman 12.50 30.00
SS6 Martin Brodeur 12.50 30.00
SS7 Jason Spezza 5.00 12.00
SS8 Mike Modano 6.00 15.00
SS9 Mario Lemieux 15.00 40.00
SS10 Jaromir Jagr 6.00 15.00
SS11 Todd Bertuzzi 4.00 10.00
SS12 Dany Heatley 5.00 12.00
SS13 Patrick Roy 15.00 40.00
SS14 Bobby Orr 20.00 50.00
SS15 Gordie Howe 12.50 30.00

2003-04 Upper Deck Team Essentials

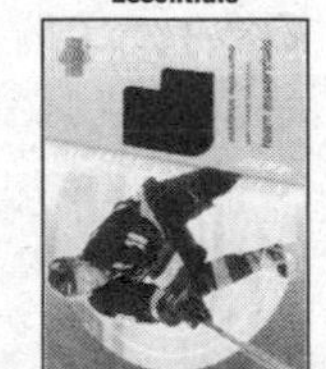

TL/TP STATED ODDS 1:96
TS STATED ODDS 1:288
*MULT.COLOR SWATCH: .5X TO 1.25X
TLJS Joe Sakic 10.00 25.00
TLJT Joe Thornton 8.00 20.00
TLML Mario Lemieux 15.00 40.00
TLMN Markus Naslund 6.00 15.00
TLMP Michael Peca 6.00 15.00
TLMS Mats Sundin 6.00 15.00
TLSS Scott Stevens 6.00 15.00
TLSY Steve Yzerman 12.50 30.00
TPAM Al MacInnis 6.00 15.00
TPDA Daniel Alfredsson 6.00 15.00
TPDH Dany Heatley 8.00 20.00
TPJT Joe Thornton 8.00 20.00
TPML Mario Lemieux 12.50 30.00
TPMM Mike Modano 8.00 20.00
TPMS Miroslav Satan 6.00 15.00
TPPF Peter Forsberg 10.00 25.00
TPPK Paul Kariya 6.00 15.00
TPVL Vincent Lecavalier 6.00 15.00
TSDH Dany Heatley 10.00 25.00
TSJJ Jaromir Jagr 12.50 30.00
TSMH Milan Hejduk 8.00 20.00
TSMH Marian Hossa 8.00 20.00
TSPB Pavel Bure 8.00 20.00
TSTB Todd Bertuzzi 8.00 20.00

2003-04 Upper Deck Three Stars

COMPLETE SET (15) 20.00 40.00
STATED ODDS 1:14
TS1 Paul Kariya .60 1.50
TS2 Marian Hossa .60 1.50
TS3 Dany Heatley .75 2.00
TS4 Alexei Yashin .60 1.50
TS5 Jaromir Jagr .75 2.00
TS6 Martin Brodeur 1.50 4.00
TS7 Marian Gaborik 1.00 2.50
TS8 Ziggy Palffy .60 1.50
TS9 Marty Turco .60 1.50
TS10 Mats Sundin .60 1.50
TS11 Jean-Sebastien Giguere .60 1.50
TS12 Mario Lemieux 3.00 8.00
TS13 Jarome Iginla .75 2.00
TS14 Markus Naslund .60 1.50
TS15 Joe Thornton .75 2.00

2003-04 Upper Deck Tough Customers

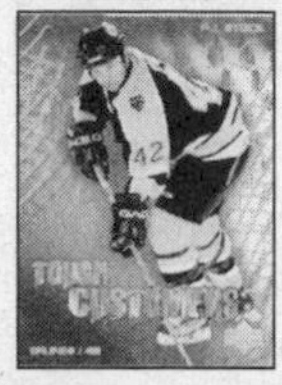

COMPLETE SET (15) 12.00 25.00
STATED ODDS 1:14
TC1 Jody Shelley .75 2.00
TC2 Andrei Nazarov .75 2.00
TC3 Reed Low .75 2.00
TC4 Andrew Peters .75 2.00
TC5 Wade Belak .75 2.00
TC6 Darren McCarty 1.00 2.50
TC7 Krzysztof Oliwa .75 2.00
TC8 P.J. Stock .75 2.00
TC9 Matt Johnson .75 2.00
TC10 Chris Neil .75 2.00
TC11 Garrett Burnett .75 2.00
TC12 Georges Laraque 1.00 2.50
TC13 Tie Domi 1.00 2.50
TC14 Jason Strudwick .75 2.00
TC15 Donald Brashear .75 2.00

2003-04 Upper Deck UD Exclusives

This 230-card set paralleled cards 246-475 of the base set. Cards 246-445 were serial-numbered out of 50 and cards 446-475 were serila-numbered out of 10. Each card carried an "Exclusive" foil stamp.

*STARS: 6X TO 15X BASIC CARDS
446-475 NOT PRICED DUE TO SCARCITY

2004-05 Upper Deck

This 210-card set was released in just one series for the 2004-05 season that was ultimately canceled due to the labor dispute. The set consisted of 180 veteran cards and 30 Young Gun subset cards inserted at 1:4. Due to a lack of a true rookie class, many of the Young Gun cards were "flashbacks" of veteran players in their rookie season.

COMPLETE SET (210) 125.00 250.00
COMP.SET w/o SP's (180) 15.00 30.00
COMMON CARD (1-210) .02 .10
1 Petr Sykora .02 .10
2 Andy McDonald .02 .10
3 Sandis Ozolinsh .02 .10
4 Sergei Fedorov .25 .60
5 Joffrey Lupul .02 .10
6 Jean-Sebastien Giguere .15 .40
7 Dany Heatley .25 .60
8 Ilya Kovalchuk .25 .60
9 Patrik Stefan .02 .10
10 Jaroslav Modry .02 .10
11 Serge Aubin .02 .10
12 Kari Lehtonen .40 1.00
13 Joe Thornton .30 .75
14 Sergei Gonchar .02 .10
15 Patrice Bergeron .15 .40
16 Nick Boynton .02 .10
17 Sergei Samsonov .15 .40
18 Andrew Raycroft .15 .40
19 Daniel Briere .02 .10
20 Miroslav Satan .15 .40
21 Mika Noronen .15 .40
22 JP Dumont .02 .10
23 Maxim Afinogenov .02 .10
24 Martin Biron .15 .40
25 Chris Simon .02 .10
26 Jarome Iginla .25 .60
27 Robyn Regehr .02 .10
28 Jordan Leopold .02 .10
29 Chuck Kobasew .02 .10
30 Miikka Kiprusoff .15 .40
31 Jeff O'Neill .02 .10
32 Ron Francis .15 .40
33 Aaron Ward .02 .10
34 Erik Cole .02 .10
35 Eric Staal .02 .10
36 Martin Gerber .15 .40
37 Matthew Barnaby .02 .10
38 Kyle Calder .02 .10
39 Tyler Arnason .02 .10
40 Eric Daze .15 .40
41 Jocelyn Thibault .15 .40
42 Peter Forsberg .50 1.25
43 Alex Tanguay .15 .40
44 Milan Hejduk .20 .50
45 Rob Blake .15 .40
46 Paul Kariya .20 .50
47 Teemu Selanne .20 .50
48 David Aebischer .15 .40
49 Luke Richardson .02 .10
50 Rick Nash .25 .60
51 Rostislav Klesla .02 .10
52 Nikolai Zherdev .20 .50
53 Marc Denis .15 .40
54 Mike Modano .20 .50
55 Sergei Zubov .02 .10
56 Bill Guerin .15 .40
57 Jason Arnott .02 .10
58 Niko Kapanen .02 .10
59 Marty Turco .15 .40
60 Kirk Maltby .02 .10
61 Nicklas Lidstrom .20 .50
62 Kris Draper .02 .10
63 Brendan Shanahan .20 .50
64 Pavel Datsyuk .20 .50
65 Robert Lang .02 .10
66 Steve Yzerman 1.00 2.50
67 Curtis Joseph .15 .40
68 Ryan Smyth .02 .10
69 Jason Smith .02 .10
70 Ales Hemsky .15 .40
71 Eric Brewer .02 .10
72 Raffi Torres .02 .10
73 Ty Conklin .15 .40
74 Mike Van Ryn .02 .10
75 Kristian Huselius .02 .10
76 Stephen Weiss .02 .10
77 Jay Bouwmeester .02 .10
78 Roberto Luongo .25 .60
79 Craig Conroy .02 .10
80 Aaron Miller .02 .10
81 Luc Robitaille .15 .40
82 Martin Straka .02 .10
83 Mattias Norstrom .02 .10
84 Roman Cechmanek .15 .40
85 Marian Gaborik .30 .75
86 Pascal Dupuis .02 .10
87 Alexander Daigle .02 .10
88 Pierre-Marc Bouchard .02 .10
89 Filip Kuba .02 .10
90 Manny Fernandez .15 .40
91 Saku Koivu .20 .50
92 Michael Ryder .02 .10
93 Marcel Hossa .02 .10
94 Mike Ribeiro .02 .10
95 Jose Theodore .20 .50
96 Sheldon Souray .02 .10
97 David Legwand .15 .40
98 Steve Sullivan .02 .10
99 Marek Zidlicky .02 .10
100 Martin Erat .02 .10
101 Tomas Vokoun .15 .40
102 Patrik Elias .15 .40
103 Jeff Friesen .02 .10
104 Brian Rafalski .02 .10
105 Scott Niedermayer .02 .10
106 Scott Stevens .15 .40
107 Martin Brodeur 1.00 2.50
108 Oleg Kvasha .02 .10
109 Mark Parrish .02 .10
110 Michael Peca .02 .10
111 Adrian Aucoin .02 .10
112 Rick DiPietro .15 .40
113 Trent Hunter .02 .10
114 Eric Lindros .20 .50
115 Tom Poti .02 .10
116 Mark Messier .20 .50
117 Jaromir Jagr .30 .75
118 Bobby Holik .02 .10
119 Mike Dunham .15 .40
120 Marian Hossa .20 .50
121 Martin Havlat .15 .40
122 Zdeno Chara .02 .10
123 Daniel Alfredsson .15 .40
124 Jason Spezza .20 .50
125 Dominik Hasek .40 1.00
126 Jeremy Roenick .25 .60
127 Tony Amonte .15 .40
128 Keith Primeau .15 .40
129 Simon Gagne .20 .50
130 Danny Markov .02 .10
131 Robert Esche .15 .40
132 Shane Doan .02 .10
133 Mike Comrie .02 .10
134 Ladislav Nagy .02 .10
135 Brett Hull .25 .60
136 Derek Morris .02 .10
137 Brian Boucher .15 .40
138 Mario Lemieux 1.25 3.00
139 Mark Recchi .02 .10
140 Ryan Malone .02 .10
141 Dick Tarnstrom .02 .10
142 Rico Fata .02 .10
143 Marc-Andre Fleury .50 1.25
144 Alyn McCauley .15 .40
145 Marco Sturm .02 .10
146 Patrick Marleau .15 .40
147 Scott Hannan .02 .10
148 Kyle McLaren .02 .10
149 Evgeni Nabokov .15 .40
150 Al MacInnis .15 .40
151 Petr Cajanek .02 .10
152 Keith Tkachuk .20 .50
153 Barret Jackman .02 .10
154 Chris Pronger .15 .40
155 Patrick Lalime .15 .40
156 Vincent Lecavalier .20 .50
157 Dave Andreychuk .02 .10
158 Brad Richards .15 .40
159 Pavel Kubina .02 .10
160 Ruslan Fedotenko .02 .10
161 Nikolai Khabibulin .20 .50
162 Alexander Mogilny .15 .40
163 Owen Nolan .15 .40
164 Gary Roberts .02 .10
165 Brian McCabe .02 .10
166 Ed Belfour .20 .50
167 Joe Nieuwendyk .15 .40
168 Markus Naslund .20 .50
169 Brendan Morrison .15 .40
170 Todd Bertuzzi .20 .50
171 Ed Jovanovski .15 .40
172 Trevor Linden .02 .10
173 Dan Cloutier .15 .40
174 Jeff Halpern .02 .10
175 Dainius Zubrus .02 .10
176 Jason Doig .02 .10
177 Brendan Witt .02 .10
178 Olaf Kolzig .15 .40
179 Wayne Gretzky CL 1.50 4.00
180 Gordie Howe CL 1.00 2.50
181 Brad Fast YG RC 2.00 5.00
182 Brennan Evans YG RC 2.00 5.00
183 Wayne Gretzky YG 15.00 40.00
184 Mark Messier YG 6.00 15.00
185 Peter Forsberg YG 6.00 15.00
186 Steve Yzerman YG 8.00 20.00
187 Ron Francis YG 4.00 10.00
188 Patrick Roy YG 10.00 25.00
189 Mario Lemieux YG 10.00 25.00
190 Dave Andreychuk YG 4.00 10.00
191 Luc Robitaille YG 4.00 10.00
192 Gordie Howe YG 8.00 20.00
193 Don Cherry YG 8.00 20.00
194 Hobey Baker YG RC 2.00 5.00
195 Mike Modano YG 4.00 10.00
196 Denis Brodeur YG 2.00 5.00
197 Keith Tkachuk YG 2.00 5.00
198 Bob Goodenow YG 2.00 5.00
199 Cammi Granato YG RC 4.00 10.00
200 Foster Hewitt YG 2.00 5.00
201 Mike Keenan YG 2.00 5.00
202 Dick Irvin Jr. YG 2.00 5.00
203 Jeremy Roenick YG 4.00 10.00
204 James Norris YG 2.00 5.00
205 Alexander Ragulin YG RC 2.00 5.00
206 Brendan Shanahan YG 4.00 10.00
207 Lord Stanley YG 2.00 5.00
208 Gary Thorne YG 2.00 5.00
209 Scott Stevens YG 4.00 10.00
210 Joe Sakic YG 6.00 15.00

2004-05 Upper Deck 1997 Game Jerseys

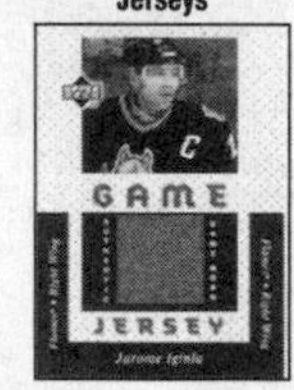

This insert set recaptured the design of Upper Deck's first jersey cards from the 1997-98 season. Cards were inserted at a rate of 1:288 and carried a "97" prefix.

KNOWN PRINT RUNS LISTED BELOW
LOWER PRINT RUNS NOT PRICED DUE TO SCARCITY
BB Joe Thornton 15.00 40.00
BS Brendan Shanahan/100 25.00 60.00
GH Gordie Howe/15
JI Jarome Iginla 15.00 40.00
JS Jason Spezza 10.00 25.00
MB Martin Brodeur 25.00 60.00
MM Mike Modano 12.50 30.00
MS Martin St. Louis 10.00 25.00
PF Peter Forsberg/50 25.00 60.00
PR Patrick Roy/50 30.00 80.00
SF Sergei Fedorov 15.00 40.00
SK Saku Koivu 10.00 25.00
SU Mats Sundin 10.00 25.00
WG2 Wayne Gretzky/25

2004-05 Upper Deck Big Playmakers

STATED PRINT RUN 50 SER.#'d SETS
BPAT Alex Tanguay 10.00 25.00
BPBH Brett Hull 12.00 30.00
BPEF Sergei Fedorov 12.00 30.00
BPGH Gordie Howe 150.00 250.00
BPHE Milan Hejduk 10.00 25.00
BPHO Marian Hossa 10.00 25.00
BPIK Ilya Kovalchuk 15.00 40.00
BPJI Jarome Iginla 15.00 40.00
BPJJ Jaromir Jagr 20.00 50.00
BPJR Jeremy Roenick 12.00 30.00
BPJS Joe Sakic 20.00 50.00
BPKP Keith Primeau 10.00 25.00
BPKT Keith Tkachuk 10.00 25.00
BPML Mario Lemieux 40.00 100.00
BPMM Mike Modano 12.00 30.00
BPMN Markus Naslund 10.00 25.00
BPMS Martin St. Louis 10.00 25.00
BPPB Pavel Bure 12.00 30.00
BPPD Pavel Datsyuk 12.00 30.00
BPSU Mats Sundin 12.00 30.00
BPTH Joe Thornton 15.00 40.00
BPWG Wayne Gretzky 100.00 200.00

2004-05 Upper Deck Canadian Exclusives

*1-180 EXCL.: 10X TO 25X
1-180 PRINT RUN 50 SER.#'d SETS
*181-210 YG EXCL.: 2X TO 5X
181-210 PRINT RUN 25 SER.#'d SETS

2004-05 Upper Deck Clutch Performers

COMPLETE SET (7) 12.50 25.00
STATED ODDS 1:24
CP1 Jarome Iginla 1.50 4.00
CP2 Brad Richards .75 2.00
CP3 Joe Sakic 2.00 5.00
CP4 Joe Thornton 1.50 4.00
CP5 Keith Primeau .75 2.00
CP6 Nikolai Khabibulin 1.25 3.00
CP7 Mario Lemieux 4.00 10.00

2004-05 Upper Deck Hardware Heroes

COMPLETE SET (14) 15.00 30.00
STATED ODDS 1:12
AW1 Scott Niedermeyer .75 2.00
Norris
AW2 Martin St. Louis .75 2.00
Art Ross
AW3 Brad Richards .75 2.00
Conn Smythe
AW4 Andrew Raycroft .75 2.00
Calder
AW5 Martin Brodeur 2.50 6.00
Vezina
AW6 Iginla/Nash/Kovalchuk/Richard 2.00 5.00
AW7 Martin St. Louis .75 2.00
Hart
AW8 Brad Richards .75 2.00
Lady Byng
AW9 Kris Draper .75 2.00
Selke
AW10 Bryan Berard .75 2.00
Masterton
AW11 Jarome Iginla 1.00 2.50
Clancy
AW12 Martin Brodeur 2.50 6.00
Jennings
AW13 Detroit Red Wings 2.00 5.00
President's Trophy
AW14 Tampa Bay Lightning 2.50 6.00
Stanley Cup

2004-05 Upper Deck Heritage Classic

Inserted at 1:288, this 15-card set featured jersey swatches of players who played in the 2003-04 Heritage Classic.

KNOWN PRINT RUNS LISTED BELOW
CCAH Ales Hemsky 15.00 40.00
CCEB Eric Brewer 12.00 30.00
CCGF Grant Fuhr 40.00 80.00
CCJK Jari Kurri 30.00 80.00
CCJT Jose Theodore/75 30.00 80.00
CCLU Guy Lafleur/82 50.00 125.00
CCMM Mark Messier/25 250.00 400.00
CCMR Mike Ribeiro 12.00 30.00
CCPC Paul Coffey/75 40.00 100.00
CCRS Ryan Smyth 20.00 50.00
CCRT Raffi Torres 12.00 30.00
CCRY Michael Ryder 20.00 50.00
CCSK Saku Koivu 20.00 50.00
CCSS Steve Shutt 12.00 30.00
CCTC Ty Conklin 12.00 30.00

2004-05 Upper Deck HG Glossy Gold

STATED PRINT RUN 5 SER.#'d SETS
NOT PRICED DUE TO SCARCITY

2004-05 Upper Deck HG Glossy Silver

STATED PRINT RUN 10 SER.#'d SETS
NOT PRICED DUE TO SCARCITY

2004-05 Upper Deck Jersey Autographs

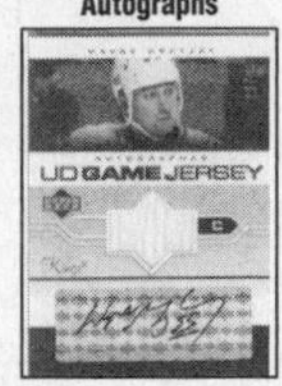

STATED ODDS 1:288
SINGLE PRINT RUN 25 SER.#'d SETS
DUAL JSY PRINT RUN 10 SER.#'d SETS
DUAL NOT PRICED DUE TO SCARCITY
GJAAA Arron Asham 12.00 40.00
GJAAF Alexander Frolov 25.00 60.00
GJAAH Adam Hall 15.00 30.00
GJAAL Ales Hemsky 25.00 60.00
GJAAS Alexander Svitov 15.00 40.00
GJAAY Alexei Yashin 15.00 40.00
GJABO Brooks Orpik 15.00 40.00
GJABU Pavel Bure 30.00 80.00
GJACK Chuck Kobasew 15.00 40.00
GJADA David Aebischer 20.00 50.00
GJAGH Gordie Howe 125.00 250.00
GJAHO Marcel Hossa 15.00 30.00
GJAHS Marian Hossa 25.00 60.00
GJAIK Ilya Kovalchuk 60.00 150.00
GJAJG Jean-Sebastien Giguere 15.00 40.00
GJAJI Jarome Iginla 60.00 150.00
GJAJL John LeClair 15.00 40.00
GJAJR Jeremy Roenick 40.00 100.00
GJAJS Jason Spezza 60.00 150.00
GJAMC Mike Comrie
GJAMG Marian Gaborik 60.00 150.00
GJAMH Martin Havlat 20.00 50.00
GJAMK Markus Naslund 30.00 80.00
GJAMN Markus Naslund 30.00 80.00
GJAMP Mark Parrish 12.00 40.00
GJAMT Marty Turco 25.00 60.00
GJAPB Pavel Bure 40.00 100.00
GJAPE Michael Peca 15.00 30.00
GJAPH Phil Esposito 30.00 80.00
GJAPR Patrick Roy 125.00 300.00
GJARD Rick DiPietro 25.00 60.00
GJARF Ron Francis 25.00 60.00
GJARL Roberto Luongo 40.00 100.00
GJARN Rick Nash 50.00 125.00
GJASF Sergei Fedorov 30.00 80.00
GJATB Todd Bertuzzi 25.00 60.00
GJATH Joe Thornton 50.00 125.00
GJAWG Wayne Gretzky 225.00 500.00
GJAJR/JL Jeremy Roenick/John LeClair
GJAPA/MP Mark Parrish/Michael Peca
GJAPB/MN Pavel Bure/Markus Naslund
GJAMB/PR M.Brodeur/P.Roy
GJAWG/GH Wayne Gretzky/Gordie Howe
GJAPR/RL Patrick Roy/Roberto Luongo
GJAIL/PB Ilya Kovalchuk/Pavel Bure
GJAPR/DA Patrick Roy/David Aebischer
GJAMT/JG Marty Turco/JS Giguere
GJAJS/AY Jason Spezza/Alexei Yashin
GJAWG/RN Wayne Gretzky/Rick Nash
GJATB/MN Todd Bertuzzi/Markus Naslund
GJAHO/HS Marcel Hossa/Marian Hossa

2004-05 Upper Deck NHL's Best

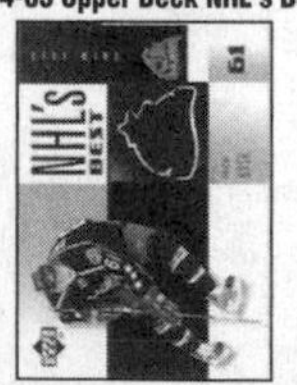

STATED ODDS 1:96
KNOWN PRINT RUNS LISTED BELOW
NBBL Brian Leetch 6.00 15.00
NBEB Ed Belfour 6.00 15.00
NBGH Gordie Howe/15
NBJT Jose Theodore 8.00 20.00
NBMB Martin Brodeur 10.00 25.00
NBML Mario Lemieux/50 30.00 80.00
NBNL Nicklas Lidstrom 6.00 15.00
NBPF Peter Forsberg/75 15.00 40.00
NBPR Patrick Roy/50 40.00 100.00
NBRB Rob Blake 6.00 15.00
NBRN Rick Nash 8.00 20.00
NBSG Sergei Gonchar 6.00 15.00
NBSN Scott Niedermayer 6.00 15.00
NBTB Todd Bertuzzi 8.00 15.00
NBWG Wayne Gretzky/25 150.00 300.00

2004-05 Upper Deck Patches

NMBR PATCH ODDS 1:2500
LOGO PATCH ODDS 1:5000
NAME PATCH ODDS 1:7500
NOT PRICED DUE TO SCARCITY
GJPABB Joe Thornton/11
GJPAJJ Jaromir Jagr/7
GJPAJR Jeremy Roenick/8
GJPAJS Joe Sakic/8
GJPAMB Martin Brodeur/5
GJPAML Mario Lemieux/5
GJPAMM Mark Messier/5
GJPAMO Mike Modano/10
GJPAMS Martin St. Louis/8
GJPAPF Peter Forsberg/5
GJPAPK Paul Kariya
GJPASY Steve Yzerman/5
GJPATB Todd Bertuzzi/8
GJPAWG Wayne Gretzky/5
GJPLBB Joe Thornton/10
GJPLJJ Jaromir Jagr/15
GJPLJR Jeremy Roenick/13
GJPLJS Joe Sakic/8
GJPLMB Martin Brodeur/8
GJPLML Mario Lemieux/5
GJPLMM Mark Messier/8
GJPLMO Mike Modano/15
GJPLMS Martin St. Louis/13
GJPLPF Peter Forsberg/8
GJPLPK Paul Kariya/3
GJPLSY Steve Yzerman/8
GJPLTB Todd Bertuzzi/12
GJPLWG Wayne Gretzky/5
GJPNBB Joe Thornton/23
GJPNJJ Jaromir Jagr/23
GJPNJR Jeremy Roenick/20
GJPNJS Joe Sakic/20
GJPNMB Martin Brodeur/23
GJPNML Mario Lemieux/15
GJPNMM Mark Messier/17
GJPNMO Mike Modano/23
GJPNMS Martin St. Louis/23
GJPNPF Peter Forsberg/20
GJPNPK Paul Kariya/2
GJPNSY Steve Yzerman/20
GJPNTB Todd Bertuzzi/23
GJPNWG Wayne Gretzky/5

2004-05 Upper Deck School of Hard Knocks

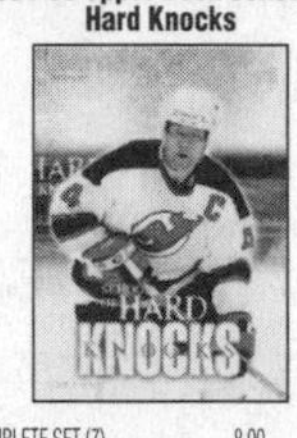

COMPLETE SET (7) 8.00 15.00
STATED ODDS 1:24
SHK1 Brendan Shanahan 1.00 2.50
SHK2 Scott Stevens 1.00 2.50
SHK3 Gary Roberts 1.00 2.50
SHK4 Jeremy Roenick 1.50 4.00
SHK5 Zdeno Chara 1.00 2.50
SHK6 Ed Jovanovski 1.00 2.50
SHK7 Todd Bertuzzi 1.00 2.50

2004-05 Upper Deck Swatch of Six

STATED ODDS 1:96
KNOWN PRINT RUNS LISTED BELOW
SSAR Andrew Raycroft 8.00 20.00
SSBS Brendan Shanahan 8.00 20.00
SSEB Ed Belfour 8.00 20.00
SSGH Gordie Howe/15
SSGR Gary Roberts 6.00 15.00
SSJJ Jaromir Jagr/50 15.00 40.00
SSJO Jocelyn Thibault 6.00 15.00
SSJT Jose Theodore 10.00 25.00
SSMM Mark Messier/25 100.00 200.00
SSPD Pavel Datsyuk 8.00 20.00
SSSK Saku Koivu 8.00 20.00
SSSY Steve Yzerman 15.00 40.00
SSTH Joe Thornton 12.50 30.00
SSTR Tuomo Ruutu 8.00 20.00
SSWG Wayne Gretzky/25 150.00 300.00

2004-05 Upper Deck Three Stars

COMPLETE SET (14) 15.00 30.00
STATED ODDS 1:12
AS1 Steve Yzerman 1.50 4.00
AS2 Joe Sakic 1.25 3.00
AS3 Mats Sundin .60 1.50
AS4 Mike Modano .75 2.00
AS5 Jarome Iginla .75 2.00
AS6 Jeremy Roenick .75 2.00
AS7 Martin Brodeur 1.50 4.00
AS8 Vincent Lecavalier .60 1.50
AS9 Markus Naslund .60 1.50
AS10 Jaromir Jagr .75 2.00
AS11 Mario Lemieux 3.00 8.00
AS12 Patrick Roy 1.50 4.00
AS13 Wayne Gretzky 3.00 8.00
AS14 Gordie Howe 1.50 4.00

2004-05 Upper Deck World's Best

This 30-card retail only set featured players who have represented their countries in international competition.

COMPLETE SET (30) 12.50 30.00
WB1 Joe Sakic .60 1.50
WB2 Jarome Iginla .40 1.00
WB3 Martin St. Louis .25 .60
WB4 Martin Brodeur 1.25 3.00
WB5 Mario Lemieux 1.50 4.00
WB6 Joe Thornton .50 1.25
WB7 Dany Heatley .40 1.00
WB8 Milan Hejduk .30 .75
WB9 Jaromir Jagr .50 1.25
WB10 Tomas Kaberle .25 .60
WB11 Tomas Vokoun .25 .60
WB12 Saku Koivu .30 .75
WB13 Kari Lehtonen .40 1.00
WB14 Teemu Selanne .30 .75
WB15 Olaf Kolzig .25 .60
WB16 Jochen Hecht .25 .60
WB17 Sergei Gonchar .25 .60
WB18 Ilya Kovalchuk .40 1.00
WB19 Pavel Datsyuk .30 .75
WB20 Zdeno Chara .25 .60
WB21 Pavel Demitra .25 .60
WB22 Marian Hossa .30 .75
WB23 Marian Gaborik .60 1.50
WB24 Mats Sundin .30 .75
WB25 Peter Forsberg .75 2.00
WB26 Nicklas Lidstrom .30 .75
WB27 Robert Esche .25 .60
WB28 Chris Chelios .30 .75
WB29 Mike Modano .50 1.25
WB30 Keith Tkachuk .30 .75

2004-05 Upper Deck World Cup Tribute

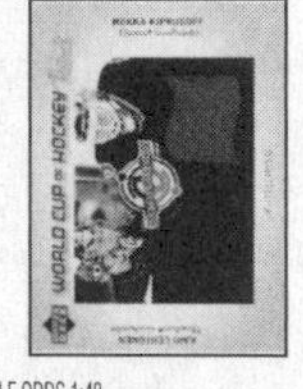

SINGLE ODDS 1:48
DUAL JSY ODDS 1:72
TRIPLE JSY ODDS 1:700
TRIPLE JSY PRINT RUN 25 SER.#'d SETS
AK Alex Kovalev 5.00 10.00
BB Joe Thornton 10.00 25.00
BG Bill Guerin 3.00 8.00
BH Brett Hull SP 12.00 30.00
BL Brian Leetch 4.00 10.00
BR Brad Richards 3.00 8.00
CC Chris Chelios 4.00 10.00
CD Chris Drury 3.00 8.00
DH Dany Heatley SP 12.00 30.00
HE Milan Hejduk 4.00 10.00
IK Ilya Kovalchuk SP 15.00 40.00
JB Jay Bouwmeester 3.00 8.00
JH Jochen Hecht 3.00 8.00
JI Jarome Iginla 5.00 12.00
JJ Jaromir Jagr 12.00 30.00
JS Joe Sakic 15.00 40.00
MB Martin Brodeur 20.00 50.00
MH Marian Hossa 4.00 10.00
MK Miikkaa Kiprusoff 10.00 25.00
ML Martin St. Louis 5.00 10.00
MM Mike Modano 8.00 20.00
MS Mats Sundin 4.00 10.00
NL Nicklas Lidstrom 4.00 10.00
OK Olaf Kolzig 3.00 8.00
PD Pavel Datsyuk 5.00 10.00
PE Patrik Elias 3.00 8.00
PF Peter Forsberg SP 15.00 40.00
RD Rick DiPietro 3.00 8.00
RE Robert Esche 3.00 8.00
RL Roberto Luongo 8.00 20.00
SK Saku Koivu SP 10.00 25.00
VL Vincent Lecavalier 5.00 12.00
ZC Zdeno Chara 3.00 8.00
BLBR Brian Leetch/Brian Ralfalski 8.00 20.00
CCTA Chris Chelios/Tony Amonte 8.00 20.00
IKAK Ilya Kovalchuk/Alexei Kovalev 15.00 40.00
JBAF Jay Bouwmeester/Adam Foote 8.00 20.00
JHOK Jochen Hecht/Olaf Kolzig 8.00 20.00
KLMK Kari Lehtonen/Miikkaa Kiprusoff 12.00 30.00
MBRL M.Brodeur/R.Luongo SP 20.00 50.00
NLMO Nicklas Lidstrom/Mattias Ohlund 8.00 20.00
RCTV Roman Cechmanek/Tomas Vokoun 8.00 20.00
SNEJ Scott Niedermeyer/Ed Jovanovski 8.00 20.00
WREB Wade Redden/Eric Brewer 8.00 20.00
ZCMG Z.Chara/M.Gaborik 8.00 20.00
AKAYSS Alexei Kovalev/Alexei Yashin
/Sergei Samsonov 20.00 50.00
CCRELDH Chris Chelios/Robert Esche
/Brian Leetch 30.00 80.00
DHPMSD Dany Heatley/Patrick Marleau
/Shane Doan 30.00 80.00
DWMOCD Doug Weight/Mike Modano
/Chris Drury 40.00 100.00
EBEJWR Eric Brewer/Ed Jovanoski
/Wade Redden 20.00 50.00
HZTSNL Henrik Zetterberg/Tommy Salo
/Nicklas Lidstrom
JSMLJI Sakic/Lemieux/Iginla 125.00 300.00
KLJPTR Kari Lehtonen/Joni Pitkanen
/Tuomo Ruutu 25.00 60.00
KTDWBH Keith Tkachuk/Doug Weight
/Brett Hull 50.00 125.00
MBRLJT Martin Brodeur/Roberto Luongo
/Jose Theodore 125.00 300.00
MGHOMI Gaborik/Hossa/Satan 50.00 125.00
MHSKTV Martin Havlat/Martin Straka
/Tomas Vokoun 20.00 50.00
MSVLBR Martin St. Louis/Vincent Lecavalier
/Brad Richards 75.00 200.00
OJSKTS Olli Jokinen/Saku Koivu
/Teemu Selanne 50.00 125.00
PBPDZC Peter Bondra/Pavol Demitra
/Zdeno Chara 25.00 60.00
PDMAIK Pavel Datsyuk/Maxim Afinogenov
/Ilya Kovalchuk 50.00 100.00
PEJJHE Elias/Jagr/Hejduk 75.00 200.00

PFSUDA Peter Forsberg/Mats Sundin
/Daniel Alfredsson 60.00 150.00
SGTHRS Simon Gagne/Joe Thornton
/Ryan Smyth 75.00 150.00
TASGBG Tony Amonte/Scott Gomez
/Bill Guerin 40.00 100.00
TCRDRE Ty Conklin/Rick DiPietro
/Robert Esche 25.00 60.00

2004-05 Upper Deck YoungStars

STATED ODDS 1:72
YSAR Andrew Raycroft 8.00 20.00
YSES Eric Staal 8.00 20.00
YSJC Jonathan Cheechoo 15.00 40.00
YSJL Joffrey Lupul 4.00 10.00
YSMR Michael Ryder 6.00 15.00
YSMS Matt Stajan 5.00 12.00
YSNZ Nikolai Zherdev 6.00 15.00
YSPB Patrice Bergeron 12.50 30.00
YSPS Philippe Sauve 4.00 10.00
YSRT Raffi Torres 4.00 10.00
YSTH Trent Hunter 4.00 10.00
YSTR Tuomo Ruutu 8.00 20.00

2005-06 Upper Deck

This 487-card set was issued over two series. The set was released in eight-card packs, with an $2.99 SRP, which came 24 packs to a box and 12 boxes to a case. Both series had a Young Guns (Rookie Cards) subset which were inserted at a stated rate of one in four. Those cards comprise cards numbered 201-242 and 443-487.

COMPLETE SET (487) 400.00 750.00
COMP.SER 1 w/o SP's (200) 12.00 25.00
COMPLETE SERIES 1 (242) 300.00 600.00
COMP.SER 2 w/o SP's (200) 12.00 25.00
COMPLETE SERIES 2 (245) 250.00 500.00
YG STATED ODDS 1:4
1 Sergei Fedorov .25 .60
2 Sandis Ozolinsh .05 .15
3 Rob Niedermayer .05 .15
4 Andy McDonald .05 .15
5 Joffrey Lupul .05 .15
6 Jean-Sebastien Giguere .15 .40
7 Ilya Kovalchuk .25 .60
8 Patrik Stefan .05 .15
9 Kari Lehtonen .15 .40
10 Marc Savard .05 .15
11 Andy Sutton .05 .15
12 Niclas Havelid .05 .15
13 Nick Boynton .05 .15
14 Joe Thornton .30 .75
15 Andrew Raycroft .15 .40
16 P.J. Axelsson .05 .15
17 Patrice Bergeron .15 .40
18 Sergei Samsonov .15 .40
19 Chris Drury .15 .40
20 Derek Roy .05 .15
21 Maxim Afinogenov .05 .15
22 Daniel Briere .05 .15
23 Mika Noronen .15 .40
24 Jean-Pierre Dumont .05 .15
25 Jarome Iginla .25 .60
26 Jordan Leopold .05 .15
27 Robyn Regehr .05 .15
28 Marcus Nilson .05 .15
29 Shean Donovan .05 .15
30 Miikka Kiprusoff .25 .60
31 Erik Cole .05 .15
32 Bret Hedican .05 .15
33 Josef Vasicek .05 .15
34 Radim Vrbata .05 .15
35 Niclas Wallin .05 .15
36 Justin Williams .05 .15
37 Mark Bell .05 .15
38 Tuomo Ruutu .05 .15
39 Eric Daze .15 .40
40 Kyle Calder .05 .15
41 Matthew Barnaby .05 .15
42 Tyler Arnason .05 .15
43 Joe Sakic .75 2.00
44 Rob Blake .15 .40
45 Alex Tanguay .15 .40
46 Dan Hinote .05 .15
47 J-M Liles .05 .15
48 Steve Konowalchuk .05 .15
49 David Aebischer .15 .40
50 Riku Hahl .05 .15
51 Rick Nash .25 .60
52 Marc Denis .15 .40
53 Jody Shelley .05 .15
54 David Vyborny .05 .15
55 Manny Malhotra .05 .15
56 Todd Marchant .05 .15
57 Geoff Sanderson .05 .15
58 Bill Guerin .15 .40
59 Brenden Morrow .15 .40
60 Sergei Zubov .05 .15
61 Jaroslav Svoboda .05 .15
62 Steve Ott .05 .15
63 Jason Arnott .05 .15
64 Niko Kapanen .05 .15
65 Stu Barnes .05 .15
66 Steve Yzerman 1.00 2.50
67 Nicklas Lidstrom .20 .50
68 Robert Lang .05 .15
69 Manny Legace .15 .40
70 Tomas Holmstrom .05 .15
71 Kris Draper .05 .15
72 Jiri Fischer .05 .15
73 Henrik Zetterberg .20 .50
74 Ty Conklin .15 .40
75 Raffi Torres .05 .15
76 Jason Smith .05 .15
77 Radek Dvorak .05 .15
78 Ales Hemsky .15 .40
79 Shawn Horcoff .05 .15
80 Roberto Luongo .25 .60
81 Mike Van Ryn .05 .15
82 Olli Jokinen .15 .40
83 Jay Bouwmeester .05 .15
84 Nathan Horton .05 .15
85 Niklas Hagman .05 .15
86 Luc Robitaille .15 .40
87 Mathieu Garon .05 .15
88 Lubomir Visnovsky .05 .15
89 Trent Klatt .05 .15
90 Mattias Norstrom .05 .15
91 Dustin Brown .05 .15
92 Dwayne Roloson .15 .40
93 Marian Gaborik .40 1.00
94 Pascal Dupuis .05 .15
95 Filip Kuba .05 .15
96 Pierre-Marc Bouchard .05 .15
97 Alexandre Daigle .05 .15
98 Saku Koivu .20 .50
99 Richard Zednik .05 .15
100 Michael Ryder .05 .15
101 Sheldon Souray .05 .15
102 Craig Rivet .05 .15
103 Jan Bulis .05 .15
104 Pierre Dagenais .05 .15
105 Tomas Vokoun .15 .40
106 David Legwand .15 .40
107 Steve Sullivan .15 .40
108 Adam Hall .05 .15
109 Jordin Tootoo .05 .15
110 Dennis Arkhipov .05 .15
111 Scott Gomez .05 .15
112 Patrik Elias .15 .40
113 Scott Stevens .15 .40
114 Sergei Brylin .05 .15
115 John Madden .05 .15
116 Jeff Friesen .05 .15
117 Paul Martin .05 .15
118 Alexei Yashin .15 .40
119 Trent Hunter .05 .15
120 Mark Parrish .05 .15
121 Garth Snow .15 .40
122 Jason Blake .05 .15
123 Janne Niinimaa .05 .15
124 Jamie Lundmark .05 .15
125 Tom Poti .05 .15
126 Jaromir Jagr .30 .75
127 Darius Kasparaitis .05 .15
128 Michael Nylander .05 .15
129 Kevin Weekes .15 .40
130 Daniel Alfredsson .15 .40
131 Dominik Hasek .40 1.00
132 Wade Redden .05 .15
133 Jason Spezza .20 .50
134 Chris Phillips .05 .15
135 Vaclav Varada .05 .15
136 Zdeno Chara .05 .15
137 Simon Gagne .20 .50
138 Joni Pitkanen .05 .15
139 Keith Primeau .05 .15
140 Michal Handzus .05 .15
141 Kim Johnsson .05 .15
142 Sami Kapanen .05 .15
143 Donald Brashear .05 .15
144 Brett Hull .25 .60
145 Tyson Nash .05 .15
146 Shane Doan .05 .15
147 Derek Morris .05 .15
148 Mike Johnson .05 .15
149 Paul Mara .05 .15
150 Mario Lemieux 1.25 3.00
151 Mark Recchi .05 .15
152 Ryan Malone .05 .15
153 Rico Fata .05 .15
154 Lasse Pirjeta .05 .15
155 Dick Tarnstrom .05 .15
156 Jonathan Cheechoo .08 .20
157 Marco Sturm .05 .15
158 Evgeni Nabokov .15 .40
159 Alyn McCauley .05 .15
160 Kyle McLaren .05 .15
161 Brad Stuart .05 .15
162 Wayne Primeau .05 .15
163 Christian Ehrhoff .05 .15
164 Keith Tkachuk .20 .50
165 Barret Jackman .05 .15
166 Patrick Lalime .15 .40
167 Dallas Drake .05 .15
168 Mark Rycroft .05 .15
169 Christian Backman .05 .15
170 Brad Richards .15 .40
171 Fredrik Modin .05 .15
172 Martin St. Louis .15 .40
173 Ruslan Fedotenko .05 .15
174 Darryl Sydor .05 .15
175 Pavel Kubina .05 .15
176 Tim Taylor .05 .15
177 Mats Sundin .20 .50
178 Matt Stajan .05 .15
179 Bryan McCabe .05 .15
180 Darcy Tucker .05 .15
181 Tomas Kaberle .05 .15
182 Owen Nolan .15 .40
183 Nikolai Antropov .05 .15
184 Ken Klee .05 .15
185 Ed Jovanovski .15 .40
186 Dan Cloutier .15 .40
187 Trevor Linden .05 .15
188 Matt Cooke .05 .15
189 Todd Bertuzzi .20 .50
190 Alex Auld .05 .15
191 Sami Salo .05 .15
192 Mattias Ohlund .05 .15
193 Olaf Kolzig .15 .40
194 Brendan Witt .05 .15
195 Jeff Halpern .05 .15
196 Dainius Zubrus .05 .15
197 Alexander Semin .05 .15
198 Boyd Gordon .05 .15
199 Joe Thornton CL .30 .75
200 Jarome Iginla CL .25 .60
201 Sidney Crosby YG RC 175.00 350.00
202 Mike Richards YG RC 8.00 20.00
203 Dion Phaneuf YG RC 12.00 30.00
204 Corey Perry YG RC 5.00 12.00
205 Alexander Steen YG RC 4.00 10.00
206 Zach Parise YG RC 8.00 20.00
207 Rostislav Olesz YG RC 3.00 8.00
208 Matt Foy YG RC 3.00 8.00
209 Brent Seabrook YG RC 5.00 12.00
210 Jeff Hoggan YG RC 3.00 8.00
211 Petteri Nokelainen YG RC 3.00 8.00
212 Andrew Wozniewski YG RC 3.00 8.00
213 Peter Budaj YG RC 3.00 8.00
214 Chris Campoli YG RC 3.00 8.00
215 Jim Howard YG RC 6.00 15.00
216 Henrik Lundqvist YG RC 15.00 40.00
217 David Leneveu YG RC 3.00 8.00
218 George Parros YG RC 3.00 8.00
219 Kevin Dallman YG RC 3.00 8.00
220 Jeff Woywitka YG RC 3.00 8.00
221 Rene Bourque YG RC 3.00 8.00
222 Jim Slater YG RC 3.00 8.00
223 Niklas Nordgren YG RC 3.00 8.00
224 Jay McClement YG RC 3.00 8.00
225 Andrew Alberts YG RC 3.00 8.00
226 Alexander Perezhogin YG RC 4.00 10.00
227 Yann Danis YG RC 4.00 10.00
228 Andrej Meszaros YG RC 3.00 8.00
229 Cam Ward YG RC 6.00 15.00
230 Duncan Keith YG RC 5.00 12.00
231 Timo Helbling YG RC 3.00 8.00
232 Keith Ballard YG RC 3.00 8.00
233 Braydon Coburn YG RC 3.00 8.00
234 Ryane Clowe YG RC 3.00 8.00
235 Ryan Hollweg YG RC 3.00 8.00
236 Maxime Talbot YG RC 3.00 8.00
237 Brett Lebda YG RC 3.00 8.00
238 Brandon Bochenski YG RC 3.00 8.00
239 Jaroslav Balastik YG RC 3.00 8.00
240 Wojtek Wolski YG RC 5.00 12.00
241 Hannu Toivonen YG RC 4.00 10.00
242 S.Crosby/C.Perry YG CL 4.00 10.00
243 Teemu Selanne .30 .75
244 Scott Niedermayer .20 .50
245 Ilya Bryzgalov .15 .40
246 Todd Fedoruk .05 .15
247 Chris Kunitz .10 .25
248 Petr Sykora .10 .25
249 Keith Carney .10 .25
250 Marian Hossa .25 .60
251 Peter Bondra .25 .60
252 Bobby Holik .20 .50
253 Mike Dunham .15 .40
254 Vyacheslav Kozlov .10 .25
255 Steve Shields .15 .40
256 Glen Murray .20 .50
257 Brian Leetch .30 .75
258 Brad Boyes .10 .25
259 Jiri Slegr .10 .25
260 Travis Green .10 .25
261 Hal Gill .10 .25
262 Marco Sturm .20 .50
263 Brad Stuart .20 .50
264 Ryan Miller .15 .40
265 Teppo Numminen .10 .25
266 Jochen Hecht .10 .25
267 Martin Biron .25 .60
268 Paul Gaustad .10 .25
269 Ales Kotalik .10 .25
270 Tim Connolly .10 .25
271 Mike Grier .10 .25
272 Tony Amonte .25 .60
273 Philippe Sauve .25 .60
274 Daymond Langkow .10 .25
275 Chuck Kobasew .20 .50
276 Chris Simon .10 .25
277 Matthew Lombardi .20 .50
278 Roman Hamrlik .10 .25
279 Stephane Yelle .10 .25
280 Eric Staal .25 .60
281 Rod Brind'Amour .25 .60
282 Cory Stillman .20 .50
283 Martin Gerber .25 .60
284 Glen Wesley .20 .50
285 Oleg Tverdovsky .20 .50
286 Nikolai Khabibulin .30 .75
287 Pavel Vorobiev .10 .25
288 Martin Lapointe .10 .25
289 Adrian Aucoin .20 .50
290 Matt Ellison .10 .25
291 Jaroslav Spacek .10 .25
292 Milan Hejduk .30 .75
293 Pierre Turgeon .20 .50
294 Ian Laperriere .10 .25
295 Marek Svatos .10 .25
296 Patrice Brisebois .10 .25
297 Antti Laaksonen .10 .25
298 Nikolai Zherdev .25 .60
299 Bryan Berard .20 .50
300 Pascal Leclaire .15 .40
301 Adam Foote .10 .25
302 Sergei Fedorov .30 .75
303 Trevor Letowski .10 .25
304 Dan Fritsche .10 .25
305 Mike Modano .30 .75
306 Marty Turco .25 .60
307 Jere Lehtinen [illegible] [illegible]
308 Johan Hedberg .15 .40
309 Philippe Boucher .10 .25
310 Antti Miettinen .10 .25
311 Trevor Daley .10 .25
312 Brendan Shanahan .30 .75
313 Chris Osgood .15 .40
314 Pavel Datsyuk .30 .75
315 Chris Chelios .30 .75
316 Jason Williams .10 .25
317 Mikael Samuelsson .10 .25
318 Mathieu Schneider .10 .25
319 Ryan Smyth .25 .60
320 Chris Pronger .25 .60
321 Jussi Markkanen .10 .25
322 Georges Laraque .10 .25
323 Michael Peca .20 .50
324 Marc-Andre Bergeron .10 .25
325 Jarret Stoll .10 .25
326 Jani Rita .10 .25
327 Stephen Weiss .20 .50
328 Joe Nieuwendyk .25 .60
329 Gary Roberts .10 .25
330 Martin Gelinas .10 .25
331 Chris Gratton .10 .25
332 Juraj Kolnik .10 .25
333 Lukas Krajicek .10 .25
334 Jeremy Roenick .30 .75
335 Alexander Frolov .25 .60
336 Pavol Demitra .25 .60
337 Craig Conroy .10 .25
338 Jason LaBarbera .15 .40
339 Mike Cammalleri .10 .25
340 Tim Gleason .10 .25
341 Manny Fernandez .25 .60
342 Marc Chouinard .10 .25
343 Brian Rolston .10 .25
344 Todd White .10 .25
345 Nick Schultz .10 .25
346 Brent Burns .10 .25
347 Jose Theodore .30 .75
348 Mike Ribeiro .20 .50
349 Steve Begin .10 .25
350 Alex Kovalev .15 .40
351 Tomas Plekanec .10 .25
352 Andrei Markov .10 .25
353 Radek Bonk .10 .25
354 Chris Higgins .10 .25
355 Paul Kariya .30 .75
356 Yanic Perreault .10 .25
357 Scott Hartnell .10 .25
358 Kimmo Timonen .20 .50
359 Scott Walker .20 .50
360 Dan Hamhuis .10 .25
361 Martin Erat .10 .25
362 Martin Brodeur .75 2.00
363 David Hale .10 .25
364 Brian Gionta .10 .25
365 Viktor Kozlov .10 .25
366 Scott Clemmensen .15 .40
367 Jamie Langenbrunner .10 .25
368 Brian Rafalski .20 .50
369 Miroslav Satan .20 .50
370 Rick DiPietro .25 .60
371 Alexei Zhitnik .10 .25
372 Mike York .10 .25
373 Brent Sopel .20 .50
374 Martin Rucinsky .10 .25
375 Martin Straka .10 .25
376 Steve Rucchin .20 .50
377 Marcel Hossa .10 .25
378 Fedor Tjutin .10 .25
379 Dominic Moore .10 .25
380 Dany Heatley .30 .75
381 Martin Havlat .25 .60
382 Peter Schaefer .10 .25
383 Bryan Smolinski .10 .25
384 Antoine Vermette .10 .25
385 Anton Volchenkov .10 .25
386 Peter Forsberg .50 1.25
387 Robert Esche .25 .60
388 Mike Rathje .10 .25
389 Eric Desjardins .10 .25
390 Patrick Sharp .10 .25
391 Mike Knuble .10 .25
392 Curtis Joseph .30 .75
393 Ladislav Nagy .20 .50
394 Geoff Sanderson .20 .50
395 Mike Comrie .15 .40
396 Oleg Saprykin .10 .25
397 Petr Nedved .20 .50
398 Zigmund Palffy .25 .60
399 John LeClair .30 .75
400 Marc-Andre Fleury .25 .60
401 Sergei Gonchar .10 .25
402 Jocelyn Thibault .15 .40
403 Sebastien Caron .10 .25
404 Patrick Marleau .15 .40
405 Vesa Toskala .15 .40
406 Marcel Goc .10 .25
407 Joe Thornton .50 1.25
408 Milan Michalek .10 .25
409 Niko Dimitrakos .10 .25
410 Doug Weight .25 .60
411 Petr Cajanek .10 .25
412 Reinhard Divis .10 .25
413 Jamal Mayers .10 .25
414 Scott Young .10 .25
415 Eric Brewer .10 .25
416 Vincent Lecavalier .30 .75
417 Sean Burke .25 .60
418 Vaclav Prospal .10 .25
419 Dave Andreychuk .20 .50
420 Cory Sarich .10 .25
421 John Grahame .15 .40
422 Ed Belfour .30 .75
423 Jason Allison .20 .50
424 Jeff O'Neill .20 .50
425 Eric Lindros .30 .75
426 Tie Domi .25 .60
427 Kyle Wellwood .15 .40
428 Mikael Tellqvist .15 .40
429 Markus Naslund .30 .75
430 Henrik Sedin .10 .25
431 Daniel Sedin .10 .25
432 Ryan Kesler .20 .50
433 Brendan Morrison .20 .50
434 Anson Carter .25 .60
435 Jeff Friesen .20 .50
436 Steve Eminger .10 .25
437 Jamie Heward .10 .25
438 Mike Green RC 2.50 6.00
439 Andrew Cassels .10 .25
440 Shaone Morrisonn .10 .25
441 Peter Forsberg CL .50 1.25
442 Dany Heatley CL .30 .75
443 Alexander Ovechkin RC 60.00 120.00
444 Jeff Carter RC 6.00 15.00
445 Cam Barker RC 3.00 8.00
446 Gilbert Brule RC 4.00 10.00
447 Brad Winchester RC 6.00 15.00
448 Eric Nystrom RC 3.00 8.00
449 R.J. Umberger RC 6.00 15.00
450 Mikko Koivu RC 4.00 10.00
451 Robert Nilsson RC 3.00 8.00
452 Ryan Getzlaf RC 6.00 15.00
453 Anthony Stewart RC 3.00 8.00
454 Ryan Suter RC 4.00 10.00
455 Al Montoya RC 4.00 10.00
456 Johan Franzen RC 15.00 40.00
457 Thomas Vanek RC 6.00 15.00
458 Patrick Eaves RC 4.00 10.00
459 Jussi Jokinen RC 3.00 8.00
460 Christoph Schubert RC 3.00 8.00
461 Ryan Whitney RC 4.00 10.00
462 Evgeny Artyukhin RC 3.00 8.00
463 Jordan Sigalet RC 3.00 8.00
464 Milan Jurcina RC 6.00 15.00
465 Dimitri Patzold RC 3.00 8.00
466 Staffan Kronwall RC 3.00 8.00
467 Erik Christensen RC 3.00 8.00
468 Kyle Brodziak RC 6.00 15.00
469 Ryan Craig RC 3.00 8.00
470 Steve Bernier RC 4.00 10.00
471 Matt Greene RC 3.00 8.00
472 Barry Tallackson RC 10.00 25.00
473 Jakub Klepis RC 3.00 8.00
474 Maxim Lapierre RC 3.00 8.00
475 Danny Richmond RC 3.00 8.00
476 Tomas Fleischmann RC 3.00 8.00
477 Adam Berkhoel RC 6.00 15.00
478 Kevin Bieksa RC 3.00 8.00
479 Greg Jacina RC 3.00 8.00
480 Gerald Coleman RC 3.00 8.00
481 Jeremy Colliton RC 3.00 8.00
482 Andrei Kostitsyn RC 4.00 10.00
483 Valtteri Filppula RC 3.00 8.00
484 Dennis Wideman RC 3.00 8.00
485 Brad Richardson RC 3.00 8.00
486 Jeff Tambellini RC 3.00 8.00
487 Alexander Ovechkin 5.00 12.00
Jeff Carter CL

2005-06 Upper Deck All-Time Greatest

COMPLETE SET (90) 20.00 50.00
1 Jean-Sebastien Giguere .40 1.00
2 Paul Kariya .50 1.25
3 Ilya Kovalchuk .60 1.50
4 Dany Heatley .60 1.50
5 Joe Thornton .75 2.00
6 Cam Neely .50 1.25
7 Dominik Hasek .75 2.00
8 Gilbert Perreault .50 1.25
9 Jarome Iginla .60 1.50
10 Lanny McDonald .40 1.00
11 Rod Brind'Amour .40 1.00
12 Gary Roberts .25 .60
13 Tony Esposito .50 1.25
14 Stan Mikita .50 1.25
15 Joe Sakic 1.00 2.50
16 Patrick Roy 2.00 5.00
17 Rick Nash .60 1.50
18 Marc Denis .40 1.00
19 Mike Modano .60 1.50
20 Ed Belfour .50 1.25
21 Gordie Howe 1.25 3.00
22 Steve Yzerman 1.50 4.00
23 Wayne Gretzky 3.00 8.00
24 Jari Kurri .50 1.25
25 Roberto Luongo .60 1.50
26 Olli Jokinen .40 1.00
27 Wayne Gretzky 3.00 8.00
28 Luc Robitaille .25 .60
29 Marian Gaborik .75 2.00
30 Dwayne Roloson .40 1.00
31 Patrick Roy 2.00 5.00
32 Jose Theodore .60 1.50
33 Steve Sullivan .25 .60
34 Tomas Vokoun .40 1.00
35 Martin Brodeur 1.50 4.00
36 Patrik Elias .40 1.00
37 Mike Bossy .50 1.25
38 Alexei Yashin .25 .60
39 Jaromir Jagr .75 2.00
40 Brian Leetch .75 2.00
41 Daniel Alfredsson .40 1.00
42 Jason Spezza .50 1.25
43 Keith Tkachuk .50 1.25
44 Shane Doan .25 .60
45 Bobby Clarke .50 1.25
46 Ron Hextall .25 .60
47 Mario Lemieux 2.00 5.00
48 Jaromir Jagr .75 2.00
49 Doug Weight .40 1.00
50 Chris Pronger .40 1.00
51 Patrick Marleau .40 1.00
52 Evgeni Nabokov .40 1.00
53 Martin St. Louis .40 1.00
54 Vincent Lecavalier .50 1.25
55 Mats Sundin .50 1.25
56 Darryl Sittler .50 1.25
57 Markus Naslund .50 1.25
58 Trevor Linden .25 .60
59 Olaf Kolzig .40 1.00
60 Peter Bondra .40 1.00
61 Dany Heatley .60 1.50
62 Ray Bourque .60 1.50
63 Andrew Raycroft .40 1.00
64 Gilbert Perreault .40 1.00
65 Jarome Iginla .60 1.50
66 Tony Esposito .50 1.25
67 Ed Belfour .50 1.25
68 Rick Nash .60 1.50
69 Paul Kariya .50 1.25
70 Gordie Howe 1.25 3.00
71 Steve Yzerman 1.50 4.00
72 Sergei Fedorov .50 1.25
73 Wayne Gretzky 3.00 8.00
74 Luc Robitaille .40 1.00
75 Mike Modano .75 2.00
76 Guy Lafleur .60 1.50
77 Patrick Roy 2.00 5.00
78 Martin Brodeur 1.50 4.00
79 Mike Bossy .50 1.25
80 Brian Leetch .50 1.25
81 Daniel Alfredsson .40 1.00
82 Ron Hextall .40 1.00
83 Eric Lindros .50 1.25
84 Sidney Crosby 4.00 10.00
85 Mario Lemieux 2.00 5.00
86 Joe Sakic 1.00 2.50
87 Peter Forsberg .75 2.00
88 Peter Stastny .25 .60
89 Evgeni Nabokov .40 1.00
90 Teemu Selanne .50 1.25

2005-06 Upper Deck Big Playmakers

PRINT RUN 50 SER.#'d SETS
BBMO Bryan McCabe 10.00 25.00
BBNI Rob Niedermayer 10.00 25.00
BJOL Jordan Leopold 10.00 25.00
BDAE David Aebischer 15.00 40.00
BMBO Martin Biron 10.00 25.00
BMDU Mike Dunham 10.00 25.00
BDHA Dominik Hasek 25.00 60.00
BSSA Sergei Samsonov 15.00 40.00
BBMC Brendan Morrison 10.00 25.00
BMST Martin St. Louis 15.00 40.00
BMBI Mike Bossy
BMHO Marian Hossa 15.00 40.00
BJEL Jamie Lundmark 10.00 25.00
BMPA Michael Peca 10.00 25.00
BMPE Mark Parrish 10.00 25.00
BDAR Denis Arkhipov 10.00 25.00
BDHE Dany Heatley 15.00 40.00
BMAH Marcel Hossa 10.00 25.00
BMSU Mats Sundin 15.00 40.00
BMRI Mike Ribeiro 10.00 25.00
BJLU Jere Lehtinen 10.00 25.00
BSST Scott Stevens 10.00 25.00
BMME Mark Messier 25.00 60.00
BJBL Jay Bouwmeester 10.00 25.00
BROB Rob Blake 15.00 40.00
BMHA Martin Havlat 12.00 30.00
BMRE Mark Recchi 10.00 25.00
BMDE Marc Denis 10.00 25.00
BMRY Michael Ryder
BJBO Jason Blake 10.00 25.00
BPBO Peter Bondra 10.00 25.00
BAC Anson Carter 10.00 25.00
BAF Alexander Frolov 10.00 25.00
BAH Adam Hall 10.00 25.00
BAM Al MacInnis 12.00 30.00
BAT Alexander Mogilny 12.00 30.00
BAT Alex Tanguay 15.00 40.00
BAY Alexei Yashin 12.00 30.00
BBC Bobby Clarke 20.00 50.00
BBG Bill Guerin 12.00 30.00
BBH Brett Hull 15.00 40.00
BBJ Barret Jackman 10.00 25.00
BBS Brendan Shanahan 15.00 40.00
BCC Chris Chelios 12.00 30.00
BCD Chris Drury 12.00 30.00
BCJ Curtis Joseph 15.00 40.00
BCN Cam Neely 20.00 40.00
BCP Chris Pronger 15.00 40.00
BCS Chris Simon 10.00 25.00
BDB Daniel Briere 15.00 40.00
BDC Dan Cloutier 10.00 25.00
BDL David Legwand 10.00 25.00
BDW Doug Weight 12.00 30.00
BEB Ed Belfour 15.00 40.00
BED Eric Daze 10.00 25.00
BEJ Ed Jovanovski 10.00 25.00
BEL Eric Lindros 15.00 40.00
BES Eric Staal 20.00 50.00
BGM Glen Murray 12.00 30.00
BGO Scott Gomez 10.00 25.00
BGS Geoff Sanderson 10.00 25.00
BHJ Milan Hejduk 15.00 40.00
BIK Ilya Kovalchuk 25.00 60.00
BJA Jason Allison 10.00 25.00
BJC Jonathan Cheechoo 15.00 40.00
BJG Jean-Sebastien Giguere 12.00 30.00
BJI Jarome Iginla 25.00 60.00
BJJ Jaromir Jagr 25.00 60.00
BJK Jari Kurri 15.00 40.00
BJL John LeClair 12.00 30.00
BJN Joe Nieuwendyk
BJO Jose Theodore 20.00 50.00
BJP Joni Pitkanen 10.00 25.00
BJR Jeremy Roenick 15.00 40.00
BJS Jason Smith 10.00 25.00
BJT Joe Thornton 25.00 60.00
BJW Justin Williams 12.00 30.00
BKP Keith Primeau 12.00 30.00
BKT Keith Tkachuk 12.00 30.00
BLR Luc Robitaille 12.00 30.00
BMA Maxim Afinogenov 12.00 30.00
BMB Martin Brodeur [illegible] [illegible]
BMF Manny Fernandez 15.00 40.00
BMG Marian Gaborik 25.00 60.00
BML Mario Lemieux 50.00 125.00
BMM Mike Modano 20.00 50.00
BMN Markus Naslund 15.00 40.00
BMO Mattias Ohlund 10.00 25.00
BMS Martin Straka 10.00 25.00
BMT Marty Turco 15.00 40.00
BNA Nik Antropov 10.00 25.00
BNK Nikolai Khabibulin 15.00 40.00
BNL Nicklas Lidstrom 15.00 40.00
BOJ Olli Jokinen 10.00 25.00
BOK Olaf Kolzig 15.00 40.00
BON Owen Nolan 12.00 30.00
BPB Patrice Bergeron 15.00 40.00
BPD Pavel Datsyuk 15.00 40.00
BPE Patrik Elias 12.00 30.00
BPF Peter Forsberg 25.00 60.00
BPK Paul Kariya 15.00 40.00
BPL Patrick Lalime 10.00 25.00
BPM Patrick Marleau
BPR Patrick Roy 40.00 100.00
BRB Ray Bourque 20.00 50.00
BRF Ruslan Fedotenko 10.00 25.00
BRH Ron Hextall 20.00 50.00
BRK Rostislav Klesla 10.00 25.00
BRL Roberto Luongo 25.00 60.00
BRN Rick Nash 20.00 40.00
BRS Ryan Smyth 15.00 40.00
BSB Sean Burke 10.00 25.00
BSD Shane Doan 10.00 25.00
BSF Sergei Fedorov 15.00 40.00
BSG Simon Gagne 15.00 40.00
BSH Scott Hartnell 10.00 25.00
BSK Saku Koivu 15.00 40.00
BSO Sandis Ozolinsh 10.00 25.00
BSP Jason Spezza 15.00 40.00
BSY Steve Yzerman 30.00 80.00
BSZ Sergei Zubov 10.00 25.00
BTA Tony Amonte 15.00 40.00
BTB Todd Bertuzzi 15.00 40.00
BTC Ty Conklin 10.00 25.00
BTH Trent Hunter 10.00 25.00
BTP Tom Poti 10.00 25.00
BTR Tuomo Ruutu 15.00 40.00
BTV Tomas Vokoun 15.00 40.00
BVD Vincent Damphousse 10.00 25.00
BVL Vincent Lecavalier 15.00 40.00
BVN Ville Nieminen 10.00 25.00
BWG Wayne Gretzky 100.00 250.00
BZC Zdeno Chara 10.00 25.00

2005-06 Upper Deck Destined for the Hall

COMPLETE SET (7) 12.00 25.00
ODDS 1:24
DH1 Steve Yzerman 4.00 10.00
DH2 Martin Brodeur 4.00 10.00
DH3 Joe Sakic 3.00 8.00
DH4 Dominik Hasek 2.00 5.00
DH5 Jaromir Jagr 2.50 6.00
DH6 Mario Lemieux 6.00 15.00
DH7 Brendan Shanahan 1.50 4.00

2005-06 Upper Deck Diary of a Phenom

COMPLETE SET (30) 15.00 40.00
COMMON CARD (DP1-DP30) .50 1.25
ONE PER RETAIL PACK

2005-06 Upper Deck Goal Celebrations

COMPLETE SETS (7) 8.00 15.00
ODDS 1:12
GC1 Ilya Kovalchuk 2.00 5.00
GC2 Dany Heatley 1.50 4.00
GC3 Jaromir Jagr 2.50 6.00
GC4 Jarome Iginla 1.25 3.00
GC5 Martin St. Louis 1.25 3.00
GC6 Rick Nash 2.00 5.00
GC7 Mats Sundin 1.50 4.00

2005-06 Upper Deck Goal Rush

COMPLETE SET (14) 10.00 20.00
STATED ODDS 1:12
GR1 Rick Nash .75 2.00
GR2 Martin St. Louis .60 1.50
GR3 Milan Hejduk .60 1.50
GR4 Steve Yzerman 1.50 4.00
GR5 Joe Sakic 1.25 3.00
GR6 Wayne Gretzky 3.00 8.00
GR7 Mario Lemieux 3.00 8.00
GR8 Ilya Kovalchuk .75 2.00

GR9 Patrice Bergeron .60 1.50
GR10 Markus Naslund .60 1.50
GR11 Marian Hossa .60 1.50
GR12 Mike Modano 1.00 2.50
GR13 Jarome Iginla .75 2.00
GR14 Dany Heatley .75 2.00

2005-06 Upper Deck HG Glossy

PRINT RUN 10 SER.#'d SETS
NOT PRICED DUE TO SCARCITY

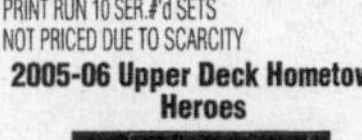

2005-06 Upper Deck Hometown Heroes

COMPLETE SET (28) 20.00 40.00
STATED ODDS 1:12
HH1 Joe Sakic 1.50 4.00
HH2 Martin Brodeur 2.00 5.00
HH3 Joe Thornton 1.25 3.00
HH4 Jarome Iginla .60 1.50
HH5 Mats Sundin .75 2.00
HH6 Steve Yzerman 2.00 5.00
HH7 Saku Koivu .75 2.00
HH8 Jaromir Jagr 1.25 3.00
HH9 Ilya Kovalchuk 1.00 2.50
HH10 Mike Modano .75 2.00
HH11 Martin St. Louis .60 1.50
HH12 Mark Messier .50 1.25
HH13 Mario Lemieux 3.00 8.00
HH14 Keith Tkachuk .75 2.00
HH15 Daniel Alfredsson .40 1.00
HH16 Evgeni Nabokov .60 1.50
HH17 Jaromir Jagr 1.25 3.00
HH18 Rick Nash 1.00 2.50
HH19 Peter Forsberg 1.25 3.00
HH20 Paul Kariya .75 2.00
HH21 Jean-Sebastien Giguere .60 1.50
HH22 Nikolai Khabibulin .75 2.00
HH23 Alexei Yashin .40 .60
HH24 Shane Doan .40 1.00
HH25 Markus Naslund .75 2.00
HH26 Dany Heatley .75 2.00
HH27 Eric Lindros .75 2.00
HH28 Olaf Kolzig .60 1.50

2005-06 Upper Deck Jerseys

STATED ODDS 1:12
JMPE Michael Peca 8.00 20.00
JAHE Ales Hemsky 8.00 20.00
JDAR Denis Arkhipov 2.50 6.00
JBHU Brett Hull 6.00 15.00
JNIB Nick Boynton 8.00 20.00
JDBR Donald Brashear 2.50 6.00
JMST Matt Stajan 8.00 20.00
JBGE Bernie Geoffrion SP 75.00 150.00
JRHX Ron Hextall SP 15.00 40.00
JPAS Patrick Stefan 8.00 20.00
JDSE Daniel Sedin 4.00 10.00
JDSA Denis Savard SP 15.00 40.00
JMLO Matthew Lombardi 8.00 20.00
JJLE Jere Lehtinen 6.00 15.00
JMPA Mark Parrish 8.00 20.00
JMHE Milan Hejduk 8.00 20.00
JRLU Roberto Luongo 15.00 40.00
JRIH Riku Hahl 4.00 10.00
JHSE Henrik Sedin 4.00 10.00
JSOZ Sandis Ozolinsh 8.00 20.00
JTSE Teemu Selanne 10.00 25.00
JPSY Petr Sykora 8.00 20.00
JBHO Bobby Holik 8.00 20.00
JMBI Martin Biron 6.00 15.00
JTRU Tuomo Ruutu 8.00 20.00
JSST Scott Stevens 4.00 10.00
JMGR Mike Grier 4.00 10.00
JBMC Bryan McCabe 8.00 20.00
JRBK Radek Bonk 4.00 10.00
JDAE David Aebischer 6.00 15.00
JMNI Marcus Nilson 4.00 10.00
JMRY Michael Ryder 6.00 15.00
JJAB Jay Bouwmeester 8.00 20.00
JSTR Steven Reinprecht 2.50 6.00
JGUL Georges Laraque 4.00 10.00
JSGA Simon Gagne 10.00 25.00
JTDO Tie Domi 6.00 15.00
JMAD Marc Denis 6.00 15.00
JSKA Sami Kapanen 8.00 20.00
JPDE Pavol Demitra 6.00 15.00
JJOL Joffrey Lupul 8.00 20.00
JMCA Mike Cammalleri 4.00 10.00
JJAR Jason Arnott 4.00 10.00
JSSA Sergei Samsonov 6.00 15.00
JMCO Mike Comrie 4.00 10.00
JSKO Steve Konowalchuk 4.00 10.00
JMAH Marcel Hossa 8.00 20.00
JSGO Scott Gomez 6.00 15.00
JSOT Steve Ott 4.00 10.00
JMGA Mathieu Garon 6.00 15.00
JAA Adrian Aucoin 5.00 12.00
JAF Adam Foote 2.50 6.00
JAK Alexei Kovalev 2.50 6.00
JAM Alexander Mogilny 6.00 15.00
JAY Alexei Yashin 8.00 20.00
JBC Bobby Clarke SP 75.00 150.00
JBG Bill Guerin SP 5.00 12.00
JBL Rob Blake 6.00 15.00
JBM Brendan Morrison 5.00 12.00
JBR Dustin Brown 5.00 12.00
JBT Bryan Trottier 6.00 15.00
JBW Brendan Witt 5.00 12.00
JCC Chris Chelios SP 15.00 40.00
JCD Chris Drury 6.00 15.00
JCJ Curtis Joseph 10.00 25.00
JCK Chuck Kobasew 5.00 12.00
JCO Chris Osgood 4.00 10.00
JCP Chris Pronger 6.00 15.00
JDB Daniel Briere 10.00 25.00
JDH Dany Heatley 10.00 25.00
JDL David Legwand 6.00 15.00
JDO Dominik Hasek 8.00 20.00
JDW Doug Weight 6.00 15.00
JEB Ed Belfour 6.00 15.00
JEJ Ed Jovanovski 6.00 15.00
JEL Eric Lindros 10.00 25.00
JGF Grant Fuhr SP 20.00 50.00
JGL Guy Lafleur SP 40.00 80.00
JGM Glen Murray 8.00 20.00
JGR Gary Roberts 4.00 10.00
JHA Dan Hamhuis 4.00 10.00
JJF Jeff Friesen 5.00 12.00
JJG Jean-Sebastien Giguere 6.00 15.00
JJH Jani Hurme 4.00 10.00
JJI Jarome Iginla 8.00 20.00
JJO Jose Theodore 8.00 20.00
JJP Joni Pitkanen SP 8.00 20.00
JJR Jeremy Roenick 8.00 20.00
JJS Jason Smith 4.00 10.00
JJS Joe Sakic SP 12.50 30.00
JJT Joe Thornton 12.00 30.00
JJW Justin Williams 6.00 15.00
JKD Kris Draper 4.00 10.00
JKL Kari Lehtonen SP 25.00 60.00
JKP Keith Primeau 5.00 12.00
JKT Keith Tkachuk 10.00 25.00
JLR Luc Robitaille 6.00 15.00
JMA Maxim Afinogenov 8.00 20.00
JMB Martin Brodeur 12.50 30.00
JMD Mike Dunham 4.00 10.00
JMK Miikka Kiprusoff 8.00 20.00
JML Mario Lemieux SP 20.00 50.00
JMM Mike Modano 8.00 20.00
JMO Mattias Ohlund 8.00 20.00
JMR Mark Recchi 6.00 15.00
JMS Mats Sundin 10.00 25.00
JNA Nik Antropov 8.00 20.00
JNH Nathan Horton 8.00 20.00
JNK Nikolai Khabibulin 8.00 20.00
JNS Nathan Smith 4.00 10.00
JOJ Olli Jokinen 6.00 15.00
JOK Olaf Kolzig 6.00 15.00
JON Owen Nolan 4.00 10.00
JPD Pavel Datsyuk 10.00 25.00
JPF Peter Forsberg 8.00 20.00
JPK Paul Kariya SP 8.00 20.00
JPR Patrick Roy 15.00 40.00
JPT Pierre Turgeon 8.00 20.00
JRB Ray Bourque SP 15.00 40.00
JRE Robert Esche 6.00 15.00
JRM Ryan Miller 4.00 10.00
JRN Rob Niedermayer 8.00 20.00
JRT Raffi Torres 8.00 20.00
JSC Stanislav Chistov 4.00 10.00
JSF Sergei Fedorov 10.00 25.00
JSH Scott Hartnell 4.00 10.00
JSK Saku Koivu 10.00 25.00
JSM Scott Mellanby 4.00 10.00
JSP Jason Spezza 6.00 15.00
JSU Scottie Upshall 4.00 10.00
JSY Steve Yzerman 12.50 30.00
JSZ Sergei Zubov 8.00 20.00
JTA Tony Amonte 6.00 15.00
JTC Ty Conklin 6.00 15.00
JTO Jordin Tootoo 4.00 10.00
JTP Tom Poti 8.00 20.00
JVB Valeri Bure 4.00 10.00
JVK Viktor Kozlov 4.00 10.00
JVL Vincent Lecavalier 10.00 25.00
JVN Ville Nieminen 4.00 10.00
JWG Wayne Gretzky SP 60.00 120.00

2005-06 Upper Deck Jerseys Series II

ODDS 1:12
J2AA Alex Auld 2.50 6.00
J2AC Anson Carter 4.00 10.00
J2AF Alexander Frolov 6.00 15.00
J2AK Alex Kovalev 4.00 10.00
J2AR Andrew Raycroft 6.00 15.00
J2AT Alex Tanguay 6.00 15.00
J2BG Bill Guerin 5.00 12.00
J2BI Martin Biron 6.00 15.00
J2BJ Barret Jackman 5.00 12.00
J2BL Brian Leetch 10.00 25.00
J2BM Brendan Morrison 5.00 12.00
J2BR Brad Richards 8.00 20.00
J2BS Brendan Shanahan 10.00 25.00
J2CK Matt Cooke 2.50 6.00
J2CM Mike Comrie 2.50 6.00
J2CO Chris Osgood 4.00 10.00
J2CP Chris Pronger 6.00 15.00
J2CS Cory Stillman 8.00 20.00
J2CY Tim Connolly 4.00 10.00
J2DA Daniel Alfredsson 6.00 15.00
J2DC Dan Cloutier 6.00 15.00
J2DM Dominic Moore 4.00 10.00
J2DW Doug Weight 6.00 15.00
J2DY Trevor Daley 2.50 6.00
J2EB Ed Belfour 10.00 25.00
J2EJ Ed Jovanovski 6.00 15.00
J2EL Eric Lindros 10.00 25.00
J2ES Eric Staal 8.00 20.00
J2FT Fedor Tjutin 2.50 6.00
J2GA Simon Gagne 10.00 25.00
J2GE Martin Gerber 6.00 15.00
J2GI Brian Gionta 4.00 10.00
J2GM Glen Murray 8.00 20.00
J2GO Scott Gomez 6.00 15.00
J2HJ Milan Hejduk 10.00 25.00
J2HO Marcel Hossa 5.00 12.00
J2HZ Michal Handzus 2.50 6.00
J2HZ Henrik Zetterberg 10.00 25.00
J2IK Ilya Kovalchuk 12.00 30.00
J2JA Jason Allison 8.00 20.00
J2JB Jay Bouwmeester 8.00 20.00
J2JC Jonathan Cheechoo 8.00 20.00
J2JE Jere Lehtinen 6.00 15.00
J2JG Jean-Sebastien Giguere 6.00 15.00
J2JH Jeff Halpern 2.50 6.00
J2JI Jarome Iginla 8.00 20.00
J2JJ Jaromir Jagr 30.00 60.00
J2JO Jose Theodore 10.00 25.00
J2JP Joni Pitkanen 5.00 12.00
J2JR Jeremy Roenick 10.00 25.00
J2JS Joe Sakic 20.00 50.00
J2JU Justin Williams 6.00 15.00
J2JW Jason Williams 4.00 10.00
J2KC Kyle Calder 8.00 20.00
J2KD Kris Draper 4.00 10.00
J2KL Kari Lehtonen 10.00 25.00
J2KP Keith Primeau 5.00 12.00
J2LE Jordan Leopold 8.00 20.00
J2LO Matthew Lombardi 6.00 15.00
J2LR Luc Robitaille 6.00 15.00
J2LU Joffrey Lupul 8.00 20.00
J2LX Mario Lemieux SP 75.00 150.00
J2MA Maxim Afinogenov 8.00 20.00
J2MB Martin Brodeur 12.00 30.00
J2MC Bryan McCabe 8.00 20.00
J2MG Marian Gaborik 12.00 30.00
J2MH Martin Havlat 6.00 15.00
J2MK Miikka Kiprusoff 10.00 25.00
J2ML Manny Legace 10.00 25.00
J2MM Mike Modano 10.00 25.00
J2MN Markus Naslund 10.00 25.00
J2MO Mattias Ohlund 8.00 20.00
J2MP Michael Peca 8.00 20.00
J2MR Mike Ribeiro 8.00 20.00
J2MS Miroslav Satan 5.00 12.00
J2MT Marty Turco 6.00 15.00
J2MW Brenden Morrow 8.00 20.00
J2NA Nik Antropov 5.00 12.00
J2NB Nick Boynton 5.00 12.00
J2NI Rob Niedermayer 5.00 12.00
J2NK Nikolai Khabibulin SP 75.00 125.00
J2NL Nicklas Lidstrom 10.00 25.00
J2NO Mika Noronen 6.00 15.00
J2NZ Nikolai Zherdev 6.00 15.00
J2OK Olaf Kolzig 6.00 15.00
J2ON Jeff O'Neill 8.00 20.00
J2PA Mark Parrish 5.00 12.00
J2PB Peter Bondra 6.00 15.00
J2PE Patrik Elias 6.00 15.00
J2PF Peter Forsberg 10.00 25.00
J2PK Paul Kariya 10.00 25.00
J2PS Patrick Sharp 4.00 10.00
J2PT Pierre Turgeon 5.00 12.00
J2RD Rick DiPietro 6.00 15.00
J2RE Robert Esche 6.00 15.00
J2RF Ruslan Fedotenko 8.00 20.00
J2RK Brian Rafalski 5.00 12.00
J2RL Roberto Luongo 15.00 40.00
J2RN Rick Nash 12.00 30.00
J2RO Brian Rolston 4.00 10.00
J2RS Ryan Smyth 10.00 25.00
J2RT Raffi Torres 5.00 12.00
J2RY Ryan Miller 4.00 10.00
J2SA Philippe Sauve 4.00 10.00
J2SB Sean Burke 6.00 15.00
J2SD Shane Doan 8.00 20.00
J2SH Shawn Horcoff 4.00 10.00
J2SK Sami Kapanen 8.00 20.00
J2SL Martin St. Louis 6.00 15.00
J2SN Scott Niedermayer 8.00 20.00
J2SO Sandis Ozolinsh 8.00 20.00
J2SP Jason Spezza 10.00 25.00
J2SR Marc Savard 8.00 20.00
J2SS Steve Sullivan 8.00 20.00
J2SU Mats Sundin 10.00 25.00
J2SV Sergei Samsonov 6.00 15.00
J2SW Stephen Weiss 8.00 20.00
J2SY Steve Yzerman SP 50.00 125.00
J2TB Todd Bertuzzi 12.00 30.00
J2TC Ty Conklin 6.00 15.00
J2TD Tie Domi 6.00 15.00
J2TH Trent Hunter 5.00 12.00
J2TL Trevor Linden 8.00 20.00
J2TO Tony Amonte 6.00 15.00
J2TP Tom Poti 8.00 20.00
J2TS Teemu Selanne 10.00 25.00
J2TV Tomas Vokoun 6.00 15.00
J2VK Viktor Kozlov 4.00 10.00
J2VL Vincent Lecavalier 10.00 25.00
J2VP Vaclav Prospal 2.50 6.00
J2WR Wade Redden 8.00 20.00
J2ZC Zdeno Chara 6.00 15.00
J2ZP Zigmund Palffy 6.00 15.00

2005-06 Upper Deck Majestic Materials

PRINT RUN 50 SER.#'d SETS
MMAF Alexander Frolov 8.00 20.00
MMAO Alexander Ovechkin 75.00 175.00
MMAP Alexander Perezhogin 12.00 30.00
MMAR Andrew Raycroft 15.00 40.00
MMAS Alexander Steen 20.00 50.00
MMAT Alex Tanguay 12.00 30.00
MMAY Alexei Yashin 15.00 40.00
MMBG Bill Guerin 8.00 20.00
MMBR Brad Richards 20.00 50.00
MMBS Brendan Shanahan 15.00 40.00

MMCH Jonathan Cheechoo 15.00 40.00
MMCP Chris Pronger 12.00 30.00
MMDA Daniel Alfredsson 15.00 40.00
MMDP Dion Phaneuf 40.00 80.00
MMDW Doug Weight 8.00 20.00
MMEB Ed Belfour 15.00 40.00
MMEJ Ed Jovanovski 8.00 20.00
MMEL Eric Lindros 15.00 40.00
MMES Eric Staal 15.00 40.00
MMGB Gilbert Brule 12.00 30.00
MMGI Brian Gionta 15.00 40.00
MMHE Milan Hejduk 8.00 20.00
MMHK Dominik Hasek 20.00 50.00
MMHL Henrik Lundqvist 30.00 80.00
MMHT Hannu Toivonen 15.00 40.00
MMHV Martin Havlat 8.00 20.00
MMHZ Henrik Zetterberg 15.00 40.00
MMIK Ilya Kovalchuk 20.00 50.00
MMJA Jason Allison 12.00 30.00
MMJB Jay Bouwmeester 15.00 40.00
MMJC Jeff Carter 20.00 50.00
MMJG Jean-Sebastien Giguere 8.00 20.00
MMJI Jarome Iginla 30.00 60.00
MMJJ Jaromir Jagr 25.00 60.00
MMJL Joffrey Lupul 8.00 20.00
MMJO Jose Theodore 20.00 50.00
MMJR Jeremy Roenick 15.00 40.00
MMJS Joe Sakic/40 30.00 60.00
MMJT Joe Thornton 25.00 60.00
MMKL Kari Lehtonen
MMKP Keith Primeau 8.00 20.00
MMKT Keith Tkachuk 8.00 20.00
MMLE Manny Legace
MMLR Luc Robitaille 15.00 40.00
MMMB Martin Brodeur 30.00 80.00
MMMG Marian Gaborik 25.00 60.00
MMML Mario Lemieux 50.00 125.00
MMMM Mike Modano 30.00 60.00
MMMN Markus Naslund 8.00 20.00
MMMP Michael Peca 8.00 20.00
MMMR Michael Ryder 8.00 20.00
MMMS Martin St.Louis 12.00 30.00
MMMT Marty Turco 20.00 40.00
MMMW Brenden Morrow 8.00 20.00
MMNL Nicklas Lidstrom 8.00 20.00
MMNZ Nikolai Zherdev 15.00 40.00
MMOK Olaf Kolzig 15.00 40.00
MMPB Patrice Bergeron 15.00 40.00
MMPD Pavel Datsyuk 12.50 30.00
MMPE Patrik Elias 8.00 20.00
MMPF Peter Forsberg 25.00 60.00
MMPK Paul Kariya 20.00 50.00
MMRB Rob Blake 8.00 20.00
MMRD Rick DiPietro 20.00 50.00
MMRE Mark Recchi 8.00 20.00
MMRI Mike Richards 12.00 30.00
MMRL Roberto Luongo 12.00 30.00
MMRM Ryan Miller 12.00 30.00
MMRN Rick Nash 25.00 60.00
MMRO Mike Ribeiro 8.00 20.00
MMRS Ryan Smyth 15.00 40.00
MMSA Miroslav Satan 12.00 30.00
MMSC Sidney Crosby 125.00 250.00
MMSD Shane Doan 15.00 40.00
MMSG Simon Gagne 20.00 50.00
MMSH Shawn Horcoff 8.00 20.00
MMSK Saku Koivu 15.00 40.00
MMSN Scott Niedermayer 15.00 40.00
MMSP Jason Spezza 20.00 50.00
MMSS Steve Sullivan 8.00 20.00
MMST Matt Stajan 20.00 50.00
MMSU Mats Sundin
MMSW Stephen Weiss 12.00 30.00
MMSY Steve Yzerman 30.00 80.00
MMTB Todd Bertuzzi 15.00 40.00
MMTC Ty Conklin 10.00 25.00
MMTS Teemu Selanne 12.00 30.00
MMTV Tomas Vokoun 15.00 40.00
MMVA Thomas Vanek 20.00 50.00
MMVL Vincent Lecavalier 12.00 30.00
MMZC Zdeno Chara 8.00 20.00
MMZP Zigmund Palffy 15.00 40.00

2005-06 Upper Deck NHL Generations

DUAL ODDS 1:144
TRIPLE ODDS 1:288
DAR J. Arnott/M.Ryder 5.00 12.00
DBB R.Bourque/J.Bouwmeester 8.00 20.00
DBT M.Brodeur/J.Theodore 20.00 50.00
DFD S.Fedorov/P.Datsyuk 8.00 20.00
DGB B.Guerin/D.Brown 5.00 12.00
DGL W.Gretzky/M.Lemieux 125.00 250.00
DGR S.Gagne/M.Ribeiro 5.00 12.00
DHV D.Hasek/T.Vokoun 10.00 25.00
DIN J.Iginla/R.Nash 12.00 30.00
DJH J.Jagr/M.Havlat 10.00 25.00
DKS J.Kurri/T.Selanne 15.00 40.00
DKZ I.Kovalchuk/N.Zherdev
DLH J.Lehtinen/R.Hahl 5.00 12.00
DML M.Messier/V.Lecavalier 10.00 25.00
DNZ M.Naslund/H.Zetterberg 8.00 20.00
DRB W.Redden/N.Boynton 5.00 12.00
DSC S.Stevens/Z.Chara 5.00 12.00
DST B.Shanahan/J.Thornton 12.50 30.00
DTC M.Turco/T.Conklin 8.00 20.00
DYS S.Yzerman/J.Spezza 25.00 60.00
TBLL Brodeur/Luongo/Lehtonen 30.00 60.00
TBTN Bossy/Thornton/Nash
TCGP Clarke/Gagne/Primeau 15.00 40.00
TFKA Fedorov/Kovalchuk/Afinogenov 20.00 50.00
TGYS Gretzky/Yzerman/Sakic 250.00 400.00
TLKR LaFleur/Koivu/Ribeiro 15.00 40.00
TMST Messier/Shanahan/Thornton 20.00 50.00
TNSN Neely/Shanahan/Nash 20.00 50.00
TRBL Roy/Brodeur/Luongo 75.00 150.00
TSFZ Sundin/Forsberg/Zetterberg 15.00 40.00
TSHT Sakic/Hejduk/Tanguay 20.00 50.00
TSIR Sakic/Iginla/Ribeiro 20.00 50.00
TSKJ Selanne/Koivu/Jokinen 15.00 40.00
TSTP Sakic/Thornton/Spezza 25.00 60.00

2005-06 Upper Deck Notable Numbers

STATED ODDS 1:288
PRINT RUNS VARY
UNDER 23 NOT PRICED DUE TO SCARCITY
NJTH Jocelyn Thibault/41 20.00 50.00
NMAS Marco Sturm/19 20.00 50.00
NMSA Miroslav Satan/81 10.00 25.00
NBRA Brian Rafalski/28 15.00 40.00
NMBA Matthew Barnaby/38 12.00 30.00
NNIK Niko Kapanen/39
NJLI John-Michael Liles/26 20.00 50.00
NPLE Pascal Leclaire/31 20.00 50.00
NJEO Jeff O'Neill/92 10.00 25.00
NMHA Michal Handzus/26
NRBL Rob Blake/4
NMPH Mark Parrish/37 25.00 60.00
NPMB P-M Bouchard/96 10.00 25.00
NMBY Mike Bossy/22
NCCO Carlo Colaiacovo/45 15.00 40.00
NPHS Philippe Sauve/30 15.00 40.00
NMRI Mike Ricci/40
NJAR Jani Rita/22
NMCO Matt Cooke/24
NCCH Chris Chelios/24
NRON Rob Niedermayer/44 15.00 40.00
NPSY Petr Sykora/39
NCRC Craig Conroy/22
NDLW Daymond Langkow/11
NMNY Michael Nylander/92 8.00 20.00
NMBR Martin Brodeur/30 75.00 200.00
NJAR Jason Arnott/44 15.00 40.00
NMDI Marcel Dionne/16
NSGO Sergei Gonchar/55
NJAL Jamie Lundmark/21
NRBO Ray Bourque/77 40.00 80.00
NSGZ Scott Gomez/23
NMGA Mathieu Garon/30
NTSA Tony Salmelainen/42 15.00 40.00
NDUB Dustin Brown/23 20.00 50.00
NMDE Marc Denis/30
NJAL Jason Allison/41
NMGE Martin Gerber/29 30.00 80.00
NAA Adrian Aucoin/33
NAC Anson Carter/11
NAE David Aebischer/1
NAF Marc-Andre Fleury/29 75.00 150.00
NAH Ales Hemsky/83 12.00 30.00
NAL Daniel Alfredsson/11
NAN Nikolai Antropov/80 12.00 30.00
NAR Andrew Raycroft/1
NAT Alex Tanguay/18 50.00 100.00
NAY Alexei Yashin/79 10.00 25.00
NBA Milan Bartovic/15
NBB Brad Boyes/26 20.00 50.00
NBC Bobby Clarke/16
NBI Martin Biron/43 15.00 40.00
NBL Brian Leetch/2
NBR Brad Richards/19
NBS Borje Salming/21
NBY Bryan McCabe/24 30.00 80.00
NCA Mike Cammalleri/13
NCB Christian Backman/55 6.00 15.00
NCD Chris Drury/23
NCE Christian Ehrhoff/44 12.00 30.00
NCK Chuck Kobasew/7
NCO Chris Osgood/30 20.00 50.00
NCP Chris Pronger/44 25.00 60.00
NCS Cory Stillman/61 10.00 25.00
NDA Dave Andreychuk/25
NDB Daniel Briere/48 20.00 50.00
NDC Dan Cloutier/39 20.00 50.00
NDF Dan Fritsche/49 10.00 25.00
NDH Dominik Hasek/39 40.00 100.00
NDL David Legwand/11
NDM Darren McCarty/25
NDR Dwayne Roloson/30 20.00 50.00
NDS Darryl Sittler/27
NDW Doug Weight/39 20.00 50.00
NEB Ed Belfour/20
NEC Erik Cole/26 25.00 60.00
NED Eric Daze/55 12.00 30.00
NEJ Ed Jovanovski/55 15.00 40.00
NEN Evgeni Nabokov/20
NES Eric Staal/12
NFP Fernando Pisani/34
NFR Alexander Frolov/24 25.00 60.00
NFT Fedor Tjutin/51 10.00 25.00
NGC Gerry Cheevers/30 30.00 80.00
NGF Grant Fuhr/31 30.00 80.00
NGH Gordie Howe/9
NGI Jean-Sebastien Giguere/35 15.00 40.00
NGL Georges Laraque/27 20.00 50.00
NGM Glen Murray/27 20.00 40.00
NHE Dany Heatley/15 25.00
NHJ Milan Hejduk/23 20.00 40.00
NHO Marcel Hossa/81 10.00 25.00
NHV Martin Havlat/9
NHZ Henrik Zetterberg/40 25.00 60.00
NIK Ilya Kovalchuk/17
NIL Ian Laperriere/22
NJB Jay Bouwmeester/4
NJC Jonathan Cheechoo/14
NJH Jochen Hecht/55 6.00 15.00
NJI Jarome Iginla/12
NJK Jari Kurri/17
NJL Joffrey Lupul/15
NJO Jose Theodore/60 20.00 50.00
NJP Joni Pitkanen/44 20.00 50.00
NJS Jason Spezza/19 125.00 200.00
NJT Joe Thornton/19
NJV Josef Vasicek/63 8.00 20.00
NJW Justin Williams/11
NKD Kris Draper/33 15.00 40.00
NKH Kristian Huselius/22
NKL Kari Lehtonen/32 25.00 60.00
NKP Keith Primeau/25 20.00 50.00
NKT Kimmo Timonen/44 8.00 20.00
NKW Kevin Weekes/80 8.00 20.00
NLM Larry Murphy/55 12.00 30.00
NLN Ladislav Nagy/17
NLO Stephen Weiss/9
NLR Luc Robitaille/20
NMA Maxim Afinogenov/61 15.00 40.00
NMB Brendan Morrison/7
NMC Mike Comrie/89 8.00 20.00
NMG Marian Gaborik/10
NMH Marian Hossa/18
NMJ Matt Stajan/14
NML Manny Legace/34 20.00 50.00
NMM Mike Modano/9
NMN Markus Naslund/19
NMO Olaf Kolzig/37 50.00 100.00
NMP Michael Peca/27 25.00 60.00
NMR Mike Ribeiro/71 12.00 30.00
NMS Martin St. Louis/26 20.00 50.00
NMT Marty Turco/35 20.00 50.00
NNA Owen Nolan/11
NNB Nick Boynton/44
NND Niko Dimitrakos/23
NNH Nathan Horton/16
NNK Nikolai Khabibulin/53 20.00 50.00
NNO Mika Noronen/35 20.00 50.00
NNZ Nikolai Zherdev/13
NPB Patrice Bergeron/37 20.00 50.00
NPD Pavol Demitra/38
NPE Phil Esposito/7
NPM Patrick Marleau/12
NPO Mark Popovic/33 10.00 25.00
NPW Peter Worrell/28 15.00 40.00
NRE Robert Esche/42 15.00 40.00
NRF Ruslan Fedotenko/17
NRH Riku Hahl/32
NRL Roberto Luongo/1
NRM Ryan Miller/30 15.00 60.00
NRN Rick Nash/61 30.00 80.00
NRO Jeremy Roenick/97 20.00 50.00
NRS Ryan Smyth/94 20.00 50.00
NRT Roman Turek/1
NRV Rogie Vachon/30 30.00 60.00
NRY Michael Ryder/73 15.00 40.00
NRZ Richard Zednik/20
NSB Sean Burke/41 10.00 25.00
NSD Shane Doan/19 20.00 50.00
NSG Simon Gagne/12
NSK Saku Koivu/11
NSN Scott Niedermayer/27 20.00 50.00
NSS Sheldon Souray/44 10.00 25.00
NSU Mats Sundin/13
NSZ Sergei Zubov/56 6.00 15.00
NTA Tyler Arnason/39 10.00 25.00
NTB Todd Bertuzzi/44 25.00 60.00
NTC Ty Conklin/1
NTE Tony Esposito/35 25.00 60.00
NTG Tim Gleason/42 12.00 30.00
NTL Trevor Linden/16
NTN Tyson Nash/18
NTO Terry O'Reilly/24 30.00 60.00
NTR Tuomo Ruutu/15
NTV Steve Sullivan/26 10.00 25.00
NVL Vincent Lecavalier/4
NVP Vaclav Prospal/20 20.00 40.00
NVR Mike Van Ryn/26 10.00 25.00
NWG Wayne Gretzky/99 150.00 250.00
NZC Zdeno Chara/3

2005-06 Upper Deck Patches

PRINT RUN 15 SER.#'d SETS
NOT PRICED DUE TO SCARCITY

2005-06 Upper Deck Patches Series II

PRINT RUN 15 SER.#'d SETS
NOT PRICED DUE TO SCARCITY

2005-06 Upper Deck Playoff Performers

COMPLETE SET (7) 12.00 25.00
STATED ODDS 1:24
PP1 Jarome Iginla 1.00 2.50
PP2 Martin St. Louis .75 2.00
PP3 Peter Forsberg 2.00 5.00
PP4 Wayne Gretzky 4.00 10.00
PP5 Jarome Iginla 1.00 2.50
PP6 Joe Sakic 1.50 4.00
PP7 Mario Lemieux 4.00 10.00

2005-06 Upper Deck Rookie Ink

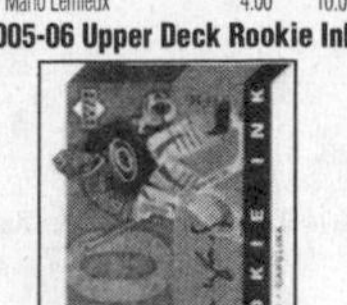

RIAA Andrew Alberts /41 12.00 30.00
RIAM Andrej Meszaros /14 60.00 100.00
RIAO Alexander Ovechkin /8
RIAP Alexander Perezhogin /42 20.00 50.00
RIAS Anthony Stewart /57 12.00 30.00
RIAW Andrew Wozniewski /55 12.00 30.00
RIBB Brandon Bochenski /10
RIBC Braydon Coburn /4
RIBS Brent Seabrook /7
RIBW Brad Winchester /26 20.00 50.00
RICB Cam Barker /25
RICC Chris Campoli /14
RICP Corey Perry /61 25.00 50.00
RICW Cam Ward /30 60.00 125.00
RIDL David Leneveu /30 20.00 50.00
RIDP Dion Phaneuf /3
RIEN Eric Nystrom /23 25.00 60.00
RIGB Gilbert Brule /17
RIGP George Parros /57 12.00 30.00
RIHL Henrik Lundqvist /30 75.00 150.00
RIHO Jeff Hoggan /22 15.00 40.00
RIHT Hannu Toivonen /33 30.00 80.00
RIJB Jaroslav Balastik /29 20.00 50.00
RIJC Jeff Carter /17 50.00 100.00
RIJF Johan Franzen /39 40.00 80.00
RIJG Josh Gorges /6
RIJH Jim Howard /35 25.00 60.00
RIJJ Jussi Jokinen /36 25.00 60.00
RIJM Jay McClement /9
RIJS Jim Slater /23 20.00 50.00
RIJW Jeff Woywitka /29 20.00 50.00
RIKB Keith Ballard /2
RIKD Kevin Dallman /58 10.00 25.00
RIKN Kevin Nastiuk /35 20.00 50.00
RIMF Matt Foy /83 10.00 25.00
RIMJ Milan Jurcina /68 12.00 30.00
RIMK Mikko Koivu /21 60.00 100.00
RIMO Alvaro Montoya /29 25.00 60.00
RIMR Mike Richards /18 40.00 100.00
RIMT Maxime Talbot /25 30.00 80.00
RIPB Peter Budaj /31 50.00 100.00
RIPE Patrick Eaves /7
RIPN Petteri Nokelainen /29 20.00 50.00
RIPP Petr Prucha /25 40.00 100.00
RIRB Rene Bourque /14
RIRC Ryane Clowe /29 20.00 50.00
RIRG Ryan Getzlaf /51 40.00 80.00
RIRH Ryan Hollweg /44 15.00 40.00
RIRI Raitis Ivanans /3
RIRN Robert Nilsson /21
RIRO Rostislav Olesz /85 12.00 30.00
RIRS Ryan Suter /20 40.00 80.00
RIRU R.J. Umberger /20 25.00 60.00
RIRW Ryan Whitney /19
RISC Sidney Crosby /87 300.00 500.00
RIST Alexander Steen /10
RITV Thomas Vanek /26 75.00 125.00
RIWW Wojtek Wolski /8
RIYD Yann Danis /75 15.00 40.00
RIZP Zach Parise /9

2005-06 Upper Deck Rookie Showcase

Available only via the Upper Deck website and one per customer, this 36-card set featured rookies making their debut in the 2005-06 season. Print run was limited to 1000 copies each.

COMMON CARD (RS1-RS36) 3.00 8.00
STATED PRINT RUN 1000 COPIES
RS1 Corey Perry 10.00 25.00
RS2 Braydon Coburn 3.00 8.00
RS3 Hannu Toivonen 5.00 12.00
RS4 Thomas Vanek 12.00 30.00
RS5 Dion Phaneuf 25.00 60.00
RS6 Cam Ward 6.00 15.00
RS7 Brent Seabrook 3.00 8.00
RS8 Wojtek Wolski 5.00 12.00
RS9 Gilbert Brule 8.00 20.00
RS10 Jussi Jokinen 5.00 12.00
RS11 Jim Howard 5.00 12.00
RS12 Brad Winchester 3.00 8.00
RS13 Rostislav Olesz 5.00 12.00
RS14 George Parros 3.00 8.00
RS15 Matt Foy 3.00 8.00
RS16 Alexander Perezhogin 5.00 12.00
RS17 Ryan Suter 5.00 12.00
RS18 Zach Parise 5.00 12.00
RS19 Robert Nilsson 5.00 12.00
RS20 Henrik Lundqvist 25.00 60.00
RS21 Andrej Meszaros 3.00 8.00
RS22 Jeff Carter 12.00 30.00
RS23 David Leneveu 5.00 12.00
RS24 Sidney Crosby 30.00 60.00
RS25 Ryane Clowe 3.00 8.00
RS26 Jeff Woywitka 3.00 8.00
RS27 Evgeni Artyukhin 3.00 8.00

RS28 Alexander Steen 5.00 12.00
RS29 Rob McVicar 3.00 8.00
RS30 Alexander Ovechkin 15.00 40.00
RS31 Yann Danis 5.00 12.00
RS32 Eric Nystrom 5.00 12.00
RS33 Mike Richards 12.00 30.00
RS34 Ryan Getzlaf 20.00 50.00
RS35 Johan Franzen 3.00 8.00
RS36 Brandon Bochenski 3.00 8.00

2005-06 Upper Deck Rookie Showcase Beckett Promos

This 36-card set was available only in copies of Beckett Hockey #180. The cards paralleled the regular Rookie Showcase cards but with a subtle color shift from gold backgrounds and details to pewter.

RS1 Corey Perry 6.00 15.00
RS2 Braydon Coburn 3.00 8.00
RS3 Hannu Toivonen 5.00 12.00
RS4 Thomas Vanek 8.00 20.00
RS5 Dion Phaneuf 15.00 40.00
RS6 Cam Ward 4.00 10.00
RS7 Brent Seabrook 3.00 8.00
RS8 Wojtek Wolski 5.00 12.00
RS9 Gilbert Brule 6.00 15.00
RS10 Jussi Jokinen 3.00 8.00
RS11 Jim Howard 8.00 20.00
RS12 Brad Winchester 3.00 8.00
RS13 Rostislav Olesz 3.00 8.00
RS14 George Parros 3.00 8.00
RS15 Matt Foy 3.00 8.00
RS16 Alexander Perezhogin 5.00 12.00
RS17 Ryan Suter 4.00 10.00
RS18 Zach Parise 10.00 25.00
RS19 Robert Nilsson 4.00 10.00
RS20 Henrik Lundqvist 15.00 40.00
RS21 Andrej Meszaros 3.00 8.00
RS22 Jeff Carter 8.00 20.00
RS23 David Leneveu 3.00 8.00
RS24 Sidney Crosby 20.00 50.00
RS25 Ryane Clowe 3.00 8.00
RS26 Jeff Woywitka 3.00 8.00
RS27 Evgeny Artyukhin 3.00 8.00
RS28 Alexander Steen 5.00 12.00
RS29 Rob McVicar 3.00 8.00
RS30 Alexander Ovechkin 15.00 40.00
RS31 Yann Danis 3.00 8.00
RS32 Eric Nystrom 3.00 8.00
RS33 Mike Richards 6.00 15.00
RS34 Ryan Getzlaf 12.00 30.00
RS35 Johan Franzen 3.00 8.00
RS36 Brandon Bochenski 3.00 8.00

2005-06 Upper Deck Rookie Threads

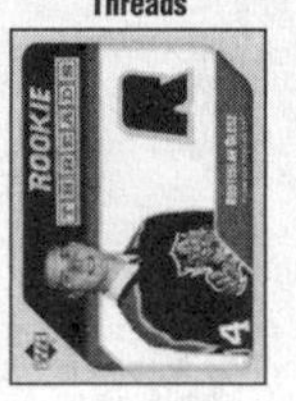

ODDS 1:24
RTAA Andrew Alberts 6.00 15.00
RTAM Andrej Meszaros 6.00 15.00
RTAO Alexander Ovechkin 30.00 60.00
RTAP Alexander Perezhogin 10.00 25.00
RTAS Anthony Stewart 8.00 20.00
RTAW Andrew Wozniewski 6.00 15.00
RTBB Brandon Bochenski 6.00 15.00
RTBC Braydon Coburn 8.00 20.00
RTBL Brett Lebda 6.00 15.00
RTBS Brent Seabrook 12.00 30.00
RTBW Brad Winchester 6.00 15.00
RTCB Cam Barker 8.00 20.00
RTCP Corey Perry 10.00 25.00
RTCW Cam Ward 8.00 20.00
RTDK Duncan Keith 15.00 40.00
RTDL David Leneveu 8.00 20.00
RTDP Dion Phaneuf 30.00 80.00
RTEN Eric Nystrom 8.00 20.00
RTGB Gilbert Brule 10.00 25.00
RTGP George Parros 6.00 15.00
RTHL Henrik Lundqvist 30.00 80.00
RTHO Jim Howard 15.00 40.00
RTHT Hannu Toivonen 10.00 25.00
RTJB Jaroslav Balastik 6.00 15.00
RTJC Jeff Carter 8.00 20.00
RTJF Johan Franzen 20.00 50.00
RTJG Josh Gorges 6.00 15.00
RTJH Jeff Hoggan 6.00 15.00
RTJJ Jussi Jokinen 10.00 25.00
RTJM Jay McClement 6.00 15.00
RTJS Jim Slater 8.00 20.00
RTJW Jeff Woywitka 6.00 15.00
RTKB Keith Ballard 6.00 15.00
RTKD Kevin Dallman 6.00 15.00
RTKN Kevin Nastiuk 8.00 20.00
RTMF Matt Foy 6.00 15.00
RTMJ Milan Jurcina 6.00 15.00
RTMO Alvaro Montoya 12.00 30.00
RTMR Mike Richards 10.00 25.00
RTMT Maxime Talbot 6.00 15.00
RTNN Niklas Nordgren 6.00 15.00
RTPB Peter Budaj 8.00 20.00
RTPE Patrick Eaves 8.00 20.00
RTPN Petteri Nokelainen 6.00 15.00
RTPP Petr Prucha 8.00 20.00
RTRB Rene Bourque 6.00 15.00
RTRC Ryane Clowe 6.00 15.00
RTRG Ryan Getzlaf 20.00 50.00
RTRH Ryan Hollweg 6.00 15.00
RTRI Raitis Ivanans 6.00 15.00
RTRN Robert Nilsson 8.00 20.00
RTRO Rostislav Olesz 8.00 20.00
RTRS Ryan Suter 8.00 20.00
RTSC Sidney Crosby 75.00 150.00
RTST Alexander Steen 10.00 25.00
RTTH Timo Helbling 6.00 15.00
RTTV Thomas Vanek 8.00 20.00
RTWW Wojtek Wolski 10.00 25.00
RTYD Yann Danis 8.00 20.00
RTZP Zach Parise 20.00 50.00

2005-06 Upper Deck Rookie Threads Autographs

*AUTO: 1.5X TO 4X JSY HI
PRINT RUN 75 SER.#'d SETS
UNLESS NOTED BELOW
ARTAO Alexander Ovechkin
ARTAP Alexander Perezhogin
ARTCP Corey Perry
ARTHL Henrik Lundqvist
ARTJC Jeff Carter
ARTMR Mike Richards
ARTRG Ryan Getzlaf
ARTSC Sidney Crosby
ARTST Alexander Steen
ARTTV Thomas Vanek

2005-06 Upper Deck School of Hard Knocks

COMPLETE SET (7) 5.00 10.00
STATED ODDS 1:24
HK1 Scott Stevens .75 2.00
HK2 Chris Pronger .75 2.00
HK3 Chris Simon .75 2.00
HK4 Jeremy Roenick 1.00 2.50
HK5 Tie Domi .75 2.00
HK6 Ed Jovanovski .75 2.00
HK7 Brendan Shanahan .75 2.00

2005-06 Upper Deck Scrapbooks

COMPLETE SET (30) 10.00 25.00
COMMON CARD .15 .40
RANDOM INSERT IN RETAIL PACKS
HS1 Ilya Kovalchuk .40 1.00
HS2 Wayne Gretzky 1.25 3.00
HS3 Joe Thornton .50 1.25
HS4 Kari Lehtonen .30 .75
HS5 Dominik Hasek .40 1.00
HS6 Mario Lemieux 1.25 3.00
HS7 Jose Theodore .30 .75
HS8 Paul Kariya .30 .75
HS9 Mike Modano .30 .75
HS10 Rick Nash .40 1.00
HS11 Mark Messier .40 1.00
HS12 Jarome Iginla .25 .60
HS13 Peter Forsberg .50 1.25
HS14 Nikolai Khabibulin .30 .75
HS15 Dany Heatley .30 .75
HS16 Brett Hull .25 .60
HS17 Marian Gaborik .40 1.00
HS18 Mats Sundin .30 .75
HS19 Steve Yzerman .75 2.00
HS20 Joe Sakic .60 1.50
HS21 Marian Hossa .25 .60
HS22 Markus Naslund .30 .75
HS23 Jaromir Jagr .50 1.25
HS24 Andrew Raycroft .25 .60
HS25 Ed Belfour .30 .75
HS26 Martin St. Louis .25 .60
HS27 Jeremy Roenick .30 .75
HS28 Brendan Shanahan .30 .75
HS29 Sergei Fedorov .30 .75
HS30 Martin Brodeur .75 2.00

2005-06 Upper Deck Shooting Stars

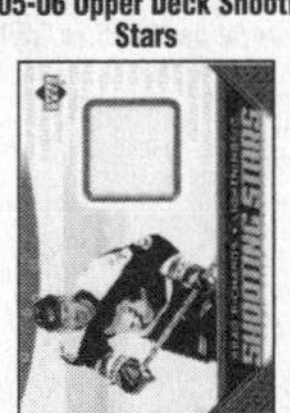

STATED ODDS 1:32
SMME Mark Messier 10.00 25.00
SMMO Mike Modano 6.00 15.00
SMHO Marian Hossa 4.00 10.00
SMRY Michael Ryder 4.00 10.00
SMHA Martin Havlat 4.00 10.00
SMRI Mike Ribeiro 3.00 8.00
SMAM Alexander Mogilny 3.00 8.00
SBG Bill Guerin 3.00 8.00
SBH Brett Hull 5.00 12.00
SBR Brad Richards 4.00 10.00
SBS Brendan Shanahan 4.00 10.00
SCD Chris Drury 3.00 8.00
SDA Daniel Alfredsson 4.00 10.00
SDH Dany Heatley 6.00 15.00
SEL Eric Lindros 4.00 10.00
SGM Glen Murray 3.00 8.00
SHZ Henrik Zetterberg 4.00 10.00
SIK Ilya Kovalchuk 6.00 15.00
SJI Jarome Iginla 6.00 15.00
SJJ Jaromir Jagr SP 40.00 100.00
SJL John LeClair 3.00 8.00
SJR Jeremy Roenick 4.00 10.00
SJS Joe Sakic 8.00 20.00
SJT Joe Thornton 6.00 15.00
SKP Keith Primeau 3.00 8.00
SKT Keith Tkachuk 3.00 8.00
SLR Luc Robitaille 4.00 10.00
SMG Marian Gaborik 6.00 15.00
SMH Milan Hejduk 3.00 8.00
SML Mario Lemieux SP 30.00 80.00
SMN Markus Naslund 4.00 10.00
SMP Michael Peca 3.00 8.00
SMP Mark Parrish 4.00 10.00
SMS Mats Sundin 4.00 10.00
SMS Martin St. Louis 4.00 10.00
SPB Peter Bondra 3.00 8.00
SPE Patrik Elias 4.00 10.00
SPK Paul Kariya 4.00 10.00
SRB Rob Blake 3.00 8.00
SRE Mark Recchi 4.00 10.00
SRN Rick Nash
SRS Ryan Smyth 3.00 8.00
SSF Sergei Fedorov 4.00 10.00
SSG Simon Gagne 4.00 10.00
SSS Sergei Samsonov 3.00 8.00
SSY Steve Yzerman 12.00 30.00
STA Tony Amonte 3.00 8.00
SVL Vincent Lecavalier 5.00 12.00
SZP Zigmund Palffy 4.00 10.00

2005-06 Upper Deck Sportsfest

COMPLETE SET (3) 30.00
NHL1 Sidney Crosby 10.00 25.00
NHL2 Alexander Ovechkin 15.00
NHL3 Wayne Gretzky 10.00
NHLAU Sidney Crosby AU 1/1

2005-06 Upper Deck Stars in the Making

COMPLETE SET (14) 25.00 50.00
SM1 Sidney Crosby 8.00 20.00
SM2 Alexander Ovechkin 6.00 15.00
SM3 Jeff Carter 4.00 10.00
SM4 Corey Perry 3.00 8.00
SM5 Thomas Vanek 5.00 12.00
SM6 Henrik Lundqvist 10.00 25.00
SM7 Alexander Perezhogin 2.50 6.00
SM8 Dion Phaneuf 10.00 25.00
SM9 Hannu Toivonen 3.00 8.00
SM10 Alexander Steen 3.00 8.00
SM11 Gilbert Brule 4.00 10.00
SM12 Mike Richards 3.00 8.00
SM13 Zach Parise 6.00 15.00
SM14 Wojtek Wolski 3.00 8.00

2006-07 Upper Deck

This 495-card set was issued in two series during the 2006-07 season. The first series of 245 cards was released in eight-card packs, with a $2.99 SRP which came 24 packs to a box and 12 boxes to a case. There are two Young Guns subsets in this product (201-250, 451-495) both of which were inserted into packs at a stated rate of one in four.

COMPLETE SET (495) 300.00 600.00
COMP. SER. 1 w/o SPs 10.00 25.00
COMP. SER. 2 w/o SPs 10.00 25.00
YG ODDS 1:4
1 Corey Perry .20 .50
2 Ilya Bryzgalov .25 .60
3 Teemu Selanne .25 .60
4 Andy McDonald .15 .40
5 Ryan Getzlaf .20 .50
6 Francois Beauchemin .07 .20
7 Scott Niedermayer .15 .40
8 Kari Lehtonen .25 .60
9 Marian Hossa .20 .50
10 Slava Kozlov .15 .40
11 Jim Slater .07 .20
12 Garnet Exelby .15 .40
13 Bobby Holik .15 .40
14 Niclas Havelid .07 .20
15 Brad Boyes .15 .40
16 Brad Stuart .15 .40
17 Tim Thomas .25 .60
18 Marco Sturm .15 .40
19 Hannu Toivonen .25 .60
20 Glen Murray .15 .40
21 Ryan Miller .25 .60
22 Thomas Vanek .12 .30
23 Chris Drury .20 .50
24 Henrik Tallinder .07 .20
25 Jochen Hecht .07 .20
26 Brian Campbell .07 .20
27 Derek Roy .15 .40
28 Jarome Iginla .50 1.25
29 Dion Phaneuf .40 1.00
30 Robyn Regehr .07 .20
31 Jamie Lundmark .07 .20
32 Darren McCarty .07 .20
33 Kristian Huselius .15 .40
34 Chuck Kobasew .15 .40
35 Eric Staal .20 .50
36 Cam Ward .40 1.00
37 Justin Williams .07 .20
38 Glen Wesley .07 .20
39 Mike Commodore .15 .40
40 Cory Stillman .15 .40
41 Ray Whitney .07 .20
42 Tuomo Ruutu .15 .40
43 Radim Vrbata .07 .20
44 Duncan Keith .30 .75
45 Nikolai Khabibulin .25 .60
46 Rene Bourque .15 .40
47 Patrick Sharp .07 .20
48 Jose Theodore .25 .60
49 Milan Hejduk .20 .50
50 Pierre Turgeon .15 .40
51 Andrew Brunette .15 .40
52 Wojtek Wolski .15 .40
53 John-Michael Liles .15 .40
54 Joe Sakic .60 1.50
55 Rick Nash .30 .75
56 Pascal Leclaire .25 .60
57 Adam Foote .07 .20
58 Alexandre Picard .07 .20
59 Bryan Berard .15 .40
60 Sergei Fedorov .25 .60
61 Marty Turco .20 .50
62 Brenden Morrow .20 .50
63 Jussi Jokinen .15 .40
64 Sergei Zubov .15 .40
65 Jere Lehtinen .07 .20
66 Steve Ott .15 .40
67 Philippe Boucher .07 .20
68 Pavel Datsyuk .25 .60
69 Mikael Samuelsson .07 .20
70 Tomas Holmstrom .15 .40
71 Kris Draper .07 .20
72 Jason Williams .07 .20
73 Chris Osgood .25 .60
74 Robert Lang .07 .20
75 Ales Hemsky .15 .40
76 Fernando Pisani .15 .40
77 Jarret Stoll .15 .40
78 Marc-Andre Bergeron .07 .20
79 Dwayne Roloson .20 .50
80 Ethan Moreau .07 .20
81 Raffi Torres .07 .20
82 Joe Nieuwendyk .20 .50
83 Jay Bouwmeester .15 .40
84 Nathan Horton .15 .40
85 Rostislav Olesz .15 .40
86 Martin Gelinas .07 .20
87 Stephen Weiss .07 .20
88 Mathieu Garon .20 .50
89 Mike Cammalleri .15 .40
90 Alexander Frolov .15 .40
91 Lubomir Visnovsky .15 .40
92 George Parros .07 .20
93 Dustin Brown .15 .40
94 Marian Gaborik .50 1.25
95 Wes Walz .07 .20
96 Pierre-Marc Bouchard .15 .40
97 Nick Schultz .15 .40
98 Derek Boogaard .15 .40
99 Todd White .15 .40
100 Saku Koivu .25 .60
101 Cristobal Huet .30 .75
102 Alex Kovalev .15 .40
103 Chris Higgins .15 .40
104 Andrei Markov .15 .40
105 Alexander Perezhogin .15 .40
106 Mathieu Dandenault .07 .20
107 Steve Sullivan .15 .40
108 Tomas Vokoun .20 .50
109 David Legwand .15 .40
110 Marek Zidlicky .07 .20
111 Kimmo Timonen .15 .40
112 Ryan Suter .15 .40
113 Jordin Tootoo .12 .30
114 Martin Brodeur 1.00 2.50
115 Brian Gionta .15 .40
116 Zach Parise .20 .50
117 Brian Rafalski .15 .40
118 Jamie Langenbrunner .07 .20
119 John Madden .07 .20
120 Jay Pandolfo .07 .20
121 Miroslav Satan .15 .40
122 Rick DiPietro .25 .60
123 Alexei Zhitnik .07 .20
124 Jeff Tambellini .07 .20
125 Chris Campoli .15 .40
126 Jason Blake .15 .40
127 Trent Hunter .15 .40
128 Jaromir Jagr .50 1.25
129 Petr Prucha .15 .40
130 Kevin Weekes .12 .30
131 Sandis Ozolinsh .07 .20
132 Ryan Hollweg .07 .20
133 Darius Kasparaitis .07 .20
134 Martin Straka .15 .40
135 Jason Spezza .25 .60
136 Ray Emery .25 .60
137 Andrej Meszaros .07 .20
138 Patrick Eaves .15 .40
139 Daniel Alfredsson .20 .50
140 Antoine Vermette .15 .40
141 Chris Phillips .15 .40
142 Peter Forsberg .50 1.25
143 Robert Esche .20 .50
144 Mike Knuble .15 .40
145 Joni Pitkanen .15 .40
146 Mike Richards .25 .60
147 R.J. Umberger .15 .40
148 Sami Kapanen .07 .20
149 Shane Doan .07 .20
150 Keith Ballard .15 .40
151 Ladislav Nagy .15 .40
152 Mike Ricci .07 .20
153 Oleg Saprykin .07 .20
154 David Leneveu .20 .50
155 Sidney Crosby 1.50 4.00
156 Colby Armstrong .15 .40
157 John LeClair .20 .50
158 Sergei Gonchar .07 .20
159 Ryan Whitney .15 .40
160 Ryan Malone .15 .40
161 Joe Thornton .50 1.25
162 Vesa Toskala .20 .50
163 Milan Michalek .15 .40
164 Marcel Goc .07 .20
165 Steve Bernier .15 .40
166 Jonathan Cheechoo .25 .60
167 Christian Ehrhoff .07 .20
168 Keith Tkachuk .20 .50
169 Barret Jackman .07 .20
170 Curtis Sanford .20 .50
171 Lee Stempniak .15 .40
172 Petr Cajanek .15 .40
173 Dallas Drake .07 .20
174 Martin St. Louis .25 .60
175 Vaclav Prospal .15 .40
176 Dan Boyle .15 .40
177 Ryan Craig .07 .20
178 Ruslan Fedotenko .15 .40
179 Paul Ranger .07 .20
180 Sean Burke .12 .30
181 Mats Sundin .25 .60
182 Darcy Tucker .15 .40
183 Alexander Steen .20 .50
184 Mikael Tellqvist .25 .60
185 Tomas Kaberle .15 .40
186 Nikolai Antropov .07 .20
187 Bryan McCabe .15 .40
188 Markus Naslund .25 .60
189 Henrik Sedin .15 .40
190 Mattias Ohlund .15 .40
191 Daniel Sedin .15 .40
192 Matt Cooke .07 .20
193 Sami Salo .15 .40
194 Ryan Kesler .15 .40
195 Brooks Laich .07 .20
196 Shaone Morrisonn .07 .20
197 Chris Clark .15 .40
198 Alexander Semin .12 .30
199 Sidney Crosby 1.50 4.00
200 Jaromir Jagr .50 1.25
201 Shane O'Brien RC 2.00 5.00
202 Ryan Shannon RC 2.00 5.00
203 Yan Stastny RC 2.00 5.00
204 Phil Kessel RC 10.00 25.00
205 Carsen Germyn RC 2.00 5.00
206 Dustin Byfuglien RC 6.00 15.00
207 Paul Stastny RC 12.00 30.00
208 Fredrik Norrena RC 3.00 8.00
209 Filip Novak RC 2.00 5.00
210 Loui Eriksson RC 3.00 8.00
211 Tomas Kopecky RC 3.00 8.00
212 Marc-Antoine Pouliot RC 3.00 8.00
213 Ladislav Smid RC 2.00 5.00
214 Patrick Thoresen RC 3.00 8.00
215 Patrick O'Sullivan RC 4.00 10.00
216 Anze Kopitar RC 15.00 40.00
217 Konstantin Pushkarev RC 2.00 5.00
218 Erik Reitz RC 2.00 5.00
219 Miroslav Kopriva RC 2.00 5.00
220 Niklas Backstrom RC 6.00 15.00
221 Guillaume Latendresse RC 8.00 20.00
222 Shea Weber RC 3.00 8.00
223 Mikko Lehtonen RC 2.00 5.00
224 Frank Doyle RC 2.00 5.00
225 Travis Zajac RC 3.00 8.00
226 John Oduya RC 2.00 5.00
227 Ryan Caldwell RC 2.00 5.00
228 Masi Marjamaki RC 2.00 5.00
229 Matt Koalska RC 2.00 5.00
230 Jarkko Immonen RC 2.00 5.00
231 Nigel Dawes RC 2.00 5.00
232 Ryan Potulny RC 2.00 5.00
233 David Printz RC 2.00 5.00
234 Bill Thomas RC 2.00 5.00
235 Joel Perrault RC 2.00 5.00
236 Patrick Fischer RC 2.00 5.00
237 Noah Welch RC 2.00 5.00
238 Michel Ouellet RC 3.00 8.00
239 Jordan Staal RC 20.00 50.00
240 Kristopher Letang RC 3.00 8.00
241 Matt Carle RC 3.00 8.00
242 Marc-Edouard Vlasic RC 3.00 8.00
243 D.J. King RC 2.00 5.00
244 Ben Ondrus RC 2.00 5.00
245 Brendan Bell RC 2.00 5.00
246 Ian White RC 2.00 5.00
247 Jeremy Williams RC 2.00 5.00
248 Luc Bourdon RC 3.00 8.00
249 Eric Fehr RC 3.00 8.00
250 Phil Kessel CL 3.00 8.00
251 Chris Pronger .20 .50
252 Todd Fedoruk .07 .20
253 Chris Kunitz .15 .40
254 Jean-Sebastien Giguere .25 .60
255 Rob Niedermayer .07 .20
256 Todd Marchant .07 .20
257 Samuel Pahlsson .07 .20
258 Ilya Kovalchuk .30 .75
259 Steve Rucchin .15 .40
260 Niko Kapanen .07 .20
261 Greg de Vries .07 .20
262 Johan Hedberg .12 .30
263 Andy Sutton .07 .20
264 Scott Mellanby .07 .20
265 Patrice Bergeron .20 .50
266 Zdeno Chara .15 .40
267 Andrew Alberts .07 .20
268 P.J. Axelsson .07 .20
269 Marc Savard .15 .40
270 Paul Mara .07 .20
271 Wayne Primeau .15 .40
272 Daniel Briere .20 .50
273 Ales Kotalik .15 .40
274 Jiri Novotny .07 .20
275 Martin Biron .20 .50
276 Jason Pominville .07 .20
277 Maxim Afinogenov .15 .40
278 Jaroslav Spacek .07 .20
279 Alex Tanguay .20 .50
280 Daymond Langkow .15 .40
281 Roman Hamrlik .07 .20
282 Miikka Kiprusoff .25 .60
283 Jeff Friesen .07 .20
284 Andrew Ference .07 .20
285 Stephane Yelle .07 .20
286 Rod Brind'Amour .20 .50
287 Erik Cole .15 .40
288 Andrew Ladd .15 .40
289 John Grahame .12 .30
290 Tim Gleason .07 .20
291 Kevyn Adams .15 .40
292 Martin Havlat .20 .50
293 Brent Seabrook .15 .40
294 Adrian Aucoin .15 .40
295 Brian Boucher .12 .30
296 Bryan Smolinski .15 .40
297 Martin Lapointe .07 .20
298 Michal Handzus .07 .20
299 Marek Svatos .15 .40
300 Mark Rycroll .07 .20
301 Tyler Arnason .07 .20
302 Peter Budaj .20 .50
303 Patrice Brisebois .07 .20
304 Antti Laaksonen .07 .20
305 Ian Laperriere .07 .20
306 Fredrik Modin .15 .40
307 Rostislav Klesla .15 .40
308 Nikolai Zherdev .15 .40
309 Gilbert Brule .15 .40
310 David Vyborny .15 .40
311 Manny Malhotra .15 .40
312 Jody Shelley .15 .40
313 Mike Modano .25 .60
314 Antti Miettinen .07 .20
315 Jeff Halpern .15 .40
316 Patrik Stefan .07 .20
317 Mike Ribeiro .15 .40
318 Eric Lindros .25 .60
319 Dominik Hasek .30 .75
320 Chris Chelios .12 .30
321 Johan Franzen .15 .40
322 Mathieu Schneider .07 .20
323 Henrik Zetterberg .25 .60
324 Nicklas Lidstrom .25 .60
325 Ryan Smyth .20 .50
326 Steve Staios .07 .20
327 Jussi Markkanen .12 .30
328 Joffrey Lupul .15 .40
329 Jason Smith .15 .40
330 Shawn Horcoff .15 .40
331 Petr Sykora .07 .20
332 Olli Jokinen .15 .40
333 Ed Belfour .60 1.50
334 Mike Van Ryn .15 .40
335 Jozef Stumpel .07 .20
336 Alexander Auld .20 .50
337 Todd Bertuzzi .20 .50
338 Gary Roberts .07 .20
339 Rob Blake .20 .50
340 Craig Conroy .15 .40
341 Dan Cloutier .12 .30
342 Mattias Norstrom .15 .40
343 Sean Avery .15 .40
344 Oleg Tverdovsky .07 .20
345 Manny Fernandez .25 .60
346 Brian Rolston .15 .40
347 Mikko Koivu .15 .40
348 Kim Johnsson .07 .20
349 Pavol Demitra .15 .40
350 Mark Parrish .15 .40
351 Kurtis Foster .15 .40
352 Michael Ryder .20 .50
353 David Aebischer .20 .50
354 Sergei Samsonov .20 .50
355 Sheldon Souray .15 .40
356 Mike Johnson
357 Craig Rivet .07 .20
358 Radek Bonk .07 .20
359 Paul Kariya .25 .60
360 Scott Hartnell .07 .20
361 Martin Erat .07 .20
362 Jason Arnott .15 .40
363 Chris Mason .12 .30
364 J.P. Dumont .15 .40
365 Patrik Elias .15 .40
366 Scott Gomez .15 .40
367 Colin White .07 .20
368 Sergei Brylin .07 .20
369 Paul Martin .07 .20
370 Cam Janssen .07 .20
371 Alexei Yashin .15 .40
372 Mike Sillinger .15 .40
373 Arron Asham .07 .20
374 Mike York .07 .20
375 Mike Dunham .12 .30
376 Brendan Witt .07 .20
377 Henrik Lundqvist .40 1.00
378 Adam Hall .07 .20
379 Wayne Gretzky 1.00 2.50
380 Matt Cullen .15 .40
381 Michal Rozsival .07 .20
382 Michael Nylander .15 .40
383 Brendan Shanahan .25 .60
384 Dany Heatley .25 .60
385 Joe Corvo .07 .20
386 Peter Schaefer .07 .20
387 Chris Neil .07 .20
388 Wade Redden .15 .40
389 Martin Gerber .25 .60
390 Mike Fisher .07 .20
391 Simon Gagne .25 .60
392 Jeff Carter .25 .60
393 Antero Niittymaki .25 .60
394 Geoff Sanderson .07 .20
395 Fredrick Meyer .07 .20
396 Kyle Calder .15 .40
397 Curtis Joseph .25 .60
398 Ed Jovanovski .15 .40
399 Mike Comrie .15 .40
400 Nick Boynton .07 .20
401 Jeremy Roenick .25 .60
402 Georges Laraque .07 .20
403 Owen Nolan .20 .50
404 Marc-Andre Fleury .25 .60
405 Nils Ekman .07 .20
406 Jarkko Ruutu .07 .20
407 Mark Eaton .07 .20
408 Dominic Moore .07 .20
409 Mark Recchi .15 .40
410 Patrick Marleau .20 .50
411 Scott Hannan .07 .20
412 Josh Gorges .15 .40
413 Mike Grier .07 .20
414 Mark Bell .15 .40
415 Evgeni Nabokov .20 .50
416 Doug Weight .15 .40
417 Dennis Wideman .07 .20
418 Jay McClement .07 .20
419 Manny Legace .20 .50
420 Bill Guerin .15 .40
421 Jay McKee .07 .20
422 Vincent Lecavalier .25 .60
423 Marc Denis .20 .50
424 Filip Kuba .07 .20
425 Tim Taylor .15 .40
426 Brad Richards .25 .60
427 Dimitry Afanasenkov .07 .20
428 Andrew Raycroft .20 .50
429 Kyle Wellwood .15 .40
430 Michael Peca .15 .40
431 Alexei Ponikarovsky .07 .20
432 Jeff O'Neill .07 .20
433 Jean-Sebastien Aubin .12 .30
434 Matt Stajan .15 .40
435 Dany Sabourin .12 .30
436 Roberto Luongo .50 1.25
437 Willie Mitchell .07 .20
438 Jan Bulis .07 .20
439 Brendan Morrison .15 .40
440 Trevor Linden .07 .20
441 Lukas Krajicek .07 .20
442 Alexander Ovechkin 1.00 2.50
443 Olaf Kolzig .30 .75
444 Richard Zednik .07 .20
445 Brian Pothier .15 .40
446 Donald Brashear .07 .20
447 Dainius Zubrus .15 .40
448 Ben Clymer .07 .20
449 Miikka Kiprusoff .25 .60
450 Wayne Gretzky 1.00 2.50
451 David McKee RC 2.00 5.00
452 Mark Stuart RC 2.00 5.00
453 Matt Lashoff RC 2.00 5.00
454 Mike Brown RC 2.00 5.00
455 Nate Thompson RC 2.00 5.00
456 Drew Stafford RC 5.00 12.00
457 Adam Dennis RC 2.00 5.00
458 Mike Card RC 2.00 5.00
459 Michael Funk RC 2.00 5.00
460 Michael Ryan RC 2.00 5.00
461 Dustin Boyd RC 3.00 8.00
462 Brandon Prust RC 2.00 5.00
463 Dave Bolland RC 4.00 10.00
464 Michael Blunden RC 2.00 5.00
465 Adam Burish RC 2.50 6.00
466 Stefan Liv RC 2.00 5.00
467 Alexei Mikhnov RC 2.00 5.00
468 Jeff Deslauriers RC 2.00 5.00
469 Jan Hejda RC 2.00 5.00
470 David Booth RC 2.00 5.00
471 Drew Larman RC 2.00 5.00
472 Peter Harrold RC 2.00 5.00
473 Barry Brust RC 2.00 5.00
474 Karri Ramo RC 2.00 5.00
475 Benoit Pouliot RC 3.00 8.00
476 Alex Radulov RC 10.00 25.00
477 Alex Brooks RC 2.00 5.00
478 Alexei Kaigorodov RC 2.00 5.00
479 Kelly Guard RC 2.00 5.00
480 Jussi Timonen RC 2.00 5.00
481 Martin Houle RC 2.00 5.00
482 Lars Jonsson RC 2.00 5.00
483 Triston Grant RC 2.00 5.00
484 Enver Lisin RC 2.00 5.00
485 Keith Yandle RC 2.00 5.00
486 Evgeni Malkin RC 50.00 100.00
487 Joe Pavelski RC 8.00 20.00
488 Roman Polak RC 2.00 5.00
489 Blair Jones RC 2.00 5.00
490 J-F Racine RC 2.00 5.00
491 Alexander Edler RC 2.00 5.00
492 Jesse Schultz RC 2.00 5.00
493 Nathan McIver RC 2.00 5.00
494 Patrick Coulombe RC 2.00 5.00
495 Evgeni Malkin 4.00 10.00

2006-07 Upper Deck Exclusives Parallel

VALUE: 10X TO 25X BASE HI
PRINT RUN 100 #'d SETS
YOUNG GUNS: 1.2X TO 3 X HI
204 Phil Kessel 20.00 50.00
207 Paul Stastny 30.00 80.00
215 Patrick O'Sullivan 15.00 40.00
216 Anze Kopitar 25.00 60.00
220 Niklas Backstrom 15.00 40.00
221 Guillaume Latendresse 20.00 50.00
225 Travis Zajac 15.00 40.00
239 Jordan Staal 40.00 100.00
241 Matt Carle 15.00 40.00
486 Evgeni Malkin 125.00 250.00

2006-07 Upper Deck High Gloss Parallel

PRINT RUN 10 SER. #'d SETS
NOT PRICED DUE TO SCARCITY

2006-07 Upper Deck All-Time Greatest

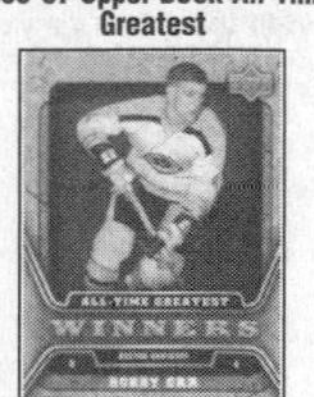

COMPLETE SET (28) 15.00 40.00
STATED ODDS 1:12 SER. 2 PACKS
ATG1 Teemu Selanne .75 2.00
ATG2 Ilya Kovalchuk 1.00 2.50
ATG3 Bobby Orr 2.50 6.00
ATG4 Gilbert Perreault .50 1.25
ATG5 Joe Sakic 1.50 4.00
ATG6 Rick Nash .75 2.00
ATG7 Mike Modano .75 2.00
ATG8 Ted Lindsay .50 1.25
ATG9 Wayne Gretzky 2.50 6.00

ATG10 Marcel Dionne .50 1.25
ATG11 Marian Gaborik 1.25 3.00
ATG12 Tomas Vokoun .60 1.50
ATG13 Martin Brodeur 2.00 5.00
ATG14 Andy Bathgate .25 .60
ATG15 Daniel Alfredsson .60 1.50
ATG16 Bobby Clarke .75 2.00
ATG17 Shane Doan .60 1.50
ATG18 Mario Lemieux 2.00 5.00
ATG19 Evgeni Nabokov .60 1.50
ATG20 Martin St. Louis .75 2.00
ATG21 Darryl Sittler .50 1.25
ATG22 Alexander Ovechkin 1.50 4.00
ATG23 Tony Esposito 1.25 3.00
ATG24 Mario Lemieux 2.00 5.00
ATG25 Guy Lafleur .75 2.00
ATG26 Gilbert Perreault .50 1.25
ATG27 Wayne Gretzky 2.50 6.00
ATG28 Johnny Bower 1.25 3.00

2006-07 Upper Deck All World

COMPLETE SET (30) 200.00 350.00
STATED ODDS 1:24 SER. 2 PACKS
AW1 Mike Modano 3.00 8.00
AW2 Nicklas Lidstrom 3.00 8.00
AW3 Joe Thornton 5.00 12.00
AW4 Teemu Selanne 3.00 8.00
AW5 Kari Lehtonen 3.00 8.00
AW6 Zdeno Chara 2.00 5.00
AW7 Jarome Iginla 5.00 12.00
AW8 Eric Staal 2.50 6.00
AW9 Martin Havlat 2.50 6.00
AW10 Milan Hejduk 2.50 6.00
AW11 Sergei Fedorov 3.00 8.00
AW12 Rick Nash 3.00 8.00
AW13 Henrik Zetterberg 3.00 8.00
AW14 Olli Jokinen 2.00 5.00
AW15 Marian Gaborik 5.00 12.00
AW16 Saku Koivu 3.00 8.00
AW17 Tomas Vokoun 2.50 6.00
AW18 Paul Kariya 3.00 8.00
AW19 Martin Gerber 3.00 8.00
AW20 Markus Naslund 3.00 8.00
AW21 Ilya Kovalchuk 15.00 40.00
AW22 Miikka Kiprusoff 20.00 50.00
AW23 Joe Sakic 30.00 80.00
AW24 Dominik Hasek 20.00 40.00
AW25 Martin Brodeur 20.00 50.00
AW26 Jaromir Jagr 20.00 50.00
AW27 Peter Forsberg 10.00 25.00
AW28 Sidney Crosby 30.00 80.00
AW29 Mats Sundin 15.00 30.00
AW30 Alexander Ovechkin 20.00 50.00

2006-07 Upper Deck Award Winners

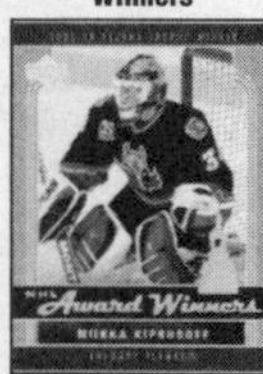

COMPLETE SET (7) 8.00 20.00
STATED ODDS 1:24 .75 2.00
AW1 Joe Thornton 1.50 4.00
AW2 Miikka Kiprusoff 1.25 3.00
AW3 Nicklas Lidstrom .75 2.00
AW4 Alexander Ovechkin 2.00 5.00
AW5 Jaromir Jagr 1.50 4.00
AW6 Rod Brind'Amour .75 2.00
AW7 Cam Ward .75 2.00

2006-07 Upper Deck Century Marks

COMPLETE SET (7) 10.00 25.00
STATED ODDS 1:24 SER. 2 PACKS
CM1 Joe Thornton 2.00 5.00
CM2 Alexander Ovechkin 5.00 12.00
CM3 Dany Heatley 1.25 3.00
CM4 Jaromir Jagr 2.00 5.00
CM5 Sidney Crosby 5.00 12.00
CM6 Eric Staal 1.00 2.50
CM7 Daniel Alfredsson 1.00 2.50

2006-07 Upper Deck Diary of a Phenom

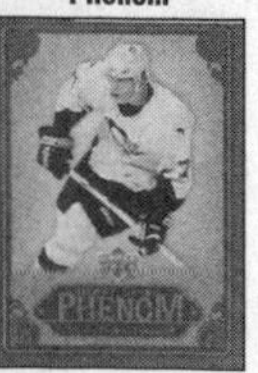

COMPLETE SET (25) 20.00 50.00
COMMON MALKIN 1.25 3.00
ONE PER SER. 2 FAT PACK
DP1 Evgeni Malkin 1.25 3.00
DP2 Evgeni Malkin 1.25 3.00
DP3 Evgeni Malkin 1.25 3.00
DP4 Evgeni Malkin 1.25 3.00
DP5 Evgeni Malkin 1.25 3.00
DP6 Evgeni Malkin 1.25 3.00
DP7 Evgeni Malkin 1.25 3.00
DP8 Evgeni Malkin 1.25 3.00
DP9 Evgeni Malkin 1.25 3.00
DP10 Evgeni Malkin 1.25 3.00
DP11 Evgeni Malkin 1.25 3.00
DP12 Evgeni Malkin 1.25 3.00
DP13 Evgeni Malkin 1.25 3.00
DP14 Evgeni Malkin 1.25 3.00
DP15 Evgeni Malkin 1.25 3.00
DP16 Evgeni Malkin 1.25 3.00
DP17 Evgeni Malkin 1.25 3.00
DP18 Evgeni Malkin 1.25 3.00
DP19 Evgeni Malkin 1.25 3.00
DP20 Evgeni Malkin 1.25 3.00
DP21 Evgeni Malkin 1.25 3.00
DP22 Evgeni Malkin 1.25 3.00
DP23 Evgeni Malkin 1.25 3.00
DP24 Evgeni Malkin 1.25 3.00
DP25 Evgeni Malkin 1.25 3.00

2006-07 Upper Deck Game Dated Moments

STATED ODDS 1:288
GD1 Sidney Crosby 30.00 80.00
GD2 Alexander Ovechkin 20.00 50.00
GD3 Luc Robitaille 15.00 40.00
GD4 Dion Phaneuf 12.00 30.00
GD5 Miikka Kiprusoff 12.00 30.00
GD6 Jaromir Jagr 15.00 40.00
GD7 Jonathan Cheechoo 10.00 25.00
GD8 Martin Brodeur 20.00 50.00
GD9 Ilya Bryzgalov 6.00 15.00
GD10 Joffrey Lupul 6.00 15.00
GD11 Ryan Miller 10.00 25.00
GD12 Cam Ward 8.00 20.00
GD13 Teemu Selanne 12.00 30.00
GD14 Pierre Turgeon 6.00 15.00
GD15 Joe Thornton 15.00 40.00
GD16 Brian Leetch 12.00 30.00
GD17 Henrik Lundqvist 15.00 40.00
GD18 Alexander Ovechkin 20.00 50.00
GD19 Sidney Crosby 30.00 80.00
GD20 Ilya Kovalchuk 15.00 40.00
GD21 Sidney Crosby 30.00 80.00
GD22 Alexander Ovechkin 20.00 50.00
GD23 Joe Thornton 15.00 40.00
GD24 Fernando Pisani 6.00 15.00
GD25 Ryan Smyth 10.00 25.00
GD26 Rod Brind'Amour 10.00 25.00
GD27 Shawn Horcoff 6.00 15.00
GD28 Jose Theodore 12.00 30.00
GD29 Patrick Marleau 10.00 25.00
GD30 Daniel Briere 10.00 25.00
GD31 Chris Drury 10.00 25.00
GD32 Cam Ward 10.00 25.00
GD33 Martin Havlat 6.00 15.00
GD34 Michael Ryder 10.00 25.00
GD35 Martin Brodeur 20.00 50.00
GD36 R.J. Umberger 8.00 20.00
GD37 Jarome Iginla 12.00 30.00
GD38 Marian Gaborik 12.00 30.00
GD39 Marek Svatos 6.00 15.00
GD40 Joe Sakic 15.00 40.00
GD41 Cristobal Huet 15.00 40.00
GD42 Patrice Bergeron 10.00 25.00

2006-07 Upper Deck Game Jerseys

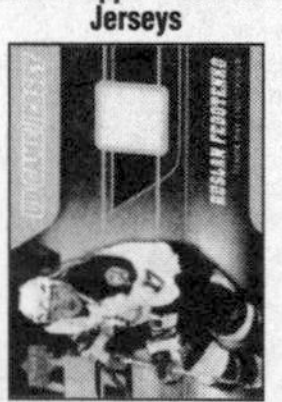

COMMON CARD 3.00 8.00
STATED ODDS 1:12
JAA Arron Asham 3.00 8.00
JAF Alexander Frolov 4.00 10.00
JAH Ales Hemsky 4.00 10.00
JAK Alex Kovalev 3.00 8.00
JAL Jason Allison 3.00 8.00
JAM Andrej Meszaros 3.00 8.00
JAO Alexander Ovechkin SP 25.00 50.00
JAT Alex Tanguay 6.00 15.00
JAY Alexei Yashin 3.00 8.00
JBA Barret Jackman 3.00 8.00
JBB Brad Boyes 3.00 8.00
JBE Patrice Bergeron 6.00 15.00
JBG Bill Guerin 4.00 10.00
JBI Martin Biron 5.00 12.00
JBL Rob Blake 5.00 12.00
JBM Mark Bell 3.00 8.00
JBR Brian Rolston 3.00 8.00
JBS Brad Stuart 3.00 8.00
JBT Barry Tallackson 3.00 8.00
JBU Peter Budaj 5.00 12.00
JCC Chris Chelios 5.00 12.00
JCD Chris Drury 4.00 10.00
JCJ Curtis Joseph 6.00 15.00
JCO Chris Osgood 5.00 12.00
JCP Corey Perry 5.00 12.00
JCS Curtis Sanford 5.00 12.00
JDA Daniel Alfredsson 5.00 12.00
JDE Pavol Demitra 3.00 8.00
JDK Duncan Keith 3.00 8.00
JDP Daniel Paille 3.00 8.00
JDW Doug Weight 4.00 10.00
JEB Ed Belfour 6.00 15.00
JEJ Ed Jovanovski 3.00 8.00
JEL Eric Lindros 6.00 15.00
JGA Simon Gagne 5.00 12.00
JGL Georges Laraque 3.00 8.00
JHA Martin Havlat 5.00 12.00
JHE Milan Hejduk 5.00 12.00
JHO Marcel Hossa 3.00 8.00
JIK Ilya Kovalchuk SP 20.00 50.00
JJA Jason Arnott 3.00 8.00
JJB Jay Bouwmeester 4.00 10.00
JJC Jonathan Cheechoo 5.00 12.00
JJF Jeff Friesen 3.00 8.00
JJG Jean-Sebastien Giguere 5.00 12.00
JJI Jarome Iginla 8.00 20.00
JJJ Jaromir Jagr 8.00 20.00
JJL Joffrey Lupul 3.00 8.00
JJN Joe Nieuwendyk 5.00 12.00
JJO Jordan Leopold 3.00 8.00
JJS Jason Spezza 6.00 15.00
JJT Joe Thornton 8.00 20.00
JJW Jason Williams 3.00 8.00
JKD Kris Draper 3.00 8.00
JKP Keith Primeau 3.00 8.00
JKS Andrei Kostitsyn 3.00 8.00
JKT Keith Tkachuk 5.00 12.00
JLA Andrew Ladd 3.00 8.00
JLE Jere Lehtinen 4.00 10.00
JLU Jamie Lundmark 3.00 8.00
JLX Mario Lemieux SP 20.00 50.00
JMB Martin Brodeur 10.00 25.00
JMC Mike Comrie 3.00 8.00
JME Martin Erat 3.00 8.00
JMG Marian Gaborik 8.00 20.00
JMH Marian Hossa 6.00 15.00
JMI Mike Komisarek 3.00 8.00
JMK Miikka Kiprusoff 8.00 20.00
JML Manny Legace 3.00 8.00
JMM Mike Modano 8.00 20.00
JMN Markus Naslund 6.00 15.00
JMO Brendan Morrison 3.00 8.00
JMP Michael Peca 4.00 10.00
JMR Mark Recchi 4.00 10.00
JMS Marc Savard 4.00 10.00
JNK Nikolai Khabibulin 5.00 12.00
JPB Peter Bondra 5.00 12.00
JPD Pavel Datsyuk 5.00 12.00
JPF Peter Forsberg 8.00 20.00
JPP Petr Prucha 3.00 8.00
JRB Rod Brind'Amour 5.00 12.00
JRF Ruslan Fedotenko 3.00 8.00
JRH Ryan Hollweg 3.00 8.00
JRI Brad Richards 6.00 15.00
JRM Ryan Miller 6.00 15.00
JRU R.J. Umberger 3.00 8.00
JSC Sidney Crosby SP 200.00 350.00
JSG Scott Gomez 4.00 10.00
JSH Brendan Shanahan 6.00 15.00
JSM Matt Stajan 3.00 8.00
JSN Scott Niedermayer 4.00 10.00
JSS Sergei Samsonov 5.00 12.00
JST Steve Sullivan 3.00 8.00
JSU Scottie Upshall 3.00 8.00
JSW Stephen Weiss 3.00 8.00
JTC Ty Conklin 5.00 12.00
JTL Trevor Linden 6.00 15.00
JTP Tom Poti 3.00 8.00
JVL Vincent Lecavalier SP 15.00 30.00
JWR Wade Redden 3.00 8.00
J2AP Alexander Perezhogin 4.00 10.00
J2AR Andrew Raycroft 6.00 15.00
J2AS Alexander Steen 4.00 10.00
J2BB Brandon Bochenski 3.00 8.00
J2BC Bobby Clarke 5.00 12.00
J2BG Brian Gionta 4.00 10.00
J2BM Brenden Morrow 4.00 10.00
J2BP Brad Park 4.00 10.00
J2BR Bryan McCabe 3.00 8.00
J2BW Brendan Witt 3.00 8.00
J2CA Mike Cammalleri 4.00 10.00
J2CH Cristobal Huet 5.00 12.00
J2CK Chuck Kobasew 3.00 8.00
J2CN Cam Neely 6.00 15.00
J2CP Chris Pronger 4.00 10.00
J2CW Cam Ward 4.00 10.00
J2DB Daniel Briere 4.00 10.00
J2DC Dan Cloutier 3.00 8.00
J2DH Dominik Hasek 8.00 20.00
J2DP Dion Phaneuf 6.00 15.00
J2DR Dwayne Roloson 5.00 12.00
J2DS Daniel Sedin 4.00 10.00
J2DT Darcy Tucker 3.00 8.00
J2DU Ron Duguay 4.00 10.00
J2DW Dave Williams 6.00 15.00
J2EC Erik Cole 3.00 8.00
J2ES Eric Staal 6.00 15.00
J2GM Glen Murray 4.00 10.00
J2GR Gary Roberts 4.00 10.00
J2HE Dany Heatley 5.00 12.00
J2HL Henrik Lundqvist 5.00 12.00
J2HS Henrik Sedin 4.00 10.00
J2HZ Henrik Zetterberg 6.00 15.00
J2JB Jason Bacashihua 4.00 10.00
J2JC Jeff Carter 6.00 15.00
J2JJ Jussi Jokinen 4.00 10.00
J2JK Jakub Klepis 3.00 8.00
J2JP Joni Pitkanen 3.00 8.00
J2JR Jeremy Roenick 5.00 12.00
J2JS Joe Sakic 10.00 25.00
J2JT Jose Theodore 6.00 15.00
J2JW Justin Williams 3.00 8.00
J2KB Kevin Bieksa 3.00 8.00
J2KC Kyle Calder 3.00 8.00
J2KL Kari Lehtonen 6.00 15.00
J2KM Kirk Muller 3.00 8.00
J2KO Saku Koivu 6.00 15.00
J2LA Lanny McDonald 5.00 12.00
J2LM Larry Murphy 3.00 8.00
J2LX Mario Lemieux 15.00 40.00
J2MA Martin St. Louis 5.00 12.00
J2MC Mike Commodore 3.00 8.00
J2MF Manny Fernandez 5.00 12.00
J2MG Mike Grier 3.00 8.00
J2MH Michal Handzus 3.00 8.00
J2MJ Milan Jurcina 3.00 8.00
J2MP Mark Parrish 3.00 8.00
J2MR Michael Ryder 5.00 12.00
J2MS Marek Svatos 3.00 8.00
J2MT Marty Turco 5.00 12.00
J2MY Mike York 3.00 8.00
J2NH Nathan Horton 3.00 8.00
J2NL Nicklas Lidstrom 5.00 12.00
J2OJ Olli Jokinen 3.00 8.00
J2OK Olaf Kolzig 5.00 12.00
J2PE Patrik Elias/15 8.00 20.00
J2PK Paul Kariya 5.00 12.00
J2PM Patrick Marleau 5.00 12.00
J2PR Bob Probert 5.00 12.00
J2PS Peter Stastny 4.00 10.00
J2RB Ray Bourque 6.00 15.00
J2RD Rick DiPietro 5.00 12.00
J2RE Ron Ellis 3.00 8.00
J2RI Mike Ribeiro 3.00 8.00
J2RK Ryan Kesler 3.00 8.00
J2RL Roberto Luongo 15.00
J2RN Rick Nash/15 8.00 20.00
J2RO Patrick Roy 15.00 40.00
J2RS Ryan Smyth 5.00 12.00
J2SA Miroslav Satan 4.00 10.00
J2SB Steve Bernier 4.00 10.00
J2SC Stanislav Chistov 3.00 8.00
J2SD Shane Doan 4.00 10.00
J2SF Sergei Federov 5.00 12.00
J2SH Jody Shelley 4.00 10.00
J2SK Steve Konowalchuk 3.00 8.00
J2SO Sandis Ozolinsh 3.00 8.00
J2SS Sergei Samsonov 3.00 8.00
J2ST Jarret Stoll 3.00 8.00
J2SU Mats Sundin 5.00 12.00
J2SZ Sergei Zubov 3.00 8.00
J2TF Tomas Fleischmann 3.00 8.00
J2TH Tomas Holmstrom 4.00 10.00
J2TS Teemu Selanne 6.00 15.00
J2TT Tim Thomas 5.00 12.00
J2TV Tomas Vokoun 12.00
J2WG Wayne Gretzky SP 75.00 175.00
J2ZC Zdeno Chara 4.00 10.00

2006-07 Upper Deck Game Patches

STATED PRINT RUN 15 SER. #'d SETS
NOT PRICED DUE TO SCARCITY
PAA Arron Asham
PAH Ales Hemsky
PAK Alex Kovalev
PAL Jason Allison
PAM Andrej Meszaros
PAO Alexander Ovechkin
PAT Alex Tanguay
PAY Alexei Yashin
PBA Barret Jackman
PBB Brad Boyes
PBE Patrice Bergeron
PBG Bill Guerin
PBI Martin Biron
PBL Rob Blake
PBM Mark Bell
PBR Brian Rolston
PBS Brad Stuart
PBT Barry Tallackson
PBU Peter Budaj
PCC Chris Chelios
PCD Chris Drury
PCJ Curtis Joseph
PCO Chris Osgood
PCP Corey Perry
PCS Curtis Sanford
PDA Daniel Alfredsson
PDE Pavol Demitra
PDK Duncan Keith
PDP Daniel Paille
PDW Doug Weight
PEB Ed Belfour
PEJ Ed Jovanovski
PEL Eric Lindros
PGA Simon Gagne
PGL Georges Laraque
PHA Martin Havlat
PHE Milan Hejduk
PHO Marcel Hossa
PIK Ilya Kovalchuk
PJA Jason Arnott
PJB Jay Bouwmeester
PJC Jonathan Cheechoo
PJF Jeff Friesen
PJG Jean-Sebastien Giguere
PJI Jarome Iginla
PJJ Jaromir Jagr
PJL Joffrey Lupul
PJN Joe Nieuwendyk
PJO Jordan Leopold
PJS Jason Spezza
PJT Joe Thornton
PJW Jason Williams
PKD Kris Draper
PKP Keith Primeau
PKS Andrei Kostitsyn
PKT Keith Tkachuk
PLA Andrew Ladd
PLE Jere Lehtinen
PLU Jamie Lundmark
PLX Mario Lemieux
PMB Martin Brodeur
PMC Mike Comrie
PME Martin Erat
PMG Marian Gaborik
PMH Marian Hossa
PMI Mike Komisarek
PMK Miikka Kiprusoff
PML Manny Legace
PMM Mike Modano
PMN Markus Naslund
PMO Brendan Morrison
PMP Michael Peca
PMR Mark Recchi
PMS Marc Savard
PNK Nikolai Khabibulin
PPB Peter Bondra
PPD Pavel Datsyuk
PPF Peter Forsberg
PPP Petr Prucha
PRB Rod Brind'Amour
PRF Ruslan Fedotenko
PRH Ryan Hollweg
PRI Brad Richards
PRM Ryan Miller
PRU R.J. Umberger
PSC Sidney Crosby
PSG Scott Gomez
PSH Brendan Shanahan
PSN Scott Niedermayer
PSS Sergei Samsonov
PST Matt Stajan
PSU Steve Sullivan
PSW Stephen Weiss
PTC Ty Conklin
PTL Trevor Linden
PTP Tom Poti
PUP Scottie Upshall
PVL Vincent Lecavalier
PWR Wade Redden

2006-07 Upper Deck Generations Duals

PRINT RUN 100 SER. #'d SETS
G2BL Martin Brodeur 30.00 60.00
Roberto Luongo
G2BP Rob Blake 12.00 30.00
Dion Phaneuf
G2BW Ed Belfour 10.00 25.00
Cam Ward
G2DH Shane Doan 10.00 25.00
Nathan Horton
G2EG Patrik Elias 10.00 25.00
Marian Gaborik
G2FD Pavel Datsyuk 12.00 30.00
Sergei Fedorov
G2FK Alexander Frolov 8.00 20.00
Alex Kovalev
G2FS Peter Forsberg 15.00 40.00
Alexander Steen
G2GB Bill Guerin 8.00 20.00
Dustin Brown
G2GC Wayne Gretzky 100.00 200.00
Sidney Crosby
G2HH Marian Hossa 8.00 20.00
Ales Hemsky
G2HS Milan Hejduk 8.00 20.00
Marek Svatos
G2IL Jarome Iginla 12.00 30.00
Joffrey Lupul
G2JK Olli Jokinen 8.00 20.00
Mikko Koivu
G2JO Jaromir Jagr 30.00 60.00
Alexander Ovechkin
G2KD Saku Koivu 12.00 30.00
Pavel Datsyuk
G2KL Miikka Kiprusoff 15.00 40.00
Kari Lehtonen
G2LP Nicklas Lidstrom 12.00 30.00
Joni Pitkanen
G2NB Scott Niedermayer 8.00 20.00
Jay Bouwmeester
G2NZ Markus Naslund 10.00 25.00
Henrik Zetterberg
G2PG Keith Primeau 10.00 25.00
Ryan Getzlaf
G2RM Wade Redden 8.00 20.00
Andrej Meszaros
G2SN Brendan Shanahan 10.00 25.00
Rick Nash
G2SS Joe Sakic 20.00 50.00
Jason Spezza
G2TS Joe Thornton 15.00 40.00
Eric Staal
G2VH Tomas Vokoun 12.00 30.00
Dominik Hasek
G2PJD Joe Sakic 20.00 50.00
Dany Heatley
G2PSH Miroslav Satan 10.00 25.00
Martin Havlat

2006-07 Upper Deck Generations Triples

PRINT RUN 25 SER. #'d SETS
NOT PRICED DUE TO SCARCITY
G3BPB Rob Blake
Dion Phaneuf
Ray Bourque
G3BTW Ed Belfour
Marty Turco
Cam Ward
G3GCL Wayne Gretzky
Sidney Crosby
Mario Lemieux
G3HSS Milan Hejduk
Miroslav Satan
Marek Svatos
G3IML Jarome Iginla
Brenden Morrow
Joffrey Lupul
G3KJK Saku Koivu
Olli Jokinen
Mikko Koivu
G3KTL Miikka Kiprusoff
Kari Lehtonen
Hannu Toivonen
G3LTS Vincent Lecavalier
Joe Thornton
Eric Staal
G3NZS Markus Naslund
Henrik Zetterberg
Alexander Steen
G3SKO Teemu Selanne
Ilya Kovalchuk
Alexander Ovechkin
G3SSC Joe Sakic
Jason Spezza
Jeff Carter

2006-07 Upper Deck Generations Patches Dual

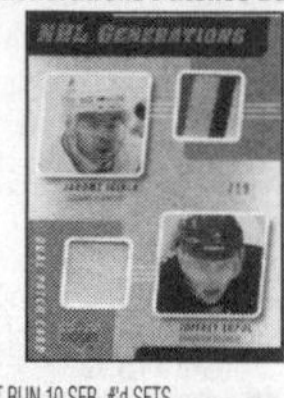

PRINT RUN 10 SER. #'d SETS
NOT PRICED DUE TO SCARCITY
G2PBL Martin Brodeur
Roberto Luongo
G2PBP Rob Blake
Dion Phaneuf
G2PBW Ed Belfour
Cam Ward
G2PDH Shane Doan
Nathan Horton
G2PEG Patrik Elias
Marian Gaborik
G2PFD Pavel Datsyuk
Sergei Fedorov
G2PFS Peter Forsberg
Alexander Steen
G2PGB Bill Guerin
Dustin Brown
G2PGC Sidney Crosby
Wayne Gretzky
G2PHH Marian Hossa
Ales Hemsky
G2PHS Milan Hejduk
Marek Svatos
G2PIL Jarome Iginla
Joffrey Lupul
G2PJD Joe Sakic
Dany Heatley
G2PJK Olli Jokinen
Mikko Koivu
G2PJO Jaromir Jagr
Alexander Ovechkin
G2PKD Saku Koivu
Pavel Datsyuk
G2PKL Miikka Kiprusoff
Kari Lehtonen
G2PLP Nicklas Lidstrom
Joni Pitkanen
G2PNB Scott Niedermayer
Jay Bouwmeester
G2PNZ Markus Naslund
Henrik Zetterberg
G2PPG Keith Primeau
Ryan Getzlaf
G2PRM Wade Redden
Andrej Meszaros
G2PSH Miroslav Satan
Martin Havlat
G2PSN Brendan Shanahan
Rick Nash
G2PSS Joe Sakic
Jason Spezza
G2PTS Joe Thornton
Eric Staal
G2PVH Tomas Vokoun
Dominik Hasek

2006-07 Upper Deck Generations Patches Triple

PRINT RUN 5 SER. #'d SETS
NOT PRICED DUE TO SCARCITY
G3PBPB Rob Blake
Dion Phaneuf
Ray Bourque
G3PBTW Ed Belfour
Marty Turco
Cam Ward
G3PGCL Mario Lemieux
Sidney Crosby
Wayne Gretzky
G3PHSS Milan Hejduk
Miroslav Satan
Marek Svatos
G3PIML Jarome Iginla
Brenden Morrow
Joffrey Lupul
G3PKJK Saku Koivu
Olli Jokinen
Mikko Koivu
G3PKTL Miikka Kiprusoff
Kari Lehtonen
Hannu Toivonen
G3PLTS Vincent Lecavalier
Joe Thornton
Eric Staal
G3PNZS Markus Naslund
Henrik Zetterberg
Alexander Steen
G3PSKO Teemu Selanne
Ilya Kovalchuk
Alexander Ovechkin
G3PSSC Joe Sakic
Jason Spezza
Jeff Carter

2006-07 Upper Deck Goal Rush

COMPLETE SET (14) 10.00 25.00
ODDS 1:24 SER. 2 PACKS
GR1 Jonathan Cheechoo 1.00 2.50
GR2 Jaromir Jagr 1.50 4.00
GR3 Dany Heatley 1.00 2.50
GR4 Ilya Kovalchuk 1.25 3.00
GR5 Rick Nash 1.00 2.50
GR6 Marian Gaborik 1.50 4.00

GR7 Markus Naslund 1.00 2.50
GR8 Jarome Iginla 1.50 4.00
GR9 Alexander Ovechkin 1.25 3.00
GR10 Simon Gagne 1.00 2.50
GR11 Eric Staal .75 2.00
GR12 Teemu Selanne 1.00 2.50
GR13 Brendan Shanahan 1.00 2.50
GR14 Sidney Crosby 2.50 6.00

2006-07 Upper Deck Hometown Heroes

COMPLETE SET (28) 20.00 50.00
STATED ODDS 1:12
HH29 Teemu Selanne 1.00 2.50
HH30 Patrice Bergeron .75 2.00
HH31 Ryan Miller 1.00 2.50
HH32 Miikka Kiprusoff 1.00 2.50
HH33 Eric Staal .75 2.00
HH34 Henrik Zetterberg 1.00 2.50
HH35 Michael Ryder .75 2.00
HH36 Henrik Lundqvist 1.50 4.00
HH37 Jason Spezza 1.00 2.50
HH38 Simon Gagne 1.00 2.50
HH39 Sidney Crosby 4.00 10.00
HH40 Jonathan Cheechoo 1.00 2.50
HH41 Darcy Tucker .60 1.50
HH42 Alexander Ovechkin 4.00 10.00
HH43 Milan Hejduk .75 2.00
HH44 Patrick Marleau .75 2.00
HH45 Cristobal Huet 1.00 2.50
HH46 Cam Ward 1.50 4.00
HH47 Vincent Lecavalier 1.00 2.50
HH48 Kari Lehtonen 1.00 2.50
HH49 Nicklas Lidstrom 1.00 2.50
HH50 Roberto Luongo 2.00 5.00
HH51 Rob Blake .75 2.00
HH52 Marian Gaborik 1.50 4.00
HH53 Alexander Steen .75 2.00
HH54 Doug Weight .60 1.50
HH55 Marc-Andre Fleury 1.00 2.50
HH56 Dion Phaneuf 1.25 3.00

2006-07 Upper Deck Masterpieces

STATED PRINT RUN 1 SER.#'d SET
NOT PRICED DUE TO SCARCITY

2006-07 Upper Deck Oversized Wal-Mart Exclusives

251 Chris Pronger 1.50 4.00
254 Jean-Sebastien Giguere 2.00 5.00
258 Ilya Kovalchuk 2.50 6.00
265 Patrice Bergeron 1.50 4.00
279 Alex Tanguay 1.50 4.00
282 Miikka Kiprusoff 2.00 5.00
286 Rod Brind'Amour 1.50 4.00
292 Martin Havlat 1.50 4.00
299 Marek Svatos 1.25 3.00
309 Gilbert Brule 1.25 3.00
313 Mike Modano 2.00 5.00
318 Eric Lindros 2.00 5.00
319 Dominik Hasek 2.50 6.00
323 Henrik Zetterberg 2.00 5.00
324 Nicklas Lidstrom 2.00 5.00
325 Ryan Smyth
333 Ed Belfour 5.00 12.00
337 Todd Bertuzzi 1.50 4.00
339 Rob Blake 1.50 4.00
345 Manny Fernandez
352 Michael Ryder
359 Paul Kariya
365 Patrik Elias 1.25 3.00
377 Henrik Lundqvist 3.00 8.00
379 Wayne Gretzky 4.00 10.00
383 Brendan Shanahan 2.00 5.00
384 Dany Heatley 2.00 5.00
391 Simon Gagne 2.00 5.00
392 Jeff Carter 2.00 5.00
401 Jeremy Roenick 2.00 5.00
403 Owen Nolan 1.50 4.00
404 Marc-Andre Fleury 2.00 5.00
409 Mark Recchi 1.50 4.00
410 Patrick Marleau 1.50 4.00
415 Evgeni Nabokov 1.50 4.00
417 Doug Weight 1.25 3.00
422 Vincent Lecavalier 2.00 5.00
426 Brad Richards 2.00 5.00
428 Andrew Raycroft 1.50 4.00
430 Michael Peca 1.25 3.00
436 Roberto Luongo 4.00 10.00
442 Alexander Ovechkin 4.00 10.00

2006-07 Upper Deck Rookie Game Dated Moments

ODDS 1:288
RGD1 Ryan Shannon 5.00 12.00
RGD2 Phil Kessel 12.00 30.00
RGD3 Mark Stuart 5.00 12.00
RGD4 Yan Stastny 5.00 12.00
RGD5 Paul Stastny 15.00 40.00
RGD6 Loui Eriksson 5.00 12.00
RGD7 Tomas Kopecky 10.00 25.00

Card	Low	High
RGD8 Patrick Thoresen	6.00	15.00
RGD9 Ladislav Smid	6.00	15.00
RGD10 Marc-Antoine Pouliot	6.00	15.00
RGD11 Patrick O'Sullivan	10.00	25.00
RGD12 Anze Kopitar	15.00	40.00
RGD13 Guillaume Latendresse	12.00	30.00
RGD14 Shea Weber	5.00	12.00
RGD15 Mikko Lehtonen	5.00	12.00
RGD16 Travis Zajac	6.00	15.00
RGD17 Nigel Dawes	5.00	12.00
RGD18 Alexei Kaigorodov	5.00	12.00
RGD19 Ryan Potulny	5.00	12.00
RGD20 Joel Perrault	5.00	12.00
RGD21 Evgeni Malkin	25.00	60.00
RGD22 Jordan Staal	15.00	40.00
RGD23 Kristopher Letang	5.00	12.00
RGD24 Noah Welch	5.00	12.00
RGD25 Marc-Edouard Vlasic	5.00	12.00
RGD26 Matt Carle	6.00	15.00
RGD27 Ian White	5.00	12.00
RGD28 Ben Ondrus	5.00	12.00
RGD29 Luc Bourdon	6.00	15.00
RGD30 Eric Fehr	5.00	12.00

2006-07 Upper Deck Rookie Headliners

Card	Low	High
COMPLETE SET (30)	100.00	175.00
ONE PER SER. 2 FAT PACK		
RH1 Patrick O'Sullivan	2.00	5.00
RH2 Loui Eriksson	2.50	6.00
RH3 Enver Lisin	2.50	6.00
RH4 Luc Bourdon	2.00	5.00
RH5 Noah Welch	2.50	6.00
RH6 Travis Zajac	2.50	6.00
RH7 Ladislav Smid	2.50	6.00
RH8 Ryan Potulny	2.00	5.00
RH9 Marc-Antoine Pouliot	2.00	5.00
RH10 Dave Bolland	5.00	12.00
RH11 Nigel Dawes	2.50	6.00
RH12 Marc-Edouard Vlasic	2.50	6.00
RH13 Patrick Thoresen	1.50	4.00
RH14 Matt Lashoff	2.50	6.00
RH15 Ian White	2.50	6.00
RH16 Alexei Mikhnov	2.50	6.00
RH17 Tomas Kopecky	2.00	5.00
RH18 Kristopher Letang	2.50	6.00
RH19 Michael Blunden	2.50	6.00
RH20 Brandon Prust	2.50	6.00
RH21 Evgeni Malkin SP	15.00	40.00
RH22 Phil Kessel SP	20.00	50.00
RH23 Jordan Staal SP	10.00	25.00
RH24 Guillaume Latendresse SP	12.00	30.00
RH25 Anze Kopitar SP	15.00	40.00
RH26 Matt Carle SP	8.00	20.00
RH27 Paul Stastny SP	12.00	30.00
RH28 Alexander Radulov SP	12.00	30.00
RH29 Dustin Boyd SP	10.00	25.00
RH30 Drew Stafford SP	4.00	10.00

2006-07 Upper Deck Rookie Materials

Card	Low	High
STATED ODDS 1:24		
RMBB Brendan Bell	4.00	10.00
RMBO Ben Ondrus	4.00	10.00
RMBT Billy Thompson	4.00	10.00
RMCG Carsen Germyn	4.00	10.00
RMDB Dustin Byfuglien	8.00	20.00
RMDK D.J. King	2.00	5.00
RMEF Eric Fehr	5.00	12.00
RMEM Evgeni Malkin	15.00	40.00
RMFN Filip Novak	4.00	10.00
RMGL Guillaume Latendresse	8.00	20.00
RMIW Ian White	4.00	10.00
RMJI Jarkko Immonen	4.00	10.00
RMJS Jordan Staal	8.00	20.00
RMJW Jeremy Williams	4.00	10.00
RMKL Kristopher Letang	6.00	15.00
RMKO Anze Kopitar	6.00	15.00
RMKP Konstantin Pushkaryov	4.00	10.00
RMKY Keith Yandle	4.00	10.00
RMLB Luc Bourdon	5.00	12.00
RMLE Loui Eriksson	4.00	10.00
RMLS Ladislav Smid	4.00	10.00
RMMC Matt Carle	4.00	10.00
RMMP MarcAntoine Pouliot	4.00	10.00
RMMS Mark Stuart	4.00	10.00
RMMV MarcEdouard Vlasic	4.00	10.00
RMNB Niklas Backstrom	3.00	8.00
RMND Nigel Dawes	4.00	10.00
RMNO Fredrik Norrena	4.00	10.00
RMNW Noah Welch	4.00	10.00
RMPK Phil Kessel	8.00	20.00
RMPO Patrick O'Sullivan	3.00	8.00
RMPS Paul Stastny	8.00	20.00
RMPT Patrick Thoresen	4.00	10.00
RMRO Roman Polak	2.00	5.00
RMRP Ryan Potulny	5.00	12.00
RMRS Ryan Shannon	4.00	10.00
RMSO Shane O'Brien	4.00	10.00
RMSW Shea Weber	4.00	10.00
RMTK Tomas Kopecky	4.00	10.00
RMTZ Travis Zajac	5.00	12.00
RMYS Yan Stastny	4.00	10.00

2006-07 Upper Deck Rookie Materials Patches

PRINT RUN 15 #'d SETS
NOT PRICED DUE TO SCARCITY

RMBB Brendan Bell
RMBO Ben Ondrus
RMBT Billy Thompson
RMCG Carsen Germyn
RMDB Dustin Byfuglien
RMDK D.J. King
RMEF Eric Fehr
RMEM Evgeni Malkin
RMFN Filip Novak
RMGL Guillaume Latendresse
RMIW Ian White
RMJI Jarkko Immonen
RMJS Jordan Staal
RMJW Jeremy Williams
RMKL Kristopher Letang
RMKO Anze Kopitar
RMKP Konstantin Pushkaryov
RMKY Keith Yandle
RMLB Luc Bourdon
RMLE Loui Eriksson
RMLS Ladislav Smid
RMMC Matt Carle
RMMP MarcAntoine Pouliot
RMMS Mark Stuart
RMMV MarcEdouard Vlasic
RMNB Niklas Backstrom
RMND Nigel Dawes
RMNO Fredrik Norrena
RMNW Noah Welch
RMPK Phil Kessel
RMPO Patrick O'Sullivan
RMPS Paul Stastny
RMPT Patrick Thoresen
RMRO Roman Polak
RMRP Ryan Potulny
RMRS Ryan Shannon
RMSO Shane O'Brien
RMSW Shea Weber
RMTK Tomas Kopecky
RMTZ Travis Zajac
RMYS Yan Stastny

2006-07 Upper Deck Shootout Artists

Card	Low	High
COMPLETE SET (14)	10.00	25.00
STATED ODDS 1:12		
SA1 Jussi Jokinen	.60	1.50
SA2 Miroslav Satan	.60	1.50
SA3 Brad Richards	.75	2.00
SA4 Alexander Ovechkin	2.00	5.00
SA5 Paul Kariya	1.00	2.50
SA6 Ales Hemsky	.75	2.00
SA7 Mikko Koivu	.75	2.00
SA8 Alexander Frolov	.60	1.50
SA9 Jason Williams	.60	1.50
SA10 Slava Kozlov	.60	1.50
SA11 Brian Gionta	.60	1.50
SA12 Vincent Lecavalier	1.00	2.50
SA13 Jaroslav Balastik	.30	.75
SA14 Sergei Zubov	.60	1.50

2006-07 Upper Deck Signatures

Card	Low	High
PRINT RUN 25 COPIES EXCEPT FOR SPs		
RANDOM INSERTS IN SER. 2 PACKS		
SAO Alexander Ovechkin SP	400.00	600.00
SAP Alexander Perezhogin	10.00	25.00
SAR Andrew Raycroft	15.00	40.00
SAT Alex Tanguay	20.00	50.00
SBB Brad Boyes	10.00	25.00
SBC Braydon Coburn	10.00	25.00
SBL Brett Lebda	10.00	25.00
SBO Jay Bouwmeester		
SCP Corey Perry SP		
SCS Cory Stillman	10.00	25.00
SCT Chris Thorburn	10.00	25.00
SDC Dan Cloutier	10.00	25.00
SDH Dany Heatley SP	60.00	100.00
SDL David Legwand SP		
SDP Daniel Paille	10.00	25.00
SDW Doug Weight SP		
SEC Erik Cole	10.00	25.00
SEL Enver Lisin	10.00	25.00
SEM Evgeni Malkin	60.00	150.00
SEN Eric Nystrom	10.00	25.00
SES Eric Staal SP		
SFP Fernando Pisani	10.00	25.00
SGB Gilbert Brule	20.00	40.00
SGH Gordie Howe SP	75.00	125.00
SGL Guillaume Latendresse	20.00	40.00
SGM Glen Murray	15.00	40.00
SHL Henrik Lundqvist	30.00	80.00
SHZ Henrik Zetterberg	40.00	80.00
SJI Jarome Iginla SP		
SJR Jeremy Roenick	25.00	50.00
SJS Jordan Staal	60.00	125.00
SJT Jeff Tambellini SP	12.00	30.00
SJW Justin Williams	10.00	25.00
SMB Martin Brodeur SP	125.00	200.00
SMG Marian Gaborik SP	75.00	125.00
SMM Mike Modano SP	40.00	80.00
SMN Markus Naslund	20.00	50.00
SMP Michael Peca	10.00	25.00
SMR Mike Ribeiro	10.00	25.00
SMS Martin St. Louis	15.00	40.00
SNK Nikolai Khabibulin	12.00	30.00
SPB Patrice Bergeron	20.00	50.00
SPH Dion Phaneuf	15.00	40.00
SPK Phil Kessel	25.00	60.00
SRH Ryan Hollweg	10.00	25.00
SRK Ryan Kesler	10.00	25.00
SRL Roberto Luongo	50.00	125.00
SSB Steve Bernier	12.00	30.00
SSC Sidney Crosby	200.00	300.00
SSG Simon Gagne	20.00	50.00
SSS Sergei Samsonov	10.00	25.00
SST Matt Stajan	15.00	40.00
STA Tyler Arnason	10.00	25.00
STV Thomas Vanek	25.00	60.00
SVL Vincent Lecavalier SP	200.00	300.00
SWG Wayne Gretzky SP		
SYD Yann Danis	10.00	25.00
SZP Zach Parise	25.00	60.00

2006-07 Upper Deck Signature Sensations

Card	Low	High
STATED ODDS 1:288		
SSAA Aaron Asham	3.00	8.00
SSAF Alexander Frolov	8.00	20.00
SSAH Adam Hall	3.00	8.00
SSAR Andrew Raycroft	8.00	20.00
SSAS Alexander Steen	8.00	20.00
SSAT Alex Tanguay	12.00	30.00
SSBB Brad Boyes	6.00	15.00
SSBL Brian Leetch	25.00	50.00
SSBO Jay Bouwmeester	10.00	25.00
SSBR Brian Rafalski	3.00	8.00
SSBW Brad Winchester		
SSCH Chris Higgins	12.00	30.00
SSCK Chris Kunitz	8.00	20.00
SSCP Chris Phillips	3.00	8.00
SSDW Doug Weight	6.00	15.00
SSEJ Ed Jovanovski	5.00	12.00
SSEN Evgeni Nabokov	12.00	30.00
SSFL Marc-Andre Fleury	25.00	60.00
SSFS Fredrik Sjostrom	3.00	8.00
SSGM Glen Murray	6.00	15.00
SSHA Michal Handzus		
SSHE Milan Hejduk		
SSHT Hannu Toivonen	10.00	25.00
SSJB Jason Blake	3.00	8.00
SSJP Joni Pitkanen	12.00	30.00
SSJR Jeremy Roenick	12.00	30.00
SSJT Jose Theodore	8.00	20.00
SSKB Keith Ballard	3.00	8.00
SSKL Kari Lehtonen	12.00	30.00
SSKP Keith Primeau	3.00	8.00
SSKT Kimmo Timonen		
SSMC Mike Comrie	3.00	8.00
SSMG Marian Gaborik	20.00	50.00
SSMH Martin Havlat	10.00	25.00
SSMK Miikka Kiprusoff	25.00	50.00
SSML Mario Lemieux	100.00	150.00
SSMP Mark Parrish	3.00	8.00
SSMS Miroslav Satan	5.00	12.00
SSNK Nikolai Khabibulin	15.00	40.00
SSPB Pierre-Marc Bouchard	6.00	15.00
SSPM Patrick Marleau		
SSPR Chris Pronger	12.00	30.00
SSRB Rene Bourque	3.00	8.00
SSRF Ruslan Fedotenko	3.00	8.00
SSRN Rick Nash	20.00	50.00
SSRS Ryan Smyth	12.00	30.00
SSRU R.J. Umberger	6.00	12.00
SSRW Ryan Whitney	8.00	20.00
SSSC Sidney Crosby	150.00	250.00
SSSD Shane Doan	6.00	12.00
SSSG Scott Gomez	8.00	20.00
SSSH Shawn Horcoff		
SSSS Steve Sullivan	3.00	8.00
SSTA Tyler Arnason	3.00	8.00
SSTL Trevor Linden	20.00	50.00
SSVT Vesa Toskala	12.00	30.00
SSWG Wayne Gretzky SP		
SSWR Wade Redden	3.00	8.00
SSWW Wojtek Wolski	6.00	15.00

2006-07 Upper Deck Statistical Leaders

Card	Low	High
COMPLETE SET (7)	10.00	25.00
STATED ODDS 1:24		
SL1 Joe Thornton	2.00	5.00
SL2 Jonathan Cheechoo	.75	2.00
SL3 Alexander Ovechkin	4.00	10.00
SL4 Wade Redden	.75	2.00
SL5 Martin Brodeur	3.00	8.00
SL6 Miikka Kiprusoff	2.00	5.00
SL7 Sean Avery	.40	1.00

2006-07 Upper Deck Zero Men

Card	Low	High
COMPLETE SET (7)	8.00	20.00
ODDS 1:24 SER. 2 PACKS		
ZM1 Martin Brodeur	3.00	8.00
ZM2 Dominik Hasek	2.00	5.00
ZM3 Roberto Luongo	1.25	3.00
ZM4 Miikka Kiprusoff	1.25	3.00
ZM5 Marty Turco	1.00	2.50
ZM6 Cam Ward	1.00	2.50
ZM7 Ed Belfour	1.00	2.50

2007-08 Upper Deck

This set, which was issued over two series, was released in November, 2007 and February, 2008. The set was issued into the hobby in eight-card packs, with a $2.99 SRP, which came 24 packs to a box and 12 boxes to a case. As in previous years, the primary subset is a Young Guns (Rookie Cards) subsets which are found in packs at a stated rate of one in four. The Young Guns subsets comprise cards 201-250 and 451-500.

Card	Low	High
COMP.SER.1 SET w/o SPs (200)	20.00	50.00
COMP.SER.2 SET w/o SPs (200)	20.00	50.00
YOUNG GUNS STATED ODDS 1:4		
1 Nicklas Lidstrom	.30	.75
2 Dan Cleary	.25	.60
3 Kris Draper	.25	.60
4 Dominik Hasek	.40	1.00
5 Henrik Zetterberg	.30	.75
6 Jiri Hudler	.20	.50
7 Brett Lebda	.20	.50
8 J.P. Dumont	.20	.50
9 Steve Sullivan	.20	.50
10 Shea Weber	.20	.50
11 Martin Erat	.20	.50
12 Alexander Radulov	.30	.75
13 David Legwand	.20	.50
14 Manny Legace	.25	.60
15 Lee Stempniak	.20	.50
16 Jay McClement	.20	.50
17 Eric Brewer	.20	.50
18 Brad Boyes	.25	.60
19 Barret Jackman	.20	.50
20 Rick Nash	.30	.75
21 Fredrik Norrena	.25	.60
22 Rostislav Klesla	.20	.50
23 Gilbert Brule	.20	.50
24 David Vyborny	.20	.50
25 Manny Malhotra	.20	.50
26 Martin Havlat	.25	.60
27 Rene Bourque	.20	.50
28 Patrick Lalime	.25	.60
29 Jason Williams	.20	.50
30 Cam Barker	.20	.50
31 Patrick Sharp	.20	.60
32 Duncan Keith	.30	.75
33 Markus Naslund	.30	.75
34 Ryan Kesler	.20	.50
35 Matt Cooke	.20	.50
36 Kevin Bieksa	.20	.50
37 Henrik Sedin	.20	.50
38 Brendan Morrison	.20	.50
39 Mattias Ohlund	.20	.50
40 Marian Gaborik	.40	1.00
41 Stephane Veilleux	.20	.50
42 Kim Johnsson	.20	.50
43 Niklas Backstrom	.25	.60
44 Brian Rolston	.20	.50
45 Mikko Koivu	.20	.50
46 Derek Boogaard	.20	.50
47 Miikka Kiprusoff	.40	1.00
48 Matthew Lombardi	.20	.50
49 Dion Phaneuf	.30	.75
50 Craig Conroy	.20	.50
51 Alex Tanguay	.25	.60
52 Wayne Primeau	.20	.50
53 Robyn Regehr	.20	.50
54 Joe Sakic	.60	1.50
55 Brett Clark	.20	.50
56 Ian Laperriere	.20	.50
57 Marek Svatos	.20	.50
58 Peter Budaj	.25	.60
59 John-Michael Liles	.20	.50
60 Paul Stastny	.30	.75
61 Dwayne Roloson	.25	.60
62 Jarret Stoll	.20	.50
63 Ladislav Smid	.20	.50
64 Raffi Torres	.20	.50
65 Marc-Antoine Pouliot	.20	.50
66 Ales Hemsky	.20	.50
67 Fernando Pisani	.20	.50
68 Ryan Getzlaf	.25	.60
69 Andy McDonald	.20	.50
70 Chris Pronger	.30	.75
71 Ilya Bryzgalov	.30	.75
72 Chris Kunitz	.20	.50
73 Francois Beauchemin	.20	.50
74 Dustin Penner	.20	.50
75 Joe Thornton	.40	1.00
76 Milan Michalek	.20	.50
77 Matt Carle	.20	.50
78 Evgeni Nabokov	.25	.60
79 Steve Bernier	.20	.50
80 Mike Grier	.20	.50
81 Joe Pavelski	.20	.50
82 Mike Modano	.30	.75
83 Sergei Zubov	.20	.50
84 Mike Smith	.25	.60
85 Mike Ribeiro	.20	.50
86 Brenden Morrow	.25	.60
87 Jussi Jokinen	.20	.50
88 Jeff Halpern	.20	.50
89 Anze Kopitar	.30	.75
90 Dan Cloutier	.25	.60
91 Dustin Brown	.20	.50
92 Mike Cammalleri	.25	.60
93 Rob Blake	.25	.60
94 Patrick O'Sullivan	.25	.60
95 Shane Doan	.20	.50
96 Mikael Tellqvist	.25	.60
97 Zbynek Michalek	.20	.50
98 Keith Ballard	.20	.50
99 Kevyn Adams	.20	.50
100 Ed Jovanovski	.20	.50
101 Patrik Elias	.20	.50
102 Travis Zajac	.20	.50
103 Jay Pandolfo	.20	.50
104 Paul Martin	.20	.50
105 Brian Gionta	.20	.50
106 John Madden	.20	.50
107 Zach Parise	.25	.60
108 Sidney Crosby	1.50	4.00
109 Jordan Staal	.40	1.00
110 Jocelyn Thibault	.25	.60
111 Sergei Gonchar	.20	.50
112 Gary Roberts	.20	.50
113 Erik Christensen	.20	.50
114 Evgeni Malkin	.75	2.00
115 Jaromir Jagr	.50	1.25
116 Petr Prucha	.20	.50
117 Marek Malik	.20	.50
118 Sean Avery	.20	.50
119 Marcel Hossa	.20	.50
120 Michal Rozsival	.20	.50
121 Ryan Hollweg	.20	.50
122 Miroslav Satan	.20	.50
123 Trent Hunter	.20	.50
124 Mike Sillinger	.20	.50
125 Marc-Andre Bergeron	.20	.50
126 Rick DiPietro	.25	.60
127 Brendan Witt	.20	.50
128 Martin Biron	.25	.60
129 Jeff Carter	.20	.50
130 Ben Eager	.20	.50
131 Simon Gagne	.30	.75
132 R.J. Umberger	.20	.50
133 Scottie Upshall	.20	.50
134 Ryan Miller	.30	.75
135 Thomas Vanek	.25	.60
136 Derek Roy	.20	.50
137 Brian Campbell	.20	.50
138 Drew Stafford	.25	.60
139 Maxim Afinogenov	.20	.50
140 Jason Pominville	.20	.50
141 Dany Heatley	.40	1.00
142 Wade Redden	.20	.50
143 Chris Kelly	.20	.50
144 Ray Emery	.25	.60
145 Chris Neil	.20	.50
146 Mike Fisher	.25	.60
147 Chris Phillips	.20	.50
148 Darcy Tucker	.25	.60
149 Ian White	.20	.50
150 Alexei Ponikarovsky	.20	.50
151 Alexander Steen	.20	.50
152 Andrew Raycroft	.25	.60
153 Bryan McCabe	.20	.50
154 Matt Stajan	.20	.50
155 Michael Ryder	.20	.50
156 Guillaume Latendresse	.25	.60
157 Cristobal Huet	.25	.60
158 Alex Kovalev	.20	.50
159 Mark Streit	.20	.50
160 Chris Higgins	.25	.60
161 Tomas Plekanec	.20	.50
162 Patrice Bergeron	.30	.75
163 Hannu Toivonen	.25	.60
164 Zdeno Chara	.20	.50
165 Phil Kessel	.30	.75
166 Chuck Kobasew	.20	.50
167 P.J. Axelsson	.20	.50
168 Glen Murray	.20	.50
169 Ilya Kovalchuk	.40	1.00
170 Jim Slater	.20	.50
171 Johan Hedberg	.25	.60
172 Marian Hossa	.30	.75
173 Bobby Holik	.20	.50
174 Alexei Zhitnik	.20	.50
175 Vincent Lecavalier	.30	.75
176 Dan Boyle	.20	.50
177 Ryan Craig	.20	.50
178 Vaclav Prospal	.20	.50
179 Marc Denis	.25	.60
180 Brad Richards	.25	.60
181 Eric Staal	.30	.75
182 Rod Brind'Amour	.25	.60
183 Cory Stillman	.20	.50
184 Mike Commodore	.20	.50
185 Erik Cole	.20	.50
186 John Grahame	.25	.60
187 Olli Jokinen	.20	.50
188 Nathan Horton	.20	.50
189 Stephen Weiss	.20	.50
190 Jay Bouwmeester	.20	.50
191 Alex Auld	.25	.60
192 Rostislav Olesz	.20	.50
193 Alexander Semin	.30	.75
194 Chris Clark	.20	.50
195 Olaf Kolzig	.30	.75
196 Mike Green	.20	.50
197 Brian Pothier	.20	.50
198 Milan Jurcina	.20	.50
199 Nicklas Lidstrom CL	.30	.75
200 Sidney Crosby CL	1.50	4.00
201 Drew Miller RC	3.00	8.00
202 Bobby Ryan RC	12.00	30.00
203 Ryan Carter RC	4.00	10.00
204 Jonas Hiller RC	8.00	20.00
205 Bryan Little RC	5.00	12.00
206 Tobias Enstrom RC	5.00	12.00
207 Milan Lucic RC	8.00	20.00
208 David Krejci RC	6.00	15.00
209 Curtis McElhinney RC	4.00	10.00
210 Patrick Kane RC	30.00	60.00
211 Magnus Johansson RC	3.00	8.00
212 Jaroslav Hlinka RC	4.00	10.00
213 Tyler Weiman RC	4.00	10.00
214 Kris Russell RC	5.00	12.00
215 Jared Boll RC	3.00	8.00
216 Matt Niskanen RC	3.00	8.00
217 Matt Ellis RC	3.00	8.00
218 Sam Gagner RC	6.00	15.00
219 Rob Schremp RC	4.00	10.00
220 Tom Gilbert RC	4.00	10.00
221 Cory Murphy RC	3.00	8.00
222 Jack Johnson RC	5.00	12.00
223 Jonathan Bernier RC	8.00	20.00
224 Lauri Tukonen RC	3.00	8.00
225 Brady Murray RC	3.00	8.00
226 Petr Kalus RC	3.00	8.00
227 Carey Price RC	30.00	60.00
228 Jaroslav Halak RC	10.00	25.00
229 Ville Koistinen RC	3.00	8.00
230 Nicklas Bergfors RC	4.00	10.00
231 Andy Greene RC	3.00	8.00
232 Frans Nielsen RC	3.00	8.00
233 Ryan Callahan RC	5.00	12.00
234 Marc Staal RC	8.00	20.00
235 Brandon Dubinsky RC	5.00	12.00
236 Daniel Girardi RC	3.00	8.00
237 Brian Elliott RC	4.00	10.00
238 Nick Foligno RC	5.00	12.00
239 Denis Tolpeko RC	3.00	8.00
240 Peter Mueller RC	10.00	25.00
241 Daniel Winnik RC	3.00	8.00
242 Torrey Mitchell RC	4.00	10.00
243 Erik Johnson RC	6.00	15.00
244 Steve Wagner RC	3.00	8.00
245 Matt Smaby RC	3.00	8.00
246 Mike Lundin RC	3.00	8.00
247 Mason Raymond RC	8.00	20.00
248 Jannik Hansen RC	3.00	8.00
249 Nicklas Backstrom RC	12.00	30.00
250 Patrick Kane RC	3.00	8.00
Carey Price		
Erik Johnson RC		
251 Pavel Datsyuk	.30	.75
252 Chris Osgood	.25	.60
253 Brian Rafalski	.20	.50
254 Henrik Zetterberg	.30	.75
255 Tomas Holmstrom	.25	.60
256 Chris Chelios	.20	.50
257 Johan Franzen	.20	.50
258 Chris Mason	.25	.60
259 Dan Hamhuis	.20	.50
260 Radek Bonk	.20	.50
261 Jordin Tootoo	.25	.60
262 Jason Arnott	.20	.50
263 Ryan Suter	.20	.50
264 Marek Zidlicky	.20	.50
265 Paul Kariya	.30	.75
266 Christian Backman	.20	.50
267 Doug Weight	.20	.50
268 Martin Rucinsky	.20	.50
269 Jay McKee	.20	.50
270 Keith Tkachuk	.25	.60
271 Pascal Leclaire	.25	.60
272 Nikolai Zherdev	.20	.50
273 Jason Chimera	.20	.50
274 Adam Foote	.20	.50
275 Rick Nash	.30	.75
276 Sergei Fedorov	.30	.75
277 Fredrik Modin	.20	.50
278 Nikolai Khabibulin	.30	.75
279 Yanic Perreault	.20	.50
280 Tuomo Ruutu	.20	.50
281 Robert Lang	.20	.50
282 Brent Sopel	.20	.50
283 Brent Seabrook	.20	.50
284 Sergei Samsonov	.20	.50
285 Roberto Luongo	.50	1.25
286 Willie Mitchell	.20	.50
287 Taylor Pyatt	.20	.50
288 Aaron Miller	.20	.50
289 Markus Naslund	.30	.75
290 Lukas Krajicek	.20	.50
291 Daniel Sedin	.20	.50
292 Pavol Demitra	.20	.50
293 Kurtis Foster	.20	.50
294 Marian Gaborik	.40	1.00
295 Pierre-Marc Bouchard	.20	.50
296 Josh Harding	.25	.60
297 Mark Parrish	.20	.50
298 Jarome Iginla	.50	1.25
299 Adrian Aucoin	.20	.50
300 Marcus Nilson	.20	.50
301 Daymond Langkow	.20	.50
302 Cory Sarich	.20	.50
303 Kristian Huselius	.20	.50
304 Owen Nolan	.25	.60
305 Jose Theodore	.30	.75
306 Milan Hejduk	.25	.60
307 Joe Sakic	.60	1.50
308 Scott Hannan	.20	.50
309 Wojtek Wolski	.20	.50
310 Tyler Arnason	.20	.50
311 Ryan Smyth	.25	.60
312 Joni Pitkanen	.20	.50
313 Ethan Moreau	.20	.50
314 Dustin Penner	.20	.50
315 Ales Hemsky	.20	.50
316 Shawn Horcoff	.20	.50
317 Matt Greene	.20	.50
318 Geoff Sanderson	.20	.50
319 Jean-Sebastien Giguere	.30	.75
320 Todd Bertuzzi	.25	.60
321 Scott Niedermayer	.20	.50
322 Corey Perry	.25	.60
323 Travis Moen	.20	.50
324 Mathieu Schneider	.20	.50
325 Sean O'Donnell	.20	.50
326 Jonathan Cheechoo	.25	.60
327 Marc-Edouard Vlasic	.20	.50
328 Ryane Clowe	.20	.50
329 Craig Rivet	.20	.50
330 Joe Thornton	.40	1.00
331 Patrick Marleau	.25	.60
332 Joe Pavelski	.20	.50
333 Marty Turco	.30	.75
334 Philippe Boucher	.20	.50
335 Loui Eriksson	.20	.50
336 Mattias Norstrom	.20	.50
337 Mike Modano	.30	.75
338 Jere Lehtinen	.20	.50
339 Alexander Frolov	.20	.50
340 Lubomir Visnovsky	.20	.50
341 Michal Handzus	.20	.50
342 Brad Stuart	.20	.50
343 Tom Preissing	.20	.50
344 Ladislav Nagy	.20	.50
345 Niko Kapanen	.20	.50
346 Shane Doan	.20	.50
347 Nick Boynton	.20	.50
348 Fredrik Sjostrom	.20	.50
349 Derek Morris	.20	.50
350 Steven Reinprecht	.20	.50
351 Martin Brodeur	.75	2.00
352 Johnny Oduya	.20	.50
353 Arron Asham	.20	.50
354 Sergei Brylin	.20	.50
355 Kevin Weekes	.25	.60
356 Dainius Zubrus	.20	.50
357 Marc-Andre Fleury	.30	.75
358 Ryan Malone	.20	.50
359 Darryl Sydor	.20	.50
360 Petr Sykora	.20	.50
361 Evgeni Malkin	.75	2.00
362 Colby Armstrong	.20	.50
363 Mark Recchi	.20	.50
364 Henrik Lundqvist	.40	1.00
365 Chris Drury	.25	.60
366 Colton Orr	.20	.50
367 Scott Gomez	.20	.50
368 Michal Rozsival	.20	.50
369 Brendan Shanahan	.30	.75
370 Martin Straka	.20	.50
371 Bill Guerin	.20	.50
372 Wade Dubielewicz	.25	.60
373 Chris Campoli	.20	.50
374 Ruslan Fedotenko	.20	.50
375 Bruno Gervais	.20	.50
376 Mike Comrie	.20	.50
377 Daniel Briere	.30	.75
378 Mike Richards	.40	1.00
379 Kimmo Timonen	.20	.50
380 Antero Niittymaki	.25	.60
381 Simon Gagne	.30	.75
382 Joffrey Lupul	.20	.50
383 Scott Hartnell	.20	.50
384 Tim Connolly	.20	.50
385 Daniel Paille	.20	.50
386 Jochen Hecht	.20	.50
387 Ales Kotalik	.20	.50
388 Ryan Miller	.30	.75
389 Andrew Peters	.20	.50
390 Daniel Alfredsson	.25	.60
391 Dany Heatley	.40	1.00
392 Patrick Eaves	.20	.50
393 Antoine Vermette	.20	.50
394 Martin Gerber	.25	.60
395 Jason Spezza	.30	.75
396 Anton Volchenkov	.20	.50
397 Vesa Toskala	.25	.60
398 Nikolai Antropov	.20	.50
399 Tomas Kaberle	.20	.50
400 Jason Blake	.20	.50
401 Simon Gamache	.20	.50
402 Mats Sundin	.30	.75
403 Kris Newbury	.20	.50
404 Roman Hamrlik	.20	.50
405 Bryan Smolinski	.20	.50
406 Mike Komisarek	.20	.50
407 Saku Koivu	.25	.60
408 Andrei Kostitsyn	.20	.50
409 Maxim Lapierre	.20	.50
410 Josh Gorges	.20	.50
411 Manny Fernandez	.25	.60
412 Brandon Bochenski	.20	.50
413 Patrice Bergeron	.30	.75
414 Marco Sturm	.20	.50
415 Dennis Wideman	.20	.50
416 Tim Thomas	.40	1.00
417 Marc Savard	.20	.50
418 Kari Lehtonen	.30	.75
419 Ken Klee	.20	.50
420 Ilya Kovalchuk	.40	1.00
421 Garnet Exelby	.20	.50
422 Todd White	.20	.50
423 Slava Kozlov	.20	.50
424 Johan Holmqvist	.25	.60
425 Chris Gratton	.20	.50
426 Filip Kuba	.20	.50
427 Michel Ouellet	.20	.50
428 Paul Ranger	.20	.50
429 Martin St. Louis	.25	.60
430 Cam Ward	.30	.75
431 Ray Whitney	.20	.50
432 Eric Staal	.30	.75
433 Tim Gleason	.20	.50
434 Andrew Ladd	.20	.50
435 Glen Wesley	.20	.50
436 Justin Williams	.20	.50
437 Tomas Vokoun	.30	.75
438 Brett McLean	.20	.50
439 Noah Welch	.20	.50
440 Jozef Stumpel	.20	.50
441 Steve Montador	.20	.50
442 Mike Van Ryn	.20	.50
443 Richard Zednik	.20	.50
444 Alexander Ovechkin	1.00	2.50
445 Tom Poti	.20	.50
446 Viktor Kozlov	.20	.50
447 Donald Brashear	.20	.50
448 Michael Nylander	.20	.50
449 Joe Thornton	.40	1.00
450 Evgeni Malkin	.75	2.00
451 Petteri Wirtanen RC	3.00	8.00
452 Kent Huskins RC	3.00	8.00
453 Ondrej Pavelec RC	5.00	12.00
454 Brett Sterling RC	3.00	8.00
455 Jonathan Sigalet RC	3.00	8.00
456 Tuukka Rask RC	8.00	20.00
457 Matt Hunwick RC	4.00	10.00

458 Vladimir Sobotka RC 4.00 10.00
459 Mark Mancari RC 4.00 10.00
460 Mike Weber RC 3.00 8.00
461 Matt Keetley RC 4.00 10.00
462 Jonathan Toews RC 40.00 80.00
463 Petri Kontiola RC 3.00 8.00
464 Jake Dowell RC 3.00 8.00
465 T.J. Hensick RC 4.00 10.00
466 Tomas Popperle RC 4.00 10.00
467 Marc Methot RC 3.00 8.00
468 Tobias Stephan RC 4.00 10.00
469 Chris Conner RC 3.00 8.00
470 Andrew Cogliano RC 8.00 20.00
471 Bryan Young RC 3.00 8.00
472 Zach Stortini RC 3.00 8.00
473 Martin Lojek RC 3.00 8.00
474 Stefan Meyer RC 3.00 8.00
475 Tanner Glass RC 3.00 8.00
476 Matt Moulson RC 3.00 8.00
477 James Sheppard RC 3.00 8.00
478 Cal Clutterbuck RC 3.00 8.00
479 Kyle Chipchura RC 5.00 12.00
480 Rich Peverley RC 3.00 8.00
481 Mark Fraser RC 3.00 8.00
482 David Clarkson RC 3.00 8.00
483 Rod Pelley RC 3.00 8.00
484 Greg Moore RC 3.00 8.00
485 Ivan Baranka RC 3.00 8.00
486 Alexander Nikulin RC 4.00 10.00
487 Steve Downie RC 4.00 10.00
488 Riley Cote RC 4.00 10.00
489 Martin Hanzal RC 4.00 10.00
490 Craig Weller RC 3.00 8.00
491 Daniel Carcillo RC 4.00 10.00
492 Tyler Kennedy RC 5.00 12.00
493 Devin Setoguchi RC 6.00 15.00
494 Lukas Kaspar RC 3.00 8.00
495 Thomas Greiss RC 5.00 12.00
496 David Perron RC 5.00 12.00
497 Jiri Tlusty RC 8.00 20.00
498 Anton Stralman RC 4.00 10.00
499 Chris Bourque RC 4.00 10.00
500 Jonathan Toews 2.50 6.00
Jiri Tlusty
Devin Setoguchi CL

2007-08 Upper Deck Printing Plates Black

STATED PRINT RUN 1 SER.#'d SETS
NOT PRICED DUE TO SCARCITY

2007-08 Upper Deck Printing Plates Cyan

STATED PRINT RUN 1 SER.#'d SETS
NOT PRICED DUE TO SCARCITY

2007-08 Upper Deck Printing Plates Magenta

STATED PRINT RUN 1 SER.#'d SETS
NOT PRICED DUE TO SCARCITY

2007-08 Upper Deck Printing Plates Yellow

STATED PRINT RUN 1 SER.#'d SETS
NOT PRICED DUE TO SCARCITY

2007-08 Upper Deck Exclusives Parallel

* EXCLUSIVES: 10X TO 25X
*YOUNG GUNS: 1X TO 2.5X
STATED PRINT RUN 100 SERIAL #'d SETS
210 Patrick Kane 60.00 150.00
227 Carey Price 60.00 150.00
250 Carey Price 8.00 20.00
Patrick Kane
Erik Johnson

2007-08 Upper Deck High Gloss Parallel

STATED PRINT RUN 10 SER.#'d SETS
NOT PRICED DUE TO SCARCITY

2007-08 Upper Deck All-Star Highlights

COMPLETE SET (21) 12.00 30.00
ONE PER SER. 1 FAT PACK
AS1 Zach Parise .50 1.25
AS2 Andy McDonald .40 1.00
AS3 Zdeno Chara .40 1.00
AS4 Roberto Luongo 1.00 2.50
AS5 Daniel Briere .60 1.50
AS6 Sidney Crosby 3.00 8.00
AS7 Alexander Ovechkin 2.00 5.00
AS8 Joe Sakic 1.25 3.00
AS9 Rick Nash .60 1.50
AS10 Brian Rolston .40 1.00
AS11 Dany Heatley .75 2.00
AS12 Marian Hossa .60 1.50
AS13 Dion Phaneuf .60 1.50
AS14 Phil Kessel .60 1.50
AS15 Ryan Getzlaf .50 1.25
AS16 Anze Kopitar .60 1.50
AS17 Eric Staal .60 1.50
AS18 Martin Brodeur 1.50 4.00
AS19 Evgeni Malkin 1.50 4.00
AS20 Ryan Miller .60 1.50
AS21 Joe Thornton .75 2.00

2007-08 Upper Deck All-World Team

COMPLETE SET (35)
AW1 Jarome Iginla 3.00 8.00
AW2 Martin Brodeur 5.00 12.00
AW3 Joe Thornton 2.50 6.00
AW4 Dany Heatley 2.50 6.00
AW5 Tomas Vokoun 2.00 5.00
AW6 Dominik Hasek 2.50 6.00
AW7 Saku Koivu 1.50 4.00
AW8 Miikka Kiprusoff 2.50 6.00
AW9 Ilya Kovalchuk 2.50 6.00
AW10 Alexander Ovechkin 6.00 15.00
AW11 Marian Gaborik 2.50 6.00
AW12 Henrik Lundqvist 2.50 6.00
AW13 Nicklas Lidstrom 2.00 5.00
AW14 Doug Weight 1.25 3.00
AW15 Ryan Miller 2.00 5.00
AW16 Sidney Crosby SP 30.00 80.00
AW17 Vincent Lecavalier SP 6.00 15.00
AW18 Michael Ryder 1.25 3.00
AW19 Eric Staal SP 6.00 15.00
AW20 Rick Nash SP 6.00 15.00
AW21 Jonathan Cheechoo SP 5.00 12.00
AW22 Patrik Elias 1.25 3.00
AW23 Martin Havlat 1.50 4.00
AW24 Milan Hejduk 1.50 4.00
AW25 Ales Hemsky 1.25 3.00
AW26 Kari Lehtonen 2.00 5.00
AW27 Ilya Kovalchuk SP 8.00 20.00
AW28 Evgeni Malkin SP 15.00 40.00
AW29 Miroslav Satan 1.25 3.00
AW30 Anze Kopitar 2.00 5.00
AW31 Henrik Zetterberg SP 6.00 15.00
AW32 Tomas Holmstrom 1.50 4.00
AW33 Dwayne Roloson 1.50 4.00
AW34 Zach Parise SP 5.00 12.00
AW35 Mike Modano SP 6.00 15.00

2007-08 Upper Deck All-World Team Autographs

STATED PRINT RUN 5 SER.#'d SETS
NOT PRICED DUE TO SCARCITY

2007-08 Upper Deck Big Playmakers

STATED PRINT RUN 50 SER.#'d SETS
BPAA Alex Auld 10.00 25.00
BPAF Alexander Frolov 8.00 20.00
BPAH Ales Hemsky 8.00 20.00
BPAK Alex Kovalev 8.00 20.00
BPAM Andrej Meszaros 8.00 20.00
BPAN Anze Kopitar 12.00 30.00
BPAO Alexander Ovechkin 40.00 100.00
BPAR Alexander Radulov 12.00 30.00
BPAS Alexander Steen 8.00 20.00
BPAT Alex Tanguay 10.00 25.00
BPAY Alexei Yashin 8.00 20.00
BPBG Bill Guerin 8.00 20.00
BPBI Martin Biron 10.00 25.00
BPBL Rob Blake 10.00 25.00
BPBM Brendan Morrison 8.00 20.00
BPBO Peter Bondra 8.00 20.00
BPBR Brad Richards 10.00 25.00
BPBS Brendan Shanahan 12.00 30.00
BPBU Peter Budaj 10.00 25.00
BPCA Matt Carle 8.00 20.00
BPCH Chris Higgins 10.00 25.00
BPCW Cam Ward 12.00 30.00
BPDA Daniel Alfredsson 10.00 25.00
BPDH Dany Heatley 15.00 40.00
BPDL David Legwand 8.00 20.00
BPDR Dwayne Roloson 10.00 25.00
BPDW Doug Weight 8.00 20.00
BPEJ Ed Jovanovski 8.00 20.00
BPEL Eric Lindros 12.00 30.00
BPEN Evgeni Nabokov 10.00 25.00
BPES Eric Staal 12.00 30.00
BPFL Marc-Andre Fleury 12.00 30.00
BPGA Simon Gagne 12.00 30.00
BPGM Glen Murray 8.00 20.00
BPHA Dominik Hasek 15.00 40.00
BPHL Henrik Lundqvist 15.00 40.00
BPHS Henrik Sedin 8.00 20.00
BPIK Ilya Kovalchuk 15.00 40.00
BPJA Jason Arnott 8.00 20.00
BPJB Jay Bouwmeester 8.00 20.00
BPJC Jeff Carter 8.00 20.00
BPJG Jean-Sebastien Giguere 12.00 30.00
BPJI Jarome Iginla 20.00 50.00
BPJJ Jaromir Jagr 20.00 50.00
BPJL Jere Lehtinen 8.00 20.00
BPJS Jason Spezza 12.00 30.00
BPJT Joe Thornton 15.00 40.00
BPJW Justin Williams 8.00 20.00
BPKC Kyle Calder 8.00 20.00
BPKL Kari Lehtonen 12.00 30.00
BPKO Andrei Kostitsyn 8.00 20.00
BPKT Keith Tkachuk 10.00 25.00
BPLE Mario Lemieux 40.00 100.00
BPLN Ladislav Nagy 8.00 20.00
BPMA Maxim Afinogenov 8.00 20.00
BPMB Martin Brodeur 30.00 80.00
BPMC Bryan McCabe 8.00 20.00
BPMF Manny Fernandez 10.00 25.00
BPMG Marian Gaborik 15.00 40.00
BPMH Marian Hossa 12.00 30.00
BPMI Mikko Koivu 8.00 20.00
BPMK Miikka Kiprusoff 15.00 40.00
BPML Manny Legace 10.00 25.00
BPMM Milan Michalek 8.00 20.00
BPMN Markus Naslund 12.00 30.00
BPMO Mike Modano 12.00 30.00
BPMR Mark Recchi 8.00 20.00
BPMS Marc Savard 8.00 20.00
BPMT Marty Turco 12.00 30.00
BPNL Nicklas Lidstrom 12.00 30.00
BPPB Patrice Bergeron 12.00 30.00
BPPD Pavol Demitra 8.00 20.00
BPPE Patrik Elias 8.00 20.00
BPPF Peter Forsberg 15.00 40.00
BPPK Paul Kariya 12.00 30.00
BPPM Patrick Marleau 10.00 25.00
BPPR Patrick Roy 40.00 100.00
BPRA Andrew Raycroft 10.00 25.00
BPRB Ray Bourque 15.00 40.00
BPRD Rick DiPietro 10.00 25.00
BPRI Mike Ribeiro 8.00 20.00
BPRL Roberto Luongo 20.00 50.00
BPRM Ryan Miller 12.00 30.00
BPRN Rick Nash 12.00 30.00
BPRO Rod Brind'Amour 10.00 25.00
BPRS Ryan Smyth 10.00 25.00
BPSA Joe Sakic 25.00 60.00
BPSC Sidney Crosby 60.00 150.00
BPSD Shane Doan 8.00 20.00
BPSF Sergei Fedorov 12.00 30.00
BPSG Scott Gomez 8.00 20.00
BPSK Saku Koivu 10.00 25.00
BPSM Miroslav Satan 8.00 20.00
BPSN Scott Niedermayer 8.00 20.00
BPSU Mats Sundin 12.00 30.00
BPSV Marek Svatos 8.00 20.00
BPSW Shea Weber 8.00 20.00
BPTB Todd Bertuzzi 10.00 25.00
BPTS Teemu Selanne 12.00 30.00
BPVL Vincent Lecavalier 12.00 30.00

2007-08 Upper Deck Big Playmakers Patches

STATED PRINT RUN 10 SER.#'d SETS
NOT PRICED DUE TO SCARCITY

2007-08 Upper Deck Clear Cut Winners

STATED PRINT RUN 100 SER.#'d SETS
CCW1 Jean-Sebastien Giguere 12.00 30.00
CCW2 Ryan Getzlaf 10.00 25.00
CCW3 Ilya Kovalchuk 15.00 40.00
CCW4 Marian Hossa 12.00 30.00
CCW5 Patrice Bergeron 12.00 30.00
CCW6 Bobby Orr 50.00 120.00
CCW7 Ryan Miller 12.00 30.00
CCW8 Thomas Vanek 10.00 25.00
CCW9 Jarome Iginla 20.00 50.00
CCW10 Miikka Kiprusoff 15.00 40.00
CCW11 Dion Phaneuf 12.00 30.00
CCW12 Eric Staal 12.00 30.00
CCW13 Patrick Roy 40.00 100.00
CCW14 Joe Sakic 25.00 60.00
CCW15 Rick Nash 12.00 30.00
CCW16 Mike Modano 12.00 30.00
CCW17 Nicklas Lidstrom 12.00 30.00
CCW18 Henrik Zetterberg 12.00 30.00
CCW19 Gordie Howe 30.00 80.00
CCW20 Ales Hemsky 8.00 20.00
CCW21 Wayne Gretzky 60.00 150.00
CCW22 Olli Jokinen 8.00 20.00
CCW23 Anze Kopitar 12.00 30.00
CCW24 Marian Gaborik 15.00 40.00
CCW25 Saku Koivu 10.00 25.00
CCW26 Martin Brodeur 30.00 80.00
CCW27 Miroslav Satan 8.00 20.00
CCW28 Jaromir Jagr 20.00 50.00
CCW29 Henrik Lundqvist 15.00 40.00
CCW30 Mark Messier 25.00 60.00
CCW31 Ray Emery 10.00 25.00
CCW32 Dany Heatley 15.00 40.00
CCW33 Simon Gagne 12.00 30.00
CCW34 Shane Doan 8.00 20.00
CCW35 Marc-Andre Fleury 12.00 30.00
CCW36 Sidney Crosby 60.00 150.00
CCW37 Mario Lemieux 40.00 100.00
CCW38 Joe Thornton 15.00 40.00
CCW39 Vincent Lecavalier 12.00 30.00
CCW40 Mats Sundin 12.00 30.00
CCW41 Roberto Luongo 20.00 50.00
CCW42 Alexander Ovechkin 40.00 100.00
CCW43 Chris Pronger 12.00 30.00
CCW44 Scott Niedermayer 8.00 20.00
CCW45 Kari Lehtonen 12.00 30.00
CCW46 Phil Kessel 12.00 30.00
CCW47 Ray Bourque 15.00 40.00
CCW48 Marc Savard 8.00 20.00
CCW49 Jason Pominville 8.00 20.00
CCW50 Gilbert Perreault 10.00 25.00
CCW51 Alex Tanguay 10.00 25.00
CCW52 Cam Ward 12.00 30.00
CCW53 Justin Williams 8.00 20.00
CCW54 Ryan Smyth 10.00 25.00
CCW55 Paul Stastny 12.00 30.00
CCW56 Sergei Fedorov 12.00 30.00
CCW57 Marty Turco 12.00 30.00
CCW58 Pavel Datsyuk 12.00 30.00
CCW59 Dominik Hasek 15.00 40.00
CCW60 Dwayne Roloson 10.00 25.00
CCW61 Tomas Vokoun 12.00 30.00
CCW62 Alexander Frolov 8.00 20.00
CCW63 Mikko Koivu 8.00 20.00
CCW64 Michael Ryder 8.00 20.00
CCW65 Guillaume Latendresse 10.00 25.00
CCW66 Patrik Elias 8.00 20.00
CCW67 Bill Guerin 8.00 20.00
CCW68 Rick DiPietro 10.00 25.00
CCW69 Brendan Shanahan 12.00 30.00
CCW70 Chris Drury 10.00 25.00
CCW71 Jason Spezza 12.00 30.00
CCW72 Daniel Alfredsson 10.00 25.00
CCW73 Daniel Briere 12.00 30.00
CCW74 Jeff Carter 8.00 20.00
CCW75 Ed Jovanovski 8.00 20.00
CCW76 Evgeni Malkin 30.00 80.00
CCW77 Jordan Staal 15.00 40.00
CCW78 Jonathan Cheechoo 10.00 25.00
CCW79 Patrick Marleau 10.00 25.00
CCW80 Vesa Toskala 10.00 25.00
CCW81 Darcy Tucker 10.00 25.00
CCW82 Markus Naslund 12.00 30.00
CCW83 Daniel Sedin 8.00 20.00
CCW84 Alexander Semin 12.00 30.00

2007-08 Upper Deck Clutch Performers

COMPLETE SET (7) 8.00 20.00
STATED ODDS 1:16
CP1 Martin Brodeur 2.50 6.00
CP2 Alexander Ovechkin 3.00 8.00
CP3 Mats Sundin 1.00 2.50
CP4 Dominik Hasek 1.25 3.00
CP5 Jean-Sebastien Giguere 1.00 2.50
CP6 Joe Sakic 2.00 5.00
CP7 Jaromir Jagr 1.50 4.00

2007-08 Upper Deck Fab Four Fabrics

STATED ODDS 1:288
STATED PRINT RUN 100 SER.#'d SETS
FFBEGP Martin Brodeur 30.00 80.00
Patrik Elias
Brian Gionta
Zach Parise
FFBLCM Martin Brodeur 60.00 150.00
Nicklas Lidstrom
Sidney Crosby
Evgeni Malkin
FFBNFK Rob Blake 12.00 30.00
Ladislav Nagy
Alexander Frolov
Anze Kopitar
FFBRSS Mark Bell 10.00 25.00
Andrew Raycroft
Matt Stajan
Alexander Steen
FFCAMV Tim Connolly 12.00 30.00
Maxim Afinogenov
Ryan Miller
Thomas Vanek
FFDGBK Pavol Demitra 15.00 40.00
Marian Gaborik
Pierre-Marc Bouchard
Mikko Koivu
FFFCBK Manny Fernandez 12.00 30.00
Zdeno Chara
Patrice Bergeron
Phil Kessel
FFGBLC Simon Gagne 12.00 30.00
Daniel Briere
Joffrey Lupul
Jeff Carter
FFGSWD Bill Guerin 10.00 25.00
Miroslav Satan
Brendan Witt
Rick DiPietro
FFHLDZ Dominik Hasek 15.00 40.00
Nicklas Lidstrom
Pavel Datsyuk
Henrik Zetterberg
FFHRKK Martin Havlat 12.00 30.00
Tuomo Ruutu
Duncan Keith
Nikolai Khabibulin
FFITKP Jarome Iginla 20.00 50.00
Alex Tanguay
Miikka Kiprusoff
Dion Phaneuf
FFJHHE Jaromir Jagr 20.00 50.00
Dominik Hasek
Milan Hejduk
Patrik Elias
FFKGOK Olaf Kolzig 40.00 100.00
Mike Green
Alexander Ovechkin
Jakub Klepis
FFKTHN Paul Kariya 15.00 40.00
Alex Tanguay
Dany Heatley
Rick Nash
FFKWTL Paul Kariya 12.00 30.00
Doug Weight
Keith Tkachuk
Manny Legace
FFLCGM Mario Lemieux 60.00 150.00
Sidney Crosby
Wayne Gretzky
Mark Messier
FFLMKB Roberto Luongo 20.00 50.00
Brendan Morrison
Ryan Kesler
Kevin Bieksa
FFLNZF Pascal Leclaire 12.00 30.00
Rick Nash
Nikolai Zherdev
Sergei Fedorov
FFLRSD Vincent Lecavalier 12.00 30.00
Brad Richards
Martin St. Louis
Marc Denis
FFLSWR David Legwand 12.00 30.00
Steve Sullivan
Shea Weber
Alexander Radulov
FFMTMJ Mike Modano 12.00 30.00
Marty Turco
Brenden Morrow
Jussi Jokinen
FFMWTM Mike Modano 12.00 30.00
Doug Weight
Keith Tkachuk
Ryan Miller
FFNKFO Evgeni Nabokov 40.00 100.00
Ilya Kovalchuk
Sergei Fedorov
Alexander Ovechkin
FFNLSS Markus Naslund 20.00 50.00
Roberto Luongo
Henrik Sedin
Daniel Sedin
FFRBLG Patrick Roy 40.00 100.00
Martin Brodeur
Roberto Luongo
Jean-Sebastien Giguere
FFRFCM Mark Recchi 60.00 150.00
Marc-Andre Fleury
Sidney Crosby
Evgeni Malkin
FFRJDB Jeremy Roenick 8.00 20.00
Ed Jovanovski
Shane Doan
Brendan Bell
FFSHRH Jarret Stoll 10.00 25.00
Shawn Horcoff
Dwayne Roloson
Ales Hemsky
FFSHTS Joe Sakic 25.00 60.00
Milan Hejduk
Jose Theodore
Ryan Smyth
FFSJSL Brendan Shanahan 20.00 50.00
Jaromir Jagr
Martin Straka
Henrik Lundqvist
FFSLFA Mats Sundin 15.00 40.00
Nicklas Lidstrom
Peter Forsberg
Daniel Alfredsson
FFSLKJ Teemu Selanne 12.00 30.00
Jere Lehtinen
Saku Koivu
Olli Jokinen
FFSLLS Joe Sakic 25.00 60.00
Eric Lindros
Vincent Lecavalier
Jason Spezza
FFSNGG Teemu Selanne 12.00 30.00
Scott Niedermayer
Jean-Sebastien Giguere
Ryan Getzlaf
FFSSJS Joe Sakic 25.00 60.00
Brendan Shanahan
Jaromir Jagr
Mats Sundin
FFSTMT Mats Sundin 12.00 30.00
Darcy Tucker
Bryan McCabe
Vesa Toskala
FFTKNL Vesa Toskala 15.00 40.00
Miikka Kiprusoff
Antero Niittymaki
Kari Lehtonen
FFTNCM Joe Thornton 15.00 40.00
Evgeni Nabokov
Jonathan Cheechoo
Milan Michalek
FFVJBH Tomas Vokoun 12.00 30.00
Olli Jokinen
Jay Bouwmeester
Nathan Horton
FFWBSW Justin Williams 12.00 30.00
Rod Brind'Amour
Eric Staal
Cam Ward

2007-08 Upper Deck Game Jerseys

STATED ODDS 1:12
JAA Arron Asham 3.00 8.00
JAH Ales Hemsky 3.00 8.00
JAK Alex Kovalev 3.00 8.00
JAM Al MacInnis 4.00 10.00
JAO Alexander Ovechkin 15.00 40.00
JAP Alexander Perezhogin 3.00 8.00
JAR Andrew Raycroft 4.00 10.00
JAS Alexander Steen 3.00 8.00
JAT Alex Tanguay 4.00 10.00
JAY Alexei Yashin 3.00 8.00
JBB Brad Boyes 4.00 10.00
JBF Bernie Federko 3.00 8.00
JBG Bill Guerin 3.00 8.00
JBJ Barret Jackman 3.00 8.00
JBM Brendan Morrison 3.00 8.00
JBO Ray Bourque 6.00 15.00
JBR Bill Ranford 4.00 10.00
JBS Billy Smith 5.00 12.00
JCH Chris Higgins 4.00 10.00
JCI Dino Ciccarelli 4.00 10.00
JCJ Jonathan Cheechoo 4.00 10.00
JCP Chris Pronger 5.00 12.00
JCS Curtis Sanford 4.00 10.00
JCW Cam Ward 5.00 12.00
JDA Daniel Alfredsson 4.00 10.00
JDB Dustin Brown 3.00 8.00
JDC Dan Cloutier 4.00 10.00
JDH Dale Hawerchuk 4.00 10.00
JDK Duncan Keith 5.00 12.00
JDL David Legwand 3.00 8.00
JDP Daniel Paille 3.00 8.00
JDR Dwayne Roloson 4.00 10.00
JDS Daniel Sedin 3.00 8.00
JDW Doug Weight 3.00 8.00
JEJ Ed Jovanovski 3.00 8.00
JEL Eric Lindros 5.00 12.00
JEM Evgeni Malkin 12.00 30.00
JEN Evgeni Nabokov 4.00 10.00
JES Eric Staal 5.00 12.00
JGI Brian Gionta 3.00 8.00
JGM Glen Murray 3.00 8.00
JHA Dominik Hasek 6.00 15.00
JHE Dany Heatley 6.00 15.00
JHL Henrik Lundqvist 6.00 15.00
JHT Hannu Toivonen 4.00 10.00
JIK Ilya Kovalchuk 6.00 15.00
JJA Jay Bouwmeester 6.00 15.00
JJB Jason Bacashihua 4.00 10.00
JJC Jeff Carter 3.00 8.00
JJD J.P. Dumont 3.00 8.00
JJG Jean-Sebastien Giguere 5.00 12.00
JJH Jeff Hoggan 3.00 8.00
JJI Jarome Iginla 8.00 20.00
JJJ Jaromir Jagr 8.00 20.00
JJL Jamie Lundmark 3.00 8.00
JJO Joe Sakic 10.00 25.00
JJS Jarret Stoll 3.00 8.00
JJT Joe Thornton 6.00 15.00
JJW Justin Williams 3.00 8.00
JKC Kyle Calder 3.00 8.00
JKL Kari Lehtonen 5.00 12.00
JKO Andrei Kostitsyn 3.00 8.00
JKT Keith Tkachuk 4.00 10.00
JLR Larry Robinson 6.00 15.00
JLU Joffrey Lupul 3.00 8.00
JMA Mark Stuart 3.00 8.00
JMB Martin Brodeur 12.00 30.00
JMC Bryan McCabe 3.00 8.00
JME Andrej Meszaros 3.00 8.00
JMF Manny Fernandez 4.00 10.00
JMG Marian Gaborik 6.00 15.00
JMH Marian Hossa 5.00 12.00
JMI Milan Michalek 3.00 8.00
JMJ Milan Jurcina 3.00 8.00
JML Mario Lemieux 15.00 40.00
JMM Mike Modano 5.00 12.00
JMN Markus Naslund 5.00 12.00
JMO Brenden Morrow 4.00 10.00
JMR Michael Ryder 3.00 8.00
JMS Marek Svatos 3.00 8.00
JMT Marty Turco 5.00 12.00
JNL Nicklas Lidstrom 5.00 12.00
JON Ben Ondrus 3.00 8.00
JPB Patrice Bergeron 5.00 12.00
JPE Corey Perry 4.00 10.00
JPF Peter Forsberg 6.00 15.00
JPK Paul Kariya 5.00 12.00
JPS Patrik Stefan 3.00 8.00
JRB Rod Brind'Amour 4.00 10.00
JRI Brad Richards 4.00 10.00
JRS Ryan Smyth 4.00 10.00
JSA Borje Salming 4.00 10.00
JSC Sidney Crosby 25.00 60.00
JSH Brendan Shanahan 5.00 12.00
JSI Darryl Sittler 4.00 10.00
JSK Saku Koivu 4.00 10.00
JSP Jason Spezza 5.00 12.00
JST Brad Stuart 3.00 8.00
JSU Mats Sundin 5.00 12.00
JTW Tiger Williams 4.00 10.00
GJ2AF Alexander Frolov 3.00 8.00
GJ2AK Alex Kovalev 3.00 8.00
GJ2AL Andrew Ladd 3.00 8.00
GJ2BR Brian Rafalski 3.00 8.00
GJ2CC Carlo Colaiacovo 3.00 8.00
GJ2CD Chris Drury 4.00 10.00
GJ2CH Chris Chelios 3.00 8.00
GJ2CJ Curtis Joseph 4.00 10.00
GJ2CO Chris Osgood 4.00 10.00
GJ2DB Daniel Briere 5.00 12.00
GJ2DP Dion Phaneuf 5.00 12.00
GJ2DT Darcy Tucker 4.00 10.00
GJ2GO Scott Gomez 3.00 8.00
GJ2GR Gary Roberts 3.00 8.00
GJ2HS Henrik Sedin 3.00 8.00
GJ2HZ Henrik Zetterberg 5.00 12.00
GJ2JA Jason Arnott 3.00 8.00
GJ2JJ Jaromir Jagr 8.00 20.00
GJ2JL Jere Lehtinen 3.00 8.00
GJ2JP Joni Pitkanen 3.00 8.00
GJ2JS Jordan Staal 6.00 15.00
GJ2KB Kevin Bieksa 3.00 8.00
GJ2KO Anze Kopitar 5.00 12.00
GJ2LN Ladislav Nagy 3.00 8.00
GJ2MA Martin Brodeur 12.00 30.00
GJ2MB Mark Bell 3.00 8.00
GJ2MF Marc-Andre Fleury 5.00 12.00
GJ2ML Mario Lemieux 15.00 40.00
GJ2MM Mark Messier 10.00 25.00
GJ2OJ Olli Jokinen 3.00 8.00
GJ2OK Olaf Kolzig 5.00 12.00
GJ2PB Pierre-Marc Bouchard 3.00 8.00
GJ2PD Pavel Datsyuk 5.00 12.00
GJ2PF Peter Forsberg 6.00 15.00
GJ2PK Phil Kessel 5.00 12.00
GJ2PP Petr Prucha 3.00 8.00
GJ2PR Patrick Roy 15.00 40.00
GJ2RB Rob Blake 4.00 10.00
GJ2RD Rick DiPietro 4.00 10.00
GJ2RG Ryan Getzlaf 4.00 10.00
GJ2RL Roberto Luongo 8.00 20.00
GJ2RM Ryan Miller 5.00 12.00
GJ2RN Rick Nash 5.00 12.00
GJ2RS Ryan Smyth 4.00 10.00
GJ2RT Raffi Torres 3.00 8.00
GJ2SC Sidney Crosby 25.00 60.00
GJ2SD Shane Doan 3.00 8.00
GJ2SF Sergei Fedorov 5.00 12.00
GJ2SG Simon Gagne 5.00 12.00
GJ2SN Scott Niedermayer 3.00 8.00
GJ2SS Steve Sullivan 3.00 8.00
GJ2SW Stephen Weiss 3.00 8.00
GJ2TB Todd Bertuzzi 4.00 10.00
GJ2TS Teemu Selanne 5.00 12.00
GJ2TV Tomas Vokoun 5.00 12.00
GJ2VL Vincent Lecavalier 5.00 12.00
GJ2VT Vesa Toskala 4.00 10.00
GJ2WE Shea Weber 3.00 8.00

2007-08 Upper Deck Game Patches

STATED PRINT RUN 15 SER.#'d SETS
NOT PRICED DUE TO SCARCITY

2007-08 Upper Deck Generation Next

COMPLETE SET (30) 12.00 30.00
RANDOM INSERTS IN TARGET PACKS
GN1 Alexander Ovechkin 2.50 6.00
GN2 Cam Ward .75 2.00
GN3 Corey Perry .60 1.50
GN4 Dion Phaneuf .75 2.00
GN5 Evgeni Malkin 2.00 5.00
GN6 Gilbert Brule .50 1.25
GN7 Guillaume Latendresse .60 1.50
GN8 Jordan Staal 1.00 2.50
GN9 Thomas Vanek .60 1.50
GN10 Phil Kessel .75 2.00
GN11 Ryan Getzlaf .60 1.50
GN12 Kari Lehtonen .75 2.00
GN13 Sidney Crosby 4.00 10.00
GN14 Steve Bernier .50 1.25
GN15 Zach Parise .60 1.50
GN16 Alexander Radulov .75 2.00
GN17 Alexander Semin .75 2.00
GN18 Anze Kopitar .75 2.00
GN19 Jack Johnson .75 2.00
GN20 Jeff Carter .50 1.25
GN21 Josh Harding .60 1.50
GN22 Kevin Bieksa .50 1.25
GN23 Lee Stempniak .50 1.25
GN24 Matt Carle .50 1.25
GN25 Mikko Koivu .50 1.25
GN26 Milan Michalek .50 1.25
GN27 Patrick Eaves .50 1.25
GN28 Paul Stastny .75 2.00
GN29 Rob Schremp .60 1.50
GN30 Wojtek Wolski .50 1.25

2007-08 Upper Deck Generation Next Autographs

STATED PRINT RUN 5 SER.#'d SETS
NOT PRICED DUE TO SCARCITY

2007-08 Upper Deck Hometown Heroes

COMPLETE SET (28) 20.00 50.00
STATED ODDS 1:24
HH57 Marian Hossa 1.50 4.00
HH58 Thomas Vanek 1.25 3.00
HH59 Rick DiPietro 1.25 3.00
HH60 Pavel Datsyuk 1.50 4.00
HH61 Evgeni Malkin 4.00 10.00
HH62 Ray Emery 1.25 3.00
HH63 Paul Stastny 1.50 4.00
HH64 Zach Parise 1.25 3.00
HH65 Ryan Getzlaf 1.25 3.00
HH66 Alexander Semin 1.50 4.00
HH67 Dwayne Roloson 1.25 3.00
HH68 Marty Turco 1.50 4.00
HH69 Guillaume Latendresse 1.25 3.00
HH70 Andrew Raycroft 1.25 3.00
HH71 Daniel Briere 1.50 4.00
HH72 Ryan Smyth 1.25 3.00
HH73 Paul Kariya 1.50 4.00
HH74 Tomas Vokoun 1.50 4.00
HH75 Alexander Radulov 1.50 4.00
HH76 Miroslav Satan 1.00 2.50
HH77 Mark Recchi 1.00 2.50
HH78 Phil Kessel 1.50 4.00
HH79 Chris Chelios 1.00 2.50
HH80 Anze Kopitar 1.50 4.00
HH81 Justin Williams 1.00 2.50
HH82 Joe Thornton 2.00 5.00
HH83 Mikko Koivu 1.00 2.50
HH84 Brad Richards 1.25 3.00

2007-08 Upper Deck Lord Stanley's Heroes

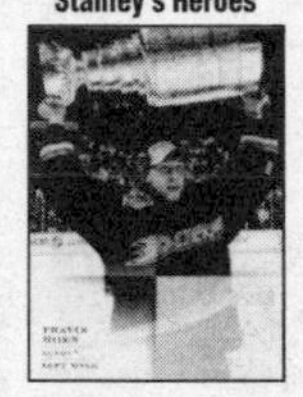

COMPLETE SET (7) 5.00 12.00
STATED ODDS 1:24
LSH1 Teemu Selanne 1.50 4.00
LSH2 Jean-Sebastien Giguere 1.50 4.00
LSH3 Chris Pronger 1.50 4.00
LSH4 Scott Niedermayer 1.00 2.50
LSH5 Andy McDonald 1.00 2.50
LSH6 Ryan Getzlaf 1.25 3.00
LSH7 Travis Moen 1.00 2.50

2007-08 Upper Deck NHL's Best

COMPLETE SET (14) 20.00 50.00
STATED ODDS 1:24
B1 Sidney Crosby 8.00 20.00
B2 Martin Brodeur 4.00 10.00
B3 Dany Heatley 2.00 5.00
B4 Alexander Ovechkin 5.00 12.00
B5 Joe Thornton 2.00 5.00
B6 Jarome Iginla 2.50 6.00
B7 Vincent Lecavalier 1.50 4.00
B8 Roberto Luongo 2.50 6.00
B9 Joe Sakic 3.00 8.00
B10 Jaromir Jagr 2.50 6.00
B11 Teemu Selanne 1.50 4.00
B12 Ilya Kovalchuk 2.00 5.00
B13 Ryan Miller 1.50 4.00
B14 Eric Staal 1.50 4.00

2007-08 Upper Deck NHL Award Winners

COMPLETE SET (7) 12.00 30.00
STATED ODDS 1:24
AW1 Sidney Crosby 8.00 20.00
AW2 Martin Brodeur 4.00 10.00
AW3 Nicklas Lidstrom 1.50 4.00

AW4 Evgeni Malkin	4.00	10.00
AW5 Rod Brind'Amour	1.25	3.00
AW6 Pavel Datsyuk	1.50	4.00
AW7 Phil Kessel	1.50	4.00

2007-08 Upper Deck Oversize Cards

WILL BE PRICED AT A LATER DATE
INSUFFICIENT MARKET DATA

2007-08 Upper Deck Rookie Headliners

RH1 Jonathan Toews SP	20.00	50.00
RH2 Patrick Kane SP	20.00	50.00
RH3 Carey Price SP	15.00	40.00
RH4 Devin Setoguchi SP	6.00	15.00
RH5 Jiri Tlusty SP	8.00	20.00
RH6 Jack Johnson SP	5.00	12.00
RH7 Bobby Ryan SP	12.00	30.00
RH8 Peter Mueller SP	10.00	25.00
RH9 Bryan Little SP	4.00	10.00
RH10 Sam Gagner SP	6.00	15.00
RH11 Andrew Cogliano	2.00	5.00
RH12 Jonathan Bernier	2.00	5.00
RH13 Nicklas Backstrom	3.00	8.00
RH14 Marc Staal	2.00	5.00
RH15 Erik Johnson	1.50	4.00
RH16 Milan Lucic	2.00	5.00
RH17 James Sheppard	.75	2.00
RH18 Nicklas Bergfors	1.00	2.50
RH19 Nick Foligno	1.25	3.00
RH20 Kyle Chipchura	1.25	3.00

2007-08 Upper Deck Rookie Materials

STATED ODDS 1:24

RMAC Andrew Cogliano	8.00	20.00
RMAG Andy Greene	3.00	8.00
RMAS Anton Stralman	4.00	10.00
RMBA Nicklas Backstrom	12.00	30.00
RMBL Bryan Little	4.00	10.00
RMBR Bobby Ryan	12.00	30.00
RMBS Brett Sterling	3.00	8.00
RMCM Curtis McElhinney	4.00	10.00
RMCP Carey Price	15.00	40.00
RMDK David Krejci	6.00	15.00
RMDM Drew Miller	3.00	8.00
RMDP David Perron	5.00	12.00
RMDS Devin Setoguchi	6.00	15.00
RMEJ Erik Johnson	6.00	15.00
RMFN Frans Nielsen	3.00	8.00
RMJB Jonathan Bernier	8.00	20.00
RMJH Jaroslav Halak	10.00	25.00
RMJJ Jack Johnson	5.00	12.00
RMJS James Sheppard	3.00	8.00
RMJT Jonathan Toews	20.00	50.00
RMKA Petr Kalus	3.00	8.00
RMKC Kyle Chipchura	5.00	12.00
RMMH Martin Hanzal	4.00	10.00
RMML Milan Lucic	8.00	20.00
RMMN Matt Niskanen	3.00	8.00
RMMR Mason Raymond	8.00	20.00
RMMS Marc Staal	8.00	20.00
RMNB Nicklas Bergfors	4.00	10.00
RMNF Nick Foligno	5.00	12.00
RMOP Ondrej Pavelec	5.00	12.00
RMPK Patrick Kane	20.00	50.00
RMPM Peter Mueller	10.00	25.00
RMRC Ryan Callahan	5.00	12.00
RMRP Ryan Parent	4.00	10.00
RMRS Rob Schremp	4.00	10.00
RMSG Sam Gagner	6.00	15.00
RMTL Jiri Tlusty	8.00	20.00
RMTM Torrey Mitchell	4.00	10.00
RMVK Ville Koistinen	3.00	8.00

2007-08 Upper Deck Rookie Materials Patches

STATED PRINT RUN 15 SER.#'d SETS
NOT PRICED DUE TO SCARCITY
RMAC Andrew Cogliano
RMAG Andy Greene
RMAS Anton Stralman
RMBA Nicklas Backstrom
RMBL Bryan Little
RMBR Bobby Ryan
RMBS Brett Sterling
RMCM Curtis McElhinney
RMCP Carey Price
RMDK David Krejci
RMDM Drew Miller
RMDP David Perron
RMDS Devin Setoguchi
RMEJ Erik Johnson
RMFN Frans Nielsen
RMJB Jonathan Bernier
RMJH Jaroslav Halak
RMJJ Jack Johnson
RMJS James Sheppard
RMJT Jonathan Toews
RMKA Petr Kalus
RMKC Kyle Chipchura
RMMH Martin Hanzal
RMML Milan Lucic
RMMN Matt Niskanen
RMMR Mason Raymond
RMMS Marc Staal
RMNB Nicklas Bergfors
RMNF Nick Foligno
RMOP Ondrej Pavelec
RMPK Patrick Kane
RMPM Peter Mueller
RMRC Ryan Callahan
RMRP Ryan Parent
RMRS Rob Schremp
RMSG Sam Gagner
RMTL Jiri Tlusty
RMTM Torrey Mitchell
RMVK Ville Koistinen

2007-08 Upper Deck Signature Sensations

STATED ODDS 1:288

SSAK Andrei Kostitsyn	4.00	10.00
SSAO Alex Ovechkin SP	125.00	200.00
SSAR Andrew Raycroft	5.00	12.00
SSAT Alex Tanguay		
SSBM Brenden Morrow	5.00	12.00
SSBO Bobby Orr SP		
SSBP Benoit Pouliot	4.00	10.00
SSBR Brad Richardson	4.00	10.00
SSBW Ben Walter	4.00	10.00
SSCK Chuck Kobasew	4.00	10.00
SSCO Erik Cole		
SSCT Chris Thorburn	4.00	10.00
SSDB Daniel Briere		
SSDH Dany Heatley		
SSDK Duncan Keith	6.00	15.00
SSDP Dion Phaneuf	6.00	15.00
SSDS Drew Stafford	5.00	12.00
SSEC Erik Christensen	4.00	10.00
SSEM Evgeni Malkin	15.00	40.00
SSEN Evgeni Nabokov	5.00	12.00
SSES Eric Staal	6.00	15.00
SSFN Filip Novak	4.00	10.00
SSFP Fernando Pisani	4.00	10.00
SSGE Martin Gerber	5.00	12.00
SSGL Guillaume Latendresse	5.00	12.00
SSGM Glen Murray		
SSGO Scott Gomez	4.00	10.00
SSHA Dominik Hasek	8.00	20.00
SSHZ Henrik Zetterberg	6.00	15.00
SSIK Ilya Kovalchuk	8.00	20.00
SSIM Jarkko Immonen		
SSIW Ian White	4.00	10.00
SSJA Jay Bouwmeester	4.00	10.00
SSJC Jonathan Cheechoo	5.00	12.00
SSJF Johan Franzen	4.00	10.00
SSJG Jean-Sebastien Giguere	6.00	15.00
SSJI Jarome Iginla	10.00	25.00
SSJL John-Michael Liles	4.00	10.00
SSJM Jay McClement	4.00	10.00
SSJO Jeff O'Neill	4.00	10.00
SSJT Joe Thornton	8.00	20.00
SSJW Jeremy Williams	4.00	10.00
SSKC Kyle Calder	4.00	10.00
SSKE Ryan Kesler	4.00	10.00
SSKL Kari Lehtonen	6.00	15.00
SSKO Anze Kopitar SP		
SSKU Chris Kunitz		
SSLA Maxim Lapierre		
SSLB Luc Bourdon		
SSMA Maxim Afinogenov	4.00	10.00
SSME Marc-Edouard Vlasic	4.00	10.00
SSMG Marian Gaborik	8.00	20.00
SSMH Marcel Hossa	4.00	10.00
SSMI Michal Handzus	4.00	10.00
SSMK Miikka Kiprusoff SP	40.00	80.00
SSML Mario Lemieux SP	60.00	120.00
SSMM Mark Messier SP		
SSMP Michael Peca	4.00	10.00
SSMS Marek Svatos	4.00	10.00
SSMT Mikael Tellqvist	5.00	12.00
SSNA Nikolai Antropov	4.00	10.00
SSON Ben Ondrus	4.00	10.00
SSPB Pierre-Marc Bouchard		
SSPE Patrick Eaves	4.00	10.00
SSPK Phil Kessel	6.00	15.00
SSPR Brandon Prust	4.00	10.00
SSPS Paul Stastny	6.00	15.00
SSRE Robert Esche	5.00	12.00
SSRK Rostislav Klesla	4.00	10.00
SSRM Ryan Malone	4.00	10.00
SSRN Rick Nash	6.00	15.00
SSRS Ryan Smyth	5.00	12.00
SSSC Sidney Crosby SP	100.00	200.00
SSSG Simon Gagne	6.00	15.00
SSSH Shawn Horcoff	4.00	10.00
SSSS Steve Sullivan		
SSST Martin St. Louis		
SSTM Travis Moen	4.00	10.00
SSTR Tuomo Ruutu	4.00	10.00
SSTV Thomas Vanek	5.00	12.00
SSVL Vincent Lecavalier	6.00	15.00
SSWG Wayne Gretzky SP		
SSWR Wade Redden	4.00	10.00
SSYS Yan Stastny	4.00	10.00

2007-08 Upper Deck Stars In The Making

COMPLETE SET (14)	8.00	20.00
STATED ODDS 1:16		
SM1 Zach Parise	.75	2.00
SM2 Mikko Koivu	.60	1.50
SM3 Jordan Staal	1.25	3.00
SM4 Thomas Vanek	.75	2.00
SM5 Phil Kessel	1.00	2.50
SM6 Alexander Semin	1.00	2.50
SM7 Drew Stafford	.75	2.00
SM8 Ryan Getzlaf	.75	2.00
SM9 Alexander Radulov	1.00	2.50
SM10 Steve Bernier	.60	1.50
SM11 Dion Phaneuf	1.00	2.50
SM12 Paul Stastny	1.00	2.50
SM13 Anze Kopitar	1.00	2.50
SM14 Brent Seabrook	.60	1.50

2007-08 Upper Deck Super Snipers

COMPLETE SET (21)	20.00	50.00
SN1 Vincent Lecavalier	1.25	3.00
SN2 Dany Heatley	1.50	4.00
SN3 Jonathan Cheechoo	1.00	2.50
SN4 Martin St. Louis	1.00	2.50
SN5 Ilya Kovalchuk	1.50	4.00
SN6 Joe Sakic	2.50	6.00
SN7 Jaromir Jagr	2.00	5.00
SN8 Jarome Iginla	2.00	5.00
SN9 Marian Hossa	1.25	3.00
SN10 Martin Havlat	1.00	2.50
SN11 Teemu Selanne	1.25	3.00
SN12 Alexander Ovechkin	4.00	10.00
SN13 Jason Spezza	1.25	3.00
SN14 Thomas Vanek	1.00	2.50
SN15 Sidney Crosby	6.00	15.00
SN16 Mike Modano	1.25	3.00
SN17 Henrik Zetterberg	1.25	3.00
SN18 Markus Naslund	1.25	3.00
SN19 Marian Gaborik	1.50	4.00
SN20 Rick Nash	1.25	3.00
SN21 Mats Sundin	1.25	3.00

2007-08 Upper Deck The Men Behind The Mask

COMPLETE SET (15)	25.00	60.00
ONE PER SER. 2 FAT PACK		
BM1 Cam Ward	2.50	6.00
BM2 Dominik Hasek	3.00	8.00
BM3 Dwayne Roloson	2.00	5.00
BM4 Henrik Lundqvist	3.00	8.00
BM5 Jean-Sebastien Giguere	2.50	6.00
BM6 Kari Lehtonen	2.50	6.00
BM7 Marc-Andre Fleury	2.50	6.00
BM8 Martin Brodeur	6.00	15.00
BM9 Marty Turco	2.50	6.00
BM10 Miikka Kiprusoff	3.00	8.00
BM11 Ray Emery	2.00	5.00
BM12 Roberto Luongo	4.00	10.00
BM13 Ryan Miller	2.50	6.00
BM14 Tomas Vokoun	2.50	6.00
BM15 Vesa Toskala	2.00	5.00

2007-08 Upper Deck Top Picks

COMPLETE SET (7)	8.00	20.00
STATED ODDS 1:16		
TP1 Sidney Crosby	5.00	12.00
TP2 Alexander Ovechkin	3.00	8.00
TP3 Marc-Andre Fleury	1.00	2.50
TP4 Rick Nash	1.00	2.50
TP5 Ilya Kovalchuk	1.25	3.00
TP6 Vincent Lecavalier	1.00	2.50
TP7 Joe Thornton	1.25	3.00

2007-08 Upper Deck UD Signatures

STATED ODDS 1:288

UDSAK Andrei Kostitsyn	6.00	15.00
UDSAM Al Montoya	8.00	20.00
UDSAO Alexander Ovechkin SP	100.00	150.00
UDSBC Blake Comeau	6.00	15.00
UDSBO Bobby Orr SP		
UDSBP Benoit Pouliot	6.00	15.00
UDSBR Mike Brown	6.00	15.00
UDSCC Chris Campoli	6.00	15.00
UDSCS Cory Stillman SP		
UDSDB Daniel Briere	10.00	25.00
UDSDH Dominik Hasek SP	20.00	50.00
UDSDS Drew Stafford	8.00	20.00
UDSEM Evgeni Malkin SP	125.00	200.00
UDSGH Gordie Howe SP		
UDSIK Ilya Kovalchuk SP	15.00	40.00
UDSJB Jaroslav Balastik	6.00	15.00
UDSJC Jeff Carter SP	20.00	50.00
UDSJF Johan Franzen	6.00	15.00
UDSJG Jean-Sebastien Giguere SP		
UDSJJ Jack Johnson	10.00	25.00
UDSJK Jakub Klepis	6.00	15.00
UDSJM Jay McClement	6.00	15.00
UDSJS Jordan Staal SP	15.00	30.00
UDSJW Jeremy Williams	6.00	15.00
UDSKB Kevin Bieksa	6.00	15.00
UDSKO Anze Kopitar	10.00	25.00
UDSLA Maxim Lapierre	6.00	15.00
UDSLN Ladislav Nagy	6.00	15.00
UDSLT Lauri Tukonen	6.00	15.00
UDSML Mario Lemieux SP	100.00	200.00
UDSMM Mark Messier SP		
UDSMR Mike Ribeiro SP	12.00	30.00
UDSNB Niklas Backstrom	8.00	20.00
UDSNK Nikolai Khabibulin SP		
UDSPH Dion Phaneuf	10.00	25.00
UDSPK Phil Kessel SP		
UDSPM Paul Mara	6.00	15.00
UDSPS Paul Stastny SP		
UDSRI Mike Richards	12.00	30.00
UDSRK Rostislav Klesla	6.00	15.00
UDSRM Ryan Miller	10.00	25.00
UDSRN Rick Nash SP	30.00	60.00
UDSRO Rob Schremp	8.00	20.00
UDSRS Ryan Smyth SP		
UDSSC Sidney Crosby SP	150.00	300.00
UDSSS Steve Sullivan SP		
UDSSW Stephen Weiss	6.00	15.00
UDSTB Todd Bertuzzi SP	10.00	25.00
UDSTV Thomas Vanek	8.00	20.00
UDSWR Wade Redden SP		
UDSZP Zach Parise	8.00	20.00

2007-08 Upper Deck Young Guns Retro Oversized

COMPLETE SET (14)	60.00	120.00
YG1 Patrick Kane	15.00	40.00
YG2 Carey Price	12.00	30.00
YG3 Erik Johnson	5.00	12.00
YG4 Bobby Ryan	10.00	25.00
YG5 Marc Staal	6.00	15.00
YG6 Nicklas Backstrom	10.00	25.00
YG7 Jonathan Bernier	6.00	15.00
YG8 Bryan Little	3.00	8.00
YG9 Sam Gagner	5.00	12.00
YG10 Nick Foligno	4.00	10.00
YG11 Peter Mueller	8.00	20.00
YG12 Jack Johnson	4.00	10.00
YG13 Nicklas Bergfors	3.00	8.00
YG14 Rob Schremp	3.00	8.00

2008-09 Upper Deck

This base set consists of 500 cards. Series 1 (cards 1-250) was released on November 11, 2008. Cards 1-200 feature veterans, and cards 201-250 are rookies. Series 2 (cards 251-500) was released on February 10, 2009. Cards 251-450 feature veterans, and cards 451-500 are rookies.

COMP.SER.1 SET (250)	200.00	350.00
COMP.SER.1 SET w/o SPs (200)	15.00	40.00
YG STATED ODDS 1:4		
1 Nicklas Backstrom	.60	1.50
2 Alexander Semin	.30	.75
3 Mike Green	.20	.50
4 Viktor Kozlov	.20	.50
5 Jeff Schultz	.20	.50
6 Boyd Gordon	.20	.50
7 Mattias Ohlund	.20	.50
8 Roberto Luongo	.50	1.25
9 Alexander Edler	.25	.60
10 Mason Raymond	.20	.50
11 Daniel Sedin	.30	.75
12 Henrik Sedin	.30	.75
13 Curtis Sanford	.20	.50
14 Ryan Kesler	.20	.50
15 Pavel Kubina	.20	.50
16 Vesa Toskala	.30	.75
17 Alexander Steen	.30	.75
18 Tomas Kaberle	.20	.50
19 Jiri Tlusty	.30	.75
20 Nik Antropov	.25	.60
21 Ian White	.20	.50
22 Paul Ranger	.20	.50
23 Martin St. Louis	.30	.75
24 Jussi Jokinen	.20	.50
25 Mike Smith	.25	.60
26 Jeff Halpern	.20	.50
27 Mike Lundin	.20	.50
28 Lee Stempniak	.20	.50
29 Paul Kariya	.30	.75
30 Erik Johnson	.40	1.00
31 Manny Legace	.25	.60
32 Brad Boyes	.25	.60
33 Andy McDonald	.20	.50
34 David Perron	.25	.60
35 Joe Thornton	.50	1.25
36 Devin Setoguchi	.30	.75
37 Evgeni Nabokov	.30	.75
38 Jonathan Cheechoo	.30	.75
39 Milan Michalek	.20	.50
40 Torrey Mitchell	.30	.75
41 Mike Grier	.20	.50
42 Sidney Crosby	1.50	4.00
43 Marc-Andre Fleury	.30	.75
44 Kristopher Letang	.20	.50
45 Tyler Kennedy	.25	.60
46 Jordan Staal	.50	1.25
47 Sergei Gonchar	.30	.75
48 Petr Sykora	.20	.50
49 Peter Mueller	.40	1.00
50 Ilya Bryzgalov	.20	.50
51 Zbynek Michalek	.20	.50
52 Martin Hanzal	.25	.60
53 Daniel Carcillo	.20	.50
54 Ed Jovanovski	.20	.50
55 Riley Cote	.20	.50
56 Simon Gagne	.25	.60
57 Mike Richards	.50	1.25
58 Martin Biron	.25	.60
59 Kimmo Timonen	.20	.50
60 Joffrey Lupul	.20	.50
61 Mike Knuble	.30	.75
62 Daniel Alfredsson	.25	.60
63 Chris Phillips	.20	.50
64 Mike Fisher	.20	.50
65 Antoine Vermette	.20	.50
66 Andrej Meszaros	.20	.50
67 Jason Spezza	.40	1.00
68 Chris Neil	.20	.50
69 Stephen Valiquette	.25	.60
70 Nigel Dawes	.20	.50
71 Marc Staal	.40	1.00
72 Brandon Dubinsky	.25	.60
73 Scott Gomez	.25	.60
74 Henrik Lundqvist	.60	1.50
75 Bill Guerin	.20	.50
76 Rick DiPietro	.30	.75
77 Blake Comeau	.20	.50
78 Trent Hunter	.20	.50
79 Brendan Witt	.20	.50
80 Mike Sillinger	.20	.50
81 Martin Brodeur	.60	1.50
82 Patrik Elias	.20	.50
83 Johnny Oduya	.20	.50
84 Brian Gionta	.30	.75
85 Paul Martin	.20	.50
86 John Madden	.20	.50
87 Radek Bonk	.20	.50
88 Martin Erat	.30	.75
89 Shea Weber	.20	.50
90 David Legwand	.25	.60
91 Ryan Suter	.20	.50
92 Francis Bouillon	.25	.60
93 Saku Koivu	.30	.75
94 Guillaume Latendresse	.25	.60
95 Carey Price	1.00	2.50
96 Tomas Plekanec	.20	.50
97 Mike Komisarek	.25	.60
98 Sergei Kostitsyn	.30	.75
99 Andrei Kostitsyn	.25	.60
100 Josh Harding	.25	.60
101 Marian Gaborik	.50	1.25
102 Mikko Koivu	.30	.75
103 James Sheppard	.30	.75
104 Nick Schultz	.20	.50
105 Pierre-Marc Bouchard	.20	.50
106 Benoit Pouliot	.20	.50
107 Anze Kopitar	.30	.75
108 Jack Johnson	.25	.60
109 Jason LaBarbera	.25	.60
110 Dustin Brown	.20	.50
111 Patrick O'Sullivan	.25	.60
112 Tomas Vokoun	.30	.75
113 Stephen Weiss	.20	.50
114 Nathan Horton	.20	.50
115 Jay Bouwmeester	.25	.60
116 David Booth	.20	.50
117 Rostislav Olesz	.20	.50
118 Fernando Pisani	.20	.50
119 Andrew Cogliano	.50	1.25
120 Shawn Horcoff	.20	.50
121 Sheldon Souray	.20	.50
122 Ales Hemsky	.20	.50
123 Mathieu Garon	.30	.75
124 Robert Nilsson	.20	.50
125 Dustin Penner	.20	.50
126 Henrik Zetterberg	.60	1.50
127 Chris Osgood	.30	.75
128 Nicklas Lidstrom	.30	.75
129 Kris Draper	.20	.50
130 Jiri Hudler	.20	.50
131 Niklas Kronwall	.25	.60
132 Tomas Holmstrom	.25	.60
133 Mike Modano	.30	.75
134 Sergei Zubov	.20	.50
135 Brenden Morrow	.25	.60
136 Brad Richards	.25	.60
137 Trevor Daley	.20	.50
138 Matt Niskanen	.20	.50
139 Steve Ott	.25	.60
140 Rick Nash	.30	.75
141 Pascal Leclaire	.25	.60
142 Jared Boll	.25	.60
143 Rostislav Klesla	.30	.75
144 Kris Russell	.30	.75
145 Michael Peca	.25	.60
146 Ole-Kristian Tollefsen	.20	.50
147 Paul Stastny	.30	.75
148 John-Michael Liles	.20	.50
149 Marek Svatos	.20	.50
150 Peter Budaj	.25	.60
151 Ryan Smyth	.25	.60
152 Milan Hejduk	.25	.60
153 Jordan Leopold	.20	.50
154 Wojtek Wolski	.20	.50
155 Jonathan Toews	1.00	2.50
156 Patrick Sharp	.20	.50
157 Adam Burish	.25	.60
158 Cam Barker	.20	.50
159 Martin Havlat	.25	.60
160 Duncan Keith	.25	.60
161 Robert Lang	.20	.50
162 Eric Staal	.50	1.25
163 Tuomo Ruutu	.30	.75
164 Joe Corvo	.20	.50
165 Rod Brind'Amour	.25	.60
166 Matt Cullen	.20	.50
167 Ray Whitney	.20	.50
168 Daymond Langkow	.20	.50
169 Jarome Iginla	.60	1.50
170 Dion Phaneuf	.30	.75
171 Matthew Lombardi	.20	.50
172 Cory Sarich	.20	.50
173 Adrian Aucoin	.20	.50
174 Maxim Afinogenov	.20	.50
175 Ryan Miller	.30	.75
176 Derek Roy	.20	.50
177 Jason Pominville	.25	.60
178 Jaroslav Spacek	.20	.50
179 Drew Stafford	.30	.75
180 Phil Kessel	.30	.75
181 Tim Thomas	.30	.75
182 Zdeno Chara	.20	.50
183 Manny Fernandez	.30	.75
184 Milan Lucic	.60	1.50
185 Mark Stuart	.20	.50
186 Chuck Kobasew	.20	.50
187 Kari Lehtonen	.20	.50
188 Tobias Enstrom	.30	.75
189 Ilya Kovalchuk	.40	1.00
190 Colby Armstrong	.20	.50
101 Todd White	.20	.60
192 Erik Christensen	.20	.50
193 Ryan Getzlaf	.40	1.00
194 Chris Kunitz	.20	.50
195 Scott Niedermayer	.20	.50
196 Bobby Ryan	.50	1.25
197 Francois Beauchemin	.20	.50
198 Jean-Sebastien Giguere	.30	.75
199 Martin Brodeur CL	.60	1.50
200 Sidney Crosby CL	1.50	4.00
201 Zach Bogosian YG RC	6.00	15.00
202 Blake Wheeler YG RC	8.00	20.00
203 Adam Pardy YG RC	3.00	8.00
204 Brandon Sutter YG RC	4.00	10.00
205 Jakub Voracek YG RC	6.00	15.00
206 Adam Pineault YG RC	3.00	8.00
207 Derick Brassard YG RC	6.00	15.00
208 Steve Mason YG RC	8.00	20.00
209 James Neal YG RC	5.00	12.00
210 Mark Fistric YG RC	2.50	6.00
211 Justin Abdelkader YG RC	6.00	15.00
212 Jonathan Ericsson YG RC	5.00	12.00
213 Darren Helm YG RC	5.00	12.00
214 Mattias Ritola YG RC	4.00	10.00
215 Tom Sestito YG RC	2.50	6.00
216 Chris Porter YG RC	3.00	8.00
217 Michael Frolik YG RC	6.00	15.00
218 T.J. Oshie YG RC	8.00	20.00
219 Shawn Matthias YG RC	3.00	8.00
220 Drew Doughty YG RC	10.00	25.00
221 Wayne Simmonds YG RC	3.00	8.00
222 Oscar Moller YG RC	3.00	8.00
223 Erik Ersberg YG RC	3.00	8.00
224 Colton Gillies YG RC	3.00	8.00
225 Matt D'Agostini YG RC	5.00	12.00
226 Ryan Jones YG RC	4.00	10.00
227 Patric Hornqvist YG RC	3.00	8.00
228 Anssi Salmela YG RC	4.00	10.00
229 Kyle Okposo YG RC	6.00	15.00
230 Lauri Korpikoski YG RC	3.00	8.00
231 Brian Lee YG RC	3.00	8.00
232 Ilya Zubov YG RC	3.00	8.00
233 Jared Ross YG RC	4.00	10.00
234 Luca Sbisa YG RC	5.00	12.00
235 Claude Giroux YG RC	6.00	15.00
236 Kyle Turris YG RC	6.00	15.00
237 Mikkel Boedker YG RC	5.00	12.00
238 Alex Goligoski YG RC	6.00	15.00
239 Jon Filewich YG RC	2.50	6.00
240 Ryan Stone YG RC	3.00	8.00
241 Alex Pietrangelo YG RC	5.00	12.00
242 Patrik Berglund YG RC	8.00	20.00
243 Vladimir Mihalik YG RC	3.00	8.00
244 Janne Niskala YG RC	3.00	8.00
245 Steven Stamkos YG RC	25.00	60.00
246 John Mitchell YG RC	3.00	8.00
247 Robbie Earl YG RC	2.50	6.00
248 Luke Schenn YG RC	10.00	25.00
249 Mike Brown YG RC	4.00	10.00
250 Drew Doughty Steven Stamkos Alex Pietrangelo CL	6.00	15.00
251 Teemu Selanne	.30	.75
252 Chris Pronger	.25	.60
253 Kent Huskins	.20	.50
254 Jonas Hiller	.30	.75
255 Corey Perry	.30	.75
256 Mathieu Schneider	.20	.50
257 Brett Sterling	.25	.60
258 Johan Hedberg	.25	.60
259 Niclas Havelid	.20	.50
260 Slava Kozlov	.20	.50
261 Bryan Little	.20	.50
262 Jason Williams	.20	.50
263 Ron Hainsey	.20	.50
264 P.J. Axelsson	.20	.50
265 Tuukka Rask	.30	.75
266 Patrice Bergeron	.30	.75
267 Dennis Wideman	.20	.50
268 Marc Savard	.20	.50
269 David Krejci	.25	.60
270 Marco Sturm	.20	.50
271 Thomas Vanek	.30	.75
272 Teppo Numminen	.25	.60
273 Jochen Hecht	.20	.50
274 Tim Connolly	.20	.50
275 Toni Lydman	.20	.50
276 Daniel Paille	.25	.60
277 Paul Gaustad	.25	.60
278 Patrick Lalime	.20	.50
279 Craig Rivet	.20	.50
280 Todd Bertuzzi	.30	.75
281 Robyn Regehr	.20	.50
282 Mike Cammalleri	.30	.75
283 Miikka Kiprusoff	.30	.75
284 Cam Ward	.30	.75
285 Patrick Eaves	.20	.50
286 Joni Pitkanen	.20	.50
287 Sergei Samsonov	.20	.50
288 Scott Walker	.20	.50
289 Tim Gleason	.20	.50
290 Patrick Kane	.75	2.00
291 Nikolai Khabibulin	.30	.75
292 Dustin Byfuglien	.25	.60
293 Brent Seabrook	.25	.60
294 Jack Skille	.25	.60
295 Brian Campbell	.50	1.25
296 Cristobal Huet	.30	.75
297 Joe Sakic	.50	1.25
298 Peter Forsberg	.50	1.25
299 Ian Laperriere	.20	.50
300 Adam Foote	.20	.50
301 Darcy Tucker	.25	.60
302 Andrew Raycroft	.30	.75
303 Kristian Huselius	.20	.50
304 Fedor Tyutin	.20	.50
305 R.J. Umberger	.20	.50
306 Fredrik Norrena	.30	.75
307 Jason Chimera	.20	.50
308 Fredrik Modin	.20	.50
309 Mike Commodore	.20	.50
310 Jere Lehtinen	.20	.50
311 Mike Ribeiro	.20	.50
312 Philippe Boucher	.20	.50
313 Marty Turco	.25	.60
314 Stephane Robidas	.20	.50
315 Toby Petersen	.20	.50
316 Loui Eriksson	.20	.50
317 Sean Avery	.25	.60
318 Pavel Datsyuk	.30	.75
319 Chris Chelios	.40	1.00
320 Mikael Samuelsson	.20	.50
321 Dan Cleary	.30	.75
322 Johan Franzen	.20	.50
323 Brian Rafalski	.20	.50
324 Valtteri Filppula	.20	.50
325 Marian Hossa	.50	1.25
326 Ty Conklin	.25	.60
327 Dwayne Roloson	.25	.60
328 Lubomir Visnovsky	.20	.50
329 Tom Gilbert	.20	.50
330 Sam Gagner	.50	1.25
331 Zach Stortini	.20	.50
332 Erik Cole	.20	.50
333 Craig Anderson	.20	.50
334 Richard Zednik	.20	.50
335 Keith Ballard	.20	.50
336 Nick Boynton	.20	.50
337 Brett McLean	.20	.50
338 Cory Murphy	.20	.50
339 Cory Stillman	.20	.50
340 Jarret Stoll	.25	.60
341 Jonathan Bernier	.40	1.00
342 Alexander Frolov	.20	.50
343 Kyle Calder	.20	.50
344 Derek Armstrong	.20	.50
345 Michal Handzus	.20	.50
346 Tom Preissing	.20	.50
347 Andrew Brunette	.20	.50
348 Niklas Backstrom	.30	.75
349 Owen Nolan	.30	.75
350 Brent Burns	.20	.50
351 Eric Belanger	.20	.50
352 Derek Boogaard	.20	.50
353 Kim Johnsson	.20	.50
354 Marek Zidlicky	.20	.50
355 Andrei Markov	.25	.60
356 Jaroslav Halak	.30	.75
357 Chris Higgins	.20	.50
358 Alex Kovalev	.30	.75
359 Roman Hamrlik	.20	.50
360 Alex Tanguay	.25	.60
361 Marc Denis	.30	.75
362 Jason Arnott	.20	.50
363 J.P. Dumont	.20	.50
364 Dan Ellis	.20	.50
365 Jordin Tootoo	.30	.75
366 Rich Peverley	.20	.50
367 Bobby Holik	.20	.50
368 Zach Parise	.30	.75
369 Jamie Langenbrunner	.20	.50
370 Dainius Zubrus	.20	.50
371 David Clarkson	.20	.50
372 Travis Zajac	.20	.50
373 Brian Rolston	.20	.50
374 Doug Weight	.20	.50
375 Mark Streit	.20	.50
376 Jeff Tambellini	.20	.50
377 Mike Comrie	.20	.50
378 Chris Campoli	.25	.60
379 Sean Bergenheim	.20	.50
380 Richard Park	.20	.50
381 Chris Drury	.30	.75
382 Aaron Voros	.20	.50
383 Nikolai Zherdev	.20	.50
384 Michal Rozsival	.20	.50
385 Daniel Girardi	.20	.50
386 Wade Redden	.20	.50
387 Dany Heatley	.40	1.00
388 Martin Gerber	.25	.60
389 Chris Kelly	.20	.50
390 Chris Phillips	.20	.50
391 Nick Foligno	.30	.75
392 Jeff Carter	.30	.75
393 Antero Niittymaki	.30	.75
394 Braydon Coburn	.20	.50
395 Riley Cote	.20	.50
396 Daniel Briere	.30	.75
397 Scott Hartnell	.25	.60
398 Randy Jones	.20	.50
399 Shane Doan	.20	.50
400 Olli Jokinen	.20	.50
401 Mikael Tellqvist	.30	.75
402 Steven Reinprecht	.30	.75
403 Derek Morris	.20	.50
404 Eric Godard	.20	.50
405 Miroslav Satan	.20	.50
406 Hal Gill	.20	.50
407 Evgeni Malkin	.75	2.00
408 Maxime Talbot	.25	.60
409 Ryan Whitney	.20	.50
410 Patrick Marleau	.25	.60
411 Jeremy Roenick	.30	.75
412 Mike Grier	.20	.50
413 Rob Blake	.30	.75
414 Brad Winchester	.20	.50
415 Keith Tkachuk	.25	.60
416 Chris Mason	.25	.60
417 David Backes	.20	.50
418 Barret Jackman	.20	.50
419 Yan Stastny	.25	.60
420 Mark Recchi	.25	.60
421 Radim Vrbata	.20	.50
422 Ryan Malone	.20	.50
423 Vaclav Prospal	.20	.50
424 Vincent Lecavalier	.30	.75
425 Andrej Meszaros	.20	.50
426 Evgeni Artyukhin	.20	.50
427 Gary Roberts	.20	.50
428 Olaf Kolzig	.30	.75
429 Jeff Finger	.20	.50
430 Curtis Joseph	.30	.75
431 Jason Blake	.20	.50
432 Niklas Hagman	.20	.50
433 Matt Stajan	.25	.60
434 Alexei Ponikarovsky	.20	.50
435 Pavol Demitra	.20	.50
436 Curtis Sanford	.20	.50
437 Cam Colo	.20	.50
438 Kevin Bieksa	.20	.50
439 Steve Bernier	.20	.50
440 Taylor Pyatt	.20	.50
441 Alexandre Burrows	.25	.60
442 Willie Mitchell	.20	.50
443 Jose Theodore	.30	.75
444 Alexander Ovechkin	1.25	3.00
445 Sergei Fedorov	.50	1.25
446 Tom Poti	.20	.50
447 Michael Nylander	.25	.60
448 Brooks Laich	.25	.60
449 Evgeni Malkin CL	.75	2.00
450 Alexander Ovechkin CL	1.25	3.00
451 Andrew Ebbett YG RC	3.00	8.00
452 Brett Festerling YG RC	2.50	6.00
453 Nathan Oystrick YG RC	3.00	8.00
454 Boris Valabik YG RC	4.00	10.00
455 Nathan Gerbe YG RC	6.00	15.00
456 Justin Peters YG RC	3.00	8.00
457 Zach Boychuk YG RC	5.00	12.00
458 Dwight Helminen YG RC	3.00	8.00
459 Patrick Dwyer YG RC	3.00	8.00
460 Simeon Varlamov YG RC	15.00	40.00
461 Joe Jensen YG RC	3.00	8.00
462 Chris Stewart YG RC	4.00	10.00
463 Dan LaCosta YG RC	4.00	10.00
464 Nikita Filatov YG RC	12.00	30.00
465 Derek Dorsett YG RC	4.00	10.00
466 Andrew Murray YG RC	2.50	6.00
467 Fabian Brunnstrom YG RC	5.00	12.00
468 Steve MacIntyre YG RC	3.00	8.00
469 Theo Peckham YG RC	3.00	8.00
470 Michal Repik YG RC	4.00	10.00
471 Jason Garrison YG RC	3.00	8.00
472 Brian Boyle YG RC	3.00	8.00
473 Teddy Purcell YG RC	3.00	8.00
474 Danny Taylor YG RC	3.00	8.00
475 Matthew Halischuk YG RC	4.00	10.00
476 Petr Vrana YG RC	4.00	10.00
477 Patrick Davis YG RC	2.50	6.00
478 Pierre-Luc Letourneau-Leblond YG RC	2.00	5.00
479 Josh Bailey YG RC	5.00	12.00
480 Brett Skinner YG RC	2.50	6.00
481 Mitch Fritz YG RC	2.50	6.00
482 Jesse Winchester YG RC	3.00	8.00
483 Andreas Nodl YG RC	3.00	8.00
484 Kenndal McArdle YG RC	3.00	8.00
485 Darrel Powe YG RC	3.00	8.00
486 Viktor Tikhonov YG RC	3.00	8.00
487 Kevin Porter YG RC	2.50	6.00
488 Janne Pesonen YG RC	2.50	6.00
489 John Curry YG RC	4.00	10.00
490 Jamie McGinn YG RC	3.00	8.00
491 Brad Staubitz YG RC	2.50	6.00
492 Tom Cavanagh YG RC	2.50	6.00

493 Ben Bishop YG RC 5.00 12.00
494 Justin Pogge YG RC 6.00 15.00
495 Nikolai Kulemin YG RC 3.00 8.00
496 Jonas Frogren YG RC 4.00 10.00
497 Cory Schneider YG RC 6.00 15.00
498 Tyler Sloan YG RC 4.00 10.00
499 Karl Alzner YG RC 5.00 12.00
500 Fabian Brunnstrom 4.00 10.00
Viktor Tikhonov
Nikita Filatov CL

2008-09 Upper Deck Exclusives Parallel

*EXCLUSIVES: 2.5X TO 6X BASE
*EXCLUSIVES YG: 1X TO 2.5X BASE
STATED PRINT RUN 100 SERIAL #'d SETS
245 Steven Stamkos YG 100.00 175.00

2008-09 Upper Deck High Gloss Parallel

STATED PRINT RUN 10 SERIAL #'d SETS
NOT PRICED DUE TO SCARCITY

2008-09 Upper Deck All-Stars

COMPLETE SET (30) 40.00 100.00
STATED ODDS 1:
SP STATED ODDS 1:
AS1 Tomas Kaberle .60 1.50
AS2 Daniel Alfredsson .75 2.00
AS3 Marian Hossa 1.50 4.00
AS4 Eric Staal 1.50 4.00
AS5 Rick DiPietro 1.00 2.50
AS6 Anze Kopitar 1.00 2.50
AS7 Zdeno Chara .60 1.50
AS8 Henrik Sedin 1.00 2.50
AS9 Jason Spezza 1.25 3.00
AS10 Shawn Horcoff .60 1.50
AS11 Marian Gaborik 1.50 4.00
AS12 Andrei Markov .75 2.00
AS13 Martin St. Louis 1.00 2.50
AS14 Nicklas Lidstrom 1.00 2.50
AS15 Pavel Datsyuk 1.00 2.50
AS16 Rick Nash 1.00 2.50
AS17 Mike Ribeiro .60 1.50
AS18 Ryan Getzlaf 1.25 3.00
AS19 Tomas Vokoun 1.00 2.50
AS20 Vincent Lecavalier 1.00 2.50
AS21 Joe Thornton SP 5.00 12.00
AS22 Evgeni Nabokov SP 3.00 8.00
AS23 Dion Phaneuf SP 3.00 8.00
AS24 Jarome Iginla SP 6.00 15.00
AS25 Chris Pronger SP 2.50 6.00
AS26 Mike Richards SP 5.00 12.00
AS27 Chris Osgood SP 3.00 8.00
AS28 Evgeni Malkin SP 8.00 20.00
AS29 Alexander Ovechkin SP 12.00 30.00
AS30 Ilya Kovalchuk SP 4.00 10.00

2008-09 Upper Deck All-World Team

COMPLETE SET (20) 60.00 120.00
STATED ODDS 1:
SP STATED ODDS 1:
AWT1 Sidney Crosby 6.00 15.00
AWT2 Alexander Ovechkin 5.00 12.00
AWT3 Evgeni Malkin 3.00 8.00
AWT4 Nicklas Lidstrom 1.25 3.00
AWT5 Martin Brodeur 2.50 6.00
AWT6 Henrik Zetterberg 2.50 6.00
AWT7 Jarome Iginla 2.50 6.00
AWT8 Mike Modano 1.25 3.00
AWT9 Ilya Kovalchuk 1.50 4.00
AWT10 Marian Gaborik 2.00 5.00
AWT11 Joe Thornton SP 8.00 20.00
AWT12 Anze Kopitar SP 5.00 12.00
AWT13 Miikka Kiprusoff SP 5.00 12.00
AWT14 Ales Hemsky SP 3.00 8.00
AWT15 Patrick Kane SP 12.00 30.00
AWT16 Michael Ryder SP 4.00 10.00
AWT17 Scott Gomez SP 4.00 10.00
AWT18 Saku Koivu SP 5.00 12.00
AWT19 Evgeni Nabokov SP 5.00 12.00
AWT20 Markus Naslund SP 5.00 12.00

2008-09 Upper Deck All-World Team Autographs

STATED PRINT RUN 5 SERIAL #'d SETS
NOT PRICED DUE TO SCARCITY

2008-09 Upper Deck Big Game Hunters

COMPLETE SET (30) 125.00 250.00
BGHAK Alex Kovalev 4.00 10.00
BGHAO Alexander Ovechkin SP 15.00 40.00
BGHBR Brad Richards 3.00 8.00
BGHCO Chris Osgood 4.00 10.00
BGHCP Chris Pronger 3.00 8.00
BGHDB Daniel Briere 4.00 10.00
BGHDP Dion Phaneuf 4.00 10.00
BGHEM Evgeni Malkin SP 10.00 25.00
BGHES Eric Staal 6.00 15.00
BGHHZ Henrik Zetterberg SP 8.00 20.00
BGHJF Johan Franzen 2.50 6.00
BGHJG Jean-Sebastien Giguere 4.00 10.00
BGHJI Jarome Iginla SP 8.00 20.00
BGHJS Joe Sakic SP 6.00 15.00
BGHJT Joe Thornton SP 6.00 15.00
BGHMB Martin Brodeur SP 8.00 20.00
BGHMG Marian Gaborik 6.00 15.00
BGHMH Marian Hossa 6.00 15.00
BGHMM Mike Modano 4.00 10.00
BGHMT Marty Turco 3.00 8.00
BGHNL Nicklas Lidstrom 4.00 10.00
BGHPE Patrik Elias 2.50 6.00
BGHPR Carey Price 10.00 25.00
BGHSC Sidney Crosby SP 15.00 40.00
BGHSG Scott Gomez 3.00 8.00
BGHSN Scott Niedermayer 2.50 6.00
BGHST Martin St. Louis 4.00 10.00
BGHTO Jonathan Toews SP 12.00 30.00
BGHTS Teemu Selanne 4.00 10.00
BGHVL Vincent Lecavalier SP 4.00 10.00

2008-09 Upper Deck Biography of a Season

1 Alexander Ovechkin 1.50 4.00
2 Henrik Zetterberg .75 2.00
3 Detroit Red Wings .40 1.00
Nicklas Lidstrom
4 Steven Stamkos 3.00 8.00
5 Fabian Brunnstrom 1.50 4.00
6 Rangers v. Lightning .75 2.00
Henrik Lundqvist
Marc Staal
7 Penguins v. Senators 2.00 5.00
Sidney Crosby
8 Montreal Canadiens 1.25 3.00
Carey Price
9 Jordan Staal .60 1.50
10 Roberto Luongo .60 1.50
11 Patrick Marleau .30 .75
12 Alexander Ovechkin 1.50 4.00
13 Sidney Crosby 2.00 5.00
14 Keith Tkachuk .30 .75
15 Thomas Vanek .40 1.00
16 Scott Hartnell .30 .75
17 Steve Mason 1.00 2.50
18 Henrik Zetterberg .75 2.00
19 Doug Weight .25 .60
20 Carey Price 1.25 3.00
21 Mats Sundin .40 1.00
22 Dion Phaneuf .40 1.00
23 Blake Wheeler 1.00 2.50
24 Alex Kovalev .40 1.00
25 Martin Brodeur .75 2.00
26 Mike Green .25 .60
27 Jarome Iginla .75 2.00
28 Steven Stamkos 3.00 8.00
29 Evgeni Malkin 1.00 2.50
30 Alexander Ovechkin 1.50 4.00

2008-09 Upper Deck Captains Calling

COMPLETE SET (7) 6.00 15.00
STATED ODDS 1:
CPT1 Sidney Crosby 4.00 10.00
CPT2 Jarome Iginla 1.50 4.00
CPT3 Joe Sakic 1.25 3.00
CPT4 Nicklas Lidstrom .75 2.00
CPT5 Saku Koivu .75 2.00
CPT6 Brenden Morrow .60 1.50
CPT7 Rick Nash .75 2.00

2008-09 Upper Deck Clear Cut Duos

STATED PRINT RUN 25 SERIAL #'d SETS
CD1 Mario Lemieux 50.00 120.00
Sidney Crosby
CD2 Evgeni Malkin 25.00 60.00
Jordan Staal
CD3 Wayne Gretzky 50.00 120.00
Mark Messier
CD4 Bobby Orr 30.00 80.00
Phil Esposito
CD5 Ryan Getzlaf 12.00 30.00
Jean-Sebastien Giguere
CD6 Patrick Roy 30.00 80.00
Carey Price
CD7 Teemu Selanne 10.00 25.00
Scott Niedermayer
CD8 Ilya Kovalchuk 12.00 30.00
Kari Lehtonen
CD9 Patrice Bergeron 10.00 25.00
Marc Savard
CD10 Ryan Miller 10.00 25.00
Thomas Vanek
CD11 Jarome Iginla 20.00 50.00
Miikka Kiprusoff
CD12 Eric Staal 15.00 40.00
Cam Ward
CD13 Joe Sakic 15.00 40.00
Paul Stastny
CD14 Rick Nash 25.00 60.00
Steve Mason
CD15 Jonathan Toews 30.00 80.00
Patrick Kane
CD16 Mike Modano 10.00 25.00
Marty Turco
CD17 Henrik Zetterberg 20.00 50.00
Pavel Datsyuk
CD18 Sam Gagner 15.00 40.00
Andrew Cogliano
CD19 Tomas Vokoun 10.00 25.00
Nathan Horton
CD20 Anze Kopitar 10.00 25.00
Jack Johnson
CD21 Marian Gaborik 15.00 40.00
Josh Harding
CD22 Carey Price 30.00 80.00
Saku Koivu
CD23 Jason Arnott 6.00 15.00
J.P. Dumont
CD24 Martin Brodeur 10.00 25.00
Zach Parise
CD25 Gordie Howe 40.00 100.00
Henrik Zetterberg
CD26 Henrik Lundqvist 20.00 50.00
Chris Drury
CD27 Mark Messier 12.00 30.00
Brian Leetch
CD28 Jason Spezza 12.00 30.00
Dany Heatley
CD29 Simon Gagne 10.00 25.00
Daniel Briere
CD30 Shane Doan 12.00 30.00
Peter Mueller
CD31 Sidney Crosby 50.00 120.00
Evgeni Malkin
CD32 Joe Thornton 15.00 40.00
Evgeni Nabokov
CD33 Paul Kariya 10.00 25.00
Brad Boyes
CD34 Vincent Lecavalier 10.00 25.00
Martin St. Louis
CD35 Mats Sundin 10.00 25.00
Alexander Steen
CD36 Roberto Luongo 15.00 40.00
Henrik Sedin
CD37 Alexander Ovechkin 40.00 100.00
Nicklas Backstrom
CD38 Ryan Getzlaf 12.00 30.00
Corey Perry
CD39 Chris Osgood 10.00 25.00
Nicklas Lidstrom
CD40 Mats Sundin 10.00 25.00
Tomas Kaberle
CD41 Joe Thornton 15.00 40.00
Patrick Marleau
CD42 Mike Modano 10.00 25.00
Brad Richards

2008-09 Upper Deck Clear Cut Rookies

STATED ODDS 1:288
STATED PRINT RUN 100 SERIAL #'d SETS
CCR1 Ilya Zubov 6.00 15.00
CCR2 Blake Wheeler 25.00 60.00
CCR3 Petr Vrana 8.00 20.00
CCR4 Jakub Voracek 12.00 30.00
CCR5 Kyle Turris 12.00 30.00
CCR6 Viktor Tikhonov 6.00 15.00
CCR7 Brandon Sutter 8.00 20.00
CCR8 Steven Stamkos 40.00 100.00
CCR9 Luke Schenn 25.00 60.00
CCR10 Luca Sbisa 10.00 25.00
CCR11 Mattias Ritola 8.00 20.00
CCR12 Kevin Porter 5.00 12.00
CCR13 Matt D'Agostini 10.00 25.00
CCR14 Alex Pietrangelo 10.00 25.00
CCR15 Nathan Oystrick 6.00 15.00
CCR16 T.J. Oshie 25.00 60.00
CCR17 Kyle Okposo 12.00 30.00
CCR18 Andreas Nodl 6.00 15.00
CCR19 James Neal 10.00 25.00
CCR20 Oscar Moller 6.00 15.00
CCR21 Vladimir Mihalik 6.00 15.00
CCR22 Shawn Matthias 6.00 15.00
CCR23 Steve Mason 40.00 100.00
CCR24 Nikolai Kulemin 6.00 15.00
CCR25 Ryan Jones 8.00 20.00
CCR26 Patric Hornqvist 6.00 15.00
CCR27 Darren Helm 10.00 25.00
CCR28 Alex Goligoski 12.00 30.00
CCR29 Claude Giroux 12.00 30.00
CCR30 Colton Gillies 6.00 15.00
CCR31 Michael Frolik 12.00 30.00
CCR32 Nikita Filatov 25.00 60.00
CCR33 Erik Ersberg 6.00 15.00
CCR34 Robbie Earl 5.00 12.00
CCR35 Drew Doughty 20.00 50.00
CCR36 Fabian Brunnstrom 40.00 100.00
CCR37 Derick Brassard 12.00 30.00
CCR38 Zach Boychuk 10.00 25.00
CCR39 Zach Bogosian 12.00 30.00
CCR40 Mikkel Boedker 10.00 25.00
CCR41 Patrik Berglund 15.00 40.00
CCR42 Justin Abdelkader 12.00 30.00

2008-09 Upper Deck Clear Cut Winners

STATED PRINT RUN 100 SERIAL #'d SETS

2008-09 Upper Deck Fab Four Fabrics

STATED PRINT RUN 100 SERIAL #'d SETS
FFANA Teemu Selanne 12.00 30.00
Ryan Getzlaf
Jean-Sebastien Giguere
Scott Niedermayer
FFASG Sidney Crosby 50.00 120.00
Joe Sakic
Joe Thornton
Vincent Lecavalier
FFATL Ilya Kovalchuk 12.00 30.00
Kari Lehtonen
Colby Armstrong
Tobias Enstrom
FFBOS Patrice Bergeron 10.00 25.00
Marc Savard
Phil Kessel
Zdeno Chara
FFBUF Thomas Vanek 10.00 25.00
Ryan Miller
Drew Stafford
Tim Connolly
FFCAN Jarome Iginla 20.00 50.00
Michael Ryder
Jonathan Cheechoo
Mike Ribeiro
FFCAR Eric Staal 15.00 40.00
Cam Ward
Justin Williams
Rod Brind'Amour
FFCEN Eric Staal 15.00 40.00
Jason Spezza
Mike Richards
Patrice Bergeron
FFCGY Jarome Iginla 20.00 50.00
Dion Phaneuf
Miikka Kiprusoff
Mike Cammalleri
FFCHI Jonathan Toews 30.00 80.00
Patrick Kane
Duncan Keith
Nikolai Khabibulin
FFCLB Rick Nash 8.00 20.00
Pascal Leclaire
Alexandre Picard
Michael Peca
FFCOL Joe Sakic 15.00 40.00
Peter Forsberg
Paul Stastny
Wojtek Wolski
FFCZS Marian Hossa 15.00 40.00
Milan Hejduk
Patrik Elias
Milan Michalek
FFDAL Mike Modano 10.00 25.00
Marty Turco
Brad Richards
Brenden Morrow
FFDEF Dion Phaneuf 12.00 30.00
Jack Johnson
Erik Johnson
Shea Weber
FFDET Henrik Zetterberg 20.00 50.00
Pavel Datsyuk
Nicklas Lidstrom
Chris Chelios
FFEDM Sam Gagner 15.00 40.00
Ales Hemsky
Gilbert Brule
Dwayne Roloson
FFFIN Teemu Selanne 10.00 25.00
Saku Koivu
Olli Jokinen
Mikko Koivu
FFFLA Tomas Vokoun 10.00 25.00
Nathan Horton
Jay Bouwmeester
Stephen Weiss
FFLAK Anze Kopitar 10.00 25.00
Alexander Frolov
Jack Johnson
Dustin Brown
FFMIN Marian Gaborik 10.00 25.00
Mikko Koivu
Pierre-Marc Bouchard
Owen Nolan
FFMTL Alex Kovalev 10.00 25.00
Alex Tanguay
Guillaume Latendresse
Saku Koivu
FFNAS Jason Arnott 8.00 20.00
Shea Weber
J.P. Dumont
David Legwand
FFNET Marty Turco 10.00 25.00
Manny Legace
Dwayne Roloson
Tim Thomas
FFNJD Martin Brodeur 10.00 25.00
Zach Parise
Brian Gionta
Patrik Elias
FFNYI Rick DiPietro 10.00 25.00
Doug Weight
Bill Guerin
Mike Comrie
FFNYR Henrik Lundqvist 20.00 50.00
Nikolai Zherdev
Scott Gomez
Chris Drury
FFOTT Dany Heatley 12.00 30.00
Jason Spezza
Daniel Alfredsson
Chris Phillips
FFPHI Simon Gagne 15.00 40.00
Mike Richards
Daniel Briere
Jeff Carter
FFPHX Peter Mueller 12.00 30.00
Shane Doan
Olli Jokinen
Ed Jovanovski
FFPIT Sidney Crosby 50.00 120.00
Evgeni Malkin
Jordan Staal
Ryan Whitney
FFQUE Martin Brodeur 20.00 50.00
Roberto Luongo
Marc-Andre Fleury
Jose Theodore
FFRUS Alexander Ovechkin 40.00 100.00
Evgeni Malkin
Ilya Kovalchuk
Sergei Fedorov
FFSJS Joe Thornton 15.00 40.00
Jonathan Cheechoo
Patrick Marleau
Milan Michalek
FFSTL Paul Kariya 10.00 25.00
Brad Boyes
Keith Tkachuk
Manny Legace
FFSWE Mats Sundin 20.00 50.00
Markus Naslund
Nicklas Backstrom
Henrik Zetterberg
FFTBL Vincent Lecavalier 10.00 25.00
Martin St. Louis
Paul Ranger
Jussi Jokinen
FFTOR Mats Sundin 10.00 25.00
Alexander Steen
Jason Blake
Vesa Toskala
FFUSA Jeremy Roenick 12.00 30.00
Mike Modano
Keith Tkachuk
Chris Chelios
FFVAN Roberto Luongo 15.00 40.00
Daniel Sedin
Henrik Sedin
Steve Bernier
FFWAS Alexander Ovechkin 40.00 100.00
Nicklas Backstrom
Alexander Semin
Mike Green
FFWNG Rick Nash 12.00 30.00
Dany Heatley
Simon Gagne
Martin St. Louis

2008-09 Upper Deck Favourite Sons

COMPLETE SET (14) 12.00 30.00
BASIC SER.2 INSERT ODDS 1:4

2008-09 Upper Deck Game Jerseys

STATED ODDS 1:12
GJAA Alex Auld 3.00 8.00
GJAE Alexander Edler 4.00 10.00
GJAH Ales Hemsky 3.00 8.00
GJAK Alex Kovalev 5.00 12.00
GJAL Alexander Steen 5.00 12.00
GJAM Andrej Meszaros 3.00 8.00
GJAN Antero Niittymaki 5.00 12.00
GJAO Alexander Ovechkin 20.00 50.00
GJAP Alexandre Picard 3.00 8.00
GJAS Alexander Semin 5.00 12.00
GJAT Alex Tanguay 4.00 10.00
GJBB Brad Boyes 4.00 10.00
GJBE Brendan Bell 3.00 8.00
GJBG Bill Guerin 3.00 8.00
GJBM Brenden Morrow 4.00 10.00
GJBR Brad Richards 4.00 10.00
GJCA Colby Armstrong 3.00 8.00
GJCC Chris Chelios 6.00 15.00
GJCD Chris Drury 5.00 12.00
Wearing a White Uniform
GJCP Chris Phillips 3.00 8.00
GJCW Cam Ward 5.00 12.00
GJDA Daniel Alfredsson 4.00 10.00
GJDB Daniel Briere 5.00 12.00
GJDH Dany Heatley 6.00 15.00
GJDK Duncan Keith 4.00 10.00
GJDL David Legwand 4.00 10.00
GJDP Dion Phaneuf 5.00 12.00
GJDR Dwayne Roloson 4.00 10.00
GJDS Daniel Sedin 5.00 12.00
GJDT Darcy Tucker 4.00 10.00
GJDW Doug Weight 3.00 8.00
GJEC Erik Cole 3.00 8.00
GJEN Evgeni Nabokov 5.00 12.00
GJES Eric Staal 8.00 20.00
GJGA Marian Gaborik 8.00 20.00
GJGB Gilbert Brule 5.00 12.00
GJGI Brian Gionta 5.00 12.00
GJGM Glen Murray 3.00 8.00
GJGR Gary Roberts 3.00 8.00
GJHT Hannu Toivonen 4.00 10.00
GJHZ Henrik Zetterberg 10.00 25.00
GJIK Ilya Kovalchuk 6.00 15.00
Wearing a white uniform
GJIW Ian White 3.00 8.00
GJJA Jason Arnott 3.00 8.00
GJJB Jay Bouwmeester 4.00 10.00
GJJC Jonathan Cheechoo 5.00 12.00
GJJE Jeff Carter 5.00 12.00
GJJG Jean-Sebastien Giguere 5.00 12.00
GJJI Jarome Iginla 10.00 25.00
GJJO Jussi Jokinen 3.00 8.00
GJJP Joni Pitkanen 3.00 8.00
GJJR Jeremy Roenick 5.00 12.00
GJJS Jason Spezza 6.00 15.00
GJJT Joe Thornton 8.00 20.00
GJKA Patrick Kane 12.00 30.00
GJKL Kari Lehtonen 3.00 8.00
GJKO Anze Kopitar 5.00 12.00
GJKT Keith Tkachuk 4.00 10.00
GJLE Manny Legace 4.00 10.00
GJLS Lee Stempniak 3.00 8.00
GJMA Marc Savard 3.00 8.00
GJMB Martin Brodeur 10.00 25.00
GJMC Mike Cammalleri 5.00 12.00
GJMG Mike Green 3.00 8.00
GJMK Miikka Kiprusoff 5.00 12.00
GJML Mario Lemieux 12.00 30.00
GJMM Mark Messier 10.00 25.00
GJMN Markus Naslund 5.00 12.00
GJMO Mike Modano 5.00 12.00
GJMR Mark Recchi 4.00 10.00
GJMS Matt Stajan 4.00 10.00
GJMT Marty Turco 4.00 10.00
GJNZ Nikolai Zherdev 3.00 8.00
GJOJ Olli Jokinen 3.00 8.00
GJPA Patrice Bergeron 5.00 12.00
GJPB Pierre-Marc Bouchard 3.00 8.00
GJPF Peter Forsberg 8.00 20.00
GJPK Paul Kariya 5.00 12.00
GJPL Pascal Leclaire 4.00 10.00
GJPR Patrick Roy 15.00 40.00
GJPS Paul Stastny 5.00 12.00
GJRA Andrew Raycroft 5.00 12.00
GJRB Brian Rafalski 3.00 8.00
GJRI Mike Richards 8.00 20.00
GJRL Roberto Luongo 8.00 20.00
GJRN Rick Nash 5.00 12.00
GJRY Michael Ryder 4.00 10.00
GJSA Joe Sakic 8.00 20.00
GJSC Sidney Crosby 25.00 60.00
GJSM Ladislav Smid 3.00 8.00
GJST Martin St. Louis 5.00 12.00
GJSU Mats Sundin 5.00 12.00
Blue Uniform
GJTH Jose Theodore 5.00 12.00
GJTI Kimmo Timonen 3.00 8.00
GJTS Teemu Selanne 5.00 12.00
GJTV Thomas Vanek 5.00 12.00
GJWG Wayne Gretzky 25.00 60.00
GJ2AA Arron Asham 4.00 10.00
GJ2AF Maxim Afinogenov 3.00 8.00
GJ2AL Andrew Ladd 3.00 8.00
GJ2AO Alexander Ovechkin 20.00 50.00
GJ2AV Nik Antropov 4.00 10.00
GJ2AW Andrew Wozniewski 5.00 12.00
GJ2BB Brandon Bochenski 4.00 10.00
GJ2BD Martin Brodeur 10.00 25.00
GJ2BL Brian Leetch 6.00 15.00
GJ2BM Brendan Morrison 3.00 8.00
GJ2BS Brad Stuart 3.00 8.00
GJ2CA Matt Carle 3.00 8.00
GJ2CC Chris Campoli 4.00 10.00
GJ2CD Chris Drury 5.00 12.00
Wearing a Blue Uniform
GJ2CJ Curtis Joseph 5.00 12.00
GJ2CP Carey Price 15.00 40.00
GJ2CS Curtis Sanford 3.00 8.00
GJ2DB Donald Brashear 3.00 8.00
GJ2DT Darcy Tucker 4.00 10.00
GJ2EC Erik Cole 3.00 8.00
GJ2EJ Ed Jovanovski 3.00 8.00
GJ2EM Evgeni Malkin 12.00 30.00
GJ2ES Eric Staal 8.00 20.00
GJ2FZ Manny Fernandez 5.00 12.00
GJ2HA Martin Havlat 4.00 10.00
GJ2HE Milan Hejduk 4.00 10.00
GJ2HL Henrik Lundqvist 10.00 25.00
GJ2HO Marian Hossa 8.00 20.00
GJ2IK Ilya Kovalchuk 6.00 15.00
Wearing a blue uniform
GJ2JS Jarret Stoll 4.00 10.00
GJ2JT Jeff Tambellini 3.00 8.00
GJ2JW Justin Williams 3.00 8.00
GJ2KC Kyle Calder 3.00 8.00
GJ2KZ Viktor Kozlov 3.00 8.00
GJ2MA Mark Stuart 3.00 8.00
GJ2MC Bryan McCabe 3.00 8.00
GJ2MD Marc Denis 5.00 12.00
GJ2ME Martin Erat 5.00 12.00
GJ2MF Marc-Andre Fleury 8.00 20.00
GJ2MG Martin Gerber 4.00 10.00
GJ2MK Mikko Koivu 5.00 12.00
GJ2ML Milan Lucic 10.00 25.00
GJ2MM Mark Messier 10.00 25.00
GJ2MN Matt Niskanen 3.00 8.00
GJ2MO Mattias Ohlund 3.00 8.00
GJ2MP Marc-Antoine Pouliot 5.00 12.00
GJ2MR Mark Recchi 4.00 10.00
GJ2MS Marc Savard 3.00 8.00
GJ2MT Marty Turco 4.00 10.00
GJ2OJ Olli Jokinen 3.00 8.00
GJ2PE Michael Peca 4.00 10.00
GJ2PH Chris Phillips 3.00 8.00
GJ2PM Peter Mueller 6.00 15.00
GJ2PY Corey Perry 5.00 12.00
GJ2RB Mike Ribeiro 3.00 8.00
GJ2RO Patrick Roy 15.00 40.00
GJ2RU Tuomo Ruutu 5.00 12.00
GJ2SB Steve Bernier 3.00 8.00
GJ2SE Brent Seabrook 4.00 10.00
GJ2SG Simon Gagne 4.00 10.00
GJ2SH Brendan Shanahan 5.00 12.00
GJ2ST Jordan Staal 8.00 20.00
GJ2SU Mats Sundin 5.00 12.00
White Uniform
GJ2SV Marek Svatos 3.00 8.00
GJ2SW Shea Weber 3.00 8.00
GJ2TO Jonathan Toews 15.00 40.00
GJ2TW Tiger Williams 3.00 8.00
GJ2VL Vincent Lecavalier 5.00 12.00

2008-09 Upper Deck Game Patches

STATED PRINT RUN 15 SERIAL #'d SETS
NOT PRICED DUE TO SCARCITY

2008-09 Upper Deck Hat Trick Heroes

COMPLETE SET (14) 6.00 15.00
STATED ODDS 1:
HT1 Alexander Ovechkin 2.50 6.00
HT2 Teemu Selanne .60 1.50
HT3 Jarome Iginla 1.25 3.00
HT4 Joe Sakic 1.00 2.50
HT5 Thomas Vanek .60 1.50
HT6 Evgeni Malkin 1.50 4.00
HT7 Ilya Kovalchuk .75 2.00
HT8 Vincent Lecavalier .60 1.50
HT9 Henrik Zetterberg 1.25 3.00
HT10 Dany Heatley .75 2.00
HT11 Rick Nash .60 1.50
HT12 Marian Gaborik 1.00 2.50
HT13 Marian Hossa 1.00 2.50
HT14 Eric Staal 1.00 2.50

2008-09 Upper Deck Hockey Heroes Sidney Crosby

COMPLETE SET (10) 75.00 150.00
COMP.SET w/o SPs (8) 12.00 30.00
COMMON CROSBY (HH1-HH8) 3.00 8.00
STATED ODD 1:
HH9 Sidney Crosby Painting 20.00 50.00
HHSCA Sidney Crosby AU/87 175.00 300.00
HHSC Sidney Crosby Header Card 40.00 80.00

2008-09 Upper Deck Masked Men

COMPLETE SET (30) 25.00 60.00
STATED ODDS 1:
SP STATED ODDS 1:
MM1 Martin Brodeur 2.00 5.00
MM2 Miikka Kiprusoff 1.00 2.50
MM3 Roberto Luongo 1.50 4.00
MM4 Chris Osgood 1.00 2.50
MM5 Carey Price 3.00 8.00
MM6 Henrik Lundqvist 2.00 5.00
MM7 Ryan Miller 1.00 2.50
MM8 Vesa Toskala 1.00 2.50
MM9 Jean-Sebastien Giguere 1.00 2.50
MM10 Evgeni Nabokov 1.00 2.50
MM11 Marty Turco .75 2.00
MM12 Manny Legace .75 2.00
MM13 Mathieu Garon 1.00 2.50
MM14 Martin Gerber .75 2.00
MM15 Josh Harding .75 2.00
MM16 Tomas Vokoun 1.00 2.50
MM17 Rick DiPietro 1.00 2.50
MM18 Kari Lehtonen .60 1.50
MM19 Marc-Andre Fleury 1.00 2.50
MM20 Cam Ward 1.00 2.50
MM21 Pascal Leclaire SP 1.00 2.50
MM22 Peter Budaj SP 1.00 2.50
MM23 Martin Biron SP 1.00 2.50
MM24 Tim Thomas SP 1.25 3.00
MM25 Cristobal Huet SP 1.25 3.00
MM26 Mike Smith SP 1.00 2.50
MM27 Chris Mason SP 1.00 2.50
MM28 Nikolai Khabibulin SP 1.25 3.00

MM29 Ilya Bryzgalov SP .75 2.00
MM30 Jason LaBarbera SP 1.00 2.50

2008-09 Upper Deck Rookie Impressions

COMPLETE SET (30) 100.00 200.00

2008-09 Upper Deck Rookie Materials

COMPLETE SET (30)
OVERALL SER.2 MEM ODDS 1:12

2008-09 Upper Deck Rookie Materials Patches

STATED PRINT RUN 15 SERIAL #'d SETS
NOT PRICED DUE TO SCARCITY

2008-09 Upper Deck Rookie Playmakers

STATED ODDS 1:288
STATED PRINT RUN 100 SERIAL #'d SETS
RPAG Alex Goligoski 12.00 30.00
RPAP Alex Pietrangelo 10.00 25.00
RPBB Brian Boyle 6.00 15.00
RPBG Zach Bogosian 12.00 30.00
RPBL Brian Lee 6.00 15.00
RPBS Brandon Sutter 8.00 20.00
RPBW Blake Wheeler 15.00 40.00
RPCG Colton Gillies 6.00 15.00
RPDB Derick Brassard 12.00 30.00
RPDD Drew Doughty 20.00 50.00
RPEE Erik Ersberg 6.00 15.00
RPFB Fabian Brunnstrom 10.00 25.00
RPFR Michael Frolik 12.00 30.00
RPGI Claude Giroux 12.00 30.00
RPIZ Ilya Zubov 6.00 15.00
RPJA Justin Abdelkader 12.00 30.00
RPJN James Neal 10.00 25.00
RPJV Jakub Voracek 12.00 30.00
RPKO Kyle Okposo 12.00 30.00
RPKP Kevin Porter 5.00 12.00
RPKT Kyle Turris 12.00 30.00
RPLK Lauri Korpikoski 6.00 15.00
RPLS Luca Sbisa 10.00 25.00
RPMA Shawn Matthias 6.00 15.00
RPMB Mikkel Boedker 10.00 25.00
RPMF Mark Fistric 5.00 12.00
RPNF Nikita Filatov 25.00 60.00
RPNK Nikolai Kulemin 6.00 15.00
RPOM Oscar Moller 6.00 15.00
RPPB Patrik Berglund 15.00 40.00
RPPH Patric Hornqvist 6.00 15.00
RPPV Petr Vrana 8.00 20.00
RPRE Robbie Earl 5.00 12.00
RPRS Ryan Stone 6.00 15.00
RPSC Luke Schenn 25.00
RPSM Steve Mason 25.00 60.00
RPSS Steven Stamkos 50.00 120.00
RPTO T.J. Oshie 15.00 40.00
RPTS Tom Sestito 5.00 12.00
RPVM Vladimir Mihalik 6.00 15.00
RPVT Viktor Tikhonov 6.00 15.00
RPZB Zach Boychuk 10.00 25.00

2008-09 Upper Deck Signature Sensations

STATED ODDS 1:288
CARD NUMBERS SS2 ARE FROM SER.2
SSAC Andrew Cogliano 12.00 30.00
SSAO Alexander Ovechkin
SSBB Brendan Bell Coyotes 5.00 12.00
SSBC Blake Comeau
SSBD Brandon Dubinsky road 10.00 25.00
SSBM Bryan McCabe 6.00 15.00
SSBO Johnny Boychuk 5.00 12.00
SSBR Bobby Ryan skating 12.00 30.00
SSCB Casey Borer 8.00 20.00
SSCH Chris Higgins
SSCL Dan Cleary 15.00 40.00
SSCM Cory Murphy
SSCP Chris Phillips 5.00 12.00
SSCS Cory Stillman home 5.00 12.00
SSDA Daniel Sedin 8.00 20.00
SSDB Dan Boyle 6.00 15.00
SSDC Daniel Carcillo road 5.00 12.00
SSDG Daniel Girardi 10.00 25.00
SSDI Dimitri Patzold 5.00 12.00
SSDJ David Jones 5.00 12.00
SSDL Drew Larman 5.00 12.00
SSDM Drew MacIntyre 8.00 20.00
SSDP Dustin Penner
SSDS Drew Stafford 8.00 20.00
SSGH Gordie Howe
SSGL Guillaume Latendresse 15.00 40.00
SSGM Greg Moore 5.00 12.00
SSHA Jaroslav Halak 8.00 20.00
SSHE T.J. Hensick 10.00 25.00
SSHI Jonas Hiller 8.00 20.00
SSHJ Jannik Hansen 8.00 20.00
SSHS Henrik Sedin 15.00 40.00
SSJA Jared Boll 6.00 15.00
SSJB Jonathan Bernier skating 10.00 25.00
SSJD Jeff Drouin-Deslauriers 10.00 25.00
SSJG Jean-Sebastien Giguere
SSJH Josh Harding road 6.00 15.00
SSJL John-Michael Liles 5.00 12.00
SSJO Joe Thornton
SSJP Jason Pominville 12.00 30.00
SSJS Jordan Staal 12.00 30.00
SSJT Jonathan Toews 20.00 50.00
SSKN Kevin Nastiuk 5.00 12.00
SSKQ Kyle Quincey
SSKR Kris Russell
SSLK Lukas Kaspar 5.00 12.00
SSLT Lauri Tukonen 5.00 12.00
SSLU Joffrey Lupul
SSMA Mark Mancari
SSME Matt Ellis Kings 5.00 12.00
SSMF Mark Fraser portrait 6.00 15.00
SSMH Michal Handzus 5.00 12.00
SSMI Milan Michalek 12.00 30.00
SSMK Mike Knuble 8.00 20.00
SSML Milan Lucic 15.00 40.00
SSMM Marc Methot 5.00 12.00
SSMN Matt Niskanen face front 5.00 12.00
SSMO Mike Modano
SSMP Marc-Antoine Pouliot 8.00 20.00
SSMR Mason Raymond 5.00 12.00
SSMS Marek Schwarz profile view 8.00 20.00
SSNA Markus Naslund
SSNK Nikolai Khabibulin profile view 12.00 30.00
SSNW Noah Welch
SSPA Ryan Parent 10.00 25.00
SSPD Daniel Paille road 6.00 15.00
SSPE Rod Pelley 5.00 12.00
SSPK Patrick Kane 20.00 50.00
SSPM Peter Mueller 10.00 25.00
SSPS Paul Stastny
SSRB Rene Bourque 8.00 20.00
SSRC Ryane Clowe 10.00 25.00
SSRI Rich Peverley 5.00 12.00
SSRK Rostislav Klesla 8.00 20.00
SSRP Ryan Potulny
SSRS Ryan Smyth boards 6.00 15.00
SSSC Sidney Crosby road 75.00 150.00
SSSD Steve Downie 8.00 20.00
SSSE Devin Setoguchi 8.00 20.00
SSSJ Jack Skille
SSSM Stefan Meyer 5.00 12.00
SSST Marco Sturm 5.00 12.00
SSSW Stephen Weiss 5.00 12.00
SSTG Tom Gilbert 10.00 25.00
SSTH Tomas Holmstrom
SSTK Tyler Kennedy 6.00 15.00
SSTL Jiri Tlusty boards w/crowd 8.00 20.00
SSTP Tomas Plihal
SSTS Tobias Stephan 15.00 40.00
SSTV Thomas Vanek
SSTZ Travis Zajac road 5.00 12.00
SS2AB Adam Burish 10.00 25.00
SS2AG Andy Greene 6.00 15.00
SS2AR Andrew Raycroft 8.00 20.00
SS2BB Brad Boyes 6.00 15.00
SS2BD Brandon Dubinsky home 10.00 25.00
SS2BH Bobby Hull
SS2BL Brendan Bell Senators 5.00 12.00
SS2BO Martin Brodeur
SS2BQ Rene Bourque 8.00 20.00
SS2BR Bobby Ryan standing 12.00 30.00
SS2BS Brett Sterling 6.00 15.00
SS2CB Chris Bourque 6.00 15.00
SS2CD Chris Drury
SS2CH Chuck Kobasew 5.00 12.00
SS2CK Chris Kunitz
SS2CO Jiri Tlusty boards 8.00 20.00
SS2CS Cory Stillman road 5.00 12.00
SS2DA Daniel Sedin home 8.00 20.00
SS2DC Daniel Carcillo home 5.00 12.00
SS2DP Daniel Paille home 6.00 15.00
SS2DR Dwayne Roloson 6.00 15.00
SS2DS Derek Sanderson 12.00 30.00
SS2DS2 Drew Stafford road 8.00 20.00
SS2DT Darcy Tucker 6.00 15.00
SS2DV David Perron 6.00 15.00
SS2EM Evgeni Malkin
SS2EN Evgeni Nabokov 8.00 20.00
SS2GH Gordie Howe
SS2HG Josh Harding home 6.00 15.00
SS2IK Marc-Antoine Pouliot road 8.00 20.00
SS2JB Jonathan Bernier in-goal 10.00 25.00
SS2JG Jean-Sebastien Giguere 25.00 60.00
SS2JH Jannik Hansen 8.00 20.00
SS2JL John-Michael Liles 5.00 12.00
SS2JM Jay McClement 5.00 12.00
SS2JP Jason Pominville
SS2JS Jordan Staal home 12.00 30.00
SS2KA Petr Kalus 6.00 15.00
SS2KB Nikolai Khabibulin face front 12.00 30.00
SS2KC Kyle Chipchura 5.00 12.00
SS2ME Matt Ellis Sabres 5.00 12.00
SS2MH Milan Hejduk 15.00 40.00
SS2ML Mike Lundin 5.00 12.00
SS2MN Matt Niskanen profile view 5.00 12.00
SS2MO Brendan Morrison
SS2MR Mike Richards
SS2MS Mark Fraser in-action 6.00 15.00
SS2MY Stefan Meyer 5.00 12.00
SS2NW Noah Welch 5.00 12.00
SS2NZ Nikolai Zherdev 10.00 25.00
SS2OR Bobby Orr 75.00 150.00
SS2PA Patrick Kane
SS2PK Phil Kessel
SS2PV Rich Peverley 5.00 12.00
SS2PY Ryan Potulny 5.00 12.00
SS2RA Mason Raymond 5.00 12.00
SS2RI Mike Ribeiro
SS2RK Rostislav Klesla 8.00 20.00
SS2RS Ryan Smyth boards w/crowd 6.00 15.00
SS2SC Sidney Crosby home 75.00 150.00
SS2SE Devin Setoguchi road 8.00 20.00
SS2SH James Sheppard 8.00 20.00
SS2SJ Jack Skille road 6.00 15.00
SS2SM Matt Smaby 6.00 15.00
SS2ST Marc Staal 10.00 25.00
SS2SW Marek Schwarz face front 8.00 20.00
SS2TE Tobias Enstrom 8.00 20.00
SS2TJ T.J. Hensick 10.00 25.00
SS2TM Torrey Mitchell 8.00 20.00
SS2TP Tomas Popperle 6.00 15.00
SS2TR Tuukka Rask 20.00 50.00
SS2TZ Travis Zajac home 5.00 12.00
SS2WG Wayne Gretzky

2008-09 Upper Deck Sophomore Sensations

COMPLETE SET (7) 8.00 20.00
STATED ODDS 1:
SS1 Patrick Kane 2.50 6.00
SS2 Jonathan Toews 3.00 8.00
SS3 Carey Price 3.00 8.00
SS4 Marc Staal 1.25 3.00
SS5 Sam Gagner 1.50 4.00
SS6 Peter Mueller 1.25 3.00
SS7 Nicklas Backstrom 2.00 5.00

2008-09 Upper Deck Spectacular Saves

COMPLETE SET (7) 8.00 20.00
BASIC SER.2 INSERTS 1:4
SAVE1 Chris Osgood 1.25 3.00
SAVE2 Evgeni Nabokov 1.25 3.00
SAVE3 Henrik Lundqvist 2.50 6.00
SAVE4 Jean-Sebastien Giguere 1.25 3.00
SAVE5 Martin Brodeur 2.50 6.00
SAVE6 Marty Turco 1.00 2.50
SAVE7 Roberto Luongo 2.00 5.00

2008-09 Upper Deck Super Skills

COMPLETE SET (20) 150.00 300.00
STATED ODDS 1:
SP STATED ODDS 1:
SS1 Martin Brodeur 6.00 15.00
SS2 Sidney Crosby 15.00 40.00
SS3 Alexander Ovechkin 12.00 30.00
SS4 Joe Thornton 5.00 12.00
SS5 Jarome Iginla 6.00 15.00
SS6 Martin St. Louis 3.00 8.00
SS7 Ilya Kovalchuk 4.00 10.00
SS8 Jonathan Toews 10.00 25.00
SS9 Evgeni Malkin 8.00 20.00
SS10 Henrik Zetterberg 6.00 15.00
SS11 Rick Nash SP 6.00 15.00
SS12 Carey Price SP 20.00 50.00
SS13 Ryan Getzlaf SP 8.00 20.00
SS14 Mike Richards SP 10.00 25.00
SS15 Paul Stastny SP 6.00 15.00
SS16 Andrew Cogliano SP 10.00 25.00
SS17 Peter Mueller SP 8.00 20.00
SS18 Anze Kopitar SP 6.00 15.00
SS19 Nicklas Backstrom SP 12.00 30.00
SS20 Eric Staal SP 10.00 25.00

2008-09 Upper Deck Super Skills Autographs

STATED PRINT RUN 5 SERIAL #'d SETS
NOT PRICED DUE TO SCARCITY

2008-09 Upper Deck Tales of the Cup

COMPLETE SET (7) 4.00 10.00
BASIC INSERTS SER.2 1:4
TC1 Peter Forsberg 1.25 3.00
TC2 Mark Messier 1.50 4.00
TC3 Doug Weight .50 1.25
TC4 Ted Lindsay .75 2.00
TC5 Clark Gillies .60 1.50
TC6 Montreal Canadiens .60 1.50
TC7 Ottawa Senators .60 1.50

2008-09 Upper Deck The New Guard

COMPLETE SET (14) 15.00 40.00
BASIC INSERTS SER.2 1:4
NE1 Anze Kopitar 1.00 2.50
NE2 Alexander Ovechkin 4.00 10.00
NE3 Marian Gaborik 1.50 4.00
NE4 Carey Price 3.00 8.00
NE5 Dion Phaneuf 1.00 2.50
NE6 Evgeni Malkin 2.50 6.00
NE7 Eric Staal 1.50 4.00
NE8 Henrik Lundqvist 2.00 5.00
NE9 Ilya Kovalchuk 1.25 3.00
NE10 Jonathan Toews 3.00 8.00
NE11 Nicklas Backstrom 2.00 5.00
NE12 Patrick Kane 2.50 6.00
NE13 Ryan Getzlaf 1.25 3.00
NE14 Sidney Crosby 5.00 12.00

2008-09 Upper Deck Winter Classic

COMPLETE SET (14) 15.00 40.00
STATED ODDS 1:
WC1 Sidney Crosby 10.00 25.00
WC2 Ryan Miller 2.00 5.00
WC3 Colby Armstrong 1.25 3.00
WC4 Ales Kotalik 1.25 3.00
WC5 Kristopher Letang 1.25 3.00
WC6 Thomas Vanek 2.00 5.00
WC7 Evgeni Malkin
WC8 Brian Campbell 3.00 8.00
WC9 Ty Conklin 1.50 4.00
WC10 Jason Pominville 1.50 4.00
WC11 Ryan Malone 1.25 3.00
WC12 Maxim Afinogenov 1.25 3.00
WC13 Jordan Staal 3.00 8.00
WC14 Tim Connolly 1.25 3.00

2008-09 Upper Deck Young Guns Oversized

COMPLETE SET (14) 30.00 75.00
STATED ODDS ONE PER BLASTER BOX
OYG1 Zach Bogosian 2.00 5.00
OYG2 Blake Wheeler 2.50 6.00
OYG3 Brandon Sutter 1.25 3.00
OYG4 Jakub Voracek 2.00 5.00
OYG5 James Neal 1.50 4.00
OYG6 Drew Doughty 3.00 8.00
OYG7 Colton Gillies 1.00 2.50
OYG8 Kyle Okposo 2.00 5.00
OYG9 Luca Sbisa 1.50 4.00
OYG10 Mikkel Boedker 1.50 4.00
OYG11 Kyle Turris 2.00 5.00
OYG12 Alex Pietrangelo 1.50 4.00
OYG13 Steven Stamkos 8.00 20.00
OYG14 Luke Schenn 3.00 8.00

2009-10 Upper Deck

COMPLETE SET (500) 300.00 600.00
COMP.SER.1 SET (250) 200.00 350.00
COMP.SER.1 SET w/o SPs (200) 15.00 40.00
COMP.SER.2 SET (250) 125.00 250.00
COMP.SER.2 SET w/o SPs (200) 15.00 40.00
YG STATED ODDS 1:4
1 Phil Kessel .30 .75
2 David Krejci .25 .60
3 Mark Recchi .25 .60
4 Zdeno Chara .20 .50
5 Tim Thomas .30 .75
6 Blake Wheeler .40 1.00
7 Dennis Wideman .20 .50
8 Tim Connolly .20 .50
9 Ryan Miller .30 .75
10 Craig Rivet .20 .50
11 Derek Roy .30 .75
12 Nathan Gerbe .40 1.00
13 Daniel Paille .25 .60
14 Chris Butler .30 .75
15 Andrei Markov .25 .60
16 Maxim Lapierre .20 .50
17 Andrei Kostitsyn .25 .60
18 Carey Price .75 2.00
19 Josh Gorges .20 .50
20 Tomas Plekanec .25 .60
21 Georges Laraque .20 .50
22 Jason Spezza .40 1.00
23 Daniel Alfredsson .30 .75
24 Nick Foligno .30 .75
25 Chris Phillips .20 .50
26 Jarkko Ruutu .20 .50
27 Jesse Winchester .25 .60
28 Brian Lee .30 .75
29 Mikhail Grabovski .25 .60
30 Luke Schenn .50 1.25
31 Vesa Toskala .30 .75
32 Matt Stajan .25 .60
33 Alexei Ponikarovsky .20 .50
34 Ian White .20 .50
35 Nikolai Kulemin .25 .60
36 Jeff Carter .30 .75
37 Claude Giroux .60 1.50
38 Ryan Parent .25 .60
39 Simon Gagne .30 .75
40 Daniel Carcillo .30 .75
41 Matt Carle .20 .50
42 Scott Hartnell .20 .50
43 Sidney Crosby 1.50 4.00
44 Maxime Talbot .30 .75
45 Sergei Gonchar .20 .50
46 Ruslan Fedotenko .20 .50
47 Marc-Andre Fleury .30 .75
48 Evgeni Malkin .75 2.00
49 Bill Guerin .20 .50
50 Martin Brodeur .75 2.00
51 Paul Martin .20 .50
52 Patrik Elias .25 .60
53 Johnny Oduya .20 .50
54 David Clarkson .20 .50
55 Jamie Langenbrunner .20 .50
56 Josh Bailey .25 .60
57 Rick DiPietro .30 .75
58 Mark Streit .20 .50
59 Kyle Okposo .30 .75
60 Bruno Gervais .20 .50
61 Doug Weight .20 .50
62 Henrik Lundqvist .60 1.50
63 Sean Avery .20 .50
64 Wade Redden .20 .50
65 Chris Drury .25 .60
66 Michal Rozsival .20 .50
67 Brandon Dubinsky .30 .75
68 Marc Staal .40 1.00
69 Nathan Horton .20 .50
70 David Booth .20 .50
71 Bryan McCabe .25 .60
72 Stephen Weiss .20 .50
73 Keith Ballard .20 .50
74 Michael Frolik .25 .60
75 Bryan Little .30 .75
76 Zach Bogosian .40 1.00
77 Kari Lehtonen .30 .75
78 Todd White .20 .50
79 Tobias Enstrom .30 .75
80 Colby Armstrong .20 .50
81 Rod Brind'Amour .25 .60
82 Eric Staal .40 1.00
83 Joe Corvo .20 .50
84 Chad LaRose .20 .50
85 Jussi Jokinen .30 .75
86 Joni Pitkanen .25 .60
87 Martin St. Louis .30 .75
88 Mike Smith .25 .60
89 Paul Ranger .20 .50
90 Steven Stamkos .75 2.00
91 Ryan Malone .20 .50
92 Noah Welch .20 .50
93 Nicklas Backstrom .60 1.50
94 Mike Green .60 1.50
95 Simeon Varlamov .60 1.50
96 Brooks Laich .25 .60
97 Tom Poti .20 .50
98 Alexander Semin .30 .75
99 Eric Fehr .30 .75
100 Paul Kariya .30 .75
101 Chris Mason .25 .60
102 Jeff Woywitka .20 .50
103 David Perron .25 .60
104 Patrik Berglund .60 1.50
105 T.J. Oshie .50 1.25
106 Keith Tkachuk .25 .60
107 Jonathan Toews .75 2.00
108 Brian Campbell .25 .60
109 Patrick Sharp .25 .60
110 Cristobal Huet .30 .75
111 Cam Barker .20 .50
112 Dustin Byfuglien .25 .60
113 Kris Versteeg .40 1.00
114 Steve Mason .50 1.25
115 R.J. Umberger .25 .60
116 Jakub Voracek .30 .75
117 Mike Commodore .20 .50
118 Derick Brassard .30 .75
119 Rick Nash .30 .75
120 Pavel Datsyuk .30 .75
121 Brian Rafalski .20 .50
122 Johan Franzen .20 .50
123 Chris Osgood .40 1.00
124 Darren Helm .40 1.00
125 Niklas Kronwall .25 .60
126 Nicklas Lidstrom .40 1.00
127 Jason Arnott .20 .50
128 J.P. Dumont .20 .50
129 Steve Sullivan .20 .50
130 Shea Weber .25 .60
131 Jordin Tootoo .30 .75
132 Pekka Rinne .25 .60
133 Anze Kopitar .30 .75
134 Jack Johnson .25 .60
135 Jonathan Quick .50 1.25
136 Dustin Brown .20 .50
137 Jarret Stoll .25 .60
138 Drew Doughty .60 1.50
139 Mike Modano .30 .75
140 Stephane Robidas .20 .50
141 Brenden Morrow .25 .60
142 Mike Ribeiro .20 .50
143 Matt Niskanen .20 .50
144 Loui Eriksson .20 .50
145 Teemu Selanne .30 .75
146 Jonas Hiller .40 1.00
147 Bobby Ryan .40 1.00
148 Ryan Getzlaf .50 1.25
149 Ryan Whitney .20 .50
150 George Parros .20 .50
151 Scott Niedermayer .25 .60
152 Joe Thornton .60 1.50
153 Joe Pavelski .20 .50
154 Dan Boyle .20 .50
155 Rob Blake .30 .75
156 Torrey Mitchell .30 .75
157 Ryane Clowe .20 .50
158 Evgeni Nabokov .30 .75
159 Peter Mueller .40 1.00
160 Keith Yandle .30 .75
161 Mikkel Boedker .25 .60
162 Matthew Lombardi .20 .50
163 Scottie Upshall .20 .50
164 Kyle Turris .40 1.00
165 Roberto Luongo .75 2.00
166 Daniel Sedin .40 1.00
167 Kevin Bieksa .20 .50
168 Mason Raymond .20 .50
169 Steve Bernier .20 .50
170 Ryan Kesler .20 .50
171 Alexandre Burrows .30 .75
172 Jarome Iginla .60 1.50
173 Rene Bourque .20 .50
174 Craig Conroy .20 .50
175 Cory Sarich .20 .50
176 Olli Jokinen .25 .60
177 Daymond Langkow .20 .50
178 Robyn Regehr .25 .60
179 Paul Stastny .30 .75
180 John-Michael Liles .25 .60
181 Peter Budaj .30 .75
182 Cody McLeod .20 .50
183 Darcy Tucker .25 .60
184 Milan Hejduk .30 .75
185 Chris Stewart .30 .75
186 Niklas Backstrom .30 .75
187 Brent Burns .30 .75
188 Owen Nolan .20 .50
189 Mikko Koivu .25 .60
190 Marek Zidlicky .20 .50
191 James Sheppard .30 .75
192 Sam Gagner .40 1.00
193 Tom Gilbert .20 .50
194 Ethan Moreau .20 .50
195 Patrick O'Sullivan .25 .60
196 Sheldon Souray .20 .50
197 Shawn Horcoff .20 .50
198 Ales Hemsky .25 .60
199 Roberto Luongo CL .75 2.00
200 Sidney Crosby CL 1.50 4.00
201 John Tavares YG RC 30.00 60.00
202 Victor Hedman YG RC 6.00 15.00
203 Matt Duchene YG RC 15.00 40.00
204 Ville Leino YG RC 4.00 10.00
205 Evander Kane YG RC 8.00 20.00
206 Michael Del Zotto YG RC 6.00 15.00
207 James Van Riemsdyk YG RC 8.00 20.00
208 Viktor Stalberg YG RC 5.00 12.00
209 Sergei Shirokov YG RC 5.00 12.00
210 Erik Karlsson YG RC 10.00 25.00
211 Dmitri Kulikov YG RC 3.00 8.00
212 Jamie Benn YG RC 5.00 12.00
213 Ryan O'Reilly YG RC 6.00 15.00
214 Tyler Myers YG RC 12.00 30.00
215 Jason Demers YG RC 2.50 6.00
216 Jay Rosehill YG RC 2.00 5.00
217 Brian Salcido YG RC 2.50 6.00
218 Luca Caputi YG RC 4.00 10.00
219 Spencer Machacek YG RC 2.50 6.00
220 Yannick Weber YG RC 4.00 10.00
221 Artem Anisimov YG RC 4.00 10.00
222 Ivan Vishnevskiy YG RC 4.00 10.00
223 Riku Helenius YG RC 3.00 8.00
224 Peter Regin YG RC 4.00 10.00
225 Antti Niemi YG RC 10.00 25.00
226 Byron Bitz YG RC 2.50 6.00
227 John Negrin YG RC 2.50 6.00
228 Ray Macias YG RC 3.00 8.00
229 Taylor Chorney YG RC 3.00 8.00
230 Mika Pyorala YG RC 3.00 8.00
231 Alec Martinez YG RC 2.00 5.00
232 Grant Lewis YG RC 2.50 6.00
233 Cal O'Reilly YG RC 3.00 8.00
234 Jesse Joensuu YG RC 4.00 10.00
235 Michal Neuvirth YG RC 8.00 20.00
236 John Scott YG RC 3.00 8.00
237 Benn Ferriero YG RC 3.00 8.00
238 Teemu Laakso YG RC 2.00 5.00
239 Jhonas Enroth YG RC 4.00 10.00
240 Matt Beleskey YG RC 3.00 8.00
241 T.J. Galiardi YG RC 4.00 10.00
242 Kris Chucko YG RC 2.50 6.00
243 James Wright YG RC 4.00 10.00
244 Joel Rechlicz YG RC 3.00 8.00
245 Matt Pelech YG RC 3.00 8.00
246 Christian Hanson YG RC 4.00 10.00
247 Matt Hendricks YG RC 2.50 6.00
248 Mike Santorelli YG RC 2.00 5.00
249 Frazer McLaren YG RC 2.00 5.00
250 Matt Duchene 6.00 15.00
Victor Hedman
John Tavares CL
251 Milan Lucic .30 .75
252 Patrice Bergeron .30 .75
253 Michael Ryder .25 .60
254 Andrew Ference .20 .50
255 Marco Sturm .20 .50
256 Marc Savard .20 .50
257 Daniel Paille .25 .60
258 Thomas Vanek .30 .75
259 Jason Pominville .30 .75
260 Mike Grier .20 .50
261 Jochen Hecht .20 .50
262 Henrik Tallinder .20 .50
263 Adam Mair .20 .50
264 Clarke MacArthur .20 .50
265 Scott Gomez .30 .75
266 Mike Cammalleri .25 .60
267 Roman Hamrlik .20 .50
268 Max Pacioretty .30 .75
269 Sergei Kostitsyn .30 .75
270 Guillaume Latendresse .25 .60
271 Brian Gionta .30 .75
272 Alex Kovalev .30 .75
273 Chris Kelly .20 .50
274 Chris Neil .20 .50
275 Pascal Leclaire .30 .75
276 Mike Fisher .20 .50
277 Filip Kuba .20 .50
278 Jonathan Cheechoo .30 .75
279 Jason Blake .20 .50
280 Phil Kessel .30 .75
281 Francois Beauchemin .20 .50
282 John Mitchell .25 .60
283 Tomas Kaberle .20 .50
284 Niklas Hagman .20 .50
285 Mike Komisarek .25 .60
286 Mike Richards .60 1.50
287 Chris Pronger .25 .60
288 Ian Laperriere .20 .50
289 Braydon Coburn .20 .50
290 Kimmo Timonen .25 .60
291 Ray Emery .25 .60
292 Daniel Briere .20 .50
293 Evgeni Malkin .75 2.00
294 Pascal Dupuis .20 .50
295 Alex Goligoski .25 .60
296 Chris Kunitz .30 .75
297 Tyler Kennedy .30 .75
298 Brooks Orpik .20 .50
299 Jordan Staal .40 1.00
300 Zach Parise .30 .75
301 Travis Zajac .30 .75
302 Andy Greene .20 .50
303 Jay Pandolfo .20 .50
304 Dainius Zubrus .20 .50
305 Rob Niedermayer .20 .50
306 Frederick Meyer .20 .50
307 Sean Bergenheim .20 .50
308 Dwayne Roloson .30 .75
309 Brendan Witt .20 .50
310 Trent Hunter .20 .50
311 Martin Biron .20 .50
312 Marian Gaborik .50 1.25
313 Vaclav Prospal .30 .75
314 Daniel Girardi .20 .50
315 Stephen Valiquette .20 .50
316 Donald Brashear .20 .50
317 Aaron Voros .20 .50
318 Chris Higgins .20 .50
319 Tomas Vokoun .20 .50
320 Jordan Leopold .20 .50
321 Rostislav Olesz .20 .50
322 Bryan Allen .20 .50
323 Nik Tarnasky .20 .50
324 Cory Stillman .20 .50
325 Nik Antropov .25 .60
326 Slava Kozlov .20 .50
327 Boris Valabik .20 .50
328 Johan Hedberg .25 .60
329 Jim Slater .20 .50
330 Ilya Kovalchuk .40 1.00
331 Cam Ward .30 .75
332 Tuomo Ruutu .20 .50
333 Manny Legace .25 .60
334 Brandon Sutter .30 .75
335 Ray Whitney .20 .50
336 Erik Cole .20 .50
337 Vincent Lecavalier .40 1.00
338 Mattias Ohlund .20 .50
339 Antero Niittymaki .30 .75
340 Lukas Krajicek .20 .50
341 Steve Downie .20 .50
342 Alex Tanguay .25 .60
343 Alexander Ovechkin 1.25 3.00
344 Karl Alzner .20 .50
345 Chris Clark .20 .50
346 Jose Theodore .30 .75
347 Michael Nylander .20 .50
348 Mike Knuble .30 .75
349 Brendan Morrison .25 .60
350 Brad Boyes .25 .60
351 Andy McDonald .20 .50
352 Eric Brewer .20 .50
353 Alexander Steen .20 .50
354 Ty Conklin .25 .60
355 Erik Johnson .25 .60
356 David Backes .25 .60
357 Patrick Kane .60 1.50
358 Andrew Ladd .30 .75
359 Dave Bolland .25 .60
360 Duncan Keith .25 .60
361 Marian Hossa .50 1.25
362 John Madden .20 .50
363 Brent Seabrook .25 .60
364 Samuel Pahlsson .20 .50
365 Kristian Huselius .20 .50
366 Kris Russell .20 .50
367 Raffi Torres .20 .50
368 Rostislav Klesla .30 .75
369 Fredrik Modin .20 .50
370 Henrik Zetterberg .60 1.50
371 Todd Bertuzzi .30 .75
372 Valtteri Filppula .30 .75
373 Tomas Holmstrom .25 .60
374 Kirk Maltby .20 .50
375 Jason Williams .20 .50
376 Dan Cleary .30 .75
377 Dan Ellis .20 .50
378 David Legwand .25 .60
379 Ryan Suter .20 .50
380 Marcel Goc .20 .50
381 Dan Hamhuis .20 .50
382 Martin Erat .30 .75
383 Ryan Smyth .30 .75
384 Justin Williams .20 .50
385 Oscar Moller .25 .60
386 Wayne Simmonds .30 .75
387 Raitis Ivanans .20 .50
388 Alexander Frolov .25 .60
389 Marty Turco .25 .60
390 James Neal .30 .75
391 Steve Ott .20 .50
392 Jere Lehtinen .25 .60
393 Fabian Brunnstrom .30 .75
394 Brad Richards .25 .60
395 Saku Koivu .30 .75
396 Luca Sbisa .40 1.00
397 Mike Brown .20 .50
398 Joffrey Lupul .20 .50
399 Corey Perry .30 .75
400 Evgeni Artyukhin .20 .50
401 Jean-Sebastien Giguere .30 .75
402 Patrick Marleau .30 .75
403 Jed Ortmeyer .20 .50
404 Scott Nichol .20 .50
405 Devin Setoguchi .25 .60
406 Jody Shelley .20 .50
407 Marc-Edouard Vlasic .20 .50
408 Dany Heatley .60 1.50
409 Shane Doan .20 .50
410 Ed Jovanovski .20 .50
411 Ilya Bryzgalov .25 .60
412 Martin Hanzal .25 .60
413 Vernon Fiddler .20 .50
414 Viktor Tikhonov .30 .75
415 Henrik Sedin .50 1.25
416 Willie Mitchell .20 .50
417 Alexandre Burrows .25 .60
418 Christian Ehrhoff .20 .50
419 Kyle Wellwood .20 .50
420 Sami Salo .20 .50
421 Mathieu Schneider .20 .50
422 Miikka Kiprusoff .30 .75
423 Curtis Glencross .25 .60
424 David Moss .25 .60
425 Dion Phaneuf .50 1.25
426 Dustin Boyd .20 .50
427 Fredrik Sjostrom .20 .50
428 Jay Bouwmeester .30 .75
429 Wojtek Wolski .30 .75
430 Craig Anderson .25 .60
431 T.J. Hensick .20 .50
432 Kyle Quincey .20 .50
433 Marek Svatos .20 .50
434 Scott Hannan .20 .50
435 Adam Foote .20 .50
436 Pierre-Marc Bouchard .25 .60
437 Martin Havlat .25 .60
438 Josh Harding .25 .60
439 Antti Miettinen .20 .50
440 Eric Belanger .20 .50
441 Colton Gillies .40 1.00
442 Andrew Cogliano .40 1.00
443 Steve Staios .20 .50
444 Fernando Pisani .20 .50
445 Lubomir Visnovsky .20 .50
446 Dustin Penner .20 .50
447 Ladislav Smid .20 .50
448 Nikolai Khabibulin .30 .75
449 Evgeni Malkin CL .75 2.00
450 Alexander Ovechkin CL 1.25 3.00
451 MacGregor Sharp YG RC 3.00 8.00
452 Brad Marchand YG RC 4.00 10.00
453 Tyler Ennis YG RC 8.00 20.00
454 Mikael Backlund YG RC 5.00 12.00
455 Ryan Wilson YG RC 3.00 8.00
456 Ryan Stoa YG RC 3.00 8.00
457 Philippe Dupuis YG RC 3.00 8.00
458 Perttu Lindgren YG RC 3.00 8.00
459 Aaron Gagnon YG RC 2.00 5.00
460 Daniel Larsson YG RC 4.00 10.00
461 Ryan O'Marra YG RC 2.50 6.00
462 Devan Dubnyk YG RC 4.00 10.00

463 Colin McDonald YG RC 3.00 8.00
464 Alexander Salak YG RC 3.00 8.00
465 Jakub Kindl YG RC 4.00 10.00
466 Andrei Loktionov YG RC 4.00 10.00
467 Scott Parse YG RC 3.00 8.00
468 Danny Irmen YG RC 2.50 6.00
469 Anton Khudobin YG RC 3.00 8.00
470 David Desharnais YG RC 5.00 12.00
471 Tom Pyatt YG RC 4.00 10.00
472 Mathieu Carle YG RC 4.00 10.00
473 Ryan White YG RC 4.00 10.00
474 Colin Wilson YG RC 6.00 15.00
475 Cody Franson YG RC 3.00 8.00
476 Peter Olvecky YG RC 3.00 8.00
477 Andreas Thuresson YG RC 2.50 6.00
478 Matthew Corrente YG RC 3.00 8.00
479 Vladimir Zharkov YG RC 3.00 8.00
480 Tyler Eckford YG RC 2.50 6.00
481 Matt Gilroy YG RC 4.00 10.00
482 Bobby Sanguinetti YG RC 2.50 6.00
483 Ryan Keller YG RC 3.00 8.00
484 Oskars Bartulis YG RC 5.00 12.00
485 David Laliberte YG RC 3.00 8.00
486 Mark Letestu YG RC 3.00 8.00
487 Logan Couture YG RC 6.00 15.00
488 Steven Zalewski YG RC 2.50 6.00
489 Lars Eller YG RC 5.00 12.00
490 Jonas Gustavsson YG RC 15.00 40.00
491 Tyler Bozak YG RC 8.00 20.00
492 Carl Gunnarsson YG RC 5.00 12.00
493 James Reimer YG RC 3.00 8.00
494 Michael Grabner YG RC 4.00 10.00
495 Mario Bliznak YG RC 3.00 8.00
496 Guillaume Desbiens YG RC 3.00 8.00
497 John Carlson YG RC 6.00 15.00
498 Mathieu Perreault YG RC 4.00 10.00
499 Braden Holtby YG RC 4.00 10.00
500 Jonas Gustavsson 4.00 10.00
Colin Wilson
Logan Couture YG CL

2009-10 Upper Deck Exclusives

*SINGLES: 3X TO 8X BASIC CARDS
*YG SINGLES: 1.5X TO 4X BASIC CARDS
STATED PRINT RUN 100 SER.#'d SETS
201 John Tavares YG 100.00 200.00
203 Matt Duchene YG 50.00 100.00
204 Ville Leino YG 30.00 60.00
205 Evander Kane YG 50.00 100.00
206 Michael Del Zotto YG 50.00 100.00
207 James Van Riemsdyk YG 40.00 80.00

2009-10 Upper Deck High Gloss

STATED PRINT RUN 10 SER.#'d SETS
NOT PRICED DUE TO SCARCITY

2009-10 Upper Deck All World

COMPLETE SET (40) 75.00 150.00
COMP.SET w/o SPs (30) 12.00 30.00
STATED ODDS 1:12
AW1 Marian Hossa 2.50 6.00
AW2 Martin Brodeur 4.00 10.00
AW3 Marc-Andre Fleury 1.50 4.00
AW4 Alexander Semin 1.50 4.00
AW5 Mike Green 3.00 8.00
AW6 Johan Franzen 1.00 2.50
AW7 Mikko Koivu 1.50 4.00
AW8 Pavel Datsyuk 1.50 4.00
AW9 Jarome Iginla 3.00 8.00
AW10 Evgeni Nabokov 1.50 4.00
AW11 Zdeno Chara 1.00 2.50
AW12 Henrik Lundqvist 3.00 8.00
AW13 Niklas Backstrom 1.50 4.00
AW14 Jason Spezza 2.00 5.00
AW15 Patrick Kane 3.00 8.00
AW16 Carey Price 4.00 10.00
AW17 Eric Staal 2.00 5.00
AW18 Shea Weber 1.25 3.00
AW19 Anze Kopitar 1.50 4.00
AW20 Pekka Rinne 1.25 3.00
AW21 Jonas Hiller 2.00 5.00
AW22 Martin St. Louis 1.50 4.00
AW23 Ales Hemsky 1.25 3.00
AW24 Miikka Kiprusoff 1.50 4.00
AW25 Mike Richards 3.00 8.00
AW26 Joe Thornton 3.00 8.00
AW27 Jeff Carter 1.50 4.00
AW28 Daniel Sedin 2.00 5.00
AW29 Henrik Sedin 2.50 6.00
AW30 Daniel Alfredsson 1.50 4.00
AW31 Zach Parise SP 2.50 6.00
AW32 Sidney Crosby SP 12.00 30.00
AW33 Evgeni Malkin SP 5.00 12.00
AW34 Ilya Kovalchuk SP 3.00 8.00
AW35 Alexander Ovechkin SP 10.00 25.00
AW36 Tim Thomas SP 2.50 6.00
AW37 Henrik Zetterberg SP 5.00 12.00
AW38 Dany Heatley SP 5.00 12.00
AW39 Rick Nash SP 2.50 6.00
AW40 Jonathan Toews SP 6.00 15.00

2009-10 Upper Deck Ambassadors of the Game

COMPLETE SET (30) 50.00 100.00
COMP.SET w/o SPs (20) 12.00 30.00
STATED ODDS 1:4
AG1 Steve Sullivan 1.25 3.00
AG2 Jason Blake 1.25 3.00
AG3 Phil Kessel 2.00 5.00
AG4 Teemu Selanne 2.00 5.00
AG5 Saku Koivu 2.00 5.00
AG6 Bobby Clarke 3.00 8.00
AG7 Lanny McDonald 2.00 5.00
AG8 Patrice Bergeron 2.00 5.00
AG9 Rod Brind'Amour 1.50 4.00
AG10 Daniel Alfredsson 2.00 5.00
AG11 Shane Doan 1.50 4.00
AG12 Tim Thomas 2.00 5.00
AG13 Vincent Lecavalier 2.50 6.00
AG14 Eric Staal 2.50 6.00
AG15 Rick Nash 2.00 5.00
AG16 Dustin Brown 1.50 4.00
AG17 Marty Turco 1.50 4.00
AG18 Alex Kovalev 2.00 5.00
AG19 Luc Robitaille 2.00 5.00
AG20 Mike Modano 2.00 5.00
AG21 Steve Yzerman SP 8.00 20.00
AG22 Cam Neely SP 4.00 10.00
AG23 Mario Lemieux SP 6.00 15.00
AG24 Jarome Iginla SP 5.00 12.00
AG25 Ray Bourque SP 4.00 10.00
AG26 Alexander Ovechkin SP 10.00 25.00
AG27 Wayne Gretzky SP 12.00 30.00
AG28 Gordie Howe SP 10.00 25.00
AG29 Bobby Orr SP 10.00 25.00
AG30 Bobby Hull SP 6.00 15.00
AG31 Scott Niedermayer 1.25 3.00
AG32 Zdeno Chara 1.25 3.00
AG33 Ryan Miller 2.00 5.00
AG34 Dion Phaneuf 3.00 8.00
AG35 Cam Ward 2.00 5.00
AG36 Kris Versteeg 2.50 6.00
AG37 Kris Draper 1.25 3.00
AG38 Pavel Datsyuk 2.00 5.00
AG39 Sheldon Souray 1.25 3.00
AG40 Ryan Smyth 2.00 5.00
AG41 Georges Laraque 1.25 3.00
AG42 Chris Drury 1.50 4.00
AG43 Don Cherry 2.00 5.00
AG44 Barry Melrose 2.00 5.00
AG45 Jason Spezza 2.50 6.00
AG46 Daniel Alfredsson 2.00 5.00
AG47 Simon Gagne 2.00 5.00
AG48 Marc-Andre Fleury 2.00 5.00
AG49 Paul Kariya 2.00 5.00
AG50 Mike Green 4.00 10.00
AG51 Ilya Kovalchuk SP 3.00 8.00
AG52 Jonathan Toews SP 6.00 15.00
AG53 Tony Esposito SP 4.00 10.00
AG54 Patrick Roy SP 8.00 20.00
AG55 Martin Brodeur SP 6.00 15.00
AG56 John Tavares SP 12.00 30.00
AG57 Mark Messier SP 5.00 12.00
AG58 Mike Richards SP 5.00 12.00
AG59 Jordan Staal SP 3.00 8.00
AG60 Roberto Luongo SP 6.00 15.00

2009-10 Upper Deck Big Playmakers

STATED PRINT RUN 75 SER.#'d SETS
BP96 Wayne Gretzky/25 125.00 200.00
BPAF Alexander Frolov 6.00 15.00
BPAK Alex Kovalev 8.00 20.00
BPAO Alexander Ovechkin 30.00 80.00
BPBC Brian Campbell/25
BPBD Brandon Dubinsky 6.00 15.00
BPBL Bryan Little 8.00 20.00
BPBR Derick Brassard 8.00 20.00
BPCH Cristobal Huet 8.00 20.00
BPCN Cam Neely 12.00 30.00
BPCP Carey Price 20.00 50.00
BPCW Cam Ward 8.00 20.00
BPDB Dave Bolland 6.00 15.00
BPDD Drew Doughty 15.00 40.00
BPDM J.P. Dumont 5.00 12.00
BPDP David Perron 6.00 15.00
BPDR Derek Roy 8.00 20.00
BPDU Dustin Brown 6.00 15.00
BPEM Evgeni Malkin 20.00 50.00
BPES Eric Staal 10.00 25.00
BPIK Ilya Kovalchuk 10.00 25.00
BPJB Jay Bouwmeester 8.00 20.00
BPJO Jordan Staal 8.00 20.00
BPJP Jason Pominville 8.00 20.00
BPJS Jason Spezza 10.00 25.00
BPJV Jakub Voracek 8.00 20.00
BPKL Kari Lehtonen 8.00 20.00
BPLU Milan Lucic/25 10.00 25.00
BPMB Martin Brodeur 100.00 175.00
BPMF Michael Frolik 6.00 15.00
BPMG Marian Gaborik 12.00 30.00
BPMH Marian Hossa 12.00 30.00
BPMI Mikkel Boedker 6.00 15.00
BPNB Nicklas Backstrom 15.00 40.00
BPNK Nikolai Khabibulin 8.00 20.00
BPNL Nicklas Lidstrom 10.00 25.00
BPOJ Olli Jokinen/25 8.00 20.00
BPPD Pavel Datsyuk 8.00 20.00
BPPE Pekka Rinne 6.00 15.00
BPPH Dion Phaneuf 12.00 30.00
BPPK Patrick Kane 15.00 40.00
BPPL Paul Stastny/100 8.00 20.00
BPPM Peter Mueller 10.00 25.00
BPPR Patrick Roy 25.00 60.00
BPRB Ray Bourque 10.00 25.00
BPRI Mike Richards 15.00 40.00
BPRM Ryan Miller 8.00 20.00
BPRN Rick Nash 8.00 20.00
BPSD Shane Doan 8.00 20.00
BPSG Sam Gagner 10.00 25.00
BPSP Patrick Sharp 6.00 15.00
BPST Drew Stafford 6.00 15.00
BPSW Stephen Weiss 5.00 12.00
BPTO Jonathan Toews 20.00 50.00
BPTP Tomas Plekanec 6.00 15.00
BPTV Thomas Vanek 8.00 20.00
BPVL Vincent Lecavalier 10.00 25.00
BPVO Tomas Vokoun 8.00 20.00
BPZP Zach Parise 8.00 20.00

2009-10 Upper Deck Captain's Calling

COMPLETE SET (9) 10.00 25.00
STATED ODDS 1:4
CC1 Sidney Crosby 4.00 10.00
CC2 Jonathan Toews 2.00 5.00
CC3 Jarome Iginla 1.50 4.00
CC4 Roberto Luongo 2.00 5.00
CC5 Rick Nash .75 2.00
CC6 Nicklas Lidstrom 1.00 2.50
CC7 Vincent Lecavalier 1.00 2.50
CC8 Ilya Kovalchuk 1.00 2.50
CC9 Mike Richards 1.50 4.00

2009-10 Upper Deck Clearcut Trios

STATED PRINT RUN 25 SER.#'d SETS
CT1 Patrick Marleau 20.00 50.00
Joe Thornton
Devin Setoguchi
CT2 Corey Perry 15.00 40.00
Bobby Ryan
Ryan Getzlaf
CT3 Olli Jokinen 20.00 50.00
Jarome Iginla
Miikka Kiprusoff
CT4 Jonathan Toews 25.00 60.00
Patrick Kane
Brian Campbell
CT5 Pavel Datsyuk 20.00 50.00
Nicklas Lidstrom
Henrik Zetterberg
CT6 Martin Brodeur 25.00 60.00
Zach Parise
Patrik Elias
CT7 Sidney Crosby 50.00 120.00
Evgeni Malkin
Marc-Andre Fleury
CT8 Glenn Anderson 50.00 120.00
Wayne Gretzky
Jari Kurri
CT9 Vincent Lecavalier 25.00 60.00
Martin St. Louis
Steven Stamkos
CT10 Henrik Zetterberg 40.00 100.00
Gordie Howe
Steve Yzerman
CT11 Steve Yzerman 30.00 80.00
Mark Messier
Mario Lemieux
CT12 Nikolai Kulemin 8.00 20.00
Matt Stajan
Luke Schenn
CT13 Roberto Luongo 25.00 60.00
Daniel Sedin
Henrik Sedin
CT14 Nicklas Backstrom 40.00 100.00
Alexander Semin
Alexander Ovechkin
CT15 Phil Esposito 40.00 100.00
Johnny Bucyk
Bobby Orr
CT16 Larry Robinson 15.00 40.00
Guy Lafleur
Steve Shutt
CT17 Patrick Kane 25.00 60.00
Jonathan Toews
Bobby Hull
CT18 Rogie Vachon 15.00 40.00
Frank Mahovlich
Jean Beliveau
CT19 Patrick Roy 25.00 60.00
Carey Price
Martin Brodeur
CT20 Ryan Miller 20.00 50.00
Henrik Lundqvist
Rick DiPietro
CT21 Miikka Kiprusoff 25.00 60.00
Roberto Luongo
Niklas Backstrom

2009-10 Upper Deck Clearly Canadian

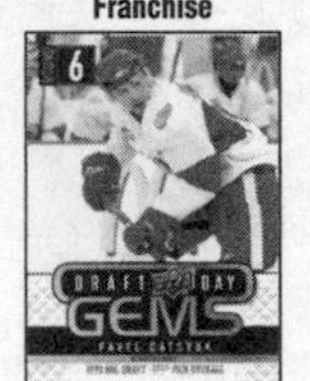

STATED PRINT RUN 100 SER.#'d SETS
CANAF Adam Foote 6.00 15.00
CANAM Al MacInnis 10.00 25.00
CANBC Bobby Clarke 15.00 40.00
CANBM Brenden Morrow 8.00 20.00
CANBO Bobby Orr 40.00 100.00
CANBR Brad Richards 8.00 20.00
CANCW Cam Ward 10.00 25.00
CANDH Dany Healley 20.00 50.00
CANDP Denis Potvin 8.00 20.00
CANDR Derek Roy 10.00 25.00
CANES Eric Staal 12.00 30.00
CANFY Marc-Andre Fleury 10.00 25.00
CANGF Grant Fuhr 12.00 30.00
CANGL Guy Lafleur 15.00 40.00
CANGP Gilbert Perreault 10.00 25.00
CANJB Jay Bouwmeester 10.00 25.00
CANJI Jarome Iginla 20.00 50.00
CANJS Joe Sakic 20.00 50.00
CANJT Jonathan Toews 25.00 60.00
CANKD Kris Draper 6.00 15.00
CANLR Luc Robitaille 10.00 25.00
CANMB Martin Brodeur 25.00 60.00
CANMG Mike Green 20.00 50.00
CANML Mario Lemieux 25.00 60.00
CANMM Mark Messier 20.00 50.00
CANMR Mike Richards 20.00 50.00
CANMS Martin St. Louis 10.00 25.00
CANPR Patrick Roy 30.00 80.00
CANPS Patrick Sharp 8.00 20.00
CANRB Ray Bourque 15.00 40.00
CANRG Ryan Getzlaf 15.00 40.00
CANRL Roberto Luongo 25.00 60.00
CANRN Rick Nash 10.00 25.00
CANRR Robyn Regehr 8.00 20.00
CANRS Ryan Smyth 10.00 25.00
CANSC Sidney Crosby 50.00 120.00
CANSG Simon Gagne 10.00 25.00
CANSM Steve Mason 15.00 40.00
CANTH Joe Thornton 20.00 50.00
CANVL Vincent Lecavalier 12.00 30.00
CANWG Wayne Gretzky 50.00 120.00
CANYZ Steve Yzerman 30.00 80.00

2009-10 Upper Deck Draft Class

STATED PRINT RUN 10 SER.#'d SETS
NOT PRICED DUE TO SCARCITY
DC1 Jonathan Toews
Phil Kessel
DC2 Steve Yzerman
Cam Neely
DC3 Matt Duchene
John Tavares
DC4 John Tavares
Victor Hedman
DC5 Jonathan Toews
Jordan Staal
DC6 Mario Lemieux
Patrick Roy
DC7 Carey Price
Sidney Crosby
DC8 Evgeni Malkin
Alexander Ovechkin

2009-10 Upper Deck Draft Day Gems

COMPLETE SET (14) 8.00 20.00
STATED ODDS 1:4
GEM1 Henrik Zetterberg 2.00 5.00
GEM2 Pavel Datsyuk 1.00 2.50
GEM3 Tomas Kaberle .60 1.50
GEM4 Andrei Markov .75 2.00
GEM5 Luc Robitaille 1.00 2.50
GEM6 Theoren Fleury 1.50 4.00
GEM7 Ron Hextall 2.00 5.00
GEM8 Dominik Hasek 1.00 2.50
GEM9 Evgeni Nabokov 1.00 2.50
GEM10 Marty Turco .75 2.00
GEM11 Henrik Lundqvist 2.00 5.00
GEM12 Ryan Miller 1.00 2.50
GEM13 Pekka Rinne .75 2.00
GEM14 Mark Messier 2.00 5.00
GEM15 Tim Thomas 1.00 2.50
GEM16 Mark Recchi .75 2.00
GEM17 Patrick Roy 3.00 8.00
GEM18 Milan Hejduk 1.00 2.50
GEM19 Cristobal Huet 1.00 2.50
GEM20 Tomas Vokoun 1.00 2.50
GEM21 Doug Gilmour 1.00 2.50
GEM22 Nikolai Khabibulin 1.00 2.50
GEM23 Michael Ryder .75 2.00
GEM24 Miikka Kiprusoff 1.00 2.50
GEM25 Nicklas Lidstrom 1.25 3.00
GEM26 Jari Kurri 1.00 2.50
GEM27 Brian Campbell .75 2.00
GEM28 Daniel Alfredsson 1.00 2.50
GEM29 Dustin Byfuglien .75 2.00
GEM30 Mark Streit .60 1.50

2009-10 Upper Deck Fab Four Fabrics

STATED PRINT RUN 100 SER.#'d SETS
F4F-BRUN Patrice Bergeron 8.00 20.00
Phil Kessel
Milan Lucic
Michael Ryder
F4F-CANE Cam Ward 10.00 25.00
Rod Brind'Amour
Tuomo Ruutu
Eric Staal
F4F-CAPS Milan Jurcina 30.00 80.00
Alexander Ovechkin
Brendan Morrison
Jose Theodore
F4F-CATS Nathan Horton 8.00 20.00
David Booth
Stephen Weiss
Tomas Vokoun
F4F-CNKS Steve Bernier 20.00 50.00
Roberto Luongo
Daniel Sedin
Henrik Sedin
F4F-DEVL David Clarkson 20.00 50.00
Zach Parise
Martin Brodeur
Patrik Elias
F4F-FLAM Jarome Iginla 12.00 30.00
Olli Jokinen
Miikka Kiprusoff
Dion Phaneuf
F4F-FLYR Jeff Carter 15.00 40.00
Mike Richards
Ray Emery
Simon Gagne
F4F-GRTS Mark Messier 60.00 120.00
Wayne Gretzky
Steve Yzerman
Sidney Crosby
F4F-HWKS Patrick Kane 20.00 50.00
Jonathan Toews
Patrick Sharp
Brian Campbell
F4F-ISLE Kyle Okposo 8.00 20.00
Josh Bailey
Rick DiPietro
Doug Weight
F4F-KNGS Dustin Brown 15.00 40.00
Alexander Frolov
Drew Doughty
Anze Kopitar
F4F-LEAF Luke Schenn 12.00 30.00
Mike Komisarek
Ryan Hollweg
Vesa Toskala
F4F-OILR Nikolai Khabibulin 10.00 25.00
Andrew Cogliano
Sam Gagner
Patrick O'Sullivan
F4F-RNGR Marian Gaborik 10.00 25.00
Chris Drury
Henrik Lundqvist
Marc Staal
F4F-SABR Jason Pominville
Thomas Vanek
Drew Stafford
Ryan Miller
F4F-SC00 Scott Gomez 20.00 50.00
Jason Arnott
Martin Brodeur
Patrik Elias
F4F-SC01 Chris Drury 6.00 15.00
Patrick Roy
Alex Tanguay
Ray Bourque
F4F-SC06 Eric Staal 10.00 25.00
Justin Williams
Cory Stillman
Cam Ward
F4F-SC89 Lanny McDonald 8.00 20.00
Joe Mullen
Doug Gilmour
Al MacInnis
F4F-SC90 Mark Messier 15.00 40.00
Jari Kurri
Grant Fuhr
Glenn Anderson
F4F-SENS Jason Spezza 15.00 40.00
Daniel Alfredsson
Dany Heatley
Alex Kovalev
F4F-STAR Mike Ribeiro 12.00 30.00
Mike Modano
Jere Lehtinen
Marty Turco
F4F-WING Nicklas Lidstrom 15.00 40.00
Henrik Zetterberg
Pavel Datsyuk
Tomas Holmstrom

2009-10 Upper Deck Face of the Franchise

COMPLETE SET (14) 10.00 25.00
STATED ODDS 1:4
FF1 Sidney Crosby 4.00 10.00
FF2 Alexander Ovechkin 3.00 8.00
FF3 Carey Price 2.00 5.00
FF4 Ales Hemsky .60 1.50
FF5 Roberto Luongo 2.00 5.00
FF6 Marc Savard .50 1.25
FF7 Henrik Lundqvist 1.50 4.00
FF8 Jarome Iginla 1.50 4.00
FF9 Mike Richards 1.50 4.00
FF10 Jonathan Toews 2.00 5.00
FF11 Jason Spezza 1.00 2.50
FF12 Luke Schenn 1.25 3.00
FF13 Joe Thornton 1.50 4.00
FF14 Martin Brodeur 2.00 5.00

2009-10 Upper Deck Game Jerseys

STATED ODDS 1:12
GJAK Anze Kopitar 6.00 15.00
GJAO Alexander Ovechkin 25.00 60.00
GJBB Bob Bourne 5.00 12.00
GJBC Brian Campbell 5.00 12.00
GJBG Butch Goring 6.00 15.00
GJBM Brendan Morrison 5.00 12.00
GJBN Bernie Nicholls 4.00 10.00
GJBO Brooks Orpik 4.00 10.00
GJBP Bob Probert 4.00 10.00
GJBR Brad Richards 5.00 12.00
GJCC Carlo Colaiacovo 4.00 10.00
GJCH Cristobal Huet 6.00 15.00
GJCN Cam Neely 10.00 25.00
GJCO Chris Osgood 8.00 20.00
GJCP Carey Price 15.00 40.00
GJDA David Booth 4.00 10.00
GJDB Dave Bolland 5.00 12.00
GJDC Dino Ciccarelli 4.00 10.00
GJDD Drew Doughty 12.00 30.00
GJDE Derick Brassard 6.00 15.00
GJDH Dale Hawerchuk 6.00 15.00
GJDO Donald Brashear 4.00 10.00
GJDP Dion Phaneuf 10.00 25.00
GJDR Derek Roy 6.00 15.00
GJDS Daniel Sedin 8.00 20.00
GJDU Dustin Brown 5.00 12.00
GJEC Erik Cole 4.00 10.00
GJEM Evgeni Malkin 15.00 40.00
GJES Eric Staal 8.00 20.00
GJFB Francis Bouillon 4.00 10.00
GJFR Michael Frolik 5.00 12.00
GJGA Glenn Anderson 6.00 15.00
GJGC Guy Carbonneau 10.00 25.00
GJGF Grant Fuhr 8.00 20.00
GJGG Simon Gagne 6.00 15.00
GJIK Ilya Kovalchuk 8.00 20.00
GJJB Jay Bouwmeester 6.00 15.00
GJJC Jonathan Cheechoo 6.00 15.00
GJJH Jeff Halpern 4.00 10.00
GJJL Joffrey Lupul 6.00 15.00
GJJO Jordin Tootoo 6.00 15.00
GJJP Jason Pominville 6.00 15.00
GJJS Jason Spezza 8.00 20.00
GJJT Jeff Tambellini 4.00 10.00
GJJV Jakub Voracek 6.00 15.00
GJKL Kari Lehtonen 6.00 15.00
GJKT Kimmo Timonen 5.00 12.00
GJLG Robert Lang 4.00 10.00
GJLM Lanny McDonald 6.00 15.00
GJLX Mario Lemieux 15.00 40.00
GJMA Matt Carle 4.00 10.00
GJMB Martin Brodeur 15.00 40.00
GJMC Bryan McCabe 5.00 12.00
GJMD Marc Denis 4.00 10.00
GJMF Manny Fernandez 5.00 12.00
GJMG Marian Gaborik 10.00 25.00
GJMH Marian Hossa 10.00 25.00
GJML Mike Lundin 4.00 10.00
GJMM Mark Messier 20.00 50.00
GJMP Marc-Antoine Pouliot 5.00 12.00
GJMR Mason Raymond 4.00 10.00
GJMS Marc Staal 8.00 20.00
GJMT Marty Turco 5.00 12.00
GJMU Larry Murphy 4.00 10.00
GJNB Nicklas Backstrom 12.00 30.00
GJNH Nathan Horton 4.00 10.00
GJPA Patrice Brisebois 4.00 10.00
GJPB Patrice Bergeron 6.00 15.00
GJPD Pavel Datsyuk 6.00 15.00
GJPE Peter Stastny 6.00 15.00
GJPK Patrick Kane 12.00 30.00
GJPO Patrick O'Sullivan 5.00 12.00
GJPR Patrick Roy 20.00 50.00
GJPS Patrick Sharp 5.00 12.00
GJRA Paul Ranger 4.00 10.00
GJRB Richard Brodeur 6.00 15.00
GJRI Mike Richards 12.00 30.00
GJRL Roberto Luongo 15.00 40.00
GJRM Ryan Miller 6.00 15.00
GJRN Rick Nash 6.00 15.00
GJSA Borje Salming 6.00 15.00
GJSC Sidney Crosby 20.00 50.00
GJSD Shane Doan 5.00 12.00
GJSG Sam Gagner 8.00 20.00
GJSI Darryl Sittler 8.00 20.00
GJSK Saku Koivu 6.00 15.00
GJSP Paul Stastny 6.00 15.00
GJSS Steve Shutt 6.00 15.00
GJST Drew Stafford 6.00 15.00
GJSU Steve Sullivan 4.00 10.00
GJSW Shea Weber 5.00 12.00
GJSY Steve Yzerman 50.00 100.00
GJTO Jonathan Toews 15.00 40.00
GJTV Thomas Vanek 6.00 15.00
GJTW Tiger Williams 5.00 12.00
GJVO Tomas Vokoun 5.00 12.00
GJVT Vesa Toskala 6.00 15.00
GJWE Stephen Weiss 4.00 10.00
GJWG Wayne Gretzky 75.00 150.00
GJWR Wade Redden 4.00 10.00
GJ2AC Andrew Cogliano 8.00 20.00
GJ2AF Alexander Frolov 5.00 12.00
GJ2AH Adam Hall 4.00 10.00
GJ2AK Anze Kopitar 6.00 15.00
GJ2BA Josh Bailey 5.00 12.00
GJ2BC Brian Campbell 5.00 12.00
GJ2BM Brendan Morrison 5.00 12.00
GJ2BS Borje Salming 6.00 15.00
GJ2CH Jonathan Cheechoo 6.00 15.00
GJ2DH Dale Hawerchuk 6.00 15.00
GJ2DS Devin Setoguchi 5.00 12.00
GJ2DT Dave Taylor 8.00 20.00
GJ2ES Eric Staal 8.00 20.00
GJ2GA Simon Gagne 6.00 15.00
GJ2GH Gordie Howe 125.00 200.00
GJ2HZ Henrik Zetterberg 12.00 30.00
GJ2IK Ilya Kovalchuk 8.00 20.00
GJ2JA Jason Arnott 4.00 10.00
GJ2JC Jeff Carter 6.00 15.00
GJ2JD J.P. Dumont 4.00 10.00
GJ2JI Jarome Iginla 12.00 30.00
GJ2JL Joffrey Lupul 6.00 15.00
GJ2JT Jonathan Toews 15.00 40.00
GJ2KE Phil Kessel 6.00 15.00
GJ2KO Kyle Okposo 6.00 15.00
GJ2LM Lanny McDonald 6.00 15.00
GJ2MC Bryan McCabe 5.00 12.00
GJ2MK Mike Komisarek 5.00 12.00
GJ2ML Milan Lucic 6.00 15.00
GJ2MM Mike Modano 6.00 15.00
GJ2MP Marc-Antoine Pouliot 5.00 12.00
GJ2MR Michael Ryder 5.00 12.00
GJ2MS Marc Staal 8.00 20.00
GJ2OJ Olli Jokinen 4.00 10.00
GJ2PK Paul Kariya 6.00 15.00
GJ2PM Peter Mueller 8.00 20.00
GJ2PS Paul Stastny 6.00 15.00
GJ2RB Rob Blake 6.00 15.00
GJ2RE Ray Emery 5.00 12.00
GJ2RG Ryan Getzlaf 10.00 25.00
GJ2RH Roman Hamrlik 4.00 10.00
GJ2RS Ryan Smyth 6.00 15.00
GJ2SD Shane Doan 5.00 12.00
GJ2SG Scott Gomez 6.00 15.00
GJ2SR Steven Reinprecht 4.00 10.00
GJ2ST Drew Stafford 6.00 15.00
GJ2SY Steve Yzerman 20.00 50.00
GJ2TF Tomas Fleischmann 4.00 10.00
GJ2TH Tomas Holmstrom 6.00 15.00
GJ2TR Tuomo Ruutu 4.00 10.00
GJ2TS Teemu Selanne 6.00 15.00
GJ2VP Vaclav Prospal 4.00 10.00
GJ2VT Vesa Toskala 6.00 15.00

2009-10 Upper Deck Game Patches

STATED PRINT RUN 15 SER.#'d SETS
NOT PRICED DUE TO SCARCITY

2009-10 Upper Deck Hockey Heroes Mark Messier

HH27 Mark Messier Header 10.00 25.00
HH28 Mark Messier Painted 10.00 25.00
HH-MM Mark Messier AU/30 150.00 250.00

2009-10 Upper Deck Hockey Heroes Martin Brodeur

COMPLETE SET (10) 40.00 80.00
COMP.SET w/o SPs (8) 10.00 25.00
COMMON BRODEUR 2.50 6.00
HH18 Martin Brodeur Painting 10.00 25.00
HHMB Martin Brodeur Header 12.00 30.00
HHMB Martin Brodeur AU/30 150.00 250.00

2009-10 Upper Deck Netminders

COMPLETE SET (30) 50.00 100.00
COMP.SET w/o SPs (20) 12.00 30.00
STATED ODDS 1:4
NET1 Marty Turco 1.25 3.00
NET2 Jean-Sebastien Giguere 1.50 4.00
NET3 Nikolai Khabibulin 1.50 4.00
NET4 Chris Mason 1.25 3.00
NET5 Vesa Toskala 1.50 4.00
NET6 Pascal Leclaire 1.50 4.00
NET7 Tomas Vokoun 1.50 4.00
NET8 Mike Smith 1.25 3.00
NET9 Pekka Rinne 1.25 3.00
NET10 Kari Lehtonen 1.50 4.00
NET11 Jonathan Quick 2.50 6.00
NET12 Evgeni Nabokov 1.50 4.00
NET13 Rick DiPietro 1.50 4.00
NET14 Ilya Bryzgalov 1.25 3.00
NET15 Cristobal Huet 1.50 4.00
NET16 Simeon Varlamov 3.00 8.00
NET17 Ray Emery 1.25 3.00
NET18 Niklas Backstrom 1.50 4.00
NET19 Chris Osgood 2.00 5.00
NET20 Peter Budaj 1.50 4.00
NET21 Martin Brodeur SP 5.00 12.00
NET22 Miikka Kiprusoff SP 2.00 5.00
NET23 Roberto Luongo SP 5.00 12.00
NET24 Steve Mason SP 3.00 8.00
NET25 Carey Price SP 5.00 12.00
NET26 Henrik Lundqvist SP 4.00 10.00
NET27 Marc-Andre Fleury SP 2.00 5.00
NET28 Cam Ward SP 2.00 5.00
NET29 Tim Thomas SP 2.00 5.00
NET30 Ryan Miller SP 2.00 5.00

2009-10 Upper Deck Playoff Performers

COMPLETE SET (16) 12.00 30.00
STATED ODDS 1:4
PP1 Alexander Ovechkin 3.00 8.00
PP2 Cam Ward .75 2.00
PP3 Evgeni Malkin 2.00 5.00
PP4 Henrik Zetterberg 1.50 4.00
PP5 Jarome Iginla 1.50 4.00
PP6 Johan Franzen .50 1.25
PP7 Jonas Hiller 1.00 2.50
PP8 Marc-Andre Fleury .75 2.00
PP9 Martin Brodeur 2.00 5.00
PP10 Patrick Kane 1.50 4.00
PP11 Roberto Luongo 2.00 5.00
PP12 Scott Niedermayer .50 1.25
PP13 Sidney Crosby 4.00 10.00
PP14 Tim Thomas .75 2.00
PP15 Chris Osgood 1.00 2.50
PP16 Eric Staal 1.00 2.50

2009-10 Upper Deck Rookie Breakouts

STATED PRINT RUN 100 SER.#'d SETS
RB1 John Tavares 25.00 60.00
RB2 Victor Hedman 10.00 25.00
RB3 Matt Duchene 20.00 50.00
RB4 James Van Riemsdyk 12.00 30.00
RB5 Jonas Gustavsson 12.00 30.00
RB6 Evander Kane 12.00 30.00
RB7 Colin Wilson 8.00 20.00
RB8 Michael Grabner 6.00 15.00
RB9 Tyler Myers 20.00 50.00
RB10 Jamie Benn 8.00 20.00
RB11 Dmitry Kulikov 5.00 12.00
RB12 Mikael Backlund 8.00 20.00
RB13 Artem Anisimov 6.00 15.00
RB14 Antti Niemi 15.00 40.00
RB15 Michael Del Zotto 10.00 25.00
RB16 Tyler Bozak 12.00 30.00
RB17 Erik Karlsson 15.00 40.00
RB18 Ryan O'Reilly 10.00 25.00
RB19 Ville Leino 6.00 15.00
RB20 Yannick Weber 6.00 15.00
RB21 Christian Hanson 6.00 15.00
RB22 Cody Franson 5.00 12.00
RB23 Ivan Vishnevskiy 6.00 15.00
RB24 Luca Caputi 6.00 15.00
RB25 Jhonas Enroth 6.00 15.00
RB26 Matt Pelech 5.00 12.00
RB27 Matt Gilroy 6.00 15.00
RB28 Viktor Stalberg 8.00 20.00
RB29 James Wright 6.00 15.00
RB30 Sergei Shirokov 8.00 20.00
RB31 Alec Martinez 3.00 8.00
RB32 Spencer Machacek 4.00 10.00
RB33 T.J. Galiardi 6.00 15.00
RB34 Jason Demers 4.00 10.00

2009-10 Upper Deck Rookie Debuts

COMPLETE SET (9) 15.00 40.00
STATED ODDS 1:4
RD1 John Tavares 4.00 10.00
RD2 James Van Riemsdyk 2.00 5.00

RD3 Victor Hedman 1.50 4.00
RD4 Matt Duchene 3.00 8.00
RD5 Jonas Gustavsson 2.00 5.00
RD6 Jamie Benn 1.25 3.00
RD7 Evander Kane 2.00 5.00
RD8 Colin Wilson 1.25 3.00
RD9 Michael Del Zotto 1.50 4.00

2009-10 Upper Deck Rookie Headliners

COMPLETE SET (30) 50.00 100.00
COMP.SET w/o SPs (20) 15.00 40.00
STATED ODDS 1:4
RH1 Matt Pelech .75 2.00
RH2 Kris Chucko .60 1.50
RH3 Antti Niemi 2.50 6.00
RH4 Ryan O'Reilly 1.50 4.00
RH5 T.J. Galiardi 1.00 2.50
RH6 Perttu Lindgren .75 2.00
RH7 Ivan Vishnevskiy 1.00 2.50
RH8 Ville Leino 1.00 2.50
RH9 Dmitry Kulikov .75 2.00
RH10 Yannick Weber 1.00 2.50
RH11 Cody Franson .75 2.00
RH12 Michael Del Zotto 1.50 4.00
RH13 Matt Gilroy 1.00 2.50
RH14 Artem Anisimov 1.00 2.50
RH15 Erik Karlsson 2.50 6.00
RH16 Tyler Bozak 2.00 5.00
RH17 Viktor Stalberg 1.25 3.00
RH18 Christian Hanson 1.00 2.50
RH19 Michael Grabner 1.00 2.50
RH20 Sergei Shirokov 1.25 3.00
RH21 Evander Kane SP 3.00 8.00
RH22 Tyler Myers SP 5.00 12.00
RH23 Mikael Backlund SP 2.00 5.00
RH24 Matt Duchene SP 5.00 12.00
RH25 Jamie Benn SP 2.00 5.00
RH26 Colin Wilson SP 2.00 5.00
RH27 John Tavares SP 6.00 15.00
RH28 James Van Riemsdyk SP 3.00 8.00
RH29 Victor Hedman SP 2.50 6.00
RH30 Jonas Gustavsson SP 3.00 8.00

2009-10 Upper Deck Rookie Materials

STATED ODDS 1:12
RMAM Alec Martinez 4.00 10.00
RMAN Antti Niemi 20.00 50.00
RMBE Matt Beleskey 6.00 15.00
RMBF Benn Ferriero 6.00 15.00
RMBM Brad Marchand 8.00 20.00
RMBS Brian Salcido 5.00 12.00
RMCB Chris Butler 6.00 15.00
RMCF Cody Franson 6.00 15.00
RMCO Cal O'Reilly 6.00 15.00
RMCW Colin Wilson 10.00 25.00
RMDK Dmitry Kulikov 6.00 15.00
RMDU Matt Duchene 15.00 40.00
RMEK Erik Karlsson 20.00 50.00
RMIV Ivan Vishnevskiy 8.00 20.00
RMJB Jamie Benn 10.00 25.00
RMJD Jason Demers 5.00 12.00
RMJE Jhonas Enroth 8.00 20.00
RMJG Jonas Gustavsson 15.00 40.00
RMJJ Jesse Joensuu 8.00 20.00
RMJS John Scott 6.00 15.00
RMJT John Tavares 20.00 50.00
RMJV James van Riemsdyk 15.00 40.00
RMKA Evander Kane 15.00 40.00
RMKC Kris Chucko 5.00 12.00
RMLC Luca Caputi 8.00 20.00
RMLO Logan Couture 12.00 30.00
RMMA Andrew MacDonald 5.00 12.00
RMMB Mikael Backlund 10.00 25.00
RMMD Michael Del Zotto 12.00 30.00
RMMG Michael Grabner 8.00 20.00
RMMP Matt Pelech 6.00 15.00
RMMS Mike Santorelli 4.00 10.00
RMPL Perttu Lindgren 6.00 15.00
RMRE Joel Rechlicz 6.00 15.00
RMRH Riku Helenius 6.00 15.00
RMRM Ray Macias 6.00 15.00
RMRO Ryan O'Reilly 12.00 30.00
RMSA Michael Sauer 5.00 12.00
RMSM Spencer Machacek 5.00 12.00
RMSS Sergei Shirokov 10.00 25.00
RMTB Tyler Bozak 15.00 40.00
RMTG T.J. Galiardi 8.00 20.00
RMTM Tyler Myers 15.00 40.00
RMVH Victor Hedman 12.00 30.00
RMVL Ville Leino 8.00 20.00
RMYW Yannick Weber 8.00 20.00

2009-10 Upper Deck Rookie Materials Patches

*SINGLES: .8X TO 2X BASIC INSERTS
STATED PRINT RUN 25 SER.#'d SETS
RM-DU Matt Duchene 50.00 100.00
RM-JG Jonas Gustavsson 75.00 150.00
RM-JT John Tavares 100.00 200.00
RM-TM Tyler Myers 75.00 150.00

2009-10 Upper Deck Season Highlights

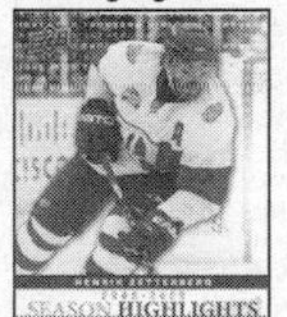

COMPLETE SET (7) 6.00 15.00
STATED ODDS 1:4
SH1 Sidney Crosby 2.00 5.00
SH2 Martin Brodeur 1.00 2.50
SH3 Tim Thomas .40 1.00
SH4 Alexander Ovechkin 1.50 4.00
SH5 Henrik Lundqvist .75 2.00
SH6 Evgeni Malkin 1.00 2.50
SH7 Henrik Zetterberg .75 2.00

2009-10 Upper Deck Signatures

STATED ODDS 1:288
UDSAE Andrew Ebbett 6.00 15.00
UDSAM Andrei Markov 6.00 15.00
UDSAO Alexander Ovechkin
UDSAP Alex Pietrangelo 6.00 15.00
UDSBM Brendan Mikkelson 5.00 12.00
UDSBO Bobby Orr 150.00 250.00
UDSBR Bobby Ryan 10.00 25.00
UDSBV Boris Valabik 8.00 20.00
UDSBW Blake Wheeler 10.00 25.00
UDSBY Brad Boyes 6.00 15.00
UDSCD Chris Drury 6.00 15.00
UDSCG Claude Giroux 15.00 40.00
UDSCR Sidney Crosby 150.00 250.00
UDSDH Darren Helm 10.00 25.00
UDSDP Dion Phaneuf 12.00 30.00
UDSFB Fabian Brunnstrom 8.00 20.00
UDSFI Mark Fistric 5.00 12.00
UDSFO Nick Foligno 8.00 20.00
UDSGB Gilbert Brule 10.00 25.00
UDSGH Gordie Howe
UDSHZ Henrik Zetterberg
UDSJB Josh Bailey
UDSJE Jonathan Ericsson 8.00 20.00
UDSJG Jean-Sebastien Giguere
UDSJH Josh Harding
UDSJI Jarome Iginla
UDSJP Justin Pogge 15.00 40.00
UDSJT Joe Thornton
UDSKA Karl Alzner 8.00 20.00
UDSLS Luke Schenn 12.00 30.00
UDSMD Matt D'Agostini 10.00 25.00
UDSME Matt Ellis 5.00 12.00
UDSMF Marc-Andre Fleury 25.00 50.00
UDSMI Mike Iggulden 5.00 12.00
UDSMP Max Pacioretty 8.00 20.00
UDSMR Mattias Ritola 6.00 15.00
UDSNF Nikita Filatov 15.00 40.00
UDSNK Nikolai Kulemin
UDSOM Oscar Moller 6.00 15.00
UDSPD Pavel Datsyuk 50.00 100.00
UDSPE Michael Peca 25.00 50.00
UDSPK Phil Kessel 20.00 40.00
UDSPR Patrick Roy
UDSRO Rostislav Olesz 5.00 12.00
UDSRP Ryan Parent 6.00 15.00
UDSRS Ryan Smyth 25.00 50.00
UDSRY Ryan Potulny 5.00 12.00
UDSSC Cory Schneider 12.00 30.00
UDSSS Steven Stamkos 40.00 80.00
UDSSY Steve Yzerman 100.00 200.00
UDSTK Tim Kennedy 8.00 20.00
UDSTS Tom Sestito 5.00 12.00
UDSTV Thomas Vanek 8.00 20.00
UDSTW Ty Wishart 8.00 20.00
UDSWG Wayne Gretzky

2009-10 Upper Deck Signature Sensations

STATED ODDS 1:288
SSAB Adam Burish 10.00 25.00
SSAE Andrew Ebbett 6.00 15.00
SSAM Al MacInnis
SSAN Andreas Nodl 5.00 12.00
SSAO Adam Oates 8.00 20.00
SSAP Alexandre Picard 6.00 15.00
SSAT Alex Tanguay 6.00 15.00
SSBB Brian Boyle 6.00 15.00
SSBE Brendan Bell
SSBO Brad Boyes
SSCG Clark Gillies
SSCN Cam Neely 12.00 30.00
SSDC Don Cherry
SSDH Dominik Hasek
SSDL Dan LaCosta 6.00 15.00
SSDN Marcel Dionne 10.00 25.00
SSDP Dimitri Patzold 6.00 15.00
SSDS Darryl Sittler
SSEF Eric Fehr 8.00 20.00
SSEL Patrik Elias 6.00 15.00
SSEM Evgeni Malkin
SSEP Phil Esposito 15.00 40.00
SSFL Marc-Andre Fleury
SSFN Fredrik Norrena 20.00 50.00
SSGB Gilbert Brule 10.00 25.00
SSGH Gordie Howe 125.00 200.00
SSHA Jannik Hansen 5.00 12.00
SSHE Dany Heatley
SSHZ Henrik Zetterberg 40.00 80.00
SSJB Jean Beliveau 40.00 80.00
SSJD Jeff Drouin-Deslauriers
SSJE Jonathan Ericsson 8.00 20.00
SSJG Jean-Sebastien Giguere 40.00 80.00
SSJH Josh Hennessy 5.00 12.00
SSJK Jari Kurri 8.00 20.00
SSJL John-Michael Liles 6.00 15.00
SSJS Jarret Stoll 6.00 15.00
SSJT Joe Thornton 15.00 40.00
SSKN Mike Knuble
SSKQ Kyle Quincey 5.00 12.00
SSKT Kyle Turris 10.00 25.00
SSLA Drew Larman 5.00 12.00
SSLR Larry Robinson 10.00 25.00
SSLT Lauri Tukonen 5.00 12.00
SSLU Joffrey Lupul 8.00 20.00
SSMD Matt D'Agostini 10.00 25.00
SSME Matt Ellis 5.00 12.00
SSMF Mark Fistric 5.00 12.00
SSMI Mike Iggulden 5.00 12.00
SSMK Matt Keetley 5.00 12.00
SSML Mike Lundin 5.00 12.00
SSMM Mark Mancari 5.00 12.00
SSMO Mike Modano 40.00 80.00
SSMP Michael Peca 6.00 15.00
SSMR Mattias Ritola 5.00 12.00
SSND Nigel Dawes 5.00 12.00
SSNK Nikolai Khabibulin 8.00 20.00
SSOP Ondrej Pavelec 6.00 15.00
SSOV Alexander Ovechkin 125.00 250.00
SSPA Daniel Paille 6.00 15.00
SSPE Rich Peverley 6.00 15.00
SSPI Adam Pineault 6.00 15.00
SSPR Patrick Roy 125.00 200.00
SSPY Ryan Potulny 5.00 12.00
SSRH Ron Hextall 15.00 40.00
SSRK Rostislav Klesla
SSRO Rostislav Olesz 5.00 12.00
SSRU R.J. Umberger 6.00 15.00
SSRY Michael Ryder 6.00 15.00
SSSB Scotty Bowman 30.00 60.00
SSSC Sidney Crosby 200.00 300.00
SSSM Stefan Meyer 6.00 15.00
SSST Martin St. Louis
SSSW Steve Wagner 5.00 12.00
SSTC Ty Conklin 6.00 15.00
SSTL Jiri Tlusty 6.00 15.00
SSTO Tobias Stephan 5.00 12.00
SSTS Tom Sestito 5.00 12.00
SSTV Thomas Vanek 8.00 20.00
SSTW Tyler Weiman 8.00 20.00
SSVF Valtteri Filppula 8.00 20.00
SSWG Wayne Gretzky
SSZC Zdeno Chara 20.00 50.00

2009-10 Upper Deck The Champions

COMPLETE SET (40) 40.00 80.00
STATED ODDS 1:2
CHAB Amanda Beard 2.00 5.00
CHAC Alissa Czisny 2.00 5.00
CHAG Alexe Gilles 2.00 5.00
CHAN Miki Ando 2.00 5.00
CHBA Ben Agosto 2.00 5.00
CHBM Bode Miller 2.00 5.00
CHBS Becky Scott 2.00 5.00
CHBT Jennifer Botterill 2.00 5.00
CHCC Cassie Campbell 2.50 6.00
CHCG Cammie Granato 2.00 5.00
CHCO Sasha Cohen 2.00 5.00
CHDD Derrick Delmore 2.00 5.00
CHGB Gaetan Boucher 2.00 5.00
CHGI Todd Gilles 2.00 5.00
CHGZ Greg Zuerlein 2.00 5.00
CHHW Hayley Wickenheiser 2.00 5.00
CHJA Jeremy Abbott 2.00 5.00
CHJB Jean Luc Brassard 2.00 5.00
CHJC Julie Chu 2.50 6.00
CHJE Jeremy Bloom 2.00 5.00
CHJJ Jojo Starbuck 2.00 5.00
CHJM Julia Mancuso 2.00 5.00
CHKG Kerrin Lee Gartner 2.00 5.00
CHMC Madison Chock 2.00 5.00
CHME Melissa Gregory 2.00 5.00
CHMR Brandon Mroz 2.00 5.00
CHND Natalie Darwitz 2.00 5.00
CHNK Nancy Kerrigan 2.00 5.00
CHNO Nobunari Oda 2.00 5.00
CHPE Denis Petukhov 2.00 5.00
CHPG Piper Gilles 2.00 5.00
CHRF Rachael Flatt 2.00 5.00
CHSB Shae-Lynn Bourne 2.00 5.00
CHSP Kim St-Pierre 2.00 5.00
CHST Jane Summersett 2.00 5.00
CHTB Tanith Belbin 2.00 5.00
CHTG Timothy Goebel 2.00 5.00
CHWE Johnny Weir 2.00 5.00
CHYU Yuka Sato 2.00 5.00
CHZD Zach Donahue 2.00 5.00

2009-10 Upper Deck The Champions Autographs

CHAB Amanda Beard 15.00 40.00
CHAG Alexe Gilles 10.00 25.00
CHAN Miki Ando 90.00 150.00
CHBA Ben Agosto 15.00 40.00
CHCG Cammi Granato 15.00 40.00
CHDP Denis Petukhov 10.00 25.00
CHGB Gaetan Boucher 12.00 30.00
CHGZ Greg Zuerlein
CHHW Haley Wickenheiser 30.00 60.00
CHJB Jeremy Bloom 10.00 25.00
CHJM Julia Mancuso 10.00 25.00
CHJS Jane Summersett 10.00 25.00
CHKS Kim St. Pierre 20.00 50.00
CHMC Madison Chock
CHME Melissa Gregory 10.00 25.00
CHND Natalie Darwitz 10.00 25.00
CHPG Piper Gilles 12.00 30.00
CHRF Rachael Flatt 15.00 40.00
CHRR Ross Rebagliati
CHTB Tanith Belbin 15.00 40.00
CHTG Todd Gilles 10.00 25.00
CHBM Bode Miller 15.00 40.00
CHBT Jennifer Botterill 15.00 40.00
CHCC Cassie Campbell 15.00 40.00
CHDD Derrick Delmore 12.00 30.00
CHJC Julie Chu 15.00 40.00
CHKG Kerrin Lee Gartner 15.00 40.00
CHNK Nancy Kerrigan 25.00 60.00

2009-10 Upper Deck Top Guns

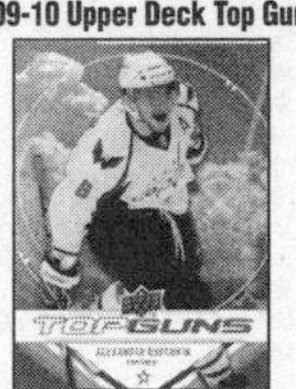

COMPLETE SET (7) 6.00 15.00
STATED ODDS 1:4
TG1 Alexander Semin .60 1.50
TG2 Zach Parise .60 1.50
TG3 Evgeni Malkin 1.50 4.00
TG4 Eric Staal .75 2.00
TG5 Jarome Iginla 1.25 3.00
TG6 Thomas Vanek .60 1.50
TG7 Alexander Ovechkin 2.50 6.00

2009-10 Upper Deck Winter Classic Oversized

COMPLETE SET (14) 10.00 25.00
WC1 Dustin Byfuglien .75 2.00
WC2 Patrick Kane 2.00 5.00
WC3 Brian Campbell .75 2.00
WC4 Patrick Sharp .75 2.00
WC5 Jonathan Toews 2.50 6.00
WC6 Kris Versteeg 1.25 3.00
WC7 Ben Eager .60 1.50
WC8 Marian Hossa 1.50 4.00
WC9 Nicklas Lidstrom 1.25 3.00
WC10 Brian Rafalski .60 1.50
WC11 Ty Conklin .75 2.00
WC12 Jiri Hudler .60 1.50
WC13 Pavel Datsyuk 1.00 2.50
WC14 Henrik Zetterberg 2.00 5.00

2009-10 Upper Deck Young Guns Oversized

XL1 Evander Kane 5.00 12.00
XL2 Tyler Myers 8.00 20.00
XL3 Matt Duchene 8.00 20.00
XL4 Jamie Benn 3.00 8.00
XL5 Ville Leino 2.50 6.00
XL6 Yannick Weber 2.50 6.00
XL7 John Tavares 30.00 60.00
XL8 Michael Del Zotto 4.00 10.00
XL9 Artem Anisimov 2.50 6.00
XL10 Erik Karlsson 6.00 15.00
XL11 James Van Riemsdyk 5.00 12.00
XL12 Victor Hedman 4.00 10.00
XL13 Viktor Stalberg 3.00 8.00
XL14 Sergei Shirokov 3.00 8.00

2007 Upper Deck BAP Draft Redemption Premium

TYSC Sidney Crosby 4.00 10.00

2006 Upper Deck Rookie Showdown

RSSCAO Sidney Crosby 3.00 8.00
Alexander Ovechkin

2003 Upper Deck All-Star Promos

Handed out in packs at the Upper Deck booth during the 2003 NHL All-Star Block Party, this 21-card set resembled the base UD set but card fronts carried a special All-Star logo and each card (except the checklists) was serial-numbered out of 500. Each pack contained 5-cards including the checklist card. Cards S1-S6 were randomly inserted into packs and carried authentic player autographs and were rumored to be limited to just 30 copies each..

COMP.SET w/o AUTOS (15) 16.00 40.00
S1 Rick Nash 80.00 200.00
S2 Stanislav Chistov 16.00 40.00
S3 Jason Spezza 20.00 70.00
S4 Alexander Frolov 12.00 20.00
S5 Jay Bouwmeester 16.00 40.00
S6 Jordan Leopold 10.00 20.00
AS1 Joe Thornton CL .40 2.00
AS2 Rick Nash 4.00 10.00
AS3 Stanislav Chistov 2.40 5.00
AS4 Chuck Kobasew 1.60 3.00
AS5 Stephen Weiss .60 2.00
AS6 Martin Brodeur CL .80 2.00
AS7 Jason Spezza 3.20 8.00
AS8 Alexander Frolov 2.00 3.00
AS9 Carlo Colaiacovo 1.20 2.00
AS10 Alexander Svitov 1.20 2.00
AS11 Nikolai Khabibulin CL .40 1.00
AS12 Henrik Zetterberg 4.00 10.00
AS13 Jordan Leopold .80 2.00
AS14 Jay Bouwmeester 2.40 5.00
AS15 P-M Bouchard 2.40 5.00

2004 Upper Deck All-Star Promos

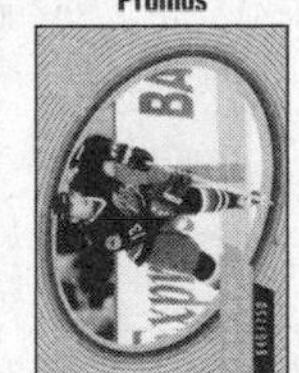

Available only via wrapper redemption at the Upper Deck booth during the 2004 NHL All-Star Fantest, this 15-card set featured perennial all-stars as well as popular prospects. Each card was serial-numbered out of 750.

COMPLETE SET (15)
BB Brent Burns 4.00 15.00
CB Christoph Brandner 4.00 10.00
ES Eric Staal 6.00 15.00
FS Fredrik Sjostrom 4.00 10.00
GH Gordie Howe 5.00 15.00
JP Joni Pitkanen 4.00 10.00
JS Jason Spezza 5.00 15.00
JT Joe Thornton 6.00 15.00
MF Marc-Andre Fleury 12.50 30.00
MG Marian Gaborik 6.00 15.00
NH Nathan Horton 6.00 15.00
NZ Nikolai Zherdev 8.00 20.00
PB Patrice Bergeron 10.00 30.00
PR Patrick Roy 8.00 30.00
TO Jordin Tootoo 6.00 15.00

2007 Upper Deck All-Star Game Redemptions

Single cards were available as wrapper redemptions over the course of the three-day card show held in conjunction with the 2007 NHL All-Star Game in Dallas.

AS1 Martin Brodeur 4.00 10.00
AS2 Phil Kessel 2.00 5.00
AS3 Eric Lindros 1.50 4.00
AS4 Joe Sakic 3.00 8.00
AS5 Jordan Staal 4.00 10.00
AS6 Marty Turco 1.25 3.00
AS7 Sidney Crosby 8.00 20.00
AS8 Alexander Radulov 2.00 5.00
AS9 Brenden Morrow 1.25 3.00
AS10 Alexander Ovechkin 4.00 10.00
AS11 Evgeni Malkin 6.00 15.00
AS12 Mike Modano 2.00 5.00

2000 Upper Deck AS Sittler

This card was given away at the 2000 All-Star Fan Fest. The card features Darryl Sittler.

1 Darryl Sittler 1.20 3.00

2001 Upper Deck Avalanche NHL All-Star Game

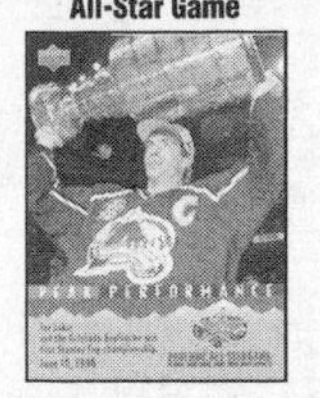

This 15-card set was produced by Upper Deck as a wrapper redemption for the 2001 All-Star Fan Fest and feature members of the host Avalanche. The cards were distributed in three-card packs, with each card serial numbered out of 500. A Wayne Gretzky e-card was given away also, these cards carried an interactive number that could be entered at the Upper Deck website to see if it "evolved" into a memorabilia card winner. The e-card is listed, but not considered part of the complete set.

COMPLETE SET (15) 50.00 125.00
CA1 Ray Bourque 6.00 15.00
CA2 Adam Foote .80 2.00
CA3 Adam Deadmarsh .80 2.00
CA4 Alex Tanguay 4.00 10.00
CA5 Aaron Miller .40 1.00
CA6 Stephane Yelle .40 1.00
HH1 David Aebischer 8.00 20.00
Patrick Roy
HH2 Milan Hejduk 6.00 15.00
Peter Forsberg
HH3 Joe Sakic 6.00 15.00
Raymond Bourque
PP1 Patrick Roy 8.00 20.00
PP2 Joe Sakic 4.80 12.00
PP3 Peter Forsberg 6.00 15.00
PP4 Chris Drury 4.00 10.00
PP5 Milan Hejduk 4.00 10.00
PP6 David Aebischer 4.00 10.00
WG Wayne Gretzky e-Card 2.00 5.00

1999-00 Upper Deck Century Legends

Released as an 89-card base set, Upper Deck Century Legends commemorates the NHL's timeless players spanning to the beginning of the century. Base cards feature action photography, a right side silver foil border and gold foil highlights. Card number 23 was not released. Century Legends was packaged in 24-pack boxes with 12 cards per pack and carried a suggested retail price of $4.99.

COMPLETE SET (89) 30.00 60.00
1 Wayne Gretzky 1.25 3.00
2 Bobby Orr 1.00 2.50
3 Gordie Howe .75 2.00
4 Mario Lemieux 1.00 2.50
5 Maurice Richard .50 1.25
6 Jean Beliveau .30 .75
7 Doug Harvey .20 .50
8 Bobby Hull .40 1.00
9 Jacques Plante .40 1.00
10 Eddie Shore .20 .50
11 Guy Lafleur .30 .75
12 Mark Messier .20 .50
13 Terry Sawchuk .40 1.00
14 Howie Morenz .15 .40
15 Denis Potvin .15 .40
16 Ray Bourque .30 .75
17 Glenn Hall .25 .60
18 Stan Mikita .30 .75
19 Phil Esposito .40 1.00
20 Mike Bossy .25 .60
21 Ted Lindsay .20 .50
22 Red Kelly .15 .40
24 Bobby Clarke .25 .60
25 Larry Robinson .20 .50
26 Milt Schmidt .15 .40
27 Frank Mahovlich .20 .50
28 Henri Richard .15 .40
29 Paul Coffey .20 .50
30 Bryan Trottier .15 .40
31 Dickie Moore .15 .40
32 Newsy Lalonde .15 .40
33 Syl Apps .15 .40
34 Bill Durnan .15 .40
35 Patrick Roy 1.00 2.50
36 Peter Stastny .20 .50
37 Jaromir Jagr .30 .75
38 Charlie Conacher .15 .40
39 Marcel Dionne .20 .50
40 Tim Horton .20 .50
41 Joe Malone .15 .40
42 Chris Chelios .20 .50
43 Bernie Geoffrion .30 .75
44 Dit Clapper .15 .40
45 Bill Cook .15 .40
46 Johnny Bucyk .15 .40
47 Serge Savard .20 .50
48 Jari Kurri .20 .50
49 Max Bentley .15 .40
50 Gilbert Perreault .15 .40
51 Dominik Hasek .40 1.00
52 Jaromir Jagr .30 .75
53 Peter Forsberg .50 1.25
54 Paul Kariya .20 .50
55 Patrick Roy 1.00 2.50
56 Steve Yzerman 1.00 2.50
57 Ray Bourque .30 .75
58 Pavel Bure .20 .50
59 Teemu Selanne .20 .50
60 Mike Modano .30 .75
61 Eric Lindros .20 .50
62 Brett Hull .25 .60
63 Martin Brodeur .50 1.25
64 Keith Tkachuk .20 .50
65 Joe Sakic .40 1.00
66 Mats Sundin .20 .50
67 John LeClair .20 .50
68 Alexei Yashin .02 .10
69 Peter Bondra .15 .40
70 Brendan Shanahan .20 .50
71 Sergei Samsonov .15 .40
72 Vincent Lecavalier .20 .50
73 Marian Hossa .20 .50
74 Chris Drury .15 .40
75 Milan Hejduk .20 .50
76 Paul Mara .02 .10
77 David Legwand .15 .40
78 Joe Thornton .30 .75
79 Pavel Rosa .02 .10
80 Patrik Elias .15 .40
81 Wayne Gretzky .75 2.00
82 Wayne Gretzky .75 2.00
83 Wayne Gretzky .75 2.00
84 Wayne Gretzky .75 2.00
85 Wayne Gretzky .75 2.00
86 Wayne Gretzky .75 2.00
87 Wayne Gretzky .75 2.00
88 Wayne Gretzky .75 2.00
89 Wayne Gretzky .75 2.00
90 Wayne Gretzky .75 2.00

1999-00 Upper Deck Century Legends Century Collection

Randomly inserted in packs, this 90-card die cut and holographic foil enhanced set parallels the base Century Legends set. Each card is sequentially numbered to 100.

*CENTURY COLL: 20X TO 50X BASIC CARDS

1999-00 Upper Deck Century Legends All Century Team

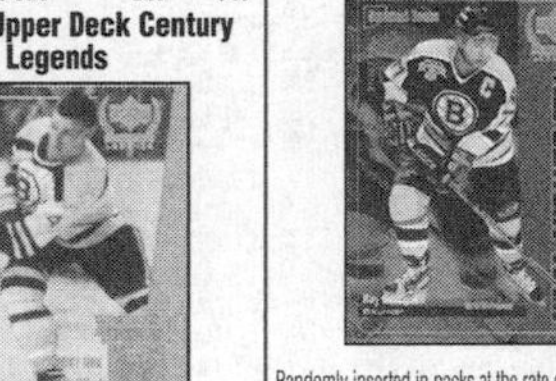

Randomly inserted in packs at the rate of 1:11, this 12-card set picks an All-Century first and second team.

COMPLETE SET (12) 40.00 80.00
AC1 Wayne Gretzky 6.00 15.00
AC2 Gordie Howe 4.00 10.00
AC3 Bobby Hull 2.50 6.00
AC4 Bobby Orr 5.00 12.00
AC5 Doug Harvey 2.00 5.00
AC6 Jacques Plante 2.00 5.00
AC7 Mario Lemieux 5.00 12.00
AC8 Maurice Richard 3.00 8.00
AC9 Ted Lindsay 2.00 5.00
AC10 Eddie Shore 2.00 5.00
AC11 Ray Bourque 4.00 10.00
AC12 Terry Sawchuk 2.50 6.00

1999-00 Upper Deck Century Legends Century Artifacts

Randomly inserted in packs, these 10 cards were issued as redemptions. Each card was redeemable for a one of one card that featured either a game used stick, jersey, autograph, cut autograph, or a Wayne Gretzky lithograph. The 1/1 cards and the lithograph are not priced due to scarcity.

UNPRICED ARTIFACTS PRINT RUN 1
C1 W.Gretzky Stick/1
C2 W.Gretzky Oilers Jersey/1
C3 W.Gretzky Rngrs Jersey/1
C4 Auto'd Card Collection/1
C5 Auto'd Puck Collection/1
C6 B.Orr Bruins Jersey/1
C7 G.Howe Wings Jersey/1
C8 W.Gretzky Litho/1
C9 J.Plante Cut Piece/1
C10 T.Sawchuk Cut Piece/1

1999-00 Upper Deck Century Legends Epic Signatures

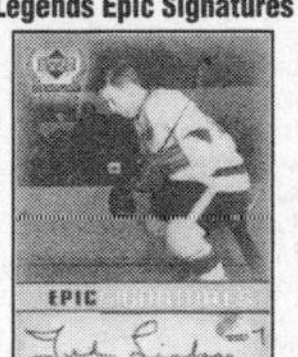

Randomly inserted in packs at the rate of 1:23, this 23-card set features authentic autographs of hockey's all time greats. The Gretzky card originally checklisted was never issued.

BC Bobby Clarke 12.50 30.00
BH Bobby Hull 20.00 50.00
BO Bobby Orr 150.00 300.00
BP Brad Park 6.00 15.00
FM Frank Mahovlich 6.00 15.00
GC Gerry Cheevers 10.00 25.00
GH Gordie Howe 75.00 150.00
JB John Bucyk 6.00 15.00
LR Larry Robinson 25.00 60.00
MB Mike Bossy 10.00 25.00
MD Marcel Dionne 8.00 20.00
ML Mario Lemieux 75.00 200.00
MR Maurice Richard 100.00 175.00
PB Pavel Bure 8.00 20.00
PE Phil Esposito 25.00 60.00
RB Ray Bourque 40.00 80.00
SM Stan Mikita 10.00 25.00
SS Sergei Samsonov 8.00 20.00
TE Tony Esposito 8.00 20.00
TL Ted Lindsay 6.00 15.00
BRH Brett Hull 15.00 40.00
JEB Jean Beliveau 12.50 30.00

1999-00 Upper Deck Century Legends Epic Signatures Gold 100

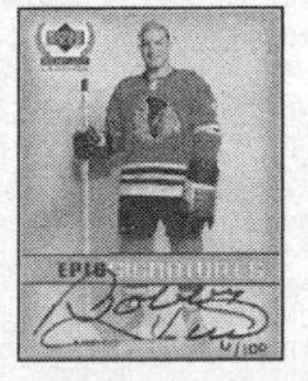

Randomly seeded in packs, this 23-card set parallels the regular Epic Signature set. Each card is sequentially numbered out of 100.

*GOLD/100: 1X TO 2.5X SILVER AU
BO Bobby Orr 150.00 400.00
GH Gordie Howe 125.00 250.00
ML Mario Lemieux 150.00 300.00
WG Wayne Gretzky 250.00 600.00

1999-00 Upper Deck Century Legends Essence of the Game

Randomly inserted in packs at the rate of 1:11, this 8-card set couples a player of the past with a present player. The "past" side of the card is in black and white, and the "present" side of the card is in color.

COMPLETE SET (8) 25.00 50.00
E1 Wayne Gretzky 5.00 12.00
Paul Kariya
E2 Bobby Orr 5.00 12.00
Ray Bourque
E3 Mario Lemieux 4.00 10.00
Jaromir Jagr
E4 Gordie Howe 2.50 6.00
Eric Lindros
E5 Jacques Plante 5.00 12.00
Patrick Roy
E6 Maurice Richard 2.50 6.00
Pavel Bure
E7 Bobby Hull 3.00 8.00
Brett Hull
E8 Ted Lindsay 2.50 6.00
Keith Tkachuk

1999-00 Upper Deck Century Legends Greatest Moments

Randomly inserted in packs at the rate of 1:23, this 10-card set pays tribute to the career of Wayne Gretzky.

COMPLETE SET (10) 60.00 125.00
COMMON GRETZKY (GM1-GM10) 6.00 15.00

1999-00 Upper Deck Century Legends Jerseys of the Century

Randomly inserted in packs at the rate of 1:475, this 6-card set features swatches of game used jersey coupled with a player photo. Bobby Clark and Mario Lemieux cards are signed and numbered out of 25. Note: set price does not include JCA1 and JCA2.

JC1 Bobby Clarke 30.00 80.00
JC2 Mike Bossy 30.00 80.00
JC3 Larry Robinson 30.00 80.00
JC4 Ray Bourque 30.00 80.00
JC5 Mario Lemieux 75.00 200.00
JC6 Wayne Gretzky 125.00 300.00
JCA1 Bobby Clarke AU/25 150.00 400.00
JCA2 Mario Lemieux AU/25 500.00 1000.00

2008-09 Upper Deck Champ's

This set was released on March 26, 2009. The base set consists of 200 cards.

COMPLETE SET (200) 75.00 150.00
COMP.SET w/o SPs 12.00 30.00
1 Ales Hemsky .20 .50
2 Alex Kovalev .30 .75
3 Alex Tanguay .25 .60
4 Alexander Frolov .20 .50
5 Alexander Ovechkin 1.25 3.00
6 Anze Kopitar .30 .75
7 Bobby Hull .60 1.50
8 Bobby Orr 1.00 2.50
9 Brad Boyes .25 .60

10 Brad Richards .25 .60
11 Brenden Morrow .25 .60
12 Brian Campbell .50 1.25
13 Brian Leetch .40 1.00
14 Cam Ward .30 .75
15 Carey Price 1.00 2.50
16 Chris Drury .30 .75
17 Chris Osgood .30 .75
18 Chris Pronger .25 .60
19 Corey Perry .30 .75
20 Cristobal Huet .30 .75
21 Dan Ellis .20 .50
22 Daniel Alfredsson .25 .60
23 Daniel Briere .30 .75
24 Daniel Sedin .30 .75
25 Dany Heatley .40 1.00
26 Derek Roy .20 .50
27 Dion Phaneuf .30 .75
28 Eric Staal .50 1.25
29 Evgeni Malkin .75 2.00
30 Evgeni Nabokov .30 .75
31 Gordie Howe 1.25 3.00
32 Guy Lafleur .60 1.50
33 Henrik Lundqvist .60 1.50
34 Henrik Sedin .30 .75
35 Henrik Zetterberg .60 1.50
36 Ilya Kovalchuk .40 1.00
37 Jari Kurri .30 .75
38 Jarome Iginla .60 1.50
39 Jason Arnott .20 .50
40 Jason Pominville .25 .60
41 Jason Spezza .40 1.00
42 Jean-Sebastien Giguere .30 .75
43 Joe Sakic .50 1.25
44 Joe Thornton .50 1.25
45 Johan Franzen .20 .50
46 Jonathan Toews 1.00 2.50
47 Jordan Staal .50 1.25
48 Kari Lehtonen .20 .50
49 Marc Savard .20 .50
50 Marc-Andre Fleury .30 .75
51 Marian Gaborik .50 1.25
52 Marian Hossa .50 1.25
53 Mario Lemieux .75 2.00
54 Mark Messier .60 1.50
55 Martin Brodeur .60 1.50
56 Martin St. Louis .30 .75
57 Marty Turco .25 .60
58 Mats Sundin .30 .75
59 Miikka Kiprusoff .30 .75
60 Mike Bossy .30 .75
61 Mike Modano .30 .75
62 Mike Ribeiro .20 .50
63 Mike Richards .50 1.25
64 Nathan Horton .20 .50
65 Nicklas Backstrom .60 1.50
66 Nicklas Lidstrom .30 .75
67 Niklas Backstrom .30 .75
68 Olli Jokinen .20 .50
69 Pascal Leclaire .25 .60
70 Patrick Kane .75 2.00
71 Patrick Roy 1.00 2.50
72 Patrick Sharp .20 .50
73 Patrik Elias .20 .50
74 Paul Kariya .30 .75
75 Paul Stastny .30 .75
76 Pavel Datsyuk .30 .75
77 Ryan Smyth .25 .60
78 Peter Mueller .40 1.00
79 Phil Esposito .50 1.25
80 Rick DiPietro .30 .75
81 Rick Nash .30 .75
82 Roberto Luongo .50 1.25
83 Rod Brind' Amour .25 .60
84 Ron Hextall .30 .75
85 Ryan Getzlaf .40 1.00
86 Ryan Miller .30 .75
87 Saku Koivu .30 .75
88 Scott Niedermayer .20 .50
89 Shane Doan .20 .50
90 Shawn Horcoff .20 .50
91 Sidney Crosby 1.50 4.00
92 Simon Gagne .25 .60
93 Thomas Vanek .30 .75
94 Tomas Kaberle .20 .50
95 Tomas Vokoun .30 .75
96 Tony Esposito .30 .75
97 Vesa Toskala .30 .75
98 Vincent Lecavalier .30 .75
99 Wayne Gretzky 1.50 4.00
100 Zach Parise .30 .75
101 Ilya Zubov RC 2.00 5.00
102 Ty Wishart RC 2.00 5.00
103 John Mitchell RC 2.00 5.00
104 Boris Valabik RC 2.50 6.00
105 Kyle Turris RC 4.00 10.00
106 Danny Taylor RC 2.00 5.00
107 Brendan Mikkelson RC 1.25 3.00
108 Justin Pogge RC 4.00 10.00
109 Janne Pesonen RC 1.50 4.00
110 Tom Sestito RC 1.50 4.00
111 Mattias Ritola RC 2.50 6.00
112 Kenndal McArdle RC 2.00 5.00
113 Teddy Purcell RC 2.00 5.00
114 Cory Schneider RC 4.00 10.00
115 Adam Pineault RC 2.00 5.00
116 Pascal Pelletier RC 1.50 4.00
117 Theo Peckham RC 2.00 5.00
118 Kyle Okposo RC 4.00 10.00
119 Michal Repik RC 2.50 6.00
120 Andrew Murray RC 1.50 4.00
121 Trevor Smith RC 1.50 4.00
122 Brett Skinner RC 1.50 4.00
123 Patrick Davis RC 1.50 4.00
124 Adam Pardy RC 2.00 5.00
125 Shawn Matthias RC 2.00 5.00
126 Steve Mason RC 5.00 12.00
127 Paul Bissonnette RC 2.50 6.00
128 Sami Lepisto RC 2.00 5.00
129 Brian Lee RC 2.00 5.00
130 Tim Kennedy RC 3.00 8.00
131 Dan LaCosta RC 2.50 6.00
132 Joe Jensen RC 2.00 5.00
133 Anssi Salmela RC 2.50 6.00
134 Niklas Hjalmarsson RC 3.00 8.00
135 Brad Staubitz RC 1.50 4.00
136 Max Pacioretty RC 5.00 12.00
137 Darren Helm RC 3.00 8.00
138 Brett Sutter RC 2.00 5.00
139 Jonas Frogren RC 2.50 6.00
140 Alex Goligoski RC 4.00 10.00
141 Claude Giroux RC 4.00 10.00
142 Simeon Varlamov RC 10.00 25.00
143 Derek Joslin RC 4.00 10.00
144 Mark Fistric RC 1.50 4.00
145 Karl Alzner RC 3.00 8.00
146 Erik Ersberg RC 2.00 5.00
147 Jonathan Ericsson RC 3.00 8.00
148 Andrew Ebbett RC 2.00 5.00
149 Robbie Earl RC 1.50 4.00
150 Tyler Sloan RC 2.50 6.00
151 Matt D'Agostini RC 3.00 8.00
152 Ben Maxwell RC 3.00 8.00
153 Trevor Lewis RC 2.00 5.00
154 Tom Cavanagh RC 1.50 4.00
155 Mike Brown RC 2.50 6.00
156 David Brine RC 1.50 4.00
157 Derick Brassard RC 4.00 10.00
158 Brian Boyle RC 2.00 5.00
159 Darryl Boyce RC 1.50 4.00
160 Justin Abdelkader RC 4.00 10.00
161 Wayne Simmonds RC 2.00 5.00
162 Zach Bogosian RC 4.00 10.00
163 Nathan Oystrick RC 2.00 5.00
164 Blake Wheeler RC 5.00 12.00
165 Zach Boychuk RC 3.00 8.00
166 Brandon Sutter RC 2.50 6.00
167 Nikita Filatov RC 8.00 20.00
168 Jakub Voracek RC 4.00 10.00
169 James Neal RC 3.00 8.00
170 Michael Frolik RC 4.00 10.00
171 Oscar Moller RC 2.00 5.00
172 Colton Gillies RC 2.00 5.00
173 Patric Hornqvist RC 2.00 5.00
174 Ryan Jones RC 2.50 6.00
175 Matthew Halischuk RC 2.50 6.00
176 Petr Vrana RC 2.50 6.00
177 Andreas Nodl RC 2.00 5.00
178 Luca Sbisa RC 3.00 8.00
179 Ben Bishop RC 3.00 8.00
180 T.J. Oshie RC 5.00 12.00
181 Patrik Berglund RC 5.00 12.00
182 Chris Porter RC 2.00 5.00
183 Jamie McGinn RC 2.00 5.00
184 Vladimir Mihalik RC 2.00 5.00
185 Luke Schenn RC 6.00 15.00
186 Nikolai Kulemin RC 2.00 5.00
187 Dwight Helminen RC 2.00 5.00
188 Patrick Dwyer RC 2.00 5.00
189 Alex Pietrangelo RC 3.00 8.00
190 Derek Dorsett RC 2.50 6.00
191 Steve MacIntyre RC 2.00 5.00
192 Darrel Powe RC 2.00 5.00
193 Chris Stewart RC 2.50 6.00
194 Dustin Jeffrey RC 3.00 8.00
195 Drew Doughty RC 6.00 15.00
196 Kevin Porter RC 1.50 4.00
197 Viktor Tikhonov RC 2.00 5.00
198 Mikkel Boedker RC 3.00 8.00
199 Fabian Brunnstrom RC 3.00 8.00
200 Steven Stamkos RC 15.00 40.00

2008-09 Upper Deck Champ's Mini

COMP.BASE w/o SPs (200) 15.00 40.00
NATURAL HISTORY STATED ODDS 1:3
C1 Ales Hemsky .40 1.00
C2 Alex Kovalev .60 1.50
C3 Alex Tanguay .50 1.25
C4 Alexander Frolov .40 1.00
C5 Alexander Ovechkin 2.50 6.00
C6 Alexander Semin .60 1.50
C7 Andrei Kostitsyn .50 1.25
C8 Andrew Cogliano 1.00 2.50
C9 Anze Kopitar .60 1.50
C10 Bill Guerin .40 1.00
C11 Brad Boyes .50 1.25
C12 Brad Richards .50 1.25
C13 Brendan Morrison .40 1.00
C14 Aaron Voros .40 1.00
C15 Brenden Morrow .50 1.25
C16 Brian Campbell 1.00 2.50
C17 Brian Gionta .60 1.50
C18 Brian Rolston .40 1.00
C19 Cam Ward .60 1.50
C20 Carey Price 2.00 5.00
C21 Chris Drury .60 1.50
C22 Chris Higgins .60 1.50
C23 Chris Kunitz .40 1.00
C24 Chris Osgood .60 1.50
C25 Chris Pronger .50 1.25
C26 Colby Armstrong .40 1.00
C27 Corey Perry .60 1.50
C28 Cristobal Huet .60 1.50
C29 Dan Boyle .60 1.50
C30 Dan Cleary .60 1.50
C31 Dan Ellis .40 1.00
C32 Daniel Alfredsson .50 1.25
C33 Daniel Briere .60 1.50
C34 Daniel Carcillo .40 1.00
C35 Daniel Sedin .60 1.50
C36 Dany Heatley .75 2.00
C37 Darcy Tucker .50 1.25
C38 David Legwand .50 1.25
C39 Daymond Langkow .40 1.00
C40 Derek Roy .40 1.00
C41 Dion Phaneuf .60 1.50
C42 Doug Weight .40 1.00
C43 Drew Stafford .60 1.50
C44 Duncan Keith .50 1.25
C45 Dustin Brown .40 1.00
C46 Dustin Penner .40 1.00
C47 Dwayne Roloson .50 1.25
C48 Ed Jovanovski .40 1.00
C49 Eric Staal 1.00 2.50
C50 Erik Cole .40 1.00
C51 Erik Johnson .75 2.00
C52 Evgeni Malkin 1.50 4.00
C53 Evgeni Nabokov .60 1.50
C54 George Parros .40 1.00
C55 Sheldon Souray .40 1.00
C56 David Krejci .50 1.25
C57 Guillaume Latendresse .50 1.25
C58 Henrik Lundqvist 1.25 3.00
C59 Henrik Sedin .60 1.50
C60 Henrik Zetterberg 1.25 3.00
C61 Ilya Bryzgalov .40 1.00
C62 Ilya Kovalchuk .75 2.00
C63 J.P. Dumont .40 1.00
C64 Jack Johnson .50 1.25
C65 Jarome Iginla 1.25 3.00
C66 Jarret Stoll .50 1.25
C67 Jason Arnott .40 1.00
C68 Jason LaBarbera .50 1.25
C69 Jason Pominville .50 1.25
C70 Jason Spezza .75 2.00
C71 Jay Bouwmeester .50 1.25
C72 Jean-Sebastien Giguere .60 1.50
C73 Jeff Carter .60 1.50
C74 Jere Lehtinen .40 1.00
C75 Joe Sakic 1.00 2.50
C76 Joe Thornton 1.00 2.50
C77 Johan Franzen .40 1.00
C78 Johan Hedberg .50 1.25
C79 Loui Eriksson .40 1.00
C80 Jonathan Cheechoo .60 1.50
C81 Jonathan Toews 2.00 5.00
C82 Jordan Staal 1.00 2.50
C83 Josh Harding .50 1.25
C84 Jussi Jokinen .40 1.00
C85 Justin Williams .40 1.00
C86 Kari Lehtonen .40 1.00
C87 Keith Tkachuk .50 1.25
C88 Kristian Huselius .40 1.00
C89 Lee Stempniak .40 1.00
C90 Manny Legace .50 1.25
C91 Marc Savard .40 1.00
C92 Marc Staal .75 2.00
C93 Marc-Andre Fleury .60 1.50
C94 Marek Zidlicky .40 1.00
C95 Marian Gaborik 1.00 2.50
C96 Marian Hossa 1.00 2.50
C97 Markus Naslund .60 1.50
C98 Martin Biron .50 1.25
C99 Martin Brodeur 1.25 3.00
C100 Martin Erat .60 1.50
C101 Martin Gerber .50 1.25
C102 Martin Hanzal .50 1.25
C103 Martin Havlat .50 1.25
C104 Martin St. Louis .60 1.50
C105 Marty Turco .60 1.50
C106 Mats Sundin .60 1.50
C107 Matt Stajan .50 1.25
C108 Matthew Lombardi .40 1.00
C109 Michael Peca .40 1.00
C110 Michael Ryder .50 1.25
C111 Michal Rozsival .40 1.00
C112 Miikka Kiprusoff .60 1.50
C113 Mike Cammalleri .60 1.50
C114 Mike Comrie .40 1.00
C115 Mike Knuble .60 1.50
C116 Mike Modano .60 1.50
C117 Mike Ribeiro .40 1.00
C118 Mike Richards 1.00 2.50
C119 Mike Smith .60 1.50
C120 Mikko Koivu .60 1.50
C121 Milan Hejduk .50 1.25
C122 Milan Lucic 1.25 3.00
C123 Milan Michalek .40 1.00
C124 Miroslav Satan .40 1.00
C125 Nathan Horton .40 1.00
C126 Nicklas Backstrom 1.25 3.00
C127 Nicklas Lidstrom .60 1.50
C128 Niklas Backstrom .60 1.50
C129 Nik Antropov .50 1.25
C130 Nikolai Khabibulin .60 1.50
C131 Nikolai Zherdev .40 1.00
C132 Olli Jokinen .40 1.00
C133 Pascal Leclaire .60 1.50
C134 Patrice Bergeron .60 1.50
C135 Patrick Kane 1.50 4.00
C136 Patrick Marleau .50 1.25
C137 Patrick O'Sullivan .50 1.25
C138 Patrick Sharp .40 1.00
C139 Patrik Elias .40 1.00
C140 Paul Kariya .60 1.50
C141 Paul Stastny .60 1.50
C142 Pavel Datsyuk .60 1.50
C143 Peter Budaj .50 1.25
C144 John-Michael Liles .40 1.00
C145 Peter Mueller .75 2.00
C146 Phil Kessel .60 1.50
C147 Pierre-Marc Bouchard .40 1.00
C148 R.J. Umberger .40 1.00
C149 Mark Recchi .50 1.25
C150 Ray Whitney .50 1.25
C151 Rick DiPietro .60 1.50
C152 Rick Nash .60 1.50
C153 Robert Lang .40 1.00
C154 Roberto Luongo 1.00 2.50
C155 Rod Brind' Amour .50 1.25
C156 Ryan Getzlaf .75 2.00
C157 Ryan Kesler .40 1.00
C158 Ryan Malone .40 1.00
C159 Ryan Miller .60 1.50
C160 Ryan Smyth .60 1.50
C161 Ryan Suter .40 1.00
C162 Saku Koivu .60 1.50
C163 Sam Gagner 1.00 2.50
C164 Scott Gomez .50 1.25
C165 Scott Niedermayer .40 1.00
C166 Sergei Fedorov 1.00 2.50
C167 Sergei Zubov .60 1.50
C168 Shane Doan .50 1.25
C169 Shawn Horcoff .40 1.00
C170 Shea Weber .40 1.00
C171 Sidney Crosby 3.00 8.00
C172 Simon Gagne .50 1.25
C173 Slava Kozlov .40 1.00
C174 Steve Bernier .40 1.00
C175 Teemu Selanne .60 1.50
C176 Thomas Vanek .60 1.50
C177 Tim Thomas .60 1.50
C178 Tobias Enstrom .60 1.50
C179 Todd White .40 1.00
C180 Tomas Holmstrom .50 1.25
C181 Tomas Kaberle .40 1.00
C182 Tomas Vokoun .60 1.50
C183 Trent Hunter .40 1.00
C184 Ty Conklin .50 1.25
C185 Vaclav Prospal .40 1.00
C186 Valtteri Filppula .40 1.00
C187 Vesa Toskala .60 1.50
C188 Vincent Lecavalier .60 1.50
C189 Wade Redden .40 1.00
C190 Wojtek Wolski .40 1.00
C191 Zach Parise .60 1.50
C192 Zdeno Chara .40 1.00
C193 Adam Pardy .60 1.50
C194 Adam Pineault .60 1.50
C195 Simeon Varlamov 3.00 8.00
C196 Alex Goligoski 1.25 3.00
C197 Alex Pietrangelo 1.00 2.50
C198 Andreas Nodl .60 1.50
C199 Andrew Ebbett .60 1.50
C200 Andrew Murray .50 1.25
C201 Anssi Salmela 3.00 8.00
C202 Max Pacioretty 6.00 15.00
C203 Ben Bishop 4.00 10.00
C204 Blake Wheeler 6.00 15.00
C205 Boris Valabik 3.00 8.00
C206 Brad Staubitz 1.25 3.00
C207 Tim Kennedy 4.00 10.00
C208 Brandon Sutter 3.00 8.00
C209 Brett Skinner 2.00 5.00
C210 Brian Boyle 2.50 6.00
C211 Brian Lee 2.50 6.00
C212 Chris Porter 2.50 6.00
C213 Claude Giroux 5.00 12.00
C214 Colton Gillies 2.50 6.00
C215 Kenndal McArdle 2.50 6.00
C216 Darren Helm 4.00 10.00
C217 Cory Schneider 5.00 12.00
C218 David Brine 2.00 5.00
C219 Derek Dorsett 3.00 8.00
C220 Derick Brassard 5.00 12.00
C221 Drew Doughty 8.00 20.00
C222 Dwight Helminen 2.50 6.00
C223 Erik Ersberg 2.50 6.00
C224 Fabian Brunnstrom 4.00 10.00
C225 Ilya Zubov 2.50 6.00
C226 Jakub Voracek 5.00 12.00
C227 James Neal 4.00 10.00
C228 Jamie McGinn 2.50 6.00
C229 Janne Pesonen 2.00 5.00
C230 Ty Wishart 2.50 6.00
C231 Joe Jensen 2.50 6.00
C232 John Mitchell 2.50 6.00
C233 Justin Pogge 5.00 12.00
C234 Jonas Frogren 3.00 8.00
C235 Jonathan Ericsson 4.00 10.00
C236 Trevor Lewis 2.50 6.00
C237 Brendan Mikkelson 1.50 4.00
C238 Justin Abdelkader 5.00 12.00
C239 Kevin Porter 2.00 5.00
C240 Brett Sutter 2.50 6.00
C241 Kyle Okposo 5.00 12.00
C242 Kyle Turris 5.00 12.00
C243 Luca Sbisa 4.00 10.00
C244 Luke Schenn 8.00 20.00
C245 Mark Fistric 2.00 5.00
C246 Matt D'Agostini 4.00 10.00
C247 Matthew Halischuk 3.00 8.00
C248 Mattias Ritola 3.00 8.00
C249 Michael Frolik 5.00 12.00
C250 Mike Brown 3.00 8.00
C251 Mikkel Boedker 4.00 10.00
C252 Trevor Smith 2.00 5.00
C253 Josh Bailey 4.00 10.00
C254 Nathan Oystrick 2.50 6.00
C255 Nikita Filatov 10.00 25.00
C256 Niklas Hjalmarsson 4.00 10.00
C257 Nikolai Kulemin 2.50 6.00
C258 Oscar Moller 2.50 6.00
C259 Pascal Pelletier 2.00 5.00
C260 Patric Hornqvist 2.50 6.00
C261 Patrick Davis 2.00 5.00
C262 Patrick Dwyer 2.50 6.00
C263 Patrik Berglund 6.00 15.00
C264 Chris Stewart 3.00 8.00
C265 Petr Vrana 3.00 8.00
C266 Dustin Jeffrey 4.00 10.00
C267 Robbie Earl 2.00 5.00
C268 Ryan Jones 3.00 8.00
C269 Karl Alzner 4.00 10.00
C270 Sami Lepisto 2.50 6.00
C271 Shawn Matthias 2.50 6.00
C272 Steve MacIntyre 2.50 6.00
C273 Steve Mason 6.00 15.00
C274 Steven Stamkos 20.00 50.00
C275 T.J. Oshie 6.00 15.00
C276 Teddy Purcell 2.50 6.00
C277 Theo Peckham 2.50 6.00
C278 Michal Repik 3.00 8.00
C279 Ben Maxwell 4.00 10.00
C280 Tom Sestito 2.00 5.00
C281 Tyler Plante 2.50 6.00
C282 Tyler Sloan 3.00 8.00
C283 Viktor Tikhonov 2.50 6.00
C284 Vladimir Mihalik 2.50 6.00
C285 Wayne Simmonds 2.50 6.00
C286 Zach Bogosian 5.00 12.00
C287 Zach Boychuk 4.00 10.00
C288 Derek Joslin 2.00 5.00
C289 Great White Shark 1.25 3.00
C290 Tiger Shark 1.25 3.00
C291 Acrocanthosaurus 1.25 3.00
C292 African Elephant 1.25 3.00
C293 African Leopard 1.25 3.00
C294 African Lion 1.25 3.00
C295 African Wild Dog 1.25 3.00
C296 Hammerhead Shark 1.25 3.00
C297 Albertosaurus 1.25 3.00
C298 Alectrosaurus 1.25 3.00
C299 Allosaurus 1.25 3.00
C300 Amargasaurus 1.25 3.00
C301 American Alligator 1.25 3.00
C302 American Lion 1.25 3.00
C303 Bull Shark 1.25 3.00
C304 Shortfin Mako Shark 1.25 3.00
C305 Anchiceratops 1.25 3.00
C306 Ankylosaur 1.25 3.00
C307 Sand Tiger Shark 1.25 3.00
C308 Apatosaurus 1.25 3.00
C309 Archelon 1.25 3.00
C310 Archaeopteryx 1.25 3.00
C311 Arctic fox 1.25 3.00
C312 Auroch 1.25 3.00
C313 Baiji Dolphin 1.25 3.00
C314 Bald Eagle 1.25 3.00
C315 Baryonyx 1.25 3.00
C316 Oceanic Whitetip Shark 1.25 3.00
C317 Bird of Paradise 1.25 3.00
C318 Black Rhino 1.25 3.00
C319 Blue Whale 1.25 3.00
C320 Bowhead Whale 1.25 3.00
C321 Brachiosaurus 1.25 3.00
C322 Brontops 1.25 3.00
C323 Brontosaurus 1.25 3.00
C324 Brown Bear 1.25 3.00
C325 Brown Pelican 1.25 3.00
C326 Burgess Shale 1.25 3.00
C327 California Condor 1.25 3.00
C328 Cambropallas Trilobite 1.25 3.00
C329 Cape Buffalo 1.25 3.00
C330 Carcharodontosaurus 1.25 3.00
C331 Carrier Pigeon 1.25 3.00
C332 Cave Bear 1.25 3.00
C333 Cheetah 1.25 3.00
C334 Chimpanzee 1.25 3.00
C335 Chinese Alligator 1.25 3.00
C336 Chinook Salmon 1.25 3.00
C337 Blue Shark 1.25 3.00
C338 Clouded Leopard 1.25 3.00
C339 Piranha 1.25 3.00
C340 Compsognathus 1.25 3.00
C341 Corythosaurus 1.25 3.00
C342 Barracuda 1.25 3.00
C343 Cro-Magnon Man 1.25 3.00
C344 Moray Eel 1.25 3.00
C345 Electric Eel 1.25 3.00
C346 Deinonychus 1.25 3.00
C347 Diatryma 1.25 3.00
C348 Dilong 1.25 3.00
C349 Dimetrodon 1.25 3.00
C350 Dimorphodon 1.25 3.00
C351 Australopithecus robustus 1.25 3.00
C352 Diplodocus 1.25 3.00
C353 Dire Wolf 1.25 3.00
C354 Dodo 1.25 3.00
C355 Dromaeosaurus 1.25 3.00
C356 Dunkleosteus 1.25 3.00
C357 Edmontosaurus 1.25 3.00
C358 Einiosaurus 1.25 3.00
C359 Elasmosaurus 1.25 3.00
C360 Emperor Penguin 1.25 3.00
C361 Euoplocephalus 1.25 3.00
C362 Fin Whale 1.25 3.00
C363 Fox 1.25 3.00
C364 Galapagos Hawk 1.25 3.00
C365 Galapagos Penguin 1.25 3.00
C366 Galapagos Tortoise 1.25 3.00
C367 Black Widow 1.25 3.00
C368 Giant Panda 1.25 3.00
C369 Giganotosaurus 1.25 3.00
C370 Portuguese Man O'War 1.25 3.00
C371 Glyptodon 1.25 3.00
C372 Gorgosaurus 1.25 3.00
C373 Gray Wolf 1.25 3.00
C374 Ground Sloth 1.25 3.00
C375 Hesperornis 1.25 3.00
C376 Hippopotamus 1.25 3.00
C377 Hominids 1.25 3.00
C378 Hoplophoncus 1.25 3.00
C379 Humpback Whale 1.25 3.00
C380 Hyaenodon 1.25 3.00
C381 Ichthyosaurus 1.25 3.00
C382 Coelacanth 1.25 3.00
C383 Iguanodon 1.25 3.00
C384 Jaguar 1.25 3.00
C385 Jobaria 1.25 3.00
C386 Kakapo 1.25 3.00
C387 Killer Whale 1.25 3.00
C388 Golden-Mantled Tree Kangaroo 1.25 3.00
C389 Komodo Dragon 1.25 3.00
C390 Lambeosaurus 1.25 3.00
C391 Lannacus Trilobite 1.25 3.00
C392 Box Jellyfish 1.25 3.00
C393 Leopard Seal 1.25 3.00
C394 Leptoceratops 1.25 3.00
C395 Lesothosaurus 1.25 3.00
C396 Maiasaura 1.25 3.00
C397 Mastodon 1.25 3.00
C398 Marbled Cone Snail 1.25 3.00
C399 Megalodon 1.25 3.00
C400 Megalosaurus 1.25 3.00
C401 Megatherium 1.25 3.00
C402 Australopithecus africanus 1.25 3.00
C403 Blue Ringed Octopus 1.25 3.00
C404 Microraptor 1.25 3.00
C405 Death Stalker Scorpion 1.25 3.00
C406 Moa 1.25 3.00
C407 Stonefish 1.25 3.00
C408 Moose 1.25 3.00
C409 Mountain Lion 1.25 3.00
C410 Muttaburrasaurus 1.25 3.00
C411 Sydney Funnel Web Spider 1.25 3.00
C412 Neanderthal Man 1.25 3.00
C413 Inland Taipan 1.25 3.00
C414 Ocelot 1.25 3.00
C415 Orangutan 1.25 3.00
C416 King Cobra 1.25 3.00
C417 Ornithomimus 1.25 3.00
C418 Ouranosaurus 1.25 3.00
C419 Oviraptor 1.25 3.00
C420 Brazilian Wandering Spider 1.25 3.00
C421 Panther 1.25 3.00
C422 Paradoxides trilobite 1.25 3.00
C423 Parasaurolophus 1.25 3.00
C424 Puffer Fish 1.25 3.00
C425 Homo habilis 1.25 3.00
C426 Plateosaurus 1.25 3.00
C427 Plesiosaurus 1.25 3.00
C428 Polacanthus 1.25 3.00
C429 Polar Bear 1.25 3.00
C430 Prairie Dog 1.25 3.00
C431 Pterodactyl 1.25 3.00
C432 Pterosaur 1.25 3.00
C433 Quetzalcoatlus 1.25 3.00
C434 Red Deer 1.25 3.00
C435 Red Wolf 1.25 3.00
C436 Rhoetosaurus 1.25 3.00
C437 Right Whale 1.25 3.00
C438 Royal Bengal Tiger 1.25 3.00
C439 Australopithecus afarensis 1.25 3.00
C440 Saber-Toothed Cat 1.25 3.00
C441 Salt Water Crocodile 1.25 3.00
C442 Saltasaurus 1.25 3.00
C443 Sarcosuchus 1.25 3.00
C444 Sea Otter 1.25 3.00
C445 Sea Turtle 1.25 3.00
C446 Seismosaurus 1.25 3.00
C447 Homo ergaster 1.25 3.00
C448 Poison Dart Frog 1.25 3.00
C449 Sinornithosaurus 1.25 3.00
C450 Sinosauropteryx 1.25 3.00
C451 Snow Leopard 1.25 3.00
C452 Sperm Whale 1.25 3.00
C453 Spider Monkey 1.25 3.00
C454 Spinosaurus 1.25 3.00
C455 Spotted Hyena 1.25 3.00
C456 Homo heidelbergensis 1.25 3.00
C457 Steelhead 1.25 3.00
C458 Stegosaurus 1.25 3.00
C459 Sturgeon 1.25 3.00
C460 Styracosaurus 1.25 3.00
C461 Sun Bear 1.25 3.00
C462 Tasmanian Devil 1.25 3.00
C463 Tasmanian Tiger 1.25 3.00
C464 Homo erectus 1.25 3.00
C465 Torosaurus 1.25 3.00
C466 Toxodon 1.25 3.00
C467 Triceratops 1.25 3.00
C468 Troodon 1.25 3.00
C469 Tropeognathus 1.25 3.00
C470 Tylosaurus 1.25 3.00
C471 Tyrannosaurus Rex 1.25 3.00
C472 Velociraptor 1.25 3.00
C473 Western Gorilla 1.25 3.00
C474 Whooping Crane 1.25 3.00
C475 Wolverine 1.25 3.00
C476 Woodpecker 1.25 3.00
C477 Woolly Mammoth 1.25 3.00
C478 Woolly Rhino 1.25 3.00
C479 Zebra 1.25 3.00
C480 Sahelanthropus tchadensis 1.25 3.00

2008-09 Upper Deck Champ's Mini Blue Backs

*SINGLES: 3X TO 8X BASIC CARDS
STATED ODDS 1:288

2008-09 Upper Deck Champ's Mini Brown Backs

*SINGLES: 1X TO 2.5X BASIC CARDS
STATED ODDS 1:25

2008-09 Upper Deck Champ's Mini Purple Backs

*SINGLES: X TO X BASIC CARDS
STATED ODDS 1:576

2008-09 Upper Deck Champ's Mini Red Backs

*SINGLES: 3X TO 8X BASIC CARDS
STATED ODDS 1:144

2008-09 Upper Deck Champ's Fossils and Artifacts

FAAT Aterian Scraper 75.00 150.00
FAAU Auroch Femur 50.00 100.00
FANE Neolithic Stone Tools 200.00 300.00
FANM Neanderthal Mousterian Flint Knife
FAPT Pterosaur Tooth
FAST Spinosaurus Teeth
FATT Tyrannosaurus Rex Tooth
FAWM Woolly Mammoth Femur 50.00 100.00
FAWR Woolly Rhino Humerus 50.00 100.00

2008-09 Upper Deck Champ's Hall of Legends Sports Memorabilia

HOLAN Glenn Anderson 8.00 20.00
HOLBT Bryan Trottier 8.00 20.00
HOLCN Cam Neely 12.00 30.00
HOLDH Dale Hawerchuk 10.00 25.00
HOLDS Darryl Sittler
HOLFM Frank Mahovlich 10.00 25.00
HOLGF Grant Fuhr 10.00 25.00
HOLGH Gordie Howe 40.00 100.00
HOLGP Gilbert Perreault 10.00 25.00
HOLHK Dominik Hasek 15.00 40.00
HOLJB Johnny Bucyk 10.00 25.00
HOLJI Jarome Iginla 20.00 50.00
HOLJK Jari Kurri 10.00 25.00
HOLLY Larry Robinson 10.00 25.00
HOLML Mario Lemieux 25.00 60.00
HOLMM Mark Messier 20.00 50.00
HOLMW Mike Weir 15.00 40.00
HOLPE Phil Esposito 15.00 40.00
HOLPR Patrick Roy 30.00 80.00
HOLRB Ray Bourque 20.00 50.00
HOLTE Tony Esposito 10.00 25.00
HOLTW Tiger Woods 250.00 400.00
HOLWG Wayne Gretzky 50.00 120.00

2008-09 Upper Deck Champ's Mini Signatures

STATED ODDS 1:12
WOODS SP IS UNPRICED DUE TO SCARCITY
CSAG Alex Goligoski 12.00 30.00
CSBK Mikkel Boedker 10.00 25.00
CSBY Brad Boyes 5.00 12.00
CSCM Cory Murphy 4.00 10.00
CSDC Dan Cleary 6.00 15.00
CSDD Drew Doughty 20.00 50.00
CSDH Dany Heatley 8.00 20.00
CSDN Daniel Negreanu 60.00 100.00
CSEE Erik Ersberg 6.00 15.00
CSEM Evgeni Malkin 30.00 60.00
CSES Eric Staal 10.00 25.00
CSFB Fabian Brunnstrom 12.00 30.00
CSFW Jon Filewich 5.00 12.00
CSGH Gordie Howe 75.00 150.00
CSGU Guillaume Latendresse 5.00 12.00
CSHI Jonas Hiller 6.00 15.00
CSIZ Ilya Zubov 6.00 15.00
CSJD Jordan Staal 10.00 25.00
CSJG Jean-Sebastien Giguere 12.00 30.00
CSJI Jarome Iginla 12.00 30.00
CSJP J.P. Dumont 4.00 10.00
CSJT Jonathan Toews 20.00 50.00
CSKO Kyle Okposo 12.00 30.00
CSKT Kyle Turris 12.00 30.00
CSKU Nikolai Kulemin 6.00 15.00
CSKY Tyler Kennedy 5.00 12.00
CSLS Les Stroud 40.00 80.00
CSLU Luke Schenn 15.00 40.00
CSMB Martin Brodeur 75.00 150.00
CSMF Mark Fistric 5.00 12.00
CSMG Marc-Andre Gragnani 5.00 12.00
CSMI Mike Iggulden 5.00 12.00
CSML Mario Lemieux 60.00 120.00
CSMM Mark Messier 50.00 100.00
CSNK Niklas Kronwall 5.00 12.00
CSOR Bobby Orr 100.00 200.00
CSPK Patrick Kane 15.00 40.00
CSPM Peter Mueller 8.00 20.00
CSRE Robbie Earl 5.00 12.00
CSRK Red Kelly 8.00 20.00
CSRN Rick Nash 6.00 15.00
CSSC Sidney Crosby 100.00 200.00
CSSE Shannon Elizabeth 50.00 100.00
CSSF Drew Stafford 6.00 15.00
CSSM Steve Mason 15.00 40.00
CSSS Steven Stamkos 50.00 120.00
CSTB Tobias Stephan 5.00 12.00
CSTH Tomas Holmstrom 5.00 12.00
CSTI Jennifer Tilly
CSTW Tiger Woods SP
CSVL Vincent Lecavalier 20.00 50.00
CSVN Thomas Vanek 6.00 15.00
CSWG Wayne Gretzky 150.00 250.00
CSWO Willie O'Ree 6.00 15.00
CSWT Walt Tkaczuk 4.00 10.00

2008-09 Upper Deck Champ's Mini Signatures Blue Backs

*SINGLES: .6X TO 1.5X BASIC INSERTS
STATED ODDS 1:576
CSGH Gordie Howe 150.00 300.00
CSOR Bobby Orr 200.00 350.00
CSSC Sidney Crosby 200.00 350.00
CSVL Vincent Lecavalier 60.00 120.00
CSWG Wayne Gretzky 350.00 600.00

2008-09 Upper Deck Champ's Mini Signatures Purple Backs

STATED ODDS 1:1152
NOT PRICED DUE TO SCARCITY

2008-09 Upper Deck Champ's Mini Signatures Red Backs

*SINGLES: .5X TO 1.2X BASIC INSERTS
STATED ODDS 1:288
CSGH Gordie Howe 125.00 250.00
CSVL Vincent Lecavalier 40.00 80.00
CSWG Wayne Gretzky 200.00 400.00

2008-09 Upper Deck Champ's Mini Threads

STATED ODDS 1:24
CTAN Antero Niittymaki 5.00 12.00
CTAO Alexander Ovechkin 20.00 50.00
CTAP Alex Pietrangelo 8.00 20.00
CTBB Bob Bourne 3.00 8.00
CTBD Brandon Sutter 6.00 15.00
CTBG Brian Gionta 5.00 12.00
CTBK Mikkel Boedker 8.00 20.00
CTBN Bernie Nicholls 3.00 8.00
CTBO Ray Bourque 10.00 25.00
CTBS Billy Smith 4.00 10.00
CTBT Bryan Trottier 4.00 10.00
CTBW Blake Wheeler 12.00 30.00
CTCG Colton Gillies 5.00 12.00
CTCJ Curtis Joseph 5.00 12.00
CTDB Derick Brassard 10.00 25.00
CTDC Dino Ciccarelli 3.00 8.00
CTDD Drew Doughty 15.00 40.00
CTDG Doug Gilmour 6.00 15.00
CTDP Dion Phaneuf 5.00 12.00
CTEC Erik Cole 3.00 8.00
CTES Eric Staal 8.00 20.00
CTFB Fabian Brunnstrom 8.00 20.00
CTGA Glenn Anderson 4.00 10.00
CTHA Dale Hawerchuk 5.00 12.00
CTIK Ilya Kovalchuk 6.00 15.00
CTJL Jere Lehtinen 3.00 8.00
CTJS Joe Sakic 8.00 20.00
CTJV Jakub Voracek 10.00 25.00
CTKL Kari Lehtonen 3.00 8.00
CTLM Lanny McDonald 5.00 12.00
CTLR Luc Robitaille 4.00 10.00
CTMB Martin Brodeur 10.00 25.00
CTMF Manny Fernandez 5.00 12.00
CTMG Marian Gaborik 8.00 20.00
CTMH Marian Hossa 8.00 20.00
CTMK Mikko Koivu 5.00 12.00
CTML Mario Lemieux 12.00 30.00
CTMR Mike Ribeiro 3.00 8.00
CTMS Mats Sundin 5.00 12.00
CTMT Marty Turco 4.00 10.00
CTNZ Nikolai Zherdev 3.00 8.00
CTOA Adam Oates 5.00 12.00
CTOJ Olli Jokinen 3.00 8.00
CTOK Olaf Kolzig 5.00 12.00
CTPB Pierre-Marc Bouchard 3.00 8.00
CTPF Peter Forsberg 8.00 20.00
CTPS Peter Stastny 5.00 12.00
CTRB Rod Brind' Amour 4.00 10.00
CTRL Roberto Luongo 8.00 20.00
CTRM Ryan Malone 3.00 8.00
CTRN Rick Nash 5.00 12.00
CTRT Raffi Torres 3.00 8.00
CTRU Tuomo Ruutu 5.00 12.00

CTRY Michael Ryder 4.00 10.00
CTSB Steve Bernier 3.00 8.00
CTSC Sidney Crosby 15.00 40.00
CTSF Sergei Fedorov 8.00 20.00
CTSG Simon Gagne 4.00 10.00
CTSK Saku Koivu 5.00 12.00
CTSS Steve Shutt 5.00 12.00
CTST Steven Stamkos 15.00 40.00
CTSW Shea Weber 3.00 8.00
CTTF Theoren Fleury 6.00 15.00
CTTR Tuukka Rask 5.00 12.00
CTTW Tiger Williams 3.00 8.00
CTUM R.J. Umberger 3.00 8.00
CTVT Vesa Toskala 5.00 12.00
CTWR Wade Redden 3.00 8.00
CTWW Wojtek Wolski 3.00 8.00
CTZP Zach Parise 5.00 12.00

2009-10 Upper Deck Champ's

COMPLETE SET (580)
COMP.SET w/o SPs (100) 15.00 40.00
ROOKIE STATED ODDS 1:4
MINI STATED ODDS 1:2
W/H STATED ODDS 1:2
HF STATED ODDS 1:2
1 Ryan Getzlaf .50 1.25
2 Bobby Ryan .40 1.00
3 Scott Niedermayer .20 .50
4 Ilya Kovalchuk .40 1.00
5 Bryan Little .30 .75
6 Milan Lucic .30 .75
7 Terry O'Reilly .25 .60
8 Blake Wheeler .40 1.00
9 Ray Bourque .50 1.25
10 Bobby Orr 1.25 3.00
11 Gilbert Perreault .30 .75
12 Derek Roy .30 .75
13 Thomas Vanek .30 .75
14 Ryan Miller .30 .75
15 Miikka Kiprusoff .30 .75
16 Al MacInnis .30 .75
17 Dion Phaneuf .50 1.25
18 Jarome Iginla .60 1.50
19 Eric Staal .40 1.00
20 Cam Ward .30 .75
21 Jonathan Toews .75 2.00
22 Tony Esposito .50 1.25
23 Denis Savard .30 .75
24 Patrick Kane .60 1.50
25 Bobby Hull .75 2.00
26 Paul Stastny .30 .75
27 Craig Anderson .25 .60
28 Milan Hejduk .30 .75
29 Steve Mason .50 1.25
30 Rick Nash .30 .75
31 Derick Brassard .30 .75
32 Mike Modano .30 .75
33 Brad Richards .25 .60
34 James Neal .30 .75
35 Marty Turco .25 .60
36 Henrik Zetterberg .60 1.50
37 Nicklas Lidstrom .40 1.00
38 Red Kelly .30 .75
39 Steve Yzerman 1.00 2.50
40 Gordie Howe 1.25 3.00
41 Alex Delvecchio .40 1.00
42 Ted Lindsay .30 .75
43 Jari Kurri .30 .75
44 Sam Gagner .40 1.00
45 Nikolai Khabibulin .30 .75
46 Ales Hemsky .25 .60
47 Sheldon Souray .20 .50
48 Michael Frolik .25 .60
49 Drew Doughty .60 1.50
50 Anze Kopitar .30 .75
51 Ryan Smyth .30 .75
52 Mikko Koivu .30 .75
53 Martin Havlat .25 .60
54 Niklas Backstrom .30 .75
55 Carey Price .75 2.00
56 Scotty Bowman .30 .75
57 Patrick Roy 1.00 2.50
58 Mike Cammalleri .25 .60
59 Pekka Rinne .25 .60
60 Jason Arnott .20 .50
61 Martin Brodeur .75 2.00
62 Zach Parise .30 .75
63 Mike Bossy .30 .75
64 Clark Gillies .30 .75
65 Kyle Okposo .30 .75
66 Mark Messier .60 1.50
67 Marian Gaborik .50 1.25
68 Brandon Dubinsky .25 .60
69 Henrik Lundqvist .60 1.50
70 Wayne Gretzky 1.50 4.00
71 Brian Leetch .30 .75
72 Jason Spezza .40 1.00
73 Daniel Alfredsson .30 .75
74 Mike Richards .60 1.50
75 Bobby Clarke .50 1.25
76 Jeff Carter .30 .75
77 Simon Gagne .30 .75
78 Daniel Carcillo .30 .75
79 Shane Doan .25 .60
80 Mario Lemieux .75 2.00
81 Marc-Andre Fleury .30 .75
82 Evgeni Malkin .75 2.00
83 Sidney Crosby 1.50 4.00
84 Joe Thornton .60 1.50
85 Dany Heatley .60 1.50
86 Patrik Berglund .60 1.50
87 Vincent Lecavalier .40 1.00
88 Martin St. Louis .30 .75
89 Steven Stamkos .75 2.00
90 Phil Kessel .30 .75
91 Lanny McDonald .30 .75
92 Doug Gilmour .30 .75
93 Roberto Luongo .75 2.00
94 Markus Naslund .30 .75
95 Ryan Kesler .25 .60
96 Alexander Ovechkin 1.25 3.00
97 Mike Green .60 1.50
98 Alexander Semin .30 .75
99 Simeon Varlamov .60 1.50
100 Dale Hawerchuk .30 .75
101 Jakub Kindl RC 2.50 6.00
102 Alec Martinez RC 1.25 3.00
103 John Carlson RC 4.00 10.00
104 Andrew MacDonald RC 1.50 4.00
105 Antti Niemi RC 6.00 15.00
106 Artem Anisimov RC 2.50 6.00
107 Ben Lovejoy RC 3.00 8.00
108 Benn Ferriero RC 1.50 4.00
109 Brandon Segal RC 1.50 4.00
110 Brian Salcido RC 1.50 4.00
111 Bryan Rodney RC 1.50 4.00
112 Byron Bitz RC 1.50 4.00
113 Cal O'Reilly RC 2.00 5.00
114 Chris Durno RC 1.50 4.00
115 Christian Hanson RC 2.50 6.00
116 Dan Turple RC 2.50 6.00
117 David Schlemko RC 1.50 4.00
118 David Sloane RC 2.50 6.00
119 David Van Der Gulik RC 1.50 4.00
120 Davis Drewiske RC 2.00 5.00
121 Derek Peltier RC 1.25 3.00
122 Dmitry Kulikov RC 2.00 5.00
123 Erik Karlsson RC 6.00 15.00
124 Evander Kane RC 5.00 12.00
125 Frazer McLaren RC 1.25 3.00
126 Geoff Kinrade RC 2.00 5.00
127 Lars Eller RC 3.00 8.00
128 Ivan Vishnevskiy RC 2.50 6.00
129 Matthew Corrente RC 2.00 5.00
130 Jakub Petruzalek RC 2.00 5.00
131 James van Riemsdyk RC 5.00 12.00
132 Jamie Benn RC 3.00 8.00
133 Jamie Fraser RC 1.50 4.00
134 Jamie Fritsch RC 2.00 5.00
135 Jason Demers RC 1.50 4.00
136 Jay Beagle RC 2.00 5.00
137 Jay Rosehill RC 1.25 3.00
138 Jesse Joensuu RC 2.50 6.00
139 Jhonas Enroth RC 2.50 6.00
140 Joel Rechlicz RC 2.00 5.00
141 Johan Backlund RC 2.00 5.00
142 John Negrin RC 1.50 4.00
143 John Scott RC 2.00 5.00
144 John Tavares RC 15.00 40.00
145 Jonas Gustavsson RC 5.00 12.00
146 Kevin Quick RC 1.25 3.00
147 Devan Dubnyk RC 2.50 6.00
148 Kris Chucko RC 1.50 4.00
149 Kurtis McLean RC 1.50 4.00
150 Luca Caputi RC 2.50 6.00
151 Matt Beleskey RC 2.00 5.00
152 Matt Climie RC 1.50 4.00
153 Matt Duchene RC 8.00 20.00
154 Matt Gilroy RC 2.50 6.00
155 Matt Hendricks RC 1.50 4.00
156 Matt Pelech RC 2.00 5.00
157 Michael Del Zotto RC 4.00 10.00
158 Michael Sauer RC 1.50 4.00
159 Michael Vernace RC 1.50 4.00
160 Michal Neuvirth RC 5.00 12.00
161 Mika Pyorala RC 2.00 5.00
162 Mikael Backlund RC 3.00 8.00
163 Ryan O'Marra RC 1.50 4.00
164 Mike Santorelli RC 1.25 3.00
165 Per Ledin RC 2.00 5.00
166 Peter Regin RC 2.50 6.00
167 Phil Oreskovic RC 2.00 5.00
168 Ray Macias RC 2.00 5.00
169 Riku Helenius RC 2.00 5.00
170 Bobby Sanguinetti RC 1.50 4.00
171 Ryan O'Reilly RC 4.00 10.00
172 Ryan Vesce RC 1.50 4.00
173 Scott Lehman RC 1.25 3.00
174 Sean Bentivoglio RC 1.50 4.00
175 Sean Collins RC 1.50 4.00
176 Sergei Shirokov RC 3.00 8.00
177 Spencer Machacek RC 1.50 4.00
178 T.J. Galiardi RC 2.50 6.00
179 Taylor Chorney RC 2.00 5.00
180 Teemu Laakso RC 1.25 3.00
181 Tim Stapleton RC 2.00 5.00
182 Tim Wallace RC 1.25 3.00
183 Tom Wandell RC 6.00 15.00
184 Tyler Bozak RC 5.00 12.00
185 Tyler Myers RC 8.00 20.00
186 Tyson Strachan RC 1.25 3.00
187 Victor Hedman RC 4.00 10.00
188 Viktor Stalberg RC 3.00 8.00
189 Ville Leino RC 2.50 6.00
190 Wes O'Neill RC 2.00 5.00
191 Yannick Weber RC 2.50 6.00
192 Logan Couture RC 4.00 10.00
193 Michael Grabner RC 2.50 6.00
194 Brad Marchand RC 2.50 6.00
195 Cody Franson RC 2.00 5.00
196 Colin Wilson RC 4.00 10.00
197 Ryan Getzlaf 1.00 2.50
198 Bobby Ryan .75 2.00
199 Scott Niedermayer .40 1.00
200 Ilya Kovalchuk .75 2.00
201 Bryan Little .60 1.50
202 Milan Lucic .60 1.50
203 Terry O'Reilly .50 1.25
204 Blake Wheeler .75 2.00
205 Ray Bourque 1.00 2.50
206 Bobby Orr 2.50 6.00
207 Gilbert Perreault .60 1.50
208 Derek Roy .60 1.50
209 Thomas Vanek .60 1.50
210 Ryan Miller .60 1.50
211 Miikka Kiprusoff .60 1.50
212 Al MacInnis .60 1.50
213 Dion Phaneuf 1.00 2.50
214 Jarome Iginla 1.25 3.00
215 Eric Staal .75 2.00
216 Cam Ward .60 1.50
217 Jonathan Toews 1.50 4.00
218 Tony Esposito 1.00 2.50
219 Denis Savard .60 1.50
220 Patrick Kane 1.25 3.00
221 Bobby Hull 1.50 4.00
222 Paul Stastny .60 1.50
223 Craig Anderson .50 1.25
224 Milan Hejduk .60 1.50
225 Steve Mason 1.00 2.50
226 Rick Nash .60 1.50
227 Derick Brassard .60 1.50
228 Mike Modano .60 1.50
229 Brad Richards .50 1.25
230 James Neal .60 1.50
231 Marty Turco .50 1.25
232 Henrik Zetterberg 1.25 3.00
233 Nicklas Lidstrom .75 2.00
234 Red Kelly .60 1.50
235 Steve Yzerman 2.00 5.00
236 Gordie Howe 2.50 6.00
237 Alex Delvecchio .75 2.00
238 Ted Lindsay .60 1.50
239 Jari Kurri .60 1.50
240 Sam Gagner .75 2.00
241 Nikolai Khabibulin .60 1.50
242 Ales Hemsky .50 1.25
243 Sheldon Souray .40 1.00
244 Michael Frolik .50 1.25
245 Drew Doughty 1.25 3.00
246 Anze Kopitar .60 1.50
247 Ryan Smyth .60 1.50
248 Mikko Koivu .60 1.50
249 Martin Havlat .50 1.25
250 Niklas Backstrom .60 1.50
251 Carey Price 1.50 4.00
252 Scotty Bowman .60 1.50
253 Patrick Roy 2.00 5.00
254 Brian Gionta .60 1.50
255 Pekka Rinne .50 1.25
256 Jason Arnott .40 1.00
257 Martin Brodeur 1.50 4.00
258 Zach Parise .60 1.50
259 Mike Bossy .60 1.50
260 Clark Gillies .60 1.50
261 Kyle Okposo .60 1.50
262 Mark Messier 1.25 3.00
263 Marian Gaborik 1.00 2.50
264 Brandon Dubinsky .50 1.25
265 Henrik Lundqvist 1.25 3.00
266 Wayne Gretzky 3.00 8.00
267 Brian Leetch .60 1.50
268 Jason Spezza .75 2.00
269 Daniel Alfredsson .60 1.50
270 Mike Richards 1.25 3.00
271 Bobby Clarke 1.00 2.50
272 Jeff Carter .60 1.50
273 Simon Gagne .60 1.50
274 Daniel Carcillo .60 1.50
275 Shane Doan .50 1.25
276 Mario Lemieux 1.50 4.00
277 Marc-Andre Fleury .60 1.50
278 Evgeni Malkin 1.50 4.00
279 Sidney Crosby 3.00 8.00
280 Joe Thornton 1.25 3.00
281 Dany Heatley 1.25 3.00
282 Patrik Berglund 1.25 3.00
283 Vincent Lecavalier .75 2.00
284 Martin St. Louis .60 1.50
285 Steven Stamkos 1.50 4.00
286 Phil Kessel .60 1.50
287 Lanny McDonald .60 1.50
288 Doug Gilmour .60 1.50
289 Roberto Luongo 1.50 4.00
290 Markus Naslund .60 1.50
291 Ryan Kesler .50 1.25
292 Alexander Ovechkin 2.50 6.00
293 Mike Green 1.25 3.00
294 Alexander Semin .60 1.50
295 Simeon Varlamov 1.25 3.00
296 Dale Hawerchuk .60 1.50
297 Jay Bouwmeester .60 1.50
298 Olli Jokinen .40 1.00
299 Robyn Regehr .50 1.25
300 Tuomo Ruutu .40 1.00
301 Marian Hossa 1.00 2.50
302 Dustin Byfuglien .50 1.25
303 Marek Svatos .40 1.00
304 Loui Eriksson .40 1.00
305 Brenden Morrow .50 1.25
306 Fabian Brunnstrom .60 1.50
307 Zdeno Chara .40 1.00
308 Mike Cammalleri .50 1.25
309 Ryan Malone .40 1.00
310 Mike Smith .50 1.25
311 Mike Knuble .60 1.50
312 Jussi Jokinen .60 1.50
313 Brent Burns .40 1.00
314 Don Cherry .60 1.50
315 Dino Ciccarelli .40 1.00
316 J.P. Dumont .40 1.00
317 Ryan Suter .40 1.00
318 Chris Pronger .50 1.25
319 Scott Hartnell .40 1.00
320 Daniel Briere .60 1.50
321 Ray Emery .50 1.25
322 Kris Versteeg .75 2.00
323 Nik Antropov .50 1.25
324 Ilya Bryzgalov .50 1.25
325 Peter Mueller .75 2.00
326 Devin Setoguchi .50 1.25
327 Evgeni Nabokov .60 1.50
328 Jordan Staal .75 2.00
329 Bill Guerin .40 1.00
330 Patrick Marleau .60 1.50
331 Rob Blake .60 1.50
332 Dan Boyle .40 1.00
333 Alex Kovalev .60 1.50
334 Frank Mahovlich .75 2.00
335 Darryl Sittler .75 2.00
336 Matt Stajan .50 1.25
337 Tomas Kaberle .40 1.00
338 Alexei Ponikarovsky .40 1.00
339 Luke Schenn 1.00 2.50
340 Paul Kariya .60 1.50
341 T.J. Oshie 1.00 2.50
342 Chris Mason .50 1.25
343 Andy McDonald .40 1.00
344 Shea Weber .50 1.25
345 Nikita Filatov 1.25 3.00
346 Fedor Tyutin .40 1.00
347 Jack Johnson .50 1.25
348 Bernie Federko .50 1.25
349 Joe Mullen .50 1.25
350 Jakub Voracek .60 1.50
351 Marc Staal .75 2.00
352 Patrik Elias .50 1.25
353 David Clarkson .40 1.00
354 Paul Martin .40 1.00
355 Chris Drury .50 1.25
356 Ales Kotalik .40 1.00
357 Doug Weight .40 1.00
358 Willie Mitchell .40 1.00
359 Daniel Sedin .75 2.00
360 Tomas Vokoun .60 1.50
361 Nathan Horton .40 1.00
362 David Booth .40 1.00
363 Jonathan Quick 1.00 2.50
364 Dustin Brown .50 1.25
365 Rod Brind'Amour .50 1.25
366 Henrik Sedin 1.00 2.50
367 Ryan Kesler .50 1.25
368 Alexandre Burrows .50 1.25
369 Ryane Clowe .40 1.00
370 Joe Pavelski .40 1.00
371 Chris Neil .40 1.00
372 Ed Jovanovski .40 1.00
373 Jody Shelley .40 1.00
374 Donald Brashear .40 1.00
375 George Parros .40 1.00
376 Georges Laraque .40 1.00
377 Eric Godard .40 1.00
378 Grant Fuhr .75 2.00
379 Glenn Anderson .60 1.50
380 Drew Stafford .60 1.50
381 Jason Pominville .60 1.50
382 Dennis Wideman .40 1.00
383 Tim Thomas .60 1.50
384 Zach Bogosian .75 2.00
385 Kari Lehtonen .60 1.50
386 Jonas Hiller .75 2.00
387 Saku Koivu .60 1.50
388 Teemu Selanne .60 1.50
389 Great Pyramid of Giza 1.25 3.00
390 Hanging Gardens of Babylon 1.25 3.00
391 Statue of Zeus at Olympia 1.25 3.00
392 Temple of Artemis at Ephesus 1.25 3.00
393 Mausoleum at Halicarnassus 1.25 3.00
394 Colossus of Rhodes 1.25 3.00
395 Lighthouse of Alexandria 1.25 3.00
396 Chichen Itza 1.25 3.00
397 Christ the Redeemer 1.25 3.00
398 Colosseum 1.25 3.00
399 Great Wall of China 1.25 3.00
400 Machu Picchu 1.25 3.00
401 Petra 1.25 3.00
402 Taj Mahal 1.25 3.00
403 Grand Canyon 1.25 3.00
404 Great Barrier Reef 1.25 3.00
405 Harbour of Rio de Janeiro 1.25 3.00
406 Mount Everest 1.25 3.00
407 Aurora 1.25 3.00
408 Parcutin Volcano 1.25 3.00
409 Victoria Falls 1.25 3.00
410 Palau 1.25 3.00
411 Belize Barrier Reef 1.25 3.00
412 Great Barrier Reef 1.25 3.00
413 Deep-Sea Vents 1.25 3.00
414 Galpagos Islands 1.25 3.00
415 Lake Baikal 1.25 3.00
416 Northern Red Sea 1.25 3.00
417 Niagara Falls 1.25 3.00
418 Bay of Fundy, the Maritimes 1.25 3.00
419 Rocky Mountains British Columbia /Alberta 1.25 3.00
420 Nahanni National Park Reserve 1.25 3.00
421 Gros Morne National Park 1.25 3.00
422 Dinosaur Provincial Park 1.25 3.00
423 Richer- Perce 1.25 3.00
424 Nichollsia borealis 1.25 3.00
425 Torosaurus 1.25 3.00
426 Saurornitholestes 1.25 3.00
427 Troodon 1.25 3.00
428 Dromaeosaurus 1.25 3.00
429 Tyrannosaurus rex 1.25 3.00
430 Pachyrhinosaurus canadensis 1.25 3.00
431 Arrhinoceratops brachyops 1.25 3.00
432 Anchiceratops ornatus 1.25 3.00
433 Panoplosaurus 1.25 3.00
434 Euoplocephalus tutus 1.25 3.00
435 Edmontonia longiceps 1.25 3.00
436 Saurolophus osborni 1.25 3.00
437 Hypacrosaurus altispinus 1.25 3.00
438 Triceratops 1.25 3.00
439 Stegoceras edmontonense 1.25 3.00
440 Parksosaurus warreni 1.25 3.00
441 Velociraptorinae 1.25 3.00
442 Struthiomimus altus 1.25 3.00
443 Ornithomimus edmontonicus 1.25 3.00
444 Pachycephalosauridae 1.25 3.00
445 Daspletosaurus 1.25 3.00
446 Chirostenotes pergracilis 1.25 3.00
447 Aublysodon 1.25 3.00
448 Albertosaurus 1.25 3.00
449 Styracosaurus albertensis 1.25 3.00
450 Leptoceratops 1.25 3.00
451 Chasmosaurus 1.25 3.00
452 Ankylosauria 1.25 3.00
453 Richardoestesia 1.25 3.00
454 Gorgosaurus 1.25 3.00
455 Edmontosaurus saskatchewanensis 1.25 3.00
456 Orodromeus 1.25 3.00
457 Ornithomimidae 1.25 3.00
458 Montanoceratops cerorhynchus 1.25 3.00
459 Dawson's Caribou 1.25 3.00
460 Sea Mink 1.25 3.00
461 Great Auk 1.25 3.00
462 Labrador Duck 1.25 3.00
463 Passenger Pigeon 1.25 3.00
464 Deepwater Cisco 1.25 3.00
465 Longjaw Cisco 1.25 3.00
466 Banff Longnose Dace 1.25 3.00
467 Blue Walleye 1.25 3.00
468 Grizzly Bear 1.25 3.00
469 Black-Footed Ferret 1.25 3.00
470 Swift Fox 1.25 3.00
471 Walrus 1.25 3.00
472 Gray Whale 1.25 3.00
473 Pygmy Short-horned Lizard 1.25 3.00
474 Gravel Chub 1.25 3.00
475 Paddlefish 1.25 3.00
476 Eastern Cougar 1.25 3.00
477 Vancouver Island Marmot 1.25 3.00
478 Bowhead Whale 1.25 3.00
479 Right Whale 1.25 3.00
480 Beluga Whale 1.25 3.00
481 Wolverine 1.25 3.00
482 Whooping Crane 1.25 3.00
483 Eskimo Curlew 1.25 3.00
484 Aurora Trout 1.25 3.00
485 Anatum Peregrine Falcon 1.25 3.00
486 Blanchard's Cricket Frog 1.25 3.00
487 Leatherback Turtle 1.25 3.00
488 Lake Erie Water Snake 1.25 3.00
489 White Trillium 1.25 3.00
490 Common Loon 1.25 3.00
491 Blue Flag Iris 1.25 3.00
492 Snowy Owl 1.25 3.00
493 Mayflower 1.25 3.00
494 Osprey 1.25 3.00
495 Purple Violet 1.25 3.00
496 Black Capped Chickadee 1.25 3.00
497 Prairie Crocus 1.25 3.00
498 Great Grey Owl 1.25 3.00
499 Pacific Dogwood 1.25 3.00
500 Steller's Jay 1.25 3.00
501 Pink Lady's Slipper 1.25 3.00
502 Blue Jay 1.25 3.00
503 Western Red Lily 1.25 3.00
504 Sharp Tailed Grouse 1.25 3.00
505 Wild Rose 1.25 3.00
506 Great Horned Owl 1.25 3.00
507 Pitcher Plant 1.25 3.00
508 Atlantic Puffin 1.25 3.00
509 Mountain Avens 1.25 3.00
510 Gyrfalcon 1.25 3.00
511 Fireweed 1.25 3.00
512 Common Raven 1.25 3.00
513 Purple Saxifrage 1.25 3.00
514 Rock Ptarmigan 1.25 3.00
515 Sir John A. Macdonald 1.50 4.00
516 Alexander Mackenzie 1.50 4.00
517 Sir John Abbott 1.50 4.00
518 Sir John Thompson 1.50 4.00
519 Sir Mackenzie Bowell 1.50 4.00
520 Sir Charles Tupper 1.50 4.00
521 Sir Wilfrid Laurier 1.50 4.00
522 Sir Robert Borden 1.50 4.00
523 Arthur Meighen 1.50 4.00
524 William Lyon Mackenzie King 1.50 4.00
525 Richard Bedford Bennett 1.50 4.00
526 Louis St. Laurent 1.50 4.00
527 John Diefenbaker 1.50 4.00
528 Lester B. Pearson 1.50 4.00
529 Pierre Trudeau 1.50 4.00
530 Joe Clark 1.50 4.00
531 John Turner 1.50 4.00
532 Brian Mulroney 1.50 4.00
533 Kim Campbell 1.50 4.00
534 Jean Chrtien 1.50 4.00
535 Paul Martin 1.50 4.00
536 Stephen Harper 1.50 4.00
537 George Washington 2.00 5.00
538 John Adams 1.50 4.00
539 Thomas Jefferson 2.00 5.00
540 James Madison 1.50 4.00
541 James Monroe 1.50 4.00
542 John Quincy Adams 1.50 4.00
543 Andrew Jackson 1.50 4.00
544 Martin Van Buren 1.50 4.00
545 William Henry Harrison 1.50 4.00
546 John Tyler 1.50 4.00
547 James K. Polk 1.50 4.00
548 Zachary Taylor 1.50 4.00
549 Millard Fillmore 1.50 4.00
550 Franklin Pierce 1.50 4.00
551 James Buchanon 1.50 4.00
552 Abraham Lincoln 2.00 5.00
553 Andrew Johnson 1.50 4.00
554 Ulysses S. Grant 1.50 4.00
555 Rutherford B. Hayes 1.50 4.00
556 James A. Garfield 1.50 4.00
557 Chester Arthur 1.50 4.00
558 Grover Cleveland 1.50 4.00
559 Benjamin Harrison 1.50 4.00
560 Grover Cleveland 1.50 4.00
561 William McKinley 1.50 4.00
562 Theodore Roosevelt 1.50 4.00
563 William Howard Taft 1.50 4.00
564 Woodrow Wilson 1.50 4.00
565 Warren G. Harding 1.50 4.00
566 Calvin Coolidge 1.50 4.00
567 Herbert Hoover 1.50 4.00
568 Franklin Delano Roosevelt 1.50 4.00
569 Harry Truman 1.50 4.00
570 Dwight D. Eisenhower 1.50 4.00
571 John F. Kennedy 3.00 8.00
572 Lyndon B. Johnson 1.50 4.00
573 Richard Nixon 1.50 4.00
574 Gerald Ford 1.50 4.00
575 Jimmy Carter 1.50 4.00
576 Ronald Reagan 2.00 5.00
577 George H.W. Bush 2.00 5.00
578 Bill Clinton 2.00 5.00
579 George W. Bush 2.00 5.00
580 Barack Obama 3.00 8.00

2009-10 Upper Deck Champ's Green

COMPLETE SET (100) 40.00 100.00
*SINGLES: 1.5X TO 4X BASIC CARDS
STATED ODDS 1:4

2009-10 Upper Deck Champ's Red

COMPLETE SET (100) 125.00 250.00
*SINGLES: 2.5X TO 6X BASIC CARDS
STATED ODDS 1:10

2009-10 Upper Deck Champ's Yellow

COMPLETE SET (100) 200.00 400.00
*SINGLES: 4X TO 10X BASIC CARDS
STATED ODDS 1:20

2009-10 Upper Deck Champ's Mini Blue Backs

*ROOKIES: .8X TO 2X BASIC
ROOKIES STATED ODDS 1:360
VETERANS: 4X TO 10X BASIC
VETERANS STATED ODDS 1:80

2009-10 Upper Deck Champ's Mini Green Backs

*ROOKIES: 1.2X TO 3X BASIC
ROOKIES STATED ODDS 1:640
VETERANS: 5X TO 12X BASIC
VETERANS STATED ODDS 1:160

2009-10 Upper Deck Champ's Mini Parkhurst Backs

ROOKIES STATED ODDS 1:5000
ROOKIES NOT PRICED DUE TO SCARCITY
VETERANS: 6X TO 15X BASIC
VETERANS STATED ODDS 1:320

2009-10 Upper Deck Champ's Mini Red Backs

*ROOKIES: .5X TO 1.2X BASIC
ROOKIES STATED ODDS 1:240
VETERANS: 2X TO 5X BASIC
VETERANS STATED ODDS 1:20

2009-10 Upper Deck Champ's Hall of Legends Memorabilia

STATED ODDS 1:160
HLAO Alexander Ovechkin 30.00 80.00
HLBO Bo Jackson 20.00 50.00
HLBS Borje Salming 8.00 20.00
HLCB Chris Bosh 8.00 20.00
HLCN Cam Neely 12.00 30.00
HLCR Cal Ripken Jr.
HLDH Dale Hawerchuk 8.00 20.00
HLDM Dan Marino 25.00 60.00
HLFH Franco Harris 12.00 30.00
HLGA Glenn Anderson 8.00 20.00
HLGH Gordie Howe 30.00 80.00
HLJA Bo Jackson 20.00 50.00
HLJE Julius Erving 12.00 30.00
HLJR Jerry Rice 15.00 40.00
HLKB Kobe Bryant 25.00 60.00
HLLB Larry Bird 20.00 50.00
HLLJ LeBron James 40.00 80.00
HLLM Lanny McDonald 8.00 20.00
HLMB Martin Brodeur 20.00 50.00
HLMG Magic Johnson 15.00 40.00
HLMJ Michael Jordan 50.00 100.00
HLMS Mike Schmidt 20.00 50.00
HLNR Nolan Ryan 25.00 60.00
HLPR Patrick Roy 25.00 60.00
HLRL Rod Langway 6.00 15.00
HLSB Scotty Bowman 8.00 20.00
HLSC Sidney Crosby 40.00 100.00
HLSN Steve Nash 8.00 20.00
HLSS Steve Shutt 8.00 20.00
HLSY Steve Yzerman 25.00 60.00
HLTW Tiger Woods 100.00 200.00
HLWG Wayne Gretzky 30.00 80.00
HLWM Warren Moon 10.00 25.00

2009-10 Upper Deck Champ's Signatures

STATED ODDS 1:15
CSAA Artem Anisimov 8.00 20.00
CSAC Andrew Cogliano
CSAE Andrew Ebbett 5.00 12.00
CSAM Andrei Markov 5.00 12.00
CSAO Alexander Ovechkin 50.00 100.00
CSAP Alex Pietrangelo
CSBA Mikael Backlund 10.00 25.00
CSBF Bob Feller 40.00 80.00
CSBL Brian Leetch 6.00 15.00
CSBO Bobby Orr 75.00 150.00
CSBR Martin Brodeur EXCH 40.00 80.00
CSBS Brandon Sutter 6.00 15.00
CSCH Christian Hanson 8.00 20.00
CSCP Carey Price 15.00 40.00
CSCR Cal Ripken Jr. 125.00 200.00
CSCS Chris Stewart 6.00 15.00
CSDB David Backes 5.00 12.00
CSDC Daniel Carcillo 6.00 15.00
CSDF Doug Flutie 40.00 80.00
CSDR Derrick Rose 25.00 50.00
CSEK Evander Kane 15.00 40.00
CSEM Evgeni Malkin 15.00 40.00
CSEN Jhonas Enroth 8.00 20.00
CSER Jonathan Ericsson 6.00 15.00
CSFA Fabian Brunnstrom 6.00 15.00
CSFO Nick Foligno 6.00 15.00
CSGA Marian Gaborik 10.00 25.00
CSGH Gordie Howe 60.00 120.00
CSHZ Henrik Zetterberg 12.00 30.00
CSJA Jason Arnott 4.00 10.00
CSJB Josh Bailey 5.00 12.00
CSJD J.P. Dumont 4.00 10.00
CSJG Jonas Gustavsson 15.00 40.00
CSJH Josh Harding 5.00 12.00
CSJN John Tavares 50.00 100.00
CSJR Jerry Rice 75.00 150.00
CSJS James Sheppard 6.00 15.00
CSJT Jonathan Toews 15.00 40.00
CSLB Larry Bird 60.00 120.00
CSLJ LeBron James
CSLS Luke Schenn 10.00 25.00
CSMA Mark Streit 4.00 10.00
CSMB Mikkel Boedker 5.00 12.00
CSMD Matt Duchene 25.00 60.00
CSMJ Michael Jordan
CSMP Max Pacioretty 6.00 15.00
CSMR Mike Richards 12.00 30.00
CSMS Mike Schmidt 20.00 40.00
CSMT Maxime Talbot 6.00 15.00
CSNB Nicklas Backstrom 12.00 30.00
CSNG Nathan Gerbe 8.00 20.00
CSNL Nicklas Lidstrom 20.00 50.00
CSNR Nolan Ryan 125.00 200.00
CSOA Adam Oates 6.00 15.00
CSOM Oscar Moller 5.00 12.00
CSPK Phil Kessel 6.00 15.00
CSPL Pascal Leclaire 6.00 15.00
CSPM Peter Mueller 8.00 20.00
CSRN Rick Nash
CSRY Bobby Ryan 8.00 20.00
CSSA Barry Sanders
CSSC Sidney Crosby 60.00 120.00
CSSH Sergei Shirokov 10.00 25.00
CSSN Steve Nash
CSSS Steven Stamkos 15.00 40.00
CSST Matt Stajan 5.00 12.00
CSSW Shea Weber 5.00 12.00
CSSY Steve Yzerman
CSTH Joe Thornton 12.00 30.00
CSTK Tim Kennedy 6.00 15.00
CSTM Tracy McGrady
CSTV Thomas Vanek
CSVH Victor Hedman 12.00 30.00
CSVL Ville Leino 8.00 20.00
CSVR James van Riemsdyk 15.00 40.00
CSWG Wayne Gretzky 100.00 200.00
CSWM Warren Moon 75.00 150.00
CSYM Yao Ming 40.00 80.00

2009-10 Upper Deck Champ's Threads

STATED ODDS 1:9
MTAO Alexander Ovechkin 12.00 30.00
MTAS Alexander Semin 3.00 8.00
MTBL Brian Leetch 3.00 8.00
MTCG Andrew Cogliano 4.00 10.00
MTCN Cam Neely 5.00 12.00
MTCO Chris Osgood 4.00 10.00
MTCP Carey Price 8.00 20.00
MTCW Cam Ward 3.00 8.00
MTDA Daniel Alfredsson 3.00 8.00
MTDB Derick Brassard 3.00 8.00
MTDG Doug Gilmour 3.00 8.00
MTDP Dion Phaneuf 5.00 12.00
MTEM Evgeni Malkin
MTGA Glenn Anderson 3.00 8.00
MTGB Marian Gaborik 5.00 12.00
MTGF Grant Fuhr 4.00 10.00
MTGH Gordie Howe 12.00 30.00
MTGP Gilbert Perreault 3.00 8.00
MTGR Sergei Gonchar 2.00 5.00
MTHL Henrik Lundqvist 6.00 15.00
MTHZ Henrik Zetterberg 6.00 15.00
MTIK Ilya Kovalchuk 4.00 10.00
MTJB Josh Bailey 2.50 6.00
MTJC Jeff Carter 3.00 8.00
MTJF Johan Franzen 2.00 5.00
MTJI Jarome Iginla 6.00 15.00
MTJM Joe Mullen 2.50 6.00
MTKI Miikka Kiprusoff 3.00 8.00
MTKL Kristopher Letang 3.00 8.00
MTLR Larry Robinson 4.00 10.00
MTMB Martin Brodeur 8.00 20.00
MTMF Marc-Andre Fleury 3.00 8.00
MTML Milan Lucic 3.00 8.00
MTMM Mike Modano 3.00 8.00
MTMR Mike Richards 6.00 15.00
MTMT Marty Turco 2.50 6.00
MTNA Nik Antropov 2.50 6.00
MTNH Nathan Horton 2.00 5.00
MTNL Nicklas Lidstrom 4.00 10.00
MTPD Pavel Datsyuk 3.00 8.00
MTPK Phil Kessel 3.00 8.00
MTPR Patrick Roy 10.00 25.00
MTPS Paul Stastny 3.00 8.00
MTRK Ryan Kesler 2.50 6.00
MTRL Roberto Luongo 8.00 20.00
MTRN Rick Nash 3.00 8.00
MTSB Steve Bernier 2.00 5.00
MTSC Sidney Crosby 15.00 40.00
MTSG Simon Gagne
MTSH Steve Shutt 3.00 8.00
MTSP Patrick Sharp 2.50 6.00
MTSS Steven Stamkos 8.00 20.00
MTST Jordan Staal 4.00 10.00
MTSW Shea Weber
MTTK Tomas Kaberle 2.00 5.00
MTVO Tomas Vokoun 3.00 8.00
MTWW Wojtek Wolski 2.00 5.00

2009-10 Upper Deck Champ's Yellow Animal Icon

COMPLETE SET (100) 500.00 1000.00
*SINGLES: 8X TO 20X BASIC CARDS
STATED ODDS 1:80

2002-03 Upper Deck Classic Portraits

Released in February, this 138-card set consisted of 100 veteran base cards (#1-100), and 38 shortprinted rookie cards (#101-138). Cards 131-138 were only available in UD Rookie Update packs. Rookies were serial-numbered to 1500 copies each.

COMPLETE SET (138) 125.00 250.00
COMP.SET w/o SP's (100) 25.00 50.00
1 Jean-Sebastien Giguere .30 .75
2 Paul Kariya .40 1.00
3 Mike LeClerc .10 .30
4 Dany Heatley .50 1.25
5 Ilya Kovalchuk .50 1.25
6 Milan Hnilicka .30 .75
7 Joe Thornton .60 1.50
8 Brian Rolston .10 .30
9 Sergei Samsonov .30 .75
10 Miroslav Satan .30 .75
11 Martin Biron .30 .75
12 Tim Connolly .30 .75
13 Roman Turek .30 .75
14 Jarome Iginla .50 1.25
15 Craig Conroy .10 .30
16 Arturs Irbe .30 .75

17 Ron Francis .30 .75
18 Rod Brind'Amour .30 .75
19 Jeff O'Neill .10 .30
20 Alexei Zhamnov .10 .30
21 Eric Daze .30 .75
22 Jocelyn Thibault .30 .75
23 Rob Blake .30 .75
24 Patrick Roy 2.00 5.00
25 Joe Sakic .75 2.00
26 Peter Forsberg 1.00 2.50
27 Chris Drury .30 .75
28 Marc Denis .30 .75
29 Espen Knutsen .10 .30
30 Rostislav Klesla .10 .30
31 Marty Turco .30 .75
32 Brenden Morrow .30 .75
33 Mike Modano .60 1.50
34 Steve Yzerman 2.00 5.00
35 Nicklas Lidstrom .40 1.00
36 Sergei Fedorov .60 1.50
37 Brendan Shanahan .40 1.00
38 Curtis Joseph .40 1.00
39 Mike Comrie .30 .75
40 Tommy Salo .30 .75
41 Ryan Smyth .10 .30
42 Roberto Luongo .50 1.25
43 Viktor Kozlov .10 .30
44 Kristian Huselius .10 .30
45 Zigmund Palffy .30 .75
46 Felix Potvin .40 1.00
47 Jason Allison .10 .30
48 Manny Fernandez .30 .75
49 Andrew Brunette .10 .30
50 Marian Gaborik .75 2.00
51 Saku Koivu .40 1.00
52 Yanic Perreault .10 .30
53 Jose Theodore .50 1.25
54 Denis Arkhipov .10 .30
55 Scott Hartnell .10 .30
56 Mike Dunham .30 .75
57 Martin Brodeur 1.00 2.50
58 Patrik Elias .30 .75
59 Joe Nieuwendyk .30 .75
60 Scott Niedermayer .10 .30
61 Alexei Yashin .10 .30
62 Michael Peca .10 .30
63 Chris Osgood .30 .75
64 Eric Lindros .40 1.00
65 Pavel Bure .40 1.00
66 Brian Leetch .30 .75
67 Dan Blackburn .30 .75
68 Martin Havlat .30 .75
69 Marian Hossa .40 1.00
70 Daniel Alfredsson .30 .75
71 John LeClair .40 1.00
72 Jeremy Roenick .40 1.00
73 Keith Primeau .10 .30
74 Simon Gagne .40 1.00
75 Tony Amonte .30 .75
76 Sean Burke .30 .75
77 Daniel Briere .10 .30
78 Alexei Kovalev .30 .75
79 Johan Hedberg .30 .75
80 Mario Lemieux 2.50 6.00
81 Patrick Marleau .30 .75
82 Teemu Selanne .40 1.00
83 Evgeni Nabokov .30 .75
84 Owen Nolan .30 .75
85 Chris Pronger .30 .75
86 Doug Weight .30 .75
87 Keith Tkachuk .40 1.00
88 Brad Richards .30 .75
89 Nikolai Khabibulin .40 1.00
90 Vincent Lecavalier .40 1.00
91 Mats Sundin .40 1.00
92 Gary Roberts .10 .30
93 Ed Belfour .40 1.00
94 Alexander Mogilny .30 .75
95 Todd Bertuzzi .40 1.00
96 Brendan Morrison .30 .75
97 Markus Naslund .40 1.00
98 Jaromir Jagr .60 1.50
99 Peter Bondra .30 .75
100 Olaf Kolzig .30 .75
101 Alexei Smirnov RC 2.00 5.00
102 Stanislav Chistov RC 2.00 5.00
103 Martin Gerber RC 3.00 8.00
104 Kurt Sauer RC 2.00 5.00
105 Chuck Kobasew RC 2.00 5.00
106 Micki Dupont RC 2.00 5.00
107 Shawn Thornton RC 2.00 5.00
108 Jeff Paul RC 2.00 5.00
109 Rick Nash RC 6.00 15.00
110 Lasse Pirjeta RC 2.00 5.00
111 Henrik Zetterberg RC 6.00 15.00
112 Dmitri Bykov RC 2.00 5.00
113 Ales Hemsky RC 4.00 10.00
114 Mike Cammalleri RC 2.00 5.00
115 Ivan Majesky RC 2.00 5.00
116 Jay Bouwmeester RC 3.00 8.00
117 Alexander Frolov RC 4.00 10.00
118 P-M Bouchard RC 4.00 10.00
119 Ron Hainsey RC 2.00 5.00
120 Adam Hall RC 2.00 5.00
121 Scottie Upshall RC 2.00 5.00
122 Anton Volchenkov RC 2.00 5.00
123 Dennis Seidenberg RC 2.00 5.00
124 Patrick Sharp RC 2.00 5.00
125 Jeff Taffe RC 2.00 5.00
126 Jason Spezza RC 6.00 15.00
127 Tom Koivisto RC 2.00 5.00
128 Alexander Svitov RC 2.00 5.00
129 Carlo Colaiacovo RC 2.00 5.00
130 Steve Eminger RC 2.00 5.00
131 Jared Aulin RC 2.00 5.00
132 Pascal LeClaire RC 3.00 8.00
133 Steve Ott RC 2.00 5.00
134 Brooks Orpik RC 2.00 5.00
135 Ari Ahonen RC 2.00 5.00
136 Mike Komisarek RC 2.00 5.00
137 Ryan Miller RC 5.00 12.00
138 Ray Emery RC 2.00 5.00

2002-03 Upper Deck Classic Portraits Etched in Time

COMPLETE SET (15) 15.00 30.00
STATED ODDS 1:12
ET1 Paul Kariya .50 1.25
ET2 Joe Sakic 1.00 2.50
ET3 Patrick Roy 2.50 6.00
ET4 Mike Modano .75 2.00
ET5 Steve Yzerman 2.50 6.00
ET6 Brendan Shanahan .75 2.00
ET7 Brett Hull .60 1.50
ET8 Mike Comrie .40 1.00
ET9 Jose Theodore .50 1.25
ET10 Martin Brodeur 1.25 3.00
ET11 Pavel Bure .60 1.50
ET12 Simon Gagne .50 1.25
ET13 Mario Lemieux 3.00 8.00
ET14 Teemu Selanne .50 1.25
ET15 Mats Sundin .50 1.25

2002-03 Upper Deck Classic Portraits Genuine Greatness

COMPLETE SET (7) 20.00 40.00
STATED ODDS 1:24
GG1 Paul Kariya 1.00 2.50
GG2 Peter Forsberg 1.50 4.00
GG3 Patrick Roy 3.00 8.00
GG4 Steve Yzerman 3.00 8.00
GG5 Wayne Gretzky 4.00 10.00
GG6 Pavel Bure 1.00 2.50
GG7 Jaromir Jagr 1.00 2.50

2002-03 Upper Deck Classic Portraits Headliners

This 12-card set featured dual jersey swatches. Cards were inserted at a rate of 1:48. A limited parallel was also created and serial-numbered out of 25.

*MULT.COLOR SWATCH: .75X TO 1.5X
*LTD: 1X TO 2.5X BASE HI
DZ Eric Daze 4.00 10.00
Alexei Zhamnov
FS Peter Forsberg 15.00 40.00
Joe Sakic
JB Jaromir Jagr 4.00 10.00
Peter Bondra
KF Paul Kariya 4.00 10.00
Jeff Friesen
LF Nicklas Lidstrom 10.00 25.00
Sergei Fedorov
LK Claude Lemieux 4.00 10.00
Krys Kolanos
LM M.Lemieux/A.Morozov 12.50 30.00
RA Patrick Roy 15.00 40.00
David Aebischer
RG Jeremy Roenick 5.00 12.00
Simon Gagne
ST Sergei Samsonov 6.00 15.00
Joe Thornton
TK Jose Theodore 12.50 30.00
Saku Koivu
YH Steve Yzerman 12.50 30.00
Dominik Hasek

2002-03 Upper Deck Classic Portraits Hockey Royalty

This 30-card set featured three jersey swatches per card. Each card was serial-numbered to just 90 copies. A limited parallel was also created and serial-numbered out of 25. As of press time, not all cards have been verified.

*MULT.COLOR SWATCH: .75X TO 1.5X
*LTD: 1.25X TO 3X BASE HI
BLB Sean Burke 12.50 30.00
Claude Lemieux
Daniel Briere
BPT Martin Brodeur 25.00 60.00
Felix Potvin
Jocelyn Thibault
DLH Mike Dunham 12.50 30.00
David Legwand
Scott Hartnell
DPP Adam Deadmarsh 12.50 30.00
Felix Potvin
Zigmund Palffy
DZT Eric Daze 12.50 30.00
Alexei Zhamnov
Jocelyn Thibault
GLS Gretzky/M.Lemieux/Sakic 60.00 150.00
GTD Simon Gagne 12.50 30.00
Alex Tanguay
Eric Daze
GTM Bill Guerin 20.00 50.00
Joe Thornton
Glen Murray
GWA Doug Weight 12.50 30.00
Tony Amonte
Bill Guerin
HBK Jeff Halpern 12.50 30.00
Peter Bondra
Olaf Kolzig
JHL Jaromir Jagr 12.50 30.00
Milan Hejduk
Robert Lang
KFB Sergei Fedorov 20.00 50.00
Pavel Bure
Ilya Kovalchuk
KFG Paul Kariya
Jeff Friesen
Jean-Sebastien Giguere EXISTS?
KGJ Steve Konowalchuk 12.50 30.00
Sergei Gonchar
Jaromir Jagr
KSJ Paul Kariya 30.00 80.00
Joe Sakic
Jarome Iginla
KTK Espen Knutsen 12.50 30.00
Ron Tugnutt
Rostislav Klesla
LBL Eric Lindros 12.50 30.00
Pavel Bure
Brian Leetch
LLN M.Lemieux/Lang/Nieminen 25.00 60.00
LLT M.Lemieux/Lindros/Thornton 30.00 80.00
LRR John LeClair 20.00 50.00
Jeremy Roenick
Mark Recchi
MML Mike Modano 20.00 50.00
Brenden Morrow
Jere Lehtinen
PGF Keith Primeau 12.50 30.00
Simon Gagne
Ruslan Fedotenko
RBT Martin Brodeur 40.00 100.00
Patrick Roy
Jose Theodore
RDF Steven Reinprecht 15.00 40.00
Chris Drury
Peter Forsberg
SCA Miroslav Satan 12.50 30.00
Tim Connolly
Maxim Afinogenov
SIT Marc Savard 12.50 30.00
Jarome Iginla
Roman Turek
SLN Teemu Selanne 12.50 30.00
Jere Lehtinen
Ville Nieminen
SNL Markus Naslund 15.00 40.00
Nicklas Lidstrom
Mats Sundin
SYL Brendan Shanahan 30.00 80.00
Steve Yzerman
Nicklas Lidstrom
TSH Alex Tanguay 12.50 30.00
Joe Sakic
Dan Hinote

2002-03 Upper Deck Classic Portraits Mini-Busts

Inserted one per box, these mini-busts stood approximately 12 in. high and carried a player likeness on top of a column base. Each player had several variations including; home, away, glass and marble. Several players also had autographed versions and alternate jersey versions. Individual print runs for autographs are listed below, print runs of less than 25 are not priced due to scarcity.

1 Brendan Shanahan A 8.00 20.00
2 Brendan Shanahan G 8.00 20.00
3 Brendan Shanahan H 6.00 15.00
4 Brendan Shanahan M 6.00 15.00
5 Curtis Joseph A 8.00 20.00
6 Curtis Joseph A AU/31 40.00 100.00
7 Curtis Joseph G 8.00 20.00
8 Curtis Joseph G AU/10
9 Curtis Joseph H 6.00 15.00
10 Curtis Joseph H AU 30.00 80.00
11 Curtis Joseph M 6.00 15.00
12 Curtis Joseph M AU/25 40.00 100.00
13 Dany Heatley A 8.00 20.00
14 Dany Heatley A AU/15
15 Dany Heatley G 8.00 20.00
16 Dany Heatley G AU/10
17 Dany Heatley H 6.00 15.00
18 Dany Heatley H AU 20.00 50.00
19 Dany Heatley M 6.00 15.00
20 Dany Heatley M AU/25 30.00 80.00
21 Dominik Hasek A 8.00 20.00
22 Dominik Hasek G 8.00 20.00
23 Dominik Hasek H 6.00 15.00
24 Dominik Hasek M 6.00 15.00
25 Dominik Hasek Third 6.00 15.00
26 Gordie Howe A 20.00 50.00
27 Gordie Howe A AU/9
28 Gordie Howe G 20.00 50.00
29 Gordie Howe G AU/10
30 Gordie Howe H 15.00 40.00
31 Gordie Howe H AU SP 50.00 125.00
32 Gordie Howe M 15.00 40.00
33 Gordie Howe M AU/25 100.00 250.00
34 Gordie Howe Third 15.00 40.00
35 Gordie Howe Third AU/50 60.00 150.00
36 Ilya Kovalchuk A 8.00 20.00
37 Ilya Kovalchuk A AU/17
38 Ilya Kovalchuk G 8.00 20.00
39 Ilya Kovalchuk G AU/10
40 Ilya Kovalchuk H 6.00 15.00
41 Ilya Kovalchuk H AU 20.00 50.00
42 Ilya Kovalchuk M 6.00 15.00
43 Ilya Kovalchuk M AU/25 30.00 80.00
44 Jarome Iginla A 8.00 20.00
45 Jarome Iginla A AU/12
46 Jarome Iginla G 8.00 20.00
47 Jarome Iginla G AU/10
48 Jarome Iginla H 6.00 15.00
49 Jarome Iginla H AU 12.50 30.00
50 Jarome Iginla M 6.00 15.00
51 Jarome Iginla M AU/25 20.00 50.00
52 Jaromir Jagr A 8.00 20.00
53 Jaromir Jagr G 8.00 20.00
54 Jaromir Jagr H 6.00 15.00
55 Jaromir Jagr M 12.50 30.00
56 Jason Spezza A 8.00 20.00
57 Jason Spezza A AU/39 50.00 125.00
58 Jason Spezza G 8.00 20.00
59 Jason Spezza G AU/10
60 Jason Spezza H 6.00 15.00
61 Jason Spezza H AU 25.00 60.00
62 Jason Spezza M 10.00 25.00
63 Jason Spezza M AU/25 40.00 100.00
64 Jason Spezza Third 6.00 15.00
65 Jason Spezza Third AU/50 30.00 80.00
66 Joe Sakic A 20.00 50.00
67 Joe Sakic G 20.00 50.00
68 Joe Sakic H 12.50 30.00
69 Joe Sakic M 15.00 40.00
70 Joe Sakic Third 15.00 40.00
71 Joe Thornton A 8.00 20.00
72 Joe Thornton A AU/19
73 Joe Thornton G 8.00 20.00
74 Joe Thornton G AU/10
75 Joe Thornton H 6.00 15.00
76 Joe Thornton H AU 30.00 80.00
77 Joe Thornton M 6.00 15.00
78 Joe Thornton M AU/25 50.00 125.00
79 Joe Thornton Third 6.00 15.00
80 Joe Thornton Third AU/50 40.00 100.00
81 Mario Lemieux H 50.00 125.00
82 Mario Lemieux G 60.00 150.00
83 Martin Brodeur A 25.00 60.00
84 Martin Brodeur A AU/30 50.00 125.00
85 Martin Brodeur G 25.00 60.00
86 Martin Brodeur G AU/10
87 Martin Brodeur H 12.50 30.00
88 Martin Brodeur H AU 50.00 125.00
89 Martin Brodeur M 15.00 40.00
90 Martin Brodeur M AU/25 75.00 200.00
91 Patrick Roy A 30.00 80.00
92 Patrick Roy A AU/33 125.00 300.00
93 Patrick Roy G 30.00 80.00
94 Patrick Roy G AU/10
95 Patrick Roy H 20.00 50.00
96 Patrick Roy H AU SP 75.00 200.00
97 Patrick Roy M 25.00 60.00
98 Patrick Roy M AU/25 125.00 300.00
99 Patrick Roy Third 25.00 60.00
100 Patrick Roy Third AU/50 100.00 250.00
101 Paul Kariya A 8.00 20.00
102 Paul Kariya G 8.00 20.00
103 Paul Kariya H 6.00 15.00
104 Paul Kariya M 6.00 15.00
105 Pavel Bure A 8.00 20.00
106 Pavel Bure A AU/9
107 Pavel Bure G 8.00 20.00
108 Pavel Bure G AU/10
109 Pavel Bure H 6.00 15.00
110 Pavel Bure H AU SP 30.00 80.00
111 Pavel Bure M 6.00 15.00
112 Pavel Bure M AU/25 60.00 150.00
113 Pavel Bure Third 6.00 15.00
114 Pavel Bure Third AU/50 40.00 100.00
115 Ray Bourque Bos.A 20.00 50.00
116 Ray Bourque Bos.A AU/77 50.00 125.00
117 Ray Bourque G 20.00 50.00
118 Ray Bourque G AU/10
119 Ray Bourque Bos.H 12.50 30.00
120 Ray Bourque Bos.H AU SP 40.00 100.00
121 Ray Bourque M 15.00 40.00
122 Ray Bourque M AU/25 60.00 150.00
123 Ray Bourque Col.Third 15.00 40.00
124 Ray Bourque Col.Third AU/50 50.00 125.00

2002-03 Upper Deck Classic Portraits Pillars of Strength

COMPLETE SET (10) 10.00 20.00
STATED ODDS 1:18
PS1 Ilya Kovalchuk .60 1.50
PS2 Jarome Iginla .50 1.25
PS3 Joe Sakic 1.00 2.50
PS4 Mike Modano .75 2.00
PS5 Brendan Shanahan .75 2.00
PS6 Martin Brodeur 1.25 3.00
PS7 Eric Lindros .40 1.00
PS8 Mario Lemieux 3.00 8.00
PS9 Teemu Selanne .40 1.00
PS10 Olaf Kolzig .40 1.00

2002-03 Upper Deck Classic Portraits Portrait of a Legend

This 10-card set was dedicated to the career of Bobby Orr. Cards were inserted at 1:18.

COMPLETE SET (10) 20.00 40.00
COMMON ORR (PL1-PL10) 2.00 5.00

2002-03 Upper Deck Classic Portraits Starring Cast

This 15-card memorabilia set was inserted at 1:48. A limited parallel was also created and serial-numbered out of 50.

*MULT.COLOR SWATCH: .75X TO 1.5X
*LTD: .6X TO 1.5X BASE HI
CAT Alex Tanguay 4.00 10.00
CBG Bill Guerin 4.00 10.00
CBS Brendan Shanahan 5.00 12.00
CFP Felix Potvin 5.00 12.00
CJR Jeremy Roenick 5.00 12.00
CKT Keith Tkachuk 5.00 12.00
CMM Mike Modano 6.00 15.00
CMN Markus Naslund 5.00 12.00
CMS Mats Sundin 5.00 12.00
CPK Paul Kariya 5.00 12.00
CSA Miroslav Satan 4.00 10.00
CSB Sean Burke 4.00 10.00
CSG Simon Gagne 5.00 12.00
CSY Steve Yzerman 12.50 30.00
CZP Zigmund Palffy 4.00 10.00

2002-03 Upper Deck Classic Portraits Stitches

This 15-card memorabilia set was inserted at 1:24. A limited parallel was also created and serial-numbered out of 75.

*MULT.COLOR SWATCH: .75X TO 1.5X
*LTD: .5X TO 1.25X BASE HI
CAD Adam Deadmarsh 3.00 8.00
CBO Peter Bondra 3.00 8.00
CCD Chris Drury 3.00 8.00
CJF Jeff Friesen 3.00 8.00
CJI Jarome Iginla 5.00 12.00
CJT Joe Thornton 8.00 20.00
CKK Krys Kolanos 3.00 8.00
CMD Mike Dunham 3.00 8.00
CPB Pavel Bure 4.00 10.00
CRS Rostislav Klesla 3.00 8.00
CSF Sergei Fedorov 6.00 15.00
CSG Simon Gagne 4.00 10.00
CSR Steven Reinprecht 3.00 8.00
CSS Sergei Samsonov 3.00 8.00
CTH Jose Theodore 5.00 12.00

2003-04 Upper Deck Classic Portraits

Released in late-October, this 188-card set consisted of 100 veteran cards, 15 "Etched in Time" subset cards (101-115) serial-numbered to 1100, 18 Patrick Roy "Portrait of a Legend" cards (116-135) serial-numbered to 600, 25 "Pillars of Strength" subset cards (136-160) serial-numbered to 650, 6 pack issued rookies (161-166); 20 shortprinted rookies available via exchange cards (167-188) and 8 shortprinted rookies (189-196) available in packs of UD Rookie Update. Cards 161-196 were serial-numbered out of 1150.

COMP.SET w/o SP's (100) 15.00 30.00
1 Sergei Fedorov .40 1.00
2 Stanislav Chistov .10 .25
3 Jean-Sebastien Giguere .25 .60
4 Dany Heatley .40 1.00
5 Ilya Kovalchuk .40 1.00
6 Joe Thornton .50 1.25
7 Glen Murray .10 .25
8 Sergei Samsonov .25 .60
9 Miroslav Satan .25 .60
10 Maxim Afinogenov .25 .60
11 Chris Drury .25 .60
12 Jarome Iginla .40 1.00
13 Steve Reinprecht .10 .25
14 Roman Turek .25 .60
15 Ron Francis .25 .60
16 Jeff O'Neill .10 .25
17 Alexei Zhamnov .10 .25
18 Kyle Calder .10 .25
19 Jocelyn Thibault .25 .60
20 Teemu Selanne .30 .75
21 Peter Forsberg .75 2.00
22 Paul Kariya .30 .75
23 Joe Sakic .60 1.50
24 David Aebischer .25 .60
25 Rick Nash .40 1.00
26 Marc Denis .25 .60
27 Todd Marchant .10 .25
28 Mike Modano .50 1.25
29 Bill Guerin .25 .60
30 Marty Turco .25 .60
31 Brendan Shanahan .30 .75
32 Henrik Zetterberg .30 .75
33 Steve Yzerman 1.50 4.00
34 Dominik Hasek .50 1.25
35 Ryan Smyth .10 .25
36 Mike Comrie .25 .60
37 Ales Hemsky .25 .60
38 Tommy Salo .25 .60
39 Olli Jokinen .25 .60
40 Stephen Weiss .10 .25
41 Jay Bouwmeester .10 .25
42 Roberto Luongo .40 1.00
43 Zigmund Palffy .25 .60
44 Alexander Frolov .10 .25
45 Roman Cechmanek .25 .60
46 Marian Gaborik .60 1.50
47 P-M Bouchard .10 .25
48 Manny Fernandez .25 .60
49 Dwayne Roloson .25 .60
50 Saku Koivu .30 .75
51 Marcel Hossa .10 .25
52 Jose Theodore .40 1.00
53 Michael Komisarek .10 .25
54 David Legwand .25 .60
55 Tomas Vokoun .25 .60
56 Patrik Elias .25 .60
57 Jamie Langenbrunner .10 .25
58 Scott Stevens .25 .60
59 Martin Brodeur .75 2.00
60 Alexei Yashin .10 .25
61 Rick DiPietro .25 .60
62 Alex Kovalev .25 .60
63 Eric Lindros .30 .75
64 Pavel Bure .30 .75
65 Mike Dunham .25 .60
66 Marian Hossa .30 .75
67 Daniel Alfredsson .25 .60
68 Jason Spezza .30 .75
69 Patrick Lalime .25 .60
70 Jeremy Roenick .40 1.00
71 Tony Amonte .25 .60
72 John LeClair .30 .75
73 Simon Gagne .30 .75
74 Mike Johnson .10 .25
75 Chris Gratton .10 .25
76 Sean Burke .25 .60
77 Mario Lemieux 2.00 5.00
78 Martin Straka .10 .25
79 Sebastien Caron .25 .60
80 Mike Ricci .10 .25
81 Nicholas Dimitrakos .10 .25
82 Evgeni Nabokov .25 .60
83 Al MacInnis .25 .60
84 Keith Tkachuk .25 .60
85 Chris Pronger .25 .60
86 Chris Osgood .25 .60
87 Vincent Lecavalier .30 .75
88 Martin St. Louis .25 .60
89 Nikolai Khabibulin .30 .75
90 Alexander Mogilny .25 .60
91 Mats Sundin .30 .75
92 Owen Nolan .25 .60
93 Ed Belfour .25 .60
94 Alexander Auld .10 .25
95 Markus Naslund .30 .75
96 Todd Bertuzzi .30 .75
97 Ed Jovanovski .25 .60
98 Jaromir Jagr .50 1.25
99 Peter Bondra .25 .60
100 Olaf Kolzig .25 .60
101 Jean-Sebastien Giguere ET .50 1.25
102 Joe Thornton ET 1.00 2.50
103 Mario Lemieux ET 4.00 10.00
104 Peter Forsberg ET 1.50 4.00
105 Steve Yzerman ET 3.00 8.00
106 Eric Lindros ET .60 1.50
107 Marian Gaborik ET 1.25 3.00
108 Paul Kariya ET .60 1.50
109 Joe Sakic ET 1.25 3.00
110 Martin Brodeur ET 1.50 4.00
111 Ed Belfour ET .60 1.50
112 Marian Hossa ET .60 1.50
113 Gordie Howe ET 5.00 12.00
114 Wayne Gretzky ET 5.00 12.00
115 Bobby Orr ET 6.00 15.00
116 Patrick Roy PL 8.00 20.00
117 Patrick Roy PL 8.00 20.00
118 Patrick Roy PL 8.00 20.00
119 Patrick Roy PL 8.00 20.00
120 Patrick Roy PL 8.00 20.00
121 Patrick Roy PL 8.00 20.00
122 Patrick Roy PL 8.00 20.00
123 Patrick Roy PL 8.00 20.00
124 Patrick Roy PL 8.00 20.00
125 Patrick Roy PL 8.00 20.00
126 Patrick Roy PL 8.00 20.00
127 Patrick Roy PL 8.00 20.00
128 Patrick Roy PL 8.00 20.00
129 Patrick Roy PL 8.00 20.00
130 Patrick Roy PL 8.00 20.00
131 Patrick Roy PL 8.00 20.00
132 Patrick Roy PL 8.00 20.00
133 Patrick Roy PL 8.00 20.00
J-S Giguere
134 Patrick Roy 8.00 20.00
Martin Brodeur PL
135 Jean-Sebastien Giguere PL 8.00 20.00
136 Mario Lemieux PS 6.00 15.00
137 Gordie Howe PS 6.00 15.00
138 Keith Tkachuk PS .75 2.00
139 Peter Forsberg PS 2.50 6.00
140 Jeremy Roenick PS 1.25 3.00
141 Eric Lindros PS 1.00 2.50
142 Jaromir Jagr PS 1.50 4.00
143 Zdeno Chara PS .30 .75
144 Owen Nolan PS .75 2.00
145 Martin Brodeur PS 2.50 6.00
146 Ed Belfour PS 1.00 2.50
147 Marian Hossa PS 1.00 2.50
148 Jarome Iginla PS 1.00 2.50
149 Jocelyn Thibault PS .75 2.00
150 Marian Gaborik PS 2.00 5.00
151 Vincent Lecavalier PS .75 2.00
152 Joe Thornton PS 1.50 4.00
153 Rick Nash PS .75 2.00
154 Joe Sakic PS 2.00 5.00
155 Mike Modano PS 1.50 4.00
156 Jean-Sebastien Giguere PS .75 2.00
157 Olli Jokinen PS .75 2.00
158 Steve Yzerman PS 5.00 12.00
159 Jason Spezza PS .75 2.00
160 Chris Pronger PS .75 2.00
161 Joe DiPenta RC 2.50 6.00
162 Milan Bartovic RC 2.50 6.00
163 Rick Mrozik RC 2.50 6.00
164 Kent McDonell RC 2.50 6.00
165 Peter Sejna RC 2.50 6.00
166 Matt Stajan RC 3.00 8.00
167 Marc-Andre Fleury RC 8.00 20.00
168 Nathan Horton RC 4.00 10.00
169 Eric Staal RC 8.00 20.00
170 Joffrey Lupul RC 3.00 8.00
171 Dustin Brown RC 2.50 6.00
172 Jordin Tootoo RC 4.00 10.00
173 Joni Pitkanen RC 3.00 8.00
174 Milan Michalek RC 4.00 10.00
175 Pavel Vorobiev RC 2.50 6.00
176 Tuomo Ruutu RC 4.00 10.00
177 Patrice Bergeron RC 5.00 12.00
178 Antoine Vermette RC 20.00 50.00
179 Antti Miettinen RC 2.50 6.00
180 Dan Hamhuis RC 2.50 6.00
181 Sean Bergenheim RC 2.50 6.00
182 Maxim Kondratiev RC 2.50 6.00
183 Chris Higgins RC 5.00 12.00
184 John-Michael Liles RC 2.50 6.00
185 Brent Burns RC 2.50 6.00
186 Marek Svatos RC 3.00 8.00
187 Boyd Gordon RC 2.50 6.00
188 Cody McCormick RC 2.50 6.00
189 Alexander Semin RC 6.00 15.00
190 Timofei Shishkanov RC 2.50 6.00
191 Mikhail Yakubov RC 2.50 6.00
192 Ryan Kesler RC 2.50 6.00
193 Fredrik Sjostrom RC 2.50 6.00
194 Nikolai Zherdev RC 2.50 6.00
195 Derek Roy RC 3.00 8.00
196 Tomas Plekanec RC 3.00 8.00

2003-04 Upper Deck Classic Portraits Classic Colors

PRINT RUN 50 SERIAL #'d SETS
CCAM Al MacInnis 8.00 20.00
CCBH Brett Hull 20.00 50.00
CCBS Brendan Shanahan 12.50 30.00
CCCD Chris Drury 8.00 20.00
CCCJ Curtis Joseph 12.50 30.00
CCCO Chris Osgood 8.00 20.00
CCDW Doug Weight 8.00 20.00
CCEL Eric Lindros 12.50 30.00
CCJA Jason Allison 8.00 20.00
CCJB Jay Bouwmeester 8.00 20.00
CCJJ Jaromir Jagr 20.00 50.00
CCJS Jason Spezza 20.00 50.00
CCJS Joe Sakic 30.00 80.00
CCMD Mike Dunham 8.00 20.00
CCON Ed Belfour 12.50 30.00
CCPK Paul Kariya 12.50 30.00
CCRN Rick Nash 25.00 60.00
CCTA Tony Amonte 8.00 20.00
CCTS Teemu Selanne 12.50 30.00
CCWG Wayne Gretzky 75.00 200.00

2003-04 Upper Deck Classic Portraits Classic Stitches

*MULT.COLOR SWATCH: .75X TO 1.5X
STATED ODDS 1:18
CSAD Adam Deadmarsh 3.00 8.00
CSBB Brian Boucher 3.00 8.00
CSCP Chris Pronger 3.00 8.00
CSEB Ed Belfour 5.00 12.00
CSGM Glen Murray 3.00 8.00
CSJT Joe Thornton 8.00 20.00
CSMA Maxim Afinogenov 3.00 8.00
CSSK Saku Koivu 5.00 12.00
CSSY Steve Yzerman 12.50 30.00
CSTH Jocelyn Thibault 3.00 8.00

2003-04 Upper Deck Classic Portraits Genuine Greatness

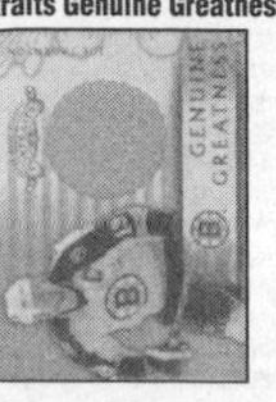

*MULT.COLOR SWATCH: .75X TO 1.5X
PRINT RUN 75 SERIAL #'d SETS
GGDH Dany Heatley 10.00 25.00
GGGR Wayne Gretzky 50.00 125.00
GGJR Jeremy Roenick 10.00 25.00
GGJS Jason Spezza 12.50 30.00
GGJT Joe Thornton 12.50 30.00
GGMB Martin Brodeur 15.00 40.00
GGML Mario Lemieux 20.00 50.00
GGPR Patrick Roy 20.00 50.00
GGRN Rick Nash 12.50 30.00
GGSY Steve Yzerman 15.00 40.00
GGWG Wayne Gretzky 50.00 125.00

2003-04 Upper Deck Classic Portraits Headliners

*MULT.COLOR SWATCH: .75X TO 1.5X
STATED ODDS 1:36
HHEL Eric Lindros 8.00 20.00
HHHA Marcel Hossa 5.00 12.00
HHJJ Jaromir Jagr 10.00 25.00
HHJT Joe Thornton 8.00 20.00
HHMG Marian Gaborik 8.00 20.00
HHML Mario Lemieux 12.50 30.00
HHMN Markus Naslund 6.00 15.00
HHPK Paul Kariya 6.00 15.00
HHVB Valeri Bure 5.00 12.00

2003-04 Upper Deck Classic Portraits Hockey Royalty

PRINT RUN 99 SERIAL #'d SETS
BLC Bure/Lindros/Kovalev 10.00 25.00
BNM Bertuzzi/Naslund/Morrison 10.00 25.00
BSM Belfour/Sundin/Mogilny 15.00 40.00
DSB Domi/Stock/Brashear 15.00 40.00
FSK Forsberg/Sakic/Kariya 25.00 60.00
KTH Koivu/Theodore/Hossa 15.00 40.00
LYG Lemieux/Yzerman/Gilmour 30.00 80.00
PLB Pronger/Lidstrom/Bowmster 12.00 30.00
RLA Roenick/LeClair/Amonte 10.00 25.00
YHS Yzerman/Hull/Shanahan 30.00 80.00

2003-04 Upper Deck Classic Portraits Mini-Busts

Inserted one per box, these ceramic busts carried two themes; Stanley Cup Winners and 500 Goal scorers. A bronze version was also created and limited to 25 copies each.

*BRONZE: 1X TO 2.5X
1 Patrick Roy COL 15.00 40.00
2 Patrick Roy MON/50 25.00 60.00
3 Gordie Howe SC 15.00 40.00
4 Martin Brodeur SC 15.00 40.00
5 Mike Modano SC 15.00 40.00
6 Joe Sakic SC 15.00 40.00
7 Peter Forsberg SC 15.00 40.00
8 Brett Hull DET 15.00 40.00
9 Brett Hull DAL/50 20.00 50.00
10 Ray Bourque SC 15.00 40.00
11 Jaromir Jagr PITT 15.00 40.00
12 Mario Lemieux SC 25.00 60.00
13 Steve Yzerman SC 20.00 50.00
14 Mark Messier NYR SC 15.00 40.00
15 Mark Messier EDM SC/50 20.00 50.00
16 Phil Esposito SC 15.00 40.00
17 Terry Sawchuk DET 15.00 40.00
18 Terry Sawchuk TOR/50 20.00 50.00
19 Bryan Trottier NYI SC 15.00 40.00
20 Bryan Trottier PITT SC/50 15.00 40.00
21 Bobby Clarke SC 15.00 40.00
22 Guy Lafleur SC 15.00 40.00
23 Scotty Bowman DET 20.00 50.00
24 Scotty Bowman MON/50 20.00 50.00
25 Scotty Bowman PITT/50 20.00 50.00
26 Phil Esposito 500 15.00 40.00
27 Steve Yzerman 500 20.00 50.00
28 Guy Lafleur 500 25.00 60.00
29 Mario Lemieux 500 25.00 60.00
30 Brett Hull 500 15.00 40.00
31 Jaromir Jagr 500 15.00 40.00
32 Gordie Howe 500 15.00 40.00
33 Mark Messier 500 15.00 40.00
34 Bryan Trottier 500 15.00 40.00
35 Joe Sakic 500 15.00 40.00

2003-04 Upper Deck Classic Portraits Mini-Busts Signed

This 21-card set partially parallels the regular bust but carried authentic player autographs. The busts in the 500 Goal Scorers subset were limited to 50 copies each and the Sawchuk busts were 1 of 1's. A bronze version was also created and limited to 10 copies or less each. Those busts are not priced due to scarcity.

BRONZE PRINT RUN 10 OR LESS
1 Patrick Roy COL 100.00 250.00
2 Patrick Roy MON/25 250.00 500.00
3 Gordie Howe SC 60.00 150.00
4 Martin Brodeur SC 60.00 150.00
10 Ray Bourque SC 40.00 100.00
11 Jaromir Jagr PITT 40.00 100.00
16 Phil Esposito SC 40.00 100.00
17 Terry Sawchuk DET/1
18 Terry Sawchuk TOR/1
19 Bryan Trottier NYI SC 40.00 100.00
20 Bryan Trottier PITT SC/25 100.00 200.00
21 Bobby Clarke SC 25.00 60.00
22 Guy Lafleur SC 50.00 125.00
23 Scotty Bowman DET 40.00 100.00
24 Scotty Bowman MON
25 Scotty Bowman PITT/25 50.00 125.00
26 Phil Esposito 500 30.00 80.00
28 Guy Lafleur 500 50.00 125.00
31 Jaromir Jagr 500 75.00 200.00
32 Gordie Howe 500 150.00 300.00
34 Bryan Trottier 500 75.00 200.00

2003-04 Upper Deck Classic Portraits Premium Portraits

*MULT.COLOR SWATCH: .75X TO 1.5X
PRINT RUN 25 SERIAL #'d SETS
PPJT Joe Thornton 25.00 60.00
PPMB Martin Brodeur 30.00 80.00
PPMH Gordie Howe 40.00 100.00
PPML Mario Lemieux 40.00 100.00
PPPF Peter Forsberg 25.00 60.00
PPPR Patrick Roy 40.00 100.00
PPSY Steve Yzerman 40.00 100.00
PPWG Wayne Gretzky 60.00 150.00

2003-04 Upper Deck Classic Portraits Starring Cast

*MULT.COLOR SWATCH: .75X TO 1.5X
STATED ODDS 1:36
SCCD Chris Drury 4.00 10.00
SCJG Jean-Sebastien Giguere 4.00 10.00
SCJH Johan Hedberg 4.00 10.00
SCMB Martin Brodeur 12.50 30.00
SCMM Mike Modano 8.00 20.00
SCPR Patrick Roy 12.50 30.00
SCRN Rick Nash 8.00 20.00
SCTA Tony Amonte 4.00 10.00
SCTB Todd Bertuzzi 4.00 10.00

1991-92 Upper Deck Czech World Juniors

This 100 card standard-size set featured players from the 1991 World Junior Championships. Two Wayne Gretzky Holograms were inserted into the set. They are priced at the end of the listings but are not included in the set price. Inside white borders, the fronts display glossy color action photos of the players in their national team uniforms. The player's name and position appear on the top, while the World Junior Tournament logo and an emblem of their national flag overlay the bottom. The backs have a second color player photo; alongside in a gray box, the player's position and a brief profile are printed in English and Czech. The cards are sequenced in this way: C.I.S. (1-23), Switzerland (24-31), Finland (32-40), Germany (41-46), Canada (47-65), U.S.A. (66-86), Czechoslovakia (87-99). These cards were designed for distribution in Eastern Europe. An album (valued at about $5) was also made to house the set.

COMPLETE SET (100) 10.00 25.00
1 Description Card .02 .10
2 Vladislav Boulin .02 .10
3 Ravil Gusmanov .02 .10
4 Denis Vinokurov .02 .10
5 Mikhail Volkov .02 .10
6 Alexei Troschinsky .02 .10
7 Andrei Nikolishin .20 .50
8 Alexander Sverzlov .02 .10
9 Artem Kopot .02 .10
10 Ildar Mukhometov .02 .10
11 Darius Kasparaitis .20 .50
12 Alexei Yashin .20 .50
13 Nikolai Khabibulin .50 1.25
14 Denis Metlyuk .02 .10
15 Konstantin Korotkov .02 .10
16 Alexei Kovalev .60 1.50
17 Alexander Kuzminsky .02 .10
18 Alexander Cherbayev .02 .10
19 Sergei Krivokrasov .20 .50
20 Sergei Zholtok .20 .50
21 Alexei Zhitnik .30 .75
22 Sandis Ozolinsh .30 .75
23 Boris Mironov .30 .75
24 Pauli Jaks .02 .10
25 Gaetan Voisard .02 .10
26 Nicola Celio .02 .10
27 Marc Weber .02 .10
28 Bernhard Schumperli .02 .10
29 Laurent Bucher .02 .10
30 Michael Blaha .02 .10
31 Tiziano Gianini .02 .10
32 Tero Lehtera .02 .10
33 Mikko Luovi .02 .10
34 Marko Kiprusoff .02 .10
35 Janne Gronvall .02 .10
36 Juha Ylonen .20 .50
37 Sami Kapanen .20 .50
38 Marko Tuomainen .02 .10
39 Jarkko Varvio .02 .10
40 Tuomas Gronman .02 .10
41 Andreas Naumann .02 .10
42 Steffen Ziesche .02 .10
43 Jens Schwabe .02 .10
44 Thomas Schubert .02 .10
45 Hans-Jorg Mayer .02 .10
46 Marc Seliger .20 .50
47 Ryan Hughes .02 .10
48 Richard Matvichuk .20 .50
49 David St. Pierre .02 .10
50 Paul Kariya 2.00 5.00
51 Patrick Poulin .20 .50
52 Mike Fountain .20 .50
53 Scott Niedermayer .20 .50
54 John Slaney .02 .10
55 Brad Bombardir .02 .10
56 Andy Schneider .02 .10
57 Steve Junker .02 .10
58 Trevor Kidd .40 1.00
59 Martin Lapointe .40 1.00
60 Tyler Wright .20 .50
61 Kimbi Daniels .02 .10
62 Karl Dykhuis .20 .50
63 Jeff Nelson .02 .10
64 Jassen Cullimore .02 .10
65 Turner Stevenson .20 .50
66 Brian Mueller .02 .10
67 Chris Tucker .02 .10
68 Marty Schriner .02 .10
69 Mike Prendergast .02 .10
70 John Lilley .02 .10
71 Jim Campbell .20 .50
72 Brian Holzinger .20 .50
73 Steve Konowalchuk .20 .50
74 Chris Ferraro .02 .10
75 Chris Imes .02 .10
76 Rich Brennan .02 .10
77 Todd Hall .02 .10
78 Brian Rafalski .20 .50
79 Scott Lachance .20 .50
80 Mike Dunham .40 1.00
81 Brent Bilodeau .02 .10
82 Ryan Sittler .02 .10
83 Peter Ferraro .02 .10
84 Pat Peake .02 .10
85 Keith Tkachuk .75 2.00
86 Brian Rolston .40 1.00
87 Milan Hnilicka .20 .50
88 Roman Hamrlik .20 .50
89 Milan Nedoma .02 .10
90 Patrik Luza .02 .10
91 Jan Caloun .20 .50
92 Viktor Ujcik .02 .10
93 Robert Petrovicky .20 .50
94 Roman Meluzin .02 .10
95 Jan Vopat .02 .10
96 Martin Prochazka .20 .50
97 Zigmund Palffy .60 1.50
98 Ivan Droppa .02 .10
99 Martin Straka .20 .50
100 Checklist 1-100 .02 .10
NNO W.Gretzky Hologram 1.50 4.00
NNO W.Gretzky Hologram 1.50 4.00

1997-98 Upper Deck Diamond Vision

This 25-card set was distributed in one-card packs with a suggested retail price of $7.99. The cards feature actual NHL game footage of the named player on each card combined with the latest technology to create fluid action sequences. Inserted one in every 500 packs is a Wayne Gretzky REEL Time card which displays his greatest moments in frame-by-frame action imagery.

COMPLETE SET (25) 50.00 125.00
1 Wayne Gretzky 10.00 25.00
2 Patrick Roy 8.00 20.00
3 Jaromir Jagr 3.00 8.00
4 Steve Yzerman 6.00 15.00
5 Martin Brodeur 5.00 12.00
6 Paul Kariya 2.00 5.00
7 John Vanbiesbrouck 1.25 3.00
8 Ray Bourque 2.00 5.00
9 Theo Fleury 1.25 3.00
10 Pavel Bure 1.50 4.00
11 Brendan Shanahan 2.00 5.00
12 Brian Leetch 1.25 3.00
13 Owen Nolan 1.25 3.00
14 Peter Forsberg 3.00 8.00
15 Doug Weight 1.25 3.00
16 Teemu Selanne 2.00 5.00
17 Mats Sundin 2.00 5.00
18 Keith Tkachuk 1.25 3.00
19 Tony Amonte 1.25 3.00
20 Joe Sakic 4.00 10.00
21 Zigmund Palffy 1.25 3.00
22 Eric Lindros 1.50 4.00
23 Sergei Fedorov 2.00 5.00
24 Dominik Hasek 4.00 10.00
25 Brett Hull 2.00 5.00
RT1 Wayne Gretzky 100.00 250.00
REEL TIME

1997-98 Upper Deck Diamond Vision Signature Moves

Randomly inserted in packs at the rate of 1:5, this 25-card set is parallel to the regular Diamond Vision set only with a facsimile signature of the player pictured on the card.

*SIGN.MOVES: 1X TO 2X BASIC CARDS

1997-98 Upper Deck Diamond Vision Defining Moments

Randomly inserted in packs at the rate of 1:40, this six-card set features incredible action technology to show the memorable highlights of the pictured player's career.

DM1 Wayne Gretzky 50.00 120.00
DM2 Patrick Roy 40.00 100.00
DM3 Steve Yzerman 40.00 100.00
DM4 Jaromir Jagr 12.50 30.00
DM5 Joe Sakic 15.00 40.00
DM6 Brendan Shanahan 8.00 20.00

2006 Upper Deck Entry Draft

Set was issued as a wrapper redemption exclusively at the 2006 NHL Entry Draft in Vancouver.

COMPLETE SET (6) 15.00 30.00
DR6 Joe Thornton 1.50 4.00
DR5 Ilya Kovalchuk 1.50 4.00
DR4 Rick Nash 1.50 4.00
DR3 Marc-Andre Fleury 1.25 3.00
DR2 Alexander Ovechkin 4.00 10.00
DR1 Sidney Crosby 6.00 15.00

1999-00 Upper Deck Gold Reserve

1999-00 Upper Deck Gold Reserve was packaged as a two-series release. Series one contained 170 cards and series two contained 180 cards. Base cards use the same design as the 2000 Upper Deck release but are enhanced with an all-foil card stock and gold foil highlights. Prospect cards in both series were short printed and numbered out of 2500. This release was packaged in 24-pack boxes where packs contained 10 cards and carried a suggested retail price of $2.99.

COMPLETE SET (350) 200.00 400.00
COMP.SERIES 1 (170) 75.00 150.00
COMP.SER.1 w/o SP's (135) 20.00 40.00
COMP.SERIES 2 (180) 100.00 250.00
COMP.SER.2 w/o SP's (150) 15.00 30.00
*GOLD RES VETS: .8X TO 2X BASIC UD
*GOLD RES SP: .8X TO 2X BASIC UD SP

1999-00 Upper Deck Gold Reserve Game-Used Souvenirs

Randomly inserted in Gold Reserve Update packs at the rate of 1:480, this 7-card set features NHL players coupled with a swatch of a game-used puck.

GRBH Brett Hull 20.00 50.00
GREL Eric Lindros 15.00 40.00
GRPB Pavel Bure 15.00 40.00
GRPK Paul Kariya 15.00 40.00
GRPR Patrick Roy 30.00 80.00
GRSY Steve Yzerman 25.00 60.00
GRWG Wayne Gretzky 40.00 100.00

1999-00 Upper Deck Gold Reserve UD Authentics

Randomly seeded in packs at the rate of 1:480, this 6-card set features authentic player autographs on the card front. Cards that carry the "UPD" suffix are found in Gold Reserve Update packs.

BH Brett Hull 25.00 50.00
BL Brian Leetch UPD 8.00 20.00
BM Bill Muckalt 6.00 15.00
CD Chris Drury 8.00 20.00
CJ Curtis Joseph 8.00 20.00
DL David Legwand 8.00 20.00
PB Pavel Bure 8.00 20.00
PS Patrik Stefan UPD 6.00 15.00
SS Sergei Samsonov UPD 8.00 20.00
SY Steve Yzerman UPD 30.00 80.00

1998-99 Upper Deck Gold Reserve

Distributed as a predominately retail product, this brand mirrored the regular Upper Deck brand in look and checklist, the only difference being that this set carried gold foil where Upper Deck was silver.

COMPLETE SET (420) 100.00 200.00
COMP.SER.1 SET (210) 60.00 120.00
COMP.SER.2 SET (210) 40.00 80.00
*1-30 GOLD SR/RR: .6X TO 1.5X BASIC CARDS
*31-390 GOLD VETS: 1.2X TO 3X BASIC CARDS
*391-412 GOLD PE: .6X TO 1.5X UPPER DECK
*413-420 GOLD CC: .6X TO 1.5X UPPER DECK
SY S.Yzerman Stick/200 75.00 200.00
SY S.Yzerman Stick AU/19
WG W.Gretzky Stick/200 75.00 200.00
WG W.Gretzky Stick AU/99 250.00 600.00
NNO1 W.Gretzky AU/200 200.00 500.00
NNO2 S.Yzerman AU/200 60.00 150.00

1999-00 Upper Deck Gretzky Exclusives

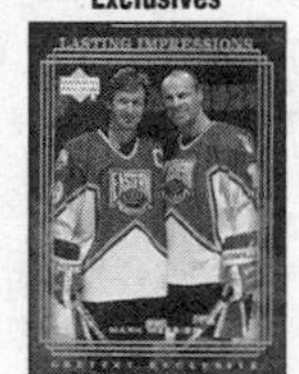

Inserted one pack per box of Upper Deck, these cards featured special tributes to Wayne Gretzky's career. Gold and platinum parallels to the set were also created and inserted randomly. Gold parallels were numbered to just 99. Platinum parallels were numbered 1/1 and are not priced due to scarcity.

COMPLETE SET (99) 125.00 250.00
COMMON GRETZKY (1-99) 1.25 3.00
*GOLD/99: 6X TO 15X BASIC INSERTS 20.00 50.00
UNPRICED PLATINUM PRINT RUN 1
NNO Gretzky Blues AU/99 150.00 400.00
NNO Gretzky Kings AU/99 150.00 400.00
NNO Gretzky Oilers AU/50 300.00 800.00
NNO Gretzky Rangers AU/25 400.00 1000.00

1999-00 Upper Deck Gretzky Game Jersey Autographs

These cards were randomly inserted in packs of Upper Deck Century Legend , Upper Deck Retro, and Upper Deck MVP. Each product had one version of the card numbered to 40 sets. The cards contain an actual piece of a game worn Wayne Gretzy jersey embedded in the cards and an authentic autograph.

WGJ W.Gretzky GJ AU/40 300.00 800.00
WGJ W.Gretzky GJ AU/40 300.00 800.00
WGJ W.Gretzky GJ AU/40 300.00 800.00

1994 Upper Deck Gretzky 24K Gold

Issued in a heavy Plexiglas holder, this card measures the standard size and commemorates Wayne Gretzky's record-breaking 802nd goal. On a black background, the horizontal front features a 24-karat gold photo and a facsimile autograph of Gretzky, along with "802" printed in large silver numbers on the left. On the same black background, the horizontal back carries Gretzky's biography and stats in gold print. The card's serial number and the production run figure (3,500) round out the back.

1 Wayne Gretzky 40.00 100.00

2002 Upper Deck Gretzky All-Star Game

This three-card set was available via wrapper redemption from the Upper Deck booth at the NHL All-Star Fantasy in Los Angeles. The cards were individually serial numbered out of 2002 and featured highlights of Wayne Gretzky's career.

COMPLETE SET (3) 10.00 25.00
AS1 Wayne Gretzky 4.00 10.00
All-Time Leading Scorer
AS2 Wayne Gretzky 4.00 10.00
All-Time Leading Goal Scorer
AS3 Wayne Gretzky 4.00 10.00
All-Star Game Goals in a Single Period Record

2001-02 Upper Deck Gretzky Expo e-Card

Available at the Upper Deck booth during the Toronto Fall Expo, these cards featured Wayne Gretzky on the card front and a scratch-off code that could be entered into the Upper Deck web site to win prizes. A Gretzky jersey card serial-numbered out of 200 was one of the prizes and was created especially for this promotion.

WG Wayne Gretzky Jsy/200 60.00 150.00
NNO Wayne Gretzky

2005 Upper Deck Hawaii Trade Conference Signature Supremacy *

SSP12 Wayne Gretzky H
SSP13 Wayne Gretzky A

2005-06 Upper Deck Hockey Showcase

Cards were issued via a special online redemption offer through Upper Deck over an eight-week period. The stated print run was 1,000 copies of each card.

HS1 Peter Forsberg 6.00 15.00
HS2 Chris Pronger 3.00 8.00
HS3 Adam Foote 1.25 3.00
HS4 Gary Roberts 1.25 3.00
HS5 Sergei Gonchar 1.25 3.00
HS6 Brian Leetch 4.00 10.00
HS7 Darren McCarty 2.50 6.00
HS8 Michael Peca 2.50 6.00
HS9 Bobby Holik 2.50 6.00
HS10 Eric Brewer 1.25 3.00
HS11 Paul Kariya 4.00 10.00
HS12 Jason Allison 2.50 6.00
HS13 Derian Hatcher 1.25 3.00
HS14 Sean Burke 3.00 8.00
HS15 Adrian Aucoin 2.50 6.00
HS16 Jeremy Roenick 4.00 10.00
HS17 Jocelyn Thibault 3.00 8.00
HS18 Alexander Mogilny 3.00 8.00
HS19 Pierre Turgeon 2.50 6.00
HS20 Anson Carter 3.00 8.00
HS21 Tony Amonte 3.00 8.00
HS22 Curtis Joseph 4.00 10.00
HS23 Miroslav Satan 2.50 6.00
HS24 Teemu Selanne 4.00 10.00
HS25 Mike York 1.25 3.00
HS26 Dany Heatley 4.00 10.00
HS27 Zigmund Palffy 3.00 8.00
HS28 Scott Niedermayer 2.50 6.00
HS29 Jeff O'Neill 2.50 6.00
HS30 Joe Nieuwendyk 3.00 8.00
HS31 Marian Hossa 3.00 8.00
HS32 Eric Lindros 4.00 10.00
HS33 Nikolai Khabibulin 4.00 10.00
HS34 Martin Straka 1.25 3.00
HS35 Chris Osgood 2.00 5.00
HS36 Pavol Demitra 3.00 8.00
HS37 Peter Bondra 3.00 8.00
HS38 John LeClair 4.00 10.00
HS39 Cory Stillman 2.50 6.00
HS40 Alexei Zhamnov 1.25 3.00

2005-06 Upper Deck Hockey Showcase Beckett Promos

Issued as a premium in an issue of Beckett Hockey, these cards featured a background that was more bronze than the one seen on the online offer cards. Although no print run was announced, there are significantly lower copies of this version of the card.

HS1 Peter Forsberg 6.00 15.00
HS2 Chris Pronger 3.00 8.00
HS3 Adam Foote 1.25 3.00
HS4 Gary Roberts 1.25 3.00
HS5 Sergei Gonchar 1.25 3.00
HS6 Brian Leetch 4.00 10.00
HS7 Darren McCarty 2.50 6.00
HS8 Michael Peca 2.50 6.00
HS9 Bobby Holik 2.50 6.00
HS10 Eric Brewer 1.25 3.00
HS11 Paul Kariya 4.00 10.00
HS12 Jason Allison
HS13 Derian Hatcher 1.25 3.00
HS14 Sean Burke 3.00 8.00
HS15 Adrian Aucoin
HS16 Jeremy Roenick 4.00 10.00
HS17 Jocelyn Thibault 3.00 8.00
HS18 Alexander Mogilny 3.00 8.00
HS19 Pierre Turgeon
HS20 Anson Carter 3.00 8.00
HS21 Tony Amonte 3.00 8.00
HS22 Curtis Joseph 4.00 10.00
HS23 Miroslav Satan 2.50 6.00
HS24 Teemu Selanne 4.00 10.00
HS25 Mike York 1.25 3.00
HS26 Dany Heatley 4.00 10.00
HS27 Zigmund Palffy 3.00 8.00
HS28 Scott Niedermayer 2.50 6.00
HS29 Jeff O'Neill 2.50 6.00
HS30 Joe Nieuwendyk 3.00 8.00
HS31 Marian Hossa 3.00 8.00
HS32 Eric Lindros 4.00 10.00
HS33 Nikolai Khabibulin 4.00 10.00
HS34 Martin Straka 1.25 3.00
HS35 Chris Osgood 2.00 5.00
HS36 Pavol Demitra 3.00 8.00
HS37 Peter Bondra 3.00 8.00
HS38 John LeClair 4.00 10.00
HS39 Cory Stillman 2.50 6.00
HS40 Alexei Zhamnov 1.25 3.00

1999-00 Upper Deck HoloGrFx

The 1999-00 Upper Deck HoloGrFx set was released as a 60-card one series set. The cards themselves feature NHL players on a silver rainbow foil holographic card with background color to match each player's team colors. This set was packaged as a 36-pack box with packs containing three cards at a suggested retail price of $1.99.

COMPLETE SET (60) 15.00 30.00
1 Teemu Selanne .25 .60
2 Paul Kariya .25 .60
3 Patrik Stefan RC 1.50 4.00
4 Sergei Samsonov .20 .50
5 Ray Bourque .40 1.00
6 Dominik Hasek .50 1.25
7 Brian Campbell RC .07 .20
8 Marc Savard .07 .20
9 Oleg Saprykin RC 1.50 4.00
10 Sami Kapanen .07 .20
11 Keith Primeau .07 .20
12 Tony Amonte .20 .50
13 J-P Dumont .20 .50
14 Peter Forsberg .60 1.50
15 Joe Sakic .50 1.25
16 Chris Drury .20 .50
17 Patrick Roy 1.25 3.00
18 Brett Hull .30 .75
19 Mike Modano .40 1.00
20 Ed Belfour .25 .60
21 Steve Yzerman 1.25 3.00
22 Brendan Shanahan .25 .60
23 Sergei Fedorov .40 1.00
24 Doug Weight .20 .50
25 Bill Guerin .07 .20
26 Pavel Bure .25 .60
27 Mark Parrish .07 .20
28 Luc Robitaille .20 .50
29 Zigmund Palffy .20 .50
30 Mike Ribeiro .20 .50
31 David Legwand .20 .50
32 Scott Gomez .07 .20
33 Martin Brodeur .60 1.50
34 Vadim Sharifijanov .07 .20
35 Jorgen Jonsson RC .07 .20
36 Eric Brewer .20 .50
37 Tim Connolly .07 .20
38 Theo Fleury .07 .20
39 Brian Leetch .25 .60
40 Mike Richter .25 .60
41 Marian Hossa .25 .60
42 Simon Gagne .25 .60
43 Eric Lindros .25 .60
44 John LeClair .25 .60
45 Keith Tkachuk .25 .60
46 Jeremy Roenick .30 .75
47 Jaromir Jagr .40 1.00
48 Niklas Sundstrom .07 .20
49 Jeff Friesen .07 .20
50 Brad Stuart .20 .50
51 Pavol Demitra .20 .50
52 Al MacInnis .20 .50
53 Paul Mara .20 .50
54 Vincent Lecavalier .25 .60
55 Mats Sundin .25 .60
56 Sergei Berezin .20 .50
57 Curtis Joseph .25 .60
58 Steve Kariya RC 1.00 2.50
59 Peter Bondra .20 .50
60 Olaf Kolzig .20 .50

1999-00 Upper Deck HoloGrFx Ausome

Randomly inserted in packs at 1:17, this gold parallel set features the base card enhanced with a gold foil background. Card backs carry an "AU" prefix.

*AUSOME: 5X TO 12X BASIC CARDS

1999-00 Upper Deck HoloGrFx Gretzky GrFx

Randomly inserted in packs at 1:3, this 15-card set pays tribute to The Great One by following his career from Edmonton to New York on the base HoloGrFx card stock. An AU-SOME parallel was also released for this set that featured a gold foil background. Parallels were inserted randomly at 1:105.

COMPLETE SET (15) 15.00 30.00
COMMON GRETZKY (GG1-GG15) 1.25 3.00
*AUSOME: 3X TO 8X BASIC INSERTS 10.00 25.00

1999-00 Upper Deck HoloGrFx Impact Zone

Randomly inserted in packs at 1:34, this 6-card set showcases some of the NHL's top players. The right 1/3 of the card front is black with the HoloGrFx logo and the players name, and the rest of the card features the player set against a silver rainbow foil background that has a laser etching effect. Card backs carry an "IZ" prefix. An AU-SOME gold foil parallel of this set was also released and inserted at 1:431.

COMPLETE SET (6) 15.00 30.00
*AUSOME: 2.5X TO 6X BASIC INSERTS
IZ1 Dominik Hasek 2.50 6.00
IZ2 Jaromir Jagr 2.00 5.00

IZ3 Eric Lindros 2.50 6.00
IZ4 Patrick Roy 6.00 15.00
IZ5 Paul Kariya 2.50 6.00
IZ6 Peter Forsberg 3.00 8.00

1999-00 Upper Deck HoloGrFx Pure Skill

Randomly inserted in packs at 1:17, this 9-card set pictures some of the NHL's most dominating offensive threats and goalies on a silver holographic foil card. Card backs carry a "PS" prefix. A gold foil AU-SOME parallel of this set was also seeded in packs at 1:210.

COMPLETE SET (9) 12.00 25.00
*AUSOME: 2.5X TO 6X BASIC INSERTS
PS1 Paul Kariya .75 2.00
PS2 Peter Forsberg 2.00 5.00
PS3 Dominik Hasek 1.50 4.00
PS4 Sergei Samsonov .75 2.00
PS5 Teemu Selanne .75 2.00
PS6 Patrick Roy 4.00 10.00
PS7 Brett Hull 1.00 2.50
PS8 Eric Lindros .75 2.00
PS9 Jaromir Jagr 1.25 3.00

1999-00 Upper Deck HoloGrFx UD Authentics

Randomly inserted in packs, this set features autographed cards of some of the NHL's top veterans and up and coming youngsters.

BH Brett Hull 15.00 40.00
BM Bill Muckalt 6.00 15.00
CD Chris Drury 10.00 25.00
DL David Legwand 6.00 15.00
PB Pavel Bure 6.00 15.00
PS Patrik Stefan 6.00 15.00
RB Ray Bourque 40.00 80.00
WG Wayne Gretzky 150.00 300.00
WG2 Wayne Gretzky Kings 150.00 300.00

1996-97 Upper Deck Ice

This retail-only set was issued in one series totaling 150 cards. Each pack contained three see-through cel cards and carried a suggested retail price of $3.99. The set is broken down into four subsets: Ice Performers (1-75), Ice Phenoms (76-105), Ice Legends (106-115), and World Juniors (116-150).

COMPLETE SET (150) 30.00 80.00
1 Kevin Todd .20 .50
2 Adam Oates .40 1.00
3 Bill Ranford .20 .50
4 Rick Tocchet .40 1.00
5 Dominik Hasek .75 2.00
6 Richard Smehlik .20 .50
7 Derek Plante .20 .50
8 Joel Bouchard .20 .50
9 Theo Fleury .20 .50
10 Chris Chelios .40 1.00
11 Ed Belfour .40 1.00
12 Eric Weinrich .20 .50
13 Tony Amonte .40 1.00
14 Greg Adams .20 .50
15 Jamie Langenbrunner .20 .50
16 Sergei Zubov .20 .50
17 Pat Verbeek .20 .50
18 Chris Osgood .40 1.00
19 Rem Murray RC .40 1.00
20 Jason Arnott .20 .50
21 Curtis Joseph .60 1.50
22 Bill Lindsay .20 .50
23 Ray Sheppard .20 .50
24 Martin Straka .20 .50
25 Jean-Sebastien Giguere RC 2.50 6.00
26 Sean Burke .40 1.00
27 Keith Primeau .20 .50
28 Geoff Sanderson .20 .50
29 Rob Blake .40 1.00
30 Ian Laperriere .20 .50
31 Byron Dafoe .40 1.00
32 Vincent Damphousse .20 .50
33 Darcy Tucker .20 .50
34 Brian Savage .20 .50
35 Bill Guerin .20 .50
36 Scott Niedermayer .20 .50
37 Steve Thomas .20 .50
38 Valeri Zelepukin .20 .50
39 Bryan Smolinski .20 .50
40 Derek King .20 .50
41 Mike Richter .60 1.50
42 Daniel Goneau RC .20 .50
43 Brian Leetch .40 1.00
44 Adam Graves .20 .50
45 Damian Rhodes .40 1.00
46 Mikael Renberg .20 .50
47 Eric Desjardins .20 .50
48 Rod Brind'Amour .40 1.00
49 Janne Niinimaa .40 1.00
50 Dale Hawerchuk .40 1.00
51 Jeremy Roenick .75 2.00
52 Mike Gartner .40 1.00
53 Cliff Ronning .20 .50
54 Patrick Lalime RC 1.00 2.50
55 Ron Francis .40 1.00
56 Petr Nedved .40 1.00
57 Bernie Nicholls .20 .50
58 Jeff Friesen .20 .50
59 Owen Nolan .40 1.00
60 Marty McSorley .20 .50
61 Pierre Turgeon .40 1.00
62 Grant Fuhr .40 1.00
63 Chris Pronger .40 1.00
64 Jim Campbell .20 .50
65 Chris Gratton .20 .50
66 Dino Ciccarelli .40 1.00
67 Felix Potvin .20 .50
68 Tie Domi .40 1.00
69 Doug Gilmour .40 1.00
70 Trevor Linden .40 1.00
71 Corey Hirsch .20 .50
72 Jim Carey .20 .50
73 Chris Simon .20 .50
74 Mark Tinordi .20 .50
75 Sergei Gonchar .20 .50
76 Paul Kariya .40 1.00
77 Teemu Selanne .40 1.00
78 Jarome Iginla .75 2.00
79 Eric Daze .20 .50
80 Sandis Ozolinsh .20 .50
81 Peter Forsberg .75 2.00
82 Mike Modano .60 1.50
83 Anders Eriksson .20 .50
84 Sergei Fedorov .40 1.00
85 Brendan Shanahan .60 1.50
86 Mike Grier RC .60 1.50
87 Doug Weight .40 1.00
88 Ed Jovanovski .20 .50
89 Saku Koivu .60 1.50
90 Jose Theodore .60 1.50
91 Jocelyn Thibault .40 1.00
92 Martin Brodeur 1.00 2.50
93 Bryan Berard .20 .50
94 Zigmund Palffy .40 1.00
95 Daniel Alfredsson .40 1.00
96 Alexei Yashin .20 .50
97 Wade Redden .20 .50
98 John LeClair .40 1.00
99 Oleg Tverdovsky .20 .50
100 Keith Tkachuk .40 1.00
101 Jaromir Jagr .75 2.00
102 Roman Hamrlik .20 .50
103 Sergei Berezin RC .40 1.00
104 Alexander Mogilny .40 1.00
105 Pavel Bure .60 1.50
106 Ray Bourque .60 1.50
107 Patrick Roy 1.25 3.00
108 Joe Sakic .75 2.00
109 Steve Yzerman 1.00 2.50
110 John Vanbiesbrouck .40 1.00
111 Mark Messier .60 1.50
112 Wayne Gretzky 1.50 4.00
113 Eric Lindros .60 1.50
114 Mario Lemieux 1.25 3.00
115 Brett Hull .60 1.50
116 Joe Thornton RC 6.00 15.00
117 Marc Denis .20 .50
118 Martin Biron RC 1.50 4.00
119 Jason Doig .20 .50
120 Daniel Briere RC 3.00 8.00
121 Trevor Letowski RC .40 1.00
122 Boyd Devereaux RC .40 1.00
123 Dwayne Hay RC .40 1.00
124 Hugh Hamilton RC .40 1.00
125 Brad Isbister RC .40 1.00
126 Shane Willis RC .40 1.00
127 Trent Whitfield RC .40 1.00
128 Jesse Wallin RC .40 1.00
129 Alyn McCauley .20 .50
130 Cameron Mann RC .40 1.00
131 Jeff Ware .20 .50
132 Corey Sarich .20 .50
133 Richard Jackman RC .20 .50
134 Brad Larsen .20 .50
135 Peter Schaefer RC .60 1.50
136 Christian Dube .20 .50
137 Chris Phillips .20 .50
138 Sergei Samsonov .40 1.00
139 Alexei Morozov .20 .50
140 Sergei Fedotov RC .40 1.00
141 Denis Khlopotnov RC .40 1.00
142 Andrei Markov RC .75 2.00
143 Andrei Petrunin .20 .50
144 Roman Liachenko RC .40 1.00
145 Joe Corvo RC .40 1.00
146 Erik Rasmussen .20 .50
147 Mike York RC .60 1.50
148 Brian Boucher .40 1.00
149 Paul Mara RC .40 1.00
150 Marty Reasoner .20 .50

1996-97 Upper Deck Ice Acetate Parallel

This 115-card set is a partial parallel version of the regular Upper Deck Ice set and features a special Light F/X acetate card design. The set contains three subsets: Ice Performers (1-75) inserted at the rate of 1:9 with a bronze design, Ice Phenoms (76-105) inserted at the rate of 1:47 with a silver design, and Ice Legends (106-115) inserted at the rate of 1:325 with a gold design. The World Juniors subset, present in the regular issue, is not included in the parallel version, leaving the set complete at 115 cards.

*PERF.VETS: 3X TO 8X BASIC CARDS
*PERF.ROOKIES: 1.5X TO 4X
*PHENOM VETS: 6X TO 15X BASIC CARDS
*PHENOM ROOKIES: 2.5X TO 6X
*LEGENDS: 10X TO 25X BASIC CARDS

1996-97 Upper Deck Ice Stanley Cup Foundation

Randomly inserted in packs at a rate of 1:96, this 10-card set features color player photos of winning teammate pairs in colored borders on an acetate card. Dynasty parallels were also inserted randomly at 1:960.

COMPLETE SET (10) 125.00 250.00
*DYNASTY: 1.5X TO 4X BASIC INSERTS
S1 Wayne Gretzky 20.00 50.00
Mark Messier
S2 Brendan Shanahan 15.00 40.00
Steve Yzerman
S3 John Vanbiesbrouck 6.00 15.00
Ed Jovanovski
S4 Jocelyn Thibault 15.00 40.00
Saku Koivu
S5 Joe Sakic 20.00 50.00
Patrick Roy
S6 Paul Kariya 6.00 15.00
Teemu Selanne
S7 Mario Lemieux 20.00 50.00
Jaromir Jagr
S8 Jeremy Roenick 12.00 30.00
Keith Tkachuk
S9 Doug Weight 6.00 15.00
Jason Arnott
S10 John LeClair 15.00 40.00
Eric Lindros

1997-98 Upper Deck Ice

The 1997-98 Upper Deck Ice set was issued in one series totaling 90 cards and was distributed in three-card packs with a suggested retail price of $4.99. The fronts feature color action player photos printed on acetate card stock. The backs carry player information.

COMPLETE SET (90) 40.00 80.00
1 Nelson Emerson .15 .40
2 Derian Hatcher .15 .40
3 Mike Richter .50 1.25
4 Sergei Berezin .15 .40
5 Nicklas Lidstrom .50 1.25
6 Ryan Smyth .15 .40
7 Martin Brodeur 1.25 3.00
8 Geoff Sanderson .40 1.00
9 Doug Weight .40 1.00
10 Owen Nolan .40 1.00
11 Daniel Alfredsson .40 1.00
12 Peter Bondra .40 1.00
13 Jim Campbell .15 .40
14 Rob Niedermayer .15 .40
15 Daymond Langkow .40 1.00
16 Zigmund Palffy .40 1.00
17 Adam Oates .40 1.00
18 Adam Deadmarsh .15 .40
19 Brian Holzinger .15 .40
20 Jarome Iginla .50 1.25
21 Janne Niinimaa .40 1.00
22 Dino Ciccarelli .15 .40
23 Mark Recchi .40 1.00
24 Sandis Ozolinsh .15 .40
25 Keith Primeau .15 .40
26 Ed Jovanovski .40 1.00
27 Jeremy Roenick .60 1.50
28 Alexei Yashin .15 .40
29 Felix Potvin .50 1.25
30 Chris Osgood .40 1.00
31 Marc Denis .40 1.00
32 Tyler Moss RC .15 .40
33 Kevin Hodson .40 1.00
34 Jamie Storr .40 1.00
35 Roman Turek .40 1.00
36 Jose Theodore .50 1.25
37 Magnus Arvedson .15 .40
38 Daniel Cleary .15 .40
39 Mike Knuble .15 .40
40 Jaroslav Svejkovsky .40 1.00
41 Patrick Marleau .75 2.00
42 Mattias Ohlund .40 1.00
43 Sergei Samsonov .40 1.00
44 Espen Knutsen RC .75 2.00
45 Vaclav Prospal RC .50 1.25
46 Joe Thornton 1.25 3.00
47 Chris Phillips .15 .40
48 Mike Johnson RC .50 1.25
49 Dainius Zubrus .50 1.25
50 Wade Redden .15 .40
51 Derek Morris RC .60 1.50
52 Marco Sturm RC .75 2.00
53 Don MacLean .15 .40
54 Bryan Berard .15 .40
55 Richard Zednik .15 .40
56 Alexei Morozov .40 1.00
57 Erik Rasmussen .15 .40
58 Olli Jokinen RC 1.00 2.50
59 Jan Bulis RC .15 .40
60 Patrik Elias RC 2.00 5.00
61 Peter Forsberg 1.25 3.00
62 Mike Modano .50 1.25
63 Tony Amonte .40 1.00
64 Theo Fleury .15 .40
65 Ron Francis .40 1.00
66 Brett Hull .60 1.50
67 Chris Chelios .50 1.25
68 Jaromir Jagr .75 2.00
69 Sergei Fedorov .75 2.00
70 Keith Tkachuk .50 1.25
71 Mark Messier .50 1.25
72 Pat LaFontaine .50 1.25
73 Mats Sundin .50 1.25
74 John Vanbiesbrouck .40 1.00
75 John LeClair .50 1.25
76 Brian Leetch .50 1.25
77 Ray Bourque .75 2.00
78 Saku Koivu .50 1.25
79 Joe Sakic 1.00 2.50
80 Teemu Selanne .50 1.25
81 Curtis Joseph .50 1.25
82 Doug Gilmour .40 1.00
83 Patrick Roy 2.50 6.00
84 Brendan Shanahan .50 1.25
85 Paul Kariya .50 1.25
86 Pavel Bure .50 1.25
87 Dominik Hasek 1.00 2.50
88 Eric Lindros .50 1.25
89 Steve Yzerman 2.50 6.00
90 Wayne Gretzky 3.00 8.00

1997-98 Upper Deck Ice Parallel

This 90-card set is a parallel version of the base set and is divided into three partial parallel sets. Ice Performers consists of cards 1-30 with an insertion rate of 1:2; Ice Phenoms consists of cards 31-60 with an insertion rate of 1:5; Ice Legends consists of the top 30 NHL players whose cards are 61-90 and have an insertion rate of 1:11.

*VETS: .6X TO 1.5X BASIC CARDS
*PHENOMS: .8X TO 2X BASIC CARDS
*LEGENDS: 2X TO 5X BASIC CARDS

1997-98 Upper Deck Ice Champions

Randomly inserted in packs at the rate of 1:47 and numbered out of 100, this 20-card set features color player head photos and action images printed with a Light FX/litho/acetate combination. An Ice Champions 2 Die Cuts parallel was also produced and limited to 100 copies each.

COMPLETE SET (20) 150.00 300.00
*DIE CUT/100: 3X TO 8X BASIC INSERTS
IC1 Wayne Gretzky 30.00 80.00
IC2 Patrick Roy 25.00 60.00
IC3 Eric Lindros 5.00 12.00
IC4 Saku Koivu 5.00 12.00
IC5 Dominik Hasek 10.00 25.00
IC6 Joe Thornton 8.00 20.00
IC7 Martin Brodeur 12.50 30.00
IC8 Teemu Selanne 5.00 12.00
IC9 Paul Kariya 5.00 12.00
IC10 Joe Sakic 10.00 25.00
IC11 Mark Messier 5.00 12.00
IC12 Peter Forsberg 12.50 30.00
IC13 Mats Sundin 5.00 12.00
IC14 Brendan Shanahan 5.00 12.00
IC15 Keith Tkachuk 5.00 12.00
IC16 Brett Hull 6.00 15.00
IC17 John Vanbiesbrouck 5.00 12.00
IC18 Jaromir Jagr 8.00 20.00
IC19 Steve Yzerman 15.00 40.00
IC20 Sergei Samsonov 5.00 12.00

1997-98 Upper Deck Ice Lethal Lines

Randomly inserted in packs at the rate of 1:11, this 30-card set features ten sets of three cards each displaying an action player photo which create an interlocking complete die-cut "lethal line" card when placed side-by-side in the correct order. A lethal line 2 parallel was also created and inserted at 1:120.

COMPLETE SET (30) 60.00 150.00
*LETHAL LINES 2: 2X TO 5X BASIC INSERTS
LETHAL LINES 2 STATED ODDS 1:120
L1A Paul Kariya 2.00 5.00
L1B Wayne Gretzky 10.00 25.00
L1C Joe Thornton 4.00 10.00
L2A Brendan Shanahan 2.00 5.00
L2B Eric Lindros 2.00 5.00
L2C Jaromir Jagr 3.00 8.00
L3A Keith Tkachuk 1.25 3.00
L3B Mark Messier 2.00 5.00
L3C Owen Nolan 1.25 3.00
L4A Daniel Alfredsson 1.25 3.00
L4B Peter Forsberg 5.00 12.00
L4C Mats Sundin 2.00 5.00
L5A Ryan Smyth 1.25 3.00
L5B Steve Yzerman 8.00 20.00
L5C Jarome Iginla 2.50 6.00
L6A Sergei Samsonov 1.25 3.00
L6B Igor Larionov 1.25 3.00
L6C Sergei Fedorov 2.50 6.00
L7A Patrik Elias 2.00 5.00
L7B Alexei Morozov .40 1.00
L7C Vaclav Prospal .40 1.00
L8A John LeClair 1.25 3.00
L8B Mike Modano 2.50 6.00
L8C Brett Hull 2.50 6.00
L9A Olli Jokinen 1.25 3.00
L9B Saku Koivu 2.50 6.00
L9C Teemu Selanne 2.50 6.00
L10A Brian Leetch 1.25 3.00
L10B Patrick Roy 8.00 20.00
L10C Nicklas Lidstrom 1.25 3.00

1997-98 Upper Deck Ice Power Shift

Randomly inserted in packs at the rate of 1:23, this 90-card set is a gold foil parallel version of the base set.

*VETS: 5X TO 12X BASIC CARDS
*ROOKIES: 2.5X TO 6X BASIC CARDS

2000-01 Upper Deck Ice

Released in mid-September, Upper Deck Ice featured a 60-card set comprised of 40 Veterans, 14 Fresh Faces cards die cut and sequentially numbered to 1500, and six Prime Performers cards die cut and sequentially numbered to 1500. Base cards were printed on clear acetate plastic card stock. Ice was released in 18-pack boxes with each pack containing four cards and carried a suggested retail price of $3.99. There was an update set that included an additional 63 cards, which was packaged along with other Upper Deck product updates.

COMPLETE SET (60) 200.00 400.00
COMP.SET w/o SP's (40) 7.50 15.00
COMP.SET w/UPDATE (123) 250.00 500.00
1 Paul Kariya .40 1.00
2 Teemu Selanne .40 1.00
3 Patrik Stefan .10 .25
4 Joe Thornton .60 1.50
5 Dominik Hasek .75 2.00
6 Michael Peca .10 .25
7 Valeri Bure .10 .25
8 Ron Francis .30 .75
9 Tony Amonte .30 .75
10 Patrick Roy 2.00 5.00
11 Ray Bourque .75 2.00
12 Milan Hejduk .40 1.00
13 Peter Forsberg .75 2.00
14 Brett Hull .50 1.25
15 Mike Modano .60 1.50
16 Brendan Shanahan .40 1.00
17 Chris Osgood .30 .75
18 Steve Yzerman 1.50 4.00
19 Doug Weight .30 .75
20 Pavel Bure .40 1.00
21 Luc Robitaille .30 .75
22 Jose Theodore .50 1.25
23 David Legwand .30 .75
24 Martin Brodeur 1.00 2.50
25 Scott Gomez .10 .25
26 Tim Connolly .10 .25
27 Mike York .10 .25
28 Marian Hossa .40 1.00
29 Brian Boucher .40 1.00
30 John LeClair .40 1.00
31 Jeremy Roenick .50 1.25
32 Jaromir Jagr .60 1.50
33 Steve Shields .30 .75
34 Chris Pronger .30 .75
35 Roman Turek .30 .75
36 Vincent Lecavalier .40 1.00
37 Curtis Joseph .40 1.00
38 Mats Sundin .40 1.00
39 Mark Messier .40 1.00
40 Olaf Kolzig .30 .75
41 Matt Pettinger RC 2.00 5.00
42 Chris Nielsen RC 2.00 5.00
43 Dany Heatley RC 15.00 40.00
44 Matt Zultek RC 2.00 5.00
45 Dmitri Afanasenkov RC 2.00 5.00
46 Tyler Bouck RC 2.50 6.00
47 Jonas Andersson RC 2.00 5.00
48 Marc-Andre Thinel RC 2.00 5.00
49 Jaroslav Svoboda RC 2.00 5.00
50 Josef Vasicek RC 2.00 5.00
51 Andrew Raycroft RC 5.00 12.00
52 Juraj Kolnik RC 2.00 5.00
53 Zdenek Blatny RC 2.00 5.00
54 Sebastien Caron RC 2.00 5.00
55 Eric Nickulas RC 2.00 5.00
56 Serge Aubin RC 2.00 5.00
57 Steven Reinprecht RC 2.00 5.00
58 David Gosselin RC 2.00 5.00
59 Colin White RC 2.00 5.00
60 Steve Valiquette RC 2.00 5.00
61 Jeff Friesen .10 .25
62 Bill Guerin .30 .75
63 J-P Dumont .10 .25
64 Oleg Saprykin .10 .25
65 Shane Willis .10 .25
66 Josef Vasicek .10 .25
67 Steve Reinprecht .10 .25
68 Marc Denis .30 .75
69 Marty Turco RC 6.00 15.00
70 Sergei Fedorov .60 1.50
71 Adam Deadmarsh .10 .25
72 Keith Tkachuk .40 1.00
73 Mark Messier .40 1.00
74 Alexei Yashin .10 .25
75 Mario Lemieux 2.00 5.00
76 Evgeni Nabokov .30 .75
77 Brad Richards .30 .75
78 Henrik Sedin .10 .25
79 Daniel Sedin .10 .25
80 Matt Pettinger .10 .25
81 Marc Chouinard RC 2.00 5.00
82 Bryan Adams RC 2.00 5.00
83 Martin Brochu RC 2.00 5.00
84 Craig Adams RC 2.00 5.00
85 David Aebischer RC 5.00 12.00
86 Rostislav Klesla RC 2.00 5.00
87 Shawn Horcoff RC 4.00 10.00
88 Mike Comrie RC 4.00 10.00
89 Eric Belanger RC 2.00 5.00
90 Marian Gaborik RC 12.00 30.00
91 Eric Landry RC 2.00 5.00
92 Scott Hartnell RC 4.00 10.00
93 Chris Mason RC 4.00 10.00
94 Rick DiPietro RC 8.00 20.00
95 Martin Havlat RC 6.00 15.00
96 Roman Cechmanek RC 2.00 5.00
97 Justin Williams RC 4.00 10.00
98 Ruslan Fedotenko RC 2.00 5.00
99 Jean-Guy Trudel RC 2.00 5.00
100 Reed Low RC 2.00 5.00
101 Alexei Ponikarovsky RC 2.00 5.00
102 Rob Blake .30 .75
103 Andy McDonald RC 4.00 10.00
104 Petr Tenkrat RC 2.00 5.00
105 Brad Tapper RC 2.00 5.00
106 Darcy Hordichuk RC 2.00 5.00
107 J.P. Vigier RC 2.00 5.00
108 Pavel Kolarik RC 2.00 5.00
109 Jarno Kultanen RC 2.00 5.00
110 Eric Manlow RC 2.00 5.00
111 Eric Boulton RC 2.00 5.00
112 Brian Swanson RC 2.00 5.00
113 Lubomir Sekeras RC 2.00 5.00
114 Greg Classen RC 2.00 5.00
115 Jiri Bicek RC 2.00 5.00
116 Jeff Ulmer RC 2.00 5.00
117 Johan Holmqvist RC 3.00 8.00
118 Shane Hnidy RC 2.00 5.00
119 Ossi Vaananen RC 2.00 5.00
120 Johan Hedberg RC 3.00 8.00
121 Mark Smith RC 2.00 5.00
122 Alexander Khavanov RC 2.00 5.00
123 Bryce Salvador RC 2.00 5.00

2000-01 Upper Deck Ice Immortals

Randomly inserted in packs, this 60-card set parallels the Series I set sequentially numbered to 25.

*STARS: 30X TO 80X BASIC CARDS
*SP's: 2X TO 4X BASIC CARDS
43 Dany Heatley 150.00 300.00

2000-01 Upper Deck Ice Legends

Randomly inserted in packs, this 60-card set parallels the Series I set and is sequentially numbered to 150.

*STARS: 6X TO 15X BASIC CARDS
*SP's: .75X TO 1.5X BASIC CARDS
43 Dany Heatley 75.00 150.00

2000-01 Upper Deck Ice Stars

Randomly inserted in packs, this 60-card set parallels the Series I set enhanced with gold foil stamping and is sequentially numbered to 500.

*STARS STARS: 2X TO 5X BASIC CARDS
*STARS SP's: .5X TO 1.25X BASIC CARDS
43 Dany Heatley 40.00 100.00

2000-01 Upper Deck Ice Champions

COMPLETE SET (6) 15.00 30.00
STATED ODDS 1:18
IC1 Patrick Roy 5.00 12.00
IC2 Mike Modano 2.00 5.00
IC3 Steve Yzerman 5.00 12.00
IC4 Martin Brodeur 2.50 6.00
IC5 John LeClair 1.50 4.00
IC6 Jaromir Jagr 1.50 4.00

2000-01 Upper Deck Ice Clear Cut Autographs

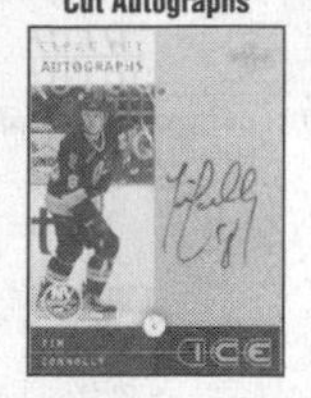

Randomly inserted in packs at the rate of 1:108, this 10-card set features authentic player autographs on the right side of the card on a gray background, and full color player action shots on the right.

BH Brett Hull 15.00 40.00
BL Brian Leetch 8.00 20.00
CJ Curtis Joseph 10.00 25.00
MY Mike York 4.00 10.00
PB Pavel Bure 10.00 25.00
PS Patrik Stefan 4.00 10.00
RT Roman Turek 4.00 10.00
SG Scott Gomez 4.00 10.00
SY Steve Yzerman 30.00 80.00
TC Tim Connolly 4.00 10.00

2000-01 Upper Deck Ice Cool Competitors

Randomly inserted in packs at the rate of 1:53, this six card set features player action shots on clear acetate plastic card stock with gold foil highlights.

COMPLETE SET (6) 40.00 80.00
CC1 Paul Kariya 4.00 10.00
CC2 Peter Forsberg 10.00 25.00
CC3 Pavel Bure 5.00 12.00
CC4 Scott Gomez 4.00 10.00
CC5 Jaromir Jagr 6.00 15.00
CC6 Curtis Joseph 4.00 10.00

2000-01 Upper Deck Ice Gallery

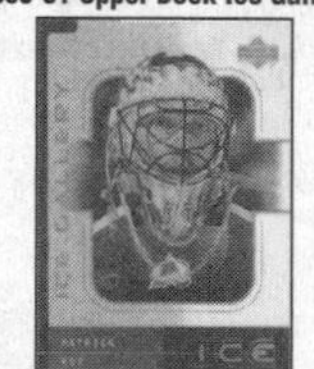

COMPLETE SET (9) 15.00 30.00
STATED ODDS 1:6
IG1 Teemu Selanne .75 2.00
IG2 Patrick Roy 4.00 10.00
IG3 Brendan Shanahan 1.25 3.00
IG4 Pavel Bure 1.00 2.50
IG5 Scott Gomez .75 2.00
IG6 John LeClair 1.00 2.50
IG7 Jaromir Jagr 1.25 3.00
IG8 Vincent Lecavalier .75 2.00
IG9 Curtis Joseph .75 2.00

2000-01 Upper Deck Ice Game Jerseys

Randomly inserted in UD Ice packs at the rate of 1:45 and 1:60 in UD Update packs this 20-card set features swatches of authentic game jerseys on acetate plastic card stock. The backs of these cards are clear as well, so the jersey swatch can be viewed from both sides of the card. Update cards are marked below.

*MULT.COLOR SWATCH: .75X TO 1.5X
JCAC Anson Carter 4.00 10.00
JCBH Brett Hull 5.00 12.00
JCBS Brendan Shanahan 4.00 10.00
JCCO Chris Osgood 4.00 10.00
JCDL David Legwand 4.00 10.00
JCJJ Jaromir Jagr 6.00 15.00
JCJL John LeClair 4.00 10.00
JCJN Joe Nieuwendyk 4.00 10.00
JCMB Martin Brodeur 12.50 30.00
JCMH Michal Handzus 4.00 10.00
JCMM Mike Modano 6.00 15.00
JCMS Miroslav Satan 4.00 10.00
JCPB Pavel Bure 4.00 10.00
JCPD Pavol Demitra 4.00 10.00
JCPK Paul Kariya 4.00 10.00
JCRB Ray Bourque 10.00 25.00
JCSF Sergei Fedorov 5.00 12.00
JCSS Sergei Samsonov 4.00 10.00
JCTC Tim Connolly 4.00 10.00
JCTS Teemu Selanne 4.00 10.00
IFO Peter Forsberg Upd 10.00 25.00
IJT Joe Thornton Upd 5.00 12.00
ILE John LeClair Upd 4.00 10.00
IMO Mike Modano Upd 6.00 15.00
IRO Patrick Roy Upd 15.00 40.00
ISA Joe Sakic Upd 10.00 25.00
ISH Brendan Shanahan Upd 4.00 10.00

ITH Jocelyn Thibault Upd 4.00 10.00
ITK Keith Tkachuk Upd 4.00 10.00

2000-01 Upper Deck Ice Rink Favorites

COMPLETE SET (9) 15.00 30.00
STATED ODDS 1:9
FP1 Paul Kariya 1.00 2.50
FP2 Peter Forsberg 2.00 5.00
FP3 Ray Bourque 1.50 4.00
FP4 Mike Modano 1.25 3.00
FP5 Steve Yzerman 4.00 10.00
FP6 Pavel Bure 1.00 2.50
FP7 Martin Brodeur 2.00 5.00
FP8 John LeClair 1.00 2.50
FP9 Jaromir Jagr 1.25 3.00

2001-02 Upper Deck Ice

Released in early September 2001, this 151-card set featured all acetate card stock and carried an SRP of $3.99 for a 4-card pack. Ice was originally released as a 84-card set of 44 regular base cards and 40 Fresh Faces redemption cards which entitled the holder to a first year card of a rookie who made his debut during the 2001-02 season. Cards 85-151 were available in random packs of UD Rookie Update. Cards 43-84 were serial-numbered to 1500 and cards 127-151 were serial-numbered to 1000 copies each.

COMPLETE SET w/o SP's 25.00 50.00
1 Paul Kariya .40 1.00
2 Joe Thornton .60 1.50
3 Sergei Samsonov .30 .75
4 Martin Biron .30 .75
5 Jarome Iginla .50 1.25
6 Arturs Irbe .30 .75
7 Tony Amonte .30 .75
8 Patrick Roy 2.00 5.00
9 Peter Forsberg 1.00 2.50
10 Ray Bourque .75 2.00
11 Ron Tugnutt .30 .75
12 Mike Modano .60 1.50
13 Ed Belfour .40 1.00
14 Brett Hull .50 1.25
15 Steve Yzerman 2.00 5.00
16 Dominik Hasek 1.00 2.50
17 Sergei Fedorov .60 1.50
18 Tommy Salo .30 .75
19 Mike Comrie .30 .75
20 Pavel Bure .40 1.00
21 Adam Deadmarsh .10 .25
22 Zigmund Palffy .30 .75
23 Marian Gaborik .75 2.00
24 Manny Fernandez .30 .75
25 Jose Theodore .50 1.25
26 Mike Dunham .30 .75
27 Martin Brodeur 1.00 2.50
28 Patrik Elias .30 .75
29 Rick DiPietro .30 .75
30 Mark Messier .40 1.00
31 Martin Havlat .30 .75
32 Marian Hossa .40 1.00
33 Jeremy Roenick .50 1.25
34 Sean Burke .30 .75
35 Johan Hedberg .40 1.00
36 Mario Lemieux 2.50 6.00
37 Evgeni Nabokov .30 .75
38 Keith Tkachuk .40 1.00
39 Vincent Lecavalier .40 1.00
40 Curtis Joseph .40 1.00
41 Markus Naslund .40 1.00
42 Jaromir Jagr .75 2.00
43 Ilja Bryzgalov RC 4.00 10.00
44 Ilya Kovalchuk RC 12.00 30.00
45 Zdenek Kutlak RC 2.50 6.00
46 Ales Kotalik RC 4.00 10.00
47 Scott Nichol RC 2.50 6.00
48 Erik Cole RC 4.00 10.00
49 Casey Hankinson RC 2.50 6.00
50 Vaclav Nedorost RC 2.50 6.00
51 Martin Spanhel RC 2.50 6.00
52 Niko Kapanen RC 2.50 6.00
53 Pavel Datsyuk RC 15.00 30.00
54 Ty Conklin RC 2.50 6.00
55 Kristian Huselius RC 4.00 10.00
56 Jaroslav Bednar RC 2.50 6.00
57 Nick Schultz RC 2.50 6.00
58 Martti Jarventie RC 2.50 6.00
59 Martin Erat RC 2.50 6.00
60 Andreas Salomonsson RC 2.50 6.00
61 Radek Martinek RC 2.50 6.00
62 Dan Blackburn RC 2.50 6.00
63 Ivan Ciernik RC 2.50 6.00
64 Jiri Dopita RC 2.50 6.00
65 Krys Kolanos RC 2.50 6.00
66 Bill Tibbetts RC 2.50 6.00
67 Jeff Jillson RC 2.50 6.00
68 Mark Rycroft RC 2.50 6.00
69 Nikita Alexeev RC 2.50 6.00
70 Bob Wren RC 2.50 6.00
71 Pat Kavanagh RC 2.50 6.00
72 Brian Sutherby RC 2.50 6.00
73 Timo Parssinen RC 2.50 6.00
74 Kamil Piros RC 2.50 6.00
75 Jukka Hentunen RC 2.50 6.00
76 Niklas Hagman RC 2.50 6.00
77 Travis Roche RC 2.50 6.00
78 Pavel Skrbek RC 2.50 6.00
79 Scott Clemmensen RC 2.50 6.00
80 Chris Neil RC RC 2.50 6.00
81 Vaclav Pletka RC 2.50 6.00
82 Josef Boumedienne RC 2.50 6.00
83 Ryan Tobler RC 2.50 6.00
84 Chris Corrinet RC 2.50 6.00
85 Dany Heatley .50 1.25
86 Glen Murray .10 .25
87 Jozef Stumpel .10 .25
88 Tim Connolly .10 .25
89 Roman Turek .30 .75
90 Joe Sakic .75 2.00
91 Radim Vrbata .30 .75
92 Milan Hejduk .40 1.00
93 Brenden Morrow .30 .75
94 Pierre Turgeon .30 .75
95 Brett Hull .50 1.25
96 Luc Robitaille .30 .75
97 Brendan Shanahan .40 1.00
98 Nicklas Lidstrom .40 1.00
99 Sandis Ozolinsh .10 .25
100 Jason Allison .10 .25
101 Felix Potvin .40 1.00
102 Donald Audette .10 .25
103 Chris Osgood .30 .75
104 Alexei Yashin .10 .25
105 Mark Parrish .10 .25
106 Eric Lindros .40 1.00
107 Theo Fleury .10 .25
108 Barrett Heisten .10 .25
109 Daniel Alfredsson .30 .75
110 Donald Brashear .10 .25
111 Luke Richardson .10 .25
112 John LeClair .40 1.00
113 Brian Boucher .30 .75
114 Alexei Kovalev .30 .75
115 Teemu Selanne .40 1.00
116 Owen Nolan .30 .75
117 Pavol Demitra .30 .75
118 Chris Pronger .30 .75
119 Doug Weight .30 .75
120 Sheldon Keefe .10 .25
121 Nikolai Khabibulin .40 1.00
122 Mats Sundin .40 1.00
123 Jan Hlavac .10 .25
124 Trevor Linden .10 .25
125 Peter Bondra .40 1.00
126 Olaf Kolzig .30 .75
127 Pasi Nurminen RC 2.50 6.00
128 Ivan Huml RC 2.50 6.00
129 Tony Tuzzolino RC 2.50 6.00
130 Steve Montador RC 2.50 6.00
131 Mike Peluso RC 2.50 6.00
132 Steve Poapst RC 2.50 6.00
133 Riku Hahl RC 2.50 6.00
134 Blake Bellefeuille RC 2.50 6.00
135 David Ling RC 2.50 6.00
136 John Erskine RC 2.50 6.00
137 Brad Norton RC 2.50 6.00
138 Nick Smith RC 2.50 6.00
139 Ryan Flinn RC 2.50 6.00
140 Pascal Dupuis RC 2.50 6.00
141 Olivier Michaud RC 2.50 6.00
142 Marcel Hossa RC 4.00 10.00
143 Raffi Torres RC 5.00 12.00
144 Mikael Samuelsson RC 2.50 6.00
145 Christian Berglund RC 2.50 6.00
146 Shane Endicott RC 2.50 6.00
147 Eric Meloche RC 2.50 6.00
148 Steve Bancroft RC 2.50 6.00
149 Martin Cibak RC 2.50 6.00
150 Dean Melanson RC 2.50 6.00
151 Mike Farrell RC 2.50 6.00

2001-02 Upper Deck Ice Autographs

Inserted at 1:179 in UD Ice and 1:180 in UD Update, this 22-card set featured authentic player autographs on acetate card stock. Update cards are marked below.

KNOWN PRINT RUNS LISTED BELOW
AI Arturs Irbe Upd 8.00 20.00
CJ Curtis Joseph Upd/31 20.00 50.00
DH Dany Heatley Upd 15.00 40.00
DS Daniel Sedin 8.00 20.00
HS Henrik Sedin 8.00 20.00
IK Ilya Kovalchuk Upd/10
JI Jarome Iginla Upd 15.00 40.00
KH Kristian Huselius Upd 6.00 15.00
KK Krys Kolanos Upd 6.00 15.00
MB Martin Brodeur 30.00 80.00
MC Mike Comrie Upd 8.00 20.00
MC Mike Comrie 8.00 20.00
MG Marian Gaborik Upd/20
MH Milan Hejduk Upd 8.00 20.00
MK Milan Kraft 6.00 15.00
MM Mike Modano 15.00 40.00
PB Peter Bondra Upd 8.00 20.00
PS Petr Sykora 6.00 16.00
RK Rostislav Klesla Upd 6.00 15.00
RL Roberto Luongo 12.50 30.00
SY Steve Yzerman 40.00 100.00
WG Wayne Gretzky 125.00 250.00

2001-02 Upper Deck Ice Combos

Inserted at 1:179, this 10-card set featured swatches of game-used jerseys coupled with a piece of game-used stick from the featured player. Cards were produced on all acetate stock. A gold parallel was also produced and serial-numbered to just 25 copies each.

*MULT.COLOR SWATCH: 1X TO 1.5X
*GOLD: 1X TO 2X HI COLUMN
JJ Jaromir Jagr 12.50 30.00
JL John LeClair 8.00 20.00
JR Jeremy Roenick 15.00 40.00
JS Joe Sakic 12.50 30.00
ML Mario Lemieux 30.00 80.00
MM Mike Modano 12.50 30.00
PK Paul Kariya 10.00 25.00
PR Patrick Roy 20.00 50.00
SF Sergei Fedorov 12.50 30.00
SY Steve Yzerman 20.00 50.00

2001-02 Upper Deck Ice First Rounders

Inserted at 1:36, this 7-card set featured swatches of game-used jersey of former first round draft picks.

*MULT.COLOR SWATCH: .75X TO 1.5X HI
FJJ Jaromir Jagr 8.00 20.00
FJR Jeremy Roenick 8.00 20.00
FJS Joe Sakic 8.00 20.00
FMM Mike Modano 6.00 15.00
FPK Paul Kariya 5.00 12.00
FPS Patrik Stefan 5.00 12.00
FSY Steve Yzerman 10.00 25.00

2001-02 Upper Deck Ice Jerseys

Inserted at 1:32, this 8-card set featured swatches of game-worn jersey on all acetate card stock.

*MULT.COLOR SWATCH: .75X TO 1.5X HI
JBH Brett Hull 5.00 12.00
JDW Doug Weight 6.00 15.00
JED Eric Daze 6.00 15.00
JJL John LeClair 4.00 10.00
JMS Marc Savard 4.00 10.00
JPR Patrick Roy 12.50 30.00
JSA Serge Aubin 4.00 10.00
JSF Sergei Fedorov 6.00 15.00

2003-04 Upper Deck Ice

Upper Deck Ice was re-introduced in 2003-04 as a 130-card set featuring 90 veteran base cards (1-90); 30 Tier 1 rookie cards (91-120) serial-numbered to 999 and 10 Tier 2 Rookie cards serial-numbered to 99.

COMP.SET w/o SP's (90) 12.50 25.00
1 Sergei Fedorov .30 .75
2 Vaclav Prospal .10 .25
3 Jean-Sebastien Giguere .20 .50
4 Dany Heatley .30 .75
5 Ilya Kovalchuk .30 .75
6 Andrew Raycroft .20 .50
7 Joe Thornton .40 1.00
8 Sergei Samsonov .20 .50
9 Mika Noronen .20 .50
10 Chris Drury .20 .50
11 Daniel Briere .10 .25
12 Roman Turek .20 .50
13 Jarome Iginla .30 .75
14 Justin Williams .10 .25
15 Ron Francis .20 .50
16 Bryan Berard .10 .25
17 Alexei Zhamnov .10 .25
18 Jocelyn Thibault .20 .50
19 Joe Sakic .50 1.25
20 Paul Kariya .25 .60
21 Peter Forsberg .60 1.50
22 David Aebischer .10 .25
23 Todd Marchant .10 .25
24 Rick Nash .30 .75
25 Marc Denis .20 .50
26 Mike Modano .40 1.00
27 Marty Turco .20 .50
28 Bill Guerin .20 .50
29 Brett Hull .30 .75
30 Pavel Datsyuk .25 .60
31 Henrik Zetterberg .25 .60
32 Steve Yzerman 1.25 3.00
33 Adam Oates .20 .50
34 Tommy Salo .20 .50
35 Raffi Torres .10 .25
36 Ales Hemsky .10 .25
37 Olli Jokinen .20 .50
38 Roberto Luongo .30 .75
39 Jay Bouwmeester .10 .25
40 Martin Straka .10 .25
41 Roman Cechmanek .10 .25
42 Zigmund Palffy .20 .50
43 Marian Gaborik .50 1.25
44 Alexandre Daigle .10 .25
45 Manny Fernandez .20 .50
46 Mike Ribeiro .10 .25
47 Saku Koivu .25 .60
48 Jose Theodore .25 .60
49 David Legwand .20 .50
50 Tomas Vokoun .20 .50
51 Patrik Elias .20 .50
52 Martin Brodeur .60 1.50
53 Scott Stevens .20 .50
54 Scott Gomez .10 .25
55 Rick DiPietro .20 .50
56 Alexei Yashin .10 .25
57 Trent Hunter .10 .25
58 Mark Messier .25 .60
59 Eric Lindros .25 .60
60 Jaromir Jagr .40 1.00
61 Patrick Lalime .20 .50
62 Jason Spezza .25 .60
63 Marian Hossa .25 .60
64 Sean Burke .20 .50
65 Jeremy Roenick .30 .75
66 Tony Amonte .20 .50
67 Ladislav Nagy .10 .25
68 Mike Comrie .20 .50
69 Mario Lemieux 1.50 4.00
70 Rico Fata .10 .25
71 Vincent Damphousse .10 .25
72 Patrick Marleau .20 .50
73 Evgeni Nabokov .20 .50
74 Keith Tkachuk .25 .60
75 Chris Osgood .20 .50
76 Doug Weight .20 .50
77 Pavol Demitra .20 .50
78 Vincent Lecavalier .25 .60
79 Nikolai Khabibulin .25 .60
80 Ed Belfour .25 .60
81 Mats Sundin .25 .60
82 Alexander Mogilny .20 .50
83 Owen Nolan .20 .50
84 Todd Bertuzzi .25 .60
85 Ed Jovanovski .20 .50
86 Jason King .10 .25
87 Markus Naslund .20 .50
88 Peter Bondra .20 .50
89 Anson Carter .20 .50
90 Olaf Kolzig .20 .50
91 Pavel Vorobiev RC 2.00 5.00
92 Antti Miettinen RC 2.00 5.00
93 Chris Higgins RC 8.00 20.00
94 Dan Hamhuis RC 2.00 5.00
95 Marek Zidlicky RC 2.00 5.00
96 Mikhail Yakubov RC 2.00 5.00
97 Antoine Vermette RC 2.00 5.00
98 Jiri Hudler RC 5.00 12.00
99 Milan Michalek RC 6.00 15.00
100 Peter Sejna RC 2.00 5.00
101 Matt Stajan RC 6.00 15.00
102 Maxim Kondratiev RC 2.00 5.00
103 Alexander Semin RC 12.00 30.00
104 Sergei Zinovjev RC 2.00 5.00
105 Julien Vauclair RC 2.00 5.00
106 Dominic Moore RC 2.00 5.00
107 Tony Salmelainen RC 2.00 5.00
108 Rastislav Stana RC 2.00 5.00
109 Peter Sarno RC 2.00 5.00
110 Jed Ortmeyer RC 2.00 5.00
111 Nathan Smith RC 2.00 5.00
112 Matthew Lombardi RC 2.00 5.00
113 Dustin Brown RC 4.00 10.00
114 John-Michael Liles RC 2.00 5.00
115 Tim Gleason RC 2.00 5.00
116 Boyd Gordon RC 2.00 5.00
117 Greg Campbell RC 2.00 5.00
118 Ryan Kesler RC 2.00 5.00
119 Trevor Daley RC 2.00 5.00
120 John Pohl RC 2.00 5.00
121 Joffrey Lupul RC 30.00 80.00
122 Patrice Bergeron RC 75.00 125.00
123 Eric Staal RC 100.00 200.00
124 Tuomo Ruutu RC 30.00 60.00
125 Nikolai Zherdev RC 40.00 80.00
126 Nathan Horton RC 60.00 125.00
127 Fredrik Sjostrom RC 15.00 40.00
128 Jordin Tootoo RC 40.00 80.00
129 Joni Pitkanen RC 20.00 50.00
130 Marc-Andre Fleury RC 150.00 300.00
90P Marc-Andre Fleury PROMO .40 1.00

2003-04 Upper Deck Ice Glass Parallel

This 40-card set paralleled the rookie cards in the base set on clear acetate stock cards. Each card was serial-numbered out of 25.

*ROOKIES 91-120: 1.25X TO 3X BASE HI
*121-130: .3X TO .75X

2003-04 Upper Deck Ice Gold

This 90-card set paralleled the first 90 cards in the base set. Each card was serial-numbered out of 40.

*STARS: 4X TO 10X

2003-04 Upper Deck Ice Authentics

This 26-card memorabilia set featured certified autographs and jersey swatches. They were inserted at 1:80.

*MULT.COLOR SWATCH: .5X TO 1.25X
IAAC Anson Carter 10.00 25.00
IAAH Ales Hemsky 10.00 25.00
IACK Chuck Kobasew 6.00 15.00
IADA David Aebischer 15.00 40.00
IAHA Marcel Hossa 6.00 15.00
IAHZ Henrik Zetterberg 15.00 40.00
IAIK Ilya Kovalchuk 25.00 60.00
IAJI Jarome Iginla 25.00 60.00
IAJR Jeremy Roenick 15.00 40.00
IAJS Jason Spezza 15.00 40.00
IAJT Joe Thornton 25.00 60.00
IAMB Martin Brodeur 75.00 150.00
IAMH Gordie Howe 75.00 150.00
IAMH Marian Hossa 15.00 40.00
IAMN Markus Naslund 15.00 40.00
IAMT Marty Turco SP 50.00 125.00
IAON Owen Nolan 8.00 20.00
IAPR Patrick Roy SP 75.00 200.00
IARD Rick DiPietro 15.00 40.00
IARL Roberto Luongo 20.00 50.00
IARN Rick Nash 25.00 60.00
IASK Saku Koivu 15.00 40.00
IATB Todd Bertuzzi 15.00 40.00
IATH Jose Theodore 25.00 60.00
IAWG Wayne Gretzky 150.00 300.00
IAZP Zigmund Palffy 8.00 20.00

2003-04 Upper Deck Ice Breakers

This 42-card set featured swatches of jersey on acetate card stock. Each card was serial-numbered out of 75. A patch parallel was also created and serial-numbered out of 25

*MULT.COLOR SWATCH: .6X TO 1.5X
*PATCHES: 1.5X TO 4X
IBAH Ales Hemsky 6.00 15.00
IBBG Bill Guerin 6.00 15.00
IBBH Brett Hull 8.00 20.00
IBBL Brian Leetch 6.00 15.00
IBBS Brendan Shanahan 6.00 15.00
IBDA David Aebischer 6.00 15.00
IBDH Dominik Hasek 10.00 25.00
IBEB Ed Belfour 10.00 25.00
IBHK Milan Hejduk 4.00 10.00
IBIK Ilya Kovalchuk 8.00 20.00
IBJJ Jaromir Jagr 10.00 25.00
IBJK Jason King 4.00 10.00
IBJR Jeremy Roenick 8.00 20.00
IBJS Joe Sakic 12.50 30.00
IBJT Joe Thornton 8.00 20.00
IBJSG Jean-Sebastien Giguere 6.00 15.00
IBKT Keith Tkachuk 6.00 15.00
IBMB Martin Brodeur 15.00 40.00
IBMH Marian Hossa 6.00 15.00
IBML Mario Lemieux 20.00 50.00
IBMM Mike Modano 8.00 20.00
IBMN Markus Naslund 6.00 15.00
IBMR Mark Messier 8.00 20.00
IBMS Mats Sundin 6.00 15.00
IBMT Marty Turco 6.00 15.00
IBNL Nicklas Lidstrom 4.00 10.00
IBPF Peter Forsberg 10.00 25.00
IBPK Paul Kariya 6.00 15.00
IBPR Patrick Roy 20.00 50.00
IBRB Rob Blake 4.00 10.00
IBRF Ron Francis 6.00 15.00
IBRN Rick Nash 10.00 25.00
IBRT Raffi Torres 4.00 10.00
IBSG Scott Gomez 4.00 10.00
IBSP Jason Spezza 6.00 15.00
IBSS Sergei Samsonov 6.00 15.00
IBST Scott Stevens 4.00 10.00
IBSY Steve Yzerman 15.00 40.00
IBTB Todd Bertuzzi 6.00 15.00
IBTH Jose Theodore 8.00 20.00
IBVL Vincent Lecavalier 6.00 15.00
IBZP Zigmund Palffy 6.00 15.00

2003-04 Upper Deck Ice Clear Cut Winners

This 20-card set featured jersey swatches on acetate card stock. Cards from this set were inserted at 1:10. A patch parallel was also created and serial-numbered to 25.

*MULT.COLOR SWATCH: .6X TO 1.5X
*PATCHES: 1.5X TO 4X
CCBH Brett Hull 4.00 10.00
CCBL Brian Leetch 3.00 8.00
CCBS Brendan Shanahan 6.00 15.00
CCDH Dominik Hasek 6.00 15.00
CCEB Ed Belfour 6.00 15.00
CCJJ Jaromir Jagr 5.00 12.00
CCJS Joe Sakic 8.00 20.00
CCMB Martin Brodeur 12.50 30.00
CCMH Milan Hejduk 6.00 15.00
CCML Mario Lemieux 16.00 40.00
CCMM Mike Modano 5.00 12.00
CCMR Mark Messier 6.00 15.00
CCNL Nicklas Lidstrom 6.00 15.00
CCPF Peter Forsberg 8.00 20.00
CCPR Patrick Roy 12.50 30.00
CCRB Rob Blake 3.00 8.00
CCRF Ron Francis 3.00 8.00
CCSG Scott Gomez 3.00 8.00
CCSS Scott Stevens 3.00 8.00
CCSY Steve Yzerman 12.50 30.00

2003-04 Upper Deck Ice Frozen Fabrics

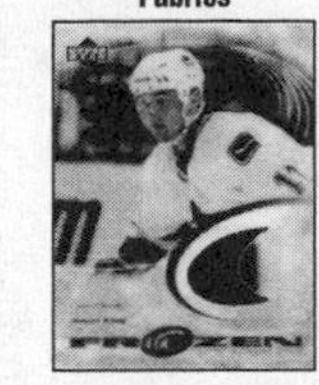

This 20-card set featured swatches of jersey on acetate card stock. A patch parallel was also created and serial-numbered to 25.

COMPLETE SET (20)
*MULT.COLOR SWATCH: .6X TO 1.5X
*PATCHES: 2X TO 5X
FFAH Ales Hemsky 4.00 10.00
FFBG Bill Guerin 4.00 10.00
FFDA David Aebischer 4.00 10.00
FFJK Jason King 4.00 10.00
FFJR Jeremy Roenick 5.00 12.00
FFJS Jason Spezza 5.00 12.00
FFJT Joe Thornton 6.00 15.00
FFJSG Jean-Sebastien Giguere 4.00 10.00
FFKT Keith Tkachuk 4.00 10.00
FFMH Marian Hossa 4.00 10.00
FFMN Markus Naslund 4.00 10.00
FFMS Mats Sundin 4.00 10.00
FFMT Marty Turco 4.00 10.00
FFPK Paul Kariya 4.00 10.00
FFRN Rick Nash 6.00 15.00
FFRT Raffi Torres 4.00 10.00
FFSS Sergei Samsonov 4.00 10.00
FFTB Todd Bertuzzi 4.00 10.00
FFTH Jose Theodore 5.00 12.00
FFZP Zigmund Palffy 4.00 10.00

2003-04 Upper Deck Ice Icons

COMPLETE SET (10) 20.00 50.00
STATED ODDS 1:40
IAM Al MacInnis 2.00 5.00
IBL Brian Leetch 2.00 5.00
IEB Ed Belfour 2.00 5.00
IJR Jeremy Roenick 2.50 6.00
IJS Joe Sakic 4.00 10.00
IMB Martin Brodeur 5.00 12.00
IML Mario Lemieux 6.00 15.00
IMM Mike Modano 3.00 8.00
ISY Steve Yzerman 5.00 12.00
ITD Tie Domi 2.00 5.00

2003-04 Upper Deck Ice Icons Jerseys

*MULT.COLOR SWATCH: .5X TO 1.25X
STATED ODDS 1:40
IAM Al MacInnis 4.00 10.00
IBL Brian Leetch 4.00 10.00
IEB Ed Belfour 6.00 15.00
IJR Jeremy Roenick 5.00 12.00
IMB Martin Brodeur 12.50 30.00
IML Mario Lemieux 12.50 30.00
IMM Mike Modano 5.00 12.00
ISY Steve Yzerman 12.50 30.00
ITD Tie Domi 4.00 10.00

2003-04 Upper Deck Ice Under Glass Autographs

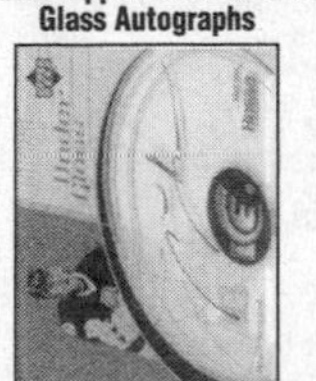

This 20-card set featured certified player autographs on thick acetate card stock. Cards in this set were inserted at 1:160.

UGAH Ales Hemsky 15.00 40.00
UGBO Bobby Orr 150.00 250.00
UGDC Don Cherry 25.00 60.00
UGEL Eric Lindros SP 50.00 100.00
UGHA Marian Hossa 15.00 40.00
UGHZ Henrik Zetterberg 20.00 50.00
UGIK Ilya Kovalchuk 30.00 80.00
UGJR Jeremy Roenick 25.00 60.00
UGJS Jason Spezza 40.00 100.00
UGJT Joe Thornton 30.00 80.00
UGMB Martin Brodeur 150.00 250.00
UGMG Marian Gaborik 40.00 100.00
UGMH Gordie Howe 75.00 200.00
UGON Owen Nolan 15.00 40.00
UGPR Patrick Roy SP 250.00 400.00
UGRD Rick DiPietro 20.00 50.00
UGRL Roberto Luongo 30.00 80.00
UGRN Rick Nash 25.00 60.00
UGTB Todd Bertuzzi 15.00 40.00
UGWG Wayne Gretzky 300.00 500.00

2005-06 Upper Deck Ice

COMP. SET w/o SP's (1-100) 12.50 30.00
101-106 PRINT RUN 99 #'d SETS
107-118 PRINT RUN 999 #'d SETS
119-142 PRINT RUN 1,999 #'d SETS
143-268 PRINT RUN 2,999 #'d SETS
1 Joffrey Lupul .30 .75
2 Scott Niedermayer .30 .75
3 Jean-Sebastien Giguere .40 1.00
4 Teemu Selanne .50 1.25
5 Ilya Kovalchuk .60 1.50
6 Kari Lehtonen .50 1.25
7 Marian Hossa .40 1.00
8 Andrew Raycroft .40 1.00
9 Patrice Bergeron .50 1.25
10 Brian Leetch .50 1.25
11 Glen Murray .30 .75
12 Ryan Miller .25 .60
13 Chris Drury .40 1.00
14 Jarome Iginla .40 1.00
15 Miikka Kiprusoff .50 1.25
16 Jordan Leopold .30 .75
17 Tony Amonte .40 1.00
18 Erik Cole .30 .75
19 Eric Staal .40 1.00
20 Nikolai Khabibulin .50 1.25
21 Tuomo Ruutu .30 .75
22 Joe Sakic 1.00 2.50
23 Milan Hejduk .50 1.25
24 Alex Tanguay .40 1.00
25 David Aebischer .40 1.00
26 Rick Nash .60 1.50
27 Sergei Fedorov .50 1.25
28 Mike Modano .50 1.25
29 Marty Turco .40 1.00
30 Bill Guerin .30 .75
31 Steve Yzerman 1.25 3.00
32 Pavel Datsyuk .50 1.25
33 Brendan Shanahan .50 1.25
34 Nicklas Lidstrom .50 1.25
35 Henrik Zetterberg .50 1.25
36 Chris Pronger .40 1.00
37 Ty Conklin .40 1.00
38 Ryan Smyth .40 1.00
39 Michael Peca .30 .75
40 Roberto Luongo .75 2.00
41 Joe Nieuwendyk .40 1.00
42 Jay Bouwmeester .30 .75
43 Stephen Weiss .30 .75
44 Jeremy Roenick .50 1.25
45 Luc Robitaille .40 1.00
46 Alexander Frolov .40 1.00
47 Marian Gaborik .60 1.50
48 Dwayne Roloson .40 1.00
49 Jose Theodore .50 1.25
50 Saku Koivu .50 1.25
51 Michael Ryder .40 1.00
52 Mike Ribeiro .30 .75
53 Steve Sullivan .30 .75
54 Paul Kariya .50 1.25
55 Tomas Vokoun .40 1.00
56 Martin Brodeur 1.25 3.00
57 Patrik Elias .40 1.00
58 Brian Gionta .15 .40
59 Alexei Yashin .30 .75
60 Miroslav Satan .30 .75
61 Rick DiPietro .40 1.00
62 Jaromir Jagr .75 2.00
63 Kevin Weekes .40 1.00
64 Tom Poti .30 .75
65 Dany Heatley .50 1.25
66 Dominik Hasek .60 1.50
67 Martin Havlat .40 1.00
68 Jason Spezza .50 1.25
69 Daniel Alfredsson .50 1.25
70 Robert Esche .40 1.00
71 Peter Forsberg .75 2.00
72 Keith Primeau .30 .75
73 Simon Gagne .50 1.25
74 Shane Doan .30 .75
75 Curtis Joseph .50 1.25
76 Mario Lemieux 2.00 5.00
77 Zigmund Palffy .40 1.00
78 Mark Recchi .40 1.00
79 Marc-Andre Fleury .40 1.00
80 Joe Thornton .75 2.00
81 Jonathan Cheechoo .50 1.25
82 Evgeni Nabokov .40 1.00
83 Patrick Marleau .40 1.00
84 Keith Tkachuk .50 1.25
85 Doug Weight .40 1.00
86 Martin St. Louis .40 1.00
87 Brad Richards .40 1.00
88 Sean Burke .40 1.00
89 Vincent Lecavalier .50 1.25
90 Mats Sundin .50 1.25
91 Nik Antropov .30 .75

92 Eric Lindros .50 1.25
93 Ed Belfour .50 1.25
94 Jason Allison .30 .75
95 Markus Naslund .50 1.25
96 Todd Bertuzzi .60 1.50
97 Brendan Morrison .30 .75
98 Ed Jovanovski .40 1.00
99 Jeff Friesen .30 .75
100 Olaf Kolzig .40 1.00
101 Gilbert Brule RC 150.00 300.00
102 Thomas Vanek RC 175.00 350.00
103 Alexander Ovechkin RC 800.00 1200.00
104 Jeff Carter RC 200.00 400.00
105 Corey Perry RC 175.00 350.00
106 Sidney Crosby RC 2000.00 3500.00
107 Ryan Getzlaf RC 10.00 25.00
108 Hannu Toivonen RC 6.00 15.00
109 Dion Phaneuf RC 20.00 40.00
110 Cam Ward RC 8.00 20.00
111 Wojtek Wolski RC 8.00 20.00
112 Jim Howard RC 10.00 25.00
113 Rostislav Olesz RC 4.00 10.00
114 Alexander Perezhogin RC 4.00 10.00
115 Zach Parise RC 12.00 30.00
116 Mikko Koivu RC 6.00 15.00
117 Mike Richards RC 10.00 25.00
118 Alexander Steen RC 8.00 20.00
119 Braydon Coburn RC 3.00 8.00
120 Andrew Alberts RC 2.00 5.00
121 Eric Nystrom RC 3.00 8.00
122 Kevin Nastiuk RC 3.00 8.00
123 Brent Seabrook RC 3.00 8.00
124 R.J. Umberger RC 5.00 12.00
125 Cam Barker RC 3.00 8.00
126 Peter Budaj RC 5.00 12.00
127 Jussi Jokinen RC 3.00 8.00
128 Johan Franzen RC 8.00 20.00
129 Brad Winchester RC 2.00 5.00
130 Anthony Stewart RC 3.00 8.00
131 Matt Foy RC 2.00 5.00
132 Yann Danis RC 5.00 12.00
133 Ryan Suter RC 4.00 10.00
134 Petteri Nokelainen RC 2.00 5.00
135 Chris Campoli RC 2.00 5.00
136 Al Montoya RC 5.00 12.00
137 Henrik Lundqvist RC 12.00 30.00
138 Ryan Whitney RC 4.00 10.00
139 Andrej Meszaros RC 3.00 8.00
140 Keith Ballard RC 3.00 8.00
141 David Leneveu RC 3.00 8.00
142 Jeff Woywitka RC 2.00 5.00
143 Jim Slater RC 3.00 8.00
144 Adam Berkhoel RC 3.00 8.00
145 Kevin Dallman RC 2.00 5.00
146 Milan Jurcina RC 2.00 5.00
147 Niklas Nordgren RC 2.00 5.00
148 Duncan Keith RC 5.00 12.00
149 Jaroslav Balastik RC 2.00 5.00
150 Brett Lebda RC 2.00 5.00
151 Kyle Brodziak RC 2.00 5.00
152 George Parros RC 2.00 5.00
153 Derek Boogaard RC 3.00 8.00
154 Mark Streit RC 2.00 5.00
155 Raitis Ivanans RC 2.00 5.00
156 Ryan Hollweg RC 2.00 5.00
157 Chris Holt RC 2.00 5.00
158 Petr Prucha RC 4.00 10.00
159 Brian McGrattan RC 2.00 5.00
160 Patrick Eaves RC 4.00 10.00
161 Wade Skolney RC 2.00 5.00
162 Maxime Talbot RC 2.00 5.00
163 Ryane Clowe RC 2.00 5.00
164 Josh Gorges RC 2.00 5.00
165 Andy Roach RC 2.00 5.00
166 Jay McClement RC 2.00 5.00
167 Jeff Hoggan RC 2.00 5.00
168 Lee Stempniak RC 2.00 5.00
169 Colin Hemingway RC 2.00 5.00
170 Timo Helbling RC 2.00 5.00
171 Paul Ranger RC 2.00 5.00
172 Andrew Wozniewski RC 2.00 5.00
173 Robert Nilsson RC 3.00 8.00
174 Rene Bourque RC 2.00 5.00
175 Brandon Bochenski RC 2.00 5.00
176 Steve Bernier RC 4.00 10.00
177 Evgeny Artyukhin RC 2.00 5.00
178 Christoph Schubert RC 2.00 5.00
179 Jakub Klepis RC 2.00 5.00
180 Dimitri Patzold RC 3.00 8.00
181 Vojtech Polak RC 2.00 5.00
182 Rob McVicar RC 2.00 5.00
183 Staffan Kronwall RC 2.00 5.00
184 Jordan Sigalet RC 3.00 8.00
185 Dustin Penner RC 4.00 10.00
186 Michael Wall RC 2.00 5.00
187 Zenon Konopka RC 2.00 5.00
188 Jay Leach RC 2.00 5.00
189 Danny Richmond RC 2.00 5.00
190 Martin St. Pierre RC 2.00 5.00
191 Andrew Penner RC 2.00 5.00
192 Steve Goertzen RC 2.00 5.00
193 Ole-Kristian Tollefsen RC 2.00 5.00
194 Junior Lessard RC 2.00 5.00
195 Danny Syvret RC 2.00 5.00
196 Greg Jacina RC 2.00 5.00
197 Jeff Giuliano RC 2.00 5.00
198 Adam Hauser RC 3.00 8.00
199 Maxim Lapierre RC 2.00 5.00
200 Barry Tallackson RC 2.00 5.00
201 Cam Janssen RC 2.00 5.00
202 Kevin Colley RC 2.00 5.00
203 Jeremy Colliton RC 2.00 5.00
204 Yanick Lehoux RC 2.00 5.00
205 Erik Christensen RC 3.00 8.00
206 Dennis Wideman RC 2.00 5.00
207 Nick Tarnasky RC 2.00 5.00
208 Brian Eklund RC 2.00 5.00
209 Gerald Coleman RC 3.00 8.00
210 Tomas Fleischmann RC 2.00 5.00
211 Brad Richardson RC 2.00 5.00
212 Mark Cullen RC 2.00 5.00
213 Jean-Philippe Cote RC 2.00 5.00
214 Andrei Kostitsyn RC 5.00 12.00
215 Matt Jones RC 2.00 5.00

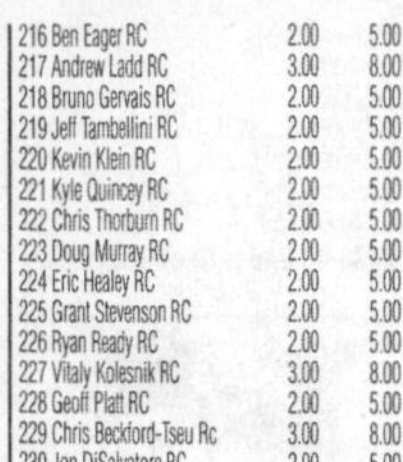

216 Ben Eager RC 2.00 5.00
217 Andrew Ladd RC 3.00 8.00
218 Bruno Gervais RC 2.00 5.00
219 Jeff Tambellini RC 2.00 5.00
220 Kevin Klein RC 2.00 5.00
221 Kyle Quincey RC 2.00 5.00
222 Chris Thorburn RC 2.00 5.00
223 Doug Murray RC 2.00 5.00
224 Eric Healey RC 2.00 5.00
225 Grant Stevenson RC 2.00 5.00
226 Ryan Ready RC 2.00 5.00
227 Vitaly Kolesnik RC 3.00 8.00
228 Geoff Platt RC 2.00 5.00
229 Chris Beckford-Tseu RC 3.00 8.00
230 Jon DiSalvatore RC 2.00 5.00
231 Ben Walter RC 2.00 5.00
232 Jonathan Ferland RC 2.00 5.00
233 Kevin Bieksa RC 2.50 6.00
234 Rick Rypien RC 2.00 5.00
235 Alexandre Burrows RC 2.00 5.00
236 David Steckel RC 2.00 5.00
237 Mike Green RC 5.00 12.00
238 Richie Regehr RC 2.00 5.00
239 Josh Gratton RC 2.00 5.00
240 Chad Larose RC 2.00 5.00
241 Petr Kanko RC 2.00 5.00
242 Matt Ryan RC 2.00 5.00
243 Connor James RC 2.00 5.00
244 Richard Petiot RC 2.00 5.00
245 Darren Reid RC 2.00 5.00
246 Ryan Craig RC 3.00 8.00
247 Matt Greene RC 2.00 5.00
248 Rob Globke RC 2.00 5.00
249 Colby Armstrong RC 4.00 10.00
250 Greg Zanon RC 2.00 5.00
251 Pekka Rinne RC 3.00 8.00
252 Valtteri Filppula RC 3.00 8.00
253 Daniel Paille RC 2.00 5.00
254 Nathan Paetsch RC 2.00 5.00
255 Jiri Novotny RC 2.00 5.00
256 Petr Taticek RC 2.00 5.00
257 Alexandre Picard RC 2.00 5.00
258 Keith Aucoin RC 2.00 5.00
259 Alexandre Picard RC 3.00 8.00
260 Corey Crawford RC 3.00 8.00
261 Jason Ryznar RC 2.00 5.00
262 Doug O'Brien RC 2.00 5.00
263 Mike Glumac RC 2.00 5.00
264 Jay Harrison RC 2.00 5.00
265 Ben Guite RC 2.00 5.00
266 Mark Giordano RC 2.00 5.00
267 David Gove RC 2.00 5.00
268 J-F Jacques RC 2.00 5.00

2005-06 Upper Deck Ice Rainbow

RAINBOW: 6X to 15X HI
PRINT RUN 100 SER. #'d SETS
31 Steve Yzerman 12.00 30.00
56 Martin Brodeur 12.00 30.00
76 Mario Lemieux 12.00 30.00

2005-06 Upper Deck Ice Cool Threads

STATED ODDS 1:36
CTAO Alexander Ovechkin 15.00 40.00
CTAP Alexander Perezhogin 3.00 8.00
CTAR Andrew Raycroft 3.00 8.00
CTAS Alexander Steen 3.00 8.00
CTBS Brent Seabrook 3.00 8.00
CTCP Corey Perry 4.00 10.00
CTCW Cam Ward 6.00 15.00
CTDP Dion Phaneuf 6.00 15.00
CTGB Gilbert Brule 4.00 10.00
CTHL Henrik Lundqvist 6.00 15.00
CTHT Hannu Toivonen 3.00 8.00
CTJB Jay Bouwmeester 2.00 5.00
CTJC Jeff Carter 5.00 12.00
CTJJ Jaromir Jagr 4.00 10.00
CTJK Jussi Jokinen 3.00 8.00
CTJO Jose Theodore 3.00 8.00
CTJT Joe Thornton 4.00 10.00
CTMB Martin Brodeur 5.00 12.00
CTMH Milan Hejduk 2.00 5.00
CTML Matthew Lombardi 2.00 5.00
CTMM Mike Modano 2.00 5.00
CTMN Markus Naslund 2.00 5.00
CTMP Michael Peca 2.00 5.00
CTMR Mike Richards 3.00 8.00
CTMV Martin Havlat 2.00 5.00
CTNH Nathan Horton 2.00 5.00
CTNI Robert Nilsson 3.00 8.00
CTPB Patrice Bergeron 3.00 8.00
CTPE Patrik Elias 3.00 8.00
CTRG Ryan Getzlaf 6.00 15.00
CTRL Roberto Luongo 4.00 10.00
CTRN Rick Nash 4.00 10.00
CTRS Ryan Suter 4.00 10.00
CTSC Sidney Crosby 40.00 100.00
CTSG Simon Gagne 3.00 8.00
CTTR Tuomo Ruutu 3.00 8.00
CTTV Thomas Vanek 4.00 10.00
CTVO Tomas Vokoun 3.00 8.00
CTZC Zdeno Chara 2.00 5.00
CTZP Zach Parise 4.00 10.00

2005-06 Upper Deck Ice Cool Threads Autographs

PRINT RUN 35 SER. #'d SETS
ACTAO Alexander Ovechkin 125.00 250.00
ACTAP Alexander Perezhogin 15.00 40.00
ACTAR Andrew Raycroft 20.00 50.00
ACTAS Alexander Steen 40.00 80.00
ACTBS Brent Seabrook 15.00 40.00

ACTCP Corey Perry
ACTCW Cam Ward 25.00 60.00
ACTDP Dion Phaneuf 50.00 100.00
ACTGB Gilbert Brule 30.00 60.00
ACTHL Henrik Lundqvist 50.00 100.00
ACTHT Hannu Toivonen 15.00 40.00
ACTJB Jay Bouwmeester 10.00 25.00
ACTJC Jeff Carter 25.00 60.00
ACTJK Jussi Jokinen
ACTJO Jose Theodore 25.00 60.00
ACTJT Joe Thornton
ACTMB Martin Brodeur 40.00 100.00
ACTMH Milan Hejduk 12.50 30.00
ACTMM Mike Modano 20.00 40.00
ACTMN Markus Naslund 20.00 50.00
ACTMP Michael Peca
ACTMR Mike Richards 20.00 40.00
ACTMV Martin Havlat 20.00 40.00
ACTNH Nathan Horton
ACTNI Robert Nilsson 15.00 40.00
ACTPB Patrice Bergeron
ACTRG Ryan Getzlaf 20.00 50.00
ACTRL Roberto Luongo
ACTRN Rick Nash
ACTRS Ryan Suter 10.00 25.00
ACTSC Sidney Crosby 350.00 500.00
ACTSD Shane Doan 10.00 25.00
ACTSG Simon Gagne 12.00 30.00
ACTTR Tuomo Ruutu 25.00 60.00
ACTTV Thomas Vanek 20.00 50.00
ACTZC Zdeno Chara 12.50 30.00
ACTZP Zach Parise 25.00 60.00

2005-06 Upper Deck Ice Cool Threads Glass

CTAO Alexander Ovechkin 20.00 50.00
CTAP Alexander Perezhogin 6.00 15.00
CTAR Andrew Raycroft 6.00 15.00
CTAS Alexander Steen 6.00 15.00
CTBS Brent Seabrook 6.00 15.00
CTCP Corey Perry 8.00 20.00
CTCW Cam Ward 8.00 20.00
CTDP Dion Phaneuf 12.50 30.00
CTGB Gilbert Brule 8.00 20.00
CTHL Henrik Lundqvist 12.00 30.00
CTHT Hannu Toivonen 6.00 15.00
CTJB Jay Bouwmeester 4.00 10.00
CTJC Jeff Carter 10.00 25.00
CTJJ Jaromir Jagr 12.00 30.00
CTJK Jussi Jokinen 6.00 15.00
CTJO Jose Theodore 8.00 20.00
CTJT Joe Thornton 10.00 25.00
CTMB Martin Brodeur 15.00 40.00
CTMH Milan Hejduk 6.00 15.00
CTML Matthew Lombardi 4.00 10.00
CTMM Mike Modano 6.00 15.00
CTMN Markus Naslund 8.00 20.00
CTMP Michael Peca 6.00 15.00
CTMR Mike Richards 6.00 15.00
CTMV Martin Havlat 6.00 15.00
CTNH Nathan Horton 4.00 10.00
CTNI Robert Nilsson 4.00 10.00
CTPB Patrice Bergeron 8.00 20.00
CTPE Patrik Elias 6.00 15.00
CTRG Ryan Getzlaf 6.00 15.00
CTRL Roberto Luongo 10.00 25.00
CTRN Rick Nash 10.00 25.00
CTRS Ryan Suter 6.00 15.00
CTSC Sidney Crosby 30.00 75.00
CTSD Shane Doan 6.00 15.00
CTSG Simon Gagne 6.00 15.00
CTTR Tuomo Ruutu 6.00 15.00
CTTV Thomas Vanek 10.00 25.00
CTVO Tomas Vokoun 8.00 20.00
CTZC Zdeno Chara 6.00 15.00
CTZP Zach Parise 6.00 15.00

2005-06 Upper Deck Ice Cool Threads Patches

CTPAO Alexander Ovechkin 60.00 150.00
CTPAP Alexander Perezhogin
CTPAR Andrew Raycroft 12.50 30.00
CTPAS Alexander Steen 20.00 50.00
CTPBS Brent Seabrook 20.00 50.00
CTPCP Corey Perry 12.00 30.00
CTPCW Cam Ward 20.00 50.00
CTPDP Dion Phaneuf 30.00 60.00
CTPGB Gilbert Brule 20.00 50.00
CTPHL Henrik Lundqvist 20.00 50.00
CTPHT Hannu Toivonen 20.00 50.00
CTPJB Jay Bouwmeester 15.00 40.00
CTPJC Jeff Carter 20.00 50.00
CTPJJ Jaromir Jagr 25.00 60.00
CTPJK Jussi Jokinen
CTPJO Jose Theodore 15.00 40.00
CTPJT Joe Thornton 25.00 60.00
CTPMB Martin Brodeur 50.00 125.00
CTPMH Milan Hejduk 12.00 30.00
CTPML Matthew Lombardi 10.00 25.00
CTPMM Mike Modano 15.00 40.00
CTPMN Markus Naslund 12.50 30.00
CTPMP Michael Peca 15.00 40.00
CTPMR Mike Richards 15.00 40.00
CTPMV Martin Havlat 20.00 50.00
CTPNH Nathan Horton 20.00 50.00
CTPNI Robert Nilsson 10.00 25.00
CTPPB Patrice Bergeron 20.00 50.00
CTPPE Patrik Elias 10.00 25.00
CTPRG Ryan Getzlaf 12.00 30.00
CTPRL Roberto Luongo 25.00 60.00
CTPRN Rick Nash 20.00 50.00
CTPRS Ryan Suter 12.00 30.00
CTPSC Sidney Crosby 125.00 250.00
CTPSD Shane Doan 10.00 25.00
CTPSG Simon Gagne 10.00 25.00
CTPTR Tuomo Ruutu 15.00 40.00
CTPTV Thomas Vanek 12.50 30.00
CTPVO Tomas Vokoun 30.00 80.00
CTPZC Zdeno Chara 15.00 40.00
CTPZP Zach Parise 12.00 30.00

2005-06 Upper Deck Ice Fresh Ice

FIAF Alexander Frolov 2.00 5.00
FIAH Adam Hall 2.00 5.00
FIAS Anthony Stewart 3.00 8.00
FIBB Brandon Bochenski 3.00 8.00
FIBC Braydon Coburn 3.00 8.00
FIBS Brent Seabrook 3.00 8.00
FIBU Peter Budaj 3.00 8.00
FIBW Brad Winchester 3.00 8.00
FIDB Dustin Brown 2.00 5.00
FIEN Eric Nystrom 3.00 8.00
FIGP George Parros 3.00 8.00
FIHE Ales Hemsky 2.00 5.00
FIHV Martin Havlat 3.00 8.00
FIHZ Henrik Zetterberg 4.00 10.00
FIJB Jay Bouwmeester 2.00 5.00
FIJF Johan Franzen 3.00 8.00
FIJJ Jussi Jokinen 3.00 8.00
FIJL Jordan Leopold 2.00 5.00
FIJP Joni Pitkanen 2.00 5.00
FIKL Kari Lehtonen 3.00 8.00
FILU Joffrey Lupul 2.00 5.00
FIMC Jay McClement 2.00 5.00
FIMH Marcel Hossa 2.00 5.00
FIMJ Milan Jurcina 2.00 5.00
FIMM Milan Michalek 2.00 5.00
FIMR Mike Richards 4.00 10.00
FIMT Maxime Talbot 2.00 5.00
FIPB Patrice Bergeron 4.00 10.00
FIPN Petteri Nokelainen 3.00 8.00
FIPP Petr Prucha 3.00 8.00
FIPS Philippe Sauve 3.00 8.00
FIRC Ryane Clowe 2.00 5.00
FIRG Ryan Getzlaf 4.00 12.00
FIRI Mike Ribeiro 2.00 5.00
FIRK Ryan Kesler 2.00 5.00
FIRM Ryan Miller 4.00 10.00
FIRS Ryan Suter 3.00 8.00
FIRT Raffi Torres 2.00 5.00
FIYD Yann Danis 3.00 8.00
FIZP Zach Parise 4.00 10.00

2005-06 Upper Deck Ice Fresh Ice Glass

FIAF Alexander Frolov 4.00 10.00
FIAH Adam Hall 4.00 10.00
FIAS Anthony Stewart 6.00 15.00
FIBB Brandon Bochenski 6.00 15.00
FIBC Braydon Coburn 6.00 15.00
FIBS Brent Seabrook 6.00 15.00
FIBU Peter Budaj 6.00 15.00
FIBW Brad Winchester 4.00 10.00
FIDB Dustin Brown 4.00 10.00
FIEN Eric Nystrom 6.00 15.00
FIGP George Parros 6.00 15.00
FIHE Ales Hemsky 4.00 10.00
FIHV Martin Havlat 6.00 15.00
FIHZ Henrik Zetterberg 8.00 20.00
FIJB Jay Bouwmeester 4.00 10.00
FIJF Johan Franzen 6.00 15.00
FIJJ Jussi Jokinen 6.00 15.00
FIJL Jordan Leopold 4.00 10.00
FIJP Joni Pitkanen 4.00 10.00
FIKL Kari Lehtonen 6.00 15.00
FILU Joffrey Lupul 4.00 10.00
FIMC Jay McClement 4.00 10.00
FIMH Marcel Hossa 4.00 10.00
FIMJ Milan Jurcina 4.00 10.00
FIMM Milan Michalek 4.00 10.00
FIMR Mike Richards 8.00 20.00
FIMT Maxime Talbot 4.00 10.00
FINH Nathan Horton 4.00 10.00
FIPB Patrice Bergeron 8.00 20.00
FIPN Petteri Nokelainen 6.00 15.00
FIPP Petr Prucha 6.00 15.00
FIPS Philippe Sauve 6.00 15.00
FIRC Ryane Clowe 4.00 10.00
FIRG Ryan Getzlaf 8.00 20.00
FIRI Mike Ribeiro 4.00 10.00
FIRK Ryan Kesler 4.00 10.00
FIRM Ryan Miller 8.00 20.00
FIRS Ryan Suter 6.00 15.00
FIRT Raffi Torres 4.00 10.00
FIYD Yann Danis 6.00 15.00
FIZP Zach Parise 8.00 20.00

2005-06 Upper Deck Ice Fresh Ice Glass Patches

FIPAF Alexander Frolov 15.00 40.00
FIPAH Adam Hall 12.50 30.00
FIPAS Anthony Stewart 12.50 30.00
FIPBB Brandon Bochenski 12.50 30.00
FIPBC Braydon Coburn 12.50 30.00
FIPBS Brent Seabrook 20.00 50.00
FIPBU Peter Budaj 25.00 60.00
FIPBW Brad Winchester 12.50 30.00
FIPDB Dustin Brown 12.50 30.00
FIPEN Eric Nystrom 12.50 30.00
FIPGP George Parros 12.50 30.00
FIPHE Ales Hemsky 12.50 30.00
FIPHV Martin Havlat 15.00 40.00
FIPHZ Henrik Zetterberg 25.00 60.00
FIPJB Jay Bouwmeester 12.50 30.00
FIPJF Johan Franzen 12.50 30.00
FIPJJ Jussi Jokinen 15.00 40.00
FIPJL Jordan Leopold 12.50 30.00
FIPJP Joni Pitkanen 12.50 30.00
FIPKL Kari Lehtonen 15.00 40.00
FIPLU Joffrey Lupul 12.50 30.00
FIPMC Jay McClement/35 12.50 30.00
FIPMH Marcel Hossa 12.50 30.00
FIPMJ Milan Jurcina 12.50 30.00
FIPMM Milan Michalek 12.50 30.00
FIPMR Mike Richards 20.00 40.00
FIPMT Maxime Talbot 15.00 40.00
FIPPB Patrice Bergeron 25.00 60.00
FIPPN Petteri Nokelainen 12.50 30.00
FIPPP Petr Prucha 15.00 40.00
FIPRC Ryane Clowe 12.50 30.00
FIPRG Ryan Getzlaf 15.00 40.00
FIPRI Mike Ribeiro 12.50 30.00
FIPRK Ryan Kesler 12.50 30.00
FIPRM Ryan Miller 25.00 60.00
FIPRS Ryan Suter 12.50 30.00
FIPRT Raffi Torres 12.50 30.00
FIPYD Yann Danis 12.50 30.00
FIPZP Zach Parise 15.00 40.00

2005-06 Upper Deck Ice Frozen Fabrics

FFAT Alex Tanguay 4.00 10.00
FFAY Alexei Yashin 3.00 8.00
FFBS Brendan Shanahan 5.00 12.00
FFCO Chris Osgood 2.50 6.00
FFCP Chris Pronger 2.00 5.00
FFDA Daniel Alfredsson 4.00 10.00
FFDH Dany Heatley 5.00 12.00
FFDW Doug Weight 4.00 10.00
FFEB Ed Belfour 5.00 12.00
FFGM Glen Murray 3.00 8.00
FFIK Ilya Kovalchuk 6.00 15.00
FFJI Jarome Iginla 4.00 10.00
FFJP Joni Pitkanen 3.00 8.00
FFJR Jeremy Roenick 5.00 12.00
FFJS Joe Sakic 5.00 15.00
FFJT Jocelyn Thibault 4.00 10.00
FFKP Keith Primeau 3.00 8.00
FFKT Keith Tkachuk 5.00 12.00
FFMB Martin Brodeur 8.00 20.00
FFMK Miikka Kiprusoff 5.00 12.00
FFML Mario Lemieux 8.00 20.00
FFMM Milan Michalek 1.50 4.00
FFMS Mats Sundin 5.00 12.00
FFMT Marty Turco 4.00 10.00
FFNK Nikolai Khabibulin 5.00 12.00
FFPD Pavel Datsyuk 5.00 12.00
FFPF Peter Forsberg 8.00 20.00
FFPK Paul Kariya 5.00 12.00
FFPM Patrick Marleau 4.00 10.00
FFPR Patrick Roy 5.00 12.00
FFRB Ray Bourque 5.00 12.00
FFRS Ryan Smyth 4.00 10.00
FFSC Sidney Crosby 30.00 80.00
FFSK Saku Koivu 5.00 12.00
FFSL Martin St. Louis 4.00 10.00
FFSP Jason Spezza 5.00 12.00
FFSY Steve Yzerman 8.00 20.00
FFSZ Sergei Zubov 3.00 8.00
FFTB Todd Bertuzzi 6.00 15.00
FFVL Vincent Lecavalier 6.00 15.00
FFZP Zigmund Palffy 4.00 10.00

2005-06 Upper Deck Ice Frozen Fabrics Autographs

PRINT RUN 35 SER. #'d SETS
AFFAT Alex Tanguay
AFFAY Alexei Yashin 12.00 30.00
AFFCO Chris Osgood 15.00 40.00
AFFCP Chris Pronger 15.00 40.00
AFFDA Daniel Alfredsson

AFFDH Dany Heatley
AFFDW Doug Weight 12.00 30.00
AFFEB Ed Belfour 30.00 80.00
AFFGM Glen Murray 15.00 40.00
AFFIK Ilya Kovalchuk 20.00 50.00
AFFJI Jarome Iginla 20.00 50.00
AFFJP Joni Pitkanen 12.00 30.00
AFFJR Jeremy Roenick 20.00 50.00
AFFJT Jocelyn Thibault
AFFKP Keith Primeau
AFFMB Martin Brodeur 60.00 125.00
AFFMM Milan Michalek
AFFMS Mats Sundin
AFFMT Marty Turco
AFFPR Patrick Roy 100.00 200.00
AFFRB Ray Bourque 40.00 75.00
AFFRS Ryan Smyth 25.00 60.00
AFFSC Sidney Crosby 300.00 500.00
AFFSK Saku Koivu 20.00 50.00
AFFSL Martin St. Louis 12.50 30.00
AFFSP Jason Spezza 15.00 40.00
AFFSZ Sergei Zubov
AFFTB Todd Bertuzzi 15.00 40.00
AFFVL Vincent Lecavalier 40.00 80.00
AFFZP Zigmund Palffy 15.00 40.00

2005-06 Upper Deck Ice Frozen Fabrics Glass

FFAT Alex Tanguay 5.00 12.00
FFAY Alexei Yashin 5.00 12.00
FFBS Brendan Shanahan 5.00 12.00
FFCO Chris Osgood 5.00 12.00
FFCP Chris Pronger 5.00 12.00
FFDA Daniel Alfredsson 5.00 12.00
FFDH Dany Heatley 8.00 20.00
FFDW Doug Weight 5.00 12.00
FFEB Ed Belfour 5.00 12.00
FFGM Glen Murray 5.00 12.00
FFIK Ilya Kovalchuk 8.00 20.00
FFJI Jarome Iginla 8.00 20.00
FFJP Joni Pitkanen 5.00 12.00
FFJR Jeremy Roenick 5.00 12.00
FFJS Joe Sakic 12.00 30.00
FFJT Jocelyn Thibault 5.00 12.00
FFKP Keith Primeau 5.00 12.00
FFKT Keith Tkachuk 5.00 12.00
FFMB Martin Brodeur 12.00 30.00
FFMK Miikka Kiprusoff 8.00 20.00
FFML Mario Lemieux 15.00 40.00
FFMM Milan Michalek 5.00 12.00
FFMS Mats Sundin 5.00 12.00
FFMT Marty Turco 5.00 12.00
FFPD Pavel Datsyuk 5.00 12.00
FFPF Peter Forsberg 8.00 20.00
FFPK Paul Kariya 6.00 15.00
FFPM Patrick Marleau 5.00 12.00
FFPR Patrick Roy 20.00 50.00
FFRB Ray Bourque 8.00 20.00
FFRS Ryan Smyth 5.00 12.00
FFSC Sidney Crosby 75.00 125.00
FFSK Saku Koivu 6.00 15.00
FFSL Martin St. Louis 5.00 12.00
FFSP Jason Spezza 6.00 15.00
FFSY Steve Yzerman 12.00 30.00
FFSZ Sergei Zubov 5.00 12.00
FFTB Todd Bertuzzi 5.00 12.00
FFVL Vincent Lecavalier 6.00 15.00
FFZP Zigmund Palffy 6.00 15.00

2005-06 Upper Deck Ice Frozen Fabrics Patches

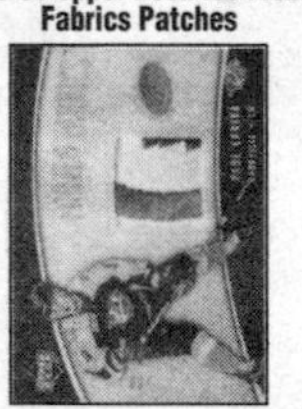

FFPAT Alex Tanguay 15.00 40.00
FFPAY Alexei Yashin
FFPBS Brendan Shanahan 20.00 50.00
FFPCO Chris Osgood 12.00 30.00
FFPCP Chris Pronger
FFPDA Daniel Alfredsson 12.00 30.00
FFPDH Dany Heatley 15.00 40.00
FFPDW Doug Weight 10.00 25.00
FFPEB Ed Belfour 20.00 50.00
FFPGM Glen Murray 10.00 25.00
FFPIK Ilya Kovalchuk 25.00 60.00
FFPJI Jarome Iginla 25.00 60.00
FFPJP Joni Pitkanen 10.00 25.00
FFPJR Jeremy Roenick 20.00 50.00
FFPJS Joe Sakic 30.00 75.00
FFPJT Jocelyn Thibault 12.00 30.00
FFPKP Keith Primeau 12.00 30.00
FFPKT Keith Tkachuk 15.00 40.00
FFPMB Martin Brodeur 40.00 100.00
FFPMK Miikka Kiprusoff 25.00 60.00
FFPML Mario Lemieux 40.00 100.00
FFPMM Milan Michalek 12.00 30.00
FFPMS Mats Sundin 15.00 40.00
FFPMT Marty Turco 20.00 50.00
FFPNK Nikolai Khabibulin 20.00 50.00
FFPPD Pavel Datsyuk 20.00 50.00
FFPPF Peter Forsberg 20.00 50.00
FFPPK Paul Kariya 15.00 40.00
FFPPM Patrick Marleau 12.00 30.00
FFPPR Patrick Roy 75.00 150.00

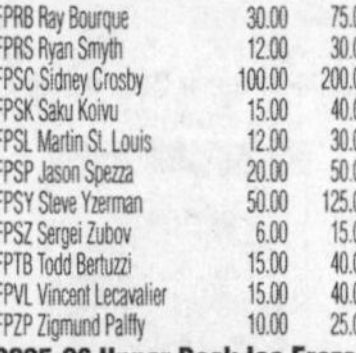

FFPRB Ray Bourque 30.00 75.00
FFPRS Ryan Smyth 12.00 30.00
FFPSC Sidney Crosby 100.00 200.00
FFPSK Saku Koivu 15.00 40.00
FFPSL Martin St. Louis 12.00 30.00
FFPSP Jason Spezza 20.00 50.00
FFPSY Steve Yzerman 50.00 125.00
FFPSZ Sergei Zubov 6.00 15.00
FFPTB Todd Bertuzzi 15.00 40.00
FFPVL Vincent Lecavalier 15.00 40.00
FFPZP Zigmund Palffy 10.00 25.00

2005-06 Upper Deck Ice Frozen Fabrics Patch Autographs

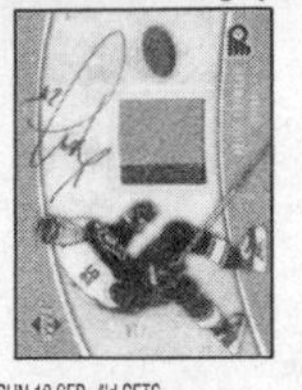

PRINT RUN 10 SER. #'d SETS
NOT PRICED DUE TO SCARCITY

2005-06 Upper Deck Ice Glacial Graphs

GGAF Alexander Frolov 4.00 10.00
GGAO Alexander Ovechkin 75.00 150.00
GGAP Alex Perezhogin 6.00 15.00
GGAR Andrew Raycroft 5.00 12.00
GGCB Cam Barker 5.00 12.00
GGCP Corey Perry 8.00 20.00
GGCW Cam Ward 12.00 30.00
GGDP Dion Phaneuf 20.00 50.00
GGEN Eric Nystrom 4.00 10.00
GGGB Gilbert Brule 8.00 20.00
GGGH Gordie Howe SP 75.00 150.00
GGHO Marian Hossa 6.00 15.00
GGHT Hannu Toivonen 4.00 10.00
GGHV Martin Havlat 6.00 15.00
GGIK Ilya Kovalchuk 20.00 50.00
GGJB Jay Bouwmeester 4.00 10.00
GGJC Jeff Carter 10.00 25.00
GGJI Jarome Iginla 15.00 30.00
GGKB Keith Ballard 4.00 10.00
GGMB Martin Brodeur 40.00 80.00
GGMM Mike Modano SP 30.00 80.00
GGMP Michael Peca 6.00 15.00
GGMR Mike Ribeiro 4.00 10.00
GGMS Matt Stajan 4.00 10.00
GGMT Marty Turco 8.00 20.00
GGNA Rick Nash 12.00 30.00
GGRB Rob Blake SP 15.00 40.00
GGRI Mike Richards 10.00 25.00
GGRK Ryan Kesler 4.00 10.00
GGRL Roberto Luongo 20.00 50.00
GGRM Ryan Miller 15.00 30.00
GGRN Robert Nilsson 4.00 10.00
GGSC Sidney Crosby 250.00 400.00
GGSD Shane Doan 4.00 10.00
GGST Alexander Steen 6.00 15.00
GGTA Tyler Arnason 4.00 10.00
GGTH Trent Hunter 4.00 10.00
GGTL Trevor Linden 8.00 20.00
GGTV Thomas Vanek 10.00 25.00
GGWG Wayne Gretzky SP 750.00 1500.00
GGWW Wojtek Wolski 8.00 20.00
GGZP Zach Parise 6.00 15.00

2005-06 Upper Deck Ice Glacial Graphs Labels

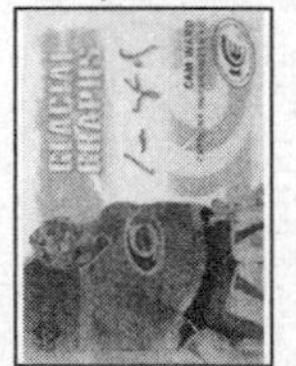

GGCB Cam Barker 8.00 20.00
GGCW Cam Ward 20.00 50.00
GGEN Eric Nystrom 8.00 20.00
GGHT Hannu Toivonen 12.50 30.00
GGJB Jay Bouwmeester 8.00 20.00
GGKB Keith Ballard 8.00 20.00
GGMS Matt Stajan 8.00 20.00
GGRK Ryan Kesler 8.00 20.00
GGRN Robert Nilsson 8.00 20.00
GGTA Tyler Arnason 8.00 20.00
GGTH Trent Hunter 8.00 20.00
GGTV Thomas Vanek 20.00 50.00
GGWW Wojtek Wolski 20.00 50.00
GGZP Zach Parise 12.50 30.00

2005-06 Upper Deck Ice Premieres Auto Patches

PRINT RUN 10 SER. #'d SETS
NOT PRICED DUE TO SCARCITY
AIPAA Andrew Alberts
AIPAM Andrej Meszaros
AIPAO Alexander Ovechkin
AIPAP Alexander Perezhogin
AIPAS Alexander Steen
AIPAW Andrew Wozniewski
AIPBB Brandon Bochenski

AIPBC Braydon Coburn
AIPBL Brett Lebda
AIPBS Brent Seabrook
AIPBT Barry Tallackson
AIPBW Brad Winchester
AIPCB Cam Barker
AIPCC Chris Campoli
AIPCP Corey Perry
AIPCW Cam Ward
AIPDB Derek Boogaard
AIPDK Duncan Keith
AIPDL David Leneveu
AIPDP Dion Phaneuf
AIPEN Eric Nystrom
AIPGB Gilbert Brule
AIPGP George Parros
AIPHL Henrik Lundqvist
AIPHO Jeff Hoggan
AIPHT Hannu Toivonen
AIPJB Jaroslav Balastik
AIPJC Jeff Carter
AIPJF Johan Franzen
AIPJG Josh Gorges
AIPJH Jim Howard
AIPJJ Jussi Jokinen
AIPJK Jakub Klepis
AIPJM Jay McClement
AIPJS Jim Slater
AIPJW Jeff Woywitka
AIPKB Keith Ballard
AIPKD Kevin Dallman
AIPKN Kevin Nastiuk
AIPMF Matt Foy
AIPMJ Milan Jurcina
AIPMK Mikko Koivu
AIPMO Alvaro Montoya
AIPMR Mike Richards
AIPMT Maxime Talbot
AIPNN Niklas Nordgren
AIPPB Peter Budaj
AIPPE Patrick Eaves
AIPPN Petteri Nokelainen
AIPPP Petr Prucha
AIPRB Rene Bourque
AIPRC Ryane Clowe
AIPRG Ryan Getzlaf
AIPRH Ryan Hollweg
AIPRI Raitis Ivanans
AIPRN Robert Nilsson
AIPRO Rostislav Olesz
AIPRS Ryan Suter
AIPSC Sidney Crosby
AIPST Anthony Stewart
AIPTF Tomas Fleischmann
AIPTH Timo Helbling
AIPTV Thomas Vanek
AIPWW Wojtek Wolski
AIPYD Yann Danis
AIPZP Zach Parise

2005-06 Upper Deck Ice Signature Swatches

SSAO Alexander Ovechkin 100.00 175.00
SSAS Alexander Steen 20.00 50.00
SSAT Alex Tanguay 20.00 50.00
SSBL Brian Leetch 20.00 50.00
SSBO Mike Bossy SP 30.00 80.00
SSCP Chris Pronger 25.00 60.00
SSCW Cam Ward 20.00 50.00
SSDH Dominik Hasek SP 75.00 125.00
SSDW Doug Weight 15.00 40.00
SSEB Ed Belfour SP 25.00 60.00
SSGB Gilbert Brule 15.00 40.00
SSHE Dany Heatley SP 40.00 80.00
SSHZ Henrik Zetterberg 25.00 60.00
SSIK Ilya Kovalchuk/50 SP 40.00 100.00
SSJC Jeff Carter 20.00 50.00
SSJI Jarome Iginla 40.00 75.00
SSJK Jari Kurri/100 SP 30.00 80.00
SSJR Jeremy Roenick SP 25.00 60.00
SSJS Jason Spezza/25 SP 100.00 200.00
SSJT Joe Thornton Sp 30.00 80.00
SSLC Luc Robitaille 20.00 50.00
SSMB Martin Brodeur SP 250.00 400.00
SSMH Milan Hejduk 15.00 40.00
SSMM Mike Modano/50 SP 50.00 100.00
SSMN Markus Naslund 20.00 50.00
SSMS Martin St. Louis SP 25.00 60.00
SSNZ Nikolai Zherdev 15.00 40.00
SSPB Patrice Bergeron 15.00 40.00
SSPR Patrick Roy/10 SP
SSRB Ray Bourque SP 60.00 125.00
SSRN Rick Nash/25 SP 100.00 200.00
SSSC Sidney Crosby/100 SP 300.00 600.00
SSSG Simon Gagne 20.00 50.00
SSSK Saku Koivu SP 30.00 80.00
SSSU Mats Sundin/15 SP
SSTB Todd Bertuzzi 20.00 50.00
SSTH Jose Theodore 20.00 50.00
SSVL Vincent Lecavalier SP 60.00 125.00
SSZP Zigmund Palffy/55 SP 40.00 100.00

2007-08 Upper Deck Ice

This set was released on March 14, 2008. The base set consists of 226 cards. Cards 1-100 feature veterans, cards 101-142 are rookies serial numbered of 1999, cards 143-184 are rookies serial numbered of 999, cards 185-210 are rookies serial numbered of 499, and cards 211-226 are rookies serial numbered of 99.

COMP.SET w/o SPs (100) 15.00 40.00
(101-142) PRINT RUN 1999 SER.#'d SETS
(143-184) PRINT RUN 999 SER.#'d SETS
(185-210) PRINT RUN 499 SER.#'d SETS
(211-226) PRINT RUN 99 SER.#'d SETS
1 Martin Brodeur 1.25 3.00
2 Zach Parise .40 1.00
3 Patrik Elias .30 .75
4 Rick DiPietro .40 1.00
5 Bill Guerin .30 .75
6 Miroslav Satan .30 .75
7 Jaromir Jagr .75 2.00
8 Henrik Lundqvist .60 1.50
9 Chris Drury .40 1.00
10 Brendan Shanahan .50 1.25
11 Simon Gagne .50 1.25
12 Daniel Briere .50 1.25
13 Jeff Carter .30 .75
14 Sidney Crosby 2.50 6.00
15 Marc-Andre Fleury .50 1.25
16 Evgeni Malkin 1.25 3.00
17 Jordan Staal .60 1.50
18 Patrice Bergeron .50 1.25
19 Phil Kessel .50 1.25
20 Marc Savard .30 .75
21 Thomas Vanek .40 1.00
22 Ryan Miller .50 1.25
23 Jason Pominville .30 .75
24 Saku Koivu .40 1.00
25 Michael Ryder .30 .75
26 Guillaume Latendresse .40 1.00
27 Cristobal Huet .40 1.00
28 Jason Spezza .50 1.25
29 Daniel Alfredsson .40 1.00
30 Ray Emery .40 1.00
31 Dany Heatley .60 1.50
32 Mats Sundin .50 1.25
33 Darcy Tucker .40 1.00
34 Alexander Steen .30 .75
35 Vesa Toskala .40 1.00
36 Kari Lehtonen .50 1.25
37 Ilya Kovalchuk .60 1.50
38 Marian Hossa .50 1.25
39 Eric Staal .50 1.25
40 Cam Ward .50 1.25
41 Justin Williams .30 .75
42 Tomas Vokoun .50 1.25
43 Nathan Horton .30 .75
44 Olli Jokinen .30 .75
45 Vincent Lecavalier .50 1.25
46 Martin St. Louis .50 1.25
47 Brad Richards .40 1.00
48 Alexander Ovechkin 1.50 4.00
49 Olaf Kolzig .50 1.25
50 Alexander Semin .50 1.25
51 Martin Havlat .40 1.00
52 Nikolai Khabibulin .50 1.25
53 Sergei Samsonov .30 .75
54 Rick Nash .50 1.25
55 Sergei Fedorov .50 1.25
56 David Vyborny .30 .75
57 Gilbert Brule .30 .75
58 Henrik Zetterberg .50 1.25
59 Nicklas Lidstrom .50 1.25
60 Dominik Hasek .60 1.50
61 Pavel Datsyuk .50 1.25
62 Alexander Radulov .50 1.25
63 Chris Mason .40 1.00
64 Jason Arnott .30 .75
65 Paul Kariya .50 1.25
66 Doug Weight .30 .75
67 Keith Tkachuk .40 1.00
68 Jarome Iginla .75 2.00
69 Miikka Kiprusoff .60 1.50
70 Alex Tanguay .50 1.25
71 Dion Phaneuf .50 1.25
72 Joe Sakic 1.00 2.50
73 Milan Hejduk .40 1.00
74 Paul Stastny .50 1.25
75 Ryan Smyth .40 1.00
76 Ales Hemsky .30 .75
77 Dwayne Roloson .40 1.00
78 Joni Pitkanen .30 .75
79 Jarret Stoll .30 .75
80 Marian Gaborik .60 1.50
81 Pavol Demitra .30 .75
82 Mikko Koivu .30 .75
83 Roberto Luongo .75 2.00
84 Markus Naslund .50 1.25
85 Daniel Sedin .30 .75
86 Henrik Sedin .30 .75
87 Ryan Getzlaf .60 1.50
88 Jean-Sebastien Giguere .40 1.00
89 Corey Perry .30 .75
90 Mike Ribeiro .30 .75
91 Mike Modano .50 1.25
92 Marty Turco .50 1.25
93 Rob Blake .40 1.00
94 Anze Kopitar .50 1.25
95 Alexander Frolov .30 .75
96 David Aebischer .40 1.00
97 Shane Doan .30 .75
98 Patrick Marleau .40 1.00
99 Jonathan Cheechoo .40 1.00
100 Joe Thornton .60 1.50
101 Tomi Maki/1999 RC 3.00 8.00
102 Tomas Plihal/1999 RC 4.00 10.00
103 Sheldon Brookbank/1999 RC 3.00 8.00
104 Shay Stephenson/1999 RC 3.00 8.00
105 Sebastien Bisaillon/1999 RC 3.00 8.00
106 Scott Munroe/1999 RC 3.00 8.00
107 Riley Cote/1999 RC 4.00 10.00
108 Rich Peverley/1999 RC 3.00 8.00
109 Pierre Parenteau/1999 RC 3.00 8.00
110 Olli Malmivaara/1999 RC 3.00 8.00
111 Nathan Guenin/1999 RC 3.00 8.00
112 Matt Ellis/1999 RC 3.00 8.00
113 Martin Lojek/1999 RC 3.00 8.00
114 Mark Mancari/1999 RC 4.00 10.00
115 Magnus Johansson/1999 RC 3.00 8.00
116 Krys Barch/1999 RC 3.00 8.00
117 Kent Huskins/1999 RC 3.00 8.00
118 Jonas Nordqvist/1999 RC 3.00 8.00
119 Joel Ward/1999 RC 3.00 8.00
120 Joel Lundqvist/1999 RC 3.00 8.00
121 Joe Piskula/1999 RC 3.00 8.00
122 Jamie Hunt/1999 RC 3.00 8.00
123 Gabe Gauthier/1999 RC 3.00 8.00
124 Duncan Milroy/1999 RC 3.00 8.00
125 Drew Fata/1999 RC 3.00 8.00
126 David Koci/1999 RC 3.00 8.00
127 Darcy Campbell/1999 RC 3.00 8.00
128 Danny Bois/1999 RC 3.00 8.00
129 Curtis Glencross/1999 RC 3.00 8.00
130 Colin Fraser/1999 RC 3.00 8.00
131 Bryan Young/1999 RC 3.00 8.00
132 Bryan Bickell/1999 RC 3.00 8.00
133 Bjorn Melin/1999 RC 3.00 8.00
134 Aaron Rome/1999 RC 3.00 8.00
135 Chris Bourque/1999 RC 4.00 10.00
136 Matt Hunwick/1999 RC 4.00 10.00
137 Tanner Glass/1999 RC 3.00 8.00
138 Aaron Voros/1999 RC 3.00 8.00
139 Alexander Nikulin/1999 RC 4.00 10.00
140 Vladimir Sobotka/1999 RC 4.00 10.00
141 Thomas Greiss/1999 RC 5.00 12.00
142 Ivan Baranka/1999 RC 3.00 8.00
143 Jonathan Sigalet/999 RC 4.00 10.00
144 Tom Gilbert/999 RC 5.00 12.00
145 Jeff Schultz/999 RC 4.00 10.00
146 Mark Fraser/999 RC 4.00 10.00
147 David Krejci/999 RC 8.00 20.00
148 David Moss/999 RC 6.00 15.00
149 Petteri Wirtanen/999 RC 4.00 10.00
150 Tomas Popperle/999 RC 5.00 12.00
151 Daniel Girardi/999 RC 4.00 10.00
152 Ryan Parent/999 RC 5.00 12.00
153 Tobias Stephan/999 RC 5.00 12.00
154 Marc Methot/999 RC 4.00 10.00
155 David Clarkson/999 RC 4.00 10.00
156 Tyler Weiman/999 RC 5.00 12.00
157 Mike Lundin/999 RC 4.00 10.00
158 Ryan Carter/999 RC 5.00 12.00
159 Mike Weber/999 RC 4.00 10.00
160 Daniel Winnik/999 RC 4.00 10.00
161 Tobias Enstrom/999 RC 6.00 15.00
162 Jared Boll/999 RC 4.00 10.00
163 Matt Keetley/999 RC 5.00 12.00
164 Stefan Meyer/999 RC 4.00 10.00
165 Patrick Kaleta/999 RC 4.00 10.00
166 Rod Pelley/999 RC 4.00 10.00
167 Jonas Hiller/999 RC 10.00 25.00
168 Brandon Dubinsky/999 RC 6.00 15.00
169 Jaroslav Hlinka/999 RC 5.00 12.00
170 Cory Murphy/999 RC 4.00 10.00
171 Denis Tolpeko/999 RC 4.00 10.00
172 Craig Weller/999 RC 4.00 10.00
173 Steve Wagner/999 RC 4.00 10.00
174 Jeff Finger/999 RC 4.00 10.00
175 Chris Conner/999 RC 4.00 10.00
176 Lukas Kaspar/999 RC 4.00 10.00
177 Ville Koistinen/999 RC 4.00 10.00
178 Zach Stortini/999 RC 4.00 10.00
179 Brady Murray/999 RC 4.00 10.00
180 Tyler Kennedy/999 RC 6.00 15.00
181 Matt Moulson/999 RC 4.00 10.00
182 John Zeiler/999 RC 4.00 10.00
183 Cal Clutterbuck/999 RC 4.00 10.00
184 Daniel Carcillo/999 RC 5.00 12.00
185 Kris Russell/499 RC 8.00 20.00
186 Matt Niskanen/499 RC 8.00 20.00
187 Nicklas Bergfors/499 RC 6.00 15.00
188 Brett Sterling/499 RC 6.00 15.00
189 Martin Hanzal/499 RC 6.00 15.00
190 Matt Smaby/499 RC 5.00 12.00
191 Petr Kalus/499 RC 5.00 12.00
192 Andy Greene/499 RC 5.00 12.00
193 Frans Nielsen/499 RC 5.00 12.00
194 Rob Schremp/499 RC 6.00 15.00
195 Kyle Chipchura/499 RC 8.00 20.00
196 Jonathan Bernier/499 RC 15.00 40.00
197 Tuukka Rask/499 RC 15.00 40.00
198 Lauri Tukonen/499 RC 5.00 12.00
199 Ondrej Pavelec/499 RC 8.00 20.00
200 Mason Raymond/499 RC 12.00 30.00
201 Ryan Callahan/499 RC 8.00 20.00
202 Curtis McElhinney/499 RC 8.00 20.00
203 Brian Elliott/499 RC 6.00 15.00
204 Drew Miller/499 RC 5.00 12.00
205 David Perron/499 RC 8.00 20.00
206 Anton Stralman/499 RC 6.00 15.00
207 Torrey Mitchell/499 RC 6.00 15.00
208 Jaroslav Halak/499 RC 20.00 50.00
209 Jannik Hansen/499 RC 5.00 12.00
210 Milan Lucic/499 RC 12.00 30.00
211 Bobby Ryan/99 RC 125.00 200.00
212 Jonathan Toews/99 RC 200.00 400.00
213 Sam Gagner/99 RC 125.00 250.00
214 Carey Price/99 RC 650.00 900.00
215 Jiri Tlusty/99 RC 60.00 120.00
216 Erik Johnson/99 RC 100.00 175.00
217 Nicklas Backstrom/99 RC 150.00 300.00
218 Jack Johnson/99 RC 75.00 150.00
219 Devin Setoguchi/99 RC 60.00 120.00
220 Bryan Little/99 RC 75.00 150.00
221 Patrick Kane/99 RC 200.00 400.00
222 Andrew Cogliano/99 RC 100.00 200.00
223 Marc Staal/99 RC 60.00 120.00
224 Nick Foligno/99 RC 50.00 100.00
225 Peter Mueller/99 RC 100.00 200.00
226 James Sheppard/99 RC 50.00 100.00

2007-08 Upper Deck Ice Black Ice Jerseys

BIAO Alexander Ovechkin 50.00 120.00
BIAT Alex Tanguay 8.00 20.00
BIBC Bobby Clarke 10.00 25.00
BIBR Martin Brodeur
BIBS Borje Salming 8.00 20.00
BIDH Dany Heatley 12.00 30.00
BIEM Evgeni Malkin 25.00 60.00
BIES Eric Staal 10.00 25.00
BIGF Grant Fuhr 15.00 40.00
BIGP Gilbert Perreault 8.00 20.00
BIHA Dominik Hasek 12.00 30.00
BIIK Ilya Kovalchuk 12.00 30.00
BIJG Jean-Sebastien Giguere 10.00 25.00
BIJI Jarome Iginla 15.00 40.00
BIJS Jordan Staal 12.00 30.00
BIJT Joe Thornton 12.00 30.00
BILR Larry Robinson 12.00 30.00
BIMB Mike Bossy 8.00 20.00
BIMD Marcel Dionne 5.00 12.00
BIMG Marian Gaborik 8.00 20.00
BIML Mario Lemieux SP 25.00 60.00
BIMM Mark Messier SP 15.00 40.00
BIMN Markus Naslund 5.00 12.00
BIMO Mike Modano 6.00 15.00
BIMR Michael Ryder 6.00 15.00
BIMS Martin St. Louis 5.00 12.00
BINL Nicklas Lidstrom 6.00 15.00
BIPB Patrice Bergeron 10.00 25.00
BIPR Patrick Roy SP 50.00 125.00
BIRB Ray Bourque 12.00 30.00
BIRG Ryan Getzlaf 8.00 20.00
BIRM Ryan Miller 6.00 15.00
BIRN Rick Nash 6.00 15.00
BISC Sidney Crosby 40.00 100.00
BISD Shane Doan 5.00 12.00
BISG Simon Gagne 6.00 15.00
BISM Stan Mikita 6.00 15.00
BITV Thomas Vanek 5.00 12.00
BIVL Vincent Lecavalier 6.00 15.00
BIVO Tomas Vokoun 10.00 25.00
BIWG Wayne Gretzky SP
BIZP Zach Parise 5.00 12.00

2007-08 Upper Deck Ice Black Ice Jerseys Autographs

BIAO Alexander Ovechkin 300.00 450.00
BIAT Alex Tanguay 25.00 60.00
BIBC Bobby Clarke 30.00 80.00
BIBR Martin Brodeur 150.00 300.00
BIBS Borje Salming 25.00 60.00
BIDH Dany Heatley 40.00 100.00
BIEM Evgeni Malkin 100.00 200.00
BIES Eric Staal 30.00 80.00
BIGF Grant Fuhr 50.00 120.00
BIGP Gilbert Perreault 25.00 60.00
BIHA Dominik Hasek 50.00 120.00
BIIK Ilya Kovalchuk 50.00 120.00
BIJG Jean-Sebastien Giguere 30.00 80.00
BIJI Jarome Iginla 40.00 80.00
BIJS Jordan Staal 40.00 100.00
BIJT Joe Thornton 30.00 80.00
BILR Larry Robinson 40.00 100.00
BIMB Mike Bossy 25.00 60.00
BIMD Marcel Dionne 15.00 40.00
BIMG Marian Gaborik 30.00 60.00
BIML Mario Lemieux SP 250.00 350.00
BIMM Mark Messier SP
BIMN Markus Naslund 15.00 40.00
BIMO Mike Modano 40.00 80.00
BIMR Michael Ryder 15.00 40.00
BIMS Martin St. Louis 30.00 60.00
BINL Nicklas Lidstrom 20.00 50.00
BIPB Patrice Bergeron 20.00 50.00
BIPR Patrick Roy SP 300.00 450.00
BIRB Ray Bourque 60.00 120.00
BIRG Ryan Getzlaf 15.00 40.00
BIRM Ryan Miller 20.00 50.00
BIRN Rick Nash 30.00 80.00
BISC Sidney Crosby 350.00 500.00
BISD Shane Doan 15.00 40.00
BISG Simon Gagne 20.00 50.00
BISM Stan Mikita 30.00 60.00
BITV Thomas Vanek 15.00 40.00
BIVL Vincent Lecavalier 30.00 80.00
BIVO Tomas Vokoun 30.00 80.00
BIWG Wayne Gretzky SP 500.00 800.00
BIZP Zach Parise 15.00 40.00

2007-08 Upper Deck Ice Fresh Threads

FTAC Andrew Cogliano 10.00 25.00
FTAG Andy Greene 4.00 10.00
FTBA Nicklas Backstrom 8.00 20.00
FTBD Brandon Dubinsky 5.00 12.00
FTBE Brian Elliott 5.00 12.00
FTBL Bryan Little 5.00 12.00
FTBR Bobby Ryan 15.00 40.00
FTBS Brett Sterling 4.00 10.00
FTCA Ryan Callahan 6.00 15.00
FTCM Curtis McElhinney 5.00 12.00
FTCP Carey Price 8.00 20.00
FTDK David Krejci 8.00 20.00
FTDM Drew Miller 4.00 10.00
FTDP David Perron 6.00 15.00
FTEJ Erik Johnson 8.00 20.00
FTFN Frans Nielsen 4.00 10.00
FTHA Jaroslav Halak 10.00 25.00
FTJA Jannik Hansen 4.00 10.00
FTJB Jonathan Bernier 8.00 20.00
FTJH Jaroslav Hlinka 5.00 12.00
FTJJ Jack Johnson 6.00 15.00
FTJS James Sheppard 4.00 10.00
FTJT Jonathan Toews 8.00 20.00
FTKA Petr Kalus 4.00 10.00
FTKC Kyle Chipchura 6.00 15.00
FTKR Kris Russell 5.00 12.00
FTLT Lauri Tukonen 4.00 10.00
FTMH Martin Hanzal 5.00 12.00
FTML Milan Lucic 10.00 25.00
FTMN Matt Niskanen 4.00 10.00
FTMR Mason Raymond 10.00 25.00
FTMS Matt Smaby 2.00 5.00
FTNB Nicklas Bergfors 5.00 12.00
FTNF Nick Foligno 4.00 10.00
FTPK Patrick Kane 8.00 20.00
FTPM Peter Mueller 10.00 25.00
FTRC Ryan Carter 5.00 12.00
FTRP Ryan Parent 5.00 12.00
FTRS Rob Schremp 5.00 12.00
FTSG Sam Gagner 4.00 10.00
FTTG Tom Gilbert 5.00 12.00
FTTM Torrey Mitchell 5.00 12.00

2007-08 Upper Deck Ice Fresh Threads Black Parallel

FTAC Andrew Cogliano 30.00 80.00
FTAG Andy Greene 12.00 30.00
FTBA Nicklas Backstrom 20.00 50.00
FTBD Brandon Dubinsky 15.00 40.00
FTBE Brian Elliott 15.00 40.00
FTBL Bryan Little 15.00 40.00
FTBR Bobby Ryan 50.00 120.00
FTBS Brett Sterling 12.00 30.00
FTCA Ryan Callahan 20.00 50.00
FTCM Curtis McElhinney 15.00 40.00
FTCP Carey Price 40.00 100.00
FTDK David Krejci 25.00 60.00
FTDM Drew Miller 12.00 30.00
FTDP David Perron 20.00 50.00
FTEJ Erik Johnson 25.00 60.00
FTFN Frans Nielsen 12.00 30.00
FTHA Jaroslav Halak 15.00 40.00
FTJA Jannik Hansen 12.00 30.00
FTJB Jonathan Bernier 15.00 40.00
FTJH Jaroslav Hlinka 15.00 40.00
FTJJ Jack Johnson 20.00 50.00
FTJS James Sheppard 12.00 30.00
FTJT Jonathan Toews 30.00 80.00
FTKA Petr Kalus 12.00 30.00
FTKC Kyle Chipchura 20.00 50.00
FTKR Kris Russell 15.00 40.00
FTLT Lauri Tukonen 12.00 30.00
FTMH Martin Hanzal 15.00 40.00
FTML Milan Lucic 30.00 80.00
FTMN Matt Niskanen 12.00 30.00
FTMR Mason Raymond 30.00 80.00
FTMS Matt Smaby 12.00 30.00
FTNB Nicklas Bergfors 15.00 40.00
FTNF Nick Foligno 20.00 50.00
FTPK Patrick Kane 30.00 80.00
FTPM Peter Mueller 15.00 40.00
FTRC Ryan Carter 15.00 40.00
FTRP Ryan Parent 15.00 40.00
FTRS Rob Schremp 15.00 40.00
FTSG Sam Gagner 12.00 30.00
FTTG Tom Gilbert 15.00 40.00
FTTM Torrey Mitchell 15.00 40.00

2007-08 Upper Deck Ice Fresh Threads Parallel

FTAC Andrew Cogliano 12.00 30.00
FTAG Andy Greene 6.00 15.00
FTBA Nicklas Backstrom 10.00 25.00
FTBD Brandon Dubinsky 6.00 15.00
FTBE Brian Elliott 8.00 20.00
FTBL Bryan Little 8.00 20.00
FTBR Bobby Ryan 20.00 50.00
FTBS Brett Sterling 6.00 15.00
FTCA Ryan Callahan 10.00 25.00
FTCM Curtis McElhinney 8.00 20.00
FTCP Carey Price 10.00 25.00
FTDK David Krejci 12.00 30.00
FTDM Drew Miller 6.00 15.00
FTDP David Perron 8.00 20.00
FTEJ Erik Johnson 12.00 30.00
FTFN Frans Nielsen 6.00 15.00
FTHA Jaroslav Halak 12.00 30.00
FTJA Jannik Hansen 6.00 15.00
FTJB Jonathan Bernier 10.00 25.00
FTJH Jaroslav Hlinka 8.00 20.00
FTJJ Jack Johnson 10.00 25.00
FTJS James Sheppard 6.00 15.00
FTJT Jonathan Toews 10.00 25.00
FTKA Petr Kalus 6.00 15.00
FTKC Kyle Chipchura 10.00 25.00
FTKR Kris Russell 8.00 20.00
FTLT Lauri Tukonen 6.00 15.00
FTMH Martin Hanzal 8.00 20.00
FTML Milan Lucic 15.00 40.00
FTMN Matt Niskanen 6.00 15.00
FTMR Mason Raymond 15.00 40.00
FTMS Matt Smaby 6.00 15.00
FTNB Nicklas Bergfors 8.00 20.00
FTNF Nick Foligno 10.00 25.00
FTPK Patrick Kane 10.00 25.00
FTPM Peter Mueller 10.00 25.00
FTRC Ryan Carter 8.00 20.00
FTRP Ryan Parent 8.00 20.00
FTRS Rob Schremp 8.00 20.00
FTSG Sam Gagner 6.00 15.00
FTTG Tom Gilbert 8.00 20.00
FTTM Torrey Mitchell 8.00 20.00

2007-08 Upper Deck Ice Fresh Threads Patches

STATED PRINT RUN 25 #'d SETS
NOT PRICED DUE TO LACK OF MARKET INFORMATION
FTAC Andrew Cogliano
FTAG Andy Greene
FTBA Nicklas Backstrom
FTBD Brandon Dubinsky
FTBE Brian Elliott
FTBL Bryan Little
FTBR Bobby Ryan
FTBS Brett Sterling
FTCA Ryan Callahan
FTCM Curtis McElhinney
FTCP Carey Price
FTDK David Krejci
FTDM Drew Miller
FTDP David Perron
FTEJ Erik Johnson
FTFN Frans Nielsen
FTHA Jaroslav Halak
FTJA Jannik Hansen
FTJB Jonathan Bernier
FTJH Jaroslav Hlinka
FTJJ Jack Johnson
FTJS James Sheppard
FTJT Jonathan Toews
FTKA Petr Kalus
FTKC Kyle Chipchura
FTKR Kris Russell
FTLT Lauri Tukonen
FTMH Martin Hanzal
FTML Milan Lucic
FTMN Matt Niskanen
FTMR Mason Raymond
FTMS Matt Smaby
FTNB Nicklas Bergfors
FTNF Nick Foligno
FTPK Patrick Kane
FTPM Peter Mueller
FTRC Ryan Carter
FTRP Ryan Parent
FTRS Rob Schremp
FTSG Sam Gagner
FTTG Tom Gilbert
FTTM Torrey Mitchell

2007-08 Upper Deck Ice Frozen Fabrics

FFAE David Aebischer 5.00 12.00
FFAH Ales Hemsky 2.00 5.00
FFAO Alexander Ovechkin 20.00 50.00
FFAT Alex Tanguay 5.00 12.00
FFBB Brad Boyes 5.00 12.00
FFBR Brad Richards 5.00 12.00
FFBS Brendan Shanahan 6.00 15.00
FFCD Chris Drury 5.00 12.00
FFDA Daniel Alfredsson 3.00 8.00
FFDB Daniel Briere 6.00 15.00
FFDH Dany Heatley 5.00 12.00
FFDR Dwayne Roloson 5.00 12.00
FFDW Doug Weight 4.00 10.00
FFES Eric Staal 6.00 15.00
FFHE Milan Hejduk 5.00 12.00
FFHZ Henrik Zetterberg 6.00 15.00
FFIK Ilya Kovalchuk 8.00 20.00
FFJB Jay Bouwmeester 4.00 10.00
FFJG Jean-Sebastien Giguere 6.00 15.00
FFJI Jarome Iginla 10.00 25.00
FFJJ Jaromir Jagr 10.00 25.00
FFJS Jason Spezza 6.00 15.00
FFJT Joe Thornton 8.00 20.00
FFKL Kari Lehtonen 6.00 15.00
FFKT Keith Tkachuk 5.00 12.00
FFMB Martin Brodeur 12.00 30.00
FFMG Marian Gaborik 5.00 12.00
FFMH Marian Hossa 6.00 15.00
FFMK Miikka Kiprusoff 8.00 20.00
FFMN Markus Naslund 6.00 15.00
FFMS Mats Sundin 6.00 15.00
FFPB Patrice Bergeron 6.00 15.00
FFPD Pavel Datsyuk 6.00 15.00
FFPF Peter Forsberg 5.00 12.00
FFPK Paul Kariya 6.00 15.00
FFPM Patrick Marleau 3.00 8.00
FFRL Roberto Luongo 10.00 25.00
FFRS Ryan Smyth 3.00 8.00
FFSA Joe Sakic 8.00 20.00
FFSC Sidney Crosby 20.00 50.00
FFSF Sergei Fedorov 6.00 15.00
FFZP Zach Parise 5.00 12.00

2007-08 Upper Deck Ice Frozen Fabrics Patches

STATED PRINT RUN 25 #'d SETS
NOT PRICED DUE TO INSUFFICIENT MARKET DATA
FFAE David Aebischer
FFAH Ales Hemsky
FFAO Alexander Ovechkin
FFAT Alex Tanguay
FFBB Brad Boyes
FFBR Brad Richards
FFBS Brendan Shanahan
FFCD Chris Drury
FFDA Daniel Alfredsson
FFDB Daniel Briere
FFDH Dany Heatley
FFDR Dwayne Roloson
FFDW Doug Weight
FFES Eric Staal
FFHE Milan Hejduk
FFHZ Henrik Zetterberg
FFIK Ilya Kovalchuk
FFJB Jay Bouwmeester
FFJG Jean-Sebastien Giguere
FFJI Jarome Iginla
FFJJ Jaromir Jagr
FFJS Jason Spezza
FFJT Joe Thornton
FFKL Kari Lehtonen
FFKT Keith Tkachuk
FFMB Martin Brodeur
FFMG Marian Gaborik
FFMH Marian Hossa
FFMK Miikka Kiprusoff
FFMN Markus Naslund
FFMS Mats Sundin
FFPB Patrice Bergeron
FFPD Pavel Datsyuk
FFPF Peter Forsberg
FFPK Paul Kariya
FFPM Patrick Marleau
FFRL Roberto Luongo
FFRS Ryan Smyth
FFSA Joe Sakic
FFSC Sidney Crosby
FFSF Sergei Fedorov
FFZP Zach Parise

2007-08 Upper Deck Ice Frozen Fabrics Patches Black Parallel

STATED PRINT RUN 10 #'d SETS
NOT PRICED DUE TO SCARCIY

2007-08 Upper Deck Ice Frozen Foursomes

STATED PRINT RUN 5 #'d SETS
NOT PRICED DUE TO SCARCITY
F4BEGP Martin Brodeur
Patrik Elias
Brian Gionta
Zach Parise
F4BGBS Gilbert Brule
Ryan Getzlaf
Steve Bernier
Jordan Staal
F4BPSS Mike Bossy
Gilbert Perreault
Darryl Sittler
Steve Shutt
F4CFCK Kyle Calder
Alexander Frolov
Mike Cammalleri
Anze Kopitar
F4EMMH Phil Esposito
Stan Mikita
Frank Mahovlich
Gordie Howe
F4FAMS Marc-Andre Fleury
Colby Armstrong
Evgeni Malkin
Jordan Staal
F4FKGM Grant Fuhr
Jari Kurri
Wayne Gretzky
Mark Messier
F4GDLP Scott Gomez
Chris Drury
Henrik Lundqvist
Petr Prucha
F4GLRC Simon Gagne
Joffrey Lupul
Mike Richards
Jeff Carter
F4HLHD Dominik Hasek
Nicklas Lidstrom
Tomas Holmstrom
Kris Draper
F4HTSW Milan Hejduk
Jose Theodore
Marek Svatos
Wojtek Wolski
F4IGSC Jarome Iginla
Simon Gagne
Martin St. Louis
Jonathan Cheechoo
F4IMTM Jarome Iginla
Lanny McDonald
Alex Tanguay
Al MacInnis
F4IWHN Jarome Iginla
Justin Williams
Dany Heatley
Rick Nash
F4KLRR Saku Koivu
Guy Lafleur
Michael Ryder
Larry Robinson
F4KOMR Evgeni Malkin
Alexander Radulov
Ilya Kovalchuk
Alexander Ovechkin
F4LDMC Mario Lemieux
Marcel Dionne
Stan Mikita
Bobby Clarke
F4LGHM Mario Lemieux
Wayne Gretzky
Gordie Howe
Mark Messier
F4LNZB Pascal Leclaire
Rick Nash
Nikolai Zherdev
Gilbert Brule
F4LTSS Vincent Lecavalier
Joe Thornton
Marc Savard
Eric Staal
F4MDPM Mike Modano
Chris Drury
Zach Parise
Joe Mullen
F4MRTM Mike Modano
Mike Ribeiro
Marty Turco
Brenden Morrow
F4MSWV Stan Mikita
Denis Savard
Doug Wilson
Rick Vaive
F4MTCB Patrick Marleau
Joe Thornton
Jonathan Cheechoo
Steve Bernier
F4NLHL Markus Naslund
Nicklas Lidstrom
Tomas Holmstrom
Henrik Lundqvist
F4NMKB Markus Naslund
Brendan Morrison
Ryan Kesler
Kevin Bieksa
F4NSSZ Ladislav Nagy
Miroslav Satan
Marek Svatos
Marek Zidlicky
F4PDAC Corey Perry
Steve Bernier
Colby Armstrong
Jordan Staal

F4RBGF Patrick Roy
Martin Brodeur
Jean-Sebastien Giguere
Marc-Andre Fleury
F4RLMW Andrew Raycroft
Henrik Lundqvist
Ryan Miller
Cam Ward
F4RTLM Patrick Roy
Marty Turco
Henrik Lundqvist
Ryan Miller
F4SKBK Marc Savard
Chuck Kobasew
Patrice Bergeron
Phil Kessel
F4SRPP Jarret Stoll
Dwayne Roloson
Joni Pitkanen
Marc-Antoine Pouliot
F4VHNL Tomas Vokoun
Dominik Hasek
Evgeni Nabokov
Henrik Lundqvist
F4VZWH Tomas Vokoun
Richard Zednik
Stephen Weiss
Nathan Horton
F4WSWC Ryan Whitney
Mark Stuart
Ian White
Matt Carle

2007-08 Upper Deck Ice Glacial Graphs

GGAK Anze Kopitar 12.00 30.00
GGAO Adam Oates 8.00 20.00
GGAR Alexander Radulov 8.00 20.00
GGAT Alex Tanguay 6.00 15.00
GGBC Blake Comeau 4.00 10.00
GGBD Brandon Dubinsky 8.00 20.00
GGBH Bobby Hull SP 20.00 50.00
GGBO Dustin Boyd 8.00 20.00
GGCA Mike Cammalleri 10.00 25.00
GGCH Cristobal Huet 10.00 25.00
GGCM Clarke MacArthur 8.00 20.00
GGCP Chris Phillips 4.00 10.00
GGCW Cam Ward 12.00 30.00
GGDB Dustin Brown 8.00 20.00
GGDH Dany Heatley 12.00 30.00
GGDS Drew Stafford 10.00 25.00
GGDT Darcy Tucker 10.00 25.00
GGEM Evgeni Malkin 30.00 60.00
GGES Eric Staal 12.00 30.00
GGGA Simon Gagne 12.00 30.00
GGGH Gordie Howe SP 100.00 200.00
GGHA Dominik Hasek SP 40.00 100.00
GGHL Henrik Lundqvist 15.00 40.00
GGIK Ilya Kovalchuk 15.00 40.00
GGIW Ian White 8.00 20.00
GGJC Jonathan Cheechoo 10.00 25.00
GGJG Jean-Sebastien Giguere 12.00 30.00
GGJI Jarome Iginla 20.00 50.00
GGJJ Jack Johnson 12.00 30.00
GGJL John-Michael Liles 8.00 20.00
GGJS Jarret Stoll 8.00 20.00
GGJT Joe Thornton SP 30.00 80.00
GGJW Jeremy Williams 8.00 20.00
GGKB Kevin Bieksa 8.00 20.00
GGKD Kris Draper 10.00 25.00
GGKE Phil Kessel 12.00 30.00
GGLT Lauri Tukonen 8.00 20.00
GGMA Martin St. Louis 6.00 15.00
GGMB Martin Brodeur SP EXCH 75.00 125.00
GGMC Matt Carle 8.00 20.00
GGMF Marc-Andre Fleury 8.00 20.00
GGMG Marian Gaborik 8.00 20.00
GGMI Miroslav Satan 4.00 10.00
GGML Mario Lemieux SP EXCH 150.00 250.00
GGMM Mark Messier SP 300.00 400.00
GGMN Markus Naslund 6.00 15.00
GGMO Mike Modano 6.00 15.00
GGMP Marc-Antoine Pouliot 8.00 20.00
GGMR Michael Ryder 8.00 20.00
GGMS Marek Schwarz 6.00 15.00
GGMT Marty Turco 12.00 30.00
GGNL Nicklas Lidstrom 8.00 20.00
GGNW Noah Welch 8.00 20.00
GGOV A. Ovechkin SP EXCH 100.00 175.00
GGPB Patrice Bergeron 12.00 30.00
GGPE Corey Perry 6.00 15.00
GGPI Pierre-Marc Bouchard 4.00 10.00
GGPK Petr Kalus 8.00 20.00
GGPO Patrick O'Sullivan 6.00 15.00
GGPR Patrick Roy SP EXCH
GGRA Andrew Raycroft 6.00 15.00
GGRI Mike Richards 12.00 30.00
GGRM Ryan Miller 12.00 30.00
GGRN Rick Nash 8.00 20.00
GGRP Ryan Parent 4.00 10.00
GGRS Rob Schremp 10.00 25.00
GGRY Ryan Potulny 4.00 10.00
GGSA Marc Savard 4.00 10.00
GGSB Steve Bernier 8.00 20.00
GGSC Sidney Crosby SP 175.00 250.00
GGSD Shane Doan 4.00 10.00
GGSG Scott Gomez 8.00 20.00
GGSK Saku Koivu SP
GGST Jordan Staal 15.00 40.00
GGSW Shea Weber 8.00 20.00
GGTH Jose Theodore 12.00 30.00
GGTV Tomas Vokoun 12.00 30.00
GGVF Valtteri Filppula 8.00 20.00
GGVL Vincent Lecavalier 12.00 30.00
GGWG Wayne Gretzky SP 400.00 600.00
GGWI Justin Williams 8.00 20.00
GGWW Wojtek Wolski 8.00 20.00

2007-08 Upper Deck Ice Premieres Autographed Patches

STATED PRINT RUN 10 SER.#'d SETS
NOT PRICED DUE TO SCARCITY
185 Kris Russell
186 Matt Niskanen
187 Nicklas Bergfors
188 Brett Sterling
189 Martin Hanzal
190 Matt Smaby
191 Petr Kalus
192 Andy Greene
193 Frans Nielsen
194 Rob Schremp
195 Kyle Chipchura
196 Jonathan Bernier
198 Lauri Tukonen
200 Mason Raymond
201 Ryan Callahan
202 Curtis McElhinney
203 Brian Elliott
204 Drew Miller
207 Torrey Mitchell
208 Jaroslav Halak
209 Jannik Hansen
210 Milan Lucic
211 Bobby Ryan
212 Jonathan Toews
213 Sam Gagner
214 Carey Price
216 Erik Johnson
217 Nicklas Backstrom
218 Jack Johnson
220 Bryan Little
221 Patrick Kane
222 Andrew Cogliano
223 Marc Staal
224 Nick Foligno
225 Peter Mueller
226 James Sheppard

2007-08 Upper Deck Ice Signature Swatches

STATED ODDS 1:320
SSAO Alexander Ovechkin 60.00 120.00
SSBB Brad Boyes 25.00 60.00
SSCW Cam Ward 15.00 40.00
SSDH Dany Heatley 25.00 60.00
SSDS Drew Stafford 25.00 60.00
SSES Eric Staal 15.00 40.00
SSGA Simon Gagne 15.00 40.00
SSIK Ilya Kovalchuk 30.00 80.00
SSJC Jonathan Cheechoo 25.00 60.00
SSJI Jarome Iginla 40.00 100.00
SSJL Joffrey Lupul 20.00 50.00
SSJP Joni Pitkanen 20.00 50.00
SSJT Joe Thornton 20.00 50.00
SSJW Justin Williams 20.00 50.00
SSMB Martin Brodeur 60.00 120.00
SSMC Mike Cammalleri 25.00 60.00
SSMG Marian Gaborik 30.00 80.00
SSML Mario Lemieux 100.00 175.00
SSMM Mike Modano 20.00 50.00
SSMN Markus Naslund 30.00 80.00
SSMS Martin St. Louis 25.00 60.00
SSMT Marty Turco 30.00 80.00
SSNL Nicklas Lidstrom 25.00 60.00
SSPB Patrice Bergeron 25.00 60.00
SSPK Phil Kessel 25.00 60.00
SSPR Patrick Roy 100.00 175.00
SSRM Ryan Miller 25.00 60.00
SSRN Rick Nash 25.00 60.00
SSSC Sidney Crosby 250.00 400.00
SSSG Scott Gomez 20.00 50.00
SSTH Tomas Holmstrom 25.00 60.00
SSTV Tomas Vokoun 30.00 80.00
SSVL Vincent Lecavalier 25.00 60.00
SSWG Wayne Gretzky 300.00 500.00

2008-09 Upper Deck Ice

This set was released on March 10, 2009. The base set consists of 226 cards.

COMP.SET w/o SPs (100) 12.00 30.00
(101-121) PRINT RUN 1999 SERIAL #'d SETS
(122-142) PRINT RUN 999 SERIAL #'d SETS
(143-168) PRINT RUN 499 SERIAL #'d SETS
(169-184) PRINT RUN 99 SERIAL #'d SETS
(185-226) PRINT RUN 10 SERIAL #'d SETS
185-226 NOT PRICED DUE TO SCARCITY
1 Ales Hemsky .30 .75
2 Alex Kovalev .50 1.25
3 Alex Tanguay .40 1.00
4 Alexander Frolov .30 .75
5 Alexander Ovechkin 2.00 5.00
6 Anze Kopitar .50 1.25
7 Brad Boyes .40 1.00
8 Brad Richards .40 1.00
9 Alexander Semin .50 1.25
10 Brenden Morrow .40 1.00
11 Cam Ward .50 1.25
12 Carey Price 1.50 4.00
13 Chris Drury .50 1.25
14 Chris Osgood .50 1.25
15 Chris Pronger .40 1.00
16 Corey Perry .50 1.25
17 Cristobal Huet .30 .75
18 Dan Ellis .30 .75
19 Daniel Alfredsson .40 1.00
20 Daniel Briere .50 1.25
21 Daniel Carcillo .30 .75
22 Daniel Sedin .50 1.25
23 Dany Heatley .60 1.50
24 Derek Roy .30 .75
25 Dion Phaneuf .50 1.25
26 Eric Staal .75 2.00
27 Evgeni Malkin 1.25 3.00
28 Evgeni Nabokov .50 1.25
29 Henrik Lundqvist 1.00 2.50
30 Henrik Zetterberg 1.00 2.50
31 Ilya Kovalchuk .60 1.50
32 J.P. Dumont .30 .75
33 Jarome Iginla 1.00 2.50
34 Jason Arnott .30 .75
35 Jason Pominville .40 1.00
36 Jason Spezza .60 1.50
37 Jean-Sebastien Giguere .50 1.25
38 Joe Sakic .75 2.00
39 Joe Thornton .75 2.00
40 Jonathan Cheechoo .50 1.25
41 Jonathan Toews 1.50 4.00
42 Joni Pitkanen .30 .75
43 Jordan Staal .75 2.00
44 Kari Lehtonen .30 .75
45 Manny Legace .40 1.00
46 Marc Savard .30 .75
47 Marc-Andre Fleury .50 1.25
48 Marek Svatos .30 .75
49 Marian Gaborik .75 2.00
50 Markus Naslund .50 1.25
51 Martin Biron .40 1.00
52 Martin Brodeur 1.00 2.50
53 Martin St. Louis .50 1.25
54 Marty Turco .40 1.00
55 Mikhail Grabovski .75 2.00
56 Miikka Kiprusoff .50 1.25
57 Mike Comrie .30 .75
58 Mike Green .30 .75
59 Mike Modano .50 1.25
60 Mike Ribeiro .30 .75
61 Mike Richards .75 2.00
62 Milan Hejduk .40 1.00
63 Nathan Horton .30 .75
64 Nicklas Backstrom 1.00 2.50
65 Nicklas Lidstrom .50 1.25
66 Nikolai Zherdev .30 .75
67 Olli Jokinen .30 .75
68 Patrice Bergeron .50 1.25
69 Patrick Kane 1.25 3.00
70 Patrick Sharp .30 .75
71 Patrik Elias .30 .75
72 Paul Kariya .50 1.25
73 Paul Martin .30 .75
74 Paul Stastny .50 1.25
75 Pavel Datsyuk .50 1.25
76 Peter Mueller .60 1.50
77 Phil Kessel .60 1.50
78 Pierre-Marc Bouchard .30 .75
79 Rick DiPietro .50 1.25
80 Rick Nash .50 1.25
81 Roberto Luongo .75 2.00
82 Ryan Getzlaf .60 1.50
83 Ryan Miller .50 1.25
84 Saku Koivu .50 1.25
85 Sam Gagner .75 2.00
86 Sean Avery .40 1.00
87 Shane Doan .30 .75
88 Shawn Horcoff .30 .75
89 Sidney Crosby 2.50 6.00
90 Simon Gagne .40 1.00
91 Thomas Vanek .50 1.25
92 Tim Thomas .50 1.25
93 Tobias Enstrom .50 1.25
94 Tomas Kaberle .30 .75
95 Tomas Vokoun .50 1.25
96 Vesa Toskala .50 1.25
97 Vincent Lecavalier .50 1.25
98 Wade Redden .30 .75
99 Zach Parise .50 1.25
100 Zdeno Chara .30 .75
101 Jack Hillen RC 2.00 5.00
102 Mark Fistric RC 2.00 5.00
103 Tom Cavanagh RC 2.00 5.00
104 Dane Byers RC 2.00 5.00
105 Dwight Helminen RC 2.50 6.00
106 Jason Garrison RC 2.50 6.00
107 Pierre-Luc Letourneau-Leblond RC 1.50 4.00
108 Tyler Sloan RC 2.00 5.00
109 Simeon Varlamov RC 12.00 30.00
110 Janne Pesonen RC 2.00 5.00
111 Brad Staubitz RC 2.00 5.00
112 Patrick Davis RC 2.00 5.00
113 Cam Paddock RC 1.50 4.00
114 Karl Alzner RC 4.00 10.00
115 John Curry RC 3.00 8.00
116 Zack Smith RC 2.00 5.00
117 Jonathon Kalinski RC 2.50 6.00
118 Tim Sestito RC 2.00 5.00
119 Joey Crabb RC 2.00 5.00
120 Andre Deveaux RC 2.50 6.00
121 Alexandre Bolduc RC 2.00 5.00
122 Brian Boyle RC 3.00 8.00
123 Mike Brown RC 4.00 10.00
124 Ben Maxwell RC 5.00 12.00
125 Matt D'Agostini RC 5.00 12.00
126 Robbie Earl RC 2.50 6.00
127 Jonathan Ericsson RC 5.00 12.00
128 Erik Ersberg RC 3.00 8.00
129 Justin Pogge RC 6.00 15.00
130 Cory Schneider RC 6.00 15.00
131 Jonas Frogren RC 4.00 10.00
132 Alex Goligoski RC 6.00 15.00
133 Shawn Matthias RC 3.00 8.00
134 John Mitchell RC 3.00 8.00
135 Brian Lee RC 3.00 8.00
136 Adam Pardy RC 3.00 8.00
137 Theo Peckham RC 3.00 8.00
138 Teddy Purcell RC 3.00 8.00
139 Mattias Ritola RC 4.00 10.00
140 Tom Sestito RC 2.50 6.00
141 Ryan Stone RC 3.00 8.00
142 Ilya Zubov RC 3.00 8.00
143 T.J. Oshie RC 10.00 25.00
144 Andreas Nodl RC 3.00 8.00
145 Kyle Okposo RC 8.00 20.00
146 Vladimir Mihalik RC 4.00 10.00
147 Darrel Powe RC 4.00 10.00
148 Alex Pietrangelo RC 6.00 15.00
149 Patrik Berglund RC 10.00 25.00
150 Steve Mason RC 25.00 60.00
151 Wayne Simmonds RC 4.00 10.00
152 Drew Doughty RC 12.00 30.00
153 Kevin Porter RC 3.00 8.00
154 Ryan Jones RC 5.00 12.00
155 Matthew Halischuk RC 5.00 12.00
156 Luca Sbisa RC 6.00 15.00
157 Oscar Moller RC 4.00 10.00
158 Patric Hornqvist RC 4.00 10.00
159 Jamie McGinn RC 4.00 10.00
160 Petr Vrana RC 5.00 12.00
161 Claude Giroux RC 8.00 20.00
162 Derek Dorsett RC 5.00 12.00
163 Lauri Korpikoski RC 4.00 10.00
164 Steve MacIntyre RC 4.00 10.00
165 Nikolai Kulemin RC 4.00 10.00
166 Viktor Tikhonov RC 4.00 10.00
167 Justin Abdelkader RC 8.00 20.00
168 Ben Bishop RC 6.00 15.00
169 Jakub Voracek RC 40.00 100.00
170 Josh Bailey RC 30.00 80.00
171 Mikkel Boedker RC 30.00 80.00
172 James Neal RC 30.00 80.00
173 Derick Brassard RC 75.00 150.00
174 Zach Boychuk RC 30.00 80.00
175 Nikita Filatov RC 60.00 120.00
176 Colton Gillies RC 20.00 50.00
177 Luke Schenn RC 125.00 250.00
178 Blake Wheeler RC 100.00 200.00
179 Brandon Sutter RC 25.00 60.00
180 Kyle Turris RC 75.00 150.00
181 Michael Frolik RC 40.00 100.00
182 Fabian Brunnstrom RC 50.00 100.00
183 Zach Bogosian RC 40.00 100.00
184 Steven Stamkos RC 250.00 400.00
185 T.J. Oshie PATCH AU
186 Robbie Earl PATCH AU
187 Marc-Andre Gragnani PATCH AU
188 Vladimir Mihalik PATCH AU
189 Ryan Stone PATCH AU
190 Tom Sestito PATCH AU
191 Patrik Berglund PATCH AU
192 Steve Mason PATCH AU
193 Mark Fistric PATCH AU
194 Jonathan Ericsson PATCH AU
195 Kevin Porter PATCH AU
196 Shawn Matthias PATCH AU
197 Ilya Zubov PATCH AU
198 Luca Sbisa PATCH AU
199 Oscar Moller PATCH AU
200 Patric Hornqvist PATCH AU
201 Brian Lee PATCH AU
202 Jon Filewich PATCH AU
203 Claude Giroux PATCH AU
204 Erik Ersberg PATCH AU
205 Lauri Korpikoski PATCH AU
206 Brian Boyle PATCH AU
207 Tyler Plante PATCH AU
208 Viktor Tikhonov PATCH AU
209 Justin Abdelkader PATCH AU
210 Alex Goligoski PATCH AU
211 Jakub Voracek PATCH AU
212 Drew Doughty PATCH AU
213 Mikkel Boedker PATCH AU
214 James Neal PATCH AU
215 Derick Brassard PATCH AU
216 Kyle Okposo PATCH AU
217 Alex Pietrangelo PATCH AU
218 Colton Gillies PATCH AU
219 Luke Schenn PATCH AU
220 Blake Wheeler PATCH AU
221 Brandon Sutter PATCH AU
222 Kyle Turris PATCH AU
223 Michael Frolik PATCH AU
224 Nikolai Kulemin PATCH AU
225 Zach Bogosian PATCH AU
226 Steven Stamkos PATCH AU

2008-09 Upper Deck Ice Fresh Threads

FTAG Alex Goligoski 6.00 15.00
FTAN Andreas Nodl 3.00 8.00
FTAP Alex Pietrangelo 5.00 12.00
FTBB Brian Boyle 3.00 8.00
FTBL Brian Lee 3.00 8.00
FTBO Zach Bogosian 6.00 15.00
FTBS Brandon Sutter 4.00 10.00
FTBW Blake Wheeler 8.00 20.00
FTCG Colton Gillies 3.00 8.00
FTDB Derick Brassard 6.00 15.00
FTDD Drew Doughty 10.00 25.00
FTFB Fabian Brunnstrom 5.00 12.00
FTFI Mark Fistric 2.50 6.00
FTGI Claude Giroux 6.00 15.00
FTIZ Ilya Zubov 3.00 8.00
FTJA Justin Abdelkader 6.00 15.00
FTJE Jonathan Ericsson 5.00 12.00
FTJF Jon Filewich 2.50 6.00
FTJN James Neal 5.00 12.00
FTJV Jakub Voracek 6.00 15.00
FTKO Kyle Okposo 6.00 15.00
FTKP Kevin Porter 2.50 6.00
FTKT Kyle Turris 6.00 15.00
FTLK Lauri Korpikoski 3.00 8.00
FTLS Luke Schenn 10.00 25.00
FTMA Steve Mason 8.00 20.00
FTMB Mikkel Boedker 5.00 12.00
FTMF Michael Frolik 6.00 15.00
FTMH Matthew Halischuk 4.00 10.00
FTNF Nikita Filatov 12.00 30.00
FTNK Nikolai Kulemin 3.00 8.00
FTOM Oscar Moller 3.00 8.00
FTPB Patrik Berglund 8.00 20.00
FTPH Patric Hornqvist 3.00 8.00
FTPV Petr Vrana 4.00 10.00
FTSB Luca Sbisa 5.00 12.00
FTSM Shawn Matthias 3.00 8.00
FTSS Steven Stamkos 25.00 60.00
FTTO T.J. Oshie 8.00 20.00
FTVM Vladimir Mihalik 3.00 8.00
FTVT Viktor Tikhonov 3.00 8.00
FTZB Zach Boychuk 5.00 12.00

2008-09 Upper Deck Ice Fresh Threads Black Parallel

*BLACK: .6X TO 1.5X BASE
STATED PRINT RUN 25 SERIAL #'d SETS

2008-09 Upper Deck Ice Fresh Threads Parallel

*PARALLEL: .5X TO 1.2X BASE
STATED PRINT RUN 100 SERIAL #'d SETS

2008-09 Upper Deck Ice Fresh Threads Patches

*PATCHES: .8X TO 2X BASE
STATED PRINT RUN 25 SERIAL #'d SETS

2008-09 Upper Deck Ice Fresh Threads Patches Black Parallel

STATED PRINT RUN 10 SERIAL #'d SETS
NOT PRICED DUE TO SCARCITY

2008-09 Upper Deck Ice Frozen Fabrics

FFAK Alex Kovalev 5.00 12.00
FFBD Brendan Shanahan 5.00 12.00
FFDG Doug Gilmour 6.00 15.00
FFDP Dion Phaneuf 5.00 12.00
FFEM Evgeni Malkin 12.00 30.00
FFES Eric Staal 8.00 20.00
FFFV Sergei Fedorov 8.00 20.00
FFGZ Scott Gomez 4.00 10.00
FFHW Dale Hawerchuk 5.00 12.00
FFIK Ilya Kovalchuk 6.00 15.00
FFJC Jonathan Cheechoo 5.00 12.00
FFJJ Joe Sakic 8.00 20.00
FFKL Kari Lehtonen 3.00 8.00
FFLR Larry Robinson 5.00 12.00
FFLW Rod Langway 6.00 15.00
FFMB Martin Brodeur 10.00 25.00
FFMH Marian Hossa 8.00 20.00
FFMK Mikko Koivu 5.00 12.00
FFMS Mats Sundin 5.00 12.00
FFNL Nicklas Lidstrom 5.00 12.00
FFOK Olaf Kolzig 5.00 12.00
FFOV Alexander Ovechkin 20.00 50.00
FFPE Patrik Elias 3.00 8.00
FFPF Peter Forsberg 8.00 20.00
FFPK Paul Kariya 5.00 12.00
FFPL Pascal Leclaire 4.00 10.00
FFPS Patrice Stastny 5.00 12.00
FFRD Rod Brind'Amour 4.00 10.00
FFRN Rick Nash 5.00 12.00
FFSC Sidney Crosby 25.00 60.00
FFSD Shane Doan 3.00 8.00
FFSG Simon Gagne 4.00 10.00
FFSS Steve Shutt 5.00 12.00
FFST Jordan Staal 8.00 20.00
FFTB Todd Bertuzzi 5.00 12.00
FFTR Tuomo Ruutu 5.00 12.00
FFTS Teemu Selanne 5.00 12.00
FFVT Vesa Toskala 5.00 12.00
FFWB Shea Weber 3.00 8.00
FFWR Wade Redden 3.00 8.00
FFWW Wojtek Wolski 3.00 8.00
FFZP Zach Parise 5.00 12.00

2008-09 Upper Deck Ice Frozen Fabrics Black Parallel

*BLACK: .6X TO 1.5X BASE
STATED PRINT RUN 25 SERIAL #'d SETS

2008-09 Upper Deck Ice Frozen Fabrics Parallel

*PARALLEL: .5X TO 1.2X BASE
STATED PRINT RUN 100 SERIAL #'d SETS

2008-09 Upper Deck Ice Frozen Fabrics Patches

*PATCHES: 1X TO 2.5X BASE
STATED PRINT RUN 25 SERIAL #'d SETS

2008-09 Upper Deck Ice Frozen Fabrics Patches Black Parallel

STATED PRINT RUN 10 SERIAL #'d SETS
NOT PRICED DUE TO SCARCITY

2008-09 Upper Deck Ice Frozen Foursomes

STATED PRINT RUN 5 SERIAL #'d SETS
NOT PRICED DUE TO SCARCITY

2008-09 Upper Deck Ice Glacial Graphs

GGAE Alexander Edler 6.00 15.00
GGAP Alex Pietrangelo 12.00 30.00
GGAR Andrew Raycroft 8.00 20.00
GGCA Jeff Carter 8.00 20.00
GGCD Daniel Carcillo
GGCM Cory Murphy 5.00 12.00
GGDA Daniel Paille 6.00 15.00
GGDC Dan Cleary 8.00 20.00
GGDD Drew Doughty 20.00 50.00
GGDH Eddie Shack 8.00 20.00
GGDJ David Jones 5.00 12.00
GGDS Devin Setoguchi 8.00 20.00
GGEM Evgeni Malkin 20.00 50.00
GGES Eric Staal 12.00 30.00
GGHS Henrik Sedin 8.00 20.00
GGJH Jonas Hiller 8.00 20.00
GGJL Joffrey Lupul 5.00 12.00
GGJP Jason Pominville 6.00 15.00
GGJS Jordan Staal 12.00 30.00
GGJT Joe Thornton 12.00 30.00
GGJV Jakub Voracek 15.00 40.00
GGLS Luke Schenn 25.00 60.00
GGMB Mikkel Boedker 15.00 40.00
GGMC Marty McSorley 5.00 12.00
GGMF Marc-Andre Fleury
GGMH Milan Hejduk 6.00 15.00
GGMN Matt Niskanen 5.00 12.00
GGMT Maxime Talbot 6.00 15.00
GGND Nigel Dawes 5.00 12.00
GGNZ Nikolai Zherdev 5.00 12.00
GGOR Bobby Orr
GGPA Patrick Kane 20.00 50.00
GGPM Peter Mueller 10.00 25.00
GGPN Dustin Penner 5.00 12.00
GGPR Carey Price 25.00 60.00
GGRG Ryan Getzlaf 10.00 25.00
GGRL Rod Langway 10.00 25.00
GGRO Rob Schremp 6.00 15.00
GGRP Rod Pelley 5.00 12.00
GGSB Steve Bernier 5.00 12.00
GGSC Sidney Crosby 100.00 175.00
GGSE Daniel Sedin 8.00 20.00
GGSS Steven Stamkos 40.00 100.00
GGTH Tomas Holmstrom 6.00 15.00
GGTK Tyler Kennedy 6.00 15.00
GGTL Jiri Tlusty 8.00 20.00
GGTV Tomas Vokoun 8.00 20.00
GGTW Jonathan Toews 25.00 60.00
GGWG Wayne Gretzky
GGZB Zach Bogosian 15.00 40.00
GGZB2 Henrik Zetterberg 15.00 40.00

2008-09 Upper Deck Ice Pride of Canada

GOLD1 Bobby Clarke 8.00 20.00
GOLD2 Bobby Hull 15.00 40.00
GOLD3 Bobby Orr 25.00 60.00
GOLD4 Bryan Trottier 6.00 15.00
GOLD5 Darryl Sittler 8.00 20.00
GOLD6 Denis Potvin 6.00 15.00
GOLD7 Gilbert Perreault 8.00 20.00
GOLD8 Guy Lafleur 15.00 40.00
GOLD9 Jarome Iginla 15.00 40.00
GOLD10 Joe Sakic 12.00 30.00
GOLD11 Jonathan Toews 25.00 60.00
GOLD12 Marcel Dionne 8.00 20.00
GOLD13 Mario Lemieux 20.00 50.00
GOLD14 Martin Brodeur 15.00 40.00
GOLD15 Mike Bossy 8.00 20.00
GOLD16 Dany Heatley 10.00 25.00
GOLD17 Paul Coffey 10.00 25.00
GOLD18 Phil Esposito 12.00 30.00
GOLD19 Sidney Crosby 75.00 150.00
GOLD20 Steve Yzerman 25.00 60.00
GOLD21 Wayne Gretzky 100.00 175.00

2009-10 Upper Deck Ice

COMP.SET w/o SPS (100) 15.00 40.00
(101-121) PRINT RUN 1999 SER.#'d SETS
(122-142) PRINT RUN 999 SER.#'d SETS
(143-168) PRINT RUN 499 SER.#'d SETS
(169-184) PRINT RUN 99 SER.#'d SETS
1 Zdeno Chara .30 .75
2 Patrice Bergeron .50 1.25
3 Tim Thomas .50 1.25
4 Marc Savard .30 .75
5 Alexander Ovechkin 2.00 5.00
6 Alexander Semin .50 1.25
7 Mike Green 1.00 2.50
8 Nicklas Backstrom 1.00 2.50
9 Martin Brodeur 1.25 3.00
10 Zach Parise .50 1.25
11 Patrik Elias .40 1.00
12 Sidney Crosby 2.50 6.00
13 Evgeni Malkin 1.25 3.00
14 Jordan Staal .60 1.50
15 Marc-Andre Fleury .50 1.25
16 Simon Gagne .50 1.25
17 Mike Richards 1.00 2.50
18 Jeff Carter .60 1.50
19 Daniel Briere .50 1.25
20 Eric Staal .60 1.50
21 Cam Ward .50 1.25
22 Jussi Jokinen .50 1.25
23 Henrik Lundqvist 1.00 2.50
24 Marian Gaborik .75 2.00
25 Chris Drury .40 1.00
26 Sean Avery .40 1.00
27 Carey Price 1.25 3.00
28 Scott Gomez .50 1.25
29 Andrei Markov .40 1.00
30 Nathan Horton .30 .75
31 Tomas Vokoun .50 1.25
32 David Booth .30 .75
33 Thomas Vanek .50 1.25
34 Ryan Miller .50 1.25
35 Jason Pominville .50 1.25
36 Derek Roy .50 1.25
37 Jason Spezza .60 1.50
38 Jonathan Cheechoo .50 1.25
39 Daniel Alfredsson .50 1.25
40 Luke Schenn .75 2.00
41 Mikhail Grabovski .40 1.00
42 Vesa Toskala .50 1.25
43 Phil Kessel .50 1.25
44 Ilya Kovalchuk .60 1.50
45 Kari Lehtonen .50 1.25
46 Bryan Little .50 1.25
47 Vincent Lecavalier .60 1.50
48 Martin St. Louis .50 1.25
49 Steven Stamkos 1.25 3.00
50 Doug Weight .30 .75
51 Rick DiPietro .50 1.25
52 Kyle Okposo .50 1.25
53 Joe Thornton 1.00 2.50
54 Patrick Marleau .50 1.25
55 Evgeni Nabokov .50 1.25
56 Dany Heatley 1.00 2.50
57 Henrik Zetterberg 1.00 2.50
58 Nicklas Lidstrom .60 1.50
59 Pavel Datsyuk .60 1.50
60 Chris Osgood .60 1.50
61 Roberto Luongo 1.25 3.00
62 Ryan Kesler .40 1.00
63 Daniel Sedin .60 1.50
64 Henrik Sedin .75 2.00
65 Patrick Kane 1.00 2.50
66 Jonathan Toews 1.25 3.00
67 Brian Campbell .40 1.00
68 Marian Hossa .75 2.00
69 Jarome Iginla 1.00 2.50
70 Dion Phaneuf .75 2.00
71 Olli Jokinen .30 .75
72 Miikka Kiprusoff .50 1.25
73 David Perron .40 1.00
74 Paul Kariya .50 1.25
75 Patrik Berglund 1.00 2.50
76 Rick Nash .50 1.25
77 Steve Mason .75 2.00
78 Derick Brassard .50 1.25
79 Ryan Getzlaf .75 2.00
80 Bobby Ryan .60 1.50
81 Saku Koivu .50 1.25
82 Mikko Koivu .50 1.25
83 Niklas Backstrom .50 1.25
84 Owen Nolan .50 1.25
85 Jason Arnott .30 .75
86 Pekka Rinne .40 1.00
87 Shea Weber .40 1.00
88 Sam Gagner .60 1.50
89 Andrew Cogliano .60 1.50
90 Nikolai Khabibulin .50 1.25
91 James Neal .50 1.25
92 Mike Ribeiro .30 .75
93 Marty Turco .40 1.00
94 Shane Doan .40 1.00
95 Peter Mueller .60 1.50
96 Drew Doughty 1.00 2.50
97 Anze Kopitar .50 1.25
98 Paul Stastny .50 1.25
99 Wojtek Wolski .30 .75
100 Milan Hejduk .50 1.25
101 Scott Parse RC 2.50 6.00
102 Phil Oreskovic RC 2.50 6.00
103 Andreas Thuresson RC 2.00 5.00
104 Philippe Dupuis RC 2.50 6.00
105 Jaime Sifers RC 2.00 5.00
106 Matt Hendricks RC 2.00 5.00
107 Teemu Laakso RC 1.50 4.00
108 Ilkka Pikkarainen RC 2.50 6.00
109 Grant Lewis RC 2.00 5.00
110 Peter Olvecky RC 2.50 6.00
111 Byron Bitz RC 2.00 5.00
112 John Scott RC 2.50 6.00
113 Francis Wathier RC 2.00 5.00
114 James Reimer RC 2.50 6.00
115 Peter Regin RC 3.00 8.00
116 Matt Climie RC 2.00 5.00
117 Taylor Chorney RC 2.00 5.00
118 Davis Drewiske RC 2.50 6.00
119 Mika Pyorala RC 2.50 6.00
120 Victor Oreskovich RC 2.00 5.00
121 Tom Wandell RC 8.00 20.00
122 Michal Neuvirth RC 8.00 20.00
123 Mathieu Carle RC 4.00 10.00
124 Lars Eller RC 5.00 12.00
125 Alexander Salak RC 3.00 8.00
126 John Negrin RC 2.50 6.00
127 Aaron Gagnon RC 2.50 6.00
128 Mario Bliznak RC 3.00 8.00
129 Anton Khudobin RC 3.00 8.00
130 Jakub Kindl RC 4.00 10.00
131 Matthew Corrente RC 3.00 8.00
132 Steven Zalewski RC 2.50 6.00
133 David Laliberte RC 3.00 8.00
134 Bobby Sanguinetti RC 2.50 6.00
135 Devan Dubnyk RC 4.00 10.00
136 Matt Pelech RC 3.00 8.00
137 Alexander Sulzer RC 2.00 5.00
138 Frazer McLaren RC 2.00 5.00
139 Michael Sauer RC 2.50 6.00
140 Ryan Wilson RC 3.00 8.00
141 Danny Irmen RC 2.50 6.00
142 Braden Holtby RC 4.00 10.00
143 Brian Salcido RC 3.00 8.00
144 Luca Caputi RC 5.00 12.00
145 Spencer Machacek RC 3.00 8.00
146 T.J. Galiardi RC 5.00 12.00
147 Yannick Weber RC 5.00 12.00
148 Christian Hanson RC 5.00 12.00
149 Jhonas Enroth RC 5.00 12.00
150 Ivan Vishnevskiy RC 5.00 12.00
151 Riku Helenius RC 4.00 10.00
152 Kris Chucko RC 3.00 8.00
153 Perttu Lindgren RC 4.00 10.00
154 Ryan O'Reilly RC 8.00 20.00
155 Dmitry Kulikov RC 4.00 10.00
156 Matt Gilroy RC 5.00 12.00
157 Sergei Shirokov RC 6.00 15.00
158 Benn Ferriero RC 4.00 10.00
159 Alec Martinez RC 2.50 6.00
160 Erik Karlsson RC 12.00 30.00
161 Cal O'Reilly RC 4.00 10.00
162 Matt Beleskey RC 4.00 10.00
163 Ville Leino RC 5.00 12.00
164 Artem Anisimov RC 5.00 12.00
165 Antti Niemi RC 25.00 60.00
166 Jason Demers RC 3.00 8.00
167 Cody Franson RC 4.00 10.00
168 Ray Macias RC 4.00 10.00
169 Tyler Myers RC 125.00 200.00
170 Jamie Benn RC 30.00 80.00
171 Michael Del Zotto RC 40.00 100.00
172 Brad Marchand RC 25.00 60.00
173 Mikael Backlund RC 40.00 100.00
174 Tyler Bozak RC 50.00 120.00
175 Logan Couture RC 40.00 100.00
176 Michael Grabner RC 40.00 100.00
177 Viktor Stalberg RC 40.00 100.00
178 Jonas Gustavsson RC 60.00 120.00
179 Colin Wilson RC 40.00 100.00
180 James van Riemsdyk RC 125.00 200.00
181 Evander Kane RC 60.00 120.00
182 Victor Hedman RC 40.00 100.00
183 Matt Duchene RC 200.00 300.00
184 John Tavares RC 350.00 500.00

2009-10 Upper Deck Ice Rookie Patch Autographs

STATED PRINT RUN 10 SER.#'d SETS
NOT PRICED DUE TO SCARCITY

2009-10 Upper Deck Ice Fresh Threads

OVERALL AU/MEM ODDS 1:7
FTAA Artem Anisimov 6.00 15.00
FTAC Andrew Cogliano 6.00 15.00
FTAN Antti Niemi 15.00 40.00
FTBA Mikael Backlund 8.00 20.00
FTBF Benn Ferriero 5.00 12.00
FTBW Blake Wheeler 6.00 15.00
FTCB Chris Butler 5.00 12.00
FTCF Cody Franson 5.00 12.00
FTCG Claude Giroux 10.00 25.00
FTCW Colin Wilson 10.00 25.00
FTDD Drew Doughty 10.00 25.00
FTDK Dmitry Kulikov 5.00 12.00
FTDS Drew Stafford 5.00 12.00
FTDU Matt Duchene 12.00 30.00
FTEK Erik Karlsson 15.00 40.00
FTIV Ivan Vishnevskiy 6.00 15.00
FTJB Jamie Benn 8.00 20.00
FTJE Jhonas Enroth 6.00 15.00
FTJG Jonas Gustavsson 8.00 20.00
FTJT John Tavares 15.00 40.00
FTJV Jakub Voracek 5.00 12.00
FTKA Evander Kane 8.00 20.00

FTKC Kris Chucko 4.00 10.00
FTLC Luca Caputi 6.00 15.00
FTMD Michael Del Zotto 10.00 25.00
FTMG Michael Grabner 6.00 15.00
FTPL Perttu Lindgren 5.00 12.00
FTPO Patrick O'Sullivan 4.00 10.00
FTRH Riku Helenius 5.00 12.00
FTRO Ryan O'Reilly 10.00 25.00
FTSM Spencer Machacek 4.00 10.00
FTSS Sergei Shirokov 8.00 20.00
FTTB Tyler Bozak 8.00 20.00
FTTG T.J. Galiardi 6.00 15.00
FTTM Tyler Myers 12.00 30.00
FTVA James van Riemsdyk 12.00 30.00
FTVH Victor Hedman 8.00 20.00
FTVL Ville Leino 6.00 15.00
FTVS Viktor Stalberg 8.00 20.00
FTYW Yannick Weber 6.00 15.00

2009-10 Upper Deck Ice Fresh Threads Autographs

STATED PRINT RUN 35 SER.#'d SETS
FTAC Andrew Cogliano 12.00 30.00
FTAN Antti Niemi 30.00 80.00
FTBA Mikael Backlund 15.00 40.00
FTBF Benn Ferriero 10.00 25.00
FTBW Blake Wheeler 12.00 30.00
FTCF Cody Franson 10.00 25.00
FTCG Claude Giroux 20.00 50.00
FTCW Colin Wilson
FTDB Derick Brassard 10.00 25.00
FTDD Drew Doughty 20.00 50.00
FTDS Drew Stafford 10.00 25.00
FTDU Matt Duchene 75.00 150.00
FTEK Erik Karlsson 30.00 80.00
FTIV Ivan Vishnevskiy 12.00 30.00
FTJB Jamie Benn 20.00 50.00
FTJE Jhonas Enroth 12.00 30.00
FTJG Jonas Gustavsson 25.00 50.00
FTJT John Tavares 50.00 120.00
FTJV Jakub Voracek 10.00 25.00
FTKA Evander Kane
FTKC Kris Chucko 8.00 20.00
FTLC Luca Caputi 12.00 30.00
FTMD Michael Del Zotto
FTMG Michael Grabner
FTMR Mason Raymond 6.00 15.00
FTPK Patrick Kane 30.00 60.00
FTPL Perttu Lindgren
FTPO Patrick O'Sullivan 8.00 20.00
FTRH Riku Helenius 10.00 25.00
FTRO Ryan O'Reilly 20.00 50.00
FTSM Spencer Machacek 8.00 20.00
FTSS Sergei Shirokov 15.00 40.00
FTTB Tyler Bozak
FTTC Taylor Chorney
FTTG T.J. Galiardi 12.00 30.00
FTTM Tyler Myers 50.00 100.00
FTTO Jonathan Toews
FTVA James van Riemsdyk 25.00 60.00
FTVH Victor Hedman 20.00 50.00
FTVL Ville Leino 12.00 30.00
FTVS Viktor Stalberg
FTYW Yannick Weber 12.00 30.00

2009-10 Upper Deck Ice Fresh Threads Patches

STATED PRINT RUN 15 SER.#'d SETS
NOT PRICED DUE TO SCARCITY

2009-10 Upper Deck Ice Fresh Threads Patches Autographs

STATED PRINT RUN 5 SER.#'d SETS
NOT PRICED DUE TO SCARCITY

2009-10 Upper Deck Ice Frozen Fabrics

OVERALL STATED AU/MEM ODDS 1:7
FRAF Alexander Frolov 4.00 10.00
FRAK Anze Kopitar 5.00 12.00
FRBB Bob Bourne 4.00 10.00
FRBC Brian Campbell 4.00 10.00
FRBS Borje Salming 5.00 12.00
FRCH Cristobal Huet 5.00 12.00
FRCN Cam Neely 8.00 20.00
FRCP Carey Price 12.00 30.00
FRCW Cam Ward 5.00 12.00
FRDB Dustin Brown 4.00 10.00
FRDG Doug Gilmour 5.00 12.00
FRDH Dale Hawerchuk 5.00 12.00
FRDP Dion Phaneuf 8.00 20.00
FRDR Derek Roy 5.00 12.00
FRGA Glenn Anderson 5.00 12.00
FRHZ Henrik Zetterberg 10.00 25.00
FRIK Ilya Kovalchuk 6.00 15.00
FRJB Jay Bouwmeester 5.00 12.00
FRJC Jeff Carter 5.00 12.00
FRJI Jarome Iginla 10.00 25.00
FRJL Jordan Leopold 3.00 8.00
FRJP Jason Pominville 5.00 12.00
FRJT Joe Thornton 10.00 25.00
FRKT Kimmo Timonen 4.00 10.00
FRLM Lanny McDonald 5.00 12.00
FRMB Martin Brodeur 12.00 30.00
FRMR Mike Richards 10.00 25.00
FRNH Nathan Horton 3.00 8.00
FRPD Pavel Datsyuk 5.00 12.00
FRRD Rick DiPietro 5.00 12.00
FRRG Ryan Getzlaf 8.00 20.00
FRRM Ryan Miller 5.00 12.00
FRRN Rick Nash 5.00 12.00
FRSC Sidney Crosby 25.00 60.00
FRSK Saku Koivu 5.00 12.00
FRSP Jason Spezza 6.00 15.00
FRSS Steve Shutt 5.00 12.00
FRST Peter Stastny 5.00 12.00
FRSY Steve Yzerman 15.00 40.00
FRTV Thomas Vanek 5.00 12.00
FRVL Vincent Lecavalier 6.00 15.00
FRVO Tomas Vokoun 5.00 12.00

2009-10 Upper Deck Ice Frozen Fabrics Autographs

STATED PRINT RUN 35 SER.#'d SETS
FRAK Anze Kopitar 12.00 30.00
FRBB Bob Bourne
FRBS Borje Salming 25.00 60.00
FRCN Cam Neely 20.00 50.00
FRCP Carey Price 30.00 80.00
FRCW Cam Ward 12.00 30.00
FRDG Doug Gilmour 12.00 30.00
FRDH Dale Hawerchuk 12.00 30.00
FRDP Dion Phaneuf 20.00 50.00
FREM Evgeni Malkin 30.00 80.00
FRHZ Henrik Zetterberg 25.00 60.00
FRIK Ilya Kovalchuk 15.00 40.00
FRJC Jeff Carter 12.00 30.00
FRJI Jarome Iginla 25.00 60.00
FRJP Jason Pominville 12.00 30.00
FRJT Joe Thornton 25.00 60.00
FRLM Lanny McDonald 12.00 30.00
FRMB Martin Brodeur 30.00 80.00
FRNH Nathan Horton 8.00 20.00
FRPB Patrice Bergeron 12.00 30.00
FRPD Pavel Datsyuk 12.00 30.00
FRRM Ryan Miller 12.00 30.00
FRRN Rick Nash 12.00 30.00
FRSC Sidney Crosby 125.00 200.00
FRSD Shane Doan 10.00 25.00
FRSS Steve Shutt 12.00 30.00
FRST Peter Stastny 12.00 30.00
FRSY Steve Yzerman 40.00 100.00
FRTV Thomas Vanek
FRVL Vincent Lecavalier 15.00 40.00
FRVO Tomas Vokoun 12.00 30.00

2009-10 Upper Deck Ice Frozen Fabrics Patches

STATED PRINT RUN 15 SER.#'d SETS
NOT PRICED DUE TO SCARCITY

2009-10 Upper Deck Ice Frozen Fabrics Patches Autographs

STATED PRINT RUN 5 SER.#'d SETS
NOT PRICED DUE TO SCARCITY

2009-10 Upper Deck Ice Frozen Foursomes

STATED PRINT RUN 4 SER.#'d SETS
NOT PRICED DUE TO SCARCITY

2009-10 Upper Deck Ice Glacial Graphs

OVERALL AU/MEM ODDS 1:7
GGAC Andrew Cogliano 8.00 20.00
GGAD Alex Delvecchio
GGAE Andrew Ebbett 5.00 12.00
GGBA Josh Bailey 5.00 12.00
GGBE Jamie Benn 10.00 25.00
GGBL Brian Lee 6.00 15.00
GGBO Bobby Orr 100.00 175.00
GGBR Bobby Ryan 8.00 20.00
GGBS Brian Sutter 6.00 15.00
GGBW Blake Wheeler
GGCB Cam Barker
GGCG Colton Gillies 8.00 20.00
GGCH Chris Stewart 6.00 15.00
GGCS Cory Schneider 10.00 25.00
GGDD Dick Duff
GGDO Drew Doughty
GGDS Darryl Sutter 5.00 12.00
GGDU Matt Duchene 25.00 60.00
GGDZ Michael Del Zotto 12.00 30.00
GGEK Evander Kane 15.00 40.00
GGER Erik Karlsson 20.00 50.00
GGFB Fabian Brunnstrom 6.00 15.00
GGGC Guy Carbonneau 10.00 25.00
GGGH Gordie Howe 75.00 150.00
GGGI Claude Giroux 12.00 30.00
GGJA Justin Abdelkader 6.00 15.00
GGJC Jeff Carter
GGJE Jonathan Ericsson 6.00 15.00
GGJG Jonas Gustavsson 25.00 60.00
GGJJ Jack Johnson 5.00 12.00
GGJN James Neal
GGJS Jordan Staal 8.00 20.00
GGJV Jakub Voracek 6.00 15.00
GGKA Karl Alzner 6.00 15.00
GGKM Kenndal McArdle 5.00 12.00
GGKR Niklas Kronwall 5.00 12.00
GGLM Lanny McDonald
GGLS Luke Schenn 10.00 25.00
GGMB Mike Bossy
GGMF Mike Foligno 4.00 10.00
GGMG Mike Green
GGMK Mikael Backlund
GGML Mario Lemieux
GGMP Max Pacioretty 6.00 15.00
GGMR Mike Ribeiro 4.00 10.00
GGMT Maxime Talbot 6.00 15.00
GGMY Tyler Myers 25.00 60.00
GGNB Nicklas Backstrom 12.00 30.00
GGNF Nikita Filatov
GGNG Nathan Gerbe 8.00 20.00
GGNK Nikolai Kulemin 5.00 12.00
GGPB Patrice Bergeron
GGPD Pavel Datsyuk
GGPE Phil Esposito 25.00 60.00
GGPR Patrick Roy 75.00 150.00
GGPS Peter Stastny 6.00 15.00
GGRI Mike Richards
GGRM Rick MacLeish
GGRN Rick Nash
GGRS Ron Sutter 8.00 20.00
GGRV Rogie Vachon
GGSB Scotty Bowman 15.00 40.00
GGSC Sidney Crosby 75.00 150.00
GGSK Steven Stamkos 15.00 40.00
GGSM Steve Mason 10.00 25.00
GGSS Steve Shutt 6.00 15.00
GGST Paul Stastny 6.00 15.00
GGSU Brandon Sutter 6.00 15.00
GGSY Steve Yzerman
GGTA John Tavares 75.00 150.00
GGTF Theoren Fleury
GGTH Tomas Holmstrom
GGTJ T.J. Galiardi 8.00 20.00
GGTK Tim Kennedy 6.00 15.00
GGTL Ted Lindsay 12.00 30.00
GGTO T.J. Oshie
GGTV Thomas Vanek 6.00 15.00
GGVH Victor Hedman 12.00 30.00
GGVL Ville Leino 8.00 20.00
GGVR James van Riemsdyk 15.00 40.00
GGVT Viktor Tikhonov
GGWG Wayne Gretzky
GGZA Zach Boychuk 8.00 20.00

2009-10 Upper Deck Ice Rinkside Signings

OVERALL AU/MEM ODDS 1:7
RSAK Anze Kopitar 25.00 50.00
RSHL Henrik Lundqvist 40.00 80.00
RSHZ Henrik Zetterberg
RSMG Marian Gaborik 25.00 50.00
RSMM Mike Modano 25.00 50.00
RSNB Nicklas Backstrom 30.00 60.00
RSNL Nicklas Lidstrom 25.00 50.00
RSPK Patrick Kane 50.00 100.00
RSRM Ryan Miller 30.00 60.00

2009-10 Upper Deck Ice Rinkside Signings Canadian

OVERALL AU/MEM ODDS 1:7
RSBO Bobby Orr 200.00 300.00
RSBR Bobby Ryan 15.00 40.00
RSCP Carey Price
RSCW Cam Ward 12.00 30.00
RSDD Drew Doughty EXCH 40.00 80.00
RSDH Dany Heatley 20.00 50.00
RSGH Gordie Howe
RSJB Jean Beliveau
RSJC Jeff Carter EXCH 15.00 40.00
RSJI Jarome Iginla 20.00 50.00
RSJS Jordan Staal 15.00 40.00
RSJT Jonathan Toews 50.00 100.00
RSLS Luke Schenn 20.00 50.00
RSMB Martin Brodeur
RSME Mark Messier
RSML Mario Lemieux 75.00 150.00
RSMS Martin St. Louis
RSPS Paul Stastny 25.00 50.00
RSRB Ray Bourque
RSRN Rick Nash EXCH 25.00 50.00
RSSC Sidney Crosby EXCH 200.00 300.00
RSSD Shane Doan
RSSG Simon Gagne
RSSM Steve Mason 15.00 40.00
RSSS Steven Stamkos 40.00 80.00
RSSY Steve Yzerman 200.00 300.00
RSTE Tony Esposito 30.00 80.00
RSTH Joe Thornton 25.00 50.00
RSVL Vincent Lecavalier EXCH 25.00 50.00
RSWG Wayne Gretzky 175.00 350.00

2009-10 Upper Deck Ice Signature Swatches

OVERALL AU/MEM ODDS 1:7
SSBL Brian Leetch 12.00 30.00
SSCN Cam Neely 20.00 50.00
SSCP Carey Price 30.00 80.00
SSDD Drew Doughty EXCH 25.00 60.00
SSDP Dion Phaneuf EXCH 20.00 50.00
SSEM Evgeni Malkin 30.00 80.00
SSGF Grant Fuhr 15.00 40.00
SSHZ Henrik Zetterberg EXCH 25.00 60.00
SSIK Ilya Kovalchuk EXCH 15.00 40.00
SSJC Jeff Carter EXCH 12.00 30.00
SSJI Jarome Iginla 25.00 60.00
SSJK Jari Kurri
SSJT Joe Thornton 25.00 60.00
SSKE Phil Kessel EXCH 12.00 30.00
SSLS Luke Schenn EXCH 20.00 50.00
SSMB Martin Brodeur EXCH 50.00 100.00
SSMF Marc-Andre Fleury 12.00 30.00
SSML Mario Lemieux 60.00 120.00
SSMR Mike Richards EXCH 25.00 60.00
SSMT Marty Turco 10.00 25.00
SSNB Nicklas Backstrom 25.00 60.00
SSPD Pavel Datsyuk 25.00 50.00
SSPK Patrick Kane EXCH 50.00 100.00
SSPR Patrick Roy
SSRM Ryan Miller 25.00 50.00
SSRN Rick Nash 12.00 30.00
SSSC Sidney Crosby 200.00 350.00
SSSS Steven Stamkos EXCH 30.00 80.00
SSSY Steve Yzerman EXCH 75.00 150.00
SSTO Jonathan Toews 50.00 100.00
SSTV Thomas Vanek 12.00 30.00
SSVL Vincent Lecavalier EXCH 15.00 40.00
SSWG Wayne Gretzky EXCH 200.00 350.00

2000-01 Upper Deck Jason Spezza Giveaways

These cards were given away at the Upper Deck booth at the 2000 and 2001 Toronto Expos. The version numbered to 300 was given away at the Fall Expo while the version numbered to 600 was given away at the Spring Expo. In order to receive a card, one had to open a box of Upper Deck product at the booth. Differently numbered and unnumbered varitions have also surfaced fueling speculation that some cards were distributed differently.

1 Jason Spezza AU/300 25.00 60.00
2 Jason Spezza AU/600 15.00 40.00

2000-01 Upper Deck Legends

Released in mid November 2000, Upper Deck Legends features a 135-card set where base design features both color and black and white photos of the greats of hockey. Base cards are enhanced with blue foil highlights and a white border that fades to each respective player's team color along the bottom. Legends was packaged in 24-pack boxes with each pack containing five cards and carried a suggested retail price of $4.99.

COMPLETE SET (135) 25.00 50.00
1 Paul Kariya .15 .40
2 Teemu Selanne .15 .40
3 Paul Kariya .15 .40
Teemu Selanne
4 Patrik Stefan .02 .10
5 Patrik Stefan .02 .10
Damian Rhodes
6 Bobby Orr .60 1.50
7 Phil Esposito .30 .75
8 Johnny Bucyk .12 .30
9 Cam Neely .15 .40
10 Eddie Shore .15 .40
11 Joe Thornton .25 .60
12 Sergei Samsonov .12 .30
13 Cam Neely .25 .60
Joe Thornton
14 Gilbert Perreault .12 .30
15 Pat LaFontaine .20 .50
16 Dominik Hasek .30 .75
17 Doug Gilmour .12 .30
18 Gilbert Perreault .30 .75
Dominik Hasek
19 Lanny McDonald .12 .30
20 Valeri Bure .02 .10
21 Theoren Fleury .02 .10
Valeri Bure
22 Ron Francis .12 .30
23 Arturs Irbe .12 .30
24 Ron Francis .12 .30
Arturs Irbe
25 Bobby Hull .30 .75
26 Stan Mikita .25 .60
27 Tony Esposito .25 .60
28 Glenn Hall .15 .40
29 Tony Amonte .12 .30
30 Bobby Hull .20 .50
Tony Amonte
31 Patrick Roy .75 2.00
32 Ray Bourque .25 .60
33 Chris Drury .12 .30
34 Peter Forsberg .40 1.00
35 Milan Hejduk .15 .40
36 Patrick Roy .75 2.00
Peter Forsberg
37 Brett Hull .20 .50
38 Ed Belfour .15 .40
39 Mike Modano .25 .60
40 M.Modano/E.Belfour .25 .60
41 Gordie Howe .60 1.50
42 Ted Lindsay .15 .40
43 Terry Sawchuk .30 .75
44 Brendan Shanahan .15 .40
45 Chris Osgood .12 .30
46 Steve Yzerman .75 2.00
47 Gordie Howe .75 2.00
Steve Yzerman
48 Grant Fuhr .15 .40
49 Wayne Gretzky 1.00 2.50
50 Jari Kurri .15 .40
51 Mark Messier .15 .40
52 Paul Coffey .15 .40
53 Doug Weight .12 .30
54 Wayne Gretzky 1.00 2.50
Doug Weight
55 Pavel Bure .15 .40
56 Viktor Kozlov .12 .30
57 John Vanbiesbrouck .25 .60
Pavel Bure
58 Marcel Dionne .20 .50
59 Zigmund Palffy .12 .30
60 Luc Robitaille .12 .30
61 Wayne Gretzky .75 2.00
Luc Robitaille
62 Dino Ciccarelli .12 .30
63 Saku Koivu .15 .40
64 Jean Beliveau .15 .40
65 Doug Harvey .25 .60
66 Jacques Plante .20 .50
67 Guy Lafleur .25 .60
68 Serge Savard .15 .40
69 Larry Robinson .15 .40
70 Eric Weinrich .02 .10
71 Bernie Geoffrion .15 .40
72 Jose Theodore .20 .50
73 Guy Lafleur .75 2.00
Patrick Roy
74 David Legwand .12 .30
75 David Legwand .12 .30
Mike Dunham
76 Martin Brodeur .40 1.00
77 Scott Gomez .02 .10
78 Scott Stevens .12 .30
79 Scott Stevens .40 1.00
Martin Brodeur
80 Denis Potvin .15 .40
81 Mike Bossy .20 .50
82 Bryan Trottier .12 .30
83 Butch Goring .12 .30
84 Bob Nystrom .12 .30
85 Chico Resch .12 .30
86 Clark Gillies .12 .30
87 Tim Connolly .02 .10
88 Bryan Trottier .02 .10
Tim Connolly
89 Ed Giacomin .12 .30
90 Rod Gilbert .15 .40
91 Theo Fleury .02 .10
92 Mark Messier .20 .50
Brian Leetch
93 Marian Hossa .15 .40
94 Radek Bonk .02 .10
95 Radek Bonk .02 .10
Marian Hossa
96 Bobby Clarke .20 .50
97 Bernie Parent .15 .40
98 Eric Lindros .15 .40
99 Brian Boucher .15 .40
100 John LeClair .15 .40
101 Bobby Clarke .20 .50
John LeClair
102 Jeremy Roenick .20 .50
103 Keith Tkachuk .15 .40
104 Jeremy Roenick .15 .40
Keith Tkachuk
105 Mario Lemieux .75 2.00
106 Joe Mullen .12 .30
107 Jaromir Jagr .25 .75
108 Mario Lemieux .40 1.00
Jaromir Jagr
109 Peter Stastny .15 .40
110 Michel Goulet .12 .30
111 Steve Shields .12 .30
112 Jeff Friesen .02 .10
113 Owen Nolan .02 .10
Jeff Friesen
114 Bernie Federko .12 .30
115 Chris Pronger .12 .30
116 Roman Turek .12 .30
117 Brett Hull .20 .50
Pavol Demitra
118 Vincent Lecavalier .15 .40
119 Vincent Lecavalier .15 .40
Paul Mara
120 Frank Mahovlich .15 .40
121 Syl Apps .12 .30
122 Tim Horton .15 .40
123 Eddie Shack .15 .40
124 Curtis Joseph .15 .40
125 Mats Sundin .15 .40
126 Frank Mahovlich .20 .50
Curtis Joseph
127 Richard Brodeur .12 .30
128 Richard Brodeur .02 .10
Markus Naslund
129 Mike Gartner .12 .30
130 Adam Oates .12 .30
131 Olaf Kolzig .12 .30
132 Mike Gartner .12 .30
Olaf Kolzig
133 Dale Hawerchuk .12 .30
134 Wayne Gretzky CL .40 1.00
135 Steve Yzerman CL .30 .75

2000-01 Upper Deck Legends Legendary Collection Bronze

Randomly inserted in packs, this 135-card set parallels the base Legends set enhanced with bronze foil highlights and cards are sequentially numbered to 25.

*BRONZE: 50X TO 120X BASIC CARDS

2000-01 Upper Deck Legends Legendary Collection Gold

Randomly inserted in packs, this 135-card set parallels the base Legends set enhanced with gold foil highlights and cards are sequentially numbered to 375.

*GOLD: 5X TO 12X BASIC CARDS

2000-01 Upper Deck Legends Legendary Collection Silver

Randomly inserted in packs, this 135-card set parallels the base Legends set enhanced with silver foil highlights and cards are sequentially numbered to 100.

*SILVER: 8X TO 20X BASIC CARDS

2000-01 Upper Deck Legends Enshrined Stars

Randomly inserted in packs at the rate of 1:12, this 15-card set features Hall of Famers on a foil bordered card with silver foil highlights.

COMPLETE SET (15) 30.00 60.00
ES1 Wayne Gretzky 6.00 15.00
ES2 Gordie Howe 4.00 10.00
ES3 Mario Lemieux 5.00 12.00
ES4 Bobby Hull 2.50 6.00
ES5 Marcel Dionne 1.50 4.00
ES6 Denis Potvin 1.50 4.00
ES7 Guy Lafleur 2.00 5.00
ES8 Mike Bossy 1.50 4.00
ES9 Bobby Clarke 1.50 4.00
ES10 Frank Mahovlich 1.50 4.00
ES11 Gilbert Perreault 1.50 4.00
ES12 Phil Esposito 2.50 6.00
ES13 Tony Esposito 2.00 5.00
ES14 Stan Mikita 2.00 5.00
ES15 Ted Lindsay 1.50 4.00

2000-01 Upper Deck Legends Epic Signatures

Randomly inserted in packs at the rate of 1:23, this 43-card set features player photography and authentic player autographs.

BC Bobby Clarke 12.50 30.00
BG Bernie Geoffrion 15.00 40.00
BH Brett Hull 15.00 40.00
BO Bobby Orr 100.00 200.00
BT Bryan Trottier 6.00 15.00
CJ Curtis Joseph 10.00 25.00
CN Cam Neely 12.00 30.00
DH Dale Hawerchuk 6.00 15.00
DP Denis Potvin 6.00 15.00
FM Frank Mahovlich 8.00 20.00
GH Gordie Howe 60.00 150.00
GL Guy Lafleur 12.00 30.00
GP Gilbert Perreault 8.00 20.00
JB John Bucyk 6.00 15.00
JK Jari Kurri 10.00 25.00
JL John LeClair 4.00 10.00
JM Joe Mullen 6.00 15.00
JN Joe Nieuwendyk 8.00 20.00
JT Joe Thornton 12.50 30.00
KT Keith Tkachuk 4.00 10.00
LM Lanny McDonald 8.00 20.00
LR Larry Robinson 8.00 20.00
MB Mike Bossy 6.00 15.00
MD Marcel Dionne 6.00 15.00
MG Mike Gartner 6.00 15.00
ML Mario Lemieux 75.00 150.00
MM Mark Messier 60.00 120.00
PB Pavel Bure 6.00 15.00
PE Phil Esposito 20.00 50.00
PL Pat LaFontaine 6.00 15.00
PS Patrik Stefan 4.00 10.00
PV Pat Verbeek 10.00 25.00
SF Sergei Fedorov 20.00 50.00
SM Stan Mikita 10.00 25.00
SS Sergei Samsonov 4.00 10.00
SY Steve Yzerman 50.00 100.00
TE Tony Esposito 12.50 30.00
TL Ted Lindsay 8.00 20.00
WG Wayne Gretzky 100.00 200.00
BHU Bobby Hull 25.00 60.00
JBE Jean Beliveau 10.00 25.00
MBR Martin Brodeur 60.00 100.00
MGO Michel Goulet 6.00 15.00
PBO Peter Bondra 5.00 10.00

2000-01 Upper Deck Legends Essence of the Game

Randomly inserted in packs at the rate of 1:23, this 8-card set combines a star from yesterday with a star from today on this all foil insert card with silver foil highlights.

COMPLETE SET (8) 30.00 60.00
EG1 Guy Lafleur 1.50 4.00
Paul Kariya
EG2 Jaromir Jagr 4.00 10.00
Wayne Gretzky
EG3 Pavel Bure 1.50 4.00
Mike Bossy
EG4 Patrick Roy 5.00 12.00
Terry Sawchuk
EG5 Martin Brodeur 2.50 6.00
Bernie Parent
EG6 Cam Neely 1.50 4.00
Brendan Shanahan
EG7 Raymond Bourque 5.00 12.00
Bobby Orr
EG8 Steve Yzerman 5.00 12.00
Gordie Howe

2000-01 Upper Deck Legends Legendary Game Jerseys

Randomly inserted in packs at the rate of 1:23, this 36-card set features both color and black and white player photos, silver foil highlights, and a swatch of an authentic game jersey in the lower right hand corner of the card front.

JAM Al MacInnis 6.00 15.00
JBG Butch Goring 5.00 12.00
JBH Brett Hull 8.00 20.00
JBN Bob Nystrom 5.00 12.00
JBO Bobby Orr SP 50.00 100.00
JBT Bryan Trottier 6.00 15.00
JCG Clark Gillies 5.00 12.00
JCR Chico Resch 5.00 12.00
JDG Doug Gilmour 6.00 15.00
JDH Dominik Hasek 8.00 20.00
JDP Denis Potvin 6.00 15.00
JGF Grant Fuhr SP 15.00 40.00
JGH Gordie Howe 20.00 50.00
JJJ Jaromir Jagr 6.00 15.00
JJK Jari Kurri SP 10.00 25.00
JJL John LeClair 6.00 15.00
JJS Joe Sakic 8.00 20.00
JKT Keith Tkachuk 6.00 15.00
JLR Larry Robinson SP 6.00 15.00
JMB Mike Bossy 8.00 20.00
JMD Marcel Dionne SP 10.00 25.00
JMG Mike Gartner 6.00 15.00
JML Mario Lemieux 12.50 30.00
JMM Mike Modano 6.00 15.00
JMS Mats Sundin 6.00 15.00
JPB Pavel Bure 6.00 15.00
JPF Peter Forsberg 10.00 25.00
JPK Paul Kariya 6.00 15.00
JPL Pat LaFontaine 5.00 12.00
JPR Patrick Roy 12.50 30.00
JRB Ray Bourque 8.00 20.00
JSF Sergei Fedorov 6.00 15.00
JSY Steve Yzerman 12.50 30.00
JTS Teemu Selanne 6.00 15.00
JWG Wayne Gretzky 40.00 80.00
JMBR Martin Brodeur 10.00 25.00

2000-01 Upper Deck Legends of the Cage

Randomly inserted in packs at the rate of 1:18, this 10-card set showcases the greatest goalies to grace the game of hockey. Base cards feature and all-foil backdrop with player action photography and silver foil highlights.

COMPLETE SET (10) 20.00 40.00
LC1 Patrick Roy 5.00 12.00
LC2 Martin Brodeur 3.00 8.00
LC3 Dominik Hasek 2.50 6.00
LC4 Curtis Joseph 1.25 3.00
LC5 Ed Belfour 1.50 4.00
LC6 Grant Fuhr 1.25 3.00
LC7 Mike Richter 1.25 3.00
LC8 Jacques Plante 1.50 4.00
LC9 Terry Sawchuk 2.50 6.00
LC10 Tony Esposito 2.00 5.00

2000-01 Upper Deck Legends Playoff Heroes

Randomly inserted in packs at the rate of 1:15, this 12-card set showcases NHL players who year after year stepped it up in the playoffs. Cards feature 3 action panels along the center of the card set against an all foil backdrop with a close up photo of the featured player. Cards have silver foil highlights.

COMPLETE SET (12) 30.00 60.00
PH1 Patrick Roy 5.00 12.00
PH2 Steve Yzerman 5.00 12.00
PH3 Jaromir Jagr 1.50 4.00
PH4 Mike Modano 2.00 5.00
PH5 Peter Forsberg 2.50 6.00
PH6 Mark Messier 1.50 4.00
PH7 Wayne Gretzky 6.00 15.00
PH8 Brett Hull 1.50 4.00
PH9 Gordie Howe 4.00 10.00
PH10 Bobby Hull 2.50 6.00
PH11 Bryan Trottier 1.50 4.00
PH12 Phil Esposito 2.50 6.00

2000-01 Upper Deck Legends Supreme Milestones

Randomly inserted in packs at the rate of 1:4, this 15-card set spotlights NHL legends and highlights some of their most significant career achievements on an all holo-foil card with silver foil highlights. Player photos are set against a larger "faded" player photo in the background.

COMPLETE SET (15) 25.00 50.00
SM1 Wayne Gretzky 4.00 10.00
SM2 Gordie Howe 2.50 6.00
SM3 Bobby Hull 1.50 4.00

SM4 Wayne Gretzky 4.00 10.00
SM5 Steve Yzerman 2.50 6.00
SM6 Brett Hull .75 2.00
SM7 Joe Sakic 1.25 3.00
SM8 Mark Messier .75 2.00
SM9 Patrick Roy 3.00 8.00
SM10 Luc Robitaille .75 2.00
SM11 Mario Lemieux 3.00 8.00
SM12 Mike Bossy 1.00 2.50
SM13 Phil Esposito 1.50 4.00
SM14 Tony Esposito 1.25 3.00
SM15 Ray Bourque 1.00 2.50

2001-02 Upper Deck Legends

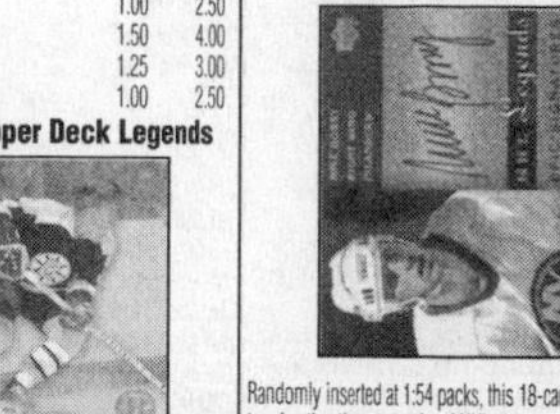

Issued in early-December 2001, this 100-card set carried an SRP of $4.99 for a 5-card pack. The set focused on legendary NHL players of the past.

COMPLETE SET (100) 25.00 50.00
1 Bobby Orr 1.25 3.00
2 Eddie Shore .40 1.00
3 Phil Esposito .60 1.50
4 Johnny Bucyk .30 .75
5 Cam Neely .40 1.00
6 Gerry Cheevers .40 1.00
7 Gilbert Perreault .30 .75
8 Rene Robert .10 .25
9 Lanny McDonald .30 .75
10 Al Secord .10 .25
11 Bobby Hull .75 2.00
12 Glenn Hall .40 1.00
13 Stan Mikita .40 1.00
14 Tony Esposito .40 1.00
15 Gordie Howe 1.25 3.00
16 Terry Sawchuk .60 1.50
17 Ted Lindsay .40 1.00
18 Sid Abel .10 .25
19 Red Kelly .40 1.00
20 Alex Delvecchio .40 1.00
21 Glenn Anderson .10 .25
22 Wayne Gretzky 1.50 4.00
23 Jari Kurri .30 .75
24 Grant Fuhr .30 .75
25 Bill Ranford .30 .75
26 Gordie Howe 1.25 3.00
27 Marcel Dionne .30 .75
28 Butch Goring .10 .25
29 Rogie Vachon .30 .75
30 Maurice Richard .75 2.00
31 Jean Beliveau .40 1.00
32 Serge Savard .40 1.00
33 Jacques Plante .60 1.50
34 Guy Lafleur .40 1.00
35 Yvan Cournoyer .40 1.00
36 Steve Shutt .10 .25
37 Rick Green .10 .25
38 Henri Richard .40 1.00
39 Bernie Geoffrion .40 1.00
40 Guy Lapointe .10 .25
41 Denis Potvin .30 .75
42 Mike Bossy .30 .75
43 Bryan Trottier .30 .75
44 Clark Gillies .10 .25
45 Billy Smith .30 .75
46 Ed Giacomin .40 1.00
47 Jean Ratelle .10 .25
48 Lester Patrick .10 .25
49 William Jennings .10 .25
50 Ray Bourque .75 2.00
51 Frank Calder .10 .25
52 Andy van Hellemond .10 .25
53 Bobby Clarke .30 .75
54 Bernie Parent .40 1.00
55 Bill Barber .10 .25
56 Syl Apps .10 .25
57 Bernie Federko .10 .25
58 Frank Mahovlich .40 1.00
59 Darryl Sittler .40 1.00
60 Tim Horton .40 1.00
61 Rick Vaive .10 .25
62 Frank Selke .10 .25
63 Conn Smythe .10 .25
64 King Clancy .10 .25
65 Tony Tanti .10 .25
66 Mike Ridley .10 .25
67 Rod Langway .10 .25
68 Mike Gartner .30 .75
69 Kent Nilsson .10 .25
70 Reggie Leach .10 .25
71 Dennis Maruk .10 .25
72 Wilf Paiement .10 .25
73 Barry Beck .10 .25
74 Simon Nolet .10 .25
75 Don Beaupre .10 .25
76 Peter Stastny .30 .75
77 Michel Goulet .30 .75
78 Dale Hawerchuk .30 .75
79 Gerry Cheevers .40 1.00
80 Glenn Hall .40 1.00
81 Jerry Sawchuk .60 1.50
82 Grant Fuhr .30 .75
83 Bernie Parent .40 1.00
84 Jacques Plante .60 1.50
85 Ed Giacomin .40 1.00
86 Bill Ranford .30 .75
87 Billy Smith .30 .75
88 Tony Esposito .40 1.00
89 Bobby Orr 1.25 3.00
90 Bobby Hull .75 2.00
91 Gordie Howe 1.25 3.00
92 Wayne Gretzky 1.50 4.00
93 Marcel Dionne .30 .75
94 Maurice Richard .75 2.00
95 Guy Lafleur .50 1.25
96 Mike Bossy .30 .75
97 Jari Kurri .40 1.00
98 Mike Gartner .40 1.00
99 Gordie Howe CL .60 1.50
100 Wayne Gretzky CL .75 2.00

2001-02 Upper Deck Legends Epic Signatures

Randomly inserted at 1:54 packs, this 18-card set featured authentic autographs of NHL alums.

AD Alex Delvecchio 12.50 30.00
BC Bobby Clarke 12.50 30.00
BH Bobby Hull 20.00 50.00
BO Bobby Orr 125.00 250.00
BT Bryan Trottier 12.50 30.00
CN Cam Neely 15.00 40.00
FM Frank Mahovlich 12.50 30.00
GH Gordie Howe 60.00 150.00
GL Guy Lafleur 15.00 40.00
GP Gilbert Perreault 12.50 30.00
JB Jean Beliveau 15.00 40.00
MB Mike Bossy 12.50 30.00
MD Marcel Dionne 12.50 30.00
PE Phil Esposito 12.50 30.00
SM Stan Mikita 12.50 30.00
TE Tony Esposito 15.00 40.00
TL Ted Lindsay 12.50 30.00
WG Wayne Gretzky 125.00 250.00

2001-02 Upper Deck Legends Fiorentino Collection

Randomly inserted at 1:18, this 15-card set featured reproductions of photographs taken by renowned sports photographer James Fiorentino.

COMPLETE SET (15) 40.00 80.00
FCBC Bobby Clarke 1.50 4.00
FCBH Bobby Hull 2.50 6.00
FCBO Bobby Orr 6.00 15.00
FCBT Bryan Trottier 1.50 4.00
FCGH Gordie Howe 3.00 8.00
FCGL Guy Lafleur 1.50 4.00
FCJP Jacques Plante 1.50 4.00
FCMB Mike Bossy 1.50 4.00
FCMD Marcel Dionne 1.50 4.00
FCMR Maurice Richard 3.00 8.00
FCPE Phil Esposito 1.50 4.00
FCSM Stan Mikita 1.50 4.00
FCTE Tony Esposito 1.50 4.00
FCTS Terry Sawchuk 1.50 4.00
FCWG Wayne Gretzky 6.00 15.00

2001-02 Upper Deck Legends Jerseys

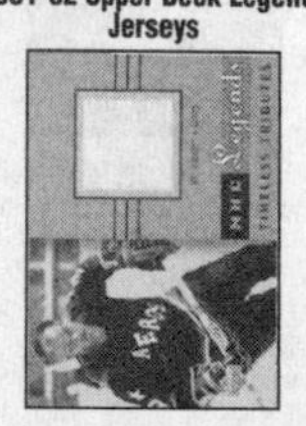

Randomly inserted at 1:18 packs, this 27-card set featured game-worn jersey swatches form the player(s) featured on the card fronts. A platinum parallel was also created and serial-numbered to 100 copies each.

*MULT.COLOR SWATCH: .75X TO 2X HI
*PLATINUM: .5X TO 1.25X HI
TTBB Bill Barber 5.00 12.00
TTBH Bobby Hull 10.00 25.00
TTBR Bill Ranford 5.00 12.00
TTBS Billy Smith 5.00 12.00
TTBT Bryan Trottier 5.00 12.00
TTCG Clark Gillies 5.00 12.00
TTCN Cam Neely 12.50 30.00
TTDP Denis Potvin 5.00 12.00
TTFL Guy Lafleur Que. 5.00 12.00
TTGC Gerry Cheevers 5.00 12.00
TTGH Gordie Howe 12.50 30.00
TTGL Guy Lafleur AS 5.00 12.00
TTGP Gilbert Perreault 5.00 12.00
TTLA Guy Lafleur Mon. 5.00 12.00
TTLF Guy Lafleur NY 5.00 12.00
TTMG Mike Gartner 5.00 12.00
TTPE Phil Esposito 5.00 12.00
TTSM Stan Mikita 5.00 12.00
TTSS Steve Shutt 5.00 12.00
TTVH Andy van Hellemond 5.00 12.00
TTWG Wayne Gretzky 25.00 60.00
TTGU Guy Lafleur Mon./Que. 12.50 30.00
TTGY Guy Lafleur NY/AS 12.50 30.00
TTHM Bobby Hull 20.00 50.00
Stan Mikita
TTSL Steve Shutt 15.00 40.00
Guy Lafleur
TTST Billy Smith 15.00 40.00
Bryan Trottier

2001-02 Upper Deck Legends Milestones

Randomly inserted at 1:18, this 16-card set honored past players and the different career milestones they achieved. Each card carried a swatch of game-used jersey from the featured player. A platinum parallel was also created and serial-numbered to just 25 copies each. The platinum parallel was not priced due to scarcity.

MBB Bill Barber 8.00 20.00
MBC Bobby Clarke 12.50 30.00
MBS Brent Sutter 8.00 20.00
MBT Bryan Trottier 8.00 20.00
MCN Cam Neely 8.00 20.00
MDP Denis Potvin 8.00 20.00
MGP Gilbert Perreault 8.00 20.00
MLM Lanny McDonald 8.00 20.00
MMB Mike Bossy 8.00 20.00
MMG Mike Gartner 8.00 20.00
MNB Neal Broten 8.00 20.00
MSS Steve Shutt 8.00 20.00
MSY Steve Yzerman 12.50 30.00
MWG Wayne Gretzky 25.00 60.00

2001-02 Upper Deck Legends Sticks

Randomly inserted at 1:18, this 29-card set featured a piece of game-used stick from the pictured player.

PHBC Bobby Clarke 12.50 30.00
PHBH Bobby Hull 12.50 30.00
PHBO Bobby Orr 60.00 125.00
PHBS Billy Smith 8.00 20.00
PHBT Bryan Trottier 8.00 20.00
PHDP Denis Potvin 8.00 20.00
PHDS Darryl Sittler 8.00 20.00
PHES Phil Esposito 8.00 20.00
PHFM Frank Mahovlich 8.00 20.00
PHGC Gerry Cheevers 8.00 20.00
PHGH Gordie Howe Det. 15.00 40.00
PHGL Guy Lafleur 8.00 20.00
PHGR Wayne Gretzky LA 40.00 100.00
PHHU Bobby Hull 15.00 40.00
PHJB Jean Beliveau 12.50 30.00
PHJK Jari Kurri 15.00 40.00
PHJP Jacques Plante 15.00 40.00
PHJR Jean Ratelle 8.00 20.00
PHMB Mike Bossy 8.00 20.00
PHMD Marcel Dionne 8.00 20.00
PHMG Mike Gartner 8.00 20.00
PHMH Gordie Howe NE 15.00 40.00
PHMR Maurice Richard 15.00 40.00
PHPE Phil Esposito 8.00 20.00
PHRA Ray Bourque Col. 15.00 40.00
PHRB Ray Bourque Bos. 12.50 30.00
PHSM Stan Mikita 8.00 20.00
PHTE Tony Esposito 8.00 20.00
PHWG Wayne Gretzky Edm. 50.00 125.00

1993 Upper Deck Locker All-Stars

This 60-card standard-size set was issued as the 1992-93 Upper Deck NHL All-Star Locker Series. The set came in a plastic locker box. Personally signed Gordie Howe "Hockey Heroes" cards were randomly inserted throughout the locker boxes; the odds of finding one are one in 120 boxes. The fronts feature full-bleed, color, action player photos. The player's name is printed in gold foil above a blue and gold-foil curving stripe at the bottom. The 44th NHL All-Star game logo overlaps the stripe and is printed in the lower right corner. The backs carry a small, close-up picture within a bright blue rough-edged border that gives the effect of torn paper. This photo overlaps a gray panel with the same rough-edge look. This panel carries player profile information. After presenting the NHL All-Stars by conference, Campbell Conference All-Stars (1-18) and Wales Conference All-Stars (19-36), the set features the following special subsets, All-Star Skills Winners (37-40), All-Star Heroes (41-50), and Future All-Stars (51-60). The card pictures for this set were taken during the 1993 NHL All-Star Weekend in Montreal.

COMPLETE SET (60) 6.00 15.00
1 Peter Bondra .20 .50
2 Steve Duchesne .01 .05
3 Jaromir Jagr .60 1.50
4 Pat LaFontaine .20 .50
5 Brian Leetch .20 .50
6 Mario Lemieux 1.00 2.50
7 Mark Messier .25 .60
8 Alexander Mogilny .08 .25
9 Kirk Muller .01 .05
10 Adam Oates .08 .25
11 Mark Recchi .08 .25
12 Patrick Roy 1.00 2.50
13 Joe Sakic .40 1.00
14 Kevin Stevens .01 .05
15 Scott Stevens .08 .25
16 Rick Tocchet .01 .05
17 Pierre Turgeon .08 .25
18 Zarley Zalapski .01 .05
19 Ed Belfour .20 .50
20 Brian Bradley .01 .05
21 Pavel Bure .40 1.00
22 Chris Chelios .20 .50
23 Paul Coffey .20 .50
24 Doug Gilmour .20 .50
25 Wayne Gretzky 1.25 3.00
26 Phil Housley .08 .25
27 Brett Hull .25 .60
28 Kelly Kisio .01 .05
29 Jari Kurri .20 .50
30 Dave Manson .01 .05
31 Mike Modano .25 .60
32 Gary Roberts .08 .25
33 Luc Robitaille .08 .25
34 Jeremy Roenick .20 .50
35 Teemu Selanne .40 1.00
36 Steve Yzerman .60 1.50
37 Al Iafrate .08 .25
38 Mike Gartner .08 .25
39 Ray Bourque .25 .60
40 Jon Casey .08 .25
41 Bob Gainey .08 .25
42 Gordie Howe .40 1.00
43 Bobby Hull .30 .75
44 Frank Mahovlich .20 .50
45 Lanny McDonald .08 .25
46 Stan Mikita .15 .40
47 Henri Richard .10 .30
48 Larry Robinson .20 .50
49 Glen Sather .08 .25
50 Bryan Trottier .08 .25
51 Tony Amonte .08 .25
52 Pat Falloon .01 .05
53 Joe Juneau .08 .25
54 Alexei Kovalev .08 .25
55 Dmitri Kvartalnov .01 .05
56 Eric Lindros .50 1.25
57 Vladimir Malakhov .01 .05
58 Felix Potvin .20 .50
59 Mats Sundin .20 .50
60 Alexei Zhamnov .08 .25
AU Gordie Howe AU 60.00 125.00
(Certified autograph)

2007-08 Upper Deck Lucky Shot Arena Giveaways

These cards were issued as arena giveaways over the second half of the 2007-08 season. Each team gave away a five-card set at a single home game. The sixth card for each team could be acquired with the purchase of a specified number of Upper Deck packs at the team's pro shop on the night of that game. As a result, the sixth card for each team tends to sell for a much higher rate.

LA1 Dustin Brown 1.50 4.00
LA2 Mike Cammalleri 2.00 5.00
LA3 Rob Blake 2.00 5.00
LA4 Alexander Frolov 1.50 4.00
LA5 Lubomir Visnovsky 1.50 4.00
LA6 Anze Kopitar 8.00 20.00
NJ1 Travis Zajac 1.50 4.00
NJ2 Jay Pandolfo 1.50 4.00
NJ3 Brian Gionta 1.50 4.00
NJ4 Sergei Brylin 1.50 4.00
NJ5 Dainius Zubrus 1.50 4.00
NJ6 Martin Brodeur 20.00 50.00
SJ1 Joe Pavelski 1.50 4.00
SJ2 Jonathan Cheechoo 2.00 5.00
SJ3 Marc-Edouard Vlasic 1.50 4.00
SJ4 Craig Rivet 1.50 4.00
SJ5 Patrick Marleau 2.00 5.00
SJ6 Joe Thornton 10.00 25.00
TB1 Dan Boyle 1.50 4.00
TB2 Ryan Craig 1.50 4.00
TB3 Vaclav Prospal 1.50 4.00
TB4 Marc Denis 2.00 5.00
TB5 Brad Richards 2.00 5.00
TB6 Vincent Lecavalier 8.00 20.00
ANA1 Andy McDonald 1.50 4.00
ANA2 Chris Pronger 2.50 6.00
ANA3 Chris Kunitz 1.50 4.00
ANA4 Jean-Sebastien Giguere 2.50 6.00
ANA5 Corey Perry 2.00 5.00
ANA6 Ryan Getzlaf 6.00 15.00
ATL1 Ilya Kovalchuk 3.00 8.00
ATL2 Marian Hossa 2.50 6.00
ATL3 Bobby Holik 1.50 4.00
ATL4 Kari Lehtonen 2.50 6.00
ATL5 Slava Kozlov 1.50 4.00
ATL6 Garnet Exelby 5.00 12.00
BOS1 Zdeno Chara 1.50 4.00
BOS2 Phil Kessel 2.50 6.00
BOS3 Glen Murray 1.50 4.00
BOS4 Marco Sturm 1.50 4.00
BOS5 Marc Savard 1.50 4.00
BOS6 Tim Thomas 10.00 25.00
BUF1 Thomas Vanek 2.00 5.00
BUF2 Derek Roy 1.50 4.00
BUF3 Brian Campbell 1.50 4.00
BUF4 Maxim Afinogenov 1.50 4.00
BUF5 Jason Pominville 1.50 4.00
BUF6 Ryan Miller 8.00 20.00
CAR1 Cory Stillman 1.50 4.00
CAR2 Ray Whitney 1.50 4.00
CAR3 Eric Staal 2.50 6.00
CAR4 Glen Wesley 1.50 4.00
CAR5 Justin Williams 1.50 4.00
CAR6 Cam Ward 8.00 20.00
CGY1 Miikka Kiprusoff 3.00 8.00
CGY2 Dion Phaneuf 2.50 6.00
CGY3 Alex Tanguay 2.00 5.00
CGY4 Daymond Langkow 1.50 4.00
CGY5 Kristian Huselius 1.50 4.00
CGY6 Jarome Iginla 12.00 30.00
CHI1 Patrick Kane 10.00 25.00
CHI2 Martin Havlat 2.00 5.00
CHI3 Patrick Sharp 1.50 4.00
CHI4 Nikolai Khabibulin 2.50 6.00
CHI5 Tuomo Ruutu 1.50 4.00
CHI6 Jonathan Toews 15.00 40.00
CLB1 Pascal Leclaire 2.00 5.00
CLB2 Nikolai Zherdev 1.50 4.00
CLB3 Adam Foote 1.50 4.00
CLB4 Sergei Fedorov 2.50 6.00
CLB5 Fredrik Modin 1.50 4.00
CLB6 Rick Nash 8.00 20.00
COL1 Joe Sakic 5.00 12.00
COL2 Ian Laperriere 1.50 4.00
COL3 Milan Hejduk 2.00 5.00
COL4 Scott Hannan 1.50 4.00
COL5 Ryan Smyth 2.00 5.00
COL6 Paul Stastny 8.00 20.00
DAL1 Sergei Zubov 1.50 4.00
DAL2 Mike Ribeiro 1.50 4.00
DAL3 Brenden Morrow 2.00 5.00
DAL4 Marty Turco 2.50 6.00
DAL5 Jere Lehtinen 1.50 4.00
DAL6 Mike Modano 8.00 20.00
DET1 Nicklas Lidstrom 2.50 6.00
DET2 Kris Draper 2.00 5.00
DET3 Pavel Datsyuk 2.50 6.00
DET4 Tomas Holmstrom 2.00 5.00
DET5 Chris Chelios 1.50 4.00
DET6 Henrik Zetterberg 8.00 20.00
EDM1 Dwayne Roloson 2.00 5.00
EDM2 Jarret Stoll 1.50 4.00
EDM3 Dustin Penner 1.50 4.00
EDM4 Shawn Horcoff 1.50 4.00
EDM5 Ethan Moreau 1.50 4.00
EDM6 Ales Hemsky 5.00 12.00
FLA1 Olli Jokinen 1.50 4.00
FLA2 Nathan Horton 1.50 4.00
FLA3 Stephen Weiss 1.50 4.00
FLA4 Jay Bouwmeester 1.50 4.00
FLA5 Tomas Vokoun 2.50 6.00
FLA6 Rostislav Olesz 5.00 12.00
MIN1 Pavol Demitra 1.50 4.00
MIN2 Kurtis Foster 1.50 4.00
MIN3 Pierre-Marc Bouchard 1.50 4.00
MIN4 Josh Harding 2.00 5.00
MIN5 Mark Parrish 1.50 4.00
MIN6 Marian Gaborik 10.00 25.00
MTL1 Guillaume Latendresse 2.00 5.00
MTL2 Cristobal Huet 2.00 5.00
MTL3 Mark Streit 1.50 4.00
MTL4 Chris Higgins 2.00 5.00
MTL5 Roman Hamrlik 1.50 4.00
MTL6 Saku Koivu 6.00 15.00
NAS1 J.P. Dumont 1.50 4.00
NAS2 Martin Erat 1.50 4.00
NAS3 David Legwand 1.50 4.00
NAS4 Chris Mason 2.00 5.00
NAS5 Jason Arnott 1.50 4.00
NAS6 Alexander Radulov 8.00 20.00
NYI1 Mike Sillinger 1.50 4.00
NYI2 Rick DiPietro 2.00 5.00
NYI3 Brendan Witt 1.50 4.00
NYI4 Bill Guerin 1.50 4.00
NYI5 Mike Comrie 1.50 4.00
NYI6 Miroslav Satan 5.00 12.00
NYR1 Jaromir Jagr 4.00 10.00
NYR2 Sean Avery 1.50 4.00
NYR3 Chris Drury 2.00 5.00
NYR4 Scott Gomez 1.50 4.00
NYR5 Brendan Shanahan 2.50 6.00
NYR6 Henrik Lundqvist 10.00 25.00
OTT1 Daniel Alfredsson 2.00 5.00
OTT2 Dany Heatley 3.00 8.00
OTT3 Antoine Vermette 1.50 4.00
OTT4 Jason Spezza 2.50 6.00
OTT5 Anton Volchenkov 1.50 4.00
OTT6 Martin Gerber 6.00 15.00
PHI1 Martin Biron 2.00 5.00
PHI2 Simon Gagne 1.50 4.00
PHI3 Daniel Briere 2.50 6.00
PHI4 Mike Richards 3.00 8.00
PHI5 Kimmo Timonen 1.50 4.00
PHI6 Scottie Upshall 5.00 12.00
PHX1 Zbynek Michalek 1.50 4.00
PHX2 Keith Ballard 1.50 4.00
PHX3 Ed Jovanovski 1.50 4.00
PHX4 Nick Boynton 1.50 4.00
PHX5 Derek Morris 1.50 4.00
PHX6 Shane Doan 5.00 12.00
PIT1 Sidney Crosby 12.00 30.00
PIT2 Sergei Gonchar 1.50 4.00
PIT3 Marc-Andre Fleury 2.50 6.00
PIT4 Petr Sykora 1.50 4.00
PIT5 Evgeni Malkin 6.00 15.00
PIT6 Jordan Staal 10.00 25.00
STL1 Manny Legace 2.00 5.00
STL2 Barret Jackman 1.50 4.00
STL3 Paul Kariya 2.50 6.00
STL4 Doug Weight 1.50 4.00
STL5 Keith Tkachuk 2.00 5.00
STL6 Brad Boyes 6.00 15.00
TOR1 Darcy Tucker 2.00 5.00
TOR2 Bryan McCabe 1.50 4.00
TOR3 Matt Stajan 1.50 4.00
TOR4 Jason Blake 1.50 4.00
TOR5 Mats Sundin 2.50 6.00
TOR6 Tomas Kaberle 5.00 12.00
VAN1 Markus Naslund 2.50 6.00
VAN2 Henrik Sedin 1.50 4.00
VAN3 Mattias Ohlund 1.50 4.00
VAN4 Willie Mitchell 1.50 4.00
VAN5 Daniel Sedin 1.50 4.00
VAN6 Roberto Luongo 12.00 30.00
WAS1 Alexander Semin 2.50 6.00
WAS2 Chris Clark 1.50 4.00
WAS3 Olaf Kolzig 2.50 6.00
WAS4 Alexander Ovechkin 8.00 20.00
WAS5 Michael Nylander 1.50 4.00
WAS6 Donald Brashear 5.00 12.00

2000-01 Upper Deck Mario Lemieux Return to Excellence

Available in various Upper Deck products, this set features game-used jersey swatches from Mario Lemieux and each card was serial numbered out of 66. Cards ML1-ML3 were randomly available in Upper Deck Pros & Prospects, cards ML4-ML6 were randomly available in SP Authentic, and cards ML7-ML9were randomly available in Upper Deck Rookie Update.

COMMON CARD (ML1-9) 100.00 200.00

2008-09 Upper Deck Montreal Canadiens Centennial

COMPLETE SET (300) 175.00 300.00
COMP.SET w/o SP's (200) 40.00 100.00
(201-300) STATED ODDS 1 PER PACK
1 Toe Blake .20 .50
2 Jean Beliveau .50 1.25
3 Donnie Marshall .20 .50
4 Bill Nyrop .20 .50
5 Mickey Redmond .20 .50
6 Yvan Cournoyer .40 1.00
7 Dick Duff .30 .75
8 Ken Dryden .50 1.25
9 Bill Durnan .40 1.00
10 Bob Gainey .30 .75
11 Herb Gardiner .20 .50
12 Bernard Geoffrion .20 .50
13 George Hainsworth .50 1.25
14 Doug Harvey .30 .75
15 Tom Johnson .20 .50
16 Aurele Joliat .30 .75
17 Elmer Lach .50 1.25
18 Guy Lafleur .60 1.50
19 Newsy Lalonde .25 .60
20 Rod Langway .40 1.00
21 Jacques Laperriere .50 1.25
22 Guy Lapointe .25 .60
23 Jack Laviolette .25 .60
24 Jacques Lemaire .20 .50
25 Frank Mahovlich .30 .75
26 Joe Malone .25 .60
27 Sylvio Mantha .40 1.00
28 Dickie Moore .25 .60
29 Howie Morenz .20 .50
30 Buddy O'Connor .20 .50
31 Bert Olmstead .20 .50
32 Didier Pitre .20 .50
33 Jacques Plante .50 1.25
34 Ken Reardon .20 .50
35 Henri Richard .40 1.00
36 Larry Robinson .30 .75
37 Maurice Richard .60 1.50
38 Mark Recchi .25 .60
39 Patrick Roy 1.00 2.50
40 Denis Savard .30 .75
41 Serge Savard .50 1.25
42 Albert Siebert .25 .60
43 Steve Shutt .30 .75
44 Georges Vezina .60 1.50
45 Butch Bouchard .40 1.00
46 Chris Nilan .20 .50
47 Doug Jarvis .20 .50
48 Pete Mahovlich .40 1.00
49 Mats Naslund .25 .60
50 Claude Provost .20 .50
51 Pierre Mondou .20 .50
52 Craig Ludwig .20 .50
53 Karl Dykhuis .20 .50
54 Ken Mosdell .20 .50
55 Georges Mantha .20 .50
56 Mark Napier .30 .75
57 Peter Popovic .20 .50
58 Vladimir Malakhov .20 .50
59 Cliff Goupille .20 .50
60 Lyle Odelein .30 .75
61 Ted Harris .20 .50
62 Gerry McNeil .20 .50
63 Murph Chamberlain .20 .50
64 Mike McPhee .20 .50
65 Andre Pronovost .20 .50
66 Kirk Muller .25 .60
67 Scott Thornton .20 .50
68 Keith Acton .20 .50
69 Brian Engblom .20 .50
70 Ralph Backstrom .20 .50
71 John Ambrose O'Brien .20 .50
72 Marcel Bonin .30 .75
73 Pierre Bouchard .30 .75
74 Armand Mondou .20 .50
75 Benoit Brunet .20 .50
76 Valeri Bure .20 .50
77 Walter Buswell .20 .50
78 Guy Carbonneau .40 1.00
79 Albert LeDuc .25 .60
80 Chris Chelios .40 1.00
81 Sprague Cleghorn .50 1.25
82 Bob Fillion .20 .50
83 Shayne Corson .20 .50
84 Russ Courtnall .20 .50
85 Billy Coutu .20 .50
86 Wilf Cude .40 1.00
87 Floyd Curry .20 .50
88 Leo Lamoureux .20 .50
89 Jean-Jacques Daigneault .25 .60
90 Vincent Damphousse .25 .60
91 Lorne Worsley .25 .60
92 Dave Balon .20 .50
93 Eric Desjardins .25 .60
94 Patrick Poulin .20 .50
95 John Ferguson .20 .50
96 Johnny Gagnon .20 .50
97 Jimmy Gardner .20 .50
98 Ray Getliffe .20 .50
99 Brent Gilchrist .25 .60
100 Gaston Gingras .20 .50
101 Phil Goyette .25 .60
102 Rick Green .20 .50
103 Howard McNamara .20 .50
104 Glen Harmon .20 .50
105 Terry Harper .20 .50
106 Bill Hicke .20 .50
107 Charlie Hodge .25 .60
108 Rejean Houle .30 .75
109 Marty Burke .20 .50
110 Joe Juneau .20 .50
111 Mike Keane .25 .60
112 Ab McDonald .25 .60
113 Patrice Brisebois .20 .50
114 Marc Tardif .25 .60
115 Yvon Lambert .30 .75
116 Wildor Larochelle .20 .50
117 Michel Larocque .20 .50
118 Claude Larose .20 .50
119 Pierre Larouche .25 .60
120 Stephan Lebeau .20 .50
121 John LeClair .30 .75
122 Roman Hamrlik .20 .50
123 Claude Lemieux .25 .60
124 Pit Lepine .40 1.00
125 Francis Bouillon .25 .60
126 Billy Reay .20 .50
127 Stephane Richer .25 .60
128 Doug Risebrough .25 .60
129 Craig Rivet .20 .50
130 Jim Roberts .20 .50
131 Bud MacPherson .20 .50
132 Bobby Rousseau .20 .50
133 Martin Rucinsky .20 .50
134 Brian Savage .20 .50
135 Mathieu Schneider .20 .50
136 Brian Skrudland .20 .50
137 Bobby Smith .20 .50
138 Turner Stevenson .20 .50
139 Petr Svoboda .20 .50
140 Jean-Guy Talbot .25 .60
141 Jose Theodore .30 .75
142 Gilles Tremblay .50 1.25
143 Jean-Claude Tremblay .20 .50
144 Mario Tremblay .40 1.00
145 Pierre Turgeon .30 .75
146 Rogie Vachon .30 .75
147 Ryan Walter .20 .50
148 Paul Meger .20 .50
149 Dick Irvin .20 .50
150 Murray Wilson .30 .75
151 Joe Hall .20 .50
152 William Northey .20 .50
153 Senator Donat Raymond .20 .50
154 Leo Dandurand .20 .50
Jos Cattarinich
Louis Letourneau
155 Hartland De Montarville Molson .20 .50
156 Sam Pollock .20 .50
157 Frank J. Selke .20 .50
158 Tom P. Gorman .20 .50
159 Bob Turner .20 .50
160 Scotty Bowman .30 .75
161 Calum MacKay .20 .50
162 Paul Haynes .20 .50
163 Youppi MASCOT .20 .50
164 Toe Blake .20 .50
165 Oleg Petrov .20 .50
166 Stephane Quintal .20 .50
167 Saku Koivu .30 .75
168 Carey Price 1.00 2.50
169 Alex Kovalev .30 .75
170 Tomas Plekanec .20 .50
171 Andrei Markov .25 .60
172 Andrei Kostitsyn .25 .60
173 Christopher Higgins .20 .50
174 Rick Chartraw .20 .50
175 Dollard St. Laurent .20 .50
176 Mike Komisarek .25 .60
177 Coupe Stanley Cup .20 .50
178 Coupe Stanley Cup .20 .50
179 Coupe Stanley Cup .20 .50
180 Coupe Stanley Cup .20 .50
181 Coupe Stanley Cup .20 .50
182 Coupe Stanley Cup .20 .50
183 Coupe Stanley Cup .20 .50
184 Coupe Stanley Cup .20 .50
185 Coupe Stanley Cup .20 .50
186 Coupe Stanley Cup .20 .50
187 Coupe Stanley Cup .20 .50
188 Coupe Stanley Cup .20 .50
189 Coupe Stanley Cup .20 .50
190 Coupe Stanley Cup .20 .50
191 Coupe Stanley Cup .20 .50
192 Coupe Stanley Cup .20 .50
193 Coupe Stanley Cup .20 .50
194 Coupe Stanley Cup .20 .50
195 Coupe Stanley Cup .20 .50
196 Coupe Stanley Cup .20 .50
197 Coupe Stanley Cup .20 .50
198 Coupe Stanley Cup .20 .50
199 Coupe Stanley Cup .20 .50
200 Coupe Stanley Cup .20 .50
201 Jack Laviolette 1.50 4.00
202 Newsy Lalonde 1.50 4.00
203 Jimmy Gardner 1.25 3.00
204 Howard McNamara 1.25 3.00
205 Sprague Cleghorn 3.00 8.00
206 Billy Coutu 1.25 3.00
207 Sylvio Mantha 2.50 6.00
208 George Hainsworth 3.00 8.00
209 Albert Siebert 1.50 4.00
210 Walter Buswell 1.25 3.00
211 Toe Blake 1.25 3.00
212 Bill Durnan 2.50 6.00
213 Butch Bouchard 2.50 6.00
214 Maurice Richard 4.00 10.00
215 Doug Harvey 2.00 5.00
216 Jean Beliveau 3.00 8.00
217 Henri Richard 2.50 6.00
218 Yvan Cournoyer 2.50 6.00
219 Serge Savard 3.00 8.00
220 Bob Gainey 2.00 5.00
221 Chris Chelios 2.50 6.00
222 Guy Carbonneau 2.50 6.00
223 Kirk Muller 1.50 4.00
224 Mike Keane 1.50 4.00
225 Pierre Turgeon 2.00 5.00
226 Vincent Damphousse 1.50 4.00
227 Saku Koivu 2.00 5.00
228 Arena Jubilee Arena 1.25 3.00
229 Arena Westmount Arena 1.25 3.00
230 Arena Mont-Royal Arena 1.25 3.00
231 Forum - 1924 1.25 3.00
232 Forum - 1949 1.25 3.00
233 Forum - 1949 1.25 3.00
234 Centre Bell Centre 1.25 3.00
235 Henri Richard 2.50 6.00
236 Maurice Richard 4.00 10.00
237 Guy Lafleur 4.00 10.00
238 Guy Lafleur 4.00 10.00
239 Chris Nilan 1.25 3.00
240 Maurice Richard 4.00 10.00
241 Jacques Plante 3.00 8.00

242 George Hainsworth 3.00 8.00
243 Larry Robinson 2.00 5.00
244 Henri Richard 2.50 6.00
245 Jean Beliveau 3.00 8.00
246 Doug Jarvis 1.25 3.00
247 George Hainsworth 3.00 8.00
248 Henri Richard 2.50 6.00
249 Maurice Richard 4.00 10.00
250 Guy Lafleur 4.00 10.00
251 Newsy Lalonde 1.50 4.00
252 Howie Morenz 1.25 3.00
253 Toe Blake 1.25 3.00
254 Elmer Lach 3.00 8.00
255 Bernard Geoffrion 1.25 3.00
256 Guy Lafleur 4.00 10.00
257 Ken Dryden 3.00 8.00
258 Doug Harvey 2.00 5.00
259 Guy Carbonneau 2.50 6.00
260 Jacques Plante 3.00 8.00
261 Jean Beliveau 3.00 8.00
262 Bob Gainey 2.00 5.00
263 Bill Durnan 2.50 6.00
264 George Hainsworth 3.00 8.00
265 Dickie Moore 1.50 4.00
266 Jacques Laperriere 3.00 8.00
267 Michel Larocque 1.25 3.00
268 Serge Savard 3.00 8.00
269 Charlie Hodge 1.50 4.00
270 Lorne Worsley 1.50 4.00
271 Patrick Roy 6.00 15.00
272 Larry Robinson 2.00 5.00
273 Jacques Plante 3.00 8.00
274 Doug Harvey 2.00 5.00
275 Jean Beliveau 3.00 8.00
276 Bernard Geoffrion 1.25 3.00
277 Howie Morenz 1.25 3.00
278 Maurice Richard 4.00 10.00
279 Guy Lafleur 4.00 10.00
280 Dickie Moore 1.50 4.00
281 Yvan Cournoyer 2.50 6.00
282 Henri Richard 2.50 6.00
283 Serge Savard 3.00 8.00
284 Larry Robinson 2.00 5.00
285 Ken Dryden 3.00 8.00
286 Bob Gainey 2.00 5.00
287 Georges Vezina 4.00 10.00
288 Howie Morenz 1.25 3.00
289 Jean Beliveau 3.00 8.00
290 Maurice Richard 4.00 10.00
291 Elmer Lach 3.00 8.00
292 Jacques Plante 3.00 8.00
293 Bernard Geoffrion 1.25 3.00
294 Henri Richard 2.50 6.00
295 Guy Lafleur 4.00 10.00
296 Bob Gainey 2.00 5.00
297 Patrick Roy 6.00 15.00
298 Guy Carbonneau 2.50 6.00
299 Maurice Richard 4.00 10.00
300 Saku Koivu 2.00 5.00

2008-09 Upper Deck Montreal Canadiens Centennial Parallel 100

*PARALLEL (1-200): 5X TO 12X BASIC CARDS
*PARALLEL (201-300): .8X TO 2X BASIC CARDS
STATED PRINT RUN 100 SERIAL #'d SETS

2008-09 Upper Deck Montreal Canadiens Centennial AKA Signings

STATED PRINT RUN 25 SER.#'d SETS
AKAAK Alex Kovalev 60.00 120.00
AKABG Bob Gainey 75.00 150.00
AKACN Chris Nilan
AKADD Dick Duff 40.00 80.00
AKADM Dickie Moore 60.00 120.00
AKAGC Guy Carbonneau 50.00 100.00
AKAGL Guy Lafleur 60.00 120.00
AKAHR Henri Richard 40.00 80.00
AKAJB Jean Beliveau 125.00 250.00
AKAJL Jacques Laperriere 40.00 80.00
AKALA Guy Lapointe 50.00 100.00
AKALE Jacques Lemaire
AKALR Larry Robinson 75.00 150.00
AKAMT Mario Tremblay 40.00 80.00
AKAPB Patrice Brisebois 40.00 80.00
AKAPR Patrick Roy 300.00 450.00
AKARH Rejean Houle 50.00 100.00
AKASS Serge Savard 125.00 200.00
AKAYC Yvan Cournoyer 75.00 150.00

2008-09 Upper Deck Montreal Canadiens Centennial Habs INKS

HABSAK Alex Kovalev 12.00 30.00
HABSAM Andrei Markov 10.00 25.00
HABSBB Benoit Brunet 8.00 20.00
HABSBG Bob Gainey 12.00 30.00
HABSCH Chris Chelios 15.00 40.00
HABSCL Claude Larose 8.00 20.00
HABSCN Chris Nilan 100.00 200.00
HABSCP Carey Price 25.00 60.00
HABSDD Dick Duff 12.00 30.00
HABSDJ Doug Jarvis 8.00 20.00
HABSDM Dickie Moore 10.00 25.00
HABSDR Doug Risebrough 10.00 25.00
HABSDS Denis Savard 12.00 30.00
HABSED Eric Desjardins 10.00 25.00
HABSFB Francis Bouillon 10.00 25.00
HABSGC Guy Carbonneau 15.00 40.00
HABSGG Gaston Gingras 8.00 20.00
HABSGL Guy Lafleur 25.00 60.00
HABSGT Gilles Tremblay 20.00 50.00
HABSHA Roman Hamrlik 8.00 20.00
HABSHI Christopher Higgins 8.00 20.00
HABSHR Henri Richard 15.00 40.00
HABSJA Jacques Lemaire
HABSJB Jean Beliveau 50.00 100.00
HABSJD Jean-Jacques Daigneault 10.00 25.00
HABSJL Jacques Laperriere 20.00 50.00
HABSJO John LeClair 12.00 30.00
HABSJT Jean-Guy Talbot 10.00 25.00
HABSKA Keith Acton 8.00 20.00
HABSKM Kirk Muller 10.00 25.00
HABSKO Andrei Kostitsyn 10.00 25.00
HABSKS Saku Koivu 12.00 30.00
HABSLA Guy Lapointe
HABSLE Claude Lemieux 10.00 25.00
HABSLO Lyle Odelein 12.00 30.00
HABSLR Larry Robinson
HABSMB Marcel Bonin 12.00 30.00
HABSMI Mike Komisarek 10.00 25.00
HABSMN Mark Napier 12.00 30.00
HABSMO Pierre Mondou 8.00 20.00
HABSMT Mario Tremblay 15.00 40.00
HABSMW Murray Wilson 12.00 30.00
HABSPB Patrice Brisebois 8.00 20.00
HABSPG Phil Goyette 10.00 25.00
HABSPI Pierre Bouchard 12.00 30.00
HABSPL Pierre Larouche 12.00 30.00
HABSPM Pete Mahovlich 15.00 40.00
HABSPR Patrick Roy 100.00 175.00
HABSPT Pierre Turgeon 12.00 30.00
HABSRH Rejean Houle 12.00 30.00
HABSRL Rod Langway 15.00 40.00
HABSRV Rogie Vachon 12.00 30.00
HABSSA Brian Savage 8.00 20.00
HABSSB Scotty Bowman 100.00 175.00
HABSSH Steve Shutt 12.00 30.00
HABSSK Brian Skrudland 8.00 20.00
HABSSQ Stephane Quintal 8.00 20.00
HABSSR Stephane Richer 10.00 25.00
HABSSS Serge Savard 20.00 50.00
HABSTP Tomas Plekanec 8.00 20.00
HABSVD Vincent Damphousse 10.00 25.00
HABSY Youppi MASCOT 15.00 40.00
HABSYC Yvan Cournoyer 15.00 40.00
HABSYI Youppi MASCOT 15.00 40.00
HABSYL Yvon Lambert 12.00 30.00

2008-09 Upper Deck Montreal Canadiens Centennial HOF Induction INKS

STATED PRINT RUN 66-106 SER.#'d SETS
HOFBB Butch Bouchard/66 25.00 60.00
HOFBG Bob Gainey/92 25.00 60.00
HOFBO Bert Olmstead/85 25.00 60.00
HOFDD Dick Duff/106 20.00 50.00
HOFDS Denis Savard/100 20.00 50.00
HOFEL Elmer Lach/66 40.00 80.00
HOFGL Guy Lapointe/93 25.00 60.00
HOFGU Guy Lafleur/88 50.00 100.00
HOFHR Henri Richard/79 40.00 80.00
HOFJB Jean Beliveau/72 50.00 100.00
HOFJL Jacques Lemaire/84 40.00 80.00
HOFLA Jacques Laperriere/87 25.00 60.00
HOFLR Larry Robinson/95 40.00 80.00
HOFPR Patrick Roy/106 125.00 250.00
HOFRL Rod Langway/102 20.00 50.00
HOFSA Serge Savard/86 40.00 80.00
HOFSB Scotty Bowman/91 50.00 100.00
HOFSS Steve Shutt/93 20.00 50.00
HOFYC Yvan Cournoyer/82 25.00 60.00

2008-09 Upper Deck Montreal Canadiens Centennial Immortal Cuts

ICAJ Aurele Joliat/1
ICBG Bernard Geoffrion/3
ICBR Billy Reay/1
ICDH Doug Harvey/2
ICFC Floyd Curry/2
ICFS Frank Selke/2
ICGM Gerry McNeil/5
ICGW Gump Worsley/3
ICJF John Ferguson/5
ICJP Jacques Plante/1
ICJT Jean-Claude Tremblay/1
ICKM Kenny Mosdell/4
ICMR Maurice Richard/5
ICSP Sam Pollock/1
ICTB Toe Blake/2
ICTJ Tom Johnson/4

2008-09 Upper Deck Montreal Canadiens Centennial Le Bleu Blanc Rouge Jerseys

LBBRAK Alex Kovalev 10.00 25.00
LBBRAL Alex Kovalev 10.00 25.00
LBBRAM Andrei Markov
LBBRBO Francis Bouillon
LBBRCH Christopher Higgins 6.00 15.00
LBBRCP Carey Price 25.00 60.00
LBBRFB Francis Bouillon 8.00 20.00
LBBRFR Francis Bouillon 8.00 20.00
LBBRGL Guy Lapointe 8.00 20.00
LBBRHA Roman Hamrlik 6.00 15.00
LBBRJB Jean Beliveau
LBBRKO Andrei Kostitsyn 8.00 20.00
LBBRKV Saku Koivu 10.00 25.00
LBBRMA Andrei Markov 8.00 20.00
LBBRMI Mike Komisarek 8.00 20.00
LBBRMK Mike Komisarek 8.00 20.00
LBBRPB Patrice Brisebois 6.00 15.00
LBBRPL Tomas Plekanec 6.00 15.00
LBBRRH Roman Hamrlik 6.00 15.00
LBBRSK Saku Koivu 10.00 25.00
LBBRTP Tomas Plekanec 6.00 15.00

2008-09 Upper Deck Montreal Canadiens Centennial Mini Banners

COMPLETE SET (24) 350.00 500.00
1 Stanley Cup 1915-16 10.00 25.00
2 Stanley Cup 1923-24 10.00 25.00
3 Stanley Cup 1929-30 10.00 25.00
4 Stanley Cup 1930-31 10.00 25.00
5 Stanley Cup 1943-44 10.00 25.00
6 Stanley Cup 1945-46 10.00 25.00
7 Stanley Cup 1952-53 10.00 25.00
8 Stanley Cup 1955-56 10.00 25.00
9 Stanley Cup 1956-57 10.00 25.00
10 Stanley Cup 1957-58 10.00 25.00
11 Stanley Cup 1958-59 10.00 25.00
12 Stanley Cup 1959-60 10.00 25.00
13 Stanley Cup 1964-65 10.00 25.00
14 Stanley Cup 1965-66 10.00 25.00
15 Stanley Cup 1967-68 10.00 25.00
16 Stanley Cup 1968-69 10.00 25.00
17 Stanley Cup 1970-71 10.00 25.00
18 Stanley Cup 1972-73 10.00 25.00
19 Stanley Cup 1975-76 10.00 25.00
20 Stanley Cup 1976-77 10.00 25.00
21 Stanley Cup 1977-78 10.00 25.00
22 Stanley Cup 1978-79 10.00 25.00
23 Stanley Cup 1985-86 10.00 25.00
24 Stanley Cup 1992-93 10.00 25.00

2008-09 Upper Deck Montreal Canadiens Centennial Signatures Dual

STATED PRINT RUN 50 SERIAL #'d SETS
DUALAA Andrei Kostitsyn
Alex Kovalev
DUALBB Butch Bouchard
Pierre Bouchard
DUALBH Francis Bouillon 15.00 40.00
Roman Hamrlik
DUALBL Jacques Laperriere 30.00 80.00
Patrice Brisebois
DUALBS Scotty Bowman 30.00 80.00
Serge Savard
DUALCC Guy Carbonneau
Chris Chelios
DUALCG Bob Gainey 25.00 60.00
Guy Carbonneau
DUALCN Claude Lemieux
Chris Nilan
DUALDL Dick Duff 20.00 50.00
Jacques Lemaire
DUALGA Guy Lapointe
Andrei Markov
DUALHL Rejean Houle 20.00 50.00
Yvon Lambert
DUALHM Kirk Muller 15.00 40.00
Christopher Higgins
DUALHR Rejean Houle 20.00 50.00
Doug Risebrough
DUALJG Bob Gainey 20.00 50.00
Doug Jarvis
DUALJR Doug Jarvis 15.00 40.00
Doug Risebrough
DUALKB Jean Beliveau 30.00 80.00
Saku Koivu
DUALKD Vincent Damphousse 20.00 50.00
Saku Koivu
DUALKP Mike Komisarek 60.00 150.00
Carey Price
DUALKS Serge Savard 30.00 80.00
Mike Komisarek
DUALLK Guy Lafleur 40.00 100.00
Alex Kovalev
DUALLN Pierre Larouche 20.00 50.00
Mark Napier
DUALLR Guy Lafleur 40.00 100.00
Stephane Richer
DUALMC Yvan Cournoyer 25.00 60.00
Dickie Moore
DUALMD Kirk Muller
Vincent Damphousse
DUALMH Dickie Moore 15.00 40.00
Christopher Higgins
DUALMP Andrei Markov
Carey Price
DUALMT Pierre Mondou 25.00 60.00
Mario Tremblay
DUALON Chris Nilan
Lyle Odelein
DUALPC Yvan Cournoyer 25.00 60.00
Tomas Plekanec
DUALQB Stephane Quintal
Patrice Brisebois
DUALRB Jean Beliveau
Henri Richard
DUALRH Larry Robinson 20.00 50.00
Roman Hamrlik
DUALRL Henri Richard 50.00 100.00
Elmer Lach
DUALTL Mario Tremblay 30.00 80.00
Jacques Lemaire

2008-09 Upper Deck Montreal Canadiens Centennial Signatures Triple

STATED PRINT RUN 15 SERIAL #'d SETS
NOT PRICED DUE TO SCARCITY
TRIOBGK Butch Bouchard
Bob Gainey
Saku Koivu
TRIOCJG Bob Gainey
Guy Carbonneau
Doug Jarvis
TRIOKHP Mike Komisarek
Christopher Higgins
Carey Price
TRIOKLM Pete Mahovlich
Jacques Lemaire
Saku Koivu
TRIOKPK Alex Kovalev
Andrei Kostitsyn
Tomas Plekanec
TRIOLMD Vincent Damphousse
Kirk Muller
John LeClair
TRIOLRT Yvon Lambert
Doug Risebrough
Mario Tremblay
TRIOMLS Serge Savard
Rod Langway
Andrei Markov
TRIORLC Patrick Roy
Claude Lemieux
Guy Carbonneau

2008-09 Upper Deck Montreal Canadiens Centennial Signatures Quad

STATED PRINT RUN 5 SERIAL #'d SETS
NOT PRICED DUE TO SCARCITY
QUADHKKP Carey Price
Andrei Kostitsyn
Mike Komisarek
Christopher Higgins
QUADKMCG Guy Carbonneau
Saku Koivu
Bob Gainey
Kirk Muller
QUADMKRS Larry Robinson
Serge Savard
Andrei Markov
Mike Komisarek
QUADRBBC Henri Richard
Jean Beliveau
Butch Bouchard
Yvan Cournoyer

1998-99 Upper Deck MVP

The 1998-99 new Upper Deck MVP set was issued in one series totaling 220 cards and distributed in ten-card packs with a suggested retail price of $1.59. The fronts feature color action player photos printed on internally die-cut, double laminated cards with player information on the backs.

COMPLETE SET (220) 15.00 30.00
1 Paul Kariya .10 .30
2 Teemu Selanne .10 .30
3 Tomas Sandstrom .05 .15
4 Johan Davidsson .05 .15
5 Mike Crowley RC .05 .15
6 Guy Hebert .08 .25
7 Marty McInnis .05 .15
8 Steve Rucchin .05 .15
9 Ray Bourque .20 .50
10 Sergei Samsonov .08 .25
11 Cameron Mann .05 .15
12 Joe Thornton .20 .50
13 Jason Allison .05 .15
14 Byron Dafoe .08 .25
15 Kyle McLaren .05 .15
16 Dimitri Khristich .05 .15
17 Hal Gill .05 .15
18 Anson Carter .08 .25
19 Miroslav Satan .08 .25
20 Brian Holzinger .05 .15
21 Dominik Hasek .25 .60
22 Matthew Barnaby .05 .15
23 Erik Rasmussen .05 .15
24 Geoff Sanderson .08 .25
25 Michal Grosek .05 .15
26 Michael Peca .08 .25
27 Rico Fata .05 .15
28 Derek Morris .05 .15
29 Phil Housley .05 .15
30 Valeri Bure .05 .15
31 Ed Ward .05 .15
32 Jean-Sebastien Giguere .08 .25
33 Jeff Shantz .05 .15
34 Jarome Iginla .15 .40
35 Ron Francis .08 .25
36 Trevor Kidd .08 .25
37 Keith Primeau .05 .15
38 Sami Kapanen .05 .15
39 Martin Gelinas .05 .15
40 Jeff O'Neill .05 .15
41 Gary Roberts .05 .15
42 Jocelyn Thibault .08 .25
43 Doug Gilmour .08 .25
44 Chris Chelios .10 .30
45 Tony Amonte .08 .25
46 Bob Probert .05 .15
47 Daniel Cleary .05 .15
48 Eric Daze .08 .25
49 Mike Maneluk RC .05 .15
50 Remi Royer RC .05 .15
51 Peter Forsberg .30 .75
52 Patrick Roy .60 1.50
53 Joe Sakic .25 .60
54 Chris Drury .08 .25
55 Milan Hejduk RC .60 1.50
56 Greg DeVries .05 .15
57 Theo Fleury .05 .15
58 Adam Deadmarsh .05 .15
59 Brett Hull .15 .40
60 Ed Belfour .10 .30
61 Mike Modano .20 .50
62 Darryl Sydor .05 .15
63 Joe Nieuwendyk .08 .25
64 Grant Marshall .05 .15
65 Sergei Zubov .05 .15
66 Derian Hatcher .05 .15
67 Jere Lehtinen .08 .25
68 Sergei Fedorov .20 .50
69 Steve Yzerman .60 1.50
70 Nicklas Lidstrom .10 .30
71 Chris Osgood .08 .25
72 Brendan Shanahan .10 .30
73 Darren McCarty .05 .15
74 Tomas Holmstrom .05 .15
75 Norm Maracle RC .20 .50
76 Doug Brown .05 .15
77 Doug Weight .08 .25
78 Janne Niinimaa .05 .15
79 Tom Poti .05 .15
80 Bill Guerin .08 .25
81 Mike Grier .05 .15
82 Ryan Smyth .08 .25
83 Roman Hamrlik .05 .15
84 Kevin Brown .05 .15
85 Pavel Bure .10 .30
86 Jaroslav Spacek .05 .15
87 Rob Niedermayer .05 .15
88 Robert Svehla .05 .15
89 Ray Whitney .05 .15
90 Peter Worrell RC .15 .40
91 Mark Parrish RC .08 .25
92 Oleg Kvasha RC .10 .30
93 Steve Duchesne .08 .25
94 Rob Blake .08 .25
95 Olli Jokinen .08 .25
96 Donald Audette .05 .15
97 Luc Robitaille .08 .25
98 Josh Green .08 .25
99 Philippe Boucher .05 .15
100 Matt Johnson .05 .15
101 Vincent Damphousse .05 .15
102 Dainius Zubrus .05 .15
103 Terry Ryan .05 .15
104 Saku Koivu .10 .30
105 Brett Clark RC .05 .15
106 Dave Morissette RC .05 .15
107 Eric Weinrich .05 .15
108 Brian Savage .05 .15
109 Shayne Corson .05 .15
110 Mike Dunham .08 .25
111 Greg Johnson .05 .15
112 Cliff Ronning .05 .15
113 Andrew Brunette .08 .25
114 Sergei Krivokrasov .05 .15
115 Sebastien Bordeleau .05 .15
116 Scott Stevens .08 .25
117 Martin Brodeur .30 .75
118 Brendan Morrison .08 .25
119 Patrik Elias .08 .25
120 Scott Niedermayer .05 .15
121 Bobby Holik .05 .15
122 Jason Arnott .05 .15
123 Jay Pandolfo .05 .15
124 Eric Brewer .05 .15
125 Zigmund Palffy .08 .25
126 Felix Potvin .10 .30
127 Robert Reichel .05 .15
128 Mike Watt .05 .15
129 Tommy Salo .08 .25
130 Kenny Jonsson .05 .15
131 Trevor Linden .08 .25
132 Wayne Gretzky .75 2.00
133 Brian Leetch .10 .30
134 Manny Malhotra .08 .25
135 Mike Richter .10 .30
136 Mike Knuble .05 .15
137 Niklas Sundstrom .05 .15
138 Todd Harvey .05 .15
139 Alexei Yashin .05 .15
140 Damian Rhodes .08 .25
141 Daniel Alfredsson .08 .25
142 Magnus Arvedson .05 .15
143 Shawn McEachern .05 .15
144 Chris Phillips .05 .15
145 Vaclav Prospal .05 .15
146 Wade Redden .05 .15
147 Eric Lindros .10 .30
148 John LeClair .10 .30
149 John Vanbiesbrouck .08 .25
150 Keith Jones .08 .25
151 Colin Forbes .05 .15
152 Mark Recchi .08 .25
153 Dan McGillis .05 .15
154 Eric Desjardins .08 .25
155 Rod Brind'Amour .08 .25
156 Keith Tkachuk .10 .30
157 Daniel Briere .05 .15
158 Nikolai Khabibulin .08 .25
159 Brad Isbister .05 .15
160 Jeremy Roenick .15 .40
161 Oleg Tverdovsky .05 .15
162 Rick Tocchet .08 .25
163 Jaromir Jagr .20 .50
164 Tom Barrasso .08 .25
165 Alexei Morozov .08 .25
166 Robert Dome .05 .15
167 Stu Barnes .05 .15
168 Martin Straka .05 .15
169 German Titov .10 .30
170 Patrick Marleau .08 .25
171 Andrei Zyuzin .05 .15
172 Marco Sturm .08 .25
173 Owen Nolan .08 .25
174 Jeff Friesen .05 .15
175 Bob Rouse .05 .15
176 Mike Vernon .08 .25
177 Mike Ricci .08 .25
178 Marty Reasoner .08 .25
179 Al MacInnis .08 .25
180 Chris Pronger .08 .25
181 Pierre Turgeon .08 .25
182 Michal Handzus RC .08 .25
183 Jim Campbell .05 .15
184 Tony Twist .05 .15
185 Pavol Demitra .08 .25
186 Daren Puppa .08 .25
187 Vincent Lecavalier .30 .75
188 Bill Ranford .08 .25
189 Alexandre Daigle .05 .15
190 Wendel Clark .08 .25
191 Rob Zamuner .05 .15
192 Chris Gratton .05 .15
193 Fredrik Modin .05 .15
194 Curtis Joseph .10 .30
195 Mats Sundin .10 .30
196 Steve Thomas .05 .15
197 Tomas Kaberle RC .15 .40
198 Alyn McCauley .05 .15
199 Mike Johnson .08 .25
200 Bryan Berard .05 .15
201 Mark Messier .10 .30
202 Jason Strudwick RC .05 .15
203 Mattias Ohlund .08 .25
204 Alexander Mogilny .08 .25
205 Bill Muckalt RC .05 .15
206 Ed Jovanovski .08 .25
207 Josh Holden .05 .15
208 Peter Schaefer .05 .15
209 Peter Bondra .08 .25
210 Olaf Kolzig .08 .25
211 Sergei Gonchar .05 .15
212 Adam Oates .08 .25
213 Brian Bellows .05 .15
214 Matt Herr RC .05 .15
215 Richard Zednik .05 .15
216 Joe Juneau .05 .15
217 Jaroslav Svejkovski .05 .15
218 Wayne Gretzky CL .40 1.00
219 Wayne Gretzky CL .40 1.00
220 Wayne Gretzky CL .40 1.00
NNO Wayne Gretzky Retire/99 150.00 400.00

1998-99 Upper Deck MVP Gold Script

Randomly inserted in hobby packs only, this 220-card set is a gold foil hobby parallel version of the base set. Only 100 sequentially numbered sets were produced.

*VETS: 20X TO 50X BASIC CARDS
*ROOKIES: 10X TO 25X BASIC CARDS

1998-99 Upper Deck MVP Silver Script

Randomly inserted into packs at the rate of 1:2, this 220-card set is a silver foil parallel version of the base set.

COMPLETE SET (220) 75.00 150.00
*VETS: .8X TO 2X BASIC CARDS
*ROOKIES: .5X TO 1.2X BASIC CARDS

1998-99 Upper Deck MVP Super Script

Randomly inserted into hobby packs only, this 220-card set is a hobby limited edition, holographic foil parallel version of the base set. Only 25 sequentially numbered sets were produced.

*VETS: 40X TO 100X BASIC CARDS
*ROOKIES: 12X TO 30X BASIC CARDS

1998-99 Upper Deck MVP Dynamics

Randomly inserted into packs at a ratio of 1:28, this set commemorates the brilliant career of Wayne Gretzky.

COMPLETE SET (15) 75.00 150.00
COMMON GRETZKY (D1-D15) 5.00 12.00

1998-99 Upper Deck MVP Game Souvenirs

Randomly inserted in hobby packs only at the rate of 1:144, this 10-card set features color action player photos with actual pieces of game used memorabilia right on the cards.

BH Brett Hull 12.50 30.00
BS Brendan Shanahan 8.00 20.00
EL Eric Lindros 8.00 20.00
JL John LeClair 8.00 20.00
MM Mike Modano 15.00 40.00
PR Patrick Roy 25.00 60.00
RB Ray Bourque 15.00 40.00
SF Sergei Fedorov 20.00 50.00
SS Sergei Samsonov 8.00 20.00
SY Steve Yzerman 25.00 60.00
VL Vincent Lecavalier 12.50 30.00
WG Wayne Gretzky 40.00 100.00
SYA S.Yzerman AU/19 500.00 1000.00
VLA V.Lecavalier AU/14 250.00 500.00

1998-99 Upper Deck MVP OT Heroes

COMPLETE SET (15) 20.00 40.00
STATED ODDS 1:9
OT1 Steve Yzerman 4.00 10.00
OT2 Patrick Roy 4.00 10.00
OT3 Jaromir Jagr 1.25 3.00
OT4 Ray Bourque 1.25 3.00
OT5 Wayne Gretzky 5.00 12.00
OT6 Sergei Samsonov .60 1.50
OT7 Dominik Hasek 1.50 4.00
OT8 Peter Forsberg 2.00 5.00
OT9 Paul Kariya .75 2.00
OT10 Eric Lindros .75 2.00
OT11 Pavel Bure .75 2.00
OT12 Keith Tkachuk .75 2.00
OT13 Brendan Shanahan .75 2.00
OT14 John LeClair .75 2.00
OT15 Joe Sakic 1.50 4.00

1998-99 Upper Deck MVP Power Game

COMPLETE SET (15) 12.00 25.00
STATED ODDS 1:9
PG1 Brendan Shanahan .75 2.00
PG2 Keith Tkachuk .75 2.00
PG3 Eric Lindros .75 2.00
PG4 Mike Modano 1.25 3.00
PG5 Vincent Lecavalier 2.00 5.00
PG6 John LeClair .75 2.00
PG7 Mark Messier .75 2.00
PG8 Mats Sundin .75 2.00
PG9 Peter Forsberg 2.00 5.00
PG10 Jaromir Jagr 1.25 3.00
PG11 Keith Primeau .40 1.00
PG12 Mark Parrish .60 1.50
PG13 Patrick Marleau .40 1.00
PG14 Bill Guerin .60 1.50
PG15 Jeremy Roenick 1.00 2.50

1998-99 Upper Deck MVP ProSign

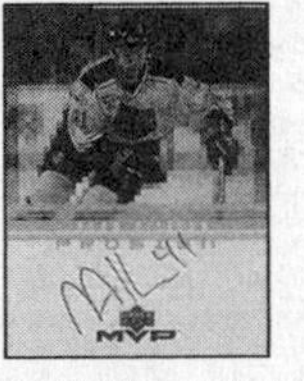

Randomly inserted in retail packs only at the rate of 1:216, this 23-card set features color action photos of the NHL's superstars with the player's autograph in the wide bottom margin. These cards were among this years toughest autograph pulls.

AM Alyn McCauley 4.00 10.00
BB Brian Bellows 4.00 10.00
BM Brendan Morrison 4.00 10.00
CD Chris Drury 5.00 12.00
DN Dmitri Nabokov 4.00 10.00
DW Doug Weight 5.00 12.00
EB Eric Brewer 4.00 10.00
ER Erik Rasmussen 4.00 10.00
JA Jason Allison 4.00 10.00
JI Jarome Iginla 12.50 30.00
JT Jose Theodore 12.50 30.00
MD Mike Dunham 4.00 10.00
MJ Mike Johnson 4.00 10.00
MM Manny Malhotra 4.00 10.00
MP Mark Parrish 4.00 10.00
OT Oleg Tverdovsky 4.00 10.00
RF Rico Fata 4.00 10.00
RN Rob Niedermayer 4.00 10.00
SY Steve Yzerman 40.00 100.00
VL Vincent Lecavalier 10.00 25.00
WG Wayne Gretzky 125.00 300.00
WR Wade Redden 4.00 10.00
JAR Jason Arnott 4.00 10.00

1998-99 Upper Deck MVP Snipers

COMPLETE SET (12) 10.00 20.00
STATED ODDS 1:6
S1 Vincent Lecavalier 1.00 2.50
S2 Wayne Gretzky 2.50 6.00
S3 Sergei Samsonov .30 .75
S4 Teemu Selanne .40 1.00
S5 Peter Forsberg 1.00 2.50
S6 Paul Kariya .40 1.00
S7 Eric Lindros .40 1.00
S8 Pavel Bure .40 1.00
S9 Peter Bondra .30 .75
S10 Joe Sakic .75 2.00
S11 Steve Yzerman 2.00 5.00
S12 Sergei Fedorov .60 1.50

1998-99 Upper Deck MVP Special Forces

COMPLETE SET (15) 30.00 60.00
STATED ODDS 1:14
F1 Brett Hull 1.25 3.00
F2 Sergei Samsonov .75 2.00
F3 Vincent Lecavalier 2.50 6.00
F4 Dominik Hasek 2.00 5.00
F5 Eric Lindros 1.00 2.50
F6 Paul Kariya 1.00 2.50
F7 Steve Yzerman 5.00 12.00
F8 Brendan Shanahan 1.00 2.50
F9 Martin Brodeur 2.50 6.00
F10 Teemu Selanne 1.00 2.50
F11 Jaromir Jagr 1.50 4.00
F12 Wayne Gretzky 6.00 15.00
F13 Patrick Roy 5.00 12.00
F14 Peter Forsberg 2.50 6.00
F15 Joe Sakic 2.00 5.00

1999-00 Upper Deck MVP

Released as a 220-card set, Upper Deck MVP featured white bordered cards with enhanced bronze foil stamping. The base set is composed of 218 regular cards and two Wayne Gretzky checklist cards. Also released with this set is a special Wayne Gretzky autographed Game Jersey card limited to just 40. MVP was packaged in 28-pack boxes of 10 card packs and carried a suggested retail price of $1.59.

COMPLETE SET (220)	12.50	25.00
1 Wayne Gretzky	.75	2.00
2 Damian Rhodes	.08	.25
3 Jody Hull	.02	.10
4 Paul Kariya	.10	.30
5 Teemu Selanne	.10	.30
6 Guy Hebert	.08	.25
7 Matt Cullen	.02	.10
8 Steve Rucchin	.08	.25
9 Oleg Tverdovsky	.02	.10
10 Johan Davidsson	.02	.10
11 Ray Bourque	.20	.50
12 Sergei Samsonov	.08	.25
13 Joe Thornton	.20	.50
14 Anson Carter	.08	.25
15 Jason Allison	.02	.10
16 Kyle McLaren	.02	.10
17 Byron Dafoe	.08	.25
18 Shawn Bates	.02	.10
19 Jonathan Girard	.02	.10
20 Hal Gill	.02	.10
21 Dominik Hasek	.25	.60
22 Joe Juneau	.08	.25
23 Michal Peca	.08	.25
24 Cory Sarich	.02	.10
25 Martin Biron	.08	.25
26 Miroslav Satan	.08	.25
27 Dixon Ward	.02	.10
28 Michal Grosek	.02	.10
29 Valeri Bure	.02	.10
30 Phil Housley	.08	.25
31 Derek Morris	.02	.10
32 Jarome Iginla	.15	.40
33 Wade Belak	.02	.10
34 Rico Fata	.02	.10
35 Jean-Sebastien Giguere	.08	.25
36 Rene Corbet	.02	.10
37 Arturs Irbe	.08	.25
38 Keith Primeau	.02	.10
39 Sami Kapanen	.02	.10
40 Ron Francis	.08	.25
41 Shane Willis	.08	.25
42 Gary Roberts	.02	.10
43 Bates Battaglia	.02	.10
44 J-P Dumont	.08	.25
45 Ty Jones	.02	.10
46 Tony Amonte	.08	.25
47 Jocelyn Thibault	.08	.25
48 Doug Gilmour	.08	.25
49 Remi Royer	.02	.10
50 Alexei Zhamnov	.02	.10
51 Joe Sakic	.30	.75
52 Peter Forsberg	.30	.75
53 Theo Fleury	.02	.10
54 Chris Drury	.08	.25
55 Patrick Roy	.60	1.50
56 Sandis Ozolinsh	.02	.10
57 Adam Deadmarsh	.02	.10
58 Milan Hejduk	.10	.30
59 Mike Modano	.20	.50
60 Brett Hull	.15	.40
61 Darryl Sydor	.02	.10
62 Ed Belfour	.10	.30
63 Jere Lehtinen	.08	.25
64 Jamie Langenbrunner	.02	.10
65 Derian Hatcher	.02	.10
66 Jon Sim RC	.02	.10
67 Joe Nieuwendyk	.08	.25
68 Sergei Fedorov	.20	.50
69 Steve Yzerman	.60	1.50
70 Brendan Shanahan	.10	.30
71 Chris Osgood	.08	.25
72 Nicklas Lidstrom	.10	.30
73 Chris Chelios	.10	.30
74 Igor Larionov	.02	.10
75 Tomas Holmstrom	.02	.10
76 Vyacheslav Kozlov	.08	.25
77 Josef Beranek	.02	.10
78 Bill Guerin	.08	.25
79 Doug Weight	.08	.25
80 Tommy Salo	.08	.25
81 Mike Grier	.08	.25
82 Tom Poti	.02	.10
83 Fredrik Lindquist	.02	.10
84 Mark Parrish	.02	.10
85 Pavel Bure	.10	.30
86 Viktor Kozlov	.02	.10
87 Ray Whitney	.08	.25
88 Rob Niedermayer	.08	.25
89 Oleg Kvasha	.08	.25
90 Scott Mellanby	.08	.25
91 Chris Allen RC	.08	.25
92 Rob Blake	.08	.25
93 Pavel Rosa	.02	.10
94 Jamie Storr	.08	.25
95 Donald Audette	.02	.10
96 Luc Robitaille	.08	.25
97 Jozef Stumpel	.08	.25
98 Vladimir Tsyplakov	.02	.10
99 Manny Legace	.15	.40
100 Saku Koivu	.10	.30
101 Martin Rucinsky	.02	.10
102 Vladimir Malakhov	.02	.10
103 Eric Weinrich	.02	.10
104 Jeff Hackett	.08	.25
105 Arron Asham	.02	.10
106 Trevor Linden	.08	.25
107 Brian Savage	.02	.10
108 Cliff Ronning	.08	.25
109 Sergei Krivokrasov	.02	.10
110 David Legwand	.08	.25
111 Kimmo Timonen	.02	.10
112 Mark Mowers RC	.02	.10
113 Mike Dunham	.08	.25
114 Scott Stevens	.08	.25
115 Martin Brodeur	.30	.75
116 Patrik Elias	.08	.25
117 Brendan Morrison	.08	.25
118 Scott Niedermayer	.02	.10
119 Petr Sykora	.02	.10
120 Jason Arnott	.02	.10
121 Vadim Sharifijanov	.02	.10
122 John Madden RC	.25	.60
123 Mariusz Czerkawski	.02	.10
124 Felix Potvin	.10	.30
125 Mike Watt	.02	.10
126 Eric Brewer	.08	.25
127 Dmitri Nabokov	.02	.10
128 Claude Lapointe	.02	.10
129 Kenny Jonsson	.02	.10
130 Zdeno Chara	.02	.10
131 Wayne Gretzky	.75	2.00
132 Brian Leetch	.10	.30
133 Mike Richter	.10	.30
134 Petr Nedved	.08	.25
135 Adam Graves	.02	.10
136 Manny Malhotra	.08	.25
137 John MacLean	.02	.10
138 Alexei Yashin	.02	.10
139 Magnus Arvedson	.02	.10
140 Daniel Alfredsson	.08	.25
141 Wade Redden	.02	.10
142 Ron Tugnutt	.08	.25
143 Sami Salo	.08	.25
144 Marian Hossa	.10	.30
145 Shawn McEachern	.02	.10
146 Eric Lindros	.10	.30
147 Jean-Marc Pelletier	.08	.25
148 John LeClair	.10	.30
149 Rod Brind'Amour	.08	.25
150 Mark Recchi	.08	.25
151 Keith Jones	.02	.10
152 Eric Desjardins	.08	.25
153 Ryan Bast RC	.02	.10
154 Brian Wesenberg RC	.02	.10
155 John Vanbiesbrouck	.08	.25
156 Jeremy Roenick	.15	.40
157 Robert Reichel	.02	.10
158 Keith Tkachuk	.10	.30
159 Rick Tocchet	.08	.25
160 Robert Esche RC	.10	.30
161 Nikolai Khabibulin	.08	.25
162 Daniel Briere	.02	.10
163 Greg Adams	.02	.10
164 Trevor Letowski	.02	.10
165 Jaromir Jagr	.20	.50
166 Martin Straka	.02	.10
167 German Titov	.02	.10
168 Tom Barrasso	.08	.25
169 Jan Hrdina	.02	.10
170 Alexei Kovalev	.02	.10
171 Matthew Barnaby	.08	.25
172 Jean-Sebastien Aubin	.08	.25
173 Vincent Damphousse	.02	.10
174 Owen Nolan	.02	.10
175 Jeff Friesen	.02	.10
176 Patrick Marleau	.08	.25
177 Marco Sturm	.08	.25
178 Mike Ricci	.08	.25
179 Gary Suter	.02	.10
180 Scott Hannan	.02	.10
181 Andy Sutton	.02	.10
182 Pavol Demitra	.08	.25
183 Al MacInnis	.08	.25
184 Pierre Turgeon	.08	.25
185 Grant Fuhr	.08	.25
186 Chris Pronger	.08	.25
187 Lubos Bartecko	.02	.10
188 Jochen Hecht RC	.30	.75
189 Michal Handzus	.08	.25
190 Vincent Lecavalier	.10	.30
191 Paul Mara	.08	.25
192 Darcy Tucker	.02	.10
193 Chris Gratton	.02	.10
194 Pavel Kubina	.02	.10
195 Kevin Hodson	.08	.25
196 Mats Sundin	.10	.30
197 Daniil Markov	.02	.10
198 Curtis Joseph	.10	.30
199 Sergei Berezin	.08	.25
200 Steve Thomas	.02	.10
201 Bryan Berard	.08	.25
202 Mike Johnson	.02	.10
203 Tomas Kaberle	.02	.10
204 Mark Messier	.10	.30
205 Bill Muckalt	.08	.25
206 Markus Naslund	.10	.30
207 Mattias Ohlund	.02	.10
208 Kevin Weekes	.08	.25
209 Ed Jovanovski	.02	.10
210 Alexander Mogilny	.08	.25
211 Josh Holden	.08	.25
212 Richard Zednik	.02	.10
213 Jaroslav Svejkovsky	.02	.10
214 Adam Oates	.08	.25
215 Peter Bondra	.08	.25
216 Sergei Gonchar	.02	.10
217 Olaf Kolzig	.08	.25
218 Jan Bulis	.02	.10
219 Wayne Gretzky CL	.40	1.00
220 Wayne Gretzky CL	.40	1.00

1999-00 Upper Deck MVP Gold Script

Randomly inserted in packs, this 220-card set parallels the base MVP set on cards enhanced with gold foil highlights and feature a foil facsimile signature of the respective player. For several players, signatures were not available, therefore these cards appear with just the gold foil highlights.

*GOLD SCRIPT: 30X TO 80X BASIC CARDS

1 Wayne Gretzky	30.00	80.00
55 Patrick Roy	25.00	60.00
69 Steve Yzerman	25.00	60.00
131 Wayne Gretzky	30.00	80.00
219 Wayne Gretzky CL	30.00	80.00
220 Wayne Gretzky CL	30.00	80.00

1999-00 Upper Deck MVP Silver Script

Randomly inserted in packs, this 220-card set parallels the base MVP set on cards enhanced with silver foil highlights and feature a facsimile signature of the respective player. For several players, signatures were not available, therefore these cards appear with just the silver foil highlights.

COMPLETE SET (220)	75.00	150.00

*SILVER SCRIPT: 1.2X TO 3X BASIC CARDS

1999-00 Upper Deck MVP Super Script

Randomly inserted in packs, this 220-card set parallels the base MVP set on cards enhanced with holographic foil highlights and feature a holographic foil facsimile signature of the respective player. For several players, signatures were not available, therefore these cards appear with just the holographic foil highlights. Each Super Script card is sequentially numbered to 25.

*SUPER SCRIPT: 50X TO 120X BASIC CARDS

1999-00 Upper Deck MVP 21st Century NHL

COMPLETE SET (10)	5.00	10.00
STATED ODDS 1:13		
1 David Legwand	.30	.75
2 Sergei Samsonov	.30	.75
3 Paul Kariya	.40	1.00
4 Peter Forsberg	1.00	2.50
5 Vincent Lecavalier	.40	1.00
6 Jaromir Jagr	.60	1.50
7 Paul Mara	.30	.75
8 Marian Hossa	.40	1.00
9 Pavel Bure	.50	1.25
10 Chris Drury	.30	.75

1999-00 Upper Deck MVP 90's Snapshots

Randomly inserted in packs at the rate of 1:27, this 10-card set features multiple snapshots on the card front that highlight each player's accomplishments during the '90's.

COMPLETE SET (10)	15.00	40.00
S1 Wayne Gretzky	6.00	15.00
S2 Jaromir Jagr	1.50	4.00
S3 Patrick Roy	4.00	10.00
S4 Eric Lindros	1.50	4.00
S5 Brendan Shanahan	1.50	4.00
S6 Peter Forsberg	2.00	5.00
S7 Steve Yzerman	3.00	8.00
S8 Teemu Selanne	1.50	4.00
S9 Dominik Hasek	2.00	5.00
S10 Pavel Bure	1.25	3.00

1999-00 Upper Deck MVP Draft Report

Randomly inserted in packs at the rate of 1:6, this 10-card set showcases some of the hottest new stars from the 1999 amateur draft. Each card features a top pick on the card front and a brief report about him and three other draftees for the same team on the card back.

COMPLETE SET (10)	2.50	6.00
DR1 Damian Rhodes	.20	.50
DR2 Bill Muckalt	.20	.50
DR3 Wayne Gretzky	1.50	4.00
DR4 Eric Brewer	.20	.50
DR5 David Legwand	.30	.75
DR6 Peter Bondra	.40	1.00
DR7 Rico Fata	.20	.50
DR8 Mark Parrish	.20	.50
DR9 Tom Poti	.20	.50
DR10 Jeff Friesen	.20	.50

1999-00 Upper Deck MVP Draw Your Own Trading Card

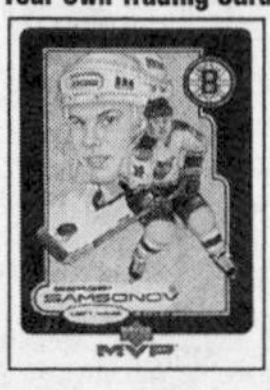

Randomly inserted in packs, this 30-card set features the winning artwork from Upper Deck's Draw Your Own Trading Card contest.

COMPLETE SET (45)	15.00	30.00
W1 Joey Kocur	.08	.25
W2 Mike Richter	.10	.30
W3 Wayne Gretzky	1.25	3.00
W4 Dominik Hasek	.40	1.00
W5 Steve Yzerman	1.00	2.50
W6 Ray Bourque	.30	.75
W7 Arturs Irbe	.08	.25
W8 Wayne Gretzky	1.25	3.00
W9 Martin Brodeur	.50	1.25
W10 Patrick Roy	1.00	2.50
W11 Wayne Gretzky	1.25	3.00
W12 Paul Kariya	.20	.50
W13 Wayne Gretzky	1.25	3.00
W14 Jaromir Jagr	.30	.75
W15 Wayne Gretzky	1.25	3.00
W16 Felix Potvin	.10	.30
W17 Marc Denis	.08	.25
W18 Dominik Hasek	.40	1.00
W19 Patrick Roy	.75	2.00
W20 Robert Svehla	.08	.25
W21 Joe Juneau	.08	.25
W22 Mattias Ohlund	.08	.25
W23 Kirk Muller	.08	.25
W24 Peter Forsberg	.50	1.25
W25 Stu Barnes	.08	.25
W26 Nikolai Khabibulin	.08	.25
W27 Sergei Samsonov	.08	.25
W28 Jeremy Roenick	.15	.40
W29 Wayne Gretzky	1.25	3.00
W30 Sergei Fedorov	.40	1.00
W31 Wayne Gretzky	.75	2.00
W32 Wayne Gretzky	.75	2.00
W33 Wayne Gretzky	.75	2.00
W34 Wayne Gretzky	.75	2.00
W35 Wayne Gretzky	.75	2.00
W36 Wayne Gretzky	.75	2.00
W37 Wayne Gretzky	.75	2.00
W38 Wayne Gretzky	.75	2.00
W39 Wayne Gretzky	.75	2.00
W40 Wayne Gretzky	.75	2.00
W41 Wayne Gretzky	.75	2.00
W42 Wayne Gretzky	.75	2.00
W43 Wayne Gretzky	.75	2.00
W44 Wayne Gretzky	.75	2.00
W45 Wayne Gretzky	.75	2.00

1999-00 Upper Deck MVP Game-Used Souvenirs

Randomly inserted in packs at the rate of 1:130, this 30-card set features swatches from game used pucks or game used sticks coupled with an image of the featured player. Autographed cards of Wayne Gretzky and Pavel Bure were limited to a print run of 25.

GU1 Paul Kariya P	6.00	15.00
GU2 Teemu Selanne P	6.00	15.00
GU3 Brett Hull P	8.00	20.00
GU4 Pavel Bure P	6.00	15.00
GU5 Marian Hossa P	6.00	15.00
GU6 Wayne Gretzky P	25.00	60.00
GU7 Brendan Shanahan P	6.00	15.00
GU8 Sergei Samsonov P	6.00	15.00
GU9 Eric Lindros P	6.00	15.00
GU10 Keith Tkachuk P	6.00	15.00
GU11 Steve Yzerman P	20.00	50.00
GU12 Jaromir Jagr P	10.00	25.00
GU13 Alexei Yashin P	6.00	15.00
GU14 Curtis Joseph P	6.00	15.00
GU15 Paul Kariya S	8.00	20.00
GU16 Teemu Selanne S	8.00	20.00
GU17 Dominik Hasek S	15.00	40.00
GU18 Pavel Bure S	8.00	20.00
GU19 Peter Forsberg S	15.00	40.00
GU20 Wayne Gretzky S	30.00	80.00
GU21 Brendan Shanahan S	8.00	20.00
GU22 Joe Sakic S	15.00	40.00
GU23 Eric Lindros S	8.00	20.00
GU24 Keith Tkachuk S	8.00	20.00
GU25 Jeremy Roenick S	10.00	25.00
GU26 Alexei Yashin S	8.00	20.00
GU27 Curtis Joseph S	8.00	20.00
GU28 Steve Yzerman S	25.00	60.00
GUS1 W.Gretzky AU/25	250.00	550.00
GUS2 P.Bure AU/25	125.00	250.00

1999-00 Upper Deck MVP Hands of Gold

COMPLETE SET (10)	12.00	25.00
STATED ODDS 1:9		
H1 Wayne Gretzky	2.50	6.00
H2 Brett Hull	.50	1.25
H3 Pavel Bure	.60	1.50
H4 Teemu Selanne	.60	1.50
H5 Sergei Samsonov	.30	.75
H6 Peter Forsberg	1.00	2.50
H7 Eric Lindros	.60	1.50
H8 Paul Kariya	.60	1.50
H9 Jaromir Jagr	.60	1.50
H10 Steve Yzerman	2.00	5.00
H11 Mike Modano	.60	1.50

1999-00 Upper Deck MVP Last Line

COMPLETE SET (10)	5.00	10.00
STATED ODDS 1:9		
LL1 Dominik Hasek	.75	2.00
LL2 Martin Brodeur	1.00	2.50
LL3 Patrick Roy	2.00	5.00
LL4 Byron Dafoe	.30	.75
LL5 Ed Belfour	.40	1.00
LL6 Curtis Joseph	.30	.75
LL7 John Vanbiesbrouck	.30	.75
LL8 Tom Barrasso	.30	.75
LL9 Chris Osgood	.30	.75
LL10 Nikolai Khabibulin	.30	.75

1999-00 Upper Deck MVP Legendary One

Randomly inserted in packs at the rate of 1:27, this 10-card set pays tribute to Wayne Gretzky and highlights some of the greatest moments of his career. Card backs carry an "LO" prefix.

COMPLETE SET (10)	30.00	60.00
COMMON GRETZKY (LO1-LO10)	3.00	8.00

1999-00 Upper Deck MVP ProSign

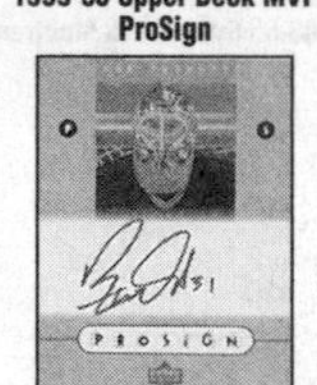

Randomly inserted in retail packs at the rate of 1:144, this 30-card set features authentic player autographs coupled with an action photo.

BH Brett Hull	12.00	30.00
BM Bill Muckalt	2.00	5.00
CD Chris Drury	5.00	12.00
DA Donald Audette	2.00	5.00
DM Derek Morris	2.00	5.00
GM Glen Murray	4.00	10.00
IL Igor Larionov	4.00	10.00
JF Jeff Friesen	4.00	10.00
JH Jeff Hackett	5.00	12.00
JR Jeremy Roenick	12.00	30.00
JT Joe Thornton	12.00	30.00
LR Luc Robitaille	8.00	20.00
MC Matt Cullen	2.00	5.00
PB Pavel Bure	8.00	20.00
PD Pavol Demitra	5.00	12.00
RB Ray Bourque	30.00	80.00
RT Ron Tugnutt	5.00	12.00
SG Sergei Gonchar	2.00	5.00
SK Sami Kapanen	2.00	5.00
SY Steve Yzerman	40.00	80.00
TF Theo Fleury	4.00	10.00
TK Tomas Kaberle	2.00	5.00
TL Trevor Linden	4.00	10.00
TP Tom Poti	2.00	5.00
WC Wendel Clark	4.00	10.00
WG Wayne Gretzky	125.00	250.00
JHR Jan Hrdina	2.00	5.00
RBR Rod Brind'Amour	5.00	12.00

1999-00 Upper Deck MVP Talent

Randomly inserted in packs at the rate of 1:13, this 10-card set identifies some of the most likely candidates for the 1999-00 Hart Trophy.

COMPLETE SET (10)	10.00	20.00
MVP1 Wayne Gretzky	2.50	6.00
MVP2 Paul Kariya	.75	2.00
MVP3 Dominik Hasek	.75	2.00
MVP4 Eric Lindros	.60	1.50
MVP5 Ray Bourque	.60	1.50
MVP6 Steve Yzerman	2.00	5.00
MVP7 Patrick Roy	2.00	5.00
MVP8 Jaromir Jagr	.75	2.00
MVP9 Martin Brodeur	1.25	3.00
MVP10 Mike Modano	.60	1.50

2000-01 Upper Deck MVP

Released in late September 2000, Upper Deck MVP features a 220-card base set comprised of 183 veteran player cards and 35 NHL Prospect cards. Base cards are white bordered and have copper foil highlights. MVP was packaged in 28-pack boxes with each pack containing 10 cards and carried a suggested retail price of $1.59.

COMPLETE SET (220)	12.50	25.00
1 Antti Aalto	.02	.10
2 Matt Cullen	.02	.10
3 Oleg Tverdovsky	.02	.10
4 Paul Kariya	.10	.30
5 Steve Rucchin	.02	.10
6 Teemu Selanne	.10	.30
7 Maxim Balmochnykh	.02	.10
8 Andrew Brunette	.08	.20
9 Damian Rhodes	.08	.20
10 Dean Sylvester	.02	.10
11 Donald Audette	.02	.10
12 Patrik Stefan	.02	.10
13 Ray Ferraro	.02	.10
14 Brian Rolston	.02	.10
15 Sergei Samsonov	.08	.20
16 Jason Allison	.08	.20
17 Joe Thornton	.20	.50
18 Kyle McLaren	.02	.10
19 Byron Dafoe	.08	.20
20 Hal Gill	.02	.10
21 Curtis Brown	.02	.10
22 Stu Barnes	.02	.10
23 Dominik Hasek	.25	.60
24 Doug Gilmour	.08	.20
25 Maxim Afinogenov	.02	.10
26 Michael Peca	.08	.20
27 Miroslav Satan	.08	.20
28 Chris Gratton	.02	.10
29 Derek Morris	.02	.10
30 Fred Brathwaite	.08	.20
31 Jarome Iginla	.15	.40
32 Marc Savard	.08	.20
33 Phil Housley	.08	.20
34 Valeri Bure	.08	.20
35 Arturs Irbe	.08	.20
36 Dave Tanabe	.08	.20
37 Jeff O'Neill	.02	.10
38 Rod Brind'Amour	.08	.20
39 Ron Francis	.08	.20
40 Sami Kapanen	.08	.20
41 Alexei Zhamnov	.02	.10
42 Eric Daze	.08	.20
43 Jocelyn Thibault	.08	.20
44 Michael Nylander	.02	.10
45 Steve Sullivan	.02	.10
46 Tony Amonte	.08	.20
47 Chris Drury	.08	.20
48 Joe Sakic	.30	.75
49 Milan Hejduk	.10	.30
50 Patrick Roy	.60	1.50
51 Peter Forsberg	.30	.75
52 Ray Bourque	.25	.60
53 Adam Deadmarsh	.02	.10
54 Alex Tanguay	.08	.20
55 Marc Denis	.08	.20
56 Brenden Morrow	.08	.20
57 Brett Hull	.15	.40
58 Derian Hatcher	.02	.10
59 Ed Belfour	.10	.30
60 Jamie Langenbrunner	.02	.10
61 Mike Modano	.20	.50
62 Sergei Zubov	.02	.10
63 Joe Nieuwendyk	.08	.20
64 Brendan Shanahan	.10	.30
65 Chris Chelios	.10	.30
66 Chris Osgood	.08	.20
67 Nicklas Lidstrom	.10	.30
68 Pat Verbeek	.02	.10
69 Sergei Fedorov	.20	.50
70 Steve Yzerman	.60	1.50
71 Darren McCarty	.02	.10
72 Tom Poti	.02	.10
73 Bill Guerin	.08	.20
74 Doug Weight	.08	.20
75 Mike Grier	.02	.10
76 Ryan Smyth	.08	.20
77 Tommy Salo	.08	.20
78 Bret Hedican	.02	.10
79 Pavel Bure	.10	.30
80 Ray Whitney	.08	.20
81 Scott Mellanby	.02	.10
82 Trevor Kidd	.08	.20
83 Viktor Kozlov	.08	.20
84 Bryan Smolinski	.02	.10
85 Stephane Fiset	.08	.20
86 Jozef Stumpel	.08	.20
87 Luc Robitaille	.08	.20
88 Rob Blake	.08	.20
89 Zigmund Palffy	.08	.20
90 Brian Savage	.02	.10
91 Dainius Zubrus	.02	.10
92 Jose Theodore	.15	.40
93 Martin Rucinsky	.02	.10
94 Saku Koivu	.10	.30
95 Sergei Zholtok	.02	.10
96 Manny Fernandez	.08	.20
97 Cliff Ronning	.02	.10
98 David Legwand	.08	.20
99 Drake Berehowsky	.02	.10
100 Vitali Yachmenev	.02	.10
101 Mike Dunham	.08	.20
102 Patric Kjellberg	.02	.10
103 Alexander Mogilny	.08	.20
104 Claude Lemieux	.02	.10
105 John Madden	.02	.10
106 Martin Brodeur	.30	.75
107 Patrik Elias	.08	.20
108 Scott Gomez	.02	.10
109 Scott Stevens	.08	.20
110 Dave Scatchard	.02	.10
111 Kenny Jonsson	.02	.10
112 Mariusz Czerkawski	.02	.10
113 Mathieu Biron	.08	.20
114 Tim Connolly	.02	.10
115 Claude Lapointe	.02	.10
116 Adam Graves	.02	.10
117 Brian Leetch	.08	.20
118 Mike York	.02	.10
119 Mike Richter	.10	.30
120 Petr Nedved	.08	.20
121 Theo Fleury	.02	.10
122 Daniel Alfredsson	.08	.20
123 Patrick Lalime	.08	.20
124 John LeClair	.10	.30
125 Marian Hossa	.10	.30
126 Keith Primeau	.02	.10
127 Radek Bonk	.02	.10
128 Shawn McEachern	.02	.10
129 Andreas Dackell	.02	.10
130 Brian Boucher	.10	.30
131 Mark Recchi	.08	.20
132 Simon Gagne	.10	.30
133 Eric Desjardins	.08	.20
134 Jeremy Roenick	.15	.40
135 Keith Tkachuk	.10	.30
136 Teppo Numminen	.02	.10
137 Eric Lindros	.10	.30
138 Shane Doan	.02	.10
139 Travis Green	.02	.10
140 Trevor Letowski	.02	.10
141 Alexei Kovalev	.02	.10
142 Jan Hrdina	.02	.10
143 Jaromir Jagr	.20	.50
144 Jean-Sebastien Aubin	.08	.20
145 Martin Straka	.02	.10
146 Matthew Barnaby	.02	.10
147 Brad Stuart	.08	.20
148 Jeff Friesen	.02	.10
149 Mike Ricci	.02	.10
150 Owen Nolan	.08	.20
151 Steve Shields	.08	.20
152 Vincent Damphousse	.02	.10
153 Al MacInnis	.08	.20
154 Chris Pronger	.08	.20
155 Jochen Hecht	.02	.10
156 Pavol Demitra	.08	.20
157 Pierre Turgeon	.08	.20
158 Roman Turek	.08	.20
159 Dan Cloutier	.08	.20
160 Fredrik Modin	.02	.10
161 Mike Johnson	.02	.10
162 Paul Mara	.02	.10
163 Vincent Lecavalier	.10	.30
164 Petr Svoboda	.02	.10
165 Curtis Joseph	.10	.30
166 Darcy Tucker	.02	.10
167 Mats Sundin	.10	.30
168 Nikolai Antropov	.02	.10
169 Sergei Berezin	.08	.20
170 Steve Thomas	.02	.10
171 Dimitri Yushkevich	.02	.10
172 Brendan Morrison	.08	.20
173 Ed Jovanovski	.02	.10
174 Felix Potvin	.10	.30
175 Harold Druken	.02	.10
176 Todd Bertuzzi	.10	.30
177 Markus Naslund	.10	.30
178 Adam Oates	.08	.20
179 Chris Simon	.02	.10
180 Jeff Halpern	.08	.20
181 Olaf Kolzig	.08	.20
182 Peter Bondra	.10	.30
183 Sergei Gonchar	.02	.10
184 Vitali Vishnevsky	.02	.10
185 Andreas Karlsson	.02	.10
186 Eric Nickulas RC	.40	1.00
187 Brandon Smith RC	.40	1.00
188 Dimitri Kalinin	.02	.10
189 Chris Herperger	.02	.10
190 Serge Aubin RC	.40	1.00
191 Alan Letang	.08	.20
192 Keith Aldridge RC	.40	1.00
193 Steven Reinprecht RC	.40	1.00
194 Brad Chartrand	.02	.10
195 David Gosselin RC	.40	1.00
196 Colin White RC	.40	1.00
197 Willie Mitchell RC	.40	1.00
198 Jason Krog	.08	.20
199 Steve Valiquette RC	.40	1.00
200 Petr Schastlivy	.02	.10
201 Andy Delmore	.08	.20
202 Mark Eaton	.02	.10
203 Evgeni Nabokov	.08	.20
204 Ladislav Nagy	.08	.20
205 Kyle Freadrich RC	.40	1.00
206 Greg Andrusak RC	.40	1.00
207 Alfie Michaud	.40	1.00
208 Brent Sopel RC	.40	1.00
209 Matt Pettinger RC	.40	1.00

210 Chris Nielsen RC .40 1.00
211 Dany Heatley RC 4.00 10.00
212 Josef Vasicek RC .40 1.00
213 Matt Zultek RC .40 1.00
214 Dmitri Afanasenkov RC .40 1.00
215 Tyler Bouck RC .40 1.00
216 Jonas Andersson RC .40 1.00
217 Juraj Kolnik RC .40 1.00
218 Andrew Raycroft RC 1.50 4.00
219 Pavel Bure CL .10 .30
220 Steve Yzerman CL .10 .30

2000-01 Upper Deck MVP Excellence

Randomly inserted in packs at the rate of 1:18, this 10-card set pairs up top NHL players on an all foil card with holographic foil highlights. Full color action shots are set side to side on the card front.

COMPLETE SET (10) 15.00 30.00
ME1 Curtis Joseph / Roberto Luongo 1.25 3.00
ME2 Pavel Bure / Pavel Brendl 1.25 3.00
ME3 Sergei Samsonov / Oleg Saprykin 1.25 3.00
ME4 Milan Hejduk / Ivan Novoseltsev 1.25 3.00
ME5 S.Yzerman/P.Verbeek 4.00 10.00
ME6 Roman Turek / Martin Biron 1.25 3.00
ME7 Henrik Sedin / Daniel Sedin 2.00 5.00
ME8 Patrik Stefan / Ladislav Nagy 1.25 3.00
ME9 Manny Malhotra / Mike York 1.25 3.00
ME10 Wayne Gretzky / Raymond Bourque 6.00 15.00

2000-01 Upper Deck MVP First Stars

Randomly inserted in Hobby packs, this 218-card set parallels the base MVP set on cards enhanced with a single star along the right side. Each card is sequentially numbered to 25.

*STARS: 75X TO 200X BASIC CARDS
*ROOKIES: 25X TO 60X BASIC CARDS
211 Dany Heatley 60.00 150.00

2000-01 Upper Deck MVP Game-Used Souvenirs

Randomly inserted in packs at the rate of 1:83, this 29-card set features cards with swatches of game used sticks. Cards with a "C" prefix were found in Canadian hobby packs only.

CGCJ Curtis Joseph 6.00 15.00
CGCO Chris Osgood 6.00 15.00
CGEB Ed Belfour 6.00 15.00
CGFP Felix Potvin 6.00 15.00
CGMB Martin Brodeur 15.00 40.00
CGMS Mats Sundin 6.00 15.00
CGWG Wayne Gretzky 25.00 60.00
GSAI Arturs Irbe 6.00 15.00
GSBS Brendan Shanahan 6.00 15.00
GSCC Chris Chelios 6.00 15.00
GSDH Dominik Hasek 10.00 25.00
GSEL Eric Lindros 6.00 15.00
GSJA Jason Allison 6.00 15.00
GSJJ Jaromir Jagr 10.00 25.00
GSJL John LeClair 6.00 15.00
GSKT Keith Tkachuk 6.00 15.00
GSMM Mark Messier 6.00 15.00
GSMR Mike Richter 10.00 25.00
GSPB Pavel Bure 6.00 15.00
GSPF Peter Forsberg 12.50 30.00
GSPK Paul Kariya 6.00 15.00
GSPR Patrick Roy 15.00 40.00
GSRB Ray Bourque 12.50 30.00
GSRL Roberto Luongo 10.00 25.00
GSSF Sergei Fedorov 10.00 25.00
GSSY Steve Yzerman 15.00 40.00
GSTS Teemu Selanne 6.00 15.00
GSWG Wayne Gretzky 25.00 60.00
GSZP Zigmund Palffy 6.00 15.00

2000-01 Upper Deck MVP Mark of Excellence

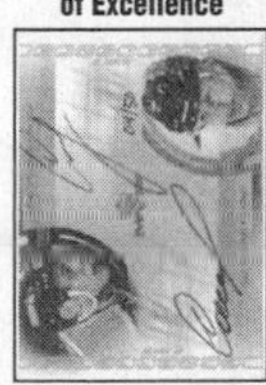

Randomly inserted in packs, this 10-card set parallels the base Excellence insert set. Each card is autographed by both players and is sequentially numbered to 50. The original checklist included a Gretzky/Bourque card which does not exist.

SGBB Pavel Bure / Pavel Brendl 20.00 50.00
SGHN Milan Hejduk / Ivan Novoseltsev 15.00 40.00
SGJL Curtis Joseph / Roberto Luongo 40.00 100.00
SGMY Manny Malhotra / Mike York 12.00 30.00
SGSE Henrik Sedin / Daniel Sedin 125.00 300.00
SGSL Patrik Stefan / Ladislav Nagy 15.00 40.00
SGSS Sergei Samsonov / Oleg Saprykin 20.00 50.00
SGTB Roman Turek / Martin Biron 15.00 40.00
SGYV S.Yzerman/P.Verbeek 75.00 200.00

2000-01 Upper Deck MVP Masked Men

COMPLETE SET (10) 15.00 30.00
STATED ODDS 1:18
MM1 Dominik Hasek 2.00 5.00
MM2 Patrick Roy 5.00 12.00
MM3 Ed Belfour 1.00 2.50
MM4 Chris Osgood .75 2.00
MM5 Martin Brodeur 2.50 6.00
MM6 Brian Boucher 1.00 2.50
MM7 Steve Shields .75 2.00
MM8 Roman Turek .75 2.00
MM9 Curtis Joseph 1.00 2.50
MM10 Olaf Kolzig .75 2.00

2000-01 Upper Deck MVP ProSign

Randomly inserted in retail packs, this 18-card set features a small portrait player photo centered that fades into a white-out background and authentic player autographs. The Boucher card has never been confirmed and probably does not exist.

AM Al MacInnis 8.00 20.00
BM Brenden Morrow 8.00 20.00
CB Curtis Brown 6.00 15.00
CJ Curtis Joseph 25.00 50.00
DL David Legwand 8.00 20.00
IV Ivan Novoseltsev 6.00 15.00
LN Ladislav Nagy 6.00 15.00
MJ Mike Johnson 6.00 15.00
MM Manny Malhotra 6.00 15.00
MR Mike Ribeiro 6.00 15.00
MY Mike York 6.00 15.00
OS Oleg Saprykin 6.00 15.00
PB Pavel Bure 10.00 25.00
PS Patrik Stefan 6.00 15.00
RL Roberto Luongo 8.00 20.00
RT Roman Turek 8.00 20.00
SM Steven McCarthy 6.00 15.00
SS Sergei Samsonov 8.00 20.00

2000-01 Upper Deck MVP Second Stars

Randomly inserted in Hobby packs, this 218-card set parallels the base MVP set on cards enhanced with two stars along the right side. Each card is sequentially numbered to 100.

*STARS: 30X TO 80X BASIC CARDS
*ROOKIES: 12.5X TO 30X BASIC CARDS
211 Dany Heatley 30.00 80.00

2000-01 Upper Deck MVP Super Game-Used Souvenirs

Randomly inserted in packs, this 29-card set parallels the base souvenirs set on cards enhanced with both a swatch of a game used stick and a game used puck. Each card is sequentially numbered to 50.

*SUPER: 1.25X TO 2.5X BASIC INSERTS

2000-01 Upper Deck MVP Talent

COMPLETE SET (15) 10.00 20.00
STATED ODDS 1:6
M1 Paul Kariya .30 .75
M2 Teemu Selanne .30 .75
M3 Ray Bourque .60 1.50
M4 Joe Sakic .60 1.50
M5 Patrick Roy 1.50 4.00
M6 Brett Hull .40 1.00
M7 Sergei Fedorov .60 1.50
M8 Pavel Bure .40 1.00
M9 Zigmund Palffy .30 .75
M10 Martin Brodeur .75 2.00
M11 Theo Fleury .30 .75
M12 Eric Lindros .50 1.25
M13 John LeClair .40 1.00
M14 Jaromir Jagr .50 1.25
M15 Jeremy Roenick .40 1.00

2000-01 Upper Deck MVP Third Stars

Randomly inserted in packs at the rate of 1:2, this 218-card set parallels the base MVP set on cards enhanced with a silver border, silver foil stamping, and three white stars along the right edge.

*STARS: 1.25X TO 3X BASIC CARDS
*ROOKIES: .75X TO 2X BASIC CARDS

2000-01 Upper Deck MVP Top Draws

COMPLETE SET (10) 5.00 10.00
STATED ODDS 1:9
TD1 Teemu Selanne .30 .75
TD2 Dominik Hasek .60 1.50
TD3 Peter Forsberg .75 2.00
TD4 Brendan Shanahan .50 1.25
TD5 Pavel Bure .40 1.00
TD6 Scott Gomez .30 .75
TD7 Eric Lindros .50 1.25
TD8 John LeClair .40 1.00
TD9 Keith Tkachuk .30 .75
TD10 Jaromir Jagr .50 1.25

2000-01 Upper Deck MVP Top Playmakers

COMPLETE SET (10) 15.00 30.00
STATED ODDS 1:18
TP1 Paul Kariya .75 2.00
TP2 Dominik Hasek 1.50 4.00
TP3 Peter Forsberg 2.00 5.00
TP4 Mike Modano 1.25 3.00
TP5 Steve Yzerman 4.00 10.00
TP6 Pavel Bure 1.00 2.50
TP7 Scott Gomez .75 2.00
TP8 Eric Lindros 1.25 3.00
TP9 Jaromir Jagr 1.25 3.00
TP10 Jeremy Roenick 1.00 2.50

2000-01 Upper Deck MVP Valuable Commodities

COMPLETE SET (10) 20.00 40.00
STATED ODDS 1:18
VC1 Paul Kariya .75 2.00
VC2 Patrick Roy 4.00 10.00
VC3 Peter Forsberg 2.00 5.00
VC4 Mike Modano 1.25 3.00
VC5 Steve Yzerman 4.00 10.00
VC6 Martin Brodeur 2.00 5.00
VC7 Theo Fleury .75 2.00
VC8 Eric Lindros 1.25 3.00
VC9 Jaromir Jagr 1.25 3.00
VC10 Curtis Joseph .75 2.00

2001-02 Upper Deck MVP

Released in late September, this 233-card set was originally released as a smaller 220-card set. Cards 221-233 were randomly available in UD Rookie Update packs.

COMP.SERIES I SET (220) 15.00 30.00
COMP.SET w/UPDATE (233) 40.00 80.00
1 Jean-Sebastien Giguere .08 .20
2 Paul Kariya .10 .25
3 Jeff Friesen .02 .10

4 Oleg Tverdovsky .02 .10
5 Mike Leclerc .02 .10
6 Milan Hnilicka .08 .20
7 Patrik Stefan .02 .10
8 Ray Ferraro .02 .10
9 Jiri Slegr .02 .10
10 Hnat Domenichelli .02 .10
11 Jason Allison .02 .10
12 Joe Thornton .20 .50
13 Bill Guerin .08 .20
14 Sergei Samsonov .08 .20
15 Kyle McLaren .02 .10
16 Jonathan Girard .02 .10
17 Maxim Afinogenov .02 .10
18 Stu Barnes .02 .10
19 Doug Gilmour .08 .20
20 Chris Gratton .02 .10
21 Martin Biron .08 .20
22 J-P Dumont .02 .10
23 Miroslav Satan .08 .20
24 Craig Conroy .02 .10
25 Jarome Iginla .12 .30
26 Rico Fata .02 .10
27 Derek Morris .02 .10
28 Marc Savard .02 .10
29 Oleg Saprykin .02 .10
30 Arturs Irbe .08 .20
31 Shane Willis .02 .10
32 Rod Brind'Amour .08 .20
33 Jeff O'Neill .02 .10
34 Sami Kapanen .02 .10
35 Ron Francis .08 .20
36 Dave Tanabe .02 .10
37 Steve Sullivan .02 .10
38 Tony Amonte .08 .20
39 Jaroslav Spacek .02 .10
40 Eric Daze .08 .20
41 Michael Nylander .02 .10
42 Alexei Zhamnov .02 .10
43 Joe Sakic .25 .60
44 Peter Forsberg .30 .75
45 Milan Hejduk .10 .25
46 Chris Drury .08 .20
47 Rob Blake .08 .20
48 Ray Bourque .25 .60
49 Patrick Roy .60 1.50
50 Alex Tanguay .08 .20
51 Geoff Sanderson .02 .10
52 Espen Knutsen .02 .10
53 Ray Whitney .02 .10
54 Rostislav Klesla .02 .10
55 Ron Tugnutt .08 .20
56 Tyler Wright .02 .10
57 Mike Modano .20 .50
58 Jere Lehtinen .08 .20
59 Sergei Zubov .02 .10
60 Brenden Morrow .08 .20
61 Ed Belfour .10 .25
62 Joe Nieuwendyk .08 .20
63 Pierre Turgeon .08 .20
64 Steve Yzerman .60 1.50
65 Brendan Shanahan .10 .25
66 Brett Hull .15 .40
67 Luc Robitaille .08 .20
68 Sergei Fedorov .20 .50
69 Dominik Hasek .30 .75
70 Darren McCarty .02 .10
71 Mike Grier .02 .10
72 Ryan Smyth .02 .10
73 Anson Carter .08 .20
74 Tom Poti .02 .10
75 Tommy Salo .08 .20
76 Mike Comrie .08 .20
77 Todd Marchant .02 .10
78 Pavel Bure .10 .25
79 Viktor Kozlov .02 .10
80 Marcus Nilson .02 .10
81 Kevyn Adams .02 .10
82 Roberto Luongo .12 .30
83 Denis Shvidki .02 .10
84 Zigmund Palffy .08 .20
85 Jozef Stumpel .02 .10
86 Adam Deadmarsh .02 .10
87 Mathieu Schneider .02 .10
88 Bryan Smolinski .02 .10
89 Eric Belanger .02 .10
90 Lubomir Visnovsky .02 .10
91 Marian Gaborik .20 .50
92 Lubomir Sekeras .02 .10
93 Wes Walz .02 .10
94 Manny Fernandez .08 .20
95 Roman Simicek .02 .10
96 Stacy Roest .02 .10
97 Saku Koivu .10 .25
98 Oleg Petrov .02 .10
99 Patrice Brisebois .02 .10
100 Jose Theodore .12 .30
101 Richard Zednik .02 .10
102 Martin Rucinsky .02 .10
103 Andrei Markov .02 .10
104 David Legwand .08 .20
105 Cliff Ronning .02 .10
106 Mike Dunham .08 .20
107 Kimmo Timonen .02 .10
108 Scott Walker .02 .10
109 Patric Kjellberg .02 .10
110 Martin Brodeur .30 .75
111 Scott Stevens .08 .20
112 Patrik Elias .08 .20
113 Scott Niedermayer .02 .10
114 Petr Sykora .02 .10
115 Jason Arnott .02 .10
116 Scott Gomez .02 .10
117 Rick DiPietro .08 .20
118 Mark Parrish .02 .10
119 Roman Hamrlik .02 .10
120 Mariusz Czerkawski .02 .10
121 Kenny Jonsson .02 .10
122 Dave Scatchard .02 .10
123 Mark Messier .10 .25
124 Brian Leetch .08 .20
125 Jan Hlavac .02 .10
126 Theo Fleury .02 .10
127 Eric Lindros .10 .25
128 Petr Nedved .02 .10
129 Daniel Alfredsson .08 .20
130 Radek Bonk .02 .10
131 Marian Hossa .10 .25
132 Shawn McEachern .02 .10
133 Patrick Lalime .08 .20
134 Wade Redden .02 .10
135 Magnus Arvedson .02 .10
136 Martin Havlat .08 .20
137 Simon Gagne .10 .25
138 Roman Cechmanek .08 .20
139 Justin Williams .02 .10
140 John LeClair .10 .25
141 Mark Recchi .08 .20
142 Eric Desjardins .02 .10
143 Jeremy Roenick .15 .40
144 Paul Mara .02 .10
145 Shane Doan .02 .10
146 Landon Wilson .02 .10
147 Sean Burke .08 .20
148 Michal Handzus .02 .10
149 Ladislav Nagy .02 .10
150 Mario Lemieux .75 2.00
151 Jan Hrdina .02 .10
152 Johan Hedberg .08 .20
153 Robert Lang .02 .10
154 Alexei Kovalev .08 .20
155 Martin Straka .02 .10
156 Owen Nolan .08 .20
157 Vincent Damphousse .02 .10
158 Brad Stuart .02 .10
159 Teemu Selanne .10 .25
160 Evgeni Nabokov .08 .20
161 Mike Ricci .02 .10
162 Chris Pronger .08 .20
163 Keith Tkachuk .10 .25
164 Scott Young .02 .10
165 Pavol Demitra .08 .20
166 Doug Weight .08 .20
167 Al MacInnis .08 .20
168 Cory Stillman .02 .10
169 Vincent Lecavalier .10 .25
170 Brad Richards .08 .20
171 Nikolai Khabibulin .10 .25
172 Fredrik Modin .02 .10
173 Mats Sundin .10 .25
174 Gary Roberts .02 .10
175 Curtis Joseph .10 .25
176 Nikolai Antropov .02 .10
177 Darcy Tucker .02 .10
178 Jonas Hoglund .02 .10
179 Markus Naslund .10 .25
180 Brendan Morrison .08 .20
181 Todd Bertuzzi .10 .25
182 Daniel Sedin .02 .10
183 Ed Jovanovski .08 .20
184 Peter Bondra .10 .25
185 Sergei Gonchar .02 .10
186 Jeff Halpern .02 .10
187 Olaf Kolzig .08 .20
188 Jaromir Jagr .20 .50
189 Gregg Naumenko .02 .10
190 Dan Snyder RC .50 1.25
191 Zdenek Kutlak RC .50 1.25
192 Niclas Wallin .02 .10
193 Michel Larocque RC .50 1.25
194 Casey Hankinson RC .50 1.25
195 Chris Nielsen .02 .10
196 Martin Spanhel RC .50 1.25
197 Mathieu Darche RC .50 1.25
198 Matt Davidson RC .50 1.25
199 Brad Larsen .02 .10
200 Steve Gainey .02 .10
201 Jason Chimera RC .50 1.25
202 Andrej Podkonicky RC .50 1.25
203 Mike Matteucci RC .50 1.25
204 Pascal Dupuis RC .50 1.25
205 Francis Belanger RC .50 1.25
206 Mike Jefferson RC .50 1.25
207 Stanislav Gron RC .50 1.25
208 Peter Smrek RC .50 1.25
209 Joel Kwiatkowski RC .50 1.25
210 Kirby Law RC .50 1.25
211 Tomas Divisek RC .50 1.25
212 David Cullen RC .50 1.25
213 Billy Tibbetts RC .50 1.25
214 Dan Lacouture .02 .10
215 Jaroslav Obsut RC .50 1.25
216 Dale Clarke RC .50 1.25
217 Thomas Ziegler RC .50 1.25
218 Mike Brown .02 .10
219 Steve Yzerman CL .10 .25
220 Curtis Joseph CL .02 .10
221 Ilya Kovalchuk RC 4.00 10.00
222 Erik Cole RC 1.50 4.00
223 Pavel Datsyuk RC 3.00 8.00
224 Kristian Huselius RC 1.50 4.00
225 Marcel Hossa RC 1.50 4.00
226 Martin Erat RC 1.50 4.00
227 Christian Berglund RC 1.50 4.00
228 Raffi Torres RC 1.50 4.00
229 Dan Blackburn RC 1.50 4.00
230 Jiri Dopita RC 1.50 4.00
231 Krys Kolanos RC 1.50 4.00
232 Brian Sutherby RC 1.50 4.00
233 Olivier Michaud RC 2.00 5.00

2001-02 Upper Deck MVP Goalie Sticks

Randomly inserted in 1:288 hobby and 1:240 retail packs, this 15-card set featured pieces of game-used sticks from the goalie pictured.

GAI Arturs Irbe 12.50 30.00
GBD Byron Dafoe 12.50 30.00
GCJ Curtis Joseph 20.00 50.00
GCO Chris Osgood 12.50 30.00
GDH Dominik Hasek 30.00 80.00
GEB Ed Belfour 20.00 50.00
GJT Jose Theodore 25.00 60.00
GMB Martin Brodeur 30.00 80.00
GMR Mike Richter 20.00 50.00
GNK Nikolai Khabibulin 20.00 50.00
GOK Olaf Kolzig 12.50 30.00
GPR Patrick Roy 40.00 100.00
GRC Roman Cechmanek 12.50 30.00
GRD Rick DiPietro 12.50 30.00
GTS Tommy Salo 12.50 30.00

2001-02 Upper Deck MVP Masked Men

This 14-card set was randomly inserted at 1:12 packs.

COMPLETE SET (14) 10.00 20.00
MM1 Martin Brodeur 1.50 4.00
MM2 Ed Belfour .60 1.50
MM3 Patrick Roy 3.00 8.00
MM4 Jocelyn Thibault .50 1.25
MM5 Tommy Salo .50 1.25
MM6 Olaf Kolzig .50 1.25
MM7 Johan Hedberg .50 1.25
MM8 Evgeni Nabokov .50 1.25
MM9 Patrick Lalime .50 1.25
MM10 Sean Burke .50 1.25
MM11 Curtis Joseph .60 1.50
MM12 Arturs Irbe .50 1.25
MM13 Roman Cechmanek .50 1.25
MM14 Felix Potvin .60 1.50

2001-02 Upper Deck MVP Morning Skate Jerseys

Randomly inserted in 1:96 hobby and 1:120 retail packs, this 15-card set featured swatches of player worn practice jerseys.

*MULT.COLOR SWATCHES: 1X TO 1.5X
JBB Brian Boucher 4.00 10.00
JEL Eric Lindros 4.00 10.00
JJA Jarome Iginla 6.00 15.00
JJI Jarome Iginla 6.00 15.00
JJJ Jaromir Jagr 8.00 20.00
JJL John LeClair 4.00 10.00
JJO John LeClair 4.00 10.00
JJS Joe Sakic 8.00 20.00
JKP Keith Primeau 4.00 10.00
JMH Milan Hejduk 4.00 10.00
JMM Mike Modano 6.00 15.00
JMR Mark Recchi 4.00 10.00
JPF Peter Forsberg 8.00 20.00
JRB Rod Brind'Amour 4.00 10.00
JSG Simon Gagne 4.00 10.00

2001-02 Upper Deck MVP Morning Skate Jersey Autographs

Serial-numbered to 100 copies each, this 10-card set partially paralleled the base morning skate jersey set but included authentic player autographs.

SJBB Brian Boucher 15.00 40.00
SJJA Jarome Iginla 30.00 60.00
SJJI Jarome Iginla 30.00 60.00
SJJL John LeClair 15.00 40.00
SJKP Keith Primeau 15.00 40.00
SJMH Milan Hejduk 15.00 40.00
SJMM Mike Modano 30.00 60.00
SJMR Mark Recchi 15.00 40.00
SJRB Rod Brind'Amour 15.00 40.00
SJSG Simon Gagne 15.00 40.00

2001-02 Upper Deck MVP Souvenirs

Randomly inserted into hobby packs only, this 30-card set featured game-used swatches of equipment. Cards with a "C" prefix carried two pieces of memorabilia and cards with a "S" prefix carried one. Dual souvenir cards were inserted at 1:288 and single souvenir cards were inserted at 1:96. A gold parallel serial-numbered to 50 copies each was also created.

*GOLD: 2X TO 4X HI BASIC CARDS
CAM Al MacInnis 10.00 25.00
CDA Daniel Alfredsson 10.00 25.00
CJR Jeremy Roenick 12.50 30.00
CJS Joe Sakic 15.00 40.00
CMM Mike Modano 15.00 40.00
CPB Pavel Bure 8.00 20.00
CSS Sergei Samsonov 10.00 25.00
CVL Vincent Lecavalier 10.00 25.00
CWG Wayne Gretzky 75.00 150.00
CZP Zigmund Palffy 10.00 25.00
SAM Alexander Mogilny 6.00 15.00
SBH Brett Hull 12.50 30.00
SBS Brendan Shanahan 8.00 20.00
SJA Jason Allison 6.00 15.00
SJJ Jaromir Jagr 12.50 30.00
SJL John LeClair 8.00 20.00
SKT Keith Tkachuk 8.00 20.00
SLR Luc Robitaille 6.00 15.00
SML Mario Lemieux 40.00 100.00
SMM Mark Messier 8.00 20.00
SMR Mark Recchi 6.00 15.00
SMS Mats Sundin 8.00 20.00
SPB Peter Bondra 8.00 20.00
SPF Peter Forsberg 25.00 60.00
SPS Patrik Stefan 6.00 15.00
SRB Ray Bourque 12.50 30.00
SSH Scott Hartnell 6.00 15.00
SSY Steve Yzerman 20.00 50.00
STA Tony Amonte 6.00 15.00
STS Teemu Selanne 8.00 20.00

2001-02 Upper Deck MVP Talent

This 14-card set was randomly inserted at 1:12 packs.

COMPLETE SET (14) 15.00 30.00
MT1 Peter Forsberg 1.25 3.00
MT2 Joe Sakic 1.00 2.50
MT3 Mike Modano .75 2.00
MT4 Mario Lemieux 3.00 8.00
MT5 Sergei Fedorov 1.00 2.50
MT6 Steve Yzerman 2.50 6.00
MT7 Pavel Bure .60 1.50
MT8 Paul Kariya .40 1.00
MT9 Teemu Selanne .40 1.00
MT10 Patrik Elias .30 .75
MT11 Zigmund Palffy .30 .75
MT12 John LeClair .60 1.50
MT13 Chris Pronger .30 .75
MT14 Martin Brodeur 1.25 3.00

2001-02 Upper Deck MVP Valuable Commodities

This 7-card set was randomly inserted at 1:24 packs.

COMPLETE SET (7) 15.00 30.00
VC1 Steve Yzerman 3.00 8.00
VC2 Pavel Bure .75 2.00
VC3 Joe Sakic 1.25 3.00
VC4 Martin Brodeur 1.50 4.00
VC5 Mario Lemieux 4.00 10.00
VC6 Peter Forsberg 1.50 4.00
VC7 Mike Modano 1.00 2.50

2001-02 Upper Deck MVP Watch

This 7-card set was randomly inserted at 1:24 packs.

COMPLETE SET (7) 10.00 20.00
MW1 Mario Lemieux 4.00 10.00
MW2 Joe Sakic 1.25 3.00
MW3 Jaromir Jagr 1.00 2.50
MW4 Brett Hull .75 2.00
MW5 Sergei Fedorov 1.25 3.00
MW6 Mark Messier .75 2.00
MW7 Chris Pronger .40 1.00

2002-03 Upper Deck MVP

Released in September, this 220-card set carried an SRP of $1.99 for an 8-card pack, and had 24 packs per box.

COMPLETE SET (220) 20.00 40.00
1 Mike LeClerc .02 .10
2 Jean-Sebastien Giguere .08 .20

3 Matt Cullen .02 .10
4 Andy McDonald .02 .10
5 Jason York .02 .10
6 Paul Kariya .10 .25
7 Frantisek Kaberle .02 .10
8 Dany Heatley .12 .30
9 Pasi Nurminen .02 .10
10 Ilya Kovalchuk .15 .40
11 Patrik Stefan .02 .10
12 Pascal Rheaume .02 .10
13 Sergei Samsonov .08 .20
14 Joe Thornton .20 .50
15 Brian Rolston .02 .10
16 Martin Lapointe .02 .10
17 Nick Boynton .02 .10
18 Jozef Stumpel .02 .10
19 Stu Barnes .02 .10
20 J-P Dumont .02 .10
21 Miroslav Satan .08 .20
22 Tim Connolly .02 .10
23 Maxim Afinogenov .02 .10
24 Martin Biron .08 .20
25 Craig Conroy .02 .10
26 Roman Turek .08 .20
27 Derek Morris .02 .10
28 Marc Savard .02 .10
29 Jarome Iginla .12 .30
30 Igor Kravchuk .02 .10
31 Sami Kapanen .02 .10
32 Bates Battaglia .02 .10
33 Ron Francis .08 .20
34 Erik Cole .02 .10
35 Jeff O'Neill .02 .10
36 Arturs Irbe .08 .20
37 Rod Brind'Amour .08 .20
38 Alexei Zhamnov .02 .10
39 Michael Nylander .02 .10
40 Steve Sullivan .02 .10
41 Jocelyn Thibault .08 .20
42 Kyle Calder .02 .10
43 Eric Daze .08 .20
44 Patrick Roy .60 1.50
45 Milan Hejduk .10 .25
46 Peter Forsberg .30 .75
47 Rob Blake .08 .20
48 Chris Drury .08 .20
49 Joe Sakic .30 .75
50 Steven Reinprecht .02 .10
51 Brad Moran .02 .10
52 Jaroslav Spacek .02 .10
53 Marc Denis .08 .20
54 Ray Whitney .02 .10
55 Rostislav Klesla .02 .10
56 Espen Knutsen .02 .10
57 Marty Turco .08 .20
58 Jere Lehtinen .08 .20
59 Mike Modano .20 .50
60 Derian Hatcher .02 .10
61 Brenden Morrow .08 .20
62 Jason Arnott .02 .10
63 Dominik Hasek .30 .75
64 Brendan Shanahan .10 .25
65 Curtis Joseph .10 .25
66 Brett Hull .15 .40
67 Steve Yzerman .60 1.50
68 Nicklas Lidstrom .10 .25
69 Pavel Datsyuk .10 .25
70 Ryan Smyth .02 .10
71 Anson Carter .08 .20
72 Mike Comrie .08 .20
73 Tommy Salo .08 .20
74 Eric Brewer .02 .10
75 Todd Marchant .02 .10
76 Roberto Luongo .12 .30
77 Kristian Huselius .02 .10
78 Marcus Nilsson .02 .10
79 Viktor Kozlov .02 .10
80 Sandis Ozolinsh .02 .10
81 Valeri Bure .02 .10
82 Jason Allison .02 .10
83 Zigmund Palffy .08 .20
84 Adam Deadmarsh .02 .10
85 Felix Potvin .10 .25
86 Mathieu Schneider .02 .10
87 Bryan Smolinski .02 .10
88 Jim Dowd .02 .10
89 Marian Gaborik .20 .50
90 Manny Fernandez .08 .20
91 Andrew Brunette .02 .10
92 Wes Walz .02 .10
93 Antti Laaksonen .02 .10
94 Yanic Perreault .02 .10
95 Richard Zednik .02 .10
96 Jose Theodore .12 .30
97 Oleg Petrov .02 .10
98 Donald Audette .02 .10
99 Saku Koivu .10 .25
100 Kimmo Timonen .02 .10
101 Stu Grimson .02 .10
102 Denis Arkhipov .02 .10
103 Scott Hartnell .02 .10
104 Mike Dunham .08 .20
105 Andy Delmore .02 .10
106 Brian Rafalski .02 .10
107 John Madden .02 .10
108 Martin Brodeur .30 .75
109 Scott Stevens .08 .20
110 Patrik Elias .08 .20
111 Scott Niedermayer .02 .10
112 Joe Nieuwendyk .08 .20
113 Mark Parrish .02 .10
114 Michael Peca .02 .10
115 Alexei Yashin .02 .10
116 Adrian Aucoin .02 .10
117 Chris Osgood .08 .20
118 Stephen Webb .02 .10
119 Eric Lindros .10 .25
120 Brian Leetch .08 .20
121 Tom Poti .02 .10
122 Pavel Bure .10 .25
123 Petr Nedved .02 .10
124 Dan Blackburn .08 .20
125 Daniel Alfredsson .08 .20
126 Patrick Lalime .08 .20
127 Marian Hossa .10 .25
128 Martin Havlat .08 .20
129 Zdeno Chara .02 .10
130 Radek Bonk .02 .10
131 Wade Redden .02 .10
132 Keith Primeau .02 .10
133 John LeClair .10 .25
134 Mark Recchi .08 .20
135 Eric Desjardins .02 .10
136 Jeremy Roenick .15 .40
137 Justin Williams .02 .10
138 Simon Gagne .10 .25
139 Tony Amonte .08 .20
140 Daniel Briere .02 .10
141 Sean Burke .08 .20
142 Ladislav Nagy .02 .10
143 Shane Doan .02 .10
144 Teppo Numminen .02 .10
145 Alexei Kovalev .08 .20
146 Johan Hedberg .08 .20
147 Jan Hrdina .02 .10
148 Mario Lemieux .75 2.00
149 Martin Straka .02 .10
150 Hans Jonsson .02 .10
151 Vincent Damphousse .02 .10
152 Owen Nolan .08 .20
153 Adam Graves .02 .10
154 Evgeni Nabokov .08 .20
155 Mike Ricci .02 .10
156 Patrick Marleau .08 .20
157 Teemu Selanne .10 .25
158 Brent Johnson .08 .20
159 Doug Weight .08 .20
160 Keith Tkachuk .10 .25
161 Al MacInnis .08 .20
162 Chris Pronger .08 .20
163 Pavol Demitra .02 .10
164 Tyson Nash .02 .10
165 Nikolai Khabibulin .10 .25
166 Vincent Lecavalier .10 .25
167 Martin St. Louis .08 .20
168 Fredrik Modin .02 .10
169 Brad Richards .08 .20
170 Shane Willis .02 .10
171 Alyn McCauley .02 .10
172 Gary Roberts .02 .10
173 Darcy Tucker .02 .10
174 Ed Belfour .10 .25
175 Mats Sundin .10 .25
176 Alexander Mogilny .08 .20
177 Todd Bertuzzi .10 .25
178 Brendan Morrison .08 .20
179 Markus Naslund .10 .25
180 Dan Cloutier .08 .20
181 Daniel Sedin .02 .10
182 Henrik Sedin .02 .10
183 Sergei Gonchar .02 .10
184 Jaromir Jagr .20 .50
185 Peter Bondra .10 .25
186 Olaf Kolzig .08 .20
187 Robert Lang .02 .10
188 Steve Konowalchuk .02 .10
189 Patrick Roy .60 1.50
190 Steve Yzerman .60 1.50
191 Mark Hartigan .02 .10
192 Mike Weaver .02 .10
193 Frederic Cassivi .08 .20
194 Andy Hilbert .02 .10
195 Chris Kelleher .02 .10
196 Henrik Tallinder .02 .10
197 Micki Dupont RC .02 .10
198 Tyler Arnason .08 .20
199 Riku Hahl .02 .10
200 Andrej Nedorost .02 .10
201 Sean Avery .02 .10
202 Stephen Weiss .02 .10
203 Lukas Krajicek .02 .10
204 Kyle Rossiter .02 .10
205 Eric Beaudoin .02 .10
206 Tony Virta .02 .10
207 Marcel Hossa .02 .10
208 Jan Lasak .02 .10
209 Trent Hunter .02 .10
210 Ray Schultz RC .02 .10
211 Martin Prusek .08 .20
212 Chris Bala .02 .10
213 Neil Little .02 .10
214 Guillaume Lefebvre .02 .10
215 Hannes Hyvonen .02 .10
216 Gaetan Royer .02 .10
217 Martin Cibak .02 .10
218 Sebastien Centomo .08 .20
219 Karel Pilar .02 .10
220 Sebastien Charpentier .02 .10

2002-03 Upper Deck MVP Gold

This 220-card hobby only set directly paralleled the base set but was serial-numbered to 100 copies each.

*GOLD: 8X TO 20X BASIC CARDS

2002-03 Upper Deck MVP Classics

This 220-card set paralleled the base set with silver borders and was inserted at odds of 1:2.

*CLASSICS: .75X TO 1.5X BASIC CARDS

2002-03 Upper Deck MVP Golden Classics

This 220-card hobby only set paralleled the base set with gold borders and was serial-numbered to 50 copies each.

*GLDN CLASSICS: 12.5X TO 30X BASIC CARDS

2002-03 Upper Deck MVP Highlight Nights

COMPLETE SET (7) 8.00 15.00
STATED ODDS 1:18
HN1 Ilya Kovalchuk .75 2.00
HN2 Joe Thornton 1.00 2.50
HN3 Jarome Iginla .50 1.25
HN4 Brendan Shanahan .75 2.00
HN5 Eric Lindros .40 1.00
HN6 Mario Lemieux 3.00 8.00
HN7 Markus Naslund .40 1.00

2002-03 Upper Deck MVP Masked Men

COMPLETE SET (7) 10.00 20.00
STATED ODDS 1:18
MM1 Patrick Roy 3.00 8.00
MM2 Dominik Hasek 1.50 4.00
MM3 Jose Theodore .75 2.00
MM4 Martin Brodeur 2.00 5.00
MM5 Mike Richter .75 2.00
MM6 Sean Burke .50 1.25
MM7 Olaf Kolzig .50 1.25

2002-03 Upper Deck MVP Overdrive

COMPLETE SET (14) 6.00 12.00
STATED ODDS 1:9
SO1 Paul Kariya .50 1.25
SO2 Ilya Kovalchuk .60 1.50
SO3 Jarome Iginla .60 1.50
SO4 Sami Kapanen .40 1.00
SO5 Chris Drury .40 1.00
SO6 Peter Forsberg 1.00 2.50
SO7 Mike Modano .60 1.50
SO8 Sergei Fedorov .60 1.50
SO9 Sandis Ozolinsh .40 1.00
SO10 Marian Hossa .50 1.25
SO11 Simon Gagne .50 1.25
SO12 Alexei Kovalev .40 1.00
SO13 Markus Naslund .50 1.25
SO14 Peter Bondra .50 1.25

2002-03 Upper Deck MVP Prosign

Inserted at 1:144, this 15-card set featured authentic player autographs. The Henrik Sedin card was originally issued as an exchange card. Known print runs were provided by UD.

BO Bobby Orr 125.00 300.00
CJ Curtis Joseph 25.00 50.00
DH Dany Heatley 10.00 25.00
DS Daniel Sedin 6.00 15.00
GH Gordie Howe 75.00 200.00
HS Henrik Sedin/33 10.00 25.00
KH Kristian Huselius 6.00 15.00
MF Manny Fernandez 6.00 15.00
MO Maxime Ouellet 6.00 15.00
PB Pavel Bure/145 6.00 15.00
PR Patrick Roy 100.00 200.00
RB Ray Bourque 50.00 125.00
SE Teemu Selanne 8.00 20.00
TS Tommy Salo 10.00 25.00
WG Wayne Gretzky 100.00 250.00

2002-03 Upper Deck MVP Skate Around Jerseys

This 57-card set featured swatches of practice-worn jerseys from the players featured alongside color action photos. Single jersey cards were inserted at 1:72, dual jersey cards were inserted at 1:288 and triple jersey cards were serial-numbered out of 100. Dual jersey cards were hobby exclusives.

SAAD Adam Deadmarsh 4.00 10.00
SACD Chris Drury 4.00 10.00
SAEK Espen Knutsen 4.00 10.00
SAEL Eric Lindros 5.00 12.00
SAFP Felix Potvin 5.00 12.00
SAJI Jarome Iginla 6.00 15.00
SAJL John LeClair 4.00 10.00
SAJS Joe Sakic 10.00 25.00
SAJT Joe Thornton 8.00 20.00
SAKP Keith Primeau 4.00 10.00
SAMM Mike Modano 8.00 20.00
SAOK Olaf Kolzig 5.00 12.00
SAPF Peter Forsberg 10.00 25.00
SAPK Paul Kariya 5.00 12.00
SAPR Patrick Roy 12.50 30.00
SDBK Rob Blake / Rostislav Klesla 8.00 20.00
SDBN Rod Brind'Amour / Joe Nieuwendyk 8.00 20.00
SDBP Ed Belfour / Felix Potvin 10.00 25.00
SDCB Roman Cechmanek / Brian Boucher 8.00 20.00
SDDB J-P Dumont / Martin Biron 8.00 20.00
SDDG Chris Drury / Simon Gagne 10.00 25.00
SDDH Chris Drury / Milan Hejduk 10.00 25.00
SDDL Adam Deadmarsh / John LeClair 8.00 20.00
SDFL Peter Forsberg / Eric Lindros 15.00 40.00
SDHP Milan Hejduk / Zigmund Palffy 10.00 25.00
SDHR Dan Hinote / Steven Reinprecht 8.00 20.00
SDJM Jaromir Jagr / Mark Messier 12.00 30.00
SDKC Olaf Kolzig / Roman Cechmanek 10.00 25.00
SDKR Alexei Kovalev / Mark Recchi 8.00 20.00
SDLC John LeClair / Roman Cechmanek 8.00 20.00
SDLF Eric Lindros / Theo Fleury 10.00 25.00
SDLP John LeClair / Keith Primeau 8.00 20.00
SDMS M.Modano/T.Selanne 10.00 25.00
SDMT M.Modano/M.Turco 10.00 25.00
SDNL Joe Nieuwendyk / Eric Lindros 8.00 20.00
SDPO Felix Potvin / Chris Osgood 15.00 40.00
SDPP Zigmund Palffy / Felix Potvin 8.00 20.00
SDRA Patrick Roy / David Aebischer 40.00 100.00
SDRG Mark Recchi / Simon Gagne 8.00 20.00
SDSD Joe Sakic / Chris Drury 20.00 50.00
SDTBE Marty Turco / Ed Belfour 10.00 25.00
SDTBL Alex Tanguay / Rob Blake 8.00 20.00
SDTD Ron Tugnutt / Marc Denis 8.00 20.00
SDWF Justin Williams / Ruslan Fedotenko 8.00 20.00
SDWG Justin Williams / Simon Gagne 8.00 20.00
STDAP Adam Deadmarsh / Jason Allison / Zigmund Palffy 12.50 30.00
STDSB J-P Dumont / Miroslav Satan / Martin Biron 12.50 30.00
STKFS Alexei Kovalev / Theo Fleury / Miroslav Satan 12.50 30.00
STLNT Eric Lindros / Joe Nieuwendyk / Joe Thornton 15.00 40.00
STLPR John LeClair / Keith Primeau / Mark Recchi 12.50 30.00
STMMT Mess./Mdno/Thornton 25.00 60.00
STSFR Joe Sakic / Peter Forsberg / Patrick Roy 25.00 60.00
STSHP Teemu Selanne / Milan Hejduk / Zigmund Palffy 12.50 30.00
STSMJ Teemu Selanne / Mike Modano / Jaromir Jagr 20.00 50.00
STTDG Joe Thornton / Chris Drury / Simon Gagne 12.50 30.00
STTDH Alex Tanguay / Chris Drury / Milan Hejduk 12.50 30.00
STWKT Ray Whitney / Rostislav Klesla / Ron Tugnutt 12.50 30.00

2002-03 Upper Deck MVP Souvenirs

Inserted at 1:48, this 27-card set featured swatches of practice-worn jerseys alongside color action photos of the featured player.

SAK Alexei Kovalev 4.00 10.00
SAT Alex Tanguay 6.00 15.00
SBB Brian Boucher 4.00 10.00
SBR Rod Brind'Amour 4.00 10.00
SCO Chris Osgood 6.00 15.00
SDH Dan Hinote 4.00 10.00
SDU Mike Dunham 4.00 10.00
SEB Ed Belfour 6.00 15.00
SJJ Jaromir Jagr 10.00 25.00
SJN Joe Nieuwendyk 4.00 10.00
SJW Justin Williams 4.00 10.00
SMB Martin Biron 4.00 10.00
SMD Marc Denis 4.00 10.00
SMM Mark Messier 8.00 20.00
SMO Mike Modano 10.00 25.00
SMR Mark Recchi 4.00 10.00
SMS Miroslav Satan 4.00 10.00
SMT Marty Turco 6.00 15.00
SRB Rob Blake 4.00 10.00
SRC Roman Cechmanek 4.00 10.00
SRK Rostislav Klesla 4.00 10.00
SRT Ron Tugnutt 4.00 10.00
SSG Simon Gagne 6.00 15.00
STFO Theo Fleury 6.00 15.00
STS Teemu Selanne 6.00 15.00
SVN Ville Nieminen 4.00 10.00
SZP Zigmund Palffy 6.00 15.00

2002-03 Upper Deck MVP Vital Forces

COMPLETE SET (14) 15.00 30.00
STATED ODDS 1:9
VF1 Paul Kariya .40 1.00
VF2 Ilya Kovalchuk .60 1.50
VF3 Joe Thornton .60 1.50
VF4 Jarome Iginla .50 1.25
VF5 Patrick Roy 2.00 5.00
VF6 Joe Sakic .75 2.00
VF7 Mike Modano .60 1.50
VF8 Dominik Hasek .75 2.00
VF9 Steve Yzerman 2.00 5.00
VF10 Eric Lindros .40 1.00
VF11 Jeremy Roenick .50 1.25
VF12 Mario Lemieux 2.50 6.00
VF13 Teemu Selanne .40 1.00
VF14 Jaromir Jagr .60 1.50

2003-04 Upper Deck MVP

This 470-card set consisted of 440 base cards and 30 rookie cards that were available only via redemption cards found in packs. Three different redemption cards represented groups of 10 rookies. Groups "A" and "B" were inserted at 1:35 while Group "C" was inserted at 1:72 hobby packs.

COMPLETE SET (470) 30.00 60.00
COMP.SET w/o SP's (440) 20.00 40.00
1 Jason Krog .04 .10
2 Petr Sykora .08 .20
3 Steve Rucchin .04 .10
4 Cam Severson .04 .10
5 Sandis Ozolinsh .04 .10
6 Steve Thomas .04 .10
7 Stanislav Chistov .04 .10
8 Sergei Fedorov .15 .40
9 Rob Niedermayer .04 .10
10 Keith Carney .04 .10
11 Alexei Smirnov .04 .10
12 Kurt Sauer .04 .10
13 Martin Gerber .08 .20
14 Jean-Sebastien Giguere .08 .20
15 Dany Heatley .15 .40
16 Slava Kozlov .04 .10
17 Ilya Kovalchuk .15 .40
18 Marc Savard .04 .10
19 Patrik Stefan .04 .10
20 Yannick Tremblay .04 .10
21 Shawn McEachern .04 .10
22 Frantisek Kaberle .04 .10
23 Andy Sutton .04 .10
24 Lubos Bartecko .04 .10
25 Jeff Odgers .04 .10
26 Pasi Nurminen .08 .20
27 Simon Gamache .04 .10
28 Byron Dafoe .08 .20
29 Garnet Exelby .04 .10
30 Joe DiPenta RC 1.00 2.50
31 Joe Thornton .20 .50
32 Glen Murray .04 .10
33 Mike Knuble .04 .10
34 Brian Rolston .08 .20
35 Ivan Huml .04 .10
36 Bryan Berard .04 .10
37 P-J Axelsson .04 .10
38 Nick Boynton .04 .10
39 Jonathan Girard .04 .10
40 Dan McGillis .04 .10
41 Michal Grosek .04 .10
42 Hal Gill .04 .10
43 Sergei Samsonov .08 .20
44 P.J. Stock .04 .10
45 Martin Lapointe .04 .10
46 Jeff Jillson .04 .10
47 Andrew Raycroft .08 .20
48 Martin Samuelsson .04 .10
49 Krzysztof Oliwa .04 .10
50 Steve Shields .08 .20
51 Miroslav Satan .08 .20
52 Daniel Briere .04 .10
53 Ales Kotalik .04 .10
54 J-P Dumont .04 .10
55 Curtis Brown .04 .10
56 Taylor Pyatt .04 .10
57 Jochen Hecht .04 .10
58 Chris Drury .08 .20
59 Alexei Zhitnik .04 .10
60 Maxim Afinogenov .04 .10
61 Martin Biron .08 .20
62 Mika Noronen .04 .10
63 Ryan Miller .08 .20
64 Milan Bartovic RC 1.00 2.50
65 Jarome Iginla .12 .30
66 Craig Conroy .04 .10
67 Steve Reinprecht .04 .10
68 Martin Gelinas .04 .10
69 Oleg Saprykin .04 .10
70 Dave Lowry .04 .10
71 Dean McAmmond .04 .10
72 Jordan Leopold .04 .10
73 Chuck Kobasew .04 .10
74 Roman Turek .08 .20
75 Jamie McLennan .04 .10
76 Rick Mrozik RC .04 .10
77 Jeff O'Neill .04 .10
78 Ron Francis .08 .20
79 Rod Brind'Amour .08 .20
80 Radim Vrbata .04 .10
81 Sean Hill .04 .10
82 Erik Cole .04 .10
83 Jan Hlavac .04 .10
84 Ryan Bayda .04 .10
85 Jaroslav Svoboda .04 .10
86 Pavel Brendl .04 .10
87 Aaron Ward .04 .10
88 Patrick DesRochers .04 .10
89 Kevin Weekes .08 .20
90 Steve Sullivan .04 .10
91 Alexei Zhamnov .04 .10
92 Eric Daze .04 .10
93 Kyle Calder .04 .10
94 Tyler Arnason .08 .20
95 Mark Bell .04 .10
96 Chris Simon .04 .10
97 Alexander Karpovtsev .04 .10
98 Igor Radulov .04 .10
99 Michael Leighton .08 .20
100 Jocelyn Thibault .08 .20
101 Peter Forsberg .30 .75
102 Milan Hejduk .10 .25
103 Alex Tanguay .08 .20
104 Joe Sakic .30 .75
105 Paul Kariya .10 .25
106 Derek Morris .04 .10
107 Rob Blake .08 .20
108 Adam Foote .04 .10
109 Eric Messier .04 .10
110 Teemu Selanne .10 .25
111 Dan Hinote .04 .10
112 David Aebischer .08 .20
113 Patrick Roy .60 1.50
114 Ray Whitney .04 .10
115 Andrew Cassels .04 .10
116 Geoff Sanderson .04 .10
117 David Vyborny .04 .10
118 Jaroslav Spacek .04 .10
119 Mike Sillinger .04 .10
120 Rick Nash .12 .30
121 Tyler Wright .04 .10
122 Todd Marchant .04 .10
123 Rostislav Klesla .04 .10
124 Jody Shelley .04 .10
125 Marc Denis .08 .20
126 Kent McDonell RC 1.00 2.50
127 Mike Modano .20 .50
128 Sergei Zubov .04 .10
129 Bill Guerin .08 .20
130 Jere Lehtinen .08 .20
131 Jason Arnott .04 .10
132 Brenden Morrow .08 .20
133 Scott Young .04 .10
134 Darryl Sydor .04 .10
135 Niko Kapanen .04 .10
136 Don Sweeney .04 .10
137 Steve Ott .04 .10
138 Jason Bacashihua .08 .20
139 Marty Turco .08 .20
140 Stephane Robidas .04 .10
141 Ron Tugnutt .08 .20
142 Sergei Fedorov .15 .40
143 Brett Hull .15 .40
144 Brendan Shanahan .10 .25
145 Nicklas Lidstrom .10 .25
146 Pavel Datsyuk .10 .25
147 Mathieu Schneider .04 .10
148 Henrik Zetterberg .10 .25
149 Igor Larionov .04 .10
150 Tomas Holmstrom .04 .10
151 Jason Woolley .04 .10
152 Darren McCarty .04 .10
153 Derian Hatcher .04 .10
154 Chris Chelios .10 .25
155 Dominik Hasek .30 .75
156 Steve Yzerman .60 1.50
157 Jiri Fischer .04 .10
158 Manny Legace .08 .20
159 Curtis Joseph .10 .25
160 Ryan Smyth .04 .10
161 Marty Reasoner .04 .10
162 Mike York .04 .10
163 Mike Comrie .08 .20
164 Radek Dvorak .04 .10
165 Ales Hemsky .08 .20
166 Eric Brewer .04 .10
167 Brad Isbister .04 .10
168 Fernando Pisani .04 .10
169 Georges Laraque .04 .10
170 Alexei Semenov .04 .10
171 Raffi Torres .04 .10
172 Jani Rita .04 .10
173 Jarret Stoll .04 .10
174 Cory Cross .04 .10
175 Jason Chimera .04 .10
176 Tommy Salo .08 .20
177 Olli Jokinen .08 .20
178 Viktor Kozlov .04 .10
179 Kristian Huselius .04 .10
180 Marcus Nilson .04 .10
181 Ivan Novoseltsev .04 .10
182 Stephen Weiss .04 .10
183 Jay Bouwmeester .04 .10
184 Valeri Bure .04 .10
185 Denis Shvidki .04 .10
186 Jaroslav Bednar .04 .10
187 Peter Worrell .04 .10
188 Roberto Luongo .12 .30
188J Roberto Luongo JUMBO 1.50 4.00
189 Jani Hurme .08 .20
190 Zigmund Palffy .08 .20
191 Jaroslav Modry .04 .10
192 Eric Belanger .04 .10
193 Alexander Frolov .04 .10
194 Jason Allison .04 .10
195 Lubomir Visnovsky .04 .10
196 Ian Laperriere .04 .10
197 Adam Deadmarsh .04 .10
198 Maxim Kuznetsov .04 .10
199 Joe Corvo .04 .10
200 Mike Cammalleri .04 .10
201 Aaron Miller .04 .10
202 Mattias Norstrom .04 .10
203 Jared Aulin .04 .10
204 Jozef Stumpel .04 .10
205 Roman Cechmanek .08 .20
206 Cristobal Huet .08 .20
207 Marian Gaborik .20 .50
208 Pascal Dupuis .04 .10
209 Cliff Ronning .04 .10
210 Andrew Brunette .04 .10
211 Sergei Zholtok .04 .10
212 Wes Walz .04 .10
213 Filip Kuba .04 .10
214 P-M Bouchard .04 .10
215 Willie Mitchell .04 .10
216 Matt Johnson .04 .10
217 Darby Hendrickson .04 .10
218 Andrei Zyuzin .04 .10
219 Manny Fernandez .08 .20
220 Dwayne Roloson .08 .20
221 Saku Koivu .10 .25
222 Richard Zednik .04 .10
223 Yanic Perreault .04 .10
224 Jan Bulis .04 .10
225 Andrei Markov .04 .10
226 Niklas Sundstrom .04 .10
227 Joe Juneau .04 .10
228 Mike Ribeiro .04 .10
229 Marcel Hossa .04 .10
230 Stephane Quintal .04 .10
231 Jose Theodore .12 .30
232 Michael Komisarek .04 .10
233 Mathieu Garon .08 .20
234 Ron Hainsey .04 .10
235 David Legwand .08 .20
236 Kimmo Timonen .04 .10
237 Andreas Johansson .04 .10
238 Denis Arkhipov .04 .10
239 Darren Haydar .04 .10
240 Scott Hartnell .04 .10
241 Scott Walker .04 .10
242 Adam Hall .04 .10
243 Greg Johnson .04 .10
244 Scottie Upshall .04 .10
245 Tomas Vokoun .08 .20
246 Brian Finley .08 .20
247 Patrik Elias .08 .20
248 Jamie Langenbrunner .04 .10
249 Scott Gomez .04 .10
250 Jeff Friesen .04 .10
251 Joe Nieuwendyk .08 .20
252 John Madden .04 .10
253 Brian Rafalski .04 .10
254 Scott Niedermayer .04 .10
255 Grant Marshall .04 .10
256 Brian Gionta .04 .10
257 Scott Stevens .08 .20
258 Colin White .04 .10
259 Michael Rupp .04 .10
260 Martin Brodeur .30 .75
261 Corey Schwab .08 .20
262 Ken Daneyko .04 .10
263 Alexei Yashin .04 .10
264 Jason Blake .04 .10
265 Mark Parrish .04 .10
266 Dave Scatchard .04 .10
267 Michael Peca .04 .10
268 Roman Hamrlik .04 .10
269 Adrian Aucoin .04 .10
270 Arron Asham .04 .10
271 Janne Niinimaa .04 .10
272 Mattias Weinhandl .04 .10
273 Rick DiPietro .08 .20
274 Garth Snow .08 .20
275 Eric Godard .04 .10
276 Alex Kovalev .08 .20
277 Anson Carter .08 .20
278 Petr Nedved .04 .10
279 Eric Lindros .10 .25
280 Tom Poti .04 .10
281 Bobby Holik .04 .10
282 Matthew Barnaby .04 .10
283 Pavel Bure .10 .25
284 Vladimir Malakhov .04 .10
285 Jamie Lundmark .04 .10
286 Mike Dunham .08 .20
287 Dan Blackburn .08 .20
288 Marian Hossa .10 .25
289 Daniel Alfredsson .08 .20
290 Todd White .04 .10
291 Martin Havlat .08 .20
292 Radek Bonk .08 .20
293 Wade Redden .04 .10

294 Zdeno Chara .04 .10
295 Magnus Arvedson .04 .10
296 Shaun Van Allen .04 .10
297 Karel Rachunek .04 .10
298 Peter Schaefer .04 .10
299 Jason Spezza .10 .25
300 Vaclav Varada .04 .10
301 Anton Volchenkov .04 .10
302 Patrick Lalime .08 .20
303 Ray Emery .08 .20
304 Jody Hull .04 .10
305 Jeremy Roenick .15 .40
306 Mark Recchi .08 .20
307 Tony Amonte .08 .20
308 Keith Primeau .08 .20
309 Michal Handzus .04 .10
310 Kim Johnsson .04 .10
311 Eric Desjardins .04 .10
312 Sami Kapanen .04 .10
313 John LeClair .10 .25
314 Simon Gagne .10 .25
315 Donald Brashear .04 .10
316 Justin Williams .04 .10
317 Eric Weinrich .04 .10
318 Jeff Hackett .08 .20
319 Robert Esche .08 .20
320 Mike Johnson .04 .10
321 Shane Doan .04 .10
322 Ladislav Nagy .04 .10
323 Daymond Langkow .04 .10
324 Chris Gratton .04 .10
325 Jan Hrdina .04 .10
326 Teppo Numminen .04 .10
327 Branko Radivojevic .04 .10
328 Paul Mara .04 .10
329 Tyson Nash .04 .10
330 Jeff Taffe .04 .10
331 Brian Boucher .08 .20
332 Sean Burke .08 .20
333 Mario Lemieux .75 2.00
334 Martin Straka .04 .10
335 Dick Tarnstrom .04 .10
336 Aleksey Morozov .04 .10
337 Mikael Samuelsson .04 .10
338 Ville Nieminen .04 .10
339 Rico Fata .04 .10
340 Dan Focht .04 .10
341 Johan Hedberg .08 .20
342 Sebastien Caron .08 .20
343 Brooks Orpik .04 .10
344 Vincent Damphousse .04 .10
345 Patrick Marleau .08 .20
346 Marco Sturm .04 .10
347 Mike Ricci .04 .10
348 Scott Hannan .04 .10
349 Jim Fahey .04 .10
350 Todd Harvey .04 .10
351 Adam Graves .04 .10
352 Jonathan Cheechoo .05 .12
353 Brad Stuart .04 .10
354 Niko Dimitrakos .04 .10
355 Kyle McLaren .04 .10
356 Miikka Kiprusoff .08 .20
357 Evgeni Nabokov .08 .20
358 Pavol Demitra .08 .20
359 Al MacInnis .08 .20
360 Eric Boguniecki .04 .10
361 Doug Weight .08 .20
362 Scott Mellanby .04 .10
363 Keith Tkachuk .10 .25
364 Petr Cajanek .04 .10
365 Alexander Khavanov .04 .10
366 Barret Jackman .08 .20
367 Steve Martins .04 .10
368 Bryce Salvador .04 .10
369 Dallas Drake .04 .10
370 Ryan Johnson .04 .10
371 Reed Low .04 .10
372 Chris Pronger .08 .20
373 Brent Johnson .08 .20
374 Chris Osgood .08 .20
375 Peter Sejna RC 1.00 2.50
376 Vaclav Prospal .04 .10
377 Vincent Lecavalier .10 .25
378 Brad Richards .08 .20
379 Martin St. Louis .08 .20
380 Dan Boyle .04 .10
381 Fredrik Modin .04 .10
382 Dave Andreychuk .04 .10
383 Pavel Kubina .04 .10
384 Alexander Svitov .04 .10
385 Nikita Alexeev .04 .10
386 Nikolai Khabibulin .10 .25
387 John Grahame .08 .20
388 Chris Dingman .04 .10
389 Tim Taylor .04 .10
390 Alexander Mogilny .08 .20
391 Mats Sundin .10 .25
392 Owen Nolan .08 .20
393 Tomas Kaberle .04 .10
394 Nik Antropov .04 .10
395 Ed Belfour .10 .25
396 Darcy Tucker .04 .10
397 Doug Gilmour .08 .20
398 Tie Domi .08 .20
399 Phil Housley .04 .10
400 Aki Berg .04 .10
401 Bryan McCabe .04 .10
402 Gary Roberts .04 .10
403 Carlo Colaiacovo .04 .10
404 Jyrki Lumme .04 .10
405 Mikael Tellqvist .08 .20
406 Trevor Kidd .08 .20
407 Matt Stajan RC 2.50 6.00
408 Markus Naslund .10 .25
409 Todd Bertuzzi .10 .25
410 Brendan Morrison .08 .20
411 Ed Jovanovski .08 .20
412 Matt Cooke .04 .10
413 Trevor Linden .04 .10
414 Henrik Sedin .04 .10
415 Brent Sopel .04 .10
416 Daniel Sedin .04 .10
417 Mattias Ohlund .04 .10
418 Brandon Reid .04 .10
419 Marek Malik .04 .10
420 Bryan Allen .04 .10
421 Jarkko Ruutu .04 .10
422 Alexander Auld .04 .10
423 Dan Cloutier .08 .20
424 Jaromir Jagr .20 .50
425 Robert Lang .04 .10
426 Sergei Gonchar .04 .10
427 Michael Nylander .04 .10
428 Peter Bondra .08 .20
429 Sergei Berezin .04 .10
430 Jeff Halpern .04 .10
431 Mike Grier .04 .10
432 Steve Konowalchuk .04 .10
433 Ivan Ciernik .04 .10
434 Steve Eminger .04 .10
435 Olaf Kolzig .08 .20
436 Sebastien Charpentier .08 .20
437 Joe Thornton CL .20 .50
438 Martin Brodeur CL .30 .75
439 Dany Heatley CL .12 .30
440 Jean-Sebastien Giguere CL .08 .20
441 Eric Staal RC 5.00 12.00
442 Boyd Gordon RC 1.00 2.50
443 Joni Pitkanen RC 2.00 5.00
444 Christopher Brandner RC 1.00 2.50
445 Joffrey Lupul RC 2.00 5.00
446 Matthew Lombardi RC 1.00 2.50
447 Cody McCormick RC 1.00 2.50
448 Tim Gleason RC 1.00 2.50
449 Jiri Hudler RC 2.50 6.00
450 Antoine Vermette RC 1.00 2.50
451 Alexander Semin RC 1.25 3.00
452 Tuomo Ruutu RC 2.50 6.00
453 Dan Hamhuis RC 1.00 2.50
454 Sean Bergenheim RC 1.00 2.50
455 Brent Burns RC 1.00 2.50
456 Dan Fritsche RC 1.00 2.50
457 Antti Miettinen RC 1.00 2.50
458 Nathan Horton RC 2.50 6.00
459 Maxim Kondratiev RC 1.00 2.50
460 Matthew Spiller RC 1.00 2.50
461 Marc-Andre Fleury RC 8.00 20.00
462 David Hale RC 1.00 2.50
463 Marek Svatos RC 1.00 2.50
464 Milan Michalek RC 1.00 2.50
465 John-Michael Liles RC 1.00 2.50
466 Dustin Brown RC 1.00 2.50
467 Chris Higgins RC 1.00 2.50
468 Patrice Bergeron RC 6.00 15.00
469 Pavel Vorobiev RC 1.00 2.50
470 Jordin Tootoo RC 5.00 12.00

2003-04 Upper Deck MVP Gold Script

COMMON CARD (1-440) 5.00 12.00
*STARS: 30X TO 80X BASIC CARDS
*ROOKIES: 1.5X TO 4X
GOLD PRINT RUN 25 SER.#'d SETS

2003-04 Upper Deck MVP Silver Script

*STARS: 6X TO 15X BASE HI
*ROOKIES: .6X TO 1.5X
STATED PRINT RUN 150 SER.#'d SETS

2003-04 Upper Deck MVP Canadian Exclusives

COMMON CARD (1-440) 6.00 15.00
*STARS: 30X TO 80X BASIC CARDS
*ROOKIES: 1.5X TO 4X
CAN.EXCL.PRINT RUN 25 SER.#'d SETS

2003-04 Upper Deck MVP Clutch Performers

COMPLETE SET (7) 8.00 15.00
STATED ODDS 1:24
CP1 Patrick Roy 2.50 6.00
CP2 Markus Naslund .60 1.50
CP3 Martin Brodeur 2.00 5.00
CP4 Joe Thornton .75 2.00
CP5 Jean-Sebastien Giguere .60 1.50
CP6 Marian Gaborik .75 2.00
CP7 Steve Yzerman 2.00 5.00

2003-04 Upper Deck MVP Lethal Lineups

STAT.PRINT RUN 50 SER.#'d SETS
LL1 Milan Hejduk 60.00 150.00
Joe Sakic
Peter Forsberg
LL2 Tony Amonte 30.00 80.00
Jeremy Roenick
John LeClair
LL3 Joe Thornton 30.00 80.00
Sergei Samsonov
Glen Murray
LL4 Markus Naslund 30.00 80.00
Todd Bertuzzi
Trevor Linden
LL5 Doug Gilmour 30.00 80.00
Mats Sundin
Owen Nolan
LL6 Brendan Shanahan 60.00 150.00
Brett Hull
Steve Yzerman

2003-04 Upper Deck MVP Masked Men

STATED ODDS 1:18
MM1 Martin Brodeur 2.00 5.00
MM2 Patrick Roy 2.50 6.00
MM3 Nikolai Khabibulin .50 1.25
MM4 Jocelyn Thibault .50 1.25

MM5 Jean-Sebastien Giguere .50 1.25
MM6 Patrick Lalime .50 1.25
MM7 Roberto Luongo .60 1.50
MM8 Ed Belfour .50 1.25
MM9 David Aebischer .50 1.25
MM10 Marty Turco .50 1.25

2003-04 Upper Deck MVP ProSign

This 19-card set featured certified player autographs on diamond-mirrored stickers affixed to the card fronts. Cards from this set were inserted at a rate of 1:480. Please note that the Gretzky card has been confirmed to exist though there is not significant market information to price it currently; the Joseph card has yet to be confirmed.

PSBO Bobby Orr 125.00 300.00
PSCJ Curtis Joseph EXISTS?
PSDH Dany Heatley 15.00 40.00
PSEC Erik Cole 6.00 15.00
PSGH Gordie Howe 100.00 250.00
PSHZ Henrik Zetterberg 20.00 50.00
PSJT Joe Thornton 30.00 80.00
PSMA Maxim Afinogenov 6.00 15.00
PSMB Martin Brodeur 125.00 300.00
PSMC Mike Comrie 20.00 50.00
PSMH Martin Havlat 12.00 30.00
PSMN Markus Naslund 20.00 50.00
PSRB Ray Bourque 75.00 200.00
PSRD Rick DiPietro 15.00 40.00
PSRM Adam Hall 6.00 15.00
PSSC Stanislav Chistov 8.00 20.00
PSSG Simon Gagne 12.50 30.00
PSSH Scott Hartnell 10.00 25.00
PSWG Wayne Gretzky 400.00 600.00

2003-04 Upper Deck MVP Souvenirs

This 26-card set featured swatches of practice-worn jerseys. Cards were randomly inserted at 1:24.

S1 Chris Drury 5.00 12.00
S2 Joe Sakic 10.00 25.00
S3 Patrick Roy 15.00 40.00
S4 Rob Blake 5.00 12.00
S5 Ray Whitney 5.00 12.00
S6 Jaromir Jagr 8.00 20.00
S7 Olaf Kolzig 5.00 12.00
S8 Peter Bondra 5.00 12.00
S9 Paul Kariya 5.00 12.00
S10 John LeClair 5.00 12.00
S11 Keith Primeau 5.00 12.00
S12 Mark Recchi 5.00 12.00
S13 Roman Cechmanek 5.00 12.00
S14 Felix Potvin 5.00 12.00
S15 Jason Allison 5.00 12.00
S16 Zigmund Palffy 5.00 12.00
S17 Peter Forsberg 10.00 25.00
S18 Alex Kovalev 5.00 12.00
S19 J-P Dumont 5.00 12.00
S20 Maxim Afinogenov 5.00 12.00
S21 Brett Hull 6.00 15.00
S22 Simon Gagne 5.00 12.00
S23 Brian Boucher 5.00 12.00
S24 Ville Nieminen 5.00 12.00
S25 Eric Lindros 5.00 12.00
S26 Jarome Iginla 6.00 15.00

2003-04 Upper Deck MVP SportsNut

This 91-card set featured a scratch off area that revealed a game code. Collectors could enter the code on the cards at the UD website to accumulate points redeemable for UD merchandise.

SN1 Jean-Sebastien Giguere .50 1.25
SN2 Paul Kariya .60 1.50
SN3 Petr Sykora .50 1.25
SN4 Pasi Numminen .50 1.25
SN5 Ilya Kovalchuk 1.00 2.50
SN6 Dany Heatley 1.00 2.50
SN7 Jeff Hackett .50 1.25
SN8 Joe Thornton 1.25 3.00
SN9 Glen Murray .25 .60
SN10 Sergei Samsonov .50 1.25
SN11 Martin Biron .50 1.25
SN12 Miroslav Satan .50 1.25
SN13 Maxim Afinogenov .25 .60
SN14 Roman Turek .50 1.25
SN15 Jarome Iginla .75 2.00
SN16 Chris Drury .50 1.25
SN17 Pavel Brendl .25 .60
SN18 Jeff O'Neill .25 .60
SN19 Jocelyn Thibault .50 1.25
SN20 Eric Daze .25 .60
SN21 David Aebischer .50 1.25
SN22 Peter Forsberg 2.00 5.00
SN23 Joe Sakic 2.00 5.00
SN24 Milan Hejduk .60 1.50
SN25 Marc Denis .50 1.25
SN26 Rick Nash .75 2.00
SN27 Marty Turco .50 1.25
SN28 Mike Modano 1.25 3.00
SN29 Bill Guerin .50 1.25
SN30 Dominik Hasek 2.00 5.00
SN31 Steve Yzerman 4.00 10.00
SN32 Sergei Fedorov 1.00 2.50
SN33 Brett Hull 1.00 2.50
SN34 Tommy Salo .50 1.25
SN35 Mike Comrie .50 1.25
SN36 Ryan Smyth .25 .60
SN37 Ales Hemsky .50 1.25
SN38 Roberto Luongo .75 2.00
SN39 Olli Jokinen .50 1.25
SN40 Stephen Weiss .25 .60
SN41 Roman Cechmanek .50 1.25
SN42 Zigmund Palffy .50 1.25
SN43 Dwayne Roloson .50 1.25
SN44 Manny Fernandez .50 1.25
SN45 Marian Gaborik 1.25 3.00
SN46 Jose Theodore .75 2.00
SN47 Saku Koivu .60 1.50
SN48 Marcel Hossa .25 .60
SN49 Tomas Vokoun .50 1.25
SN50 Martin Brodeur 2.00 5.00
SN51 Jamie Langenbrunner .25 .60
SN52 Patrik Elias .50 1.25
SN53 Garth Snow .50 1.25
SN54 Alexei Yashin .25 .60
SN55 Mike Dunham .50 1.25
SN56 Dan Blackburn .50 1.25
SN57 Eric Lindros .60 1.50
SN58 Pavel Bure .60 1.50
SN59 Alex Kovalev .50 1.25
SN60 Patrick Lalime .50 1.25
SN61 Marian Hossa .60 1.50
SN62 Daniel Alfredsson .50 1.25
SN63 Jason Spezza .60 1.50
SN64 Robert Esche .50 1.25
SN65 Jeremy Roenick 1.00 2.50
SN66 John LeClair .60 1.50
SN67 Tony Amonte .50 1.25
SN68 Sean Burke .50 1.25
SN69 Mike Johnson .25 .60
SN70 Johan Hedberg .50 1.25
SN71 Mario Lemieux 5.00 12.00
SN72 Martin Straka .25 .60
SN73 Evgeni Nabokov .50 1.25
SN74 Vincent Damphousse .25 .60
SN75 Chris Osgood .50 1.25
SN76 Keith Tkachuk .60 1.50
SN77 Al MacInnis .50 1.25
SN78 Nikolai Khabibulin .60 1.50
SN79 Vincent Lecavalier .60 1.50
SN80 Martin St. Louis .50 1.25
SN81 Ed Belfour .60 1.50
SN82 Mats Sundin .60 1.50
SN83 Owen Nolan .50 1.25
SN84 Alexander Mogilny .50 1.25
SN85 Alexander Auld .25 .60
SN86 Todd Bertuzzi .60 1.50
SN87 Markus Naslund .60 1.50
SN88 Ed Jovanovski .50 1.25
SN89 Olaf Kolzig .50 1.25
SN90 Jaromir Jagr 1.25 3.00
SN91 Peter Bondra .50 1.25

2003-04 Upper Deck MVP Talent

COMPLETE SET (15) 15.00 30.00
STATED ODDS 1:12
MT1 Mario Lemieux 3.00 8.00
MT2 Martin Brodeur 2.00 5.00
MT3 Markus Naslund .50 1.25
MT4 Marian Gaborik 1.50 4.00
MT5 Dany Heatley 1.00 2.50
MT6 Joe Thornton 1.25 3.00
MT7 Steve Yzerman 2.50 6.00
MT8 Marian Hossa .50 1.25
MT9 Ed Belfour .50 1.25
MT10 Pavel Bure .50 1.25
MT11 Peter Forsberg 2.00 5.00
MT12 Ilya Kovalchuk 1.00 2.50
MT13 Jaromir Jagr 1.25 3.00
MT14 Zigmund Palffy .50 1.25
MT15 Mike Modano 1.25 3.00

2003-04 Upper Deck MVP Threads

STAT.PRINT RUN 100 SER.#'d SETS
TC1 Al MacInnis 12.50 30.00
TC2 Bill Guerin 12.50 30.00
TC3 Brendan Shanahan 15.00 40.00
TC4 Brett Hull 20.00 50.00
TC5 Chris Osgood 12.50 30.00
TC6 Ed Belfour 15.00 40.00
TC7 Jaromir Jagr 20.00 50.00
TC8 Keith Primeau 12.50 30.00
TC9 Patrick Roy 40.00 100.00
TC10 Ray Bourque 25.00 60.00

2003-04 Upper Deck MVP Wal-Mart Jumbos

8 Sergei Fedorov
14 Jean-Sebastien Giguere
15 Dany Heatley
31 Joe Thornton
63 Ryan Miller
65 Jarome Iginla
74 Roman Turek
100 Jocelyn Thibault
101 Peter Forsberg
104 Joe Sakic
105 Paul Kariya
120 Rick Nash
139 Marty Turco
156 Steve Yzerman
160 Ryan Smyth
163 Mike Comrie
165 Ales Hemsky
188 Roberto Luongo
207 Marian Gaborik
221 Saku Koivu
229 Marcel Hossa
231 Jose Theodore
232 Mike Komisarek
260 Martin Brodeur
277 Anson Carter
288 Marian Hossa
289 Daniel Alfredsson
302 Patrick Lalime
333 Mario Lemieux
363 Keith Tkachuk
375 Peter Sejna
377 Vincent Lecavalier
390 Alexander Mogilny
391 Mats Sundin
392 Owen Nolan
395 Ed Belfour
407 Matt Stajan
408 Markus Naslund
409 Todd Bertuzzi
411 Ed Jovanovski
418 Brandon Reid
424 Jaromir Jagr

2003-04 Upper Deck MVP Winning Formula

COMPLETE SET (10) 10.00 20.00
STATED ODDS 1:18
WF1 Rick Nash .60 1.50
WF2 Todd Bertuzzi .50 1.25
WF3 Jeremy Roenick .60 1.50
WF4 Steve Yzerman 2.50 6.00
WF5 Jason Spezza .50 1.25
WF6 Brett Hull 1.00 2.50
WF7 Jean-Sebastien Giguere .50 1.25
WF8 Mike Modano 1.25 3.00
WF9 Paul Kariya .50 1.25
WF10 Henrik Zetterberg .50 1.25

2005-06 Upper Deck MVP

This 445-card set was issued into the hobby in eight-card packs, with a $1.99 SRP, which came 24 to a box. Cards numbered 1-392 feature veterans in alphabetical team order while cards 393-437 are Rookie Cards and the set concludes with Checklist cards from 438-445.

COMPLETE SET (445) 75.00 150.00
1 Sergei Fedorov .20 .50
2 Sandis Ozolinsh .12 .30
3 Scott Niedermayer .12 .30
4 Rob Niedermayer .12 .30
5 Teemu Selanne .20 .50
6 Jean-Sebastien Giguere .15 .40
7 Ruslan Salei .05 .15
8 Joffrey Lupul .12 .30
9 Andy McDonald .05 .15
10 Keith Carney .05 .15
11 Vitali Vishnevsky .05 .15
12 Petr Sykora .12 .30
13 Marian Hossa .15 .40
14 Patrik Stefan .12 .30
15 Kari Lehtonen .20 .50
16 Bobby Holik .12 .30
17 Andy Sutton .05 .15
18 Serge Aubin .05 .15
19 Marc Savard .12 .30
20 Peter Bondra .15 .40
21 Jaroslav Modry .05 .15
22 Niclas Havelid .05 .15
23 Mike Dunham .10 .25
24 Slava Kozlov .05 .15
25 Scott Mellanby .05 .15
26 Ilya Kovalchuk .25 .60
27 Glen Murray .12 .30
28 Joe Thornton .30 .75
29 Andrew Raycroft .15 .40
30 Patrice Bergeron .20 .50
31 Hal Gill .05 .15
32 P.J. Axelsson .05 .15
33 Shawn McEachern .12 .30
34 Brian Leetch .20 .50
35 Alexei Zhamnov .05 .15
36 Nick Boynton .12 .30
37 Brad Isbister .05 .15
38 Jiri Slegr .05 .15
39 Brad Boyes .05 .15
40 Travis Green .05 .15
41 Tom Fitzgerald .05 .15
42 Dave Scatchard .05 .15
43 Chris Drury .15 .40
44 Martin Biron .15 .40
45 Maxim Afinogenov .12 .30
46 Daniel Briere .15 .40
47 Mika Noronen .15 .40
48 Jean-Pierre Dumont .12 .30
49 Derek Roy .12 .30
50 Mike Grier .05 .15
51 Jochen Hecht .05 .15
52 Jeff Jillson .05 .15
53 Teppo Numminen .05 .15
54 Ryan Miller .10 .25
55 Tim Connolly .05 .15
56 Jarome Iginla .15 .40
57 Jordan Leopold .12 .30
58 Tony Amonte .15 .40
59 Chris Simon .05 .15
60 Shean Donovan .05 .15
61 Roman Hamrlik .05 .15
62 Chuck Kobasew .12 .30
63 Darren McCarty .12 .30
64 Robyn Regehr .12 .30
65 Phillippe Sauve .15 .40
66 Stephane Yelle .05 .15
67 Daymond Langkow .05 .15
68 Matthew Lombardi .12 .30
69 Marcus Nilson .05 .15
70 Jason Wiemer .05 .15
71 Erik Cole .12 .30
72 Glen Wesley .12 .30
73 Josef Vasicek .05 .15
74 Radim Vrbata .05 .15
75 Niclas Wallin .05 .15
76 Martin Gerber .15 .40
77 Rod Brind'Amour .15 .40
78 Eric Staal .15 .40
79 Justin Williams .15 .40
80 Ray Whitney .05 .15
81 Oleg Tverdovsky .12 .30
82 Bret Hedican .05 .15
83 Jesse Boulerice .05 .15
84 Cory Stillman .12 .30
85 Nikolai Khabibulin .20 .50
86 Tuomo Ruutu .12 .30
87 Eric Daze .15 .40
88 Kyle Calder .12 .30
89 Matthew Barnaby .05 .15
90 Adrian Aucoin .12 .30
91 Tyler Arnason .12 .30
92 Martin Lapointe .05 .15
93 Jaroslav Spacek .05 .15
94 Curtis Brown .05 .15
95 Mark Bell .12 .30
96 Pavel Vorobiev .05 .15
97 Joe Sakic .40 1.00
98 Rob Blake .15 .40
99 Alex Tanguay .15 .40
100 Milan Hejduk .20 .50
101 John-Michael Liles .12 .30
102 Steve Konowalchuk .05 .15
103 David Aebischer .15 .40
104 Brad May .05 .15
105 Patrice Brisebois .05 .15
106 Pierre Turgeon .12 .30
107 Andrew Brunette .05 .15
108 Antti Laaksonen .05 .15
109 Riku Hahl .05 .15
110 Dan Hinote .05 .15
111 Karlis Skrastins .05 .15
112 Rick Nash .25 .60
113 Marc Denis .15 .40
114 Todd Marchant .05 .15
115 David Vyborny .05 .15
116 Manny Malhotra .05 .15
117 Tyler Wright .05 .15
118 Jan Hrdina .05 .15
119 Nikolai Zherdev .15 .40
120 Bryan Berard .12 .30
121 Adam Foote .05 .15
122 Luke Richardson .05 .15
123 Trevor Letowski .05 .15
124 Jody Shelley .05 .15
125 Mike Modano .20 .50
126 Brenden Morrow .15 .40
127 Sergei Zubov .12 .30
128 Marty Turco .15 .40
129 Steve Ott .05 .15
130 Jason Arnott .05 .15
131 Bill Guerin .12 .30
132 Stu Barnes .05 .15
133 Jere Lehtinen .15 .40
134 Jaroslav Svoboda .05 .15
135 Phillippe Boucher .05 .15
136 Johan Hedberg .10 .25
137 Trevor Daley .05 .15
138 Martin Skoula .05 .15
139 Steve Yzerman .50 1.25
140 Chris Chelios .20 .50
141 Robert Lang .05 .15
142 Chris Osgood .10 .25
143 Tomas Holmstrom .05 .15
144 Kris Draper .05 .15
145 Jiri Fischer .05 .15
146 Brendan Shanahan .20 .50
147 Nicklas Lidstrom .20 .50
148 Manny Legace .20 .50
149 Henrik Zetterberg .20 .50
150 Mathieu Schneider .05 .15
151 Pavel Datsyuk .20 .50
152 Ty Conklin .15 .40
153 Ryan Smyth .15 .40
154 Jason Smith .05 .15
155 Ales Hemsky .12 .30
156 Michael Peca .12 .30
157 Chris Pronger .15 .40
158 Radek Dvorak .05 .15
159 Georges Laraque .05 .15
160 Raffi Torres .12 .30
161 Alexei Semenov .05 .15
162 Todd Harvey .05 .15
163 Igor Ulanov .05 .15
164 Jani Rita .05 .15
165 Roberto Luongo .30 .75
166 Jay Bouwmeester .12 .30
167 Olli Jokinen .15 .40
168 Sean Hill .05 .15
169 Nathan Horton .12 .30
170 Stephen Weiss .12 .30
171 Chris Gratton .05 .15
172 Joe Nieuwendyk .15 .40
173 Gary Roberts .05 .15
174 Jamie McLennan .05 .15
175 Mike Van Ryn .05 .15
176 Martin Gelinas .05 .15
177 Jozef Stumpel .05 .15
178 Luc Robitaille .15 .40
179 Mathieu Garon .15 .40
180 Lubomir Visnovsky .05 .15
181 Jeremy Roenick .20 .50
182 Mattias Norstrom .05 .15
183 Dustin Brown .12 .30
184 Alexander Frolov .15 .40
185 Valeri Bure .05 .15
186 Pavol Demitra .15 .40
187 Mike Cammalleri .05 .15
188 Aaron Miller .05 .15
189 Manny Fernandez .15 .40
190 Marian Gaborik .25 .60
191 Brian Rolston .05 .15
192 Filip Kuba .12 .30
193 P-M Bouchard .12 .30
194 Andrei Zyuzin .05 .15
195 Pascal Dupuis .05 .15
196 Alexandre Daigle .12 .30
197 Dwayne Roloson .15 .40
198 Marc Chouinard .05 .15
199 Nick Schultz .05 .15
200 Saku Koivu .20 .50
201 Richard Zednik .12 .30
202 Michael Ryder .15 .40
203 Radek Bonk .05 .15
204 Alexei Kovalev .10 .25
205 Jan Bulis .05 .15
206 Pierre Dagenais .05 .15
207 Mike Ribeiro .12 .30
208 Jose Theodore .20 .50
209 Mike Komisarek .05 .15
210 Sheldon Souray .12 .30
211 Niklas Sundstrom .05 .15
212 Mathieu Dandenault .05 .15
213 Andrei Markov .05 .15
214 Craig Rivet .05 .15
215 Tomas Vokoun .15 .40
216 David Legwand .15 .40
217 Steve Sullivan .12 .30
218 Adam Hall .05 .15
219 Scott Walker .12 .30
220 Martin Erat .05 .15
221 Paul Kariya .20 .50
222 Scott Hartnell .05 .15
223 Scott Nichol .05 .15
224 Randy Robitaille .05 .15
225 Kimmo Timonen .12 .30
226 Danny Markov .05 .15
227 Jordin Tootoo .05 .15
228 Scott Gomez .15 .40
229 Patrik Elias .15 .40
230 Martin Brodeur .40 1.00
231 Sergei Brylin .05 .15
232 John Madden .12 .30
233 Dan McGillis .05 .15
234 Paul Martin .05 .15
235 Alexander Mogilny .15 .40
236 Brian Rafalski .12 .30
237 Brian Gionta .05 .15
238 Viktor Kozlov .05 .15
239 Jamie Langenbrunner .05 .15
240 Jay Pandolfo .05 .15
241 Erik Rasmussen .05 .15
242 Alexei Yashin .12 .30
243 Rick DiPietro .15 .40
244 Alexei Zhitnik .05 .15
245 Brent Sopel .12 .30
246 Jason Blake .05 .15
247 Janne Niinimaa .05 .15
248 Mark Parrish .12 .30
249 Miroslav Satan .12 .30
250 Trent Hunter .12 .30
251 Garth Snow .10 .25
252 Mike York .05 .15
253 Shawn Bates .05 .15
254 Tom Poti .12 .30
255 Martin Straka .05 .15
256 Jaromir Jagr .30 .75
257 Darius Kasparaitis .05 .15
258 Michael Nylander .05 .15
259 Kevin Weekes .15 .40
260 Steve Rucchin .12 .30
261 Fedor Tyutin .05 .15
262 Martin Rucinsky .05 .15
263 Ville Nieminen .05 .15
264 Jason Ward .05 .15
265 Marcel Hossa .12 .30
266 Dany Heatley .20 .50
267 Dominik Hasek .25 .60
268 Wade Redden .12 .30
269 Jason Spezza .20 .50
270 Chris Phillips .05 .15
271 Bryan Smolinski .05 .15
272 Zdeno Chara .15 .40

Card	Low	High
273 Daniel Alfredsson	.15	.40
274 Martin Havlat	.15	.40
275 Vaclav Varada	.05	.15
276 Peter Schaefer	.05	.15
277 Antoine Vermette	.05	.15
278 Mike Fisher	.05	.15
279 Simon Gagne	.20	.50
280 Peter Forsberg	.30	.75
281 Keith Primeau	.12	.30
282 Derian Hatcher	.05	.15
283 Kim Johnsson	.12	.30
284 Sami Kapanen	.12	.30
285 Mike Knuble	.05	.15
286 Eric Desjardins	.05	.15
287 Robert Esche	.15	.40
288 Donald Brashear	.05	.15
289 Joni Pitkanen	.12	.30
290 Mike Rathje	.05	.15
291 Chris Therien	.05	.15
292 Michal Handzus	.05	.15
293 Geoff Sanderson	.05	.15
294 Curtis Joseph	.20	.50
295 Mike Ricci	.12	.30
296 Derek Morris	.05	.15
297 Mike Johnson	.05	.15
298 Petr Nedved	.12	.30
299 Oleg Saprykin	.05	.15
300 Shane Doan	.12	.30
301 Ladislav Nagy	.12	.30
302 Tyson Nash	.05	.15
303 Mike Comrie	.10	.25
304 Brad Ference	.05	.15
305 Paul Mara	.05	.15
306 Mario Lemieux	.75	2.00
307 Zigmund Palffy	.15	.40
308 Ryan Malone	.12	.30
309 Rico Fata	.05	.15
310 John LeClair	.20	.50
311 Lasse Pirjeta	.05	.15
312 Konstantin Koltsov	.05	.15
313 Mark Recchi	.15	.40
314 Jocelyn Thibault	.15	.40
315 Sergei Gonchar	.05	.15
316 Lyle Odelein	.05	.15
317 Dick Tarnstrom	.05	.15
318 Jonathan Cheechoo	.20	.50
319 Marco Sturm	.12	.30
320 Evgeni Nabokov	.15	.40
321 Alyn McCauley	.05	.15
322 Milan Michalek	.05	.15
323 Brad Stuart	.12	.30
324 Wayne Primeau	.05	.15
325 Patrick Marleau	.15	.40
326 Scott Thornton	.05	.15
327 Vesa Toskala	.10	.25
328 Marcel Goc	.05	.15
329 Kyle McLaren	.05	.15
330 Christian Ehrhoff	.05	.15
331 Keith Tkachuk	.20	.50
332 Barret Jackman	.12	.30
333 Patrick Lalime	.15	.40
334 Doug Weight	.15	.40
335 Mark Rycroft	.12	.30
336 Christian Backman	.05	.15
337 Dallas Drake	.12	.30
338 Mike Sillinger	.05	.15
339 Jamal Mayers	.05	.15
340 Eric Brewer	.05	.15
341 Scott Young	.05	.15
342 Dean McAmmond	.05	.15
343 Brad Richards	.15	.40
344 Fredrik Modin	.12	.30
345 Martin St. Louis	.15	.40
346 Ruslan Fedotenko	.12	.30
347 Dave Andreychuk	.12	.30
348 Pavel Kubina	.12	.30
349 Tim Taylor	.05	.15
350 Vincent Lecavalier	.20	.50
351 Sean Burke	.15	.40
352 Darryl Sydor	.05	.15
353 Vaclav Prospal	.05	.15
354 Mats Sundin	.20	.50
355 Tie Domi	.15	.40
356 Bryan McCabe	.12	.30
357 Darcy Tucker	.05	.15
358 Tomas Kaberle	.05	.15
359 Kyle Wellwood	.05	.15
360 Nikolai Antropov	.12	.30
361 Ken Klee	.05	.15
362 Ed Belfour	.20	.50
363 Matt Stajan	.12	.30
364 Eric Lindros	.20	.50
365 Jason Allison	.12	.30
366 Jeff O'Neill	.12	.30
367 Mariusz Czerkawski	.05	.15
368 J-S Aubin	.05	.15
369 Markus Naslund	.20	.50
370 Dan Cloutier	.15	.40
371 Trevor Linden	.12	.30
372 Anson Carter	.15	.40
373 Todd Bertuzzi	.25	.60
374 Daniel Sedin	.05	.15
375 Sami Salo	.05	.15
376 Mattias Ohlund	.12	.30
377 Henrik Sedin	.05	.15
378 Jarkko Ruutu	.05	.15
379 Brendan Morrison	.12	.30
380 Ed Jovanovski	.15	.40
381 Jason King	.05	.15
382 Alex Auld	.05	.15
383 Matt Cooke	.05	.15
384 Olaf Kolzig	.15	.40
385 Brendan Witt	.12	.30
386 Jeff Halpern	.05	.15
387 Dainius Zubrus	.05	.15
388 Alexander Semin	.05	.15
389 Jeff Friesen	.12	.30
390 Andrew Cassels	.05	.15
391 Brian Willsie	.12	.30
392 Boyd Gordon	.05	.15
393 Sidney Crosby RC	20.00	50.00
394 Alexander Ovechkin RC	12.00	30.00
395 Gilbert Brule RC	4.00	10.00
396 Wojtek Wolski RC	3.00	8.00
397 Rene Bourque RC	2.50	6.00
398 Jeff Woywitka RC	2.50	6.00
399 Hannu Toivonen RC	2.50	6.00
400 Yann Danis RC	3.00	8.00
401 Alexander Perezhogin RC	2.00	5.00
402 David Leneveu RC	3.00	8.00
403 Zach Parise RC	8.00	20.00
404 Dion Phaneuf RC	12.00	30.00
405 Eric Nystrom RC	3.00	8.00
406 Mike Richards RC	3.00	8.00
407 Jeff Carter RC	5.00	12.00
408 Cam Ward RC	6.00	15.00
409 Kevin Nastiuk RC	3.00	8.00
410 Petteri Nokelainen RC	2.50	6.00
411 Robert Nilsson RC	3.00	8.00
412 Andy Wozniewski RC	2.50	6.00
413 Alexander Steen RC	4.00	10.00
414 Ryan Getzlaf RC	10.00	25.00
415 Corey Perry RC	4.00	10.00
416 Rostislav Olesz RC	3.00	8.00
417 Ryan Suter RC	3.00	8.00
418 Henrik Lundqvist RC	10.00	25.00
419 Petr Prucha RC	2.50	6.00
420 Jimmy Howard RC	4.00	10.00
421 Johan Franzen RC	5.00	12.00
422 Thomas Vanek RC	6.00	15.00
423 Brandon Bochenski RC	2.50	6.00
424 Andrej Meszaros RC	2.50	6.00
425 Ryane Clowe RC	2.50	6.00
426 Jussi Jokinen RC	2.50	6.00
427 Braydon Coburn RC	3.00	8.00
428 Jim Slater RC	3.00	8.00
429 Matthew Foy RC	2.50	6.00
430 Peter Budaj RC	3.00	8.00
431 Brent Seabrook RC	5.00	12.00
432 Lee Stempniak RC	2.50	6.00
433 Andrew Alberts RC	2.50	6.00
434 Keith Ballard RC	2.50	6.00
435 Duncan Keith RC	6.00	15.00
436 Milan Jurcina RC	2.50	6.00
437 Chris Campoli RC	2.50	6.00
438 Joe Sakic CL	.40	1.00
439 Joe Thornton CL	.30	.75
440 Jarome Iginla CL	.15	.40
441 Steve Yzerman CL	.50	1.25
442 Martin Brodeur CL	.40	1.00
443 Peter Forsberg CL	.30	.75
444 Mario Lemieux CL	.75	2.00
445 Martin St. Louis CL	.15	.40

2005-06 Upper Deck MVP Gold

*STARS: 10X TO 25X BASE HI
*ROOKIES: 1.25X TO 3X BASE HI
PRINT RUN 100 SER.#'d SETS

Card	Low	High
393 Sidney Crosby	100.00	250.00
394 Alexander Ovechkin	80.00	200.00

2005-06 Upper Deck MVP Platinum

*STARS: 30X TO 80 BASE HI
*ROOKIES: 4X TO 10X
PRINT RUN 25 SER.#'d SETS

2005-06 Upper Deck MVP Materials

STATED ODDS 1:24

Card	Low	High
MAA Aaron Asham	3.00	8.00
MAF Adam Foote	3.00	8.00
MAH Adam Hall	3.00	8.00
MBB Brian Boucher	3.00	8.00
MBO Brooks Orpik	3.00	8.00
MCO Chris Osgood	3.00	8.00
MCS Chris Simon	3.00	8.00
MDC Dan Cloutier	3.00	8.00
MDH Derian Hatcher	3.00	8.00
MDR Derek Roy	3.00	8.00
MED Eric Daze	3.00	8.00
MGM Glen Murray	3.00	8.00
MJA Jason Arnott	3.00	8.00
MJB Jason Blake	3.00	8.00
MJJ Jaromir Jagr	5.00	12.00
MJL John LeClair	3.00	8.00
MJR Jarkko Ruutu	3.00	8.00
MKJ Kenny Jonsson	3.00	8.00
MLO Lyle Odelein	3.00	8.00
MMD Marc Denis	3.00	8.00
MMF Manny Fernandez	3.00	8.00
MMP Mark Parrish	3.00	8.00
MMR Mark Recchi	3.00	8.00
MMS Martin Straka	3.00	8.00
MPD Pavol Demitra	3.00	8.00
MPE Patrik Elias	3.00	8.00
MPL Patrick Lalime	3.00	8.00
MRB Rob Blake	3.00	8.00
MRF Ruslan Fedotenko	3.00	8.00
MRK Ryan Kesler	3.00	8.00
MRL Robert Lang	3.00	8.00
MSK Steve Konowalchuk	3.00	8.00
MSN Scott Niedermayer	3.00	8.00
MSS Scott Stevens	3.00	8.00
MSW Stephen Weiss	3.00	8.00
MSY Steve Yzerman SP	60.00	100.00
MTA Tony Amonte	3.00	8.00
MTB Todd Bertuzzi	3.00	8.00
MTP Tom Poti	3.00	8.00
MVD Vincent Damphousse	3.00	8.00
MVK Viktor Kozlov	3.00	8.00
MZC Zdeno Chara	3.00	8.00

2005-06 Upper Deck MVP Materials Duals

STATED PRINT RUN 100 SER.#'d SETS

Card	Low	High
DCO Zedno Chara	8.00	20.00
Lyle Odelein		
DDR Pavol Demitra	8.00	20.00
Mark Recchi		
DHH M.Havlat/M.Hejduk	12.00	30.00
DJF E.Jovanovski/A.Foote	8.00	20.00
DLC T.Linden/D.Cloutier	20.00	50.00
DLJ Mario Lemieux	30.00	80.00
Jaromir Jagr		
DPB Mike Peca	8.00	20.00
Rob Blake		
DPD Keith Primeau	8.00	20.00
Eric Daze		
DRN Wade Redden	8.00	20.00
Scott Niedermayer		
DSH Joe Sakic	20.00	50.00
Dan Hinote		

2005-06 Upper Deck MVP Materials Triples

STATED PRINT RUN 25 SER.#'d SETS

Card	Low	High
TTFD Theodore/Fernandez/Denis	40.00	100.00
TVAN Markus Naslund	40.00	100.00
Trevor Linden		
Ed Jovanovski		
TGST Wayne Gretzky	100.00	250.00
Joe Sakic		
Joe Thornton		
TSKF Joe Sakic	50.00	125.00
Paul Kariya		
Peter Forsberg		
TLKF Martin St. Louis	30.00	80.00
Nikolai Khabibulin		
Rusian Fedotenko		
TGPD Gaborik/Palffy/Demitra	40.00	100.00

2005-06 Upper Deck MVP Monumental Moments

Card	Low	High
COMPLETE SET (7)	8.00	20.00
STATED ODDS 1:24		
MM1 Wayne Gretzky	3.00	8.00
MM2 Gordie Howe	2.50	6.00
MM3 Brett Hull	.60	1.50
MM4 Steve Yzerman	2.00	5.00
MM5 Mario Lemieux	3.00	8.00
MM6 Jaromir Jagr	1.25	3.00
MM7 Dominik Hasek	1.00	2.50

2005-06 Upper Deck MVP ProSign

STATED ODDS 1:480

Card	Low	High
PAL Daniel Alfredsson SP	20.00	50.00
PBG Boyd Gordon	6.00	15.00
PBM Bryan McCabe	10.00	25.00
PDA David Aebischer	15.00	40.00
PDH Dany Heatley SP		
PDM Darren McCarty	15.00	40.00
PDW Doug Weight	10.00	25.00
PEC Erik Cole	10.00	25.00
PED Eric Daze	6.00	15.00
PJI Jarome Iginla SP		
PJL John-Michael Liles	10.00	25.00
PJR Jeremy Roenick	20.00	50.00
PJT Joe Thornton SP	30.00	80.00
PMA Maxim Afinogenov		
PMB Martin Biron	10.00	25.00
PMC Mike Cammalleri	10.00	25.00
PMH Milan Hejduk SP	15.00	40.00
PMO Brendan Morrison	12.00	30.00
PMP Michael Peca	10.00	25.00
PMW Brenden Morrow	10.00	25.00
PNA Nikolai Antropov	6.00	15.00
POK Olaf Kolzig	10.00	25.00
PON Owen Nolan	20.00	50.00
PPO Mark Popovic	6.00	15.00
PRB Rob Blake	15.00	40.00
PRE Robert Esche	10.00	25.00
PRK Ryan Kesler	6.00	15.00
PRN Rick Nash SP	40.00	80.00
PRS Ryan Smyth	10.00	25.00
PSD Shane Doan	10.00	25.00
PSG Simon Gagne	15.00	40.00
PSL Martin St. Louis	20.00	50.00
PSS Sheldon Souray	6.00	15.00
PSU Steve Sullivan	6.00	15.00
PTA Tyler Arnason	6.00	15.00
PTH Trent Hunter	6.00	15.00
PTL Trevor Linden	20.00	50.00
PTP Tom Poti	6.00	15.00
PTS Tony Salmelainen	6.00	15.00
PWG Wayne Gretzky SP		
PZC Zdeno Chara	10.00	25.00
TMR Mike Ribeiro	6.00	15.00

2005-06 Upper Deck MVP Rising to the Occasion

Card	Low	High
COMPLETE SET (14)	8.00	20.00
STATED ODDS 1:12		
RO1 Joe Sakic	1.25	3.00
RO2 Mario Lemieux	2.50	6.00
RO3 Martin St. Louis	.50	1.25
RO4 Jarome Iginla	.50	1.25
RO5 Martin Brodeur	1.50	4.00
RO6 Steve Yzerman	1.50	4.00
RO7 Dominik Hasek	.75	2.00
RO8 Peter Forsberg	1.00	2.50
RO9 Mike Modano	.60	1.50
RO10 Jose Theodore	.60	1.50
RO11 Jaromir Jagr	1.00	2.50
RO12 Ed Belfour	.60	1.50
RO13 Wayne Gretzky	2.50	6.00
RO14 Ilya Kovalchuk	.75	2.00

2005-06 Upper Deck MVP Rookie Breakthrough

Card	Low	High
COMPLETE SET (14)	25.00	60.00
STATED ODDS 1:12		
RB1 Sidney Crosby	8.00	20.00
RB2 Alexander Ovechkin	4.00	10.00
RB3 Jeff Carter	3.00	8.00
RB4 Gilbert Brule	2.50	6.00
RB5 Wojtek Wolski	2.00	5.00
RB6 Alexander Perezhogin	2.00	5.00
RB7 Zach Parise	4.00	10.00
RB8 Dion Phaneuf	6.00	15.00
RB9 Corey Perry	2.50	6.00
RB10 Alexander Steen	2.00	5.00
RB11 Thomas Vanek	4.00	10.00
RB12 Hannu Toivonen	2.00	5.00
RB13 Mike Richards	2.50	6.00
RB14 Robert Nilsson	2.00	5.00

2005-06 Upper Deck MVP Tribute to Greatness

Card	Low	High
COMPLETE SET (7)	10.00	25.00
COMMON CARD (TG1-TG7)	2.00	5.00
STATED ODDS 1:24		
TG1 Wayne Gretzky	2.00	5.00
TG2 Wayne Gretzky	2.00	5.00
TG3 Wayne Gretzky	2.00	5.00
TG4 Wayne Gretzky	2.00	5.00
TG5 Wayne Gretzky	2.00	5.00
TG6 Wayne Gretzky	2.00	5.00
TG7 Wayne Gretzky	2.00	5.00

2006-07 Upper Deck MVP

This 360-card set was issued into the hobby in 10-card packs, with an $1.99 SRP, which came 24 packs to a box. Cards numbered 1-297 are veterans sequenced in team alphabetical order while cards numbered from 298-356 are Rookie Cards. The set concludes with a checklist subset from cards 397-400.

Card	Low	High
COMPLETE SET (360)	75.00	150.00
1 Chris Pronger	.25	.60
2 Ilya Bryzgalov	.30	.75
3 Andy McDonald	.20	.50
4 Teemu Selanne	.30	.75
5 Francois Beauchemin	.10	.25
6 Chris Kunitz	.20	.50
7 Corey Perry	.25	.60
8 Scott Niedermayer	.20	.50
9 Ryan Getzlaf	.25	.60
10 Jean-Sebastien Giguere	.30	.75
11 Ilya Kovalchuk	.40	1.00
12 Jim Slater	.10	.25
13 Slava Kozlov	.20	.50
14 Kari Lehtonen	.30	.75
15 Bobby Holik	.20	.50
16 Marian Hossa	.25	.60
17 Niko Kapanen	.10	.25
18 Steve Rucchin	.10	.25
19 Johan Hedberg	.15	.40
20 Brad Boyes	.25	.60
21 Hannu Toivonen	.30	.75
22 Zdeno Chara	.20	.50
23 Tim Thomas	.30	.75
24 Marco Sturm	.20	.50
25 Patrice Bergeron	.25	.60
26 Brad Stuart	.20	.50
27 Marc Savard	.20	.50
28 Glen Murray	.20	.50
29 Paul Mara	.10	.25
30 Daniel Briere	.25	.60
31 Chris Drury	.25	.60
32 Ryan Miller	.30	.75
33 Ales Kotalik	.20	.50
34 Thomas Vanek	.25	.60
35 Jaroslav Spacek	.10	.25
36 Maxim Afinogenov	.20	.50
37 Jason Pominville	.10	.25
38 Derek Roy	.20	.50
39 Jochen Hecht	.10	.25
40 Martin Biron	.25	.60
41 Miikka Kiprusoff	.30	.75
42 Alex Tanguay	.25	.60
43 Jamie Lundmark	.10	.25
44 Jeff Friesen	.10	.25
45 Jarome Iginla	.50	1.25
46 Dion Phaneuf	.40	1.00
47 Tony Amonte	.10	.25
48 Chuck Kobasew	.20	.50
49 Kristian Huselius	.20	.50
50 Daymond Langkow	.20	.50
51 Cam Ward	.50	1.25
52 Rod Brind'Amour	.25	.60
53 Erik Cole	.20	.50
54 Mike Commodore	.20	.50
55 Andrew Ladd	.20	.50
56 Eric Staal	.25	.60
57 Cory Stillman	.20	.50
58 Justin Williams	.20	.50
59 Ray Whitney	.10	.25
60 Frantisek Kaberle	.10	.25
61 Nikolai Khabibulin	.30	.75
62 Michal Handzus	.10	.25
63 Pavel Vorobiev	.10	.25
64 Rene Bourque	.20	.50
65 Martin Havlat	.25	.60
66 Duncan Keith	.40	1.00
67 Bryan Smolinski	.10	.25
68 Tuomo Ruutu	.20	.50
69 Brandon Bochenski	.20	.50
70 Joe Sakic	.60	1.50
71 Jose Theodore	.20	.50
72 John-Michael Liles	.10	.25
73 Marek Svatos	.10	.25
74 Brad Richardson	.10	.25
75 Wojtek Wolski	.20	.50
76 Milan Hejduk	.25	.60
77 Pierre Turgeon	.20	.50
78 Andrew Brunette	.20	.50
79 Peter Budaj	.25	.60
80 Patrice Brisebois	.10	.25
81 Rick Nash	.30	.75
82 Rostislav Klesla	.20	.50
83 Gilbert Brule	.20	.50
84 Pascal Leclaire	.30	.75
85 Bryan Berard	.20	.50
86 Fredrik Modin	.20	.50
87 David Vyborny	.20	.50
88 Sergei Fedorov	.30	.75
89 Nikolai Zherdev	.20	.50
90 Adam Foote	.10	.25
91 Jody Shelley	.20	.50
92 Marty Turco	.25	.60
93 Brenden Morrow	.25	.60
94 Sergei Zubov	.20	.50
95 Eric Lindros	.30	.75
96 Jussi Jokinen	.20	.50
97 Mike Modano	.30	.75
98 Jere Lehtinen	.20	.50
99 Steve Ott	.20	.50
100 Jeff Halpern	.20	.50
101 Pavel Datsyuk	.30	.75
102 Tomas Holmstrom	.20	.50
103 Kris Draper	.20	.50
104 Dominik Hasek	.40	1.00
105 Nicklas Lidstrom	.30	.75
106 Henrik Zetterberg	.30	.75
107 Robert Lang	.10	.25
108 Mikael Samuelsson	.10	.25
109 Chris Chelios	.15	.40
110 Mathieu Schneider	.10	.25
111 Jason Williams	.10	.25
112 Dwayne Roloson	.25	.60
113 Ales Hemsky	.20	.50
114 Fernando Pisani	.20	.50
115 Shawn Horcoff	.20	.50
116 Jarret Stoll	.20	.50
117 Jason Smith	.20	.50
118 Ryan Smyth	.25	.60
119 Raffi Torres	.10	.25
120 Jussi Markkanen	.15	.40
121 Joffrey Lupul	.20	.50
122 Marc-Andre Bergeron	.10	.25
123 Nathan Horton	.20	.50
124 Stephen Weiss	.20	.50
125 Alex Auld	.25	.60
126 Olli Jokinen	.25	.60
127 Todd Bertuzzi	.25	.60
128 Joe Nieuwendyk	.25	.60
129 Ed Belfour	.75	2.00
130 Jay Bouwmeester	.20	.50
131 Rostislav Olesz	.20	.50
132 Alexander Frolov	.20	.50
133 Dan Cloutier	.15	.40
134 Mike Cammalleri	.20	.50
135 Rob Blake	.25	.60
136 Craig Conroy	.20	.50
137 Lubomir Visnovsky	.20	.50
138 Mathieu Garon	.25	.60
139 Sean Avery	.20	.50
140 Dustin Brown	.20	.50
141 Marian Gaborik	.50	1.25
142 Mark Parrish	.20	.50
143 Pierre-Marc Bouchard	.20	.50
144 Mikko Koivu	.20	.50
145 Wes Walz	.10	.25
146 Brian Rolston	.20	.50
147 Manny Fernandez	.30	.75
148 Pavol Demitra	.20	.50
149 Kim Johnsson	.10	.25
150 Todd White	.20	.50
151 Cristobal Huet	.20	.50
152 Saku Koivu	.30	.75
153 Chris Higgins	.20	.50
154 Andrei Markov	.20	.50
155 Mike Ribeiro	.20	.50
156 David Aebischer	.25	.60
157 Alex Kovalev	.20	.50
158 Sergei Samsonov	.25	.60
159 Michael Ryder	.20	.50
160 Sheldon Souray	.20	.50
161 Alexander Perezhogin	.10	.25
162 Paul Kariya	.30	.75
163 Jason Arnott	.20	.50
164 Jordin Tootoo	.15	.40
165 J.P. Dumont	.20	.50
166 Steve Sullivan	.20	.50
167 Tomas Vokoun	.25	.60
168 Marek Zidlicky	.10	.25
169 Martin Erat	.10	.25
170 Scott Hartnell	.10	.25
171 Martin Brodeur	1.00	2.50
172 Brian Gionta	.20	.50
173 John Madden	.10	.25
174 Zach Parise	.25	.60
175 Brian Rafalski	.20	.50
176 Patrik Elias	.20	.50
177 Sergei Brylin	.10	.25
178 Scott Gomez	.20	.50
179 Jamie Langenbrunner	.10	.25
180 Paul Martin	.10	.25
181 Miroslav Satan	.20	.50
182 Mike Sillinger	.20	.50
183 Tom Poti	.20	.50
184 Jason Blake	.20	.50
185 Trent Hunter	.20	.50
186 Alexei Yashin	.20	.50
187 Rick DiPietro	.30	.75
188 Alexei Zhitnik	.10	.25
189 Shawn Bates	.20	.50
190 Jeff Tambellini	.20	.50
191 Jaromir Jagr	.50	1.25
192 Brendan Shanahan	.30	.75
193 Martin Straka	.20	.50
194 Marek Malik	.10	.25
195 Petr Prucha	.20	.50
196 Henrik Lundqvist	.50	1.25
197 Sandis Ozolinsh	.10	.25
198 Matt Cullen	.20	.50
199 Michael Nylander	.20	.50
200 Fedor Tyutin	.10	.25
201 Jason Spezza	.30	.75
202 Ray Emery	.30	.75
203 Wade Redden	.20	.50
204 Patrick Eaves	.20	.50
205 Daniel Alfredsson	.25	.60
206 Martin Gerber	.30	.75
207 Dany Heatley	.30	.75
208 Andrej Meszaros	.20	.50
209 Mike Fisher	.10	.25
210 Peter Schaefer	.10	.25
211 Simon Gagne	.30	.75
212 Joni Pitkanen	.20	.50
213 Jeff Carter	.30	.75
214 R.J. Umberger	.20	.50
215 Peter Forsberg	.50	1.25
216 Antero Niittymaki	.20	.50
217 Mike Richards	.30	.75
218 Mike Knuble	.20	.50
219 Robert Esche	.25	.60
220 Kyle Calder	.20	.50
221 Geoff Sanderson	.10	.25
222 Shane Doan	.25	.60
223 Ed Jovanovski	.20	.50
224 Ladislav Nagy	.20	.50
225 Curtis Joseph	.30	.75
226 Jeremy Roenick	.30	.75
227 Keith Ballard	.20	.50
228 Mike Comrie	.20	.50
229 David Leneveu	.25	.60
230 Owen Nolan	.20	.50
231 Sidney Crosby	1.50	4.00
232 Mark Recchi	.20	.50
233 Nils Ekman	.10	.25
234 Ryan Whitney	.20	.50
235 Colby Armstrong	.20	.50
236 John LeClair	.25	.60
237 Marc-Andre Fleury	.30	.75
238 Sergei Gonchar	.10	.25
239 Ryan Malone	.20	.50
240 Joe Thornton	.50	1.25
241 Vesa Toskala	.25	.60
242 Mark Bell	.20	.50
243 Steve Bernier	.20	.50
244 Christian Ehrhoff	.10	.25
245 Jonathan Cheechoo	.30	.75
246 Patrick Marleau	.25	.60
247 Mike Grier	.10	.25
248 Milan Michalek	.20	.50
249 Evgeni Nabokov	.25	.60
250 Keith Tkachuk	.25	.60
251 Manny Legace	.25	.60
252 Martin Rucinsky	.10	.25
253 Bill Guerin	.20	.50
254 Lee Stempniak	.20	.50
255 Petr Cajanek	.20	.50
256 Doug Weight	.20	.50
257 Jay McKee	.10	.25
258 Martin St. Louis	.30	.75
259 Marc Denis	.25	.60
260 Vaclav Prospal	.20	.50
261 Brad Richards	.30	.75
262 Paul Ranger	.10	.25
263 Ruslan Fedotenko	.20	.50
264 Vincent Lecavalier	.30	.75
265 Filip Kuba	.10	.25
266 Ryan Craig	.10	.25
267 Dan Boyle	.30	.75
268 Mats Sundin	.30	.75
269 Michael Peca	.20	.50
270 Alexander Steen	.25	.60
271 Bryan McCabe	.20	.50
272 Tomas Kaberle	.20	.50
273 Andrew Raycroft	.25	.60
274 Nikolai Antropov	.10	.25
275 Kyle Wellwood	.20	.50
276 Mikael Tellqvist	.30	.75
277 Darcy Tucker	.20	.50
278 Matt Stajan	.20	.50
279 Jeff O'Neill	.10	.25
280 Matt Cooke	.10	.25
281 Sami Salo	.20	.50
282 Roberto Luongo	.60	1.50
283 Markus Naslund	.30	.75
284 Daniel Sedin	.20	.50
285 Mattias Ohlund	.20	.50
286 Ryan Kesler	.20	.50
287 Henrik Sedin	.20	.50
288 Brendan Morrison	.20	.50
289 Mika Noronen	.15	.40
290 Brian Sutherby	.10	.25
291 Steve Eminger	.20	.50
292 Alexander Ovechkin	1.25	3.00
293 Olaf Kolzig	.40	1.00
294 Richard Zednik	.10	.25
295 Dainius Zubrus	.20	.50
296 Brent Johnson	.15	.40
297 Chris Clark	.20	.50
298 Patrick O'Sullivan RC	2.50	6.00
299 Phil Kessel RC	5.00	12.00
300 Guillaume Latendresse RC	2.50	6.00
301 Jordan Staal RC	5.00	12.00
302 Paul Stastny RC	4.00	10.00
303 Evgeni Malkin RC	8.00	20.00
304 Luc Bourdon RC	2.50	6.00
305 Alexei Kaigorodov RC	2.50	6.00
306 Anze Kopitar RC	3.00	8.00
307 Travis Zajac RC	3.00	8.00
308 Nigel Dawes RC	2.50	6.00
309 Kristopher Letang RC	3.00	8.00
310 Marc-Edouard Vlasic RC	2.50	6.00
311 Patrick Thoresen RC	2.00	5.00
312 Ladislav Smid RC	2.00	5.00
313 Loui Eriksson RC	2.50	6.00
314 Shane O'Brien RC	2.50	6.00
315 Ryan Shannon RC	2.50	6.00
316 John Oduya RC	2.50	6.00
317 Fredrik Norrena RC	2.00	5.00
318 Niklas Backstrom RC	2.00	5.00
319 D.J. King RC	1.25	3.00
320 Patrick Fischer RC	1.25	3.00
321 Mikko Lehtonen RC	1.25	3.00
322 Roman Polak RC	1.25	3.00
323 Ben Ondrus RC	2.50	6.00
324 Bill Thomas RC	2.50	6.00
325 Billy Thompson RC	2.00	5.00
326 Brendan Bell RC	2.50	6.00
327 Carsen Germyn RC	2.00	5.00
328 Keith Yandle RC	2.50	6.00
329 Dan Jancevski RC	2.50	6.00
330 David Liffiton RC	2.50	6.00
331 David Printz RC	2.50	6.00
332 Dustin Byfuglien RC	5.00	12.00
333 Eric Fehr RC	2.50	6.00
334 Erik Reitz RC	2.50	6.00
335 Filip Novak RC	2.50	6.00
336 Frank Doyle RC	2.50	6.00
337 Ian White RC	2.50	6.00
338 Jarkko Immonen RC	2.00	5.00
339 Jeremy Williams RC	2.50	6.00
340 Joel Perrault RC	2.50	6.00
341 Jonas Johansson RC	1.25	3.00
342 Konstantin Pushkarev RC	2.50	6.00
343 Marc-Antoine Pouliot RC	2.50	6.00
344 Mark Stuart RC	2.50	6.00
345 Masi Marjamaki RC	2.50	6.00
346 Matt Carle RC	2.50	6.00
347 Matt Koalska RC	2.50	6.00
348 Michel Ouellet RC	3.00	8.00
349 Miroslav Kopriva RC	2.00	5.00
350 Noah Welch RC	2.50	6.00
351 Rob Collins RC	2.50	6.00
352 Ryan Caldwell RC	2.50	6.00
353 Ryan Potulny RC	2.50	6.00
354 Shea Weber RC	2.50	6.00
355 Enver Lisin RC	2.50	6.00
356 Tomas Kopecky RC	2.50	6.00
357 Yan Stastny RC	2.50	6.00
358 Joe Thornton CL	.50	1.25
359 Martin St. Louis CL	.30	.75
360 Peter Forsberg CL	.50	1.25

2006-07 Upper Deck MVP Gold Script

*GOLD 8X TO 20X BASE HI
*ROOKIES .75X TO 2X BASE HI
PRINT RUN 100 SETS

2006-07 Upper Deck MVP Super Script

*SUPER SCRIPT: 12X TO 30X BASE HI
*RCS: 2X TO 5X BASE HI
STATED PRINT RUN 25 #'d SETS

Card	Low	High
231 Sidney Crosby	125.00	250.00
303 Evgeni Malkin	100.00	200.00

2006-07 Upper Deck MVP Autographs

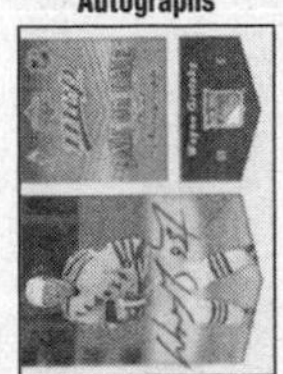

STATED ODDS 1:240
OAAT Nikolai Antropov 12.00 30.00
Mikael Tellqvist
OABK Rene Bourque 8.00 20.00
Duncan Keith
OABM Steve Bernier 12.00 30.00
Milan Michalek
OABP Pierre-Marc Bouchard 12.00 30.00
Mark Parrish
OABS Brad Boyes 12.00 30.00
Yan Stastny
OACL Erik Cole 8.00 20.00
Andrew Ladd
OACR Jeff Carter 30.00 80.00
Mike Richards
OACS Zdeno Chara 12.00 30.00
Mark Stuart
OADA Chris Drury 12.00 30.00
Maxim Afinogenov
OADO Kris Draper 15.00 40.00
Chris Osgood
OAEE Robert Esche 8.00 20.00
Ben Eager
OAEG Patrik Elias 12.00 30.00
Brian Gionta
OAFC Alexander Frolov 12.00 30.00
Mike Cammalleri
OAFQ Valtteri Filppula 12.00 30.00
Kyle Quincey
OAGA Martin Gerber 25.00 60.00
David Aebischer SP
OAGL Wayne Gretzky
Mario Lemieux SP
OAHC Dany Heatley 25.00 60.00
Jonathan Cheechoo SP
OAHH Martin Havlat 12.00 30.00
Michal Handzus
OAHT Milan Hejduk 15.00 40.00
Jose Theodore
OAKL Miikka Kiprusoff 40.00 80.00
Roberto Luongo SP
OALH Joffrey Lupul 8.00 20.00
Shawn Horcoff
OALS David Leneveu 8.00 20.00
Philippe Sauve
OALW Manny Legace 8.00 20.00
Jeff Woywitka
OALZ Nicklas Lidstrom
Henrik Zetterberg SP
OAMC Ryan Malone 12.00 30.00
Erik Christensen
OAMK Andy McDonald 8.00 20.00
Chris Kunitz
OANI Rick Nash 00.00 100.00
Jarome Iginla SP
OANM Markus Naslund 12.00 30.00
Brendan Morrison
OAPK Dion Phaneuf 20.00 50.00
Chuck Kobasew SP
OAPT Michael Peca 20.00 50.00
Darcy Tucker SP
OARK Mike Ribeiro 15.00 40.00
Andrei Kostitsyn SP
OARL Brad Richardson 8.00 20.00
John-Michael Liles
OARS Michael Ryder 12.00 30.00
Sergei Samsonov SP
OASC Miroslav Satan 8.00 20.00
Jeremy Colliton
OATM Joe Thornton 25.00 60.00
Patrick Marleau
OAVV Tomas Vokoun 20.00 50.00
Josef Vasicek SP

2006-07 Upper Deck MVP Clutch Performers

COMPLETE SET (25) 10.00 25.00
STATED ODDS 1:8
CP1 Cam Ward 1.00 2.50
CP2 Peter Forsberg 1.00 2.50
CP3 Joe Sakic 1.25 3.00
CP4 Martin Brodeur 2.00 5.00
CP5 Jarome Iginla 1.00 2.50
CP6 Jaromir Jagr 1.00 2.50
CP7 Mats Sundin .60 1.50
CP8 Dany Heatley .60 1.50
CP9 Ryan Miller .60 1.50
CP10 Alexander Ovechkin 1.50 4.00
CP11 Eric Staal .50 1.25
CP12 Mike Modano .60 1.50
CP13 Martin St. Louis .60 1.50
CP14 Ryan Smyth .50 1.25
CP15 Chris Pronger .50 1.25
CP16 Henrik Zetterberg .60 1.50
CP17 Jonathan Cheechoo .60 1.50
CP18 Ilya Kovalchuk .75 2.00
CP19 Marian Gaborik 1.00 2.50
CP20 Shane Doan .75 2.00
CP21 Rick Nash .60 1.50
CP22 Sidney Crosby 3.00 8.00
CP23 Markus Naslund .60 1.50
CP24 Dominik Hasek .75 2.00
CP25 Mario Lemieux 2.00 5.00

2006-07 Upper Deck MVP Gotta Have Hart

COMPLETE SET (25) 10.00 25.00
STATED ODDS 1:8
HH1 Joe Thornton 1.00 2.50
HH2 Peter Forsberg 1.00 2.50
HH3 Martin St. Louis .60 1.50
HH4 Jose Theodore .60 1.50
HH5 Joe Sakic 1.25 3.00
HH6 Chris Pronger .50 1.25
HH7 Jaromir Jagr 1.00 2.50
HH8 Mario Lemieux 2.00 5.00
HH9 Wayne Gretzky 3.00 8.00
HH10 Eric Lindros .60 1.50
HH11 Sergei Fedorov .60 1.50
HH12 Alexander Ovechkin 1.50 4.00
HH13 Sidney Crosby 3.00 8.00
HH14 Jarome Iginla 1.00 2.50
HH15 Eric Staal .50 1.25
HH16 Martin Brodeur 2.00 5.00
HH17 Miikka Kiprusoff .60 1.50
HH18 Rick Nash .60 1.50
HH19 Ilya Kovalchuk .75 2.00
HH20 Dominik Hasek .75 2.00
HH21 Marian Gaborik 1.00 2.50
HH22 Patrice Bergeron .50 1.25
HH23 Mats Sundin .60 1.50
HH24 Markus Naslund .60 1.50
HH25 Dany Heatley .60 1.50

2006-07 Upper Deck MVP International Icons

COMPLETE SET (25)
STATED ODDS 1:8
II1 Teemu Selanne .60 1.50
II2 Ilya Kovalchuk .75 2.00
II3 Marian Hossa .50 1.25
II4 Marco Sturm .40 1.00
II5 Milan Hejduk .50 1.25
II6 Sergei Fedorov .60 1.50
II7 Mike Modano .60 1.50
II8 Nicklas Lidstrom .60 1.50
II9 Dominik Hasek .75 2.00
II10 Olli Jokinen .40 1.00
II11 Marian Gaborik 1.00 2.50
II12 Saku Koivu .60 1.50
II13 Tomas Vokoun .50 1.25
II14 Martin Brodeur 2.00 5.00
II15 Miroslav Satan .40 1.00
II16 Rick DiPietro .60 1.50
II17 Jaromir Jagr 1.00 2.50
II18 Martin Gerber .60 1.50
II19 Peter Forsberg 1.00 2.50
II20 Sidney Crosby 3.00 8.00
II21 Vincent Lecavalier .60 1.50
II22 Mats Sundin .60 1.50
II23 Nikolai Antropov .20 .50
II24 Alexander Ovechkin 2.50 6.00
II25 Olaf Kolzig .75 2.00

2006-07 Upper Deck MVP Jerseys

COMPLETE SET (97)
STATED ODDS 1:24
OJAB Alexandre Picard 4.00 10.00
Brandon Bochenski
OJAR David Aebischer 6.00 15.00
Andrew Raycroft
OJBJ Jay Bouwmeester 4.00 10.00
Olli Jokinen
OJBK Pierre-Marc Bouchard 4.00 10.00
Ryan Kesler
OJBL Martin Brodeur 15.00 40.00
Henrik Lundqvist
OJBN Martin Brodeur 12.00 30.00
Antero Niittymaki
OJBR Patrice Bergeron 6.00 15.00
Michael Ryder
OJCF Sidney Crosby 40.00 80.00
Peter Forsberg SP
OJCG Jeff Carter 6.00 15.00
Scott Gomez
OJCJ Chuck Kobasew 4.00 10.00
Jarret Stoll
OJCO Sidney Crosby 75.00 150.00
Alexander Ovechkin SP
OJCR Zdeno Chara 4.00 10.00
Wade Redden
OJCS Jonathan Cheechoo 8.00 20.00
Teemu Selanne
OJDH Pavol Demitra 4.00 10.00
Ales Hemsky
OJDK Chris Drury 4.00 10.00
Alex Kovalev
OJDM Shane Doan 6.00 15.00
Brenden Morrow
OJDP Kris Draper 4.00 10.00
Michael Peca
OJDR Martin Brodeur 15.00 40.00
Jaromir Jagr
OJEP Patrik Elias 4.00 10.00
Petr Prucha
OJER Eric Staal 6.00 15.00
Ryan Smyth
OJES Patrik Elias 4.00 10.00
Miroslav Satan
OJEV Eric Staal 8.00 20.00
Vincent Lecavalier
OJFA Sergei Fedorov 6.00 15.00
Jason Arnott
OJFD Sergei Fedorov 8.00 20.00
Pavel Datsyuk
OJFM Fernando Pisani 4.00 10.00
Matthew Lombardi
OJFN Alexander Frolov 6.00 15.00
Ladislav Nagy
OJFR Manny Fernandez 6.00 15.00
Dwayne Roloson
OJGC Ryan Getzlaf 4.00 10.00
Mike Cammalleri
OJGH Marian Gaborik 10.00 25.00
Martin Havlat
OJGL Wayne Gretzky 150.00 300.00
Mario Lemieux SP
OJHB Dany Heatley 15.00 40.00
Daniel Briere SP
OJHF Marian Hossa 4.00 10.00
Ruslan Fedotenko
OJHH Milan Hejduk 4.00 10.00
Ales Hemsky
OJHL Nathan Horton 4.00 10.00
Andrew Ladd
OJHM Trent Hunter 4.00 10.00
Ryan Malone
OJHS Dany Heatley 8.00 20.00
Alexander Steen
OJHV Dominik Hasek 10.00 25.00
Tomas Vokoun
OJIS Jarome Iginla 8.00 20.00
Ryan Smyth
OJJC Curtis Joseph 6.00 15.00
Dan Cloutier
OJJF Jaromir Jagr 10.00 25.00
Peter Forsberg
OJJJ Jarret Stoll 4.00 10.00
Jeff Friesen
OJJL Ed Jovanovski 4.00 10.00
Jordan Leopold
OJJM Jarret Stoll 4.00 10.00
Marek Svatos
OJJS Jaromir Jagr 10.00 25.00
Miroslav Satan
OJKD Olaf Kolzig 6.00 15.00
Marc Denis
OJKL Miikka Kiprusoff 15.00 40.00
Roberto Luongo
OJKR Mikko Koivu 6.00 15.00
Tuomo Ruutu
OJKS Jason Spezza 6.00 15.00
Saku Koivu
OJKW Paul Kariya 6.00 15.00
Doug Weight
OJKZ Paul Kariya 8.00 20.00
Henrik Zetterberg
OJLD Henrik Lundqvist 10.00 25.00
Rick DiPietro
OJLF Andrew Ladd 4.00 10.00
Tomas Fleischmann
OJLJ Vincent Lecavalier 6.00 15.00
Olli Jokinen
OJLK Kari Lehtonen 6.00 15.00
Olaf Kolzig
OJLM Nicklas Lidstrom 10.00 25.00
Bryan McCabe
OJLS Robert Lang 4.00 10.00
Steve Sullivan
OJLZ Nicklas Lidstrom 6.00 15.00
Sergei Zubov
OJMJ Andrej Meszaros 4.00 10.00
Milan Jurcina
OJMS Martin St. Louis 6.00 15.00
Simon Gagne
OJMT Mike Modano 6.00 15.00
Pierre Turgeon
OJNJ Scott Niedermayer 4.00 10.00
Ed Jovanovski
OJNT Rick Nash 6.00 15.00
Keith Tkachuk
OJOC Chris Osgood 6.00 15.00
Ty Conklin
OJOK Alexander Ovechkin 20.00 50.00
Ilya Kovalchuk
OJOT Jason Spezza 10.00 25.00
Mats Sundin
OJPB Chris Pronger 6.00 15.00
Rob Blake
OJPJ Corey Perry 4.00 10.00
Jussi Jokinen
OJPL Dion Phaneuf 10.00 25.00
John-Michael Liles
OJPN Dion Phaneuf 6.00 15.00
Scott Niedermayer
OJPO Joni Pitkanen 4.00 10.00
Sandis Ozolinsh
OJPR Joni Pitkanen 4.00 10.00
Brian Rafalski
OJRB Brad Richards 6.00 15.00
Rod Brind'Amour
OJRL Jeremy Roenick 8.00 20.00
Eric Lindros
OJRM Roberto Luongo 6.00 15.00
Manny Fernandez
OJRW Brian Rafalski 4.00 10.00
Brendan Witt
OJSA Sergei Samsonov 4.00 10.00
Maxim Afinogenov
OJSC Steve Sullivan 4.00 10.00
Kyle Calder
OJSD Marc Savard 4.00 10.00
Chris Drury
OJSF Teemu Selanne 6.00 15.00
Alexander Frolov
OJSG Brendan Shanahan 8.00 20.00
Simon Gagne
OJSH Martin St. Louis 6.00 15.00
Nathan Horton
OJSK Mats Sundin 6.00 15.00
Saku Koivu
OJSL Brendan Shanahan 15.00 40.00
John LeClair SP
OJSM Joe Sakic 10.00 25.00
Mike Modano
OJSN Sergei Samsonov 4.00 10.00
Nikolai Antropov
OJSS Miroslav Satan 4.00 10.00
Martin Straka
OJST Joe Sakic 12.00 30.00
Joe Thornton
OJSV Marek Svatos 4.00 10.00
Joffrey Lupul
OJTG Marty Turco 8.00 20.00
Jean-Sebastien Giguere
OJTH Keith Tkachuk 4.00 10.00
Martin Havlat
OJTN Alex Tanguay 6.00 15.00
Markus Naslund
OJWA Doug Weight 4.00 10.00
Jason Arnott
OJWC Doug Weight 4.00 10.00
Kyle Calder
OJWD Cam Ward 8.00 20.00
Marc Denis
OJWL Cam Ward 8.00 20.00
Kari Lehtonen
OJWW Justin Williams 4.00 10.00
Stephen Weiss
OJZN Henrik Zetterberg 8.00 20.00
Rick Nash

2006-07 Upper Deck MVP Last Line of Defense

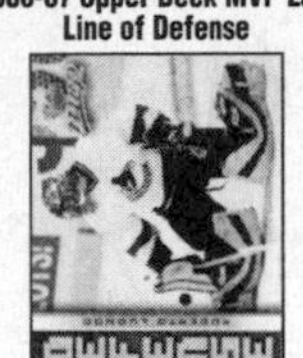

COMPLETE SET (25) 10.00 25.00
STATED ODDS 1:8
LL1 Martin Brodeur 2.50 6.00
LL2 Miikka Kiprusoff 1.00 2.50
LL3 Henrik Lundqvist 1.50 4.00
LL4 Marty Turco .75 2.00
LL5 Cristobal Huet 1.00 2.50
LL6 Marc-Andre Fleury 1.00 2.50
LL7 Roberto Luongo 2.00 5.00
LL8 Cam Ward 1.50 4.00
LL9 Ryan Miller 1.00 2.50
LL10 Nikolai Khabibulin 1.00 2.50
LL11 Kari Lehtonen 1.00 2.50
LL12 Tomas Vokoun .75 2.00
LL13 Dwayne Roloson .75 2.00
LL14 Olaf Kolzig 1.25 3.00
LL15 Ed Belfour 2.50 6.00
LL16 Vesa Toskala .75 2.00
LL17 Jose Theodore 1.00 2.50
LL18 Curtis Joseph 1.00 2.50
LL19 Manny Fernandez 1.00 2.50
LL20 Dominik Hasek 1.25 3.00
LL21 Martin Gerber 1.00 2.50
LL22 Andrew Raycroft .75 2.00
LL23 Rick DiPietro 1.00 2.50
LL24 Hannu Toivonen 1.00 2.50
LL25 Manny Legace .75 2.00

2007-08 Upper Deck MVP

This 350-card set was released in October, 2007. The set was issued into the hobby in eight-card packs, with a $1.99 SRP, which came 24-packs to a box. Cards numbered 1-300 feature veterans while cards 301-350 are Rookie Cards which were inserted into packs at a stated rate of onein two. In addition, Cards numbered 351-380 were issued as three-card packs as redemptions from packs which were inserted at a stated rate of one in 24. By February 2008, all the MVP redeemed rookies were live and we have notated that information in our checklist.

COMPLETE SET (380) 75.00 150.00
COMP.SET w/o RCs (300) 15.00 40.00
(351-380) ISSUED AS 3 CARD RED.PACKS
1 Joe Sakic .60 1.50
2 Brett Clark .20 .50
3 Peter Budaj .25 .60
4 Marek Svatos .20 .50
5 Andrew Brunette .20 .50
6 Paul Stastny .30 .75
7 Milan Hejduk .25 .60
8 Wojtek Wolski .20 .50
9 John-Michael Liles .20 .50
10 Tyler Arnason .20 .50
11 Jose Theodore .30 .75
12 Martin Havlat .25 .60
13 Patrick Sharp .20 .50
14 Nikolai Khabibulin .30 .75
15 Duncan Keith .30 .75
16 Jason Williams .20 .50
17 Radim Vrbata .20 .50
18 Brent Seabrook .20 .50
19 Patrick Lalime .25 .60
20 Jeff Hamilton .20 .50
21 Tuomo Ruutu .20 .50
22 Rick Nash .30 .75
23 Fredrik Norrena .25 .60
24 Fredrik Modin .20 .50
25 Gilbert Brule .20 .50
26 Jody Shelley .20 .50
27 David Vyborny .20 .50
28 Pascal Leclaire .25 .60
29 Sergei Fedorov .30 .75
30 Nikolai Zherdev .20 .50
31 Rostislav Klesla .20 .50
32 Doug Weight .20 .50
33 Jay McClement .20 .50
34 Manny Legace .25 .60
35 Barret Jackman .20 .50
36 David Backes .20 .50
37 Lee Stempniak .20 .50
38 Brad Boyes .25 .60
39 Eric Brewer .20 .50
40 Jason Bacashihua .25 .60
41 Patrice Bergeron .30 .75
42 Zdeno Chara .20 .50
43 Tim Thomas .40 1.00
44 Marco Sturm .20 .50
45 Chuck Kobasew .20 .50
46 Glen Murray .20 .50
47 Phil Kessel .30 .75
48 Hannu Toivonen .25 .60
49 Marc Savard .20 .50
50 Dennis Wideman .20 .50
51 Saku Koivu .25 .60
52 Chris Higgins .25 .60
53 Andrei Markov .25 .60
54 Cristobal Huet .25 .60
55 Guillaume Latendresse .25 .60
56 Sheldon Souray .20 .50
57 Tomas Plekanec .20 .50
58 Alex Kovalev .20 .50
59 Michael Ryder .20 .50
60 Maxim Lapierre .20 .50
61 Andrei Kostitsyn .20 .50
62 Roberto Luongo .50 1.25
63 Markus Naslund .30 .75
64 Sami Salo .20 .50
65 Taylor Pyatt .20 .50
66 Daniel Sedin .20 .50
67 Henrik Sedin .20 .50
68 Kevin Bieksa .20 .50
69 Brendan Morrison .20 .50
70 Ryan Kesler .20 .50
71 Mattias Ohlund .20 .50
72 Trevor Linden .25 .60
73 Alexander Ovechkin 1.00 2.50
74 Mike Green (Wa Capitals) .20 .50
75 Brent Johnson .25 .60
76 Jiri Novotny .20 .50
77 Chris Clark .20 .50
78 Matt Pettinger .20 .50
79 Brian Pothier .20 .50
80 Alexander Semin .30 .75
81 Olaf Kolzig .30 .75
82 Shane Doan .20 .50
83 Mikael Tellqvist .25 .60
84 Zbynek Michalek .20 .50
85 Keith Ballard .20 .50
86 Owen Nolan .25 .60
87 Steven Reinprecht .20 .50
88 Derek Morris .20 .50
89 Ed Jovanovski .20 .50
90 Curtis Joseph .25 .60
91 Martin Brodeur .75 2.00
92 Scott Gomez .20 .50
93 Travis Zajac .20 .50
94 Brian Rafalski .20 .50
95 Patrik Elias .20 .50
96 Jamie Langenbrunner .20 .50
97 Brian Gionta .20 .50
98 Johnny Oduya .20 .50
99 Jay Pandolfo .20 .50
100 John Madden .20 .50
101 Teemu Selanne .30 .75
102 Chris Pronger .30 .75
103 Ilya Bryzgalov .30 .75
104 Dustin Penner .20 .50
105 Ryan Getzlaf .25 .60
106 Scott Niedermayer .20 .50
107 Chris Kunitz .20 .50
108 Corey Perry .25 .60
109 Andy McDonald .20 .50
110 Jean-Sebastien Giguere .30 .75
111 Jarome Iginla .50 1.25
112 Matthew Lombardi .20 .50
113 Daymond Langkow .20 .50
114 Miikka Kiprusoff .40 1.00
115 Robyn Regehr .20 .50
116 Dion Phaneuf .30 .75
117 Kristian Huselius .20 .50
118 Stephane Yelle .20 .50
119 Alex Tanguay .25 .60
120 Roman Hamrlik .20 .50
121 Tony Amonte .20 .50
122 Simon Gagne .30 .75
123 Martin Biron .25 .60
124 Joni Pitkanen .20 .50
125 R.J. Umberger .20 .50
126 Jeff Carter .20 .50
127 Mike Knuble .20 .50
128 Ben Eager .20 .50
129 Mike Richards .40 1.00
130 Antero Niittymaki .25 .60
131 Eric Staal .30 .75
132 Ray Whitney .20 .50
133 Mike Commodore .20 .50
134 Cory Stillman .20 .50
135 John Grahame .25 .60
136 Rod Brind'Amour .25 .60
137 Erik Cole .20 .50
138 Cam Ward .30 .75
139 Glen Wesley .20 .50
140 Justin Williams .20 .50
141 Alexei Yashin .20 .50
142 Rick DiPietro .25 .60
143 Ryan Smyth .25 .60
144 Brendan Witt .20 .50
145 Jason Blake .20 .50
146 Chris Simon .20 .50
147 Viktor Kozlov .20 .50
148 Mike Sillinger .20 .50
149 Miroslav Satan .20 .50
150 Alexander Frolov .20 .50
151 Dan Cloutier .25 .60
152 Rob Blake .25 .60
153 Dustin Brown .20 .50
154 Patrick O'Sullivan .25 .60
155 Lubomir Visnovsky .20 .50
156 Anze Kopitar .30 .75
157 Mike Cammalleri .25 .60
158 Derek Armstrong .20 .50
159 Vincent Lecavalier .30 .75
160 Marc Denis .25 .60
161 Dan Boyle .20 .50
162 Eric Perrin .20 .50
163 Filip Kuba .20 .50
164 Brad Richards .25 .60
165 Ruslan Fedotenko .20 .50
166 Vaclav Prospal .20 .50
167 Martin St. Louis .25 .60
168 Johan Holmqvist .25 .60
169 Mats Sundin .30 .75
170 Ian White .20 .50
171 Matt Stajan .20 .50
172 Darcy Tucker .25 .60
173 Bryan McCabe .20 .50
174 Andrew Raycroft .25 .60
175 Kyle Wellwood .25 .60
176 Alexei Ponikarovsky .20 .50
177 Alexander Steen .20 .50
178 Tomas Kaberle .20 .50
179 Vesa Toskala .25 .60
180 Dwayne Roloson .25 .60
181 Petr Sykora .20 .50
182 Marc-Antoine Pouliot .20 .50
183 Raffi Torres .20 .50
184 Joffrey Lupul .20 .50
185 Steve Staios .20 .50
186 Jussi Markkanen .25 .60
187 Shawn Horcoff .20 .50
188 Jarret Stoll .20 .50
189 Ladislav Smid .20 .50
190 Ales Hemsky .20 .50
191 Olli Jokinen .20 .50
192 Rostislav Olesz .20 .50
193 Jay Bouwmeester .20 .50
194 Alex Auld .25 .60
195 Nathan Horton .20 .50
196 Mike Van Ryn .20 .50
197 Jozef Stumpel .20 .50
198 Stephen Weiss .20 .50
199 Tomas Vokoun .30 .75
200 Sidney Crosby 1.50 4.00
201 Evgeni Malkin .75 2.00
202 Ryan Whitney .25 .60
203 Mark Recchi .20 .50
204 Marc-Andre Fleury .30 .75
205 Sergei Gonchar .20 .50
206 Michel Ouellet .20 .50
207 Jordan Staal .40 1.00
208 Colby Armstrong .20 .50
209 Erik Christensen .20 .50
210 Peter Forsberg .40 1.00
211 Paul Kariya .30 .75
212 Chris Mason .25 .60
213 Shea Weber .20 .50
214 Jason Arnott .20 .50
215 Alexander Radulov .30 .75
216 J.P. Dumont .20 .50
217 Steve Sullivan .20 .50
218 Kimmo Timonen .20 .50
219 David Legwand .20 .50
220 Jaromir Jagr .50 1.25
221 Sean Avery .20 .50
222 Petr Prucha .20 .50
223 Henrik Lundqvist .40 1.00
224 Martin Straka .20 .50
225 Michael Nylander .20 .50
226 Michal Rozsival .20 .50
227 Marek Malik .20 .50
228 Matt Cullen .20 .50
229 Brendan Shanahan .30 .75
230 Dominik Hasek .40 1.00
231 Pavel Datsyuk .30 .75
232 Robert Lang .20 .50
233 Dan Cleary .25 .60
234 Nicklas Lidstrom .30 .75
235 Johan Franzen .20 .50
236 Tomas Holmstrom .25 .60
237 Kris Draper .25 .60
238 Mathieu Schneider .20 .50
239 Jiri Hudler .20 .50
240 Henrik Zetterberg .30 .75
241 Daniel Briere .30 .75
242 Thomas Vanek .25 .60
243 Ryan Miller .30 .75
244 Brian Campbell .20 .50
245 Chris Drury .25 .60
246 Andrew Peters .20 .50
247 Maxim Afinogenov .20 .50
248 Derek Roy .20 .50
249 Jason Pominville .20 .50
250 Drew Stafford .25 .60
251 Dany Heatley .40 1.00
252 Ray Emery .25 .60
253 Wade Redden .20 .50
254 Chris Neil .20 .50
255 Mike Fisher .25 .60
256 Patrick Eaves .20 .50
257 Jason Spezza .30 .75
258 Daniel Alfredsson .25 .60
259 Martin Gerber .25 .60
260 Antoine Vermette .20 .50
261 Chris Phillips .20 .50
262 Joe Thornton .40 1.00
263 Evgeni Nabokov .25 .60
264 Patrick Marleau .25 .60
265 Bill Guerin .20 .50
266 Milan Michalek .20 .50
267 Steve Bernier .20 .50
268 Matt Carle .20 .50
269 Jonathan Cheechoo .25 .60
270 Marc-Edouard Vlasic .20 .50
271 Joe Pavelski .20 .50
272 Mike Modano .30 .75
273 Jere Lehtinen .20 .50
274 Marty Turco .30 .75
275 Mike Ribeiro .20 .50
276 Sergei Zubov .20 .50
277 Brenden Morrow .25 .60
278 Jussi Jokinen .20 .50
279 Philippe Boucher .20 .50
280 Eric Lindros .30 .75
281 Kari Lehtonen .30 .75
282 Marian Hossa .30 .75
283 Keith Tkachuk .25 .60
284 Alexei Zhitnik .20 .50
285 Bobby Holik .20 .50
286 Slava Kozlov .20 .50
287 Ilya Kovalchuk .40 1.00
288 Eric Belanger .20 .50
289 Mark Parrish .20 .50
290 Marian Gaborik .40 1.00
291 Pavol Demitra .20 .50
292 Manny Fernandez .25 .60
293 Brian Rolston .20 .50
294 Mikko Koivu .20 .50
295 Pierre-Marc Bouchard .20 .50
296 Derek Boogaard .20 .50
297 Niklas Backstrom .25 .60
298 Roberto Luongo CL .50 1.25
299 Vincent Lecavalier CL .30 .75
300 Sidney Crosby CL 1.50 4.00
301 Jeff Finger RC .75 2.00
302 Colin Fraser RC .75 2.00
303 Pierre Parenteau RC .75 2.00
304 Bryan Bickell RC .75 2.00
305 Tomas Popperle RC 1.00 2.50
306 Curtis Glencross RC .75 2.00
307 Marc Methot RC .75 2.00
308 David Krejci RC 1.50 4.00
309 Jonathan Sigalet RC .75 2.00
310 Petr Kalus RC .75 2.00
311 Jaroslav Halak RC 2.50 6.00
312 Duncan Milroy RC .75 2.00
313 Jannik Hansen RC .75 2.00
314 Jeff Schultz RC .75 2.00
315 Jamie Hunt RC .75 2.00
316 Daniel Carcillo RC 1.00 2.50
317 Andy Greene RC .75 2.00
318 Mark Fraser RC .75 2.00
319 Rod Pelley RC .75 2.00
320 David Clarkson RC .75 2.00
321 Aaron Rome RC .75 2.00
322 Drew Miller RC .75 2.00
323 David Moss RC 1.25 3.00
324 Tomi Maki RC .75 2.00
325 Scott Munroe RC .75 2.00
326 Ryan Parent RC 1.00 2.50
327 Frans Nielsen RC .75 2.00
328 Lauri Tukonen RC .75 2.00
329 Yutaka Fukufuji RC 1.00 2.50
330 John Zeiler RC .75 2.00
331 Joe Piskula RC .75 2.00
332 Jack Johnson RC 1.25 3.00
333 Tom Gilbert RC 1.00 2.50
334 Mathieu Roy RC .75 2.00
335 Zack Stortini RC .75 2.00
336 Bryan Young RC .75 2.00
337 Sebastien Bisaillon RC .75 2.00
338 Rob Schremp RC 1.00 2.50
339 Martin Lojek RC .75 2.00
340 Rich Peverley RC .75 2.00
341 Ryan Callahan RC 1.25 3.00
342 Daniel Girardi RC .75 2.00
343 Brandon Dubinsky RC 1.25 3.00
344 Matt Ellis RC .75 2.00
345 Patrick Kaleta RC .75 2.00
346 Mark Mancari RC 1.00 2.50
347 Danny Bois RC .75 2.00
348 Thomas Plihal RC 1.00 2.50
349 Tobias Stephan RC 1.00 2.50
350 Krys Barch RC .75 2.00
351 Jonathan Toews RC 8.00 20.00
352 Carey Price RC 8.00 12.00
353 Bobby Ryan RC 4.00 10.00
354 Sam Gagner RC 2.00 5.00
355 Patrick Kane RC 6.00 15.00
356 Nicklas Bergfors RC 1.25 3.00
357 Erik Johnson RC 2.00 5.00
358 Nicklas Backstrom RC 4.00 10.00
359 Anton Stralman RC 1.25 3.00
360 Jonathan Bernier RC 2.50 6.00
361 Bryan Little RC 1.25 3.00
362 Kris Russell RC 1.25 3.00
363 Andrew Cogliano RC 2.50 6.00
364 Marc Staal RC 2.50 6.00
365 Nick Foligno RC 1.50 4.00
366 Peter Mueller RC 3.00 8.00
367 Ondrej Pavelec RC 1.50 4.00
368 Martin Hanzal RC 1.25 3.00
369 Matt Smaby RC 1.00 2.50
370 Brian Elliott RC 1.25 3.00
371 Brett Sterling RC 1.00 2.50
372 Matt Niskanen RC 1.00 2.50
373 Devin Setoguchi RC 2.00 5.00
374 James Sheppard RC 1.00 2.50
375 Kyle Chipchura RC 1.50 4.00

376 Tyler Kennedy RC 1.50 4.00
377 Jiri Tlusty RC 2.50 6.00
378 Mason Raymond RC 2.50 6.00
379 David Perron RC 1.50 4.00
380 Milan Lucic RC 2.50 6.00

2007-08 Upper Deck MVP Gold Script

*GOLD (1-300): 6X TO 15X
*GOLD ROOKIES (301-350): 1.2X TO 3X
*GOLD ROOKIES (351-380): 1.2X TO 3X
STATED PRINT RUN 100 SER.#'d SETS

2007-08 Upper Deck MVP Super Script

*SUPER (1-300): 12X TO 30X
*SUPER ROOKIES (301-350): 4X TO 10X
STATED PRINT RUN 25 SER.#'d SETS
*SUPER ROOKIES (351-380): 4X TO 10X

2007-08 Upper Deck MVP Game Faces

COMPLETE SET (7) 6.00 15.00
STATED ODDS 1:8
GF1 Sidney Crosby 2.50 6.00
GF2 Jaromir Jagr .75 2.00
GF3 Jarome Iginla .75 2.00
GF4 Ilya Kovalchuk .60 1.50
GF5 Peter Forsberg .60 1.50
GF6 Joe Thornton .60 1.50
GF7 Alexander Ovechkin 1.50 4.00

2007-08 Upper Deck MVP Hart Candidates

COMPLETE SET (7) 6.00 15.00
STATED ODDS 1:8
HC1 Roberto Luongo .75 2.00
HC2 Sidney Crosby 2.50 6.00
HC3 Martin Brodeur 1.25 3.00
HC4 Joe Thornton .60 1.50
HC5 Vincent Lecavalier .50 1.25
HC6 Miikka Kiprusoff .60 1.50
HC7 Dany Heatley .60 1.50

2007-08 Upper Deck MVP Monumental Moments

COMPLETE SET (14) 8.00 20.00
STATED ODDS 1:8
MM1 Joe Sakic 1.00 2.50
MM2 Mats Sundin .50 1.25
MM3 Sidney Crosby 2.50 6.00
MM4 Martin Brodeur 1.25 3.00
MM5 Evgeni Malkin 1.25 3.00
MM6 Mark Recchi .30 .75
MM7 Mike Modano .50 1.25
MM8 Joe Thornton .60 1.50
MM9 Brendan Shanahan .50 1.25
MM10 Daniel Briere .50 1.25
MM11 Roberto Luongo .75 2.00
MM12 Vincent Lecavalier .50 1.25
MM13 Daniel Alfredsson .40 1.00
MM14 Scott Niedermayer .30 .75

2007-08 Upper Deck MVP New World Order

COMPLETE SET (14) 8.00 20.00
STATED ODDS 1:8
NW1 Sidney Crosby 2.50 6.00
NW2 Alexander Ovechkin 1.50 4.00
NW3 Milan Michalek .30 .75
NW4 Ryan Miller .50 1.25
NW5 Marian Gaborik .60 1.50
NW6 Anze Kopitar .50 1.25
NW7 Mikko Koivu .30 .75
NW8 Henrik Zetterberg .50 1.25
NW9 Evgeni Malkin 1.25 3.00
NW10 Thomas Vanek .40 1.00
NW11 Marc-Andre Fleury .50 1.25
NW12 Henrik Lundqvist .60 1.50
NW13 Kari Lehtonen .50 1.25
NW14 Zach Parise .40 1.00

2007-08 Upper Deck MVP One on One Autographs

STATED ODDS 1:288
OABF Pierre-Marc Bouchard
Matt Foy
OABR Brendan Morrison
Ryan Kesler
OABS Daniel Briere 12.00 30.00
Drew Stafford
OABV Steve Bernier
Marc-Edouard Vlasic
OABW Peter Budaj 40.00 80.00
Wojtek Wolski
OACA Chris Higgins 10.00 25.00
Andrei Kostitsyn
OACK Phil Kessel 12.00 30.00
Zdeno Chara
OACS Erik Cole
Eric Staal
OADB Chris Drury
Daniel Briere
OADM Chris Drury
Ryan Miller
OAEM Alexander Edler 8.00 20.00
Nathan McIver
OAFK Alexander Frolov 12.00 30.00
Anze Kopitar
OAGP Scott Gomez 40.00 80.00
Zach Parise
OAHH Ales Hemsky 8.00 20.00
Shawn Horcoff
OAHK Ilya Kovalchuk
Marian Hossa
OAHL Milan Hejduk 10.00 25.00
John-Michael Liles
OAHS Milan Hejduk 12.00 30.00
Paul Stastny
OAHZ Dominik Hasek 40.00 80.00
Henrik Zetterberg
OAIK Ilya Kovalchuk 15.00 40.00
Kari Lehtonen
OAIP Jarome Iginla 25.00 60.00
Dion Phaneuf
OAJF Jarret Stoll 8.00 20.00
Fernando Pisani
OAJS Milan Jurcina 8.00 20.00
Mark Stuart
OAJW Olli Jokinen 8.00 20.00
Stephen Weiss
OAKK Nikolai Khabibulin 12.00 30.00
Duncan Keith
OALB Derek Boogaard
Georges Laraque
OALM Mario Lemieux 150.00 250.00
Evgeni Malkin
OALP Petr Prucha 15.00 40.00
Henrik Lundqvist
OAMK Andy McDonald
Chris Kunitz
OAMR Bryan McCabe 10.00 25.00
Andrew Raycroft
OAMV Milan Michalek 8.00 20.00
Marc-Edouard Vlasic
OANZ Rick Nash
Nikolai Zherdev
OAOB Bobby Orr
Ray Bourque
OAOM Alexander Ovechkin 150.00 250.00
Evgeni Malkin
OAPB Pierre-Marc Bouchard 8.00 20.00
Mark Parrish
OAPD Nigel Dawes 8.00 20.00
Petr Prucha
OAPG Corey Perry 10.00 25.00
Ryan Getzlaf
OAPK Andrei Kostitsyn
Alexander Perezhogin
OARG Wade Redden 10.00 25.00
Martin Gerber
OARL Guillaume Latendresse 40.00 80.00
Michael Ryder
OARS Andrew Raycroft 10.00 25.00
Alexander Steen
OASS Peter Stastny
Paul Stastny
OAST Rob Schremp 10.00 25.00
Patrick Thoresen
OASZ Steve Sullivan 8.00 20.00
Marek Zidlicky
OATC Joe Thornton 50.00 100.00
Jonathan Cheechoo
OATK Alex Tanguay 15.00 40.00
Miikka Kiprusoff
OATM Brenden Morrow
Marty Turco
OATW Darcy Tucker 10.00 25.00
Jeremy Williams
OAVM Thomas Vanek 10.00 25.00
Clarke MacArthur
OAZB Gilbert Brule 8.00 20.00
Nikolai Zherdev

2007-08 Upper Deck MVP One on One Jerseys

STATED ODDS 1:24
OOAJ Alex Tanguay 4.00 10.00
Joffrey Lupul
OOAK Nikolai Antropov 3.00 8.00
Andrei Kostitsyn
OOBL Martin Brodeur 12.00 30.00
Henrik Lundqvist
OOBP Brad Boyes 4.00 10.00
Alexandre Picard
OOBS Daniel Briere 5.00 12.00
Marc Savard
OOBW Ed Belfour 5.00 12.00
Cam Ward
OOCB Sidney Crosby 100.00 175.00
Martin Brodeur
OOCK Carlo Colaiacovo 3.00 8.00
Mike Komisarek
OOCM Zdeno Chara 3.00 8.00
Andrej Meszaros
OOCP Jeff Carter 4.00 10.00
Zach Parise
OOCV Matthew Lombardi 3.00 8.00
Ryan Kesler
OODE Rick DiPietro 4.00 10.00
Robert Esche
OODI Brian Rafalski 3.00 8.00
Brendan Witt
OODL Pavel Datsyuk 5.00 12.00
Jere Lehtinen
OODM Shane Doan 4.00 10.00
Brenden Morrow
OOFL Peter Forsberg 6.00 15.00
Nicklas Lidstrom
OOFT Manny Fernandez 5.00 12.00
Jose Theodore
OOGC Jean-Sebastien Giguere 5.00 12.00
Corey Perry
Ryan Getzlaf
OOGG Simon Gagne 5.00 12.00
Brian Gionta
OOGH Marian Gaborik 6.00 15.00
Milan Hejduk
OOHG Cristobal Huet 4.00 10.00
Martin Gerber
OOHK Dany Heatley 6.00 15.00
Ilya Kovalchuk
OOHM Shawn Horcoff 3.00 8.00
Brendan Morrison
OOHR Dany Heatley 6.00 15.00
Michael Ryder
OOHT Dany Heatley 6.00 15.00
Alex Tanguay
OOHV Dominik Hasek 6.00 15.00
Tomas Vokoun
OOIN Jarome Iginla 8.00 20.00
Markus Naslund
OOJD Jay Bouwmeester 3.00 8.00
Dan Hamhuis
OOJE Jaromir Jagr 8.00 20.00
Patrik Elias
OOJT Curtis Joseph 5.00 12.00
Marty Turco
OOKD Olaf Kolzig 5.00 12.00
Marc Denis
OOKN Paul Kariya 5.00 12.00
Rick Nash
OOLC Andrew Ladd 3.00 8.00
Ryan Craig
OOLJ Vincent Lecavalier 5.00 12.00
Olli Jokinen
OOLK Roberto Luongo 8.00 20.00
Miikka Kiprusoff
OOLL Pascal Leclaire 4.00 10.00
Manny Legace
OOLN Kari Lehtonen 5.00 12.00
Antero Niittymaki
OOLR Roberto Luongo 8.00 20.00
Dwayne Roloson
OOLW Robert Lang 3.00 8.00
Jason Williams
OOMH Brendan Morrison 3.00 8.00
Adam Hall
OOMK Glen Murray 3.00 8.00
Alex Kovalev
OOMM Patrick Marleau 5.00 12.00
Mike Modano
OOMR Bryan McCabe 3.00 8.00
Wade Redden
OONM Ladislav Nagy 3.00 8.00
Milan Michalek
OONY Martin Straka 3.00 8.00
Miroslav Satan
OOOH Ben Ondrus 3.00 8.00
Jeff Hoggan
OOOL Chris Osgood 4.00 10.00
Patrick Lalime
OOOM Alexander Ovechkin 15.00 40.00
Evgeni Malkin
OOPJ Chris Pronger 5.00 12.00
Ed Jovanovski
OORH Martin Havlat 4.00 10.00
Brian Rolston
OORS Rod Brind'Amour 4.00 10.00
Stephen Weiss
OORT Andrew Raycroft 6.00 15.00
Tim Thomas
OOSA Mats Sundin 5.00 12.00
Daniel Alfredsson
OOSC Teemu Selanne 5.00 12.00
Jonathan Cheechoo
OOSF Joe Sakic 10.00 25.00
Peter Forsberg
OOSS Brendan Shanahan 5.00 12.00
Ryan Smyth
OOTL Joe Thornton 6.00 15.00
Eric Lindros
OOTM Raffi Torres 3.00 8.00
Darren McCarty
OOVS Thomas Vanek 4.00 10.00
Alexander Steen
OOWH Doug Weight 3.00 8.00
Michal Handzus

2008-09 Upper Deck MVP

This set was released on December 2, 2008. The base set consists of 392 cards. Cards 1-300 feature veterans, and cards 301-392 are rookies.

COMPLETE SET (392) 150.00 300.00
COMP.SET w/o RCs (300) 15.00 40.00
1 Ryan Getzlaf .40 1.00
2 Corey Perry .30 .75
3 Teemu Selanne .30 .75
4 Jean-Sebastien Giguere .25 .60
5 Chris Pronger .25 .60
6 Mathieu Schneider .20 .50
7 George Parros .20 .50
8 Scott Niedermayer .20 .50
9 Chris Kunitz .20 .50
10 Brendan Morrison .20 .50
11 Ilya Kovalchuk .40 1.00
12 Eric Perrin .20 .50
13 Tobias Enstrom .30 .75
14 Eric Boulton .20 .50
15 Colby Armstrong .20 .50
16 Bryan Little .20 .50
17 Erik Christensen .20 .50
18 Kari Lehtonen .20 .50
19 Johan Hedberg .25 .60
20 Jason Williams .20 .50
21 Patrice Bergeron .30 .75
22 Marc Savard .20 .50
23 Zdeno Chara .20 .50
24 Chuck Kobasew .20 .50
25 Phil Kessel .30 .75
26 Tim Thomas .30 .75
27 Marco Sturm .20 .50
28 Milan Lucic .60 1.50
29 Tuukka Rask .30 .75
30 Derek Roy .20 .50
31 Jason Pominville .25 .60
32 Thomas Vanek .30 .75
33 Maxim Afinogenov .20 .50
34 Jochen Hecht .20 .50
35 Ales Kotalik .20 .50
36 Ryan Miller .30 .75
37 Drew Stafford .30 .75
38 Andrew Peters .20 .50
39 Daniel Paille .25 .60
40 Craig Rivet .20 .50
41 Patrick Lalime .20 .50
42 Todd Bertuzzi .30 .75
43 Robyn Regehr .20 .50
44 Jarome Iginla .60 1.50
45 Dion Phaneuf .30 .75
46 Daymond Langkow .20 .50
47 Miikka Kiprusoff .30 .75
48 Matthew Lombardi .20 .50
49 Adrian Aucoin .20 .50
50 Mike Cammalleri .30 .75
51 Eric Staal .50 1.25
52 Ray Whitney .20 .50
53 Rod Brind'Amour .25 .60
54 Matt Cullen .20 .50
55 Justin Williams .20 .50
56 Cam Ward .30 .75
57 Scott Walker .20 .50
58 Sergei Samsonov .20 .50
59 Joni Pitkanen .20 .50
60 Patrick Kane .75 2.00
61 Jonathan Toews 1.00 2.50
62 Patrick Sharp .20 .50
63 Dustin Byfuglien .25 .60
64 Adam Burish .25 .60
65 Nikolai Khabibulin .30 .75
66 Duncan Keith .25 .60
67 Martin Havlat .25 .60
68 James Wisniewski .20 .50
69 Brian Campbell .50 1.25
70 Cristobal Huet .30 .75
71 Paul Stastny .30 .75
72 Joe Sakic .50 1.25
73 Peter Forsberg .50 1.25
74 Ryan Smyth .20 .50
75 Wojtek Wolski .20 .50
76 Milan Hejduk .25 .60
77 Marek Svatos .20 .50
78 Ian Laperriere .20 .50
79 Peter Budaj .25 .60
80 T.J. Hensick .25 .60
81 Darcy Tucker .25 .60
82 Kristian Huselius .20 .50
83 Rick Nash .30 .75
84 Michael Peca .25 .60
85 Pascal Leclaire .25 .60
86 Fredrik Norrena .30 .75
87 Jared Boll .25 .60
88 Kris Russell .30 .75
89 R.J. Umberger .20 .50
90 Mike Ribeiro .20 .50
91 Mike Modano .30 .75
92 Brad Richards .25 .60
93 Marty Turco .25 .60
94 Sergei Zubov .20 .50
95 Jere Lehtinen .20 .50
96 Steve Ott .25 .60
97 Brenden Morrow .25 .60
98 Sean Avery .25 .60
99 Philippe Boucher .20 .50
100 Ty Conklin .25 .60
101 Niklas Kronwall .25 .60
102 Jiri Hudler .20 .50
103 Valtteri Filppula .20 .50
104 Mikael Samuelsson .20 .50
105 Chris Osgood .20 .50
106 Henrik Zetterberg .60 1.50
107 Pavel Datsyuk .30 .75
108 Nicklas Lidstrom .30 .75
109 Brian Rafalski .20 .50
110 Dan Cleary .20 .50
111 Tomas Holmstrom .25 .60
112 Johan Franzen .20 .50
113 Marian Hossa .50 1.25
114 Erik Cole .20 .50
115 Gilbert Brule .30 .75
116 Ales Hemsky .30 .75
117 Shawn Horcoff .20 .50
118 Sam Gagner .50 1.25
119 Dustin Penner .20 .50
120 Andrew Cogliano .50 1.25
121 Zach Stortini .20 .50
122 Robert Nilsson .20 .50
123 Mathieu Garon .30 .75
124 Dwayne Roloson .25 .60
125 Lubomir Visnovsky .20 .50
126 Nathan Horton .20 .50
127 Stephen Weiss .20 .50
128 Jay Bouwmeester .25 .60
129 Tomas Vokoun .30 .75
130 David Booth .20 .50
131 Brett McLean .20 .50
132 Rostislav Olesz .20 .50
133 Cory Stillman .20 .50
134 Jarret Stoll .25 .60
135 Anze Kopitar .30 .75
136 Alexander Frolov .20 .50
137 Dustin Brown .20 .50
138 Patrick O'Sullivan .25 .60
139 Jason LaBarbera .25 .60
140 Jack Johnson .25 .60
141 Andrew Brunette .20 .50
142 Marian Gaborik .50 1.25
143 Pierre-Marc Bouchard .20 .50
144 Brent Burns .20 .50
145 James Sheppard .30 .75
146 Mikko Koivu .30 .75
147 Niklas Backstrom .20 .50
148 Josh Harding .25 .60
149 Derek Boogaard .30 .75
150 Marek Zidlicky .20 .50
151 Alex Tanguay .25 .60
152 Alex Kovalev .30 .75
153 Tomas Plekanec .20 .50
154 Andrei Markov .25 .60
155 Saku Koivu .30 .75
156 Andrei Kostitsyn .25 .60
157 Sergei Kostitsyn .25 .60
158 Chris Higgins .20 .50
159 Carey Price 1.00 2.50
160 Kyle Chipchura .20 .50
161 Guillaume Latendresse .25 .60
162 Georges Laraque .25 .60
163 Jason Arnott .20 .50
164 J.P. Dumont .20 .50
165 Shea Weber .20 .50
166 Martin Erat .30 .75
167 David Legwand .25 .60
168 Dan Ellis .20 .50
169 Jordin Tootoo .30 .75
170 Ryan Suter .20 .50
171 Brian Rolston .20 .50
172 Zach Parise .30 .75
173 Patrik Elias .20 .50
174 Brian Gionta .20 .50
175 Martin Brodeur .60 1.50
176 David Clarkson .20 .50
177 John Madden .20 .50
178 Jamie Langenbrunner .20 .50
179 Dainius Zubrus .20 .50
180 Travis Zajac .30 .75
181 Mark Streit .20 .50
182 Mike Comrie .20 .50
183 Bill Guerin .20 .50
184 Trent Hunter .20 .50
185 Rick DiPietro .30 .75
186 Chris Campoli .25 .60
187 Sean Bergenheim .25 .60
188 Jeff Tambellini .25 .60
189 Blake Comeau .25 .60
190 Doug Weight .20 .50
191 Nikolai Zherdev .20 .50
192 Scott Gomez .25 .60
193 Brendan Shanahan .30 .75
194 Chris Drury .30 .75
195 Brandon Dubinsky .25 .60
196 Henrik Lundqvist .60 1.50
197 Colton Orr .20 .50
198 Stephen Valiquette .25 .60
199 Marc Staal .40 1.00
200 Wade Redden .20 .50
201 Markus Naslund .30 .75
202 Jason Spezza .40 1.00
203 Daniel Alfredsson .25 .60
204 Dany Heatley .40 1.00
205 Antoine Vermette .20 .50
206 Mike Fisher .20 .50
207 Filip Kuba .20 .50
208 Chris Neil .20 .50
209 Chris Phillips .20 .50
210 Martin Gerber .25 .60
211 Mike Richards .50 1.25
212 Daniel Briere .30 .75
213 Mike Knuble .30 .75
214 Jeff Carter .30 .75
215 Martin Biron .25 .60
216 Joffrey Lupul .20 .50
217 Kimmo Timonen .20 .50
218 Riley Cote .20 .50
219 Scott Hartnell .25 .60
220 Olli Jokinen .25 .60
221 Ilya Bryzgalov .20 .50
222 Shane Doan .20 .50
223 Peter Mueller .40 1.00
224 Ed Jovanovski .20 .50
225 Martin Hanzal .25 .60
226 Daniel Winnik .20 .50
227 Daniel Carcillo .20 .50
228 Mikael Tellqvist .30 .75
229 Eric Godard .20 .50
230 Miroslav Satan .20 .50
231 Sidney Crosby 1.50 4.00
232 Evgeni Malkin .75 2.00
233 Jordan Staal .50 1.25
234 Sergei Gonchar .30 .75
235 Ryan Whitney .30 .75
236 Petr Sykora .20 .50
237 Marc-Andre Fleury .30 .75
238 Tyler Kennedy .25 .60
239 Rob Blake .30 .75
240 Doug Murray .20 .50
241 Joe Thornton .50 1.25
242 Milan Michalek .20 .50
243 Patrick Marleau .25 .60
244 Joe Pavelski .20 .50
245 Jonathan Cheechoo .30 .75
246 Jeremy Roenick .30 .75
247 Evgeni Nabokov .30 .75
248 Devin Setoguchi .30 .75
249 Dan Boyle .25 .60
250 Chris Mason .25 .60
251 Brad Boyes .25 .60
252 Paul Kariya .30 .75
253 Manny Legace .25 .60
254 David Backes .20 .50
255 Erik Johnson .40 1.00
256 David Perron .20 .50
257 Keith Tkachuk .25 .60
258 Andy McDonald .20 .50
259 Lee Stempniak .20 .50
260 Radim Vrbata .20 .50
261 Ryan Malone .20 .50
262 Vincent Lecavalier .30 .75
263 Martin St. Louis .30 .75
264 Mike Smith .25 .60
265 Michel Ouellet .20 .50
266 Paul Ranger .20 .50
267 Shane O'Brien .20 .50
268 Jussi Jokinen .20 .50
269 Andrej Meszaros .20 .50
270 Mats Sundin .30 .75
271 Nikolai Antropov .25 .60
272 Tomas Kaberle .20 .50
273 Pavel Kubina .20 .50
274 Jason Blake .20 .50
275 Alexander Steen .25 .60
276 Jiri Tlusty .30 .75
277 Vesa Toskala .20 .50
278 Matt Stajan .25 .60
279 Steve Bernier .20 .50
280 Pavol Demitra .25 .60
281 Daniel Sedin .30 .75
282 Henrik Sedin .30 .75
283 Ryan Kesler .20 .50
284 Alexander Edler .25 .60
285 Kevin Bieksa .25 .60
286 Roberto Luongo .50 1.25
287 Taylor Pyatt .20 .50
288 Alexandre Burrows .25 .60
289 Jason Blake .20 .50
290 Jose Theodore .30 .75
291 Alexander Ovechkin 1.25 3.00
292 Nicklas Backstrom .60 1.50
293 Mike Green .30 .75
294 Viktor Kozlov .20 .50
295 Alexander Semin .30 .75
296 Donald Brashear .20 .50
297 Sergei Fedorov .50 1.25
298 Jarome Iginla CL .60 1.50
299 Evgeni Malkin CL .75 2.00
300 Alexander Ovechkin CL 1.25 3.00
301 Tyler Plante RC 1.25 3.00
302 Tom Sestito RC 1.00 2.50
303 Tom Cavanagh RC 1.00 2.50
304 Tim Ramholt RC 1.00 2.50
305 Tim Conboy RC 1.00 2.50
306 Theo Peckham RC 1.00 2.50
307 Teddy Purcell RC 1.25 3.00
308 Steve Mason RC 3.00 8.00
309 Shawn Matthias RC 1.25 3.00
310 Sami Lepisto RC 1.25 3.00
311 Ryan Stone RC 1.25 3.00
312 Robbie Earl RC 1.00 2.50
313 Zach Bogosian RC 2.50 6.00
314 Pascal Pelletier RC 1.00 2.50
315 Niklas Hjalmarsson RC 2.00 5.00
316 Mike Mole RC 1.00 2.50
317 Mike Iggulden RC 1.00 2.50
318 Mike Brown RC 1.50 4.00
319 Mattias Ritola RC 1.50 4.00
320 Matt D'Agostini RC 2.00 5.00
321 Mark Fistric RC 1.00 2.50
322 Marc-Andre Gragnani RC 1.00 2.50
323 Lauri Korpikoski RC 1.25 3.00
324 Kyle Turris RC 2.50 6.00
325 Kyle Okposo RC 2.50 6.00
326 Kyle Greentree RC 1.50 4.00
327 Blake Wheeler RC 3.00 8.00
328 Justin Abdelkader RC 2.50 6.00
329 Jordan LaVallee RC 1.25 3.00
330 Jordan Hendry RC 1.00 2.50
331 Jonathan Ericsson RC 2.00 5.00
332 Jon Filewich RC 1.00 2.50
333 Joey Mormina RC 1.00 2.50
334 Joe Jensen RC 1.25 3.00
335 Jesse Winchester RC 1.25 3.00
336 Jack Hillen RC 1.00 2.50
337 Ilya Zubov RC 1.25 3.00
338 Garrett Stafford RC 1.50 4.00
339 Erik Ersberg RC 1.25 3.00
340 Derick Brassard RC 2.50 6.00
341 David Brine RC 1.00 2.50
342 Darryl Boyce RC 1.00 2.50
343 Darren Helm RC 2.00 5.00
344 Danny Taylor RC 1.25 3.00
345 Dan LaCosta RC 1.50 4.00
346 Corey Locke RC 1.25 3.00
347 Colin Stuart RC 1.00 2.50
348 Cody McLeod RC 1.00 2.50
349 Clay Wilson RC .75 2.00
350 Claude Giroux RC 2.50 6.00
351 Chris Minard RC 1.25 3.00
352 Brian Lee RC 1.25 3.00
353 Brian Boyle RC 1.25 3.00
354 Brandon Nolan RC 1.50 4.00
355 Boris Valabik RC 1.50 4.00
356 B.J. Crombeen RC 1.00 2.50
357 Andrew Murray RC 1.00 2.50
358 Andrew Ebbett RC 1.25 3.00
359 Alex Goligoski RC 2.50 6.00
360 Alex Foster RC 1.00 2.50
361 Adam Pineault RC 1.25 3.00
362 Adam Pardy RC 1.25 3.00
363 Brandon Sutter RC 1.50 4.00
364 Jakub Voracek RC 2.50 6.00
365 Michael Frolik RC 2.50 6.00
366 James Neal RC 2.00 5.00
367 Drew Doughty RC 4.00 10.00
368 Wayne Simmonds RC 1.25 3.00
369 Oscar Moller RC 1.25 3.00
370 Colton Gillies RC 1.25 3.00
371 Ryan Jones RC 1.50 4.00
372 Patric Hornqvist RC 1.25 3.00
373 Anssi Salmela RC 1.50 4.00
374 Luca Sbisa RC 2.00 5.00
375 Jared Ross RC 1.50 4.00
376 Mikkel Boedker RC 2.00 5.00
377 Patrik Berglund RC 3.00 8.00
378 Chris Porter RC 1.25 3.00
379 T.J. Oshie RC 3.00 8.00
380 Alex Pietrangelo RC 2.00 5.00
381 Steven Stamkos RC 10.00 25.00
382 Vladimir Mihalik RC 1.25 3.00
383 Janne Niskala RC 1.25 3.00
384 Nikolai Kulemin RC 1.25 3.00
385 Luke Schenn RC 4.00 10.00
386 John Mitchell RC 1.25 3.00
387 Jonas Frogren RC 1.50 4.00
388 Derek Dorsett RC 1.50 4.00
389 Viktor Tikhonov RC 1.25 3.00
390 Kevin Porter RC 1.00 2.50
391 Paul Bissonnette RC 1.50 4.00
392 Zach Fitzgerald RC 1.25 3.00

2008-09 Upper Deck MVP Gold Script

*GOLD: 2.5X TO 6X BASE
*GOLD RC: .8X TO 2X BASE
STATED PRINT RUN 100 SERIAL #'d SETS
381 Steven Stamkos 30.00 60.00

2008-09 Upper Deck MVP Super Script

*SUPER: 5X TO 12X BASE
*SUPER RC: 2X TO 5X BASE
STATED PRINT RUN 25 SERIAL #'d SETS
381 Steven Stamkos 60.00 120.00

2008-09 Upper Deck MVP Alexander the Gr8

COMPLETE SET (8) 6.00 15.00
COMMON OVECHKIN (AO1-AO8) 1.25 3.00
STATED ODDS 1:

2008-09 Upper Deck MVP First Line Phenoms

COMPLETE SET (15) 8.00 20.00
STATED ODDS 1:
FL1 Alexander Ovechkin 2.00 5.00
FL2 Marian Gaborik .75 2.00
FL3 Andrei Kostitsyn .40 1.00
FL4 Evgeni Malkin 1.25 3.00
FL5 Jonathan Toews 1.50 4.00

FL6 Mike Richards .75 2.00
FL7 Nicklas Backstrom 1.00 2.50
FL8 Patrick Kane 1.25 3.00
FL9 Paul Stastny .50 1.25
FL10 Peter Mueller .60 1.50
FL11 Ryan Getzlaf .60 1.50
FL12 Sam Gagner .75 2.00
FL13 Sidney Crosby 2.50 6.00
FL14 Thomas Vanek .50 1.25
FL15 Zach Parise .50 1.25

2008-09 Upper Deck MVP Magnificent Sevens

COMPLETE SET (7) 8.00 20.00
STATED ODDS 1:
M7CP Carey Price 2.50 6.00
M7CW Cam Ward .75 2.00
M7GL Guy Lafleur 1.50 4.00
M7MB Martin Brodeur 1.50 4.00
M7PL Pat LaFontaine .75 2.00
M7TB Turk Broda .75 2.00
M7WG Wayne Gretzky 4.00 10.00

2008-09 Upper Deck MVP Marked by Valor

COMPLETE SET (15) 10.00 25.00
STATED ODDS 1:

2008-09 Upper Deck MVP One on One Autographs

STATED ODDS 1:
ABC Dan Cleary 12.00 30.00
Brad Boyes
ABD Brandon Dubinsky 15.00 40.00
David Clarkson
ABF Martin Brodeur
Marc-Andre Fleury
ABJ Jack Johnson
Brendan Bell
ABN Rick Nash
Brad Boyes
ABW Dan Boyle 6.00 15.00
Noah Welch
ACB Nicklas Backstrom
Jeff Carter
ACF Nick Foligno
Kyle Chipchura
ACS Andrew Cogliano
James Sheppard
ADC Jeff Carter
Chris Drury
ADD Steve Downie 15.00 40.00
Brandon Dubinsky
ADH Josh Harding
Jeff Drouin-Deslauriers
ADJ Devin Setoguchi 12.00 30.00
Joe Pavelski
ADK Chris Drury
Phil Kessel
AED Erik Johnson 10.00 25.00
Dustin Byfuglien
AES Patrik Elias
Miroslav Satan
AFG Daniel Girardi 10.00 25.00
Mark Fraser
AFM Evgeni Malkin
Marc-Andre Fleury
AFT Jiri Tlusty 15.00 40.00
Nick Foligno
AGP Jason Pominville
Scott Gomez
AGR Greg Moore 15.00 40.00
Rod Pelley
AHB Peter Budaj
Milan Hejduk
AHM Ryan Malone 12.00 30.00
Nathan Horton
AHR Mason Raymond 15.00 40.00
Jannik Hansen
AHS James Sheppard 12.00 30.00
T.J. Hensick
AHV Dany Heatley
Thomas Vanek
AIG Jarome Iginla
Sam Gagner
AJB Jonathan Bernier 12.00 30.00
Jack Johnson
AKK Andrei Kostitsyn
Sergei Kostitsyn
AKL Guillaume Latendresse 15.00 40.00
Phil Kessel
AKP Patrick Kane
David Perron
AKS Eric Staal
Ilya Kovalchuk
AKT David Krejci 15.00 40.00
Jiri Tlusty
ALK Nicklas Lidstrom
Tomas Kaberle
ALS Eric Staal
Vincent Lecavalier
AMG Ryan Getzlaf
Brenden Morrow
AMK Milan Michalek
Lukas Kaspar
ANY Marc Staal 10.00 25.00
Ryan Callahan
AOM Alexander Ovechkin
Evgeni Malkin
APA Peter Mueller
Anze Kopitar
APK Corey Perry
Anze Kopitar
APM Chris Phillips
Bryan McCabe
APP Dustin Penner
Marc-Antoine Pouliot
APR Carey Price
Tuukka Rask
APS Paul Stastny
Dustin Penner
APT Carey Price
Jiri Tlusty
ARG Sam Gagner
Mason Raymond
ARM Mike Ribeiro
Brenden Morrow
ARP Kris Russell
Alexandre Picard
ART Ryan Smyth
T.J. Hensick
ASD Daniel Sedin 12.00 30.00
Henrik Sedin
ASH Matt Stajan
Chris Higgins
ASS Marc Staal
Jordan Staal
ATG Joe Thornton
Ryan Getzlaf
ATK Patrick Kane 50.00 100.00
Jonathan Toews
AVL Kari Lehtonen
Tomas Vokoun
AWH Nathan Horton
Stephen Weiss
AZC Travis Zajac 12.00 30.00
David Clarkson
AZT Jonathan Toews
Henrik Zetterberg

2008-09 Upper Deck MVP Two on Two Jerseys

STATED ODDS 1:
J2AWLS Jason Arnott 6.00 15.00
Shea Weber
David Legwand
Steve Sullivan
J2BDLP Martin Brodeur 15.00 40.00
Zach Parise
Henrik Lundqvist
Chris Drury
J2BEGP Martin Brodeur 8.00 20.00
Zach Parise
Patrik Elias
Brian Gionta
J2BGRC Simon Gagne 12.00 30.00
Mike Richards
Jeff Carter
Martin Biron
J2BNLE Tobias Enstrom 8.00 20.00
Matt Niskanen
Kevin Bieksa
Mike Lundin
J2BTTL Vesa Toskala 15.00 40.00
Jason Blake
Tim Thomas
Milan Lucic
J2CHSN Sidney Crosby 25.00 60.00
Dany Heatley
Jason Spezza
Rick Nash
J2DCKM Shane Doan 10.00 25.00
Peter Mueller
Anze Kopitar
Kyle Calder
J2DSTC Chris Drury 8.00 20.00
Brendan Shanahan
Jeff Tambellini
Mike Comrie
J2DZSK Henrik Zetterberg 20.00 50.00
Pavel Datsyuk
Patrick Kane
Patrick Sharp
J2FCMS Sidney Crosby 40.00 100.00
Evgeni Malkin
Marc-Andre Fleury
Jordan Staal
J2FGOB Alexander Ovechkin 30.00 80.00
Nicklas Backstrom
Mike Green
Sergei Fedorov
J2GBSC Sidney Crosby
Miroslav Satan
Daniel Briere
Simon Gagne
J2GBSO Simon Gagne 30.00 80.00
Daniel Briere
Alexander Ovechkin
Tomas Fleischmann
J2GCDA Scott Gomez 8.00 20.00
Chris Drury
Tim Connolly
Maxim Afinogenov
J2GCOM Sidney Crosby 60.00 120.00
Evgeni Malkin
Alexander Ovechkin
Mike Green
J2HDSK Dominik Hasek 12.00 30.00
Kris Draper
Patrick Sharp
Nikolai Khabibulin
J2HHSB Chris Osgood 8.00 20.00
Tomas Holmstrom
Marek Svatos
Peter Budaj
J2HLDZ Henrik Zetterberg 15.00 40.00
Nicklas Lidstrom
Dominik Hasek
Pavel Datsyuk
J2JSDL Henrik Lundqvist 15.00 40.00
Nikolai Zherdev
Rick DiPietro
Trent Hunter
J2KGBK Marian Gaborik 8.00 20.00
Mikko Koivu
Steve Bernier
Ryan Kesler
J2KKSJ Saku Koivu 8.00 20.00
Alex Kovalev
Mats Sundin
Curtis Joseph
J2KPKL Saku Koivu 8.00 20.00
Tomas Plekanec
Guillaume Latendresse
Alex Kovalev
J2KSLW Eric Staal 12.00 30.00
Cam Ward
Ilya Kovalchuk
Kari Lehtonen
J2KTAW Paul Kariya 8.00 20.00
Keith Tkachuk
Jason Arnott
Shea Weber
J2KTBP Paul Kariya 8.00 20.00
Brad Boyes
Keith Tkachuk
David Perron
J2LBSD Roberto Luongo 12.00 30.00
Steve Bernier
Daniel Sedin
Pavol Demitra
J2LJLT Roberto Luongo 12.00 30.00
Curtis Joseph
Pascal Leclaire
Tim Thomas
J2LNCP Dion Phaneuf 8.00 20.00
Nicklas Lidstrom
Scott Niedermayer
Zdeno Chara
J2LOHG Roberto Luongo 12.00 30.00
Mattias Ohlund
Sam Gagner
Shawn Horcoff
J2LSBS Eric Staal 12.00 30.00
Rod Brind'Amour
Vincent Lecavalier
Martin St. Louis
J2MMNT Evgeni Nabokov 8.00 20.00
Patrick Marleau
Marty Turco
Mike Modano
J2MTNC Joe Thornton 12.00 30.00
Jonathan Cheechoo
Patrick Marleau
Evgeni Nabokov
J2MZLI Mike Modano 8.00 20.00
Marty Turco
Jere Lehtinen
Sergei Zubov
J2NGKJ Ryan Getzlaf 10.00 25.00
Scott Niedermayer
Anze Kopitar
Jack Johnson
J2PDGB Marian Gaborik 12.00 30.00
Pierre-Marc Bouchard
Steve Bernier
Pavol Demitra
J2PRRC Dion Phaneuf 8.00 20.00
Robyn Regehr
Dwayne Roloson
Erik Cole
J2RDTG Martin Brodeur 15.00 40.00
Rick DiPietro
Vesa Toskala
Martin Gerber
J2SBHR Martin St. Louis 6.00 15.00
Paul Ranger
Nathan Horton
Jay Bouwmeester
J2SCBK Patrice Bergeron 8.00 20.00
Phil Kessel
Marc Savard
Zdeno Chara
J2SDRC Mike Richards 8.00 20.00
Jeff Carter
Chris Drury
Brendan Shanahan
J2SHSW Joe Sakic 12.00 30.00
Milan Hejduk
Wojtek Wolski
Ryan Smyth
J2SHVS Jason Spezza 8.00 20.00
Dany Heatley
Thomas Vanek
Drew Stafford
J2SHZS Henrik Zetterberg 15.00 40.00
Tomas Holmstrom
Mats Sundin
Alexander Steen
J2SJGL Zach Parise 8.00 20.00
Brian Rolston
Brendan Shanahan
Scott Gomez
J2SKHG Marian Gaborik 8.00 20.00
Mikko Koivu
Joe Sakic
Milan Hejduk
J2SMRG Ryan Getzlaf 10.00 25.00
Teemu Selanne
Mike Modano
Mike Ribeiro
J2SNGG Teemu Selanne 10.00 25.00
Ryan Getzlaf
Scott Niedermayer
Jean-Sebastien Giguere
J2SSHA Mats Sundin 6.00 15.00
Nik Antropov
Dany Heatley
Jason Spezza
J2SSTS Mats Sundin 8.00 20.00
Alexander Steen
Vesa Toskala
Matt Stajan
J2STMA Mats Sundin 8.00 20.00
Vesa Toskala
Ryan Miller
Maxim Afinogenov
J2TCKJ Jonathan Cheechoo
Joe Thornton
Anze Kopitar
Jack Johnson
J2TCPG Joe Thornton 12.00 30.00
Jonathan Cheechoo
Ryan Getzlaf
Corey Perry
J2THGS Dany Heatley 10.00 25.00
Martin Gerber
Alexander Steen
Vesa Toskala
J2TLLN Keith Tkachuk 8.00 20.00
Manny Legace
Rick Nash
Pascal Leclaire
J2TRBK Patrice Bergeron 8.00 20.00
Phil Kessel
Tim Thomas
Michael Ryder
J2VWKL Ilya Kovalchuk 10.00 25.00
Kari Lehtonen
Tomas Vokoun
Stephen Weiss
J2WBSW Eric Staal 12.00 30.00
Rod Brind'Amour
Cam Ward
Justin Williams

2008-09 Upper Deck MVP Winter Classic

COMPLETE SET (20) 20.00 50.00
STATED ODDS 1:
WC1 Winter Classic 1.00 2.50
WC2 Chris Chelios 2.00 5.00
WC3 Pavel Datsyuk 1.50 4.00
WC4 Johan Franzen 1.00 2.50
WC5 Tomas Holmstrom 1.25 3.00
WC6 Marian Hossa 2.50 6.00
WC7 Nicklas Lidstrom 1.50 4.00
WC8 Chris Osgood 1.50 4.00
WC9 Brian Rafalski 1.00 2.50
WC10 Henrik Zetterberg 3.00 8.00
WC11 Brian Campbell 2.50 6.00
WC12 Martin Havlat 1.25 3.00
WC13 Cristobal Huet 1.50 4.00
WC14 Duncan Keith 1.25 3.00
WC15 Patrick Kane 4.00 10.00
WC16 Dustin Byfuglien 1.25 3.00
WC17 Brent Seabrook 1.25 3.00
WC18 Patrick Sharp 1.00 2.50
WC19 Jonathan Toews 5.00 12.00
WC20 Wrigley Field 1.00 2.50

2009-10 Upper Deck MVP

COMPLETE SET (394) 250.00 400.00
COMP.SET w/o SPS (300) 12.00 30.00
RC STATED ODDS 1:2
1 Alexander Ovechkin 1.25 3.00
2 Nicklas Backstrom .60 1.50
3 Alexander Semin .30 .75
4 Mike Green .60 1.50
5 Brooks Laich .25 .60
6 Tomas Fleischmann .20 .50
7 Jose Theodore .30 .75
8 Michael Nylander .20 .50
9 Eric Fehr .30 .75
10 Karl Alzner .30 .75
11 Roberto Luongo .75 2.00
12 Ryan Kesler .25 .60
13 Pavol Demitra .25 .60
14 Henrik Sedin .50 1.25
15 Kevin Bieksa .20 .50
16 Alexander Edler .20 .50
17 Steve Bernier .20 .50
18 Daniel Sedin .40 1.00
19 Willie Mitchell .20 .50
20 Mason Raymond .20 .50
21 Jason Blake .20 .50
22 Alexei Ponikarovsky .20 .50
23 Francois Beauchemin .20 .50
24 Mikhail Grabovski .25 .60
25 Lee Stempniak .20 .50
26 Tomas Kaberle .20 .50
27 Nikolai Kulemin .25 .60
28 Luke Schenn .50 1.25
29 Vesa Toskala .30 .75
30 Mike Komisarek .25 .60
31 Martin St. Louis .30 .75
32 Vincent Lecavalier .40 1.00
33 Steven Stamkos .75 2.00
34 Steve Downie .20 .50
35 Ryan Malone .20 .50
36 Mike Smith .25 .60
37 Alex Tanguay .25 .60
38 Lukas Krajicek .20 .50
39 Paul Ranger .20 .50
40 Brad Boyes .25 .60
41 David Backes .25 .60
42 David Perron .25 .60
43 Patrik Berglund .60 1.50
44 T.J. Oshie .50 1.25
45 Paul Kariya .30 .75
46 Chris Mason .25 .60
47 Andy McDonald .20 .50
48 Keith Tkachuk .25 .60
49 Ty Conklin .25 .60
50 Joe Thornton .60 1.50
51 Patrick Marleau .30 .75
52 Devin Setoguchi .25 .60
53 Joe Pavelski .20 .50
54 Rob Blake .30 .75
55 Evgeni Nabokov .30 .75
56 Dan Boyle .20 .50
57 Ryane Clowe .20 .50
58 Jonathan Cheechoo .30 .75
59 Marc-Edouard Vlasic .20 .50
60 Evgeni Malkin .75 2.00
61 Sidney Crosby 1.50 4.00
62 Chris Kunitz .30 .75
63 Jordan Staal .40 1.00
64 Tyler Kennedy .30 .75
65 Marc-Andre Fleury .30 .75
66 Maxime Talbot .30 .75
67 Pascal Dupuis .20 .50
68 Kristopher Letang .30 .75
69 Brooks Orpik .20 .50
70 Shane Doan .25 .60
71 Matthew Lombardi .20 .50
72 Ed Jovanovski .20 .50
73 Peter Mueller .40 1.00
74 Scottie Upshall .20 .50
75 Martin Hanzal .25 .60
76 Mikkel Boedker .25 .60
77 Kyle Turris .40 1.00
78 Ilya Bryzgalov .25 .60
79 Viktor Tikhonov .30 .75
80 Jeff Carter .30 .75
81 Mike Richards .60 1.50
82 Simon Gagne .30 .75
83 Scott Hartnell .20 .50
84 Chris Pronger .25 .60
85 Claude Giroux .60 1.50
86 Daniel Briere .30 .75
87 Kimmo Timonen .25 .60
88 Braydon Coburn .20 .50
89 Daniel Carcillo .30 .75
90 Daniel Alfredsson .30 .75
91 Jason Spezza .40 1.00
92 Dany Heatley .60 1.50
93 Nick Foligno .30 .75
94 Brian Elliott .25 .60
95 Pascal Leclaire .30 .75
96 Jarkko Ruutu .20 .50
97 Filip Kuba .20 .50
98 Mike Fisher .20 .50
99 Alex Kovalev .30 .75
100 Marian Gaborik .50 1.25
101 Sean Avery .25 .60
102 Chris Drury .25 .60
103 Chris Higgins .20 .50
104 Brandon Dubinsky .25 .60
105 Ryan Callahan .20 .50
106 Michal Rozsival .20 .50
107 Henrik Lundqvist .60 1.50
108 Wade Redden .20 .50
109 Marc Staal .40 1.00
110 Mark Streit .20 .50
111 Kyle Okposo .30 .75
112 Doug Weight .20 .50
113 Frans Nielsen .20 .50
114 Trent Hunter .20 .50
115 Josh Bailey .25 .60
116 Rick DiPietro .30 .75
117 Blake Comeau .20 .50
118 Richard Park .20 .50
119 Martin Brodeur .75 2.00
120 Zach Parise .30 .75
121 Patrik Elias .25 .60
122 Jamie Langenbrunner .20 .50
123 Travis Zajac .20 .50
124 Dainius Zubrus .20 .50
125 David Clarkson .20 .50
126 Paul Martin .20 .50
127 Brian Rolston .20 .50
128 Colin White .20 .50
129 Pekka Rinne .25 .60
130 J.P. Dumont .20 .50
131 Jason Arnott .20 .50
132 Shea Weber .25 .60
133 Martin Erat .30 .75
134 Ryan Suter .20 .50
135 David Legwand .25 .60
136 Jordin Tootoo .30 .75
137 Dan Hamhuis .20 .50
138 Dan Ellis .20 .50
139 Andrei Markov .25 .60
140 Andrei Kostitsyn .25 .60
141 Carey Price .75 2.00
142 Tomas Plekanec .25 .60
143 Maxim Lapierre .20 .50
144 Guillaume Latendresse .25 .60
145 Scott Gomez .30 .75
146 Max Pacioretty .30 .75
147 Roman Hamrlik .20 .50
148 Brian Gionta .30 .75
149 Mikko Koivu .30 .75
150 Andrew Brunette .20 .50
151 Pierre-Marc Bouchard .25 .60
152 Niklas Backstrom .30 .75
153 Colton Gillies .40 1.00
154 Owen Nolan .30 .75
155 James Sheppard .30 .75
156 Marek Zidlicky .20 .50
157 Antti Miettinen .20 .50
158 Cal Clutterbuck .25 .60
159 Anze Kopitar .30 .75
160 Alexander Frolov .25 .60
161 Dustin Brown .25 .60
162 Jarret Stoll .25 .60
163 Drew Doughty .60 1.50
164 Jack Johnson .25 .60
165 Jonathan Quick .50 1.25
166 Erik Ersberg .25 .60
167 Justin Williams .20 .50
168 Ryan Smyth .30 .75
169 Tomas Vokoun .30 .75
170 Stephen Weiss .20 .50
171 David Booth .20 .50
172 Cory Stillman .20 .50
173 Nathan Horton .20 .50
174 Michael Frolik .25 .60
175 Bryan McCabe .25 .60
176 Keith Ballard .20 .50
177 Gregory Campbell .20 .50
178 Brett McLean .20 .50
179 Ales Hemsky .25 .60
180 Sheldon Souray .20 .50
181 Shawn Horcoff .20 .50
182 Tom Gilbert .20 .50
183 Patrick O'Sullivan .25 .60
184 Sam Gagner .40 1.00
185 Andrew Cogliano .40 1.00
186 Ethan Moreau .20 .50
187 Lubomir Visnovsky .20 .50
188 Nikolai Khabibulin .30 .75
189 Pavel Datsyuk .30 .75
190 Henrik Zetterberg .60 1.50
191 Nicklas Lidstrom .40 1.00
192 Brian Rafalski .20 .50
193 Valtteri Filppula .30 .75
194 Tomas Holmstrom .25 .60
195 Kris Draper .20 .50
196 Chris Osgood .40 1.00
197 Niklas Kronwall .25 .60
198 Johan Franzen .20 .50
199 Mike Ribeiro .20 .50
200 Loui Eriksson .20 .50
201 Brad Richards .25 .60
202 Mike Modano .30 .75
203 Steve Ott .20 .50
204 James Neal .30 .75
205 Matt Niskanen .20 .50
206 Krys Barch .20 .50
207 Brenden Morrow .25 .60
208 Marty Turco .25 .60
209 Steve Mason .50 1.25
210 Rick Nash .30 .75
211 Kristian Huselius .20 .50
212 R.J. Umberger .25 .60
213 Jakub Voracek .30 .75
214 Antoine Vermette .20 .50
215 Derick Brassard .30 .75
216 Mike Commodore .20 .50
217 Marc Methot .20 .50
218 Fedor Tyutin .20 .50
219 David Jones .20 .50
220 Milan Hejduk .30 .75
221 Wojtek Wolski .20 .50
222 Paul Stastny .30 .75
223 John-Michael Liles .25 .60
224 Chris Stewart .30 .75
225 T.J. Hensick .20 .50
226 Cody McLeod .20 .50
227 Peter Budaj .30 .75
228 Patrick Kane .60 1.50
229 Jonathan Toews .75 2.00
230 Kris Versteeg .40 1.00
231 Cristobal Huet .30 .75
232 Brian Campbell .25 .60
233 Patrick Sharp .25 .60
234 Duncan Keith .25 .60
235 Dustin Byfuglien .25 .60
236 Marian Hossa .50 1.25
237 Cam Barker .20 .50
238 Ray Whitney .20 .50
239 Eric Staal .40 1.00
240 Tuomo Ruutu .20 .50
241 Rod Brind'Amour .25 .60
242 Sergei Samsonov .20 .50
243 Jussi Jokinen .30 .75
244 Cam Ward .30 .75
245 Joe Corvo .20 .50
246 Brandon Sutter .30 .75
247 Anton Babchuk .25 .60
248 Jarome Iginla .60 1.50
249 Olli Jokinen .20 .50
250 Daymond Langkow .20 .50
251 Miikka Kiprusoff .30 .75
252 Craig Conroy .20 .50
253 Dion Phaneuf .50 1.25
254 Rene Bourque .20 .50
255 Dustin Boyd .20 .50
256 Jay Bouwmeester .30 .75
257 Cory Sarich .20 .50
258 Derek Roy .30 .75
259 Jason Pominville .30 .75
260 Thomas Vanek .30 .75
261 Tim Connolly .20 .50
262 Ryan Miller .30 .75
263 Drew Stafford .30 .75
264 Clarke MacArthur .20 .50
265 Daniel Paille .25 .60
266 Paul Gaustad .25 .60
267 Jochen Hecht .20 .50
268 Marc Savard .20 .50
269 Tim Thomas .30 .75
270 David Krejci .25 .60
271 Phil Kessel .30 .75
272 Michael Ryder .25 .60
273 Zdeno Chara .20 .50
274 Blake Wheeler .40 1.00
275 Patrice Bergeron .30 .75
276 Milan Lucic .30 .75
277 Dennis Wideman .20 .50
278 Ilya Kovalchuk .40 1.00
279 Slava Kozlov .20 .50
280 Todd White .20 .50
281 Bryan Little .30 .75
282 Rich Peverley .25 .60
283 Colby Armstrong .20 .50
284 Kari Lehtonen .30 .75
285 Zach Bogosian .40 1.00
286 Nik Antropov .25 .60
287 Tobias Enstrom .30 .75
288 Ryan Getzlaf .50 1.25
289 Corey Perry .30 .75
290 Bobby Ryan .40 1.00
291 Teemu Selanne .30 .75
292 Saku Koivu .30 .75
293 George Parros .20 .50
294 Jonas Hiller .40 1.00
295 Jean-Sebastien Giguere .30 .75
296 Andrew Ebbett .25 .60
297 Scott Niedermayer .20 .50
298 Alexander Ovechkin CL 1.25 3.00
299 Carey Price CL .75 2.00
300 Sidney Crosby CL 1.50 4.00
301 Brian Salcido RC 1.00 2.50
302 Luca Caputi RC 1.50 4.00
303 Spencer Machacek RC 1.00 2.50
304 Matt Beleskey RC 1.25 3.00
305 T.J. Galiardi RC 1.50 4.00
306 Michael Sauer RC 1.00 2.50
307 Yannick Weber RC 1.50 4.00
308 Jesse Joensuu RC 1.50 4.00
309 Cal O'Reilly RC 1.25 3.00
310 Grant Lewis RC 1.00 2.50
311 Tim Stapleton RC 1.25 3.00
312 Christian Hanson RC 1.50 4.00
313 Mikael Backlund RC 2.00 5.00
314 Artem Anisimov RC 1.50 4.00
315 Jhonas Enroth RC 1.50 4.00
316 Ivan Vishnevskiy RC 1.50 4.00
317 Riku Helenius RC 1.25 3.00
318 Kris Chucko RC 1.00 2.50
319 Matt Pelech RC 1.25 3.00
320 Michal Neuvirth RC 3.00 8.00
321 Ray Macias RC 1.25 3.00
322 Ville Leino RC 1.50 4.00
323 Taylor Chorney RC 1.25 3.00
324 John Negrin RC 1.00 2.50
325 Alexander Sulzer RC .75 2.00
326 Mike Santorelli RC .75 2.00
327 Tom Wandell RC 4.00 10.00
328 Andrew MacDonald RC 1.00 2.50
329 Kevin Quick RC .75 2.00
330 David Van Der Gulik RC 1.00 2.50
331 Jakub Petruzalek RC 1.25 3.00
332 Chris Durno RC 1.00 2.50
333 Peter Regin RC 1.50 4.00
334 Kurtis McLean RC 1.00 2.50
335 John Scott RC 1.25 3.00
336 Bryan Rodney RC 1.00 2.50
337 Riley Armstrong RC 1.00 2.50
338 Ryan Vesce RC 1.00 2.50
339 Brandon Segal RC 1.00 2.50
340 Antti Niemi RC 4.00 10.00
341 Derek Peltier RC .75 2.00
342 Matt Hendricks RC 1.00 2.50
343 Mike McKenna RC 1.00 2.50
344 Aaron MacKenzie RC 1.50 4.00
345 David Sloane RC 1.50 4.00
346 Jamie Fritsch RC 1.25 3.00
347 Geoff Kinrade RC 1.25 3.00
348 Tyson Strachan RC .75 2.00
349 Troy Bodie RC 1.00 2.50
350 Kevin Westgarth RC 1.00 2.50
351 Byron Bitz RC 1.00 2.50
352 Tim Wallace RC .75 2.00
353 Ben Lovejoy RC 2.00 5.00
354 Jaime Sifers RC 1.00 2.50
355 Sean Collins RC 1.00 2.50
356 Davis Drewiske RC 1.25 3.00
357 David Schlemko RC 1.00 2.50
358 Jay Beagle RC 1.25 3.00
359 Phil Oreskovic RC 1.25 3.00
360 Joel Rechlicz RC 1.25 3.00
361 Michael Vernace RC 1.00 2.50
362 Scott Lehman RC .75 2.00
363 Dan Turple RC 1.50 4.00
364 Matt Climie RC 1.00 2.50
365 Jamie Fraser RC 1.00 2.50
366 Per Ledin RC 1.25 3.00
367 Wes O'Neill RC 1.25 3.00
368 Sean Bentivoglio RC 1.00 2.50
369 Evander Kane RC 3.00 8.00
370 Tyler Myers RC 5.00 12.00
371 Matt Duchene RC 5.00 12.00
372 Ryan O'Reilly RC 2.50 6.00
373 Jamie Benn RC 2.00 5.00
374 Dmitri Kulikov RC 1.25 3.00
375 Alec Martinez RC .75 2.00
376 Teemu Laakso RC .75 2.00
377 John Tavares RC 20.00 50.00
378 Matt Gilroy RC 1.50 4.00
379 Michael Del Zotto RC 2.50 6.00
380 Erik Karlsson RC 4.00 10.00
381 James Van Riemsdyk RC 3.00 8.00
382 Johan Backlund RC 1.25 3.00
383 Mika Pyorala RC 1.25 3.00
384 Jason Demers RC 1.00 2.50
385 Benn Ferriero RC 1.25 3.00
386 Frazer McLaren RC .75 2.00
387 Victor Hedman RC 2.50 6.00
388 Viktor Stalberg RC 2.00 5.00
389 Jay Rosehill RC .75 2.00
390 Jonas Gustavsson RC 10.00 25.00
391 Sergei Shirokov RC 2.00 5.00
392 Ilkka Pikkarainen RC 1.25 3.00
393 Colin Wilson RC 2.00 5.00
394 Tyler Bozak RC 3.00 8.00

2009-10 Upper Deck MVP Gold Script

*SINGLES: 2.5X TO 6X BASIC CARDS
*ROOKIES: 1.2X TO 3X BASIC CARDS
STATED PRINT RUN 100 SER.#'d SETS
377 John Tavares 30.00 80.00
390 Jonas Gustavsson 15.00 40.00

2009-10 Upper Deck MVP Super Script

*SINGLES: 5X TO 12X BASIC CARDS
*ROOKIES: 2.5X TO 6X BASIC CARDS
STATED PRINT RUN 25 SER.#'d SETS
377 John Tavares 100.00 200.00
390 Jonas Gustavsson 40.00 100.00

2009-10 Upper Deck MVP Hart Candidates

COMPLETE SET (30) 12.00 30.00
STATED ODDS 1:4
HC1 Tim Thomas .75 2.00
HC2 Nicklas Backstrom 1.50 4.00
HC3 Zach Parise .75 2.00
HC4 Evgeni Malkin 2.00 5.00
HC5 Jeff Carter .75 2.00
HC6 Eric Staal 1.00 2.50

HC7 Henrik Lundqvist 1.50 4.00
HC8 Carey Price 2.00 5.00
HC9 Tomas Vokoun .75 2.00
HC10 Thomas Vanek .75 2.00
HC11 Jason Spezza 1.00 2.50
HC12 Luke Schenn 1.25 3.00
HC13 Ilya Kovalchuk 1.00 2.50
HC14 Steven Stamkos 2.00 5.00
HC15 Rick DiPietro .75 2.00
HC16 Evgeni Nabokov .75 2.00
HC17 Henrik Zetterberg 1.50 4.00
HC18 Roberto Luongo 2.00 5.00
HC19 Jonathan Toews 2.00 5.00
HC20 Jarome Iginla 1.50 4.00
HC21 David Perron .60 1.50
HC22 Rick Nash .75 2.00
HC23 Ryan Getzlaf 1.25 3.00
HC24 Niklas Backstrom .75 2.00
HC25 Pekka Rinne .60 1.50
HC26 Sam Gagner 1.00 2.50
HC27 Mike Ribeiro .50 1.25
HC28 Peter Mueller 1.00 2.50
HC29 Anze Kopitar .75 2.00
HC30 Paul Stastny .75 2.00

2009-10 Upper Deck MVP Hart Winners

COMPLETE SET (10) 20.00 50.00
STATED ODDS 1:4
HW1 Alexander Ovechkin 4.00 10.00
HW2 Sidney Crosby 5.00 12.00
HW3 Joe Thornton 2.00 5.00
HW4 Martin St. Louis 1.00 2.50
HW5 Mark Messier 2.00 5.00
HW6 Bobby Hull 2.50 6.00
HW7 Gordie Howe 4.00 10.00
HW8 Mario Lemieux 2.50 6.00
HW9 Bobby Orr 4.00 10.00
HW10 Wayne Gretzky 5.00 12.00

2009-10 Upper Deck MVP One on One Autographs

STATED ODDS 1:240
AAB Zach Bogosian/Karl Alzner 12.00 30.00
ABB Fabian Brunnstrom/Mikkel Boedker 10.00 25.00
ACR Daniel Cleary/Michael Ryder 10.00 25.00
AES Andrew Ebbett/Wayne Simmonds 10.00 25.00
AFD Drew Doughty/Mark Fistric 20.00 50.00
AFS Michael Frolik/Steven Stamkos 25.00 60.00
AGR Scott Gomez/Michael Ryder 10.00 25.00
AGS Colton Gillies/Chris Stewart 12.00 30.00
AHB Patric Hornqvist/Patrik Berglund 20.00 50.00
AKG Chris Kunitz/Claude Giroux 20.00 50.00
APA Ales Hemsky/Paul Stastny 10.00 25.00
APW Blake Wheeler/Jason Pominville 12.00 30.00
ARG Wade Redden/Mike Green 20.00 50.00
ARS Devin Setoguchi/Bobby Ryan 12.00 30.00
ASO Alexander Ovechkin/Eric Staal 40.00 100.00
AVM Tomas Vokoun/Steve Mason 15.00 40.00

2009-10 Upper Deck MVP Two on Two Jerseys

STATED ODDS 1:24
JBDLP Henrik Lundqvist 15.00 40.00
Chris Drury
Zach Parise
Martin Brodeur
JBFCP Zach Parise 25.00 60.00
Martin Brodeur
Sidney Crosby
Marc-Andre Fleury
JBOCR Steve Bernier 8.00 20.00
Mason Raymond
Patrick O'Sullivan
Andrew Cogliano
JBSOF Tomas Fleischmann 25.00 60.00
Alexander Ovechkin
Eric Staal
Rod Brind'Amour
JCOMB Evgeni Malkin 30.00 80.00
Sidney Crosby
Alexander Ovechkin
Nicklas Backstrom
JCTHS Luke Schenn 10.00 25.00
Vesa Toskala
Brian Campbell
Cristobal Huet
JKLHV Nathan Horton 6.00 15.00
Tomas Vokoun
Ilya Kovalchuk
Kari Lehtonen
JLDHS Patrick Sharp 15.00 40.00
Cristobal Huet
Roberto Luongo
Pavol Demitra
JMCFB Dustin Brown 6.00 15.00
Alexander Frolov
Jonathan Cheechoo
Patrick Marleau
JMDTS Devin Setoguchi 12.00 30.00
Joe Thornton
Shane Doan
Peter Mueller
JMFBS Michael Frolik 15.00 40.00
David Booth
Steven Stamkos
Ryan Malone
JRRDM Brad Richards 8.00 20.00
Mike Ribeiro
Shane Doan
Peter Mueller
JRTCS Matt Carle 8.00 20.00
Kimmo Timonen
Marc Staal
Wade Redden
JSBHJ Cory Stillman 6.00 15.00
Nathan Horton
Jussi Jokinen
Rod Brind'Amour
JTJLS Milan Jurcina 8.00 20.00
Jose Theodore
Henrik Lundqvist
Marc Staal
JTWCG Wojtek Wolski 8.00 20.00
Darcy Tucker
Sam Gagner
Andrew Cogliano

2009-10 Upper Deck MVP Winter Classic

WC1 Jeff Carter 1.00 2.50
WC2 Daniel Briere 1.00 2.50
WC3 Chris Pronger .75 2.00
WC4 Ray Emery .75 2.00
WC5 Mike Richards 2.00 5.00
WC6 Simon Gagne 1.00 2.50
WC7 Claude Giroux 2.00 5.00
WC8 Daniel Carcillo 1.00 2.50
WC9 Scott Hartnell .60 1.50
WC10 Michael Ryder .75 2.00
WC11 Tim Thomas 1.00 2.50
WC12 Blake Wheeler 1.25 3.00
WC13 Zdeno Chara .60 1.50
WC14 Milan Lucic 1.00 2.50
WC15 Marc Savard .60 1.50
WC16 David Krejci .75 2.00
WC17 Mark Recchi .75 2.00
WC18 Patrice Bergeron 1.00 2.50
WC19 City of Boston .60 1.50
WC20 Wrigley Field .60 1.50

1999-00 Upper Deck MVP SC Edition

Released late in the 1999-00 hockey season, the 1999-00 Upper Deck MVP Stanley Cup Edition set features 193 regular cards, 25 CHL Prospects cards, and 2 Checklists to comprise the 220-card set. MVP Stanley Cup Edition was packaged in boxes containing 28-packs with 10-cards per pack, and carried a suggested retail price of $1.59.

COMPLETE SET (220) 20.00 40.00
1 Teemu Selanne .10 .30
2 Paul Kariya .10 .30
3 Guy Hebert .08 .25
4 Oleg Tverdovsky .05 .15
5 Tony Hrkac .05 .15
6 Mike Leclerc .05 .15
7 Ladislav Kohn .05 .15
8 Ray Ferraro .05 .15
9 Ed Ward .05 .15
10 Norm Maracle .08 .25
11 Dean Sylvester RC .08 .25
12 Yannick Tremblay .05 .15
13 Patrik Stefan RC .40 1.00
14 Johan Garpenlov .05 .15
15 Per-Johan Axelsson .05 .15
16 Joe Thornton .20 .50
17 Sergei Samsonov .08 .25
18 Jay Henderson RC .05 .15
19 Byron Dafoe .08 .25
20 Steve Heinze .05 .15
21 Marty McSorley .05 .15
22 Dominik Hasek .25 .60
23 Miroslav Satan .08 .25
24 Curtis Brown .05 .15
25 Martin Biron .08 .25
26 Jason Woolley .05 .15
27 Michael Peca .08 .25
28 Wayne Primeau .05 .15
29 Valeri Bure .05 .15
30 Derek Morris .08 .25
31 Cory Stillman .05 .15
32 Fred Brathwaite .08 .25
33 Jarome Iginla .15 .40
34 Andre Nazarov .05 .15
35 Jeff Shantz .05 .15
36 Ron Francis .05 .15
37 Jeff O'Neill .05 .15
38 Arturs Irbe .08 .25
39 Sami Kapanen .05 .15
40 Sean Hill .05 .15
41 Byron Ritchie RC .08 .25
42 Tommy Westlund RC .05 .15
43 Tony Amonte .08 .25
44 Doug Gilmour .08 .25
45 Blair Atcheynum .05 .15
46 Alexei Zhamnov .05 .15
47 Dean Mcammond .05 .15
48 Michael Nylander .05 .15
49 Aaron Miller .05 .15
50 Milan Hejduk .10 .30
51 Patrick Roy .60 1.50
52 Joe Sakic .30 .75
53 Chris Drury .08 .25
54 Peter Forsberg .30 .75
55 Ray Bourque .20 .50
56 Marc Denis .08 .25
57 Brett Hull .15 .40
58 Mike Modano .20 .50
59 Ed Belfour .10 .30
60 Kirk Muller .05 .15
61 Brenden Morrow .10 .30
62 Mike Keane .05 .15
63 Brad Lukowich RC .05 .15
64 Sergei Fedorov .20 .50
65 Steve Yzerman .60 1.50
66 Chris Osgood .08 .25
67 Brendan Shanahan .10 .30
68 Martin Lapointe .08 .25
69 Pat Verbeek .05 .15
70 Stacy Roest .05 .15
71 Tommy Salo .08 .25
72 Doug Weight .08 .25
73 Alexander Selivanov .05 .15
74 Ryan Smyth .05 .15
75 Boyd Devereaux .05 .15
76 Ethan Moreau .05 .15
77 Pavel Bure .10 .30
78 Viktor Kozlov .05 .15
79 Mike Vernon .08 .25
80 Ivan Novoseltsev RC .25 .60
81 Ray Whitney .08 .25
82 Filip Kuba RC .05 .15
83 Ray Sheppard .05 .15
84 Zigmund Palffy .08 .25
85 Luc Robitaille .08 .25
86 Bryan Smolinski .08 .25
87 Rob Blake .08 .25
88 Jere Karalahti RC .05 .15
89 Marko Tuomainen .05 .15
90 Garry Galley .05 .15
91 Saku Koivu .10 .30
92 Dainius Zubrus .05 .15
93 Jose Theodore .15 .40
94 Karl Dykhuis .05 .15
95 Sergei Zholtok .05 .15
96 Francis Bouillon RC .05 .15
97 David Legwand .08 .25
98 Mike Dunham .08 .25
99 Robert Valicevic RC .05 .15
100 Cliff Ronning .08 .25
101 Drake Berehowsky .05 .15
102 Greg Johnson .05 .15
103 Patric Kjellberg .05 .15
104 Martin Brodeur .30 .75
105 Scott Stevens .08 .25
106 Claude Lemieux .05 .15
107 Scott Gomez .05 .15
108 Partik Elias .08 .25
109 Randy McKay .05 .15
110 Sergei Brylin .05 .15
111 Tim Connolly .05 .15
112 Roberto Luongo .15 .40
113 Dave Scatchard .05 .15
114 Kenny Jonsson .05 .15
115 Vladimir Orszagh RC .05 .15
116 Ted Drury .05 .15
117 Theo Fleury .05 .15
118 Mike Richter .10 .30
119 Mike York .05 .15
120 Brian Leetch .10 .30
121 Petr Nedved .05 .15
122 Radek Dvorak .05 .15
123 Jan Hlavac .05 .15
124 Marian Hossa .10 .30
125 Radek Bonk .05 .15
126 Daniel Alfredsson .08 .25
127 Ron Tugnutt .08 .25
128 Rob Zamuner .05 .15
129 Jason York .05 .15
130 Shaun Van Allen .05 .15
131 Eric Lindros .10 .30
132 John LeClair .10 .30
133 Simon Gagne .10 .30
134 Mark Recchi .08 .25
135 Keith Primeau .05 .15
136 Daymond Langkow .08 .25
137 Brian Boucher .10 .30
138 Luke Richardson .05 .15
139 Keith Tkachuk .10 .30
140 Jeremy Roenick .15 .40
141 Travis Green .05 .15
142 Dallas Drake .05 .15
143 Jyrki Lumme .05 .15
144 Shane Doan .05 .15
145 Sean Burke .08 .25
146 Jaromir Jagr .20 .50
147 Alexei Kovalev .05 .15
148 Tom Barrasso .08 .25
149 Martin Sonnenberg RC .05 .15
150 Robert Lang .05 .15
151 Robert Dome .05 .15
152 Darius Kasparaitis .05 .15
153 Owen Nolan .08 .25
154 Jeff Friesen .05 .15
155 Steve Shields .08 .25
156 Vincent Damphousse .05 .15
157 Mike Rathje .05 .15
158 Alexander Korolyuk .05 .15
159 Todd Harvey .08 .25
160 Pavol Demitra .08 .25
161 Pierre Turgeon .08 .25
162 Roman Turek .08 .25
163 Chris Pronger .08 .25
164 Jochen Hecht RC .50 1.25
165 Todd Reirden RC .05 .15
166 Scott Young .05 .15
167 Vincent Lecavalier .10 .30
168 Dan Cloutier .08 .25
169 Chris Gratton .05 .15
170 Todd Warriner .05 .15
171 Mike Sillinger .05 .15
172 Petr Svoboda .05 .15
173 Mats Sundin .10 .30
174 Curtis Joseph .10 .30
175 Jonas Hoglund .05 .15
176 Sergei Berezin .05 .15
177 Nathan Dempsey RC .05 .15
178 Nikolai Antropov RC .50 1.25
179 Alyn McCauley .05 .15
180 Alexander Karpovtsev .05 .15
181 Steve Kariya RC .30 .75
182 Mark Messier .10 .30
183 Markus Naslund .10 .30
184 Adrian Aucoin .05 .15
185 Andrew Cassels .05 .15
186 Artem Chubarov .05 .15
187 Brad May .08 .25
188 Peter Bondra .10 .30
189 Olaf Kolzig .08 .25
190 Dmitri Mironov .05 .15
191 Jeff Halpern RC .30 .75
192 Andrei Nikolishin .05 .15
193 Terry Yake .08 .25
194 Pavel Brendl RC .50 1.25
195 Sheldon Keefe RC .40 1.00
196 Branislav Mezei RC .08 .25
197 Milan Kraft RC .50 1.25
198 Ryan Jardine RC .30 .75
199 Kristian Kudroc RC .05 .15
200 Alexander Buturlin RC .15 .40
201 Jaroslav Kristek RC .10 .30
202 Andrei Shefer RC .10 .30
203 Brad Moran RC .15 .40
204 Brett Lysak RC .08 .25
205 Michal Sivek RC .15 .40
206 Luke Sellars RC .08 .25
207 Brad Ralph RC .08 .25
208 Bryan Kazarian RC .08 .25
209 Barret Jackman .08 .25
210 Brian Finley .08 .25
211 Jamie Lundmark .08 .25
212 Denis Shvidki .08 .25
213 Taylor Pyatt .08 .25
214 Kris Beech .05 .15
215 Michael Zigomanis .08 .25
216 Justin Papineau .08 .25
217 Daniel Sedin .05 .15
218 Henrik Sedin .05 .15
219 Checklist .05 .15
220 Checklist .05 .15

1999-00 Upper Deck MVP SC Edition Gold Script

Randomly seeded in packs, this 220-card set parallels the base set and is enhanced with gold foil instead of bronze, and on the regular cards, a gold-foil signature. Cards are serial numbered out of 100.

*GOLD SCRIPT: 30X TO 80X BASIC CARDS

1999-00 Upper Deck MVP SC Edition Silver Script

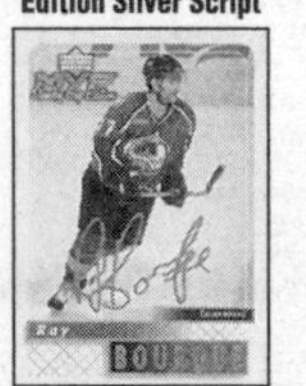

Randomly seeded in packs at 1:2, this 220-card set parallels the base set and is enhanced with silver foil instead of bronze, and on the regular cards, a silver-foil signature.

*SILVER SCRIPT: 1.2X TO 3X BASIC CARDS

1999-00 Upper Deck MVP SC Edition Super Script

Randomly inserted in packs, this 220-card set parallels the base set and features a printed signature on the front of the regular cards. Each card is serial numbered out of 25.

*SUPER SCRIPT: 50X TO 120X BASIC CARDS

1999-00 Upper Deck MVP SC Edition Clutch Performers

Randomly inserted in packs at 1:28, this 10-card set showcases some of the NHL's key clutch players.

COMPLETE SET (10) 15.00 30.00
CP1 Paul Kariya 1.00 2.50
CP2 Ray Bourque 1.50 4.00
CP3 Joe Sakic 2.00 5.00
CP4 Steve Yzerman 5.00 12.00
CP5 Luc Robitaille .75 2.00
CP6 Martin Brodeur 2.50 6.00
CP7 Theo Fleury .75 2.00
CP8 John LeClair 1.25 3.00
CP9 Jaromir Jagr 1.50 4.00
CP10 Curtis Joseph 1.00 2.50

1999-00 Upper Deck MVP SC Edition Cup Contenders

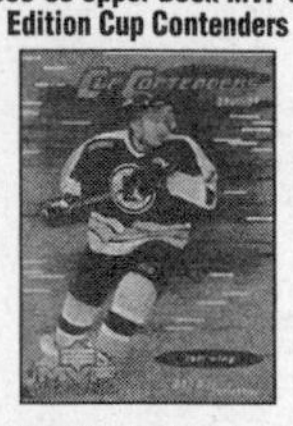

Randomly inserted in packs at 1:9, this 10-card set features emerging NHL superstars.

COMPLETE SET (10) 5.00 10.00
CC1 Patrik Stefan .75 2.00
CC2 Sergei Samsonov .60 1.50
CC3 Milan Hejduk .75 2.00
CC4 Chris Drury .60 1.50
CC5 David Legwand .40 1.00
CC6 Scott Gomez .50 1.25
CC7 Marian Hossa .60 1.50
CC8 Jeff Friesen .50 1.25
CC9 Vincent Lecavalier .50 1.25
CC10 Steve Kariya .50 1.25

1999-00 Upper Deck MVP SC Edition Game-Used Souvenirs

Randomly inserted in packs at the rate of 1:130, this 18-card set features players with swatches of game-used sticks. Super Game Used Souvenirs came inserted into Canadian packs at the rate of 1:130, and feature two swatches of material instead of one.

GUBH Brett Hull 6.00 15.00
GUBJ Barret Jackman 3.00 8.00
GUCJ Curtis Joseph 5.00 12.00
GUDS Denis Shvidki 3.00 8.00
GUEL Eric Lindros 6.00 15.00
GUJC John LeClair 5.00 12.00
GUJS Joe Sakic 10.00 25.00
GUKB Kris Beech 3.00 8.00
GUMK Milan Kraft 3.00 8.00
GUMO Maxime Ouellet 3.00 8.00
GUPB Pavel Brendl 3.00 8.00
GUPF Peter Forsberg 10.00 25.00
GUPV Pavel Bure 6.00 15.00
GURB Ray Bourque 10.00 25.00
GUSK Scott Kelman 3.00 8.00
GUSY Steve Yzerman 12.50 30.00
GUTP Taylor Pyatt 3.00 8.00
GUTS Teemu Selanne 5.00 12.00
SGDS Denis Shvidki Super 4.00 10.00
SGKB Kris Beech Super 4.00 10.00
SGMK Milan Kraft Super 4.00 10.00
SGPB Pavel Brendl Super 4.00 10.00

1999-00 Upper Deck MVP SC Edition Golden Memories

Randomly inserted in packs at 1:14, this 10-card set spotlights outstanding moments in NHL post-season play.

COMPLETE SET (10) 12.00 25.00
GM1 Paul Kariya .50 1.25
GM2 Patrick Roy 2.50 6.00
GM3 Peter Forsberg 1.25 3.00
GM4 Mike Modano .75 2.00
GM5 Steve Yzerman 2.50 6.00
GM6 Martin Brodeur 1.25 3.00
GM7 Theo Fleury .50 1.25
GM8 Eric Lindros .75 2.00
GM9 Jaromir Jagr .75 2.00
GM10 Curtis Joseph .50 1.25

1999-00 Upper Deck MVP SC Edition Great Combinations

Randomly inserted in packs at the rate of 1:196, this 16-card set showcases some of the NHL's most dominating teammates. Parallels numbered to just 25 were also randomly inserted in packs.

*GOLD/25: 1.2X TO 3X SILVER
GCBK Pavel Bure 10.00 25.00
Viktor Kozlov
GCGL Wayne Gretzky 25.00 60.00
Brian Leetch
GCGR Wayne Gretzky 20.00 50.00
Mike Richter
GCHM B.Hull/M.Modano 12.50 30.00
GCHP Dominik Hasek 8.00 20.00
Michael Peca
GCJS Jaromir Jage 10.00 25.00
Martin Straka
GCKS Paul Kariya 10.00 25.00
Teemu Selanne
GCLL Eric Lindros 10.00 25.00
John LeClair
GCLS Vincent Lecavalier 8.00 20.00
Petr Svoboda
GCRF Patrick Roy 25.00 60.00
Peter Forsberg
GCSF Brendan Shanahan 10.00 25.00
Sergei Fedorov
GCSJ Mats Sundin 8.00 20.00
Curtis Joseph
GCSR Patrik Stefan 8.00 20.00
Damian Rhodes
GCTR Keith Tkachuk 8.00 20.00
Jeremy Roenick
GCTS Joe Thornton 12.50 30.00
Sergei Samsonov
GCYO Steve Yzerman 15.00 40.00
Chris Osgood

1999-00 Upper Deck MVP SC Edition Playoff Heroes

Randomly seeded in packs at the rate of 1:72, this 10-card set pays tribute to the rare superstars who have performed exceptionally in the post season.

COMPLETE SET (10) 40.00 80.00
PH1 Paul Kariya 3.00 8.00
PH2 Dominik Hasek 5.00 12.00
PH3 Patrick Roy 12.50 30.00
PH4 Mike Modano 4.00 10.00
PH5 Sergei Fedorov 5.00 12.00
PH6 Pavel Bure 3.00 8.00
PH7 Martin Brodeur 6.00 15.00
PH8 Eric Lindros 4.00 10.00
PH9 Jaromir Jagr 4.00 10.00
PH10 Mark Messier 3.00 8.00

1999-00 Upper Deck MVP SC Edition ProSign

Randomly inserted in reatil packs at the rate of 1:144, this 24-card set featured an authentic autograph.

AM Al MacInnis 6.00 15.00
AT Alex Tanguay 6.00 15.00
BF Brian Finley 4.00 10.00
BH Brett Hull 15.00 40.00
BJ Barret Jackman 6.00 15.00
BL Brian Leetch 6.00 15.00
CJ Curtis Joseph 20.00 50.00
DA Dave Andreychuk 4.00 10.00
DL David Legwand 4.00 10.00
DS Denis Shvidki 2.00 5.00
JH Jochen Hecht 4.00 10.00
JS Jozef Stumpel 2.00 5.00
KB Kris Beech 2.00 5.00
MB Martin Biron 4.00 10.00
MK Milan Kraft 2.00 5.00
MO Maxime Ouellet 4.00 10.00
PB Pavel Bure 6.00 15.00
PS Patrik Stefan 2.00 5.00
SG Simon Gagne 6.00 15.00
SK Scott Kelman 2.00 5.00
SS Sergei Samsonov 6.00 15.00
SY Steve Yzerman 100.00 175.00
TP Taylor Pyatt 6.00 15.00
PBR Pavel Brendl 4.00 10.00

1999-00 Upper Deck MVP SC Edition Second Season Snipers

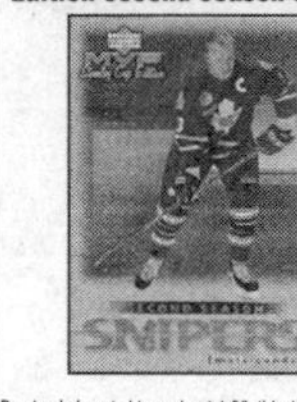

Randomly inserted in packs at 1:28, this 12-card set spotlights players that have a knack for scoring clutch goals.

COMPLETE SET (12) 12.00 25.00
SS1 Teemu Selanne 1.00 2.50
SS2 Joe Thornton 1.00 2.50
SS3 Peter Forsberg 2.50 6.00
SS4 Brendan Shanahan 1.00 2.50
SS5 Pavel Bure 1.00 2.50
SS6 Claude Lemieux .75 2.00
SS7 Eric Lindros 1.00 2.50
SS8 John LeClair 1.00 2.50
SS9 Keith Tkachuk 1.00 2.50
SS10 Jaromir Jagr 1.50 4.00
SS11 Mats Sundin 1.00 2.50
SS12 Mark Messier 1.00 2.50

1999-00 Upper Deck MVP SC Edition Stanley Cup Talent

Inserted at a rate of 1:5 packs, this 20-card set features elite players of top teams in full color action photos on the card fronts, and a breakdown of individual stats on card backs.

COMPLETE SET (20) 8.00 15.00
SC1 Paul Kariya .30 .75
SC2 Teemu Selanne .30 .75
SC3 Ray Bourque .50 1.25
SC4 Joe Sakic .60 1.50
SC5 Patrick Roy 1.50 4.00
SC6 Brett Hull .40 1.00
SC7 Sergei Fedorov .50 1.25
SC8 Pavel Bure .30 .75
SC9 Zigmund Palffy .25 .60
SC10 Martin Brodeur .75 2.00
SC11 Theo Fleury .20 .50
SC12 Eric Lindros .30 .75
SC13 John LeClair .30 .75
SC14 Jaromir Jagr .50 1.25
SC15 Jeremy Roenick .40 1.00
SC16 Keith Tkachuk .30 .75
SC17 Steve Shields .20 .50
SC18 Mats Sundin .30 .75
SC19 Mark Messier .30 .75
SC20 Peter Bondra .20 .50

2002 Upper Deck National Convention *

COMPLETE SET (3) 40.00
N8 Wayne Gretzky 20.00
N9 Bobby Orr 20.00
N10 Gordie Howe 10.00

2008-09 Upper Deck National Hockey Card Day

COMPLETE SET (15) 8.00 20.00
HCD1 Steven Stamkos 5.00 12.00
HCD2 Kyle Turris 1.25 3.00
HCD3 Josh Bailey 1.00 2.50
HCD4 Colton Gillies .60 1.50
HCD5 Derick Brassard 1.25 3.00
HCD6 Sidney Crosby 3.00 8.00
HCD7 Vincent Lecavalier .60 1.50
HCD8 Jarome Iginla 1.25 3.00
HCD9 Joe Sakic 1.00 2.50
HCD10 Martin Brodeur 1.25 3.00
HCD11 Wayne Gretzky 3.00 8.00
HCD12 Mario Lemieux 1.50 4.00
HCD13 Gordie Howe 2.50 6.00
HCD14 Bobby Orr 2.00 5.00
HCD15 Don Cherry 1.50 4.00

2009-10 Upper Deck National Hockey Card Day

COMPLETE SET (15) 10.00 25.00
HCD1 John Tavares 2.00 5.00
HCD2 Matt Duchene 1.50 4.00
HCD3 Jamie Benn .60 1.50
HCD4 Evander Kane 1.00 2.50
HCD5 Logan Couture .75 2.00
HCD6 Sidney Crosby 2.00 5.00
HCD7 Vincent Lecavalier .50 1.25
HCD8 Martin Brodeur 1.00 2.50
HCD9 Mike Richards .75 2.00
HCD10 Rick Nash .40 1.00
HCD11 Jarome Iginla .75 2.00
HCD12 Jonathan Toews 1.00 2.50
HCD13 Roberto Luongo 1.00 2.50
HCD14 Wayne Gretzky 2.00 5.00
HCD15 Steve Yzerman 1.25 3.00

1994 Upper Deck NHLPA/Be A Player

This special 45-card set features the NHL's top players in unique settings. Upper Deck sent three top photographers, including Walter Iooss, to capture on film players in off-ice situations. The first 18 cards bear Iooss' photos (Walter Iooss Collection) and are arranged alphabetically. Cards 19-40 are also arranged alphabetically and carry photos of the other photographers. The final five cards feature Doug Gilmour: A Canadian Hero (41-45).

COMPLETE SET (45) 12.00 30.00
1 Tony Amonte .20 .50
2 Chris Chelios .30 .75
3 Alexandre Daigle .08 .25
4 Dave Ellett .08 .25
5 Sergei Fedorov .60 1.50
6 Chris Gratton .08 .25
7 Wayne Gretzky 2.00 5.00
8 Brett Hull .40 1.00
9 Brian Leetch .30 .75
10 Rob Niedermayer .20 .50
11 Felix Potvin .30 .75
12 Luc Robitaille .20 .50
13 Jeremy Roenick .30 .75
14 Joe Sakic .60 1.50
15 Teemu Selanne .60 1.50
16 Brendan Shanahan .40 1.00
17 Alexei Yashin .20 .50
18 Steve Yzerman 1.50 4.00
Detroit R
19 Jason Arnott .20 .50
20 Pavel Bure .60 1.50
21 Theo Fleury .30 .75
22 Mike Gartner .20 .50
23 Kevin Haller .08 .25
24 Derian Hatcher .08 .25
25 Mark Howe .30 .75
Gordie Howe
26 Al Iafrate .08 .25
27 Joe Juneau .20 .50
28 Pat LaFontaine .20 .50
29 Eric Lindros .60 1.50
30 Dave Manson .08 .25
31 Mike Modano .40 1.00
32 Scott Niedermayer .20 .50
33 Owen Nolan .20 .50
34 Joel Otto .08 .25
35 Chris Pronger .20 .50
36 Scott Stevens .20 .50

37 Pierre Turgeon	.20	.50
38 Pat Verbeek	.08	.25
39 Doug Weight	.20	.50
40 Terry Yake	.08	.25
41 Doug Gilmour (Two-Year Old Doug With A Hockey Stick)	.30	.75
42 Doug Gilmour (Nine-Year Old Doug On The Ice)	.30	.75
43 Doug Gilmour (Standing Next To A Little Girl)	.30	.75
44 Doug Gilmour (Sitting On Motorcycle)	.30	.75
45 Doug Gilmour (With Fishing Rod)	.30	.75

2000-01 Upper Deck NHLPA

These cards were produced by UD at the behest of the Players' Association to ensure that every member of the PA earned a card in the 2000-01 season. Approximately 100 copies of each card were produced, with all copies going to the individual player for them to do with as they wish. Therefore, there were no sets available and likely none exist outside of the NHLPA repository. The cards share the same design as the base 2000-01 UD set. Because we have seen so few singles trade hands, the cards are checklisted but not priced. Thanks to collector Aaron Brownley for providing the checklist.

COMPLETE SET (90)
PA1 Mike Crowley
PA2 Ruslan Salei
PA3 Pascal Trepanier
PA4 David Harlock
PA5 Jeff Odgers
PA6 Yves Sarault
PA7 Ken Belanger
PA8 Jay Henderson
PA9 Cameron Mann
PA10 Denis Hamel
PA11 Jason Holland
PA12 Rob Ray
PA13 Dallas Eakins
PA14 Denis Gauthier
PA15 Dwayne Hay
PA16 Dave Karpa
PA17 Darren Langdon
PA18 Tyler Moss
PA19 Kevin Dean
PA20 Mark Janssens
PA21 Rob Tallas
PA22 Chris Dingman
PA23 Greg DeVries
PA24 Dave Reid
PA25 Kevin Dahl
PA26 Frantisek Kucera
PA27 Steve Maltais
PA28 Sami Helenius
PA29 Brad Lukowich
PA30 Kirk Muller
PA31 Yuri Butsayev
PA32 Maxim Kuznetsov
PA33 Aaron Ward
PA34 Rem Murray
PA35 Frank Musil
PA36 Dominic Pittis
PA37 Len Barrie
PA38 Dan Boyle
PA39 John Jakopin
PA40 Philippe Boucher
PA41 Steve Passmore
PA42 Scott Thomas
PA43 J.J. Daigneault
PA44 Matt Johnson
PA45 Stacy Roest
PA46 Francois Bouillon
PA47 Eric Fichaud
PA48 Stephane Robidas
PA49 Cale Hulse
PA50 Ville Peltonen
PA51 Mike Watt
PA52 Ken Daneyko
PA53 Jim McKenzie
PA54 Ed Ward
PA55 Jesse Belanger
PA56 Anders Myrvold
PA57 Steve Webb
PA58 Jason Doig
PA59 Bert Robertsson
PA60 David Wilkie
PA61 John Emmons
PA62 David Oliver
PA63 Jamie Rivers
PA64 Chris McAllister
PA65 Paul Ranheim
PA66 P.J. Stock
PA67 Joel Bouchard
PA68 Landon Wilson
PA69 Juha Ylonen
PA70 Marc Bergevin
PA71 Bob Boughner
PA72 Rene Corbet
PA73 Bobby Dollas
PA74 Tony Granato
PA75 Jim Montgomery
PA76 Vladimir Chebaturkin
PA77 Pascal Rheaume
PA78 Reid Simpson
PA79 Ben Clymer
PA80 Nils Ekman
PA81 Craig Miller
PA82 Donald MacLean
PA83 Alyn McCauley
PA84 Glenn Healy
PA85 Bob Essensa
PA86 Scott Lachance
PA87 Denis Pederson
PA88 Craig Billington
PA89 Dmitri Mironov
PA90 Joe Sacco

1999-00 Upper Deck Ovation

Released as a 90-card set, Ovation was comprised of 60 regular issue base cards and 30 short prints. The short prints were divided up into Premier Prospects seeded at one in three and Superstar Spotlights seeded at one in six packs. Base cards featured an embossed border molded to look like a used ice rink and silver foil stamping.

COMPLETE SET (90)	60.00	125.00
1 Paul Kariya	.30	.75
2 Teemu Selanne	.30	.75
3 Patrik Stefan RC	1.25	3.00
4 Sergei Samsonov	.25	.60
5 Ray Bourque	.50	1.25
6 Dominik Hasek	.60	1.50
7 Michael Peca	.25	.60
8 Miroslav Satan	.25	.60
9 Oleg Saprykin RC	1.25	3.00
10 Valeri Bure	.08	.25
11 Ron Francis	.25	.60
12 Dave Tanabe	.08	.25
13 Tony Amonte	.25	.60
14 J-P Dumont	.25	.60
15 Patrick Roy	1.50	4.00
16 Alex Tanguay	.25	.60
17 Joe Sakic	.60	1.50
18 Peter Forsberg	.75	2.00
19 Mike Modano	.50	1.25
20 Ed Belfour	.30	.75
21 Brett Hull	.40	1.00
22 Sergei Fedorov	.50	1.25
23 Chris Osgood	.25	.60
24 Steve Yzerman	1.50	4.00
25 Doug Weight	.25	.60
26 Tom Poti	.08	.25
27 Pavel Bure	.30	.75
28 Ivan Novoseltsev RC	.60	1.50
29 Luc Robitaille	.25	.60
30 Zigmund Palffy	.25	.60
31 Mike Ribeiro	.25	.60
32 David Legwand	.25	.60
33 Martin Brodeur	.75	2.00
34 Scott Gomez	.08	.25
35 Tim Connolly	.08	.25
36 Theo Fleury	.08	.25
37 Mike Richter	.30	.75
38 Brian Leetch	.30	.75
39 Marian Hossa	.30	.75
40 Daniel Alfredsson	.25	.60
41 Eric Lindros	.30	.75
42 John LeClair	.30	.75
43 Simon Gagne	.30	.75
44 Keith Tkachuk	.40	1.00
45 Jeremy Roenick	.40	1.00
46 Jaromir Jagr	.50	1.25
47 Alexei Kovalev	.08	.25
48 Pavol Demitra	.25	.60
49 Al MacInnis	.25	.60
50 Owen Nolan	.25	.60
51 Brad Stuart	.25	.60
52 Steve Shields	.25	.60
53 Vincent Lecavalier	.30	.75
54 Paul Mara	.25	.60
55 Curtis Joseph	.30	.75
56 Mats Sundin	.30	.75
57 Steve Kariya RC	.75	2.00
58 Mark Messier	.30	.75
59 Peter Bondra	.30	.75
60 Olaf Kolzig	.25	.60
61 Pavel Brendl PP SP RC	3.00	8.00
62 Daniel Sedin PP SP	.75	2.00
63 Henrik Sedin PP SP	.75	2.00
64 Sheldon Keefe PP SP RC	1.25	3.00
65 Jeff Heerema PP SP	.75	2.00
66 Norm Milley PP SP	.75	2.00
67 Branislav Mezei PP SP RC	.75	2.00
68 Denis Shvidki PP SP	.75	2.00
69 Brian Finley PP SP	.75	2.00
70 Taylor Pyatt PP SP	.75	2.00
71 Jamie Lundmark PP SP	.75	2.00
72 Milan Kraft SP RC	3.00	8.00
73 Kris Beech PP SP	.75	2.00
74 Alexei Volkov PP SP	.75	2.00
75 Mathieu Chouinard PP SP	.75	2.00
76 Justin Papineau PP SP	.75	2.00
77 Brad Moran PP SP RC	.75	2.00
78 Jonathan Cheechoo PP SP	.75	2.00
79 Mark Bell PP SP	.75	2.00
80 Mattias Weinhandl PP SP	.75	2.00
81 Jaromir Jagr SS SP	1.50	4.00
82 Steve Kariya SS SP	1.00	2.50
83 Dominik Hasek SS SP	2.00	5.00
84 Paul Kariya SS SP	1.25	3.00
85 Eric Lindros SS SP	1.00	2.50
86 Patrick Roy SS SP	5.00	12.00
87 Steve Yzerman SS SP	5.00	12.00
88 Pavel Bure SS SP	1.00	2.50
89 Theo Fleury SS SP	1.00	2.50
90 Patrik Stefan SS SP	1.50	4.00

1999-00 Upper Deck Ovation Standing Ovation

Randomly inserted in packs, this 90-card set parallels the base Ovation set. Each card is enhanced with gold foil highlights and is sequentially numbered to 60.

*VETS 1-60: 25X TO 60X BASIC CARDS
*PP/SS 61-90: 8X TO 20X BASIC SP

61 Pavel Brendl PP	100.00	175.00
72 Milan Kraft PP	100.00	175.00

1999-00 Upper Deck Ovation A Piece Of History

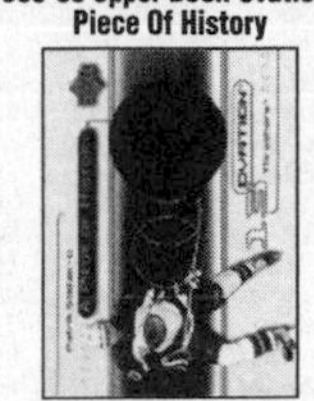

Randomly seeded in packs at the rate of 1:118, and autographs numbered to 25, this 16-card set features swatches of game used memorabilia.

BH Brett Hull	12.50	30.00
CJ Curtis Joseph	8.00	20.00
JJ Jaromir Jagr	12.50	30.00
MB Martin Brodeur	20.00	50.00
MR Mike Ribeiro	8.00	20.00
PB Pavel Bure	8.00	20.00
PK Paul Kariya	8.00	20.00
PR Patrick Roy	20.00	50.00
PS Patrik Stefan	8.00	20.00
SK Steve Kariya	8.00	20.00
SS Sergei Samsonov	8.00	20.00
TC Tim Connolly	8.00	20.00
WG Wayne Gretzky	25.00	60.00
BHS Brett Hull AU/25	150.00	300.00
CJS Curtis Joseph AU/25	125.00	250.00
PBS Pavel Bure AU/25	200.00	400.00
PSS Patrik Stefan AU/25	30.00	75.00

1999-00 Upper Deck Ovation Center Stage

Randomly inserted in packs as a tiered insert set, card numbers 1-10 are seeded at one in nine and feature silver foil highlights, card-numbers 11-20 are seeded at one in 39 and feature gold foil highlights, and card numbers 21-30 are seeded at one in 99 and feature rainbow holofoil highlights.

COMMON GRETZKY (CS1-CS5)	2.00	5.00
COMMON HOWE (CS6-CS10)	1.25	3.00
COMMON GRETZY (CS11-CS20)	6.00	15.00
COMMON HOWE (CS16-CS19)	4.00	10.00
COMMON GRETZKY (CS22-CS25)	20.00	50.00
COMMON HOWE (CS26-CS27)	12.50	30.00
COMMON DUAL (CS21/CS28-CS30)	25.00	60.00

1999-00 Upper Deck Ovation Lead Performers

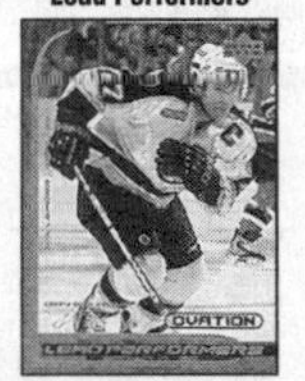

COMPLETE SET (20)	15.00	30.00
STATED ODDS 1:4		
LP1 Mike Modano	.75	2.00
LP2 Theo Fleury	.25	.60
LP3 Paul Kariya	.50	1.25
LP4 Peter Forsberg	1.25	3.00
LP5 Pavel Bure	.60	1.50
LP6 John LeClair	.60	1.50
LP7 Keith Tkachuk	.50	1.25
LP8 Jaromir Jagr	.75	2.00
LP9 Patrik Stefan	.25	.60
LP10 Steve Kariya	.25	.60
LP11 Ray Bourque	.75	2.00
LP12 Teemu Selanne	.50	1.25
LP13 Zigmund Palffy	.50	1.25
LP14 Steve Yzerman	2.50	6.00
LP15 Eric Lindros	.75	2.00
LP16 Dominik Hasek	1.00	2.50
LP17 Martin Brodeur	1.25	3.00
LP18 Brendan Shanahan	.75	2.00
LP19 Ed Belfour	.50	1.25
LP20 Patrick Roy	2.50	6.00

1999-00 Upper Deck Ovation Super Signatures

Randomly inserted in packs, this set features Wayne Gretzky and Gordie Howe autographs. Base versions are sequentially numbered to 99, Gold versions are sequentially numbered to 50, Rainbow versions are numbered to 25, and the Rainbow Combination card is numbered to nine. Wayne Gretzky SS1 was issued as a redemption. The Gretzky/Howe card is not priced due to scarcity.

SS1 Wayne Gretzky/99	150.00	400.00
SS2 Gordie Howe/99	60.00	150.00
SSG1 Wayne Gretzky GOLD/50	300.00	600.00
SSG2 Gordie Howe GOLD/50	150.00	300.00
SSR1 Wayne Gretzky RAINBOW/25	500.00	1000.00
SSR2 Gordie Howe RAINBOW/25	300.00	500.00
SSRC Wayne Gretzky Gordie Howe/9		

1999-00 Upper Deck Ovation Superstar Theater

COMPLETE SET (10)	10.00	20.00
STATED ODDS 1:9		
ST1 Paul Kariya	.60	1.50
ST2 Sergei Fedorov	1.00	2.50
ST3 Brett Hull	.60	1.50
ST4 Patrick Roy	2.50	6.00
ST5 Dominik Hasek	1.00	2.50
ST6 Eric Lindros	.75	2.00
ST7 Jaromir Jagr	.75	2.00
ST8 Martin Brodeur	1.25	3.00
ST9 Pavel Bure	.60	1.50
ST10 Teemu Selanne	.60	1.50

2006-07 Upper Deck Ovation

COMPLETE SET (200)	75.00	125.00
DISTRIBUTED IN FOUR RETAIL TINS		
1 Jean-Sebastien Giguere	.40	1.00
2 Teemu Selanne	.40	1.00
3 Slava Kozlov	.25	.60
4 Brad Boyes	.25	.60
5 Hannu Toivonen	.40	1.00
6 Thomas Vanek	.30	.75
7 Ales Kotalik	.25	.60
8 Miikka Kiprusoff	.40	1.00
9 Erik Cole	.25	.60
10 Nikolai Khabibulin	.40	1.00
11 Tuomo Ruutu	.25	.60
12 Alex Tanguay	.30	.75
13 Jose Theodore	.40	1.00
14 David Vyborny	.25	.60
15 Jason Arnott	.25	.60
16 Brendan Shanahan	.40	1.00
17 Pavol Datsyuk	.40	1.00
18 Nicklas Lidstrom	.40	1.00
19 Chris Pronger	.30	.75
20 Jarret Stoll	.25	.60
21 M-A Pouliot RC	1.50	4.00
22 Joe Nieuwendyk	.30	.75
23 Lubomir Visnovsky	.25	.60
24 Manny Fernandez	.40	1.00
25 Erik Reitz RC	1.25	3.00
26 Mike Ribeiro	.25	.60
27 Chris Higgins	.25	.60
28 Martin Brodeur	1.25	3.00
29 Brian Gionta	.25	.60
30 Miroslav Satan	.25	.60
31 Jason Blake	.25	.60
32 Petr Prucha	.25	.60
33 Jason Spezza	.40	1.00
34 Filip Novak RC	1.25	3.00
35 Simon Gagne	.40	1.00
36 Robert Esche	.30	.75
37 Ryan Potulny RC	1.50	4.00
38 Mike Comrie	.25	.60
39 Bill Thomas RC	1.25	3.00
40 Marc-Andre Fleury	.40	1.00
41 Sergei Gonchar	.12	.30
42 Evgeni Nabokov	.40	1.00
43 Keith Tkachuk	.30	.75
44 Martin St. Louis	.40	1.00
45 Mike Commodore	.25	.60
46 Bryan McCabe	.25	.60
47 Alexander Steen	.30	.75
48 Markus Naslund	.40	1.00
49 Ed Jovanovski	.25	.60
50 Dainius Zubrus	.25	.60
51 Scott Niedermayer	.25	.60
52 Joffrey Lupul	.25	.60
53 Ilya Kovalchuk	.50	1.25
54 Brian Leetch	.25	.60
55 Marco Sturm	.25	.60
56 Martin Biron	.30	.75
57 Dion Phaneuf	.50	1.25
58 Daymond Langkow	.25	.60
59 Cam Ward	.60	1.50
60 Kyle Calder	.25	.60
61 Dustin Byfuglien RC	2.50	6.00
62 Milan Hejduk	.30	.75
63 Rick Nash	.40	1.00
64 Sergei Fedorov	.40	1.00
65 Nikolai Zherdev	.25	.60
66 Sergei Zubov	.25	.60
67 Henrik Zetterberg	.40	1.00
68 Kris Draper	.25	.60
69 Tomas Kopecky RC	1.50	4.00
70 Dwayne Roloson	.30	.75
71 Roberto Luongo	.75	2.00
72 Jay Bouwmeester	.25	.60
73 Nathan Horton	.25	.60
74 Mathieu Garon	.30	.75
75 Pierre-Marc Bouchard	.25	.60
76 Cristobal Huet	.40	1.00
77 Steve Sullivan	.25	.60
78 Scott Gomez	.25	.60
79 Alexei Yashin	.25	.60
80 Mike York	.12	.30
81 Ryan Caldwell RC	1.25	3.00
82 Jaromir Jagr	.60	1.50
83 Jason Spezza	.40	1.00
84 Ray Emery	.40	1.00
85 Jeff Carter	.40	1.00
86 Mike Knuble	.25	.60
87 Keith Ballard	.25	.60
88 Joel Perrault RC	1.25	3.00
89 John LeClair	.30	.75
90 Joe Thornton	.60	1.50
91 Matt Carle RC	1.50	4.00
92 Scott Young	.12	.30
93 Vincent Lecavalier	.40	1.00
94 Brad Richards	.40	1.00
95 Vaclav Prospal	.25	.60
96 Darcy Tucker	.25	.60
97 Ian White RC	1.25	3.00
98 Brendan Morrison	.25	.60
99 Olaf Kolzig	.50	1.25
100 Jeff Halpern	.25	.60
101 Corey Perry	.30	.75
102 Ryan Getzlaf	.30	.75
103 Kari Lehtonen	.40	1.00
104 Marian Hossa	.30	.75
105 Tim Thomas	.40	1.00
106 Mark Stuart RC	1.25	3.00
107 Ryan Miller	.40	1.00
108 Maxim Afinogenov	.25	.60
109 Chuck Kobasew	.25	.60
110 Carsen Germyn RC	1.25	3.00
111 Eric Staal	.30	.75
112 Rod Brind'Amour	.30	.75
113 Mark Bell	.25	.60
114 Rob Blake	.30	.75
115 Pascal Leclaire	.40	1.00
116 Mike Modano	.40	1.00
117 Brenden Morrow	.30	.75
118 Jussi Jokinen	.25	.60
119 Tomas Holmstrom	.25	.60
120 Ryan Smyth	.30	.75
121 Raffi Torres	.12	.30
122 Alexander Frolov	.25	.60
123 Mike Cammalleri	.25	.60
124 Konstantin Pushkarev RC	1.25	3.00
125 Marian Gaborik	.60	1.50
126 Brian Rolston	.25	.60
127 Alex Kovalev	.25	.60
128 Tomas Vokoun	.25	.60
129 Scott Hartnell	.12	.30
130 Brian Rafalski	.25	.60
131 Henrik Lundqvist	.60	1.50
132 Michael Nylander	.25	.60
133 David Liffiton RC	1.25	3.00
134 Daniel Alfredsson	.30	.75
135 Wade Redden	.25	.60
136 Billy Thompson RC	1.25	3.00
137 Peter Forsberg	.60	1.50
138 Keith Primeau	.25	.60
139 Ladislav Nagy	.25	.60
140 Sidney Crosby	5.00	12.00
141 Jonathan Cheechoo	.40	1.00
142 Vesa Toskala	.30	.75
143 Petr Cajanek	.25	.60
144 Fredrik Modin	.25	.60
145 Mats Sundin	.40	1.00
146 Kyle Wellwood	.25	.60
147 Alexander Steen	.30	.75
148 Brendan Bell	.25	.60
149 Daniel Sedin	.25	.60
150 Eric Fehr RC	1.50	4.00
151 Marc Savard	.25	.60
152 Patrice Bergeron	.30	.75
153 Glen Murray	.25	.60
154 Phil Kessel RC	4.00	10.00
155 Chris Drury	.30	.75
156 Daniel Briere	.30	.75
157 Jarome Iginla	.60	1.50
158 Doug Weight	.25	.60
159 Justin Williams	.25	.60
160 Brent Seabrook	.25	.60
161 Joe Sakic	.75	2.00
162 Marek Svatos	.25	.60
163 Paul Stastny RC	3.00	8.00
164 Marty Turco	.30	.75
165 Jere Lehtinen	.25	.60
166 Fernando Pisani	.25	.60
167 Ales Hemsky	.25	.60
168 Shawn Horcoff	.25	.60
169 Olli Jokinen	.25	.60
170 Pavol Demitra	.25	.60
171 Mikko Koivu	.25	.60
172 Guillaume Latendresse RC	2.00	5.00
173 Saku Koivu	.40	1.00
174 Michael Ryder	.30	.75
175 David Aebischer	.25	.60
176 Paul Kariya	.40	1.00
177 Mike Sillinger	.25	.60
178 Shea Weber RC	1.50	4.00
179 Patrik Elias	.25	.60
180 Rick DiPietro	.40	1.00
181 Steve Regier RC	1.25	3.00
182 Masi Marjamaki RC	1.25	3.00
183 Martin Straka	.25	.60
184 Jarkko Immonen XRC	1.25	3.00
185 Patrick O'Sullivan RC	1.50	4.00
186 Martin Havlat	.30	.75
187 Antero Niittymaki	.40	1.00
188 Shane Doan	.30	.75
189 Curtis Joseph	.40	1.00
190 Colby Armstrong	.25	.60
191 Jordan Staal RC	3.00	8.00
192 Evgeni Malkin RC	6.00	15.00
193 Patrick Marleau	.30	.75
194 Steve Bernier	.25	.60
195 Curtis Sanford	.30	.75
196 Ruslan Fedotenko	.25	.60
197 Andrew Raycroft	.30	.75
198 Henrik Sedin	.25	.60
199 Luc Bourdon RC	1.50	4.00
200 Alexander Ovechkin	1.50	4.00

2007-08 Upper Deck Ovation

COMPLETE SET (225)	60.00	120.00
1 Olaf Kolzig	.40	1.00
2 Daniel Sedin	.25	.60
3 Henrik Sedin	.25	.60
4 Alexander Steen	.25	.60
5 Bryan McCabe	.25	.60
6 Brad Richards	.30	.75
7 Manny Legace	.30	.75
8 Jonathan Cheechoo	.30	.75
9 Joe Pavelski	.25	.60
10 Mark Recchi	.25	.60
11 Sidney Crosby	2.00	5.00
12 Shane Doan	.25	.60
13 Jeff Carter	.25	.60
14 Jason Spezza	.40	1.00
15 Martin Straka	.25	.60
16 Brendan Shanahan	.40	1.00
17 Rick DiPietro	.30	.75
18 Martin Brodeur	1.00	2.50
19 Travis Zajac	.25	.60
20 Kimmo Timonen	.25	.60
21 Peter Forsberg	.50	1.25
22 Cristobal Huet	.30	.75
23 Guillaume Latendresse	.30	.75
24 Manny Fernandez	.30	.75
25 Pavol Demitra	.25	.60
26 Anze Kopitar	.40	1.00
27 Jay Bouwmeester	.25	.60
28 Ales Hemsky	.25	.60
29 Rob Schremp RC	.30	.75
30 Tomas Holmstrom	.25	.60
31 Nicklas Lidstrom	.40	1.00
32 Mike Ribeiro	.25	.60
33 Brenden Morrow	.30	.75
34 David Vyborny	.25	.60
35 Pascal Leclaire	.30	.75
36 Paul Stastny	.40	1.00
37 Marek Svatos	.25	.60
38 Tuomo Ruutu	.25	.60
39 Duncan Keith	.40	1.00
40 Justin Williams	.25	.60
41 Erik Cole	.25	.60
42 Daymond Langkow	.25	.60
43 Jarome Iginla	.60	1.50
44 Thomas Vanek	.30	.75
45 Daniel Briere	.40	1.00
46 Marc Savard	.25	.60
47 Petr Kalus RC	.50	1.25
48 Marian Hossa	.40	1.00
49 Andy McDonald	.25	.60
50 Ryan Getzlaf	.30	.75
51 Alexander Ovechkin	1.25	3.00
52 Brendan Morrison	.25	.60
53 Trevor Linden	.30	.75
54 Owen Nolan	.30	.75
55 Andrew Raycroft	.30	.75
56 Yanic Perreault	.25	.60
57 Vincent Lecavalier	.40	1.00
58 Brad Boyes	.30	.75
59 Barret Jackman	.25	.60
60 Vesa Toskala	.25	.60
61 Bill Guerin	.25	.60
62 Marc-Andre Fleury	.40	1.00
63 Jordan Staal	.50	1.25
64 Zbynek Michalek	.25	.60
65 Simon Gagne	.40	1.00
66 Daniel Alfredsson	.30	.75
67 Ray Emery	.30	.75
68 Michael Nylander	.25	.60
69 Michal Rozsival	.25	.60
70 Jason Blake	.25	.60
71 Alexei Yashin	.25	.60
72 Zach Parise	.30	.75
73 Scott Gomez	.25	.60
74 Paul Kariya	.40	1.00
75 Jason Arnott	.25	.60
76 Alex Kovalev	.25	.60
77 Jaroslav Halak RC	.75	2.00
78 Mikko Koivu	.25	.60
79 Mike Cammalleri	.30	.75
80 Jack Johnson RC	.40	1.00
81 Nathan Horton	.25	.60
82 Olli Jokinen	.25	.60
83 Shawn Horcoff	.25	.60
84 Joffrey Lupul	.25	.60
85 Dominik Hasek	.50	1.25
86 Kris Draper	.30	.75
87 Mike Modano	.40	1.00
88 Rick Nash	.40	1.00
89 Peter Budaj	.30	.75
90 Wojtek Wolski	.25	.60
91 Nikolai Khabibulin	.40	1.00
92 Eric Staal	.40	1.00
93 Dion Phaneuf	.40	1.00
94 Matthew Lombardi	.25	.60
95 Ryan Miller	.40	1.00
96 Jason Pominville	.25	.60
97 Patrice Bergeron	.40	1.00
98 Kari Lehtonen	.40	1.00
99 Scott Niedermayer	.40	1.00
100 Corey Perry	.30	.75
101 Chris Clark	.25	.60
102 Eric Fehr	.25	.60
103 Markus Naslund	.40	1.00
104 Tomas Kaberle	.25	.60
105 Jeff O'Neill	.25	.60
106 Johan Holmqvist	.30	.75
107 Vaclav Prospal	.25	.60
108 Lee Stempniak	.25	.60
109 Jay McClement	.25	.60
110 Patrick Marleau	.30	.75
111 Evgeni Nabokov	.30	.75
112 Evgeni Malkin	1.00	2.50
113 Sergei Gonchar	.25	.60
114 Curtis Joseph	.30	.75
115 Ryan Parent	.30	.75
116 Mike Richards	.50	1.25
117 Mike Fisher	.30	.75
118 Wade Redden	.25	.60
119 Henrik Lundqvist	.50	1.25
120 Ryan Smyth	.30	.75
121 Brian Rafalski	.25	.60
122 Brian Gionta	.25	.60
123 Steve Sullivan	.25	.60
124 Chris Mason	.30	.75
125 Saku Koivu	.30	.75
126 Brian Rolston	.25	.60
127 P-M Bouchard	.25	.60
128 Lauri Tukonen RC	.25	.60
129 Alexander Frolov	.25	.60
130 Stephen Weiss	.25	.60
131 Jozef Stumpel	.25	.60
132 Jarret Stoll	.25	.60
133 Pavel Datsyuk	.40	1.00
134 Philippe Boucher	.25	.60
135 Eric Lindros	.40	1.00
136 Gilbert Brule	.25	.60
137 Fredrik Modin	.25	.60
138 Andrew Brunette	.25	.60
139 Joe Sakic	.75	2.00
140 Martin Havlat	.30	.75
141 Cam Ward	.40	1.00
142 Miikka Kiprusoff	.50	1.25
143 Maxim Afinogenov	.25	.60
144 Brian Campbell	.25	.60
145 Glen Murray	.25	.60
146 Phil Kessel	.40	1.00
147 Slava Kozlov	.25	.60
148 Ilya Kovalchuk	.50	1.25
149 Jean-Sebastien Giguere	.40	1.00
150 Chris Pronger	.40	1.00
151 Alexander Semin	.40	1.00
152 Nicklas Backstrom RC	1.00	2.50
153 Roberto Luongo	.60	1.50
154 Sami Salo	.25	.60
155 Darcy Tucker	.30	.75
156 Mats Sundin	.40	1.00
157 Dan Boyle	.25	.60
158 Erik Johnson RC	.50	1.25
159 Doug Weight	.25	.60
160 Joe Thornton	.50	1.25
161 Peter Mueller RC	.75	2.00
162 Ed Jovanovski	.25	.60
163 Martin Biron	.30	.75
164 Nick Foligno RC	.40	1.00
165 Dany Heatley	.50	1.25
166 Marc Staal RC	.60	1.50
167 Viktor Kozlov	.25	.60
168 Miroslav Satan	.25	.60
169 Nicklas Bergfors RC	.30	.75
170 Carey Price RC	1.25	3.00
171 Chris Higgins	.30	.75
172 Michael Ryder	.25	.60
173 Mark Parrish	.25	.60
174 Marian Gaborik	.50	1.25
175 Jack Johnson RC	.40	1.00
176 Jonathan Bernier RC	.60	1.50
177 Ed Belfour	.40	1.00
178 Sam Gagner RC	.50	1.25
179 Petr Sykora	.25	.60
180 Andrew Cogliano RC	.60	1.50
181 Henrik Zetterberg	.40	1.00
182 Marty Turco	.40	1.00
183 Ladislav Nagy	.25	.60
184 Sergei Fedorov	.40	1.00
185 Fredrik Norrena	.30	.75
186 Milan Hejduk	.30	.75
187 Patrick Kane RC	1.50	4.00
188 Jason Williams	.25	.60
189 Radim Vrbata	.25	.60
190 Ray Whitney	.25	.60
191 Rod Brind'Amour	.30	.75
192 Alex Tanguay	.30	.75
193 Chris Drury	.30	.75
194 Derek Roy	.25	.60
195 Zdeno Chara	.25	.60
196 Bryan Little RC	.40	1.00
197 Keith Tkachuk	.30	.75
198 Brett Sterling RC	.25	.60
199 Bobby Ryan RC	1.00	2.50
200 Teemu Selanne	.40	1.00
201 Vincent Lecavalier	.40	1.00
202 Daniel Alfredsson	.30	.75
203 Evgeni Malkin	1.00	2.50
204 Ilya Kovalchuk	.50	1.25
205 Alexander Ovechkin	1.25	3.00
206 Eric Staal	.40	1.00
207 Jason Spezza	.40	1.00
208 Martin St. Louis	.30	.75
209 Andrei Markov	.30	.75
210 Tomas Kaberle	.25	.60
211 Dion Phaneuf	.40	1.00
212 Nicklas Lidstrom	.40	1.00
213 Scott Niedermayer	.25	.60
214 Jarome Iginla	.60	1.50
215 Joe Thornton	.50	1.25
216 Rick Nash	.40	1.00
217 Tuukka Rask RC	.60	1.50
218 T.J. Hensick RC	.30	.75
219 Jonathan Toews RC	1.50	4.00
220 Steve Downie RC	.25	.60
221 Devin Setoguchi RC	.50	1.25
222 David Perron RC	.40	1.00
223 Jiri Tlusty RC	.60	1.50
224 James Sheppard RC	.25	.60
225 Sergei Kostitsyn	.75	2.00

2007-08 Upper Deck Ovation 3x5s

XL1 Alexander Ovechkin	6.00	15.00
XL4 Andrew Raycroft	1.50	4.00
XL6 Vincent Lecavalier	2.00	5.00
XL7 Patrick Marleau	1.50	4.00
XL8 Sidney Crosby	10.00	25.00
XL10 Jason Spezza	2.00	5.00
XL11 Dany Heatley	2.50	6.00
XL12 Martin Brodeur	5.00	12.00
XL13 Guillaume Latendresse	1.50	4.00
XL18 Rick Nash	2.00	5.00
XL20 Eric Staal	2.00	5.00
XL21 Jarome Iginla	3.00	8.00
XL22 Dion Phaneuf	2.00	5.00
XL24 Thomas Vanek	2.00	5.00

2007-08 Upper Deck Ovation Autographed 3x5s

NOT PRICED DUE TO SCARCITY
XLAAO Alexander Ovechkin
XLAAR Andrew Raycroft
XLADP Dion Phaneuf
XLAGL Guillaume Latendresse
XLAJI Jarome Iginla
XLARN Rick Nash
XLASC Sidney Crosby
XLATV Thomas Vanek

2008-09 Upper Deck Ovation

COMPLETE SET (200) 75.00 150.00
COMP.FACT.SER.1 (50) 15.00 40.00
COMP.FACT.SER.2 (50) 15.00 40.00
COMP.FACT.SER.3 (50) 15.00 40.00
COMP.FACT.SER.4 (50) 20.00 50.00
1 Teemu Selanne .40 1.00
2 Jean-Sebastien Giguere .40 1.00
3 Tobias Enstrom .40 1.00
4 Phil Kessel .40 1.00
5 Zdeno Chara .25 .60
6 Marc-Andre Gragnani .25 .60
7 Jason Pominville .30 .75
8 Alex Tanguay .30 .75
9 Kristian Huselius .25 .60
10 Erik Cole .25 .60
11 Patrick Kane 1.00 2.50
12 Duncan Keith .30 .75
13 Ryan Smyth .30 .75
14 Wojtek Wolski .25 .60
15 Steve Mason RC 3.00 8.00
16 Rick Nash .40 1.00
17 Mike Modano .40 1.00
18 Brenden Morrow .30 .75
19 Dominik Hasek .60 1.50
20 Valtteri Filppula .25 .60
21 Dwayne Roloson .30 .75
22 Shawn Matthias RC .40 1.00
23 Tomas Vokoun .40 1.00
24 Jay Bouwmeester .30 .75
25 Pierre-Marc Bouchard .25 .60
26 Carey Price 1.25 3.00
27 Saku Koivu .40 1.00
28 Alex Kovalev .40 1.00
29 Andrei Markov .30 .75
30 Martin Erat .40 1.00
31 Martin Brodeur .75 2.00
32 Travis Zajac .25 .60
33 Bill Guerin .25 .60
34 Henrik Lundqvist .75 2.00
35 Chris Drury .40 1.00
36 Ray Emery .30 .75
37 Simon Gagne .30 .75
38 Daniel Briere .40 1.00
39 Ilya Bryzgalov .25 .60
40 Jon Filewich RC .30 .75
41 Evgeni Malkin 1.00 2.50
42 Jordan Staal .60 1.50
43 Evgeni Nabokov .40 1.00
44 Lee Stempniak .25 .60
45 Martin St. Louis .40 1.00
46 Johan Holmqvist .30 .75
47 Robbie Earl RC .30 .75
48 Nikolai Antropov .30 .75
49 Darcy Tucker .30 .75
50 Alexander Edler .30 .75
51 Corey Perry .40 1.00
52 Bryan Little .25 .60
53 Ilya Kovalchuk .50 1.25
54 Derek Roy .25 .60
55 Thomas Vanek .40 1.00
56 Dion Phaneuf .40 1.00
57 Justin Williams .25 .60
58 Martin Havlat .30 .75
59 Joe Sakic .60 1.50
60 Paul Stastny .40 1.00
61 Nikolai Zherdev .25 .60
62 Mark Fistric RC .30 .75
63 Marty Turco .30 .75
64 Sergei Zubov .25 .60
65 Henrik Zetterberg .75 2.00
66 Ales Hemsky .25 .60
67 Dustin Penner .25 .60
68 Nathan Horton .25 .60
69 Anze Kopitar .40 1.00
70 Brian Boyle RC .40 1.00
71 Mikko Koivu .40 1.00
72 Andrei Kostitsyn .30 .75
73 Michael Ryder .30 .75
74 David Legwand .30 .75
75 Jason Arnott .25 .60
76 John Madden .25 .60
77 Mike Comrie .25 .60
78 Miroslav Satan .25 .60
79 Jaromir Jagr .50 1.25
80 Scott Gomez .30 .75
81 Daniel Alfredsson .30 .75
82 Ilya Zubov RC .40 1.00
83 Nick Foligno .40 1.00
84 Claude Giroux RC .75 2.00
85 Mike Knuble .40 1.00
86 R.J. Umberger .25 .60
87 Ed Jovanovski .25 .60
88 Shane Doan .25 .60
89 Marian Hossa .60 1.50
90 Ryan Stone RC .40 1.00
91 Joe Thornton .60 1.50
92 Jonathan Cheechoo .40 1.00
93 Milan Michalek .25 .60
94 Erik Johnson .50 1.25
95 Dan Boyle .30 .75
96 Tomas Kaberle .25 .60
97 Daniel Sedin .40 1.00
98 Markus Naslund .40 1.00
99 Alexander Ovechkin 1.50 4.00
100 Mike Green .25 .60
101 Chris Pronger .30 .75
102 Ryan Getzlaf .50 1.25
103 Kari Lehtonen .25 .60
104 Johan Hedberg .30 .75
105 Marco Sturm .25 .60
106 Ryan Miller .40 1.00
107 Jarome Iginla .75 2.00
108 Daymond Langkow .25 .60
109 Eric Staal .60 1.50
110 Rod Brind'Amour .30 .75
111 Jonathan Toews 1.25 3.00
112 Nikolai Khabibulin .40 1.00
113 Milan Hejduk .30 .75
114 Peter Budaj .30 .75
115 Derick Brassard RC .75 2.00
116 Pascal Leclaire .30 .75
117 Jonathan Ericsson RC .60 1.50
118 Nicklas Lidstrom .40 1.00
119 Dan Cleary .40 1.00
120 Sam Gagner .60 1.50
121 Shawn Horcoff .25 .60
122 Olli Jokinen .25 .60
123 Teddy Purcell RC .40 1.00
124 Alexander Frolov .25 .60
125 Jack Johnson .30 .75
126 Marian Gaborik .60 1.50
127 Brian Rolston .25 .60
128 Chris Higgins .25 .60
129 Alexander Radulov .40 1.00
130 J.P. Dumont .25 .60
131 Patrik Elias .25 .60
132 Trent Hunter .25 .60
133 Brendan Shanahan .40 1.00
134 Brandon Dubinsky .30 .75
135 Dany Heatley .50 1.25
136 Patrick Sharp .25 .60
137 Jeff Carter .40 1.00
138 Peter Mueller .50 1.25
139 Kyle Turris RC .75 2.00
140 Alex Goligoski RC .75 2.00
141 Mike Iggulden .30 .75
142 Brad Boyes .30 .75
143 David Perron .30 .75
144 Vincent Lecavalier .40 1.00
145 Paul Ranger .25 .60
146 Vesa Toskala .40 1.00
147 Henrik Sedin .40 1.00
148 Nicklas Backstrom .75 2.00
149 Alexander Semin .40 1.00
150 Viktor Kozlov .25 .60
151 Scott Niedermayer .25 .60
152 Zach Bogosian RC .75 2.00
153 Tim Thomas .40 1.00
154 Patrice Bergeron .40 1.00
155 Marc Savard .25 .60
156 Chuck Kobasew .25 .60
157 Drew Stafford .40 1.00
158 Miikka Kiprusoff .40 1.00
159 Matthew Lombardi .25 .60
160 Cam Ward .40 1.00
161 Brandon Sutter RC .50 1.25
162 Robert Lang .25 .60
163 Peter Forsberg .60 1.50
164 Marek Svatos .25 .60
165 James Neal RC .60 1.50
166 Brad Richards .30 .75
167 Pavel Datsyuk .40 1.00
168 Tomas Holmstrom .30 .75
169 Andrew Cogliano .60 1.50
170 Mathieu Garon .40 1.00
171 Stephen Weiss .25 .60
172 Dustin Brown .25 .60
173 Drew Doughty RC 1.25 3.00
174 Josh Harding .30 .75
175 Colton Gillies RC .40 1.00
176 Guillaume Latendresse .30 .75
177 Chris Mason .30 .75
178 Zach Parise .40 1.00
179 Brian Gionta .40 1.00
180 Rick DiPietro .40 1.00
181 Kyle Okposo RC .75 2.00
182 Michal Rozsival .25 .60
183 Martin Gerber .30 .75
184 Jason Spezza .50 1.25
185 Mike Richards .60 1.50
186 Mikkel Boedker RC .60 1.50
187 Sidney Crosby 2.00 5.00
188 Marc-Andre Fleury .40 1.00
189 Ryan Whitney .25 .60
190 Patrick Marleau .30 .75
191 T.J. Oshie RC 1.00 2.50
192 Alex Pietrangelo RC .60 1.50
193 Steven Stamkos RC 4.00 10.00
194 Nikolai Kulemin RC .40 1.00
195 Matt Stajan .30 .75
196 Luke Schenn RC 4.00 10.00
197 Roberto Luongo .60 1.50
198 Brendan Morrison .25 .60
199 Sergei Fedorov .60 1.50
200 Cristobal Huet .40 1.00

2008-09 Upper Deck Ovation Jumbo

STATED ODDS 1 PER TIN
XL1 Teemu Selanne 1.00 2.50
XL2 Patrick Kane 2.50 6.00
XL3 Dominik Hasek 1.50 4.00
XL4 Carey Price 3.00 8.00
XL5 Martin Brodeur 2.00 5.00
XL6 Evgeni Malkin 2.50 6.00
XL7 Joe Sakic 1.50 4.00
XL8 Henrik Zetterberg 2.00 5.00
XL9 Jaromir Jagr 1.25 3.00
XL10 Daniel Alfredsson .75 2.00
XL11 Joe Thornton 1.50 4.00
XL12 Alexander Ovechkin 4.00 10.00
XL13 Jarome Iginla 2.00 5.00
XL14 Eric Staal 1.50 4.00
XL15 Sam Gagner 1.50 4.00
XL16 Marian Gaborik 1.50 4.00
XL17 Dany Heatley 1.25 3.00
XL18 Vincent Lecavalier 1.00 2.50
XL19 Patrice Bergeron 1.00 2.50
XL20 Miikka Kiprusoff 1.00 2.50
XL21 Peter Forsberg 1.50 4.00
XL22 Sidney Crosby 5.00 12.00
XL23 Steven Stamkos 8.00 20.00
XL24 Roberto Luongo 1.50 4.00

2008-09 Upper Deck Ovation Jumbo Autographs

XLANB Nicklas Backstrom 15.00 40.00

2009-10 Upper Deck Ovation

COMPLETE SET (150) 25.00 60.00
1 Corey Perry .30 .75
2 Ryan Getzlaf .50 1.25
3 Brian Salcido RC .25 .60
4 Matt Beleskey RC .30 .75
5 Ilya Kovalchuk .40 1.00
6 Bryan Little .30 .75
7 Spencer Machacek RC .25 .60
8 Tim Thomas .30 .75
9 Phil Kessel .30 .75
10 Zdeno Chara .20 .50
11 Marc Savard .20 .50
12 David Krejci .25 .60
13 Byron Bitz RC .25 .60
14 Blake Wheeler .40 1.00
15 Thomas Vanek .30 .75
16 Ryan Miller .30 .75
17 Jason Pominville .30 .75
18 Jhonas Enroth RC .40 1.00
19 Derek Roy .30 .75
20 Dion Phaneuf .50 1.25
21 Jarome Iginla .60 1.50
22 Miikka Kiprusoff .30 .75
23 Olli Jokinen .20 .50
24 Daymond Langkow .20 .50
25 Kris Chucko RC .25 .60
26 Mikael Backlund RC .50 1.25
27 Eric Staal .40 1.00
28 Cam Ward .30 .75
29 Erik Cole .20 .50
30 Jonathan Toews .75 2.00
31 Patrick Sharp .25 .60
32 Patrick Kane .60 1.50
33 Dustin Byfuglien .25 .60
34 Brian Campbell .25 .60
35 Kris Versteeg .40 1.00
36 Paul Stastny .30 .75
37 Milan Hejduk .30 .75
38 T.J. Galiardi RC .40 1.00
39 Steve Mason .50 1.25
40 Rick Nash .30 .75
41 Derick Brassard .30 .75
42 Brenden Morrow .25 .60
43 Evander Kane RC .75 2.00
44 Marty Turco .25 .60
45 Henrik Zetterberg .60 1.50
46 Pavel Datsyuk .60 1.50
47 Johan Franzen .20 .50
48 Nicklas Lidstrom .40 1.00
49 Tomas Holmstrom .25 .60
50 Chris Osgood .40 1.00
51 Ville Leino RC .40 1.00
52 Sheldon Souray .20 .50
53 Ales Hemsky .25 .60
54 Sam Gagner .40 1.00
55 Andrew Cogliano .40 1.00
56 Dustin Penner .25 .60
57 Dwayne Roloson .25 .60
58 Shawn Horcoff .20 .50
59 Tomas Vokoun .30 .75
60 Nathan Horton .20 .50
61 David Booth .20 .50
62 Anze Kopitar .30 .75
63 Drew Doughty .60 1.50
64 Alexander Frolov .25 .60
65 Brent Burns .20 .50
66 Niklas Backstrom .30 .75
67 Mikko Koivu .30 .75
68 Andrei Markov .25 .60
69 Carey Price .75 2.00
70 John Tavares RC 4.00 10.00
71 Saku Koivu .30 .75
72 Tomas Plekanec .25 .60
73 James Van Riemsdyk RC .75 2.00
74 Yannick Weber RC .40 1.00
75 J.P. Dumont .20 .50
76 Pekka Rinne .25 .60
77 Jason Arnott .25 .60
78 Cal O'Reilly RC .30 .75
79 Mike Santorelli RC .30 .75
80 Martin Brodeur .75 2.00
81 Zach Parise .30 .75
82 Brian Gionta .30 .75
83 Jamie Langenbrunner .20 .50
84 Travis Zajac .20 .50
85 Kyle Okposo .30 .75
86 Rick DiPietro .30 .75
87 Jesse Joensuu RC .40 1.00
88 Henrik Lundqvist .60 1.50
89 Nik Antropov .25 .60
90 Matt Duchene RC 1.25 3.00
91 Scott Gomez .30 .75
92 Artem Anisimov RC .40 1.00
93 Victor Hedman RC .60 1.50
94 Sean Avery .25 .60
95 Dany Heatley .60 1.50
96 Jason Spezza .40 1.00
97 Brian Elliott .25 .60
98 Filip Kuba .20 .50
99 Daniel Alfredsson .30 .75
100 Mike Fisher .20 .50
101 Ryan Shannon .25 .60
102 Mike Richards .60 1.50
103 Jeff Carter .30 .75
104 Martin Biron .25 .60
105 Daniel Briere .30 .75
106 Scott Hartnell .20 .50
107 Daniel Carcillo .30 .75
108 Sergei Shirokov RC .50 1.25
109 Peter Mueller .40 1.00
110 Shane Doan .25 .60
111 Jonas Gustavsson RC .75 2.00
112 Ilya Bryzgalov .25 .60
113 Sidney Crosby 1.50 4.00
114 Evgeni Malkin .75 2.00
115 Jordan Staal .40 1.00
116 Marc-Andre Fleury .30 .75
117 Chris Kunitz .30 .75
118 Luca Caputi RC .40 1.00
119 Joe Thornton .60 1.50
120 Evgeni Nabokov .30 .75
121 Patrick Marleau .30 .75
122 Rob Blake .30 .75
123 Dan Boyle .20 .50
124 Devin Setoguchi .25 .60
125 Joe Pavelski .20 .50
126 Brad Boyes .25 .60
127 Patrik Berglund .60 1.50
128 David Backes .25 .60
129 Chris Mason .25 .60
130 Riku Helenius RC .30 .75
131 Steven Stamkos .75 2.00
132 Martin St. Louis .30 .75
133 Vincent Lecavalier .40 1.00
134 Luke Schenn .50 1.25
135 Matt Stajan .25 .60
136 Alexei Ponikarovsky .20 .50
137 Tomas Kaberle .20 .50
138 Nikolai Kulemin .20 .50
139 Niklas Hagman .20 .50
140 Justin Pogge .60 1.50
141 Willie Mitchell .20 .50
142 Ryan Kesler .25 .60
143 Alexandre Burrows .25 .60
144 Kyle Wellwood .20 .50
145 Roberto Luongo .75 2.00
146 Michal Neuvirth RC .75 2.00
147 Alexander Ovechkin 1.25 3.00
148 Alexander Semin .30 .75
149 Nicklas Backstrom .60 1.50
150 Mike Green .60 1.50

2009-10 Upper Deck Ovation Spotlight

COMPLETE SET (30) 15.00 40.00
OS1 Saku Koivu 1.00 2.50
OS2 Alexander Ovechkin 4.00 10.00
OS3 Marc-Andre Fleury 1.00 2.50
OS4 Steven Stamkos 2.50 6.00
OS5 Thomas Vanek 1.00 2.50
OS6 Carey Price 2.50 6.00
OS7 Jeff Carter 1.00 2.50
OS8 Jason Spezza 1.25 3.00
OS9 Evgeni Malkin 2.50 6.00
OS10 Miikka Kiprusoff 1.00 2.50
OS11 Martin Brodeur 2.50 6.00
OS12 Jonathan Toews 2.50 6.00
OS13 Dany Heatley 2.00 5.00
OS14 Henrik Lundqvist 2.00 5.00
OS15 Jarome Iginla 2.00 5.00
OS16 Mike Green 2.00 5.00
OS17 Joe Thornton 2.00 5.00
OS18 Henrik Zetterberg 2.00 5.00
OS19 Dion Phaneuf 1.50 4.00
OS20 Sidney Crosby 5.00 12.00
OS21 Ales Hemsky .75 2.00
OS22 Alexandre Burrows .75 2.00
OS23 Pavel Datsyuk 1.00 2.50
OS24 Luke Schenn 1.50 4.00
OS25 Patrick Kane 2.00 5.00
OS26 Mike Richards 2.00 5.00
OS27 Justin Pogge 2.00 5.00
OS28 Ilya Kovalchuk 1.25 3.00
OS29 Roberto Luongo 2.50 6.00
OS30 Rick Nash 1.00 2.50

2009-10 Upper Deck Ovation Spotlight Autographs

NOT PRICED DUE TO LACK OF MARKET INFO

2001 Upper Deck Pearson Awards

These three extremely rare cards were handed out only to attendees of the 2001 NHLPA Pearson Awards Banquet. It is commonly believed that most were either thrown out or stashed away, and that very few got into circulation within the hobby.

COMPLETE SET (3) 400.00 700.00
LPBJJ Jaromir Jagr 100.00 200.00
LPBML Mario Lemieux 200.00 400.00
LPBJS Joe Sakic 100.00 200.00

2002 Upper Deck Pearson Awards

Like the set from the previous year, these three cards were available exclusively to attendees of the annual NHLPA Pearson Awards Banquet. Their relative scarcity makes them very unique and desirable.

COMPLETE SET (3) 250.00 500.00
1 Patrick Roy 200.00 400.00
2 Jarome Iginla 75.00 150.00
3 Sean Burke 30.00 75.00

2004 Upper Deck Pearson Awards

Like the sets from previous years, these three cards were available exclusively to attendees of the annual NHLPA Pearson Awards Banquet. Their relative scarcity makes them very unique and desirable.

COMPLETE SET (3) 250.00 400.00
JS Joe Sakic 100.00 200.00
MSL Martin St.Louis 30.00 75.00
RL Roberto Luongo 100.00 200.00

1999 Upper Deck PowerDeck Athletes of the Century

4 Wayne Gretzky

1999-00 Upper Deck PowerDeck

The 1999-00 Upper Deck PowerDeck set was released as a 20-card base set featuring digital CD cards. Packaged at four cards per pack and 24-packs per box, PowerDeck carried a suggested retail price of $4.99. Auxiliary parallels were released as a paper parallel to the CD base cards, this 20-card set is randomly inserted in packs. The card backs carry an "AUX" prefix.

COMPLETE SET (20) 25.00 60.00
1 Paul Kariya 1.25 3.00
2 Teemu Selanne 1.25 3.00
3 Patrik Stefan 1.00 2.50
4 Ray Bourque 2.00 5.00
5 Sergei Samsonov 1.25 3.00
6 Dominik Hasek 2.00 5.00
7 Peter Forsberg 2.00 5.00
8 Patrick Roy 5.00 12.00
9 Brett Hull 1.50 4.00
10 Mike Modano 2.00 5.00
11 Steve Yzerman 4.00 10.00
12 Pavel Bure 1.25 3.00
13 David Legwand 1.00 2.50
14 Martin Brodeur 2.50 6.00
15 Theo Fleury 1.25 3.00
16 Eric Lindros 1.25 3.00
17 Jaromir Jagr 1.50 4.00
18 Bobby Orr 6.00 15.00
19 Gordie Howe 4.00 10.00
20 Wayne Gretzky 6.00 15.00

1999-00 Upper Deck PowerDeck Auxiliary

Released as a paper parallel to the CD base cards, this 20-card set is randomly inserted in packs. The card backs carry an "AUX" prefix.

COMPLETE SET (20) 30.00 60.00
*AUXILIARY: .2X TO .5X BASIC CARDS

1999-00 Upper Deck PowerDeck Auxiliary 1 of 1

Randomly inserted in packs, this 20-card paper parallel set is serial numbered one of one.

UNPRICED AUXILIARY 1 OF 1 ISSUED

1999-00 Upper Deck PowerDeck Powerful Moments

Randomly inserted in packs at 1:23, this 4-card CD set features great moments from Wayne Gretzky's career. The card backs carry a "PM" prefix.

COMPLETE SET (4) 20.00 40.00
COMMON GRETZKY (PM1-PM4) 6.00 15.00
*AUXILIARY: .4X TO 1X BASIC INSERTS

1999-00 Upper Deck PowerDeck Time Capsule

Randomly inserted in packs at 1:7, this 8-card CD set features a digital flashback of current players as well as some of yesterday's greats. Card backs carry a "T" prefix. Auxiliary parallels were released as a paper parallels to the CD base cards, and inserted at 1:7.

COMPLETE SET (8) 20.00 50.00
*AUXILIARY: .4X TO 1X
UNPRICED AUXILIARY 1 OF 1 ISSUED
T1 Jaromir Jagr 2.00 5.00
T2 Paul Kariya 2.00 5.00
T3 Patrick Roy 6.00 15.00
T4 Bobby Orr 8.00 20.00
T5 Dominik Hasek 3.00 8.00
T6 Gordie Howe 4.00 10.00
T7 Brett Hull 2.00 5.00
T8 Steve Yzerman 5.00 12.00

2008-09 Upper Deck Power Play

This box set (cards 1-300) was released on November 18, 2008. The update set (cards 301-400) was released on March 23, 2009.

COMPLETE SET (400) 30.00 80.00
COMP.FACT.SET (300) 25.00 50.00
COMP.FACT.UPDATE (100) 12.00 30.00
1 Francois Beauchemin .10 .25
2 George Parros .10 .25
3 Bobby Ryan .25 .60
4 Ryan Getzlaf .20 .50
5 Jean-Sebastien Giguere .15 .40
6 Corey Perry .15 .40
7 Teemu Selanne .15 .40
8 Chris Pronger .12 .30
9 Chris Kunitz .10 .25
10 Scott Niedermayer .12 .30
11 Brendan Morrison .10 .25
12 Slava Kozlov .10 .25
13 Todd White .10 .25
14 Ilya Kovalchuk .20 .50
15 Eric Perrin .10 .25
16 Colby Armstrong .10 .25
17 Kari Lehtonen .10 .25
18 Bryan Little .10 .25
19 Tobias Enstrom .15 .40
20 Jason Williams .10 .25
21 David Krejci .12 .30
22 Milan Lucic .30 .75
23 Peter Schaefer .10 .25
24 Patrice Bergeron .15 .40
25 Marc Savard .10 .25
26 Tim Thomas .15 .40
27 Zdeno Chara .10 .25
28 Marco Sturm .10 .25
29 Phil Kessel .15 .40
30 Aaron Ward .10 .25
31 Michael Ryder .12 .30
32 Jochen Hecht .10 .25
33 Ales Kotalik .10 .25
34 Tim Connolly .10 .25
35 Thomas Vanek .15 .40
36 Ryan Miller .15 .40
37 Derek Roy .10 .25
38 Jason Pominville .12 .30
39 Drew Stafford .15 .40
40 Eric Nystrom .10 .25
41 Cory Sarich .10 .25
42 Adrian Aucoin .10 .25
43 Todd Bertuzzi .15 .40
44 Miikka Kiprusoff .15 .40
45 Jarome Iginla .30 .75
46 Daymond Langkow .10 .25
47 Dion Phaneuf .15 .40
48 Matthew Lombardi .10 .25
49 Robyn Regehr .10 .25
50 Mike Cammalleri .15 .40
51 Sergei Samsonov .10 .25
52 Matt Cullen .10 .25
53 Eric Staal .25 .60
54 Rod Brind'Amour .12 .30
55 Cam Ward .15 .40
56 Justin Williams .10 .25
57 Ray Whitney .10 .25
58 Joni Pitkanen .10 .25
59 Adam Burish .12 .30
60 Dustin Byfuglien .12 .30
61 Patrick Kane .40 1.00
62 Nikolai Khabibulin .15 .40
63 Patrick Sharp .10 .25
64 Brent Seabrook .12 .30
65 Jonathan Toews .50 1.25
66 Martin Havlat .12 .30
67 Duncan Keith .12 .30
68 Brian Campbell .25 .60
69 Cristobal Huet .15 .40
70 John-Michael Liles .10 .25
71 T.J. Hensick .12 .30
72 David Jones .10 .25
73 Joe Sakic .25 .60
74 Ryan Smyth .12 .30
75 Milan Hejduk .12 .30
76 Marek Svatos .10 .25
77 Paul Stastny .15 .40
78 Wojtek Wolski .10 .25
79 Andrew Raycroft .15 .40
80 Darcy Tucker .12 .30
81 Kristian Huselius .10 .25
82 Derick Brassard RC .30 .75
83 Steve Mason RC 3.00 8.00
84 Jason Chimera .10 .25
85 Fredrik Norrena .15 .40
86 Rick Nash .15 .40
87 Kris Russell .15 .40
88 Pascal Leclaire .12 .30
89 Rostislav Klesla .10 .25
90 Jared Boll .12 .30
91 R.J. Umberger .10 .25
92 Loui Eriksson .10 .25
93 Sergei Zubov .10 .25
94 Stephane Robidas .10 .25
95 Mike Modano .15 .40
96 Brad Richards .12 .30
97 Marty Turco .12 .30
98 Mike Ribeiro .10 .25
99 Brenden Morrow .12 .30
100 Jere Lehtinen .10 .25
101 Sean Avery .12 .30
102 Johan Franzen .10 .25
103 Jiri Hudler .10 .25
104 Mikael Samuelsson .10 .25
105 Kris Draper .10 .25
106 Andreas Lilja .10 .25
107 Nicklas Lidstrom .15 .40
108 Pavel Datsyuk .15 .40
109 Chris Osgood .15 .40
110 Henrik Zetterberg .30 .75
111 Dan Cleary .15 .40
112 Tomas Holmstrom .12 .30
113 Valtteri Filppula .12 .30
114 Ty Conklin .10 .25
115 Marian Hossa .25 .60
116 Erik Cole .10 .25
117 Sheldon Souray .10 .25
118 Sam Gagner .25 .60
119 Ales Hemsky .15 .40
120 Mathieu Garon .15 .40
121 Shawn Horcoff .10 .25
122 Dustin Penner .10 .25
123 Andrew Cogliano .25 .60
124 Dwayne Roloson .12 .30
125 Shawn Matthias RC .15 .40
126 Craig Anderson .10 .25
127 Brett McLean .10 .25
128 Rostislav Olesz .10 .25
129 Tomas Vokoun .15 .40
130 Nathan Horton .10 .25
131 David Booth .10 .25
132 Stephen Weiss .10 .25
133 Jay Bouwmeester .12 .30
134 Jarret Stoll .12 .30
135 Jack Johnson .12 .30
136 Jason LaBarbera .12 .30
137 Anze Kopitar .15 .40
138 Alexander Frolov .12 .30
139 Dustin Brown .10 .25
140 Patrick O'Sullivan .12 .30
141 Andrew Brunette .10 .25
142 Brent Burns .10 .25
143 James Sheppard .15 .40
144 Derek Boogaard .10 .25
145 Marian Gaborik .25 .60
146 Niklas Backstrom .15 .40
147 Pierre-Marc Bouchard .10 .25
148 Josh Harding .12 .30
149 Mikko Koivu .15 .40
150 Mark Zidlicky .10 .25
151 Alex Tanguay .12 .30
152 Andrei Kostitsyn .12 .30
153 Sergei Kostitsyn .15 .40
154 Maxim Lapierre .10 .25
155 Saku Koivu .15 .40
156 Carey Price .50 1.25
157 Tomas Plekanec .10 .25
158 Alex Kovalev .15 .40
159 Chris Higgins .10 .25
160 Andrei Markov .12 .30
161 Guillaume Latendresse .12 .30
162 Dan Ellis .10 .25
163 Shea Weber .10 .25
164 Ryan Suter .10 .25
165 Jason Arnott .10 .25
166 Martin Erat .15 .40
167 J.P. Dumont .10 .25
168 David Legwand .12 .30
169 Bobby Holik .10 .25
170 Brian Rolston .10 .25
171 Paul Martin .10 .25
172 Jamie Langenbrunner .10 .25
173 Johnny Oduya .10 .25
174 Martin Brodeur .30 .75
175 Zach Parise .15 .40
176 Patrik Elias .15 .40
177 Brian Gionta .15 .40
178 John Madden .10 .25
179 Travis Zajac .15 .40
180 Kyle Okposo RC .30 .75
181 Mike Sillinger .10 .25
182 Blake Comeau .10 .25
183 Rick DiPietro .15 .40
184 Mike Comrie .10 .25
185 Bill Guerin .10 .25
186 Trent Hunter .10 .25
187 Nikolai Zherdev .10 .25
188 Stephen Valiquette .12 .30
189 Nigel Dawes .10 .25
190 Lauri Korpikoski RC .15 .40
191 Henrik Lundqvist .30 .75
192 Chris Drury .15 .40
193 Scott Gomez .12 .30
194 Brendan Shanahan .15 .40
195 Marc Staal .20 .50
196 Brandon Dubinsky .12 .30
197 Wade Redden .10 .25
198 Markus Naslund .15 .40
199 Chris Phillips .10 .25
200 Chris Neil .10 .25
201 Filip Kuba .10 .25
202 Anton Volchenkov .10 .25
203 Jason Spezza .20 .50
204 Dany Heatley .20 .50
205 Nick Foligno .15 .40
206 Antoine Vermette .10 .25
207 Mike Fisher .12 .30
208 Daniel Alfredsson .12 .30
209 Martin Gerber .12 .30
210 Kimmo Timonen .10 .25
211 Scottie Upshall .10 .25
212 Claude Giroux RC .30 .75
213 Mike Richards .25 .60
214 Martin Biron .12 .30
215 Daniel Briere .15 .40
216 Simon Gagne .12 .30
217 Mike Knuble .15 .40
218 Jeff Carter .15 .40
219 Olli Jokinen .10 .25
220 Kyle Turris RC .30 .75
221 Steven Reinprecht .15 .40
222 Daniel Carcillo .10 .25
223 Daniel Winnik .10 .25
224 Peter Mueller .20 .50
225 Shane Doan .10 .25
226 Ilya Bryzgalov .15 .40
227 Ed Jovanovski .10 .25
228 Martin Hanzal .12 .30
229 Miroslav Satan .10 .25
230 Ruslan Fedotenko .10 .25
231 Tyler Kennedy .12 .30
232 Brooks Orpik .10 .25
233 Maxime Talbot .12 .30
234 Sidney Crosby .75 2.00
235 Marc-Andre Fleury .15 .40
236 Evgeni Malkin .40 1.00
237 Sergei Gonchar .12 .30
238 Jordan Staal .25 .60
239 Ryan Whitney .15 .40
240 Rob Blake .15 .40
241 Ryane Clowe .10 .25
242 Joe Pavelski .10 .25
243 Torrey Mitchell .15 .40
244 Joe Thornton .25 .60
245 Evgeni Nabokov .15 .40
246 Jonathan Cheechoo .15 .40
247 Milan Michalek .15 .40
248 Patrick Marleau .12 .30
249 Dan Boyle .12 .30
250 Chris Mason .12 .30
251 Andy McDonald .10 .25
252 David Backes .10 .25
253 David Perron .12 .30
254 Paul Kariya .15 .40

255 Manny Legace .12 .30
256 Erik Johnson .20 .50
257 Brad Boyes .12 .30
258 Lee Stempniak .10 .25
259 Keith Tkachuk .12 .30
260 Radim Vrbata .10 .25
261 Ryan Malone .10 .25
262 Mark Recchi .12 .30
263 Vaclav Prospal .10 .25
264 Jussi Jokinen .10 .25
265 Michel Ouellet .10 .25
266 Vincent Lecavalier .15 .40
267 Mike Smith .12 .30
268 Matt Carle .10 .25
269 Martin St. Louis .15 .40
270 Paul Ranger .10 .25
271 Andrej Meszaros .10 .25
272 Olaf Kolzig .15 .40
273 Ian White .10 .25
274 Pavel Kubina .10 .25
275 Jason Blake .10 .25
276 Robbie Earl RC .12 .30
277 Mats Sundin .15 .40
278 Vesa Toskala .15 .40
279 Alexander Steen .15 .40
280 Tomas Kaberle .10 .25
281 Nikolai Antropov .12 .30
282 Matt Stajan .12 .30
283 Jiri Tlusty .15 .40
284 Steve Bernier .10 .25
285 Pavol Demitra .10 .25
286 Taylor Pyatt .10 .25
287 Kevin Bieksa .10 .25
288 Roberto Luongo .25 .60
289 Daniel Sedin .15 .40
290 Ryan Kesler .10 .25
291 Alexander Edler .12 .30
292 Henrik Sedin .15 .40
293 Jose Theodore .15 .40
294 Brooks Laich .12 .30
295 Tomas Fleischmann .10 .25
296 Alexander Ovechkin .60 1.50
297 Nicklas Backstrom .30 .75
298 Sergei Fedorov .25 .60
299 Mike Green .10 .25
300 Alexander Semin .15 .40
301 Brett Festerling RC .20 .50
302 Andrew Ebbett RC .25 .60
303 Zach Bogosian RC .50 1.25
304 Boris Valabik RC .30 .75
305 Nathan Oystrick RC .25 .60
306 Blake Wheeler RC .60 1.50
307 Nathan Gerbe RC .50 1.25
308 Adam Pardy RC .25 .60
309 Brandon Sutter RC .30 .75
310 Zach Boychuk RC .40 1.00
311 Cristobal Huet .25 .60
312 Kris Versteeg .40 1.00
313 Brian Campbell .40 1.00
314 Chris Stewart RC .30 .75
315 Nikita Filatov RC 1.00 2.50
316 Jakub Voracek RC .50 1.25
317 Adam Pineault RC .25 .60
318 Dan LaCosta RC .30 .75
319 Tom Sestito RC .20 .50
320 Derek Dorsett RC .30 .75
321 Mike Commodore .15 .40
322 Fabian Brunnstrom RC .40 1.00
323 Mark Fistric RC .20 .50
324 James Neal RC .40 1.00
325 Mark Parrish .15 .40
326 Marian Hossa .40 1.00
327 Justin Abdelkader RC .50 1.25
328 Jonathan Ericsson RC .40 1.00
329 Darren Helm RC .40 1.00
330 Jeff Drouin-Deslauriers .15 .40
331 Steve MacIntyre RC .25 .60
332 Theo Peckham RC .25 .60
333 Michael Frolik RC .50 1.25
334 Kenndal McArdle RC .25 .60
335 Michal Repik RC .30 .75
336 Drew Doughty RC .75 2.00
337 Brian Boyle RC .25 .60
338 Oscar Moller RC .25 .60
339 Trevor Lewis RC .25 .60
340 Erik Ersberg RC .25 .60
341 Wayne Simmonds RC .25 .60
342 Colton Gillies RC .25 .60
343 Antti Miettinen .15 .40
344 Alex Tanguay .20 .50
345 Matt D'Agostini RC .40 1.00
346 Ben Maxwell RC .40 1.00
347 Patric Hornqvist RC .25 .60
348 Ryan Jones RC .30 .75
349 Petr Vrana RC .30 .75
350 Scott Clemmensen .15 .40
351 Matthew Halischuk RC .30 .75
352 Patrick Davis RC .20 .50
353 Josh Bailey RC .40 1.00
354 Mark Streit .15 .40
355 Peter Mannino RC .15 .40
356 Mitch Fritz RC .20 .50
357 Markus Naslund .20 .50
358 Brian Lee RC .25 .60
359 Ilya Zubov RC .25 .60
360 Alex Auld .15 .40
361 Jared Ross RC .20 .50
362 Luca Sbisa RC .40 1.00
363 Nate Raduns RC .15 .40
364 Andreas Nodl RC .25 .60
365 Jonathon Kalinski RC .25 .60
366 Olli Jokinen .15 .40
367 Mikkel Boedker RC .40 1.00
368 Viktor Tikhonov RC .25 .60
369 Kevin Porter RC .20 .50
370 Janne Pesonen RC .20 .50
371 Paul Bissonnette RC .30 .75
372 Alex Goligoski RC .50 1.25
373 Jon Filewich RC .20 .50
374 Ryan Stone RC .25 .60
375 Miroslav Satan .15 .40
376 Brad Staubitz RC .20 .50
377 Rob Blake .25 .60
378 Devin Setoguchi .25 .60
379 Jamie McGinn RC .25 .60
380 Alex Pietrangelo RC .40 1.00
381 Patrik Berglund RC .60 1.50
382 T.J. Oshie RC .60 1.50
383 Ben Bishop RC .40 1.00
384 Chris Porter RC .25 .60
385 Cam Paddock RC .15 .40
386 Radek Smolenak RC .30 .75
387 Steven Stamkos RC 3.00 8.00
388 Vladimir Mihalik RC .25 .60
389 Luke Schenn RC .75 2.00
390 Nikolai Kulemin RC .25 .60
391 Niklas Hagman .15 .40
392 Mikhail Grabovski .40 1.00
393 Andre Deveaux RC .25 .60
394 Jonas Frogren RC .30 .75
395 John Mitchell RC .25 .60
396 Justin Pogge RC .50 1.25
397 Cory Schneider RC .50 1.25
398 Mats Sundin .25 .60
399 Tyler Sloan RC .30 .75
400 Karl Alzner RC .40 1.00

2008-09 Upper Deck Power Play Jerseys

STATED ODDS 1 PER FACT.SET
PPAO Alexander Ovechkin 20.00 50.00
PPEM Evgeni Malkin 12.00 30.00
PPHL Henrik Lundqvist 10.00 25.00
PPHZ Henrik Zetterberg 10.00 25.00
PPIK Ilya Kovalchuk 6.00 15.00
PPJC Jonathan Cheechoo 5.00 12.00
PPJG Jean-Sebastien Giguere 5.00 12.00
PPJI Jarome Iginla 10.00 25.00
PPJS Jason Spezza 6.00 15.00
PPJT Joe Thornton 8.00 20.00
PPKL Kari Lehtonen 3.00 8.00
PPKT Keith Tkachuk 4.00 10.00
PPMA Marc-Andre Fleury 5.00 12.00
PPMB Martin Brodeur 10.00 25.00
PPMG Marian Gaborik 8.00 20.00
PPMM Mike Modano 5.00 12.00
PPMN Markus Naslund 5.00 12.00
PPMR Mike Richards 8.00 20.00
PPMS Mats Sundin 5.00 12.00
PPMT Marty Turco
PPNL Nicklas Lidstrom
PPPB Patrice Bergeron 5.00 12.00
PPPD Pavel Datsyuk 5.00 12.00
PPPK Paul Kariya 5.00 12.00
PPRL Roberto Luongo 8.00 20.00
PPRM Ryan Miller 5.00 12.00
PPRN Rick Nash
PPSC Sidney Crosby 25.00 60.00
PPSK Saku Koivu 5.00 12.00
PPVL Vincent Lecavalier 5.00 12.00

1999-00 Upper Deck Retro

Released as a 109-card set, Upper Deck Retro features players from both today and yesterday on a "throw-back" style base card enhanced with bronze foil stamping. Each Retro box was packaged in an actual Wayne Gretzky lunchbox, contained 24-packs per box with six cards per pack and carried a suggested retail price of $4.99. Card number 82 was supposed to be Gordie Howe, but a licensing agreement was never reached. A few of the Howe cards are known to exist with a crimp of Jeff Gordon over Howe's head.

COMPLETE SET (109) 20.00 40.00
1 Paul Kariya .20 .50
2 Teemu Selanne .20 .50
3 Jim McKenzie .02 .10
4 Ray Bourque .20 .50
5 Sergei Samsonov .15 .40
6 Joe Thornton .20 .50
7 Dominik Hasek .40 1.00
8 Miroslav Satan .15 .40
9 Michael Peca .15 .40
10 Todd Simpson .02 .10
11 Valeri Bure .02 .10
12 Jarome Iginla .25 .60
13 Kent Manderville .25 .60
14 Keith Primeau .02 .10
15 Sami Kapanen .02 .10
16 Mark Janssens .02 .10
17 Tony Amonte .15 .40
18 Doug Gilmour .15 .40
19 Peter Forsberg .50 1.25
20 Patrick Roy 1.00 2.50
21 Joe Sakic .40 1.00
22 Theo Fleury .02 .10
23 Chris Drury .15 .40
24 Mike Modano .20 .50
25 Brett Hull .20 .50
26 Ed Belfour .20 .50
27 Steve Yzerman 1.00 2.50
28 Sergei Fedorov .30 .75
29 Brendan Shanahan .20 .50
30 Chris Chelios .20 .50
31 Doug Weight .15 .40
32 Bill Guerin .15 .40
33 Tom Poti .02 .10
34 Gord Murphy .02 .10
35 Pavel Bure .20 .50
36 Mark Parrish .15 .40
37 Rob Blake .15 .40
38 Pavel Rosa .02 .10
39 Luc Robitaille .15 .40
40 Stephane Quintal .02 .10
41 Saku Koivu .20 .50
42 Bob Boughner .02 .10
43 David Legwand .15 .40
44 Mike Dunham .15 .40
45 Martin Brodeur .50 1.25
46 Scott Stevens .15 .40
47 John Madden RC .20 .50
48 Vadim Sharifijanov .02 .10
49 Wayne Gretzky 1.25 3.00
50 Manny Malhotra .02 .10
51 Brian Leetch .15 .40
52 Mike Richter .20 .50
53 Eric Brewer .02 .10
54 Alexei Yashin .02 .10
55 Marian Hossa .20 .50
56 Chris Phillips .02 .10
57 Eric Lindros .20 .50
58 John LeClair .20 .50
59 Mark Recchi .15 .40
60 Jeremy Roenick .30 .75
61 Keith Tkachuk .20 .50
62 Nikolai Khabibulin .15 .40
63 Robert Esche RC .15 .40
64 Jaromir Jagr .30 .75
65 Martin Straka .02 .10
66 Jeff Friesen .02 .10
67 Vincent Damphousse .02 .10
68 Chris Pronger .15 .40
69 Pavol Demitra .15 .40
70 Al MacInnis .15 .40
71 Paul Mara .02 .10
72 Vincent Lecavalier .20 .50
73 Sergei Berezin .02 .10
74 Mats Sundin .20 .50
75 Curtis Joseph .20 .50
76 Markus Naslund .20 .50
77 Mark Messier .20 .50
78 Bill Muckalt .02 .10
79 Peter Bondra .20 .50
80 Adam Oates .15 .40
81 Bobby Orr 1.00 2.50
82 Gordie Howe SP
(embossed with Gordon profile)
83 Mario Lemieux 1.00 2.50
84 Maurice Richard .50 1.25
85 Jean Beliveau .20 .50
86 Bobby Hull .40 1.00
87 Terry Sawchuk .40 1.00
88 Eddie Shore .25 .60
89 Alex Delvecchio .25 .60
90 Jacques Plante .25 .60
91 Stan Mikita .20 .50
92 Gerry Cheevers .40 1.00
93 Glenn Hall .25 .60
94 Phil Esposito .40 1.00
95 Lanny McDonald .25 .60
96 Mike Bossy .25 .60
97 Ted Lindsay .25 .60
98 Red Kelly .25 .60
99 Bobby Clarke .25 .60
100 Larry Robinson .25 .60
101 Ken Dryden .50 1.25
102 Vladislav Tretiak RC .50 1.25
103 Marcel Dionne .25 .60
104 Bernie Geoffrion .20 .50
105 Johnny Bucyk .25 .60
106 Brad Park .25 .60
107 Tony Esposito .20 .50
108 Jari Kurri .25 .60
109 Henri Richard .25 .60
110 Mike Gartner .25 .60

1999-00 Upper Deck Retro Gold

Randomly inserted in packs, this 109-card set parallels the base Retro set and is enhanced with gold foil highlights. Each card is sequentially numbered to 150.

*GOLD: 12X TO 30X BASIC CARDS

1999-00 Upper Deck Retro Platinum

Randomly inserted in packs, this 109-card set parallels the base Retro set and is enhanced with platinum silver foil highlights. Each card is numbered one of one.

UNPRICED PLATINUM PRINT RUN 1

1999-00 Upper Deck Retro Distant Replay

Randomly inserted in packs at the rate on 1:11, this 14-card set features black and white photography on a card enhanced with gold foil highlights. Card number DR11 was not released. Level 2 parallels were also released and inserted randomly, these cards were numbered out of 100.

COMPLETE SET (14) 30.00 60.00
*LEVEL 2/100: 6X TO 15X BASIC INSERTS
DR1 Ray Bourque 1.50 4.00
DR2 Martin Brodeur 2.50 6.00
DR3 Jaromir Jagr 1.50 4.00
DR4 Paul Kariya 1.00 2.50
DR5 Steve Yzerman 5.00 12.00
DR6 Mark Messier 1.00 2.50
DR7 Patrick Roy 5.00 12.00
DR8 Dominik Hasek 2.50 5.00
DR9 Wayne Gretzky 6.00 15.00
DR10 Bobby Orr 5.00 12.00
DR12 Mario Lemieux 5.00 12.00
DR13 Lanny McDonald 1.00 2.50
DR14 Maurice Richard 3.00 8.00
DR15 Vladislav Tretiak 2.00 5.00

1999-00 Upper Deck Retro Epic Gretzky

Randomly inserted in packs at the rate of 1:23, this 10-card set spotlights Wayne Gretzky. Base cards feature action photography set against a blue background with gold foil highlights. Level 2 parallels were also released and inserted randomly, these cards were numbered out of 50.

COMPLETE SET (10) 75.00 150.00
COMMON GRETZKY (EG1-EG10) 8.00 15.00
*LEVEL 2/50: 3X TO 8X BASIC INSERTS 50.00 125.00

1999-00 Upper Deck Retro Generation

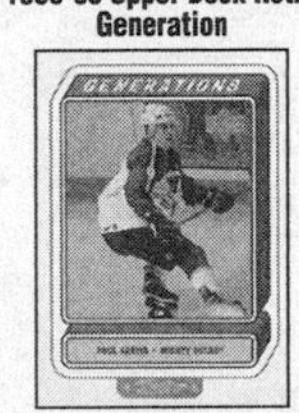

Randomly inserted in packs at the rate of 1:3, this 29-card set features tow players of the past on separate cards paired with another card featuring a player of today who has assumed a modern day role of a legend. Card number G2A was not released. Level 2 parallels were also released and inserted randomly, these cards were numbered out of 500.

COMPLETE SET (29) 20.00 40.00
*LEVEL 2/500: 1.5X TO 4X BASIC INSERTS
G1A Bobby Orr 2.50 6.00
G1B Brian Leetch .40 1.00
G1C Bryan Berard .40 1.00
G2B Bobby Clarke .75 2.00
G2C Keith Tkachuk .75 2.00
G3A Glenn Hall .75 2.00
G3B Patrick Roy 2.50 6.00
G3C Jean-Marc Pelletier .40 1.00
G4A Eddie Shore .75 2.00
G4B Bobby Orr 2.50 6.00
G4C Ray Bourque .75 2.00
G5A Jean Beliveau 1.00 2.50
G5B Mario Lemieux 2.50 6.00
G5C Vincent Lecavalier .75 2.00
G6A Maurice Richard 1.50 4.00
G6B Pavel Bure .75 2.00
G6C Sergei Samsonov .40 1.00
G7A Stan Mikita 1.00 2.50
G7B Theo Fleury .40 1.00
G7C Paul Kariya .75 2.00
G8A Jari Kurri .75 2.00
G8B Teemu Selanne .75 2.00
G8C Olli Jokinen .40 1.00
G9A Phil Esposito 1.25 3.00
G9B Brendan Shanahan .75 2.00
G9C Mark Parrish .40 1.00
G10A Terry Sawchuk 1.25 3.00
G10B Dominik Hasek 1.00 2.50
G10C Jean-Sebastien Giguere .40 1.00

1999-00 Upper Deck Retro Inkredible

Randomly inserted in packs at the rate of 1:23, this 29-card set features authentic player autographs.

AD Alex Delvecchio 8.00 20.00
BC Bobby Clarke 12.50 30.00
BG Bernie Geoffrion 15.00 40.00
BO Bobby Orr 175.00 350.00
BP Brad Park 8.00 20.00
DW Doug Weight 4.00 10.00
GC Gerry Cheevers 12.50 30.00
KP Keith Primeau 4.00 10.00
LM Lanny McDonald 8.00 20.00
MB Mike Bossy 8.00 20.00
MD Marcel Dionne 8.00 20.00
ML Mario Lemieux 150.00 250.00
PE Phil Esposito 15.00 40.00
RB Ray Bourque 25.00 60.00
SM Stan Mikita 10.00 25.00
SS Sergei Samsonov 4.00 10.00
SY Steve Yzerman 50.00 100.00
TA Tony Amonte 4.00 10.00
TE Tony Esposito 10.00 25.00
TL Ted Lindsay 8.00 20.00
VL Vincent Lecavalier 12.50 30.00
VT Vladislav Tretiak 25.00 60.00
WG Wayne Gretzky 200.00 400.00
BOH Bobby Hull 15.00 40.00
BRH Brett Hull 12.00 30.00
JEB Jean Beliveau 15.00 40.00
JOB John Bucyk 8.00 20.00
MAR Maurice Richard 100.00 200.00
PAB Pavel Bure 8.00 20.00

1999-00 Upper Deck Retro Inkredible Level 2

Parallel to the regular Inkredible set, these cards are randomly inserted into packs, and feature a serial number out of 25.

*LEVEL 2/25: 1.5X TO 4X BASIC INSERTS
BO Bobby Orr 250.00 600.00
ML Mario Lemieux 200.00 400.00
SY Steve Yzerman 200.00 400.00
WG Wayne Gretzky 600.00 1000.00
MAR Maurice Richard 150.00 400.00

1999-00 Upper Deck Retro Lunchboxes

Each box of Retro was packaged in a Wayne Gretzky lunchbox showcasing the great one in his Kings, Oilers, Ranger jerseys, as well as a special tribute lunchbox.

COMPLETE SET (4) 35.00 70.00
1 Wayne Gretzky Kings 7.50 15.00
2 Wayne Gretzky Oilers 7.50 15.00
3 Wayne Gretzky Rangers 7.50 15.00
4 Wayne Gretzky Tribute 15.00 40.00

1999-00 Upper Deck Retro Memento

Randomly inserted in packs, this 5-card set features hockey's greats coupled with a swatch of game used memorabilia.

RM1 Wayne Gretzky 100.00 200.00
RM2 Marcel Dionne 12.00 30.00
RM3 Mario Lemieux 50.00 100.00
RM4 Phil Esposito 50.00 100.00
RM5 Ken Dryden 75.00 150.00

1999-00 Upper Deck Retro Turn of the Century

Randomly inserted in packs at the rate of 1:23, this 14-card set features Light F/X holofoil technology and players from the past and present.

COMPLETE SET (14) 40.00 80.00
TC1 Vincent Lecavalier 2.00 5.00
TC2 Martin Brodeur 2.50 6.00
TC3 Jaromir Jagr 1.50 4.00
TC4 Paul Kariya 2.00 5.00
TC5 Steve Yzerman 5.00 12.00
TC6 Ray Bourque 1.50 4.00
TC7 Patrick Roy 5.00 12.00
TC8 Dominik Hasek 2.00 5.00
TC9 Wayne Gretzky 6.00 15.00
TC10 Bobby Clarke .75 2.00
TC11 Larry Robinson .75 2.00
TC13 Mario Lemieux 5.00 12.00
TC14 Maurice Richard 2.50 6.00
TC15 Bobby Orr 5.00 12.00

2006-07 Upper Deck Rookie Class

COMPLETE SET (50) 6.00 15.00
1 Shea Weber .30 .75
2 Matt Carle .30 .75
3 Patrick O'Sullivan .40 1.00
4 Phil Kessel .75 2.00
5 Guillaume Latendresse .75 2.00
6 Loui Eriksson .30 .75
7 Luc Bourdon .30 .75
8 Enver Lisin .10 .25
9 Evgeni Malkin 2.00 5.00
10 Dustin Boyd .30 .75
11 Mark Stuart .10 .25
12 Eric Fehr .10 .25
13 Noah Welch .10 .25
14 Anze Kopitar 1.25 3.00
15 Travis Zajac .40 1.00
16 Jordan Staal 1.50 4.00
17 Ladislav Smid .10 .25
18 Alexander Radulov .75 2.00
19 Ryan Potulny .10 .25
20 Marc-Antoine Pouliot .10 .25
21 Jarkko Immonen .10 .25
22 Paul Stastny 1.25 3.00
23 Alexei Kaigorodov .10 .25
24 Dave Bolland .10 .25
25 Nigel Dawes .10 .25
26 Jeremy Williams .10 .25
27 Marc-Edouard Vlasic .10 .25
28 Keith Yandle .10 .25
29 Matt Lashoff .10 .25
30 Ian White .10 .25
31 Alexei Mikhnov .10 .25
32 Tomas Kopecky .20 .50
33 Konstantin Pushkaryov .10 .25
34 Kristopher Letang .10 .25
35 Michael Blunden .10 .25
36 Brandon Prust .10 .25
37 Dustin Byfuglien .10 .25
38 Ben Ondrus .10 .25
39 Brendan Bell .10 .25
40 Janis Sprukts .10 .25
41 Ryan Shannon .10 .25
42 Shane O'Brien .10 .25
43 Patrick Thoresen .10 .25
44 Nathan McIver .10 .25
45 Drew Stafford .60 1.50
46 Alexander Edler .10 .25
47 Yan Stastny .10 .25
48 Kelly Guard .10 .25
49 Nate Thompson .10 .25
50 Adam Burish .10 .25

2007-08 Upper Deck Rookie Class

COMPLETE SET (50) 8.00 20.00
COMP.FACT.SET (51) 10.00 25.00
1 Bobby Ryan .60 1.50
2 Ondrej Pavelec .25 .60
3 Patrick Kane 1.00 2.50
4 Kris Russell .20 .50
5 Matt Niskanen .15 .40
6 Andrew Cogliano .40 1.00
7 Jonathan Bernier .40 1.00
8 Marc Staal .40 1.00
9 Nick Foligno .25 .60
10 Peter Mueller .50 1.25
11 Jiri Tlusty .40 1.00
12 Brett Sterling .15 .40
13 Petr Kalus .15 .40
14 Rob Schremp .20 .50
15 Andy Greene .15 .40
16 Frans Nielsen .15 .40
17 Martin Hanzal .20 .50
18 Devin Setoguchi .30 .75
19 Matt Smaby .15 .40
20 James Sheppard .15 .40
21 Kyle Chipchura .25 .60
22 Ryan Parent .20 .50
23 David Krejci .30 .75
24 Lauri Tukonen .15 .40
25 Anton Stralman .20 .50
26 Tobias Enstrom .25 .60
27 Tyler Kennedy .25 .60
28 Mason Raymond .40 1.00
29 Thomas Greiss .25 .60
30 Drew Miller .15 .40
31 Curtis McElhinney .25 .60
32 Ryan Callahan .25 .60
33 Brian Elliott .20 .50
34 Vladimir Sobotka .20 .50
35 Jonathan Sigalet .15 .40
36 Ville Koistinen .15 .40
37 Torrey Mitchell .20 .50
38 David Perron .25 .60
39 Jannik Hansen .15 .40
40 Chris Bourque .20 .50
41 Milan Lucic .40 1.00
42 Tuukka Rask .40 1.00
43 Jonathan Toews 1.00 2.50
44 Sam Gagner .30 .75
45 Jack Johnson .25 .60
46 Carey Price .75 2.00
47 Nicklas Bergfors .20 .50
48 Erik Johnson .30 .75
49 Bryan Little .20 .50
50 Nicklas Backstrom .60 1.50

2007-08 Upper Deck Rookie Class C-Card Insert

STATED ODDS 1 PER BOX SET
CC1 Jonathan Toews 2.50 6.00
CC2 Patrick Kane 2.50 6.00
CC3 Carey Price 2.00 5.00
CC4 Jack Johnson .60 1.50
CC5 Nicklas Backstrom 1.50 4.00
CC6 Sam Gagner .75 2.00

2008-09 Upper Deck Rookie Class

This set was released on February 13, 2009. The base set consists of 50 cards.

COMP.FACT.SET (51) 10.00 25.00
COMPLETE SET (50) 8.00 20.00
1 Steven Stamkos 2.00 5.00
2 Michael Frolik .50 1.25
3 Drew Doughty .75 2.00
4 Claude Giroux .50 1.25
5 Zach Bogosian .50 1.25
6 Mark Fistric .20 .50
7 Alex Pietrangelo .40 1.00
8 Vladimir Mihalik .25 .60
9 Luke Schenn .75 2.00
10 Nikita Filatov 1.00 2.50
11 Patrik Berglund .60 1.50
12 Karl Alzner .40 1.00
13 Mikkel Boedker .40 1.00
14 Justin Abdelkader .50 1.25
15 Brian Boyle .25 .60
16 Adam Pineault .25 .60
17 Jonathan Ericsson .40 1.00
18 Shawn Matthias .25 .60
19 Zach Boychuk .40 1.00
20 Cory Schneider .50 1.25
21 Josh Bailey .40 1.00
22 Oscar Moller .25 .60
23 Colton Gillies .25 .60
24 Matt D'Agostini .40 1.00
25 Luca Sbisa .40 1.00
26 Lauri Korpikoski .25 .60
27 Robbie Earl .20 .50
28 Andreas Nodl .25 .60
29 Blake Wheeler .60 1.50
30 Dan LaCosta .30 .75
31 Steve Mason .60 1.50
32 Viktor Tikhonov .25 .60
33 Tom Sestito .20 .50
34 Fabian Brunnstrom .40 1.00
35 Teddy Purcell .25 .60
36 Kyle Okposo .50 1.25
37 Brian Lee .25 .60
38 Kyle Turris .50 1.25
39 Alex Goligoski .50 1.25
40 Patric Hornqvist .25 .60
41 Petr Vrana .30 .75
42 T.J. Oshie .60 1.50
43 Nikolai Kulemin .25 .60
44 Boris Valabik .30 .75
45 Brandon Sutter .30 .75
46 Derick Brassard .50 1.25
47 Jakub Voracek .50 1.25
48 James Neal .40 1.00
49 Darren Helm .40 1.00
50 Ilya Zubov .25 .60

2008-09 Upper Deck Rookie Class Autographs

UNPRICED AUTO ODDS 1:20 FACT.SET
1 Steven Stamkos
2 Michael Frolik
3 Drew Doughty
5 Zach Bogosian
6 Mark Fistric
7 Alex Pietrangelo
8 Vladimir Mihalik
9 Luke Schenn
10 Nikita Filatov
11 Patrik Berglund
13 Mikkel Boedker
14 Justin Abdelkader
15 Brian Boyle
16 Adam Pineault
17 Jonathan Ericsson
18 Shawn Matthias
19 Zach Boychuk
22 Oscar Moller
23 Colton Gillies
25 Luca Sbisa
26 Lauri Korpikoski
27 Robbie Earl
29 Blake Wheeler
30 Dan LaCosta
31 Steve Mason 100.00 200.00
32 Viktor Tikhonov
33 Tom Sestito
34 Fabian Brunnstrom
37 Brian Lee
38 Kyle Turris
40 Patric Hornqvist
41 Petr Vrana
42 T.J. Oshie
43 Nikolai Kulemin
44 Boris Valabik
45 Brandon Sutter
46 Derick Brassard
47 Jakub Voracek
48 James Neal
49 Darren Helm
50 Ilya Zubov

2008-09 Upper Deck Rookie Class C-Card Insert

ONE PER FACTORY SET
C1 Steven Stamkos 5.00 12.00
C2 Kyle Turris 1.25 3.00
C3 Drew Doughty 2.00 5.00
C4 Luke Schenn 2.00 5.00
C5 Blake Wheeler 1.50 4.00
C6 Derick Brassard 1.25 3.00
C7 Cory Schneider 1.25 3.00
C8 Colton Gillies .60 1.50
C9 Fabian Brunnstrom 1.00 2.50
C10 Kyle Okposo 1.25 3.00
C11 Nikita Filatov 2.50 6.00
C12 Nikolai Kulemin .60 1.50
C13 Jakub Voracek 1.25 3.00
C14 Brandon Sutter .75 2.00

2000-01 Upper Deck Rookie Update

This product updated several Upper Deck sets. All cards are listed with their parent set.

CARDS LISTED UNDER ORIGINAL BASE SETS

2001-02 Upper Deck Rookie Update Signs of History

This limited autograph card was randomly inserted into packs of UD Rookie Update. Little is known about the card other than it's serial-numbering out of 33.

STATED PRINT RUN 33 SER.#'d SETS
1 Patrick Roy AU

2002-03 Upper Deck Rookie Update

Released in May 2003, Rookie Update consisted of a 176-card base set, a jersey card insert set, an autograph insert set and update cards for SP Authentic, SPx, UD Foundations and UD Classic Portraits. In the base set, cards 101-116 were serial-numbered to 999, cards 117-148 and 173-176 were serial-numbered to 1500, and cards 163-171 were serial-numbered to 199. Cards 163-171 carried dual autographs. Cards 149-162 had three different versions, A, B and C. Each version was serial-numbered with the 'A' cards being serial-numbered from 1 to 400; the 'B' cards being serial-numbered 401-800 and the 'C' versions serial-numbered 801-1200 for a total of 1200 cards. Cards 149-162 carried jersey swatches of each player pictured.

COMP.SET w/o SP's (100) 20.00 40.00
1 Paul Kariya .30 .75
2 Adam Oates .25 .60
3 Jean-Sebastien Giguere .25 .60
4 Sandis Ozolinsh .10 .25
5 Dany Heatley .40 1.00

6 Ilya Kovalchuk .40 1.00
7 Patrik Stefan .10 .25
8 Dan McGillis .10 .25
9 Joe Thornton .50 1.25
10 Sergei Samsonov .25 .60
11 Jeff Hackett .25 .60
12 Glen Murray .10 .25
13 Miroslav Satan .25 .60
14 Martin Biron .25 .60
15 Daniel Briere .10 .25
16 Chris Drury .25 .60
17 Jarome Iginla .40 1.00
18 Roman Turek .25 .60
19 Pavel Brendl .10 .25
20 Rod Brind'Amour .25 .60
21 Ron Francis .25 .60
22 Tyler Arnason .25 .60
23 Jocelyn Thibault .25 .60
24 Bryan Marchment .10 .25
25 Joe Sakic .60 1.50
26 Peter Forsberg .75 2.00
27 Patrick Roy 1.50 4.00
28 Rob Blake .25 .60
29 Geoff Sanderson .10 .25
30 Marc Denis .25 .60
31 Mike Modano .50 1.25
32 Bill Guerin .25 .60
33 Marty Turco .25 .60
34 Steve Yzerman 1.50 4.00
35 Brendan Shanahan .30 .75
36 Brett Hull .40 1.00
37 Curtis Joseph .30 .75
38 Nicklas Lidstrom .30 .75
39 Sergei Fedorov .50 1.25
40 Mathieu Schneider .10 .25
41 Mike Comrie .25 .60
42 Tommy Salo .25 .60
43 Olli Jokinen .25 .60
44 Kristian Huselius .10 .25
45 Roberto Luongo .40 1.00
46 Adam Deadmarsh .10 .25
47 Zigmund Palffy .25 .60
48 Felix Potvin .30 .75
49 Marian Gaborik .60 1.50
50 Gordie Howe 1.50 4.00
51 Pascal Dupuis .10 .25
52 Saku Koivu .30 .75
53 Marcel Hossa .10 .25
54 Jose Theodore .40 1.00
55 David Legwand .25 .60
56 Scott Hartnell .10 .25
57 Tomas Vokoun .25 .60
58 John Madden .10 .25
59 Scott Gomez .10 .25
60 Martin Brodeur .75 2.00
61 Alexei Yashin .10 .25
62 Mark Parrish .10 .25
63 Janne Niinimaa .10 .25
64 Alex Kovalev .25 .60
65 Pavel Bure .30 .75
66 Mike Dunham .25 .60
67 Mark Messier .30 .75
68 Brian Leetch .25 .60
69 Daniel Alfredsson .25 .60
70 Marian Hossa .30 .75
71 Patrick Lalime .25 .60
72 Jeremy Roenick .40 1.00
73 John LeClair .30 .75
74 Tony Amonte .25 .60
75 Gordie Howe 1.50 4.00
76 Roman Cechmanek .25 .60
77 Brian Boucher .25 .60
78 Shane Doan .10 .25
79 Mario Lemieux 2.00 5.00
80 Martin Straka .10 .25
81 Sebastien Caron .25 .60
82 Alexei Morozov .10 .25
83 Doug Weight .30 .75
84 Keith Tkachuk .30 .75
85 Chris Osgood .25 .60
86 Teemu Selanne .30 .75
87 Kyle McLaren .10 .25
88 Evgeni Nabokov .25 .60
89 Martin St. Louis .25 .60
90 Nikolai Khabibulin .30 .75
91 Doug Gilmour .25 .60
92 Mats Sundin .30 .75
93 Owen Nolan .25 .60
94 Ed Belfour .30 .75
95 Todd Bertuzzi .30 .75
96 Markus Naslund .30 .75
97 Dan Cloutier .25 .60
98 Jaromir Jagr .50 1.25
99 Olaf Kolzig .25 .60
100 Michael Nylander .10 .25
101 Gordie Howe RRM 3.00 8.00
102 Wayne Gretzky RRM 4.00 10.00
103 Bobby Orr RRM 8.00 20.00
104 Patrick Roy RRM 3.00 8.00
105 Mario Lemieux RRM 4.00 10.00
106 Joe Thornton RRM 1.00 2.50
107 Martin Brodeur RRM 1.50 4.00
108 Steve Yzerman RRM 3.00 8.00
109 Jaromir Jagr RRM 1.00 2.50
110 Paul Kariya RRM .60 1.50
111 Jarome Iginla RRM 1.00 2.50
112 Joe Sakic RRM 1.25 3.00
113 Mats Sundin RRM .60 1.50
114 Ilya Kovalchuk RRM .75 2.00
115 Marian Gaborik RRM .75 2.00
116 Mike Modano RRM 1.00 2.50
117 Carlo Colaiacovo RC 2.00 5.00
118 Jay Bouwmeester RC 4.00 10.00
119 Ari Ahonen RC 2.00 5.00
120 Patrick Boileau RC 2.00 5.00
121 Mike Komisarek RC 2.00 5.00
122 Cristobal Huet RC 8.00 20.00
123 Josh Harding RC 12.00 30.00
124 Chris Schmidt RC 2.00 5.00
125 Niko Dimitrakos RC 2.00 5.00
126 Ryan Bayda RC 2.00 5.00
127 Radoslav Hecl RC 2.00 5.00
128 Burke Henry RC 2.00 5.00
129 Frederic Cloutier RC 2.00 5.00
130 Tomas Kurka RC 2.00 5.00
131 John Tripp RC 2.00 5.00
132 Francois Beauchemin RC 2.00 5.00
133 Brandon Reid RC 2.00 5.00
134 Tomas Surovy RC 2.00 5.00
135 Chad Wiseman RC 2.00 5.00
136 Jason Bacashihua RC 2.00 5.00
137 Jesse Fibiger RC 2.00 5.00
138 Marc-Andre Bergeron RC 2.00 5.00
139 Ryan Miller RC 10.00 25.00
140 Ryan Kraft RC 2.00 5.00
141 Simon Gamache RC 2.00 5.00
142 Rob Davison RC 2.00 5.00
143 Jason King RC 2.00 5.00
144 Brad Defauw RC 2.00 5.00
145 Miroslav Zalesak RC 2.00 5.00
146 Sean McMorrow RC 2.00 5.00
147 Mike Siklenka RC 2.00 5.00
148 Doug Janik RC 2.00 5.00
149A A.Svitov RC/B.Shanahan 4.00 10.00
149B A.Svitov RC/T.Bertuzzi 4.00 10.00
149C A.Svitov RC/J.LeClair 4.00 10.00
150A A.Smirnov RC/A.Yashin 4.00 10.00
150B A.Smirnov RC/T.Bertuzzi 4.00 10.00
150C A.Smirnov RC/J.LeClair 4.00 10.00
151A B.Orpik RC/R.Blake 4.00 10.00
151B B.Orpik RC/E.Jovanoski 4.00 10.00
151C B.Orpik RC/S.Stevens 4.00 10.00
152A A.Hall RC/J.LeClair 4.00 10.00
152B A.Hall RC/A.Deadmarsh 4.00 10.00
152C A.Hall RC/J.Iginla 6.00 15.00
153A J.Taffe RC/C.Drury 4.00 10.00
153B J.Taffe RC/M.York 4.00 10.00
153C J.Taffe RC/J.Roenick 4.00 10.00
154A S.Eminger RC/N.Lidstrom 6.00 15.00
154B S.Eminger RC/S.Gonchar 4.00 10.00
154C S.Eminger RC/B.Leetch 4.00 10.00
155A J.Leopold RC/A.MacInnis 4.00 10.00
155B J.Leopold RC/B.Leetch 6.00 15.00
155C J.Leopold RC/S.Niedermayer 4.00 10.00
156A P.Sharp RC/S.Reinprecht 4.00 10.00
156B P.Sharp RC/M.Peca 4.00 10.00
156C P.Sharp RC/J.Roenick 6.00 15.00
157A S.Ott RC/P.Kariya 6.00 15.00
157B S.Ott RC/S.Samsonov 4.00 10.00
157C S.Ott RC/T.Fleury 4.00 10.00
158A A.Hemsky RC/J.Jagr 10.00 25.00
158B A.Hemsky RC/M.Hejduk 8.00 20.00
158C A.Hemsky RC/P.Elias 6.00 15.00
159A A.Frolov RC/J.LeClair 6.00 15.00
159B A.Frolov RC/A.Yashin 6.00 15.00
159C A.Frolov RC/J.Jagr 10.00 25.00
160A J.Stoll RC/J.LeClair 6.00 15.00
160B J.Stoll RC/K.Tkachuk 6.00 15.00
160C J.Stoll RC/B.Guerin 6.00 15.00
161A A.Volchenkov RC/R.Blake 4.00 10.00
161B A.Volchenkov RC/S.Stevens 4.00 10.00
161C A.Volchenkov RC/E.Jovanoski 4.00 10.00
162A D.Bykov RC/B.Leetch 4.00 10.00
162B D.Bykov RC/N.Lidstrom 6.00 15.00
162C D.Bykov RC/S.Gonchar 4.00 10.00
163 J.Spezza RC/W.Gretzky 300.00 450.00
164 P.Bouchard RC/S.Samsonov 15.00 40.00
165 R.Hainsey RC/R.Bourque 25.00 60.00
166 S.Chistov RC/P.Bure 15.00 40.00
167 C.Kobasew RC/J.Iginla 15.00 40.00
168 H.Zetterberg RC/G.Howe 150.00 250.00
169 S.Upshall RC/M.Comrie 12.00 30.00
170 P.LeClaire RC/P.Roy 75.00 175.00
171 M.Tellqvist RC/E.Belfour 25.00 60.00
172 R.Nash RC/J.Thornton 100.00 200.00
173 Igor Radulov RC 2.00 5.00
174 Paul Gaustad RC 2.00 5.00
175 Christian Backman RC 2.00 5.00
176 Cam Severson RC 2.00 5.00

2002-03 Upper Deck Rookie Update Autographs

Inserted in packs at 1:144, this 29-card set featured authentic player autographs inset vertically on the card fronts. As of press time, not all cards have been verified. Print run totals below were provided by UD, cards with print runs under 25 are not priced due to scarcity.

STATED ODDS 1:144
BO Bobby Orr/9
BR Pavel Brendl 10.00 25.00
CJ Curtis Joseph 20.00 50.00
CK Chuck Kobasew/24
DH Dany Heatley 15.00 40.00
EC Erik Cole 10.00 25.00
GH Gordie Howe/24
HZ Henrik Zetterberg/24 50.00 100.00
IK Ilya Kovalchuk 15.00 40.00
JA Jason Spezza/24
JB Jay Bouwmeester/24 15.00 40.00
JI Jarome Iginla 15.00 40.00
JL John LeClair 10.00 25.00
MA Maxim Afinogenov 10.00 25.00
MC Mike Comrie 10.00 25.00
MH Martin Havlat 12.50 30.00
MN Markus Naslund 10.00 25.00
MT Mikael Tellqvist/24 60.00 100.00
PB Pavel Bure 10.00 25.00
PM P-M Bouchard/24 20.00 50.00
PR Patrick Roy/24 100.00 150.00
RB Ray Bourque/24 40.00 80.00
RH Ron Hainsey/24 20.00 40.00
SC Stanislav Chistov/24 10.00 25.00
SG Simon Gagne 10.00 25.00
SO Steve Ott 10.00 25.00
SS Sergei Samsonov 10.00 25.00
SY Steve Yzerman 30.00 80.00
WG Wayne Gretzky 150.00 250.00

2002-03 Upper Deck Rookie Update Jerseys

Randomly insrted in packs, this 42-card set consisted of 36 single jersey cards and 6 dual jersey cards. Single jersey cards were serial-numbered out of 299 and dual cards were serial-numbered out of 99.

*MULT.COLOR SWATCH: .75X TO 1.5X
DAY Alexei Yashin 4.00 10.00
DBG Bill Guerin 4.00 10.00
DBS Brendan Shanahan 5.00 12.00
DCO Chris Osgood 4.00 10.00
DDH Dany Heatley 6.00 15.00
DEL Eric Lindros 6.00 15.00
DFP Felix Potvin 5.00 12.00
DHO Marian Hossa 4.00 10.00
DIK Ilya Kovalchuk 6.00 15.00
DJG Jean-Sebastien Giguere 10.00 25.00
DJI Jarome Iginla 6.00 15.00
DJJ Jaromir Jagr 8.00 20.00
DJR Jeremy Roenick 6.00 15.00
DJS Joe Sakic 8.00 20.00
DJT Joe Thornton 8.00 20.00
DKP Keith Primeau 4.00 10.00
DMD Mike Dunham 4.00 10.00
DMH Milan Hejduk 4.00 10.00
DML Mario Lemieux 12.50 30.00
DMM Mike Modano 6.00 15.00
DMS Mats Sundin 4.00 10.00
DOK Olaf Kolzig 4.00 10.00
DPB Pavel Bure 5.00 12.00
DPD Pavol Demitra 4.00 10.00
DPK Paul Kariya 5.00 12.00
DPR Patrick Roy 12.50 30.00
DRC Roman Cechmanek 4.00 10.00
DRL Roberto Luongo 6.00 15.00
DRT Roman Turek 4.00 10.00
DSK Saku Koivu 4.00 10.00
DSS Sergei Samsonov 4.00 10.00
DSY Steve Yzerman 12.50 30.00
DTB Todd Bertuzzi 4.00 10.00
DTH Jose Theodore 6.00 15.00
DTS Tommy Salo 4.00 10.00
DZP Zigmund Palffy 4.00 10.00
SJK Jaromir Jagr 12.50 30.00
Olaf Kolzig
SKH Ilya Kovalchuk 15.00 40.00
Dany Heatley
SLB Eric Lindros 12.50 30.00
Pavel Bure
SRS Patrick Roy 20.00 50.00
Joe Sakic
STS Joe Thornton 12.50 30.00
Sergei Samsonov
SYS Steve Yzerman 20.00 50.00
Brendan Shanahan

2002-03 Upper Deck Rookie Update Jerseys Gold

This 42-card set directly paralleled the base jersey set but featured gold foil highlights. Single jersey cards were serial-numbered to 125 and dual jersey cards were serial-numbered to 10. Dual jersey cards were not priced due to scarcity.

*SINGLE JSY: .6X TO 1.5X BASIC CARD
DUAL JSY NOT PRICED DUE TO SCARCITY

2003-04 Upper Deck Rookie Update

This 217-card set consisted of 90-veteran base cards, 65 base rookies (91-150 and 166-172) numbered to 999, 10 dual-jersey cards (151-158 and 173-174) numbered to 999 that featured both a rookie and a veteran, 8 dual-autograph cards (159-165 and 175) numbered to 199 that featured a rookie and a veteran and an additional 43 rookie cards (176-217) serial-numbered to 199 that were available only via a redemption card good for all 43 cards.

COMP.SET w/o SP's (90) 25.00 50.00
1 Petr Sykora .10 .25
2 Jean-Sebastien Giguere .25 .60
3 Sergei Fedorov .40 1.00
4 Dany Heatley .40 1.00
5 Ilya Kovalchuk .40 1.00
6 Sergei Samsonov .25 .60
7 Joe Thornton .50 1.25
8 Andrew Raycroft .25 .60
9 Chris Drury .25 .60
10 Daniel Briere .10 .25
11 Mika Noronen .25 .60
12 Jarome Iginla .40 1.00
13 Miikka Kiprusoff .25 .60
14 Justin Williams .10 .25
15 Ron Francis .25 .60
16 Jocelyn Thibault .25 .60
17 Bryan Berard .10 .25
18 Mark Bell .10 .25
19 Joe Sakic .60 1.50
20 Paul Kariya .30 .75
21 Peter Forsberg .60 1.50
22 David Aebischer .25 .60
23 Todd Marchant .10 .25
24 Rick Nash .40 1.00
25 Marc Denis .25 .60
26 Bill Guerin .25 .60
27 Marty Turco .25 .60
28 Mike Modano .40 1.00
29 Pavel Datsyuk .30 .75
30 Henrik Zetterberg .30 .75
31 Brett Hull .40 1.00
32 Steve Yzerman 1.50 4.00
33 Adam Oates .25 .60
34 Tommy Salo .25 .60
35 Raffi Torres .10 .25
36 Ales Hemsky .25 .60
37 Roberto Luongo .40 1.00
38 Jay Bouwmeester .10 .25
39 Olli Jokinen .25 .60
40 Martin Straka .10 .25
41 Roman Cechmanek .25 .60
42 Zigmund Palffy .25 .60
43 Marian Gaborik .60 1.50
44 Alexandre Daigle .10 .25
45 Manny Fernandez .25 .60
46 Jose Theodore .40 1.00
47 Saku Koivu .30 .75
48 Mike Ribeiro .10 .25
49 Steve Sullivan .10 .25
50 Tomas Vokoun .25 .60
51 Patrik Elias .25 .60
52 Scott Gomez .10 .25
53 Martin Brodeur .75 2.00
54 Scott Stevens .25 .60
55 Alexei Yashin .10 .25
56 Trent Hunter .10 .25
57 Rick DiPietro .25 .60
58 Jaromir Jagr .50 1.25
59 Mark Messier .30 .75
60 Peter Bondra .25 .60
61 Jason Spezza .30 .75
62 Marian Hossa .30 .75
63 Patrick Lalime .25 .60
64 Sean Burke .25 .60
65 Jeremy Roenick .40 1.00
66 Alexei Zhamnov .10 .25
67 Brian Boucher .25 .60
68 Mike Comrie .25 .60
69 Mario Lemieux 2.00 5.00
70 Sebastien Caron .25 .60
71 Vincent Damphousse .10 .25
72 Evgeni Nabokov .25 .60
73 Patrick Marleau .25 .60
74 Chris Osgood .25 .60
75 Doug Weight .25 .60
76 Pavol Demitra .25 .60
77 Keith Tkachuk .30 .75
78 Nikolai Khabibulin .30 .75
79 Vincent Lecavalier .30 .75
80 Mats Sundin .30 .75
81 Alexander Mogilny .25 .60
82 Owen Nolan .25 .60
83 Ed Belfour .30 .75
84 Todd Bertuzzi .30 .75
85 Ed Jovanovski .25 .60
86 Markus Naslund .30 .75
87 Jason King .10 .25
88 Dan Cloutier .25 .60
89 Anson Carter .25 .60
90 Olaf Kolzig .25 .60
91 Niklas Kronwall RC 4.00 10.00
92 Doug Doull RC 2.00 5.00
93 Fedor Tyutin RC 2.00 5.00
94 Dwayne Zinger RC 2.00 5.00
95 Jason MacDonald RC 2.00 5.00
96 Ryan Malone RC 3.00 8.00
97 Rob Skrlac RC 2.00 5.00
98 Jame Pollock RC 2.00 5.00
99 Grant McNeill RC 2.00 5.00
100 Noah Clarke RC 2.00 5.00
101 Joey MacDonald RC 2.00 5.00
102 John Pohl RC 2.00 5.00
103 Tony Martensson RC 2.00 5.00
104 Antti Miettinen RC 2.00 5.00
105 Ryan Barnes RC 2.00 5.00
106 Graham Mink RC 2.00 5.00
107 Patrick Leahy RC 2.00 5.00
108 Sergei Zinovjev RC 2.00 5.00
109 Steve McLaren RC 2.00 5.00
110 Seamus Kotyk RC 2.00 5.00
111 Tim Jackman RC 2.00 5.00
112 Andrew Hutchinson RC 2.00 5.00
113 Andy Chiodo RC 2.00 5.00
114 Timofei Shishkanov RC 2.00 5.00
115 Milan Michalek RC 4.00 10.00
116 Trevor Daley RC 2.00 5.00
117 Jeff MacMillan RC 2.00 5.00
118 Jason Pominville RC 4.00 10.00
119 Mikko Luoma RC 2.00 5.00
120 Brad Boyes RC 4.00 10.00
121 Michael Morrison RC 2.00 5.00
122 Tomas Plekanec RC 3.00 8.00
123 Mike Stuart RC 2.00 5.00
124 Tuomas Pihlman RC 2.00 5.00
125 Darcy Verot RC 2.00 5.00
126 Mark Popovic RC 2.00 5.00
127 Erik Westrum RC 2.00 5.00
128 Aaron Johnson RC 2.00 5.00
129 Doug Lynch RC 2.00 5.00
130 Randy Jones RC 2.00 5.00
131 Nathan Smith RC 2.00 5.00
132 Aleksander Suglobov RC 2.00 5.00
133 Kyle Wellwood RC 3.00 8.00
134 Chris Kunitz RC 3.00 8.00
135 Jeff Hamilton RC 2.00 5.00
136 Garth Murray RC 2.00 5.00
137 Peter Sejna RC 2.00 5.00
138 Mike Smith RC 6.00 15.00
139 Antero Niittymaki RC 5.00 12.00
140 Carl Corazzini RC 2.00 5.00
141 Anton Babchuk RC 2.00 5.00
142 Julien Vauclair RC 2.00 5.00
143 Nathan Robinson RC 2.00 5.00
144 Dan Ellis RC 2.00 5.00
145 Colton Orr RC 2.00 5.00
146 Rastislav Stana RC 2.00 5.00
147 Gavin Morgan RC 2.00 5.00
148 Dan Hamhuis RC 3.00 8.00
149 Nolan Schaefer RC 2.00 5.00
150 Pat Rissmiller RC 2.00 5.00
151 Bergeron J RC/Thornton J 8.00 20.00
152 J.Hudler J RC/S.Yzerman J 10.00 25.00
153 R.Kesler J RC/T.Bertuzzi J 5.00 12.00
154 A.Semin J RC/P.Bure J 10.00 25.00
155 C.Higgins J RC/S.Koivu J 8.00 20.00
156 J.Lupul J RC/S.Fedorov J 6.00 15.00
157 D. Brown J RC/Z.Palffy J 5.00 12.00
158 J.Pitkanen J RC/J. Roenick J 5.00 12.00
159 M.Fleury AU RC/P.Roy AU 175.00 300.00
160 T.Ruutu AU RC/S.Koivu AU 40.00 80.00
161 E.Staal AU RC/W.Gretzky AU 175.00 350.00
162 N.Horton AU RC/G.Howe AU 75.00 150.00
163 N.Zherdev AU RC/R.Nash AU 60.00 120.00
164 F.Sjostrom RC/M.Naslund AU 15.00 40.00
165 J.Tootoo AU RC/O.Nolan AU 20.00 50.00
166 Zbynek Michalek RC 2.00 5.00
167 Lawrence Nycholat RC 2.00 5.00
168 Fred Meyer RC 2.00 5.00
169 Mike Bishai RC 2.00 5.00
170 Mike Green RC 2.00 5.00
171 Matt Ellison RC 2.00 5.00
172 Joe Motzko RC 2.00 5.00
173 Derek Roy JSY RC 4.00 10.00
Chris Drury JSY
174 D.Fritsche J RC/R.Nash J 6.00 15.00
175 Matt Stajan AU RC 30.00 60.00
Owen Nolan AU
176 Kari Lehtonen RC 30.00 80.00
177 Goran Bezina RC 4.00 10.00
178 Owen Fussey RC 4.00 10.00
179 Josh Olson RC 4.00 10.00
180 Michal Barinka RC 4.00 10.00
181 Bryce Lampman RC 4.00 10.00
182 Matt Hussey RC 4.00 10.00
183 Mike Stutzel RC 4.00 10.00
184 Roman Tvrdon RC 4.00 10.00
185 Matthew Yeats RC 4.00 10.00
186 Thomas Pock RC 4.00 10.00
187 Wade Dubielewicz RC 4.00 10.00
188 Greg Mauldin RC 4.00 10.00
189 Mike Pandolfo RC 4.00 10.00
190 Eric Perrin RC 4.00 10.00
191 Christoph Brandner RC 4.00 10.00
192 Matthew Lombardi RC 6.00 15.00
193 John-Michael Liles RC 6.00 15.00
194 Marek Svatos RC 15.00 40.00
195 Tony Salmelainen RC 4.00 10.00
196 Dominic Moore RC 4.00 10.00
197 Brooks Laich RC 4.00 10.00
198 Cory Larose RC 4.00 10.00
199 Adam Munro RC 4.00 10.00
200 Mikhail Kuleshov RC 4.00 10.00
201 Matt Keith RC 4.00 10.00
202 Denis Grebeshkov RC 4.00 10.00
203 Quintin Laing RC 4.00 10.00
204 Benoit Dusablon RC 4.00 10.00
205 Matt Underhill RC 4.00 10.00
206 Jozef Balej RC 4.00 10.00
207 Robert Scuderi RC 4.00 10.00
208 Libor Pivko RC 4.00 10.00
209 Mikhail Yakubov RC 4.00 10.00
210 Tom Preissing RC 4.00 10.00
211 Cody McCormick RC 4.00 10.00
212 Pavel Vorobiev RC 4.00 10.00
213 Matt Murley RC 4.00 10.00
214 Matthew Spiller RC 4.00 10.00
215 Marek Zidlicky RC 4.00 10.00
216 Christian Ehrhoff RC 4.00 10.00
217 Brent Burns RC 6.00 15.00
RR1 Rookie Redemption

2003-04 Upper Deck Rookie Update All-Star Lineup

This 12-card set featured swatches of game-used jersey and each card was serial-numbered out of 25. As of press time, all cards have not been verified.

*MULT.COLOR SWATCH: .5X TO 1.25X
AS1 Martin Brodeur 25.00 60.00
AS2 Ilya Kovalchuk 15.00 40.00
AS3 Joe Thornton 20.00 50.00
AS4 Marian Hossa 10.00 25.00
AS5 Scott Niedermayer 8.00 20.00
AS6 Zdeno Chara
AS7 Marty Turco 8.00 20.00
AS8 Markus Naslund 10.00 25.00
AS9 Joe Sakic 12.50 30.00
AS10 Brett Hull 20.00 50.00
AS11 Rob Blake 12.50 30.00
AS12 Nicklas Lidstrom 10.00 25.00

2003-04 Upper Deck Rookie Update Skills

*MULT.COLOR SWATCH: .5X TO 1.25X
PRINT RUN 75 SER.#'d SETS
SKJSG Jean-Sebastien Giguere 3.00 8.00
SKAH Ales Hemsky 3.00 8.00
SKAY Alexei Yashin 3.00 8.00
SKBG Bill Guerin 3.00 8.00
SKBH Brett Hull 5.00 12.00
SKCD Chris Drury 3.00 8.00
SKDA David Aebischer 3.00 8.00
SKDH Dany Heatley 5.00 12.00
SKDW Doug Weight 3.00 8.00
SKEB Ed Belfour 4.00 10.00
SKEL Eric Lindros 4.00 10.00
SKGM Glen Murray 3.00 8.00
SKJJ Jaromir Jagr 6.00 15.00
SKJR Jeremy Roenick 5.00 12.00
SKJS Jason Spezza 4.00 10.00
SKJT Jose Theodore 5.00 12.00
SKMB Martin Brodeur 12.50 30.00
SKMF Manny Fernandez 3.00 8.00
SKMG Marian Gaborik 6.00 20.00
SKMH Marian Hossa 4.00 10.00
SKMK Mark Messier 4.00 10.00
SKML Mario Lemieux 12.50 30.00
SKMM Mike Modano 6.00 15.00
SKMN Markus Naslund 4.00 10.00
SKMS Mats Sundin 4.00 10.00
SKMT Marty Turco 3.00 8.00
SKNK Nikolai Khabibulin 4.00 10.00
SKON Owen Nolan 3.00 8.00
SKPF Peter Forsberg 10.00 25.00
SKPK Paul Kariya 4.00 10.00
SKPL Patrick Lalime 3.00 8.00
SKRN Rick Nash 5.00 12.00
SKSA Joe Sakic 8.00 20.00
SKSB Sean Burke 3.00 8.00
SKSF Sergei Fedorov 6.00 15.00
SKSK Saku Koivu 3.00 8.00
SKSY Steve Yzerman 12.50 30.00
SKTA Tony Amonte 4.00 10.00
SKTB Todd Bertuzzi 4.00 10.00
SKTH Joe Thornton 6.00 15.00
SKVL Vincent Lecavalier 3.00 8.00
SKZP Zigmund Palffy 3.00 8.00

2003-04 Upper Deck Rookie Update Super Stars

*MULT.COLOR SWATCH: .5X TO 1.25X
PRINT RUN 75 SER.#'d SETS
SSHJK Milan Hejduk 4.00 10.00
SSMSL Martin St. Louis 3.00 8.00
SSAF Alexander Frolov 3.00 8.00
SSAM Alexander Mogilny 3.00 8.00
SSBH Brett Hull 5.00 12.00
SSBM Brendan Morrison 3.00 8.00
SSDA David Aebischer 3.00 8.00
SSDH Dany Heatley 5.00 12.00
SSDW Doug Weight 3.00 8.00
SSEB Ed Belfour 4.00 10.00
SSGM Glen Murray 3.00 8.00
SSHZ Henrik Zetterberg 4.00 10.00
SSJB Jay Bouwmeester 3.00 8.00
SSJI Jarome Iginla 5.00 12.00
SSJL John LeClair 4.00 10.00
SSJO Joe Sakic 8.00 20.00
SSJR Jeremy Roenick 6.00 15.00
SSJS Jason Spezza 4.00 10.00
SSJT Joe Thornton 6.00 15.00
SSKT Keith Tkachuk 4.00 10.00
SSLR Luc Robitaille 3.00 8.00
SSMB Martin Brodeur 12.50 30.00
SSMF Manny Fernandez 3.00 8.00
SSMG Marian Gaborik 8.00 20.00
SSMH Marian Hossa 4.00 10.00
SSMK Mark Messier 4.00 10.00
SSML Mario Lemieux 12.50 30.00
SSMM Mike Modano 6.00 15.00
SSMS Mats Sundin 4.00 10.00
SSMT Marty Turco 3.00 8.00
SSON Owen Nolan 3.00 8.00
SSPD Pavol Demitra 3.00 8.00
SSPF Peter Forsberg 10.00 25.00
SSPL Patrick Lalime 3.00 8.00
SSRC Roman Cechmanek 3.00 8.00
SSSD Shane Doan 3.00 8.00
SSSF Sergei Fedorov 6.00 15.00
SSSK Saku Koivu 4.00 10.00
SSSS Sergei Samsonov 3.00 8.00
SSSY Steve Yzerman 12.50 30.00
SSVL Vincent Lecavalier 3.00 8.00
SSZP Zigmund Palffy 3.00 8.00

2003-04 Upper Deck Rookie Update Top Draws

This 20-card autograph set featured "cut" autographs of current stars. Cards in this set were inserted at odds of 1:72.

KNOWN PRINT RUNS LISTED BELOW
PRINT RUNS UNDER 25 NOT
PRICED DUE TO SCARCITY
TD1 Evgeni Nabokov 6.00 15.00
TD2 Teemu Selanne 8.00 20.00
TD3 Todd Bertuzzi SP 20.00 50.00
TD4 Wayne Gretzky/14
TD5 Gordie Howe/14
TD6 Jason Spezza SP 75.00 150.00
TD7 Rick DiPietro 6.00 15.00
TD8 Jean-Sebastien Giguere 50.00 100.00
TD9 Nikolai Zherdev 6.00 15.00
TD10 Ales Hemsky 6.00 15.00
TD11 Ilya Kovalchuk SP 20.00 50.00
TD12 Pascal Leclaire 6.00 15.00
TD13 Rick Nash 12.50 30.00
TD14 Nikolai Khabibulin SP 25.00 60.00
TD15 Steve Yzerman 30.00 80.00
TD16 John LeClair 8.00 15.00
TD17 Patrick Roy 60.00 150.00
TD18 Jay Bouwmeester 6.00 15.00
TD19 Alexander Svitov 6.00 15.00
TD20 Fredrik Sjostrom 6.00 15.00

2003-04 Upper Deck Rookie Update YoungStars

*MULT.COLOR SWATCH: .5X TO 1.25X
PRINT RUN 99 SER.#'d SETS
YS1 Michael Ryder 8.00 20.00
YS2 Eric Staal 12.00 30.00
YS2A Eric Staal 12.00 30.00
YS3 Patrice Bergeron 10.00 25.00
YS3A Patrice Bergeron 12.00 30.00
YS4 Trent Hunter 4.00 10.00
YS5 Ryan Malone 5.00 12.00
YS6 Derek Roy 4.00 10.00
YS6A Derek Roy 4.00 10.00
YS7 Matt Stajan 6.00 15.00
YS7A Matt Stajan 6.00 15.00
YS8 Joni Pitkanen 5.00 12.00
YS8A Joni Pitkanen 5.00 12.00
YS9 Paul Martin 4.00 10.00
YS10 Brooks Orpik 4.00 10.00
YS11 Andrew Raycroft 8.00 20.00
YS11A Andrew Raycroft 8.00 20.00
YS12 Pierre-Marc Bouchard 4.00 10.00
YS13 Joffrey Lupul 6.00 15.00
YS14 Matthew Lombardi 4.00 10.00
YS15 Tuomo Ruutu 8.00 20.00
YS15A Tuomo Ruutu 8.00 20.00
YS16 Raffi Torres 4.00 10.00
YS17 Nikolai Zherdev 8.00 20.00
YS17A Nikolai Zherdev 8.00 20.00
YS18 Jonathan Cheechoo 12.00 30.00
YS19 Christian Ehrhoff 4.00 10.00
YS20 Dan Hamhuis 5.00 12.00
YS21 Alexei Semenov 4.00 10.00
YS22 Philippe Sauve 4.00 10.00

2005-06 Upper Deck Rookie Update

This 277-card set was issued into the hobby in five-card packs which came 24 packs to a box and 12 boxes to a case. Cards numbered 1-100 feature veteran players in team alphabetical order while cards 101-277 feature single player Rookie Cards (101-195) and multi-player Rookie Cards (196-275) which feature both a rookie and a veteran player and has two game-worn jersey swatches. The set concludes with a Sidney Crosby Rookie Card which is issued to a stated print run of 199 serial numbered copies. All cards 101-275 are serial numbered with cards 101-195 being issued to a stated print run of 1999 serial numbered sets, cards 196-254 issued to a stated print run of 999 serial numbered sets; cards numbered 255-273 issued to a stated print run of 499 serial numbered sets and cards 274, 275 and 276 were also issued to a stated print run of 199 serial numbered sets. In addition, Rookie Cards not already issued in five products were also inserted into this set. The products which had updated Rookie Cards inserted were: SP Game Used, Trilogy, Black Diamond, SPx and Artifacts. There are two versions of card number 276 with the more common version serial numbered to 199 and a second version serial numbered to 23.

COMPLETE SET w/o SPs (100) 8.00 20.00
101-195 PRINT RUN 1,999 #'d SETS
196-254 PRINT RUN 999 #'d SETS
255-273 PRINT RUN 499 #'d SETS
274-276 PRINT RUN 199 #'d SETS
CROSBY/23 IS PART OF 199 PRINT RUN
1 Jean-Sebastien Giguere .30 .75
2 Teemu Selanne .40 1.00
3 Joffrey Lupul .25 .60
4 Ilya Kovalchuk .50 1.25
5 Marian Hossa .30 .75
6 Kari Lehtonen .40 1.00
7 Andrew Raycroft .30 .75
8 Brian Leetch .40 1.00
9 Patrice Bergeron .40 1.00
10 Glen Murray .25 .60
11 Chris Drury .30 .75
12 Ryan Miller .20 .50
13 Jarome Iginla .30 .75
14 Miikka Kiprusoff .40 1.00
15 Daymond Langkow .12 .30

16 Eric Staal .30 .75
17 Martin Gerber .30 .75
18 Doug Weight .30 .75
19 Erik Cole .25 .60
20 Nikolai Khabibulin .40 1.00
21 Tuomo Ruutu .25 .60
22 Jose Theodore .40 1.00
23 Alex Tanguay .30 .75
24 Joe Sakic .75 2.00
25 Marek Svatos .12 .30
26 Milan Hejduk .40 1.00
27 Rob Blake .30 .75
28 Rick Nash .50 1.25
29 Sergei Fedorov .40 1.00
30 Mike Modano .40 1.00
31 Brenden Morrow .30 .75
32 Marty Turco .30 .75
33 Steve Yzerman 1.00 2.50
34 Pavel Datsyuk .40 1.00
35 Henrik Zetterberg .40 1.00
36 Brendan Shanahan .40 1.00
37 Nicklas Lidstrom .40 1.00
38 Ryan Smyth .30 .75
39 Chris Pronger .30 .75
40 Ales Hemsky .25 .60
41 Roberto Luongo .60 1.50
42 Nathan Horton .25 .60
43 Olli Jokinen .30 .75
44 Alexander Frolov .30 .75
45 Jeremy Roenick .40 1.00
46 Pavol Demitra .30 .75
47 Luc Robitaille .30 .75
48 Marian Gaborik .50 1.25
49 Manny Fernandez .30 .75
50 Saku Koivu .40 1.00
51 David Aebischer .30 .75
52 Michael Ryder .30 .75
53 Mike Ribeiro .25 .60
54 Paul Kariya .40 1.00
55 Tomas Vokoun .30 .75
56 Martin Brodeur 1.00 2.50
57 Patrik Elias .30 .75
58 Brian Gionta .12 .30
59 Scott Gomez .30 .75
60 Alexei Yashin .25 .60
61 Miroslav Satan .25 .60
62 Rick DiPietro .30 .75
63 Jaromir Jagr .60 1.50
64 Martin Straka .12 .30
65 Dominik Hasek .50 1.25
66 Dany Heatley .40 1.00
67 Daniel Alfredsson .30 .75
68 Jason Spezza .40 1.00
69 Wade Redden .25 .60
70 Peter Forsberg .60 1.50
71 Simon Gagne .40 1.00
72 Antero Niittymaki .20 .50
73 Keith Primeau .25 .60
74 Joni Pitkanen .25 .60
75 Curtis Joseph .40 1.00
76 Shane Doan .25 .60
77 Ladislav Nagy .25 .60
78 Mario Lemieux 1.50 4.00
79 Ryan Malone .25 .60
80 Marc-Andre Fleury .30 .75
81 Joe Thornton .60 1.50
82 Patrick Marleau .30 .75
83 Evgeni Nabokov .30 .75
84 Jonathan Cheechoo .40 1.00
85 Keith Tkachuk .40 1.00
86 Barret Jackman .25 .60
87 Vincent Lecavalier .40 1.00
88 Martin St. Louis .30 .75
89 Brad Richards .30 .75
90 Vaclav Prospal .12 .30
91 Mats Sundin .40 1.00
92 Ed Belfour .40 1.00
93 Jason Allison .25 .60
94 Bryan McCabe .25 .60
95 Eric Lindros .40 1.00
96 Markus Naslund .40 1.00
97 Alex Auld .12 .30
98 Todd Bertuzzi .50 1.25
99 Brendan Morrison .25 .60
100 Olaf Kolzig .30 .75
101 Dustin Penner RC 3.00 8.00
102 Michael Wall RC 2.50 6.00
103 Zenon Konopka RC 1.50 4.00
104 Adam Berkhoel RC 4.00 10.00
105 Jay Leach RC 1.50 4.00
106 Eric Healey RC 1.50 4.00
107 Ben Guite RC 1.50 4.00
108 Ben Walter RC 1.50 4.00
109 Brian Eklund RC 2.50 6.00
110 Nathan Paetsch RC 1.50 4.00
111 Jiri Novotny RC 1.50 4.00
112 Mark Giordano RC 1.50 4.00
113 Richie Regehr RC 1.50 4.00
114 Chad Larose RC 1.50 4.00
115 Keith Aucoin RC 1.50 4.00
116 David Gove RC 1.50 4.00
117 Mark Cullen RC 1.50 4.00
118 Rene Bourque RC 3.00 8.00
119 Martin St. Pierre RC 1.50 4.00
120 Corey Crawford RC 2.50 6.00
121 James Wisniewski RC 1.50 4.00
122 Vitaly Kolesnik RC 2.50 6.00
123 Andrew Penner RC 1.50 4.00
124 Steven Goertzen RC 1.50 4.00
125 Geoff Platt RC 1.50 4.00
126 Joakim Lindstrom RC 1.50 4.00
127 Junior Lessard RC 1.50 4.00
128 Vojtech Polak RC 1.50 4.00
129 Brett Lebda RC 3.00 8.00
130 Kyle Brodziak RC 3.00 8.00
131 Danny Syvret RC 1.50 4.00
132 Matt Greene RC 1.50 4.00
133 J-F Jacques RC 1.50 4.00
134 Mathieu Roy RC 2.50 6.00
135 Greg Jacina RC 1.50 4.00
136 Rob Globke RC 1.50 4.00
137 Petr Taticek RC 1.50 4.00
138 Adam Hauser RC 2.50 6.00
139 George Parros RC 3.00 8.00
140 Yanick Lehoux RC 1.50 4.00
141 Petr Kanko RC 2.50 6.00
142 Jeff Giuliano RC 1.50 4.00
143 Matt Ryan RC 1.50 4.00
144 Connor James RC 1.50 4.00
145 Richard Petiot RC 1.50 4.00
146 Derek Boogaard RC 4.00 10.00
147 Matt Foy RC 3.00 8.00
148 Raitis Ivanans RC 3.00 8.00
149 Mark Streit RC 3.00 8.00
150 Jonathan Ferland RC 1.50 4.00
151 J-P Cote RC 1.50 4.00
152 Kevin Klein RC 1.50 4.00
153 Pekka Rinne RC 2.50 6.00
154 Greg Zanon RC 1.50 4.00
155 Cam Janssen RC 1.50 4.00
156 Jason Ryznar RC 1.50 4.00
157 Bruno Gervais RC 1.50 4.00
158 Kevin Colley RC 1.50 4.00
159 Ryan Hollweg RC 3.00 8.00
160 Chris Holt RC 3.00 8.00
161 Brian McGrattan RC 3.00 8.00
162 Wade Skolney RC 3.00 8.00
163 Josh Gratton RC 1.50 4.00
164 Ryan Ready RC 1.50 4.00
165 Alexandre Picard RC 1.50 4.00
166 Stefan Ruzicka RC 1.50 4.00
167 Matt Jones RC 1.50 4.00
168 Colby Armstrong RC 3.00 8.00
169 Doug Murray RC 1.50 4.00
170 Grant Stevenson RC 1.50 4.00
171 Kevin Dallman RC 3.00 8.00
172 Andy Roach RC 3.00 8.00
173 Jon DiSalvatore RC 1.50 4.00
174 Dennis Wideman RC 1.50 4.00
175 Jeff Hoggan RC 3.00 8.00
176 Colin Hemingway RC 1.50 4.00
177 Chris Beckford-Tseu RC 3.00 8.00
178 Mike Glumac RC 1.50 4.00
179 Timo Helbling RC 3.00 8.00
180 Nick Tarnasky RC 1.50 4.00
181 Gerald Coleman RC 2.50 6.00
182 Paul Ranger RC 3.00 8.00
183 Darren Reid RC 1.50 4.00
184 Doug O'Brien RC 1.50 4.00
185 Staffan Kronwall RC 1.50 4.00
186 Jay Harrison RC 1.50 4.00
187 Rick Rypien RC 1.50 4.00
188 Rob McVicar RC 2.50 6.00
189 Alexandre Burrows RC 1.50 4.00
190 Tomas Mojzis RC 1.50 4.00
191 Prestin Ryan RC 1.50 4.00
192 David Steckel RC 1.50 4.00
193 Mike Green RC 5.00 12.00
194 Joey Tenute RC 1.50 4.00
195 Louis Robitaille RC 2.50 6.00
196 Braydon Coburn 4.00 10.00
Jay Bouwmeester
197 Jim Slater 4.00 10.00
Kris Draper
198 Milan Jurcina 4.00 10.00
Zdeno Chara
199 Jordan Sigalet 8.00 20.00
Andrew Raycroft
200 Eric Nystrom 4.00 10.00
Tony Amonte
201 Kevin Nastiuk 6.00 15.00
Martin Biron
202 Danny Richmond 4.00 10.00
Brian Rafalski
203 Brent Seabrook 4.00 10.00
Ed Jovanovski
204 Cam Barker 6.00 15.00
Rob Blake
205 Peter Budaj 8.00 20.00
Tomas Vokoun
206 Brad Richardson 10.00 25.00
Joe Sakic
207 Jussi Jokinen 6.00 15.00
Jere Lehtinen
208 Jim Howard 6.00 15.00
Ty Conklin
209 Johan Franzen 10.00 25.00
Henrik Zetterberg
210 Brad Winchester 6.00 15.00
Keith Tkachuk
211 Anthony Stewart 4.00 10.00
Shane Doan
212 Jeff Tambellini 4.00 10.00
Martin St. Louis
213 Yann Danis 6.00 15.00
Jose Theodore
214 Maxim Lapierre 4.00 10.00
Pierre Turgeon
215 Ryan Suter 4.00 10.00
Chris Chelios
216 Zach Parise 6.00 15.00
Jeremy Roenick
217 Barry Tallackson 4.00 10.00
Bill Guerin
218 Petteri Nokelainen 4.00 10.00
Olli Jokinen
219 Robert Nilsson 4.00 10.00
Markus Naslund
220 Chris Campoli 4.00 10.00
Bryan McCabe
221 Al Montoya 6.00 15.00
Robert Esche
222 Christoph Schubert 4.00 10.00
Joni Pitkanen
223 Brandon Bochenski 4.00 10.00
Mark Parrish
224 Patrick Eaves 4.00 10.00
Michael Peca
225 R.J. Umberger 6.00 15.00
Keith Primeau
226 Keith Ballard 4.00 10.00
Scott Niedermayer
227 David Leneveu 6.00 15.00
Curtis Joseph
228 Maxime Talbot 4.00 10.00
Brendan Morrison
229 Ryan Whitney 6.00 15.00
Brian Leetch
230 Steve Bernier 8.00 20.00
Dany Heatley
231 Ryane Clowe 8.00 20.00
Jonathan Cheechoo
232 Jeff Woywitka 4.00 10.00
Adam Foote
233 Lee Stempniak 6.00 15.00
Patrice Bergeron
234 Evgeny Artyukin 6.00 15.00
Jaromir Jagr
235 Andrew Wozniewski 4.00 10.00
Derian Hatcher
236 Jakub Klepis 4.00 10.00
Ales Hemsky
237 Tomas Fleischmann 6.00 15.00
Milan Hejduk
238 Andrew Alberts 4.00 10.00
Nick Boynton
239 Ben Eager 4.00 10.00
Eric Daze
240 Alexandre Picard 6.00 15.00
Luc Robitaille
241 Ole-Kristian Tollefsen 4.00 10.00
Rostislav Klesla
242 Daniel Paille 4.00 10.00
Cory Stillman
243 Erik Christensen 6.00 15.00
Eric Staal
244 Dimitri Patzold 6.00 15.00
Evgeni Nabokov
245 Ryan Craig 6.00 15.00
Vincent Lecavalier
246 Kevin Bieksa 4.00 10.00
Barret Jackman
247 Jeremy Colliton 4.00 10.00
Trent Hunter
248 Jay McClement 4.00 10.00
Jason Arnott
249 Josh Gorges 4.00 10.00
Dan Hamhuis
250 Kyle Quincey 4.00 10.00
Robyn Regehr
251 Chris Thorburn 4.00 10.00
Rod Brind'Amour
252 Niklas Nordgren 4.00 10.00
Tomas Holmstrom
253 Duncan Keith 5.00 12.00
Brad Stuart
254 Jaroslav Balastik 4.00 10.00
Vaclav Prospal
255 Petr Prucha 8.00 20.00
Martin Straka
256 Ryan Getzlaf 25.00 60.00
Jason Spezza
257 Corey Perry 15.00 40.00
Alex Tanguay
258 Hannu Toivonen 20.00 50.00
Miikka Kiprusoff
259 Thomas Vanek 30.00 60.00
Jarome Iginla
260 Alexander Steen 25.00 60.00
Mats Sundin
261 Andrew Ladd 12.00 30.00
Todd Bertuzzi
262 Cam Ward 15.00 40.00
Marty Turco
263 Wojtek Wolski 15.00 40.00
Ryan Smyth
264 Gilbert Brule 15.00 40.00
Simon Gagne
265 Valtteri Filppula 12.00 30.00
Tuomo Ruutu
266 Rostislav Olesz 10.00 25.00
Martin Havlat
267 Mikko Koivu 15.00 40.00
Saku Koivu
268 Alexander Perezhogin 12.00 30.00
Alexei Yashin
269 Andrei Kostitsyn 15.00 40.00
Alexander Frolov
270 Henrik Lundqvist 40.00 80.00
Dominik Hasek
271 Andrej Meszaros 12.00 30.00
Wade Redden
272 Jeff Carter 25.00 60.00
Joe Thornton
273 Mike Richards 25.00 60.00
Olli Jokinen
274 Dion Phaneuf 60.00 120.00
Chris Pronger SP
275 Alexander Ovechkin 175.00 350.00
Ilya Kovalchuk SP
276 Sidney Crosby RC SP 1200.00 1500.00
276B Sidney Crosby RC SP 1400.00 1800.00

2005-06 Upper Deck Rookie Update Inspirations Patch Rookies

PRINT RUN 25 SER. #'d SETS
NOT PRICED DUE TO SCARCITY

2008-09 Upper Deck Fall Expo Priority Signings

STATED PRINT RUN 75 UNLESS NOTED
PSAO Adam Oates 6.00 15.00
PSBE Brendan Bell
PSBB Brad Boyes 6.00 15.00
PSBL Bryan Little
PSCP Corey Perry/50 6.00 15.00
PSDG Doug Gilmour/10
PSDP Denis Potvin/10
PSPA Daniel Paille/10
PSEM Evgeni Malkin/25 40.00 80.00
PSGA Glenn Anderson/5
PSGH Gordie Howe/5
PSGL Guy Lafleur/10
PSJI Jarome Iginla/10
PSJT Joe Thornton/5
PSME Matt Ellis 6.00 15.00
PSMF Mark Fraser 6.00 15.00
PSMP Michael Peca 6.00 15.00
PSMR Mason Raymond 6.00 15.00
PSPE Phil Esposito/5
PSPR Patrick Roy/5
PSPS Paul Stastny/50
PSRC Ryane Clowe 6.00 15.00
PSRE Ron Ellis/40 6.00 15.00
PSRH Ron Hextall/5
PSRS Ryan Smyth/15
PSRV Rogie Vachon/15
PSSC Sidney Crosby/25
PSST Stefan Meyer 6.00 15.00
PSSM Stan Mikita/5
PSWG Wayne Gretzky/5
PSNH Nathan Horton

2003-04 Upper Deck Trilogy

Released in early December 2003, this 181-card set consisted of 100 veteran base cards; two different rookie subsets and the Crest of Honor subset. Crest cards carried miniature felt emblems on the card fronts. Cards 142-171 were serial-numbered to 999 sets and cards 172-181 were serial-numbered to 499 each. Cards 182-189 were only available in packs of UD Rookie Update and were serial numbered to 999. Please note that two cards carry the number 17 on the cardbacks.

COMP.SET w/o SP's 50.00 100.00
COH 123-141 ODDS 1:9
1 Sergei Fedorov .75 2.00
2 Stanislav Chistov .30 .75
3 Jean-Sebastien Giguere .50 1.25
4 Dany Heatley .75 2.00
5 Ilya Kovalchuk .75 2.00
6 Joe Thornton 1.00 2.50
7 Glen Murray .30 .75
8 Bobby Orr 6.00 15.00
9 Miroslav Satan .50 1.25
10 Maxim Afinogenov .30 .75
11 Chris Drury .50 1.25
12 Jarome Iginla .75 2.00
13 Lanny McDonald .75 2.00
14 Roman Turek .50 1.25
15 Ron Francis .50 1.25
16 Jeff O'Neill .30 .75
17 Alexei Zhamnov .30 .75
17 Kyle Calder .30 .75
19 Jocelyn Thibault .50 1.25
20 Teemu Selanne .60 1.50
21 Peter Forsberg 1.50 4.00
22 Paul Kariya .60 1.50
23 Joe Sakic 1.25 3.00
24 Patrick Roy 3.00 8.00
25 Rick Nash .75 2.00
26 Marc Denis .50 1.25
27 Todd Marchant .30 .75
28 Mike Modano 1.00 2.50
29 Bill Guerin .50 1.25
30 Marty Turco .50 1.25
31 Brendan Shanahan .60 1.50
32 Gordie Howe 3.00 8.00
33 Steve Yzerman 3.00 8.00
34 Dominik Hasek 1.25 3.00
35 Ryan Smyth .30 .75
36 Mike Comrie .50 1.25
37 Ales Hemsky .50 1.25
38 Wayne Gretzky 5.00 12.00
39 Olli Jokinen .50 1.25
40 Stephen Weiss .30 .75
41 Jay Bouwmeester .30 .75
42 Roberto Luongo .75 2.00
43 Zigmund Palffy .50 1.25
44 Alexander Frolov .30 .75
45 Roman Cechmanek .50 1.25
46 Marian Gaborik 1.25 3.00
47 Pierre-Marc Bouchard .30 .75
48 Manny Fernandez .50 1.25
49 Dwayne Roloson .50 1.25
50 Saku Koivu .60 1.50
51 Marcel Hossa .30 .75
52 Jose Theodore .75 2.00
53 Guy Lafleur 1.00 2.50
54 David Legwand .50 1.25
55 Tomas Vokoun .50 1.25
56 Patrik Elias .50 1.25
57 Jamie Langenbrunner .30 .75
58 Scott Stevens .50 1.25
59 Martin Brodeur 1.50 4.00
60 Alexei Yashin .30 .75
61 Rick DiPietro .50 1.25
62 Alex Kovalev .50 1.25
63 Eric Lindros .60 1.50
64 Pavel Bure .60 1.50
65 Mike Dunham .50 1.25
66 Marian Hossa .60 1.50
67 Daniel Alfredsson .50 1.25
68 Jason Spezza .60 1.50
69 Patrick Lalime .50 1.25
70 Jeremy Roenick .75 2.00
71 Tony Amonte .50 1.25
72 John LeClair .60 1.50
73 Bobby Clarke 1.00 2.50
74 Mike Johnson .30 .75
75 Chris Gratton .30 .75
76 Sean Burke .50 1.25
77 Mario Lemieux 4.00 10.00
78 Martin Straka .30 .75
79 Sebastien Caron .50 1.25
80 Mike Ricci .30 .75
81 Niko Dimitrakos .30 .75
82 Evgeni Nabokov .50 1.25
83 Al MacInnis .50 1.25
84 Keith Tkachuk .60 1.50
85 Chris Pronger .50 1.25
86 Chris Osgood .50 1.25
87 Vincent Lecavalier .60 1.50
88 Martin St. Louis .50 1.25
89 Nikolai Khabibulin .60 1.50
90 Alexander Mogilny .50 1.25
91 Mats Sundin .60 1.50
92 Owen Nolan .50 1.25
93 Ed Belfour .60 1.50
94 Alexander Auld .30 .75
95 Markus Naslund .60 1.50
96 Todd Bertuzzi .60 1.50
97 Ed Jovanovski .50 1.25
98 Jaromir Jagr 1.00 2.50
99 Peter Bondra .50 1.25
100 Olaf Kolzig .50 1.25
101 Joe Thornton COH 8.00 20.00
102 Sergei Fedorov COH 5.00 12.00
103 Dany Heatley COH 6.00 15.00
104 Steve Yzerman COH 8.00 20.00
105 Henrik Zetterberg COH 6.00 15.00
106 Patrick Roy COH 15.00 40.00
107 Peter Forsberg COH 6.00 15.00
108 Jean-Sebastien Giguere COH 4.00 10.00
109 Marian Gaborik COH 6.00 15.00
110 Markus Naslund COH 6.00 15.00
111 Jeremy Roenick COH 6.00 15.00
112 Mario Lemieux COH 15.00 40.00
113 Mats Sundin COH 6.00 15.00
114 Ed Belfour COH 4.00 10.00
115 Ilya Kovalchuk COH 8.00 20.00
116 Marian Hossa COH 4.00 10.00
117 Eric Lindros COH 4.00 10.00
118 Jocelyn Thibault COH 4.00 10.00
119 Jose Theodore COH 6.00 15.00
120 Mike Modano COH 6.00 15.00
121 Jason Spezza COH 6.00 15.00
122 Rick Nash COH 6.00 15.00
123 Jean Beliveau COH 6.00 15.00
124 Mike Bossy COH 6.00 15.00
125 Johnny Bucyk COH 4.00 10.00
126 Marcel Dionne COH 4.00 10.00
127 Grant Fuhr COH 10.00 25.00
128 Michel Goulet COH 4.00 10.00
129 Jari Kurri COH 4.00 10.00
130 Guy Lafleur COH 4.00 10.00
131 Ted Lindsay COH 4.00 10.00
132 Scotty Bowman COH 4.00 10.00
133 Lanny McDonald COH 4.00 10.00
134 Stan Mikita COH 6.00 15.00
135 Denis Potvin COH 4.00 10.00
136 Ray Bourque COH 8.00 20.00
137 Don Cherry COH 10.00 25.00
138 Bobby Orr COH 20.00 40.00
139 Gordie Howe COH 12.50 30.00
140 Bobby Clarke COH 8.00 20.00
141 Phil Esposito COH 6.00 15.00
142 Jiri Hudler RC 3.00 8.00
143 Patrice Bergeron RC 8.00 20.00
144 Matthew Lombardi RC 2.00 5.00
145 Lasse Kukkonen RC 2.00 5.00
146 John-Michael Liles RC 2.00 5.00
147 Marek Svatos RC 4.00 10.00
148 Cody McCormick RC 2.00 5.00
149 Dan Fritsche RC 2.00 5.00
150 Antti Miettinen RC 2.00 5.00
151 Esa Pirnes RC 2.00 5.00
152 Tim Gleason RC 2.00 5.00
153 Brent Burns RC 2.00 5.00
154 Christoph Brandner RC 2.00 5.00
155 Chris Higgins RC 5.00 12.00
156 Dan Hamhuis RC 2.00 5.00
157 Marek Zidlicky RC 2.00 5.00
158 Wade Brookbank RC 2.00 5.00
159 David Hale RC 2.00 5.00
160 Paul Martin RC 2.00 5.00
161 Sean Bergenheim RC 2.00 5.00
162 Antoine Vermette RC 4.00 10.00
163 Matthew Spiller RC 2.00 5.00
164 Ryan Malone RC 4.00 10.00
165 Christian Ehrhoff RC 2.00 5.00
166 Alexander Semin RC 8.00 20.00
167 Tom Preissing RC 2.00 5.00
168 Peter Sejna RC 2.00 5.00
169 Maxim Kondratiev RC 2.00 5.00
170 Matt Stajan RC 4.00 10.00
171 Boyd Gordon RC 2.00 5.00
172 Joffrey Lupul RC 4.00 10.00
173 Eric Staal RC 10.00 25.00
174 Tuomo Ruutu RC 5.00 12.00
175 Pavel Vorobiev RC 2.00 5.00
176 Nathan Horton RC 6.00 15.00
177 Dustin Brown RC 4.00 10.00
178 Jordin Tootoo RC 8.00 20.00
179 Joni Pitkanen RC 2.00 5.00
180 Marc-Andre Fleury RC 15.00 40.00
181 Milan Michalek RC 5.00 12.00
182 Mikhail Yakubov RC 2.00 5.00
183 Trevor Daley RC 2.00 5.00
184 Ryan Kesler RC 2.00 5.00
185 Fredrik Sjostrom RC 2.00 5.00
186 Nikolai Zherdev RC 4.00 10.00
187 Timofei Shishkanov RC 2.00 5.00
188 Niklas Kronwall RC 2.50 6.00
189 Fedor Tyutin RC 2.00 5.00

2003-04 Upper Deck Trilogy Authentic Patches

These jersey patch cards were inserted at 1:27.

*SINGLE COLOR SWATCH: .5X TO 1X
AP1 Wayne Gretzky 100.00 250.00
AP2 Jean-Sebastien Giguere 15.00 40.00
AP3 Mike Modano 20.00 50.00
AP4 Jaromir Jagr 20.00 50.00
AP5 Steve Yzerman 30.00 80.00
AP6 Jose Theodore 25.00 60.00

AP7 Joe Sakic 20.00 50.00
AP8 Mario Lemieux 30.00 80.00
AP9 Marian Hossa 15.00 40.00
AP10 Martin Brodeur 25.00 60.00
AP11 Dominik Hasek 15.00 40.00
AP12 Mats Sundin 15.00 40.00
AP13 Milan Hejduk 15.00 40.00
AP14 Jeremy Roenick 20.00 50.00
AP15 Ray Bourque 25.00 60.00
AP16 Markus Naslund 15.00 40.00
AP17 Pavol Demitra 15.00 40.00
AP18 Doug Gilmour 15.00 40.00
AP19 Joe Thornton 20.00 50.00
AP20 Peter Forsberg 25.00 60.00
AP21 Scott Gomez 15.00 40.00
AP22 Sergei Fedorov 20.00 50.00
AP23 Pavel Bure 15.00 40.00
AP24 Dany Heatley 20.00 50.00
AP25 Teemu Selanne 15.00 40.00
AP26 John LeClair 15.00 40.00
AP27 Zigmund Palffy 15.00 40.00
AP28 Guy Lafleur 20.00 50.00
AP29 Ed Belfour 15.00 40.00
AP30 Jari Kurri 25.00 60.00
AP31 Marcel Dionne 15.00 40.00
AP32 Tony Amonte 15.00 40.00
AP33 Patrick Roy 40.00 100.00
AP34 Eric Lindros 15.00 40.00
AP35 Sergei Samsonov 15.00 40.00
AP36 Keith Tkachuk 15.00 40.00
AP37 Grant Fuhr 15.00 40.00
AP38 Guy Lafleur 15.00 40.00
AP39 Wayne Gretzky 100.00 250.00
AP40 Nicklas Lidstrom 15.00 40.00
AP41 Ray Bourque 25.00 60.00
AP42 Patrick Roy 40.00 100.00

2003-04 Upper Deck Trilogy Crest Variations

This parallel to the "Crest of Honor" subset carried different emblems on the card fronts. Cards 101-122 carried the player's jersey number and were limited to that number of copies. Cards 123-141 carried an image of the Stanley Cup, print runs were based on the last year the player won the Cup and are listed below. The cards of Marcel Dionne and Michel Goulet carried alternate team emblems since neither won a Cup during their career. The Don Cherry card carried a cherries emblem.

PRINT RUNS PROVIDED BY UD
101 Joe Thornton JSY#/19
102 Sergei Fedorov JSY#/91 20.00 50.00
103 Dany Heatley JSY#/15
104 Steve Yzerman JSY#/19
105 Henrik Zetterberg JSY#/40 25.00 60.00
106 Patrick Roy JSY#/33 75.00 200.00
107 Peter Forsberg JSY#/21
108 Jean-Sebastien Giguere JSY#/35 30.00 60.00
109 Marian Gaborik JSY#/10
110 Markus Naslund JSY#/19
111 Jeremy Roenick JSY#/97 15.00 40.00
112 Mario Lemieux JSY#/66 40.00 100.00
113 Mats Sundin JSY#/13
114 Ed Belfour JSY#/20 60.00 150.00
115 Ilya Kovalchuk JSY#/17
116 Marian Hossa JSY#/18
117 Eric Lindros JSY#/88 12.50 30.00
118 Jocelyn Thibault JSY#/41 20.00 50.00
119 Jose Theodore JSY#/60 20.00 50.00
120 Mike Modano JSY#/9
121 Jason Spezza JSY#/39 50.00 100.00
122 Rick Nash JSY#/61 15.00 40.00
123 Jean Beliveau SC/72 15.00 40.00
124 Mike Bossy SC/91 12.50 30.00
125 Johnny Bucyk SC/81 15.00 40.00
126 Marcel Dionne DET/92 15.00 40.00
127 Grant Fuhr SC/3
128 Michel Goulet QUE/98 12.00 30.00
129 Jari Kurri SC/1
130 Guy Lafleur SC/88 15.00 40.00
131 Ted Lindsay SC/66 12.50 30.00
132 Scotty Bowman SC/91 15.00 40.00
133 Lanny McDonald SC/92 12.50 30.00
134 Stan Mikita SC/83 15.00 40.00
135 Denis Potvin SC/91 15.00 40.00
136 Ray Bourque SC/77 20.00 50.00
137 Don Cherry 20.00 50.00
Cherries/99
138 Bobby Orr SC/79 50.00 100.00
139 Gordie Howe SC/72 30.00 80.00
140 Bobby Clarke SC/87 12.50 30.00
141 Wayne Gretzky SC/99
141 Phil Esposito CO/04 12.50 30.00

2003-04 Upper Deck Trilogy Limited

*STARS: 8X TO 20X BASE HI
*CRESTS: 2X TO 5X
*ROOKIES: 1.25X TO 3X
STATED PRINT RUN 30 SER.#'d SETS

2003-04 Upper Deck Trilogy Limited Threads

This 30-card set featured a replica felt team logo on one side of the card front and a swatch of game-used jersey on the other. Cards were serial-numbered out of 50.

STATED PRINT RUN 50 SER.#'d SETS
LT1 Jaromir Jagr 30.00 80.00
LT2 Scott Stevens 15.00 40.00
LT3 Mario Lemieux 75.00 150.00
LT4 Jarome Iginla 50.00 100.00
LT5 Roman Turek 15.00 40.00
LT6 Patrick Roy 75.00 150.00
LT7 Steve Yzerman 60.00 120.00
LT8 Mats Sundin 15.00 40.00
LT9 Mike Modano 25.00 60.00
LT10 Zigmund Palffy 15.00 40.00
LT11 Peter Forsberg 30.00 80.00
LT12 Pavel Bure 15.00 40.00
LT13 Todd Bertuzzi 20.00 50.00
LT14 Jason Spezza 25.00 60.00
LT15 Scott Stevens 20.00 50.00
LT16 Jocelyn Thibault 15.00 40.00
LT17 Joe Sakic 50.00 100.00
LT18 Henrik Zetterberg 25.00 60.00
LT19 Joe Thornton 30.00 80.00
LT20 Patrick Lalime 15.00 40.00
LT21 Adam Deadmarsh 15.00 40.00
LT22 Markus Naslund 15.00 40.00
LT23 Ed Belfour 20.00 50.00
LT24 Scott Gomez 15.00 40.00
LT25 Marian Hossa 15.00 40.00
LT26 Alexei Yashin 15.00 40.00
LT27 Sergei Samsonov 15.00 40.00
LT28 Martin Brodeur 50.00 100.00
LT29 Martin Brodeur 50.00 100.00
LT30 Marian Gaborik

2003-04 Upper Deck Trilogy Scripts

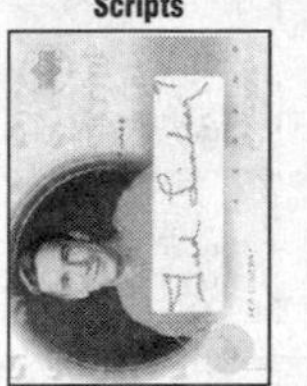

This autographed insert set consisted of 4 distinct subsets. Script 1 cards were rookies and prospects, Script 2 cards were current stars, Script 3 cards were retired greats. The Custom Scripts subset included special "customized" autographs of the featured player. Please note that several of the "Custom" cards on this checklist have yet to be confirmed while different, un-catalogued version appear frequently. Any further information can be sent to hockeymag@beckett.com.-

SCRIPTS 1-3 ODDS 1:4
CUSTOM ODDS 1:45
S1AH Ales Hemsky 4.00 10.00
S1BO Brooks Orpik 3.00 8.00
S1HL Adam Hall 3.00 8.00
S1HZ Henrik Zetterberg 12.50 30.00
S1JA Jared Aulin 3.00 8.00
S1JB Jay Bouwmeester 8.00 20.00
S1JL Jordan Leopold 3.00 8.00
S1JS Jason Spezza 12.50 30.00
S1PB P-M Bouchard 5.00 12.00
S1PL Pascal Leclaire 4.00 10.00
S1RH Ron Hainsey 3.00 8.00
S1SO Steve Ott 5.00 12.00
S2CJ Curtis Joseph 10.00 25.00
S2EC Erik Cole 3.00 8.00
S2IK Ilya Kovalchuk EXCH
S2JG Jean-Sebastien Giguere 4.00 10.00
S2JL John LeClair 6.00 15.00
S2JT Joe Thornton 25.00 60.00
S2JT Jose Theodore 12.00 30.00
S2JW Justin Williams 5.00 12.00
S2MA Maxim Afinogenov 5.00 12.00
S2MB Martin Brodeur 60.00 150.00
S2MH Martin Havlat 6.00 15.00
S2MH Marian Hossa 6.00 15.00
S2MN Markus Naslund 6.00 15.00
S2MT Marty Turco 8.00 20.00
S2PR Patrick Roy 75.00 200.00
S2SS Sergei Samsonov 4.00 10.00
S2TB Todd Bertuzzi 6.00 15.00
S3BC Bobby Clarke 12.50 30.00
S3BK Johnny Bucyk AS 8.00 20.00
S3BO Bobby Orr 100.00 200.00
S3BY Mike Bossy AS 10.00 25.00
S3DC Don Cherry 15.00 40.00
S3DP Denis Potvin NYI 6.00 15.00
S3G1 Wayne Gretzky AS 100.00 200.00
S3GF Grant Fuhr 8.00 20.00
S3GH Gordie Howe HAR 30.00 80.00
S3GL Guy Lafleur 12.50 30.00
S3GR Wayne Gretzky AS 100.00 200.00
S3GT Michel Goulet AS 5.00 12.00
S3GY Wayne Gretzky NYR 100.00 200.00
S3JB Jean Beliveau 15.00 40.00
S3JK Jari Kurri 10.00 25.00
S3JK Johnny Bucyk BOS 8.00 20.00
S3LM Lanny McDonald 5.00 12.00
S3MB Mike Bossy NYI 10.00 25.00
S3MD Marcel Dionne 5.00 12.00

S3MG Michel Goulet CHI 5.00 12.00
S3MH Gordie Howe DET 50.00 125.00
S3PE Phil Esposito 15.00 40.00
S3PN Denis Potvin AS 6.00 15.00
S3RB Ray Bourque 15.00 40.00
S3SB Scotty Bowman 15.00 40.00
S3SM Stan Mikita 6.00 15.00
S3TL Ted Lindsay 10.00 25.00
S3WA Wayne Gretzky LA 100.00 200.00
S3WG Wayne Gretzky EDM 100.00 200.00
S399 Wayne Gretzky HOF 100.00 200.00
CSBC Bobby Clarke HOF 20.00 50.00
CSBC2 Bobby Clarke Broad Street Bullies 30.00 80.00
CSBU Jean Beliveau LeGros Bill 25.00 60.00
CSBU2 J.Beliveau HOF 25.00 60.00
CSBU3 J.Beliveau SC
CSBY M.Bossy HOF 10.00 25.00
CSBY2 M.Bossy SC 25.00 60.00
CSDC D.Cherry Grapes 20.00 50.00
CSGH Gordie Howe
CSGL Guy Lafleur HOF 20.00 50.00
CSGL2 G.Lafleur SC
CSJB J.Bucyk Chief 15.00 40.00
CSJG J.Giguere Jiggy 12.50 30.00
CSMC Mike Comrie 8.00 20.00
CSMH G.Howe HOF 50.00 125.00
CSMH2 G.Howe Mr.Elbows 50.00 125.00
CSMH3 G.Howe SC 50.00 125.00
CSMH4 Gordie Howe Production Line 50.00 125.00
CSRN R.Nash #1 Pick 20.00 50.00
CSSB S.Bowman HOF 30.00 80.00
CSSO S.Ott Otter 8.00 20.00
CSTB T.Bertuzzi Bert 20.00 50.00
CSTL T.Lindsay Prod.Line 15.00 40.00
CSTL2 T.Lindsay Art Ross 15.00 40.00
CSTL3 T.Lindsay HOF 15.00 40.00
CSTL4 T.Lindsay SC Winner 15.00 40.00
CSZP Z.Palffy Ziggy 15.00 40.00

2003-04 Upper Deck Trilogy Scripts Limited

This partial-parallel to the basic Scripts set carried a gold foil "Limited" stamp on the card fronts and serial-numbering out of 30.

COMMON GRETZKY 100.00 250.00

2003-04 Upper Deck Trilogy Scripts Red

This unannounced partial-parallel set to the basic Scripts set carried red ink signatures and hand written serial-numbering (listed below). Please note that the Gretzky cards were signed in blue ink, not red and that Gordie Howe signed all of his cards in this product with red ink.

PRINT RUNS UNDER 27
NOT PRICED DUE TO SCARCITY
S1HL Adam Hall/31 15.00 40.00
S1JB Jay Bouwmeester/31 20.00 50.00
S1JL Jordan Leopold/2
S1PL Pascal Leclaire/31 15.00 40.00
S1RH Ron Hainsey/2
S1SO Steve Ott/6
S2CJ Curtis Joseph/30 20.00 50.00
S2IK Ilya Kovalchuk/30 40.00 100.00
S2JT Joe Thornton/7
S2JW Justin Williams/2
S2MN Markus Naslund/30 30.00 80.00
S2MT Marty Turco/13
S2PR Patrick Roy/27 150.00 250.00
S2SS Sergei Samsonov/17
S2TB Todd Bertuzzi/22
S3BC Bobby Clarke/30 20.00 50.00
S3BO Bobby Orr/30 125.00 250.00
S3DC Don Cherry/30 60.00 150.00
S3DP Denis Potvin/30 25.00 60.00
S3GF Grant Fuhr/30 30.00 80.00
S3GL Guy Lafleur/30 30.00 80.00
S3JB Jean Beliveau/30 25.00 60.00
S3JB Johnny Bucyk/30 15.00 40.00
S3JK Jari Kurri/30
S3LM Lanny McDonald/30 15.00 40.00
S3MB Mike Bossy/30 20.00 50.00
S3MD Marcel Dionne/30 20.00 50.00
S3MG Michel Goulet/30 20.00 50.00
S3MH Gordie Howe/30 60.00 125.00
S3RB Ray Bourque/30 40.00 100.00
S3SB Scotty Bowman/30 40.00 100.00
S3SM Stan Mikita/30 30.00 80.00
S3TL Ted Lindsay/30 25.00 60.00
S3WG W.Gretzky EDM Blue/30 300.00 500.00

2005-06 Upper Deck Trilogy

This 320-card was issued through both product specific unopened and inserts in the Rookie Update product. Cards numbered 1-220 were in the unopened product while cards 221-320 were in the Rookie Update product. The unopened product were five-cards packs which came nine packs to a box. Cards numbered 1-90 feature veterans in alphabetical team order while cards 91-170 is a veteran Frozen in Time subset. The pack issued set concludes with Rookie cards from 171-220. All cards numbered 90 and up were serial numbered: Cards 91-170 were issued to a stated print run of 599 serial numbered sets while cards 221-320 were issued to a stated print run of 999 serial numbered sets.

COMP.SET w/o SP's (90) 20.00 40.00
FIT PRINT RUN 599 SER.#'d SETS
RC PRINT RUN 999 SER.#'d SETS
1 Jean-Sebastien Giguere .75 2.00
2 Joffrey Lupul .60 1.50
3 Sergei Fedorov 1.00 2.50
4 Marian Hossa .75 2.00
5 Ilya Kovalchuk 1.25 3.00
6 Kari Lehtonen 1.00 2.50
7 Andrew Raycroft .75 2.00
8 Joe Thornton 1.50 4.00
9 Patrice Bergeron 1.00 2.50
10 Glen Murray .60 1.50
11 Brian Leetch 1.00 2.50
12 Daniel Briere .75 2.00
13 Chris Drury .75 2.00
14 Maxim Afinogenov .60 1.50
15 Jarome Iginla .75 2.00
16 Jordan Leopold .60 1.50
17 Miikka Kiprusoff 1.00 2.50
18 Eric Staal .75 2.00
19 Erik Cole .60 1.50
20 Nikolai Khabibulin 1.00 2.50
21 Tuomo Ruutu .60 1.50
22 David Aebischer .75 2.00
23 Joe Sakic 2.00 5.00
24 Rob Blake .75 2.00
25 Milan Hejduk 1.00 2.50
26 Alex Tanguay .75 2.00
27 Rick Nash 1.25 3.00
28 Nikolai Zherdev .75 2.00
29 Mike Modano 1.00 2.50
30 Bill Guerin .60 1.50
31 Marty Turco .75 2.00
32 Manny Legace 1.00 2.50
33 Pavel Datsyuk 1.00 2.50
34 Brendan Shanahan 1.00 2.50
35 Steve Yzerman 2.50 6.00
36 Henrik Zetterberg 1.00 2.50
37 Ty Conklin .75 2.00
38 Ryan Smyth .75 2.00
39 Chris Pronger .75 2.00
40 Roberto Luongo 1.50 4.00
41 Stephen Weiss .60 1.50
42 Luc Robitaille .75 2.00
43 Jeremy Roenick 1.00 2.50
44 Marian Gaborik 1.25 3.00
45 Mike Ribeiro .60 1.50
46 Michael Ryder .75 2.00
47 Jose Theodore 1.00 2.50
48 Saku Koivu 1.00 2.50
49 Paul Kariya 1.00 2.50
50 Steve Sullivan .60 1.50
51 Tomas Vokoun .75 2.00
52 Martin Brodeur 2.50 6.00
53 Scott Gomez .75 2.00
54 Patrik Elias .75 2.00
55 Jaromir Jagr 1.50 4.00
56 Kevin Weekes .75 2.00
57 Alexei Yashin .60 1.50
58 Miroslav Satan .60 1.50
59 Rick DiPietro .75 2.00
60 Daniel Alfredsson .75 2.00
61 Dany Heatley 1.00 2.50
62 Jason Spezza 1.00 2.50
63 Martin Havlat .75 2.00
64 Peter Forsberg 1.50 4.00
65 Keith Primeau .60 1.50
66 Simon Gagne 1.00 2.50
67 Robert Esche .75 2.00
68 Ladislav Nagy .75 2.00
69 Curtis Joseph 1.00 2.50
70 Shane Doan .60 1.50
71 Zigmund Palffy .75 2.00
72 Mario Lemieux 4.00 10.00
73 Mark Recchi .75 2.00
74 Evgeni Nabokov .75 2.00
75 Patrick Marleau .75 2.00
76 Jonathan Cheechoo 1.00 2.50
77 Patrick Lalime .75 2.00
78 Doug Weight .75 2.00
79 Keith Tkachuk 1.00 2.50
80 Brad Richards .75 2.00
81 Sean Burke .75 2.00
82 Martin St. Louis .75 2.00
83 Vincent Lecavalier 1.00 2.50
84 Ed Belfour 1.00 2.50
85 Mats Sundin 1.00 2.50
86 Eric Lindros 1.00 2.50
87 Kyle Wellwood .30 .75
88 Markus Naslund 1.00 2.50
89 Ed Jovanovski .75 2.00
90 Olaf Kolzig .75 2.00
91 Jean-Sebastien Giguere FIT 6.00 15.00
92 Sergei Fedorov FIT 4.00 10.00
93 Sergei Fedorov FIT 4.00 10.00
94 Ilya Kovalchuk FIT 5.00 12.00
95 Joe Thornton FIT 6.00 12.00
96 Ray Bourque FIT 5.00 12.00
97 Chris Drury FIT 6.00 15.00
98 Jarome Iginla FIT 5.00 12.00
99 Miikka Kiprusoff FIT 4.00 10.00
100 Eric Staal FIT 4.00 10.00
101 Tuomo Ruutu FIT 5.00 12.00
102 Joe Sakic FIT 6.00 15.00
103 Patrick Roy FIT 12.00 30.00
104 Paul Kariya FIT 5.00 12.00
105 Peter Forsberg FIT 5.00 12.00
106 Nikolai Zherdev FIT 5.00 12.00
107 Rick Nash FIT 4.00 10.00
108 Mike Modano FIT 4.00 10.00
109 Gordie Howe FIT 8.00 20.00
110 Pavel Datsyuk FIT 5.00 12.00
111 Steve Yzerman FIT 10.00 25.00
112 Henrik Zetterberg FIT 5.00 12.00
113 Wayne Gretzky FIT 15.00 40.00
114 Marian Gaborik FIT 5.00 12.00
115 Jose Theodore FIT 3.00 8.00
116 Saku Koivu FIT 6.00 15.00
117 Martin Brodeur FIT 8.00 20.00
118 Jaromir Jagr FIT 6.00 12.00
119 Mark Messier FIT 4.00 10.00
120 Jason Spezza FIT 6.00 15.00
121 Jeremy Roenick FIT 4.00 10.00
122 Marc-Andre Fleury FIT 6.00 15.00
123 Mario Lemieux FIT 12.00 30.00
124 Chris Pronger FIT 5.00 12.00
125 Brad Richards FIT 5.00 12.00
126 Martin St. Louis FIT 5.00 12.00
127 Vincent Lecavalier FIT 6.00 15.00
128 Ed Belfour FIT 6.00 15.00
129 Mats Sundin FIT 6.00 15.00
130 Markus Naslund FIT 6.00 15.00
131 Kari Lehtonen FIT 6.00 15.00
132 Andrew Raycroft FIT 5.00 12.00
133 Patrice Bergeron FIT 5.00 12.00
134 Alex Tanguay FIT 5.00 12.00
135 Milan Hejduk FIT 5.00 12.00
136 Marty Turco FIT 5.00 12.00
137 Bill Guerin FIT 3.00 8.00
138 Brendan Shanahan FIT 5.00 12.00
139 Ryan Smyth FIT 5.00 12.00
140 Roberto Luongo FIT 5.00 12.00
141 Luc Robitaille FIT 5.00 12.00
142 Michael Ryder FIT 5.00 12.00
143 Tomas Vokoun FIT 5.00 12.00
144 Patrik Elias FIT 5.00 12.00
145 Rick DiPietro FIT 5.00 12.00
146 Daniel Alfredsson FIT 5.00 12.00
147 Marian Hossa FIT 5.00 12.00
148 Keith Primeau FIT 4.00 10.00
149 Brett Hull FIT 5.00 12.00
150 Evgeni Nabokov FIT 5.00 12.00
151 Patrick Marleau FIT 5.00 12.00
152 Doug Weight FIT 5.00 12.00
153 Keith Tkachuk FIT 5.00 12.00
154 Todd Bertuzzi FIT 6.00 15.00
155 Olaf Kolzig FIT 5.00 12.00
156 Cam Neely FIT 4.00 10.00
157 Gilbert Perreault FIT 4.00 10.00
158 Denis Savard FIT 3.00 8.00
159 Tony Esposito FIT 3.00 8.00
160 Jari Kurri FIT 3.00 8.00
161 Grant Fuhr FIT 3.00 8.00
162 Mike Ribeiro FIT 3.00 8.00
163 Guy LaFleur FIT 4.00 10.00
164 Mike Bossy FIT 4.00 10.00
165 Alexei Yashin FIT 4.00 10.00
166 Phil Esposito FIT 4.00 10.00
167 Dominik Hasek FIT 6.00 15.00
168 Martin Havlat FIT 5.00 12.00
169 Simon Gagne FIT 6.00 15.00
170 Ed Jovanovski FIT 5.00 12.00
171 Corey Perry RC 5.00 12.00
172 Ryan Getzlaf RC 8.00 20.00
173 Braydon Coburn RC 4.00 8.00
174 Jim Slater RC 4.00 8.00
175 Hannu Toivonen RC 3.00 8.00
176 Milan Jurcina RC 5.00 12.00
177 Andrew Alberts RC 5.00 12.00
178 Thomas Vanek RC 8.00 20.00
179 Dion Phaneuf RC 12.00 30.00
180 Eric Nystrom RC 6.00 15.00
181 Cam Ward RC 6.00 15.00
182 Brent Seabrook RC 10.00 25.00
183 Rene Bourque RC 5.00 12.00
184 Cam Barker RC 4.00 8.00
185 Wojtek Wolski RC 5.00 12.00
186 Peter Budaj RC 6.00 15.00
187 Gilbert Brule RC 4.00 10.00
188 Jussi Jokinen RC 4.00 10.00
189 Jim Howard RC 6.00 15.00
190 Johan Franzen RC 10.00 25.00
191 Brett Lebda RC 5.00 12.00
192 Rostislav Olesz RC 4.00 8.00
193 Anthony Stewart RC 6.00 15.00
194 Alexander Perezhogin RC 4.00 10.00
195 Yann Danis RC 2.50 6.00
196 Mark Streit RC 5.00 12.00
197 Ryan Suter RC 4.00 10.00
198 Zach Parise RC 6.00 15.00
199 Robert Nilsson RC 2.50 6.00
200 Petteri Nokelainen RC 5.00 12.00
201 Chris Campoli RC 5.00 12.00
202 Henrik Lundqvist RC 12.00 30.00
203 Petr Prucha RC 4.00 10.00
204 Al Montoya RC 4.00 10.00
205 Andrej Meszaros RC 5.00 12.00
206 Brandon Bochenski RC 5.00 12.00
207 Jeff Carter RC 8.00 20.00
208 Mike Richards RC 4.00 10.00
209 David Leneveu RC 6.00 15.00
210 Keith Ballard RC 5.00 12.00
211 Sidney Crosby RC 100.00 200.00
212 Maxime Talbot RC 5.00 12.00
213 Ryane Clowe RC 5.00 12.00
214 Jeff Woywitka RC 5.00 12.00
215 Jay McClement RC 6.00 15.00
216 Lee Stempniak RC 4.00 10.00
217 Jeff Hoggan RC 5.00 12.00
218 Alexander Steen RC 3.00 10.00
219 Andrew Wozniewski RC 2.50 6.00
220 Alexander Ovechkin RC 60.00 120.00
221 Dustin Penner RC 4.00 10.00
222 Zenon Konopka RC 2.50 6.00
223 Michael Wall RC 4.00 10.00
224 Adam Berkhoel RC 4.00 10.00
225 Jordan Sigalet RC 4.00 10.00
226 Ben Walter RC 2.50 6.00
227 Chris Thorburn RC 2.50 6.00
228 Daniel Paille RC 2.50 6.00
229 Nathan Paetsch RC 2.50 6.00
230 Jiri Novotny RC 2.50 6.00
231 Richie Regehr RC 2.50 6.00
232 Mark Giordano RC 2.50 6.00
233 Andrew Ladd RC 4.00 8.00
234 Chad Larose RC 2.50 6.00
235 Niklas Nordgren RC 5.00 12.00
236 Danny Richmond RC 2.50 6.00
237 Martin St. Pierre RC 2.50 6.00
238 Corey Crawford RC 4.00 10.00
239 James Wisniewski RC 2.50 6.00
240 Duncan Keith RC 5.00 12.00
241 Brad Richardson RC 2.50 6.00
242 Vitaly Kolesnik RC 4.00 8.00
243 Andrew Penner RC 2.50 6.00
244 Ole-Kristian Tollefsen RC 2.50 6.00
245 Alexandre Picard RC 3.00 8.00
246 Joakim Lindstrom RC 2.50 6.00
247 Steven Goertzen RC 2.50 6.00
248 Geoff Platt RC 2.50 6.00
249 Jaroslav Balastik RC 5.00 12.00
250 Junior Lessard RC 2.50 6.00
251 Vojtech Polak RC 2.50 6.00
252 Kyle Quincey RC 2.50 6.00
253 Valtteri Filppula RC 2.50 6.00
254 Brad Winchester RC 5.00 12.00
255 Matt Greene RC 2.50 6.00
256 Kyle Brodziak RC 5.00 12.00
257 J-F Jacques RC 2.50 6.00
258 Mathieu Roy RC
259 Danny Syvret RC 2.50 6.00
260 Greg Jacina RC 2.50 6.00
261 Rob Globke RC 2.50 6.00
262 Petr Taticek RC 2.50 6.00
263 Jeff Tambellini RC 2.50 6.00
264 Petr Kanko RC 3.00 8.00
265 Yanick Lehoux RC 2.50 6.00
266 Richard Petiot RC 2.50 6.00
267 Matt Ryan RC 2.50 6.00
268 Connor James RC 2.50 6.00
269 Mikko Koivu RC 3.00 8.00
270 Derek Boogaard RC 3.00 8.00
271 Maxim Lapierre RC 2.50 6.00
272 Andrei Kostitsyn RC 5.00 12.00
273 J-P Cote RC 2.50 6.00
274 Jonathan Ferland RC 2.50 6.00
275 Kevin Klein RC 2.50 6.00
276 Pekka Rinne RC 3.00 8.00
277 Barry Tallackson RC 8.00 20.00
278 Cam Janssen RC 2.50 6.00
279 Jason Ryznar RC 2.50 6.00
280 Jeremy Colliton RC 2.50 6.00
281 Bruno Gervais RC 2.50 6.00
282 Ryan Hollweg RC 5.00 12.00
283 Chris Holt RC 5.00 12.00
284 Patrick Eaves RC 3.00 8.00
285 Christoph Schubert RC 2.50 6.00
286 Brian McGrattan RC 5.00 12.00
287 R.J. Umberger RC 5.00 12.00
288 Ben Eager RC 2.50 6.00
289 Alexandre Picard RC 2.50 6.00
290 Stefan Ruzicka RC 2.50 6.00
291 Matt Jones RC 2.50 6.00
292 Ryan Whitney RC 2.50 6.00
293 Erik Christensen RC 3.00 8.00
294 Colby Armstrong RC 3.00 8.00
295 Steve Bernier RC 4.00 10.00
296 Dimitri Patzold RC 3.00 8.00
297 Grant Stevenson RC 2.50 6.00
298 Doug Murray RC 2.50 6.00
299 Josh Gorges RC 5.00 12.00
300 Dennis Wideman RC 2.50 6.00
301 Chris Beckford-Tseu RC 3.00 8.00
302 Colin Hemingway RC 2.50 6.00
303 Jon DiSalvatore RC 2.50 6.00
304 Evgeny Artyukhin RC 2.50 6.00
305 Gerald Coleman RC 3.00 8.00
306 Ryan Craig RC 2.50 6.00
307 Nick Tarnasky RC 2.50 6.00
308 Paul Ranger RC 5.00 12.00
309 Darren Reid RC 2.50 6.00
310 Doug O'Brien RC 2.50 6.00
311 Staffan Kronwall RC 2.50 6.00
312 Jay Harrison RC 2.50 6.00
313 Kevin Bieksa RC 2.50 6.00
314 Rob McVicar RC 3.00 8.00
315 Tomas Mojzis RC 2.50 6.00
316 Tomas Fleischmann RC 2.50 6.00
317 Jakub Klepis RC 2.50 6.00
318 Mike Green RC 8.00 20.00
319 David Steckel RC 2.50 6.00
320 Joey Tenute RC 2.50 6.00

2005-06 Upper Deck Trilogy Crystal

*STARS: 1.5X TO 4X BASE HI
PRINT RUN 25 SER.#'d SETS

2005-06 Upper Deck Trilogy Crystal Autographs

PRINT RUN 10 SER.#'d SETS
NOT PRICED DUE TO SCARCITY
91 Jean-Sebastien Giguere
93 Dany Heatley
94 Ilya Kovalchuk
95 Joe Thornton
96 Ray Bourque
98 Jarome Iginla
100 Tuomo Ruutu
109 Gordie Howe
111 Henrik Zetterberg
113 Wayne Gretzky
114 Marian Gaborik
115 Jose Theodore
116 Saku Koivu
117 Martin Brodeur
120 Jason Spezza
121 Jeremy Roenick
126 Martin St. Louis
127 Vincent Lecavalier
129 Mats Sundin
130 Markus Naslund

2005-06 Upper Deck Trilogy Honorary Swatches

STATED ODDS 1:3
SCRIPTS PRINT RUN 10 SER.#'d SETS
SCRIPTS NOT PRICED DUE TO SCARCITY
PATCHES PRINT RUN 10 SER.#'d SETS
PATCHES NOT PRICED DUE TO SCARCITY
PATCH SCRIPT PRINT RUN 5 SER.#'d SETS
PATCH SCRIPT NOT PRICED DUE TO SCARCITY
HSCP Chris Pronger 5.00 12.00
HSRS Ryan Smyth 5.00 12.00
HSEJ Ed Jovanovski 5.00 12.00
HSZP Zigmund Palffy 5.00 12.00
HSNL Nicklas Lidstrom 6.00 15.00
HSTC Ty Conklin 5.00 12.00
HSCJ Curtis Joseph 6.00 15.00
HSIK Ilya Kovalchuk 8.00 20.00
HSMS Mats Sundin 6.00 15.00
HSJL John LeClair 6.00 15.00
HSWG Wayne Gretzky 30.00 80.00
HSAR Andrew Raycroft 5.00 12.00
HSRL Roberto Luongo 10.00 25.00
HSBL Brian Leetch 6.00 15.00
HSKD Kris Draper 2.00 5.00
HSKL Kari Lehtonen 6.00 15.00
HSMG Marian Gaborik 8.00 20.00
HSAF Alexander Frolov 5.00 12.00
HSVL Vincent Lecavalier 6.00 15.00
HSKP Keith Primeau 4.00 10.00
HSTR Tuomo Ruutu 4.00 10.00
HSSG Simon Gagne 6.00 15.00
HSAT Alex Tanguay 5.00 12.00
HSSK Saku Koivu 6.00 15.00
HSAL Daniel Alfredsson 5.00 12.00
HSJB Jay Bouwmeester 4.00 10.00
HSRN Rick Nash 8.00 20.00
HSJC Jonathan Cheechoo 4.00 10.00
HSPE Patrik Elias 5.00 12.00
HSMD Marc Denis 5.00 12.00
HSOK Olaf Kolzig 5.00 12.00
HSSF Sergei Fedorov 6.00 15.00
HSDB Daniel Briere 5.00 12.00
HSMO Mike Modano 6.00 15.00
HSTK Keith Tkachuk 6.00 15.00
HSMN Markus Naslund 6.00 15.00
HSRE Robert Esche 5.00 12.00
HSBR Brad Richards SP 5.00 12.00
HSSY Steve Yzerman 10.00 25.00
HSJO Jose Theodore 5.00 12.00
HSGM Glen Murray 4.00 10.00
HSCC Chris Chelios 6.00 15.00
HSAM Al MacInnis 3.00 8.00
HSJR Jeremy Roenick 5.00 12.00
HSJI Jarome Iginla 5.00 12.00
HSMT Marty Turco 5.00 12.00
HSNH Nathan Horton 4.00 10.00
HSMK Miikka Kiprusoff 4.00 10.00
HSJT Joe Thornton 10.00 25.00
HSJJ Jaromir Jagr 8.00 20.00
HSBG Bill Guerin 4.00 10.00
HSAH Ales Hemsky 4.00 10.00
HSLU Joffrey Lupul 4.00 10.00
HSSS Scott Stevens 3.00 8.00
HSML Mario Lemieux 15.00 40.00
HSMP Michael Peca 4.00 10.00
HSEL Eric Lindros 6.00 15.00
HSHK Dominik Hasek 8.00 20.00
HSMB Martin Brodeur 10.00 25.00
HSDA David Aebischer 5.00 12.00
HSTB Todd Bertuzzi 8.00 20.00
HSDL David Legwand 5.00 12.00
HSNZ Nikolai Zherdev 5.00 12.00
HSJS Joe Sakic 12.00 30.00
HSSP Jason Spezza 6.00 15.00
HSMH Milan Hejduk 6.00 15.00
HSJW Justin Williams 5.00 12.00
HSDC Dan Cloutier 5.00 12.00
HSRI Mike Ribeiro 4.00 10.00
HSPF Peter Forsberg 6.00 15.00
HSHO Marian Hossa 5.00 12.00
HSRY Michael Ryder 5.00 12.00
HSJG Jean-Sebastien Giguere 5.00 12.00
HSSV Sergei Samsonov 5.00 12.00
HSPK Paul Kariya 6.00 15.00
HSNK Nikolai Khabibulin 6.00 15.00
HSED Eric Daze 5.00 12.00
HSHA Martin Havlat 5.00 12.00
HSMM Mark Messier 4.00 10.00
HSDW Doug Weight 5.00 12.00

2005-06 Upper Deck Trilogy Ice Scripts

STATED ODDS 1:9
ISAH Ales Hemsky 8.00 20.00
ISAT Alex Tanguay 8.00 20.00
ISAR Andrew Raycroft 8.00 20.00
ISBC Bobby Clarke 30.00 80.00
ISCN Cam Neely 15.00 40.00
ISAL Daniel Alfredsson 75.00 150.00
ISDB Daniel Briere 12.00 30.00
ISDH Dany Heatley 20.00 50.00
ISDA David Aebischer 6.00 15.00
ISDC Don Cherry 20.00 50.00
ISGC Gerry Cheevers 12.00 30.00
ISGP Gilbert Perreault 10.00 25.00
ISHL Glenn Hall 20.00 50.00
ISGH Gordie Howe 60.00 125.00
ISIK Ilya Kovalchuk 30.00 60.00
ISJI Jarome Iginla 20.00 50.00
ISJT Joe Thornton 20.00 50.00
ISJO Jose Theodore 12.00 30.00
ISJG Jean-Sebastien Giguere 8.00 20.00
ISLR Luc Robitaille 15.00 40.00
ISMF Marc-Andre Fleury 12.00 30.00
ISHS Marcel Hossa 6.00 15.00
ISMG Marian Gaborik 15.00 40.00
ISHO Marian Hossa 10.00 25.00
ISMN Markus Naslund 10.00 25.00
ISMB Martin Brodeur 100.00 200.00
ISHA Martin Havlat 8.00 20.00
ISSL Martin St. Louis 12.00 30.00
ISMT Marty Turco 12.00 30.00
ISMS Mats Sundin SP 200.00 300.00
ISBO Mike Bossy 15.00 40.00
ISMM Mike Modano 15.00 40.00
ISMH Milan Hejduk 8.00 20.00
ISRB Ray Bourque SP 50.00 100.00
ISRN Rick Nash 15.00 40.00
ISRS Ryan Smyth 15.00 40.00
ISSK Saku Koivu SP 150.00 400.00
ISSW Stephen Weiss 6.00 15.00
ISVL Vincent Lecavalier 60.00 150.00
ISWG Wayne Gretzky 150.00 300.00

2005-06 Upper Deck Trilogy Legendary Scripts

STATED ODDS 1:45
LEGBC Bobby Clarke 12.00 30.00
LEGBH Bobby Hull SP 30.00 80.00
LEGCG Clark Gillies 6.00 15.00
LEGCN Cam Neely 10.00 25.00
LEGDC Don Cherry 15.00 40.00
LEGDS Denis Savard 6.00 15.00
LEGGA Glenn Anderson 6.00 15.00
LEGGC Gerry Cheevers 12.00 30.00
LEGGH Gordie Howe SP 60.00 125.00
LEGGL Guy Lafleur SP 60.00 125.00
LEGGP Gilbert Perreault 12.00 30.00
LEGJK Jari Kurri 12.00 30.00
LEGLM Lanny McDonald 6.00 15.00
LEGMD Marcel Dionne 10.00 25.00
LEGPE Phil Esposito SP 30.00 80.00
LEGRB Ray Bourque SP 60.00 125.00
LEGRR Rene Robert 6.00 15.00
LEGSM Stan Mikita SP 12.00 30.00
LEGTE Tony Esposito SP 20.00 50.00
LEGTL Ted Lindsay 12.00 30.00
LEGWG Wayne Gretzky SP 350.00 500.00

2005-06 Upper Deck Trilogy Personal Scripts

STATED ODDS 1:90
PERBC Bobby Clarke SP 20.00 50.00
PERBH Bobby Hull SP 25.00 60.00
PERCN Cam Neely SP 25.00 60.00
PERDS Denis Savard SP 12.00 30.00
PERGF Grant Fuhr 20.00 50.00
PERGH Gordie Howe 75.00 200.00
PERGL Guy Lafleur SP 50.00 100.00
PERGP Gilbert Perreault SP 25.00 50.00
PERLM Lanny McDonald 10.00 25.00
PERMB Martin Brodeur SP 200.00 300.00
PERMD Marcel Dionne 15.00 40.00
PERMF Marc-Andre Fleury 15.00 40.00
PERPE Phil Esposito SP 40.00 80.00
PERRB Ray Bourque SP 75.00 200.00
PERRH Ron Hextall 20.00 50.00
PERRN Rick Nash 15.00 40.00
PERRR Rene Robert SP 10.00 25.00
PERSM Stan Mikita SP 25.00 60.00
PERSP Jason Spezza 10.00 25.00
PERTE Tony Esposito SP 30.00 60.00
PERGC1 G.Cheevers No Inscrip. 12.50 30.00
PERGC2 Gerry Cheevers Cheesy 20.00 50.00

2005-06 Upper Deck Trilogy Scripts

FS1 ODDS 1:9
CS2 ODDS 1:27
SS3 PRINT RUN 50 SER.#'d SETS
SCSAY Alexei Yashin 5.00 12.00
SCSCD Chris Drury 5.00 12.00
SCSJG Jean-Sebastien Giguere 8.00 20.00
SCSJL John LeClair 5.00 12.00
SCSJS Jason Spezza 10.00 25.00
SCSMN Markus Naslund 6.00 15.00
SCSMP Mark Parrish 5.00 12.00
SCSMT Marty Turco 6.00 15.00
SCSPB Pavel Bure 6.00 15.00
SCSPE Michael Peca 5.00 12.00
SCSRL Roberto Luongo 6.00 15.00
SCSRN Rick Nash 12.50 30.00
SCSRS Ryan Smyth 8.00 20.00
SCSTB Todd Bertuzzi 8.00 20.00
SCSTR Tuomo Ruutu 5.00 12.00
SFSAF Alexander Frolov 4.00 10.00
SFSAH Ales Hemsky 3.00 8.00
SFSAM Antti Miettinen 3.00 8.00
SFSAR Andrew Raycroft 4.00 10.00
SFSBB Brad Boyes 3.00 8.00
SFSBG Boyd Gordon 3.00 8.00
SFSBM Brenden Morrow 4.00 10.00
SFSCK Chuck Kobasew 3.00 8.00
SFSDA David Aebischer 4.00 10.00
SFSDB Dustin Brown 3.00 8.00
SFSFS Fredrik Sjostrom 3.00 8.00
SFSJB Jay Bouwmeester 3.00 8.00
SFSJL Joffrey Lupul 3.00 8.00
SFSJP Joni Pitkanen 3.00 8.00
SFSKL Kari Lehtonen 6.00 15.00
SFSLN Ladislav Nagy 3.00 8.00
SFSMA Maxim Afinogenov 3.00 8.00
SFSMC Mike Cammalleri 3.00 8.00
SFSMF Marc-Andre Fleury 15.00 40.00
SFSMH Martin Havlat 4.00 10.00
SFSMR Mike Ribeiro 3.00 8.00
SFSMS Matt Stajan 3.00 8.00
SFSNA Nik Antropov 3.00 8.00
SFSNH Nathan Horton 3.00 8.00
SFSNS Nathan Smith 3.00 8.00
SFSNZ Nikolai Zherdev 4.00 10.00
SFSPS Philippe Sauve 4.00 10.00
SFSRF Ruslan Fedotenko 3.00 8.00
SFSRK Ryan Kesler 3.00 8.00
SFSRM Ryan Miller 6.00 15.00
SFSSB Sean Bergenheim 3.00 8.00
SFSTC Ty Conklin 4.00 10.00
SFSTH Trent Hunter 3.00 8.00
SFSTM Travis Moen 3.00 8.00
SFSTP Tom Poti 3.00 8.00
SSSDH Dominik Hasek 25.00 60.00
SSSGL Guy Lafleur 20.00 50.00
SSSIK Ilya Kovalchuk 25.00 60.00
SSSJI Jarome Iginla 20.00 50.00
SSSJO Jose Theodore 12.50 30.00
SSSJT Joe Thornton 15.00 40.00
SSSMB Martin Brodeur 75.00 150.00
SSSMG Marian Gaborik 15.00 40.00
SSSRB Ray Bourque 40.00 100.00
SSSWG Wayne Gretzky 150.00 250.00

2006-07 Upper Deck Trilogy

This 160-card set was issued into the hobby in five-card packs, with an $19.99 SRP which came nine packs to a box. Cards numbered 1-100 feature veterans in team alphabetical order while cards 101-160 feature Rookie Cards also in team alphabetical order. The Rookie Cards were issued to a stated print run of 999 serial numbered sets.

1 Chris Pronger .75 2.00
2 Teemu Selanne 1.00 2.50
3 Jean-Sebastien Giguere 1.00 2.50
4 Ilya Kovalchuk 1.25 3.00
5 Kari Lehtonen 1.00 2.50
6 Marian Hossa .75 2.00
7 Hannu Toivonen 1.00 2.50
8 Zdeno Chara .60 1.50
9 Patrice Bergeron .75 2.00
10 Brad Boyes .60 1.50
11 Ryan Miller 1.00 2.50
12 Chris Drury .75 2.00
13 Daniel Briere .75 2.00
14 Miikka Kiprusoff 1.00 2.50
15 Jarome Iginla 1.50 4.00
16 Alex Tanguay .75 2.00
17 Dion Phaneuf 1.25 3.00
18 Eric Staal .75 2.00
19 Cam Ward 1.50 4.00
20 Rod Brind'Amour .75 2.00
21 Martin Havlat .75 2.00
22 Nikolai Khabibulin 1.00 2.50
23 Tuomo Ruutu .60 1.50
24 Joe Sakic 2.00 5.00
25 Jose Theodore 1.00 2.50
26 Milan Hejduk .75 2.00
27 Marek Svatos .60 1.50
28 Pascal Leclaire 1.00 2.50
29 Rick Nash 1.00 2.50
30 Fredrik Modin .60 1.50
31 Sergei Fedorov 1.00 2.50
32 Mike Modano 1.00 2.50
33 Marty Turco .75 2.00
34 Eric Lindros 1.00 2.50
35 Pavel Datsyuk 1.00 2.50
36 Henrik Zetterberg 1.00 2.50
37 Nicklas Lidstrom 1.00 2.50
38 Dominik Hasek 1.25 3.00
39 Ryan Smyth .75 2.00
40 Joffrey Lupul .60 1.50
41 Ales Hemsky .60 1.50
42 Dwayne Roloson .75 2.00
43 Todd Bertuzzi .75 2.00
44 Olli Jokinen .60 1.50
45 Ed Belfour 2.50 6.00
46 Rob Blake .75 2.00
47 Alexander Frolov .60 1.50
48 Marian Gaborik 1.50 4.00
49 Pavol Demitra .60 1.50
50 Manny Fernandez 1.00 2.50
51 Saku Koivu 1.00 2.50
52 Cristobal Huet 1.00 2.50
53 Michael Ryder .75 2.00
54 Alex Kovalev .60 1.50
55 Tomas Vokoun .75 2.00
56 Paul Kariya 1.00 2.50
57 Jason Arnott .60 1.50
58 Martin Brodeur 2.50 6.00
59 Patrik Elias .60 1.50
60 Brian Gionta .60 1.50
61 Miroslav Satan .60 1.50
62 Rick DiPietro 1.00 2.50
63 Alexei Yashin .60 1.50

64 Jaromir Jagr 1.50 4.00
65 Henrik Lundqvist 1.50 4.00
66 Brendan Shanahan 1.00 2.50
67 Daniel Alfredsson .75 2.00
68 Jason Spezza 1.00 2.50
69 Dany Heatley 1.00 2.50
70 Martin Gerber 1.00 2.50
71 Peter Forsberg 1.50 4.00
72 Jeff Carter 1.00 2.50
73 Simon Gagne 1.00 2.50
74 Mike Richards 1.00 2.50
75 Shane Doan .75 2.00
76 Curtis Joseph 1.00 2.50
77 Jeremy Roenick 1.00 2.50
78 Mark Recchi .60 1.50
79 Sidney Crosby 4.00 10.00
80 Marc-Andre Fleury 1.00 2.50
81 Joe Thornton 1.50 4.00
82 Vesa Toskala .75 2.00
83 Patrick Marleau .75 2.00
84 Jonathan Cheechoo 1.00 2.50
85 Keith Tkachuk .75 2.00
86 Doug Weight .60 1.50
87 Manny Legace .75 2.00
88 Brad Richards 1.00 2.50
89 Vincent Lecavalier 1.00 2.50
90 Martin St. Louis 1.00 2.50
91 Mats Sundin 1.00 2.50
92 Andrew Raycroft .75 2.00
93 Michael Peca .60 1.50
94 Alexander Steen .75 2.00
95 Roberto Luongo 2.00 5.00
96 Markus Naslund 1.00 2.50
97 Henrik Sedin .60 1.50
98 Daniel Sedin .60 1.50
99 Alexander Ovechkin 3.00 8.00
100 Olaf Kolzig 1.25 3.00
101 Shane O'Brien RC 4.00 10.00
102 Ryan Shannon RC 4.00 10.00
103 Yan Stastny RC 4.00 10.00
104 Mark Stuart RC 4.00 10.00
105 Phil Kessel RC 12.00 30.00
106 Carsen Germyn RC 4.00 10.00
107 Dustin Byfuglien RC 8.00 20.00
108 Paul Stastny RC 10.00 25.00
109 Filip Novak RC 4.00 10.00
110 Fredrik Norrena RC 4.00 10.00
111 Loui Eriksson RC 4.00 10.00
112 Tomas Kopecky RC 6.00 15.00
113 Marc-Antoine Pouliot RC 6.00 15.00
114 Patrick Thoresen RC 4.00 10.00
115 Ladislav Smid RC 4.00 10.00
116 Konstantin Pushkarev RC 4.00 10.00
117 Patrick O'Sullivan RC 5.00 12.00
118 Anze Kopitar RC 10.00 25.00
119 Erik Reitz RC 4.00 10.00
120 Miroslav Kopriva RC 4.00 10.00
121 Niklas Backstrom RC 4.00 10.00
122 Dan Jancevski RC 4.00 10.00
123 Guillaume Latendresse RC 10.00 25.00
124 Shea Weber RC 5.00 12.00
125 Mikko Lehtonen RC 2.00 5.00
126 Frank Doyle RC 6.00 15.00
127 John Oduya RC 4.00 10.00
128 Travis Zajac RC 6.00 15.00
129 Rob Collins RC 4.00 10.00
130 Steve Regier RC 4.00 10.00
131 Matt Koalska RC 4.00 10.00
132 Ryan Caldwell RC 4.00 10.00
133 Masi Marjamaki RC 4.00 10.00
134 Keith Yandle RC 4.00 10.00
135 Enver Lisin RC 4.00 10.00
136 Jarkko Immonen RC 4.00 10.00
137 David Liffiton RC 4.00 10.00
138 Nigel Dawes RC 4.00 10.00
139 Alexei Kaigorodov RC 4.00 10.00
140 Ryan Potulny RC 6.00 15.00
141 David Printz RC 4.00 10.00
142 Bill Thomas RC 4.00 10.00
143 Joel Perrault RC 4.00 10.00
144 Patrick Fischer RC 2.00 5.00
145 Noah Welch RC 4.00 10.00
146 Michel Ouellet RC 5.00 12.00
147 Jordan Staal RC 12.00 30.00
148 Kristopher Letang RC 8.00 20.00
149 Evgeni Malkin RC 40.00 80.00
150 Matt Carle RC 5.00 12.00
151 Marc-Edouard Vlasic RC 4.00 10.00
152 D.J. King RC 2.00 5.00
153 Roman Polak RC 2.00 5.00
154 Ben Ondrus RC 4.00 10.00
155 Brendan Bell RC 4.00 10.00
156 Ian White RC 4.00 10.00
157 Jeremy Williams RC 4.00 10.00
158 Luc Bourdon RC 5.00 12.00
159 Eric Fehr RC 5.00 12.00
160 Jonas Johansson RC 2.00 5.00

2006-07 Upper Deck Trilogy Combo Autographed Jerseys

PRINT RUN 15 #'d SETS
NOT PRICED DUE TO SCARCITY
CJBS Mike Bossy
Billy Smith
CJCL Guy Lafleur
Bobby Clarke
CJGP Marian Gaborik
Mark Parrish
CJHK Ilya Kovalchuk
Marian Hossa
CJHL Ales Hemsky
Joffrey Lupul
CJHN Rick Nash
Dany Heatley
CJHT Jose Theodore
Milan Hejduk
CJIT Jarome Iginla
Alex Tanguay
CJKL Miikka Kiprusoff
Kari Lehtonen
CJKR Saku Koivu
Michael Ryder
CJLG Wayne Gretzky
Mario Lemieux
CJLZ Henrik Zetterberg
Nicklas Lidstrom
CJNB Cam Neely
Patrice Bergeron
CJNL Roberto Luongo
Markus Naslund
CJRB Patrick Roy
Martin Brodeur
CJRD Jeremy Roenick
Shane Doan
CJTC Joe Thornton
Jonathan Cheechoo
CJTM Marty Turco
Brenden Morrow
CJVH Dominik Hasek
Tomas Vokoun

2006-07 Upper Deck Trilogy Combo Autographed Patches

PRINT RUN 5 #'d SETS
NOT PRICED DUE TO SCARCITY
CJBS Mike Bossy
Billy Smith
CJCL Guy Lafleur
Bobby Clarke
CJGP Marian Gaborik
Mark Parrish
CJHK Ilya Kovalchuk
Marian Hossa
CJHL Ales Hemsky
Joffrey Lupul
CJHN Rick Nash
Dany Heatley
CJHT Jose Theodore
Milan Hejduk
CJIT Jarome Iginla
Alex Tanguay
CJKL Miikka Kiprusoff
Kari Lehtonen
CJKR Saku Koivu
Michael Ryder
CJLG Wayne Gretzky
Mario Lemieux
CJLZ Henrik Zetterberg
Nicklas Lidstrom
CJNB Cam Neely
Patrice Bergeron
CJNL Roberto Luongo
Markus Naslund
CJRB Patrick Roy
Martin Brodeur
CJRD Jeremy Roenick
Shane Doan
CJTC Joe Thornton
Jonathan Cheechoo
CJTM Marty Turco
Brenden Morrow
CJVH Dominik Hasek
Tomas Vokoun

2006-07 Upper Deck Trilogy Combo Clearcut Autographs

DOUBLE AU PRINT RUN 100 #'d SETS
TRIPLE AU PRINT RUN 25 #'d SETS
C2AR Ryan Smyth 12.00 30.00
Ales Hemsky
C2BB Brad Boyes 12.00 30.00
Patrice Bergeron
C2CK Kyle Calder 12.00 30.00
Nikolai Khabibulin
C2EE Phil Esposito 30.00 80.00
Tony Esposito
C2GP Scott Gomez 15.00 40.00
Zach Parise
C2HS Milan Hejduk 12.00 30.00
Marek Svatos
C2KK Saku Koivu 15.00 40.00
Mikko Koivu
C2KN Miikka Kiprusoff 20.00 50.00
Antero Niittymaki
C2LJ Roberto Luongo 15.00 40.00
Olli Jokinen
C2LS Vincent Lecavalier 40.00 80.00
Martin St. Louis
C2LZ Manny Legace 20.00 50.00
Henrik Zetterberg
C2MM Lanny McDonald 12.00 30.00
Joe Mullen
C2MV Ryan Miller 15.00 40.00
Thomas Vanek
C2NM Markus Naslund 12.00 30.00
Brendan Morrison
C2PG Corey Perry 20.00 50.00
Ryan Getzlaf
C2PM Patrick Marleau 15.00 40.00
Milan Michalek
C2RC Wade Redden 15.00 40.00
Zdeno Chara
C2SH Billy Smith 25.00 60.00
Ron Hextall
C2VS Tomas Vokoun 20.00 50.00
Steve Sullivan
C3BLS Jean Beliveau 90.00 150.00
Guy Lafleur
Steve Shutt
C3BPS Mike Bossy 60.00 125.00
Denis Potvin
Billy Smith
C3CGS Erik Cole 40.00 80.00
Martin Gerber
Eric Staal
C3CLP Bobby Clarke
Reggie Leach
Bernie Parent
C3FCB Alexander Frolov 50.00 100.00
Mike Cammalleri
Dustin Brown
C3FEC Grant Fuhr 60.00 125.00
Tony Esposito
Gerry Cheevers
C3HTT Milan Hejduk 60.00 125.00
Jose Theodore
Alex Tanguay
C3IKP Jarome Iginla 100.00 200.00
Miikka Kiprusoff
Dion Phaneuf
C3LDZ Manny Legace 100.00 200.00
Kris Draper
Henrik Zetterberg
C3MSS Lanny McDonald
Darryl Sittler
Borje Salming
C3MTC Patrick Marleau
Joe Thornton
Jonathan Cheechoo
C3MTM Mike Modano 50.00 100.00
Marty Turco
Brenden Morrow
C3NOB Cam Neely 75.00 150.00
Terry O'Reilly
Ray Bourque
C3NZB Rick Nash
Nikolai Zherdev
Gilbert Brule
C3PGC Keith Primeau 30.00 60.00
Simon Gagne
Jeff Carter
C3RBH Patrick Roy 250.00 400.00
Martin Brodeur
Dominik Hasek
C3RHH Wade Redden 40.00 80.00
Martin Havlat
Dany Heatley

2006-07 Upper Deck Trilogy Frozen In Time

COMPLETE SET (20) 150.00 250.00
PRINT RUN 999 #'d SETS
FT1 Alexander Ovechkin 8.00 20.00
FT2 Bobby Clarke 3.00 8.00
FT3 Brendan Shanahan 3.00 8.00
FT4 Cam Neely 4.00 10.00
FT5 Dominik Hasek 5.00 12.00
FT6 Gordie Howe 8.00 20.00
FT7 Guy Lafleur 4.00 10.00
FT8 Jaromir Jagr 6.00 15.00
FT9 Jean Beliveau 3.00 8.00
FT10 Joe Sakic 6.00 15.00
FT11 Martin Brodeur 8.00 20.00
FT12 Mats Sundin 3.00 8.00
FT13 Mike Bossy 3.00 8.00
FT14 Mike Modano 3.00 8.00
FT15 Patrick Roy 10.00 25.00
FT16 Ray Bourque 4.00 10.00
FT17 Sidney Crosby 15.00 40.00
FT18 Steve Yzerman 8.00 20.00
FT19 Tony Esposito 3.00 8.00
FT20 Wayne Gretzky 15.00 40.00

2006-07 Upper Deck Trilogy Honorary Scripted Patches

PRINT RUN 10 #'d SETS
NOT PRICED DUE TO SCARCITY
HSAH Ales Hemsky
HSPAF Alexander Frolov
HSPAO Alexander Ovechkin
HSPAR Andrew Raycroft
HSPAT Alex Tanguay
HSPBB Brad Boyes
HSPBG Brian Gionta
HSPBL Rob Blake
HSPBM Brenden Morrow
HSPBO Borje Salming
HSPBR Bill Ranford
HSPBS Billy Smith
HSPCA Jeff Carter
HSPCD Chris Drury
HSPCK Chuck Kobasew
HSPCN Cam Neely
HSPCO Corey Perry
HSPDA David Aebischer
HSPDB Dustin Brown
HSPDC Dan Cloutier
HSPDG Doug Gilmour
HSPDH Dany Heatley
HSPDR Dwayne Roloson
HSPDS Darryl Sittler
HSPDW Doug Weight
HSPEB Ed Belfour
HSPES Eric Staal
HSPGA Simon Gagne
HSPGL Guy Lafleur
HSPHA Dominik Hasek
HSPHE Milan Hejduk
HSPHV Martin Havlat
HSPHZ Henrik Zetterberg
HSPIK Ilya Kovalchuk
HSPJA Jarret Stoll
HSPJB Jay Bouwmeester
HSPJI Jarome Iginla
HSPJL Joffrey Lupul
HSPJP Joni Pitkanen
HSPJR Jeremy Roenick
HSPJS Jason Spezza
HSPJT Joe Thornton
HSPJW Justin Williams
HSPKC Kyle Calder
HSPKD Kris Draper
HSPKL Kari Lehtonen
HSPKP Keith Primeau
HSPLE Mario Lemieux
HSPLM Lanny McDonald
HSPMB Martin Brodeur
HSPMC Mike Cammalleri
HSPMG Martin Gerber
HSPMH Marian Hossa
HSPMK Miikka Kiprusoff
HSPML Manny Legace
HSPMN Markus Naslund
HSPMP Michael Peca
HSPMR Michael Ryder
HSPMS Marek Svatos
HSPMT Marty Turco
HSPNH Nathan Horton
HSPNK Nikolai Khabibulin
HSPNL Nicklas Lidstrom
HSPON Owen Nolan
HSPPB Patrice Bergeron
HSPPE Patrik Elias
HSPPI Pierre-Marc Bouchard
HSPPM Patrick Marleau
HSPPR Patrick Roy
HSPRB Ray Bourque
HSPRE Robert Esche
HSPRL Roberto Luongo
HSPRM Ryan Miller
HSPRN Rick Nash
HSPRS Ryan Smyth
HSPSA Miroslav Satan
HSPSC Sidney Crosby
HSPSD Shane Doan
HSPSG Scott Gomez
HSPSK Saku Koivu
HSPSN Scott Niedermayer
HSPSS Sergei Samsonov
HSPST Martin St. Louis
HSPSU Steve Sullivan
HSPTB Todd Bertuzzi
HSPTV Tomas Vokoun
HSPVL Vincent Lecavalier
HSPWG Wayne Gretzky
HSPWI Doug Wilson

2006-07 Upper Deck Trilogy Honorary Scripted Swatches

STATED PRINT RUN 25 #'d SETS
HSAH Ales Hemsky 25.00 60.00
HSAF Alexander Frolov 25.00 60.00
HSAO Alexander Ovechkin 60.00 125.00
HSAR Andrew Raycroft 25.00 60.00
HSAT Alex Tanguay 25.00 60.00
HSBB Brad Boyes 25.00 60.00
HSBG Brian Gionta 25.00 60.00
HSBL Rob Blake 25.00 60.00
HSBM Brenden Morrow 25.00 60.00
HSBO Borje Salming 15.00 40.00
HSBR Bill Ranford 50.00 120.00
HSBS Billy Smith 40.00 100.00
HSCA Jeff Carter 30.00 80.00
HSCD Chris Drury 30.00 80.00
HSCK Chuck Kobasew 25.00 60.00
HSCN Cam Neely 20.00 50.00
HSCO Corey Perry 25.00 60.00
HSDA David Aebischer 25.00 60.00
HSDB Dustin Brown 25.00 60.00
HSDC Dan Cloutier 15.00 40.00
HSDG Doug Gilmour 20.00 50.00
HSDH Dany Heatley 25.00 60.00
HSDR Dwayne Roloson 25.00 60.00
HSDS Darryl Sittler 20.00 50.00
HSDW Doug Weight 25.00 60.00
HSEB Ed Belfour 80.00 200.00
HSES Eric Staal 25.00 60.00
HSGA Simon Gagne 30.00 80.00
HSGH Gordie Howe 75.00 150.00
HSGL Guy Lafleur 60.00 150.00
HSHA Dominik Hasek 30.00 80.00
HSHE Milan Hejduk 30.00 80.00
HSHV Martin Havlat 25.00 60.00
HSHZ Henrik Zetterberg 30.00 80.00
HSIK Ilya Kovalchuk 20.00 50.00
HSJA Jarret Stoll 15.00 40.00
HSJB Jay Bouwmeester 25.00 60.00
HSJI Jarome Iginla 50.00 120.00
HSJL Joffrey Lupul 25.00 60.00
HSJP Joni Pitkanen 25.00 60.00
HSJR Jeremy Roenick 25.00 60.00
HSJS Jason Spezza 30.00 80.00
HSJT Joe Thornton 30.00 80.00
HSJW Justin Williams 25.00 60.00
HSKC Kyle Calder 25.00 60.00
HSKD Kris Draper 25.00 60.00
HSKL Kari Lehtonen 30.00 80.00
HSKP Keith Primeau 25.00 60.00
HSLE Mario Lemieux 75.00 200.00
HSLM Lanny McDonald 25.00 60.00
HSMB Martin Brodeur 60.00 125.00
HSMC Mike Cammalleri 25.00 60.00
HSMG Martin Gerber 30.00 80.00
HSMH Marian Hossa 25.00 60.00
HSMK Miikka Kiprusoff 30.00 80.00
HSML Manny Legace 25.00 60.00
HSMN Markus Naslund 30.00 80.00
HSMP Michael Peca 25.00 60.00
HSMR Michael Ryder 25.00 60.00
HSMS Marek Svatos 25.00 60.00
HSMT Marty Turco 25.00 60.00
HSNH Nathan Horton 25.00 60.00
HSNK Nikolai Khabibulin 30.00 80.00
HSNL Nicklas Lidstrom 30.00 80.00
HSON Owen Nolan 25.00 60.00
HSPB Patrice Bergeron 25.00 60.00
HSPE Patrik Elias 25.00 60.00
HSPI Pierre-Marc Bouchard 25.00 60.00
HSPM Patrick Marleau 25.00 60.00
HSPR Patrick Roy 75.00 200.00
HSRB Ray Bourque 40.00 100.00
HSRE Robert Esche 25.00 60.00
HSRL Roberto Luongo 60.00 150.00
HSRM Ryan Miller 30.00 80.00
HSRN Rick Nash 30.00 80.00
HSRS Ryan Smyth 25.00 60.00
HSSA Miroslav Satan 25.00 60.00
HSSC Sidney Crosby 200.00 350.00
HSSD Shane Doan 30.00 80.00
HSSG Scott Gomez 25.00 60.00
HSSK Saku Koivu 30.00 80.00
HSSN Scott Niedermayer 25.00 60.00
HSSS Sergei Samsonov 25.00 60.00
HSST Martin St. Louis 30.00 80.00
HSSU Steve Sullivan 25.00 60.00
HSTB Todd Bertuzzi 25.00 60.00
HSTV Tomas Vokoun 25.00 60.00
HSVL Vincent Lecavalier 40.00 100.00
HSWG Wayne Gretzky 150.00 300.00
HSWI Doug Wilson 25.00 60.00

2006-07 Upper Deck Trilogy Honorary Swatches

STATED ODDS 1:3
HSAH Ales Hemsky 5.00 12.00
HSAO Alexander Ovechkin 12.00 30.00
HSBM Brenden Morrow 8.00 20.00
HSBO Ray Bourque 6.00 15.00
HSBR Bill Ranford 12.00 30.00
HSBS Borje Salming 4.00 10.00
HSCD Chris Drury 6.00 15.00
HSCN Cam Neely 6.00 15.00
HSCW Cam Ward 4.00 10.00
HSDG Doug Gilmour 5.00 12.00
HSDH Dany Heatley 8.00 20.00
HSDS Darryl Sittler 5.00 12.00
HSEB Ed Belfour 20.00 50.00
HSES Eric Staal 6.00 15.00
HSGH Gordie Howe 12.00 30.00
HSGL Guy Lafleur 10.00 25.00
HSGO Scott Gomez 5.00 12.00
HSHA Dominik Hasek 10.00 25.00
HSHO Marian Hossa 8.00 20.00
HSHZ Henrik Zetterberg 8.00 20.00
HSIK Ilya Kovalchuk 10.00 25.00
HSIM Jarkko Immonen 3.00 6.00
HSIW Ian White
HSJG Jean-Sebastien Giguere 4.00 10.00
HSJI Jarome Iginla 12.00 30.00
HSJS Jason Spezza 8.00 20.00
HSJT Joe Thornton 10.00 25.00
HSJW Justin Williams 5.00 12.00
HSKD Kris Draper 5.00 12.00
HSKL Kari Lehtonen 10.00 25.00
HSKP Keith Primeau 5.00 12.00
HSLE Manny Legace 8.00 20.00
HSLM Lanny McDonald 8.00 20.00
HSMB Martin Brodeur 15.00 40.00
HSMH Milan Hejduk 6.00 15.00
HSMK Miikka Kiprusoff 8.00 20.00
HSML Mario Lemieux 15.00 40.00
HSMN Markus Naslund 8.00 20.00
HSMP Marc-Antoine Pouliot 2.50 6.00
HSMR Michael Ryder 8.00 20.00
HSMS Marek Svatos 5.00 12.00
HSMT Marty Turco 8.00 20.00
HSPB Patrice Bergeron 6.00 15.00
HSPR Patrick Roy 10.00 25.00
HSRB Rob Blake 8.00 20.00
HSRL Roberto Luongo 15.00 40.00
HSRM Ryan Miller 8.00 20.00
HSRN Rick Nash 8.00 20.00
HSRS Ryan Smyth 8.00 20.00
HSSA Miroslav Satan 5.00 12.00
HSSC Sidney Crosby 30.00 80.00
HSSG Simon Gagne 8.00 20.00
HSSK Saku Koivu 8.00 20.00
HSSM Billy Smith 10.00 25.00
HSSN Scott Niedermayer 5.00 12.00
HSST Martin St. Louis 10.00 25.00
HSVL Vincent Lecavalier 8.00 20.00
HSWG Wayne Gretzky 40.00 80.00

2006-07 Upper Deck Trilogy Ice Scripts

STATED ODDS 1:9
ISAH Ales Hemsky 15.00 40.00
ISAK Andrei Kostitsyn 15.00 40.00
ISAL Andrew Ladd 12.00 30.00
ISAN Antero Niittymaki 10.00 25.00
ISAO Alexander Ovechkin 40.00 100.00
ISBB Brad Boyes 12.00 30.00
ISBH Bobby Hull 40.00 100.00
ISBR Dustin Brown 12.00 30.00
ISCD Chris Drury 20.00 50.00
ISCK Chuck Kobasew 12.00 30.00
ISCP Chris Pronger 25.00 60.00
ISDA David Aebischer 15.00 40.00
ISDB Daniel Briere 20.00 50.00
ISDC Don Cherry 20.00 50.00
ISDH Dominik Hasek 30.00 80.00
ISDR Dwayne Roloson 10.00 25.00
ISGF Grant Fuhr 40.00 100.00
ISGH Gordie Howe 40.00 80.00
ISGL Guy Lafleur 50.00 100.00
ISHE Dany Heatley 20.00 50.00
ISJB Johnny Bucyk 12.00 30.00
ISJC Jonathan Cheechoo 20.00 50.00
ISJI Jarome Iginla 30.00 80.00
ISJL Joffrey Lupul 12.00 30.00
ISJO Joe Thornton 20.00 50.00
ISJT Jose Theodore 15.00 40.00
ISKD Kris Draper 15.00 40.00
ISMA Martin Brodeur 75.00 150.00
ISMB Mike Bossy 20.00 50.00
ISMC Mike Cammalleri 12.00 30.00
ISMF Marc-Andre Fleury 30.00 80.00
ISMG Marian Gaborik 40.00 100.00
ISMH Milan Hejduk 20.00 50.00
ISMI Miikka Kiprusoff 25.00 60.00
ISMK Mikko Koivu 15.00 40.00
ISMM Milan Michalek 15.00 40.00
ISMN Markus Naslund 10.00 25.00
ISMR Mike Ribeiro 12.00 30.00
ISMS Marek Svatos 15.00 40.00
ISOJ Olli Jokinen 15.00 40.00
ISPB Patrice Bergeron 10.00 25.00
ISPE Phil Esposito 20.00 50.00
ISPR Patrick Roy 150.00 250.00
ISRB Ray Bourque 40.00 100.00
ISRM Ryan Malone 20.00 50.00
ISRY Ryan Miller 25.00 60.00
ISSB Scotty Bowman 50.00 100.00
ISSC Sidney Crosby 175.00 300.00
ISSH Shawn Horcoff 12.00 30.00
ISSK Saku Koivu 20.00 50.00
ISTV Thomas Vanek 30.00 80.00
ISVL Vincent Lecavalier 25.00 60.00
ISVO Tomas Vokoun 15.00 40.00
ISWG Wayne Gretzky 150.00 300.00

2006-07 Upper Deck Trilogy Legendary Scripts

PRINT RUN 50 UNLESS OTHERWISE NOTED
LSBC Bobby Clarke 25.00 60.00
LSBR Richard Brodeur 20.00 50.00
LSBS Billy Smith 15.00 40.00
LSCN Cam Neely 25.00 60.00
LSDC Don Cherry 25.00 60.00
LSDS Denis Savard 10.00 25.00
LSGA Glenn Anderson 6.00 15.00
LSGC Gerry Cheevers 15.00 40.00
LSGF Grant Fuhr 15.00 40.00
LSGH Gordie Howe/25 75.00 150.00
LSGL Guy Lafleur/25 30.00 80.00
LSJB Jean Beliveau 30.00 80.00
LSJM Joe Mullen 6.00 15.00
LSMB Mike Bossy 20.00 50.00
LSML Mario Lemieux/25 75.00 200.00
LSPE Phil Esposito 20.00 50.00
LSRD Ray Bourque/25 40.00 80.00
LSRH Ron Hextall 25.00 60.00
LSRL Reggie Leach 20.00 50.00
LSSB Scotty Bowman 25.00 50.00
LSTE Tony Esposito 15.00 40.00
LSTL Ted Lindsay 8.00 20.00
LSWG Wayne Gretzky/25 200.00 350.00

2006-07 Upper Deck Trilogy Scripts

UNDER 20 NOT LISTED DUE TO SCARCITY
S1AO Alexander Ovechkin/1
S1BC Bobby Clarke/15
S1BR Martin Brodeur/13
S1DH Dany Heatley/4
S1DP Dion Phaneuf/1
S1GC Gerry Cheevers/12
S1GH Gordie Howe/26 75.00 150.00
S1GL Guy Lafleur/17 100.00 200.00
S1HA Dominik Hasek/14
S1IK Ilya Kovalchuk/4
S1JB Jean Beliveau/19
S1KL Kari Lehtonen/2
S1MB Mike Bossy/10
S1MF Marc-Andre Fleury/2
S1MG Marian Gaborik/5
S1ML Mario Lemieux/17 150.00 250.00
S1NL Nicklas Lidstrom/14
S1PB Patrice Bergeron/2
S1PR Patrick Roy/19 150.00 300.00
S1RB Ray Bourque/23 40.00 80.00
S1RL Roberto Luongo/6
S1RN Rick Nash/3
S1SC Sidney Crosby/1
S1VL Vincent Lecavalier/7
S1WG Wayne Gretzky/20 200.00 400.00
S2CH Cristobal Huet/7
S2CN Cam Neely/3
S2DH Dominik Hasek/6
S2DS Darryl Sittler/10
S2ES Eric Staal/28 20.00 50.00
S2GH Gordie Howe/6
S2GL Guy Lafleur/3
S2HZ Henrik Zetterberg/39 20.00 50.00
S2IK Ilya Kovalchuk/27 25.00 60.00
S2JB Jean Beliveau/10
S2JC Jonathan Cheechoo/5
S2JI Jarome Iginla/2
S2JT Jose Theodore/1
S2MB Martin Brodeur/5
S2MK Miikka Kiprusoff/10
S2ML Mario Lemieux/6
S2MS Marek Svatos/9
S2NL Nicklas Lidstrom/4
S2PE Phil Esposito/5
S2PM Patrick Marleau/7
S2PR Patrick Roy/3
S2RB Ray Bourque/5
S2SC Sidney Crosby/3
S2TH Joe Thornton/1
S2WG Wayne Gretzky/9
S3AR Andrew Raycroft/25 20.00 40.00
S3DH Dany Heatley/25 25.00 60.00
S3ES Eric Staal/25 20.00 50.00
S3HA Dominik Hasek/25 40.00 80.00
S3HZ Henrik Zetterberg/25 30.00 60.00
S3IK Ilya Kovalchuk/25 25.00 60.00
S3JC Jonathan Cheechoo/25 20.00 50.00
S3JI Jarome Iginla/25 25.00 60.00
S3JR Jeremy Roenick/25 25.00 60.00
S3JT Joe Thornton/25 40.00 80.00
S3MB Martin Brodeur/25
S3MG Marian Gaborik/25 25.00 60.00
S3MK Miikka Kiprusoff/25 25.00 50.00
S3MN Markus Naslund/25 25.00 50.00
S3MT Marty Turco/25
S3NL Nicklas Lidstrom/25 25.00 60.00
S3PB Patrice Bergeron/25 15.00 40.00
S3RB Rob Blake/25 20.00 50.00
S3RL Roberto Luongo/25 25.00 60.00
S3RN Rick Nash/25 20.00 50.00
S3SC Sidney Crosby/25 250.00 400.00
S3SK Saku Koivu/25 20.00 50.00
S3TH Jose Theodore/25 20.00 40.00
S3TV Tomas Vokoun/25 20.00 50.00
S3VL Vincent Lecavalier/25 40.00 80.00
TSAA Adrian Aucoin 3.00 8.00
TSAF Alexander Frolov 5.00 12.00
TSAH Ales Hemsky 5.00 12.00
TSAL Andrew Ladd 3.00 8.00
TSAN Antero Niittymaki 6.00 15.00
TSAP Alexandre Picard 3.00 8.00
TSBD Brad Doyes 8.00 20.00
TSBR Dustin Brown 8.00 20.00
TSBS Billy Smith SP 20.00 50.00
TSCD Chris Drury 10.00 25.00
TSCK Chuck Kobasew 6.00 15.00
TSCN Cam Neely SP 12.00 30.00
TSDA David Aebischer 12.00 30.00
TSDB Daniel Briere SP 25.00 60.00
TSDC Dan Cloutier 5.00 12.00
TSDL David Leneveu 8.00 20.00
TSDO Doug Wilson 6.00 15.00
TSDP Dion Phaneuf SP 30.00 80.00
TSDR Danny Richmond 3.00 8.00
TSDS Derek Sanderson 8.00 20.00
TSDT Dave Taylor 4.00 10.00
TSDW Doug Weight 6.00 15.00
TSED Eric Daze 3.00 8.00
TSGH Gordie Howe SP 30.00 60.00
TSHO Shawn Horcoff 8.00 20.00
TSHZ Henrik Zetterberg
TSJB Johnny Bucyk 6.00 15.00
TSJC Jonathan Cheechoo 12.00 30.00
TSJH Jeff Halpern 6.00 15.00
TSJI Jarome Iginla SP 30.00 80.00
TSJL Jason Labarbera 4.00 10.00
TSJM Joe Mullen SP 8.00 20.00
TSJP Joni Pitkanen 8.00 20.00
TSJT Jose Theodore SP 15.00 40.00
TSKC Kyle Calder 6.00 15.00
TSKD Kris Draper 8.00 20.00
TSKL Kari Lehtonen SP 25.00 60.00
TSKM Kirk Muller SP 8.00 20.00
TSKU Chris Kunitz 6.00 15.00
TSLI John-Michael Liles 6.00 15.00
TSLN Ladislav Nagy 6.00 15.00
TSLS Lee Stempniak 6.00 15.00
TSLU Joffrey Lupul SP 12.00 30.00
TSMB Martin Biron 8.00 20.00
TSMC Mike Cammalleri 10.00 25.00
TSMF Marc-Andre Fleury SP 25.00 50.00
TSMG Marian Gaborik SP 30.00 80.00
TSMH Marcel Hossa 3.00 8.00
TSMI Ryan Miller 15.00 40.00
TSMK Miikka Kiprusoff SP
TSML Manny Legace 8.00 20.00
TSMM Milan Michalek 8.00 20.00
TSMN Markus Naslund SP 20.00 50.00
TSMP Mark Parrish 6.00 15.00
TSMR Mike Ribeiro 6.00 15.00
TSMS Marc Savard 8.00 20.00
TSMT Mikael Tellqvist 10.00 25.00
TSNA Nikolai Antropov 3.00 8.00
TSPM Patrick Marleau SP 25.00 60.00
TSPO Denis Potvin SP 25.00 60.00
TSPS Philippe Sauve 4.00 10.00
TSRB Richard Brodeur SP 12.00 30.00
TSRF Ruslan Fedotenko 6.00 15.00
TSRG Ryan Getzlaf 12.00 30.00
TSRH Ron Hextall 10.00 25.00
TSRL Reggie Leach SP 15.00 40.00
TSRM Ryan Malone 12.00 30.00
TSRV Rogie Vachon 25.00 60.00
TSRY Michael Ryder 8.00 20.00
TSSA Denis Savard 5.00 12.00
TSSC Sidney Crosby SP 125.00 250.00
TSSG Scott Gomez 6.00 15.00
TSSH Scott Hartnell 3.00 8.00
TSSS Steve Shutt 10.00 25.00
TSSW Stephen Weiss 3.00 8.00
TSTA Jeff Tambellini 6.00 15.00
TSTC Ty Conklin 5.00 12.00
TSTE Tony Esposito SP
TSTL Ted Lindsay SP 15.00 40.00
TSTV Tomas Vokoun 10.00 25.00
TSVA Rick Vaive 8.00 20.00
TSWC Wayne Cashman 5.00 12.00
TSWG Wayne Gretzky SP 125.00 200.00
TSWI Dave Williams 8.00 20.00

TSWR Wade Redden 8.00 20.00
TSZC Zdeno Chara 8.00 20.00

2007-08 Upper Deck Trilogy

This 180-card set was released in January, 2008. The set was issued into the hobby in five-card packs, with a $19.99 SRP, which came nine packs to a box and 10 boxes to a case. Cards numbered 1-100 feature veterans while cards numbered 101-120 are a Frozen in Time subset which was issued to a stated print run of 799 serial numbered sets and cards 121-180 are Rookie Cards which were issued to a stated print run of 999 serial numbered sets.

COMP.SET w/o SPs (100) 15.00 40.00
FIT PRINT RUN 799 SER.#'d SETS
ROOKIE PRINT RUN 999 SER.#'d SETS
1 Ryan Getzlaf .50 1.25
2 Jean-Sebastien Giguere .60 1.50
3 Chris Pronger .60 1.50
4 Teemu Selanne .60 1.50
5 Ilya Kovalchuk .75 2.00
6 Kari Lehtonen .60 1.50
7 Marian Hossa .60 1.50
8 Phil Kessel .60 1.50
9 Manny Fernandez .50 1.25
10 Patrice Bergeron .60 1.50
11 Ryan Miller .60 1.50
12 Thomas Vanek .50 1.25
13 Jason Pominville .40 1.00
14 Drew Stafford .50 1.25
15 Miikka Kiprusoff .75 2.00
16 Dion Phaneuf .60 1.50
17 Jarome Iginla 1.00 2.50
18 Alex Tanguay .50 1.25
19 Cam Ward .50 1.25
20 Eric Staal .60 1.50
21 Justin Williams .40 1.00
22 Nikolai Khabibulin .60 1.50
23 Martin Havlat .50 1.25
24 Tuomo Ruutu .40 1.00
25 Joe Sakic 1.25 3.00
26 Ryan Smyth .60 1.50
27 Paul Stastny .60 1.50
28 Milan Hejduk .50 1.25
29 Rick Nash .60 1.50
30 David Vyborny .40 1.00
31 Sergei Fedorov .60 1.50
32 Mike Modano .60 1.50
33 Marty Turco .60 1.50
34 Mike Ribeiro .40 1.00
35 Henrik Zetterberg .60 1.50
36 Kris Draper .50 1.25
37 Pavel Datsyuk .60 1.50
38 Nicklas Lidstrom .60 1.50
39 Dwayne Roloson .50 1.25
40 Joni Pitkanen .40 1.00
41 Shawn Horcoff .40 1.00
42 Ales Hemsky .40 1.00
43 Tomas Vokoun .60 1.50
44 Olli Jokinen .40 1.00
45 Nathan Horton .40 1.00
46 Alexander Frolov .40 1.00
47 Anze Kopitar .60 1.50
48 Rob Blake .50 1.25
49 Marian Gaborik .75 2.00
50 Niklas Backstrom .50 1.25
51 Mikko Koivu .40 1.00
52 Saku Koivu .50 1.25
53 Cristobal Huet .60 1.50
54 Michael Ryder .40 1.00
55 Guillaume Latendresse .50 1.25
56 Alexander Radulov .60 1.50
57 Chris Mason .50 1.25
58 Steve Sullivan .40 1.00
59 Martin Brodeur 1.50 4.00
60 Zach Parise .50 1.25
61 Patrik Elias .40 1.00
62 Rick DiPietro .50 1.25
63 Miroslav Satan .40 1.00
64 Trent Hunter .40 1.00
65 Jaromir Jagr 1.00 2.50
66 Chris Drury .50 1.25
67 Henrik Lundqvist .75 2.00
68 Dany Heatley .75 2.00
69 Ray Emery .50 1.25
70 Daniel Alfredsson .50 1.25
71 Jason Spezza .60 1.50
72 Daniel Briere .60 1.50
73 Simon Gagne .60 1.50
74 Jeff Carter .40 1.00
75 Shane Doan .40 1.00
76 Ed Jovanovski .40 1.00
77 Sidney Crosby 3.00 8.00
78 Evgeni Malkin 1.50 4.00
79 Marc-Andre Fleury .60 1.50
80 Jordan Staal .75 2.00
81 Joe Thornton .75 2.00
82 Patrick Marleau .50 1.25
83 Jonathan Cheechoo .50 1.25
84 Paul Kariya .60 1.50
85 Doug Weight .40 1.00
86 Keith Tkachuk .50 1.25
87 Martin St. Louis .60 1.50
88 Vincent Lecavalier .60 1.50
89 Brad Richards .50 1.25
90 Mats Sundin .60 1.50
91 Darcy Tucker .50 1.25
92 Vesa Toskala .50 1.25
93 Jason Blake .40 1.00
94 Henrik Sedin .40 1.00
95 Daniel Sedin .40 1.00
96 Roberto Luongo 1.00 2.50
97 Markus Naslund .60 1.50
98 Alexander Semin .60 1.50
99 Olaf Kolzig .60 1.50
100 Alexander Ovechkin 2.00 5.00
101 Alexander Ovechkin/799 8.00 20.00
102 Bobby Hull/799 4.00 10.00
103 Bobby Orr/799 10.00 25.00
104 Evgeni Malkin/799 6.00 15.00
105 Gordie Howe/799 6.00 15.00
106 Jarome Iginla/799 4.00 10.00
107 Jaromir Jagr/799 4.00 10.00
108 Joe Sakic/799 5.00 12.00
109 Joe Thornton/799 3.00 8.00
110 Larry Robinson/799 3.00 8.00
111 Mario Lemieux/799 8.00 20.00
112 Martin Brodeur/799 6.00 15.00
113 Mats Sundin/799 2.50 6.00
114 Nicklas Lidstrom/799 2.50 6.00
115 Patrick Roy/799 8.00 20.00
116 Phil Esposito/799 4.00 10.00
117 Roberto Luongo/799 4.00 10.00
118 Sidney Crosby/799 12.00 30.00
119 Vincent Lecavalier/799 2.50 6.00
120 Wayne Gretzky/799 12.00 30.00
121 Bobby Ryan RC 12.00 30.00
122 Drew Miller RC 3.00 8.00
123 Ryan Carter RC 4.00 10.00
124 Jonas Hiller RC 8.00 20.00
125 Bryan Little RC 5.00 12.00
126 Brett Sterling RC 5.00 12.00
127 Tobias Enstrom RC 5.00 12.00
128 David Krejci RC 6.00 15.00
129 Milan Lucic RC 8.00 20.00
130 Jonathan Sigalet RC 3.00 8.00
131 Curtis McElhinney RC 4.00 10.00
132 Jonathan Toews RC 20.00 50.00
133 Patrick Kane RC 15.00 40.00
134 Magnus Johansson RC 3.00 8.00
135 Tyler Weiman RC 4.00 10.00
136 Jaroslav Hlinka RC 4.00 10.00
137 Kris Russell RC 5.00 12.00
138 Jared Boll RC 3.00 8.00
139 Marc Methot RC 3.00 8.00
140 Matt Niskanen RC 3.00 8.00
141 Tobias Stephan RC 4.00 10.00
142 Matt Ellis RC 3.00 8.00
143 Sam Gagner RC 6.00 15.00
144 Andrew Cogliano RC 8.00 20.00
145 Rob Schremp RC 4.00 10.00
146 Tom Gilbert RC 4.00 10.00
147 Cory Murphy RC 3.00 8.00
148 Jack Johnson RC 5.00 12.00
149 Jonathan Bernier RC 8.00 20.00
150 Lauri Tukonen RC 3.00 8.00
151 Brady Murray RC 3.00 8.00
152 Petr Kalus RC 3.00 8.00
153 James Sheppard RC 3.00 8.00
154 Carey Price RC 20.00 50.00
155 Kyle Chipchura RC 5.00 12.00
156 Jaroslav Halak RC 10.00 25.00
157 Ville Koistinen RC 3.00 8.00
158 Nicklas Bergfors RC 4.00 10.00
159 Andy Greene RC 3.00 8.00
160 Frans Nielsen RC 3.00 8.00
161 Marc Staal RC 8.00 20.00
162 Brandon Dubinsky RC 5.00 12.00
163 Ryan Callahan RC 5.00 12.00
164 Daniel Girardi RC 3.00 8.00
165 Nick Foligno RC 5.00 12.00
166 Brian Elliott RC 4.00 10.00
167 Ryan Parent RC 4.00 10.00
168 Denis Tolpeko RC 3.00 8.00
169 Peter Mueller RC 10.00 25.00
170 Martin Hanzal RC 4.00 10.00
171 Craig Weller RC 3.00 8.00
172 Daniel Winnik RC 3.00 8.00
173 Torrey Mitchell RC 4.00 10.00
174 Erik Johnson RC 6.00 15.00
175 Steve Wagner RC 3.00 8.00
176 Matt Smaby RC 3.00 8.00
177 Mike Lundin RC 3.00 8.00
178 Mason Raymond RC 8.00 20.00
179 Jannik Hansen RC 3.00 8.00
180 Nicklas Backstrom RC 12.00 30.00

2007-08 Upper Deck Trilogy Combo Clearcut Autographs

STATED PRINT RUN 100 SERIAL #'d SETS
CC2BH Martin Brodeur 50.00 120.00
Cristobal Huet/25
CC2GL Mario Lemieux 350.00 600.00
Wayne Gretzky/25
CC2HE Tony Esposito 30.00 80.00
Bobby Hull/25
CC2HL Ted Lindsay 60.00 150.00
Gordie Howe/100
CC2HN Dany Heatley
Rick Nash/25
CC2IC Jarome Iginla 30.00 80.00
Jonathan Cheechoo/25
CC2MS Ryan Miller 12.00 30.00
Drew Stafford/100
CC2MT Mike Modano 20.00 50.00
Marty Turco/25
CC2OC Bobby Orr 150.00 250.00
Don Cherry/100
CC2OM Alexander Ovechkin
Evgeni Malkin/25
CC2RF Patrick Roy
Grant Fuhr/25
CC2RP Denis Potvin 15.00 40.00
Larry Robinson/100
CC2SD Peter Stastny
Marcel Dionne/100
CC2SR Steve Shutt 10.00 25.00
Michael Ryder/100
CC2SS Eric Staal 15.00 40.00
Jordan Staal/100
CC2TL Vincent Lecavalier
Joe Thornton/25

2007-08 Upper Deck Trilogy Honorary Scripted Patches

STATED PRINT RUN 10 SER.#'d SETS
NOT PRICED DUE TO SCARCITY

2007-08 Upper Deck Trilogy Honorary Scripted Swatches

STATED PRINT RUN 50 #'d SETS
SSAH Ales Hemsky 12.00 30.00
SSAM Al MacInnis 15.00 40.00
SSAO Alexander Ovechkin 60.00 150.00
SSAR Andrew Raycroft 15.00 40.00
SSBE Patrice Bergeron 20.00 50.00
SSBG Brian Gionta 12.00 30.00
SSCN Cam Neely 20.00 50.00
SSDH Dale Hawerchuk 15.00 40.00
SSGF Grant Fuhr 30.00 80.00
SSGH Gordie Howe/10
SSHA Dominik Hasek 25.00 60.00
SSHE Dany Heatley 25.00 60.00
SSHL Henrik Lundqvist 25.00 60.00
SSIK Ilya Kovalchuk 25.00 60.00
SSJC Jonathan Cheechoo 15.00 40.00
SSJI Jarome Iginla 30.00 80.00
SSJT Joe Thornton 25.00 60.00
SSKL Kari Lehtonen 20.00 50.00
SSMB Martin Brodeur 50.00 120.00
SSMF Marc-Andre Fleury 20.00 50.00
SSMG Marian Gaborik 25.00 60.00
SSML Mario Lemieux/10
SSMR Michael Ryder 12.00 30.00
SSMT Marty Turco 20.00 50.00
SSNL Nicklas Lidstrom 20.00 50.00
SSPB Pierre-Marc Bouchard 12.00 30.00
SSPM Patrick Marleau 15.00 40.00
SSPR Patrick Roy/10
SSPS Peter Stastny 15.00 40.00
SSRB Ray Bourque 25.00 60.00
SSRM Ryan Miller 20.00 50.00
SSRN Rick Nash 20.00 50.00
SSSC Sidney Crosby 150.00 300.00
SSSG Simon Gagne 20.00 50.00
SSTV Tomas Vokoun 20.00 50.00
SSVL Vincent Lecavalier 20.00 50.00
SSWG Wayne Gretzky/10

2007-08 Upper Deck Trilogy Honorary Swatches

STATED ODDS 1:3
HSAH Ales Hemsky 3.00 8.00
HSAM Al MacInnis 4.00 10.00
HSAO Alexander Ovechkin 15.00 40.00
HSAR Andrew Raycroft 4.00 10.00
HSAY Alexei Yashin 3.00 8.00
HSBC Bobby Clarke 5.00 12.00
HSBF Bernie Federko 3.00 8.00
HSBG Bill Guerin 3.00 8.00
HSBL Rob Blake 4.00 10.00
HSBO Pierre-Marc Bouchard 3.00 8.00
HSBR Brad Richards 4.00 10.00
HSBS Billy Smith 5.00 12.00
HSCH Jonathan Cheechoo 4.00 10.00
HSCJ Curtis Joseph 4.00 10.00
HSCN Cam Neely 5.00 12.00
HSCP Chris Pronger 5.00 12.00
HSCW Cam Ward 5.00 12.00
HSDA Daniel Alfredsson 4.00 10.00
HSDB Daniel Briere 5.00 12.00
HSDC Dino Ciccarelli 4.00 10.00
HSDE Denis Savard 4.00 10.00
HSDG Doug Gilmour 4.00 10.00
HSDH Dale Hawerchuk 4.00 10.00
HSDS Darryl Sittler 4.00 10.00
HSDW Doug Weight 3.00 8.00
HSEB Ed Belfour 5.00 12.00
HSEL Eric Lindros 5.00 12.00
HSES Eric Staal 5.00 12.00
HSFL Marc-Andre Fleury 5.00 12.00
HSGF Grant Fuhr 8.00 20.00
HSGH Gordie Howe 12.00 30.00
HSGI Brian Gionta 3.00 8.00
HSGL Guy Lafleur 12.00 30.00
HSHA Dominik Hasek 6.00 15.00
HSHE Dany Heatley 6.00 15.00
HSHL Henrik Lundqvist 6.00 15.00
HSIK Ilya Kovalchuk 6.00 15.00
HSJC Jeff Carter 3.00 8.00
HSJG Jean-Sebastien Giguere 5.00 12.00
HSJI Jarome Iginla 8.00 20.00
HSJJ Jaromir Jagr 8.00 20.00
HSJO Joe Sakic 10.00 25.00
HSJS Jason Spezza 5.00 12.00
HSJT Joe Thornton 6.00 15.00
HSKL Kari Lehtonen 5.00 12.00
HSKO Mikko Koivu 3.00 8.00
HSKT Keith Tkachuk 4.00 10.00
HSLM Lanny McDonald 4.00 10.00
HSLR Larry Robinson 6.00 15.00
HSMB Martin Brodeur 12.00 30.00
HSMF Manny Fernandez 4.00 10.00
HSMG Marian Gaborik 6.00 15.00
HSMH Marian Hossa 5.00 12.00
HSMK Miikka Kiprusoff 6.00 15.00
HSML Mario Lemieux 15.00 40.00
HSMM Mike Modano 6.00 15.00
HSMN Markus Naslund 5.00 12.00
HSMR Mark Recchi 3.00 8.00
HSMS Marek Svatos 3.00 8.00
HSMT Marty Turco 5.00 12.00
HSNH Nathan Horton 3.00 8.00
HSNK Nikolai Khabibulin 5.00 12.00
HSNL Nicklas Lidstrom 5.00 12.00
HSOK Olaf Kolzig 5.00 12.00
HSPB Patrice Bergeron 5.00 12.00
HSPD Pavel Datsyuk 5.00 12.00
HSPE Patrik Elias 3.00 8.00
HSPF Peter Forsberg 6.00 15.00
HSPK Paul Kariya 5.00 12.00
HSPM Patrick Marleau 4.00 10.00
HSPR Patrick Roy 15.00 40.00
HSPS Peter Stastny 4.00 10.00
HSRB Ray Bourque 6.00 15.00
HSRD Rick DiPietro 4.00 10.00
HSRH Ron Hextall 8.00 20.00
HSRL Roberto Luongo 8.00 20.00
HSRM Ryan Miller 5.00 12.00
HSRN Rick Nash 5.00 12.00
HSRS Ryan Smyth 4.00 10.00
HSRY Michael Ryder 3.00 8.00
HSSA Borje Salming 4.00 10.00
HSSC Sidney Crosby 25.00 60.00
HSSD Shane Doan 3.00 8.00
HSSF Sergei Fedorov 5.00 12.00
HSSG Simon Gagne 5.00 12.00
HSSH Brendan Shanahan 5.00 12.00
HSSK Saku Koivu 4.00 10.00
HSSN Scott Niedermayer 3.00 8.00
HSSS Steve Shutt 4.00 10.00
HSST Jordan Staal 6.00 15.00
HSSU Mats Sundin 5.00 12.00
HSSZ Sergei Zubov 3.00 8.00
HSTB Todd Bertuzzi 4.00 10.00
HSTS Teemu Selanne 5.00 12.00
HSTV Thomas Vanek 4.00 10.00
HSVL Vincent Lecavalier 5.00 12.00
HSVO Tomas Vokoun 5.00 12.00
HSWG Wayne Gretzky 25.00 60.00
HSWI Doug Wilson 6.00 15.00
HSZC Zdeno Chara 3.00 8.00

2007-08 Upper Deck Trilogy Ice Scripts

STATED ODDS 1:9
ISAH Ales Hemsky 8.00 20.00
ISAK Anze Kopitar 12.00 30.00
ISAM Al MacInnis 10.00 25.00
ISAO Alexander Ovechkin 75.00 150.00
ISAR Andrew Raycroft 10.00 25.00
ISBH Bobby Hull 20.00 50.00
ISBO Bobby Orr 150.00 250.00
ISBP Benoit Pouliot 8.00 20.00
ISCH Cristobal Huet 10.00 25.00
ISCI Dino Ciccarelli 10.00 25.00
ISCP Corey Perry 10.00 25.00
ISDH Dany Heatley 15.00 40.00
ISDP Denis Potvin 10.00 25.00
ISDS Drew Stafford 10.00 25.00
ISEM Evgeni Malkin 30.00 80.00
ISES Eric Staal 12.00 30.00
ISGF Grant Fuhr 20.00 50.00
ISGH Gordie Howe 60.00 120.00
ISGP Gilbert Perreault 10.00 25.00
ISJB Johnny Bower
ISJC Jonathan Cheechoo 10.00 25.00
ISJG Jean-Sebastien Giguere 12.00 30.00
ISJH Jaroslav Halak 25.00 60.00
ISJI Jarome Iginla 20.00 50.00
ISJK Jari Kurri 12.00 30.00
ISJS Jordan Staal 15.00 40.00
ISJT Joe Thornton
ISLR Larry Robinson 15.00 40.00
ISLT Lauri Tukonen 8.00 20.00
ISMB Martin Brodeur 100.00 200.00
ISMD Marcel Dionne 8.00 20.00
ISMF Marc-Andre Fleury 12.00 30.00
ISMG Marian Gaborik 15.00 40.00
ISML Mario Lemieux 125.00 200.00
ISMR Michael Ryder 8.00 20.00
ISMT Marty Turco 12.00 30.00
ISND Nigel Dawes 8.00 20.00
ISNL Nicklas Lidstrom 12.00 30.00
ISPK Phil Kessel 12.00 30.00
ISPR Patrick Roy 75.00 150.00
ISRH Ron Hextall 20.00 50.00
ISRM Ryan Miller 12.00 30.00
ISRN Rick Nash 12.00 30.00
ISSC Sidney Crosby 100.00 200.00
ISSG Simon Gagne 12.00 30.00
ISSS Steve Shutt 10.00 25.00
ISSV Marek Svatos 8.00 20.00
ISTE Tony Esposito 20.00 50.00
ISTL Ted Lindsay 10.00 25.00
ISTV Tomas Vokoun 12.00 30.00
ISVL Vincent Lecavalier 12.00 30.00
ISWG Wayne Gretzky 150.00 250.00
ISWW Wojtek Wolski 8.00 20.00

2007-08 Upper Deck Trilogy Personal Scripts

STATED PRINT RUN 25 SERIAL #'d SETS
PSAH Ales Hemsky
PSAK Anze Kopitar 50.00 100.00
PSAM Al MacInnis
PSAT Alex Tanguay 15.00 40.00
PSBC Bobby Clarke 20.00 50.00
PSBF Bernie Federko 12.00 30.00
PSBH Bobby Hull 30.00 80.00
PSBN Bob Nystrom 12.00 30.00
PSBO Bobby Orr/10 400.00 500.00
PSCP Corey Perry
PSCW Cam Ward 20.00 50.00
PSDH Dany Heatley 25.00 60.00
PSEM Evgeni Malkin 75.00 125.00
PSGF Grant Fuhr 30.00 80.00
PSGH Gordie Howe 40.00 100.00
PSGP Gilbert Perreault 15.00 40.00
PSHA Dominik Hasek 25.00 60.00
PSHO Gordie Howe 40.00 100.00
PSJC Jonathan Cheechoo 15.00 40.00
PSJG Jean-Sebastien Giguere 20.00 50.00
PSJI Jarome Iginla
PSJK Jari Kurri
PSJS Jordan Staal 25.00 60.00
PSJT Joe Thornton 25.00 60.00
PSLM Lanny McDonald 15.00 40.00
PSLR Larry Robinson 25.00 60.00
PSMB Martin Brodeur 75.00 150.00
PSME Mark Messier/10 150.00 300.00
PSMF Marc-Andre Fleury 20.00 50.00
PSML Mario Lemieux
PSMM Mark Messier/75 150.00 300.00
PSMR Michael Ryder 12.00 30.00
PSMS Martin St. Louis 15.00 40.00
PSMT Marty Turco 20.00 50.00
PSNL Nicklas Lidstrom 75.00 150.00
PSPE Phil Esposito
PSPK Phil Kessel 20.00 50.00
PSPR Patrick Roy
PSRB Ray Bourque 25.00 60.00
PSRH Ron Hextall 30.00 80.00
PSRM Ryan Miller 20.00 50.00
PSSC Sidney Crosby 250.00 400.00
PSSG Simon Gagne 20.00 50.00
PSTE Tony Esposito 30.00 80.00
PSVL Vincent Lecavalier 20.00 50.00

2007-08 Upper Deck Trilogy Scripts

S1AB Alex Brooks 6.00 15.00
S1AD Adam Dennis SP
S1AK Anze Kopitar 10.00 25.00
S1BC Blake Comeau 6.00 15.00
S1BE Benoit Pouliot 6.00 15.00
S1BJ Blair Jones 6.00 15.00
S1BO Dave Bolland 6.00 15.00
S1BP Brandon Prust 6.00 15.00
S1BR Brad Boyes 8.00 20.00
S1CH Chris Higgins 8.00 20.00
S1CK Chris Kunitz 6.00 15.00
S1CP Corey Perry 8.00 20.00
S1CW Cam Ward 10.00 25.00
S1DB Dustin Boyd 6.00 15.00
S1DS Drew Stafford 8.00 20.00
S1EC Erik Christensen 6.00 15.00
S1EF Eric Fehr 6.00 15.00
S1EM Evgeni Malkin SP
S1HL Henrik Lundqvist SP
S1HT Hannu Toivonen 8.00 20.00
S1IW Ian White 6.00 15.00
S1JC Jeff Carter
S1JG Josh Gorges 6.00 15.00
S1JH Josh Hennessy 6.00 15.00
S1JO Johnny Oduya 6.00 15.00
S1JP Joe Pavelski 6.00 15.00
S1JS Jordan Staal 12.00 30.00
S1MC Matt Carle 6.00 15.00
S1MJ Milan Jurcina 6.00 15.00
S1MP Marc-Antoine Pouliot SP
S1MR Mike Richards 12.00 30.00
S1MS Marek Svatos 6.00 15.00
S1NW Noah Welch SP
S1PK Phil Kessel SP
S1PN Petteri Nokelainen 6.00 15.00
S1PO Patrick O'Sullivan 8.00 20.00
S1PP Petr Prucha 6.00 15.00
S1PR Paul Ranger 6.00 15.00
S1PS Paul Stastny 10.00 25.00
S1RG Ryan Getzlaf 8.00 20.00
S1RK Ryan Kesler 6.00 15.00
S1RM Ryan Miller
S1RO Roman Polak 6.00 15.00
S1RP Ryan Potulny SP
S1RS Ryan Shannon 6.00 15.00
S1SB Steve Bernier 6.00 15.00
S1SO Shane O'Brien 6.00 15.00
S1TK Tomas Kopecky 8.00 20.00
S1TZ Travis Zajac SP
S1VF Valtteri Filppula 6.00 15.00
S1WW Wojtek Wolski 6.00 15.00
S1YS Yan Stastny 6.00 15.00
S2AF Alexander Frolov 6.00 15.00
S2AO Alexander Ovechkin SP 75.00 150.00
S2AT Alex Tanguay 8.00 20.00
S2DH Dominik Hasek SP 40.00 100.00
S2DR Dwayne Roloson 8.00 20.00
S2ES Eric Staal 10.00 25.00
S2GO Scott Gomez 6.00 15.00
S2HE Dany Heatley 12.00 30.00
S2IK Ilya Kovalchuk 12.00 30.00
S2JC Jonathan Cheechoo 8.00 20.00
S2JG Jean-Sebastien Giguere SP
S2JI Jarome Iginla
S2JT Joe Thornton SP 30.00 60.00
S2MB Martin Brodeur SP
S2MF Marc-Andre Fleury 10.00 25.00
S2MG Marian Gaborik 12.00 30.00
S2MR Michael Ryder 6.00 15.00
S2NL Nicklas Lidstrom 10.00 25.00
S2PB Patrice Bergeron 10.00 25.00
S2RN Rick Nash 10.00 25.00
S2SC Sidney Crosby 90.00 150.00
S2SD Shane Doan SP
S2SG Simon Gagne 10.00 25.00
S2ST Martin St. Louis 8.00 20.00
S2TV Tomas Vokoun 10.00 25.00
S2VL Vincent Lecavalier 10.00 25.00
S2VT Vesa Toskala 8.00 20.00
S3AM Al MacInnis 8.00 20.00
S3BC Bobby Clarke 10.00 25.00
S3CN Cam Neely 10.00 25.00
S3GC Gerry Cheevers 15.00 40.00
S3GF Grant Fuhr 15.00 40.00
S3GH Gordie Howe SP 100.00 175.00
S3JK Jari Kurri 10.00 25.00
S3LM Lanny McDonald 8.00 20.00
S3LR Larry Robinson 12.00 30.00

2007-08 Upper Deck Trilogy Triple Clearcut Autographs

STATED PRINT RUN 10 SER.#'d SETS
NOT PRICED DUE TO SCARCITY
CC3DWK Alexander Ovechkin
Evgeni Malkin
Ilya Kovalchuk
CC3GCR Simon Gagne
Jonathan Cheechoo
Michael Ryder
CC3GHE Marian Gaborik
Ales Hemsky
Patrik Elias
CC3GHO Bobby Orr
Wayne Gretzky
Gordie Howe
CC3INH Jarome Iginla
Dany Heatley
Rick Nash
CC3MFS Marc-Andre Fleury
Evgeni Malkin
Jordan Staal
CC3ORL Patrick Roy
Mario Lemieux
Bobby Orr
CC3PMA Peter Stastny
Anton Stastny
Marian Stastny
CC3SSS Brian Sutter
Darryl Sutter
Duane Sutter

2008-09 Upper Deck Trilogy

This set was released on December 30, 2008. The base set consists of 175 cards. Cards 1-100 feature veterans, and cards 101-175 are rookies.

COMPLETE SET (175)
COMP.SET w/o SPs (100) 15.00 40.00
STATED PRINT RUN 999 SERIAL #'d SETS
STATED PRINT RUN 499 SERIAL #'d SETS
OVERALL RC STATED ODDS 1:3
1 Ales Hemsky .60 1.50
2 Alex Kovalev 1.00 2.50
3 Alexander Frolov .60 1.50
4 Alexander Ovechkin 4.00 10.00
5 Andrew Cogliano 1.50 4.00
6 Anze Kopitar 1.00 2.50
7 Brad Boyes .75 2.00
8 Brad Richards .75 2.00
9 Brenden Morrow .75 2.00
10 Brian Campbell 1.50 4.00
11 Cam Ward 1.00 2.50
12 Carey Price 3.00 8.00
13 Chris Drury 1.00 2.50
14 Chris Osgood 1.00 2.50
15 Chris Pronger .75 2.00
16 Corey Perry 1.00 2.50
17 Cristobal Huet 1.00 2.50
18 Daniel Alfredsson .75 2.00
19 Daniel Briere 1.00 2.50
20 Daniel Sedin 1.00 2.50
21 Dany Heatley 1.25 3.00
22 Derek Roy .60 1.50
23 Dion Phaneuf 1.00 2.50
24 Eric Staal 1.50 4.00
25 Evgeni Malkin 2.50 6.00
26 Evgeni Nabokov 1.00 2.50
27 Henrik Lundqvist 2.00 5.00
28 Henrik Sedin 1.00 2.50
29 Henrik Zetterberg 2.00 5.00
30 Ilya Kovalchuk 1.25 3.00
31 J.P. Dumont .60 1.50
32 Jarome Iginla 2.00 5.00
33 Jason Arnott .60 1.50
34 Jason Pominville .75 2.00
35 Jason Spezza 1.25 3.00
36 Jean-Sebastien Giguere 1.00 2.50
37 Joe Sakic 1.50 4.00
38 Joe Thornton 1.50 4.00
39 Jonathan Cheechoo 1.00 2.50
40 Jonathan Toews 3.00 8.00
41 Jordan Staal 1.50 4.00
42 Jose Theodore 1.00 2.50
43 Justin Williams .60 1.50
44 Kari Lehtonen .60 1.50
45 Manny Legace .75 2.00
46 Marc-Andre Fleury 1.00 2.50
47 Marian Gaborik 1.50 4.00
48 Marian Hossa 1.50 4.00
49 Mark Streit .60 1.50
50 Markus Naslund 1.00 2.50
51 Martin Brodeur 2.00 5.00
52 Martin St. Louis 1.00 2.50
53 Marty Turco .75 2.00
54 Mats Sundin 1.00 2.50
55 Miikka Kiprusoff 1.00 2.50
56 Mike Comrie .60 1.50
57 Mike Green .60 1.50
58 Mike Modano 1.00 2.50
59 Mike Ribeiro .60 1.50
60 Mike Richards 1.50 4.00
61 Mikko Koivu 1.00 2.50
62 Nathan Horton .60 1.50
63 Nicklas Backstrom 2.00 5.00
64 Nicklas Lidstrom 1.00 2.50
65 Nik Antropov .75 2.00
66 Niklas Backstrom 1.00 2.50
67 Nikolai Zherdev .60 1.50
68 Olli Jokinen .60 1.50
69 Pascal Leclaire .75 2.00
70 Patrice Bergeron 1.00 2.50
71 Patrick Kane 2.50 6.00
72 Patrick Sharp .60 1.50
73 Patrik Elias .60 1.50
74 Paul Kariya 1.00 2.50
75 Paul Stastny 1.00 2.50
76 Pavel Datsyuk 1.00 2.50
77 Peter Mueller 1.25 3.00
78 Phil Kessel 1.00 2.50
79 Rick DiPietro 1.00 2.50
80 Rick Nash 1.00 2.50
81 Roberto Luongo 1.50 4.00
82 Ryan Getzlaf 1.25 3.00
83 Ryan Malone .60 1.50
84 Ryan Miller 1.00 2.50
85 Ryan Smyth .75 2.00
86 Saku Koivu 1.00 2.50
87 Sam Gagner 1.50 4.00
88 Scott Gomez .75 2.00
89 Shane Doan .60 1.50
90 Shawn Horcoff .60 1.50
91 Sidney Crosby 5.00 12.00
92 Simon Gagne .75 2.00
93 Thomas Vanek 1.00 2.50
94 Tim Thomas 1.00 2.50
95 Tobias Enstrom 1.00 2.50
96 Tomas Kaberle .60 1.50
97 Tomas Vokoun 1.00 2.50
98 Vesa Toskala 1.00 2.50
99 Vincent Lecavalier 1.00 2.50
100 Zach Parise 1.00 2.50
101 Sami Lepisto RC 4.00 10.00
102 Mike Brown RC 5.00 12.00
103 Zach Fitzgerald RC 4.00 10.00
104 Alex Foster RC 3.00 8.00
105 Darryl Boyce RC 3.00 8.00
106 John Mitchell RC 4.00 10.00
107 Robbie Earl RC 3.00 8.00
108 Jonas Frogren RC 5.00 12.00
109 Vladimir Mihalik RC 4.00 10.00
110 Janne Niskala RC 4.00 10.00
111 Tom Cavanagh RC 3.00 8.00
112 Alex Goligoski RC 8.00 20.00
113 Jon Filewich RC 3.00 8.00
114 Ryan Stone RC 4.00 10.00
115 Kevin Porter RC 3.00 8.00
116 Kyle Turris RC 8.00 20.00
117 Claude Giroux RC 8.00 20.00
118 Tim Ramholt RC 3.00 8.00
119 Brian Lee RC 4.00 10.00
120 Ilya Zubov RC 4.00 10.00
121 Jesse Winchester RC 4.00 10.00
122 Kyle Okposo RC 8.00 20.00
123 Mike Iggulden RC 3.00 8.00
124 Anssi Salmela RC 5.00 12.00
125 Ryan Jones RC 5.00 12.00
126 Matt D'Agostini RC 6.00 15.00
127 James Neal RC 6.00 15.00
128 Brian Boyle RC 4.00 10.00
129 Oscar Moller RC 4.00 10.00
130 Danny Taylor RC 4.00 10.00
131 Erik Ersberg RC 4.00 10.00
132 Wayne Simmonds RC 8.00 20.00
133 Michael Frolik RC 8.00 20.00
134 Shawn Matthias RC 4.00 10.00
135 Viktor Tikhonov RC 4.00 10.00
136 Patrik Berglund RC 10.00 25.00
137 Darren Helm RC 6.00 15.00
138 Jonathan Ericsson RC 6.00 15.00
139 Justin Abdelkader RC 8.00 20.00
140 Mattias Ritola RC 5.00 12.00
141 B.J. Crombeen RC 3.00 8.00
142 Garrett Stafford RC 5.00 12.00
143 Mark Fistric RC 4.00 10.00
144 Adam Pineault RC 4.00 10.00
145 Andrew Murray RC 3.00 8.00
146 Dan LaCosta RC 5.00 12.00
147 Derick Brassard RC 8.00 20.00
148 Derek Dorsett RC 5.00 12.00
149 Steve Mason RC 10.00 25.00
150 Tom Sestito RC 3.00 8.00
151 Cody McLeod RC 3.00 8.00
152 Jordan Hendry RC 3.00 8.00
153 Brandon Nolan RC 5.00 12.00
154 Joe Jensen RC 4.00 10.00
155 Tim Conboy RC 4.00 10.00
156 Kyle Greentree RC 5.00 12.00
157 Luca Sbisa RC 6.00 15.00
158 Pascal Pelletier RC 3.00 8.00
159 Boris Valabik RC 5.00 12.00
160 Andrew Ebbett RC 4.00 10.00
161 Luke Schenn RC 15.00 40.00
162 Nikolai Kulemin RC 5.00 12.00
163 Steven Stamkos RC 40.00 100.00
164 Alex Pietrangelo RC 8.00 20.00
165 T.J. Oshie RC 12.00 30.00
166 Zach Boychuk RC 8.00 20.00
167 Mikkel Boedker RC 8.00 20.00
168 Nikita Filatov RC 20.00 50.00
169 Fabian Brunnstrom RC 8.00 20.00
170 Drew Doughty RC 15.00 40.00
171 Colton Gillies RC 5.00 12.00
172 Jakub Voracek RC 10.00 25.00
173 Brandon Sutter RC 6.00 15.00
174 Blake Wheeler RC 12.00 30.00
175 Zach Bogosian RC 8.00 20.00

2008-09 Upper Deck Trilogy Combo Clearcut Autographs

STATED PRINT RUN 100 SERIAL #'d SETS
CC2BG Mike Bossy 20.00 50.00
Clark Gillies/25
CC2BO Bobby Orr
Johnny Bucyk/25
CC2BT Walt Tkaczuk 15.00 40.00
Andy Bathgate/100
CC2HD Henrik Sedin 15.00 40.00
Daniel Sedin/100
CC2HN Dany Heatley
Rick Nash/25
CC2JJ Erik Johnson 20.00 50.00
Jack Johnson/100

C2KP Carey Price
Saku Koivu/25
C2LM Mark Messier
Brian Leetch/25
C2LS Nicklas Lidstrom
Borje Salming/25
C2OB Alexander Ovechkin
Nicklas Backstrom/25
C2PG Ryan Getzlaf 20.00 50.00
Corey Perry/100
C2SB Martin St. Louis
Dan Boyle/100
C2SS Peter Stastny 15.00 40.00
Paul Stastny/100
C2TK Patrick Kane 60.00 120.00
Jonathan Toews/100
C2TN Joe Thornton 30.00 80.00
Evgeni Nabokov/25
C2VH Tomas Vokoun 15.00 40.00
Nathan Horton/100

2008-09 Upper Deck Trilogy Frozen in Time

COMPLETE SET (20) 150.00 300.00
STATED ODDS 1:12
STATED PRINT RUN 799 SERIAL #'d SETS

2008-09 Upper Deck Trilogy Honorary Swatches

OVERALL G-U STATED ODDS 1:3
HSBD Rod Brind'Amour 4.00 10.00
HSBS Brendan Shanahan 5.00 12.00
HSCP Carey Price 15.00 40.00
HSEM Evgeni Malkin 12.00 30.00
HSES Eric Staal 8.00 20.00
HSHL Henrik Lundqvist 10.00 25.00
HSIK Ilya Kovalchuk 6.00 15.00
HSJS Jason Spezza 6.00 15.00
HSJT Joe Thornton 8.00 20.00
HSKN Patrick Kane 12.00 30.00
HSMB Martin Brodeur 10.00 25.00
HSMG Marian Gaborik 8.00 20.00
HSMH Marian Hossa 8.00 20.00
HSMM Mike Modano 5.00 12.00
HSMS Martin St. Louis 5.00 12.00
HSNB Nicklas Backstrom 10.00 25.00
HSNZ Nikolai Zherdev 3.00 8.00
HSPK Phil Kessel 5.00 12.00
HSPM Pierre-Marc Bouchard 3.00 8.00
HSPS Paul Stastny 5.00 12.00
HSRB Rob Blake 5.00 12.00
HSRD Rick DiPietro 5.00 12.00
HSRL Roberto Luongo 8.00 20.00
HSRM Ryan Miller 5.00 12.00
HSRN Rick Nash 5.00 12.00
HSSC Sidney Crosby 25.00 60.00
HSSK Saku Koivu 5.00 12.00
HSSU Mats Sundin 5.00 12.00
HSSW Shea Weber 3.00 8.00
HSTO Jonathan Toews 15.00 40.00

2008-09 Upper Deck Trilogy Ice Scripts

STATED ODDS 1:9
OVERALL AU STAED ODDS 1:3
ISAC Andrew Cogliano 15.00 40.00
ISAD Alex Delvecchio 12.00 30.00
ISAO Alexander Ovechkin 50.00 100.00
ISBB Brad Boyes 8.00 20.00
ISBO Bobby Orr 125.00 250.00
ISCD Chris Drury 10.00 25.00
ISCG Claude Giroux 20.00 50.00
ISCP Carey Price 30.00 80.00
ISDB Derick Brassard 20.00 50.00
ISDC Don Cherry 125.00 250.00
ISDP David Perron 8.00 20.00
ISDS Daniel Sedin 10.00 25.00
ISEJ Erik Johnson 12.00 30.00
ISEM Evgeni Malkin 60.00 120.00
ISGH Gordie Howe
ISGI Clark Gillies 8.00 20.00
ISGP Gilbert Perreault 10.00 25.00
ISHS Henrik Sedin 10.00 25.00
ISHZ Henrik Zetterberg 20.00 50.00
ISJB Johnny Bucyk 10.00 25.00
ISJC Jeff Carter 15.00 40.00
ISJH Josh Harding 8.00 20.00
ISJJ Jack Johnson 8.00 20.00
ISJO Joe Thornton 15.00 40.00
ISJS Jordan Staal 15.00 40.00
ISJT Jonathan Toews 30.00 80.00
ISKE Phil Kessel 10.00 25.00
ISLI Ted Lindsay 10.00 25.00
ISMB Martin Brodeur 60.00 120.00
ISML Mario Lemieux 125.00 250.00
ISMM Mark Messier 75.00 150.00
ISMO Mike Modano 10.00 25.00
ISMR Mike Ribeiro 6.00 15.00
ISMS Marc Staal
ISMT Marty Turco 8.00 20.00
ISNB Nicklas Backstrom 20.00 50.00
ISNF Nick Foligno 10.00 25.00
ISNH Nathan Horton 6.00 15.00
ISPK Patrick Kane 25.00 60.00
ISPM Peter Mueller 12.00 30.00
ISPO Denis Potvin 8.00 20.00
ISPR Patrick Roy 40.00 100.00
ISPS Paul Stastny 10.00 25.00
ISRB Ray Bourque 40.00 100.00
ISRE Robbie Earl 8.00 20.00
ISRG Ryan Getzlaf 12.00 30.00
ISRL Rod Langway 12.00 30.00
ISSB Scotty Bowman 40.00 100.00
ISSC Sidney Crosby 125.00 250.00
ISSG Sam Gagner 15.00 40.00
ISSM Steve Mason 25.00 60.00
ISSS Steve Shutt 10.00 25.00
ISST Peter Stastny 10.00 25.00
ISTE Tony Esposito 20.00 50.00
ISTL Jiri Tlusty 10.00 25.00
ISTR Tuukka Rask 10.00 25.00
ISTV Tomas Vokoun 10.00 25.00
ISWG Wayne Gretzky
ISWT Walt Tkaczuk 6.00 15.00

2008-09 Upper Deck Trilogy Quad Clearcut Autographs

STATED PRINT RUN 5 SERIAL #'d SETS
NOT PRICED DUE TO SCARCITY

2008-09 Upper Deck Trilogy Rivals

STATED ODDS 1:90
ANACOL Jean-Sebastien Giguere 30.00 80.00
Chris Pronger
ANASJS Ryan Getzlaf 30.00 80.00
Scott Niedermayer
Jean-Sebastien Giguere
Joe Thornton
Jonathan Cheechoo
Evgeni Nabokov
BOSNYR Patrice Bergeron 20.00 50.00
Zdeno Chara
Marc Savard
Chris Drury
Scott Gomez
Nikolai Zherdev
CARTBY Cam Ward 30.00 80.00
Eric Staal
Rod Brind'Amour
Vincent Lecavalier
Martin St. Louis
Jussi Jokinen
CGYEDM Dion Phaneuf 30.00 80.00
Miikka Kiprusoff
Mike Cammalleri
Sam Gagner
Dwayne Roloson
Erik Cole
CGYVAN Dion Phaneuf 30.00 80.00
Miikka Kiprusoff
Mike Cammalleri
Roberto Luongo
Daniel Sedin
Pavol Demitra
DETCHI Henrik Zetterberg
Pavel Datsyuk
Nicklas Lidstrom
Jonathan Toews
Patrick Kane
Duncan Keith
EDMCGY Mark Messier 40.00 100.00
Jari Kurri
Grant Fuhr
Theoren Fleury
Al MacInnis
Joe Mullen
EDMVAN Sam Gagner 30.00 80.00
Shawn Horcoff
Erik Cole
Roberto Luongo
Pavol Demitra
Steve Bernier
LAKANA Anze Kopitar
Dustin Brown
Kyle Calder
Ryan Getzlaf
Chris Pronger
Teemu Selanne
MONBOS Carey Price 60.00 150.00
Alex Kovalev
Saku Koivu
Phil Kessel
Tim Thomas
Michael Ryder
NJDNYR Martin Brodeur
Zach Parise
Patrik Elias
Henrik Lundqvist
Chris Drury
Scott Gomez
NYRNYI Henrik Lundqvist
Markus Naslund
Scott Gomez
Rick DiPietro
Mike Comrie
Jeff Tambellini
NYRPIT Henrik Lundqvist 40.00 100.00
Wade Redden
Marc Staal
Marc-Andre Fleury
Sergei Gonchar
Jordan Staal
OTTMON Dany Heatley 60.00 150.00
Jason Spezza
Martin Gerber
Alex Kovalev
Carey Price
Saku Koivu
PITPHI Sidney Crosby 100.00 250.00
Evgeni Malkin
Marc-Andre Fleury
Daniel Briere
Mike Richards
Martin Biron
SJSDAL Joe Thornton 30.00 80.00
Patrick Marleau
Jonathan Cheechoo
Brad Richards
Jere Lehtinen
Mike Ribeiro
TORBUF Mats Sundin 20.00 50.00
Vesa Toskala
Matt Stajan
Ryan Miller
Maxim Afinogenov
Drew Stafford
TORMON Mats Sundin 60.00 150.00
Vesa Toskala
Nikolai Antropov
Carey Price
Saku Koivu
Alex Kovalev

2008-09 Upper Deck Trilogy Scripted Swatches First Star

STATED PRINT RUN 10 SERIAL #'d SETS
NOT PRICED DUE TO SCARCITY

2008-09 Upper Deck Trilogy Scripted Swatches Second Star

*SECOND STAR: .6X TO 1.5X THIRD STAR
STATED PRINT RUN 25 SERIAL #'d SETS

2008-09 Upper Deck Trilogy Scripted Swatches Third Star

STATED PRINT RUN 100 SERIAL #'d SETS
3RDAM Al MacInnis 12.00 30.00
3RDAO Alexander Ovechkin 40.00 100.00
3RDCP Carey Price 30.00 80.00
3RDCW Cam Ward 10.00 25.00
3RDDC Dino Ciccarelli 6.00 15.00
3RDEM Evgeni Malkin 30.00 80.00
3RDES Eric Staal 15.00 40.00
3RDGP Gilbert Perreault 10.00 25.00
3RDHA Dominik Hasek 15.00 40.00
3RDHE Milan Hejduk 8.00 20.00
3RDHZ Henrik Zetterberg EXCH 20.00 50.00
3RDIK Ilya Kovalchuk 12.00 30.00
3RDJC Jonathan Cheechoo 10.00 25.00
3RDJG Jean-Sebastien Giguere 10.00 25.00
3RDJL Joffrey Lupul 6.00 15.00
3RDJT Joe Thornton 15.00 40.00
3RDKL Kari Lehtonen 6.00 15.00
3RDLR Luc Robitaille 8.00 20.00
3RDMB Martin Brodeur 20.00 50.00
3RDMF Marc-Andre Fleury 10.00 25.00
3RDMH Marian Hossa 15.00 40.00
3RDMM Mike Modano 10.00 25.00
3RDMN Markus Naslund 10.00 25.00
3RDMT Marty Turco 8.00 20.00
3RDNH Nathan Horton EXCH 6.00 15.00
3RDNL Nicklas Lidstrom 10.00 25.00
3RDNZ Nikolai Zherdev 6.00 15.00
3RDPK Patrick Kane 25.00 60.00
3RDPS Paul Stastny 10.00 25.00
3RDRG Ryan Getzlaf 12.00 30.00
3RDRM Ryan Miller 10.00 25.00
3RDRN Rick Nash 10.00 25.00
3RDSC Sidney Crosby 50.00 120.00
3RDSG Simon Gagne 8.00 20.00
3RDSK Saku Koivu 10.00 25.00
3RDSM Sam Gagner 15.00 40.00
3RDTO Jonathan Toews 30.00 80.00
3RDVO Tomas Vokoun 10.00 25.00

2008-09 Upper Deck Trilogy Superstar Scripts

STATED ODDS 1:9
SSAO Alexander Ovechkin 40.00 100.00
SSAT Alex Tanguay 8.00 20.00
SSBB Brad Boyes 8.00 20.00
SSBM Brenden Morrow 8.00 20.00
SSCD Chris Drury 10.00 25.00
SSCN Cam Neely 12.00 30.00
SSCP Corey Perry 10.00 25.00
SSCW Cam Ward 10.00 25.00
SSDB Dan Boyle 8.00 20.00
SSDC Dan Cleary 10.00 25.00
SSDS Daniel Sedin 10.00 25.00
SSDT Darcy Tucker 8.00 20.00
SSEM Evgeni Malkin 40.00 100.00
SSES Eric Staal
SSGO Scott Gomez 8.00 20.00
SSHE Dany Heatley
SSHL Henrik Lundqvist 20.00 50.00
SSHO Marian Hossa
SSHS Henrik Sedin 10.00 25.00
SSHZ Henrik Zetterberg 20.00 50.00
SSJA Jason Arnott 6.00 15.00
SSJC Jonathan Cheechoo 10.00 25.00
SSJG Jean-Sebastien Giguere 10.00 25.00
SSJI Jarome Iginla
SSLR Luc Robitaille 8.00 20.00
SSMH Milan Hejduk 8.00 20.00
SSMK Mike Knuble 10.00 25.00
SSMM Milan Michalek 6.00 15.00
SSMN Markus Naslund 10.00 25.00
SSMO Mike Modano
SSMR Mike Ribeiro 6.00 15.00
SSMT Marty Turco 8.00 20.00
SSNL Nicklas Lidstrom 10.00 25.00
SSOA Adam Oates
SSPE Patrik Elias 6.00 15.00
SSPM Pierre-Marc Bouchard 6.00 15.00
SSPS Paul Stastny 10.00 25.00
SSRG Ryan Getzlaf 12.00 30.00
SSRM Ryan Miller 10.00 25.00
SSRS Ryan Smyth 8.00 20.00
SSSC Sidney Crosby 50.00 120.00
SSSG Simon Gagne
SSTV Tomas Vokoun 10.00 25.00
SSVA Thomas Vanek 10.00 25.00

2008-09 Upper Deck Trilogy Three Star Spotlights

OVERALL G-U STATED ODDS 1:3
3SADW Jason Arnott 4.00 10.00
J.P. Dumont
Shea Weber
3SBPP Ray Bourque 12.00 30.00
Dion Phaneuf
Chris Pronger
3SCNT Sidney Crosby 30.00 80.00
Rick Nash
Joe Thornton
3SCOM Sidney Crosby 25.00 60.00
Alexander Ovechkin
Evgeni Malkin
3SDMF Marc-Andre Fleury 6.00 15.00
Rick DiPietro
Ryan Miller
3SDSL Roberto Luongo 10.00 25.00
Daniel Sedin
Pavol Demitra
3SFMM Theoren Fleury 8.00 20.00
Al MacInnis
Lanny McDonald
3SFSS Marc-Andre Fleury 10.00 25.00
Jordan Staal
Petr Sykora
3SGHL Wayne Gretzky
Gordie Howe
Mario Lemieux
3SGNB Marian Gaborik 10.00 25.00
Owen Nolan
Pierre-Marc Bouchard
3SGSP Ryan Getzlaf 8.00 20.00
Teemu Selanne
Corey Perry
3SHGP Marian Hossa 10.00 25.00
Marian Gaborik
Zach Parise
3SHSG Dany Heatley 8.00 20.00
Jason Spezza
Martin Gerber
3SKAA Ilya Kovalchuk 8.00 20.00
Maxim Afinogenov
Nik Antropov
3SKMF Mark Messier 12.00 30.00
Jari Kurri
Grant Fuhr
3SKPM Patrick Kane 15.00 40.00
Zach Parise
Peter Mueller
3SKSK Saku Koivu 6.00 15.00
Steve Shutt
Alex Kovalev
3SLBN Roberto Luongo 12.00 30.00
Martin Brodeur
Evgeni Nabokov
3SLLN Martin St. Louis 6.00 15.00
Vincent Lecavalier
Rick Nash
3SLMP Henrik Lundqvist 12.00 30.00
Ryan Miller
Rick DiPietro
3SLNK Roberto Luongo 10.00 25.00
Evgeni Nabokov
Miikka Kiprusoff
3SLPP Nicklas Lidstrom 6.00 15.00
Dion Phaneuf
Chris Pronger
3SMKA Mark Messier 12.00 30.00
Jari Kurri
Glenn Anderson
3SMKG Evgeni Malkin 15.00 40.00
Alex Kovalev
Sergei Gonchar
3SMRL Mike Modano 6.00 15.00
Mike Ribeiro
Jere Lehtinen
3SNGS Markus Naslund 5.00 12.00
Scott Gomez
Brendan Shanahan
3SNPL Rick Nash 5.00 12.00
Michael Peca
Pascal Leclaire
3SOMK Alexander Ovechkin 25.00 60.00
Evgeni Malkin
Ilya Kovalchuk
3SPBC Dion Phaneuf 6.00 15.00
Todd Bertuzzi
Mike Cammalleri
3SRBG Mike Richards 10.00 25.00
Daniel Briere
Simon Gagne
3SRBP Patrick Roy 20.00 50.00
Carey Price
Martin Brodeur
3SSFS Paul Stastny 10.00 25.00
Joe Sakic
Peter Forsberg
3SSGS Borje Salming 8.00 20.00
Doug Gilmour
Mats Sundin
3SSSF Mats Sundin 10.00 25.00
Joe Sakic
Peter Forsberg
3SSSG Eric Staal 10.00 25.00
Ryan Getzlaf
Martin St. Louis
3SSTA Mats Sundin 5.00 12.00
Vesa Toskala
Nikolai Antropov
3SSTC Marc Savard 6.00 15.00
Tim Thomas
Zdeno Chara
3STKB Jonathan Toews 20.00 50.00
Patrick Kane
Nicklas Backstrom
3STTN Jonathan Toews 20.00 50.00
Joe Thornton
Rick Nash
3SZHL Henrik Zetterberg 12.00 30.00
Tomas Holmstrom
Nicklas Lidstrom

2008-09 Upper Deck Trilogy Tri-Color Tandems

STATED ODDS 1:45
TCTBF Martin Brodeur
Marc-Andre Fleury
TCTCH Erik Cole
Shawn Horcoff
TCTCM Sidney Crosby 80.00 200.00
Evgeni Malkin
TCTCO Sidney Crosby
Alexander Ovechkin
TCTDM Shane Doan
Peter Mueller
TCTEJ Eric Staal
Jordan Staal
TCTEP Zach Parise 15.00 40.00
Patrik Elias
TCTGB Marian Gaborik 25.00 60.00
Pierre-Marc Bouchard
TCTHG Dany Heatley 20.00 50.00
Martin Gerber
TCTJM Evgeni Malkin 40.00 100.00
Jordan Staal
TCTJP David Perron
Erik Johnson
TCTJS Joe Sakic 25.00 60.00
Paul Stastny
TCTKJ Anze Kopitar
Jack Johnson
TCTKK Saku Koivu 15.00 40.00
Alex Kovalev
TCTKL Ilya Kovalchuk 20.00 50.00
Kari Lehtonen
TCTKM Evgeni Malkin 40.00 100.00
Ilya Kovalchuk
TCTKS Paul Kariya 15.00 40.00
Teemu Selanne
TCTLD Roberto Luongo
Pavol Demitra
TCTLL Kari Lehtonen
Jere Lehtinen
TCTLP Nicklas Lidstrom 15.00 40.00
Dion Phaneuf
TCTLS Vincent Lecavalier
Martin St. Louis
TCTLW Cam Ward
Pascal Leclaire
TCTMD Ryan Miller 15.00 40.00
Rick DiPietro
TCTNC Evgeni Nabokov 15.00 40.00
Jonathan Cheechoo
TCTOB Alexander Ovechkin 60.00 150.00
Nicklas Backstrom
TCTPG Ryan Getzlaf 40.00 100.00
Dion Phaneuf
TCTPL Carey Price 50.00 120.00
Henrik Lundqvist
TCTPN Chris Pronger 12.00 30.00
Scott Niedermayer
TCTPR Peter Forsberg 25.00 60.00
Rob Blake
TCTRB Mike Richards
Daniel Briere
TCTSD Daniel Sedin 15.00 40.00
Pavol Demitra
TCTSF Mats Sundin 25.00 60.00
Peter Forsberg
TCTSK Marc Savard 15.00 40.00
Phil Kessel
TCTSN Rick Nash
Jason Spezza
TCTTD Joe Thornton 25.00 60.00
Shane Doan
TCTTK Patrick Kane 50.00 120.00
Jonathan Toews
TCTVH Nathan Horton 15.00 40.00
Tomas Vokoun
TCTWA Shea Weber 10.00 25.00
Jason Arnott
TCTZD Henrik Zetterberg
Pavel Datsyuk

2008-09 Upper Deck Trilogy Triple Clearcut Autographs

STATED PRINT RUN 5 SERIAL #'d SETS
NOT PRICED DUE TO SCARCITY

2008-09 Upper Deck Trilogy Two-Way Threads

OVERALL G-U STATED ODDS 1:3
2WAO Alexander Ovechkin 25.00 60.00
2WAR Jason Arnott 4.00 10.00
2WBM Brendan Morrison 4.00 10.00
2WCP Chris Pronger 5.00 12.00
2WDP Dion Phaneuf 6.00 15.00
2WDW Doug Weight 4.00 10.00
2WEC Erik Cole 4.00 10.00
2WHZ Henrik Zetterberg 12.00 30.00
2WJL Jere Lehtinen 4.00 10.00
2WJS Jordan Staal 10.00 25.00
2WJT Joe Thornton 10.00 25.00
2WKD Kris Draper 4.00 10.00
2WMA Maxim Afinogenov
2WMP Michael Peca 5.00 12.00
2WNH Nathan Horton 4.00 10.00
2WNL Nicklas Lidstrom 6.00 15.00
2WOJ Olli Jokinen 4.00 10.00
2WPE Patrik Elias 4.00 10.00
2WPF Peter Forsberg 10.00 25.00
2WPM Patrick Marleau 5.00 12.00
2WPS Patrick Sharp 4.00 10.00
2WRB Rod Brind'Amour 5.00 12.00
2WRG Ryan Getzlaf 8.00 20.00
2WSD Shane Doan 4.00 10.00
2WSF Sergei Fedorov 10.00 25.00
2WSK Joe Sakic 10.00 25.00
2WTH Tomas Holmstrom 5.00 12.00
2WVL Vincent Lecavalier 6.00 15.00
2WZC Zdeno Chara 4.00 10.00
2WZP Zach Parise 6.00 15.00

2008-09 Upper Deck Trilogy Young Star Scripts

STATED ODDS 1:9
YSAB Adam Burish 6.00 15.00
YSAC Andrew Cogliano 12.00 30.00
YSBC Blake Comeau 5.00 12.00
YSBD Brandon Dubinsky 6.00 15.00
YSBE Jonathan Bernier 10.00 25.00
YSCB Cam Barker 5.00 12.00
YSCK Chris Kunitz 5.00 12.00
YSCL David Clarkson 5.00 12.00
YSCP Carey Price 25.00 60.00
YSDC Daniel Carcillo 5.00 12.00
YSDP Dustin Penner 5.00 12.00
YSDS Devin Setoguchi 8.00 20.00
YSEC Erik Christensen 5.00 12.00
YSEJ Erik Johnson 10.00 25.00
YSJB Jared Boll 6.00 15.00
YSJC Jeff Carter 8.00 20.00
YSJH Josh Harding 6.00 15.00
YSJJ Jack Johnson 6.00 15.00
YSJP Jason Pominville 6.00 15.00
YSJS Jordan Staal 12.00 30.00
YSJT Jiri Tlusty 8.00 20.00
YSKC Kyle Chipchura 5.00 12.00
YSKL Kari Lehtonen 5.00 12.00
YSKO Kyle Okposo 15.00 40.00
YSKT Kyle Turris 15.00 40.00
YSMF Marc-Andre Fleury 8.00 20.00
YSML Milan Lucic 15.00 40.00
YSMR Mike Richards 12.00 30.00
YSNB Nicklas Backstrom 15.00 40.00
YSND Nigel Dawes 5.00 12.00
YSNZ Nikolai Zherdev 5.00 12.00
YSPK Patrick Kane 20.00 50.00
YSPM Peter Mueller 10.00 25.00
YSPN David Perron 6.00 15.00
YSPS Paul Stastny 8.00 20.00
YSRS Rob Schremp 6.00 15.00
YSSB Steve Bernier 5.00 12.00
YSSG Sam Gagner 12.00 30.00
YSSM Steve Mason 20.00 50.00
YSST Drew Stafford 8.00 20.00
YSSW Shea Weber 6.00 15.00
YSTE Tobias Enstrom 8.00 20.00
YSTH T.J. Hensick 6.00 15.00
YSTK Tyler Kennedy 6.00 15.00
YSTO Jonathan Toews 25.00 60.00
YSVF Valtteri Filppula 5.00 12.00

2009-10 Upper Deck Trilogy

COMP.SET w/o SPS (100)
FIT PRINT RUN 599 SER.#'d SETS
121-155 PRINT RUN 799 SER.#'d SETS
156-170 PRINT RUN 499 SER.#'d SETS
OVERALL RC ODDS 1:3
FROZEN IN TIME ODDS 1:12
1 Roberto Luongo 2.50 6.00
2 Luke Schenn 1.50 4.00
3 Dion Phaneuf 1.50 4.00
4 Bobby Orr 4.00 10.00
5 Nicklas Lidstrom 1.25 3.00
6 Shea Weber .75 2.00
7 Phil Esposito 2.00 5.00
8 Alexander Ovechkin 4.00 10.00
9 Zach Parise 1.00 2.50
10 Corey Perry 1.00 2.50
11 Jordan Staal 1.25 3.00
12 Jarome Iginla 2.00 5.00
13 Pavel Datsyuk 1.00 2.50
14 Jonathan Cheechoo 1.00 2.50
15 Ryan Getzlaf 1.50 4.00
16 Devin Setoguchi .75 2.00
17 Jeff Carter 1.00 2.50
18 Mike Richards 2.00 5.00
19 Jonathan Toews 2.50 6.00
20 Evgeni Nabokov 1.00 2.50
21 Olli Jokinen .60 1.50
22 Dan Boyle .60 1.50
23 Chris Drury .75 2.00
24 Nathan Horton .60 1.50
25 Chris Pronger .75 2.00
26 Paul Stastny 1.00 2.50
27 Ilya Kovalchuk 1.25 3.00
28 Alexander Semin 1.00 2.50
29 Marc-Andre Fleury 1.00 2.50
30 Martin Brodeur 2.50 6.00
31 Carey Price 2.50 6.00
32 Niklas Backstrom 1.00 2.50
33 Patrick Roy 3.00 8.00
34 Miikka Kiprusoff 1.00 2.50
35 Marty Turco .75 2.00
36 Jussi Jokinen 1.00 2.50
37 J.P. Dumont .60 1.50
38 Daniel Sedin 1.25 3.00
39 Rick DiPietro 1.00 2.50
40 Henrik Zetterberg 2.00 5.00
41 Nikolai Kulemin .75 2.00
42 Josh Bailey .75 2.00
43 Mikko Koivu 1.00 2.50
44 Sheldon Souray .60 1.50
45 Marian Hossa 1.50 4.00
46 Daniel Alfredsson 1.00 2.50
47 Marian Gaborik 1.50 4.00
48 Daniel Briere 1.00 2.50
49 Thomas Vanek 1.00 2.50
50 Chris Mason .75 2.00
51 Brian Campbell .75 2.00
52 Mike Green 2.00 5.00
53 Bobby Ryan 1.25 3.00
54 Eric Staal 1.25 3.00
55 Jason Blake .60 1.50
56 Shane Doan .75 2.00
57 David Perron .75 2.00
58 James Neal 1.00 2.50
59 Joe Thornton 2.00 5.00
60 Henrik Sedin 1.50 4.00
61 Rick Nash 1.00 2.50
62 Martin St. Louis 1.00 2.50
63 Kris Versteeg 1.25 3.00
64 Mike Modano 1.00 2.50
65 Andrew Cogliano 1.25 3.00
66 Mario Lemieux 2.50 6.00
67 Michael Frolik .75 2.00
68 Bryan Little 1.00 2.50
69 Henrik Lundqvist 2.00 5.00
70 Derek Roy 1.00 2.50
71 Evgeni Malkin 2.50 6.00
72 Patrik Elias .75 2.00
73 Michael Ryder .75 2.00
74 T.J. Oshie 1.50 4.00
75 Tomas Vokoun 1.00 2.50
76 Kyle Okposo 1.00 2.50
77 Ray Bourque 1.50 4.00
78 Cam Ward 1.00 2.50
79 Andrei Markov .75 2.00
80 Jason Arnott .60 1.50
81 Phil Kessel 1.00 2.50
82 Mike Cammalleri .75 2.00
83 Ales Hemsky .75 2.00
84 Mikhail Grabovski .75 2.00
85 Dany Heatley 2.00 5.00
86 Scott Gomez 1.00 2.50
87 Sidney Crosby 5.00 12.00
88 Patrick Kane 2.00 5.00
89 Sam Gagner 1.25 3.00
90 Ryan Miller 1.00 2.50
91 Steven Stamkos 2.50 6.00
92 Simeon Varlamov 2.00 5.00
93 Jakub Voracek 1.00 2.50
94 Ryan Smyth 1.00 2.50
95 Patrik Berglund 2.00 5.00
96 Pierre-Marc Bouchard .75 2.00
97 Steve Mason 1.50 4.00
98 Peter Mueller 1.25 3.00
99 Wayne Gretzky 5.00 12.00
100 Jason Spezza 1.25 3.00
101 Alexander Ovechkin FIT 12.00 30.00
102 Bobby Orr FIT 12.00 30.00
103 Carey Price FIT 8.00 20.00
104 Evgeni Malkin FIT 8.00 20.00
105 Gordie Howe FIT 12.00 30.00
106 Ilya Kovalchuk FIT 4.00 10.00
107 Joe Thornton FIT 6.00 15.00
108 Jonathan Toews FIT 8.00 20.00
109 Mario Lemieux FIT 8.00 20.00
110 Mark Messier FIT 6.00 15.00
111 Martin Brodeur FIT 8.00 20.00
112 Mike Richards FIT 6.00 15.00
113 Nicklas Backstrom FIT 6.00 15.00
114 Patrick Kane FIT 6.00 15.00
115 Patrick Roy FIT 10.00 25.00
116 Roberto Luongo FIT 8.00 20.00
117 Ron Hextall FIT 6.00 15.00
118 Sidney Crosby FIT 15.00 40.00
119 Vincent Lecavalier FIT 4.00 10.00
120 Wayne Gretzky FIT 15.00 40.00
121 Michael Sauer RC 3.00 8.00
122 Tyler Bozak RC 10.00 25.00
123 Spencer Machacek RC 3.00 8.00
124 Jhonas Enroth RC 5.00 12.00
125 Benn Ferriero RC 4.00 10.00
126 Matt Hendricks RC 3.00 8.00
127 Cal O'Reilly RC 4.00 10.00
128 Michael Grabner RC 5.00 12.00
129 Mike Santorelli RC 2.50 6.00
130 Tom Wandell RC 12.00 30.00
131 Jay Rosehill RC 2.50 6.00
132 Luca Caputi RC 5.00 12.00
133 T.J. Galiardi RC 5.00 12.00
134 Frazer McLaren RC 2.50 6.00
135 Riku Helenius RC 4.00 10.00
136 Joel Rechlicz RC 4.00 10.00
137 Alec Martinez RC 2.50 6.00
138 Dmitry Kulikov RC 4.00 10.00
139 Matt Beleskey RC 4.00 10.00
140 Ivan Vishnevskiy RC 5.00 12.00
141 Antti Niemi RC 12.00 30.00
142 James Wright RC 5.00 12.00
143 Mikael Backlund RC 6.00 15.00
144 Teemu Laakso RC 2.50 6.00
145 Erik Karlsson RC 12.00 30.00
146 Michal Neuvirth RC 10.00 25.00
147 Mika Pyorala RC 4.00 10.00
148 Jason Demers RC 3.00 8.00
149 Taylor Chorney RC 4.00 10.00
150 John Negrin RC 3.00 8.00
151 Matt Gilroy RC 5.00 12.00
152 Yannick Weber RC 5.00 12.00
153 Christian Hanson RC 5.00 12.00
154 Artem Anisimov RC 5.00 12.00
155 Sergei Shirokov RC 6.00 15.00
156 Colin Wilson SP RC 8.00 20.00

157 Ryan O'Reilly SP RC 10.00 25.00
158 Brad Marchand SP RC 6.00 15.00
159 Ville Leino SP RC 6.00 15.00
160 Michael Del Zotto SP RC 10.00 25.00
161 Victor Hedman SP RC 10.00 25.00
162 Evander Kane SP RC 12.00 30.00
163 Matt Duchene SP RC 20.00 50.00
164 James van Riemsdyk SP RC 12.00 30.00
165 Jonas Gustavsson SP RC 12.00 30.00
166 Jamie Benn SP RC 8.00 20.00
167 Viktor Stalberg SP RC 8.00 20.00
168 Tyler Myers SP RC 20.00 50.00
169 Logan Couture SP RC 10.00 25.00
170 John Tavares SP RC 40.00 80.00

2009-10 Upper Deck Trilogy Classic Confrontations

STATED ODDS 1:45
CCBOBU Grant Fuhr 20.00 50.00
Pat LaFontaine
Dale Hawerchuk
Ray Bourque
Adam Oates
Cam Neely
CCCANJ Cam Ward 30.00 80.00
Rod Brind'Amour
Eric Staal
Patrik Elias
Zach Parise
Martin Brodeur
CCCGMT Doug Gilmour
Al MacInnis
Lanny McDonald
Guy Carbonneau
Chris Chelios
Patrick Roy
CCCHSL Tony Esposito 20.00 50.00
Denis Savard
Doug Wilson
Doug Gilmour
Joe Mullen
Bernie Federko
CCCODA Milan Hejduk 25.00 60.00
Chris Drury
Joe Sakic
Mike Modano
Sergei Zubov
Jere Lehtinen
CCCONJ Joe Sakic 30.00 80.00
Patrick Roy
Martin Brodeur
Scott Niedermayer
Patrik Elias
Ray Bourque
CCDECH Brian Campbell
Patrick Kane
Jonathan Toews
Nicklas Lidstrom
Tomas Holmstrom
Henrik Zetterberg
CCDECO Brendan Shanahan 25.00 60.00
Sergei Fedorov
Joe Sakic
Patrick Roy
Milan Hejduk
Chris Osgood
CCDEPH Brendan Shanahan 25.00 60.00
Sergei Fedorov
Chris Osgood
Rod Brind'Amour
Ron Hextall
Dale Hawerchuk
CCDEPI Marian Hossa 75.00 150.00
Pavel Datsyuk
Henrik Zetterberg
Jordan Staal
Evgeni Malkin
Sidney Crosby
CCDESL Dino Ciccarelli 25.00 60.00
Chris Pronger
Al MacInnis
Dale Hawerchuk
Kris Draper
Sergei Fedorov
CCDETO Sergei Fedorov 25.00 60.00
Nicklas Lidstrom
Glenn Anderson
Wendel Clark
Doug Gilmour
Dino Ciccarelli
CCEDCG Lanny McDonald 25.00 60.00
Doug Gilmour
Joe Mullen
Mark Messier
Grant Fuhr
Jari Kurri
CCEDDA Ryan Smyth 30.00 80.00
Curtis Joseph
Jason Arnott
Jere Lehtinen
Mike Modano
Sergei Zubov
CCEDNY Grant Fuhr 15.00 40.00
Glenn Anderson
Jari Kurri
Mike Bossy
Bob Bourne
Denis Potvin
CCHABO Cam Neely 20.00 50.00
Adam Oates
Ray Bourque
Bobby Holik
Chris Pronger
Brendan Shanahan
CCLAED Wayne Gretzky 60.00 120.00
Bernie Nicholls
Luc Robitaille
Mark Messier
Grant Fuhr
Jari Kurri
CCLATO Luc Robitaille 40.00 100.00
Jari Kurri
Wayne Gretzky
Glenn Anderson
Wendel Clark
Doug Gilmour
CCMTBO Guy Lafleur 25.00 60.00
Larry Robinson
Steve Shutt
Brad Park
Johnny Bucyk
Phil Esposito
CCMTCG Steve Shutt 20.00 50.00
Guy Lafleur
Larry Robinson
Ron Ellis
Borje Salming
Lanny McDonald
CCNJPH Patrik Elias 30.00 80.00
Scott Niedermayer
Martin Brodeur
Rod Brind'Amour
Simon Gagne
Mark Recchi
CCNYNJ Mark Messier 40.00 100.00
Glenn Anderson
Brian Leetch
Martin Brodeur
Bill Guerin
Scott Niedermayer
CCNYPH Pat LaFontaine
Denis Potvin
Bobby Clarke
Ron Hextall
Mark Howe
Mike Bossy
CCPHNY Ron Hextall 25.00 60.00
Mark Recchi
Rod Brind'Amour
Brian Leetch
Sergei Zubov
Mark Messier
CCPIPH Mark Recchi 30.00 80.00
Rod Brind'Amour
Ron Hextall
Mario Lemieux
Larry Murphy
Joe Mullen
CCPIWA Sergei Gonchar 50.00 100.00
Evgeni Malkin
Sidney Crosby
Nicklas Backstrom
Alexander Ovechkin
Mike Green
CCTOMT Glenn Anderson
Grant Fuhr
Doug Gilmour
Patrick Roy
Denis Savard
Guy Carbonneau
CCWANY Chris Drury 60.00 120.00
Scott Gomez
Marc Staal
Mike Green
Nicklas Backstrom
Alexander Ovechkin

2009-10 Upper Deck Trilogy Combo Clearcut Autographs

OVERALL AUTO ODDS 1:3
PRINT RUN 100 SER.#'d SETS UNLESS NOTED
CC2BP Denis Potvin 15.00 40.00
Mike Bossy
CC2CG Sam Gagner 15.00 40.00
Andrew Cogliano
CC2EB Ray Bourque 30.00 80.00
Phil Esposito
CC2GB Nicklas Backstrom 25.00 60.00
Mike Green
CC2GG Clark Gillies 15.00 40.00
Colton Gillies
CC2GR Ryan Getzlaf 20.00 50.00
Bobby Ryan
CC2IP Jarome Iginla 25.00 60.00
Dion Phaneuf
CC2JD Jack Johnson 25.00 60.00
Drew Doughty
CC2LD Alex Delvecchio 15.00 40.00
Ted Lindsay
CC2MS Lanny McDonald 15.00 40.00
Borje Salming
CC2NK Phil Kessel 25.00 60.00
Cam Neely
CC2NL Henrik Lundqvist 30.00 80.00
Markus Naslund
CC2NM Rick Nash 25.00 60.00
Steve Mason
CC2OB Kyle Okposo 12.00 30.00
Josh Bailey
CC2PS Justin Pogge 25.00 60.00
Luke Schenn
CC2RC Mike Richards 30.00 80.00
Jeff Carter
CC2SW Ty Wishart 30.00 80.00
Steven Stamkos
CC2TK Patrick Kane 40.00 100.00
Jonathan Toews
CC2TS Joe Thornton 30.00 80.00
Devin Setoguchi

2009-10 Upper Deck Trilogy Hat Trick Heroes

OVERALL MEM ODDS 1:3
HTHAK Andrei Kostitsyn 5.00 12.00
HTHAO Alexander Ovechkin 25.00 60.00
HTHBL Bryan Little 6.00 15.00
HTHBW Blake Wheeler 8.00 20.00
HTHCD Chris Drury 6.00 15.00
HTHDB David Booth 4.00 10.00
HTHDU Dustin Brown 6.00 15.00
HTHEM Evgeni Malkin 15.00 40.00
HTHES Eric Staal 8.00 20.00
HTHIK Ilya Kovalchuk 8.00 20.00
HTHJC Jeff Carter 6.00 15.00
HTHJN James Neal 6.00 15.00
HTHJS Jason Spezza 8.00 20.00
HTHKE Phil Kessel 6.00 15.00
HTHMC Mike Cammalleri 5.00 12.00
HTHML Milan Lucic 6.00 15.00
HTHMM Mark Messier 12.00 30.00
HTHOJ Olli Jokinen 4.00 10.00
HTHPK Patrick Kane 12.00 30.00
HTHPS Petr Sykora 4.00 10.00
HTHRN Rick Nash 6.00 15.00
HTHSC Sidney Crosby 30.00 80.00
HTHSG Sam Gagner 8.00 20.00
HTHST Jordan Staal 8.00 20.00
HTHTS Teemu Selanne 6.00 15.00
HTHTV Thomas Vanek 6.00 15.00
HTHWG Wayne Gretzky 30.00 80.00

2009-10 Upper Deck Trilogy Hat Trick Heroes Autographs

STATED PRINT RUN 5 SER.#'d SETS
NOT PRICED DUE TO SCARCITY
HTHAO Alexander Ovechkin
HTHBW Blake Wheeler
HTHCD Chris Drury
HTHEM Evgeni Malkin
HTHES Eric Staal
HTHIK Ilya Kovalchuk
HTHJC Jeff Carter
HTHJN James Neal
HTHKE Phil Kessel
HTHMM Mark Messier
HTHPK Patrick Kane
HTHRN Rick Nash
HTHSC Sidney Crosby
HTHSG Sam Gagner
HTHST Jordan Staal
HTHTV Thomas Vanek
HTHWG Wayne Gretzky

2009-10 Upper Deck Trilogy Hat Trick Heroes Gold

*SINGLES: .5X TO 1.2X BASIC INSERTS
STATED PRINT RUN 50 SER.#'d SETS

2009-10 Upper Deck Trilogy Hat Trick Heroes Platinum

STATED PRINT RUN 10 SER.#'d SETS
NOT PRICED DUE TO SCARCITY

2009-10 Upper Deck Trilogy Honorary Swatches

OVERALL MEM ODDS 1:3
HSAO Alexander Ovechkin 25.00 60.00
HSBL Brian Leetch 6.00 15.00
HSBS Borje Salming 6.00 15.00
HSCN Cam Neely 10.00 25.00
HSCP Carey Price 15.00 40.00
HSDC Dino Ciccarelli 4.00 10.00
HSDG Doug Gilmour 6.00 15.00
HSDH Dale Hawerchuk 6.00 15.00
HSDS Denis Savard 6.00 15.00
HSEM Evgeni Malkin 15.00 40.00
HSES Eric Staal 8.00 20.00
HSFM Frank Mahovlich 8.00 20.00
HSGA Glenn Anderson 6.00 15.00
HSGF Grant Fuhr 8.00 20.00
HSGH Gordie Howe 25.00 60.00
HSGP Gilbert Perreault 6.00 15.00
HSIK Ilya Kovalchuk 8.00 20.00
HSJB Johnny Bucyk 10.00 25.00
HSJK Jari Kurri 6.00 15.00
HSJT Jonathan Toews 15.00 40.00
HSLM Lanny McDonald 6.00 15.00
HSLR Larry Robinson 8.00 20.00
HSMB Martin Brodeur 15.00 40.00
HSMK Miikka Kiprusoff 6.00 15.00
HSML Mario Lemieux 15.00 40.00
HSMM Mark Messier 12.00 30.00
HSMO Mike Modano 6.00 15.00
HSMT Marty Turco 5.00 12.00
HSNL Nicklas Lidstrom 8.00 20.00
HSPE Phil Esposito 12.00 30.00
HSPK Patrick Kane 12.00 30.00
HSPR Patrick Roy 20.00 50.00
HSRB Ray Bourque 10.00 25.00
HSRH Ron Hextall 12.00 30.00
HSRL Roberto Luongo 15.00 40.00
HSRN Rick Nash 6.00 15.00
HSRO Luc Robitaille 6.00 15.00
HSSC Sidney Crosby 30.00 80.00
HSTE Tony Esposito 10.00 25.00
HSWG Wayne Gretzky 30.00 80.00

2009-10 Upper Deck Trilogy Honorary Swatches Autographs

STATED PRINT RUN 5 SER.#'d SETS
NOT PRICED DUE TO SCARCITY
HSAO Alexander Ovechkin
HSBL Brian Leetch
HSBS Borje Salming
HSCN Cam Neely
HSCP Carey Price
HSDH Dale Hawerchuk
HSDS Denis Savard
HSEM Evgeni Malkin
HSES Eric Staal
HSGF Grant Fuhr
HSGH Gordie Howe
HSGP Gilbert Perreault
HSIK Ilya Kovalchuk
HSJB Johnny Bucyk
HSJK Jari Kurri
HSJT Jonathan Toews
HSLM Lanny McDonald
HSLR Larry Robinson
HSMB Martin Brodeur
HSML Mario Lemieux
HSMM Mark Messier
HSMO Mike Modano
HSMT Marty Turco
HSNL Nicklas Lidstrom
HSPE Phil Esposito
HSPK Patrick Kane
HSPR Patrick Roy
HSRB Ray Bourque
HSRH Ron Hextall
HSRN Rick Nash
HSRO Luc Robitaille
HSSC Sidney Crosby
HSTE Tony Esposito
HSWG Wayne Gretzky

2009-10 Upper Deck Trilogy Honorary Swatches Gold

*SINGLES: .5X TO 1.2X BASIC INSERTS
STATED PRINT RUN 50 SER.#'d SETS

2009-10 Upper Deck Trilogy Honorary Swatches Platinum

STATED PRINT RUN 10 SER.#'d SETS
NOT PRICED DUE TO SCARCITY

2009-10 Upper Deck Trilogy Ice Scripts

STATED ODDS 1:10
ISAC Andrew Cogliano 10.00 25.00
ISBA Josh Bailey 6.00 15.00
ISBH Bobby Hull SP 25.00 60.00
ISBL Brian Leetch 8.00 20.00
ISBO Bobby Orr SP 150.00 250.00
ISBR Bobby Ryan 10.00 25.00
ISBS Brandon Sutter 8.00 20.00
ISCN Cam Neely SP 25.00 60.00
ISDD Drew Doughty 15.00 40.00
ISDH Dany Heatley 15.00 40.00
ISDP Dion Phaneuf 12.00 30.00
ISES Eric Staal 10.00 25.00
ISGH Gordie Howe SP 60.00 120.00
ISHL Henrik Lundqvist 15.00 40.00
ISHZ Henrik Zetterberg SP 20.00 50.00
ISIK Ilya Kovalchuk SP 12.00 30.00
ISJB Jean Beliveau SP 75.00 150.00
ISJI Jarome Iginla SP 20.00 50.00
ISJK Jari Kurri 8.00 20.00
ISJN James Neal 8.00 20.00
ISJP Justin Pogge 15.00 40.00
ISJT Joe Thornton SP 20.00 50.00
ISKA Karl Alzner 8.00 20.00
ISKM Kenndal McArdle 6.00 15.00
ISLS Luke Schenn 12.00 30.00
ISMB Martin Brodeur SP 50.00 100.00
ISMF Marc-Andre Fleury 15.00 40.00
ISML Mario Lemieux SP EXCH 50.00 100.00
ISMP Max Pacioretty 8.00 20.00
ISMR Mike Richards 15.00 40.00
ISNB Nicklas Backstrom 15.00 40.00
ISNL Nicklas Lidstrom 10.00 25.00
ISPB Patrice Bergeron 8.00 20.00
ISPD Pavel Datsyuk SP 25.00 50.00
ISPE Phil Esposito SP 40.00 80.00
ISPH Chris Phillips 5.00 12.00
ISPK Patrick Kane 15.00 40.00
ISPR Patrick Roy SP
ISPS Paul Stastny 8.00 20.00
ISRB Ray Bourque SP 40.00 80.00
ISRM Ryan Miller 20.00 40.00
ISRN Rick Nash 8.00 20.00
ISSB Scotty Bowman SP 50.00 100.00
ISSC Sidney Crosby SP 125.00 200.00
ISSG Clark Gillies 8.00 20.00
ISSK Saku Koivu 15.00 40.00
ISSM Steve Mason 12.00 30.00
ISSS Steven Stamkos 20.00 50.00
ISTE Tony Esposito SP 25.00 60.00
ISTO Jonathan Toews 20.00 50.00
ISWG Wayne Gretzky SP EXCH 300.00 400.00
ISZB Zach Bogosian 10.00 25.00

2009-10 Upper Deck Trilogy Line Mates

OVERALL MEM ODDS 1:3
LMAD J.P. Dumont 4.00 10.00
Jason Arnott
LMAM Mark Messier 12.00 30.00
Glenn Anderson
LMBK Anze Kopitar 6.00 15.00
Dustin Brown
LMCG Sam Gagner 8.00 20.00
Andrew Cogliano
LMHD Pavel Datsyuk 6.00 15.00
Tomas Holmstrom
LMHS Milan Hejduk 6.00 15.00
Paul Stastny
LMJI Olli Jokinen 12.00 30.00
Jarome Iginla
LMKL Ilya Kovalchuk 8.00 20.00
Bryan Little
LMLL Vincent Lecavalier 8.00 20.00
Martin St. Louis
LMLS Steve Shutt 10.00 25.00
Guy Lafleur
LMMN Mike Modano 6.00 15.00
James Neal
LMMS Lanny McDonald 8.00 20.00
Darryl Sittler
LMMT Joe Thornton 12.00 30.00
Patrick Marleau
LMNO Adam Oates 10.00 25.00
Cam Neely
LMOB Alexander Ovechkin 25.00 60.00
Nicklas Backstrom
LMRG Mike Richards 12.00 30.00
Simon Gagne
LMRL Brian Rafalski 8.00 20.00
Nicklas Lidstrom
LMRS Tuomo Ruutu 8.00 20.00
Eric Staal
LMRV Thomas Vanek 6.00 15.00
Derek Roy
LMRW Blake Wheeler 8.00 20.00
Michael Ryder
LMSC Jason Spezza 8.00 20.00
Jonathan Cheechoo
LMSH Dany Heatley
Jason Spezza
LMSM Miroslav Satan 30.00 80.00
Sidney Crosby
LMSS Paul Stastny 6.00 15.00
Marek Svatos
LMTK Patrick Kane 15.00 40.00
Jonathan Toews
LMWF Michael Frolik 5.00 12.00
Stephen Weiss
LMWL Luc Robitaille 30.00 80.00
Wayne Gretzky

2009-10 Upper Deck Trilogy Line Mates Autographs

STATED PRINT RUN 5 SER.#'d SETS
NOT PRICED DUE TO SCARCITY
LMAD J.P. Dumont
Jason Arnott
LMCG Sam Gagner
Andrew Cogliano
LMHD Pavel Datsyuk
Tomas Holmstrom
LMLL Vincent Lecavalier
Martin St. Louis
LMLS Steve Shutt
Guy Lafleur
LMMN Mike Modano
James Neal
LMNO Adam Oates
Cam Neely
LMOB Alexander Ovechkin
Nicklas Backstrom
LMRG Mike Richards
Simon Gagne
LMRW Blake Wheeler
Michael Ryder
LMSS Paul Stastny
Marek Svatos
LMTK Patrick Kane
Jonathan Toews
LMWL Luc Robitaille
Wayne Gretzky

2009-10 Upper Deck Trilogy Line Mates Gold

*SINGLES: .5X TO 1.2X BASIC INSERTS
STATED PRINT RUN 50 SER.#'d SETS

2009-10 Upper Deck Trilogy Line Mates Platinum

STATED PRINT RUN 10 SER.#'d SETS
NOT PRICED DUE TO SCARCITY

2009-10 Upper Deck Trilogy Quad Clearcut Autographs

STATED PRINT RUN 5 SER.#'d SETS
NOT PRICED DUE TO SCARCITY
CC41CHI Jack Skille
Patrick Kane
Jonathan Toews
Cam Barker
CC41KPT Bobby Hull
Jean Beliveau
Alex Delvecchio
Gordie Howe
CC41MTL Saku Koivu
Chris Higgins
Carey Price
Max Pacioretty
CC41NYI Josh Bailey
Kyle Okposo
Denis Potvin
Clark Gillies
CC41TOR Jiri Tlusty
Justin Pogge
Luke Schenn
Lanny McDonald
CC4BEST Mario Lemieux
Wayne Gretzky
Gordie Howe
Bobby Orr
CC4CBOS Terry O'Reilly
Joe Thornton
Johnny Bucyk
Ray Bourque
CC4CCHI Jonathan Toews
Denis Savard
Doug Gilmour
Darryl Sutter
CC4CDET Gordie Howe
Alex Delvecchio
Nicklas Lidstrom
Ted Lindsay
CC4CLDR Drew Doughty
Patrik Berglund
Steve Mason
Kris Versteeg
CC4CMTL Jean Beliveau
Saku Koivu
Butch Bouchard
Guy Carbonneau
CC4CNYR Mark Messier
Harry Howell
Chris Drury
Brian Leetch
CC4DPTS Ray Bourque
Bobby Orr
Al MacInnis
Denis Potvin
CC4EAST Martin Brodeur
Patrice Bergeron
Mike Richards
Carey Price
CC4NTMR Patrick Roy
Tony Esposito
Martin Brodeur
Rogie Vachon
CC4WEST Jonathan Toews
Pavel Datsyuk
Joe Thornton
Jarome Iginla

2009-10 Upper Deck Trilogy Superstar Scripts

STATED ODDS 1:10
SSAC Andrew Cogliano 10.00 25.00
SSAM Al MacInnis 8.00 20.00
SSAO Alexander Ovechkin 50.00 100.00
SSCB Cam Barker 5.00 12.00
SSCC Cal Clutterbuck 6.00 15.00
SSCK Chris Kunitz 8.00 20.00
SSCL David Clarkson 5.00 12.00
SSCW Cam Ward 8.00 20.00
SSDC Dan Cleary 8.00 20.00
SSDP David Perron 6.00 15.00
SSEL Patrik Elias 6.00 15.00
SSEM Evgeni Malkin 20.00 50.00
SSHZ Henrik Zetterberg 15.00 40.00
SSJA Jason Arnott 5.00 12.00
SSJC Jeff Carter 8.00 20.00
SSJD J.P. Dumont 5.00 12.00
SSJH Josh Harding 6.00 15.00
SSJI Jarome Iginla 15.00 40.00
SSJJ Jack Johnson 6.00 15.00
SSJP Jason Pominville 8.00 20.00
SSMF Marc-Andre Fleury 15.00 40.00
SSMG Mike Green 30.00 60.00
SSMR Mike Richards 15.00 40.00
SSMS Matt Stajan 6.00 15.00
SSMT Maxime Talbot 8.00 20.00
SSNB Nicklas Backstrom 15.00 40.00
SSPB Peter Budaj 8.00 20.00
SSPD Pavel Datsyuk 20.00 40.00
SSPE Dustin Penner 5.00 12.00
SSPH Dion Phaneuf 12.00 30.00
SSPK Phil Kessel 8.00 20.00
SSPO Denis Potvin 6.00 15.00
SSRS Ryan Smyth 8.00 20.00
SSSB Steve Bernier 5.00 12.00
SSSC Sidney Crosby 75.00 150.00
SSSG Simon Gagne 8.00 20.00
SSSS Steve Shutt 8.00 20.00
SSSW Stephen Weiss 5.00 12.00
SSTH Tomas Holmstrom 6.00 15.00
SSTV Thomas Vanek 8.00 20.00

2009-10 Upper Deck Trilogy Triple Clearcut Autographs

STATED PRINT RUN 10 SER.#'d SETS
NOT PRICED DUE TO SCARCITY
CC303D Eric Staal
Marc-Andre Fleury
Nathan Horton
CC304D Evgeni Malkin
Blake Wheeler
Cam Barker
CC305D Carey Price
Devin Setoguchi
Bobby Ryan
CC306D Jordan Staal
Jonathan Toews
Nicklas Backstrom
CC307D Karl Alzner
Patrick Kane
Kyle Turris
CC308D Drew Doughty
Zach Bogosian
Steven Stamkos
CC372C Bobby Clarke
Phil Esposito
Gilbert Perreault
CC376C Bobby Orr
Bobby Hull
Steve Shutt
CC3C81 Steve Shutt
Ray Bourque
Clark Gillies
CC3C87 Doug Gilmour
Ron Hextall
Dale Hawerchuk
CC3C91 Mark Messier
Luc Robitaille
Theoren Fleury
CC3CAN Joe Thornton
Rick Nash
Jarome Iginla
CC3CZE Jakub Voracek
Patrik Elias
Milan Hejduk
CC3J07 Jonathan Toews
Karl Alzner
Steve Downie
CC3J08 Steven Stamkos
Claude Giroux
Kyle Turris
CC3RUS Evgeni Malkin
Pavel Datsyuk
Ilya Kovalchuk
CC3SLV Marian Hossa
Peter Budaj
Marian Gaborik
CC3SWE Nicklas Lidstrom
Nicklas Backstrom
Henrik Lundqvist
CC3USA Patrick Kane
Phil Kessel
Peter Mueller
CC3WJG Steve Mason
Martin Brodeur
Carey Price

2009-10 Upper Deck Trilogy Young Star Scripts

STATED ODDS 1:10
YSAE Andrew Ebbett 5.00 12.00
YSAN Andreas Nodl 4.00 10.00
YSBB Ben Bishop 6.00 15.00
YSBL Brian Lee 6.00 15.00
YSBM Brendan Mikkelson 4.00 10.00
YSBO Brian Boyle 5.00 12.00
YSBS Brandon Sutter 6.00 15.00
YSBV Boris Valabik 6.00 15.00
YSBW Blake Wheeler 8.00 20.00
YSCG Colton Gillies 8.00 20.00
YSCS Chris Stewart 6.00 15.00
YSDD Drew Doughty 15.00 40.00
YSDL Dan LaCosta 5.00 12.00
YSDO Derek Dorsett 5.00 12.00
YSDT Danny Taylor 5.00 12.00
YSEE Erik Ersberg 5.00 12.00
YSFB Fabian Brunnstrom 6.00 15.00
YSGI Claude Giroux 12.00 30.00
YSJB Josh Bailey 5.00 12.00
YSJE Jonathan Ericsson 6.00 15.00
YSJF Jonas Frogren 5.00 12.00
YSJM John Mitchell 5.00 12.00
YSJP Justin Pogge 12.00 30.00
YSJT John Tavares 75.00 150.00
YSJV Jakub Voracek 6.00 15.00
YSKA Karl Alzner 6.00 15.00
YSKM Kenndal McArdle 5.00 12.00
YSKO Kyle Okposo 6.00 15.00
YSKP Kevin Porter 4.00 10.00
YSLS Luke Schenn 10.00 25.00
YSMA Ben Maxwell 10.00 25.00
YSMB Mikkel Boedker 5.00 12.00
YSMC Jamie McGinn 5.00 12.00
YSMD Matt D'Agostini 8.00 20.00
YSMH Matthew Halischuk 5.00 12.00
YSMP Max Pacioretty 6.00 15.00
YSMR Michal Repik 5.00 12.00
YSNF Nikita Filatov 12.00 30.00
YSNO Nathan Oystrick 4.00 10.00
YSOM Oscar Moller 5.00 12.00
YSPI Alex Pietrangelo 5.00 12.00
YSPV Petr Vrana 8.00 20.00
YSRJ Ryan Jones 4.00 10.00
YSRY Bobby Ryan 8.00 20.00
YSSC Cory Schneider 10.00 25.00
YSSM Shawn Matthias 6.00 15.00
YSSS Steven Stamkos 15.00 40.00
YSST Steve Mason 10.00 25.00
YSTK Tim Kennedy 6.00 15.00
YSTL Trevor Lewis 4.00 10.00
YSTO T.J. Oshie 10.00 25.00
YSTP Tyler Plante 5.00 12.00
YSTS Tom Sestito 4.00 10.00
YSTW Ty Wishart 6.00 15.00
YSVT Viktor Tikhonov 6.00 15.00
YSWS Wayne Simmonds 6.00 15.00
YSZA Zach Boychuk 8.00 20.00
YSZB Zach Bogosian 8.00 20.00

2006 Upper Deck National NHL

COMPLETE SET (3) 25.00 50.00
NHL1 Sidney Crosby 15.00 40.00
NHL2 Wayne Gretzky 6.00 15.00
NHL3 Alexander Ovechkin 6.00 15.00

2006 Upper Deck National NHL Autographs

Randomly inserted in VIP packages at the National Convention. Limited print runs preclude us from giving pricing.

COMPLETE SET (2)
NHL1 Sidney Crosby
NHL2 Wayne Gretzky

2006 Upper Deck National NHL VIP

COMPLETE SET (6) 30.00 60.00
1 Alexander Ovechkin 6.00 15.00
2 Wayne Gretzky 6.00 15.00
3 Sidney Crosby 15.00 40.00
4 Martin Brodeur 4.00 10.00
5 Steve Yzerman 4.00 10.00
6 Jean-Sebastian Giguere .75 2.00

2002 Upper Deck USHL Gordie Howe

This rare single was given away at the USHL All-Star Game in Sioux Falls. It commemorated Mr. Howe as the honorary spokesman for Upper Deck.

1 Gordie Howe AU 300.00

1999-00 Upper Deck Victory

Released as a 440-card set, 1999-00 Upper Deck Victory was comprised of 265 regular cards, 12 All Victory team cards showcasing top players, 30 Season Leaders, 40 Victory Prospects, 15 Stacking the Pads cards, 50 Hockey Legacy cards, and 28 Team Checklist cards. Base cards are white bordered with a red "Victory" logo. This brand contains no insert cards. Victory was packaged in 36-pack boxes where packs contained 12 cards and carried a suggested retail price of $.99.

COMPLETE SET (440) 40.00 80.00
1 Paul Kariya CL .10 .30
2 Paul Kariya .10 .30
3 Teemu Selanne .10 .30
4 Matt Cullen .02 .10
5 Steve Rucchin .02 .10
6 Oleg Tverdovsky .02 .10
7 Guy Hebert .08 .25
8 Fredrik Olausson .02 .10
9 Ted Donato .02 .10
10 Marty McInnis .02 .10
11 Damian Rhodes CL .08 .25
12 Jody Hull .02 .10
13 Damian Rhodes .08 .25
14 Kelly Buchberger .02 .10
15 Scott Langkow RC .08 .25
16 Norm Maracle .08 .25
17 Jason Botterill .02 .10
18 Randy Robitaille .02 .10
19 Ray Ferraro .02 .10
20 Ray Bourque CL .08 .25
21 Ray Bourque .20 .50
22 Sergei Samsonov .08 .25
23 Joe Thornton .20 .50
24 Shawn Bates .02 .10
25 Byron Dafoe .08 .25
26 Jonathan Girard .02 .10
27 Jason Allison .02 .10
28 Anson Carter .08 .25
29 Hal Gill .02 .10
30 Kyle McLaren .02 .10
31 Don Sweeney .02 .10
32 Dominik Hasek CL .08 .25
33 Dominik Hasek .25 .60
34 Michael Peca .08 .25
35 Miroslav Satan .08 .25
36 Dixon Ward .02 .10

Card	Low	High
37 Martin Biron	.08	.25
38 Joe Juneau	.08	.25
39 Cory Sarich	.02	.10
40 Brian Holzinger	.02	.10
41 Rhett Warrener	.02	.10
42 Alexei Zhitnik	.02	.10
43 Jean-Sebastien Giguere CL	.08	.25
44 Valeri Bure	.02	.10
45 Jean-Sebastien Giguere	.08	.25
46 Jarome Iginla	.15	.40
47 Rico Fata	.02	.10
48 Derek Morris	.02	.10
49 Rene Corbet	.02	.10
50 Phil Housley	.08	.25
51 Tyrone Garner RC	.02	.10
52 Marc Savard	.02	.10
53 Keith Primeau CL	.02	.10
54 Sami Kapanen	.02	.10
55 Bates Battaglia	.02	.10
56 Arturs Irbe	.08	.25
57 Keith Primeau	.02	.10
58 Gary Roberts	.02	.10
59 Ron Francis	.08	.25
60 Paul Coffey	.10	.30
61 Martin Gelinas	.02	.10
62 Jeff O'Neill	.02	.10
63 Glen Wesley	.02	.10
64 Tony Amonte CL	.02	.10
65 Tony Amonte	.08	.25
66 J-P Dumont	.08	.25
67 Doug Gilmour	.08	.25
68 Ty Jones	.02	.10
69 Anders Eriksson	.02	.10
70 Remi Royer	.02	.10
71 Jocelyn Thibault	.08	.25
72 Alexei Zhamnov	.02	.10
73 Eric Daze	.08	.25
74 Bryan McCabe	.02	.10
75 Peter Forsberg CL	.08	.25
76 Chris Drury	.08	.25
77 Peter Forsberg	.30	.75
78 Patrick Roy	.60	1.50
79 Joe Sakic	.25	.60
80 Milan Hejduk	.10	.30
81 Adam Deadmarsh	.02	.10
82 Adam Foote	.02	.10
83 Sandis Ozolinsh	.02	.10
84 Claude Lemieux	.02	.10
85 Brett Hull CL	.08	.25
86 Ed Belfour	.10	.30
87 Brett Hull	.15	.40
88 Mike Modano	.20	.50
89 Derian Hatcher	.02	.10
90 Jamie Langenbrunner	.02	.10
91 Joe Nieuwendyk	.08	.25
92 Jon Sim RC	.08	.25
93 Jere Lehtinen	.08	.25
94 Darryl Sydor	.02	.10
95 Sergei Zubov	.02	.10
96 Steve Yzerman CL	.08	.25
97 Brendan Shanahan	.10	.30
98 Steve Yzerman	.60	1.50
99 Chris Chelios	.10	.30
100 Sergei Fedorov	.20	.50
101 Vyacheslav Kozlov	.02	.10
102 Igor Larionov	.02	.10
103 Nicklas Lidstrom	.10	.30
104 Tomas Holmstrom	.02	.10
105 Chris Osgood	.08	.25
106 Kris Draper	.02	.10
107 Darren McCarty	.02	.10
108 Doug Weight CL	.02	.10
109 Bill Guerin	.08	.25
110 Tom Poti	.02	.10
111 Mike Grier	.02	.10
112 Tommy Salo	.08	.25
113 Doug Weight	.08	.25
114 Jozef Beranek	.02	.10
115 Fredrik Lindquist	.02	.10
116 Roman Hamrlik	.02	.10
117 Todd Marchant	.02	.10
118 Janne Niinimaa	.02	.10
119 Pavel Bure CL	.08	.25
120 Pavel Bure	.10	.30
121 Mark Parrish	.02	.10
122 Scott Mellanby	.02	.10
123 Viktor Kozlov	.02	.10
124 Oleg Kvasha	.02	.10
125 Rob Niedermayer	.02	.10
126 Bret Hedican	.02	.10
127 Trevor Kidd	.08	.25
128 Robert Svehla	.02	.10
129 Peter Worrell	.02	.10
130 Rob Blake CL	.02	.10
131 Rob Blake	.08	.25
132 Pavel Rosa	.02	.10
133 Donald Audette	.02	.10
134 Luc Robitaille	.08	.25
135 Vladimir Tsyplakov	.02	.10
136 Jozef Stumpel	.08	.25
137 Nathan Lafayette	.02	.10
138 Glen Murray	.02	.10
139 Zigmund Palffy	.08	.25
140 Bryan Smolinski	.02	.10
141 Jamie Storr	.08	.25
142 Saku Koivu CL	.10	.30
143 Saku Koivu	.10	.30
144 Arron Asham	.02	.10
145 Jeff Hackett	.08	.25
146 Trevor Linden	.02	.10
147 Eric Weinrich	.02	.10
148 Vladimir Malakhov	.02	.10
149 Martin Rucinsky	.02	.10
150 Brian Savage	.02	.10
151 Shayne Corson	.02	.10
152 Scott Lachance	.02	.10
153 Jose Theodore	.15	.40
154 David Legwand CL	.08	.25
155 Mike Dunham	.08	.25
156 David Legwand	.08	.25
157 Sergei Krivokrasov	.02	.10
158 Cliff Ronning	.02	.10
159 Kimmo Timonen	.02	.10
160 Bob Boughner	.02	.10
161 Mark Mowers RC	.02	.10
162 Patrick Cote	.02	.10
163 Tomas Vokoun	.08	.25
164 Jan Vopat	.02	.10
165 Martin Brodeur CL	.08	.25
166 Martin Brodeur	.30	.75
167 John Madden RC	.25	.60
168 Vadim Sharifijanov	.02	.10
169 Patrik Elias	.08	.25
170 Scott Stevens	.08	.25
171 Petr Sykora	.02	.10
172 Jason Arnott	.02	.10
173 Brendan Morrison	.08	.25
174 Scott Niedermayer	.02	.10
175 Bobby Holik	.02	.10
176 Eric Brewer CL	.02	.10
177 Eric Brewer	.02	.10
178 Zdeno Chara	.02	.10
179 Kenny Jonsson	.02	.10
180 Dmitri Nabokov	.02	.10
181 Mariusz Czerkawski	.02	.10
182 Brad Isbister	.02	.10
183 Olli Jokinen	.08	.25
184 Felix Potvin	.10	.30
185 Mike Watt	.02	.10
186 Claude Lapointe	.02	.10
187 Brian Leetch CL	.02	.10
188 Manny Malhotra	.08	.25
189 Mike Richter	.10	.30
190 Theo Fleury	.02	.10
191 Adam Graves	.02	.10
192 Brian Leetch	.10	.30
193 Petr Nedved	.08	.25
194 Brent Fedyk	.02	.10
195 Barry Richter	.02	.10
196 Valeri Kamensky	.08	.25
197 Kirk McLean	.08	.25
198 Kevin Stevens	.02	.10
199 Alexei Yashin CL	.02	.10
200 Marian Hossa	.10	.30
201 Alexei Yashin	.02	.10
202 Shawn McEachern	.02	.10
203 Sami Salo	.02	.10
204 Daniel Alfredsson	.08	.25
205 Magnus Arvedson	.02	.10
206 Wade Redden	.02	.10
207 Ron Tugnutt	.08	.25
208 Chris Phillips	.02	.10
209 Vaclav Prospal	.02	.10
210 Eric Lindros CL	.08	.25
211 John LeClair	.10	.30
212 Eric Lindros	.10	.30
213 Mark Recchi	.08	.25
214 Rod Brind'Amour	.02	.10
215 Eric Desjardins	.02	.10
216 Jean-Marc Pelletier	.08	.25
217 Ryan Bast RC	.02	.10
218 Keith Jones	.02	.10
219 John Vanbiesbrouck	.08	.25
220 Brian Wesenberg RC	.02	.10
221 Dan McGillis	.02	.10
222 Keith Tkachuk CL	.08	.25
223 Robert Esche RC	.08	.25
224 Keith Tkachuk	.10	.30
225 Nikolai Khabibulin	.08	.25
226 Trevor Letowski	.02	.10
227 Robert Reichel	.02	.10
228 Jeremy Roenick	.15	.40
229 Greg Adams	.02	.10
230 Daniel Briere	.02	.10
231 Rick Tocchet	.08	.25
232 Stanislav Neckar	.02	.10
233 Teppo Numminen	.02	.10
234 Jaromir Jagr CL	.10	.30
235 Jaromir Jagr	.20	.50
236 Matthew Barnaby	.02	.10
237 Tom Barrasso	.08	.25
238 Jan Hrdina	.02	.10
239 Martin Straka	.02	.10
240 Jean-Sebastien Aubin	.02	.10
241 Alexei Kovalev	.02	.10
242 German Titov	.02	.10
243 Kevin Hatcher	.02	.10
244 Kip Miller	.02	.10
245 Alexei Morozov	.02	.10
246 Jeff Friesen CL	.02	.10
247 Vincent Damphousse	.02	.10
248 Jeff Friesen	.02	.10
249 Scott Hannan	.02	.10
250 Patrick Marleau	.10	.30
251 Mike Ricci	.02	.10
252 Owen Nolan	.08	.25
253 Marco Sturm	.02	.10
254 Gary Suter	.02	.10
255 Jeff Norton	.02	.10
256 Steve Shields	.02	.10
257 Mike Vernon	.08	.25
258 Al MacInnis CL	.02	.10
259 Pavol Demitra	.08	.25
260 Al MacInnis	.08	.25
261 Lubos Bartecko	.02	.10
262 Jochen Hecht RC	1.50	4.00
263 Chris Pronger	.08	.25
264 Grant Fuhr	.08	.25
265 Michal Handzus	.08	.25
266 Pierre Turgeon	.08	.25
267 Jim Campbell	.02	.10
268 Roman Turek	.08	.25
269 Vincent Lecavalier CL	.08	.25
270 Vincent Lecavalier	.10	.30
271 Paul Mara	.02	.10
272 Kevin Hodson	.08	.25
273 Dan Cloutier	.08	.25
274 Chris Gratton	.02	.10
275 Pavel Kubina	.02	.10
276 Darcy Tucker	.02	.10
277 Alexandre Daigle	.02	.10
278 Stephane Richer	.02	.10
279 Niklas Sundstrom	.02	.10
280 Mats Sundin CL	.08	.25
281 Mats Sundin	.10	.30
282 Bryan Berard	.08	.25
283 Sergei Berezin	.02	.10
284 Curtis Joseph	.10	.30
285 Tomas Kaberle	.02	.10
286 Daniil Markov	.02	.10
287 Steve Thomas	.02	.10
288 Mike Johnson	.02	.10
289 Tie Domi	.08	.25
290 Yanic Perreault	.02	.10
291 Derek King	.02	.10
292 Mark Messier CL	.08	.25
293 Mark Messier	.10	.30
294 Bill Muckalt	.02	.10
295 Josh Holden	.02	.10
296 Markus Naslund	.10	.30
297 Kevin Weekes	.08	.25
298 Ed Jovanovski	.02	.10
299 Alexander Mogilny	.08	.25
300 Mattias Ohlund	.02	.10
301 Todd Bertuzzi	.10	.30
302 Peter Schaefer	.02	.10
303 Peter Bondra CL	.02	.10
304 Peter Bondra	.08	.25
305 Adam Oates	.08	.25
306 Jan Bulis	.02	.10
307 Jaroslav Svejkovsky	.02	.10
308 Sergei Gonchar	.02	.10
309 Olaf Kolzig	.08	.25
310 Richard Zednik	.02	.10
311 Benoit Gratton RC	.02	.10
312 Matt Herr	.02	.10
313 Nolan Baumgartner	.02	.10
314 Peter Forsberg	.10	.30
315 Jaromir Jagr	.10	.30
316 Paul Kariya	.10	.30
317 Ray Bourque	.10	.30
318 Al MacInnis	.08	.25
319 Dominik Hasek	.10	.30
320 Steve Yzerman	.10	.30
321 Teemu Selanne	.10	.30
322 Brett Hull	.10	.30
323 Chris Pronger	.08	.25
324 Nicklas Lidstrom	.10	.30
325 Patrick Roy	.10	.30
326 Teemu Selanne	.10	.30
327 Tony Amonte	.08	.25
328 Jaromir Jagr	.10	.30
329 Alexei Yashin	.02	.10
330 John LeClair	.10	.30
331 Jaromir Jagr	.10	.30
332 Peter Forsberg	.10	.30
333 Paul Kariya	.10	.30
334 Teemu Selanne	.10	.30
335 Joe Sakic	.10	.30
336 Jaromir Jagr	.10	.30
337 Teemu Selanne	.10	.30
338 Paul Kariya	.10	.30
339 Peter Forsberg	.10	.30
340 Joe Sakic	.10	.30
341 Al MacInnis	.08	.25
342 Nicklas Lidstrom	.10	.30
343 Ray Bourque	.10	.30
344 Fredrik Olausson	.02	.10
345 Brian Leetch	.10	.30
346 Martin Brodeur	.10	.30
347 Robert Lang	.02	.10
348 Curtis Joseph	.10	.30
349 Chris Osgood	.08	.25
350 Patrick Roy	.10	.30
351 Milan Hejduk	.10	.30
352 Brendan Morrison	.08	.25
353 Chris Drury	.08	.25
354 Jan Hrdina	.02	.10
355 Mark Parrish	.02	.10
356 Oleg Saprykin RC	1.25	3.00
357 Patrik Stefan RC	1.25	3.00
358 Pavel Brendl RC	2.50	6.00
359 Roberto Luongo	.15	.40
360 Scott Gomez	.02	.10
361 Sheldon Keefe RC	.75	2.00
362 Simon Gagne	.10	.30
363 Steve Kariya RC	.75	2.00
364 Alex Tanguay	.08	.25
365 Brad Stuart	.10	.30
366 Branislav Mezei RC	.10	.30
367 Brian Campbell RC	.08	.25
368 Daniel Sedin	.02	.10
369 Henrik Sedin	.02	.10
370 Mike Ribeiro	.10	.30
371 Ivan Novoseltsev RC	.60	1.50
372 Nick Boynton	.08	.25
373 Nikos Tselios	.08	.25
374 Tim Connolly	.10	.30
375 J.F. Damphousse RC	.10	.30
376 Patrick Roy	.10	.30
377 Ed Belfour	.10	.30
378 Chris Osgood	.08	.25
379 Arturs Irbe	.08	.25
380 Nikolai Khabibulin	.08	.25
381 Dominik Hasek	.10	.30
382 Byron Dafoe	.08	.25
383 Jean-Sebastien Giguere	.08	.25
384 Olaf Kolzig	.08	.25
385 John Vanbiesbrouck	.08	.25
386 Martin Brodeur	.10	.30
387 Dan Cloutier	.08	.25
388 Damian Rhodes	.08	.25
389 Curtis Joseph	.10	.30
390 Mike Richter	.10	.30
391 Wayne Gretzky	.30	.75
392 Wayne Gretzky	.30	.75
393 Wayne Gretzky	.30	.75
394 Wayne Gretzky	.30	.75
395 Wayne Gretzky	.30	.75
396 Wayne Gretzky	.30	.75
397 Wayne Gretzky	.30	.75
398 Wayne Gretzky	.30	.75
399 Wayne Gretzky	.30	.75
400 Wayne Gretzky	.30	.75
401 Wayne Gretzky	.30	.75
402 Wayne Gretzky	.30	.75
403 Wayne Gretzky	.30	.75
404 Wayne Gretzky	.30	.75
405 Wayne Gretzky	.30	.75
406 Wayne Gretzky	.30	.75
407 Wayne Gretzky	.30	.75
408 Wayne Gretzky	.30	.75
409 Wayne Gretzky	.30	.75
410 Wayne Gretzky	.30	.75
411 Wayne Gretzky	.30	.75
412 Wayne Gretzky	.30	.75
413 Wayne Gretzky	.30	.75
414 Wayne Gretzky	.30	.75
415 Wayne Gretzky	.30	.75
416 Wayne Gretzky	.30	.75
417 Wayne Gretzky	.30	.75
418 Wayne Gretzky	.30	.75
419 Wayne Gretzky	.30	.75
420 Wayne Gretzky	.30	.75
421 Wayne Gretzky	.30	.75
422 Wayne Gretzky	.30	.75
423 Wayne Gretzky	.30	.75
424 Wayne Gretzky	.30	.75
425 Wayne Gretzky	.30	.75
426 Wayne Gretzky	.30	.75
427 Wayne Gretzky	.30	.75
428 Wayne Gretzky	.30	.75
429 Wayne Gretzky	.30	.75
430 Wayne Gretzky	.30	.75
431 Wayne Gretzky	.30	.75
432 Wayne Gretzky	.30	.75
433 Wayne Gretzky	.30	.75
434 Wayne Gretzky	.30	.75
435 Wayne Gretzky	.30	.75
436 Wayne Gretzky	.30	.75
437 Wayne Gretzky	.30	.75
438 Wayne Gretzky	.30	.75
439 Wayne Gretzky	.30	.75
440 Wayne Gretzky	.30	.75

2000-01 Upper Deck Victory

Released as a 330-card set, Upper Deck Victory features 210 regular player cards, 20 Season Highlight cards, 30 Team Checklist cards, 20 NHL Prospect cards, and 50 NHL's Best cards. Victory was released in mid September and was packaged in 36-pack boxes with packs containing 12 cards and carried a suggested retail price of $.99. A contest card was also included in most packs, it allowed the collector to visit the Upper Deck website and enter a contest to win a Pavel Bure autographed jersey.

Card	Low	High
COMPLETE SET (330)	25.00	50.00
1 Paul Kariya CL	.08	.20
2 Ladislav Kohn	.02	.10
3 Vitali Vishnevsky	.02	.10
4 Steve Rucchin	.02	.10
5 Oleg Tverdovsky	.02	.10
6 Guy Hebert	.08	.20
7 Teemu Selanne	.15	.40
8 Paul Kariya	.15	.40
9 Patrik Stefan CL	.10	.25
10 Andrew Brunette	.02	.10
11 Patrik Stefan	.02	.10
12 Donald Audette	.02	.10
13 Damian Rhodes	.08	.20
14 Maxim Galanov	.02	.10
15 Dean Sylvester	.02	.10
16 Ray Ferraro	.02	.10
17 Joe Thornton CL	.10	.25
18 Brian Rolston	.02	.10
19 Sergei Samsonov	.08	.20
20 Joe Thornton	.25	.60
21 Byron Dafoe	.08	.20
22 Jason Allison	.02	.10
23 Anson Carter	.08	.20
24 Hal Gill	.02	.10
25 Dominik Hasek CL	.15	.40
26 Dominik Hasek	.30	.75
27 Michael Peca	.08	.20
28 Miroslav Satan	.08	.20
29 Doug Gilmour	.08	.20
30 Chris Gratton	.02	.10
31 Curtis Brown	.02	.10
32 Maxim Afinogenov	.02	.10
33 Jay McKee	.02	.10
34 Valeri Bure CL	.02	.10
35 Valeri Bure	.02	.10
36 Fred Brathwaite	.08	.20
37 Jarome Iginla	.20	.50
38 Phil Housley	.08	.20
39 Derek Morris	.02	.10
40 Cory Stillman	.02	.10
41 Marc Savard	.02	.10
42 Ron Francis CL	.02	.10
43 Sami Kapanen	.02	.10
44 Arturs Irbe	.08	.20
45 Rod Brind'Amour	.08	.20
46 Gary Roberts	.02	.10
47 Ron Francis	.08	.20
48 Paul Coffey	.15	.40
49 Jeff O'Neill	.02	.10
50 Tony Amonte CL	.02	.10
51 Tony Amonte	.08	.20
52 Steve Sullivan	.02	.10
53 Michael Grosek	.08	.20
54 Boris Mironov	.02	.10
55 Jocelyn Thibault	.08	.20
56 Alexei Zhamnov	.02	.10
57 Eric Daze	.08	.20
58 Peter Forsberg CL	.20	.50
59 Chris Drury	.08	.20
60 Peter Forsberg	.40	1.00
61 Patrick Roy	.75	2.00
62 Joe Sakic	.30	.75
63 Ray Bourque	.30	.75
64 Adam Deadmarsh	.02	.10
65 Milan Hejduk	.15	.40
66 Sandis Ozolinsh	.02	.10
67 Alex Tanguay	.08	.20
68 Adam Foote	.02	.10
69 Blue Jackets CL	.08	.20
70 Mike Modano CL	.12	.30
71 Ed Belfour	.15	.40
72 Brett Hull	.20	.50
73 Sergei Zubov	.02	.10
74 Brenden Morrow	.08	.20
75 Jamie Langenbrunner	.02	.10
76 Joe Nieuwendyk	.08	.20
77 Mike Modano	.25	.60
78 Derian Hatcher	.02	.10
79 Jere Lehtinen	.08	.20
80 Roman Lyashenko	.02	.10
81 Steve Yzerman CL	.40	1.00
82 Brendan Shanahan	.15	.40
83 Steve Yzerman	.75	2.00
84 Chris Chelios	.15	.40
85 Sergei Fedorov	.25	.60
86 Slava Kozlov	.02	.10
87 Pat Verbeek	.02	.10
88 Nicklas Lidstrom	.15	.40
89 Tomas Holmstrom	.02	.10
90 Chris Osgood	.08	.20
91 Martin Lapointe	.02	.10
92 Doug Weight CL	.02	.10
93 Bill Guerin	.08	.20
94 Tom Poti	.02	.10
95 Mike Grier	.02	.10
96 Tommy Salo	.08	.20
97 Doug Weight	.08	.20
98 Ryan Smyth	.08	.20
99 Alexander Selivanov	.08	.20
100 Pavel Bure CL	.12	.30
101 Pavel Bure	.15	.40
102 Mark Parrish	.02	.10
103 Scott Mellanby	.02	.10
104 Viktor Kozlov	.08	.20
105 Oleg Kvasha	.02	.10
106 Ray Whitney	.02	.10
107 Trevor Kidd	.08	.20
108 Rob Blake CL	.02	.10
109 Rob Blake	.08	.20
110 Jere Karalahti	.02	.10
111 Luc Robitaille	.08	.20
112 Jozef Stumpel	.02	.10
113 Glen Murray	.02	.10
114 Zigmund Palffy	.08	.20
115 Bryan Smolinski	.02	.10
116 Wild CL	.08	.20
117 Saku Koivu CL	.08	.20
118 Saku Koivu	.15	.40
119 Sergei Zholtok	.02	.10
120 Eric Weinrich	.02	.10
121 Jose Theodore	.20	.50
122 Martin Rucinsky	.02	.10
123 Brian Savage	.02	.10
124 Shayne Corson	.02	.10
125 Dainius Zubrus	.02	.10
126 David Legwand CL	.02	.10
127 Mike Dunham	.08	.20
128 David Legwand	.08	.20
129 Greg Johnson	.02	.10
130 Cliff Ronning	.02	.10
131 Kimmo Timonen	.02	.10
132 Patric Kjellberg	.02	.10
133 Drake Berehowsky	.02	.10
134 Martin Brodeur CL	.20	.50
135 Martin Brodeur	.40	1.00
136 John Madden	.02	.10
137 Scott Gomez	.02	.10
138 Patrik Elias	.08	.20
139 Scott Stevens	.08	.20
140 Jason Arnott	.02	.10
141 Alexander Mogilny	.08	.20
142 Tim Connolly CL	.02	.10
143 Dave Scatchard	.02	.10
144 Tim Connolly	.02	.10
145 Kenny Jonsson	.02	.10
146 Claude Lapointe	.02	.10
147 Mariusz Czerkawski	.02	.10
148 Brad Isbister	.02	.10
149 Olli Jokinen	.08	.20
150 Theo Fleury CL	.08	.20
151 Mike Richter	.15	.40
152 Theo Fleury	.02	.10
153 Adam Graves	.02	.10
154 Brian Leetch	.08	.20
155 Petr Nedved	.02	.10
156 Radek Dvorak	.02	.10
157 Mike York	.02	.10
158 Marian Hossa CL	.02	.10
159 Marian Hossa	.15	.40
160 Radek Bonk	.02	.10
161 Shawn McEachern	.02	.10
162 Vaclav Prospal	.02	.10
163 Daniel Alfredsson	.08	.20
164 Magnus Arvedson	.02	.10
165 Wade Redden	.02	.10
166 John LeClair CL	.08	.25
167 John LeClair	.15	.40
168 Eric Lindros	.15	.40
169 Mark Recchi	.08	.20
170 Keith Primeau	.02	.10
171 Eric Desjardins	.02	.10
172 Brian Boucher	.08	.20
173 Daymond Langkow	.08	.20
174 Simon Gagne	.15	.40
175 Jeremy Roenick CL	.25	.50
176 Daniel Briere	.02	.10
177 Keith Tkachuk	.15	.40
178 Sean Burke	.08	.20
179 Trevor Letowski	.02	.10
180 Shane Doan	.02	.10
181 Jeremy Roenick	.20	.50
182 Travis Green	.02	.10
183 Jaromir Jagr CL	.12	.30
184 Jaromir Jagr	.25	.60
185 Matthew Barnaby	.02	.10
186 Robert Lang	.02	.10
187 Jan Hrdina	.02	.10
188 Martin Straka	.02	.10
189 Ron Tugnutt	.08	.20
190 Alexei Kovalev	.08	.20
191 Jeff Friesen CL	.02	.10
192 Vincent Damphousse	.02	.10
193 Jeff Friesen	.02	.10
194 Brad Stuart	.08	.20
195 Patrick Marleau	.08	.20
196 Mike Ricci	.02	.10
197 Owen Nolan	.08	.20
198 Steve Shields	.08	.20
199 Chris Pronger CL	.02	.10
200 Pavol Demitra	.08	.20
201 Al MacInnis	.08	.20
202 Lubos Bartecko	.02	.10
203 Jochen Hecht	.02	.10
204 Chris Pronger	.08	.20
205 Roman Turek	.08	.20
206 Michal Handzus	.02	.10
207 Pierre Turgeon	.08	.20
208 Vincent Lecavalier CL	.08	.20
209 Vincent Lecavalier	.15	.40
210 Paul Mara	.02	.10
211 Mike Johnson	.02	.10
212 Dan Cloutier	.08	.20
213 Wayne Primeau	.02	.10
214 Pavel Kubina	.02	.10
215 Fredrik Modin	.02	.10
216 Mats Sundin CL	.08	.20
217 Mats Sundin	.15	.40
218 Darcy Tucker	.02	.10
219 Sergei Berezin	.02	.10
220 Curtis Joseph	.15	.40
221 Jonas Hoglund	.02	.10
222 Nikolai Antropov	.02	.10
223 Steve Thomas	.02	.10
224 Tie Domi	.08	.20
225 Mark Messier CL	.10	.25
226 Mark Messier	.15	.40
227 Andrew Cassels	.02	.10
228 Brendan Morrison	.08	.20
229 Markus Naslund	.15	.40
230 Felix Potvin	.15	.40
231 Ed Jovanovski	.02	.10
232 Harold Druken	.02	.10
233 Olaf Kolzig CL	.02	.10
234 Peter Bondra	.15	.40
235 Adam Oates	.08	.20
236 Jan Bulis	.02	.10
237 Jeff Halpern	.02	.10
238 Sergei Gonchar	.02	.10
239 Olaf Kolzig	.08	.20
240 Chris Simon	.02	.10
241 P.Bure/V.Bure HL	.15	.40
242 P.Kariya/S.Kariya HL	.15	.40
243 Dominik Hasek HL	.15	.40
244 Patrick Roy HL	.40	1.00
245 Joe Sakic HL	.15	.40
246 Ray Bourque HL	.15	.40
247 Brett Hull HL	.10	.25
248 Brendan Shanahan HL	.12	.30
249 Steve Yzerman HL	.40	1.00
250 Pat Verbeek HL	.02	.10
251 Pavel Bure HL	.12	.30
252 Scott Gomez HL	.02	.10
253 John LeClair HL	.08	.25
254 Brian Boucher HL	.02	.10
255 Jeremy Roenick HL	.25	.50
256 Jaromir Jagr HL	.12	.30
257 Chris Pronger HL	.02	.10
258 Roman Turek HL	.02	.10
259 Curtis Joseph HL	.10	.25
260 Wayne Gretzky HL	1.00	2.50
261 Serge Aubin RC Dan Hinote	.30	.75
262 Brandon Smith RC Andre Savage	.08	.20
263 Keith Aldridge RC Ryan Christie	.08	.20
264 Steven Reinprecht RC Brad Chartrand	.75	2.00
265 Petr Mika RC Jason Krog	.08	.20
266 Steve Valiquette RC Vladimir Orszagh	.15	.40
267 Kyle Freadrich RC Corey Sarich	.08	.20
268 Eric Nickulas RC Joel Prpic	.08	.20
269 David Gosselin RC Richard Lintner	.08	.20
270 Greg Andrusak RC Nathan Dempsey	.08	.20
271 Brent Sopel RC Alfie Michaud	.10	.25
272 Jeremy Stevenson RC Maxim Balmochnykh	.08	.20
273 Andreas Karlsson Scott Fankhouser	.08	.20
274 Dave Tanabe Byron Ritchie	.08	.20
275 Steven McCarthy Kyle Calder	.08	.20
276 Petr Schastlivy Mike Fisher	.08	.20
277 Andy Delmore Mark Eaton	.08	.20
278 Evgeni Nabokov Scott Hannan	.15	.40
279 Dany Heatley RC Jaroslav Svoboda RC	1.00	2.50
280 Matt Pettinger RC Chris Nielsen RC	.08	.20
281 Teemu Selanne NB	.08	.20
282 Paul Kariya NB	.15	.40
283 Patrik Stefan NB	.10	.25
284 Sergei Samsonov NB	.08	.20
285 Joe Thornton NB	.10	.25
286 Dominik Hasek NB	.15	.40
287 Doug Gilmour NB	.08	.20
288 Valeri Bure NB	.02	.10
289 Ron Francis NB	.02	.10
290 Tony Amonte NB	.08	.20
291 Peter Forsberg NB	.20	.50
292 Patrick Roy NB	.40	1.00
293 Joe Sakic NB	.15	.40
294 Ray Bourque NB	.15	.40
295 Milan Hejduk NB	.10	.25
296 Ed Belfour NB	.08	.20
297 Brett Hull NB	.10	.25
298 Mike Modano NB	.12	.30
299 Brendan Shanahan NB	.12	.30
300 Steve Yzerman NB	.40	1.00
301 Sergei Fedorov NB	.15	.40
302 Chris Osgood NB	.08	.20
303 Doug Weight NB	.02	.10
304 Pavel Bure NB	.12	.30
305 Zigmund Palffy NB	.08	.20
306 Rob Blake NB	.02	.10
307 Saku Koivu NB	.08	.20
308 David Legwand NB	.02	.10
309 Martin Brodeur NB	.20	.50
310 Scott Gomez NB	.02	.10
311 Tim Connolly NB	.02	.10
312 Theo Fleury NB	.08	.20
313 Marian Hossa NB	.15	.40
314 John LeClair NB	.08	.25
315 Eric Lindros NB	.12	.30
316 Keith Tkachuk NB	.08	.20
317 Jeremy Roenick NB	.25	.50
318 Jaromir Jagr NB	.12	.30
319 Jeff Friesen NB	.02	.10
320 Owen Nolan NB	.02	.10
321 Al MacInnis NB	.02	.10
322 Pavol Demitra NB	.02	.10
323 Chris Pronger NB	.02	.10
324 Roman Turek NB	.02	.10
325 Vincent Lecavalier NB	.08	.20
326 Mats Sundin NB	.08	.20
327 Curtis Joseph NB	.10	.25
328 Mark Messier NB	.10	.25
329 Peter Bondra NB	.15	.40
330 Olaf Kolzig NB	.02	.10
WCB Pavel Bure Jer Contest	.02	.10

2001-02 Upper Deck Victory

Released in mid-August 2001, this 453-card set carried an SRP of $3.99 for a 10-card pack. The set was originally released as a 440-card set, and cards 441-453 were available in random packs of UD Rookie Update.

Card	Low	High
COMP.SERIES I SET (440)	30.00	60.00
COMP.SET w/UPDATE (453)	50.00	100.00
1 Jean-Sebastien Giguere CL	.02	.10
2 Steve Rucchin	.02	.10
3 Oleg Tverdovsky	.02	.10
4 Matt Cullen	.02	.10
5 Vitali Vishnevsky	.02	.10
6 Jean-Sebastien Giguere	.08	.20
7 Mike LeClerc	.02	.10
8 Petr Tenkrat	.02	.10
9 Paul Kariya	.12	.30
10 Samuel Pahlsson	.02	.10
11 Jeff Friesen	.02	.10
12 Milan Hnilicka CL	.02	.10
13 Patrik Stefan	.02	.10
14 Andrew Brunette	.02	.10
15 Hnat Domenichelli	.02	.10
16 Jiri Slegr	.02	.10
17 Tomi Kallio	.02	.10
18 Steve Staios	.02	.10
19 Steve Guolla	.02	.10
20 Milan Hnilicka	.08	.20
21 Ray Ferraro	.02	.10
22 Frantisek Kaberle	.02	.10
23 Ladislav Kohn	.02	.10
24 Byron Dafoe CL	.08	.20
25 Sergei Samsonov	.08	.20
26 Joe Thornton	.25	.60
27 Per Johan Axelsson	.02	.10
28 Brian Rolston	.02	.10
29 Mikko Eloranta	.02	.10
30 Jason Allison	.02	.10
31 Mike Knuble	.02	.10
32 Eric Weinrich	.02	.10
33 Byron Dafoe	.08	.20
34 Bill Guerin	.08	.20
35 Kyle McLaren	.02	.10
36 Dominik Hasek CL	.15	.40
37 Curtis Brown	.02	.10
38 Miroslav Satan	.08	.20
39 Dominik Hasek	.30	.75
40 Maxim Afinogenov	.02	.10
41 Stu Barnes	.02	.10
42 J-P Dumont	.02	.10
43 Martin Biron	.08	.20
44 Alexei Zhitnik	.02	.10
45 Dimitri Kalinin	.02	.10
46 Chris Gratton	.02	.10
47 Denis Hamel	.02	.10
48 Mike Vernon CL	.02	.10
49 Jarome Iginla	.15	.40
50 Marc Savard	.02	.10
51 Jeff Cowan	.02	.10
52 Derek Morris	.02	.10
53 Dave Lowry	.02	.10
54 Craig Conroy	.02	.10
55 Robyn Regehr	.02	.10
56 Oleg Saprykin	.02	.10
57 Clarke Wilm	.02	.10
58 Toni Lydman	.02	.10
59 Arturs Irbe CL	.08	.20
60 Rod Brind'Amour	.08	.20
61 Ron Francis	.08	.20
62 Sami Kapanen	.02	.10
63 Jeff O'Neill	.02	.10
64 Sandis Ozolinsh	.02	.10
65 Arturs Irbe	.08	.20
66 Dave Tanabe	.02	.10
67 Shane Willis	.02	.10
68 Josef Vasicek	.02	.10

69 Tommy Westlund .02 .10
70 Bates Battaglia .02 .10
71 Jocelyn Thibault CL .02 .10
72 Steve Sullivan .02 .10
73 Tony Amonte .08 .20
74 Eric Daze .08 .20
75 Steven McCarthy .02 .10
76 Alexei Zhamnov .02 .10
77 Jaroslav Spacek .02 .10
78 Jocelyn Thibault .08 .20
79 Michael Nylander .02 .10
80 Kyle Calder .02 .10
81 Chris Herperger .02 .10
82 Ryan Vandenbussche .02 .10
83 Patrick Roy CL .40 1.00
84 Peter Forsberg .40 1.00
85 Ray Bourque .30 .75
86 Milan Hejduk .12 .30
87 Alex Tanguay .08 .20
88 David Aebischer .08 .20
89 Chris Drury .08 .20
90 Rob Blake .08 .20
91 Joe Sakic .30 .75
92 Patrick Roy .75 2.00
93 Ville Nieminen .02 .10
94 Steven Reinprecht .02 .10
95 Adam Foote .02 .10
96 Ron Tugnutt CL .02 .10
97 Geoff Sanderson .02 .10
98 Serge Aubin .02 .10
99 David Vyborny .02 .10
100 Ron Tugnutt .08 .20
101 Espen Knutsen .02 .10
102 Tyler Wright .02 .10
103 Lyle Odelein .02 .10
104 Marc Denis .08 .20
105 Blake Sloan .02 .10
106 Jean-Luc Grand-Pierre .02 .10
107 Mike Maneluk .02 .10
108 Ed Belfour CL .08 .20
109 Mike Modano .25 .60
110 Brett Hull .20 .50
111 Brenden Morrow .08 .20
112 Joe Nieuwendyk .08 .20
113 Sergei Zubov .02 .10
114 Ed Belfour .12 .30
115 Derian Hatcher .02 .10
116 Jamie Langenbrunner .02 .10
117 Grant Marshall .02 .10
118 Marty Turco .08 .20
119 Jere Lehtinen .08 .20
120 Darryl Sydor .02 .10
121 Chris Osgood CL .08 .20
122 Sergei Fedorov .25 .60
123 Steve Yzerman .75 2.00
124 Nicklas Lidstrom .12 .30
125 Mathieu Dandenault .02 .10
126 Slava Kozlov .02 .10
127 Chris Osgood .08 .20
128 Darren McCarty .02 .10
129 Kirk Maltby .02 .10
130 Boyd Devereaux .02 .10
131 Manny Legace .08 .20
132 Brendan Shanahan .12 .30
133 Tomas Holmstrom .02 .10
134 Tommy Salo CL .02 .10
135 Anson Carter .08 .20
136 Todd Marchant .02 .10
137 Ryan Smyth .02 .10
138 Tommy Salo .08 .20
139 Doug Weight .08 .20
140 Janne Niinimaa .02 .10
141 Rem Murray .02 .10
142 Daniel Cleary .02 .10
143 Tom Poti .02 .10
144 Georges Laraque .02 .10
145 Mike Grier .02 .10
146 Roberto Luongo CL .02 .10
147 Kevyn Adams .02 .10
148 Viktor Kozlov .08 .20
149 Marcus Nillson .02 .10
150 Robert Svehla .02 .10
151 Pavel Bure .12 .30
152 Anders Eriksson .02 .10
153 Vaclav Prospal .02 .10
154 Roberto Luongo .15 .40
155 Denis Shvidki .02 .10
156 Peter Worrell .02 .10
157 Olli Jokinen .08 .20
158 Felix Potvin CL .08 .20
159 Luc Robitaille .08 .20
160 Zigmund Palffy .08 .20
161 Jozef Stumpel .02 .10
162 Bryan Smolinski .02 .10
163 Glen Murray .02 .10
164 Aaron Miller .02 .10
165 Adam Deadmarsh .02 .10
166 Jaroslav Modry .02 .10
167 Felix Potvin .12 .30
168 Eric Belanger .02 .10
169 Ian Laperriere .02 .10
170 Manny Fernandez CL .02 .10
171 Marian Gaborik .25 .60
172 Stacy Roest .02 .10
173 Wes Walz .02 .10
174 Lubomir Sekeras .02 .10
175 Manny Fernandez .08 .20
176 Darby Hendrickson .02 .10
177 Aaron Gavey .02 .10
178 Roman Simicek .02 .10
179 Jamie McLennan .02 .10
180 Antti Laaksonen .02 .10
181 Andy Sutton .02 .10
182 Jose Theodore CL .12 .30
183 Richard Zednik .02 .10
184 Martin Rucinsky .02 .10
185 Saku Koivu .12 .30
186 Jose Theodore .15 .40
187 Brian Savage .02 .10
188 Oleg Petrov .02 .10
189 Patrice Brisebois .02 .10
190 Chad Kilger .02 .10
191 Craig Darby .02 .10
192 Andrei Markov .02 .10
193 Mike Dunham CL .02 .10
194 Cliff Ronning .02 .10
195 Vitali Yachmenev .02 .10
196 Scott Walker .02 .10
197 Kimmo Timonen .02 .10
198 Patric Kjellberg .02 .10
199 Mike Dunham .08 .20
200 Greg Johnson .02 .10
201 David Legwand .08 .20
202 Scott Hartnell .02 .10
203 Tom Fitzgerald .02 .10
204 Tomas Vokoun .02 .10
205 Martin Brodeur CL .20 .50
206 Scott Stevens .08 .20
207 Patrik Elias .08 .20
208 Randy McKay .02 .10
209 Jason Arnott .02 .10
210 Alexander Mogilny .08 .20
211 Petr Sykora .02 .10
212 Scott Gomez .02 .10
213 Sergei Brylin .02 .10
214 Bobby Holik .02 .10
215 Martin Brodeur .40 1.00
216 John Madden .02 .10
217 Scott Niedermayer .02 .10
218 Rick DiPietro CL .02 .10
219 Mariusz Czerkawski .02 .10
220 Jason Krog .02 .10
221 Roman Hamrlik .02 .10
222 Jason Blake .02 .10
223 Rick DiPietro .08 .20
224 Dave Scatchard .02 .10
225 Brad Isbister .02 .10
226 Mark Parrish .02 .10
227 Kenny Jonsson .02 .10
228 Oleg Kvasha .02 .10
229 Mike Richter CL .08 .20
230 Mark Messier .12 .30
231 Mike York .02 .10
232 Theo Fleury .02 .10
233 Brian Leetch .08 .20
234 Petr Nedved .02 .10
235 Radek Dvorak .02 .10
236 Jan Hlavac .02 .10
237 Mike Richter .12 .30
238 Manny Malhotra .02 .10
239 Tomas Kloucek .02 .10
240 Sandy McCarthy .02 .10
241 Patrick Lalime CL .02 .10
242 Marian Hossa .12 .30
243 Shawn McEachern .02 .10
244 Wade Redden .02 .10
245 Daniel Alfredsson .08 .20
246 Radek Bonk .02 .10
247 Martin Havlat .08 .20
248 Patrick Lalime .08 .20
249 Magnus Arvedson .02 .10
250 Karel Rachunek .02 .10
251 Sami Salo .02 .10
252 Jani Hurme .08 .20
253 Roman Cechmanek CL .02 .10
254 John LeClair .12 .30
255 Daymond Langkow .08 .20
256 Keith Primeau .02 .10
257 Justin Williams .02 .10
258 Simon Gagne .12 .30
259 Roman Cechmanek .08 .20
260 Mark Recchi .08 .20
261 Ruslan Fedotenko .08 .20
262 Dan McGillis .02 .10
263 Eric Desjardins .02 .10
264 Brian Boucher .08 .20
265 Sean Burke CL .02 .10
266 Shane Doan .02 .10
267 Mike Johnson .02 .10
268 Michal Handzus .02 .10
269 Landon Wilson .02 .10
270 Jeremy Roenick .15 .40
271 Mika Alatalo .02 .10
272 Sean Burke .08 .20
273 Daniel Briere .02 .10
274 Trevor Letowski .02 .10
275 Teppo Numminen .02 .10
276 Ladislav Nagy .02 .10
277 Johan Hedberg CL .02 .10
278 Jaromir Jagr .25 .75
279 Jan Hrdina .02 .10
280 Mario Lemieux 1.00 2.50
281 Alexei Kovalev .08 .20
282 Robert Lang .02 .10
283 Martin Straka .02 .10
284 Alexei Morozov .02 .10
285 Janne Laukkanen .02 .10
286 Rene Corbet .02 .10
287 Jean-Sebastien Aubin .02 .10
288 Darius Kasparaitis .02 .10
289 Evgeni Nabokov CL .02 .10
290 Teemu Selanne .12 .30
291 Patrick Marleau .02 .10
292 Owen Nolan .08 .20
293 Marcus Ragnarsson .02 .10
294 Brad Stuart .08 .20
295 Mike Ricci .02 .10
296 Vincent Damphousse .02 .10
297 Scott Thornton .02 .10
298 Mike Rathje .02 .10
299 Marco Sturm .02 .10
300 Evgeni Nabokov .08 .20
301 Alexander Korolyuk .02 .10
302 Brent Johnson CL .08 .20
303 Keith Tkachuk .12 .30
304 Cory Stillman .02 .10
305 Chris Pronger .08 .20
306 Scott Young .02 .10
307 Pavol Demitra .08 .20
308 Al MacInnis .08 .20
309 Jochen Hecht .02 .10
310 Pierre Turgeon .08 .20
311 Tyson Nash .02 .10
312 Jamal Mayers .02 .10
313 Dallas Drake .02 .10
314 Kevin Weekes CL .02 .10
315 Vincent Lecavalier .12 .30
316 Brad Richards .08 .20
317 Brian Holzinger .02 .10
318 Fredrik Modin .02 .10
319 Kevin Weekes .08 .20
320 Pavel Kubina .02 .10
321 Andrei Zyuzin .02 .10
322 Martin St. Louis .08 .20
323 Matthew Barnaby .08 .20
324 Nikolai Khabibulin .12 .30
325 Curtis Joseph CL .10 .25
326 Mats Sundin .12 .30
327 Gary Roberts .02 .10
328 Bryan McCabe .02 .10
329 Curtis Joseph .12 .30
330 Tomas Kaberle .02 .10
331 Jonas Hoglund .02 .10
332 Darcy Tucker .02 .10
333 Nikolai Antropov .02 .10
334 Tie Domi .08 .20
335 Aki Berg .02 .10
336 Dimitri Yushkevich .02 .10
337 Dan Cloutier CL .10 .25
338 Markus Naslund .12 .30
339 Donald Brashear .02 .10
340 Andrew Cassels .02 .10
341 Todd Bertuzzi .12 .30
342 Ed Jovanovski .02 .10
343 Brendan Morrison .08 .20
344 Daniel Sedin .02 .10
345 Henrik Sedin .02 .10
346 Dan Cloutier .08 .20
347 Peter Schaefer .02 .10
348 Harold Druken .02 .10
349 Olaf Kolzig CL .02 .10
350 Peter Bondra .12 .30
351 Sergei Gonchar .02 .10
352 Steve Konowalchuk .02 .10
353 Chris Simon .02 .10
354 Adam Oates .08 .20
355 Olaf Kolzig .08 .20
356 Jeff Halpern .02 .10
357 Trevor Linden .02 .10
358 Calle Johansson .02 .10
359 Dainius Zubrus .02 .10
360 Andrei Nikolishin .02 .10
361 Gregg Naumenko .02 .10
362 Brad Tapper .08 .20
J.P. Vigier
Dan Snyder RC
363 Zdenek Kutlak RC .08 .20
Lee Goren
Pavel Kolarik
364 Mika Noronen .08 .20
365 Marty Murray .08 .20
Rico Fata
Ronald Petrovicky
366 Casey Hankinson RC .08 .20
Michel Larocque RC
Mark Bell
367 Yuri Babenko .08 .20
Rob Shearer
368 Steve Gainey .02 .10
369 Jason Williams .08 .20
Maxim Kuznetsov
370 Jason Chimera .08 .20
Mike Comrie
Chris Hajt
371 Jody Shelley RC .08 .20
Martin Spanhel RC
Rostislav Klesla
372 Mathieu Darche .08 .20
Matt Davidson
373 Andrej Podkonicky RC .08 .20
Rocky Thompson
374 Travis Scott .08 .20
Andreas Lilja
375 Pascal Dupuis RC .02 .10
376 Mike Matteucci RC .08 .20
Derek Gustafson
377 Francis Belanger RC .08 .20
378 Chris Mason .08 .20
Pavel Skrbek RC
379 Pierre Dagenais .08 .20
Mike Jefferson RC
380 Juraj Kolnik .02 .10
381 Peter Smrek .08 .20
Jeff Ulmer
Vitali Yeremeyev
382 Joel Kwiatkowski RC .08 .20
383 Maxime Ouellet .08 .20
384 David Cullen RC .02 .10
385 Bill Tibbetts RC .12 .30
Greg Crozier
Johan Hedberg
386 Miikka Kiprusoff .08 .20
Mikael Samuelsson RC
387 Jaroslav Obsut .08 .20
Mike Van Ryn
388 Thomas Ziegler RC .08 .20
Dmitri Afanasenkov
389 Alexei Ponikarovsky .08 .20
Jeff Farkas
390 Kris Beech .02 .10
Matt Pettinger
391 Mario Lemieux MHG 1.25 3.00
392 Jaromir Jagr MHG .30 .75
393 Chris Pronger MHG .10 .25
394 Peter Forsberg MHG .50 1.25
395 Pavel Bure MHG .25 .60
396 Patrick Roy MHG 1.00 2.50
397 Joe Sakic MHG .40 1.00
398 Dominik Hasek MHG .40 1.00
399 John Leclair MHG .25 .60
400 Sergei Fedorov MHG .40 1.00
401 Nicklas Lidstrom MHG .15 .40
402 Martin Brodeur MHG .50 1.25
403 Ed Belfour MHG .15 .40
404 Steve Yzerman MHG .50 1.25
405 Owen Nolan MHG .10 .25
406 Keith Tkachuk MHG .15 .40
407 Olaf Kolzig MHG .10 .25
408 Rob Blake MHG .10 .25
409 Brett Hull MHG .25 .60
410 Brian Leetch MHG .10 .25
411 Ray Bourque MHG .40 1.00
412 Pierre Turgeon MHG .10 .25
413 Alexei Yashin MHG .05 .15
414 Mike Modano MHG .30 .80
415 Curtis Joseph MHG .15 .40
416 Alexei Kovalev MHG .10 .25
417 Marian Hossa MHG .15 .40
418 Milan Hejduk MHG .15 .40
419 Markus Naslund MHG .15 .40
420 Theo Fleury MHG .05 .15
421 Bill Guerin MHG .10 .25
422 Doug Weight MHG .10 .25
423 Luc Robitaille MHG .10 .25
424 Zigmund Palffy MHG .10 .25
425 Jeremy Roenick MHG .20 .50
426 Mats Sundin MHG .15 .40
427 Alexander Mogilny MHG .10 .25
428 Ed Jovanovski MHG .05 .15
429 Adam Foote MHG .05 .15
430 Peter Bondra MHG .15 .40
431 Mark Recchi MHG .10 .25
432 Radek Bonk MHG .05 .15
433 Simon Gagne MHG .15 .40
434 Scott Stevens MHG .10 .25
435 Steve Sullivan MHG .05 .15
436 Martin Straka MHG .05 .15
437 Evgeni Nabokov MHG .10 .25
438 Keith Primeau MHG .05 .15
439 Brendan Shanahan MHG .30 .80
440 Vincent Lecavalier MHG .15 .40
441 Ilya Kovalchuk RC 3.00 8.00
442 Erik Cole RC 1.50 4.00
443 Pavel Datsyuk RC 4.00 10.00
444 Kristian Huselius RC 1.50 4.00
445 Marcel Hossa RC 1.50 4.00
446 Martin Erat RC 1.50 4.00
447 Christian Berglund RC 1.50 4.00
448 Raffi Torres RC 1.50 4.00
449 Dan Blackburn RC 1.50 4.00
450 Jiri Dopita RC 1.50 4.00
451 Krys Kolanos RC 1.50 4.00
452 Brian Sutherby RC 1.50 4.00
453 Olivier Michaud RC 1.50 4.00

2001-02 Upper Deck Victory Gold

Randomly inserted at 1:2 packs, this 440-card set paralleled the Series I base set but was printed on gold card stock.

*STARS: .75X TO 1.5X BASIC CARDS

2002-03 Upper Deck Victory

Released in late-July 2002, this 220-card set had an SRP of $.99 for a 10-card pack. A bronze bordered parallel was also created and inserted in 1:2 packs.

COMPLETE SET (220) 20.00 40.00
*BRONZE: .5X to 1.25 X BASIC CARD
1 Vitali Vishnevsky .02 .10
2 Paul Kariya .12 .30
3 Jeff Friesen .02 .10
4 Jean-Sebastien Giguere .08 .20
5 Oleg Tverdovsky .02 .10
6 Matt Cullen .02 .10
7 Mike LeClerc .02 .10
8 Pasi Nurminen .02 .10
9 Dany Heatley .15 .40
10 Ilya Kovalchuk .20 .50
11 Pascal Rheaume .02 .10
12 Lubos Bartecko .02 .10
13 Mark Hartigan .02 .10
14 Frederic Cassivi .08 .20
15 Jozef Stumpel .02 .10
16 Sergei Samsonov .08 .20
17 P.J. Stock .02 .10
18 Joe Thornton .25 .60
19 Nick Boynton .02 .10
20 Brian Rolston .02 .10
21 Martin Lapointe .02 .10
22 Maxim Afinogenov .02 .10
23 Martin Biron .08 .20
24 J-P Dumont .02 .10
25 Stu Barnes .02 .10
26 Tim Connolly .02 .10
27 Miroslav Satan .08 .20
28 Taylor Pyatt .02 .10
29 Craig Conroy .02 .10
30 Roman Turek .08 .20
31 Jarome Iginla .15 .40
32 Dean McAmmond .02 .10
33 Marc Savard .02 .10
34 Derek Morris .02 .10
35 Micki Dupont RC .02 .10
36 Sami Kapanen .02 .10
37 Jeff O'Neill .02 .10
38 Ron Francis .08 .20
39 Rod Brind'Amour .08 .20
40 Erik Cole .02 .10
41 Bates Battaglia .02 .10
42 Arturs Irbe .08 .20
43 Alexei Zhamnov .02 .10
44 Jocelyn Thibault .08 .20
45 Eric Daze .02 .10
46 Steve Sullivan .02 .10
47 Phil Housley .02 .10
48 Kyle Calder .02 .10
49 Bob Probert .02 .10
50 Patrick Roy .75 2.00
51 Radim Vrbata .02 .10
52 Chris Drury .08 .20
53 Joe Sakic .30 .75
54 Milan Hejduk .12 .30
55 Alex Tanguay .08 .20
56 Peter Forsberg .40 1.00
57 Rob Blake .08 .20
58 Ray Whitney .02 .10
59 Espen Knutsen .02 .10
60 Marc Denis .08 .20
61 Rostislav Klesla .02 .10
62 Ron Tugnutt .08 .20
63 Mike Sillinger .02 .10
64 Chris Nielsen .02 .10
65 Jason Arnott .02 .10
66 Marty Turco .08 .20
67 Jere Lehtinen .08 .20
68 Sergei Zubov .02 .10
69 Mike Modano .25 .60
70 Brenden Morrow .08 .20
71 Pierre Turgeon .08 .20
72 Derian Halcher .02 .10
73 Brendan Shanahan .12 .30
74 Dominik Hasek .30 .75
75 Sergei Fedorov .25 .60
76 Pavel Datsyuk .12 .30
77 Steve Yzerman .75 2.00
78 Brett Hull .20 .50
79 Chris Chelios .12 .30
80 Luc Robitaille .08 .20
81 Mike Comrie .08 .20
82 Anson Carter .08 .20
83 Ryan Smyth .02 .10
84 Tommy Salo .08 .20
85 Jochen Hecht .02 .10
86 Eric Brewer .02 .10
87 Mike York .02 .10
88 Kristian Huselius .02 .10
89 Stephen Weiss .02 .10
90 Roberto Luongo .15 .40
91 Sandis Ozolinsh .02 .10
92 Valeri Bure .02 .10
93 Marcus Nilsson .02 .10
94 Niklas Hagman .02 .10
95 Adam Deadmarsh .02 .10
96 Felix Potvin .12 .30
97 Jason Allison .02 .10
98 Eric Belanger .02 .10
99 Zigmund Palffy .08 .20
100 Cliff Ronning .02 .10
101 Mathieu Schneider .02 .10
102 Andrew Brunette .02 .10
103 Sylvain Blouin RC .02 .10
104 Marian Gaborik .25 .60
105 Wes Walz .02 .10
106 Filip Kuba .02 .10
107 Manny Fernandez .08 .20
108 Tony Virta .02 .10
109 Jose Theodore .15 .30
110 Saku Koivu .12 .30
111 Mike Ribeiro .02 .10
112 Yanic Perreault .02 .10
113 Oleg Petrov .02 .10
114 Joe Juneau .02 .10
115 Marcel Hossa .02 .10
116 Denis Arkhipov .02 .10
117 Scott Hartnell .02 .10
118 David Legwand .08 .20
119 Mike Dunham .08 .20
120 Kimmo Timonen .02 .10
121 Greg Johnson .02 .10
122 Andy Delmore .02 .10
123 Petr Sykora .02 .10
124 Scott Stevens .08 .20
125 Brian Gionta .02 .10
126 Scott Niedermayer .02 .10
127 Martin Brodeur .40 1.00
128 Patrik Elias .08 .20
129 Joe Nieuwendyk .08 .20
130 Scott Gomez .02 .10
131 Ray Schultz RC .02 .10
132 Mark Parrish .02 .10
133 Raffi Torres .02 .10
134 Alexei Yashin .02 .10
135 Chris Osgood .08 .20
136 Michael Peca .02 .10
137 Shawn Bates .02 .10
138 Pavel Bure .12 .30
139 Mark Messier .12 .30
140 Eric Lindros .12 .30
141 Brian Leetch .08 .20
142 Petr Nedved .02 .10
143 Tom Poti .02 .10
144 Dan Blackburn .08 .20
145 Mike Richter .12 .30
146 Martin Havlat .08 .20
147 Patrick Lalime .08 .20
148 Daniel Alfredsson .08 .20
149 Marian Hossa .12 .30
150 Radek Bonk .02 .10
151 Wade Redden .02 .10
152 Magnus Arvedson .02 .10
153 Todd White .02 .10
154 Roman Cechmanek .08 .20
155 Mark Recchi .08 .20
156 Simon Gagne .12 .30
157 Jeremy Roenick .15 .40
158 John LeClair .12 .30
159 Keith Primeau .02 .10
160 Justin Williams .02 .10
161 Brian Boucher .08 .20
162 Krys Kolanos .02 .10
163 Sean Burke .08 .20
164 Teppo Numminen .02 .10
165 Shane Doan .02 .10
166 Ladislav Nagy .02 .10
167 Daymond Langkow .08 .20
168 Daniel Briere .02 .10
169 Kris Beech .02 .10
170 Johan Hedberg .08 .20
171 Martin Straka .02 .10
172 Mario Lemieux 1.00 2.50
173 Alexei Kovalev .08 .20
174 Jan Hrdina .02 .10
175 Alexei Morozov .02 .10
176 Vincent Damphousse .02 .10
177 Owen Nolan .08 .20
178 Patrick Marleau .08 .20
179 Evgeni Nabokov .08 .20
180 Brad Stuart .02 .10
181 Mike Ricci .02 .10
182 Scott Thornton .02 .10
183 Al MacInnis .08 .20
184 Pavol Demitra .08 .20
185 Chris Pronger .08 .20
186 Brent Johnson .08 .20
187 Doug Weight .08 .20
188 Keith Tkachuk .12 .30
189 Scott Young .02 .10
190 Cory Stillman .02 .10
191 Sheldon Keefe .02 .10
192 Brad Richards .08 .20
193 Nikolai Khabibulin .12 .30
194 Martin St. Louis .08 .20
195 Vincent Lecavalier .12 .30
196 Fredrik Modin .02 .10
197 Pavel Kubina .02 .10
198 Alexander Mogilny .08 .20
199 Tomas Kaberle .02 .10
200 Mats Sundin .12 .30
201 Gary Roberts .02 .10
202 Mikael Renberg .02 .10
203 Tie Domi .08 .20
204 Darcy Tucker .02 .10
205 Brendan Morrison .08 .20
206 Brent Sopel .02 .10
207 Trevor Linden .02 .10
208 Dan Cloutier .08 .20
209 Todd Bertuzzi .12 .30
210 Ed Jovanovski .08 .20
211 Markus Naslund .12 .30
212 Sergei Gonchar .02 .10
213 Jaromir Jagr .25 .60
214 Peter Bondra .08 .20
215 Steve Konowalchuk .02 .10
216 Dainius Zubrus .02 .10
217 Brian Sutherby .02 .10
218 Olaf Kolzig .08 .20
219 Patrick Roy CL .40 1.00
220 Pavel Bure CL .12 .30

2002-03 Upper Deck Victory Bronze

This 220-card set paralleled the base set with bronze trim and was inserted at 1:2 packs.

*BRONZE: X TO X BASIC CARD

2002-03 Upper Deck Victory Gold

This 220-card set paralleled the base set with gold trim. Each card was serial-numbered to 100.

*GOLD: 8X TO 20X BASIC CARD

2002-03 Upper Deck Victory Silver

This 220-card set paralleled the base set with silver trim and was inserted at 1:36.

*SILVER: 4X TO 10X BASIC CARD

2002-03 Upper Deck Victory National Pride

Inserted at 1:4, this 60-card set featured small color player photos over larger silhouettes.

COMPLETE SET 20.00 40.00
NP1 Ruslan Salei .15 .40
NP2 Paul Kariya .30 .75
NP3 Jarome Iginla .40 1.00
NP4 Joe Sakic .60 1.50
NP5 Rob Blake .25 .60
NP6 Steve Yzerman 1.50 4.00
NP7 Brendan Shanahan .50 1.25
NP8 Martin Brodeur .75 2.00
NP9 Eric Lindros .30 .75
NP10 Simon Gagne .30 .75
NP11 Mario Lemieux 2.00 5.00
NP12 Chris Pronger .25 .60
NP13 Curtis Joseph .30 .75
NP14 Milan Hejduk .30 .75
NP15 Dominik Hasek .60 1.50
NP16 Patrik Elias .25 .60
NP17 Petr Sykora .15 .40
NP18 Martin Rucinsky .15 .40
NP19 Marian Hossa .25 .60
NP20 Robert Lang .15 .40
NP21 Jaromir Jagr .50 1.25
NP22 Sami Kapanen .15 .40
NP23 Ville Nieminen .15 .40
NP24 Jere Lehtinen .25 .60
NP25 Jani Hurme .25 .60
NP26 Teppo Numminen .15 .40
NP27 Teemu Selanne .30 .75
NP28 Jochen Hecht .15 .40
NP29 Marco Sturm .15 .40
NP30 Olaf Kolzig .25 .60
NP31 Ilya Kovalchuk .40 1.00
NP32 Sergei Samsonov .25 .60
NP33 Alexei Zhamnov .15 .40
NP34 Sergei Fedorov .60 1.50
NP35 Pavel Bure .50 1.25
NP36 Alexei Yashin .15 .40
NP37 Alexei Kovalev .25 .60
NP38 Nikolai Khabibulin .30 .75
NP39 Sergei Gonchar .15 .40
NP40 Miroslav Satan .25 .60
NP41 Zigmund Palffy .25 .60
NP42 Marian Hossa .30 .75
NP43 Pavol Demitra .25 .60
NP44 Nicklas Lidstrom .30 .75
NP45 Tomas Holmstrom .15 .40
NP46 Tommy Salo .25 .60
NP47 Daniel Alfredsson .25 .60
NP48 Kim Johnsson .15 .40
NP49 Mats Sundin .30 .75
NP50 Markus Naslund .30 .75
NP51 Bill Guerin .25 .60
NP52 Tony Amonte .25 .60
NP53 Chris Drury .25 .60
NP54 Mike Modano .50 1.25
NP55 Chris Chelios .30 .75
NP56 Mike Dunham .25 .60
NP57 Mike Richter .30 .75
NP58 Jeremy Roenick .40 1.00
NP59 Keith Tkachuk .30 .75
NP60 Doug Weight .25 .60

2003-04 Upper Deck Victory

Released in September, this 210-card set featured 200 base cards and a 10-card rookie redemption set. The rookie redemption exchange card was inserted to 1:72. Please note that card #15 does not exist and card #27 was duplicated.

COMP.SET w/o ROOK.RED (200) 25.00 50.00
COMMON RC (201-210) 1.50 4.00
1 Paul Kariya .12 .30
2 Petr Sykora .02 .10
3 Adam Oates .08 .20
4 Stanislav Chistov .02 .10
5 Jean-Sebastien Giguere .08 .20
6 Dany Heatley .15 .40
7 Ilya Kovalchuk .20 .50
8 Marc Savard .02 .10
9 Patrik Stefan .02 .10
10 Simon Gamache .02 .10
11 Joe DiPenta RC .60 1.50
12 Joe Thornton .25 .60
13 Glen Murray .02 .10
14 Bryan Berard .02 .10
16 P.J. Stock .02 .10
17 Jeff Hackett .02 .10
18 Steve Shields .08 .20
19 Miroslav Satan .08 .20
20 Daniel Briere .02 .10
21 Ales Kotalik .02 .10
22 Milan Bartovic RC .60 1.50
23 Maxim Afinogenov .02 .10
24 Martin Biron .08 .20
25 Ryan Miller .08 .20
26 Rick Mrozik RC .02 .10
27 Jarome Iginla .15 .40
27 Sergei Samsonov .08 .20
28 Chris Drury .08 .20
29 Jordan Leopold .02 .10
30 Roman Turek .08 .20
31 Jamie McLennan .02 .10
32 Jeff O'Neill .02 .10
33 Ron Francis .08 .20
34 Rod Brind'Amour .08 .20
35 Erik Cole .02 .10
36 Pavel Brendl .02 .10
37 Steve Sullivan .02 .10
38 Alexei Zhamnov .02 .10
39 Eric Daze .02 .10
40 Kyle Calder .02 .10
41 Igor Radulov .02 .10
42 Jocelyn Thibault .08 .20
43 Peter Forsberg .40 1.00
44 Milan Hejduk .12 .30
45 Alex Tanguay .08 .20
46 Joe Sakic .30 .75
47 Rob Blake .08 .20
48 David Aebischer .08 .20
49 Patrick Roy .75 2.00
50 Ray Whitney .02 .10
51 Andrew Cassels .02 .10
52 Geoff Sanderson .02 .10
53 Rick Nash .15 .40
54 Marc Denis .08 .20
55 Kent McDonell RC .40 1.00
56 Mike Modano .25 .60
57 Bill Guerin .08 .20
58 Jere Lehtinen .08 .20
59 Jason Arnott .02 .10
60 Steve Ott .02 .10
61 Marty Turco .08 .20
62 Sergei Fedorov .15 .40
63 Brett Hull .15 .40
64 Brendan Shanahan .12 .30
65 Nicklas Lidstrom .12 .30
66 Pavel Datsyuk .12 .30
67 Henrik Zetterberg .12 .30

68 Steve Yzerman .75 2.00
69 Manny Legace .08 .20
70 Curtis Joseph .12 .30
71 Ryan Smyth .02 .10
72 Todd Marchant .02 .10
73 Mike Comrie .08 .20
74 Ales Hemsky .08 .20
75 Eric Brewer .02 .10
76 Fernando Pisani .02 .10
77 Tommy Salo .08 .20
78 Olli Jokinen .08 .20
79 Viktor Kozlov .02 .10
80 Stephen Weiss .02 .10
81 Jay Bouwmeester .02 .10
82 Roberto Luongo .15 .40
83 Zigmund Palffy .08 .20
84 Alexander Frolov .02 .10
85 Jason Allison .02 .10
86 Adam Deadmarsh .02 .10
87 Jamie Storr .08 .20
88 Cristobal Huet .08 .20
89 Marian Gaborik .30 .75
90 Pascal Dupuis .02 .10
91 P-M Bouchard .02 .10
92 Manny Fernandez .08 .20
93 Dwayne Roloson .08 .20
94 Wes Walz .02 .10
95 Saku Koivu .12 .30
96 Richard Zednik .02 .10
97 Marcel Hossa .02 .10
98 Jose Theodore .15 .40
99 Michael Komisarek .02 .10
100 Mathieu Garon .08 .20
101 Ron Hainsey .02 .10
102 David Legwand .08 .20
103 Denis Arkhipov .02 .10
104 Scott Hartnell .02 .10
105 Scottie Upshall .02 .10
106 Tomas Vokoun .08 .20
107 Patrik Elias .08 .20
108 Jamie Langenbrunner .02 .10
109 Scott Gomez .02 .10
110 Joe Nieuwendyk .08 .20
111 John Madden .02 .10
112 Scott Stevens .08 .20
113 Martin Brodeur .75 2.00
114 Alexei Yashin .02 .10
115 Jason Blake .02 .10
116 Dave Scatchard .02 .10
117 Michael Peca .02 .10
118 Janne Niinimaa .02 .10
119 Rick DiPietro .08 .20
120 Garth Snow .02 .10
121 Alex Kovalev .08 .20
122 Anson Carter .08 .20
123 Eric Lindros .12 .30
124 Tom Poti .02 .10
125 Mark Messier .12 .30
126 Pavel Bure .12 .30
127 Brian Leetch .08 .20
128 Mike Dunham .08 .20
129 Dan Blackburn .08 .20
130 Marian Hossa .12 .30
131 Daniel Alfredsson .08 .20
132 Todd White .02 .10
133 Zdeno Chara .02 .10
134 Jason Spezza .12 .30
135 Patrick Lalime .08 .20
136 Ray Emery .08 .20
137 Jeremy Roenick .15 .40
138 Mark Recchi .08 .20
139 Tony Amonte .08 .20
140 Keith Primeau .02 .10
141 John LeClair .12 .30
142 Simon Gagne .12 .30
143 Robert Esche .08 .20
144 Mike Johnson .02 .10
145 Shane Doan .02 .10
146 Ladislav Nagy .02 .10
147 Chris Gratton .02 .10
148 Sean Burke .08 .20
149 Mario Lemieux 1.00 2.50
150 Martin Straka .02 .10
151 Rico Fata .02 .10
152 Johan Hedberg .08 .20
153 Sebastien Caron .08 .20
154 Brooks Orpik .02 .10
155 Teemu Selanne .12 .30
156 Vincent Damphousse .02 .10
157 Patrick Marleau .08 .20
158 Jim Fahey .02 .10
159 Niko Dimitrakos .02 .10
160 Kyle McLaren .02 .10
161 Evgeni Nabokov .08 .20
162 Peter Sejna RC 1.50 4.00
163 Pavol Demitra .08 .20
164 Al MacInnis .08 .20
165 Doug Weight .08 .20
166 Keith Tkachuk .12 .30
167 Chris Pronger .08 .20
168 Chris Osgood .08 .20
169 Barret Jackman .08 .20
170 Vaclav Prospal .02 .10
171 Vincent Lecavalier .12 .30
172 Martin St. Louis .08 .20
173 Alexander Svitov .02 .10
174 Nikolai Khabibulin .12 .30
175 Matt Stajan RC 1.00 2.50
176 Alexander Mogilny .08 .20
177 Mats Sundin .12 .30
178 Owen Nolan .08 .20
179 Nik Antropov .02 .10
180 Doug Gilmour .08 .20
181 Tie Domi .08 .20
182 Gary Roberts .02 .10
183 Ed Belfour .12 .30
184 Carlo Colaiacovo .02 .10
185 Alexander Auld .02 .10
186 Markus Naslund .12 .30
187 Todd Bertuzzi .12 .30
188 Brendan Morrison .08 .20
189 Ed Jovanovski .08 .20
190 Matt Cooke .02 .10
191 Trevor Linden .02 .10
192 Henrik Sedin .02 .10
193 Daniel Sedin .02 .10
194 Dan Cloutier .08 .20
195 Jaromir Jagr .25 .60
196 Sergei Gonchar .02 .10
197 Michael Nylander .02 .10
198 Peter Bondra .08 .20
199 Mike Grier .02 .10
200 Olaf Kolzig .08 .20
201 Jeffrey Lupul RC 2.00 5.00
202 Eric Staal RC 2.50 6.00
203 Tuomo Ruutu RC 2.00 5.00
204 Nathan Horton RC 2.00 5.00
205 Dustin Brown RC 1.50 4.00
206 Jordin Tootoo RC 2.00 5.00
207 Joni Pitkanen RC 1.50 4.00
208 Milan Michalek RC 1.50 4.00
209 Sean Bergenheim RC 1.50 4.00
210 Marc-Andre Fleury RC 1.50 4.00

2003-04 Upper Deck Victory Bronze

*STARS: 2X TO 5X BASIC CARDS
*ROOKIES: .4X TO 1X
STATED PRINT RUN 199 SER.#'d SETS

2003-04 Upper Deck Victory Gold

*STARS: 12X TO 30X BASIC CARDS
*ROOKIES: 1.5X TO 4X
STATED PRINT RUN 25 SER.#'d SETS

2003-04 Upper Deck Victory Silver

*STARS: 8X TO 20X BASIC CARDS
*ROOKIES: .75X TO 2X
STATED PRINT RUN 50 SER.#'d SETS

2003-04 Upper Deck Victory Freshman Flashback

COMPLETE SET (50) 15.00 30.00
STATED ODDS 1:2
FF1 Paul Kariya .20 .50
FF2 Stanislav Chistov .15 .40
FF3 Ilya Kovalchuk .40 1.00
FF4 Dany Heatley .30 .75
FF5 Joe Thornton .50 1.25
FF6 Sergei Samsonov .15 .40
FF7 Ryan Miller .15 .40
FF8 Jarome Iginla .25 .60
FF9 Jordan Leopold .15 .40
FF10 Jocelyn Thibault .15 .40
FF11 Igor Radulov .15 .40
FF12 Peter Forsberg .75 2.00
FF13 Joe Sakic .60 1.50
FF14 Patrick Roy 1.50 4.00
FF15 Rick Nash .25 .60
FF16 Mike Modano .50 1.25
FF17 Henrik Zetterberg .20 .50
FF18 Brett Hull .40 1.00
FF19 Brendan Shanahan .20 .50
FF20 Dmitri Bykov .15 .40
FF21 Roberto Luongo .25 .60
FF22 Jay Bouwmeester .15 .40
FF23 Zigmund Palffy .15 .40
FF24 Cristobal Huet .15 .40
FF25 Marian Gaborik .60 1.50
FF26 Mike Komisarek .15 .40
FF27 Martin Brodeur .75 2.00
FF28 Alex Kovalev .15 .40
FF29 Pavel Bure .20 .50
FF30 Marian Hossa .20 .50
FF31 Jason Spezza .20 .50
FF32 Ray Emery .15 .40
FF33 John LeClair .20 .50
FF34 Tony Amonte .15 .40
FF35 Jeremy Roenick .25 .60
FF36 Mario Lemieux 2.00 5.00
FF37 Teemu Selanne .20 .50
FF38 Jim Fahey .15 .40
FF39 Niko Dimitrakos .15 .40
FF40 Chris Pronger .15 .40
FF41 Keith Tkachuk .20 .50
FF42 Vincent Lecavalier .20 .50
FF43 Owen Nolan .15 .40
FF44 Mats Sundin .20 .50
FF45 Alexander Mogilny .15 .40
FF46 Jaromir Jagr .50 1.25
FF47 Bobby Orr 2.00 5.00
FF48 Ray Bourque .60 1.50
FF49 Wayne Gretzky 2.00 5.00
FF50 Gordie Howe 1.50 4.00

2003-04 Upper Deck Victory Game Breakers

COMPLETE SET (50) 12.50 25.00
STATED ODDS 1:2
GB1 Peter Forsberg .75 2.00
GB2 Paul Kariya .20 .50
GB3 Ilya Kovalchuk .25 .60
GB4 Martin Brodeur 1.00 2.50
GB5 Sean Burke .15 .40
GB6 Bill Guerin .15 .40
GB7 Owen Nolan .15 .40
GB8 Alexei Yashin .15 .40
GB9 Marty Turco .15 .40
GB10 Dany Heatley .25 .60
GB11 Joe Sakic .40 1.00
GB12 Mike Comrie .15 .40
GB13 Jason Blake .15 .40
GB14 Nikolai Khabibulin .20 .50
GB15 Ed Belfour .20 .50
GB16 Chris Pronger .15 .40
GB17 Rick Nash .25 .60
GB18 Jaromir Jagr .30 .75
GB19 Vincent Lecavalier .20 .50
GB20 Olli Jokinen .15 .40
GB21 Alex Kovalev .15 .40
GB22 Mike Modano .30 .75
GB23 Henrik Zetterberg .20 .50
GB24 Roberto Luongo .25 .60
GB25 Teemu Selanne .20 .50
GB26 John LeClair .20 .50
GB27 Tie Domi .15 .40
GB28 Todd Bertuzzi .20 .50
GB29 Pavel Bure .20 .50
GB30 Mario Lemieux 1.25 3.00
GB31 Al MacInnis .15 .40
GB32 Joe Thornton .30 .75
GB33 Mats Sundin .20 .50
GB34 Keith Tkachuk .20 .50
GB35 Alexander Mogilny .15 .40
GB36 Marian Hossa .20 .50
GB37 Brett Hull .25 .60
GB38 Marian Gaborik .40 1.00
GB39 Tony Amonte .15 .40
GB40 Zigmund Palffy .15 .40
GB41 Patrick Roy 1.00 2.50
GB42 Sergei Samsonov .15 .40
GB43 Sergei Fedorov .25 .60
GB44 Markus Naslund .20 .50
GB45 Brendan Shanahan .20 .50
GB46 Saku Koivu .20 .50
GB47 Jarome Iginla .25 .60
GB48 Jocelyn Thibault .15 .40
GB49 Jason Spezza .20 .50
GB50 Jeremy Roenick .25 .60

2005-06 Upper Deck Victory

Victory was released in late-summer 2005, this 300-card set was one of the first of the 2005-06 season. The final 100 cards in the series were found in Upper Deck Series 2 packs.

COMP.SET w/o UPDATE (200) 15.00 30.00
COMP.UPDATE SET (100) 40.00 80.00
UPDATE FOUND IN UDII PACKS
1 Jean-Sebastien Giguere .20 .50
2 Joffrey Lupul .15 .40
3 Sergei Fedorov .20 .50
4 Stanislav Chistov .07 .20
5 Sandis Ozolinsh .15 .40
6 Steve Rucchin .15 .40
7 Dany Heatley .25 .60
8 Ilya Kovalchuk .30 .75
9 Kari Lehtonen .25 .60
10 Shawn McEachern .15 .40
11 Marc Savard .15 .40
12 Patrik Stefan .15 .40
13 Glen Murray .15 .40
14 Patrice Bergeron .25 .60
15 Andrew Raycroft .15 .40
16 Nick Boynton .15 .40
17 Sergei Gonchar .07 .20
18 Sergei Samsonov .20 .50
19 Joe Thornton .40 1.00
20 Miroslav Satan .15 .40
21 Chris Drury .20 .50
22 Martin Biron .20 .50
23 Jochen Hecht .07 .20
24 Daniel Briere .20 .50
25 Maxim Afinogenov .15 .40
26 Mike Grier .07 .20
27 Jarome Iginla .25 .60
28 Martin Gelinas .07 .20
29 Jordan Leopold .15 .40
30 Miikka Kiprusoff .25 .60
31 Chris Simon .07 .20
32 Ville Nieminen .07 .20
33 Jeff O'Neill .15 .40
34 Martin Gerber .07 .20
35 Rod Brind'Amour .15 .40
36 Erik Cole .15 .40
37 Eric Staal .20 .50
38 Josef Vasicek .07 .20
39 Bryan Berard .15 .40
40 Eric Daze .20 .50
41 Jocelyn Thibault .20 .50
42 Tyler Arnason .15 .40
43 Mark Bell .15 .40
44 Tuomo Ruutu .15 .40
45 Joe Sakic .30 .75
46 Peter Forsberg .40 1.00
47 David Aebischer .20 .50
48 Rob Blake .20 .50
49 Milan Hejduk .20 .50
50 Alex Tanguay .20 .50
51 Paul Kariya .25 .60
52 Adam Foote .07 .20
53 Teemu Selanne .25 .60
54 Rick Nash .30 .75
55 Rostislav Klesla .15 .40
56 Geoff Sanderson .07 .20
57 Nikolai Zherdev .20 .50
58 Marc Denis .20 .50
59 Pascal LeClaire .12 .30
60 Mike Modano .25 .60
61 Bill Guerin .15 .40
62 Marty Turco .20 .50
63 Brenden Morrow .20 .50
64 Jere Lehtinen .20 .50
65 Jason Arnott .07 .20
66 Sergei Zubov .15 .40
67 Steve Yzerman .60 1.50
68 Brendan Shanahan .25 .60
69 Chris Chelios .25 .60
70 Pavel Datsyuk .25 .60
71 Henrik Zetterberg .25 .60
72 Robert Lang .07 .20
73 Nicklas Lidstrom .20 .50
74 Kris Draper .07 .20
75 Curtis Joseph .25 .60
76 Gordie Howe .75 2.00
77 Wayne Gretzky 1.00 2.50
78 Raffi Torres .15 .40
79 Ty Conklin .20 .50
80 Ryan Smyth .20 .50
81 Jason Smith .07 .20
82 Georges Laraque .07 .20
83 Mike York .07 .20
84 Stephen Weiss .15 .40
85 Roberto Luongo .40 1.00
86 Olli Jokinen .20 .50
87 Mike Van Ryn .07 .20
88 Kristian Huselius .07 .20
89 Jay Bouwmeester .15 .40
90 Eric Belanger .07 .20
91 Luc Robitaille .20 .50
92 Mathieu Garon .20 .50
93 Zigmund Palffy .20 .50
94 Lubomir Visnovsky .07 .20
95 Mike Cammalleri .07 .20
96 Marian Gaborik .30 .75
97 Pascal Dupuis .07 .20
98 Andrew Brunette .07 .20
99 Brian Rolston .07 .20
100 Manny Fernandez .20 .50
101 Dwayne Roloson .20 .50
102 Jose Theodore .25 .60
103 Saku Koivu .25 .60
104 Michael Ryder .20 .50
105 Mike Ribeiro .15 .40
106 Sheldon Souray .15 .40
107 Richard Zednik .15 .40
108 Yanic Perreault .07 .20
109 David Legwand .20 .50
110 Scott Walker .15 .40
111 Tomas Vokoun .20 .50
112 Steve Sullivan .15 .40
113 Kimmo Timonen .15 .40
114 Martin Erat .07 .20
115 Martin Brodeur .75 2.00
116 Scott Stevens .12 .30
117 Scott Gomez .20 .50
118 Brian Rafalski .07 .20
119 Scott Niedermayer .15 .40
120 Patrik Elias .20 .50
121 Rick DiPietro .20 .50
122 Alexei Yashin .15 .40
123 Mark Parrish .15 .40
124 Michael Peca .15 .40
125 Trent Hunter .15 .40
126 Adrian Aucoin .15 .40
127 Bobby Holik .15 .40
128 Mark Messier .15 .40
129 Mike Dunham .12 .30
130 Jaromir Jagr .40 1.00
131 Jamie Lundmark .15 .40
132 Tom Poti .15 .40
133 Daniel Alfredsson .20 .50
134 Martin Havlat .20 .50
135 Dominik Hasek .30 .75
136 Jason Spezza .25 .60
137 Marian Hossa .20 .50
138 Peter Bondra .20 .50
139 Wade Redden .15 .40
140 Jeremy Roenick .25 .60
141 Simon Gagne .20 .50
142 Keith Primeau .15 .40
143 John LeClair .25 .60
144 Robert Esche .20 .50
145 Tony Amonte .20 .50
146 Donald Brashear .07 .20
147 Michal Handzus .07 .20
148 Brett Hull .20 .50
149 Shane Doan .20 .50
150 Ladislav Nagy .15 .40
151 Brian Boucher .12 .30
152 Mike Comrie .12 .30
153 Mike Ricci .15 .40
154 Milan Kraft .07 .20
155 Mario Lemieux 1.00 2.50
156 Marc-Andre Fleury .20 .50
157 Mark Recchi .20 .50
158 Dick Tarnstrom .07 .20
159 Ryan Malone .15 .40
160 Patrick Marleau .20 .50
161 Nils Ekman .07 .20
162 Jonathan Cheechoo .25 .60
163 Evgeni Nabokov .20 .50
164 Marco Sturm .15 .40
165 Alyn McCauley .07 .20
166 Doug Weight .20 .50
167 Keith Tkachuk .25 .60
168 Chris Pronger .20 .50
169 Al MacInnis .12 .30
170 Patrick Lalime .20 .50
171 Pavol Demitra .20 .50
172 Barret Jackman .15 .40
173 Brad Richards .20 .50
174 Vincent Lecavalier .25 .60
175 Fredrik Modin .15 .40
176 Nikolai Khabibulin .25 .60
177 Ruslan Fedotenko .15 .40
178 Cory Stillman .15 .40
179 Martin St. Louis .20 .50
180 Dan Boyle .07 .20
181 Mats Sundin .25 .60
182 Bryan McCabe .20 .50
183 Joe Nieuwendyk .20 .50
184 Gary Roberts .07 .20
185 Tie Domi .20 .50
186 Ed Belfour .25 .60
187 Brian Leetch .25 .60
188 Darcy Tucker .10 .20
189 Markus Naslund .25 .60
190 Brendan Morrison .15 .40
191 Dan Cloutier .20 .50
192 Ed Jovanovski .20 .50
193 Matt Cooke .07 .20
194 Brent Sopel .15 .40
195 Trevor Linden .15 .40
196 Olaf Kolzig .20 .50
197 Jeff Halpern .07 .20
198 Alexander Semin .07 .20
199 Rastislav Stana .12 .30
200 Brendan Witt .15 .40
201 Teemu Selanne .25 .60
202 Scott Niedermayer .15 .40
203 Marian Hossa .20 .50
204 Peter Bondra .20 .50
205 Brian Leetch .25 .60
206 Brad Boyes .07 .20
207 Ryan Miller .12 .30
208 Tony Amonte .20 .50
209 Justin Williams .20 .50
210 Nikolai Khabibulin .25 .60
211 Pavel Vorobiev .07 .20
212 Pierre Turgeon .15 .40
213 Sergei Fedorov .25 .60
214 Antti Miettinen .07 .20
215 Niko Kapanen .07 .20
216 Manny Legace .25 .60
217 Jason Williams .07 .20
218 Chris Pronger .20 .50
219 Ales Hemsky .15 .40
220 Joe Nieuwendyk .20 .50
221 Nathan Horton .15 .40
222 Jeremy Roenick .25 .60
223 Pavol Demitra .20 .50
224 Pierre-Marc Bouchard .15 .40
225 Alex Kovalev .15 .40
226 Paul Kariya .25 .60
227 Scott Hartnell .07 .20
228 Brian Gionta .07 .20
229 Jamie Langenbrunner .07 .20
230 Miroslav Satan .15 .40
231 Alexei Zhitnik .07 .20
232 Steve Rucchin .15 .40
233 Kevin Weekes .20 .50
234 Dany Heatley .25 .60
235 Zdeno Chara .07 .20
236 Peter Forsberg .40 1.00
237 Joni Pitkanen .15 .40
238 Curtis Joseph .25 .60
239 Geoff Sanderson .07 .20
240 Sergei Gonchar .07 .20
241 John LeClair .25 .60
242 Milan Michalek .07 .20
243 Petr Cajanek .07 .20
244 Sean Burke .20 .50
245 Vaclav Prospal .07 .20
246 Eric Lindros .25 .60
247 Jason Allison .15 .40
248 Jeff O'Neill .15 .40
249 Todd Bertuzzi .30 .75
250 Jeff Friesen .15 .40
251 Peter Budaj RC .40 1.00
252 Wojtek Wolski RC 1.00 2.50
253 Brent Seabrook RC .40 1.00
254 Cam Barker RC .60 1.50
255 Gilbert Brule RC 1.00 2.50
256 Jay McClement RC .40 1.00
257 Jeff Woywitka RC .40 1.00
258 Andrew Alberts RC .40 1.00
259 Hannu Toivonen RC .75 2.00
260 Yann Danis RC .40 1.00
261 Alexander Perezhogin RC .75 2.00
262 Brad Winchester RC .40 1.00
263 Kyle Brodziak RC .40 1.00
264 Alexander Ovechkin RC 8.00 20.00
265 Jakub Klepis RC .40 1.00
266 Keith Ballard RC .40 1.00
267 David Leneveu RC .60 1.00
268 Zach Parise RC 1.25 3.00
269 Dion Phaneuf RC 1.50 4.00
270 Eric Nystrom RC .40 1.50
271 Mike Richards RC 1.00 2.50
272 Jeff Carter RC 1.50 4.00
273 R.J. Umberger RC .60 1.50
274 Cam Ward RC 2.00 5.00
275 Robert Nilsson RC .60 1.50
276 Chris Campoli RC .40 1.00
277 George Parros RC .40 1.00
278 Evgeny Artyukhin RC .40 1.00
279 Alexander Steen RC 1.00 2.50
280 Ryan Getzlaf RC 1.25 3.00
281 Corey Perry RC 1.00 2.50
282 Rostislav Olesz RC .60 1.50
283 Anthony Stewart RC .60 1.50
284 Ryan Whitney RC .40 1.00
285 Sidney Crosby RC 12.00 30.00
286 Maxime Talbot RC .40 1.00
287 Ryan Suter RC .60 1.50
288 Henrik Lundqvist RC 1.50 4.00
289 Alvaro Montoya RC .75 2.00
290 Jim Howard RC 2.00 5.00
291 Johan Franzen RC 1.25 3.00
292 Thomas Vanek RC 1.25 3.00
293 Andrej Meszaros RC .40 1.00
294 Christoph Schubert RC .40 1.00
295 Patrick Eaves RC .60 1.50
296 Steve Bernier RC .75 2.00
297 Jussi Jokinen RC .75 2.00
298 Braydon Coburn RC .60 1.50
299 Matt Foy RC .40 1.00
300 Mikko Koivu RC .75 2.00

2005-06 Upper Deck Victory Black

PRINT RUN 5 SER.#'d SETS
NOT PRICED DUE TO SCARCITY

2005-06 Upper Deck Victory Gold

*GOLD: 6X TO 15X BASE HI
*ROOKIES: 3X TO 8X BASE HI
PRINT RUN 100 SER.#'d SETS
264 Alexander Ovechkin 50.00 125.00
269 Dion Phaneuf 10.00 25.00
285 Sidney Crosby 150.00 250.00

2005-06 Upper Deck Victory Silver

*SILVER: 3X TO 8X BASE HI
PRINT RUN 250 SER.#'d SETS

2005-06 Upper Deck Victory Game Breakers

COMPLETE SET (45) 6.00 12.00
STATED ODDS 1:2
GB1 Sergei Fedorov .25 .60
GB2 Dany Heatley .25 .60
GB3 Ilya Kovalchuk .25 .60
GB4 Glen Murray .15 .40
GB5 Joe Thornton .30 .75
GB6 Chris Drury .15 .40
GB7 Eric Daze .15 .40
GB8 Tuomo Ruutu .15 .40
GB9 Peter Forsberg .75 2.00
GB10 Joe Sakic .40 1.00
GB11 Milan Hejduk .20 .50
GB12 Paul Kariya .20 .50
GB13 Rick Nash .25 .60
GB14 Mike Modano .30 .75
GB15 Bill Guerin .15 .40
GB16 Brendan Shanahan .20 .50
GB17 Steve Yzerman 1.00 2.50
GB18 Kris Draper .15 .40
GB19 Henrik Zetterberg .20 .50
GB20 Ryan Smyth .15 .40
GB21 Olli Jokinen .15 .40
GB22 Zigmund Palffy .15 .40
GB23 Marian Gaborik .30 .75
GB24 Michael Ryder .15 .40
GB25 Saku Koivu .20 .50
GB26 Steve Sullivan .15 .40
GB27 Alexei Yashin .15 .40
GB28 Jaromir Jagr .30 .75
GB29 Marian Hossa .20 .50
GB30 Martin Havlat .15 .40
GB31 Peter Bondra .15 .40
GB32 Keith Primeau .15 .40
GB33 Simon Gagne .20 .50
GB34 Brett Hull .25 .60
GB35 Shane Doan .15 .40
GB36 Mario Lemieux 1.25 3.00
GB37 Patrick Marleau .15 .40
GB38 Pavol Demitra .15 .40
GB39 Keith Tkachuk .20 .50
GB40 Martin St. Louis .15 .40
GB41 Vincent Lecavalier .20 .50
GB42 Brad Richards .15 .40
GB43 Alexander Mogilny .15 .40
GB44 Mats Sundin .20 .50
GB45 Markus Naslund .20 .50

2005-06 Upper Deck Victory Stars on Ice

COMPLETE SET (45) 6.00 12.00
SI1 Jean-Sebastien Giguere .15 .40
SI2 Dany Heatley .25 .60
SI3 Ilya Kovalchuk .25 .60
SI4 Joe Thornton .30 .75
SI5 Andrew Raycroft .15 .40
SI6 Miroslav Satan .15 .40
SI7 Jarome Iginla .25 .60
SI8 Miikka Kiprusoff .25 .60
SI9 Jeff O'Neill .15 .40
SI10 Jocelyn Thibault .15 .40
SI11 Joe Sakic .40 1.00
SI12 Peter Forsberg .75 2.00
SI13 Alex Tanguay .15 .40
SI14 Rob Blake .15 .40
SI15 David Aebischer .15 .40
SI16 Rick Nash .25 .60
SI17 Marty Turco .15 .40
SI18 Sergei Zubov .15 .40
SI19 Mike Modano .30 .75
SI20 Nicklas Lidstrom .20 .50
SI21 Steve Yzerman 1.00 2.50
SI22 Robert Lang .15 .40
SI23 Roberto Luongo .25 .60
SI24 Luc Robitaille .15 .40
SI25 Jose Theodore .25 .60
SI26 Martin Brodeur 1.00 2.50
SI27 Scott Stevens .15 .40
SI28 Eric Lindros .20 .50
SI29 Dominik Hasek .40 1.00
SI30 Daniel Alfredsson .15 .40
SI31 Jason Spezza .20 .50
SI32 Jeremy Roenick .25 .60
SI33 John LeClair .20 .50
SI34 Brett Hull .25 .60
SI35 Mario Lemieux 1.25 3.00
SI36 Evgeni Nabokov .15 .40
SI37 Keith Tkachuk .20 .50
SI38 Doug Weight .15 .40
SI39 Martin St. Louis .15 .40
SI40 Nikolai Khabibulin .20 .50
SI41 Ed Belfour .20 .50
SI42 Brian Leetch .20 .50
SI43 Mats Sundin .20 .50
SI44 Markus Naslund .20 .50
SI45 Ed Jovanovski .15 .40

2006-07 Upper Deck Victory

COMPLETE SET (230) 15.00 40.00
COMPLETE UDATE SET (100)
231-330 FOUND IN UD2 PACKS
1 Jean-Sebastien Giguere .30 .75
2 Joffrey Lupul .20 .50
3 Teemu Selanne .30 .75
4 Andy McDonald .20 .50
5 Scott Niedermayer .20 .50
6 Corey Perry .25 .60
7 Ilya Kovalchuk .40 1.00
8 Kari Lehtonen .30 .75
9 Marian Hossa .25 .60
10 Marc Savard .20 .50
11 Slava Kozlov .20 .50
12 Patrice Bergeron .25 .60
13 Tim Thomas .30 .75
14 Brian Leetch .20 .50
15 Glen Murray .20 .50
16 Brad Boyes .20 .50
17 Marco Sturm .20 .50
18 Brad Stuart .20 .50
19 Andrew Raycroft .25 .60
20 Chris Drury .25 .60
21 Ryan Miller .30 .75
22 Thomas Vanek .25 .60
23 Tim Connolly .10 .25
24 Maxim Afinogenov .20 .50
25 Martin Biron .25 .60
26 Ales Kotalik .20 .50
27 Daniel Briere .25 .60
28 Miikka Kiprusoff .30 .75
29 Jarome Iginla .50 1.25
30 Dion Phaneuf .40 1.00
31 Daymond Langkow .20 .50
32 Chuck Kobasew .20 .50
33 Kristian Huselius .20 .50
34 Cam Ward .50 1.25
35 Eric Staal .25 .60
36 Mark Recchi .25 .60
37 Doug Weight .20 .50
38 Justin Williams .20 .50
39 Erik Cole .20 .50
40 Rod Brind'Amour .25 .60
41 Tuomo Ruutu .20 .50
42 Nikolai Khabibulin .30 .75
43 Kyle Calder .20 .50
44 Brent Seabrook .20 .50
45 Mark Bell .20 .50
46 Pavel Vorobiev .10 .25
47 Joe Sakic .60 1.50
48 Jose Theodore .30 .75
49 Marek Svatos .30 .75
50 Milan Hejduk .25 .60
51 Alex Tanguay .25 .60
52 Rob Blake .25 .60
53 Andrew Brunette .20 .50
54 Rick Nash .30 .75
55 David Vyborny .20 .50
56 Marc Denis .25 .60
57 Nikolai Zherdev .20 .50
58 Sergei Fedorov .30 .75
59 Pascal Leclaire .30 .75
60 Mike Modano .30 .75
61 Marty Turco .25 .60
62 Jussi Jokinen .20 .50
63 Brenden Morrow .25 .60
64 Sergei Zubov .20 .50
65 Jere Lehtinen .20 .50
66 Bill Guerin .20 .50
67 Jason Arnott .20 .50
68 Steve Yzerman 1.00 2.50
69 Pavel Datsyuk .30 .75
70 Brendan Shanahan .30 .75
71 Manny Legace .25 .60
72 Nicklas Lidstrom .30 .75
73 Henrik Zetterberg .30 .75
74 Tomas Holmstrom .20 .50
75 Kris Draper .20 .50
76 Ryan Smyth .25 .60
77 Shawn Horcoff .20 .50
78 Ales Hemsky .20 .50
79 Chris Pronger .25 .60
80 Dwayne Roloson .25 .60
81 Michael Peca .20 .50
82 Raffi Torres .10 .25
83 Roberto Luongo .60 1.50
84 Nathan Horton .20 .50
85 Olli Jokinen .20 .50
86 Jay Bouwmeester .20 .50
87 Mike Van Ryn .20 .50
88 Joe Nieuwendyk .20 .50
89 Mathieu Garon .25 .60
90 Dustin Brown .20 .50
91 Alexander Frolov .20 .50
92 Pavol Demitra .20 .50
93 Craig Conroy .20 .50
94 Mike Cammalleri .20 .50
95 Lubomir Visnovsky .20 .50
96 Marian Gaborik .50 1.25

97 Manny Fernandez .30 .75
98 Brian Rolston .20 .50
99 Pierre-Marc Bouchard .20 .50
100 Wes Walz .10 .25
101 Mikko Koivu .20 .50
102 David Aebischer .25 .60
103 Saku Koivu .30 .75
104 Alex Kovalev .20 .50
105 Michael Ryder .25 .60
106 Chris Higgins .20 .50
107 Mike Ribeiro .20 .50
108 Cristobal Huet .30 .75
109 Paul Kariya .30 .75
110 Tomas Vokoun .25 .60
111 Steve Sullivan .20 .50
112 Martin Erat .10 .25
113 Kimmo Timonen .20 .50
114 Scott Hartnell .10 .25
115 David Legwand .20 .50
116 Martin Brodeur 1.00 2.50
117 Brian Gionta .20 .50
118 Scott Gomez .20 .50
119 Patrik Elias .20 .50
120 Brian Rafalski .20 .50
121 Zach Parise .25 .60
122 Alexei Yashin .20 .50
123 Rick DiPietro .30 .75
124 Miroslav Satan .20 .50
125 Jason Blake .20 .50
126 Mike York .10 .25
127 Alexei Zhitnik .10 .25
128 Trent Hunter .20 .50
129 Henrik Lundqvist .50 1.25
130 Jaromir Jagr .50 1.25
131 Martin Straka .20 .50
132 Petr Prucha .20 .50
133 Michael Nylander .20 .50
134 Fedor Tyutin .10 .25
135 Jason Spezza .30 .75
136 Dany Heatley .30 .75
137 Dominik Hasek .40 1.00
138 Daniel Alfredsson .25 .60
139 Zdeno Chara .20 .50
140 Wade Redden .20 .50
141 Martin Havlat .25 .60
142 Ray Emery .30 .75
143 Peter Forsberg .50 1.25
144 Antero Niittymaki .30 .75
145 Simon Gagne .30 .75
146 Joni Pitkanen .20 .50
147 Keith Primeau .20 .50
148 Jeff Carter .30 .75
149 Mike Richards .30 .75
150 Robert Esche .25 .60
151 Shane Doan .25 .60
152 Curtis Joseph .30 .75
153 Ladislav Nagy .20 .50
154 Mike Comrie .20 .50
155 Geoff Sanderson .10 .25
156 Keith Ballard .20 .50
157 Sidney Crosby 1.50 4.00
158 Ryan Malone .20 .50
159 Marc-Andre Fleury .30 .75
160 Sergei Gonchar .10 .25
161 Colby Armstrong .20 .50
162 Ryan Whitney .20 .50
163 Joe Thornton .50 1.25
164 Evgeni Nabokov .25 .60
165 Patrick Marleau .25 .60
166 Jonathan Cheechoo .30 .75
167 Vesa Toskala .25 .60
168 Steve Bernier .25 .60
169 Curtis Sanford .25 .60
170 Lee Stempniak .20 .50
171 Keith Tkachuk .25 .60
172 Scott Young .10 .25
173 Petr Cajanek .20 .50
174 Barret Jackman .10 .25
175 Evgeni Artyukhin .20 .50
176 Vaclav Prospal .20 .50
177 Martin St. Louis .30 .75
178 Vincent Lecavalier .30 .75
179 Sean Burke .15 .40
180 Brad Richards .30 .75
181 Fredrik Modin .20 .50
182 Tie Domi .10 .25
183 Mats Sundin .30 .75
184 Ed Belfour .75 2.00
185 Eric Lindros .30 .75
186 Bryan McCabe .20 .50
187 Alexander Steen .25 .60
188 Darcy Tucker .20 .50
189 Jason Allison .10 .25
190 Henrik Sedin .20 .50
191 Alex Auld .25 .60
192 Markus Naslund .30 .75
193 Brendan Morrison .20 .50
194 Ed Jovanovski .20 .50
195 Mattias Ohlund .20 .50
196 Daniel Sedin .20 .50
197 Jeff Halpern .20 .50
198 Dainius Zubrus .20 .50
199 Alexander Ovechkin 1.25 3.00
200 Olaf Kolzig .40 1.00
201 Tomas Kopecky RC 1.00 2.50
202 Billy Thompson RC .75 2.00
203 Dustin Byfuglien RC 1.50 4.00
204 Yan Stastny RC .75 2.00
205 Eric Fehr RC 1.00 2.50
206 Ben Ondrus RC .75 2.00
207 Rob Collins RC .75 2.00
208 Brendan Bell RC .75 2.00
209 Frank Doyle RC 1.00 2.50
210 Noah Welch RC .75 2.00
211 Filip Novak RC .75 2.00
212 Ian White RC .75 2.00
213 Konstantin Pushkaryov RC .75 2.00
214 Dan Jancevski RC .75 2.00
215 Shea Weber RC 1.00 2.50
216 Michel Ouellet RC 1.25 3.00
217 Marc-Antoine Pouliot RC 1.00 2.50
218 Carsen Germyn RC .75 2.00
219 Matt Carle RC 1.00 2.50
220 Steve Regier RC .75 2.00
221 Mark Stuart RC .75 2.00
222 Bill Thomas RC .75 2.00
223 Jarkko Immonen RC .75 2.00
224 Erik Reitz RC .75 2.00
225 Joel Perrault RC .75 2.00
226 Ryan Potulny RC 1.00 2.50
227 Jeremy Williams RC .75 2.00
228 Masi Marjamaki RC .75 2.00
229 Miroslav Kopriva RC .75 2.00
230 Matt Koalska RC .75 2.00
231 Chris Pronger .20 .50
232 Zdeno Chara .40
233 Marc Savard .20 .50
234 Hannu Toivonen .30 .75
235 Alex Tanguay .25 .60
236 Martin Havlat .25 .60
237 Michal Handzus .10 .25
238 Wojtek Wolski .20 .50
239 Jordan Leopold .20 .50
240 Fredrik Modin .20 .50
241 Gilbert Brule .20 .50
242 Anson Carter .10 .25
243 Mike Ribeiro .20 .50
244 Eric Lindros .30 .75
245 Patrik Stefan .10 .25
246 Jeff Halpern .20 .50
247 Dominik Hasek .40 1.00
248 Joffrey Lupul .20 .50
249 Petr Sykora .10 .25
250 Todd Bertuzzi .25 .60
251 Ed Belfour .75 2.00
252 Alexander Auld .25 .60
253 Rob Blake .25 .60
254 Dan Cloutier .15 .40
255 Pavol Demitra .20 .50
256 Mark Parrish .20 .50
257 Sergei Samsonov .25 .60
258 Jason Arnott .20 .50
259 Mike Sillinger .20 .50
260 Brendan Shanahan .30 .75
261 Matt Cullen .20 .50
262 Martin Gerber .30 .75
263 Kyle Calder .20 .50
264 Geoff Sanderson .10 .25
265 Owen Nolan .25 .60
266 Ed Jovanovski .20 .50
267 Jeremy Roenick .30 .75
268 Mark Recchi .20 .50
269 Nils Ekman .10 .25
270 Mark Bell .20 .50
271 Mike Grier .10 .25
272 Doug Weight .20 .50
273 Bill Guerin .20 .50
274 Manny Legace .25 .60
275 Marc Denis .25 .60
276 Andrew Raycroft .25 .60
277 Michael Peca .20 .50
278 Kyle Wellwood .20 .50
279 Roberto Luongo .60 1.50
280 Alexander Semin .15 .40
281 Shane O'Brien RC .75 2.00
282 Jonas Johansson RC .40 1.00
283 Ryan Shannon RC .75 2.00
284 Patrick O'Sullivan RC 1.00 2.50
285 Anze Kopitar RC 2.00 5.00
286 John Oduya RC .75 2.00
287 Travis Zajac RC 1.25 3.00
288 Fredrik Norrena RC .75 2.00
289 Phil Kessel RC 3.00 8.00
290 Guillaume Latendresse RC 2.50 6.00
291 Nigel Dawes RC .75 2.00
292 Jordan Staal RC 3.00 8.00
293 Kristopher Letang RC 1.25 3.00
294 Paul Stastny RC 5.00 12.00
295 Niklas Backstrom RC .75 2.00
296 D.J. King RC .40 1.00
297 Marc-Edouard Vlasic RC .75 2.00
298 Patrick Thoresen RC .75 2.00
299 Ladislav Smid RC .75 2.00
300 Loui Eriksson RC .75 2.00
301 Patrick Fischer RC .40 1.00
302 Mikko Lehtonen RC .40 1.00
303 Roman Polak RC .40 1.00
304 Evgeni Malkin RC 6.00 15.00
305 Luc Bourdon RC 1.00 2.50
306 Alexei Kaigorodov RC .75 2.00
307 Alex Brooks RC .40 1.00
308 Nate Thompson RC .40 1.00
309 Janis Sprukts RC .40 1.00
310 Alexander Radulov RC 2.00 5.00
311 Keith Yandle RC .75 2.00
312 Enver Lisin RC .75 2.00
313 Cole Jarrett RC .40 1.00
314 Ryan Caldwell RC .75 2.00
315 David Printz RC .75 2.00
316 David Liffiton RC .75 2.00
317 Adam Burish RC .75 2.00
318 Dave Bolland RC 1.50 4.00
319 Michael Blunden RC .75 2.00
320 Matt Lashoff RC .75 2.00
321 Alexei Mikhnov RC .75 2.00
322 Jan Hejda RC .40 1.00
323 Lars Jonsson RC .40 1.00
324 Triston Grant RC .40 1.00
325 Alexander Edler RC .75 2.00
326 Brandon Prust RC .75 2.00
327 Dustin Boyd RC 1.00 2.50
328 Drew Stafford RC 1.25 3.00
329 Kelly Guard RC 1.00 2.50
330 Nathan McIver RC .40 1.00

2006-07 Upper Deck Victory Black

STATED ODDS 1:720
NOT PRICED DUE TO SCARCITY

2006-07 Upper Deck Victory Gold

COMMON CARD 2.00 5.00
*STARS: 5X TO 12X HI
* ROOKIES: 1.5X TO 4X HI
68 Steve Yzerman 12.00 30.00
116 Martin Brodeur 10.00 25.00
157 Sidney Crosby 12.00 30.00
199 Alexander Ovechkin 10.00 25.00

2006-07 Upper Deck Victory GameBreakers

ODDS 1:4 PACKS
GB1 Jean-Sebastien Giguere 1.50 4.00
GB2 Ilya Kovalchuk 2.00 5.00
GB3 Marian Hossa 1.25 3.00
GB4 Patrice Bergeron 1.25 3.00
GB5 Jarome Iginla 2.50 6.00
GB6 Miikka Kiprusoff 1.50 4.00
GB7 Eric Staal 1.25 3.00
GB8 Martin Gerber 1.50 4.00
GB9 Nikolai Khabibulin 1.50 4.00
GB10 Joe Sakic 3.00 8.00
GB11 Alex Tanguay 1.25 3.00
GB12 Marek Svatos 1.00 2.50
GB13 Rick Nash 1.50 4.00
GB14 Mike Modano 1.50 4.00
GB15 Marty Turco 1.25 3.00
GB16 Henrik Zetterberg 1.50 4.00
GB17 Pavel Datsyuk 1.50 4.00
GB18 Brendan Shanahan 1.50 4.00
GB19 Roberto Luongo 3.00 8.00
GB20 Olli Jokinen 1.00 2.50
GB21 Alexander Frolov 1.00 2.50
GB22 Marian Gaborik 2.50 6.00
GB23 Saku Koivu 1.50 4.00
GB24 Alex Kovalev 1.00 2.50
GB25 Michael Ryder 1.25 3.00
GB26 Paul Kariya 1.50 4.00
GB27 Tomas Vokoun 1.25 3.00
GB29 Patrik Elias 1.00 2.50
GB30 Jaromir Jagr 2.50 6.00
GB31 Henrik Lundqvist 2.00 5.00
GB32 Jason Spezza 1.50 4.00
GB33 Dany Heatley 1.50 4.00
GB34 Daniel Alfredsson 1.25 3.00
GB35 Dominik Hasek 2.00 5.00
GB36 Simon Gagne 1.50 4.00
GB37 Jeff Carter 1.50 4.00
GB38 Peter Forsberg 2.50 6.00
GB39 Shane Doan 1.25 3.00
GB40 Sidney Crosby 4.00 10.00
GB41 Marc-Andre Fleury 1.50 4.00
GB42 Joe Thornton 2.50 6.00
GB43 Patrick Marleau 1.25 3.00
GB44 Jonathan Cheechoo 1.50 4.00
GB45 Martin St. Louis 1.50 4.00
GB46 Vincent Lecavalier 1.50 4.00
GB47 Ed Belfour 4.00 10.00
GB48 Mats Sundin 1.50 4.00
GB49 Markus Naslund 1.50 4.00
GB50 Alexander Ovechkin 3.00 8.00

2006-07 Upper Deck Victory Next In Line

ODDS 1:4
NL1 Corey Perry .75 2.00
NL2 Joffrey Lupul .75 2.00
NL3 Ryan Getzlaf .75 2.00
NL4 Ilya Kovalchuk 1.25 3.00
NL5 Kari Lehtonen 1.00 2.50
NL6 Patrice Bergeron 1.00 2.50
NL7 Andrew Raycroft .75 2.00
NL8 Brad Boyes .60 1.50
NL9 Thomas Vanek .60 1.50
NL10 Ryan Miller .75 2.00
NL11 Dion Phaneuf 1.50 4.00
NL12 Eric Staal 1.25 3.00
NL13 Cam Ward 1.00 2.50
NL14 Tuomo Ruutu .60 1.50
NL15 Marek Svatos .60 1.50
NL16 Rick Nash 1.25 3.00
NL17 Nikolai Zherdev .60 1.50
NL18 Gilbert Brule 1.25 3.00
NL19 Jussi Jokinen .60 1.50
NL20 Henrik Zetterberg 1.00 2.50
NL21 Ales Hemsky .60 1.50
NL22 Jarret Stoll .60 1.50
NL23 Nathan Horton .60 1.50
NL24 Rostislav Olesz .60 1.50
NL25 Alexander Frolov .60 1.50
NL26 Mike Cammalleri .60 1.50
NL27 Marian Gaborik 2.00 5.00
NL28 Mikko Koivu .75 2.00
NL29 Yann Danis .75 2.00
NL30 Alexander Perezhogin .75 2.00
NL31 Zach Parise .75 2.00
NL32 Rick DiPietro .75 2.00
NL33 Henrik Lundqvist 2.00 5.00
NL34 Petr Prucha .60 1.50
NL35 Jason Spezza 1.00 2.50
NL36 Dany Heatley 1.25 3.00
NL37 Jeff Carter .75 2.00
NL38 Mike Richards .75 2.00
NL39 Joni Pitkanen .60 1.50
NL40 Marc-Andre Fleury .75 2.00
NL41 Sidney Crosby 4.00 10.00
NL42 Jonathan Cheechoo 1.00 2.50
NL43 Evgeni Artyukhin .60 1.50
NL44 Matt Stajan .60 1.50
NL45 Alexander Steen .75 2.00
NL46 Ryan Kesler .60 1.50
NL47 Alex Auld .75 2.00
NL48 Alexander Ovechkin 3.00 8.00
NL49 Erik Cole .60 1.50
NL50 Kyle Wellwood .60 1.50

2007-08 Upper Deck Victory

This 345-card set was released in August, 2007. The first 245 cards were issued into the hobby in six-card packs, with a 99 cent SRP, which came 36 packs to a box and 20 boxes to a case. In the first series, cards numbered 1-200 are veterans while cards 201-245 are Rookie Cards. There was an update set later issued, split into 50 veteran cards and 50 Rookie Cards. These cards were inserted one per Upper Deck Series 2 pack.

COMPLETE SET (345) 30.00 60.00
COMP.SET w/o SPs (200) 12.00 30.00
1 Martin Brodeur .60 1.50
2 Zach Parise .20 .50
3 Brian Rafalski .15 .40
4 Scott Gomez .15 .40
5 Brian Gionta .15 .40
6 Travis Zajac .15 .40
7 Patrik Elias .15 .40
8 Marc-Andre Fleury .25 .60
9 Evgeni Malkin .60 1.50
10 Mark Recchi .15 .40
11 Jordan Staal .30 .75
12 Ryan Whitney .20 .50
13 Sergei Gonchar .15 .40
14 Sidney Crosby 1.25 3.00
15 Rick DiPietro .20 .50
16 Jason Blake .15 .40
17 Viktor Kozlov .15 .40
18 Ryan Smyth .20 .50
19 Alexei Yashin .15 .40
20 Miroslav Satan .15 .40
21 Henrik Lundqvist .30 .75
22 Martin Straka .15 .40
23 Brendan Shanahan .25 .60
24 Michael Nylander .15 .40
25 Sean Avery .15 .40
26 Jaromir Jagr .40 1.00
27 Martin Biron .20 .50
28 Jeff Carter .15 .40
29 Joni Pitkanen .15 .40
30 Mike Knuble .15 .40
31 Mike Richards .30 .75
32 Simon Gagne .15 .40
33 Ryan Miller .25 .60
34 Maxim Afinogenov .15 .40
35 Thomas Vanek .20 .50
36 Drew Stafford .20 .50
37 Jason Pominville .15 .40
38 Chris Drury .15 .40
39 Derek Roy .15 .40
40 Daniel Briere .25 .60
41 Ray Emery .20 .50
42 Jason Spezza .25 .60
43 Mike Fisher .20 .50
44 Wade Redden .15 .40
45 Daniel Alfredsson .20 .50
46 Dany Heatley .30 .75
47 Cristobal Huet .15 .40
48 Alex Kovalev .15 .40
49 Guillaume Latendresse .20 .50
50 Sheldon Souray .15 .40
51 Michael Ryder .15 .40
52 Chris Higgins .20 .50
53 Saku Koivu .15 .40
54 Andrew Raycroft .15 .40
55 Alexander Steen .15 .40
56 Tomas Kaberle .15 .40
57 Darcy Tucker .15 .40
58 Jeff O'Neill .15 .40
59 Bryan McCabe .15 .40
60 Mats Sundin .25 .60
61 Tim Thomas .30 .75
62 Marc Savard .15 .40
63 Marco Sturm .15 .40
64 Zdeno Chara .15 .40
65 Glen Murray .15 .40
66 Phil Kessel .25 .60
67 Patrice Bergeron .25 .60
68 Johan Holmqvist .20 .50
69 Dan Boyle .15 .40
70 Brad Richards .20 .50
71 Vaclav Prospal .15 .40
72 Vincent Lecavalier .25 .60
73 Martin St. Louis .20 .50
74 Kari Lehtonen .15 .40
75 Slava Kozlov .15 .40
76 Keith Tkachuk .20 .50
77 Marian Hossa .15 .40
78 Scott Mellanby .15 .40
79 Ilya Kovalchuk .30 .75
80 Cam Ward .25 .60
81 Erik Cole .15 .40
82 Justin Williams .15 .40
83 Cory Stillman .15 .40
84 Rod Brind'Amour .20 .50
85 Eric Staal .25 .60
86 Ed Belfour .25 .60
87 Nathan Horton .15 .40
88 Jay Bouwmeester .15 .40
89 Stephen Weiss .15 .40
90 Jozef Stumpel .15 .40
91 Olli Jokinen .15 .40
92 Olaf Kolzig .15 .40
93 Alexander Semin .25 .60
94 Chris Clark .15 .40
95 Matt Pettinger .15 .40
96 Eric Fehr .15 .40
97 Alexander Ovechkin .75 2.00
98 Dominik Hasek .30 .75
99 Tomas Holmstrom .20 .50
100 Pavel Datsyuk .25 .60
101 Nicklas Lidstrom .25 .60
102 Dan Cleary .15 .40
103 Kris Draper .20 .50
104 Henrik Zetterberg .25 .60
105 Tomas Vokoun .25 .60
106 Paul Kariya .25 .60
107 Chris Mason .20 .50
108 Kimmo Timonen .15 .40
109 Jason Arnott .15 .40
110 Steve Sullivan .15 .40
111 Peter Forsberg .30 .75
112 Manny Legace .15 .40
113 Brad Boyes .20 .50
114 Doug Weight .15 .40
115 Lee Stempniak .15 .40
116 Barret Jackman .15 .40
117 Jay McClement .15 .40
118 Nikolai Khabibulin .25 .60
119 Jason Williams .15 .40
120 Tuomo Ruutu .15 .40
121 Duncan Keith .25 .60
122 Radim Vrbata .15 .40
123 Martin Havlat .20 .50
124 Fredrik Norrena .15 .40
125 David Vyborny .15 .40
126 Sergei Fedorov .20 .50
127 Fredrik Modin .15 .40
128 Pascal Leclaire .20 .50
129 Gilbert Brule .15 .40
130 Rick Nash .25 .60
131 Roberto Luongo .40 1.00
132 Daniel Sedin .15 .40
133 Brendan Morrison .15 .40
134 Henrik Sedin .15 .40
135 Sami Salo .15 .40
136 Trevor Linden .20 .50
137 Markus Naslund .20 .50
138 Manny Fernandez .15 .40
139 Brian Rolston .15 .40
140 Pierre-Marc Bouchard .15 .40
141 Mikko Koivu .15 .40
142 Pavol Demitra .20 .50
143 Niklas Backstrom .15 .40
144 Marian Gaborik .30 .75
145 Miikka Kiprusoff .30 .75
146 Daymond Langkow .15 .40
147 Craig Conroy .15 .40
148 Dion Phaneuf .25 .60
149 Alex Tanguay .20 .50
150 Matthew Lombardi .15 .40
151 Jarome Iginla .40 1.00
152 Petr Budaj .20 .50
153 Paul Stastny .25 .60
154 Milan Hejduk .20 .50
155 Wojtek Wolski .15 .40
156 Andrew Brunette .15 .40
157 Marek Svatos .15 .40
158 Jose Theodore .25 .60
159 Joe Sakic .50 1.25
160 Dwayne Roloson .20 .50
161 Raffi Torres .15 .40
162 Jarret Stoll .15 .40
163 Shawn Horcoff .15 .40
164 Joffrey Lupul .15 .40
165 Petr Sykora .15 .40
166 Ales Hemsky .15 .40
167 Jean-Sebastien Giguere .25 .60
168 Andy McDonald .15 .40
169 Scott Niedermayer .15 .40
170 Chris Kunitz .15 .40
171 Ryan Getzlaf .20 .50
172 Chris Pronger .25 .60
173 Corey Perry .20 .50
174 Teemu Selanne .25 .60
175 Vesa Toskala .20 .50
176 Jonathan Cheechoo .20 .50
177 Bill Guerin .15 .40
178 Evgeni Nabokov .20 .50
179 Milan Michalek .15 .40
180 Patrick Marleau .20 .50
181 Joe Thornton .30 .75
182 Marty Turco .15 .40
183 Philippe Boucher .15 .40
184 Mike Ribeiro .15 .40
185 Eric Lindros .20 .50
186 Brenden Morrow .15 .40
187 Ladislav Nagy .15 .40
188 Mike Modano .15 .40
189 Mathieu Garon .20 .50
190 Lubomir Visnovsky .15 .40
191 Rob Blake .20 .50
192 Anze Kopitar .25 .60
193 Mike Cammalleri .20 .50
194 Alexander Frolov .15 .40
195 Curtis Joseph .20 .50
196 Owen Nolan .20 .50
197 Shane Doan .15 .40
198 Ed Jovanovski .15 .40
199 Mikael Tellqvist .20 .50
200 Zbynek Michalek .15 .40
201 Jack Johnson RC 1.00 2.50
202 Mark Mancari RC .75 2.00
203 Daniel Girardi RC .60 1.50
204 Rich Peverley RC .60 1.50
205 David Clarkson RC .60 1.50
206 Tomi Maki RC .60 1.50
207 Petr Kalus RC .60 1.50
208 Bryan Bickell RC .60 1.50
209 Marc Methot RC .60 1.50
210 Robbie Schremp RC .75 2.00
211 Yutaka Fukufuji RC .75 2.00
212 Frans Nielsen RC .60 1.50
213 Colin Fraser RC .60 1.50
214 Aaron Rome RC .60 1.50
215 Martin Lojek RC .60 1.50
216 Ryan Parent RC .75 2.00
217 David Moss RC 1.00 2.50
218 Ryan Callahan RC 1.00 2.50
219 Patrick Kaleta RC .60 1.50
220 Mark Fraser RC .60 1.50
221 Tobias Stephan RC .75 2.00
222 Tomas Popperle RC .75 2.00
223 Jeff Schultz RC .60 1.50
224 Tom Gilbert RC .75 2.00
225 Jonathan Sigalet RC .60 1.50
226 Brandon Dubinsky RC 1.00 2.50
227 Jaroslav Halak RC 2.00 5.00
228 David Krejci RC 1.25 3.00
229 Andy Greene RC .60 1.50
230 Lauri Tukonen RC .60 1.50
231 Jeff Finger RC .60 1.50
232 Daniel Carcillo RC .75 2.00
233 Kent Huskins RC .60 1.50
234 John Zeiler RC .60 1.50
235 Zack Stortini RC .60 1.50
236 Matt Ellis RC .60 1.50
237 Joel Lundqvist RC .60 1.50
238 Duncan Milroy RC .60 1.50
239 Bryan Young RC .60 1.50
240 Danny Bois RC .60 1.50
241 Drew Fata RC .60 1.50
242 Krys Barch RC .60 1.50
243 Pierre Parenteau RC .60 1.50
244 Mathieu Roy RC .60 1.50
245 Jannik Hansen RC .60 1.50
246 Dainius Zubrus .15 .40
247 Petr Sykora .15 .40
248 Darryl Sydor .15 .40
249 Bill Guerin .15 .40
250 Mike Comrie .15 .40
251 Chris Drury .20 .50
252 Scott Gomez .15 .40
253 Daniel Briere .25 .60
254 Joffrey Lupul .15 .40
255 Tim Connolly .15 .40
256 Andrew Peters .15 .40
257 Patrick Eaves .15 .40
258 Chris Neil .15 .40
259 Bryan Smolinski .15 .40
260 Roman Hamrlik .15 .40
261 Vesa Toskala .20 .50
262 Jason Blake .15 .40
263 Manny Fernandez .15 .40
264 Michel Ouellet .15 .40
265 Todd White .15 .40
266 Ray Whitney .15 .40
267 Mike Commodore .15 .40
268 Tomas Vokoun .25 .60
269 Richard Zednik .15 .40
270 Viktor Kozlov .15 .40
271 Michael Nylander .15 .40
272 Brian Rafalski .15 .40
273 Mikael Samuelsson .15 .40
274 Alexander Radulov .25 .60
275 Paul Kariya .25 .60
276 Keith Tkachuk .20 .50
277 Robert Lang .15 .40
278 Sergei Samsonov .15 .40
279 Nikolai Zherdev .15 .40
280 Brendan Morrison .15 .40
281 Mark Parrish .15 .40
282 Owen Nolan .20 .50
283 Adrian Aucoin .15 .40
284 Ryan Smyth .20 .50
285 Joni Pitkanen .15 .40
286 Geoff Sanderson .15 .40
287 Todd Bertuzzi .20 .50
288 Mathieu Schneider .15 .40
289 Matt Carle .15 .40
290 Jere Lehtinen .15 .40
291 Jussi Jokinen .15 .40
292 Ladislav Nagy .15 .40
293 Kyle Calder .15 .40
294 Fredrik Sjostrom .15 .40
295 Nick Boynton .15 .40
296 Andrew Cogliano RC 1.50 4.00
297 Anton Stralman RC .75 2.00
298 Bobby Ryan RC 2.50 6.00
299 Brett Sterling RC .60 1.50
300 Brian Elliott RC .75 2.00
301 Bryan Little RC 1.00 2.50
302 Cal Clutterbuck RC .60 1.50
303 Carey Price RC 3.00 8.00
304 Cory Murphy RC .60 1.50
305 Curtis McElhinney RC .75 2.00
306 Daniel Winnik RC .60 1.50
307 David Perron RC 1.00 2.50
308 Denis Tolpeko RC .60 1.50
309 Devin Setoguchi RC 1.25 3.00
310 Erik Johnson RC 1.25 3.00
311 James Sheppard RC .60 1.50
312 Jared Boll RC .60 1.50
313 Jaroslav Hlinka RC .75 2.00
314 Jiri Tlusty RC 1.50 4.00
315 Jonathan Bernier RC 1.50 4.00
316 Jonathan Toews RC 4.00 10.00
317 Kris Russell RC 1.00 2.50
318 Kyle Chipchura RC 1.00 2.50
319 Lukas Kaspar RC .60 1.50
320 Marc Staal RC 1.50 4.00
321 Martin Hanzal RC .75 2.00
322 Mason Raymond RC 1.50 4.00
323 Matt Keetley RC .75 2.00
324 Matt Moulson RC .60 1.50
325 Matt Niskanen RC .60 1.50
326 Matt Smaby RC .60 1.50
327 Mike Lundin RC .60 1.50
328 Mike Weber RC .60 1.50
329 Milan Lucic RC 1.50 4.00
330 Nick Foligno RC 1.00 2.50
331 Nicklas Backstrom RC 2.50 6.00
332 Nicklas Bergfors RC .75 2.00
333 Olli Malmivaara RC .60 1.50
334 Ondrej Pavelec RC 1.00 2.50
335 Patrick Kane RC 4.00 10.00
336 Peter Mueller RC 2.00 5.00
337 Petteri Wirtanen RC .60 1.50
338 Sam Gagner RC 1.25 3.00
339 Stefan Meyer RC .60 1.50
340 Steve Wagner RC .60 1.50
341 Tobias Stephan RC .75 2.00
342 Torrey Mitchell RC .75 2.00
343 Tyler Kennedy RC 1.00 2.50
344 Tyler Weiman RC .75 2.00
345 Ville Koistinen RC .60 1.50

2007-08 Upper Deck Victory Black

STATED ODDS 1:720
NOT PRICED DUE TO SCARCITY

2007-08 Upper Deck Victory Gold

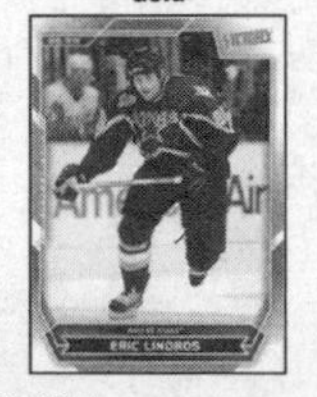

*GOLD: 6X TO 15X
GOLD (1-200) ODDS 1:24
*GOLD RCs 3X TO 8X
GOLD (201-245) ODDS 1:240

2007-08 Upper Deck Victory EA Sports Face-Off

COMPLETE SET (6) 1.50 4.00
STATED ODDS 1:8
FO1 Jarome Iginla .75 2.00
FO2 Henrik Lundqvist .60 1.50
FO3 Eric Staal .50 1.25
FO4 Kris Draper .40 1.00
FO5 Chris Pronger .50 1.25
FO6 Dion Phaneuf .50 1.25

2007-08 Upper Deck Victory GameBreakers

COMPLETE SET (50) 15.00 40.00
STATED ODDS 1:4
GB1 Sidney Crosby 3.00 8.00
GB2 Martin Brodeur 1.50 4.00
GB3 Joe Thornton .75 2.00
GB4 Saku Koivu .50 1.25
GB5 Daniel Alfredsson .50 1.25
GB6 Roberto Luongo 1.00 2.50
GB7 Chris Drury .50 1.25
GB8 Henrik Zetterberg .60 1.50
GB9 Ilya Kovalchuk .75 2.00
GB10 Jean-Sebastien Giguere .60 1.50
GB11 Mike Modano .60 1.50
GB12 Daniel Briere .60 1.50
GB13 Kari Lehtonen .60 1.50
GB14 Simon Gagne .60 1.50
GB15 Paul Kariya .60 1.50
GB16 Milan Hejduk .50 1.25
GB17 Dominik Hasek .75 2.00
GB18 Jonathan Cheechoo .50 1.25
GB19 Joe Sakic 1.25 3.00
GB20 Vincent Lecavalier .60 1.50
GB21 Cam Ward .60 1.50
GB22 Mats Sundin .60 1.50
GB23 Patrik Elias .40 1.00
GB24 Ryan Miller .60 1.50
GB25 Teemu Selanne .60 1.50
GB26 Jason Spezza .60 1.50
GB27 Tomas Vokoun .60 1.50
GB28 Ales Hemsky .40 1.00
GB29 Marian Hossa .60 1.50
GB30 Marc-Andre Fleury .60 1.50
GB31 Evgeni Malkin 1.50 4.00
GB32 Anze Kopitar .60 1.50
GB33 Olli Jokinen .40 1.00
GB34 Patrick Marleau .50 1.25
GB35 Dany Heatley .75 2.00
GB36 Paul Stastny .60 1.50
GB37 Marty Turco .60 1.50
GB38 Jarome Iginla 1.00 2.50
GB39 Eric Staal .60 1.50
GB40 Peter Forsberg .75 2.00
GB41 Andrew Raycroft .50 1.25
GB42 Martin St. Louis .50 1.25
GB43 Thomas Vanek .50 1.25
GB44 Pavel Datsyuk .60 1.50
GB45 Markus Naslund .60 1.50
GB46 Jaromir Jagr 1.00 2.50
GB47 Miikka Kiprusoff .75 2.00

GB48 Patrice Bergeron .60 1.50
GB49 Henrik Lundqvist .75 2.00
GB50 Alexander Ovechkin 2.00 5.00

2007-08 Upper Deck Victory Oversize Cards

COMPLETE SET (42) 30.00 60.00
OS1 Martin Brodeur 2.00 5.00
OS2 Marc-Andre Fleury .75 2.00
OS3 Evgeni Malkin 2.00 5.00
OS4 Sidney Crosby 4.00 10.00
OS5 Rick DiPietro .60 1.50
OS6 Henrik Lundqvist 1.00 2.50
OS7 Brendan Shanahan .75 2.00
OS8 Jaromir Jagr 1.25 3.00
OS9 Simon Gagne .75 2.00
OS10 Ryan Miller .75 2.00
OS11 Thomas Vanek .60 1.50
OS12 Jason Spezza .75 2.00
OS13 Dany Heatley 1.00 2.50
OS14 Michael Ryder .50 1.25
OS15 Saku Koivu .60 1.50
OS16 Andrew Raycroft .60 1.50
OS17 Mats Sundin .75 2.00
OS18 Patrice Bergeron .75 2.00
OS19 Vincent Lecavalier .75 2.00
OS20 Martin St. Louis .60 1.50
OS21 Kari Lehtonen .75 2.00
OS22 Ilya Kovalchuk 1.00 2.50
OS23 Eric Staal .75 2.00
OS24 Alexander Ovechkin 2.50 6.00
OS25 Dominik Hasek 1.00 2.50
OS26 Pavel Datsyuk .75 2.00
OS27 Henrik Zetterberg .75 2.00
OS28 Paul Kariya .75 2.00
OS29 Peter Forsberg 1.00 2.50
OS30 Rick Nash .75 2.00
OS31 Roberto Luongo 1.25 3.00
OS32 Markus Naslund .75 2.00
OS33 Marian Gaborik 1.00 2.50
OS34 Miikka Kiprusoff 1.00 2.50
OS35 Jarome Iginla 1.25 3.00
OS36 Joe Sakic 1.50 4.00
OS37 Dwayne Roloson .60 1.50
OS38 Jean-Sebastien Giguere .75 2.00
OS39 Jonathan Cheechoo .60 1.50
OS40 Joe Thornton 1.00 2.50
OS41 Mike Modano .75 2.00
OS42 Shane Doan .50 1.25

2007-08 Upper Deck Victory Stars on Ice

COMPLETE SET (50) 12.00 30.00
STATED ODDS 1:4
SI1 Roberto Luongo .75 2.00
SI2 Joe Thornton .60 1.50
SI3 Dion Phaneuf .50 1.25
SI4 Ryan Miller .50 1.25
SI5 Nicklas Lidstrom .50 1.25
SI6 Phil Kessel .50 1.25
SI7 Sergei Fedorov .50 1.25
SI8 Alexander Ovechkin 1.50 4.00
SI9 Jason Spezza .50 1.25
SI10 Brian Gionta .30 .75
SI11 Dany Heatley .60 1.50
SI12 Eric Staal .50 1.25
SI13 Teemu Selanne .50 1.25
SI14 Jonathan Cheechoo .40 1.00
SI15 Cristobal Huet .40 1.00
SI16 Jaromir Jagr .75 2.00
SI17 Ilya Kovalchuk .60 1.50
SI18 Saku Koivu .40 1.00
SI19 Joe Sakic 1.00 2.50
SI20 Andy McDonald .30 .75
SI21 Jay Bouwmeester .30 .75
SI22 Ryan Getzlaf .40 1.00
SI23 Dominik Hasek .60 1.50
SI24 Scott Niedermayer .30 .75
SI25 Simon Gagne .50 1.25
SI26 Martin St. Louis .40 1.00
SI27 Marian Hossa .50 1.25
SI28 Mats Sundin .50 1.25
SI29 Ryan Smyth .40 1.00
SI30 Martin Brodeur 1.25 3.00
SI31 Jordan Staal .60 1.50
SI32 Milan Hejduk .40 1.00
SI33 Rick Nash .50 1.25
SI34 Miikka Kiprusoff .60 1.50
SI35 Marty Turco .50 1.25
SI36 Patrice Bergeron .50 1.25
SI37 Vincent Lecavalier .50 1.25
SI38 Markus Naslund .50 1.25
SI39 Jarome Iginla .75 2.00
SI40 Henrik Zetterberg .50 1.25
SI41 Evgeni Malkin 1.25 3.00
SI42 Martin Havlat .40 1.00
SI43 Brendan Shanahan .50 1.25
SI44 Michael Ryder .30 .75
SI45 Patrick Marleau .40 1.00
SI46 Zach Parise .40 1.00
SI47 Daniel Briere .50 1.25
SI48 Marc-Andre Fleury .50 1.25
SI49 Tomas Kaberle .30 .75
SI50 Sidney Crosby 2.50 6.00

2008-09 Upper Deck Victory

COMPLETE SET (350) 25.00 60.00
COMP.SET w/o SPs (200) 15.00 40.00
RC STATED ODDS 1:4
UPDATED STATED ODDS 1 PER UD SER.2 PACK
RC UPDATE STATED ODDS 1:4 UD SER.2
1 Olaf Kolzig .25 .60
2 Alexander Ovechkin 1.00 2.50
3 Nicklas Backstrom .50 1.25
4 Alexander Semin .25 .60
5 Cristobal Huet .25 .60
6 Sergei Fedorov .40 1.00
7 Roberto Luongo .40 1.00
8 Daniel Sedin .25 .60
9 Henrik Sedin .25 .60
10 Ryan Kesler .15 .40
11 Alexander Edler .20 .50
12 Markus Naslund .25 .60
13 Brendan Morrison .15 .40
14 Mats Sundin .25 .60
15 Vesa Toskala .25 .60
16 Matt Stajan .20 .50
17 Darcy Tucker .20 .50
18 Tomas Kaberle .15 .40
19 Nikolai Antropov .20 .50
20 Alexander Steen .25 .60
21 Vincent Lecavalier .25 .60
22 Mike Smith .20 .50
23 Martin St. Louis .25 .60
24 Paul Ranger .15 .40
25 Jussi Jokinen .15 .40
26 Paul Kariya .25 .60
27 Manny Legace .20 .50
28 Lee Stempniak .15 .40
29 Erik Johnson .30 .75
30 Keith Tkachuk .20 .50
31 Brad Boyes .20 .50
32 Joe Thornton .40 1.00
33 Milan Michalek .15 .40
34 Evgeni Nabokov .25 .60
35 Jonathan Cheechoo .25 .60
36 Patrick Marleau .20 .50
37 Brian Campbell .40 1.00
38 Sidney Crosby 1.25 3.00
39 Marc-Andre Fleury .25 .60
40 Ryan Malone .15 .40
41 Evgeni Malkin .60 1.50
42 Jordan Staal .40 1.00
43 Ty Conklin .20 .50
44 Marian Hossa .40 1.00
45 Ilya Bryzgalov .15 .40
46 Shane Doan .15 .40
47 Peter Mueller .30 .75
48 Radim Vrbata .15 .40
49 Ed Jovanovski .15 .40
50 Martin Hanzal .20 .50
51 Mike Richards .40 1.00
52 Daniel Briere .25 .60
53 Mike Knuble .25 .60
54 Martin Biron .20 .50
55 Jeff Carter .25 .60
56 R.J. Umberger .15 .40
57 Simon Gagne .20 .50
58 Daniel Alfredsson .20 .50
59 Jason Spezza .30 .75
60 Ray Emery .20 .50
61 Wade Redden .15 .40
62 Dany Heatley .30 .75
63 Martin Gerber .20 .50
64 Henrik Lundqvist .50 1.25
65 Scott Gomez .20 .50
66 Jaromir Jagr .30 .75
67 Chris Drury .25 .60
68 Brendan Shanahan .25 .60
69 Marc Staal .30 .75
70 Michal Rozsival .15 .40
71 Rick DiPietro .25 .60
72 Bill Guerin .15 .40
73 Miroslav Satan .15 .40
74 Trent Hunter .15 .40
75 Mike Comrie .15 .40
76 Ruslan Fedotenko .15 .40
77 Martin Brodeur .50 1.25
78 Brian Gionta .25 .60
79 Travis Zajac .15 .40
80 Patrik Elias .15 .40
81 John Madden .15 .40
82 Zach Parise .25 .60
83 Jason Arnott .15 .40
84 Dan Ellis .15 .40
85 David Legwand .20 .50
86 J.P. Dumont .15 .40
87 Alexander Radulov .25 .60
88 Martin Erat .25 .60
89 Carey Price .75 2.00
90 Saku Koivu .25 .60
91 Andrei Kostitsyn .20 .50
92 Guillaume Latendresse .20 .50
93 Michael Ryder .20 .50
94 Alex Kovalev .25 .60
95 Chris Higgins .15 .40
96 Marian Gaborik .40 1.00
97 Josh Harding .20 .50
98 Mikko Koivu .25 .60
99 Pierre-Marc Bouchard .15 .40
100 Brian Rolston .15 .40
101 Niklas Backstrom .25 .60
102 Anze Kopitar .25 .60
103 Jack Johnson .20 .50
104 Patrick O'Sullivan .20 .50
105 Alexander Frolov .15 .40
106 Mike Cammalleri .25 .60
107 Dustin Brown .15 .40
108 Jason LaBarbera .20 .50
109 Olli Jokinen .15 .40
110 Tomas Vokoun .25 .60
111 Jay Bouwmeester .20 .50
112 Nathan Horton .15 .40
113 Stephen Weiss .15 .40
114 David Booth .15 .40
115 Dustin Penner .15 .40
116 Ales Hemsky .15 .40
117 Dwayne Roloson .20 .50
118 Sam Gagner .40 1.00
119 Shawn Horcoff .15 .40
120 Jarret Stoll .20 .50
121 Andrew Cogliano .40 1.00
122 Dominik Hasek .40 1.00
123 Nicklas Lidstrom .25 .60
124 Dan Cleary .25 .60
125 Pavel Datsyuk .25 .60
126 Chris Osgood .25 .60
127 Valtteri Filppula .15 .40
128 Tomas Holmstrom .20 .50
129 Henrik Zetterberg .50 1.25
130 Johan Holmqvist .20 .50
131 Brad Richards .20 .50
132 Mike Modano .25 .60
133 Marty Turco .20 .50
134 Brenden Morrow .20 .50
135 Jere Lehtinen .15 .40
136 Sergei Zubov .15 .40
137 Mike Ribeiro .15 .40
138 Pascal Leclaire .20 .50
139 Rick Nash .25 .60
140 Nikolai Zherdev .15 .40
141 Gilbert Brule .25 .60
142 Michael Peca .20 .50
143 Peter Budaj .20 .50
144 Ryan Smyth .20 .50
145 Joe Sakic .40 1.00
146 Peter Forsberg .40 1.00
147 Milan Hejduk .20 .50
148 Paul Stastny .25 .60
149 Wojtek Wolski .15 .40
150 Patrick Kane .60 1.50
151 Nikolai Khabibulin .25 .60
152 Martin Havlat .20 .50
153 Jonathan Toews .75 2.00
154 Patrick Sharp .15 .40
155 Duncan Keith .20 .50
156 Robert Lang .15 .40
157 Cam Ward .25 .60
158 Ray Whitney .15 .40
159 Eric Staal .40 1.00
160 Justin Williams .15 .40
161 Rod Brind'Amour .20 .50
162 Erik Cole .15 .40
163 Miikka Kiprusoff .25 .60
164 Jarome Iginla .50 1.25
165 Matthew Lombardi .15 .40
166 Dion Phaneuf .25 .60
167 Kristian Huselius .15 .40
168 Daymond Langkow .15 .40
169 Alex Tanguay .20 .50
170 Steve Bernier .15 .40
171 Derek Roy .15 .40
172 Ryan Miller .25 .60
173 Drew Stafford .25 .60
174 Jason Pominville .20 .50
175 Thomas Vanek .25 .60
176 Ales Kotalik .15 .40
177 Tim Thomas .25 .60
178 Patrice Bergeron .25 .60
179 Milan Lucic .50 1.25
180 Zdeno Chara .15 .40
181 Phil Kessel .25 .60
182 Glen Murray .15 .40
183 Marc Savard .15 .40
184 Colby Armstrong .15 .40
185 Ilya Kovalchuk .30 .75
186 Kari Lehtonen .15 .40
187 Slava Kozlov .15 .40
188 Bobby Holik .15 .40
189 Todd White .15 .40
190 Johan Hedberg .20 .50
191 Teemu Selanne .25 .60
192 Ryan Getzlaf .30 .75
193 Scott Niedermayer .15 .40
194 Jean-Sebastien Giguere .25 .60
195 Corey Perry .25 .60
196 Chris Kunitz .15 .40
197 Chris Pronger .20 .50
198 George Parros .15 .40
199 Sidney Crosby CL 1.25 3.00
200 Alexander Ovechkin CL 1.00 2.50
201 Derick Brassard RC 1.25 3.00
202 Mark Fistric RC .50 1.25
203 Alex Goligoski RC 1.25 3.00
204 Claude Giroux RC 1.25 3.00
205 Jon Filewich RC .50 1.25
206 Robbie Earl RC .50 1.25
207 Ilya Zubov RC .60 1.50
208 Steve Mason RC 1.50 4.00
209 Brian Boyle RC .60 1.50
210 Shawn Matthias RC .60 1.50
211 Ryan Stone RC .60 1.50
212 Teddy Purcell RC .60 1.50
213 Mike Iggulden RC .50 1.25
214 Tim Ramholt RC .50 1.25
215 Dan LaCosta RC .75 2.00
216 Sami Lepisto RC .60 1.50
217 Danny Taylor RC .60 1.50
218 Tom Cavanagh RC .50 1.25
219 Andrew Murray RC .50 1.25
220 Kevin Doell RC .40 1.00
221 Tim Conboy RC .50 1.25
222 Pascal Pelletier RC .50 1.25
223 Chris Minard RC .60 1.50
224 Joey Mormina RC .50 1.25
225 Darryl Boyce RC .50 1.25
226 Cody McLeod RC .50 1.25
227 Jordan Hendry RC .50 1.25
228 Corey Locke RC .60 1.50
229 Mike Brown RC .50 1.25
230 B.J. Crombeen RC .50 1.25
231 David Brine RC .50 1.25
232 Joe Jensen RC .60 1.50
233 Kyle Greentree RC .75 2.00
234 Peter Vandermeer RC .40 1.00
235 Marc-Andre Gragnani RC .50 1.25
236 Andrew Ebbett RC .60 1.50
237 Erik Ersberg RC .60 1.50
238 Jonathan Ericsson RC 1.00 2.50
239 Theo Peckham RC .60 1.50
240 Darren Helm RC 1.00 2.50
241 Mattias Ritola RC .75 2.00
242 Clay Wilson RC .40 1.00
243 Brian Lee RC .60 1.50
244 Alex Foster RC .50 1.25
245 Kyle Okposo RC 1.25 3.00
246 Kyle Turris RC 1.25 3.00
247 Tyler Plante RC .60 1.50
248 Matt D'Agostini RC 1.00 2.50
249 Adam Pineault RC .60 1.50
250 Boris Valabik RC .75 2.00
251 Brendan Morrison .15 .40
252 Mathieu Schneider .15 .40
253 Ron Hainsey .15 .40
254 Patrick Lalime .15 .40
255 Todd Bertuzzi .25 .60
256 Mike Cammalleri .25 .60
257 Joni Pitkanen .15 .40
258 Brian Campbell .40 1.00
259 Cristobal Huet .25 .60
260 Adam Foote .15 .40
261 Darcy Tucker .20 .50
262 Andrew Raycroft .25 .60
263 Kristian Huselius .15 .40
264 R.J. Umberger .15 .40
265 Sean Avery .20 .50
266 Marian Hossa .40 1.00
267 Ty Conklin .20 .50
268 Lubomir Visnovsky .15 .40
269 Erik Cole .15 .40
270 Keith Ballard .15 .40
271 Cory Stillman .15 .40
272 Jarret Stoll .20 .50
273 Andrew Brunette .15 .40
274 Owen Nolan .25 .60
275 Marek Zidlicky .15 .40
276 Georges Laraque .20 .50
277 Alex Tanguay .20 .50
278 Brian Rolston .15 .40
279 Doug Weight .15 .40
280 Mark Streit .15 .40
281 Markus Naslund .25 .60
282 Nikolai Zherdev .15 .40
283 Wade Redden .15 .40
284 Olli Jokinen .15 .40
285 Eric Godard .20 .50
286 Miroslav Satan .15 .40
287 Ruslan Fedotenko .15 .40
288 Rob Blake .25 .60
289 Chris Mason .20 .50
290 Mark Recchi .20 .50
291 Radim Vrbata .15 .40
292 Ryan Malone .15 .40
293 Andrej Meszaros .15 .40
294 Matt Carle .15 .40
295 Gary Roberts .15 .40
296 Olaf Kolzig .25 .60
297 Curtis Joseph .25 .60
298 Pavol Demitra .15 .40
299 Steve Bernier .25 .60
300 Jose Theodore .25 .60
301 Steve MacIntyre RC .60 1.50
302 Jason Garrison RC .60 1.50
303 Darrel Powe RC .60 1.50
304 Mitch Fritz RC .60 1.50
305 Fabian Brunnstrom RC 1.00 2.50
306 Petr Vrana RC .75 2.00
307 Nathan Oystrick RC .60 1.50
308 Brett Skinner RC .50 1.25
309 Matthew Halischuk RC .75 2.00
310 Pierre-Luc Letourneau-Leblond RC .40 1.00
311 Paul Bissonnette RC .75 2.00
312 Brad Staubitz RC .50 1.25
313 Tyler Sloan RC .75 2.00
314 Andreas Nodl RC .60 1.50
315 Derek Dorsett RC .75 2.00
316 Nikita Filatov RC 2.50 6.00
317 Dwight Helminen RC .60 1.50
318 Nikolai Kulemin RC .60 1.50
319 Viktor Tikhonov RC .60 1.50
320 Kevin Porter RC .50 1.25
321 Zach Boychuk RC 1.00 2.50
322 Patrik Berglund RC 1.50 4.00
323 Mikkel Boedker RC 1.00 2.50
324 Zach Bogosian RC 1.25 3.00
325 Drew Doughty RC 2.00 5.00
326 Michael Frolik RC 1.25 3.00
327 Colton Gillies RC .60 1.50
328 Jamie McGinn RC .60 1.50
329 Patric Hornqvist RC .60 1.50
330 Ryan Jones RC .75 2.00
331 Steve Mason RC 1.50 4.00
332 Ben Bishop RC 1.00 2.50
333 Vladimir Mihalik RC .60 1.50
334 Jonas Frogren RC .75 2.00
335 Oscar Moller RC .60 1.50
336 James Neal RC 1.00 2.50
337 Janne Niskala RC .60 1.50
338 T.J. Oshie RC 1.50 4.00
339 Adam Pardy RC .60 1.50
340 Alex Pietrangelo RC 1.00 2.50
341 Chris Porter RC .60 1.50
342 Jared Ross RC .75 2.00
343 Anssi Salmela RC .75 2.00
344 Luca Sbisa RC 1.00 2.50
345 Luke Schenn RC 2.00 5.00
346 Wayne Simmonds RC .60 1.50
347 Blake Wheeler RC 1.50 4.00
348 Brandon Sutter RC .75 2.00
349 Jakub Voracek RC 1.25 3.00
350 Steven Stamkos RC 5.00 12.00

2008-09 Upper Deck Victory Black

STATED ODDS 1:720
UPDATE STATED ODDS 1:288
NOT PRICED DUE TO SCARCITY

2008-09 Upper Deck Victory Gold

*GOLD: 4X TO 10X BASE
UPDATE STATED ODDS 1:24
*GOLD RCs: 2X TO 5X BASE

2008-09 Upper Deck Victory Game Breakers

COMPLETE SET (50) 15.00 40.00
GB1 Sidney Crosby 2.50 6.00
GB2 Alexander Ovechkin 2.00 5.00
GB3 Roberto Luongo .75 2.00
GB4 Vincent Lecavalier .50 1.25
GB5 Miikka Kiprusoff .50 1.25
GB6 Joe Thornton .75 2.00
GB7 Ilya Kovalchuk .60 1.50
GB8 Martin Brodeur 1.00 2.50
GB9 Marian Gaborik .75 2.00
GB10 Henrik Zetterberg 1.00 2.50
GB11 Eric Staal .75 2.00
GB12 Mats Sundin .50 1.25
GB13 Anze Kopitar .50 1.25
GB14 Jaromir Jagr .60 1.50
GB15 Rick Nash .50 1.25
GB16 Patrick Kane 1.25 3.00
GB17 Dany Heatley .60 1.50
GB18 Paul Kariya .50 1.25
GB19 Jarome Iginla 1.00 2.50
GB20 Joe Sakic .75 2.00
GB21 Evgeni Malkin 1.25 3.00
GB22 Peter Mueller .60 1.50
GB23 Patrik Elias .30 .75
GB24 Jean-Sebastien Giguere .50 1.25
GB25 Marian Hossa .75 2.00
GB26 Josh Harding .40 1.00
GB27 Marc-Andre Fleury .50 1.25
GB28 Nicklas Backstrom 1.00 2.50
GB29 Michael Ryder .40 1.00
GB30 Carey Price 1.50 4.00
GB31 Sam Gagner .75 2.00
GB32 Jonathan Cheechoo .50 1.25
GB33 Patrice Bergeron .50 1.25
GB34 Tomas Vokoun .50 1.25
GB35 Daniel Sedin .50 1.25
GB36 Phil Kessel .50 1.25
GB37 Daniel Alfredsson .40 1.00
GB38 Olli Jokinen .30 .75
GB39 Jack Johnson .40 1.00
GB40 Paul Stastny .50 1.25
GB41 Ryan Miller .50 1.25
GB42 Pavel Datsyuk .50 1.25
GB43 Jonathan Toews 1.50 4.00
GB44 Simon Gagne .40 1.00
GB45 Teemu Selanne .50 1.25
GB46 Mike Richards .75 2.00
GB47 Shane Doan .30 .75
GB48 Martin St. Louis .50 1.25
GB49 Henrik Lundqvist 1.00 2.50
GB50 Alexander Radulov .50 1.25

2008-09 Upper Deck Victory Oversize Cards

COMPLETE SET (42) 40.00 100.00
STATED ODDS 1:
OS1 Alexander Ovechkin 4.00 10.00
OS2 Roberto Luongo 1.50 4.00
OS3 Mats Sundin 1.00 2.50
OS4 Vincent Lecavalier 1.00 2.50
OS5 Martin St. Louis 1.00 2.50
OS6 Paul Kariya 1.00 2.50
OS7 Joe Thornton 1.50 4.00
OS8 Sidney Crosby 5.00 12.00
OS9 Evgeni Malkin 2.50 6.00
OS10 Peter Mueller 1.25 3.00
OS11 Simon Gagne .75 2.00
OS12 Jason Spezza 1.25 3.00
OS13 Dany Heatley 1.25 3.00
OS14 Jaromir Jagr 1.25 3.00
OS15 Brendan Shanahan 1.00 2.50
OS16 Martin Brodeur 2.00 5.00
OS17 Carey Price 3.00 8.00
OS18 Saku Koivu 1.00 2.50
OS19 Marian Gaborik 1.50 4.00
OS20 Anze Kopitar 1.00 2.50
OS21 Ales Hemsky .60 1.50
OS22 Sam Gagner 1.50 4.00
OS23 Dominik Hasek 1.50 4.00
OS24 Pavel Datsyuk 1.00 2.50
OS25 Henrik Zetterberg 2.00 5.00
OS26 Mike Modano 1.00 2.50
OS27 Marty Turco .75 2.00
OS28 Rick Nash 1.00 2.50
OS29 Joe Sakic 1.50 4.00
OS30 Peter Forsberg 1.00 2.50
OS31 Paul Stastny 1.00 2.50
OS32 Patrick Kane 2.50 6.00
OS33 Jonathan Toews 3.00 8.00
OS34 Eric Staal 1.50 4.00
OS35 Miikka Kiprusoff 1.00 2.50
OS36 Jarome Iginla 2.00 5.00
OS37 Ryan Miller 1.00 2.50
OS38 Thomas Vanek 1.00 2.50
OS39 Patrice Bergeron 1.00 2.50
OS40 Ilya Kovalchuk 1.25 3.00
OS41 Teemu Selanne 1.00 2.50
OS42 Ryan Getzlaf 1.25 3.00

2008-09 Upper Deck Victory Stars of the Game

COMPLETE SET (50) 20.00 50.00
STATED ODDS 1:
SG1 Teemu Selanne .50 1.25
SG2 Ilya Kovalchuk .60 1.50
SG3 Jonathan Toews 1.50 4.00
SG4 Jarome Iginla 1.00 2.50
SG5 Dominik Hasek .75 2.00
SG6 Marian Gaborik .75 2.00
SG7 Jason Spezza .60 1.50
SG8 Thomas Vanek .50 1.25
SG9 Henrik Lundqvist 1.00 2.50
SG10 Simon Gagne .40 1.00
SG11 Brad Boyes .40 1.00
SG12 Sidney Crosby 2.50 6.00
SG13 Anze Kopitar .50 1.25
SG14 Martin Brodeur 1.00 2.50
SG15 Patrice Bergeron .50 1.25
SG16 Vincent Lecavalier .50 1.25
SG17 Saku Koivu .50 1.25
SG18 Roberto Luongo .75 2.00
SG19 Rick Nash .50 1.25
SG20 Henrik Zetterberg 1.00 2.50
SG21 Michael Ryder .40 1.00
SG22 Joe Sakic .75 2.00
SG23 Jaromir Jagr .60 1.50
SG24 Dany Heatley .60 1.50
SG25 Ryan Miller .50 1.25
SG26 Eric Staal .75 2.00
SG27 Mats Sundin .50 1.25
SG28 Sam Gagner .75 2.00
SG29 Joe Thornton .75 2.00
SG30 Alexander Ovechkin 2.00 5.00
SG31 Miikka Kiprusoff .50 1.25
SG32 Mike Modano .50 1.25
SG33 Rick DiPietro .50 1.25
SG34 Paul Kariya .50 1.25
SG35 Patrick Kane 1.25 3.00
SG36 Alexander Radulov .50 1.25
SG37 Marty Turco .40 1.00
SG38 Ryan Getzlaf .60 1.50
SG39 Shane Doan .30 .75
SG40 Evgeni Malkin 1.25 3.00
SG41 Pavel Datsyuk .50 1.25
SG42 Markus Naslund .50 1.25
SG43 Martin St. Louis .50 1.25
SG44 Paul Stastny .50 1.25
SG45 Tomas Vokoun .50 1.25
SG46 Zach Parise .50 1.25
SG47 Daniel Alfredsson .40 1.00
SG48 Marian Hossa .75 2.00
SG49 Carey Price 1.50 4.00
SG50 Brendan Shanahan .50 1.25

2009-10 Upper Deck Victory

COMPLETE SET (340) 75.00 150.00
COMP.SET (250) 40.00 100.00
COMP.SET w/o SPs (200) 15.00 40.00
COMP.UPDATE SET (90) 25.00 60.00
RC STATED ODDS 1:2
UPDATE ODDS 1 PER UD2 PACK
1 Ryan Getzlaf .40 1.00
2 Scott Niedermayer .15 .40
3 Jean-Sebastien Giguere .25 .60
4 Corey Perry .25 .60
5 Chris Pronger .20 .50
6 Bryan Little .25 .60
7 Ilya Kovalchuk .30 .75
8 Kari Lehtonen .25 .60
9 Colby Armstrong .15 .40
10 Todd White .15 .40
11 Slava Kozlov .15 .40
12 Michael Ryder .20 .50
13 David Krejci .20 .50
14 Patrice Bergeron .25 .60
15 Blake Wheeler .30 .75
16 Zdeno Chara .15 .40
17 Phil Kessel .25 .60
18 Tim Thomas .25 .60
19 Marc Savard .15 .40
20 Clarke MacArthur .15 .40
21 Derek Roy .25 .60
22 Ryan Miller .25 .60
23 Drew Stafford .25 .60
24 Jason Pominville .25 .60
25 Thomas Vanek .25 .60
26 David Moss .20 .50
27 Mike Cammalleri .20 .50
28 Jarome Iginla .50 1.25
29 Todd Bertuzzi .25 .60
30 Dion Phaneuf .40 1.00
31 Miikka Kiprusoff .25 .60
32 Daymond Langkow .15 .40
33 Rene Bourque .15 .40
34 Olli Jokinen .15 .40
35 Cam Ward .25 .60
36 Ray Whitney .15 .40
37 Eric Staal .30 .75
38 Brandon Sutter .25 .60
39 Rod Brind'Amour .20 .50
40 Tuomo Ruutu .15 .40
41 Patrick Kane .50 1.25
42 Nikolai Khabibulin .25 .60
43 Martin Havlat .20 .50
44 Jonathan Toews .60 1.50
45 Patrick Sharp .20 .50
46 Brian Campbell .20 .50
47 Kris Versteeg .30 .75
48 John-Michael Liles .20 .50
49 Ryan Smyth .25 .60
50 T.J. Hensick .15 .40
51 Peter Budaj .25 .60
52 Milan Hejduk .25 .60
53 Paul Stastny .25 .60
54 Wojtek Wolski .15 .40
55 Jakub Voracek .25 .60
56 Derick Brassard .25 .60
57 Rick Nash .25 .60
58 Steve Mason .40 1.00
59 R.J. Umberger .20 .50
60 Kristian Huselius .15 .40
61 Marty Turco .20 .50
62 Brad Richards .20 .50
63 Mike Modano .25 .60
64 Loui Eriksson .15 .40
65 Brenden Morrow .20 .50
66 Mike Ribeiro .15 .40
67 Fabian Brunnstrom .25 .60
68 Johan Franzen .15 .40
69 Nicklas Lidstrom .30 .75
70 Jiri Hudler .15 .40
71 Pavel Datsyuk .25 .60
72 Ty Conklin .20 .50
73 Marian Hossa .40 1.00
74 Tomas Holmstrom .20 .50
75 Henrik Zetterberg .50 1.25
76 Ales Kotalik .15 .40
77 Andrew Cogliano .30 .75
78 Ales Hemsky .20 .50
79 Sheldon Souray .15 .40
80 Sam Gagner .30 .75
81 Shawn Horcoff .15 .40
82 Dustin Penner .15 .40
83 Dwayne Roloson .20 .50
84 Michael Frolik .20 .50
85 Tomas Vokoun .25 .60
86 Jay Bouwmeester .25 .60
87 Nathan Horton .15 .40
88 Stephen Weiss .15 .40
89 David Booth .15 .40
90 Anze Kopitar .25 .60
91 Jack Johnson .20 .50
92 Alexander Frolov .20 .50
93 Drew Doughty .50 1.25
94 Dustin Brown .20 .50
95 Erik Ersberg .20 .50
96 Marian Gaborik .40 1.00
97 Marek Zidlicky .15 .40
98 Mikko Koivu .25 .60
99 Andrew Brunette .15 .40
100 Niklas Backstrom .25 .60
101 Antti Miettinen .15 .40
102 Andrei Kostitsyn .20 .50
103 Carey Price .60 1.50
104 Saku Koivu .25 .60
105 Andrei Markov .20 .50
106 Robert Lang .15 .40
107 Alex Tanguay .20 .50
108 Alex Kovalev .25 .60
109 Max Pacioretty .25 .60
110 Jason Arnott .15 .40
111 Dan Ellis .15 .40
112 Ryan Suter .15 .40
113 J.P. Dumont .15 .40
114 Shea Weber .20 .50
115 Martin Erat .25 .60
116 Martin Brodeur .60 1.50
117 Brian Gionta .25 .60
118 Travis Zajac .15 .40
119 Patrik Elias .20 .50
120 Scott Clemmensen .20 .50
121 Zach Parise .25 .60
122 Josh Bailey .20 .50
123 Rick DiPietro .20 .50
124 Doug Weight .15 .40
125 Kyle Okposo .25 .60
126 Mark Streit .15 .40
127 Henrik Lundqvist .50 1.25
128 Scott Gomez .25 .60
129 Wade Redden .15 .40
130 Chris Drury .20 .50
131 Marc Staal .30 .75
132 Nikolai Zherdev .15 .40
133 Markus Naslund .25 .60
134 Nik Antropov .20 .50
135 Daniel Alfredsson .25 .60
136 Jason Spezza .30 .75
137 Filip Kuba .15 .40
138 Antoine Vermette .15 .40
139 Dany Heatley .50 1.25
140 Alex Auld .20 .50
141 Mike Richards .50 1.25
142 Martin Biron .20 .50
143 Mike Knuble .25 .60
144 Daniel Briere .25 .60
145 Jeff Carter .25 .60
146 Scott Hartnell .15 .40
147 Simon Gagne .25 .60
148 Shane Doan .20 .50
149 Peter Mueller .30 .75
150 Mikkel Boedker .20 .50
151 Ilya Bryzgalov .20 .50
152 Kyle Turris .30 .75
153 Chris Kunitz .25 .60
154 Bill Guerin .15 .40
155 Petr Sykora .15 .40
156 Marc-Andre Fleury .25 .60
157 Miroslav Satan .15 .40
158 Evgeni Malkin .60 1.50
159 Jordan Staal .30 .75
160 Sidney Crosby 1.25 3.00
161 Alex Goligoski .20 .50
162 Devin Setoguchi .20 .50

163 Joe Pavelski .15 .40
164 Ryane Clowe .15 .40
165 Evgeni Nabokov .25 .60
166 Patrick Marleau .25 .60
167 Dan Boyle .15 .40
168 Joe Thornton .50 1.25
169 Manny Legace .20 .50
170 Paul Kariya .25 .60
171 Patrik Berglund .50 1.25
172 Keith Tkachuk .25 .60
173 Brad Boyes .20 .50
174 Vincent Lecavalier .30 .75
175 Vaclav Prospal .15 .40
176 Steven Stamkos .60 1.50
177 Martin St. Louis .25 .60
178 Mike Smith .20 .50
179 Luke Schenn .40 1.00
180 Matt Stajan .20 .50
181 Mikhail Grabovski .20 .50
182 Vesa Toskala .25 .60
183 Tomas Kaberle .15 .40
184 Alexei Ponikarovsky .15 .40
185 Nikolai Kulemin .20 .50
186 Kevin Bieksa .15 .40
187 Daniel Sedin .30 .75
188 Henrik Sedin .40 1.00
189 Ryan Kesler .20 .50
190 Roberto Luongo .60 1.50
191 Mats Sundin .25 .60
192 Steve Bernier .15 .40
193 Mike Green .50 1.25
194 Alexander Ovechkin 1.00 2.50
195 Nicklas Backstrom .50 1.25
196 Alexander Semin .25 .60
197 Semen Varlamov .50 1.25
198 Sergei Fedorov .50 1.25
199 Sidney Crosby CL 1.25 3.00
200 Alexander Ovechkin CL 1.00 2.50
201 Chris Durno RC .50 1.25
202 Peter Regin RC .75 2.00
203 Kevin Quick RC .40 1.00
204 Taylor Chorney RC .60 1.50
205 Mike Santorelli RC .40 1.00
206 Alexander Sulzer RC .40 1.00
207 Troy Bodie RC .50 1.25
208 Matt Beleskey RC .60 1.50
209 Kevin Westgarth RC .50 1.25
210 John Scott RC .60 1.50
211 Mikael Backlund RC 1.00 2.50
212 Byron Bitz RC .60 1.50
213 Matt Pelech RC .60 1.50
214 Tim Wallace RC .40 1.00
215 Ben Lovejoy RC 1.00 2.50
216 Riley Armstrong RC .50 1.25
217 Christian Hanson RC .75 2.00
218 Sean Collins RC .50 1.25
219 Riku Helenius RC .60 1.50
220 Ville Leino RC .75 2.00
221 Michal Neuvirth RC 1.50 4.00
222 Artem Anisimov RC .75 2.00
223 Davis Drewiske RC .60 1.50
224 David Schlemko RC .50 1.25
225 Luca Caputi RC .75 2.00
226 Jakub Petruzalek RC .60 1.50
227 Ryan Vesce RC .50 1.25
228 Jay Beagle RC .60 1.50
229 Jhonas Enroth RC .75 2.00
230 Brandon Segal RC .50 1.25
231 Tim Stapleton RC .60 1.50
232 Jesse Joensuu RC .75 2.00
233 John Negrin RC .50 1.25
234 Grant Lewis RC .50 1.25
235 Cal O'Reilly RC .60 1.50
236 Brian Salcido RC .60 1.50
237 Phil Oreskovic RC .60 1.50
238 Kris Chucko RC .50 1.25
239 Joel Rechlicz RC .60 1.50
240 Andrew MacDonald RC .50 1.25
241 Antti Niemi RC 2.00 5.00
242 Ivan Vishnevskiy RC .75 2.00
243 Mike McKenna RC .50 1.25
244 Spencer Machacek RC .50 1.25
245 Tom Wandell RC 2.00 5.00
246 Michael Vernace RC .50 1.25
247 Yannick Weber RC .75 2.00
248 Matt Hendricks RC .50 1.25
249 Scott Lehman RC .40 1.00
250 T.J. Galiardi RC .75 2.00
251 Saku Koivu .25 .60
252 Joffrey Lupul .25 .60
253 Nik Antropov .20 .50
254 Maxim Afinogenov .15 .40
255 Mark Recchi .25 .60
256 Daniel Paille .20 .50
257 Tim Connolly .15 .40
258 Jay Bouwmeester .25 .60
259 Nigel Dawes .15 .40
260 Jussi Jokinen .20 .50
261 Marian Hossa .40 1.00
262 Dustin Byfuglien .20 .50
263 Craig Anderson .20 .50
264 Antoine Vermette .15 .40
265 James Neal .25 .60
266 Jim Howard .30 .75
267 Dan Cleary .25 .60
268 Nikolai Khabibulin .25 .60
269 Patrick O'Sullivan .20 .50
270 Jordan Leopold .15 .40
271 Ryan Smyth .25 .60
272 Jonathan Quick .40 1.00
273 Owen Nolan .25 .60
274 Martin Havlat .20 .50
275 Mike Cammalleri .20 .50
276 Scott Gomez .25 .60
277 Brian Gionta .25 .60
278 Pekka Rinne .20 .50
279 Jamie Langenbrunner .15 .40
280 Matt Moulson .15 .40
281 Dwayne Roloson .20 .50
282 Marian Gaborik .40 1.00
283 Vaclav Prospal .15 .40
284 Jonathan Cheechoo .25 .60
285 Alex Kovalev .25 .60
286 Milan Michalek .15 .40
287 Chris Pronger .20 .50
288 Ray Emery .20 .50
289 Matthew Lombardi .15 .40
290 Tyler Kennedy .25 .60
291 Dany Heatley .50 1.25
292 Chris Mason .20 .50
293 Alex Tanguay .20 .50
294 Mattias Ohlund .15 .40
295 Mike Komisarek .20 .50
296 Francois Beauchemin .15 .40
297 Christian Ehrhoff .15 .40
298 Mikael Samuelsson .15 .40
299 Mike Knuble .25 .60
300 Brendan Morrison .20 .50
301 Evander Kane RC 1.50 4.00
302 Brad Marchand RC .75 2.00
303 Tyler Myers RC 2.50 6.00
304 Chris Butler RC .60 1.50
305 Matt Duchene RC 2.50 6.00
306 Ryan O'Reilly RC 1.25 3.00
307 Ryan Wilson RC .60 1.50
308 Jamie Benn RC 1.00 2.50
309 Perttu Lindgren RC .60 1.50
310 Aaron Gagnon RC .40 1.00
311 Francis Wathier RC .50 1.25
312 Dmitry Kulikov RC .60 1.50
313 Jakub Kindl RC .75 2.00
314 Teemu Laakso RC .40 1.00
315 Colin Wilson RC 1.25 3.00
316 Cody Franson RC .60 1.50
317 Ilkka Pikkarainen RC .60 1.50
318 John Tavares RC 5.00 12.00
319 Matt Gilroy RC .75 2.00
320 Michael Del Zotto RC 1.25 3.00
321 Erik Karlsson RC 2.00 5.00
322 James Van Riemsdyk RC 1.50 4.00
323 Johan Backlund RC .60 1.50
324 Lars Eller RC 1.00 2.50
325 Jason Demers RC .50 1.25
326 Benn Ferriero RC .60 1.50
327 Frazer McLaren RC .40 1.00
328 Steven Zalewski RC .50 1.25
329 Logan Couture RC 1.25 3.00
330 James Wright RC .75 2.00
331 Victor Hedman RC 1.25 3.00
332 Viktor Stalberg RC 1.00 2.50
333 Jay Rosehill RC .40 1.00
334 Jonas Gustavsson RC 3.00 8.00
335 Tyler Bozak RC 1.50 4.00
336 James Reimer RC .60 1.50
337 Sergei Shirokov RC 1.00 2.50
338 Guillaume Desbiens RC .60 1.50
339 Michael Grabner RC .75 2.00
340 Braden Holtby RC .75 2.00

2009-10 Upper Deck Victory Black

STATED ODDS 1:720
RC STATED ODDS 1:1,440
UPDATE ODDS 1:288
NOT PRICED DUE TO SCARCITY

2009-10 Upper Deck Victory Gold

*GOLD: 4X TO 10X BASE
STATED ODDS 1:36
*GOLD RCs: 1.5X TO 4X BASE
RCs STATED ODDS 1:144
*GOLD UPDATE: 4X TO 10X BASE
*GOLD UPDATE RCs: 1.2X TO 3X BASE
GOLD UPDATE ODDS 1:24 UD2
318 John Tavares 8.00 20.00
334 Jonas Gustavsson 5.00 12.00

2009-10 Upper Deck Victory Game Breakers

COMPLETE SET (50) 15.00 40.00
STATED ODDS 1:4
GB1 Sidney Crosby 2.50 6.00
GB2 Patrick Sharp .40 1.00
GB3 Rick Nash .50 1.25
GB4 Phil Kessel .50 1.25
GB5 Brad Richards .40 1.00
GB6 Joe Thornton 1.00 2.50
GB7 Eric Staal .60 1.50
GB8 Simon Gagne .50 1.25
GB9 Paul Stastny .50 1.25
GB10 Thomas Vanek .50 1.25
GB11 Vincent Lecavalier .60 1.50
GB12 Martin St. Louis .50 1.25
GB13 Ilya Kovalchuk .60 1.50
GB14 David Krejci .40 1.00
GB15 Brad Boyes .40 1.00
GB16 Alex Tanguay .40 1.00
GB17 Jeff Carter .50 1.25
GB18 Patrick Kane 1.00 2.50
GB19 Devin Setoguchi .40 1.00
GB20 Jarome Iginla 1.00 2.50
GB21 Marian Gaborik .75 2.00
GB22 Pavel Datsyuk .50 1.25
GB23 Mikko Koivu .50 1.25
GB24 Markus Naslund .50 1.25
GB25 Loui Eriksson .30 .75
GB26 Chris Drury .40 1.00
GB27 Dany Heatley 1.00 2.50
GB28 Jason Arnott .30 .75
GB29 Evgeni Malkin 1.25 3.00
GB30 Peter Mueller .60 1.50
GB31 Bryan Little .50 1.25
GB32 Patrik Elias .40 1.00
GB33 Mats Sundin .50 1.25
GB34 Patrick Marleau .50 1.25
GB35 Patrice Bergeron .50 1.25
GB36 Shane Doan .40 1.00
GB37 Marian Hossa .75 2.00
GB38 Nicklas Backstrom 1.00 2.50
GB39 Alex Kovalev .50 1.25
GB40 Ryan Getzlaf .75 2.00
GB41 Mike Cammalleri .40 1.00
GB42 David Booth .30 .75
GB43 Jason Spezza .60 1.50
GB44 Jonathan Toews 1.25 3.00
GB45 Zach Parise .50 1.25
GB46 Ryane Clowe .30 .75
GB47 Daniel Sedin .60 1.50
GB48 Henrik Zetterberg 1.00 2.50
GB49 Paul Kariya .50 1.25
GB50 Alexander Ovechkin 2.00 5.00

2009-10 Upper Deck Victory Oversize Cards

COMPLETE SET (42) 40.00 100.00
OS1 Ryan Getzlaf 1.50 4.00
OS2 Ilya Kovalchuk 1.25 3.00
OS3 Phil Kessel 1.00 2.50
OS4 Ryan Miller 1.00 2.50
OS5 Thomas Vanek 1.00 2.50
OS6 Jarome Iginla 2.00 5.00
OS7 Dion Phaneuf 1.50 4.00
OS8 Eric Staal 1.25 3.00
OS9 Patrick Kane 2.00 5.00
OS10 Jonathan Toews 2.50 6.00
OS11 Paul Stastny 1.00 2.50
OS12 Rick Nash 1.00 2.50
OS13 Steve Mason 1.50 4.00
OS14 Marty Turco .75 2.00
OS15 Mike Modano 1.00 2.50
OS16 Nicklas Lidstrom 1.25 3.00
OS17 Pavel Datsyuk 1.00 2.50
OS18 Henrik Zetterberg 2.00 5.00
OS19 Sam Gagner 1.25 3.00
OS20 Anze Kopitar 1.00 2.50
OS21 Drew Doughty 2.00 5.00
OS22 Marian Gaborik 1.50 4.00
OS23 Carey Price 2.50 6.00
OS24 Saku Koivu 1.00 2.50
OS25 Shea Weber .75 2.00
OS26 Martin Brodeur 2.50 6.00
OS27 Zach Parise 1.00 2.50
OS28 Rick DiPietro 1.00 2.50
OS29 Henrik Lundqvist 2.00 5.00
OS30 Jason Spezza 1.25 3.00
OS31 Dany Heatley 2.00 5.00
OS32 Mike Richards 2.00 5.00
OS33 Jeff Carter 1.00 2.50
OS34 Peter Mueller 1.25 3.00
OS35 Marc-Andre Fleury 1.00 2.50
OS36 Evgeni Malkin 2.50 6.00
OS37 Sidney Crosby 5.00 12.00
OS38 Joe Thornton 2.00 5.00
OS39 Vincent Lecavalier 1.25 3.00
OS40 Luke Schenn 1.50 4.00
OS41 Roberto Luongo 2.50 6.00
OS42 Alexander Ovechkin 4.00 10.00

2009-10 Upper Deck Victory Stars of the Game

COMPLETE SET (50) 20.00 50.00
STATED ODDS 1:4
SG1 Carey Price 1.25 3.00
SG2 Patrice Bergeron .50 1.25
SG3 Ilya Kovalchuk .60 1.50
SG4 Zach Parise .50 1.25
SG5 Vincent Lecavalier .60 1.50
SG6 Nicklas Lidstrom .60 1.50
SG7 Jean-Sebastien Giguere .50 1.25
SG8 Alexander Ovechkin 2.00 5.00
SG9 Joe Thornton 1.00 2.50
SG10 Patrick Kane 1.00 2.50
SG11 Marty Turco .40 1.00
SG12 Simon Gagne .50 1.25
SG13 Dany Heatley 1.00 2.50
SG14 Mats Sundin .50 1.25
SG15 Henrik Lundqvist .60 1.50
SG16 Eric Staal .60 1.50
SG17 Evgeni Malkin 1.25 3.00
SG18 Peter Mueller .60 1.50
SG19 Tomas Vokoun .50 1.25
SG20 Alex Kovalev .50 1.25
SG21 Henrik Zetterberg 1.00 2.50
SG22 Marian Gaborik .75 2.00
SG23 Martin Brodeur 1.25 3.00
SG24 Marc Savard .30 .75
SG25 Jarome Iginla 1.00 2.50
SG26 Vesa Toskala .50 1.25
SG27 Rick Nash .50 1.25
SG28 Pavel Datsyuk .50 1.25
SG29 Miikka Kiprusoff .50 1.25
SG30 Alex Tanguay .40 1.00
SG31 Patrick Marleau .50 1.25
SG32 Jonathan Toews 1.25 3.00
SG33 Roberto Luongo 1.25 3.00
SG34 Thomas Vanek .50 1.25
SG35 Martin St. Louis .50 1.25
SG36 Jason Spezza .60 1.50
SG37 Paul Stastny .50 1.25
SG38 Marc-Andre Fleury .50 1.25
SG39 Alexander Semin .50 1.25
SG40 Mike Richards 1.00 2.50
SG41 Ryan Getzlaf .75 2.00
SG42 Mike Modano .50 1.25
SG43 Steve Mason .75 2.00
SG44 Markus Naslund .50 1.25
SG45 Marian Hossa .75 2.00
SG46 Anze Kopitar .50 1.25
SG47 Rick DiPietro .50 1.25
SG48 Saku Koivu .50 1.25
SG49 Paul Kariya .50 1.25
SG50 Sidney Crosby 2.50 6.00

2010-11 Upper Deck Victory

COMPLETE SET (250)
COMP.SET w/o SPs (200) 12.00 30.00
STATED ODDS 1:2
1 Ryan Getzlaf .40 1.00
2 Jonas Hiller .30 .75
3 Corey Perry .25 .60
4 Bobby Ryan .30 .75
5 Lubomir Visnovsky .15 .40
6 Nik Antropov .20 .50
7 Zach Bogosian .30 .75
8 Evander Kane .60 1.50
9 Bryan Little .25 .60
10 Rich Peverley .15 .40
11 Patrice Bergeron .25 .60
12 Zdeno Chara .15 .40
13 David Krejci .20 .50
14 Milan Lucic .25 .60
15 Marc Savard .15 .40
16 Tim Thomas .25 .60
17 Blake Wheeler .30 .75
18 Tim Connolly .15 .40
19 Ryan Miller .25 .60
20 Tyler Myers .60 1.50
21 Jason Pominville .25 .60
22 Derek Roy .25 .60
23 Drew Stafford .25 .60
24 Thomas Vanek .25 .60
25 Erik Cole .15 .40
26 Jussi Jokinen .25 .60
27 Joni Pitkanen .20 .50
28 Eric Staal .30 .75
29 Brandon Sutter .25 .60
30 Cam Ward .25 .60
31 Jay Bouwmeester .25 .60
32 Rene Bourque .15 .40
33 Niklas Hagman .15 .40
34 Jarome Iginla .50 1.25
35 Miikka Kiprusoff .25 .60
36 Daymond Langkow .15 .40
37 Matt Stajan .20 .50
38 Marian Hossa .40 1.00
39 Patrick Kane .50 1.25
40 Duncan Keith .20 .50
41 Brent Seabrook .20 .50
42 Patrick Sharp .20 .50
43 Jonathan Toews .60 1.50
44 Kris Versteeg .30 .75
45 Derick Brassard .25 .60
46 Kristian Huselius .15 .40
47 Steve Mason .40 1.00
48 Rick Nash .25 .60
49 Antoine Vermette .15 .40
50 Jakub Voracek .25 .60
51 Craig Anderson .20 .50
52 Matt Duchene .60 1.50
53 T.J. Galiardi .20 .50
54 Milan Hejduk .25 .60
55 Ryan O'Reilly .30 .75
56 Paul Stastny .25 .60
57 Chris Stewart .25 .60
58 Jamie Benn .25 .60
59 Loui Eriksson .15 .40
60 Kari Lehtonen .25 .60
61 Brenden Morrow .20 .50
62 James Neal .25 .60
63 Mike Ribeiro .15 .40
64 Brad Richards .20 .50
65 Dan Cleary .25 .60
66 Pavel Datsyuk .25 .60
67 Johan Franzen .15 .40
68 Jim Howard .30 .75
69 Nicklas Lidstrom .30 .75
70 Brian Rafalski .15 .40
71 Henrik Zetterberg .50 1.25
72 Andrew Cogliano .30 .75
73 Sam Gagner .30 .75
74 Ales Hemsky .20 .50
75 Shawn Horcoff .15 .40
76 Nikolai Khabibulin .25 .60
77 Dustin Penner .15 .40
78 David Booth .15 .40
79 Michael Frolik .20 .50
80 Nathan Horton .15 .40
81 Cory Stillman .15 .40
82 Tomas Vokoun .25 .60
83 Stephen Weiss .15 .40
84 Dustin Brown .20 .50
85 Drew Doughty .50 1.25
86 Michal Handzus .15 .40
87 Anze Kopitar .25 .60
88 Jonathan Quick .40 1.00
89 Wayne Simmonds .25 .60
90 Ryan Smyth .25 .60
91 Niklas Backstrom .25 .60
92 Andrew Brunette .15 .40
93 Brent Burns .15 .40
94 Cal Clutterbuck .15 .40
95 Martin Havlat .20 .50
96 Mikko Koivu .25 .60
97 Guillaume Latendresse .20 .50
98 Mike Cammalleri .20 .50
99 Scott Gomez .25 .60
100 Brian Gionta .25 .60
101 Jaroslav Halak .50 1.25
102 Andrei Markov .20 .50
103 Tomas Plekanec .20 .50
104 Carey Price .50 1.25
105 Jason Arnott .15 .40
106 J.P. Dumont .15 .40
107 Martin Erat .25 .60
108 Patric Hornqvist .20 .50
109 Pekka Rinne .20 .50
110 Steve Sullivan .15 .40
111 Shea Weber .20 .50
112 Martin Brodeur .60 1.50
113 Patrik Elias .20 .50
114 Ilya Kovalchuk .30 .75
115 Jamie Langenbrunner .15 .40
116 Zach Parise .25 .60
117 Brian Rolston .15 .40
118 Travis Zajac .15 .40
119 Josh Bailey .20 .50
120 Blake Comeau .20 .50
121 Matt Moulson .15 .40
122 Kyle Okposo .25 .60
123 Mark Streit .15 .40
124 John Tavares 1.00 2.50
125 Ryan Callahan .15 .40
126 Chris Drury .20 .50
127 Brandon Dubinsky .20 .50
128 Marian Gaborik .40 1.00
129 Henrik Lundqvist .50 1.25
130 Vaclav Prospal .15 .40
131 Marc Staal .30 .75
132 Daniel Alfredsson .25 .60
133 Mike Fisher .15 .40
134 Alex Kovalev .25 .60
135 Filip Kuba .15 .40
136 Brian Elliott .15 .40
137 Milan Michalek .15 .40
138 Jason Spezza .30 .75
139 Daniel Briere .25 .60
140 Jeff Carter .25 .60
141 Claude Giroux .50 1.25
142 Scott Hartnell .15 .40
143 Chris Pronger .20 .50
144 Mike Richards .50 1.25
145 James van Riemsdyk .40 1.00
146 Ilya Bryzgalov .20 .50
147 Shane Doan .20 .50
148 Scottie Upshall .15 .40
149 Radim Vrbata .15 .40
150 Wojtek Wolski .15 .40
151 Keith Yandle .15 .40
152 Sidney Crosby 1.25 3.00
153 Marc-Andre Fleury .25 .60
154 Tyler Kennedy .25 .60
155 Kristopher Letang .20 .50
156 Evgeni Malkin .60 1.50
157 Jordan Staal .30 .75
158 Maxime Talbot .25 .60
159 Dan Boyle .15 .40
160 Ryane Clowe .15 .40
161 Dany Heatley .30 .75
162 Patrick Marleau .25 .60
163 Joe Pavelski .15 .40
164 Devin Setoguchi .20 .50
165 Joe Thornton .50 1.25
166 David Backes .25 .60
167 Brad Boyes .20 .50
168 Erik Johnson .20 .50
169 Andy McDonald .20 .50
170 T.J. Oshie .40 1.00
171 David Perron .20 .50
172 Steve Downie .15 .40
173 Victor Hedman .30 .75
174 Vincent Lecavalier .30 .75
175 Ryan Malone .15 .40
176 Martin St. Louis .25 .60
177 Steven Stamkos .75 2.00
178 Tyler Bozak .50 1.25
179 Jean-Sebastien Giguere .25 .60
180 Jonas Gustavsson .60 1.50
181 Phil Kessel .25 .60
182 Nikolai Kulemin .20 .50
183 Dion Phaneuf .30 .75
184 Luke Schenn .40 1.00
185 Alexandre Burrows .20 .50
186 Alexander Edler .15 .40
187 Ryan Kesler .20 .50
188 Roberto Luongo .60 1.50
189 Mason Raymond .15 .40
190 Daniel Sedin .30 .75
191 Henrik Sedin .40 1.00
192 Nicklas Backstrom .50 1.25
193 Tomas Fleischmann .15 .40
194 Mike Green .50 1.25
195 Mike Knuble .25 .60
196 Alexander Ovechkin 1.00 2.50
197 Alexander Semin .25 .60
198 Semyon Varlamov .50 1.25
199 Ryan Miller CL .25 .60
200 Steven Stamkos CL .75 2.00
201 Nick Bonino RC 1.00 2.50
202 Arturs Kulda RC 1.25 3.00
203 Andrew Bodnarchuk RC .60 1.50
204 Zach Hamill RC .75 2.00
205 Adam McQuaid RC .75 2.00
206 Jeff Penner RC .60 1.50
207 Jamie McBain RC .60 1.50
208 Jerome Samson RC 1.00 2.50
209 Justin Mercier RC .60 1.50
210 Brandon Yip RC 1.50 4.00
211 Grant Clitsome RC .75 2.00
212 Tomas Kana RC .60 1.50
213 Maxime Fortunus RC .75 2.00
214 Philip Larsen RC .60 1.50
215 Raymond Sawada RC .50 1.25
216 Dean Arsene RC 1.00 2.50
217 Johan Motin RC .60 1.50
218 Bryan Pitton RC .75 2.00
219 Alex Plante RC .75 2.00
220 Evgeny Dadonov RC 1.00 2.50
221 Mike Duco RC .60 1.50
222 Richard Clune RC 1.00 2.50
223 Cody Almond RC .75 2.00
224 Justin Falk RC .60 1.50
225 Maxim Noreau RC .60 1.50
226 Clayton Stoner RC 1.00 2.50
227 Casey Wellman RC .75 2.00
228 P.K. Subban RC 2.50 6.00
229 Brock Trotter RC 1.25 3.00
230 J.T. Wyman RC .75 2.00
231 Nick Spaling RC .50 1.25
232 Nick Palmieri RC .60 1.50
233 Dustin Kohn RC .50 1.25
234 Dylan Reese RC .60 1.50
235 Ilkka Heikkinen RC .75 2.00
236 Matt Zaba RC .75 2.00
237 Bobby Butler RC .60 1.50
238 Jared Cowen RC 1.00 2.50
239 Kaspars Daugavins RC 1.50 4.00
240 Derek Smith RC .50 1.25
241 Jeremy Duchesne RC .50 1.25
242 Nick Johnson RC .60 1.50
243 Alexander Pechurski RC 1.25 3.00
244 Eric Tangradi RC 1.00 2.50
245 John McCarthy RC .50 1.25
246 Dustin Tokarski RC .50 1.25
247 Brayden Irwin RC 1.00 2.50
248 Nazem Kadri RC 2.50 6.00
249 Evan Oberg RC 1.25 3.00
250 Kyle Wilson RC 1.25 3.00

2010-11 Upper Deck Victory Black

(1-200) STATED ODDS 1:720
(201-250) STATED ODDS 1:1440
NOT PRICED DUE TO SCARCITY

2010-11 Upper Deck Victory Gold

*GOLD: 4X TO 10X BASE
STATED ODDS 1:36
*GOLD RCs: 1.5X TO 4X BASE
RCs STATED ODDS 1:144

2010-11 Upper Deck Victory Red

*RED: 6X TO 15X BASE
*RED RCs: 4X TO 10X BASE

2010-11 Upper Deck Victory Game Breakers

COMPLETE SET (50) 25.00 50.00
STATED ODDS 1:2
GBAK Anze Kopitar .40 1.00
GBAO Alexander Ovechkin 1.50 4.00
GBAS Alexander Semin .40 1.00
GBBA Nicklas Backstrom .75 2.00
GBCP Corey Perry .40 1.00
GBDA Daniel Alfredsson .40 1.00
GBDD Drew Doughty .75 2.00
GBDH Dany Heatley .50 1.25
GBDR Derek Roy .40 1.00
GBDS Daniel Sedin .50 1.25
GBDU Pascal Dupuis .25 .60
GBEM Evgeni Malkin 1.00 2.50
GBES Eric Staal .50 1.25
GBGL Guillaume Latendresse .30 .75
GBHS Henrik Sedin .60 1.50
GBHZ Henrik Zetterberg .75 2.00
GBIK Ilya Kovalchuk .50 1.25
GBJC Jeff Carter .40 1.00
GBJI Jarome Iginla .75 2.00
GBJJ Jussi Jokinen .40 1.00
GBJT John Tavares 1.50 4.00
GBJV James van Riemsdyk .60 1.50
GBKA Patrick Kane .75 2.00
GBMC Mike Cammalleri .30 .75
GBMD Matt Duchene 1.00 2.50
GBMF Mike Fisher .25 .60
GBMG Marian Gaborik .60 1.50
GBMH Michal Handzus .25 .60
GBMK Mikko Koivu .40 1.00
GBMM Matt Moulson .25 .60
GBMR Mike Richards .75 2.00
GBMS Martin St. Louis .40 1.00
GBNB Nicklas Bergfors .30 .75
GBPB Patrice Bergeron .40 1.00
GBPD Pavel Datsyuk .40 1.00
GBPH Patric Hornqvist .30 .75
GBPK Phil Kessel .40 1.00
GBPM Patrick Marleau .40 1.00
GBRG Ryan Getzlaf .60 1.50
GBRM Ryan Malone .25 .60
GBRN Rick Nash .40 1.00
GBRP Rich Peverley .25 .60
GBSC Sidney Crosby 2.00 5.00
GBSD Shane Doan .30 .75
GBSS Steven Stamkos 1.25 3.00
GBTB Troy Brouwer .25 .60
GBTH Joe Thornton .75 2.00
GBTO Jonathan Toews 1.00 2.50
GBWW Wojtek Wolski .25 .60
GBZP Zach Parise .40 1.00

2010-11 Upper Deck Victory Stars of the Game

COMPLETE SET (50) 25.00 50.00
STATED ODDS 1:2
SOGAK Anze Kopitar .40 1.00
SOGAM Andrei Markov .30 .75
SOGAO Alexander Ovechkin 1.50 4.00
SOGBB Brad Boyes .30 .75
SOGBR Bobby Ryan .50 1.25
SOGCP Carey Price .75 2.00
SOGDA Daniel Alfredsson .40 1.00
SOGDD Drew Doughty .75 2.00
SOGDH Dany Heatley .50 1.25
SOGDS Daniel Sedin .50 1.25
SOGEM Evgeni Malkin 1.00 2.50
SOGES Eric Staal .50 1.25
SOGGA Marian Gaborik .60 1.50
SOGHL Henrik Lundqvist .75 2.00
SOGHS Henrik Sedin .60 1.50
SOGHZ Henrik Zetterberg .75 2.00
SOGIB Ilya Bryzgalov .30 .75
SOGJC Jeff Carter .40 1.00
SOGJI Jarome Iginla .75 2.00
SOGJS Jason Spezza .50 1.25
SOGJT John Tavares 1.50 4.00
SOGKE Phil Kessel .40 1.00
SOGMB Martin Brodeur 1.00 2.50
SOGMD Matt Duchene 1.00 2.50
SOGMF Marc-Andre Fleury .40 1.00
SOGMG Mike Green .75 2.00
SOGMK Mikko Koivu .40 1.00
SOGMR Mike Richards .75 2.00
SOGMS Martin St. Louis .40 1.00
SOGNB Nicklas Backstrom .75 2.00
SOGPB Patrice Bergeron .40 1.00
SOGPD Pavel Datsyuk .40 1.00
SOGPE Corey Perry .40 1.00
SOGPK Patrick Kane .75 2.00
SOGPR Chris Pronger .30 .75
SOGPS Paul Stastny .40 1.00
SOGRG Ryan Getzlaf .60 1.50
SOGRI Brad Richards .30 .75
SOGRL Roberto Luongo 1.00 2.50
SOGRM Ryan Miller .40 1.00
SOGRN Rick Nash .40 1.00
SOGSC Sidney Crosby 2.00 5.00
SOGSD Shane Doan .30 .75
SOGSS Steven Stamkos 1.25 3.00
SOGSW Shea Weber .30 .75
SOGTH Joe Thornton .75 2.00
SOGTM Tyler Myers 1.00 2.50
SOGTO Jonathan Toews 1.00 2.50
SOGZC Zdeno Chara .25 .60
SOGZP Zach Parise .40 1.00

2000-01 Upper Deck Vintage

Released in mid January 2001, Upper Deck Vintage is a 400-card set comprised of 340 regular cards, 30 prospect cards and 30 triple player team checklists. Base cards are thick cardboard with a throwback vintage design. Backgrounds are white with a colored nameplate along the bottom. Vintage was packaged in 24-pack boxes with packs containing 10 cards and carried a suggested retail price of $1.99. NOTE: The Curtis Joseph promo was handed out as a single to announce the upcoming arrival of the product. It is numbered 31 (the P was added on our end as a database sorter) and has the word sample written across the back.

COMPLETE SET (400) 30.00 60.00
1 German Titov .08 .20
2 Teemu Selanne .25 .60
3 Matt Cullen .08 .20
4 Oleg Tverdovsky .08 .20
5 Jean-Sebastien Giguere .20 .50
6 Guy Hebert .08 .20
7 Mike Leclerc .08 .20
8 Jason Marshall .08 .20
9 Paul Kariya .25 .60
10 Steve Rucchin .08 .20
11 Paul Kariya .25 .60
Guy Hebert
Teemu Selanne
12 Paul Kariya .25 .60
Guy Hebert
13 Patrik Stefan .08 .20
14 Damian Rhodes .08 .20
15 Donald Audette .08 .20
16 Yannick Tremblay .08 .20
17 Hnat Domenichelli .08 .20
18 Dean Sylvester .08 .20
19 Steve Guolla .08 .20
20 Petr Buzek .08 .20
21 Andrew Brunette .08 .20
22 Ray Ferraro .08 .20
23 Patrik Stefan .08 .20
Damian Rhodes
Denny Lambert
24 Patrik Stefan .08 .20
Damian Rhodes
25 Joe Thornton .40 1.00
26 Brian Rolston .08 .20
27 Kyle McLaren .08 .20
28 Sergei Samsonov .20 .50
29 Paul Coffey .25 .60
30 Andrei Kovalenko .08 .20
31 Jason Allison .08 .20
31P Curtis Joseph PROMO
32 Bill Guerin .20 .50
33 Byron Dafoe .08 .20
34 Mikko Eloranta .08 .20
35 Don Sweeney .08 .20
36 Joe Thornton .08 .20
Byron Dafoe
Kyle McLaren
37 Joe Thornton .08 .20
Byron Dafoe
38 Miroslav Satan .20 .50
39 Dominik Hasek .50 1.25
40 Stu Barnes .08 .20
41 Chris Gratton .08 .20
42 Doug Gilmour .20 .50
43 Curtis Brown .08 .20
44 James Patrick .08 .20
45 Alexei Zhitnik .08 .20
46 Rhett Warrener .08 .20
47 Dave Andreychuk .20 .50
48 Maxim Afinogenov .08 .20
49 Miroslav Satan .25 .60
Dominik Hasek
Rob Ray
50 Miroslav Satan .30 .75
Dominik Hasek
51 Valeri Bure .08 .20
52 Mike Vernon .20 .50
53 Marc Savard .08 .20
54 Clarke Wilm .08 .20
55 Phil Housley .08 .20
56 Fred Brathwaite .20 .50
57 Cory Stillman .08 .20
58 Derek Morris .08 .20
59 Robyn Regehr .08 .20
60 Jarome Iginla .30 .75
61 Valeri Bure .08 .20
Fred Brathwaite
Jason Wiemer
62 Valeri Bure .08 .20
Fred Brathwaite
63 Bates Battaglia .08 .20
64 Sandis Ozolinsh .08 .20
65 Jeff O'Neill .08 .20
66 Ron Francis .20 .50
67 Sami Kapanen .08 .20
68 Martin Gelinas .08 .20
69 Arturs Irbe .20 .50
70 Dave Tanabe .08 .20
71 Rod Brind'Amour .20 .50
72 Glen Wesley .08 .20
73 Jeff O'Neill .08 .20

Arturs Irbe
Ron Francis
74 Ron Francis .08 .20
Arturs Irbe
75 Tony Amonte .20 .50
76 Steve Sullivan .08 .20
77 Eric Daze .20 .50
78 Boris Mironov .08 .20
79 Jocelyn Thibault .20 .50
80 Jean-Yves Leroux .08 .20
81 Valeri Zelepukin .08 .20
82 Alexei Zhamnov .08 .20
83 Josef Marha .08 .20
84 Michael Nylander .08 .20
85 Tony Amonte .08 .20
Jocelyn Thibault
Bob Probert
86 Tony Amonte .08 .20
Jocelyn Thibault
87 Patrick Roy 1.25 3.00
88 Joe Sakic .50 1.25
89 Jon Klemm .08 .20
90 Adam Deadmarsh .08 .20
91 Ray Bourque .50 1.25
92 Peter Forsberg .60 1.50
93 Milan Hejduk .25 .60
94 Chris Drury .20 .50
95 Alex Tanguay .20 .50
96 Adam Foote .08 .20
97 Dave Reid .08 .20
98 Joe Sakic .60 1.50
Patrick Roy
Raymond Bourque
99 Joe Sakic .60 1.50
Patrick Roy
100 Marc Denis .20 .50
101 Geoff Sanderson .08 .20
102 Ron Tugnutt .20 .50
103 Lyle Odelein .08 .20
104 Krzysztof Oliwa .08 .20
105 Kevyn Adams .08 .20
106 Steve Heinze .08 .20
107 Jamie Pushor .08 .20
108 Bruce Gardiner .08 .20
109 Jan Caloun .08 .20
110 Kevyn Adams .08 .20
Marc Denis
Krzysztof Oliwa
111 Geoff Sanderson .08 .20
Ron Tugnutt
112 Mike Modano .40 1.00
113 Jere Lehtinen .20 .50
114 Brett Hull .30 .75
115 Sergei Zubov .08 .20
116 Jamie Langenbrunner .08 .20
117 Shaun Van Allen .08 .20
118 Ed Belfour .25 .60
119 Brenden Morrow .20 .50
120 Darryl Sydor .08 .20
121 Joe Nieuwendyk .20 .50
122 Derian Hatcher .08 .20
123 Mike Modano .08 .20
Ed Belfour
Derian Hatcher
124 M.Modano/E.Belfour .25 .60
125 Steve Yzerman 1.25 3.00
126 Nicklas Lidstrom .25 .60
127 Sergei Fedorov .40 1.00
128 Chris Osgood .20 .50
129 Brendan Shanahan .25 .60
130 Larry Murphy .08 .20
131 Darren McCarty .08 .20
132 Chris Chelios .25 .60
133 Kris Draper .08 .20
134 Tomas Holmstrom .08 .20
135 Slava Kozlov .08 .20
136 Steve Yzerman 1.00 2.50
Chris Osgood
Brendan Shanahan
137 Steve Yzerman 1.00 2.50
Chris Osgood
138 Doug Weight .20 .50
139 Todd Marchant .08 .20
140 Eric Brewer .08 .20
141 Mike Grier .08 .20
142 Tom Poti .08 .20
143 Ryan Smyth .08 .20
144 Tommy Salo .20 .50
145 Janne Niinimaa .08 .20
146 Daniel Cleary .08 .20
147 Bill Guerin .20 .50
148 Doug Weight .08 .20
Tommy Salo
Georges Laraque
149 Doug Weight .08 .20
Tommy Salo
150 Pavel Bure .25 .60
151 Ray Whitney .08 .20
152 Viktor Kozlov .08 .20
153 Igor Larionov .08 .20
154 Scott Mellanby .08 .20
155 Trevor Kidd .20 .50
156 Rob Niedermayer .20 .50
157 Robert Svehla .08 .20
158 Roberto Luongo .30 .75
159 Mike Sillinger .08 .20
160 Pavel Bure .25 .60
Roberto Luongo
Peter Worrell
161 Pavel Bure .25 .60
Trevor Kidd
162 Zigmund Palffy .20 .50
163 Luc Robitaille .20 .50
164 Stephane Fiset .08 .20
165 Rob Blake .20 .50
166 Bryan Smolinski .08 .20
167 Glen Murray .08 .20
168 Mattias Norstrom .08 .20
169 Jamie Storr .20 .50
170 Craig Johnson .08 .20
171 Nelson Emerson .08 .20
172 Zigmund Palffy .08 .20
Jamie Storr
Rob Blake
173 Luc Robitaille .08 .20
Stephane Fiset
174 Stacy Roest .08 .20
175 Manny Fernandez .20 .50
176 Jim Dowd .08 .20
177 Curtis Leschyshyn .08 .20
178 Jeff Nielsen .08 .20
179 Aaron Gavey .08 .20
180 Sergei Krivokrasov .08 .20
181 Brad Bombardir .08 .20
182 Cam Stewart .08 .20
183 Scott Pellerin .08 .20
184 Pellerin/Frnandz/Gaborik CL .20 .50
185 Sergei Krivokrasov .08 .20
Manny Fernandez
186 Saku Koivu .25 .60
187 Eric Weinrich .08 .20
188 Sergei Zholtok .08 .20
189 Dainius Zubrus .08 .20
190 Brian Savage .08 .20
191 Jeff Hackett .08 .20
192 Patrick Poulin .08 .20
193 Jose Theodore .30 .75
194 Christian Laflamme .08 .20
195 Martin Rucinsky .08 .20
196 Linden/Theodore/Koivu CL .25 .60
197 S.Koivu/J.Theodore .25 .60
198 Greg Johnson .08 .20
199 Cliff Ronning .08 .20
200 Drake Berehowsky .08 .20
201 Mike Dunham .08 .20
202 David Legwand .20 .50
203 Tom Fitzgerald .08 .20
204 Patric Kjellberg .08 .20
205 Scott Walker .08 .20
206 Kimmo Timonen .08 .20
207 Bill Houlder .08 .20
208 David Legwand .08 .20
Mike Dunham
Todd Fitzgerald
209 David Legwand .08 .20
Mike Dunham
210 Scott Stevens .20 .50
211 Martin Brodeur .60 1.50
212 Jason Arnott .08 .20
213 Patrik Elias .20 .50
214 Alexander Mogilny .20 .50
215 Scott Gomez .08 .20
216 John Madden .08 .20
217 Bobby Holik .08 .20
218 Petr Sykora .08 .20
219 Ken Sutton .08 .20
220 Randy McKay .08 .20
221 Scott Gomez .25 .60
Martin Brodeur
Scott Stevens
222 Scott Gomez .30 .75
Martin Brodeur
223 Tim Connolly .08 .20
224 Kevin Haller .08 .20
225 Brad Isbister .20 .50
226 Mariusz Czerkawski .08 .20
227 Roman Hamrlik .08 .20
228 Claude Lapointe .08 .20
229 Bill Muckalt .08 .20
230 John Vanbiesbrouck .20 .50
231 Kenny Jonsson .08 .20
232 Mark Parrish .08 .20
233 Tim Connolly .08 .20
John Vanbiesbrouck
Kenny Jonsson
234 Tim Connolly .08 .20
John Vanbiesbrouck
235 Theo Fleury .08 .20
236 Brian Leetch .20 .50
237 Mark Messier .25 .60
238 Adam Graves .08 .20
239 Mike Richter .25 .60
240 Vladimir Malakhov .08 .20
241 Mike York .08 .20
242 Radek Dvorak .08 .20
243 Petr Nedved .08 .20
244 Jan Hlavac .08 .20
245 Tim Taylor .08 .20
246 Mark Messier .25 .60
Mike Richter
Adam Graves
247 Mark Messier .25 .60
Mike Richter
248 Radek Bonk .08 .20
249 Marian Hossa .25 .60
250 Jason York .08 .20
251 Wade Redden .08 .20
252 Patrick Lalime .20 .50
253 Daniel Alfredsson .20 .50
254 Shawn McEachern .08 .20
255 Sami Salo .08 .20
256 Petr Schastlivy .08 .20
257 Vaclav Prospal .08 .20
258 Alexei Yashin .10 .30
Patrick Lalime
Marian Hossa
259 Marian Hossa .10 .30
Patrick Lalime
260 John LeClair .25 .60
261 Rick Tocchet .08 .20
262 Daymond Langkow .20 .50
263 Simon Gagne .25 .60
264 Keith Primeau .08 .20
265 Eric Desjardins .20 .50
266 Brian Boucher .25 .60
267 Andy Delmore .08 .20
268 Mark Recchi .20 .50
269 Keith Jones .08 .20
270 Chris Therien .08 .20
271 John LeClair .25 .60
Brian Boucher
Rick Tocchet
272 John LeClair .20 .60
Brian Boucher
273 Jeremy Roenick .30 .75
274 Teppo Numminen .08 .20
275 Brad May .08 .20
276 Keith Tkachuk .25 .60
277 Trevor Letowski .08 .20
278 Shane Doan .08 .20
279 Jyrki Lumme .08 .20
280 Joe Juneau .08 .20
281 Sean Burke .20 .50
282 Travis Green .08 .20
283 Jeremy Roenick .10 .30
Sean Burke
Keith Tkachuk
284 Keith Tkachuk .10 .30
Sean Burke
285 Jean-Sebastien Aubin .20 .50
286 Jaromir Jagr .40 1.00
287 Alexei Morozov .08 .20
288 Josef Beranek .08 .20
289 Jan Hrdina .08 .20
290 Milan Kraft .08 .20
291 Alexei Kovalev .20 .50
292 Robert Lang .08 .20
293 Janne Laukkanen .08 .20
294 Martin Straka .08 .20
295 Jaromir Jagr .25 .60
Jean-Sebastien Aubin
Darius Kasparaitis
296 Jaromir Jagr .20 .50
Jean-Sebastien Aubin
297 Niklas Sundstrom .08 .20
298 Owen Nolan .20 .50
299 Jeff Friesen .08 .20
300 Vincent Damphousse .08 .20
301 Brad Stuart .20 .50
302 Marco Sturm .08 .20
303 Alexander Korolyuk .08 .20
304 Mike Ricci .08 .20
305 Patrick Marleau .20 .50
306 Steve Shields .20 .50
307 Jeff Friesen .08 .20
Steve Shields
Owen Nolan
308 Jeff Friesen .08 .20
Steve Shields
309 Chris Pronger .20 .50
310 Pavol Demitra .20 .50
311 Marty Reasoner .08 .20
312 Jochen Hecht .08 .20
313 Michal Handzus .08 .20
314 Al MacInnis .20 .50
315 Roman Turek .20 .50
316 Lubos Bartecko .08 .20
317 Jamal Mayers .08 .20
318 Dallas Drake .08 .20
319 Pierre Turgeon .20 .50
320 Pavol Demitra .08 .20
Roman Turek
Chris Pronger
321 Chris Pronger .08 .20
Roman Turek
322 Vincent Lecavalier .25 .60
323 Mike Johnson .08 .20
324 Brad Richards .08 .20
325 Dan Cloutier .08 .20
326 Paul Mara .08 .20
327 Fredrik Modin .08 .20
328 Bryan Muir .08 .20
329 Jassen Cullimore .08 .20
330 Todd Warriner .08 .20
331 Petr Svoboda .08 .20
332 Vincent Lecavalier .10 .30
Dan Cloutier
Petr Svoboda
333 Vincent Lecavalier .10 .30
Dan Cloutier
334 Mats Sundin .25 .60
335 Sergei Berezin .08 .20
336 Nikolai Antropov .20 .50
337 Steve Thomas .08 .20
338 Curtis Joseph .25 .60
339 Jonas Hoglund .08 .20
340 Dimitri Yushkevich .08 .20
341 Darcy Tucker .08 .20
342 Gary Roberts .08 .20
343 Jeff Farkas .08 .20
344 Tie Domi .20 .50
345 Mats Sundin .15 .40
Curtis Joseph
Tie Domi
346 Mats Sundin .15 .40
Curtis Joseph
347 Markus Naslund .25 .60
348 Brendan Morrison .20 .50
349 Todd Bertuzzi .25 .60
350 Adrian Aucoin .08 .20
351 Donald Brashear .08 .20
352 Murray Baron .08 .20
353 Daniel Sedin .08 .20
354 Andrew Cassels .08 .20
355 Henrik Sedin .08 .20
356 Mattias Ohlund .08 .20
357 Markus Naslund .08 .20
Felix Potvin
Donald Brashear
358 Markus Naslund .08 .20
Felix Potvin
359 Chris Simon .08 .20
360 Olaf Kolzig .25 .60
361 Jeff Halpern .08 .20
362 Andrei Nikolishin .08 .20
363 Steve Konowalchuk .08 .20
364 Peter Bondra .25 .60
365 Adam Oates .20 .50
366 Richard Zednik .08 .20
367 Sergei Gonchar .08 .20
368 Brendan Witt .08 .20
369 Peter Bondra .08 .20
Olaf Kolzig
Chris Simon
370 Adam Oates .08 .20
Olaf Kolzig
371 Rostislav Klesla RC .60 1.50
372 Jonas Ronnqvist RC .40 1.00
373 Eric Nickulas RC .40 1.00
374 Andrew Raycroft RC 2.00 5.00
375 Jeff Cowan RC .40 1.00
376 Reto Von Arx RC .40 1.00
377 Serge Aubin RC .40 1.00
378 Tyler Bouck RC .40 1.00
379 Michel Riesen RC .40 1.00
380 Eric Belanger RC .40 1.00
381 Marian Gaborik RC 2.50 6.00
382 Scott Hartnell RC .60 1.50
383 Greg Classen RC .40 1.00
384 Willie Mitchell RC .40 1.00
385 Colin White RC .40 1.00
386 Steve Valiquette RC .40 1.00
387 Jani Hurme RC .60 1.50
388 Martin Havlat RC 2.00 5.00
389 Justin Williams RC .60 1.50
390 Petr Hubacek RC .40 1.00
391 Roman Simicek RC .40 1.00
392 Matt Elich RC .40 1.00
393 Brent Sopel RC .40 1.00
394 Marc-Andre Thinel RC .40 1.00
395 Zdenek Blatny RC .40 1.00
396 Michael Ryder RC 5.00 12.00
397 Jason Jaspers RC .40 1.00
398 Jordan Krestanovich RC .40 1.00
399 Fedor Fedorov RC .40 1.00
400 Jeff Bateman RC .40 1.00

2000-01 Upper Deck Vintage All UD Team

COMPLETE SET (10) 6.00 15.00
STATED ODDS 1:23
UD1 Patrick Roy 2.00 5.00
UD2 Martin Brodeur 1.00 2.50
UD3 Chris Pronger .25 .60
UD4 Ray Bourque .75 2.00
UD5 Paul Kariya .25 .60
UD6 John LeClair .50 1.25
UD7 Steve Yzerman 2.00 5.00
UD8 Peter Forsberg 1.00 2.50
UD9 Jaromir Jagr .60 1.50
UD10 Pavel Bure .50 1.25

2000-01 Upper Deck Vintage Dynasty: A Piece of History

Randomly inserted in packs at the rate of 1:72, this 11-card set features two swatches of game worn jerseys from some of the NHL's most dominating teams and player combinations. Two player photos are pictured in the middle of the card's horizontal design with jersey swatches on the outsides. Gold parallels to this set were also created and inserted randomly, these cards were numbered to just 50.

*MULTI-COLOR SWATCH: 1X TO 1.5X
*GOLD: 1X TO 1.5X BASIC CARDS
BG Bob Bourne 8.00 20.00
Clark Gillies
BK Mike Bossy 8.00 20.00
Anders Kallur
GC Butch Goring 8.00 20.00
Billy Carroll
GH Clark Gillies 8.00 20.00
Mats Hallin
GK Wayne Gretzky 60.00 150.00
Mark Messier
LJ Mario Lemieux 25.00 60.00
Jaromir Jagr
LL Pat Lafontaine 8.00 20.00
Dave Langevin
NS Bobby Nystrom 8.00 20.00
Brent Sutter
PR Denis Potvin 12.50 30.00
Chico Resch
TP Bryan Trottier 8.00 20.00
Stefan Persson
YO Steve Yzerman 15.00 40.00
Chris Osgood

2000-01 Upper Deck Vintage Great Gloves

COMPLETE SET (20) 4.00 10.00
STATED ODDS 1:12
GG1 Guy Hebert .40 1.00
GG2 Byron Dafoe .40 1.00
GG3 Dominik Hasek 1.25 2.50
GG4 Fred Brathwaite .40 1.00
GG5 Arturs Irbe .40 1.00
GG6 Patrick Roy 2.50 6.00
GG7 Ed Belfour .50 1.25
GG8 Chris Osgood .40 1.00
GG9 Tommy Salo .40 1.00
GG10 Trevor Kidd .40 1.00
GG11 Jose Theodore .60 1.50
GG12 Mike Richter .40 1.00
GG13 Brian Boucher .40 1.00
GG14 Jean-Sebastien Aubin .40 1.00
GG15 Steve Shields .40 1.00
GG16 Roman Turek .40 1.00
GG17 Dan Cloutier .40 1.00
GG18 Curtis Joseph .50 1.25
GG19 Felix Potvin .50 1.25
GG20 Olaf Kolzig .40 1.00

2000-01 Upper Deck Vintage Messier Heroes of Hockey

Randomly inserted in packs at the rate of 1:23, this 10-card set pays tribute to Mark Messier. Base cards are while bordered with an action photo set inside the NHL logo shield. The bottom of the card features a blue box containing the Mark Messier Heroes of Hockey logo.

COMPLETE SET (10) 10.00 20.00
COMMON MESSIER 1.25 3.00

2000-01 Upper Deck Vintage National Heroes

Randomly inserted in packs at the rate of 1:4, this 20-card set features top NHL players in action on a card with each respective player's home country flag set against a yellow background.

COMPLETE SET (20) 6.00 15.00
NH1 Paul Kariya .25 .60
NH2 Teemu Selanne .25 .60
NH3 Patrik Stefan .20 .50
NH4 Sergei Samsonov .20 .50
NH5 Dominik Hasek .50 1.25
NH6 Valeri Bure .20 .50
NH7 Tony Amonte .20 .50
NH8 Patrick Roy 1.25 3.00
NH9 Peter Forsberg .60 1.50
NH10 Mike Modano .40 1.00
NH11 Steve Yzerman 1.25 3.00
NH12 Pavel Bure .30 .75
NH13 Saku Koivu .25 .60
NH14 Martin Brodeur .60 1.50
NH15 Scott Gomez .20 .50
NH16 Mark Messier .30 .75
NH17 John LeClair .30 .75
NH18 Jeremy Roenick .30 .75
NH19 Jaromir Jagr .40 1.00
NH20 Mats Sundin .25 .60

2000-01 Upper Deck Vintage Original 6: A Piece of History

Randomly inserted in packs at the rate of 1:72, this six card set features six top players from yesterday and today, each representing one of the NHL's original six teams. Cards have player action shots and a circular jersey swatch in the middle of the number six on the right side of the card front. Gold parallels to this set were also created and inserted randomly, these cards were limited to just 67 sets.

*MULTI-COLOR SWATCH: 1X TO 1.5X
STATED ODDS 1:72
*GOLD: 1.5X TO 3X BASIC CARDS
OCJ Curtis Joseph 6.00 15.00
OJT Jose Theodore 8.00 20.00
OMY Mike York 6.00 15.00
OSS Sergei Samsonov 6.00 15.00
OSY Steve Yzerman 12.50 30.00
OTE Tony Esposito 10.00 25.00

2000-01 Upper Deck Vintage Star Tandems

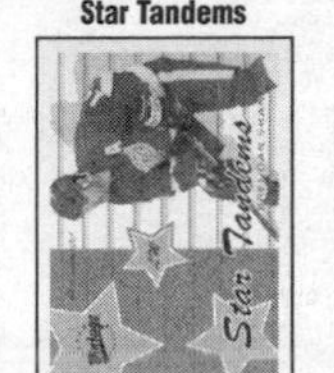

COMPLETE SET (10) 10.00 20.00
STATED ODDS 1:23
S1A Paul Kariya .50 1.25
S1B Teemu Selanne .50 1.25
S2A Joe Sakic .75 2.00
S2B Patrick Roy 2.00 5.00
S3A Steve Yzerman 2.00 5.00
S3B Brendan Shanahan .60 1.50
S4A Scott Gomez .50 1.25
S4B Martin Brodeur 1.00 2.50
S5A John LeClair .50 1.25
S5B Brian Boucher .50 1.25

2001-02 Upper Deck Vintage

Issued in late-December 2001, this 300-card set carried an SRP of $1.99 for a 10-card pack.

COMPLETE SET (300) 40.00 80.00
1 Jean-Sebastien Giguere .20 .50
2 Jeff Friesen .08 .20
3 Paul Kariya .25 .60
4 Oleg Tverdovsky .08 .20
5 Steve Rucchin .08 .20
6 Mike Leclerc .08 .20
7 Dan Bylsma .08 .20
8 Paul Kariya .25 .60
9 Paul Kariya .08 .20
Mike Leclerc
Oleg Tverdovsky
Marty McInnis
10 Patrik Stefan .08 .20
11 Tomi Kallio .08 .20
12 Chris Tamer .08 .20
13 Milan Hnilicka .20 .50
14 Ray Ferraro .08 .20
15 Stephen Guolla .08 .20
16 Ray Ferraro .08 .20
17 Patrik Stefan .08 .20
Ray Ferraro
Milan Hnilicka
Tommi Kallio
18 Kyle McLaren .08 .20
19 Brian Rolston .08 .20
20 Byron Dafoe .20 .50
21 Mikko Eloranta .08 .20
22 Sergei Samsonov .20 .50
23 Joe Thornton .40 1.00
24 Bill Guerin .20 .50
25 Joe Thornton .40 1.00
26 Bill Guerin .08 .20
Joe Thornton
Sergei Samsonov
Byron Dafoe
27 Martin Biron .20 .50
28 Maxim Afinogenov .08 .20
29 J-P Dumont .08 .20
30 Chris Gratton .08 .20
31 Rhett Warrener .08 .20
32 Miroslav Satan .20 .50
33 Curtis Brown .08 .20
34 Miroslav Satan .20 .50
35 Chris Gratton .08 .20
Miroslav Satan
J.P. Dumont
Curtis Brown
36 Marc Savard .08 .20
37 Jarome Iginla .30 .75
38 Derek Morris .08 .20
39 Oleg Saprykin .08 .20
40 Jeff Shantz .08 .20
41 Craig Conroy .08 .20
42 Jarome Iginla .30 .75
43 Marc Savard .25 .60
Derek Morris
Jarome Iginla
Oleg Saprykin
44 Jeff O'Neill .08 .20
45 Arturs Irbe .20 .50
46 Shane Willis .08 .20
47 Dave Tanabe .08 .20
48 Rod Brind'Amour .20 .50
49 Sami Kapanen .08 .20
50 Ron Francis .20 .50
51 Jeff O'Neill .08 .20
52 Arturs Irbe .08 .20
Sami Kapanen
Jeff O'Neill
Rod Brind'Amour
53 Eric Daze .20 .50
54 Alexei Zhamnov .08 .20
55 Jaroslav Spacek .08 .20
56 Michael Nylander .08 .20
57 Tony Amonte .20 .50
58 Steve Sullivan .08 .20
59 Kevin Dean .08 .20
60 Steve Sullivan .08 .20
61 Tony Amonte .08 .20
Eric Daze
Alexei Zhamnov
Steve Sullivan
62 Chris Drury .20 .50
63 Rob Blake .20 .50
64 Joe Sakic .50 1.25
65 Peter Forsberg .60 1.50
66 Ray Bourque .50 1.25
67 Milan Hejduk .25 .60
68 Patrick Roy 1.25 3.00
69 Joe Sakic .50 1.25
70 Patrick Roy .25 .60
Joe Sakic
Peter Forsberg
Milan Hejduk
71 Ron Tugnutt .20 .50
72 Geoff Sanderson .08 .20
73 Espen Knutsen .08 .20
74 Tyler Wright .08 .20
75 Rostislav Klesla .08 .20
76 Jamie Heward .08 .20
77 Geoff Sanderson .08 .20
78 Ron Tugnutt .08 .20
Espen Knutsen
Geoff Sanderson
Rostislav Klesla
79 Mike Modano .40 1.00
80 Ed Belfour .25 .60
81 Pierre Turgeon .20 .50
82 Joe Nieuwendyk .20 .50
83 Sergei Zubov .08 .20
84 Jere Lehtinen .20 .50
85 Donald Audette .08 .20
86 Mike Modano .40 1.00
87 Mike Modano .08 .20
Ed Belfour
Joe Nieuwendyk
Sergei Zubov
88 Steve Yzerman 1.25 3.00
89 Brendan Shanahan .25 .60
90 Sergei Fedorov .40 1.00
91 Luc Robitaille .20 .50
92 Dominik Hasek .50 1.25
93 Nicklas Lidstrom .25 .60
94 Darren McCarty .08 .20
95 Brendan Shanahan .40 1.00
96 Steve Yzerman .25 .60
Nicklas Lidstrom
Brendan Shanahan
Tomas Holmstrom
97 Tommy Salo .20 .50
98 Mike Comrie .20 .50
99 Tom Poti .08 .20
100 Mike Grier .08 .20
101 Janne Niinimaa .08 .20
102 Ryan Smyth .08 .20
103 Anson Carter .20 .50
104 Ryan Smyth .08 .20
105 Tommy Salo .08 .20
Mike Comrie
Ryan Smyth
Tom Poti
106 Pavel Bure .25 .60
107 Viktor Kozlov .08 .20
108 Marcus Nilsson .08 .20
109 Denis Shvidki .08 .20
110 Bret Hedican .08 .20
111 Roberto Luongo .30 .75
112 Pavel Bure .40 1.00
113 Pavel Bure .25 .60
Roberto Luongo
Viktor Kozlov
Marcus Nilsson
114 Zigmund Palffy .20 .50
115 Felix Potvin .25 .60
116 Adam Deadmarsh .08 .20
117 Glen Murray .08 .20
118 Eric Belanger .08 .20
119 Jason Holland .08 .20
120 Jozef Stumpel .08 .20
121 Zigmund Palffy .20 .50
122 Felix Potvin .08 .20
Zigmund Palffy
Adam Deadmarsh
Jozef Stumpel
123 Marian Gaborik .50 1.25
124 Manny Fernandez .20 .50
125 Brad Bombardir .08 .20
126 Lubomir Sekeras .08 .20
127 Wes Walz .08 .20
128 Antti Laaksonen .08 .20
129 Marian Gaborik .50 1.25
130 Wild CL .08 .20
131 Saku Koivu .25 .60
132 Oleg Petrov .08 .20
133 Martin Rucinsky .08 .20
134 Jose Theodore .30 .75
135 Brian Savage .08 .20
136 Andrei Markov .08 .20
137 Richard Zednik .08 .20
138 Saku Koivu .25 .60
139 Andre Savage .25 .60
Jose Theodore
Martin Rucinsky
Saku Koivu
140 David Legwand .20 .50
141 Mike Dunham .20 .50
142 Scott Walker .08 .20
143 Cliff Ronning .08 .20
144 Patric Kjellberg .08 .20
145 Greg Johnson .08 .20
146 Vitali Yachmenev .08 .20
147 Cliff Ronning .08 .20
148 Mike Dunham .08 .20
David Legwand
Scott Walker
Cliff Ronning
149 Martin Brodeur .60 1.50
150 Patrik Elias .20 .50
151 Jason Arnott .08 .20
152 Scott Niedermayer .08 .20
153 Petr Sykora .08 .20
154 Scott Gomez .08 .20
155 Scott Stevens .20 .50
156 Patrik Elias .20 .50
157 Martin Brodeur .08 .20
Scott Stevens
Jason Arnott
Bobby Holik
158 Michael Peca .08 .20
159 Rick DiPietro .20 .50
160 Mariusz Czerkawski .08 .20
161 Roman Hamrlik .08 .20
162 Dave Scatchard .08 .20
163 Brad Isbister .08 .20
164 Mark Parrish .08 .20
165 Rick DiPietro .08 .20
Mariusz Czerkawski
Roman Hamrlik
Dave Scatchard
166 Mark Messier .25 .60
167 Theo Fleury .08 .20
168 Mike Richter .25 .60
169 Brian Leetch .20 .50
170 Kim Johnsson .08 .20

171 Radek Dvorak .08 .20
172 Theo Fleury .08 .20
173 Mark Messier .08 .20
Brian Leetch
Mike Richter
Theo Fleury
174 Marian Hossa .25 .60
175 Radek Bonk .08 .20
176 Martin Havlat .20 .50
177 Daniel Alfredsson .20 .50
178 Magnus Arvedson .08 .20
179 Patrick Lalime .20 .50
180 Shawn McEachern .08 .20
181 Radek Bonk .08 .20
182 Marian Hossa .08 .20
Daniel Alfredsson
Radek Bonk
Magnus Arvedson
183 Jeremy Roenick .30 .75
184 Roman Cechmanek .20 .50
185 Keith Primeau .08 .20
186 John LeClair .25 .60
187 Kent Manderville .08 .20
188 Mark Recchi .20 .50
189 Eric Desjardins .08 .20
190 Mark Recchi .20 .50
191 Keith Primeau .08 .20
John LeClair
Roman Cechmanek
Mark Recchi
192 Sean Burke .20 .50
193 Shane Doan .08 .20
194 Michal Handzus .08 .20
195 Teppo Numminen .08 .20
196 Ladislav Nagy .08 .20
197 Landon Wilson .08 .20
198 Sean Burke .20 .50
199 Michal Handzus .08 .20
Sean Burke
Shane Doan
Teppo Numminen
200 Alexei Kovalev .20 .50
201 Mario Lemieux 1.50 4.00
202 Johan Hedberg .20 .50
203 Robert Lang .08 .20
204 Martin Straka .08 .20
205 Andrew Ference .08 .20
206 Kevin Stevens .08 .20
207 Alexei Kovalev .20 .50
208 Mario Lemieux .08 .20
Alexei Kovalev
Martin Straka
Johan Hedberg
209 Evgeni Nabokov .20 .50
210 Teemu Selanne .25 .60
211 Owen Nolan .20 .50
212 Mike Ricci .08 .20
213 Scott Thornton .08 .20
214 Vincent Damphousse .08 .20
215 Brad Stuart .08 .20
216 Evgeni Nabokov .20 .50
217 Owen Nolan .08 .20
Teemu Selanne
Vincent Damphousse
Brad Stuart
218 Chris Pronger .20 .50
219 Keith Tkachuk .25 .60
220 Doug Weight .20 .50
221 Pavol Demitra .20 .50
222 Cory Stillman .08 .20
223 Al MacInnis .20 .50
224 Bryce Salvador .08 .20
225 Scott Young .08 .20
226 Chris Pronger .08 .20
Pavol Demitra
Keith Tkachuk
Al MacInnis
227 Brad Richards .20 .50
228 Vincent Lecavalier .25 .60
229 Nikolai Khabibulin .25 .60
230 Fredrik Modin .08 .20
231 Martin St. Louis .20 .50
232 Pavel Kubina .08 .20
233 Brad Richards .20 .50
234 Vincent Lecavalier .08 .20
Brad Richards
Fredrik Modin
Nikolai Khabibulin
235 Curtis Joseph .25 .60
236 Mats Sundin .25 .60
237 Shayne Corson .08 .20
238 Darcy Tucker .08 .20
239 Nikolai Antropov .08 .20
240 Gary Roberts .08 .20
241 Bryan McCabe .08 .20
242 Mats Sundin .25 .60
243 Curtis Joseph .08 .20
Darcy Tucker
Mats Sundin
Gary Roberts
244 Markus Naslund .25 .60
245 Daniel Sedin .08 .20
246 Peter Schaefer .08 .20
247 Andrew Cassels .08 .20
248 Brendan Morrison .20 .50
249 Todd Bertuzzi .25 .60
250 Markus Naslund .25 .60
251 Marcus Naslund .08 .20
Daniel Sedin
Henrik Sedin
Todd Bertuzzi
252 Steve Konowalchuk .08 .20
253 Sergei Gonchar .08 .20
254 Calle Johansson .08 .20
255 Peter Bondra .25 .60
256 Jaromir Jagr .40 1.00
257 Olaf Kolzig .20 .50
258 Andrei Nikolishin .08 .20
259 Olaf Kolzig .20 .50
260 Peter Bondra .08 .20
Olaf Kolzig
Sergei Gonchar
Steve Konowalchuk
261 Pavel Bure .40 1.00
Joe Sakic
Jaromir Jagr
262 Jaromir Jagr .40 1.00
Adam Oates
Martin Straka
263 Jaromir Jagr .40 1.00
Joe Sakic
Patrik Elias
264 Peter Bondra .40 1.00
Pavel Bure
Joe Sakic
265 Joe Sakic .40 1.00
Patrik Elias
Scott Stevens
266 Matthew Barnaby .40 1.00
Peter Worrell
Stu Grimson
267 M.Brodeur/P.Roy/D.Hasek 1.50 4.00
268 Roman Cechmanek .40 1.00
Manny Legace
Marty Turco
269 Mike Dunham .40 1.00
SeanBurke
Marty Turco
270 Dominik Hasek .40 1.00
Roman Cechmanek
Martin Brodeur
271 Timo Parssinen RC 1.50 4.00
272 Ilja Bryzgalov RC 1.50 4.00
273 Kevin Sawyer RC 1.50 4.00
274 Kamil Piros RC 1.50 4.00
275 Ilya Kovalchuk RC 2.00 5.00
276 Brian Pothier RC 1.50 4.00
277 Zdenek Kutlak RC 1.50 4.00
278 Vaclav Nedorost RC 1.50 4.00
279 Jaroslav Obsut RC 1.50 4.00
280 Niko Kapanen RC .40 1.00
281 Kristian Huselius RC 1.50 4.00
282 Jaroslav Bednar RC 1.50 4.00
283 Martin Erat RC 1.50 4.00
284 Josef Boumedienne RC 1.50 4.00
285 Scott Clemmensen RC 1.50 4.00
286 Andreas Salomonsson RC 1.50 4.00
287 Radek Martinek RC 1.50 4.00
288 Mikael Samuelsson RC 1.50 4.00
289 Peter Smrek RC 1.50 4.00
290 Ivan Ciernik RC 1.50 4.00
291 Chris Neil RC 1.50 4.00
292 Jiri Dopita RC 1.50 4.00
293 David Cullen RC 1.50 4.00
294 Krys Kolanos RC 1.50 4.00
295 Jeff Jillson RC 1.50 4.00
296 Mark Rycroft RC 1.50 4.00
297 Nikita Alexeev RC 1.50 4.00
298 Thomas Ziegler RC 1.50 4.00
299 Bob Wren RC 1.50 4.00
300 Brian Sutherby RC 1.50 4.00

2001-02 Upper Deck Vintage Jerseys

Randomly inserted at 1:144 packs, this 16-card set featured swatches of game-worn jerseys of the featured players. This set consisted of three subsets: Golden Goalies (denoted by a "GG" prefix), Stars of the Decades (denoted by a "SD" prefix), and Stanley Cup Stars (denoted by a "SC" prefix).

GGAM Andy Moog 10.00 25.00
GGBS Billy Smith 12.50 30.00
GGGC Gerry Cheevers 10.00 25.00
GGGF Grant Fuhr 10.00 25.00
GGRV Rogie Vachon 12.50 30.00
SCBS Billy Smith 10.00 25.00
SCBT Bryan Trottier 10.00 25.00
SCMB Mike Bossy 10.00 25.00
SCSY Steve Yzerman 10.00 25.00
SCWG Wayne Gretzky 40.00 100.00
SDBC Bobby Clarke 15.00 40.00
SDGH Gordie Howe 12.50 30.00
SDGL Guy Lafleur 10.00 25.00
SDGP Gilbert Perreault 10.00 25.00
SDMB Mike Bossy 10.00 25.00
SDPE Phil Esposito 10.00 25.00

2001-02 Upper Deck Vintage Next In Line

Serial-numbered to just 50-copies each, this 6-card set featured game-worn jersey swatches of NHL legends and their heir-apparents.

NLBL Ray Bourque 60.00 125.00
Nicklas Lidstrom
NLCO Gerry Cheevers 25.00 60.00
Maxime Ouellet
NLGS Wayne Gretzky 125.00 250.00
Joe Sakic
NLHY Gordie Howe 150.00 300.00
Steve Yzerman
NLLK Guy Lafleur 25.00 60.00
Paul Kariya
NLSC Billy Smith 25.00 60.00
Roman Cechmanek

2001-02 Upper Deck Vintage Sweaters of Honor

Inserted randomly in 1:96 hobby packs, this 4-card set featured game-used jersey swatches of the pictured players.

SHGL Guy Lafleur 8.00 20.00
SHLA Guy Lapointe 8.00 20.00
SHML Michel Larocque 6.00 15.00
SHSS Steve Shutt 6.00 15.00

2002-03 Upper Deck Vintage

This 350-card set consisted of 305 base cards (1-260, 291-305 and 321-350); 30 checklist cards (261-290) and 15 statistical leaders cards (306-320). SP's were inserted at 1:5.

COMPLETE SET (350) 50.00 100.00
1 Vitali Vishnevski .08 .20
2 Paul Kariya SP .20 .50
3 Samuel Pahlsson .08 .20
4 Mike LeClerc .08 .20
5 Matt Cullen .08 .20
6 Ruslan Salei .08 .20
7 Jean-Sebastien Giguere .15 .40
8 Andy McDonald .08 .20
9 Patrik Stefan .08 .20
10 Milan Hnilicka .15 .40
11 Lubos Bartecko .08 .20
12 Jeff Cowan .08 .20
13 Ilya Kovalchuk .25 .60
14 Frantisek Kaberle .08 .20
15 Dany Heatley .25 .60
16 Daniel Tjarnqvist .08 .20
17 Sergei Samsonov .15 .40
18 P.J. Stock .08 .20
19 Nick Boynton .08 .20
20 Martin Lapointe .08 .20
21 Jozef Stumpel .08 .20
22 John Grahame .15 .40
23 Joe Thornton SP .50 1.25
24 Glen Murray .08 .20
25 Brian Rolston .08 .20
26 Hal Gill .08 .20
27 Stu Barnes .08 .20
28 Tim Connolly .08 .20
29 Miroslav Satan .15 .40
30 Maxim Afinogenov .08 .20
31 Martin Biron .15 .40
32 Jay McKee .08 .20
33 J-P Dumont .08 .20
34 Curtis Brown .08 .20
35 Alexei Zhitnik .08 .20
36 Roman Turek .15 .40
37 Rob Niedermayer .08 .20
38 Marc Savard .08 .20
39 Jarome Iginla SP .30 .75
40 Derek Morris .08 .20
41 Denis Gauthier .08 .20
42 Dave Lowry .08 .20
43 Craig Conroy .08 .20
44 Sami Kapanen .08 .20
45 Ron Francis .15 .40
46 Rod Brind'Amour .15 .40
47 Niclas Wallin .08 .20
48 Josef Vasicek .08 .20
49 Jeff O'Neill .08 .20
50 Erik Cole .08 .20
51 Dave Tanabe .08 .20
52 Arturs Irbe .15 .40
53 Steve Sullivan .08 .20
54 Ryan VandenBussche .08 .20
55 Michael Nylander .08 .20
56 Mark Bell .08 .20
57 Kyle Calder .08 .20
58 Jocelyn Thibault .15 .40
59 Eric Daze .15 .40
60 Alexei Zhamnov .08 .20
61 Steve Reinprecht .08 .20
62 Stephane Yelle .08 .20
63 Rob Blake .15 .40
64 Peter Forsberg .50 1.25
65 Patrick Roy SP 1.50 4.00
66 Milan Hejduk .20 .50
67 Joe Sakic SP .60 1.50
68 Greg DeVries .08 .20
69 Chris Drury .15 .40
70 Alex Tanguay .15 .40
71 Adam Foote .08 .20
72 David Vyborny .08 .20
73 Rostislav Klesla .08 .20
74 Marc Denis .15 .40
75 Ray Whitney .08 .20
76 Jody Shelley .08 .20
77 Jean-Luc Grand-Pierre .08 .20
78 Geoff Sanderson .08 .20
79 Espen Knutsen .08 .20
80 Pierre Turgeon .15 .40
81 Mike Modano SP .50 1.25
82 Marty Turco .15 .40
83 Bill Guerin .15 .40
84 Jere Lehtinen .15 .40
85 Jason Arnott .08 .20
86 Derian Hatcher .08 .20
87 Brenden Morrow .15 .40
88 Steve Yzerman SP 1.50 4.00
89 Sergei Fedorov .30 .75
90 Pavel Datsyuk .20 .50
91 Nicklas Lidstrom .20 .50
92 Luc Robitaille .15 .40
93 Kris Draper .08 .20
94 Curtis Joseph .20 .50
95 Dominik Hasek SP .60 1.50
96 Brett Hull .25 .60
97 Brendan Shanahan .20 .50
98 Boyd Devereaux .08 .20
99 Tommy Salo .15 .40
100 Ryan Smyth .08 .20
101 Mike York .08 .20
102 Mike Comrie SP .25 .60
103 Georges Laraque .08 .20
104 Ethan Moreau .08 .20
105 Daniel Cleary .08 .20
106 Anson Carter .15 .40
107 Viktor Kozlov .08 .20
108 Valeri Bure .08 .20
109 Olli Jokinen .15 .40
110 Sandis Ozolinsh .08 .20
111 Roberto Luongo .25 .60
112 Peter Worrell .08 .20
113 Niklas Hagman .08 .20
114 Kristian Huselius .08 .20
115 Zigmund Palffy .15 .40
116 Mattias Norstrom .08 .20
117 Mathieu Schneider .08 .20
118 Jason Allison .08 .20
119 Felix Potvin .20 .50
120 Bryan Smolinski .08 .20
121 Adam Deadmarsh .08 .20
122 Aaron Miller .08 .20
123 Richard Park .08 .20
124 Nick Schultz .08 .20
125 Marian Gaborik SP .50 1.25
126 Jim Dowd .08 .20
127 Hnat Domenichelli .08 .20
128 Filip Kuba .08 .20
129 Manny Fernandez .15 .40
130 Andrew Brunette .08 .20
131 Yanic Perreault .08 .20
132 Saku Koivu .20 .50
133 Richard Zednik .08 .20
134 Jose Theodore SP .40 1.00
135 Donald Audette .08 .20
136 Craig Rivet .08 .20
137 Andrei Markov .08 .20
138 Andreas Dackell .08 .20
139 Stu Grimson .08 .20
140 Scott Hartnell .08 .20
141 Mike Dunham .15 .40
142 Martin Erat .08 .20
143 Kimmo Timonen .08 .20
144 Denis Arkhipov .08 .20
145 David Legwand .15 .40
146 Andy Delmore .08 .20
147 Sergei Brylin .08 .20
148 Scott Stevens .15 .40
149 Scott Niedermayer .08 .20
150 John Madden .08 .20
151 Patrik Elias .15 .40
152 Martin Brodeur SP .75 2.00
153 Joe Nieuwendyk .15 .40
154 Brian Rafalski .08 .20
155 Roman Hamrlik .08 .20
156 Raffi Torres .08 .20
157 Michael Peca .08 .20
158 Mark Parrish .08 .20
159 Oleg Kvasha .08 .20
160 Eric Cairns .08 .20
161 Dave Scatchard .08 .20
162 Chris Osgood .15 .40
163 Alexei Yashin SP .15 .40
164 Tom Poti .08 .20
165 Sandy McCarthy .08 .20
166 Radek Dvorak .08 .20
167 Petr Nedved .08 .20
168 Pavel Bure SP .20 .50
169 Matthew Barnaby .08 .20
170 Mark Messier .20 .50
171 Eric Lindros .20 .50
172 Dan Blackburn .15 .40
173 Brian Leetch .15 .40
174 Wade Redden .08 .20
175 Radek Bonk .08 .20
176 Patrick Lalime .15 .40
177 Mike Fisher .08 .20
178 Martin Havlat .15 .40
179 Marian Hossa .20 .50
180 Magnus Arvedson .08 .20
181 Daniel Alfredsson .15 .40
182 Simon Gagne SP .30 .75
183 Kim Johnsson .08 .20
184 Roman Cechmanek .15 .40
185 Mark Recchi .15 .40
186 Keith Primeau .08 .20
187 Justin Williams .08 .20
188 John LeClair .20 .50
189 Jeremy Roenick .25 .60
190 Eric Weinrich .08 .20
191 Donald Brashear .08 .20
192 Teppo Numminen .08 .20
193 Shane Doan .08 .20
194 Sean Burke .15 .40
195 Ladislav Nagy .08 .20
196 Daymond Langkow .08 .20
197 Daniel Briere .08 .20
198 Claude Lemieux .15 .40
199 Tony Amonte .08 .20
200 Ville Nieminen .08 .20
201 Martin Straka .08 .20
202 Mario Lemieux SP 2.00 5.00
203 Johan Hedberg .15 .40
204 Jan Hrdina .08 .20
205 Andrew Ference .08 .20
206 Alexei Kovalev .15 .40
207 Alexei Morozov .08 .20
208 Vincent Damphousse .08 .20
209 Scott Thornton .08 .20
210 Patrick Marleau .15 .40
211 Owen Nolan .15 .40
212 Mike Ricci .08 .20
213 Marcus Ragnarsson .08 .20
214 Marco Sturm .08 .20
215 Evgeni Nabokov SP .25 .60
216 Brad Stuart .08 .20
217 Tyson Nash .08 .20
218 Shjon Podein .08 .20
219 Pavol Demitra .15 .40
220 Keith Tkachuk SP .25 .60
221 Doug Weight .15 .40
222 Cory Stillman .08 .20
223 Chris Pronger .15 .40
224 Brent Johnson .15 .40
225 Al MacInnis .15 .40
226 Vincent Lecavalier .20 .50
227 Vaclav Prospal .08 .20
228 Shane Willis .08 .20
229 Pavel Kubina .08 .20
230 Nikolai Khabibulin .20 .50
231 Martin St. Louis .15 .40
232 Fredrik Modin .08 .20
233 Brad Richards .15 .40
234 Tomas Kaberle .08 .20
235 Tie Domi .15 .40
236 Shayne Corson .08 .20
237 Mats Sundin SP .30 .75
238 Gary Roberts .08 .20
239 Darcy Tucker .08 .20
240 Ed Belfour .20 .50
241 Bryan McCabe .08 .20
242 Alyn McCauley .08 .20
243 Alexander Mogilny .15 .40
244 Trevor Linden .08 .20
245 Todd Bertuzzi .20 .50
246 Markus Naslund .20 .50
247 Henrik Sedin .08 .20
248 Ed Jovanovski .15 .40
249 Daniel Sedin .08 .20
250 Dan Cloutier .15 .40
251 Brendan Morrison .15 .40
252 Brendan Witt .08 .20
253 Steve Konowalchuk .08 .20
254 Sergei Gonchar .08 .20
255 Peter Bondra .15 .40
256 Olaf Kolzig .15 .40
257 Jeff Halpern .08 .20
258 Jaromir Jagr SP .50 1.25
259 Andrei Nikolishin .08 .20
260 Robert Lang .08 .20
261 Paul Kariya .15 .40
Vitali Vishnevski
Jean-Sebastien Giguere
Mike LeClerc
262 Ilya Kovalchuk .15 .40
Dany Heatley
Milan Hnilicka
Patrik Stefan
263 Sergei Samsonov .15 .40
Joe Thornton
Nick Boynton
Glen Murray
264 Tim Connolly .15 .40
Stu Barnes
Miroslav Satan
Martin Biron
265 Jarome Iginla .15 .40
Roman Turek
Marc Savard
Derek Morris
266 Jeff O'Neill .15 .40
Ron Francis
Arturs Irbe
Erik Cole
267 Eric Daze .15 .40
Kyle Calder
Jocelyn Thibault
Alexei Zhamnov
268 Joe Sakic .20 .50
Peter Forsberg
Patrick Roy
Rob Blake
269 Geoff Sanderson .15 .40
Rostislav Klesla
Marc Denis
Jody Shelley
270 Pierre Turgeon .15 .40
Mike Modano
Marty Turco
Derian Hatcher
271 Steve Yzerman .15 .40
Sergei Fedorov
Brendan Shanahan
Nicklas Lidstrom
272 Mike Comrie .15 .40
Ryan Smyth
Tommy Salo
Georges Laraque
273 Viktor Kozlov .15 .40
Stephen Weiss
Roberto Luongo
Peter Worrell
274 Zigmund Palffy .15 .40
Jason Allison
Felix Potvin
Adam Deadmarsh
275 Wild CL .15 .40
276 Saku Koivu .15 .40
Donald Audette
Jose Theodore
Yanic Perreault
277 Scott Hartnell .15 .40
Martin Erat
Mike Dunham
Stu Grimson
278 Patrik Elias .15 .40
Brian Rafalski
Martin Brodeur
Scott Stevens
279 Mike Peca .15 .40
Alexei Yashin
Chris Osgood
Eric Cairns
280 Pavel Bure .15 .40
Eric Lindros
Mike Richter
Mark Messier
281 Marian Hossa .15 .40
Daniel Alfredsson
Patrick Lalime
Martin Havlat
282 Simon Gagne .15 .40
Jeremy Roenick
Roman Cechmanek
Donald Brashear
283 Daniel Briere .15 .40
Teppo Numminen
Sean Burke
Tony Amonte
284 Penguins CL .15 .40
285 Patrick Marleau .15 .40
Owen Nolan
Evgeni Nabokov
Mike Ricci
286 Pavol Demitra .15 .40
Chris Pronger
Brent Johnson
Tyson Nash
287 Vincent Lecavalier .20 .50
Brad Richards
Nikolai Khabibulin
Pavel Kubina
288 Mats Sundin .15 .40
Alexander Mogilny
Ed Belfour
Tie Domi
289 Todd Bertuzzi .15 .40
Markus Naslund
Dan Cloutier
Trevor Linden
290 Peter Bondra .15 .40
Jaromir Jagr
Olaf Kolzig
Sergei Gonchar
291 Joe Sakic .40 1.00
292 Patrick Roy 1.00 2.50
293 Mike Modano .30 .75
294 Brendan Shanahan .20 .50
295 Steve Yzerman 1.00 2.50
296 Detroit Red Wings .20 .50
297 Joe Nieuwendyk .15 .40
298 Martin Brodeur .50 1.25
299 Pavel Bure .20 .50
300 Brian Leetch .15 .40
301 Jeremy Roenick .25 .60
302 Mark Recchi .15 .40
303 Mario Lemieux 1.25 3.00
304 Teemu Selanne .20 .50
305 Peter Bondra .15 .40
306 Jarome Iginla .15 .40
Glen Murray
Mats Sundin
307 Adam Oates .15 .40
Jason Allison
Joe Sakic
308 Jarome Iginla .15 .40
Markus Naslund
Todd Bertuzzi
309 Peter Bondra .15 .40
Jarome Iginla
Alexei Yashin
310 Sergei Gonchar .15 .40
Nicklas Lidstrom
Rob Blake
311 Brian Rolston .15 .40
Mike Peca
Miroslav Satan
312 Chris Chelios .15 .40
Jeremy Roenick
Simon Gagne
313 Peter Worrell .15 .40
Brad Ference
Chris Neil
314 Daniel Briere .15 .40
Jan Hrdina
Adam Deadmarsh
315 Dany Heatley .25 .60
Ilya Kovalchuk
Kristian Huselius
316 Dominik Hasek .20 .50
Martin Brodeur
Evgeni Nabokov
317 Patrick Roy .20 .50
Roman Cechmanek
Marty Turco
318 Jose Theodore .20 .50
Patrick Roy
Roman Cechmanek
319 Patrick Roy .25 .60
Jose Theodore
Nikolai Khabibulin
320 Dan Blackburn .15 .40
Mikka Kiprusoff
Mika Noronen
321 Pasi Numminen .08 .20
322 Mark Hartigan .08 .20
323 Henrik Tallinder .08 .20
324 Micki Dupont RC .40 1.00
325 Jaroslav Svoboda .08 .20
326 Jordan Krestanovich .08 .20
327 Kelly Fairchild .08 .20
328 Riku Hahl .08 .20
329 Andrej Nedorost .08 .20
330 Blake Bellefeuille .08 .20
331 Ales Pisa .08 .20
332 Jani Rita .08 .20
333 Stephen Weiss .08 .20
334 Lukas Krajicek .08 .20
335 Sylvain Blouin RC .40 1.00
336 Marcel Hossa .08 .20
337 Adam Hall RC .40 1.00
338 Jonas Andersson .08 .20
339 Jan Lasak .08 .20
340 Ray Schultz RC .40 1.00
341 Trent Hunter .08 .20
342 Martin Prusek .15 .40
343 Branko Radivojevic .08 .20
344 Shane Endicott .08 .20
345 Sebastien Centomo .15 .40
346 Karel Pilar .08 .20
347 Sebastien Charpentier .08 .20
348 Jean-Francois Fortin .08 .20
349 Ales Kotalik .08 .20
350 Kyle Rossiter .08 .20

2002-03 Upper Deck Vintage Jerseys

OS STAT.ODDS 1:96 RETAIL
SO/EE/HS ODDS 1:96 HBBY/RETAIL
FS STAT.ODDS 1:96 HOBBY
EEBB Brian Boucher 4.00 10.00
EEDA David Aebischer 4.00 10.00
EEFP Felix Potvin 6.00 15.00
EEMB Martin Biron 4.00 10.00
EEMD Mike Dunham 4.00 10.00
EEMO Maxime Ouellet 4.00 10.00
EEMT Marty Turco 6.00 15.00
EEOK Olaf Kolzig 6.00 15.00
EERC Roman Cechmanek 4.00 10.00
EERT Ron Tugnutt 4.00 10.00
FSBM Brenden Morrow 6.00 15.00
FSCD Chris Drury 6.00 15.00
FSJJ Jaromir Jagr 8.00 20.00
FSKP Keith Primeau 4.00 10.00
FSMH Milan Hejduk 4.00 10.00
FSSY Steve Yzerman 12.00 30.00
HSJD J-P Dumont 4.00 10.00
HSJW Justin Williams 4.00 10.00
HSMD Marc Denis 4.00 10.00
HSPB Peter Bondra 6.00 15.00
HSRB Ray Bourque 8.00 20.00
HSRF Ruslan Fedotenko 4.00 10.00
HSRK Rostislav Klesla 4.00 10.00
HSSG Simon Gagne 6.00 15.00
HSSK Steve Konowalchuk 4.00 10.00
HSVN Ville Nieminen 4.00 10.00
OSED Eric Daze 4.00 10.00
OSGM Glen Murray 4.00 10.00
OSJT Jose Theodore SP 8.00 20.00
OSMS Mats Sundin 6.00 15.00
OSRD Radek Dvorak 4.00 10.00
OSSY Steve Yzerman 12.00 30.00
SOCD Chris Drury 6.00 15.00
SOEL Eric Lindros 6.00 15.00
SOJH Jeff Halpern 4.00 10.00
SOJI Jarome Iginla SP 8.00 20.00
SOJJ Jaromir Jagr SP 10.00 25.00
SOJL John LeClair 4.00 10.00
SOKP Keith Primeau 4.00 10.00
SOMR Mark Recchi 4.00 10.00
SOPF Peter Forsberg 8.00 20.00
SOPK Paul Kariya 6.00 15.00

2002-03 Upper Deck Vintage Jerseys Gold

*GOLD: 1.25X TO 3X BASIC CARDS
GOLD PRINT RUN 50 SER.#'d SETS

2002-03 Upper Deck Vintage Tall Boys

Inserted 2 per hobby box, this 70-card set partially paralleled the base set on oversized cards. A gold version numbered out of 99 was also created.

COMPLETE SET (70) 40.00 100.00
*GOLD: 1.25X TO 3X BASE HI
T1 Paul Kariya .75 2.00
T2 Jean-Sebastien Giguere .60 1.50
T3 Dany Heatley 1.00 2.50
T4 Ilya Kovalchuk 1.00 2.50
T5 Joe Thornton 1.25 3.00
T6 Sergei Samsonov .60 1.50
T7 Miroslav Satan .60 1.50
T8 Maxim Afinogenov .60 1.50
T9 Roman Turek .60 1.50
T10 Jarome Iginla 1.00 2.50
T11 Arturs Irbe .60 1.50
T12 Ron Francis .60 1.50
T13 Eric Daze .60 1.50
T14 Jocelyn Thibault .60 1.50
T15 Patrick Roy 4.00 10.00
T16 Peter Forsberg 2.00 5.00
T17 Joe Sakic 1.50 4.00
T18 Chris Drury .60 1.50
T19 Alex Tanguay .60 1.50
T20 Espen Knutsen .60 1.50
T21 Rostislav Klesla .60 1.50
T22 Mike Modano 1.25 3.00
T23 Jason Arnott .60 1.50
T24 Steve Yzerman 4.00 10.00
T25 Brendan Shanahan .75 2.00
T26 Sergei Fedorov 1.25 3.00
T27 Curtis Joseph .75 2.00
T28 Mike Comrie .60 1.50
T29 Tommy Salo .60 1.50
T30 Roberto Luongo 1.00 2.50
T31 Stephen Weiss .60 1.50

T32 Jason Allison .60 1.50
T33 Zigmund Palffy .60 1.50
T34 Marian Gaborik 1.50 4.00
T35 Jose Theodore 1.00 2.50
T36 Saku Koivu .75 2.00
T37 Mike Dunham .60 1.50
T38 Scott Hartnell .60 1.50
T39 Martin Brodeur 2.00 5.00
T40 Patrik Elias .60 1.50
T41 Michael Peca .60 1.50
T42 Chris Osgood .60 1.50
T43 Eric Lindros .75 2.00
T44 Pavel Bure .75 2.00
T45 Daniel Alfredsson .60 1.50
T46 Marian Hossa .75 2.00
T47 Jeremy Roenick 1.00 2.50
T48 Simon Gagne .75 2.00
T49 Sean Burke .60 1.50
T50 Daniel Briere .60 1.50
T51 Tony Amonte .60 1.50
T52 Mario Lemieux 5.00 12.00
T53 Johan Hedberg .60 1.50
T54 Owen Nolan .60 1.50
T55 Evgeni Nabokov .60 1.50
T56 Keith Tkachuk .75 2.00
T57 Chris Pronger .60 1.50
T58 Vincent Lecavalier .75 2.00
T59 Nikolai Khabibulin .75 2.00
T60 Mats Sundin .75 2.00
T61 Alexander Mogilny .60 1.50
T62 Markus Naslund .75 2.00
T63 Todd Bertuzzi .75 2.00
T64 Jaromir Jagr 1.25 3.00
T65 Olaf Kolzig .60 1.50
T66 Gordie Howe 5.00 12.00
T67 Gordie Howe 5.00 12.00
T68 Gordie Howe 5.00 12.00
T69 Gordie Howe 5.00 12.00
T70 Gordie Howe with Coleen Howe 5.00 12.00

2000 Upper Deck Wayne Gretzky Master Collection

Released as a box set limited in production to 300 total sets (150 US and 150 Canada) the Upper Deck Wayne Gretzky Collection includes an 18-card base set where each card is sequentially numbered to 150, eight insert cards consisting of jersey cards and signed jersey cards sequentially numbered to 50, and one mystery pack containing an autograph, memorabilia card, or an autographed memorabilia card. Canadian versions are differentiated by the maple leaf they carry along the side of the card. US and Canadian versions carry the same value.

COMPLETE SET (18) 240.00 600.00
COMMON GRETZKY (1-18) 16.00 40.00

2000 Upper Deck Wayne Gretzky Master Collection Inserts

Three versions of each card were released. Each Master Collection contains one of each of these three versions: One Edmonton autographed jersey card in Canadian issues and one unautographed Edmonton jersey card in USA sets, one Los Angeles jersey card, one All-Star jersey card, and one New York jersey card in Canadian sets and one autographed New York jersey card in American sets. Each card is sequentially numbered to 50. As of press time, not all cards have been verified for pricing.

1 Gretzky Ed.AU/50 Can 320.00 800.00
2 Gretzky Ed.AU/50 Can 320.00 800.00
3 Gretzky Ed.AU/50 Can 320.00 800.00
4 Gretzky Ed/50 USA 100.00 200.00
5 Gretzky Ed/50 USA 100.00 200.00
6 Gretzky Ed/50 USA 100.00 200.00
7 Gretzky LA/50 100.00 200.00
8 Gretzky LA/50 100.00 200.00
9 Gretzky LA/50 100.00 200.00
10 Gretzky AS/50 100.00 200.00
11 Gretzky AS/50 100.00 200.00
12 Gretzky AS/50 100.00 200.00
13 Gretzky NY AU/50 USA 300.00 750.00
14 Gretzky NY AU/50 USA 300.00 750.00
15 Gretzky NY AU/50 USA 300.00 750.00
16 Gretzky NY/50 Can 100.00 200.00
17 Gretzky NY/50 Can 100.00 200.00
18 Gretzky NY/50 Can 100.00 200.00

2000 Upper Deck Wayne Gretzky Master Collection Mystery Pack

One Mystery Pack was inserted into each Wayne Gretzky Master Collection which contained one of the following: one of 18 different Ultimate Gretzky Autograph 1/1's, one Great Gretzky Jersey card sequentially numbered to 99 , one Great Gretzky Signed Jersey card, one Great Gretzky Patch card, or one Great Gretzky Signed Patch card. Lower print runs are not priced due to scarcity.

ULTIMATE AU's #'D 1/1
US AND CANADA SAME VALUE
19 Gretzky Jersey/99 250.00 400.00
20 Gretzky Jersey AU/9
21 Gretzky Patch/15
22 Gretzky Patch AU/9

2000 Upper Deck Wayne Gretzky Retirement Set

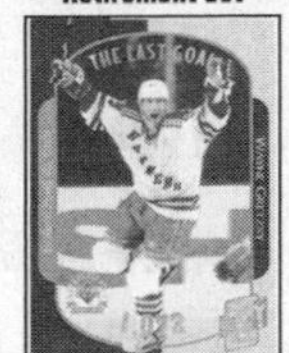

Released by Upper Deck Authenticated as a tribute to Wayne Gretzky, this 16-card set features 3 1/2" X 5" cards highlighting Wayne's career. Cards contain gold foil highlights and the date of Gretzky's retirement. Card number 16 is printed on black and gold card stock and lists the Grand total of Gretzky's NHL goals. This set was offered at retail price of $19.99.

COMPLETE SET (16) 12.00 30.00
COMMON GRETZKY (1-16) .80 2.00

2005-06 Upper Deck Where's Sidney?

We have no pricing information on this card.

NNO Sidney Crosby Redemption Card

1924 V-122

This set features athletes from a variety of sports and was inserted along with Willard's Chocolates. The cards measure 1 3/8 by 3 7/8 and feature black and white photography. The four hockey players in the set, all members of the 1924 gold medal-winning Canadian Olympic team, are listed below. Although the set is designated as a 1923-24 issue by the ACC, our research suggests it was not released until the summer of 1924.

COMPLETE SET (4) 375.00 750.00
43 Harry Watson 125.00 250.00
45 Ernie Collett RC 75.00 150.00
47 Hooley Smith 125.00 250.00
52 Dunc Munro RC 100.00 200.00

1924-26 V128-1 Paulin's Candy

This 70-card set was issued during the 1923-24 season and featured players from the WCHL. The horizontal back explains how to obtain either a hockey stick or a box of Paulin's chocolates by collecting and sending in the complete Famous Hockey Players set. The cards were to be returned to the collector with the hockey stick or chocolates. The cards are in black and white and measure approximately 1 3/8" by 2 3/4".

COMPLETE SET (70) 4500.00 9000.00
1 Bill Borland 75.00 150.00
2 Pete Speirs 50.00 100.00
3 Jack Hughes 50.00 100.00
4 Errol Gillis 50.00 100.00
5 Cecil Browne 50.00 100.00
6 W. Roberts 50.00 100.00
7 Howard Brandon 50.00 100.00
8 Fred Comfort 50.00 100.00
9 Cliff O'Meara 50.00 100.00
10 Leo Benard 50.00 100.00
11 Lloyd Harvey 50.00 100.00
12 Bobby Connors 50.00 100.00
13 Daddy Dalman 50.00 100.00
14 Dub Mackie 50.00 100.00
15 Lorne Chabot 150.00 300.00
16 Phat Wilson 62.50 125.00
17 Wilf L'Heureux 50.00 100.00
18 Danny Cox 50.00 100.00
19 Bill Brydge 50.00 100.00
20 Alex Gray 50.00 100.00
21 Albert Pudas 50.00 100.00
22 Jack Irwin 50.00 100.00
23 Puss Traub 50.00 100.00
24 Red McCusker 62.50 125.00
25 Jack Asseltine 62.50 125.00
26 Duke Dutkowski 50.00 100.00
27 Charley McVeigh 50.00 100.00
28 George Hay 125.00 250.00
29 Amby Moran 50.00 100.00
30 Barney Stanley 150.00 300.00
31 Art Gagne 50.00 100.00
32 Louis Berlinquette 50.00 100.00
33 P.C. Stevens 50.00 100.00
34 W.D. Elmer 50.00 100.00
35 Bill Cook 175.00 350.00
36 Leo Reise 50.00 100.00
37 Curly Headley 125.00 250.00
38 Newsy Lalonde 300.00 600.00
39 George Hainsworth 300.00 600.00
40 Laurie Scott 50.00 100.00
41 Joe Simpson 175.00 350.00
42 Bob Trapp 50.00 100.00
43 Joe McCormick 50.00 100.00
44 Ty Arbour 50.00 100.00
45 Duke Keats 62.50 125.00
46 Hal Winkler 50.00 100.00
47 Johnny Sheppard 50.00 100.00
48 Crutchy Morrison 50.00 100.00
49 Spunk Sparrow 50.00 100.00
50 Percy McGregor 50.00 100.00
51 Harry Tuckwell 50.00 100.00
52 Chubby Scott 50.00 100.00
53 Scotty Fraser 50.00 100.00
54 Bob Davis 50.00 100.00
55 Clucker White 50.00 100.00
56 Bob Armstrong 50.00 100.00
57 Doc Longtry 50.00 100.00
58 Darb Sommers 50.00 100.00
59 Frank Hacquoil 50.00 100.00
60 Stan Evans 50.00 100.00
61 Ed Oatman 50.00 100.00
62 Mervyn(Red) Dutton 200.00 400.00
63 Herb Gardiner 125.00 250.00
64 Bernie Morris 50.00 100.00
65 Bobbie Benson 50.00 100.00
66 Ernie Anderson 50.00 100.00
67 Cully Wilson 50.00 100.00
68 Charlie Reid 62.50 125.00
69 Harry Oliver 125.00 250.00
70 Rusty Crawford 100.00 200.00

1928-29 V128-2 Paulin's Candy

This scarce set of 90 black and white cards was produced and distributed in Western Canada and features Western Canadian teams and players. The cards are numbered on the back and measure approximately 1 3/8" by 2 5/8". The card back details an offer (expiring June 1st, 1929) of a hockey stick prize (or box of chocolates for girls) if someone could bring in a complete set of 90 cards. Players on the Calgary Jimmies are not explicitly identified on the card so they are listed below without a specific player name.

COMPLETE SET (90) 2750.00 5500.00
1 Univ. of Man. Girls Hockey Team 50.00 100.00
2 Elgin Hockey Team 40.00 80.00
3 Brandon Schools Boy Champions 40.00 80.00
4 Port Arthur Hockey Team 40.00 80.00
5 Enderby Hockey Team 40.00 80.00
6 Humboldt High School Team 40.00 80.00
7 Regina Collegiate Hockey Team 40.00 80.00
8 Weyburn Beavers 40.00 80.00
9 Moose Jaw College Junior Hockey Team 50.00 100.00
10 M.A.C. Junior Hockey 40.00 80.00
11 Vermillion Agricultural School 40.00 80.00
12 Rovers& Cranbrook B.C. 40.00 80.00
13 Empire School& Moose Jaw 40.00 80.00
14 Arts Senior Hockey 40.00 80.00
15 Juvenile Varsity Hockey 40.00 80.00
16 St. Peter's College Hockey 40.00 80.00
17 Arts Girls Hockey 50.00 100.00
18 Swan River Hockey Team 40.00 80.00
19 U.M.S.U. Junior Hockey Team 40.00 80.00
20 Campion College Hockey Team 50.00 100.00
21 Drinkwater Hockey Team 40.00 80.00
22 Elks Hockey Team Biggar, Saskatchewan 40.00 80.00
23 South Calgary High School 40.00 80.00
24 Meota Hockey 40.00 80.00
25 Chartered Accountants 50.00 100.00
26 Nutana Collegiate Hockey Team 40.00 80.00
27 MacLeod Hockey Team 50.00 100.00
28 Arts Junior Hockey 40.00 80.00
29 Fort William Juniors 40.00 80.00
30 Swan Lake Hockey Team 40.00 80.00
31 Dauphin Hockey Team 40.00 80.00
32 Mount Royal Hockey Team 40.00 80.00
33 Port Arthur W. End Junior Hockey 40.00 80.00
34 Hanna Hockey Club 40.00 80.00
35 Vermillion Junior Hockey 40.00 80.00
36 Smithers Hockey Team 40.00 80.00
37 Lloydminster High School 40.00 80.00
38 Winnipeg Rangers 50.00 100.00
39 Delisle Intermediate Hockey 40.00 80.00
40 Moose Jaw College Senior Hockey 40.00 80.00
41 Art Bonneyman 25.00 50.00
42 Jimmy Graham 25.00 50.00
43 Pat O'Hunter 25.00 50.00
44 Leo Moret 25.00 50.00
45 Blondie McLennen 25.00 50.00
46 Red Beattie 40.00 80.00
47 Frank Peters 40.00 80.00
48 Lloyd McIntyre 25.00 50.00
49 Art Somers 40.00 80.00
50 Ikey Morrison 25.00 50.00
51 Calgary Jimmies 25.00 50.00
52 Don Cummings 25.00 50.00
53 Calgary Jimmies 25.00 50.00
54 P. Gerlitz 25.00 50.00
55 A. Kay 25.00 50.00
56 Paul Runge 40.00 80.00
57 J. Gerlitz 25.00 50.00
58 H. Gerlitz 25.00 50.00
59 C. Biles 25.00 50.00
60 Jimmy Evans 25.00 50.00
61 Ira Stuart 25.00 50.00
62 Berg Irving 50.00 100.00
63 Cecil Browne 40.00 80.00
64 Nick Wasnie 40.00 80.00
65 Gordon Teal 40.00 80.00
66 Jack Hughes 40.00 80.00
67 D. Yeatman 40.00 80.00
68 Connie Johanneson 25.00 50.00
69 S. Walters 25.00 50.00
70 Harold McMunn 40.00 80.00
71 Smokey Harris 25.00 50.00
72 Calgary Jimmies 25.00 50.00
73 Bernie Morris 25.00 50.00
74 J. Fowler 40.00 80.00
75 Calgary Jimmies 25.00 50.00
76 Pete Spiers 25.00 50.00
77 Bill Borland 40.00 80.00
78 Cliff O'Meara 40.00 80.00
79 F. Porteous 40.00 80.00
80 W. Brooks 40.00 80.00
81 Everett McGowan 25.00 50.00
82 Calgary Jimmies 25.00 50.00
83 George Dame 25.00 50.00
84 Calgary Jimmies 25.00 50.00
85 Calgary Jimmies 25.00 50.00
86 Calgary Jimmies 25.00 50.00
87 Heck Fowler 40.00 80.00
88 Jimmy Hoyle 25.00 50.00
89 Charlie Gardiner 75.00 150.00
90 Calgary Jimmies 25.00 50.00

1933-34 V129

This 50-card set was issued anonymously during the 1933-34 season. Recent research may link the cards' distribution to British Consul Cigarettes. This has yet to be confirmed. The cards are sepia toned and measure approximately 1 5/8" by 2 7/8". The cards are numbered on the back with the capsule biography both in French and in English. Card number 39 is now known to exist but is quite scarce as it was the card that the company (allegedly) short-printed in order to make it difficult to complete the set. The short-printed Oliver card is not included in the complete set price below.

COMPLETE SET (49) 7500.00 15000.00
1 Red Horner RC 250.00 500.00
2 Hap Day 175.00 350.00
3 Ace Bailey RC 250.00 500.00
4 Buzz Boll RC 75.00 150.00
5 Charlie Conacher RC 500.00 1000.00
6 Busher Jackson RC 250.00 500.00
7 Joe Primeau RC 250.00 500.00
8 King Clancy 500.00 1000.00
9 Alex Levinsky RC 100.00 200.00
10 Bill Thoms RC 75.00 150.00
11 Andy Blair RC 75.00 150.00
12 Harold Cotton RC 100.00 200.00
13 George Hainsworth 250.00 500.00
14 Ken Doraty RC 75.00 150.00
15 Fred Robertson RC 75.00 150.00
16 Charlie Sands RC 75.00 150.00
17 Hec Kilrea RC 75.00 150.00
18 John Roach 100.00 200.00
19 Larry Aurie RC 75.00 150.00
20 Ebbie Goodfellow RC 150.00 300.00
21 Normie Himes RC 100.00 200.00
22 Bill Brydge RC 75.00 150.00
23 Mervyn Dutton RC 150.00 300.00
24 Cooney Weiland RC 200.00 400.00
25 Bill Beveridge RC 100.00 200.00
26 Frank Finnigan 100.00 200.00
27 Albert Leduc RC 100.00 200.00
28 Babe Siebert RC 200.00 400.00
29 Murray Murdoch RC 75.00 150.00
30 Butch Keeling RC 75.00 150.00
31 Bill Cook 150.00 300.00
32 Cecil Dillon RC 75.00 150.00
33 Ivan Johnson RC 200.00 400.00
34 Ott Heller RC 100.00 200.00
35 Red Beattie RC 75.00 150.00
36 Dit Clapper 300.00 600.00
37 Eddie Shore RC 1000.00 2000.00
38 Marty Barry RC 150.00 300.00
39 Harry Oliver SP RC 7500.00 15000.00
40 Bob Gracie RC 75.00 150.00
41 Howie Morenz 1500.00 3000.00
42 Pit Lepine RC 75.00 150.00
43 Johnny Gagnon RC 75.00 150.00
44 Armand Mondou RC 75.00 150.00
45 Lorne Chabot RC 150.00 300.00
46 Dun Cook RC 150.00 300.00
47 Alex Smith RC 75.00 150.00
48 Danny Cox RC 75.00 150.00
49 Baldy Northcott RC UER 100.00 200.00
50 Paul Thompson RC 100.00 200.00

1924-25 V130 Maple Crispette

This 30-card set was issued during the 1924-25 season in the Montreal area. The cards are in black and white and measure approximately 1 3/8" by 2 3/8". There was a prize offer detailed on the reverse of every card offering a pair of hockey skates for a complete set of the cards. Card number 15 apparently was the "impossible" card that prevented most collectors of that day from ever getting the skates. The cards are numbered on the front in the lower right hand corner. The set is considered complete without the short-printed Cleghorn.

COMPLETE SET (29) 4000.00 8000.00
1 Capt. Dunc Munro 100.00 200.00
2 Clint Benedict 200.00 400.00
3 Norman Fowler 100.00 200.00
4 Curly Headley 75.00 150.00
5 Alf Skinner 75.00 150.00
6 Bill Cook 150.00 300.00
7 Smokey Harris 75.00 150.00
8 Jim Herberts 75.00 150.00
9 Carson Cooper 75.00 150.00
10 Red Green 75.00 150.00
11 Billy Boucher 75.00 150.00
12 Howie Morenz 1000.00 2000.00
13 Georges Vezina 700.00 1400.00
14 Aurel Joliat 400.00 800.00
15 Sprague Cleghorn SP 6000.00 12000.00
16 Dutch Cain 75.00 150.00
17 Charlie Dinsmore 75.00 150.00
18 Punch Broadbent 150.00 300.00
19 Sam Rothschild 75.00 150.00
20 George Carroll 75.00 150.00
21 Billy Burch 150.00 300.00
22 Shorty Green 150.00 300.00
23 Mickey Roach 75.00 150.00
24 Ken Randall 75.00 150.00
25 Vernon Forbes 100.00 200.00
26 Charlie Langlois 75.00 150.00
27 Newsy Lalonde 300.00 600.00
28 Fred (Frock) Lowrey 75.00 150.00
29 Ganton Scott 75.00 150.00
30 Louis Berlinguette 100.00 200.00

1923-24 V145-1

This relatively unattractive 40-card set is printed in sepia tone. The cards measure approximately 2" by 3 1/4". The cards have blank backs. The cards are numbered on the front in the lower left corner. The player's name, team, and National Hockey League are at the bottom of each card. The issuer of the set is not indicated in any way on the card, although speculation suggests it was William Patterson, Ltd, a Canadian confectioner. This set is easily confused with the other V145 set. Except for the tint and size differences and the different card name/number correspondence, these sets are essentially the same. Thankfully the only player with the same number in both sets is number 3 King Clancy. The Bert Corbeau card (#25) is extremely difficult to find in any condition, as it most likely was short printed. It is not included in the complete set price below.

COMPLETE SET (40) 6000.00 12000.00
1 Eddie Gerard 125.00 250.00
2 Frank Nighbor RC 175.00 350.00
3 King Clancy RC 900.00 1800.00
4 Jack Darragh 100.00 200.00
5 Harry Helman RC 50.00 100.00
6 George Boucher RC 100.00 200.00
7 Clint Benedict 150.00 300.00
8 Lionel Hitchman RC 100.00 200.00
9 Punch Broadbent 125.00 250.00
10 Cy Denneny RC 200.00 400.00
11 Sprague Cleghorn 150.00 300.00
12 Sylvio Mantha RC 125.00 250.00
13 Joe Malone 200.00 400.00
14 Aurel Joliat RC 650.00 1300.00
15 Howie Morenz RC 1500.00 3000.00
16 Billy Boucher RC 60.00 125.00
17 Billy Coutu RC 60.00 125.00
18 Odie Cleghorn 60.00 125.00
19 Georges Vezina 750.00 1500.00
20 Amos Arbour RC 50.00 100.00
21 Lloyd Andrews RC 50.00 100.00
22 Red Stuart RC 60.00 125.00
23 Cecil Dye RC 150.00 300.00
24 Jack Adams RC 200.00 400.00
25 Bert Corbeau RC SP 10000.00 20000.00
26 Reg Noble RC 150.00 300.00
27 Stan Jackson RC 50.00 100.00
28 John Roach RC 60.00 125.00
29 Vernon Forbes RC 60.00 125.00
30 Shorty Green RC 100.00 200.00
31 Red Green RC 50.00 100.00
32 Goldie Prodgers 50.00 100.00
33 Leo Reise RC 50.00 100.00
34 Ken Randall RC 50.00 100.00
35 Billy Burch RC 100.00 200.00
36 Jesse Spring RC 50.00 100.00
37 Eddie Bouchard RC 50.00 100.00
38 Mickey Roach RC 50.00 100.00
39 Chas. Fraser RC 50.00 100.00
40 Corbett Denneny RC 100.00 200.00

1924-25 V145-2

This 60-card set was issued anonymously during the 1924-25 season. The cards have a green-black tint and measure approximately 1 3/4" by 3 1/4". Cards are numbered in the lower left corner and have a blank back. The player's name, team, and National Hockey League are at the bottom of each card. The issuer of the set is not indicated in any way on the card, although speculation points to William Patterson, Ltd., a Canadian confectioner. This set is easily confused with the other V145 set. Except for the tint and size differences and the different card name/number correspondence, these sets are essentially the same. Thankfully the only player with the same number in both sets is number 3 King Clancy.

COMPLETE SET (60) 6000.00 12000.00
1 Joe Ironstone RC 125.00 250.00
2 George Boucher 100.00 200.00
3 King Clancy 750.00 1500.00
4 Lionel Hitchman 75.00 150.00
5 Howie Smith RC 125.00 250.00
6 Frank Nighbor 100.00 200.00
7 Cy Denneny 125.00 250.00
8 Spill Campbell RC 50.00 100.00
9 Frank Finnigan RC 75.00 150.00
10 Alex Connell RC 125.00 250.00
11 Vernon Forbes 60.00 125.00
12 Ken Randall 50.00 100.00
13 Billy Burch 100.00 200.00
14 Shorty Green 100.00 200.00
15 Red Green 50.00 100.00
16 Alex McKinnon RC 50.00 100.00
17 Charlie Langlois RC 50.00 100.00
18 Mickey Roach 50.00 100.00
19 Eddie Bouchard 50.00 100.00
20 Jesse Spring 50.00 100.00
21 Carson Cooper RC 50.00 100.00
22 Smokey Harris RC 50.00 100.00
23 Gopher Headley RC 50.00 100.00
24 Bill Cook RC 200.00 400.00
25 Jim Herberts RC 50.00 100.00
26 Werner Schnarr RC 50.00 100.00
27 Alf Skinner RC 50.00 100.00
28 George Redding RC 50.00 100.00
29 Herbie Mitchell RC 50.00 100.00
30 Hek Fowler RC 60.00 125.00
31 Red Stuart 50.00 100.00
32 Clint Benedict 100.00 200.00
33 Gerald Munro RC 50.00 100.00
34 Dunc Munro RC 60.00 125.00
35 Dutch Cain RC 50.00 100.00
36 Fred Lowrey RC 50.00 100.00
37 Sam Rothschild RC 50.00 100.00
38 Ganton Scott RC 50.00 100.00
39 Punch Broadbent 125.00 250.00
40 Charlie Dinsmore RC 50.00 100.00
41 Louis Berlinquette RC 50.00 100.00
42 George Carroll RC 50.00 100.00
43 Georges Vezina 600.00 1200.00
44 Billy Coutu 50.00 100.00
45 Odie Cleghorn 60.00 125.00
46 Billy Boucher 75.00 150.00
47 Howie Morenz 1000.00 2000.00
48 Aurel Joliat 500.00 1000.00
49 Sprague Cleghorn 125.00 250.00
50 Billy Mantha RC 75.00 150.00
51 Reg Noble 100.00 200.00
52 John Roach 60.00 125.00
53 Jack Adams 125.00 250.00
54 Cecil Dye 100.00 200.00
55 Reg Reid RC 50.00 100.00
56 Albert Holway RC 50.00 100.00
57 Bert McCaffery RC 50.00 100.00
58 Bert Corbeau 100.00 200.00
59 Lloyd Andrews RC 50.00 100.00
60 Stan Jackson 75.00 150.00

1933-34 V252 Canadian Gum

This unnumbered set of 50 cards was designated V252 by the American Card Catalog. Cards are black and white pictures with a red border. Backs are written in both French and English. Cards measure approximately 2 1/2" by 3 1/4" including a 3/4" tab at the bottom describing a premium (contest) offer and containing one large letter. When enough of these letters were saved so that the collector could spell out the names of five NHL teams, they could be redeemed for a free home hockey game according to the details given on the card backs. The cards are checklisted in alphabetical order.

COMPLETE SET (50) 4500.00 9000.00
1 Clarence Abel RC 100.00 200.00
2 Larry Aurie RC 90.00 150.00
3 Ace Bailey RC 200.00 400.00
4 Helge Bostrom RC 50.00 100.00
5 Bill Brydge RC 50.00 100.00
6 Glyn Brydson RC 50.00 100.00
7 Marty Burke RC 50.00 100.00
8 Gerald Carson RC 75.00 125.00
9 Lorne Chabot RC 200.00 400.00
10 King Clancy 450.00 800.00
11 Dit Clapper RC 200.00 400.00
12 Charlie Conacher RC 400.00 750.00
13 Lionel Conacher RC 200.00 400.00
14 Alex Connell 100.00 175.00
15 Bun Cook RC 100.00 175.00
16 Danny Cox RC 50.00 100.00
17 Hap Day 100.00 200.00
18 Cecil Dillon RC 50.00 100.00
19 Lorne Duguid RC 75.00 125.00
20 Duke Dutkowski RC 50.00 100.00
21 Mervyn Dutton RC 100.00 175.00
22 Hap Emms RC 75.00 125.00
23 Frank Finnigan 75.00 125.00
24 Chuck Gardiner RC 100.00 175.00
25 Ebbie Goodfellow RC 100.00 175.00
26 Johnny Gottselig RC 75.00 125.00
27 Bob Gracie RC 50.00 100.00
28 George Hainsworth 200.00 400.00
29 Ott Heller RC 50.00 100.00
30 Normie Himes RC 75.00 125.00
31 Red Horner RC 150.00 300.00
32 Busher Jackson RC 200.00 400.00
33 Walter Jackson RC 50.00 100.00
34 Aurel Joliat 400.00 750.00
35 Dave Kerr RC 75.00 125.00
36 Pit Lepine RC 50.00 100.00
37 Georges Mantha RC 50.00 100.00
38 Howie Morenz 1000.00 2000.00
39 Murray Murdoch RC 50.00 100.00
40 Baldy Northcott RC 75.00 125.00
41 John Roach 90.00 150.00
42 Johnny Sheppard 50.00 100.00
43 Babe Siebert RC 125.00 250.00
44 Alex Smith RC 50.00 100.00
45 John Sorrell RC 90.00 150.00
46 Nelson Stewart RC 200.00 400.00
47 Dave Trottier RC 50.00 100.00
48 Bill Touhey RC 50.00 100.00
49 Jimmy Ward RC 50.00 100.00
50 Nick Wasnie RC 50.00 100.00

1933-34 V288 Hamilton Gum

This skip-numbered set of 21 cards was designated V288 by the American Card Catalog. Cards are black and white pictures with a beige, blue, green, or orange background. Backs are written in both French and English. Cards measure approximately 2 3/8" by 2 3/4".

COMPLETE SET (21) 3000.00 6000.00
1 Nick Wasnie 62.50 125.00
2 Joe Primeau 200.00 400.00
3 Marty Burke 50.00 100.00
7 Bill Thoms 50.00 100.00
8 Howie Morenz 1000.00 2000.00
9 Andy Blair 50.00 100.00
11 Ace Bailey 175.00 350.00
14 Wildor Larochelle 50.00 100.00
17 King Clancy 400.00 800.00
18 Sylvio Mantha 87.50 175.00
21 Red Horner 150.00 300.00
23 Pit Lepine 50.00 100.00
27 Aurel Joliat 400.00 800.00
29 Harvey(Busher) Jackson 175.00 350.00
30 Lorne Chabot 100.00 200.00
33 Clarence(Hap) Day 100.00 200.00
36 Alex Levinsky 62.50 125.00
39 Harold Cotton 75.00 150.00
42 Ebbie Goodfellow 87.50 175.00
44 Larry Aurie 50.00 100.00
49 Charlie Conacher 400.00 800.00

1937-38 V356 Worldwide Gum

These rather crude greenish-gray cards feature the player's name and card number on the front and the card number, the player's name, his position and biographical data (in both English and French) on the back. Cards are approximately 2 3/8" by 2 7/8". Although the backs of the cards state that the cards were printed in Canada, no mention of the issuer, World Wide Gum, is apparent anywhere on the card.

COMPLETE SET (135) 11000.00 22000.00
1 Charlie Conacher 500.00 1000.00
2 Jimmy Ward 50.00 100.00
3 Babe Siebert 175.00 350.00
4 Marty Barry 100.00 200.00
5 Eddie Shore 750.00 1500.00
6 Paul Thompson 50.00 100.00
7 Roy Worters 150.00 300.00
8 Red Horner 100.00 200.00
9 Wilfred Cude 75.00 150.00
10 Lionel Conacher 175.00 350.00
11 Ebbie Goodfellow 125.00 250.00
12 Tiny Thompson 150.00 300.00
13 Harold March RC 60.00 125.00
14 Mervyn (Red) Dutton 100.00 200.00
15 Butch Keeling 50.00 100.00
16 Frank Boucher RC 100.00 200.00
17 Tommy Gorman RC 50.00 100.00
18 Howie Morenz 1250.00 2500.00
19 Marvin Wentworth 75.00 150.00
20 Hooley Smith 100.00 200.00
21 Ching Johnson RC 150.00 300.00
22 Baldy Northcott 75.00 150.00
23 Syl Apps 400.00 800.00
24 Hec Kilrea 50.00 100.00
25 John Sorrell 50.00 100.00
26 Lorne Carr RC 50.00 100.00
27 Charlie Sands 50.00 100.00
28 Nick Metz 50.00 100.00
29 King Clancy 500.00 1000.00
30 Russ Blinco 50.00 100.00
31 Pete Martin RC 50.00 100.00
32 Walter Buswell RC 50.00 100.00
33 Paul Haynes 50.00 100.00
34 Wildor Larochelle 60.00 125.00
35 Harold Cotton 60.00 125.00
36 Dit Clapper 200.00 400.00
37 Joe Lamb 50.00 100.00
38 Bob Gracie 50.00 100.00
39 Jack Shill 50.00 100.00
40 Buzz Boll 50.00 100.00
41 John Gallagher 50.00 100.00
42 Art Chapman 50.00 100.00
43 Tom Cook RC 50.00 100.00
44 Bill MacKenzie 50.00 100.00
45 Georges Mantha 50.00 100.00
46 Herb Cain 60.00 125.00
47 Mud Bruneteau RC 75.00 150.00
48 Bob Davidson 50.00 100.00
49 Doug Young RC 50.00 100.00
50 Paul Drouin RC 50.00 100.00
51 Busher Jackson 200.00 400.00
52 Hap Day 150.00 300.00
53 Dave Kerr 100.00 200.00
54 Al Murray 50.00 100.00
55 Johnny Gottselig 60.00 125.00
56 Andy Blair 50.00 100.00
57 Lynn Patrick 200.00 400.00
58 Sweeney Schriner 125.00 250.00
59 Hap Emms 60.00 125.00
60 Allan Shields 50.00 100.00
61 Alex Levinsky 60.00 125.00
62 Flash Hollett 50.00 100.00
63 Peggy O'Neil RC 50.00 100.00
64 Herbie Lewis RC 100.00 200.00
65 Aurel Joliat 400.00 800.00
66 Carl Voss RC 100.00 200.00
67 Stew Evans 50.00 100.00
68 Bun Cook 125.00 250.00
69 Cooney Weiland 125.00 250.00
70 Dave Trottier 50.00 100.00
71 Louis Trudel RC 50.00 100.00
72 Marty Burke 50.00 100.00
73 Leroy Goldsworthy 50.00 100.00
74 Normie Smith RC 50.00 100.00
75 Syd Howe 150.00 300.00
76 Gordon Pettinger RC 50.00 100.00
77 Jack McGill 50.00 100.00
78 Pit Lepine 50.00 100.00
79 Sammy McManus RC 50.00 100.00
80 Phil Watson RC 75.00 150.00
81 Paul Runge 50.00 100.00
82 Bill Beveridge 60.00 125.00
83 Johnny Gagnon 50.00 100.00
84 Bucko MacDonald RC 60.00 125.00
85 Earl Robinson 50.00 100.00
86 Pep Kelly 50.00 100.00
87 Ott Heller 50.00 100.00
88 Murray Murdoch 50.00 100.00
89 Mac Colville RC 50.00 100.00
90 Alex Shibicky 75.00 150.00
91 Neil Colville 125.00 250.00
92 Normie Himes 60.00 125.00
93 Charley McVeigh 50.00 100.00
94 Lester Patrick 200.00 400.00
95 Connie Smythe 200.00 400.00
96 Art Ross 200.00 400.00
97 Cecil M.Hart RC 125.00 250.00
98 Dutch Gainor RC 50.00 100.00
99 Jack Adams 150.00 300.00
100 Howie Morenz Jr. 150.00 300.00
101 Buster Mundy RC 50.00 100.00
102 Johnny Wing RC 50.00 100.00
103 Morris Croghan RC 50.00 100.00
104 Pete Jotkus RC 50.00 100.00
105 Doug MacQuisten RC 50.00 100.00
106 Lester Brennan RC 50.00 100.00
107 Jack O'Connell RC 50.00 100.00
108 Ray Malenfant RC 50.00 100.00
109 Ken Murray RC 50.00 100.00
110 Frank Stangle RC 50.00 100.00
111 Dave Neville RC 50.00 100.00
112 Claude Burke RC 50.00 100.00
113 Herman Murray RC 50.00 100.00
114 Buddy O'Connor RC 125.00 250.00
115 Albert Perreault RC 50.00 100.00
116 Johnny Taugher RC 50.00 100.00
117 Rene Boudreau RC 50.00 100.00
118 Kenny McKinnon RC 50.00 100.00
119 Alex Bolduc RC 50.00 100.00
120 Jimmy Keiller RC 50.00 100.00
121 Lloyd McIntyre RC 50.00 100.00
122 Emile Fortin RC 50.00 100.00
123 Mike Karakas 60.00 125.00
124 Arl Wiebe 50.00 100.00
125 Louis St. Denis RC 50.00 100.00
126 Stan Pratt RC 50.00 100.00
127 Jules Cholette RC 50.00 100.00
128 Jimmy Muir RC 50.00 100.00
129 Pete Morin RC 50.00 100.00

130 Jimmy Heffernan RC 50.00 100.00
131 Morris Bastien RC 50.00 100.00
132 Tuffy Griffiths RC 50.00 100.00
133 Johnny Mahaffey RC 50.00 100.00
134 Trueman Donnelly RC 50.00 100.00
135 Bill Stewart RC 75.00 150.00

1933-34 V357 Ice Kings

This interesting and attractive set of 72 cards features black and white photos on the front, upon which the head of the player portrayed has been tinted in flesh tones. The cards measure approximately 2 3/8" by 2 7/8". The player's name appears on the front of the card. The card number, position, team and player's name is listed on the back as are brief biographies in both French and English. Some cards appear with the resumes in English only. Printed in Canada and issued by World Wide Gum, the catalog designation for this set is V357.

COMP.SET (72) 9000.00 15000.00
1 Dit Clapper RC 350.00 600.00
2 Bill Brydge RC 50.00 100.00
3 Aurel Joliat UER 500.00 800.00
4 Andy Blair 50.00 100.00
5 Earl Robinson RC 50.00 100.00
6 Paul Haynes RC 50.00 100.00
7 Ronnie Martin RC 50.00 100.00
8 Babe Siebert RC 175.00 300.00
9 Archie Wilcox RC 50.00 100.00
10 Clarence(Hap) Day 150.00 250.00
11 Roy Worters RC 200.00 350.00
12 Nels Stewart RC 350.00 600.00
13 King Clancy 600.00 1000.00
14 Marty Burke RC 125.00 200.00
15 Cecil Dillon RC 50.00 100.00
16 Red Horner RC 175.00 300.00
17 Armand Mondou RC 50.00 100.00
18 Paul Raymond RC 50.00 100.00
19 Dave Kerr RC 75.00 125.00
20 Butch Keeling RC 50.00 100.00
21 Johnny Gagnon RC 50.00 100.00
22 Ace Bailey RC 300.00 500.00
23 Harry Oliver RC 150.00 250.00
24 Gerald Carson RC 50.00 100.00
25 Red Dutton RC 150.00 250.00
26 Georges Mantha RC 50.00 100.00
27 Marty Barry RC 150.00 250.00
28 Wildor Larochelle RC 75.00 125.00
29 Red Beattie RC 50.00 100.00
30 Bill Cook 150.00 250.00
31 Hooley Smith 150.00 250.00
32 Art Chapman RC 50.00 100.00
33 Harold Cotton RC 125.00 200.00
34 Lionel Hitchman 125.00 200.00
35 George Patterson RC 50.00 100.00
36 Howie Morenz 1200.00 2000.00
37 Jimmy Ward RC 50.00 100.00
38 Charley McVeigh RC 75.00 125.00
39 Glen Brydson RC 75.00 125.00
40 Joe Primeau RC 300.00 500.00
41 Joe Lamb RC 90.00 150.00
42 Sylvio Mantha 125.00 200.00
43 Cy Wentworth RC 75.00 125.00
44 Normie Himes RC 75.00 125.00
45 Doug Brennan RC 50.00 100.00
46 Pit Lepine RC 50.00 100.00
47 Alex Levinsky RC 75.00 125.00
48 Baldy Northcott RC 75.00 125.00
49 Ken Doraty RC 75.00 125.00
50 Bill Thoms RC 75.00 125.00
51 Vernon Ayres RC 75.00 125.00
52 Lorne Duguid RC 75.00 125.00
53 Wally Kilrea RC 75.00 125.00
54 Vic Ripley RC 75.00 125.00
55 Hap Emms RC 75.00 125.00
56 Duke Dutkowski RC 75.00 125.00
57 Tiny Thompson RC 300.00 500.00
58 Charlie Sands RC 75.00 125.00
59 Larry Aurie RC 75.00 125.00
60 Bill Beveridge RC 75.00 125.00
61 Bill McKenzie RC 75.00 125.00
62 Earl Roche RC 75.00 125.00
63 Bob Gracie RC 75.00 125.00
64 Hec Kilrea RC 75.00 125.00
65 Cooney Weiland RC 250.00 400.00
66 Bun Cook RC 200.00 350.00
67 John Roach 90.00 150.00
68 Murray Murdoch RC 75.00 125.00
69 Danny Cox RC 75.00 125.00
70 Desse Roche RC 75.00 125.00
71 Lorne Chabot RC 175.00 300.00
72 Syd Howe RC 250.00 400.00

1933-34 V357-2 Ice Kings Premiums

These six black-and-white large cards are actually premiums. The cards measure approximately 7" by 9". The cards are unnumbered and rather difficult to find now.

COMPLETE SET (6) 2000.00 4000.00
1 King Clancy 500.00 1000.00
2 Clarence(Hap) Day 175.00 350.00
3 Aurel Joliat 400.00 800.00
4 Howie Morenz 1000.00 2000.00
5 Allan Shields 87.50 175.00
6 Reginald(Hooley) Smith 125.00 250.00

1983-84 Vachon

This set of 140 standard-size cards was issued by Vachon Foods as panels of two cards. The set includes players from the seven Canadian NHL teams. The cards were also available as a set directly from Vachon. The first printing contained an error in that number 96 pictures Peter Ihnacek instead of Walt Poddubny. The error was corrected for the second printing. The card

backs are written in French and English. The Vachon logo is on the front of every card in the lower right corner. The set is difficult to collect in uncut panels of two; the prices below are for individual cards, the panel prices are 50 percent greater than the prices listed below.

COMPLETE SET (140) 80.00 200.00
1 Paul Baxter .30 .75
2 Ed Beers .20 .50
3 Steve Bozek .20 .50
4 Mike Eaves .20 .50
5 Don Edwards .40 1.00
6 Kari Eloranta .20 .50
7 Dave Hindmarch .20 .50
8 Jamie Hislop .20 .50
9 Steve Konroyd .20 .50
10 Reggie Lemelin .40 1.00
11 Hakan Loob .75 2.00
12 Jamie Macoun .20 .50
13 Lanny McDonald 1.25 3.00
14 Kent Nilsson .75 2.00
15 Colin Patterson .20 .50
16 Jim Peplinski .40 1.00
17 Paul Reinhart .40 1.00
18 Doug Risebrough .40 1.00
19 Steve Tambellini .20 .50
20 Mickey Volcan .20 .50
21 Glenn Anderson 1.50 4.00
22 Paul Coffey 5.00 12.00
23 Lee Fogolin .20 .50
24 Grant Fuhr 2.00 5.00
25 Randy Gregg .20 .50
26 Wayne Gretzky 20.00 50.00
27 Charlie Huddy .30 .75
28 Pat Hughes .20 .50
29 Dave Hunter .20 .50
30 Don Jackson .20 .50
31 Jari Kurri 3.00 8.00
32 Willy Lindstrom .20 .50
33 Ken Linseman .30 .75
34 Kevin Lowe .60 1.50
35 Dave Lumley .20 .50
36 Mark Messier 10.00 25.00
37 Andy Moog 2.00 5.00
38 Jaroslav Pouzar .20 .50
39 Tom Roulston .20 .50
40 Dave Semenko .30 .75
41 Guy Carbonneau 1.25 3.00
42 Kent Carlson .20 .50
43 Gilbert Delorme .20 .50
44 Bob Gainey .75 2.00
45 Jean Hamel .20 .50
46 Mark Hunter .20 .50
47 Guy Lafleur 2.50 6.00
48 Craig Ludwig .20 .50
49 Pierre Mondou .20 .50
50 Mats Naslund .75 2.00
51 Chris Nilan .40 1.00
52 Greg Paslawski .20 .50
53 Larry Robinson .75 2.00
54 Richard Sevigny .40 1.00
55 Steve Shutt .75 2.00
56 Bobby Smith .40 1.00
57 Mario Tremblay .30 .75
58 Ryan Walter .30 .75
59 Rick Wamsley .40 1.00
60 Doug Wickenheiser .20 .50
61 Bo Berglund .20 .50
62 Dan Bouchard .40 1.00
63 Alain Cote .20 .50
64 Brian Ford .20 .50
65 Michel Goulet 1.00 2.50
66 Dale Hunter .75 2.00
67 Mario Marois .30 .75
68 Tony McKegney .30 .75
69 Randy Moller .20 .50
70 Wilf Paiement .40 1.00
71 Pat Price .20 .50
72 Normand Rochefort .20 .50
73 Andre Savard .20 .50
74 Louis Sleigher .20 .50
75 Anton Stastny .30 .75
76 Marian Stastny .30 .75
77 Peter Stastny 2.50 6.00
78 John Van Boxmeer .20 .50
79 Wally Weir .20 .50
80 Blake Wesley .20 .50
81 John Anderson .30 .75
82 Jim Benning .20 .50
83 Dan Daoust .20 .50
84 Bill Derlago .30 .75
85 Dave Farrish .20 .50
86 Miroslav Frycer .20 .50
87 Stewart Gavin .30 .75
88 Gaston Gingras .20 .50
89 Billy Harris .20 .50
90 Peter Ihnacak .40 1.00
91 Jim Korn .20 .50
92 Terry Martin .20 .50
93 Dale McCourt .20 .50
94 Gary Nylund .20 .50
95 Mike Palmateer .75 2.00
96A Walt Poddubny ERR 4.00 10.00
(Photo actually
Peter Ihnacek
no mustache)
96B Walt Poddubny COR 1.00 2.50
(With mustache)
97 Borje Salming 1.25 3.00
98 Rick St.Croix .40 1.00
99 Greg P. Terrion .20 .50
100 Rick Vaive .40 1.00
101 Richard Brodeur .60 1.50
102 Jiri Bubla .20 .50
103 Garth Butcher .20 .50
104 Ron Delorme .20 .50
105 John Garrett .60 1.50
106 Jere Gillis .20 .50
107 Thomas Gradin .40 1.00
108 Doug Halward .20 .50
109 Mark Kirton .20 .50
110 Rick Lanz .20 .50
111 Gary Lupul .20 .50
112 Kevin McCarthy .20 .50
113 Lars Molin .20 .50
114 Jim Nill .20 .50
115 Darcy Rota .20 .50
116 Stan Smyl .40 1.00
117 Harold Snepsts .60 1.50
118 Patrik Sundstrom .40 1.00
119 Tony Tanti .40 1.00
120 Dave(Tiger) Williams .75 2.00
121 Scott Arniel .20 .50
122 Dave Babych .40 1.00
123 Laurie Boschman .20 .50
124 Wade Campbell .20 .50
125 Lucien DeBlois .20 .50
126 Dale Hawerchuk 3.00 8.00
127 Brian Hayward .40 1.00
128 Jim Kyte .30 .75
129 Morris Lukowich .20 .50
130 Bengt Lundholm .20 .50
131 Paul MacLean .40 1.00
132 Moe Mantha .20 .50
133 Andrew McBain .20 .50
134 Brian Mullen .20 .50
135 Robert Picard .20 .50
136 Doug Smail .40 1.00
137 Doug Soetaert .40 1.00
138 Thomas Steen .60 1.50
139 Tim Watters .20 .50
140 Tim Young .30 .75

1973-74 Vancouver Blazers

This set features the Blazers of the WHA. The cards are actually oversized black and white photos and were issued as a promotional item by the team. The Archambault and Cardiff cards were recently confirmed by collector M.R. LaFleche. No pricing information is available for these singles at this time.

COMPLETE SET (21) 25.00 50.00
1 Jim Adair 1.50 3.00
2 Yves Archambault
3 Don Burgess 2.00 4.00
4 Bryan Campbell 2.00 4.00
5 Colin Campbell 2.50 5.00
6 Jim Cardiff
7 Mike Chernoff 1.50 3.00
8 Peter Donnelly 1.50 3.00
9 George Gardner 1.50 3.00
10 Sam Gellard 1.50 3.00
11 Ed Hatoum 1.50 3.00
12 Dave Hutchison 2.00 4.00
13 Danny Lawton 1.50 3.00
14 Ralph MacSweyn 1.50 3.00
15 Denis Meloche 1.50 3.00
16 John Migneault 1.50 3.00
17 Murray Myers 1.50 3.00
18 Michel Plante 1.50 3.00
19 Ron Plumb 2.00 4.00
20 Claude St. Sauveur 1.50 3.00
21 Irv Spencer 2.00 4.00

2000-01 Vanguard

In 2000-01 Pacific Vanguard was released as a 151-card set with cards 101-150 released as short-printed cards. The base set design consisted of card fronts that featured laser-etched technology to silhouette the player with silver blending into a team color. The short printed cards were serial numbered to 390.

COMP.SET w/o SP's (101) 15.00 40.00
1 Guy Hebert .50 1.25
2 Paul Kariya .60 1.50
3 Teemu Selanne .60 1.50
4 Ray Ferraro .20 .50
5 Damian Rhodes .20 .50
6 Patrik Stefan .20 .50
7 Jason Allison .20 .50
8 Bill Guerin .50 1.25
9 Sergei Samsonov .50 1.25
10 Joe Thornton 1.00 2.50
11 Maxim Afinogenov .20 .50
12 Doug Gilmour .50 1.25
13 Dominik Hasek 1.25 3.00
14 Miroslav Satan .50 1.25
15 Valeri Bure .20 .50
16 Jarome Iginla .75 2.00
17 Marc Savard .20 .50
18 Rod Brind'Amour .50 1.25
19 Ron Francis .50 1.25
20 Arturs Irbe .50 1.25
21 Sami Kapanen .20 .50
22 Tony Amonte .50 1.25
23 Jocelyn Thibault .50 1.25
24 Alexei Zhamnov .20 .50
25 Ray Bourque 1.25 3.00
26 Chris Drury .50 1.25
27 Peter Forsberg 1.25 3.00
28 Milan Hejduk .60 1.50
29 Patrick Roy 3.00 6.00
30 Joe Sakic 1.25 3.00
31 Geoff Sanderson .20 .50
32 Ron Tugnutt .50 1.25
33 Ed Belfour .60 1.50
34 Brett Hull .75 2.00
35 Mike Modano 1.00 2.50
36 Joe Nieuwendyk .50 1.25
37 Sergei Fedorov 1.00 2.50
38 Nicklas Lidstrom .60 1.50
39 Chris Osgood .50 1.25
40 Brendan Shanahan .60 1.50
41 Steve Yzerman 3.00 6.00
42 Anson Carter .50 1.25
43 Tommy Salo .50 1.25
44 Doug Weight .50 1.25
45 Pavel Bure .60 1.50
46 Viktor Kozlov .50 1.25
47 Ray Whitney .20 .50
48 Ziggy Palffy .50 1.25
49 Luc Robitaille .50 1.25
50 Sergei Krivokrasov .20 .50
51 Saku Koivu .60 1.50
52 Trevor Linden .50 1.25
53 Jose Theodore .75 2.00
54 David Legwand .50 1.25
55 Randy Robitaille .20 .50
56 Jason Arnott .20 .50
57 Martin Brodeur 1.50 4.00
58 Patrik Elias .50 1.25
59 Scott Gomez .20 .50
60 Alexander Mogilny .50 1.25
61 Tim Connolly .20 .50
62 Mariusz Czerkawski .20 .50
63 John Vanbiesbrouck .50 1.25
64 Theo Fleury .20 .50
65 Brian Leetch .50 1.25
66 Mark Messier .60 1.50
67 Mike Richter .60 1.50
68 Daniel Alfredsson .60 1.50
69 Marian Hossa .60 1.50
70 Alexei Yashin .20 .50
71 Brian Boucher .60 1.50
72 Simon Gagne .60 1.50
73 John LeClair .60 1.50
74 Eric Lindros .60 1.50
75 Shane Doan .20 .50
76 Jeremy Roenick .75 2.00
77 Keith Tkachuk .60 1.50
78 Jean-Sebastien Aubin .50 1.25
79 Jan Hrdina .20 .50
80 Jaromir Jagr 1.00 2.50
81 Martin Straka .20 .50
82 Al MacInnis .50 1.25
83 Chris Pronger .50 1.25
84 Roman Turek .50 1.25
85 Pierre Turgeon .50 1.25
86 Vincent Damphousse .20 .50
87 Jeff Friesen .20 .50
88 Owen Nolan .50 1.25
89 Mike Johnson .20 .50
90 Vincent Lecavalier .60 1.50
91 Nik Antropov .20 .50
92 Tie Domi .50 1.25
93 Curtis Joseph .60 1.50
94 Mats Sundin .60 1.50
95 Andrew Cassels .20 .50
96 Markus Naslund .60 1.50
97 Felix Potvin .60 1.50
98 Peter Bondra .60 1.50
99 Olaf Kolzig .50 1.25
100 Adam Oates .50 1.25
101 Samuel Pahlsson SP 1.50 4.00
102 Jonas Ronnqvist RC 1.50 4.00
103 Milan Hnilicka SP 1.50 4.00
104 Andrew Raycroft RC 10.00 25.00
105 Dimitri Kalinin SP 1.50 4.00
106 Mika Noronen SP 1.50 4.00
107 Oleg Saprykin SP 1.50 4.00
108 Josef Vasicek RC 2.50 6.00
109 Shane Willis SP 1.50 4.00
110 Steve McCarthy SP 1.50 4.00
111 David Aebischer RC 8.00 20.00
112 Serge Aubin RC 1.50 4.00
113 Marc Denis SP 2.50 6.00
114 Rostislav Klesla RC 2.50 6.00
115 David Vyborny SP 1.50 4.00
116 Tyler Bouck RC 1.50 4.00
117 Marty Turco RC 10.00 25.00
118 Joaquin Gage SP 1.50 4.00
119 Michel Riesen RC 1.50 4.00
120 Brian Swanson RC 1.50 4.00
121 Roberto Luongo SP 2.50 6.00
122 Ivan Novoseltsev SP 1.50 4.00
123 Eric Belanger RC 1.50 4.00
124 Steven Reinprecht RC 1.50 4.00
125 Lubomir Visnovsky RC 1.50 4.00
126 Manny Fernandez SP 1.50 4.00
127 Marian Gaborik RC 8.00 20.00
128 Filip Kuba SP 1.50 4.00
129 Mathieu Garon SP 1.50 4.00
130 Andrei Markov SP 1.50 4.00
131 Scott Hartnell RC 2.50 6.00
132 Colin White RC 1.50 4.00
133 Rick DiPietro RC 10.00 25.00
134 Taylor Pyatt SP 1.50 4.00
135 Martin Havlat RC 8.00 20.00
136 Jani Hurme RC 2.50 6.00
137 Roman Cechmanek RC 2.50 4.00
138 Justin Williams RC 6.00 15.00
139 Robert Esche SP 1.50 4.00
140 Wyatt Smith SP 1.50 4.00
141 Ossi Vaananen RC 1.50 4.00
142 Milan Kraft SP 1.50 4.00
143 Brent Johnson SP 1.50 4.00
144 Ladislav Nagy SP 2.50 6.00
145 Evgeni Nabokov SP 2.50 6.00
146 Sheldon Keefe SP 1.50 4.00
147 Brad Richards SP 2.50 6.00
148 Petr Svoboda RC 1.50 4.00
149 Daniel Sedin SP 1.50 4.00
150 Henrik Sedin SP 1.50 4.00
151 Mario Lemieux 4.00 10.00

2000-01 Vanguard Premiere Date

These cards were random inserts in 2000-01 Pacific Vanguard. This parallel set had the serial numbers on the bottom right corner on the front of the card. The cards were serial numbered to 100.

*STARS:3X TO 6X BASIC CARDS

2000-01 Vanguard Cosmic Force

Randomly inserted in packs at a rate of 1:73, this 10-card set featured some of the top players from the NHL. The card design had a foilboard card front and used 30-point styrene. There was a photo of the players head over laying a full body photo faintly seen in the background.

COMPLETE SET (10) 30.00 80.00
1 Paul Kariya 2.50 6.00
2 Dominik Hasek 4.00 10.00
3 Peter Forsberg 4.00 10.00
4 Patrick Roy 10.00 25.00
5 Steve Yzerman 8.00 20.00
6 Pavel Bure 2.50 6.00
7 Martin Brodeur 6.00 15.00
8 Eric Lindros 2.50 6.00
9 Jaromir Jagr 4.00 10.00
10 Curtis Joseph 2.50 6.00

2000-01 Vanguard Dual Game-Worn Jerseys

These cards were inserted into packs of Pacific Vanguard at a rate of 2 per box. The 20-card set featured the some of the top players from the NHL. The cards featured 2 jersey swatches per card, one on the front and one on the back. The cards were highlighted with silver-foil markings. The cards were serial numbered and the print runs vary, please see below for actual print runs.

*MULT.COLOR SWATCH: 1X TO 2X
1 Joe Thornton 6.00 15.00
Sergei Samsonov/1500
2 Peter Forsberg 25.00 60.00
Mats Sundin/125
3 Joe Sakic 15.00 40.00
Eric Lindros/250
4 Derian Hatcher 6.00 15.00
Mike Modano/1500
5 Brendan Shanahan 6.00 15.00
Chris Chelios/1500
6 Sergei Fedorov 8.00 20.00
Chris Osgood/400
7 Doug Weight 6.00 15.00
Ryan Smyth/1500
8 Bobby Holik 6.00 15.00
Mariusz Czerkawski/1500
9 John Vanbiesbrouck 25.00 60.00
Mike Richter/50
10 Alexei Zhamnov 6.00 15.00
Cory Stillman/1500
11 Cliff Ronning 6.00 15.00
Vitali Yachmenev/1500
12 Tom Fitzgerald 6.00 15.00
Kimmo Timonen/1400
13 Byron Dafoe 6.00 15.00
Darren McCarty/1400
14 Kyle McLaren 6.00 15.00
Don Sweeney/1400
15 Jere Lehtinen 6.00 15.00
Jamie Langenbrunner/400
16 Eric Daze 6.00 15.00
Marty McInnis/300
17 Andreas Dackell 6.00 15.00
Ulf Dahlen/400
18 Shayne Corson 6.00 15.00
Jeff Hackett/400
19 Chris Terreri 6.00 15.00
Guy Hebert/400
20 Scott Niedermayer 6.00 15.00
Claude Lapointe/400

2000-01 Vanguard Dual Game-Worn Patches

The 20-card set featured the some of the top players from the NHL. The cards featured 2 jersey-patch swatches per card, one on the front and one on the back. The cards were highlighted with silver-foil markings. The cards were serial numbered and the print runs vary, please see below for actual print runs. Note that card 9 does not exist. Lower print run cards not priced due to scarcity.

1 Joe Thornton 20.00 50.00
Sergei Samsonov/300
2 Peter Forsberg 50.00 125.00
Mats Sundin/100
3 Joe Sakic 25.00 60.00
Eric Lindros/100
4 Derian Hatcher 15.00 40.00
Mike Modano/300
5 Brendan Shanahan 25.00 60.00
Chris Chelios/125
6 Sergei Fedorov
Chris Osgood/25
7 Doug Weight 10.00 25.00
Ryan Smyth/300
8 Bobby Holik 10.00 25.00
Mariusz Czerkawski/300
10 Alexei Zhamnov 10.00 25.00
Cory Stillman/300
11 Cliff Ronning 10.00 25.00
Vitali Yachmenev/300
12 Tom Fitzgerald 10.00 25.00
Kimmo Timonen/300
13 Byron Dafoe 10.00 25.00
Darren McCarty/300
14 Kyle McLaren 10.00 25.00
Don Sweeney/300
15 Jere Lehtinen 10.00 25.00
Jamie Langenbrunner/100
16 Eric Daze
Marty McInnis/15
17 Andreas Dackell 10.00 25.00
Ulf Dahlen/75
18 Shayne Corson 10.00 25.00
Jeff Hackett/75
19 Chris Terreri 10.00 25.00
Guy Hebert/75
20 Scott Niedermayer 10.00 25.00
Claude Lapointe/100

2000-01 Vanguard High Voltage

These cards were randomly inserted in 2000-01 Pacific Vanguard at a rate of 1:1. The set consisted of 36 cards that featured some of the most prolific player from the NHL. Four different colored parallels were also created and randomly inserted. Parallel values can be found by using the multipliers below. Red parallels were serial numbered out of 299, gold parallels were serial numbered out of 199, green parallels were serial numbered out of 99, and silver parallels were serial numbered to just 10. Silver parallels are not priced due to scarcity.

COMPLETE SET (36) 10.00 20.00
*RED: 2X TO 4X BASIC CARDS
*GOLD: 3X TO 6X BASIC CARDS
*GREEN: 4X TO 8X BASIC CARDS
1 Paul Kariya .30 .75
2 Teemu Selanne .30 .75
3 Joe Thornton .40 1.00
4 Jason Allison .25 .60
5 Dominik Hasek .60 1.50
6 Ray Bourque .60 1.50
7 Peter Forsberg .75 2.00
8 Patrick Roy 1.50 4.00
9 Joe Sakic .60 1.50
10 Ed Belfour .30 .75
11 Brett Hull .40 1.00
12 Mike Modano .50 1.25
13 Brendan Shanahan .30 .75
14 Steve Yzerman 1.50 4.00
15 Doug Weight .25 .60
16 Pavel Bure .30 .75
17 Zigmund Palffy .25 .60
18 Marian Gaborik 2.00 5.00
19 Martin Brodeur .75 2.00
20 Scott Gomez .25 .60
21 Rick DiPietro 2.00 5.00
22 Theo Fleury .25 .60
23 Mark Messier .30 .75
24 Marian Hossa .30 .75
25 John LeClair .30 .75
26 Eric Lindros .30 .75
27 Jeremy Roenick .40 1.00
28 Keith Tkachuk .30 .75
29 Jaromir Jagr .50 1.25
30 Pierre Turgeon .25 .60
31 Vincent Lecavalier .30 .75
32 Curtis Joseph .30 .75
33 Mats Sundin .30 .75
34 Daniel Sedin .25 .60
35 Henrik Sedin .25 .60
36 Peter Bondra .30 .75

2000-01 Vanguard Holographic Gold

These cards were randomly inserted into packs of 2000-01 Pacific Vanguard retail at a rate of 1:25. These 100 cards were a parallel to the base set of Vanguard, and they were serial numbered to 60.

*STARS: 10X TO 20X BASIC CARDS

2000-01 Vanguard Holographic Purple

These cards were randomly inserted into packs of 2000-01 Pacific Vanguard hobby at a rate of 1:24. These 100 cards were a parallel to the base set of Vanguard, and they were serial numbered to 105.

*STARS: 3X TO 6X BASIC CARDS

2000-01 Vanguard In Focus

COMPLETE SET (20) 20.00 40.00
STATED ODDS 1:25
1 Paul Kariya .60 1.50
2 Teemu Selanne .60 1.50
3 Jason Allison .50 1.25
4 Ray Bourque 1.25 3.00
5 Peter Forsberg 1.50 4.00
6 Patrick Roy 3.00 8.00
7 Brett Hull .75 2.00
8 Sergei Fedorov 1.25 3.00
9 Steve Yzerman 3.00 8.00
10 Pavel Bure .75 2.00
11 Marian Gaborik 3.00 8.00
12 Martin Brodeur 1.50 4.00
13 Theo Fleury .50 1.25
14 John LeClair .75 2.00
15 Jaromir Jagr 1.00 2.50
16 Vincent Lecavalier .60 1.50
17 Curtis Joseph .60 1.50
18 Mats Sundin .60 1.50
19 Daniel Sedin .50 1.25
20 Henrik Sedin .50 1.25

2000-01 Vanguard Press East/West

Randomly inserted in packs of 2000-01 Pacific Vanguard, this 20-card set featured some of the top players from the NHL split into hobby-only cards and retail-only cards. The split was done on an East/West basis, the West players were hobby-only and the East players were retail-only. They were found in packs at a rate of 2:25 for either distribution channel.

COMPLETE SET (20) 30.00 60.00
1 Paul Kariya .60 1.50
2 Teemu Selanne .60 1.50
3 Peter Forsberg 1.50 4.00
4 Patrick Roy 3.00 8.00
5 Brett Hull .75 2.00
6 Sergei Fedorov 1.25 3.00
7 Steve Yzerman 3.00 8.00
8 Zigmund Palffy .50 1.25
9 Jeremy Roenick .75 2.00
10 Pierre Turgeon .50 1.25
11 Joe Thornton 2.50 6.00
12 Dominik Hasek 3.00 8.00
13 Pavel Bure 2.00 5.00
14 Martin Brodeur 4.00 10.00
15 Mark Messier 2.00 5.00
16 Alexei Yashin 1.50 4.00
17 Eric Lindros 1.50 4.00
18 Jaromir Jagr 2.50 6.00
19 Vincent Lecavalier 1.50 4.00
20 Curtis Joseph 1.50 4.00

2001-02 Vanguard

Released in early-February 2002, this 130-card set consisted of 100 regular base cards and 30 cards of first year players serial-numbered to 404 copies each.

COMP.SET w/o SP's (100) 20.00 50.00
1 Jeff Friesen .20 .50
2 Paul Kariya .40 1.00
3 Dany Heatley .75 2.00
4 Milan Hnilicka .30 .75
5 Byron Dafoe .30 .75
6 Glen Murray .20 .50
7 Sergei Samsonov .30 .75
8 Joe Thornton .75 2.00
9 Martin Biron .30 .75
10 Tim Connolly .20 .50
11 J-P Dumont .20 .50
12 Jarome Iginla .75 2.00
13 Marc Savard .20 .50
14 Roman Turek .30 .75
15 Ron Francis .30 .75
16 Arturs Irbe .30 .75
17 Jeff O'Neill .20 .50
18 Tony Amonte .30 .75
19 Mark Bell .20 .50
20 Kyle Calder .20 .50
21 Eric Daze .30 .75
22 Jocelyn Thibault .30 .75
23 Rob Blake .30 .75
24 Chris Drury .30 .75
25 Milan Hejduk .40 1.00
26 Patrick Roy 2.50 6.00
27 Joe Sakic 1.25 3.00
28 Alex Tanguay .30 .75
29 Rostislav Klesla .20 .50
30 Ron Tugnutt .30 .75
31 Ed Belfour .40 1.00
32 Mike Modano .75 2.00
33 Pierre Turgeon .30 .75
34 Sergei Fedorov .60 1.50
35 Dominik Hasek 1.25 3.00
36 Brett Hull .60 1.50
37 Brendan Shanahan .40 1.00
38 Steve Yzerman 2.50 6.00
39 Mike Comrie .30 .75
40 Tommy Salo .30 .75
41 Ryan Smyth .20 .50
42 Pavel Bure .40 1.00
43 Roberto Luongo .75 2.00
44 Jason Allison .20 .50
45 Zigmund Palffy .30 .75
46 Felix Potvin .40 1.00
47 Manny Fernandez .30 .75
48 Marian Gaborik .75 2.00
49 Doug Gilmour .30 .75
50 Yanic Perreault .20 .50
51 Brian Savage .20 .50
52 Jose Theodore .60 1.50
53 Mike Dunham .30 .75
54 David Legwand .30 .75
55 Jason Arnott .20 .50
56 Martin Brodeur 1.50 4.00
57 Patrik Elias .30 .75
58 Rick DiPietro .30 .75
59 Chris Osgood .30 .75
60 Mark Parrish .20 .50
61 Michael Peca .20 .50
62 Alexei Yashin .20 .50
63 Brian Leetch .30 .75

64 Eric Lindros .40 1.00
65 Mark Messier .40 1.00
66 Mike Richter .40 1.00
67 Daniel Alfredsson .30 .75
68 Martin Havlat .30 .75
69 Marian Hossa .40 1.00
70 Patrick Lalime .30 .75
71 Pavel Brendl .30 .75
72 Roman Cechmanek .30 .75
73 John LeClair .40 1.00
74 Jeremy Roenick .60 1.50
75 Sean Burke .30 .75
76 Shane Doan .20 .50
77 Daymond Langkow .20 .50
78 Kris Beech .20 .50
79 Johan Hedberg .30 .75
80 Mario Lemieux 3.00 8.00
81 Brent Johnson .30 .75
82 Chris Pronger .30 .75
83 Keith Tkachuk .40 1.00
84 Doug Weight .30 .75
85 Patrick Marleau .30 .75
86 Evgeni Nabokov .30 .75
87 Owen Nolan .30 .75
88 Teemu Selanne .40 1.00
89 Vincent Lecavalier .40 1.00
90 Brad Richards .30 .75
91 Martin St. Louis .30 .75
92 Curtis Joseph .40 1.00
93 Alexander Mogilny .30 .75
94 Mats Sundin .40 1.00
95 Dan Cloutier .30 .75
96 Brendan Morrison .30 .75
97 Markus Naslund .40 1.00
98 Peter Bondra .40 1.00
99 Jaromir Jagr 1.00 2.50
100 Olaf Kolzig .30 .75
101 Ilja Bryzgalov RC 4.00 10.00
102 Timo Parssinen RC 2.00 5.00
103 Ilya Kovalchuk RC 15.00 40.00
104 Brian Pothier RC 2.00 5.00
105 Jukka Hentunen RC 2.00 5.00
106 Erik Cole RC 4.00 10.00
107 Vaclav Nedorost RC 2.00 5.00
108 Niko Kapanen RC 2.00 5.00
109 Pavel Datsyuk RC 10.00 25.00
110 Jason Chimera RC 2.00 5.00
111 Ty Conklin RC 2.00 5.00
112 Jussi Markkanen SP 2.00 5.00
113 Niklas Hagman RC 2.00 5.00
114 Kristian Huselius RC 4.00 10.00
115 Jaroslav Bednar RC 2.00 5.00
116 Pascal Dupuis RC 2.00 5.00
117 Nick Schultz RC 2.00 5.00
118 Martin Erat RC 2.00 5.00
119 Andreas Salomonsson RC 2.00 5.00
120 Radek Martinek RC 2.00 5.00
121 Raffi Torres RC 4.00 10.00
122 Dan Blackburn RC 2.00 5.00
123 Chris Neil RC 2.00 5.00
124 Jiri Dopita RC 2.00 5.00
125 David Cullen RC 2.00 5.00
126 Krystofer Kolanos RC 2.00 5.00
127 Mark Rycroft RC 2.00 5.00
128 Jeff Jillson RC 2.00 5.00
129 Nikita Alexeev RC 2.00 5.00
130 Brian Sutherby RC 2.00 5.00

2001-02 Vanguard Blue

Inserted in 1:49 hobby and 1:25 retail packs, this 130-card set paralleled the base set with blue foil highlights replacing the silver. Each card was serial-numbered out of 89.

*STARS: 4X TO 8X BASIC CARD
*SP's: .25X TO .75X BASIC CARD

2001-02 Vanguard Red

Randomly inserted at 1:96 hobby and retail packs, this 130-card set paralleled the base set with red foil replacing the silver. Cards in this set were serial-numbered out of 38.

*STARS: 5X TO 12X BASIC CARD
*SP's: .5X TO 1X BASIC CARD

2001-02 Vanguard East Meets West

This 10-card set was randomly inserted at 1:97 packs.

COMPLETE SET (10) 20.00 50.00
1 M.Lemieux/J.Jagr 5.00 12.00
2 Patrick Roy 5.00 12.00
Dominik Hasek
3 Joe Sakic 4.00 10.00
Peter Forsberg
4 Martin Brodeur 4.00 10.00
Johan Hedberg
5 Eric Lindros 2.00 5.00
Alexei Yashin
6 Paul Kariya 2.00 5.00
Teemu Selanne
7 Steve Yzerman 4.00 10.00
Sergei Fedorov
8 Brendan Shanahan 2.00 5.00
Pavel Bure
9 Jarome Iginla 2.50 6.00
Mats Sundin
10 Chris Pronger 2.00 5.00
Nicklas Lidstrom

2001-02 Vanguard In Focus

This 10-card set was randomly inserted at a rate of 1:481 hobby packs. Each card was serial-numbered to 55 copies each.

1 Patrick Roy 20.00 50.00
2 Joe Sakic 12.50 30.00
3 Dominik Hasek 12.50 30.00
4 Brendan Shanahan 10.00 25.00
5 Steve Yzerman 20.00 50.00
6 Pavel Bure 8.00 20.00
7 Martin Brodeur 15.00 40.00
8 Mario Lemieux 25.00 60.00
9 Mats Sundin 8.00 10.00
10 Jaromir Jagr 10.00 25.00

2001-02 Vanguard Memorabilia

This 50-card set featured pieces of game-used equipment. Cards 1-41 and 43-44 carried dual swatches of game jerseys. Card #42 carried a swatch of jersey and a piece of game-used stick. Cards 45-50 carried a piece of the goal net from the NHL All-Star game. Cards 1-44 were inserted at 2:25 hobby and 1:25 retail. Cards 45-50 were inserted at 1:97 hobby packs only.

*MULT.COLOR SWATCH: 1X TO 1.5X HI
1 Paul Kariya 3.00 8.00
Oleg Tverdovsky
2 Paul Kariya 3.00 8.00
Guy Hebert
3 Sergei Samsonov 2.00 5.00
Don Sweeney
4 Jarome Iginla 3.00 8.00
Marc Savard
5 Fred Brathwaite 2.00 5.00
Roman Turek
6 Craig Stillman 2.00 5.00
Cory Conroy
7 Boris Mironov 2.00 5.00
Michael Nylander
8 Tony Amonte 5.00 12.00
Steve Sullivan SP
9 Joe Sakic 10.00 20.00
Peter Forsberg
10 Patrick Roy 15.00 40.00
Joe Sakic
11 Mike Modano 4.00 10.00
Derian Hatcher
12 Jamie Langenbrunner 2.00 5.00
Darryl Sydor
13 Steve Yzerman 12.00 30.00
Chris Chelios
14 Niklas Lidstrom 12.00 30.00
Sergei Fedorov SP
15 Saku Koivu 6.00 15.00
Teemu Selanne
16 Cliff Ronning 2.00 5.00
Vitali Yachmenev
17 Bobby Holik 2.00 5.00
Scott Niedermayer
18 Mariusz Czerkawski 2.00 5.00
Shawn Bates
19 Eric Lindros 3.00 8.00
Pavel Brendl
20 Mike Richter 12.00 30.00
Mike York
21 Jeremy Roenick 5.00 12.00
Eric Weinrich
22 Jeremy Lehtinen 2.00 5.00
Jyrki Lumme
23 Martin Straka 2.00 5.00
Josef Beranek
24 Jan Hrdina 2.00 5.00
Bob Boughner
25 Alexei Kovalev 2.00 5.00
Darius Kasparaitis
26 M.Lemieux/R.Lang 15.00 40.00
27 Martin Straka 2.00 5.00
Rich Parent
28 Dallas Drake 2.00 5.00
Mike Eastwood
29 Jochen Hecht 2.00 5.00
Jamie McLennan
30 Pierre Turgeon 4.00 10.00
Vincent Lecavalier
31 J-P Dumont 2.00 5.00
Scott Young
32 Curtis Joseph 12.00 30.00
Jose Theodore
33 Jaromir Jagr 10.00 25.00
Peter Bondra
34 Mats Sundin 3.00 8.00
Andrew Cassels
35 Olaf Kolzig 5.00 12.00
Dan Cloutier
36 Claude Lapointe 2.00 5.00
Mats Lindgren
37 Greg DeVries 5.00 12.00
Eric Messier
38 Steve Yzerman 20.00 50.00
Eric Lindros
39 Alexei Kovalev 2.00 5.00
Kip Miller
40 Lyle Odelein 2.00 5.00
Andre Savage
41 Marc Savard 2.00 5.00
Roman Turek
42 Jaromir Jagr 15.00 40.00
Ilya Kovalchuk STK/200
43 Patrick Roy 15.00 40.00
Jose Theodore
44 M.Lemieux/M.Sundin 15.00 40.00
45 Theo Fleury 10.00 25.00
Marian Hossa NET
46 Brett Hull 25.00 60.00
Pavel Bure NET
47 Doug Weight 10.00 25.00
Peter Forsberg NET
48 Jason Allison 10.00 25.00
Zigmund Palffy NET
49 Rob Blake 12.00 30.00
Milan Hejduk NET
50 Martin Brodeur 30.00 80.00
Dominik Hasek NET

2001-02 Vanguard Patches

Randomly inserted at 1:97 hobby packs, this 16-card set partially paralleled the base memorabilia set but featured swatches of jersey patches. The set is skip-numbered.

3 Sergei Samsonov 12.50 30.00
Don Sweeney/35
5 Fred Brathwaite 12.50 30.00
Roman Turek/181
6 Cory Stillman 12.50 30.00
Craig Conroy
10 Patrick Roy 30.00 80.00
Joe Sakic/55
12 Jamie Langenbrunner 12.50 30.00
Darryl Sydor
21 Jeremy Roenick 20.00 50.00
Eric Weinrich
22 Jeremy Lehtinen 12.50 30.00
Jyrki Lumme
23 Martin Straka 12.50 30.00
Josef Beranek
25 Alexei Kovalev 12.50 30.00
Darius Kasparaitis
27 Martin Straka 12.50 30.00
Rich Parent
28 Dallas Drake 12.50 30.00
Mike Eastwood
33 Jaromir Jagr 25.00 60.00
Peter Bondra
37 Greg DeVries 12.50 30.00
Eric Messier
38 Steve Yzerman 30.00 80.00
Eric Lindros/25
39 Alexei Kovalev 12.50 30.00
Kip Miller
41 Marc Savard 12.50 30.00
Roman Turek

2001-02 Vanguard Premiere Date

Randomly inserted into hobby packs, this 130-card set paralleled the base set but each card carried a "Premier Date" stamp on the card front. Cards from this set were serial-numbered to 83 copies each.

*STARS: 4X TO 10X BASIC CARD
*SP's: .25X TO .75X BASIC CARD

2001-02 Vanguard Prime Prospects

This 20-card set was randomly inserted at 1:25 packs.

COMPLETE SET (20) 30.00 60.00
1 Dany Heatley 3.00 8.00
2 Ilya Kovalchuk 4.00 10.00
3 Vaclav Nedorost .75 2.00
4 Rostislav Klesla .75 2.00
5 Pavel Datsyuk 3.00 8.00
6 Mike Comrie 1.25 3.00
7 Kristian Huselius .75 2.00
8 Jaroslav Bednar .75 2.00
9 Marian Gaborik 3.00 8.00
10 Martin Erat .75 2.00
11 Rick DiPietro 2.00 5.00
12 Dan Blackburn .75 2.00
13 Martin Havlat 2.00 5.00
14 Pavel Brendl .75 2.00
15 Krystofer Kolanos .75 2.00
16 Brent Johnson 1.25 3.00
17 Jeff Jillson .75 2.00
18 Nikita Alexeev .75 2.00
19 Daniel Sedin 2.00 5.00
20 Henrik Sedin 2.00 5.00

2001-02 Vanguard Quebec Tournament Heroes

Cards from this 20-card set were split distributed. Cards 1-10 were found in packs at 1:25. Cards11-20 were distributed as giveaways to fans attending the Quebec Tournament in Feb. 2002.

COMPLETE HOBBY SET (10) 20.00 40.00
1 Brett Hull 1.25 3.00
2 Mario Lemieux 5.00 12.00

3 Patrick Roy 4.00 10.00
4 Steve Yzerman 4.00 10.00
5 Mike Modano 1.50 4.00
6 Jeremy Roenick 1.25 3.00
7 Brendan Shanahan 1.50 4.00
8 Felix Potvin 1.00 2.50
9 Doug Weight 1.00 2.50
10 Eric Lindros 1.50 4.00
11 Jocelyn Thibault 4.00 10.00
12 Jason Allison 2.00 5.00
13 Chris Drury 2.00 5.00
14 Jeff O'Neill 2.00 5.00
15 Sergei Samsonov 10.00 25.00
16 Alex Tanguay 4.00 10.00
17 Marian Hossa 10.00 25.00
18 Simon Gagne 10.00 25.00
19 Vincent Lecavalier 6.00 15.00
20 Rick DiPietro 6.00 15.00

2001-02 Vanguard Stonewallers

This 20-card set was randomly inserted at 1:49 packs.

COMPLETE SET (20) 40.00 80.00
1 Milan Hnilicka 1.25 3.00
2 Byron Dafoe 1.25 3.00
3 Martin Biron 1.25 3.00
4 Roman Turek 1.25 3.00
5 Patrick Roy 6.00 15.00
6 Ed Belfour 1.50 4.00
7 Dominik Hasek 3.00 8.00
8 Tommy Salo 1.25 3.00
9 Roberto Luongo 2.00 5.00
10 Jose Theodore 2.00 5.00
11 Martin Brodeur 4.00 10.00
12 Chris Osgood 1.25 3.00
13 Mike Richter 1.50 4.00
14 Patrick Lalime 1.25 3.00
15 Roman Cechmanek 1.25 3.00
16 Johan Hedberg 1.25 3.00
17 Evgeni Nabokov 1.25 3.00
18 Nikolai Khabibulin 1.50 4.00
19 Curtis Joseph 1.50 4.00
20 Olaf Kolzig 1.25 3.00

2001-02 Vanguard V-Team

This 20-card set was randomly inserted at 1:25 hobby and retail packs. Cards 1-10 were hobby exclusives and cards 11-20 were retail exclusives.

COMPLETE SET (20) 40.00 80.00
1 Roman Turek .60 1.50
2 Patrick Roy 4.00 10.00
3 Ed Belfour .75 2.00
4 Dominik Hasek 1.50 4.00
5 Martin Brodeur 2.00 5.00
6 Chris Osgood .60 1.50
7 Roman Cechmanek .60 1.50
8 Johan Hedberg .60 1.50
9 Evgeni Nabokov .60 1.50
10 Curtis Joseph .75 2.00
11 Jarome Iginla 1.00 2.50
12 Joe Sakic 1.50 4.00
13 Brendan Shanahan 1.25 3.00
14 Steve Yzerman 4.00 10.00
15 Pavel Bure 1.00 2.50
16 Eric Lindros 1.25 3.00
17 Mario Lemieux 5.00 12.00
18 Teemu Selanne .75 2.00
19 Mats Sundin .75 2.00
20 Jaromir Jagr 1.25 3.00

2002-03 Vanguard

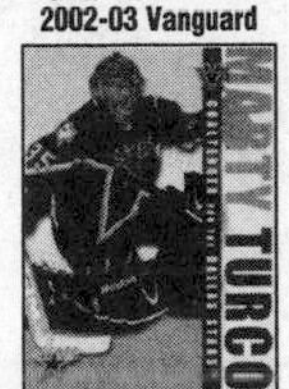

Released in March, this 136-card set consisted of 100 veteran base cards and 36 shortprinted rookie cards. Rookies were serial-numbered out of 1650. There were 6 cards per pack and 24 packs per box.

COMPLETE SET (136) 75.00 200.00
COMP.SET w/o SP's (100) 15.00 40.00
1 Jean-Sebastien Giguere .20 .50
2 Paul Kariya .30 .75
3 Steve Rucchin .10 .25
4 Byron Dafoe .20 .50
5 Dany Heatley .40 1.00
6 Ilya Kovalchuk .40 1.00
7 Glen Murray .10 .25
8 Brian Rolston .20 .50
9 Steve Shields .20 .50
10 Joe Thornton .75 2.00
11 Martin Biron .20 .50
12 Chris Gratton .10 .25
13 Jochen Hecht .10 .25
14 Chris Drury .20 .50
15 Jarome Iginla .40 1.00
16 Roman Turek .20 .50
17 Rod Brind'Amour .20 .50
18 Ron Francis .20 .50
19 Jeff O'Neill .10 .25
20 Kevin Weekes .20 .50
21 Tyler Arnason .20 .50
22 Eric Daze .20 .50
23 Theo Fleury .10 .25
24 Jocelyn Thibault .20 .50
25 Peter Forsberg 1.50 4.00
26 Milan Hejduk .30 .75
27 Patrick Roy 2.00 5.00
28 Joe Sakic 1.00 2.50
29 Andrew Cassels .10 .25
30 Marc Denis .20 .50
31 Geoff Sanderson .10 .25
32 Bill Guerin .20 .50
33 Mike Modano .75 2.00
34 Marty Turco .20 .50
35 Sergei Fedorov .75 2.00
36 Brett Hull .40 1.00
37 Curtis Joseph .30 .75
38 Nicklas Lidstrom .30 .75
39 Brendan Shanahan .30 .75
40 Steve Yzerman 2.00 5.00
41 Anson Carter .20 .50
42 Mike Comrie .20 .50
43 Tommy Salo .20 .50
44 Kristian Huselius .10 .25
45 Olli Jokinen .20 .50
46 Roberto Luongo .40 1.00
47 Jason Allison .10 .25
48 Adam Deadmarsh .10 .25
49 Ziggy Palffy .20 .50
50 Felix Potvin .30 .75
51 Andrew Brunette .10 .25
52 Marian Gaborik .75 2.00
53 Dwayne Roloson .20 .50
54 Jeff Hackett .20 .50
55 Saku Koivu .30 .75
56 Yanic Perreault .10 .25
57 Jose Theodore .40 1.00
58 Andreas Johansson .10 .25
59 David Legwand .20 .50
60 Martin Brodeur 1.50 4.00
61 Patrik Elias .20 .50
62 Jamie Langenbrunner .10 .25
63 Mark Parrish .10 .25
64 Michael Peca .10 .25
65 Alexei Yashin .10 .25
66 Dan Blackburn .20 .50
67 Pavel Bure .30 .75
68 Eric Lindros .30 .75
69 Daniel Alfredsson .20 .50
70 Marian Hossa .30 .75
71 Patrick Lalime .20 .50
72 Roman Cechmanek .20 .50
73 Simon Gagne .30 .75
74 John LeClair .30 .75
75 Jeremy Roenick .40 1.00
76 Tony Amonte .20 .50
77 Brian Boucher .20 .50
78 Mike Johnson .10 .25
79 Johan Hedberg .20 .50
80 Alexei Kovalev .20 .50
81 Mario Lemieux 2.50 6.00
82 Eric Boguniecki .10 .25
83 Cory Stillman .10 .25
84 Doug Weight .20 .50
85 Evgeni Nabokov .20 .50
86 Owen Nolan .20 .50
87 Teemu Selanne .30 .75
88 Nikolai Khabibulin .30 .75
89 Vincent Lecavalier .30 .75
90 Martin St. Louis .30 .75
91 Ed Belfour .30 .75
92 Alexander Mogilny .20 .50
93 Mats Sundin .30 .75
94 Todd Bertuzzi .30 .75
95 Dan Cloutier .20 .50
96 Brendan Morrison .20 .50
97 Markus Naslund .30 .75
98 Peter Bondra .20 .50
99 Jaromir Jagr .75 2.00
100 Olaf Kolzig .20 .50
101 Stanislav Chistov RC 1.50 4.00
102 Martin Gerber RC 1.50 4.00
103 Alexei Smirnov RC 1.00 2.50
104 Tim Thomas RC 2.00 5.00
105 Ryan Miller RC 4.00 10.00
106 Chuck Kobasew RC 1.50 4.00
107 Jordan Leopold RC 1.50 4.00
108 Pascal Leclaire RC 2.00 5.00
109 Rick Nash RC 8.00 20.00
110 Lasse Pirjeta RC 1.00 2.50
111 Steve Ott RC 1.50 4.00
112 Dmitri Bykov RC 1.00 2.50
113 Henrik Zetterberg RC 6.00 15.00
114 Ales Hemsky RC 2.00 5.00
115 Jay Bouwmeester RC 2.00 5.00
116 Mike Cammalleri RC 1.50 4.00
117 Alexander Frolov RC 2.00 5.00
118 P-M Bouchard RC 2.00 5.00
119 Stephane Veilleux RC 1.00 2.50
120 Sylvain Blouin RC 1.00 2.50
121 Ron Hainsey RC 1.00 2.50
122 Adam Hall RC 1.50 4.00
123 Scottie Upshall RC 1.50 4.00
124 Jason Spezza RC 6.00 15.00
125 Anton Volchenkov RC 1.50 4.00
126 Dennis Seidenberg RC 1.00 2.50
127 Patrick Sharp RC 1.00 2.50
128 Radovan Somik RC 1.00 2.50
129 Jeff Taffe RC 1.00 2.50
130 Dick Tarnstrom RC 1.00 2.50
131 Tom Koivisto RC 1.00 2.50
132 Curtis Sanford RC 1.50 4.00
133 Lynn Loyns RC 1.00 2.50
134 Alexander Svitov RC 1.00 2.50
135 Carlo Colaiacovo RC 1.00 2.50
136 Steve Eminger RC 1.50 4.00

2002-03 Vanguard LTD

Inserted at 1:5 hobby, this 136-card set paralleled the base set but each card was serial-numbered to 450.

*STARS: 3X TO 8X BASIC CARDS
*ROOKIES: .5X TO 1.25X

2002-03 Vanguard East Meets West

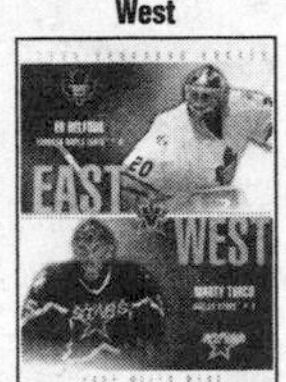

COMPLETE SET (10) 15.00 30.00
STATED ODDS 1:13
1 Ilya Kovalchuk 2.00 5.00
Markus Naslund
2 Joe Thornton 2.50 6.00
Jarome Iginla
3 M.Lemieux/S.Yzerman 4.00 10.00
4 Pavel Bure 2.00 5.00
Sergei Fedorov
5 J.LeClair/M.Modano 2.00 5.00
6 Mats Sundin 2.00 5.00
Peter Forsberg
7 Vincent Lecavalier 2.00 5.00
Joe Sakic
8 M.Hossa/M.Gaborik 2.00 5.00
9 M.Brodeur/P.Roy 4.00 10.00
10 Ed Belfour 2.00 5.00
Marty Turco

2002-03 Vanguard In Focus

COMPLETE SET (10) 20.00 40.00
STATED ODDS 1:25
1 Paul Kariya 1.25 3.00
2 Ilya Kovalchuk 2.00 5.00
3 Peter Forsberg 2.00 5.00
4 Joe Sakic 2.00 5.00
5 Rick Nash 3.00 8.00
6 Steve Yzerman 4.00 10.00
7 Marian Gaborik 2.00 5.00
8 Jason Spezza 3.00 8.00
9 Mario Lemieux 4.00 10.00
10 Jaromir Jagr 1.50 4.00

2002-03 Vanguard Jerseys

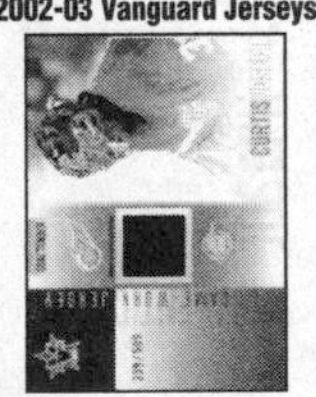

*MULT.COLOR SWATCH: .5X TO 1.25X
STATED ODDS 3:25
1 Adam Oates 2.00 5.00
2 Dany Heatley 5.00 12.00
3 Ilya Kovalchuk 5.00 12.00
4 Patrik Stefan 2.00 5.00
5 Joe Thornton 6.00 15.00
6 J-P Dumont 2.00 5.00
7 Chris Drury 2.00 5.00
8 Jamie McLennan 2.00 5.00
9 Rod Brind'Amour 2.00 5.00
10 Sergei Berezin 2.00 5.00
11 Theo Fleury 3.00 8.00
12 Alexei Zhamnov SP 3.00 8.00
13 Joe Sakic 6.00 15.00
14 Rostislav Klesla 2.00 5.00
15 Mike Modano 6.00 15.00
16 Pierre Turgeon 2.00 5.00
17 Sergei Fedorov 4.00 10.00
18 Brett Hull 4.00 10.00
19 Curtis Joseph 3.00 8.00
20 Ryan Smyth 3.00 8.00
21 Kristian Huselius 2.00 5.00
22 Ziggy Palffy 3.00 8.00
23 Yanic Perreault 2.00 5.00
24 Jose Theodore 4.00 10.00
25 Scott Walker 2.00 5.00
26 Martin Brodeur 10.00 25.00
27 Scott Gomez 2.00 5.00
28 Michael Peca 2.00 5.00
29 Pavel Bure 3.00 8.00
30 Mark Messier 3.00 8.00
31 Daniel Alfredsson 3.00 8.00
32 Patrick Lalime 2.00 5.00
33 John LeClair 2.00 5.00
34 Tomi Kallio 2.00 5.00
35 Krystofer Kolanos 2.00 5.00
36 Johan Hedberg 2.00 5.00
37 Mario Lemieux 12.50 30.00
38 Pavol Demitra 2.00 5.00
39 Keith Tkachuk 2.00 5.00
40 Patrick Marleau 3.00 8.00
41 Evgeni Nabokov 3.00 8.00
42 Nikolai Khabibulin 3.00 8.00
43 Alexander Mogilny 2.00 5.00
44 Gary Roberts 2.00 5.00
45 Darcy Tucker 2.00 5.00
46 Dan Cloutier 2.00 5.00
47 Brendan Morrison 2.00 5.00
48 Markus Naslund 3.00 8.00
49 Peter Bondra 3.00 8.00
50 Jaromir Jagr 6.00 15.00

2002-03 Vanguard Jerseys Gold

*GOLD: 1X TO 2.5X BASE HI
GOLD PRINT RUN 50 SER.#'d SETS

2002-03 Vanguard Prime Prospects

COMPLETE SET (20) 15.00 40.00
STATED ODDS 1:7
1 Stanislav Chistov .75 2.00
2 Alexei Smirnov .75 2.00
3 Ivan Huml .75 2.00
4 Ryan Miller 2.00 5.00
5 Chuck Kobasew 1.25 3.00
6 Jordan Leopold .75 2.00
7 Tyler Arnason .75 2.00
8 Rick Nash 4.00 10.00
9 Henrik Zetterberg 3.00 8.00
10 Ales Hemsky 1.50 4.00
11 Jay Bouwmeester 1.50 4.00
12 Stephen Weiss .75 2.00
13 Alexander Frolov 1.50 4.00
14 P-M Bouchard 1.50 4.00
15 Scottie Upshall .75 2.00
16 Justin Mapletoft .75 2.00
17 Jamie Lundmark .75 2.00
18 Jason Spezza 3.00 8.00
19 Petr Cajanek .75 2.00
20 Barret Jackman .75 2.00

2002-03 Vanguard Stonewallers

COMPLETE SET (12) 10.00 20.00
STATED ODDS 1:9
1 Patrick Roy 4.00 10.00
2 Marty Turco .60 1.50
3 Curtis Joseph .75 2.00
4 Roberto Luongo 1.00 2.50
5 Felix Potvin .75 2.00
6 Jose Theodore 1.00 2.50
7 Martin Brodeur 2.00 5.00
8 Mike Richter .75 2.00
9 Patrick Lalime .60 1.50
10 Roman Cechmanek .60 1.50
11 Nikolai Khabibulin .75 2.00
12 Ed Belfour .75 2.00

2002-03 Vanguard V-Team

Inserted at odds of 1:25, this 12-card set had split insertion. Cards 1-6 were found in hobby packs while cards 7-12 were found in retail packs.

COMPLETE SET (12) 20.00 40.00
1 Patrick Roy 4.00 10.00
2 Marty Turco .60 1.50
3 Curtis Joseph .75 2.00
4 Jose Theodore 1.00 2.50
5 Martin Brodeur 2.00 5.00
6 Ed Belfour .75 2.00
7 Ilya Kovalchuk 1.00 2.50
8 Joe Thornton 1.25 3.00
9 Joe Sakic 1.50 4.00
10 Steve Yzerman 4.00 10.00
11 Mario Lemieux 5.00 12.00
12 Jaromir Jagr 1.25 3.00

1999-00 Wayne Gretzky Hockey

This Upper Deck-produced set features the top players in the NHL. Company spokesman Gretzky offered comments on each player on the card back. The product was packaged in 24-pack boxes with packs containing eight cards and carried a suggested retail price of $2.49. Please note that although card #GM1 was supposed to carry a piece of game-used puck, there have been several singles found with stick pieces instead.

COMPLETE SET (181) 20.00 40.00
1 Paul Kariya .20 .50
2 Guy Hebert .15 .40
3 Steve Rucchin .15 .40
4 Teemu Selanne .20 .50
5 Oleg Tverdovsky .15 .40
6 Matt Cullen .08 .25
7 Jeff Nielsen .08 .25
8 Patrik Stefan RC .50 1.25
9 Kelly Buchberger .08 .25
10 Andrew Brunette .15 .40
11 Ray Ferraro .08 .25
12 Nelson Emerson .08 .25
13 Damian Rhodes .15 .40
14 Sergei Samsonov .15 .40
15 John Grahame RC .50 1.25
16 Joe Thornton .30 .75
17 Jason Allison .08 .25
18 Kyle McLaren .08 .25
19 Rob DiMaio .08 .25
20 Ray Bourque .30 .75
21 Dominik Hasek .40 1.00
22 Miroslav Satan .15 .40
23 Alexei Zhitnik .08 .25
24 Stu Barnes .08 .25
25 Curtis Brown .08 .25
26 Brian Campbell RC .08 .25
27 Michael Peca .15 .40
28 Marc Savard .08 .25
29 Valeri Bure .08 .25
30 Phil Housley .08 .25
31 Grant Fuhr .15 .40
32 Cory Stillman .08 .25
33 Oleg Saprykin RC .50 1.25
34 Sami Kapanen .08 .25
35 Bates Battaglia .08 .25
36 Dave Tanabe .15 .40
37 Ron Francis .15 .40
38 Arturs Irbe .15 .40
39 Keith Primeau .08 .25
40 Doug Gilmour .15 .40
41 J-P Dumont .15 .40
42 Eric Daze .15 .40
43 Tony Amonte .15 .40
44 Alexei Zhamnov .15 .40
45 Kyle Calder RC .20 .50
46 Joe Sakic .40 1.00
47 Chris Drury .15 .40
48 Milan Hejduk .20 .50
49 Adam Deadmarsh .08 .25
50 Patrick Roy 1.00 2.50
51 Peter Forsberg .50 1.25
52 Alex Tanguay .15 .40
53 Mike Modano .30 .75
54 Brett Hull .25 .60
55 Ed Belfour .20 .50
56 Jamie Langenbrunner .08 .25
57 Pavel Patera RC .08 .25
58 Joe Nieuwendyk .15 .40
59 Jere Lehtinen .15 .40
60 Steve Yzerman 1.00 2.50
61 Jiri Fischer .08 .25
62 Brendan Shanahan .20 .50
63 Chris Osgood .15 .40
64 Chris Chelios .20 .50
65 Sergei Fedorov .30 .75
66 Nicklas Lidstrom .20 .50
67 Doug Weight .15 .40
68 Mike Grier .08 .25
69 Ryan Smyth .15 .40
70 Jason Smith .08 .25
71 Tom Poti .08 .25
72 Pavel Bure .20 .50
73 Mark Parrish .08 .25
74 Ivan Novoseltsev RC .40 1.00
75 Trevor Kidd .15 .40
76 Viktor Kozlov .15 .40
77 Scott Mellanby .08 .25
78 Rob Blake .15 .40
79 Ian Lapperiere .08 .25
80 Zigmund Palffy .15 .40
81 Luc Robitaille .15 .40
82 Jozef Stumpel .15 .40
83 Aki Berg .08 .25
84 Stephane Fiset .15 .40
85 Saku Koivu .20 .50
86 Brian Savage .08 .25
87 Trevor Linden .08 .25
88 Jeff Hackett .15 .40
89 Eric Weinrich .08 .25
90 David Legwand .15 .40
91 Sergei Krivokrasov .08 .25
92 Randy Robitaille .08 .25
93 Kimmo Timonen .08 .25
94 Mike Dunham .15 .40
95 Brendan Morrison .15 .40
96 Scott Stevens .15 .40
97 Sheldon Souray .08 .25
98 Petr Sykora .08 .25
99 Wayne Gretzky 1.25 3.00
100 Martin Brodeur .50 1.25
101 Scott Niedermayer .08 .25
102 Patrik Elias .15 .40
103 Tim Connolly .08 .25
104 Jorgen Jonsson RC .08 .25
105 Mathieu Biron .15 .40
106 Claude Lapointe .08 .25
107 Kenny Jonsson .08 .25
108 Roberto Luongo .25 .60
109 Theo Fleury .08 .25
110 Petr Nedved .15 .40
111 Valeri Kamensky .15 .40
112 Adam Graves .08 .25
113 Manny Malhotra .15 .40
114 Brian Leetch .20 .50
115 Mike Richter .20 .50
116 Marian Hossa .20 .50
117 Radek Bonk .08 .25
118 Joe Juneau .08 .25
119 Wade Redden .08 .25
120 Ron Tugnutt .15 .40
121 Daniel Alfredsson .15 .40
122 Eric Lindros .20 .50
123 John LeClair .20 .50
124 Marc Bureau .08 .25
125 Simon Gagne .20 .50
126 Mark Recchi .15 .40
127 Rod Brind'Amour .15 .40
128 John Vanbiesbrouck .15 .40
129 Keith Tkachuk .20 .50
130 Jeremy Roenick .25 .60
131 Daniel Briere .08 .25
132 Bob Essensa .15 .40
133 J.J. Daigneault .08 .25
134 Mika Alatalo RC .15 .40
135 Travis Green .08 .25
136 Jaromir Jagr .30 .75
137 Martin Straka .08 .25
138 Alexei Morozov .15 .40
139 Jan Hrdina .08 .25
140 Alexei Kovalev .08 .25
141 Peter Skudra .08 .25
142 John Slaney .08 .25
143 Pierre Turgeon .15 .40
144 Roman Turek .15 .40
145 Pavol Demitra .15 .40
146 Al MacInnis .15 .40
147 Chris Pronger .15 .40
148 Jochen Hecht RC 1.00 2.50
149 Jeff Friesen .08 .25
150 Steve Shields .15 .40
151 Patrick Marleau .15 .40
152 Vincent Damphousse .08 .25
153 Marco Sturm .15 .40
154 Brad Stuart .15 .40
155 Darcy Tucker .08 .25
156 Vincent Lecavalier .20 .50
157 Andrei Zyuzin .08 .25
158 Chris Gratton .08 .25
159 Fredrik Modin .08 .25
160 Mats Sundin .20 .50
161 Steve Thomas .08 .25
162 Sergei Berezin .15 .40
163 Mike Johnson .15 .40
164 Dimitri Khristich .08 .25
165 Bryan Berard .08 .25
166 Curtis Joseph .20 .50
167 Mark Messier .20 .50
168 Alexander Mogilny .15 .40
169 Garth Snow .15 .40
170 Markus Naslund .20 .50
171 Steve Kariya RC .50 1.25
172 Peter Schaefer .08 .25
173 Peter Bondra .20 .50
174 Joe Sacco .08 .25
175 Adam Oates .15 .40
176 Olaf Kolzig .15 .40
177 Jan Bulis .08 .25
178 Alexander Volchkov RC .15 .40
179 Wayne Gretzky CL .08 .25
180 Curtis Joseph CL .08 .25
GM1 W.Gretzky PUCK or STICK 30.00 80.00

1999-00 Wayne Gretzky Hockey Changing The Game

Randomly inserted in packs at the rate of 1:27, this 10-card set highlights 10 top NHL stars who have left their mark on hockey. Each card is enhanced with silver foil stamping.

COMPLETE SET (10) 15.00 30.00
CG1 Peter Forsberg 2.50 6.00
CG2 Eric Lindros 1.00 2.50
CG3 Paul Kariya 1.00 2.50
CG4 Jaromir Jagr 1.50 4.00
CG5 Dominik Hasek 2.00 5.00
CG6 Sergei Samsonov .75 2.00
CG7 Theo Fleury .75 2.00
CG8 Al MacInnis .75 2.00
CG9 Pavel Bure 1.00 2.50
CG10 Patrick Roy 5.00 12.00

1999-00 Wayne Gretzky Hockey Elements of the Game

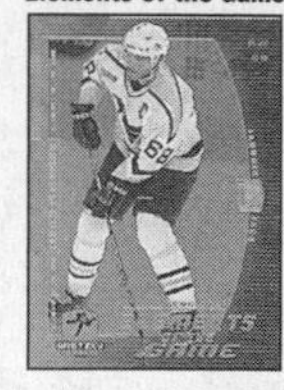

Randomly seeded in packs at the rate of 1:6, this 15-card set showcases top players on a card with purple foil borders with enhanced silver foil highlights.

COMPLETE SET (15) 8.00 15.00
EG1 Teemu Selanne .40 1.00
EG2 Mike Peca .30 .75
EG3 Sergei Samsonov .30 .75
EG4 Sergei Fedorov .60 1.50
EG5 Peter Forsberg 1.00 2.50
EG6 Brett Hull .50 1.25
EG7 Eric Lindros .40 1.00
EG8 Pavel Bure .40 1.00
EG9 Theo Fleury .30 .75
EG10 Martin Brodeur 1.00 2.50
EG11 Jaromir Jagr .60 1.50
EG12 Keith Tkachuk .40 1.00
EG13 Peter Bondra .40 1.00
EG14 Joe Sakic .75 2.00
EG15 Curtis Joseph .40 1.00

1999-00 Wayne Gretzky Hockey Great Heroes

Randomly inserted in packs at the rate of 1:27, this 10-card set showcases modern day heroes on a card with silver and purple foil borders and silver foil stamping.

COMPLETE SET (10) 20.00 40.00
GH1 Jaromir Jagr 1.50 4.00
GH2 Paul Kariya 2.00 5.00
GH3 Joe Sakic 2.00 5.00
GH4 Dominik Hasek 2.00 5.00
GH5 Patrick Roy 5.00 12.00
GH6 Steve Yzerman 5.00 12.00
GH7 Eric Lindros 1.50 4.00
GH8 Patrik Stefan 1.50 4.00
GH9 Teemu Selanne 2.00 5.00
GH10 Pavel Bure 1.25 3.00

1999-00 Wayne Gretzky Hockey Hall of Fame Career

Inserted one per pack this 30-card set traced Wayne Gretzky's career on a card with purple foil borders and silver foil stamping.

COMPLETE SET (30) 12.00 25.00
COMMON GRETZKY .40 1.00

1999-00 Wayne Gretzky Hockey Signs of Greatness

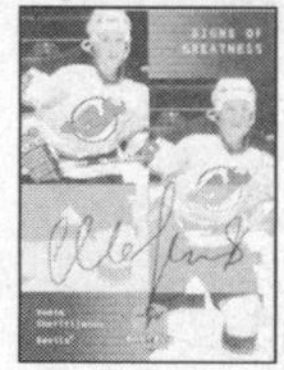

Randomly inserted in Retail packs at the rate of 1:15, this 15-card set features portrait photography and authentic player signatures.

AI Arturs Irbe 6.00 15.00
BH Brett Hull SP 30.00 60.00
CD Chris Drury 6.00 15.00
CJ Curtis Joseph SP 40.00 80.00
CO Chris Osgood 6.00 15.00
DL David Legwand 6.00 15.00
MP Mark Parrish 6.00 15.00
NK Nikolai Khabibulin 10.00 25.00
PB Pavel Bure SP 25.00 60.00
PM Paul Mara 6.00 15.00
PS Patrik Stefan 6.00 15.00
RB Ray Bourque 25.00 60.00
SS Sergei Samsonov SP 12.00 30.00
VS Vadim Sharifijanov 6.00 15.00
WG Wayne Gretzky SP 200.00 400.00

1999-00 Wayne Gretzky Hockey Tools of Greatness

Randomly inserted in Hobby packs at the rate of 1:139, this 20-card set features action player photography coupled with a swatch of a game used stick.

TGAI Arturs Irbe 10.00 25.00
TGBH Brett Hull 12.50 30.00
TGBS Brendan Shanahan 10.00 25.00
TGCJ Curtis Joseph 10.00 25.00
TGDW Doug Weight 10.00 25.00
TGEB Ed Belfour 10.00 25.00
TGEL Eric Lindros 10.00 25.00
TGLR Luc Robitaille 10.00 25.00
TGMR Mike Richter 10.00 25.00
TGMS Mats Sundin 10.00 25.00
TGNK Nikolai Khabibulin 10.00 25.00
TGPB Pavel Bure 10.00 25.00
TGPF Peter Forsberg 20.00 50.00
TGPK Paul Kariya 10.00 25.00
TGPR Patrick Roy 20.00 50.00
TGRB Ray Bourque 15.00 40.00
TGSS Sergei Samsonov 10.00 25.00
TGTA Tony Amonte 10.00 25.00
TGTS Teemu Selanne 10.00 25.00

1999-00 Wayne Gretzky Hockey Visionary

Randomly inserted in packs at the rate of 1:167, this 10-card set features none other than the Great One on an acetate holofoil insert card. Cards carry a "V" prefix

COMPLETE SET (10) 75.00 150.00
COMMON GRETZKY (V1-V10) 10.00 25.00

1999-00 Wayne Gretzky Hockey Will to Win

Randomly seeded in packs at the rate of 1:13, this 10-card set features ten of the most dominant stars of the NHL. Cards are enhanced with silver foil highlights.

COMPLETE SET (10) 12.00 25.00
W1 Paul Kariya .60 1.50
W2 Steve Yzerman 3.00 8.00
W3 Jaromir Jagr 1.00 2.50
W4 Dominik Hasek 1.25 3.00
W5 Patrick Roy 3.00 8.00
W6 Jeremy Roenick .75 2.00
W7 Ray Bourque 1.00 2.50
W8 John LeClair .75 2.00
W9 Mats Sundin .60 1.50
W10 Mark Messier .75 2.00

1999 Wayne Gretzky Living Legend

Released as a 99-card set, Wayne Gretzky Living Legend traces The Great One's course of life from beginning to New York. Base cards feature both portrait and action photography with enhanced gold foil stamping. Wayne Gretzky Living Legend was packaged in 24-pack boxes with packs containing six cards and carried a suggested retail price of $1.99. One Wayne Gretzky bonus pack was inserted in every box.

COMMON GRETZKY (1-99) .20 .50

1999 Wayne Gretzky Living Legend A Leader by Example

Randomly inserted in Wayne Gretzky bonus packs at the rate of 1:23, this 6-card set photos Gretzky in each of his NHL as well as some All-Star jerseys.

COMPLETE SET (6) 15.00 30.00
COMMON GRETZKY (L1-L6) 2.00 5.00

1999 Wayne Gretzky Living Legend Authentics

Randomly inserted in packs at the rate of 1:288 for pucks, 1:1196 for sticks, and jerseys autographed and sequentially numbered to 99, this 10-card set features swatches of authentic game used items.

COMMON WG PUCK (P1-P6) 15.00 40.00
COMMON WG STICK (S1-S2) 25.00 60.00
C1 W.Gretzky Collection/99 AU 150.00 300.00
GJ1 Wayne Gretzky Jersey/99 AU 150.00 300.00

1999 Wayne Gretzky Living Legend Goodwill Ambassador

Randomly inserted in packs at the rate of 1:11, this nine card set showcases Wayne Gretzky not just as a player of the game, but as a spokesman and ambassador of hockey. Cards are enhanced with holofoil borders and gold foil stamping.

COMMON GRETZKY (GW1-GW9) 1.50 4.00

1999 Wayne Gretzky Living Legend Great Accolades

Randomly seeded in packs at the rate of 1:6, this 45-card set highlights some of Wayne Gretzky's greatest achievements. Cards are enhanced with silver foil stamping.

COMMON GRETZKY (GA1-GA45) 2.50 6.00

1999 Wayne Gretzky Living Legend Great Stats

Randomly inserted in Wayne Gretzky bonus packs at the rate of 1:23, this six card set features Wayne in all of his professional Hockey and All-Star jerseys. Cards are enhanced with holofoil borders and gold foil highlights.

COMMON GRETZKY (GS1-GS6) 2.00 5.00

1999 Wayne Gretzky Living Legend Magic Moments

Randomly inserted in Wayne Gretzky bonus packs at the rate of 1:23, this six card set highlights some of Wayne Gretzky's greatest NHL achievements. Cards are enhanced with holofoil borders and gold foil stamping.

COMMON GRETZKY (MM1-MM6) 2.00 5.00

1999 Wayne Gretzky Living Legend More Than a Number

Randomly inserted in packs, this 99-card set parallels the base Wayne Gretzky Living Legend set on cards that are sequentially numbered to 99.

COMMON GRETZKY (1-99) 25.00 60.00

1999 Wayne Gretzky Living Legend Only One 99

Randomly inserted in packs, this 99-card set parallels the base Wayne Gretzky Living Legend set. As the cards are each one-of-ones, they are not priced below.

NOT PRICED DUE TO SCARCITY

1999 Wayne Gretzky Living Legend The Great One

Randomly inserted in packs at the rate of 1:2, this 9-card set highlights Wayne Gretzkys impact on the sport of hockey. Cards are enhanced with holofoil borders and gold foil stamping.

COMMON GRETZKY (GO1-GO9) .75 2.00

1999 Wayne Gretzky Living Legend Wearing the Leaf

Randomly inserted in Wayne Gretzky bonus packs at the rate of 1:23, this six card holofoil set features Gretzky in his Team Canada jersey. Cards are enhanced with holofoil borders and gold foil stamping.

COMMON GRETZKY (WL1-WL6) 2.00 5.00

1999 Wayne Gretzky Living Legend Year of the Great One

Randomly inserted in packs, this 99-card set parallels the base Wayne Gretzky Living Legend set on die cut cards. Each card is serial numbered out of 1999.

COMMON GRETZKY (1-99) 1.50 4.00

1927 Werner and Mertz Field Hockey

Cards measure approximately 2 1/2 x 4 1/2 and feature full color drawings of field hockey action shots. Produced in Germany by Werner & Mertz Aktiengesellschaft, Mainz.

COMPLETE SET (6) 62.50 125.00
1 Womens Field Hockey 12.50 25.00
2 Womens Field Hockey 12.50 25.00
3 Mens Field Hockey 12.50 25.00
Scrum at midfield
4 Mens Field Hockey 12.50 25.00
Chasing the ball
5 Mens Field Hockey 12.50 25.00
Pileup
6 Mens Field Hockey 12.50 25.00
Goalie action shot

1982-83 Whalers Junior Hartford Courant

Sponsored by the Hartford Courant, this 23-card set measures approximately 3 1/4" by 6 3/8". The fronts feature borderless color action player photos. and the sponsor's name. The white backs carry a black-and-white headshot, player's name, jersey number, biography and statistics. The cards are unnumbered and checklisted below in alphabetical order. The card of Ron Francis appears in his Rookie Card year.

COMPLETE SET (22) 14.00 75.00
1 Greg Adams 1.50 4.00
2 Russ Anderson .75 2.00
3 Ron Francis 10.00 25.00
4 Michel Galarneau .75 2.00
5 Dan Fridgen .75 2.00
6 Archie Henderson .75 2.00
7 Ed Hospodar .75 2.00
8 Mark Johnson 1.25 3.00
9 Chris Kotsopoulos .75 2.00
10 Pierre Larouche 1.50 4.00
11 George Lyle .75 2.00
12 Greg Millen 2.00 5.00
13 Warren Miller .75 2.00
14 Ray Neufeld 1.25 3.00
15 Mark Renaud .75 2.00
16 Risto Siltanen 1.25 3.00
17 Stuart Smith .75 2.00
18 Blaine Stoughton 1.50 4.00
19 Doug Sulliman .75 2.00
20 Bob Sullivan .75 2.00
21 Mike Veisor 1.25 3.00
22 Mickey Volcan .75 2.00
23 Blake Wesley .75 2.00

1983-84 Whalers Junior Hartford Courant

Sponsored by the Hartford Courant, this 22-card set measures approximately 3 3/4" by 8 1/4". The fronts feature color action player photos and the sponsor's name. The white backs carry a black-and-white headshot, player's name, jersey number, biography and statistics. The cards are unnumbered and checklisted below in alphabetical order.

COMPLETE SET (22) 10.00 25.00
1 Bob Crawford .40 1.00
2 Mike Crombeen .40 1.00
3 Richie Dunn .40 1.00
4 Normand Dupont .40 1.00
5 Ron Francis 3.00 8.00
6 Ed Hospodar .40 1.00
7 Marty Howe .75 2.00
8 Mark Johnson .60 1.50
9 Chris Kotsopoulos .40 1.00
10 Pierre Lacroix .60 1.50
11 Greg Malone .60 1.50
12 Greg Malone .60 1.50
13 Ray Neufeld .40 1.00
14 Joel Quenneville .60 1.50
15 Torrie Robertson .60 1.50
16 Risto Siltanen .40 1.00
17 Blaine Stoughton .75 2.00
18 Steve Stoyanovich .40 1.00
19 Doug Sulliman .40 1.00
20 Sylvain Turgeon .60 1.50
21 Mike Veisor .60 1.50
22 Mike Zuke .40 1.00

1984-85 Whalers Junior Wendy's

This 22-card set was sponsored by Wendy's and The Civic Center Mall. The cards measure approximately 3 3/4" by 8 1/4" and feature color action player photos. The backs have a black and white head shot, biography, 1983-84 season summary, career summary, miscellaneous player information, and statistics. The cards are unnumbered and checklisted below in alphabetical order.

COMPLETE SET (22) 10.00 25.00
1 Jack Brownschidle .40 1.00
2 Sylvain Cote .40 1.00
3 Bob Crawford .40 1.00
4 Mike Crombeen .40 1.00
5 Tony Currie .40 1.00
6 Ron Francis 2.50 6.00
7 Mark Fusco .40 1.00
8 Dave Jensen .40 1.00
9 Mark Johnson .60 1.50
10 Chris Kotsopoulos .40 1.00
11 Greg Malone .60 1.50
12 Greg Millen .75 2.00
13 Ray Neufeld .40 1.00
14 Randy Pierce .40 1.00
15 Joel Quenneville .60 1.50
16 Torrie Robertson .60 1.50
17 Ulf Samuelsson 1.50 4.00
18 Risto Siltanen .40 1.00
19 Dave Tippett .40 1.00
20 Sylvain Turgeon .40 1.00
21 Steve Weeks .75 2.00
22 Mike Zuke .60 1.50

1985-86 Whalers Junior Wendy's

Sponsored by Wendy's, this 23-card set measures approximately 3 3/4" by 8 1/4". The fronts feature full-bleed color action player photos, along with the sponsor's name. The white backs carry a black-and-white headshot, biography, 1984-85 season summary, career summary, personal information, and statistics. The cards were issued to members of the team's Kid's Club. Since they are unnumbered, the cards are checklisted below in alphabetical order.

COMPLETE SET (23) 12.00 30.00
1 Jack Brownschidle .40 1.00
2 Sylvain Cote .40 1.00
3 Bob Crawford .40 1.00
4 Kevin Dineen 1.50 4.00
5 Paul Fenton .40 1.00
6 Ray Ferraro 1.25 3.00
7 Ron Francis 2.00 5.00
8 Scott Kleinendorst .40 1.00
9 Paul Lawless .40 1.00
10 Mike Liut 1.25 3.00
11 Paul MacDermid .40 1.00
12 Greg Malone .40 1.00
13 Dana Murzyn .40 1.00
14 Ray Neufeld .40 1.00
15 Jorgen Pettersson .40 1.00
16 Joel Quenneville .40 1.00
17 Torrie Robertson .60 1.50
18 Ulf Samuelsson 1.25 3.00
19 Risto Siltanen .40 1.00
20 Dave Tippett .40 1.00
21 Sylvain Turgeon .60 1.50
22 Steve Weeks .60 1.50
23 Mike Zuke .40 1.00

1986-87 Whalers Junior Thomas'

Sponsored by Thomas', this 23-card set measures approximately 3 3/4" by 8 1/4". The cards were issued only to members of the team's Kid's Club. The fronts feature color action player photos, along with the team and sponsor name. The white backs carry a black-and-white headshot, player's name, jersey number, biography, 1985-86 season summary, career summary, personal information, and statistics. The cards are unnumbered and checklisted below in alphabetical order.

COMPLETE SET (23) 12.00 30.00
1 John Anderson .40 1.00
2 Dave Babych .75 2.00
3 Wayne Babych .40 1.00
4 Sylvain Cote .40 1.00
5 Kevin Dineen 1.25 3.00
6 Dean Evason .40 1.00
7 Ray Ferraro .40 1.00
8 Ron Francis 2.50 6.00
9 Bill Gardner .40 1.00
10 Stewart Gavin .40 1.00
11 Doug Jarvis .40 1.00
12 Scot Kleinendorst .40 1.00
13 Paul Lawless .40 1.00
14 Mike Liut 1.25 3.00
15 Paul MacDermid .40 1.00
16 Mike McEwen .40 1.00
17 Dana Murzyn .40 1.00
18 Joel Quenneville .40 1.00
19 Torrie Robertson .50 1.25
20 Ulf Samuelsson 1.25 3.00
21 Dave Tippett .40 1.00
22 Sylvain Turgeon .40 1.00
23 Steve Weeks .60 1.50

1987-88 Whalers Jr. Burger King/Pepsi

This 21-card set was sponsored by Burger King restaurants and Pepsi Cola and measures approximately 3 3/4" by 8 1/4". The fronts feature color action player photos with the team name and sponsors' logos at the bottom. The backs carry a small headshot, biography, season summary, career summary, miscellaneous player information, and statistics. The cards, which were issued only to members of the team's Kid's Club, are unnumbered and checklisted below in alphabetical order.

COMPLETE SET (21) 10.00 25.00
1 John Anderson .40 1.00
2 Dave Babych .75 2.00
3 Sylvain Cote .40 1.00
4 Kevin Dineen 1.00 2.50
5 Dean Evason .40 1.00
6 Ray Ferraro 1.00 2.50
7 Ron Francis 1.50 4.00
8 Stew Gavin .40 1.00
9 Doug Jarvis .40 1.00
10 Scott Kleinendorst .40 1.00
11 Randy Ladouceur .40 1.00
12 Paul Lawless .40 1.00
13 Mike Liut 1.00 2.50
14 Paul MacDermid .40 1.00
15 Dana Murzyn .40 1.00
16 Joel Quenneville .40 1.00
17 Torrie Robertson .40 1.00
18 Ulf Samuelsson .75 2.00
19 Dave Tippett .40 1.00
20 Sylvain Turgeon .40 1.00
21 Steve Weeks .60 1.50

1988-89 Whalers Junior Ground Round

This 18-card set of Hartford Whalers was sponsored by Ground Round restaurants. The cards measure approximately 3 11/16" by 8 1/4". The front features a borderless full color photo of the player. The team logo and a Ground Round advertisement appear in the blue and green stripes that cut across the bottom of the card face. The back has a black and white head shot of the player at the upper left hand corner as well as extensive player information and career statistics. Another Ground Round advertisement and a Ground Round Drug Tip (an anti-drug and alcohol message) appear at the bottom of the card. The cards were issued to members of the team's Kid's Club. They are unnumbered and hence are checklisted below in alphabetical order.

COMPLETE SET (18) 8.00 20.00
1 John Anderson .40 1.00
2 Dave Babych .60 1.50
3 Sylvain Cote .40 1.00
4 Kevin Dineen .75 2.00

5 Dean Evason	.40	1.00
6 Ray Ferraro	.75	2.00
7 Ron Francis	1.50	4.00
8 Scot Kleinendorst	.40	1.00
9 Randy Ladouceur	.40	1.00
10 Mike Liut	.75	2.00
11 Paul MacDermid	.40	1.00
12 Brent Peterson	.40	1.00
13 Joel Quenneville	.40	1.00
14 Torrie Robertson	.40	1.00
15 Ulf Samuelsson	.75	2.00
16 Dave Tippett	.40	1.00
17 Sylvain Turgeon	.40	1.00
18 Carey Wilson	.40	1.00

1989-90 Whalers Junior Milk

This 23-card set of Hartford Whalers was sponsored by Milk and issued to members of the team's Kid's Club. The cards measure approximately 3 11/16" by 8 1/4". The front features a borderless full color photo of the player. The team logo and a Milk advertisement appear in the blue and green stripes that cut across the bottom of the card face. The back has a black and white head shot of the player in the upper left hand corner as well as extensive player information and career statistics. A Junior Whaler Nutrition Tip and another Milk advertisement appear at the bottom of the card's reverse. The cards are unnumbered and hence are checklisted below in alphabetical order. Three cards (11, 12, 21) were added to the set at the end of the season and are marked as SP in the checklist below.

COMPLETE SET (23)	8.00	20.00
1 Mikael Andersson	.20	.50
2 Dave Babych	.30	.75
3 Sylvain Cote	.20	.50
4 Randy Cunneyworth	.20	.50
5 Kevin Dineen	.60	1.50
6 Dean Evason	.20	.50
7 Ray Ferraro	.40	1.00
8 Ron Francis	1.25	3.00
9 Jody Hull	.20	.50
10 Grant Jennings	.20	.50
11 Ed Kastelic SP	.75	2.00
12 Todd Krygier SP	.75	2.00
13 Randy Ladouceur	.20	.50
14 Mike Liut	.60	1.50
15 Paul MacDermid	.20	.50
16 Joel Quenneville	.20	.50
17 Ulf Samuelsson	.60	1.50
18 Brad Shaw	.30	.75
19 Peter Sidorkiewicz	.30	.75
20 Dave Tippett	.20	.50
21 Mike Tomlak SP	.75	2.00
22 Pat Verbeek	.60	1.50
23 Scott Young	.40	1.00

1990-91 Whalers Jr. 7-Eleven

This 27-card set of Hartford Whalers was issued by 7-Eleven and sent out as a premium to all members of the Hartford Junior Whalers. This set features full-color photographs on the front while the backs contain the same information about the players that is available in the media guides. The set has been checklisted alphabetically for convenient reference. The set measures approximately 3 3/4" by 8 1/4" and has the players of the Hartford Whalers along with a special Gordie Howe card. Four cards (3, 12, 19, 20) were added to the set at the end of the season and their backs are blank.

COMPLETE SET (27)	8.00	20.00
1 Mikael Andersson	.20	.50
2 Dave Babych	.30	.75
3 Rob Brown SP	.75	2.00
4 Yvon Corriveau	.20	.50
5 Sylvain Cote	.20	.50
6 Doug Crossman	.20	.50
7 Randy Cunneyworth	.20	.50
8 Paul Cyr	.20	.50
9 Kevin Dineen	.40	1.00
10 Dean Evason	.20	.50
11 Ron Francis	.75	2.00
12 Chris Govedaris SP	.75	2.00
13 Bobby Holik	.40	1.00
14 Gordie Howe	2.00	5.00
15 Grant Jennings	.20	.50
16 Ed Kastelic	.20	.50
17 Todd Krygier	.20	.50
18 Randy Ladouceur	.20	.50
19 Jim McKenzie SP	.75	2.00
20 Daryl Reaugh SP	1.00	2.50
21 Ulf Samuelsson	.40	1.00
22 Brad Shaw	.30	.75
23 Peter Sidorkiewicz	.30	.75
24 Mike Tomlak	.20	.50
25 Pat Verbeek	.60	1.50
26 Carey Wilson	.20	.50
27 Scott Young	.30	.75

1991-92 Whalers Jr. 7-Eleven

This 28-card set of Hartford Whalers was issued by 7-Eleven and sent out as a premium to all members of the Hartford Junior Whalers. This set features full-color photographs on the front while the backs contain the same information about the players that is available in the media guides. The set has been checklisted alphabetically for convenient reference. The set measures approximately 3 3/4" by 8 1/4" and contains the players of the Hartford Whalers. Six cards (3, 6, 10, 12, 18, 19) were issued late in the season and their backs are blank.

COMPLETE SET (28)	8.00	20.00
1 Mikael Andersson	.20	.50
2 Marc Bergevin	.20	.50
3 James Black SP	.60	1.50
4 Rob Brown	.25	.60
5 Adam Burt	.20	.50
6 Andrew Cassels SP	1.25	3.00
7 Murray Craven	.30	.75
8 John Cullen	.40	1.00
9 Randy Cunneyworth	.20	.50
10 Paul Cyr SP	.60	1.50
11 Joe Day	.20	.50
12 Paul Gillis SP	.60	1.50
13 Mark Greig	.20	.50
14 Bobby Holik	.30	.75
15 Doug Houda	.20	.50
16 Mark Hunter	.20	.50
17 Ed Kastelic	.20	.50
18 Dan Keczmer SP	.75	2.00
19 Steve Konroyd SP	.60	1.50
20 Randy Ladouceur	.20	.50
21 Jim McKenzie	.20	.50
22 Michel Picard	.20	.50
23 Geoff Sanderson	2.00	5.00
24 Brad Shaw	.25	.60
25 Peter Sidorkiewicz	.30	.75
26 Pat Verbeek	.60	1.50
27 Kay Whitmore	.30	.75
28 Zarley Zalapski	.30	.75

1992-93 Whalers Dairymart

Sponsored by Dairymart, this 26-card set was issued to members of the team's Kid's Club. Each features a white-bordered glossy color studio head shot on a card that measures approximately 2 3/8" by 3 1/2". The Dairymart and Whalers logos are displayed above the player photo, and the player's name and position, along with "1992-93 Hartford Whalers," appear beneath his image. The white horizontal back carries the player's name, uniform number, position, and biography above a stat table. The cards are unnumbered and checklisted below in alphabetical order.

COMPLETE SET (26)	7.20	18.00
1 Jim Agnew	.20	.50
2 Sean Burke	.60	1.50
3 Adam Burt	.20	.50
4 Andrew Cassels	.40	1.00
5 Murray Craven	.25	.60
6 Randy Cunneyworth	.20	.50
7 Paul Gillis	.20	.50
8 Paul Holmgren CO	.20	.50
9 Doug Houda	.20	.50
10 Mark Janssens	.20	.50
11 Tim Kerr	.30	.75
12 Steve Konroyd	.20	.50
13 Nick Kypreos	.20	.50
14 Randy Ladouceur	.20	.50
15 Jim McKenzie	.20	.50
16 Michael Nylander	.40	1.00
17 Allen Pedersen	.20	.50
18 Robert Petrovicky	.20	.50
19 Frank Pietrangelo	.30	.75
20 Patrick Poulin	.20	.50
21 Geoff Sanderson	1.50	4.00
22 Pat Verbeek	.60	1.50
23 Eric Weinrich	.20	.50
24 Terry Yake	.20	.50
25 Zarley Zalapski	.20	.50
26 Junior Whalers Member Card	.08	.25

1993-94 Whalers Coke

Sponsored by Coca-Cola, this 24-card set features white-bordered color studio head shots on cards that measure approximately 2 3/8" by 3 1/2". The white horizontal backs carry the player's name, uniform number, position, and biography above a stat table. The cards were issued to members of the Junior Whalers club, and as they are unnumbered, they are checklisted below in alphabetical order.

COMPLETE SET (24)	7.20	18.00
1 Sean Burke	.75	2.00
2 Adam Burt	.20	.50
3 Andrew Cassels	.40	1.00
4 Randy Cunneyworth	.20	.50
5 Alexander Godynyuk	.20	.50
6 Mark Greig	.20	.50
7 Mark Janssens	.20	.50
8 Robert Kron	.20	.50
9 Bryan Marchment	.20	.50
10 Brad McCrimmon	.20	.50
11 Pierre McGuire CO	.08	.25
12 Michael Nylander	.30	.75
13 James Patrick	.20	.50
14 Frank Pietrangelo	.30	.75
15 Marc Potvin	.20	.50
16 Chris Pronger	1.25	3.00
17 Brian Propp	.30	.75
18 Jeff Reese	.30	.75
19 Geoff Sanderson	.75	2.00
20 Jim Sandlak	.20	.50
21 Jim Storm	.20	.50
22 Darren Turcotte	.30	.75
23 Pat Verbeek	.60	1.50
24 Zarley Zalapski	.20	.50

1995-96 Whalers Bob's Stores

This set features the Whalers of the NHL. The standard-sized cards were issued to members of the team's Junior Whalers kid's club. The cards are unnumbered, and so are listed below in alphabetical order.

COMPLETE SET (27)	4.80	12.00
1 Sean Burke	.30	.75
2 Adam Burke	.15	.40
3 Andrew Cassels	.15	.40
4 Kelly Chase	.15	.40
5 Scott Daniels	.15	.40
6 Gerald Diduck	.15	.40
7 Nelson Emerson	.25	.60
8 Glen Featherstone	.15	.40
9 Brian Glynn	.15	.40
10 Mark Janssens	.15	.40
11 Robert Kron	.15	.40
12 Frantisek Kucera	.15	.40
13 Jocelyn Lemieux	.15	.40
14 Marek Malik	.15	.40
15 Steve Martins	.15	.40
16 Paul Maurice CO	.08	.25
17 Brad McCrimmon	.15	.40
18 Jason Muzzatti	.15	.40
19 Andrei Nikolishin	.15	.40
20 Jeff O'Neill	.15	.40
21 Paul Ranheim	.15	.40
22 Steven Rice	.15	.40
23 Geoff Sanderson	.60	1.50
24 Brendan Shanahan	1.25	3.00
25 Kevin Smyth	.15	.40
26 Glen Wesley	.25	.60
27 Kids Club Discount Card	.02	.10

1996-97 Whalers Kid's Club

This set features the Whalers of the NHL. The cards were produced by the team for distribution to members of its Kid's Club. The cards of Steve Chiasson and Kent Manderville were available only in sets issued late in the season. The Kevin Brown card is not necessary for the complete set. The photo features him with the Springfield Falcons, the Whalers' farm team, the background is a different color, and the stock is noticeably thinner.

COMPLETE SET (28)	14.00	35.00
1 Sean Burke	.75	2.00
2 Jason Muzzatti	.60	1.50
3 Kevin Dineen	.60	1.50
4 Geoff Sanderson	.60	1.50
5 Keith Primeau	.75	2.00
6 Jeff O'Neill	.75	2.00
7 Marek Malik	.40	1.00
8 Paul Ranheim	.40	1.00
9 Alexander Godynyuk	.40	1.00
10 Robert Kron	.40	1.00
11 Gerald Diduck	.40	1.00
12 Kelly Chase	.40	1.00
13 Glen Wesley	.40	1.00
14 Andrew Cassels	.60	1.50
15 Hnat Domenichelli	.40	1.00
16 Sami Kapanen	.75	2.00
17 Nelson Emerson	.60	1.50
18 Mark Janssens	.40	1.00
19 Stu Grimson	.75	2.00
20 Nolan Pratt	.40	1.00
21 Glen Featherstone	.40	1.00
22 Curtis Leschyshyn	.40	1.00
23 Jeff Brown	.40	1.00
24 Adam Burt	.40	1.00
25 Steven Rice	.40	1.00
26 Kevin Brown	1.25	3.00
27 Steve Chiasson	1.25	3.00
28 Kent Manderville	1.25	3.00

1960-61 Wonder Bread Labels

Similar to Wonder Bread Premium Photos, these are the actual labels that were wrapped around the Wonder Bread packages. Little is known about them, and few are confirmed to exist, so no prices have been established.

1 Gordie Howe
2 Bobby Hull
3 Dave Keon
4 Maurice Richard

1960-61 Wonder Bread Premium Photos

Produced and issued in Canada, the 1960-61 Wonder Bread set features four hockey stars. This set of premium photos measure approximately 5" by 7" and are unnumbered. There were actually two sets produced: Bread Labels and Premium Photos. The bread labels are valued at 50 to 100 percent of the values listed below. Reportedly the premium photo was inside the bread package and there was also a small picture of the player on the end of the bread wrapper. Keon's photo is noteworthy for preceding his RC by one year.

COMPLETE SET (4)	300.00	600.00
1 Gordie Howe	150.00	300.00
2 Bobby Hull	100.00	200.00
3 Dave Keon	40.00	80.00
4 Maurice Richard	100.00	200.00

2001-02 Wild Crime Prevention

These eight cards are part of a larger 24-card set that also features players from the Minnesota Twins and Vikings. The cards are standard sized and were issued by local police.

COMPLETE SET (8)	4.00	20.00
17 Willie Mitchell	.40	1.00
18 Marian Gaborik	2.00	15.00
19 Darby Hendrickson	.40	1.00
20 Andrew Brunette	.40	1.00
21 Sergei Zholtok	.40	1.00
22 Jim Dowd	.40	1.00
23 Manny Fernandez	.60	1.50
24 Nick Schultz	.40	1.00

2001-02 Wild Team Issue

These oversized (5X8) team issues feature player photos on the front and stats on the back. The sponsor (SBC) appears on all three, but just two (Fernandez and Mitchell) have text reading Limited Edition, 1 of 2,500. It's not known whether these cards actually are from the same set (which is assumed) or not. The checklist is far from complete -- if you know of additional cards, please email us at hockeymag@beckett.com.

COMPLETE SET (?)	
1 Manny Fernandez	2.00
2 Stacy Roest	1.00
3 Willie Mitchell	1.00

2003-04 Wild Law Enforcement Cards

These cards were handed out by local police in the St. Paul area. They are unnumbered and listed below in alphabetical order. It's quite likely that more cards exist. Please contact us at hockeymag@beckett.com if you can confirm.

COMPLETE SET (11)	
1 Brad Bombardir	1.00
2 Pierre-Marc Bouchard	3.00
3 Marian Gaborik	3.00
4 Filip Kuba	1.00
5 Willie Mitchell	1.00
6 Richard Park	1.00
7 Dwayne Roloson	2.00
8 Nick Schultz	1.00
9 Wes Walz	1.00
10 Sergei Zholtok	1.00
11 McGruff the Crime Dog	.10

2006-07 Wild Crime Prevention

1 Pavol Demitra	.40	1.00
2 Kim Johnsson	.40	1.00
3 Keith Carney	.40	1.00
4 Mark Parrish	.40	1.00
5 Brian Rolston	.40	1.00
6 Kurtis Foster	.40	1.00
7 Mikko Koivu	.75	2.00
8 Marian Gaborik	2.00	5.00
9 McGruff the Crime Dog	.10	.25

2007-08 Wild Crime Prevention

COMPLETE SET (9)	5.00	10.00
1 McGruff The Crime Dog	.10	.25
2 Niklas Backstrom	.75	2.00
3 Brent Burns	.60	1.50
4 Pierre-Marc Bouchard	.60	1.50
5 Nick Schultz	.60	1.50
6 Stephane Veilleux	.40	1.00
7 Josh Harding	.75	2.00
8 Petteri Nummelin	.40	1.00
9 Branko Radivojevic	.40	1.00

1960-61 York Photos

This set of 37 photos is very difficult to put together. These unnumbered photos measure approximately 5" by 7" and feature members of the Montreal Canadiens (MC) and Toronto Maple Leafs (TML). The checklist below is ordered alphabetically. These large black and white cards were supposedly available from York Peanut Butter as a mail-in premium in return for two proofs of purchase; unfortunately there are no identifying marking on the photo that indicate the producer or the year of issue. The photos are action shots with a facsimile autograph of the player on the photo. The cards were apparently issued very late in the 1960-61 season since the set includes Eddie Shack as a Maple Leaf (he was acquired by Toronto from the Rangers during the 1960-61 season). Gilles Tremblay (his first NHL season was 1960-61 with the Canadiens), and several players (Jean-Guy Gendron, Larry Regan, Bob Turner) who were with other teams for the 1961-62 season.

COMPLETE SET (37)	1200.00	2400.00
1 George Armstrong TML	30.00	60.00
2 Ralph Backstrom MC	25.00	50.00
3 Bob Baun TML	30.00	60.00
4 Jean Beliveau MC	87.50	175.00
5 Marcel Bonin MC	17.50	35.00
6 Johnny Bower TML	62.50	125.00
7 Carl Brewer TML	25.00	50.00
8 Dick Duff TML	25.00	50.00
9 Jean-Guy Gendron MC	17.50	35.00
10 Boom Boom Geoffrion MC	62.50	125.00
11 Phil Goyette MC	17.50	35.00
12 Billy Harris TML	17.50	35.00
13 Doug Harvey MC	50.00	100.00
14 Bill Hicke MC	17.50	35.00
15 Larry Hillman TML	17.50	35.00
16 Charlie Hodge MC	25.00	50.00
17 Tim Horton TML	87.50	175.00
18 Tom Johnson MC	25.00	50.00
19 Red Kelly TML	30.00	60.00
20 Dave Keon TML	62.50	125.00
21 Albert Langlois MC	17.50	35.00
22 Frank Mahovlich TML	62.50	125.00
23 Don Marshall MC	25.00	50.00
24 Dickie Moore MC	30.00	60.00
25 Bob Nevin TML	17.50	35.00
26 Bert Olmstead TML	30.00	60.00
27 Jacques Plante MC	175.00	350.00
28 Claude Provost MC	25.00	50.00
29 Bob Pulford TML	30.00	60.00
30 Larry Regan TML	17.50	35.00
31 Henri Richard MC	62.50	125.00
32 Eddie Shack TML	50.00	100.00
33 Allan Stanley TML	30.00	60.00
34 Ron Stewart TML	17.50	35.00
35 Jean-Guy Talbot MC	25.00	50.00
36 Gilles Tremblay MC	25.00	50.00
37 Bob Turner MC	17.50	35.00

1961-62 York Yellow Backs

This set of 42 octagonal cards was issued by York Peanut Butter. The cards are numbered on the backs at the top. An album was originally available as a send-in offer or at certain food stores for 25 cents. The cards measure approximately 2 1/2" in diameter. The set can be dated as a 1961-62 set by referring to the career totals given on the back of each player's cards. The card backs were written in both French and English. The set is considered complete without the album.

COMPLETE SET (42)	300.00	600.00
1 Bob Baun	7.50	15.00
2 Dick Duff	6.00	12.00
3 Frank Mahovlich	12.50	25.00
4 Gilles Tremblay	5.00	10.00
5 Dickie Moore	7.50	15.00
6 Don Marshall	5.00	10.00
7 Tim Horton	15.00	30.00
8 Johnny Bower	10.00	20.00
9 Allan Stanley	7.50	15.00
10 Jean Beliveau	20.00	40.00
11 Tom Johnson	7.50	15.00
12 Jean-Guy Talbot	6.00	12.00
13 Carl Brewer	5.00	10.00
14 Bob Pulford	7.50	15.00
15 Billy Harris	5.00	10.00
16 Bill Hicke	5.00	10.00
17 Claude Provost	6.00	12.00
18 Henri Richard	12.50	25.00
19 Bert Olmstead	7.50	15.00
20 Ron Stewart	5.00	10.00
21 Red Kelly	7.50	15.00
22 Toe Blake CO	7.50	15.00
23 Jacques Plante	25.00	50.00
24 Ralph Backstrom	6.00	12.00
25 Eddie Shack	10.00	20.00
26 Bob Nevin	5.00	10.00
27 Dave Keon	20.00	40.00
28 Boom Boom Geoffrion	10.00	20.00
29 Marcel Bonin	5.00	10.00
30 Phil Goyette	5.00	10.00
31 Larry Hillman	5.00	10.00
32 Larry Keenan	5.00	10.00
33 Al Arbour	7.50	15.00
34 J.C. Tremblay	6.00	12.00
35 Bobby Rousseau	5.00	10.00
36 Al McNeil	5.00	10.00
37 George Armstrong	7.50	15.00
38 Punch Imlach CO	6.00	12.00
39 King Clancy	10.00	20.00
40 Lou Fontinato	5.00	10.00
41 Cesare Maniago	7.50	15.00
42 Jean Gauthier	5.00	10.00
xx Album	20.00	40.00

1962-63 York Iron-On Transfers

These iron-on transfers are very difficult to find. They measure approximately 2 1/4" by 4 1/4". There is some dispute with regard to the year of issue but the 1962-63 season seems to be a likely date based on the careers of the players included in the set. These transfers are numbered at the bottom.

COMPLETE SET (36)	900.00	1800.00
1 Johnny Bower	25.00	50.00
2 Jacques Plante	75.00	150.00
3 Tim Horton	50.00	100.00
4 Jean-Guy Talbot	15.00	30.00
5 Carl Brewer	15.00	30.00
6 J.C. Tremblay	15.00	30.00
7 Dick Duff	15.00	30.00
8 Jean Beliveau	50.00	100.00
9 Dave Keon	25.00	50.00
10 Henri Richard	40.00	80.00
11 Frank Mahovlich	40.00	80.00
12 BoomBoom Geoffrion	25.00	50.00
13 Kent Douglas	12.50	25.00
14 Claude Provost	15.00	30.00
15 Bob Pulford	15.00	30.00
16 Ralph Backstrom	15.00	30.00
17 George Armstrong	20.00	40.00
18 Bobby Rousseau	12.50	25.00
19 Gordie Howe	125.00	250.00
20 Red Kelly	20.00	40.00
21 Alex Delvecchio	20.00	40.00
22 Dickie Moore	20.00	40.00
23 Marcel Pronovost	15.00	30.00
24 Doug Barkley	12.50	25.00
25 Terry Sawchuk	50.00	100.00
26 Billy Harris	12.50	25.00
27 Parker MacDonald	12.50	25.00
28 Don Marshall	12.50	25.00
29 Norm Ullman	25.00	50.00
30A Andre Pronovost	12.50	25.00
30B Vic Stasiuk	12.50	25.00
31 Bill Gadsby	15.00	30.00
32 Eddie Shack	25.00	50.00
33 Larry Jeffrey	12.50	25.00
34 Gilles Tremblay	12.50	25.00
35 Howie Young	12.50	25.00
36 Bruce MacGregor	12.50	25.00

1963-64 York White Backs

This set of 54 octagonal cards was issued with York Peanut Butter and York Salted Nuts. The cards are numbered on the backs at the top. The cards measure approximately 2 1/2" in diameter. The set can be dated as a 1963-64 set by referring to the career totals given on the back of each player's card. The card backs were written in both French and English. An album was originally available for holding the set; the set is considered complete without the album.

COMPLETE SET (54)	375.00	750.00
1 Tim Horton	20.00	40.00
2 Johnny Bower	12.50	25.00
3 Ron Stewart	7.50	15.00
4 Eddie Shack	12.50	25.00
5 Frank Mahovlich	15.00	30.00
6 Dave Keon	15.00	30.00
7 Bob Baun	7.50	15.00
8 Bob Nevin	7.50	15.00
9 Dick Duff	7.50	15.00
10 Billy Harris	7.50	15.00
11 Larry Hillman	7.50	15.00
12 Red Kelly	10.00	20.00
13 Kent Douglas	7.50	15.00
14 Allan Stanley	7.50	15.00
15 Don Simmons	7.50	15.00
16 George Armstrong	10.00	20.00
17 Carl Brewer	7.50	15.00
18 Bob Pulford	7.50	15.00
19 Henri Richard	15.00	30.00
20 BoomBoom Geoffrion	12.50	25.00
21 Gilles Tremblay	7.50	15.00
22 Gump Worsley	12.50	25.00
23 Jean-Guy Talbot	7.50	15.00
24 J.C. Tremblay	7.50	15.00
25 Bobby Rousseau	7.50	15.00
26 Jean Beliveau	20.00	40.00
27 Ralph Backstrom	7.50	15.00
28 Claude Provost	7.50	15.00
29 Jean Gauthier	7.50	15.00
30 Bill Hicke	7.50	15.00
31 Terry Harper	7.50	15.00
32 Marc Reaume	7.50	15.00
33 Dave Balon	7.50	15.00
34 Jacques Laperriere	10.00	20.00
35 John Ferguson	10.00	20.00
36 Red Berenson	7.50	15.00
37 Terry Sawchuk	25.00	50.00
38 Marcel Pronovost	7.50	15.00
39 Bill Gadsby	10.00	20.00
40 Parker MacDonald	7.50	15.00
41 Larry Jeffrey	7.50	15.00
42 Floyd Smith	7.50	15.00
43 Andre Pronovost	7.50	15.00
44 Art Stratton	7.50	15.00
45 Gordie Howe	50.00	100.00
46 Doug Barkley	7.50	15.00
47 Norm Ullman	10.00	20.00
48 Eddie Joyal	7.50	15.00
49 Alex Faulkner	15.00	30.00
50 Alex Delvecchio	10.00	20.00
51 Bruce MacGregor	7.50	15.00
52 Ted Hampson	7.50	15.00
53 Pete Goegan	7.50	15.00
54 Ron Ingram	7.50	15.00
xx Album	20.00	40.00

1967-68 York Action Octagons

This 36-card set was issued by York Peanut Butter. Only cards 13-36 are numbered. The twelve unnumbered cards have been assigned the numbers 1-12 based on alphabetizing the names of the first player listed on each card. Each card shows an action scene involving two or three players. Uniform numbers are also given on the cards. The card backs give the details of a send-in contest ending June 30, 1968. Collecting four cards spelling "YORK" entitled one to receive a Bobby Hull Hockey Game. These octagonal cards measure approximately 2 7/8" in diameter. The card backs were written in both French and English.

COMPLETE SET (36)	300.00	600.00
1 Brian Conacher 22 Allan Stanley 26 Leon Rochefort 25	7.50	15.00
2 Terry Harper 19 Gump Worsley 30 Mike Walton 16	10.00	20.00
3 Tim Horton 7 George Armstrong 10 Jean Beliveau 4	20.00	40.00
4 Dave Keon 14 George Armstrong 10 Claude Provost 14	10.00	20.00
5 Jacques Laperriere 2 Rogatien Vachon 29 Bob Pulford 20	10.00	20.00
6 Bob Pulford 20 Brian Conacher 22 Claude Provost 14	6.00	12.00
7 Bob Pulford 20 Jim Pappin 18 Terry Harper 19	6.00	12.00
8 Pete Stemkowski 12 Jim Pappin 18 Harris 10	6.00	12.00
9 J.C. Tremblay 3 Rogatien Vachon 29 Pete Stemkowski 12	7.50	15.00
10 Rogatien Vachon 29 Ralph Backstrom 6 Bob Pulford 20	10.00	20.00
11 Rogatien Vachon 29 Jacques Laperriere 2 Mike Walton 16	10.00	20.00
12 Mike Walton 16 Pete Stemkowski 12 J.C. Tremblay 3	6.00	12.00
13 Dave Keon 14 Mike Walton 16 J.C. Tremblay 3	7.50	15.00
14 Pete Stemkowski 12 Ralph Backstrom 6	5.00	10.00
15 Rogatien Vachon 29 Bob Pulford 20	7.50	15.00
16 Johnny Bower 1 Ron Ellis 8 John Ferguson 22	7.50	15.00
17 Ron Ellis 8 Gump Worsley 30	7.50	15.00
18 Gump Worsley 30 Jacques Laperriere 2 Frank Mahovlich 27	12.50	25.00
19 J.C. Tremblay 3 Dave Keon 14	7.50	15.00
20 Claude Provost 14 Frank Mahovlich 27	10.00	20.00
21 John Ferguson 22 Tim Horton 7	10.00	20.00
22 Gump Worsley 30 Ron Ellis 8	7.50	15.00
23 Johnny Bower 1 Mike Walton 16 Jean Beliveau 4	10.00	20.00
24 J.C. Tremblay 3 Gump Worsley 30 Bob Pulford 20	7.50	15.00
25 Tim Horton 7 Johnny Bower 1 Jean Beliveau 4	15.00	30.00
26 Allan Stanley 26 Johnny Bower 1 Dick Duff 8	7.50	15.00
27 Ralph Backstrom 6 Johnny Bower 1	7.50	15.00
28 Yvan Cournoyer 12 Jean Beliveau 4 Frank Mahovlich 27	20.00	40.00
29 Johnny Bower 1 Larry Hillman 2 Yvan Cournoyer 12	10.00	20.00
30 Johnny Bower 1 Yvan Cournoyer 12	10.00	20.00
31 Tim Horton 7 Rogatien Vachon 29	10.00	20.00
32 Jim Pappin 18 Bob Pulford 20 Rogatien Vachon 29	7.50	15.00
33 Terry Harper 19 Bobby Rousseau 15 Pronovost 3	5.00	10.00
34 Johnny Bower 1 Pronovost 3 Ralph Backstrom 6	6.00	12.00
35 Frank Mahovlich 27 Gump Worsley 30	12.50	25.00
36 Claude Provost 14 Johnny Bower 1	6.00	12.00

1992-93 Zeller's Masters of Hockey

This seven-card "Signature Series" standard-size set, featuring former NHL greats, was a promotion by Zeller's. According to the certificate of authenticity, the production run was 1,000 sets. The cards have posed color player photos inside white borders. A blue stripe above the picture carries the player's name and is accented by a thin mustard stripe. A silver foil facsimile signature is inscribed across the picture. The backs have the blue and mustard stripes running down the left side and carrying the player's jersey number. In English and French, biography, career highlights, and statistics are included on a white background. A close-up color player photo with a shadow border partially overlaps the stripe near the top. The cards are unnumbered and checklisted below in alphabetical order. There was also a large Marcel Dionne card reportedly given out at various store signings.

COMPLETE SET (7)	8.00	20.00
1 Johnny Bower	1.25	3.00
2 Rod Gilbert	1.25	3.00
3 Ted Lindsay	1.25	3.00
4 Frank Mahovlich	1.50	4.00
5 Stan Mikita	1.50	4.00
6 Maurice Richard	2.50	6.00
7 Certificate of Authenticity		.01

1992-93 Zeller's Masters of Hockey Signed

This set features cards signed by former NHL greats and was distributed by Canadian retailing giant Zeller's. It is believed that approximately 1,000 copies exist of each card. We cannot confirm exactly how they were distributed at this point, although it is believed they could be acquired through a Zeller's customer loyalty program. Any further information can be forwarded to hockeymag@beckett.com.

COMPLETE SET (7)	50.00	125.00
1 Johnny Bower	6.00	15.00
2 Rod Gilbert	6.00	15.00
3 Ted Lindsay	6.00	15.00
4 Frank Mahovlich	8.00	20.00
5 Stan Mikita	8.00	20.00
6 Maurice Richard	25.00	60.00
7 Certificate of Authenticity		.01

1993-94 Zeller's Masters of Hockey

Featuring former NHL greats, this 8-card "Signature Series" marks the second consecutive year a promotion was issued by Zellers. The cards measure the standard size and have posed color player photos inside white borders. A blue stripe above the picture carries the player's name and is accented by a thin mustard stripe. A silver foil facsimile signature is inscribed across the picture. The backs have the blue and mustard stripes running down the left side and carrying the player's jersey number. In English and French, biography, career highlights, and statistics are included on a white background. A close-up color player photo with a shadow border partially overlaps the stripe near the top. The cards are unnumbered and checklisted below in alphabetical order.

COMPLETE SET (8)	6.00	15.00
1 Andy Bathgate	.40	1.00
2 Johnny Bucyk	.75	2.00
3 Yvan Cournoyer	.75	2.00
4 Marcel Dionne	.75	2.00
5 Bobby Hull	1.50	4.00
6 Brad Park	.75	2.00
7 Jean Ratelle	.75	2.00
8 Gump Worsley	1.00	2.50
NNO Marcel Dionne Large	.40	1.00

1993-94 Zeller's Masters of Hockey Signed

This set features cards signed by former NHL greats and was distributed by Canadian retailing giant Zeller's. It is believed that approximately 2,000 copies exist of each card. We cannot confirm exactly how they were distributed at this point, although it is believed they could be acquired through a Zeller's customer loyalty program. Any further information can be forwarded to hockeymag@beckett.com.

COMPLETE SET (8)	60.00	150.00
1 Andy Bathgate	6.00	15.00
2 Johnny Bucyk	10.00	25.00
3 Yvan Cournoyer	10.00	25.00
4 Marcel Dionne	10.00	25.00
5 Bobby Hull	15.00	40.00
6 Brad Park	10.00	25.00
7 Jean Ratelle	6.00	15.00
8 Gump Worsley	10.00	25.00
NNO Marcel Dionne Large		

1994-95 Zeller's Masters of Hockey

For the third consecutive year, Zeller's issued an 8-card "Signature Series" set, featuring former NHL greats. The cards measure the standard size and have posed color player photos inside white borders. A blue stripe above the picture carries the player's name and is accented by a thin mustard stripe. A silver foil facsimile signature is inscribed across the picture. The backs have the blue and mustard stripes running down the left side and carrying the player's jersey number. In English and French, biography, career highlights, and statistics are included on a white background. A close-up color player photo with a shadow border partially overlaps the stripe near the top. The cards are unnumbered and checklisted below in alphabetical order.

COMPLETE SET (8)	4.00	10.00
1 Jean Beliveau	1.50	4.00
2 Gerry Cheevers	.75	2.00
3 Red Kelly	.75	2.00
4 Dave Keon	.75	2.00
5 Lanny McDonald	.40	1.00
6 Pierre Pilote	.40	1.00
7 Henri Richard	.75	2.00
8 Norm Ullman	.75	2.00
NNO Jean Beliveau Large	.75	2.00

1994-95 Zeller's Masters of Hockey Signed

This set features cards signed by former NHL greats and was distributed by Canadian retailing giant Zeller's. It is believed that approximately 1,100 copies exist of each card. We cannot confirm exactly how they were distributed at this point, although it is believed they could be acquired through a Zeller's customer loyalty program. Any further information can be forwarded to hockeymag@beckett.com.

COMPLETE SET (8) 50.00 125.00
1 Jean Beliveau 12.00 30.00
2 Gerry Cheevers 6.00 15.00
3 Red Kelly 6.00 15.00
4 Dave Keon 6.00 15.00
5 Lanny McDonald 6.00 15.00
6 Pierre Pilote 6.00 15.00
7 Henri Richard 8.00 20.00
8 Norm Ullman 6.00 15.00

1995-96 Zeller's Masters of Hockey Signed

This set features cards signed by former NHL greats and was distributed by Canadian retailing giant Zeller's. It is believed that approximately 3,500 copies exist of each card. Unlike previous years, it is thought that there were no un-signed versions released. We cannot confirm exactly how they were distributed at this point, although it is believed they could be acquired through a Zeller's customer loyalty program. Any further information can be forwarded to hockeymag@beckett.com.

COMPLETE SET (8) 70.00 175.00
1 Mike Bossy 10.00 25.00
2 Eddie Giacomin 6.00 15.00
3 Gordie Howe 20.00 50.00
4 Jacques Laperriere 6.00 15.00
5 Gilbert Perreault 8.00 20.00
6 Serge Savard 6.00 15.00
7 Steve Shutt 6.00 15.00
8 Darryl Sittler 8.00 20.00

1995-96 Zenith

The 1995-96 Zenith set was issued in one series totaling 150 standard-size cards. The 6-card packs had a suggested retail of $3.99. The set features 24-point card stock with exclusive Dufex all-foil printing.

COMPLETE SET (150) 15.00 40.00
1 Brett Hull .30 .75
2 Paul Coffey .25 .60
3 Jaromir Jagr .40 1.00
4 Joe Murphy .08 .25
5 Jim Carey .15 .40
6 Eric Lindros .25 .60
7 Ulf Dahlen .08 .25
8 Mark Recchi .15 .40
9 Pavel Bure .25 .60
10 Adam Oates .15 .40
11 Theo Fleury .08 .25
12 Martin Brodeur .75 2.00
13 Wayne Gretzky 2.00 5.00
14 Geoff Sanderson .08 .25
15 Chris Gratton .08 .25
16 Owen Nolan .15 .40
17 Paul Kariya .25 .60
18 Mark Messier .25 .60
19 Mats Sundin .25 .60
20 Brian Savage .08 .25
21 Mathieu Schneider .08 .25
22 Alexandre Daigle .08 .25
23 Jason Arnott .08 .25
24 Mike Modano .40 1.00
25 Scott Mellanby .08 .25
26 Alexei Zhamnov .15 .40
27 Scott Niedermayer .08 .25
28 Chris Pronger .25 .60
29 Ray Bourque .30 .75
30 Sergei Fedorov .60 1.50
31 Alexander Mogilny .15 .40
32 Brian Leetch .15 .40
33 Adam Graves .08 .25
34 Jocelyn Thibault .25 .60
35 Ron Francis .15 .40
36 John Vanbiesbrouck .15 .40
37 Chris Chelios .25 .60
38 Pierre Turgeon .15 .40
39 Stephane Richer .15 .40
40 Al MacInnis .15 .40
41 Dave Andreychuk .15 .40
42 Mikael Renberg .15 .40
43 Nelson Emerson .08 .25
44 Kevin Hatcher .08 .25
45 Kirk Muller .08 .25
46 Bernie Nicholls .08 .25
47 Bill Ranford .15 .40
48 Luc Robitaille .15 .40
49 Peter Bondra .15 .40
50 Jari Kurri .25 .60
51 Dino Ciccarelli .15 .40
52 Kevin Stevens .08 .25
53 Mike Richter .25 .60
54 Doug Gilmour .15 .40
55 Kelly Hrudey .15 .40
56 Dave Gagner .08 .25
57 Kirk McLean .15 .40
58 Geoff Courtnall .08 .25
59 John LeClair .25 .60
60 Mike Vernon .15 .40
61 Cam Neely .25 .60
62 Mike Gartner .15 .40
63 Igor Korolev .08 .25
64 Joe Sakic .60 1.50
65 Jeff Friesen .08 .25
66 Sergei Zubov .08 .25
67 Trevor Kidd .15 .40
68 Rod Brind'Amour .15 .40
69 John MacLean .15 .40
70 Peter Forsberg .60 1.50
71 Oleg Tverdovsky .08 .25
72 Jeremy Roenick .30 .75
73 Gary Suter .08 .25
74 Keith Tkachuk .25 .60
75 Todd Harvey .15 .40
76 Felix Potvin .25 .60
77 Vincent Damphousse .08 .25
78 Blaine Lacher .15 .40
79 Tomas Sandstrom .08 .25
80 Chris Osgood .15 .40
81 Arturs Irbe .15 .40
82 Pat Verbeek .08 .25
83 Keith Primeau .08 .25
84 Brett Lindros .08 .25
85 Pat LaFontaine .25 .60
86 Brendan Shanahan .25 .60
87 Trevor Linden .15 .40
88 Rob Blake .15 .40
89 Scott Stevens .15 .40
90 Tom Barrasso .15 .40
91 Mike Ricci .15 .40
92 Ray Sheppard .08 .25
93 Steve Yzerman 1.00 2.50
94 Wendel Clark .15 .40
95 Ed Belfour .25 .60
96 Joe Juneau .08 .25
97 Ron Hextall .15 .40
98 Shayne Corson .08 .25
99 Guy Hebert .15 .40
100 Sean Burke .15 .40
101 Sandis Ozolinsh .08 .25
102 Teemu Selanne .25 .60
103 Petr Nedved .15 .40
104 Phil Housley .15 .40
105 Andy Moog .25 .60
106 Larry Murphy .15 .40
107 Grant Fuhr .25 .60
108 Mario Lemieux 1.25 3.00
109 Dominik Hasek .60 1.50
110 Rob Niedermayer .15 .40
111 Steve Duchesne .08 .25
112 Joe Nieuwendyk .15 .40
113 Yanic Perreault .08 .25
114 Steve Thomas .15 .40
115 Russ Courtnall .08 .25
116 Claude Lemieux .08 .25
117 Patrick Roy 1.25 3.00
118 Rick Tocchet .15 .40
119 Stephane Fiset .15 .40
120 Daren Puppa .15 .40
121 Ed Jovanovski .25 .60
122 Eric Daze .15 .40
123 Cory Stillman RC .08 .25
124 Brendan Witt .08 .25
125 Valeri Bure .08 .25
126 Brian Holzinger RC .15 .40
127 Kyle McLaren RC .08 .25
128 Niklas Sundstrom .15 .40
129 Jamie Langenbrunner .15 .40
130 Jeff O'Neill .08 .25
131 Vitali Yachmenev .08 .25
132 Shane Doan RC 1.25 3.00
133 Byron Dafoe RC .15 .40
134 Corey Hirsch .15 .40
135 Antti Tormanen RC .08 .25
136 Jason Bonsignore .08 .25
137 Ryan Smyth .15 .40
138 Bryan McCabe RC .08 .25
139 Chad Kilger RC .08 .25
140 Todd Bertuzzi RC 1.25 3.00
141 Marcus Ragnarsson RC .15 .40
142 Marty Murray .08 .25
143 Daymond Langkow RC .25 .60
144 Saku Koivu .25 .60
145 Jere Lehtinen .15 .40
146 Aki Berg RC .15 .40
147 Radek Dvorak RC .25 .60
148 Robert Svehla RC .08 .25
149 Daniel Alfredsson RC 1.25 3.00
150 Miroslav Satan RC .40 1.00

1995-96 Zenith Gifted Grinders

Randomly inserted in packs at a rate of 1:6, this 18-card set showcases some of the best tough-play wingers in the game.

COMPLETE SET (18) 6.00 15.00
1 Keith Tkachuk .60 1.50
2 Kevin Stevens .40 1.00
3 Wendel Clark .60 1.50
4 Claude Lemieux .40 1.00
5 Rick Tocchet .40 1.00
6 Trevor Linden .60 1.50
7 John LeClair .40 1.00
8 Mikael Renberg .40 1.00
9 Owen Nolan .40 1.00
10 Todd Harvey .40 1.00
11 Dave Gagner .40 1.00
12 Dale Hunter .40 1.00
13 Dave Andreychuk .40 1.00
14 Mark Recchi .40 1.00
15 Jason Arnott .40 1.00
16 Dino Ciccarelli .40 1.00
17 Adam Graves .40 1.00
18 Steve Thomas .40 1.00

1995-96 Zenith Rookie Roll Call

Randomly inserted in packs at a rate of 1:24, this 18-card set features the hottest 1995-96 rookies highlighted by the Dufex technology. A note on the card backs alluded to the total production run of these cards being no greater than 1,200 total sets.

COMPLETE SET (18) 8.00 20.00
1 Saku Koivu 1.25 3.00
2 Radek Dvorak .40 1.00
3 Brendan Witt .40 1.00
4 Antti Tormanen .40 1.00
5 Brian Holzinger .40 1.00
6 Aki-Petteri Berg .40 1.00
7 Ed Jovanovski .75 2.00
8 Marcus Ragnarsson .40 1.00
9 Todd Bertuzzi 1.25 3.00
10 Daniel Alfredsson 1.25 3.00
11 Vitali Yachmenev .40 1.00
12 Chad Kilger .40 1.00
13 Eric Daze .40 1.00
14 Niklas Sundstrom .40 1.00
15 Shane Doan 1.25 3.00
16 Cory Stillman .40 1.00
17 Kyle McLaren .40 1.00
18 Jeff O'Neill .40 1.00

1995-96 Zenith Z-Team

Randomly inserted in packs at a rate of 1:72, this 18-card set depicts the best players in hockey, using a modified Dufex-type foil style. Based on stated insertion odds and the information given on the backs of the Rookie Roll Call singles, it is believed that no more than 400 of each Z-Team card is in existence.

COMPLETE SET (18) 50.00 100.00
STATED ODDS 1:72
1 Patrick Roy 6.00 15.00
2 Martin Brodeur 4.00 10.00
3 Mario Lemieux 6.00 15.00
4 Wayne Gretzky 10.00 25.00
5 Mark Messier 2.50 6.00
6 Jeremy Roenick 2.00 5.00
7 Eric Lindros 2.00 5.00
8 Peter Forsberg 3.00 8.00
9 Sergei Fedorov 2.00 5.00
10 Mike Modano 2.00 5.00
11 Jaromir Jagr 3.00 8.00
12 Pavel Bure 2.00 5.00
13 Joe Sakic 4.00 10.00
14 Paul Kariya 2.00 5.00
15 Brett Hull 2.00 5.00
16 Brendan Shanahan 2.00 5.00
17 Felix Potvin 2.00 5.00
18 Jim Carey 2.00 5.00
S2 Martin Brodeur-SAMPLE 2.00 5.00

1996-97 Zenith

The 1996-97 Zenith set was issued in one series totaling 150 cards and was distributed in six-card packs. Printed on thick card stock, the fronts feature color action player images on a gold foil background. The backs carry in-depth player statistics. Dainius Zubrus and Sergei Berezin are the key rookies in the set.

COMPLETE SET (150) 12.00 30.00
1 Mike Modano .30 .75
2 Martin Brodeur .75 2.00
3 Pavel Bure .20 .50
4 Ray Bourque .30 .75
5 Steve Yzerman 1.25 3.00
6 Keith Tkachuk .20 .50
7 Jim Carey .20 .50
8 Valeri Kamensky .08 .25
9 Valeri Bure .05 .15
10 Ron Francis .08 .25
11 Trevor Kidd .08 .25
12 Doug Weight .08 .25
13 Wayne Gretzky 2.00 5.00
14 Todd Gill .05 .15
15 Dominik Hasek .60 1.50
16 Scott Mellanby .08 .25
17 John LeClair .20 .50
18 Al MacInnis .08 .25
19 Derian Hatcher .05 .15
20 Stephane Fiset .08 .25
21 Alexander Selivanov .05 .15
22 Vyacheslav Kozlov .05 .15
23 Alexei Yashin .05 .15
24 Wendel Clark .08 .25
25 Ed Belfour .20 .50
26 Travis Green .08 .25
27 Joe Juneau .05 .15
28 Teemu Selanne .20 .50
29 Jeff O'Neill .05 .15
30 Jeremy Roenick .30 .75
31 Felix Potvin .20 .50
32 Bernie Nicholls .05 .15
33 Steve Thomas .05 .15
34 Alexander Mogilny .20 .50
35 Patrick Roy 1.25 3.00
36 Luc Robitaille .08 .25
37 Owen Nolan .08 .25
38 Sergei Zubov .05 .15
39 Pierre Turgeon .08 .25
40 Nikolai Khabibulin .08 .25
41 Adam Oates .08 .25
42 Stephane Richer .08 .25
43 Daren Puppa .08 .25
44 Joe Sakic .60 1.50
45 Ed Jovanovski .08 .25
46 Ron Hextall .08 .25
47 Doug Gilmour .08 .25
48 Paul Coffey .20 .50
49 Craig Janney .08 .25
50 Brendan Witt .05 .15
51 Jere Lehtinen .05 .15
52 Vitali Yachmenev .05 .15
53 Damian Rhodes .08 .25
54 Petr Nedved .08 .25
55 Theo Fleury .05 .15
56 Petr Sykora .05 .15
57 Kelly Hrudey .08 .25
58 Saku Koivu .20 .50
59 Brian Bradley .05 .15
60 Arturs Irbe .08 .25
61 Eric Lindros .20 .50
62 Michal Pivonka .05 .15
63 Joe Nieuwendyk .08 .25
64 Mats Sundin .20 .50
65 Jason Arnott .05 .15
66 Mike Richter .20 .50
67 Brett Hull .30 .75
68 Chris Chelios .20 .50
69 Jocelyn Thibault .20 .50
70 Oleg Tverdovsky .08 .25
71 Peter Bondra .08 .25
72 Bill Ranford .08 .25
73 Scott Stevens .08 .25
74 Jaromir Jagr .50 1.25
75 Corey Hirsch .08 .25
76 Peter Forsberg .50 1.25
77 Brendan Shanahan .20 .50
78 Antti Tormanen .05 .15
79 Marcus Ragnarsson .05 .15
80 Sergei Fedorov .30 .75
81 Todd Bertuzzi .20 .50
82 Grant Fuhr .08 .25
83 Pat LaFontaine .20 .50
84 Rob Niedermayer .08 .25
85 Brian Leetch .20 .50
86 Yanic Perreault .05 .15
87 Dino Ciccarelli .08 .25
88 Dimitri Khristich .05 .15
89 Jeff Friesen .05 .15
90 Paul Kariya .20 .50
91 John Vanbiesbrouck .08 .25
92 Roman Hamrlik .08 .25
93 Pat Verbeek .05 .15
94 Mark Messier .20 .50
95 Trevor Linden .08 .25
96 Igor Larionov .05 .15
97 Zigmund Palffy .08 .25
98 Tom Barrasso .08 .25
99 Eric Daze .08 .25
100 Vincent Damphousse .05 .15
101 Keith Primeau .05 .15
102 Claude Lemieux .05 .15
103 Daniel Alfredsson .08 .25
104 Ryan Smyth .20 .50
105 Chris Osgood .08 .25
106 Bill Guerin .05 .15
107 Shayne Corson .05 .15
108 Alexei Zhamnov .08 .25
109 Mikael Renberg .08 .25
110 Andy Moog .08 .25
111 Larry Murphy .08 .25
112 Curtis Joseph .20 .50
113 Cory Stillman .05 .15
114 Mario Lemieux 1.25 3.00
115 Scott Young .05 .15
116 Eric Fichaud .08 .25
117 Jonas Hoglund .05 .15
118 Tomas Holmstrom RC .75 2.00
119 Jarome Iginla .40 1.00
120 Richard Zednik RC .30 .75
121 Andreas Dackell RC .08 .25
122 Anson Carter .08 .25
123 Dainius Zubrus RC .40 1.00
124 Janne Niinimaa .20 .50
125 Jason Allison .05 .15
126 Bryan Berard .20 .50
127 Sergei Berezin RC .30 .75
128 Wade Redden .05 .15
129 Jim Campbell .05 .15
130 Darcy Tucker .05 .15
131 Harry York RC .20 .50
132 Brandon Convery .05 .15
133 Ethan Moreau RC .20 .50
134 Mattias Timander RC .05 .15
135 Christian Dube .05 .15
136 Kevin Hodson RC .20 .50
137 Anders Eriksson .05 .15
138 Chris O'Sullivan .05 .15
139 Jamie Langenbrunner .05 .15
140 Steve Sullivan RC .30 .75
141 Daymond Langkow .08 .25
142 Landon Wilson .05 .15
143 Scott Bailey RC .05 .15
144 Terry Ryan RC .05 .15
145 Curtis Brown .05 .15
146 Rem Murray RC .05 .15
147 Jamie Pushor .05 .15
148 Daniel Goneau RC .05 .15
149 Mike Prokopec RC .05 .15
150 Brad Smyth RC .05 .15

1996-97 Zenith Artist's Proofs

Randomly inserted in packs at a rate of 1:48, this 150-card set is parallel to the regular set and is similar in design. The difference is found in the gold, rainbow holographic foil stamp on each card.

*VETS: 20X TO 50X BASIC CARDS
*ROOKIES: 8X TO 20X

1996-97 Zenith Assailants

Randomly inserted in packs at a rate of 1:10, this 15-card set features color photos of some of the NHL's most deadly snipers (as well as a couple of guys who couldn't hit water from the beach) and is printed on silver, micro-etched, poly-laminate card stock.

COMPLETE SET (15) 10.00 25.00
1 Alexei Yashin .75 2.00
2 Mike Modano 2.00 5.00
3 Jason Arnott .75 2.00
4 Mikael Renberg .75 2.00
5 Saku Koivu 1.25 3.00
6 Todd Bertuzzi 1.25 3.00
7 Zigmund Palffy 1.25 3.00
8 Eric Lindros 1.25 3.00
9 Pat LaFontaine .75 2.00
10 John LeClair .75 2.00
11 Theo Fleury .75 2.00
12 Pierre Turgeon .75 2.00
13 Petr Nedved .75 2.00
14 Owen Nolan 1.25 3.00
15 Valeri Bure .75 2.00

1996-97 Zenith Champion Salute

Randomly inserted in packs at a rate of 1:23, this special commemorative insert set honors superstar veteran players who have played on a Stanley Cup championship team. The fronts feature color player photos printed on micro-etched, silver poly-laminate card stock, along with a faux "diamond" chip embedded in the Stanley Cup ring icon. A parallel to this set, entitled Champion Salute Extra, included an actual diamond chip.

COMPLETE SET (15) 20.00 50.00
*DIAMOND: 2.5X TO 6X BASIC INSERTS
DIAMOND STATED ODDS 1:350
1 Mark Messier .75 2.00
2 Wayne Gretzky 5.00 12.00
3 Grant Fuhr .75 2.00
4 Paul Coffey .75 2.00
5 Mario Lemieux 4.00 10.00
6 Jaromir Jagr 1.25 3.00
7 Ron Francis .75 2.00
8 Joe Sakic 1.50 4.00
9 Peter Forsberg 1.50 4.00
10 Claude Lemieux .75 2.00
11 Patrick Roy 3.00 8.00
12 Chris Chelios .75 2.00
13 Doug Gilmour .75 2.00
14 Mike Richter .75 2.00
15 Martin Brodeur 2.00 5.00
P3 Grant Fuhr PROMO 1.50 4.00
P9 Peter Forsberg PROMO 3.00 8.00
P15 Martin Brodeur PROMO 4.00 10.00

1996-97 Zenith Z-Team

Randomly inserted packs at a rate of 1:71, this 18-card set honors some of the NHL superstars by combining embossing, micro-etching, rainbow holographic and gold foil stamping on clear plastic card stock.

COMPLETE SET (18) 40.00 100.00
1 Eric Lindros 4.00 10.00
2 Paul Kariya 4.00 10.00
3 Teemu Selanne 4.00 10.00
4 Brendan Shanahan 4.00 10.00
5 Sergei Fedorov 4.00 10.00
6 Steve Yzerman 12.00 30.00
7 Brett Hull 6.00 15.00
8 Pavel Bure 4.00 10.00
9 Alexander Mogilny 2.00 5.00
10 Jeremy Roenick 4.00 10.00
11 Jocelyn Thibault 2.00 5.00
12 Keith Tkachuk 2.00 5.00
13 Daniel Alfredsson 2.00 5.00
14 Eric Daze 2.00 5.00
15 Jim Carey 2.00 5.00
16 Felix Potvin 4.00 10.00
17 John Vanbiesbrouck 2.00 5.00
18 Chris Osgood 2.00 5.00

1997-98 Zenith

The 1997-98 Zenith set was issued in one series totaling 100 cards and was distributed in packs of three 5" by 7" cards with one regular size card inside each of the jumbo cards. The jumbo cards had to be torn open to get to the regular cards inside. The fronts feature action color player photos. The backs carry player information and another photo.

COMPLETE SET (100) 50.00 125.00
1 Jarome Iginla .60 1.50
2 Peter Forsberg .60 1.50
3 Brendan Shanahan .50 1.25
4 Wayne Gretzky 2.00 5.00
5 Steve Yzerman 1.25 3.00
6 Eric Lindros .50 1.25
7 Keith Tkachuk .50 1.25
8 John LeClair .50 1.25
9 John Vanbiesbrouck .30 .75
10 Patrick Roy 1.25 3.00
11 Ray Bourque .60 1.50
12 Theo Fleury .20 .50
13 Brian Leetch .50 1.25
14 Chris Chelios .50 1.25
15 Paul Kariya .50 1.25
16 Mark Messier .50 1.25
17 Curtis Joseph .50 1.25
18 Mike Richter .60 1.50
19 Jeremy Roenick .50 1.25
20 Dominik Hasek .75 2.00
21 Martin Brodeur 1.00 2.50
22 Sergei Fedorov .60 1.50
23 Pierre Turgeon .30 .75
24 Teemu Selanne .50 1.25
25 Brett Hull .60 1.50
26 Saku Koivu .50 1.25
27 Owen Nolan .30 .75
28 Jozef Stumpel .20 .50
29 Joe Sakic .75 2.00
30 Zigmund Palffy .30 .75
31 Jaromir Jagr .75 2.00
32 Adam Oates .30 .75
33 Jeff Friesen .20 .50
34 Pavel Bure .50 1.25
35 Chris Osgood .30 .75
36 Mark Recchi .30 .75
37 Mike Modano .60 1.50
38 Felix Potvin .50 1.25
39 Vincent Damphousse .20 .50
40 Byron Dafoe .30 .75
41 Luc Robitaille .30 .75
42 Peter Bondra .30 .75
43 Daniel Alfredsson .30 .75
44 Pat LaFontaine .20 .50
45 Mikael Renberg .30 .75
46 Doug Gilmour .30 .75
47 Dino Ciccarelli .20 .50
48 Mats Sundin .50 1.25
49 Ed Belfour .50 1.25
50 Ron Francis .30 .75
51 Miroslav Satan .30 .75
52 Cory Stillman .20 .50
53 Bryan Berard .20 .50
54 Keith Primeau .20 .50
55 Eric Daze .30 .75
56 Chris Gratton .30 .75
57 Claude Lemieux .20 .50
58 Nicklas Lidstrom .50 1.25
59 Olaf Kolzig .30 .75
60 Grant Fuhr .30 .75
61 Jamie Langenbrunner .20 .50
62 Doug Weight .30 .75
63 Joe Nieuwendyk .20 .50
64 Yanic Perreault .20 .50
65 Jocelyn Thibault .30 .75
66 Guy Hebert .20 .50
67 Shayne Corson .20 .50
68 Bobby Holik .20 .50
69 Sami Kapanen .20 .50
70 Robert Reichel .20 .50
71 Ryan Smyth .20 .50
72 Alexei Yashin .20 .50
73 Trevor Linden .20 .50
74 Rod Brind'Amour .30 .75
75 Dave Gagner .20 .50
76 Nikolai Khabibulin .30 .75
77 Tom Barrasso .30 .75
78 Tony Amonte .30 .75
79 Alexander Mogilny .30 .75
80 Jason Allison .20 .50
81 Patrik Elias RC 1.00 2.50
82 Mike Johnson RC .30 .75
83 Richard Zednik .30 .75
84 Patrick Marleau .30 .75
85 Mattias Ohlund .30 .75
86 Sergei Samsonov .30 .75
87 Marco Sturm RC .75 2.00
88 Alyn McCauley .30 .75
89 Chris Phillips .30 .75
90 Brendan Morrison RC .75 2.00
91 Vaclav Prospal RC .40 1.00
92 Joe Thornton 1.50 4.00
93 Boyd Devereaux .30 .75
94 Alexei Morozov .30 .75
95 Vincent Lecavalier RC 15.00 40.00
96 Manny Malhotra RC .40 1.00
97 Roberto Luongo RC 15.00 40.00
98 Mathieu Garon .30 .75
99 Alex Tanguay RC 3.00 8.00
100 Josh Holden .30 .75

1997-98 Zenith Z-Gold

Randomly inserted in packs, this 100-card set is a parallel version of the base set printed on gold-foil card stock and sequentially numbered to 100.

*VETS: 15X TO 40X BASIC CARDS
*PROSPECTS: 10X TO 25X
4 Wayne Gretzky 150.00 300.00
95 Vincent Lecavalier 125.00 200.00
97 Roberto Luongo 125.00 250.00

1997-98 Zenith Z-Silver

Randomly inserted in packs at the rate of 1:7, this 100-card set is a parallel version of the base set printed on silver-foil board.

COMPLETE SET (100)
*VETS: 2X TO 5X BASIC CARDS
*PROSPECTS: 1X TO 2.5X
4 Wayne Gretzky 15.00 40.00
95 Vincent Lecavalier 20.00 50.00
97 Roberto Luongo 25.00 60.00

1997-98 Zenith 5x7

This 80-card set measuring 5" by 7" was distributed in three-card packs with a regular size card inside each jumbo card. The fronts feature color action player photos with another photo and player information on the backs.

COMPLETE SET (80) 75.00 150.00
1 Wayne Gretzky 4.00 10.00
2 Eric Lindros .60 1.50
3 Patrick Roy 3.00 8.00
4 John Vanbiesbrouck .50 1.25
5 Martin Brodeur 1.50 4.00
6 Teemu Selanne .60 1.50
7 Joe Sakic 1.25 3.00
8 Jaromir Jagr 1.00 2.50
9 Brendan Shanahan .60 1.50
10 Ed Belfour .60 1.50
11 Guy Hebert .50 1.25
12 Doug Gilmour .50 1.25
13 Keith Primeau .25 .60
14 Grant Fuhr .50 1.25
15 Joe Nieuwendyk .50 1.25
16 Ryan Smyth .50 1.25
17 Chris Osgood .50 1.25
18 Keith Tkachuk .60 1.50
19 Peter Forsberg 1.50 4.00
20 Jarome Iginla .75 2.00
21 Steve Yzerman 3.00 8.00
22 Jeremy Roenick .75 2.00
23 Jozef Stumpel .50 1.25
24 Mark Recchi .50 1.25
25 Daniel Alfredsson .60 1.50
26 Pat LaFontaine .60 1.50
27 Zigmund Palffy .50 1.25
28 Jason Allison .25 .60
29 Yanic Perreault .25 .60
30 Olaf Kolzig .50 1.25
31 Mikael Renberg .50 1.25
32 Bryan Berard .50 1.25
33 Jocelyn Thibault .50 1.25
34 Shayne Corson .50 1.25
35 Dave Gagner .25 .60
36 Claude Lemieux .25 .60
37 Saku Koivu .60 1.50
38 Curtis Joseph .60 1.50
39 Chris Chelios .60 1.50
40 Ray Bourque 1.00 2.50
41 Adam Oates .50 1.25
42 Felix Potvin .60 1.50
43 Peter Bondra .50 1.25
44 Sergei Fedorov 1.00 2.50
45 Paul Kariya .60 1.50
46 Theo Fleury .25 .60
47 John LeClair .60 1.50
48 Brett Hull .75 2.00
49 Rod Brind'Amour .50 1.25
50 Doug Weight .50 1.25
51 Jamie Langenbrunner .25 .60
52 Mats Sundin .60 1.50
53 Pavel Bure .50 1.25
54 Eric Daze .50 1.25
55 Nicklas Lidstrom .60 1.50
56 Luc Robitaille .50 1.25
57 Vincent Damphousse .25 .60
58 Mike Modano 1.00 2.50
59 Pavel Bure .60 1.50
60 Owen Nolan .50 1.25
61 Pierre Turgeon .50 1.25
62 Dominik Hasek 1.25 3.00
63 Mike Richter .60 1.50
64 Mark Messier .60 1.50
65 Brian Leetch .60 1.50
66 Sergei Samsonov .30 .75
67 Alexei Morozov .30 .75
68 Marco Sturm RC 1.25 3.00
69 Patrik Elias RC 1.00 2.50
70 Eric Messier RC .30 .75
71 Alyn McCauley .30 .75
72 Richard Zednik .30 .75
73 Mattias Ohlund .30 .75
74 Joe Thornton 1.50 4.00
75 Vincent Lecavalier RC 8.00 20.00
76 Manny Malhotra RC .75 2.00
77 Roberto Luongo RC 12.50 25.00
78 Mathieu Garon .30 .75
79 Alex Tanguay RC 2.50 6.00
80 Josh Holden .30 .75

1997-98 Zenith 5x7 Gold Impulse

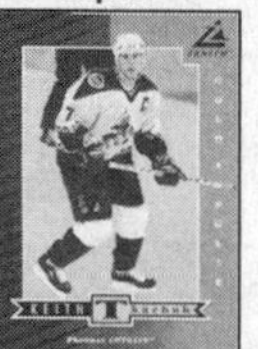

Randomly inserted in packs, this 80-card set is a gold foil parallel version of the base set and is sequentially numbered to 100.

*VETS: 10X TO 25X BASIC 5x7
*PROSPECTS: 2X TO 5X BASIC 5x7

1997-98 Zenith 5x7 Silver Impulse

Randomly inserted in packs at the rate of 1:7, this 80-card set is a silver foil parallel version of the base set.

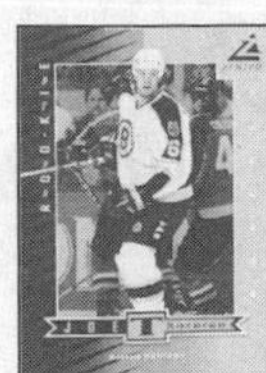

*VETS: 2X TO 5X BASIC 5x7
*PROSPECTS: .3X TO .8X BASIC 5x7

1997-98 Zenith Chasing The Cup

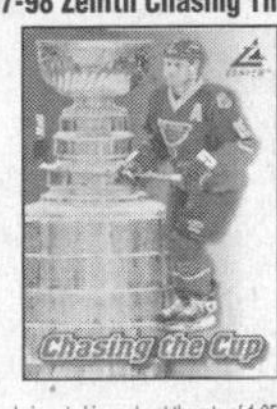

Randomly inserted in packs at the rate of 1:25, this 15-card set features color photos of top players printed on rainbow-hued holographic foil with an image of the trophy in the background.

COMPLETE SET (15) 50.00 125.00
1 Patrick Roy 12.00 30.00
2 Wayne Gretzky 15.00 40.00
3 Jaromir Jagr 4.00 10.00
4 Eric Lindros 2.00 5.00
5 Mike Modano 4.00 10.00
6 Brendan Shanahan 2.00 5.00
7 Brett Hull 3.00 8.00
8 John LeClair 1.25 3.00
9 Jocelyn Thibault 1.25 3.00
10 Ed Belfour 2.00 5.00
11 Martin Brodeur 8.00 20.00
12 Peter Forsberg 6.00 15.00
13 Saku Koivu 2.00 5.00
14 Pat LaFontaine 1.25 3.00
15 Steve Yzerman 12.00 30.00

1997-98 Zenith Rookie Reign

Randomly inserted in packs at the rate of 1:25, this 15-card set features color photos of top young players printed on holographic foil.

COMPLETE SET (15) 30.00 60.00
1 Sergei Samsonov 4.00 10.00
2 Joe Thornton 8.00 20.00
3 Erik Rasmussen 1.25 3.00
4 Brendan Morrison 2.00 5.00
5 Magnus Arvedson 1.25 3.00
6 Vaclav Prospal 1.25 3.00
7 Brad Isbister 1.25 3.00
8 Alexei Morozov 1.25 3.00
9 Marco Sturm 2.00 5.00
10 Patrick Marleau 4.00 10.00
11 Alyn McCauley 2.00 5.00
12 Mike Johnson 1.25 3.00
13 Mattias Ohlund 1.25 3.00
14 Patrik Elias 2.00 5.00
15 Richard Zednik 1.25 3.00

1997-98 Zenith Z-Team

Randomly inserted in packs at the rate of 1:35 for cards #1-9 and 1:58 for #10-18, this 18-card set features color action photos of top NHL players and rookies in white, black, and colored borders. The backs carry player information.

COMPLETE SET (18) 100.00 200.00
*5X7: .5X TO 1.2X BASIC INSERTS
5X7 STATED ODDS 1:35
*GOLDS: 1X TO 2.5X BASIC INSERTS
GOLD STATED ODDS 1:175
1 Teemu Selanne 3.00 8.00
2 Wayne Gretzky 20.00 50.00
3 Patrick Roy 12.00 30.00
4 Eric Lindros 3.00 8.00
5 Peter Forsberg 6.00 15.00
6 Paul Kariya 3.00 8.00
7 John LeClair 2.00 5.00
8 Martin Brodeur 8.00 20.00
9 Brendan Shanahan 3.00 8.00
10 Joe Thornton 6.00 15.00
11 Mattias Ohlund 2.00 5.00
12 Mike Johnson 2.00 5.00
13 Vaclav Prospal 2.00 5.00
14 Sergei Samsonov 2.00 5.00
15 Marco Sturm 2.00 5.00
16 Patrik Elias 2.00 5.00
17 Richard Zednik 2.00 5.00
18 Alexei Morozov 2.00 5.00

1956 Austrian Platnik and Shone

This single comes from an Austrian-issued multi-sport series. The cards are oversized and feature black and white fronts with blue and white backs, highlighted by the Olympic rings.

NNO Ice Hockey 12.50 25.00

1995-96 Austrian National Team

This 24-card set of the Austrian national team was sold at the 1996 World Championships in Vienna. The cards measure approximately 2 7/8" by 4" and feature color player cut-outs on the left with a head shot and player information printed on the right. The backs are blank. The cards are unnumbered and checklisted below in alphabetical order.

COMPLETE SET (28) 6.00 15.00
1 Christoph Brander .40 1.00
2 Thomas Cijan .20 .50
3 Claus Dalpiaz .30 .75
4 Reinhard Divis 1.25 3.00
5 Konrad Dorn .20 .50
6 Robin Doyle .20 .50
7 Michael Guntner .20 .50
8 Karl Heinzle .20 .50
9 Herbert Hohenberger .30 .75
10 Dieter Kalt .20 .50
11 Peter Kasper .20 .50
12 Werner Kerth .20 .50
13 Martin Krainz .20 .50
14 Gunter Lanzinger .20 .50
15 Engelbert Linder .20 .50
16 Arthur Marczell .20 .50
17 Manfred Muhr .20 .50
18 Rick Nasheim .20 .50
19 Kraig Nienhuis .40 1.00
20 Christian Perthaler .20 .50
21 Michael Puschacher .20 .50
22 Gerhard Puschnik .20 .50
23 Andreas Puschnig .20 .50
24 Gerald Ressmann .20 .50
25 Mario Schaden .20 .50
26 Michael Shea .20 .50
27 Wolfgang Strauss .20 .50
28 Martin Ulrich .20 .50

1937 British Sporting Personalities

Card features black and white front with biographical information on back.

37 Joe Beaton 10.00 20.00

1932 Bulgaria Zigaretten Sport Photos

Cards measure approximately 1 1/2 x 2 1/2 and are black and white photos. Cards were meant to be glued onto strips along with the appropriate caption. There were 272 cards in this multi-sport set.

142 Field Hockey 5.00 10.00
143 Field Hockey 5.00 10.00
144 Field Hockey 5.00 10.00
148 Ice Hockey 12.50 25.00
149 Dr. B. Watson Canada 10.00 20.00
150 Ice Hockey Goalie 12.50 25.00

1994-95 Czech APS Extraliga

This 303-card set measures the standard size and features the players of the Czech Elite League. Several prominent NHLers, including Jaromir Jagr and Martin Straka appear in this set. They returned to their homeland to play for their old club teams during the 1994 NHL lockout.

COMPLETE SET (303) 60.00 150.00
1 Pavel Cagas .30 .75
2 Ladislav Blazek .20 .50
3 Ales Flasar .08 .25
4 Petr Tejkl .08 .25
5 Jaromir Latal .08 .25
6 Ales Tomasek .08 .25
7 Jiri Kuntos .08 .25
8 Jan Vavrecka .08 .25
9 Martin Smetak .08 .25
10 Patrik Rimmel .08 .25
11 Michal Slavik .08 .25
12 Milan Navratil .08 .25
13 Petr Fabian .15 .40
14 Zdenek Eichenmann .08 .25
15 Miroslav Chalanek .08 .25
16 Pavel Nohel .08 .25
17 Radim Radevic .08 .25
18 Tomas Martinec .08 .25
19 Ales Zima .08 .25
20 Ivo Hrstka .08 .25
21 Richard Brancik .08 .25
22 Martin Jenacek .08 .25
23 Robert Holy .08 .25
24 Radovan Biegl .20 .50
25 Dusan Salficky .30 .75
26 Jiri Malinsky .08 .25
27 Jan Filip .08 .25
28 Jaroslav Spelda .08 .25
29 Petr Jancarik .08 .25
30 Robert Kostka .08 .25
31 Kamil Toupal .08 .25
32 Tomas Pacal .08 .25
33 Ales Pisa .15 .40
34 Milan Hejduk 15.00 40.00
35 Josef Zajic .20 .50
36 Stanislav Prochazka .08 .25
37 Jiri Sejba .20 .50
38 Marek Zadina .08 .25
39 Milan Filipi .08 .25
40 David Pospisil .08 .25
41 Tomas Blazek .20 .50
42 Patrik Weber .15 .40
43 Richard Kral .15 .40
44 Martin Sekera .08 .25
45 Ladislav Lubina .08 .25
46 Jiri Provaznik .08 .25
47 Michal Chlad .20 .50
48 Tomas Vokoun 4.00 10.00
49 Pavel Trnka .30 .75
50 Petr Kuda .08 .25
51 Frantisek Kaberle .30 .75
52 Libor Prochazka .30 .75
53 Jan Dlouhy .08 .25
54 Otakar Cerny .08 .25
55 Martin Ancicka .08 .25
56 Marek Zidlicky .75 2.00
57 Martin Prochazka .20 .50
58 Pavel Patera .30 .75
59 Otakar Vejvoda .30 .75
60 Jan Blaha .08 .25
61 David Cermak .15 .40
62 Petr Ton .08 .25
63 Miroslav Mach .08 .25
64 Patrik Elias 6.00 15.00
65 Martin Stepanek .08 .25
66 Tomas Mikolasek .08 .25
67 Milan Ruchar .15 .40
68 Jaromir Jagr 20.00 50.00
69 Milos Kajer .08 .25
70 Jaromir Sindel .40 1.00
71 Ivo Capek .20 .50
72 Jan Bohacek .08 .25
73 Zdenek Touzimsky .08 .25
74 Jan Krulis .08 .25
75 Frantisek Musil .20 .50
76 Jaroslav Nedved .08 .25
77 Frantisek Ptacek .08 .25
78 Pavel Taborsky .08 .25
79 Frantisek Kucera .20 .50
80 Pavel Srek .08 .25
81 Martin Simek .08 .25
82 Zbynek Kukacka .08 .25
83 Jiri Zelenka .15 .40
84 Jan Hlavac .75 2.00
85 Patrik Martinec .08 .25
86 David Bruk .08 .25
87 Pavel Geffert .20 .50
88 Michal Sup .08 .25
89 Jaromir Kverka .08 .25
90 Miroslav Hlinka .08 .25
91 Milan Kastner .20 .50
92 Andrej Potajcuk .08 .25
93 Roman Turek 2.00 5.00
94 Ladislav Gula .20 .50
95 Robert Slavik .20 .50
96 Jiri Hala .08 .25
97 Jaroslav Modry .20 .50
98 Petr Sedy .08 .25
99 Petr Hodek .08 .25
100 Petr Mainer .08 .25
101 Michael Kubicek .08 .25
102 Milan Nedoma .20 .50
103 Rudolf Suchanek .08 .25
104 Libor Zabransky .20 .50
105 Jaroslav Brabec .08 .25
106 Lubos Rob .15 .40
107 Zdenek Sperger .08 .25
108 Ondrej Vosta .08 .25
109 Filip Turek .08 .25
110 Radek Belohlav .20 .50
111 Frantisek Sevcik .08 .25
112 Roman Bozek .15 .40
113 Roman Horak .08 .25
114 Pavel Pycha .08 .25
115 Arpad Gyori .08 .25
116 Tomas Vasicek .20 .50
117 Michal Hlinka .20 .50
118 Daniel Kysela .08 .25
119 Rudolf Wolf .08 .25
120 Antonin Planovsky .08 .25
121 Tomas Kramny .08 .25
122 Vitezslav Skuta .20 .50
123 Pavel Marecek .08 .25
124 Miroslav Javin .08 .25
125 Kamil Pribyla .08 .25
126 Michal Cerny .08 .25
127 Juris Opulskis .08 .25
128 Richard Smehlik .30 .75
129 Ales Badal .08 .25
130 Robert Simicek .08 .25
131 Vladimir Vujtek .20 .50
132 Tomas Chlubna .08 .25
133 Michal Piskor .15 .40
134 Petr Folta .15 .40
135 Roman Kadera .15 .40
136 Lumir Kotala .08 .25
137 Jan Peterek .15 .40
138 Roman Rysanek .08 .25
139 Rudolf Pejchar .20 .50
140 Jiri Kucera .20 .50
141 Stanislav Benes .08 .25
142 Karel Smid .20 .50
143 Martin Kovarik .08 .25
144 Jiri Jonak .08 .25
145 Alexander Savickij .08 .25
146 Vaclav Ruprecht .08 .25
147 Ivan Vlcek .08 .25
148 Jaroslav Spacek .20 .50
149 Peter Veselovsky .08 .25
150 Milan Cerny .08 .25
151 Milan Volak .08 .25
152 Dusan Huml .08 .25
153 Tomas Kucharcik .08 .25
154 Martin Zivny .08 .25
155 Martin Straka .75 2.00
156 Michal Straka .08 .25
157 Jiri Beranek .15 .40
158 Ondrej Steiner .08 .25
159 Josef Rybar .40 1.00
160 Jaroslav Kreuzmann .08 .25
161 David Trachta .08 .25
162 Marek Novotny .20 .50
163 Pavel Falta .20 .50
164 Antonin Necas .08 .25
165 Roman Cech .08 .25
166 Pavel Zmrhal .08 .25
167 Petr Buzek .20 .50
168 Jaroslav Benak .08 .25
169 Michael Vyhlidal .08 .25
170 Petr Kuchyna .08 .25
171 Josef Marha .40 1.00
172 Leos Pipa .08 .25
173 Jiri Poukar .08 .25
174 Libor Dolana .08 .25
175 Viktor Ujcik .30 .75
176 Ladislav Prokupek .20 .50
177 Jiri Cihlar .20 .50
178 Patrik Fink .08 .25
179 Oldrich Valek .08 .25
180 Zdenek Cely .08 .25
181 Jaroslav Kames .30 .75
182 Pavel Malac .20 .50
183 Martin Maskarinec .08 .25
184 Pavel Rajnoha .15 .40
185 Pavel Kowalczyk .08 .25
186 Miloslav Guren .20 .50
187 Radim Tesarik .08 .25
188 Jan Krajicek .08 .25
189 Patrik Hucko .08 .25
190 Roman Kankovsky .08 .25
191 Jaroslav Hub .08 .25
192 Petr Kankovsky .08 .25
193 Pavel Janku .20 .50
194 Miroslav Okal .08 .25
195 Zdenek Okal .08 .25
196 Roman Mejzlik .15 .40
197 Juraj Jurik .08 .25
198 Roman Meluzin .08 .25
199 Josef Straub .20 .50
200 Martin Kotasek .08 .25
201 Zdenek Sedlak .08 .25
202 Petr Cajanek 1.25 3.00
203 Zdenek Orct .40 1.00
204 Petr Franek .20 .50
205 Petr Svoboda .40 1.00
206 Angel Nikolov .20 .50
207 Petr Molnar .08 .25
208 Kamil Prachar .20 .50
209 Jiri Slegr .40 1.00
210 Radek Mrazek .08 .25
211 Jan Vopat .20 .50
212 Ondrej Zetek .08 .25
213 Martin Stelcich .08 .25
214 Zdenek Skorepa .08 .25
215 Stanislav Rosa .08 .25
216 Radek Sip .20 .50
217 Martin Rousek .08 .25
218 Tomas Vlasak .20 .50
219 Radim Piroutek .08 .25
220 Robert Kysela .08 .25
221 Martin Rucinsky .40 1.00
222 Robert Lang .75 2.00
223 Ivo Prorok .08 .25
224 Jan Alinc .15 .40
225 Vladimir Machulda .08 .25
226 Kamil Kolacek .08 .25
227 David Balazs .08 .25
228 Roman Cechmanek 4.00 10.00
229 Ivo Pesat .20 .50
230 Antonin Stavjana .20 .50
231 Pavel Augusta .08 .25
232 Daniel Vrla .08 .25
233 Alexej Jaskin .08 .25
234 Radek Mesicek .08 .25
235 Marek Tichy .08 .25
236 Stanislav Pavelec .08 .25
237 Jan Srdinko .08 .25
238 Zbynek Marak .08 .25
239 Andrej Galkin .08 .25
240 Miroslav Stavjana .08 .25
241 Libor Forch .08 .25
242 Roman Stantien .08 .25
243 Josef Beranek .30 .75
244 Lubos Jenacek .08 .25
245 Michal Tomek .08 .25
246 Rostislav Vlach .08 .25
247 Miroslav Barus .08 .25
248 Josef Podlaha .08 .25
249 Pavel Rohlik .08 .25
250 Martin Altrichter .20 .50
251 Radek Toth .30 .75
252 Vladimir Hudacek .20 .50
253 Miloslav Horava .20 .50
254 Petr Macek .08 .25
255 Pavel Blaha .08 .25
256 Radomir Brazda .08 .25
257 Jiri Hes .08 .25
258 Tomas Arnost .08 .25
259 Miroslav Husek .08 .25
260 Jan Penk .08 .25
261 Tomas Jelinek .20 .50
262 Jiri Hlinka .08 .25
263 Lubos Pazler .08 .25
264 Roman Blazek .08 .25
265 Vladimir Ruzicka .40 1.00
266 Tomas Kupka .08 .25
267 Lubos Dopita .08 .25
268 Ladislav Slizek .08 .25
269 Milan Antos .08 .25
270 Vadim Kulabuchov .08 .25
271 Anatolij Najda .08 .25
272 Tomas Hyka .08 .25
273 Vaclav Eiselt .08 .25
274 Tomas Placatka .08 .25
275 Jan Nemecek .20 .50
276 Josef Augusta CO .08 .25
277 Lubomir Fischer CO .08 .25
278 Jaromir Precechtel CO .08 .25
279 Marek Sykora CO .08 .25
280 Petr Hemsky CO .08 .25
281 Jan Neliba CO .08 .25
282 Zdenek Muller CO .08 .25
283 Frantisek Vyborny CO .08 .25
284 Stanislav Berger CO .08 .25
285 Karel Prazak CO .08 .25
286 Vladimir Caldr CO .08 .25
287 Alois Hadamczik CO .08 .25
288 Bretislav Bochensky CO .08 .25
289 Karel Trachta CO .08 .25
290 Jindrich Setikovsky CO .08 .25
291 Jaroslav Holik CO .08 .25
292 Jan Hrbaty CO .08 .25
293 Vladimir Vujtek CO .08 .25
294 Zdenek Cech CO .08 .25
295 Frantisek Vorlicek CO .08 .25
296 Ondrej Weissmann CO .08 .25
297 Horst Valasek CO .08 .25
298 Zdislav Tabara CO .08 .25
299 Pavel Richter CO .08 .25
300 Bretislav Kopriva CO .08 .25
NNO Checklist 1 .02 .10
NNO Checklist 2 .02 .10
NNO Checklist 3 .02 .10

1995-96 Czech APS Extraliga

This 400-card set features color action player photos of members of the Czech Republic's Extraliga.

COMPLETE SET (400) 50.00 125.00
1 Horst Valasek CO .08 .25
2 Zdislav Tabara CO .08 .25
3 Roman Cechmanek 1.50 4.00
4 Ivo Pesat .30 .75
5 Alexej Jaskin .08 .25
6 Stanislav Pavelec .08 .25
7 Jan Srdinko .08 .25
8 Antonin Stavjana .20 .50
9 Pavel Taborsky .08 .25
10 Jiri Veber .08 .25
11 Daniel Vrla .08 .25
12 Miroslav Barus .08 .25
13 Ivan Padelek .08 .25
14 Libor Forch .08 .25
15 Andrej Galkin .08 .25
16 Lubos Jenacek .08 .25
17 Tomas Srsen .08 .25
18 Rostislav Vlach .08 .25
19 Zbynek Marak .08 .25
20 Jiri Dopita .40 1.00
21 Ales Polcar .30 .75
22 Roman Stantien .08 .25
23 Michal Tomek .08 .25
24 Jiri Zadrazil .08 .25
25 Pavel Augusta .08 .25
26 Tomas Jakes .08 .25
27 Vladimir Vujtek CO .20 .50
28 Zdenek Cech CO .08 .25
29 Jaroslav Kames .30 .75
30 Pavel Malac .30 .75
31 Jan Vavrecka .08 .25
32 Miroslav Javin .08 .25
33 Stanislav Medrik .08 .25
34 Pavel Kowalczyk .08 .25
35 Miloslav Guren .20 .50
36 Radim Tesarik .08 .25
37 Jan Krajicek .08 .25
38 Jiri Marusak .08 .25
39 Josef Straub .30 .75
40 Pavel Janku .08 .25
41 Roman Meluzin .30 .75
42 Miroslav Okal .08 .25
43 Zdenek Okal .08 .25
44 David Bruk .08 .25
45 Jaroslav Hub .08 .25
46 Petr Cajanek .40 1.00
47 Tomas Nemcicky .08 .25
48 Martin Kotasek .08 .25
49 Zdenek Sedlak .08 .25
50 Petr Leska .08 .25
51 Vladimir Caldr CO .08 .25
52 Jaroslav Liska .08 .25
53 Oldrich Svoboda .08 .25
54 Robert Slavik .20 .50
55 Rudolf Suchanek .08 .25
56 Milan Nedoma .30 .75
57 Lukas Zib .08 .25
58 Karel Soudek .08 .25
59 Petr Sedy .30 .75
60 Libor Zabransky .20 .50
61 Kamil Toupal .08 .25
62 Michal Kubicek .08 .25
63 Martin Masak .08 .25
64 Radek Belohlav .20 .50
65 Radek Toupal .15 .40
66 Pavel Pycha .08 .25
67 Lubos Rob .15 .40
68 Filip Turek .08 .25
69 Ondrej Vosta .20 .50
70 Roman Bozek .15 .40
71 Jaroslav Brabec .08 .25
72 Petr Sailer .08 .25
73 Martin Strba .08 .25
74 Zdenek Sperger .08 .25
75 Jan Neliba CO .08 .25
76 Zdenek Muller CO .08 .25
77 Martin Chlad .30 .75
78 Jiri Kucera .08 .25
79 Jan Dlouhy .08 .25
80 Tomas Kaberle .75 2.00
81 Petr Kasik .08 .25
82 Jan Krulis .08 .25
83 Petr Kuda .08 .25
84 Libor Prochazka .20 .50
85 Martin Stepanek .08 .25
86 Marek Zidlicky .40 1.00
87 Jiri Beranek .15 .40
88 Jiri Burger .08 .25
89 David Cermak .08 .25
90 Milos Kajer .08 .25
91 Miroslav Mach .08 .25
92 Tomas Mikolasek .08 .25
93 Pavel Patera .30 .75
94 Martin Prochazka .30 .75
95 Petr Ton .08 .25
96 Otakar Vejvoda .30 .75
97 Josef Zajic .30 .75
98 Josef Augusta CO .08 .25
99 Lubomir Fischer CO .08 .25
100 Jaromir Precechtel CO .08 .25
101 Pavel Cagas .20 .50
102 Ladislav Blazek .20 .50
103 Jaromir Latal .08 .25
104 Jiri Latal .15 .40
105 Petr Tejkl .08 .25
106 Jiri Kuntos .08 .25
107 Patrik Rimmel .08 .25
108 Robert Machalek .08 .25
109 Jiri Polak .08 .25
110 Martin Bakula .08 .25
111 Michal Slavik .08 .25
112 Pavel Nohel .08 .25
113 Igor Cikl .08 .25
114 Zdenek Eichenmann .08 .25
115 Milan Navratil .08 .25
116 Ales Zima .08 .25
117 Tomas Martinec .15 .40
118 Richard Brancik .08 .25
119 Ondrej Kratena .30 .75
120 Michal Bros .20 .50
121 Juraj Jurik .08 .25
122 Jan Tomajko .08 .25
123 Richard Farda .15 .40
124 Bretislav Kopriva CO .08 .25
125 Martin Altrichter .30 .75
126 Radek Toth .20 .50
127 Miloslav Horava .30 .75
128 Martin Maskarinec .08 .25
129 Jakub Ficenec .20 .50
130 Jiri Hes .08 .25
131 Andrej Jakovenko .15 .40
132 Petr Macek .08 .25
133 Jan Penk .08 .25
134 Robert Kostka .08 .25
135 Vladimir Ruzicka .30 .75
136 Viktor Ujcik .30 .75
137 Ivo Prorok .08 .25
138 Tomas Jelinek .20 .50
139 Michal Sup .08 .25
140 Milan Antos .08 .25
141 Roman Blazek .08 .25
142 Jiri Hlinka .08 .25
143 Tomas Kupka .08 .25
144 Vaclav Eiselt .08 .25
145 Jaroslav Bednar .75 2.00
146 Ladislav Svoboda .08 .25
147 Ladislav Kudrna .08 .25
148 Josef Beranek .20 .50
149 Vladimir Kyhos .08 .25
150 Zdenek Orct .30 .75
151 Petr Franek .30 .75
152 Kamil Prachar .15 .40
153 Angel Nikolov .20 .50
154 Ondrej Zetek .08 .25
155 Tomas Arnost .08 .25
156 Normunds Sejejs .08 .25
157 Petr Kratky .08 .25
158 Sergej Butko .08 .25
159 Petr Molnar .08 .25
160 Radek Mrazek .08 .25
161 Radim Piroutek .08 .25
162 David Balazs .08 .25
163 Jindrich Kotrla .08 .25
164 Jaroslav Buchal .08 .25
165 Josef Straka .30 .75
166 Michail Fadejev .08 .25
167 Radek Sip .08 .25
168 Martin Rousek .08 .25
169 Tomas Vlasak .20 .50
170 Robert Kysela .30 .75
171 Jan Alinc .15 .40
172 Vladimir Machulda .08 .25
173 Vladimir Jerabek .08 .25
174 Frantisek Vorlicek CO .08 .25
175 Jan Hrbaty CO .08 .25
176 Marek Novotny .20 .50
177 Lukas Sablik .08 .25
178 Roman Kankovsky .08 .25
179 Michael Vyhlidal .08 .25
180 Jan Bohacek .08 .25
181 Roman Cech .30 .75
182 Zdenek Touzimsky .08 .25
183 Marek Posmyk .20 .50
184 Pavel Rajnoha .15 .40
185 Martin Tupa .08 .25
186 Libor Dolana .08 .25
187 Petr Vlk .15 .40
188 Petr Kankovsky .08 .25
189 Jiri Cihlar .30 .75
190 Jiri Poukar .08 .25
191 Jaromir Kverka .08 .25
192 Leos Pipa .08 .25
193 Ladislav Prokupek .30 .75
194 Patrik Fink .08 .25
195 Marek Melenovsky .30 .75
196 Jiri Holik .08 .25
197 Miroslav Bruna .08 .25
198 Jaroslav Walter .08 .25
199 Otto Zelezny .08 .25
200 Libor Barta .08 .25
201 Pavel Nestak .08 .25
202 Leo Gudas .08 .25
203 Karel Beran .08 .25
204 Richard Adam .08 .25
205 Pavel Zubicek .08 .25
206 Alexandr Elsner .08 .25
207 Robert Kantor .08 .25
208 Ladislav Tresl .20 .50
209 Frantisek Sevcik .20 .50
210 Michal Konecny .08 .25
211 Richard Sebestu .08 .25
212 Roman Mejzlik .15 .40
213 Zdenek Cely .08 .25
214 Jiri Vitek .08 .25
215 Radek Haman .08 .25
216 Tomas Krasny .08 .25
217 Jiri Suhrada .08 .25
218 Jaroslav Smolik .08 .25
219 Alois Hadamczik CO .08 .25
220 Karel Suchanek .08 .25
221 Michal Hlinka .30 .75
222 Josef Lucak .08 .25
223 Karel Pavlik CO .08 .25
224 Stanislav Meciar .30 .75
225 Petr Mainer .08 .25
226 Petr Pavlas .08 .25
227 Lubomir Sekeras .40 1.00
228 Roman Sindel .20 .50
229 Vaclav Slaby .08 .25
230 Miroslav Cihal .08 .25
231 Martin Palinek .08 .25
232 Petr Zajonc .08 .25
233 Michal Piskor .15 .40
234 Roman Kadera .30 .75
235 Marek Zadina .08 .25
236 Richard Kral .15 .40
237 Miroslav Skovira .08 .25
238 Vladimir Michalek .08 .25
239 Libor Zatopek .08 .25
240 Dusan Adamcik .08 .25
241 Jiri Novotny .08 .25
242 Karel Trachta CO .08 .25
243 Jindrich Setikovsky CO .08 .25
244 Rudolf Pejchar .30 .75
245 Michal Marik .08 .25
246 Karel Smid .30 .75
247 Martin Kovarik .08 .25
248 Jiri Hanzlik .08 .25
249 Jaroslav Spacek .20 .50
250 Stanislav Benes .08 .25
251 Robert Jindrich .20 .50
252 Vaclav Ruprecht .08 .25
253 Tomas Kucharcik .08 .25
254 Michal Straka .08 .25
255 Ondrej Steiner .20 .50
256 Tomas Klimt .20 .50
257 Martin Zivny .08 .25
258 Milan Volak .08 .25
259 Pavel Metlicka .08 .25
260 Josef Rybar .30 .75
261 Jaroslav Kreuzmann .08 .25
262 David Trachta .08 .25
263 Anatolij Najda .08 .25
264 Tomas Ruprecht .08 .25
265 Dalibor Sanda .08 .25
266 Jaroslav Brabec .08 .25
267 Frantisek Vyborny CO .08 .25
268 Stanislav Berger CO .08 .25
269 Ivo Capek .30 .75
270 David Volek .30 .75
271 Jiri Vykoukal .20 .50
272 Vaclav Burda .08 .25
273 Petr Kuchyna .08 .25
274 Pavel Srek .08 .25
275 Frantisek Ptacek .08 .25
276 Radek Hamr .15 .40
277 Jiri Krocak .08 .25
278 Jaroslav Nedved .08 .25
279 Jiri Zelenka .15 .40
280 David Vyborny .30 .75
281 Checklist 1 .02 .10
282 Checklist 2 .02 .10
283 Checklist 3 .02 .10
284 Checklist 4 .02 .10
285 Zbynek Kukacka .08 .25
286 Miroslav Hlinka .08 .25
287 Jaroslav Hlinka .08 .25
288 Jan Hlavac .40 1.00
289 Andrej Potajcuk .08 .25
290 Richard Zemlicka .40 1.00
291 Vladimir Stransky .08 .25
292 Ladislav Svozil .08 .25
293 Martin Prusek 4.00 10.00
294 Vladimir Hudacek .15 .50
295 Pavel Marecek .08 .25
296 Rudolf Wolf .08 .25
297 Tomas Kramny .08 .25
298 Pavel Kubina 1.25 3.00
299 Rene Sevecek .08 .25
300 Filip Kuba .30 .75
301 Ales Tomasek .08 .25
302 Roman Rysanek .08 .25
303 Vladimir Vujtek .20 .50
304 Petr Folta .08 .25
305 Jan Peterek .08 .25
306 Roman Simicek .20 .50
307 Pavel Zulalial .08 .25
308 Pavel Sebesta .08 .25
309 David Moravec .40 1.00
310 Tomas Chlubna .08 .25
311 Ludek Krayzel .08 .25
312 Waldemar Klisiak .08 .25
313 Petr Fabian .08 .25
314 Josef Palacek .08 .25
315 Florian Strida .08 .25
316 Radovan Biegl .08 .25
317 Dusan Salficky .30 .75
318 Petr Jancarik .08 .25
319 Tomas Pacal .08 .25
320 Radomir Brazda .08 .25
321 Radek Mesicek .08 .25
322 Jiri Antonin .08 .25
323 Alexander Terechov .08 .25
324 Milan Beranek .08 .25
325 Ladislav Lubina .08 .25
326 David Pospisil .08 .25
327 Milan Kastner .08 .25
328 Stanislav Prochazka .08 .25
329 Patrik Weber .08 .25
330 Milan Hejduk 10.00 20.00
331 Tomas Blazek .08 .25
332 Jiri Janlovsky .08 .25
333 Jaroslav Kudrna .08 .25
334 Tomas Pisa .08 .25
335 Ales Pisa .08 .25
336 Ivan Vasilev .08 .25
337 Milan Hnilicka 2.00 5.00
338 Ales Flasar .08 .25
339 Martin Smetak .08 .25
340 Libor Polasek .20 .50
341 Vitezslav Skuta .08 .25
342 Ladislav Benysek .40 1.00
343 Jaroslav Smolik .08 .25
344 Igor Cikl .08 .25
345 Jan Czerlinski .08 .25
346 Marek Vorel .08 .25
347 Martin Ancicka .08 .25
348 Pavel Skrbek .20 .50
349 Petr Kadlec .08 .25
350 Tomas Kucharcik .08 .25
351 Ludek Bukac .30 .75
352 Zdenek Uher .08 .25
353 Roman Cechmanek 1.50 4.00
354 Roman Turek .75 2.00
355 Petr Briza .75 2.00
356 Jaroslav Kames .30 .75
357 Florian Otevjeno .20 .50
358 Dedrich Scerban .30 .75
359 Petr Kuchyna .08 .25
360 Jiri Vykoukal .30 .75
361 Frantisek Kaberle .30 .75
362 Jan Vopat .30 .75
363 Libor Prochazka .20 .50

1995-96 Czech APS Extraliga

364 Jiri Kucera	.20	.50
365 Tomas Jelinek	.20	.50
366 Richard Zemlicka	.40	1.00
367 Martin Hostak	.20	.50
368 Tomas Srsen	.08	.25
369 Jiri Dopita	.40	1.00
370 Martin Prochazka	.30	.75
371 Pavel Patera	.20	.50
372 Otakar Vejvoda	.30	.75
373 Roman Horak	.08	.25
374 Radek Belohlav	.20	.50
375 Pavel Geffert	.08	.25
376 Jan Alinc	.08	.25
377 Roman Kadera	.08	.25
378 Viktor Ujcik	.30	.75
379 Roman Meluzin	.20	.50
380 Pavel Janku	.08	.25
381 Tomas Kucharcik	.08	.25
382 Zbynek Marak	.08	.25
383 Ales Zima	.08	.25
384 Jaromir Jagr	10.00	25.00
385 Pavel Patera	.30	.75
386 Martin Prochazka	.30	.75
387 Pavel Janku	.08	.25
388 Roman Cechmanek	1.50	4.00
389 Antonin Stavjana	.20	.50
390 Rostislav Vlach	.08	.25
391 Lubos Jenacek	.08	.25
392 Dominik Hasek	6.00	15.00
393 Jiri Holik	.08	.25
394 Frantisek Pospisil	.08	.25
395 Ivan Hlinka	.30	.75
396 Vladimir Martinec	.08	.25
397 Jaroslav Pouzar	.08	.25
398 Karel Gut	.08	.25
399 Jan Benda	.30	.75
400 unknown	.08	.25

1996-97 Czech APS Extraliga

This 350-card set features the players of the top division in the Czech Republic, the Extraliga. They were produced by APS cards and sponsored by Fuji Film. Key cards in the set include Roman Turek, Marek Posmyk and Robert Reichel.

COMPLETE SET (350)	36.00	90.00
1 Marek Sykora CO	.02	.10
2 Vladimir Kolek	.02	.10
3 Rudolf Pejchar	.15	.40
4 Ladislav Kudrna	.15	.40
5 Miroslav Horava	.08	.25
6 Petr Kadlec	.08	.25
7 Jaromir Latal	.08	.25
8 Jiri Hes	.08	.25
9 Andrei Jakovenko	.08	.25
10 Martin Maskarinec	.08	.25
11 Jaroslav Horacek	.08	.25
12 Robert Kostka	.08	.25
13 Jiri Dolezal	.08	.25
14 Tomas Kucharcik	.08	.25
15 Ivo Prorok	.08	.25
16 Roman Kadera	.08	.25
17 Jiri Hlinka	.08	.25
18 Tomas Kupka	.08	.25
19 Viktor Ujcik	.30	.75
20 Vladimir Ruzicka	.15	.40
21 Ladislav Slizek	.08	.25
22 Jaroslav Bednar	.40	1.00
23 Michal Sup	.08	.25
24 Radek Matejovsky	.08	.25
25 Horst Valasek	.02	.10
26 Jiri Vodak	.02	.10
27 Jaroslav Kames	.30	.75
28 Petr Kubena	.15	.40
29 Petr Kuchyna	.08	.25
30 Jiri Marusak	.08	.25
31 Radim Tesarik	.08	.25
32 Vadim Podrezov	.08	.25
33 Stanislav Medrik	.08	.25
34 Jan Krajicek	.08	.25
35 Pavel Kowalczyk	.08	.25
36 David Bruk	.08	.25
37 Tomas Nemcicky	.08	.25
38 Zdenek Sedlak	.08	.25
39 Ales Zima	.08	.25
40 Zbynek Marak	.08	.25
41 Ales Polcar	.08	.25
42 Roman Meluzin	.08	.25
43 Pavel Janku	.08	.25
44 Miroslav Okal	.08	.25
45 Petr Cajanek	.40	1.00
46 Martin Kotasek	.08	.25
47 Petr Leska	.08	.25
48 Alois Hadamczik CO	.02	.10
49 Ales Mach	.02	.10
50 Radovan Biegl	.20	.50
51 Josef Lukac	.20	.50
52 Petr Jancarik	.08	.25
53 Lubomir Sekeras	.40	1.00
54 Jiri Kuntos	.08	.25
55 Stanislav Pavelec	.08	.25
56 Patrik Hucko	.08	.25
57 Miroslav Cihal	.08	.25
58 Karel Pavlik	.08	.25
59 Ondrej Zetek	.08	.25
60 Richard Kral	.08	.25
61 Petr Folta	.08	.25
62 Josef Straub	.08	.25
63 Petr Zajonc	.08	.25
64 Roman Kontsek	.08	.25
65 Marek Zadina	.08	.25
66 Roman Blazek	.08	.25
67 Michal Piskor	.08	.25
68 Jozef Dano	.08	.25
69 Vladimir Machulda	.08	.25
70 Jiri Novotny	.08	.25
71 Petr Lipina	.08	.25
72 Jan Novotny CO	.02	.10
73 Lubomir Bauer	.02	.10
74 Milan Hnilicka	2.00	5.00
75 Martin Chlad	.20	.50
76 Petr Kasik	.08	.25
77 Jan Krulis	.08	.25
78 Libor Prochazka	.20	.50
79 Jan Dlouhy	.08	.25
80 Marek Zidlicky	.40	1.00
81 Tomas Kaberle	.60	1.50
82 Pavel Skrbek	.20	.50
83 Tomas Trachta	.08	.25
84 Zdenek Eichenmann	.08	.25
85 Josef Zajic	.20	.50
86 David Cermak	.08	.25
87 Ladislav Svoboda	.08	.25
88 Tomas Mikolasek	.08	.25
89 Petr Ton	.08	.25
90 Jiri Beranek	.15	.40
91 Vaclav Eiselt	.08	.25
92 Jiri Burger	.08	.25
93 Petr Tenkrat	.30	.75
94 Petr Vogeltanz	.08	.25
95 Filip Klapac	.08	.25
96 Karel Suchanek	.08	.25
97 Kamil Konecny	.08	.25
98 Rostislav Haas	.08	.25
99 Roman Stupina	.08	.25
100 Milos Hrubes	.08	.25
101 Petr Tejkl	.08	.25
102 Martin Bakula	.08	.25
103 Radek Mesicek	.08	.25
104 Karel Frydl	.08	.25
105 David Galvas	.08	.25
106 Denis Tsygurov	.15	.40
107 Juraj Jurik	.08	.25
108 Petr Fabian	.08	.25
109 Radim Radevic	.08	.25
110 Jiri Zadrazil	.08	.25
111 Martin Filip	.08	.25
112 Karel Horny	.08	.25
113 Zdenek Pavelek	.08	.25
114 Eduard Gorbachev	.15	.40
115 Valerij Belov	.08	.25
116 Dalibor Rimsky	.08	.25
117 Marek Harazim	.08	.25
118 David Dostal	.08	.25
119 Slavomir Lener CO	.15	.40
120 Vaclav Sykora	.08	.25
121 Robert Schistad	.15	.40
122 Martin Cinibulk	.08	.25
123 Jiri Vykoukal	.20	.50
124 Jan Bohacek	.08	.25
125 Jaroslav Nedved	.08	.25
126 Jiri Krocak	.08	.25
127 Vaclav Burda	.08	.25
128 Radek Hamr	.15	.40
129 Frantisek Ptacek	.08	.25
130 Roman Horak	.08	.25
131 Pavel Geffert	.08	.25
132 Richard Zemlicka	.20	.50
133 Jiri Zelenka	.15	.40
134 Patrik Martinec	.08	.25
135 David Vyborny	.20	.50
136 Miroslav Hlinka	.08	.25
137 Martin Hostak	.15	.40
138 Jan Hlavac	.40	1.00
139 Jaroslav Hinka	.08	.25
140 Jan Benda	.15	.40
141 Josef Palecek	.08	.25
142 Milos Riha CO	.08	.25
143 Libor Barta	.08	.25
144 Dusan Salficky	.30	.75
145 Radomir Brazda	.08	.25
146 Pavel Augusta	.08	.25
147 Jiri Malinsky	.08	.25
148 Tomas Pacal	.08	.25
149 Ales Pisa	.08	.25
150 Pavel Kriz	.15	.40
151 Alexander Tsyplakov	.20	.50
152 Petr Mudroch	.08	.25
153 Ladislav Lubina	.08	.25
154 David Pospisil	.08	.25
155 Stanislav Prochazka	.08	.25
156 Tomas Martinec	.08	.25
157 Milan Hejduk	7.50	15.00
158 Tomas Martinec	.08	.25
159 Jiri Jantovsky	.08	.25
160 Martin Koudelka	.08	.25
161 Pavel Kabrt	.08	.25
162 Petr Sykora	.20	.50
163 Milan Prochazka	.15	.40
164 Karel Plasek	.08	.25
165 Josef Beranek	.20	.50
166 Vladimir Kyhos	.08	.25
167 Zdenek Orct	.30	.75
168 Richard Hrazdira	.08	.25
169 Kamil Prachar	.15	.40
170 Radek Mrazek	.08	.25
171 Roman Cech	.20	.50
172 Angel Nikolov	.20	.50
173 Martin Stepanek	.08	.25
174 Sergej Butko	.08	.25
175 Normunds Sejejs	.08	.25
176 Petr Kratky	.08	.25
177 Vladimir Jerabek	.08	.25
178 Kamil Kastak	.15	.40
179 Robert Kysela	.08	.25
180 Petr Hrbek	.08	.25
181 Martin Rousek	.08	.25
182 Tomas Krasny	.08	.25
183 Tomas Vlasak	.20	.50
184 David Balazs	.08	.25
185 Jindrich Kotrla	.08	.25
186 Josef Straka	.20	.50
187 Jaroslav Buchal	.08	.25
188 Kamil Piros	.60	1.50
189 Vladimir Vujtek CO	.08	.25
190 Ladislav Svozil	.08	.25
191 Martin Prusek	2.00	5.00
192 Tomas Vasicek	.08	.25
193 Jiri Jonak	.08	.25
194 Ales Tomasek	.08	.25
195 Daniel Kysela	.08	.25
196 Vitezslav Skuta	.08	.25
197 Tomas Kramny	.08	.25
198 Rene Sevecek	.08	.25
199 Dmitrij Jerofejev	.08	.25
200 Pavel Kumstat	.08	.25
201 Roman Rysanek	.08	.25
202 Roman Simicek	.20	.50
203 Martin Smetak	.08	.25
204 Tomas Chlubna	.08	.25
205 Ludek Krayzel	.08	.25
206 David Moravec	.20	.50
207 Alexander Prokopjev	.08	.25
208 Ales Kratoska	.08	.25
209 Libor Pavlis	.08	.25
210 Radek Klauda	.08	.25
211 Libor Polasek	.15	.40
212 Jan Neliba CO	.08	.25
213 Zdislav Tabara CO	.08	.25
214 Roman Cechmanek	.75	2.00
215 Ivo Pesat	.20	.50
216 Antonin Stavjana	.08	.25
217 Bedrich Scerban	.15	.40
218 Jiri Veber	.08	.25
219 Alexej Jaskin	.08	.25
220 Jan Srdinko	.08	.25
221 Tomas Jakes	.08	.25
222 Petr Kubos	.08	.25
223 Michal Divisek	.08	.25
224 Rostislav Vlach	.08	.25
225 Michal Tomek	.08	.25
226 Oto Hascak	.20	.50
227 Tomas Kapusta	.20	.50
228 Tomas Srsen	.08	.25
229 Roman Stantien	.08	.25
230 Jiri Dopita	.30	.75
231 Ivan Padelek	.08	.25
232 Andrej Galkin	.08	.25
233 Ondrej Kratena	.20	.50
234 David Hruska	.08	.25
235 Daniel Tesarik	.08	.25
236 Lukas Duba	.08	.25
237 Vladimir Caldr CO	.08	.25
238 Jaroslav Liska	.08	.25
239 Oldrich Svoboda	.08	.25
240 Robert Slavik	.20	.50
241 Rudolf Suchanek	.08	.25
242 Karel Soudek	.08	.25
243 Milan Nedoma	.20	.50
244 Kamil Toupal	.08	.25
245 Petr Sedy	.08	.25
246 Lukas Zib	.08	.25
247 Martin Masak	.08	.25
248 Radek Martinek	.40	1.00
249 Vladimir Antipin	.08	.25
250 Radek Toupal	.15	.40
251 Pavel Pycha	.08	.25
252 Lubos Rob	.15	.40
253 Filip Turek	.08	.25
254 Arpad Gyori	.08	.25
255 Radek Belohlav	.20	.50
256 Ondrej Vosta	.08	.25
257 Milan Navratil	.08	.25
258 Frantisek Sevcik	.08	.25
259 Petr Sailer	.08	.25
260 Michal Horak	.08	.25
261 Kamil Brabenec	.15	.40
262 Miroslav Barus	.08	.25
263 Jiri Latal	.15	.40
264 Miroslav Venkrbec	.08	.25
265 Ladislav Blazek	.20	.50
266 Robert Horyna	.15	.40
267 Petr Pavlas	.08	.25
268 Roman Veber	.08	.25
269 Marek Tichy	.08	.25
270 Jergus Baca	.15	.40
271 Ladislav Benysek	.20	.50
272 Jiri Polak	.08	.25
273 Marek Cernosek	.08	.25
274 Michal Slavik	.08	.25
275 Pavel Nohel	.08	.25
276 Radek Sip	.08	.25
277 Jan Tomajko	.08	.25
278 Michal Bros	.15	.40
279 Radek Prochazka	.08	.25
280 Radek Svoboda	.08	.25
281 Michal Dvorak	.08	.25
282 Ales Lipensky	.08	.25
283 Filip Dvorak	.08	.25
284 Milan Jurak	.08	.25
285 Adam Drabek	.08	.25
286 Bohuslav Ebermann	.08	.25
287 Radim Rulik	.08	.25
288 Martin Altrichter	.20	.50
289 Michal Marik	.08	.25
290 Ivan Vlcek	.08	.25
291 Josef Reznicek	.08	.25
292 Karel Smid	.20	.50
293 Vaclav Ruprecht	.08	.25
294 Jaroslav Spacek	.20	.50
295 Jiri Hanzlik	.08	.25
296 Robert Jindrich	.20	.50
297 Tomas Jelinek	.08	.25
298 Milan Volak	.08	.25
299 Radek Kampf	.08	.25
300 Miroslav Mach	.08	.25
301 Petr Korinek	.20	.50
302 Jiri Kucera	.15	.40
303 Michal Straka	.08	.25
304 Tomas Klimt	.20	.50
305 Josef Rybar	.20	.50
306 Dalibor Sanda	.08	.25
307 Jiri Novotny	.08	.25
308 Pavel Vostrak	.08	.25
309 Frantisek Vorlicek CO	.08	.25
310 Jan Hrbaty CO	.08	.25
311 Ivo Capek	.20	.50
312 Marek Novotny	.08	.25
313 Roman Kankovsky	.08	.25
314 Miroslav Javin	.08	.25
315 Michael Vyhlidal	.08	.25
316 Zdenek Touzimsky	.08	.25
317 Martin Tupa	.08	.25
318 Marian Morava	.08	.25
319 Filip Vanecek	.08	.25
320 Marek Posmyk	.20	.50
321 Libor Dolana	.08	.25
322 Petr Vlk	.15	.40
323 Petr Kankovsky	.08	.25
324 Jaroslav Hub	.08	.25
325 Jiri Poukar	.08	.25
326 Leos Pipa	.08	.25
327 Ladislav Prokupek	.20	.50
328 Patrik Fink	.08	.25
329 Marek Melenovsky	.15	.40
330 Milan Antos	.08	.25
331 Jiri Holik	.08	.25
332 Miroslav Bruna	.08	.25
333 Michail Fadejev	.08	.25
334 Ludek Bukac CO	.15	.40
335 Slavomir Lener CO	.15	.40
336 Zdenek Uher	.08	.25
337 Roman Cechmanek	.75	2.00
338 Roman Turek	.75	2.00
339 Robert Sysela	.08	.25
340 Jiri Veber	.08	.25
341 Pavel Patera	.20	.50
342 Radek Bonk	.40	1.00
343 Radek Belohlav	.20	.50
344 Drahomir Kadlec	.15	.40
345 Michal Sykora	.20	.50
346 Jiri Vykoukal	.20	.50
347 Viktor Ujcik	.20	.50
348 Stanislav Neckar	.20	.50
349 Robert Reichel	.30	.75
350 Roman Meluzin	.15	.40

1997-98 Czech APS Extraliga

This standard-sized set features the players of the Czech Republic's Extraliga and was produced by APS. The set features early or even first cards of several top NHLers including Milan Hejduk, Patrik Stefan and Roman Cechmanek.

COMPLETE SET (380)	50.00	125.00
1 Slavomir Lener CO	.20	.50
2 Vaclav Sykora CO	.08	.25
3 Milan Hnilicka	2.00	5.00
4 Martin Cinibulk	.08	.25
5 Frantisek Ptacek	.08	.25
6 Frantisek Kucera	.08	.25
7 Jaroslav Nedved	.08	.25
8 Jiri Krocak	.08	.25
9 Martin Holy	.08	.25
10 Jaromir Kverka	.08	.25
11 Jiri Zelenka	.08	.25
12 Richard Zemlicka	.20	.50
13 Jaroslav Hlinka	.08	.25
14 Jaroslav Bednar	.40	1.00
15 Ivo Novotny	.08	.25
16 Radek Duda	.20	.50
17 Michal Sivek	.75	2.00
18 Jan Hlavac	.40	1.00
19 Miroslav Hlinka	.08	.25
20 Patrik Stefan ERC	1.25	3.00
21 Vaclav Burda	.08	.25
22 Patrik Martinec	.08	.25
23 Ladislav Benysek	.20	.50
24 Jiri Vykoukal	.20	.50
25 Petr Nedved	.75	2.00
26 Jan Neliba CO	.08	.25
27 Zdislav Tabara CO	.08	.25
28 Roman Cechmanek	2.00	5.00
29 Ivo Pesat	.30	.75
30 Radim Tesarik	.08	.25
31 Antonin Stavjana	.20	.50
32 Jiri Veber	.08	.25
33 Michal Bros	.08	.25
34 Alexej Jaskin	.08	.25
35 Andrej Galkin	.08	.25
36 Rostislav Vlach	.08	.25
37 Ivan Padelek	.08	.25
38 Tomas Srsen	.08	.25
39 Jiri Dopita	.30	.75
40 Ondrej Kratena	.08	.25
41 Tomas Kapusta	.08	.25
42 Pavel Zubicek	.08	.25
43 Radek Belohlav	.20	.50
44 Tomas Demel	.08	.25
45 Michal Divisek	.08	.25
46 Michal Safarik	.08	.25
47 Josef Beranek	.20	.50
48 Jan Tomajko	.08	.25
49 Jan Srdinko	.08	.25
50 Roman Stantien	.08	.25
51 Eduard Novak CO	.08	.25
52 Zdenek Cech CO	.08	.25
53 Jaroslav Kames	.40	1.00
54 Robert Hamrla	.08	.25
55 Pavel Kowalczyk	.08	.25
56 Jan Krajicek	.08	.25
57 Petr Kuchyna	.08	.25
58 Pavel Rajnoha	.08	.25
59 Martin Hamrlik	.08	.25
60 Jiri Marusak	.08	.25
61 Karel Rachunek	.40	1.00
62 Roman Meluzin	.20	.50
63 Ales Zima	.08	.25
64 Pavel Janku	.20	.50
65 Tomas Nemcicky	.08	.25
66 Petr Cajanek	.30	.75
67 Miroslav Okal	.08	.25
68 Zdenek Sedlak	.08	.25
69 Ales Polcar	.08	.25
70 Petr Leska	.08	.25
71 Martin Spanhel	.30	.75
72 Branislav Janos	.08	.25
73 Marek Vorel	.08	.25
74 Tomas Zizka	.20	.50
75 Ondrej Weissman CO	.08	.25
76 Vladimir Jerabek CO	.08	.25
77 Zdenek Orct	.30	.75
78 Richard Hrazdira	.08	.25
79 Angel Nikolov	.08	.25
80 Drahomir Kadlec	.30	.75
81 Frantisek Prochazka	.08	.25
82 Radek Mrazek	.08	.25
83 Petr Molnar	.08	.25
84 Martin Stepanek	.08	.25
85 Roman Cech	.08	.25
86 Vladimir Gyna	.08	.25
87 Tomas Vlasak	.08	.25
88 Robert Kysela	.08	.25
89 Martin Rousek	.08	.25
90 Petr Hrbek	.08	.25
91 Vladimir Petrovka	.08	.25
92 Ivo Prorok	.08	.25
93 Tomas Krasny	.08	.25
94 David Balazs	.08	.25
95 Josef Straka	.08	.25
96 Kamil Piros	.40	1.00
97 Denis Afinogenov	.20	.50
98 Rail Muftijev	.08	.25
99 Dmitrij Denisov	.08	.25
100 Karel Franek CO	.08	.25
101 Petr Pelucha CO	.08	.25
102 Rostislav Haas	.08	.25
103 Pavel Nestak	.08	.25
104 Martin Maskarinec	.08	.25
105 David Galvas	.08	.25
106 Milos Hrubes	.08	.25
107 Pavel Sebesta	.08	.25
108 Tomas Kramny	.08	.25
109 Pavel Marecek	.08	.25
110 Vaclav Slaby	.08	.25
111 Petr Suchanek	.08	.25
112 Zbynek Marak	.08	.25
113 Michal Tomek	.08	.25
114 Michal Piskor	.08	.25
115 Juraj Jurik	.08	.25
116 Karel Horny	.08	.25
117 Jiri Zurek	.08	.25
118 Martin Sychra	.08	.25
119 Zdenek Pavelek	.08	.25
120 Richard Brancik	.08	.25
121 Milan Ministr	.08	.25
122 Martin Sekera	.08	.25
123 Vladimir Vujtek CO	.20	.50
124 Ladislav Svozil CO	.08	.25
125 Martin Prusek	1.50	4.00
126 Zdenek Dobes	.08	.25
127 Jiri Jonak	.08	.25
128 Vitezslav Skuta	.08	.25
129 Dmitrij Jerofejev	.08	.25
130 Petr Jurecka	.08	.25
131 Pavel Kumstat	.08	.25
132 Roman Simicek	.20	.50
133 Roman Rysanek	.08	.25
134 David Moravec	.30	.75
135 Alexander Prokopjev	.08	.25
136 Alexander Cherbajev	.20	.50
137 Libor Pavlis	.08	.25
138 Jan Matejny	.08	.25
139 Libor Polasek	.08	.25
140 Martin Kotasek	.08	.25
141 Petr Zajonc	.08	.25
142 Martin Lamich	.08	.25
143 Daniel Vilasek	.08	.25
144 Martin Tomasek	.08	.25
145 Ales Kratoska	.08	.25
146 Richard Farda CO	.08	.25
147 Ladislav Slizek CO	.08	.25
148 Martin Altrichter	.20	.50
149 Ladislav Blazek	.20	.50
150 Robert Kostka	.08	.25
151 Jiri Hes	.08	.25
152 Andrej Jakovenko	.08	.25
153 Pavel Kolarik	.20	.50
154 Martin Bakula	.08	.25
155 Petr Kadlec	.08	.25
156 Jan Novak	.08	.25
157 Jan Hejda	.20	.50
158 Vladimir Ruzicka	.20	.50
159 Viktor Ujcik	.20	.50
160 Jiri Dolezal	.08	.25
161 Jiri Poukar	.08	.25
162 Tomas Kucharcik	.08	.25
163 Michal Sup	.08	.25
164 Jiri Hlinka	.08	.25
165 Tomas Kupka	.08	.25
166 Radek Matejovsky	.08	.25
167 Robert Kucera	.08	.25
168 Jan Fadrny	.08	.25
169 Jan Sochor	.08	.25
170 Marek Sykora CO	.08	.25
171 Radim Rulik CO	.08	.25
172 Michal Marik	.08	.25
173 Dusan Salficky	.40	1.00
174 Josef Reznicek	.08	.25
175 Ivan Vlcek	.08	.25
176 Robert Jindrich	.20	.50
177 Jiri Hanzlik	.08	.25
178 Pavel Srek	.08	.25
179 Ondrej Zetek	.08	.25
180 Pavel Geffert	.08	.25
181 David Pospisil	.08	.25
182 Martin Filip	.08	.25
183 Tomas Jelinek	.08	.25
184 Michal Straka	.08	.25
185 Milan Volak	.08	.25
186 Pavel Vostrak	.08	.25
187 Dalibor Sanda	.08	.25
188 Milan Navratil	.08	.25
189 Mojmir Musil	.08	.25
190 Milan Kraft	2.00	5.00
191 Jiri Jelen	.08	.25
192 Martin Cech	.08	.25
193 Jan Novotny CO	.08	.25
194 Lubomir Bauer CO	.08	.25
195 Radek Toth	.08	.25
196 Martin Bilek	.08	.25
197 Jan Krulis	.08	.25
198 Marek Zidlicky	.08	.25
199 Tomas Kaberle	1.25	3.00
200 Pavel Skrbek	.20	.50
201 Jan Penk	.08	.25
202 Jan Dlouhy	.08	.25
203 Jan Hranac	.08	.25
204 Josef Zajic	.08	.25
205 Zdenek Eichenmann	.08	.25
206 Petr Ton	.08	.25
207 Jiri Beranek	.08	.25
208 Ladislav Svoboda	.08	.25
209 Vaclav Eiselt	.08	.25
210 Jiri Burger	.08	.25
211 Petr Tenkrat	.30	.75
212 Jiri Kuchler	.08	.25
213 Tomas Trachta	.08	.25
214 Jiri Holsan	.08	.25
215 Milan Novy	.08	.25
216 Jiri Kloboucek	.08	.25
217 Tomas Mikolasek	.08	.25
218 Milan Kasparek CO	.08	.25
219 Karel Trachta CO	.08	.25
220 Vladimir Hudacek	.08	.25
221 Robert Horyna CO	.08	.25
222 Petr Pavlas	.08	.25
223 Petr Mainer	.08	.25
224 Ales Tomasek	.08	.25
225 Pavel Blaha	.08	.25
226 Jiri Polak	.08	.25
227 Martin Richter	.08	.25
228 Martin Rejthar	.08	.25
229 Michal Cerny	.08	.25
230 Zbynek Kukacka	.08	.25
231 Ondrej Steiner	.08	.25
232 Pavel Metlicka	.08	.25
233 Martin Streit	.08	.25
234 Radek Prochazka	.08	.25
235 Radek Svoboda	.08	.25
236 Michal Porak	.08	.25
237 Michal Horak	.08	.25
238 Jan Lipiansky	.08	.25
239 Jaroslav Buchal	.08	.25
240 Tomas Klimt	.20	.50
241 Petr Fical	.08	.25
242 Milos Riha CO	.08	.25
243 Josef Palecek CO	.08	.25
244 Libor Barta	.08	.25
245 Adam Svoboda	.40	1.00
246 Patrik Rozsival	.08	.25
247 Jiri Malinsky	.08	.25
248 Ales Pisa	.08	.25
249 Tomas Pacal	.08	.25
250 Pavel Kriz	.20	.50
251 Pavel Augusta	.08	.25
252 Petr Murdoch	.08	.25
253 Robert Pospisil	.08	.25
254 Tomas Blazek	.20	.50
255 Milan Hejduk	8.00	20.00
256 Jiri Jantovsky	.08	.25
257 Stanislav Prochazka	.08	.25
258 Tomas Martinec	.08	.25
259 Pavel Kabrt	.08	.25
260 Jaroslav Kudrna	.20	.50
261 Karel Plasek	.08	.25
262 Petr Sykora	2.00	5.00
263 Lukas Palecek	.08	.25
264 Vladimir Caldr CO	.08	.25
265 Jaroslav Liska CO	.08	.25
266 Oldrich Svoboda	.40	1.00
267 Robert Slavik	.08	.25
268 Rudolf Suchanek	.08	.25
269 Karel Soudek	.08	.25
270 Milan Nedoma	.08	.25
271 Kamil Toupal	.08	.25
272 Lukas Zib	.08	.25
273 Jan Bohacek	.08	.25
274 Filip Vanecek	.08	.25
275 Radek Martinek	.30	.75
276 Radek Toupal	.08	.25
277 Lubos Rob	.08	.25
278 Pavel Pycha	.08	.25
279 David Bruk	.08	.25
280 Filip Turek	.08	.25
281 Ondrej Vosta	.08	.25
282 Arpad Gyori	.08	.25
283 Petr Sailer	.08	.25
284 Martin Strba	.08	.25
285 Petr Sachl	.08	.25
286 Miroslav Barus	.08	.25
287 Vaclav Kral	.08	.25
288 Ales Kotalik ERC	2.00	5.00
289 Josef Augusta CO	.20	.50
290 Karel Dvorak CO	.08	.25
291 Marek Novotny	.20	.50
292 Lukas Sablik	.08	.25
293 Michael Vyhlidal	.08	.25
294 Miroslav Javin	.08	.25
295 Martin Tupa	.08	.25
296 Marian Morava	.08	.25
297 Jaroslav Horacek	.08	.25
298 Tomas Jakes	.08	.25
299 Daniel Zapotocny	.08	.25
300 Miroslav Duben	.08	.25
301 Petr Vlk	.08	.25
302 Roman Mejzlik	.08	.25
303 Jiri Cihlar	.08	.25
304 Jaroslav Hub	.08	.25
305 Leos Pipa	.08	.25
306 Ladislav Prokupek	.08	.25
307 Marek Melenovsky	.08	.25
308 Milan Antos	.08	.25
309 Vaclav Adamec	.08	.25
310 Ales Sochorec	.08	.25
311 Ales Polcar	.08	.25
312 Daniel Hodek	.08	.25
313 Alois Hadamczik CO	.08	.25
314 Kamil Konecny CO	.08	.25
315 Radovan Biegl	.20	.50
316 Vlastimil Lakosil	.08	.25
317 Lubomir Sekeras	.30	.75
318 Miroslav Cihal	.08	.25
319 Petr Jancarik	.08	.25
320 Stanislav Pavelec	.08	.25
321 Jiri Kuntos	.08	.25
322 Patrik Hucko	.08	.25
323 Petr Gregorek	.08	.25
324 Filip Stefanka	.08	.25
325 Vladimir Machulda	.08	.25
326 Marek Zadina	.08	.25
327 Richard Kral	.08	.25
328 Jozef Dano	.08	.25
329 Ladislav Lubina	.08	.25
330 Tomas Chlubna	.08	.25
331 Jan Peterek	.08	.25
332 Petr Folta	.08	.25
333 Josef Straub	.08	.25
334 Roman Kadera	.08	.25
335 Marian Kacir	.08	.25
336 Robert Kantor	.08	.25
337 Roman Kontsek	.08	.25
338 Miroslav Horava	.08	.25
339 Ladislav Kudrna	.08	.25
340 Ivan Hlinka CO	.30	.75
341 Slavomir Lener CO	.08	.25
342 Roman Cechmanek	2.00	5.00
343 Milan Hnilicka	2.00	5.00
344 Martin Prusek	1.50	4.00
345 Frantisek Kaberle	.20	.50
346 Jiri Slegr	.20	.50
347 Jiri Vykoukal	.20	.50
348 Jiri Veber	.08	.25
349 Ladislav Benysek	.20	.50
350 Frantisek Kucera	.08	.25
351 Libor Prochazka	.08	.25
352 Jaroslav Spacek	.20	.50
353 Vlastimil Kroupa	.08	.25
354 Robert Reichel	.30	.75
355 Robert Lang	.40	1.00
356 Pavel Patera	.20	.50
357 Martin Prochazka	.20	.50
358 Jiri Dopita	.30	.75
359 Josef Beranek	.20	.50
360 Viktor Ujcik	.20	.50
361 David Vyborny	.20	.50
362 Vladimir Vujtek	.20	.50
363 Roman Simicek	.20	.50
364 Jan Alinc	.08	.25
365 Rostislav Vlach	.08	.25
366 Ondrej Kratena	.08	.25
367 Richard Zemlicka	.20	.50
368 Dominik Hasek POY	4.00	10.00
369 Jiri Dopita	.30	.75
370 Roman Cechmanek	2.00	5.00
371 Roman Horak	.08	.25
372 Richard Zemlicka	.08	.25
373 Antonin Stavjana	.20	.50
374 Ondrej Kratena	.08	.25
375 Richard Farda	.08	.25
376 Frantisek Cernik	.08	.25
377 Ludek Cajka	.08	.25
378 Vlastimil Bubnik	.08	.25
379 Josef Mikolas	.08	.25
380 Stanislav Konopasek	.08	.25

1997-98 Czech DS Extraliga

This set features the top players of the Czech Extraliga. The first 13 cards are short printed. Card No. 1, Roman Cechmanek Super Chase, was issued 1:48, while the Golden All-Stars cards No. 2-12 came 1:4.

COMPLETE SET (120)	20.00	75.00
1 Roman Cechmanek	4.00	10.00
2 Milan Hnilicka	4.00	10.00
3 Josef Beranek	.30	.75
4 Milan Nedoma	.40	1.00
5 Lubomir Sekeras	.40	1.00
6 Jiri Vykoukal	.75	2.00
7 Jiri Dopita	.75	2.00
8 Robert Kysela	.40	1.00
9 Roman Meluzin	.75	2.00
10 Roman Simicek	.20	.50
11 Petr Ton	.40	1.00
12 Viktor Ujcik	.75	2.00
13 Vladimir Hudacek	.20	.50
14 Petr Pavlas	.08	.25
15 Ales Tomasek	.08	.25
16 Pavel Blaha	.08	.25
17 Pavel Nohel	.08	.25
18 Tomas Klimt	.08	.25
19 Radek Prochazka	.20	.50
20 Rostislav Haas	.08	.25
21 Karel Smid	.20	.50
22 Milos Hrubes	.08	.25
23 Martin Maskarinec	.08	.25
24 Zbynek Marak	.08	.25
25 Michal Tomek	.08	.25
26 Juraj Jurik	.08	.25
27 Oldrich Svoboda	.40	1.00
28 Rudolf Suchanek	.08	.25
29 Karel Soudek	.08	.25
30 Radek Martinek	.30	.75
31 Radek Toupal	.08	.25
32 Lubos Rob	.08	.25
33 Pavel Pycha	.08	.25
34 Marek Novotny	.08	.25
35 Michael Vyhlidal	.08	.25
36 Petr Vlk	.08	.25
37 Roman Mejzlik	.08	.25
38 Jiri Cihlar	.08	.25
39 Jaroslav Hub	.08	.25
40 Marek Melenovsky	.08	.25
41 Zdenek Orct	.30	.75
42 Angel Nikolov	.20	.50

43 Frantisek Prochazka .08 .25
44 Martin Stepanek .08 .25
45 Tomas Vlasak .08 .25
46 Martin Rousek .08 .25
47 Petr Hrbek .08 .25
48 Ivo Prorok .08 .25
49 Dusan Salficky .30 .75
50 Josef Reznicek .08 .25
51 Ivan Vlcek .08 .25
52 Robert Jindrich .20 .50
53 Pavel Geffert .08 .25
54 Tomas Jelinek .08 .25
55 David Pospisil .08 .25
56 Milan Volak .08 .25
57 Antonin Stavjana .20 .50
58 Radim Tesarik .08 .25
59 Alexej Jaskin .08 .25
60 Tomas Srsen .08 .25
61 Tomas Kapusta .08 .25
62 Radek Belohlav .20 .50
63 Ondrej Kratena .08 .25
64 Jan Tomajko .08 .25
65 Michal Bros .08 .25
66 Rostislav Vlach .08 .25
67 Libor Barta .08 .25
68 Pavel Augusta .08 .25
69 Tomas Blazek .08 .25
70 Milan Hejduk 4.00 10.00
71 Stanislav Prochazka .08 .25
72 Tomas Martinec .08 .25
73 Jaroslav Kudrna .20 .50
74 Ladislav Blazek .08 .25
75 Martin Bakula .08 .25
76 Vladimir Ruzicka .20 .50
77 Jiri Dolezal .08 .25
78 Jiri Poukar .08 .25
79 Tomas Kucharcik .08 .25
80 Frantisek Kucera .08 .25
81 Vaclav Burda .08 .25
82 Jaroslav Nedved .08 .25
83 Richard Zemlicka .20 .50
84 Jiri Zelenka .08 .25
85 Patrik Martinec .08 .25
86 Jan Hlavac .40 1.00
87 Patrik Stefan ERC .75 2.00
88 Jaroslav Bednar .40 1.00
89 Radek Toth .08 .25
90 Jan Krulis .08 .25
91 Pavel Skrbek .20 .50
92 Josef Zajic .08 .25
93 Zdenek Eichenmann .08 .25
94 Ladislav Svoboda .08 .25
95 Martin Prusek .75 2.00
96 Jiri Jonak .08 .25
97 Vitezslav Skuta .08 .25
98 Dimitri Jerofejev .08 .25
99 Roman Rysanek .08 .25
100 David Moravec .20 .50
101 Alexander Prokopjev .08 .25
102 Jaroslav Kames .30 .75
103 Pavel Kowalczyk .08 .25
104 Petr Kuchyna .08 .25
105 Ales Zima .08 .25
106 Pavel Janku .08 .25
107 Tomas Nemcicky .08 .25
108 Petr Cajanek .40 1.00
109 Branislav Janos .08 .25
110 Radovan Biegl .20 .50
111 Richard Kral .08 .25
112 Roman Kontsek .08 .25
113 Jozef Dano .08 .25
114 Ladislav Lubina .08 .25
115 Tomas Chlubna .08 .25
116 Jozef Straub .08 .25
117 Roman Kadera .08 .25
118 Marek Zadina .08 .25
119 Checklist .02 .10
120 Premium card

1997-98 Czech DS Stickers

This set of stickers features many of the players in the Czech Republic Extraliga. The stickers are about 1/3 the size of a standard card. Because many of them were placed into sticker albums, they are difficult to find in their original condition.

COMPLETE SET (283) 35.00 90.00
1 Roman Cechmanek .60 1.50
2 Jiri Veber .08 .25
3 Jiri Vykoukal .20 .50
4 Miloslav Horava .08 .25
5 Martin Stepanek .08 .25
6 Antonin Stavjana .20 .50
7 Bedrich Scerban .08 .25
8 Radek Belohlav .20 .50
9 League Logo .08 .25
10 Jiri Dopita .30 .75
11 David Vyborny .20 .50
12 Josef Beranek .20 .50
13 Vladimir Jerabek .08 .25
14 Viktor Ujcik .20 .50
15 Roman Meluzin .20 .50
16 Jiri Kucera .08 .25
17 Robert Lang .40 1.00
18 Roman Cechmanek .60 1.50
19 Antonin Stavjana .20 .50
20 Tomas Jakes .08 .25
21 Alexej Jaskin .08 .25
22 Jan Srdinko .08 .25
23 Jiri Veber .08 .25
24 Bedrich Scerban .08 .25
25 Ivan Padelek .08 .25
26 HC Petra Vsetin Logo .08 .25
27 HC Petra Vsetin Team Card .08 .25
28 HC Petra Vsetin Team Card .08 .25
29 Rostislav Vlach .08 .25
30 Josef Beranek .20 .50
31 Ondrej Kratena .08 .25
32 Jiri Dopita .30 .75
33 Tomas Kapusta .08 .25
34 Tomas Srsen .08 .25
35 Andrej Galkin .08 .25
36 Oto Hascak .08 .25
37 Zdenek Orct .30 .75
38 Martin Stepanek .08 .25
39 Normunds Sejejs .08 .25
40 Sergej Butko .08 .25
41 Roman Cech .08 .25
42 Radek Mrazek .08 .25
43 Angel Nikolov .20 .50
44 Robert Kysela .08 .25
45 HC Litvinov Logo .08 .25
46 HC Litvinov Team Card .08 .25
47 HC Litvinov Team Card .08 .25
48 Vladimir Jerabek .08 .25
49 Martin Rousek .08 .25
50 Jaroslav Buchal .08 .25
51 Petr Hrbek .08 .25
52 Tomas Vlasak .08 .25
53 Tomas Krasny .08 .25
54 Josef Straka .08 .25
55 Kamil Kastak .08 .25
56 Robert Schistad .08 .25
57 Radek Hamr .08 .25
58 Jaroslav Nedved .08 .25
59 Jan Bohacek .08 .25
60 Vaclav Burda .08 .25
61 Jiri Vykoukal .20 .50
62 Frantisek Ptacek .08 .25
63 Jan Benda .08 .25
64 HC Sparta Praha Logo .08 .25
65 HC Sparta Praha Team Card .08 .25
66 HC Sparta Praha Team Card .08 .25
67 Richard Zemlicka .20 .50
68 Roman Horak .20 .50
69 Patrik Martinec .08 .25
70 Martin Hostak .08 .25
71 David Vyborny .20 .50
72 Pavel Geffert .08 .25
73 Robert Lang .40 1.00
74 Andrej Potajcuk .08 .25
75 Oldrich Svoboda .40 1.00
76 Karel Soudek .08 .25
77 Kamil Toupal .08 .25
78 Milan Nedoma .08 .25
79 Radek Martinek .20 .50
80 Vladimir Antipin .08 .25
81 Rudolf Suchanek .08 .25
82 Pavel Pycha .08 .25
83 HC Ceske Budejovice Logo .08 .25
84 HC Ceske Budejovice Team .08 .25
85 HC Ceske Budejovice Team .08 .25
86 Radek Toupal .08 .25
87 Lubos Rob .08 .25
88 Milan Navratil .08 .25
89 Filip Turek .08 .25
90 Radek Belohlav .20 .50
91 Miroslav Barus .08 .25
92 Frantisek Sevcik .08 .25
93 Arpad Györi .08 .25
94 Jaroslav Kames .30 .75
95 Petr Kuchyna .08 .25
96 Pavel Kowalczyk .08 .25
97 Stanislav Medrik .08 .25
98 Jan Krajicek .08 .25
99 Radim Tesarik .08 .25
100 Jiri Marusak .08 .25
101 Pavel Janku .08 .25
102 HC ZPS Zlin Logo .08 .25
103 HC ZPS Zlin Team Card .08 .25
104 HC ZPS Zlin Team Card .08 .25
105 Ales Polcar .08 .25
106 David Bruk .08 .25
107 Zbynek Marak .08 .25
108 Ales Zima .08 .25
109 Roman Meluzin .20 .50
110 Miroslav Okal .08 .25
111 Petr Cajanek .40 1.00
112 Tomas Nemcicky .08 .25
113 Rudolf Pejchar .08 .25
114 Jaromir Latal .08 .25
115 Robert Kostka .08 .25
116 Jiri Hes .08 .25
117 Petr Kadlec .08 .25
118 Martin Maskarinec .08 .25
119 Michal Horava .08 .25
120 Roman Kadera .08 .25
121 HC Slavia Praha Logo .08 .25
122 HC Slavia Praha Team Card .08 .25
123 HC Slavia Praha Team Card .08 .25
124 Tomas Kucharcik .08 .25
125 Jiri Dolezal .08 .25
126 Jaroslav Bednar .40 1.00
127 Ladislav Slizek .08 .25
128 Tomas Kupka .08 .25
129 Viktor Ujcik .20 .50
130 Vladimir Ruzicka .20 .50
131 Ivo Prorok .08 .25
132 Milan Hnilicka .60 1.50
133 Jan Krulis .08 .25
134 Jan Dlouhy .08 .25
135 Libor Prochazka .08 .25
136 Tomas Kaberle .60 1.50
137 Marek Zidlicky .40 1.00
138 Petr Kasik .08 .25
139 Jiri Beranek .08 .25
140 HC Poldi Kladno Logo .08 .25
141 HC Poldi Kladno Team Card .08 .25
142 HC Poldi Kladno Team Card .08 .25
143 Josef Zajic .08 .25
144 Tomas Mikulasek .08 .25
145 Ladislav Svoboda .08 .25
146 Zdenek Eichenmann .08 .25
147 Vaclav Eiselt .08 .25
148 Petr Ton .08 .25
149 Jiri Burger .08 .25
150 David Cermak .08 .25
151 Ivo Capek .08 .25
152 Marian Morava .08 .25
153 Michael Vyhlidal .08 .25
154 Roman Kankovsky .08 .25
155 Zdenek Touzimsky .08 .25
156 Marek Posmyk .08 .25
157 Miroslav Javin .08 .25
158 Miroslav Bruna .08 .25
159 HC Dukla Jihlava Logo .08 .25
160 HC Dukla Jihlava Team Card .08 .25
161 HC Dukla Jihlava Team Card .08 .25
162 Jaroslav Hub .08 .25
163 Petr Vlk .08 .25
164 Jiri Poukar .08 .25
165 Petr Kankovsky .08 .25
166 Ladislav Prokupek .08 .25
167 Milan Antos .08 .25
168 Leos Pipa .08 .25
169 Michail Fadejev .08 .25
170 Ladislav Blazek .08 .25
171 Petr Pavlas .20 .50
172 Marek Cernosek .08 .25
173 Ladislav Benysek .20 .50
174 Jergus Baca .08 .25
175 Marek Tichy .08 .25
176 Roman Veber .08 .25
177 Martin Streit .08 .25
178 Hockey Olomouc Logo .08 .25
179 Hockey Olomouc Team Card .08 .25
180 Hockey Olomouc Team Card .08 .25
181 Michal Bros .08 .25
182 Radek Svoboda .08 .25
183 Pavel Nohel .08 .25
184 Radek Prochazka .08 .25
185 Jan Tomajko .08 .25
186 Michal Slavik .08 .25
187 Radek Sip .08 .25
188 Filip Dvorak .08 .25
189 Martin Prusek .60 1.50
190 Jiri Jonak .08 .25
191 Pavel Kumstat .08 .25
192 Vitezslav Skuta .08 .25
193 Dmitri Jerofejev .08 .25
194 Rene Sevecek .08 .25
195 Ales Tomasek .08 .25
196 Roman Simicek .20 .50
197 HC Vitkovice Logo .08 .25
198 HC Vitkovice Team Card .08 .25
199 HC Vitkovice Team Card .08 .25
200 Alexander Prokopjev .08 .25
201 Jan Peterek .08 .25
202 David Moravec .20 .50
203 Tomas Chlubna .08 .25
204 Libor Polasek .08 .25
205 Ales Kratoska .08 .25
206 Roman Rysanek .08 .25
207 Martin Smetak .08 .25
208 Martin Altrichter .08 .25
209 Karel Smid .20 .50
210 Josef Reznicek .08 .25
211 Jaroslav Spacek .20 .50
212 Ivan Vlcek .08 .25
213 Jiri Hanzlik .08 .25
214 Robert Jindrich .20 .50
215 Milan Volak .08 .25
216 HC ZKZ Plzen Logo .08 .25
217 HC ZKZ Plzen Team Card .08 .25
218 HC ZKZ Plzen Team Card .08 .25
219 Jiri Kucera .08 .25
220 Tomas Klimt .20 .50
221 Tomas Jelinek .08 .25
222 Michal Straka .08 .25
223 Miroslav Mach .08 .25
224 Pavel Vostrak .08 .25
225 Petr Korinek .08 .25
226 Radek Kampf .08 .25
227 Radovan Biegl .20 .50
228 Jiri Kuntos .08 .25
229 Lubomir Sekeras .30 .75
230 Petr Jancarik .08 .25
231 Stanislav Pavelec .08 .25
232 Ondrej Zetek .08 .25
233 Patrik Hucko .08 .25
234 Vladimir Machulda .08 .25
235 HC Zelezarny Trinec Logo .08 .25
236 HC Zelezarny Trinec Team .08 .25
237 HC Zelezarny Trinec Team .08 .25
238 Jozef Dano .08 .25
239 Roman Blazek .08 .25
240 Marek Zadina .08 .25
241 Richard Kral .08 .25
242 Petr Folta .08 .25
243 Michal Piskor .08 .25
244 Josef Straub .08 .25
245 Petr Zajonc .08 .25
246 Dusan Salficky .30 .75
247 Pavel Augusta .08 .25
248 Tomas Pacal .08 .25
249 Jiri Malinsky .08 .25
250 Pavel Kriz .08 .25
251 Radomir Brazda .08 .25
252 Ales Pisa .08 .25
253 Ladislav Lubina .08 .25
254 HC IB Pardubice Logo .08 .25
255 HC IB Pardubice Team .08 .25
256 HC IB Pardubice Team .08 .25
257 Tomas Blazek .08 .25
258 Jiri Jantovsky .08 .25
259 Milan Hejduk 4.00 10.00
260 Tomas Martinec .08 .25
261 David Pospisil .08 .25
262 Stanislav Prochazka .08 .25
263 Milan Prochazka .08 .25
264 Milan Kastner .08 .25
265 Rostislav Haas .08 .25
266 Denis Tsygurov .08 .25
267 Martin Bakula .08 .25
268 David Galvas .08 .25
269 Petr Tejkl .08 .25
270 Radek Mesicek .08 .25
271 Milos Hrubes .08 .25
272 Eduard Gorbachev .08 .25
273 HC Slezan Opava Logo .08 .25
274 HC Slezan Opava Team .08 .25
275 HC Slezan Opava Team .08 .25
276 Petr Fabian .08 .25
277 Zdenek Pavelek .08 .25
278 Karel Horny .08 .25
279 Martin Filip .08 .25
280 Juraj Jurik .08 .25
281 Radim Radevic .08 .25
282 Jan Zurek .08 .25
283 Valerij Belov .08 .25

1998-99 Czech DS

This set features the top players of the Czech Republic's Extraliga. The set features several short prints. Card no. 1 is 1:125, cards no. 2-11 are 1:30 and cards no. 12-25 are 1:20.

COMPLETE SET (125) 75.00 150.00
1 Jiri Dopita 10.00 25.00
2 Pavel Patera 2.00 5.00
3 Martin Prochazka 2.00 5.00
4 Martin Rucinsky 2.00 5.00
5 Vladimir Vujtek 2.00 5.00
6 David Moravec 2.00 5.00
7 Libor Prochazka 2.00 5.00
8 Viktor Ujcik 2.00 5.00
9 Vladimir Ruzicka 2.00 5.00
10 Frantisek Kucera 2.00 5.00
11 David Vyborny 2.00 5.00
12 Rudolf Pejchar 4.00 10.00
13 Oldrich Svoboda 2.00 5.00
14 Marek Novotny 2.00 5.00
15 Zdenek Orct 2.00 5.00
16 Libor Barta 2.00 5.00
17 Dusan Salficky 2.00 5.00
18 Pavel Cagas 2.00 5.00
19 Ladislav Blazek 2.00 5.00
20 Roman Cechmanek 2.00 5.00
21 Milan Hnilicka 2.00 5.00
22 Martin Cinibulk 2.00 5.00
23 Martin Prusek 2.00 5.00
24 Jaroslav Kames 2.00 5.00
25 Radovan Biegl 2.00 5.00
26 Petr Pavlas .08 .25
27 Ondrej Steiner .08 .25
28 Pavel Janku .08 .25
29 Jaromir Kverka .08 .25
30 Martin Rousek .08 .25
31 Milan Nedoma .08 .25
32 Radek Martinek .20 .50
33 Rudolf Suchanek .08 .25
34 Radek Toupal .15 .40
35 Filip Turek .08 .25
36 Miroslav Barus .08 .25
37 Miroslav Duben .08 .25
38 Petr Vlk .08 .25
39 Marek Melenovsky .08 .25
40 Jiri Cihlar .08 .25
41 Roman Mejzlik .08 .25
42 Ales Polcar .20 .50
43 Angel Nikolov .20 .50
44 Martin Stepanek .08 .25
45 Petr Hrbek .08 .25
46 Ivo Prorok .08 .25
47 Vladimir Petrovka .08 .25
48 Robert Kysela .08 .25
49 Josef Straka .08 .25
50 Ales Pisa .08 .25
51 Pavel Kriz .08 .25
52 Tomas Blazek .08 .25
53 Tomas Martinec .08 .25
54 Jiri Jantovsky .08 .25
55 Stanislav Prochazka .08 .25
56 Jaroslav Kudrna .08 .25
57 Josef Reznicek .08 .25
58 Pavel Geffert .08 .25
59 Petr Korinek .15 .40
60 Pavel Vostrak .08 .25
61 Michal Straka .08 .25
62 David Pospisil .08 .25
63 Milan Volak .08 .25
64 Milan Navratil .08 .25
65 Vitezslav Skuta .08 .25
66 Michael Vyhlidal .08 .25
67 Petr Kuchyna .08 .25
68 Drahomir Kadlec .08 .25
69 Petr Kadlec .08 .25
70 Martin Bakula .08 .25
71 Andrej Jakovenko .08 .25
72 Marian Kacir .20 .50
73 Vladimir Machulda .08 .25
74 Michal Sup .08 .25
75 Jiri Dolezal .15 .40
76 Tomas Kucharcik .08 .25
77 Jiri Veber .08 .25
78 Jan Srdinko .08 .25
79 Radim Tesarik .08 .25
80 Ondrej Kratena .08 .25
81 Michal Bros .08 .25
82 Jan Tomajko .08 .25
83 Tomas Srsen .08 .25
84 Zbynek Marak .08 .25
85 Radek Belohlav .15 .40
86 Roman Stantien .08 .25
87 Alexej Jaskin .08 .25
88 Vaclav Burda .08 .25
89 Ladislav Benysek .20 .50
90 Frantisek Ptacek .08 .25
91 Roman Horak .08 .25
92 Richard Zemlicka .20 .50
93 Jan Hlavac .40 1.00
94 Jiri Zelenka .08 .25
95 Patrik Martinec .08 .25
96 Jaroslav Bednar .40 1.00
97 Marek Zidlicky .40 1.00
98 Ladislav Svoboda .08 .25
99 Vaclav Eiselt .08 .25
100 Zdenek Eichenmann .08 .25
101 Jiri Burger .08 .25
102 Ales Tomasek .08 .25
103 Tomas Jelinek .08 .25
104 Rene Sevecek .08 .25
105 Pavel Kowalczyk .08 .25
106 Alexander Cherbajev .08 .25
107 Martin Kotasek .08 .25
108 Ales Kratoska .08 .25
109 Martin Hamrlik .08 .25
110 Roman Meluzin .08 .25
111 Petr Cajanek .40 1.00
112 Tomas Nemcicky .15 .40
113 Josef Straub .08 .25
114 Miroslav Okal .08 .25
115 Lubomir Sekeras .30 .75
116 Jiri Kuntos .08 .25
117 Stanislav Pavelec .08 .25
118 Richard Kral .08 .25
119 Ladislav Lubina .08 .25
120 Roman Kadera .08 .25
121 Jozef Dano .08 .25
122 Tomas Chlubna .08 .25
123 Ales Zima .08 .25
124 Branislav Janos .08 .25
125 Checklist .02 .10

1998-99 Czech DS Stickers

This set features many of the top stars of the Czech Extraliga in fun sticker form. The stickers are approximately 1-by-1 1/2 inches and feature color fronts and blank backs.

COMPLETE SET 30.00 60.00
1 HC Petra Vsetin .08 .25
2 HC Petra Vsetin .08 .25
3 HC Petra Vsetin .08 .25
4 HC Petra Vsetin .08 .25
5 HC Petra Vsetin .08 .25
6 HC Petra Vsetin .08 .25
7 League Logo .08 .25
8 Roman Cechmanek .40 1.00
9 unknown
10 Antonin Stavjana .15 .40
11 Milan Nedoma .08 .25
12 Jiri Vykoukal .20 .50
13 unknown
14 Martin Stepanek .08 .25
15 Vitezslav Skuta .08 .25
16 Jiri Zelenka .08 .25
17 Robert Lang .40 1.00
18 Ondrej Kratena .08 .25
19 Viktor Ujcik .15 .40
20 unknown
21 unknown
22 unknown
23 unknown
24 Team Logo .02 .10
25 Team Photo .08 .25
26 Team Photo .08 .25
27 Vladimir Hudacek .20 .50
28 Robert Horyna .08 .25
29 Petr Pavlas .08 .25
30 Ales Tomasek .08 .25
31 Pavel Blaha .08 .25
32 Jiri Polak .08 .25
33 Martin Richter .08 .25
34 Marek Cernosek .08 .25
35 Pavel Nohel .08 .25
36 Michal Cerny .08 .25
37 Tomas Klimt .20 .50
38 Ondrej Steiner .08 .25
39 Zbynek Kukacka .08 .25
40 Martin Streit .08 .25
41 Radek Prochazka .08 .25
42 Radek Svoboda .08 .25
43 Jan Lipiansky .08 .25
44 Team Logo .02 .10
45 Team Photo .08 .25
46 Team Photo .08 .25
47 Rostislav Haas .08 .25
48 Pavel Nestak .08 .25
49 Martin Maskarinec .08 .25
50 David Galvas .08 .25
51 Milos Hrubes .08 .25
52 Karel Smid .20 .50
53 Tomas Kramny .08 .25
54 Pavel Marecek .08 .25
55 Zbynek Marak .08 .25
56 Michal Tomek .08 .25
57 Juraj Jurik .08 .25
58 Michal Piskor .08 .25
59 Karel Horny .08 .25
60 Pavel Sebesta .08 .25
61 Martin Sychra .08 .25
62 Zdenek Pavelek .08 .25
63 Milan Kubis .08 .25
64 Team Logo .02 .10
65 Team Photo .08 .25
66 Team Photo .08 .25
67 Oldrich Svoboda .20 .50
68 Rudolf Suchanek .08 .25
69 Karel Soudek .08 .25
70 Milan Nedoma .08 .25
71 Radek Martinek .20 .50
72 Jan Bohacek .20 .50
73 Kamil Toupal .08 .25
74 Radek Toupal .08 .25
75 Lubos Rob .08 .25
76 Pavel Pycha .08 .25
77 Filip Turek .08 .25
78 David Bruk .08 .25
79 Ondrej Vosta .08 .25
80 Arpad Györi .08 .25
81 Miroslav Barus .08 .25
82 Petr Sailer .08 .25
83 Petr Sachl .08 .25
84 Team Logo .02 .10
85 Team Photo .08 .25
86 Team Photo .08 .25
87 Zdenek Orct .30 .75
88 Richard Hrazdira .08 .25
89 Frantisek Prochazka .08 .25
90 Angel Nikolov .20 .50
91 Martin Stepanek .08 .25
92 Roman Cech .08 .25
93 Radek Mrazek .08 .25
94 Robert Kysela .08 .25
95 Tomas Vlasak .08 .25
96 Martin Rousek .08 .25
97 Petr Hrbek .08 .25
98 Vladimir Petrovka .08 .25
99 Ivo Prorok .08 .25
100 Denis Afinogenov .20 .50
101 Rail Muftijev .08 .25
102 Dmitrij Denisov .08 .25
103 Kamil Piros .40 1.00
104 Team Logo .02 .10
105 Team Photo .08 .25
106 Team Photo .08 .25
107 Marek Novotny .08 .25
108 Lukas Sablik .08 .25
109 Michael Vyhlidal .08 .25
110 Miroslav Javin .08 .25
111 Martin Tupa .08 .25
112 Marian Morava .08 .25
113 Tomas Jakes .08 .25
114 Miroslav Duben .08 .25
115 Petr Vlk .08 .25
116 Roman Mejzlik .08 .25
117 Jiri Cihlar .08 .25
118 Jaroslav Hub .08 .25
119 Leos Pipa .08 .25
120 Ladislav Prokupek .08 .25
121 Marek Melenovsky .08 .25
122 Milan Antos .08 .25
123 Miroslav Stavjana .08 .25
124 Team Logo .02 .10
125 Team Photo .08 .25
126 Team Photo .08 .25
127 Libor Barta .08 .25
128 Adam Svoboda .30 .75
129 Michal Sykora .15 .40
130 Pavel Augusta .08 .25
131 Tomas Pacal .08 .25
132 Ales Pisa .08 .25
133 Petr Mudroch .08 .25
134 Alexander Cypljakov .08 .25
135 Jiri Malinsky .08 .25
136 Milan Hejduk 4.00 10.00
137 Tomas Blazek .08 .25
138 Jaroslav Kudrna .08 .25
139 Tomas Maskarinec .08 .25
140 Stanislav Prochazka .08 .25
141 Jiri Jantovsky .08 .25
142 Pavel Kabrt .08 .25
143 Martin Koudelka .08 .25
144 Team Logo .02 .10
145 Team Photo .08 .25
146 Team Photo .08 .25
147 Dusan Salficky .30 .75
148 Michal Marik .08 .25
149 Josef Reznicek .08 .25
150 Ivan Vlcek .08 .25
151 Robert Jindrich .20 .50
152 Martin Cech .08 .25
153 Jiri Hanzlik .08 .25
154 Pavel Srek .08 .25
155 Tomas Jelinek .08 .25
156 Pavel Geffert .08 .25
157 David Pospisil .08 .25
158 Martin Filip .08 .25
159 Milan Volak .08 .25
160 Michal Straka .08 .25
161 Milan Navratil .08 .25
162 Mojmir Musil .08 .25
163 Pavel Vostrak .08 .25
164 Team Logo .02 .10
165 Team Photo .08 .25
166 Team Photo .08 .25
167 Roman Cechmanek .40 1.00
168 Antonin Stavjana .15 .40
169 Jan Srdinko .08 .25
170 Radim Tesarik .08 .25
171 Alexej Jaskin .08 .25
172 Michal Divisek .08 .25
173 Pavel Zubicek .08 .25
174 Rostislav Vlach .08 .25
175 Jiri Dopita .30 .75
176 Tomas Srsen .08 .25
177 Radek Belohlav .15 .40
178 Tomas Kapusta .08 .25
179 Ondrej Kratena .08 .25
180 Michal Bros .08 .25
181 Jan Tomajko .08 .25
182 Andrej Galkin .08 .25
183 Josef Beranek .20 .50
184 Team Logo .02 .10
185 Team Photo .08 .25
186 Team Photo .08 .25
187 Ladislav Blazek .20 .50
188 Martin Altrichter .08 .25
189 Robert Kostka .08 .25
190 Andrej Jakovenko .08 .25
191 Pavel Kolarik .20 .50
192 Martin Bakula .08 .25
193 Petr Kadlec .08 .25
194 Jan Hejda .08 .25
195 Vladimir Ruzicka .20 .50
196 Viktor Ujcik .15 .40
197 Jiri Dolezal .15 .40
198 Jiri Poukar .08 .25
199 Tomas Kucharcik .08 .25
200 Michal Sup .08 .25
201 Jiri Hlinka .08 .25
202 Tomas Kupka .08 .25
203 Radek Matejovsky .08 .25
204 Team Logo .02 .10
205 Team Photo .08 .25
206 Team Photo .08 .25
207 Milan Hnilicka .75 2.00
208 Martin Cinibulk .08 .25
209 Jiri Vykoukal .20 .50
210 Vaclav Burda .08 .25
211 Frantisek Kucera .08 .25
212 Jaroslav Nedved .08 .25
213 Frantisek Ptacek .08 .25
214 Richard Zemlicka .20 .50
215 Jiri Zelenka .08 .25
216 Patrik Martinec .08 .25
217 Jaroslav Bednar .40 1.00
218 Jaromir Kverka .08 .25
219 Jan Hlavac .40 1.00
220 Miroslav Hlinka .08 .25
221 Jaroslav Hlinka .08 .25
222 Patrik Stefan .75 2.00
223 Petr Nedved .40 1.00
224 Team Logo .02 .10
225 Team Photo .08 .25
226 Team Photo .08 .25
227 Radek Toth .08 .25
228 Martin Bilek .20 .50
229 Jan Krulis .08 .25
230 Marek Zidlicky .40 1.00
231 Tomas Kaberle .40 1.00
232 Pavel Skrbek .20 .50
233 Jan Penk .08 .25
234 Jan Dlouhy .08 .25
235 Josef Zajic .08 .25
236 Zdenek Eichenmann .08 .25
237 Petr Ton .08 .25
238 Jiri Beranek .08 .25
239 Tomas Mikolasek .08 .25
240 Ladislav Svoboda .08 .25
241 Vaclav Eiselt .08 .25
242 Jiri Burger .08 .25
243 Petr Tenkrat .40 1.00
244 Team Logo .02 .10
245 Team Photo .08 .25
246 Team Photo .08 .25
247 Martin Prusek .75 2.00
248 Zdenek Dobes .08 .25
249 Vitezslav Skuta .08 .25
250 Pavel Kumstat .08 .25
251 Jiri Jonak .08 .25
252 Rene Sevecek .08 .25
253 Dmitrij Jerofejev .08 .25
254 Petr Jurecka .08 .25
255 Roman Simicek .20 .50
256 Roman Rysanek .08 .25
257 David Moravec .20 .50
258 Alexander Prokopjev .08 .25
259 Libor Polasek .08 .25
260 Martin Kotasek .08 .25
261 Alexander Cherbajev .08 .25
262 Libor Pavlis .08 .25
263 Petr Zajonc .08 .25
264 Team Logo .02 .10
265 Team Photo .08 .25
266 Team Photo .08 .25
267 Radovan Biegl .20 .50
268 Lubomir Sekeras .30 .75
269 Jiri Kuntos .08 .25
270 Stanislav Pavelec .08 .25
271 Patrik Hucko .08 .25
272 Petr Jancarik .08 .25
273 Robert Kantor .08 .25
274 Richard Kral .08 .25
275 Ladislav Lubina .08 .25
276 Tomas Chlubna .08 .25
277 Roman Kadera .08 .25
278 Josef Straub .08 .25
279 Jozef Dano .08 .25
280 Roman Kontsek .08 .25
281 Marek Zadina .08 .25
282 Petr Folta .08 .25
283 Jan Peterek .08 .25
284 Team Logo .02 .10
285 Team Photo .08 .25
286 Team Photo .08 .25
287 Jaroslav Kames .30 .75
288 Pavel Kowalczyk .08 .25
289 Jan Krajicek .08 .25
290 Petr Kuchyna .08 .25
291 Martin Hamrlik .08 .25
292 Pavel Rajnoha .08 .25
293 Jiri Marusak .08 .25
294 Roman Meluzin .20 .50
295 Pavel Janku .08 .25
296 Ales Zima .08 .25
297 Miroslav Okal .08 .25
298 Petr Cajanek .40 1.00
299 Tomas Nemcicky .08 .25
300 Branislav Janos .08 .25
301 Ales Polcar .08 .25
302 Zdenek Sedlak .08 .25
303 Petr Leska .08 .25

1998-99 Czech OFS

This expansive set covers the entire Czech Extraliga. Cards 1-249 comprise Series I, while cards 250-490 make up Series II. Each series also has four NNO checklists. The set is noteworthy for including early cards of Martin Havlat and Roman Cechmanek, among others.

COMPLETE SET (490) 60.00 150.00

1 Ondrej Weissmann .08 .25
2 Zdenek Orct .20 .50
3 Angel Nikolov .20 .50
4 Radek Mrazek .08 .25
5 Martin Stepanek .08 .25
6 Sergej Butko .08 .25
7 Oleg Romanov .08 .25
8 Marian Menhart .20 .50
9 Vladimir Petrovka .08 .25
10 Ivo Prorok .08 .25
11 Jindrich Kotrla .08 .25
12 Josef Straka .08 .25
13 Vadim Bekbulatov .08 .25
14 Daniel Branda .08 .25
15 Vojtech Kubincak .08 .25
16 Michal Travnicek .20 .50
17 Zdenek Venera .08 .25
18 Jaroslav Kames .30 .75
19 Pavel Augusta .08 .25
20 Patrik Hucko .08 .25
21 Martin Hamrlik .08 .25
22 Jiri Marusak .08 .25
23 Pavel Mojzis .08 .25
24 Tomas Zizka .08 .25
25 Roman Meluzin .08 .25
26 Michal Tomek .08 .25
27 Josef Straub .08 .25
28 Tomas Nemcicky .15 .40
29 Petr Cajanek .40 1.00
30 Miroslav Okal .08 .25
31 Petr Leska .08 .25
32 Petr Vala .08 .25
33 Radim Rulik .08 .25
34 Dusan Salficky .30 .75
35 Josef Reznicek .08 .25
36 Robert Jindrich .20 .50
37 Jiri Hanzlik .08 .25
38 Ondrej Kriz .08 .25
39 Vladimir Zajic .08 .25
40 Pavel Geffert .08 .25
41 David Pospisil .08 .25
42 Milan Antos .08 .25
43 Petr Korinek .15 .40
44 Michal Straka .08 .25
45 Milan Volak .08 .25
46 Pavel Vostrak .08 .25
47 Milan Navratil .08 .25
48 Martin Spanhel .40 1.00
49 Josef Augusta .08 .25
50 Jaroslav Suchan .08 .25
51 Martin Tupa .08 .25
52 Marian Morava .08 .25
53 Michal Divisek .08 .25
54 Petr Svoboda .15 .40
55 Zdenek Fuksa .08 .25
56 Petr Vlk .08 .25
57 Jiri Cihlar .08 .25
58 Leos Pipa .08 .25
59 Marek Melenovsky .08 .25
60 Miroslav Bruna .08 .25
61 Petr Mokrejs .08 .25
62 Vaclav Adamec .08 .25
63 Richard Cachnin .08 .25
64 Jan Kloboucek .08 .25
65 Stanislav Nevesely .08 .25
66 Radek Masny .08 .25
67 Jan Krajicek .08 .25
68 Ales Tomasek .08 .25
69 Vladimir Holik .08 .25
70 Tomas Jelinek .08 .25
71 Pavel Nohel .08 .25
72 Jaroslav Hub .08 .25
73 Robert Kucera .08 .25
74 Andrej Galkin .08 .25
75 Pavel Selingr .08 .25
76 Pavel Bacho .08 .25
77 Jiri Zurek .08 .25
78 Pavel Zdrahal .08 .25
79 Bogdan Savenko .08 .25
80 Zdenek Sedlak .08 .25
81 Karel Trachta .08 .25
82 Rudolf Pejchar .20 .50
83 Petr Pavlas .08 .25
84 Pavel Blaha .08 .25
85 Martin Richter .08 .25
86 Jan Snopek .15 .40
87 Martin Filip .08 .25
88 Jaromir Kverka .08 .25
89 Pavel Janku .08 .25
90 Martin Rousek .08 .25
91 Ondrej Steiner .08 .25
92 Pavel Metlicka .08 .25
93 Streit Martin .08 .25
94 Ladislav Prokupek .08 .25
95 Richard Richter .08 .25
96 Martin Maskarinec .08 .25
97 Zdislav Tabara .08 .25
98 Miroslav Venkrbec .08 .25
99 Roman Cechmanek .40 1.00
100 Jiri Veber .08 .25
101 Radim Tesarik .08 .25
102 Jan Srdinko .08 .25
103 Alexej Jaskin .08 .25
104 Pavel Zubicek .08 .25
105 Jiri Dopita .30 .75
106 Martin Prochazka .20 .50
107 Pavel Patera .20 .50
108 Radek Belohlav .15 .40
109 Ondrej Kratena .08 .25
110 Michal Bros .08 .25
111 Jan Tomajko .08 .25
112 Roman Slantien .08 .25
113 Ladislav Svozil .08 .25
114 Jiri Trvaj .08 .25
115 Rene Sevecek .08 .25
116 Vitezslav Skuta .08 .25
117 Pavel Kowalczyk .08 .25
118 Radek Philipp .08 .25
119 Vladimir Vujtek .20 .50
120 Alexander Cherbajev .08 .25
121 Libor Pavlis .08 .25
122 Libor Polasek .08 .25
123 Martin Kotasek .08 .25
124 Zdenek Pavelek .08 .25
125 Martin Lamich .08 .25
126 Igor Varickij .08 .25
127 Petr Hubacek .08 .25
128 Zbynek Irgl .08 .25
129 Julius Supler .08 .25
130 Milan Hnilicka .40 1.00
131 Frantisek Ptacek .08 .25
132 Ladislav Benysek .20 .50
133 Richard Adam .08 .25
134 Frantisek Kucera .08 .25
135 Pavel Srek .08 .25
136 Jiri Zelenka .08 .25
137 David Vyborny .20 .50
138 Patrik Martinec .08 .25
139 Jaroslav Bednar .40 1.00
140 Jan Hlavac .40 1.00
141 Miroslav Hlinka .08 .25
142 Jaroslav Hlinka .08 .25
143 Martin Chabada .08 .25
144 Vaclav Novak .08 .25
145 Michal Chalupa .08 .25
146 Adam Svoboda .30 .75
147 Jiri Malinsky .08 .25
148 Ales Pisa .08 .25
149 Tomas Pacal .08 .25
150 Pavel Kriz .08 .25
151 Petr Jancarik .08 .25
152 Petr Mudroch .08 .25
153 Tomas Blazek .08 .25
154 Jiri Jantovsky .08 .25
155 Stanislav Prochazka .08 .25
156 Tomas Martinec .08 .25
157 Pavel Kabrt .08 .25
158 Jaroslav Kudrna .20 .50
159 Karel Plasek .08 .25
160 Michal Mikeska .08 .25
161 Zdenek Sindler .08 .25
162 Martin Cinibulk .20 .50
163 Marek Zidlicky .40 1.00
164 Jan Dlouhy .08 .25
165 Pavel Taborsky .08 .25
166 Michal Madl .08 .25
167 Jiri Jelinek .08 .25
168 Tomas Mikolasek .08 .25
169 Ladislav Svoboda .08 .25
170 Jiri Burger .08 .25
171 Petr Tenkrat .40 1.00
172 Tomas Kupka .08 .25
173 Marke Vorel .08 .25
174 Michal Kanka .08 .25
175 Tomas Horna .08 .25
176 Zdenek Mraz .08 .25
177 Kamil Konecny .08 .25
178 Radovan Biegl .20 .50
179 Stanislav Pavelec .08 .25
180 Jiri Kuntos .08 .25
181 Petr Gregorek .08 .25
182 Miroslav Cihal .08 .25
183 Robert Prochazka .08 .25
184 Viktor Ujcik .20 .50
185 Ladislav Lubina .08 .25
186 Jan Peterek .08 .25
187 Petr Folta .08 .25
188 Ales Zima .08 .25
189 Roman Kadera .08 .25
190 Vaclav Pletka .20 .50
191 Patrik Moskal .08 .25
192 David Appel .08 .25
193 Jaroslav Parizek CO .08 .25
194 Michal Marik .08 .25
195 Rudolf Suchanek .08 .25
196 Milan Nedoma .08 .25
197 Kamil Toupal .08 .25
198 Roman Cech .08 .25
199 Radek Martinek .20 .50
200 Vladimir Sicak .08 .25
201 Radek Toupal .15 .40
202 Filip Turek .08 .25
203 Petr Sailer .08 .25
204 Martin Strba .08 .25
205 Miroslav Barus .08 .25
206 Vaclav Kral .08 .25
207 Milan Filipi .08 .25
208 Peter Barlos .08 .25
209 Richard Farda .08 .25
210 Roman Malek .08 .25
211 Robert Kostka .08 .25
212 Pavel Kolarik .20 .50
213 Martin Bakula .08 .25
214 Petr Kadlec .08 .25
215 Jan Novak .08 .25
216 Vladimir Ruzicka .20 .50
217 Jiri Dolezal .15 .40
218 Tomas Kucharcik .08 .25
219 Michal Sup .08 .25
220 Vladimir Machulda .08 .25
221 Petr Mika .30 .75
222 Tomas Divisek .30 .75
223 Jan Kopecky .08 .25
224 Jiri Polak .08 .25
225 Ivan Hlinka OLY .30 .75
226 Slavomir Lener OLY .15 .40
227 Dominik Hasek OLY 4.00 10.00
228 Roman Cechmanek OLY .40 1.00
229 Milan Hnilicka OLY .40 1.00
230 Richard Smehlik OLY .15 .40
231 Petr Svoboda OLY .15 .40
232 Roman Hamrlik OLY .30 .75
233 Jiri Slegr OLY .15 .40
234 Frantisek Kucera OLY .08 .25
235 Libor Prochazka OLY .20 .50
236 Jaroslav Spacek OLY .20 .50
237 Robert Reichel OLY .40 1.00
238 Robert Lang OLY .40 1.00
239 Pavel Patera OLY .40 1.00
240 Martin Prochazka OLY .30 .75
241 Jiri Dopita OLY .30 .75
242 Josef Beranek OLY .20 .50
243 David Moravec OLY .30 .75
244 Jan Caloun OLY .30 .75
245 Martin Rucinsky OLY .30 .75
246 Martin Straka OLY .40 1.00
247 Jaromir Jagr OLY 8.00 20.00
248 Vladimir Ruzicka OLY .20 .50
249 Milan Hejduk OLY 4.00 10.00
250 Ladislav Slizek .08 .25
251 Ladislav Blazek .08 .25
252 Andrej Jakovenko .08 .25
253 Jan Hejda .08 .25
254 Marian Kacir .20 .50
255 Robin Bacul .08 .25
256 Jan Sochor .08 .25
257 Petr Hrbek .08 .25
258 Jan Sebor .08 .25
259 Michal Slavik .08 .25
260 Vladimir Jerabek .08 .25
261 Marek Pinc .08 .25
262 Vladimir Gyna .08 .25
263 Martin Znojemsky .08 .25
264 Robert Kysela .08 .25
265 Petr Hrbek .08 .25
266 Kamil Piros .40 1.00
267 Viktor Hubl .08 .25
268 Marian Kacir .20 .50
269 Miloslav Horava .08 .25
270 Michal Pinc .08 .25
271 Zdenek Skorepa .08 .25
272 Vaclav Sykora .08 .25
273 Antonin Stavjana .15 .40
274 Richard Hrazdira .08 .25
275 Karel Rachunek .40 1.00
276 David Brezik .08 .25
277 Marek Zadina .08 .25
278 Jaroslav Balastik .08 .25
279 Martin Ambruz .08 .25
280 Ondrej Vesely .08 .25
281 Tomas Kapusta .08 .25
282 Tomas Martinek .08 .25
283 Ivan Rachunek .20 .50
284 Karel Sefcik .08 .25
285 Marek Sykora .08 .25
286 Vladimir Hudacek .20 .50
287 Ivan Vlcek .08 .25
288 Martin Cech .08 .25
289 Michal Vasicek .08 .25
290 Michal Jelinek .08 .25
291 Vladimir Bednar .08 .25
292 Pavel Augusta .08 .25
293 Ladislav Slizek .08 .25
294 Karel Dvorak .08 .25
295 Marek Novotny .08 .25
296 Lukas Sablik .08 .25
297 Daniel Zapotocny .08 .25
298 Miroslav Duben .08 .25
299 Ales Polcar .08 .25
300 Roman Mejzlik .08 .25
301 Radek Matejovsky .08 .25
302 Daniel Hodek .08 .25
303 Ales Padelek .08 .25
304 Ivan Padelek .08 .25
305 Pavel Rajnoha .08 .25
306 Richard Adam .08 .25
307 Vladimir Caldr .08 .25
308 Jiri Dobrovolny .08 .25
309 Lukas Novak .08 .25
310 Ivo Novotny .08 .25
311 Jan Smarda .08 .25
312 Lubomir Oslizlo .08 .25
313 Pavel Cagas .20 .50
314 Petr Kuchyna .08 .25
315 Drahomir Kadlec .08 .25
316 Michael Vyhlidal .08 .25
317 Miroslav Javin .08 .25
318 Petr Suchanek .08 .25
319 Vitezslav Skuta .08 .25
320 Libor Polasek .08 .25
321 Jiri Poukar .08 .25
322 Michal Cech .08 .25
323 Lukas Fiala .08 .25
324 Milota Florian .08 .25
325 Milan Kubis .08 .25
326 Jiri Latal .08 .25
327 Libor Pavlis .08 .25
328 Ivan Puncochar .08 .25
329 Rostislav Vlach .08 .25
330 Tomas Zapletal .08 .25
331 Josef Beranek .20 .50
332 Robert Hamrla .08 .25
333 Marek Cernosek .08 .25
334 Normunds Sejejs .08 .25
335 Tomas Klimt .08 .25
336 Radek Prochazka .08 .25
337 Radek Svoboda .08 .25
338 Michal Horak .08 .25
339 Jakub Kraus .08 .25
340 Ivo Pesat .20 .50
341 Tomas Jakes .08 .25
342 Michal Safarik .08 .25
343 Tomas Srsen .08 .25
344 Zbynek Marak .08 .25
345 Tomas Demel .08 .25
346 Ondrej Kavulic .08 .25
347 Petr Suchy .08 .25
348 Libor Zabransky .15 .40
349 Vladimir Vujtek .20 .50
350 Martin Prusek .40 1.00
351 Lukas Galvas .08 .25
352 Petr Jurecka .08 .25
353 Vadim Brezgunov .08 .25
354 Lukas Zatopek .08 .25
355 David Moravec .20 .50
356 Ludek Krayzel .08 .25
357 Ales Kratoska .08 .25
358 Ales Tomasek .08 .25
359 Milos Holan .15 .40
360 Roman Kelner .08 .25
361 Frantisek Vyborny .08 .25
362 Petr Prikryl .08 .25
363 Zdenek Touzimsky .08 .25
364 Vaclav Burda .08 .25
365 Vaclav Benak .08 .25
366 Michal Dobron .08 .25
367 Richard Zemlicka .20 .50
368 Roman Horak .08 .25
369 Michal Sivek .40 1.00
370 Jaroslav Kalla .08 .25
371 Pavel Richter .08 .25
372 Jaroslav Roubik .08 .25
373 Michal Sykora .15 .40
374 Milos Riha .08 .25
375 Libor Barta .08 .25
376 Alexander Cypljakov .08 .25
377 Robert Pospisil .08 .25
378 Petr Caslava .08 .25
379 Martin Koudelka .08 .25
380 Patrik Rozsival .08 .25
381 Michal Tvrdik .08 .25
382 Tomas Vak .08 .25
383 Alois Hadamczik CO .08 .25
384 Vlastimil Lakosil .08 .25
385 Lubomir Sekeras .20 .50
386 Libor Prochazka .20 .50
387 Robert Kantor .08 .25
388 Mario Cartelli .08 .25
389 Richard Kral .08 .25
390 Jozef Dano .08 .25
391 Branislav Janos .08 .25
392 Tomas Chlubna .08 .25
393 Martin Havlat 10.00 25.00
394 Jaroslav Jagr .20 .50
395 Lubomir Bauer .08 .25
396 Martin Bilek .20 .50
397 Lubos Horcicka .08 .25
398 Jiri Krocak .08 .25
399 Martin Taborsky .08 .25
400 Zdenek Eichenmann .08 .25
401 Vaclav Eiselt .08 .25
402 Premysl Sedlak .08 .25
403 Jiri Holsan .08 .25
404 Jiri Kames .08 .25
405 Jiri Habacek .08 .25
406 Stanislav Lapacek .08 .25
407 Lukas Poznik .08 .25
408 Otakar Vejvoda .15 .40
409 Jaroslav Liska .08 .25
410 Oldrich Svoboda .20 .50
411 Lukas Zib .08 .25
412 Michal Klimes .08 .25
413 Kamil Brabenec .08 .25
414 Ales Kotalik 1.00 2.50
415 Jiri Broz .08 .25
416 Zdenek Kutlak .20 .50
417 Vaclav Nedorost .40 1.00
418 Lubos Rob .10 .25
419 Martin Prusek .40 1.00
420 Frantisek Kaberle .20 .50
421 Jiri Vykoukal .20 .50
422 Jiri Veber .08 .25
423 Ladislav Benysek .20 .50
424 Martin Stepanek .08 .25
425 Jan Srdinko .08 .25
426 Radek Belohlav .15 .40
427 David Vyborny .20 .50
428 Viktor Ujcik .20 .50
429 Roman Meluzin .08 .25
430 Vladimir Vujtek .20 .50
431 Ondrej Kratena .08 .25
432 Michal Bros .08 .25
433 Marian Kacir .20 .50
434 Jan Hlavac .40 1.00
435 Richard Kral .08 .25
436 Roman Kadera .08 .25
437 Ivan Hlinka .40 1.00
438 Roman Cechmanek .40 1.00
439 Milan Hnilicka .40 1.00
440 Libor Prochazka .20 .50
441 Pavel Patera .20 .50
442 Martin Prochazka .20 .50
443 Josef Augusta .08 .25
444 Pavel Richter .08 .25
445 Marek Sykora .08 .25
446 Milan Hnilicka .40 1.00
447 Dusan Salficky .30 .75
448 Frantisek Kucera .08 .25
449 Ladislav Benysek .20 .50
450 Josef Reznicek .08 .25
451 Martin Richter .08 .25
452 Ales Pisa .08 .25
453 Ivan Vlcek .08 .25
454 Martin Stepanek .08 .25
455 Petr Jancarik .08 .25
456 David Vyborny .20 .50
457 Jan Hlavac .40 1.00
458 Jiri Zelenka .08 .25
459 Petr Tenkrat .40 1.00
460 Vaclav Kral .08 .25
461 David Pospisil .08 .25
462 Vaclav Eiselt .08 .25
463 Tomas Kucharcik .08 .25
464 Petr Korinek .15 .40
465 Pavel Janku .08 .25
466 Radek Toupal .15 .40
467 Ivo Prorok .08 .25
468 Zdislav Tabara .08 .25
469 Jaroslav Jagr .20 .50
470 Roman Cechmanek .40 1.00
471 Libor Prochazka .20 .50
472 Jiri Veber .08 .25
473 Milos Holan .15 .40
474 Jan Srdinko .08 .25
475 Robert Kantor .08 .25
476 Ales Tomasek .08 .25
477 Miroslav Duben .08 .25
478 Jiri Dopita .30 .75
479 Martin Prochazka .20 .50
480 Pavel Patera .20 .50
481 Radek Belohlav .15 .40
482 David Moravec .20 .50
483 Roman Meluzin .08 .25
484 Jiri Poukar .08 .25
485 Andrej Galkin .08 .25
486 Ivo Padelek .08 .25
487 Marek Zadina .08 .25
488 Petr Cajanek .40 1.00
489 Miroslav Javin .08 .25
490 Ondrej Kratena .08 .25
NNO Checklist .02 .10
NNO Checklist .02 .10
NNO Checklist .02 .10
NNO Checklist .02 .10
NNO Checklist .02 .10
NNO Checklist .02 .10
NNO Checklist .02 .10
NNO Checklist .02 .10

1998-99 Czech OFS Legends

This series of insert cards honoring some of the greatest players in Czech history were randomly included in series II packs.

COMPLETE SET (20) 12.00 30.00
1 Vaclav Nedomansky .75 2.00
2 Miroslav Horava .75 2.00
3 Peter Stastny 4.00 10.00
4 Jiri Sejba .40 1.00
5 Ivan Hlinka 1.25 3.00
6 Vladimir Martinec .40 1.00
7 Jaroslav Pouzar .40 1.00
8 Jiri Holecek .40 1.00
9 Ludek Cajka .40 1.00
10 Ludek Bukac .40 1.00
11 Milan Novy .75 2.00
12 Jiri Kralik .40 1.00
13 Jiri Hrdina .40 1.00
14 Frantisek Cernik .40 1.00
15 Frantisek Pospisil .40 1.00
16 Jiri Lala .40 1.00
17 Antonin Stavjana .75 2.00
18 Jaromir Sindel .75 2.00
19 Vincent Lukac .40 1.00
20 Dusan Pasek 1.25 3.00

1998-99 Czech OFS Olympic Winners

This insert series commemorates the members of the Czech Republic's gold medal-winning Olympic squad. Cards 1-10 were found in Series I packs, while cards 11-20 were found in Series II.

COMPLETE SET (20) 30.00 75.00
1 Jiri Dopita .75 2.00
2 Dominik Hasek 8.00 20.00
3 Jaromir Jagr 15.00 40.00
4 Frantisek Kucera .75 2.00
5 Pavel Patera .75 2.00
6 Robert Reichel .75 2.00
7 Martin Rucinsky .75 2.00
8 Vladimir Ruzicka .75 2.00
9 Jiri Slegr .75 2.00
10 Petr Svoboda .75 2.00
11 David Moravec .75 2.00
12 Richard Smehlik .75 2.00
13 Jaroslav Spacek .75 2.00
14 Martin Prochazka .75 2.00
15 Roman Hamrlik .75 2.00
16 Ivan Hlinka .75 2.00
17 Roman Cechmanek 1.25 3.00
18 Josef Beranek .75 2.00
19 Robert Lang 1.25 3.00
20 Martin Straka 1.25 3.00

1998 Czech Bonaparte

This unusual set features many members of the 1998 Czech Gold medal winning Olympic team. The cards are the size of playing cards, feature a photo on the front, and the word Bonaparte on the back. The numbering assigned to each is found on the front of the cards.

COMPLETE SET (33) 14.00 35.00
1A Martin Prochazka .20 .50
1B Robert Reichel .20 .50
1C Robert Lang .20 .50
1D Milan Hejduk 1.50 4.00
2A Martin Rucinsky .20 .50
2B Jaromir Jagr 2.00 5.00
2C Richard Smehlik .20 .50
2D Dominik Hasek 1.25 3.00
3A Josef Beranek .20 .50
3B Jaroslav Spacek .20 .50
3C Jaromir Jagr 2.00 5.00
3D Jiri Slegr .20 .50
4A Vladimir Ruzicka .20 .50
4B Roman Cechmanek .40 1.00
4C Jan Caloun .20 .50
4D Milan Hnilicka .75 2.00
5A Jiri Dopita .30 .75
5B Frantisek Kucera .20 .50
5C Jaromir Jagr 2.00 5.00
5D Petr Svoboda .20 .50
6A Petr Svoboda .20 .50
6B Ivan Hlinka .20 .50
6C Slavomir Lener .20 .50
6D Jaromir Jagr 2.00 5.00
7A Jiri Slegr .20 .50
7B Martin Straka .20 .50
7C Pavel Patera .20 .50
7D David Moravec .20 .50
8A Vladimir Ruzicka .20 .50
8B Libor Prochazka .20 .50
8C Roman Hamrlik .20 .50
8D Dominik Hasek 1.25 3.00
HOKEJ Jaromir Jagr

1998 Czech Bonaparte Tall

These Tall Boy-type cards feature Czech's Olympic champs from 1998. The cards have a small colour photo surrounded by plenty of white space, a large Czech flag and the Bonaparte 1998. Only three cards are confirmed to exist to this point. Please forward additional information to hockeymag@beckett.com.

COMPLETE SET ?
1 Dominik Hasek
2 Jaromir Jagr
3 Robert Reichel

1998 Czech Pexeso

This set of undersized cards features members of the Olympic Gold medal-winning Czech squad. It is believed that the cards were issued as a premium with some sort of food item.

COMPLETE SET (28) 8.00 20.00
1 Martin Prochazka .08 .25
2 Robert Reichel .20 .50
3 Robert Lang .20 .50
4 Milan Hejduk 1.50 4.00
5 Martin Rucinsky .08 .25
6 Richard Smehlik .08 .25
7 Dominik Hasek 1.25 3.00
8 Josef Beranek .08 .25
9 Jaroslav Spacek .08 .25
10 Jaromir Jagr 2.00 5.00
11 Roman Cechmanek .40 1.00
12 Martin Rucinsky .08 .25
13 Jiri Slegr .08 .25
14 Jan Caloun .08 .25
15 Milan Hnilicka .75 2.00
16 Jiri Dopita .20 .50
17 Jiri Kucera .08 .25
18 Jaromir Jagr 2.00 5.00
19 Petr Svoboda .08 .25
20 Ivan Hlinka .08 .25
21 Slavomir Lener .08 .25
22 Jiri Slegr .08 .25
23 Martin Straka .08 .25
24 Pavel Patera .08 .25
25 David Moravec .08 .25
26 Libor Prochazka .08 .25
27 Roman Hamrlik .08 .25
28 Dominik Hasek 1.25 3.00

1998 Czech Spaghetti

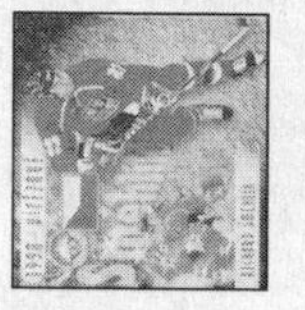

This undersized set honors the members of the Czech team that won the Olympic Gold medal. The cards were issued as a premium on boxes of pasta products, and were licensed by the NHLPA.

COMPLETE SET (12) 8.00 20.00
1 Jaromir Jagr 4.00 10.00
2 Dominik Hasek 2.00 5.00
3 Josef Beranek .40 1.00
4 Roman Hamrlik .40 1.00
5 Robert Lang .60 1.50
6 Martin Straka .60 1.50
7 Robert Reichel .60 1.50
8 Martin Rucinsky .60 1.50
9 Jiri Slegr .40 1.00
10 Petr Svoboda .40 1.00
11 Richard Smehlik .40 1.00
12 Martin Prochazka .40 1.00

1999-00 Czech DS

This set features the stars of the Czech Republic's top league. The set includes cards of NHLers Patrik Elias and Brendan Morrison, who began that season in the Czech league whilst in the midst of a contract dispute. Checklist courtesy of Hockey Heaven.

COMPLETE SET (196) 30.00 75.00
1 Richard Hrazdira .20 .50
2 Vladimir Hudacek .20 .50
3 Roman Hamrlik .30 .75
4 Martin Hamrlik .08 .25
5 Jiri Marusak .08 .25
6 Tomas Zizka .08 .25
7 Petr Cajanek .30 .75
8 Miroslav Okal .08 .25
9 Josef Straub .08 .25
10 Petr Leska .08 .25
11 Michal Tomek .08 .25
12 Martin Kotasek .08 .25
13 Ondrej Vesely .08 .25
14 Petr Vala .08 .25
15 Rudolf Pejchar .08 .25
16 Zdenek Smid .30 .75
17 Martin Richter .08 .25
18 Petr Pavlas .08 .25
19 Martin Maskarinec .08 .25
20 Jan Snopek .08 .25
21 Michal Divisek .08 .25
22 Pavel Janku .08 .25
23 Jaromir Kverka .08 .25
24 Martin Rousek .08 .25
25 Miroslav Barus .08 .25
26 Martin Streit .08 .25
27 Martin Filip .08 .25
28 Radek Prochazka .08 .25
29 Ivo Capek .20 .50
30 Michal Marik .08 .25
31 Milan Nedoma .08 .25
32 Radek Martinek .20 .50
33 Rudolf Suchanek .20 .50
34 Roman Cech .08 .25
35 Vaclav Kral .08 .25
36 Filip Turek .08 .25
37 Peter Bartos .08 .25
38 Radek Toupal .08 .25
39 Lubos Rob .08 .25
40 Martin Strba .08 .25
41 Petr Sailer .08 .25
42 Kamil Brabenec .08 .25
43 Pavel Cagas .20 .50
44 Robert Horyna .08 .25
45 Michael Vyhlidal .08 .25
46 Miroslav Javin .08 .25
47 Libor Pivko .08 .25
48 Ales Tomasek .08 .25
49 Roman Horak .20 .50
50 Pavel Nohel .08 .25
51 Ales Alma .08 .25
52 Marek Melanovsky .08 .25
53 Jaroslav Hub .08 .25
54 Pavel Zdrahal .08 .25
55 Bogdan Savenko .08 .25
56 Robert Kantor .08 .25
57 Zdenek Orct .20 .50
58 Marek Pinc .08 .25
59 Miloslav Horava .08 .25
60 Angel Nikolov .20 .50
61 Petr Kratky .08 .25
62 Radek Mrazek .08 .25
63 Robert Reichel .20 .50
64 Robert Kysela .08 .25
65 Ivo Prorok .08 .25
66 Jan Alinc .20 .50
67 Jindrich Kotrla .08 .25
68 Zdenek Skorepa .20 .50
69 Josef Straka .08 .25
70 Michal Travnicek .20 .50
71 Libor Barta .08 .25
72 Adam Svoboda .30 .75
73 Ales Pisa .08 .25
74 Tomas Pacal .08 .25
75 Jiri Malinsky .08 .25
76 Petr Jancarik .08 .25
77 Patrik Elias .75 2.00
78 Brendan Morrison 1.25 3.00
79 Radek Bonk .40 1.00
80 Jaroslav Kudrna .20 .50
81 Tomas Blazek .08 .25
82 Ladislav Lubina .08 .25
83 Stanislav Prochazka .08 .25
84 Jiri Jantovsky .08 .25
85 Dusan Salficky .30 .75
86 Radek Masny .08 .25
87 Josef Reznicek .08 .25
88 Ivan Vlcek .08 .25
89 Martin Cech .08 .25
90 Jiri Hanzlik .08 .25
91 Martin Spanhel .30 .75
92 Michal Straka .08 .25
93 Zdenek Sedlak .08 .25
94 Pavel Vostrak .08 .25
95 Petr Korinek .20 .50
96 Pavel Geffert .08 .25
97 David Pospisil .08 .25
98 Milan Volak .08 .25
99 Vlastimil Lakosil .20 .50
100 Marek Novotny .08 .25
101 Jiri Kuntos .08 .25
102 Petr Gregorek .08 .25
103 Milos Holan .08 .25
104 Lubomir Sekeras .20 .50
105 Richard Kral .08 .25
106 Marek Zadina .08 .25
107 Martin Havlat 6.00 15.00
108 Roman Dadera .08 .25
109 Tomas Chlubna .08 .25
110 Petr Folta .08 .25
111 Ondrej Zetek .08 .25
112 Branislav Janos .08 .25
113 Ladislav Blazek .08 .25
114 Roman Malek .08 .25
115 Vitezslav Skuta .08 .25
116 Jan Krajicek .08 .25
117 Pavel Kolarik .20 .50
118 Martin Bakula .08 .25
119 Vladimir Ruzicka .20 .50
120 Tomas Kucharcik .08 .25
121 Michal Sup .08 .25
122 Jiri Dolezal .08 .25
123 Jan Kopecky .08 .25
124 Petr Hrbek .08 .25
125 Radek Matejovsky .08 .25
126 Vladimir Machulda .08 .25
127 Roman Cechmanek .40 1.00
128 Ivo Pesat .08 .25
129 Jan Srdinko .08 .25
130 Libor Zabransky .08 .25
131 Jiri Veber .08 .25
132 Radim Tesarik .08 .25
133 Jiri Dopita .20 .50
134 Radek Belohlav .15 .40
135 Jan Tomajko .08 .25
136 Jan Pardavy .08 .25
137 Roman Stantien .08 .25
138 Zbynek Marak .08 .25
139 Alexej Jaskin .08 .25
140 Pavel Zubicek .08 .25
141 Petr Briza .30 .75
142 Petr Prikryl .08 .25
143 Frantisek Kucera .07 .20
144 Ladislav Benysek .20 .50
145 Michal Sykora .20 .50
146 Jaroslav Nedved .08 .25
147 David Vyborny .20 .50
148 Patrik Martinec .08 .25
149 Jaroslav Hlinka .08 .25
150 Ondrej Kratena .08 .25
151 Michal Bros .08 .25
152 Richard Zemlicka .20 .50
153 Jiri Zelenka .08 .25
154 Vaclav Eiselt .08 .25

155 Martin Bilek .20 .50
156 Lubos Horcicka .08 .25
157 Michal Madl .08 .25
158 Jan Krulis .08 .25
159 Jiri Krocak .08 .25
160 Jan Dlouhy .08 .25
161 Tomas Horna .08 .25
162 Ladislav Svoboda .08 .25
163 Zdenek Eichenmann .08 .25
164 Jiri Burger .08 .25
165 Tomas Kupka .08 .25
166 Jiri Kames .20 .50
167 Juri Holdan .08 .25
168 Ondrej Kriz .08 .25
169 Martin Prusek .75 2.00
170 Jiri Trvaj .08 .25
171 Dmitrij Jerofejev .08 .25
172 Lukas Galvas .08 .25
173 Pavel Kowalczyk .08 .25
174 Petr Jurecka .08 .25
175 Ludik Krayzel .08 .25
176 Libor Polasek .08 .25
177 Martin Lamich .08 .25
178 Petr Hubacek .08 .25
179 Serej Petrenko .08 .25
180 Zdenik Pavelek .08 .25
181 Martin Tomasek .08 .25
182 Zbynik Irgi .08 .25
183 Ladislav Kudrna .20 .50
184 Pavol Rybar .20 .50
185 Pavel Kumstat .08 .25
186 Tomas Jakes .08 .25
187 Karel Soudek .08 .25
188 Jiri Hes .08 .25
189 Petr Kankovsky .08 .25
190 Milan Kastner .08 .25
191 Jiri Poukar .08 .25
192 Peter Pucher .08 .25
193 Marek Vorel .08 .25
194 Radek Haman .08 .25
195 Karel Plasek .08 .25
196 Milan Prochazka .08 .25
GC Jaromir Jagr Gold 20.00 50.00

1999-00 Czech DS Goalies

This set, featuring the top goalies of the Czech league, were random inserts in packs. The set includes a key pre-NHL card of Roman Cechmanek.

COMPLETE SET (14) 16.00 40.00
G1 Richard Hrazdira 1.25 3.00
G2 Rudolf Pejchar 1.25 3.00
G3 Ivo Capek 1.25 3.00
G4 Pavel Cagas 1.25 3.00
G5 Zdenek Orct 1.25 3.00
G6 Libor Barta 1.25 3.00
G7 Dusan Salficky 1.50 4.00
G8 Vlastimil Lakosil 1.25 3.00
G9 Ladislav Blazek 1.25 3.00
G10 Roman Cechmanek 1.50 4.00
G11 Petr Briza 1.50 4.00
G12 Martin Bilek 1.25 3.00
G13 Martin Prusek 4.00 10.00
G14 Pavol Rybar 1.25 3.00

1999-00 Czech DS National Stars

These cards, featuring the members of the Czech Republic's gold medal winning team, were randomly inserted in packs.

COMPLETE SET (23) 50.00 125.00
NS1 Dominik Hasek 8.00 20.00
NS2 Milan Hnilicka 2.00 5.00
NS3 Jaromir Jagr 15.00 40.00
NS4 Jiri Slegr 1.25 3.00
NS5 Jaroslav Spacek 1.25 3.00
NS6 Frantisek Kucera 1.25 3.00
NS7 Roman Hamrlik 1.50 4.00
NS8 Petr Svoboda 1.50 4.00
NS9 Viktor Ujcik 1.25 3.00
NS10 Frantisek Kaberle 1.25 3.00
NS11 Libor Prochazka 1.25 3.00
NS12 Robert Reichel 1.25 3.00
NS13 Martin Rucinsky 1.25 3.00
NS14 Martin Straka 1.50 4.00
NS15 Martin Prochazka 1.25 3.00
NS16 Pavel Patera 1.25 3.00
NS17 Vladimir Ruzicka 1.25 3.00
NS18 Josef Beranek 1.25 3.00
NS19 David Moravec 1.25 3.00
NS20 Jan Hlavac 1.50 4.00
NS21 David Vyborny 1.25 3.00
NS22 Jiri Dopita 1.25 3.00
NS23 Petr Sykora 2.00 5.00

1999-00 Czech DS Premium

This insert set features the top Czech-born players and was randomly seeded into packs. The cards were limited to 150 copies each.

COMPLETE SET (12) 36.00 75.00
P1 Dominik Hasek 10.00 25.00
P2 Roman Turek 1.50 4.00
P3 Roman Cechmanek 1.50 4.00
P4 Milan Hnilicka 2.00 5.00
P5 Martin Prochazka 1.25 3.00
P6 Jaromir Jagr 20.00 50.00
P7 Jiri Slegr 1.25 3.00
P8 Jaroslav Spacek 1.25 3.00
P9 Pavel Patera 1.25 3.00
P10 Jiri Dopita 1.25 3.00
P11 Robert Reichel 1.25 3.00
P12 Martin Rucinsky 1.50 4.00

1999-00 Czech OFS

This set features every player from the Czech Elite League.

COMPLETE SET (560) 30.00 75.00
1 Libor Barta .08 .25
2 Martin Bilek .20 .50
3 Ladislav Blazek .08 .25
4 Petr Briza .30 .75
5 Ivo Capek .20 .50
6 Roman Cechmanek .40 1.00
7 Robert Horyna .20 .50
8 Vladimir Hudacek .20 .50
9 Ladislav Kudrna .20 .50
10 Vlastimil Lakosil .20 .50
11 Michal Marik .20 .50
12 Zdenek Orct .20 .50
13 Rudolf Pejchar .20 .50
14 Martin Prusek .75 2.00
15 Dusan Salficky .30 .75
16 Richard Farda .07 .20
17 Marian Jelinek .07 .20
18 Josef Beranek .07 .20
19 Leo Gudas .07 .20
20 Milan Hnilicka .40 1.00
21 Milos Holan .07 .20
22 Jan Hrdina .75 2.00
23 Jaromir Jagr 4.00 10.00
24 Frantisek Kaberle .20 .50
25 Tomas Kaberle .30 .75
26 Pavel Kubina .40 1.00
27 Marek Malik .07 .20
28 Pavel Patera .20 .50
29 Martin Prochazka .07 .20
30 Vaclav Prospal .20 .50
31 Robert Reichel .20 .50
32 Martin Rucinsky .20 .50
33 Vladimir Ruzicka .20 .50
34 Pavel Skrbek .20 .50
35 Jiri Slegr .20 .50
36 Jaroslav Spacek .20 .50
37 Martin Straka .40 1.00
38 Vaclav Varada .20 .50
39 David Volek .20 .50
40 Jan Vopat .20 .50
41 Vladimir Caldr .07 .20
42 Martin Bakula .07 .20
43 Miroslav Hajek .07 .20
44 Petr Hrbek .07 .20
45 Petr Kadlec .07 .20
46 Jan Kopecky .07 .20
47 Jan Krajicek .07 .20
48 Angel Krstev .07 .20
49 Radek Matejovsky .07 .20
50 Jan Novak .07 .20
51 Vladimir Pojkar .07 .20
52 Vladimir Ruzicka .20 .50
53 Jan Slavik .07 .20
54 Jan Sochor .07 .20
55 Michal Sup .07 .20
56 Zdislav Tabara .07 .20
57 Jiri Dopita .20 .50
58 Ondrej Kavulic .07 .20
59 Petr Kubos .07 .20
60 Radim Kucharczyk .07 .20
61 Marko Palo .07 .20
62 Jukka Seppo .07 .20
63 Lukas Slaby .07 .20
64 Roman Stantien .07 .20
65 Petr Suchy .07 .20
66 Radim Tesarik .07 .20
67 Jan Tomajko .07 .20
68 Martin Vozdecky .07 .20
69 Petr Zajgla .07 .20
70 Pavel Zubicek .07 .20
71 Pavel Pazourek .07 .20
72 Petr Belohlavek .07 .20
73 Radim Freibauer .07 .20
74 Radek Haman .07 .20
75 David Havir .07 .20
76 Jiri Hes .07 .20
77 Jiri Hradecky .07 .20
78 Jan Klobouoek .07 .20
79 David Pazourek .07 .20
80 David Petlak .07 .20
81 Karel Plasek .07 .20
82 Jiri Poukar .07 .20
83 Milan Prochazka .07 .20
84 Peter Pucher .07 .20
85 Marek Vorel .07 .20
86 Pavel Marek .07 .20
87 Martin Barek .07 .20
88 Tomas Blazek .07 .20
89 Jan Dusanek .07 .20
90 Patrik Elias .75 2.00
91 Petr Jancarik .07 .20
92 Jaroslav Kudrna .20 .50
93 Tomas Martinec .07 .20
94 Brendan Morrison .40 1.00
95 Andrej Novotny .07 .20
96 Tomas Pacal .07 .20
97 Rastislav Palov .07 .20
98 Patrik Rozsival .07 .20
99 Michael Tvrdik .07 .20
100 Tomas Vak .07 .20
101 Pavel Richter .07 .20
102 Michal Bros .08 .25
103 Vaclav Eiselt .07 .20
104 Petr Havelka .07 .20
105 Martin Holy .07 .20
106 Pavel Kasparik .07 .20
107 Ondrej Kratena .08 .25
108 Frantisek Kucera .07 .20
109 Jaroslav Nedved .07 .20
110 Frantisek Ptacek .07 .20
111 Miha Rebolj .07 .20
112 Pavel Srek .07 .20
113 David Vyborny .07 .20
114 Jiri Zelenka .07 .20
115 Richard Zemlicka .20 .50
116 Marek Sykora .07 .20
117 Milan Antos .07 .20
118 Martin Cech .07 .20
119 Marek Cernosek .07 .20
120 Petr Chvojka .07 .20
121 Pavel Geffert .07 .20
122 Jiri Hanzlik .07 .20
123 Jiri Jelen .07 .20
124 Michal Jelinek .07 .20
125 Petr Korinek .07 .20
126 Josef Reznicek .07 .20
127 Radek Svoboda .07 .20
128 Petr Ulehla .07 .20
129 Ivan Vlcek .07 .20
130 Pavel Vostrak .07 .20
131 Martin Pesout .07 .20
132 Michal Dobron .07 .20
133 Martin Filip .07 .20
134 Pavel Janku .07 .20
135 Jaroslav Kalla .07 .20
136 Jan Kostal .07 .20
137 Jaromir Kverka .07 .20
138 Petr Macek .07 .20
139 Martin Maskarinec .07 .20
140 Petr Pavlas .07 .20
141 Josef Podlaha .07 .20
142 Michal Porak .07 .20
143 Martin Richter .07 .20
144 Jan Snopek .07 .20
145 Martin Streit .07 .20
146 Vaclav Sykora .07 .20
147 David Balazs .07 .20
148 Viktor Hubl .07 .20
149 Petr Kratky .07 .20
150 Vojtech Kubincak .07 .20
151 Robert Kysela .07 .20
152 Marian Menhart .20 .50
153 Radek Mrazek .07 .20
154 Angel Nikolov .20 .50
155 Karel Pilar .40 1.00
156 Ivo Prorok .07 .20
157 Robert Reichel .20 .50
158 Zdenek Skorepa .20 .50
159 Josef Straka .20 .50
160 Martin Strbak .07 .20
161 Otakar Vejvoda .07 .20
162 Jan Dlouhy .07 .20
163 Zdenek Eichenmann .07 .20
164 Jiri Holsan .07 .20
165 Tomas Horna .07 .20
166 Ondrej Kriz .07 .20
167 Jiri Krocak .07 .20
168 Tomas Kupka .07 .20
169 Michal Madl .07 .20
170 Milan Novy .07 .20
171 Tomas Polansky .07 .20
172 Lukas Poznik .07 .20
173 Ladislav Svoboda .07 .20
174 Tomas Ullrych .07 .20
175 Martin Vejvoda .07 .20
176 Jaroslav Liska .07 .20
177 Kamil Brabenec .07 .20
178 Roman Cech .07 .20
179 Milan Filipi .07 .20
180 Stanislav Jasecko .07 .20
181 Josef Jindra .07 .20
182 Michal Klimes .07 .20
183 Zdenek Kutlak .20 .50
184 Milan Nedoma .07 .20
185 David Nedorost .07 .20
186 Lubos Rob .07 .20
187 Petr Sailer .07 .20
188 Jiri Simanek .07 .20
189 Rudolf Suchanek .07 .20
190 Radek Toupal .07 .20
191 Alois Hadamczik CO .07 .20
192 Mario Cartelli .07 .20
193 Petr Gregorek .07 .20
194 Martin Havlat 6.00 15.00
195 Branislav Janos .07 .20
196 Roman Kadera .07 .20
197 Richard Kral .07 .20
198 Jiri Kuntos .07 .20
199 David Nosek .07 .20
200 Vaclav Pletka .20 .50
201 Pavel Selinger .07 .20
202 Petr Svoboda .15 .40
203 Viktor Ujcik .15 .40
204 Marek Zadina .07 .20
205 Jiri Zurck .07 .20
206 Antonin Stavjana .07 .20
207 Jaroslav Balastik .07 .20
208 Roman Hamrlik .30 .75
209 Lubomir Korhon .07 .20
210 Martin Kotasek .07 .20
211 Petr Leska .07 .20
212 Patrik Luza .07 .20
213 Jiri Marusak .07 .20
214 Pavel Mojzis .07 .20
215 Milan Navratil .07 .20
216 Miroslav Okal .07 .20
217 Michal Tomek .07 .20
218 Petr Vala .07 .20
219 Pavol Valko .07 .20
220 Tomas Zizka .07 .20
221 Vladimir Vujtek .07 .20
222 Lukas Galvas .07 .20
223 Dmitrij Gogolev .07 .20
224 Zbynek Irgl .07 .20
225 Dmitri Jerofejev .07 .20
226 Petr Jurecka .07 .20
227 Ludek Krayzel .07 .20
228 Daniel Kysela .07 .20
229 Zdenek Pavelek .07 .20
230 Sergei Petrenko .07 .20
231 Daniel Seman .07 .20
232 Lukas Smolka .07 .20
233 Vaclav Varada .20 .50
234 Jan Vytisk .07 .20
235 Lukas Zatopek .07 .20
236 Richard Farda .07 .20
237 Michal Cech .07 .20
238 Vladimir Holik .07 .20
239 Andrei Yakovenko .07 .20
240 Marek Melenovsky .07 .20
241 Martin Miklik .07 .20
242 Pavel Nohel .07 .20
243 Libor Pivko .07 .20
244 Bogdan Savenko .07 .20
245 Petr Suchanek .07 .20
246 Kamil Suchanek .07 .20
247 Petr Tejkl .07 .20
248 Petr Vlasanek .07 .20
249 Michael Vyhlidal .20 .50
250 Tomas Zapletal .07 .20
251 Josef Augusta .07 .20
252 Ivan Hlinka .07 .20
253 Vladimir Martinec .07 .20
254 Roman Cechmanek .40 1.00
255 Martin Prusek .75 2.00
256 Radek Belohlav .15 .40
257 Ladislav Benysek .20 .50
258 Petr Cajanek .30 .75
259 Jan Caloun .20 .50
260 Jiri Dopita .20 .50
261 Vaclav Kral .07 .20
262 Frantisek Kucera .07 .20
263 Tomas Kucharcik .07 .20
264 Radek Martinek .20 .50
265 Ales Pisa .07 .20
266 Robert Reichel .20 .50
267 Martin Richter .07 .20
268 Roman Simicek .20 .50
269 Jan Srdinko .07 .20
270 Martin Stepanek .07 .20
271 Petr Tenkrat .30 .75
272 Jan Tomajko .07 .20
273 Viktor Ujcik .15 .40
274 Tomas Vlasak .07 .20
275 David Vyborny .07 .20
276 Jiri Vykoukal .07 .20
277 Jaroslav Parizek CO .07 .20
278 Peter Bartos .07 .20
279 Jiri Broz .07 .20
280 Ales Kotalik 1.25 3.00
281 Lukas Zib .07 .20
282 Vaclav Kral .07 .20
283 Radek Martinek .20 .50
284 Vaclav Nedorost .75 2.00
285 Martin Strba .07 .20
286 Filip Turek .07 .20
287 Ivo Pestuka CO .07 .20
288 Jaroslav Hub .07 .20
289 Miroslav Javin .07 .20
290 Roman Kontsek .07 .20
291 Rostislav Pilavka .07 .20
292 Ivan Puncochar .07 .20
293 Roman Rysanek .07 .20
294 Petr Sykora .07 .20
295 Ales Tomasek .07 .20
296 Daniel Vilasek .07 .20
297 David Kriz .07 .20
298 Michal Mikeska .07 .20
299 Pavel Pekarik .07 .20
300 Jan Peterek .07 .20
301 Radek Philipp .07 .20
302 Pavel Zdrahal .07 .20
303 Ales Zima .07 .20
304 Filip Stefanka .07 .20
305 Tomas Sykora .07 .20
306 Marcel Hanzal .07 .20
307 Roman Horak .07 .20
308 Milos Riha CO .07 .20
309 Ladislav Prokupek .07 .20
310 Roman Prosek .07 .20
311 Martin Rousek .07 .20
312 Miroslav Darus .07 .20
313 Michal Divisek .07 .20
314 David Hruska .07 .20
315 Pavel Metlicka .07 .20
316 Radek Prochazka .07 .20
317 Tomas Martinec .07 .20
318 Zdenek Pavelek .07 .20
319 Jiri Polak .07 .20
320 Tomas Chlubna .07 .20
321 Jiri Malinsky .07 .20
322 Petr Fiala .07 .20
323 Eduard Novak CO .07 .20
324 Lubomir Bauer .07 .20
325 Petr Bohunicky .07 .20
326 Jiri Burger .07 .20
327 Jiri Hubacek .07 .20
328 Jiri Kames .07 .20
329 Michal Kanka .07 .20
330 Petr Kounovsky .07 .20
331 Jan Krulis .07 .20
332 Radim Skuhrovec .07 .20
333 Martin Taborsky .07 .20
334 Ladislav Vlcek .07 .20
335 Radek Gardon .07 .20
336 Vladimir Jerabek CO .07 .20
337 Jan Alinc .07 .20
338 Vladimir Gyna .07 .20
339 Jindrich Kotrla .07 .20
340 Michal Travnicek .07 .20
341 Lukas Bednarik .07 .20
342 Daniel Branda .07 .20
343 Marek Cernosek .07 .20
344 Jan Liska .07 .20
345 Kamil Piros .40 1.00
346 Petr Rosol .07 .20
347 Josef Palecek CO .07 .20
348 Petr Hemsky CO .07 .20
349 Milan Chalupa CO .07 .20
350 Ales Hemsky 8.00 20.00
351 Jiri Jantovsky .07 .20
352 Robert Kantor .07 .20
353 Marek Cernosek .07 .20
354 Jiri Malinsky .07 .20
355 Miroslav Mosnar .07 .20
356 Ales Pisa .07 .20
357 Stanislav Prochazka .07 .20
358 Petr Sykora .07 .20
359 Jan Archalous .07 .20
360 Martin Filip .07 .20
361 Pavel Kabrt .07 .20
362 Jan Koliar .07 .20
363 Martin Koudelka .07 .20
364 Radek Matejovsky .07 .20
365 Michal Mikeska .07 .20
366 Petr Mudroch .07 .20
367 Petr Caslava .07 .20
368 Radim Rulik CO .07 .20
369 Jiri Dobrovolny .07 .20
370 Mojmir Musil .07 .20
371 David Pospisil .07 .20
372 Martin Spanhel .40 1.00
373 Jaroslav Spelda .07 .20
374 Michal Straka .07 .20
375 Milan Volak .07 .20
376 Zdenek Sedlak .07 .20
377 Jan Fiala .07 .20
378 Petr Kadlec .07 .20
379 Josef Straka .07 .20
380 Jiri Kalous CO .07 .20
381 Josef Beranek CO .07 .20
382 Jiri Dolezal .07 .20
383 Jan Hejda .07 .20
384 Pavel Kolarik .20 .50
385 Tomas Kucharcik .07 .20
386 Vladimir Machulda .07 .20
387 Jan Bohac .07 .20
388 Pavel Geffert .07 .20
389 Jiri Jantovsky .07 .20
390 Zdenek Skorepa .07 .20
391 Vitezslav Skuta .07 .20
392 Robin Bacul .07 .20
393 Marek Tomica .07 .20
394 Frantisek Vyborny CO .07 .20
395 Ladislav Benysek .20 .50
396 Jaroslav Hlinka .07 .20
397 Vaclav Novak .07 .20
398 Patrik Martinec .07 .20
399 Vaclav Novak .07 .20
400 Josef Slanec .07 .20
401 Michal Sykora .08 .25
402 Vladimir Vujtek .07 .20
403 Kamil Konecny CO .07 .20
404 Jozef Dano .07 .20
405 Petr Folta .07 .20
406 Tomas Chlubna .07 .20
407 Robert Kantor .07 .20
408 Jan Marek .07 .20
409 Lubomir Sekeras .20 .50
410 Ondrej Zetek .07 .20
411 David Appel .07 .20
412 Pavel Janku .07 .20
413 Dmitrij Jerofejev .07 .20
414 David Nosek .07 .20
415 Vladimir Vlk .07 .20
416 Kamil Konecny .07 .20
417 Jan Sterbak CO .07 .20
418 Mojmir Trlicik .07 .20
419 Pavel Bacho .07 .20
420 Ondrej Zetek .07 .20
421 Roman Kadera .07 .20
422 Petr Hubacek .07 .20
423 Roman Kelner .07 .20
424 Pavel Kowalczyk .07 .20
425 Martin Lamich .07 .20
426 Jan Matejny .07 .20
427 Libor Pavlis .07 .20
428 Radek Philipp .07 .20
429 Libor Polasek .07 .20
430 Martin Tomasek .07 .20
431 Libor Gelacek .07 .20
432 Martin Louzek .07 .20
433 Martin Maskarinec .07 .20
434 David Moravec .20 .50
435 Ivan Padelek .07 .20
436 Martin Sivelt .07 .20
437 Miroslav Venkrbec .07 .20
438 Radek Belohlav .15 .40
439 Alexej Jaskin .07 .20
440 Zbynek Marak .07 .20
441 Oleg Antonenko .07 .20
442 Josef Mikes .07 .20
443 Jan Pardavy .07 .20
444 Jan Srdinko .07 .20
445 Jiri Veber .07 .20
446 Libor Zabransky .07 .20
447 Pavel Patera .20 .50
448 Martin Prochazka .07 .20
449 Zbynek Spitzer .07 .20
450 S. Prikryl CO .07 .20
451 Petr Cajanek .30 .75
452 Jiri David .07 .20
453 Martin Hamrlik .07 .20
454 Marek Ivan .07 .20
455 Josef Straub .07 .20
456 Ondrej Vesely .07 .20
457 Martin Ambruz .07 .20
458 Jan Homer .07 .20
459 Rostislav Malena .07 .20
460 S. Barada CO .07 .20
461 Pavol Valko .07 .20
462 Marek Uram .07 .20
463 Patrik Fink .07 .20
464 Tomas Hradecky .07 .20
465 Tomas Jakes .07 .20
466 Petr Kankovsky .07 .20
467 Milan Kastner .07 .20
468 David Kudelka .07 .20
469 Pavel Kumstat .07 .20
470 Karel Soudek .07 .20
471 Jan Kopecky .07 .20
472 Michal Bros .08 .25
473 Martin Cech .07 .20
474 Petr Gregorek .07 .20
475 Jiri Hanzlik .07 .20
476 Jaroslav Hlinka .07 .20
477 Petr Korinek .07 .20
478 Lukas Krajicek .07 .20
479 David Moravec .20 .50
480 Angel Nikolov .20 .50
481 Pavel Patera .20 .50
482 Kamil Piros .40 1.00
483 Vaclav Pletka .20 .50
484 Martin Spanhel .40 1.00
485 Radim Tesarik .07 .20
486 Libor Zabransky .07 .20
487 Petr Briza .30 .75
488 Dusan Salficky .30 .75
489 Roman Cechmanek .40 1.00
490 Vladimir Hudacek .20 .50
491 Petr Bartos .07 .20
492 Vladimir Vujtek .07 .20
493 David Vyborny .07 .20
494 Ladislav Benysek .20 .50
495 Tomas Blazek .08 .25
496 Frantisek Kucera .07 .20
497 Jiri Burger .07 .20
498 Jan Kopecky .07 .20
499 Vaclav Kral .07 .20
500 Jan Krulis .07 .20
501 Ivo Prorok .07 .20
502 Radek Martinek .20 .50
503 Jaroslav Nedved .07 .20
504 Petr Pavlas .07 .20
505 Ales Pisa .07 .20
506 Michal Sykora .08 .25
507 Robert Reichel .20 .50
508 Miroslav Buras .07 .20
509 Martin Spanhel .40 1.00
510 Michal Sup .07 .20
511 Petr Cajanek .40 1.00
512 Jiri Dopita .20 .50
513 Martin Hamrlik .07 .20
514 Roman Horak .07 .20
515 Zbynek Irgl .07 .20
516 Tomas Jakes .07 .20
517 Ludek Krayzel .07 .20
518 Jiri Kuntos .07 .20
519 Petr Leska .07 .20
520 Jiri Marusak .07 .20
521 David Moravec .20 .50
522 Jan Pardavy .07 .20
523 Pavel Patera .20 .50
524 Jan Peterek .07 .20
525 Martin Prochazka .07 .20
526 Karel Soudek .07 .20
527 Jan Srdinko .07 .20
528 Radim Tesarik .07 .20
529 Viktor Ujcik .15 .40
530 Libor Zabransky .08 .25
531 Pavel Cagas .20 .50
532 Zdenek Smid .30 .75
533 Lubos Horcicka .20 .50
534 Pavel Krizek .20 .50
535 Marek Pinc .20 .50
536 Petr Jez .08 .25
537 Radek Masny .20 .50
538 Roman Malek .20 .50
539 Tomas Duba .20 .50
540 Petr Prikryl .20 .50
541 Jiri Kratochvil .20 .50
542 Marek Novotny .08 .25
543 Jiri Trvaj .20 .50
544 Ivo Pesat .20 .50
545 Richard Hrazdira .20 .50
546 Petr Kubena .20 .50
547 Pavol Rybar .20 .50
548 Adam Svoboda .30 .75
549 Radek Masny .20 .50
550 Petr Tucek .20 .50
551 Vladimir Hudacek .20 .50
552 Dusan Salficky .30 .75
NNO Vladimir Hudacek CL .20 .50
NNO Rudolf Pejchar CL .40 1.00
NNO Zdenek Orct CL .40 1.00
NNO Petr Briza CL .30 .75
NNO Ladislav Blazek CL .08 .25
NNO Martin Prusek CL .40 1.00
NNO Roman Cechmanek CL .40 1.00
NNO Dusan Salficky CL .30 .75

1999-00 Czech OFS All-Star Game Blue

A blue-foil enhanced parallel to the 44-card All-Star Game subset. These cards were random inserts in packs.

COMPLETE SET (44) 15.00 25.00
487 Petr Briza .40 1.00
488 Dusan Salficky .40 1.00
489 Roman Cechmanek .75 2.00
490 Vladimir Hudacek .20 .50
491 Peter Bartos .20 .50
492 Vladimir Vujtek .20 .50
493 David Vyborny .20 .50
494 Ladislav Benysek .40 1.00
495 Tomas Blazek .40 1.00
496 Frantisek Kucera .20 .50
497 Jiri Burger .20 .50
498 Jan Kopecky .20 .50
499 Vaclav Kral .20 .50
500 Jan Krulis .20 .50
501 Ivo Prorok .20 .50
502 Radek Martinek .40 1.00
503 Jaroslav Nedved .20 .50
504 Petr Pavlas .20 .50
505 Ales Pisa .20 .50
506 Michal Sykora .20 .50
507 Robert Reichel .40 1.00
508 Miroslav Buras .20 .50
509 Martin Spanhel .30 .75
510 Michal Sup .20 .50
511 Petr Cajanek 1.25 3.00
512 Jiri Dopita .40 1.00
513 Martin Hamrlik .20 .50
514 Roman Horak .20 .50
515 Zbynek Irgl .20 .50
516 Tomas Jakes .20 .50
517 Ludek Krayzel .20 .50
518 Jiri Kuntos .20 .50
519 Petr Leska .20 .50
520 Jiri Marusak .20 .50
521 David Moravec .20 .50
522 Jan Pardavy .20 .50
523 Pavel Patera .20 .50
524 Jan Peterek .20 .50
525 Martin Prochazka .20 .50
526 Karel Soudek .20 .50
527 Jan Srdinko .20 .50
528 Radim Tesarik .20 .50
529 Viktor Ujcik .20 .50
530 Libor Zabransky .30 .75

1999-00 Czech OFS Goalie Die-Cuts

These randomly inserted cards parallel the first 15 cards in the base set and feature a distinctive die-cutting.

COMPLETE SET (15) 40.00 80.00
1 Libor Barta 2.00 5.00
2 Martin Bilek 2.00 5.00
3 Ladislav Blazek 2.00 5.00
4 Petr Briza 3.00 8.00
5 Ivo Capek 2.00 5.00
6 Roman Cechmanek 4.00 10.00
7 Robert Horyna 2.00 5.00
8 Vladimir Hudacek 2.00 5.00
9 Ladislav Kudrna 2.00 5.00
10 Vlastimil Lakosil 2.00 5.00
11 Michal Marik 2.00 5.00
12 Zdenek Orct 2.00 5.00
13 Rudolf Pejchar 2.00 5.00
14 Martin Prusek 8.00 20.00
15 Dusan Salficky 3.00 8.00

1999-00 Czech OFS Jagr Team Embossed

This set parallels cards #16-40 of the base OFS set, which features the Jagr Team subset. The cards are distinguishable from base cards by an embossed feature.

COMPLETE SET (25) 15.00 30.00
16 Richard Farda .20 .50
17 Marian Jelinek .20 .50
18 Josef Beranek .20 .50
19 Leo Gudas .20 .50
20 Milan Hnilicka 1.25 3.00
21 Milos Holan .20 .50
22 Jan Hrdina .75 2.00
23 Jaromir Jagr 8.00 20.00
24 Frantisek Kaberle .20 .50
25 Tomas Kaberle .60 1.50
26 Pavel Kubina .75 2.00
27 Marek Malik .20 .50
28 Pavel Patera .20 .50
29 Martin Prochazka .20 .50
30 Vaclav Prospal .40 1.00
31 Robert Reichel .40 1.00
32 Martin Rucinsky .40 1.00
33 Vladimir Ruzicka .20 .50
34 Pavel Skrbek .40 1.00
35 Jiri Slegr .40 1.00
36 Jaroslav Spacek .40 1.00
37 Martin Straka .75 2.00
38 Vaclav Varada .40 1.00
39 David Volek .40 1.00
40 Jan Vopat .40 1.00

1999-00 Czech Score Blue 2000

This set features players from the Czech second division. The set is noteworthy for the inclusion of cards of NHLers Brendan Morrison and Patrik Elias, who were holding out from the New Jersey Devils at the time. A parallel version of the set, Red Ice 2000, also exists. At this time, we believe there is no price difference between the two versions.

COMPLETE SET (165) 20.00 50.00
1 Roman Malek .30 .75
2 Roman Hrubes .20 .50
3 Ladislav Slizek .20 .50
4 Jaroslav Roubik .20 .50
5 Jiri Kuchler .20 .50
6 Petr Mudroch .20 .50
7 Jiri Cmunt .20 .50
8 Lukas Palecek .20 .50
9 Pavel Malecek .20 .50
10 Vaclav Drabek .20 .50
11 Dalibor Sanda .20 .50
12 Jiri Novotny .20 .50
13 Dalimil Svoboda .20 .50
14 Petr Kubena .20 .50
15 Martin Svetlik .20 .50
16 Jakub Zeska .20 .50
17 Richard Kolacek .20 .50
18 Tomas Trachta .20 .50
19 Patrik Weber .20 .50
20 Ales Sochorec .20 .50
21 Alexandr Elsner .20 .50
22 Michal Safarik .20 .50
23 Michal Safarik .20 .50
24 Tomas Mikolasek .20 .50
25 Pavel Malac .20 .50
26 Kamil Jarina .20 .50
27 Petr Martinek .20 .50
28 Ladislav Bousek .20 .50
29 Kamil Kolacek .20 .50
30 Jiri Gombar .20 .50
31 David Hajek .20 .50
32 Martin Tupa .20 .50
33 Stanislav Stavensky .20 .50
34 Martin Stelcich .20 .50
35 Radek Sip .20 .50
36 Petr Altrichter .20 .50
37 Lukas Stabl .20 .50
38 Lukas Sablik .20 .50
39 Marian Morava .20 .50
40 Zdenek Fuksa .20 .50
41 Petr Mokrejs .20 .50
42 Miroslav Duben .20 .50
43 Jiri Cihlar .20 .50
44 Vaclav Adamec .20 .50
45 Daniel Hodek .20 .50
46 Ales Polcar .20 .50
47 Daniel Zapotocny .20 .50
48 Richard [illegible] .20 .50
49 Roman Spiler .20 .50
50 Filip Sindelar .20 .50
51 Petr Jaros .20 .50
52 Marek Dvorak .20 .50
53 Jaroslav Mares .20 .50
54 Robert Vavroch .20 .50

55 Vratislav Hreben .20 .50
56 Petr Cerveny .20 .50
57 Jaroslav Kocar .20 .50
58 Ales Skokan .20 .50
59 Michal Horak .20 .50
60 Jakub Kraus .20 .50
61 Marcel Kucera .20 .50
62 Miroslav Sedlacek .20 .50
63 Richard Richter .20 .50
64 Rudolf Mudra .20 .50
65 Jaroslav Muller .20 .50
66 Evzen Gal .20 .50
67 Petr Spojcar .20 .50
68 Jaroslav Kreuzman .20 .50
69 Premysl Sedlak .20 .50
70 Martin Nosek .20 .50
71 Tomas Vyskocil .20 .50
72 Michal Lanicek .20 .50
73 Pavel Malac .20 .50
74 Ales Vala .20 .50
75 Martin Vyborny .20 .50
76 Tomas Vozka .20 .50
77 Petr Hocicka .20 .50
78 Jan Plodek .20 .50
79 Oldrich Nyc .20 .50
80 Filip Pesan .20 .50
81 Milan Plodek .20 .50
82 Jiri Matousek .20 .50
83 Vitezslav Jankovych .20 .50
84 Petr Kus .20 .50
85 Martin Chlad .20 .50
86 Hiroyuki Murakami .20 .50
87 Lukas Bednarik .20 .50
88 Michal Oliverius .20 .50
89 Tomas Pisa .20 .50
90 Jan Hranac .20 .50
91 Jan Bohacek .20 .50
92 Tomas Klimt .20 .50
93 Martin Zivny .20 .50
94 Michal Havel .20 .50
95 Martin Rejthar .20 .50
96 Karl Rakovsky .20 .50
97 Martin Vojtek .20 .50
98 Robert Prochazka .20 .50
99 Daniel Vilasek .20 .50
100 Jan Kasik .20 .50
101 Jevgenij Alipov .20 .50
102 Ales Kretinsky .20 .50
103 Pavel Sebesta .20 .50
104 David Kostelnak .20 .50
105 Karel Harazim .20 .50
106 Richard Brancik .20 .50
107 Petr Rozum .20 .50
108 Michal Pinkas .20 .50
109 Robert Slavik .20 .50
110 Josef Vachulka .20 .50
111 Lubos Pindiak .20 .50
112 Robert Zak .20 .50
113 David Mika .20 .50
114 Jiri Kudrna .20 .50
115 Vaclav Benak .20 .50
116 Roman Bezpalec .20 .50
117 Pavel Hejl .20 .50
118 Michal Janiga .20 .50
119 Vladimir Mizera .20 .50
120 David Plsek .20 .50
121 Petr Tucek .20 .50
122 Martin Palinek .20 .50
123 Jiri Polak .20 .50
124 Michal Cerny .20 .50
125 Milan Ministr .20 .50
126 Tomas Hradecky .20 .50
127 David Svec .20 .50
128 Filip Janecek .20 .50
129 Tomas Hradecky .20 .50
130 Radomir Brazda .20 .50
131 Petr Hrachovina .20 .50
132 Martin Altrichter .20 .50
133 Jaromir Pichal .20 .50
134 Jiri Bures .20 .50
135 Jiri Mifek .20 .50
136 Jaroslav Smolik .20 .50
137 Milota Florian .20 .50
138 Robert Holy .20 .50
139 Josef Drabek .20 .50
140 Michal Slavik .20 .50
141 Tomas Kramny .20 .50
142 Jan Konecny .20 .50
143 Radek Lukes .20 .50
144 Robert Hamrla .20 .50
145 Petr Lustinec .20 .50
146 Radek Kucera .20 .50
147 Petr Sakarov .20 .50
148 Pavel Kormunda .20 .50
149 Petr Suchy .20 .50
150 David Brezik .20 .50
151 Michal Nohejl .20 .50
152 Martin Jenacek .20 .50
153 Dusan Barica .20 .50
154 Zdenek Kucirek .20 .50
155 Stanislav Neruda .20 .50
156 Robert Pospisil .20 .50
157 Brendan Morrison .75 2.00
158 Frantisek Sevcik .20 .50
159 Roman Hlouch .20 .50
160 Patrik Elias .75 2.00
161 Oldrich Bakus .20 .50
162 Jiri Oliva .20 .50
163 Karel Sefcik .20 .50
164 Marcel Hrbacek .20 .50
165 Rostislav Malena .20

2000-01 Czech DS Extraliga

This set features the top players of the Czech Elite league. The cards feature an action photo on the front surrounded by a white border, with two more photos and stats on the back.

COMPLETE SET (168) 25.00 60.00
1 Petr Briza• .40 1.00
2 Petr Prikryl• .20 .50
3 Libor Zabransky• .20 .50
4 Vlastimil Kroupa• .20 .50
5 Frantisek Ptacek• .20 .50
6 Michal Dobron• .20 .50
7 Vladimir Vujtek• .20 .50
8 Jaroslav Hlinka• .20 .50
9 Martin Chabada• .20 .50
10 Ondrej Kratena• .20 .50
11 Michal Bros• .20 .50
12 Richard Zemlicka• .30 .75
13 Jaroslav Kames• .40 1.00
14 Ivo Pesat• .20 .50
15 Jan Srdinko• .20 .50
16 Milan Nedoma• .20 .50
17 Martin Strbak• .20 .50
18 Radim Tesarik• .20 .50
19 Jan Pardavy• .20 .50
20 Jiri Dopita• .40 1.00
21 Jan Sochor• .20 .50
22 Jan Lipiansky• .20 .50
23 Jiri Hudler• 6.00 15.00
24 Ondrej Vesely• .20 .50
25 Dusan Salficky• .40 1.00
26 Petr Kus• .20 .50
27 Josef Reznicek• .20 .50
28 Martin Cech• .20 .50
29 Ivan Vlcek• .20 .50
30 Jiri Hanzlik• .20 .50
31 Pavel Vostrak• .20 .50
32 Petr Korinek• .20 .50
33 Milan Volak• .20 .50
34 Michal Straka• .20 .50
35 David Pospisil• .20 .50
36 Milan Antos• .20 .50
37 Zdenek Orct• .40 1.00
38 Michal Podolka• .40 1.00
39 Angel Nikolov• .30 .75
40 Karel Pilar• .40 1.00
41 Radek Mrazek• .20 .50
42 Vladimir Gyna• .20 .50
43 Robert Reichel• .30 .75
44 Petr Rosol• .20 .50
45 Vojtech Kubincak• .20 .50
46 Kamil Piros• .40 1.00
47 Vesa Karjalainen• .20 .50
48 Robert Kysela• .20 .50
49 Vladimir Hudacek• .40 1.00
50 Richard Hrazdira• .20 .50
51 Tomas Zizka• .40 1.00
52 Jiri Marusak• .20 .50
53 Martin Hamrlik• .20 .50
54 Miroslav Barus• .20 .50
55 Miroslav Okal• .20 .50
56 Petr Cajanek• .30 .75
57 Jaroslav Balastik• .20 .50
58 Petr Vala• .20 .50
59 Martin Ambruz• .20 .50
60 Petr Leska• .20 .50
61 Marek Novotny• .20 .50
62 Vlastimil Lakosil• .40 1.00
63 Marek Zadina• .20 .50
64 Mario Cartelli• .20 .50
65 Vladimir Vlk• .20 .50
66 Jiri Kuntos• .20 .50
67 Richard Kral• .20 .50
68 Viktor Ujcik• .30 .75
69 Jozef Dano• .20 .50
70 Petr Gregorek• .20 .50
71 Richard Kapus• .20 .50
72 Pavel Janku• .20 .50
73 Michal Marik• .20 .50
74 Ivo Capek• .40 1.00
75 Radek Martinek• .40 1.00
76 Rudolf Suchanek• .20 .50
77 Stanislav Jasecko• .20 .50
78 Vaclav Kral• .20 .50
79 Filip Turek• .20 .50
80 Lubos Rob• .20 .50
81 Radek Belohlav• .30 .75
82 Jiri Simanek• .20 .50
83 Ales Kotalik• .20 .50
84 Kamil Brabenec• .20 .50
85 Libor Barta• .20 .50
86 Adam Svoboda• .40 1.00
87 Ales Pisa• .40 1.00
88 Jiri Malinsky• .20 .50
89 Petr Jancarik• .20 .50
90 Otakar Janecky• .30 .75
91 Ladislav Lubina• .20 .50
92 Tomas Blazek• .20 .50
93 Jaroslav Kudrna• .30 .75
94 Michal Mikeska• .20 .50
95 Stanislav Prochazka• .20 .50
96 Michal Tvrdik• .20 .50
97 Oldrich Svoboda• .40 1.00
98 Ladislav Kudrna• .20 .50
99 Tomas Jakes• .20 .50
100 Jiri Hes• .20 .50
101 Pavel Kumstat• .20 .50
102 Karel Soudek• .20 .50
103 Petr Pucher• .20 .50
104 David Havir• .20 .50
105 Zbynek Marak• .20 .50
106 Milan Prochazka• .20 .50
107 Radek Haman• .20 .50
108 David Pazourek• .20 .50
109 Ladislav Blazek• .20 .50
110 Roman Malek• .40 1.00
111 Petr Kadlec• .20 .50
112 Jan Novak• .20 .50
113 Angel Krstev• .20 .50
114 Jan Snopek• .20 .50
115 Daniel Branda• .20 .50
116 Jan Alinc• .20 .50
117 Viktor Hubl• .20 .50
118 Petr Hrbek• .20 .50
119 Jan Bohac• .20 .50
120 Zdenek Skorepa• .20 .50
121 Petr Franek• .20 .50
122 Zdenek Smid• .40 1.00
123 Libor Prochazka• .20 .50
124 Normunds Sejejs• .20 .50
125 Jiri Polak• .20 .50
126 Roman Zak• .20 .50
127 Jaromir Kverka• .20 .50
128 Tomas Chlubna• .20 .50
129 Radek Prochazka• .20 .50
130 David Hruska• .20 .50
131 Robert Tomik• .20 .50
132 Pavel Kasparik• .20 .50
133 Lubos Horcicka• .20 .50
134 Marek Pinc• .30 .75
135 Jan Krulis• .20 .50
136 Michal Madl• .20 .50
137 Radek Gardon• .20 .50
138 Jan Bohacek• .20 .50
139 Ladislav Svoboda• .20 .50
140 Tomas Horna• .20 .50
141 Jiri Holsan• .20 .50
142 Ondrej Kriz• .20 .50
143 Ladislav Vlcek• .20 .50
144 Jozef Voskar• .20 .50
145 Radovan Biegl• .30 .75
146 Radek Masny• .20 .50
147 Michael Vyhlidal• .20 .50
148 Miroslav Javin• .20 .50
149 Petr Pavlas• .20 .50
150 Tomas Srsen• .20 .50
151 Petr Folta• .20 .50
152 Libor Pivko• .20 .50
153 Daniel Bohac• .20 .50
154 Roman Horak• .20 .50
155 Jan Peterek• .20 .50
156 Richard Pavlikovsky• .20 .50
157 Martin Prusek• .40 1.00
158 Jiri Trvaj• .20 .50
159 Zdenek Pavelek• .20 .50
160 Vitezslav Skuta• .20 .50
161 Dimitri Jerofejev• .20 .50
162 David Moravec• .40 1.00
163 Roman Kadera• .20 .50
164 Zbynek Irgl• .20 .50
165 Marek Ivan• .20 .50
166 Martin Prochazka• .30 .75
167 Josef Straub• .20 .50
168 Ivan Padelek• .20 .50

2000-01 Czech DS Extraliga Best of the Best

This insert set features the two best Czech-born players ever. The autograph cards are serial numbered out of 200.

COMPETE SET (4) 25.00 60.00
PRINT RUN 200 SER.#'d SETS
BBH1 Dominik Hasek 4.00 10.00
BBH2 Dominik Hasek 4.00 10.00
BBJ1 Jaromir Jagr 6.00 15.00
BBJ2 Jaromir Jagr 6.00 15.00
BBH1 D.Hasek AU/200 40.00 100.00
BBJ2 J.Jagr AU/200 60.00 150.00

2000-01 Czech DS Extraliga Goalies

This insert set features the top stoppers in the Czech Extraliga.

COMPLETE SET (14) 25.00 60.00
G1 Petr Briza• 3.00 8.00
G2 Jaroslav Kames• 2.00 5.00
G3 Dusan Salficky• 2.00 5.00
G4 Zdenek Orct• 2.00 5.00
G5 Vladimir Hudacek• 2.00 5.00
G6 Vlastimil Lakosil• 2.00 5.00
G7 Ivo Capek• 2.00 5.00
G8 Adam Svoboda• 2.00 5.00
G9 Oldrich Svoboda• 2.00 5.00
G10 Roman Malek• 2.00 5.00
G11 Zdenek Smid• 2.00 5.00
G12 Marek Pinc• 2.00 5.00
G13 Radovan Biegl• 2.00 5.00
G14 Martin Prusek• 4.00 10.00

2000-01 Czech DS Extraliga National Team

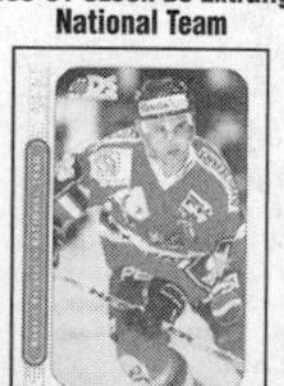

This insert set features members of the Czech Republic's gold medal-winning World Championships team.

COMPLETE SET (10) 25.00 60.00
NT1 Dusan Salficky• 2.00 5.00
NT2 Roman Cechmanek• 3.00 7.50
NT3 Martin Stepanek• 1.25 3.00
NT4 Vladimir Vujtek• 1.25 3.00
NT5 Robert Reichel• 2.00 5.00
NT6 Jiri Dopita• 2.00 5.00
NT7 Martin Rucinsky• 2.00 5.00
NT8 Martin Havlat• 10.00 25.00
NT9 Tomas Vlasak• 1.25 3.00
NT10 Michal Bros• 1.25 3.00

2000-01 Czech DS Extraliga Team Jagr

This players for this insert set were chosen by Jagr himself as his favorite Czech stars. The cards are slightly thicker than the base cards of this season.

COMPLETE SET (16) 40.00 80.00
JT1 Roman Turek• 2.00 5.00
JT2 Milan Hnilicka• 2.00 5.00
JT3 Petr Sykora• 1.50 4.00
JT4 Roman Hamrlik• 1.25 3.00
JT5 Martin Straka• 1.50 4.00
JT6 Pavel Kubina• 1.25 3.00
JT7 Petr Nedved• 1.50 4.00
JT8 Martin Prochazka• 1.25 3.00
JT9 Vaclav Prospal• 1.25 3.00
JT10 David Volek• 1.25 3.00
JT11 Milan Hejduk• 6.00 15.00
JT12 Jaromir Jagr• 8.00 25.00
JT13 Jan Hlavac• 1.50 4.00
JT14 Pavel Patera• 1.25 3.00
JT15 Tomas Vlasak• 1.25 3.00
JT16 Vaclav Varada• 1.25 3.00

2000-01 Czech DS Extraliga Team Jagr Parallel

This partial parallel set features Jagr's favorite Czech players in the NHL. The cards were serial numbered out of 300.

COMPLETE SET (9) 50.00 125.00
STATED PRINT RUN 300 SER.#'d SETS
JT1 Roman Turek• 8.00 20.00
JT2 Milan Hnilicka• 4.00 10.00
JT3 Petr Sykora• 4.00 15.00
JT4 Roman Hamrlik• 4.00 10.00
JT5 Martin Straka• 4.00 10.00
JT6 Petr Nedved• 4.00 10.00
JT7 Milan Hejduk• 12.50 30.00
JT8 Jaromir Jagr• 20.00 50.00
JT9 Jan Hlavac• 4.00 10.00

2000-01 Czech DS Extraliga Top Stars

This set features the first All-Star team of the Czech Extraliga.

TS1 Petr Briza• 3.00 8.00
TS2 Radek Martinek• 2.00 5.00
TS3 Petr Cajanek• 2.00 5.00
TS4 Jiri Dopita• 3.00 8.00
TS5 Robert Reichel• 3.00 8.00
TS6 Martin Prochazka• 2.00 5.00

2000-01 Czech DS Extraliga Valuable Players

Yet another insert set featuring the Extraliga's top stars.

COMPLETE SET (6) 12.00 20.00
VP1 Vladimir Hudacek• 2.00 5.00
VP2 Frantisek Kucera• 1.00 3.00
VP3 Michal Sykora• 1.00 3.00
VP4 Robert Reichel• 2.00 5.00
VP5 Jiri Dopita• 2.00 5.00
VP6 Petr Cajanek• 1.00 3.00

2000-01 Czech DS Extraliga World Champions

This insert set features more members of the Czech World Championship team.

COMPLETE SET (11) 30.00 75.00
WCH1 Roman Cechmanek• 6.00 8.00
WCH2 Dusan Salficky• 2.00 5.00
WCH3 Radek Martinek• 2.00 5.00
WCH4 Martin Stepanek• 2.00 5.00
WCH5 Frantisek Kucera• 2.00 5.00
WCH6 Michal Sykora• 2.00 5.00
WCH7 Martin Havlat• 10.00 25.00
WCH8 Robert Reichel• 2.00 5.00
WCH9 Tomas Vlasak• 2.00 5.00
WCH10 David Vyborny• 2.00 5.00
WCH11 Michal Bros• 2.00 5.00

2000-01 Czech OFS

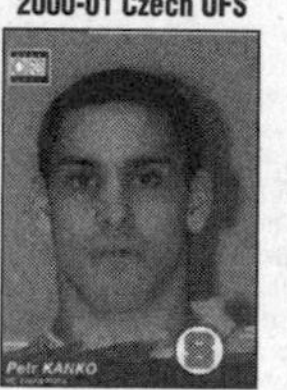

This set was released in pack form in the Czech Republic and features every member of that country's elite league.

COMPLETE SET (421) 32.00 80.00
1 Team Logo .04 .10
2 Jaroslav Liska CO .04 .10
3 Jaroslav Parizek CO .04 .10
4 Jan Tlacil CO .04 .10
5 Jaroslav Pouzar CO .04 .10
6 Michal Marik .10 .25
7 Ivo Capek .20 .50
8 Radek Martinek .30 .50
9 Rudolf Suchanek .20 .50
10 Stanislav Jasecko .10 .25
11 Pavel Mojzis .10 .25
12 Vaclav Benak .10 .25
13 Ladislav Cierny .20 .50
14 Josef Jindra .10 .25
15 Vaclav Kral .10 .25
16 Filip Turek .10 .25
17 Lubos Rob .10 .25
18 Radek Belohlav .15 .40
19 Ales Kotalik .75 2.00
20 Kamil Brabenec .10 .25
21 Jiri Simanek .10 .25
22 Martin Strba .10 .25
23 Petr Sailer .10 .25
24 Milan Filipi .04 .25
25 Jiri Broz .10 .25
26 Jiri Novotny .20 .50
27 Michal Vondrka .10 .25
28 Team Logo .04 .10
29 Josef Palacek CO .04 .10
30 Petr Hemsky CO .04 .10
31 Libor Barta .20 .25
32 Adam Svoboda .30 .75
33 Martin Barek .10 .25
34 Ales Pisa .10 .25
35 Jiri Malinsky .10 .25
36 Petr Jancarik .10 .25
37 Miroslav Duben .10 .25
38 Tomas Pacal .10 .25
39 Michal Divisek .10 .25
40 Andrej Novotny .10 .25
41 Petr Mudroch .10 .25
42 Otakar Janecky .20 .50
43 Ladislav Lubina .10 .25
44 Tomas Blazek .20 .25
45 Jaroslav Kudrna .20 .50
46 Michal Mikeska .10 .25
47 Stanislav Prochazka .10 .25
48 Michal Tvrdik .10 .25
49 Martin Filip .10 .25
50 Martin Koudelka .10 .25
51 Pavel Kabrt .10 .25
52 Petr Sykora .20 .50
53 Tomas Rolinek .10 .25
54 Jan Kolar .10 .25
55 Team Logo .04 .10
56 Marek Sykora CO .04 .10
57 Dusan Salficky .30 .75
58 Petr Kus .10 .25
59 Josef Reznicek .10 .25
60 Martin Cech .10 .25
61 Ivan Vlcek .10 .25
62 Jiri Hanzlik .10 .25
63 Jaroslav Spelda .10 .25
64 Zdenek Touzimsky .10 .25
65 Jiri Dobrovolny .10 .25
66 Jan Choteborsky .10 .25
67 Pavel Vostrak .10 .25
68 Petr Korinek .20 .50
69 Milan Volak .10 .25
70 Michal Straka .10 .25
71 David Pospisil .10 .25
72 Josef Straka .10 .25
73 Milan Antos .10 .25
74 Andrej Nedorost .40 1.00
75 Vaclav Eiselt .10 .25
76 Jiri Jelen .10 .25
77 Michal Dvorak .10 .25
78 Jiri Zurek .10 .25
79 Dusan Andrasovsky .10 .25
80 Team Logo .04 .10
81 Jaromir Sindel CO .10 .25
82 Ondrej Weissmann CO .04 .10
83 Ladislav Blazek .20 .25
84 Roman Malek .10 .25
85 Petr Kadlec .10 .25
86 Jan Novak .10 .25
87 Angel Krstev .10 .25
88 Jan Snopek .10 .25
89 Jan Kloboucek .10 .25
90 Jan Hejda .10 .25
91 Petr Martinek .10 .25
92 Jan Slavik .10 .25
93 Daniel Branda .10 .25
94 Jan Alinc .20 .50
95 Viktor Hubl .10 .25
96 Jan Kopecky .10 .25
97 Jan Bohac .10 .25
98 Zdenek Skorepa .20 .50
99 Michal Sup .10 .25
100 Radek Matejovsky .10 .25
101 Robin Bacul .10 .25
102 Leos Cermak .10 .25
103 Petr Jira .10 .25
104 Marek Tomica .10 .25
105 Petr Hrbek .10 .25
106 Team Logo .04 .10
107 Eduard Novak CO .04 .10
108 Petr Fiala CO .04 .10
109 Lubos Horcicka .10 .25
110 Marek Pinc .10 .25
111 Jan Pospisil .10 .25
112 Jan Krulis .10 .25
113 Michal Madl .10 .25
114 Ondrej Kriz .10 .25
115 Jan Bohacek .10 .25
116 David Hajek .10 .25
117 Jan Dlouhy .10 .25
118 Martin Taborsky .10 .25
119 Jiri Kames .20 .50
120 Ladislav Svoboda .10 .25
121 Pavel Geffert .10 .25
122 Tomas Horna .10 .25
123 Jiri Holsan .10 .25
124 Radek Gardon .10 .25
125 Ladislav Vlcek .10 .25
126 Jozef Voskar .10 .25
127 Tomas Klimt .20 .50
128 Premysl Sedlak .10 .25
129 Tomas Plekanec ERC .10 .25
130 Michal Havel .10 .25
131 Vaclav Skuhravy .10 .25
132 Team Logo .04 .10
133 Vaclav Sykora CO .04 .10
134 Otakar Vejvoda CO .04 .10
135 Zdenek Orct .20 .50
136 Michal Podolka .30 .75
137 Angel Nikolov .20 .50
138 Karel Pilar .40 1.00
139 Radek Mrazek .10 .25
140 Marek Cernosek .10 .25
141 Vladimir Gyna .10 .25
142 Martin Tupa .10 .25
143 Jan Hranac .10 .25
144 Petr Suchy .10 .25
145 Robert Reichel .31 .50
146 Petr Rosol .10 .25
147 Vojtech Kubincak .10 .25
148 Kamil Piros .40 1.00
149 Jindrich Kotrla .10 .25
150 Vesa Karjalainen .10 .25
151 Robert Kysela .10 .25
152 Stanislav Slavensky .10 .25
153 Tomas Martinec .10 .25
154 Zdenek Zak .10 .25
155 Martin Tvrznik .10 .25
156 Lukas Bednarik .10 .25
157 Team Logo .04 .10
158 Radim Rulik CO .04 .10
159 Martin Pesout CO .04 .10
160 Petr Franek .10 .25
161 Zdenek Smid .30 .75
162 Pavel Csipka .10 .25
163 Libor Prochazka .10 .25
164 Robert Kantor .10 .25
165 Jiri Polak .10 .25
166 Normunds Sejejs .10 .25
167 Roman Prosek .10 .25
168 Roman Zak .10 .25
169 Ivan Puncochar .10 .25
170 Petr Puncochar .10 .25
171 Jakub Grof .10 .25
172 Jaromir Kverka .10 .25
173 Tomas Chlubna .10 .25
174 Radek Prochazka .10 .25
175 David Hruska .10 .25
176 Robert Tomik .10 .25
177 Pavel Kasparik .10 .25
178 Martin Rousek .10 .25
179 Jaroslav Kalla .10 .25
180 Peter Bohunicky .10 .25
181 Jan Kostal .10 .25
182 Petr Domin .10 .25
183 Petr Sinagl .10 .25
184 Team Logo .04 .10
185 Milan Chalupa CO .10 .25
186 Pavel Pazourek CO .04 .10
187 Oldrich Svoboda .10 .25
188 Ladislav Kudrna .20 .50
189 Miloslav Bahensky .10 .25
190 Tomas Jakes .10 .25
191 Jiri Hes .10 .25
192 Pavel Kumstat .10 .25
193 Karel Soudek .10 .25
194 Pavol Valko .10 .25
195 David Havir .10 .25
196 David Petlak .10 .25
197 Vladimir Holik .10 .25
198 Peter Pucher .10 .25
199 Marek Uram .10 .25
200 Karel Plasek .10 .25
201 Zbynek Marak .10 .25
202 Milan Prochazka .10 .25
203 Patrik Fink .10 .25
204 David Pazourek .10 .25
205 Marek Vorel .10 .25
206 Radek Haman .10 .25
207 Petr Lipina .10 .25
208 Petr Kumstat .10 .25
209 Team Logo .04 .10
210 Vladimir Vujtek CO .04 .10
211 Ales Mach CO .04 .10
212 Marek Novotny .10 .25
213 Vlastimil Lakosil .20 .50
214 Mario Cartelli .10 .25
215 Vladimir Vlk .10 .25
216 Jiri Kuntos .10 .25
217 Petr Gregorek .10 .25
218 Robert Prochazka .10 .25
219 Ondrej Zetek .10 .25
220 David Nosek .10 .25
221 Tomas Houdek .10 .25
222 Tomas Harant .10 .25
223 Richard Kral .10 .25
224 Viktor Ujcik .15 .40
225 Jozef Dano .10 .25
226 Richard Kapus .10 .25
227 Pavel Janku .20 .25
228 Marek Zadina .10 .25
229 Branislav Janos .10 .25
230 Tomas Nemcicky .10 .25
231 Patrik Moskal .10 .25
232 David Appel .10 .25
233 Jan Marek .10 .25
234 Jiri Hasek .10 .25
235 Team Logo .04 .10
236 Alois Hadamczik CO .04 .10
237 Kamil Konecny CO .04 .10
238 Mojmir Trlicik CO .04 .10
239 Martin Prusek .75 2.00
240 Jiri Trvaj .10 .25
241 Lukas Smolka .10 .25
242 Vitezslav Skuta .10 .25
243 Dmitrij Jerofejev .10 .25
244 Daniel Kapotocny .10 .25
245 Petr Jurecka .10 .25
246 Radek Philipp .10 .25
247 Lukas Zatopek .10 .25
248 Daniel Seman .10 .25
249 Jan Vytisk .10 .25
250 David Moravec .20 .50
251 Martin Prochazka .10 .25
252 Ivan Padelek .10 .25
253 Josef Straub .10 .25
254 Roman Kadera .10 .25
255 Marek Ivan .10 .25
256 Zdenek Pavelek .10 .25
257 Martin Tomasek .10 .25
258 Pavel Selinger .10 .25
259 Jan Pleva .10 .25
260 Ales Padelek .10 .25
261 Team Logo .04 .10
262 Ivo Pestuka CO .04 .10
263 Jiri Roznar CO .04 .10
264 Radovan Biegl .10 .25
265 Radek Masny .10 .25
266 Michael Vyhlidal .10 .25
267 Miroslav Javin .10 .25
268 Richard Pavlikovsky .10 .25
269 Petr Pavlas .10 .25
270 Patrik Rimmel .10 .25
271 Ales Tomasek .10 .25
272 Petr Suchanek .10 .25
273 Tomas Srsen .10 .25
274 Petr Folta .10 .25
275 Libor Pivko .10 .25
276 Daniel Bohac .10 .25
277 Roman Horak .20 .50
278 Jan Peterek .10 .25
279 Marek Melenovsky .10 .25
280 Pavel Zdrahal .10 .25
281 Roman Kontsek .10 .25
282 Michal Cech .10 .25
283 Tomas Sykora .10 .25
284 Martin Streit .10 .25
285 Milos Melicherik .10 .25
286 Team Logo .04 .10
287 Milos Riha CO .04 .10
288 Frantisek Vyborny CO .04 .10
289 Pavel Hynek CO .04 .10
290 Petr Briza .30 .75
291 Petr Prikryl .10 .25
292 Tomas Duba .10 .25
293 Libor Zabransky .20 .25
294 Vlastimil Kroupa .20 .50
295 Frantisek Ptacek .10 .25
296 Michal Dobron .10 .25
297 Pavel Srek .10 .25
298 Jaroslav Nedved .10 .25
299 Martin Holy .10 .25
300 Miha Rebolj .10 .25
301 Jan Hanzlik .10 .25
302 Vladimir Vujtek .20 .50
303 Jaroslav Hlinka .10 .25
304 Martin Chabada .10 .25
305 Ondrej Kratena .10 .25
306 Michal Bros .20 .25
307 Patrik Martinec .10 .25
308 Richard Zemlicka .20 .50
309 Jiri Zelenka .10 .25
310 Vaclav Novak .10 .25
311 Petr Havelka .10 .25
312 Michal Sivek .60 1.50
313 Petr Hrbek .10 .25
314 Radek Duda .10 .25
315 Josef Slanec .10 .25
316 Petr Kanko .75 2.00
317 Team Logo .04 .10
318 Zdislav Tabara CO .04 .10
319 Miroslav Venkrbec CO .04 .10
320 Jaroslav Kames .30 .75
321 Ivo Pesat .10 .25
322 Lukas Plsek .10 .25
323 Jan Srdinko .10 .25
324 Milan Nedoma .10 .25
325 Martin Strbak .10 .25
326 Radim Tesarik .10 .25
327 Pavel Zubicek .10 .25
328 Alexej Jaskin .10 .25
329 Petr Kubos .10 .25
330 Zbynek Spitzer .10 .25
331 Michal Safarik .10 .25
332 Pavel Augusta .10 .25
333 Jan Pardavy .10 .25
334 Jiri Dopita .20 .50
335 Jan Tomajko .10 .25
336 Roman Stantien .10 .25
337 Jan Sochor .10 .25
338 Martin Paroulek .10 .25
339 Jan Lipiansky .10 .25
340 Jiri Hudler ERC 6.00 15.00
341 Ondrej Vesely .10 .25
342 Jiri Jantovsky .10 .25
343 Petr Zajgla .10 .25
344 Tomas Demel .10 .25
345 Petr Vampola .10 .25
346 Team Logo .04 .10
347 Antonin Stavjana CO .10 .25
348 Zdenek Venera CO .04 .10
349 Vladimir Hudacek .20 .50
350 Richard Hrazdira .20 .50
351 Petr Tucek .10 .25
352 Tomas Zizka .10 .25
353 Jiri Marusak .10 .25
354 Martin Hamrlik .10 .25
355 Patrik Luza .10 .25
356 Rostislav Malena .08 .20
357 Jan Homer .10 .25
358 Lukas Zib .10 .25
359 Boris Zabka .10 .25
360 Miroslav Okal .08 .20
361 Petr Cajanek .30 .75
362 Jaroslav Balastik .10 .25
363 Petr Vala .10 .25
364 Martin Ambruz .10 .25
365 Petr Leska .10 .25
366 Miroslav Barus .10 .25
367 Martin Kotasek .10 .25
368 Lubomir Korhon .20 .50
369 Ivan Rachunek .40 1.00
370 Radovan Somik .10 .25
371 Filip Cech .10 .25
372 Martin Jenacek .10 .25
373 Pavel Mojzis .10 .25
374 Milan Navratil .10 .25
375 Michal Safarik .10 .25
376 Miroslav Blatak .10 .25
377 Team Logo .04 .10
378 Roman Turek .40 1.00
379 Milan Hnilicka .40 1.00
380 Tomas Kaberle .30 .75
381 Frantisek Kaberle .20 .50
382 Roman Hamrlik .30 .75
383 Pavel Kubina .40 1.00
384 Jaromir Jagr 2.00 5.00
385 Patrik Elias .75 2.00
386 Milan Hejduk 2.00 5.00
387 Radek Dvorak .40 1.00
388 Petr Nedved .30 .75
389 Vaclav Prospal .40 1.00
390 Pavel Patera .20 .50
391 Petr Sykora 1.25 3.00
392 Vaclav Varada .20 .50
393 Martin Straka .40 1.00
394 Jan Hrdina .40 1.00
395 David Volek .20 .50
396 Tomas Vlasak .10 .25
397 Michal Rozsival .30 .75
398 Team Logo .04 .10
399 Ladislav Blazek .20 .25
400 Milos Horava .10 .25
401 Frantisek Kucera .20 .20
402 Lubomir Sekeras .20 .50
403 Petr Kadlec .10 .25
404 Jaroslav Spacek .20 .50
405 Frantisek Prochazka .20 .50
406 Antonin Stavjana .10 .25
407 Vladimir Ruzicka .20 .50
408 Petr Rosol .10 .25
409 Robert Reichel .31 .50
410 Martin Rucinsky .20 .50
411 Josef Beranek .20 .50

412 Viktor Ujcik .15 .40
413 Michal Sup .10 .25
414 Ivo Prorok .10 .25
415 Zdeno Ciger .20 .50
416 Jiri Hrdina .10 .25
417 J.Jagr/V.Ruzicka 2.00 5.00
418 Checklist .04 .10
419 Checklist .04 .10
420 Checklist .04 .10
421 Checklist .04 .10

2000-01 Czech OFS Star Emerald

This is one of three versions of this insert set, found exclusively in packs of Czech OFS. The Emerald version was found 1:2 packs. The Violet parallels were found 1:3 packs and the Pink parallels were found 1:6 packs.

COMPLETE SET (36) 10.00 25.00
EMERALD ODDS 1:2
VIOLET PARALLELS: 1X to 2X
VIOLET ODDS 1:3
PINK PARALLELS : 2X to 3X
PINK ODDS 1:6
1 Jaroslav Kames .40 1.00
2 Jiri Dopita .40 1.00
3 Jan Pardavy .20 .50
4 Vladimir Hudacek .20 .50
5 Petr Cajanek .75 2.00
6 Richard Hrazdira .40 1.00
7 Petr Briza .75 2.00
8 Jiri Zelenka .20 .50
9 Richard Zemlicka .40 1.00
10 Libor Barta .40 1.00
11 Adam Svoboda .40 1.00
12 Otakar Janecky .40 1.00
13 Vaclav Kral .20 .50
14 Rudolf Suchanek .40 1.00
15 Michal Marik .20 .50
16 Dusan Salficky .60 1.50
17 Petr Korinek .40 1.00
18 Ivan Vlcek .20 .50
19 Zdenek Orct .40 1.00
20 Robert Reichel .40 1.00
21 Petr Franek .20 .50
22 Libor Prochazka .20 .50
23 Vlastimil Lakosil .40 1.00
24 Richard Kral .20 .50
25 Viktor Ujcik .20 .50
26 Martin Prusek 1.00 2.50
27 Martin Prochazka .20 .50
28 Josef Straub .20 .50
29 Radek Gardon .20 .50
30 Lubos Horcicka .20 .50
31 Tomas Srsen .20 .50
32 Radovan Biegl .20 .50
33 Oldrich Svoboda .20 .50
34 Marek Uram .20 .50
35 Ladislav Blazek .40 1.00
36 Roman Malek .20 .50

2000 Czech Stadion

This set was issued in conjunction with Stadion, a Czech sports magazine. It was released in two series totaling 216 cards and featuring athletes of several different sports. The hockey cards from the set are listed below in checklist order.

COMPLETE SET (216) 100.00 200.00
5 Dominik Hasek 2.00 3.00
13 Roman Turek 1.20 .50
57 Jaromir Jagr 2.00 5.00
61 Mike Ricci .20 .50
64 Marty McSorley .20 .50
65 Martin Brodeur 2.00 10.00
66 Olaf Kolzig 1.20 1.50
67 Mark Messier 1.60 4.00
68 Eric Lindros 2.00 3.00
69 Robert Lang .20 .50
71 Milan Hejduk 1.60 3.00
72 Alexei Yashin .40 .50
74 Owen Nolan 1.20 1.00
75 Patrick Roy 6.00 15.00
76 Petr Svoboda .10 .25
77 Martin Straka .20 .50
79 Mario Lemieux 6.00 15.00
80 Petr Nedved .40 .50
81 Mats Sundin 1.20 3.00
82 Wayne Gretzky 8.00 25.00
83 Jaromir Jagr 2.00 5.00
84 Saku Koivu 1.20 3.00
85 Steve Yzerman 6.00 15.00
87 Mike Modano 1.60 3.00
90 Brian Leetch 1.20 2.00
91 Patrik Stefan 1.20 .50
92 Ed Belfour 1.60 4.00
93 Curtis Joseph 1.60 3.00
94 Brett Hull 1.60 4.00
95 Scott Stevens .80 1.00
96 Patrik Elias 1.20 1.00
99 Pavel Bure 2.00 3.00
109 Roman Turek .80 .50
110 Arturs Irbe .20 .50
111 Radek Dvorak .20 .50
112 Valeri Kamensky .20 .50
113 Jiri Slegr .20 .50
114 Alexander Mogilny .40 1.00
115 Peter Forsberg 3.20 5.00
116 Martin Havlat 4.00 10.00
117 Daniel Alfredsson .40 1.00
118 Theo Fleury 1.20 2.00
119 Sergei Brylin .10 .25
120 Patrick Roy 6.00 15.00
121 Patrick Lalime .80 1.50
122 Tomas Vokoun .40 1.50
123 Marian Hossa 1.20 3.00
124 Zigmund Palffy .80 1.00
125 Evgeni Nabokov 2.00 2.00
126 Jaroslav Modry .10 .25
145 Rob Blake 1.20 1.00
146 Jaromir Jagr 2.00 5.00
147 Mario Lemieux 6.00 15.00
148 Mario Lemieux 6.00 15.00
149 Al MacInnis .80 1.00
150 Mark Messier 1.60 4.00
151 Chris Pronger 1.20 2.00
152 Mike Richter 1.20 3.00
153 Brian Savage .20 .50
154 Maxim Afinogenov .40 1.00
155 Martin Biron 1.20 2.00
156 Martin Brodeur 2.00 10.00
157 Paul Coffey 1.20 2.00
158 Mariusz Czerkawski .20 .50
159 Wayne Gretzky 8.00 25.00
160 Michal Grosek .10 .25
161 Adam Graves .20 .50
162 J.Jagr/M.Lemieux 6.00 15.00
190 Dominik Hasek 2.00 3.00
191 Milan Hnilicka .80 1.00
192 Joe Sakic 2.00 5.00
193 Jocelyn Thibault 1.20 2.00
194 Vladimir Chebaturkin .10 .25
195 Bill Guerin 1.20 1.00
196 Krzysztof Oliwa .80 1.00
197 Bob Probert .80 2.00
198 Rick Tocchet .80 1.00

2001-02 Czech DS

COMPLETE SET (61) 15.00 30.00
1 Dominik Hasek 2.00 5.00
2 Vladimir Hudacek .20 .50
3 Roman Malek .10 .25
4 Mario Cartelli .10 .25
5 Tomas Kaberle .30 .75
6 Petr Kadlec .10 .25
7 Angel Nikolov .20 .50
8 Radek Philipp .10 .25
9 Libor Prochazka .10 .25
10 Michal Sykora .10 .25
11 Libor Zabransky .10 .25
12 Kamil Brabenec .10 .25
13 Michal Bros .10 .25
14 Jiri Burger .10 .25
15 Petr Cajanek .30 .75
16 Jaroslav Hlinka .10 .25
17 Viktor Hubl .10 .25
18 David Moravec .20 .50
19 Martin Prochazka .10 .25
20 Petr Sykora .10 .25
21 Jan Tomajko .10 .25
22 Viktor Ujcik .15 .35
23 Pavel Vostrak .10 .25
24 Jaroslav Bednar .20 .50
25 Martin Rucinsky .20 .50
26 Tomas Vokoun 1.25 3.00
27 Milan Hnilicka .20 .50
28 Josef Melichar .20 .50
29 Michal Rozsival .20 .50
30 Karel Pilar .20 .50
31 Jan Horacek .10 .25
32 Robert Schnabel .20 .50
33 Pavel Kolarik .20 .50
34 Petr Mika .20 .50
35 Petr Tenkrat .20 .50
36 Jaromir Jagr 2.00 5.00
37 Pavel Patera .20 .50
38 Josef Beranek .20 .50
39 Martin Straka .30 .75
40 Petr Nedved .30 .75
41 Martin Rucinsky .20 .50
42 Robert Reichel .20 .50
43 David Vyborny .40 1.00
44 Roman Hamrlik .30 .75
45 Milan Hejduk 1.25 3.00
46 Patrik Elias .75 2.00
47 Vaclav Prospal .20 .50
48 Vaclav Varada .20 .50
49 Petr Sykora .10 .25
50 Dusan Salficky .30 .75
51 Petr Briza .30 .75
52 Martin Prusek .40 1.00
53 Radek Martinek .20 .50
54 Karel Pilar .20 .50
55 Viktor Ujcik .15 .35
56 Vaclav Nedorost .40 1.00
57 Ales Kotalik .60 1.50
58 Jiri Dopita .20 .50
59 Robert Reichel .20 .50
60 Petr Cajanek .30 .75
61 David Moravec .20 .50

2001-02 Czech DS Best of the Best

COMPLETE SET (9) 5.00 10.00
STATED ODDS 1:3
BB1 Dominik Hasek 2.00 5.00
BB2 Tomas Kaberle .60 1.50
BB3 Michal Sykora .20 .50
BB4 Petr Cajanek .60 1.50
BB5 David Moravec .40 1.00
BB6 Martin Prochazka .20 .50
BB7 Martin Rucinsky .40 1.00
BB8 Robert Reichel .40 1.00
BB9 Jiri Dopita .40 1.00

2001-02 Czech DS Goalies

COMPLETE SET (5) 6.00 15.00
STATED ODDS 1:4
G1 Dominik Hasek 4.00 10.00
G2 Milan Hnilicka .75 2.00
G3 Petr Briza .75 2.00
G4 Roman Cechmanek .75 2.00
G5 Roman Malek .75 2.00

2001-02 Czech DS Ice Heroes

COMPLETE SET (10) 8.00 15.00
STATED ODDS 1:2
IH1 Tomas Vokoun 2.00 5.00
IH2 Jaromir Jagr 3.00 8.00
IH3 Pavel Patera .40 1.00
IH4 Josef Beranek .40 1.00
IH5 Martin Straka .75 2.00
IH6 Petr Nedved .60 1.50
IH7 Martin Rucinsky .40 1.00
IH8 Robert Reichel .40 1.00
IH9 David Vyborny .20 .50
IH10 Petr Tenkrat .60 1.50

2001-02 Czech DS Legends

COMPLETE SET (12) 3.00 6.00
STATED ODDS 1:2
L1 Jiri Holocek .40 1.00
L2 Jiri Kralik .20 .50
L3 Vlastimil Bubnik .40 1.00
L4 Vaclav Rozinak .20 .50
L5 Vladimir Zabrodsky .40 1.00
L6 Vladimir Martinec .40 1.00
L7 Ivan Hlinka .40 1.00
L8 Jan Havel .20 .50
L9 Frantisek Pospisil .20 .50
L10 Jaroslav Holik .20 .50
L11 Milan Novy .40 1.00
L12 Jiri Lala .20 .50

2001-02 Czech DS Top Gallery

COMPLETE SET (2) 8.00 15.00
STATED ODDS 1:10
1 Jaromir Jagr 4.00 10.00
2 Jaromir Jagr 4.00 10.00

2001-02 Czech National Team Postcards

COMPLETE SET (16) 20.00 40.00
1 Josef Beranek .75 2.00
2 Petr Briza .75 2.00
3 Josef Beranek .75 2.00
4 Radek Duda .75 2.00
5 Jiri Hudler 2.00 5.00
6 Jaromir Jagr 4.00 10.00
7 Richard Kral .75 2.00
8 Frantisek Kucera .75 2.00
9 David Moravec .75 2.00
10 Karel Rachunek .75 2.00
11 Martin Richter .75 2.00
12 Dusan Salficky .75 2.00
13 Michal Sykora .75 2.00
14 Viktor Ujcik .75 2.00
15 Tomas Vlasak .75 2.00
16 Vladimir Vujtek .75 2.00
17 Michal Bros .75 2.00

2001-02 Czech OFS

This set features the top players of the Czech Elite League. The cards were sold in pack form. The set is noteworthy for including an early card of Jiri Hudler.

COMPLETE SET (284) 25.00 50.00
1 Lukas Hronek .08 .20
2 Petr Martinek .08 .20
3 Petr Kadlec .08 .20
4 Roman Malek .08 .20
5 Jan Alinc .20 .50
6 Josef Beranek .20 .50
7 Viktor Hubl .08 .20
8 Martin Rousek .08 .20
9 Radek Matejovsky .08 .20
10 Jan Kloboucek .08 .20
11 Daniel Brandl .08 .20
12 Viktor Ujcik .20 .50
13 Milan Antos .08 .20
14 Radek Belohlav .08 .20
15 Michal Bros .20 .50
16 Petr Briza .20 .50
17 Radek Hamr .08 .20
18 Jaroslav Hlinka .08 .20
19 Martin Chabada .08 .20
20 Pavel Kasparik .08 .20
21 Marek Ivan .08 .20
22 Lukas Galvas .08 .20
23 Radek Simicek .08 .20
24 Robert Tomanek .08 .20
25 Jan Tomajko .08 .20
26 Ivan Padelek .08 .20
27 Zdenek Pavelek .08 .20
28 Radek Philipp .08 .20
29 Pavel Srek .08 .20
30 David Moravec .20 .50
31 Jan Srdinko .08 .20
32 Marek Melenovsky .20 .50
33 Frantisek Ptacek .08 .20
34 Vaclav Novak .08 .20
35 Jaroslav Nedved .20 .50
36 Ludek Krayzel .08 .20
37 Roman Kadera .08 .20
38 Petr Jurecka .08 .20
39 Lukas Smolka .08 .20
40 Vitezslav Skuta .08 .20
41 Josef Straub .08 .20
42 Jiri Trvaj .08 .20
43 Jan Vytisk .08 .20
44 Daniel Zapotocny .08 .20
45 Pavel Selingr .08 .20
46 Martin Prochazka .20 .50
47 Vlastimil Lakosil .08 .20
48 Petr Gregorek .08 .20
49 Mario Cartelli .08 .20
50 Miloslav Guren .20 .50
51 Petr Jancarik .08 .20
52 Libor Prochazka .20 .50
53 Jan Slavik .08 .20
54 Pavel Janku .08 .20
55 Branislav Janos .08 .20
56 Marek Zadina .08 .20
57 Jiri Polak .08 .20
58 Ondrej Nemec .08 .20
59 Petr Kubos .08 .20
60 Slavomir Hrina .08 .20
61 Ivo Pesat .08 .20
62 Radovan Biegl .20 .50
63 Zdenek Skorepa .20 .50
64 Roman Meluzin .08 .20
65 Jan Marek .08 .20
66 Richard Kral .08 .20
67 Rostislav Vlach .08 .20
68 Ondrej Vetchy .08 .20
69 Petr Vampola .08 .20
70 Lukas Valko .08 .20
71 Michal Sararcik .08 .20
72 Martin Streit .08 .20
73 Radim Kucharczyk .08 .20
74 Jiri Hudler 8.00 20.00
75 Jiri Burger .08 .20
76 Martin Strbak .08 .20
77 Martin Ambruz .08 .20
78 Jakub Blazek .08 .20
79 Pavel Mojzis .08 .20
80 Jiri Marusak .08 .20
81 Rostislav Malena .08 .20
82 Jan Homer .08 .20
83 Martin Hamrlik .08 .20
84 Petr Tucek .08 .20
85 Vladimir Hubacek .08 .20
86 Ales Zacha .08 .20
87 Radovan Somik .08 1.00
88 Ivan Rachunek .08 .20
89 Libor Pivko .08 .20
90 Milan Ministr .08 .20
91 Petr Leska .08 .20
92 Martin Jenacek .08 .20
93 Petr Cajanek .30 .75
94 Karol Bartanus .20 .50
95 Jaroslav Balastik .08 .20
96 Petr Havelka .08 .20
97 Jan Hanzlik .08 .20
98 Petr Prikryl .08 .20
99 Libor Zabransky .20 .50
100 David Hnat .08 .20
101 David Pazourek .08 .20
102 Zbynek Marak .08 .20
103 Radek Haman .08 .20
104 Karel Soudek .08 .20
105 Pavel Kumstat .08 .20
106 Tomas Jakes .08 .20
107 Vladimir Holik .08 .20
108 Jiri Hes .08 .20
109 David Havir .08 .20
110 Oldrich Svoboda .20 .50
111 Ladislav Kudrna .20 .50
112 Valdemar Jirus .08 .20
113 Miroslav Okal .08 .20
114 Peter Bohunicky .08 .20
115 Patrik Hucko .08 .20
116 Miroslav Blatak .08 .20
117 Tomas Netik .08 .20
118 Richard Zemlicka .20 .50
119 Marek Uram .08 .20
120 Peter Pucher .08 .20
121 Lukas Krajicek ERC .75 2.00
122 Michal Klimes .08 .20
123 Josef Jindra .08 .20
124 Ladislav Cierny .08 .20
125 Michal Marik .08 .20
126 Josef Kucera .08 .20
127 Michal Kolarik .08 .20
128 Jiri Hasek .08 .20
129 David Nosek .08 .20
130 Martin Vojtek .08 .20
131 Milan Nedoma .08 .20
132 Rudolf Suchanek .08 .20
133 Filip Vanecek .08 .20
134 Pavel Zubicek .08 .20
135 Kamil Brabenec .08 .20
136 Jiri Broz .08 .20
137 Dan Hlavka .08 .20
138 Stepan Hrebejk .08 .20
139 Roman Horak .08 .20
140 Milan Michalek ERC 6.00 15.00
141 Peter Bartos .20 .50
142 Michal Vondrka .08 .20
143 Jiri Simanek .08 .20
144 Petr Sailer .08 .20
145 Lubos Rob .08 .20
146 Jan Rehor .08 .20
147 Martin Strba .08 .20
148 Marek Pinc .08 .20
149 Vladimir Gyna .08 .20
150 Jan Hranac .08 .20
151 Martin Nosek .08 .20
152 Lukas Pozivil .08 .20
153 Vojtech Kubincak .08 .20
154 Anton Lezo .08 .20
155 Martin Tupa .08 .20
156 Vlastimil Kroupa .20 .50
157 Jindrich Kotrla .08 .20
158 David Hruska .08 .20
159 Petr Jira .08 .20
160 Michal Oliverius .08 .20
161 Lukas Havel .08 .20
162 Jaroslav Buchal .08 .20
163 Jan Sulc .08 .20
164 Pavol Rieciciar .08 .20
165 Petr Klima .20 .50
166 Jiri Gombar .08 .20
167 Tomas Kaberle .20 .50
168 Ladislav Svoboda .08 .20
169 Pavel Geffert .08 .20
170 Tomas Horna .08 .20
171 Zdenek Orct .20 .50
172 Robert Kysela .08 .20
173 Radek Gardon .08 .20
174 Ondrej Kriz .20 .50
175 Tomas Klimt .20 .50
176 Jan Bohacek .20 .50
177 Michal Havel .08 .20
178 David Hajek .08 .20
179 Vaclav Skuhravy .08 .20
180 Radim Skuhrovec .08 .20
181 Tomas Plekanec .08 .20
182 Jan Dlouhy .08 .20
183 David Patera .08 .20
184 Jan Krulis .08 .20
185 Jan Pospisil .08 .20
186 David Appel .08 .20
187 Jakub Kraus .08 .20
188 Petr Machulda .08 .20
189 Petr Franek .08 .20
190 Jaromir Kverka .08 .20
191 Michal Madl .08 .20
192 Marcel Kucera .08 .20
193 Jakub Grof .08 .20
194 Michal Dobron .08 .20
195 Jan Kopecky .08 .20
196 Dmitrij Rodine .08 .20
197 David Balasz .08 .20
198 Roman Prosek .08 .20
199 Jan Kostal .08 .20
200 Petr Domin .08 .20
201 Jan Choteborsky .08 .20
202 Vaclav Benak .08 .20
203 Miroslav Simonovic .08 .20
204 Jiri Hanzlik .08 .20
205 Josef Reznicek .08 .20
206 Ivan Vlcek .08 .20
207 Libor Barta .08 .20
208 Ondrej Steiner .08 .20
209 Dusan Andrasovsky .08 .20
210 Martin Vyborny .08 .20
211 Juraj Stefanka .08 .20
212 Radek Duda .08 .20
213 Josef Slanec .08 .20
214 Michal Dvorak .08 .20
215 Libor Pavlis .08 .20
216 Vaclav Eiselt .08 .20
217 Tomas Nemcicky .08 .20
218 Petr Mudroch .08 .20
219 Patrik Moskal .08 .20
220 Zdenek Sedlak .08 .20
221 Pavel Vostrak .08 .20
222 Milan Volak .08 .20
223 Petr Mudroch .08 .20
224 Jiri Malinsky .08 .20
225 Jan Svik .08 .20
226 Petr Caslava .08 .20
227 Michal Straka .08 .20
228 Adam Svoboda .20 .50
229 Josef Straka .20 .50
230 Patrik Rimmel .08 .20
231 Petr Pavlas .08 .20
232 Michael Prochazka .20 .50
233 Miroslav Javin .08 .20
234 Robin Bacul .08 .20
235 Marek Cernosek .08 .20
236 Petr Folta .08 .20
237 Pavel Malac .08 .20
238 Radek Krestan .08 .20
239 Lubomir Korhon .08 .20
240 Pavel Cagas .20 .50
241 Radoslav Kropac .08 .20
242 Dusan Pohorelec .08 .20
243 Petr Vala .08 .20
244 Pavel Zdrahal .08 .20
245 Otakar Janecky .20 .50
246 Tomas Blazek .20 .50
247 Michael Vyhlidal .20 .50
248 Michal Sykora .20 .50
249 Tomas Pacal .08 .20
250 Andrej Novotny .08 .20
251 Tomas Rolinek .08 .20
252 Stanislav Prochazka .08 .20
253 David Pospisil .08 .20
254 Michal Mikeska .08 .20
255 Ladislav Lubina .08 .20
256 Jaroslav Kudrna .20 .50
257 Tomas Vak .08 .20
258 Michal Tvrdik .08 .20
259 Petr Sykora .20 .50
260 Jan Bokoc .08 .20
261 Milan Prochazka .08 .20
262 Patrik Fink .08 .20
263 Richard Kuckrek .08 .20
264 Marek Vorel .08 .20
265 Tomas Klimes .08 .20
266 Premysl Sedlak .08 .20
267 David Hajek .08 .20
268 Ladislav Vlcek .08 .20
269 Jiri Kames .20 .50
270 Radek Krestan .08 .20
271 Jan Hejda .08 .20
272 Borek Stagma .08 .20
273 Leos Cermak .08 .20
274 Jan Novak .08 .20
275 Zbynek Tuma .08 .20
276 Daniel Bohac .08 .20
277 Michal Sup .08 .20
278 Jan Snopek .08 .20
279 Adam Saffer .08 .20
280 David Pojkar .08 .20
281 Marek Tomica .08 .20
282 Petr Jurecka .08 .20
283 Lukas Krenzelok .08 .20
284 Michael Prochazka .20 .50

2001-02 Czech OFS All Stars

These cards were randomly inserted into packs of Czech OFS.

COMPLETE SET (41) 17.78 44.44
1 Martin Hamrlik .40 1.00
2 Petr Gregorek .40 1.00
3 Oldrich Svoboda .80 2.00
4 Radim Tesarik .40 1.00
5 Jiri Dopita 1.20 3.00
6 Petr Cajanek .80 2.00
7 Marek Uram .40 1.00
8 Michael Vyhlidal .40 1.00
9 Mario Cartelli .40 1.00
10 Pavel Zdrahal .40 1.00
11 Libor Prochazka .80 2.00
12 Ales Pisa .80 2.00
13 Robert Reichel .80 2.00
14 Josef Reznicek .40 1.00
15 Karel Pilar 1.20 3.00
16 Dusan Salficky .80 2.00
17 Patrik Martinec .40 1.00
18 Rudolf Suchanek .40 1.00
19 Jaromir Kverka .40 1.00
20 Ladislav Svoboda .40 1.00
21 Daniel Branda .40 1.00
22 Jan Pardavy .40 1.00
23 David Moravec .80 2.00
24 Zbynek Marak .40 1.00
25 Petr Leska .40 1.00
26 Jiri Marusak .40 1.00
27 Roman Stantien .40 1.00
28 Jan Srdinko .40 1.00
29 Martin Prusek 2.00 5.00
30 Libor Pivko .40 1.00
31 Zdenek Pavelek .40 1.00
32 Jaroslav Hlinka .40 1.00
33 Otakar Janecky .80 2.00
34 Petr Kadlec .80 2.00
35 Ales Kotalik 1.20 3.00
36 Jan Krulis .40 1.00
37 Robert Tomik .40 1.00
38 Petr Sykora .80 2.00
39 Ivan Vlcek .40 1.00
40 Pavel Vostrak .40 1.00
41 Vladimir Vujtek .40 1.00

2001-02 Czech OFS Gold Inserts

These cards were randomly inserted into packs of Czech OFS. We have no confirmation on insertion rate.

COMPLETE SET (11) 20.00 40.00
G1 Roman Malek 2.00 5.00
G2 Petr Franek 2.00 5.00
G3 Petr Prikryl 2.00 5.00
G4 Vlastimil Lakosil 2.00 5.00
G5 Radovan Biegl 2.00 5.00
G6 Vladimir Hudacek 2.00 5.00
G7 Oldrich Svoboda 2.00 5.00
G8 Josef Kucera 2.00 5.00
G9 Michal Marik 2.00 5.00
G10 Miroslav Simonovic 2.00 5.00
G11 Pavel Malac 2.00 5.00

2001-02 Czech OFS H Inserts

These cards were randomly inserted into packs of Czech OFS. We have no confirmation on insertion rate.

COMPLETE SET (15) 25.00 50.00
H1 Lukas Hronek 1.50 4.00
H2 Marcel Kucera 1.50 4.00
H3 Zdenek Orct 2.00 5.00
H4 Martin Vojtek 1.50 4.00
H5 Jan Pospisil 1.50 4.00
H6 Lukas Smolka 1.50 4.00
H7 Jiri Trvaj 1.50 4.00
H8 Ivo Pesat 1.50 4.00
H9 Petr Tucek 1.50 4.00
H10 Ladislav Kudrna 1.50 4.00
H11 Marek Pinc 1.50 4.00
H12 Pavel Cagas 1.50 4.00
H13 Adam Svoboda 2.00 5.00
H14 Libor Barta 1.50 4.00
H15 Petr Briza 2.50 6.00

2001-02 Czech OFS Red Inserts

These cards were randomly inserted into packs of Czech OFS. We have no confirmation on insertion rate.

COMPLETE SET (24) 50.00
RE1D Viktor Ujcik .75 2.00
RE2D Josef Beranek .75 2.00
RE3D Tomas Plekanec .75 2.00
RE4D Tomas Kaberle 1.25 3.00
RE5D Jiri Zelenka .75 2.00
RE6D Martin Prochazka .75 2.00
RE7D David Moravec .75 2.00
RE8D Petr Klima .75 2.00
RE9D Rudolf Suchanek .75 2.00
RE10D Frantisek Kucera .75 2.00
RE11D Michal Sykora .75 2.00
RE12D Otakar Janecky .75 2.00
RE13D Pavel Zdrahal .75 2.00
RE14D Radoslav Kropac .75 2.00
RE15D Rostislav Vlach .75 2.00
RE16D Marek Uram .75 2.00
RE17D Petr Leska .75 2.00
RE18D Petr Cajanek 1.25 3.00
RE19D Ondrej Kratena 1.25 3.00
RE20D Petr Korinek .75 2.00
RE21D Jiri Hudler 6.00 15.00
RE22D Pavel Janku 2.00
RE23D Richard Kral 2.00
RE24D Miloslav Guren 2.00

2001 Czech Stadion

This set was issued in conjunction with the Czech sports magazine Stadion. It is a multi-sport issue. We have only included hockey players, so it is listed below in skip-numbered form.

COMPLETE SET (45) 30.00 60.00
217 Ray Bourque 2.00 5.00
218 Patrik Elias .75 2.00
219 Milan Hejduk .75 2.00
220 Bobby Holik .40 1.00
221 Tomas Kaberle .40 1.00
222 Nick Lidstrom 1.25 3.00
223 Petr Sykora .40 1.00
224 Martin Skoula .40 1.00
225 Alex Tanguay .75 2.00
226 Daniel Alfredsson .75 2.00
227 Jason Allison .40 1.00
228 Adam Deadmarsh .40 1.00
229 Chris Drury .75 2.00
230 Bob Essensa .40 1.00
231 Scott Gomez .40 1.00
233 Tomas Holmstrom .75 2.00
234 Darius Kasparaitis .40 1.00
235 Pavel Brendl .40 1.00
236 Eric Lindros 1.25 3.00
237 Rostislav Klesla .40 1.00
238 Scott Niedermayer .40 1.00
239 Brett Hull 1.25 3.00
240 Paul Kariya 1.25 3.00
241 Chris Gratton .40 1.00
242 Doug Gilmour .75 2.00
243 Alexei Yashin .40 1.00
244 Saku Koivu .75 2.00
245 Randy McKay .40 1.00
246 Markus Naslund .75 2.00
247 Keith Primeau .40 1.00
248 Dainius Zubrus .40 1.00
249 Dominik Hasek 1.50 4.00
250 Frantisek Kaberle .40 1.00
251 Jaromir Jagr 2.00 5.00
252 Jaromir Jagr (Tennis) 2.00 5.00
253 Rob Blake .40 1.00
254 Adam Oates .40 1.00
255 Joe Sakic 2.00 5.00
256 Alexei Kovalev .40 1.00
257 Ivan Hlinka .40 1.00
258 Martin Straka .40 1.00
259 Milan Hnilicka .40 1.00
260 Miroslav Satan .40 1.00
261 Peter Bondra .40 1.00
324 John Leclair .40 1.00

2002-03 Czech DS

This set features the top Czech players in the world. The first 40 cards in the set are base cards. 41-54 are Young Heroes (1:2); 55-75 are Jagr Team base cards; 76-82 are Goalies (1:3); 83-89 are Best Shooters (1:3); 90-96 are Power Stars (1:3) and 97-100 are Stanley Cup Champs (1:7).

COMPLETE SET (100) 30.00 60.00
41-54 ODDS 1:2
55-96 ODDS 1:3
97-100 ODDS 1:7
1 Milan Hnilicka .40 1.00
2 Dusan Salficky .30 .75
3 Petr Briza .30 .75
4 Adam Svoboda .30 .75
5 Frantisek Kucera .10 .25
6 Petr Kadlec .10 .25
7 Karel Rachunek .30 .75
8 Richard Kral .10 .25
9 Josef Beranek .20 .50
10 Radek Duda .10 .25
11 Petr Mudroch .10 .25
12 Milan Michalek 2.00 5.00
13 Tomas Kucharcik .10 .25
14 Frantisek Kaberle .10 .25
15 Rostislav Klesla .75 2.00
16 Filip Kuba .20 .50
17 Pavel Kubina .30 .75
18 Jaroslav Spacek .20 .50
19 Michal Sykora .10 .25
20 Martin Richter .10 .25
21 Michal Bros .10 .25
22 Petr Cajanek .30 .75
23 Jaroslav Hlinka .10 .25
24 Jan Hrdina .40 1.00
25 Jaromir Jagr 2.00 5.00
26 David Moravec .20 .50
27 Pavel Patera .20 .50
28 Martin Prochazka .10 .25
29 Zdenek Sedlak .10 .25
30 Viktor Ujcik .20 .50
31 Tomas Vlasak .10 .25
32 Ondrej Kratena .10 .25
33 David Vyborny .10 .25
34 Vladimir Vujtek .20 .50
35 Petr Leska .10 .25

36 Marek Zidlicky .30 .75
37 Jaroslav Balastik .10 .25
38 Libor Pivko .10 .25
39 David Hruska .10 .25
40 Jiri Marusak .10 .25
41 Milan Hnilicka 2.00 5.00
42 Tomas Vokoun .20 .50
43 Jaroslav Spacek .20 .50
44 Jaroslav Bednar .10 .25
45 Martin Rucinsky .10 .25
46 Jaromir Jagr .20 .50
47 Karel Pilar 2.00 5.00
48 David Vyborny .10 .25
49 Frantisek Kaberle .20 .50
50 Tomas Kaberle .10 .25
51 Vaclav Prospal .40 1.00
52 Jan Hrdina .10 .25
53 Robert Reichel .20 .50
54 Josef Melichar .10 .25
55 Jan Hlavac .40 1.00
56 Jiri Fischer .75 2.00
57 Milan Hejduk .20 .50
58 Jiri Dopita .40 1.00
59 Vaclav Varada .20 .50
60 Patrik Stefan 2.00 5.00
61 Milan Kraft .20 .50
62 Jiri Hudler .10 .25
63 Libor Ustrnul .10 .25
64 Lukas Hronek .30 .75
65 Miroslav Blatak .20 .50
66 Jan Hanzlik .40 1.00
67 Jiri Novotny .20 .50
68 Ales Hemsky .20 .50
69 Tomas Plekanec .20 .50
70 Filip Novak .75 2.00
71 Miloslav Horava 1.50 4.00
72 Lukas Krajicek .20 .50
73 Tomas Mojzis .20 .50
74 Jiri Jakes .40 1.00
75 Jan Bohac .40 1.00
76 Milan Hnilicka .40 1.00
77 Dusan Salficky .30 .75
78 Roman Malek .10 .25
79 Tomas Vokoun .75 2.00
80 Lukas Hronek .10 .25
81 Petr Briza .30 .75
82 Adam Svoboda .30 .75
83 Viktor Ujcik .20 .50
84 Martin Prochazka .10 .25
85 Petr Cajanek .30 .75
86 Pavel Patera .20 .50
87 Radek Duda .10 .25
88 Tomas Vlasak .10 .25
89 Jaromir Jagr 2.00 5.00
90 Jaromir Jagr 2.00 5.00
91 Robert Reichel .20 .50
92 Frantisek Kaberle .10 .25
93 Jaroslav Spacek .20 .50
94 Jan Hlavac .20 .50
95 Martin Rucinsky .20 .50
96 Tomas Kaberle .30 .75
97 Dominik Hasek 1.25 3.00
98 Dominik Hasek 1.25 3.00
99 Dominik Hasek 1.25 3.00
100 Checklist .10 .25

2002-03 Czech OFS Plus

COMPLETE SET (369) 75.00 125.00
1 Daniel Branda .20 .50
2 Michal Bros .20 .50
3 Petr Briza .30 .75
4 Jan Hanzlik .20 .50
5 Petr Havelka .20 .50
6 Valdemar Jirus .20 .50
7 Pavel Kasparik .20 .50
8 Ondrej Kratena .20 .50
9 Petr Leska .20 .50
10 Patrik Martinec .20 .50
11 Jaroslav Nedved .20 .50
12 Petr Prikryl .20 .50
13 Frantisek Ptacek .20 .50
14 Martin Richter .20 .50
15 Jan Srdinko .20 .50
16 Martin Spanhel .20 .50
17 Pavel Srek .20 .50
18 Jan Tomajko .20 .50
19 Robert Tomik .20 .50
20 Roman Vondracek .20 .50
21 Jiri Zelenka .20 .50
22 Richard Zemlicka .20 .50
23 Jaroslav Balastik .60 1.50
24 Miroslav Blatak .20 .50
25 Martin Cech .20 .50
26 Lukas Galvas .20 .50
27 Martin Hamrlik .20 .50
28 Jan Homer .20 .50
29 Slavomir Hrina .20 .50
30 Petr Hubacek .20 .50
31 Patrik Hucko .20 .50
32 Martin Jenacek .20 .50
33 Jiri Marusak .20 .50
34 Milan Ministr .20 .50
35 Petr Mokrejs .20 .50
36 Miroslav Okal .20 .50
37 Ivo Pesat .20 .50
38 Libor Pivko .20 .50
39 Ivan Rachunek .20 .50
40 Petr Tucek .20 .50
41 Ondrej Vesely .20 .50
42 Rostislav Vlach .20 .50
43 Ladislav Vlcek .20 .50
44 Martin Zahorovsky .20 .50
45 Pavel Zubicek .20 .50
46 Jiri Burger .20 .50
47 Marek Cernosek .20 .50
48 Martin Falter .20 .50
49 Stanislav Gron .40 1.00
50 Jakub Hulva .20 .50
51 Lukas Chmelir .20 .50
52 Zbynek Irgl .30 .75
53 Petr Jurecka .20 .50
54 Roman Kadera .20 .50
55 Ludek Krayzel .20 .50
56 Leszek Laszkiewicz .20 .50
57 Marek Melenovsky .20 .50
58 David Moravec .20 .50
59 Ales Padelek .20 .50
60 Ivan Padelek .20 .50
61 Radek Philipp .20 .50
62 Martin Ambruz .20 .50
63 Peter Bartek .20 .50
64 Radovan Biegl .30 .75
65 Tomas Demel .20 .50
66 Marek Dubec .20 .50
67 Jiri Hudler 10.00 25.00
68 Alexej Jaskin .20 .50
69 Petr Kubos .20 .50
70 Radim Kucharczyk .20 .50
71 Patrik Luza .20 .50
72 Ondrej Nemec .20 .50
73 Lukas Plsek .20 .50
74 Jiri Polak .20 .50
75 Bohuslav Ptacek .20 .50
76 Jan Sochor .20 .50
77 Roman Stantien .20 .50
78 Martin Streit .20 .50
79 Tomas Vak .20 .50
80 Lukas Valko .20 .50
81 Petr Vampola .20 .50
82 Jiri Hasek .20 .50
83 Lubos Horcicka .20 .50
84 Tomas Houdek .20 .50
85 Jiri Hunkes .20 .50
86 Marek Ivan .20 .50
87 Petr Jancarik .20 .50
88 Pavel Janku .20 .50
89 Richard Kral .20 .50
90 Vlastimil Lakosil .20 .50
91 Jiri Malinsky .20 .50
92 Jan Marek .20 .50
93 Rostislav Martynek .20 .50
94 Roman Meluzin .20 .50
95 Marian Morava .20 .50
96 David Nosek .20 .50
97 Zdenek Pavelek .20 .50
98 Gregor Poloncic .20 .50
99 Libor Prochazka .20 .50
100 Marek Zadina .20 .50
101 Tomas Zboril .20 .50
102 Boris Zabka .20 .50
103 Martin Altrichter .20 .50
104 Miroslav Barus .20 .50
105 Vaclav Benak .20 .50
106 Roman Erat .20 .50
107 Radek Haman .20 .50
108 David Havir .20 .50
109 Ales Kretinsky .20 .50
110 Pavel Kumstat .20 .50
111 Petr Kumstat .20 .50
112 David Ludvik .20 .50
113 Jan Mikulik .20 .50
114 Karel Plasek .20 .50
115 Jan Plch .20 .50
116 Milan Prochazka .20 .50
117 Peter Pucher .20 .50
118 Jaroslav Sklenar .20 .50
119 Jan Snopek .20 .50
120 Karel Soudek .20 .50
121 Oldrich Svoboda .20 .50
122 Milan Toman .20 .50
123 Marek Uram .20 .50
124 Marek Vorel .20 .50
125 Lukas Bednarik .20 .50
126 Daniel Bohac .20 .50
127 Jakub Cech .20 .50
128 Michal Cech .20 .50
129 Vratislav Cech .20 .50
130 Ales Cerny .20 .50
131 Juraj Durco .20 .50
132 Martin Filip .20 .50
133 Petr Folta .20 .50
134 Tomas Harant .20 .50
135 Martin Holy .20 .50
136 Jan Kopecky .20 .50
137 Jiri Kucera .20 .50
138 Michal Marik .20 .50
139 Petr Pavlas .20 .50
140 Albin Podstavek .20 .50
141 Radek Prochazka .20 .50
142 Rene Pucher .20 .50
143 Tomas Srsen .20 .50
144 Ales Stanek .20 .50
145 Vaclav Studeny .20 .50
146 Filip Stefanka .20 .50
147 Milan Beranek .20 .50
148 Martin Cakajik .20 .50
149 Pavel Falta .20 .50
150 Miroslav Hajek .20 .50
151 Jan Holub .20 .50
152 Vitezslav Jankovych .20 .50
153 Pavel Kabrt .20 .50
154 Vaclav Koci .20 .50
155 Radoslav Kropac .20 .50
156 Angel Krstev .20 .50
157 Vojtech Kubincak .20 .50
158 Jiri Kudrna .20 .50
159 Pavel Malecek .20 .50
160 Jiri Moravec .20 .50
161 Mojmir Musil .20 .50
162 Vaclav Novak .20 .50
163 Jan Plodek .20 .50
164 Robert Pospisil .20 .50
165 Stanislav Prochazka .20 .50
166 Patrik Rozsival .20 .50
167 Michal Straka .20 .50
168 Daniel Babka .20 .50
169 Michal Barinka .20 .50
170 Petr Bartos .20 .50
171 Jiri Broz .20 .50
172 Petr Gregorek .20 .50
173 Stepan Hrebejk .20 .50
174 Vladimir Hudacek .20 .50
175 Josef Jindra .20 .50
176 Ivo Kotaska .20 .50
177 Josef Kucera .20 .50
178 Milan Michalek 4.00 10.00
179 Frantisek Mrazek .20 .50
180 Jan Mucha .20 .50
181 Milan Nedoma .20 .50
182 Zdenek Ondrej .20 .50
183 Lubos Rob .20 .50
184 Petr Sailer .20 .50
185 Rudolf Suchanek .20 .50
186 Jiri Simanek .20 .50
187 Martin Strba .20 .50
188 Filip Turek .20 .50
189 Michal Vondrka .20 .50
190 Jan Alinc .20 .50
191 Jiri Gombar .20 .50
192 Vladimir Gyna .20 .50
193 Lukas Havel .20 .50
194 Jan Hranac .20 .50
195 Petr Klima .20 .50
196 Jan Kloboucek .20 .50
197 Jindrich Kotrla .20 .50
198 Vlastimil Kroupa .20 .50
199 Jiri Kuntos .20 .50
200 Petr Macholda .20 .50
201 Tomas Martinec .20 .50
202 Marek Pinc .20 .50
203 Michal Podolka .20 .50
204 Lukas Pozivil .20 .50
205 Ivo Prorok .20 .50
206 Lukas Riha .20 .50
207 Stanislav Stavensky .20 .50
208 Jiri Slegr .20 .50
209 Jan Sulc .20 .50
210 Martin Tupa .20 .50
211 Martin Barek .20 .50
212 Jakub Barton .20 .50
213 Tomas Blazek .20 .50
214 Tomas Divisek .40 1.00
215 Miroslav Duben .20 .50
216 Otakar Janecky .20 .50
217 Jan Kolar .20 .50
218 Petr Koukal .20 .50
219 Ladislav Lubina .20 .50
220 Michal Mikeska .20 .50
221 Petr Mocek .20 .50
222 Petr Mudroch .20 .50
223 Andrej Novotny .20 .50
224 Lubomir Pistek .20 .50
225 David Pospisil .20 .50
226 Petr Prucha ERC 6.00 15.00
227 Tomas Rolinek .20 .50
228 Petr Caslava .20 .50
229 Adam Svoboda .30 .75
230 Michal Sykora .20 .50
231 Petr Sykora .20 .50
232 Michael Vyhlidal .20 .50
233 Milan Antos .20 .50
234 Josef Beranek .20 .50
235 Dominik Granak .20 .50
236 Jan Hejda .40 1.00
237 Lukas Hronek .20 .50
238 David Hruska .20 .50
239 Petr Jaros .20 .50
240 Petr Kadlec .20 .50
241 Jakub Klepis ERC 1.25 3.00
242 Pavel Kolarik .20 .50
243 Frantisek Kucera .20 .50
244 Roman Malek .20 .50
245 Petr Mika .30 .75
246 Jan Novak .20 .50
247 Marek Posmyk .20 .50
248 Ondrej Steiner .20 .50
249 Michal Sup .20 .50
250 Adam Saffer .20 .50
251 Josef Straub .20 .50
252 Marek Tomica .20 .50
253 Viktor Ujcik .20 .50
254 Dusan Andrasovsky .20 .50
255 Libor Barta .20 .50
256 Michal Dobron .20 .50
257 Radek Duda .20 .50
258 Michal Dvorak .20 .50
259 Robert Hamrla .20 .50
260 Jiri Hanzlik .20 .50
261 Petr Chvojka .20 .50
262 Vaclav Kral .20 .50
263 Ales Kratoska .20 .50
264 Radek Matejovsky .20 .50
265 Josef Reznicek .20 .50
266 Josef Straka .20 .50
267 Jaroslav Spelda .20 .50
268 Juraj Stefanka .20 .50
269 Jan Svik .20 .50
270 Ivan Vlcek .20 .50
271 Milan Voboril .20 .50
272 Milan Volak .20 .50
273 Josef Voskar .20 .50
274 Martin Vyborny .20 .50
275 Robin Bacul .20 .50
276 David Balasz .20 .50
277 Richard Bauer .20 .50
278 Petr Franek .20 .50
279 Jakub Grof .20 .50
280 Martin Hlavacka .20 .50
281 Jan Kostal .20 .50
282 Lukas Krajicek .60 1.50
283 Jakub Kraus .20 .50
284 Marcel Kucera .20 .50
285 Jaromir Kverka .20 .50
286 Michal Madl .20 .50
287 Tomas Nemcicky .20 .50
288 Martin Opatovsky .20 .50
289 Libor Pavlis .20 .50
290 Petr Puncochar .20 .50
291 Dmitri Rodine .20 .50
292 Vaclav Skuhravy .20 .50
293 Ladislav Svoboda .20 .50
294 Petr Sinagl .20 .50
295 Marek Topoli .20 .50
296 Kamil Tvrdek .20 .50
297 Pavel Selinger .20 .50
298 Radim Tesarik .20 .50
299 Jiri Trvaj .20 .50
300 Jan Vytisk .20 .50
301 Danniel Zapotocny .20 .50
302 Michal Divisek .20 .50
303 Jiri Dobrovolny .20 .50
304 Michal Kello .20 .50
305 Radek Krestan .20 .50
306 Tomas Micka .20 .50
307 Petr Mika .20 .50
308 Jan Dresler .20 .50
309 Rostislav Olesz ERC 4.00 10.00
310 Lukas Zatopek .20 .50
311 Vaclav Pletka .30 .75
312 Lukas Krenzelok .20 .50
313 Lukas Smolka .20 .50
314 Jaroslav Sklenar .20 .50
315 Richard Bordowski .20 .50
316 Mario Cartelli .20 .50
317 Tomas Horna .20 .50
318 Petr Hrbek .20 .50
319 Martin Kotasek .20 .50
320 Jan Korotvicka .20 .50
321 Michal Tvrdik .20 .50
322 David Pojkar .20 .50
323 Martin Adamsky .20 .50
324 Jaroslav Kracik .20 .50
325 Miloslav Topol .20 .50
326 Vojtech Polak .20 .50
327 Lukas Pech .20 .50
328 Jaroslav Hasek .20 .50
329 Jan Kudrna .20 .50
330 Jan Visek .20 .50
331 Patrik Moskal .20 .50
332 Zdenek Smid .20 .50
333 Michal Travnicek .20 .50
334 Martin Nosek .20 .50
335 Zdenek Skorepa .20 .50
336 Jan Horacek .20 .50
337 David Appel .20 .50
338 Petr Svoboda .20 .50
339 Jan Nemecek .20 .50
340 Jan Kotatko .20 .50
341 Ales Vala .20 .50
342 Radek Mrazek .20 .50
343 Viktor Hubl .20 .50
344 Jaroslav Kudrna .20 .50
345 Tomas Pacal .20 .50
346 David Mazanec .20 .50
347 Radek Prochazka .20 .50
348 Ales Kratoska .20 .50
349 Michal Marik .20 .50
350 Ladislav Vlcek .20 .50
351 Jiri Hanzlik .20 .50
352 Jaroslav Hubl .20 .50
353 Martin Tuma .20 .50
354 Petr Martinek .20 .50
355 Michal Divisek .20 .50
356 Lubomir Hurtaj .20 .50
357 Jakub Koreis ERC .75 2.00
358 Ondrej Kubes .20 .50
359 Viktor Ujcik .20 .50
360 Radek Dlouhy .20 .50
361 Radek Duda .20 .50
362 Milan Kopecky .20 .50
363 Patrik Stejskal .20 .50
364 Vaclav Pletka .30 .75
365 Radek Masny .20 .50
366 Zbynek Spitzer .20 .50
367 Tomas Frolo .20 .50
368 Martin Filip .20 .50
369 Ivan Rachunek .30 .75
370 Tomas Klimes .20 .50

2002-03 Czech OFS Plus All-Star Game

COMPLETE SET (43) 30.00 75.00
H1 Jaroslav Balastik 2.00 5.00
H2 Jiri Burger .75 2.00
H3 Petr Cajanek 1.25 3.00
H4 Petr Gregorek .75 2.00
H5 Miloslav Guren .75 2.00
H6 Martin Hamrlik .75 2.00
H7 Vladimir Hudacek .75 2.00
H8 Jiri Hudler 4.00 10.00
H9 Tomas Jakes .75 2.00
H10 Miroslav Javin .75 2.00
H11 Lubomir Korhon .75 2.00
H12 Richard Kral .75 2.00
H13 Petr Leska .75 2.00
H14 Jiri Marusak .75 2.00
H15 Marek Melenovsky .75 2.00
H16 David Moravec .75 2.00
H17 David Nosek .75 2.00
H18 Karel Soudek .75 2.00
H19 Jiri Trvaj .75 2.00
H20 Marek Uram .75 2.00
H21 Petr Vala .75 2.00
H22 Ondrej Vesely .75 2.00
H23 Petr Bartos .75 2.00
H24 Petr Briza 1.25 3.00
H25 Vladimir Gyna .75 2.00
H26 Martin Hlavacka .75 2.00
H27 Jaroslav Hlinka .75 2.00
H28 Otakar Janecky .75 2.00
H29 Petr Kadlec .75 2.00
H30 Ladislav Lubina .75 2.00
H31 Jaroslav Nedved .75 2.00
H32 Tomas Nemcicky .75 2.00
H33 Josef Reznicek .75 2.00
H34 Vaclav Skuhravy .75 2.00
H35 Jan Srdinko .75 2.00
H36 Josef Straka .75 2.00
H37 Adam Svoboda 1.25 3.00
H38 Ladislav Svoboda .75 2.00
H39 Michal Sykora .75 2.00
H40 Viktor Ujcik .75 2.00
H41 Unknown .75 2.00
H42 Jiri Zelenka .75 2.00
H43 Daniel Branda .75 2.00

2002-03 Czech OFS Plus Checklists

COMPLETE SET (12) 5.00 10.00
C1 Jakub Cech .40 1.00
C2 Marek Pinc .40 1.00
C3 Pavel Falta .40 1.00
C4 Petr Prikril .40 1.00
C5 Lukas Hronek .40 1.00
C6 Robert Hamrla .40 1.00
C7 Adam Svoboda .75 2.00
C8 Petr Franek .40 1.00
C9 Petr Tucek .40 1.00
C10 Lubos Horcicka .40 1.00
C11 Jiri Trvaj .40 1.00
C12 Radovan Biegl .75 2.00

2002-03 Czech OFS Plus Masks

COMPLETE SET (?)
M1 Unknown
M2 Ivo Pesat 4.00 10.00
M3 Petr Tucek 4.00 10.00
M4 Jiri Trvaj 4.00 10.00
M5 Lukas Plsek 4.00 10.00
M6 Radovan Biegl 4.00 10.00
M7 Marek Pinc 4.00 10.00
M8 Petr Prikril 4.00 10.00
M9 Lukas Hronek 4.00 10.00
M10 Roman Malek 4.00 10.00
M11 Pavel Falta 4.00 10.00
M12 Unknown
M13 Unknown
M14 Vladimir Hudacek 4.00 10.00
M15 Unknown
M16 Adam Svoboda 6.00 15.00
M17 Robert Hamrla 4.00 10.00
M18 Marcel Kucera 4.00 10.00
M19 Unknown
M20 Unknown
M21 Unknown
M22 Unknown
M23 Unknown
M24 Jakub Cech 4.00 10.00

2002-03 Czech OFS Plus Trios

STATED ODDS 1:8
T1 Vladimir Hudacek 2.50 6.00
Rudolf Suchanek
Peter Bartos
T2 Michal Marik 2.50 6.00
Filip Stefanka
Michal Cech
T3 Jakub Cech 2.50 6.00
Tomas Harant
Daniel Bohac
T4 Petr Franek 2.50 6.00
Dmitri Rodine
TomasNemcicky
T5 Pavel Falta 2.50 6.00
Angel Krstev
Vitezslav Jankovych
T6 Marek Pinc 2.50 6.00
Jiri Slegr
Martin Rucinsky
T7 Michal Podolka 2.50 6.00
I Petr Martinek
Petr Klima
T8 Adam Svoboda 2.50 6.00
Michal Sykora
Petr Sykora
T9 Tomas Maly 2.50 6.00
Michael Vyhlidal
Ladislav Lubina
T10 Libor Barta 2.50 6.00
Josef Reznicek
Radek Duda
T11 Robert Hamrla 2.50 6.00
Ivan Vlcek
Josef Straka
T12 Roman Malek 2.50 6.00
Frantisek Kucera
Josef Beranek
T13 Lukas Hronek 2.50 6.00
Petr Kadlec
Viktor Ujcik
T14 Petr Briza 2.50 6.00
Jaroslav Nedved
Richard Zemlicka
T15 Petr Prikril 2.50 6.00
Jan Srdinko
Petr Leska
T16 Vlastimil Lakosil 2.50 6.00
Libor Prochazka
Richard Kral
T17 Lubos Horcicka 2.50 6.00
David Nosek
Vaclav Pletka
T18 Jiri Trvaj 2.50 6.00
Radim Tesarik
David Moravec
T19 Martin Falter 2.50 6.00
Marek Cernosek
Roman Kadera
T20 Radovan Biegl 8.00 20.00
Alexej Jaskin
Jiri Hudler
T21 Radek Masny 2.50 6.00
Petr Kubos
Radim Kucharczyk
T22 Ivo Pesat 2.50 6.00
Martin Hamrlik
Miroslav Okal
T23 Petr Tucek 2.50 6.00
Jirin Marusak
Ladislav Vlach
T24 Petr Svoboda 2.50 6.00
Jan Snopek
Peter Pucher
T25 Martin Altrichter 2.50 6.00
Karel Soudek
Marek Uram

2002-03 Czech OFS Plus Znaky Klubu

COMPLETE SET (14) 5.00 10.00
Z1 Ceske Budejovice .40 1.00
Z2 Havirov Panthers .40 1.00
Z3 Energie Karlovy Vary .40 1.00
Z4 Bili Tygri Liberec .40 1.00
Z5 Chemopetrol Litvinov .40 1.00
Z6 IPB Pojistovna Pardubice .40 1.00
Z7 Keramika Plzen .40 1.00
Z8 Slavia Praha .40 1.00
Z9 Sparta Praha .40 1.00
Z10 Ocelari Trinec .40 1.00
Z11 Vitkovice .40 1.00
Z12 Vsetin .40 1.00
Z13 Hame Zlin .40 1.00
Z14 ME Znojemsti Orli .40 1.00

2002-03 Czech OFS Plus Duos

COMPLETE SET (25) 40.00 80.00
STATED ODDS 1:8
D1 Radovan Biegl 6.00 15.00
Jiri Hudler
D2 Petr Briza 2.00 5.00
Jiri Zelenka
D3 Martin Richter 2.00 5.00
Jan Tomajko
D4 Josef Beranek 2.00 5.00
Roman Malek
D5 Frantisek Kucera 2.00 5.00
Viktor Ujcik
D6 Jiri Trvaj 2.00 5.00
David Moravec
D7 Jiri Burger 2.00 5.00
Roman Kadera
D8 Libor Prochazka 2.00 5.00
Richard Kral
D9 Vaclav Pletka 2.00 5.00
Vlastimil Lakocil
D10 Adam Svoboda 2.00 5.00
Michal Vyhlidal
D11 Michal Sykora 2.00 5.00
Ladislav Lubina
D12 Oldrich Svoboda 3.00 8.00
Marek Uram
D13 Peter Pucher 2.00 5.00
Martin Altrichter
D14 Martin Vyborny 2.00 5.00
Libor Barta
D15 Radek Duda 2.00 5.00
Robert Hamrla
D16 Martin Hamrlik 2.00 5.00
Jiri Marusak
D17 Rostislav Vlach 2.00 5.00
Petr Tucek
D18 Petr Ranek 2.00 5.00
Robin Bacul
D19 Vladimir Hudacek 2.00 5.00
Milan Nedoma
D20 Vlastimil Kroupa 2.00 5.00
Marek Pinc
D21 Martin Rucinsky 2.00 5.00
Jiri Slegr
D22 Radoslav Kropac 2.00 5.00
Pavel Falta
D23 Angel Krstev 2.00 5.00
Vitezslav Jankovych
D24 Tomas Srsen 2.00 5.00
Jakub Cech
D25 Jan Kopecky 2.00 5.00
Michal Marik

2002 Czech IQ Sports Blue

We have no pricing information on these cards, but present the complete checklist for you below.

COMPLETE SET (29)
1 Dominik Hasek
2 Josef Beranek
3 Jan Caloun
4 Roman Cechmanek
5 Jiri Dopita
6 Roman Hamrlik
7 Dominik Hasek
8 Dominik Hasek
9 Dominik Hasek
10 Milan Hejduk
11 Roman Simicek
12 Jaromir Jagr
13 Frantisek Kaberle
14 Frantisek Kucera
15 Frantisek Kucera
16 Robert Lang
17 David Moravec
18 Pavel Patera
19 Libor Prochazka
20 Martin Prochazka
21 Robert Reichel
22 Martin Rucinsky
23 Vladimir Ruzicka
24 Vladimir Ruzicka
25 Jiri Slegr
26 Richard Smehlik
27 Jaroslav Spacek
28 Martin Straka
29 Petr Svoboda

2002 Czech IQ Sports Yellow

We have no pricing information for these cards, but present the complete checklist for you below.

COMPLETE SET (29)
1 Jaromir Jagr
2 Josef Beranek
3 Jan Caloun
4 Roman Cechmanek
5 Jiri Dopita
6 Roman Hamrlik
7 Roman Hamrlik
8 Milan Hnilicka
9 Dominik Hasek
10 Dominik Hasek
11 Dominik Hasek
12 Milan Hejduk
13 Jaromir Jagr
14 Jaromir Jagr
15 Petr Sykora
16 Frantisek Kucera
17 Robert Lang
18 David Moravec
19 Pavel Patera
20 Martin Prochazka
21 Libor Prochazka
22 Robert Reichel
23 Martin Rucinsky
24 Vladimir Ruzicka
25 Jiri Slegr
26 Jiri Slegr
27 Richard Smehlik
28 Jaroslav Spacek
29 Petr Svoboda

2002 Czech National Team Postcards

COMPLETE SET (15) 10.00 20.00
1 Jaroslav Balastik .75 2.00
2 Jaroslav Bednar .75 2.00
3 Petr Briza .75 2.00
4 Jan Hlavac .75 2.00
5 Jindrich Kotrla .40 1.00
6 Tomas Kucharcik .40 1.00
7 Jan Marek .40 1.00
8 Zbynek Michalek 1.25 3.00
9 Jaroslav Modry .40 1.00
10 Vaclav Pletka .40 1.00
11 Jaroslav Spacek .40 1.00
12 Petr Tenkrat .40 1.00
13 Radim Tesarik .40 1.00
14 Marek Vorel .40 1.00
15 David Vyborny .75 2.00

2002 Czech Stadion Cup Finals

This set features stars from the World Cup and Stanley Cup. Only hockey players are listed below.

COMPLETE SET (9)
484 Scotty Bowman .75 2.00
485 Jiri Fischer .75 2.00
486 Ron Francis .75 2.00
487 Dominik Hasek 2.00 5.00
488 Arturs Irbe .75 2.00
489 Marek Malik .40 1.00
490 Jaroslav Svoboda .40 1.00
491 Jiri Slegr .40 1.00
492 Josef Vasicek .40 1.00

2002 Czech Stadion Olympics

This set was issued in conjunction with the Czech sports magazine Stadion. It features athletes who represented the Czech Republic at the 2002 Winter Olympics. We only include hockey players, so the set is listed in skip-number form below.

325 Petr Cajanek .75 2.00
326 Roman Cechmanek .40 1.00
327 Jiri Dopita .40 1.00
328 Radek Dvorak .40 1.00
329 Patrik Elias 1.25 3.00
330 Roman Hamrlik .40 1.00
331 Milan Hejduk 1.25 3.00
332 Martin Havlat 2.00 5.00
333 Dominik Hasek 2.00 5.00
334 Jan Hrdina .40 1.00
335 Jaromir Jagr 2.00 5.00
336 Tomas Kaberle .75 2.00
337 Pavel Patera .40 1.00
338 Robert Lang .40 1.00
339 Pavel Kubina .40 1.00
340 Petr Sykora .40 1.00
341 Martin Rucinsky .40 1.00
342 Robert Reichel .40 1.00
347 Roman Turek .40 1.00
348 Jaroslav Spacek .40 1.00
349 Richard Smehlik .40 1.00
350 Martin Skoula .40 1.00
351 Michal Sykora .40 1.00

2003-04 Czech National Team

This partial checklist represents what appears to be a set produced by World Sport of the 2003-04 Czech National Team. If anyone has additional information, please forward it to hockeymag@beckett.com

COMPLETE SET (?)
1 Dusan Salficky .40 1.00
2 Jan Hejda .20 .50
3 Martin Cech .20 .50
4 Pavel Patera .20 .50

2003-04 Czech OFS Plus

COMPLETE SET (398) 40.00 80.00
1 Jiri Burger .20 .50
2 Marek Cernosek .20 .50
3 Jan Dresler .20 .50
4 Martin Falter .20 .50
5 Petr Hubacek .20 .50
6 Jakub Hulva .20 .50
7 Lukas Chmelir .20 .50
8 Zbynek Irgl .20 .50
9 Roman Kadera .20 .50
10 Rostislav Olesz 1.25 3.00
11 Ludek Krayzel .20 .50
12 Lukas Krenzelok .20 .50
13 Pavel Kumstat .20 .50
14 Jiri Trvaj .20 .50
15 Petr Vala .20 .50
16 Ales Padelek .20 .50
17 Ivan Padelek .20 .50
18 Tomas Ficenc .20 .50
19 Pavel Kowalczyk .20 .50
20 Petr Mika .20 .50
21 Daniel Zapotocny .20 .50
22 Daniel Seman .20 .50
23 Martin Tomasek .20 .50
24 Martin Ambruz .20 .50
25 Marek Dubec .20 .50
26 Radovan Biegl .30 .75
27 Michal Horak .20 .50
28 Tomas Demel .20 .50
29 Radim Hruska .20 .50
30 Petr Kubos .20 .50
31 Alexej Jaskin .20 .50
32 Ondrej Nemec .20 .50
33 Jiri Polak .20 .50
34 Roman Stantien .20 .50
35 Jan Sochor .20 .50
36 Radek Masny .20 .50
37 Tomas Vak .20 .50
38 Petr Vampola .20 .50
39 Pavel Selinger .20 .50
40 Jiri Hasek .20 .50
41 Michal Hudec .20 .50
42 Lubomir Stach .20 .50

Card	Low	High
43 Martin Vyrubalik	.20	.50
44 Patrik Luza	.20	.50
45 Otakar Janecky	.20	.50
46 Martin Barek	.20	.50
47 Tomas Blazek	.20	.50
48 Petr Caslava	.20	.50
49 Tomas Divisek	.20	.50
50 Miroslav Duben	.20	.50
51 Petr Koukal	.20	.50
52 Jaroslav Kudrna	.20	.50
53 Frantisek Mrazek	.20	.50
54 Petr Mudroch	.20	.50
55 Andrej Novotny	.20	.50
56 Tomas Pacal	.20	.50
57 Lubomir Pistek	.20	.50
58 Petr Prucha	2.00	5.00
59 Adam Svoboda	.30	.75
60 Jan Kolar	.20	.50
61 Michal Sykora	.20	.50
62 Petr Sykora	.20	.50
63 Jiri Dopita	.20	.50
64 Peter Podhradsky	.20	.50
65 Tomas Razingar	.20	.50
66 Jan Alinc	.20	.50
67 Robin Bacul	.20	.50
68 Richard Bauer	.20	.50
69 Lukas Bednarik	.20	.50
70 Jakub Kraus	.20	.50
71 Lukas Galvas	.20	.50
72 Jan Kostal	.20	.50
73 Lukas Krajicek	.40	1.00
74 Petr Kumstat	.20	.50
75 Tomas Mencicky	.20	.50
76 Rudolf Pejchar	.20	.50
77 Dmitrij Rodin	.20	.50
78 Vaclav Skuhravy	.20	.50
79 Frantisek Ptacek	.20	.50
80 Vojtech Polak	.20	.50
81 Ladislav Svoboda	.20	.50
82 Michal Tvrdik	.20	.50
83 Lukas Sablik	.20	.50
84 Tomas Netik	.20	.50
85 Miroslav Vantroba	.20	.50
86 Martin Kivon	.20	.50
87 Jan Lipiansky	.20	.50
88 David Balaze	.20	.50
89 Frantisek Bojnic	.20	.50
90 Viktor Hubl	.20	.50
91 Jan Hranac	.20	.50
92 Jiri Gombar	.20	.50
93 Lukas Havel	.20	.50
94 Marian Kacir	.20	.50
95 Lukas Kaspar	.20	.50
96 Jan Kloboucek	.20	.50
97 Vlastimil Kroupa	.20	.50
98 Vojtech Kubincak	.20	.50
99 Tomas Martinec	.20	.50
100 Petr Martinek	.20	.50
101 Lukas Riha	.20	.50
102 Richard Zemlicka	.20	.50
103 Tomas Rolinek	.20	.50
104 Miha Rebolj	.20	.50
105 Michal Travnicek	.20	.50
106 Marek Pinc	.20	.50
107 Lukas Pozivil	.20	.50
108 Ivo Prorok	.20	.50
109 Martin Cakajik	.20	.50
110 Miroslav Hajek	.20	.50
111 Jan Holub	.20	.50
112 Richard Jares	.20	.50
113 Waldemar Jirus	.20	.50
114 Pavel Kasparik	.20	.50
115 Vaclav Koci	.20	.50
116 Radoslav Kropac	.20	.50
117 Angel Krstev	.20	.50
118 Vaclav Novak	.20	.50
119 Jiri Moravec	.20	.50
120 Lukas Pabiska	.20	.50
121 Mojmir Musil	.20	.50
122 Jan Plodek	.20	.50
123 Stanislav Prochazka	.20	.50
124 Patrik Rozsival	.20	.50
125 Michal Straka	.20	.50
126 Oldrich Svoboda	.20	.50
127 Ladislav Smid ERC	2.00	5.00
128 Lubomir Korhon	.20	.50
129 Rudolf Vercik	.20	.50
130 Jaroslav Balastik	.40	1.00
131 Miroslav Blatak	.20	.50
132 Martin Cech	.20	.50
133 Martin Cech	.20	.50
134 Martin Hamrlik	.20	.50
135 Martin Jenacek	.20	.50
136 Petr Leska	.20	.50
137 Petr Macholda	.20	.50
138 Petr Mokrejs	.20	.50
139 Martin Nosek	.20	.50
140 Miroslav Okal	.20	.50
141 Martin Altrichter	.20	.50
142 Radim Tesarik	.20	.50
143 Petr Tucek	.20	.50
144 Ondrej Vesely	.20	.50
145 Rostislav Vlach	.20	.50
146 Martin Zahorovsky	.20	.50
147 Pavel Zubicek	.20	.50
148 Peter Barinka	.20	.50
149 Erik Weissemann	.20	.50
150 Pavel Zavrtalek	.20	.50
151 Michal Bros	.20	.50
152 Petr Briza	.30	.75
153 Jan Hanzlik	.20	.50
154 Jaroslav Mrazek	.20	.50
155 Jakub Sindel	.30	.75
156 Ondrej Kratena	.30	.75
157 Jan Marek	.20	.50
158 Martin Paroulek	.20	.50
159 Petr Ton	.20	.50
160 David Vrbata	.20	.50
161 Libor Prochazka	.20	.50
162 Josef [illegible]	.20	.50
163 Marek Schwarz ERC	2.00	5.00
164 Jan Srdinko	.20	.50
165 Jan Tomajko	.20	.50
166 Roman Vondracek	.20	.50
167 Jan Vytisk	.20	.50
168 Karel Hromas	.20	.50
169 Jiri Jakes	.20	.50
170 Radek Mika	.20	.50
171 Milan Antos	.20	.50
172 Josef Beranek	.20	.50
173 Radek Dlouhy	.20	.50
174 Jan Fadrny	.20	.50
175 Dominik Granak	.20	.50
176 Lukas Hronek	.20	.50
177 David Hruska	.20	.50
178 Jiri Kuntos	.20	.50
179 Roman Malek	.20	.50
180 Patrik Martinec	.20	.50
181 Petr Jaros	.20	.50
182 Jakub Klepis	.40	1.00
183 Pavel Kolarik	.20	.50
184 Milan Kopecky	.20	.50
185 Frantisek Kucera	.20	.50
186 Jan Novak	.20	.50
187 David Pojkar	.20	.50
188 Ondrej Slanek	.20	.50
189 Michal Sup	.20	.50
190 Adam Saffer	.20	.50
191 Stanislav Gron	.40	1.00
192 Petr Kadlec	.20	.50
193 Marek Tomica	.20	.50
194 Leos Cermak	.20	.50
195 Ivan Dropa	.20	.50
196 Martin Adamsky	.20	.50
197 Michal Dobron	.20	.50
198 Michal Dvorak	.20	.50
199 Libor Barta	.20	.50
200 Mario Cartelli	.20	.50
201 Jiri Hanzlik	.20	.50
202 Ales Kratoska	.20	.50
203 Ondrej Kubes	.20	.50
204 Josef Straka	.20	.50
205 Radek Matejovsky	.20	.50
206 Jan Svik	.20	.50
207 Milan Voboril	.20	.50
208 Milan Volak	.20	.50
209 Zdenek Smid	.20	.50
210 David Pospisil	.20	.50
211 Roman Bilek	.20	.50
212 Jiri Dobrovolny	.20	.50
213 Michal Duraz	.20	.50
214 Patrik Rimmel	.20	.50
215 Zdenek Sedlak	.20	.50
216 Vitezslav Bilek	.20	.50
217 Jakub Evan	.20	.50
218 Martin Frolik	.20	.50
219 Radek Gardon	.20	.50
220 Tomas Horna	.20	.50
221 Miloslav Horava	.20	.50
222 Vitezslav Jankovych	.20	.50
223 Jaroslav Kalla	.20	.50
224 David Pazourek	.20	.50
225 Jan Pospisil	.20	.50
226 Tomas Klimt	.20	.50
227 Jan Krulis	.20	.50
228 Robert Kysela	.20	.50
229 Rostislav Malena	.20	.50
230 Zdenek Orct	.20	.50
231 Jiri Zeman	.20	.50
232 Jan Dlouhy	.20	.50
233 Petr Horava	.20	.50
234 Petr Kasik	.20	.50
235 Miroslav Lazo	.20	.50
236 Martin Prochazka	.20	.50
237 Juraj Stefanka	.20	.50
238 Miroslav Barus	.20	.50
239 Vaclav Benak	.20	.50
240 Roman Eral	.20	.50
241 Radek Haman	.20	.50
242 David Havir	.20	.50
243 Ales Kretinsky	.20	.50
244 David Ludvik	.20	.50
245 Roman Nemecek	.20	.50
246 Karel Plasek	.20	.50
247 Jan Snopek	.20	.50
248 Milan Prochazka	.20	.50
249 Peter Pucher	.20	.50
250 Robert Slavik	.20	.50
251 Pavel Mojzis	.20	.50
252 Tomas Duba	.20	.50
253 Igor Rataj	.20	.50
254 Jan Pardavy	.20	.50
255 Lukas Vomela	.20	.50
256 Daniel Babka	.20	.50
257 Radek Belohlav	.20	.50
258 Stepan Hrebejk	.20	.50
259 Vladimir Hudacek	.20	.50
260 Stanislav Jasecko	.20	.50
261 Josef Jindra	.20	.50
262 Vaclav Koci	.20	.50
263 Jaroslav Kristek	.20	.50
264 Josef Kucera	.20	.50
265 Lukas Kveton	.20	.50
266 Jan Mucha	.20	.50
267 Zbynek Neckar	.20	.50
268 Zdenek Ondrej	.20	.50
269 Ivan Rachunek	.20	.50
270 Lubos Rob	.20	.50
271 Petr Sailer	.20	.50
272 Jiri Simanek	.20	.50
273 Vladimir Skoda	.20	.50
274 Rudolf Suchanek	.20	.50
275 Filip Turek	.20	.50
276 Michal Vondra	.20	.50
277 Robert Prochazka	.20	.50
278 Marek Schwarz	2.00	5.00
279 Zdenek Skorepa	.20	.50
280 Filip Stefanka	.20	.50
281 Richard Bordowski	.20	.50
282 Michal Holes	.20	.50
283 Lubos Horcicka	.20	.50
284 Tomas Houdek	.20	.50
285 Jiri Hunkes	.20	.50
286 [illegible]	.20	.50
287 Petr Jancarik	.20	.50
288 Pavel Janku	.20	.50
289 Richard Kral	.20	.50
290 Jan Kudrna	.20	.50
291 Vlastimil Lakosil	.20	.50
292 Marek Melenovsky	.20	.50
293 Jiri Malinsky	.20	.50
294 Rostislav Martynek	.20	.50
295 Roman Meluzin	.20	.50
296 Zdenek Pavelek	.20	.50
297 Vaclav Pletka	.20	.50
298 Michal Podolka	.20	.50
299 Jiri Polansky	.20	.50
300 Gregor Polencic	.20	.50
301 Josef Vitek	.20	.50
302 Boris Zabka	.20	.50
303 Marek Zadina	.20	.50
304 Tomas Zboril	.20	.50
305 Tomas Frolo	.20	.50
306 Martin Vyborny	.20	.50
307 Marek Posmyk	.20	.50
308 Milan Nedoma	.20	.50
309 Dusan Andrasovsky	.20	.50
310 Ladislav Lubina	.20	.50
311 Alexandr Hylak	.20	.50
312 Jaroslav Nedved	.20	.50
313 Pavel Falta	.20	.50
314 Leos Cermak	.20	.50
315 Tomas Vlcek	.20	.50
316 Igor Murin	.20	.50
317 Tomas Karny	.20	.50
318 Patrik Hucko	.20	.50
319 Michal Mikeska	.20	.50
320 Pavel Srek	.20	.50
321 Gabriel Spilar	.20	.50
322 Petr Havelka	.20	.50
323 Martin Richter	.20	.50
324 Radovan Sloboda	.20	.50
325 Peter Bartos	.20	.50
326 Vladimir Gyna	.20	.50
327 Jan Chabera	.20	.50
328 Andrej Mezin	.20	.50
329 Jan Rehor	.20	.50
330 Martin Strba	.20	.50
331 Miroslav Durak	.20	.50
332 Kamil Jarina	.20	.50
333 Roman Kadera	.20	.50
334 Angel Krstev	.20	.50
335 Michal Marik	.20	.50
336 Jakub Petruzalek	.20	.50
337 Lubos Bartecko	.20	.50
338 Petr Buzek	.20	.50
339 Vaclav Eiselt	.20	.50
340 Martin Chabada	.20	.50
341 Tomas Popperle	.20	.50
342 Zdenek Sedlak	.20	.50
343 Ladislav Svoboda	.20	.50
344 Roman Simicek	.20	.50
345 Martin Havlat	2.00	5.00
346 Martin Vojtek	.20	.50
347 Martin Jurecka	.20	.50
348 Petr Jurecka	.20	.50
349 David Mocek	.20	.50
350 Patrik Rimmel	.20	.50
351 Juraj Stefanka	.20	.50
352 Filip Turek	.20	.50
353 Pavel Zdrahal	.20	.50
354 Daniel Mracka	.20	.50
355 Libor Pavlis	.20	.50
356 Tomaz Razingar	.20	.50
357 Pavel Sebesta	.20	.50
358 Dalibor Sochorek	.20	.50
359 Radim Tesarik	.20	.50
360 Juraj Prokop	.20	.50
361 Josef Hrabal	.20	.50
362 Stefan Zigardy	.20	.50
363 Jan Kudrna	.20	.50
364 Vaclav Skuhravy	.20	.50
365 Ivan Droppa	.20	.50
366 Michal Hreus	.20	.50
367 Radim Skuhrovec	.20	.50
368 Jiri Veber	.20	.50
369 Jan Dlouhy	.20	.50
370 Marek Dubec	.20	.50
371 Miroslav Hlinka	.20	.50
372 Jiri Beroun	.20	.50
373 Tomas Duba	.20	.50
374 Tomas Hradecky	.20	.50
375 Jaroslav Mares	.20	.50
376 Petr Puncochar	.20	.50
377 Michal Straka	.20	.50
378 Marek Uram	.20	.50
379 Jakub Kindl	.20	.50
380 Libor Zabransky	.20	.50
381 Lubomir Jurtaj	.20	.50
382 Petr Jez	.20	.50
383 Robert Jindrich	.20	.50
384 Roman Malek	.20	.50
385 Martin Paroulek	.20	.50
386 Adam Saffer	.20	.50
387 Michal Straka	.20	.50
388 Martin Klaus	.20	.50
389 Tomas Kapusta	.20	.50
390 Lubomir Vosatko	.20	.50
391 Jiri Hanzlik	.20	.50
392 Jiri Hasek	.20	.50
393 Ctibor Jech	.20	.50
394 Ctirad Ovcacik	.20	.50
395 Tomas Rolinek	.20	.50
396 Martin Tupa	.20	.50
397 Libor Barta	.20	.50
398 Jiri Jantovsky	.20	.50
399 Petr Jaros	.20	.50
400 Martin Havlat CL	.75	2.00

2003-04 Czech OFS Plus All-Star Game

Card	Low	High
COMPLETE SET (45)	30.00	75.00
H1 Miroslav Simonovic	.75	2.00
H2 Normunds Sejejs	.75	2.00
H3 Jiri Hes	.75	2.00
H4 Marcel Hanzal	.75	2.00
H5 Roman Kukumberg	.75	2.00
H6 Arne Krotak	.75	2.00
H7 Karol Krizan	.75	2.00
H8 Juraj Kledrowetz	.75	2.00
H9 Miroslav Vantroba	.75	2.00
H10 Miroslav Skovira	.75	2.00
H11 Jaroslav Kmit	.75	2.00
H12 Lubomir Kolnik	.75	2.00
H13 Pavel Kowalczyk	.75	2.00
H14 Martin Ivicic	.75	2.00
H15 Branislav Janos	.75	2.00
H16 Zdeno Ciger	.75	2.00
H17 Petr Korinek	.75	2.00
H18 Tomas Starosta	.75	2.00
H19 Tomas Nadazdi	.75	2.00
H20 Igor Rataj	.75	2.00
H21 Richard Kapus	.75	2.00
H22 Erik Weissmann	.75	2.00
H23 Adam Svoboda	1.25	3.00
H24 Michal Sykora	.75	2.00
H25 Petr Sykora	.75	2.00
H26 Roman Malek	1.25	3.00
H27 Petr Kadlec	.75	2.00
H28 Jan Hejda	.75	2.00
H29 Michal Sup	.75	2.00
H30 Frantisek Kucera	.75	2.00
H31 Frantisek Ptacek	.75	2.00
H32 Ondrej Kratena	.75	2.00
H33 Libor Prochazka	.75	2.00
H34 Richard Kral	.75	2.00
H35 Marek Zadina	.75	2.00
H36 Jan Marek	.75	2.00
H37 Vaclav Pletka	.75	2.00
H38 Martin Hlavacka	.75	2.00
H39 Jan Vytisk	.75	2.00
H40 David Moravec	.75	2.00
H41 Jiri Burger	.75	2.00
H42 Jiri Hudler	6.00	15.00
H43 Marek Uram	.75	2.00
H44 Peter Pucher	.75	2.00
H45 A.Svoboda/M.Sykora CL	.75	2.00

2003-04 Czech OFS Plus Checklists

Card	Low	High
COMPLETE SET (14)	15.00	30.00
1 Jiri Trvaj	1.25	3.00
2 Radovan Biegl	1.25	3.00
3 Adam Svoboda	1.25	3.00
4 Petr Franek	1.25	3.00
5 Marek Pinc	1.25	3.00
6 Oldrich Svoboda	1.25	3.00
7 Petr Tucek	1.25	3.00
8 Petr Briza	1.25	3.00
9 Roman Malek	1.25	3.00
10 Libor Barta	1.25	3.00
11 Josef Kucera	1.25	3.00
12 Martin Altrichter	1.25	3.00
13 Josef Kucera	1.25	3.00
14 Vlastimil Lakosil	1.25	3.00

2003-04 Czech OFS Plus Insert B

We have no pricing information on this series.

B1 Roman Malek
B2 Petr Briza
B3 Adam Svoboda
B4 Marek Pinc
B5 Jiri Trvaj
B6 Vlastimil Lakosil
B7 Petr Franek
B8 Martin Altrichter
B9 Vladimir Hudacek
B10 Radovan Biegl
B11 Petr Tucek
B12 Libor Barta
B13 Lubos Horcicka
B14 Pavel Falta
B15 Petr Briza
Zdenek Orct CL

2003-04 Czech OFS Plus Insert C

We have no pricing information on this series.

C1 Lubos Rob
C2 Ladislav Svoboda
C3 Radek Gardon
C4 Michal Straka
C5 Richard Zemlicka
C6 Jiri Dopita
C7 Jiri Hanzlik
C8 Josef Beranek
C9 Ondrej Kratena
C10 Richard Kral
C11 Roman Kadera
C12 Josef Straub
C13 Miroslav Okal
C14 Rene Pucher

2003-04 Czech OFS Plus Insert G

We have no pricing information on this series.

G1 Lubos Rob
G2 Michal Sup
G3 Radoslav Kropac
G4 Marek Zadina
G5 Jan Marek
G6 Roman Kadera
G7 Viktor Ujcik
G8 Richard Kral
G9 Marek Uram
G10 Pavel Janku

2003-04 Czech OFS Plus Insert H

We have no pricing information on this series.

H1 Josef Kucera
H2 Jiri Trvaj
H3 Roman Kadera
H4 Pavel Falta
H5 Jaroslav Nedved
H6 Igor Murin
H7 Jan Pardavy
H8 Jan Snopek
H9 Richard Kral
H10 Vaclav Pletka
H11 Zdenek Pavelek
H12 Roman Stantien
H13 Richard Zemlicka
H14 Marek Pinc
H15 Tomas Horna
H16 Michal Mikeska
H17 Adam Svoboda
H18 Michal Sykora
H19 Petr Briza
H20 Dusan Andrasovsky
H21 Marek Posmyk
H22 Radovan Sloboda
H23 Lukas Hronek
H24 Michal Sup
H25 David Hruska

2003-04 Czech OFS Plus Insert M

We have no pricing information on this series.

M1 Josef Straka
M2 Jiri Dopita
M3 Ladislav Lubina
M4 Petr Sykora
M5 Josef Beranek
M6 Jakub Klepis
M7 Roman Malek
M8 Tomas Klimt
M9 Zdenek Orct
M10 Jiri Hasek
M11 Tomas Martinec
M12 Jan Marek
M13 Ondrej Kratena
M14 Zdenek Skorepa
M15 Rostislav Martynek
M16 Martin Cakajik
M17 Martin Altrichter
M18 Martin Hamrlik
M19 Tomas Duba
M20 Peter Pucher
M21 Jiri Burger
M22 Ivan Padelek
M23 Lukas Sablik
M24 Jan Alinc
M25 Jaroslav Kristek
M26 Jiri Dopita CL

2003-04 Czech OFS Plus Insert P

We have no pricing information on this series.

P1 Roman Malek
P2 Petr Briza
P3 Petr Franek
P4 Adam Svoboda
P5 Marek Pinc
P6 Jiri Trvaj
P7 Vlastimil Lakosil
P8 Martin Altrichter
P9 Radovan Biegl
P10 Libor Barta
P11 Lubos Horcicka
P12 Petr Tucek
P13 Vladimir Hudacek
P14 Pavel Falta
P15 Roman Malek
Jiri Trvaj CL

2003-04 Czech OFS Plus Insert S

We have no pricing information on this series.

S1 Richard Kral
S2 Jan Marek
S3 Jiri Burger
S4 David Moravec
S5 Zdenek Pavelek
S6 Lubos Rob
S7 Marek Zadina
S8 Radoslav Kropac
S9 Jiri Hudler
S10 Roman Kadera

2003-04 Czech OFS Plus MS Praha

Card	Low	High
COMPLETE SET (50)	30.00	75.00
SE1 Martin Havlat	4.00	10.00
SE2 Roman Simicek	.75	2.00
SE3 Petr Briza	1.25	3.00
SE4 Jan Marek	.75	2.00
SE5 Petr Buzek	.75	2.00
SE6 Ondrej Kratena	.75	2.00
SE7 Michal Sykora	.75	2.00
SE8 Petr Sykora	.75	2.00
SE9 Adam Svoboda	1.25	3.00
SE10 Jiri Dopita	.75	2.00
SE11 Michal Mikeska	.75	2.00
SE12 Petr Prucha	4.00	10.00
SE13 Martin Prochazka	.75	2.00
SE14 Zdenek Orct	1.25	3.00
SE15 Petr Leska	.75	2.00
SE16 Jaroslav Balastik	1.25	3.00
SE17 Jan Snopek	.75	2.00
SE18 Jiri Burger	.75	2.00
SE19 Rostislav Olesz	4.00	10.00
SE20 Jiri Trvaj	.75	2.00
SE21 Zdenek Pavelek	.75	2.00
SE22 Frantisek Ptacek	.75	2.00
SE23 Roman Malek	.75	2.00
SE24 Marek Posmyk	.75	2.00
SE25 Petr Kadlec	.75	2.00
SE26 Oldrich Svoboda	.75	2.00
SE27 Josef Beranek	.75	2.00
SE28 Michal Travnicek	.75	2.00
SE29 Lukas Havel	.75	2.00
SE30 Jiri Hudler	4.00	10.00
SE31 David Moravec	.75	2.00
SE32 Radim Tesarik	.75	2.00
SE33 Jan Hejda	.75	2.00
SE34 Vlastimil Lakosil	.75	2.00
SE35 Martin Chabada	.75	2.00
SE36 Petr Franek	.75	2.00
SE37 Radovan Biegl	1.25	3.00
SE38 Tomas Duba	.75	2.00
SE39 Lukas Hronek	.75	2.00
SE40 Jan Novak	.75	2.00
SE41 Martin Altrichter	.75	2.00
SE42 Marek Schwarz	2.00	5.00
SE43 Josef Kucera	.75	2.00
SE44 Tomas Divisek	.75	2.00
SE45 Jakub Klepis	2.00	5.00
SE46 Michal Sup	.75	2.00
SE47 Michal Marik	.75	2.00
SE48 Richard Kral	.75	2.00
SE49 Marek Pinc	.75	2.00
SE50 Pavel Falta	.75	2.00

2003-04 Czech Pardubice Postcards

This team-issued set features postcard sized (4X6) collectibles of the Pardubice squad from the Czech Elite League. They are listed below in alphabetical order.

Card	Low	High
COMPLETE SET (16)	8.00	15.00
1 Martin Barek	.40	1.00
2 Tomas Blazek	.40	1.00
3 Tomas Divisek	.40	1.00
4 Jiri Dopita	.40	1.00
5 Otakar Janecky	.40	1.00
6 Petr Koukal	.40	1.00
7 Jaroslav Kudrna	.40	1.00
8 Ladislav Lubina	.40	1.00
9 Michal Mikeska	.40	1.00
10 Frantisek Mrazek	.40	1.00
11 Andrej Novotny	.40	1.00
12 Tomas Pacal	.40	1.00
13 Petr Prucha	2.00	5.00
14 Tomaz Razingar	.40	1.00
15 Adam Svoboda	.75	2.00
16 Michal Sykora	.40	1.00

2003-04 Czech Stadion

These cards were issued as part of a multi-sport set by a Czech athletic magazine.

Card	Low	High
601 Scott Stevens	.75	2.00
603 Patrik Elias	.75	2.00
604 Jeff Friesen	.40	1.00
605 Grant Marshall	.40	1.00
606 Jamie Langenbrunner	.40	1.00
607 Martin Brodeur	4.00	10.00
608 Scott Niedermayer	.40	1.00
609 Mike Rupp	.40	1.00
610 Ruslan Salei	.40	1.00
611 Guy Lafleur	1.50	4.00
612 Petr Sykora	.40	1.00
613 Steve Rucchin	.40	1.00
614 Jean-Sebastien Giguere	1.25	3.00
615 Adam Oates	.40	1.00
616 Paul Kariya	1.50	4.00
617 Steve Thomas	.40	1.00
618 Rob Niedermayer	.40	1.00
622 Vladimir Zabrodsky	.40	1.00
637 Vsevolod Bobrov	.40	1.00
638 Vlastimil Bubnik	.40	1.00
639 Leif Holmqvist	.40	1.00
640 Vladimir Dzurilla	.75	2.00
641 Anatoli Firsov	.40	1.00
642 Josef Golonka	.40	1.00
643 Jiri Holecek	.40	1.00
644 Jaroslav Holik	.40	1.00
645 Jiri Holik	.40	1.00
646 Bobby Hull	2.00	5.00
647 Alexander Yakushev	.75	2.00
648 Sven Tumba Johansson	.40	1.00
649 Alexander Maltsev	.75	2.00
650 Vaclav Nedomansky	.40	1.00
651 Alexander Ragulin	.75	2.00
652 Maurice Richard	2.00	5.00
653 Vladimir Martinek	.40	1.00
654 Frantisek Pospisil	.40	1.00

2003 Czech National Team Postcards

This postcard-sized issue features members of the Czech team from the 2003 World Championships.

Card	Low	High
COMPLETE SET (17)	20.00	40.00
17 David Vyborny	1.25	3.00
1 Jaroslav Balastik	1.25	3.00
2 Jan Hejda	.75	2.00
3 Milan Hejduk	2.00	5.00
4 Jan Hlavac	.75	2.00
5 Ivan Hlinka CO	.40	1.00
6 Jiri Hudler	4.00	10.00
7 Frantisek Kaberle	.75	2.00
8 Jindrich Kotrla	.75	2.00
9 Jaroslav Modry	.75	2.00
10 Robert Reichel	.75	2.00
11 Martin Straka	.75	2.00
12 Radek Sup	.75	2.00
13 Martin Tomasek	.75	2.00
14 Josef Vasicek	.75	2.00
15 Tomas Vokoun	2.00	5.00
16 Radim Vrbata	1.25	3.00
18 Tomas Kaberle	2.00	5.00
19 Michal Sup	.75	2.00
20 Jaroslav Hlinka	.75	2.00

2003 Czech Stadion

This multi-sport set was issued in conjunction with the Czech magazine Stadion. It is listed below in skip-numbered form.

Card	Low	High
COMPLETE SET	15.00	40.00
529 Anson Carter	.40	1.00
530 Peter Bondra	.40	1.00
531 Magnus Arvedson	.40	1.00
532 Sandy McCarthy	.40	1.00
533 Mikko Eloranta	.40	1.00
534 Bates Battaglia	.40	1.00
534 Tie Domi	.75	2.00
536 Jaromir Jagr Mario Lemieux	4.00	10.00
537 Darcy Tucker	.40	1.00
538 Brian Rafalski	.40	1.00
539 Jozef Stumpel	.40	1.00
540 Marco Sturm	.40	1.00
541 Eric Lindros	1.25	3.00
542 Ed Jovanovski	.40	1.00
543 Darren McCarty	.40	1.00
544 Zigmund Palffy	.40	1.00
545 Luc Robitaille	1.25	3.00
546 Keith Primeau	.40	1.00
547 Bobby Clarke	.40	1.00
548 Marcel Dionne	.40	1.00
549 Ken Dryden	2.00	5.00
550 Frank Mahovlich	.75	2.00
551 Valeri Kharlamov	.75	2.00
552 Phil Esposito	2.00	5.00
553 Boris Mikhailov	.75	2.00
554 Stan Mikita	.75	2.00
555 Bobby Orr	4.00	10.00
556 Vladimir Petrov	.40	1.00
557 Vladislav Tretiak	1.25	3.00
562 Chuck Kobasew	.40	1.00
565 Bobby Holik	.40	1.00

2004-05 Czech HC Plzen Postcards

This postcard issue features members of HC Plzen, one of the top teams in the Czech Extraliga. The set is noteworthy for the inclusion of several NHLers who joined the team during the 2004-05 lockout.

Card	Low	High
COMPLETE SET (23)	10.00	20.00
1 Martin Adamsky	.40	1.00
2 Dusan Andrasovsky	.40	1.00
3 Mario Cartelli	.40	1.00
4 Martin Cibak	.60	1.50
5 Tomas Duba	.40	1.00
6 Michal Duras	.40	1.00
7 Robert Jindrich	.60	1.50
8 Jaroslav Kracik	.40	1.00
9 Jaroslav Kudrna	.40	1.00
10 Radek Matejovsky	.40	1.00
11 Frank Mrazek	.40	1.00
12 Milan Nedoma	.40	1.00
13 Martin Paroulek	.40	1.00
14 Rudolf Pejchar	.40	1.00
15 David Pospisil	.40	1.00
16 Jaroslav Spacek	.40	1.00
17 Pavel Srek	.40	1.00
18 Josef Straka	.40	1.00
19 Martin Straka	.60	1.50
20 Michal Straka	.40	1.00
21 Pavel Trnka	.40	1.00
22 Martin Vyborny	.40	1.00
23 Jan Vytisk	.40	1.00

2004-05 Czech HC Slavia Praha Postcards

This postcard issue features HC Slavia Praha from the Czech Extraliga. The set is noteworthy for the inclusion of several well-known NHL stars who played with the team during the 2004-05 lockout. but if you know of others, please contact us via email at hockeymag@beckett.com.

Card	Low	High
COMPLETE SET (12)	15.00	25.00
1 Milan Antos	.40	1.00
2 Radek Duda	.40	1.00
3 Petr Franek	.40	1.00
4 Petr Kadlec	.40	1.00
5 Tomas Kloucek	.60	1.50
6 Zigmund Palffy	1.50	4.00
7 Vladimir Ruzicka	.40	1.00
8 Jozef Stumpel	.60	1.50
9 Radek Sup	.40	1.00
10 Josef Vasicek	.60	1.50
11 Tomas Vlasak	.40	1.00
12 Team Card	.60	1.50
13 Josef Beranek	.40	1.00
14 Jan Novak	.40	1.00
15 Pavel Kolarik	.40	1.00
16 David Hruska	.40	1.00
17 Michal Sup	.40	1.00
18 Jaroslav Spacek	.40	1.00
19 Dominik Granak	.40	1.00
20 Lukas Havel	.40	1.00
21 Zdenek Smid	.40	1.00
22 Tomas Zizka	.40	1.00

2004-05 Czech HC Sparta Praha Postcards

This postcard issue features Sparta Praha, a top team in the Czech Extraliga. It features a number of well-known NHLers who ventured overseas during the lockout of 2004-05.

Card	Low	High
COMPLETE SET (24)	15.00	30.00
1 Petr Briza	.75	2.00
2 Michal Bros	.40	1.00
3 Martin Chabada	.40	1.00
4 Michal Dobron	.40	1.00
5 Michal Dragoun	.40	1.00
6 Jan Hanzlik	.40	1.00
7 Jan Hlavac	.75	2.00
8 Pavel Kasparik	.40	1.00
9 Jindrich Kotrla	.40	1.00
10 Ondrej Kratena	.40	1.00
11 Jan Marek	.40	1.00
12 Petr Nedved	.75	2.00
13 Tomas Netik	.40	1.00
14 Rostislav Olesz	1.25	3.00
15 Karel Pilar	.75	2.00
16 Tomas Popperle	.40	1.00
17 Libor Prochazka	.40	1.00
18 Jozef Reznicek	.40	1.00
19 Martin Richter	.40	1.00
20 Robert Schnabel	.40	1.00

Card	Low	High
21 Jakub Sindel	.40	1.00
22 Michal Sivek	.75	2.00
23 Petr Ton	.40	1.00
24 David Vyborny	.75	2.00

2004-05 Czech NHL ELH Postcards

This series of 16 postcards features NHL players who spent all or part of the 2004-05 season in the Czech Extraliga. The cards feature full-colour photos on the fronts showing the players in their Czech sweaters. The cards are unnumbered and listed below alphabetically.

Card	Low	High
COMPLETE SET (16)	15.00	30.00
1 Jan Bulis	.75	2.00
2 Petr Cajanek	.75	2.00
3 Roman Hamrlik	.75	2.00
4 Milan Hejduk	1.50	4.00
5 Ales Hemsky	1.50	4.00
6 Jan Hlavac	.75	2.00
7 Jaromir Jagr	2.00	5.00
8 Ales Kotalik	.75	2.00
9 Petr Nedved	.75	2.00
10 Karel Pilar	.75	2.00
11 Robert Reichel	.75	2.00
12 Martin Rucinsky	.75	2.00
13 Jiri Slegr	.75	2.00
14 Jaroslav Spacek	.75	2.00
15 Martin Straka	.75	2.00
16 David Vyborny	.75	2.00

2004-05 Czech OFS

Card	Low	High
COMPLETE SET (372)	40.00	100.00
1 Petr Altrichter	.08	.20
2 Oldrich Bakus	.08	.20
3 Petr Buzek	.08	.20
4 Tomas Cachotsky	.08	.20
5 Dusan Devecka	.08	.20
6 Jiri Dobrovolny	.08	.20
7 Tomas Ficenc	.08	.20
8 Marian Havel	.08	.20
9 Roman Hlouch	.08	.20
10 Lukas Hronek	.08	.20
11 Jiri Jantovsky	.08	.20
12 Petr Kuchyna	.08	.20
13 Rostislav Malena	.08	.20
14 Jaroslav Mares	.08	.20
15 Ales Padelek	.08	.20
16 Vojtech Polak	.08	.20
17 Petr Puncochar	.08	.20
18 Ladislav Rytnauer	.08	.20
19 Jaroslav Suchan	.08	.20
20 Petr Vala	.08	.20
21 Rudolf Vercik	.08	.20
22 Martin Zajac	.08	.20
23 Richard Bauer	.08	.20
24 Michal Dvorak	.08	.20
25 Martin Hlavacka	.08	.20
26 Martin Kivon	.08	.20
27 Jan Kostal	.08	.20
28 Petr Kumstat	.08	.20
29 Edgars Masalskis	.08	.20
30 Petr Mika	.08	.20
31 Lukas Pech	.08	.20
32 Milan Prochazka	.08	.20
33 Frantisek Ptacek	.08	.20
34 Vaclav Skuhravy	.08	.20
35 Zdenek Smid	.08	.20
36 Dmitrij Suur	.08	.20
37 Robert Tomik	.08	.20
38 Jiri Polak	.08	.20
39 Lukas Krajicek	.40	1.00
40 Lukas Bednarik	.08	.20
41 Jakub Kraus	.08	.20
42 Jan Alinc	.08	.20
43 Jan Lipiansky	.08	.20
44 Lubomir Hurtaj	.08	.20
45 Zdenek Kutlak	.08	.20
46 Lukas Mensator	.20	.50
47 Vitezslav Bilek	.08	.20
48 Vratislav Cech	.08	.20
49 Jakub Evan	.08	.20
50 Martin Frolik	.08	.20
51 Michael Frolik	2.00	5.00
52 Radek Gardon	.08	.20
53 Miloslav Horava	.08	.20
54 Petr Horava	.08	.20
55 Tomas Horna	.08	.20
56 Jaromir Jagr	2.00	5.00
57 Jiri Jelinek	.08	.20
58 Tomas Kaberle	.20	.50
59 Jaroslav Kalla	.08	.20
60 Tomas Klimt	.08	.20
61 Jakub Lev	.08	.20
62 Zdenek Orct	.20	.50
63 Pavel Patera	.08	.20
64 Martin Prochazka	.08	.20
65 Martin Sevc	.08	.20
66 Jaroslav Spelda	.08	.20
67 Josef Zajic	.08	.20
68 Jan Holub	.08	.20
69 Richard Jares	.08	.20
70 Valdemar Jirus	.08	.20
71 Ales Kotalik	.60	1.50
72 Jiri Moravec	.08	.20
73 Vaclav Nedorost	.40	1.00
74 Vaclav Novak	.08	.20
75 Jan Plodek	.08	.20
76 Andrej Podkonicky	.08	.20
77 Stanislav Prochazka	.08	.20
78 Igor Rataj	.08	.20
79 Patrik Rozsival	.08	.20
80 Ladislav Smid ERC	.75	2.00
81 Jan Tomajko	.08	.20
82 Lubomir Vaic	.20	.50
83 Radim Vrbata	.40	1.00
84 Pavel Falta	.08	.20
85 Leos Cermak	.08	.20
86 Miroslav Duben	.08	.20
87 Milan Hnilicka	.40	1.00
88 Jiri Hanzlik	.08	.20
89 David Balaze	.08	.20
90 Frantisek Bombic	.08	.20
91 Daniel Branda	.08	.20
92 Jiri Gombar	.08	.20
93 Lukas Havel	.08	.20
94 Viktor Hubl	.08	.20
95 Kamil Jarina	.08	.20
96 Jan Kloboucek	.08	.20
97 Vlastimil Kroupa	.08	.20
98 Vojtech Kubincak	.08	.20
99 Tomas Kurka	.08	.20
100 Michal Marik	.08	.20
101 Lukas Pozivil	.08	.20
102 Robert Reichel	.20	.50
103 Lukas Riha	.08	.20
104 Martin Rucinsky	.20	.50
105 Zbynek Sklenicka	.08	.20
106 Martin Skoula	.20	.50
107 Radim Skuhrovec	.08	.20
108 Jiri Slegr	.08	.20
109 Michal Travnicek	.08	.20
110 Martin Tupa	.08	.20
111 Tomas Blazek	.08	.20
112 Jan Bulis	.08	.20
113 Petr Caslava	.08	.20
114 Tomas Divisek	.20	.50
115 Jiri Dopita	.20	.50
116 David Havir	.08	.20
117 Milan Hejduk	.75	2.00
118 Alexandr Hylak	.08	.20
119 Jaroslav Kames	.20	.50
120 Jan Kolar	.08	.20
121 Petr Koukal	.08	.20
122 Tomas Linhart	.08	.20
123 Ladislav Lubina	.08	.20
124 Michal Mikeska	.08	.20
125 Petr Mudroch	.08	.20
126 Andrej Novotny	.08	.20
127 Tomas Pacal	.08	.20
128 Petr Prucha	.75	2.00
129 Tomaz Razingar	.08	.20
130 Tomas Rolinek	.08	.20
131 Jan Snopek	.08	.20
132 Petr Sykora	.40	1.00
133 Jan Lasak	.75	2.00
134 Ales Hemsky	1.25	3.00
135 Michal Tvrdik	.08	.20
136 Lubomir Korhon	.08	.20
137 Martin Adamsky	.08	.20
138 Dusan Andrasovsky	.08	.20
139 Mario Cartelli	.08	.20
140 Tomas Duba	.08	.20
141 Michal Duraz	.08	.20
142 Petr Havelka	.08	.20
143 Robert Jindrich	.20	.50
144 Josef Straka	.08	.20
145 Jaroslav Kracik	.08	.20
146 Milan Kraft	.40	1.00
147 Martin Straka	.40	1.00
148 Radek Matejovsky	.08	.20
149 Michal Straka	.08	.20
150 Milan Nedoma	.08	.20
151 Rudolf Pejchar	.08	.20
152 David Pospisil	.08	.20
153 Adam Saffer	.08	.20
154 Jaroslav Spacek	.08	.20
155 Pavel Trnka	.08	.20
156 Martin Vyborny	.08	.20
157 Jan Vytisk	.08	.20
158 Milan Antos	.08	.20
159 Radek Dlouhy	.08	.20
160 Radek Duda	.08	.20
161 Petr Franek	.08	.20
162 Dominik Granak	.08	.20
163 David Hruska	.08	.20
164 Petr Kadlec	.08	.20
165 Tomas Kloucek	.20	.50
166 Pavel Kolarik	.08	.20
167 Milan Kopecky	.08	.20
168 Ales Kratoska	.08	.20
169 Frantisek Kucera	.08	.20
170 Lukas Musil	.08	.20
171 Jan Novak	.08	.20
172 Zigmund Palffy	.75	2.00
173 Jozef Stumpel	.20	.50
174 Michal Sup	.08	.20
175 Marek Tomica	.08	.20
176 Josef Vasicek	.20	.50
177 Michal Vondrka	.08	.20
178 Boris Zabka	.08	.20
179 Petr Jaros	.08	.20
180 David Pojkar	.08	.20
181 Patrik Martinec	.08	.20
182 Vladimir Sobotka	.08	.20
183 Petr Briza	.20	.50
184 Michal Dobron	.08	.20
185 Jan Hanzlik	.08	.20
186 Jan Hlavac	.20	.50
187 Martin Chabada	.08	.20
188 Pavel Kasparik	.08	.20
189 Jindrich Kotrla	.08	.20
190 Jan Marek	.08	.20
191 Petr Nedved	.20	.50
192 Tomas Netik	.08	.20
193 Rostislav Olesz	1.25	3.00
194 Karel Pilar	.20	.50
195 Tomas Popperle	.08	.20
196 Libor Prochazka	.08	.20
197 Josef Reznicek	.08	.20
198 Martin Richter	.08	.20
199 Robert Schnabel	.08	.20
200 Jakub Sindel	.08	.20
201 Michal Sivek	.08	.20
202 Petr Ton	.08	.20
203 David Vyborny	.20	.50
204 Radek Bonk	.20	.50
205 Richard Bordowski	.08	.20
206 Martin Cakajik	.08	.20
207 Miroslav Durak	.08	.20
208 Jiri Hasek	.08	.20
209 Pavel Janku	.08	.20
210 Vladislav Koutsky	.08	.20
211 Richard Kral	.08	.20
212 Vlastimil Lakosil	.08	.20
213 Jiri Malinsky	.08	.20
214 Rostislav Martynek	.08	.20
215 Marek Melenovsky	.08	.20
216 Zdenek Pavelek	.08	.20
217 Jan Peterek	.08	.20
218 Vaclav Pletka	.20	.50
219 Peter Podhradsky	.08	.20
220 Jiri Polansky	.08	.20
221 Michal Rozsival	.20	.50
222 Zdenek Skorepa	.08	.20
223 Filip Stefanka	.08	.20
224 Jiri Burger	.08	.20
225 Marek Cernosek	.08	.20
226 Petr Hubacek	.08	.20
227 Stanislav Hudec	.08	.20
228 Jakub Hulva	.08	.20
229 Zbynek Irgl	.08	.20
230 Martin Krayzel	.08	.20
231 Lukas Krenzelok	.08	.20
232 Pavel Kumstat	.08	.20
233 Marek Malik	.08	.20
234 David Moravec	.08	.20
235 Ivan Padelek	.08	.20
236 Radek Philipp	.08	.20
237 Marek Pinc	.08	.20
238 Martin Prusek	.40	1.00
239 Patrik Rimmel	.08	.20
240 Martin Tomasek	.08	.20
241 Filip Turek	.08	.20
242 Vaclav Varada	.20	.50
243 Kamil Brabenec	.08	.20
244 Roman Cechmanek	.20	.50
245 Tomas Demel	.08	.20
246 Marek Dubec	.08	.20
247 Tomas Frolo	.08	.20
248 Ladislav Gengel	.08	.20
249 Josef Hrabal	.08	.20
250 Alexej Jaskin	.08	.20
251 Rostislav Klesla	.40	1.00
252 Robin Kovar	.08	.20
253 Pavel Kowalczyk	.08	.20
254 Radek Masny	.08	.20
255 Ondrej Nemec	.08	.20
256 Libor Pavlis	.08	.20
257 Lukas Plsek	.08	.20
258 Branko Radivojevic	.40	1.00
259 Pavel Selingr	.08	.20
260 Roman Stantien	.08	.20
261 Tomas Vak	.08	.20
262 Martin Vasut	.08	.20
263 Rostislav Vlach	.08	.20
264 Marek Zadina	.08	.20
265 Robert Horak	.08	.20
266 Radovan Somik	.08	.20
267 Jan Koroptvicka	.08	.20
268 Ondrej Vesely	.08	.20
269 Martin Altrichter	.08	.20
270 Martin Ambruz	.08	.20
271 Jaroslav Balastik	.40	1.00
272 Peter Barinka	.20	.50
273 Miroslav Blatak	.08	.20
274 Petr Cajanek	.20	.50
275 Martin Cech	.08	.20
276 Martin Erat	.40	1.00
277 Lukas Galvas	.08	.20
278 Roman Hamrlik	.20	.50
279 Martin Jenacek	.08	.20
280 Miroslav Kovacik	.08	.20
281 Jaroslav Kristek	.08	.20
282 Tomas Kudelka	.08	.20
283 Petr Leska	.08	.20
284 Petr Mokrejs	.08	.20
285 Igor Murin	.08	.20
286 David Nosek	.08	.20
287 Miroslav Okal	.08	.20
288 Radim Tesarik	.08	.20
289 Martin Vosatko	.08	.20
290 Martin Zahorovsky	.08	.20
291 Pavel Zubicek	.08	.20
292 Vaclav Benak	.08	.20
293 Radim Bicanek	.08	.20
294 Roman Erat	.08	.20
295 Radek Haman	.08	.20
296 Tomas Kucharcik	.08	.20
297 Branislav Kvetan	.08	.20
298 Zdenek Ondrej	.08	.20
299 Jan Pardavy	.08	.20
300 Peter Pucher	.08	.20
301 Ivan Rachunek	.08	.20
302 Milan Toman	.08	.20
303 Marek Vorel	.08	.20
304 Marek Uram	.08	.20
305 Karel Plasek	.08	.20
306 Ales Kretinsky	.08	.20
307 Miroslav Barus	.08	.20
308 David Ludvik	.08	.20
309 Robert Slavik	.08	.20
310 Pavel Mojzis	.08	.20
311 Tomas Vokoun	1.25	3.00
312 Patrik Elias	.40	1.00
313 Martin Havlat	.75	2.00
314 David Vsetecka	.08	.20
315 Josef Vitek	.08	.20
316 Jiri Hunkes	.08	.20
317 Radim Kucharczyk	.08	.20
318 Branislav Mezei	.20	.50
319 Karel Rachunek	.20	.50
320 Ivan Majesky	.20	.50
321 David Vrbata	.08	.20
322 Jaroslav Kasik	.08	.20
323 Ondrej Malinsky	.08	.20
324 Michal Dragoun	.08	.20
325 Michal Bros	.08	.20
326 Ondrej Kratena	.08	.20
327 Petr Kasik	.08	.20
328 Jiri Zeman	.08	.20
329 Miroslav Kopriva	.08	.20
330 Robert Kysela	.08	.20
331 Frantisek Kaberle	.08	.20
332 Jan Hrdina	.20	.50
333 Jiri Jelinek	.08	.20
334 Milan Hluchy	.08	.20
335 Jiri Stejskal	.08	.20
336 Jiri Fischer	.20	.50
337 Angel Krstev	.08	.20
338 Tomas Klimenta	.08	.20
339 Lukas Pabiska	.08	.20
340 Petr Vampola	.08	.20
341 Jan Visek	.08	.20
342 Jaroslav Modry	.20	.50
343 Martin Strba	.08	.20
344 David Stich	.08	.20
345 Jakub Korinek	.08	.20
346 Martin Paroulek	.08	.20
347 Frantisek Mrazek	.08	.20
348 Martin Cibak	.20	.50
349 David Moravec	.08	.20
350 Lukas Pulpan	.08	.20
351 Josef Beranek	.08	.20
352 Tomas Vlasak	.08	.20
353 Tomas Zizka	.08	.20
354 Vladimir Vujtek	.08	.20
355 Daniel Seman	.08	.20
356 Roman Simicek	.08	.20
357 Juraj Stefanka	.08	.20
358 Tomas Dolana	.08	.20
359 Pavel Vostrak	.08	.20
360 Radovan Biegl	.20	.50
361 Karol Sloboda	.08	.20
362 Vladimir Gyna	.08	.20
363 Petr Gregorek	.08	.20
364 Jiri Hudler	1.50	4.00
365 Pavel Kubina	.40	1.00
366 Ludek Krayzel	.08	.20
367 Martin Hamrlik	.08	.20
368 Michal Hrazdira	.08	.20
369 Connor Dunlop	.40	1.00
370 Miroslav Hanuljak	.08	.20
371 Miroslav Zalesak	.40	1.00
372 Radovan Biegl	.20	.50
373 Martin Vojtek	.08	.20
374 Tomáš Zboril	.08	.20
375 Tomáš Kloucek	.20	.50
376 Tomáš Pospíšil	.20	.50
377 Jaroslav Kudrna	.20	.50
378 Tomáš Harant	.20	.50
379 Milan Kraft	.20	.50
380 Radim Kucharczyk	.08	.20
381 Roman Málek	.20	.50
382 Andrej Nedorost	.20	.50
383 Vojtech Polák	.30	.75
384 František Mrázek	.08	.20
385 Jan Caloun	.08	.20
386 Radek Fiala	.08	.20
387 Martin Heinisch	.08	.20
388 Peter Jansky	.08	.20
389 Jindrich Kotrla	.08	.20
390 Jaroslav Špacek	.08	.20
391 Matej Badiura	.08	.20
392 Štepán Hrebejk	.08	.20
393 Radek Hubácek	.08	.20
394 Radek Hubácek	.08	.20
395 Mojmír Musil	.08	.20
396 Robert Najdek	.08	.20
397 Michal Nedbálek	.08	.20
398 Michal Šafarík	.08	.20
399 Radek Bonk	.20	.50
400 Ondrej Veselý	.08	.20
401 Martin Ambruz	.08	.20
402 Jirí Beroun	.08	.20
403 Martin Cakajík	.08	.20
404 Petr Kuboš	.08	.20
405 Milan Mikulík	.08	.20
406 Roman Nemecek	.08	.20
407 Ondrej Šmach	.08	.20
408 Josef Straka	.08	.20
409 Róbert Filc	.08	.20
410 Pavel Mojžiš	.08	.20
411 Jan Peterek	.08	.20
412 Radek Procházka	.08	.20
NNO Frantisek Kaberle CL	.08	.20

2004-05 Czech OFS Assist Leaders

Card	Low	High
COMPLETE SET (15)	15.00	35.00
1 Josef Beranek	1.25	3.00
2 Petr Leska	1.25	3.00
3 Peter Pucher	1.25	3.00
4 Josef Straka	1.25	3.00
5 Jan Marek	1.25	3.00
6 Zdenek Pavelek	1.25	3.00
7 Jiri Dopita	1.25	3.00
8 Jiri Burger	1.25	3.00
9 Martin Hamrlik	1.25	3.00
10 Michal Bros	1.25	3.00
11 Pavel Janku	1.25	3.00
12 Marek Uram	1.25	3.00
13 Tomas Divisek	1.25	3.00
14 Dusan Andrasovsky	1.25	3.00
15 Petr Sykora	1.25	3.00

2004-05 Czech OFS Checklist Cards

Card	Low	High
COMPLETE SET	10.00	25.00
1 Petr Buzek	.75	2.00
2 Frantisek Ptacek	.75	2.00
3 Jaromir Jagr	2.00	5.00
4 Patrik Rozsival	.75	2.00
5 Martin Skoula	.75	2.00
6 Milan Hejduk	1.25	3.00
7 Jaroslav Spacek	.75	2.00
8 Zigmund Palffy	1.25	3.00
9 Petr Nedved	.75	2.00
10 Radek Bonk	.75	2.00
11 David Moravec	.75	2.00
12 Rostislav Klesla	.75	2.00
13 Petr Cajanek	.75	2.00
14 Patrik Elias	1.25	3.00

2004-05 Czech OFS Czech/Slovak

Card	Low	High
COMPLETE SET (46)	20.00	40.00
1 Jaroslav Balastik	.75	2.00
2 Jiri Burger	.40	1.00
3 Tomas Demel	.40	1.00
4 Michal Dobron	.40	1.00
5 Jiri Dopita	.40	1.00
6 Tomas Duba	.40	1.00
7 Martin Chabada	.40	1.00
8 Waldemar Jirus	.40	1.00
9 Jiri Malinsky	.40	1.00
10 Jan Novak	.40	1.00
11 Frantisek Ptacek	.40	1.00
12 Peter Pucher	.40	1.00
13 Petr Sailer	.40	1.00
14 Jan Srdinko	.40	1.00
15 Josef Straka	.40	1.00
16 Michal Sup	.40	1.00
17 Adam Svoboda	.75	2.00
18 Michal Sykora	.40	1.00
19 Petr Sykora	.40	1.00
20 Michal Travnicek	.40	1.00
21 Marek Uram	.40	1.00
22 Libor Zabransky	.40	1.00
23 Daniel Babka	.40	1.00
24 Martin Bartek	.40	1.00
25 Zdeno Ciger	.40	1.00
26 Peter Fabus	.40	1.00
27 Miroslav Hala	.40	1.00
28 Juraj Halaj	.40	1.00
29 Richard Hartmann	.40	1.00
30 Jiri Hes	.40	1.00
31 Martin Ivicic	.40	1.00
32 Juraj Kledrowetz	.40	1.00
33 Jaroslav Kmit	.40	1.00
34 Arne Krotak	.40	1.00
35 Roman Kukumberg	.40	1.00
36 Igor Majesky	.40	1.00
37 Petr Pavlas	.40	1.00
38 Slavomir Pavlicko	.40	1.00
39 Pavol Rybar	.40	1.00
40 Michal Segla	.40	1.00
41 Richard Sechny	.40	1.00
42 Marcel Simurda	.40	1.00
43 Tomas Starosta	.40	1.00
44 Rastislav Stork	.40	1.00
45 Adam Svoboda CL	.75	2.00
46 Pavol Rybar CL	.40	1.00

2004-05 Czech OFS Defence Points

Card	Low	High
COMPLETE SET (15)	15.00	25.00
1 Martin Hamrlik	1.00	2.50
2 David Havir	1.00	2.50
3 Jan Novak	1.00	2.50
4 Stanislav Jasecko	1.00	2.50
5 Michal Sykora	1.00	2.50
6 Josef Reznicek	1.00	2.50
7 Frantisek Ptacek	1.00	2.50
8 Alexej Jaskin	1.00	2.50
9 Valdemar Jirus	1.00	2.50
10 Petr Kadlec	1.00	2.50
11 Jiri Malinsky	1.00	2.50
12 Patrik Luza	1.00	2.50
13 Radim Tesarik	1.00	2.50
14 Pavel Kowalczyk	1.00	2.50
15 Petr Jancarik	1.00	2.50

2004-05 Czech OFS Goals-Against Leaders

Card	Low	High
COMPLETE SET (16)	25.00	60.00
1 Igor Murin	2.00	5.00
2 Adam Svoboda	2.50	6.00
3 Petr Briza	2.00	5.00
4 Jiri Trvaj	2.00	5.00
5 Roman Malek	2.00	5.00
6 Petr Franek	2.00	5.00
7 Radovan Biegl	2.00	5.00
8 Tomas Duba	2.00	5.00
9 Zdenek Orct	2.00	5.00
10 Lukas Hronek	2.00	5.00
11 Martin Vojtek	2.00	5.00
12 Martin Altrichter	2.00	5.00
13 Oldrich Svoboda	2.00	5.00
14 Michal Marik	2.00	5.00
15 Marek Pinc	2.00	5.00
NNO Altrichter/Murin CL	2.00	5.00

2004-05 Czech OFS Goals Leaders

Card	Low	High
COMPLETE SET (15)	12.00	30.00
1 Jaroslav Balastik	1.50	4.00
2 Michal Sup	1.00	2.50
3 Marek Uram	1.00	2.50
4 Josef Straka	1.00	2.50
5 Jiri Burger	1.00	2.50
6 Petr Sykora	1.00	2.50
7 Marek Melenovsky	1.00	2.50
8 Jan Marek	1.00	2.50
9 Lukas Havel	1.00	2.50
10 Jiri Dopita	1.00	2.50
11 Tomas Divisek	1.00	2.50
12 Peter Barinka	1.00	2.50
13 Zbynek Irgl	1.00	2.50
14 David Hruska	1.00	2.50
15 Ondrej Vesely	1.00	2.50

2004-05 Czech OFS Jaromir Jagr

Card	Low	High
COMPLETE SET (6)	20.00	50.00
JO1 Jaromir Jagr	4.00	10.00
JO2 Jaromir Jagr	4.00	10.00
JO3 Jaromir Jagr	4.00	10.00
JO4 Jaromir Jagr	4.00	10.00
JO5 Jaromir Jagr	4.00	10.00
JO6 Jaromir Jagr	4.00	10.00

2004-05 Czech OFS Points Leaders

Card	Low	High
COMPLETE SET (15)	20.00	40.00
1 Josef Beranek	1.25	3.00
2 Petr Leska	1.25	3.00
3 Josef Straka	1.25	3.00
4 Peter Pucher	1.25	3.00
5 Jan Marek	1.25	3.00
6 Marek Uram	1.25	3.00
7 Jiri Burger	1.25	3.00
8 Jiri Dopita	1.25	3.00
9 Jaroslav Balastik	1.25	3.00
10 Petr Sykora	1.25	3.00
11 Michal Sup	1.25	3.00
12 Tomas Divisek	1.25	3.00
13 Marek Melenovsky	1.25	3.00
14 Zdenek Pavelek	1.25	3.00
15 Michal Bros	1.25	3.00

2004-05 Czech OFS Save Percentage Leaders

Card	Low	High
COMPLETE SET (15)	25.00	60.00
1 Igor Murin	2.00	5.00
2 Petr Briza	2.00	5.00
3 Zdenek Orct	2.00	5.00
4 Petr Franek	2.00	5.00
5 Roman Malek	2.00	5.00
6 Jiri Trvaj	2.00	5.00
7 Adam Svoboda	2.50	6.00
8 Radovan Biegl	2.00	5.00
9 Martin Vojtek	2.00	5.00
10 Tomas Duba	2.00	5.00
11 Martin Altrichter	2.00	5.00
12 Marek Pinc	2.00	5.00
13 Lukas Hronek	2.00	5.00
14 Libor Barta	2.00	5.00
15 Michal Marik	2.00	5.00

2004-05 Czech OFS Stars

Card	Low	High
COMPLETE SET (51)	30.00	60.00
1 Tomas Kaberle	.75	2.00
2 Jaromir Jagr	4.00	10.00
3 Radim Vrbata	1.25	3.00
4 Vaclav Nedorost	.75	2.00
5 Tomas Kurka	.40	1.00
6 Martin Rucinsky	.40	1.00
7 Martin Skoula	.40	1.00
8 Robert Reichel	.40	1.00
9 Jiri Slegr	.40	1.00
10 Jan Bulis	.40	1.00
11 Milan Hejduk	1.50	4.00
12 Ales Hemsky	2.00	5.00
13 Jiri Dopita	.40	1.00
14 Jan Lasak	.75	2.00
15 Martin Straka	.40	1.00
16 Jaroslav Spacek	.40	1.00
17 Milan Kraft	.75	2.00
18 Zigmund Palffy	1.25	3.00
19 Josef Stumpel	.40	1.00
20 Josef Vasicek	.40	1.00
21 Tomas Kloucek	.40	1.00
22 Radek Duda	.40	1.00
23 Jan Hlavac	.40	1.00
24 Karel Pilar	.40	1.00
25 David Vyborny	.75	2.00
26 Petr Nedved	.40	1.00
27 Michal Rozsival	.40	1.00
28 Radek Bonk	.40	1.00
29 Branislav Mezei	.40	1.00
30 Martin Prusek	.75	2.00
31 Marek Malik	.40	1.00
32 Pavel Kubina	.40	1.00
33 Vaclav Varada	.40	1.00
34 Rostislav Klesla	.40	1.00
35 Roman Cechmanek	.40	1.00
36 Branko Radivojevic	.40	1.00
37 Radovan Somik	.40	1.00
38 Martin Erat	.40	1.00
39 Roman Hamrlik	.40	1.00
40 Petr Cajanek	.40	1.00
41 Patrik Elias	.75	2.00
42 Martin Havlat	1.50	4.00
43 Karel Rachunek	.40	1.00
44 Tomas Vokoun	2.00	5.00
45 Petr Buzek	.40	1.00
46 David Moravec	.40	1.00
47 Martin Hlavacka	.40	1.00
48 Ales Kotalik	1.25	3.00
49 Robert Schnabel	.40	1.00
50 Michal Sivek	.40	1.00
51 Jaromir Jagr CL	4.00	10.00

2004-05 Czech OFS Stars II

Card	Low	High
COMPLETE SET (8)	20.00	50.00
1 Frantisek Kaberle	1.50	4.00
2 Jan Hrdina	1.50	4.00
3 Ivan Majesky	1.50	4.00
4 Jiri Hudler	6.00	15.00
5 Connor Dunlop	1.50	4.00
6 Vladimir Vujtek	1.50	4.00
7 Josef Beranek	1.50	4.00
8 Tomas Vlasak	1.50	4.00
9 Roman Malek	1.50	4.00
10 Jan Caloun	1.50	4.00
11 Jiri Fischer	2.00	5.00
12 Jaroslav Modry	1.50	4.00
13 Roman Simicek	1.50	4.00
14 Tomas Harant	1.50	4.00
15 Martin Hamrlik	1.50	4.00
16 Pavel Kubina CL	1.50	4.00

2004-05 Czech OFS Team Cards

Card	Low	High
COMPLETE SET (14)	6.00	15.00
1 Jaroslav Suchan	.40	1.00
2 Zdenek Smid	.40	1.00
3 Zdenek Orct	.75	2.00
4 Milan Hnilicka	.75	2.00
5 Michal Marik	.40	1.00
6 Jan Lasak	1.25	3.00
7 Tomas Duba	.40	1.00
8 Petr Franek	.40	1.00
9 Petr Briza	.75	2.00
10 Vlastimil Lakosil	.40	1.00
11 Martin Prusek	.75	2.00
12 Roman Cechmanek	.75	2.00
13 Martin Altrichter	.40	1.00
14 Robert Slavik	.40	1.00

2004 Czech DS Stars

1 Jaromir Jagr
Looking Down
2 Jaromir Jagr
Skating to right side
3 Jaromir Jagr
Stick Up Looking Left
4 Tomas Kaberle
5 Jan Hrdina
6 Jiri Slegr
7 Martin Havlat
8 Josef Melichar
9 Martin Rucinsky
10 Frantisek Kaberle
11 Petr Nedved
12 Vaclav Prospal
13 Ivan Huml
14 Jan Hlavac
15 David Vyborny
16 Tomas Vokoun
(Horizontal
17 Tomas Vokoun
(Vertical
18 Milan Kraft
19 Robert Schnabel
20 Martin Altrichter
(Looking to Side
21 Martin Altrichter
(Looking Down

2004 Czech World Championship Postcards

This series was issued to commemorate the 2004 World Championships, which were held in Prague and Ostrava, Czech Republic. They are postcard sized and unnumbered.

Card	Low	High
COMPLETE SET (24)	10.00	25.00
1 Josef Beranek	.40	1.00
2 Roman Cechmanek	.60	1.50
3 Jiri Dopita	.40	1.00
4 Radek Dvorak	.40	1.00
5 Radek Hamr	.40	1.00
6 Roman Hamrlik	.40	1.00
7 Jan Hejda	.40	1.00
8 Jan Hlavac	.40	1.00
9 Jaroslav Hlinka	.40	1.00
10 Jaromir Jagr	2.00	5.00
11 Frantisek Kaberle	.40	1.00
12 Milan Kraft	.40	1.00
13 Jan Novak	.40	1.00
14 Vaclav Prospal	.40	1.00
15 Petr Prucha	1.50	4.00
16 Martin Rucinsky	.40	1.00
17 Dusan Salficky	.60	1.50
18 Jiri Slegr	.40	1.00
19 Jaroslav Spacek	.40	1.00
20 Martin Straka	.40	1.00
21 Michal Sup	.40	1.00
22 Tomas Vokoun	1.50	4.00
23 David Vyborny	.60	1.50

2005 Czech World Champions Postcards

Standard postcard-sized issue was released to commemorate the Czech Republic's victory at the 2005 WC. The cards are unnumbered.

Card	Low	High
COMPLETE SET (23)		
1 Frantisek Kaberle	.40	1.00
2 Jiri Slegr	.40	1.00
3 David Vyborny	.40	1.00
4 Jiri Fischer	.40	1.00
5 Jan Hlavac	.40	1.00
6 Josef Vasicek	.40	1.00
7 Vaclav Prospal	.40	1.00
8 Vaclav Varada	.40	1.00
9 Pavel Kubina	.40	1.00
10 Radek Dvorak	.40	1.00
11 Ales Hemsky	1.50	4.00
12 Radim Vrbata	.75	2.00
13 Martin Rucinsky	.40	1.00
14 Martin Straka	.40	1.00
15 Jaromir Jagr	4.00	10.00
16 Marek Zidlicky	.40	1.00
17 Milan Hnilicka	.75	2.00
18 Petr Sykora	.40	1.00
19 Tomas Kaberle	.40	1.00
20 Petr Cajanek	.40	1.00
21 Tomas Vokoun	2.00	5.00
22 Jaroslav Spacek	.40	1.00
23 Jan Hejda	.40	1.00

2005 Czech Stadion

673 Jaromir Jagr
675 Martin Havlat
676 Robert Reichel
677 Tomas Vokoun
678 Martin Brodeur
679 Mario Lemieux
680 Keith Tkachuk
681 Teemu Selanne
682 Ruslan Fedotenko
683 Nikolai Khabibulin
684 Jarome Iginla
685 Mikka Kiprusoff
686 Pavel Kubina
687 Vincent Lecavalier
688 Robyn Regehr
689 Brad Richards
690 Martin St. Louis

2005-06 Czech HC Ceski Budejovice

Card	Low	High
COMPLETE SET (16)	8.00	20.00
1 Kamil Brabenec	.60	1.50
2 Petr Gregorek	.60	1.50
3 Tomas Harant	.60	1.50
4 Stepan Hrebejk	.60	1.50
5 Viktor Hubl	.60	1.50
6 Michal Hudec	.60	1.50
7 Milan Kopecky	.60	1.50
8 Jindrich Kotrla	.60	1.50
9 Ales Kratoska	.60	1.50
10 Zdenek Kutlak	.60	1.50
11 Jan Moucha	.60	1.50
12 Marek Posmyk	.60	1.50
13 Petr Sailer	.60	1.50
14 Roman Turek	.75	2.00
15 Tomas Vak	.60	1.50
16 Rene Vydareny	.60	1.50

2005-06 Czech HC Hame Zlin

Card	Low	High
COMPLETE SET (16)	8.00	20.00
1 Martin Altrichter	.60	1.50
2 Petr Barinka	.60	1.50
3 Jan Benda	.60	1.50
4 Miroslav Blatak	.60	1.50
5 Lukas Galvas	.60	1.50
6 Martin Hamrlik	.60	1.50
7 Richard Kral	.60	1.50

8 Petr Leska .60 1.50
9 Marek Melenovsky .60 1.50
10 Petr Mokrejs .60 1.50
11 Igor Murin .60 1.50
12 David Nosek .60 1.50
13 Miroslav Okal .60 1.50
14 Ivan Rachunek .60 1.50
15 Michal Travnicek .60 1.50
16 Martin Zahorovsky .60 1.50

2005-06 Czech HC Karlovy Vary

COMPLETE SET (16) 8.00 20.00
1 Jan Alinc .60 1.50
2 Roman Cechmanek .75 2.00
3 Miroslav Duben .60 1.50
4 Michal Dvorak .60 1.50
5 Lubomir Hurtaj .60 1.50
6 Jan Kostal .60 1.50
7 Lukas Krajicek .60 1.50
8 Petr Kumstat .60 1.50
9 Lukas Mensator .60 1.50
10 Andrej Nedorost .60 1.50
11 Ondrej Nemec .60 1.50
12 Lukas Pech .60 1.50
13 Frantisek Ptacek .60 1.50
14 Josef Reznicek .60 1.50
15 Vaclav Skuhravy .60 1.50
16 Libor Ustrnul .60 1.50

2005-06 Czech HC Kladno

COMPLETE SET (15) 109.00 25.00
1 Jan Besser .60 1.50
2 Martin Frolik .60 1.50
3 Michael Frolik 2.00 5.00
4 Radek Gardon .60 1.50
5 Tomas Horna .60 1.50
6 Ivan Huml 1.00 2.50
7 Jaroslav Kalla .60 1.50
8 Jakub Lev .60 1.50
9 Zdenek Orct .75 2.00
10 Libor Prochazka .60 1.50
11 Martin Prochazka .60 1.50
12 Jaroslav Spelda .60 1.50
13 Ladislav Vlcek .60 1.50
14 Josef Zajic .60 1.50
15 Jiri Zeman .60 1.50

2005-06 Czech HC Liberec

COMPLETE SET (16) 8.00 20.00
1 Leos Cermak .60 1.50
2 Pavel Falta .60 1.50
3 Jiri Hanzlik .60 1.50
4 Milan Hnilicka .75 2.00
5 Valdemar Jirus .60 1.50
6 Angel Krstev .60 1.50
7 Lukas Pabiska .60 1.50
8 Andrej Podkonicky .60 1.50
9 Stanislav Prochazka .60 1.50
10 Igor Rataj .60 1.50
11 Martin Richtr .60 1.50
12 Patrik Rozsival .60 1.50
13 Martin Rygl .60 1.50
14 Jan Tomajko .60 1.50
15 Lubomir Vaic .60 1.50
16 Petr Vampola .60 1.50

2005-06 Czech HC Pardubice

COMPLETE SET (16) 8.00 20.00
1 Tomas Blazek .60 1.50
2 Jan Caloun .60 1.50
3 Petr Caslava .60 1.50
4 David Havir .60 1.50
5 Robert Kantor .60 1.50
6 Jan Kolar .60 1.50
7 Lubomir Korhon .60 1.50
8 Jan Lasak 1.25 3.00
9 Ladislav Lubina .60 1.50
10 Michal Mikeska .60 1.50
11 Frantisek Mrazek .60 1.50
12 Petr Mudroch .75 2.00
13 Andrej Novotny .75 2.00
14 Tomas Rolinek .60 1.50
15 Jan Snopek .60 1.50
16 Michal Tvrdik .60 1.50

2005-06 Czech HC Plzen

COMPLETE SET (16) 8.00 20.00
1 Martin Adamsky .60 1.50
2 Mario Cartelli .60 1.50
3 Michal Duras .60 1.50
4 Petr Jez .60 1.50
5 Robert Jindrich .60 1.50
6 Jaroslav Kracik .60 1.50
7 Roman Malek .60 1.50
8 Radek Matejovsky .60 1.50
9 David Moravec .60 1.50
10 Martin Stepanek .60 1.50
11 Josef Straka .60 1.50
12 Michal Straka .60 1.50
13 Pavel Trnka .60 1.50
14 Matej Trojovsky .60 1.50
15 Roman Tvrdon .60 1.50
16 Marek Vorel .60 1.50

2005-06 Czech HC Slavia Praha

COMPLETE SET (16) 8.00 20.00
1 Jaroslav Bednar .60 1.50
2 Josef Beranek .60 1.50
3 Roman Cervenka .60 2.00
4 Radek Dlouhy .60 1.50
5 Jiri Drtina .60 1.50
6 Radek Duda .60 1.50
7 Petr Franek .60 1.50
8 David Hruska .60 1.50
9 Petr Kadlec .60 1.50
10 Pavel Kolarik .60 1.50
11 Jan Novak .60 1.50
12 Michal Sup .60 1.50
13 Tomas Vlasak .60 1.50
14 Michal Vondrka .60 1.50
15 Boris Zabka .60 1.50
16 Tomas Zizka .60 1.50

2005-06 Czech HC Sparta Praha

COMPLETE SET (16) 8.00 20.00
1 Petr Briza 1.25 3.00
2 Marek Cernosek .60 1.50
3 Michal Dobron .60 1.50
4 Jan Hanzlik .60 1.50
5 Martin Hlavacka .60 1.50
6 Martin Chabada .60 1.50
7 Ondrej Kratena .60 1.50
8 Jan Marek .60 1.50
9 Jakub Sindel .60 1.50
10 Michal Sivek .75 2.00
11 Martin Spanhel .75 2.00
12 Josef Straka .60 1.50
13 Milan Toman .60 1.50
14 Petr Ton .60 1.50
15 Roman Vopat .60 1.50
16 Jiri Vykoukal .60 1.50

2005-06 Czech HC Trinec

COMPLETE SET (15) 8.00 20.00
1 Richard Bordowski .60 1.50
2 Lukas Danecek .60 1.50
3 Jiri Hasek .60 1.50
4 Jiri Hunkes .60 1.50
5 Tomas Jurdic .60 1.50
6 Jaroslav Kudrna .60 1.50
7 Tomas Pacal .60 1.50
8 Jan Peterek .60 1.50
9 Lubomir Pistek .60 1.50
10 Vaclav Pletka 1.00 2.50
11 Jiri Polansky .60 1.50
12 Radim Tesarik .60 1.50
13 David Vsetecka .60 1.50
14 Martin Vojtek .60 1.50
15 Tomas Zboril .60 1.50

2005-06 Czech HC Vitkovice

COMPLETE SET (16) 8.00 20.00
1 Jiri Burger .60 1.50
2 Jan Dresler .60 1.50
3 Petr Hubacek .60 1.50
4 Stanislav Hudec .60 1.50
5 Jakub Hulva .60 1.50
6 Zbynek Irgl .60 1.50
7 Petr Jurecka .60 1.50
8 Jaroslav Kames .75 2.00
9 Bedrich Kohler .60 1.50
10 Lukas Krenzelok .60 1.50
11 Radoslav Kropac .60 1.50
12 Radek Philipp .60 1.50
13 Marek Pinc .75 2.00
14 Radek Prochazka .60 1.50
15 Roman Simicek .60 1.50
16 Martin Tomasek .60 1.50

2005-06 Czech HC Vsetin

COMPLETE SET (15) 8.00 20.00
1 Richard Bauer .60 1.50
2 Tomas Demel .60 1.50
3 Roman Gorev .60 1.50
4 Michal Horak .60 1.50
5 Josef Hrabal .60 1.50
6 Ondrej Hruska .60 1.50
7 Radim Hruska .60 1.50
8 Josef Kucera .60 1.50
9 David Kveton .60 1.50
10 Havi Sasu .60 1.50
11 Zdenek Spitzer .60 1.50
12 Roman Stantien .60 1.50
13 Filip Stefanka .60 1.50
14 Ondrej Steiner .60 1.50
15 Patrik Luza .60 1.50

2005-06 Czech HC Znojmo

COMPLETE SET (14) 8.00 20.00
1 Radim Bicanek .60 1.50
2 Martin Cakajik .60 1.50
3 Jiri Dopita .60 1.50
4 Roman Erat .60 1.50
5 Radek Haman .60 1.50
6 Richard Jares .60 1.50
7 Ales Kretinsky .60 1.50
8 Milan Ministr .60 1.50
9 Pavel Mojzis .60 1.50
10 Zdenek Ondrej .60 1.50
11 Karel Plasek .60 1.50
12 Peter Pucher .60 1.50
13 Jiri Trvaj .60 1.50
14 Marek Uram .60 1.50

2006-07 Czech CP Cup Postcards

COMPLETE SET (23) 20.00 40.00
1 Miroslav Blatak .75 2.00
2 Jiri Burger .75 2.00
3 Radek Hamr .75 2.00
4 Jaroslav Hlinka .75 2.00
5 Milan Hnilicka 1.25 3.00
6 Miloslav Horava .75 2.00
7 Petr Hubacek .75 2.00
8 Jiri Hunkes .75 2.00
9 Martin Chabada .75 2.00
10 Zbynek Irgl .75 2.00
11 Zdenek Kutlak .75 2.00
12 Roman Malek .75 2.00
13 Jan Marek .75 2.00
14 Josef Marha .75 2.00
15 Vaclav Pletka .75 2.00
16 Tomas Rolinek .75 2.00
17 Michal Sivek .75 2.00
18 Vaclav Skuhravy .75 2.00
19 Petr Sykora .75 2.00
20 Martin Sevc .75 2.00
21 Ivan Rachunek .75 2.00
22 Lukas Zib .75 2.00
23 Tomas Zizka .75 2.00

2006-07 Czech HC Ceske Budejovice Postcards

COMPLETE SET (14) 15.00 25.00
1 Petr Gregorek .75 2.00
2 Viktor Hubl .75 2.00
3 Michal Hudec .75 2.00
4 Jindrich Kotrla .75 2.00
5 Jan Mucha .75 2.00
6 Vaclav Nedorost 1.25 3.00
7 Petr Sailer .75 2.00
8 Jiri Simanek .75 2.00
9 Milan Toman .75 2.00
10 Roman Turek 1.25 3.00
11 Martin Vagner .75 2.00
12 Tomas Vak .75 2.00
13 Ondrej Vesely .75 2.00
14 Rene Vydareny .75 2.00

2006-07 Czech HC Kladno Postcards

It is quite likely that this checklist is incomplete. If you know if additional postcards, please email us at hockeymag@beckett.com.

COMPLETE SET (11) 10.00 20.00
1 Ales Pavlas .75 2.00
2 Jakub Lev .75 2.00
3 Jaroslav Kalla .75 2.00
4 Martin Frolik .75 2.00
5 Martin Prochazka .75 2.00
6 Martin Sevc .75 2.00
7 Michal Havel .75 2.00
8 Milan Hluchy .75 2.00
9 Pavel Patera .75 2.00
10 Radek Gardon .75 2.00
11 Zdenek Orct 1.25 3.00

2006-07 Czech HC Liberec Postcards

It is likely this checklist is incomplete. Please forward additional information to hockeymag@beckett.com.

COMPLETE SET (12) 10.00 20.00
1 Jakub Cutta .75 2.00
2 Ondrej Hruska .75 2.00
3 Waldemar Jirus .75 2.00
4 Angel Krstev .75 2.00
5 Michal Nedvidek .75 2.00
6 Vaclav Novak .75 2.00
7 Vaclav Pletka .75 2.00
8 Filip Sindelar .75 2.00
9 Jan Tomajko .75 2.00
10 Lubomir Vaic .75 2.00
11 Jan Visek .75 2.00
12 Lukas Zib .75 2.00

2006-07 Czech HC Pardubice Postcards

COMPLETE SET (23) 20.00 40.00
1 Dusan Andrasovsky .75 2.00
2 Tomas Blazek 1.25 3.00
3 Jan Caloun 1.25 3.00
4 Petr Caslava .75 2.00
5 David Havir .75 2.00
6 Miroslav Hlinka .75 2.00
7 Jan Kolar .75 2.00
8 Jaroslav Koma .75 2.00
9 Petr Koukal .75 2.00
10 Vladislav Koutsky .75 2.00
11 Jan Lasak 1.25 3.00
12 Tomas Linhart .75 2.00
13 Frantisek Mrazek .75 2.00
14 Andrej Novotny .75 2.00
15 Ales Pisa .75 2.00
16 Libor Pivko .75 2.00
17 Tomas Rolinek .75 2.00
18 Michal Seda .75 2.00
19 Jan Snopek .75 2.00
20 Adam Svoboda 1.25 3.00
21 Petr Sykora .75 2.00
22 Michal Tvrdik .75 2.00
23 Jan Stary .75 2.00

2006-07 Czech HC Plzen Postcards

COMPLETE SET (16) 15.00 30.00
1 Adam Saffer .75 2.00
2 Ales Padelek .75 2.00
3 David Ludvik .75 2.00
4 Jiri Malinsky .75 2.00
5 Jiri Zelenka .75 2.00
6 Lukas Derner .75 2.00
7 Lukas Pulpan .75 2.00
8 Roman Malek 1.25 3.00
9 Martin Adamsky .75 2.00
10 Michal Duras .75 2.00
11 Milan Nedoma .75 2.00
12 Peter Fabus .75 2.00
13 Petr Jez .75 2.00
14 Tomas Divisek .75 2.00
15 Tomas Kubalik .75 2.00
16 Vaclav Benak .75 2.00

2006-07 Czech HC Slavia Praha Postcards

COMPLETE SET (16) 15.00 30.00
1 Jaroslav Bednar .75 2.00
2 Josef Beranek .75 2.00
3 Leos Cermak .75 2.00
4 Roman Cervenka .75 2.00
5 Radek Dlouhy .75 2.00
6 Jiri Drtina .75 2.00
7 Dominik Granak .75 2.00
8 Martin Hlavacka .75 2.00
9 David Hruska .75 2.00
10 Pavel Kolarik .75 2.00
11 Igor Rataj .75 2.00
12 Vladimir Sobotka .75 2.00
13 Michal Sup .75 2.00
14 Adam Svoboda 1.25 3.00
15 Tomas Vlasak .75 2.00
16 Tomas Zizka .75 2.00

2006-07 Czech HC Sparta Praha Postcards

COMPLETE SET (15) 15.00 30.00
1 Ladislav Benysek .75 2.00
2 Marek Cernosek .75 2.00
3 David Vrbata .75 2.00
4 Dusan Salficky 1.25 3.00
5 Frantisek Ptacek .75 2.00
6 Jan Hanzlik .75 2.00
7 Jan Hlavac 1.25 3.00
8 Jaroslav Hlinka .75 2.00
9 Jakub Langhammer .75 2.00
10 Michal Sivek 1.25 3.00
11 Ondrej Kratena .75 2.00
12 Petr Ton .75 2.00
13 Martin Strba .75 2.00
14 Tomas Netik .75 2.00
15 Tomas Protivny .75 2.00

2006-07 Czech HC Vsetin Postcards

This set is likely to be incomplete. If you have additional information, please email hockeymag@beckett.com.

COMPLETE SET (12) 10.00
1 Lukas Bolf .75 2.00
2 Guntis Galvins .75 2.00
3 Josef Hrabal .75 2.00
4 Jiri Kucny .75 2.00
5 Lukas Duba .75 2.00
6 Lubos Rob .75 2.00
7 Lubomir Sabol .75 2.00
8 Vladimir Skoda .75 2.00
9 Lubomir Stach .75 2.00
10 Roman Stantien .75 2.00
11 Martin Stefl .75 2.00
12 Tomas Demel .75 2.00

2006-07 Czech HC Zlin Hame Postcards

COMPLETE SET (15) 15.00 30.00
1 Martin Cech .75 2.00
2 Martin Hamrlik .75 2.00
3 Jan Horacek .75 2.00
4 Robin Kovar .75 2.00
5 Jaroslav Kristek .75 2.00
6 Pavel Kubis .75 2.00
7 Petr Leska .75 2.00
8 Marek Melenovsky 1.25 3.00
9 Igor Murin .75 2.00
10 Roman Psurny .75 2.00
11 Ivan Rachunek .75 2.00
12 Robert Tomik .75 2.00
13 Lubomir Sekeras .75 2.00
14 Martin Zahorovsky .75 2.00
15 Pavel Zubicek .75 2.00

2006-07 Czech IIHF World Championship Postcards

COMPLETE SET (23) 20.00 40.00
1 Jaroslav Balastik .75 2.00
2 Jaroslav Bednar .60 1.50
3 Jan Bulis .60 1.50
4 Martin Erat .75 2.00
5 Jan Hejda .60 1.50
6 Jan Hlavac .60 1.50
7 Jaroslav Hlinka .60 1.50
8 Milan Hnilicka .75 2.00
9 Petr Hubacek .60 1.50
10 Zbynek Irgl .60 1.50
11 Tomas Kaberle .75 2.00
12 Lukas Krajicek .75 2.00
13 Zdenek Kutlak .60 1.50
14 Zbynek Michalek .60 1.50
15 Tomas Plekanec 1.25 3.00
16 Ivo Prorok .60 1.50
17 Martin Richter .60 1.50
18 Tomas Rolinek .60 1.50
19 Martin Skoula .60 1.50
20 Patrik Stefan .60 1.50
21 Adam Svoboda .60 1.50
22 Petr Tenkrat .60 1.50
23 David Vyborny .75 2.00

2006-07 Czech LG Hockey Games Postcards

COMPLETE SET (22) 15.00 30.00
1 Jaroslav Balastik .75 2.00
2 Jaroslav Bednar .40 1.00
3 Miroslav Blatak .40 1.00
4 Petr Hubacek .40 1.00
5 Jiri Hunkes .40 1.00
6 Zbynek Irgl .75 2.00
7 Jaroslav Kracik .40 1.00
8 Lukas Krajicek .75 2.00
9 Jaroslav Kudrna .75 2.00
10 Zdenek Kutlak .40 1.00
11 Jan Marek .40 1.00
12 Zbynek Michalek .40 1.00
13 Jan Novak .40 1.00
14 Jan Peterek .40 1.00
15 Tomas Popperle .75 2.00
16 Ivo Prorok .40 1.00
17 Tomas Rolinek .40 1.00
18 Martin Sevc .40 1.00
19 Martin Skoula .40 1.00
20 Patrik Stefan .40 1.00
21 Adam Svoboda .75 2.00
22 Petr Tenkrat .40 1.00

2006-07 Czech OFS

COMPLETE SET (326) 75.00 125.00
1 Kamil Brabenec .20 .50
2 Petr Gregorek .20 .50
3 Milan Gulas .20 .50
4 Stepan Hrebejk .20 .50
5 Viktor Hubl .20 .50
6 Michal Hudec .20 .50
7 Jan Chabera .30 .75
8 Jindrich Kotrla .20 .50
9 Zdenek Kutlak .30 .75
10 Lukas Kveton .20 .50
11 Petr Machacek .20 .50
12 Jan Mucha .20 .50
13 Vaclav Nedorost .40 1.00
14 Marek Posmyk .30 .75
15 Petr Sailer .20 .50
16 Jiri Simanek .20 .50
17 Milan Toman .20 .50
18 Roman Turek .40 1.00
19 Martin Vagner .30 .75
20 Tomas Vak .20 .50
21 Ondrej Vesely .20 .50
22 Rene Vydareny .20 .50
23 David Balasz .20 .50
24 Michal Borovansky .20 .50
25 Michal Dobron .20 .50
26 Miroslav Duben .20 .50
27 Michal Dvorak .20 .50
28 Jiri Hanzlik .20 .50
29 Vojtech Kloz .20 .50
30 Jan Kostal .20 .50
31 Milan Kraft .40 1.00
32 Petr Kumstat .20 .50
33 Vladimir Machulda .20 .50
34 Lukas Mensator .30 .75
35 Petr Mudroch .20 .50
36 Ondrej Nemec .20 .50
37 Lukas Pech .20 .50
38 Milan Prochazka .20 .50
39 Josef Reznicek .20 .50
40 Lukas Sablik .30 .75
41 Frantisek Skladany .20 .50
42 Vaclav Skuhravy .20 .50
43 Kamil Tvrdek .20 .50
44 Libor Ustrnul .30 .75
45 Jiri Burger .20 .50
46 Jan Dresler .20 .50
47 Michal Gulasi .20 .50
48 Petr Hubacek .20 .50
49 Stanislav Hudec .20 .50
50 Lukas Chmelir .20 .50
51 Zbynek Irgl .30 .75
52 Stanislav Jasecko .20 .50
53 Petr Jurecka .20 .50
54 Tomas Kana .20 .50
55 Bedrich Kohler .20 .50
56 Lukas Krenzelok .20 .50
57 Radoslav Kropac .20 .50
58 Petr Kubos .20 .50
59 Milan Mikulik .20 .50
60 Marek Pinc .30 .75
61 Radek Prochazka .20 .50
62 Filip Seman .20 .50
63 Roman Simicek .20 .50
64 Jakub Stepanek .30 .75
65 Martin Tomasek .20 .50
66 Lukas Klimek .20 .50
67 Jiri Vykoukal .20 .50
68 David Vrbata .20 .50
69 Petr Ton .20 .50
70 Jan Tabacek .20 .50
71 Michal Sivek .40 1.00
72 Dusan Salficky .60 1.50
73 Frantisek Ptacek .20 .50
74 Petr Prikryl .30 .75
75 Tomas Protivny .20 .50
76 Martin Podlesak .20 .50
77 Tomas Netik .20 .50
78 Jaroslav Mrazek .20 .50
79 Jakub Langhammer .20 .50
80 Ondrej Kratena .30 .75
81 Karel Hromas .20 .50
82 Jaroslav Hlinka .20 .50
83 Jan Hlavac .40 1.00
84 Jan Hanzlik .20 .50
85 Michal Dragoun .20 .50
86 Marek Cernosek .20 .50
87 Ladislav Benysek .20 .50
88 Jan Holub .20 .50
89 Ondrej Hruska .20 .50
90 Ctibor Jech .20 .50
91 Valdemar Jirus .20 .50
92 Tomas Klimenta .20 .50
93 Vaclav Koci .20 .50
94 Angel Krstev .20 .50
95 Jiri Moravec .20 .50
96 Michal Nedvidek .30 .75
97 Lukas Pabiska .20 .50
98 Rok Pajic .20 .50
99 Vaclav Pletka .30 .75
100 Jan Plodek .20 .50
101 Andrej Podkonicky .20 .50
102 Stanislav Prochazka .20 .50
103 Jiri Stejskal .30 .75
104 Petr Sachl .20 .50
105 Lubomir Vaic .20 .50
106 Petr Vampola .20 .50
107 Jan Visek .20 .50
108 Lukas Zib .20 .50
109 Boris Zabka .20 .50
110 Dusan Andrasovsky .20 .50
111 Tomas Blazek .20 .50
112 Jan Caloun .30 .75
113 Petr Caslava .20 .50
114 David Havir .20 .50
115 Miroslav Hlinka .20 .50
116 Jan Kolar .20 .50
117 Jaroslav Koma .20 .50
118 Petr Koukal .20 .50
119 Vladislav Koutsky .30 .75
120 Jan Lasak .75 2.00
121 Tomas Linhart .20 .50
122 Andrej Novotny .20 .50
123 Zdenek Ondrej .20 .50
124 Tomas Rolinek .20 .50
125 Jan Snopek .20 .50
126 Petr Sykora .20 .50
127 Michal Seda .20 .50
128 Lukas Bednarik .20 .50
129 Jan Benda .20 .50
130 Frantisek Bombic .20 .50
131 Daniel Branda .20 .50
132 Jakub Cerny .20 .50
133 Vladimir Gyna .20 .50
134 Jan Hranac .20 .50
135 Jaroslav Hubl .30 .75
136 Peter Jansky .20 .50
137 Martin Jenacek .20 .50
138 Milan Kopecky .20 .50
139 Vojtech Kubincak .20 .50
140 Frantisek Lukes .20 .50
141 Marian Morava .20 .50
142 Angel Nikolov .20 .50
143 Lukas Pozivil .20 .50
144 Ivo Prorok .20 .50
145 Robert Reichel .40 1.00
146 Zbynek Sklenicka .20 .50
147 Radim Skuhrovec .20 .50
148 Jiri Slegr .30 .75
149 Michal Travnicek .20 .50
150 Michal Podolka .40 1.00
151 Jaroslav Barton .20 .50
152 Radovan Biegl .30 .75
153 Jan Danecek .20 .50
154 Lukas Danecek .40 1.00
155 Tomas Frolo .20 .50
156 Jiri Hasek .20 .50
157 Alexandr Hegegy .20 .50
158 Marcin Kolusz .30 .75
159 Lubomir Korhon .20 .50
160 Vlastimil Kroupa .20 .50
161 Jaroslav Kudrna .20 .50
162 Rostislav Martynek .20 .50
163 Tomas Pacal .20 .50
164 Jan Peterek .20 .50
165 Jiri Polansky .20 .50
166 Tomas Razingar .20 .50
167 Zdenek Skorepa .20 .50
168 Radim Tesarik .20 .50
169 Roman Tomas .20 .50
170 Tomas Vrba .20 .50
171 Jan Vytisk .20 .50
172 Stefan Zigardy .30 .75
173 Armands Berzins .20 .50
174 Lukas Bolf .20 .50
175 Martin Davidek .20 .50
176 Tomas Demel .20 .50
177 Lukas Duba .20 .50
178 Marek Dubec .20 .50
179 Guntis Galvins .20 .50
180 Marek Grill .20 .50
181 Michal Horak .20 .50
182 Josef Hrabal .20 .50
183 Jakub Kraus .20 .50
184 Jiri Kucny .20 .50
185 David Kveton .20 .50
186 Radim Ostrcil .20 .50
187 Lubos Rob .20 .50
188 Lubomir Sabol .20 .50
189 Petr Sakrajda .20 .50
190 Roman Stantien .20 .50
191 Matej Strilesky .20 .50
192 Vladimir Skoda .20 .50
193 Lubomir Stach .20 .50
194 Martin Stefl .20 .50
195 Simo Vehvilainen .30 .75
196 Dusan Brincko .20 .50
197 Waldemar Pelikovsky .20 .50
198 Jiri Beroun .20 .50
199 Radim Bicanek .20 .50
200 Martin Cakajik .20 .50
201 Jiri Dopita .30 .75
202 Roman Erat .20 .50
203 Radek Haman .20 .50
204 Christoph Harand .20 .50
205 Richard Jares .20 .50
206 Ivo Kotaska .20 .50
207 Radim Kucharczyk .20 .50
208 Pavel Mojzis .20 .50
209 Roman Nemecek .20 .50
210 Karel Plasek .20 .50
211 Peter Pucher .20 .50
212 Martin Ruzicka .20 .50
213 Pavel Selingr .20 .50
214 Jaroslav Svoboda .20 .50
215 Ondrej Smach .20 .50
216 Jiri Trvaj .30 .75
217 David Turon .20 .50
218 Lubomir Vaskovic .20 .50
219 David Adamec .30 .75
220 Stanislav Balan .20 .50
221 Jakub Cech .30 .75
222 Martin Cech .20 .50
223 Lukas Galvas .20 .50
224 Martin Hamrlik .20 .50
225 Jan Horacek .20 .50
226 Pavel Kasparik .20 .50
227 Robin Kovar .20 .50
228 Jaroslav Kristek .20 .50
229 Pavel Kubis .20 .50
230 Petr Leska .20 .50
231 Martin Lucka .20 .50
232 Jiri Marusak .20 .50
233 Marek Melenovsky .20 .50
234 Pavel Mokrejs .20 .50
235 Igor Murin .30 .75
236 David Nosek .20 .50
237 Miroslav Okal .20 .50
238 Michal Psurny .20 .50
239 Roman Psurny .20 .50
240 Ivan Rachunek .20 .50
241 Dalibor Sedlar .30 .75
242 Lubomir Sekeras .20 .50
243 Robert Tomik .20 .50
244 Lubomir Vosatko .20 .50
245 Martin Zahorovsky .20 .50
246 Pavel Zubicek .20 .50
247 Vitezslav Bilek .20 .50
248 Vratislav Cech .20 .50
249 Marek Curilla .20 .50
250 Richard Divis .20 .50
251 Martin Frolik .20 .50
252 Radek Gardon .20 .50
253 David Hajek .20 .50
254 Michal Havel .20 .50
255 Milan Hluchy .20 .50
256 Tomas Horna .20 .50
257 Petr Jaros .20 .50
258 Jaroslav Kalla .20 .50
259 Jiri Kuchler .20 .50
260 Jakub Lev .30 .75
261 Zdenek Orct .30 .75
262 Pavel Patera .20 .50
263 Ales Pavlas .20 .50
264 Libor Prochazka .20 .50
265 Martin Prochazka .20 .50
266 Martin Sevc .20 .50
267 Martin Stepanek .20 .50
268 Jiri Zeman .20 .50
269 Vaclav Benak .20 .50
270 Mario Cartelli .20 .50
271 Michal Duraz .20 .50
272 Jan Herman .20 .50
273 Petr Jez .30 .75
274 Richard Kepl .20 .50
275 Richard Kral .20 .50
276 Roman Malek .30 .75
277 Jiri Malinsky .20 .50
278 Radek Matejovsky .20 .50
279 David Mazanec .20 .50
280 Milan Nedoma .20 .50
281 Ales Padelek .20 .50
282 Igor Rataj .20 .50
283 Adam Saffer .20 .50
284 Jakub Sindel .20 .50
285 Pavel Trnka .20 .50
286 Milan Voboril .20 .50
287 Jiri Zelenka .20 .50
288 Jaroslav Bednar .40 1.00
289 Josef Beranek .20 .50
290 Roman Cervenka .20 .50
291 Tomas Divisek .40 1.00
292 Radek Dlouhy .20 .50
293 Jiri Drtina .20 .50
294 Petr Franek .30 .75
295 Dominik Granak .20 .50
296 Lukas Hronek .30 .75
297 David Hruska .20 .50
298 Jiri Jebavy .20 .50
299 Petr Kadlec .20 .50
300 David Pojkar .20 .50
301 Vladimir Ruzicka .20 .50
302 Jakub Sklenar .20 .50
303 Vladimir Sobotka .20 .50
304 Michal Sup .20 .50
305 Tomas Spila .20 .50
306 Tomas Vlasak .20 .50
307 Michal Vondrka .20 .50
308 Tomas Zizka .20 .50
309 Radek Hubacek .20 .50
310 Petr Tucek .30 .75
311 Andrej Novotny .20 .50
312 Petr Puncochar .20 .50
313 Jan Stary .20 .50
314 Michal Tvrdik .20 .50
315 Libor Pivko .20 .50
316 Jan Kolar .20 .50
317 Martin Cech .20 .50
318 Jan Kana .20 .50
319 Tomas Voracek .20 .50
320 Marek Novotny .20 .50
321 Tomas Brnak .20 .50
322 Martin Zatovic .30 .75
323 Tomas Chrenko .20 .50
324 Ales Pisa .20 .50
325 Frantisek Mrazek .20 .50
326 Josef Kucera .20 .50

2006-07 Czech OFS All Stars

1 Milan Hnilicka 2.00 5.00
2 Roman Malek 2.00 5.00
3 Jan Novak 1.50 4.00
4 Miroslav Blatak 1.50 4.00
5 Frantisek Ptacek 1.50 4.00
6 Josef Reznicek 1.50 4.00
7 Radim Tesarik 1.50 4.00
8 Stanislav Hudec 1.50 4.00
9 Valdemar Jirus 1.50 4.00
10 Martin Richter 1.50 4.00
11 Ivan Rachunek 1.50 4.00
12 Lubomir Vaic 1.50 4.00
13 Petr Sykora 1.50 4.00
14 Michal Mikeska 1.50 4.00
15 Jan Marek 1.50 4.00
16 Marek Tomica 1.50 4.00
17 Jiri Burger 1.50 4.00
18 Michal Travnicek 1.50 4.00
19 Radek Gardon 1.50 4.00
20 David Moravec 1.50 4.00
21 Jan Peterek 1.50 4.00
22 Ales Kretinsky 1.50 4.00

2006-07 Czech OFS Brothers

1 Martin Herman 2.00 5.00
Jan Herman
2 Jan Kana 2.00 5.00
Tomas Kana
3 Lukas Danecek 2.00 5.00
Jan Danecek
4 Radek Hubacek 2.00 5.00
Petr Hubacek
5 Michal Psurny 2.00 5.00
Roman Psurny

2006-07 Czech OFS Coaches

1 Ernest Bokros .40 1.00
2 Milos Holan .40 1.00
3 Miloslav Horava .40 1.00
4 Josef Jandac .40 1.00
5 Jiri Jurik .40 1.00
6 Zdenek Müller .40 1.00
7 Josef Palecek .40 1.00
8 Vladimir Ruzicka .40 1.00
9 Milos Riha .40 1.00
10 Marek Sykora .40 1.00
11 Vaclav Sykora .40 1.00
12 Zdenek Venera .40 1.00
13 Rostislav Vlach .40 1.00
14 Frantisek Vyborny .40 1.00

2006-07 Czech OFS Defenders

1 Martin Hamrlik .75 2.00
2 Jan Novak .75 2.00
3 Stanislav Hudec .75 2.00
4 Martin Richter .75 2.00
5 Valdemar Jirus .75 2.00
6 Petr Gregorek .75 2.00
7 Marek Posmyk .75 2.00
8 Martin Sevc .75 2.00
9 Josef Reznicek .75 2.00
10 Miroslav Blatak .75 2.00
11 Petr Kadlec .75 2.00
12 Radim Tesarik .75 2.00
13 Angel Krstev .75 2.00
14 Radim Bicanek .75 2.00
15 Frantisek Ptacek .75 2.00

2006-07 Czech OFS Goalies I

1 Igor Murin 2.00 5.00
2 Lukas Mensator 2.00 5.00
3 Petr Franek 2.00 5.00
4 Milan Hnilicka 2.00 5.00
5 Jiri Trvaj 2.00 5.00
6 Marek Pinc 2.00 5.00
7 Roman Malek 2.00 5.00
8 Jan Chabera 2.00 5.00
9 Radek Fiala 2.00 5.00
10 Sasu Hovi 2.00 5.00
11 Jan Lasak 2.50 6.00
12 Kamil Jarina 2.00 5.00
13 Petr Briza 2.50 6.00
14 Martin Altrichter 2.00 5.00
15 Roman Turek 2.00 5.00

2006-07 Czech OFS Goalies II

1 Milan Hnilicka 2.00 5.00
2 Igor Murin 2.00 5.00
3 Petr Franek 2.00 5.00
4 Jan Chabera 2.00 5.00
5 Jiri Trvaj 2.00 5.00
6 Lukas Mensator 2.00 5.00
7 Marek Pinc 2.00 5.00
8 Roman Turek 2.00 5.00
9 Radek Fiala 2.00 5.00
10 Roman Malek 2.00 5.00
11 Kamil Jarina 2.00 5.00
12 Martin Altrichter 2.00 5.00
13 Jan Lasak 2.50 6.00
14 Petr Briza 2.50 6.00
15 Radovan Biegl 2.00 5.00

2006-07 Czech OFS Goals Leaders

1 Petr Ton 1.25 3.00
2 Michal Sup 1.25 3.00
3 Jan Marek 1.25 3.00
4 Jaroslav Kudrna 1.25 3.00
5 Jaroslav Bednar 1.25 3.00
6 Ales Padelek 1.25 3.00
7 Lubomir Vaic 1.25 3.00
8 Jan Caloun 1.25 3.00
9 Igor Rataj 1.25 3.00
10 Peter Pucher 1.25 3.00
11 Radek Duda 1.25 3.00
12 Petr Hubacek 1.25 3.00
13 Ondrej Kratena 1.25 3.00
14 Jiri Zelenka 1.25 3.00
15 Jan Benda 1.25 3.00

2006-07 Czech OFS Jagr Team

1 Marek Schwarz 4.00 10.00
2 Jaroslav Kames 1.25 3.00
3 Jiri Tlusty 4.00 10.00
4 Petr Taticek 1.25 3.00
5 Jakub Koreis 2.00 5.00
6 Jiri Novotny 1.25 3.00
7 Lukas Krajicek 1.25 3.00
8 Martin Richter 1.25 3.00
9 Rostislav Klesla 1.25 3.00
10 Josef Melichar 1.25 3.00
11 Michal Rozsival 1.25 3.00
12 Petr Tenkrat 1.25 3.00
13 Tomas Plekanec 2.50 6.00
14 Jaroslav Hlinka 1.25 3.00
15 Jan Hrdina 1.25 3.00
16 Ales Kotalik 2.00 5.00
17 Tomas Kaberle 2.00 5.00
18 David Vyborny 1.25 3.00
19 Martin Straka 1.25 3.00
20 Martin Rucinsky 1.25 3.00
21 Jaromir Jagr 4.00 10.00
22 Jaroslav Svoboda 1.25 3.00
23 Jiri Hudler 2.50 6.00

2006-07 Czech OFS Points Leaders

1 Jan Marek 1.25 3.00
2 Lubomir Vaic 1.25 3.00
3 Josef Beranek 1.25 3.00
4 Petr Ton 1.25 3.00
5 Jaroslav Kudrna 1.25 3.00
6 Jaroslav Bednar 1.25 3.00
7 Radek Duda 1.25 3.00
8 Jan Peterek 1.25 3.00
9 Peter Pucher 1.25 3.00
10 Jan Benda 1.25 3.00
11 Petr Hubacek 1.25 3.00
12 Jan Caloun 1.25 3.00
13 Tomas Vlasak 1.25 3.00
14 Martin Strba 1.25 3.00
15 Michal Sup 1.25 3.00

2006-07 Czech OFS Stars

1 Jiri Stejskal 1.25 3.00
2 Andrej Podkonicky 1.25 3.00
3 Daniel Branda 1.25 3.00
4 Lukas Mensator 1.25 3.00
5 Milan Kraft 1.25 3.00
6 Igor Murin 1.25 3.00
7 Petr Leska 1.25 3.00
8 Martin Hamrlik 1.25 3.00
9 Roman Malek 1.25 3.00
10 Richard Kral 1.25 3.00
11 Petr Sykora 1.25 3.00
12 Miroslav Hlinka 1.25 3.00
13 Roman Turek 1.50 4.00
14 Vaclav Nedorost 1.25 3.00
15 Jiri Polansky 1.25 3.00
16 Zdenek Orct 1.50 4.00
17 Jaroslav Bednar 1.25 3.00
18 Dusan Salficky 1.50 4.00
19 Jiri Vykoukal 1.25 3.00
20 Tomas Demel 1.25 3.00
21 Martin Stefl 1.25 3.00
22 Roman Erat 1.25 3.00
23 Pavol Mojzis 1.25 3.00
24 Jiri Trvaj 1.50 4.00
25 Zbynek Irgl 1.50 4.00

2006-07 Czech OFS Team Cards

1 Roman Turek 1.50 4.00
Vaclav Nedorost
2 Lukas Mansator 1.50 4.00
Petr Kumstat
3 Pavel Patera 1.50 4.00
Zdenek Orct
4 Jiri Stejskal 1.50 4.00
Jan Plodek
5 Robert Reichel 1.50 4.00
Jaroslav Hübl
6 Petr Sykora 2.00 5.00
Jan Lasak
7 Jiri Zelenka 1.50 4.00
Roman Malek
8 Tomas Vlasak 1.50 4.00
Petr Franek
9 Dusan Salficky 1.50 4.00
Jaroslav Hlinka
10 Radovan Biegl 1.50 4.00
Jan Vytisk
11 Marek Pinc 1.50 4.00
Jiri Burger
12 Martin Stefl 1.50 4.00
Roman Stantien
13 Igor Murin 1.50 4.00
Petr Leska
14 Jiri Trvaj 1.50 4.00
Jiri Dopita

2006-07 Czech NHL ELH Postcards

COMPLETE SET (15) 15.00 30.00
1 Martin Havlat .75 2.00
2 Milan Hnilicka .75 2.00
3 Jan Hrdina .75 2.00
4 Milan Kraft .75 2.00
5 Pavel Kubina .75 2.00
6 Jason Marshall .75 2.00
7 Vaclav Nedorost .75 2.00
8 Zigmund Palffy 1.25 3.00
9 Michal Rozsival .75 2.00
10 Jaroslav Spacek .75 2.00
11 Josef Stumpel .75 2.00
12 Pavel Trnka .75 2.00
13 Vaclav Varada .75 2.00
14 Radim Vrbata .75 2.00
15 Josef Vasicek .75 2.00

2006-07 Czech Super Six Postcards

1 Niklas Backstrom 2.00 5.00
2 Michal Bros .75 2.00
3 Mikhail Grabovskij 1.25 3.00
4 David Havir .75 2.00
5 Miroslav Hlinka .75 2.00
6 Robert Kantor .75 2.00
7 Jan Lasak 1.25 3.00
8 Michal Mikeska .75 2.00
9 Vaclav Pletka .75 2.00
10 Tomasz Razingar 1.25 3.00
11 Tomas Rolinek .75 2.00
12 Pavel Rosa .75 2.00
13 Maxim Susinskij .75 2.00
14 Petr Tenkrat .75 2.00
15 Viktor Ujcik .75 2.00
16 Jiri Vluhkola .75 2.00

1998-99 Danish Hockey League

We know little about this set, beyond the checklist provided by collector Vinnie Montalbano. As a result, we have no pricing. If you have additional information, please contact us at hockeymag@beckett.com.

COMPLETE SET (239)
1 Ola Persson
2 Kenneth Jensen
3 Jesper Skov
4 Henrik Benjaminsen
5 Mikkel Bjerrum
6 Keld Frederiksen
7 Kristian Lodberg
8 Jukka Vilander
9 Jesper Pedersen
10 Oleg Starkov
11 Soren Jensen
12 Andreas Andreasen
13 Magnus Sorensen
14 Ken Peters
15 Kasper Kristensen
16 Torbin Benjaminsen
17 Thomas Bjerrum
18 Bjorn Eden
19 Jesper Madsen
20 Thomas Kjogx
21 Preben Bertram
22 Anders Johansson
23 Alexei Salomatin
24 Daniel Jardemyr
25 Rolf Nilsson
26 Morten Evensen
27 Jens Terkelsen
28 Anders V. Jensen
29 Morten Dahlmann
30 Randy Maxwell
31 Soren True
32 Leonid Truhno
33 Mads True
34 Morten Green
35 Nikolai Clausen
36 Alexander Alexeev
37 Pavel Kostichkin
38 Thomas Johansen
39 Jens Johansson
40 Nicklas Monberg
41 Jesper Gram
42 Mikkel Schmidt
43 Kent Aalborg
44 Christian Mourier
45 Ole Valipirtti
46 G. Karlstrom
47 Jiri Podesva
48 Michael Thomsen
49 Not produced?
50 Thomas Pedersen
51 Bo Nordby Andersen
52 Jan Jakobsen
53 Nick Lamia
54 Karel Krecek
55 Kasper Sorensen
56 Johan Moller Jensen
57 Tomas Klima
58 Tomas Pedersen
59 Rico Larsen
61 Jacek Nowakowski
62 Kasper Haslund Knudsen
63 Martin Struzinski
64 Michael Steffensen
65 Gert Andreasen
66 Jens Christian Gregersen
67 Rasmus Christiansen
68 Kristian L. Hansen
69 Henning Ludvigsen
69 Mads Moller
70 Valeri Shilov
71 Christian De Brass
72 Mikkel Quistgaard Lund
73 Rasmus Aradsson
74 Peter Hjort
75 Morten Ahlberg
76 Steen Bengtson
77 Andreas Mattsson
78 Brian Holse
79 Jeppe Ahlberg
80 Alexander Sundberg
81 Rasmus Olsen
82 Poul B. Andersen
83 Simon Petersen
84 Claus Esmark
85 Markku Tiemonen
86 Jens Maribo
87 Claus Tauson
88 Dennis Olsson
89 Andre Clausen
90 Johan Allringer
91 Casper Nilsson
92 Soren Tranholm
93 David Moore
94 Rene B. Madsen
95 Jens Hellsten
96 Lars Oxholm
97 Marten Rasten
98 Randy Murphy
99 Henrik Oxholm
100 Jonas Hansson
101 Rene Jensen
102 Per Apollo
103 Flemming Jensen
104 Marku Kyllonen
105 Peter Skraem
106 Dmitri Lavrentiev
107 Ntsika Shange
108 Curt Regnier
109 David Moore
110 Rasmus Holst
111 Hans Hansson
112 Not produced?
113 Andrejs Zinkovs
114 Thomas Ingvordsen
115 Konstantins Grigorjevs
116 Morten Rasmussen
117 Rasmus Jacobsen
118 Thor Dresler
119 Tom Dibbern
120 Ronni Thomassen
121 Christian Fabricius
122 Brian Schultz
123 Filip Faurholm
124 Sergejs Cubars
125 Peter F. Hansen
126 Johan Marklund
127 Dennis Olsson
128 Torben Schultz
129 Kenneth Madsen
130 Ulrich Hansen
131 Rene Sloth
132 Jesper Andersen
133 Aigars Razgals
134 Yuri Agureikin
135 Johan Westermark
136 Mads Johnsen
137 Rasmus Norgaard
138 Christian Schioldan
139 Karel Smid
140 Jesper Pedersen
141 Klaus Nielsen
142 Rasmus Christiansen
143 Soren Jensen
144 Martin E. Andersen
145 Niklas Rinaldo
146 Andreas Borup
147 Thomas Englund
148 Jorn Ole Bertelsen
149 Thomas Reinert
150 Bent Christensen
151 Anders Thomsen
152 Sergejs Senins
153 Soren Pedersen
154 Ilya Dubkov
155 Mike Grey
156 Jimmy Nielsson
157 Tomas Placatka
158 Jan Justra
159 Peter Therkildsen
160 Kim Fonnesbech
161 Rasmus Pander
162 Claus Mortensen
163 Jan Phillipsen
164 Jesper Molby
165 Lars Molgaard
166 Ulrik Thomsen
167 Petri Skriko
168 Martin Kristiansen
169 Lasse Degn
170 Daniel Nielsen
171 Erkki Makela
172 Henrik Toft
173 Todd Bjorkstrand
174 Claus Damgaard
175 Anders Pyndt
176 Dan Jensen
177 Rasmus Hartung
178 Kasper Degn
179 Jarmo Makitalo
180 Jarmo Kuusisto
181 Seppo Repo
182 Not produced?
183 Dan Jensen
184 Ulrick Nielsen
185 Claus Jensen
186 Mikael Wiklander
187 Kim Foder
188 Mats Diberius
189 Ole Christiansen
190 Brian Foder
191 Dennis Blom
192 Soren Gerber
193 Lars Bach
194 Kim Jensen
195 Rasmus Kubel
196 Jan Jensen
197 Soren Nielsen
198 Todd Sparks
199 Morten Callesen
200 Ian Hebert
201 Jesper Gaarde
202 Henrik Lundin
203 Mika Nyqvist
204 Daniel Ullbors
205 Bill Morrison
206 Michael Senderovitz
207 Igor A. Knyazev
208 Lars Bundgaard
209 Jens Edmund
210 Ruby Flomo
211 Magnus Sundquist
212 Morten Ovesen
213 Boris Bykovsky
214 Martin Sorensen
215 Lars Eller
216 Bo Larsen
217 Soren Koziol
218 Martin Skygge
219 Rasmus Edmund
220 Michael Thomsen
221 Soren Lykke-Jorgensen
222 Mathies Stengaard
223 Henrik Borner
224 Jannik Sonderby
225 Sergei Solomatov
226 Ulrick Sinding Olsen
227 Anatoli Chistyakov
228 Olaf Eller
229 Ken Ruddick
NNO Esbjerg Pirates
NNO Gentofte
NNO Vojens Lions
NNO Aalborg
NNO Frederikshavn Hawks
NNO Herning Blue Fox
NNO Rodovre
NNO Rungsted Cobras
NNO Hvidovre
NNO Odense Bulldogs

1999-00 Danish Hockey League

Little is known about this set beyond the checklist and thus it is not priced. Several cards are marked below as unknown. If you have information about the identities of these cards or have sales information, write hockeymag@beckett.com.

COMPLETE SET (225)
1 Jan Jensen
2 Kenneth Jensen
3 Torben Schultz
4 Michael Pedersen
5 Henrik Benjaminsen
6 Mikkel Bjerrum
7 Todd Sparks
8 Keld Frederiksen
9 Alexander Weinrich
10 Kristian Lodberg
11 Lars T. Pedersen
12 Oleg Starkov
13 Andreas Andreasen
14 Mikko Suvanto
15 Anders Skov
16 Jacques Joubert
17 Thomas Bjerrum
18 Bjorn Eden
19 Jesper Madsen
20 Thomas Kjogx
21 Anders Johansson
22 Mats Diberius
23 Bill Stewart
24 Robert Nordberg
25 Peter Nordstrom
26 Rasmus Aradsson
27 Ole Valipirtti
28 Mathias Frelin
29 Bo Larsen
30 Mikko Niemi
31 Michel Olsen
32 Rasmus Jacobsen
33 Jens Maribo
34 Brian Jensen
35 Claus Esmark
36 Rasmus Olsen
37 Brian Schultz
38 Christian Jorgensen
39 Johan Marklund
40 Rene Sloth
41 Ronni Dahlsten
42 Ronni Thomassen
43 Thor Dresler
44 Poul B. Andersson
45 Steen Bengtson
46 Peter Therkildsen
47 unknown
48 Claus Mortensen
49 Daniel Nielsen
50 Jan Philipsen
51 Kasper Degn
52 Martin Kristiansen
53 Jarmo Kuusisto
54 unknown
55 Rasmus Hartung
56 Todd Bjorkstrand
57 Rico Larsen
58 unknown
59 Martin Struzinski
60 Christian Kjaergaard
61 Jesper Molby
62 Rasmus Pander
63 Dan Jensen
64 Lasse Degn
65 Sami Wikstrom
66 unknown
67 Michael Madsen
68 Mikael Wiklander
69 Lars Bach
70 Christian Erntgaard
71 unknown
72 Claus Jensen
73 Henrik Lundin
74 Mikko Honkonen
75 Morten Callesen
76 Ray Podloski
77 Sami Simonen
78 Stefan Nyman
79 Soren Nielsen
80 Valeri Chierny
81 Brian Foder
82 Rasmus Kubel
83 Jan Jensen
84 Ole Christiansen
85 Kim Foder
86 Dan Jensen
87 Thomas Carlsson
88 Jiri Podesva
89 Jens Sonny Thomsen
90 Alexanders Shishkovich
91 Jesper Pedersen
92 Carsten Ronnest
93 Alexanders Macijevskis'
94 Jacek Nowakowski
95 Mads Moller
96 unknown
97 Ronnie Sorensen
98 Thomas Englund
99 Tomas Placatka
100 unknown
101 Kasper Haslund Knudsen
102 Thomas Mortensen
103 Bo Nordby Andersen
104 Rasmus Kristiansen
105 Jens Christian Gregersen
106 Jesper Pedersen
107 Thomas Pedersen
108 Johan Allringer
109 Casper Nilsson
110 Peter Skraem
111 Henrik B. Madsen
112 Curt Regnier
113 Dean Seymour
114 Mario Simioni
115 Jens Hellsten
116 Hernik Oxholm
117 Ntsika Shange
118 Dmitri Lavrentiev
119 Marku Kyllonen
120 Lars Oxholm
121 Pavel Tolstik
122 Anders Holst
123 Rasmus Holst
124 Pierre Dufour
125 Soren Tranholm
126 unknown
127 Rene B. Madsen
128 Rene Jensen
129 Bill Morrison
130 Michael Senderovitz
131 Michael Sauffaus
132 Christian Fabricius
133 Pavel Lazerev
134 unknown
135 Soren Koziol
136 Boris Bykovsky
137 Igor A. Knyazev
138 Henrik Borner
139 Jannik Sonderby
140 Michael Thomsen
141 Magnus Sorensen
142 Anatoli Chistyakov
143 Filip Faurholm
144 Ulrich Hansen
145 Magnus Sundquist
146 Soren Lykke-Jorgensen
147 unknown
148 Ulrick Sinding Olsen
149 Martin Skygge
150 Rasmus Nielsen
151 Lars Bundgaard
152 Johan Westermark
153 Mads Johnsen
154 Mike Grey
155 Anders Thomsen
156 Kasper Kristensen
157 Lars Molgaard
158 Karel Smid
159 Soren Jensen
160 Martin E. Andersen
161 Ilja Dubkov
162 Mads Brandt
163 Radim Piroutek
164 Thomas Reinert
165 Christian Schioldan
166 Bent Christensen
167 Sergejs Senins
168 Hasse Olsen
169 Simon Pedersen
170 Klaus Nielsen
171 Torbin Benjaminsen
172 Andreas Borup
173 Henrik Bjerring
174 unknown
175 Anders V. Jensen
176 Michael Widenborg
177 Ruby Flomo
178 unknown
179 Marco Poulsen
180 unknown
181 Sergejs Cubars
182 Andreas Sabroe
183 Christian Dall-Hansen
184 unknown
185 Lars-Peter Drewsen
186 Michael Lauridsen
187 Morten Ovesen
188 Thomas Hansen
189 Dan Vollertzen
190 unknown
191 Casper Brandis
192 Casper Skovby
193 unknown
194 Thomas Wahlgren
195 Dan Jensen
196 Thomas Robbert
197 Benny Nielsen
198 Troels Biltoft
199 unknown
200 Jimmy Nielsson
201 Mikkel Schmidt
202 Anders Hansen
203 unknown
204 Morten Hagen
205 unknown
206 Morten Dahlmann
207 Nicklas Plampeck
208 Randy Maxwell
209 Soren True
210 Leronid Truhno
211 Mads True
212 Nikolai Clausen
213 Alexander Alexeev
214 Pavel Kostichkin
215 Thomas Johansen
216 Jens Johansson
217 Jesper Gram
218 Alexander Sundberg
219 Christian Mourier
220 Kristian Just Petersen
221 Dennis Olsson
222 Andreas Mattsson
223 Andre Clausen
224 Hakan Falkenhall
225 Nicklas Monberg

2008-09 Dinamo Riga Team Issue

1 Logo Card
2 Rodrigo Lavins
3 Marsell Hossa
4 Martin Prusek
5 Sergejs Naumovs
6 Lauris Darzins
7 Armands Berzins
8 Mikelis Redlihs
9 Aleksandrs Nizivijs
10 Matt Ellison
11 Mark Hartigan
12 Ronald Petrovicky
13 Filip Novak
14 Duvie Westcott
15 Martins Cipulis
16 Atvars Tribuncovs
17 Aleksejs Sirokovs
18 Guntis Galvins
19 Olegs Sorokins
20 Girts Ankipans
21 Gints Meija
22 Kristaps Sotnieks
23 Krisjanis Redlihs
24 Aigars Cipruss
25 Viktors Blinovs
26 Edgars Masalskis
27 Daniel Sperrle
28 Sergejs Pecura
29 Juris Stals
30 Edijs Brahmanis
31 Toms Hartmanis
32 Georgijs Pujacs
33 Agris Saviels
34 Miroslav Mikloshovich COA
35 Artis Abols coach
36 Julius Shupler Head COA
37 Logo Card
38 Maksims Sirokovs
39 Raimonds Danilics
40 Ervins Mustukovs
41 Edgars Brancis
42 Janis Straupe
43 Nauris Enkuzens
44 Gvido Kauss
45 Renars Valters
46 Miks Indrasis
47 Raimonds Vilkoits
48 Janis Ozolinsh
49 Kriss Grundmanis
50 Ronalds Cinks
51 Renars Demiters
52 Karlis Rozkalns
53 Ronalds Ozolinsh COA
54 Haralds Vasiljevs COA
55 Armands Berzins
56 Aleksandrs Nizivijs
57 Aleksejs Sirokovs
58 Duvie Westcott
59 Filip Novak
60 Girts Ankipans
61 Guntis Galvins
62 Kristaps Sotnieks
63 Lauris Darzins
64 Martins Cipulis
65 Matt Ellison
66 Mark Hartigan
67 Marsell Hossa
68 Martin Prusek
69 Mikelis Redlihs
70 Olegs Sorokins
71 Rodrigo Lavins
72 Sergejs Naumovs

2005-06 Dutch Vadeko Flyers

COMPLETE SET (20) 8.00 15.00
1 Kevin Bruijsten .30 .75
2 Andriy Butochnov .30 .75
3 Anton Butochnov .30 .75
4 Sander Dijkstra .30 .75
5 James Easter .30 .75
6 Brent Janssen .30 .75
7 Matt Korthuis .30 .75
8 Petr Kratky .30 .75
9 Hans Kroon .30 .75
10 Paul Kroon .30 .75
11 Jacco Landman .30 .75
12 Don Nichols .30 .75
13 Marcel Nijland .30 .75
14 Tyler Palmiscno .30 .75
15 Marco Postma .30 .75
16 Brad Smulders .30 .75
17 Ruud vander Holst .30 .75
18 Jeroen van Olphen .30 .75
19 Stanislav Vernikov .30 .75
20 Brain de Bruijn HC .10 .25

1965-66 Finnish Hellas

This vintage set is the earliest confirmed to feature members of the Finnish SM-Liiga. The cards were apparently issued in packs by a company named Hellas, which is the parent company for Leaf. Because of the age and limited availability of these cards, we have no pricing information and are presenting them below for checklisting purposes only.

COMPLETE SET (160)
1 Lasse Kiili
2 Ilkka Mesikammen
3 Jorma Laapas
4 Esko Reijonen
5 Juhani Iso Eskeli
6 Pertti Nieminen
7 Kari Aro
8 Juhani Wahlsten
9 Rauno Heinonen
10 Kalevi Leppanen
11 Pertti Karelius
12 Pekka Oikkonen
13 Kari Sillanpaa
14 Jarmo Rantanen
15 Heikki Heimo
16 Jorma Valtonen
17 Risto Kaitala
18 Kalevi Virkku
19 Heikko Stenvall
20 Teppo Rastio
21 Seppo Vainio
22 Pentti Jokinen
23 Matti Keinonen
24 Matti Koivunen
25 Esa Isaksson
26 Juhani Jylha
27 Pentti Rautalin
28 Simo Saimo
29 Hannu Torma
30 Olli Malmivuori
31 Matti Saurio
32 Mikko Erholm
33 Anto Virtanen
34 Juha Rantasila
35 Jaakko Honkanen
36 Antti Heikkila
37 Lasse Heikkila
38 Veli-Pekka Ketola
39 Keijo Koistinen
40 Mikko Myllyniemi
41 Matti Salmi
42 Tuomo Pirskanen
43 Matti Jansson
44 Erkki Saine
45 Erkki Harju
46 Kaj Matalamaki
47 Seppo Nystrom
48 Timo Jussila
49 Jorma Rikala
50 Tapio Raunio
51 Pekka Korjakoff
52 Jorma Borgstrom
53 Jorma Kyntola
54 Jyrki Malmio
55 Aarno Heikkaranta
56 Kalevi Salo
57 Martti Kuokkanen
58 Seppo Ikola
59 Hannu Kyllastinen
60 Pentti Katainen
61 Harri Linnonmaa
62 Kyosti Wall
63 Kari Kinnunen
64 Martti Kallionpaa
65 Pekka Kuusisto
66 Johannes Karttunen
67 Heikki Veravainen
68 Pentti Riitahaara
69 Lauri Lehtonen
70 Matti Harju
71 Pertti Kontto
72 Timo Makela
73 Tapio Rautalammi
74 Kimmo Kivela
75 Raimo Maattanen
76 Kari Rajala
77 Tapani Suominen
78 Heimo Tervo
79 Raimo Kilpio
80 Matti Lampainen
81 Raimo Helppolainen
82 Esko Nenonen
83 Lalli Partinen
84 Leo Haakana
85 Hannu Lemander
86 Leevi Ryhanen
87 Yrjo Hakala
88 Pauli Hyvari
89 Jorma Hietanen
90 Juhani Pyyhtia
91 Timo Vaatamoinen
92 Heikki Juselius
93 Pentti Hyvari
94 Antti Ravi
95 Markku Eiskonen
96 Martti Sinkkonen
97 Tapio Majaniemi
98 Matti Reunamaki
99 Rauno Heinonen
100 Rauno Lehtio
101 Risto Lehtio
102 Juhani Tamminen
103 Matti Kautto
104 Pekka Lehtolainen
105 Markku Pulli
106 Eero Hopalainen
107 Aaro Nurminen
108 Kalevi Pulli
109 Jorma Suokko
110 Erkki Suokko
111 Heino Pulli
112 Seppo Nikkila
113 Pentti Pynnonen
114 Lasse Oksanen

115 Olli Wirzenius
116 Pentti Uotila
117 Jaakko Jaskari
118 Markku Hakanen
119 Illka Halme
120 Pekka Alfors
121 Tauno Niemi
122 Erkan Nasib
123 Veikko Ukkonen
124 Jarmo Wasama
125 Juhani Lahtinen
126 Jorma Peltonen
127 Kari Palooja
128 Reijo Hakanen
129 Esko Kaonpaa
130 Kimmo Heino
131 Jaako Siren
132 Seppo Naukkarinen
133 Rainer Kolehmainen
134 Henrik Granholm
135 Erkki Partanen
136 Heikki Jarn
137 Jerry Sullivan
138 Jaakko Marttinen
139 Ulf Lindholm
140 Pentti Lindegren
141 Pentti Kotkas
142 Pekka Perttula
143 Esko Rekomaa
144 Christer Thun
145 Matti Kaski
146 Pekka Marjamaki
147 Antti Virtanen
148 Matti Peltonen
149 Reijo Ojanen
150 Timo Ahlqvist
151 Seppo Makinen
152 Jouni Seistamo
153 Harri Harvela
154 Kari Makinen
155 Heikki Koskimies
156 Timo Jussila
157 Pertti Ansakorpi
158 Hannu Elo
159 Mikko Holopainen
160 Kalevi Numminen

1966 Finnish Jaakiekkosarja

This early Finnish set is presented for checklisting purposes only. We have no confirmed sales info and thus the set is unpriced. If you have additional info on this series, please forward it to hockeymag@beckett.com.

COMPLETE SET (220)
COMMON CARD (1-220)
1 Jukka Haapala
2 Simo Saimo
3 Hannu Torma
4 Jukka Savunen
5 Tenho Lotila
6 Tapani Koskimaki
7 Matti Saurio
8 Risto Kaitala
9 Raimo Tiainen
10 Esa Isaksson
11 Pentti Rautalin
12 Heikko Stenvall
13 Teppo Rastio
14 Jorma Vehmanen
15 Raimo Kilpio
16 Veikko Ukkonen
17 Lauri Lehtonen
18 Heikki Veravainen
19 Pentti Riitahaara
20 Pekka Kuusisto
21 Tapio Raulalammi
22 Raimo Tuli
23 Matti Paivinen
24 Matti Harju
25 Kari Sillanpaa
26 Matti Keinonen
27 Pekka Lahti
28 Johannes Karttunen
29 Sakari Isomaki
30 Samu Leikko
31 Tapani Suominen
32 Esa Vesslin
33 Pekka Jalava
34 Pertti Makela
35 Juha Rantasila
36 Jukka Haanpaa
37 Teuvo Helenius
38 Anto Virtanen
39 Kimmo Nokikuru
40 Jaakko Honkanen
41 Seppo Nystrom
42 Tuomo Pirskainen
43 Matti Jansson
44 Alpo Suhonen
45 Matti Varpela
46 Kaj Matalamaki
47 Antti Heikkila
48 Jaakko Jaskari
49 Jouko Ojansuu
50 Mikko Myllyniemi
51 Veli-Pekka Ketola
52 Matti Salmi
53 Pentti Vihanto
54 Hannu Luojola
55 Seppo Parikka
56 Martti Salonen
57 Risto Forss
58 Hannu Niittoaho
59 Kari Johansson
60 Henry Leppa
61 Jarmo Rantanen
62 Kari Torkkel
63 Seppo Vikstrom
64 Veijo Saarinen
65 Pekka Lahtela
66 Risto Vainio
67 Reijo Paksal
68 Erkan Nasib
69 Matti Breilin
70 Voitto Soini
71 Urpo Ylonen
72 Rauno Heinonen
73 Heikki Heino
74 Lasse Killi
75 Ilkka Mesikammen
76 Timo Nummelin
77 Pertti Kuismanen
78 Juhani Wahlsten
79 Rauli Ottila
80 Pertti Karelius
81 Teuvo Andelmin
82 Kari Varjanen
83 Kalevi Leppanen
84 Juhani Iso-Eskeli
85 Hannu Koivunen
86 Yrjo Hakala
87 Kari Ruontimo
88 Raimo Lohko
89 Markku Eiskonen
90 Hannu Lemander
91 Timo Vaatamoinen
92 Pekka Moisio
93 Martti Makia
94 Risto Heinvirta
95 Taisto Jahma
96 Veikko Makia
97 Raimo Helppolainen
98 Lalli Partinen
99 Keijo Sinkkonen
100 Antti Ravi
101 Martti Sinkkonen
102 Heikki Juselius
103 Timo Rantala
104 Heikki Mikkola
105 Jaakko Siren
106 Matti Korhonen
107 Erkki Mononen
108 Pertti Valkonen
109 Ilpo Koskela
110 Bengt Wilenius
111 Hannu Lindberg
112 Kristen Bertell
113 Veikko Kuusisto
114 Tapio Majaniemi
115 Leo Vankka
116 Pentti Harju
117 Ari Myllymaki
118 Matti Koskinen
119 Pentti Andersson
120 Pentti Heikkinen
121 Pekka Peltoniemi
122 Jouko Jarvinen
123 Matti Vartiainen
124 Esko Reijonen
125 Erkki Rasanen
126 Timo Viskari
127 Raimo Turkulainen
128 Paavo Tirkkonen
129 Orvo Paatero
130 Juhani Leirivaara
131 Jyrki Turunen
132 Timo Tuomainen
133 Pentti Karkkainen
134 Jussi Piuhola
135 Pentti Pihlapuro
136 Pentti Pennanen
137 Esa Viskari
138 Timo Luostarinen
139 Seppo Iivonen
140 Risto Alho
141 Esko Kiuru
142 Jaakko Hovinheimo
143 Jaakko Koikkalainen
144 Juhani Sodervik
145 Seppo Makinen
146 Teuvo Peltola
147 Antti Alenius
148 Kalevi Numminen
149 Esko Kaonpaa
150 Lauri Salomaa
151 Risto Pirttiaho
152 Antti Leppanen
153 Kari Makinen
154 Jorma Oksala
155 Pekka Marjamaki
156 Jouni Seistamo
157 Pertti Ansakorpi
158 Erkki Jarkko
159 Juhani Peltola
160 Erkki Mannikko
161 Keijo Mannisto
162 Matti Peltonen
163 Hannu Heikkonen
164 Pentti Hyytiainen
165 Antti Virtanen
166 Seppo Nurmi
167 Matti Reunamaki
168 Mikko Raikkonen
169 Esko Rantanen
170 Eero Holopainen
171 Juhani Ruohonen
172 Veikko Savolainen
173 Heikki Sivonen
174 Markku Pulli
175 Pekka Uitus
176 Heikki Keinonen
177 Jorma Saarikorpi
178 Rauno Lehtio
179 Kalevi Toivonen
180 Jorma Vilen
181 Pentti Kuusinen
182 Olavi Haapalainen
183 Seppo Nikkila
184 Jorma Suokko
185 Heino Pulli
186 Risto Lehtio
187 Pekka Lehtolainen
188 Timo Hirsimaki
189 Kari Palo-Oja
190 Pekka Leimu
191 Ali Saadetin
192 Erkki Jarvinen
193 Markku Hakanen
194 Jorma Kallio
195 Vaino Kolkka
196 Timo Saari
197 Jorma Peltonen
198 Pentti Pynnonen
199 Pentti Uotila
200 Timo Lahtinen
201 Juhani Lahtinen
202 Reijo Hakanen
203 Lasse Oksanen
204 Juhani Aromaki
205 Jukka Alkula
206 Pekka Olkkonen
207 Tapani Salo
208 Vesa Kartsalo
209 Antti Komsi
210 Asko Sallamaa
211 Juhani Tarkiainen
212 Antero Hakala
213 Ulf Slotte
214 Raimo Savolainen
215 Matias Savolainen
216 Risto Savolainen
217 Keijo Makinen
218 Tapio Makinen
219 Ossi Peltoniemi
220 Matti Valikangas

1970-71 Finnish Jaakiekko

This early Finnish set is presented for checklisting purposes only. We have no confirmed sales information at this time.

COMPLETE SET (384)
1 Vitali Davydov
2 Anatoli Firsov
3 Valeri Kharlamov
4 Aleksandr Yakushev
5 Viktor Konovalenko
6 Vladimir Lutshenko
7 Aleksandr Maltsev
8 Boris Mikhailov
9 Jevgeni Mishakov
10 Valeri Nikitin
11 Vladimir Petrov
12 Jevgeni Paladjev
13 Viktor Polupanov
14 Aleksandr Ragulin
15 Igor Romishevski
16 Vladimir Shadrin
17 Viatjeslav Starsinov
18 Vladislav Tretjak
19 Valeri Vasiljev
20 Vladimir Vikulov
21 Tommy Abrahamsson
22 Gunnar Backman
23 Arne Carlsson
24 Anders Hagstrom
25 Anders Hedberg
26 Leif Holmqvist
27 Nils Johansson
28 Stig-Goran Johansson
29 Stefan Karlsson
30 Hans Lindberg
31 Tord Lundstrom
32 Kjell-Rune Milton
33 Lars-Goran Nilsson
34 Anders Nordin
35 Roger Olsson
36 Bjorn Palmqvist
37 Lars-Erik Sjoberg
38 Ulf Sterner
39 Lennart Svedberg
40 Hakan Wickberg
41 Vladimir Bednar
42 Josef Cerny
43 Vladimir Dzurilla
44 Richard Farda
45 Julius Haas
46 Ivan Hlinka
47 Jaroslav Holik
48 Jiri Holik
49 Josef Horesovsky
50 Jan Hrbaty
51 Jiri Kochta
52 Miroslav Lacky
53 Oldrich Machac
54 Vladislav Martinec
55 Vaclav Nedomansky
56 Frantisek Pospisil
57 Stanislav Pryl
58 Frantisek Sevcik
59 Jan Suchy
60 Lubomir Ujvary
61 Matti Keinonen
62 Veli-Pekka Ketola
63 Vaino Kolkka
64 Ilpo Koskela
65 Pekka Leimu
66 Seppo Lindstrom
67 Harri Linnonmaa
68 Pekka Marjamaki
69 Lauri Mononen
70 Matti Murto
71 Lasse Oksanen
72 Lalli Partinen
73 Esa Peltonen
74 Jorma Peltonen
75 Juha Rantasila
76 Heikki Riihiranta
77 Juhani Tamminen
78 Jorma Valtonen
79 Jorma Vehmanen
80 Urpo Ylonen
81 Rolf Bielas
82 Frank Braun
83 Dieter Dewitz
84 Lothar Fuchs
85 Bernd Hiller
86 Klaus Hirche
87 Reinhard Karger
88 Bernd Karrenbauer
89 Hartmut Nickel
90 Rudiger Noack
91 Helmut Novy
92 Rainer Patschinski
93 Dietmar Peters
94 Wolfgang Plotka
95 Peter Prusa
96 Dieter Purschel
97 Wilfried Rohrbach
98 Dieter Rohl
99 Peter Slapke
100 Joachim Ziesche
101 Juhani Bostrom
102 Henrik Granholm
103 Matti Harju
104 Kimmo Heino
105 Esa Isaksson
106 Juhani Jylha
107 Heikki Riihiranta
108 Mauri Kaukokari
109 Vaino Kolkka
110 Harri Linnonmaa
111 Matti Murto
112 Lalli Partinen
113 Juha Rantasila
114 Heikki Riihiranta
115 Jorma Rikala
116 Jorma Thusberg
117 Matti Vaisanen
118 Sakari Ahlberg
119 Jorma Aro
120 Esko Eriksson
121 Markku Hakanen
122 Matti Hakanen
123 Reijo Hakanen
124 Pentti Hartin
125 Timo Hirsimaki
126 Jorma Kallio
127 Pekka Kuusisto
128 Juhani Lahtinen
129 Timo Lahtinen
130 Pekka Leimu
131 Jukka Mattila
132 Esko Makinen
133 Lasse Oksanen
134 Kari Palo-oja
135 Jorma Peltonen
136 Ali Saadetdin
137 Timo Saari
138 Heikki Hurme
139 Matti Jakonen
140 Kari Johansson
141 Keijo Jarvinen
142 Reijo Leppanen
143 Seppo Lindstrom
144 Hannu Luojola
145 Hannu Niittoaho
146 Reijo Paksal
147 Seppo Parikka
148 Jarmo Rantanen
149 Martti Salonen
150 Voitto Soini
151 Kari Torkkel
152 Risto Vainio
153 Pentti Vihanto
154 Urpo Ylonen
155 Rauno Heinonen
156 Lauri Jamsen
157 Lasse Killi
158 Hannu Koivunen
159 Jarmo Koivunen
160 Pertti Kuismanen
161 Pekka Lahtela
162 Harry Luoto
163 Jaakko Marttinen
164 Timo Nummelin
165 Rauli Ottila
166 Matti Rautee
167 Pekka Rautee
168 Jouni Samuli
169 Rauli Tammelin
170 Juhani Tamminen
171 Kari Varjanen
172 Pertti Ahokas
173 Pertti Hiirros
174 Eero Holopainen
175 Veli-Pekka Ketola
176 Kari Kinnunen
177 Ilpo Koskela
178 Osmo Kuusisto
179 Timo Kyntola
180 Henry Leppa
181 Erkki Mononen
182 Lauri Mononen
183 Pertti Nurmi
184 Antti Perttula
185 Seppo Peraoja
186 Timo Relas
187 Alpo Suhonen
188 Timo Turunen
189 Tapio Flinck
190 Jaakko Honkanen
191 Antti Heikkila
192 Matti Jansson
193 Esa Kari
194 Raimo Kilpio
195 Tapio Koskinen
196 Kaj Matalamaki
197 Ilkka Mesikammen
198 Pertti Makela
199 Jaakko Nurminen
200 Pekka Rautakallio
201 Tapio Rautalammi
202 Markku Riihimaki
203 Matti Salmi
204 Kari-Pekka Toivonen
205 Jorma Valtonen
206 Anto Virtanen
207 Erkki Vakiparta
208 Pertti Ansakorpi
209 Pertti Koivulahti
210 Ilpo Kuisma
211 Harri Lappalainen
212 Pekka Marjamaki
213 Mikko Myntinen
214 Kari Makinen
215 Pekka Makinen
216 Seppo Makinen
217 Keijo Mannisto
218 Jorma Oksala
219 Matti Peltonen
220 Tuomo Rautiainen
221 Lauri Salomaa
222 Risto Seesvuori
223 Jorma Siitarinen
224 Teemu Sistonen
225 Lasse Aaltonen
226 Mikko Erholm
227 Jukka Haapala
228 Veikko Ihalainen
229 Matti Keinonen
230 Tapani Koskimaki
231 Arto Laine
232 Hannu Lunden
233 Pentti Rautalin
234 Paavo Riekkinen
235 Kai Rosvall
236 Matti Saurio
237 Jukka Savunen
238 Hannu Siivonen
239 Heikko Stenvall
240 Jorma Vehmanen
241 Hannu Haapalainen
242 Timo Jarvinen
243 Heikki Keinonen
244 Heimo Keinonen
245 Rauno Lehtio
246 Tapio Nummela
247 Seppo Nurmi
248 Markku Pulli
249 Esko Rantanen
250 Juhani Ruohonen
251 Mikko Raikkonen
252 Jorma Saarikorpi
253 Veikko Savolainen
254 Leo Seppanen
255 Pertti Sihvonen
256 Pekka Uitus
257 Jorma Vilen
258 Tapio Virhimo
259 Jaakko Koikkalainen
260 Jorma Muikku
261 Ossi Oksala
262 Pekka Parikka
263 Pentti Pennanen
264 Jussi Piuhola
265 Seppo Repo
266 Erkki Rasanen
267 Juhani Sodervik
268 Heikki Tirkkonen
269 Paavo Tirkkonen
270 Timo Tuomainen
271 Raimo Turkulainen
272 Jyrki Turunen
273 Martti Turunen
274 Timo Viskari
275 Antero Vaatamoinen
276 Juhani Aaltonen
277 Matti Ahvenharju
278 Hannu Auvinen
279 Jorma Borgstrom
280 Seppo Laakkio
281 Jarmo Laukkanen
282 Hannu Lindberg
283 Reijo Myyrylainen
284 Raimo Maattanen
285 Esa Peltonen
286 Keijo Puhakka
287 Antti Ravi
288 Erkki Suni
289 Henrik Wahl
290 Stig Wetzell
291 Olli Viilma
292 Esa Willberg
293 Kauko Fomin
294 Risto Forss
295 Rauno Karlsson
296 Jarmo Kiprusoff
297 Matti Koivunen
298 Timo Kokkonen
299 Timo Lehtonen
300 Kalevi Leppanen
301 Hans Martin
302 Timo Nurminen
303 Jari Rosberg
304 Veijo Saarinen
305 Simo Suoknuuti
306 Veikko Suominen
307 Seppo Wikstrom
308 Juha-Pekka Aho
309 Seppo Aro
310 Kari Jokinen
311 Pekka Karhunen
312 Pertti Kettunen
313 Lauri Kosonen
314 Jyrki Kahonen
315 Marko Lepaus
316 Matti Lisko
317 Marko Niemi
318 Hannu Pohja
319 Jarmo Ronkainen
320 Mikko Silvasti
321 Jari Suokas
322 Kimmo Turunen
323 Jari Viitala
324 Mikko Viitanen
325 Jaakko Virtanen
326 Jarmo Viteli
327 Kari Anttila
328 Harri Hiltunen
329 Arto Javanainen
330 Tapio Jylhasaari
331 Jorma Korkeamaki
332 Kari Koskinen
333 Martti Lunden
334 Petri Niskanen
335 Jari Nystrom
336 Ari Peltola
337 Jari Peltonen
338 Petri Salminen
339 Juha Salo
340 Esa Salosensaari
341 Rauli Siimes
342 Esa Suvanto
343 Jukka Tuli
344 Jukka Virtanen
345 Pertti Vaisanen
346 Timo Hyrsky
347 Jorma Jokinen
348 Jari Kokkola
349 Pentti Kuosmanen
350 Pekka Laukkanen
351 Tom Lund
352 Jouni Niemela
353 Kari Rantanen
354 Pekka Reimola
355 Teijo Salminen
356 Veli-Matti Tammi
357 Juhani Tamminen
358 Risto Valhinen
359 Antti Vanne
360 Ari Vanne
361 Hannu Vehmanen
362 Heikki Virta
363 Hannu Virtanen
364 Jyrki Valimaki
365 Pekka Anttila
366 Jouni Honkanen
367 Kari Jalonen
368 Ari Kaikkonen
369 Timo Kajula
370 Jorma Kinnunen
371 Esa Kontio
372 Tapio Kuiri
373 Pekka Kyllonen
374 Ari Mustaniemi
375 Jukka Pajala
376 Pentti Perhomaa
377 Reijo Raatesalmi
378 Markku Ruotsalainen
379 Reijo Ruotsalainen ERC
380 Jarmo Tauriainen
381 Ari Timosaari
382 Pekka Tuomisto
383 Timo Vahanen
384 Sakari Valiharju

1971-72 Finnish Suomi Stickers

COMPLETE SET (384) 200.00 400.00
1 Vitaly Davydov .30 .75
2 Anatoli Firsov 2.00 5.00
3 Valeri Kharlamov 6.00 15.00
4 Viktor Konovalenko .30 .75
5 Viktor Kuzkin .30 .75
6 Yuri Liapkin .40 1.00
7 Vladimir Lutchenko .30 .75
8 Alexander Maltsev 2.00 5.00
9 Alexander Martiniuk .40 1.00
10 Boris Mikhailov 2.00 5.00
11 Evgeni Mishakov .30 .75
12 Vladimir Petrov 2.00 5.00
13 Alexander Ragulin .75 2.00
14 Igor Romishevski .30 .75
15 Vladimir Shadrin .40 1.00
16 Viatjeslav Starshinov .40 1.00
17 Vladislav Tretiak 10.00 20.00
18 Gennady Tsygankov .40 1.00
19 Vladimir Vikulov .40 1.00
20 Evgeni Zimin .40 1.00
21 Bedrich Brunschk .20 .50
22 Jiri Bubla .75 2.00
23 Josef Cerny .30 .75
24 Richard Farda .20 .50
25 Jan Havel .20 .50
26 Ivan Hnlicka .20 .50
27 Jiri Holecek .40 1.00
28 Jiri Holik .30 .75
29 Josef Horesovsky .20 .50
30 Jiri Kochta .20 .50
31 Oldrich Machac .20 .50
32 Vladimir Martinec .30 .75
33 Vaclav Nedomansky .75 2.00
34 Eduard Novak .20 .50
35 Frantisek Panchartek .20 .50
36 Frantisek Pospisil .30 .75
37 Marcel Sakac .20 .50
38 Bohuslav Stastny .40 1.00
39 Jan Suchy .30 .75
40 Christer Abrahamsson .75 2.00
41 Thommy Abrahamsson .40 1.00
42 Thommie Bergman 1.25 3.00
43 Arne Carlsson .20 .50
44 Inge Hammarstrom 4.00 10.00
45 Anders Hedberg 3.00 8.00
46 Leif Holmqvist .75 2.00
47 Stig-Goran Johansson .40 1.00
48 Stefan Karlsson .20 .50
49 Hans Lindberg .20 .50
50 Tord Lundstrom .20 .50
51 William Lofqvist .40 1.00
52 Kjell-Rune Milton .20 .50
53 Lars-Goran Nilsson .20 .50
54 Bert-Ola Nordlander .40 1.00
55 Hakan Nygren .20 .50
56 Bjorn Palmqvist .20 .50
57 Hakan Pettersson .20 .50
58 Ulf Sterner .20 .50
59 Lennart Svedberg .40 1.00
60 Hakan Wickberg .20 .50
61 Esa Isaksson .20 .50
62 Heikki Jarn .20 .50
63 Veli-Pekka Ketola .75 2.00
64 Ilpo Koskela .20 .50
65 Seppo Lindstrom .20 .50
66 Harri Linnonmaa .20 .50
67 Hannu Luojola .20 .50
68 Pekka Mononen .20 .50
69 Erkki Mononen .20 .50
70 Lauri Mononen .20 .50
71 Matti Murto .40 1.00
72 Lasse Oksanen .20 .50
73 Esa Peltonen .20 .50
74 Seppo Repo .20 .50
75 Tommi Salmelainen .20 .50
76 Juhani Tamminen .20 .50
77 Jorma Valtonen .40 1.00
78 Jorma Vehmanen .20 .50
79 Urpo Ylonen .40 1.00
80 Jouko Oystila .20 .50
81 Tapio Flinck .20 .50
82 Antti Heikkila .20 .50
83 Reijo Heinonen .20 .50
84 Jaakko Honkanen .20 .50
85 Veli-Pekka Ketola .75 2.00
86 Raimo Kilpio .20 .50
87 Tapio Koskinen .20 .50
88 Kaj Matalamaki .20 .50
89 Pertti Makela .20 .50
90 Pekka Rautakallio .20 .50
91 Markku Riihimaki .20 .50
92 Matti Salmi .20 .50
93 Jorma Valtonen .40 1.00
94 Anto Virtanen .20 .50
95 Erkki Vakiparta .20 .50
96 Pertti Ahokas .20 .50
97 Pertti Arvaja .20 .50
98 Olli Hietanen .20 .50
99 Pentti Hiiros .20 .50
100 Eero Holopainen .20 .50
101 Kari Kinnunen .20 .50
102 Ilpo Koskela .20 .50
103 Timo Kyntola .20 .50
104 Henry Leppa .20 .50
105 Erkki Mononen .20 .50
106 Pertti Nurmi .20 .50
107 Timo Relas .20 .50
108 Timo Sutinen .20 .50
109 Timo Turunen .20 .50
110 Jouko Oystila .20 .50
111 Juhani Bostrom .20 .50
112 Kimmo Heino .20 .50
113 Esa Isaksson .20 .50
114 Juhani Jylha .20 .50
115 Heikki Jarn .20 .50
116 Mauri Kaukorari .20 .50
117 Vaino Kolkka .20 .50
118 Harri Linnonmaa .20 .50
119 Jaakko Marttinen .20 .50
120 Matti Murto .40 1.00
121 Lalli Partinen .20 .50
122 Juha Rantasila .20 .50
123 Heikki Riihiranta .20 .50
124 Jorma Rikala .20 .50
125 Tommi Salmelainen .20 .50
126 Jorma Thusberg .20 .50
127 Matti Vaisanen .20 .50
128 Jukka Alkula .20 .50
129 Pertti Ansakorpi .20 .50
130 Keijo Jarvinen .20 .50
131 Pertti Koivulahti .20 .50
132 Ilpo Kuisma .20 .50
134 Antti Leppanen .20 .50
135 Pekka Marjamaki .20 .50
136 Mikko Mynttien .20 .50
137 Pekka Makinen .20 .50
138 Seppo Makinen .20 .50
139 Keijo Mannisto .20 .50
140 Antti Perttula .20 .50
141 Tuomo Rautiainen .20 .50
142 Juhani Saarelainen .20 .50
143 Jorma Saarikorpi .20 .50
144 Risto Seesvuori .20 .50
145 Jorma Siitarinen .20 .50
146 Raimo Suoniemi .20 .50
147 Juhani Aaltonen .20 .50
148 Matti Ahvenharju .20 .50
149 Hannu Auvinen .20 .50
150 Jorma Borgstrom .20 .50
151 Martti Immonen .20 .50
152 Matti Keinonen .20 .50
153 Seppo Laakkio .20 .50
154 Timo Lahtinen .20 .50
155 Esa Peltonen .20 .50
156 Keijo Puhakka .20 .50
157 Antti Ravi .20 .50
158 Timo Saari .20 .50
159 Esa Siren .20 .50
160 Erkki Suni .20 .50
161 Seppo Suoraniemi .20 .50
162 Juhani Tamminen .20 .50
163 Jorma Vehmanen .20 .50
164 Stig Wetzell .20 .50
165 Olli Viilma .20 .50
166 Leo Aikas .20 .50
167 Sakari Ahlberg .20 .50
168 Seppo Ahokainen .20 .50
169 Jorma Aro .20 .50
170 Esko Eriksson .20 .50
171 Marku Hakanen .20 .50
172 Matti Hakanen .20 .50
173 Reijo Hakanen .20 .50
174 Martti Helle .20 .50
175 Timo Hirsimaki .20 .50
176 Jorma Kallio .20 .50
177 Esko Kaonpaa .20 .50
178 Pentti Koskela .20 .50
179 Pekka Kuusisto .20 .50
180 Pekka Leimu .20 .50
181 Jukka Mattila .20 .50
182 Lasse Oksanen .20 .50
183 Kari Palooja .20 .50
184 Jorma Peltonen .40 1.00
185 Tuomo Sillman .20 .50
186 Jaakko Siren .20 .50
187 Veikkoi Suominen .20 .50
188 Matti Jakonen .20 .50
189 Kari Johansson .20 .50
190 Arto Kaunonen .20 .50
191 Timo Kokkonen .20 .50
192 Reijo Leppanen .20 .50
193 Seppo Lindstrom .20 .50
194 Hannu Luojola .20 .50
195 Hannu Niittoaho .20 .50
196 Reijo Paksal .20 .50
197 Seppo Parikka .20 .50
198 Jarmo Rantanen .20 .50
199 Veijo Saarinen .20 .50
200 Martti Salonen .20 .50
201 Voitto Soini .20 .50
202 Kari Torkkel .20 .50
203 Risto Vainio .20 .50

204 Pentti Vihanto .20 .50
205 Seppo Wikstrom .20 .50
206 Urpo Ylonen .40 1.00
207 Hannu Haapalainen .20 .50
208 Jukka-Pekka Jarvenpaa .20 .50
209 Timo Jarvinen .20 .50
210 Heikki Keinonen .20 .50
211 Heimo Keinonen .20 .50
212 Rauno Lehtio .20 .50
213 Markku Moisio .20 .50
214 Seppo Nurmi .20 .50
215 Esko Rantanen .20 .50
216 Juhani Ruohonen .20 .50
217 Mikko Raikkonen .20 .50
218 Lauri Salomaa .20 .50
219 Veikko Savolainen .20 .50
220 Leo Seppanen .20 .50
221 Pekka Uitus .20 .50
222 Jorma Vilen .20 .50
223 Tapio Virhimo .20 .50
224 Kauko Fomin .20 .50
225 Heikki Hurme .20 .50
226 Eero Juntunen .20 .50
227 Lauri Jamsen .20 .50
228 Lasse Kiili .20 .50
229 Hannu Koivunen .20 .50
230 Jarmo Koivunen .20 .50
231 Pekka Lahtela .20 .50
232 Ilkka Mesikammen .20 .50
233 Timo Nummelin .20 .50
234 Rauli Ottila .20 .50
235 Matti Rautee .20 .50
236 Pekka Rautee .20 .50
237 Jari Rosberg .20 .50
238 Jouni Samuli .20 .50
239 Harry Silver .20 .50
240 Rauli Tammelin .20 .50
241 Bengt Wilenius .20 .50
242 Mikko Erholm .20 .50
243 Veikko Ihalainen .20 .50
244 Heikki Kauhanen .20 .50
245 Tapani Koskimaki .20 .50
246 Antti Laine .20 .50
247 Arto Laine .20 .50
248 Timo Lehtorinne .20 .50
249 Hannu Lunden .20 .50
250 Teppo Rastio .20 .50
251 Pentti Rautalin .20 .50
252 Kai Rosvall .20 .50
253 Ilkka Saarikko .20 .50
254 Jari Sarronlahti .20 .50
255 Matti Saurio .20 .50
256 Hannu Siivonen .20 .50
257 Erkki Sundelin .20 .50
258 Simo Suoknuuti .20 .50
259 Martti Haapala .20 .50
260 Yrjo Hakulinen .20 .50
261 Pentti Hirvonen .20 .50
262 Antero Honkanen .20 .50
263 Pekka Lavkainen .20 .50
264 Pentti Lavkainen .20 .50
265 Pertti Martikainen .20 .50
266 Pentti Martikainen .20 .50
267 Seppo Nevalainen .20 .50
268 Tapio Pohtinen .20 .50
269 Kari Puustinen .20 .50
270 Markku Rouhiainen .20 .50
271 Jarmo Sahlmann .20 .50
272 Seppo Saros .20 .50
273 Juha Silvennoinen .20 .50
274 Unto Turpeinen .20 .50
275 Kari Viitakahti .20 .50
276 Erkki Airaksinen .20 .50
277 Kauko Alkunen .20 .50
278 Jarmo Gummerus .20 .50
279 Bjorn Herbert .20 .50
280 Jarmo Jaakkola .20 .50
281 Hannu Kapanen .20 .50
282 Matti Koskinen .20 .50
283 Martti Kuokkanen .20 .50
284 Juhani Laine .20 .50
285 Heikki Leppik .20 .50
286 Juhani Langstrom .20 .50
287 Osmo Lotjonen .20 .50
288 Lauri Mononen .20 .50
289 Christer Nordblad .20 .50
290 Juha Poikolainen .20 .50
291 Kimmo Rantanen .20 .50
292 Seppo Repo .20 .50
293 Ilpo Ruokosalmi .20 .50
294 Arto Siisala .20 .50
295 Bo Sjostedt .20 .50
296 Pentti Viitanen .20 .50
297 Pekka Arbelius .40 1.00
298 Olli Engvist .20 .50
299 Hannu Hiltunen .20 .50
300 Paavo Holopainen .20 .50
301 Juha Huikari .20 .50
302 Ari Jalonen .20 .50
303 Kari Jalonen .20 .50
304 Ari Kaikkonen .20 .50
305 Ari Kalmokoski .20 .50
306 Arto Lehtinen .20 .50
307 Markku Narhi .20 .50
308 Ilkka Okkonen .20 .50
309 Matti Perhonma .20 .50
310 Juha-Pekka Porvari .20 .50
311 Arto Ruotanen .20 .50
312 Reijo Ruotsalainen .20 .50
313 Matti Ruutti .20 .50
314 Pertti Raisanen .20 .50
315 Ari Timosaari .20 .50
316 Janne Oro .20 .50
317 Anssi Eronen .20 .50
318 Seppo Hirvonen .20 .50
319 Jari Hannu Hamalainen .20 .50
320 Jari Pekka Hamalainen .20 .50
321 Timo Harkonen .40 1.00
322 Jouko Ikonen .20 .50
323 Lasse Kaiponen .20 .50
324 Jyri Kemppinen .20 .50
325 Jouni Kostiainen .20 .50
326 Kai Kulhoranta .20 .50
327 Olli Lemola .20 .50
328 Jari Lopponen .20 .50
329 Pasi Makkonen .20 .50
330 Vesa Massinen .20 .50
331 Timo Minkkila .20 .50
332 Petri Pellinen .20 .50
333 Juhan Rasanen .20 .50
334 Pasi Sallinen .20 .50
335 Kauko Tamminen .20 .50
336 Olli Teijonmaa .20 .50
337 Ismo Tolvanen .20 .50
338 Timo Vaahtoluoto .20 .50
339 Kari Heikkila .20 .50
340 Pekka Helander .20 .50
341 Jari Hirsimaki .20 .50
342 Jari Huotari .20 .50
343 Ilkka Huura .20 .50
344 Tero Juojarvi .20 .50
345 Jari Jarvinen .20 .50
346 Mika Laine .20 .50
347 Marko Lepaus .20 .50
348 Pertti Lundberg .20 .50
349 Tino Minetti .20 .50
350 Jarom Partanen .20 .50
351 Olli-Pekka Perala .20 .50
352 Ari Ruuska .20 .50
353 Kai Saario .20 .50
354 Olli-Pekka Turunen .20 .50
355 Veli-Matti Uusimaa .20 .50
356 Mauri Viita .20 .50
357 Timo Virtanen .20 .50
358 Jarmo Viteli .20 .50
359 Petri Viteli .20 .50
360 Ari Havukainen .20 .50
361 Ismo Heinonen .20 .50
362 Riku Hoyden .20 .50
363 Jari Jokinen .20 .50
364 Timo Joutsenvuori .20 .50
365 Jyrki Jantti .20 .50
366 Kimmo Jantti .20 .50
367 Toni Ketola .20 .50
368 Juha Korhonen .20 .50
369 Ari Laine .20 .50
370 Kari Lainio .20 .50
371 Juha Makinen .20 .50
372 Reima Numminen .20 .50
373 Mika Pirila .20 .50
374 Kai Pulli .20 .50
375 Tero Tommila .20 .50
376 Harri Tuohimaa .20 .50
377 Pasi Tuohimaa .20 .50
378 Ari Veijalainen .20 .50
379 Jean Beliveau 10.00 25.00
380 Phil Esposito 15.00 40.00
381 Tony Esposito 15.00 40.00
382 Gordie Howe 30.00 60.00
383 Bobby Hull 15.00 40.00
384 Bobby Orr 50.00 100.00

1972-73 Finnish Jaakiekko

COMPLETE SET (360) 100.00 200.00
1 Vladimir Bednar .40 1.00
2 Jiri Bubla .40 1.00
3 Vladimir Dzurilla 1.25 3.00
4 Richard Farda .20 .50
5 Julius Haas .20 .50
6 Ivan Hlinka .75 2.00
7 Jiri Holecek .75 2.00
8 Jaroslav Holik .40 1.00
9 Jiri Holik .40 1.00
10 Josef Horesovsky .20 .50
11 Jan Klapac .20 .50
12 Jiri Kochta .20 .50
13 Milan Kuzela .20 .50
14 Oldrich Machac .20 .50
15 Vladimir Martinec .20 .50
16 Vaclav Nedomansky 2.00 5.00
17 Josef Palecek .20 .50
18 Frantisek Pospisil .20 .50
19 Bohuslav Stastny .20 .50
20 Rudolf Tajcnar .20 .50
21 Vjatsjeslav Anisin .40 1.00
22 Juri Blinov .40 1.00
23 Aleksandr Gusev .75 2.00
24 Valeri Kharlamov 6.00 15.00
25 Aleksandr Yakushev 4.00 10.00
26 Viktor Kuzkin .40 1.00
27 Vladimir Lutshenko .40 1.00
28 Aleksandr Maltsev 2.00 5.00
29 Boris Mikhailov 2.00 5.00
30 Jevgeni Mishakov .75 2.00
31 Vladimir Petrov 2.00 5.00
32 Aleksandr Ragulin .75 2.00
33 Igor Romishevski .40 1.00
34 Vladimir Shadrin .75 2.00
35 Vladimir Shepovalov .40 1.00
36 Vjatsjeslav Solodukhin .40 1.00
37 Vladislav Tretjak 8.00 20.00
38 Gennadi Tsigankov .40 1.00
39 Valeri Vasiljev 2.00 5.00
40 Vladimir Vikulov .40 1.00
41 Christer Abrahamsson 1.25 3.00
42 Tommy Abrahamsson 1.25 3.00
43 Thommie Bergman 2.00 5.00
44 Inge Hammarstrom 3.00 8.00
45 Anders Hedberg 3.00 8.00
46 Leif Holmqvist .75 2.00
47 Bjorn Johansson .20 .50
48 Stig-Goran Johansson .40 1.00
49 Stefan Karlsson .20 .50
50 Stig Larsson .20 .50
51 Mats Lind .20 .50
52 Tord Lundstrom .20 .50
53 Lars-Goran Johansson .20 .50
54 Bjorn Palmqvist .20 .50
55 Hakan Pettersson .20 .50
56 Borje Salming 8.00 20.00
57 Lars-Erik Sjoberg 1.25 3.00
58 Carl Sundqvist .20 .50
59 Hakan Wickberg .20 .50
60 Stig Ostling .20 .50
61 Seppo Ahokainen .20 .50
62 Matti Keinonen .20 .50
63 Veli-Pekka Ketola 1.25 3.00
64 Harri Linnonmaa .20 .50
65 Pekka Marjamaki .20 .50
66 Lauri Mononen .20 .50
67 Matti Murto .20 .50
68 Timo Nummelin .20 .50
69 Lasse Oksanen .20 .50
70 Esa Peltonen .20 .50
71 Juha Rantasila .20 .50
72 Pekka Rautakallio 1.25 3.00
73 Seppo Repo .20 .50
74 Heikki Riihiranta .20 .50
75 Juhani Tamminen .40 1.00
76 Timo Turunen .20 .50
77 Pertti Valkeapaa .20 .50
78 Jorma Valtonen .20 .50
79 Stig Wetzell .20 .50
80 Jouko Oystila .20 .50
81 Juhani Bostrom .20 .50
82 Kimmo Heino .20 .50
83 Penti Karlsson .20 .50
84 Mauri Kaukokari .20 .50
85 Jarmo Koivunen .20 .50
86 Heikki Kojola .20 .50
87 Vaino Kolkka .20 .50
88 Harri Linnonmaa .20 .50
89 Jaakko Marttinen .20 .50
90 Matti Murto .20 .50
91 Lalli Partinen .20 .50
92 Juha Rantasila .20 .50
93 Heikki Riihiranta .20 .50
94 Jorma Rikala .20 .50
95 Henry Saleva .20 .50
96 Tommi Salmelainen .20 .50
97 Jorma Thusberg .20 .50
98 Jorma Virtanen .20 .50
99 Matti Vaisanen .20 .50
100 Juhani Aaltonen .20 .50
101 Jorma Immonen .20 .50
102 Martti Immonen .20 .50
103 Heikki Jarn .20 .50
104 Matti Keinonen .20 .50
105 Seppo Laakkio .20 .50
106 Timo Lahtinen .20 .50
107 Esa Peltonen .20 .50
108 Keijo Puhakka .20 .50
109 Seppo Raiilio .20 .50
110 Antti Ravi .20 .50
111 Timo Saari .20 .50
112 Esa Siren .20 .50
113 Seppo Suoraniemi .20 .50
114 Juhani Tamminen .20 .50
115 Jorma Vehmanen .20 .50
116 Stig Wetzell .20 .50
117 Leo Aikas .20 .50
118 Sakari Ahlberg .20 .50
119 Seppo Ahokainen .20 .50
120 Jorma Aro .20 .50
121 Esko Eriksson .20 .50
122 Markku Hakanen .20 .50
123 Timo Hirsimaki .20 .50
124 Jorma Kallio .20 .50
125 Esko Kaonpaa .20 .50
126 Pentti Koskela .20 .50
127 Pekka Kuusisto .20 .50
128 Pekka Leimu .20 .50
129 Len Lunde .20 .50
130 Jukka Mattila .20 .50
131 Lasse Oksanen .20 .50
132 Hannu Palmu .20 .50
133 Kari Palo-oja .20 .50
134 Jorma Peltonen .20 .50
135 Tuomo Sillman .20 .50
136 Veikko Suominen .20 .50
137 Pertti Ahokass .20 .50
138 Pertti Arvaja .20 .50
139 Christer Bergenheim .20 .50
140 Jorma Borgstrom .20 .50
141 Olli Hietanen .20 .50
142 Pentti Hiiros .20 .50
143 Eero Holopainen .20 .50
144 Kari Kinnunen .20 .50
145 Keijo Koivunen .20 .50
146 Ilpo Koskela .20 .50
147 Timo Kyntola .20 .50
148 Henry Leppa .20 .50
149 Erkki Mononen .20 .50
150 Pertti Nurmi .20 .50
151 Tero Raty .20 .50
152 Timo Sutinen .20 .50
153 Timo Turunen .20 .50
154 Jouko Oystila .20 .50
155 Hannu Haapalainen .20 .50
156 Olavi Haapalainen .20 .50
157 Jukka-Pekka Jarvenpaa .20 .50
158 Heimo Keinonen .20 .50
159 Markku Moisio .20 .50
160 Heikki Nurmi .20 .50
161 Seppo Nurmi .20 .50
162 Oiva Oijennus .20 .50
163 Reino Pulkkinen .20 .50
164 Esko Rantanen .20 .50
165 Juhani Ruohonen .20 .50
166 Mikko Raikkonen .20 .50
167 Lauri Salomaa .20 .50
168 Leo Seppanen .20 .50
169 Pekka Uitus .20 .50
170 Jorma Vilen .20 .50
171 Tapio Virhimo .20 .50
172 Leo Haakana .20 .50
173 Seppo Hyvonen .20 .50
174 Heikki Juselius .20 .50
175 Hannu Lemander .20 .50
176 Kyosti Lahde .20 .50
177 Ari Mikkola .20 .50
178 Martti Makia .20 .50
179 Martti Narinen .20 .50
180 Pekka Nieminen .20 .50
181 Teijo Rasanen .20 .50
182 Timo Sartiala .20 .50
183 Pekka Sartjarvi .20 .50
184 Keijo Sinkkonen .20 .50
185 Martti Sinkkonen .20 .50
186 Arto Summanen .20 .50
187 Erkki Suni .20 .50
188 Seppo Urpalainen .20 .50
189 Matti Vaatamoinen .20 .50
190 Timo Vaatamoinen .20 .50
191 Jukka Alkula .20 .50
192 Pertti Ansakorpi .20 .50
193 Keijo Jarvinen .20 .50
194 Pertti Koivulahti .20 .50
195 Ilpo Kuisma .20 .50
196 Vesa Lehtoranta .20 .50
197 Antti Leppanen .20 .50
198 Pekka Marjamaki .20 .50
199 Mikko Myntinen .20 .50
200 Pekka Makinen .20 .50
201 Seppo Makinen .20 .50
202 Antti Perttula .20 .50
203 Tuomo Rautiainen .20 .50
204 Jorma Saarikorpi .20 .50
205 Jorma Siitarinen .20 .50
206 Raimo Suoniemi .20 .50
207 Pertti Valkeapaa .20 .50
208 Kari Horkko .20 .50
209 Eero Juntunen .20 .50
210 Lauri Jamsen .20 .50
211 Kari Kauppila .20 .50
212 Lasse Kiili .20 .50
213 Olli Kokkonen .20 .50
214 Pekka Lahtela .20 .50
215 Robert Lamoureux .20 .50
216 Ilkka Mesikammen .20 .50
217 Timo Nummelin .20 .50
218 Rauli Ottila .20 .50
219 Matti Rautee .20 .50
220 Pekka Rautee .20 .50
221 Jari Rosberg .20 .50
222 Jouni Samuli .20 .50
223 Harri Silver .20 .50
224 Rauli Tammelin .20 .50
225 Bengt Wilenius .20 .50
226 Pertti Hasanen .20 .50
227 Kari Johansson .20 .50
228 Arto Kaunonen .20 .50
229 Timo Kokkonen .20 .50
230 Reijo Leppanen .20 .50
231 Seppo Lindstrom .20 .50
232 Hannu Luojola .20 .50
233 Hannu Niittoaho .20 .50
234 Reijo Paksal .20 .50
235 Seppo Parikka .20 .50
236 Jarmo Rantanen .20 .50
237 Kari Salonen .20 .50
238 Tapani Sura .20 .50
239 Kari Torkkel .20 .50
240 Risto Vainio .20 .50
241 Pentti Vihanto .20 .50
242 Seppo Wikstrom .20 .50
243 Urpo Ylonen .20 .50
244 Tapio Flinck .20 .50
245 Antti Heikkila .20 .50
246 Reijo Heinonen .20 .50
247 Jaakko Honkanen .20 .50
248 Veli-Pekka Ketola 1.25 3.00
249 Raimo Kilpio .20 .50
250 Tapio Koskinen .20 .50
251 Jarkko Levonen .20 .50
252 Kaj Matalamaki .20 .50
253 Pertti Makela .20 .50
254 Hannu Pulkkinen .20 .50
255 Pekka Rautakallio 1.25 3.00
256 Markku Riihimaki .20 .50
257 Matti Salmi .20 .50
258 Jorma Valtonen .20 .50
259 Anto Virtanen .20 .50
260 Erkki Vakiparta .20 .50
261 Martti Jarkko .20 .50
262 Torsti Jarvenpaa .20 .50
263 Tapio Kallio .20 .50
264 Jussi Kiansten .20 .50
265 Kimmo Korpela .20 .50
266 Jarmo Kuisma .20 .50
267 Antero Lehtonen .20 .50
268 Mikko Leinonen .20 .50
269 Tuomas Leinonen .20 .50
270 Lasse Litma .20 .50
271 Seppo Makinen .20 .50
272 Heikki Niemi .20 .50
273 Reijo Narvanen .20 .50
274 Kalevi Paakkonen .20 .50
275 Reijo Rossi .20 .50
276 Seppo Sevon .20 .50
277 Jorma Siren .20 .50
278 Risto Sirkkola .20 .50
279 Risto Hevonkorpi .20 .50
280 Veijo Hukkanen .20 .50
281 Timo Hytti .20 .50
282 Kalle Impola .20 .50
283 Pertti Jarvenpaa .20 .50
284 Rauno Jarvinen .20 .50
285 Antti Kaivola .20 .50
286 Jorma Karvonen .20 .50
287 Pekka Karvonen .20 .50
288 Seppo Kettunen .20 .50
289 Kari Niemi .20 .50
290 Timo Niiniviita .20 .50
291 Jari Nurminen .20 .50
292 Pentti Poussu .20 .50
293 Matti Rautiainen .20 .50
294 Vesa Ronkainen .20 .50
295 Mauri Salminen .20 .50
296 Kari Silius .20 .50
297 Kimo Turtiainen .20 .50
298 Juha Wikman .20 .50
299 Juha-Pekka Aho .20 .50
300 Matti Estola .20 .50
301 Markku Heinonen .20 .50
302 Mauri Heinonen .20 .50
303 Jukka Hirsimaki .20 .50
304 Jarmo Huhtala .20 .50
305 Harri Huotari .20 .50
306 Kari Jarvinen .20 .50
307 Jari Kaarela .20 .50
308 Kai Lehto .20 .50
309 Jari Leppanen .20 .50
310 Jarmo Liilius .20 .50
311 Markus Matsson .20 .50
312 Jari Niinimaki .20 .50
313 Hannu Oksanen .20 .50
314 Sakari Pehu .20 .50
315 Mika Rajala .20 .50
316 Risto Siltanen .20 .50
317 Jarmo Siro .20 .50
318 Jukka Siro .20 .50
319 Jari Uusikartano .20 .50
320 Seppo Vartiainen .20 .50
321 Mika Weissman .20 .50
322 Seppo Aro .20 .50
323 Jari Huotari .20 .50
324 Ilkka Huura .20 .50
325 Jari Hytti .20 .50
326 Jarmo Jamalainen .20 .50
327 Jari Jokinen .20 .50
328 Tero Juojarvi .20 .50
329 Jari Jarvinen .20 .50
330 Lauri Kosonen .20 .50
331 Aki Laakso .20 .50
332 Ismo Laine .20 .50
333 Matti Lisko .20 .50
334 Dale Lunde .20 .50
335 Markku Pirkkalanniemi .20 .50
336 Rauno Saarnio .20 .50
337 Jukka Silander .20 .50
338 Olli-Pekka Turunen .20 .50
339 Mauri Unkila .20 .50
340 Jarmo Viteli .20 .50
341 Jukka Ahonen .20 .50
342 Jari Hallila .20 .50
343 Jari Helle .20 .50
344 Jari Hirsimaki .20 .50
345 Petri Jokinen .20 .50
346 Kari Jarvinen .20 .50
347 Arto Laine .20 .50
348 Ari Leinonen .20 .50
349 Jukka Oksanen .20 .50
350 Sten Pakarinen .20 .50
351 Jyrki Seppa .20 .50
352 Jari Simola .20 .50
353 Olli Sarkilahti .20 .50
354 Kari-Pekka Tarko .20 .50
355 Timo Toivonen .20 .50
356 Veli-Matti Uusimaa .20 .50
357 Risto Viljanen .20 .50
358 Timo Virtanen .20 .50
359 Teppo Valimaki .20 .50
360 Juha Yrjola .20 .50

1972 Finnish Hellas

This vintage Finnish set appears to feature players who appeared in the previous World Championships.

COMPLETE SET (99) 50.00 125.00
1 Seppo Ahokainen .20 .50
2 Veli-Pekka Ketola .60 1.50
3 Henry Leppa .20 .50
4 Harri Linnonmaa .20 .50
5 Pekka Marjamaki .20 .50
6 Lauri Mononen .20 .50
7 Matti Murto .20 .50
8 Timo Nummelin .20 .50
9 Lasse Oksanen .20 .50
10 Esa Peltonen .20 .50
11 Pekka Rautakallio .60 1.50
12 Seppo Repo .20 .50
13 Heikki Riihiranta .40 1.00
14 Tommi Salmelainen .20 .50
15 Leo Seppanen .20 .50
16 Juhani Tamminen .40 1.00
17 Timo Turunen .20 .50
18 Pertti Valkeapaa .20 .50
19 Jorma Valtonen .40 1.00
20 Jouko Oystila .20 .50
21 Timo Saari .20 .50
22 Seppo Suoraniemi .20 .50
23 Leif Holmqvist .40 1.00
24 Thommy Abrahamsson .40 1.00
25 Thommie Bergman .75 2.00
26 Stig Ostling .40 1.00
27 Lars Sjoberg .75 2.00
28 Carl Sundquist .20 .50
29 Bjorn Johansson .20 .50
30 Tord Lundstrom .20 .50
31 Stig-Goran Johansson .20 .50
32 Stefan Karlsson .20 .50
33 Lars-Goran Nilsson .20 .50
34 Stig Larsson .20 .50
35 Mats Lindh .20 .50
36 Bjorn Palmqvist .20 .50
37 Inge Hammarstrom 4.00 10.00
38 Anders Hedberg 2.00 5.00
39 Kurt Larsson .20 .50
40 Hakan Pettersson .20 .50
41 Hakan Wickberg .20 .50
42 Borje Salming 6.00 15.00
43 Franz Funk .20 .50
44 Otto Schneitberger .20 .50
45 Josef Volk .20 .50
46 Rudolph Thanner .20 .50
47 Paul Langner .20 .50
48 Harald Kadow .20 .50
49 Anton Pohl .20 .50
50 Karl-Heinz Egger 2.00 5.00
51 Lorenz Funk .20 .50
52 Alois Schloder .20 .50
53 Gustav Hanig .20 .50
54 Philips Reiner .20 .50
55 Bernd Kuhn .20 .50
56 Johan Eimansberger .20 .50
57 Rainer Makatsch .20 .50
58 Michael Eibl .20 .50
59 Hans Schichti .20 .50
60 Anrton Hoffher .20 .50
61 Valdimir Lutchenko .40 1.00
62 Aleksandr Gusev .30 .75
63 Vladimir Lutchenko .40 1.00
64 Viktor Kuzkin .20 .50
65 Aleksandr Ragulin .40 1.00
66 Igor Romishevski .20 .50
67 Gennadi Tsigankov .40 1.00
68 Valeri Vasiliev .40 1.00
69 Yuri Blinov .20 .50
70 Alexander Maltsev 2.00 5.00
71 Evgeny Mishakov .30 .75
72 Boris Mikhailov 2.00 5.00
73 Vjatseslav Anisin .30 .75
74 Alexander Yakushev 2.00 5.00
75 Vladimir Petrov 1.25 3.00
76 Valeri Kharlamov 4.00 10.00
77 Vladimir Vikulov .30 .75
78 Vladimir Shadrin .30 .75
79 Vladislav Tretiak 6.00 15.00
80 Vladimir Dzurilla .60 1.50
81 Jiri Holecek .40 1.00
82 Josef Horesovsky .20 .50
83 Oldrich Machac .20 .50
84 Jaroslav Holik .30 .75
85 Rudolf Tajcnar .20 .50
86 Frantisek Pospisil .30 .75
87 Jiri Kochta .20 .50
88 Jan Klapac .20 .50
89 Vladimir Martinec .20 .50
90 Richard Farda .30 .75
91 Bohuslav Stastny .30 .75
92 Vaclav Nedomansky .60 1.50
93 Julius Haas .20 .50
94 Josef Palecek .20 .50
95 Jiri Bubla .40 1.00
96 Milan Kuzela .20 .50
97 Vladimir Bednar .20 .50
98 Jiri Holik .40 1.00
99 Ivan Hlinka .30 .75

1972 Finnish Panda Toronto

COMPLETE SET (118) 50.00 100.00
1 Juhani Bostrom .40 1.00
2 Gary Engberg .40 1.00
3 Kimmo Heino .40 1.00
4 Mauri Kaukokari .40 1.00
5 Vaino Kolkka .40 1.00
6 Harri Linnonmaa .40 1.00
7 Jaakko Marttinen .40 1.00
8 Matti Murto .40 1.00
9 Lalli Partinen .40 1.00
10 Juha Rantasila .40 1.00
11 Heikki Riihiranta .40 1.00
12 Jorma Rikala .40 1.00
13 Tommi Salmelainen .40 1.00
14 Jorma Thusberg .40 1.00
15 Jorma Virtanen .40 1.00
16 Matti Vaisanen .40 1.00
17 Sakari Ahlberg .40 1.00
18 Jorma Aro .40 1.00
19 Esko Eriksson .40 1.00
20 Markku Hakanen .40 1.00
21 Matti Hakanen .40 1.00
22 Reijo Hakanen .40 1.00
23 Timo Hirsimaki .40 1.00
24 Jorma Kallio .40 1.00
25 Esko Kaonpaa .40 1.00
26 Pentti Koskela .40 1.00
27 Pekka Kuusisto .40 1.00
28 Pekka Leimu .40 1.00
29 Lasse Oksanen .40 1.00
30 Kari Palo-oja .40 1.00
31 Jorma Peltonen .40 1.00
32 Veikko Suominen .40 1.00
33 Tapio Flinck .40 1.00
34 Pentti Hakamaki .40 1.00
35 Antti Heikkila .40 1.00
36 Reijo Heinonen .40 1.00
37 Jaakko Honkanen .40 1.00
38 Veli-Pekka Ketola .40 1.00
39 Raimo Kilpio .40 1.00
40 Tapio Koskinen .40 1.00
41 Kaj Matalamaki .40 1.00
42 Pekka Rautakallio .40 1.00
43 Matti Salmi .40 1.00
44 Kari-Pekka Toivonen .40 1.00
45 Jorma Valtonen .40 1.00
46 Anto Virtanen .40 1.00
47 Erkki Vakiparta .40 1.00
48 Vitaly Davydov .75 2.00
49 Anatoly Firsov .75 2.00
50 Valeri Kharlamov 8.00 20.00
51 Victor Konovalenko .75 2.00
52 Victor Kuzkin .75 2.00
53 Yuri Liapkin .75 2.00
54 Vladimir Lutchenko .75 2.00
55 Alexander Maltsev 2.00 5.00
56 Alexander Martyniuk .75 2.00
57 Boris Mikhailov 2.00 5.00
58 Aleksander Ragulin .75 2.00
59 Igor Romishevskyi .75 2.00
60 Vladimir Shadrin .75 2.00
61 Viacheslav Starshinov .75 2.00
62 Vladislav Tretiak 8.00 20.00
63 Evgenyi Zimin .75 2.00
64 Christer Abrahamsson .75 2.00
65 Tommy Abrahamsson .75 2.00
66 Arne Carlsson .40 1.00
67 Inge Hammarstrom 2.00 5.00
68 Leif Holmqvist .75 2.00
69 Stig-Goran Johansson .40 1.00
70 Stefan Karlsson .40 1.00
71 Hans Lindberg .40 1.00
72 Tord Lundstrom .40 1.00
73 Lars-Goran Nilsson .40 1.00
74 Bert-Ola Nordlander .40 1.00
75 Hakan Nygren .40 1.00
76 Bjorn Palmqvist .40 1.00
77 Ulf Sterner .40 1.00
78 Lennart Svedberg .40 1.00
79 Hakan Wickberg .40 1.00
80 Josef Cerny .40 1.00
81 Richard Farda .40 1.00
82 Ivan Hlinka .40 1.00
83 Jiri Holecek .40 1.00
84 Jiri Holik .40 1.00
85 Josef Horesovsky .40 1.00
86 Milan Kuzela .40 1.00
87 Oldrich Machac .40 1.00
88 Vladimir Martinec .40 1.00
89 Vladimir Nadrchal .40 1.00
90 Vaclav Nedomansky 1.50 4.00
91 Frantisek Panchartek .40 1.00
92 Frantisek Pospisil .40 1.00
93 Marcel Sakac .40 1.00
94 Bohuslav Stastny .40 1.00
95 Rudolf Tajcnar .40 1.00
96 Esa Isaksson .40 1.00
97 Heikki Jarn .40 1.00
98 Veli-Pekka Ketola 1.50 4.00
99 Ilpo Koskela .40 1.00
100 Seppo Lindstrom .40 1.00
101 Harri Linnonmaa .40 1.00
102 Pekka Marjamaki .40 1.00
103 Erkki Mononen .40 1.00
104 Lauri Mononen 1.00
105 Matti Murto .40 1.00
106 Lasse Oksanen .40 1.00
107 Esa Peltonen .40 1.00
108 Seppo Repo .40 1.00
109 Tommi Salmelainen .40 1.00
110 Jorma Valtonen .40 1.00
111 Urpo Ylonen .40 1.00
112 Jouko Oystila .40 1.00
113 Sovjet - Finland .40 1.00
114 Sverige - Tjeckoslovakien .40 1.00
115 Finland - Svergie .40 1.00
116 Tjeckoslovakien - Sovjet .40 1.00
117 USA - Sovjet .40 1.00
118 Hockey Sticks .40 1.00

1973-74 Finnish Jaakiekko

COMPLETE SET (325) 125.00 250.00
1 Vjatsjeslav Anisin .75 2.00
2 Aleksandr Bodunov .75 2.00
3 Aleksandr Gusev .75 2.00
4 Valeri Kharlamov 6.00 15.00
5 Aleksandr Yakushev 2.00 5.00
6 Juri Lebedev .75 2.00
7 Juri Liapkin .75 2.00
8 Vladimir Lutshenko .75 2.00
9 Aleksandr Maltsev 2.00 5.00
10 Aleksandr Martiniuk .75 2.00
11 Boris Mikhailov 2.00 5.00
12 Jevgeni Paladiev .75 2.00
13 Vladimir Petrov 2.00 5.00
14 Aleksandr Ragulin .75 2.00
15 Vladimir Shadrin .75 2.00
16 Aleksandr Sidelnikov .75 2.00
17 Vladislav Tretiak 8.00 20.00
18 Gennadi Tsigankov .75 2.00
19 Valeri Vasiljev 2.00 5.00
20 Vladimir Vikulov .75 2.00
21 Aleksandr Voltshkov .75 2.00
22 Christer Abrahamsson 1.25 3.00
23 Thommy Abrahamsson 1.25 3.00
24 Roland Bond .40 1.00
25 Arne Carlsson .40 1.00
26 Inge Hammarstrom 2.00 5.00
27 Anders Hedberg 2.00 5.00
28 Bjorn Johansson .40 1.00
29 Stefan Karlsson .40 1.00
30 Curt Larsson .40 1.00
31 Tord Lundstrom .40 1.00
32 William Lofqvist .40 1.00
33 Ulf Nilsson 2.00 5.00
34 Borje Salming 6.00 15.00
35 Lars-Erik Sjoberg 1.25 3.00
36 Ulf Sterner .40 1.00
37 Karl-Johan Sundqvist .40 1.00
38 Dan Soderstrom .40 1.00
39 Hakan Wickberg .40 1.00
40 Kjell-Arne Wickstrom .40 1.00
41 Dick Yderstrom .40 1.00
42 Mats Ahlberg .40 1.00
43 Peter Adamik .40 1.00
44 Jiri Bubla .40 1.00
45 Jiri Crha 1.25 3.00
46 Richard Farda .40 1.00
47 Ivan Hlinka .75 2.00
48 Jiri Holecek .75 2.00
49 Jaroslav Holik .40 1.00
50 Jiri Holik .40 1.00
51 Josef Horesovsky .40 1.00
52 Jan Klapac .40 1.00
53 Jiri Kochta .40 1.00
54 Milan Kuzela .40 1.00
55 Oldrich Machac .40 1.00
56 Vladimir Martinec .40 1.00
57 Vaclav Nedomansky 1.25 3.00
58 Jiri Novak .40 1.00
59 Josef Palecek .40 1.00
60 Frantisek Pospisil .40 1.00
61 Bohuslav Stastny .40 1.00
62 Karel Vohralik .40 1.00
63 Seppo Ahokainen .40 1.00
64 Matti Keinonen .40 1.00
65 Veli-Pekka Ketola 1.25 3.00
66 Ilpo Koskela .40 1.00
67 Ilpo Kuisma .40 1.00
68 Pekka Kuusisto .40 1.00
69 Henry Leppa .40 1.00
70 Antti Leppanen .40 1.00
71 Seppo Lindstrom .40 1.00
72 Lauri Mononen .40 1.00
73 Timo Nummelin .40 1.00
74 Lalli Partinen .40 1.00
75 Esa Peltonen .40 1.00
76 Pekka Rautakallio 1.25 3.00
77 Seppo Repo .40 1.00
78 Heikki Riihiranta .40 1.00
79 Timo Sutinen .40 1.00
80 Juhani Tamminen .40 1.00
81 Timo Turunen .40 1.00
82 Jorma Valtonen .40 1.00
83 Jorma Vehmanen .40 1.00
84 Jouko Oystila .40 1.00
85 Josef Batkiewicz .40 1.00
86 Krzysztof Bialynicki .40 1.00
87 Stefan Chowaniec .40 1.00
88 Ludwik Czachovski .40 1.00
89 Andrzej Czczepaniec .40 1.00
90 Stanislav Fryzlewicz .40 1.00
91 Robert Goralczyk .40 1.00
92 Mieczyslaw Jaskierski .40 1.00
93 Tadeusz Kacik .40 1.00
94 Adam Kopczynski .40 1.00
95 Valery Kosyl .40 1.00
96 Tadeusz Obloj .40 1.00
97 Jerzy Potz .40 1.00
98 Andrzej Slowakiewicz .40 1.00
99 Josef Slowakiewicz .40 1.00

100 Jan Szeja .40 1.00
101 Leszek Tokarz .40 1.00
102 Wieslav Tokarz .40 1.00
103 Henryk Vojtynek .40 1.00
104 Walenty Zietara .40 1.00
105 Pertti Arvaja .40 1.00
106 Olli J. Hietanen .40 1.00
107 Olli T. Hietanen .40 1.00
108 Pentti Hiiros .40 1.00
109 Eero Holopainen .40 1.00
110 Kari Kinnunen .40 1.00
111 Ilpo Koskela .40 1.00
112 Timo Kyntola .40 1.00
113 Henry Leppa .40 1.00
114 Jan Lindberg .40 1.00
115 Lauri Mononen .40 1.00
116 Mika Rajala .40 1.00
117 Pertti Nurmi .40 1.00
118 Jyrki Seivo .40 1.00
119 Jorma Siitarinen .40 1.00
120 Seppo Suoraniemi .40 1.00
121 Timo Sutinen .40 1.00
122 Timo Turunen .40 1.00
123 Jorma Valtonen .40 1.00
124 Seppo Vartiainen .40 1.00
125 Jouko Oystila .40 1.00
126 Juhani Bostrom .40 1.00
127 Matti Hagman 1.25 3.00
128 Kimmo Heino .40 1.00
129 Jorma Immonen .40 1.00
130 Pentti Karlsson .40 1.00
131 Mauri Kaukokari .40 1.00
132 Jarmo Koivunen .40 1.00
133 Vaino Kolkka .40 1.00
134 Harri Linnonmaa .40 1.00
135 Jaakko Marttinen .40 1.00
136 Matti Murto .40 1.00
137 Lalli Partinen .40 1.00
138 Esa Peltonen .40 1.00
139 Juha Rantasila .40 1.00
140 Heikki Riihiranta .40 1.00
141 Jorma Rikala .40 1.00
142 Tommi Salmelainen .40 1.00
143 Henry Saleva .40 1.00
144 Juhani Tamminen .75 2.00
145 Jorma Thusberg .40 1.00
146 Jorma Virtanen .40 1.00
147 Matti Vaisanen .40 1.00
148 Stig Wetzell .40 1.00
149 Jukka Alkula .40 1.00
150 Pertti Ansakorpi .40 1.00
151 Hannu Haapalainen .40 1.00
152 Martti Jarkko .40 1.00
153 Keijo Jarvinen .40 1.00
154 Pertti Koivulahti .40 1.00
155 Ilpo Kuisma .40 1.00
156 Antero Lehtonen .40 1.00
157 Antti Leppanen .40 1.00
158 Lasse Litma .40 1.00
159 Pekka Marjamaki .40 1.00
160 Mikko Mynttinen .40 1.00
161 Pekka Makinen .40 1.00
162 Seppo I. Makinen .40 1.00
163 Seppo S. Makinen .40 1.00
164 Keijo Mannisto .40 1.00
165 Antti Perttula .40 1.00
166 Tuomo Rautiainen .40 1.00
167 Jorma Saarikorpi .40 1.00
168 Juha Silvennoinen .40 1.00
169 Jorma Siren .40 1.00
170 Raimo Suoniemi .40 1.00
171 Pertti Valkeapaa .40 1.00
172 Sakari Ahlberg .40 1.00
173 Seppo Ahokainen .40 1.00
174 Jorma Aro .40 1.00
175 Esko Eriksson .40 1.00
176 Markku Hakanen .40 1.00
177 Reijo Hakanen .40 1.00
178 Martti Helle .40 1.00
179 Erkki Jarvinen .40 1.00
180 Jorma Kallio .40 1.00
181 Erkki Kesalainen .40 1.00
182 Pekka Kuusisto .40 1.00
183 Pekka Leimu .40 1.00
184 Jukka Mattila .40 1.00
185 Esko Makinen .40 1.00
186 Lassse Oksanen .40 1.00
187 Kari Palo-oja .40 1.00
188 Jorma Peltonen .40 1.00
189 Pekka Rampa .40 1.00
190 Heikki Salminen .40 1.00
191 Tuomo Sillman .40 1.00
192 Veikko Suominen .40 1.00
193 Tapio Virhimo .40 1.00
194 Juhani Aaltonen .40 1.00
195 Bjorn Herbert .40 1.00
196 Hannu Kapanen .40 1.00
197 Matti Keinonen .40 1.00
198 Lasse Kiili .40 1.00
199 Matti Koskinen .40 1.00
200 Martti Kuokkanen .40 1.00
201 Urpo Kuukauppi .40 1.00
202 Seppo Laakkio .40 1.00
203 Timo Lahtinen .40 1.00
204 Juhani Laine .40 1.00
205 Heikki Leppik .40 1.00
206 Osmo Lotjonen .40 1.00
207 Kyosti Majava .40 1.00
208 Keijo Puhakka .40 1.00
209 Antti Ravi .40 1.00
210 Seppo Repo .40 1.00
211 Timo Saari .40 1.00
212 Arto Siissala .40 1.00
213 Jorma Vehmanen .40 1.00
214 Pentti Viitanen .40 1.00
215 Leo Aikas .40 1.00
216 Raine Heinonen .40 1.00
217 Vladimir Jursinov .40 1.00
218 Jukka-Pekka Jarvenpaa .40 1.00
219 Pertti Jarvenpaa .40 1.00
220 Heimo Keinonen .40 1.00
221 Seppo Kettunen .40 1.00
222 Veikko Kirveskoski .40 1.00
223 Reijo Laksola .40 1.00
224 Raimo Majapuro .40 1.00
225 Markku Moisio .40 1.00
226 Heikki Nurmi .40 1.00
227 Seppo Nurmi .40 1.00
228 Oiva Oijennus .40 1.00
229 Esko Rantanen .40 1.00
230 Matti Rautiainen .40 1.00
231 Juhani Ruohonen .40 1.00
232 Mikko Raikkonen .40 1.00
233 Lauri Salomaa .40 1.00
234 Veikko Savolainen .40 1.00
235 Leo Seppanen .40 1.00
236 Veikko Seppanen .40 1.00
237 Pekka Uitus .40 1.00
238 Kari Viitalahti .40 1.00
239 Jorma Vilen .40 1.00
240 Asko Ahonen .40 1.00
241 Tapio Flinck .40 1.00
242 Matti Hakanen .40 1.00
243 Antti Heikkila .40 1.00
244 Reijo Heinonen .40 1.00
245 Jaakko Honkanen .40 1.00
246 Jari Kaski .40 1.00
247 Veli-Pekka Ketola .40 1.00
248 Raimo Kilpio .40 1.00
249 Tapio Koskinen .40 1.00
250 Jarkko Levonen .40 1.00
251 Kaj Matalamaki .40 1.00
252 Pertti Makela .40 1.00
253 Jaakko Niemi .40 1.00
254 Hannu Pulkkinen .40 1.00
255 Pekka Rautakallio .40 1.00
256 Markku Riihimaki .40 1.00
257 Anto Virtanen .40 1.00
258 Erkki Vakiparta .40 1.00
259 Pertti Hasanen .40 1.00
260 Rainer Holmroos .40 1.00
261 Kari Johansson .40 1.00
262 Arto Kaunonen .40 1.00
263 Timo Kokkonen .40 1.00
264 Reijo Leppanen .40 1.00
265 Seppo Lindstrom .40 1.00
266 Hannu Luojola .40 1.00
267 Hannu Niittoaho .40 1.00
268 Reijo Paksal .40 1.00
269 Seppo Parikka .40 1.00
270 Jarmo Rantanen .40 1.00
271 Kari Hyokki .40 1.00
272 Kari Salonen .40 1.00
273 Tapani Sura .40 1.00
274 Kari Torkkel .40 1.00
275 Risto Vainio .40 1.00
276 Pentti Vihanto .40 1.00
277 Urpo Ylonen .40 1.00
278 Lars Ellfolk .40 1.00
279 Kari Horkko .40 1.00
280 Hannu Jortikka .40 1.00
281 Eero Juntunen .40 1.00
282 Lauri Jamsen .40 1.00
283 Jari Kapanen .40 1.00
284 Jari Kauppila .40 1.00
285 Matti Kauppila .40 1.00
286 Jukka Koskilahti .40 1.00
287 Jukka Koivu .40 1.00
288 Ilkka Laaksonen .40 1.00
289 Robert Lamoureux .40 1.00
290 Hannu Lunden .40 1.00
291 Ilkka Mesikammen .40 1.00
292 Timo Nummelin .40 1.00
293 Timo Nurminen .40 1.00
294 Rauli Ottila .40 1.00
295 Matti Rautee .40 1.00
296 Pekka Rautee .40 1.00
297 Jari Rosberg .40 1.00
298 Tarmo Saarni .40 1.00
299 Asko Salminen .40 1.00
300 Jouni Samuli .40 1.00
301 Rauli Tammelin .40 1.00
302 Veijo Wahlsten .40 1.00
303 Bengt Wilenius .40 1.00
304 Denis Bavaudin .40 1.00
305 Mikko Erholm .40 1.00
306 Matti Forss .40 1.00
307 Esa Hakkarainen .40 1.00
308 Veikko Ihalainen .40 1.00
309 Esa Isaksson .40 1.00
310 Juhani Jylha .40 1.00
311 Heikki Kauhanen .40 1.00
312 Jari Laiho .40 1.00
313 Arto Laine .40 1.00
314 Jouni Peltonen .40 1.00
315 Jouni Rinne .40 1.00
316 Kai Rosvall .40 1.00
317 Seppo Santala .40 1.00
318 Jari Sarronlahti .40 1.00
319 Matti Saurio .40 1.00
320 Ari Sjoman .40 1.00
321 Erkki Sundelin .40 1.00
322 Ismo Villa .40 1.00
323 Mikko Ylaja .40 1.00
324 Veijo Ylanen .40 1.00
NNO Album 25.00 50.00

1974 Finnish Jenkki

COMPLETE SET (120) 50.00 100.00
1 Sakari Ahlberg .30 .75
2 Seppo Ahokainen .30 .75
3 Jukka Alkula .30 .75
4 Jorma Aro .30 .75
5 Hannu Haapalainen .30 .75
6 Veli-Pekka Ketola 1.25 3.00
7 Tapio Koskinen .30 .75
8 Henry Leppa .30 .75
9 Antti Leppanen .30 .75
10 Reijo Leppanen .30 .75
11 Pekka Marjamaki .30 .75
12 Matti Murto .30 .75
13 Esa Peltonen .30 .75
14 Pekka Rautakallio 1.25 3.00
15 Leo Seppanen .30 .75
16 Juha Silvennoinen .30 .75
17 Raimo Suoniemi .30 .75
18 Seppo Suoraniemi .30 .75
19 Timo Sutinen .30 .75
20 Juhani Tamminen .75 2.00
21 Pertti Valkeapaa .30 .75
22 Christer Abrahamsson 1.25 3.00
23 Thommie Bergman 1.25 3.00
24 Roland Bond .30 .75
25 Anders Hedberg 2.00 5.00
26 Bjorn Johansson .30 .75
27 Stefan Karlsson .30 .75
28 Mats Lind .30 .75
29 Tord Lundstrom .30 .75
30 William Lofqvist .30 .75
31 Ulf Nilsson 2.00 5.00
32 Bjorn Palmqvist .30 .75
33 Hakan Pettersson .30 .75
34 Lars-Erik Sjoberg .75 2.00
35 Ulf Sterner .30 .75
36 Karl-Johan Sundqvist .30 .75
37 Hakan Wickberg .30 .75
38 Kjell-Arne Wickstrom .30 .75
39 Dick Yderstrom .30 .75
40 Mats Ahlberg .30 .75
41 Stig Ostling .30 .75
42 Vjatseslav Anisin .40 1.00
43 Aleksandr Bodunov .40 1.00
44 Aleksandr Gusev .40 1.00
45 Valeri Kharlamov 6.00 15.00
46 Aleksandr Yakushev 2.00 5.00
47 Juri Liapkin .40 1.00
48 Vladimir Lutshenko .40 1.00
49 Aleksandr Maltsev 2.00 5.00
50 Aleksandr Martiniuk .40 1.00
51 Boris Mikhailov 2.00 5.00
52 Jevgeni Paladiev .40 1.00
53 Vladimir Petrov 2.00 5.00
54 Aleksandr Ragulin .40 1.00
55 Vladimir Shadrin .40 1.00
56 Aleksandr Sidelnikov .40 1.00
57 Vladislav Tretiak 6.00 15.00
58 Gennadi Tsigankov .40 1.00
59 Valeri Vasiljev 2.00 5.00
60 Vladimir Vikulov .40 1.00
61 Aleksandr Voltshkov .40 1.00
62 Julij Blinov .40 1.00
63 Vladimir Sepovalov .40 1.00
64 Josef Horesovsky .30 .75
65 Peter Adamik .30 .75
66 Vladimir Bednar .30 .75
67 Jiri Bubla .75 2.00
68 Richard Farda .30 .75
69 Julius Haas .30 .75
70 Ivan Hlinka .75 2.00
71 Jiri Holecek .75 2.00
72 Jaroslav Holik .30 .75
73 Jiri Holik .30 .75
74 Jan Klapac .30 .75
75 Jiri Kochta .30 .75
76 Milan Kuzela .30 .75
77 Oldrich Machac .30 .75
78 Vladimir Martinec .30 .75
79 Vaclav Nedomansky 1.50 4.00
80 Josef Palecek .30 .75
81 Frantisek Pospisil .30 .75
82 Bohuslav Stastny .30 .75
83 Rudolf Tajcnar .30 .75
84 Karl Vohralik .30 .75
85 Jerzy Potz .30 .75
86 Andrzej Slowakiewicz .30 .75
87 Jusef Slowakiewicz .30 .75
88 Leszek Tokarz .30 .75
89 Wieslav Tokarz .30 .75
90 Henryk Vojtynek .30 .75
91 Walenty Zietara .30 .75
92 Josef Batkiewicz .30 .75
93 Stefan Chowaniec .30 .75
94 Ludvik Czachovski .30 .75
95 Andrzej Czczepaniec .30 .75
96 Robert Goralczyk .30 .75
97 Mieczyslaw Jaskierski .30 .75
98 Tadeusz Kacik .30 .75
99 Adam Kopczynski .30 .75
100 Valery Kosyl .30 .75
101 Tadeusz Obloj .30 .75
102 Joachim Stasche .30 .75
103 Roland Peters .30 .75
104 Dietmar Peters .30 .75
105 Bernd Karrenbauer .30 .75
106 Peter Prusa .30 .75
107 Rainer Patschinski .30 .75
108 Hartmut Nickel .30 .75
109 Dieter Dewitz .30 .75
110 Harald Felber .30 .75
111 Joachim Hurbanek .30 .75
112 Wolfgang Fischer .30 .75
113 Frank Braun .30 .75
114 Dieter Huschto .30 .75
115 Ruediger Hoack .30 .75
116 Dieter Simon .30 .75
117 Hartwig Schur .30 .75
118 Jochen Philipp .30 .75
119 Rolf Bielas .30 .75
120 Peter Slapke .30 .75

1974 Finnish Typotor

COMPLETE SET (120)
1 Matti Murto .40 1.00
2 Esa Peltonen .20 .50
3 Juha Rantasila .20 .50
4 Heikki Riihiranta .75 2.00
5 Juhani Tamminen .75 2.00
6 Jorma Virtanen .20 .50
7 Seppo Ahokainen .40 1.00
8 Jorma Kallio .20 .50
9 Ari Kankaanpera .20 .50
10 Lasse Oksanen .20 .50
11 Jorma Peltonen .40 1.00
12 Tapio Virhimo .20 .50
13 Ilpo Kokela .20 .50
14 Henry Leppa .20 .50
15 Seppo Suoraniemi .20 .50
16 Timo Sutinen .20 .50
17 Timo Turunen .20 .50
18 Jorma Valtonen .40 1.00
19 Mikko Erholm .20 .50
20 Esa Isaksson .20 .50
21 Juhani Jylha .20 .50
22 Tapani Koskimaki .20 .50
23 Hannu Siivonen .20 .50
24 Jorma Vehmanen .40 1.00
25 Jukka Alkula .20 .50
26 Hannu Haapalainen .20 .50
27 Martti Jarkko .20 .50
28 Antti Leppanen .20 .50
29 Pekka Marjamaki .20 .50
30 Raimo Suoniemi .20 .50
31 Lasse Kiili .20 .50
32 Timo Nummelin .20 .50
33 Matti Rautee .20 .50
34 Pekka Rautee .20 .50
35 Seppo Repo .20 .50
36 Jouko Oystila .20 .50
37 Kari Johansson .20 .50
38 Reijo Leppanen .20 .50
39 Seppo Lindstrom .20 .50
40 Hannu Niittoaho .20 .50
41 Pentti Vihanto .20 .50
42 Urpo Ylonen .20 .50
43 Antti Heikkila .20 .50
44 Reijo Heinonen .20 .50
45 Veli-Pekka Ketola .60 1.50
46 Raimo Kilpio .20 .50
47 Tapio Koskinen .20 .50
48 Pekka Rautakallio .75 2.00
49 Seppo Ahokainen .20 .50
50 Henry Leppa .20 .50
51 Antti Leppanen .20 .50
52 Pekka Marjamaki .20 .50
53 Matti Murto .20 .50
54 Esa Peltonen .20 .50
55 Heikki Riihiranta .40 1.00
56 Timo Sutinen .20 .50
57 Juhani Tamminen .75 2.00
58 Rolf Bielas .20 .50
59 Joachim Hurbanek .20 .50
60 Reinhard Karger .20 .50
61 Hartmut Nickel .20 .50
62 Rudiger Noack .20 .50
63 Helmut Novy .20 .50
64 Dietmar Peters .20 .50
65 Peter Prusa .20 .50
66 Peter Slapke .20 .50
67 Vakeri Kharlamov 4.00 10.00
68 Alexander Yakushev 1.50 4.00
69 Alexander Maltsev 1.50 4.00
70 Boris Mikhailov 1.50 4.00
71 Vladimir Petrov 1.50 4.00
72 Vladimir Shadrin .40 1.00
73 Vladislav Tretiak 6.00 15.00
74 Gennady Tsygankov .40 1.00
75 Valeri Vasiljev 1.25 3.00
76 Per-Erik Ingier .20 .50
77 Morten Johansen .20 .50
78 Hakan Lundenes .20 .50
79 N. Nilsen .20 .50
80 Morten Sethereng .20 .50
81 T. Skar .20 .50
82 J-E. Solberg .20 .50
83 K. Thorkildsen .20 .50
84 T. Troymark .20 .50
85 J. Borovicz .20 .50
86 L. Czachowski .20 .50
87 Michael Jaskierski .20 .50
88 Tadeusz Kacik .20 .50
89 Adam Kopczynski .20 .50
90 Tadeusz Obloj .20 .50
91 Jan Szeja .20 .50
92 Leszek Tokarz .20 .50
93 Walenty Zietara .20 .50
94 Christer Abrahamsson .50 1.50
95 Tommy Abrahamsson .75 2.00
96 Anders Hedberg 1.50 4.00
97 Stefan Karlsson .20 .50
98 Kjell-Rune Milton .20 .50
99 Ulf Nilsson 1.50 4.00
100 Bjorn Palmqvist .20 .50
101 Dan Soderstrom .20 .50
102 Mats Ahlberg .30 .75
103 Guy Dubois .40 1.00
104 C. Friedrich .20 .50
105 Charly Henzen .20 .50
106 Ueli Hofmann .20 .50
107 Micro Horisberger .20 .50
108 M. Lindenmann .20 .50
109 Alfio Molina .20 .50
110 Tony Neininger .20 .50
111 U. Willimann .20 .50
112 Richard Farda .20 .50
113 Ivan Hlinka .40 1.00
114 Jiri Holecek .40 1.00
115 Jiri Holik .40 1.00
116 Josef Horesovsky .20 .50
117 Jiri Kochta .20 .50
118 Oldrich Machac .20 .50
119 Vladimir Martinec .20 .50
120 Bohuslav Stastny .30 .75

1977-79 Sportscaster Finnish *

This set mirrors the North American version in many ways in that the series features personalities from many sports and that only the hockey players are listed. Card front and back text is entirely in Finnish. The checklist may not be complete. Additional information can be forwarded to us via hockeymag@beckett.com.

12-279 MM-Kilpailut .50 1.00
14-335 Suomen Maajoukkue .50 1.00
16-364 Antti Leppanen 2.50 5.00
Jorma Valtonen
17-397 Veli-Pekka Ketola 2.50 5.00
19-436 Pekka Marjamaki 1.50 3.00
19-447 MM-Kilpailut .50 1.00
20-469 Vaclav Nedomansky 2.50 5.00
21-492 Pelaajien Varusteet .50 1.00
23-532 Hat Trick 1.50 3.00
26-673 Valeri Kharlamov 2.50 5.00
Boris Mikhailov
Vladimir Petrov
26-692 Brad Park 4.00 8.00
31-736 NHL 1.50 3.00
32-747 Matti Hagman 2.50 5.00
33-775 Porin Assat .50 1.00
33-785 Jean Beliveau 6.00 12.00
36-845 Lalli Partinen 1.00 2.00
37-869 Phil Esposito 7.50 15.00
38-891 Bobby Clarke 4.00 8.00
38-895 Guy Lafleur 5.00 10.00
40-937 Matti Keinonen 1.00 2.00
40-945 The Stanley Cup 2.50 5.00
41-961 Matti Murto 1.00 2.00
42-1008 Viivoja Jaasa .50 1.00
43-1009 HIFK 1.50 3.00
43-1031 Tommy Abrahamsson 5.00 10.00
Christer Abrahamsson
45-1075 Ilves Tampere 1.50 3.00
45-1069 Jaroslav Jirik 1.00 2.00
45-1057 Lasse Oksanen 1.50 3.00
46-1084 Juhani Tamminen 1.50 3.00
47-1125 TPS .50 1.00
47-1113 Helmut Balderis 1.50 3.00
47-1106 Pekka Rautakallio 2.50 5.00
48-1145 Ken Dryden 10.00 20.00
48-1152 Timo Nummelin 1.50 3.00
49-1174 Gerry Cheevers 5.00 10.00
49-1197 Bryan Trottier 4.00 8.00
49-1175 Esa Peltonen 2.50 5.00
50-1197 Rogie Vachon 4.00 8.00
50-1199 Teppo Rastio 1.50 3.00
50-1178 Steve Shutt 2.50 5.00
50-1190 Laman .50 1.00
50-1188 Izvestia Tournament .50 1.00
51-1214 Jokerit 1.50 3.00
51-1224 Stan Mikita 6.00 12.00
51-1212 Rangaistukset .50 1.00
51-1218 Jiri Holik 1.50 3.00
Jaroslav Holik
51-1201 Markus Mattsson 1.00 2.00
52-1232 Garry Unger 2.50 5.00
52-1243 Ilpo Koskela 2.50 5.00
52-1235 Oulun Karpat .50 1.00
52-1230 Nurkkapeli .50 1.00
53-1265 Darryl Sittler 6.00 12.00
54-1273 Antero Lehtonen 2.50 5.00
54-1290 Bryan Trottier 5.00 10.00
Clark Gillies
Mike Bossy
56-1324 Denis Potvin 4.00 8.00
57-1358 Bobby Hull 10.00 20.00
57-1356 Guy Lafleur 5.00 10.00
57-1364 Kasvosuojukset 1.00 2.00
58-1392 Yvan Cournoyer 4.00 8.00
58-1381 Bobby Hull 10.00 20.00
66-1566 Montreal Forum 6.00 12.00
68-1623 Pete Stemkowski 2.50 5.00
69-1649 Bobby Clarke 4.00 8.00
70-1663 Borje Salming 5.00 10.00
70-1670 Gordie Howe 15.00 30.00
Mark Howe
Marty Howe
71-1686 Alexander Yakushev 2.50 5.00
71-1699 Soviet Union 1.00 2.00
72-1716 Lester Patrick 1.50 3.00
72-1705 Jukka Porvari 1.50 3.00
74-1760 Seppo Repo 1.50 3.00
74-1758 Ed Giacomin 4.00 8.00
75-1796 Risto Siltanen 2.50 5.00
75-1800 Kalevi Numminen 1.00 2.00
76-1821 Mikko Leinonen 1.00 2.00
76-1801 Pertti Koivulahti 1.00 2.00
77-1848 Jari Kurri 7.50 15.00
78-1849 Tapio Levo 1.50 3.00
78-1861 Vladislav Tretiak 7.50 15.00
79-1973 Koovee .50 1.00
79-1896 Rauman Luokko .50 1.00
80-1911 Ulf Nilsson 4.00 8.00
Anders Hedberg
81-1931 Tssekoslovakia .50 1.00
81-1922 NHL and Soviet Union 1.50 3.00
82-1949 Hannu Haapalainen 2.50 5.00
82-1955 Markku Hakulinen 1.00 2.00
Yrjo Hakulinen
83-1982 Seppo Lindstrom 1.50 3.00
83-1983 Jiri Holecek 1.50 3.00
83-1970 Reijo Leppanen 1.50 3.00
84-2015 Alexander Yakushev 2.50 5.00
84-2006 Canada 5.00 10.00
84-2016 Lasse Litma 1.00 2.00
85-2024 Dave Dryden 4.00 8.00
85-2035 Jacques Lemaire 6.00 12.00
85-2017 Seppo Suoraniemi 1.50 3.00
86-2064 Hannu Koskinen 2.50 5.00
86-2041 Reijo Ruotsalainen 2.50 5.00
87-2072 Jouni Rinne 1.50 3.00
88-2103 HIFK 1.50 3.00
89-2127 Wayne Gretzky 200.00 400.00
90-2160 NHL and WHA 1.50 3.00
90-2150 Markku Kimmalainen 1.00 2.00
90-2162 Scotty Bowman 12.50 25.00
90-2169 Timo Susi 1.50 3.00
90-2148 Antero Kivela 2.50 5.00
90-2139 Real Cloutier 2.50 5.00
90-2165 Ismo Villa 1.50 3.00
90-2152 Jarmo Makitalo 1.50 3.00
103-2455 Ivan Hlinka 1.50 3.00
105-2513 Soviet Union 1.00 2.00
107-2559 Jorma Valtonen 1.50 3.00
108-2573 Henry Leppa 1.50 3.00
108-2583 Suomen Jaahallit .50 1.00
02-27 Isekkoslovakia .50 1.00
02-39 Stanley Cup .50 1.00
03-71 Olympiakiekkoilu 1960 .50 1.00
04-83 Bobby Orr 20.00 50.00
05-105 Phil Esposito 10.00 20.00
Tony Esposito
05-115 Tappara 1976-77 .50 1.00
07-152 Soviet Union 1976 1.50 3.00
07-168 Gordie Howe 12.50 25.00
08-181 Bobby Hull 10.00 20.00
UK-327 Suomen Jaakiekkoilu .50 1.00

1978-79 Finnish SM-Liiga

This set features the top players from Finland's elite league. These odd-sized cards measure 2 X 2 3/8. The set is noteworthy for including the first known card of Hall of Famer Jari Kurri. It is believed the cards were issued in pack form, but that cannot be ascertained at this point.

COMPLETE SET (240) 50.00 125.00
1 Hannu Kamppuri .40 1.00
2 Pekka Rautakallio .75 2.00
3 Timo Nummelin .20 .50
4 Pertti Valkeapaa .20 .50
5 Risto Siltanen .40 1.00
6 Hannu Haapalainen .20 .50
7 Markku Kiimalainen .20 .50
8 Tapio Levo .40 1.00
9 Lasse Litma .20 .50
10 Reijo Ruotsalainen .75 2.00
11 Jukka Porvari .20 .50
12 Matti Rautiainen .20 .50
13 Veli-Pekka Ketola .75 2.00
14 Antero Lehtonen .20 .50
15 Martti Jarkko .20 .50
16 Juhani Tamminen .75 2.00
17 Pertti Koivulahti .20 .50
18 Kari Makkonen .20 .50
19 Antero Kivela .20 .50
20 Veli-Matti Ruisma .20 .50
21 Stig Wetzell .20 .50
22 Kyosti Majava .20 .50
23 Seppo Pakelo .20 .50
24 Reijo Laksola .20 .50
25 Heikki Riihiranta .20 .50
26 Raimo Hirvonen .20 .50
27 Jorma Immonen .20 .50
28 Terry Ball .20 .50
29 Pertti Lehtonen .20 .50
30 Jaakko Marttinen .20 .50
31 Esa Peltonen .40 1.00
32 Lauri Mononen .40 1.00
33 Tommi Salmelainen .20 .50
34 Hannu Kapanen .20 .50
35 Matti Forss .20 .50
36 Harri Linnonmaa .20 .50
37 Matti Murto .20 .50
38 Juhani Bostrom .20 .50
39 Matti Hagman .40 1.00
40 Ilkka Sinisalo .75 2.00
41 Tomi Taimio .20 .50
42 Ari Lahteenmaki .20 .50
43 Tapio Virhimo .20 .50
44 Jukka Airaksinen .20 .50
45 Hannu Helander .20 .50
46 Jorma Aro .20 .50
47 Jouko Urvikko .20 .50
48 Hannu Pulkkinen .20 .50
49 Olli Pennanen .20 .50
50 Ari Kankaanpera .20 .50
51 Risto Siltanen .40 1.00
52 Jari Jarvinen .20 .50
53 Sakari Ahlberg .20 .50
54 Keijo Kivela .20 .50
55 Lasse Oksanen .20 .50
56 Risto Kankaanpera .20 .50
57 Kari Jarvinen .20 .50
58 Pekka Orimus .20 .50
59 Jarmo Huhtala .20 .50
60 Hannu Oksanen .20 .50
61 Jari Viitala .20 .50
62 Veikko Suominen .20 .50
63 Antti Heikkila .20 .50
64 Seppo Hiitela .20 .50
65 Hannu Kamppuri .40 1.00
66 Patrik Wainio .20 .50
67 Timo Blomqvist .40 1.00
68 Ilmo Uotila .20 .50
69 Pertti Savolainen .20 .50
70 Jussi Lepisto .20 .50
71 Jorma Piisinen .20 .50
72 Robert Barnes .20 .50
73 Ari Makinen .20 .50
74 David Conte .40 1.00
75 Juha Jyrkkio .20 .50
76 Jari Kurri 20.00 40.00
77 Matti Heikkila .20 .50
78 Henry Leppa .20 .50
79 Pekka Kaski .20 .50
80 Jari Kapanen .20 .50
81 Ari Mikkola .20 .50
82 Vesa Rajaniemi .20 .50
83 Ari Blomqvist .20 .50
84 Erkki Korhonen .20 .50
85 Rainer Risku .20 .50
86 Henry Saleva .20 .50
87 Leo Seppanen .20 .50
88 Rauli Sohlman .20 .50
89 Juhani Ruohonen .20 .50
90 Tuomo Martin .20 .50
91 Reijo Mansikka .20 .50
92 Reino Pulkkinen .20 .50
93 Mauri Kultakuusi .20 .50
94 Kari Saarikko .20 .50
95 Kari Viitalahti .20 .50
96 Barry Salovaara .20 .50
97 Auvo Vaananen .20 .50
98 Pauli Pyykko .20 .50
99 Ari Jortikka .20 .50
100 Jukka-Pekka Jarvenpaa .20 .50
101 Seppo Sevon .20 .50
102 Pekka Koskela .20 .50
103 Arto Jokinen .20 .50
104 Timo Niinivirta .20 .50
105 Matti Rautiainen .20 .50
106 Pertti Jarvenpaa .20 .50
107 Reima Pullinen .20 .50
108 Jukka-Pekka Vuorinen .20 .50
109 Petteri Kanerva .20 .50
110 Kalevi Rantanen .20 .50
111 Jorma Virtanen .20 .50
112 Matti Kaario .20 .50
113 Frank Neal .20 .50
114 Eero Mantere .20 .50
115 Harri Nyman .20 .50
116 Olli Saarinen .20 .50
117 Jari Saarela .20 .50
118 Pasi Virta .20 .50
119 Dave Chalk .20 .50
120 Hannu Koskinen .20 .50
121 Harri Toivonen .20 .50
122 Jarmo Makitalo .20 .50
123 Kari Makitalo .20 .50
124 Olavi Niemenranta .20 .50
125 Pekka Laine .20 .50
126 Markku Hakulinen .20 .50
127 Pekka Nissinen .20 .50
128 Yrjo Hakulinen .20 .50
129 Timo Heino .20 .50
130 Hannu Savolainen .20 .50
131 Ari Hellgren .20 .50
132 Matti Saikkonen .20 .50
133 Ilpo Kukkola .20 .50
134 Pentti Karlsson .20 .50
135 Pekka Karjala .20 .50
136 Juha Tuohimaa .20 .50
137 Pekka Makinen .20 .50
138 Reijo Ruotsalainen .75 2.00
139 Seppo Tenhunen .20 .50
140 Hannu Jalonen .20 .50
141 Jari Virtanen .20 .50
142 Juha Huikuri .20 .50
143 Veikko Torkkeli .20 .50
144 Markku Kiimalainen .20 .50
145 Kalevi Hongisto .20 .50
146 Eero Vartiainen .20 .50
147 Jouko Kamarainen .20 .50
148 Kai Suikkanen .20 .50
149 Ilkka Alatalo .20 .50
150 Markku Perkkio .20 .50
151 Jorma Torkkeli .20 .50
152 Kari Jalonen .20 .50
153 Hannu Siivonen .20 .50
154 Kari Kaupinsalo .20 .50
155 Teppo Mattsson .20 .50
156 Esa Hakkarainen .20 .50
157 Jouni Peltonen .20 .50
158 Timo Peltonen .20 .50
159 Hannu Luojola .20 .50
160 Tapani Koskimaki .20 .50
161 Tuomo Jormakka .20 .50
162 Mika Rajala .20 .50
163 Pekka Santanen .20 .50
164 Jorma Vehmanen .20 .50
165 Olli Tuominen .20 .50
166 Hannu Kemppainen .20 .50
167 Ismo Villa .20 .50
168 Matti Tynkkynen .20 .50
169 Jouni Rinne .20 .50
170 Jari Rastio .20 .50
171 Harri Tuohimaa .20 .50
172 Jari Laiho .20 .50
173 Juhani Wallenius .20 .50
174 Pekka Strander .20 .50
175 Pertti Hasanen .20 .50
176 Petri Karjalainen .20 .50
177 Jorma Kallio .20 .50
178 Pekka Marjamaki .20 .50
179 Hannu Haapalainen .20 .50
180 Pertti Valkeapaa .20 .50
181 Lasse Litma .20 .50
182 Jukka Hirsimaki .20 .50
183 Oiva Oijennus .20 .50
184 Jukka Alkula .20 .50
185 Timo Susi .20 .50
186 Jukka Porvari .20 .50
187 Erkki Lehtonen .20 .50
188 Antero Lehtonen .20 .50
189 Juha Silvennoinen .20 .50
190 Pertti Koivulahti .20 .50
191 Keijo Mannisto .20 .50
192 Jorma Sevon .20 .50
193 Martti Jarkko .20 .50
194 Jari Lindgren .20 .50
195 Tapio Kallio .20 .50
196 Tero Kapynen .20 .50
197 Urpo Ylonen .20 .50
198 Jorma Valtonen .20 .50
199 Harri Kari .20 .50
200 Hannu Jortikka .20 .50
201 Timo Nummelin .20 .50
202 Seppo Suoraniemi .20 .50
203 Ilkka Mesikammen .20 .50
204 Pertti Ahokas .20 .50
205 Hannu Niitoaho .20 .50
206 Arto Kaunonen .20 .50
207 Pekka Rautee .20 .50
208 Juhani Tamminen .20 .50
209 Timo Viljanen .20 .50
210 Kari Kauppila .20 .50
211 Bengt Willenius .20 .50
212 Reijo Leppanen .20 .50
213 Rauli Tammelin .20 .50
214 Jukka Koskilahti .20 .50
215 Markku Haapaniemi .20 .50
216 Kari Horkko .20 .50
217 Kalevi Aho .20 .50
218 Hakan Hjerpe .20 .50
219 Antero Kivela .20 .50
220 Pertti Lehti .20 .50
221 Antti Heikkila .20 .50
222 Tapio Flinck .20 .50
223 Pekka Rautakallio .75 2.00
224 Jaakko Niemi .20 .50
225 Tapio Levo .40 1.00
226 Jyrki Levonen .20 .50
227 Harry Nikander .20 .50
228 Arto Javanainen .20 .50
229 Pekka Makela .20 .50
230 Tapio Koskinen .20 .50
231 Pekka Stenfors .20 .50
232 Ari Peltola .20 .50
233 Veli-Pekka Ketola .75 2.00
234 Erkki Vakiparta .20 .50

235 Rauli Levonen .20 .50
236 Martti Nenonen .20 .50
237 Jouni Makitalo .20 .50
238 Veli-Matti Ruisma .20 .50
239 Tauno Makela .20 .50
240 Kari Makkonen .20 .50

1980 Finnish Mallasjuoma

We have no pricing information for this series and present it only for checklisting purposes.

COMPLETE SET (220)
1 Stig Wetzell
2 Seppo Pakola
3 Frank Neal
4 Heikki Riihiranta
5 Esa Peltonen
6 Tommi Salmelainen
7 Matti Forss
8 Olli Ignatius
9 Raimo Hirvonen
10 Harri Linnonmaa
11 Jorma Immonen
12 Arto Sirvio
13 Matti Murto
14 Jari Kapanen
15 Ilkka Sinisalo
16 Arto Jokinen
17 Pertti Lehtonen
18 Timo Ukkola
19 Rainer Risku
20 Ari Lahteenmaki
21 Hannu Riihimaki
22 Jarmo Vuorinen
23 Jukka Airaksinen
24 Reijo Laksola
25 Jorma Aro
26 Jari Jarvinen
27 Jouko Urvikko
28 Ari Jokinen
29 Kari Heikkila
30 Auvo Vaananen
31 Risto Jalo
32 Lasse Oksanen
33 Lasse Tasala
34 Kari Jarvinen
35 Jarmo Lilius
36 Jyrki Seppa
37 Jorma Huhtala
38 Jari Viitala
39 Antti Heikkila
40 Matti Rautiainen
41 Pertti Jarvenpaa
42 Seppo Sevon
43 Henry Lehvonen
44 Tapio Virhimo
45 Rauli Sohlman
46 Martti Tuomisto
47 Pekka Rasanen
48 Aarre Kourula
49 Timo Saari
50 Arto Laine
51 Anssi Melametsa
52 Veli-Pekka Kinnunen
53 Matti Heikkila
54 Tony Arima
55 Ismo Lehkonen
56 Matti Virmanen
57 Sakari Petajaaho
58 Antti Lehto
59 Pasi Mustonen
60 Erkki Korhonen
61 Ilmo Uotila
62 Jussi Lepisto
63 Hannu Nykvist
64 Ari Blomqvist
65 Henry Leppa
66 Ari Makinen
67 Jari Vuorio
68 Olli Saarinen
69 Matti Kaario
70 Timo Blomqvist
71 Petteri Kanerva
72 Timo Harkonen
73 Keijo Koivisto
74 Eero Mantere
75 Harri Nyman
76 Harri Toivonen
77 Harri Laine
78 Olavi Niemenranta
79 Pekka Laine
80 Harri Haapaniemi
81 Juha Silvennoinen
82 Pekka Lumela
83 Yrjo Hakulinen
84 Tom Regnier
85 Richard Regnier
86 Jukka Hoitari
87 Timo Heino
88 Hannu Koskinen
89 Ari Hellgren
90 Arto Ruotanen
91 Hannu Jalonen
92 Kari Suoraniemi
93 Hannu Hiltunen
94 Juha Tuohimaa
95 Pentti Perhomaa
96 Reijo Ruotsalainen
97 Seppo Tenhunen
98 Kari Jalonen
99 Markku Kiimalainen
100 Juha Huikari
101 Pekka Tuomisto
102 Jouni Koutuaniemi
103 Veikko Torkkeli
104 Jouko Kamarainen
105 Kai Suikkanen
106 Jorma Torkkeli
107 Mikko Leinonen
108 Ari Timosaari
109 Jarmo Taurlainen
110 Pekka Arbelius
111 Teppo Mattsson
112 Esa Hakkarainen
113 Jouni Peltonen
114 Jarmo Kuusisto
115 Timo Peltonen
116 Ari-Pekka Strander
117 Jorma Vehmanen
118 Pasi Tuohimaa
119 Olli Tuominen
120 Hannu Kemppainen
121 Ismo Villa
122 Esa Wallin
123 Matti Tynkkynen
124 Jari Rastio
125 Kari Kaupinsalo
126 Lasse Lindberg
127 Olli-Pekka Rajala
128 Harri Tuohimaa
129 Hannu Vierimaa
130 Jari Laiho
131 Juhani Wallenius
132 Jarmo Kaistakari
133 Jukka Peitsoma
134 Tuomo Martin
135 Keijo Taskula
136 Martti Immonen
137 Ilkka Kaarna
138 Pertti Ahokas
139 Ari Lehikoinen
140 Jyrki Paakkarinen
141 Jouko Kukko
142 Harri Poyhia
143 Pentti Matikainen
144 Juha Sokkanen
145 Antero Vaatamoinen
146 Pertti Heikkeri
147 Esko Heikkeri
148 Heikki Malkia
149 Tuomo Laukkanen
150 Kari Weckstrom
151 Seppo Urpalainen
152 Kari Saarikko
153 Tuomo Jormakka
154 Juha Henttonen
155 Lasse Schultz
156 Mikko Viitanen
157 Hannu Helander
158 Pertti Valkeapaa
159 Lasse Litma
160 Timo Jutila
161 Oiva Oijennus
162 Timo Susi
163 Jukka Porvari
164 Erkki Lehtonen
165 Esa Valioja
166 Pertti Koivulahti
167 Juha Nurmi
168 Hannu Kamppuri
169 Petri Karjalainen
170 Timo Pentila
171 Jari Lindgren
172 Seppo Virta
173 Jukka Hirsimaki
174 Petri Niukkanen
175 Seppo Ahokainen
176 Antero Lehtonen
177 Hannu Jortikka
178 Timo Nummelin
179 Seppo Suoraniemi
180 Pasi Virta
181 Kari Vaihinen
182 Henry Saleva
183 Jari Hytti
184 Kari Kauppila
185 Reijo Leppanen
186 Rauli Tammelin
187 Markku Haapaniemi
188 Kari Horkko
189 Martti Jarkko
190 Juhani Tamminen
191 Kalevi Aho
192 Reima Pullinen
193 Hannu Hjerppe
194 Rauno Sjoroos
195 Hannu Niitoaho
196 Jari Paavola
197 Petteri Lehto
198 Jim Bedard
199 Antero Kivela
200 Antti Heikkila
201 Tapio Flinck
202 Arto Javanainen
203 Jukka Virtanen
204 Risto Tuomi
205 Tapio Koskinen
206 Juha Jyrkkio
207 Ari Peltola
208 Tapio Levo
209 Veli-Pekka Ketola
210 Erkki Vakiparta
211 Simo Ketola
212 Rauli Levonen
213 Jari Nystrom
214 Matti Ruisma
215 Tauno Makela
216 Kari Makkonen
217 Harry Nikander
218 Pentti Rautakallio
219 Martti Nenonen
220 Kari Takko

1982 Finnish Skopbank

Little is known about this sticker set beyond the checklist and values, provided by Finnish collector Janne Harvula. The cards are unnumbered and are checklisted below in alphabetical order.

COMPLETE SET (8) 24.00 60.00
1 Pekka Arbelius 2.00 5.00
2 Ari Hellgren 2.00 5.00
3 Raimo Hirvonen 2.00 5.00
4 Hannu Kamppuri 3.00 8.00
5 Markku Kiimalainen 2.00 5.00
6 Pertti Koivulahti 2.00 5.00
7 Hannu Koskinen 2.00 5.00
8 Mikko Leinonen 2.00 5.00
9 Reijo Leppanen 2.00 5.00
10 Tapio Levo 2.00 5.00
11 Timo Nummelin 2.00 5.00
12 Jukka Porvari 2.00 5.00
13 Reijo Ruotsalainen 3.00 8.00
14 Seppo Suoraniemi 2.00 5.00
15 Timo Susi 2.00 5.00
16 Juhani Tamminen 3.00 8.00

1989 Finnish Pelimiehen

Little is known about this six-sticker set beyond the accuracy of the checklist, which was provided by collector Ray Bayless. Any additional information can be forwarded to hockeymag@beckett.com

COMPLETE SET (6) 12.00 30.00
1 Kari Eloranta 1.25 3.00
2 Jari Kurri 6.00 15.00
3 Reijo Ruotsalainen 1.25 3.00
4 Christian Ruuttu 1.25 3.00
5 Kari Takko 2.00 5.00
6 Esa Tikkanen 3.00 8.00

1990-91 Finnish Jyvas-Hyva Stickers

Size about 1 2/3 X 4 1/6. These stickers were inserted inside chocolate bar wrappers (one sticker per bar).

COMPLETE SET (12) 10.00 25.00
NNO Saipa Lappeenranta .75 2.00
NNO TPS Turku .75 2.00
NNO Jokerit .75 2.00
NNO Assat Pori .75 2.00
NNO Tappara Tampere .75 2.00
NNO JypHT Jyvaskyla .75 2.00
NNO Lukko Rauma 1.25 3.00
NNO Hockey Reipas Lahti .75 2.00
NNO Kalpa Kuopio .75 2.00
NNO Ilves Tampere .75 2.00
NNO HPK Hameenlinna .75 2.00
NNO HIFK .75 2.00

1991 Finnish Semic World Championship Stickers

These hockey stickers, which measure approximately 2 1/8" by 2 7/8", were sold five to a packet. Also an album was available to display all 250 stickers. The fronts display color posed player shots framed by a red inner border studded with yellow miniature stars and a white outer border. The team flag, the player's name, and the sticker number appear in the white border below the picture. The backs were different based on distribution; blank backs were sold in Czechoslovakia; Marabou Chocolate ads were on the backs of cards sold in Finland and Milky Way ads were on the back of cards sold in Sweden. The stickers are grouped according to country. Teemu Selanne and Nicklas Lidstrom each appears in his Rookie Card year.

COMPLETE SET (250) 50.00 100.00
1 Finnish Emblem .02 .10
2 Markus Ketterer .20 .50
3 Sakari Lindfors .20 .50
4 Jukka Tammi .20 .50
5 Jyrki Lumme .08 .25
6 Hannu Virta .08 .25
7 Simo Saarinen .08 .25
8 Jukka Marttila .08 .25
9 Ville Siren .08 .25
10 Pasi Huura .08 .25
11 Hannu Henriksson .08 .25
12 Arto Ruotanen .08 .25
13 Ari Haanpaa .08 .25
14 Pauli Jarvinen .08 .25
15 Teppo Kivela .08 .25
16 Risto Kurkinen .08 .25
17 Mika Nieminen .08 .25
18 Jari Kurri .75 2.00
19 Esa Keskinen .08 .25
20 Raimo Summanen .08 .25
21 Teemu Selanne 4.00 10.00
22 Jari Torkki .08 .25
23 Hannu Jarvenpaa .08 .25
24 Raimo Helminen .08 .25
25 Timo Peltomaa .08 .25
26 Swedish Emblem .02 .10
27 Peter Lindmark .20 .50
28 Rolf Ridderwall .20 .50
29 Tommy Soderstrom .20 .50
30 Thomas Eriksson .08 .25
31 Nicklas Lidstrom 4.00 10.00
32 Tomas Jonsson .08 .25
33 Tommy Samuelsson .08 .25
34 Fredrik Stillman .08 .25
35 Peter Andersson .08 .25
36 Peter Andersson .08 .25
37 Kenneth Kennholt .08 .25
38 Hakan Loob .40 1.00
39 Thomas Rundqvist .08 .25
40 Hakan Ahlund .08 .25
41 Jan Viktorsson .08 .25
42 Charles Berglund .08 .25
43 Mikael Johansson .08 .25
44 Robert Burakovsky .08 .25
45 Bengt-Ake Gustafsson .08 .25
46 Patrik Carnback .08 .25
47 Patrik Erickson .08 .25
48 Anders Carlsson .08 .25
49 Mats Naslund .75 2.00
50 Kent Nilsson .75 2.00
51 Canadian Emblem .40 1.00
52 Patrick Roy 10.00 25.00
53 Ed Belfour 2.00 5.00
54 Daniel Berthiaume .40 1.00
55 Ray Bourque 4.00 10.00
56 Scott Stevens .40 1.00
57 Al MacInnis .75 2.00
58 Paul Coffey .75 2.00
59 Paul Cavallini .40 1.00
60 Zarley Zalapski .40 1.00
61 Steve Duchesne .40 1.00
62 Dave Ellett .40 1.00
63 Mark Messier 4.00 10.00
64 Wayne Gretzky 12.00 30.00
65 Steve Yzerman 8.00 20.00
66 Pierre Turgeon .40 1.00
67 Bernie Nicholls .40 1.00
68 Cam Neely 2.00 5.00
69 Joe Nieuwendyk .40 1.00
70 Luc Robitaille 2.00 5.00
71 Kevin Dineen .40 1.00
72 John Cullen .40 1.00
73 Steve Larmer .40 1.00
74 Mark Recchi .75 2.00
75 Joe Sakic 4.00 10.00
76 Soviet Emblem .02 .10
77 Arturs Irbe .40 1.00
78 Alexei Marin .20 .50
79 Mikhail Shtalenkov .20 .50
80 Vladimir Malakhov .08 .25
81 Vladimir Konstantinov 1.25 3.00
82 Igor Kravchuk .08 .25
83 Ilya Byakin .08 .25
84 Dimitri Mironov .08 .25
85 Vladimir Turikov .08 .25
86 Vjatjeslav Uvajev .08 .25
87 Vladimir Fedosov .08 .25
88 Valeri Kamensky .08 .25
89 Pavel Bure 2.00 5.00
90 Vyacheslav Butsayev .08 .25
91 Igor Maslennikov .08 .25
92 Evgeny Davydov .08 .25
93 Andrei Kovalev .08 .25
94 Alexander Semak .08 .25
95 Alexei Zhamnov .08 .25
96 Sergei Nemchinov .08 .25
97 Viktor Gordijuk .08 .25
98 Vyacheslav Kozlov .08 .25
99 Andrei Khomotov .08 .25
100 Vyacheslav Bykov .08 .25
101 Czech Emblem .02 .10
102 Petr Briza .20 .50
103 Dominik Hasek 4.00 10.00
104 Eduard Hartmann .20 .50
105 Bedrich Scerban .08 .25
106 Jiri Slegr .08 .25
107 Josef Reznicek .08 .25
108 Petr Pavlas .08 .25
109 Peter Slanina .08 .25
110 Martin Maskarinec .08 .25
111 Antonin Stavjana .08 .25
112 Stanislav Medrik .08 .25
113 Dusan Pasek .08 .25
114 Jiri Lala .08 .25
115 Darius Rusnak .08 .25
116 Oto Hascak .08 .25
117 Radek Toupal .08 .25
118 Pavel Pycha .08 .25
119 Lubomir Kolnik .08 .25
120 Libor Dolana .08 .25
121 Ladislav Lubina .08 .25
122 Tomas Jelinek .08 .25
123 Petr Vlk .08 .25
124 Vladimir Petrovka .08 .25
125 Richard Zemlicka .08 .25
126 U.S.A. Emblem .02 .10
127 John Vanbiesbrouck .75 2.00
128 Mike Richter .75 2.00
129 Chris Terreri .40 1.00
130 Chris Chelios 2.00 5.00
131 Brian Leetch 1.25 3.00
132 Gary Suter .40 1.00
133 Phil Housley .40 1.00
134 Mark Howe .40 1.00
135 Al Iafrate .40 1.00
136 Kevin Hatcher .40 1.00
137 Mathieu Schneider .40 1.00
138 Pat LaFontaine .75 2.00
139 Darren Turcotte .40 1.00
140 Neal Broten .75 2.00
141 Mike Modano 2.00 5.00
142 Dave Christian .40 1.00
143 Craig Janney .40 1.00
144 Brett Hull 2.00 5.00
145 Kevin Stevens .40 1.00
146 Joe Mullen .40 1.00
147 Tony Granato .40 1.00
148 Ed Olczyk .40 1.00
149 Jeremy Roenick 2.00 5.00
150 Jimmy Carson .40 1.00
151 West German Emblem .02 .10
152 Helmut De Raaf .20 .50
153 Josef Heiss .20 .50
154 Karl Friesen .20 .50
155 Uli Hiemer .08 .25
156 Harold Kreis .08 .25
157 Udo Kiessling .08 .25
158 Michael Schmidt .08 .25
159 Michael Heidt .08 .25
160 Andreas Pokorny .08 .25
161 Bernd Wagner .08 .25
162 Uwe Krupp .08 .25
163 Gerd Truntschka .08 .25
164 Bernd Truntschka .08 .25
165 Thomas Brandl .08 .25
166 Peter Draisaitl .08 .25
167 Andreas Brockmann .08 .25
168 Ulrich Liebsch .08 .25
169 Ralf Hantschke .08 .25
170 Thomas Schinko .08 .25
171 Anton Krinner .08 .25
172 Thomas Werner .08 .25
173 Dieter Hegen .08 .25
174 Helmut Steiger .08 .25
175 Georg Franz .08 .25
176 Swiss Emblem .02 .10
177 Renato Tosio .20 .50
178 Reto Pavoni .20 .50
179 Dino Stecher .20 .50
180 Sven Leuenberger .08 .25
181 Rick Tschumi .08 .25
182 Patrice Brasey .08 .25
183 Didier Massy .08 .25
184 Sandro Bertaggia .08 .25
185 Samuel Balmer .08 .25
186 Martin Rauch .08 .25
187 Marc Leuenberger .08 .25
188 Jorg Eberle .08 .25
189 Fredy Luthi .08 .25
190 Andy Ton .08 .25
191 Raymond Walder .08 .25
192 Manuele Celio .08 .25
193 Roman Wager .08 .25
194 Felix Hollenstein .08 .25
195 Andre Rotheli .08 .25
196 Christian Weber .08 .25
197 Peter Jaks .08 .25
198 Gil Montandon .08 .25
199 Oliver Hoffmann. .08 .25
200 Thomas Vrabec .08 .25
201 Teppo Numminen .08 .25
202 Jyrki Lumme .08 .25
203 Esa Tikkanen .08 .25
204 Petri Skriko .08 .25
205 Christian Ruutu .08 .25
206 Ilkka Sinisalo .08 .25
207 Calle Johansson .08 .25
208 Tomas Sandstrom .08 .25
209 Thomas Steen .08 .25
210 Per-Erik Eklund .08 .25
211 Mats Sundin 1.25 3.00
212 Johan Garpenlov .08 .25
213 Slava Fetisov .08 .25
214 Alexei Kasatonov .08 .25
215 Mikhail Tatarinov .08 .25
216 Sergei Makarov .20 .50
217 Igor Larionov .40 1.00
218 Alexander Mogilny .40 1.00
219 Sergei Fedorov 1.25 3.00
220 Petr Klima .08 .25
221 David Volek .08 .25
222 Michal Pivonka .08 .25
223 Robert Reichel .08 .25
224 Robert Holik .08 .25
225 Jaromir Jagr 4.00 10.00
226 Urpo Ylonen .08 .25
227 Ilpo Koskela .08 .25
228 Pekka Rautakallio .20 .50
229 Lasse Oksanen .08 .25
230 Veli-Pekka Ketola .20 .50
231 Leif Holmqvist .20 .50
232 Lennart Svedberg .08 .25
233 Sven Tumba Johansson .08 .25
234 Ulf Sterner .08 .25
235 Anders Hedberg .20 .50
236 Ken Dryden 2.00 5.00
237 Bobby Orr 10.00 25.00
238 Gordie Howe 4.00 10.00
239 Bobby Hull 3.00 8.00
240 Phil Esposito 2.00 5.00
241 Vladislav Tretiak 4.00 10.00
242 Alexander Ragulin .08 .25
243 Anatoli Firsov .08 .25
244 Valeri Kharlamov 2.00 5.00
245 Alexander Maltsev .75 2.00
246 Jiri Holecek .08 .25
247 Jan Suchy .08 .25
248 Jozef Golonka .08 .25
249 Vaclav Nedomansky .08 .25
250 Ivan Hlinka .08 .25

1991-92 Finnish Jyvas-Hyva Stickers

This set features the players of Finland's SM-Liiga. The stickers were inserted as premiums in candy products. They measured 1 2/3 X 4 1/6. The set is noteworthy for the inclusion of a sticker of Teemu Selanne in his RC year. A poster on which to place the stickers was also issued for this set.

COMPLETE SET (84) 20.00 50.00
1 Sakari Lindfors .40 1.00
2 Jukka Seppo .08 .25
3 Pekka Tuomisto .05 .15
4 Harri Tuohimaa .05 .15
5 Pertti Lehtonen .05 .15
6 Simo Saarinen .05 .15
7 Timo Lehkonen .05 .15
8 Teppo Kivela .05 .15
9 Markku Piikkila .05 .15
10 Pekka Peltola .05 .15
11 Hannu Henriksson .05 .15
12 Jari Haapamaki .05 .15
13 Jukka Tammi .40 1.00
14 Risto Jalo .05 .15
15 Timo Peltomaa .05 .15
16 Raimo Summanen .40 1.00
17 Ville Siren .20 .50
18 Risto Siltanen .40 1.00
19 Markus Ketterer .30 .75
20 Pekka Jarvela .05 .15
21 Teemu Selanne 15.00 40.00
22 Keijo Sailynoja .05 .15
23 Mika Stromberg .05 .15
24 Waltteri Immonen .05 .15
25 Ari-Pekka Siekkinen .08 .25
26 Jari Lindroos .05 .15
27 Ari Haanpaa .05 .15
28 Jiri Dolezal .08 .25
29 Harri Laurila .05 .15
30 Leo Gudas .08 .25
31 Mika Rautio .05 .15
32 Pekka Tirkkonen .05 .15
33 Jarmo Kekalainen .20 .50
34 Juha Jokiharju .05 .15
35 Juha Tuohimaa .05 .15
36 Erik Hamalainen .08 .25
37 Juha Jaaskelainen .05 .15
38 Rostislav Vlach .05 .15
39 Jouni Mustonen .05 .15
40 Marku Kyllonen .05 .15
41 Antonin Stavjana .08 .25
42 Ossi Piitulainen .20 .50
43 Petr Briza .40 1.00
44 Mika Nieminen .20 .50
45 Jari Torkki .05 .15
46 Tommi Pullola .05 .15
47 Jarmo Kuusisto .05 .15
48 Pasi Huura .05 .15
49 Jaromir Sindel .20 .50
50 Marko Jantunen .08 .25
51 Erkki Laine .05 .15
52 Erkki Makela .05 .15
53 Niko Marttila .05 .15
54 Erik Kakko .05 .15
55 Jari Halme .05 .15
56 Kari Heikkinen .05 .15
57 Jiri Kucera .08 .25
58 Vesa Viitakoski .20 .50
59 Jukka Marttila .05 .15
60 Pekka Laksola .05 .15
61 Jouni Rokama .08 .25
62 Esa Keskinen .20 .50
63 Jukka Vilander .05 .15
64 Jari Pulliainen .05 .15
65 Jouko Narvanmaa .05 .15
66 Hannu Virta .08 .25
67 Kari Takko .40 1.00
68 Janne Virtanen .05 .15
69 Arto Javanainen .05 .15
70 Oleg Znarok .08 .25
71 Tapio Levo .05 .15
72 Harry Nikander .05 .15
NNO JyPHT Jyvaskyla .05 .15
NNO Assat Pori .05 .15
NNO Tappara Tampere .05 .15
NNO HIFK Helsinki .05 .15
NNO Ilves Tampere .05 .15
NNO KalPa Kupio .05 .15
NNO Hockey Reipat Lahti .05 .15
NNO Jokerit Helsinki .08 .25
NNO HPK Hameenlinna .05 .15
NNO Rauman Luoko .05 .15
NNO Turun Palloseura .05 .15
NNO Joensuun Kiekkopojat .05 .15

1992-93 Finnish Jyvas-Hyva Stickers

This sticker set features the players of the SM-Liiga. The odd-sized stickers (about 2 x 3 1/3) were inserted as premiums with candy products and came in strips of three. The set is noteworthy for early appearances of Saku Koivu and Sami Kapanen.

COMPLETE SET (204) 19.56 48.89
1 Harri Rindell .05 .15
2 Sakari Lindfors .40 1.00
3 Simo Saarinen .05 .15
4 Pertti Lehtonen .05 .15
5 Kari Laitinen .05 .15
6 Teppo Kivela .05 .15
7 Darren Boyko .20 .50
8 Kai Rautio .08 .25
9 Drahomir Kadlec .08 .25
10 Mika Kortelainen .05 .15
11 Jukka Seppo .08 .25
12 Pekka Tuomisto .05 .15
13 Pasi Sormunen .05 .15
14 Kai Tervonen .05 .15
15 Ville Peltonen .40 1.00
16 Valeri Krykov .05 .15
17 Iiro Jarvi .20 .50
18 Hannu Jortikka .05 .15
19 Timo Lehkonen .05 .15
20 Timo Nykopp .05 .15
21 Janne Laukkanen .40 1.00
22 Marko Palo .08 .25
23 Juha Ylonen 1.25 3.00
24 Jarkko Varvio .20 .50
25 Marko Allen .05 .15
26 Marko Tuulola .05 .15
27 Jarkko Nikander .08 .25
28 Radek Toupal .05 .15
29 Tommi Varjonen .05 .15
30 Niko Marttila .05 .15
31 Jari Haapamaki .05 .15
32 Pasi Kivela .05 .15
33 Tony Virta .05 .15
34 Markku Piikkila .05 .15
35 Anatoli Bogdanov .05 .15
36 Jukka Tammi .40 1.00
37 Jani Nikko .08 .25
38 Jukka Ollila .05 .15
39 Tommi Kiiski .05 .15
40 Mikko Luovi .08 .25
41 Juha Jarvenpaa .05 .15
42 Juha Lampinen .05 .15
43 Janne Siva .05 .15
44 Timo Peltomaa .08 .25
45 Mika Arvaja .05 .15
46 Esa Tommila .05 .15
47 Kristian Taubert .05 .15
48 Jarkko Glad .05 .15
49 Hannu Mattila .05 .15
50 Pasi Maattanen .05 .15
51 Petri Sullamaa .05 .15
52 Boris Majorov .05 .15
53 Markus Ketterer .40 1.00
54 Waltteri Immonen .05 .15
55 Mika Stromberg .08 .25
56 Keijo Sailynoja .05 .15
57 Otakar Janecky .08 .25
58 Jiri Sejba .08 .25
59 Kari Martikainen .05 .15
60 Erik Hamalainen .08 .25
61 Timo Norppa .05 .15
62 Pekka Jarvela .05 .15
63 Juha Salo .05 .15
64 Heikki Riihijarvi .05 .15
65 Ari Salo .05 .15
66 Hannu Jarvenpaa .20 .50
67 Jali Wahlsten .05 .15
68 Juha Jokiharju .05 .15
69 Hannu Aravirta .05 .15
70 Ari-Pekka Siekkinen .08 .25
71 Jarmo Jokilahti .05 .15
72 Harri Laurila .05 .15
73 Juha Riihijarvi .20 .50
74 Jari Lindroos .08 .25
75 Marko Virtanen .05 .15
76 Jari Munck .05 .15
77 Markku Heikkinen .05 .15
78 Lasse Nieminen .05 .15
79 Tero Lehikoinen .05 .15
80 Ari Haanpaa .05 .15
81 Jarmo Rantanen .05 .15
82 Veli-Pekka Hard .05 .15
83 Mika Paananen .08 .25
84 Joni Lius .08 .25
85 Risto Kurkinen .05 .15
86 Juha Junno .05 .15
87 Pasi Kuivalainen .20 .50
88 Jari Jarvinen .05 .15
89 Vesa Salo .05 .15
90 Vesa Karjalainen .05 .15
91 Darius Rusnak .05 .15
92 Arto Sirvio .05 .15
93 Vesa Ruotsalainen .05 .15
94 Juha Tuohimaa .05 .15
95 Jari Hamalainen .05 .15
96 Pekka Tirkkonen .05 .15
97 Jari Laukkanen .05 .15
98 Antti Tuomenoksa .05 .15
99 Janne Leppanen .05 .15
100 Marko Jantunen .08 .25
101 Dusan Pasek .40 1.00
102 Sami Kapanen 1.25 3.00
103 Martti Merra .05 .15
104 Sami Aikaa .05 .15
105 Teemu Sillanpaa .05 .15
106 Sami Nuutinen .05 .15
107 Jere Lehtinen 3.00 8.00
108 Jan Langbacka .05 .15
109 Tero Lehtera .08 .25
110 Robert Salo .05 .15
111 Jimi Helin .05 .15
112 Sami Kokko .05 .15
113 Riku Kuusisto .05 .15
114 Markku Tiinus .05 .15
115 Pasi Heinisto .05 .15
116 Petri Pulkkinen .05 .15
117 Tom Laaksonen .05 .15
118 Jarmo Muukkonen .05 .15
119 Petro Koivunen .08 .25
120 Matti Keinonen .05 .15
121 Petr Briza .40 1.00
122 Timo Kulonen .05 .15
123 Allan Measures .05 .15
124 Harri Suvanto .05 .15
125 Timo Saarikoski .05 .15
126 Mika Alatalo .75 2.00
127 Kari-Pekka Friman .05 .15
128 Jarmo Kuusisto .05 .15
129 Mika Valila .05 .15
130 Jari Torkki .05 .15
131 Pekka Peltola .05 .15
132 Pasi Huura .05 .15
133 Matti Forss .05 .15
134 Kalle Sahlstedt .08 .25
135 Tommi Pullola .05 .15
136 Tero Arkiomaa .05 .15
137 Esko Nokelainen .05 .15
138 Petri Engman .05 .15
139 Timo Kahelin .05 .15
140 Pasi Ruponen .05 .15
141 Petteri Sihvonen .05 .15
142 Toni Sihvonen .05 .15
143 Sami Wikstrom .05 .15
144 Erik Kakko .05 .15
145 Jari Parviainen .05 .15
146 Jonni Vauhkonen .08 .25
147 Jari Kauppila .05 .15
148 Erkki Makela .05 .15
149 Jarkko Hamalainen .05 .15
150 Petri Koski .05 .15
151 Sami Lekkerimaki .05 .15
152 Toni Koivunen .05 .15
153 Jani Uski .05 .15
154 Pertti Hasanen .05 .15
155 Jaromir Sindel .20 .50
156 Tommi Haapsaari .05 .15
157 Jukka Marttila .05 .15
158 Jarmo Kekalainen .20 .50
159 Tommi Pohja .05 .15
160 Pauli Jarvinen .05 .15
161 Timo Jutila .20 .50
162 Janne Gronvall .08 .25
163 Jussi-Pekka Jarvinen .05 .15
164 Kari Heikkinen .05 .15
165 Marko Ek .05 .15
166 Veli-Pekka Kautonen .05 .15
167 Pekka Laksola .05 .15
168 Pasi Forsberg .05 .15
169 Marko Lapinkoski .05 .15
170 Mikko Peltola .05 .15
171 Vladimir Jursinov .05 .15
172 Jouni Rokama .08 .25
173 Mikko Haapakoski .05 .15
174 Kari Harila .05 .15
175 Kari Kanervo .05 .15
176 Esa Keskinen .20 .50
177 Saku Koivu 6.00 15.00
178 Jouko Narvanmaa .05 .15
179 Alexander Smirnov .05 .15
180 Reijo Mikkolainen .05 .15
181 Mikko Makela .30 .75
182 Raimo Summanen .20 .50
183 Hannu Virta .08 .25
184 Jukka Virtanen .05 .15
185 German Titov .20 .50
186 Jukka Vilander .05 .15
187 Ari Vuori .05 .15
188 Vasili Tikhonov .20 .50
189 Kari Takko .40 1.00
190 Sami Saarinen .05 .15
191 Marko Sten .05 .15
192 Arto Javanainen .05 .15
193 Janne Virtanen .05 .15
194 Arto Heiskanen .05 .15
195 Jouni Vento .05 .15
196 Olli Kaski .05 .15
197 Vyacheslav Fandul .05 .15
198 Jokke Hainanen .05 .15
199 Petri Varis .20 .50
200 Harry Nikander .05 .15
201 Jarno Miikkulainen .05 .15
202 Jari Korpisalo .08 .25
203 Rauli Raitanen .05 .15
204 Jari Levonen .05 .15

1992 Finnish Semic

COMPLETE SET (288) 50.00 100.00
1 Finland .02 .10
2 Pentti Matikainen .20 .50
3 Markus Ketterer .20 .50
4 Sakari Lindfors .20 .50
5 Teppo Numminen .08 .25
6 Jyrki Lumme .08 .25

7 Janne Laukkanen .08 .25
8 Ville Siren .08 .25
9 Mikko Haapakoski .08 .25
10 Simo Saarinen .08 .25
11 Teemu Selanne 2.00 5.00
12 Petri Skriko .08 .25
13 Iiro Jarvi .08 .25
14 Esa Tikkanen .08 .25
15 Christian Ruuttu .08 .25
16 Raimo Summanen .08 .25
17 Jari Kurri .75 2.00
18 Timo Peltomaa .08 .25
19 Mika Nieminen .08 .25
20 Mikko Makela .08 .25
21 Janne Ojanen .08 .25
22 Jarmo Kekalainen .08 .25
23 Keijo Sailynoja .08 .25
24 Esa Keskinen .08 .25
25 Norge .02 .10
26 Bengt Ohlsson .20 .50
27 Jim Marthinsen .20 .50
28 Steve Allman .20 .50
29 Petter Salsten .08 .25
30 Age Ellingsen .08 .25
31 Kim Sogaard .08 .25
32 Jan Roar Fagerli .08 .25
33 Tommy Jakobsen .08 .25
34 Cato Tom Andersen .08 .25
35 Arne Billkvam .08 .25
36 Oystein Olsen .08 .25
37 Geir Hoff .08 .25
38 Erik Kristiansen .08 .25
39 Orjan Lovdal .08 .25
40 Espen Knutsen .75 2.00
41 Ole Eskild Dahlstrom .08 .25
42 Rune Gulliksen .08 .25
43 Marius Rath .08 .25
44 Petter Thoresen .08 .25
45 Tom Johansen .08 .25
46 Stephen Foyn .08 .25
47 Stig Johansen .08 .25
48 Per Christian Knold .08 .25
49 Sverige .02 .10
50 Conny Evensson .02 .10
51 Tommy Soderstrom .20 .50
52 Fredrik Andersson .20 .50
53 Thomas Eriksson .08 .25
54 Peter Andersson .08 .25
55 Peter Andersson .08 .25
56 Nicklas Lidstrom 2.00 5.00
57 Calle Johansson .08 .25
58 Ulf Samuelsson .08 .25
59 Fredrik Olausson .08 .25
60 Borje Salming .40 1.00
61 Hakan Loob .08 .25
62 Thomas Rundqvist .08 .25
63 Mats Naslund .08 .25
64 Mikael Johansson .08 .25
65 Bengt-Ake Gustavsson .08 .25
66 Peter Ottosson .08 .25
67 Markus Naslund .08 .25
68 Daniel Rydmark .08 .25
69 Tomas Sandstrom .08 .25
70 Thomas Steen .08 .25
71 Per-Erik Eklund .08 .25
72 Mats Sundin .75 2.00
73 Kanada .20 .50
74 Dave King .02 .10
75 Bill Ranford .75 2.00
76 Ed Belfour 1.25 3.00
77 Al MacInnis .75 2.00
78 Scott Stevens .40 1.00
79 Steve Smith .40 1.00
80 Ray Bourque 3.00 8.00
81 Paul Coffey .75 2.00
82 Larry Murphy .40 1.00
83 Mark Tinordi .40 1.00
84 Wayne Gretzky 10.00 25.00
85 Mark Messier 3.00 8.00
86 Mario Lemieux 8.00 20.00
87 Steve Yzerman 6.00 15.00
88 Eric Lindros 1.25 3.00
89 Luc Robitaille 1.25 3.00
90 Theoren Fleury .75 2.00
91 Steve Larmer .40 1.00
92 Brent Sutter .40 1.00
93 Shayne Corson .40 1.00
94 Dale Hawerchuk .75 2.00
95 Russ Courtnall .40 1.00
96 Rick Tocchet .40 1.00
97 Soviet .02 .10
98 Victor Tikhonov .02 .10
99 Andrei Trefilov .20 .50
100 Mikhail Shtalenkov .20 .50
101 Alexei Kasatonov .08 .25
102 Mikhail Tatarinov .08 .25
103 Igor Kravchuk .08 .25
104 Vladimir Malakhov .08 .25
105 Alex Gusarov .08 .25
106 Dimitri Filimonov .08 .25
107 Dimitri Mironov .08 .25
108 Vladimir Konstantinov .75 2.00
109 Sergei Fedorov 1.25 3.00
110 Alexei Zhamnov .08 .25
111 Vyatcheslav Kozlov .08 .25
112 Valery Kamesky .08 .25
113 Alexander Semak .08 .25
114 Vjatcheslav Butsayev .08 .25
115 Andrei Lomakin .08 .25
116 Pavel Bure 2.00 5.00
117 Andrei Kovalenko .08 .25
118 Ravil Khaidarov .08 .25
119 Victor Gordiuk .08 .25
120 Vitali Prokhorov .08 .25
121 Tjeckoslovakien .02 .10
122 Ivan Hlinka .02 .10
123 Oldrich Svoboda .20 .50
124 Dominik Hasek 4.00 10.00
125 Leo Gudas .08 .25
126 Frantisek Musil .08 .25
127 Kamil Prachar .08 .25
128 Frantisek Kucera .08 .25
129 Richard Smehlik .08 .25
130 Jergus Baca .08 .25
131 Jiri Slegr .08 .25
132 Petr Hrbek .08 .25
133 Kamil Kastak .08 .25
134 Richard Zemlicka .08 .25
135 Jaromir Jagr 3.00 8.00
136 Martin Rucinsky .08 .25
137 Josef Beranek .08 .25
138 Michael Pivonka .08 .25
139 Robert Kron .08 .25
140 Zigmund Palffy .75 2.00
141 Tomas Jelinek .08 .25
142 Robert Reichel .08 .25
143 Lubomir Kolnik .08 .25
144 Zdeno Ciger .08 .25
145 USA .02 .10
146 Tim Taylor .02 .10
147 John Vanbiesbrouck .75 2.00
148 Mike Richter .75 2.00
149 Phil Housley .08 .25
150 Brian Leetch .40 1.00
151 Kevin Hatcher .08 .25
152 Gary Suter .08 .25
153 Chris Chelios .75 2.00
154 Eric Weinrich .08 .25
155 Jim Johnson .08 .25
156 Brett Hull 2.00 5.00
157 Mike Modano 2.00 5.00
158 Jeremy Roenick 2.00 5.00
159 Pat LaFontaine .40 1.00
160 Craig Janney .08 .25
161 Ed Olczyk .08 .25
162 Tony Granato .08 .25
163 Joe Mullen .08 .25
164 Dave Christian .08 .25
165 Doug Brown .08 .25
166 Kevin Miller .08 .25
167 Joel Otto .08 .25
168 Randy Wood .08 .25
169 Tyskland .02 .10
170 Ludek Bukac .08 .25
171 Klaus Merk .08 .25
172 Josef Heiss .08 .25
173 Harold Kreiss .08 .25
174 Michael Heidt .08 .25
175 Jorg Mayr .08 .25
176 Marco Rentzsch .08 .25
177 Heinrich Schiffel .08 .25
178 Stefan Steinecker .08 .25
179 Torsten Kienass .08 .25
180 Raimund Hilger .08 .25
181 Ernst Kopf .08 .25
182 Peter Draisatl .08 .25
183 Axel Kammerer .08 .25
184 Michael Rumrich .08 .25
185 Jurgen Rumrich .08 .25
186 Georg Holzmann .08 .25
187 Lorenz Funk .08 .25
188 Thomas Schinko .08 .25
189 Andreas Lupzig .08 .25
190 Tobias Abstreiter .08 .25
191 Michael Pohl .08 .25
192 Antony Vogel .08 .25
193 Schweiz .02 .10
194 Juhani Tamminen .02 .10
195 Renato Tosio .20 .50
196 Reto Pavoni .20 .50
197 Rick Tschumi .08 .25
198 Patrice Brasey .08 .25
199 Didier Massy .08 .25
200 Sandro Bertaggia .08 .25
201 Sven Leuenberger .08 .25
202 Samuel Palmer .08 .25
203 Martin Rauch .08 .25
204 Dino Kessler .08 .25
205 Raymond Walder .08 .25
206 Peter Jaks .08 .25
207 Andy Ton .08 .25
208 Jorg Eberle .08 .25
209 Felix Hollenstein .08 .25
210 Fredy Luthi .08 .25
211 Manuele Celio .08 .25
212 Christian Weber .08 .25
213 Andre Rotheli .08 .25
214 Gil Montandon .08 .25
215 Thomas Vrabec .08 .25
216 Patrick Howald .08 .25
217 Frankrike .02 .10
218 Kjell Larsson .02 .10
219 Jean-Marc Djian .20 .50
220 Petri Ylonen .20 .50
221 Stephane Botteri .08 .25
222 Michel Leblanc .08 .25
223 Jean-Philippe Lemoine .08 .25
224 Denis Perez .08 .25
225 Bruno Saunier .08 .25
226 Steven Woodburn .08 .25
227 Serge Poudrier .08 .25
228 Michael Babin .08 .25
229 Stephane Barin .08 .25
230 Philippe Bozon .40 1.00
231 Arnaud Briand .08 .25
232 Yves Crettenand .08 .25
233 Patrick Dunn .08 .25
234 Yannick Goicoechea .08 .25
235 Benoit Laporte .08 .25
236 Christian Pouget .08 .25
237 Antoine Richer .08 .25
238 Christophe Ville .08 .25
239 Peter Almasy .08 .25
240 Pierre Pousse .08 .25
241 Italien .02 .10
242 Gene Ubriaco .02 .10
243 David Delfino .40 1.00
244 Mike Zanier .40 1.00
245 Erwin Kostner .08 .25
246 Roberto Oberrauch .08 .25
247 Jim Camazzola .08 .25
248 Anthony Circelli .08 .25
249 Michael de Angelis .08 .25
250 Giovanni Marchetti .08 .25
251 Alessandro Batiani .08 .25
252 Georg Comploi .08 .25
253 Gaetano Orlando .08 .25
254 Bruno Zarrillo .08 .25
255 Emilio Iovio .08 .25
256 Frank Nigro .08 .25
257 Marco Scapinello .08 .25
258 Giuseppe Foglietta .08 .25
259 Rick Morocco .08 .25
260 Santino Pellegrino .08 .25
261 Lucio Topatigh .08 .25
262 Mario Simioni .08 .25
263 Ivano Cloch .08 .25
264 Martino Soracreppa .08 .25
265 Polen .02 .10
266 Leszek Lejcyk .02 .10
267 Andrzej Hanisz .20 .50
268 Mariusz Kieca .20 .50
269 Henryk Gruth .08 .25
270 Janusz Syposz .08 .25
271 Robert Szopinski .08 .25
272 Mark Cholewa .08 .25
273 Jacek Zamojski .08 .25
274 Rafal Stroka .08 .25
275 Dariusz Garbocz .08 .25
276 Stanislaw Cyrwus .08 .25
277 Janusz Adamiec .08 .25
278 Miloslaw Copija .08 .25
279 Piotr Zdunek .08 .25
280 Krzysztof Bujar .08 .25
281 Ludwik Czapka .08 .25
282 Andrzej Kotonski .08 .25
283 Janusz Hajnos .08 .25
284 Slawomir Wieloch .08 .25
285 Wojciech Matczak .08 .25
286 Jedrzej Kasperczyk .08 .25
287 Wojciech Tkacs .08 .25
288 Mariusz Czerkawski .20 .50

1993-94 Finnish Jyvas-Hyva Stickers

This 349-sticker set features the players of Finland's SM-Liiga. The odd-sized stickers (1 X 1 1/2") were inserted as premiums with candy products. The set skips the following numbers: 30, 60, 90, 120, 150, 180, 210, 240, 270, 300, 330. There are no spaces for these cards in the binder produced to store the set, and the cards were never issued. The set is noteworthy for early appearances of Saku Koivu and Janne Niinimaa.

COMPLETE SET (359) 24.00 60.00
1 HIFK Team Photo .02 .10
2 HIFK Team Photo .02 .10
3 HIFK Team Photo .02 .10
4 HIFK Team Photo .02 .10
5 HIFK Team Photo .02 .10
6 HIFK Team Photo .02 .10
7 HIFK Team Photo .02 .10
8 HIFK Team Photo .02 .10
9 HIFK Team Photo .02 .10
10 HIFK Team Photo .02 .10
11 HIFK Team Photo .02 .10
12 HIFK Team Photo .02 .10
13 Harri Rindell CO .05 .15
14 Sakari Lindfors .40 1.00
15 Simo Saarinen .05 .15
16 Pertti Lehtonen .05 .15
17 Jari Laukkanen .05 .15
18 Valeri Krykov .05 .15
19 Iiro Jarvi .20 .50
20 Jari Munck .05 .15
21 Paci Sormunen .05 .15
22 Pekka Peltola .05 .15
23 Teppo Kivela .05 .15
24 Pekka Tuomisto .05 .15
25 Kai Tervonen .05 .15
26 Dan Lambert .20 .50
27 Marco Poulsen .05 .15
28 Ville Peltonen .40 1.00
29 Kim Ahlroos .05 .15
31 HPK Team Photo .02 .10
32 HPK Team Photo .02 .10
33 HPK Team Photo .02 .10
34 HPK Team Photo .02 .10
35 HPK Team Photo .02 .10
36 HPK Team Photo .02 .10
37 HPK Team Photo .02 .10
38 HPK Team Photo .02 .10
39 HPK Team Photo .02 .10
40 HPK Team Photo .02 .10
41 HPK Team Photo .02 .10
42 HPK Team Photo .02 .10
43 Pentti Matikainen .05 .15
44 Kari Rosenberg .08 .25
45 Mikko Myllykoski .05 .15
46 Janne Laukkanen .40 1.00
47 Jarkko Nikander .08 .25
48 Tomas Kapusta .05 .15
49 Mika Lartama .05 .15
50 Niko Marttila .05 .15
51 Jari Haapamaki .05 .15
52 Tommi Varjonen .05 .15
53 Tony Virta .05 .15
54 Marko Palo .08 .25
55 Marko Allen .05 .15
56 Miikka Ruokonen .05 .15
57 Jani Hassinen .05 .15
58 Pasi Kivila .05 .15
59 Markku Piikkila .05 .15
61 Ilves Team Photo .02 .10
62 Ilves Team Photo .02 .10
63 Ilves Team Photo .02 .10
64 Ilves Team Photo .02 .10
65 Ilves Team Photo .02 .10
66 Ilves Team Photo .02 .10
67 Ilves Team Photo .02 .10
68 Ilves Team Photo .02 .10
69 Ilves Team Photo .02 .10
70 Ilves Team Photo .02 .10
71 Ilves Team Photo .02 .10
72 Ilves Team Photo .02 .10
73 Jukka Jalonen CO .05 .15
74 Jukka Tammi .40 1.00
75 Jani Nikko .08 .25
76 Hannu Henriksson .05 .15
77 Juha Jarvenpaa .05 .15
78 Hannu Mattila .05 .15
79 Timo Peltomaa .08 .25
80 Jukka Ollila .05 .15
81 Juha-Matti Marijarvi .05 .15
82 Mikko Louvi .08 .25
83 Jarno Peltonen .05 .15
84 Pasi Maattanen .05 .15
85 Juha Lampinen .05 .15
86 Allan Measures .05 .15
87 Janne Seva .05 .15
88 Risto Jalo .05 .15
89 Esa Tommila .05 .15
91 Jokerit Team Photo .02 .10
92 Jokerit Team Photo .02 .10
93 Jokerit Team Photo .02 .10
94 Jokerit Team Photo .02 .10
95 Jokerit Team Photo .02 .10
96 Jokerit Team Photo .02 .10
97 Jokerit Team Photo .02 .10
98 Jokerit Team Photo .02 .10
99 Jokerit Team Photo .02 .10
100 Jokerit Team Photo .02 .10
101 Jokerit Team Photo .02 .10
102 Jokerit Team Photo .02 .10
103 Alpo Suhonen CO .20 .50
104 Ari Sulander .40 1.00
105 Kari Martikainen .08 .25
106 Erik Hamalainen .08 .25
107 Juha Jokiharju .05 .15
108 Otakar Janecky .08 .25
109 Petri Varis .20 .50
110 Waltteri Immonen .05 .15
111 Mika Stromberg .08 .25
112 Keijo Sailynoja .05 .15
113 Timo Saarikoski .05 .15
114 Juha Ylonen .75 2.00
115 Ari Salo .05 .15
116 Heikki Riihijarvi .05 .15
117 Timo Norppa .05 .15
118 Jali Wahlsten .05 .15
119 Rami Koivisto .05 .15
121 JYP HT Team Photo .02 .10
122 JYP HT Team Photo .02 .10
123 JYP HT Team Photo .02 .10
124 JYP HT Team Photo .02 .10
125 JYP HT Team Photo .02 .10
126 JYP HT Team Photo .02 .10
127 JYP HT Team Photo .02 .10
128 JYP HT Team Photo .02 .10
129 JYP HT Team Photo .02 .10
130 JYP HT Team Photo .02 .10
131 JYP HT Team Photo .02 .10
132 JYP HT Team Photo .02 .10
133 Kari Savolainen CO .05 .15
134 Ari-Pekka Siekkinen .08 .25
135 Harri Laurila .05 .15
136 Markku Heikkinen .05 .15
137 Jari Lindroos .08 .25
138 Lasse Nieminen .05 .15
139 Risto Kurkinen .05 .15
140 Jarmo Jokilahti .06 .15
141 Veli-Pekka Hard .05 .15
142 Joni Lius .08 .25
143 Jyrki Jokinen .05 .15
144 Mika Arvaja .05 .15
145 Vesa Ponto .05 .15
146 Jarmo Rantanen .05 .15
147 Mika Paananen .05 .15
148 Marko Virtanen .08 .25
149 Marko Ek .05 .15
151 Kalpa Team Photo .02 .10
152 Kalpa Team Photo .02 .10
153 Kalpa Team Photo .02 .10
154 Kalpa Team Photo .02 .10
155 Kalpa Team Photo .02 .10
156 Kalpa Team Photo .02 .10
157 Kalpa Team Photo .02 .10
158 Kalpa Team Photo .02 .10
159 Kalpa Team Photo .02 .10
160 Kalpa Team Photo .02 .10
161 Kalpa Team Photo .02 .10
162 Kalpa Team Photo .02 .10
163 Hannu Kapanen .05 .15
164 Pasi Kuivalainen .20 .50
165 Kimmo Timonen .60 1.50
166 Vesa Salo .05 .15
167 Jani Rautio .05 .15
168 Pekka Tirkkonen .05 .15
169 Dimitri Zinine .05 .15
170 Antti Tuomenoksa .05 .15
171 Jari Jarvinen .05 .15
172 Tuomas Kalliomaki .05 .15
173 Tommi Miettinen .08 .25
174 Sami Kapanen .75 2.00
175 Vesa Ruotsalainen .05 .15
176 Mikko Tavi .05 .15
177 Sami Mettovaara .05 .15
178 Veli-Pekka Pekkarinen .05 .15
179 Arto Sirvio .05 .15
181 Kiekko-Espoo Team Photo .02 .10
182 Kiekko-Espoo Team Photo .02 .10
183 Kiekko-Espoo Team Photo .02 .10
184 Kiekko-Espoo Team Photo .02 .10
185 Kiekko-Espoo Team Photo .02 .10
186 Kiekko-Espoo Team Photo .02 .10
187 Kiekko-Espoo Team Photo .02 .10
188 Kiekko-Espoo Team Photo .02 .10
189 Kiekko-Espoo Team Photo .02 .10
190 Kiekko-Espoo Team Photo .02 .10
191 Kiekko-Espoo Team Photo .02 .10
192 Kiekko-Espoo Team Photo .02 .10
193 Martti Merra .05 .15
194 Timo Maki .05 .15
195 Sami Nuutinen .05 .15
196 Teemu Sillanpaa .05 .15
197 Tero Lehtera .08 .25
198 Jan Langbacka .05 .15
199 Jukka Tiilikainen .05 .15
200 Petri Pulkkinen .05 .15
201 Robert Salo .05 .15
202 Petro Koivunen .08 .25
203 Juha Ikonen .05 .15
204 Mikko Lempiainen .05 .15
205 Marko Halonen .05 .15
206 Jimi Helin .05 .15
207 Timo Hirvonen .05 .15
208 Mikko Halonen .05 .15
209 Kimmo Maki-Kokkila .05 .15
211 Lukko Team Photo .02 .10
212 Lukko Team Photo .02 .10
213 Lukko Team Photo .02 .10
214 Lukko Team Photo .02 .10
215 Lukko Team Photo .02 .10
216 Lukko Team Photo .02 .10
217 Lukko Team Photo .02 .10
218 Lukko Team Photo .02 .10
219 Lukko Team Photo .02 .10
220 Lukko Team Photo .02 .10
221 Lukko Team Photo .02 .10
222 Lukko Team Photo .02 .10
223 Vaclav Sykora .05 .15
224 Jarmo Myllys .40 1.00
225 Kari-Pekka Friman .05 .15
226 Timo Kulonen .05 .15
227 Pasi Saarela .05 .15
228 Kalle Sahlstedt .08 .25
229 Kimmo Rintanen .20 .50
230 Jarmo Kuusisto .05 .15
231 Tuomas Gronman .08 .25
232 Tero Arkiomaa .05 .15
233 Petr Korinek .08 .25
234 Mika Alatalo .60 1.50
235 Marko Tuulola .05 .15
236 Pasi Huura .05 .15
237 Tommi Pullola .05 .15
238 Mika Valila .05 .15
239 Jari Torkki .05 .15
241 Reipas Lahti Team Photo .02 .10
242 Reipas Lahti Team Photo .02 .10
243 Reipas Lahti Team Photo .02 .10
244 Reipas Lahti Team Photo .02 .10
245 Reipas Lahti Team Photo .02 .10
246 Reipas Lahti Team Photo .02 .10
247 Reipas Lahti Team Photo .02 .10
248 Reipas Lahti Team Photo .02 .10
249 Reipas Lahti Team Photo .02 .10
250 Reipas Lahti Team Photo .02 .10
251 Reipas Lahti Team Photo .02 .10
252 Reipas Lahti Team Photo .02 .10
253 Kari Makinen CO .05 .15
254 Oldrich Svoboda .05 .15
255 Timo Kahelin .05 .15
256 Pasi Ruponen .05 .15
257 Tommy Kiviaho .05 .15
258 Jari Multanen .05 .15
259 Erkki Makela .05 .15
260 Jari Parviainen .05 .15
261 Petri Koski .05 .15
262 Jouni Vauhkonen .08 .25
263 Toni Koivunen .05 .15
264 Sami Wikstrom .05 .15
265 Jarkko Hamalainen .05 .15
266 Sami Helenius .20 .50
267 Sami Lekkerimaki .05 .15
268 Jari Kauppila .05 .15
269 Jani Uski .05 .15
271 Tappara Team Photo .02 .10
272 Tappara Team Photo .02 .10
273 Tappara Team Photo .02 .10
274 Tappara Team Photo .02 .10
275 Tappara Team Photo .02 .10
276 Tappara Team Photo .02 .10
277 Tappara Team Photo .02 .10
278 Tappara Team Photo .02 .10
279 Tappara Team Photo .02 .10
280 Tappara Team Photo .02 .10
281 Tappara Team Photo .02 .10
282 Tappara Team Photo .02 .10
283 Boris Majorov .05 .15
284 Timo Hankela .05 .15
285 Timo Jutila .20 .50
286 Samuli Rautio .05 .15
287 Ari Haanpaa .05 .15
288 Mikko Peltola .05 .15
289 Pauli Jarvinen .05 .15
290 Pekka Laksola .05 .15
291 Janne Gronvall .08 .25
292 Kari Heikkinen .05 .15
293 Tommi Pohja .05 .15
294 Petri Aaltonen .05 .15
295 Petri Kalteva .05 .15
296 Tommi Haapsaari .05 .15
297 Teemu Numminen .05 .15
298 Pasi Forsberg .05 .15
299 Veli-Pekka Kautonen .05 .15
301 TPS Team Photo .02 .10
302 TPS Team Photo .02 .10
303 TPS Team Photo .02 .10
304 TPS Team Photo .02 .10
305 TPS Team Photo .02 .10
306 TPS Team Photo .02 .10
307 TPS Team Photo .02 .10
308 TPS Team Photo .02 .10
309 TPS Team Photo .02 .10
310 TPS Team Photo .02 .10
311 TPS Team Photo .02 .10
312 TPS Team Photo .02 .10
313 Vladimir Jursinov CO .05 .15
314 Jouni Rokama .08 .25
315 Hannu Virta .08 .25
316 Erik Kakko .05 .15
317 Jukka Vilander .05 .15
318 Esa Keskinen .20 .50
319 Ari Vuori .05 .15
320 Jouko Narvanmaa .05 .15
321 Marko Kiprusoff .08 .25
322 Jere Lehtinen 2.00 5.00
323 Saku Koivu 4.00 10.00
324 Marko Jantunen .08 .25
325 Kari Harila .05 .15
326 Alexander Smirnov .05 .15
327 Toni Sihvonen .05 .15
328 Harri Sillgren .05 .15
329 Kai Nurminen .40 1.00
331 Assat Team Photo .02 .10
332 Assat Team Photo .02 .10
333 Assat Team Photo .02 .10
334 Assat Team Photo .02 .10
335 Assat Team Photo .02 .10
336 Assat Team Photo .02 .10
337 Assat Team Photo .02 .10
338 Assat Team Photo .02 .10
339 Assat Team Photo .02 .10
340 Assat Team Photo .02 .10
341 Assat Team Photo .02 .10
342 Assat Team Photo .02 .10
343 Veli-Pekka Ketola CO .08 .25
344 Kari Takko .40 1.00
345 Olli Kaski .05 .15
346 Karri Kivi .05 .15
347 Arto Heiskanen .05 .15
348 Janne Virtanen .05 .15
349 Mikael Kotkaniemi .05 .15
350 Stanislav Meciar .05 .15
351 Jarno Miikkulainen .05 .15
352 Jokke Heinanen .05 .15
353 Vjatseslav Fandul .08 .25
354 Ari Saarinen .05 .15
355 Jouni Vento .05 .15
356 Arto Javanainen .05 .15
357 Jari Korpisalo .08 .25
358 Rauli Raitanen .05 .15
359 Jari Levonen .05 .15
NNO Binder 4.00 10.00

1993-94 Finnish SISU

The 396 standard-size cards comprising this first series of players from the Finnish Hockey League feature on-ice color player photos on their fronts. The photos are bordered in a gray lithic, and each carries the player's name, uniform number, and team logo near the bottom. The gray lithic design continues on the horizontal back, which carries the player's team name in a yellow stripe across the top, followed below by his name, position, biography, and statistics. With a few exceptions, all text is in Finnish. Cards 301-396 differ from the others in that the design is orange lithic instead of gray, and some have horizontal fronts. The cards are numbered on the front. There are several new errors and variations in this edition, as provided by Finnish collector Heikki Silvennoinen.

COMPLETE SET (396) 20.00 50.00
1 Jokerit Team Card .08 .25
2 Alpo Suhonen .20 .50
3 Ari Sulander .40 1.00
4 Marko Rantanen .05 .15
5 Ari Salo .02 .10
6 Kalle Koskinen .05 .15
7 Sebastian Sulku .02 .10
8 Waltteri Immonen .05 .15
9 Mika Stromberg .08 .25
10 Heikki Riihijarvi .02 .10
11 Kari Martikainen .05 .15
12 Erik Hamalainen .08 .25
13 Juha Jokiharju .05 .15
14 Timo Norppa .02 .10
15 Rami Koivisto .02 .10
16 Antti Tormanen .30 .75
17 Keijo Sailynoja .05 .15
18 Jere Keskinen .02 .10
19 Jali Wahlsten .02 .10
20 Mikko Kontilla .02 .10
21 Juha Ylonen .60 1.50
22 Jussi Vienonen ERR .02 .10
(wrong photo
22B Jussi Vienonen COR .08 .25
23 Petri Varis .20 .50
24 Juha Lind .40 1.00
25 Timo Saarikoski .02 .10
26 Otakar Janecky .08 .25
27 TPS Team Card .05 .15
28 Vladimir Jursinov CO .02 .10
29 Jouni Rokama .05 .15
30 Kimmo Lecklin .02 .10
31 Jouko Narvanmaa .02 .10
32 Petteri Nummelin .05 .15
33 Erik Kakko .02 .10
34 Tom Koivisto .02 .10
35 Marko Kiprusoff .08 .25
36 Kari Harila .02 .10
37 Hannu Virta .08 .25
38 Aki Berg .40 1.00
39 Aleksander Smirnov .02 .10
40 Esa Keskinen .08 .25
41 Saku Koivu 4.00 10.00
42 Jukka Vilander .02 .10
43 Antti Aalto .40 1.00
44 Mika Karapuu ERR .02 .10
(wrong photo
44B Mika Karapuu COR .08 .25
45 Toni Sihvonen .02 .10
46 Pavel Torgajev .08 .25
47 Jere Lehtinen 1.25 3.00
48 Kai Nurminen .08 .25
49 Harri Sillgren .02 .10
50 Niko Mikkola .02 .10
51 Ari Vuori .02 .10
52 Lasse Pirjeta .02 .10
53 Reijo Mikkolainen .02 .10
54 Marko Jantunen .08 .25
55 Mikko Virolainen ERR .02 .10
(wrong photo
55B Mikko Virolainen COR .08 .25
56 Tappara Team Card .05 .15
57 Boris Majorov CO .05 .15
58 Jaromir Sindel .08 .25
59 Timo Hankela .02 .10
60 Teemu Kivinen .02 .10
61 Petri Kalteva .02 .10
62 Jari Harjumaki .02 .10
63 Timo Jutila .08 .25
64 Janne Gronvall .08 .25
65 Jari Gronstrand .05 .15
66 Pekka Laksola .02 .10
67 Tommi Haapsaari .02 .10
68 Veli-Pekka Kautonen .02 .10
69 Mikko Peltola .02 .10
70 Kari Heikkinen .02 .10
71 Teemu Numminen .02 .10
72 Jiri Kucera .05 .15
73 Pauli Jarvinen .02 .10
74 Pasi Forsberg .02 .10
75 Tero Toivola .02 .10
76 Ari Haanpaa .05 .15
77 Tommi Pohja .02 .10
78 Samuli Rautio .02 .10
79 Markus Oijennus .02 .10
80 Petri Aaltonen .02 .10
81 HIFK Team Card .05 .15
82 Harri Rindell CO .02 .10
83 Sakari Lindfors .08 .25
84 Mikael Granlund .02 .10
85 Kimmo Hyttinen .02 .10
86 Jere Karalahti .20 .50
87 Dan Lambert .20 .50
88 Simo Saarinen .02 .10
89 Pasi Sormunen .02 .10
90 Tommi Hamalainen .02 .10
91 Pertti Lehtonen .02 .10
92 Jari Munck .02 .10
93 Kai Tervonen .02 .10
94 Kim Ahlroos .02 .10
95 Teppo Kivela .02 .10
96 Darren Boyko .05 .15
97 Pekka Peltola .02 .10
98 Marco Poulsen .02 .10
99 Valeri Krykov .02 .10
100 Jari Laukkanen .02 .10
101 Ville Peltonen .40 1.00
102 Pekka Tuomisto .02 .10
103 Miro Haapaniemi .02 .10
104 Mika Kortelainen .02 .10
105 Marko Ojanen .02 .10
106 Iiro Jarvi .05 .15
107 Ilves Tampere Team Card .05 .15
108 Jukka Jalonen CO .02 .10
109 Jukka Tammi .20 .50
110 Mika Manninen .05 .15
111 Jani Nikko .08 .25
112 Jukka Ollila .02 .10
113 Juha Lampinen .02 .10
114 Hannu Henriksson .02 .10
115 Sami Lehtonen .02 .10
116 Mikko Niemi .02 .10
117 Juha-Matti Marijarvi .02 .10
118 Jarkko Glad .02 .10
119 Allan Measures .02 .10
120 Mikko Luovi .05 .15
121 Risto Jalo .05 .15
122 Juha Jarvenpaa .05 .15
123 Jarno Peltonen .02 .10
124 Matti Kaipainen .02 .10
125 Timo Peltomaa .05 .15
126 Esa Tommila .02 .10
127 Hannu Mattila .02 .10
128 Jari Neuvonen .02 .10
129 Pasi Maattanen .02 .10
130 Juha Hautamaa .02 .10
131 Janne Seva .02 .10
132 Sami Ahlberg .02 .10
133 Jari Virtanen .02 .10
134 JyP HT Team Card .05 .15
135 Kari Savolainen CO .02 .10
136 Ari-Pekka Siekkinen .05 .15
137 Marko Leinonen .02 .10
138 Jan Latvala .02 .10
139 Markku Heikkinen .02 .10
140 Jarmo Jokilahti .02 .10
141 Veli-Pekka Hard .02 .10
142 Kalle Koskinen .02 .10
143 Vesa Ponto .02 .10
144 Petri Kujala .02 .10
145 Jarmo Rantanen .02 .10
146 Harri Laurila .02 .10
147 Lasse Nieminen .02 .10
148 Mika Paananen .02 .10
149 Mika Arvaja .02 .10
150 Marko Virtanen .05 .15
151 Marko Ek .02 .10
152 Joni Lius .02 .10
153 Teemu Kohvakka .02 .10
154 Jari Lindroos .05 .15
155 Marko Kupari .02 .10
156 Markku Ikonen .02 .10
157 Jyrki Jokinen .02 .10
158 Risto Kurkinen .02 .10
159 KalPa Team Card .05 .15
160 Hannu Kapanen CO .02 .10
161 Pasi Kuivalainen .05 .15
162 Kimmo Kapanen .02 .10
163 Kimmo Timonen .40 1.00
164 Jari Jarvinen .02 .10
165 Mikko Tavi .02 .10
166 Jermu Pisto .02 .10
167 Antti Tuomenoksa .02 .10
168 Vesa Ruotsalainen .02 .10
169 Vesa Salo .02 .10
170 Veli-Pekka Pekkarinen .02 .10
171 Tuomas Kalliomaki .02 .10
172 Dimitri Zinine .02 .10
173 Jani Rautio .02 .10
173B Marko Virtanen ERR .08 .25
(incorrect numbering
174 Janne Kekalainen .02 .10
174B Marko Ek ERR .08 .25
(incorrect numbering
175 Arto Sirvio .02 .10
176 Sami Mettovaara .02 .10
177 Sami Simonen .02 .10
178 Pekka Tirkkonen .05 .15
179 Sami Kapanen .75 2.00
180 Jussi Tarvainen .02 .10
181 Lukko Team Card .05 .15
182 Vaclav Sykora .02 .10
183 Jarmo Myllys .40 1.00
183B Petri Kujala ERR .08 .25
(incorrect numbering
184 Kimmo Vesa .02 .10
185 Mika Yli-Maenpaa .05 .15
185B Jarmo Rantanen ERR .08 .25
(incorrect numbering
186 Jarmo Kuusisto .02 .10
187 Marko Tuulola .02 .10
188 Tuomas Gronman .08 .25
189 Timo Kulonen .02 .10
189B Mika Arvaja ERR .08 .25
(incorrect numbering
190 Kari-Pekka Friman VAR .02 .10
(name on front smaller font size

190B Kari-Pekka Friman VAR .08 .25
(name on front larger font size
191 Pasi Huura .05 .15
192 Harri Suvanto .02 .10
193 Kamil Kastak .02 .10
194 Jari Torkki .02 .10
195 Kalle Sahlstedt .05 .15
196 Tommi Pullola .02 .10
197 Mika Valila .02 .10
198 Tero Arkiomaa .02 .10
199 Pasi Saarela .02 .10
200 Matti Forss .02 .10
201 Jussi Kiuru ERR .02 .10
(wrong photo
201B Jussi Kiuru COR .08 .25
202 Mika Alatalo .75 2.00
203 Kimmo Rintanen .08 .25
204 Petri Latti ERR .02 .10
(wrong photo
204B Petri Latti COR .08 .25
205 Petr Korinek .05 .15
206 Assat Team Card .05 .15
207 Veli-Pekka Ketola CO .05 .15
208 Kari Takko .08 .25
209 Timo Jarvinen .02 .10
210 Marko Sten .02 .10
211 Pasi Peltonen .02 .10
212 Olli Kaski .02 .10
213 Jarmo Miikkulainen .02 .10
214 Jouni Vento .02 .10
215 Karri Kivi .05 .15
215B HIFK Team Card ERR .02 .10
(incorrect numbering
215C Jouni Vento ERR .08 .25
(incorrect numbering
216 Stanislav Meciar .02 .10
217 Nemo Nokkosmaki .02 .10
218 Arto Javanainen .02 .10
219 Janne Virtanen .02 .10
220 Vjatseslav Fandul .05 .15
221 Jari Levonen .02 .10
222 Jarmo Levonen .02 .10
223 Jari Korpisalo .08 .25
224 Jokke Heinanen .02 .10
225 Harri Lonnberg .02 .10
226 Ari Saarinen .02 .10
227 Kari Syvasalmi .02 .10
228 Jarmo Makela .02 .10
229 Rauli Raitanen .02 .10
230 Arto Heiskanen .02 .10
231 Mikael Kotkaniemi .02 .10
232 HPK Team Card .05 .15
233 Pentti Matikainen .02 .10
234 Kari Rosenberg .05 .15
235 Petri Vilen .02 .10
236 Marko Allen .02 .10
237 Mikko Myllykoski .02 .10
238 Kim Vahanen .02 .10
239 Janne Laukkanen .30 .75
240 Jari Haapamaki .02 .10
241 Niko Marttila .02 .10
242 Esa Sateri .02 .10
243 Toni Virta .02 .10
244 Marko Palo .05 .15
245 Markku Piikkila .02 .10
246 Jani Hassinen .02 .10
247 Jarkko Nikander .05 .15
248 Pasi Kivila .02 .10
249 Mika Lartama .02 .10
250 Tomas Kapusta .05 .15
251 Tommi Varjonen .02 .10
252 Teemu Tamminen .02 .10
253 Jukka Seppo .05 .15
254 Kiekko-Espoo Team Card .05 .15
255 Martti Merra .02 .10
256 Scott Brower .20 .50
257 Timo Maki .02 .10
258 Petri Pulkkinen .02 .10
259 Robert Salo .02 .10
260 Sami Nuutinen .02 .10
261 Teemu Sillanpaa .02 .10
262 Marko Halonen .02 .10
263 Jimi Helin .02 .10
264 Kari Haakana .02 .10
265 Jukka Tiilikainen .02 .10
266 Jan Langbacka .02 .10
267 Jarmo Muukkonen .02 .10
268 Timo Hirvonen .05 .15
269 Pasi Heinisto .02 .10
270 Kimmo Maki-Kokkila .02 .10
271 Mikko Lempiainen .02 .10
272 Tero Lehtera .05 .15
273 Hannu Jarvenpaa .05 .15
274 Riku Kuusisto .02 .10
275 Mikko Halonen .02 .10
276 Markku Takala .02 .10
277 Petro Koivunen .05 .15
278 Reipas Lahti Team Card .05 .15
279 Kari Makinen CO .02 .10
280 Oldrich Svoboda .02 .10
281 Pekka Ilmivalta .02 .10
282 Matti Vuorio .02 .10
283 Jari Parviainen .02 .10
284 Timo Kahelin .02 .10
285 Ville Skinnari .02 .10
286 Petri Koski .02 .10
287 Jarkko Hamalainen .02 .10
288 Pasi Ruponen .02 .10
289 Oldrich Valek .02 .10
290 Juha Nurminen .02 .10
291 Erkki Laine .02 .10
292 Sami Lekkerimaki .02 .10
293 Tommy Kiviaho .02 .10
293B Ville Skinnari ERR .08 .25
(incorrect numbering
294 Jyrki Poikolainen .02 .10
295 Sami Wikstrom .02 .10
296 Jonni Vauhkonen .08 .25
297 Erkki Laine .02 .10
298 Jani Uski .02 .10
299 Jari Multanen .02 .10
300 Toni Koivunen .02 .10
301 Runkosarjan 1 .02 .10
302 Runkosarjan 2 .02 .10
303 Runkosarjan 3 .02 .10
304 Runkosarjan 4 .02 .10
305 Runkosarjan 5 .02 .10
306 Runkosarjan 6 .02 .10
307 Runkosarjan 7 .02 .10
308 Runkosarjan 8 .02 .10
309 Runkosarjan 9 .02 .10
310 Runkosarjan 10 .02 .10
311 Runkosarjan 11 .02 .10
312 Runkosarjan 12 .02 .10
313 Runkosarjan 13 .02 .10
314 Runkosarjan 14 .02 .10
315 Runkosarjan 15 .02 .10
316 Runkosarjan 16 .02 .10
317 Runkosarjan 17 .02 .10
318 Runkosarjan 18 .02 .10
319 Runkosarjan 19 .02 .10
320 Runkosarjan 20 .02 .10
321 Runkosarjan 21 .02 .10
322 Runkosarjan 22 .02 .10
323 Runkosarjan 23 .02 .10
324 Runkosarjan 24 .02 .10
325 Runkosarjan 25 .02 .10
326 Runkosarjan 26 .02 .10
327 Runkosarjan 27 .02 .10
328 Runkosarjan 28 .02 .10
329 Runkosarjan 29 .02 .10
330 Runkosarjan 30 .02 .10
331 Runkosarjan 31 .02 .10
332 Runkosarjan 32 .02 .10
333 Runkosarjan 33 .02 .10
334 Runkosarjan 34 .02 .10
335 Runkosarjan 35 .02 .10
336 Runkosarjan 36 .02 .10
337 Runkosarjan 37 .02 .10
338 Runkosarjan 38 .02 .10
339 Runkosarjan 39 .02 .10
340 Runkosarjan 40 .02 .10
341 Runkosarjan 41 .02 .10
342 Runkosarjan 42 .02 .10
343 Runkosarjan 43 .02 .10
344 Runkosarjan 44 .02 .10
345 Paikallisottelut .02 .10
(HIFK/Jokerit/K-Espoo)
346 Paikallisottelut .02 .10
(Lukko/TPS/Assat)
347 Paikallisottelut .02 .10
(HPK/Ilves/Tappara)
348 Paikallisottelut .02 .10
(JyP HT/KalPa/Reipas)
349 Puolivaliera .02 .10
(HPK/Lukko)
350 Puolivaliera .02 .10
(Jokerit/Assat)
351 Puolivaliera .02 .10
(Jokerit/Assat)
352 Puolivaliera .02 .10
(TPS/Ilves)
353 Valiera .02 .10
(HPK/JyP HT)
354 Valiera .02 .10
(TPS/Assat)
355 Pronssiottelu .02 .10
356 1.Finaali .02 .10
(TPS 9& HPK 3)
357 2. Finaali .02 .10
358 3.Finaali .02 .10
(TPS 3& HPK 2)
360 Esa Keskinen LL .08 .25
361 Tomas Kapusta LL .02 .10
362 Erik Hamalainen LL .05 .15
363 Brian Tutt LL .02 .10
364 Otakar Janecky LL ERR .05 .15
364B Otakar Janecky LL COR .08 .25
365 Ville Peltonen LL .40 1.00
366 Petr Briza AS .40 1.00
367 Janne Laukkanen AS .20 .50
368 Timo Jutila AS .08 .25
369 Juha Riihijarvi AS ERR .08 .25
(card back from 384
369B Juha Riihijarvi AS COR .20 .50
370 Esa Keskinen AS ERR .08 .25
(card back from 372
370B Esa Keskinen AS COR
371 Jarkko Varvio AS .05 .15
372 Esa Keskinen AW ERR .08 .25
(card back from 370
372B Esa Keskinen AW COR .20 .50
373 Vladimir Jursinov AW .02 .10
374 Erik Hamalainen AW .05 .15
375 Timo Lehkonen AW .05 .15
376 German Titov AW .08 .25
377 Raimo Summanen AW .05 .15
378 Mikko Haapakoski AW .02 .10
379 Marko Palo AW .02 .10
380 Seppo Makela AW .02 .10
381 TPS, Turku Team Card .02 .10
382 HPK Hameenlinna .02 .10
383 JyP HT Jyvaskyla .02 .10
384 Juha Riihijarvi MVP ERR .05 .15
(card back from 369
384B Juha Riihijarvi MVP COR .08 .25
385 Jukka Virtanen .02 .10
386 Kari Jalonen .05 .15
387 Matti Forss .02 .10
388 Arto Javanainen .02 .10
389 Saku Koivu 4.00 10.00
390 Janne Niinimaa .40 1.00
391 Ville Peltonen .40 1.00
392 Jonni Vauhkonen .08 .25
393 Petri Varis .20 .50
394 Antti Aalto .40 1.00
395 Jere Karalahti .20 .50
396 Kimmo Timonen .40 1.00

1993-94 Finnish SISU Autographs

These cards were issued as random inserts in packs of 1993 94 SISU. Essentially, they are the same as the base cards, save for the autograph and serial numbering. We do not have confirmed serial numbers for any of these cards. If you can provide them, please contact us at hockeymag@beckett.com. Thanks to collector Heikki Silvennoinen for providing the checklist.

COMPLETE SET (12) 90.00 150.00
8 Walteri Immonen 4.00 10.00
41 Saku Koivu 20.00 50.00
73 Pauli Jarvinen 4.00 10.00
83 Sakari Lindfors 10.00 25.00
121 Risto Jalo 4.00 10.00
173 Marko Virtanen 4.00 10.00
178 Pekka Tirkkonen 6.00 15.00
203 Kimmo Rintanen 4.00 10.00
223 Jari Korpisalo 4.00 10.00
239 Janne Laukkanen 6.00 15.00
260 Sami Nuutinen 4.00 10.00
296 Jonni Vauhkonen 4.00 10.00

1993-94 Finnish SISU Promos

Produced by Leaf, this 12-card promo set was handed out to members of the Finnish media before the 1993-94 season to introduce North American style hockey cards to the fanatical hockey followers of Finland. The card design mirrors that of the base cards, but the cards are not numbered on the back.

COMPLETE SET (12) 50.00 125.00
NNO Rami Koivisto 4.00 10.00
NNO Janne Laukkanen 6.00 15.00
NNO Petri Skriko 6.00 15.00
NNO Rauli Raitanen 4.00 10.00
NNO Timo Peltomaa 4.00 10.00
NNO Pekka Tirkkonen 6.00 15.00
NNO Simo Saarinen 4.00 10.00
NNO Jari Lindroos 4.00 10.00
NNO Timo Jutila 4.00 10.00
NNO Pasi Ruponen 4.00 10.00
NNO German Titov 4.00 10.00
NNO Mika Alatalo 6.00 15.00

1994-95 Finnish SISU

Manufactured by Leaf in Turku, Finland, this set consists of 400 standard-size cards and features Finnish Hockey League players. The cards were sold in eight-card foil packs. The Canada Bowl Super Chase Card was inserted in first series foil packs. The Saku Koivu Super Chase Card was randomly inserted in second series foil packs at a rate of one in 192 packs. Several notable NHLers, including Teemu Selanne, Jari Kurri and Esa Tikkanen returned to Finland during the 1994 NHL lockout and thus appear in the second series.

COMPLETE SET (400) 20.00 50.00
COMPLETE SERIES 1 (200) 6.00 15.00
COMPLETE SERIES 2 (200) 14.00 35.00
1 Pasi Kuivolainen .07 .20
2 Jere Karalahti .20 .50
3 Markku Heikkinen .02 .10
4 Marko Allen .02 .10
5 Jarmo Kuusisto .02 .10
6 Marko Tuulola .02 .10
7 Marko Kiprusoff .08 .25
8 Vesa Ponto .02 .10
9 Tero Lehtera .07 .20
10 Darren Boyko .02 .10
11 Kari Heikkinen .02 .10
12 Niko Marttila .02 .10
13 Jari Torkki .02 .10
14 Jiri Kucera .07 .20
15 Jari Levonen .02 .10
16 Juha Ikonen .02 .10
17 Joni Lius .02 .10
18 Pekka Tuomisto .02 .10
19 Petri Kokku .02 .10
20 Jere Lehtinen 1.25 3.00
21 Janne Kekalainen .02 .10
22 Ari Haanpaa .02 .10
23 Hannu Jarvenpaa .07 .20
24 Waltteri Immonen .07 .20
25 Jari Lindroos .07 .20
26 Jan Langbacka .02 .10
27 Kari Takko .20 .50
28 Pasi Maattanen .02 .10
29 Jan Latvala .02 .10
30 Arto Heiskanen .02 .10
31 Iiro Jarvi .08 .25
32 Igor Boldin .02 .10
33 Sami Simonen .02 .10
34 Kari Rosenberg .07 .20
35 Sakari Lindfors .20 .50
36 Veli-Pekka Hard .02 .10
37 Jari Halme .08 .25
38 Jukka Tammi .20 .50
39 Kalle Koskinen .02 .10
40 Pekka Tirkkonen .02 .10
41 Ari Sulander .20 .50
42 Joni Hassinen .02 .10
43 Timo Peltomaa .02 .10
44 Sami Mettovaara .02 .10
45 Mika Yli-Maenpaa .08 .25
46 Toni Virta .02 .10
47 Kimmo Lecklin .07 .20
48 Rauli Raitanen .02 .10
49 Juha Lind .20 .50
50 Ari-Pekka Siekkinen .07 .20
51 Kim Ahlroos .02 .10
52 Jarkko Nikander .02 .10
53 Jouni Vento .02 .10
54 Juha Lampinen .02 .10
55 Kalle Sahlstedt .02 .10
56 Teemu Sillanpaa .02 .10
57 Lasse Nieminen .02 .10
58 Janne Niinimaa .40 1.00
59 Timo Jutila .07 .20
60 Tommi Haapsaari .02 .10
61 Allan Measures .02 .10
62 Petteri Nummelin .02 .10
63 Antti Tormanen .08 .25
64 Pekka Laksola .02 .10
65 Esa Sateri .02 .10
66 Petro Koivunen .02 .10
67 Janne Virtanen .02 .10
68 Pekka Peltola .02 .10
69 Matti Kaipainen .02 .10
70 Semi Pekki .02 .10
71 Jussi Tarvainen .02 .10
72 Jari Virtanen .02 .10
73 Kimmo Salminen .02 .10
74 Tommi Varjonen .02 .10
75 Pauli Jarvinen .02 .10
76 Hannu Mattila .02 .10
77 Aleksander Smirnov .02 .10
78 Arto Kulmala .02 .10
79 Roland Carlsson .02 .10
80 Jarma Miikkulainen .02 .10
81 Jarmo Muukkonen .02 .10
82 Mika Paananen .02 .10
83 Pasi Kivila .02 .10
84 Jari Laukkanen .02 .10
85 Tero Arkiomaa .02 .10
86 Tommi Miettinen .07 .20
87 Juha Jarvenpaa .02 .10
88 Niko Mikkola .02 .10
89 Antti Tuomenoksa .02 .10
90 Ilkka Sinisalo .08 .25
91 Otakar Janecky .07 .20
92 Arto Sirvio .02 .10
93 Robert Salo .02 .10
94 Ari Saarinen .02 .10
95 Kari Martikainen .02 .10
96 Miro Haapaniemi .02 .10
97 Fredrik Norrena .07 .20
98 Erik Hamalainen .07 .20
99 Simo Saarinen .02 .10
100 Harri Suvanto .02 .10
101 Kai Nurminen .20 .50
102 Rami Koivisto .02 .10
103 Pasi Peltonen .02 .10
104 Kari-Pekka Friman .02 .10
105 Mika Kortelainen .07 .20
106 Timo Hirvanen .02 .10
107 Jari Haapamaki .02 .10
108 Mika Manninen .02 .10
109 Ari Vuori .02 .10
110 Markku Ikonen .02 .10
111 Mikko Konttila .02 .10
112 Harri Sillgren .02 .10
113 Mikko Teui .02 .10
114 Markus Oijennus .02 .10
115 Kimmo Hyttinen .02 .10
116 Jokke Heinanen .02 .10
117 Sami Ahlberg .02 .10
118 Mika Rautio .07 .20
119 Ari Salo .07 .20
120 Juha Hautamaa .02 .10
121 Kari Haakana .02 .10
122 Sami Nuutinen .02 .10
123 Lasse Pirjeta .02 .10
124 Koijo Sailynoja .07 .20
125 Mikael Kotkaniemi .02 .10
126 Samuli Rautio .02 .10
127 Veli-Pekka Pekkarinen .02 .10
128 Hannu Henriksson .02 .10
129 Antti Aalto .30 .75
130 Jyrki Jokinen .02 .10
131 Marko Ek .02 .10
132 Marko Ojanen .02 .10
133 Mika Arvaja .02 .10
134 Karri Kivi .02 .10
135 Timo Saarikoski .02 .10
136 Toni Sihvonen .02 .10
137 Mika Laaksonen .02 .10
138 HIFK Helsinki .02 .10
Team Card
139 HPK Team Card .02 .10
140 Ilves Team Card .02 .10
141 Jokerit Team Card .08 .25
142 JyP HT Team Card .02 .10
143 KalPa Team Card .02 .10
144 Kiekko-Espoo .02 .10
Team Card
145 Lukko Team Card .02 .10
146 Tappara Team Card .02 .10
147 TPS Turku Team Card .02 .10
148 TuTo Turku .02 .10
Team Card
149 Assat Team Card .02 .10
150 Petteri Nummelin CL .02 .10
151 Kari Takko CL .08 .25
152 Vladimir Jursinov CL .02 .10
153 Juha Lind CL .08 .25
154 Marko Jantunen LL .07 .20
155 Jere Lehtinen LL .75 2.00
156 Esa Keskinen LL .08 .25
157 Jere Lehtinen LL .75 2.00
158 Timo Peltomaa LL .08 .25
159 Janne Gronval LL .08 .25
160 Jarmo Myllys AS .20 .50
161 Markko Kiprusoff AS .08 .25
162 Timo Jutila AS .07 .20
163 Sami Kapanen AS .40 1.00
164 Esa Keskinen AS .08 .25
165 Mika Alatalo AS .20 .50
166 Ville Peltonen .20 .50
167 Igor Boldin .02 .10
168 Sami Lehtonen .02 .10
169 Juha Jokiharju .02 .10
170 Harri Laurila .02 .10
171 Pekka Tirkkonen .02 .10
172 Mikko Halonen .02 .10
173 Tero Arkiomaa .02 .10
174 Jonni Vauhkonen .08 .25
175 Janne Gronvall .08 .25
176 Marko Jantunen .02 .10
177 Jouni Vento .07 .20
178 HIFK
179 HPK
180 Ilves Tampere .02 .10
181 JyP HT .02 .10
182 Jokerit .02 .10
183 KalPa .02 .10
184 Kiekko-Espoo .02 .10
185 Lukko .02 .10
186 Tappara .02 .10
187 TPS .02 .10
188 Reipas .02 .10
189 Assat .02 .10
190 Jokerit Champions .08 .25
191 Lukko 2nd Place .02 .10
192 TPS Euro Champs 1994 .08 .25
193 TPS Euro Cup Champs .08 .25
194 Playoffs .02 .10
195 Playoffs .02 .10
196 Playoffs .02 .10
197 Finals Game 1 .02 .10
198 Finals Game 2 .02 .10
199 Finals Game 3 .02 .10
200 Finals Game 4 .02 .10
201 Jouni Rokama .07 .20
202 Sami Leinonen .02 .10
203 Jani Nikko .08 .25
204 Arto Vuoti .02 .10
205 Petr Pavlas .02 .10
206 Reijo Mikkolainen .02 .10
207 Jari Kurri .75 2.00
208 Janne Ojanen .20 .50
209 Sami Kapanen .75 2.00
210 Teppo Kivela .02 .10
211 Saku Koivu 2.00 5.00
212 Pekka Virta .02 .10
213 Risto Jalo .07 .20
214 Sergei Prjakhin .08 .25
215 Aleksander Barkov .02 .10
216 Ville Peltonen .30 .75
217 Jari Korpisalo .07 .20
218 Jari Liikkanen .02 .10
219 Timo Lehkonen .07 .20
220 Juha Ylonen .20 .50
221 Harri Lonnberg .02 .10
222 Teemu Vuorinen .02 .10
223 Pertti Lehtonen .02 .10
224 Tommi Pullola .02 .10
225 Tomas Kapusta .07 .20
226 Joonas Jaaskelainen .02 .10
227 Jukka Tiilikainen .02 .10
228 Jarno Kultanen .20 .50
229 Kimmo Kapanen .08 .25
230 Jari Kauppila .02 .10
231 Jarkko Glad .02 .10
232 Nemo Nokkosmaki .02 .10
233 Petri Matikainen .02 .10
234 Christian Ruutu .20 .50
235 Martti Jarventie .30 .75
236 Sami Salo .20 .50
237 Timo Kulonen .02 .10
238 Pasi Sormunen .02 .10
239 Timo Nurmberg .02 .10
240 Jari Hirsimaki .02 .10
241 Tommi Hamalainen .02 .10
242 Vesa Salo .08 .25
243 Juha Nurminen .02 .10
244 Petr Korinek .02 .10
245 Kimmo Vesa .07 .20
246 Jukka Seppo .02 .10
247 Jarno Makela .02 .10
248 Petri Varis .20 .50
249 Marko Virtanen .02 .10
250 Risto Siltanen .08 .25
251 Juha Jarvenpaa .02 .10
252 Raimo Summanen .08 .25
253 Markus Hatinen .02 .10
254 Kimmo Nurro .02 .10
255 Timo Salonen .02 .10
256 Jari Munck .02 .10
257 Kimmo Rintanen .08 .25
258 Jarno Levonen .02 .10
259 Jarno Peltonen .02 .10
260 Valeri Krykov .02 .10
261 Kai Rautio .02 .10
262 Timo Blomqvist .08 .25
263 Teemu Selanne 2.00 5.00
264 Juha Virtanen .02 .10
265 Veli-Pekka Kautonen .02 .10
266 Mikko Koivunoro .02 .10
267 Mikko Luovi .08 .25
268 Jaroslav Otevrel .02 .10
269 Erik Kakko .02 .10
270 Peter Ahola .07 .20
271 Miikka Kemppi .02 .10
272 Toni Makiaho .02 .10
273 Pekka Poikolainen .02 .10
274 Timo Norppa .02 .10
275 Sebastian Sulku .02 .10
276 Esa Tikkanen .40 1.00
277 Pasi Saarela .02 .10
278 Ilpo Kauhanen .20 .50
279 Mika Alatalo .20 .50
280 Jukka Suomalainen .02 .10
281 Tony Arima .02 .10
282 Mika Puhakka .02 .10
283 Jussi Kiuru .02 .10
284 Jarkko Isotalo .02 .10
285 Esa Tommila .02 .10
286 Jouni Loponen .02 .10
287 Jermu Pisto .02 .10
288 Pasi Heinisto .02 .10
289 Toni Porkka .02 .10
290 Juha Vuorivirta .08 .25
291 Vesa Karjalainen .02 .10
292 Tom Koivisto .02 .10
293 Markku Hurme .02 .10
294 Mika Kannisto .02 .10
295 Marko Rantanen .07 .20
296 Petri Kalteva .02 .10
297 Pasi Huura .02 .10
298 Miikka Ruokonen .02 .10
299 Tuomo Raty .02 .10
300 Vadim Shaidullin .02 .10
301 Juha Riihijarvi .07 .20
302 Brad Turner .02 .10
303 Marko Toivola .02 .10
304 Kimmo Timonen .30 .75
305 Kai Nurminen .20 .50
306 Vesa Lehtonen .02 .10
307 Mika Niittymaki .02 .10
308 Sami Wahlsten .02 .10
309 Pavel Torgajev .08 .25
310 Pasi Kemppainen .02 .10
311 Markku Kallio .02 .10
312 Timo Maki .07 .20
313 Mika Stromberg .08 .25
314 Tuomas Gronman .08 .25
315 Tommi Rajamaki .08 .25
316 Juri Kuznetsov .07 .20
317 Mikko Myllykoski .02 .10
318 Brian Tutt .02 .10
319 Teemu Numminen .07 .20
320 Juha Jokiharju .02 .10
321 Mika Lehtinen .02 .10
322 Jari Pulliainen .02 .10
323 Kimmo Maki-Kokkila .02 .10
324 Mikko Peltola .02 .10
325 Risto Kurkinen .02 .10
326 Harri Laurila .02 .10
327 Vjatcheslav Fandul .02 .10
328 Niklas Hede .02 .10
329 Boris Rousson .20 .50
330 Jukka Ollila .08 .25
331 Jouni Tuominen .02 .10
332 Marko Harkonen .07 .20
333 Petri Engman .07 .20
334 Mikko Halonen .02 .10
335 Aki Berg .30 .75
336 Kristian Fagerstrom .02 .10
337 Jiri Veber .02 .10
338 Tommy Kiviaho .02 .10
339 Konstantin Astrahantsev .02 .10
340 Jukka Makitalo .07 .20
341 Timo Nykopp .02 .10
342 Sami Lehtonen .02 .10
343 Joni Lehto .07 .20
344 Jouko Myrra .02 .10
345 Mikko Makela .20 .50
346 Marco Poulsen .02 .10
347 Janne Seva .02 .10
348 Shawn McEachern .20 .50
349 Jarkko Varvio .07 .20
350 Mikko Konttila .02 .10
351 Veli-Pekka Ahonen .02 .10
352 Michael Nylander .30 .75
353 Kristian Taubert .02 .10
354 Ismo Kuoppala .02 .10
355 Kimmo Hyttinen .02 .10
356 Petri Latti .02 .10
357 Ted Donato .20 .50
358 Jari Harjumaki .02 .10
359 Teppo Numminen .20 .50
360 Jyrki Lumme .20 .50
361 German Titov .20 .50
362 Kari Eloranta .08 .25
363 Raimo Helminen .08 .25
364 Marko Jantunen .08 .25
365 Olli Kaski .02 .10
366 Jarmo Kekalainen .07 .20
367 Esa Keskinen .08 .25
368 Jarmo Makitalo .02 .10
369 Mika Nieminen .08 .25
370 Marko Palo .02 .10
371 Ville Siren .08 .25
372 Kari Suoraniemi .02 .10
373 Otakar Janecky PM .08 .25
374 Jari Lindroos PM .02 .10
375 Teppo Kivela PM .02 .10
376 Petri Varis PM .08 .25
377 Pekka Laksola PM .02 .10
378 Jari Korpisalo PM .07 .20
379 Iiro Jarvi PM .08 .25
380 Timo Saarikoski PM .02 .10
381 Rauli Raitanen PM .02 .10
382 Juha Riihijarvi PM .02 .10
383 Juha Jokiharju PM .02 .10
384 Vesa Salo PM .02 .10
385 Mika Nieminen CL .08 .25
386 Marko Jantunen CL .02 .10
387 Jere Lehtinen CL .40 1.00
388 Ari Sulander CL .08 .25
389 Hannu Kapanen CO .02 .10
390 Hannu Savolainen CO .02 .10
391 Heikki Vesala CO .02 .10
392 Hannu Aravirta CO .02 .10
393 Kari Savolainen CO .02 .10
394 Anatoli Bogdanov CO .02 .10
395 Harri Rindell CO .02 .10
396 Vaclav Sykora CO .02 .10
397 Boris Majorov CO .02 .10
398 Vladimir Jursinov CO .05 .15
399 Seppo Suoraniemi CO .02 .10
400 Veli-Pekka Ketola CO .08 .25
NNO1 Canada Bowl Super Chase COR 8.00 20.00
NNO1B Canada Bowl Super Chase ERR
(card back text not fully printed
NNO2 Saku Koivu Super Chase 20.00 50.00

1994-95 Finnish SISU Fire On Ice

This 20-card set highlights players who had multiple games of three or more points during the 1993-94 Finnish season. The cards were randomly inserted in first series packs.

COMPLETE SET (20) 12.00 30.00
1 Tero Arkiomoa .40 1.00
2 Igor Boldin .40 1.00
3 Vjatseslav Fandul .40 1.00
4 Otakar Janecky .75 2.00
5 Marko Jantunen .75 2.00
6 Timo Jutila .40 1.00
7 Pauli Jarvinen .40 1.00
8 Sami Kapanen 1.25 3.00
9 Tomas Kapusta .40 1.00
10 Esa Keskinen .75 2.00
11 Saku Koivu 4.00 10.00
12 Petro Koivunen .40 1.00
13 Petr Korinek .40 1.00
14 Jari Karpisolo .40 1.00
15 Risto Kurkinen .40 1.00
16 Tero Lehtera .75 2.00
17 Juha Nurminen .40 1.00
18 Kai Nurminen .75 2.00
19 Janne Ojanen .75 2.00
20 Jari Torkki .40 1.00

1994-95 Finnish SISU Guest Specials

Randomly inserted at a rate of one in thirteen series two foil packs, this 12-card standard-size set focuses on NHL stars who signed on to play in the Finnish league during the 1994 NHL lockout.

COMPLETE SET (12) 16.00 30.00
1 Ted Donato .75 2.00
2 Jari Kurri 2.00 5.00
3 Jyrki Lumme .75 2.00
4 Shawn McEachern .75 2.00
5 Mikko Makela .75 2.00
6 Teppo Numminen .75 2.00
7 Michael Nylander .75 2.00
8 Christian Ruuttu .75 2.00
9 Teemu Selanne 10.00 20.00
10 Esa Tikkanen .75 2.00
11 German Titov .40 1.00
12 Jarkko Varvio .40 1.00

1994-95 Finnish SISU Horoscopes

Randomly inserted at a rate of one in four second series foil packs, this 20-card standard-size set describes the players' personalities according to the astrological signs they were born under.

COMPLETE SET (20) 4.80 12.00
1 Juha Lind .40 1.00
2 Jukka Seppo .40 1.00
3 Antti Tuomenoksa .20 .50
4 Tuomas Gronman .40 1.00
5 Peter Ahola .20 .50
6 Ville Peltonen .75 2.00
7 Timo Saarikoski .20 .50
8 Timo Peltomaa .40 1.00
9 Jari Levonen .20 .50
10 Teppo Kivela .20 .50
11 Valeri Krykov .20 .50
12 Juha Riihijarvi .20 .50
13 Kai Nurminen .40 1.00
14 Mikko Luovi .20 .50
15 Raimo Summanen .40 1.00
16 Tommy Kiviaho .20 .50
17 Hannu Jarvenpaa .20 .50
18 Marko Virtanen .20 .50
19 Sami Lehtonen .20 .50
20 Mika Alatalo .75 2.00

1994-95 Finnish SISU Junior

These standard size cards feature ten of Finland's brightest young stars as they appeared as youth hockey players. The cards were randomly inserted into series I packs.

COMPLETE SET (10) 6.00 15.00
1 Saku Koivu 3.00 8.00
2 Jekke Heimanen .40 1.00
3 Tommi Miettinen .40 1.00
4 Jere Karalahti .75 2.00
5 Kalle Koskinen .40 1.00
6 Kari Rosenberg .40 1.00
7 Mika Manninen .40 1.00
8 Jussi Tarvainen .40 1.00
9 Mika Stromberg .40 1.00
10 Kalle Sahlstedt .40 1.00

1994-95 Finnish SISU Magic Numbers

This ten-card standard-size set was randomly inserted at a rate of one in eight second series foil packs.

COMPLETE SET (10) 4.80 12.00
STATED ODDS 1:8 SERIES 2
1 Pasi Kuivalainen .40 1.00
2 Petteri Nummelin .75 2.00
3 Jarmo Kuusisto .40 1.00
4 Janne Ojanen .40 1.00
5 Sami Kapanen 1.25 3.00
6 Pekka Virta .40 1.00
7 Antti Tormanen .40 1.00
8 Jari Korpisalo .40 1.00
9 Kimmo Salminen .40 1.00
10 Jukka Tammi 1.25 3.00

1994-95 Finnish SISU NHL Draft

Randomly inserted at a rate of one in twenty foil second series packs, this eight-card standard-size set spotlights seven Finns who were drafted by NHL teams in 1994.

COMPLETE SET (8) 2.00 5.00
STATED ODDS 1:20 SERIES 2
1 Title Card .20 .50
2 Marko Kiprusoff .40 1.00
3 Jussi Tarvainen .40 1.00
4 Arto Kuki .40 1.00
5 Tommi Rajamaki .40 1.00
6 Tero Lehtera .40 1.00
7 Tommi Miettinen .40 1.00
8 Antti Tormanen .40 1.00

1994-95 Finnish SISU NHL Phenoms

These standard size cards feature ten goaltenders who posted multiple shutouts during the 1993-94 Finnish campaign. The cards show the netminder cutout photo of the netminder over a brown backdrop.

COMPLETE SET (10) 12.00 30.00
1 Mika Manninen 1.25 3.00
2 Kari Takko 2.00 5.00
3 Ari Sulander 2.00 5.00
4 Jouni Rokama 1.25 3.00
5 Kari Rosenberg 1.25 3.00
6 Mika Rautio 1.25 3.00
7 Ari-Pekka Siekkinen 1.25 3.00
8 Allain Roy 1.25 3.00
9 Pasi Kuivalainen 1.25 3.00
10 Sakari Lindfors 1.25 3.00

1994-95 Finnish SISU Specials

These standard sized cards were random inserts in Leaf first series packs and showcase winners of the player of the month award, among other titles. The main cards are white. The B cards are black. The B suffix does not appear on the actual card: it is included here for checklisting purposes only. The Koivu Jumbo was available as a redemption to those who sent in the Koivu Super Bonus card. It mirrors the white version of the Koivu card.

COMPLETE SET (10) 8.00 20.00
1 Mika Alatalo .75 2.00
1B Mika Alatalo
2 Jarl Korpisalo .40 1.00
2B Jari Korpisalo
3 Petteri Nummelin .75 2.00
3B Petteri Nummelin
4 Janne Ojanen .40 1.00
4B Janne Ojanen
5 Sami Kapanen 1.25 3.00

5B Sami Kapanen
6 Kari Takko .75 2.00
6B Kari Takko
7 Esa Keskinen .40 1.00
7B Esa Keskinen
8 Ari Sulander .75 2.00
8B Ari Sulander
9 Jarmo Myllys .75 2.00
9B Jarmo Myllys
10 Saku Koivu 4.00 10.00
10B Saku Koivu
10J Saku Koivu JUMBO

1994 Finnish Jaa Kiekko

This 360-card set was issued in Finland by Semic in conjunction with the 1994 World Championships. The set includes players from the traditional hockey powers, as well as Great Britain, Austria, Norway and France, shown in action for their countries. A number of NHL players who had participated in previous Canada Cups or World Championships are also pictured. The cards were distributed in 5-card packets. A binder also was available to house the collection.

COMPLETE SET (360) 30.00 50.00
1 Jarmo Myllys .08 .25
2 Pasi Kuivalainen .02 .10
3 Jukka Tammi .07 .20
4 Markus Ketterer .08 .25
5 Timo Jutila .05 .15
6 Mikko Haapakoski .02 .10
7 Marko Tuulola .02 .10
8 Jyrki Lumme .08 .25
9 Kari Harila .02 .10
10 Teppo Numminen .08 .25
11 Pasi Sormunen .02 .10
12 Petteri Nummelin .02 .10
13 Harri Laurila .02 .10
14 Mika Stromberg .05 .15
15 Ville Siren .05 .15
16 Pekka Laksola .02 .10
17 Janne Laukkanen .07 .20
18 Marko Kiprusoff .05 .15
19 Waltteri Immonen .05 .15
20 Teemu Selanne .60 1.50
21 Mika Alatalo .08 .25
22 Vesa Viitakoski .05 .15
23 Tero Arkiomaa .02 .10
24 Jari Kurri .20 .50
25 Pekka Tirkkonen .02 .10
26 Jarmo Kekalainen .05 .15
27 Saku Koivu .40 1.00
28 Antti Tormanen .07 .20
29 Jere Lehtinen .20 .50
30 Raimo Helminen .05 .15
31 Mikko Makela .05 .15
32 Marko Jantunen .05 .15
33 Ville Peltonen .08 .25
34 Esa Tikkanen .08 .25
35 Janne Ojanen .05 .15
36 Mika Nieminen .02 .10
37 Marko Palo .02 .10
38 Rauli Raitanen .02 .10
39 Sami Kapanen .40 1.00
40 Juha Riihijarvi .02 .10
41 Esa Keskinen .02 .10
42 Jari Korpisalo .02 .10
43 Christian Ruuttu .05 .15
44 Jarkko Varvio .05 .15
45 Sami Wahlsten .02 .10
46 Petri Varis .08 .25
47 Timo Saarikoski .02 .10
48 Timo Norppa .02 .10
49 Marko Virtanen .02 .10
50 Pauli Jarvinen .02 .10
51 Hakan Algotsson .07 .20
52 Tommy Soderstrom .08 .25
53 Rolf Ridderwall .05 .15
54 Tomas Jonsson .05 .15
55 Christian Due-Boje .05 .15
56 Peter Popovic .05 .15
57 Fredrik Stillman .02 .10
58 Magnus Svensson .07 .20
59 Fredrik Nilsson .02 .10
60 Tommy Albelin .05 .15
61 Joacim Esbjors .02 .10
62 Roger Johansson .05 .15
63 Stefan Nilsson .02 .10
64 Hakan Loob .08 .25
65 Peter Ottosson .02 .10
66 Daniel Rydmark .05 .15
67 Mikael Renberg .08 .25
68 Patrik Juhlin .07 .20
69 Thomas Rundqvist .05 .15
70 Andreas Johansson .08 .25
71 Stefan Ornskog .05 .15
72 Niklas Eriksson .02 .10
73 Jonas Bergqvist .08 .25
74 Mats Sundin .40 1.00
75 Peter Forsberg .75 2.00
76 Stefan Elvenes .02 .10
77 Tomas Forslund .05 .15
78 Patric Kjellberg .05 .15
79 Bill Ranford .20 .50
80 Corey Hirsch .08 .25
81 Larry Murphy .08 .25
82 Mark Tinordi .05 .15
83 Scott Stevens .20 .50
84 Al MacInnis .40 1.00
85 Steve Smith .08 .25
86 Paul Coffey .40 1.00
87 Eric Desjardins .08 .25
88 Eric Lindros .60 1.50
89 Dale Hawerchuk .20 .50
90 Steve Larmer .08 .25
91 Brent Sutter .07 .20
92 Luc Robitaille .40 1.00
93 Shayne Corson .08 .25
94 Mark Messier .60 1.50
95 Rick Tocchet .20 .50
96 Theo Fleury .40 1.00
97 Dirk Graham .08 .25
98 Russ Courtnall .08 .25
99 Wayne Gretzky 2.00 5.00
100 Brendan Shanahan .60 1.50
101 Mark Recchi .40 1.00
102 David Harlock .05 .15
103 Craig Woodcroft .02 .10
104 Paul Kariya .75 2.00
105 Jason Marshall .05 .15
106 Brett Lindros .08 .25
107 Mike Richter .40 1.00
108 Mike Dunham .20 .50
109 Craig Wolanin .05 .15
110 Jim Johnson .05 .15
111 Chris Chelios .40 1.00
112 Eric Weinrich .05 .15
113 Brian Leetch .40 1.00
114 Kevin Hatcher .08 .25
115 Ed Olczyk .08 .25
116 Kevin Miller .07 .20
117 Doug Brown .02 .10
118 Joe Mullen .08 .25
119 Craig Janney .08 .25
120 Pat LaFontaine .20 .50
121 Gary Suter .08 .25
122 Jeremy Roenick .40 1.00
123 Brett Hull .60 1.50
124 Joel Otto .08 .25
125 Mike Modano .60 1.50
126 Tony Granato .08 .25
127 Dave Christian .07 .20
128 Brian Mullen .05 .15
129 Chris Ferraro .07 .20
130 John Lilley .05 .15
131 Jeff Lazaro .05 .15
132 Peter Ferraro .08 .25
133 Brian Rolston .08 .25
134 David Roberts .05 .15
135 Nikolai Khabibulin .40 1.00
136 Andrei Trefilov .08 .25
137 Vladimir Malakhov .08 .25
138 Alexander Karpovtsev .07 .20
139 Alexander Kmirnov .05 .15
140 Sergei Zubov .08 .25
141 Sergei Seljanin .02 .10
142 Sergei Shendelev .02 .10
143 Alexei Kasatonov .07 .20
144 Sergei Sorokin .02 .10
145 Vjatseslav Bykov .02 .10
146 Sergei Fedorov .60 1.50
147 Alexei Yashin .08 .25
148 Vjatseslav Butsajev .05 .15
149 Konstantin Astrahantsev .02 .10
150 Alexei Zhamnov .08 .25
151 Dimitri Frolov .02 .10
152 Slava Kozlov .08 .25
153 Sergei Pushkov .02 .10
154 Andrei Khomutov .05 .15
155 Sergei Makarov .08 .25
156 Igor Larionov .20 .50
157 Valeri Kamenski .08 .25
158 Alexander Semak .05 .15
159 Alexei Gusarov .05 .15
160 Andrei Lomakin .02 .10
161 Igor Korolev .05 .15
162 Ravil Haidarov .02 .10
163 Dominik Hasek .60 1.50
164 Oldrich Svoboda .02 .10
165 Petr Briza .08 .25
166 Leo Gudas .02 .10
167 Kamil Prachar .02 .10
168 Richard Smehlik .07 .20
169 Frantisek Kucera .05 .15
170 Drahomir Kadlec .05 .15
171 Jan Vopat .02 .10
172 Frantisek Prochazka .02 .10
173 Antonin Stavjana .02 .10
174 Bedrich Scerban .02 .10
175 Kamil Kastak .02 .10
176 Josef Beranek .08 .25
177 Martin Rucinsky .08 .25
178 Michal Pivonka .08 .25
179 Tomas Jelinek .05 .15
180 Richard Zemlicka .05 .15
181 Robert Kron .07 .20
182 Jiri Slegr .02 .10
183 Jaromir Jagr .75 2.00
184 Robert Reichel .08 .25
185 David Vyborny .05 .15
186 Robert Lang .08 .25
187 Petr Rosol .05 .15
188 Otakar Janecky .05 .15
189 Martin Hostak .02 .10
190 Jiri Kucera .05 .15
191 Eduard Hartmann .08 .25
192 Lubomir Sekeras .02 .10
193 Marian Smerciak .02 .10
194 Jan Varholik .02 .10
195 Lubomir Rybovic .02 .10
196 Miroslav Marcinko .02 .10
197 Stanislav Medrik .02 .10
198 Zdeno Ciger .07 .20
199 Jergus Baca .05 .15
200 Peter Stastny .08 .25
201 Peter Veselovsky .02 .10
202 Anton Stastny .07 .20
203 Lubomir Kolnik .05 .15
204 Roman Kontsek .02 .10
205 Rene Pucher .02 .10
206 Slavomir Ilvasky .02 .10
207 Zigmund Palffy .40 1.00
208 Vlastimil Plavucha .02 .10
209 Dusan Pohorelec .02 .10
210 Robert Petrovicky .05 .15
211 Michel Valliere .02 .10
212 Petri Ylonen .08 .25
213 Jean-Philippe Lemoine .02 .10
214 Christophe Moyon .02 .10
215 Denis Perez .02 .10
216 Bruno Saunier .02 .10
217 Stephane Botteri .02 .10
218 Michel Breistroff .02 .10
219 Gerall Guennelon .02 .10
220 Serge Poudrier .02 .10
221 Benjamin Agnel .02 .10
222 Stephane Arcangeloni .02 .10
223 Pierrick Maia .02 .10
224 Antoine Richer .02 .10
225 Christoph Ville .02 .10
226 Michael Babin .02 .10
227 Lionel Orsolini .02 .10
228 Stephane Barin .02 .10
229 Arnaud Briand .02 .10
230 Franck Pajonkowski .07 .20
231 Claus Dalpiaz .07 .20
232 Brian Stankiewicz .02 .10
233 Rob Doyle .02 .10
234 Michael Guntner .02 .10
235 Martin Krainz .02 .10
236 Michael Shea .02 .10
237 Martin Ulrich .02 .10
238 Erich Solderer .02 .10
239 Wayne Groulx .02 .10
240 Andreas Puschnig .02 .10
241 Dieter Kalt .02 .10
242 Gerhard Puschnik .02 .10
243 Werner Kerth .02 .10
244 Richard Nasheim .02 .10
245 Arno Maier .02 .10
246 Mario Schaden .02 .10
247 Reinhard Lampert .02 .10
248 Karl Heinzle .02 .10
249 Wolfgang Kromp .02 .10
250 Marty Dallman .02 .10
251 Jim Marthinsen .07 .20
252 Rob Schistad .02 .10
253 Tom Calo Andersen .02 .10
254 Anders Myrvold .07 .20
255 Svein Enok Norstebo .02 .10
256 Tommy Jakobsen .02 .10
257 Pal Kristiansen .02 .10
258 Petter Salsten .02 .10
259 Ole Eskild Dahlstrom .02 .10
260 Morten Finstad .02 .10
261 Espen Knutsen .08 .25
262 Erik Kristiansen .02 .10
263 Geir Hoff .02 .10
264 Roy Johansen .02 .10
265 Trond Magnussen .02 .10
266 Marius Rath .02 .10
267 Vegar Barlie .02 .10
268 Arne Billkvam .02 .10
269 Tom Johansen .02 .10
270 Petter Thoresen .02 .10
271 Klaus Merk .08 .25
272 Josef Heiss .07 .20
273 Rikhard Amann .02 .10
274 Torsten Kienass .02 .10
275 Mirco Ludemann .02 .10
276 Jason Meyer .02 .10
277 Uli Hiemer .02 .10
278 Karsten Mende .02 .10
279 Andreas Niederberger .02 .10
280 Thomas Brandl .02 .10
281 Benoit Doucet .05 .15
282 Robert Hock .02 .10
283 Georg Franz .02 .10
284 Ernst Kopf, Jr. .02 .10
285 Reemt Pyka .05 .15
286 Jurgen Rumrich .02 .10
287 Dieter Hegen .02 .10
288 Raimund Hilger .02 .10
289 Thomas Schinko .02 .10
290 Leo Stefan .02 .10
291 David Delfino .07 .20
292 Elmar Parth .07 .20
293 Luigi Da Corte .02 .10
294 Phil De Gaetano .02 .10
295 Ralph Di Fiore .02 .10
296 Giorgio Comploi .02 .10
297 Alexander Thaler .02 .10
298 Giovanni Marchetti .02 .10
299 Gaetano Orlando .05 .15
300 Frank Di Muzio .02 .10
301 Giuseppe Foglietta .02 .10
302 Stefano Figliuzzi .02 .10
303 John Vecchiarelli .02 .10
304 Maurizio Mansi .02 .10
305 Santino Pellegrino .02 .10
306 Lino De Toni .02 .10
307 Mario Chitarroni .02 .10
308 Bruno Zarillo .02 .10
309 Armando Chelodi .02 .10
310 Carmine Vani .02 .10
311 Martin McKay .02 .10
312 Scott O'Connor .02 .10
313 John McCrone .02 .10
314 Stephen Cooper .02 .10
315 Mike O'Connor .02 .10
316 Chris Kelland .02 .10
317 Graham Waghorn .02 .10
318 Nicky Chinn .02 .10
319 Damian Smith .02 .10
320 Tim Cranston .02 .10
321 Scott Morrisson .02 .10
322 Antony Johnson .02 .10
323 Tony Hand .05 .15
324 Kevin Conway .02 .10
325 Rick Fera .02 .10
326 Doug McEwen .02 .10
327 Scott Neil .02 .10
328 John Iredale .02 .10
329 Iain Robertson .02 .10
330 Ian Cooper .02 .10
331 Bill Ranford DT .08 .25
332 Jarmo Myllys DT .08 .25
333 Dominik Hasek DT .60 1.50
334 Tommy Soderstrom DT .08 .25
335 Teppo Numminen DT .08 .25
336 Mihail Tatarinov DT .05 .15
337 Paul Coffey DT .40 1.00
338 Chris Chelios DT .40 1.00
339 Brian Leetch DT .40 1.00
340 Al MacInnis DT .40 1.00
341 Vladimir Malakhov DT .02 .10
342 Kevin Hatcher DT .02 .10
343 Jiri Slegr DT .05 .15
344 Wayne Gretzky DT 2.00 5.00
345 Teemu Selanne DT .60 1.50
346 Jari Kurri DT .20 .50
347 Brett Hull DT .60 1.50
348 Sergei Fedorov DT .60 1.50
349 Esa Tikkanen DT .08 .25
350 Mark Messier DT .60 1.50
351 Jaromir Jagr DT .75 2.00
352 Jeremy Roenick DT .40 1.00
353 Luc Robitaille DT .40 1.00
354 Tomas Sandstrom DT .08 .25
355 Peter Forsberg DT .75 2.00
356 Alexei Zhamnov DT .08 .25
357 Theo Fleury DT .40 1.00
358 Rick Tocchet DT .20 .50
359 Pat LaFontaine DT .20 .50
360 Eric Lindros DT .60 1.50
NNO Album 4.00 10.00

1995-96 Finnish Beckett Ad Cards

This eight-card set features color action player photos on a perforated sheet which measures approximately 3" by 9". The top half of the sheet contains the photo while the bottom half is a form to subscribe to the Finnish Beckett Hockey Monthly magazine. The backs are blank. Although these look like cards, they actually were meant to be folded in half and used as a protective covering for trading cards which were dispensed through vending machines in Finland during the 1995-96 season. The cards were not manufactured by Beckett, but by Semic, the company which produced the Finnish and Swedish versions of Beckett Hockey Monthly.

COMPLETE SET (8) 10.00 25.00
1 Saku Koivu 4.00 10.00
2 Jere Lehtinen 2.00 5.00
3 Ville Peltonen .75 2.00
4 Erik Hamalainen .75 2.00
5 Sami Kapanen 2.00 5.00
6 Marko Kiprusoff .75 2.00
7 Mika Stromberg .75 2.00
8 Marko Palo .75 2.00

1995-96 Finnish Jaa Kiekko Lehti Ad Cards

This eight-card set features color action photos on a perforated sheet which measures approximately 3" by 9". The top half of the sheet contains the photo of a popular Finnish national team member, while the bottom half is a form to subscribe to Jaa Kiekko Lehti, the leading hockey magazine in that country. The backs are blank. Although these look like cards when separated, they actually were meant to be folded in half and used as a protective barrier for trading cards which were dispensed through vending machines in Finland during the 1995-96 season. The cards were produced by Semic, and were numbered out of 8 on the front.

COMPLETE SET (8) 14.00 35.00
1 Jarmo Myllys 1.25 3.00
2 Jari Kurri 1.50 4.00
3 Saku Koivu 3.00 8.00
4 Teemu Selanne 6.00 15.00
5 Esa Tikkanen 1.25 3.00
6 Christian Ruuttu .75 2.00
7 Mika Nieminen .75 2.00
8 Timo Jutila .75 2.00

1995-96 Finnish SISU

This 400-card set features the players of Finland's top hockey circuit, the SM-Liiga. The cards were distributed in two series of 200 cards each, and in packs of eight cards. The fronts feature a full-bleed photo with the player's name ghosted along the bottom. The Saku Koivu Super Chase card was randomly inserted in series 1 packs at a rate of 1:600. The Koivu Super Bonus and Niinimaa Super Chase cards were found in series 2 packs at a rate of 1:480. The latter Koivu card could be redeemed to Leaf in Finland for an exclusive Koivu SISU Specials jumbo card. If redeemed, the Super Bonus card was returned with a punch hole. These cards trade for about half the unpunched.

COMPLETE SET (400) 20.00 50.00
COMPLETE SERIES 1 (200) 12.00 30.00
COMPLETE SERIES 2 (200) 8.00 20.00
1 HIFK, Team Card .02 .10
2 Kimmo Kapanen .02 .10
3 Juri Kuznetsov .02 .10
4 Simo Saarinen .02 .10
5 Roland Carlsson .02 .10
6 Veli-Pekka Fagerstrom .02 .10
7 Kristian Fagerstrom .02 .10
8 Mika Kortelainen .02 .10
9 Jari Laukkanen .02 .10
10 Juha Nurminen .02 .10
11 Markku Hurme .02 .10
12 Sami Kapanen .40 1.00
13 Darren Boyko .02 .10
14 Marko Ojanen .02 .10
15 HPK, Team Card .02 .10
16 Kari Rosenberg .08 .25
17 Petri Engman .02 .10
18 Niko Marttila .02 .10
19 Jari Haapamaki .02 .10
20 Marko Allen .02 .10
21 Erik Kakko .02 .10
22 Mikko Myllykoski .02 .10
23 Jani Hassinen .02 .10
24 Risto Jalo .08 .25
25 Juha Jarvenpaa .02 .10
26 Jari Kauppila .02 .10
27 Toni Makiaho .08 .25
28 Ilves, Team Card .02 .10
29 Jarmo Myllys .02 .10
30 Hannu Henriksson .02 .10
31 Petri Kokko .02 .10
32 Martti Jarventie .20 .50
33 Allan Measures .40 1.00
34 Pasi Huura .40 1.00
35 Janne Seva .40 1.00
36 Timmy Kiviaho .40 1.00
37 Reijo Mikkolainen .02 .10
38 Hannu Mattila .02 .10
39 Jari Virtanen .02 .10
40 Ossi [illegible] .02 .10
41 Juha Hautamaa .60 1.50
42 Jokerit, Team Card .02 .10
43 Ari Sulander .60 1.50
44 Santeri Immonen .02 .10
45 Pasi Sormunen .02 .10
46 Waltteri Immonen .02 .10
47 Mika Stromberg .08 .25
48 Kari Martikainen .02 .10
49 Tommi Sova .08 .25
50 Juha Lind .20 .50
51 Niko Halttunen .02 .10
52 Keijo Sailynoja .08 .25
53 Otakar Janecky .08 .25
54 Timo Saarikoski .02 .10
55 JYP HT, Team Card .02 .10
56 Ari-Pekka Siekkinen .08 .25
57 Vesa Ponto .02 .10
58 Kalle Koskinen .02 .10
59 Jouni Loponen .02 .10
60 Miska Kangasniemi .08 .25
61 Mika Paananen .02 .10
62 Markku Ikonen .02 .10
63 Kimmo Salminen .02 .10
64 Joni Lius .02 .10
65 Lasse Nieminen .02 .10
66 Janne Kurjenniemi .02 .10
67 Marko Virtanen .02 .10
68 KalPa, Team Card .02 .10
69 Jarkko Kortesoja .02 .10
70 Petri Matikainen .02 .10
71 Mika Laaksonen .02 .10
72 Kai Rautio .02 .10
73 Jarno Kultanen .20 .50
74 Miikka Ruokonen .02 .10
75 Jussi Tarvainen .02 .10
76 Mikko Honkonen .02 .10
77 Sami Simonen .02 .10
78 Petr Korinek .02 .10
79 Veli-Pekka Pekkarinen .02 .10
80 Pekka Tirkkonen .02 .10
81 Kiekko-Espoo, Team Card .02 .10
82 Iiro Itamies .08 .25
83 Tommi Nyyssonen .02 .10
84 Robert Salo .02 .10
85 Sami Nuutinen .02 .10
86 Timo Blomqvist .02 .10
87 Ismo Kuoppala .02 .10
88 Mikko Koivunoro .02 .10
89 Petro Koivunen .08 .25
90 Jarmo Muukkonen .02 .10
91 Sergei Prjahin .02 .10
92 Teemu Riihijarvi .08 .25
93 Juha Ikonen .02 .10
94 Lukko, Team Card .02 .10
95 Boris Rousson .20 .50
96 Vesa Salo .08 .25
97 Toni Porkka .02 .10
98 Mika Yli-Maenpaa .08 .25
99 Juha Riihijarvi .08 .25
100 Petri Latti .02 .10
101 Veli-Pekka Ahonen .02 .10
102 Mikko Peltola .02 .10
103 Kalle Sahlstedt .08 .25
104 Jari Torkki .02 .10
105 Jussi Kiuru .02 .10
106 Sakari Palsola .02 .10
107 Tappara, Team Card .02 .10
108 Ilpo Kauhanen .20 .50
109 Sami Lehtonen .02 .10
110 Pasi Petrilainen .02 .10
111 Pekka Laksola .02 .10
112 Tommi Haapsaari .02 .10
113 Ville Nieminen 1.25 3.00
114 Arto Kulmala .02 .10
115 Valeri Krykov .02 .10
116 Timo Nurmberg .02 .10
117 Aleksander Barkov .02 .10
118 Miikka Kemppi .02 .10
119 Marko Toivola .02 .10
120 Juha Vuorivirta .08 .25
121 TPS, Team Card .02 .10
122 Miikka Kiprusoff 4.00 10.00
123 Kimmo Timonen .20 .50
124 Sami Salo .02 .10
125 Kari Harila .02 .10
126 Tuomas Gronman .08 .25
127 Vjatsheslav Fandul .02 .10
128 Mika Alatalo .20 .50
129 Jukka Tiilikainen .02 .10
130 Kimmo Rintanen .15 .40
131 Hannes Hyvonen .20 .50
132 Simo Rouvali .02 .10
133 Harri Sillgren .02 .10
134 Harri Suvanto .02 .10
135 TuTo, Team Card .02 .10
136 Markus Korhonen .02 .10
137 Sebastian Sulku .02 .10
138 Jukka Suomalainen .02 .10
139 Timo Kulonen .02 .10
140 Risto Siltanen .08 .25
141 Sami Leinonen .02 .10
142 Juha Virtanen .02 .10
143 Jari Hirsimaki .02 .10
144 Jouni Tuominen .02 .10
145 Vesa Karjalainen .02 .10
146 Pekka Virta .02 .10
147 Jouko Myrra .02 .10
148 Assat, Team Card .02 .10
149 Kari Takko .20 .50
150 Timo Nykopp .02 .10
151 Harri Laurila .02 .10
152 Jarno Miikkulainen .02 .10
153 Pasi Peltonen .02 .10
154 Jari Korpisalo .02 .10
155 Teppo Kivela .02 .10
156 Jari Levonen .02 .10
157 Janne Virtanen .02 .10
158 Jarno Makela .02 .10
159 Mikael Kotkaniemi .02 .10
160 Ari Saarinen .02 .10
161 Boris Rousson AS .20 .50
162 Joni Lehto AS .05 .15
163 Marko Kiprusoff AS .08 .25
164 Jere Lehtinen AS .40 1.00
165 Saku Koivu AS 1.25 3.00
166 Kai Nurminen AS .20 .50
167 Ari Sulander AS .20 .50
168 Mika Stromberg AS .08 .25
169 All Stars/Kuusisto .02 .10
170 All Stars/Arkiomaa .02 .10
171 Otakar Janecky AS .08 .25
172 Ville Peltonen AS .20 .50
173 Milestones/Arima .02 .10
174 Milestones/Boyko .02 .10
175 Milestones/Friman .02 .10
176 Milestones/Heiskanen .02 .10
177 Milestones/Henriksson .02 .10
178 Milestones/Hamalainen .02 .10
179 Milestones/Jalo .02 .10
180 Timo Jutila AS .07 .20
181 Milestones/Jarvenpaa .02 .10
182 Milestones/Kuusisto .02 .10
183 Milestones/Laksola .02 .10
184 Milestones/Laurila .02 .10
185 Milestones/Lehtonen .02 .10
186 Milestones/Lindroos .02 .10
187 Milestones/Mikkolainen .02 .10
188 Milestones/Tommila .02 .10
189 Milestones/Torkki .02 .10
190 Milestones/Tuomenoksa .02 .10
191 Milestones/Vuori .02 .10
192 TPS, SM-kultaa .02 .10
193 Jokerit, SM-hopeaa .02 .10
194 Assat, SM-pronssia .02 .10
195 Jokerit, EM-kultaa .02 .10
196 TPS, EM-pronssia .02 .10
197 Kai Nurminen CL .15 .40
198 Veli-Pekka Kautonen CL .02 .10
199 Koivu Checklist .40 1.00
200 Kiprusoff Checklist .08 .25
201 HIFK, Fan Card .02 .10
202 Sakari Lindfors .20 .50
203 Lauri Puolanne .02 .10
204 Pertti Lehtonen .02 .10
205 Peter Ahola .02 .10
206 Jere Karalahti .20 .50
207 Kimmo Maki-Kokkila .02 .10
208 Tom Laaksonen .02 .10
209 Tero Hamalainen .02 .10
210 Miro Haapaniemi .02 .10
211 Toni Sihvonen .02 .10
212 Sami Laine .02 .10
213 Iiro Jarvi .08 .25
214 Pekka Tuomisto .02 .10
215 HPK, Fan Card .02 .10
216 Mika Pietila .08 .25
217 Tom Koivisto .02 .10
218 Tommi Hamalainen .02 .10
219 Kai Rautio .02 .10
220 Jani Nikko .08 .25
221 Mika Kannisto .02 .10
222 Jason Miller .02 .10
223 Niklas Hede .02 .10
224 Tony Virta .02 .10
225 Aleksander Andrijevski .02 .10
226 Mika Puhakka .02 .10
227 Timo Peltomaa .02 .10
228 Toni Saarinen .02 .10
229 Ilves, Fan Card .02 .10
230 Vesa Toskala 1.25 3.00
231 Pekka Kangasalusta .02 .10
232 Juha Lampinen .02 .10
233 Pasi Saarinen .02 .10
234 Teemu Vuorinen .02 .10
235 Jarno Peltonen .02 .10
236 Matti Kaipainen .02 .10
237 Semi Pekki .02 .10
238 Sami Karjalainen .02 .10
239 Juoni Lahtinen .02 .10
240 Pasi Maatanen .02 .10
241 Petri Murtovaara .02 .10
242 Tomi Hirvonen .02 .10
243 Mikko Eloranta .20 .50
244 Mika Arvaja .02 .10
245 Juha Jarvenpaa .08 .25
246 Jokerit, Fan Card .02 .10
247 Marko Rantanen .02 .10
248 Marko Tuulola .02 .10
249 Jani-Matti Loikala .02 .10
250 Antti-Jussi Niemi .20 .50
251 Janne Niinimaa .30 .75
252 Jari Lindroos .02 .10
253 Paso Saarela .02 .10
254 Juha Ylonen .30 .75
255 Mika Asikainen .08 .25
256 Eero Somervuori .40 1.00
257 Tero Lehtera .02 .10
258 Jukka Penttinen .02 .10
259 Petri Varis .20 .50
260 JyP HT, Fan Card .02 .10
261 Marko Leinonen .02 .10
262 Jan Latvala .02 .10
263 Jukka Laamanen .02 .10
264 Pekka Poikolainen .02 .10
265 Thomas Sjogren .02 .10
266 Pasi Kangas .08 .25
267 Tini Koivunen .02 .10
268 Lasse Jamsen .02 .10
269 Petri Kujala .02 .10
270 Mikko Inkinen .02 .10
271 Kalpa, Fan Card .02 .10
272 Pasi Kuivalainen .20 .50
273 Pasi Kolehmainen .02 .10
274 Reijo Ruotsalainen .08 .25
275 Jarkko Glad .02 .10
276 Ivan Vlzek .02 .10
277 Jarmo Levonen .02 .10
278 Janne Kekalainen .02 .10
279 Veli-Pekka Nutikka .20 .50
280 Mikko Konttila .08 .25
281 Janne Virtanen .02 .10
282 Pasi Kemppainen .02 .10
283 Kiekko-Espoo, Fan Card .02 .10
284 Mika Rautio .08 .25
285 Kari Haakana .02 .10
286 Teemu Sillanpaa .02 .10
287 Timo Nykopp .02 .10
288 Mikko [illegible] .02 .10
289 Tero Tiainen .02 .10
290 Joonas Jaaskelainen .02 .10
291 Lubomir Kolnik .08 .25
292 Arto Sirvio .02 .10
293 Iikka Sinisalo .08 .25
294 Timo Hirvonen .02 .10
295 Arto Kuki .02 .10
296 Timo Norppa .02 .10
297 Lukko, Fan Card .02 .10
298 Timo Kauharren .02 .10
299 Joni Lehto .02 .10
300 Jarno Miikkulainen .02 .10
301 Kimmo Lotvonen .02 .10
302 Robert Nordmark .02 .10
303 Riku Kallioniemi .02 .10
304 Matti Raunio .02 .10
305 Tommi Turunen .02 .10
306 Jarkko Varvio .05 .15
307 Tero Arkiomaa .02 .10
308 Harri Lonnberg .08 .25
309 Mikko Luovi .02 .10
310 Tappara, Fan Card .02 .10
311 Jussi Markkanen .75 2.00
312 Timo Jutila .02 .10
313 Jukka Ollila .02 .10
314 Antti Rahkonen .02 .10
315 Derek Mayer .02 .10
316 Petri Kalteva .02 .10
317 Jarkko Nikander .02 .10
318 Pauli Jarvinen .02 .10
319 Mikko Helisten .02 .10
320 Ari Haanpaa .02 .10
321 Markus Oijennus .02 .10
322 Janne Ojanen .15 .40
323 TPS, Fan Card .02 .10
324 Fredrik Norrena .15 .40
325 Mika Lehtinen .02 .10
326 Karlis Skrastins .20 .50
327 Marru Laapas .02 .10
328 Antti Aalto .20 .50
329 Teemu Numminen .02 .10
330 Tommi Miettinen .02 .10
331 Lasse Pirjeta .02 .10
332 Miikka Rousu .02 .10
333 Marko Makinen .02 .10
334 Mikko Markkanen .02 .10
335 Tomi Kallio .40 1.00
336 Miika Elomo .20 .50
337 Sami Mettovaara .02 .10
338 TuTo, Fan Card .02 .10
339 Jukka Tammi .15 .40
340 Kari-Pekka Friman .02 .10
341 Veli-Pekka Hard .02 .10
342 Antti Tirkkonen .02 .10
343 Jukka Seppo .02 .10
344 Kim Ahlroos .02 .10
345 Marto Poulsen .02 .10
346 Juha Kuusisaari .02 .10
347 Mikko Laaksonen .02 .10
348 Tuomas Jalava .02 .10
349 Tommi Pullola .08 .25
350 Tuomas Kalliomaki .02 .10
351 Assat, Fan Card .02 .10
352 Karri Kivi .02 .10
353 Olli Kaski .02 .10
354 Jouni Vento .02 .10
355 Tommi Rajamaki .08 .25
356 Jokke Heinanen .02 .10
357 Tomas Kapusta .02 .10
358 Jaroslav Otevrel .02 .10
359 Timo Salonen .02 .10
360 Pekka Virta .02 .10
361 Vesa Goman .02 .10
362 Pekka Peltola .02 .10
363 Rauli Raitanen .02 .10
364 Pasi Tuominen .02 .10
365 Kari Syvasalmi .02 .10
366 Timo Hakanen .02 .10
367 Foreigners/Andrijevski .02 .10
368 Foreigners/Barkov .02 .10
369 Foreigners/Boyko .02 .10
370 Foreigners/Fandul .02 .10
371 Foreigners/Janecky .02 .10
372 Foreigners/Kapusta .02 .10
373 Foreigners/Kolnik .02 .10
374 Foreigners/Korinek .02 .10
375 Foreigners/Mayer .02 .10
376 Foreigners/Measures .02 .10
377 Foreigners/Miller .02 .10
378 Foreigners/Nordmark .02 .10
379 Foreigners/Otevrel .02 .10
380 Foreigners/Prjahin .02 .10
381 Foreigners/Rousson .08 .25
382 Foreigners/Sjogren .02 .10
383 Foreigners/Skrastins .02 .10
384 Foreigners/Vlzek .02 .10
385 Vladimir Jursinov CO .02 .10
386 Hannu Aravirta CO .02 .10
387 Veli-Pekka Ketola CO .08 .25
388 Vaclav Sykora CO .02 .10
389 Hannu Kapanen CO .02 .10
390 Kari Savolainen CO .02 .10
391 Harri Rindell CO .02 .10
392 Anatoli Bogdanov .02 .10
393 Sakari Pietilla .02 .10
394 Jukka Rautakorpi .02 .10
395 Harri Jalava .02 .10
396 Vladimir Jursinov Jr. .02 .10
397 Jere Lehtinen CL .20 .50
398 Checklist 251-300 .02 .10
399 Checklist 301-350 .02 .10
400 Koivu Checklist .40 1.00
NNOA Saku Koivu Super Bonus 10.00 20.00
(SISU logo upper right
NNOB Saku Koivu Super Bonus
(SISU logo upper left
NNO Saku Koivu Jumbo 2.00 5.00
NNO Janne Niinimaa Super Chase 4.00 10.00
NNO Saku Koivu Super Chase 10.00 25.00

1995-96 Finnish SISU Double Trouble

This eight card set features action shots of the top two players from the teams of the SM-Liiga. The cards were randomly inserted at a rate of 1:17 series 2 packs.

COMPLETE SET (8) 8.00 20.00
STATED ODDS 1:17 SERIES 2
1 Tuomas Gronman 1.25 3.00

Kimmo Timonen
2 Waltteri Immonen 1.25 3.00
Mika Stromberg
3 Olli Kaski 1.25 3.00
Karri Kivi
4 Joni Lehto 1.25 3.00
Robert Nordmark
5 Peter Ahola 1.25 3.00
Pertti Lehtonen
6 Timo Blomqvist 1.25 3.00
Sami Nuutinen
7 Reijo Ruotsalainen 1.25 3.00
Ivan Vizek
8 Timo Jutila 1.25 3.00
Pekka Laksola

1995-96 Finnish SISU Drafted Dozen

Randomly inserted at a rate of 1:19 series 2 packs, this set depicts a dozen players from the SM-Liiga who were selected in the NHL Entry Draft.

COMPLETE SET (12) 8.00 25.00
STATED ODDS 1:19 SERIES 2
1 Aki Berg .75 2.00
2 Teemu Riihijarvi .40 1.00
3 Miika Elomo .75 2.00
4 Marko Makinen .40 1.00
5 Tomi Kallio 1.25 3.00
6 Sami Kapanen 1.50 4.00
7 Vesa Toskala 2.00 5.00
8 Miikka Kiprusoff 6.00 15.00
9 Timo Hakanen .40 1.00
10 Juha Vuorivirta .40 1.00
11 Tomi Hirvonen .40 1.00
12 Mikko Markkanen .40 1.00

1995-96 Finnish SISU Ghost Goalies

This 10-card set focuses on the top netminders of the SM-Liiga. The cards were randomly inserted at a rate of 1:24 series 1 packs.

COMPLETE SET (10) 16.00 40.00
STATED ODDS 1:24 SERIES 1
1 Sakari Lindfors 2.00 5.00
2 Boris Rousson 1.50 4.00
3 Ari Sulander 2.00 5.00
4 Kari Takko 1.50 4.00
5 Fredrik Norrena 1.50 4.00
6 Kari Rosenberg 1.50 4.00
7 Ari-Pekka Siekkinen 1.50 4.00
8 Jukka Tammi 1.50 4.00
9 Pasi Kuivalainen 1.50 4.00
10 Ilpo Kauhanen 1.50 4.00

1995-96 Finnish SISU Gold Cards

This 24-card set celebrates the players who earned Finland's first major title by winning the 1995 World Championship. The cards were distributed over both series in a scattered (i.e., not 1-12 and 13-24) fashion. The cards were randomly inserted at a rate of 1:10 series 1 packs and 1:9 series 2 packs.

COMPLETE SET (24) 24.00 60.00
STATED ODDS 1:10 SERIES 1/1:9 SERIES 2
1 Title Card .75 2.00
2 Jarmo Myllys 1.50 4.00
3 Ari Sulander 1.50 4.00
4 Jukka Tammi 1.50 4.00
5 Erik Hamalainen .75 2.00
6 Timo Jutila .75 2.00
7 Marko Kiprusoff .75 2.00
8 Janne Niinimaa 1.50 4.00
9 Petteri Nummelin .75 2.00
10 Mika Stromberg .75 2.00
11 Hannu Virta .75 2.00
12 Raimo Helminen .75 2.00
13 Sami Kapanen 2.00 5.00
14 Esa Keskinen .75 2.00
15 Saku Koivu 6.00 15.00
16 Tero Lehtera .75 2.00
17 Jere Lehtinen 3.00 8.00
18 Mika Nieminen .75 2.00
19 Janne Ojanen .75 2.00
20 Marko Palo .75 2.00
21 Ville Peltonen 1.25 3.00
22 Raimo Summanen .75 2.00
23 Antti Tormanen .75 2.00
24 Juha Ylonen 1.25 3.00

1995-96 Finnish SISU Limited

This 108-card set is the first super-premium issue released in Europe. The cards are printed on 24-point stock and picture the elite athletes of the Finnish SM-Liiga. Production was announced as 7,500 individually numbered boxes. Each box contained 18, 5-card "packs". These packs were actually boxes themselves, and pictured either Saku Koivu, Teemu Selanne or Esa Tikkanen. The card fronts have a color photo of the player over his ghosted close-up in the background. The back contains another photo as well as a brief bio in Finnish and the Leaf trademark. Several NHLers who played here during the 1994 lockout are featured, including Selanne, Jari Kurri, and Koivu. The Koivu Line super chase card was randomly inserted 1:219 and was serial numbered out of 720.

COMPLETE SET (108) 20.00 40.00
1 Fredrik Norrena .20 .50
2 Hannu Virta .15 .40
3 Petteri Nummelin .07 .20
4 Tuomas Gronman .15 .40
5 Marko Kiprusoff .15 .40
6 Saku Koivu 2.00 5.00
7 Raimo Summanen .15 .40
8 Esa Keskinen .15 .40
9 Jere Lehtinen 1.25 3.00
10 Ari Sulander .30 .75
11 Waltteri Immonen .07 .20
12 Mika Stromberg .15 .40
13 Janne Niinimaa .40 1.00
14 Otakar Janecky .15 .40
15 Teemu Selanne 4.00 10.00
16 Jari Kurri 1.25 3.00
17 Antti Tormanen .15 .40
18 Petri Varis .30 .75
19 Kari Takko .30 .75
20 Olli Kaski .07 .20
21 Rauli Raitanen .07 .20
22 Jari Korpisalo .07 .20
23 Teppo Kivela .07 .20
24 Jokke Heinanen .07 .20
25 Arto Javanainen .07 .20
26 Jari Levonen .07 .20
27 Arto Heiskanen .07 .20
28 Jarmo Myllys .40 1.00
29 Boris Rousson .20 .50
30 Jarmo Kuusisto .07 .20
31 Joni Lehto .07 .20
32 Robert Nordmark .07 .20
33 Tero Arkiomaa .07 .20
34 Jari Torkki .07 .20
35 Juha Riihijarvi .15 .40
36 Matti Forss .07 .20
37 Sakari Lindfors .30 .75
38 Pertti Lehtonen .07 .20
39 Simo Saarinen .07 .20
40 Esa Tikkanen .40 1.00
41 Ville Peltonen .40 1.00
42 Christian Ruuttu .15 .40
43 Mika Kortelainen .07 .20
44 Darren Boyko .07 .20
45 Iiro Jarvi .15 .40
46 Ari-Pekka Siekkinen .20 .50
47 Harri Laurila .07 .20
48 Jouni Loponen .07 .20
49 Joni Lius .07 .20
50 Jari Lindroos .07 .20
51 Risto Kurkinen .07 .20
52 Thomas Sjogren .07 .20
53 Marko Virtanen .07 .20
54 Michael Nylander .40 1.00
55 Mika Rautio .20 .50
56 Sami Nuutinen .07 .20
57 Peter Ahola .07 .20
58 Timo Blomqvist .07 .20
59 Ikka Sinisalo .15 .40
60 Petro Koivunen .15 .40
61 Sergei Prjahin .07 .20
62 Tero Lehtera .07 .20
63 Mariusz Czerkawski .40 1.00
64 Pasi Kuivalainen .30 .75
65 Kimmo Timonen .40 1.00
66 Reijo Ruotsalainen .15 .40
67 Vesa Salo .15 .40
68 Petr Korinek .07 .20
69 Marko Jantunen .15 .40
70 Pekka Tirkkonen .07 .20
71 Janne Kekalainen .07 .20
72 Sami Kapanen .75 2.00
73 Timo Jutila .07 .20
74 Pekka Laksola .07 .20
75 Janne Gronvall .15 .40
76 Jiri Kucera .07 .20
77 Janne Ojanen .20 .50
78 Pauli Jarvinen .07 .20
79 Ari Haanpaa .07 .20
80 Aleksander Barkov .07 .20
81 Theo Fleury 1.25 3.00
82 Kari Rosenberg .15 .40
83 Janne Laukkanen .20 .50
84 Jani Nikko .15 .40
85 Mika Lartama .07 .20
86 Kai Nurminen .30 .75
87 Tomas Kapusta .07 .20
88 Marko Palo .07 .20
89 Jarkko Varvio .15 .40
90 Risto Jalo .15 .40
91 Jukka Tammi .20 .50
92 Risto Siltanen .15 .40
93 Teppo Numminen .30 .75
94 Marco Poulsen .07 .20
95 Jukka Seppo .07 .20
96 Vesa Karjalainen .07 .20
97 Ted Donato .15 .40
98 Juha Virtanen .07 .20
99 Jari Hirsimaki .07 .20
100 Vesa Toskala 2.50 5.00
101 Jyrki Lumme .40 1.00
102 Hannu Henriksson .07 .20
103 Allan Measures .07 .20
104 Timo Peltomaa .07 .20
105 Juha Hautamaa .07 .20
106 Mikko Makela .15 .40
107 Juha Jarvenpaa .07 .20
108 Semi Pekki .07 .20
NNO Koivu Line Super Chase 10.00 25.00

1995-96 Finnish SISU Limited Leaf Gallery

The nine cards in this set were randomly inserted at a rate of 1 in 6 packs of SISU Limited. The fronts feature a dynamic action photo surrounded by a refractive holofoil border. The cards are numbered of 9 on the front. The backs display a gold-foil etched portrait of the player.

COMPLETE SET (9) 10.00 15.00
STATED ODDS 1:6
1 Jyrki Lumme .75 2.00
2 Janne Laukkanen .75 2.00
3 Michael Nylander 1.25 3.00
4 Janne Ojanen .75 2.00
5 Peter Ahola .75 2.00
6 Kari Takko 1.25 3.00
7 Hannu Virta .75 2.00
8 Juha Lind .75 2.00
9 Sakari Lindfors 1.25 3.00

1995-96 Finnish SISU Limited Signed and Sealed

The nine cards in this set were randomly inserted at a rate of 1 in 9 SISU Limited packs. The set features a number of current and former NHLers. The cards feature an action photo printed on a silver foil background. The player's "signature" is embossed in gold foil across the bottom of the photo. The backs feature another photo and are numbered out of 9.

COMPLETE SET (9) 20.00 25.00
STATED ODDS 1:9
1 Sami Kapanen 1.25 3.00
2 Christian Ruuttu .75 2.00
3 Teemu Selanne 7.50 15.00
4 Aki Berg .75 2.00
5 Joni Lehto .75 2.00
6 Teppo Numminen .75 2.00
7 Jari Kurri 2.00 5.00
8 Esa Tikkanen 1.25 3.00
9 Theo Fleury 2.00 5.00

1995-96 Finnish SISU Painkillers

Randomly inserted in series 1 packs at a rate of 1:15, these eight cards highlight some of the dominant snipers of the SM-Liiga.

COMPLETE SET (8) 3.00 8.00
STATED ODDS 1:15 SERIES 1
1 Jokke Heinanen .40 1.00
2 Mika Alatalo .40 1.00
3 Joni Lehto .40 1.00
4 Harri Lonnberg .40 1.00
5 Ville Peltonen .75 2.00
6 Harri Sillgren .40 1.00
7 Petri Varis .75 2.00
8 Marko Virtanen .40 1.00

1995-96 Finnish SISU Specials

Randomly inserted at a rate of 1:24 series 1 packs, these cards picture some of the most popular players in the SM-Liiga, including several NHLers who played there during the 1994 lockout.

COMPLETE SET (10) 16.00 40.00
STATED ODDS 1:24 SERIES 1
1 Petri Varis 1.25 3.00
2 Boris Rousson 1.25 3.00
3 Saku Koivu 6.00 15.00
4 Jari Kurri 3.00 8.00
5 Jarmo Kuusisto .75 2.00
6 Janne Ojanen .75 2.00
7 Jere Lehtinen 3.00 8.00
8 Peter Ahola .75 2.00
9 Jukka Seppo .75 2.00
10 Michael Nylander 1.25 3.00

1995-96 Finnish SISU Spotlights

This eight-card series shines the -- yes -- spotlight on some of the most offensively gifted players in the SM-Liiga. The cards were randomly inserted in series 2 packs at a rate of 1:8.

COMPLETE SET (8) 2.00 5.00
STATED ODDS 1:8 SERIES 2
1 Otakar Janecky .40 1.00
2 Jari Korpisalo .40 1.00
3 Juha Riihijarvi .40 1.00
4 Iiro Jarvi .40 1.00
5 Thomas Sjogren .40 1.00
6 Risto Jalo .40 1.00
7 Jari Hirsimaki .40 1.00
8 Juha Hautamaa .40 1.00

1995 Finnish Karjala World Championship Labels

This unusual set is comprised of 24 odd-sized (2 1/2 by 2 1/2") labels that were issued on the front of Karjala beer bottles in Finland to commemorate that country's first World Championship. Each label features an action photo of the player superimposed over the gold medal, with his name underneath. The Finnish national team logo is in the upper left corner, and World Champions, 1995 (in Finnish) is in the right. The labels are blank backed. As they are unnumbered, the labels are listed below in alphabetical order.

COMPLETE SET (24) 16.00 40.00
1 Erik Hamalainen .40 1.00
2 Raimo Helminen .40 1.00
3 Timo Jutila .60 1.50
4 Sami Kapanen .75 2.00
5 Esa Keskinen .40 1.00
6 Marko Kiprusoff .40 1.00
7 Saku Koivu 2.00 5.00
8 Tero Lehtera .40 1.00
9 Jere Lehtinen 1.25 3.00
10 Curt Lindstrom .40 1.00
11 Jarmo Myllys .75 2.00
12 Mika Nieminen .40 1.00
13 Janne Niinimaa .75 2.00
14 Petteri Nummelin .40 1.00
15 Janne Ojanen .40 1.00
16 Marko Palo .40 1.00
17 Ville Peltonen .60 1.50
18 Mika Stromberg .40 1.00
19 Ari Sulander .75 2.00
20 Raimo Summanen .40 1.00
21 Jukka Tammi .75 2.00
22 Antti Tormanen .40 1.00
23 Hannu Virta .60 1.50
24 Juha Ylonen .60 1.50

1995 Finnish Kellogg's

This six-card set was issued as a one-card-per-box premium in Kellogg's cereals in Finland. The cards are about half the size of a standard card.

COMPLETE SET (6) 12.00 30.00
1 Jarmo Myllys 2.00 5.00
2 Marko Kiprusoff 1.25 3.00
3 Hannu Virta 1.25 3.00
4 Ville Peltonen 1.25 3.00
5 Saku Koivu 6.00 15.00
6 Sami Kapanen 2.00 5.00

1995 Finnish Semic World Championships

This 240 standard-size card set features players from Finland and other countries who have taken part in international competition. Subsets include All Stars, Maalivahti Extra and Future Stars.

COMPLETE SET (240) 20.00 50.00
1 Pasi Kuivalainen .07 .20
2 Marko Kiprusoff .05 .15
3 Tuomas Gronman .05 .15
4 Erik Hamalainen .02 .10
5 Timo Jutila .05 .15
6 Pasi Sormunen .02 .10
7 Waltteri Immonen .05 .15
8 Janne Ojanen .05 .15
9 Esa Keskinen .05 .15
10 Kimmo Timonen .08 .25
11 Saku Koivu .40 1.00
12 Janne Laukkanen .08 .25
13 Marko Palo .02 .10
14 Raimo Helminen .02 .10
15 Mika Alatalo .08 .25
16 Ville Peltonen .15 .40
17 Jari Kurri .30 .75
18 Jari Korpisalo .05 .15
19 Kimmo Rintanen .05 .15
20 Jere Lehtinen .40 1.00
21 Kalle Sahlstedt .05 .15
22 Christian Ruuttu .05 .15
23 Hannu Virta .05 .15
24 Sami Kapanen .20 .50
25 Marko Tuulola .02 .10
26 Mika Stromberg .05 .15
27 Tero Lehtera .05 .15
28 Petri Varis .05 .15
29 Mikko Peltola .02 .10
30 Jukka Tammi .08 .25
31 Tero Arkiomaa .02 .10
32 Olli Kaski .02 .10
33 Pekka Laksola .02 .10
34 Mika Valila .02 .10
35 Jarmo Myllys .08 .25
36 Harri Laurila .02 .10
37 Teppo Numminen .08 .25
38 Jyrki Lumme .07 .20
39 Petteri Nummelin .02 .10
40 Mika Nieminen .08 .25
41 Teemu Selanne .60 1.50
42 Mikko Makela .05 .15
43 Esa Tikkanen .15 .40
44 Jarkko Varvio .05 .15
45 Vesa Viitakoski .05 .15
46 Juha Riihijarvi .05 .15
47 Markus Ketterer .08 .25
48 Mikko Haapakoski .02 .10
49 Antti Tormanen .05 .15
50 Timo Peltomaa .02 .10
51 Rauli Raitanen .02 .10
52 Roger Nordstrom .02 .10
53 Tommy Salo .20 .50
54 Tommy Soderstrom .20 .50
55 Magnus Svensson .05 .15
56 Fredrik Stillman .02 .10
57 Nicklas Lidstrom .40 1.00
58 Roger Johansson .02 .10
59 Kenny Jonsson .20 .50
60 Peter Andersson .02 .10
61 Tommy Sjodin .05 .15
62 Mats Sundin .40 1.00
63 Jonas Bergqvist .05 .15
64 Peter Forsberg .75 2.00
65 Roger Hansson .02 .10
66 Jorgen Jonsson .02 .10
67 Charles Berglund .02 .10
68 Mikael Johansson .02 .10
69 Tomas Forslund .05 .15
70 Andreas Dackell .08 .25
71 Stefan Ornskog .02 .10
72 Mikael Andersson .05 .15
73 Jan Larsson .02 .10
74 Patrik Carnback .05 .15
75 Hakan Loob .08 .25
76 Patrik Juhlin .08 .25
77 Bill Ranford .20 .50
78 Ed Belfour .60 1.50
79 Rob Blake .20 .50
80 Yves Racine .05 .15
81 Steve Smith .05 .15
82 Paul Coffey .40 1.00
83 Larry Murphy .20 .50
84 Mark Tinordi .05 .15
85 Al MacInnis .40 1.00
86 Paul Kariya .75 2.00
87 Joe Sakic .75 2.00
88 Brendan Shanahan .60 1.50
89 Luc Robitaille .40 1.00
90 Rod Brind'Amour .30 .75
91 Shayne Corson .08 .25
92 Mike Ricci .08 .25
93 Mario Lemieux ERR 2.00 5.00
Name
94 Eric Lindros .75 2.00
95 Russ Courtnall .08 .25
96 Theo Fleury .40 1.00
97 Mark Messier .60 1.50
98 Rick Tocchet .20 .50
99 Wayne Gretzky 2.00 5.00
100 Steve Larmer .08 .25
101 Brett Lindros .08 .25
102 John Vanbiesbrouck .40 1.00
103 Craig Wolanin .05 .15
104 Chris Chelios .40 1.00
105 Brian Leetch .40 1.00
106 Kevin Hatcher .07 .20
107 Craig Janney .08 .25
108 Tim Sweeney .05 .15
109 Shawn Chambers .05 .15
110 Scott Young .08 .25
111 John Lilley .05 .15
112 Joe Sacco .05 .15
113 Brett Hull .60 1.50
114 Pat LaFontaine .20 .50
115 Joel Otto .08 .25
116 Mike Modano .60 1.50
117 Tony Granato .05 .15
118 Jeremy Roenick .60 1.50
119 Jeff Lazaro .05 .15
120 Brian Mullen .05 .15
121 Mihail Shtalenkov .20 .50
122 Valeri Ivannikov .02 .10
123 Andrei Nikolishin .08 .25
124 Ilya Byakin .05 .15
125 Alexander Smirnov .02 .10
126 Dimitri Yushkevich .08 .25
127 Sergei Shendelev .02 .10
128 Alexei Zhitnik .05 .15
129 Igor Ulanov .05 .15
130 Dmitri Frolov .02 .10
131 Valeri Kamensky .15 .40
132 Igor Fedulov .02 .10
133 Andrei Kovalenko .08 .25
134 Valeri Bure .20 .50
135 Sergei Berezin .15 .40
136 Alexei Yashin .20 .50
137 Vyatcheslav Kozlov .15 .40
138 Vyatcheslav Bykov .08 .25
139 Andrei Khomutov .08 .25
140 Petr Briza .08 .25
141 Dominik Hasek .60 1.50
142 Roman Turek .30 .75
143 Jan Vopat .05 .15
144 Drahomir Kadlec .05 .15
145 Petr Pavlas .02 .10
146 Frantisek Kucera .05 .15
147 Jiri Veber .02 .10
148 David Vyborny .05 .15
149 Radek Toupal .05 .15
150 Jiri Kucera .05 .15
151 Richard Zemlicka .05 .15
152 Martin Rucinsky .08 .25
153 Jiri Dolezal .02 .10
154 Josef Beranek .05 .15
155 Martin Prochazka .05 .15
156 Tomas Srsen .05 .15
157 David Bruk .02 .10
158 Jaromir Jagr .75 2.00
159 Jan Caloun .05 .15
160 Martin Straka .20 .50
161 Roman Horak .02 .10
162 Frantisek Musil .05 .15
163 Petr Hrbek .02 .10
164 Jan Alino .02 .10
165 Joseph Heiss .07 .20
166 Peter Gulda .02 .10
167 Jayson Meyer .02 .10
168 Ernst Kopf .02 .10
169 Raimund Hilger .02 .10
170 Richard Bohm .02 .10
171 Michael Rosati .08 .25
172 Michael DeAngelis .02 .10
173 Anthony Circelli .02 .10
174 Gaetano Orlando .02 .10
175 Lucio Topatigh .02 .10
176 Martin Pavlu .02 .10
177 Jim Marthinsen .08 .25
178 Petter Salsten .02 .10
179 Tommy Jacobson .02 .10
180 Morten Finsted .02 .10
181 Tom Andersen .02 .10
182 Manus Rath .02 .10
183 Michael Puschacher .05 .15
184 James Burton .02 .10
185 Michael Shea .02 .10
186 Dieter Kalt .02 .10
187 Manfred Muhr .02 .10
188 Andreas Puschnig .02 .10
189 Renato Tosio .02 .10
190 Doug Honneger .02 .10
191 Felix Hollenstein .02 .10
192 Jorg Eberle .02 .10
193 Gil Montandon .02 .10
194 Roberto Triulzi .02 .10
195 Petri Ylonen .05 .15
196 Bruno Maynort .02 .10
197 Michel LeBlanc .02 .10
198 Benoit Laborte .04 .10
199 Christophe Ville .02 .10
200 Antoine Richer .02 .10
201 Bill Ranford AS .20 .50
202 Timo Jutila AS .05 .15
203 Magnus Svensson AS .05 .15
204 Jari Kurri AS .30 .75
205 Saku Koivu AS .40 1.00
206 Paul Kariya AS .75 2.00
207 Jarmo Myllys ME .08 .25
208 Bill Ranford ME .20 .50
209 Roger Nordstrom ME .02 .10
210 Guy Hebert ME .30 .75
211 Mihail Shtalenkov ME .20 .50
212 Tommy Soderstrom ME .20 .50
213 Petr Briza ME .08 .25
214 Dominik Hasek ME .60 1.50
215 Tom Barrasso ME .15 .40
216 Jukka Tammi ME .05 .15
217 John Vanbiesbrouck ME .40 1.00
218 Mike Richter ME .40 1.00
219 Saku Koivu Special .40 1.00
220 Saku Koivu Special .40 1.00
221 Saku Koivu Special .40 1.00
222 Saku Koivu Special .40 1.00
223 Saku Koivu Special .40 1.00
224 Saku Koivu Special .40 1.00
225 Tuomas Gronman FS .05 .15
226 Jani Nikko FS .02 .10
227 Janne Niinimaa FS .40 1.00
228 Jukka Tiilikainen FS .02 .10
229 Kimmo Rintanen FS .05 .15
230 Ville Peltonen FS .15 .40
231 Sami Kapanen FS .30 .75
232 Jere Lehtinen FS .40 1.00
233 Kimmo Timonen FS .05 .15
234 Jonni Vauhkonen FS .05 .15
235 Juha Lind FS .08 .25
236 Tommi Miettinen FS .05 .15
237 Jere Karalahti FS .08 .25
238 Antti Aalto FS .08 .26
239 Teemu Kohvakka FS .02 .10
240 Niko Mikkola FS .02 .10

1996-97 Finnish SISU Redline

This set featuring players of Finland's SM-Liiga is complete at 200 cards; although a second series was intended, it was not produced as a result of disappointing sales for the first series. The Super Chase and Super Bonus cards were randomly inserted at the rate of 1:240 packs. If found, they could be exchanged by mail with Leaf for one of five Silver Signature goalie cards that were limited to 400 copies. We have no further information on these Silver Signature cards. Anyone who can provide photocopies or other documentation of these cards is asked to email hockeymag@beckett.com.

COMPLETE SET (200) 8.00 20.00
1 Checklist (1-50) .02 .10
2 Sakari Lindfors .20 .50
3 Peter Ahola .05 .15
4 Jere Karalahti .20 .50
5 Pertti Lehtonen .02 .10
6 Lauri Puolanne .02 .10
7 Sami Laine .08 .25
8 Tommy Kiviaho .02 .10
9 Markku Hurme .02 .10
10 Jari Laukkanen .02 .10
11 Tero Nyman .02 .10
12 Toni Sihvonen .02 .10
13 Mika Kortelainen .05 .15
14 Tero Hamalainen .02 .10
15 Mika Pietila .08 .25
16 Erik Kakko .02 .10
17 Tom Koivisto .02 .10
18 Jani Nikko .08 .25
19 Risto Jalo .08 .25
20 Aleksander Andrievski .05 .15
21 Jari Kauppila .02 .10
22 Jarkko Savijoki .02 .10
23 Toni Makiaho .02 .10
24 Mika Kannisto .02 .10
25 Mika Puhakka .02 .10
26 Toni Saarinen .02 .10
27 Vesa Toskala .40 1.00
28 Teemu Vuorinen .02 .10
29 Petri Kokko .02 .10
30 Pekka Kangasalusta .02 .10
31 Tommi Kahiluoto .02 .10
32 Jarno Peltonen .02 .10
33 Mika Arvaja .02 .10
34 Matti Kaipainen .02 .10
35 Hannu Mattila .02 .10
36 Tomi Hirvonen .02 .10
37 Jouni Lahtinen .02 .10
38 Jari Suorsa .02 .10
39 Juha Jarvenpaa . .07 .20
40 Semi Pekki .02 .10
41 Ari Sulander .20 .50
42 Mika Stromberg .08 .25
43 Marko Tuulola .02 .10
44 Pasi Sormunen .02 .10
45 Waltteri Immonen .05 .15
46 Jukka Penttinen .02 .10
47 Petri Varis .20 .50
48 Keijo Sailynoja .08 .25
49 Tero Lehtera .05 .15
50 Checklist (51-100) .02 .10
51 Jari Lindroos .05 .15
52 Ismo Kuoppala .02 .10
53 Juha Ylonen .20 .50
54 Pasi Saarela .05 .15
55 Marko Leinonen .02 .10
56 Kalle Koskinen .02 .10
57 J-P Laamanen .02 .10
58 Jouni Loponen .02 .10
59 Pekka Poikolainen .02 .10
60 Jan Latvala .02 .10
61 Timo Ahmaoja .02 .10
62 Mika Paananen .02 .10
63 Kimmo Salminen .02 .10
64 Lasse Jamsen .02 .10
65 Thomas Sjogren .07 .20
66 Juha Viinikainen .02 .10
67 Mikko Inkinen .02 .10
68 Toni Koivunen .02 .10
69 Pasi Kuivalainen .08 .25
70 Tommi Kovanen .02 .10
71 Jermu Pisto .02 .10
72 Ivan Vlzek .02 .10
73 Mika Laaksonen .02 .10
74 Miikka Ruokonen .02 .10
75 Sami Simonen .02 .10
76 Mikko Honkonen .02 .10
77 Veli-Pekka Nutikka .20 .50
78 Arto Sirvio .02 .10
79 Janne Kekalainen .02 .10
80 Jarno Levonen .02 .10
81 Jussi Tarvainen .02 .10
82 Iiro Itamies .08 .25
83 Tommi Nyyssonen .02 .10
84 Kari Haakana .02 .10
85 Jarmo Muukkonen .02 .10
86 Tero Nissinen .02 .10
87 Tero Tiainen .02 .10
88 Joonas Jaaskelainen .02 .10
89 Juha Ikonen .02 .10
90 Timo Norppa .02 .10
91 Teemu Riihijarvi .08 .25
92 Mikko Koivunoro .02 .10
93 Sergei Priakhin .05 .15
94 Timo Hirvonen .02 .10
95 Boris Rousson .20 .50
96 Kimmo Lotvonen .02 .10
97 Riku Kallioniemi .02 .10
98 Martti Jarventie .15 .40
99 Mikko Luovi .07 .20
100 Checklist (101-150) .02 .10
101 Kalle Sahlstedt .08 .25
102 Sakari Palsola .02 .10
103 Tommi Turunen .02 .10
104 Petri Latti .02 .10
105 Jonni Vauhkonen .05 .15
106 Veli-Pekka Ahonen .02 .10
107 Jarl Torkki .05 .15
108 Jarkko Varvio .05 .15
109 Matti Viitakoski .02 .10
110 Mikko Myllykoski .02 .10
111 Petri Peronmaa .02 .10
112 Vesa Ruotsalainen .02 .10
113 Timo Lohko .02 .10
114 Simo Liukka .02 .10
115 Juha-Pekka Rinkinen .02 .10
116 Timo Makinen .02 .10
117 Marko Ek .05 .15
118 Matti Nevalainen .02 .10
119 Ari Santanen .02 .10
120 Jonas Hemming .02 .10
121 Mika Karapuu .02 .10
122 Ilpo Kauhanen .20 .50
123 Sami-Ville Salomaa .02 .10
124 Antti Rahkonen .02 .10
125 Harri Laurilla .02 .10
126 Sami Lehtonen .02 .10
127 Pasi Petrilainen .08 .25
128 Arto Kulmala .02 .10
129 Jarkko Nikander .02 .10
130 Timo Nurmberg .02 .10
131 Tuomas Reijonen .02 .10
132 Aleksander Barkov .02 .10
133 Mika Niittymaki .02 .10
134 Valeri Krykov .02 .10
135 Fredrik Norrena .20 .50
136 Mika Lehtinen .02 .10
137 Sami Salo .20 .50
138 Riku-Petteri Lehtonen .02 .10
139 Mikko Sokka .02 .10
140 Manu Laapas .02 .10
141 Hannes Hyvonen .15 .40
142 Miikka Rousu .02 .10
143 Simo Rouvali .02 .10
144 Tommi Miettinen .02 .10
145 Kimmo Rintanen .20 .50
146 Tomi Kallio .20 .50
147 Antti Aalto .20 .50
148 Miika Elomo .20 .50
149 Kari Takko .20 .50
150 Checklist (151-200) .02 .10
151 Tommi Rajamaki .08 .25
152 Pasi Peltonen .02 .10
153 Karri Kivi .07 .20
154 Jokke Heinanen .02 .10
155 Teppo Kivela .02 .10
156 Vesa Goman .02 .10
157 Pekka Virta .02 .10
158 Pasi Tuominen .02 .10
159 Timo Hakanen .02 .10
160 Jari Levonen .02 .10
161 Jari Korpisalo .05 .15
162 Timo Salonen .02 .10
163 Jokerit .08 .25
164 Jokerit .02 .10
165 Jokerit .02 .10
166 Jokerit .02 .10
167 Jokerit .02 .10
168 Jokerit .02 .10
169 Jokerit .02 .10
170 Jokerit .02 .10
171 Jokerit .02 .10
172 Jokerit .02 .10
173 Jokerit .02 .10
174 Jokerit .02 .10
175 Ari Sulander .20 .50
176 Joni Lehto .05 .15
177 Timo Jutila .05 .15
178 Mikko Peltola .02 .10
179 Juha Riihijarvi .08 .25
180 Petri Varis .20 .50
181 Boris Rousson .20 .50
182 Kimmo Timonen .20 .50
183 Mika Stromberg .08 .25
184 Jari Korpisalo .05 .15
185 Otakar Janecky .08 .25
186 Juha Lind .08 .25
187 Aarne Honkavaara .20 .50
188 Esko Niemi .02 .10
189 Raimo Kilpio .02 .10
190 Jarmo Wasama .02 .10
191 Lalli Partinen .02 .10
192 Urpo Ylonen .08 .25
193 Ilpo Koskela .20 .50
194 Jorma Vehmanen .02 .10
195 Pekka Marjamaki .02 .10
196 Veli-Pekka Ketola .08 .25
197 Matti Murto .02 .10
198 Juhani Tamminen .08 .25
199 Matti Hagman .07 .20
200 Mask CL .08 .25
NNO Kari Takko Super Bonus 2.00 5.00
NNO Juha Riihijarvi Chase 2.00 5.00

1996-97 Finnish SISU Redline At The Gala

This set of inserts showcases the 1995-96 award winners from the SM-Liiga. The cards were randomly inserted at a rate of 1:6 packs. The card fronts display the players in the tuxedos accepting the awards, while the backs show the player in action.

COMPLETE SET (8) 5.00 10.00
STATED ODDS 1:6
1 Petri Varis .75 2.00
2 Juha Riihijarvi .40 1.00
3 Waltteri Immonen .40 1.00
4 Jani Hurme 1.25 3.00
5 Pasi Kuivalainen .75 2.00
6 Mika Stromberg .40 1.00
7 Sakari Pietila .40 1.00
8 Ari Sulander .75 2.00

1996-97 Finnish SISU Redline Foil Parallels

Little is known about these cards beyond the confirmed checklist below. The skip numbering, and the odd player selection, suggests that a complete set might exist. Any additional information can be forwarded to hockeymag@beckett.com.

COMPLETE SET (25)
1 Checklist
2 Sakari Lindfors
27 Vesa Toskala
41 Ari Sulander
50 Checklist
69 Pasi Kuivalainen
95 Timo Hirvonen
100 Checklist

122 Ilpo Kauhanen
135 Fredrik Norrena
149 Kari Takko
150 Checklist
163 Jokerit
164 Jokerit
165 Jokerit
166 Jokerit
167 Jokerit
168 Jokerit
169 Jokerit
170 Jokerit
171 Jokerit
172 Jokerit
173 Jokerit
174 Jokerit
200 Mask Checklist

1996-97 Finnish SISU Redline Keeping It Green

This most difficult of the SISU inserts (1:60) features four top netminders in a set promoting environmental awareness, as well as keeping the light behind their nets from turning red.

COMPLETE SET (4) 15.00 30.00
STATED ODDS 1:60
1 Ari Sulander 4.00 10.00
2 Jani Hurme 7.50 15.00
3 Boris Rousson 4.00 10.00
4 Mika Pietila 4.00 10.00

1996-97 Finnish SISU Redline Mighty Adversaries

This 9-card set with a two-front format was inserted at a rate of 1:8 packs. Each side featured either a forward or a goalie, with the ghosted image of the counterpart's face in the background. Each side also had text addressing their adversarial relationship.

COMPLETE SET (9) 10.00 25.00
STATED ODDS 1:8
1 K.Takko/K.Rintanen 1.25 3.00
2 B.Rousson/P.Saarela 1.25 3.00
3 I.Kauhanen/A.Andrijevski 1.25 3.00
4 A.Sulander/M.Kortelainen 1.25 3.00
5 P.Kuivalainen/T.Sjogren 1.25 3.00
6 V.Toskala/J.Ojanen 2.00 5.00
7 F.Norrena/O.Janecky 1.25 3.00
8 S.Lindfors/J.Korpisalo 1.25 3.00
9 A.Siekkinen/J.Lindroos 1.25 3.00

1996-97 Finnish SISU Redline Promos

These cards were handed out at a hockey event in Finland to promote the upcoming series. Checklist courtesy of collector Heikki Silvenoinen.

COMPLETE SET (12) 15.00
1 Mika Kortelainen .40 1.00
2 Alexander Andrievski .40 1.00
3 Vesa Toskala 1.25 3.00
4 Jari Lindroos .40 1.00
5 Thomas Sjogren .40 1.00
6 Pasi Kuivalainen .75 2.00
7 Iiro Itamies .75 2.00
8 Kalle Sahlstedt .75 2.00
9 Mika Karapuu .40 1.00
10 Valeri Krykov .40 1.00
11 Kimmo Rintanen .40 1.00
12 Jari Levonen .40 1.00

1996-97 Finnish SISU Redline Rookie Energy

This 9-card set features the top rookies from the SM-Liiga's 95-96 campaign. The cards were randomly inserted into packs at a rate of 1:6. The card fronts feature an image of the player over a colored sky highlighted by lightning bolts. The backs include a head shot as well as some text relating the player's fine season.

COMPLETE SET (9) 8.00 15.00
STATED ODDS 1:6
1 Jani Hurme 2.00 5.00
2 Mikko Eloranta .75 2.00
3 Sami Salo .75 2.00
4 Tero Hamalainen .40 1.00
5 Miika Elomo .75 2.00
6 Mika Pietila .40 1.00
7 Arto Kuki .40 1.00
8 Vesa Toskala 2.00 5.00
9 Miikka Rousu .40 1.00

1996-97 Finnish SISU Redline Silver Signatures

These cards were available as a redemption only to those who mailed in their Kari Takko Super Bonus card. Thanks to collector Heikki Silvennoinen for providing the checklist.

COMPLETE SET (5) 60.00 125.00
1 Jani Hurme 12.00 30.00
2 Pasi Kuivalainen 8.00 20.00
3 Boris Rousson 12.00 30.00
4 Ari Sulander 12.00 30.00
5 Vesa Toskala 15.00 40.00

1996-97 Finnish SISU Redline Sledgehammers

These 9 cards were randomly inserted into packs at a rate of 1:6. The cards are essentially double-fronted, with both sides picturing the player in action, superimposed over a Sledgehammer logo.

COMPLETE SET (9) 2.00 5.00
STATED ODDS 1:6
1 Hannu Henriksson .40 1.00
2 Robert Nordmark .40 1.00
3 Pasi Sormunen .40 1.00
4 Tuomas Gronman .40 1.00
5 Derek Mayer .40 1.00
6 Toni Porkka .40 1.00
7 Timo Peltomaa .40 1.00
8 Iiro Jarvi .40 1.00
9 Joni Lehto .40 1.00

1998-99 Finnish Kerailysarja

This set features many of the players of Finland's SM-Liiga. The cards feature a colour action photo on the front, while the backs feature another photo and stats.

COMPLETE SET (270) 16.00 40.00
1 Checklist 1-60 .07 .20
2 Checklist 61-120 .07 .20
3 Checklist 121-180 .07 .20
4 Checklist 181-240 .07 .20
5 Checklist 241-270 .07 .20
6 Inserts Checklist .07 .20
7 Ari-Pekka Siekkinen .15 .40
8 Jani Riihinen .07 .20
9 Riku Varjamo .07 .20
10 Jiri Vykoukal .07 .20
11 Jonas Andersson-Junkka .15 .40
12 Riku-Petteri Lehtonen .07 .20
13 Pasi Sormunen .07 .20
14 Robert Salo .07 .20
15 Juha Gustafsson .15 .40
16 Christian Ruuttu .15 .40
17 Tero Hamalainen .07 .20
18 Juha Ikonen .07 .20
19 Hannes Hyvonen .20 .50
20 Timo Hirvonen .20 .50
21 Petr Ton .07 .20
22 Nils Ekman .30 .75
23 Joonas Jaaskelainen .07 .20
24 Tommy Kiviaho .07 .20
25 Tomas Kapusta .07 .20
26 Tero Tiainen .07 .20
27 Teemu Riihijarvi .15 .40
28 Jan Lundell .07 .20
29 Niklas Backstrom .07 .20
30 Ville Siren .07 .20
31 Marko From .07 .20
32 Brian Rafalski .40 1.00
33 Jarno Kultanen .20 .50
34 Toni Lydman .20 .50
35 Jani Nikko .15 .40
36 Jere Karalahti .15 .40
37 Kari Rajala .07 .20
38 Kari Kalto .07 .20
39 Kimmo Kuhta .07 .20
40 Jan Caloun .15 .40
41 Markku Hurme .07 .20
42 Tom Laaksonen .07 .20
43 Niklas Hagman .40 1.00
44 Luciano Borsato .07 .20
45 Toni Sihvonen .07 .20
46 Mika Kortelainen .15 .40
47 Toni Makiaho .07 .20
48 Mika Nieminen .15 .40
49 Jarkko Ruutu .30 .75
50 Marko Tuomainen .15 .40
51 Pasi Nurminen 1.50 4.00
52 Kari Rosenberg .07 .20
53 Aki Heino .07 .20
54 Erik Kakko .07 .20
55 Tom Koivisto .07 .20
56 Ari Vallin .07 .20
57 Tomi Kallarsson .07 .20
58 Jaroslav Nedved .07 .20
59 Kai Rautio .07 .20
60 Mikko Kuparinen .15 .40
61 Mika Kannisto .07 .20
62 Juha Virtanen .07 .20
63 Jani Keinanen .07 .20
64 Jyrki Louhi .07 .20
65 Roman Simicek .20 .50
66 Semi Pekki .07 .20
67 Timo Parssinen .07 .20
68 Jarkko Savijoki .07 .20
69 Marko Palo .07 .20
70 Antti Virtanen .07 .20
71 Niko Kapanen .75 2.00
72 Tomas Vlasak .15 .40
73 Riku Hahl .40 1.00
74 Vesa Toskala .75 2.00
75 Markus Korhonen .07 .20
76 Timo Willman .07 .20
77 Veli-Pekka Hard .07 .20
78 Pekka Kangasalusta .07 .20
79 Oscar Ackestrom .07 .20
80 Allan Measures .07 .20
81 Pasi Puistola .07 .20
82 Pasi Saarinen .15 .40
83 Mikko Haapakoski .07 .20
84 Martti Jarventie .20 .50
85 Mika Arvaja .07 .20
86 Juha Hautamaa .07 .20
87 Raimo Helminen .15 .40
88 Tomi Hirvonen .07 .20
89 Matti Kaipainen .07 .20
90 Peter Larsson .07 .20
91 Vesa Viitakoski .15 .40
92 Mikko Peltola .07 .20
93 Timo Peltomaa .07 .20
94 Hannu Mattila .07 .20
95 Sami Ahlberg .07 .20
96 Juha Jarvenpaa .07 .20
97 Markus Ketterer .15 .40
98 Ari Kumpula .07 .20
99 Waltteri Immonen .07 .20
100 Antti-Jussi Niemi .15 .40
101 Sami Nuutinen .07 .20
102 Yves Racine .15 .40
103 Rami Alanko .07 .20
104 Mika Stromberg .15 .40
105 Ossi Vaananen .40 1.00
106 Jani Rita .40 1.00
107 Sami Mettovaara .07 .20
108 Fredrik Nilsson .07 .20
109 Kimmo Rintanen .15 .40
110 Jari Kauppila .07 .20
111 Pasi Saarela .15 .40
112 Timo Saarikoski .07 .20
113 Eero Somervuori .15 .40
114 Jukka Tiilikainen .07 .20
115 Jarkko Vaananen .07 .20
116 Otakar Janecky .15 .40
117 Patrik Juhlin .15 .40
118 Juha Lind .20 .50
119 Marko Leinonen .07 .20
120 Tommi Satosaari .07 .20
121 Mikko Luoma .07 .20
122 Jan Latvala .07 .20
123 Kevin Wortman .07 .20
124 Kalle Koskinen .07 .20
125 Jyrki Valivaara .07 .20
126 Markus Kankaanpera .07 .20
127 Jarkko Glad .07 .20
128 Marko Kauppinen .07 .20
129 Robert Nordberg .07 .20
130 Juha Viinikainen .07 .20
131 Marko Ojanen .07 .20
132 Toni Koivunen .07 .20
133 Mikko Rantala .07 .20
134 Jussi Tarvainen .07 .20
135 Tommi Turunen .07 .20
136 Timo Vertala .07 .20
137 Veli-Pekka Nutikka .15 .40
138 Stefan Ornskog .07 .20
139 Marko Virtanen .07 .20
140 Lasse Jamsen .07 .20
141 Kimmo Kapanen .07 .20
142 Ari Luostarinen .07 .20
143 Tobias Ablad .07 .20
144 Derry Menard .07 .20
145 Jermu Pisto .07 .20
146 Sebastian Sulku .07 .20
147 Timo Ahmaoja .07 .20
148 Teemu Tuomainen .07 .20
149 Pekka Poikolainen .07 .20
150 Aki Korhonen .07 .20
151 Pekka Tirkkonen .07 .20
152 Petro Koivunen .07 .20
153 Marko Levanen .07 .20
154 Janne Kekalainen .07 .20
155 Antti Riekkinen .07 .20
156 Mikko Honkonen .07 .20
157 Timo Sikkula .07 .20
158 Sami Simonen .07 .20
159 Mikko Konttila .07 .20
160 Jaakko Uhlback .07 .20
161 Lubos Rob .07 .20
162 Kimmo Vesa .07 .20
163 Sinuhe Wallinheimo .07 .20
164 Jaakko Harikkala .15 .40
165 Aivars Tribuntsovs .07 .20
166 Ismo Kuoppala .07 .20
167 Kimmo Lotvonen .07 .20
168 Marko Toivonen .07 .20
169 Erik Hamalainen .15 .40
170 Mikael Tjallden .07 .20
171 Roland Carlsson .07 .20
172 Niko Halttunen .07 .20
173 Jouni Vauhkonen .07 .20
174 Matti Raunio .07 .20
175 Ville Mikkonen .07 .20
176 Petri Pakaslahti .07 .20
177 Janne Seva .07 .20
178 Harri Sillgren .07 .20
179 Leonids Tambijevs .07 .20
180 Jari Hyvarinen .07 .20
181 Patrik Wallenberg .07 .20
182 Jarkko Nikander .07 .20
183 Aigars Cipruss .07 .20
184 Jussi Markkanen .60 1.50
185 Pasi Hakkinen .07 .20
186 Harri Tikkanen .07 .20
187 Juri Kuznetsov .07 .20
188 Riku Kallioniemi .07 .20
189 Jussi Pekkala .07 .20
190 Mikko Myllykoski .07 .20
191 Vesa Ruotsalainen .07 .20
192 Tommi Sova .07 .20
193 Dale McTavish .07 .20
194 Pasi Maattanen .07 .20
195 Aleksander Matsijevski .07 .20
196 Sami Kaartinen .07 .20
197 Ari Saarinen .07 .20
198 Joel Salonen .07 .20
199 Ari Santanen .07 .20
200 Mika Skytta .07 .20
201 Mika Kauppinen .07 .20
202 Keijo Sailynoja .07 .20
203 Eric Weilleux .07 .20
204 Ville Immonen .07 .20
205 Mika Noronen 2.00 5.00
206 Iiro Itamies .07 .20
207 Josef Boumedienne .20 .50
208 Miska Kangasniemi .15 .40
209 Mikko Tamminen .07 .20
210 Timo Jutila .07 .20
211 Janne Gronvall .15 .40
212 Sami-Ville Salomaa .07 .20
213 Janne Vuorela .07 .20
214 Pasi Petrilainen .15 .40
215 Pasi Tuominen .07 .20
216 Jani Hassinen .07 .20
217 Valeri Krykov .07 .20
218 Juha Vuorivirta .07 .20
219 Aleksander Barkov .07 .20
220 Harri Lonnberg .07 .20
221 Arto Kumala .07 .20
222 Janne Ojanen .15 .40
223 Lasse Pirjeta .07 .20
224 Sami Salonen .07 .20
225 Johannes Alanen .07 .20
226 Mikko Makela .15 .40
227 Fredrik Norrena .15 .40
228 Miikka Kiprusoff 2.00 5.00
229 Kimmo Eronen .07 .20
230 Marko Kiprusoff .07 .20
231 Jouni Loponen .07 .20
232 Ilkka Mikkola .07 .20
233 Aki Berg .20 .50
234 Tommi Rajamaki .15 .40
235 Peter Ahola .07 .20
236 Mika Lehtinen .07 .20
237 Tony Virta .07 .20
238 Joni Lius .07 .20
239 Mikko Eloranta .20 .50
240 Marco Tuokko .07 .20
241 Juha Joninen .07 .20
242 Tomi Kallio .15 .40
243 Mikko Rautio .07 .20
244 Jani Kiviharju .07 .20
245 Tommi Miettinen .20 .50
246 Simo Rouvali .07 .20
247 Kalle Sahlstedt .15 .40
248 Teemu Elomo .15 .40
249 Mika Alatalo .20 .50
250 Miika Elomo .15 .40
251 Pasi Kuivalainen .15 .40
252 Mika Lehto .07 .20
253 Joachim Esbjors .07 .20
254 Mikko Sokka .07 .20
255 Pasi Peltonen .15 .40
256 Vesa Salo .07 .20
257 Mika Laaksonen .07 .20
258 Santeri Immonen .07 .20
259 Jonas Esbjors .07 .20
260 Vjatcheslav Fandul .07 .20
261 Kimmo Salminen .07 .20
262 Jokke Heinanen .07 .20
263 Jari Levonen .07 .20
264 Niko Mikkola .07 .20
265 Andrei Potaitshuk .07 .20
266 Rauli Raitanen .07 .20
267 Timo Hakanen .07 .20
268 Jan Benda .07 .20
269 Tero Arkiomaa .15 .40
270 Marko Kivenmaki .07 .20

1998-99 Finnish Kerailysarja 90's Top 12

These inserts honor the decade's best Finnish players. They were randomly inserted into packs. Unfortunately, the wrappers do not reveal the insertion odds.

COMPLETE SET (12) 16.00 30.00
1 Jere Lehtinen 1.25 3.00
2 Pertti Lehtonen .75 2.00
3 Janne Laukkanen .75 2.00
4 Jukka Tammi .75 2.00
5 Teemu Selanne 4.00 10.00
6 Jari Lindroos .75 2.00
7 Sami Kapanen 1.25 3.00
8 Jarmo Kuusisto .75 2.00
9 Ari Santanen .75 2.00
10 Timo Jutila .75 2.00
11 Saku Koivu 2.00 5.00
12 Kari Takko .75 2.00

1998-99 Finnish Kerailysarja Dream Team

These inserts honor the best of Finland's current talent pool. The cards were randomly inserted into packs. Unfortunately, the packs do not reveal the insertion odds.

COMPLETE SET (7) 16.00 20.00
1 Jari Kurri 2.00 5.00
2 Ari Sulander 1.25 3.00
3 Jyrki Lumme .75 2.00
4 Janne Niinimaa .75 2.00
5 Jere Lehtinen 1.50 4.00
6 Saku Koivu 2.00 5.00
7 Teemu Selanne 4.00 10.00

1998-99 Finnish Kerailysarja Leijonat

These inserts honor players who have performed for The Lions, the nickname of Finland's national team. The cards were randomly inserted into packs. Unfortunately, the packs do not reveal the insertion odds.

COMPLETE SET (47) 6.00 15.00
1 Markus Ketterer .20 .50
2 Jarmo Myllys .20 .50
3 Jukka Tammi .20 .50
4 Peter Ahola .08 .25
5 Erik Hamalainen .08 .25
6 Timo Jutila .08 .25
7 Jere Karalahti .20 .50
8 Marko Kiprusoff .08 .25
9 Janne Laukkanen .20 .50
10 Joni Lehto .08 .25
11 Kaj Linna .08 .25
12 Jouni Loponen .08 .25
13 Toni Lydman .15 .40
14 Antti-Jussi Niemi .20 .50
15 Petteri Nummelin .08 .25
16 Mika Stromberg .08 .25
17 Kimmo Timonen .20 .50
18 Hannu Virta .08 .25
19 Mika Alatalo .08 .25
20 Mikko Eloranta .20 .50
21 Raimo Helminen .08 .25
22 Juha Ikonen .08 .25
23 Marko Jantunen .08 .25
24 Olli Jokinen .75 2.00
25 Joonas Jaaskelainen .08 .25
26 Sami Kapanen .75 2.00
27 Esa Keskinen .08 .25
28 Jari Korpisalo .08 .25
29 Tero Lehtera .08 .25
30 Juha Lind .08 .25
31 Joni Lius .08 .25
32 Toni Makiaho .08 .25
33 Mika Nieminen .20 .50
34 Janne Ojanen .20 .50
35 Marko Palo .08 .25
36 Ville Peltonen .30 .75
37 Juha Riihijarvi .08 .25
38 Kimmo Rintanen .08 .25
39 Christian Ruuttu .15 .40
40 Jarkko Ruutu .08 .25
41 Jukka Seppo .08 .25
42 Raimo Summanen .08 .25
43 Esa Tikkanen .40 1.00
44 Marko Tuomainen .08 .25
45 Antti Tormanen .08 .25
46 Jarkko Varvio .08 .25
47 Juha Ylonen .20 .50

1998-99 Finnish Kerailysarja Mad Masks

These inserts honor the best goalies in Finland. The cards were randomly inserted into packs. Unfortunately, the packs do not reveal the insertion odds.

COMPLETE SET (12) 24.00 75.00
1 Ari-Pekka Siekkinen 2.00 5.00
2 Jan Lundell 2.00 5.00
3 Pasi Nurminen 6.00 15.00
4 Vesa Toskala 4.00 10.00
5 Markus Ketterer 2.00 5.00
6 Marko Leinonen 2.00 5.00
7 Kimmo Kapanen 2.00 5.00
8 Sinuhe Wallinheimo 2.00 5.00
9 Jussi Markkanen 4.00 10.00
10 Mika Noronen 6.00 15.00
11 Fredrik Norrena 2.00 5.00
12 Pasi Kuivalainen 2.00 5.00

1998-99 Finnish Kerailysarja Off Duty

These inserts show players away from the ice. The cards were randomly inserted into packs. Unfortunately, the packs do not reveal the insertion odds.

COMPLETE SET (12) 8.00 20.00
1 Juha Ikonen .75 2.00
2 Toni Sihvonen .75 2.00
3 Tom Koivisto .75 2.00
4 Juha Hautamaa .75 2.00
5 Kimmo Rintanen .75 2.00
6 Marko Leinonen .75 2.00
7 Sami Simonen .75 2.00
8 Sinuhe Wallinheimo 1.25 3.00
9 Jussi Markkanen 1.50 4.00
10 Arto Kulmala .75 2.00
11 Marko Kiprusoff .75 2.00
12 Pasi Kuivalainen .75 2.00

1999-00 Finnish Cardset

This set features the top players of the Finnish SM-Liiga. It was issued in foil packs over two series. The cards feature action photos over a computer generated background. Cards #158-177 comprise a Sharpshooters subset while cards #178-200 form a Flaming Patriots subset. The Jere Lehtinen Triple Threat card was a long-odds insert that was hand serial numbered out of 1,000 copies. The Teemu Selanne Global Glory card was a long-odds insert that was hand serial numbered out of 1,000 copies as well. Neither card is considered part of the complete set.

COMPLETE SET (346) 30.00 75.00
1 Checklist 1-40 .07 .20
2 Checklist 41-80 .07 .20
3 Checklist 81-120 .07 .20
4 Checklist 121-160 .07 .20
5 Checklist 161-200 .07 .20
6 Inserts Checklist .07 .20
7 Ari-Pekka Siekkinen .15 .40
8 Jiri Vykoukal .07 .20
9 Riku Varjamo .07 .20
10 Riku-Petteri Lehtonen .07 .20
11 Juha Gustafsson .15 .40
12 Arto Laatikainen .30 .75
13 Hannes Hyvonen .20 .50
14 Timo Hirvonen .20 .50
15 Tommy Kiviaho .07 .20
16 Tero Tiainen .07 .20
17 Joonas Jaaskelainen .07 .20
18 Teemu Riihijarvi .15 .40
19 Olli Ahonen .07 .20
20 Santeri Heiskanen .07 .20
21 Jarno Kultanen .20 .50
22 Marko From .07 .20
23 Kimmo Kuhta .07 .20
24 Tom Laaksonen .07 .20
25 Kari Kalto .07 .20
26 Jan Caloun .15 .40
27 Markku Hurme .07 .20
28 Toni Makiaho .07 .20
29 Mika Nieminen .15 .40
30 Luciano Borsato .07 .20
31 Aki Heino .07 .20
32 Jonas Andersson-Junkka .15 .40
33 Tomi Kallarsson .07 .20
34 Roman Simicek .20 .50
35 Juha Virtanen .07 .20
36 Antti Virtanen .07 .20
37 Jyrki Louhi .07 .20
38 Jarkko Savijoki .07 .20
39 Jukka Hentunen .20 .50
40 Timo Parssinen .40 1.00
41 Niko Kapanen .40 1.00
42 Tomas Vlasak .15 .40
43 Kristian Antila .07 .20
44 Pasi Puistola .07 .20
45 Pasi Saarinen .15 .40
46 Pekka Kangasalusta .07 .20
47 Martti Jarventie .07 .20
48 Sami Karjalainen .07 .20
49 Riku Niemela .07 .20
50 Mikko Peltola .07 .20
51 Juha Hautamaa .07 .20
52 Raimo Helminen .15 .40
53 Tomi Hirvonen .07 .20
54 Sami Ahlberg .07 .20
55 Vesa Viitakoski .07 .20
56 Mika Arvaja .07 .20
57 Rami Alanko .07 .20
58 Antti-Jussi Niemi .15 .40
59 Antti Hulkkonen .10 .30
60 Jani Rita .40 1.00
61 Jarkko Vaananen .07 .20
62 Fredrik Nilsson .07 .20
63 Jari Kauppila .07 .20
64 Eero Somervuori .20 .50
65 Jukka Tiilikainen .07 .20
66 Patrik Juhlin .15 .40
67 Tommi Satosaari .07 .20
68 Jarkko Glad .07 .20
69 Jyrki Valivaara .07 .20
70 Markus Kankaanpera .07 .20
71 Kalle Koskinen .07 .20
72 Juha Viinikainen .07 .20
73 Marko Ojanen .07 .20
74 Toni Koivunen .07 .20
75 Veli-Pekka Nutikka .15 .40
76 Stefan Ornskog .07 .20
77 Marko Virtanen .07 .20
78 Lasse Jamsen .07 .20
79 Petri Vehanen .07 .20
80 Kimmo Lotvonen .07 .20
81 Jaakko Harikkala .15 .40
82 Ismo Kuoppala .07 .20
83 Erik Hamalainen .15 .40
84 Zdenek Nedved .07 .20
85 Harri Suvanto .07 .20
86 Jouni Vauhkonen .07 .20
87 Ville Mikkonen .07 .20
88 Janne Seva .07 .20
89 Petri Latti .07 .20
90 Harri Sillgren .07 .20
91 Leonids Tambijevs .07 .20
92 Sami Lehtinen .07 .20
93 Jussi-Antti Reimari .07 .20
94 Marko Ahonen .07 .20
95 Veli-Pekka Laitinen .07 .20
96 Mika Niskanen .07 .20
97 Jan Latvala .07 .20
98 Mika Asikainen .07 .20
99 Aigars Cipruss .07 .20
100 Michael Johansson .07 .20
101 Tomi-Pekka Kolu .07 .20
102 Jarkko Ollikainen .07 .20
103 Toni Saarinen .07 .20
104 Jussi Vienonen .07 .20
105 Jouko Myrra .07 .20
106 Jussi Markkanen .40 1.00
107 Harri Tikkanen .07 .20
108 Riku Kallioniemi .07 .20
109 Jussi Pekkala .07 .20
110 Mikko Myllykoski .07 .20
111 Vesa Ruotsalainen .07 .20
112 Tommi Sova .07 .20
113 Ari Santanen .07 .20
114 Pasi Maattanen .07 .20
115 Tero Hamalainen .07 .20
116 Mika Skytta .07 .20
117 Ville Immonen .07 .20
118 Keijo Sailynoja .07 .20
119 Miska Kangasniemi .15 .40
120 Josef Boumedienne .20 .50
121 Janne Vuorela .07 .20
122 Janne Gronvall .15 .40
123 Valeri Krykov .07 .20
124 Arto Kumala .07 .20
125 Aleksander Barkov .07 .20
126 Johannes Alanen .07 .20
127 Jani Hassinen .07 .20
128 Janne Ojanen .15 .40
129 Tuomas Reijonen .07 .20
130 Sami Salonen .07 .20
131 Fredrik Norrena .15 .40
132 Kimmo Eronen .07 .20
133 Marko Kiprusoff .08 .25
134 Jouni Loponen .07 .20
135 Ilkka Mikkola .15 .40
136 Jani Kiviharju .07 .20
137 Tony Virta .07 .20
138 Kalle Sahlstedt .15 .40
139 Tomi Kallio .40 1.00
140 Joni Lius .07 .20
141 Teemu Elomo .15 .40
142 Ville Vahalahti .07 .20
143 Marco Tuokko .07 .20
144 Kai Nurminen .15 .40
145 Petr Kuchyna .07 .20
146 Tuomo Kyha .07 .20
147 Pasi Peltonen .15 .40
148 Santeri Immonen .07 .20
149 Pauli Levokari .07 .20
150 Vesa Salo .07 .20
151 Timo Salonen .07 .20
152 Marko Kivenmaki .07 .20
153 Niko Mikkola .07 .20
154 Andrei Potaitshuk .07 .20
155 Tero Arkiomaa .15 .40
156 Timo Hakanen .07 .20
157 Jan Peterek .07 .20
158 Jan Caloun .15 .40
159 Pasi Saarela .15 .40
160 Tomas Vlasak .15 .40
161 Brian Rafalski .40 1.00
162 Peter Larsson .07 .20
163 Roman Simicek .20 .50
164 Raimo Helminen .15 .40
165 Leonids Tambijevs .07 .20
166 Mika Nieminen .15 .40
167 Janne Ojanen .15 .40
168 Otakar Janecky .15 .40
169 Juha Ikonen .07 .20
170 Jari Kauppila .07 .20
171 Jan Benda .07 .20
172 Tony Virta .07 .20
173 Niko Kapanen .40 1.00
174 Aleksander Barkov .07 .20
175 Hannes Hyvonen .20 .50
176 Lasse Pirjeta .07 .20
177 Jussi Tarvainen .07 .20
178 Miikka Kiprusoff 2.00 5.00
179 Ari Sulander .30 .75
180 Vesa Toskala .75 2.00
181 Aki Berg .20 .50
182 Jere Karalahti .20 .50
183 Marko Kiprusoff .08 .25
184 Toni Lydman .20 .50
185 Kari Martikainen .07 .20
186 Antti-Jussi Niemi .15 .40
187 Petteri Nummelin .15 .40
188 Kimmo Timonen .30 .75
189 Mikko Eloranta .20 .50
190 Raimo Helminen .15 .40
191 Olli Jokinen .40 1.00
192 Tomi Kallio .40 1.00
193 Saku Koivu 1.25 3.00
194 Juha Lind .20 .50
195 Ville Peltonen .20 .50
196 Kimmo Rintanen .15 .40
197 Teemu Selanne 2.00 5.00
198 Toni Sihvonen .07 .20
199 Marko Tuomainen .15 .40
200 Antti Tormanen .20 .50
201 Tom Draper .15 .40
202 Timo Leinonen .07 .20
203 Pasi Nurminen 1.25 3.00
204 Tommi Satosaari .07 .20
205 Mika Oksa .07 .20
206 Jermu Pisto .07 .20
207 Niclas Hedberg .15 .40
208 Peter Ahola .07 .20
209 Aki Korhonen .07 .20
210 Mikko Kaukokari .07 .20
211 Esa Pirnes .07 .20
212 Arto Kuki .07 .20
213 Dale McTavish .15 .40
214 Ari Katavisto .07 .20
215 Teemu Siren .07 .20
216 Mikael Jamsanen .07 .20
217 Otakar Janecky .15 .40
218 Niklas Backstrom .07 .20
219 Ari Ahonen ERC 1.25 3.00
220 Jere Karalahti .20 .50
221 Marek Zidlicky .07 .20
222 Toni Lydman .07 .20
223 Pekka Kangasalusta .07 .20
224 Kari Rajala .07 .20
225 Mike Gaffney .07 .20
226 Timo Ahmaoja .07 .20
227 Aki Tuominen .07 .20
228 Aki Uusikartano .07 .20
229 Mika Kortelainen .15 .40
230 Toni Sihvonen .07 .20
231 Pasi Nielikainen .07 .20
232 Lasse Pirjeta .07 .20
233 Kimmo Kapanen .07 .20
234 Ari Kumpula .07 .20
235 Kimmo Peltonen .07 .20
236 Sebastian Sulku .07 .20
237 Harri Laurila .07 .20
238 Teemu Aalto .07 .20
239 Oscar Ackestrom .07 .20
240 Antti Miettinen ERC .30 .75
241 Marko Palo .07 .20
242 Riku Hahl .40 1.00
243 Petr Tenkrat .30 .75
244 Pasi Kuivalainen .15 .40
245 Arto Tukio .07 .20
246 Hannu Henriksson .07 .20
247 Teemu Kesa .07 .20
248 Antti Bruun .07 .20
249 Tomi Pettinen .07 .20
250 Tapio Sammalkangas .07 .20
251 Rodrigo Lavins .15 .40
252 Ilkka Laitinen .07 .20
253 Tommi Miettinen .15 .40
254 Jarkko Nikander .07 .20
255 Daniel Marois .15 .40
256 Antti Hilden .07 .20
257 Kimmo Vese .07 .20
258 Pasi Nurminen 1.25 3.00
259 Ossi Vaananen .40 1.00
260 Sean Gagnon .15 .40
261 Marko Kauppinen .15 .40
262 Tuomas Gronman .15 .40
263 Tom Koivisto .07 .20
264 Tomek Valtonen .07 .20
265 Esa Tikkanen .40 1.00
266 Jan Benda .07 .20
267 Tommi Santala .07 .20
268 Petri Varis .15 .40
269 Tuomas Eskelinen .07 .20
270 Tero Lehtera .15 .40
271 Markus Hatinen .07 .20
272 Pekka Poikolainen .07 .20
273 Mikko Luoma .07 .20
274 Vesa Ponto .07 .20
275 Nik Zupancic .07 .20
276 Pasi Kangas .15 .40
277 Topi Riutta .07 .20
278 Jussi Pesonen .07 .20
279 Petr Ton .07 .20
280 Jaroslav Bednar .30 .75
281 Tom Draper .20 .50
282 Mika Laaksonen .07 .20
283 Allan Measures .07 .20
284 Martin Stepanek .07 .20
285 Marko Toivonen .07 .20
286 Petteri Lotila .07 .20
287 Jari Hyvarinen .07 .20
288 Timo Peltomaa .07 .20
289 Petri Pakaslahti .07 .20
290 Jokke Heinanen .07 .20
291 Matti Kaipainen .07 .20
292 Ville Korvula .07 .20
293 Veli-Pekka Kautonen .07 .20
294 Daniel Johansson .07 .20
295 Tommi Kovanen .07 .20
296 Roland Carlsson .07 .20

297 Jani Keinanen .07 .20
298 Mikko Juutilainen .07 .20
299 Aki Kaskinen .07 .20
300 Tommi Turunen .07 .20
301 Mathias Bosson .07 .20
302 Teemu Riihijarvi .07 .20
303 Pasi Hakkinen .07 .20
304 Jani-Matti Loikala .07 .20
305 Juri Kuznetsov .15 .40
306 Mikko Jokela .07 .20
307 Ville Hamalainen .07 .20
308 Joel Salonen .07 .20
309 Timo Saarikoski .07 .20
310 Pekka Tirkkonen .07 .20
311 Mika Kauppinen .15 .40
312 Sami Kaartinen .07 .20
313 Timo Jarvinen .07 .20
314 Jason Muzzatti .20 .50
315 Per Lofstrom .07 .20
316 Ari Vallin .07 .20
317 Asko Rantanen .07 .20
318 Tuukka Mantyla .07 .20
319 Pasi Petrilainen .20 .50
320 Pasi Tuominen .07 .20
321 Roman Meluzin .07 .20
322 Miikka Mannikko .07 .20
323 Jussi Tarvainen .07 .20
324 Timo Vertala .07 .20
325 Jaakko Uhlback .07 .20
326 Antero Niittymaki ERC 1.25 3.00
327 Kimmo Lecklin .07 .20
328 Tommi Rajamaki .07 .20
329 Mika Lehtinen .07 .20
330 Kari Harila .07 .20
331 Petri Tahtisalo .07 .20
332 Esa Keskinen .07 .20
333 Kimmo Rintanen .15 .40
334 Michael Holmkvist .20 .50
335 Mikko Rautee .07 .20
336 Mika Lehto .07 .20
337 Timo Leinonen .07 .20
338 Timo Willman .07 .20
339 Olli Kaski .07 .20
340 Samu Wesslin .07 .20
341 Mika Kannisto .07 .20
342 Ales Kratoska .07 .20
343 Marko Luomala .07 .20
344 Jaakko Makela .07 .20
345 Ondrej Steiner .07 .20
346 Markku Tahtinen .07 .20
NNO Teemu Selanne GG 10.00 25.00
NNO Jere Lehtinen TT 4.00 10.00

1999-00 Finnish Cardset Aces High

This insert set was created in the form of playing cards. Several great stars of Finland's past, as well as four cheerleaders from the SM-Liiga are featured alongside today's heroes. The fronts feature action photos with symbols in the corners of typical playing cards. As the cards are not traditionally numbered, they have been listed below according to their suits. C stands for Clubs, D for Diamonds, H for Hearts and S for Spades.

COMPLETE SET (54) 8.00 25.00
J1 Jari Kurri .75 2.00
J2 Teemu Selanne 2.00 5.00
C2 Peter Ahola .07 .20
C3 Teppo Numminen .20 .50
C4 Janne Laukkanen .07 .20
C5 Risto Siltanen .07 .20
C6 Iiro Jarvi .07 .20
C7 Antti Aalto .07 .20
C8 Theo Fleury .75 2.00
C9 Ilkka Sinisalo .07 .20
C10 Michael Nylander .07 .20
D2 Timo Blomqvist .07 .20
D3 Sami Salo .07 .20
D4 Marko Kiprusoff .07 .20
D5 Aki Berg .20 .50
D6 Jan Caloun .07 .20
D7 Olli Jokinen .40 1.00
D8 Patrik Juhlin .07 .20
D9 Dale McTavish .07 .20
D10 Sami Kapanen .40 1.00
H2 Hannu Virta .07 .20
H3 Tuomas Gronman .07 .20
H4 Timo Jutila .07 .20
H5 Jyrki Lumme .20 .50
H6 Juha Ylonen .30 .75
H7 Janne Ojanen .07 .20
H8 Juha Lind .20 .50
H9 Antti Tormanen .07 .20
H10 Jarkko Varvio .07 .20
S2 Reijo Ruotsalainen .07 .20
S3 Janne Niinimaa .20 .50
S4 Brian Rafalski .20 .50
S5 Kimmo Timonen .20 .50
S6 Kai Nurminen .07 .20
S7 Raimo Helminen .07 .20
S8 Raimo Summanen .07 .20
S9 Petri Varis .15 .40
S10 Christian Ruuttu .07 .20
CA Jani Hurme .40 1.00
CJ Mika Alatalo .20 .50
CK Ville Peltonen .15 .40
CQ Paivi Ylitalo .40 1.00
DA Jarmo Myllys .20 .50
DJ Mikko Eloranta .20 .50
DK Jere Lehtinen .60 1.50
DQ Carissa Chan .40 1.00
HA Boris Rousson .20 .50
HJ Jan Benda .07 .20
HK Saku Koivu 1.50 4.00
HQ Ann Bjorklof .40 1.00
SA Kari Takko .20 .50
SJ Marko Tuomainen .07 .20
SK Esa Tikkanen .40 1.00
SQ Satu Jokinen .40 1.00

1999-00 Finnish Cardset Blazing Patriots

This insert set is a partial parallel of the Flaming Patriots subset and features the top performers for Finland's national team. The cards were inserted at a rate of 1:10 packs.

COMPLETE SET (6) 20.00 30.00
STATED ODDS 1:10
1 Miikka Kiprusoff 4.00 10.00
2 Jere Karalahti 1.25 3.00
3 Kimmo Timonen 1.25 3.00
4 Teemu Selanne 4.00 10.00
5 Saku Koivu 4.00 8.00
6 Marko Tuomainen 1.25 3.00

1999-00 Finnish Cardset Jere Lehtinen Triple Threat

This is a single card tribute to Finnish hockey hero Jere Lehtinen. The card is hand numbered on the back out of 1,000.

1 Jere Lehtinen 4.00 10.00

1999-00 Finnish Cardset Most Wanted

This insert set features the players drafted earliest in the NHL draft. The cards were inserted at a rate of 1:4 packs.

COMPLETE SET (12) 20.00 30.00
STATED ODDS 1:4
1 Aki Berg .75 2.00
2 Olli Jokinen .75 2.00
3 Teemu Selanne 4.00 10.00
4 Teemu Riihijarvi .40 1.00
5 Jani Rita .75 2.00
6 Saku Koivu 4.00 8.00
7 Mika Noronen 2.00 5.00
8 Miika Elomo .75 2.00
9 Jukka Seppo .40 1.00
10 Ari Ahonen 2.00 5.00
11 Tuomas Gronman .40 1.00
12 Ville Siren .40 1.00

1999-00 Finnish Cardset Par Avion

This insert set focuses on some of the best Finnish players who have moved on to play in North America. The cards were inserted 1:4 packs.

COMPLETE SET (12) 14.00 25.00
STATED ODDS 1:4
1 Mika Alatalo .75 2.00
2 Toni Lydman .75 2.00
3 Brian Rafalski .75 2.00
4 Jere Karalahti .75 2.00
5 Juha Lind .75 2.00
6 Mikko Kuparinen .40 1.00
7 Marko Tuomainen .40 1.00
8 Miikka Kiprusoff 4.00 10.00
9 Mika Noronen 2.00 5.00
10 Vesa Toskala 2.00 5.00
11 Mikko Eloranta .75 2.00
12 Jarkko Ruutu .75 2.00

1999-00 Finnish Cardset Puck Stoppers

This six-card set features the top netminders in the SM-Liiga. The cards were inserted at a rate of 1:10.

COMPLETE SET (6) 12.00 25.00
STATED ODDS 1:10
1 Antero Niittymaki 4.00 10.00
2 Ari-Pekka Siekkinen 2.00 5.00
3 Pasi Kuivalainen 2.00 5.00
4 Sami Lehtinen 2.00 5.00
5 Jason Muzzatti 2.00 5.00
6 Kimmo Kapanen 2.00 5.00

1999 Finnish Valio World Championships

Little is known about this Finnish issued set other than the confirmed checklist. Any additional information can be forwarded to hockeymag@beckett.com.

COMPLETE SET (6) 6.00 15.00
1 Kari Eloranta .75 2.00
2 Jari Kurri 3.00 8.00
3 Tapio Levo .75 2.00
4 Markus Mattsson 1.25 3.00
5 Jukka Porvari .75 2.00
6 Pekka Rautakallio .75 2.00

2000-01 Finnish Cardset

This brand features the players from Finland's tip league, the SM-Liiga. It was issued in foil packs across three separate series. The cards are brightly colored with an action photo on the front, another on the back, and a bizarre ranking system on the back which tabulates how great the player is. The brand is noteworthy for including cards of several prominent Finnish players currently in the NHL, as well as several 2001 draft picks such as Mikko Koivu and Tuomo Ruutu. There were three special cards hand numbered to 1,000 copies available: Saku Koivu Millennium Thunder was found in series 1 packs, Pasi Nurminen Masked Marvel was found in series 2, and Ari Ahonen Masked Marvel card was inserted into series 3 packs.

COMPLETE SET (360) 30.00 60.00
COMMON CARD (1-360) .04 .10
SEMISTARS/GOALIES .08 .20
UNLISTED STARS .20 .50
1 Checklist .04 .10
2 Checklist .04 .10
3 Checklist .04 .10
4 Mika Oksa .04 .10
5 Peter Ahola .04 .10
6 Jermu Pisto .04 .10
7 Jiri Vykoukal .04 .10
8 Niclas Hedberg .04 .10
9 Teemu Siren .04 .10
10 Joonas Jaaskelainen .20 .50
11 Timo Hirvonen .04 .10
12 Mikko Kaukokari .04 .10
13 Ari Ahonen 1.25 3.00
14 Marek Zidlicky .04 .10
15 Jarno Kultanen .08 .20
16 Toni Sihvonen .04 .10
17 Aki Uusikartano .04 .10
18 Pasi Nielikainen .04 .10
19 Hannes Hyvonen .20 .50
20 Mika Nieminen .20 .50
21 Mika Kortelainen .04 .10
22 Kimmo Kapanen .04 .10
23 Jonas Andersson-Junkka .08 .20
24 Kimmo Peltonen .04 .10
25 Sebastian Sulku .04 .10
26 Teemu Aalto .04 .10
27 Antti Miettinen .30 .75
28 Riku Hahl .40 1.00
29 Marko Palo .04 .10
30 Juha Pitkamaki .04 .10
31 Arto Tukio .20 .50
32 Tapio Sammalkangas .04 .10
33 Tommi Pettinen .04 .10
34 Jarkko Nikander .04 .10
35 Raimo Helminen .08 .20
36 Juha Hautamaa .04 .10
37 Sami Karjalainen .04 .10
38 Pasi Nurminen .75 2.00
39 Ossi Vaananen .30 .75
40 Marko Kauppinen .20 .50
41 Tom Koivisto .04 .50
42 Rami Alanko .04 .10
43 Petri Varis .20 .50
44 Jan Benda .08 .20
45 Jani Rita .40 1.00
46 Markus Kankaanpera .20 .50
47 Jarkko Glad .04 .10
48 Jyrki Valivaara .04 .10
49 Tuomas Pihlman ERC .04 .10
50 Jussi Pesonen .04 .10
51 Petr Ton .04 .10
52 Markus Korhonen .20 .50
53 Harri Aho .04 .10
54 Karri Kivi .08 .20
55 Mikko Haapakoski .04 .10
56 Jaakko Niskavaara .08 .20
57 Niklas Hagman .40 1.00
58 Sakari Palsola .04 .10
59 Jari Laukkanen .04 .10
60 Petri Isotalus .20 .50
61 Jari Viuhkola .04 .10
62 Allan Measures .04 .10
63 Mika Laaksonen .04 .10
64 Marko Toivonen .04 .10
65 Matti Kaipainen .04 .10
66 Petri Latti .04 .10
67 Sami Torkki .04 .10
68 Jokke Hainanen .04 .10
69 Sami Lehtinen .20 .50
70 Veli-Pekka Laitinen .04 .10
71 Kaj Lindstrom .04 .10
72 Mika Niskanen .04 .10
73 Jani Keinanen .04 .10
74 Tommi Turunen .04 .10
75 Mikko Juutilainen .04 .10
76 Veli-Pekka Nutikka .08 .20
77 Mikko Jokela .20 .50
78 Martin Richter .04 .10
79 Pekka Tirkkonen .08 .20
80 Vladimir Machulda .04 .10
81 Ville Hamalainen .04 .10
82 Mika Skytta .04 .10
83 Ville Immonen .04 .10
84 Sami Kaartinen .04 .10
85 Tuukka Mantyla .20 .50
86 Miska Kangasniemi .08 .20
87 Janne Gronvall .08 .20
88 Jussi Tarvainen .08 .20
89 Janne Ojanen .08 .20
90 Jaakko Uhlback .04 .10
91 Johannes Alanen .04 .10
92 Jani Hassinen .04 .10
93 Fredrik Norrena .20 .50
94 Jouni Loponen .04 .10
95 Tommi Rajamaki .04 .10
96 Kimmo Eronen .04 .10
97 Kimmo Rintanen .04 .10
98 Tony Virta .04 .10
99 Jani Kiviharju .04 .10
100 Teemu Elomo .04 .10
101 Mikko Rautee .04 .10
102 Jim Hrivnak .20 .50
103 Pasi Peltonen .04 .10
104 Timo Willman .04 .10
105 Pauli Levokari .04 .10
106 Tuomo Kyha .04 .10
107 Janne Laitila .04 .10
108 Janne Makela .04 .10
109 Samu Wesslin .04 .10
110 Hannu Tala .04 .10
111 Vesa Toskala .40 1.00
112 Aki Berg .20 .50
113 Antti-Jussi Niemi .08 .20
114 Janne Niinimaa .20 .50
115 Ville Peltonen .30 .75
116 Olli Jokinen .40 1.00
117 Teemu Selanne 1.25 3.00
118 Marko Tuomainen .08 .20
119 Juha Lind .08 .20
120 Niko Kapanen .40 1.00
121 Checklist 1 .04 .10
122 Checklist 2 .04 .10
123 Checklist 3 .04 .10
124 Arto Laatikainen .20 .50
125 Tero Maatta .30 .50
126 Juha Gustafsson .04 .10
127 Toni Koivunen .04 .10
128 Teemu Virkkunen .04 .10
129 Valeri Krykov .04 .10
130 Frank Banham .20 .50
131 Semir Ben-Amor .04 .10
132 Jiri Burger .04 .10
133 Aki Tuominen .04 .10
134 Ray Giroux .08 .20
135 Mikko Kurvinen .04 .10
136 Patrik Hucko .04 .10
137 Jari Kauppila .04 .10
138 Tony Salmelainen .04 .10
139 Kimmo Kuhta .04 .10
140 Jaroslav Bednar .40 .50
141 Ari Vallin .04 .10
142 Sami Nuutinen .04 .10
143 Jani Virtanen .04 .10
144 Timo Ahmaoja .04 .10
145 Tomi Suoniemi .04 .10
146 Jari Kesti .04 .10
147 Tommi Santala .04 .10
148 Pavel Rosa .20 .50
149 Eero Somervuori .08 .20
150 Mika Pietila .04 .10
151 Ivan Majesky ERC .04 .10
152 Antti Bruun .04 .10
153 Matt Smith .08 .20
154 Jari-Pekka Pajula .04 .10
155 Kimmo Vaha-Ruohola .04 .10
156 Toni Dahlman .04 .10
157 Antti Hilden .04 .10
158 Timo Koskela .04 .10
159 Vesa Viitakoski .08 .20
160 Kari Haakana .04 .10
161 Pasi Saarinen .08 .20
162 Santeri Heiskanen .04 .10
163 Antti Tormanen .08 .20
164 Juha Virtanen .04 .10
165 Tuomo Ruutu ERC 4.00 10.00
166 Niko Mikkola .04 .10
167 Aigars Cipruss .04 .10
168 Mika Lehto .04 .10
169 Chris MacKenzie .08 .20
170 Pekka Poikolainen .04 .10
171 Riku Varjamo .04 .10
172 Markku Paukkunen .04 .10
173 Mika Paananen .04 .10
174 Juha-Pekka Hytonen .04 .10
175 Janne Hauhtonen .04 .10
176 Jouni Kulonen .04 .10
177 Antti Virtanen .04 .10
178 Kristian Taubert .04 .10
179 Mikko Lehtonen .20 .50
180 Lasse Kukkonen ERC .04 .10
181 Kimmo Koskenkorva .04 .10
182 Tuomo Harjula .04 .10
183 Juha Joenvaara .04 .10
184 Brett Lievers .04 .10
185 Miikka Rousu .04 .10
186 Bruce Racine .20 .50
187 Ismo Kuoppala .04 .10
188 Topi Lehtonen .04 .10
189 Toni Koivisto .04 .10
190 Jouni Vauhkonen .08 .20
191 Jimmy Provencher .04 .10
192 Pasi Saarela .04 .10
193 Pasi Kuivalainen .20 .50
194 Jussi-Antti Reimari .04 .10
195 Jan Latvala .04 .10
196 Roman Vopat .08 .20
197 Janne Sinkkonen .04 .10
198 Ales Kratoska .04 .10
200 Niklas Backstrom .04 .10
201 Oleg Romanov .04 .10
202 Riku Kallioniemi .04 .10
203 Petri Kokko .04 .10
204 Juha Pursiainen .04 .10
205 Joni Yli-Torkko .04 .10
206 Pasi Tuominen .04 .10
207 Ludek Krayzel .04 .10
208 Mika Kauppinen .08 .20
209 Jussi Markkanen .40 1.00
210 Alain Cote .08 .20
211 Pekka Saravo .04 .10
212 Niki Siren .04 .10
213 Timo Vertala .04 .10
214 Tero Lehtera .08 .20
216 Henrik Tallinder .20 .50
217 Martti Jarventie .30 .50
218 Marco Tuokko .04 .10
219 Joni Lius .04 .10
220 Jarkko Varvio .08 .20
222 Mikko Koivu ERC 6.00 15.00
223 Ari Vapola .04 .10
224 Curtis Sheptak .04 .10
225 Marcus Kristoffersson .40 1.00
226 Jari Korpisalo .04 .10
227 Gabriel Karlsson .20 .50
228 Sami Salonen .04 .10
229 Jarkko Vaananen .04 .10
230 Niklas Hede .04 .10
231 Ari Sulander .20 .50
232 Jere Karalahti .04 .10
233 Toni Lydman .20 .50
234 Petteri Nummelin .20 .50
235 Raimo Helminen .20 .50
236 Tomi Kallio .30 .50
237 Toni Sihvonen .04 .10
238 Jukka Hentunen .04 .10
239 Tony Virta .04 .10
240 Esa Tikkanen .20 .50
241 Checklist 1 .04 .10
242 Checklist 2 .04 .10
243 Checklist 3 .04 .10
244 Tom Draper .20 .50
245 Timo Willman .04 .10
246 Asko Rantanen .04 .10
247 Jukka Tiilikainen .04 .10
248 Mikael Jamsanen .04 .10
249 Kari Kalto .04 .10
250 Esa Pirnes .04 .10
251 Johan Davidsson .20 .50
252 Shayne Toporowski .20 .50
253 Sakari Lindfors .20 .50
254 Tomi Nyman .04 .10
255 Kari Rajala .04 .10
256 Martin Stepanek .04 .10
257 Veli-Pekka Kautonen .04 .10
258 Toni Makiaho .04 .10
259 Lasse Pirjeta .04 .10
260 Markku Hurme .04 .10
261 Erkki Rajamaki .04 .10
262 Jan Caloun .20 .50
263 Joonas Vihko .04 .10
264 Jan Lundell .04 .10
265 Dan Ratushny .08 .20
266 Darcy Werenka .08 .20
267 Timo Parssinen .30 .50
268 Tomas Vlasak .04 .10
269 Jyrki Louhi .04 .10
270 Pasi Maattanen .04 .10
271 Petr Kuchyna .04 .10
272 Jani Nikko .04 .10
273 Tommi Miettinen .30 .50
274 Jesse Welling .04 .10
275 Oliver Setzinger .04 .50
276 Jarno Peltonen .04 .10
277 Tony Salmelainen .04 .10
278 Kari Lehtonen ERC 8.00 20.00
279 Pauli Levokari .04 .10
280 Thomas Johansson .04 .10
281 Lee Sorochan .20 .50
282 Tomek Valtonen .04 .10
283 Jukka Hentunen .20 .50
284 Mikko Ruutu .20 .50
285 Timo Saarikoski .04 .10
286 Teemu Sainomaa .04 .10
287 Ari-Pekka Siekkinen .04 .10
288 Tomi Hirvonen .04 .10
289 Jarno Tiilikainen .04 .10
290 Radoslav Kropac .04 .10
291 Zdenek Sedlak .04 .10
292 Tuomo Jaaskelainen .04 .10
293 Antti Kangas .04 .10
294 Steve Shierreffs .04 .10
295 Pekka Kangasalusta .04 .10
296 Vjatsheslav Fandul .04 .10
297 Kimmo Salminen .04 .10
298 Sami Alalauri .04 .10
299 Andrei Potaitshuk .04 .10
300 Petri Vehanen .04 .10
301 Erik Hamalainen .04 .10
302 Tuomas Gronman .04 .10
303 Kimmo Lotvonen .04 .10
304 Janne Siivonen .04 .10
305 Marko Kivenmaki .04 .10
306 Zdenek Nedved .04 .10
307 Petri Pakaslahti .04 .10
308 Harri Sillgren .04 .10
309 Samu Isosalo .04 .10
310 Henri Laurila .04 .10
311 Jussi Salminen .04 .10
312 Kalle Koskinen .04 .10
313 Jarkko Ollikainen .04 .10
314 Toni Saarinen .04 .10
315 Teemu Riihijarvi .08 .20
316 Lasse Jamsen .04 .10
317 Jouko Myrra .04 .10
318 Pasi Hakkinen .04 .10
319 Juha Kuokkanen .04 .10
320 Roland Carlsson .20 .50
321 Harri Tikkanen .04 .10
322 Juri Kuznetsov .20 .50
323 Ville Kiiskinen .04 .10
324 Olli Sipilainen .04 .10
325 Tuomas Reijonen .04 .10
326 Joel Salonen .04 .10
327 Sami Ahlberg .04 .10
328 Sasu Hovi .04 .10
329 Janne Vourela .04 .10
330 Mikko Luoma .04 .10
331 Miro Laitinen .04 .10
332 Sami Venalainen .04 .10
333 Marko Ojanen .04 .10
334 Marko Makinen .04 .10
335 Aleksander Barkov .04 .10
336 Antero Niittymaki 1.25 3.00
337 Markus Seikola .04 .10
338 Ilkka Mikkola .04 .10
339 Mika Lehtinen .04 .10
340 Niko Kapanen .40 1.00
341 Ville Vahalahti .04 .10
342 Kalle Sahlstedt .20 .50
343 Kristian Antila .04 .10
344 Pasi Puistola .04 .10
345 Vesa Salo .04 .10
346 Veli-Pekka Hard .04 .10
347 Eric Perrin .04 .10
348 Tomas Kucharcik .04 .10
349 Markku Tahtinen .04 .10
350 Mikko Konttila .04 .10
351 Pasi Nurminen .75 2.00
352 Kimmo Timonen .20 .50
353 Jyrki Lumme .20 .50
354 Janne Laukkanen .20 .50
355 Kimmo Rintanen .20 .50
356 Saku Koivu .75 2.00
357 Jere Lehtinen .40 1.00
358 Sami Kapanen .40 1.00
359 Antti Aalto .20 .50
360 Mika Alatalo .20 .50
NNO Ari Ahonen MM 8.00 20.00
NNO Saku Koivu MT 10.00 25.00
NNO Pasi Nurminen MM 10.00 25.00

2000-01 Finnish Cardset Masquerade

These singles feature the masks of the top netminders of the SM-Liiga. They were inserted approximately 1:5 packs in series three only.

COMPLETE SET (9) 24.00 40.00
STATED ODDS 1:5 SERIES 3
1 Mika Pietila 2.00 5.00
2 Bruce Racine 4.00 10.00
3 Sami Lehtinen 2.00 5.00
4 Niklas Backstrom 2.00 5.00
5 Antero Niittymaki 6.00 15.00
6 Markus Korhonen 2.00 5.00
7 Jussi Markkanen 6.00 15.00
8 Tom Draper 4.00 10.00
9 Kristian Antila 2.00 5.00

2000-01 Finnish Cardset Master Blasters

This nine-card set honors the Finnish league's top snipers. The cards were inserted 1:5 packs in series one.

COMPLETE SET (9) 12.50 20.00
STATED ODDS 1:5 SERIES 1
1 Kai Nurminen 1.20 3.00
2 Jan Caloun 1.20 3.00
3 Petr Tenkrat 2.00 5.00
4 Jaroslav Bednar 2.00 5.00
5 Dale McTavish .80 2.00
6 Kalle Sahlstedt 1.20 3.00
7 Zdenek Nedved .80 2.00
8 Tomi Kallio 2.00 5.00
9 Timo Parssinen 2.00 5.00

2000-01 Finnish Cardset Next Generation

This set features the top newcomers to the Finnish Elite League. The cards were inserted at a rate of 1:5 packs in series two only.

COMPLETE SET (9) 30.00 30.00
STATED ODDS 1:5 SERIES 2
1 Mikko Koivu 4.00 10.00
2 Tuukka Mantyla .60 1.50
3 Tuomo Ruutu 3.00 8.00
4 Jani Rita 1.00 2.50
5 Ari Ahonen 1.50 4.00
6 Arto Tukio .60 1.50
7 Antti Miettinen 1.50 4.00
8 Markus Kankaanpera .60 1.50
9 Antero Niittymaki 2.00 5.00

2001-02 Finnish Cardset

This set features the top players of the Finnish SM-Liiga. The series was divided into two sets, with 180 cards in the first series, and 200 in the second. The set is noteworthy for containing early cards of first-rounders such as Mikko Koivu, Tuomo Ruutu and Hannu Toivonen. The autographs of Koivu and Ruutu, along with the American Dream card of Ville Nieminen, were random inserts in series 1 packs. The Niittymaki and Lehtonen autographs, along with the Kurri insert, were found in series 2 packs. There were 200 copies of each autograph, and 999 copies of the Nieminen and Kurri inserts.

COMPLETE SET (380) 35.00 70.00
1 Espoo Blues .04 .10
2 Mika Oksa .08 .20
3 Tero Maatta .20 .50
4 Jermu Pisto .08 .20
5 Niclas Hedberg .08 .20
6 Arto Laatikainen .20 .50
7 Valeri Krykov .08 .20
8 Teemu Virkkunen .08 .20
9 Teemu Siren .08 .20
10 Timo Hirvonen .08 .20
11 Mikael Jamsanen .08 .20
12 Kari Kalto .08 .20
13 HIFK Helsinki .04 .10
14 Sakari Lindfors .20 .50
15 Marek Zidlicky .40 1.00
16 Tuomas Eskelinen .08 .20
17 Aki Tuominen .08 .20
18 Mikko Kurvinen .08 .20
19 Hannes Hyvonen .20 .50
20 Kimmo Kuhta .08 .20
21 Toni Happola .08 .20
22 Pasi Nielikainen .08 .20
23 Mika Nieminen .20 .50
24 Toni Makiaho .08 .20
25 Jaroslav Bednar .20 .50
26 HPK Hameenlinna .04 .10
27 Kimmo Peltonen .08 .20
28 Teemu Aalto .08 .20
29 Eero Somervuori .08 .20
30 Riku Hahl .20 .50
31 Antti Miettinen .75 2.00
32 Tommi Santala .08 .20
33 Kasper Kenig .08 .20
34 Pasi Maattanen .08 .20
35 Ilves Tampere .04 .10
36 Mika Pietila .08 .20
37 Jani Nikko .08 .20
38 Antti Bruun .08 .20
39 Tomi Pettinen .08 .20
40 Matt Smith .08 .20
41 Oliver Setzinger .20 .50
42 Toni Dahlman .08 .20
43 Timo Koskela .08 .20
44 Kimmo Vaha-Ruohola .08 .20
45 Jarkko Nikander .08 .20
46 Jari-Pekka Pajula .08 .20
47 Antti Hilden .08 .20
48 Jokerit Helsinki .04 .10
49 Pasi Nurminen .60 1.50
50 Kari Haakana .08 .20
51 Rami Alanko .08 .20
52 Tomek Valtonen .08 .20
53 Teemu Sainomaa .08 .20
54 Antti Tormanen .08 .20
55 Timo Saarikoski .08 .20
56 Teemu Laine .20 .50
57 Mikko Ruutu .08 .20
58 Tuomo Ruutu 1.50 4.00
59 Niko Mikkola .08 .20
60 JYP Jyvaskala .04 .10
61 Mika Lehto .08 .20
62 Pekka Poikolainen .08 .20
63 Jarkko Glad .08 .20
64 Tuomo Jaaskelainen .08 .20
65 Juha-Pekka Hytonen .08 .20
66 Tuomas Pihlman .20 .50
67 Janne Hauhtonen .08 .20
68 Jouni Kulonen .08 .20
69 Tomi Hirvonen .08 .20
70 Antti Virtanen .08 .20
71 Oulun Karpat .04 .10
72 Antti Kangas .08 .20
73 Lasse Kukkonen .20 .50
74 Joni Pitkanen ERC .75 2.00
75 Harri Aho .08 .20
76 Kristian Taubert .08 .20
77 Mikko Lehtonen .20 .50
78 Kimmo Koskenkorva .08 .20
79 Jari Laukkanen .08 .20
80 Juha Joenvaara .08 .20
81 Brett Lievers .08 .20
82 Jari Viuhkola .08 .20
83 Andrei Potaitshuk .08 .20
84 Rauman Lukko .04 .10
85 Mika Laaksonen .08 .20
86 Topi Lehtonen .08 .20
87 Marko Toivonen .08 .20
88 Tuomas Gronman .08 .20
89 Petteri Lotila .08 .20
90 Toni Koivisto .08 .20
91 Sami Torkki .08 .20
92 Samu Isosalo .08 .20
93 Petri Latti .08 .20
94 Janne Siivonen .08 .20
95 Matti Kaipainen .08 .20
96 Lahden Pelicans .04 .10
97 Pasi Kuivalainen .20 .50
98 Mika Niskanen .08 .20
99 Jan Latvala .08 .20
100 Kaj Lindstrom .08 .20
101 Mikko Peltola .08 .20
102 Teemu Riihijarvi .08 .20
103 Jani Keinanen .08 .20
104 Lasse Jamsen .08 .20
105 Toni Saarinen .08 .20
106 Veli-Pekka Nutikka .08 .20
107 SaiPa Lappeenranta .04 .10
108 Harri Tikkanen .08 .20
109 Riku Kallioniemi .08 .20
110 Juri Kuznetsov .20 .50
111 Petri Kokko .08 .20
112 Mikko Jokela .20 .50
113 Ville Hamalainen .08 .20
114 Pasi Tuominen .08 .20
115 Pekka Tirkkonen .08 .20
116 Mika Kauppinen .08 .20
117 Vladimir Machulda .20 .50
118 Olli Sipilainen .08 .20
119 Joni Yli-Torkko .08 .20
120 Tappara Tampere .04 .10
121 Jussi Markkanen .40 1.00
122 Miska Kangasniemi .08 .20
123 Miikko Luoma .08 .20
124 Pekka Saravo .08 .20
125 Miro Laitinen .08 .20
126 Aleksander Barkov .08 .20
127 Jussi Tarvainen .08 .20
128 Marko Ojanen .08 .20
129 Johannes Alanen .08 .20
130 Timo Vertala .08 .20
131 Jaakko Uhlback .08 .20
132 Arto Kuki .08 .20
133 TPS Turku .04 .10
134 Antero Niittymaki .75 2.00
135 Tuomo Karjalainen .08 .20
136 Mika Lehtinen .08 .20
137 Henrik Tallinder .20 .50
138 Markus Seikola .08 .20
139 Kimmo Eronen .08 .20
140 Martti Jarventie .20 .50
141 Mikko Rautee .08 .20
142 Mikko Koivu 2.00 5.00
143 Marco Tuokko .08 .20
144 Michael Holmqvist .40 1.00
145 Ville Vahalahti .08 .20
146 Porin Assat .04 .10
147 Kristian Antila .08 .20
148 Pasi Peltonen .08 .20
149 Curtis Sheptak .08 .20
150 Sami Karjalainen .08 .20
151 Jari Korpisalo .08 .20
152 Mikko Konttila .08 .20
153 Juha Viinikainen .08 .20
154 Eric Perrin .08 .20
155 Markku Tahtinen .08 .20
156 Finnish National Team .04 .10
157 Pasi Nurminen .60 1.50
158 Miikka Kiprusoff .75 2.00
159 Jarmo Myllys .20 .50
160 Marko Kiprusoff .08 .20
161 Petteri Nummelin .20 .50
162 Kimmo Timonen .20 .50
163 Sami Salo .20 .50
164 Ossi Vaananen .20 .50
165 Aki Berg .20 .50
166 Antti-Jussi Niemi .08 .20
167 Janne Gronvall .08 .20
168 Raimo Helminen .08 .20
169 Antti Laaksonen .20 .50
170 Tomi Kallio .20 .50
171 Niko Kapanen .40 1.00
172 Sami Kapanen .40 1.00
173 Jukka Hentunen .20 .50
174 Timo Parssinen .20 .50
175 Juha Lind .20 .50
176 Toni Sihvonen .08 .20
177 Kimmo Rintanen .08 .20
178 Tony Virta .08 .20
179 Juha Ylonen .20 .50
180 Jarkko Ruutu .20 .50
181 Espoo Blues .04 .10
182 Jarmo Myllys .20 .50
183 Juha Gustafsson .08 .20
184 Matti Kuusisto .08 .20
185 Jani Virtanen .08 .20
186 Jiri Vykoukal .08 .20
187 Jan Caloun .20 .50
188 Markku Hurme .08 .20
189 Jiri Zelenka .08 .20
190 Tero Lehtera .08 .20
191 Janne Seva .08 .20
192 Teemu Elomo .08 .20
193 Filip Turek .08 .20

194 HIFK Helsinki .04 .10
195 Mikko Stromberg .08 .20
196 Antti-Pekka Lamberg .08 .20
197 Robert Kantor .08 .20
198 Jonas Junkka .08 .20
199 Mikko Ilkka .08 .20
200 Pauli Levokari .08 .20
201 Kari Rajala .08 .20
202 Joonas Vihko .08 .20
203 Carlo Grunn .08 .20
204 Jonni Vauhkonen .20 .50
205 Mika Kortelainen .08 .20
206 Kimmo Salminen .08 .20
207 Aigars Cipruss .08 .20
208 Ilkka Pikkarainen .08 .20
209 Andrej Podkonicky .20 .50
210 Kim Hirschovits .08 .20
211 HPK Hameenlinna .04 .10
212 Zdenek Smid .20 .50
213 Hannu Toivonen ERC 1.25 3.00
214 Joni Puurula .08 .20
215 Vladimir Sicak .08 .20
216 Janne Juppo .08 .20
217 Sebastian Sulku .08 .20
218 Markus Kankaanpera .20 .50
219 Marko Tuulola .08 .20
220 Tuukka Makela .40 1.00
221 Erkki Rajamaki .08 .20
222 Olli Sillanpaa .08 .20
223 Vladimir Vujtek .08 .20
224 Tomas Kucharcik .08 .20
225 Harri Suutarinen .08 .20
226 Jarkko Savijoki .08 .20
227 Zdenek Nedved .08 .20
228 Janne Lahti .08 .20
229 Ilves Tampere .04 .10
230 Bruce Racine .20 .50
231 Juha Pitkamaki .08 .20
232 Kari Takko .20 .50
233 Ville Koistinen .08 .20
234 Arto Tukio .20 .50
235 Teemu Jaaskelainen .08 .20
236 Ivan Majesky .20 .50
237 Roman Vopat .08 .20
238 Tommi Miettinen .20 .50
239 Riku Rahikainen .08 .20
240 Ville Hirvonen .08 .20
241 Tony Salmelainen .08 .20
242 Vesa Viitakoski .08 .20
243 Mika Nieminen .20 .50
244 Raimo Helminen .08 .20
245 Jokerit Helsinki .04 .10
246 Markus Helanen .08 .20
247 Jamie Ram .20 .50
248 Kari Lehtonen 4.00 10.00
249 Ari Vallin .08 .20
250 Pasi Saarinen .08 .20
251 Tuomas Luotonen .08 .20
252 Ilkka Mikkola .08 .20
253 Tom Koivisto .08 .20
254 Olli Malmivaara .08 .20
255 Rob Cowie .20 .50
256 Alex Brooks .08 .20
257 Sean Bergenheim ERC .60 1.50
258 Antti Aalto .20 .50
259 Ville Peltonen .20 .50
260 Petri Pakaslahti .08 .20
261 Petri Varis .20 .50
262 Jussi Pesonen .08 .20
263 Frank Banham .20 .50
264 Pavel Rosa .20 .50
265 JYP Jyvaskyla .04 .10
266 Tero Leinonen .08 .20
267 Jani-Matti Loikala .08 .20
268 Martin Cech .08 .20
269 Sami Siltavirta .08 .20
270 Jyri Marttinen .08 .20
271 Petri Virolainen .08 .20
272 Angel Nikolov .20 .50
273 Olli Ahonen .08 .20
274 Jari Jaaskelainen .08 .20
275 Harri Sillgren .08 .20
276 Petr Ton .08 .20
277 Tomas Chlubna .08 .20
278 Oulun Karpat .04 .10
279 Markus Korhonen .20 .50
280 Kimmo Lotvonen .08 .20
281 Mikko Myllykoski .08 .20
282 Pekka Saarenheimo .08 .20
283 Mika Pyorala .08 .20
284 Tuomo Harjula .08 .20
285 Harri Korpela .08 .20
286 Janne Pesonen .08 .20
287 Juha-Pekka Haataja .08 .20
288 Sakari Palsola .08 .20
289 Lasse Pirjeta .08 .20
290 Jussi Jokinen ERC 2.00 5.00
291 Rauman Lukko .04 .10
292 Petri Vehanen .08 .20
293 Jaakko Harikkala .08 .20
294 Mikko Purontakanen .08 .20
295 Ville Piekkola .20 .50
296 Janne Niskala .08 .20
297 Teemu Kesa .08 .20
298 Jaakko Hagelberg .08 .20
299 Jari Hyvarinen .08 .20
300 Mika Viinanen .08 .20
301 Joel Salonen .08 .20
302 Teemu Normio .08 .20
303 Hermani Vidman .08 .20
304 Aki Uusikartano .08 .20
305 Pasi Saarela .08 .20
306 Markus Jamsa .08 .20
307 Lahden Pelicans .04 .10
308 Mikko Ramo .08 .20
309 Kalle Koskinen .08 .20
310 Jussi-Antti Reimari .08 .20
311 Veli-Pekka Laitinen .08 .20
312 Henri Laurila .08 .20
313 Teemu Viherva .08 .20
314 Jussi Saarinen .08 .20
315 Olli Sinkkonen .08 .20
316 Jarkko Vaananen .08 .20
317 Jarkko Ollikainen .08 .20
318 Joonas Jaaskelainen .20 .50
319 Niki Siren .08 .20
320 Tommi Turunen .08 .20
321 Toni Koivunen .08 .20
322 SaiPa Lappeenranta .04 .10
323 Juha Kuokkanen .08 .20
324 Sami Lehtinen .20 .50
325 Tomas Duba .08 .20
326 Antti Hulkkonen .08 .20
327 Juha Pursiainen .08 .20
328 Jan Huokko .08 .20
329 Ville Immonen .08 .20
330 Mikko Kinnunen .08 .20
331 Mika Skytta .08 .20
332 Juuso Vakkilainen .08 .20
333 Jesse Welling .08 .20
334 Ville Koho .08 .20
335 Tappara Tampere .04 .10
336 Tom Draper .20 .50
337 Tuukka Mantyla .20 .50
338 Pasi Puistola .08 .20
339 Jyrki Valivaara .08 .20
340 Janne Gronvall .08 .20
341 Esa Pirnes .08 .20
342 Christian Sjogren .08 .20
343 Marko Makinen .08 .20
344 Sami Venalainen .08 .20
345 Janne Ojanen .08 .20
346 Tuomas Reijonen .08 .20
347 Jani Hassinen .08 .20
348 TPS Turku .04 .10
349 Fredrik Norrena .20 .50
350 Matti Tahkapaa .08 .20
351 Marko Kauppinen .20 .50
352 Pasi Petrilainen .08 .20
353 Pekka Kangasalusta .08 .20
354 Markku Paukkunen .08 .20
355 Chris Joseph .20 .50
356 Peter Schaefer .20 .50
357 Kai Nurminen .20 .50
358 Miika Elomo .20 .50
359 Janne Jokila .08 .20
360 Mikko Kankaanpera .08 .20
361 Tommi Hannus .08 .20
362 Mika Alatalo .20 .50
363 Rob Shearer .20 .50
364 Jani Kiviharju .08 .20
365 Porin Assat .04 .10
366 Tommi Satosaari .08 .20
367 Matti Jarvinen .08 .20
368 Mika Rontti .08 .20
369 Timo Willman .08 .20
370 Stanislav Jasecko .08 .20
371 Jukka-Pekka Laamanen .08 .20
372 Timo Ahmaoja .08 .20
373 Tapio Sammalkangas .08 .20
374 Jan Liplansky .08 .20
375 Jani Vaananen .08 .20
376 Jarkko Immonen .08 .20
377 Sandy Moger .20 .50
378 Marko Palo .08 .20
379 Semir Ben-Amor .08 .20
380 Samu Wesslin .08 .20
NNO Mikko Koivu AU 30.00 80.00
NNO Antero Niittymaki AU 12.50 30.00
NNO Tuomo Ruutu AU 25.00 60.00
NNO Ville Nieminen DREAM 2.00 5.00
NNO Kari Lehtonen AU 50.00 125.00
NNO Jari Kurri HOF 8.00 20.00

2001-02 Finnish Cardset Adrenaline Rush

This set features some of the top young talent in Finland's SM-Liiga. The odds for these series 1 inserts is not confirmed at this time.

COMPLETE SET (6) 16.00 35.00
RANDOM INSERTS IN SERIES 1 PACKS
1 Kari Lehtonen 6.00 15.00
2 Tero Maatta 2.00 3.00
3 Tuukka Mantyla 2.00 3.00
4 Tony Salmelainen 2.00 3.00
5 Mikko Koivu 4.00 10.00
6 Tuomo Ruutu 4.00 10.00

2001-02 Finnish Cardset Dueling Aces

This set features a pair of arch-enemies from the Finnish SM-Liiga. The cards were random inserts in series 2 packs. The exact odds of insertion are not confirmed at this time.

COMPLETE SET (8) 6.00 15.00
RANDOM INSERTS IN SERIES 2 PACKS
1 Joonas Jaaskelainen .80 2.00
Vladimir Machulda
2 Ville Peltonen 1.20 3.00
Janne Ojanen
3 Jan Caloun .80 2.00
Kai Nurminen
4 Toni Happola .80 2.00
Mika Viinanen
5 Vladimir Vujtek .80 2.00
Raimo Helminen
6 Petr Ton .80 2.00
Pavel Rosa
7 Marek Zidlicky .80 2.00
Jiri Vykoukal
8 Tom Draper 1.20 3.00
Jari Korpisalo

2001-02 Finnish Cardset Haltmeisters

This set features the top Finnish-born goaltenders, many of whom were employed in North America during this season. The odds on these series 1 inserts are unconfirmed at this time.

COMPLETE SET (12) 30.00 75.00
RANDOM INSERTS IN SERIES 1 PACKS
1 Pasi Nurminen 4.00 10.00
2 Miikka Kiprusoff 6.00 15.00
3 Jani Hurme 4.00 10.00
4 Vesa Toskala 6.00 15.00
5 Mika Noronen 6.00 10.00
6 Jarmo Myllys 2.00 5.00
7 Ari Sulander 2.00 5.00
8 Ari Ahonen 6.00 10.00
9 Jussi Markkanen 4.00 10.00
10 Fredrik Norrena 2.00 5.00
11 Sakari Lindfors 2.00 5.00
12 Pasi Kuivalainen 2.00 5.00

2001-02 Finnish Cardset Salt Lake City

This set features 12 members of Finland's Olympic team. The cards were inserted in series 2 packs. The odds of insertion cannot be confirmed at this time.

COMPLETE SET (12) 20.00 30.00
RANDOM INSERTS IN SERIES 2 PACKS
1 Jani Hurme 2.00 3.00
2 Miikka Kiprusoff 2.00 8.00
3 Teppo Numminen .80 2.00
4 Kimmo Timonen .80 2.00
5 Janne Niinimaa .80 2.00
6 Jyrki Lumme .80 2.00
7 Teemu Selanne 6.00 10.00
8 Juha Ylonen .80 2.00
9 Jere Lehtinen 2.00 3.00
10 Tomi Kallio .80 2.00
11 Raimo Helminen .80 2.00
12 Sami Kapanen 2.00 3.00

2001 Finnish Cardset Teemu Selanne

NNO Teemu Selanne 8.00 20.00

2002-03 Finnish Cardset

This set was issued in two series and features the top players of the SM-Liiga.

COMPLETE SET (300) 30.00 80.00
1 Peter Ahola .08 .20
2 Mika Alatalo .08 .20
3 Kristian Antila .08 .20
4 Frank Banham .25 .60
5 Jaroslav Bednar .25 .60
6 Jan Benda .08 .20
7 Frantisek Bombic .08 .20
8 Jan Caloun .08 .20
9 Martin Cech .08 .20
10 Tomas Chlubna .08 .20
11 Toni Dahlman .08 .20
12 Johan Davidsson .08 .20
13 Tom Draper .25 .60
14 Tomas Duba .08 .20
15 Miika Elomo .25 .60
16 Mikko Eloranta .25 .60
17 Vjatsheslav Fandul .08 .20
18 Theo Fleury .40 1.00
19 Janne Gronvall .08 .20
20 Kari Haakana .08 .20
21 Niklas Hagman .25 .60
22 Riku Hahl .40 1.00
23 Jaakko Harikkala .25 .60
24 Jani Hassinen .08 .20
25 Timo Hirvonen .08 .20
26 Sasu Hovi .08 .20
27 Markku Hurme .08 .20
28 Ville Immonen .08 .20
29 Otakar Janecky .25 .60
30 Olli Jokinen .25 .60
31 Martti Jarventie .25 .60
32 Erik Kakko .08 .20
33 Tomi Kallio .25 .60
34 Kimmo Kapanen .25 .60
35 Niko Kapanen .25 .60
36 Sami Kapanen .25 .60
37 Jari Kauppila .08 .20
38 Markus Ketterer .25 .60
39 Marko Kiprusoff .08 .20
40 Miikka Kiprusoff .40 1.00
41 Tom Koivisto .25 .60
42 Markus Korhonen .25 .60
43 Jari Korpisalo .08 .20
44 Mika Kortelainen .08 .20
45 Kimmo Koskenkorva .08 .20
46 Valeri Krykov .08 .20
47 Kimmo Kuhta .08 .20
48 Pasi Kuivalainen .25 .60
49 Jarno Kultanen .08 .20
50 Mikko Kuparinen .08 .20
51 Jari Kurri .40 1.00
52 Jarmo Kuusisto .08 .20
53 Juri Kuznetsov .08 .20
54 Arto Laatikainen .25 .60
55 Veli-Pekka Laitinen .08 .20
56 Peter Larsson .08 .20
57 Mikko Lehtonen .08 .20
58 Pertti Lehtonen .08 .20
59 Jari Levonen .08 .20
60 Brett Lievers .08 .20
61 Juha Lind .08 .20
62 Sakari Lindfors .25 .60
63 Kimmo Lotvonen .08 .20
64 Jyrki Lumme .25 .60
65 Petri Lätti .08 .20
66 Vladimir Machulda .08 .20
67 Ivan Majesky .25 .60
68 Olli Malmivaara .08 .20
69 Jussi Markkanen .25 .60
70 Kari Martikainen .08 .20
71 Dale McTavish .08 .20
72 Sami Mettovaara .08 .20
73 Antti Miettinen 3.00 8.00
74 Niko Mikkola .08 .20
75 Cory Murphy .08 .20
76 Jason Muzzatti .25 .60
77 Tuukka Makela .25 .60
78 Marko Mäkinen .25 .60
79 David Nemirovsky .08 .20
80 Ville Nieminen .25 .60
81 Antero Niittymaki .40 1.00
82 Angel Nikolov .08 .20
83 Janne Niskala .25 .60
84 Fredrik Norrena .25 .60
85 Petteri Nummelin .25 .60
86 Kai Nurminen .25 .60
87 Janne Ojanen .08 .20
88 Mika Oksa .08 .20
89 Pasi Pakaslahti .08 .20
90 Mikko Peltola .08 .20
91 Kimmo Peltonen .08 .20
92 Pasi Peltonen .08 .20
93 Tomi Pettinen .08 .20
94 Tuomas Pihlman .40 1.00
95 Ilkka Pikkarainen .08 .20
96 Lasse Pirjeta .08 .20
97 Esa Pirnes .08 .20
98 Andrei Potaitshuk .08 .20
99 Pasi Puistola .08 .20
100 Joni Puurula .40 1.00
101 Timo Parssinen .08 .20
102 Bruce Racine .25 .60
103 Brian Rafalski .25 .60
104 Jamie Ram .25 .60
105 Martin Richter .25 .60
106 Juha Riihijarvi .08 .20
107 Teemu Riihijarvi .08 .20
108 Kimmo Rintanen .08 .20
109 Pavel Rosa .08 .20
110 Boris Rousson .25 .60
111 Christian Ruuttu .08 .20
112 Pasi Saarela .08 .20
113 Peter Schaefer .08 .20
114 Markus Seikola .08 .20
115 Teemu Selanne .75 2.00
116 Oliver Setzinger .25 .60
117 Vladimir Sicak .08 .20
118 Ari-Pekka Siekkinen .08 .20
119 Toni Sihvonen .08 .20
121 Ari Sulander .25 .60
122 Sebastian Sulku .08 .20
123 Kari Takko .25 .60
123 Mike Stapleton .08 .20
124 Jussi Tarvainen .08 .20
125 Esa Tikkanen .25 .60
126 Harri Tikkanen .08 .20
127 Petr Ton .08 .20
128 Vesa Toskala .25 .60
129 Arto Tukio .08 .20
130 Tommi Turunen .08 .20
131 Marko Tuulola .08 .20
132 Markus Tähtinen .08 .20
133 Antti Tormanen .08 .20
134 Ville Vahalahti .08 .20
135 Ari Vallin .08 .20
136 Petri Varis .25 .60
137 Timo Vertala .08 .20
138 Joonas Vihko .08 .20
139 Mika Viinanen .08 .20
140 Vesa Viitakoski .08 .20
141 Tony Virta .08 .20
142 Tomas Vlasak .08 .20
143 Pavel Vostrak .08 .20
144 Vladimir Vujtek .08 .20
145 Jiri Vykoukal .08 .20
146 Marek Zidlicky .08 .20
147 Kari Lehtonen CL 2.50 6.00
148 Niklas Backstrom CL .08 .20
149 Petri Vehanen CL .08 .20
150 Tomas Duba CL .08 .20
151 Antti Aalto .25 .60
152 Teemu Aalto .08 .20
153 Ari Ahonen .75 2.00
154 Rami Alanko .08 .20
155 Drew Bannister .08 .20
156 Aleksander Barkov .08 .20
157 Aki Berg .25 .60
158 Sean Bergenheim .25 .60
159 Tom Bissett .25 .60
160 Niklas Backstrom .25 .60
161 Aigars Cipruss .08 .20
162 Parris Duffus .25 .60
163 Jason Elliott .25 .60
164 Teemu Elomo .08 .20
165 Jarkko Glad .08 .20
166 Carlo Grunn .08 .20
167 Tuomas Gronman .08 .20
168 Juha Gustafsson .08 .20
169 Timo Hakanen .08 .20
170 Quinn Hancock .08 .20
171 Markus Helanen .08 .20
172 Raimo Helminen .08 .20
173 Jukka Hentunen .08 .20
174 Michael Holmkvist .25 .60
175 Antti Hulkkonen .08 .20
176 Jani Hurme .40 1.00
177 Hannes Hyvonen .25 .60
178 Erik Hamalainen .08 .20
179 Toni Happola .08 .20
180 Juha Ikonen .08 .20
181 Jarkko Immonen .08 .20
182 Mikko Jokela .25 .60
183 Jussi Jokinen .40 1.00
184 Timo Jutila .08 .20
185 Lasse Jamsen .08 .20
186 Joonas Jaaskelainen .08 .20
187 Matti Kaipainen .08 .20
188 Robert Kantor .08 .20
189 Jere Karalahti .08 .20
190 Marko Kauppinen .08 .20
191 Mika Kauppinen .08 .20
192 Jani Keinanen .08 .20
193 Max Kenig .08 .20
194 Esa Keskinen .08 .20
195 Jani Kiviharju .08 .20
196 Toni Koivisto .08 .20
197 Mikko Koivu 2.00 5.00
198 Saku Koivu 1.25 3.00
199 Toni Koivunen .08 .20
200 Tomas Kucharcik .08 .20
201 Arto Kuki .08 .20
202 Lasse Kukkonen .08 .20
203 Juha Kuokkanen .08 .20
204 Janne Laakkonen .08 .20
205 Antti Laaksonen .25 .60
206 Jukka-Pekka Laamanen .08 .20
207 Scott Langkow .25 .60
208 Jan Latvala .08 .20
209 Janne Laukkanen .08 .20
210 Jari Laukkanen .25 .60
211 Tero Lehtera .25 .60
212 Jere Lehtinen .40 1.00
213 Mika Lehto .08 .20
214 Kari Lehtonen 5.00 12.00
215 Tero Leinonen .08 .20
216 Pauli Levokari .08 .20
217 Joni Lius .08 .20
218 Jouni Loponen .08 .20
219 Mikko Luoma .08 .20
220 Toni Lydman .08 .20
221 Jyri Marttinen .08 .20
222 Ilkka Mikkola .08 .20
223 Mikko Myllykoski .08 .20
224 Jere Myllyniemi .08 .20
225 Jarmo Myllys .25 .60
226 Toni Makiaho .08 .20
227 Tuukka Mantyla .08 .20
228 Tero Maatta .25 .60
229 Antti-Jussi Niemi .08 .20
230 Mika Nieminen .08 .20
231 Janne Niinimaa .25 .60
232 Jesse Niinimaki .40 1.00
233 Tuomas Nissinen .08 .20
234 Mika Noronen .40 1.00
235 Teppo Numminen .25 .60
236 Pasi Numminen .25 .60
237 Michael Nylander .25 .60
238 Matti Naatanen .08 .20
239 Marko Ojanen .08 .20
240 Marko Palo .08 .20
241 Sakari Palsola .08 .20
242 Jan Pardavy .08 .20
243 Timo Peltomaa .08 .20
244 Ville Peltonen .08 .20
245 Eric Perrin .08 .20
246 Jussi Pesonen .08 .20
247 Pasi Petrilainen .08 .20
248 Juha Pitkamaki .08 .20
249 Joni Pitkanen 1.25 3.00
250 Toni Porkka .08 .20
251 Mika Pyorala .08 .20
252 Erkki Rajamaki .08 .20
253 Jani Rita .25 .60
254 Jarkko Ruutu .25 .60
255 Mikko Ruutu .40 1.00
256 Tuomo Ruutu 1.00 2.50
257 Mikko Ramo .08 .20
258 Timo Saarikoski .08 .20
259 Pasi Saarinen .08 .20
260 Kalle Sahlstedt .25 .60
261 Teemu Sainomaa .08 .20
262 Tony Salmelainen .08 .20
263 Sami Salo .25 .60
264 Timo Salonen .08 .20
265 Tommi Santala .08 .20
266 Peter Sarno .25 .60
267 Tommi Satosaari .08 .20
268 Steve Shirreffs .08 .20
269 Harri Sillgren .08 .20
270 Roman Simicek .08 .20
271 Eero Somervuori .25 .60
272 Dave Stathos .25 .60
273 Mika Stromberg .25 .60
274 Raimo Summanen .25 .60
275 Henrik Tallinder .25 .60
276 Petr Tenkrat .25 .60
277 Tim Thomas .25 .60
278 Kimmo Timonen .08 .20
279 Pekka Tirkkonen .08 .20
280 Hannu Toivonen 1.00 2.50
281 Sami Torkki .08 .20
282 Marco Tuokko .08 .20
283 Marko Tuomainen .08 .20
284 Aki Uusikartano .08 .20
285 Lubomir Vaic .08 .20
286 Tomek Valtonen .08 .20
287 Petri Vehanen .08 .20
288 Samu Wesslin .08 .20
289 Hannu Virta .08 .20
290 Antti Virtanen .08 .20
291 Jari Viuhkola .08 .20
292 Roman Vopat .08 .20
293 Jukka Voutilainen .08 .20
294 Jyrki Valivaara .08 .20
295 Ossi Vaananen .25 .60
296 Juha Ylonen .25 .60
297 Dave Stathos .08 .20
298 Scott Langkow .25 .60
299 Tero Leinonen .08 .20
300 Mika Lehto .08 .20

2002-03 Finnish Cardset Bound for Glory

Random inserts in series two packs. Insertion odds unknown.

COMPLETE SET (10) 12.00 30.00
1 Sean Bergenheim .75 2.00
2 Jussi Jokinen 1.50 4.00
3 Mikko Koivu 3.00 8.00
4 Kari Lehtonen 4.00 10.00
5 Jesse Niinimaki .40 1.00
6 Joni Pitkanen 1.25 3.00
7 Tuomo Ruutu 2.00 5.00
8 Oliver Setzinger .40 1.00
9 Jussi Timonen .75 2.00
10 Hannu Toivonen 2.00 5.00

2002-03 Finnish Cardset Dynamic Duos

Randomly inserted in series 2 packs. Insertion ratios unknown.

COMPLETE SET (10) 15.00 40.00
1 Saku Koivu 4.00 10.00
Mikko Koivu
2 Pasi Nurminen 4.00 10.00
Kari Lehtonen
3 Sami Kapanen 2.00 5.00
Tuomo Ruutu
4 Janne Niinimaa 1.25 3.00
Joni Pitkanen
5 Olli Jokinen 1.25 3.00
Jukka Voutilainen
6 Ville Nieminen 1.25 3.00
Tuukka Mantyla
7 Tomi Kallio 1.25 3.00
Tuomas Pihlman
8 Jani Hurme 1.25 3.00
Tomas Duba
9 Niko Kapanen 2.00 5.00
Antti Miettinen
10 Teemu Selanne 4.00 10.00
Sean Bergenheim

2002-03 Finnish Cardset Kari Lehtonen Honors

Random inserts in series 2 packs. Odds unconfirmed, but believed to be 1:64.

COMPLETE SET (3) 10.00 25.00
1 Kari Lehtonen 4.00 10.00
U-18 top goalie
2 Kari Lehtonen 4.00 10.00
U-18 All-Stars
3 Kari Lehtonen 4.00 10.00
U-20 top goalie

2002-03 Finnish Cardset Kari Lehtonen Trophies

Random inserts in series 1 packs. Odds were 1:64.

COMPLETE SET (3) 10.00 25.00
1 Kari Lehtonen 4.00 10.00
2 Kari Lehtonen 4.00 10.00
3 Kari Lehtonen 4.00 10.00

2002-03 Finnish Cardset Signatures

STATED ODDS 1:128 SERIES 1
STATED PRINT RUN 120 SER.#'d SETS
1 Sean Bergenheim 10.00 25.00
2 Jussi Jokinen 15.00 40.00
3 Mikko Koivu 20.00 50.00
4 Kari Lehtonen 75.00 200.00
5 Jesse Niinimaki 10.00 25.00
6 Joni Pitkanen 20.00 50.00
7 Tuomo Ruutu 25.00 60.00
8 Oliver Setzinger 10.00 25.00
9 Jussi Timonen 10.00 25.00
10 Hannu Toivonen 15.00 40.00

2002-03 Finnish Cardset Solid Gold

COMPLETE SET (6) 15.00
STATED ODDS 1:16 SERIES 1
1 Pasi Nurminen 2.00
2 Janne Niinimaa 2.00
3 Sami Salo 2.00
4 Sami Kapanen 2.00
5 Saku Koivu 5.00
6 Teemu Selanne 5.00

2002-03 Finnish Cardset Solid Gold Six-Pack

Randomly inserted in series 2 packs. Insertion ratios unknown.

COMPLETE SET (6) 8.00
1 Jussi Markkanen 3.00
2 Toni Lydman 1.00
3 Ossi Vaananen 1.00
4 Niklas Hagman 1.00
5 Olli Jokinen 3.00
6 Niko Kapanen 3.00

2003-04 Finnish Cardset

COMPLETE SET (182) 20.00 40.00
1 Jere Myllyniemi .20 .50
2 Sami Heinonen .20 .50
3 Sebastien Sulku .08 .20
4 Tero Maatta .08 .20
5 Rami Alanko .08 .20
6 Arto Laatikainen .08 .20
7 Jan Caloun .08 .20
8 Markku Hurme .08 .20
9 Jukka Tiilikainen .08 .20
10 Ladislav Kohn .08 .20
11 Miika Elomo .08 .20
12 Bruce Gardiner .20 .50
13 Marko Tuomainen .08 .20
14 Teemu Elomo .08 .20
15 Dave Stathos .30 .75
16 Ladislav Benysek .08 .20
17 Jere Karalahti .08 .20
18 Jarno Kultanen .08 .20
19 Toni Soderholm .08 .20
20 Pasi Saarinen .08 .20
21 Kim Hirschovits .08 .20
22 Kimmo Kuhta .08 .20
23 Joonas Vihko .08 .20
24 Toni Happola .08 .20
25 Carlo Grunn .08 .20
26 Timo Parssinen .20 .50
27 Brett Harkins .20 .50
28 Martin Spanhel .08 .20
29 Joni Puurula .20 .50
30 Rob Tallas .20 .50
31 Vladimir Sicak .08 .20
32 Aki Heino .08 .20
33 Tomas Eskeleinen .08 .20
34 Marko Tuulola .08 .20
35 Teemu Aalto .08 .20
36 Jyrki Louhi .08 .20
37 Tony Virta .08 .20
38 Vladimir Vujtek .08 .20
39 Tomas Kucharcik .08 .20
40 Janne Laakkonen .08 .20
41 Janne Lahti .08 .20
42 Anders Burstrom .08 .20
43 Juha Pitkamaki .20 .50
44 Tuomas Nissinen .20 .50
45 Cory Murphy .08 .20
46 Ismo Siren .08 .20
47 Martin Hlavacka .08 .20
48 Jukka-Pekka Laamanen .08 .20
49 Jesse Niinimaki .30 .75
50 Ville Snellman .08 .20
51 Toni Dahlman .08 .20
52 Erkki Rajamaki .08 .20
53 Marek Vorel .08 .20
54 Mikko Suvanto .08 .20
55 Vesa Viitakoski .08 .20
56 Raimo Helminen .08 .20
57 Markus Helanen .20 .50
58 Pasi Hakkinen .20 .50
59 Sami Helenius .20 .50
60 Jan Latvala .08 .20
61 Martti Jarventie .20 .50
62 Arto Tukio .08 .20
63 Tomek Valtonen .08 .20
64 Petri Pakaslahti .08 .20
65 Jussi Pesonen .08 .20
66 Timo Vertala .08 .20
67 Tommi Turunen .08 .20
68 Glen Metropolit .30 .75
69 Marko Jantunen .08 .20
70 Teemu Laine .08 .20
71 Tero Leinonen .20 .50
72 Tommi Nikkila .20 .50
73 Tuomo Kortelainen .08 .20
74 Tommi Kovanen .08 .20
75 Jari Korhonen .08 .20
76 Jyri Marttinen .08 .20
77 Ilari Filppula .08 .20
78 Tuomo Jaaskelainen .08 .20
79 Alexandre Tremblay .08 .20
80 Jari Jaaskelainen .08 .20
81 Jarkko Immonen .08 .20
82 Jaakko Uhlback .08 .20
83 Antti Virtanen .08 .20
84 P.C. Drouin .20 .50
85 Niklas Backstrom .30 .75
86 Ari Vallin .08 .20
87 Ilkka Mikkola .08 .20
88 Martin Stepanek .08 .20
89 Mikko Lehtonen .08 .20
90 Kimmo Lotvonen .08 .20
91 Mikko Myllykoski .08 .20
92 Jussi Jokinen .08 .20
93 Lasse Jamsen .08 .20
94 Mika Pyorala .08 .20
95 Janne Pesonen .08 .20
96 Brett Lievers .08 .20
97 Jari Viuhkola .08 .20
98 Sakari Palsola .08 .20
99 Antti Jokela .20 .50
100 Petri Vehanen .20 .50
101 Jaakko Harikkala .08 .20
102 Toni Porkka .08 .20
103 Janne Niskala .08 .20
104 Erik Hamalainen .08 .20
105 Mikko Luovi .08 .20
106 Mika Viinanen .08 .20
107 Toni Koivisto .08 .20
108 Sami Torkki .08 .20
109 Joe Murphy .20 .50
110 Markku Tahtinen .08 .20
111 Quinn Hancock .20 .50
112 Pasi Saarela .08 .20
113 Mikko Ramo .08 .20
114 Martin Cech .08 .20
115 Tero Paappanen .08 .20
116 Santeri Heiskanen .08 .20
117 Jermu Pisto .08 .20
118 Radek Philipp .08 .20
119 Tommi Hannus .08 .20
120 Daniel Widing .08 .20
121 Jari Kauppila .08 .20
122 Ville Hirvonen .08 .20
123 Toni Saarinen .08 .20
124 Toni Makiaho .08 .20
125 Shayne Toporowski .20 .50
126 Oliver Setzinger .20 .50
127 Juha Kuokkanen .08 .20
128 Jarmo Myllys .20 .50
129 Jussi Pekkala .08 .20
130 Petri Kokko .08 .20
131 Antti Bruun .08 .20
132 Sami Kaartinen .08 .20
133 Ville Immonen .08 .20
134 Kalle Kerman .08 .20
135 Mika Kauppinen .08 .20
136 Vladimir Machulda .08 .20
137 Pasi Nielikainen .08 .20
138 Petr Sachl .08 .20
139 Aki Uusikartano .08 .20
140 Timo Hirvonen .08 .20
141 Sasu Hovi .20 .50
142 Mika Lehto .20 .50
143 Pekka Saravo .08 .20
144 Pasi Puistola .08 .20
145 Pasi Petrilainen .08 .20
146 Miska Kangasniemi .08 .20
147 Janne Ojanen .08 .20
148 Alexander Barkov .08 .20
149 Petri Varis .08 .20
150 Marko Ojanen .08 .20
151 Marko Makinen .08 .20
152 Sami Venalainen .08 .20
153 Stefan Ohman .08 .20
154 Arto Kuki .08 .20
155 Teemu Lassila .20 .50
156 Tuomo Karjalainen .20 .50
157 Kimmo Peltonen .08 .20
158 Marko Kauppinen .08 .20
159 David Schneider .08 .20
160 Jiri Vykoukal .08 .20
161 Antti Hulkkonen .08 .20
162 Mikko Koivu 1.25 3.00
163 Marko Tuokko .08 .20

164 Antti Aalto .08 .20
165 Kai Nurminen .08 .20
166 Ville Vahalahti .08 .20
167 Mikko Eloranta .08 .20
168 Niko Mikkola .08 .20
169 Scott Langkow .30 .75
170 Steve Shierrefs .20 .50
171 Pasi Peltonen .08 .20
172 Oleg Sorokin .08 .20
173 Jarkko Glad .08 .20
174 Samu Wesslin .08 .20
175 Vyacheslav Fandul .08 .20
176 Jari Korpisalo .08 .20
177 Pasi Tuominen .08 .20
178 Marko Kivenmaki .08 .20
179 Tomi Pollanen .08 .20
180 Timo Salonen .08 .20
181 Juha Kiilholma .08 .20
182 Martin Bergeron .20 .50

2003-04 Finnish Cardset D-Day

Featuring Finnish prospects drafted highly by the NHL, these cards were inserted 1:8 packs.

COMPLETE SET (16) 15.00 40.00
DD1 Sean Bergenheim .75 2.00
DD2 Mikael Holmqvist .75 2.00
DD3 Lasse Kukkonen .75 2.00
DD4 Kari Lehtonen 5.00 12.00
DD5 Mikko Luoma .40 1.00
DD6 Antti Miettinen .75 2.00
DD7 Eric Perrin 1.25 3.00
DD8 Tuomas Pihlman .75 2.00
DD9 Ilkka Pikkarainen .40 1.00
DD10 Esa Pirnes .40 1.00
DD11 Joni Pitkanen 1.25 3.00
DD12 Tuomo Ruutu 3.00 8.00
DD13 Tomi Santala .40 1.00
DD14 Eero Somervuori .40 1.00
DD15 Hannu Toivonen 3.00 8.00
DD16 Marek Zidlicky 1.25 3.00

2003-04 Finnish Cardset Globetrotters

These cards were inserted 1:16.

COMPLETE SET (9) 6.00 15.00
GR1 Toni Dahlman .75 2.00
GR2 Mikko Eloranta .75 2.00
GR3 Sami Helenius .75 2.00
GR4 Marko Jantunen .75 2.00
GR5 Jere Karalahti .75 2.00
GR6 Martin Stepanek .75 2.00
GR7 Petri Varis .75 2.00
GR8 Tony Virta .75 2.00
GR9 Vladimir Vujtek .75 2.00

2003-04 Finnish Cardset Vintage 1983

Featuring three top prospects born in 1983, these cards were inserted 1:32.

COMPLETE SET (3) 10.00 25.00
V1 Mikko Koivu 6.00 15.00
V2 Joni Pitkanen 2.00 5.00
V3 Tuomo Ruutu 4.00 10.00

2004-05 Finnish Cardset

Includes cards from a 200-card main set plus a 117-card update series.

COMPLETE SET (317) 30.00 60.00
1 Jere Myllyniemi .20 .50
2 Mika Oksa .20 .50
3 Kari Haakana .08 .20
4 Arto Laatikainen .08 .20
5 Mika Lehtinen .08 .20
6 Landon Wilson .20 .50
7 Donald MacLean .20 .50
8 Krystofer Kolanos .20 .50
9 Joni Toykkala .08 .20
10 Olli Ahonen .08 .20
11 Ladislav Kohn .08 .20
12 Lauri Tukonen ERC 1.25 3.00
13 Teemu Elomo .08 .20
14 Dave Stathos .20 .50
15 Marek Zidlicky .20 .50
16 Jere Karalahti .08 .20
17 Jarno Kultanen .08 .20
18 Toni Soderholm .08 .20
19 Pasi Saarinen .08 .20
20 Kim Hirschovits .08 .20
21 Kimmo Kuhta .08 .20
22 Joonas Vihko .08 .20
23 Jarkko Ruutu .20 .50
24 Timo Parssinen .08 .20
25 Arttu Luttinen .08 .20
26 Lennart Petrell .08 .20
27 Brett Harkins .20 .50
28 Eetu Holma .08 .20
29 Roman Vopat .08 .20
30 Miika Wiikman .20 .50
31 Vladimir Sicak .20 .50
32 Tuomas Eskelinen .08 .20
33 Mikko Jokela .08 .20
34 Veli-Pekka Laitinen .08 .20
35 Tuukka Makela .08 .20
36 Jyrki Louhi .08 .20
37 Jani Hassinen .08 .20
38 Hannu Vaisanen .08 .20
39 Riku Hahl .20 .50
40 Jani Keinanen .08 .20
41 Janne Laakkonen .08 .20
42 Jani Rita .20 .50
43 Jukka Voutilainen .08 .20
44 Toni Makiaho .08 .20
45 Oliver Setzinger .20 .50
46 Juha Pitkamaki .08 .20
47 Tuukka Rask ERC 2.00 5.00
48 Ville Koistinen .08 .20
49 Cory Murphy .08 .20
50 Sami Helenius .20 .50
51 Ismo Kuoppala .20 .50
52 Jesse Niinimaki .20 .50
53 Marko Luomala .08 .20
54 Timo Peltomaa .08 .20
55 Ville Leino .08 .20
56 Steve Kariya .40 1.00
57 Patrik Stefan .20 .50
58 Jussi Pesonen .08 .20
59 Tommi Turunen .08 .20
60 Raimo Helminen .08 .20
61 Simo Vidgren .08 .20
62 Pasi Hakkinen .20 .50
63 Tim Thomas .40 1.00
64 Kevin Kantee .08 .20
65 Kari Martikainen .08 .20
66 Jan Latvala .08 .20
67 Sami Lepisto .08 .20
68 Martti Jarventie .08 .20
69 Marko Jantunen .08 .20
70 Tomek Valtonen .08 .20
71 Toni Dahlman .08 .20
72 Petri Pakaslahti .08 .20
73 Petri Varis .08 .20
74 Juha Lind .08 .20
75 Timo Vertala .08 .20
76 Quinn Hancock .08 .20
77 Glen Metropolit .20 .50
78 Valtteri Filppula ERC .40 1.00
79 Tommi Nikkila .20 .50
80 Sinuhe Wallinheimo .20 .50
81 Tommi Kovanen .08 .20
82 Duvie Westcott .20 .50
83 Jari Korhonen .08 .20
84 Ilari Filppula .08 .20
85 Arsi Piispanen .08 .20
86 Steve Martins .20 .50
87 Jarkko Immonen .20 .50
88 Janne Hauhtonen .08 .20
89 Jaakko Uhlback .08 .20
90 Antti Virtanen .08 .20
91 Niklas Backstrom .40 1.00
92 Oskari Korpikari .08 .20
93 Lasse Kukkonen .20 .50
94 Ari Vallin .08 .20
95 Mikko Lehtonen .08 .20
96 Janne Niinimaa .08 .20
97 Jussi Jokinen .40 1.00
98 Viktor Ujcik .08 .20
99 Pekka Saarenheimo .08 .20
100 Mika Pyorala .08 .20
101 Janne Pesonen .08 .20
102 Jari Viuhkola .08 .20
103 Toni Sihvonen .08 .20
104 Sakari Palsola .08 .20
105 Petr Tenkrat .08 .20
106 Eero Somervuori .08 .20
107 Michael Nylander .20 .50
108 Dwayne Roloson .75 2.00
109 Petri Vehanen .08 .20
110 Toni Porkka .08 .20
111 Tomi Pettinen .08 .20
112 Janne Niskala .08 .20
113 Otto Honkaheimo .08 .20
114 Erik Hamalainen .08 .20
115 Steve Larouche .20 .50
116 Esa Pirnes .08 .20
117 Ville Snellman .08 .20
118 Shayne Toporowski .08 .20
119 Martin Bartek .08 .20
120 Toni Koivisto .08 .20
121 Sami Torkki .08 .20
122 Markku Tahtinen .08 .20
123 Pasi Saarela .08 .20
124 Pasi Nurminen .20 .50
125 Santeri Heiskanen .08 .20
126 Topi Lehtonen .08 .20
127 Erik Kakko .08 .20
128 Daniel Widing .08 .20
129 Sami Salonen .08 .20
130 Lasse Jamsen .08 .20
131 Ville Hirvonen .08 .20
132 Toni Saarinen .08 .20
133 Jesse Saarinen .08 .20
134 Jesse Welling .08 .20
135 Toni Koivunen .08 .20
136 Jarmo Myllys .20 .50
137 Jussi Pekkala .08 .20
138 Jussi Timonen .08 .20
139 Olli Malmivaara .20 .50
140 Petri Kokko .08 .20
141 Justin D. Forrest .08 .20
142 Eetu Qvist .08 .20
143 Kalle Kerman .08 .20
144 Mika Kauppinen .08 .20
145 Petr Sachl .08 .20
146 Petteri Nokelainen ERC 1.25 3.00
147 Timo Hirvonen .08 .20
148 Frank Banham .20 .50
149 Ville Viitaluoma .08 .20
150 Mika Lehto .20 .50
151 Anssi Salmela .08 .20
152 Pekka Saravo .08 .20
153 Juha Gustafsson .08 .20
154 Pasi Puistola .08 .20
155 Robert Kantor .08 .20
156 Mikko Myllykoski .08 .20
157 Janne Ojanen .08 .20
158 Johannes Alanen .08 .20
159 Mika Viinanen .08 .20
160 Marko Ojanen .08 .20
161 Petri Kontiola .08 .20
162 Ville Nieminen .20 .50
163 Sami Venalainen .08 .20
164 Stefan Ohman .08 .20
165 Tomas Chlubna .08 .20
166 Teemu Laine .20 .50
167 Teemu Lassila .08 .20
168 Tuomo Karjalainen .08 .20
169 Marko Kiprusoff .08 .20
170 Kimmo Eronen .08 .20
171 Markus Seikola .08 .20
172 David Schneider .08 .20
173 Jiri Vykoukal .08 .20
174 Antti Hulkkonen .08 .20
175 Marco Tuokko .08 .20
176 Antti Aalto .08 .20
177 Joni Lius .08 .20
178 Kai Nurminen .08 .20
179 Ville Vahalahti .08 .20
180 Lauri Korpikoski ERC 1.25 3.00
181 Mika Alatalo .08 .20
182 Jari Kauppila .08 .20
183 Arttu Virtanen .08 .20
184 Tuomas Nissinen .08 .20
185 Scott Langkow .20 .50
186 Pasi Peltonen .08 .20
187 Olegs Sorokins .08 .20
188 Pauli Levokari .08 .20
189 Greg Classen .20 .50
190 Samu Wesslin .08 .20
191 Mika Niemi .08 .20
192 Jari Korpisalo .08 .20
193 Jesse Joensuu .08 .20
194 Pasi Tuominen .08 .20
195 Marko Kivenmaki .08 .20
196 Teemu Virkkunen .08 .20
197 Pasi Nielikainen .08 .20
198 Jason Williams .20 .50
199 Aki Uusikartano .08 .20
200 Juha Kiilholma .08 .20
201 Janne Jalasvaara .08 .20
202 Tommi Pelkonen .08 .20
203 Tero Maatta .08 .20
204 Antti Pihlstrom .08 .20
205 Miika Elomo .08 .20
206 Jarkko Almmonen .08 .20
207 Mike Ribeiro .20 .50
208 Matti Naatanen .08 .20
209 Jani Nieminen .08 .20
210 Tomas Vokoun .75 2.00
211 Mikko Turunen .08 .20
212 Mikko Kurvinen .08 .20
213 Hannu Pikkarainen .08 .20
214 Lasse Pirjeta .08 .20
215 Juha Fagerstedt .08 .20
216 Jarmo Porthen .08 .20
217 Mikko Laine .08 .20
218 Mika Noronen .20 .50
219 Jarmo Virkki .08 .20
220 Tuomas Immonen .08 .20
221 Jukka-Pekka Laamanen .08 .20
222 Josh Holden .08 .20
223 Petteri Virtanen .08 .20
224 Joni Lappalainen .08 .20
225 Joni Lindlof .08 .20
226 Juha-Pekka Loikas .08 .20
227 Janne Lahti .08 .20
228 Juuso Riksman .08 .20
229 Teemu Jaaskelainen .08 .20
230 Henri Laurila .08 .20
231 Ossi Pellinen .08 .20
232 Antti Miettinen .40 1.00
233 Hannes Hyvonen .08 .20
234 Jukka Tiilikainen .08 .20
235 Tommi Jaminki .08 .20
236 Mikko Suvanto .08 .20
237 Samuli Jalkanen .08 .20
238 Brian Campbell .20 .50
239 Mikko Kalteva .08 .20
240 Markus Kankaanpera .08 .20
241 Tero Konttinen .08 .20
242 Ossi Vaananen .08 .20
243 Tomi Maki .08 .20
244 Arto Koivisto .08 .20
245 Arto Kuki .08 .20
246 Roni Andersson .08 .20
247 Teemu Kuusisto .08 .20
248 Petri Virolainen .08 .20
249 Ilkka Vaarasuo .08 .20
250 Carlo Grünn .08 .20
251 Juha-Pekka Hytonen .08 .20
252 Jari Jaaskelainen .08 .20
253 Ossi Louhivaara .08 .20
254 Tuomas Mikkonen .08 .20
255 Eero Hyvarinen .08 .20
256 Jody Shelley .40 1.00
257 Pekka Rinne .40 1.00
258 Ilkka Mikkola .08 .20
259 Topi Jaakola .08 .20
260 Kimmo Lotvonen .08 .20
261 Josef Boumedienne .08 .20
262 Juha-Pekka Haataja .08 .20
263 Antti Aarnio .08 .20
264 Mikael Vuorio .08 .20
265 Jaakko Harikkala .08 .20
266 Antti Bruun .08 .20
267 Ilkka Saarela .08 .20
268 Jarkko Kauvosaari .08 .20
269 Teemu Normio .08 .20
270 Janne Siivonen .08 .20
271 Juhamatti Yli-Junnila .08 .20
272 Joni Yli-Torkko .08 .20
273 Jaakko Suomalainen .08 .20
274 Karri Ramo .08 .20
275 Markus Helanen .08 .20
276 Olli Korkeavuori .08 .20
277 Antti-Pekka Lamberg .08 .20
278 Mikko Niinikoski .08 .20
279 Petri Koskinen .08 .20
280 Tommi Hannus .08 .20
281 Tuomas Santavuori .08 .20
282 Juha Kuokkanen .08 .20
283 Thomas Innerwinkler .08 .20
284 Harri Tikkanen .08 .20
285 Matti Hana .08 .20
286 Ossi-Petteri Gronholm .08 .20
287 Mike Gabinet .08 .20
288 Kalle Kaijomaa .08 .20
289 Ville Koho .08 .20
290 Mika Skytta .08 .20
291 Tuomas Vanttinen .08 .20
292 Andrew Raycroft .60 1.50
293 Sasu Hovi .08 .20
294 Mikko Pukka .08 .20
295 Kimmo Koskenkorva .08 .20
296 Teemu Nurmi .08 .20
297 Robert Tomik .08 .20
298 Jarkko Pyymaki .08 .20
299 Marko Makinen .08 .20
300 Timo Vertala .08 .20
301 Juho Santanen .08 .20
302 Simon Backman .08 .20
303 Markku Paukkunen .08 .20
304 Craig Rivet .08 .20
305 Tomi Sykko .08 .20
306 Saku Koivu .75 2.00
307 Matias Metsaranta .08 .20
308 Markus Ojala .08 .20
309 Tyler Bouck .20 .50
310 Matti Aho .08 .20
311 Marko Toivonen .08 .20
312 Mika Rontti .08 .20
313 Atte Pentikainen .08 .20
314 Aki Heino .08 .20
315 Kristian Kuusela .08 .20
316 Matti Kuparinen .08 .20
317 Juha-Pekka Ketola .08 .20

2004-05 Finnish Cardset Parallel

2X to 5X BASE CARD VALUE

2004-05 Finnish Cardset Saku Koivu Golden Signatures

Random inserts in series II packs.

COMPLETE SET (3) 10.00 25.00
1 Saku Koivu 4.00 10.00
2 Saku Koivu 4.00 10.00
3 Saku Koivu 4.00 10.00

2004-05 Finnish Cardset Signatures

Random inserts in series II packs. Inserted approximately one per box.

1 Joni Toykkala 8.00 20.00
2 Ladislav Kohn 8.00 20.00
3 Lauri Tukonen 12.00 30.00
4 Marek Zidlicky 12.00 30.00
5 Jere Karalahti 8.00 20.00
6 Jarno Kultanen 8.00 20.00
7 Brett Harkins 8.00 20.00
8 Vladimir Sicak 8.00 20.00
9 Tuomas Eskelinen 8.00 20.00
10 Riku Hahl 8.00 20.00
11 Jani Rita 8.00 20.00
12 Tuukka Rask 25.00 60.00
13 Jussi Pesonen 8.00 20.00
14 Simo Vidgren 8.00 20.00
15 Toni Dahlman 8.00 20.00
16 Valtteri Filppula 12.00 30.00
17 Duvie Westcott 12.00 30.00
18 Arsi Piispanen 8.00 20.00
19 Steve Martins 8.00 20.00
20 Jarkko Immonen 12.00 30.00
21 Niklas Backstrom 15.00 40.00
22 Jussi Jokinen 60.00
23 Dwayne Roloson 15.00 40.00
24 Esa Pirnes 8.00 20.00
25 Erik Kakko 8.00 20.00
26 Jarmo Myllys 8.00 20.00
27 Petteri Nokelainen 12.00 30.00
28 Frank Banham 12.00 30.00
29 Pekka Saravo 8.00 20.00
30 Pasi Puistola 8.00 20.00
31 Mikko Myllykoski 8.00 20.00
32 Petri Kontiola 8.00 20.00
33 Ville Nieminen 8.00 20.00
34 Marko Kiprusoff 8.00 20.00
35 David Schneider 8.00 20.00
36 Lauri Korpikoski 12.00 30.00
37 Olegs Sorokins 8.00 20.00
38 Mika Niemi 8.00 20.00
39 Jesse Joensuu 8.00 20.00
40 Teemu Virkkunen 8.00 20.00
41 Jason Williams 12.00 30.00

2004-05 Finnish Cardset Stars of the Game

COMPLETE SET (14) 25.00
1 Riku Hahl 3.00
2 Hannes Hyvonen 1.00
3 Jarkko Immonen 3.00
4 Scott Langkow 2.00
5 Teemu Lassila 1.00
6 Ville Nieminen 2.00
7 Janne Niinimaa 2.00
8 Mika Noronen 3.00
9 Pasi Nurminen 3.00
10 Michael Nylander 2.00
11 Jarkko Ruutu 2.00
12 Patrik Stefan 2.00
13 Tim Thomas 3.00
14 Marek Zidlicky 2.00

2004-05 Finnish Cardset Tribute to Koivu

Random inserts in series II packs.

COMPLETE SET (3) 25.00
1 Saku Koivu 10.00
2 Saku Koivu 10.00
3 Saku Koivu 10.00

2005 Finnish Tappara Legendat

COMPLETE SET (32) 10.00 25.00
1 Antti Leppanen .40 1.00
2 Seppo Liitsola .40 1.00
3 Aleksander Barkov .40 1.00
4 Jukka Porvari .40 1.00
5 Mikko Leinonen .40 1.00
6 Martti Jarkko .40 1.00
7 Kiira Korpi .40 1.00
8 Ville Nieminen .40 1.00
9 Esko Niemi .40 1.00
10 Teppo Numminen .40 1.00
11 Erkki Lehtonen .40 1.00
12 Jarl Ohlson .40 1.00
13 Timo Susi .40 1.00
14 Kiira Korpi .40 1.00
15 Timo Jutila .40 1.00
16 Hannu Kamppuri .75 2.00
17 Lasse Litma .40 1.00
18 Pertti Valkeapaa .40 1.00
19 Yrjo Hakala .40 1.00
20 Jouni Seistamo .40 1.00
21 Kiira Korpi .40 1.00
22 Pekka Marjamaki .40 1.00
23 Markus Mattsson .40 1.00
24 Seppo Ahokainen .40 1.00
25 Hannu Haapalainen .40 1.00
26 Esko Luostarinen .40 1.00
27 Pertti Koivulahti .40 1.00
28 Kiira Korpi .40 1.00
29 Janne Ojanen .40 1.00
30 Kalevi Numminen .40 1.00
31 Jukka Rautakorpi .40 1.00
32 Rauno Korpi .40 1.00

2005-06 Finnish Cardset

COMPLETE SET (352) 25.00 60.00
1 Janne Jalasvaara .10 .25
2 Kari Haakana .10 .25
3 Arto Laatikainen .10 .25
4 Joni Toykkala .10 .25
5 Olli Ahonen .10 .25
6 Ladislav Kohn .10 .25
7 Lauri Tukonen .20 .50
8 Mike Ribeiro .20 .50
9 Niko Nieminen .10 .25
10 Jan Lundell .10 .25
11 Marek Zidlicky .20 .50
12 Mikko Turunen .10 .25
13 Toni Lydman .10 .25
14 Mikko Kurvinen .10 .25
15 Pasi Saarinen .10 .25
16 Kim Hirschovits .10 .25
17 Joonas Vihko .10 .25
18 Toni Happola .10 .25
19 Juha Fagerstedt .10 .25
20 Turo Jarvinen .10 .25
21 Arttu Luttinen .10 .25
22 Eetu Holma .10 .25
23 Olli Jokinen .20 .50
24 Mika Noronen .20 .50
25 Miika Wiikman .10 .25
26 Tuomas Immonen .10 .25
27 Mikko Jokela .10 .25
28 Veli-Pekka Laitinen .10 .25
29 Jyrki Louhi .10 .25
30 Petteri Wirtanen .10 .25
31 Joni Lappalainen .10 .25
32 Hannu Vaisanen .10 .25
33 Riku Hahl .10 .25
34 Jani Keinanen .10 .25
35 Juha-Pekka Loikas .10 .25
36 Janne Lahti .10 .25
37 Oliver Setzinger .10 .25
38 Juha Pitkamaki .10 .25
39 Vesa Toskala .40 1.00
40 Tuukka Rask 1.25 3.00
41 Joonas Ronnberg .10 .25
42 Ville Koistinen .20 .50
43 Ossi Pellinen .10 .25
44 Marko Anttila .10 .25
45 Marko Luomala .10 .25
46 Patrik Stefan .10 .25
47 Jussi Pesonen .10 .25
48 Raimo Helminen .10 .25
49 Simo Vidgren .10 .25
50 Pasi Hakkinen .10 .25
51 Tim Thomas .75 2.00
52 Brian Campbell .20 .50
53 Markus Kankaanpera .10 .25
54 Kevin Kantee .10 .25
55 Kari Martikainen .10 .25
56 Ossi Vaananen .10 .25
57 Martti Jarventie .10 .25
58 Tomi Maki .10 .25
59 Toni Dahlman .10 .25
60 Petri Pakaslahti .10 .25
61 Petri Varis .10 .25
62 Teemu Kuusisto .10 .25
63 Tommi Nikkila .10 .25
64 Tommi Kovanen .10 .25
65 Duvie Westcott .20 .50
66 Ilkka Vaarasuo .10 .25
67 Carlo Grunn .10 .25
68 Juha-Pekka Hytonen .10 .25
69 Arsi Piispanen .10 .25
70 Jari Jaaskelainen .10 .25
71 Ossi Louhivaara .10 .25
72 Tuomas Mikkonen .10 .25
73 Jarkko Immonen .20 .50
74 Antti Virtanen .10 .25
75 Ari Luostarinen .10 .25
76 Jermu Pisto .10 .25
77 Mikko Saavinen .10 .25
78 Samuli Suhonen .10 .25
79 Ville Hamalainen .10 .25
80 Tuomas Kiiskinen .10 .25
81 Henri Huohvanainen .10 .25
82 Sami Salonen .10 .25
83 Max Kenig .10 .25
84 Saku Kekalainen .10 .25
85 Sami Kaartinen .10 .25
86 Timo Kuuluvainen .10 .25
87 Pekka Rinne .40 1.00
88 Oskari Korpikari .10 .25
89 Lasse Kukkonen .10 .25
90 Ilkka Mikkola .10 .25
91 Topi Jaakola .10 .25
92 Janne Niinimaa .10 .25
93 Jussi Jokinen .40 1.00
94 Viktor Ujcik .10 .25
95 Pekka Saarenheimo .10 .25
96 Mika Pyorala .10 .25
97 Juha-Pekka Haataja .10 .25
98 Petr Tenkrat .10 .25
99 Antti Jokela .10 .25
100 Dwayne Roloson .40 1.00
101 Toni Porkka .10 .25
102 Antti Bruun .10 .25
103 Otto Honkaheimo .10 .25
104 Ilkka Heikkinen .10 .25
105 Tommi Hannus .10 .25
106 Ville Snellman .10 .25
107 Jarkko Kauvosaari .10 .25
108 Jaakko Hagelberg .10 .25
109 Teemu Normio .10 .25
110 Markku Tahtinen .10 .25
111 Juhamatti Yli-Junnila .10 .25
112 Pasi Nurminen .15 .40
113 Olli Korkeavuori .10 .25
114 Kimmo Pikkarainen .10 .25
115 Santeri Heiskanen .10 .25
116 Matias Loppi .10 .25
117 Tuomas Santavuori .10 .25
118 Toni Sihvonen .10 .25
119 Henri Heino .10 .25
120 Marcus Paulsson .10 .25
121 Tommi Turunen .10 .25
122 Ville-Matti Koponen .10 .25
123 Jesse Saarinen .10 .25
124 Jussi Timonen .10 .25
125 Harri Tikkanen .10 .25
126 Olli Malmivaara .10 .25
127 Ossi-Petteri Gronholm .10 .25
128 Petri Kokko .10 .25
129 Kalle Kaijomaa .10 .25
130 Ville Koho .10 .25
131 Teemu Paakkarinen .10 .25
132 Mika Skytta .10 .25
133 Tuomas Vanttinen .10 .25
134 Eetu Qvist .10 .25
135 Ville Viitaluoma .10 .25
136 Mikko Silvennoinen .10 .25
137 Mika Lehto .10 .25
138 Anssi Salmela .10 .25
139 Ville Mantymaa .10 .25
140 Pasi Puistola .10 .25
141 Mikko Pukka .10 .25
142 Janne Ojanen .10 .25
143 Mika Viinanen .10 .25
144 Marko Ojanen .10 .25
145 Petri Kontiola .10 .25
146 Marko Makinen .10 .25
147 Ville Nieminen .10 .25
148 Sami Venalainen .10 .25
149 Stefan Öhman .10 .25
150 Teemu Laine .10 .25
151 Juho Santanen .10 .25
152 Tuomo Karjalainen .10 .25
153 Marko Kiprusoff .10 .25
154 Kimmo Eronen .10 .25
155 Antti Hulkkonen .10 .25
156 Saku Koivu .40 1.00
157 Antti Aalto .10 .25
158 Kai Nurminen .10 .25
159 Ville Vahalahti .10 .25
160 Lauri Korpikoski .40 1.00
161 Jari Kauppila .10 .25
162 Arttu Virtanen .10 .25
163 Matti Aho .10 .25
164 Tuomas Nissinen .10 .25
165 Pasi Peltonen .10 .25
166 Marko Toivonen .10 .25
167 Kristian Kuusela .10 .25
168 Mika Niemi .10 .25
169 Matti Kuparinen .10 .25
170 Marko Kivenmaki .10 .25
171 Pasi Nielikainen .10 .25
172 Jason Williams .40 1.00
173 Aki Uusikartano .10 .25
174 Juha Kiilholma .10 .25
175 Neil Little .40 1.00
176 Matti Kaltiainen .10 .25
177 Tuomas Eskelinen .10 .25
178 Tero Maatta .10 .25
179 Kimmo Peltonen .10 .25
180 Joakim Eriksson .10 .25
181 Esa Pirnes .10 .25
182 Markku Hurme .10 .25
183 Pentti Noyranen .10 .25
184 Steve Kariya .40 1.00
185 Timo Hirvonen .10 .25
186 Jaakko Uhlback .10 .25
187 Kari Kalto .10 .25
188 Tom Askey .20 .50
189 Robert Schnabel .10 .25
190 Jere Karalahti .10 .25
191 Hannu Pikkarainen .10 .25
192 Patrik Lostedt .10 .25
193 Tony Salmelainen .20 .50
194 Miika Jouhkimainen .10 .25
195 Jermu Porthen .10 .25
196 Janne Hauhtonen .10 .25
197 Tobias Salmelainen .10 .25
198 Lennart Petrell .10 .25
199 Pasi Salonen .10 .25
200 Heikki Laine .10 .25
201 Juha Toivonen .10 .25
202 David Schneider .10 .25
203 Juuso Hietanen .10 .25
204 Jukka-Pekka Laamanen .10 .25
205 Kaspars Astashenko .10 .25
206 Jani Hassinen .10 .25
207 Jari Sailio .10 .25
208 Mikko Laine .10 .25
209 Antti Hilden .10 .25
210 Jukka Voutilainen .10 .25
211 Janis Sprukts .10 .25
212 Ville Leino .10 .25
213 Toni Niemi .10 .25
214 Jyrki Lumme .10 .25
215 Juha Alen .10 .25
216 Mikko Kuukka .10 .25
217 Jonas Andersson .10 .25
218 Perttu Lindgren .40 1.00
219 Ville Korhonen .10 .25
220 Tommi Huhtala .10 .25
221 Toni Koivisto .10 .25
222 Jason Guerriero .10 .25
223 Tomi Hirvonen .10 .25
224 Henrik Juntunen .10 .25
225 Vesa Viitakoski .10 .25
226 Joonas Hallikainen .10 .25
227 Samuli Jalkanen .10 .25
228 Mikko Kalteva .10 .25
229 Jan Latvala .10 .25
230 Sami Lepisto .10 .25
231 Tero Konttinen .10 .25
232 Tony Virta .10 .25
233 Marko Jantunen .10 .25
234 Tomek Valtonen .10 .25
235 Jesse Niinimaki .10 .25
236 Arto Koivisto .10 .25
237 Ilari Filppula .10 .25
238 Tommi Santala .10 .25
239 Arto Kuki .10 .25
240 Sinuhe Wallinheimo .20 .50
241 Miika Huczkowski .10 .25
242 Jaako Niskavaara .10 .25
243 Eerikki Koivu .10 .25
244 Juha Salmu .10 .25
245 Jyri Marttinen .10 .25
246 Johannes Alanen .10 .25
247 Filip Riska .10 .25
248 Miikka Mannikko .10 .25
249 Valtteri Tenkanen .10 .25
250 Lucas Lawson .10 .25
251 Tero Koponen .10 .25
252 Miika Lahti .10 .25
253 Juha Jaaskelainen .10 .25
254 Kimmo Kapanen .10 .25
255 Juha Alastalo .10 .25
256 Juho Kuronen .10 .25
257 Jussi Savolainen .10 .25
258 Matti Kuusisto .10 .25
259 Mikko Hakkarainen .10 .25
260 Jani Tuppurainen .10 .25
261 Tomi Pollanen .10 .25
262 Kasper Kenig .10 .25
263 Tomas Kurka .10 .25
264 Matti Tiihonen .10 .25
265 Niklas Backstrom .75 2.00
266 Mika Pietila .10 .25
267 Antti Ylonen .10 .25
268 Ari Vallin .10 .25
269 Mikko Lehtonen .15 .40
270 Jouni Loponen .10 .25
271 Janne Pesonen .10 .25
272 Tommi Paakkolanvaara .10 .25
273 Jari Viuhkola .10 .25
274 Mikko Alikoski .10 .25
275 Michal Bros .10 .25
276 Kalle Sahlstedt .10 .25
277 Juhamatti Aaltonen .10 .25
278 Tomi Mustonen .10 .25
279 Scott Langkow .20 .50
280 Topi Lehtonen .10 .25
281 Markku Paukkunen .10 .25
282 Tuukka Makela .10 .25
283 Pauli Levokari .10 .25
284 Erik Hamalainen .10 .25
285 Jamie Wright .10 .25
286 Petri Lammassaari .10 .25
287 Shayne Toporowski .10 .25
288 Miikka Tuomainen .10 .25
289 Pasi Saarela .10 .25
290 Joni Yli-Torkko .10 .25
291 Antti Niemi .10 .25
292 Esa Saksinen .10 .25
293 Sami Helenius .10 .25
294 Jarkko Glad .10 .25
295 Erik Kakko .10 .25
296 Kari Sihvonen .10 .25
297 Toni Koivunen .10 .25
298 Olli Julkunen .10 .25
299 Jussi Saarinen .10 .25
300 Lasse Jamsen .10 .25
301 Mikko Stromberg .10 .25
302 Rob Zepp .10 .25
303 Mikko Palomaki .10 .25
304 Juha Jokiraita .10 .25
305 Joni Tuominen .10 .25
306 Kristian Kudroc .10 .25
307 Antti Pihlstrom .10 .25
308 Kimmo Koskenkorva .40 1.00
309 Jaska Vilen .10 .25
310 Morten Ask .10 .25
311 Jarkko Immonen .20 .50
312 Peter Nylander .10 .25
313 Janne Kolehmainen .10 .25
314 Teemu Seppanen .10 .25
315 Pekka Tuokkola .10 .25
316 Brian White .10 .25
317 Marko Kauppinen .10 .25
318 Tuukka Mantyla .10 .25
319 Jussi Halme .10 .25
320 Greg Hawgood .20 .50
321 Janne Gronvall .10 .25
322 Teemu Nurmi .10 .25
323 Jarkko Pyymaki .10 .25
324 Teemu Virkkunen .10 .25
325 Timo Vertala .10 .25
326 Quinn Hancock .10 .25
327 Mika Lehtinen .10 .25
328 Henri Palmroth .10 .25
329 Simon Backman .10 .25
330 Markus Seikola .10 .25
331 Tomi Sykko .10 .25
332 Joni Lius .10 .25
333 Jussi Makkonen .10 .25
334 Mika Alatalo .10 .25
335 Jarmo Jokila .10 .25
336 Daniel Widing .10 .25
337 Andreas Jamtin .10 .25
338 Tuukka Pulliainen .10 .25
339 Juuso Riksman .10 .25
340 Jussi Rynnas .10 .25
341 Justin Forrest .10 .25
342 Atte Pentikainen .10 .25
343 Matt Nickerson .20 .50
344 Jesse Saarinen .10 .25
345 Mikko Rautee .10 .25
346 Jesse Joensuu .20 .50
347 Tuomas Takala .10 .25
348 Rob Hisey .10 .25
349 Patrik Forsbacka .10 .25
350 Petteri Tasku .10 .25
351 Leo Komarov .10 .25
352 Matti Kaipainen .10 .25

2005-06 Finnish Cardset Magicmakers

OMPLETE SET (18) 15.00 40.00
TATED ODDS 1:4
Mike Ribeiro .75 2.00
Toni Lydman .75 2.00
Olli Jokinen 1.25 3.00
Jarkko Ruutu .75 2.00
Riku Hahl .75 2.00
Josh Holden .75 2.00
Steve Kariya 1.25 3.00
Patrik Stefan .75 2.00
Sami Lepistö .75 2.00
0 Ossi Väänänen .75 2.00
Valtteri Filppula 2.00 5.00
2 Jarkko Immonen 1.50 4.00
3 Jussi Jokinen 2.00 5.00
4 Jari Viuhkola .75 2.00
5 Ville Nieminen .75 2.00
6 Saku Koivu 2.00 5.00
7 Craig Rivet .75 2.00
8 Jason Williams 1.50 4.00

2005-06 Finnish Cardset Super Snatchers

OMPLETE SET (18) 20.00 50.00
TATED ODDS 1:4
Jan Lundell 1.25 3.00
Tomas Vokoun 2.50 6.00
Mika Noronen 1.25 3.00
Miika Wiikman 1.25 3.00
Juha Pitkämäki 1.25 3.00
Vesa Toskala 2.50 6.00
Tim Thomas 2.50 6.00
Sinuhe Wallinheimo 1.25 3.00
Kimmo Kapanen 1.25 3.00
0 Niklas Bäckström 1.50 4.00
1 Dwayne Roloson 1.50 4.00
2 Pasi Nurminen 1.25 3.00
3 Jarmo Myllys 1.25 3.00
4 Andrew Raycroft 2.00 5.00
5 Mika Lehto 1.25 3.00
6 Tuomo Karjalainen 1.25 3.00
7 Teemu Lassila 1.25 3.00
8 Tuomas Nissinen 1.25 3.00

2006-07 Finnish Cardset

COMPLETE SERIES 1 (180) 40.00 80.00
1 Juha Gustafsson .20 .50
2 Tuomas Eskelinen .20 .50
3 Arto Laatikainen .20 .50
4 Kimmo Peltonen .20 .50
5 Jari Korhonen .20 .50
6 Markku Hurme .20 .50
7 Olli Ahonen .20 .50
8 Ladislav Kohn .20 .50
9 Erkki Rajamäki .20 .50
10 Mikko Lehtonen .20 .50
11 Pentti Nöyränen .20 .50
12 Kari Kalto .20 .50
13 Jan Lundell .30 .75
14 Teemu Laakso .20 .50
15 Jere Karalahti .20 .50
16 Mikko Turunen .20 .50
17 Hannu Pikkarainen .20 .50
18 Tony Salmelainen .20 .50
19 Turo Järvinen .20 .50
20 Jermu Porthén .20 .50
21 Janne Hauhtonen .20 .50
22 Arttu Luttinen .20 .50
23 Pasi Salonen .20 .50
24 Heikki Laine .20 .50
25 Karri Rämö .75 2.00
26 Juha Toivonen .20 .50
27 David Schneider .20 .50
28 Juuso Hietanen .20 .50
29 Mikko Jokela .20 .50
30 Veli-Pekka Laitinen .20 .50
31 Jani Hassinen .20 .50
32 Jari Sailio .20 .50
33 Petteri Wirtanen .20 .50
34 Iivo Hokkanen .20 .50
35 Joni Lappalainen .20 .50
36 Hannu Väisänen .20 .50
37 Juha-Pekka Loikas .20 .50
38 Ville Leino .20 .50
39 Tuukka Rask 2.00 5.00
40 Toni Niemi .20 .50
41 Jyrki Lumme .20 .50
42 Ville Koistinen .20 .50
43 Juha Alén .20 .50
44 Juho Mielonen .20 .50
45 Perttu Lindgren .60 1.50
46 Marko Anttila .20 .50
47 Ville Korhonen .20 .50
48 Toni Koivisto .20 .50
49 Jussi Pesonen .20 .50
50 Tomi Hirvonen .20 .50
51 Vesa Viitakoski .20 .50
52 Raimo Helminen .20 .50
53 Joonas Hallikainen .20 .50
54 Mikko Kalteva .20 .50
55 Markus Kankaanperä .20 .50
56 Kevin Kantee .20 .50
57 Jan Latvala .20 .50
58 Sami Lepistö .20 .50
59 Tony Virta .20 .50
60 Tomek Valtonen .20 .50
61 Arto Koivisto .20 .50
62 Petri Pakaslahti .20 .50
63 Tommi Santala .20 .50
64 Petri Varis .20 .50
65 Jesse Uronen .20 .50
66 Roni Andersson .20 .50
67 Sinuhe Wallinheimo .30 .75
68 Miika Huczkowski .20 .50
69 Jaako Niskavaara .20 .50
70 Erkka Leppänen .20 .50
71 Ferikki Koivu .20 .50
72 Julia Salmu .20 .50
73 Jyrki Marttinen .20 .50
74 Carlo Grünn .20 .50
75 Johannes Alanen .20 .50
76 Miikka Männikkö .20 .50
77 Juha-Pekka Hytönen .20 .50
78 Arsi Piispanen .20 .50
79 Jari Jääskeläinen .20 .50
80 Ossi Louhivaara .20 .50
81 Kimmo Kapanen .30 .75
82 Jermu Pisto .20 .50
83 Matti Kuusisto .20 .50
84 Juha Alastalo .20 .50
85 Ville Hämäläinen .20 .50
86 Jani Tuppurainen .20 .50
87 Kasper Kenig .20 .50
88 Henri Huohvanainen .20 .50
89 Sami Salonen .20 .50
90 Tuomas Kiiskinen .20 .50
91 Sami Kaartinen .20 .50
92 Niklas Bäckström 1.50 4.00
93 Oskari Korpikari .20 .50
94 Ari Vallin .20 .50
95 Ilkka Mikkola .20 .50
96 Mikko Lehtonen .20 .50
97 Jouni Loponen .20 .50
98 Viktor Ujcik .20 .50
99 Janne Pesonen .20 .50
100 Tommi Paakkolanvaara .20 .50
101 Jyri Junnila .20 .50
102 Jari Viuhkola .20 .50
103 Michal Bros .20 .50
104 Kalle Sahlstedt .20 .50
105 Tomi Mustonen .20 .50
106 Markus Nordlund .20 .50
107 Otto Honkaheimo .20 .50
108 Tuukka Mäkelä .20 .50
109 Ilkka Heikkinen .20 .50
110 Pauli Levokari .20 .50
111 Erik Hämäläinen .20 .50
112 Tommi Hannus .20 .50
113 Ville-Vesa Vainiola .20 .50
114 Petri Lammassaari .20 .50
115 Shayne Toporowski .20 .50
116 Jarkko Kauvosaari .20 .50
117 Miikka Tuomainen .20 .50
118 Juhamatti Yli-Junnila .20 .50
119 Antti Niemi .30 .75
120 Esa Saksinen .20 .50
121 Olli Korkeavuori .20 .50
122 Sami Helenius .20 .50
123 Jarkko Glad .20 .50
124 Erik Kakko .20 .50
125 Matias Loppi .20 .50
126 Olli Julkunen .20 .50
127 Jesse Saarinen .20 .50
128 Jussi Saarinen .20 .50
129 Tuomas Santavuori .20 .50
130 Henri Heino .20 .50
131 Ville-Matti Koponen .20 .50
132 Toni Koivunen .20 .50
133 Mikko Strömberg .20 .50
134 Jussi Timonen .30 .75
135 Harri Tikkanen .20 .50
136 Mikko Palomäki .20 .50
137 Ossi-Petteri Grönholm .20 .50
138 Ville Koho .20 .50
139 Kimmo Koskenkorva .20 .50
140 Teemu Paakkarinen .20 .50
141 Jaska Vilen .20 .50
142 Jarkko Immonen .30 .75
143 Janne Kolehmainen .20 .50
144 Mika Lehto .30 .75
145 Marko Kauppinen .20 .50
146 Ville Mäntymaa .20 .50
147 Tuukka Mäntylä .20 .50
148 Mikko Pukka .20 .50
149 Janne Grönvall .20 .50
150 Teemu Nurmi .20 .50
151 Mika Viinanen .20 .50
152 Petri Kontiola .20 .50
153 Sami Venäläinen .20 .50
154 Stefan Öhman .20 .50
155 Quinn Hancock .20 .50
156 Teemu Laine .20 .50
157 Marko Kiprusoff .20 .50
158 Simon Backman .20 .50
159 Tomi Sykkö .20 .50
160 Kai Nurminen .20 .50
161 Jussi Makkonen .20 .50
162 Ville Vahalahti .20 .50
163 Lauri Korpikoski .60 1.50
164 Mika Alatalo .20 .50
165 Arttu Virtanen .20 .50
166 Matti Aho .20 .50
167 Tuukka Pulliainen .20 .50
168 Jussi Rynnäs .20 .50
169 Pasi Peltonen .20 .50
170 Marko Toivonen .20 .50
171 Mika Rontti .20 .50
172 Juhamatti Hietamäki .20 .50
173 Matt Nickerson .40 1.00
174 Kristian Kuusela .20 .50
175 Jesse Joensuu .20 .50
176 Marko Kivenmäki .20 .50
177 Matti Kuparinen .20 .50
178 Tuomas Takala .20 .50
179 Rob Hisey .20 .50
180 Patrik Forsbacka .20 .50
181 Bernd Brückler .30 .75
182 Ari Ahonen .40 1.00
183 Tomi Källarsson .20 .50
184 Kimmo Pikkarainen .20 .50
185 Ismo Kuoppala .20 .50
186 Samuli Suhonen .20 .50
187 Tomas Sinisalo .20 .50
188 Joni Töykkälä .20 .50
189 Jari Tolsa .20 .50
190 Semir Ben-Amor .20 .50
191 Ville Viitaluoma .20 .50
192 Mikko Laine .20 .50
193 Martin Kariya .20 .50
194 Toni Kähkönen .20 .50
195 Aleksis Ahlqvist .30 .75
196 Robert Schnabel .20 .50
197 Cory Murphy .20 .50
198 Patrik Lostedt .20 .50
199 Pasi Saarinen .20 .50
200 Kimmo Kuhta .20 .50
201 Miikka Jouhkimainen .20 .50
202 Raymond Murray .20 .50
203 Juha Fagerstedt .20 .50
204 Janne Laakkonen .20 .50
205 Lennart Petrell .20 .50
206 Ilkka Pikkarainen .20 .50
207 Jan Hrdina .20 .50
208 Pasi Nielikäinen .20 .50
209 Mika Oksa .30 .75
210 Miika Wiikman .30 .75
211 Risto Korhonen .20 .50
212 Mikko Mäenpää .20 .50
213 Philippe Seydoux .20 .50
214 Mika Strömberg .30 .75
215 Fredrik Svensson .20 .50
216 Jani Keinänen .20 .50
217 Janne Lahti .20 .50
218 Joonas Vihko .20 .50
219 Aki Uusikartano .20 .50
220 Antti Pihlström .20 .50
221 Jonas Andersson .20 .50
222 Toni Mäkiaho .20 .50
223 Riku Helenius .60 1.50
224 Teemu Jääskeläinen .20 .50
225 Mikko Kuukka .20 .50
226 Teppo Tuomanen .20 .50
227 Kristian Kudroc .20 .50
228 Pasi Petriläinen .20 .50
229 Mikko Peltola .20 .50
230 Sami Sandell .20 .50
231 Tommi Huhtala .20 .50
232 Pasi Määttänen .20 .50
233 Lauris Darzins .20 .50
234 Tomas Kurka .20 .50
235 Niko Hovinen .30 .75
236 Juuso Riksman .30 .75
237 Mikko Kuparinen .20 .50
238 Marko Tuulola .20 .50
239 Martti Järventie .20 .50
240 Tim Stapleton .20 .50
241 Jyrki Louhi .20 .50
242 Jani Rita .20 .50
243 Arto Kuki .20 .50
244 Kim Hirschovits .20 .50
245 Ryan VandenBussche .40 1.00
246 Jori Lehterä .20 .50
247 Samuli Jalkanen .20 .50
248 Pekka Tuokkola .20 .50
249 Miska Kangasniemi .20 .50
250 Henrik Forsberg .20 .50
251 Valtteri Tenkanen .20 .50
252 Miika Lahti .20 .50
253 Tuomas Vänttinen .20 .50
254 Samuli Piiroinen .20 .50
255 Olli Sipiläinen .20 .50
256 Riku Rahikainen .20 .50
257 Ilari Filppula .20 .50
258 Tuomas Nissinen .30 .75
259 Janne Jalasvaara .20 .50
260 Kyle Peto .20 .50
261 Mats Hansson .20 .50
262 Mikko Purontakanen .20 .50
263 Eetu Qvist .20 .50
264 Timo Koskela .20 .50
265 Martin Sonnenberg .20 .50
266 Matt Davidson .20 .50
267 Aatu Hämäläinen .20 .50
268 Jaakko Suomalainen .30 .75
269 Tuomas Tarkki .30 .75
270 Tommi Leinonen .20 .50
271 Topi Jaakola .20 .50
272 Ivan Majesky .20 .50
273 Atvars Tribuncovs .20 .50
274 Jukka-Pekka Laamanen .20 .50
275 Antti Ylönen .20 .50
276 Teemu Normio .20 .50
277 Veikko Karppinen .20 .50
278 Mika Pyörälä .20 .50
279 Antti Aarnio .20 .50
280 Juhamatti Aaltonen .20 .50
281 Markus Korhonen .30 .75
282 Petri Tähtisalo .20 .50
283 Kari Martikainen .20 .50
284 Jiri Hunkes .20 .50
285 Otto Honkaheimo .20 .50
286 Jan Platil .20 .50
287 Pekka Saarenheimo .20 .50
288 Toni Dahlman .20 .50
289 Juha-Pekka Haataja .20 .50
290 Henrik Juntunen .20 .50
291 Marko Luomala .20 .50
292 Josef Straka .20 .50
293 Tommi Satosaari .20 .50
294 Jani Forsström .20 .50
295 Mikko Heiskanen .20 .50
296 Anssi Salmela .20 .50
297 Ville Uusitalo .20 .50
298 Vili Sopanen .20 .50
299 Karo Koivunen .20 .50
300 Toni Sihvonen .20 .50
301 Kari Sihvonen .20 .50
302 Leo Komarov .20 .50
303 Marko Jantunen .20 .50
304 Rob Zepp .30 .75
305 Jarno Virkki .20 .50
306 Joonas Rönnberg .20 .50
307 Pauli Levokari .20 .50
308 Kalle Kaijomaa .20 .50
309 Henrik Petré .20 .50
310 Sami Ryhänen .20 .50
311 Petri Koskinen .20 .50
312 Mikko Hakkarainen .20 .50
313 Janne Jokila .20 .50
314 Eetu Holma .20 .50
315 Emil Lundberg .20 .50
316 Ville Snellman .20 .50
317 Jens Bergenström .20 .50
318 Tommi Nikkilä .30 .75
319 Burke Henry .20 .50
320 Matti Koistinen .20 .50
321 Harri Ilvonen .20 .50
322 Dale Clarke .20 .50
323 Teemu Aalto .20 .50
324 Janne Ojanen .20 .50
325 Niko Nieminen .20 .50
326 Jarkko Pyymäki .20 .50
327 Marko Ojanen .20 .50
328 Jonas Enlund .20 .50
329 Antti Hölli .20 .50
330 Teemu Virkkunen .20 .50
331 Juho Santanen .20 .50
332 Jani Hurme .40 1.00
333 Juho Jokinen .20 .50
334 Aki Berg .20 .50
335 Vladimir Sicak .20 .50
336 Jesse Saarinen .20 .50
337 Mikko Rautee .20 .50
338 Tommi Laine .20 .50
339 Layne Ulmer .20 .50
340 Tuomas Suominen .20 .50
341 Ivan Huml .30 .75
342 Teemu Ramstedt .20 .50
343 Joni Yli-Torkko .20 .50
344 Matti Kaltiainen .30 .75
345 Eero Kilpeläinen .30 .75
346 Peter Aston .20 .50
347 Anssi Tieranta .20 .50
348 Eetu Heikkinen .20 .50
349 Ilkka Törnvall .20 .50
350 Tapio Sammalkangas .20 .50
351 Toni Häppölä .20 .50
352 Tom Wandell .20 .50
353 Aleksandr Naurov .20 .50
354 Joonas Kemppainen .20 .50
355 Ville Hirvonen .20 .50
356 Brandon Crombeen .30 .75

2006-07 Finnish Cardset Between the Pipes

1 Ari Ahonen 3.00 8.00
2 Bernd Brückler 2.00 5.00
3 Aleksis Ahlqvist 2.00 5.00
4 Jan Lundell 2.00 5.00
5 Mika Oksa 2.00 5.00
6 Miika Wiikman 2.00 5.00
7 Riku Helenius 2.50 6.00
8 Tuukka Rask 5.00 12.00
9 Niko Hovinen 2.00 5.00
10 Juuso Riksman 2.00 5.00
11 Sinuhe Wallinheimo 2.00 5.00
12 Kimmo Kapanen 2.00 5.00
13 Tuomas Nissinen 2.00 5.00
14 Jaakko Suomalainen 2.00 5.00
15 Tuomas Tarkki 2.00 5.00
16 Markus Korhonen 2.00 5.00
17 Antti Niemi 4.00 10.00
18 Mikko Strömberg 2.00 5.00
19 Rob Zepp 2.00 5.00
20 Mika Lehto 2.00 5.00
21 Tommi Nikkilä 2.00 5.00
22 Jani Hurme 2.50 6.00
23 Matti Kaltiainen 2.00 5.00
24 Eero Kilpeläinen 2.00 5.00

2006-07 Finnish Cardset Enforcers

1 Sami Helenius 1.25 3.00
2 Kristian Kudroc 1.25 3.00
3 Ryan VandenBussche 2.00 5.00
4 Robert Schnabel 1.25 3.00
5 Burke Henry 1.25 3.00
6 Jan Platil 1.25 3.00
7 Toni Mäkiaho 1.25 3.00
8 Markus Kankaanperä 1.25 3.00
9 Aki Berg 1.25 3.00
10 Pasi Peltonen 1.25 3.00
11 Pasi Nielikäinen 1.25 3.00
12 Jere Karalahti 1.25 3.00

2006-07 Finnish Cardset Playmakers Rookies

1 Perttu Lindgren 2.00 5.00
2 Juhamatti Aaltonen 1.25 3.00
3 Jussi Makkonen 1.25 3.00
4 Pasi Salonen 1.25 3.00
5 Juuso Hietanen 1.25 3.00
6 Petteri Wirtanen 1.25 3.00
7 Petri Lammassaari 1.25 3.00
8 Patrick Forsbacka 1.25 3.00
9 Juha Alén 1.25 3.00
10 Miika Lahti 1.25 3.00
11 Jari Sailio 1.25 3.00
12 Leo Komarov 1.25 3.00

2006-07 Finnish Cardset Playmakers Rookies Gold

COMPLETE SET (12)
STATED PRINT RUN 100 SETS
1 Perttu Lindgren 6.00 15.00
2 Juhamatti Aaltonen 4.00 10.00
3 Jussi Makkonen 4.00 10.00
4 Pasi Salonen 4.00 10.00
5 Juuso Hietanen 4.00 10.00
6 Petteri Wirtanen 4.00 10.00
7 Petri Lammassaari 4.00 10.00
8 Patrick Forsbacka 4.00 10.00
9 Juha Alén 4.00 10.00
10 Miika Lahti 4.00 10.00
11 Jari Sailio 4.00 10.00
12 Leo Komarov 4.00 10.00

2006-07 Finnish Cardset Playmakers Rookies Silver

COMPLETE SET (12)
STATED PRINT RUN 200 SETS
1 Perttu Lindgren 4.00 10.00
2 Juhamatti Aaltonen 2.00 5.00
3 Jussi Makkonen 2.00 5.00
4 Pasi Salonen 2.00 5.00
5 Juuso Hietanen 2.00 5.00
6 Petteri Wirtanen 2.00 5.00
7 Petri Lammassaari 2.00 5.00
8 Patrick Forsbacka 2.00 5.00
9 Juha Alén 2.00 5.00
10 Miika Lahti 2.00 5.00
11 Jari Sailio 2.00 5.00
12 Leo Komarov 2.00 5.00

2006-07 Finnish Cardset Signature Sensations

1 Mikko Lehtonen 15.00 40.00
2 Erkki Rajamäki 15.00 40.00
3 Miika Wiikman 15.00 40.00
4 Juuso Hietanen 15.00 40.00
5 Petteri Wirtanen 15.00 40.00
6 Tuukka Rask 40.00 80.00
7 Ville Koistinen 15.00 40.00
8 Perttu Lindgren 25.00 60.00
9 Joonas Hallikainen 15.00 40.00
10 Sami Lepistö 15.00 40.00
11 Tommi Santala 15.00 40.00
12 Sinuhe Wallinheimo 15.00 40.00
13 Miika Lahti 15.00 40.00
14 Arsi Piispanen 15.00 40.00
15 Kimmo Kapanen 15.00 40.00
16 Tuomas Kiiskinen 15.00 40.00
17 Mikko Alikoski 15.00 40.00
18 Lasse Kukkonen 15.00 40.00
19 Juhamatti Aaltonen 15.00 40.00
20 Otto Honkaheimo 15.00 40.00
21 Petri Lammassaari 15.00 40.00
22 Miikka Tuomainen 15.00 40.00
23 Antti Niemi 30.00 60.00
24 Jesse Saarinen 15.00 40.00
25 Mikko Strömberg 15.00 40.00
26 Jarkko Immonen 15.00 40.00
27 Mika Lehto 15.00 40.00
28 Petri Kontiola 15.00 40.00
29 Juho Santanen 15.00 40.00
30 Jussi Makkonen 15.00 40.00
31 Tuukka Pulliainen 15.00 40.00
32 Kristian Kuusela 15.00 40.00
33 Jesse Joensuu 15.00 40.00
34 Marko Kivenmäki 15.00 40.00
35 Patrick Forsbacka 15.00 40.00

2006-07 Finnish Cardset Superior Snatchers

1 Niklas Bäckström 4.00 10.00
2 Joonas Hallikainen 2.00 5.00
3 Kimmo Kapanen 2.00 5.00
4 Mika Lehto 2.00 5.00
5 Jan Lundell 2.00 5.00
6 Antti Niemi 4.00 10.00
7 Tuukka Rask 5.00 12.00
8 Juuso Riksman 2.00 5.00
9 Karri Rämö 3.00 8.00
10 Sinuhe Wallinheimo 2.00 5.00
11 Miika Wiikman 2.00 5.00
12 Rob Zepp 2.00 5.00

2006-07 Finnish Cardset Superior Snatchers Gold

COMPLETE SET (12)
STATED PRINT RUN 100 SETS
1 Niklas Bäckström 12.00 30.00
2 Joonas Hallikainen 6.00 15.00
3 Kimmo Kapanen 6.00 15.00
4 Mika Lehto 6.00 15.00
5 Jan Lundell 6.00 15.00
6 Antti Niemi 6.00 15.00
7 Tuukka Rask 15.00 40.00
8 Juuso Riksman 6.00 15.00
9 Karri Rämö 8.00 20.00
10 Sinuhe Wallinheimo 6.00 15.00
11 Miika Wiikman 6.00 15.00
12 Rob Zepp 6.00 15.00

2006-07 Finnish Cardset Superior Snatchers Silver

COMPLETE SET (12)
STATED PRINT RUN 200 SETS
1 Niklas Bäckström 8.00 20.00
2 Joonas Hallikainen 4.00 10.00
3 Kimmo Kapanen 4.00 10.00
4 Mika Lehto 4.00 10.00
5 Jan Lundell 4.00 10.00
6 Antti Niemi 4.00 10.00
7 Tuukka Rask 12.00 30.00
8 Juuso Riksman 4.00 10.00
9 Karri Rämö 6.00 15.00
10 Sinuhe Wallinheimo 4.00 10.00
11 Miika Wiikman 4.00 10.00
12 Rob Zepp 4.00 10.00

2006-07 Finnish Cardset Trophy Winners

COMPLETE SET (7)
1 Jukka Jalonen 1.25 3.00
2 Perttu Lindgren 2.00 5.00
3 Esa Pirnes 1.25 3.00
4 Juuso Riksman 1.25 3.00
5 Lasse Kukkonen 1.25 3.00
6 Miika Wiikman 1.25 3.00
7 Tony Salmelainen 1.25 3.00

2006-07 Finnish Ilves Team Set

1 Juha Alen .20 .50
2 Juuso Antonen .20 .50
3 Marko Anttila .20 .50
4 Lauris Darzins .20 .50
5 Riku Helenius .75 2.00
6 Tomi Hirvonen .20 .50
7 Tommi Huhtala .20 .50
8 Teemu Jaaskelainen .20 .50
9 Toni Koivisto .20 .50
10 Ville Korhonen .20 .50
11 Kristian Kudroc .20 .50
12 Tomas Kurka .20 .50
13 Mikko Kuukka .20 .50
14 Jarno Laitinen .20 .50
15 Joonas Lehtivuori .20 .50
16 Perttu Lindgren .60 1.50
17 Juho Mielonen .20 .50
18 Pasi Maaltanen .20 .50
19 Toni Niemi .20 .50
20 Mikko Peltola .20 .50
21 Jussi Pesonen .20 .50
22 Pasi Petrilainen .20 .50
23 Tuukka Rask 4.00 10.00
24 Sami Sandell .20 .50
25 Teppo Tuomanen .20 .50
26 Vesa Viitakoski .20 .50
27 Kari Eloranta CO .10 .25
28 Petteri Hirvonen CO .10 .25

2006-07 Finnish Porin Assat Pelaajakortit

COMPLETE SET (32) 10.00 25.00
1 Matti Kaltiainen .30 .75
2 Eero Kilpelainen .60 1.50
3 Jussi Rynnas .30 .75
4 Pasi Peltonen .30 .75
5 Marko Toivonen .30 .75
6 Mika Rontti .30 .75
7 Peter Aston .30 .75
8 Tero Konttinen .30 .75
9 Juhamatti Hietamaki .30 .75
10 Anssi Tieranta .30 .75
11 Eetu Heikkinen .30 .75
12 Iikka Tornvall .30 .75
13 Tapio Samalkangas .30 .75
14 Toni Happola .30 .75
15 Kristian Kuusela .30 .75
16 Tom Wandell .30 .75
17 Tuomas Huhtanen .30 .75
18 Jesse Joensuu .30 .75
19 Marko Kivenmaki .30 .75
20 Matti Kuparinen .30 .75
21 Tuomas Takala .30 .75
22 Patrick Forsbacka .30 .75
23 Petteri Tasku .30 .75
24 Alexander Naurov .30 .75
25 Joonas Kemppainen .30 .75
26 Jussi Peltomaa .30 .75
27 Ville Hirvonen .30 .75
28 Brandon BJ Crombeen .40 1.00
29 Teemu Kesa .30 .75
30 Tobias Salmelainen .30 .75
31 David Bararuk .30 .75
32 Jari Harkala .30 .75

2007-08 Finnish Cardset

1 Santeri Heiskanen
2 Ismo Kuoppala
3 Arto Laatikainen
4 Samuli Suhonen
5 Matti Uusivirta
6 Joni Töykkälä
7 Erkki Rajamäki
8 Mikko Lehtonen
9 Ville Viitaluoma
10 Jaakko Uhlbäck
11 Kari Kalto
12 Jan Lundell
13 Jere Karalahti
14 Mikko Turunen
15 Joni Haverinen
16 Tommi Kovanen
17 Kimmo Kuhta
18 Stephen Guolla
19 Raymond Murray
20 Juha Fagerstedt
21 Jermu Porthén
22 Janne Laakkonen
23 Ilkka Pikkarainen
24 Janne Keränen
25 Andy Chiodo
26 Mikko Mäenpää
27 Veli-Pekka Laitinen
28 Jani Hassinen
29 Jari Sailio
30 Iivo Hokkanen
31 Hannu Väisänen
32 Juha-Pekka Loikas
33 Joonas Vihko
34 Aki Uusikartano
35 Antti Pihlström
36 Jonas Andersson
37 Toni Niemi
38 Joonas Lehtivuori
39 Teemu Jääskeläinen
40 Mikko Kuukka
41 Pasi Petriläinen
42 Mikko Peltola
43 Sami Sandell
44 Perttu Lindgren
45 Toni Koivisto
46 Lassi Mattila
47 Vesa Viitakoski
48 Pasi Määttänen
49 Marko Anttila
50 Juuso Riksman
51 Joonas Hallikainen
52 Mikko Kuparinen
53 Mikko Kalteva
54 Marko Tuulola
55 Sami Lepistö
56 Arto Koivisto
57 Tim Stapleton
58 Jyrki Louhi
59 Jani Rita
60 Ossi Saarinen
61 Kim Hirschovits
62 Samuli Jalkanen
63 Sinuhe Wallinheimo
64 Miska Kangasniemi
65 Jaako Niskavaara
66 Juha Salmu
67 Henrik Forsberg
68 Jari Jääskeläinen
69 Ossi Louhivaara
70 Tuomas Vänttinen
71 Mika Niemi
72 Samuli Piiroinen
73 Olli Sipiläinen
74 Ilari Filppula
75 Tuomas Nissinen
76 Janne Jalasvaara
77 Aku Pekkarinen
78 Matti Kuusisto
79 Juha Alastalo
80 Simo Pulkki
81 Ville Hämäläinen
82 Jani Tuppurainen
83 Henri Huohvanainen
84 Tuomas Kiiskinen
85 Jarkko Kauvosaari
86 Tuomas Tarkki
87 Ilkka Mikkola
88 Topi Jaakola
89 Jouni Loponen
90 Jukka-Pekka Laamanen
91 Hannes Hyvönen
92 Teemu Normio
93 Mikko Alikoski
94 Janne Pesonen
95 Jari Viuhkola
96 Michal Bros
97 Antti Aarnio
98 Juhamatti Aaltonen
99 Tomi Mustonen
100 Petri Tähtisalo
101 Mikko Viitanen
102 Erik Hämäläinen
103 Pekka Saarenheimo
104 Petri Lammassaari
105 Tero Koponen
106 Shayne Toporowski
107 Juha-Pekka Haataja
108 Miikka Tuomainen
109 Henrik Juntunen
110 Juhamatti Yli-Junnila
111 Ville-Vesa Vainiola
112 Tommi Satosaari
113 Joonas Jalvanti
114 Ville Uusitalo
115 Erik Kakko
116 Matias Loppi
117 Jesse Saarinen
118 Tuomas Santavuori
119 Karo Koivunen
120 Kari Sihvonen
121 Henri Heino
122 Marko Jantunen
123 Toni Koivunen
124 Joonas Rönnberg
125 Pauli Levokari
126 Ossi-Petteri Grönholm
127 Ville Koho
128 Sami Ryhänen
129 Petri Koskinen
130 Jaska Vilen
131 Mikko Hakkarainen
132 Jarkko Immonen
133 Janne Kolehmainen
134 Ville Snellman
135 Mika Lehto
136 Janne Grönvall
137 Teemu Aalto
138 Janne Ojanen
139 Niko Nieminen
140 Juha Kiilholma
141 Teemu Nurmi
142 Jarkko Pyymäki
143 Jonas Enlund
144 Petri Kontiola
145 Sami Venäläinen
146 Quinn Hancock
147 Marko Kiprusoff
148 Juho Jokinen
149 Aki Berg
150 Simon Backman
151 Jesse Saarinen
152 Mikko Rautee
153 Jussi Makkonen
154 Tuomas Suominen
155 Teemu Ramstedt
156 Matti Aho
157 Tuukka Pulliainen
158 Eero Kilpeläinen
159 Pasi Peltonen
160 Marko Toivonen
161 Juhamatti Hietamäki
162 Anssi Tieranta
163 Tapio Sammalkangas
164 Toni Häppölä
165 Tuomas Huhtanen
166 Jesse Joensuu
167 Marko Kivenmäki
168 Tuomas Takala
169 Bernd Brückler
170 Jere Myllyniemi
171 Miika Huczkowski
172 Kimmo Pikkarainen
173 Dale Clarke
174 Patrik Lostedt
175 Rami Alanko
176 Ryan Keller
177 Oskar Osala
178 Stefan Öhman
179 Camilo Miettinen
180 Arto Kuki
181 Toni Kähkönen
182 Aleksis Ahlqvist
183 Teemu Laakso
184 Hannu Pikkarainen
185 Ilkka Heikkinen
186 Lasse Korhonen
187 Charlie Cook
188 Miikka Jouhkimainen
189 Ryan Vesce
190 Jerry Ahtola
191 Eetu Pöysti
192 Lennart Petrell
193 Arttu Luttinen
194 Pasi Nielikäinen
195 Teemu Lassila
196 Harri Tikkanen
197 Tommi Leinonen
198 Cole Jarrett
199 Markus Seikola
200 Pasi Salonen
201 Pasi Tuominen
202 Kai Nurminen
203 Ossi Pellinen
204 Sami Lähteenmäki
205 Emil Lundberg
206 Toni Mäkiaho
207 Roni Andersson
208 Tero Leinonen
209 Pasi Häkkinen
210 Eric Werner
211 Kevin Kantee
212 Arto Tukio
213 Miikka Männikkö
214 Ville Korhonen
215 Sami Torkki
216 Henrik Malmström
217 Raimo Helminen

218 Mike Bishai
219 Turo Järvinen
220 Niko Hovinen
221 Jussi Markkanen
222 Sami Helenius
223 Mika Rontti
224 Marko Kauppinen
225 Mikko Jokela
226 Tony Virta
227 Tobias Salmelainen
228 Tommi Santala
229 Petri Varis
230 Clarke Wilm
231 Ville Leino
232 Pekka Tuokkola
233 Esa Saksinen
234 Ville Mäntymaa
235 Kalle Kaijomaa
236 Juha-Pekka Hytönen
237 Valtteri Tenkanen
238 Tuomas Mikkonen
239 Jarkko Immonen
240 Miika Lahti
241 Dwight Helminen
242 Antti Virtanen
243 Tuomas Pihlman
244 Tommi Hannus
245 Mika Oksa
246 Timo Seppänen
247 Ville Varakas
248 Mika Strömberg
249 Tomi Tuomainen
250 Jyri Junnila
251 Jeremy Stevenson
252 Mikko Laine
253 Tommi Jokinen
254 Toni Hyvärinen
255 Timo Salo
256 Tapio Laakso
257 Mikko Strömberg
258 Oskari Korpikari
259 Atte Ohtamaa
260 Mikko Lehtonen
261 Jere Karalahti
262 Veikko Karppinen
263 Kristian Kuusela
264 Tommi Paakkolanvaara
265 Timo Vertala
266 Kalle Sahlstedt
267 Ondrej Kratena
268 Mikael Vuorio
269 Petri Vehanen
270 Esa Lehikoinen
271 Mike Siklenka
272 Doug O'Brien
273 Markus Nordlund
274 Juha Alén
275 Janis Sprukts
276 Mika Viinanen
277 Ossipekka Lehtonen
278 Semir Ben-Amor
279 Marko Luomala
280 Antti Niemi
281 Tuukka Mäkelä
282 Jan Latvala
283 Henri Laurila
284 Jani Forsström
285 Samuli Suhonen
286 Olli Julkunen
287 Villi Sopanen
288 Jussi Saarinen
289 Evan Schwabe
290 Leo Komarov
291 Joni Puurula
292 Iiro Tarkki
293 Juho Mielonen
294 Dan Iliakis
295 Simo Mäkiä
296 Arturas Katulis
297 Jarno Lippojoki
298 Alex Nikiforuk
299 Dan Hacker
300 Eetu Holma
301 Tommi Nikkilä
302 Jussi Halme
303 André Benoit
304 Nicholas Angell
305 Atte Pentikäinen
306 Anssi Salmela
307 Timo Koskela
308 Steve Saviano
309 Arsi Piispanen
310 Jori Lehterä
311 Niclas Lucenius
312 Alexander Salak
313 Juha Kuokkanen
314 Antti Halonen
315 Lee Sweatt
316 Joonas Järvinen
317 Tommi Laine
318 Tomas Sinisalo
319 Max Kolu
320 Markku Hurme
321 David Lundbohm
322 Antti Erkinjuntti
323 Teemu Laine
324 Kimmo Kapanen
325 Tero Konttinen
326 Nick Kuiper
327 Eetu Heikkinen
328 Henrik Petré
329 Sakari Salminen
330 Matti Kuparinen
331 Petteri Tasku
332 Tommi Huhtala
333 Joonas Kemppainen
334 Markku Tähtinen
335 Veli-Matti Savinainen
336 Pasi Saarela

2009-10 Finnish Upper Deck Victory

COMPLETE SET (250) 75.00 150.00
COMP.SET w/o SPS (200) 30.00 60.00
ROOKIE STATED ODDS 1:2
1 Ryan Getzlaf .60 1.50
2 Scott Niedermayer .25 .60
3 Jean-Sebastien Giguere .40 1.00
4 Corey Perry .40 1.00
5 Chris Pronger .30 .75
6 Bryan Little .40 1.00
7 Ilya Kovalchuk .50 1.25
8 Kari Lehtonen .40 1.00
9 Colby Armstrong .25 .60
10 Todd White .25 .60
11 Slava Kozlov .25 .60
12 Michael Ryder .30 .75
13 David Krejci .30 .75
14 Patrice Bergeron .40 1.00
15 Blake Wheeler .50 1.25
16 Zdeno Chara .25 .60
17 Phil Kessel .40 1.00
18 Tim Thomas .40 1.00
19 Marc Savard .25 .60
20 Clarke MacArthur .25 .60
21 Derek Roy .40 1.00
22 Ryan Miller .40 1.00
23 Drew Stafford .40 1.00
24 Jason Pominville .40 1.00
25 Thomas Vanek .40 1.00
26 David Moss .30 .75
27 Mike Cammalleri .30 .75
28 Jarome Iginla .75 2.00
29 Todd Bertuzzi .40 1.00
30 Dion Phaneuf .60 1.50
31 Miikka Kiprusoff .40 1.00
32 Dymond Langkow .25 .60
33 Rene Bourque .25 .60
34 Olli Jokinen .25 .60
35 Cam Ward .40 1.00
36 Ray Whitney .25 .60
37 Eric Staal .50 1.25
38 Brandon Sutter .40 1.00
39 Rod Brind'Amour .30 .75
40 Tuomo Ruutu .25 .60
41 Patrick Kane .75 2.00
42 Nikolai Khabibulin .40 1.00
43 Martin Havlat .30 .75
44 Jonathan Toews 1.00 2.50
45 Patrick Sharp .30 .75
46 Brian Campbell .30 .75
47 Kris Versteeg .50 1.25
48 John-Michael Liles .30 .75
49 Ryan Smyth .40 1.00
50 T.J. Hensick .25 .60
51 Peter Budaj .40 1.00
52 Milan Hejduk .40 1.00
53 Paul Stastny .40 1.00
54 Wojtek Wolski .25 .60
55 Jakub Voracek .40 1.00
56 Derick Brassard .40 1.00
57 Rick Nash .40 1.00
58 Steve Mason .60 1.50
59 R.J. Umberger .30 .75
60 Kristian Huselius .25 .60
61 Marty Turco .30 .75
62 Brad Richards .30 .75
63 Mike Modano .60 1.50
64 Loui Eriksson .25 .60
65 Brenden Morrow .30 .75
66 Mike Ribeiro .25 .60
67 Fabian Brunnstrom .40 1.00
68 Johan Franzen .25 .60
69 Nicklas Lidstrom .50 1.25
70 Jiri Hudler .25 .60
71 Pavel Datsyuk .40 1.00
72 Ty Conklin .30 .75
73 Marian Hossa .60 1.50
74 Tomas Holmstrom .30 .75
75 Henrik Zetterberg .75 2.00
76 Ales Kotalik .25 .60
77 Andrew Cogliano .50 1.25
78 Ales Hemsky .30 .75
79 Sheldon Souray .25 .60
80 Sam Gagner .50 1.25
81 Shawn Horcoff .25 .60
82 Dustin Penner .25 .60
83 Dwayne Roloson .30 .75
84 Michael Frolik .30 .75
85 Tomas Vokoun .40 1.00
86 Jay Bouwmeester .40 1.00
87 Nathan Horton .25 .60
88 Stephen Weiss .25 .60
89 David Booth .25 .60
90 Anze Kopitar .40 1.00
91 Jack Johnson .30 .75
92 Alexander Frolov .30 .75
93 Drew Doughty .75 2.00
94 Dustin Brown .30 .75
95 Erik Ersberg .30 .75
96 Marian Gaborik .60 1.50
97 Marek Zidlicky .25 .60
98 Mikko Koivu .40 1.00
99 Andrew Brunette .25 .60
100 Niklas Backstrom .40 1.00
101 Antti Miettinen .25 .60
102 Andrei Kostitsyn .30 .75
103 Carey Price 1.00 2.50
104 Saku Koivu .40 1.00
105 Andrei Markov .30 .75
106 Robert Lang .25 .60
107 Alex Tanguay .30 .75
108 Alex Kovalev .40 1.00
109 Max Pacioretty .40 1.00
110 Jason Arnott .25 .60
111 Dan Ellis .25 .60
112 Ryan Suter .25 .60
113 Jean-Pierre Dumont .25 .60
114 Shea Weber .30 .75
115 Martin Erat .40 1.00
116 Martin Brodeur 1.00 2.50
117 Brian Gionta .40 1.00
118 Travis Zajac .25 .60
119 Patrik Elias .30 .75
120 Scott Clemmensen .30 .75
121 Zach Parise .40 1.00
122 Josh Bailey .30 .75
123 Rick DiPietro .40 1.00
124 Doug Weight .25 .60
125 Kyle Okposo .40 1.00
126 Mark Streit .25 .60
127 Henrik Lundqvist .75 2.00
128 Scott Gomez .40 1.00
129 Wade Redden .25 .60
130 Chris Drury .30 .75
131 Marc Staal .50 1.25
132 Nikolai Zherdev .25 .60
133 Markus Naslund .40 1.00
134 Nik Antropov .30 .75
135 Daniel Alfredsson .40 1.00
136 Jason Spezza .50 1.25
137 Filip Kuba .25 .60
138 Antoine Vermette .25 .60
139 Dany Heatley .75 2.00
140 Alex Auld .30 .75
141 Mike Richards .75 2.00
142 Martin Biron .30 .75
143 Mike Knuble .40 1.00
144 Daniel Briere .40 1.00
145 Jeff Carter .40 1.00
146 Scott Hartnell .25 .60
147 Simon Gagne .40 1.00
148 Shane Doan .30 .75
149 Peter Mueller .50 1.25
150 Mikkel Boedker .30 .75
151 Ilya Bryzgalov .30 .75
152 Kyle Turris .50 1.25
153 Chris Kunitz .40 1.00
154 Bill Guerin .25 .60
155 Petr Sykora .25 .60
156 Marc-Andre Fleury .40 1.00
157 Miroslav Satan .25 .60
158 Evgeni Malkin 1.00 2.50
159 Jordan Staal .50 1.25
160 Sidney Crosby 2.00 5.00
161 Alex Goligoski .30 .75
162 Devin Setoguchi .30 .75
163 Joe Pavelski .25 .60
164 Ryane Clowe .25 .60
165 Evgeni Nabokov .40 1.00
166 Patrick Marleau .40 1.00
167 Dan Boyle .25 .60
168 Joe Thornton .75 2.00
169 Manny Legace .30 .75
170 Paul Kariya .40 1.00
171 Patrik Berglund .75 2.00
172 Keith Tkachuk .30 .75
173 Brad Boyes .30 .75
174 Vincent Lecavalier .50 1.25
175 Vaclav Prospal .25 .60
176 Steven Stamkos 1.00 2.50
177 Martin St. Louis .40 1.00
178 Mike Smith .30 .75
179 Luke Schenn .60 1.50
180 Matt Stajan .30 .75
181 Mikhail Grabovski .30 .75
182 Vesa Toskala .40 1.00
183 Tomas Kaberle .25 .60
184 Alexei Ponikarovsky .25 .60
185 Nikolai Kulemin .30 .75
186 Kevin Bieksa .25 .60
187 Daniel Sedin .50 1.25
188 Henrik Sedin .60 1.50
189 Ryan Kesler .30 .75
190 Roberto Luongo 1.00 2.50
191 Mats Sundin .40 1.00
192 Steve Bernier .25 .60
193 Mike Green .75 2.00
194 Alexander Ovechkin 1.50 4.00
195 Nicklas Backstrom 1.00 2.50
196 Alexander Semin .40 1.00
197 Simeon Varlamov .75 2.00
198 Sergei Fedorov .75 2.00
199 Sidney Crosby CL 2.00 5.00
200 Alexander Ovechkin CL 1.50 4.00
201 Chris Durno .75 2.00
202 Peter Regin 1.25 3.00
203 Kevin Quick .60 1.50
204 Taylor Chorney 1.00 2.50
205 Mike Santorelli 1.00 2.50
206 Alexander Sulzer .60 1.50
207 Troy Bodie .75 2.00
208 Matt Beleskey 1.00 2.50
209 Kevin Westgarth .75 2.00
210 John Scott 1.00 2.50
211 Mikael Backlund 1.50 4.00
212 Byron Bitz .75 2.00
213 Matt Pelech 1.00 2.50
214 Tim Wallace .60 1.50
215 Ben Lovejoy 1.50 4.00
216 Riley Armstrong .75 2.00
217 Christian Hanson 1.25 3.00
218 Sean Collins .75 2.00
219 Riku Helenius 1.00 2.50
220 Ville Leino 1.25 3.00
221 Michal Neuvirth 2.50 6.00
222 Artem Anisimov 1.25 3.00
223 Davis Drewiske .75 2.00
224 David Schlemko .75 2.00
225 Luca Caputi 1.25 3.00
226 Jakub Petruzalek 1.00 2.50
227 Ryan Vesce .75 2.00
228 Jay Beagle 1.00 2.50
229 Jhonas Enroth 1.25 3.00
230 Brandon Segal .75 2.00
231 Tim Stapleton 1.00 2.50
232 Jesse Joensuu 1.25 3.00
233 John Negrin .75 2.00
234 Grant Lewis .75 2.00
235 Cal O'Reilly .75 2.00
236 Brian Salcido .75 2.00
237 Phil Oreskovic 1.00 2.50
238 Kris Chucko .75 2.00
239 Joel Rechlicz 1.00 2.50
240 Andrew MacDonald .75 2.00
241 Antti Niemi 3.00 8.00
242 Ivan Vishnevskiy 1.25 3.00
243 Mike McKenna .75 2.00
244 Spencer Machacek .75 2.00
245 Tom Wandell 3.00 8.00
246 Michael Vernace .75 2.00
247 Yannick Weber 1.25 3.00
248 Matt Hendricks .75 2.00
249 Scott Lehman .60 1.50
250 T.J. Galiardi 1.25 3.00

2009-10 Finnish Upper Deck Victory Suomalaisia Supertahtia

COMPLETE SET (20) 10.00 25.00
STATED ODDS 1 PER PACK
FF1 Kari Lehtonen .75 2.00
FF2 Niklas Hagman .50 1.25
FF3 Niklas Backstrom .75 2.00
FF4 Sami Salo .75 2.00
FF5 Jarkko Ruutu .50 1.25
FF6 Vesa Toskala .75 2.00
FF7 Antti Miettinen .50 1.25
FF8 Jere Lehtinen .60 1.50
FF9 Mikko Koivu .75 2.00
FF10 Teppo Numminen .75 2.00
FF11 Saku Koivu .75 2.00
FF12 Olli Jokinen .50 1.25
FF13 Teemu Selanne .75 2.00
FF14 Kimmo Timonen .60 1.50
FF15 Tuomo Ruutu .50 1.25
FF16 Miikka Kiprusoff .75 2.00
FF17 Joni Pitkanen .60 1.50
FF18 Valtteri Filppula .75 2.00
FF19 Pekka Rinne .60 1.50
FF20 Jussi Jokinen .75 2.00

1994-95 French National Team

These standard-size cards were made available to fans at venues where the national team was appearing in France. The cards feature simulated action photography, surrounded by red, white and blue borders. The player's name is at the top of the card, while the words "Equipe de France 94-95" line the bottom. Card backs contain a color headshot, and international statistics. The cards are unnumbered and checklisted below in alphabetical order.

COMPLETE SET (35) 8.00 20.00
1 Benjamin Agnel .20 .50
2 Richard Aimonetto .20 .50
3 Stephane Arcangeloni .20 .50
4 Mickael Babin .20 .50
5 Alain Beaule .20 .50
6 J. Francois Bonnard .20 .50
7 Arnaud Briand .20 .50
8 Karl DeWolf .20 .50
9 Serge Djelloul .20 .50
10 Roger Dube .20 .50
11 Patrick Dunn .20 .50
12 J. Christophe Filippin .20 .50
13 Michel Galarneau .20 .50
14 Gerald Guennelon .20 .50
15 Eric Lemarque .20 .50
16 J. Philippe Lemoine .20 .50
17 Fabrice L'Henry .30 .75
18 Pierrick Maia .20 .50
19 Antoine Mindjimba .75 2.00
20 Christophe Moyon .20 .50
21 Lionel Orsolini .20 .50
22 Franck Pajonkowski .30 .75
23 Denis Perez .20 .50
24 Eric Pinard .20 .50
25 Serge Poudrier .30 .75
26 Christian Pouget .20 .50
27 Pierre Pousse .20 .50
28 Antoine Richer .20 .50
29 Franck Saunier .20 .50
30 J. Marc Soghomonian .20 .50
31 Juhani Tamminen .30 .75
32 Michel Valliere .30 .75
33 Andre Vittenberg .20 .50
34 Steven Woodburn .20 .50
35 Petri Ylonen .60 1.50

1932 German Margarine Sanella

Cards measure 2 3/4 x 4 1/8 and feature full color fronts. Backs are in German.

NNO Ice Hockey 25.00 50.00
NNO Field Hockey Scrum 5.00 10.00
NNO Field Hockey Goalie 5.00 10.00

1936 German Jaszmatzi

Full color card from the Deutscher Sports series of Germany. Thin paper stock, with back in German.

208 Ice Hockey 15.00 30.00

1994-95 German DEL

This 440-card set of the German hockey league was produced (apparently) by International Hockey Archives. The cards feature an action photo on the front, with player and team name along the borders. The back contain a space for autographing, as well as another photo and player bio in German. The set includes NHL prospects Florian Keller and Jochen Hecht, as well as several ex-NHL players.

COMPLETE SET (440) 20.00 50.00
1 Int'l Hockey Association .02 .10
2 DEL 1994/95 .02 .10
3 Season 1994-95 .02 .10
4 Augsburger Panther Team .02 .10
5 Gunnar Leidborg .02 .10
6 Gary Prior .08 .25
7 Scott Campbell .02 .10
8 Dieter Medicus .02 .10
9 Duanne Moeser .02 .10
10 Daniel Naud .02 .10
11 Andy Romer .02 .10
12 Thomas Groger .02 .10
13 Sven Zywitza .02 .10
14 Fritz Meyer .02 .10
15 Christian Curth .02 .10
16 Toni Krinner .02 .10
17 Patrik Pysz .02 .10
18 Heinrich Romer .02 .10
19 Ales Polcar .02 .10
20 Philip Kukuk .02 .10
21 Dietrich Adam .02 .10
22 Tim Schnobrich .02 .10
23 Tim Ferguson .08 .25
24 Robert Heidt .02 .10
25 Alfred Burkhard .02 .10
26 Charly Fliegauf .02 .10
27 Robert Paclik .02 .10
28 Stefan Mayer .02 .10
29 Reinhard Haider .02 .10
30 Dennis Schrapp .02 .10
31 Eisbaren Berlin Team Card .02 .10
32 Walter Jaroslav .02 .10
33 Klaus Schroder .02 .10
34 Andre Dietzsch .02 .10
35 Juri Stumpf .02 .10
36 Torsten Deutscher .02 .10
37 Frank Kannewurf .02 .10
38 Thomas Graul .02 .10
39 Sven Felski .02 .10
40 Moritz Schmidt .02 .10
41 Marco Swibenko .02 .10
42 Holger Mix .02 .10
43 Jiri Dopita .40 1.00
44 Dirk Perschau .02 .10
45 Guido Hiller .02 .10
46 Daniel Held .02 .10
47 Richard Zemlicka .08 .25
48 Jan Schertz .02 .10
49 Mike Losch .02 .10
50 Patrick Solf .02 .10
51 Rupert Meister .02 .10
52 BSC Preussen Team Card .02 .10
53 Billy Flynn .08 .25
54 Tony Tanti .08 .25
55 Jochen Molling .02 .10
56 Andreas Schubert .02 .10
57 Stefan Steinecker .02 .10
58 Josef Lehner .02 .10
59 Tom O'Regan .08 .25
60 Gaetan Malo .02 .10
61 Michael Komma .02 .10
62 Marco Schinko .02 .10
63 Marco Rentzsch .02 .10
64 Georg Holzmann .02 .10
65 Mark Kosturik .02 .10
66 Jurgen Rumrich .02 .10
67 John Chabot .20 .50
68 Harald Windler .02 .10
69 Mark Teevens .08 .25
70 Klaus Merk .08 .25
71 Stephan Sinner .02 .10
72 Mark Gronau .02 .10
73 Bruce Hardy .08 .25
74 Fabian Brannstrom .02 .10
75 Daniel Poudrier .08 .25
76 Dusseldorfer EG Team Card .02 .10
77 Hans Zach .02 .10
78 Helmut DeRaaf .02 .10
79 Markus Kehle .02 .10
80 Christian Schmitz .02 .10
81 Lorenz Funk .02 .10
82 Chris Valentine .20 .50
83 Rafael Jedamzik .02 .10
84 Torsten Kienass .08 .25
85 Christopher Kreutzer .02 .10
86 Benoit Doucet .08 .25
87 Bernd Kuhnhauser .02 .10
88 Andreas Niederberger .02 .10
89 Rick Amann .08 .25
90 Thorsten Van Leyen .02 .10
91 Bruce Eakin .02 .10
92 Pierre Rioux .08 .25
93 Andreas Brockmann .02 .10
94 Uli Hiemer .02 .10
95 Bernd Truntschka .08 .25
96 Wolfgang Kummer .02 .10
97 Carsten Gossmann .02 .10
98 Ernst Kopf .08 .25
99 Robert Sterflinger .02 .10
100 Kevin LaVallee .08 .25
101 Rainer Zerwesz .02 .10
102 Frankfurt Lions Team Card .02 .10
103 Pjotr Vorobjev .02 .10
104 Peter Obresa .02 .10
105 Vladimir Quapp .02 .10
106 Florian Storf .02 .10
107 Alexander Wedl .02 .10
108 Olaf Scholz .02 .10
109 Ilya Vorobjev .02 .10
110 Ladislav Strompf .02 .10
111 Udo Dohler .02 .10
112 Alexander Wunsch .02 .10
113 Jiri Lala .02 .10
114 Andrej Jaufmann .02 .10
115 Thomas Muhlbauer .02 .10
116 Markus Kempf .02 .10
117 Igor Schultz .02 .10
118 Martin Schultz .02 .10
119 Michael Raubal .02 .10
120 Rudi Gorgenlander .02 .10
121 Jurgen Schaal .02 .10
122 Patrick Vozar .02 .10
123 Rochus Schneider .02 .10
124 Toni Raubal .02 .10
125 Stefan Koniger .02 .10
126 EC Hannover Team Card .02 .10
127 Hartmut Nickel .02 .10
128 Joachim Lempio .02 .10
129 Torsten Hanusch .02 .10
130 Thomas Jungwirth .02 .10
131 David Reierson .02 .10
132 Friedhelm Bogelsack .02 .10
133 Thomas Werner .02 .10
134 Dirk Rohrbach .02 .10
135 Harald Kuhnke .02 .10
136 Florian Funk .02 .10
137 Mark Maroste .02 .10
138 Anton Maidl .02 .10
139 Rene Reuter .02 .10
140 Rene Ledock .02 .10
141 Marco Herbst .02 .10
142 Milos Vanik .02 .10
143 Gunther Preuss .02 .10
144 Troy Tumbach .02 .10
145 Marc Wittbrock .02 .10
146 Roger Mede .02 .10
147 Craig Topolnisky .02 .10
148 Josef Schlickenrieder .02 .10
149 Marcus Bleicher .02 .10
150 EC Kassel Team Card .02 .10
151 Ross Yates .02 .10
152 Josef Kontny .02 .10
153 Milan Mokros .02 .10
154 Alexander Engel .02 .10
155 Greg Johnston .08 .25
156 Jedrzej Kasperczyk .02 .10
157 Dave Morrison .02 .10
158 Jaro Mucha .02 .10
159 Mike Millar .08 .25
160 Ireneusz Pacula .02 .10
161 Vitalij Grossmann .02 .10
162 Murray McIntosh .02 .10
163 Manfred Ahne .02 .10
164 Peter Kwasigroch .02 .10
165 Georg Guttler .02 .10
166 Falk Ozellis .02 .10
167 Mario Naster .02 .10
168 Sergej Wikulow .02 .10
169 Gerhard Hegen .02 .10
170 Brian Hannon .02 .10
171 Tino Boos .02 .10
172 Kaufbeurer Adler Team Card .02 .10
173 Peter Kathan .02 .10
174 Kenneth Karpuk .02 .10
175 Michael Olbrich .02 .10
176 Drahomir Kadlec .08 .25
177 Christian Seeberger .02 .10
178 Elmar Boiger .02 .10
179 Oto Hascak .02 .10
180 Thorsten Rau .02 .10
181 Tomas Martinec .02 .10
182 Norbert Zabel .02 .10
183 Daniel Kunce .02 .10
184 Hans-Jorg Mayer .02 .10
185 Manfred Jorde .02 .10
186 Roland Timoschuk .02 .10
187 Jim Hoffmann .02 .10
188 Andreas Volland .02 .10
189 Rolf Hammer .02 .10
190 Manuel Hess .02 .10
191 Timo Gschwill .02 .10
192 Marc Pethke .02 .10
193 Axel Kammerer .02 .10
194 Jurgen Simon .02 .10
195 Patrick Lange .02 .10
196 Ronny Martin .02 .10
197 Kolner EC Team Card .02 .10
198 Vladimir Vassiliev .02 .10
199 Bernd Haake .02 .10
200 Joseph Heiss .30 .75
201 Jorg Mayr .02 .10
202 Thomas Brandl .02 .10
203 Stephan Mann .02 .10
204 Tonny Reddo .02 .10
205 Mirco Ludemann .08 .25
206 Leo Stefan .08 .25
207 Andreas Pokorny .02 .10
208 Peter Draisaitl .08 .25
209 Ralf Dobrzynski .02 .10
210 Andreas Lupzig .02 .10
211 Karsten Mende .02 .10
212 Frank Hohenadl .02 .10
213 Marco Heinrichs .02 .10
214 Michael Rumrich .02 .10
215 Martin Ondrejka .02 .10
216 Herbert Hohenberger .08 .25
217 Thorsten Sendt .02 .10
218 Thorsten Koslowski .02 .10
219 Olaf Grundmann .02 .10
220 Franz Demmel .02 .10
221 Sergej Berezin .75 2.00
222 Krefelder EV Team Card .02 .10
223 Michael Zettel .02 .10
224 Frank Brunsing .02 .10
225 Karel Lang .02 .10
226 Markus Kranwinkel .02 .10
227 Earl Spry .02 .10
228 Andre Grein .02 .10
229 Greg Evtushevski .08 .25
230 Herberts Vasiljevs .02 .10
231 Ken Petrash .02 .10
232 Greg Thomson .02 .10
233 Reemt Pyka .08 .25
234 Brad Bergen .08 .25
235 Chris Lindberg .08 .25
236 Markus Kranwinkel .02 .10
237 Martin Gebel .02 .10
238 Francois Sills .02 .10
239 Klaus Micheller .02 .10
240 Peter Ihnacak .20 .50
241 Marek Stebnicki .02 .10
242 Johnny Walker .02 .10
243 Gunter Oswald .02 .10
244 James Hanlon .02 .10
245 Rene Bielke .02 .10
246 EV Landshut Team Card .02 .10
247 Bernhard Johnston .02 .10
248 Mark Stuckey .02 .10
249 Michael Bresagk .02 .10
250 Bernd Wagner .02 .10
251 Eduard Uvria .02 .10
252 Mike Smazal .02 .10
253 Jacek Plachta .02 .10
254 Georg Franz .02 .10
255 Stephan Retzer .02 .10
256 Henri Marcoux .02 .10
257 Andreas Loth .02 .10
258 Mike Bullard .02 .10
259 Markus Berwanger .02 .10
260 Petr Briza .40 1.00
261 Wally Schreiber .20 .50
262 Peter Gulda .02 .10
263 Ralf Hantschke .02 .10
264 Steve McNeil .02 .10
265 Christian Kunast .02 .10
266 Jorg Hendrick .02 .10
267 Helmut Steiger .02 .10
268 Udo Kiessling .02 .10
269 Mike Lay .02 .10
270 Adler Mannheim Team Card .02 .10
271 Lance Nethery .08 .25
272 Marcus Kuhl .02 .10
273 Joachim Appel .02 .10
274 Harold Kreis .02 .10
275 Mike Heidt .02 .10
276 Mario Gehrig .02 .10
277 Pavel Gross .02 .10
278 Steffen Michel .02 .10
279 Daniel Korber .02 .10
280 Robert Cimetta .08 .25
281 Dale Krentz .08 .25
282 Jochen Hecht 4.00 10.00
283 Till Feser .02 .10
284 Lars Bruggemann .02 .10
285 Toni Plattner .02 .10
286 Alexander Schuster .02 .10
287 Dieter Willmann .02 .10
288 Markus Flemming .02 .10
289 Rick Goldmann .20 .50
290 Damian Adamus .02 .10
291 Frederik Ledlin .02 .10
292 David Musial .02 .10
293 Michael Gabler .02 .10
294 Sven Valenti .02 .10
295 Maddogs Munchen Team Card .02 .10
296 Robert Murdoch .02 .10
297 Alexander Genze .02 .10
298 Greg Muller .02 .10
299 Mike Schmidt .02 .10
300 Zdenek Travnicek .02 .10
301 Christian Lukes .02 .10
302 Gordon Sherven .08 .25
303 Anthony Vogel .02 .10
304 Michael Hreuss .02 .10
305 Dale Derkatch .08 .25
306 Sergej Schendelew .02 .10
307 Christian Brittig .02 .10
308 Harald Waibel .02 .10
309 Rainer Lutz .02 .10
310 Ewald Steiger .02 .10
311 Didi Hegen .02 .10
312 Ralf Reisinger .02 .10
313 Henrik Holscher .02 .10
314 Karl Friesen .20 .50
315 Christian Frutel .02 .10
316 Tobias Abstreiter .02 .10
317 Christopher Sandner .02 .10
318 Harald Birk .02 .10
319 Chris Strausse .02 .10
320 EHC 80 Numberg Team Card .02 .10
321 Josef Golonka .02 .10
322 Christian Gerum .02 .10
323 Paul Geddes .02 .10
324 Ian Young .02 .10
325 Stefan Steinbock .02 .10
326 Doug Irwin .02 .10
327 Christian Flugge .02 .10
328 Klaus Birk .02 .10
329 Jurgen Lechl .02 .10
330 Thomas Popiesch .02 .10
331 Miroslav Maly .02 .10
332 Stephan Eder .02 .10
333 Arno Brux .02 .10
334 Jiri Dolezal .02 .10
335 Reiner Vorderbruggen .02 .10
336 Thomas Sterflinger .02 .10
337 Bernhard Engelbrecht .02 .10
338 Michael Weinfurter .02 .10
339 Sepp Wassermann .02 .10
340 Stephan Bauer .02 .10
341 Otto Sykora .02 .10
342 Ratingen Die Lowen Team Card .02 .10
343 Bill Lochead .08 .25
344 Pavel Mann .02 .10
345 Christian Kohmann .02 .10
346 Sven Prusa .02 .10
347 Otto Keresztes .02 .10
348 Frank Kovacs .02 .10
349 Jiri Smicek .02 .10
350 Richard Brodnicke .02 .10
351 Andrej Fuchs .02 .10
352 Oliver Kasper .02 .10
353 Michael Kratz .02 .10
354 Klaus Striemitzer .02 .10
355 Oliver Schwarz .02 .10
356 Boris Fuchs .02 .10
357 Christian Althoff .02 .10
358 Waldemar Novosjolov .02 .10
359 Thomas Imdahl .02 .10
360 Helmut Elters .02 .10
361 Andrej Hanisz .02 .10
362 Peter Lutter .02 .10
363 Martem Janov .02 .10
364 Mark Bassen .02 .10
365 Udo Schmid .02 .10
366 Mark Bassen .08 .25
367 Rosenheim Star Bulls Team Card .02 .10
368 Ernst Hofner .02 .10
369 Ludek Bukac .02 .10
370 Markus Wieland .02 .10
371 Andreas Schneider .02 .10
372 Raphael Kruger .02 .10
373 Michael Tattner .02 .10
374 Rick Boehm .02 .10
375 Robert Hock .02 .10
376 Joachim Reil .02 .10
377 Radek Toupal .02 .10
378 Martin Reichel .02 .10
379 Ron Fischer .02 .10
380 Raimund Hilger .08 .25
381 Petr Hrbek .02 .10
382 Oliver Hausler .02 .10
383 Christian Gegenfurther .02 .10
384 Marc Seliger .08 .25
385 Venci Sebek .02 .10
386 Florian Keller .08 .25
387 Heinrich Schiffl .02 .10
388 Michael Pohl .02 .10
389 Fuchse Sachsen Team Card .02 .10
390 Jiri Kochta .02 .10
391 Boris Capla .02 .10
392 Matthias Kliemann .02 .10
393 Josef Rednicek .02 .10
394 Branjo Heisig .02 .10
395 Jens Schwabe .08 .25

Frank Peschke .02 .10
Thomas Schubert .02 .10
Torsten Eisebitt .02 .10
Marcel Lichnovsky .02 .10
Jari Gronstrand .08 .25
Thomas Knobloch .02 .10
2 Falk Herzig .02 .10
3 Thomas Wagner .02 .10
4 Jan Tabor .02 .10
5 Sebastian Klenner .02 .10
6 Peter Hofmann .02 .10
7 Terry Cambell .08 .25
8 Antonio Fonso .02 .10
9 Thomas Bresagk .02 .10
0 Peter Franke .02 .10
1 Andreas Ott .02 .10
2 Michael Flemming .02 .10
3 Janusz Janikowski .02 .10
4 Schwenningen Wild Wings Team Card .02 .10
5 Miroslav Berek .02 .10
6 Bob Burns .02 .10
7 Thomas Gaus .02 .10
8 Richard Trojan .02 .10
9 Ilmar Toman .02 .10
0 Alan Young .02 .10
1 Michael Pastika .02 .10
2 Thomas Schadler .02 .10
3 Andrei Kovalev .02 .10
4 Alexander Horn .02 .10
5 Petr Kopta .02 .10
6 Robert Brezina .02 .10
27 Wayne Hynes .08 .25
28 Frantisek Frosch .02 .10
29 Carsten Solbach .02 .10
30 George Fritz .02 .10
31 Mike Bader .02 .10
32 Thomas Deiter .02 .10
33 Daniel Nowak .08 .25
34 Peter Heinold .02 .10
35 Matthias Hoppe .02 .10
36 Grant Martin .08 .25
37 Roger Bruns .02 .10
38 Andreas Renz .02 .10
39 Karsten Schulz .02 .10
40 Alfie Turcotte .08 .25

1994-95 German First League

This set features players of the German First League, a division one lower than the DEL. The set is noteworthy for the inclusion of several NHLers who performed briefly on this circuit during the 1994 NHL lockout, including Jaromir Jagr, Petr Klima and Vladimir Konstantinov.

COMPLETE SET (665) 30.00 80.00
33 Jorn Seuthe .08 .25
34 Pietro Vacca .08 .25
35 Gunther Eisenhut .08 .25
36 Thomas Kulzer .08 .25
37 Christian Zessak .08 .25
38 Peter Sterz .08 .25
39 Michael Maass .08 .25
40 Thomas Brandl .08 .25
41 Thomas Daffner .08 .25
42 Volker Kollmeder .08 .25
43 Thomas Haiti .08 .25
44 Hans Eberhard .08 .25
45 Enrico Kock .08 .25
46 Peter Hampl .08 .25
47 German Wolgin .08 .25
48 Andrej Balandin .08 .25
49 Rainer Wohlmann .08 .25
50 Teamcard/Checklist .08 .25
51 Michael Eibl .08 .25
52 Sven Schubert .08 .25
53 Franz Steer .08 .25
54 Ottmar Schluttenhofer .08 .25
55 Wolfgang Oswald .08 .25
56 John Samanski .08 .25
57 Marty Irvine .08 .25
58 Herbert Schadler .08 .25
59 Jeff Vaive .08 .25
60 Markus Neumuller .08 .25
61 Norbert Arians .08 .25
62 Alfred Weiss .08 .25
63 Gert Heubach .08 .25
64 Hans-Georg Eder .08 .25
65 Hansi Bader .08 .25
66 Franz Futtner .08 .25
67 Klaus Pillmaier .08 .25
68 Donar Dotzauer .08 .25
69 Bertil Filgis .08 .25
70 Roman Zaborowski .08 .25
71 Thomas Dahlem .08 .25
72 Markus Faistenhammer .08 .25
73 Teamcard/Checklist .08 .25
74 Thomas Dolak .08 .25
75 Oliver Kratt .08 .25
76 Klaus Muller .08 .25
77 Ralf Lux .08 .25
78 Igor Dorochin .08 .25
79 Ravil Khaidarov .08 .25
80 Peter Hejma .08 .25
81 Thomas Geldreich .08 .25
82 Christian Helber .08 .25
83 Marc Schonfeld .08 .25
84 Christian Wolfgramm .08 .25
85 Leos Zajic .08 .25
86 Rick Laycock .08 .25
87 Stefan Lahn .08 .25
88 Thomas Steinberg .08 .25
89 Jan Repka .08 .25
90 Joseph Peroutka .08 .25
91 Andreas Mockl .08 .25
92 Peter Salmik .08 .25
93 Jorg Lettgen .08 .25
94 Frank Furderer .08 .25
95 Christian Ott .08 .25
96 Teamcard/Checklist .08 .25
97 Rodion Pauels .08 .25
98 Aaron Strasser .08 .25
99 Ernst Messthaler .08 .25
100 Juri Starkhov .08 .25
101 Nikolai Varianov .08 .25
102 Tomas Krejcir .08 .25
103 Stefan Zellhuber .08 .25
104 Markus Gmeiner .08 .25
105 Richard Schnetz .08 .25
106 Wolfgang Koziol .08 .25
107 Christian Hauserer .08 .25
108 Gerhard Dittrich .08 .25
109 Christopher Zweng .08 .25
110 Peter Hartung .08 .25
111 Robert Scharpf .08 .25
112 Florian Schneider .08 .25
113 Tauno Zobel .08 .25
114 Matthias Sanger .08 .25
115 Peter Asanger .08 .25
116 Christian Ganseneder .08 .25
117 Hans-Jorg Stetter .08 .25
118 Thomas Frohlich .08 .25
119 Karl Streit .08 .25
120 Stefan Bardzinski .08 .25
121 Teamcard/Checklist .08 .25
122 Josef Capla .08 .25
123 Jorg Zinnecker .08 .25
124 Peter Harrer .08 .25
125 Heinrich Korph .08 .25
126 Martin Kirsch .08 .25
127 Michael Freissmann .08 .25
128 Peter Rappold .08 .25
129 Daniel Piechaczek .08 .25
130 Bernd Gessinger .08 .25
131 Michael Hogl .08 .25
132 Hubert Jellen .08 .25
133 Hans Hansch .08 .25
134 Steven Schafer .08 .25
135 Harald Wust .08 .25
136 Jean-Claude Brehm .08 .25
137 Olaf Bjorner .08 .25
138 Dusan Canik .08 .25
139 Martin Gessinger .08 .25
140 Martin Tschichoflos .08 .25
141 Ultich Liebsch .08 .25
142 Svyatoslav Khalizov .08 .25
143 Michael Pescheck .08 .25
144 Roland Seckler .08 .25
145 Teamcard/Checklist .08 .25
146 Gerd Wittmann .08 .25
147 Vladimir Macholda .08 .25
148 Sascha Bernhardt .08 .25
149 Michael Thurner .08 .25
150 Norbert Haslach .08 .25
151 Vitus ner Mitterfell .08 .25
152 Thorsten Haaf .08 .25
153 Michael Stejskal .08 .25
154 Klaus Jansen .08 .25
155 Oliver Hackert .08 .25
156 Ladislav Svozil .08 .25
157 Karsten Neumann .08 .25
158 Alexander Ulmer .08 .25
159 Joseph West .08 .25
160 Oliver Weissenberger .08 .25
161 Manfred Schuster .08 .25
162 Oliver Vost .08 .25
163 Peter Stankovic .08 .25
164 Uwe Geisert .08 .25
165 Peter Holdschick .08 .25
166 Ralf Hartfuss .08 .25
167 Bernhard Kopf .08 .25
168 Teamcard/Checklist .08 .25
169 Kim Collins .08 .25
170 Josef Wieser .08 .25
171 Frank Fischer .08 .25
172 Peter Geier .08 .25
173 Glenn Goodall .40 1.00
174 Patrick Fertich .08 .25
175 Mathias Wieser .08 .25
176 Maximilian Schindler .08 .25
177 Bastian Kammerloher .08 .25
178 James Quinlan .08 .25
179 Dirk Heick .08 .25
180 Walter Deisenberger .08 .25
181 Christoph Sauter .08 .25
182 Christian Walleitner .08 .25
183 Martin Sauter .08 .25
184 Oliver Mayer .08 .25
185 Roland Floss .08 .25
186 Maximilian Ahammer .08 .25
187 Robert Schumacher .08 .25
188 Ludvik Kopecky .08 .25
189 Florian Eder .10 .25
190 Teamcard/Checklist .08 .25
191 Ewalds Grabowskis .08 .25
192 Gerhard Petrussek .08 .25
193 Robert Bockler .08 .25
194 Markus Epple .08 .25
195 Mivhael Weisenbach .08 .25
196 Michael Billmaier .08 .25
197 Joachim Ried .08 .25
198 Holger Micheller .08 .25
199 Igor Pavlov .08 .25
200 Rudiger Weis .08 .25
201 Alexander Zittlau .08 .25
202 Michael Schaeufl .08 .25
203 Oleg Znarok .08 .25
204 Armin Fohry .08 .25
205 Franz-Xaver Ibelherr .08 .25
206 Karl Sajdl .08 .25
207 Daniel Schury .08 .25
208 Manfred Korb .08 .25
209 Christian Baier .08 .25
210 Christian Reuter .08 .25
211 Paul Haringer .08 .25
212 Erwin Haiusa .08 .25
213 Roland Hanemann .08 .25
214 Joachim Jais .08 .25
215 Teamcard/Checklist .08 .25
216 Eduard Giblak .08 .25
217 Robert Bohm .08 .25
218 Paul Greiter .08 .25
219 Max Ostermeier .08 .25
220 Florian Schmid .08 .25
221 Alexander Meyer .08 .25
222 Michael Lehmann .08 .25
223 Andi Ostermeier .08 .25
224 Manfred Braun .08 .25
225 Franz Daxner .08 .25
226 Michael Hock .08 .25
227 Oliver Kleininger .08 .25
228 Chris Clarke .08 .25
229 Andreas Paukner .08 .25
230 Florian Jager .08 .25
231 Patrick Gerber .08 .25
232 Karl Huttl .08 .25
233 Brad Belland .08 .25
234 Christian Lex .08 .25
235 Anton Hager .08 .25
236 Uli Stadier .08 .25
237 Teamcard/Checklist .08 .25
238 Florian Strida .08 .25
239 Peter Freissl .08 .25
240 Peter Engel .08 .25
241 Georg Weckerle .08 .25
242 Reiner Bauerle .08 .25
243 Johann Fischer .08 .25
244 Christian Kratzmeir .08 .25
245 Martin Strida .08 .25
246 Wolfgang Obermeier .08 .25
247 Franz Bruckl .08 .25
248 Robert Schmidt .08 .25
249 Jiri Jiroutek .08 .25
250 Bjorn Lehner .08 .25
251 Florian Rohde .08 .25
252 Paul Ruzicka .08 .25
253 Andreas Kraus .08 .25
254 Oliver Ciganovic .08 .25
255 Christian Steidl .08 .25
256 Klaus Strobl .08 .25
257 Robert Hauck .08 .25
258 Thomas Reitmeir .08 .25
259 Joachim Hagelsperger .08 .25
260 Florian Steidl .08 .25
261 Teamcard/Checklist .08 .25
262 Alexej Sulak .08 .25
263 Markus Mayer .08 .25
264 Thomas Brenzig .08 .25
265 Sven Erhart .08 .25
266 Holger Lieb .08 .25
267 Josef Maier .08 .25
268 Paul Huber .08 .25
269 Rainer Hain .08 .25
270 Peter Kothmayr .08 .25
271 Denis Hanko .08 .25
272 Manfred Muhlegger .08 .25
273 James Johannsen .08 .25
274 Michael Kteitl .08 .25
275 Reiner Sangl .08 .25
276 Rainer Hirschvogel .08 .25
277 Markus Weiss .08 .25
278 Herbert Gmeinder .08 .25
279 Gunther Hartmann .08 .25
280 Jorg Peters .08 .25
281 Sergej Boldavesko .08 .25
282 Peter Dorn .08 .25
283 Markus Kothmayr .08 .25
284 Teamcard/Checklist .08 .25
285 Georg Kink .08 .25
286 Gerhard Stranka .08 .25
287 Michael Pump .08 .25
288 Tom Gobel .08 .25
289 Vladimir Fedossov .08 .25
290 Andreas Oswald .08 .25
291 Andreas Ludwig .08 .25
292 Martin Leuthner .08 .25
293 Jurgen Reindl .08 .25
294 Karl Ostler .08 .25
295 Martin Holzer .08 .25
296 Peter Fischer .08 .25
297 Jens Feller .08 .25
298 Henry Domke .08 .25
299 Markus Kossig .08 .25
300 Andreas Maurer .08 .25
301 Georg Grunauer .08 .25
302 Andreas Wittig .08 .25
303 Andreas Gebauer .08 .25
304 Hubert Buchwieser .08 .25
305 Andreas Raubal .08 .25
306 Christian Winkler .08 .25
307 Brett Stewart .08 .25
308 Christoph Sandner .08 .25
309 Rainer Lutz .08 .25
310 Alfred Burkhard .08 .25
311 Dale Derkatch .20 .50
312 Teamcard/Checklist .08 .25
313 Rudolf Sindelar .08 .25
314 Thomas Hobek .08 .25
315 Jason Hall .08 .25
316 Jochen Hordler .08 .25
317 Mark Armstrong .08 .25
318 Peter Netsch .08 .25
319 Armin Hanke .08 .25
320 Jaroslav Peska .08 .25
321 Steve Neumann .08 .25
322 Markus Trendl .08 .25
323 Daniel Gardner .08 .25
324 Marek Kurowski .08 .25
325 Markus Albrecht .08 .25
326 Sascha Groger .08 .25
327 Stefan Leuschner .08 .25
328 Andreas Kimker .08 .25
329 Roland Schneider .08 .25
330 Elko Porzi .08 .25
331 Stefan Wegmann .08 .25
332 Holger Cocco .08 .25
333 Ralf Gaess .08 .25
334 EHC Straubing .08 .25
335 Franz Hejcik .08 .25
337 Achim Sipmeier .08 .25
338 Christian Penzkofer .08 .25
339 Thomas Schambeck .08 .25
340 Douglas Kirton .08 .25
341 Rainer Schuster .08 .25
342 Vaclav Mandous .08 .25
343 Christian Knott .08 .25
344 Edward Zawatsky .08 .25
345 Christian Heitzer .08 .25
346 Rüdiger Metsch .08 .25
347 Christian Setz .08 .25
348 Sascha Werner .08 .25
349 Martin Ebenburger .08 .25
350 Daniel Vogl .08 .25
351 Stephan Meier .08 .25
352 Sven Barnet .08 .25
353 Robert Steinmann .08 .25
354 1. EV Weiden .08 .25
355 Wilbert Duszenko .08 .25
356 Alexander Becker .08 .25
357 Frank Gentges .08 .25
358 Anton Doll .08 .25
359 Stefan Peschek .08 .25
360 Oliver Hecht .08 .25
361 Dirk Salinger .08 .25
362 Yuri Chipitsyn .08 .25
363 Marco Zimmermann .08 .25
364 Christian Martin .08 .25
365 Lubos Thur .08 .25
366 Andreas Frysztacki .08 .25
367 Sergej Agejkin .08 .25
368 Roman Bartosch .08 .25
369 Ales Volek .08 .25
370 Josef Preuß .08 .25
371 Thomas Pokorny .08 .25
372 Roman Zilka .08 .25
373 Dietmar Habnitt .08 .25
374 Horst Bärnreuther .08 .25
375 Stefan Breitner .08 .25
376 Teamcard/Checklist .08 .25
377 Ricki Alexander .08 .25
378 Ingo Schwarz .08 .25
379 Serge Lajoie .08 .25
380 Thomas Barczikowski .08 .25
381 Rik Schaefer .08 .25
382 Markus Reiter .08 .25
383 Todd Goodwin .08 .25
384 Thorsten Wolf .08 .25
385 Volker Lindenzweig .08 .25
386 Sven Paschek .08 .25
387 Markus Jehner .08 .25
388 Jurgen Engels .08 .25
389 Martin Prada .08 .25
390 Norbert Scholz .08 .25
391 Gregory Pruden .08 .25
392 Oliver Vieten .08 .25
393 Robert Vozar .08 .25
394 Martin Williams .08 .25
395 Jan Schier .08 .25
396 Michael Eckert .08 .25
397 Thomas Krebs .08 .25
398 Teamcard/Checklist .08 .25
399 Gerald Mull .08 .25
400 Juris Kruminsch .08 .25
401 Frank Strauss .08 .25
402 Peter Kaluza .08 .25
403 Dirk Sobottka .08 .25
404 Alwin Wever .08 .25
405 Jerzey Christ .08 .25
406 Andreas Kemper .08 .25
407 Andre Wilmshofer .08 .25
408 Olaf Busch .08 .25
409 Rico Petrick .08 .25
410 Kurt Wickenheiser .20 .50
411 Marc Muller .20 .50
412 Steffen Klau .08 .25
413 Zsolt Heffler .08 .25
414 Martin Bergeron .08 .25
415 Willi Tesch .08 .25
416 Frank Fischoder .08 .25
417 Darius Wonschweski .08 .25
418 Teamcard/Checklist .08 .25
419 Eduard Nocak .08 .25
420 Stephan Schafer .08 .25
421 Michael Schmitz .08 .25
422 Jochen Hecker .08 .25
423 Axel Gesser .08 .25
424 Heinz-Gerd Albers .08 .25
425 Markus Bak .08 .25
426 Bernd Deske .08 .25
427 Ron Noak .08 .25
428 Darren Colbourne .08 .25
429 Frank Pribil .08 .25
430 Holger Rimroth .08 .25
431 Lars Tannhof .08 .25
432 Ulrik Kuhnekath .08 .25
433 Jorg Deske .08 .25
434 Guy Phillips .08 .25
435 Jorg Bohme .08 .25
436 Udo Sofan .08 .25
437 Matthias Starke .08 .25
438 Oliver Walde .08 .25
439 Teamcard/Checklist .08 .25
440 Dieter Bruggemann .08 .25
441 Julian Binavince .08 .25
442 Kai Kemper .08 .25
443 Raimund Peschke .08 .25
444 Frank Besser .08 .25
445 Frank Blanke .08 .25
446 John Neeld .08 .25
447 Alexander Knoff .08 .25
448 Brad Scott .08 .25
449 Bodo Mischer .08 .25
450 Jiri Kovarik .08 .25
451 Markus Kolloch .08 .25
452 Carsten Plate .08 .25
453 Thomas Hesse .08 .25
454 Jorg Loschek .08 .25
455 Dirk Voss .08 .25
456 Detlev Ellermann .08 .25
457 Volker Loscheck .08 .25
458 Richard Drewniak .08 .25
459 Teamcard/Checklist .08 .25
460 Erwin Materna .08 .25
461 Ingmar Kracht .08 .25
462 Michael Meixner .08 .25
463 Dirk Rossbach .08 .25
464 Karsten Scherping .08 .25
465 Mark Mahon .08 .25
466 Wolfgang Hofbauer .08 .25
467 Uwe Geiselmann .08 .25
468 Sean Krakivsky .08 .25
469 Douglas Murray .08 .25
470 Marek Gajewski .08 .25
471 Mario Feigl .08 .25
472 Frank Liebert .08 .25
473 Miroslav Mago .08 .25
474 Mirsolav Sakmirda .08 .25
475 Dirk Nieleck .08 .25
476 Jan Furd .08 .25
477 Ralf Kubiak .08 .25
478 Marek Adamec .08 .25
479 Douglas Murray .08 .25
480 Teamcard/Checklist .08 .25
481 Sergej Svetlov .08 .25
482 Christian Berlin .08 .25
483 Marek Adamek .08 .25
484 Ralf Cassebaum .08 .25
485 Ingo Rdurch .08 .25
486 Sergej Hatkevitsch .08 .25
487 Thomas Otto .08 .25
488 Riccardo Siegert .08 .25
489 Willy Reinhard .08 .25
490 Jorn Sigmansky .08 .25
491 Guido Drongowski .08 .25
492 Carsten Boss .08 .25
493 Jacek Piechutta .08 .25
494 Thorsten Peters .08 .25
495 Lutz Bongers .08 .25
496 Armin Schnitzler .08 .25
497 Teamcard/Checklist .08 .25
498 Walter Koberle .08 .25
499 Carsten Lange .08 .25
500 Jurgen Schultz .08 .25
501 Jan Raspel .08 .25
502 Christoph Gelzinus .08 .25
503 Markus Kamman .08 .25
504 Markus Buchhart .08 .25
505 Holger Schmitz .08 .25
506 Ladislav Kolda .08 .25
507 Arndt Kons .08 .25
508 Boris Morsch .08 .25
509 Darius Wonschewski .08 .25
510 Benedikt Kons .08 .25
511 James Dressler .08 .25
512 Dirk Scholz .08 .25
513 Marco Scharf .08 .25
514 Mike van Hauten .08 .25
515 Max Bander .08 .25
516 Gilbert Schroder .08 .25
517 Teamcard/Checklist .08 .25
518 Alexander Wolkow .08 .25
519 Sven Schmitz .08 .25
520 Andrej Ovtschinnikov .08 .25
521 Boguslav Kuta .08 .25
522 Sergej Zaitsev .08 .25
523 Rene Naroska .08 .25
524 Markus Menschig .08 .25
525 Milos Piperski .08 .25
526 Andreas Halfmann .08 .25
527 Marcus Golabek .08 .25
528 Peter Kraus .08 .25
529 Peter Juchem .08 .25
530 Marius Cissewski .08 .25
531 Falk Elzner .08 .25
532 Jens Herget .08 .25
533 Fabian Dahlem .08 .25
534 Jurgen Trattner .08 .25
535 Daniel Walther .08 .25
536 Peter Burfant .08 .25
537 Eduard Lorer .08 .25
538 Andreas Keiler .08 .25
539 Haie Schalker GEV .08 .25
540 Charly Stenner CO .08 .25
541 Thomas Blasche .08 .25
542 Dietmar Schramm .08 .25
543 Achim Blaar .08 .25
544 Graischa Pietsch .08 .25
545 Robert Simon .08 .25
546 Bruce Bonner .08 .25
547 Ladislav Hospodar .08 .25
548 Martin Jilek .08 .25
549 Michael Scanu .08 .25
550 Phil Berger .08 .25
551 Christoph Kleckers .08 .25
552 Patrick Schmitz .08 .25
553 Gregor Wilk .08 .25
554 Jens Casten .08 .25
555 Andre Jucknischke .08 .25
556 Vladimir Kames .08 .25
557 Petr Fiala .08 .25
558 Marco Blazyczek .08 .25
559 Trajan Cazacu .08 .25
560 Robert Schutz .08 .25
561 Jaromir Jagr 20.00 50.00
562 ETC Timmendorf .08 .25
563 Jeff Pyle .08 .25
564 Gerd Vogel .08 .25
565 Andrzej Bielenink .08 .25
566 Marvin Glaser .08 .25
567 Harald Bolke .08 .25
568 Christian Spaan .08 .25
569 Henry Thom .08 .25
570 Matthias Schnabel .08 .25
571 Mike Bukowski .08 .25
572 Jeff Tomlinson .20 .50
573 Steffen Thau .08 .25
574 Mark MacKay .20 .50
575 Olaf Brull .08 .25
576 Moe Lemay .40 1.00
577 Michael Mai .08 .25
578 Peter Hiller .08 .25
579 Christoph Hadraschek .08 .25
580 Mike Wehrmann .08 .25
581 Lars Wunsche .08 .25
582 Maj Boguslaw .08 .25
583 Sven Rampf .08 .25
584 Teamcard/Checklist .08 .25
585 Helmut Bauer .08 .25
586 Guido Titzhoff .08 .25
587 Lubomir Lang .08 .25
588 Guy Rouleau .08 .25
589 Andreas Naumann .20 .50
590 Marc Otten .08 .25
591 Kenneth Filgis .08 .25
592 Dimitri Matuschow .08 .25
593 Markus Pollock .08 .25
594 Mario Plack .08 .25
595 Herbert Plattner .08 .25
596 Roman Sindelar .20 .50
597 Herbert Ott .08 .25
598 Reik Blasche .08 .25
599 Vladimir Lukscheider .08 .25
600 Christof Grunthal .08 .25
601 Hermann Retzer .08 .25
602 Adam Gedyk .08 .25
603 Ralf Lamberty .08 .25
604 Teamcard/Checklist .08 .25
605 Kevin Gaudet .08 .25
606 Dale Reinig .08 .25
607 Jorg Meyer .08 .25
608 Bruce Keller .08 .25
609 Laszlo Csata .08 .25
610 Douglas Murray .08 .25
611 Garry Schwindt .08 .25
612 Fred Carroll .08 .25
613 Len Soccio .20 .50
614 Michail Lemmer .08 .25
615 Dieter Reiss .08 .25
616 Jirko Seib .08 .25
617 Matthias Kuhnel .08 .25
618 Heinrich Synowietz .08 .25
619 Paul Synowietz .08 .25
620 Justyn Denisiuk .08 .25
621 Slawomir Osinski .08 .25
622 Jari Pasanen .08 .25
623 Marcus Beeck .08 .25
624 Vladimir Konstantinov 4.00 10.00
625 Teamcard/Checklist .08 .25
626 Josef Vimmer .08 .25
627 Torsten Kluin .08 .25
628 Dieter Frenzel .08 .25
629 Harald Hebig .08 .25
630 Jorg Volkle .08 .25
631 Alexander Gorsdorf .08 .25
632 Roman Slezak .08 .25
633 Jan Baron .08 .25
634 Sergej Jaschin .08 .25
635 Robert Eylert .08 .25
636 Anatoli Antipov .08 .25
637 Heiko Tabor .08 .25
638 Jan-Hans Pokorny .08 .25
639 Roman Blazek .08 .25
640 Alexander Purschel .08 .25
641 Bernd Timmer .08 .25
642 Tomasz Mieszkowski .08 .25
643 Vaclav Drobny .08 .25
644 Teamcard/Checklist .08 .25
645 Nikolai Besprosvannych .08 .25
646 Dimitri Ritthaler .08 .25
647 Dimitri Konjuchov .08 .25
648 Erwin Forster .08 .25
649 Olaf-Bjorn Kolle .08 .25
650 Gary Cummins .08 .25
651 Garth Bannatyne .08 .25
652 Jamie Hartnett .08 .25
653 Cory Holden .08 .25
654 Andreas Henkel .08 .25
655 Janusz Wielgus .08 .25
656 Douglas Morton .08 .25
657 Kebin McGibney .08 .25
658 Daniel Poudrier .20 .50
659 Peter Just .08 .25
660 Lumir Mikesz .08 .25
661 Kenneth Filbey .08 .25
662 Richard Jelsovsky .08 .25
663 Petr Klima .40 1.00
664 Jiri Jiroutek .08 .25
665 Mark MacKay .20 .50

1995-96 German DEL

This 450-card set features the players of Germany's top hockey division, the DEL. The cards measure the standard size, and were issued in six-card packs for 2.5 marks. The card fronts feature action photography with the player name, position and team logo along the bottom. The back includes another photo along with stats. The set is highlighted by the inclusion of several NHLers who played in the DEL during the 1994 lockout including Pavel Bure, Jeremy Roenick and Brendan Shanahan. The hologram chase card was randomly inserted in 1:375 packs. A collector's album to house the cards was available through a wrapper offer for 45 marks.

COMPLETE SET (450) 50.00 125.00
1 Gary Prior .05 .15
2 Rupert Meister .02 .10
3 Dennis Schrapp .02 .10
4 Scott Campbell .02 .10
5 Fritz Meyer .02 .10
6 Rob Mendel .02 .10
7 Ken Collins .05 .15
8 Stefan Mayer .02 .10
9 Torsten Fendt .02 .10
10 Andrei Skopintsev .05 .15
11 Bob Wilkie .02 .10
12 Duanne Moeser .02 .10
13 Martin Nagler .02 .10
14 Sven Zywitza .02 .10
15 Marc Habscheid .08 .25
16 Daniel Held .02 .10
17 Heinrich Romer .02 .10
18 Rick Laycock .02 .10
19 Robert Francz .02 .10
20 Tim Ferguson .02 .10
21 Robert Heidt .05 .15
22 Eric Dylla .02 .10
23 Harald Birk .02 .10
24 Rochus Schneider .02 .10
25 Billy Flynn .02 .10
26 Andre Dietzsch .02 .10
27 Udo Dohler .02 .10
28 Juri Stumpf .02 .10
29 Torsten Deutscher .02 .10
30 Frank Kannewurf .02 .10
31 Thomas Graul .02 .10
32 Dirk Perschau .02 .10
33 Patrick Solf .02 .10
34 Daniel Poudrier .02 .10
35 Bernhard Kaminski .02 .10
36 Christoph Hadraschek .02 .10
37 Sven Felski .02 .10
38 Marco Swibenko .02 .10
39 Holger Mix .02 .10
40 Mark Maroste .02 .10
41 Troy Tumbach .02 .10
42 Jan Schertz .02 .10
43 Mike Losch .02 .10
44 Andreas Naumann .05 .15
45 Marc Garthe .02 .10
46 Igor Dorochin .02 .10
47 Thomas Mitew .02 .10
48 Claes Lundmark .02 .10
49 Chris Panek .02 .10
50 Klaus Merk .20 .50
51 Mark Gronau .02 .10
52 Stefan Steinecker .02 .10
53 Josef Lehner .02 .10
54 Tom O'Regan .05 .15
55 Fredrik Stillmann .02 .10
56 Marco Rentzsch .02 .10
57 Stephan Sinner .02 .10
58 Andreas Schubert .05 .15
59 Tony Tanti .08 .25
60 Gaeten Malo .02 .10
61 Michael Komma .02 .10
62 Thomas Schinko .02 .10
63 Georg Holzmann .02 .10
64 Mark Kosturik .02 .10
65 Christian Brittig .02 .10
66 Jurgen Rumrich .02 .10
67 John Chabot .20 .50
68 Andreas Dimbat .02 .10
69 Ulrich Liebsch .02 .10
70 Mark Teevens .05 .15
71 Fabian Brannstom .02 .10
72 Dennis Meyer .02 .10
73 Lars Hoffmann .02 .10
74 Hardy Nilsson CO .02 .10
75 Marcus Karlsson .02 .10
76 Helmut De Raaf .08 .25
77 Kai Fischer .30 .75
78 Carsten Gossmann .02 .10
79 Torsten Kienass .08 .25
80 Christopher Kreutzer .02 .10
81 Brad Bergen .02 .10
82 Andreas Niederberger .05 .15
83 Rick Amann .02 .10
84 Uli Hiemer .05 .15
85 Sergei Sorokin .05 .15
86 Robert Sterflinger .02 .10
87 Lorenz Funk .02 .10
88 Chris Valentine .20 .50
89 Gord Sherven .05 .15
90 Boris Lingemann .02 .10
91 Benoit Doucet .08 .25
92 Bernd Kuhnhauser .02 .10
93 Bruce Eakin .05 .15
94 Dieter Hegen .08 .25
95 Andreas Brockmann .02 .10
96 Bernd Truntschka .08 .25
97 Wolfgang Kummer .02 .10
98 Mikko Makela .08 .25
99 Nikolaus Mondt .02 .10
100 Piotr Vorobjew .05 .15
101 Peter Obresa .02 .10
102 Thierry Mayer .02 .10
103 Marc Seliger .40 1.00
104 Florian Storf .02 .10
105 Ladislav Strompf .02 .10
106 Greg Thompson .02 .10
107 Sergei Schendelev .02 .10
108 Martin Duris .02 .10
109 Rudi Gorgenlander .02 .10
110 Andreas Raubal .02 .10
111 Stephan Ziesche .05 .15
112 Petr Kopta .02 .10
113 Thomas Popiesch .02 .10
114 Francois Sills .02 .10
115 Jiri Lala .05 .15
116 Robert Reichel .40 1.00
117 Markus Kempf .02 .10
118 Igor Schultz .02 .10
119 Martin Schultz .02 .10
120 Brian Hannon .02 .10
121 Jurgen Schaal .02 .10
122 Patrick Vozar .02 .10
123 Ron Kennedy .02 .10
124 Friedhelm Bogelsack .05 .15
125 Marco Herbst .02 .10
126 Josef Schlickenrieder .02 .10
127 Torsten Hanusch .02 .10
128 Thomas Jungwirth .02 .10
129 David Reierson .02 .10
130 Christian Curth .02 .10
131 Anton Maidl .02 .10
132 Marc Wittbrock .02 .10
133 Brad Schlegel .08 .25
134 Thomas Werner .02 .10
135 Dirk Rohrbach .02 .10
136 Bruce Hardy .02 .10
137 Harald Kuhnke .02 .10
138 Florian Funk .02 .10
139 Rene Reuter .02 .10
140 Milos Vaník .02 .10
141 Gunther Preuss .02 .10
142 Kevin LaVallee .05 .15
143 Marcus Bleicher .02 .10
144 Anton Krinner .02 .10
145 Harald Waibel .02 .10
146 Hans Zach .02 .10
147 Josef Kontny .02 .10
148 Gerhard Hegen .02 .10
149 Milan Mokros .02 .10
150 Venci Sebek .02 .10
151 Alexander Engel .02 .10
152 Alexander Wedl .02 .10
153 Jaro Mucha .02 .10

1995-96 German DEL

154 Murray McIntosh	.02	.10
155 Georg Guttler	.02	.10
156 Greg Johnston	.05	.15
157 Jederzej Kasperczyk	.02	.10
158 Dave Morrison	.02	.10
159 Mike Millar	.05	.15
160 Ireneusz Pacula	.02	.10
161 Vitalij Grossmann	.02	.10
162 Igor Varitsky	.02	.10
163 Peter Kwasigroch	.02	.10
164 Branjo Heisig	.02	.10
165 Greg Evtushevski	.05	.15
166 Falk Ozellis	.02	.10
167 Tino Boos	.02	.10
168 Jarmo Tolvanen	.02	.10
169 Dieter Medicus	.02	.10
170 Michael Olbrich	.02	.10
171 Marc Pethke	.02	.10
172 Drahomir Kadlec	.05	.15
173 Christian Seeberger	.02	.10
174 Georg Kunce	.02	.10
175 Daniel Kunce	.02	.10
176 Timo Gschwill	.02	.10
177 Marco Eltner	.02	.10
178 Jurgen Simon	.02	.10
179 Alexander Herbst	.02	.10
180 Elmar Boiger	.02	.10
181 Otto Hascak	.08	.25
182 Tim Schnobrich	.02	.10
183 Anthony Vogel	.02	.10
184 Tomas Martinec	.02	.10
185 Hans-Jorg Mayer	.05	.15
186 Roland Timoschuk	.02	.10
187 Jim Hoffmann	.02	.10
188 Andreas Volland	.02	.10
189 Rolf Hammer	.02	.10
190 Manuel Hess	.02	.10
191 Dale Derkatch	.20	.50
192 Sebastian Schwele	.02	.10
193 R.J. Murdoch	.08	.25
194 Bernd Haake	.02	.10
195 Joseph Heiss	.30	.75
196 Olaf Grundmann	.02	.10
197 Alexander Genze	.02	.10
198 A. von Trzcinski	.02	.10
199 Jorg Mayr	.05	.15
200 Mirco Ludemann	.08	.25
201 Andreas Pokorny	.02	.10
202 Jayson Meyer	.02	.10
203 Karsten Mende	.02	.10
204 Herbert Hohenberger	.20	.50
205 Thomas Brandl	.02	.10
206 Stefan Mann	.02	.10
207 Luciano Borsato	.08	.25
208 Leo Stefan	.08	.25
209 Peter Draisaitl	.08	.25
210 Andreas Lupzig	.08	.25
211 Ralf Reisinger	.02	.10
212 Rainer Zerwesz	.02	.10
213 Michael Rumrich	.02	.10
214 Martin Ondrejka	.02	.10
215 Tobias Abstreiter	.02	.10
216 Franz Demmel	.02	.10
217 Sergei Berezin	.40	1.00
218 Miroslav Berek CO	.02	.10
219 Karel Lang	.02	.10
220 Rene Bielke	.02	.10
221 Markus Krawinkel	.02	.10
222 Kenneth Karpuk	.02	.10
223 Klaus Micheller	.02	.10
224 Earl Spry	.02	.10
225 Andreas Ott	.02	.10
226 Petri Limatainen	.02	.10
227 Andre Grein	.02	.10
228 Ken Petrash	.02	.10
229 James Hanlon	.02	.10
230 Reemt Pyka	.08	.25
231 Thomas Imdahl	.02	.10
232 Chris Lindberg	.08	.25
233 Jay Luknowsky	.02	.10
234 Peter Ihnacak	.08	.25
235 Marek Stebnicki	.02	.10
236 Johnny Walker	.02	.10
237 Arno Brux	.02	.10
238 Robert Busch	.02	.10
239 Mark Bassen	.02	.10
240 Martin Gebel	.02	.10
241 Bernhard Johnston	.02	.10
242 Petr Briza	.30	.75
243 Christian Kunast	.02	.10
244 Michael Bresagk	.02	.10
245 Eduard Uvria	.02	.10
246 Michael Heidt	.02	.10
247 Peter Gulda	.02	.10
248 Udo Kiessling	.08	.25
249 Dieter Bloem	.02	.10
250 Thomas Vogl	.02	.10
251 Jacek Plachta	.02	.10
252 Georg Franz	.02	.10
253 Stephan Retzer	.02	.10
254 Henri Marcoux	.02	.10
255 Andreas Loth	.02	.10
256 Mike Bullard	.08	.25
257 Jose Charbonneau	.08	.25
258 Wally Schreiber	.08	.25
259 Jorg Handrick	.02	.10
260 Holger Steiger	.02	.10
261 Marco Sturm	6.00	15.00
262 Lance Nethery	.05	.15
263 Marcus Kuhl	.02	.10
264 Joachim Appel	.02	.10
265 Markus Flemming	.02	.10
266 Harold Kreis	.02	.10
267 Paul Stanton	.08	.25
268 Christian Lukes	.02	.10
269 Steffen Michel	.02	.10
270 Stephane J.G. Richer	.05	.15
271 Jorg Hanft	.02	.10
272 Erich Goldmann	.02	.10
273 Mario Gehrig	.02	.10
274 Pavel Gross	.02	.10
275 Daniel Korber	.02	.10
276 Rob Cimetta	.08	.25
277 Jochen Hecht	1.25	3.00
278 Till Feser	.02	.10
279 Alexander Serikow	.40	1.00
280 Patrik Pysz	.05	.15
281 Darian Adamus	.02	.10
282 David Musial	.02	.10
283 Michael Hreus	.02	.10
284 Chris Strausse	.02	.10
285 Sven Valenti	.02	.10
286 Sebastien Thivierge	.02	.10
287 Jan Eysselt CO	.02	.10
288 Richard Neubauer	.02	.10
289 Roman Turek	.40	1.00
290 Stefan Lahn	.02	.10
291 Christian Gerum	.02	.10
292 Heiko Smazal	.02	.10
293 Miroslav Maly	.02	.10
294 Thomas Sterflinger	.02	.10
295 Michael Weinfurter	.02	.10
296 Stephan Bauer	.02	.10
297 Lars Bruggemann	.02	.10
298 Markus Kehle	.02	.10
299 Paul Geddes	.02	.10
300 Ian Young	.02	.10
301 Stefan Steinbock	.02	.10
302 Jurgen Lechl	.02	.10
303 Markus Goerlitz	.02	.10
304 Jiri Dolezal	.08	.25
305 Henrik Holscher	.02	.10
306 Sepp Wassermann	.02	.10
307 Otto Sykora	.02	.10
308 Bil Lochead	.05	.15
309 Patrick Lange	.02	.10
310 Ian Wood	.02	.10
311 H. Thorn	.02	.10
312 Doug Irwin	.02	.10
313 Christian Schmitz	.02	.10
314 Alexander Wunsch	.02	.10
315 Cory Holden	.02	.10
316 Jamie Bartman	.02	.10
317 Peter Lutter	.02	.10
318 Pavel Mann	.02	.10
319 Greg Muller	.02	.10
320 Christian Kohmann	.02	.10
321 Paul Beraldo	.05	.15
322 Thomas Groger	.02	.10
323 Andrej Fuchs	.02	.10
324 Klaus Birk	.02	.10
325 Dave Rich	.02	.10
326 Boris Fuchs	.02	.10
327 Thomas Muhlbauer	.02	.10
328 Axel Kammerer	.02	.10
329 Jeff Lazaro	.20	.50
330 Olaf Scholz	.02	.10
331 Bobby Reynolds	.02	.10
332 Jaroslav Sevcik	.08	.25
333 P.M. Arnholt	.02	.10
334 Gerhard Stranka	.02	.10
335 Vincent Riendeau	.20	.50
336 Michael Schmidt	.02	.10
337 T. Gobel	.02	.10
338 Vladimir Fedosov	.02	.10
339 R. Jadamzik	.02	.10
340 Frank Hohenadl	.02	.10
341 Anton Raubal	.02	.10
342 C. Schonmoser	.02	.10
343 Andreas Ludwig	.02	.10
344 Karl Ostler	.02	.10
345 Markus Berwanger	.02	.10
346 Martin Holzer	.02	.10
347 Jens Feller	.02	.10
348 Henry Domke	.02	.10
349 Andreas Maurer	.02	.10
350 Andreas Gebauer	.02	.10
351 Guntar Oswald	.02	.10
352 Hubert Buchwieser	.02	.10
353 Brett Stewart	.02	.10
354 Christopher Sandner	.02	.10
355 Joachim Hagelsperger	.02	.10
356 Robert Hock	.02	.10
357 Mark Jooris	.02	.10
358 Ernst Hofner	.02	.10
359 Gary Clark CO	.02	.10
360 Karl Friesen	.30	.75
361 Klaus Dalpiaz	.08	.25
362 Markus Wieland	.02	.10
363 Chris Clarke	.02	.10
364 Markus Pottinger	.02	.10
365 Raphael Kruger	.02	.10
366 Ron Fischer	.02	.10
367 Christian Gegenfurter	.02	.10
368 Heinrich Schiffl	.02	.10
369 Andreas Schneider	.02	.10
370 Vitus Mitterfellner	.02	.10
371 Richard Bohm	.02	.10
372 Dale Krentz	.08	.25
373 Tobias Schraven	.02	.10
374 Florian Keller	.40	1.00
375 Doug Derraugh	.04	.10
376 Martin Reichel	.05	.15
377 Markus Draxler	.02	.10
378 Raimund Hilger	.05	.15
379 Michael Pohl	.02	.10
380 Martin Kropf	.02	.10
381 Joel Savage	.20	.50
382 J. Eckmaier	.02	.10
383 R.R. Burns	.02	.10
384 Gunnar Leidborg	.02	.10
385 Carsten Solbach	.02	.10
386 Matthias Hoppe	.02	.10
387 Gord Hynes	.08	.25
388 Thomas Gaus	.02	.10
389 Zdenek Travnicek	.02	.10
390 Richard Trojan	.02	.10
391 Frantisek Frosch	.02	.10
392 Daniel Nowak	.02	.10
393 Andreas Renz	.02	.10
394 Alan Young	.02	.10
395 Robert Brezina	.02	.10
396 Wayne Hynes	.02	.10
397 George Fritz	.02	.10
398 Mike Bader	.02	.10
399 Grant Martin	.02	.10
400 Karsten Schulz	.02	.10
401 Mike Lay	.02	.10
402 Jackson Penney	.05	.15
403 Rich Chernomaz	.05	.15
404 Mark MacKay	.30	.75
405 Sana Hassan	.02	.10
406 Jiri Kochta	.02	.10
407 Thomas Bresagk	.02	.10
408 Peter Franke	.02	.10
409 Jochen Molling	.02	.10
410 Frantisek Prochazka	.02	.10
411 Josef Reznicek	.02	.10
412 Thomas Schubert	.02	.10
413 Ronny Martin	.02	.10
414 Marcel Lichnovsky	.02	.10
415 Matthias Kliemann	.02	.10
416 Ronny Reddo	.02	.10
417 Frank Peschke	.02	.10
418 Torsten Eisebitt	.02	.10
419 Janusz Janikowski	.02	.10
420 Thomas Knobloch	.02	.10
421 Falk Herzig	.02	.10
422 Thomas Wagner	.02	.10
423 Jan Tabor	.05	.15
424 Jorg Pohling	.02	.10
425 Pavel Vit	.02	.10
426 Vadim Kulabuchov	.02	.10
427 D. Cup Meister 1995	.08	.25
428 Kingston/Kuhnhauser/Genze	.08	.25
429 Heiss/Lupzig	.08	.25
430 Brandl/Mann	.08	.25
431 Doucet/Nowak	.08	.25
432 Meyer/Pyka	.08	.25
433 Hegen/Kunce	.08	.25
434 Rumrich/Ludemann	.08	.25
435 Benda/Kosturik	.08	.25
436 Kienass/Brockmann/Hanft	.05	.15
437 Draisaitl/Simon/Schneider	.08	.25
438 Andreas Niederberger	.08	.25
439 Martin Reichel	.05	.15
440 Klaus Merk	.20	.50
441 Glenn Anderson	1.25	3.00
442 Pavel Bure	12.00	30.00
443 Vincent Damphousse	2.00	5.00
444 Uwe Krupp	.20	.50
445 Robert Reichel	.40	1.00
446 Jeremy Roenick	12.00	30.00
447 Brendan Shanahan	12.00	30.00
448 Jozef Stumpel	.75	2.00
449 Doug Weight	2.00	5.00
450 Scott Young	.75	2.00
NNO Hologram Karte	4.00	10.00

1996-97 German DEL

This 360-card set features the players of Germany's top division, the DEL. The cards measure the standard size and were issued in six-card packs. The card fronts feature full-bleed action photography, along with the player's name, team logo and logo of the manufacturer. The back includes another photo, affiliated logos, and stats for the '95-96 season, along with career totals and, in some cases, NHL totals. In a few instances, no stats are provided in the case of those players making their debuts in the DEL.

COMPLETE SET (360)	16.00	40.00
1 Gary Prior CO	.05	.15
2 Bruno Campese	.08	.25
3 Leonardo Conti	.05	.15
4 Scott Campbell	.05	.15
5 Robert Mendel	.05	.15
6 Serge Poudrier	.05	.15
7 Torsten Fendt	.05	.15
8 Shawn Rivers	.05	.15
9 Stefan Mayer	.05	.15
10 Michael Bakos	.05	.15
11 Tommy Jakobsen	.05	.15
12 Duanne Moeser	.05	.15
13 Tero Arkiomaa	.05	.15
14 Sven Zywitza	.05	.15
15 Craig Streu	.05	.15
16 Terry Campbell	.05	.15
17 Timothy Ferguson	.05	.15
18 Yves Heroux	.05	.15
19 Max Boldt	.05	.15
20 Andre Faust	.05	.15
21 Rochus Schneider	.05	.15
22 Ron Kennedy CO	.05	.15
23 Barry Lewis ACO	.05	.15
24 Mario Brunetta	.20	.50
25 Udo Dohler	.05	.15
26 Dirk Perschau	.05	.15
27 Darren Durdle	.05	.15
28 Greg Andrusak	.08	.25
29 Leif Carlsson	.05	.15
30 Derek Mayer	.08	.25
31 Rob Leask	.05	.15
32 Chad Biafore	.05	.15
33 Thomas Steen	.05	.15
34 Lorenz Funk	.05	.15
35 Florian Funk	.05	.15
36 Sven Felski	.05	.15
37 Peter Lee	.08	.25
38 Andrew McKim	.20	.50
39 Andrei Lomakin	.08	.25
40 Pelle Svensson	.05	.15
41 Jan Schertz	.05	.15
42 Kraig Nienhuis	.20	.50
43 Niklas Hede	.05	.15
44 Mario Chitarroni	.08	.25
45 Chris Govedaris	.20	.50
46 Pentti Matikainen CO	.05	.15
47 Jukka Tammi	.08	.25
48 Rupert Meister	.05	.15
49 Florian Storf	.05	.15
50 Greg Thomson	.05	.15
51 Toni Porkka	.05	.15
52 Sergej Schendelev	.05	.15
53 Kai Rautio	.05	.15
54 Rudi Gorgenlander	.05	.15
55 Petr Kopta	.05	.15
56 Tony Virta	.08	.25
57 Ilja Vorobjev	.05	.15
58 Thomas Popiesch	.05	.15
59 Francois Sills	.05	.15
60 Iiro Jarvi	.05	.15
61 Jurgen Schaal	.05	.15
62 Pavel Vit	.05	.15
63 Timo Peltomaa	.05	.15
64 Igor Schultz	.05	.15
65 Dave Archibald	.08	.25
66 Joni Lehto	.05	.15
67 Brad Jones	.05	.15
68 Miroslav Berek CO	.05	.15
69 Karel Lang	.05	.15
70 Peter Franke	.05	.15
71 Markus Krawinkel	.05	.15
72 Zdenek Travnicek	.05	.15
73 Martin Gebel	.05	.15
74 Klaus Micheller	.05	.15
75 Earl Spry	.05	.15
76 Frantisek Frosch	.05	.15
77 Petri Liimatainen	.05	.15
78 Andre Grein	.05	.15
79 Ken Petrash	.05	.15
80 James Hanlon	.05	.15
81 Andrej Kovalev	.05	.15
82 Reemt Pyka	.05	.15
83 Chris Lindberg	.08	.25
84 Jay Luknowsky	.05	.15
85 Peter Ihnacak	.08	.25
86 Marek Stebnicki	.05	.15
87 Johnny Walker	.05	.15
88 Danton Cole	.08	.25
89 Michael Hreus	.05	.15
90 Damian Adamus	.05	.15
91 Bill Lochead CO	.08	.25
92 Joakim Persson	.08	.25
93 Ian Wood	.05	.15
94 Pierre Jonsson	.05	.15
95 Juha Lampinen	.05	.15
96 Christian Schmitz	.05	.15
97 Cory Holden	.05	.15
98 Peter Lutter	.05	.15
99 Dieter Bloem	.05	.15
100 Maurizio Catenacci	.05	.15
101 Andrej Fuchs	.05	.15
102 Mark Montanari	.05	.15
103 Boris Fuchs	.05	.15
104 Andreas Salomonsson	.05	.15
105 Robert Reynolds	.05	.15
106 Axel Kammerer	.05	.15
107 Jeffrey Lazaro	.08	.25
108 Olaf Scholz	.05	.15
109 Tony Cimellaro	.05	.15
110 Kenneth Hodge	.08	.25
111 Gregory Burke	.05	.15
112 Tom Coolen CO	.05	.15
113 Marc Pethke	.05	.15
114 Christian Kunast	.05	.15
115 Drahomir Kadlec	.08	.25
116 Florian Kuhn	.08	.25
117 Erich Goldmann	.08	.25
118 Jurgen Simon	.05	.15
119 Jeff Winstanley	.05	.15
120 Stefano Figliuzzi	.05	.15
121 Maurice Mansi	.05	.15
122 Agostino Casale	.05	.15
123 Hans-Jorg Mayer	.05	.15
124 Dino Felicetti	.05	.15
125 Roland Timoschuk	.05	.15
126 Jim Hoffmann	.05	.15
127 John Porco	.05	.15
128 Rolf Hammer	.05	.15
129 Manuel Hess	.05	.15
130 Andy Rymsha	.08	.25
131 Wolfgang Kummer	.05	.15
132 Trevor Burgess	.05	.15
133 Daniel Kunce	.05	.15
134 Timo Sutinen CO	.05	.15
135 Petr Briza	.30	.75
136 Markus Nachtmann	.05	.15
137 Markus Wieland	.05	.15
138 Mike Heidt	.05	.15
139 Peter Gulda	.05	.15
140 Jacek Plachta	.05	.15
141 Georg Franz	.05	.15
142 Stephan Retzer	.05	.15
143 Henry Marcoux	.05	.15
144 Mike Bullard	.30	.75
145 Jose Charbonneau	.08	.25
146 Wally Schreiber	.08	.25
147 Jorg Handrick	.05	.15
148 Helmut Steiger	.05	.15
149 Marco Sturm	4.00	10.00
150 Jonas Johnsson	.05	.15
151 Vesa Salo	.05	.15
152 Gino Cavallini	.08	.25
153 Lars Hurtig	.05	.15
154 Olli Kaski	.05	.15
155 007 Charly	.05	.15
156 Lance Nethery CO	.05	.15
157 Ross Yates ACO	.05	.15
158 Joachim Appel	.05	.15
159 Mike Rosati	.20	.50
160 Harold Kreis	.05	.15
161 Paul Stanton	.08	.25
162 Christian Lukes	.05	.15
163 Robert Nardella	.05	.15
164 Alexander Erdmann	.05	.15
165 Stephane J.G. Richer	.08	.25
166 Martin Ulrich	.05	.15
167 Mike Pellegrims	.05	.15
168 Mario Gehrig	.05	.15
169 Pavel Gross	.05	.15
170 Dave Tomlinson	.08	.25
171 Daniel Korber	.05	.15
172 Francois Guay	.05	.15
173 Jochen Hecht	1.25	3.00
174 Florian Keller	.20	.50
175 Till Feser	.05	.15
176 Alexander Serikow	.20	.50
177 Christian Pouget	.05	.15
178 Dieter Kalt	.05	.15
179 Paul Beraldo	.05	.15
180 Steven Thornton	.05	.15
181 Robert Cimetta	.20	.50
182 Gary Clark CO	.05	.15
183 Bjorn Leonhardt	.05	.15
184 Claus Dalpiaz	.08	.25
185 Jesper Duus	.05	.15
186 Manuel Hiemer	.05	.15
187 Markus Pottinger	.05	.15
188 Chris Bartolone	.05	.15
189 Christian Gegenfurther	.05	.15
190 Heinrich Schiffl	.05	.15
191 Per Lundell	.05	.15
192 Joel Savage	.08	.25
193 Josef Muller	.05	.15
194 Jari Torkki	.05	.15
195 James Hiller	.05	.15
196 Doug Derraugh	.05	.15
197 Pekka Tirkkonen	.05	.15
198 Martin Reichel	.05	.15
199 Raimond Hilger	.08	.25
200 Michael Schneidawind	.05	.15
201 Scott Beattie	.05	.15
202 Paris Proft	.05	.15
203 Kevin Gaudet CO	.05	.15
204 Wayne Cowley	.05	.15
205 Marco Herbst	.05	.15
206 Andreas Schubert	.05	.15
207 Stephan Sinner	.05	.15
208 Heinrich Synowietz	.05	.15
209 Paul Synowietz	.05	.15
210 Dimitri Frolov	.05	.15
211 Andrej Saposhnikov	.05	.15
212 Jedrzej Kasperczyk	.05	.15
213 Joseph West	.05	.15
214 Fabian Ahrens	.05	.15
215 Maurice Lemay	.05	.15
216 Mark Kosturik	.05	.15
217 Mark Jooris	.05	.15
218 Len Soccio	.05	.15
219 Mark Mahon	.05	.15
220 Frank LaScala	.05	.15
221 Jari Pasanen	.05	.15
222 Ralph Vos	.05	.15
223 Anthony Cirelli	.05	.15
224 Emilio Iovio	.05	.15
225 Gerhard Brunner CO	.05	.15
226 Pavel Cagas	.05	.15
227 Jonas Eriksson	.05	.15
228 Alexander Engel	.05	.15
229 Gregory Johnston	.08	.25
230 Alexander Wedl	.05	.15
231 Jouni Vento	.05	.15
232 Roger Ohman	.05	.15
233 David Morrison	.05	.15
234 Bruce Eakin	.05	.15
235 Michael Millar	.05	.15
236 Roger Hansson	.02	.10
237 Peter Kwasigroch	.05	.15
238 Branjo Heisig	.05	.15
239 Jukka Seppo	.05	.15
240 Greg Evtushevski	.05	.15
241 Falk Ozellis	.05	.15
242 Daniel Larin	.05	.15
243 Tino Boos	.05	.15
244 Toni Krinner	.05	.15
245 Milan Mokros	.05	.15
246 Peter Ustorf CO	.05	.15
247 Klaus Merk	.08	.25
248 David Berge	.05	.15
249 Georg Holzmann	.05	.15
250 Tom O'Regan	.05	.15
251 Jochen Molling	.05	.15
252 Joseph Lehner	.05	.15
253 Marco Rentzsch	.05	.15
254 Pekka Laksola	.05	.15
255 Petri Matikainen	.05	.15
256 Tony Tanti	.30	.75
257 Gaetan Malo	.05	.15
258 Thomas Schinko	.05	.15
259 Vitali Karamnov	.05	.15
260 Gunther Oswald	.05	.15
261 Christian Brittig	.05	.15
262 Jurgen Rumrich	.05	.15
263 John Chabot	.20	.50
264 Andreas Dimbat	.05	.15
265 Mark Teevens	.05	.15
266 Veli-Pekka Kautonen	.05	.15
267 Jarno-Sakari Peltonen	.05	.15
268 Hardy Nilsson CO	.05	.15
269 Martin Karlsson ACO	.05	.15
270 Ake Lilljebjorn	.05	.15
271 Kai Fischer	.08	.25
272 Brad Bergen	.05	.15
273 Andreas Niederberger	.05	.15
274 Sergej Sorokin	.05	.15
275 Robert Sterflinger	.05	.15
276 Peter Andersson	.05	.15
277 Viktor Gordiouk	.08	.25
278 Gordon Sherven	.08	.25
279 Benoit Doucet	.20	.50
280 Bernd Kuhnhauser	.08	.25
281 Dieter Hegen	.05	.15
282 Andreas Brockmann	.05	.15
283 Ernst Kopf	.05	.15
284 Alexej Kudashov	.05	.15
285 Bernd Truntschka	.08	.25
286 Mikko Makela	.05	.15
287 Nikolaus Mondt	.05	.15
288 Boris Lingemann	.05	.15
289 Thomas Brandl	.08	.25
290 Leo Stefan	.08	.25
291 Bob Burns CO	.05	.15
292 Carsten Solbach	.05	.15
293 Matthias Hoppe	.05	.15
294 Sascha Goc	.20	.50
295 Gordon Hynes	.20	.50
296 Thomas Gaus	.05	.15
297 Brian Tutt	.05	.15
298 Richard Trojan	.05	.15
299 Daniel Nowak	.05	.15
300 Andreas Renz	.05	.15
301 Sana Hassan	.05	.15
302 Alan Young	.05	.15
303 Mike Bader	.05	.15
304 Robert Brezina	.05	.15
305 Wayne Hynes	.05	.15
306 Mark Bassen	.05	.15
307 Andrew Clark	.05	.15
308 Grant Martin	.05	.15
309 Michael Lay	.05	.15
310 Jackson Penney	.05	.15
311 Rich Chernomaz	.15	.40
312 Mark MacKay	.20	.50
313 Vladimir Fedosov	.05	.15
314 Emanuel Viveiros	.08	.25
315 Jan Eysselt CO	.05	.15
316 Michel Valliere	.05	.15
317 Stefan Lahn	.05	.15
318 Christian Gerum	.05	.15
319 Heiko Smazal	.05	.15
320 Christian Curth	.05	.15
321 Miroslav Maly	.05	.15
322 Torsten Kienass	.05	.15
323 Thomas Sterflinger	.05	.15
324 Lars Bruggemann	.05	.15
325 Paul Geddes	.05	.15
326 Rolan Ramoser	.05	.15
327 Martin Jiranek	.05	.15
328 Stefan Steinbock	.05	.15
329 Martin Ekrt	.05	.15
330 Jurgen Lechl	.05	.15
331 Dion Del Monte	.05	.15
332 Markus Welz	.05	.15
333 Henrik Holscher	.05	.15
334 Otto Sykora	.05	.15
335 Milos Vanik	.05	.15
336 Robert Murdoch CO	.05	.15
337 Bernd Haake ACO	.05	.15
338 Joseph Heiss	.08	.25
339 Olaf Grundmann	.05	.15
340 Alexander Genze	.05	.15
341 Jorg Mayr	.05	.15
342 Mirco Ludemann	.05	.15
343 Jayson Meyer	.05	.15
344 Karsten Mende	.05	.15
345 Herbert Hohenberger	.08	.25
346 Joe Cirella	.08	.25
347 Petter Nilsson	.05	.15
348 Jim Montgomery	.20	.50
349 Stefan Mann	.05	.15
350 Luciano Borsato	.08	.25
351 Dwayne Norris	.08	.25
352 Bruno Zarrillo	.05	.15
353 Peter Draisaitl	.08	.25
354 Joe Busillo	.05	.15
355 Andreas Lupzig	.05	.15
356 Rainer Zerwesz	.05	.15
357 Thomas Forslund	.08	.25
358 Tobias Abstreiter	.05	.15
359 Patrick Carnback	.08	.25
360 Franz Demmel	.05	.15

1998-99 German DEL

This set features members of Germany's top hockey circuit. The card stock is very thin, and the words Schirner Edition appear on the front. The backs feature sponsor information (including Eishockey News), stats, and a reproduced signature.

COMPLETE SET (344)	20.00	50.00
1 Burke Murphy	.07	.20
2 Marc Seliger	.20	.50
3 Jason Clark	.07	.20
4 Mike McNeill	.07	.20
5 Norm Matherson	.07	.20
6 Jeff Sebastien	.07	.20
7 Phil Huber	.07	.20
8 Todd Wtzel	.07	.20
9 Jesper Morin	.07	.20
10 Marc Pethke	.07	.20
11 Jacek Plachta	.07	.20
12 Marcus Adolfson	.07	.20
13 Christian Schmitz	.07	.20
14 Bob Marshall	.07	.20
15 Peter Lutter	.07	.20
16 Stefan Mayer	.07	.20
17 Daniel Korber	.07	.20
18 Carsten Gosdeck	.07	.20
19 Jiri Kochta	.07	.20
20 Petri Liimatainen	.07	.20
21 Thomas Brandl	.07	.20
22 Andrej Kovalev	.08	.25
23 Johnny Walker	.07	.20
24 Neil Eisenhut	.20	.50
25 Karel Lang	.07	.20
26 Marek Stebnicki	.07	.20
27 Chris Bartolone	.07	.20
28 John Van Kessel	.07	.20
29 Lars Bruggemann	.07	.20
30 Jason Meyer	.07	.20
31 Reemt Pyka	.07	.20
32 Mark Pederson	.07	.20
33 Veli-Pekka Kautonen	.07	.20
34 Tommie Hartogs	.07	.20
35 Frantisek Frosch	.07	.20
36 Leo van den Thillart	.07	.20
37 Vitali Karamnov	.08	.25
38 Stephane Barin	.07	.20
39 Roger Nordstrom	.07	.20
40 Robert Ouellet	.07	.20
41 Doug Mason	.07	.20
42 Francois Guay	.07	.20
43 Greg Johnston	.20	.50
44 Greg Evtushevski	.07	.20
45 Shane Peacock	.07	.20
46 Chris Rogles	.30	.75
47 Gunter Oswald	.07	.20
48 Jukka Seppo	.07	.20
49 Jurgen Rumrich	.07	.20
50 Roger Hansson	.07	.20
51 Stephane Robitaille	.07	.20
52 Orjan Lindmark	.07	.20
53 Jeff MacLeod	.07	.20
54 Alexander Wedl	.07	.20
55 Jochen Molling	.07	.20
56 Paul Cohen	.07	.20
57 Daniel Kreutzer	.07	.20
58 Nikolaus Mondt	.07	.20
59 John Lilley	.20	.50
60 Roland Ramoser	.07	.20
61 Thomas Dolak	.07	.20
62 Tino Boos	.07	.20
63 Tobias Abstreiter	.07	.20
64 Hans Zach	.07	.20
65 Petr Briza	.30	.75
66 Wally Schreiber	.20	.50
67 Chris Luongo	.20	.50
68 Dean Evason	.20	.50
69 David Bruce	.20	.50
70 Peter Douris	.20	.50
71 Jason Herter	.20	.50
72 Jorg Hendrick	.07	.20
73 Rob Murphy	.20	.50
74 Mike Casselmann	.07	.20
75 Steve Junker	.07	.20
76 Zbynek Kukacka	.07	.20
77 Mark Krys	.07	.20
78 Markus Wieland	.07	.20
79 Evan Marble	.07	.20
80 Jari Korpisalo	.07	.20
81 Peter Gulda	.07	.20
82 Bob Joyce	.20	.50
83 Johan Rosen	.07	.20
84 Christian Kunast	.07	.20
85 Olli Kaski	.07	.20
86 Chris Valentine	.30	.75
87 Corey Millen	.20	.50
88 Tomas Forslund	.15	.40
89 Bruno Zarrillo	.20	.50
90 Igor Alexandrov	.07	.20
91 Bob Halkidis	.20	.50
92 Petri Varis	.20	.50
93 Joseph Heiss	.20	.50
94 Greg Brown	.20	.50
95 Dwayne Norris	.20	.50
96 Mirko Ludemann	.07	.20
97 John Miner	.07	.20
98 Boris Rousson	.30	.75
99 Craig Woodcroft	.07	.20
100 Jorg Mayr	.07	.20
101 Steve Wilson	.07	.20
102 Rainer Zerwesz	.07	.20
103 Brian McReynolds	.07	.20
104 Andreas Lupzig	.07	.20
105 Giuseppe Busillo	.07	.20
106 Jeff Ricciardi	.07	.20
107 Mike Hartman	.20	.50
108 Timo Lahtinen	.07	.20
109 Stephane Morin	.20	.50
110 Paul Broten	.20	.50
111 Robert Guillet	.07	.20
112 Clayton Beddoes	.15	.40
113 Robert Cimetta	.20	.50
114 Dave MacIntyre	.07	.20
115 Johan Norgren	.07	.20
116 Todd Nelson	.07	.20
117 Guy Phillips	.07	.20
118 Craig Martin	.20	.50
119 Parris Duffus	.30	.75
120 Christian Brittig	.07	.20
121 Thomas Schinko	.07	.20
122 Mario Gehrig	.07	.20
123 Fredrik Ytfeldt	.07	.20
124 Lawrence Rucchin	.07	.20
125 Heinz Ehlers	.07	.20
126 Heinrich Schiffl	.07	.20
127 Sylvain Couturier	.08	.25
128 Hakan Galiamoutsas	.07	.20
129 David Berge	.07	.20
130 Marc Savard	.07	.20
131 Dale McCourt	.20	.50
132 Jukka Tammi	.20	.50
133 Chris Snell	.20	.50
134 John Chabot	.20	.50
135 Len Barrie	.20	.50
136 Lija Vorobjev	.07	.20
137 Steve Palmer	.07	.20
138 Fabrice L'Henry	.07	.20
139 Rob Doyle	.07	.20
140 Victor Gervais	.07	.20
141 Jose Charbonneau	.08	.25
142 Thorsten Apel	.07	.20
143 Michael Bresagk	.07	.20
144 Rick Hayward	.08	.25
145 Phil von Steffenelli	.07	.20
146 Martin Williams	.07	.20
147 Toni Porkka	.07	.20
148 Jean-Marc Richard	.07	.20
149 Douglas Kirton	.07	.20
150 Joel Savage	.20	.50
151 Ralf Hantschke	.07	.20
152 Ken Quinney	.15	.40
153 Marcus Bleicher	.07	.20
154 Bob Manno	.08	.25
155 Rob Cowie	.07	.20
156 Mike Bullard	.30	.75
157 Maren Valenti	.07	.20
158 Sven Felski	.07	.20
159 Andrew McKim	.20	.50
160 Derek Mayer	.08	.25
161 Niklas Hede	.07	.20
162 Thomas Steen	.20	.50
163 Mario Brunetta	.20	.50
164 Marc Fortier	.20	.50
165 Thomas Rhodin	.07	.20
166 Nico Pyka	.07	.20
167 Chris Govedaris	.08	.25
168 Lorenz Funk	.07	.20
169 Florian Funk	.07	.20
170 Yvon Corriveau	.20	.50
171 Mikael Wahlberg	.07	.20
172 Darren Durdle	.07	.20
173 Pelle Svensson	.07	.20
174 Greg Andrusak	.08	.25
175 Leif Carlsson	.07	.20
176 Andreas Brockmann	.07	.20
177 Robert Leask	.07	.20

Card	Low	High
178 Mario Chitaroni	.07	.20
179 Chad Biafore	.07	.20
180 Peter John Lee	.07	.20
181 Len Soccio	.20	.50
182 Jason Lafreniere	.20	.50
183 Joe West	.07	.20
184 Brent Tully	.20	.50
185 Mark Kosturik	.07	.20
186 David Haas	.07	.20
187 Darcy Martini	.07	.20
188 Gary Leeman	.20	.50
189 Lee Davidson	.07	.20
190 Scott Metcalfe	.20	.50
191 Tom Pederson	.20	.50
192 Francois Gravel	.07	.20
193 Bjorn Leonhardt	.07	.20
194 Mike Johnson	.07	.20
195 Claudio Scremin	.07	.20
196 Mike Ware	.07	.20
197 Jurgen Trattner	.07	.20
198 Dan Currie	.20	.50
199 Patrick Curcio	.20	.50
200 Patrick Senger	.07	.20
201 Frank Di Muzio	.07	.20
202 Kevin Gaudet	.07	.20
203 Mark MacKay	.20	.50
204 Claude Vilgrain	.20	.50
205 Rich Chernomaz	.07	.20
206 Daniel Laperriere	.20	.50
207 Wayne Hynes	.07	.20
208 Todd Harkins	.07	.20
209 Scott McCrory	.20	.50
210 Andrew Rymsha	.15	.40
211 Daniel Nowak	.07	.20
212 Andy Schneider	.15	.40
213 David Marcinshyn	.07	.20
214 Marc Laniel	.07	.20
215 Guy Lehoux	.07	.20
216 Matthias Vater	.07	.20
217 Jens Stramkowski	.07	.20
218 Alexander Dexheimer	.07	.20
219 Mark Bassen	.07	.20
220 Steffen Karg	.07	.20
221 Randy Perry	.07	.20
222 Robert Schistad	.20	.50
223 Andreas Renz	.07	.20
224 Matthias Hoppe	.07	.20
225 Ron Ivany	.07	.20
226 Phillippe Bozon	.40	1.00
227 Dave Tomlinson	.20	.50
228 Stephane Richer	.07	.20
229 Paul Stanton	.20	.50
230 Pavel Gross	.07	.20
231 Christian Pouget	.07	.20
232 Jackson Penney	.07	.20
233 Gordon Hynes	.20	.50
234 Jason Young	.07	.20
235 Alexander Serikow	.20	.50
236 Mike Stevens	.07	.20
237 Mike Pellegrims	.07	.20
238 Reid Simonton	.07	.20
239 Christian Lukes	.07	.20
240 Ron Pasco	.07	.20
241 Mike Hudson	.30	.75
242 Denis Perez	.07	.20
243 Sven Rampf	.07	.20
244 Danny Lorenz	.20	.50
245 Brian Tutt	.07	.20
246 Jan Alston	.07	.20
247 Lance Nethery	.07	.20
248 Sergio Momesso	.20	.50
249 Andrej Mezin	.40	1.00
250 Jarno Peltonen	.07	.20
251 Martin Reichel	.07	.20
252 Sergej Stas	.07	.20
253 Martin Jiranek	.07	.20
254 Jason Miller	.07	.20
255 Jozef Cierny	.07	.20
256 Liam Garvey	.07	.20
257 Kevin Grant	.07	.20
258 Chris Strausse	.07	.20
259 Heiko Smazal	.07	.20
260 Vadim Shakhraichuk	.07	.20
261 Leszek Laszkiewicz	.07	.20
262 Sven Valenti	.07	.20
263 Michel Valliere	.07	.20
264 Per Lundell	.07	.20
265 Dimitri Dudik	.07	.20
266 Daniel Kunce	.07	.20
267 Ivan Droppa	.07	.20
268 Peter Ihnacak	.20	.50
269 Harald Birk	.07	.20
270 Bradley Bergen	.07	.20
271 Pierre Rioux	.07	.20
272 Jim Camazzola	.07	.20
273 Klaus Merk	.20	.50
274 Rick Girard	.07	.20
275 Andre Faust	.07	.20
276 Hakan Ahlund	.07	.20
277 Kyosti Karjalainen	.20	.50
278 Leonardo Conti	.07	.20
279 Leo Gudas	.07	.20
280 Mathias Ahxner	.07	.20
281 Francois Groleau	.07	.20
282 Michael Bakos	.07	.20
283 Alan Reader	.07	.20
284 Nordin Harfaoui	.07	.20
285 Dale Craigwell	.20	.50
286 Dimitri Gromling	.07	.20
287 Duanne Moeser	.07	.20
288 Tommy Jakobsen	.07	.20
289 Patrik Degerstedt	.07	.20
290 Greg Bullock	.07	.20
291 Gunnar Leidborg	.07	.20
292 Dieter Hegen	.07	.20
293 Derek Cormier	.07	.20
294 Jim Hiller	.07	.20
295 Gordon Sherven	.08	.25
296 Eric Murano	.07	.20
297 Robert Muller	.07	.20
298 Klaus Kathan	.07	.20
299 Raimond Hilger	.07	.20
300 Christian Due-Boje	.07	.20
301 Jesper Duus	.07	.20
302 Michael Pohl	.07	.20
303 Bernd Kuhnhauser	.15	.40
304 Frank Hohenadl	.07	.20
305 Alexander Jansen	.07	.20
306 Teemu Sillanpaa	.07	.20
307 Hans Abranamsson	.07	.20
308 Claus Dalpiaz	.08	.25
309 Kari Haakana	.07	.20
310 Christian Gegenfurtner	.07	.20
311 Peter Ottosson	.07	.20
312 Wolfgang Kummer	.07	.20
313 Beppi Eckmaier	.07	.20
314 Gerhard Brunner	.07	.20
315 Mirko Ludemann	.08	.25
316 Sven Felski	.07	.20
317 Reemt Pyka	.07	.20
318 Jorg Mayr	.07	.20
319 Michael Bresagk	.07	.20
320 Andraes Lupzig	.07	.20
321 Jurgen Rumrich	.07	.20
322 Josef Lehner	.07	.20
323 Peter Draisaitl	.07	.20
324 Leo Stefan	.07	.20
325 Joseph Heiss	.08	.25
326 Klaus Kathan	.07	.20
327 Klaus Merk	.08	.25
328 Peter Gulda	.07	.20
329 Daniel Nowak	.07	.20
330 Bradley Bergen	.07	.20
331 Thomas Dolak	.07	.20
332 Martin Reichel	.07	.20
333 Alexander Serikow	.20	.50
334 Harold Birk	.07	.20
335 Michael Bakos	.07	.20
336 Mario Gehrig	.07	.20
337 Mark Mackay	.20	.50
338 Dieter Hegen	.15	.40
339 Hans Zach	.07	.20
340 Erich Kuhnackl	.15	.40
341 Ernst Hofner	.07	.20
NNO Gerhard Leinauer CL	.07	.20
NNO Rick Amann CL	.08	.25
NNO Robert Muller CL	.07	.20

1999-00 German DEL

This 434-card set features the players of Germany's elite hockey league. The regulation-sized cards feature a color photo on the front, along with two photos and stats on the back. The set was sponsored by Eishockey News and Skoda and may have been produced by a company named Eberswalder.

Card	Low	High
COMPLETE SET (434)	24.00	60.00
1 Mannheim	.05	.15
2 Gordon Hynes	.20	.50
3 Paul Stanton	.20	.50
4 Christian Lukes	.05	.15
5 Clayton Beddoes	.20	.50
6 Shawn McCosh	.05	.15
7 Dave Tomlinson	.20	.50
8 Patrice Lefebvre	.20	.50
9 Steve Junker	.20	.50
10 Ralph Intranuovo	.20	.50
11 Joel Savage	.20	.50
12 Stephane J.G. Richer	.20	.50
13 Rainer Zerwesz	.05	.15
14 Yves Racine	.20	.50
15 Mike Stevens	.20	.50
16 Markus Wieland	.05	.15
17 Bjorn Leonhardt	.05	.15
18 Mike Rosati	.20	.50
19 Philip Schumacher	.05	.15
20 Jan Alston	.05	.15
21 Kevin Grant	.05	.15
22 Chris Straube	.05	.15
23 Dennis Seidenberg	.05	.15
24 Chris Valentine TR	.20	.50
25 Nürnberg	.05	.15
26 Stefan Mann	.05	.15
27 Vadim Shakhraichuk	.05	.15
28 Roland Ramoser	.05	.15
29 Martin Jiranek	.05	.15
30 Hannes Körber	.05	.15
31 Jarno Peltonen	.05	.15
32 Dimitri Dudik	.05	.15
33 Viktors Ignatjevs	.05	.15
34 Alexander Cherbayev	.08	.25
35 Martin Reichel	.05	.15
36 Russ Romaniuk	.08	.25
37 Jason Miller	.05	.15
38 Sergej Bautin	.05	.15
39 Jozef Cierny	.05	.15
40 Marc Seliger	.40	1.00
41 Daniel Kunce	.05	.15
42 Pasi Sormunen	.05	.15
43 Christian Schönmoser	.05	.15
44 Stefan Mayer	.05	.15
45 Alain Cote	.08	.25
46 Liam Garvey	.05	.15
47 John Craighead	.05	.15
48 Petr Franek	.05	.15
49 Peter Ihnacak TR	.20	.50
50 Eisbaren	.05	.15
51 Nico Pyka	.05	.15
52 Robert Leask	.20	.50
53 Alexander Godynyuk	.08	.25
54 Lorenz Funk	.05	.15
55 Sven Felski	.05	.15
56 Giuseppe Busillo	.05	.15
57 Yvon Corriveau	.20	.50
58 Mikael Wahlberg	.05	.15
59 Udo Dohler	.05	.15
60 Sandy Smith	.20	.50
61 Jaroslav Kames	.05	.15
62 Rob Murphy	.08	.25
63 Marc Fortier	.20	.50
64 Mario Chitaroni	.05	.15
65 Leif Carlsson	.05	.15
66 Derek Mayer	.20	.50
67 Sebastian Elwing	.05	.15
68 Thomas Schinko	.05	.15
69 Rob Cowie	.05	.15
70 Thomas Rhodin	.05	.15
71 Peter Hammarstrom	.05	.15
72 Chris Govedaris	.20	.50
73 Mike Bullard	.20	.50
74 Peter John Lee TR	.05	.15
75 Frankfurt	.05	.15
76 Michael Bresagk	.05	.15
77 Joachim Appel	.05	.15
78 Rick Hayward	.20	.50
79 Robin Doyle	.05	.15
80 Christian Langer	.05	.15
81 Bob Bassen	.20	.50
82 John Chabot	.20	.50
83 Devin Edgerton	.20	.50
84 Toni Porkka	.05	.15
85 Jean-Marc Richard	.05	.15
86 Jose Charbonneau	.08	.25
87 Douglas Kirton	.05	.15
88 Andrej Vasilyev	.05	.15
89 Ralf Hantschke	.05	.15
90 Steve Palmer	.05	.15
91 Jason Ruff	.20	.50
92 Bastian Niedermeier	.05	.15
93 Chris Hynes	.05	.15
94 Victor Gervais	.05	.15
95 Ken Quinney	.20	.50
96 Mark Bassen	.05	.15
97 Chris Snell	.20	.50
98 Eldon Reddick	.20	.50
99 Peter Obresa TR	.05	.15
100 Koln	.05	.15
101 Joseph Heiss	.20	.50
102 Steve Wilson	.05	.15
103 Mario Doyon	.20	.50
104 Jorg Mayr	.05	.15
105 Marty Murray	.20	.50
106 Mirko Ludemann	.05	.15
107 Dwayne Norris	.20	.50
108 Christoph Paepke	.05	.15
109 Bruno Zarrillo	.20	.50
110 Dan Lambert	.20	.50
111 Anders Huusko	.05	.15
112 George Zajankala	.05	.15
113 Andreas Lupzig	.05	.15
114 Jean-Yves Roy	.20	.50
115 Tomas Forslund	.08	.25
116 Jason Young	.08	.25
117 Todd Hlushko	.20	.50
118 Andrew Verner	.20	.50
119 Corey Millen	.20	.50
120 Greg Brown	.05	.15
121 John Miner	.08	.25
122 Sergio Momesso	.20	.50
123 Lance Nethery TR	.05	.15
124 Krefeld	.05	.15
125 Karel Lang	.05	.15
126 Andy Roach	.05	.15
127 Tomas Brandl	.05	.15
128 Neil Eisenhut	.20	.50
129 Ilja Vorobjev	.05	.15
130 Andrey Kovalev	.05	.15
131 Mark Pederson	.08	.25
132 Shayne Wright	.05	.15
133 Reemt Pyka	.05	.15
134 Andrew Rymsha	.05	.15
135 Lars Bruggemann	.05	.15
136 Tommie Hartogs	.05	.15
137 Marek Stebnicki	.05	.15
138 Johnny Walker	.05	.15
139 Chris Bartolone	.05	.15
140 Stephane Barin	.05	.15
141 Mickey Elick	.05	.15
142 Phil von Stefenelli	.08	.25
143 Jean-Francois Jomphe	.20	.50
144 Robert Ouellet	.05	.15
145 Roger Nordstrom	.05	.15
146 Martin Lindman	.05	.15
147 Doug Mason TR	.05	.15
148 Augsburg	.05	.15
149 Vladislav Boulin	.05	.15
150 Leo Gudas	.05	.15
151 Duane Moeser	.05	.15
152 Sergej Vostrikov	.05	.15
153 Igor Maslennikov	.05	.15
154 Kyosti Karjalainen	.05	.15
155 Kurtis Miller	.05	.15
156 Bradley Borgen	.05	.15
157 Scott Allison	.05	.15
158 Hakan Ahlund	.05	.15
159 Peter Larsson	.05	.15
160 Brian Loney	.05	.15
161 Michael Bakos	.05	.15
162 Sven Rampf	.05	.15
163 Jim Camazzola	.05	.15
164 Andre Faust	.05	.15
165 Harald Birk	.05	.15
166 Tommy Jakobsen	.05	.15
167 Sergej Klimovich	.05	.15
168 Klaus Merk	.20	.50
169 Bob Manno TR	.08	.25
170 Kassel	.05	.15
171 Jochen Molling	.05	.15
172 David Cooper	.20	.50
173 Thomas Dolak	.05	.15
174 Stephane Robitaille	.05	.15
175 Jeff MacLeod	.05	.15
176 Roger Hansson	.05	.15
177 Francois Guay	.05	.15
178 Nikolaus Mondt	.05	.15
179 Andreas Loth	.05	.15
180 Ron Pasco	.05	.15
181 Jurgen Rumrich	.05	.15
182 Greg Evtushevski	.05	.15
183 Daniel Kreutzer	.05	.15
184 Brent Tully	.05	.15
185 Ivan Droppa	.05	.15
186 Tobias Abstreiter	.05	.15
187 Sylvain Turgeon	.20	.50
188 Chris Rogles	.20	.50
189 Leonardo Conti	.05	.15
190 Tino Boos	.05	.15
191 Benjamin Hinterstocker	.05	.15
192 Craig Woodcroft	.20	.50
193 Orjan Lindmark	.05	.15
194 Hans Zach TR	.05	.15
195 Schwenningen	.05	.15
196 Kevin Wortman	.05	.15
197 Marc Laniel	.20	.50
198 Daniel Laperriere	.20	.50
199 Marcel Goc	1.25	3.00
200 Guy Lehoux	.05	.15
201 Steffen Oder	.05	.15
202 Jens Stramkowski	.05	.15
203 Mark Kolesar	.15	.40
204 Scott McCrory	.05	.15
205 John Lilley	.20	.50
206 Patrik Augusta	.05	.15
207 Randy Perry	.05	.15
208 Daniel Nowak	.05	.15
209 Todd Harkins	.05	.15
210 Robert Schistad	.05	.15
211 Andreas Renz	.05	.15
212 Stephane Beauregard	.20	.50
213 Rick Girard	.05	.15
214 Iain Fraser	.20	.50
215 Andy Schneider	.20	.50
216 Mark Mackay	.20	.50
217 Rich Chernomaz TR	.20	.50
218 Hannover	.05	.15
219 Lars Jansson	.05	.15
220 Tom Pederson	.20	.50
221 Juri Gunko	.05	.15
222 Mattias Loof	.05	.15
223 Joseph West	.05	.15
224 Egor Bashkatov	.08	.25
225 Grigori Panteleyev	.20	.50
226 Mark Kosturik	.05	.15
227 Len Soccio	.05	.15
228 Dominic Lavoie	.20	.50
229 Peter Willmann	.05	.15
230 Wally Schreiber	.20	.50
231 Scott Metcalfe	.20	.50
232 David Haas	.05	.15
233 Ildar Mukhometov	.20	.50
234 Igor Chibirev	.08	.25
235 Michael Thurner	.05	.15
236 Jan Munster	.05	.15
237 Jakob Karlsson	.05	.15
238 David Sulkovsky	.05	.15
239 Brian Tutt	.05	.15
240 Igor Alexandrov	.05	.15
241 Kevin Gaudet TR	.05	.15
242 Rosenheim	.05	.15
243 Hakan Algotsson	.20	.50
244 Trevor Burgess	.05	.15
245 Christian Due-Boje	.05	.15
246 Teemu Sillanpaa	.05	.15
247 Curtis Fry	.05	.15
248 Gordon Sherven	.20	.50
249 Frank Hohenadl	.05	.15
250 Bernd Kuhnhauser	.05	.15
251 Michael Pohl	.05	.15
252 Derek Cormier	.05	.15
253 Jean-Francois Quintin	.20	.50
254 Dieter Hegen	.05	.15
255 Peter Ottosson	.05	.15
256 Raimond Hilger	.08	.25
257 Niklas Brannstrom	.05	.15
258 Wolfgang Kummer	.05	.15
259 Kari Haakana	.05	.15
260 Paul Weismann	.05	.15
261 Klaus Kathan	.05	.15
262 Sami Nuutinen	.05	.15
263 Patrik Hucko	.05	.15
264 Robert Muller	.05	.15
265 Gerhard Brunner TR	.05	.15
266 Capitals	.05	.15
267 Andrej Mezin	.40	1.00
268 Fredrik Stillman	.20	.50
269 Fredrik Ytfeldt	.05	.15
270 Markus Pottinger	.05	.15
271 Niklas Hede	.05	.15
272 Alexander Kuzminski	.05	.15
273 Thomas Sjogren	.05	.15
274 Dennis Meyer	.05	.15
275 Robert Cimetta	.20	.50
276 Jim Hiller	.05	.15
277 Doug Derraugh	.05	.15
278 Patrick Senger	.05	.15
279 Pavel Gross	.05	.15
280 Robert Guillet	.05	.15
281 Sylvain Couturier	.05	.15
282 Heinrich Schiffl	.05	.15
283 Heinz Ehlers	.05	.15
284 Larry Rucchin	.05	.15
285 Gregory Johnston	.20	.50
286 David Berge	.05	.15
287 Johan Norgren	.05	.15
288 Martin Ulrich	.05	.15
289 Benjamin Hecker	.05	.15
290 Mike Pellegrims	.05	.15
291 Michael Komma TR	.05	.15
292 Oberhausen	.05	.15
293 Peter Gulda	.05	.15
294 Jergus Baca	.05	.15
295 Bob Marshall	.05	.15
296 Mike Sullivan	.20	.50
297 Jacek Plachta	.05	.15
298 Andrej Fuchs	.05	.15
299 Mike McNeill	.20	.50
300 Aleksandrs Kerch	.05	.15
301 Robert Hock	.05	.15
302 Albert Malgin	.05	.15
303 Kai Fischer	.20	.50
304 Burke Murphy	.05	.15
305 Jeff Sebastian	.05	.15
306 Sergej Stas	.05	.15
307 Sebastian Klenner	.05	.15
308 Boris Fuchs	.05	.15
309 Ivo Jan	.05	.15
310 Francois Gravel	.05	.15
311 Alexander Makritzky	.05	.15
312 Viktor Karatchun	.05	.15
313 Gunnar Leidborg TR	.05	.15
314 Munchen	.05	.15
315 Boris Rousson	.20	.50
316 Hans Lodin	.05	.15
317 Chris Luongo	.20	.50
318 Mike Casselman	.05	.15
319 Heiko Smazal	.05	.15
320 Peter Abstreiter	.05	.15
321 Simon Wheeldon	.20	.50
322 Phil Huber	.05	.15
323 Peter Douris	.20	.50
324 Jari Korpisalo	.05	.15
325 Kent Fearns	.05	.15
326 Markus Jocher	.05	.15
327 Pelle Svensson	.05	.15
328 Sven Wiele	.05	.15
329 Wayne Hynes	.05	.15
330 Bill McDougall	.20	.50
331 Alexander Serikow	.20	.50
332 Robert Joyce	.20	.50
333 Jorg Handrick	.05	.15
334 Jason Herter	.08	.25
335 Johan Rosen	.05	.15
336 Mike Kennedy	.20	.50
337 Christian Kunast	.05	.15
338 Shane Peacock	.05	.15
339 Sean Simpson TR	.05	.15
340 Essen	.05	.15
341 Oldrich Svoboda	.05	.15
342 Bodo Mueller-Boenigk	.05	.15
343 Vlastimil Kroupa	.05	.15
344 Zdenek Touzimsky	.05	.15
345 Pavel Augusta	.05	.15
346 Christian Kohmann	.05	.15
347 Martin Sychra	.05	.15
348 Torsten Kienass	.08	.25
349 Peter Draisaitl	.05	.15
350 Marian Kacir	.05	.15
351 Terry Campbell	.05	.15
352 Roland Verwey	.05	.15
353 Radek Toth	.05	.15
354 Josef Zajic	.05	.15
355 Jochen Vollmer	.05	.15
356 Jiri Sejba	.05	.15
357 Jukka Seppo	.05	.15
358 Marc Savard	.20	.50
359 Enrico Ciccone	.08	.25
360 Michael Dvorak	.05	.15
361 Tomas Nemcicky	.05	.15
362 Andrej Nederost	.40	1.00
363 Tomas Srsen	.05	.15
364 Bedrich Scerban	.05	.15
365 Jan Benda TR	.15	.40
366 3ffi National	.05	.15
367 Robert Muller	.05	.15
368 Torsten Kienass	.08	.25
369 Markus Pottinger	.05	.15
370 Lorenz Funk	.05	.15
371 Nico Pyka	.05	.15
372 Sven Felski	.05	.15
373 Jochen Molling	.05	.15
374 Christian Langer	.05	.15
375 Nikolaus Mondt	.05	.15
376 Bernd Kuhnhauser	.05	.15
377 Jurgen Rumrich	.05	.15
378 Lars Bruggemann	.05	.15
379 Alexander Serikow	.20	.50
380 Klaus Kathan	.05	.15
381 Terry Campbell	.05	.15
382 Tino Boos	.05	.15
383 Michael Bresagk	.05	.15
384 Christian Lukes	.05	.15
385 Heiko Smazal	.05	.15
386 Tobias Abstreiter	.05	.15
387 Thomas Dolak	.05	.15
388 Udo Dohler	.05	.15
389 Andreas Loth	.05	.15
390 David Berge	.05	.15
391 Mark MacKay	.20	.50
392 Hans Zach TR	.05	.15
393 Moderatoren	.05	.15
394 Marc Hindelang	.05	.15
395 Peter Kohl	.05	.15
396 Sven Kukulies	.05	.15
397 Claus Muller	.05	.15
398 Gerhard Leinauer	.05	.15
399 Michael Leopold	.05	.15
400 Rick Amann	.05	.15
401 Schiris	.05	.15
402 Holger Gerstberger	.05	.15
403 Ralph Dimmers	.05	.15
404 Harald Deubert	.05	.15
405 Petr Chvatal	.05	.15
406 Frank Awizus	.05	.15
407 Axel Rademaker	.05	.15
408 Wolfgang Hellwig	.05	.15
409 Gerhard Muller	.05	.15
410 Gerhard Lichtnecker	.05	.15
411 Rainer Kluge	.05	.15
412 Stefan TR	.05	.15
413 Richard Schütz	.05	.15
414 Willi Schimm	.05	.15
415 Peter Slapke	.05	.15
416 TW 1	.05	.15
417 TW 2	.05	.15
418 TW 3	.05	.15
419 TW 4	.05	.15
420 TW 5	.05	.15
421 TW 6	.05	.15
422 TW 7	.05	.15
423 TW 8	.05	.15
424 TW 9	.05	.15
425 RS 1	.05	.15
426 RS 2	.05	.15
427 RS 3	.05	.15
428 RS 4	.05	.15
429 RS 5	.05	.15
430 RS 6	.05	.15
431 RS 7	.05	.15
432 RS 8	.05	.15
433 RS 9	.05	.15
434 SK	.05	.15

1999-00 German Bundesliga 2

Card	Low	High
COMPLETE SET (330)	30.00	60.00
1 EC Bad Nauheim Team Card	.02	.10
2 Darryl Olsen	.20	.50
3 Sven Gerbig	.08	.25
4 Gaetan Malo	.08	.25
5 Steffen Michel	.08	.25
6 Dennis Cardona	.08	.25
7 Marco Rentzsch	.08	.25
8 Dino Felicetti	.08	.25
9 David Matsos	.08	.25
10 Sven Paschek	.08	.25
11 Marco Heinrichs	.08	.25
12 Larry Mitchell	.08	.25
13 Ingo Schwarz	.08	.25
14 Dale Jago	.08	.25
15 Claus Dalpiaz	.20	.50
16 Marc West	.08	.25
17 Christian Seeberger	.08	.25
18 Olaf Scholz	.08	.25
19 Carsten Gosdeck	.08	.25
20 Dan Olsen	.08	.25
21 EC Bad Tölz Team Card	.02	.10
22 Christian Proulx	.20	.50
23 Michael Teltscher	.08	.25
24 Florian Keller	.08	.25
25 Christian Curth	.08	.25
26 Yanick Dube	.20	.50
27 Markus Witting	.08	.25
28 Axel Kammerer	.08	.25
29 Dave Flanagan	.08	.25
30 Ilpo Kauhanen	.20	.50
31 Johan Sälle	.08	.25
32 Ambrosius Fichtner	.08	.25
33 David St. Pierre	.08	.25
34 Mathias Hart	.08	.25
35 Franz Demmel	.08	.25
36 Markus Feierabend	.08	.25
37 Florian Zeller	.08	.25
38 Sven Valenti	.08	.25
39 Christian Gegenfurtner	.08	.25
40 Josef Schlickenrieder	.08	.25
41 SC Bietigheim-Bissingen Team Card	.02	.10
42 David Belitski	.20	.50
43 Frank Appel	.08	.25
44 Markus Rohde	.08	.25
45 Milos Vanik	.08	.25
46 Marc Mundil	.08	.25
47 Ulrich Liebsch	.08	.25
48 Darren Ritchie	.08	.25
49 Mike Bader	.08	.25
50 Daniel Held	.08	.25
51 Andrej Jaufmann	.08	.25
52 Tim Leahy	.08	.25
53 Martin Ancicka	.08	.25
54 Christian Baader	.08	.25
55 Craig Teeple	.08	.25
56 Ralf Stärk	.08	.25
57 Andreas Naumann	.08	.25
58 Stephan Sinner	.08	.25
59 Timo Nykopp	.08	.25
60 Vaclav Drobny	.08	.25
61 Thomas Mieszkowski	.08	.25
62 Tom Pokel	.08	.25
63 Braunlager EHC/Harz Team Card	.02	.10
64 Jarno Miikkulainen	.20	.50
65 Peter Lundmark	.20	.50
66 Josef Beppi Eckmair	.08	.25
67 Douglas Murray	.08	.25
68 Chris Clarke	.08	.25
69 Ron Gaudet	.08	.25
70 Sven Gerike	.08	.25
71 Marek Gajewski	.08	.25
72 Markus Draxler	.08	.25
73 Frederik Andersson	.08	.25
74 Timo Gschwill	.08	.25
75 Georg Gailer	.08	.25
76 Frank Richardt	.08	.25
77 Johan Silfwerplatz	.08	.25
78 Marcus Bleicher	.08	.25
79 Anton Krinner	.08	.25
80 Sebastian Buchwieser	.08	.25
81 Bastian Niedermeier	.08	.25
82 Anton Raubal	.08	.25
83 Peter Gailer	.08	.25
84 Düsseldorfer EG Team Card	.02	.10
85 Chad Biafore	.20	.50
86 Fabian Brännström	.20	.50
87 Zdenek Travnicek	.08	.25
88 Victor Gordiouk	.08	.25
89 Leo Stefan	.08	.25
90 Till Feser	.08	.25
91 Andreas Pokorny	.08	.25
92 Andreas Brockmann	.08	.25
93 Ralf Reisinger	.08	.25
94 Marc Dillmann	.08	.25
95 Sergej Sorokin	.08	.25
96 Peter Franke	.08	.25
97 Udo Schmid	.08	.25
98 Rafael Jedamzik	.08	.25
99 Jouni Vento	.08	.25
100 Torsten Kunz	.08	.25
101 Sebastian Odenthal	.08	.25
102 Anders Gozzi	.08	.25
103 Maurizio Mansi	.08	.25
104 Boris Lingemann	.08	.25
105 Czeslaw Panek	.08	.25
106 EHC Freiburg Team Card	.02	.10
107 Rostislav Haas	.20	.50
108 Alexander Semak	.08	.25
109 Oleg Znarok	.08	.25
110 David Danner	.08	.25
111 Igor Dorochin	.08	.25
112 Tobias Samendinger	.08	.25
113 Ravil Khaidarov	.08	.25
114 Evgeni Sultanowitsch	.08	.25
115 Thomas Jeller	.08	.25
116 Rudolf Gorgenländer	.08	.25
117 Andrej Strakhov	.08	.25
118 Vitalij Grossmann	.08	.25
119 Max Bauer	.08	.25
120 Peter Mares	.08	.25
121 Josef Peroutka	.08	.25
122 Peter Piecner	.08	.25
123 Michael Vasicek	.08	.25
124 Patrick Vozar	.08	.25
125 Frantisek Frosch	.08	.25
126 Thomas Dolak sen.	.08	.25
127 Grefrather EV Team Card	.02	.10
128 Frank Gentges	.20	.50
129 Jochen Hecker	.08	.25
130 Dirk Kuhnekath	.08	.25
131 Bill Trew	.08	.25
132 Thomas Popiesch	.08	.25
133 Christoph Kleckers	.08	.25
134 Henrik Hölscher	.08	.25
135 Arno Brux	.08	.25
136 Ashlin Halfnight	.08	.25
137 Nolan McDonald	.08	.25
138 Gilbert Schröder	.08	.25
139 Nicklas Norlander	.08	.25
140 Steve Smillie	.08	.25
141 Tobias Grossecker	.08	.25
142 Marcel Sakac	.08	.25
143 Elmar Schmitz	.08	.25
144 Hamburg Crocodiles Team Card	.02	.10
145 Alexander Genze	.08	.25
146 Derek Booth	.08	.25
147 Alexander Engel	.08	.25
148 John Johnson	.08	.25
149 Jason Dunham	.08	.25
150 Mike Millar	.08	.25
151 Jay Luknowsky	.08	.25
152 Andy Pritchard	.08	.25
153 Mark Mahon	.08	.25
154 Patrick Pysz	.08	.25
155 Karsten Mende	.08	.25
156 Phil Bourque	.20	.50
157 Jürgen Trattner	.08	.25
158 Carsten Solbach	.08	.25
159 Maurice Lemay	.30	.75
160 Jayson Meyer	.08	.25
161 Marius Cissewski	.08	.25
162 Christoph Sandner	.08	.25
163 Harald Waibel	.08	.25
164 Mario Gehrig	.08	.25
165 Ross Yates	.08	.25
166 Heilbronner EC Team Card	.02	.10
167 Mikael Granlund	.20	.50
168 Alexander Schuster	.08	.25
169 Niklas Rinaldo	.08	.25
170 Todd Sparks	.08	.25
171 Thomas Schädler	.08	.25
172 Martin Williams	.08	.25
173 Kenneth Filbey	.08	.25
174 Ronny Martin	.08	.25
175 Henri Marcoux	.08	.25
176 Christian Martin	.08	.25
177 Felix Feeser	.08	.25
178 Brad Scott	.08	.25
179 Alexander Semjonov	.08	.25
180 Michael Rumrich	.08	.25
181 Layne Roland	.08	.25
182 Björn Barta	.08	.25
183 Markus Eberl	.08	.25
184 Rainer Suchan	.08	.25
185 Johan Lindh	.08	.25
186 Gary Prior	.08	.25
187 ERC Ingolstadt Team Card	.02	.10
188 Marco Thommes	.08	.25
189 Stephane Julien	.08	.25
190 Agostino Casale	.08	.25
191 Kevin Ryan	.08	.25
192 Harald Schäller	.08	.25
193 Markus Welz	.08	.25
194 Wolfgang Fries	.08	.25
195 Petr Bares	.08	.25
196 Thomas Daffner	.08	.25
197 Clayton Young	.08	.25
198 Samuel Groleau	.08	.25
199 Philippe DeRouville	.30	.75
200 Cory Holden	.08	.25
201 Sven Zywitza	.08	.25
202 Frank Kannewurf	.08	.25
203 Fabian Dahlem	.08	.25
204 Jürgen Simon	.08	.25
205 Roland Timoschuk	.08	.25
206 Glenn Goodall	.40	1.00
207 Giacinto Boni	.08	.25
208 Iserlohner EC Team Card	.02	.10
209 Cory Laylin	.08	.25
210 Oliver Bernhardt	.08	.25
211 Robert Gratza	.08	.25
212 Collin Danielsmeier	.08	.25
213 Pat Mikesch	.08	.25
214 Tomas Martinec	.08	.25
215 Teal Fowler	.08	.25
216 Michael Hackert	.08	.25
217 Mike Muller	.08	.25
218 Oliver Hackert	.08	.25
219 Peter Hellmann	.08	.25
220 Steve Potvin	.08	.25
221 Torsten Fendt	.08	.25
222 Manuel Kofler	.08	.25
223 Lars Müller	.08	.25
224 Elvis Beslagic	.08	.25
225 Ronny Arendt	.08	.25
226 Christian Franz	.08	.25
227 Ian Wood	.20	.50
228 Greg Poss	.08	.25
229 EHC Neuwied Team Card	.02	.10
230 Juri Stumpf	.08	.25
231 Dean Fedorchuk	.08	.25
232 Andrej Teljukin	.08	.25
233 Alexander Andrievsky	.08	.25
234 Ladislav Strompf	.08	.25
235 Richard Baptist	.08	.25
236 Otto Keresztes	.08	.25
237 Klaus Micheller	.08	.25
238 Todd Johnson	.08	.25
239 Mario Naster	.08	.25
240 Jens Hergt	.08	.25
241 Falk Ozellis	.08	.25
242 Craig Streu	.08	.25
243 Marc Gronau	.08	.25
244 Ole Kopitz	.08	.25

245 Vitalij Semenchenko	.08	.25
246 Radek Vit	.08	.25
247 Sinuhe Wallinheimo	.30	.75
248 Michael Weinfurter	.08	.25
249 Petteri Lehmussaari	.08	.25
250 GEC Nordhorn Team Card	.02	.10
251 Christian von Trzcinski	.08	.25
252 Jedrzej Kasperczyk	.08	.25
253 Peter Kwasigroch	.08	.25
254 Christian Spaan	.08	.25
255 Gabriel Krüger	.08	.25
256 Moritz Schmidt	.08	.25
257 Alexej Pogodin	.08	.25
258 Markus Kempf	.08	.25
259 Sergej Zvyagin	.08	.25
260 Christian Brittig	.08	.25
261 Juris Opulskis	.08	.25
262 Andreas Morczinietz	.08	.25
263 Andrzej Hanisz	.08	.25
264 Sami Leinonen	.08	.25
265 Sergej Tchoudinov	.08	.25
266 Mikka Kemppi	.08	.25
267 Anton Weissgerber	.08	.25
268 SC Riessersee Team Card	.02	.10
269 Michael Pump	.08	.25
270 Georg Güttler	.08	.25
271 Christoph Klotz	.08	.25
272 Tim Regan	.08	.25
273 Alexander Wedl	.08	.25
274 Mika Puhakka	.08	.25
275 Martin Holzer	.08	.25
276 Hubert Buchwieser	.08	.25
277 Michael Raubal	.08	.25
278 Josef Lehner	.08	.25
279 Christian Mayr	.08	.25
280 Tobias Netter	.08	.25
281 Tom O'Grady	.08	.25
282 Samuli Peltosara	.08	.25
283 Leonhard Wild	.08	.25
284 Florian Brandl	.08	.25
285 Duane Dennis	.08	.25
286 Mark Zdan	.08	.25
287 Florian Storf	.08	.25
288 Ron Chyzowski	.08	.25
289 ES Weisswasser Team Card	.02	.10
290 Torsten Hanusch	.08	.25
291 Daniel Sikorski	.08	.25
292 Alexej Jefimov	.08	.25
293 Alexandre Vinogradov	.08	.25
294 Ronny Reddo	.08	.25
295 Frank Peschke	.08	.25
296 Ronny Glaser	.08	.25
297 Jörgen Hermansson	.08	.25
298 Robert Brezina	.08	.25
299 Sven Steinecke	.08	.25
300 David Musial	.08	.25
301 Pekka Virta	.08	.25
302 Thomas Knobloch	.08	.25
303 Daniel Bartell	.08	.25
304 Falk Herzig	.08	.25
305 Dimitri Alekhin	.08	.25
306 Joakim Wiberg	.08	.25
307 Martin Wiita	.08	.25
308 Jörg Pohling	.08	.25
309 Bror Hansson	.08	.25
310 EC Wilhelmshaven-Stickhausen Team Card	.02	.10
311 Vadim Finko	.08	.25
312 Harald Hebig	.08	.25
313 Kai Ahlroth	.08	.25
314 Boris Blank	.08	.25
315 Eduard Lewandowski	.08	.25
316 Alexander Rusch	.08	.25
317 Dimitry Dudarev	.08	.25
318 Vitali Janke	.08	.25
319 Ilia Stachenkov	.08	.25
320 Jürgen Schaal	.08	.25
321 Andrej Dmitriev	.08	.25
322 Iiro Itämies	.08	.25
323 Sergej Jaschin	.08	.25
324 Martin Ekrt	.08	.25
325 Marian Horvarth	.08	.25
326 Mario Schüssel	.08	.25
327 Alexander Herbst	.08	.25
328 Andrej Naumann	.08	.25
329 Peter Kalinowski	.08	.25
330 Anatoli Antipov	.08	.25

2000-01 German Berlin Polar Bears Postcards

This team-issued set is standard postcard size. Cards are unnumbered and listed below in alphabetical order. Thanks to collector Andy Hatzos for this and other Polar Bears checklist.

COMPLETE SET (22)	10.00	20.00
1 John Chabot	.40	1.00
2 Derek Cormier	.40	1.00
3 Rob Cowie	.40	1.00
4 Uli Egen	.40	1.00
5 Sven Felski	.40	1.00
6 Marc Fortier	.40	1.00
7 Alexander Godynyuk	.40	1.00
8 Rich Gosselin	.40	1.00
9 Peter Hammarstrom	.40	1.00
10 Todd Harkins	.40	1.00
11 Alex Hicks	.40	1.00
12 Alexander Jung	.40	1.00
13 Daniel Laperriere	.40	1.00
14 Rob Leask	.40	1.00
15 Martin Lindman	.40	1.00
16 Derek Mayer	.40	1.00
17 Klaus Merk	.40	1.00
18 Nico Pyka	.40	1.00
19 Sandy Smith	.40	1.00
20 Jeff Tomlinson	.40	1.00
21 Lubomir Vaic	.40	1.00
22 Steve Walker	.40	1.00

2000-01 German DEL

This set features the top players in Germany's elite league. The cards were produced by Upper Deck and feature an action photo on the front, with a head shot and stats on the back.

COMPLETE SET (240)	15.00	40.00
1 Gordon Hynes	.10	.25
2 Dave Tomlinson	.20	.50
3 Stephane Richer	.05	.15
4 Steve Junker	.05	.15
5 Wayne Hynes	.05	.15
6 Bradley Bergen	.05	.15
7 Devin Edgerton	.05	.15
8 Ron Pasco	.05	.15
9 Francois Groleau	.05	.15
10 Todd Hlushko	.20	.50
11 Mike Rosati	.20	.50
12 Chris Straube	.05	.15
13 Jean-Francois Jomphe	.20	.50
14 Jan Alston	.05	.15
15 Sven Rampf	.05	.15
16 Sergej Vostrikov	.05	.15
17 Igor Maslennikov	.05	.15
18 Reemt Pyka	.05	.15
19 Dave Chyzowski	.20	.50
20 Arnaud Briand	.05	.15
21 Sergej Stas	.05	.15
22 Sebastian Klenner	.05	.15
23 Vasily Pankov	.05	.15
24 Duane Moeser	.05	.15
25 Jason Muzzatti	.40	1.00
26 Herbert Hohenberger	.20	.50
27 Ryan Savoia	.05	.15
28 Jim Camazzola	.05	.15
29 Tommy Jakobsen	.05	.15
30 Andrei Mezin	.40	1.00
31 Markus Pottinger	.05	.15
32 Thomas Sjogren	.05	.15
33 Jim Hiller	.05	.15
34 Pavel Gross	.05	.15
35 Robert Guillet	.05	.15
36 Udo Dohler	.05	.15
37 Anders Huusko	.05	.15
38 Heinz Ehlers	.05	.15
39 Gregory Johnston	.20	.50
40 Petri Liimatainen	.05	.15
41 Johan Norgren	.05	.15
42 Martin Ulrich	.05	.15
43 Iain Fraser	.10	.25
44 Gary Shuchuk	.20	.50
45 Torsten Kienass	.10	.25
46 Niki Mondt	.05	.15
47 Bernd Kuhnhauser	.05	.15
48 Craig Reichert	.10	.25
49 Niclas Sundblad	.05	.15
50 Sergey Sorokin	.05	.15
51 Peter Franke	.05	.15
52 Ivan Droppa	.05	.15
53 Christopher Bartolone	.05	.15
54 Leo Stefan	.20	.50
55 Victor Gordiouk	.10	.25
56 Lorenz Funk	.05	.15
57 Boris Lingemann	.05	.15
58 Andrei Trefilov	.20	.50
59 Nico Pyka	.05	.15
60 Alexander Jung	.05	.15
61 Alexander Godynyuk	.10	.25
62 Derek Mayer	.10	.25
63 Sven Felski	.05	.15
64 Marc Fortier	.10	.25
65 John Chabot	.20	.50
66 Derek Cormier	.05	.15
67 Steve Walker	.05	.15
68 Lubomir Vaic	.10	.25
69 Klaus Merk	.20	.50
70 Dan Laperriere	.20	.50
71 Rob Cowie	.05	.15
72 Martin Lindman	.05	.15
73 Chris Govedaris	.20	.50
74 Michael Bresagk	.05	.15
75 Leonardo Conti	.05	.15
76 Robin Doyle	.05	.15
77 Toni Porkka	.05	.15
78 John Walker	.05	.15
79 Jean-Marc Richard	.20	.50
80 Jason Ruff	.10	.25
81 Jason Cirone	.10	.25
82 Jose Charbonneau	.10	.25
83 Victor Gervais	.05	.15
84 Patrice Lefebvre	.20	.50
85 Martin Gendron	.20	.50
86 Ken Quinney	.20	.50
87 Keith Aldridge	.20	.50
88 Eldon Reddick	.20	.50
89 Oscar Ackestrom	.05	.15
90 Mattias Loof	.05	.15
91 Egor Bashkatov	.10	.25
92 Mark Kosturik	.05	.15
93 Wallace Schreiber	.20	.50
94 Dominic Lavoie	.05	.15
95 Rob Murphy	.10	.25
96 Pavel Cagas	.05	.15
97 Igor Chibirev	.10	.25
98 Kevin Grant	.05	.15
99 Jan Munster	.05	.15
100 Chris Snell	.10	.25
101 Patrik Zetterberg	.05	.15
102 Colin Beardsmore	.05	.15
103 Calle Carlsson	.05	.15
104 Tomas Martinec	.05	.15
105 Teal Fowler	.05	.15
106 Alexander Kuzminski	.05	.15
107 Terence Campbell	.05	.15
108 Duane Derksen	.20	.50
109 Peter Roed	.05	.15
110 Torsten Fendt	.05	.15
111 Shawn Anderson	.05	.15
112 Manuel Kofler	.05	.15
113 Radek Toth	.05	.15
114 Steve Potvin	.05	.15
115 Brent Tully	.05	.15
116 Ted Crowley	.05	.15
117 Pat Mikesch	.05	.15
118 Stephane Robitaille	.05	.15
119 Francois Guay	.05	.15
120 Andreas Loth	.05	.15
121 Patrice Tardif	.20	.50
122 Scott Levins	.05	.15
123 Joachim Appel	.05	.15
124 Chris Rogles	.20	.50
125 Thomas Daffner	.05	.15
126 Klaus Kathan	.05	.15
127 Sylvain Turgeon	.10	.25
128 Andrew Verner	.20	.50
129 Bruno Zarrillo	.05	.15
130 Dwayne Norris	.20	.50
131 Christoph Paepke	.05	.15
132 Mirko Ludemann	.05	.15
133 Andreas Lupzig	.05	.15
134 Jason Young	.10	.25
135 Joseph Heiss	.20	.50
136 Tomas Forslund	.10	.25
137 Andre Faust	.05	.15
138 Tino Boos	.05	.15
139 John Miner	.10	.25
140 Dave McIlwain	.20	.50
141 Dieter Kalt	.05	.15
142 Corey Millen	.20	.50
143 Marc Hussey	.05	.15
144 Brent Severyn	.20	.50
145 Christian Ehrhoff	.05	.15
146 Neil Eisenhut	.10	.25
147 Ilja Vorobjev	.05	.15
148 Shayne Wright	.05	.15
149 Dan Lambert	.20	.50
150 Brad Purdie	.05	.15
151 Christoph Brandner	.05	.15
152 Roger Nordstrom	.05	.15
153 Jeff Christian	.10	.25
154 Karel Lang	.05	.15
155 Thomas Brandl	.05	.15
156 Martin Sychra	.05	.15
157 Jason McBain	.05	.15
158 Ralph Intranuovo	.20	.50
159 Jarkko Savijoki	.05	.15
160 Marc Savard	.20	.50
161 Roman Meluzin	.05	.15
162 Todd Simon	.10	.25
163 Jean-Francois Quintin	.10	.25
164 Scott Pearson	.20	.50
165 Kevin Wortman	.05	.15
166 Geoff Sarjeant	.20	.50
167 Leonard Wild	.05	.15
168 Erich Goldmann	.20	.50
169 Marc Laniel	.20	.50
170 Esa Tikkanen	.75	2.00
171 Hans Lodin	.05	.15
172 Rick Girard	.05	.15
173 Christian Kunast	.05	.15
174 Simon Wheeldon	.15	.40
175 Shane Peacock	.05	.15
176 Christoph Schubert	.05	.15
177 Peter Douris	.10	.25
178 Alexander Serikow	.20	.50
179 Peter Larsson	.05	.15
180 Thomas Dolak	.05	.15
181 Jorg Handrick	.05	.15
182 Jason Herter	.05	.15
183 Andrew Schneider	.10	.25
184 Parris Duffus	.20	.50
185 Luciano Borsato	.10	.25
186 Jurgen Rumrich	.10	.25
187 Dimitri Dudik	.05	.15
188 Alexander Cherbayev	.10	.25
189 Martin Jiranek	.05	.15
190 Martin Reichel	.05	.15
191 Mario Chitarroni	.05	.15
192 Jason Miller	.05	.15
193 Bjorn Nord	.05	.15
194 Kevin Miehm	.10	.25
195 Marc Seliger	.20	.50
196 Daniel Kunce	.05	.15
197 Paul Stanton	.10	.25
198 Peter Gulda	.05	.15
199 Christian Kohmann	.05	.15
200 Mika Arvaja	.05	.15
201 Carsten Gosdeck	.05	.15
202 Aleksandrs Kercs	.05	.15
203 Alexandre Andrievski	.10	.25
204 Robert Hock	.05	.15
205 Josef Zajic	.05	.15
206 Marek Stebnicki	.05	.15
207 Andrej Kovalev	.05	.15
208 Ladislav Karabin	.05	.15
209 Peter Draisaitl	.05	.15
210 Sinuhe Wallinheimo	.10	.25
211 Jergus Baca	.20	.50
212 Peter Allen	.05	.15
213 Alexander Duck	.05	.15
214 Marcel Goc	.60	1.50
215 Jens Stramkowski	.05	.15
216 Mark MacKay	.10	.25
217 Vadym Slivchenko	.05	.15
218 Jacek Plachta	.05	.15
219 Alexei Yegorov	.20	.50
220 Patrik Augusta	.05	.15
221 Brad Schlegel	.10	.25
222 Andreas Renz	.05	.15
223 Thomas Greilinger	.05	.15
224 Ian Gordon	.10	.25
225 Mike Bullard	.20	.50
226 Robert Muller	.05	.15
227 Mike Pellegrims	.05	.15
228 Mike Casselman	.05	.15
229 Leonardo Soccio	.05	.15
230 Andreas Pokorny	.10	.25
231 Tim Schnelle	.05	.15
232 Daniel Kreutzer	.05	.15
233 Tobias Abstreiter	.05	.15
234 Tomas Hartogs	.05	.15
235 Stephane Barin	.05	.15
236 Boris Rousson	.20	.50
237 Mike Kennedy	.10	.25
238 John Craighead	.05	.15
239 Marc Pethke	.05	.15
240 Markus Janka	.05	.15

2000-01 German DEL All-Star Class

This series was an insert found in the 2000-01 German DEL set and features the league's top scorers. They were inserted at a rate of 1:17.

COMPLETE SET (10)	8.00	20.00
STATED ODDS 1:17		
A1 Martin Jiranek	.80	2.00
A2 Patrice Lefebvre	1.60	4.00
A3 Peter Douris	.80	2.00
A4 Sergej Vostrikov	.80	2.00
A5 Gregory Johnston	1.20	3.00
A6 Chris Govedaris	.80	2.00
A7 Mike Casselman	.80	2.00
A8 Corey Millen	1.20	3.00
A9 Shawn Anderson	1.20	3.00
A10 Sylvain Turgeon	1.20	3.00

2000-01 German DEL Game Jersey

This insert set features a swatch of actual game-worn jersey on each card. Because the jerseys in the DEL are laden with ads, multi-colored swatches are plentiful. As such, they do not draw significant premiums as similar swatches might earn in North American sets. The cards were inserted 1:144 packs.

COMPLETE SET (16)	160.00	400.00
STATED ODDS 1:144		
BZ Bruno Zarrillo	16.00	40.00
DM Duane Moeser	10.00	25.00
JB Jergus Baca	12.00	30.00
JR Jurgen Rumrich	10.00	25.00
LE Leonard Soccio	12.00	30.00
LS Leo Stefan	12.00	30.00
MF Marc Fortier	12.00	30.00
MM Mark MacKay	12.00	30.00
MS Marc Savard	20.00	50.00
PG Pavel Gross	12.00	30.00
SR Stephane Richer	12.00	30.00
SW Simon Wheeldon	16.00	40.00
TA Tobias Abstreiter	16.00	40.00
TF Teal Fowler	12.00	30.00
TH Tomas Hartogs	12.00	30.00
TP Toni Porkka	10.00	25.00

2000-01 German DEL Profiles

Inserted 1:8 packs of German DEL, these cards picture the league's top performers.

COMPLETE SET (11)	8.00	20.00
STATED ODDS 1:8		
P1 Jan Alston	.80	2.00
P2 Andrei Mezin	2.00	5.00
P3 John Chabot	1.20	3.00
P4 Wallace Schreiber	1.20	3.00
P5 Shane Peacock	.80	2.00
P6 Mike Bullard	1.20	3.00
P7 Mirko Ludemann	.80	2.00
P8 Boris Rousson	1.20	3.00
P9 Andrej Kovalev	.80	2.00
P10 Mike Pellegrims	.40	1.00
P11 Andrei Trefilov	.80	2.00

2000-01 German DEL Star Attractions

This set profiles the most popular players in the German DEL. The cards were inserted 1:17 packs.

COMPLETE SET (10)	10.00	25.00
STATED ODDS 1:17		
S1 Ivan Droppa	1.20	3.00
S2 Gordon Hynes	1.20	3.00
S3 Marek Stebnicki	1.20	3.00
S4 Daniel Kreutzer	1.20	3.00
S5 Thomas Brandl	1.20	3.00
S6 Esa Tikkanen	2.00	5.00
S7 Bob Sweeney	1.20	3.00
S8 Paul Stanton	1.20	3.00
S9 Dave Tomlinson	1.20	3.00
S10 Brent Severyn	2.00	5.00

2001-02 German Adler Mannheim Eagles Postcards

1 Robert Muller	.75	2.00
2 Eric Charron	.75	2.00
3 Devin Edgerton	.75	2.00
4 Mike Rosati	.75	2.00
5 Chris Straube	.75	2.00
6 Francois Groleau	.75	2.00
7 Rene Corbet	.75	2.00
8 Stephane Richer	1.25	3.00
9 Stefan Ustorf	.75	2.00

2001-02 German Berlin Polar Bears Postcards

COMPLETE SET (27)	10.00	25.00
1 Keith Aldridge	.40	1.00
2 Alex Barta	.40	1.00
3 Boris Blank	.40	1.00
4 David Cooper	.40	1.00
5 Patrick Czajka	.40	1.00
6 Uli Egen	.40	1.00
7 Sven Felski	.40	1.00
8 Marc Fortier	.40	1.00
9 Daniel Laperriere	.40	1.00
10 Steve Larouche	.40	1.00
11 Rob Leask	.40	1.00
12 Scott Levins	.40	1.00
13 Eduard Lewandoski	.40	1.00
14 Martin Lindman	.40	1.00
15 Chris Marinucci	.40	1.00
16 Klaus Merk	.40	1.00
17 Hartmut Nickel	.40	1.00
18 Fabio Patrzek	.40	1.00
19 Ed Patterson	.40	1.00
20 Nico Pyka	.40	1.00
21 David Roberts	.40	1.00
22 Jan Schertz	.40	1.00
23 Richard Shulmistra	.40	1.00
24 Tom Skinner	.40	1.00
25 Lee Sorochan	.40	1.00
26 Jeff Tomlinson	.40	1.00
27 Steve Walker	.40	1.00

2001-02 German Upper Deck

This set features the top players of the German DEL. The cards were produced by Upper Deck and sold only in Germany. The design mirrors that of the base 2001-02 Upper Deck series.

COMPLETE SET (268)	16.00	40.00
1 Igor Alexandrov	.08	.20
2 Marc Beaucage	.16	.40
3 Eric Dylla	.20	.50
4 Mickey Elick	.16	.40
5 Magnus Eriksson	.08	.20
6 Jakub Ficenec	.20	.50
7 Robert Guillet	.08	.20
8 Tommy Jakobsen	.08	.20
9 Christian Lukes	.08	.20
10 Igor Maslennikov	.08	.20
11 Duanne Moeser	.16	.40
12 Vasily Pankov	.08	.20
13 Reemt Pyka	.08	.20
14 Reid Simonton	.16	.40
15 Sergej Vostrikov	.08	.20
16 Alexander Cherbayev	.08	.20
17 Heinz Ehlers	.08	.20
18 Ronny Arendt	.08	.20
19 Andrej Vassilyev	.08	.20
20 Francois Leroux	.20	.50
21 Andrei Mezin	.40	1.00
22 Jan Münster	.08	.20
23 Markus Pöttinger	.08	.20
24 Patrick Senger	.08	.20
25 Aleksandrs Kercs	.08	.20
26 Gordon Hynes	.20	.50
27 Greg Andrusak	.20	.50
28 Vjatcheslav Fanduls	.08	.20
29 Yvon Corriveau	.20	.50
30 Frederik Öberg	.08	.20
31 Keith Aldridge	.20	.50
32 David Cooper	.16	.40
33 Sven Felski	.08	.20
34 Marc Fortier	.20	.50
35 Dan Laperriere	.20	.50
36 Steve LaRouche	.20	.50
37 Scott Levins	.20	.50
38 Chris Marinucci	.20	.50
39 Klaus Merk	.20	.50
40 Nico Pyka	.08	.20
41 David Roberts	.20	.50
42 Jan Schertz	.08	.20
43 Richard Shulmistra	.20	.50
44 Lee Sorochan	.20	.50
45 Steve Walker	.16	.40
46 Chris Bartolone	.16	.40
48 Ivan Droppa	.08	.20
49 Neil Eisenhut	.16	.40
50 Tore Vikingstad	.08	.20
51 Torsten Kienass	.08	.20
52 Bernd Kühnhauser	.08	.20
53 Trond Magnussen	.08	.20
54 Mike Pellegrims	.16	.40
55 Jean-Francois Quintin	.16	.40
56 Ralf Reisinger	.08	.20
57 Leo Stefan	.08	.20
58 Andrej Trefilov	.20	.50
59 Martin Ulrich	.08	.20
60 Rainer Zerwesz	.08	.20
61 Frank Appel	.16	.40
62 Lars Brüggemann	.08	.20
63 Mike Casselman	.16	.40
64 Ted Crowley	.16	.40
65 Liam Garvey	.08	.20
66 Erich Goldmann	.20	.50
67 Todd Hawkins	.16	.40
68 Ralph Intranuovo	.20	.50
69 Martin Sychra	.08	.20
70 Riku-Petteri Lehtonen	.08	.20
71 Doug MacDonald	.16	.40
72 Marc Savard	.20	.50
73 Todd Simon	.16	.40
74 Jimmy Waite	.30	.75
75 Craig Woodcroft	.16	.40
76 Michael Bresagk	.08	.20
77 Brent Cullaton	.16	.40
78 Rob Doyle	.08	.20
79 Greg Evtushevski	.16	.40
80 Victor Gervais	.16	.40
81 Rick Girard	.16	.40
82 Stewart Malgunas	.16	.40
83 Rob Pearson	.20	.50
84 Eldon Reddick	.20	.50
85 Ian Fraser	.16	.40
86 Alexander Selivanov	.08	.20
87 Vadim Slivchenko	.08	.20
88 Chris Snell	.16	.40
89 Brent Tully	.16	.40
90 John Walker	.16	.40
91 Oscar Ackeström	.20	.50
92 Egor Bashkatov	.08	.20
93 Igor Chibirev	.08	.20
94 Kevin Grant	.16	.40
95 David Haas	.16	.40
96 Peter Jakobsson	.08	.20
97 Dominic Lavoie	.20	.50
98 Mattias Lööf	.08	.20
99 Rob Murphy	.16	.40
100 Mark Pederson	.16	.40
101 Wally Schreiber	.16	.40
102 Len Soccio	.20	.50
103 Andrew Verner	.20	.50
104 Steve Wilson	.16	.40
105 Patrik Zetterberg	.08	.20
106 Doug Ast	.16	.40
107 Colin Beardsmore	.16	.40
108 Guy Dupuis	.16	.40
109 Oliver Bernhardt	.08	.20
110 Rusty Fitzgerald	.20	.50
111 Terry Hollinger	.20	.50
112 Kimmo Kapanen	.08	.20
113 Dmitrij Kotschnew	.08	.20
114 Cory Laylin	.16	.40
115 Paul Dyck	.20	.50
116 Tomas Martinec	.08	.20
117 Colin Danielsmeier	.08	.20
118 David Musial	.16	.40
119 Andreas Pokorny	.08	.20
120 Sean Tallaire	.16	.40
121 Tobias Abstreiter	.20	.50
122 Thomas Daffner	.08	.20
123 Doug Derraugh	.16	.40
124 Leonid Fatikov	.08	.20
125 Tommie Hartogs	.08	.20
126 Klaus Kathan	.08	.20
127 Ilpo Kauhanen	.20	.50
128 Örjan Lindmark	.08	.20
129 Andreas Loth	.08	.20
130 Jeff MacLeod	.16	.40
131 Pat Mikesch	.08	.20
132 Jochen Molling	.08	.20
133 Brent Peterson	.20	.50
134 Shayne Wright	.16	.40
135 Jeff Tory	.16	.40
136 Tino Boos	.08	.20
137 André Faust	.20	.50
138 Alex Hicks	.20	.50
139 Petri Liimatainen	.08	.20
140 Mirko Lüdemann	.20	.50
141 Jörg Mayr	.08	.20
142 Dave McLlwain	.20	.50
143 Corey Millen	.20	.50
144 John Miner	.16	.40
145 Dwayne Norris	.16	.40
146 Toni Porkka	.08	.20
147 Andreas Renz	.08	.20
148 Chris Rogles	.20	.50
149 Niklas Sundblad	.20	.50
150 Jason Young	.16	.40
151 Patrik Augusta	.08	.20
152 Stéphane Barin	.08	.20
153 Thomas Brandl	.08	.20
154 Steffen Ziesche	.08	.20
156 Jeff Christian	.16	.40
157 Gilbert Dionne	.20	.50
158 Mario Doyon	.20	.50
159 Daniel Kunce	.08	.20
160 Dan Lambert	.30	.75
161 Roger Nordström	.08	.20
162 Brad Purdie	.20	.50
163 Gary Shuchuk	.20	.50
164 Sergej Stas	.08	.20
165 Phil von Stefenelli	.20	.50
166 Brad Bergen	.16	.40
167 Fabian Brännström	.08	.20
168 Devin Edgerton	.16	.40
169 Todd Hlushko	.20	.50
170 Wayne Hynes	.16	.40
171 François Groleau	.16	.40
172 Michel Picard	.20	.50
173 Yves Racine	.20	.50
174 Stéphane Richer	.16	.40
175 Andy Roach	.16	.40
176 Mike Rosati	.30	.75
177 Mike Stevens	.16	.40
178 Dave Tomlinson	.16	.40
179 Steve Junker	.16	.40
180 Stefan Ustorf	.20	.50
181 Kent Fearns	.16	.40
182 Jason Herter	.16	.40
183 Mike Kennedy	.20	.50
184 Derek King	.20	.50
185 Christian Künast	.08	.20
186 Hans Lodin	.08	.20
187 David Oliver	.16	.40
188 Shane Peacock	.16	.40
189 Derek Planté	.20	.50
190 Johan Rosén	.08	.20
191 Boris Rousson	.20	.50
192 Andy Schneider	.16	.40
193 Peter Douris	.20	.50
194 Heiko Smazal	.08	.20
195 Simon Wheeldon	.20	.50
196 Shawn Anderson	.16	.40
197 Luciano Borsato	.20	.50
198 Frederic Chabot	.40	1.50
199 Mario Chitarroni	.20	.50
200 Kevin Dahl	.16	.40
201 David Emma	.20	.50
202 Martin Jiranek	.08	.20
203 Chris Luongo	.20	.50
204 Guy Lehoux	.20	.50
205 Jacek Plachta	.08	.20
206 Martin Reichel	.08	.20
207 Jürgen Rumrich	.08	.20
208 Christian Schönmoser	.08	.20
209 Jan Nemecek	.08	.20
210 Bruno Zarrillo	.20	.50
211 Andreas Lupzig	.08	.20
212 Jergus Baca	.08	.20
213 Derek Cormier	.16	.40
214 John Craighead	.16	.75
215 Jesper Damgaard	.08	.20
216 Peter Gulda	.08	.20
217 Robert Hock	.08	.20
218 Martin Hohenberger	.08	.20
219 Ladislav Karabin	.08	.20
220 Christian Kohmann	.08	.20
221 Andrej Kovalev	.08	.20
222 Jason McBain	.16	.40
223 Andrei Teljukin	.08	.20
224 Sinuhe Wallinheimo	.08	.50
225 Josef Zajic	.08	.20
226 Micah Aivazoff	.30	.75
227 Peter Allen	.16	.40
228 Mike Bullard	.20	.50
229 Dave Chyzowski	.20	.50
230 Eric Dubois	.16	.40
231 Ian Gordon	.16	.40
232 Markus Janka	.08	.20
233 Mark MacKay	.20	.50
234 Neal Martin	.16	.40
235 Jeff Nelson	.16	.40
236 Jackson Penney	.16	.40
237 Kent Simpson	.16	.40
238 Jason Deleurme	.16	.40
239 Gerhard Unterluggauer	.08	.20
240 Darcy Werenka	.20	.50
241 Andreas Morczinietz	.08	.20
242 Christian Rohde	.08	.20
243 Jonas Lanier	.08	.20
244 Boris Blank	.08	.20
245 Eduard Lewandowski	.08	.20
246 Niki Mondt	.08	.20
247 Leonard Wild	.08	.20
248 Leonardo Conti	.08	.20
249 Philip Schumacher	.08	.20
250 Björn Leonhardt	.20	.50
251 Christian Franz	.20	.50
252 Manuel Kofler	.20	.50
253 Daniel Kreutzer	.20	.50
254 Markus Guggemos	.20	.50
255 Dimitri Pätzold	.20	.50
256 Benjamin Hinterstocker	.20	.50
257 Christian Ehrhoff	.20	1.00
258 Adrian Grygiel	.20	.50
259 Benjamin Voigt	.20	.50
260 Robert Müller	.20	.50
261 Dennis Seidenberg	.20	1.50
262 Peter Abstreiter	.20	.50
263 Christoph Schubert	.20	.50
264 Andrej Strakhov	.20	.50
265 Benjamin Hecker	.20	.50
266 Vitalij Aab	.20	.50
267 Carsten Gosdeck	.20	.50
268 Lasse Kopitz	.20	.50
269 Marcel Goc	1.20	2.00
270 Alexander Dück	.20	.50

2001-02 German Upper Deck Gate Attractions

This set features the most exciting players in the DEL. The cards were inserted one in every 17 packs.

COMPLETE SET (10)	10.00	25.00
STATED ODDS 1:17		
GA1 Sergej Vostrikov	1.20	3.00
GA2 Aleksandrs Kercs	1.20	3.00
GA3 Sven Felski	1.20	3.00
GA4 Mark MacKay	1.20	3.00
GA5 Alexander Selivanov	1.20	3.00
GA6 Len Soccio	2.00	5.00
GA7 Ivan Droppa	1.20	3.00
GA8 Gilbert Dionne	2.00	5.00
GA9 Stefan Ustorf	1.20	3.00
GA10 Jason Miller	1.20	3.00

2001-02 German Upper Deck Goalies in Action

This set features the top stoppers in the DEL. The cards were inserted one in every 17 packs

COMPLETE SET (10)	20.00	40.00
STATED ODDS 1:17		
G1 Andrei Mezin	3.20	6.00
G2 Klaus Merk	2.00	5.00
G3 Andrej Trefilov	3.20	6.00
G4 Andrew Verner	2.00	5.00
G5 Chris Rogles	2.00	5.00
G6 Roger Nordstrom	2.00	5.00
G7 Mike Rosati	2.00	5.00
G8 Christian Kunast	2.00	5.00
G9 Marc Seliger	4.00	8.00
G10 Sinuhe Wallinheimo	2.00	5.00

2001-02 German Upper Deck Jersey Cards

The cards in this set feature a swatch of a jersey worn in an actual DEL game. Singles were inserted one in every 144 packs. Cards that display multi-colour swatches are valued at 1X to 2X the prices below.

COMPLETE SET (6)	160.00	400.00
AMJ Andrei Mezin	20.00	50.00
ATJ Andrej Trefilov	16.00	30.00
AVJ Andrew Verner	16.00	30.00
CKJ Christian Kunast	10.00	20.00
CRJ Chris Rogles	16.00	30.00
ERJ Eldon Reddick	16.00	30.00
FCJ Frederic Chabot	20.00	50.00
IGJ Ian Gordon	10.00	20.00
JWJ Jimmy Waite	20.00	50.00
KKJ Kimmo Kapanen	10.00	20.00
LFJ Leonid Fatikov	10.00	20.00
MEJ Magnus Eriksson	10.00	20.00
MRJ Mike Rosati	16.00	30.00
RNJ Roger Nordstrom	10.00	20.00
RSJ Richard Shulmistra	16.00	30.00
SWJ Sinuhe Wallinheimo	16.00	30.00

2001-02 German Upper Deck Skilled Stars

This series features some of the DEL's top players. The cards were inserted one in every eight packs.

COMPLETE SET (11)	6.00	15.00
SS1 Robert Hock	.80	2.00
SS2 David Cooper	1.20	3.00
SS3 Brad Purdie	1.20	3.00
SS4 Todd Simon	.80	2.00
SS5 Oscar Ackestrom	.80	2.00
SS6 Tomas Martinec	.80	2.00
SS7 Pat Mikesch	.80	2.00
SS8 Mirko Ludemann	.80	2.00
SS9 Stephane Richer	.80	2.00
SS10 Shane Peacock	.80	2.00
SS11 Paul Stanton	.80	2.00

2002-03 German Adler Mannheim Eagles Postcards

Card		
1 Todd Hlushko	.40	1.00
2 Thomas Schenkel	.40	1.00
3 Danny Aus Den Birken	.40	1.00
4 Mike Rosati	.40	1.00
5 Thomas Fischer	.40	1.00
6 Klaus Kathan	.40	1.00
7 Sachar Blank	.40	1.00
8 Yannic Seidenberg	.40	1.00
9 Rico Rossi	.40	1.00
10 Bill Stewart	.40	1.00
11 Fabio Carciola	.40	1.00
12 Rene Corbet	.40	1.00
13 Sascha Goc	.40	1.00
14 Nick Naumenko	.40	1.00
15 Ilja Vorobiev	.40	1.00
16 Steve Junker	.40	1.00
17 Wayne Hynes	.40	1.00
18 Devin Edgerton	.40	1.00

2002-03 German Berlin Polar Bears Postcards

COMPLETE SET (28)	10.00	25.00
1 Keith Aldridge	.40	1.00
2 Alex Barta	.40	1.00
3 Marc Beaufait	.40	1.00
4 Brad Bergen	.40	1.00
5 Boris Blank	.40	1.00
6 David Cooper	.40	1.00
7 Yvon Corriveau	.40	1.00
8 Kelly Fairchild	.40	1.00
9 Sven Felski	.40	1.00
10 John Gruden	.40	1.00
11 Thorsten Heine	.40	1.00
12 Martin Hoffmann	.40	1.00
13 Oliver Jonas	.40	1.00
14 Florian Katz	.40	1.00
15 Florian Keller	.40	1.00
16 Mark Kosick	.40	1.00
17 Rob Leask	.40	1.00
18 Klaus Merk	.40	1.00
19 Hartmut Nickel	.40	1.00
20 Pierre Page CO	.40	1.00
21 Ricard Persson	.40	1.00
22 Daniel Pyka	.40	1.00
23 Nico Pyka	.40	1.00
24 David Roberts	.40	1.00
25 Rob Shearer	.40	1.00
26 Richard Shulmistra	.40	1.00
27 Jeff Tomlinson	.40	1.00
28 Steve Walker	.40	1.00

2002-03 German DEL City Press

COMPLETE SET (290)	50.00	100.00
1 Ronny Arendt	.20	.50
2 Philippe Audet	.20	.50
3 Bjorn Barta	.20	.50
4 Frederic Bouchard	.20	.50
6 Shawn Carter	.20	.50
7 Igor Dorochin	.20	.50
8 P.C. Drouin	.40	1.00
9 Magnus Eriksson	.20	.50
10 Thorsten Fendt	.20	.50
11 Maxim Galanov	.20	.50
12 Patrick Koslow	.20	.50
13 Greg Leeb	.40	1.00
14 Christian Lukes	.20	.50
15 Shayne McCosh	.20	.50
16 Duanne Moeser	.20	.50
17 Christopher Oravec	.20	.50
18 Reid Simonton	.20	.50
19 Andrej Strakhov	.20	.50
20 Chris Straube	.20	.50
21 Sergej Vostrikov	.20	.50
22 Keith Aldridge	.20	.50
23 Alexander Barta	.20	.50
24 Mark Beaufait	.20	.50
25 Bradley Bergen	.20	.50
26 Boris Blank	.20	.50
27 David Cooper	.20	.50
28 Yvon Corriveau	.20	.50
29 Kelly Fairchild	.20	.50
30 Sven Felski	.20	.50
31 John Gruden	.20	.50
32 Oliver Jonas	.20	.50
33 Florian Keller	.20	.50
34 Robert Leask	.20	.50
35 Ricard Persson	.20	.50
36 Nico Pyka	.20	.50
37 David Roberts	.20	.50
38 Rob Shearer	.20	.50
39 Richard Shulmistra	.20	.50
40 Jeff Tomlinson	.20	.50
41 Steve Walker	.20	.50
42 Marc Beaucage	.20	.50
43 Fabian Brannstrom	.20	.50
44 Jeff Christian	.20	.50
45 Neil Eisenhut	.20	.50
46 Jakub Ficenec	.40	1.00
47 Michael Hackert	.20	.50
48 Mathias Hart	.20	.50
49 Tommy Jakobsen	.20	.50
50 Alexander Jung	.20	.50
51 Torsten Kienass	.20	.50
52 Daniel Kreutzer	.20	.50
53 Bernd Kuhnhauser	.20	.50
54 Trond Magnussen	.20	.50
55 Nikolaus Mondt	.20	.50
56 Mike Pellegrims	.20	.50
57 Markus Pottinger	.20	.50
58 Jean-Francois Quintin	.20	.50
60 Andrei Trefilov	.20	.50
61 Martin Ulrich	.20	.50
62 Gerhard Unterluggauer	.20	.50
63 Tore Vikingstad	.20	.50
65 Greg Adams	.20	.50
66 Pascal Appel	.20	.50
67 Michael Bresagk	.20	.50
68 Robert Busch	.20	.50
69 Collin Danielsmeier	.20	.50
70 Jason Dunham	.20	.50
71 Rusty Fitzgerald	.20	.50
72 Marc Fortier	.20	.50
73 Robert Francz	.20	.50
74 Matthias Frenzel	.20	.50
75 Victor Gervais	.20	.50
76 Rick Girard	.20	.50
77 Cory Laylin	.20	.50
78 Stewart Malgunas	.20	.50
79 Jackson Penney	.20	.50
80 Marc Pethke	.20	.50
81 Stephane Richer	.20	.50
82 Dominic Roussel	.40	1.00
83 Christoph Sandner	.20	.50
84 Chris Snell	.20	.50
85 Paul Stanton	.20	.50
86 Jonas Stopfgeshoff	.20	.50
87 Peter Abstreiter	.20	.50
88 Greg Andrusak	.20	.50
89 Ted Crowley	.20	.50
90 Thomas Dolak	.20	.50
91 Ted Drury	.20	.50
92 Bobby House	.20	.50
93 Manuel Kofler	.20	.50
94 Patrick Koppchen	.20	.50
95 Christian Kunast	.20	.50
96 Bob Lachance	.20	.50
97 Jason Miller	.20	.50
98 Jacek Plachta	.20	.50
99 Boris Rousson	.40	1.00
100 Andrew Schneider	.20	.50
101 Heiko Smazal	.20	.50
102 Mike Stevens	.20	.50
103 David Sulkovsky	.20	.50
104 Jeff Tory	.20	.50
105 Christian Volk	.20	.50
106 Phil von Stefenelli	.20	.50
107 Gilbert Dionne	.20	.50
108 Patrick Ehelechner	.20	.50
109 Edvin Frylen	.20	.50
110 Lorenz Funk Jr.	.20	.50
111 Todd Hawkins	.20	.50
112 Stefan Hellkvist	.20	.50
113 Peter Jakobsson	.20	.50
114 Peter Johansson	.20	.50
115 Torbjorn Johansson	.20	.50
116 Jakob Karlsson	.20	.50
117 Sebastian Klenner	.20	.50
118 Mattias Loof	.20	.50
119 Rob Murphy	.20	.50
120 Fredrik Oberg	.20	.50
121 Daniel Reiss	.20	.50
122 Wallace Schreiber	.20	.50
123 Patrick Senger	.20	.50
124 Leonard Soccio	.20	.50
125 Andrew Verner	.20	.50
126 Steve Wilson	.20	.50
127 Chad Allan	.20	.50
128 Mike Bales	.40	1.00
129 Petr Bares	.20	.50
130 Francois Bouchard	.20	.50
131 Brad Burym	.20	.50
132 Terry Campbell	.20	.50
133 Kent Fearns	.20	.50
134 Alexander Genze	.20	.50
135 Erich Goldman	.20	.50
136 Glen Goodall	.40	1.00
137 Samuel Groleau	.20	.50
138 Jean-Francois Jomphe	.20	.50
139 Ilpo Kauhanen	.20	.50
140 Steve Lingren	.20	.50
141 Christoph Melischko	.20	.50
142 Neville Rautert	.20	.50
143 Jason Ruff	.20	.50
144 Reiner Suchan	.20	.50
145 Sean Tallaire	.20	.50
146 Shayne Toporowski	.20	.50
147 Jason Young	.20	.50
148 Igor Alexandrov	.20	.50
149 Doug Ast	.20	.50
150 Christopher Bartolone	.20	.50
151 Colin Beardsmore	.20	.50
152 Oliver Bernhardt	.20	.50
153 Lars Bruggemann	.20	.50
154 Markus Draxler	.20	.50
155 Jorgen Eriksson	.20	.50
156 Petr Fical	.20	.50
157 Christian Franz	.20	.50
158 Carsten Gosdeck	.20	.50
159 Justin Harney	.20	.50
160 Christian Hommel	.20	.50
161 Scott King	.20	.50
162 Lasse Kopitz	.20	.50
163 Dimitrij Kotschnew	.20	.50
164 Chris Lipsett	.20	.50
165 Andrej Podkonicky	.20	.50
166 Roland Verwey	.20	.50
167 Jimmy Waite	.40	1.00
168 Steve Washburn	.20	.50
169 Tobias Abstreiter	.20	.50
170 Gert Acker	.20	.50
171 Frank Appel	.20	.50
172 Alexander Cherbayev	.20	.50
173 Thomas Daffner	.20	.50
174 Doug Deraugh	.20	.50
175 Markus Janka	.20	.50
176 Lars Jonsson	.20	.50
177 Orjan Lindmark	.20	.50
178 Andreas Loth	.20	.50
179 Jeffrey John MacLeod	.20	.50
180 Pat Mikesch	.20	.50
181 Zdenek Nedved	.20	.50
182 Rich Parent	.40	1.00
183 Brent Peterson	.20	.50
184 Stephan Retzer	.20	.50
185 Stéphane Robitaille	.20	.50
186 Alexander Serikow	.20	.50
187 Andrej Teljukin	.20	.50
188 Sven Valenti	.20	.50
189 Mikael Wahlberg	.20	.50
190 Shayne Wright	.20	.50
191 Tino Boos	.20	.50
192 Mickey Elick	.20	.50
193 Sebastian Furchner	.20	.50
194 Alex Hicks	.20	.50
195 Robert Hock	.20	.50
196 Markus Jocher	.20	.50
197 Eduard Lewandowski	.20	.50
198 Mirko Ludemann	.20	.50
199 Dave McLlwain	.20	.50
200 Andreas Morczinietz	.20	.50
201 Frederik Nilsson	.20	.50
202 Dwayne Norris	.20	.50
203 Ron Pasco	.20	.50
204 Shane Peacock	.20	.50
205 Andreas Renz	.20	.50
206 Chris Rogles	.40	1.00
207 Stefan Schauer	.20	.50
208 Brad Schlegel	.20	.50
209 Niklas Sundblad	.20	.50
210 Christoph Ullmann	.20	.50
211 Darcy Werenka	.20	.50
212 Leonard Wild	.20	.50
213 Patrick Augusta	.20	.50
214 Stephane Barin	.20	.50
215 Thomas Brandl	.20	.50
216 Christoph Brandner	.20	.50
217 Mario Doyon	.20	.50
218 Paul Dyck	.20	.50
219 Christian Ehrhoff	1.25	3.00
220 Adrian Grygiel	.20	.50
221 Daniel Kunce	.20	.50
222 Dan Lambert	.20	.50
223 Jonas Lanier	.20	.50
224 Sandy Moger	.20	.50
225 Robert Muller	.20	.50
226 David Musial	.20	.50
227 Roger Nordstrom	.20	.50
228 Gunther Oswald	.20	.50
229 Brad Purdie	.20	.50
230 Andreas Raubal	.20	.50
231 Darryl Shannon	.20	.50
232 Gary Shuchuk	.20	.50
233 Sergej Stas	.20	.50
234 Steffen Ziesche	.20	.50
235 Michael Bakos	.20	.50
236 Rene Corbet	.20	.50
237 Devin Edgerton	.20	.50
238 Sascha Goc	.20	.50
239 Marcel Goc	.75	2.00
240 Francois Groleau	.20	.50
241 Todd Hlushko	.20	.50
242 Wayne Hynes	.20	.50
243 Chris Joseph	.20	.50
244 Steve Junker	.20	.50
245 Klaus Kathan	.20	.50
246 Mike Kennedy	.20	.50
247 Tomas Martinec	.20	.50
248 Anders Myrvold	.20	.50
249 Nick Naumenko	.20	.50
250 Dimitri Patzold	.75	2.00
251 Jason Podollan	.20	.50
252 Yves Racine	.20	.50
253 Andy Roach	.40	1.00
254 Mike Rosati	.40	1.00
255 Yannic Seidenberg	.20	.50
256 Stefan Ustorf	.20	.50
257 Ilja Vorobiev	.20	.50
258 Vitalij Aab	.20	.50
259 Shawn Anderson	.20	.50
260 Frederic Chabot	.75	2.00
261 Kevin Dahl	.20	.50
262 Ivan Droppa	.20	.50
263 Thomas Greilinger	.20	.50
264 Robert Guillet	.20	.50
265 Martin Jiranek	.20	.50
266 Steve Larouche	.20	.50
267 Guy Lehoux	.20	.50
268 Christopher Luongo	.20	.50
269 Martin Reichel	.20	.50
270 Jurgen Rumrich	.20	.50
271 Marc Savard	.20	.50
272 Thomas Schinko	.20	.50
273 Christian Schonmoser	.20	.50
274 Marc Seliger	.20	.50
275 Martin Sychra	.20	.50
276 Dave Tomlinson	.20	.50
277 Terry Yake	.20	.50
278 Paul Brousseau	.20	.50
279 Markus Busch	.20	.50
280 Dave Chyzowski	.20	.50
281 Alexander Duck	.20	.50
282 Mark Etz	.20	.50
283 Francois Fortier	.20	.50
284 Ian Gordon	.20	.50
285 Eric Houde	.20	.50
286 Ladislav Karabin	.20	.50
287 Steffen Karg	.20	.50
288 Rainer Kosttstorfer	.20	.50
289 Christian Kohmann	.20	.50
290 Alexander Kuzminski	.20	.50
291 Neal Martin	.20	.50
292 Jochen Molling	.20	.50
293 Curtis Sheptak	.20	.50
294 Vadim Slivchenko	.20	.50
295 Ralf Stark	.20	.50
296 Jens Stramkowski	.20	.50
297 Mathias Svedberg	.20	.50
298 Lukas Zib	.20	.50

2002-03 German DEL City Press All Stars

We have no pricing information on this series.

COMPLETE SET (16)
AS1 Alex Hicks
AS2 Vitalij Aab
AS3 David Cooper
AS4 Magnus Eriksson
AS5 Robert Muller
AS6 Mike Pellegrims
AS7 Stephane Richer
AS8 Chris Snell
AS9 Jeff Tory
AS10 Robert Hock
AS11 Thomas Martinec
AS12 Frederik Oberg
AS13 Brad Purdie
AS14 Andrew Schneider
AS15 Paul Stanton
AS16 Terry Yake

2002-03 German DEL City Press Top Scorers

We have no pricing information on this series.

COMPLETE SET (10)
TS1 Christoph Brandner
TS2 Vadim Slivchenko
TS3 Robert Guillet
TS4 Andreas Morczinietz
TS5 Leonard Soccio
TS6 Marc Fortier
TS7 Sean Tallaire
TS8 David Roberts
TS9 Trond Magnussen
TS10 Stefan Ustorf

2002-03 German DEL City Press Top Stars

We have no pricing information on this series.

COMPLETE SET (10)
GT1 Marc Seliger
GT2 Tobias Abstreiter
GT3 Christian Ehrhoff
GT4 Jurgen Rumrich
GT5 Mirko Ludemann
GT6 Christian Kunast
GT7 Sven Felski
GT8 Daniel Kreutzer
GT9 Wayne Hynes
GT10 Klaus Kathan

2003-04 German Berlin Polar Bears Postcards

COMPLETE SET (31)	10.00	25.00
1 Keith Aldridge	.40	1.00
2 Nils Antons	.40	1.00
3 Alex Barta	.40	1.00
4 Jens Baxmann	.40	1.00
5 Mark Beaufait	.40	1.00
6 Brad Bergen	.40	1.00
7 Florian Busch	.40	1.00
8 Yvon Corriveau	.40	1.00
9 Tobias Draxinger	.40	1.00
10 Micki DuPont	.40	1.00
11 Kelly Fairchild	.40	1.00
12 Sven Felski	.40	1.00
13 Tom Fiedler	.40	1.00
14 Patrick Flynn	.40	1.00
15 Mathias Forster	.40	1.00
16 Martin Hoffmann	.40	1.00
17 Frank Hordler	.40	1.00
18 Oliver Jonas	.40	1.00
19 Florian Keller	.40	1.00
20 Rob Leask	.40	1.00
21 Hartmut Nickel	.40	1.00
22 Pierre Page CO	.40	1.00
23 Rich Parent	.75	2.00
24 Denis Pederson	.40	1.00
25 Ricard Persson	.40	1.00
26 Andre Rankel	.40	1.00
27 David Roberts	.40	1.00
28 Darryl Shannon	.40	1.00
29 Rob Shearer	.40	1.00
30 Jeff Tomlinson	.40	1.00
31 Steve Walker	.40	1.00

2003-04 German Deg Metro Stars

This was a team-issued set featuring a club from the top German league.

COMPLETE SET (23)	10.00	20.00
1 Fabian Brannstrom	.40	1.00
2 Christian Brittig	.40	1.00
3 Mathias Hart	.40	1.00
4 Tommy Jakobsen	.40	1.00
5 Thomas Jorg	.40	1.00
6 Alexander Jung	.40	1.00
7 Florian Jung	.40	1.00
8 Walter Koberle	.40	1.00
9 Michael Komma	.40	1.00
10 Daniel Kreutzer	.40	1.00
11 Bobo Kuhnhauser	.40	1.00
12 Trond Magnussen	.40	1.00
13 Pat Mikesch	.40	1.00
14 Johan Molin	.40	1.00
15 Mike Pellegrims	.40	1.00
16 Markus Pottinger	.40	1.00
17 Alexander Sulzer	.40	1.00
18 Jeff Tory	.40	1.00
19 Andrej Trefilov	.40	1.00
20 Martin Ulrich	.40	1.00
21 Gerhard Unterluggauer	.40	1.00
22 Tore Vikingstad	.40	1.00
23 Clayton Young	.40	1.00

2003-04 German DEL

COMPLETE SET (210)	15.00	40.00
1 Rene Corbet	.10	.25
2 Devin Edgerton	.10	.25
3 Sascha Goc	.10	.25
4 Francois Groleau	.10	.25
5 Robert Hock	.10	.25
6 Chris Joseph	.10	.25
7 Klaus Kathan	.10	.25
8 Tomas Martinec	.10	.25
9 Jochen Molling	.10	.25
10 Derek Plante	.10	.25
11 Jason Podollan	.10	.25
12 Andy Roach	.20	.50
13 Marc Seliger	.10	.25
14 Richard Shulmistra	.10	.25
15 Christoph Ullmann	.10	.25
16 Ronny Arendt	.10	.25
17 Bjorn Barta	.10	.25
18 Colin Beardsmore	.10	.25
19 Shawn Carter	.10	.25
20 Eric Dandenault	.10	.25
21 Xavier Delisle	.10	.25
22 Magnus Eriksson	.10	.25
23 Francois Fortier	.10	.25
24 Rick Girard	.10	.25
25 John Miner	.10	.25
26 Duanne Moeser	.10	.25
27 Arvids Rekis	.10	.25
28 Marc Savard	.10	.25
29 Andrej Strakhov	.10	.25
30 Bob Wren	.10	.25
31 Fabian Brannstrom	.10	.25
32 Christian Brittig	.10	.25
33 Tommy Jakobsen	.10	.25
34 Alexander Jung	.10	.25
35 Daniel Kreutzer	.10	.25
36 Trond Magnussen	.10	.25
37 Pat Mikesch	.10	.25
38 Mike Pellegrims	.10	.25
39 Marcus Thuresson	.10	.25
40 Jeff Tory	.10	.25
41 Andrej Trefilov	.10	.25
42 Martin Ulrich	.10	.25
43 Gerhard Unterluggauer	.10	.25
44 Tore Vikingstad	.10	.25
45 Clayton Young	.10	.25
46 Peter Boon	.10	.25
47 Dany Bousquet	.10	.25
48 Olivier Coqueux	.10	.25
49 David Danner	.10	.25
50 Juraj Faith	.10	.25
51 Dusan Frosch	.10	.25
52 Rudolf Gorgenlander	.10	.25
53 Rostislav Haas	.10	.25
54 Henrik Holscher	.10	.25
55 Thomas Jetter	.10	.25
56 Ravil Khaidarov	.10	.25
57 Vadim Slivchenko	.10	.25
58 Sergej Stas	.10	.25
59 Bastian Steingross	.10	.25
60 Jiri Zelenka	.10	.25
61 Keith Aldridge	.10	.25
62 Alexander Barta	.10	.25
63 Mark Beaufait	.10	.25
64 Micki Dupont	.10	.25
65 Kelly Fairchild	.10	.25
66 Sven Felski	.10	.25
67 Oliver Jonas	.10	.25
68 Florian Keller	.10	.25
69 Robert Leask	.10	.25
70 Rich Parent	.40	1.00
71 Denis Pederson	.10	.25
72 Ricard Persson	.10	.25
73 David Roberts	.10	.25
74 Rob Shearer	.10	.25
75 Steve Walker	.10	.25
76 Doug Ast	.10	.25
77 Craig Ferguson	.10	.25
78 Jakub Ficenec	.20	.50
79 Glenn Goodall	.40	1.00
80 Samuel Groleau	.10	.25
81 Justin Harney	.10	.25
82 Cameron Mann	.40	1.00
83 Nikolaus Mondt	.10	.25
84 Gunther Oswald	.10	.25
85 Yves Racine	.10	.25
86 Thomas Schinko	.10	.25
87 Ken Sutton	.10	.25
88 Sean Tallaire	.10	.25
89 Phil von Stefenelli	.10	.25
90 Jimmy Waite	.40	1.00
91 Christian Kohmann	.10	.25
92 Jesse Belanger	.10	.25
93 Francois Bouchard	.10	.25
94 Michael Bresagk	.10	.25
95 Ian Gordon	.10	.25
96 David Gosselin	.10	.25
97 Michael Hackert	.10	.25
98 Mike Harder	.10	.25
99 Sebastian Klenner	.10	.25
100 Patrick Lebeau	.40	1.00
101 Dwayne Norris	.10	.25
102 Peter Ratchuk	.10	.25
103 Martin Reichel	.10	.25
104 Paul Stanton	.10	.25
105 Jason Young	.10	.25
106 Darren van Impe	.10	.25
107 Mark Greig	.10	.25
108 Robert House	.10	.25
109 Wayne Hynes	.10	.25
110 Christian Kunast	.10	.25
111 Patrick Koppchen	.10	.25
112 Dan Lambert	.10	.25
113 Paul Manning	.10	.25
114 Shane Peacock	.10	.25
115 Jacek Plachta	.10	.25
116 Brad Purdie	.10	.25
117 Boris Rousson	.40	1.00
118 Andrew Schneider	.10	.25
119 Heiko Smazal	.10	.25
120 Dave Tomlinson	.10	.25
121 Patrik Augusta	.10	.25
122 Bjorn Bombis	.10	.25
123 Jeff Christian	.10	.25
124 Gordon Borberg	.10	.25
125 Edvin Frylen	.10	.25
126 Lorenz Funk	.10	.25
127 David Haas	.10	.25
128 Peter Jakobsson	.10	.25
129 Ilpo Kauhanen	.10	.25
130 Mattias Loof	.10	.25
131 Zdenek Nedved	.10	.25
132 Frederik Oberg	.10	.25
133 Leonard Soccio	.10	.25
134 Andrej Teljukin	.10	.25
135 Steve Wilson	.10	.25
136 David Cooper	.10	.25
137 Bryan Adams	.10	.25
138 Chris Bartolone	.10	.25
139 James Black	.10	.25
140 Lars Bruggemann	.10	.25
141 Jason Cipolla	.10	.25
142 Michael Fountain	.10	.25
143 Erich Goldmann	.10	.25
144 Matt Henderson	.10	.25
145 Matt Higgins	.10	.25
146 Christian Hommel	.10	.25
147 Scott King	.10	.25
148 Dimitrij Kotschnew	.10	.25
149 Rob Sandrock	.10	.25
150 Roland Verwey	.10	.25
151 Tobias Abstreiter	.10	.25
152 Paul Brousseau	.10	.25
153 Ted Crowley	.10	.25
154 Josh DeWolf	.10	.25
155 Ted Drury	.10	.25
156 Joaquin Gage	.10	.25
157 Orjan Lindmark	.10	.25
158 Andreas Loth	.10	.25
159 Jeff MacLeod	.10	.25
160 Brent Peterson	.10	.25
161 Stephan Retzer	.10	.25
162 Stephane Robitaille	.10	.25
163 Alexander Serikow	.10	.25
164 Matthias Trattnig	.10	.25
165 Mikael Wahlberg	.10	.25
166 Jeremy Adduono	.10	.25
167 Tino Boos	.10	.25
168 Jeff Dessner	.10	.25
169 Mickey Elick	.10	.25
170 Sebastian Furchner	.10	.25
171 Alex Hicks	.10	.25
172 Mirko Ludemann	.10	.25
173 Eduard Lewandowski	.10	.25
174 Dave McLlwain	.10	.25
175 Andreas Morczinietz	.10	.25
176 Andreas Renz	.10	.25
177 Chris Rogles	.10	.25
178 Jean-Yves Roy	.10	.25
179 Brad Schlegel	.10	.25
180 Leo Stefan	.10	.25
181 Pascal Appel	.10	.25
182 Marc Beaucage	.10	.25
183 Eric Bertrand	.10	.25
184 Adrian Grygiel	.10	.25
185 Robert Guillet	.10	.25
186 Christopher Kelleher	.10	.25
187 Daniel Kunce	.10	.25
188 Justin Kurtz	.10	.25
189 Chris Luongo	.10	.25
190 Robert Muller	.10	.25
191 Alexander Selivanov	.10	.25
192 Stefan Ustorf	.10	.25
193 Shayne Wright	.10	.25
194 Terry Yake	.10	.25
195 Steffen Ziesche	.10	.25
196 Vitalij Aab	.10	.25
197 Frederic Chabot	.40	1.00
198 Marian Cisar	.10	.25
199 Petr Fical	.10	.25
200 Liam Garvey	.10	.25
201 Thomas Greilinger	.10	.25
202 Martin Jiranek	.10	.25
203 Stephane Julien	.10	.25
204 Lasse Kopitz	.10	.25
205 Steve Larouche	.10	.25
206 Greg Leeb	.20	.50
207 Guy Lehoux	.10	.25
208 Alfie Michaud	.10	.25
209 Yan Stastny ERC	1.25	3.00
210 Robert Tomik	.10	.25

2003-04 German DEL All-Stars

COMPLETE SET (22)	15.00	30.00
AS1 Jimmy Waite	1.25	3.00
AS2 Andrej Trefilov	1.25	3.00
AS3 Chris Rogles	1.25	3.00
AS4 Justin Harney	.75	2.00
AS5 Paul Stanton	.75	2.00
AS6 Andy Roach	1.25	3.00
AS7 Christoph Brandner	.75	2.00
AS8 Dwayne Norris	.75	2.00
AS9 Francois Fortier	.75	2.00
AS10 Philippe Audet	.75	2.00
AS11 Doug Ast	.75	2.00
AS12 Brad Purdie	.75	2.00
AS13 Kelly Fairchild	.75	2.00
AS14 Wally Schreiber	.75	2.00
AS15 Terry Yake	.75	2.00
AS16 Jean-Francois Jomphe	.75	2.00
AS17 Andrew Schneider	.75	2.00
AS18 Tommy Jakobsen	.75	2.00
AS19 Dave McLlwain	.75	2.00
AS20 Trond Magnussen	.75	2.00
AS21 Shawn Anderson	.75	2.00
AS22 Jeff Tory	.75	2.00

2003-04 German Mannheim Eagles Postcards

These 4X6 postcards were issued by the team in set form. All cards are autographed by the players, although the Sachar Blank autograph was scratched out in our set. Perhaps the auto was determined to have been signed by someone else???

COMPLETE SET (29)	30.00	75.00
1 Richard Shulmistra	1.50	4.00
2 Marc Seliger	1.50	4.00
3 Marco Schutz	1.50	4.00
4 Sachar Blank	.40	1.00
5 Yannic Seidenberg	1.50	4.00
6 Bill Stewart	1.50	4.00
7 Christoph Ullmann	1.50	4.00
8 Stefan Ustorf	1.50	4.00
9 Rico Rossi	1.50	4.00
10 Andy Roach	2.50	6.00
11 Yves Racine	1.50	4.00
12 Nico Pyka	1.50	4.00
13 Jason Podollan	2.50	6.00
14 Derek Plante	2.50	6.00
15 Jochen Molling	1.50	4.00
16 Tomas Martinec	1.50	4.00
17 Mike Kennedy	1.50	4.00
18 Klaus Kathan	1.50	4.00
19 Steve Junker	1.50	4.00
20 Chris Joseph	1.50	4.00
21 Robert Hock	1.50	4.00
22 Todd Hlushko	1.50	4.00
23 Francois Groleau	1.50	4.00
24 Sascha Goc	1.50	4.00
25 Devin Edgerton	1.50	4.00
26 Rene Corbet	1.50	4.00
27 Fabio Carciola	1.50	4.00
28 Michael Bakos	1.50	4.00
29 Danny Aus Den Birken	1.50	4.00
30 Marc Bruns	1.50	4.00
31 Markus Koch	1.50	4.00
32 Andy Roach	2.50	6.00
33 Christoph Ullmann	1.50	4.00

2003-04 German Nuremberg Ice Tigers Postcards

These 4X6 postcards were issued in set form by the team. They are unnumbered and listed below in alphabetical order.

COMPLETE SET (26)	10.00	25.00
1 Vitalij Aab	.40	1.00
2 Benjamin Barz	.40	1.00
3 Frederic Chabot	1.25	3.00
4 Marian Cisar	.40	1.00
5 Kevin Dahl	.40	1.00
6 Jon DiSalvatore	.40	1.00
7 Petr Fical	.40	1.00
8 Konstantin Firsanov	.40	1.00
9 Liam Garvey	.40	1.00
10 Thomas Greilinger	.40	1.00
11 Tobias Guttner	.40	1.00
12 Martin Jiranek	.40	1.00
13 Stephane Julien	.40	1.00
14 Lasse Kopitz	.40	1.00
15 Steve Larouche	.40	1.00
16 Greg Leeb	.75	2.00
17 Guy Lehoux	.40	1.00
18 Josef Menauer	.40	1.00
19 Alfie Michaud	.40	1.00
20 Sebastian Osterloh	.40	1.00
21 Felix Petermann	.40	1.00
22 Greg Poss	.40	1.00
23 Jurgen Rumrich	.40	1.00
24 Christian Schonmoser	.40	1.00
25 Otto Sykora GM	.40	1.00
26 Robert Tomik	.40	1.00

2004-05 German Augsburg Panthers Postcards

These cards are unnumbered and so are listed below in alphabetical order.

COMPLETE SET (27)	10.00	25.00
1 Pascal Appel	.40	1.00
2 Ronny Arendt	.40	1.00
3 Steve Bancroft	.40	1.00
4 Bjorn Barta	.40	1.00
5 Rich Brennan	.40	1.00
6 Robert Brezina	.40	1.00
7 Marc Brown	.40	1.00
8 Robert Busch	.40	1.00
9 Shawn Carter	.40	1.00
10 David Danner	.40	1.00
11 Dennis Endras	.40	1.00
12 Brian Felsner	.40	1.00
13 Torsten Fendt	.40	1.00
14 Francois Fortier	.40	1.00
15 Rick Girard	.40	1.00
16 Manuel Kopfler	.40	1.00
17 Jean-Francois Labbe	.75	2.00
18 Benoit Laporte CO	.20	.50
19 Roland Mayr	.40	1.00
20 Francois Methot	.40	1.00
21 John Miner	.40	1.00
22 Duanne Moeser	.40	1.00
23 Mike Pudlick	.40	1.00
24 Daniel Rau	.40	1.00
25 Arvids Rekis	.40	1.00
26 Steffen Tolzer	.40	1.00
27 Benjamin Voigt	.40	1.00

2004-05 German Berlin Eisbarens 50th Anniversary

Standard-sized card set features top players from the past and present of Germany's most famous team.

COMPLETE SET (75)	15.00	30.00
1 Header	.02	.10
2 Mike Losch	.20	.50
3 Dave Morrison	.20	.50
4 Roland Peters	.20	.50
5 Mario Plack	.20	.50
6 Joachim Stasche	.20	.50
7 Detlef Radant	.20	.50
8 Pelle Svensson	.20	.50
9 Egon Schmeisser	.20	.50
10 Klaus Merk	.20	.50

11 Rainer Patschinski .20 .50
12 Franz Steer .20 .50
13 Sergej Jaschin .20 .50
14 Steffen Ziesche .20 .50
15 Wolfgang Kraske .20 .50
16 Torsten Deutscher .20 .50
17 Magnus Roupe .20 .50
18 Heinz Pohland .20 .50
19 Mark Jooris .20 .50
20 Wolfgang Beuthner .20 .50
21 Uwe Geisert .20 .50
22 Rene Bielke .20 .50
23 Reinhard Fengler .20 .50
24 Dietmar Peters .20 .50
25 Helmut Senftleben .20 .50
26 Peter Prusa .20 .50
27 Thomas Swibenko .20 .50
28 Marc Fortier .20 .50
29 Andre Dietzch .20 .50
30 Holger Mix .20 .50
31 Werner Thomas .20 .50
32 Hanne Frenzel .20 .50
33 Thomas Milew .20 .50
34 Jeff Tomlinson .20 .50
35 Fred Freitag .20 .50
36 Bernd Karrenbauer .20 .50
37 Friedhelm Bogelsack .20 .50
38 Thomas Graul .20 .50
39 Sven Felski .20 .50
40 Dirk Perschau .20 .50
41 Gerhard Muller .20 .50
42 Jurgen Schmutzler .20 .50
43 Wilhelm Kopatz .20 .50
44 Dieter Janke .20 .50
45 Jurgen Geisert .20 .50
46 Rob Cowie .20 .50
47 Dieter Dewitz .20 .50
48 Joachim Lempio .20 .50
49 Leif Carlsson .20 .50
50 Joachim Hurbanek .20 .50
51 Gerhard Klugel .20 .50
52 Udo Dohler .20 .50
53 Frank Proske .20 .50
54 Wolfgang Plotka .20 .50
55 Hartmut Nickel .20 .50
56 Andrew McKim .20 .50
57 Jens Ziesche .20 .50
58 Wilfried Rohrbach .20 .50
59 Dieter Frenzel .20 .50
60 Jurgen Breitschuh .20 .50
61 Peter-John Lee .20 .50
62 Mike Bullard .20 .50
63 Guido Hiller .20 .50
64 Gunther Katzur .20 .50
65 Peter Lehnigk .20 .50
66 Matthias Dietz .20 .50
67 Harald Kuhnke .20 .50
68 Frank Krause .20 .50
69 Joachim Ziesche .20 .50
70 Dieter Voigt .20 .50
71 Thomas Steen .20 .50
72 Daniel Held .20 .50
73 Derek Mayer .20 .50
74 Nico Pyka .20 .50
75 Checklist .02 .10

2004-05 German Berlin Polar Bears Postcards

These cards are unnumbered and are listed below in alphabetical order.

COMPLETE SET (32) 10.00 25.00
1 Alexander Barta .30 .75
2 Jens Baxmann .30 .75
3 Mark Beaufait .30 .75
4 Florian Busch .30 .75
5 Erik Cole .75 2.00
6 Nathan Dempsey .40 1.00
7 Tobias Draxinger .30 .75
8 Danier Dshunussow .30 .75
9 Micki Dupont .40 1.00
10 Kelly Fairchild .40 1.00
11 Sven Felski .30 .75
12 Christoph Gawlik .30 .75
13 Shawn Heins .40 1.00
14 Martin Hoffmann .30 .75
15 Frank Hordler .30 .75
16 Kay Hurbanek .30 .75
17 Oliver Jonas .30 .75
18 Florian Keller .30 .75
19 Olaf Kolzig 2.00 5.00
20 Rob Leask .30 .75
21 Hartmut Nickel ACO .10 .25
22 Pierre Page CO .10 .25
23 Denis Pederson .40 1.00
24 Ricard Persson .30 .75
25 Andre Rankel .30 .75
26 Rob Shearer .30 .75
27 Stefan Ustorf .30 .75
28 Steve Walker .30 .75
29 Derrick Walser .40 1.00
30 Yourri Ziffzer .30 .75
31 Bully MASCOT .40 1.00
32 Team Photo .10 .25

2004-05 German Cologne Sharks Postcards

The cards are unnumbered, so they are listed below alphabetically.

COMPLETE SET (28) 10.00 25.00
1 Jeremy Adduono .40 1.00
2 Colin Beardsmore .40 1.00
3 Markus Berwanger CO .10 .25
4 Dan Bjornlie .40 1.00
5 Boris Blank .40 1.00
6 Tino Boos .40 1.00
7 Jon Coleman .40 1.00
8 Thomas Fischer .40 1.00
9 Sebastian Furchner .40 1.00
10 Philip Gogulla .40 1.00
11 Thomas Greiss .40 1.00
12 Mattias Hart .40 1.00
13 Alex Hicks .40 1.00
14 Kai Hospelt .40 1.00
15 Michael Hrstka .40 1.00

16 Stephane Julien .40 1.00
17 Eduard Lewandowski .40 1.00
18 Mirko Ludemann .40 1.00
19 Dave McLlwain .40 1.00
20 Rupert Meister ACO .10 .25
21 Moritz Muller .40 1.00
22 Andreas Renz .40 1.00
23 Chris Rogles .60 1.50
24 Jean-Yves Roy .40 1.00
25 Brad Schlegel .40 1.00
26 Yannic Seidenberg .40 1.00
27 Paul Traynor .40 1.00
28 Hans Zach CO .10 .25

2004-05 German DEL

COMPLETE SET (283) 25.00 50.00
1 Vitalij Aab .10 .25
2 Danny aus den Birken .10 .25
3 Michael Bakos .10 .25
4 Sven Butenschon .10 .25
5 Rene Corbet .20 .50
6 Andy Delmore .20 .50
7 Devin Edgerton .10 .25
8 Sascha Goc .20 .50
9 Francois Groleau .10 .25
10 Eric Healey .20 .50
11 Jochen Hecht .40 1.00
12 Christopher Joseph .10 .25
13 Steve Kelly .10 .25
14 Markus Kink .10 .25
15 Derek Plante .10 .25
16 Jason Podollan .10 .25
17 Nico Pyka .10 .25
18 John Tripp .10 .25
19 Cristobal Huet 1.25 3.00
20 Thomas Greilinger .10 .25
21 Christoph Ullmann .10 .25
22 Ronny Arendt .10 .25
23 Bjorn Barta .10 .25
24 Robert Brezina .10 .25
25 Marc Brown .10 .25
26 Shawn Carter .10 .25
27 Brian Felsner .10 .25
28 Thorsten Fendt .10 .25
29 Francois Fortier .10 .25
30 Rick Girard .10 .25
31 Manuel Kofler .10 .25
32 Jean Francois Labbe .20 .50
33 Roland Mayr .10 .25
34 Francois Methot .10 .25
35 John Miner .10 .25
36 Duanne Moeser .10 .25
37 Arvids Rekis .10 .25
38 Steve Bancroft .10 .25
39 Mike Pudlick .10 .25
40 David Danner .10 .25
41 Daniel Rau .10 .25
42 Christian Brittig .10 .25
43 Fabian Brannstrom .10 .25
44 Eric Dandenault .10 .25
45 Matt Davidson .10 .25
46 Matt Herr .20 .50
47 Tommy Jakobsen .10 .25
48 Alexander Jung .10 .25
49 Klaus Kathan .10 .25
50 Bernd Kuhnhauser .10 .25
51 Daniel Kreutzer .10 .25
52 Trond Magnussen .10 .25
53 Mike Pellegrims .10 .25
54 Andrew Schneider .10 .25
55 Jeff Tory .10 .25
56 Andrej Trefilov .20 .50
57 Martin Ulrich .10 .25
58 Tore Vikingstad .10 .25
59 Clayton Young .10 .25
60 Florian Jung .10 .25
61 Alexander Sulzer .10 .25
62 Jens Baxmann .10 .25
63 Mark Beaufait .10 .25
64 Tobias Draxinger .10 .25
65 Micki DuPont .20 .50
66 Kelly Fairchild .20 .50
67 Sven Felski .10 .25
68 Shawn Heins .20 .50
69 Frank Hordler .10 .25
70 Oliver Jonas .10 .25
71 Florian Keller .10 .25
72 Robert Leask .10 .25
73 Denis Pederson .10 .25
74 Ricard Persson .10 .25
75 Rob Shearer .10 .25
76 Stefan Ustorf .10 .25
77 Steve Walker .10 .25
78 Derrick Walser .20 .50
79 Youri Ziffzer .10 .25
80 Alexander Barta .10 .25
81 Florian Busch .10 .25
82 Chris Armstrong .10 .25
83 Doug Ast .20 .50
84 Brad Burym .10 .25
85 Craig Ferguson .10 .25
86 Jakub Ficenec .20 .50
87 Glenn Goodall .20 .50
88 Justin Harney .10 .25
89 Martin Jiranek .10 .25
90 Andreas Loth .10 .25
91 Cameron Mann .40 1.00
92 Nikolaus Mondt .10 .25
93 Gunther Oswald .10 .25
94 Aleksander Polaczek .10 .25
95 Marco Sturm .40 1.00
96 Ken Sutton .10 .25
97 Phil von Stefenelli .10 .25
98 Jimmy Waite .20 .50
99 Andy McDonald .40 1.00
100 Daniel Hilpert .10 .25
101 Christoph Melischko .10 .25
102 Boris Ackers .10 .25
103 Marc Beaucage .10 .25
104 Francois Bouchard .10 .25
105 Mihael Bresagk .10 .25
106 Ian Gordon .10 .25
107 Markus Jocher .10 .25
108 Sebastian Klenner .10 .25
109 Christian Kohmann .10 .25
110 Patrick Lebeau .20 .50
111 Mikael Magnusson .10 .25
112 Dwayne Norris .10 .25
113 Sean Pronger .10 .25
114 Peter Ratchuk .10 .25
115 Martin Reichel .10 .25
116 Andrej Strakhov .10 .25
117 David Sulkovsky .10 .25
118 Jason Young .10 .25
119 Stephane Robidas .20 .50
120 Michael Hackert .10 .25
121 Neville Rautert .10 .25
122 Nils Antons .10 .25
123 Robert Francz .10 .25
124 Robert House .10 .25
125 Wayne Hynes .10 .25
126 Craig Johnson .10 .25
127 Alan Letang .10 .25
128 Paul Manning .10 .25
129 Jochen Molling .10 .25
130 Shane Peacock .10 .25
131 Jacek Plachta .10 .25
132 Brad Purdie .10 .25
133 Brandon Reid .40 1.00
134 Boris Rousson .40 1.00
135 Jurgen Rumrich .10 .25
136 Heiko Smazal .10 .25
137 Dave Tomlinson .10 .25
138 Darren van Impe .10 .25
139 Leonhard Wild .10 .25
140 Jim Dowd .20 .50
141 Christopher Oravec .10 .25
142 Martin Walter .10 .25
143 Petr Abstreiter .10 .25
144 Patrick Augusta .10 .25
145 Gordon Borberg .10 .25
146 Lars Bruggemann .10 .25
147 Jason Cipolla .10 .25
148 Thomas Dolak .10 .25
149 Edvin Frylen .10 .25
150 Robert Hock .10 .25
151 Christian Kunast .10 .25
152 Lipo Kauhanen .10 .25
153 Patrick Koppchen .10 .25
154 Dan Lambert .10 .25
155 Andreas Morczinietz .10 .25
156 Frederik Oberg .10 .25
157 Len Soccio .10 .25
158 Andrej Teljukin .10 .25
159 Steve Wilson .10 .25
160 Michael Nemirovski .10 .25
161 Rene Rothke .10 .25
162 Benedikt Schopper .10 .25
163 Bryan Adams .10 .25
164 Igor Alexandrov .10 .25
165 Oliver Bernhardt .10 .25
166 Leonardo Conti .10 .25
167 Collin Danielsmeier .10 .25
168 Sven Gerbig .10 .25
169 Erich Goldmann .10 .25
170 Rhett Gordon .10 .25
171 Matt Higgins .20 .50
172 Ralph Intranuovo .20 .50
173 Martin Knold .10 .25
174 Dimitrij Kotschew .10 .25
175 Brett Lysak .10 .25
176 Mike Martin .10 .25
177 Kevin Mitchell .10 .25
178 Roland Verwey .10 .25
179 Brian White .10 .25
180 Mike York .20 .50
181 Mark Etz .10 .25
182 Franz Fritzmeier .10 .25
183 Tobias Abstreiter .10 .25
184 Gert Acker .10 .25
185 Dany Bousquet .20 .50
186 Daniel Corso .10 .25
187 Kirk Furey .10 .25
188 Joaquin Gage .20 .50
189 David Gosselin .10 .25
190 Christian Hommel .10 .25
191 Sebastian Jones .10 .25
192 Mark Greig .10 .25
193 Christian Laflamme .10 .25
194 Jan Munster .10 .25
195 Dean Melanson .10 .25
196 Alexander Serikow .10 .25
197 Brian Swanson .10 .25
198 Martin Sychra .10 .25
199 Sven Valenti .10 .25
200 Nick Schultz .20 .50
201 Stephan Retzer .10 .25
202 Petr Macholda .10 .25
203 Christian Retzer .10 .25
204 Jeremy Adduono .20 .50
205 Colin Beardsmore .10 .25
206 Dan Bjornlie .10 .25
207 Boris Blank .10 .25
208 Tino Boos .10 .25
209 Thomas Fischer .10 .25
210 Thomas Greiss .20 .50
211 Matthias Hart .10 .25
212 Alex Hicks .10 .25
213 Stephane Julien .10 .25
214 Mirko Ludemann .10 .25
215 Eduard Lewandowski .10 .25
216 Dave McLlwain .10 .25
217 Andreas Renz .10 .25
218 Chris Rogles .20 .50
219 Jean-Yves Roy .10 .25
220 Brad Schlegel .10 .25
221 Leo Stefan .10 .25
222 Yannic Seidenberg .10 .25
223 Sebastian Furchner .10 .25
224 Steve Brule .10 .25
225 Alexander Dueck .10 .25
226 Paul Dyck .10 .25
227 Carsten Gosdeck .10 .25
228 Robert Guillet .10 .25
229 Chris Herperger .10 .25
230 Christian Rhode .10 .25
231 Ivo Jan .10 .25
232 Markus Janka .10 .25
233 Scott King .10 .25
234 Daniel Kunce .10 .25
235 Justin Kurtz .10 .25
236 Guy Lehoux .10 .25
237 Robert Muller .10 .25
238 Florian Schnitzer .10 .25
239 Alexander Selivanov .10 .25
240 Shayne Wright .10 .25
241 Steffen Ziesche .10 .25
242 Adrian Grygiel .10 .25
243 Rainer Koltstorfer .10 .25
244 Drew Bannister .10 .25
245 Benjamin Barz .10 .25
246 Petr Fical .10 .25
247 Konstantin Firsanov .10 .25
248 Christian Franz .10 .25
249 Mike Green .10 .25
250 Lasse Kopitz .10 .25
251 Greg Leeb .10 .25
252 Tomas Martinec .10 .25
253 Ulrich Maurer .10 .25
254 Josef Menauer .10 .25
255 Stefan Schauer .10 .25
256 Lubomir Sekeras .10 .25
257 Yan Stastny 1.25 3.00
258 Adam Svoboda .20 .50
259 Sean Tallaire .10 .25
260 Brad Tapper .20 .50
261 Pascal Trepanier .20 .50
262 Bjorn Bombis .10 .25
263 Felix Petermann .10 .25
264 Ivan Ciernik .10 .25
265 Dale Clarke .10 .25
266 Xavier Delisle .10 .25
267 Alexander Genze .10 .25
268 Ladislav Karabin .10 .25
269 Andrej Kaufmann .10 .25
270 Boris Lingemann .10 .25
271 Per-Anton Lundstrom .10 .25
272 Marek Mastic .10 .25
273 David Musial .10 .25
274 Christoph Paepke .10 .25
275 Richard Pavlikovsky .10 .25
276 Marc Seliger .10 .25
277 Todd Simon .10 .25
278 Peter Smrek .10 .25
279 Rainer Suchan .10 .25
280 Roman Veber .10 .25
281 Jan Zurek .10 .25
282 Markus Guggemos .10 .25
283 Tobias Samendinger .10 .25
NNO Deutscher Meister 2004 Frankfurt Lions 4.00 10.00

2004-05 German DEL All-Stars

COMPLETE SET (19) 15.00 30.00
AS1 Jimmy Waite 2.00 5.00
AS2 Andrej Trefilov .75 2.00
AS3 Stephane Julien .75 2.00
AS4 Ricard Persson .75 2.00
AS5 Peter Ratchuk .75 2.00
AS6 Jakub Ficenec 1.25 3.00
AS7 Mike Pellegrims .75 2.00
AS8 John Miner .75 2.00
AS9 Cameron Mann 1.25 3.00
AS10 Marian Cisar .75 2.00
AS11 Ted Drury .75 2.00
AS12 Rene Corbet .75 2.00
AS13 Kelly Fairchild .75 2.00
AS14 Danny Bousquet .75 2.00
AS15 Patrick Augusta .75 2.00
AS16 Alexander Selivanov .75 2.00
AS17 Dave McLlwain .75 2.00
AS18 Brad Purdie .75 2.00
AS19 Scott King .75 2.00

2004-05 German DEL Global Players

COMPLETE SET (5) 10.00 20.00
GP1 Olaf Kolzig 4.00 10.00
GP2 Christian Ehrhoff 1.25 3.00
GP3 Jochen Hecht 1.25 3.00
GP4 Marco Sturm 1.25 3.00
GP5 Dennis Seidenberg 1.25 3.00
GP6 Checklist .40 1.00

2004-05 German DEL Superstars

COMPLETE SET (23) 20.00 40.00
SU01 Sven Butenschön .75 2.00
SU02 Jochen Hecht 1.25 3.00
SU03 Cristobal Huet 2.00 5.00
SU04 Yannick Tremblay .75 2.00
SU05 Erik Cole 1.25 3.00
SU06 Olaf Kölzig 2.00 5.00
SU07 Nathan Dempsey .75 2.00
SU08 Stephane Robidas .75 2.00
SU09 Doug Weight .75 2.00
SU10 Andy McDonald .75 2.00
SU11 Marco Sturm 1.25 3.00
SU12 Jamie Langenbrunner .75 2.00
SU13 Aaron Ward .75 2.00
SU14 Mike York .75 2.00
SU15 John-Michael Liles .75 2.00
SU16 Jean-Sebastian Giguere .75 2.00
SU17 Paul Mara .75 2.00
SU18 Nick Schultz .75 2.00
SU19 Tom Preissing .75 2.00
SU20 Krys Kolanos .75 2.00
SU21 Ty Conklin 1.25 3.00
SU22 Kevyn Adams .75 2.00
SU23 Superstars Checklist .40 1.00

2004-05 German DEL Update

We only have a partial checklist at this time. Please forward additional information to hockeymag@beckett.com.

COMPLETE SET (?)
289 Markus Pottinger .10 .25
290 Patrick Reimer .10 .25
291 Thomas Jorg .10 .25
292 DEG Metro Stars CL .02 .10
321A Paul Traynor .10 .25
322A John Coleman .10 .25
323A Kai Hospelt .10 .25
324A Andreas Loth .10 .25
325A Marquis Mathieu .40 1.00
334 Stefan Schroder .10 .25
335 Martin Hyun .10 .25
336 Martin Schymainski .10 .25
337 Vadim Slivchenko .10 .25
338 Krefeld Checklist .02 .10
339 Herbert Vasiljevs .10 .25
340 Lukas Lang .10 .25
341 Robert Tomik .10 .25
342 Nuremberg Checklist .02 .10
284 Fabio Carciola .10 .25
285 Steven Passmore .20 .50
286 Adler Manheim CL .02 .10
287 Richard Brennan .10 .25
288 Augsburger Panther CL .02 .10
293 Andre Rankel .10 .25
294 Norman Martens .10 .25
295 Christoph Gawlik .10 .25
296 Daniar Dshunussov .10 .25
297 Richard Mueller .10 .25
298 Marcus Sommerfeld .10 .25
299 Ehc EisBaren Berlin CL .02 .10
300 Mike Harder .10 .25
301 Markus Schroder .10 .25
302 Steffen Karg .10 .25
303 ERC Ingolstadt CL .02 .10
305 Chad Bassen .10 .25
306 Frankfurt Lions CL .02 .10
307 Sasha Martinovic .10 .25
308 Clayton Young .10 .25
309 Hamburg Freezers CL .02 .10
310 Todd Hlushko .10 .25
311 Marian Cisar .10 .25
312 Bastian Steingrog .02 .10
313 Alexander Serikow .10 .25
314 Jonas Lanier .10 .25
316 Wayne Hynes .10 .25
317 Rich Parent .40 1.00
318 Hannover Scorpions CL .02 .10
319 Tobias Schwab .10 .25
320 Iserlohn Roosters CL .02 .10
326 Manuel Klinge .10 .25
327 Kassel Huskies CL .02 .10
343 Sebastian Osterloh .10 .25
344 Lars Bruggemann .10 .25
345 Artjom Kostyrev .10 .25
346 Eric Wolfsburg CL .02 .10
304 Joseph Murray .10 .25
315 Michael Kozhenikov .10 .25
322B Ted Drury .20 .50
323B Corey Hirsch .20 .50
324B Peter Abstreiter .10 .25
325B Mark Kosick .10 .25
326A Manuel Klinge .10 .25
326b Kolner Haie CL .02 .10
NNO Kolner Haie Checklist .02 .10

2004-05 German Dusseldorf Metro Stars Postcards

COMPLETE SET (25) 10.00 20.00
1 Fabian Brannstrom .40 1.00
2 Christian Brittig .40 1.00
3 Eric Dandenault .40 1.00
4 Matt Davidson .40 1.00
5 Matt Herr .75 2.00
6 Tommy Jakobsen .40 1.00
7 Thomas Jorg .40 1.00
8 Alexander Jung .40 1.00
9 Florian Jung .40 1.00
10 Klaus Kathan .40 1.00
11 Walter Koberle CO .10 .25
12 Daniel Kreutzer .40 1.00
13 Bernd Kuhnhauser .40 1.00
14 Trond Magnussen .40 1.00
15 Mike Pellegrims .40 1.00
16 Markus Pottinger .40 1.00
17 Patrick Reimer .40 1.00
18 Andy Schneider .40 1.00
19 Alexander Sulzer .40 1.00
20 Jeff Tory .40 1.00
21 Andrei Trefilov .60 1.50
22 Martin Ulrich .40 1.00
23 Tore Vikingstad .40 1.00
24 Clayton Young .40 1.00
25 Dussi MASCOT .02 .10

2004-05 German Hamburg Freezers Postcards

The cards are unnumbered and so are listed below in alphabetical order.

COMPLETE SET (22) 10.00 20.00
1 Nils Antons .40 1.00
2 Robert Francz .40 1.00
3 Jean-Sebastien Giguere 2.00 5.00
4 Bobby House .40 1.00
5 Craig Johnson .40 1.00
6 Alan Letang .40 1.00
7 Paul Manning .40 1.00
8 Sasha Martinovic .40 1.00
9 Jochen Molling .40 1.00
10 Christopher Oravec .40 1.00
11 Shane Peacock .40 1.00
12 Jacek Plachta .40 1.00
13 Brad Purdie .40 1.00
14 Brandon Reid .75 2.00
15 Boris Rousson .75 2.00
16 Jorgen Rumrich .40 1.00
17 Mike Schmidt CO .40 1.00
18 Mike Smazal .40 1.00
19 Dave Tomlinson .40 1.00
20 Darren Van Impe .40 1.00
21 Martin Walter .40 1.00
22 Clayton Young .40 1.00

2004-05 German Hannover Scorpions Postcards

Cards are unnumbered and so are listed below alphabetically.

COMPLETE SET (29) 10.00 25.00
1 Peter Abstreiter .40 1.00
2 Patrik Augusta .40 1.00
3 Gordon Borberg .40 1.00
4 Lars Bruggemann .40 1.00
5 Jason Cipolla .40 1.00
6 Marian Cisar .40 1.00
7 Thomas Dolak .40 1.00
8 Edvin Frylen .40 1.00
9 Axel Hackert .40 1.00
10 Todd Hlushko .40 1.00
11 Robert Hock .40 1.00
12 Wayne Hynes .40 1.00
13 Ilpo Kauhanen .75 2.00
14 Patrick Koppchen .40 1.00
15 Mikhail Kozhevnikov .40 1.00
16 Christian Kunast .40 1.00
17 Dan Lambert .40 1.00
18 Jonas Lanier .40 1.00
19 Paul Mara .75 2.00
20 Andreas Morczinietz .40 1.00
21 Fredrik Oberg .40 1.00
22 Andy Reiss .40 1.00
23 Rene Rothke .40 1.00
24 Benedikt Schopper .40 1.00
25 Alexander Serikow .40 1.00
26 Lenny Soccio .40 1.00
27 Bastian Steingross .40 1.00
28 Andrei Teljukin .40 1.00
29 Steve Wilson .40 1.00

2004-05 German Ingolstadt Panthers

Cards are unnumbered and are listed below alphabetically.

COMPLETE SET (27) 10.00 25.00
1 Chris Armstrong .30 .75
2 Doug Ast .30 .75
3 Jamie Bartman CO .10 .25
4 Brad Burym .30 .75
5 Craig Ferguson .30 .75
6 Jakub Ficenec .30 .75
7 Glen Goodall .30 .75
8 Mike Harder .30 .75
9 Justin Harney .30 .75
10 Daniel Hilpert .30 .75
11 Martin Jiranek .30 .75
12 Steffen Karg .30 .75
13 Ron Kennedy CO .10 .25
14 Jamie Langenbrunner .30 .75
15 Cameron Mann .75 2.00
16 Andy McDonald .75 2.00
17 Christoph Melischko .30 .75
18 Nikolaus Mondt .30 .75
19 Gunther Oswald .30 .75
20 Alexander Polaczek .30 .75
21 Markus Schroder .30 .75
22 Marco Sturm 1.25 3.00
23 Ken Sutton .30 .75
24 Phil von Stefenelli .30 .75
25 Jimmy Waite .75 2.00
26 Aaron Ward .75 2.00
27 Xavier MASCOT .02 .10
28 Drew Omicioli .30 .75
29 Andreas Loth .30 .75

2004-05 German Krefeld Penguins Postcards

COMPLETE SET (24) 30.00
1 Steve Brule .60 1.50
2 Alexander Duck .60 1.50
3 Paul Dyck .60 1.50
4 Franz Fritzmeier CO .10 .25
5 Carsten Gosdeck .60 1.50
6 Adrien Grygiel .60 1.50
7 Robert Guillet .60 1.50
8 Chris Herperger .60 1.50
9 Martin Hyun .60 1.50
10 Ivo Jan .60 1.50
11 Markus Janka .60 1.50
12 Scott King .60 1.50
13 Rainer Kottstorfer .60 1.50
14 Daniel Kunce .60 1.50
15 Justin Kurtz .60 1.50
16 Guy Lehoux .60 1.50
17 Robert Muller .60 1.50
18 Christian Rohde .60 1.50
19 Florian Schnitzer .60 1.50
20 Alexander Selivanov .60 1.50
21 Mario Simioni CO .10 .25
22 Ferdinand Stradter MD .10 .25
23 Shayne Wright .60 1.50
24 Steffen Ziesche .60 1.50

2004-05 German Nuremburg Ice Tigers Postcards

Set is unnumbered and cards are listed below alphabetically.

COMPLETE SET (19) 25.00
1 Drew Bannister .60 1.50
2 Benjamin Barz .60 1.50
3 Bjorn Bombis .60 1.50
4 Robert Dietrich .60 1.50
5 Petr Fical .60 1.50
6 Konstantin Firsanov .60 1.50
7 Christian Franz .60 1.50
8 Mike Green .60 1.50
9 Lasse Kopitz .60 1.50
10 Lukas Lang .60 1.50
11 Tomas Martinec .60 1.50
12 Ulrich Maurer .60 1.50
13 Felix Petermann .60 1.50
14 Greg Poss CO .10 .25
15 Stefan Schauer .60 1.50
16 Yan Stastny 1.25 3.00
17 Adam Svoboda 1.25 3.00
18 Otto Sykora MG .10 .25
19 Brad Tapper .60 1.50

2004-05 German Weiden Blue Devils

Team-issued set from the German Second Division.

COMPLETE SET (27) 10.00 20.00
1 Florian Bartels .30 .75
2 Michal Bartosch .30 .75
3 J.F. Boutin .30 .75
4 Christian Franz .30 .75
5 Roman Goeldner .30 .75
6 Christian Grosch .30 .75
7 Peter Gruhle .30 .75
8 Benjamin Grunwald .30 .75
9 Stephan Hagn .30 .75
10 Reinhard Haider .30 .75
11 Alexander Herbst .30 .75
12 Michael Hoeck .30 .75
13 Thomas Kastner .30 .75
14 Stefan Keski-Kungas .30 .75
15 Christian Kinateder .30 .75
16 Holger Koenig .30 .75
17 Christian Meiler .30 .75
18 Florian Ondruschka .30 .75
19 Jan Penk .30 .75
20 Michal Piskor .30 .75
21 Daniel Rappl .30 .75
22 Samuel St. Pierre .30 .75
23 Daniel Strom .30 .75
24 Sebastian Wolsch .30 .75
25 Florian Zellner .30 .75
26 Josef Hefner ACO .10 .25
27 Leos Sulak CO .10 .25

2005-06 German DEL

COMPLETE SET (381) 30.00 60.00
1 Patrick Aufiero .10 .25
2 Christian Eklund .10 .25
3 Dennis Endrass .10 .25
4 Thorsten Fendt .10 .25
5 Rick Girard .10 .25
6 Scott King .20 .50
7 Manuel Kofler .10 .25
8 Martin Lindmann .10 .25
9 Roland Mayr .10 .25
10 Josef Menauer .10 .25
11 Steve Potvin .10 .25
12 Daniel Rau .10 .25
13 Arvids Rekis .10 .25
14 Rainer Suchan .10 .25
15 Jayme Filipowicz .10 .25
16 Rolf Wanhainen .10 .25
17 Stefan Endrass .10 .25
18 Brendan Yarema .10 .25
19 David Danner .10 .25
20 Konstantin Firsanov .10 .25
21 Jens Baxmann .10 .25
22 Mark Beaufait .10 .25
23 Tobias Draxinger .10 .25
24 Daniar Dshunussow .10 .25
25 Micki DuPont .20 .50
26 Kelly Fairchild .20 .50
27 Sven Felski .10 .25
28 Steve Walker .10 .25
29 Christoph Gawlik .10 .25
30 Frank Hördler .10 .25
31 Rob Leask .10 .25
32 Norman Martens .10 .25
33 Richard Mueller .10 .25
34 Rene Kramer .10 .25
35 Stefan Ustorf .10 .25
36 Derrick Walser .20 .50
37 Denis Pederson .20 .50
38 Youri Ziffzer .10 .25
39 Florian Busch .10 .25
40 Andre Rankel .10 .25
41 Steve Brule .10 .25
42 Mathieu Darche .20 .50
43 Robert Francz .10 .25
44 Thorsten Kienass .10 .25
45 Patrick Koslow .10 .25
46 Petri Kujala .10 .25
47 Trond Magnussen .10 .25
48 Shawn McNeill .20 .50
49 Stephane Robitaille .10 .25
50 Christian Rohde .10 .25
51 Martin Schymainski .10 .25
52 Niklas Sundblad .10 .25
53 Andrej Teljukin .10 .25
54 Michael Waginger .10 .25
55 Jean-Luc Grand-Pierre .20 .50
56 Radek Vit .10 .25
57 Francois Groleau .10 .25
58 Mika Puhakka .10 .25
59 Björn Reiser .10 .25
60 Anton Bader .10 .25
61 Alexander Jung .10 .25
62 Marian Bazany .10 .25
63 Fabian Brännström .10 .25
64 Chris Ferraro .20 .50
65 Florian Jung .10 .25
66 Thomas Jörg .10 .25
67 Craig Johnson .20 .50
68 Klaus Kathan .10 .25
69 Daniel Kreutzer .10 .25
70 Peter Ferraro .20 .50
71 Mike Pellegrims .10 .25
72 Chris Schmidt .10 .25
73 Andrew Schneider .20 .50
74 Jeff Tory .10 .25
75 Andrej Trefilov .20 .50
76 Tore Vikingstad .10 .25
77 Todd Reirden .10 .25
78 Tommy Jakobsen .10 .25
79 Patrick Reimer .10 .25
80 Alexander Sulzer .10 .25
81 Patrick Boileau .10 .25
82 Francois Bouchard .10 .25
83 Michael Bresagk .10 .25
84 Daniel Corso .20 .50
85 Ian Gordon .10 .25
86 David Gosselin .20 .50
87 Markus Jocher .10 .25
88 Sebastian Klenner .10 .25
89 Christian Kohmann .10 .25
90 Patrick Lebeau .20 .50

1 Dwayne Norris .20 .50
2 Philippe Plante .10 .25
3 Neville Rautert .10 .25
4 Jonas Stöpfgeshoff .10 .25
5 David Sulkovsky .10 .25
6 Jason Young .10 .25
7 Boris Ackers .10 .25
8 Chad Bassen .10 .25
9 Simon Danner .10 .25
100 Jan Barta .10 .25
101 Marc Beaucage .10 .25
102 Björn Bombis .10 .25
103 Francois Fortier .10 .25
104 Benoit Gratton .20 .50
105 Tobias Güttner .10 .25
106 Benjamin Hinterstocker .10 .25
107 Martin Hinterstocker .10 .25
108 Christian Hommel .10 .25
109 Alan Letang .10 .25
110 Paul Manning .10 .25
111 Sasa Martinovic .10 .25
112 Shane Peacock .10 .25
113 Jacek Plachta .10 .25
114 Boris Rousson .20 .50
115 Heiko Smazal .10 .25
116 Christopher Oravec .10 .25
117 Jeff Ulmer .10 .25
118 Darren van Impe .10 .25
119 Alexander Barta .10 .25
120 Martin Walter .10 .25
121 Patrick Augusta .10 .25
122 Brad Burym .10 .25
123 Jason Cipolla .10 .25
124 Thomas Dolak .10 .25
125 Sascha Goc .20 .50
126 Mike Green .20 .50
127 Shawn Heins .20 .50
128 Robert Hock .10 .25
129 Marcel Juhasz .10 .25
130 Trevor Kidd .20 .50
131 Patrick Köppchen .10 .25
132 Christian Künast .10 .25
133 Dan Lambert .20 .50
134 Andreas Morczinietz .10 .25
135 Brad Tapper .20 .50
136 Todd Warriner .20 .50
137 Jeff Finley .10 .25
138 Steve Guolla .20 .50
139 Rene Röthke .10 .25
140 Michael Höck .10 .25
141 Chris Armstrong .10 .25
142 Doug Ast .10 .25
143 Björn Barta .10 .25
144 Craig Ferguson .10 .25
145 Jakub Ficenec .20 .50
146 Glenn Goodall .20 .50
147 Daniel Hilpert .10 .25
148 Jason Holland .10 .25
149 Martin Jiranek .10 .25
150 Florian Keller .10 .25
151 Cameron Mann .20 .50
152 Christoph Melischko .10 .25
153 Günther Oswald .10 .25
154 Sebastian Vogl .10 .25
155 Ken Sutton .10 .25
156 Sean Tallaire .10 .25
157 Phil von Stefenelli .20 .50
158 Jimmy Waite .20 .50
159 Christoph Höhenleitner .10 .25
160 Yannic Seidenberg .10 .25
161 Vitalij Aab .10 .25
162 Bryan Adams .10 .25
163 Collin Danielsmeier .10 .25
164 Mark Etz .10 .25
165 Linus Fagemo .10 .25
166 Kirk Furey .10 .25
167 Erich Goldmann .10 .25
168 Michael Wolf .10 .25
169 Matt Higgins .20 .50
170 Raffaele Intranuovo .20 .50
171 Sebastian Jonas .10 .25
172 Ladislav Karabin .10 .25
173 Martin Knold .10 .25
174 Leonardo Conti .10 .25
175 Dimitrij Kotschnew .10 .25
176 Markus Pöttinger .10 .25
177 Bruce Richardson .10 .25
178 Mats Trygg .10 .25
179 Tobias Schwab .10 .25
180 Alexej Dmitriev .10 .25
181 Tobias Abstreiter .10 .25
182 Drew Bannister .20 .50
183 Eric Bertrand .10 .25
184 Joaquin Gage .20 .50
185 Sven Gerbig .10 .25
186 Domminik Hammer .10 .25
187 Justin Harney .10 .25
188 Guy Lehoux .10 .25
189 Alexander Serikow .10 .25
190 Martin Sychra .10 .25
191 Sven Valenti .10 .25
192 Steffen Ziesche .10 .25
193 Dale Clarke .10 .25
194 Danny Groulx .10 .25
195 Ryan Kraft .10 .25
196 Adam Ondraschek .10 .25
197 Jason Ulmer .10 .25
198 Alexander Heinrich .10 .25
199 Manuel Klinge .10 .25
200 Tobias Wörle .10 .25
201 Jeremy Adduono .10 .25
202 Tino Boos .10 .25
203 Ivan Ciernik .10 .25
204 Sebastian Furchner .10 .25
205 Thomas Greiss .10 .25
206 Kai Hospelt .10 .25
207 Oliver Jonas .10 .25
208 Stephane Julien .10 .25
209 Lasse Kopitz .10 .25
210 Eduard Lewandowski .10 .25
211 Mirko Lüdemann .10 .25
212 Dave McLlwain .10 .25
213 Nikolaus Mondt .10 .25
214 Andreas Renz .10 .25
215 Jean-Yves Roy .10 .25
216 Paul Traynor .10 .25
217 Brad Schlegel .10 .25
218 Alex Hicks .10 .25
219 Philip Gogulla .10 .25
220 Moritz Müller .10 .25
221 Boris Blank .10 .25
222 Alexander Dück .10 .25
223 Franz Fritzmeier .10 .25
224 Robert Guillet .10 .25
225 Chris Herperger .10 .25
226 Andre Huebscher .10 .25
227 Ivo Jan .10 .25
228 Rainer Köttsdorfer .10 .25
229 Daniel Kunce .10 .25
230 Richard Pavlikovski .10 .25
231 Ken Passmann .10 .25
232 Alexander Selivanov .10 .25
233 Herberts Vasiljevs .10 .25
234 Roland Verwey .10 .25
235 Markus Witting .10 .25
236 Robert Müller .10 .25
237 Philip Hendle .10 .25
238 Andy Hedlund .10 .25
239 Adrian Grygiel .10 .25
240 Daniel Pietta .10 .25
241 Ronny Arendt .10 .25
242 Patrick Ehelechner .20 .50
243 Michael Bakos .10 .25
244 Lonny Bohonos .20 .50
245 Shawn Carter .10 .25
246 Karl Dykhuis .10 .25
247 Devin Edgerton .10 .25
248 Pierre Hedin .10 .25
249 Steve Kelly .20 .50
250 Marcus Kink .10 .25
251 Peter Ratchuk .10 .25
252 Sefan Retzer .10 .25
253 Jeff Shantz .10 .25
254 John Tripp .10 .25
255 Marco Schütz .10 .25
256 Sachar Blank .10 .25
257 Fredrik Chabot .20 .50
258 Rene Corbet .20 .50
259 Fabio Carciola .10 .25
260 Christoph Ullmann .10 .25
261 Benjamin Barz .10 .25
262 Colin Beardsmore .10 .25
263 Rich Brennan .10 .25
264 Matt Davidson .20 .50
265 Robert Döme .20 .50
266 Petr Fical .10 .25
267 Christian Franz .10 .25
268 Lukas Lang .10 .25
269 Jean-Francois Labbe .20 .50
270 Christian Laflamme .10 .25
271 Greg Leeb .10 .25
272 Thomas Martinec .10 .25
273 Francois Methot .10 .25
274 Michel Periard .10 .25
275 Alexander Polaczek .10 .25
276 Jame Pollock .10 .25
277 Christian Retzer .10 .25
278 Brian Swanson .10 .25
279 Felix Petermann .10 .25
280 Stefan Schauer .10 .25
281 Olaf Kölzig 2.00 5.00
282 Alexander Jung .10 .25
283 Rob Leask .10 .25
284 Christian Erhoff .30 .75
285 Chritoph Schubert .10 .25
286 Andreas Renz .10 .25
287 Lasse Kopitz .10 .25
288 Dennis Seidenberg .20 .50
289 Sven Felski .10 .25
290 Jochen Hecht .40 1.00
291 Marco Sturm .40 1.00
292 Stefan Ustorf .10 .25
293 Daniel Kreutzer .10 .25
294 Alexander Barta .10 .25
295 Thomas Martinec .10 .25
296 Klaus Kathan .10 .25
297 Michael Hackert .10 .25
298 Tino Boos .10 .25
299 Andreas Morczinietz .10 .25
300 Jan Benda .10 .25
301 Patrick Buzas .10 .25
302 Jay Henderson .20 .50
303 Marc Savard .10 .25
304 Steffen Tölzer .10 .25
305 Drake Berehowsky .10 .25
306 Constantin Braun .10 .25
307 Sean Fischer .10 .25
308 Patrick Jarrett .20 .50
309 Tomás Pöpperle .10 .25
310 Deron Quint .20 .50
311 Thomas Schenkel .10 .25
312 Hugo Boisvert .10 .25
313 Patrick Ehelechner .20 .50
314 Kari Haakana .10 .25
315 Martin Hamann .10 .25
316 Michael Henrich .10 .25
317 Markus Schmidt .10 .25
318 Chris Bright .10 .25
319 Michael Hackert .10 .25
320 Steve Kelly .10 .25
321 James Patrick .10 .25
322 Martin Reichel .10 .25
323 Andrej Strakhov .10 .25
324 Roman Cechmanek .20 .50
325 Matthias Forster .10 .25
326 Niklas Hede .10 .25
327 Ryan Jardine .10 .25
328 Steffen Karg .10 .25
329 Max Lingemann .10 .25
330 Florian Schnitzer .10 .25
331 Lukas Slavetinsky .10 .25
332 Björn Bombis .10 .25
333 Dominik Hammer .10 .25
334 Jonas Lanier .10 .25
335 Marty Murray .10 .25
336 André Reiss .10 .25
337 Benedikt Schopper .10 .25
338 Wally Schreiber .10 .25
339 Matt Kinch .10 .25
340 Bastian Steingrog .10 .25
341 Rob Valicevic .20 .50
342 Mark Greig .10 .25
343 Brad Purdie .10 .25
344 Rich Parent .40 1.00
345 Steve Brule .10 .25
346 Brad Burym .10 .25
347 Martin Hlinka .10 .25
348 Sinsa Martinovic .10 .25
349 Chris Nielsen .10 .25
350 Sebastian Osterloh .10 .25
351 Torsten Ankert .10 .25
352 Daniel Hatterscheid .10 .25
353 William Lindsay .10 .25
354 Henry Martens .10 .25
355 Ted Drury .10 .25
356 Mike Pudlick .10 .25
357 Igor Alexandrov .10 .25
358 Anthony Aquino .10 .25
359 David Cespiva .10 .25
360 Daniel Del Monte .10 .25
361 Ilpo Kauhanen .20 .50
362 Stefan Langwieder .10 .25
363 Thomas Pielmeier .10 .25
364 Yannick Tremblay .10 .25
365 Gert Acker .10 .25
366 Ulrich Maurer .10 .25
367 Florian Ondruschka .10 .25
368 Björn Barta .10 .25
369 Michael Bresagk .10 .25
370 Petr Fical .10 .25
371 Sebastian Furchner .10 .25
372 Marcel Goc .20 .50
373 Dimitrij Kotschnew .10 .25
374 Eduard Lewandowski .10 .25
375 Robert Müller .10 .25
376 Alexander Sulzer .10 .25
377 Christoph Ullmann .10 .25
378 Thomas Greiss .10 .25
379 Nico Pyka .10 .25
NNO DEG Metro Stars DEB Pokalsieger 2006 4.00 10.00
NNO Eisbären Berlin Deutscher Meister 2005 4.00 10.00

2005-06 German DEL All-Star Jerseys

AS01 Andy Delmore 8.00 20.00
AS02 Micki DuPont 8.00 20.00
AS03 Jakub Ficenec 8.00 20.00
AS04 Darren van Impe 8.00 20.00
AS05 Stepahne Julien 8.00 20.00
AS06 Ladislav Karabin 8.00 20.00
AS07 Ivan Ciernik 8.00 20.00
AS08 Patrick Lebeau 8.00 20.00
AS09 Dave McLlwain 8.00 20.00
AS10 Francois Methot 8.00 20.00
AS11 Duanne Moeser 8.00 20.00
AS12 Dwayne Norris 8.00 20.00
AS13 Mike Pellegrims 8.00 20.00
AS14 Brad Purdie 8.00 20.00
AS15 Chris Rogles 8.00 20.00
AS16 Boris Rousson 10.00 25.00
AS17 Alexander Selivanov 8.00 20.00
AS18 Yan Stastny 12.00 30.00
AS19 Steve Walker 8.00 20.00
AS20 Pascal Trepanier 8.00 20.00
AS21 All Star Game 2006 20.00 50.00

2005-06 German DEL DEB-Jerseys

TR01 Jan Benda 8.00 20.00
TR02 Jochen Hecht 12.00 30.00
TR03 Olaf Kölzig 20.00 50.00
TR04 Marco Sturm 12.00 30.00

2005-06 German DEL Defender

We have no pricing data on this set.

DF01 Drew Bannister
DF02 Francois Bouchard
DF03 Micki DuPont
DF04 Karl Dykhuis
DF05 Jakub Ficenec
DF06 Francois Groleau
DF07 Andy Hedlund
DF08 Shawn Heins
DF09 Tommy Jakobsen
DF10 Stephane Julien
DF11 Martin Knold
DF12 Shane Peacock
DF13 Jame Pollock
DF14 Arvids Rekis

2005-06 German DEL Defender Promos

We have no pricing information on this set. The skip-numbered checklist is believed to be complete.

DF02 Francois Bouchard
DF03 Micki DuPont
DF04 Karl Dykhuis
DF05 Jakub Ficenec
DF10 Stephane Julien
DF12 Shane Peacock
DF13 Jame Pollock

2005-06 German DEL Goalies

COMPLETE SET (14) 20.00 40.00
G01 Roman Cechmanek 1.25 3.00
G02 Patrick Ehelechner 2.00 5.00
G03 Joaquin Gage 1.25 3.00
G04 Ian Gordon 1.25 3.00
G05 Thomas Greiss 1.25 3.00
G06 Trevor Kidd 2.00 5.00
G07 Alexander Jung 1.25 3.00
G08 Ilpo Kauhanen 1.25 3.00
G09 Jean-Francois Labbé 1.25 3.00
G10 Robert Müller 1.25 3.00
G11 Rich Parent 2.00 5.00
G12 Tomás Pöpperle 1.25 3.00
G13 Jimmy Waite 2.00 5.00
G14 Rolf Wanhainen 1.25 3.00

2005-06 German DEL Star Attack

COMPLETE SET (10) 8.00 20.00
ST01 Ivan Ciernik .75 2.00
ST02 Jochen Hecht 1.25 3.00
ST03 Daniel Kreutzer .75 2.00
ST04 Patrick Lebeau .75 2.00
ST05 Dwayne Norris .75 2.00
ST06 Yan Stastny 1.50 4.00
ST07 Brad Tapper .75 2.00
ST08 Pascal Trepanier .75 2.00
ST09 Mike York 1.25 3.00
ST10 Jason Young .75 2.00

2005-06 German DEL Team Checklists

COMPLETE SET (20) 6.00 15.00
CL01 Augsburger Panther Checklist .40 1.00
CL02 Eisbären Berlin Checklist .40 1.00
CL03 DEG Metro Stars Checklist .40 1.00
CL04 EV Duisburg Checklist .40 1.00
CL05 Frankfurt Lions Checklist .40 1.00
CL06 Hamburg Freezers Checklist .40 1.00
CL07 Hannover Scorpions Checklist .40 1.00
CL08 ERC Ingolstadt Checklist .40 1.00
CL09 Iserlohn Roosters Checklist .40 1.00
CL10 Kassel Huskies Checklist .40 1.00
CL11 Kölner Haie Checklist .40 1.00
CL12 Krefeld Pinguine Checklist .40 1.00
CL13 Adler Mannheim Checklist .40 1.00
CL14 Nürnberg Ice Tigers Checklist .40 1.00
CL15 Nationalmannschaft Checklist .40 1.00
CL16 Defender Checklist .40 1.00
CL17 Star Attack Checklist .40 1.00
CL18 Allstars'05 Checklist .40 1.00
CL19 Goalies Checklist .40 1.00
CL20 Trikotkarten DEB Checklist .40 1.00

2006-07 German DEL

1 Travis Brigley .20 .50
2 Jesper Damgaard .20 .50
3 Craig Darby .30 .75
4 Patrick Buzas .20 .50
5 Thorsten Fendt .20 .50
6 Jay Henderson .30 .75
7 Manuel Kofler .20 .50
8 Kevin Lavallee .30 .75
9 Roland Mayr .20 .50
10 Josef Menauer .20 .50
11 Arvids Rekis .20 .50
12 Rainer Suchan .20 .50
13 Rolf Wanhainen .20 .50
14 Mark Beaufait .30 .75
15 Florian Busch .20 .50
16 Cole Jarrett .30 .75
17 Kelly Fairchild .30 .75
18 Sven Felski .20 .50
19 Frank Hordler .20 .50
20 Patrick Jarrett .30 .75
21 Deron Quint .30 .75
22 Andre Rankel .20 .50
23 Andy Roach .30 .75
24 Stefan Ustorf .20 .50
25 Steve Walker .30 .75
26 Youri Ziffzer .20 .50
27 Anton Bader .20 .50
28 Martin Bartek .20 .50
29 Calle Bergstrom .20 .50
30 Daniel Del Monte .20 .50
31 Johan Forsander .20 .50
32 Robert Francz .20 .50
33 Stanislav Gron .20 .50
34 Torsten Kienass .20 .50
35 Artjom Kostyrev .20 .50
36 Christopher Oravec .20 .50
37 Thomas Schenkel .20 .50
38 Alexander Engel .20 .50
39 Levente Szuper .40 1.00
40 Marian Bazany .20 .50
41 Rob Collins .30 .75
42 Jean Luc Grand Pierre .30 .75
43 Thomas Jorg .20 .50
44 Craig Johnson .30 .75
45 Klaus Kathan .20 .50
46 Daniel Kreutzer .20 .50
47 Jeff Panzer .20 .50
48 Charlie Stephens .30 .75
49 Jamie Storr .40 1.00
50 Alexander Sulzer .20 .50
51 Darren Van Impe .20 .50
52 Ture Vikingstad .20 .50
53 Chris Armstrong .30 .75
54 Michael Bresagk .20 .50
55 Ian Gordon .30 .75
56 Steve Kelly .30 .75
57 Patrick Lebeau .40 1.00
58 Michael Hackert .20 .50
59 Dwayne Norris .30 .75
60 Shane Peacock .30 .75
61 Peter Podhradsky .20 .50
62 Martin Reichel .20 .50
63 Chris Taylor .30 .75
64 Jeff Ulmer .30 .75
65 Jason Young .30 .75
66 Vitalij Aab .20 .50
67 Alexander Barta .20 .50
68 Marc Beaucage .30 .75
69 Patrick Boileau .30 .75
70 Cory Cross .30 .75
71 Francois Fortier .30 .75
72 Alan Letang .30 .75
73 Paul Manning .30 .75
74 Jacek Plachta .20 .50
75 Boris Rousson .40 1.00
76 Florian Schnitzer .20 .50
77 Brad Smyth .30 .75
78 Christoph Brandner .20 .50
79 Thomas Dolak .20 .50
80 Rob Hisey .20 .50
81 Martin Hlinka .20 .50
82 Alexander Jung .20 .50
83 Dan Lambert .30 .75
84 Andreas Morczinietz .20 .50
85 Eric Nickulas .30 .75
86 Stephane Robitaille .20 .50
87 Brad Schlegel .20 .50
88 Eric Schneider .20 .50
89 Sascha Goc .30 .75
90 Jason Ulmer .20 .50
91 Todd Warriner .30 .75
92 Doug Ast .30 .75
93 Michael Bakos .20 .50
94 Bjorn Barta .20 .50
95 Jakub Ficenec .40 1.00
96 Glen Goodall .30 .75
97 Matt Higgins .30 .75
98 Jason Holland .20 .50
99 Florian Keller .20 .50
100 Yannic Seidenberg .20 .50
101 Jeff Tory .20 .50
102 Rob Valicevic .40 1.00
103 Michael Waginger .20 .50
104 Jimmy Waite .40 1.00
105 Jeremy Adduono .30 .75
106 Kirk Furey .20 .50
107 Erich Goldmann .20 .50
108 Mark Greig .30 .75
109 Robert Hock .20 .50
110 Jens Karlsson .20 .50
111 Dmitrij Kotschnew .20 .50
112 Brad Purdie .30 .75
113 Jimmy Roy .30 .75
114 David Sulkovsky .20 .50
115 Brad Tiley .30 .75
116 Paul Traynor .20 .50
117 Michael Wolf .20 .50
118 Tino Boos .20 .50
119 Ivan Ciernik .20 .50
120 Sebastian Furchner .20 .50
121 Philip Gogulla .40 1.00
122 Adam Hauser .40 1.00
123 Kai Hospelt .20 .50
124 Stephane Julien .20 .50
125 Lasse Kopitz .20 .50
126 Mirko Ludemann .20 .50
127 Jason Marshall .30 .75
128 Dave McLlwain .30 .75
129 Sean Tallaire .30 .75
130 Bryan Adams .30 .75
131 Boris Blank .20 .50
132 Raymond Dilauro .20 .50
133 Ted Drury .30 .75
134 Franz Fritzmeier .20 .50
135 Rainer Kottstorfer .20 .50
136 Dusan Milo .20 .50
137 Richard Pavlikovsky .20 .50
138 Reto Pavoni .30 .75
139 Daniel Pietta .20 .50
140 Alexander Selivanov .20 .50
141 Herberts Vasilijevs .30 .75
142 Roland Verwey .20 .50
143 Jan Alinc .20 .50
144 Francois Bouchard .20 .50
145 Sven Butenschon .30 .75
146 Rene Corbet .20 .50
147 Colin Forbes .30 .75
148 Jason Jaspers .30 .75
149 Eduard Lewandowski .20 .50
150 Tomas Martinec .20 .50
151 Francois Methot .20 .50
152 Robert Muller .20 .50
153 Nathan Robinson .30 .75
154 Pascal Trepanier .20 .50
155 Christoph Ullmann .20 .50
156 Martin Ancicka .20 .50
157 Rich Brennan .30 .75
158 Shawn Carter .30 .75
159 Petr Fical .30 .75
160 Adrian Grygiel .20 .50
161 Martin Jiranek .20 .50
162 Scott King .40 1.00
163 Jean-Francois Labbe .40 1.00
164 Greg Leeb .30 .75
165 Michel Periard .20 .50
166 Alexander Polaczek .20 .50
167 Jame Pollock .30 .75
168 Stefan Schauer .20 .50
169 Colin Beardsmore .20 .50
170 Peter Caspersson .20 .50
171 Jason Dunham .20 .50
172 Per Eklund .20 .50
173 Peter Abstreiter .20 .50
174 Trevor Gallant .30 .75
175 Markus Jocher .20 .50
176 Matt Kinch .30 .75
177 Josef Lehner .20 .50
178 Christoffer Norgren .20 .50
179 Gunther Oswald .20 .50
180 Cam Severson .30 .75
181 William Trew .40 1.00
182 Mike Bales .40 1.00
183 Florian Busch .20 .50
184 Petr Fical .20 .50
185 Sascha Goc .30 .75
186 Thomas Greiss .40 1.00
187 Jochen Hecht .60 1.50
188 Daniel Kreutzer .20 .50
189 Uwe Krupp .20 .50
190 Robert Muller .20 .50
191 Andreas Renz .20 .50
192 Stefan Schauer .20 .50
193 Marco Sturm .60 1.50
194 Alexander Sulzer .20 .50
195 Alexander Barta .20 .50

2006-07 German DEL All-Star Jerseys

AS1 Doug Ast 10.00 25.00
AS2 Francois Bouchard 10.00 25.00
AS3 Ivan Ciernik 10.00 25.00
AS4 Ted Drury 10.00 25.00
AS5 Jakub Ficenec 15.00 40.00
AS6 Andy Hedlund 10.00 25.00
AS7 Matt Higgins 10.00 25.00
AS8 Martin Hlinka 10.00 25.00
AS9 Stephane Julien 10.00 25.00
AS10 Trevor Kidd 15.00 40.00

2006-07 German DEL German Forwards

GF1 Tomas Martinec 1.25 3.00
GF2 Michael Hackert 1.25 3.00
GF3 Andreas Morczinietz 1.25 3.00
GF4 Daniel Kreutzer 1.25 3.00
GF5 Manuel Kofler 1.25 3.00
GF6 Sven Felski 1.25 3.00
GF7 Markus Jocher 1.25 3.00
GF8 Robert Hock 1.25 3.00
GF9 Robert Francz 1.25 3.00
GF10 Petr Fical 1.25 3.00
GF11 Tino Boos 1.25 3.00
GF12 Boris Blank 1.25 3.00
GF13 Alexander Barta 1.25 3.00
GF14 Michael Waginger 1.25 3.00

2006-07 German DEL New Arrivals

NA1 Travis Brigley 1.25 3.00
NA2 Cory Cross 1.25 3.00
NA3 Per Eklund 1.25 3.00
NA4 Scott King 1.25 3.00
NA5 Jason Marshall 1.25 3.00
NA6 Dusan Milo 1.25 3.00
NA7 Eric Nickulas 2.00 5.00
NA8 Andy Roach 2.00 5.00
NA9 Nathan Robinson 2.00 5.00
NA10 Jamie Storr 1.50 4.00
NA11 Levente Szuper 1.50 4.00
NA12 Chris Taylor 1.25 3.00
NA13 Brad Tiley 1.25 3.00
NA14 Daniel Tkaczuk 1.25 3.00

2006-07 German DEL Sonderkarten Diverse

We have no pricing information for this card.

MK1 Deutscher Meister 2006

2006-07 German DEL Team Leaders

TL1 Craig Darby 1.25 3.00
TL2 Ted Drury 1.25 3.00
TL3 Glen Goodall 2.00 5.00
TL4 Torsten Kienass 1.25 3.00
TL5 Alan Letang 1.25 3.00
TL6 Greg Leeb 1.25 3.00
TL7 Dave McIlwain 1.25 3.00
TL8 Jimmy Roy 1.25 3.00
TL9 William Trew 1.25 3.00
TL10 Stefan Ustorf 1.25 3.00
TL11 Todd Warriner 1.50 4.00
TL12 Pascal Trepanier 1.25 3.00
TL13 Craig Johnson 1.25 3.00
TL14 Jason Young 1.25 3.00

1994-95 Italian Milano

These 2 1/4 by 3 1/2 cards were apparently issued as part of a perforated sheet. The complete set size is unknown, and we have no pricing information on the cards. They are presented for checklisting purposes only. They are unnumbered and listed below in alphabetical order. If you have any additional info, please contact us at hockeymag@beckett.com.

COMPLETE SET (?)
1 Massimo Ansoldi
2 Scott Beattie
3 Georg Comploi
4 Andrea Mosele
5 Carmine Vani
6 Kim Gellert CO#)Conny Priondolo GM

2007-08 Italian Ritten Renon Team Set

COMPLETE SET (23) 4.00 10.00
1 Josh Olson .25 .60
2 Mark Smith .25 .60
3 Enrico Dorigatti .25 .60
4 Shawn Mather .25 .60
5 Dan Tudin .25 .60
6 Alex Egger .25 .60
7 Tony Tuzzolino .25 .60
8 Ingemar Gruber .25 .60
9 Kaspars Astashenko .25 .60
10 Emanuel Scelfo .25 .60
11 Jan Vodrazka .25 .60
12 Paolo Bustreo .25 .60
13 Matteo Rasom .25 .60
14 Alex Rottensteiner .25 .60
15 Lorenz Daccordo .25 .60
16 Marcus Hafner .25 .60
17 Fritz Pioner .25 .60
18 Thomas Unterfrauner .25 .60
19 Benjamin Bregenzer .25 .60
20 Frederic Cloutier .25 .60
21 Niederstaetter .25 .60
22 Paul Adey .25 .60
23 Herbert Frisch .25 .60

1992-93 Norwegian Elite Series

COMPLETE SET (242) 20.00 50.00
1 Jim Marthinsen .20 .50
2 Jarl Eriksen .07 .20
3 Erik Tveten .07 .20
4 Carl Gunnar Gundersen .07 .20
5 Nick Carone .07 .20
6 Jaromir Latal .07 .20
7 Tom Johansen .07 .20
8 Asgaut Moe .07 .20
9 Oystein Olsen .07 .20
10 Atle Olsen .07 .20
11 Roy Johansen .07 .20
12 Marius Rath .07 .20
13 Svenn Erik Bjornstad .07 .20
14 Jon Magne Karlstad .07 .20
15 Pal Kristiansen .07 .20
16 Espen Knutsen 2.00 5.00
17 Stig Johansen .07 .20
18 Geir Myhre .07 .20
19 Remo Martinsen .07 .20
20 Jan Tore Ronningen .07 .20
21 Jon Hroar Nordstrom .07 .20
22 Tom Erik Olsen .07 .20
23 Peter Madach .07 .20
24 Rune Gulliksen .07 .20
25 Carl Oscar Boe Andersen .07 .20
26 Martin Ahlberg .07 .20
27 Erik Kristiansen .07 .20
28 Tommy Larsen .07 .20
29 Age Ellingsen .07 .20
30 Patric Eide .07 .20
31 Svein Harald Arnesen .07 .20
32 Petter Thoresen .07 .20
33 Pal Marthinsen .07 .20
34 Ole Eskild Dahlstrom .07 .20
35 Nikolai Davydkin .07 .20
36 Lennart Ahlberg .07 .20
37 Tommie Eriksen .07 .20
38 Jan Roar Fagerli .07 .20
39 Erik Nerell .07 .20
40 Knut Walbye .07 .20
41 Pal Dahlstrom .07 .20
42 Martin Andresen .07 .20
43 Geir Hoff .07 .20
44 Cato Andersen .07 .20
45 Per Oddvar Walbye .07 .20
46 Cato Tom Andersen .07 .20
47 Frode Hansen .20 .50
48 Petter Salsten .07 .20
49 Arne Billkvam .07 .20
50 Jarle Friis .07 .20
51 Steve Allmann .07 .20
52 Torbjorn Orskau .07 .20
53 Christian Kjeldsberg .07 .20
54 Bjorn Mathisrud .07 .20
55 Pal Gjermundsen .07 .20
56 Ketil Martinsen .07 .20
57 Vidar Andersen .07 .20
58 Rene Hansen .07 .20
59 Martin Friis .07 .20
60 Orjan Lovdal .07 .20
61 Lars Hakon Andersen .07 .20
62 Robert Sundt .07 .20
63 Henrik Buskoven .07 .20
64 Morten Finstad .20 .50
65 Magnus Christoffersen .07 .20
66 Roar Larsen .07 .20
67 Zdenek Albrecht .07 .20
68 Oldrich Valek .07 .20
69 Fredrik Jacobsen .07 .20
70 Rune Hansen .07 .20
71 Lars Jacobsen .07 .20
72 Staffan Tholsson .07 .20
73 Lase Syversen .07 .20
74 Kim Sogaard .07 .20
75 Jan Erik Thoresen .07 .20
76 Pal Andre Eriksen .07 .20
77 Bjorn Freddy Bekkerud .07 .20
78 Kjell Erik Myreng .07 .20
79 Lars Eilertsen .07 .20
80 Reino Johansen .07 .20
81 Igor Mishukov .07 .20
82 Ole Petter Dalene .07 .20
83 Jon Gundersen .07 .20
84 Pal Raab Lien .07 .20
85 Vadim Tunikov .07 .20
86 Tommy Skaarberg .07 .20
87 Per Christian Knold .07 .20
88 Stephen Foyn .07 .20
89 Glenn Asland .07 .20
90 Bjorte Olsson .07 .20
91 Gorm Gundersen .07 .20
92 Morgan Andersen .07 .20
93 Vegar Barlie .07 .20
94 Oystein Tronrud .07 .20
95 Kim Fagerhoi .07 .20
96 Tor Nilsen .07 .20
97 Arne Bergseng .07 .20
98 Timo Laituri .07 .20
99 Sjur Robert Nilsen .07 .20
100 Mattis Haakensen .07 .20
101 Lars Dergseng .07 .20
102 Svein Enok Norstebo .20 .50
103 Tor Anders Jacobsen .07 .20
104 Jorgen Salsten .07 .20
105 Tommy Jakobsen .07 .20
106 Tim Budy .07 .20
107 Martin Wiita .07 .20
108 Lenny Eriksson .07 .20
109 Stale Berg .07 .20
110 Bjorn Anders Dahl .07 .20
111 Geir Tore Dahl .07 .20
112 Dallas Gaume .07 .20
113 Geir Haugen .07 .20
114 Roar Husby .07 .20
115 Robert Nielsen .07 .20
116 Lars Erik Lunde .07 .20
117 Kare Nordnes .07 .20
118 Magne Nordnes .07 .20
119 Geir Leknes .07 .20
120 Rob Doroshuk .07 .20
121 Roger Olsen .07 .20
122 Oyvind Sorli .07 .20
123 Gunnar Bye .07 .20
124 Per Kristian Vellan .07 .20
125 Marc Laniel .20 .50
126 Dallas Gaume .07 .20
127 Robert Schistad .07 .20
128 Jan Petter Loschbrandt .07 .20
129 Tore Kristensen .07 .20
130 Eskil Eide .07 .20
131 Erik Brodahl .07 .20
132 Morten Nordhus .07 .20
133 Erik Pettersen .07 .20
134 Hans Bekken .07 .20
135 Jan Bekken .07 .20
136 Jon Erik Haaland .07 .20
137 Richard Little .07 .20
138 Eivind Olsen .07 .20
139 Morten Gilje .07 .20
140 Sverre Hogemark .07 .20
141 Eirik Paulsen .07 .20
142 Kyle McDonough .07 .20
143 Steffen Trettenes .07 .20
144 Richard David .07 .20
145 Odd Nilsen .07 .20
146 Per Marthinsen .07 .20
147 Johnny Nilsen .07 .20
148 Per Christian Fjeldstad .07 .20
149 Christian Hafsmoe .07 .20
150 Raymond Lunde .07 .20
151 Rono Lemiro .07 .20
152 Thomas Kristiansen .07 .20
153 Vidar Wold .07 .20
154 Hans Petter Halla .07 .20
155 Michael Smithurst .07 .20
156 Lars Erik Solberg .07 .20
157 Kenneth Fjell .07 .20

158 Morten Hem .07 .20
159 Dag Hoyem .07 .20
160 Vince Guidotti .07 .20
161 Glen Engevik .07 .20
162 Joe Clarke .07 .20
163 Lars Erik Kjaer .07 .20
164 Gorm Laursen .07 .20
165 Per Reidar Johansen .07 .20
166 Anders Martinsen .07 .20
167 Jorn Arild Flatha .07 .20
168 Rune Hansen .07 .20
169 Stian Kraft .07 .20
170 Geir Svendsberget .07 .20
171 Andre Aas .07 .20
172 Erik Skoglund Nilsen .07 .20
173 Frode Sletner .07 .20
174 Petter Syversne .07 .20
175 Jarle Gundersen .07 .20
176 Terje Wikstrom .07 .20
177 Steve MacDonald .07 .20
178 Sjur Kinder .07 .20
179 Morten Fjeldstad .07 .20
180 George Tower .07 .20
181 Espen Knutsen 2.00 5.00
182 Jon Magne Karlstad .07 .20
183 Tommy Jakobsen .07 .20
184 Valerengen .02 .10
185 Trondheim .02 .10
186 Dallas Gaume .20 .50
187 Bjorn Anders Dahl .02 .10
188 Jarl Eriksen .02 .10
189 Mark Fioretti .02 .10
190 Brian Tutt .20 .50
191 Jim Marthinsen .20 .50
192 Brian Tutt .20 .50
193 Jaromir Latal .07 .20
194 Espen Knutsen 2.00 5.00
195 Dallas Gaume .20 .50
196 Oldrich Valek .07 .20
197 Bjorn Skaare .07 .20
198 Knut Walbye .07 .20
199 Age Ellingsen .07 .20
200 Espen Knutsen 2.00 5.00
201 Ole Eskild Dahlstrom .07 .20
202 Tommie Eriksen .07 .20
203 Vegar Barlie .07 .20
204 Glenn Jessesen .07 .20
205 Tor Arne Alseth .07 .20
206 Per Kristian Vellan .07 .20
207 Jone Hatteland .07 .20
208 Henrik Aaby .07 .20
209 Johnny Nilsen .07 .20
210 Geir Svendsberget .07 .20
211 Pal Kristian Eggen .07 .20
212 Andreas Brunvoll .07 .20
213 Andre Manscov Hansen .07 .20
214 Frode Christiansen .07 .20
215 Jan Morten Dahl .07 .20
216 Stian Kraft .07 .20
217 Lubos Sikela .07 .20
218 Rune Fjeldstad .07 .20
219 Sven Arild Olsen .07 .20
220 Kent Inge Kristiansen .07 .20
221 Sjur Rakstad Larsen .07 .20
222 Borre Ostvang .07 .20
223 Harald Bastiansen .07 .20
224 Jon Warset .07 .20
225 Jo Espen Leibnitz .07 .20
226 Arild Syversen .07 .20
227 Terje Haukali .07 .20
228 Geir Dalene .07 .20
229 Jonas Larsen .07 .20
230 Thomas Hansen .07 .20
231 Stig Olsen .07 .20
232 Lars Hansen .07 .20
233 Hans M. Anonsen .07 .20
234 Ketil Kristiansen .07 .20
235 Bjornar Sorensen .07 .20
236 Tom Jostne .07 .20
237 John Klears .07 .20
238 Arve Jansen .07 .20
239 Orjan Gjertsen .07 .20
240 Checklist (1-81) .02 .10
241 Checklist (82-162) .02 .10
242 Checklist (163-242) .02 .10

1999-00 Norwegian National Team

COMPLETE SET (24) 10.00 25.00
1 Robert Schistad .75 2.00
2 Geir Svendsberget .40 1.00
3 Henrik Aaby .40 1.00
4 Tommy Jacobsen .40 1.00
5 Tommy Jacobsen .40 1.00
6 Andre Manskov Hansen .40 1.00
7 Morten Fjeldstad .40 1.00
8 Lars Hakon Andersen .40 1.00
9 Marius Trygg .40 1.00
10 Svein Enok Norstebo .75 2.00
11 Carl Oscar Boe Andersen .40 1.00
12 Ole Eskild Dalstrom .40 1.00
13 Per Age Skroder .40 1.00
14 Pal Johnsen .40 1.00
15 Trond Vegar Magnussen .40 1.00
16 Mats Trygg .40 1.00
17 Ketil Wold .40 1.00
18 Sjur Robert Nilsen .40 1.00
19 Anders Myrvold .75 2.00
20 Tore Vikingstad .40 1.00
21 Bjorge Josefsen .40 1.00
22 Oyvind Sorli .40 1.00
23 Bard Sorlie .40 1.00
24 Leif Boork CO .20 .50

1969-70 Russian National Team Postcards

COMPLETE SET (27) 75.00 150.00
1 Viktor Zinger 1.50 4.00
2 Vitali Davydov 1.50 4.00
3 Vladimir Lutchenko 1.50 4.00
4 Viktor Kuzkin 1.50 4.00
5 Alexander Ragulin 4.00 10.00
6 Igor Romishevski 1.50 4.00
7 Boris Mikhailov 6.00 15.00
8 Viacheslav Starshinov 1.50 4.00

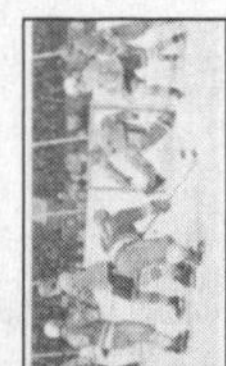

9 Evgeny Zimin 1.50 4.00
10 Alexander Maltsev 6.00 15.00
11 Anatoli Firsov 4.00 10.00
12 Evgeny Paladiev 1.50 4.00
13 Alexander Yakushev 6.00 15.00
14 Vladimir Petrov 6.00 15.00
15 Valeri Kharlamov 10.00 25.00
16 Evgeny Mishakov 1.50 4.00
17 Vladimir Vikulov 1.50 4.00
18 Vladimir Yursinov 1.50 4.00
19 Viktor Pushkov 1.50 4.00
20 Arkady Chernishev 1.50 4.00
21 Anatoli Tarasov 4.00 10.00
22 USSR vs Sweden .75 2.00
23 USSR vs Sweden .75 2.00
24 USSR vs Sweden .75 2.00
25 USSR vs Finland, Sweden .75 2.00
26 USSR vs Canada, Sweden 1.50 4.00
27 Team Photo 1.50 4.00

1970-71 Russian National Team Postcards

This set measures 3 1/2" by 5 3/4". The horizontal fronts feature a color head shot and a preprint blue ink autograph on the left, and a black and white action photo on the right. The backs look like standard postcards. A protective sleeve featuring Russia in action against Sweden is usually found with the set.

COMPLETE SET (20) 100.00 150.00
1 Viktor Konovalenko 2.00 5.00
2 Vitali Davydov 2.00 5.00
3 Vladimir Lutchenko 2.00 5.00
4 Valeri Nikitin 2.00 5.00
5 Alexander Ragulin 4.00 10.00
6 Igor Romishevski 2.00 5.00
7 Evgeni Paladiev 2.00 5.00
8 Viacheslav Starshinov 2.00 5.00
9 Viktor Polupanov 2.00 5.00
10 Alexander Maltsev 6.00 15.00
11 Anatoli Firsov 6.00 15.00
12 Evgeni Mishakov 2.00 5.00
13 Boris Mikhailov 6.00 15.00
14 Valeri Vasiliev 4.00 10.00
15 Alexander Yakushev 6.00 15.00
16 Vladimir Petrov 6.00 15.00
17 Valeri Kharlamov 10.00 25.00
18 Vladimir Vikulov 2.00 5.00
19 Vladimir Shadrin 2.00 5.00
20 Vladislav Tretiak 10.00 25.00

1973-74 Russian National Team

This set comes in a commemorative folder and features "cards" that are 4 1/16 by 5 3/4.

COMPLETE SET (25) 60.00 125.00
1 Team Photo 1.50 4.00
2 Vladislav Tretiak 8.00 20.00
3 Alexander Sidelnikov 1.50 4.00
4 Alexander Gusev 1.50 4.00
5 Valeri Vasiliev 3.00 8.00
6 Boris Mikhailov 3.00 8.00
7 Vladimir Petrov 3.00 8.00
8 Valeri Kharlamov 6.00 15.00
9 Kharlamov, Petrov, Mikhailov 4.00 10.00
10 Vladimir Lutchenko 1.50 4.00
11 Gennady Tsygankov 1.50 4.00
12 Alexander Ragulin 1.50 4.00
13 Alexander Volchkov 1.50 4.00
14 Viacheslav Anisin 1.50 4.00
15 Yuri Lebedev 1.50 4.00
16 Alexander Bodunov 1.50 4.00
17 Alexander Martinyuk 1.50 4.00
18 Vladimir Shadrin 1.50 4.00
19 Alexander Yakushev 3.00 8.00
20 Alexander Maltsev 3.00 8.00
21 Evgeny Paladiev 1.50 4.00
22 Yuri Liapkin 1.50 4.00
23 Vsevolod Bobrov CO#Boris Kulagin CO .75 2.00
24 Boris Mikhailov 3.00 8.00
25 Viktor Kuzkin 1.50 4.00

1974 Russian National Team

Unusually sized (8.25 X 3.5) postcard-type collectibles feature members of the powerful CCCP club. Often found in a folder.

COMPLETE SET (25) 50.00 100.00
1 Vyacheslav Anisin 1.50 4.00
2 Vsevolod Bobrov CO 1.50 4.00
3 Alexander Bodunov 1.50 4.00
4 Alexander Gusev 1.50 4.00
5 Sergei Kapustin 1.50 4.00
6 Valeri Kharlamov 5.00 12.00
7 Boris Kulagin CO 1.50 4.00
8 Viktor Kuzkin 1.50 4.00
9 Yuri Lebedev 1.50 4.00
10 Yuri Liapkin 1.50 4.00
11 Vladimir Lutchenko 1.50 4.00
12 Alexander Maltsev 3.00 8.00
13 Boris Mikhailov 3.00 8.00
14 Boris Mikhailov 3.00 8.00
15 Vladimir Petrov 3.00 8.00
16 Vladimir Repneev 1.50 4.00
17 Vladimir Shadrin 1.50 4.00
18 Yuri Shatalov 1.50 4.00
19 Alexander Sidelnikov 1.50 4.00
20 Vladislav Tretiak 6.00 15.00
21 Gennady Tsygankov 1.50 4.00
22 Valeri Vasiliev 3.00 8.00
23 Alexander Yakushev 3.00 8.00
24 USSR .40 1.00
25 USSR .40 1.00

1979 Russian National Team

This set features the Soviet National Team. The cards measure 8 1/4 by 5 7/8 and were issued in a folder.

COMPLETE SET (24) 37.50 100.00
1 Team Photo .50 1.00
2 Viktor Tikhonov CO 1.00 2.00
3 Vladimir Yursinov CO .50 2.00
4 Vladislav Tretiak 5.00 15.00
5 Alexander Pashkov 1.50 3.00
6 Vladimir Lutchenko 1.00 3.00
7 Valeri Vasiliev 1.00 5.00
8 Gennady Tsygankov 1.00 3.00
9 Yuri Fedorov 1.00 2.00
10 Slava Fetisov 5.00 15.00
11 Zinetula Bilyaletinov 2.50 5.00
12 Vasili Pervukhin 1.00 3.00
13 Boris Mikhailov 2.50 8.00
14 Vladimir Petrov 2.50 8.00
15 Valeri Kharlamov 5.00 15.00
16 Alexander Maltsev 2.50 8.00
17 Sergei Kapustin 1.00 3.00
18 Yuri Lebedev 1.00 2.00
19 Viktor Zhluktov 1.00 3.00
20 Helmut Balderis 1.50 5.00
21 Alexander Golikov 1.00 2.00
22 Sergei Makarov 4.00 15.00
23 Vladimir Golikov 1.00 2.00
24 Team Photo .50 1.00

1984 Russian National Team

This 23-card set presents Russian hockey players. The cards were packaged in a cardboard sleeve that displays a photo of the 1983 Russian national team. The cards measure approximately 5 1/2" by 7" and feature full-bleed head and shoulders shots of the players dressed in civilian clothing. On the left portion, the backs carry three action shots in a filmstrip format while the right portion has player information in Russian. The cards are unnumbered and checklisted below in alphabetical order.

COMPLETE SET (23) 40.00 80.00
1 Sergei Babinov .75 2.00
2 Helmut Balderis 1.25 3.00
3 Zinetula Bilyaletinov 1.25 3.00
4 Vyacheslav Bykov 2.00 5.00
5 Slava Fetisov 4.00 10.00
6 Irek Gimaev .75 2.00
7 Sergei Kapustin .75 2.00
8 Alexei Kasatonov 2.00 5.00
9 Andrei Khomotov 2.00 5.00
10 Vladimir Krutov 4.00 10.00
11 Igor Larionov 6.00 15.00
12 Sergei Makarov 4.00 10.00
13 Alexander Maltsev 2.00 5.00
14 Vladimir Myshkin 2.00 5.00
15 Vasily Pervukhin .75 2.00
16 Sergei Shepelev .75 2.00
17 Alexander Skvorstsov .75 2.00
18 Sergei Starikov 1.25 3.00
19 Viktor Tikhonov CO .75 2.00
20 Vladislav Tretiak 4.00 10.00
21 Mikhael Vasiliev .75 2.00
22 Vladimir Yursinov CO .40 1.00
23 Viktor Zhluktov .75 2.00
24 Vladimir Zubkov .75 2.00

1987 Russian National Team

This 24-card set presents Russian hockey players and is subtitled "The USSR 1987 National Hockey Team." The cards were printed in the USSR, released by Panorama Publishers (USSR), and distributed in North America by Tri-Globe International, Inc. The production run was reportedly 25,000 sets. The cards were packaged in a cardboard sleeve that displays a team photo from the world championships. The cards measure approximately 4 1/8" by 5 13/16" and feature full-bleed head and shoulders shots of the players dressed in coat and tie. The player's autograph and uniform number are printed on the lower portion of the picture in gold lettering. The backs are in Russian and present player profile and statistics. The cards are unnumbered and checklisted below in alphabetical order.

COMPLETE SET (24) 18.00 45.00
1 Sergei Ageikin .40 1.00
2 Evgeny Belosheikin .75 2.00
3 Zinetula Belyaletdinov .40 1.00
4 Vlacheslav Bykov .75 2.00
5 Slava Fetisov 2.00 5.00
6 Alexei Gusarov .60 1.50
7 Valeri Kamensky 1.25 3.00
8 Alexei Kasatonov .75 2.00
9 Yuri Khmylev .60 1.50
10 Andrei Khomutov .75 2.00
11 Vladimir Konstantinov 2.00 5.00
12 Vladimir Krutov 1.25 3.00
13 Igor Larionov 2.00 5.00
14 Sergei Makarov 1.25 3.00
15 Sergei Mylnikov .75 2.00
16 Vasili Pervukhin .40 1.00
17 Sergei Starikov .40 1.00
18 Igor Stelnov .40 1.00
19 Sergei Svetlov .40 1.00
20 Viktor Tikhonov CO .75 2.00
21 Viktor Tjumenev .40 1.00
22 Michael Varnakov .40 1.00
23 Sergei Yashin .40 1.00
24 Vladimir Yursinov CO .40 1.00

1989 Russian National Team

This set of 24 postcards was released by Plakat Publishers, USSR. The cards measure approximately 4 1/8" by 5 13/16" and features some of the best Russian players of modern years. The set features 22 player cards and two coach cards. The cards were packaged in a cardboard sleeve that displays an action photo of Valeri Kamensky. Reportedly 100,000 sets were printed but most were sold in the USSR and fewer sets made it to the U.S. and Canada. The fronts have head and shoulder shots of Russian Team players in coat and tie (street clothes) with a superimposed facsimile autograph while the backs contain biographical information in Russian. An unauthorized reprint of the set was issued in 1991, but the size was reduced to 2 1/2" by 3 1/2". The players in the reprint set who had since played in the NHL were given English biographies on labels added to the back. The cards are listed below alphabetically since they are unnumbered.

COMPLETE SET (24) 14.00 35.00
1 Ilya Byakin .30 .75
2 Vlacheslav Bykov .40 1.00
3 Alexandr Chernik .20 .50
4 Igor Dmitriev CO .20 .50
5 Sergei Fedorov 3.00 8.00
6 Slava Fetisov 1.25 3.00
7 Alexei Gusarov .30 .75
8 Arturs Irbe 2.00 5.00
9 Valeri Kamensky .75 2.00
10 Alexei Kasatonov .60 1.50
11 Svatoslav Khalizov .20 .50
12 Yuri Khmylev .30 .75
13 Andrei Khomutov .40 1.00
14 Vladimir Konstantinov 2.00 5.00
15 Vladimir Krutov .75 2.00
16 Dimitri Kvartalnov .40 1.00
17 Igor Larionov 1.50 4.00
18 Sergei Makarov .75 2.00
19 Vladimir Mishkin .40 1.00
20 Sergei Mylnikov .40 1.00
21 Sergei Nemchinov .40 1.00
22 Valeri Shirjaev .20 .50
23 Viktor Tikhonov CO .40 1.00
24 Sergei Yashin .20 .50

1991-92 Russian Stars Red Ace

This 17-card standard-size set, featuring Russian stars in the NHL, was produced by Red Ace. The cards were packaged in a box, on which it is claimed that the production run was limited to 50,000 sets. The fronts feature borderless action shots with the player's name. Printed on white cover stock, the horizontal backs feature a close-up photograph as well as biographical and statistical information in Russian and English. The cards are unnumbered and checklisted below in alphabetical order.

COMPLETE SET (17) 4.00 10.00
1 Pavel Bure 1.25 3.00
2 Evgeny Davydov .08 .25
3 Sergei Fedorov 1.25 3.00
4 Slava Fetisov .40 1.00
5 Alexei Gusarov .08 .25
6 Valeri Kamensky .30 .75
7 Alexei Kasatonov .20 .50
8 Ravil Khaidarov .08 .25
9 Vladimir Konstantinov .40 1.00
10 Igor Kravchuk .15 .40
11 Igor Larionov .40 1.00
12 Andrei Lomakin .08 .25
13 Sergei Makarov .30 .75
14 Alexander Mogilny .40 1.00
15 Sergei Nemchinov .15 .40
16 Anatoli Semenov .08 .25
17 Mikhail Tatarinov .08 .25

1991-92 Russian Tri-Globe Bure

This standard-size five-card set was produced by Tri-Globe as part of the "The Magnificent Five" series. These sets spotlight five Russian hockey stars currently playing in the NHL, with set 2 featuring Pavel Bure. It is claimed that 5,000 numbered display boxes were produced, each containing 40 sets (ten for each player). Printed in Russia on heavy laminated textured stock, card fronts feature full-color action shots in various formats and accented predominantly in green. Each set includes a checklist on the back of a Sergei Fedorov promo card.

COMPLETE SET (6) 3.00 8.00
COMMON CARD (6-10) .60 1.50
NNO Sergei Fedorov .20 .50
Checklist

1991-92 Russian Tri-Globe Fedorov

This five-card set honoring Sergei Fedorov is the product of a joint venture between Tri-Globe International, Inc. and Ivan Fiodorov Press. The cards measure approximately 2 1/2" by 3 3/4" and are printed on a grainy cardboard stock. The fronts feature color action game shots. The cards are numbered on the back. According to Tri-Globe, 600 uncut, numbered sheets were printed, producing the equivalent of 3,000 sets, as well as 1,000 uncut, numbered five-card strips. Moreover, 100,000 five-card sets were reportedly produced.

COMPLETE SET (5) 2.50 6.00
COMMON CARD (1-5) .50 1.25

1991-92 Russian Tri-Globe Irbe

This standard-size five-card set was produced by Tri-Globe as part of the "The Magnificent Five" series. These sets spotlight five Russian hockey stars currently playing in the NHL, with set four featuring Arturs Irbe.

COMPLETE SET (6) 1.50 4.00
COMMON CARD (16-20) .30 .75
NNO Sergei Fedorov .20 .50
Checklist

1991-92 Russian Tri-Globe Kamensky

This standard-size five-card set was produced by Tri-Globe as part of the "The Magnificent Five" series. These sets spotlight five Russian hockey stars currently playing in the NHL, with set 1 featuring Valeri Kamensky.

COMPLETE SET (6) .60 1.50
COMMON CARD (1-5) .30 .75
NNO Sergei Fedorov .20 .50
Checklist

1991-92 Russian Tri-Globe Semenov

This standard-size five-card set was produced by Tri-Globe as part of the "The Magnificent Five" series. These sets spotlight five Russian hockey stars currently playing in the NHL, with set three featuring Anatoli Semenov.

COMPLETE SET (6) .60 1.50
COMMON CARD (11-15) .08 .25
NNO Sergei Fedorov .20 .50
Checklist

1991 Russian Sports Unite Hearts

A boxed set of standard-sized cards of Russian players in the NHL, this issue was limited to 50,000 sets produced.

COMPLETE SET (10) 6.00 15.00
1 Sergei Fedorov 2.00 5.00
2 Slava Kozlov .75 2.00
3 Alexei Gusarov .40 1.00
4 Alexei Kasatonov .40 1.00
5 Vladimir Konstantinov .75 2.00
6 Igor Larionov .75 2.00
7 Sergei Makarov .40 1.00
8 Alexander Mogilny .75 2.00
9 Mikhail Tatarinov .40 1.00
10 Vladislav Tretiak 1.25 3.00

1991 Russian Stars in NHL

This 11-card standard-size set was reportedly printed in Leningrad by Ivan Fiodorov Press as a special limited edition; it is claimed that there were only 50,000 sets issued. The cards essentially feature Russian players in the NHL. The front has a full-color player photo, bordered on the two sides by hockey sticks (with hockey gloves below). A red banner is draped across the top of the picture, with the player's name in between USSR (sickle and hammer) and USA (US flag) emblems. In contrast to the dark purple background, the bottom is light purple and presents the message "Sports Unites Hearts" in English and Russian. The horizontally-oriented back provide player information in two colored panels (English and Russian) and has a head shot of the player as well.

COMPLETE SET (11) 3.00 8.00
1 Sergei Fedorov 1.50 4.00
2 Slava Fetisov .40 1.00
3 Alexei Gusarov .08 .25
4 Alexei Kasatonov .40 1.00
5 Vladimir Konstantinov .40 1.00
6 Igor Larionov .40 1.00
7 Sergei Makarov .40 1.00
8 Alexander Mogilny .60 1.50
9 Mikhail Tatarinov .08 .25
10 Vladislav Tretiak .75 2.00
11 Team Photo .15 .40
USSR National Team

1992-93 Russian Stars Red Ace

This 37-card, standard-size set features action color player photos bordered in white. The player's name and the Red Ace logo appear in a gradated violet stripe at the bottom. A red triangle at the upper left corner of the picture carries a white star outline. In a red box with rounded corners, the back provides biography in Cyrillic (Russian) and English. The top portion of the back has a yellow background and displays a close-up photo in a circular format and the player's name in Russian and English. The cards are numbered on the back essentially alphabetically.

COMPLETE SET (37) 2.00 5.00
1 Alexander Barkov .02 .10
2 Sergei Bautin .02 .10
3 Igor Boldin .02 .10
4 Nikolai Borchevsky .08 .25
5 Sergei Brylin .08 .25
6 Viacheslav Butsayev .02 .10
7 Alexander Cherbajev .02 .10
8 Evgeny Garanin .02 .10
9 Sergei Gonchar .20 .50
10 Alexander Karpovtsev .08 .25
11 Darius Kasparaitis .08 .25
12 Alexander Kharlamov .08 .25
13 Yuri Khmylev .08 .25
14 Sergei Klimovich .02 .10
15 Igor Korolev .08 .25
16 Andrei Kovalenko .08 .25
17 Alexei Kovalev UER .30 .75
(Back photo is Igor Korolev)
18 Dmitri Kvartalnov .08 .25
19 Vladimir Malakhov .08 .25
20 Maxim Mikhailovsky .02 .10
21 Boris Mironov .08 .25
22 Dmitri Mironov .08 .25
23 Andrei Nazarov .08 .25
24 Roman Oksyuta .02 .10
25 Artur Oktyabrev .02 .10
26 Sergei Petrenko .02 .10
27 Oleg Petrov .08 .25
28 Andrei Potaichuk .02 .10
29 Vitali Prokhorov .02 .10
30 Alexander Semak .08 .25
31 Dmitri Starostenko .02 .10
32 Ravil Yakubov .02 .10
33 Alexei Yashin .20 .50
34 Dmitri Yushkevich .08 .25
35 Alexei Zhamnov .08 .25
36 Alexei Zhitnik .08 .25
NNO Checklist Card .04 .01

1992 Russian Stars Red Ace

The 1992 Red Ace Russian Hockey Stars boxed set was co-sponsored by the World of Hockey Magazine and World Sport. The cards were sold in a light blue box with production limited supposedly to 25,000 sets. The cards are printed on thin card stock and measure approximately 2 1/2" by 3 3/8". The light blue bordered fronts feature color action player photos. The player's name appears on a light green diagonal stripe in an upper corner, accented with a red triangle containing a white star. The Red Ace logo is printed in a lower corner of the picture. The white backs display a small head shot next to the player's name on a green bar. In a pale pink panel below is the player's biography and career highlights in Russian and English. The cards are numbered on the back.

COMPLETE SET (36) 2.00 5.00
1 Darius Kasparaitis .08 .25
2 Alexei Zhamnov .08 .25
3 Dimitri Khristich .20 .50
4 Andrei Trefilov .20 .50
5 Vitali Prokhorov .02 .10
6 Dmitri Filimonov .02 .10
7 Valeri Zelepukin .08 .25
8 Alexei Kovalev .30 .75
9 Dmitri Kvartalnov .08 .25
10 Igor Korolev .08 .25
11 Nikolai Borschevsky .08 .25
12 Igor Boldin .02 .10
13 Arturs Irbe .30 .75
14 Viachesiav Butsayev .02 .10
15 Boris Mironov .08 .25
16 Sergei Bautin .02 .10
17 Alexander Kharlamov .08 .25
18 Viachesiav Kozlov .20 .50
19 Mikhail Shtalenkov .20 .50
20 Roman Oksyuta .02 .10
21 Sandis Ozolinsh .20 .50
22 Dmitri Mironov .08 .25
23 Sergei Brylin .08 .25
24 Vladimir Grachev .02 .10
25 Dmitri Starostenko .02 .10
26 Andrei Nazarov .08 .25
27 Alexei Yashin .20 .50
28 Vladimir Malakhov .08 .25
29 Ravil Jakubov .02 .10
30 Sergei Klimovich .02 .10
31 Artur Oktjabrev .02 .10
32 Lev Berdichevski .02 .10
33 Ian Kaminski .08 .25
34 Andrei Kovalenko .08 .25
35 Dmitri Yushkevich .08 .25
36 Checklist .04 .01

1992 Russian Tri-Globe From Russia With Puck

Twelve Russian hockey stars who are currently playing in the NHL are featured in this 24-card boxed standard-size set, with two cards devoted to each player. The production run was reportedly 50,000 sets. The fronts of all cards display color action player photos. On the player's first card (i.e., an odd-numbered card), his name appears at the top in a silver stripe, and red, white, and blue stripes accent the picture on three sides. On his second card (i.e., an even-numbered card), black-and-white speckled stripes edge the picture above and below. The back of the player's first card carries a second color action photo and biographical information, while the back of his second card has a close-up color photo and career statistics. All text is in French and English.

COMPLETE SET (24) 4.00 10.00
1 Igor Larionov .20 .50
2 Igor Larionov .20 .50
3 Andrei Lomakin .08 .25
4 Andrei Lomakin .08 .25
5 Pavel Bure .75 2.00
6 Pavel Bure .75 2.00
7 Alexei Zhamnov .08 .25
8 Alexei Zhamnov .08 .25
9 Sergei Krivokrasov .08 .25
10 Sergei Krivokrasov .08 .25
11 Valeri Kamensky .08 .25
12 Valeri Kamensky .08 .25
13 Viachesiav Kozlov .20 .50
14 Viachesiav Kozlov .20 .50
15 Valeri Zelepukin .08 .25
16 Valeri Zelepukin .08 .25
17 Igor Kravchuk .08 .25
18 Igor Kravchuk .08 .25
19 Vladimir Malakhov .08 .25
20 Vladimir Malakhov .08 .25
21 Boris Mironov .08 .25
22 Boris Mironov .08 .25
23 Arturs Irbe .20 .50
24 Arturs Irbe .20 .50

1998-99 Russian Hockey League

This set features the elite of the Russian Hockey League. The cards feature blue borders around action

shots. The set is notable for featuring 2001 first-overall draft pick Ilya Kovalchuk.

COMPLETE SET (167) 24.00 60.00
1 Sergei Gomolyako .20 .50
2 Sergei Zemchenok .20 .50
3 Oleg Mikulchik .20 .50
4 Evgueni Koreshkov .20 .50
5 Andrei Razin .20 .50
6 Ravil Gusmanov .20 .50
7 Dmitri Popov .20 .50
8 Valeri Karpov .30 .75
9 Andrei Sokolov .20 .50
10 Makhail Borodulin .20 .50
11 Konstantin Shafranov .30 .75
12 Vladimir Antipin .20 .50
13 Igor Zemlyanoi .20 .50
14 Sergei Tertyshny .20 .50
15 Vadim Glovatski .20 .50
16 Alexander Soltts .30 .75
17 Alexander Koreshkov .20 .50
18 Boris Tortunov .20 .50
19 Valeri Nikulin .20 .50
20 Andrei Sapoznikov .20 .50
21 Dmitri Maksimov .20 .50
22 Dmitri Mylnikov .75 2.00
23 Maxim Sushinski .40 1.00
24 Yuri Panov .20 .50
25 Alexander Terekhov .20 .50
26 Vladimir Zorkin .20 .50
27 Eduard Gorbachev .20 .50
28 Leonid Kanarekin .20 .50
29 Alexander Savchenkov .20 .50
30 Maxim Chukanov .20 .50
31 Evgueni Fedorov .20 .50
32 Yaroslav Lyuzenkov .20 .50
33 Oleg Leontiev .20 .50
34 Sergei Osipov .20 .50
35 Andrei Kudinov .20 .50
36 Dmitri Krasotkin .20 .50
37 Ravil Yakubov .40 1.00
38 Dmitri Zatonski .20 .50
39 Konstantin Maslyukov .20 .50
40 Andrei Subbotin .30 .75
41 Pavel Kamentsev .20 .50
42 Evgueni Tarasov .20 .50
43 Oleg Kryazhev .20 .50
44 Igor Nikulin .20 .50
45 Denis Arkhipov 1.25 3.00
46 Albert Loginov .20 .50
47 Andrei Samokhvalov .20 .50
48 Igor Dorofeev .20 .50
49 Sergei Bautin .20 .50
50 Evgueni Varlamov .20 .50
51 Sergei Korobkin .20 .50
52 Rafik Yakubov .20 .50
53 Alexei Chupin .20 .50
54 Dmitri Ryabikin .20 .50
55 Alexei Kudashov .20 .50
56 Alexander Trofimov .20 .50
57 Igor Andryushchenko .20 .50
58 Igor Gorbenko .20 .50
59 Dmitri Gorenko .20 .50
60 Alexander Kazakov .20 .50
61 Evgueni Kuveko .20 .50
62 Igor Nikolaev .20 .50
63 Mikhail Pereyaslov .20 .50
64 Alexander Filippov .20 .50
65 Igor Mikhailov .20 .50
66 Roman Shipulin .20 .50
67 Dmitri Shpakovski .20 .50
68 Dmitri Shulakov .20 .50
69 Konstantin Golokhvastov .20 .50
70 Yuri Fimin .20 .50
71 Sergei Yasakov .20 .50
72 Oleg Filimonov .20 .50
73 Anatoli Ustyugov .20 .50
74 Andrei Skabelka .30 .75
75 Sergei Zolotov .20 .50
76 Dmitri Bezrukov .20 .50
77 Dmitri Vanyasov .20 .50
78 Evgueni Zakharov .20 .50
79 Arat Kadyekin .20 .50
80 Evgueni Mlinchenko .20 .50
81 Leonid Labzov .20 .50
82 Andrei Mazhugin .20 .50
83 Vladislav Makarov .20 .50
84 Remir Khaidarov .20 .50
85 Pavel Agarkov .20 .50
86 Igor Belyavski .20 .50
87 Dmitri Dubrovski .20 .50
88 Vyacheslav Zavalnyuk .20 .50
89 Yuri Zuev .20 .50
90 Andrei Evstafiev .20 .50
91 Vadim Epanchintsev .40 1.00
92 Igor Zelenchev .20 .50
93 Dmitri Klevakin .20 .50
94 Alexei Koledaev .20 .50
95 Nikolai Kurochkin .20 .50
96 Boris Kuzmin .20 .50
97 Roman Kukhtinov .20 .50
98 Sergei Moskalev .20 .50
99 Evgueni Pupkov .20 .50
100 Alexei Tkachuk .20 .50
101 Rinat Khasanov .20 .50
102 Sergei Shalamai .20 .50
103 Vadim Tarasov .75 2.00
104 Vladislav Morozov .20 .50
105 Almaz Garifullin .30 .75
106 Ilnur Gizatullin .20 .50
107 Alexander Zavyalov .20 .50
108 Oleg Vevcherenko .20 .50

109 Alexander Savitski .20 .50
110 Mikhail Sarmatin .20 .50
111 Igor Stepanov .20 .50
112 Konstantin Butsenko .20 .50
113 Alexei Murzin .20 .50
114 Andrei Nikolaev .20 .50
115 Dmitri Plekhanov .20 .50
116 Roman Salnikov .20 .50
117 Vyacheslav Timchenko .20 .50
118 Anitoli Stepanishev .20 .50
119 Roman Baranov .20 .50
120 Artem Anisimov .20 .50
121 Yuri Guniko .20 .50
122 Eduard Kudermetov .20 .50
123 Dmitri Balmin .20 .50
124 Igor Dyakiv .20 .50
125 Ramil Saifullin .20 .50
126 Alexander Vyukhin .20 .50
127 Oleg Leontiev .20 .50
128 Evgueni Koreshkov .20 .50
129 Sergei Gomolyako .20 .50
130 Oleg Mikulchik .20 .50
131 Andrei Petrakov .20 .50
132 Alexei Stepanov .20 .50
133 Dmitri Verzhinin .20 .50
134 Artem Ostroushko .20 .50
135 Sergei Berdnikov .20 .50
136 Konstantin Koltsov .20 .50
137 Vladimir Tarasov .20 .50
138 Sergei Shimkovski .20 .50
139 Oleg Pchelyakov .20 .50
140 Oleg Burlutski .20 .50
141 Oleg Bratash .20 .50
142 Sergei Voronov .20 .50
143 Uldar Mukhometov .30 .75
144 Alexei Egorov .40 1.00
145 Vladimir Kopat .20 .50
146 Vladimir Kochin .20 .50
147 Alexei Putilin .20 .50
148 Andrei Rasolko .20 .50
149 Vadim Molotilov .20 .50
150 Dmitri Nazarov .20 .50
151 Igor Vyazmikin .20 .50
152 Alexei Kalyukhny .20 .50
153 Denis Kartsev .20 .50
154 Alexander Kuvaldin .20 .50
155 Alexei Troschinsky .20 .50
156 Alexander Kharitonov .40 1.00
157 Valeri Cherny .20 .50
158 Yuri Dobrishkin .20 .50
159 Evgueni Pavlov .20 .50
160 Nikolai Antropov 1.25 3.00
161 Alexander Churik .20 .50
162 Valeri Belousov .20 .50
163 Artem Chubarov .40 1.00
164 Boris Zelenko .20 .50
165 Dmitri Frolov .40 1.00
166 Vladimir Kirik .20 .50
167 Alexei Danilov .20 .50

1999-00 Russian Dynamo Moscow

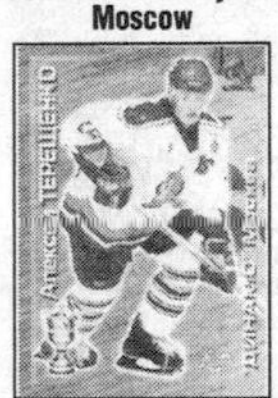

This team-issued set features Dynamo Moscow of the Russian League. The cards were sold by the team at its souvenir stands.

COMPLETE SET (27) 6.00 15.00
1 Alexei Tereshenko .20 .50
2 Igor Shadilov .20 .50
3 Alexei Ponikarovski .30 .75
4 Alexei Litvinenko .20 .50
5 Roman Zolotov .20 .50
6 Andrei Markov .40 1.00
7 Alexander Khavanov .30 .75
8 Vitali Proshkin .20 .50
9 Alexei Troschinsky .20 .50
10 Oleg Orekhovski .20 .50
11 Marat Davydov .20 .50
12 Dmitri Kokorev .20 .50
13 Alexander Kharitonov .30 .75
14 Alexander Prokopiev .20 .50
15 Mikhail Ivanov .20 .50
16 Alexei Kudashov .30 .75
17 Alexander Kuvaldin .20 .50
18 Denis Kartsev .20 .50
19 Stanislav Romanov .20 .50
20 Alexander Savchenkov .20 .50
21 Lev Berdichevski .20 .50
22 Alexei Kalyuzhni .20 .50
23 Alexander Stepanov .20 .50
24 Boris Zelenko .20 .50
25 Vitali Yeremeev .60 1.50
26 Alexei Yegorov .40 1.00
NNO Team Photo .20 .50

1999-00 Russian Hockey League

This set features the top players of the sprawling Russian Hockey League. The cards feature a color action photo on the front and player information on the back in Cyrillic. The set is noteworthy for featuring the first ever card of 2001 first overall pick, Ilya Kovalchuk.

COMPLETE SET (270) 60.00 100.00
1 Valeri Karpov .40 1.00
2 Igor Zemlyanoi .08 .25
3 Mikhail Borodulin .08 .25
4 Vladimir Antipin .08 .25
5 Vadim Glovatskin .08 .25
6 Alexei Stepanov .08 .25
7 Sergei Gomolyako .08 .25
8 Andrei Sokolov .08 .25
9 Andrei Razin .08 .25
10 Dmitri Popov .08 .25
11 Valeri Nikulin .08 .25
12 Andrei Petrakov .08 .25
13 Evgueni Koreshkov .08 .25
14 Alexander Koreshkov .08 .25
15 Andrei Sapozhnikov .20 .50
16 Oleg Mikulchik .40 1.00
17 Ravil Gusmanov .30 .75
18 Vitali Prokhorov .20 .50
19 Boris Tortunov .08 .25
20 Sergei Zemchenok .08 .25
21 Sergei Tertyshny .08 .25
22 Yuri Kuznetsov .08 .25
23 Maxim Bets .40 1.00
24 Sergei Osipov .08 .25
25 Oleg Leontiev .08 .25
26 Andrei Kudinov .08 .25
27 Konstantin Bezborodov .08 .25
28 Maxim Stepanov .08 .25
29 Alexei Lazarenko .08 .25
30 Vladimir Tyurikov .08 .25
31 Alexei Komarov .08 .25
32 Oleg Polkovnikov .08 .25
33 Dmitri Vershinin .08 .25
34 Vladimir Dumnov .08 .25
35 Oleg Smirnov .08 .25
36 Denis Ivanov .08 .25
37 Alexander Grishin .08 .25
38 Sergei Luchinkin .08 .25
39 Sergei Reshetnikov .08 .25
40 Denis Martiniuk .08 .25
41 Igor Boldin .08 .25
42 Nikolai Semin .08 .25
43 Alexander Zhdan .30 .75
44 Denis Metliuk .08 .25
45 Sergei Zolotov .08 .25
46 Yuri Dobryshkin .08 .25
47 Sergei Mylnikov, Jr. .40 1.00
48 Anton Ulyanov .08 .25
49 Yakov Deev .08 .25
50 Dmitri Bykov .08 .25
51 Dmitri Milnikov .40 1.00
52 Rinat Kasyanov .08 .25
53 Dmitri Balmin .08 .25
54 Alexei Chupin .08 .25
55 Artem Anisimov .08 .25
56 Sergei Smirnov .08 .25
57 Ivan Andriyashev .08 .25
58 Sergei Shilov .08 .25
59 Vladislav Makarov .08 .25
60 Dmitri Mylnikov .75 2.00
(Sergei Mylnikov Jr.
61 Rafik Yakubov .08 .25
62 Dmitri Shandurov .08 .25
63 Vladimir Pozdnyakov .08 .25
64 Alexei Ivashkin .08 .25
65 Valeri Ivannikov .08 .25
66 Egor Mikhailov .08 .25
67 Alexander Zibin .08 .25
68 Igor Averchenkov .08 .25
69 Alexei Sheblanov .08 .25
70 Dmitri Yachanov .08 .25
71 Oleg Romanov .08 .25
72 Denis Arkhipov 1.25 3.00
73 Almaz Garifullin .08 .25
74 Evgueni Varlamov .08 .25
75 Igor Stepanov .08 .25
76 Alexander Zavyalov .08 .25
77 Ilnur Gizhatullin .08 .25
78 Alexander Trofimov .08 .25
79 Eduard Kudermetov .08 .25
80 Remir Khaidarov .08 .25
81 Nikolai Pronin .08 .25
82 Andrei Glebov .08 .25
83 Andrei Savchenko .08 .25
84 Andrei Mukhachev .08 .25
85 Maxim Ossipov .20 .50
86 Sergei Mozyakin .08 .25
87 Alexei Gubarev .08 .25
88 Oleg Filimonov .30 .75
89 Igor Nikolaev .08 .25
90 Eduard Polyakov .08 .25
91 Konstantin Tatarintsev .08 .25
92 Anitoli Ustyugov .08 .25
93 Victor Dronov .08 .25
94 Sergei Yasakov .08 .25
95 Oleg Gorbenko .08 .25
96 Igor Andryushenko .08 .25
97 Alexei Plotinkov .08 .25
98 Igor Bakhmutov .08 .25
99 Dmitri Shandurov .08 .25
100 Dmitri Bezrukov .08 .25
101 Airat Kadeikin .08 .25
102 Leonid Labzov .08 .25
103 Alexei Vakhrushev .08 .25
104 Denis Tsigurov .08 .25
105 Roman Baranov .08 .25
106 Vladimir Zorkin .08 .25
107 Dmitri Maksimov .08 .25
108 Dmitri Kulikov .08 .25
109 Alexander Guskov .08 .25
110 Dmitri Khomutov .08 .25
111 Alexander Skugarev .08 .25
112 Mikhail Pereyaslov .08 .25
113 Artem Argokov .08 .25
114 Alexei Strakhov .08 .25
115 Dmitri Shulakov .08 .25
116 Oleg Vevcherenko .08 .25
117 Yuri Fimin .08 .25
118 Ruslan Bernikov .08 .25
119 Alexander Titov .08 .25
120 Dmitri Gorenko .08 .25
121 Alexander Filippov .08 .25
122 Konstantin Mitroshkin .08 .25
123 Alexander Zevakhin .08 .25
124 Steve Plouffe .40 1.00
125 Nikolai Tsulgin .30 .75
126 Alexei Tertyshny .08 .25
127 Nikolai Zavarykhin .30 .75
128 Evgueni Zakharov .08 .25
129 Sergei Klimentiev .20 .50
130 Pavel Duma .30 .75
131 Maxim Vasyuchkov .08 .25
132 Rustem Amirov .08 .25
133 Matvei Belousov .08 .25
134 Alexander Ochev .08 .25
135 Evgueni Muratov .08 .25
136 Andrei Buldakov .08 .25
137 Andrei Tsareev .08 .25
138 Vladimir Zavyalov .08 .25
139 Andrei Pchelyakov .08 .25
140 Igor Knyazev 1.25 3.00
141 Ilya Kovalchuk 25.00 50.00
142 Alexei Chervyakov .08 .25
143 Vladimir Kulikov .08 .25
144 Andrei Bushan .08 .25
145 Ravil Yakubov .20 .50
146 Sergei Shitkovski .08 .25
147 Sergei Berdnikov .08 .25
148 Ramil Saifullin .08 .25
149 Konstantin Golokhvastov .08 .25
150 Konstantin Maslyukov .08 .25
151 Alexei Bulatov .08 .25
152 Dmitri Kirilenko .08 .25
153 Sergei Makarov .08 .25
154 Rustem Kamaletdinov .08 .25
155 Maxim Mikhailovski .30 .75
156 Denis Khlopotnov .40 1.00
157 Albert Loginov .08 .25
158 Dmitri Nazarov .08 .25
159 Alexei Miroshnikov .08 .25
160 Sergei Zimakov .08 .25
161 Valeri Belov .08 .25
162 Alexei Kochegarov .08 .25
163 Alexei Pogonin .08 .25
164 Andrei Rasolko .08 .25
165 Dmitri Denisov .20 .50
166 Dmitri Tarasov .08 .25
167 Vadim Pokotilo .08 .25
168 Evgueni Fedorov .08 .25
169 Maxim Sushinski .30 .75
170 Alexander Popov .08 .25
171 Dmitri Parkhomenko .08 .25
172 Oleg Kryazhev .08 .25
173 Vitali Lyutkevich .08 .25
174 Dmitri Zatonski .08 .25
175 Oleg Ugolnikov .08 .25
176 Alexander Svitov 1.50 4.00
177 Dmitri Ryabkin .08 .25
178 Nikolai Babenko .08 .25
179 Yuri Panov .08 .25
180 Andrei Samokhvalov .08 .25
181 Alexander Ermakov .08 .25
182 Sergei Kagaikin .08 .25
183 Anvar Gatiyatulin .08 .25
184 Vladimir Tarasov .08 .25
185 Igor Varitskin .08 .25
186 Oleg Bolkov .08 .25
187 Rail Muftiev .08 .25
188 Vitali Yeremeev 1.25 3.00
189 Vladislav Brizgalov .30 .75
190 Dmitri Teplyakov .08 .25
191 Vladimir Kopat .08 .25
192 Denis Kuzmenko .08 .25
193 Evgueni Petrochinin .08 .25
194 Sergei Arekaev .08 .25
195 Pavel Agarkov .08 .25
196 Evgueni Pupkov .08 .25
197 Vadim Tarasov .40 1.00
198 Andrei Smirnov .08 .25
199 Alexander Maksimov .08 .25
200 Vitali Valui .08 .25
201 Sergei Petrenko .08 .25
202 Alexei Chistyakov .08 .25
203 Alexei Murzin .08 .25
204 Oleg Komissarov .08 .25
205 Mikhail Buturlin .08 .25
206 Konstantin Frolov .08 .25
207 Igor Zhelenchev .08 .25
208 Oleg Shargorodski .40 1.00
209 Sergei Selyutin .08 .25
210 Alexei Kupreenkov .08 .25
211 Roman Kukhtinov .08 .25
212 Vladislav Morozov .08 .25
213 Igor Belyavski .08 .25
214 Sergei Moskalev .08 .25
215 Alexei Tkachuk .08 .25
216 Sergei Chernyavski .08 .25
217 Vitali Kabanov .08 .25
218 Dmitri Klevakin .08 .25
219 Alexei Koledaev .08 .25
220 Oleg Glebov .08 .25
221 Georgi Evtyukhin .08 .25
222 Alexei Koznev .08 .25
223 Alexei Rubov .08 .25
224 Sergei Zinovjev 2.00 5.00
225 Evgueni Petrochinin .08 .25
226 Valeri Pokrovski .08 .25
227 Sergei Fedotov .08 .25
228 Vyacheslav Kurochkin .08 .25
229 Oleg Boltunov .08 .25
230 Alexei Baranov .08 .25
231 Igor Emeleev .08 .25
232 Roman Krivomazov .08 .25
233 Sergei Tikhonov .08 .25
234 Vladislav Brizgalov .30 .75
235 Dmitri Dubrovski .08 .25
236 Stepan Mokhov .08 .25
237 Dmitri Gogolev .08 .25
238 Evgueni Filinov .08 .25
239 Alexander Yudin .20 .50
240 Alexander Druzdelskin .08 .25
241 Sergei Shalamai .08 .25
242 Timofei Shishkanov .40 1.00
243 Alexander Sivov .08 .25
244 Vadim Musatov .08 .25
245 Andrei Chernoskutov .08 .25
246 Ruslan Shafikov .08 .25
247 Maxim Sokolov .20 .50
248 Alexander Matvichuk .08 .25
249 Andrei Evstafiev .08 .25
250 Vyacheslav Zavalnyuk .08 .25
251 Andrei Korolev .08 .25
252 Alexander Yudin .20 .50
253 Dmitri Mikhailov .08 .25
254 Artem Ostroushko .08 .25
255 Rinat Khasanov .08 .25
256 Vadim Epanchintsev .30 .75
257 Pavel Komarov .08 .25
258 Alexander Vyukhin .08 .25
259 Alfred Fatkullin .08 .25
260 Danis Zaripov .08 .25
261 Andrei Zubkov .08 .25
262 Marat Askarov .08 .25
263 Alexei Myagkikh .08 .25
264 Alexander Yudin .20 .50
265 Eduard Dmitriev .08 .25
266 Oleg Saltikov .08 .25
267 Oleg Grachev .08 .25
268 Valeri Oleinik .08 .25
269 Konstantin Koltsov .40 1.00
NNO Andrei Raiski .08 .25
NNO I.Koreshkov .20 .50
Alexander Koreshkov
Evgeni Koreshkov

1999-00 Russian Metallurg Magnetogorsk

This team set features Metallurg of the Russian Hockey League. The cards are numbered sequentially to those in the Dynamo Moscow set.

COMPLETE SET 6.00 15.00
27 Sergei Gomolyako .20 .50
28 Vadim Glovatski .20 .50
29 Sergei Tertyshny .20 .50
30 Igor Zemlyanoi .20 .50
31 Valeri Nikulin .20 .50
32 Andrei Sapozhnikov .30 .75
33 Boris Tortunov .20 .50
34 Sergei Zemchenok .20 .50
35 Oleg Mikulchuk .30 .75
36 Andrei Razin .30 .75
37 Ravil Gusmanov .30 .75
38 Maxim Bets .30 .75
39 Andrei Petrakov .20 .50
40 Andrei Kudinov .20 .50
41 Mikhail Borodulin .20 .50
42 Sergei Osipov .20 .50
43 Valeri Karpov .30 .75
44 Evgeni Koreshkov .20 .50
45 Alexander Koreshkov .20 .50
46 Dmitri Popov .20 .50
47 Andrei Sokolov .20 .50
48 Oleg Leontiev .20 .50
49 Vladimir Antipin .20 .50
50 Alexei Stelanov .20 .50
51 Vitali Prokhorov .30 .75
52 Alexander Golts .20 .50
53 Konstantin Shafranov .40 1.00
54 Team Card .20 .50

1999-00 Russian Stars of Hockey

This 42-card set was issued in May of 2000 in conjunction with the Russian Championship tournament. It was created to commemorate stars of past championship tournaments.

COMPLETE SET (42) 12.00 30.00
1 Alexei Chupin .08 .25
2 Alexander Prokopiev .08 .25
3 Alexei Kudashov .08 .25
4 Alexander Khavanov .20 .50
5 Andrei Markov .20 .50
6 Maxim Sushinski .08 .25
7 Dmitri Krasotkin .08 .25
8 Sergei Petrenko .08 .25
9 Valeri Karpov .08 .25
10 Sergei Tertyshny .08 .25
11 Ravil Gusmanov .08 .25
12 Egor Podomatski .20 .50
13 Alexei Chervyakov .08 .25
14 Valeri Ivannikov .08 .25
15 Maxim Mikhailovski .08 .25
16 Alexander Kharitonov .20 .50
17 Denis Arkhipov .30 .75
18 Yuri Dobryshkin .08 .25
19 Alexander Kuvaldin .08 .25
20 Dmitri Vlasenkov .08 .25
21 Evgeny Petrochinin .08 .25
22 Alexei Koznev .08 .25
23 Oleg Shargorodski .08 .25
24 Maxim Bets .08 .25
25 Dmitri Filimonov .08 .25
26 Alexei Yashin .20 .50
27 Pavel Bure 1.00 2.50
28 Sergei Fedorov 1.25 3.00
29 Alexander Mogilny .40 1.00
30 Alexei Kovalev .40 1.00
31 Maxim Sokolov .08 .25
32 Vyacheslav Kozlov .30 .75
33 Alexander Yakushev .40 1.00
34 Valeri Kharlamov 1.00 2.50
35 Alexei Kasatonov .20 .50
36 Vladislav Tretiak 2.00 5.00
37 Vyacheslav Fetisov .75 2.00
38 Valeri Vasiliev .40 1.00
39 Boris Mikhailov .40 1.00
40 Vyacheslav Anisin .08 .25
41 Vladimir Petrov .40 1.00
42 Alexander Maltsev .40 1.00

1999-00 Russian Stars Postcards

These postcards picture Russian stars with their club teams. It's likely that the listing below is not complete. The cards feature only the player's jersey number, so they are listed below in alphabetical order.

COMPLETE SET (32)
1 Maxim Afinogenov .75 2.00
2 Maxim Balmochnykh .40 1.00
3 Maxim Bets .40 1.00
4 Alexander Boikov .40 1.00
5 Victor Chistov .40 1.00
6 Marat Davydov .40 1.00
7 Kirill Golubev .40 1.00
8 Alexei Gorshkov .40 1.00
9 Airat Kadeikin .40 1.00
10 Svyatoslav Khalizov .40 1.00
11 Igor Khatsej .40 1.00
12 Viacheslav Kurochkin .40 1.00
13 Evgeny Kuveko .40 1.00
14 Albert Lecshev .40 1.00
15 Egor Mikhailov .75 2.00
16 Ildar Mukhametov .75 2.00
17 Andrei Pchelyakov .40 1.00
18 Sergey Petrenko .40 1.00
19 Alexander Prokopiev .40 1.00
20 Maxim Rybin .40 1.00
21 Vener Safin .40 1.00
22 Evgeny Shtepa .40 1.00
23 Dmitry Starostenko .40 1.00
24 Maxim Stepanov .40 1.00
25 Andrei Subbotin .40 1.00
26 Vadim Tarasov .75 2.00
27 Alexei Tkachuk .40 1.00
28 Andrei Tsarev .40 1.00
29 Vasily Turkovsky .40 1.00
30 Vladimir Tyurikov .40 1.00
31 Alexander Vyukhin .40 1.00
32 Sergei Yasakov .40 1.00

1999 Russian Fetisov Tribute

This set commemorates a game held in Russia in tribute of Slava Fetisov, perhaps the most important Russian-born player ever. It featured both Russian and NHL stars.

COMPLETE SET (41) 6.00 15.00
1 Alexander Korolyuk .07 .20
2 Pavel Bure .75 2.00
3 Alexei Morozov .07 .20
4 Viktor Kozlov .07 .20
5 Sergei Makarov .20 .50
6 Valeri Kamensky .07 .20
7 Maxim Afinogenov .20 .50
8 Slava Fetisov .20 .50
9 Maxim Sokolov .20 .50
10 Vladimir Malakhov .07 .20
11 Alexei Yashin .07 .20
12 Sergei Vyshedkevich .07 .20
13 Oleg Tverdovsky .07 .20
14 Sergei Brylin .07 .20
15 Vladimir Krutov .20 .50
16 Gennadi Tsygankov .07 .20
17 Egor Podomatski .20 .50
18 Vitali Vishnevski .07 .20
19 Sergei Nemchinov .07 .20
20 Daniil Markov .07 .20
21 Alexander Kharitonov .07 .20
22 Slava Bykov .07 .20
23 Bobby Carpenter .07 .20
24 Scott Stevens .20 .50
25 Ken Daneyko .07 .20
26 Jari Kurri .75 2.00
27 Slava Kozlov .20 .50
28 Anders Eriksson .07 .20
29 Darius Kasparaitis .07 .20
30 Doug Brown .07 .20
31 Ilkka Sinisalo .07 .20
32 Valeri Shiryaev .07 .20
33 Martin Brodeur 2.00 5.00
34 Christian Ruuttu .07 .20
35 Randy McKay .07 .20
36 Gino Odjick .20 .50
37 Igor Larionov .20 .50
38 Martin Lapointe .07 .20
39 Larry Robinson CO .20 .50
40 Viktor Tikhonov CO .07 .20
41 Scotty Bowman CO .20 .50

2000 Russian Champions

This Russian-produced set features players who have won the big one back in the ol' USSR.

COMPLETE SET (6) 4.00 10.00
1 Alexander Khavanov .80 2.00
2 Alexei Troschinsky .80 2.00
3 Andrei Markov .80 2.00
4 Alexander Kharitonov .80 2.00
5 Alexander Prokopiev .40 1.00
6 Vitali Yeremeyev 1.20 3.00

2000-01 Russian Dynamo Moscow

This set features players from the top Russian club team, Dynamo Moscow. The cards were produced in Russia and apparently were sold at home games. Some sets made their way to North America via the Internet.

COMPLETE SET (33) 6.00 15.00
1 Alexey Yegorov .30 .75
2 Oleg Shevtsov .20 .50
3 Alexander Yeremenko .30 .75
4 Mikhail Shtalenkov .40 1.00
5 Roman Zolotov .20 .50
6 Oleg Orekhovsky .20 .50
7 Igor Stchadilov .20 .50
8 Oleg Polkovnikov .20 .50
9 Ilya Nikulin .30 .75
10 Evgeny Gribko .20 .50
11 Marat Davydov .20 .50
12 Mikhail Donika .20 .50
13 Andrei Kuzmin .20 .50
14 Mikhail Ivanov .20 .50
15 Alexander Kuvaldin .20 .50
16 Sergei Klimovich .20 .50
17 Alexander Kharlamov .30 .75
18 Alexander Savchenkov .20 .50
19 Alexei Smirnov .40 1.00
20 Oleg Smirnov .20 .50
21 Stanislav Romanov .20 .50
22 Alexei Kudashov .30 .75
23 Boris Zelenko .20 .50
24 Alexei Tereshenko .20 .50
25 Alexander Stepanov .20 .50
26 Dmitri Dudarev .20 .50
27 Denis Kartsev .20 .50
28 Dmitri Subbotin .20 .50
29 Igor Bakhmutov .20 .50
30 Alexander Karpovtsev .30 .75
31 Alexander Klebnikov .20 .50
32 Dmitri Semenov .20 .50
33 Dmitriy Kokorev .30 .75

2000-01 Russian Dynamo Moscow Blue-White

Little is known about this Russian-produced set beyond the checklist. Additional information can be forwarded to hockeymag@beckett.com

COMPLETE SET (5) 2.50 6.00
1 Mikhail Shtalenkov 1.25 3.00
2 Alexei Kudashov .75 2.00
3 Oleg Orekhovsky .40 1.00
4 Mikhail Ivanov .40 1.00
5 Dmitri Subbotin .40 1.00

2000-01 Russian Goalkeepers

As the title suggests, this Russian-produced set features top stoppers from the RHL. Any additional information can be forwarded to hockeymag@beckett.com.

COMPLETE SET (9) 5.00 12.00
1 Maxim Sokolov .40 1.00
2 Mikhail Shtalenkov .75 2.00
3 Ilja Bryzgalov 1.50 4.00
4 Andrei Tsareev .40 1.00
5 Oleg Shevtsov .40 1.00
6 Andrei Malkov .40 1.00
7 Sergey Nikolaev .40 1.00
8 Alexei Yegorov .40 1.00
9 Maxim Mikhailovsky .40 1.00

2000-01 Russian Hockey League

This set features the top players in Russia's elite league. The set is noteworthy for including early or first cards of top Russian prospects Ilya Kovalchuk, Stan Chistov, Alexander Svitov, Andrei Medvedev, Pavel Datsyuk, etc. It is worth noting that card #260 is misnumbered at #199.

COMPLETE SET (394) 75.00 175.00
COMMON CARD (1-394) .10 .25
SEMISTARS/GOALIES .20 .50
UNLISTED STARS .30 .75
1 Oleg Filimonov .10 .25
2 Alexei Lazarenko .10 .25
3 Sergei Yasakov .10 .25
4 Steve Plouffe .30 .75
5 Alexander Tichkin .10 .25
6 Igor Boldin .10 .25
7 Vitali Evdokimov .10 .25
8 Igor Andryiotshenko .10 .25
9 Alexander Grishin .10 .25
10 Andrei Kyselev .10 .25
11 Dmitri Tarasov .10 .25
12 Anatoli Ustyugov .10 .25
13 Ruslan Bernikov .10 .25
14 Oleg Naumenko .10 .25
15 Igor Nikolaev .10 .25
16 Renat Khairetdinov .10 .25
17 Vadim Pokotilo .10 .25
18 Vladimir Tyorikov .10 .25
19 Dmitri Uchaikin .10 .25
20 Konstantin Mitroshkin .10 .25
21 Alexei Plotnikov .10 .25
22 Oleg Vevcherenko .10 .25
23 Dmitri Shulakov .10 .25
24 Sergei Butko .10 .25
25 Dmitri Levinski .10 .25
26 Vladimir Gusev .30 .75
27 Denis Martiniuk .10 .25
28 Ross Harris .10 .25
29 Nikolai Pronin .10 .25
30 Sergei Zholobov .10 .25
31 Dmitri Bykov .75 2.00
32 Remir Khaidarov .10 .25
33 Eduard Kudermetov .10 .25
34 Dmitri Yachanov .10 .25
35 Dmitri Balmin .10 .25
36 Alexander Zhdan .30 .75
37 Alexei Chupin .10 .25
38 Almaz Gariffillin .10 .25
39 Alexander Zavyalov .10 .25
40 Ilnur Gizhatullin .10 .25
41 Alexei Tertyshny .10 .25
42 Evgeni Varlamov .10 .25
43 Oleg Glebov .10 .25
44 Sergei Mylnikov Jr. .30 .75
45 Leonid Kanaryekin .10 .25
46 Ildar Yobin .10 .25
47 Anton Volchenkov ERC 2.00 5.00
48 Andrei Loginov .10 .25
49 Vitali Drindeyen .10 .25
50 Pavel Khanarski .10 .25
51 Vladimir Kramskoy .10 .25
52 Oleg Mikulchik .10 .25
53 Vyacheslav Zhavaliuk .10 .25
54 Sergei Soin ERC .75 2.00
55 Andrei Galkin .10 .25
56 Valeri Cherni .10 .25
57 Andrei Posnov .10 .25
58 Alexander Ardashev .10 .25
59 Roman Salnikov .10 .25
60 Eduard Gorbachev .10 .25
61 Sergei Martinov .10 .25
62 Dmitri Perozhkov .10 .25
63 Alexander Frolov ERC 6.00 15.00
64 Vladimir Zhavyalov .10 .25
65 Lev Berdischevski .10 .25
66 Andrei Maximenko .10 .25
67 Dmitri Teplyakov .10 .25
68 Boris Kuzmin .10 .25
69 Nikolai Ruzhenikov .10 .25
70 Maxim Ossipov .20 .50
71 Vladimir Loginov .10 .25
72 Andrei Kuzmin .20 .50
73 Ilya Dokshin .10 .25
74 Sergei Yakimovich .10 .25
75 Oleg Kuzmin .10 .25
76 Yuri Truvacheev .10 .25
77 Fedor Tjutin ERC .10 .25
78 Alexei Tsvetkov .10 .25
79 Alexander Shenkar .10 .25
80 Gyori Kabanov .10 .25
81 Vitali Chumicheev .10 .25
82 Artem Chernov .30 .75
83 Dmitri Khramchenko .20 .50
84 Andrei Sharapov .10 .25
85 Oleg Antonenko .10 .25
86 Oleg Namestnikov .10 .25
87 Andrei Poddyakon .10 .25
88 Vasili Smirnov .10 .25
89 Vitali Novopashin .10 .25
90 Roman Malov .10 .25
91 Vadim Averkin .10 .25
92 Nikolai Voevodin .10 .25
93 Vladimir Fedosov .10 .25
94 Vasili Chestokletov .10 .25
95 Anatoli Filatov .10 .25
96 Igor Safonov .10 .25
97 Mikhail Belobragin .10 .25
98 Maxim Ovchinikov .10 .25
99 Alexei Vorobiev .10 .25
100 Igor Shevtsov .10 .25
101 Sergei Fadeyev .10 .25
102 Dmitri Pankov .10 .25
103 Sergei Berdnikov .10 .25
104 Georgi Evtyiokhin .10 .25
105 Sergei Voronov .10 .25
106 Alexei Kaliozhni .10 .25
107 Yuri Kuznetsov .10 .25
108 Alexander Golts .20 .50
109 Sergei Klyshin .10 .25
110 Igor Melyakov .10 .25
111 Sergei Kiseleev .10 .25
112 Igor Karpenko .30 .75
113 Igor Karpenko .30 .75
114 Sergei Nikolayev .10 .25
115 Igor Sipchenko .10 .25
116 Valeri Pokrovski .10 .25
117 Sergei Gubernatorov .10 .25
118 Igor Samoylov .10 .25
119 Alexander Urakin .10 .25
120 Oleg Eremeyev .10 .25
121 Paolo Della Bella .20 .50
122 Slava Bezhukladnikov .10 .25
123 Alexei Troschinsky .20 .50
124 Vladimir Antipin .10 .25
125 Alexander Yudin .10 .25
126 Vitali Proshkin .10 .25
127 Ilya Kovalchuk 6.00 15.00
128 Dmitri Ryabikin .10 .25
129 Alexander Zhurik .10 .25
130 Igor Shastin .10 .25
131 Mikhail Shukaev .10 .25
132 Anvar Gatiyatulin .10 .25
133 Andrei Anisimov .10 .25
134 Maxim Soloviev .10 .25
135 Konstantin Bezborodov .10 .25
136 Ravil Yakubov .10 .25
137 Alexander Prokopiev .10 .25
138 Oleg Shargorodsky .20 .50
139 Ruslan Batyrshin .20 .50
140 Alexei Kypreyenkov .10 .25
141 Pavel Komarov .10 .25
142 Alexei Sharnin .10 .25
143 Sergei Fedotov .10 .25
144 Denis Khlistov .10 .25
145 Mikhail Potapov .10 .25
146 Alexander Semak .20 .50
147 Andrei Vasilesvki .30 .75
148 Azhat Sharipov .10 .25
149 Andrei Sidyakin .10 .25
150 Sergei Shikhanov .10 .25
151 Sergei Gomolyako .10 .25
152 Dmitri Nabokov .20 .50
153 Valentin Morozov .10 .25
154 Denis Metliuk .20 .50
155 Ilja Bryzgalov ERC 2.00 5.00
156 Alexander Lyubimov .20 .50
157 Ilya Byakin .20 .50
158 Sergei Tertyshny .10 .25
159 Valeri Karpov .20 .50
160 Andrei Tarasenko .10 .25
161 Alexander Yudin .20 .50
162 Nikolai Zavarukin .20 .50
163 Oleg Belkin .10 .25
164 Andrei Skabelka .10 .25
165 Leonid Fatikov .10 .25
166 Oleg Khmylev .10 .25
167 Denis Afinogenov .10 .25
168 Alexander Nesterov .10 .25
169 Andrei Kruchinin .10 .25
170 Andrei Petrunin .20 .50
171 Vladimir Malenkikh .10 .25
172 Sergei Shabanov .10 .25
173 Vadim Tarasov .30 .75
174 Igor Zhelenchev .10 .25
175 Sergei Shalamai .10 .25
176 Yuri Zhuev .10 .25
177 Artem Argokov .10 .25
178 Evgeni Pupkov .10 .25
179 Sergei Moskaleev .10 .25
180 Alexander Filippov .10 .25
181 Igor Dyakiv .10 .25
182 Stanislav Pinevski .10 .25
183 Alexander Agnevtshikov .10 .25
184 Sergei Sherevtsov .10 .25
185 Roman Kuhtinov .10 .25
186 Evgeni Lapin .10 .25
187 Nikolai Kurochkin .10 .25
188 Alexei Alekeev .10 .25
189 Alexei Koledaev .10 .25
190 Sergei Berenikin .10 .25
191 Denis Tyurin .10 .25
192 Rail Rozakov .10 .25
193 Vladimir Pozdnyakov .10 .25

194 Pavel Desyatkov .10 .25
195 Alexei Krovopuskov .10 .25
196 Sergei Sevastyanov .10 .25
197 Mikhail Yakubov ERC 1.50 4.00
198 Mikhail Sevastyanov .10 .25
199 Pavel Torgaev .10 .25
200 Denis Tyulyapkin .10 .25
201 Dmitri Altareev .10 .25
202 Maxim Savosin .10 .25
203 Leonid Toropchenko .10 .25
204 Stanislav Timakov .10 .25
205 Valeri Emelyanov .10 .25
206 Igor Gracheev .10 .25
207 Stanislav Udyachski .10 .25
208 Yuris Ozols .10 .25
209 Alexander Galkin .10 .25
210 Sergei C. Makarov .10 .25
211 Sergei Seliutin .10 .25
212 Alexander Popov .10 .25
213 Sergei Zhadeleyenov .10 .25
214 Alexei Litvinenko .10 .25
215 Dmitri Shulga .10 .25
216 Denis Sokolov .10 .25
217 Maxim Krayev .10 .25
218 Renat Hasanov .10 .25
219 Boris Tortunov .10 .25
220 Dmitri Krasotkin .10 .25
221 Maxim Velikov .10 .25
222 Yuri Panov .10 .25
223 Alexander Vyukhin .10 .25
224 Vadim Shakhraichuk .10 .25
225 Alexei Badyukov .10 .25
226 Alexander Korobolin .10 .25
227 Dmitri Zatonski .10 .25
228 Kirill Koltsov .75 2.00
229 Alexander Svitov 1.25 3.00
230 Ilya Gorbushin .10 .25
231 Andrei Samokhvalov .10 .25
232 Igor Nikitin .10 .25
233 Ramil Saifullin .10 .25
234 Viktor Chistov .10 .25
235 Vladimir Vorobiev .10 .25
236 Igor Niklulin .10 .25
237 Alexander Sidorovski .10 .25
238 Oleg Polkovnikov .10 .25
239 Dmitri Dudarev .10 .25
240 Andrei Sapozhnikov .10 .25
241 Andrei Kudinov .10 .25
242 Alik Gareev .10 .25
243 Ruslan Nurtdinov .10 .25
244 Alexander Ageev .10 .25
245 Andrei Yakhanov .10 .25
246 Vener Safin .10 .25
247 Sergei Komarov .10 .25
248 Nail Shayakhmetov .10 .25
249 Vladislav Ozolin .10 .25
250 Nikolai Tsuligin .10 .25
251 Albert Letsvheyev .10 .25
252 Stanislav Shalnov .10 .25
253 Maxim Orlov .10 .25
254 Alexei Chernikov .10 .25
255 Sergei B. Makarov .10 .25
256 Sergei Zimakov .20 .50
257 Gennady Savilov .10 .25
258 Vasili Turkovski .10 .25
259 Igor Mikhailov .10 .25
260 Vadim Glovatskin .10 .25
261 Alexei Tkachuk .10 .25
262 Mikhail Volkov .10 .25
263 Dmitri Gogolev .10 .25
264 Pavel Agarkov .10 .25
265 Vladimir Korsunov .10 .25
266 Andrei Medvedev 1.50 4.00
267 Dmitri Bykov .20 .50
268 Ruslan Zainullin .20 .50
269 Dmitri Starostenko .20 .50
270 Alexander Schev .10 .25
271 Andrei Petrakov .10 .25
272 Sergei Klimentiev .10 .25
273 Yuri Kuznetsov .10 .25
274 Igor Knyazev .60 1.50
275 Vladimir Tikhomirov .10 .25
276 Vladimir Repneev .10 .25
277 Alexander Boikov .10 .25
278 Sergei Voronov .10 .25
279 Rustem Kamaletdinov .10 .25
280 Konstantin Molodstov .10 .25
281 Andrei Frolkin .10 .25
282 Vladimir Terekhov .10 .25
283 Dmitri Klevakin .10 .25
284 Denis Denisov .20 .50
285 Vladislav Korneev .20 .50
286 Evgeni Muratov .20 .50
287 Pavel Duma .30 .75
288 Egor Shastin .75 2.00
289 Artem Chernov .30 .75
290 Rail Rozakov .30 .75
291 Alexander Chagodaev .30 .75
292 Alexander Buturlin .75 2.00
293 Mikhail Yakubov 1.50 4.00
294 Alexei Petrov .30 .75
295 Pavel Vorobiev ERC 1.50 4.00
296 Ilya Kovalchuk 6.00 15.00
297 Vladimir Tikhomirov .20 .50
298 Igor Bakhmutov .20 .50
299 Sergei Zholotov .20 .50
300 Vadim Tarasov .30 .75
301 Andrei Medvedev 1.50 4.00
302 Anton Volchenkov ERC 2.00 5.00
303 Denis Grebeshkov ERC .40 1.00
304 Andrei Shefer .75 2.00
305 Alexander Seluyanov .20 .50
306 Ivan Nepryaev .30 .75
307 Stanislav Chistov ERC 2.00 5.00
308 Alexander Barkunov .30 .75
309 Alexander Svitov 1.25 3.00
310 Igor Boriskov .20 .50
311 Alexander Zhdan .30 .75
312 Ilya Nikulin .20 .50
313 Mikhail Donika .20 .50
314 Andrei Kuzmin .20 .50
315 Alexei Smirnov .75 2.00
316 Vadim Brezhgunov .75 2.00
317 Mikhail Shtalenkov .30 .75
318 Sergei Klimovich .20 .50
319 Alexander Kharlamov .20 .50
320 Dmitri Subbotin .10 .25
321 Alexander Karpovstev .10 .25
322 Oleg Shevtsov .10 .25
323 Evgeni Gribko .10 .25
324 Denis Khlopotnov .30 .75
325 Pavel Boichenko .10 .25
326 Alexander Stepanov .10 .25
327 Nikolai Ignatov .10 .25
328 Alexander Skoptsov .10 .25
329 Mikhail Mikhailovski .10 .25
330 Sergei Semin .10 .25
331 Pavel Trakhanov .10 .25
332 Dmitri Riabkin .10 .25
333 Ravil Yakubov .10 .25
334 Pavel Datsyuk ERC 15.00 40.00
335 Andrei Evstafiev .10 .25
336 Andrei Razin .10 .25
337 Denis Afinogenov .10 .25
338 Oleg Orekhovsky .10 .25
339 Ilya Gorbushin .10 .25
340 Viktor Tchistov .10 .25
341 Valeri Oleinik .10 .25
342 Sergei Shumykin .10 .25
343 Oleg Romashko .10 .25
344 Yuri Bogusevich .10 .25
345 Nikolai Koptin .10 .25
346 Vladislav Pustovalov .10 .25
347 Andrei Gavrylin .10 .25
348 Dmitri Chikin .10 .25
349 Evgeni Letov .10 .25
350 Vadim Navrotskin .10 .25
351 Vitali Chumichev .10 .25
352 Sergei Mozyakin .10 .25
353 Alexei Simakov .10 .25
354 Vadim Gusev .10 .25
355 Sergei Kutyavin .10 .25
356 Lev Trifonov .10 .25
357 Roman Oksiuta .10 .25
358 Alexei Chervyakov .10 .25
359 Sergei Erkovich .10 .25
360 Oleg Volkov .10 .25
361 Sergei Gomolyako .10 .25
362 Evgeni Bobariko .10 .25
363 Evgeni Bobariko .10 .25
364 Igor Boldin .10 .25
365 Oleg Komissarov .10 .25
366 Yuri Zlov .10 .25
367 Andrei Petyakov .10 .25
368 Oleg Boltunov .10 .25
369 Nikolai Babenko .10 .25
370 Igor Varitskin .10 .25
371 Andrei Rasolko .10 .25
372 Dmitri Denisov .10 .25
373 Konstantin Maslyukov .10 .25
374 Vadim Epanchintsev .20 .50
375 Alexei Krivchenkov .10 .25
376 Maxim Sokolov .10 .25
377 Alexei Koznev .10 .25
378 Evgeni Petrochinin .10 .25
379 Vladislav Luchkin .10 .25
380 Artur Oktyabriev .10 .25
381 Vladimir Kopat .10 .25
382 Vladimir Kochin .10 .25
383 Igor Emeleev .10 .25
384 Sergei Shitkovski .10 .25
385 Andrei Kozyrev .10 .25
386 Alexander Smagin .10 .25
387 Rafik Yakubov .10 .25
388 Ildar Mukhometov .30 .75
389 Ivan Tkachenko .10 .25
390 Evgeni Akhmetov .10 .25
391 Vitali Lyutkevich .10 .25
392 Alexander Vinogradov .10 .25
393 Evgeni Artyukhin .20 .50
394 Andrei Tsarev .10 .25

2001-02 Russian Dynamo Moscow

This set features the players of Moscow's top team, Dynamo. The cards were sold in set form, apparently at home games.

COMPLETE SET (22) 15.00 35.00
1 Oleg Orekhovskiy .20 .50
2 Alexei Troschinsky .30 .75
3 Andrey Razin .20 .50
4 Dmitriy Starostenko .20 .50
5 Andrey Skopintsev .20 .50
6 Evgeniy Gribko .20 .50
7 Alexey Kudashov .20 .50
8 Evgeniy Lapin .20 .50
9 Iliy Nikulin .20 .50
10 Valeriy Karpov .20 .50
11 Alexander Kuvaldin .20 .50
12 Ravil Yakubov .20 .50
13 Alexander Nizivij .20 .50
14 Dmitriy Semenov .20 .50
15 Alexander Ovechkin 10.00 25.00
16 Marat Davydov .20 .50
17 Mikhail Shtalenkov .30 .75
18 Vladimir Korolkov .20 .50
19 Igor Mirnov .20 .50
20 Vitaliy Yeremeev .40 1.00
21 Alexander Savchenkov .20 .50
22 Sergei Vishedkevich .20 .50

2001-02 Russian Dynamo Moscow Mentos

This set also features Dynamo Moscow and is distinguishable from the other set by the prominent placement of the Mentos trademark. Little else is known about this set; additional information can be forwarded to hockeymag@beckett.com.

COMPLETE SET (16) 3.00 8.00
1 Sergey Vishedkevich .20 .50
2 Evgeniy Lapin .20 .50
3 Alexander Savtchenkov .20 .50
4 Alexander Stepanov .20 .50
5 Mikhail Ivanov .20 .50
6 Mikhail Shtalenkov .30 .75
7 Dmitriy Starostenko .20 .50
8 Alexei Troschinsky .20 .50
9 Ravil Yakubov .20 .50
10 Oleg Orekhovskiy .20 .50
11 Andrey Skopintsev .20 .50
12 Andrey Razin .20 .50
13 Marat Davydov .20 .50
14 Iliy Nikulin .20 .50
15 Alexander Yudin .20 .50
16 Evgeniy Gribko .20 .50

2001-02 Russian Hockey League

COMPLETE SET (173) 30.00 60.00
1 Dmitri Spirin .08 .20
2 Alexander Yakovenko .08 .20
3 Ivan Sakharov .08 .20
4 Andrei Mukhachev .08 .20
5 Anatoli Stepanov .08 .20
6 Nikolai Pronin .08 .20
7 Igor Boiko .08 .20
8 Alexander Borovkov .08 .20
9 Dmitri Sergeev .08 .20
10 Stepanov Brothers .08 .20
11 Renat Kharetdinov .08 .20
12 Alexander Andrievsky .08 .20
13 Evgeni Bobariko .08 .20
14 Andrei Galkin .08 .20
15 Evgeni Gamalei .08 .20
16 Oleg Grachev .08 .20
17 Dmitri Yevdokimov .08 .20
18 Andrei Yershov .08 .20
19 Sergei Kiselev .08 .20
20 Maxim Korobov .08 .20
21 Denis Kuzmenko .08 .20
22 Denis Makarov .08 .20
23 Sergei Makarov .08 .20
24 Oleg Mikulchik .08 .20
25 Roman Oksiuta .08 .20
26 Slava Polikarkin .08 .20
27 Andrei Ponomarev .08 .20
28 Dmitri Popov .08 .20
29 Vitali Prokhorov .08 .20
30 Alexander Romanov .08 .20
31 Sergei Selyutin .08 .20
32 Alexander Smirnov .75 2.00
33 Sergei Sorokin .08 .20
34 Mikhail Strelkov .08 .20
35 Stanislav Timakov .08 .20
36 Dmitri Timofeev .08 .20
37 Vladimir Fedossov .08 .20
38 Alexei Chrevyakov .08 .20
39 Vitali Chinakhov .08 .20
40 Oleg Yashin .08 .20
41 Sergei Gomolyako .08 .20
42 Vasili Chistokletov .08 .20
43 Alexander Yudin .08 .20
44 Alexander Yudin .08 .20
45 Alexander Yudin .08 .20
46 Artem Anisimov .08 .20
47 Sergei Shikhanov .08 .20
48 Evgeni Akhmetov .08 .20
49 Igor Varitsky .08 .20
50 Vladimir Antipin .08 .20
51 Vadim Sharifjanov .20 .50
52 Rail Muftiev .08 .20
53 Maxim Bets .20 .50
54 Viktor Ignatiev .20 .50
55 Yuri Trubachev .08 .20
56 Igor Shadilov .08 .20
57 Sergei Gusev .08 .20
58 Viktor Chistov .20 .50
59 Maxim Sokolov .40 1.00
60 Alexander Semak .08 .20
61 Ruslan Akhmadullin .08 .20
62 Igor Volkov .08 .20
63 Sergei Shalamai .08 .20
64 Vitali Karamnov .08 .20
65 Vladislav Ozolin .08 .20
66 Vladislav Makarov .08 .20
67 Igor Karpenko .40 1.00
68 Parris Duffus .75 2.00
69 Igor Shastin .08 .20
70 Evgeny Muratov .08 .20
71 Nikolai Bardin .08 .20
72 Roman Baranov .08 .20
73 Artem Chernov .08 .20
74 Konstantin Mikhailov .08 .20
75 Dmitri Parkhomenko .08 .20
76 Igor Mikhailov .08 .20
77 Vladimir Korsunov .08 .20
78 Alexei Livinenko .08 .20
79 Alexander Vyukhin .20 .50
80 Dmitri Zatonski .08 .20
81 Kirill Koltsov .75 2.00
82 Alexander Kharitonov .08 .20
83 Renat Kharetdinov .08 .20
84 Alexander Levenyuk .08 .20
85 Alexei Volkov .40 1.00
86 Sergei Yasakov .08 .20
87 Andrei Dylevsky .08 .20
88 Sergei Kutyavin .08 .20
89 Sergei Yerkovich .08 .20
90 Sergei Berdnikov .08 .20
91 Oleg Shargorodsky .20 .50
92 Oleg Vevcherenko .08 .20
93 Stanislav Shalnov .08 .20
94 Alexei Gorshkov .08 .20
95 Andrei Subbotin .60 1.50
96 Ramil Saifullin .08 .20
97 Ilya Gorbushin .08 .20
98 Alexander Svitov 1.25 3.00
99 Sergei Tertyshny .08 .20
100 Alexander Popov .08 .20
101 Alexander Korobolin .08 .20
102 Denis Zaripov .08 .20
103 Sergei Klimentiev .08 .20
104 Dmitri Kirilenko .08 .20
105 Maxim Rybin .08 .20
106 Konstantin Gorovikov .08 .20
107 Denis Khlystov .08 .20
108 Andrei Tsarev .20 .50
109 Alexei Chupin .08 .20
110 unknown
111 Alexander Drozdetski .08 .20
112 unknown
113 Vadim Brezgunov .08 .20
114 Alexei Podalinski .08 .20
115 Konstantin Shafronov .08 .20
116 Alexander Golts .08 .20
117 Ilya Gorokhov .08 .20
118 Dmitri Zatonski .08 .20
119 Vadim Epanchinsev .08 .20
120 Dmitri Gogolev .08 .20
121 Alexander Yudin .08 .20
122 Maxim Sokolov .40 1.00
123 Boris Tortunov .20 .50
124 Vladimir Antipov .08 .20
125 Vladimir Kretchin .08 .20
126 Sergei Zinovjev 1.25 3.00
127 Andrei Kruchinin .08 .20
128 Sergei Zhukov .08 .20
129 Yuri Kuznetsov .08 .20
130 Anton But .08 .20
131 Denis Khlopotnov .20 .50
132 Yuri Kuznetsov .08 .20
133 Oleg Shvetsov .20 .50
134 Andrei Loginov .08 .20
135 Stanislav Udiansky .08 .20
136 Denis Baev .08 .20
137 Sergei Semin .08 .20
138 Maxim Soloviev .08 .20
139 Dmitri Dubrovsky .08 .20
140 Vitali Drynin .08 .20
141 Lev Berdischevski .08 .20
142 Alexei Sergievsky .08 .20
143 Evgeni Artyukhin .08 .20
144 Alexei Kochegarov .08 .20
145 Evgeny Lapenkov .08 .20
146 Alexander Borozenko .08 .20
147 Dmitri Vershinin .08 .20
148 Yaroslav Lyuzenkov .08 .20
149 Artem Rybin .08 .20
150 Alexander Skoptsev .08 .20
151 Alexei Pogonin .08 .20
152 Vladislav Poperechny .08 .20
153 Dmitri Plekhanov .08 .20
154 Alexei Krovopuskov .08 .20
155 Alexei Yegorov .20 .50
156 Oleg Voschenikin .08 .20
157 Vitali Trigubov .20 .50
158 Jan Benda .08 .20
159 Patrik Martinec .08 .20
160 Dmitri Yachanov .20 .50
161 Almaz Garifullin .08 .20
162 Alexei Murzin .08 .20
163 Vladimir Loginov .08 .20
164 Khalim Nigmatullin .08 .20
165 Alexander Dolishnya .08 .20
166 Igor Fadeev .08 .20
167 Dmitri Kulikov .08 .20
168 Andrei Yemelin .08 .20
169 Oleg Yashin .08 .20
170 Andrei Zabolotnev .08 .20
171 Alexander Semak .08 .20
172 Sergei Askimov .08 .20
173 Rinat Khasanov .08 .20

2001-02 Russian Legions

Little is known about this set, which features top Russian players. It is believed that the checklist below is incomplete. Any additional information can be forwarded to hockeymag@beckett.com.

COMPLETE SET (3) .80 2.00
1 Alexei Troschinsky .40 1.00
2 Dmitriy Starostenko .40 1.00
3 Vladimir Tsiplakov .40 1.00

2001-02 Russian Lightnings

Little is known about this Russian set, which features top players of the RHL. Any additional information can be forwarded to hockeymag@beckett.com.

COMPLETE SET (8) 2.00 5.00
1 Maxim Sushinskiy .40 1.00
2 Igor Varitskiy .40 1.00
3 Alexey Kudashov .40 1.00
4 Andrey Razin .40 1.00
5 Dmitriy Gogolev .40 1.00
6 Dmitriy Kvartalnov .40 1.00
7 Denis Metlyuk .40 1.00
8 Andrei Kovalenko .40 1.00

2001-02 Russian Ultimate Line

Little is known about this Russian set, which features top goaltenders of the RHL. Any additional information can be forwarded to hockeymag@beckett.com.

COMPLETE SET (5)
1 Vitaliy Yeremeev .80 2.00
2 Egor Podomatskiy .80 2.00
3 Mike Fountain .80 2.00
4 Jaroslav Kamesh .40 1.00
5 Alexander Yeremenko .40 1.00

2001-02 Russian Young Lions

Little is known about this Russian set, which features top players of the RHL. Any additional information can be forwarded to hockeymag@beckett.com.

COMPLETE SET (11) 10.00 40.00
1 Ilya Kovalchuk 4.00 15.00
2 Alexander Svitov 1.20 2.00
3 Alexander Ovechkin 6.00 15.00
4 Igor Grigorenko 1.20 4.00
5 Kirill Koltsov .80 2.00
6 Anton Babchuk .80 2.00
7 Alexander Frolov 1.20 3.00
8 Nikolai Zherdev 1.25 3.00
9 Alexander Perezhogin .40 1.00
10 Ilya Nikulin .40 1.00
11 Maxim Sheviev .40 1.00

2002-03 Russian Future Stars

This Russian-produced set features many of that country's top young stars.

COMPLETE SET (20) 10.00 25.00
1 Alexander Ovechkin 6.00 15.00
2 Igor Grigorenko 1.25 3.00
3 Vladislav Evseev .75 2.00
4 Konstantin Glazachev .40 1.00
5 Fedor Tyutin .40 1.00
6 Denis Grebeshkov .40 1.00
7 Alexander Perezhogin .75 2.00
8 Kiril Koltsov .40 1.00
9 Yuri Trubachev .20 .50
10 Andrei Taratukhin .20 .50
11 Igor Mirnov .20 .50
12 Dmitri Chernykh .20 .50
13 Dmitri Shitikov .20 .50
14 Dmitri Semin .20 .50
15 Andrei Medvedev .40 1.00
16 Alexei Volkov .30 .75
17 Sergei Zinovjev .75 2.00
18 Sergei Soin .40 1.00
19 Alexei Mikhnov .20 .50
20 Ilya Nikulin .20 .50

2002-03 Russian Hockey League

This set, produced by World Sport, features the top players in the Russian circuit. Many players have multiple cards in the set from a variety of subsets including All-Stars, Team Russia and World Juniors. Card #184 appears twice.

COMPLETE SET (273) 75.00 150.00
COMMON CARD (1-273) .08 .20
SEMISTARS/GOALIES .20 .50
UNLISTED STARS .40 1.00
1 Evgeni Krutov .08 .20
2 Sergei Zhurikov .08 .20
3 Alexei Medvedev .08 .20
4 Juri Bogusevich .08 .20
5 Gleb Klimenko .08 .20
6 Alexei Petrov .08 .20
7 Andrei Tsarev .20 .50
8 Victor Lee .08 .20
9 Slava Zavalnyuk ENG .20 .50
10 Slava Zavalnyuk RUS .20 .50
11 Dmitri Klevakin .20 .50
12 Dmitri Semin .08 .20
13 Evgeny Fedorov .08 .20
14 Evgeny Fedorov .08 .20
15 Dmitri Yachanov .20 .50
16 Dmitri Balmin .08 .20
17 Konstantin Maslyukov .08 .20
18 Vitali Atyushov .08 .20
19 Denis Metliuk .08 .20
20 Andrei Kudinov .08 .20
21 Anton Babchuk ERC 1.25 3.00
22 Alexei Badyukov .08 .20
23 Dmitri Gogolev .08 .20
24 Alexei Chupin .08 .20
25 Denis Platonov .08 .20
26 Sergei Zolotov .08 .20
27 Jan Benda .08 .20
28 Steve Plouffe .75 2.00
29 Artem Chernov .08 .20
30 Dmitri Khomutov .20 .50
31 Sergei Zvyagin .20 .50
32 Vladimir Malenjkih .08 .20
33 Oleg Minakov .08 .20
34 Stanislav Yasechko .08 .20
35 Mike Fountain .75 2.00
36 Oleg Volkov .08 .20
37 Maxim Mikhailovsky .20 .50
38 Oleg Belkin .08 .20
39 Alexander Buturlin .08 .20
40 Alexander Bobkin .08 .20
41 Sergei Sevostjanov .08 .20
42 Andrei Frolkin .08 .20
43 Alexander Boikov .08 .20
44 Richard Shekhny .08 .20
45 Petr Vorobiev CO .05
46 Andrei Esipov .08 .20
47 Mikhail Sevostjanov .08 .20
48 Alexander Semin ERC 6.00 15.00
49 Alexander Yudin .08 .20
50 Rail Rozakov .08 .20
51 Sergei Berdnikov .08 .20
52 Philip Metliuk .08 .20
53 Vadim Averkin .08 .20
54 Alexander Gutov .08 .20
55 Ilya Gorokov .08 .20
56 Maxim Kondratiev .20 .50
57 Alexander Nesterov .08 .20
58 Igor Grigorenko ERC 5.00 12.00
59 Vladislav Boulin .08 .20
60 Artur Oktyabrev .08 .20
61 Ladislav Chierny .08 .20
62 Alexander Yudin .08 .20
63 Alex Westlund .75 2.00
64 Alexander Fomitchev .40 1.00
65 David MacIsaac .20 .50
66 Andrei Tsarev .20 .50
67 Maxim Splridonov .08 .20
68 Vadim Pokotilo .08 .20
69 Konstantin Chaschukhin .20 .50
70 Evgeni Safronov .08 .20
71 Albert Vishnyakov .08 .20
72 Christian Bronsard .75 2.00
73 Alexei Mikhnov .20 .50
74 Askhat Rakhmatullin .08 .20
75 Andrei Tarasenko .08 .20
76 Alexei Korshkov .08 .20
77 Leo Chermak .08 .20
78 Kirill Sidorenko .08 .20
79 Sergei Gomolyako .08 .20
80 Ildar Mukhometov .20 .50
81 Dmitri Dudarev .08 .20
82 Artem Ternavsky .08 .20
83 Igor Kamaev .08 .20
84 Sergei Rozin .08 .20
85 Roman Gorev .08 .20
86 Dmitri Kokorev .08 .20
87 Martin Tomasek .08 .20
88 Roman Popov .08 .20
89 Vladimir Antipin .08 .20
90 Vadim Tarasov .20 .50
91 Sergei Mikhailev CO .05
92 Nikolai Zherdev ERC 6.00 15.00
93 Andrei Mukhachev .08 .20
94 Ilya Byakin .08 .20
95 Miroslav Guren .08 .20
96 Nikolai Pronin .08 .20
97 Sergei Mozyakin .08 .20
98 Maxim Ossipov .08 .20
99 Alexei Kolkunov .08 .20
100 Albert Leschev .08 .20
101 Alexander Polushin ERC 2.00 5.00
102 Igor Emeleev .08 .20
103 Sergei Luchinkin .08 .20
104 Rail Muftiev .08 .20
105 Nikolai Semin .08 .20
106 Sergei Anshakov .20 .50
107 Vadim Khomitsky .08 .20
108 Pavel Trakhanov .08 .20
109 Yan Golubovsky .20 .50
110 Dusan Salficky .40 1.00
111 Dmitri Kosmachev .08 .20
112 Vladimir Kramskoy .08 .20
113 Alexander Drozdetsky .08 .20
114 Alexei Shotkov .08 .20
115 Maxim Velikov .08 .20
116 Evgeni Akhmetov .08 .20
117 Vladimir Gorbunov .08 .20
118 Pavel Patera .08 .20
119 Maxim Sokolov .40 1.00
120 Martin Prochazka .08 .20
121 Tomas Vlasak .08 .20
122 Alexander Perezhogin .75 2.00
123 Dmitri Zatonsky .08 .20
124 Andrei Subbotin .40 1.00
125 Ravil Yakubov .08 .20
126 Valeri Pokrovsky .08 .20
127 Kirill Koltsov 1.25 3.00
128 Ramil Saifullin .08 .20
129 Maxim Sokolov .40 1.00
130 Igor Varitsky .08 .20
131 Maxim Balmochnykh .20 .50
132 Marcel Cousineau .75 2.00
133 Yuri Kuznetsov .08 .20
134 Ruslan Nurtdinov .08 .20
135 Andrei Sidyakin .08 .20
136 Sergei Zvyagin .20 .50
137 Patrik Guchko .08 .20
138 Andrei Yakhanov .08 .20
139 Evgeni Muratov .08 .20
140 Alexei Simakov .08 .20
141 Roman Baranov .08 .20
142 Alexander Zavyalov .08 .20
143 Evgeni Varlamov .08 .20
144 Alexei Tertyshny .08 .20
145 Danis Zaripov .08 .20
146 Vasili Turkovsky .08 .20
147 Alexander Guskov .08 .20
148 Alexander Zhurik .08 .20
149 Yuri Kuznetsov .08 .20
150 Maxim Balmochnykh .20 .50
151 Marat Davydov .08 .20
152 Alexei Koznev .08 .20
153 Valeri Karpov .08 .20
154 Oleg Shargorodsky .20 .50
155 Sergei Gomolyako .08 .20
156 Vladimir Tikhomirov .20 .50
157 Alexei Yegorov .20 .50
158 Konstantin Simchuk .20 .50
159 Sergei Shalamai .08 .20
160 Alexei Danilov .08 .20
161 Vadim Epanchintsev .08 .20
162 Vasily Tikhonov ACO .05
163 Viktor Tikhonov CO .08 .20
164 Andrei Sapozhnikov .08 .20
165 Yuri Dobryshkin .08 .20
166 Vasili Turkovsky .08 .20
167 Evgeni Petrochinin .08 .20
168 Sergei Gimaev .08 .20
169 Alexander Yudin .08 .20
170 Alexander Shinin .08 .20
171 Yuri Trubachev .08 .20
172 Evgeny Isakov .08 .20
173 Andrei Nikitenko .08 .20
174 Alexander Shinkar .08 .20
175 Viktor Chistov .20 .50
176 Andrei Shefer .20 .50
177 Igor Shadilov .08 .20
178 Martin Brochu .75 2.00
179 Alexei Kalyuzhny .08 .20
180 Alexander Shinin .08 .20
181 Maxim Balmochnykh .20 .50
182 Vladimir Antipov .08 .20
183 Boris Tortunov .08 .20
184 Vadim Epanchintsev .08 .20
184B Yuri Trubachev .08 .20
185 Fedor Tjutin 1.25 3.00
186 Sergei Anshakov .20 .50
187 Timofei Shishkanov 2.00 5.00
188 Igor Grigorenko ERC 6.00 15.00
189 Maxim Kondratiev ERC .20 .50
190 Kirill Koltsov .75 2.00
191 Evgeny Artyukhin .08 .20
192 Konstantin Barulin ERC .40 1.00
193 Andrei Taratukhin .08 .20
194 Dmitri Fakhrutdinov .08 .20
195 Dmitri Pestunov .08 .20
196 Andrei Medvedev .75 2.00
197 Nikolai Zherdev ERC 6.00 15.00
198 Alexander Ovechkin ERC 25.00 60.00
199 Alexander Polushin ERC 2.00 5.00
200 Alexei Kaigorodov .08 .20
201 Alexander Perezhogin ERC .75 2.00
202 Mikhail Lyubushin .08 .20
203 Konstantin Korneev .20 .50
204 Denis Grebeshkov 1.25 3.00
205 Konstantin Gorovikov .08 .20
206 Vitali Proshkin .08 .20
207 Alexander Suglobov ERC .40 1.00
208 Alexei Chupin .08 .20
209 Sergei Soin .20 .50
210 Andrei Subbotin .40 1.00
211 Dmitri Vlasenkov .08 .20
212 Sergei Gusev .08 .20
213 Vladimir Vujtek .08 .20
214 Vasily Turkovsky .08 .20
215 Igor Shadilov .08 .20
216 Yuri Dobryshin .08 .20
217 Igor Podomatski .40 1.00
218 Alexander Semak .08 .20
219 Ilya Byakin .08 .20
220 Alexander Guskov .08 .20
221 Alexander Guskov .08 .20
222 Nikolai Zavarukhin .08 .20
223 Andrei Petrunin .08 .20
224 Konstantin Gorovikov .08 .20
225 Alexei Gorshkov .08 .20
226 Rustem Kamaletdinov .08 .20
227 Alexander Zavakhin .08 .20
228 Vladislav Ozolin .08 .20
229 Dmitri Krasotkin .08 .20
230 Sergei Nemchinov .20 .50
231 Alexei Chupin .08 .20
232 Andrei Kovalenko .08 .20
233 Sergei Gomolyako .08 .20
234 Vitali Yeremeyev .40 1.00
235 Sergei Zholotov .08 .20
236 Dmitri Kirilenko .08 .20
237 Sergei Askimov .08 .20
238 Ruslan Berdnikov .08 .20
239 Yuri Butsayev .08 .20
240 Sergei Zinovjev 2.00 5.00
241 Radim Tesarik .08 .20
242 Dmitri Zatonsky .08 .20
243 Konstantin Baranov .08 .20
244 Vladimir Popov CO .05
245 Sergei Piskunov .08 .20
246 Vladimir Antipin .08 .20
247 Alexander Drozdetksy .08 .20
248 Sergei Vyshedkevich .20 .50
249 Timofei Shishkanov 2.00 5.00
250 Alexander Kharitonov .08 .20
251 Dmitri Fakhrutdinov .08 .20
252 Vladimir Tsyplakov .08 .20
253 Evgeni Namestnikov .20 .50
254 Vitali Atyushov .08 .20
255 Dmitri Erofeev .08 .20
256 Sergei Korolev .08 .20
257 Dmitri Erofeev .08 .20
258 Vladislav Gushin .08 .20
259 Vadim Glovatskin .08 .20
260 Renat Khasanov .08 .20
261 Nikolai Zherdev ERC 6.00 15.00
262 Dmitri Zatonsky .08 .20
263 Yan Peterik .08 .20
264 Alexei Petrov .08 .20
265 Lev Trifonov .08 .20
266 Almaz Garifullin .08 .20
267 Mikhail Sarmatin .08 .20
268 Rail Rozakov .08 .20
269 Patrick Labrecque .75 2.00
270 Oleg Khmyl .08 .20
271 Alexander Blokhin .08 .20
272 Leonid Labzov .08 .20

2002-03 Russian Lightnings

COMPLETE SET (3) 10.00 25.00
1 Alexander Ovechkin 10.00 25.00
2 Alexander Polushin .75 2.00
3 Alexander Stepanov .20 .50

2002-03 Russian SL

Little is known about the background of this set. If you have any information, please forward it to hockeymag@beckett.com.

COMPLETE SET (52) 20.00 40.00
1 Andrei Razin .20 .50
2 Dusan Salficky .40 1.00
3 Alexander Polushin .75 2.00
4 Alexander Guskov .20 .50
5 Vladimir Vujtek CO .02 .10
6 Evgeni Varlamov .20 .50
7 Andrei Skopintsev .20 .50
8 Vladimir Plyustchev CO .02 .10
9 Valeri Karpov .20 .50
10 Igor Mirnov .20 .50
11 Egor Podomatskiy .30 .75
12 Mike Fountain .30 .75
13 Mikhail Donika .20 .50
14 Vyacheslav Butsaev .20 .50
15 Andrei Esipov .20 .50
16 Igor Grigorenko 1.25 3.00
17 Yuri Moiseev CO .02 .10
18 Alexander Zhdan .20 .50
19 Maxim Sokolov .20 .50
20 Alexander Selivanov .20 .50
21 Mikhail Ivanov .20 .50
22 Ivan Hlinka CO .08 .25
23 Andrei Tsareev .20 .50
24 Dmitriy Ryabykin .20 .50
25 Jiri Slegr .20 .50
26 Sergei Soin .30 .75
27 Anton But .20 .50
28 Alexander Ovechkin 10.00 25.00
29 Vladimir Antipov .20 .50
30 Evgeni Makarov .20 .50
31 Sergei Naumov .20 .50
32 Andrei Pyatanov CO .02 .10

33 Sergei Gusev .20 .50
34 Viktor Tikhonov CO .02 .10
35 Mikhail Lyubushin .20 .50
36 Dmitri Yachanov .20 .50
37 Tomas Vlasak .20 .50
38 Alex Westlund .40 1.00
39 Vladislav Boulin .20 .50
40 Jan Peterek .20 .50
41 Vladimir Vorobiev .20 .50
42 Petr Vorobiev CO .02 .10
43 Vasily Turkovski .20 .50
44 Nikolai Zherdev 1.50 4.00
45 Andrei Taratukhin .20 .50
46 Viktor Aleksandrov .20 .50
47 Yuri Dobryshkin .20 .50
48 Alexander Savchenkov .20 .50
49 Sergei Voronov .20 .50
50 Alexei Terestchenko .20 .50
51 Alexei Shkotov .20 .50
52 Alexander Zevakhin .20 .50

2002-03 Russian Transfert

COMPLETE SET (31) 6.00 15.00
1 Alexander Semin .40 1.00
2 Alexander Golts .20 .50
3 Georgi Evtyukhin .20 .50
4 Alexander Korolyuk .20 .50
5 Marcel Cousineau .30 .75
6 Sergei Bautin .20 .50
7 Vitali Lutkevich .20 .50
8 Valeri Zelepukin .20 .50
9 Nikolai Zherdev 1.25 3.00
10 Vladimir Vorobiev .20 .50
11 Sergei Petrenko .20 .50
12 Osmo Soutukorva .20 .50
13 Sergei Korolev .20 .50
14 Alex Westlund .20 .50
15 Denis Afinogenov .20 .50
16 Vadim Tarasov .40 1.00
17 Alexander Zhdan .20 .50
18 Alexander Selivanov .20 .50
19 Vladislav Boulin .20 .50
20 Maxim Sokolov .20 .50
21 Dmitri Gogolev .20 .50
22 Alexei Volkov .30 .75
23 Ravil Yakubov .20 .50
24 Mikhail Ivanov .20 .50
25 Alexei Egorov .20 .50
26 Viktor Gordiyuk .20 .50
27 Alexander Semak .20 .50
28 Bruce Gardiner .20 .50
29 Rodrigo Lavins .20 .50
30 Steve Plouffe .30 .75
31 Sergei Krivokrasov .20 .50

2002-03 Russian Transfert Promos

COMPLETE SET (6) 2.00 5.00
1 Vladimir Vorobiev .40 1.00
2 Osmo Soutukorvo .40 1.00
3 Vitali Lutkevich .40 1.00
4 Denis Afinogenov .40 1.00
5 Alexei Volkov .75 2.00
6 Maxim Sokolov .75 2.00

2002-03 Russian Ultimate Line

COMPLETE SET (13) 6.00 15.00
1 Sergei Zvyagin .40 1.00
2 Dusan Salficky .75 2.00
3 Alexander Yeremenko .40 1.00
4 Sergei Nikolaev .40 1.00
5 Mike Fountain 1.25 3.00
6 Steve Plouffe 1.25 3.00
7 Igor Karpenko .75 2.00
8 Oleg Glebov .40 1.00
9 Patrick Labrecque 1.25 3.00
10 Alexei Volkov .75 2.00
11 Vadim Tarasov .75 2.00
12 Andrei Medvedev .75 2.00
13 Vitali Yeremeyev .75 2.00

2002-03 Russian Young Lions

COMPLETE SET (17) 10.00 25.00
1 Dmitri Kazionov .20 .50
2 Alexander Ovechkin 6.00 15.00
3 Igor Mirnov .20 .50
4 Alexander Semin .40 1.00
5 Igor Grigorenko 1.25 3.00
6 Sergei Soin .30 .75
7 Denis Grebeshkov .40 1.00
8 Alexei Kaigorodov .20 .50
9 Dmitry Pestunov .20 .50
10 Alexander Polushin .75 2.00
11 Konstantin Mikhailov .20 .50
12 Illy Nikulin .20 .50
13 Alexander Perezhogin .75 2.00
14 Alexei Mikhnov .20 .50
15 Nikolai Zherdev 1.25 3.00
16 Fedor Tyutin .40 1.00
NNO Alexander Ovechkin PROMO 6.00 15.00

2002 Russian Olympic Faces

This set was released in Russia to celebrate key players on the Russian Olympic club. It is believed that the list below is incomplete. Please forward additional information to hockeymag@beckett.com.

COMPLETE SET (4) 2.76 6.89
1 Nikolai Khabibulin .80 2.00
2 Nikolai Khabibulin .80 2.00
3 Sergei Fedorov 1.20 2.50
4 Sergei Fedorov 1.20 2.50

2002 Russian Olympic Team

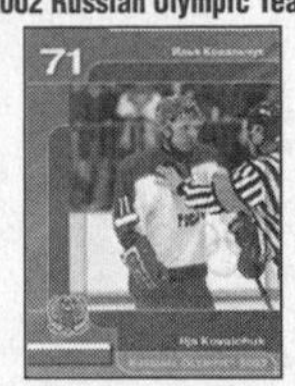

This set was released in Russia to celebrate members of its Olympic Team. It is believed that the listing below could be incomplete. Please forward information of additional cards to hockeymag@beckett.com.

COMPLETE SET (9) 6.00 15.00
1 Sergei Samsonov .80 2.00
2 Sergei Fedorov 1.25 3.00
3 Pavel Bure 1.00 2.50
4 Ilya Kovalchuk 3.00 8.00
5 Valeri Bure .20 .50
6 Alexei Kovalev .20 .50
7 Nikolai Khabibulin .80 2.00
8 Maxim Afinogenov .75 2.00
9 Darius Kasparaitis .10 .25

2002 Russian World Championships

This Russian-produced set honors members of that country's World Championship team.

COMPLETE SET (20) 3.00 8.00
1 Egor Podomatski .40 1.00
2 Alexander Yudin .20 .50
3 Maxim Sushinski .20 .50
4 Maxim Sokolov .40 1.00
5 Ivan Tkachenko .20 .50
6 Vladimir Antipov .20 .50
7 Roman Lyashenko .30 .75
8 Maxim Afinogenov .75 2.00
9 Alexander Guskov .20 .50
10 Alexei Kozniev .20 .50
11 Sergei Gusev .20 .50
12 Slava Butsayev .20 .50
13 Ravil Gusmanov .20 .50
14 Dmitri Kalinin .20 .50
15 Valeri Karpov .20 .50
16 Andrei Kovalenko .20 .50
17 Alexander Prokopiev .20 .50
18 Sergei Vyshedkevich .20 .50
19 Dmitri Zatonsky .20 .50
20 Sergei Zhukov .20 .50

2003-04 Russian Avangard Omsk

This 28-card set honours the 2002-03 champions of the Russian league. It was produced by World Sport.

COMPLETE SET (28) 4.00 10.00
1 Maxim Sokolov .20 .50
2 Konstantin Baranov .10 .25
3 Maxim Sushinski .10 .25
4 Dmitri Zatonsky .10 .25
5 Tomas Vlasak .10 .25
6 Oleg Tverdovsky .10 .25
7 Sergei Krivokrasov .10 .25
8 Stanislav Shalnov .10 .25
9 Dmitri Subbotin .10 .25
10 Dmitri Ryabikin .10 .25
11 Valeri Belousov CO .02 .10
12 Igor Nikitin .10 .25
13 Pavel Patera .10 .25
14 Alexander Popov .10 .25
15 Ramil Saifullin .10 .25
16 Yuri Yermolin .10 .25
17 Alexander Golovin .10 .25
18 Alexander Prokopiev .10 .25
19 Evgeni Khatsei .10 .25
20 Oleg Grachev .10 .25
21 Jaroslav Bednar .20 .50
22 Oleg Orekhovsky .10 .25
23 Yuri Panov .10 .25
24 Anton Kuzmin .10 .25
25 Vladimir Antipin .10 .25
26 Vitali Semenchenko .20 .50
27 Anatoli Bardin GM .02 .10
28 Checklist .02 .10

2003-04 Russian Hockey League

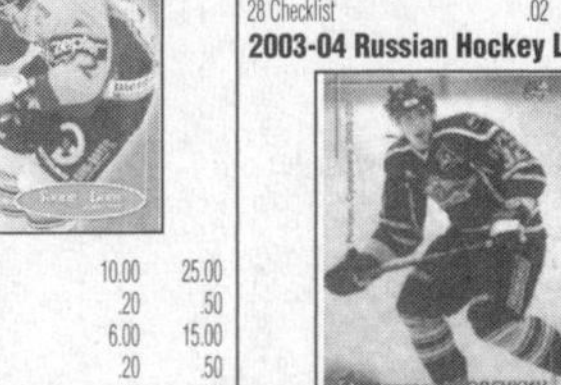

This set was produced by World Sport in Russia. Thanks to collector Darren Morris for providing the complete checklist.

COMPLETE SET (283) 50.00 125.00
1 Roman Salnikov .08 .20
2 Denis Tyrin .08 .20
3 Almaz Garifullin .08 .20
4 Sergei Shalamai .08 .20
5 Andrei Evstafiev .08 .20
6 Nikolai Zherdev 2.00 5.00
7 Mikhail Sarmatin .08 .20
8 Dusan Salficky .40 1.00
9 Sergei Mozyakin .08 .20
10 Andrei Razin .08 .20
11 Yuri Butsayev .08 .20
12 Oleg Romashko .20 .50
13 Evgeny Fedorov .08 .20
14 Denis Zaripov .08 .20
15 Gennady Razin .08 .20
16 Oleg Filimonov .20 .50
17 Dmitri Tarasov .08 .20
18 Vitali Shulakov .08 .20
19 Oleg Minakov .08 .20
20 Jan Benda .08 .20
21 Alexander Zevakhin .08 .20
22 Alexander Yudin .08 .20
23 Alexander Yudin .08 .20
24 SKA St. Pete's .02 .05
25 Dynamo Moscow .02 .05
26 Vitali Yeremeev .20 .50
27 Alexei Volkov .20 .50
28 Alexander Yeremenko .20 .50
29 Mikhail Lyubishin .08 .20
30 Ilya Zubov .08 .20
31 Alexei Troschinsky .08 .20
32 Igor Mirnov .08 .20
33 Alexander Kuvaldin .08 .20
34 Igor Schyadilov .08 .20
35 Andrei Skopintsev .08 .20
36 Alexander Kharitonov .08 .20
37 Alexei Chupin .08 .20
38 Vadim Shakhrajchuk .08 .20
39 Alexander Savchenkov .08 .20
40 Vladislav Boulin .08 .20
41 Alexei Kudashov .08 .20
42 Alexander Zhdan .08 .20
43 Alexei Tereschenko .08 .20
44 Alexander Stepanov .08 .20
45 Alexander Ovechkin 10.00 25.00
46 Sergei Vyshedkevich .20 .50
47 Miroslav Hlinka .08 .20
48 Dmitri Starostenko .08 .20
49 Alexander Stepanov .08 .20
50 Alexander Ovechkin 10.00 25.00
51 Tomas Garant .20 .50
52 Vladimir Vorobiev .08 .20
53 Yuri Babenko .08 .20
54 Ruslan Zainullin .20 .50
55 Robert Kantor .08 .20
56 Denis Kartsev .08 .20
57 Vladislav Evseev .40 1.00
58 Zinatula Bilyaletdinov CO .08 .20
59 Alexei Yegorov .20 .50
60 Sergei Naumov .40 1.00
61 Sergei Semin .08 .20
62 Valeri Pokrovski .08 .20
63 Torbjorn Johansson .08 .20
64 Artem Ostroushko .08 .20
65 Andrei Spiridonov .08 .20
66 Marat Davydov .08 .20
67 Nikolai Syrtsov .08 .20
68 Vyacheslav Zavalnyuk .08 .20
69 Alexander Kozyrev .08 .20
70 Yan Golubovsky .08 .20
71 Jan Lasak .75 2.00
72 Konstantin Kasiyanchuk .08 .20
73 Egor Bashkatov .08 .20
74 Andrei Potaichuk .08 .20
75 Egor Mikhailov .08 .20
76 Andrei Galushkin .08 .20
77 Mike Watt .20 .50
78 Alexei Akifjev .08 .20
79 Andrei Pchelyakov .08 .20
80 Evgeni Tunik .08 .20
81 Pavel Boichenko .08 .20
82 Valeri Zelepukin .08 .20
83 Oleg Boltunov .08 .20
84 Alexei Tsvetkov .08 .20
85 Boris Mikhailov CO .20 .50
86 Eduard Kudermetov .08 .20
87 Sergei Berdnikov .08 .20
88 Vladimir Antipin .08 .20
89 Oleg Tverdovsky .08 .20
90 Denis Khlopotnov .08 .20
91 Fedor Tjutin .40 1.00
92 Andrei Shurupov .08 .20
93 Evgeny Koronov .08 .20
94 Albert Leschev .08 .20
95 Sergei Yerkovich .08 .20
96 Vladimir Tyurikov .08 .20
97 Dmitri Vershinin .08 .20
98 Alexei Krutov .08 .20
99 German Titov .08 .20
100 Igor Nikolaev .08 .20
101 Maxim Shevyev .08 .20
102 Andrei Ershov .08 .20
103 Ilya Krikunov .08 .20
104 Peter Skudra .40 1.00
105 Andrei Galkin .08 .20
106 Andrei Dylevski .08 .20
107 Ondrej Steiner .08 .20
108 Vadim Brezgunov .08 .20
109 Roman Oksiuta .08 .20
110 Oleg Belkin .08 .20
111 Alexander Boikov .08 .20
112 Dmitri Kazionov .08 .20
113 Vladimir Malenkikh .08 .20
114 Ruslan Bernikov .08 .20
115 Alexander Buturlin .08 .20
116 Andrei Esipov .08 .20
117 Maxim Semenov .08 .20
118 Yakov Rachinsky .08 .20
119 Mikhail Balandin .08 .20
120 Dmitri Vorobiev .08 .20
121 J.F. Labbe .40 1.00
122 Rinat Khasanov .08 .20
123 Vladimir Loginov .08 .20
124 Alexei Deev .08 .20
125 Alexander Grishin .08 .20
126 Sergei Gomolyako .08 .20
127 Anatoli Filatov .08 .20
128 Vasili Koshechkin .20 .50
129 Alexander Seluyanov .08 .20
130 Ladislav Cherny .08 .20
131 Igor Varitski .08 .20
132 Maxim Yakutsenya .08 .20
133 Alexander Gulov .08 .20
134 Stanislav Zhmakin .08 .20
135 Mikhail Sevostjanov .08 .20
136 Alexander Skugarev .08 .20
137 Sergei Sevostjanov .08 .20
138 Petr Vorobiev CO .02 .05
139 Yevgeni Safronov .08 .20
140 Ilya Vorobiev .08 .20
141 Alexander Titov .08 .20
142 Ruslan Nurtdinov .08 .20
143 Alexander Zavjalov .08 .20
144 Vadim Epanchinsev .08 .20
145 Jamie Ram .75 2.00
146 Viktor Chistov CO .02 .05
147 Tomas Hlubna .08 .20
148 Alexander Semak .08 .20
149 Sergei Gimaev .08 .20
150 Nikolai Makarov CO .02 .05
151 Atvars Tribuntsovs .08 .20
152 Vladislav Ozolin .08 .20
153 Nikolai Semin .08 .20
154 Vitali Proshkin .08 .20
155 Vassiliy Turkovsky .08 .20
156 Denis Platonov .08 .20
157 Radek Duda .08 .20
158 Sergei Korolev .08 .20
159 Konstantin Korneev .20 .50
160 Sergei Arakaev .08 .20
161 Denis Denisov .08 .20
162 Alexander Drozdetsky .08 .20
163 Alexander Cherbayev .08 .20
164 Maxim Mikhailovsky .20 .50
165 Mikhail Tyulyapkin .08 .20
166 Valeri Kamensky .08 .20
167 Vladimir Vujtek .08 .20
168 Konstantin Glazachev .20 .50
169 Konstantin Mikhailov .08 .20
170 Egor Shastin .08 .20
171 Alexei Mikhnov .40 1.00
172 Alexander Fomitchev .30 .75
173 Daniel Branda .08 .20
174 Eric Charron .20 .50
175 Miroslav Guren .08 .20
176 Ravil Yakubov .08 .20
177 Dmitri Dudarev .08 .20
178 Ruslan Batyrshin .08 .20
179 Ruslan Shafikov .08 .20
180 Martin Cech .08 .20
181 Tero Lehtera .08 .20
182 Egor Mikhailov .08 .20
183 Valeri Pokrovsky .08 .20
184 Vadim Sharifjanov .20 .50
185 David Pospisil .08 .20
186 Yan Golubovsky .08 .20
187 Angel Nikolov .20 .50
188 Viktor Alexandrov .08 .20
189 Dmitri Pankov .08 .20
190 Jiri Marushak .08 .20
191 Oleg Gross CO .02 .05
192 Sergei Moskalev .08 .20
193 Alexei Medvedev .08 .20
194 Vadim Tarasov .30 .75
195 Evgeny Shtaiger .08 .20
196 Nikolai Soloviev CO .02 .05
197 Evgeny Lapin .08 .20
198 Mikhail Chernov .08 .20
199 Zdenek Skorepa .08 .20
200 Sergei Mikhailev CO .02 .05
201 Sergei Naumov .40 1.00
202 Evgeny Korolev .08 .20
203 Rail Rozakov .08 .20
204 Yuri Kuznetsov .20 .50
205 Sergei Berdnikov .08 .20
206 Yuri Kuznetsov .20 .50
207 Andrei Sapozhnikov .08 .20
208 Andrei Nikilenko .08 .20
209 Andrei Petrunin .08 .20
210 Yuri Dobryshkin .08 .20
211 Sergei Gimaev .08 .20
212 Alexander Astashev CO .02 .05
213 Vadim Khomitsky .08 .20
214 Maxim Yakutsenya .08 .20
215 Martin Richter .08 .20
216 Sergei Anshakov .20 .50
217 Denis Parshin .20 .50
218 Sergei Berezin .08 .20
219 Jan Hejda .08 .20
220 Dmitri Levinsky .08 .20
221 Norm Maracle .75 2.00
222 Pavel Patera .08 .20
223 Tomas Vlasak .08 .20
224 Jaroslav Bednar .20 .50
225 Konstantin Baranov .08 .20
226 Maxim Sokolov .30 .75
227 Denis Kuzmenko .20 .50
228 Oleg Burlitsky .08 .20
229 Alexei Polemkin .08 .20
230 Alexander Zhukov .08 .20
231 Ilnaz Zagitov .08 .20
232 Dmitri Yushkevich .08 .20
233 Martin Hlavacka .08 .20
234 Alexander Guskov .08 .20
235 Robert Kantor .08 .20
236 Marat Vailullin .08 .20
237 Zdenek Orct .20 .50
238 David Nemirovsky .08 .20
239 Jiri Hudler 2.00 5.00
240 Maxim Krivonozhkin .08 .20
241 Yuri Butsayev .20 .50
242 Andrei Esipov .08 .20
243 Rudolf Guna .08 .20
244 Philip Metliuk .08 .20
245 Alexander Lyubimov .08 .20
246 Jiri Trvaj .20 .50
247 Dmitri Cherhukh .08 .20
248 Renat Khairetdinov .08 .20
249 Artem Vostrikov .08 .20
250 Peter Skudra .40 1.00
251 Evgeny Malkin 15.00 40.00
252 Nikolai Tsulygin .08 .20
253 Andrei Kostitsyn 4.00 10.00
254 Denis Belsky .08 .20
255 Andrei Davletov .08 .20
256 Sergei Konkov .08 .20
257 Denis Loginov .08 .20
258 Michael Martin .08 .20
259 David Moravec .08 .20
260 Yan Peterik .08 .20
261 Lubomir Sekeras .08 .20
262 Toivo Suursoo .08 .20
263 Marat Salimov .08 .20
264 Sergei Fadeev .08 .20
265 Mikhail Shukaev .08 .20
266 Dmitri Yachanov .20 .50
267 Lukas Zib .08 .20
268 Butsayev Brothers .08 .20
269 Sergei Sevostjanov .08 .20
270 Mikhail Sevostjanov .08 .20
271 Ruslan Nurtdinov .08 .20
272 Frank Banham .20 .50
273 Herbert Vasiliev .08 .20
274 Dave Karpa .20 .50
275 Kirill Lyamin .20 .50
276 Mikhail Chernov .08 .20
277 Ildar Mukhometov .20 .50
278 Ilya Zubov .08 .20
279 Sergei Shinkar .08 .20
280 Sergei Voronov .08 .20
281 Sergei Borisov .20 .50
282 Yuri Trubachev .08 .20
283 Sergei Bernatsky .08 .20

2003-04 Russian Metallurg Magnitogorsk

COMPLETE SET (9) 3.00 8.00
1 Vitali Atyushov .40 1.00
2 Alexander Boikov .40 1.00
3 Evgeni Gladskikh .40 1.00
4 Oleg Davydov .40 1.00
5 Nikolai Ignatov .40 1.00
6 Dmitri Pestunov .40 1.00
7 Ivan Sidorov .40 1.00
8 Martin Cech .40 1.00
9 Lubomir Vaic .40 1.00

2003-04 Russian National Team

Produced by World Sport, this set highlights 36 players who wore the jersey of Russia's various national teams over the 2003-04 season.

COMPLETE SET (36) 10.00 25.00
1 Alexei Badyukov .20 .50
2 Danis Zaripov .20 .50
3 Sergei Mozyakin .20 .50
4 Andrei Mukhachev .20 .50
5 Igor Emeleev .20 .50
6 Denis Gusmanov .20 .50
7 Maxim Spiridonov .20 .50
8 Alexei Yegorov .20 .50
9 Alexander Stepanov .20 .50
10 Nikolai Semin .20 .50
11 Alexander Drozdetsky .20 .50
12 Alexander Skugarev .20 .50
13 Sergei Korolev .20 .50
14 Vladimir Chebaturkin .20 .50
15 Andrei Kovalenko .20 .50
16 Vitali Yachmenev .20 .50
17 Igor Volkov .20 .50
18 Alexander Boikov .20 .50
19 Yuri Dobryshkin .20 .50
20 Alexander Ryazantsev .20 .50
21 Maxim Sushinsky .30 .75
22 Alexander Prokopiev .20 .50
23 Oleg Tverdovsky .20 .50
24 Alexander Ovechkin 6.00 15.00
25 Viktor Tikhonov .20 .50
26 Vladimir Malenkikh .20 .50
27 Valeri Zelepukin .20 .50
28 Dmitri Yushkevich .20 .50
29 Andrei Bashkirov .20 .50
30 Alexander Buturlin .20 .50
31 Leonid Kanareikin .20 .50
32 Artur Oktyabrev .20 .50
33 Maxim Kondratiev .20 .50
34 Vyacheslav Butsayev .20 .50
35 Alexander Savchenkov .20 .50
36 Sergei Krivokrasov .20 .50

2003-04 Russian Postcards

This postcard-sized set features 12 members of Russia's national team. The cards feature only jersey numbers, so they are listed below alphabetically.

COMPLETE SET (12) 8.00 20.00
1 Viacheslav Butsayev .75 2.00
2 Alexander Guskov .75 2.00
3 Andrei Kovalenko .75 2.00
4 Sergei Mozyakin .75 2.00
5 Egor Podomatsky .75 2.00
6 Alexander Prokopiev .75 2.00
7 Maxim Sokolov .75 2.00
8 Maxim Sushinsky .75 2.00
9 Oleg Tverdovsky .75 2.00
10 Igor Volkov .75 2.00
11 Vitali Yachmenev .75 2.00
12 Dmitry Zatonsky .75 2.00

2003-04 Russian SL

COMPLETE SET (40) 15.00 30.00
1 Alexei Chupin .20 .50
2 Radek Duda .20 .50
3 Alexei Yegorov .40 1.00
4 Tomas Harant .20 .50
5 Miroslav Hlinka .20 .50
6 Tomas Hlubna .20 .50
7 J.F. Labbe .30 .75
8 Oleg Orekhovsky .20 .50
9 Alexander Ovechkin 4.00 10.00
10 Andrei Razin .20 .50
11 Dmitri Ryabykin .20 .50
12 Konstantin Simchuk .40 1.00
13 Andrei Subbotin .20 .50
14 Yuri Trubachev .20 .50
15 Ravil Yakubov .20 .50
16 Nikolai Zherdev 1.25 3.00
17 Vadim Tarasov .40 1.00
18 Sergei Naumovs .40 1.00
19 Christian Bronsard .40 1.00
20 Dmitri Kazionov .20 .50
21 Sergei Gomolyako .20 .50
22 Alexander Kuvaldin .20 .50
23 Peter Skudra .40 1.00
24 Alex Westlund .40 1.00
25 Sergei Shalamai .20 .50
26 Atvars Tribuntsovs .20 .50
27 Alexei Kudashov .20 .50
28 Ruslan Nurtdinov .20 .50
29 David Moravec .20 .50
30 Alexei Tertyshny .20 .50
31 Mikhail Shukaev .40 1.00
32 Alexei Vasiliev .20 .50
33 Kirill Lyamin .40 1.00
34 Daniel Branda .20 .50
35 Vadim Khomitsky .20 .50
36 Vitali Yeremeev .40 1.00
37 Lubomir Vaic .20 .50
38 Ruslan Zainullin .20 .50
39 Alexander Savchenkov .20 .50
40 Sergei Mozyakin .20 .50

2003-04 Russian Young Lions

COMPLETE SET (7) 5.00 12.00
1 Dmitri Chernykh .40 1.00
2 Alexander Semin .60 1.50
3 Alexander Ovechkin 4.00 10.00
4 Maxim Shevjev .40 1.00
5 Dmitri Pestunov .40 1.00
6 Maxim Krivonozhkin .40 1.00
7 Kirill Lyamin .40 1.00

2003 Russian Under-18 Team

COMPLETE SET (22) 15.00 35.00
1 Grigori Shafigulin .20 .50
2 Dmitri Petrov .20 .50
3 Alexei Ivanov .20 .50
4 Evgeni Malkin 6.00 15.00
5 Dmitri Pestunov .20 .50
6 Vitali Anikienko .20 .50
7 Dmitri Chernykh .20 .50
8 Anton Dubinin .20 .50
9 Rustan Sidikov .30 .75
10 Alexander Naurov .20 .50
11 Denis Pervyshin .20 .50
12 Alexander Ovechkin 6.00 15.00
13 Denis Ezhov .20 .50
14 Georgi Misharin .20 .50
15 Anton Belov .20 .50
16 Artem Nosov .20 .50
17 Denis Loginov .20 .50
18 Dmitri Kosmachev .20 .50
19 Konstantin Makarov .20 .50
20 Sergei Gorelov .30 .75
21 Konstantin Glazachev .60 1.50
22 Dmitri Shitikov .20 .50

2003 Russian World Championship Stars

COMPLETE SET (35) 10.00 25.00
1 Jan Benda .10 .25
2 Leonid Tambievs .10 .25
3 Jan Lasak .30 .75
4 Miroslav Hlinka .10 .25
5 Sergei Naumov .20 .50
6 Atvars Tribuntsovs .10 .25
7 Peter Forsberg 1.25 3.00
8 Tommy Salo .30 .75
9 Mats Sundin .60 1.50
10 Henrik Zetterberg .60 1.50
11 Mikael Tellqvist .60 1.50
12 Dany Heatley .75 2.00
13 Sean Burke .40 1.00
14 Mike Comrie .30 .75
15 Kris Draper .40 1.00
16 Roberto Luongo 1.25 3.00
17 Anson Carter .40 1.00
18 Miroslav Satan .40 1.00
19 Peter Bondra .40 1.00
20 Zigmund Palffy .40 1.00
21 Robert Svehla .10 .25
22 Richard Zednik .10 .25
23 Arturs Irbe .40 1.00
24 Milan Hejduk .60 1.50
25 Jiri Hudler .75 2.00
26 Robert Reichel .20 .50
27 Martin Straka .20 .50
28 Radek Duda .10 .25
29 Alexander Khavanov .10 .25
30 Ilya Kovalchuk 1.00 2.50
31 Maxim Sokolov .20 .50
32 Tomas Vokoun .60 1.50
33 Ryan Smith .60 1.50
34 Rodrigo Lavins .10 .25
35 Eric Brewer .20 .50

2003 Russian World Championship Team 2003

COMPLETE SET (24) 6.00 15.00
1 Maxim Sokolov .20 .50
2 Igor Podomatski .20 .50
3 Alexander Frolov .75 2.00
4 Alexander Semin 1.00 2.50
5 Pavel Datsyuk 1.00 2.50
6 Ivan Novoseltsev .10 .25
7 Sergei Zinovjev .40 1.00
8 Vladimir Antipov .10 .25
9 Dmitri Kalinin .10 .25
10 Vitali Proshkin .10 .25
11 Sergei Soin .10 .25
12 Alexander Suglobov .20 .50
13 Alexander Zhdan .10 .25
14 Sergei Vyshedkevich .10 .25
15 Sergei Gusev .10 .25
16 Oleg Saprykin .20 .50
17 Denis Arkhipov .20 .50
18 Dmitri Erofeev .20 .50
19 Igor Grigorenko .75 2.00
20 Alexander Guskov .10 .25
21 Vasily Turkovsky .10 .25
22 Alexander Khavanov .10 .25
23 Ilya Kovalchuk 2.00 5.00
24 Alexei Kaigorodov .40 1.00

2003 Russian World Championships Preview

COMPLETE SET (5) 6.00 15.00
1 Alexander Ovechkin 6.00 15.00
2 Pavel Datsyuk .75 2.00
3 Denis Loginov .20 .50
4 Denis Arkhipov .20 .50
5 Ilya Kovalchuk 1.50 4.00

2004-05 Russian Back to Russia

COMPLETE SET (41) 12.00 30.00
1 Alexander Frolov .75 2.00
2 Pavel Datsyuk 1.50 4.00
3 Konstantin Koltsov .20 .50
4 Andrei Markov .40 1.00
5 Slava Kozlov .40 1.00
6 Dmitri Afanasenkov .20 .50
7 Igor Korolev .20 .50
8 Ilya Kovalchuk 4.00 10.00
9 Artem Chubarov .20 .50
10 Nikolai Zherdev 1.00 2.50
11 Alexander Semin 1.50 4.00
12 Maxim Kuznetsov .20 .50
13 Andrei Nikolishin .20 .50
14 Alexei Ponikarovsky .40 1.00
15 Maxim Afinogenov .75 2.00
16 Oleg Saprykin .20 .50
17 Viktor Kozlov .40 1.00
18 Andrei Nazarov .20 .50
19 Fedor Fedorov .40 1.00
20 Maxim Kondratiev .20 .50
21 Alexei Morozov .20 .50
22 Dmitry Kalinin .20 .50
23 Alexander Karpovtsev .20 .50
24 Nikolai Khabibulin .75 2.00
25 Oleg Kvasha .20 .50
26 Vitaly Vishnevsky .40 1.00
27 Sergei Gonchar .40 1.00
28 Darius Kasparaitis .20 .50
29 Alexander Perezhogin .40 1.00
30 Kirill Safronov .20 .50
31 Fedor Tyutin .20 .50
32 Nikolai Antropov .40 1.00
33 Evgeny Nabokov 1.00 2.50
34 Sergei Brylin .20 .50
35 Alexei Kovalev .40 1.00
36 Alexei Yashin .40 1.00
37 Ruslan Salei .20 .50
38 Sergei Samsonov 1.00 2.50
39 Alexei Zhitnik .20 .50
40 Igor Radulov .20 .50
41 Denis Arkhipov .40 1.00

2004-05 Russian Hope

COMPLETE SET (6) 15.00 30.00
1 Alexander Ovechkin 8.00 20.00
2 Evgeni Malkin 8.00 20.00
3 Enver Lisin .40 1.00
4 Anton Belov .40 1.00
5 Yakov Rylov .40 1.00
6 Viacheslav Seluyanov .40 1.00

2004-05 Russian Legion

COMPLETE SET (41) 15.00 40.00
1 Pavel Rosa .20 .50
2 Jaromir Jagr 6.00 15.00
3 Lubomir Bartecko .20 .50
4 Martin Strbak .20 .50
5 Martin Havlat 1.50 4.00
6 Fred Brathwaite .75 2.00
7 Tomas Harant .20 .50
8 Vladimir Tsyplakov .20 .50
9 Joni Puurula .20 .50
10 Dainius Zubrus .20 .50
11 Vadim Shakhraichuk .20 .50
12 Jussi Markkanen .40 1.00
13 Vladimir Hudacek .20 .50
14 Curtis Murphy .20 .50
15 Roman Tomas .20 .50
16 Jiri Trvaj .20 .50
17 Jaroslav Bednar .20 .50
18 Miroslav Lipovsky .20 .50
19 Martin Cech .20 .50
20 Jaroslav Hlinka .20 .50
21 Lukas Zib .20 .50
23 Jan Hejda .20 .50
24 Vincent Lecavalier 6.00 15.00
25 Miroslav Guren .20 .50
27 Petr Sykora .40 1.00
28 Kamil Piros .20 .50
29 Patrik Elias .40 1.00
30 Petr Kubos .20 .50
31 Marc Lamothe .40 1.00
32 Roman Malek .20 .50
33 Aigars Cipruss .20 .50

34 Markus Korhonen .20 .50
35 Jan Benda .20 .50
36 Dusan Salficky .40 1.00
37 Dany Heatley 6.00 15.00
38 Mika Pietila .20 .50
39 Pauli Jaks .20 .50
41 Atvars Tribuntsovs .20 .50

2004-05 Russian Moscow Dynamo

COMPLETE SET (36) 15.00 35.00
1 Maxim Afinogenov .75 2.00
2 Yuri Babenko .20 .50
3 Lubomir Bartecko .20 .50
4 Vladislav Boulin .20 .50
5 Albert Vishnyakov .20 .50
6 Vladimir Vorobiev .20 .50
7 Sergey Vyshedkevich .20 .50
8 Martin Havlat 1.50 4.00
9 Tomas Harant .20 .50
10 Pavel Datsyuk 1.25 3.00
11 Vladislav Evseev .20 .50
12 Vitaly Yeremeev .40 1.00
13 Alexander Yeremenko .40 1.00
14 Vladimir Karpov .20 .50
15 Denis Kartsev .20 .50
16 Alexei Komarov .20 .50
17 Alexei Kudashov .20 .50
18 Maxim Kuznetsov .20 .50
19 Andrei Markov .20 .50
20 Igor Mirnov .20 .50
21 Ilya Nikulin .20 .50
22 Alexander Ovechkin 8.00 20.00
23 Oleg Orekhovsky .20 .50
24 Konstantin Romanov .20 .50
25 Pavel Rosa .20 .50
26 Yakov Rylov .20 .50
27 Alexander Savchenkov .20 .50
28 Andrei Skopintsev .20 .50
29 Alexander Stepanov .20 .50
30 Alexei Tereschenko .20 .50
31 Alexei Troschinsky .20 .50
32 Alexander Kharitonov .20 .50
33 Artem Chubarov .20 .50
34 Alexei Chupin .20 .50
35 Igor Shadilov .20 .50
36 Vladimir Krikunov CO .20 .50

2004-05 Russian RHL

COMPLETE SET (22) 15.00 30.00
1 Sergey Borisov .20 .50
2 Andrei Kovalenko .20 .50
3 Maxim Potapov .20 .50
4 Roman Sychev .20 .50
5 Andrei Taratukhin .20 .50
6 Maxim Ovchinikov .20 .50
7 Denis Mashanov .20 .50
8 Alexander Zavyzlov .20 .50
9 Andrei Petrunin .20 .50
10 Mikhail Varnakov .20 .50
11 Sergey Zhurikov .20 .50
12 Evgeni Malkin 10.00 25.00
13 Igor Grigorenko 1.25 3.00
14 Vladimir Popov .20 .50
15 Ruslan Khasanshin .20 .50
16 Dmitry Dudarev .20 .50
17 Valery Pokrovsky .20 .50
18 Andrei Tsareev .20 .50
19 Roman Malov .20 .50
20 Sergey Korolev .20 .50
21 Maxim Ossipov .20 .50
22 Vladimir Antipin .20 .50

2004 Russian Super League All-Stars

COMPLETE SET (31) 6.00 15.00
1 Egor Podomatsky .40 1.00
2 Viktor Chistov .40 1.00
3 Dmitry Krasotkin .20 .50
4 Alexei Troschinsky .20 .50
5 Vladimir Tyurikov .20 .50
6 Alexander Yudin .20 .50
7 Alexander Semak .20 .50
8 Marat Davydov .20 .50
9 Dmitry Gogolev .20 .50
10 Andrei Razin .20 .50
11 Valeri Zelepukin .20 .50
12 Egor Mikhailov .20 .50
13 Pavel Boichenko .20 .50
14 Vladimir Samylin .20 .50
15 Vladimir Vorobiev .20 .50
16 Alexei Chupin .20 .50
17 Konstantin Simchuk .40 1.00
18 Alexander Fomitchev .40 1.00
19 Sergei Klimentiev .20 .50
20 Andrei Evstafiev .20 .50
21 Jiri Marushak .20 .50
22 Nikolai Tsulygin .20 .50
23 Oleg Khmylev .20 .50
24 Jan Benda .20 .50
25 Sergei Gomolyako .20 .50
26 Igor Varitsky .20 .50
27 Andrei Skabelka .20 .50
28 Evgeny Koreshkov .20 .50
29 Sergei Moskalev .20 .50
30 Dmitri Kvartalnov .20 .50
31 Vadim Epanchintsev .20 .50

2004 Russian Under-18 Team

COMPLETE SET (23) 15.00 40.00
1 Adgur Dzhugelia .20 .50
2 Evgeni Biryukov .20 .50
3 Sergei Salnikov .20 .50
4 Kirill Lyamin .30 .75
5 Dmitri Shitikov UER .20 .50
(first name listed as Sergei
6 Rinat Ibragimov .20 .50
7 Anton Belov .20 .50
8 Sergei Shirokov .20 .50
9 Nikolai Kulemin .20 .50
10 Ivan Kasutin .30 .75
11 Evgeni Malkin 10.00 25.00
12 Roman Voloshenko .40 1.00
13 Alexander Aksenenko .20 .50
14 Sergei Karetin .20 .50
15 Enver Lisin .40 1.00
16 Denis Parshin .20 .50
17 Alexander Plyuschev .20 .50
18 Mikhail Yunkov .20 .50
19 Sergei Ogorodnikov .20 .50
20 Anton Khudobin .30 .75
21 Alexei Yemelin .20 .50
22 Alexander Radulov 4.00 10.00
NNO Checklist .02 .10

2004 Russian World Championship Team

This set, produced by World Sport, features the 2004 World Championship team.

COMPLETE SET (25) 15.00 30.00
1 Maxim Afinogenov .60 1.50
2 Alexei Yashin .20 .50
3 Nikolai Pronin .20 .50
4 Maxim Kondratiev .20 .50
5 Andrei Skopintsev .20 .50
6 Alexander Prokopiev .20 .50
7 Alexei Morozov .20 .50
8 Alexander Ovechkin 8.00 20.00
9 Maxim Sushinski .20 .50
10 Alexander Guskov .20 .50
11 Alexander Skugarev .20 .50
12 Vasili Turkovski .20 .50
13 Alexander Fomitchev .30 .75
14 Andrei Bashkirov .20 .50
15 Valeri Zelepukin .20 .50
16 Vitali Proshkin .20 .50
17 Ilya Kovalchuk 2.00 5.00
18 Maxim Sokolov .20 .50
19 Dmitri Bykov .20 .50
20 Oleg Tverdovsky .20 .50
21 Slava Butsayev .20 .50
22 Dmitri Yushkevich .20 .50
23 Dmitri Kalinin .20 .50
24 Vladimir Antipov .20 .50
25 Egor Podomatski .30 .75

2004 Russian World Junior Team

This team set was sold in Russia after the team won the WJC Gold medal in Finland. Produced by World Sport.

COMPLETE SET (22) 15.00 40.00
1 Konstantin Korneev .20 .50
2 Denis Grot .20 .50
3 Alexander Ovechkin 8.00 20.00
4 Dmitry Pestunov .20 .50
5 Alexei Shkotov .20 .50
6 Sergei Gimaev .20 .50
7 Andrei Spiridonov .20 .50
8 Ilya Krikunov .20 .50
9 Yevgeny Malkin 8.00 20.00
10 Sergei Anshakov .20 .50
11 Mikhail Tyulyapkin .20 .50
12 Sergei Karpov .20 .50
13 Grigory Shafigulin .20 .50
14 Alexander Kozhevnikov .20 .50
15 Yuri Ermolin .20 .50
16 Dmitry Kosmachev .20 .50
17 Denis Ezhov .20 .50
18 Evgeny Tunik .20 .50
19 Dmitry Kazionov .20 .50
20 Alexander Semin 1.25 3.00
21 Konstantin Barulin .40 1.00
22 Denis Khudyakov .40 1.00

2005 Russian Avangard Omsk Calendars

These oversized cards (4X3) feature players from the 2003-04 Russian champs on the front, and a calendar on the back. It's possible other cards exist in this series.

COMPLETE SET (5) 4.00 8.00
1 Alexander Prokopiev .75 2.00
2 Dmitry Subbotin .75 2.00
3 Maxim Sushinsky .75 2.00
4 Oleg Tverdovsky .75 2.00
5 Team photo .75 2.00

2005-06 Russian Hockey League RHL

COMPLETE SET (60) 20.00 40.00
1 Denis Kulyash .20 .50
2 Alexander Bumagin .20 .50
3 Alexei Kaigorodov .40 1.00
4 Anton Krysanov .20 .50
5 Alexander Budkin .20 .50
6 Denis Bodrov .20 .50
7 Stanislav Chistov .30 .75
8 Mikhail Grabovsky .30 .75
9 Nikita Alexeev .30 .75
10 Dmitri Shitikov .20 .50
11 Igor Ignatushkin .20 .50
12 Vladislav Bouljin .20 .50
13 Fred Brathwaite .40 1.00
14 Alexander Korolyuk .30 .75
15 Alexei Troschinsky .20 .50
16 Alexei Shkotov .20 .50
17 Eugeni Birukov .20 .50
18 Alexei Chupin .20 .50
19B Alexander Ryazantsev .20 .50
20 Vadim Epanchintsev .20 .50
21 Milan Kraft .30 .75
22 Andrei Mukhachev .20 .50
23 Eugeni Fedorov .30 .75
24 Alexander Semin 1.25 3.00
25 Vladimir Vorobiev .20 .50
26 Eugeni Ryasenski .20 .50
27 Did Not Issue/Unknown
28 Travis Scott .40 1.00
29 Did Not Issue/Unknown
30 Maxim Sushinsky .30 .75
31 David Nemirovsky .30 .75
32 David Ling .30 .75
33 Vyacheslav Buravchikov .20 .50
34 Sergei Zvyagin .20 .50
35 Raymond Giroux .30 .75
36 Kirill Koltsov .40 1.00
37 Eugeni Malkin 8.00 20.00
38 Atrem Bjkkinyaev .20 .50
39 Ilya Zubov .40 1.00
40 Nikolai Kulemin .40 1.00
41 Oleg Romashko .20 .50
42 Alexander Rybakov .20 .50
43 Dusan Salficky .40 1.00
44 Maxim Yakutsenya .20 .50
45 Boris Tortunov .20 .50
46 Ilya Nikulin .20 .50
47 Did Not Issue/Unknown
48 Radik Zakiyev .20 .50
49 Ruslan Nurtdinov .20 .50
50 Tyler Moss .40 1.00
51 Dmitri Obukhov .20 .50
52 Andrei Nikolishin .20 .50
53 Alexander Yunkov(+)Mikhail Yunkov .20 .50
54 Alexander Yudin .20 .50
55 Eugeni Konstantinov .40 1.00
C1 Milos Rziga .20 .50
C2 Jan Zadrulla .20 .50
C3 Vladimir Kapulovsky .20 .50

2006 Russian Sport Collection Olympic Stars

1 Maxim Afinogenov 1.00 2.50
2 Ilya Bryzgalov 1.00 2.50
3 Anton Volchenkov 1.00 2.50
4 Sergei Gonchar 1.00 2.50
5 Pavel Datsyuk 2.00 5.00
6 Darius Kasparaitis 1.00 2.50
7 Alexei Kovalev 1.00 2.50
8 Ilya Kovalchuk 4.00 10.00
9 Evgeny Malkin 8.00 20.00
10 Andrei Markov 1.00 2.50
11 Evgeny Nabokov 2.00 5.00
12 Alexander Ovechkin 8.00 20.00
13 Maxim Sokolov 1.00 2.50
14 Fedor Tyutin 1.00 2.50
15 Alexei Yashin 1.00 2.50
16 Daniel Alfredson 2.00 5.00
17 Henrik Zetterberg 2.00 5.00
18 Nicklas Lidstrom 2.00 5.00
19 Henrik Lundqvist 4.00 10.00
20 Mats Sundin 2.00 5.00
21 Peter Forsberg 4.00 10.00
22 Jussi Jokinen 1.00 2.50
23 Saku Koivu 2.00 5.00
24 Jere Lehtinen 2.00 5.00
25 Antero Niittymaki 2.00 5.00
26 Ville Peltonen 1.00 2.50
27 Teemu Selanne 4.00 10.00
28 Tomas Vokoun 2.00 5.00
29 Tomas Kaberle 1.00 2.50
30 Martin Straka 1.00 2.50
31 Milan Hejduk 2.00 5.00
32 Ales Hemsky 2.00 5.00
33 Jaromir Jagr 4.00 10.00
34 Martin Brodeur 6.00 15.00
35 Jarome Iginla 4.00 10.00
36 Vincent Lecavalier 4.00 10.00
37 Rick Nash 4.00 10.00
38 Brad Richards 2.00 5.00
39 Joe Sakic 6.00 15.00
40 Joe Thornton 4.00 10.00
41 Dany Heatley 4.00 10.00
42 Peter Bondra 1.00 2.50
43 Peter Budaj 1.00 2.50
44 Marian Gaborik 4.00 10.00
45 Pavol Demitra 1.00 2.50
46 Richard Zednik 1.00 2.50
47 Zdeno Chara 1.00 2.50
48 Marian Hossa 2.00 5.00
49 Miroslav Satan 1.00 2.50
50 Rick Dipietro 2.00 5.00
51 Mike Modano 3.00 8.00
52 Keith Tkachuk 2.00 5.00
53 Vitali Yeremeyev 1.00 2.50

2006 Russian Torino Olympic Team

COMPLETE SET (26) 15.00 25.00
1 Alexander Ovechkin 4.00 10.00
2 Evgeny Malkin 4.00 10.00
3 Maxim Sokolov .20 .50
4 Ilya Bryzgalov .40 1.00
5 Fedor Tyutin .20 .50
6 Vitaly Vishenvsky .20 .50
7 Maxim Sushinski .20 .50
8 Alexei Yashin .20 .50
9 Alexei Kovalev .40 1.00
10 Alexander Korolyuk .20 .50
11 Ilya Kovalchuk 1.25 3.00
12 Maxim Afinogenov .40 1.00
13 Alexander Kharitonov .20 .50
14 Pavel Datsyuk .75 2.00
15 Viktor Kozlov .20 .50
16 Ivan Nepryaev .20 .50
17 Andrei Markov .20 .50
18 Alexander Frolov .40 1.00
19 Sergei Zhukov .20 .50
20 Evgeny Nabokov .40 1.00
21 Darius Kasparaitis .20 .50
22 Andrei Taratukhin .20 .50
23 Sergei Gonchar .20 .50
24 Anton Volchenkov .20 .50
25 Daniil Markov .20 .50
26 Russian Team CL .02 .10

1995-96 Slovakian APS National Team

This set of 28-cards features the 1996 Slovakian national team. The cards were sold in team set form at home games. The cards feature an action photo complemented by national and federation logos. The card backs reprise the front photo along with international statistics. The set is notable for the inclusion of sniper Peter Bondra, among other NHLers.

COMPLETE SET (28) 20.00 40.00
1 Dr. Jan Mitosinka CO .02 .10
2 Dusan Pasek CO .08 .25
3 Julius Supler CO .08 .25
4 Jan Selvek .08 .25
5 Jaromir Dragan .08 .25
6 Eduard Hartmann .08 .25
7 Roman Cunderlik .08 .25
8 Stanislav Jasecko .08 .25
9 Lubomir Sekeras .40 1.00
10 Stanislav Medrik .08 .25
11 Jan Varholik .08 .25
12 Marian Smerciak .08 .25
13 Robert Svehla .40 1.00
14 Slavomir Vorobel .20 .50
15 Vlastimil Plavucha .08 .25
16 Oto Hascak .20 .50
17 Peter Bondra 6.00 15.00
18 Rene Pucher .08 .25
19 Miroslav Satan 6.00 15.00
20 Branislav Janos .08 .25
21 Lubomir Kolnik .20 .50
22 Peter Stastny 2.00 5.00
23 Zdeno Ciger .20 .50
24 Zigmund Palffy 6.00 15.00
25 Jozef Dano .08 .25
26 Robert Petrovicky .20 .50
27 Dusan Pohorelec .08 .25
28 Jozef Stumpel .75 2.00

1995 Slovakian-Quebec Pee-Wee Tournament

This 29-card set features the group of youngsters who represented Slovakia at the 1995 Quebec Pee Wee Tournament. The cards were sold at the tournament to help finance the team's trip. The cards have color player photos with red inside and faded purple outside borders. The backs carry player information. The cards are unnumbered and checklisted below in alphabetical order.

COMPLETE SET (29) 3.00 8.00
1 Jozef Balej 1.25 3.00
2 Patrik Behan .08 .25
3 Michal Bela .08 .25
4 Ivan Dobry .08 .25
5 Milan Dornic CO .02 .10
6 Vladimir Dubek .08 .25
7 Ladislav Gero CO .02 .10
8 Marian Hutyra .08 .25
9 Peter Hutyra .08 .25
10 Dr. Leopold Karafiat MG .02 .10
11 Miroslav Karafiat CO .02 .10
12 Vladimir Kulich .08 .25
13 Marek Laco .08 .25
14 Michal Loksa .08 .25
15 Igor Martak .08 .25
16 Branislav Medzihorsky .08 .25
17 Miroslav Micuda .08 .25
18 Tomas Mihalik .08 .25
19 Stanislav Mistrik .08 .25
20 Andrej Mrena .08 .25
21 Marian Nemeth .08 .25
22 Vladimir Polacek .08 .25
23 Rastislav Sendrey .08 .25
24 Norbert Skorvaga .08 .25
25 Tomas Surovy .60 1.50
26 Michal Turcer .08 .25
27 Sponsor Card .10 .01
28 Team Card .02 .10
29 Title Card .10 .01

1996 Slovakian Quebec Pee-Wee Tournament Team

This 30-card set features color player photos with red inside and faded purple outside borders. The backs carry player information. The cards are unnumbered and checklisted below in alphabetical order.

COMPLETE SET (30) 5.60 15.00
1 Jozef Balej .75 2.00
2 Michal Baranka .20 .50
3 Jan Behan CO .02 .10
4 Martin Bonda .20 .50
5 Robert Cerny .20 .50
6 Peter Duris .20 .50
7 Jan Frkan .20 .50
8 Milan Fujerik CO .02 .10
9 Michal Gunis .20 .50
10 Stefan Hlusek .20 .50
11 Peter Holecko .20 .50
12 Dr. Leopold Karafiat GM .02 .10
13 Lukas Krejci .20 .50
14 Miroslav Kristin .20 .50
15 Andrej Kucko .20 .50
16 Roman Kyndl .20 .50
17 Michal Macho .20 .50
18 Tomas Mikus .30 .75
19 Juraj Nemcak .20 .50
20 Viliam Ondrejik .20 .50
21 Miroslav Pistek .20 .50
22 Marek Pollak .30 .75
23 Tomas Psenka .20 .50
24 Milan Sitar CO .02 .10
25 Frantisek Skladany .40 1.00
26 Peter Steklac .20 .50
27 Richard Svrbik .20 .50
28 Michal Sykora .20 .50
29 Martin Wala .20 .50
30 Team Picture .02 .10

1998-99 Slovakian Eurotel

This set of cards was released in Slovakia to promote Eurotel. The slightly undersized issues feature a number of NHL stars -- primarily of European origin.

COMPLETE SET (29) 32.00 80.00
1 Peter Bondra 1.25 3.00
2 Sergei Fedorov 2.00 5.00
3 Peter Forsberg 3.00 8.00
4 Wayne Gretzky 8.00 20.00
5 Bill Guerin .75 2.00
6 Brett Hull 1.50 4.00
7 Jaromir Jagr 2.00 5.00
8 Saku Koivu 1.25 3.00
9 Jari Kurri .75 2.00
10 Pat Lafontaine .75 2.00
11 Janne Laukkanen .40 1.00
12 Robert Lang .40 1.00
13 John LeClair .75 2.00
14 Eric Lindros 1.50 4.00
15 Al MacInnis .75 2.00
16 Joe Nieuwendyk .75 2.00
17 Zigmund Palffy .75 2.00
18 Mike Richter 1.25 3.00
19 Patrick Roy 6.00 15.00
20 Joe Sakic 2.00 5.00
21 Tommy Salo .75 2.00
22 Miroslav Satan .75 2.00
23 Teemu Selanne 1.50 4.00
24 Mikhail Shtalenkov .40 1.00
25 Martin Straka .40 1.00
26 Mats Sundin .75 2.00
27 Alexei Yashin .40 1.00
28 Steve Yzerman 6.00 15.00
29 Alexei Zhamnov .40 1.00

1999-00 Slovakian Challengers

This odd-sized set was produced as a promotional incentive by a Slovakian candy bar manufacturer. The checklist for this set provided by www.hockeyheaven.com.

COMPLETE SET (30) 30.00 60.00
1 Rob Niedermayer .20 .50
2 Robert Svehla .20 .50
3 Richard Zednik .20 .50
4 Steve Sullivan .20 .50
5 Alexei Yashin .20 .50
6 Alexander Mogilny .30 .75
7 Zigmund Palffy .40 1.00
8 Martin Brodeur 6.00 15.00
9 Sandis Ozolinsh .20 .50
10 Adam Deadmarsh .30 .75
11 Peter Forsberg 2.50 6.00
12 Martin Rucinsky .20 .50
13 Shayne Corson .20 .50
14 Grant Fuhr .75 2.00
15 Al MacInnis .75 2.00
16 Paul Kariya 2.00 5.00
17 Teemu Selanne 2.00 5.00
18 Steve Yzerman 8.00 20.00
19 Chris Osgood .75 2.00
20 Brendan Shanahan 1.25 3.00
21 Vaclav Varada .20 .50
22 Brian Holzinger .20 .50
23 Dominik Hasek 2.50 6.00
24 Michael Peca .30 .75
25 Ed Belfour 1.25 3.00
26 Jere Lehtinen .75 2.00
27 Jaromir Jagr 3.00 8.00
28 Kevin Hatcher .20 .50
29 John LeClair .75 2.00
30 Alexei Zhamnov .20 .50

2001 Slovakian Kvarteto

This set features players who routinely suit up for Slovakia in key international events. The cards are shaped like playing cards, with a photo on front and the words Kvarteto on the back.

COMPLETE SET (33) 10.00 25.00
1A Jergus Baca .20 .50
1B Josef Dano .20 .50
1C Peter Bondra .40 2.00
1D Jaromir Dragan .40 1.00
2A Zdeno Ciger .20 .50
2B Peter Bondra .60 2.00
2C Pavol Demitra .60 2.00
2D Stanislav Jasecko .20 .50
3A Ivan Droppa .20 .50
3B Otto Hascak .20 .50
3C Branislav Janos .20 .50
3D Peter Bondra .60 2.00
4A Stanislav Jasecko .20 .50
4B Lubomir Kolnik .20 .50
4C Zigmund Palffy .60 2.00
4D Roman Kontsek .20 .50
5A Igor Murin .20 .50
5B Lubomir Visnovsky .30 .75
5C Lubomir Kolnik .20 .50
5D Jan Pardavy .20 .50
6A Robert Petrovicky .20 .50
6B Vlastimil Plavucha .20 .50
6C Peter Pucher .20 .50
6D Rene Pucher .20 .50
7A Pavol Rybar .20 .50
7B Miroslav Satan .60 2.00
7C Lubomir Sekeras .30 .75
7D Roman Stantien .20 .50
8A Roman Stantien .20 .50
8B Jozef Stumpel .30 .75
8C Robert Svehla .20 .50
8D Marian Varolik .20 .50
HOKEJ Peter Bondra 2.00 5.00

2002 Slovakian Kvarteto

This set features the world champion Slovaks. They look like playing cards with a player photo on the front and the word Kvarteto on the back. We have a complete list of players, but the numbering was randomly assigned. If you have the correct numbering, please get in touch.

COMPLETE SET (32) 8.00 20.00
1 Miroslav Satan .75 2.00
2 Peter Bondra .75 2.00
3 Zigmund Palffy .75 2.00
4 Jan Lasak .40 1.00
5 Rastislav Stana .40 1.00
6 Radoslav Hecl .20 .50
7 Richard Lintner .20 .50
8 Dusan Milo .20 .50
9 Peter Smrek .20 .50
10 Martin Strbak .20 .50
11 Lubomir Visnovsky .20 .50
12 Jergus Baca .20 .50
13 Michael Handzus .20 .50
14 Rastislav Pavlikovsky .20 .50
15 Robert Petrovicky .20 .50
16 Jozef Stumpel .20 .50
17 Radovan Somik .20 .50
18 Robert Tomik .20 .50
19 Miroslav Hlinka .20 .50
20 Lubos Bartecko .20 .50
21 Ladislav Nagy .40 1.00
22 Vladimir Orszagh .20 .50
23 Peter Stastny GM .20 .50
24 Samuel Petras .20 .50
25 Dalimir Jancovic .20 .50
26 Ernest Bokros .20 .50
27 Marek Uram .20 .50
28 Peter Pucher .20 .50
29 Ladislav Cierny .20 .50
30 Vladimir Stastny .20 .50
31 Miroslav Simonovic .20 .50
32 Jan Filc .20 .50

2004-05 Slovakian Poprad Team Set

COMPLETE SET (30) 10.00 25.00
1 Ladislav Svozil .30 .75
2 Vladimir Klinga .30 .75
3 Stanislav Kozuch .30 .75
4 Radovan Hurajt .30 .75
5 Miroslav Javin .30 .75
6 Stefan Rusnak .30 .75
7 Miroslav Turan .30 .75
8 Lukas Bambuch .30 .75
9 Stefan Fabian .30 .75
10 Ridvan Sadiki .30 .75
11 Tomas Jurco .30 .75
12 Radoslav Suchy .30 .75
13 Tomas Valecko .30 .75
14 Pavol Gurcik .30 .75
15 Peter Bondra 1.25 3.00
16 Miroslav Skovira .30 .75
17 Slavomir Pavlicko .30 .75
18 Juraj Halaj .30 .75
19 Pavol Zavacky .30 .75
20 Miroslav Ihnacak .30 .75
21 Juraj Faith .30 .75
22 Peter Misal' .30 .75
23 Ludovit Jurinyi .30 .75
24 Jozef Slaninak .30 .75
25 Richard Zemlicka .30 .75
26 Stefan Rusnak .30 .75
27 Miroslav Stolc .30 .75
28 Viktor Kubenko .30 .75
29 Erik Piatak .30 .75
30 Roman Soltys .30 .75

2004-05 Slovakian Skalica Team Set

COMPLETE SET (28) 10.00 25.00
1 Martin Kucera .40 1.00
2 Matej Bukna .40 1.00
3 Tibor Visnovsky .40 1.00
4 Jozef Mrena .40 1.00
5 Jaroslav Prosvic .40 1.00
6 Roman Chatrnuch .40 1.00
7 Milan Carsky .40 1.00
8 Miroslav Zalesak .60 1.50
9 Davis Galvas .40 1.00
10 Rene Jarolin .40 1.00
11 Richard Hartmann .40 1.00
12 Peter Kocak .40 1.00
13 Roman Kelner .40 1.00
14 Milan Malik .40 1.00
15 Marek Grill .40 1.00
16 Robert Liscak .40 1.00
17 Zigmund Palffy 1.25 3.00
18 Ladislav Paciga .40 1.00
19 Jozef Liska .40 1.00
20 Radovan Sloboda .40 1.00
21 Boris Flamik .40 1.00
22 Juraj Mikus .40 1.00
23 Peter Ivicic .40 1.00
24 Richard Stehlik .40 1.00
25 Martin Ivicic .40 1.00
26 Petr Tucek .40 1.00
27 Lukas Komarek .40 1.00
28 Martin Skadra .40 1.00

2004-05 South Surrey Eagles

COMPLETE SET (30) 15.00
1 Tyson Angus .50
2 Tim Crowder .50
3 Chris Delfrancescanto .50
4 Korey Diehl .50
5 Korey Diehl PROMO 1.00
6 Tyler Eckford .50
7 Tyler Eckford PROMO 1.00
8 Matthew Girling .50
9 Daniel Idema .50
10 Andrew Kozek .50
11 Andrew Kozek PROMO 1.00
12 Kyle Kuehner .50
13 Aaron McKenzie .50
14 Brock Meadows .50
15 T.J. Miller .50
16 David Moncur .50
17 Tyrell Moulton .50
18 T.J. Mulock .50
19 T.J. Mulock PROMO 1.00
20 Kyle Nason .50
21 Blake Rielly PROMO 1.00
22 Blake Rielly PROMO 1.00
23 David Rutherford .50
24 David Rutherford PROMO 1.00
25 Cody Rymut .50
26 Dustin Slade .50
27 Stewart Thiessen .50
28 Matt Wiest .50
29 Rick Hillier HC .10
30 Team Card .10

1932-33 Swedish Marabou

This multi-sport Swedish issue is believed to contain just six hockey players. The singles are very small, measuring about 1/2" by 1". It is believed that two versions of the set exist, one with white borders and another without. The fronts feature a photo, while the backs have the player's name, history, and the set name, Marabou-Sportserie. If anyone knows of other hockey players in this set, please contact us at hockeymag@beckett.com

Hockey players in set (6)
4 C. Abrahamsson
146 Herman Carlsson
147 Folke Wohlin
148 Carl-Erik Furst
149 Bertil Linde
150 Olof Johansson

1938-39 Swedish Liv's Magazine

Hockey Players In Set (2)
56 Vilhelm Petersen
57 Axel Nilsson

1955-56 Swedish Alfabilder

We have no pricing information on this early Swedish set.

COMPLETE SET (36)
COMMON CARD (1-36)
1 Lars Bjorn
2 Sven Tumba Johansson
3 Sven Lill-Cacka Andersson
4 Bertz Zetterberg
5 Yngve Johansson
6 Yngve Carlsson
7 Bengt Bingen Larsson
8 Torsten Totte Magnusson
9 Arne Boman
10 Gote Vicke Hallon Blomquist
11 Stig Carlsson
12 Erik Epa Johansson
13 Borje Lofgren
14 Birger Bigge Nilsson
15 Rune Mankan Magnusson
16 Thord Flodqvist
17 Sven Thunman
18 Lars Erik Lundvall
19 Lars Henrik Johansson
20 Arne Jern
21 Kalle Lilja
22 Yngve Casslind
23 Nisse Nilsson
24 Patrik Linder
25 Lars-Erik Soderberg
26 Per Rockstrom
27 Ake Blomberg
28 Holger Numela
29 Sune Rakan Holmgren
30 Karl-Harry Engstrom
31 Kurt Andersson
32 Hans Bjargestad
33 Ake Plutten Andersson
34 Rolf Pettersson
35 Lars Lasse Svensson
36 Ake Elgstrom

1956-57 Swedish Alfabilder

We have no pricing information on this early Swedish set.

COMPLETE SET (72)
37 Carl Gustav Gustafsson
38 Gunnar Nilas Brundin
39 Runar Soderstrom
40 Gert Blome
41 Egon Hillgren
42 Carl-Goran Lill-Stoveln Oberg
43 Bertil Bomben Carlbaum
44 Hans Stoveln Oberg
45 Sven Wikman
46 Valter Ahlen
47 Bernt Eriksson
48 Einar Granath
49 Uno Ohrlund
50 Nils-Olov Fredriksson
51 Karl-Erik Olsson
52 Jarl Sjoberg
53 Gote Almqvist
54 Stig Wallner
55 Roland Granberg
56 Folke Aronsson
57 Anders Andersson
58 Haldor Jonsson
59 Olle Larsson
60 Soren Hedlund
61 Ivan Aronsson
62 Ake Lundmark
63 Hjalle Sundqvist
64 Lennart Markgren
65 Harry Granberg
66 Gunnar Segerman
67 Lasse Pettersson
68 Torsten Pettersson
69 Sven Svard
70 Jan Gustafsson
71 Birger Adrian
72 Bertil Svard
73 Anders Fernstrom
74 Ake Nilsson
75 Bjorn Johansson
76 Sune Johansson
77 Bo Hultin
78 Sven Gote Andersson
79 Hans Pfeiffer
80 S.A. Nilsson
81 Pelle Jansson

82 Sven Ake Sahlin
83 Sven Erik Sundqvist
84 Hasse Andersson
85 Folke Gustafsson
86 Kjell Eklind
87 Rune Blomberg
88 Arne Kuben Lang
89 Mas-Ake Larsson
90 Bo Olsson
91 Evert Tysk
92 Erik Pettersson
93 Sven Kristoffersson
94 Ingvar Mattsson
95 Ake Alfvendahl
96 Jan-Erik Johansson
97 Bo Hessel
98 Lennart Astrom
99 Torsten Osterberg
100 Yngve Feldt
101 Gunnar Svensson
102 Olle Linder
103 Sven-Erik Ekdahl
104 Jan Hjelm
105 Karl-Erik Jansson
106 Nils Nord
107 Bernt Sjoqvist
108 Hans Saker

1957-58 Swedish Alfabilder

COMPLETE SET (72)
73 Eje Lindstrom
74 Lennart Andersson
75 Soren Bostrom
76 Berndt Arvidsson
77 Gote Wiklund
78 Alf Skonberg
79 Bo Eriksson
80 Ingvar Lillen Naslund
81 Lars Soderblom
82 Sune Bojan Bolin
83 Arne Pandel
84 Bert-Ola Nordlander
85 Stig Palvels
86 Gunnar Hedbys
87 Gunnar Jonses
88 Knut Knutsson
89 Vilgot Larsson
90 Per-Agne Karlstrom
91 Ingemar Lysen
92 Ake Lassas
93 Goran Lysen
94 Ingemar Brandstrom
95 Karl-Gerhard Juhlin
96 Erik Holmgren
97 Rune Holmgren
98 Arne Holmgren
99 Sune Johansson
100 Lars-Erik Jansson
101 Olsten Johansson
102 Sune Wretling
103 Anders Hemmingsson
104 Ove Dahlberg
105 Hans-Ove Norrman
106 Ake Johansson
107 Arne Falkvist
108 Olle Groning
109 Kjell Andersson
110 Ove Andersson
111 Nisse Edholm
112 Fred Andersson
113 Hans-Ove Lindberg
114 Roland Hellgren
115 Lars Andersson
116 Tor Horstad
117 Bernt-Ola Stenlund
118 Campbell Fuhrberg
119 Lennart Skarp
120 Hjalle Sundkvist
121 Rune Holmstrom
122 Kurt Lovgren
123 Kjell Adrian
124 Rickard Fagerlund
125 Bengt Nilsson
126 Sten Lindqvist
127 Roland Skarin
128 Lars Rosenstam
129 Rolf Ek
130 Bertil Andersson
131 Arne Lund
132 Sigge Broms
133 Bert-Ola Nordlander
134 Sonny Fermstrom
135 Bertil Hasselqvist
136 Bertil Carlbaum
137 Goran Wallin
138 Olle Stenar
139 Berndt Karlsson
140 Olle Westlund
141 Bertil Masen Karlsson
142 Ulf Gronberg
143 Rolf Gardin
144 Lars Jansson

1964 Swedish Coralli ISHockey

These tiny cards (1 7/8" by 1 1/4") feature players from the Swedish national team, Tre Kroner, as well as many club teams. The cards apparently were distributed as premiums in chocolate bars. According to reports, such sets existed in Sweden as far back as 1955. The card fronts have a posed player photo, name and card number. The backs offer a brief biography in Swedish. An album to hold these cards is believed to exist; this, however, has not been confirmed.

Card	Low	High
COMPLETE SET (165)	150.00	300.00
1 Sven Johansson	1.50	3.00
2 Ove Malmberg	1.00	2.00
3 Bjorn Larsson	1.00	2.00
4 Ulf Sterner	1.00	2.00
5 Bertil Karlsson	1.00	2.00
6 Leif Holmqvist	5.00	10.00
7 Uno Ohrlund	1.00	2.00
8 Mats Lonn	1.00	2.00
9 Bjorn Palmqvist	1.00	2.00
10 Nils Johansson	1.00	2.00
11 Anders Andersson	1.00	2.00
12 Lennart Haggroth	2.00	4.00
13 Hans Svedberg	1.00	2.00
14 Ronald Pettersson	1.00	2.00
15 Lars Eric Lundvall	1.00	2.00
16 Gert Blome	1.00	2.00
17 Bo Englund	1.00	2.00
18 Folke Bengtsson	1.00	2.00
19 Nils Nilsson	1.00	2.00
20 Lennart Johansson	1.00	2.00
21 Lennart Svedberg	2.50	5.00
22 Lars Ake Sivertsson	1.00	2.00
23 Hakan Wickberg	1.00	2.00
24 Tord Lundstrom	1.00	2.00
25 Ove Andersson	1.00	2.00
26 Bert Ola Nordlander	1.50	3.00
27 Jan Erik Nilsson	1.00	2.00
28 Eilert Maatta	1.00	2.00
29 Roland Stoltz	1.00	2.00
30 Kurt Thulin	1.00	2.00
31 Ove Andersson	1.00	2.00
32 Ingemar Johansson	1.00	2.00
33 Rune Lind	1.00	2.00
34 Bert-Ola Nordlander	1.50	3.00
35 Hans Eriksson	1.00	2.00
36 Antik Johansson	1.00	2.00
37 Bo Hansson	1.00	2.00
38 Jan Back	1.00	2.00
39 Lennart Soderberg	1.00	2.00
40 Benny Soderling	1.00	2.00
41 Anders Parmstrom	1.00	2.00
42 Lennart Selinder	1.00	2.00
43 Bjorn Larsson	1.00	2.00
44 Jorma Salmi	1.00	2.00
45 Berndt Arvidsson	1.00	2.00
46 P.A. Karlstrom	1.00	2.00
47 Lars Erik Sjoberg	5.00	10.00
48 Vilgot Larsson	1.00	2.00
49 Gunnar Andersson	1.00	2.00
50 Roland Bond	1.00	2.00
51 Goran Lysen	1.00	2.00
52 Bosse Englund	1.00	2.00
53 Stig Pavels	1.00	2.00
54 Bengt Bornstrom	1.00	2.00
55 Nisse Nilsson	1.00	2.00
56 Lennart Lange	1.00	2.00
57 Des Moroney	1.00	2.00
58 Folke Bengtsson	1.00	2.00
59 Olle Sjogren	1.00	2.00
60 Knut Knutsson	1.00	2.00
61 Kjell Svensson	1.00	2.00
62 Rickard Fagerlund	2.50	5.00
63 Arne Loong	1.00	2.00
64 Stig Carlsson	1.00	2.00
65 Lars Hagg	1.00	2.00
66 Olle Stenar	1.00	2.00
67 Einar Granath	1.00	2.00
68 Leif Andersson	1.00	2.00
69 Hans Soderstrom	1.00	2.00
70 Kalle Lilja	1.00	2.00
71 Soren Maatta	1.00	2.00
72 Sven Bystrom	1.00	2.00
73 Hans Karlsson	1.00	2.00
74 Stig Goran Johansson	1.50	3.00
75 Jan Allinger	1.00	2.00
76 Kjell Larsson	1.00	2.00
77 Hakan Wickberg	1.00	2.00
78 Tord Lundstrom	1.00	2.00
79 Lennart Svedberg	2.50	5.00
80 Jan Erik Lyck	1.00	2.00
81 Hans Eriksson	1.00	2.00
82 Kjell Jonsson	1.00	2.00
83 Lars Hedenstrom	1.00	2.00
84 Lars Ake Sivertsson	1.00	2.00
85 Lennart Johansson	1.00	2.00
86 Hans Sjoberg	1.00	2.00
87 Hans Dahllof	1.00	2.00
88 Leif Jansson	1.00	2.00
89 Lars Byling	1.00	2.00
90 Bertil Lindstrom	1.00	2.00
91 Arne Eriksson	1.00	2.00
92 Gert Blomer	1.00	2.00
93 Kjell Adrian	1.00	2.00
94 Jan Olsen	1.00	2.00
95 Benny Karlsson	1.00	2.00
96 Tommy Carlsson	1.00	2.00
97 Ulf Sterner	1.00	2.00
98 Kjell-Ove Gustafsson	1.00	2.00
99 Lars Erik Lundvall	1.00	2.00
100 Kjell-Ronny Pettersson	1.00	2.00
101 Ronald Pettersson	1.00	2.00
102 Kjell Jonsson	1.00	2.00
103 Gote Hansson	1.00	2.00
104 Rolf Eklof	1.00	2.00
105 Eine Olsson	1.00	2.00
106 Hans-Erik Fernstrom	1.00	2.00
107 Leif Holmqvist	1.00	2.00
108 Bo Zetterberg	1.00	2.00
109 Ake Zattlin	1.00	2.00
110 Bengt-Olov Andreasson	1.00	2.00
111 Borje Mohlander	1.00	2.00
112 Sture Sundin	1.00	2.00
113 Bertil Karlsson	1.00	2.00
114 Lars Molander	1.00	2.00
115 Benno Persson	1.00	2.00
116 Gert Nystrom	1.00	2.00
117 Sune Bohlin	1.00	2.00
118 Olle Westlund	1.00	2.00
119 Goran Wallin	1.00	2.00
120 Ingemar Persson	1.00	2.00
121 Tommy Bjorkman	1.00	2.00
122 Eddie Wingren	1.00	2.00
123 Lars Bjorn	1.00	2.00
124 Roland Stoltz	1.00	2.00
125 Sven Johansson	1.50	3.00
126 Leif Skold	1.00	2.00
127 Hans Mild	1.00	2.00
128 Kurt Thulin	1.00	2.00
129 Ake Rydberg	1.00	2.00
130 Ove Malmberg	1.00	2.00
131 Lars Lundqvist	1.00	2.00
132 Kurt Svensson	1.00	2.00
133 Gosta Westerlund	1.00	2.00
134 Lars Andersson	1.00	2.00
135 Ulf Rydin	1.00	2.00
136 Lennart Haggroth	2.00	4.00
137 Jan Hedberg	1.00	2.00
138 Karl Soren Hedlund	1.00	2.00
139 Hans Svedberg	1.00	2.00
140 Sture Hoverberg	1.00	2.00
141 Anders Ronnblom	1.00	2.00
142 Ulf Eriksson	1.00	2.00
143 Anders Andersson	1.00	2.00
144 Henrik Hedlund	1.00	2.00
145 Per Lundstrom	1.00	2.00
146 Hakan Nygren	1.00	2.00
147 Bo Berglund, Sr	2.00	4.00
148 Lars Ake Warning	1.00	2.00
149 Sven-Olov Johansson	1.00	2.00
150 Ove Stenlund	1.00	2.00
151 Ivar Larsson	1.00	2.00
152 Nils Johansson	1.00	2.00
153 Sten Olsen	1.00	2.00
154 Lars Gidlund	1.00	2.00
155 Tor Haarstad	1.00	2.00
156 Kjell-Olav Barrefjord	1.00	2.00
157 Bjorn Palmqvist	1.00	2.00
158 Soren Lindstrom	1.00	2.00
159 Henna Svensson	1.00	2.00
160 Lars Hagstrom	1.00	2.00
161 Ake Eklof	1.00	2.00
162 Ulf Lundstrom	1.00	2.00
163 Ronny Nordstrom	1.00	2.00
164 Paul Stahl	1.00	2.00
165 Kenneth Sahlen	1.50	3.00

1965 Swedish Coralli ISHockey

These tiny (1 7/8" by 1 1/4") feature players from the Swedish National Team, Tre Kroner, as well as many club teams. The cards apparently were issued as premiums with chocolate bars. The card fronts have a posed player photo, name and card number. The backs offer a brief biography in Swedish.

Card	Low	High
COMPLETE SET (214)	125.00	300.00
1 Sven Johansson	1.25	3.00
2 Ove Malmberg	.75	2.00
3 Bjorn Larsson	.75	2.00
4 Ulf Sterner	.75	2.00
5 Bertil Karlsson	1.00	3.00
6 Leif Holmqvist	4.00	8.00
7 Uno Ohrlund	.75	2.00
8 Mats Lonn	.75	2.00
9 Bjorn Palmqvist	.75	2.00
10 Nils Johansson	.75	2.00
11 Anders Andersson	.75	2.00
12 Lennart Haggroth	1.50	4.00
13 Hans Svedberg	.75	2.00
14 Ronald Pettersson	.75	2.00
15 Lars Eric Lundvall	.75	2.00
16 Gert Blome	.75	2.00
17 Bo Englund	.75	2.00
18 Folke Bengtsson	.75	2.00
19 Nils Nilsson	.75	2.00
20 Lennart Johansson	.75	2.00
21 Lennart Svedberg	1.75	4.00
22 Lars Ake Sivertsson	.75	2.00
23 Hakan Wickberg	.75	2.00
24 Tord Lundstrom	.75	2.00
25 Ove Andersson	.75	2.00
26 Bert Ola Nordlander	1.25	3.00
27 Jan Erik Nilsson	.75	2.00
28 Eilert Maatta	.75	2.00
29 Roland Stoltz	.75	2.00
30 Kurt Thulin	.75	2.00
31 Leif Holmquist	4.00	8.00
32 Ingemar Johansson	1.00	3.00
33 Rune Lind	.75	2.00
34 Bert-Ola Nordlander	1.25	3.00
35 Hans Eriksson	.75	2.00
36 Antik Johansson	.75	2.00
37 Bo Hansson	.75	2.00
38 Hans-Ake Carlsson	.75	2.00
39 Lennart Soderberg	.75	2.00
40 Benny Soderling	.75	2.00
41 Anders Parmstrom	.75	2.00
42 Lennart Selinder	.75	2.00
43 Bjorn Larsson	.75	2.00
44 Ove Hedberg	.75	2.00
45 Berndt Arvidsson	.75	2.00
46 P.A. Carlstrom	.75	2.00
47 Lars Erik Sjoberg	4.00	8.00
48 Kjell Fhinn	.75	2.00
49 Gunnar Andersson	.75	2.00
50 Roland Bond	.75	2.00
51 Goran Lysen	.75	2.00
52 Bosse Englund	.75	2.00
53 Stig Pavels	.75	2.00
54 Bengt Bornstrom	.75	2.00
55 Nisse Nilsson	.75	2.00
56 Lennart Lange	.75	2.00
57 Tommy Abrahamsson	4.00	8.00
58 Folke Bengtsson	.75	2.00
59 Olle Sjogren	.75	2.00
60 Knut Knutsson	.75	2.00
61 Kjell Svensson	.75	2.00
62 Rickard Fagerlund	1.75	4.00
63 Eilert Maatta	.75	2.00
64 Stig Carlsson	.75	2.00
65 Lars Hagg	.75	2.00
66 Ollie Stenar	.75	2.00
67 Einar Andersson	.75	2.00
68 Leif Andersson	.75	2.00
69 Percy Lind	.75	2.00
70 Gunnar Tallberg	.75	2.00
71 Soren Maatta	.75	2.00
72 Sven Bystrom	.75	2.00
73 Hans Carlsson	.75	2.00
74 Stig Goran Johansson	1.25	3.00
75 Thomas Warming	.75	2.00
76 Kjell Larsson	.75	2.00
77 Hakan Wickberg	.75	2.00
78 Tord Lundstrom	.75	2.00
79 Lennart Svedberg	2.00	4.00
80 Jan Erik Lyck	.75	2.00
81 Stefan Carlsson	.75	2.00
82 Kjell Jonsson	.75	2.00
83 Lars Hedenstrom	.75	2.00
84 Lars Ake Sivertsson	.75	2.00
85 Lennart Johansson	.75	2.00
86 Hans Sjoberg	.75	2.00
87 Hans Dahllof	.75	2.00
88 Hans Lindberg	.75	2.00
89 Lars Bylund	.75	2.00
90 Sten Edqvist	.75	2.00
91 Arne Ericsson	.75	2.00
92 Gert Blomer	.75	2.00
93 Kjell Adrian	.75	2.00
94 Jan Olsen	.75	2.00
95 Benny Karlsson	.75	2.00
96 Jorma Salmi	.75	2.00
97 Ulf Sterner	.75	2.00
98 Kjell-Ove Gustafsson	.75	2.00
99 Lars Erik Lundvall	.75	2.00
100 Kjell-Ronny Pettersson	1.00	3.00
101 Ronald Pettersson	.75	2.00
102 Kjell Jonsson	.75	2.00
103 Gote Hansson	.75	2.00
104 Ove Sterner	.75	2.00
105 Eine Olsson	.75	2.00
106 Hans-Erik Fernstrom	.75	2.00
107 Per-Olov Hardin	.75	2.00
108 Bo Zetterberg	.75	2.00
109 Ake Zettlin	.75	2.00
110 Bengt-Olov Andreasson	.75	2.00
111 Borje Molander	.75	2.00
112 Sture Sundin	.75	2.00
113 Bertil Karlsson	1.00	3.00
114 Lars Molander	.75	2.00
115 Benno Persson	.75	2.00
116 Rolf Larsson	.75	2.00
117 Ronny Francis	.75	2.00
118 Olle Westlund	.75	2.00
119 Goran Wallin	.75	2.00
120 Ingemar Persson	.75	2.00
121 Tommy Bjorkman	.75	2.00
122 Eddie Wingren	.75	2.00
123 Lars Bjorn	.75	2.00
124 Roland Stoltz	.75	2.00
125 Sven Johansson	1.25	3.00
126 Arne Loong	.75	2.00
127 Per Lundstrom		5.00
127 Hans Mild	.75	2.00
128 Kurt Thulin	.75	2.00
129 Ake Rydberg	.75	2.00
130 Ove Malmberg	.75	2.00
131 Lars Lundqvist	.75	2.00
132 Kurt Svensson	.75	2.00
133 Gosta Westerlund	.75	2.00
134 Lars Andersson	.75	2.00
135 Ulf Rydin	.75	2.00
136 Lennart Haggroth	1.50	4.00
137 Jan Hedberg	.75	2.00
138 Anders Carlberg	.75	2.00
139 Hans Svedberg	.75	2.00
140 Sture Holverberg	.75	2.00
141 Anders Ronnblom	.75	2.00
142 Ulf Eriksson	.75	2.00
143 Anders Andersson	.75	2.00
144 Henrik Hedlund	.75	2.00
145 Roger Boman	.75	2.00
146 Bo Astrom	.75	2.00
147 Bo Berglund	1.50	3.00
148 Lars Ake Warning	.75	2.00
149 Sven-Olov Johansson	.75	2.00
150 Ove Stenlund	.75	2.00
151 Ivar Larsson	.75	2.00
152 Nicke Johansson	.75	2.00
153 Sten Olsen	.75	2.00
154 Lars Gidlund	.75	2.00
155 Tor Haarstad	.75	2.00
156 Hakan Nygren	.75	2.00
157 Bjorn Palmqvist	.75	2.00
158 Soren Lindstrom	.75	2.00
159 Henry Svensson	.75	2.00
160 Lars Hagstrom	.75	2.00
161 Ake Eklof	.75	2.00
162 Ulf Lundstrom	.75	2.00
163 Ronny Nordstrom	.75	2.00
164 Paul Stahl	.75	2.00
165 Kenneth Sahlen	1.25	3.00
166 Anders Hedlund	.75	2.00
167 Ingemar Caris	.75	2.00
168 Arne Carlsson	.75	2.00
169 Gote Bostrom	.75	2.00
170 Roger Olsson	.75	2.00
171 Ole Jacobson	.75	2.00
172 Curt Edenvik	.75	2.00
173 Goran Svensson	.75	2.00
174 Eje Lindstrom	.75	2.00
175 Curt Larsson	2.50	5.00
176 Gunnar Backman	.75	2.00
177 Anders Nordin	.75	2.00
178 Ulf Torstensson	.75	2.00
179 Kent Lindgren	.75	2.00
180 Kent Sjalin	.75	2.00
181 Lars Goran Nilsson	.75	2.00
182 Heimo Klockare	.75	2.00
183 Lars Sattare	.75	2.00
184 Lars-Ake Lundell	.75	2.00
185 Kjell Savstrom	.75	2.00
186 Carl-Goran Oberg	.75	2.00
187 Bjorn Larsson	.75	2.00
188 Leif Eriksson	.75	2.00
189 Dag Olsson	.75	2.00
190 Lars Lohman	.75	2.00
191 unknown	.75	2.00
192 unknown	.75	2.00
193 unknown	.75	2.00
194 unknown	.75	2.00
195 unknown	.75	2.00
196 unknown	.75	2.00
197 unknown	.75	2.00
198 unknown	.75	2.00
199 unknown	.75	2.00
200 Hans Aleblad	.75	2.00
201 Karl Soren Hedlund	.75	2.00
202 Clarence Carlsson	.75	2.00
203 Bjorn Johansson	.75	2.00
204 Kent Persson	.75	2.00
205 Goran Thelin	.75	2.00
206 Leif Ohrlund	.75	2.00
207 Mats Davidsson	.75	2.00
208 Leif Arturson	.75	2.00
209 Karl Gunnar Backman	.75	2.00
210 Hans Mellinger	.75	2.00
211 Hans Inge Lund	.75	2.00
212 Kent Jansson	.75	2.00
213 Anders Ronnkvist	.75	2.00
214 Bo Olofsson	.75	2.00

1967-68 Swedish Hockey

This 300-card set features the skaters from the Swedish first and second division teams from the 1967-68 season, as well as the national team, Tre Kronor. The cards measure 2" by 3 1/8" and feature posed color photos on the front. The national team cards have the words Tre Kronor and the three crown logo across the top. The backs have the card number, player stats and an invitation to purchase a collectors album, all in Swedish. The album for the set includes numerous pages of text and photos about Swedish hockey, and is valued at $35. Although short on widely recognizable names, the set does include early -- if not first -- cards of Inge Hammarstrom and Christer Abrahamsson.

Card	Low	High
COMPLETE SET (300)	62.50	150.00
1 Christer Abrahamsson	2.00	4.00
2 Tommy Abrahamsson	1.00	2.00
3 Folke Bengtsson	.25	1.00
4 Arne Carlsson	.25	1.00
5 Bengt-Ake Gustavsson	.25	1.00
6 Anders Hagstrom	.25	1.00
7 Inge Hammarstrom	2.50	5.00
8 Leif Henriksson	.25	1.00
9 Leif Holmqvist	1.00	2.00
10 Per-Arne Hubinette	.25	1.00
11 Mats Hysing	.25	1.00
12 Nils Johansson	.25	1.00
13 Stig-Goran Johansson	.25	1.00
14 Hans Lindberg	.25	1.00
15 Tord Lundstrom	.25	1.00
16 Lars-Goran Nilsson	.25	1.00
17 Anders Nordin	.25	1.00
18 Bert-Ola Nordlander	.25	1.00
19 Roger Olsson	.25	1.00
20 Bjorn Palmquist	.25	1.00
21 Kjell Sundstrom	.25	1.00
22 Lennart Svedberg	.50	2.00
23 Hakan Wickberg	.25	1.00
24 Carl-Goran Oberg	.25	1.00
25 Lasse Ohman	.25	1.00
26 Curt Edenvik	.25	1.00
27 Hans Eriksson	.25	1.00
28 Rolf Hallgren	.25	1.00
29 Bo Hansson	.25	1.00
30 Ove Hedberg	.25	1.00
31 Kjell Hedman	.50	2.00
32 Leif Holmqvist	1.00	2.00
33 Anders Johansson	.25	1.00
34 Bengt Larsson	.25	1.00
35 Bjorn Larsson	.25	1.00
36 Rune Lindh	.25	1.00
37 Borje Molander	.25	1.00
38 Kjell Nilsson	.25	1.00
39 Bert-Ola Nordlander	.25	1.00
40 Anders Parmstrom	.25	1.00
41 Lennart Sellinder	.25	1.00
42 Kjell Savstrom	.25	1.00
43 Lars Bylund	.25	1.00
44 Hans Dahllof	.50	2.00
45 Lennart Gustafsson	.25	1.00
46 Lars Hedenstrom	.25	1.00
47 Lennart Johansson	.25	1.00
48 Kjell Johnsson	.25	1.00
49 Stefan Karlsson	.25	1.00
50 Nisse Larsson	.25	1.00
51 Lennart Lind	.25	1.00
52 Hans Lindberg	.25	1.00
53 Tord Lundstrom	.25	1.00
54 Jan-Erik Lyck	.25	1.00
55 Lars-Goran Nilsson	.25	1.00
56 Anders Sahlin	.50	2.00
57 Lars-Ake Sivertsson	.25	1.00
58 Hans Sjoberg	.25	1.00
59 Hakan Wickberg	.25	1.00
60 Tommy Bjorkman	.50	2.00
61 Lasse Bjorn	.25	1.00
62 Thomas Carlsson	.25	1.00
63 Roland Einarsson	.50	2.00
64 Kjell Keijser	.25	1.00
65 Stig Larsson	.25	1.00
66 Kent Lindgren	.25	1.00
67 Tommie Lindgren	.25	1.00
68 Lars-Ake Lundell	.25	1.00
69 Per Lundstrom	.25	1.00
70 Bjorn Palmquist	.25	1.00
71 Ulf Rydin	.25	1.00
72 Lars-Eric Sjoberg	2.00	4.00
73 Lars Starck	.25	1.00
74 Roland Stoltz	.25	1.00
75 Henry Svensson	.25	1.00
76 Kurt Thulin	.25	1.00
77 Gosta Westerlund	.25	1.00
78 Eddie Wingren	.25	1.00
79 Carl-Goran Oberg	.25	1.00
80 Anders Andersson	.25	1.00
81 Hasse Andersson	.25	1.00
82 Hakan Andersson	.25	1.00
83 Anders Asplund	.25	1.00
84 Hans Bergqvist	.25	1.00
85 Hans Bostrom	.25	1.00
86 Kjell Eriksson	.50	2.00
87 Conny Evensson	.50	2.00
88 Bjorn Fagerlund	.50	2.00
89 Ingemar Magnusson	.25	1.00
90 Hans-Ake Nilsson	.25	1.00
91 Rune Nilsson	.25	1.00
92 Kent Olsson	.25	1.00
93 Lars Stalberg	.25	1.00
94 Christer Sundquist	.25	1.00
95 Christer Abrahamsson	2.00	4.00
96 Tommy Abrahamsson	1.00	2.00
97 Dosse Andersson	.25	1.00
98 Gunnar Andersson	.25	1.00
99 Lars Andersson	.25	1.00
100 Folke Bengtsson	.25	1.00
101 Roland Bond	.25	1.00
102 Kjell Fihnn	.25	1.00
103 Jan-Olof Kroon	.25	1.00
104 Lennart Lange	.25	1.00
105 Sture Leksell	.50	2.00
106 Goran Lysen	.25	1.00
107 Ulf Martensson	.25	1.00
108 Nisse Nilsson	.25	1.00
109 Dag Ohlsson	.25	1.00
110 Olle Sjogren	.25	1.00
111 Ake Sunesson	.25	1.00
112 Dan Soderstrom	.25	1.00
113 Goran Winge	.25	1.00
114 Mats Ahlberg	.25	1.00
115 Olle Ost	.25	1.00
116 Gunnar Backman	.50	2.00
117 Lage Edin	.25	1.00
118 Ake Eklof	.25	1.00
119 Torbjorn Hubinette	.25	1.00
120 Nils Johansson	.25	1.00
121 Ulf Kroon	.25	1.00
122 Ivar Larsson	.50	2.00
123 Christer Nilsson	.25	1.00
124 Anders Nordin	.25	1.00
125 Hakan Nygren	.25	1.00
126 Sten Olsen	.25	1.00
127 Paul Stahl	.25	1.00
128 Gunnar Safsten	.25	1.00
129 Ulf Torstensson	.25	1.00
130 Ulf Wigren	.25	1.00
131 Lars Ohman	.25	1.00
132 Tore Ohman	.25	1.00
133 Bengt Andersson	.25	1.00
134 Nils Carlsson	.25	1.00
135 Kjell Eklind	.25	1.00
136 Allan Fernstrom	.25	1.00
137 Bengt Gustavsson	.25	1.00
138 Bengt-Ake Gustavsson	.50	2.00
139 Gote Hansson	.25	1.00
140 Per-Arne Hubinette	.25	1.00
141 Sven-Ake Jakobsson	.25	1.00
142 Goran Johansson	.50	2.00
143 Mats Lind	.25	1.00
144 Mats Lonn	.25	1.00
145 Ulf Nises	.25	1.00
146 Bo Olsson	.25	1.00
147 Lennart Svedberg	.50	2.00
148 Evert Tysk	.25	1.00
149 Stig Ostling	.25	1.00
150 Ulf Berglund	.25	1.00
151 Clarence Carlsson	.25	1.00
152 Arne Ekenberg	.25	1.00
153 Kenneth Ekman	.25	1.00
154 Tom Haugh	.50	2.00
155 Rolf Joelsson	.25	1.00
156 Bjorn Johanesson	.25	1.00
157 Arne Johansson	.25	1.00
158 Bengt-Goran Karlsson	.25	1.00
159 Kjell Larsson	.25	1.00
160 Lasse Larsson	.25	1.00
161 Barry Murman	.25	1.00
162 Klas Goran Nilsson	.25	1.00
163 Rolf Norell	.25	1.00
164 Lennart Skordaker	.25	1.00
165 Ulf Sterner	.50	2.00
166 Arne Wickstrom	.25	1.00
167 Bengt-Olov Andreasson	.50	2.00
168 Leif Eriksson	.25	1.00
169 Ove Evaldson	.25	1.00
170 Hans-Erik Fernstrom	.25	1.00
171 Kenneth Hillgren	.25	1.00
172 Per-Olof Hardin	.25	1.00
173 Bertil Karlsson	.25	1.00
174 Torsten Karlsson	.25	1.00
175 Rolf Larsson	.25	1.00
176 William Lofqvist	1.00	2.00
177 Lars Mollander	.25	1.00
178 Gert Nystrom	.25	1.00
179 Olle Westlund	.25	1.00
180 Bo Zetterberg	.25	1.00
181 Leif Andersson	.25	1.00
182 Borje Burlin	.25	1.00
183 Hans Carlsson	.25	1.00
184 Stig Carlsson	.25	1.00
185 Einar Granath	.25	1.00
186 Kjell-Ake Hedstrom	.25	1.00
187 Mats Hysing	.25	1.00
188 Stig-Goran Johansson	.25	1.00
189 Curt Larsson	1.25	2.50
190 Eilert Maatta	.25	1.00
191 Soren Maatta	.25	1.00
192 Nils-Olof Schilstrom	.25	1.00
193 Jan Schullstrom	.25	1.00
194 Kjell Svensson	.50	2.00
195 Gunnar Tallberg	.25	1.00
196 Dick Yderstrom	.25	1.00
197 Sten Andersson	.50	2.00
198 Lars Arne Bergkvist	.25	1.00
199 Anders Edstrom	.25	1.00
200 Lars Bertil Eriksson	.25	1.00
201 Charles Gustavsson	.25	1.00
202 Ake Johansson	.25	1.00
203 Lars Karestal	.25	1.00
204 Rolf Karlsson	.25	1.00
205 Erik Lindahl	.25	1.00
206 Freddy Lindfors	.50	2.00
207 Lennart Lindkvist	.25	1.00
208 Kjell Rune Milton	.25	1.00
209 Olle Nilsater	.25	1.00
210 Birger Nordlund	.25	1.00
211 Inge Tornlund	.25	1.00
212 Jan Roger Oberg	.25	1.00
213 Kjell Sture Oberg	.25	1.00
214 Tommy Andersson	.25	1.00
215 Soren Bostrom	.25	1.00
216 Anders Bryner	.25	1.00
217 Anders Claesson	.50	2.00
218 Svante Granholm	.25	1.00
219 Inge Hammarstrom	2.50	5.00
220 Borje Holmstrom	.25	1.00
221 Jan Johansson	.25	1.00
222 Antero Jonasson	.25	1.00
223 Ove Jonsson	.25	1.00
224 Lennart Lind	.50	2.00
225 Jan-Erik Nilsson	.25	1.00
226 Kurt Olofsson	.25	1.00
227 Gosta Sjokvist	.25	1.00
228 Jan Stolpe	.25	1.00
229 Kjell Westerlund	.25	1.00
230 Olle Ahman	.25	1.00
231 Jan-Ivar Bergqvist	.25	1.00
232 Lars-Ake Brannlund	.50	2.00
233 Hans Bohlmark	.25	1.00
234 Jan Christiansson	.25	1.00
235 Bengt Eriksson	.25	1.00
236 Arne Grenemo	.25	1.00
237 Lars-Olof Henriksson	.25	1.00
238 Kurt Jakobsson	.25	1.00
239 Leif Jakobsson	.25	1.00
240 Lars-Goran Johansson	.25	1.00
241 Kimo Kivela	.25	1.00
242 Borje Maatta	.25	1.00
243 Anders Rapp	.25	1.00
244 Tommy Sahlsten	.25	1.00
245 Stig-Olof Zetterbrg	.25	1.00
246 Lennart Abrahamsson	.25	1.00
247 John Andersson	.25	1.00
248 Ove Andersson	.50	2.00
249 Kjell-olov Barrefjord	.25	1.00
250 Ulf Barrefjord	.25	1.00
251 Kent Bjork	.25	1.00
252 Lars Dahlgren	.25	1.00
253 Karl-Ove Eriksson	.25	1.00
254 Osten Folkesson	.25	1.00
255 Anders Hagstrom	.25	1.00
256 Eric Jarvholm	.25	1.00
257 Ulf Larsson	.25	1.00
258 Bengt Lovgren	.25	1.00
259 Roger Nilsson	.25	1.00
260 Bengt Persson	.50	2.00
261 Kjell Sundstrom	.25	1.00
262 Roger Osterlund	.25	1.00
263 Hans Aleblad	.50	2.00
264 Ake Bolander	.25	1.00
265 Karl-Gunnar Backman	.25	1.00
266 Mats Davidsson	.25	1.00
267 Bosse Englund	.25	1.00
268 Tommy Eriksson	.25	1.00
269 Karl-Soren Hedlund	.25	1.00
270 Don Hughes	.25	1.00
271 Krister Lindgren	.25	1.00
272 Hans Mellinger	.25	1.00
273 Des Moroney	.25	1.00
274 Bo Olofsson	.25	1.00
275 Hakan Olsson	.25	1.00
276 Kent Persson	.25	1.00
277 Ove Stenlund	.25	1.00
278 Goran Thelin	.25	1.00
279 Ove Thelin	.25	1.00
280 Leif Ohrlund	.25	1.00
281 Uno Ohrlund	.25	1.00
282 Jan Ostling	.25	1.00
283 Gert Blome	.25	1.00
284 Ingemar Caris	.50	2.00
285 Arne Carlsson	.25	1.00
286 Kjell-Ove Gustafsson	.25	1.00
287 Henric Hedlund	.25	1.00
288 Leif Henriksson	.25	1.00
289 Kjell Jonsson	.25	1.00
290 Berny Karlsson	.25	1.00
291 Goran Lindberg	.25	1.00
292 Bernt Lundqvist	.25	1.00
293 Lars Eric Lundvall	.25	1.00
294 Carl-Fredrik Montan	.25	1.00
295 Eine Ohlsson	.50	2.00
296 Jan Olsen	.25	1.00
297 Roger Olsson	.25	1.00
298 Kjell-Ronnie Pettersson	.50	2.00
299 Ronald Pettersson	.25	1.00
300 Roland Sarnholm	.25	1.00

1969-70 Swedish Hockey

This 384-card set was released in Sweden by Williams Forlags AB to commemorate the players and nations competing in the World Championships, as well as club teams from Sweden. The cards measured 1 7/8" by 2 1/2" and featured a small portrait on the front, along with team name and emblem. The backs gave the player's name, vital stats (in Swedish) and sticker number. Early (first?) appearances by many legends make this set notable: look for Valeri Kharlamov, Alexander Yakushev and Ulf Nilsson. An album was available which not only housed the set, but offered stories, photos and stats to wrap up the previous season. This album is valued at $50.

Card	Low	High
COMPLETE SET (384)	200.00	400.00
1 Valerij Charlamov	7.50	15.00
2 Vitalij Davydov	.75	1.50
3 Anatolij Firsov	3.00	6.00
4 Alexander Jakusjev	5.00	10.00
5 Vladimir Jursinov	1.00	2.00
6 Victor Kuzkin	.38	.75
7 Vladimir Lutjenko	1.00	2.00
8 Alexander Maltsev	5.00	10.00
9 Boris Michailov	5.00	10.00
10 Jevgenij Misjakov	1.50	3.00
11 Vladimir Petrov	5.00	10.00
12 Jevgenij Poladjev	.38	.75
13 Victor Putjkov	.50	1.00
14 Alexander Ragulin	1.50	3.00
15 Igor Romisjevskij	.38	.75
16 Vjatjeslav Starsjinov	1.25	2.50
17 Vladimir Vikulov	.75	1.50
18 Jevgenij Zimin	.75	1.50
19 Victor Zinger	.50	1.00
20 Josef Augusta	.38	.75
21 Vladimir Bednar	.38	.75
22 Josef Cerny	.50	1.00
23 Vladimir Dzurilla	5.00	10.00
24 Richard Farda	.38	.75
25 Josef Golonka	.75	1.50
26 Jan Havel	.38	.75
27 Jaroslav Holik	.75	1.50
28 Jiri Holik	.50	1.00
20 Josef Horosovsky	.38	.75
30 Jan Hrbaty	.38	.75
31 Jaroslav Jirik	.38	.75
32 Jan Klapac	.38	.75
33 Miroslav Lacky	.75	1.50
34 Oldrich Machac	.38	.75

35 Vaclav Nedomansky 2.50 5.00
36 Frantisek Pospisil 1.00 2.00
37 Frantisek Sevcik .50 1.00
38 Jan Suchy .50 1.00
39 Ake Carlsson .38 .75
40 Curt Edenvik .38 .75
41 Hans Eriksson .38 .75
42 Bo Hansson .38 .75
43 Ove Hedberg .38 .75
44 Kjell Hedman .75 1.50
45 Leif Holmqvist 1.50 3.00
46 Anders Johansson .38 .75
47 Bjorn Larsson .38 .75
48 Borje Molander .38 .75
49 Ulf Nilsson 10.00 20.00
50 Bert-Ola Nordlander .50 1.00
51 Bo Olofsson .38 .75
52 Anders Parmstrom .38 .75
53 Lennart Selinder .38 .75
54 Hans Stromberg .38 .75
55 Kjell Savstrom .38 .75
56 Lars-Ake Warning .38 .75
57 Lars Bylund .38 .75
58 Inge Hammarstrom 2.50 5.00
59 Hans Dahllof .75 1.50
60 Lars Hedenstrom .38 .75
61 Kjell Johnsson .38 .75
62 Lennart Johansson .38 .75
63 Bertil Karlsson .38 .75
64 Stefan Karlsson .38 .75
65 Lennart Lind .38 .75
66 Hans Lindberg .38 .75
67 Tord Lundstrom .38 .75
68 Jan-Erik Lyck .38 .75
69 William Lovqvist 1.00 2.00
70 Lars-Goran Nilsson .38 .75
71 Stig Salming .50 1.00
72 Lars-Ake Sivertsson .38 .75
73 Lars-Goran Tano .38 .75
74 Hakan Wickberg .38 .75
75 Rolf Berglund .38 .75
76 Lars Alserydh .75 1.50
77 Tage Blom .38 .75
78 Alf Granstrom .38 .75
79 Lennart Haggroth .75 1.50
80 Bertil Karlsson .38 .75
81 Sven-Bertil Lindstrom .38 .75
82 Anders Lundberg .38 .75
83 Goran Lundmark .75 1.50
84 Sven-Erik Lundqvist .38 .75
85 Hans Lundstrom .38 .75
86 Kjell Lang .38 .75
87 Borje Lofstedt .38 .75
88 Olle Nilsson .38 .75
89 Jan-Olof Nordin .38 .75
90 Kjell Rehnstrom .38 .75
91 Peder Rehnstrom .38 .75
92 Leif Tjernstrom .38 .75
93 Kjell-Arne Wikstrom .38 .75
94 Anders Andren .38 .75
95 Thomas Carlsson .38 .75
96 Roland Einarsson 1.00 2.00
97 Lars Granlund .38 .75
98 Stig Larsson .38 .75
99 Lars-Ake Lundell .38 .75
100 Per Lundstrom .38 .75
101 Bjorn Palmquist .38 .75
102 Ulf Rydin .38 .75
103 Christer Sehlstedt .75 1.50
104 Lars Starck .38 .75
105 Roland Stoltz .38 .75
106 Billy Sundstrom .38 .75
107 Henry Svensson .38 .75
108 Ove Svensson .38 .75
109 Ulf Torstensson .38 .75
110 Christer Abrahamsson 2.50 5.00
111 Tommy Abrahamsson 1.00 2.00
112 Gunnar Andersson .38 .75
113 Folke Bengtsson .38 .75
114 Kjell Brus .38 .75
115 Ake Danielsson .38 .75
116 Bo Englund .38 .75
117 Lennart Gustavsson .38 .75
118 Hans Jax .38 .75
119 Jan-Olov Kroon .38 .75
120 Roger Lindqvist .38 .75
121 Gunnar Mars .75 1.50
122 Ulf Martensson .38 .75
123 Nisse Nilsson .38 .75
124 Lars-Erik Sjoberg 2.50 5.00
125 Olle Sjogren .38 .75
126 Dan Soderstrom .38 .75
127 Mats Ahlberg .38 .75
128 Gunnar Backman 1.00 2.00
129 Ulf Croon .38 .75
130 Lage Edin .38 .75
131 Ake Eklof .38 .75
132 Anders Hedberg 10.00 20.00
133 Torbjorn Hubinette .38 .75
134 Nils Johansson .38 .75
135 Ivar Larsson 1.00 2.00
136 Christer Nilsson .38 .75
137 Lennart Norberg .38 .75
138 Anders Nordin .38 .75
139 Hakan Nygren .38 .75
140 Sten Olsen .38 .75
141 Anders Schahlin .38 .75
142 Gunnar Salsten .38 .75
143 Ulf Wigren .38 .75
144 Lars Ohman .38 .75
145 Tore Ohman .38 .75
146 Nils Carlsson .38 .75
147 Kjell Eklund .38 .75
148 Bengt Gustavsson .38 .75
149 Bengt-Ake Gustavsson 1.00 2.00
150 Gote Hansson .38 .75
151 Hans Hansson .38 .75
152 Per-Arne Hubinette .38 .75
153 Sven-Ake Jakobsson .38 .75
154 Goran Johansson .75 1.50
155 Mats Lind .38 .75
156 Mats Lonn .38 .75
157 Borje Marcus .38 .75
158 Lars Mjoberg .38 .75
159 Ulf Nises .38 .75
160 Bo Olsson .38 .75
161 Erling Sundblad .38 .75
162 Lennart Svedberg 1.00 2.00
163 Evert Tysk .38 .75
164 Stig Ostling .38 .75
165 Magnus Andersson .38 .75
166 Erling Bergmark .38 .75
167 Kenneth Hellman .38 .75
168 Bjorn Johansson .38 .75
169 Ulf Johansson .38 .75
170 Berny Karlsson .38 .75
171 Nils-Erik Karlsson .38 .75
172 Rolf Larsson .38 .75
173 Tore Larsson .38 .75
174 Roland Lestander .75 1.50
175 Lennart Lindgren .38 .75
176 Finn Lundstrom .38 .75
177 Kenneth Manberg .38 .75
178 Lars Molander .38 .75
179 Lennart Rudby .38 .75
180 Sven-Ake Rudby .38 .75
181 Curt Svensson .38 .75
182 Sverker Torstensson .38 .75
183 Gunnar Backman 1.00 2.00
184 Arne Carlsson .38 .75
185 Leif Henriksson .38 .75
186 Leif Holmqvist 1.50 3.00
187 Mats Hysing .38 .75
188 Nils Johansson .38 .75
189 Stig-Goran Johansson .75 1.50
190 Stefan Karlsson .38 .75
191 Tord Lundstrom .38 .75
192 Kjell-Rune Milton .38 .75
193 Lars-Goran Nilsson .38 .75
194 Bert-Ola Nordlander .50 1.00
195 Hakan Nygren .38 .75
196 Roger Olsson .38 .75
197 Bjorn Palmquist .38 .75
198 Lars-Erik Sjoberg 2.00 4.00
199 Ulf Sterner .38 .75
200 Lennart Svedberg .75 1.50
201 Dick Yderstrom .38 .75
202 Lennart Abrahamsson .38 .75
203 Anders Bengtsson .75 1.50
204 Agne Bylund .38 .75
205 Jan Edlund .38 .75
206 Goran Hedberg .38 .75
207 Christer Johansson .75 1.50
208 Rolf Jager .38 .75
209 Per-Erik Kall .38 .75
210 Anders Norberg .38 .75
211 Janne Pettersson .75 1.50
212 Bo Sjostrom .38 .75
213 Dick Sjostrom .38 .75
214 Lasse Sjostrom .38 .75
215 Ulf Stecksen .38 .75
216 Lennart Strohm .38 .75
217 Kurt Tillander .38 .75
218 Roger Osterlund .38 .75
219 Hans-Ake Andersson .38 .75
220 Hans Bejbom .38 .75
221 Carl-Axel Berglund .38 .75
222 Goran Borell .38 .75
223 Bjarne Brostrom .38 .75
224 Per Backman .38 .75
225 Kennet Calen .38 .75
226 Lennart Carlsson .38 .75
227 Mats Davidsson .38 .75
228 Curt Ferding .38 .75
229 Lars-Olof Granstrom .38 .75
230 Rolf Hansson .38 .75
231 Rune Holmgren .38 .75
232 Rune Norrstrom .38 .75
233 Bert-Ake Olsson .38 .75
234 Olle Olsson .38 .75
235 Jan Svedman .38 .75
236 Walter Winsth .38 .75
237 Goran Akerlund .38 .75
238 Borje Burlin .38 .75
239 Hans Carlsson .38 .75
240 Stig Carlsson .38 .75
241 Gunnar Granberg .38 .75
242 Allan Helenefors .38 .75
243 Mats Hysing .38 .75
244 Bertil Jacobsson .38 .75
245 Stig-Goran Johansson .75 1.50
246 Curt Larsson 1.25 2.50
247 Eilert Maatta .38 .75
248 Soren Maatta .38 .75
249 Tommy Bergman .38 .75
250 Nils-Olof Schilstrom .38 .75
251 Jan Schullstrom .38 .75
252 Kjell Svensson .75 1.50
253 Gunnar Tallberg .38 .75
254 Borje Ulweback .38 .75
255 Dick Yderstrom .38 .75
256 Tommy Andersson .38 .75
257 Bulla Berggren .38 .75
258 Anders Bryner .38 .75
259 Anders Claesson .75 1.50
260 Jan Johansson .38 .75
261 Ove Jonsson .38 .75
262 Lennart Lind .38 .75
263 Arne Lundstrom .38 .75
264 Ake Lundstrom .38 .75
265 Jan-Erik Nilsson .38 .75
266 Lennart Norberg .38 .75
267 Sten-Olov Olsson .38 .75
268 Hakan Pettersson .38 .75
269 Stefan Pettersson .38 .75
270 Gosta Sjokvist .38 .75
271 Jan Stolpe .38 .75
272 Ake Soderberg .38 .75
273 Kjell Westerlund .38 .75
274 Olle Ahman .38 .75
275 Kristet Andersson .75 1.50
276 Bert Danielsson .38 .75
277 Gert Danielsson .38 .75
278 Bengt Eriksson .38 .75
279 Lars-Anders Gustavsson .38 .75
280 Curt Jacobsson .38 .75
281 Leif Jacobsson .38 .75
282 Lars-Erik Jakobsson .38 .75
283 Lars-Goran Johansson .38 .75
284 Des Moroney .38 .75
285 Borje Maatta .38 .75
286 Lars-Ake Nordin .38 .75
287 Kenneth Pedersen .38 .75
288 Anders Rapp .38 .75
289 Benny Runesson .38 .75
290 Jonny Ryman .38 .75
291 Ake Ryman .38 .75
292 Goran Ahstrom .75 1.50
293 John Andersson .38 .75
294 Kjell-Olov Barrefjord .38 .75
295 Ulf Barrefjord .38 .75
296 Kent Bjork .38 .75
297 Lars Dahlgren .38 .75
298 Karl-Olof Eriksson .38 .75
299 Osten Folkesson .38 .75
300 Anders Hagstrom .38 .75
301 Eric Jarvholm .38 .75
302 Ulf Larsson .38 .75
303 Bo Leong .75 1.50
304 Bengt Lofgren .38 .75
305 Roger Nilsson .38 .75
306 Bengt Persson .75 1.50
307 Ulf Stromsoe .38 .75
308 Kjell Sundstrom .38 .75
309 Leif Andersson .38 .75
310 Bernt Augustsson .75 1.50
311 Kjell Augustsson .38 .75
312 Tommy Eriksson 1.00 2.00
313 Lars-Olof Feltendahl .38 .75
314 Karl-Soren Hedlund .38 .75
315 Penti Hyytiainen .38 .75
316 Arne Johansson .38 .75
317 Bengt-Goran Karlsson .38 .75
318 Curt Lundmark 1.00 2.00
319 Hakan Olsson .75 1.50
320 Kent Persson .38 .75
321 Ove Stenlund .38 .75
322 Goran Thelin .38 .75
323 Ove Thelin .38 .75
324 Bo Astrom .38 .75
325 Hasse Mellinger .38 .75
326 Uno Ohrlund .38 .75
327 Jan Ostling .38 .75
328 Kjell Andersson .38 .75
329 Ronny Andersson 1.00 2.00
330 Gert Blome .38 .75
331 Ingemar Caris 1.00 2.00
332 Arne Carlsson .38 .75
333 Svante Granholm .38 .75
334 Henric Hedlund .38 .75
335 Leif Henriksson .38 .75
336 Anders Johansson .38 .75
337 Kjell Jonsson .38 .75
338 Bjorn Lindberg .38 .75
339 Goran Lindberg .38 .75
340 Carl-Fredrik Montan .38 .75
341 Leif Nilsson .38 .75
342 Kurt Olofsson .38 .75
343 Jan Olsen .38 .75
344 Roger Olsson .38 .75
345 Kjell-Ronnie Pettersson .38 .75
346 Ulf Sterner .38 .75
347 Rickie Bayes 1.25 2.50
348 Gary Begg .75 1.50
349 Roger Bourbonnais 1.00 2.00
350 Jack Bownass 1.00 2.00
351 Terry Caffery 1.25 2.50
352 Steve Carlyle 1.25 2.50
353 Ab Demarco 1.50 3.00
354 Ted Hargreaves 1.00 2.00
355 Bill Heindl 1.25 2.50
356 Fran Huck .75 1.50
357 Steve King 1.25 2.50
358 Chuck Lefley 2.00 4.00
359 Morris Mott 1.25 2.50
360 Terry O'Malley 1.00 2.00
361 Kevin O'Shea 1.25 2.50
362 Gerry Pinder 2.00 4.00
363 Steve Rexe 1.50 3.00
364 Ken Stephenson 1.25 2.50
365 Wayne Stephenson 5.00 10.00
366 Matti Harju .38 .75
367 Esa Isaksson .38 .75
368 Kari Johansson .38 .75
369 Juhani Jylha .38 .75
370 Matti Keinonen .38 .75
371 Veli-Pekka Ketola 1.50 3.00
372 Lasse Killi .75 1.50
373 Ilpo Koskela .38 .75
374 Pekka Leimu .38 .75
375 Seppo Lindstrom .38 .75
376 Pekka Marjamaki .38 .75
377 Lauri Mononen .38 .75
378 Lasse Oksanen .38 .75
379 Lalli Partanen .38 .75
380 Esa Peltonen .38 .75
381 Jorma Peltonen .38 .75
382 Juhani Rantasila .38 .75
383 Juhani Wahlsten .38 .75
384 Urpo Ylonen 1.25 2.50

1970-71 Swedish Hockey

This set of 384-cards was issued by Williams Forlags AB and printed by Panini in Italy. The cards, which measure approximately 2 1/2" by 1 3/4", feature teams from the Swedish first and second divisions, as well as national team members from Tre Kroner, Russia, Czechoslovakia, Finland and East Germany. The card fronts feature a small player portrait along with the team emblem. The backs give player name, a brief bio and card number. The set includes many well known international stars, most prominently the first appearance of HOFer Borje Salming. An album to house the stickers was available as well; it also included text and photos to give a brief history of the teams involved. It is valued at approximately $40. Note: Spellings are as they appear on the cards and, in the case of Russian players, are not necessarily the spellings typically used for these players.

COMPLETE SET (384) 200.00 400.00
1 Leif (Honken) Holmqvist 1.25 2.50
2 Kjell Hedman .75 1.50
3 Lars Danielsson .38 .75
4 Ake Fagerstrom .38 .75
5 Per-Arne Hubinette .38 .75
6 Hakan Lindgren .38 .75
7 Bert-Ola Nordlander .50 1.00
8 Rolf (Rattan) Edberg .75 1.50
9 Bo Hansson .38 .75
10 Jan-Olov Kroon .38 .75
11 Ulf Nilsson 5.00 10.00
12 Bosse Olofsson .38 .75
13 Lennart Selinder .38 .75
14 Hans Stromberg .38 .75
15 Kjell Savstrom .38 .75
16 Lars-Ake Warning .38 .75
17 Lars-Goran Nilsson .75 1.50
Alexander Yakushev
18 William Lofqvist .75 1.50
19 Hans Dahllof .75 1.50
20 Lars Bylund .38 .75
21 Lars Hedenstrom .38 .75
22 Kjell Johnsson .38 .75
23 Borje Salming 12.50 25.00
24 Stig Salming .38 .75
25 Stig Ostling .38 .75
26 Inge Hammarstrom 2.50 5.00
27 Lennart Johansson .38 .75
28 Stefan Karlsson .38 .75
29 Lennart Lind .38 .75
30 Hans (Virus) Lindberg .38 .75
31 Tord Lundstrom .38 .75
32 Jan-Erik Lyck .38 .75
33 Lars-Goran Nilsson .38 .75
34 Lars-Ake Sivertsson .38 .75
35 Hakan Wickberg .38 .75
36 puzzle .38 .75
37 puzzle .38 .75
38 puzzle .38 .75
39 puzzle .38 .75
40 puzzle .38 .75
41 puzzle .38 .75
42 puzzle .50 .75
43 puzzle .50 .75
44 puzzle .38 .75
45 puzzle .38 .75
46 puzzle .50 .75
47 puzzle .50 .75
48 Roland Einarsson .75 1.50
49 Ake Eklof .38 .75
50 Christer Ahlstrand .38 .75
51 Thomas Carlsson .38 .75
52 Anders Rylin .38 .75
53 Billy Sundstrom .38 .75
54 Folke Bengtsson .38 .75
55 Stig Larsson .38 .75
56 Lars-Ake Lundell .38 .75
57 Per Lundstrom .38 .75
58 Bjorn Palmqvist .38 .75
59 Ulf Rydin .38 .75
60 Ove Svensson .38 .75
61 Jan Zabrodsky .38 .75
62 Leif Holmqvist PUZ 1.00 2.00
63 Leif Holmqvist PUZ 1.00 2.00
64 Leif Holmqvist PUZ 1.00 2.00
65 Leif Holmqvist PUZ 1.00 2.00
66 Christer Abrahamsson 1.50 3.00
67 Christer Sterner .75 1.50
68 Thommy Abrahamsson .75 1.50
69 Karl-Gustaf Alander .38 .75
70 Gunnar Andersson .38 .75
71 Roland Bond .38 .75
72 Ake Danielsson .38 .75
73 Per-Olov Brasar 1.50 3.00
74 Kjell Brus .38 .75
75 Hans Jax .38 .75
76 Dan Labraaten 1.50 3.00
77 Roger Lindqvist .38 .75
78 Ulf Martensson .38 .75
79 Olle Sjogren .38 .75
80 Ingemar Snis .38 .75
81 Dan Soderstrom .38 .75
82 Mats Ahlberg .38 .75
83 Gunnar Backman .75 1.50
84 Ivar Larsson .75 1.50
85 Lage Edin .38 .75
86 Kjell-Rune Milton .38 .75
87 Ulf Torstensson .38 .75
88 Ulf Wigren .38 .75
89 Ulf Croon .38 .75
90 Hakan Dahllof .38 .75
91 Anders Hedberg 5.00 10.00
92 Torbjorn Hubinette .38 .75
93 Christer Nilsson .38 .75
94 Lennart Norberg .38 .75
95 Anders Nordin .38 .75
96 Hakan Nygren .38 .75
97 Per-Olof Uusitalo .38 .75
98 Lars Ohman .38 .75
99 Tore Ohman .38 .75
100 V. Dzurilla PUZ .75 1.50
101 V. Dzurilla PUZ .75 1.50
102 V. Dzurilla PUZ .75 1.50
103 V. Dzurilla PUZ .75 1.50
104 V. Dzurilla PUZ .75 1.50
105 V. Dzurilla PUZ .75 1.50
106 V. Dzurilla PUZ .75 1.50
107 V. Dzurilla PUZ .75 1.50
108 V. Dzurilla PUZ .75 1.50
109 V. Dzurilla PUZ .75 1.50
110 V. Dzurilla PUZ .75 1.50
111 V. Dzurilla PUZ .75 1.50
112 Bengt-Ake Gustavsson .75 1.50
113 Lars Gustavsson .75 1.50
114 Tommy Andersson .75 1.50
115 Hans-Olov Ernlund .75 1.50
116 Lars Mjoberg .38 .75
117 Gote Hansson .38 .75
118 L. Svedberg PUZ .50 1.00
119 B. Mikhailov PUZ 1.50 3.00
120 Leif Holmqvist PUZ 1.00 2.00
121 Hans Hansson .38 .75
122 Sven-Ake Jakobsson .38 .75
123 Mats Lind .38 .75
124 Mats Lonn .38 .75
125 Borje Marcus .38 .75
126 Ulf Nises .38 .75
127 Borje Skoog .38 .75
128 Erling Sundblad .38 .75
129 Kent Sundkvist .38 .75
130 Curt Larsson 1.00 2.00
131 Torbjorn Hellsing .75 1.50
132 Tommie Bergman 2.00 4.00
133 Arne Carlsson .38 .75
134 Allan Helenefors .38 .75
135 Eilert Maatta .38 .75
136 Jan Schullstrom .38 .75
137 Hans Carlsson .38 .75
138 Tommy Carlsson .38 .75
139 Gunnar Granberg .38 .75
140 Mats Hysing .38 .75
141 Bertil Jacobsson .38 .75
142 Stig-Goran Johansson .38 .75
143 Soren Maatta .38 .75
144 Nils-Olov Schilstrom .38 .75
145 Dick Yderstrom .38 .75
146 Carl-Goran Oberg .38 .75
147 Lennart Svedberg .50 1.00
148 Anders Claesson .75 1.50
149 Kent Othberg .75 1.50
150 Jan Johansson .38 .75
151 Jan-Erik Nilsson .38 .75
152 Stefan Pettersson .38 .75
153 Lennart Svedberg .75 1.50
154 Bo Berggren .38 .75
155 Arne Lundstrom .38 .75
156 Finn Lundstrom .38 .75
157 I. Romisjevskij PUZ .38 .75
158 I. Romisjevskij PUZ .50 1.00
159 Ake Lundstrom .38 .75
160 V. Tretiak PUZ 4.00 8.00
161 V. Tretiak PUZ 4.00 8.00
162 Lennart Norberg .38 .75
163 Hakan Pettersson .38 .75
164 Ake Soderberg .50 1.00
165 Olle Ahman .38 .75
166 puzzle .38 .75
167 puzzle .38 .75
168 puzzle .38 .75
169 puzzle .38 .75
170 puzzle .38 .75
171 puzzle .38 .75
172 puzzle .38 .75
173 puzzle .38 .75
174 puzzle .38 .75
175 puzzle .38 .75
176 puzzle .38 .75
177 puzzle .38 .75
178 Christer Andersson .75 1.50
179 Goran Astrom .75 1.50
180 Kenneth Ekman .38 .75
181 Lars Erik Jakobsson .38 .75
182 Des Moroney .38 .75
183 Borje Maatta .38 .75
184 Kenneth Pedersen .38 .75
185 Anders Rapp .38 .75
186 Sven Crabo .38 .75
187 Lars Anders Gustavsson .38 .75
188 Kurt Jacobsson .38 .75
189 Leif Jacobsson .38 .75
190 Lars Goran Johansson .38 .75
191 Bernt Karlsson .38 .75
192 Benny Runesson .38 .75
193 Jonny Ryman .38 .75
194 Ake Ryman .38 .75
195 Christer Grahn .75 1.50
196 Ronny Sandstrom .38 .75
197 John Andersson .38 .75
198 Karl-Olof Eriksson .38 .75
199 Anders Hagstrom .38 .75
200 Rolf Jager .38 .75
201 Erik Jarvholm .38 .75
202 Lars Nordin .38 .75
203 Ulf Barrefjord .38 .75
204 Lars Dahlgren .38 .75
205 Ulf Ingvarsson .38 .75
206 Ulf Larsson .38 .75
207 Jan Lundqvist .38 .75
208 Ulf Lundstrom .38 .75
209 Bengt Lovgren .38 .75
210 Lars SJostrom .38 .75
211 Kjell Sundstrom .38 .75
212 Ulf Stromsoe .38 .75
213 Hakan Olsson .75 1.50
214 Leif Andersson .38 .75
215 Tommy Eriksson .75 1.50
216 Karl-Soren Hedlund .38 .75
217 Curt Lundmark .75 1.50
218 Ove Nystrom .38 .75
219 Gote Gustavsson .38 .75
220 Hans Hjelm .38 .75
221 Pennti Hyytiainen .38 .75
222 Arne Johansson .38 .75
223 Bengt-Goran Karlsson .38 .75
224 Kent Persson .38 .75
225 Ove Stenlund .38 .75
226 Goran Thelin .38 .75
227 Ove Thelin .38 .75
228 Bo Astrom .38 .75
229 Jan Ostling .38 .75
230 V. Tretiak action 10.00 20.00
231 V. Konovalenko PUZ .38 .75
232 V. Konovalenko PUZ .38 .75
233 V. Konovalenko PUZ .38 .75
234 V. Konovalenko PUZ .38 .75
235 V. Konovalenko PUZ .38 .75
236 V. Konovalenko PUZ .38 .75
237 V. Konovalenko PUZ .38 .75
238 V. Konovalenko PUZ .38 .75
239 V. Konovalenko PUZ .38 .75
240 V. Konovalenko PUZ .38 .75
241 V. Konovalenko PUZ .38 .75
242 V. Konovalenko PUZ .38 .75
243 Ingemar Caris .75 1.50
244 Ronny Andersson .75 1.50
245 Gert Blome .38 .75
246 Anders Johansson .38 .75
247 Goran Lindberg .38 .75
248 Jan Olsen .38 .75
249 Lars-Erik Sjoberg 2.00 4.00
250 Kjell Andersson .38 .75
251 Svante Granholm .38 .75
252 Henrik Hedlund .38 .75
253 Leif Henriksson .38 .75
254 Bjorn Lindberg .38 .75
255 Billy Lindstrom .38 .75
256 Carl-Fredrik Montan .38 .75
257 Leif Nilsson .38 .75
258 Kurt Olofsson .38 .75
259 Roger Olsson .38 .75
260 Kjell-Ronnie Pettersson .38 .75
261 Soviet team PUZ .38 .75
262 Soviet team PUZ .38 .75
263 Soviet team PUZ .38 .75
264 Soviet team PUZ .38 .75
265 Soviet team PUZ .38 .75
266 Soviet team PUZ .38 .75
267 Soviet team PUZ .38 .75
268 Soviet team PUZ .38 .75
269 Soviet team PUZ .38 .75
270 Soviet team PUZ .38 .75
271 Soviet team PUZ .38 .75
272 Soviet team PUZ .38 .75
273 Leif Holmqvist 1.00 2.00
274 Gunnar Backman .75 1.50
275 Christer Abrahamsson 1.50 3.00
276 Thommy Abrahamsson .75 1.50
277 Arne Carlsson .38 .75
278 Nils Johansson .38 .75
279 Ljell-Rune Milton .38 .75
280 Lars-Erik Sjoberg 2.00 4.00
281 Lennart Svedberg .75 1.50
282 Anders Hedberg 5.00 10.00
283 Stig-Goran Johansson .38 .75
284 Stefan Karlsson .38 .75
285 Hans Lindberg .38 .75
286 Tord Lundstrom .38 .75
287 Lars-Goran Nilsson .38 .75
288 Anders Nordin .38 .75
289 Roger Olsson .38 .75
290 Bjorn Palmqvist .38 .75
291 Ulf Sterner .38 .75
292 Hakan Wickberg .38 .75
293 Urpo Ylonen 1.00 2.00
294 Jorma Valtonen .75 1.50
295 Ilpo Koskela .38 .75
296 Seppo Lindstrom .38 .75
297 Pekka Marjamaki .38 .75
298 Lalli Partinen .38 .75
299 Juha Rantasila .38 .75
300 Heikki Riihiranta 1.00 2.00
301 Pekka Keimu .38 .75
302 Matti Keinonen .38 .75
303 Veli-Pekka Ketola 1.50 3.00
304 Vaino Kolkka .38 .75
305 Harri Linnonmaa .38 .75
306 Lauri Mononen .38 .75
307 Matti Murto .75 1.50
308 Lasse Oksanen .38 .75
309 Esa Peltonen .38 .75
310 Jorma Peltonen .38 .75
311 Juhani Tamminen .75 1.50
312 Jorma Vehmanen .38 .75
313 Viktor Konovalenko .75 1.50
314 Vladislav Tretjak 20.00 40.00
315 Vitalij Davidov .75 1.50
316 Vladimir Lutjenko .75 1.50
317 Jevgenij Paladjev .38 .75
318 Alexander Ragulin 1.50 3.00
319 Igor Romisjevski .50 1.00
320 Valerij Vasiljev 2.50 5.00
321 Valerij Nikitin .50 1.00
322 Valerij Kharlamov 7.50 15.00
323 Anatolij Firsov 4.00 8.00
324 Alexander Jakusjev 4.00 8.00
325 Alexander Maltsev 4.00 8.00
326 Boris Michailov 4.00 8.00
327 Jevgenij Misjakov 1.25 2.50
328 Vladimir Petrov 2.50 5.00
329 Viktor Polupanov .38 .75
330 Vladimir Sjadrin 1.50 3.00
331 Vjatjeslav Starsinov 1.25 2.50
332 Vladimir Vikulov .50 1.00
333 puzzle .38 .75
334 puzzle .38 .75
335 puzzle .38 .75
336 puzzle .38 .75
337 puzzle .38 .75
338 puzzle .38 .75
339 puzzle .38 .75
340 puzzle .38 .75
341 puzzle .38 .75
342 puzzle .38 .75
343 puzzle .38 .75
344 puzzle .38 .75
345 Vladimir Dzurilla 2.50 5.00
346 Miroslav Lacky .75 1.50
347 Vladimir Bednar .38 .75
348 Josef Horesovsky .38 .75
349 Oldrich Machac .38 .75
350 Frantisek Pospisil .75 1.50
351 Jan Suchy .50 1.00
352 Lubomir Ujvary .38 .75
353 Josef Cerny .50 1.00
354 Richard Farda .38 .75
355 Julius Haas .38 .75
356 Ivan Hlinka .75 1.50
357 Jaroslav Holik .50 1.00
358 Jiri Holik .50 1.00
359 Jan Hrbaty .38 .75
360 Jiri Kochta .38 .75
361 Vladislav Martinec .38 .75
362 Vaclav Nedomansky 1.50 3.00
363 Stanislav Pryl .38 .75
364 Frantisek Sevcik .38 .75
365 Klaus Hirche .75 1.50
366 Diter Purschel .75 1.50
367 Frank Braun .38 .75
368 Dieter Dewitz .38 .75
369 Bernd Karrenbauer .38 .75
370 Helmut Novy .38 .75
371 Dietmar Peters .38 .75
372 Wolfgang Plotka .38 .75
373 Peter Slapke .38 .75
374 Rolf Bielas .38 .75
375 Lothar Fuchs .38 .75
376 Bernd Hiller .38 .75
377 Reinhard Karger .38 .75
378 Hartmut Nickel .38 .75
379 Rudiger Noack .38 .75
380 Rainer Patschinski .38 .75
381 Peter Prusa .38 .75
382 Wilfried Rohrbach .38 .75
383 Dieter Rohl .38 .75
384 Joachim Ziesche .38 .75

1970 Swedish Masterserien

This 200-card set was released in Sweden to commemorate the 1970 World Championships held in Bern and Geneva, Switzerland. The cards in the set are inconsistent in their appearance. Cards 1-50 measure approximately 2 3/4" by 3 3/4". Cards 51-100 are 3" by 4". Cards 101-200 are 3" by 3 3/4". All feature color action photos on the front, but only the first and third groupings have numbers on the front. Cards 51-100 were not numbered on the cards but only in the collector's album. The cards were distributed in 5-card, clear plastic packages. The key cards in the set are two of HOFer Ken Dryden as a member of Team Canada. The cards precede his RC by two years. An album was available to store the cards; it is valued at $30.

COMPLETE SET (200) 175.00 350.00
1 Vladimir Dzurila 4.00 8.00
2 Jozef Golonka .50 1.00
3 Jiri Holik .38 .75
4 Vaclav Nedomansky 1.25 2.50
5 Vaclav Nedomansky 1.25 2.50
6 Jaroslav Holik .50 1.00
7 Jozef Golonka .50 1.00
8 Vaclav Nedomansky 1.25 2.50
9 Vladimir Bednar .25 .50
10 Jan Havel .25 .50
11 Jan Hrbaty .25 .50
12 Jan Suchy .38 .75
13 Lasse Oksanen .25 .50
14 Urpo Ylonen .50 1.00
15 Michael Curran .75 1.50
16 Gary Begg .50 1.00
17 Carl Lackey .50 1.00
18 Terry O'Malley .75 1.50
19 Gary Gamuicci .50 1.00
20 Seppo Lindstrom .50 1.00
21 Lucenko .75 1.50
Misjakov
Davidov
22 Victor Putjkov .38 .75
23 Alexandr Ragulin 1.00 2.00
24 Gerry Pinder 1.25 2.50
25 Fran Huck .50 1.00
26 Ken Dryden 50.00 100.00
27 Viktor Zinger .38 .75
28 Vladimir Petrov 2.50 5.00
29 Igor Romisjevsky .50 1.00
Viktor Zinger
30 Valerij Charlamov 5.00 10.00
31 Alexandr Ragulin 1.00 2.00
32 Ab Demarco 1.00 2.00
33 Morris Mott .75 1.50
34 Fran Huck .50 1.00
35 Vjatjeslav Starsinov .50 1.00
36 Lars-Goran Nilsson .50 1.00
37 Stig-Goran Stisse Johansson .50 1.00
38 Leif Honken Holmqvist 1.00 2.00
39 Hakan Nygren .25 .50
40 Tord Lundstrom .25 .50
41 Ulf Sterner .25 .50
42 Lars-Erik Sjoberg 1.50 3.00
43 Kjell-Rune Milton .25 .50
44 Leif Honken Holmqvist 1.00 2.00
45 Stefan Lill-Prosten Karlsson .25 .50
46 Lennart Lill-Strimma Svedberg .50 1.00
47 Tord Lundstrom .25 .50
48 Ulf Sterner .25 .50
49 Tord Lundstrom .25 .50
50 Lennart Lill-Strimma Svedberg .50 1.00
51 Sverige (12 st) .25 .50
52 Bert-Ola Nordlander .38 .75
53 Leif Honken Holmqvist 1.00 2.00
54 Lars-Erik Sjoberg 1.50 3.00
55 Lars-Erik Sjoberg 1.50 3.00
56 Nils Nicke Johansson .25 .50
57 Ulf Sterner .25 .50
58 Ulf Sterner .25 .50
Leif Blixten Henriksson
59 Tord Lundstrom .25 .50
60 Mats Hysing .25 .50
Nils Johansson
61 Lars-Goran Nilsson .25 .50
62 Hakan Nygren .25 .50
63 Gerry Pinder 1.25 2.50
Firsov
64 Evgenij Misjakov .50 1.00
65 Vjatjeslav Starsinov .75 1.50
66 Alexandr Ragulin 1.00 2.00
67 Alexandr Maltsev 2.50 5.00
68 Anatolij Firsov 2.00 4.00
69 Vladimir Lucenko .75 1.50
70 Vladimir Petrov 2.50 5.00
71 Vladimir Petrov 2.50 5.00
72 Vjatjeslav Starsinov .75 1.50
73 Vladimir Vikulov .50 1.00
74 Vitaly Davidov .50 1.00
75 Evgenij Zimin .38 .75
76 Vladimir Bednar 1.25 2.50
Vladimir Dzurilla
77 Jan Suchy .38 .75
78 Jaroslav Holik .50 1.00
79 Josef Horesovsky .50 1.00
80 Jozef Golonka .50 1.00
81 Richard Farda .25 .50
82 Frantisek Pospisil .50 1.00
Oldrich Machac
83 Ilop Koskela .25 .50
84 Juhani Jylha .25 .50
85 Esa Peltonen .25 .50
86 Lasse Oksanen .25 .50
87 Juhani Wahlsten .25 .50
88 Juha Rantasila .25 .50

89 Bob Paradise .50 1.00
90 Bob Paradise .50 1.00
91 Tim Sheehy .50 1.00
92 Michael Curran .75 1.50
93 Ken Dryden 50.00 100.00
94 Morris Mott .75 1.50
95 Fran Huck .50 1.00
96 unknown .25 .50
97 unknown .25 .50
98 unknown .25 .50
99 unknown .25 .50
100 unknown .25 .50
101 Arne Carlsson .25 .50
102 Nils Nicke Johansson .25 .50
103 Leif Holmqvist 1.00 2.00
104 Leif Henriksson .25 .50
105 Lennart Svedberg .50 1.00
106 Hakan Wickberg .25 .50
107 Gennar Backman .25 .50
108 Roger Olsson .25 .50
109 Kjell-Rune Milton .25 .50
110 Mats Hysing .25 .50
111 Lars-Erik Sjoberg 1.50 3.00
112 Anders Hedberg 5.00 10.00
113 Bjorn Palmqvist .25 .50
114 Tord Lundstrom .25 .50
115 Ulf Sterner .25 .50
116 Stig-Goran Johansson .50 1.00
117 Lars-Goran Nilsson .25 .50
118 Stefan Karlsson .25 .50
119 Anders Nordin .25 .50
120 Hans Virus Lindberg .25 .50
121 Davidov/Stars/Polup/Jaku/Malt/Firsov .50 1.00
122 Vitaly Davidov .50 1.00
123 Alexandr Jakusjev 2.50 5.00
Valtonen O. Rantasila
124 Alexandr Maltsev 2.50 5.00
125 Valerij Charlamov 5.00 10.00
126 Alexandr Ragulin 1.00 2.00
127 Igor Romisjevskij .25 .50
128 Boris Michailov 2.50 5.00
129 Starsinov/Polupanov/Ragulin /Lucenko .50 1.00
130 Victor Konovalenko .25 .50
131 Jakusjev/Davidov/Michailov/Tretjak /Malt./Pala. 2.00 4.00
132 Lucenko/Petrov/Firsov/Niki./Romis /Viku/Jakus. 1.50 3.00
133 Alexandr Maltsev 2.50 5.00
134 Valerij Nikitin .25 .50
135 Vladimir Vikulov .50 1.00
136 Vjatjeslav Starsinov .75 1.50
137 Evgenij Paladjev .25 .50
138 Vladimir Shapovalov .25 .50
139 Anatolij Firsov 2.00 4.00
140 Victor Polupanov .25 .50
141 Jaroslav Jirik .25 .50
142 Miroslav Lacky .50 1.00
143 Jan Suchy .38 .75
144 Lubomir Ujvary .25 .50
145 Vladimir Bednar .25 .50
146 Richard Farda .25 .50
147 Josef Cernyh .38 .75
148 Vaclav Nedomansky 1.25 2.50
149 Jaroslav Holik .75 1.50
150 Jiri Holik .38 .75
151 Julius Haas .38 .75
Vladislav Martinec
152 Vaclav Nedomansky 1.25 2.50
153 Josef Horesovsky .25 .50
154 Oldrich Machac .25 .50
155 Tommy Abrahamsson .50 1.00
Jiri Kochta
156 Vladimir Dzurila 2.00 4.00
Suchy (17)
Bednar
157 Jorma Valtonen .50 1.00
158 Veli-Pekka Ketola 1.00 2.00
159 Matti Murto .25 .50
Lauri Mononen
160 Heikki Riihiranta .50 1.00
161 Pekka Leimu .25 .50
162 Lasse Oksanen .25 .50
163 J. Valtonen .25 .50
Vaino Kolkka
Pekka Marjamaki
164 Urpo Ylonen .50 1.00
165 Matti Keinonen .25 .50
166 Juha Rantasila .75 1.50
Anatolij Firsov
167 Jorma Vehmanen .25 .50
168 Matti Murto .25 .50
169 Peter Slapke .25 .50
170 Claus Hirche .25 .50
171 Frank Braun .25 .50
172 Rolf Bielas .25 .50
173 Kargar .25 .50
Hiller
Ziesche
Braun
174 Beilas .25 .50
Braun
Hirche
Kolbe
175 Wilfried Rohrbach .25 .50
Hartmut Nickel
176 Plotka .25 .50
Karrenbauer
Rohrbach
Patschinski
177 John Mayasich .25 .50
James Branch
178 Larry Skime .50 1.00
179 Paul Coppo .50 1.00
180 Larry Pleau .50 1.00
181 Bruce Riutta .50 1.00
Ron Nasland
John Lothrop
182 Jerry Lackey .50 1.00
183 Bob Paradise .75 1.50
Michael Curran
Carl Lackey
184 Paul Coppo .50 1.00
Peter Markle
185 Roger Bourbonnais .75 1.50
186 Ted Hargreaves .75 1.50
187 Fran Huck .50 1.00
188 Wayne Stephenson 2.50 5.00
189 Morris Mott .75 1.50
190 Gerry Pinder 1.25 2.50
191 Gary Begg .50 1.00
192 Ken Dryden 50.00 100.00
Blank Back
193 Felix Goralczyk .25 .50
194 Andrzej Tkacz .25 .50
195 Jan Modzelewski .25 .50
196 Marian Kajzerek .25 .50
197 Josef Stefaniak .25 .50
198 Walery Kosyl .25 .50
199 Jan Modzelewski .25 .50
200 Pajerski/Goralczyk/Chachowski/Polen .25 .50

1971-72 Swedish Hockey

This set of 400 cards was printed by Panini and released in Sweden by Williams Forlags AB. The cards--which measure approximately 2 1/2" by 1 3/4" -- feature players from Sweden's top league, as well as from several national teams and NHL clubs. The fronts offer a simple player portrait; the backs contain sticker number and a brief player bio in Swedish. An album to house the set can be found; it is valued approximately at $40. Key stars in this set include Bobby Orr, Gordie Howe and Vladislav Tretiak. NOTE: Spellings used are those found on the sticker. In the case of the Russian players, these spellings may differ from those in common usage.

COMPLETE SET (400) 225.00 450.00
1 Christer Abrahamsson 1.00 2.00
2 Leif Holmqvist .50 1.00
3 William Lofqvist .50 1.00
4 Thommy Abrahamsson .50 1.00
5 Gunnar Andersson .25 .50
6 Thommie Bergman 1.50 3.00
7 Arne Carlsson .25 .50
8 Kjell-Rune Milton .25 .50
9 Bert-Ola Nordlander .50 1.00
10 Lennart Svedberg .50 1.00
11 Lars-Erik Sjoberg 1.00 2.00
12 Stig Ostling .25 .50
13 Inge Hammarstrom 1.50 10.00
14 Anders Hedberg 4.00 8.00
15 Stig-Goran Johansson .50 1.00
16 Stefan Karlsson .25 .50
17 Dan Labraaten 1.00 2.00
18 Hans Lindberg .25 .50
19 Tord Lundstrom .25 .50
20 Lars-Goran Nilsson .25 .50
21 Hakan Nygren .25 .50
22 Bjorn Palmqvist .25 .50
23 Hakan Pettersson .25 .50
24 Ulf Sterner .25 .50
25 Hakan Wickberg .25 .50
26 Viktor Konovalenko .30 .75
27 Vladislav Tretjak 10.00 20.00
28 Gennadij Tsigankov .30 .75
29 Vitali Davidov .30 .75
30 Victor Kuskin .30 .75
31 Vladimir Lutjenko .30 .75
32 Alexander Ragulin 1.00 2.00
33 Igor Romisjevskij .30 .75
34 Valerij Kharlamov 5.00 15.00
35 Anatolij Firsov 2.50 5.00
36 Alexander Maltsev 2.50 5.00
37 Boris Michailov 2.50 5.00
38 Jevgenij Misjakov 1.00 2.00
39 Vladimir Petrov 2.50 5.00
40 Vjatjeslav Starshinov .50 1.00
41 Vladimir Vikulov .30 .75
42 Evgenij Zimin .50 1.00
43 Jiri Holecek .50 1.00
44 Josef Horesovsky .25 .50
45 Oldrich Machac .25 .50
46 Frantisek Panchartek .30 .75
47 Frantisek Pospisil .30 .75
48 Jan Suchy .30 .75
49 Josef Cerny .30 .75
50 Richard Farda .25 .50
51 Jan Havel .25 .50
52 Ivan Hlinka .50 1.00
53 Jiri Holik .30 .75
54 Jiri Kochta .25 .50
55 Vladimir Martinec .30 .75
56 Vaclav Nedomansky 1.00 2.00
57 Eduard Novak .25 .50
58 Bohuslav Stastny .50 1.00
59 Jorma Valtonen .50 1.00
60 Urpo Ylonen .50 1.00
61 Ilpo Koskela .25 .50
62 Seppo Lindstrom .25 .50
63 Hannu Luojola .25 .50
64 Pekka Marjamaki .25 .50
65 Esa Isaksson .25 .50
66 Veli-Pekka Ketola 1.00 2.00
67 Harri Linnonmaa .25 .50
68 Erkki Mononen .25 .50
69 Lauri Mononen .25 .50
70 Matti Murto .50 1.00
71 Lasse Oksanen .25 .50
72 Esa Peltonen .25 .50
73 Juhanni Tamminen .50 1.00
74 Jorma Vehmanen .25 .50
75 Leif Holmqvist .50 1.00
76 Bert Jattne .50 1.00
77 Lars Danielsson .25 .50
78 Ake Fagerstrom .25 .50
79 Per-Arne Hubinette .25 .50
80 Hakan Lindgren .25 .50
81 Bert-Ola Nordlander .50 1.00
82 Lennart Pettersson .25 .50
83 Rolf Edberg .25 .50
84 Bo Hansson .25 .50
85 Jan-Olov Kroon .25 .50
86 Gunnar Lindkvist .25 .50
87 Christer Lundberg .25 .50
88 Ulf Nilsson 4.00 8.00
89 Bo Olofsson .25 .50
90 Jan Olsson .25 .50
91 Lennart Selinder .25 .50
92 Soren Sjogren .25 .50
93 Hans Stromberg .25 .50
94 Jan Ostling .25 .50
95 Kjell Helling .50 1.00
96 William Lofqvist .50 1.00
97 Lars Bylund .25 .50
98 Kjell Johnsson .25 .50
99 Par Malmstrom .25 .50
100 Borje Salming 5.00 10.00
101 Stig Salming .25 .50
102 Stig Ostling .25 .50
103 Inge Hammarstrom 1.50 10.00
104 Lennart Johansson .25 .50
105 Stefan Karlsson .25 .50
106 Lennart Lind .25 .50
107 Hans Lindberg .25 .50
108 Tord Lundstrom .25 .50
109 Jan-Erik Lyck .25 .50
110 Lars-Goran Nilsson .25 .50
111 Leif Olsson .25 .50
112 Lars-Ake Sivertsson .25 .50
113 Hakan Wickberg .25 .50
114 Lars Oberg .25 .50
115 Roland Einarsson .50 1.00
116 Peder Nilsson .50 1.00
117 Kent Olsson .50 1.00
118 Thomas Carlsson .25 .50
119 Lars-Ake Lundell .25 .50
120 Jorgen Palm .25 .50
121 Anders Rylin .25 .50
122 Billy Sundstrom .25 .50
123 Kent Soderlund .25 .50
124 Folke Bengtsson .25 .50
125 Ake Eklof .25 .50
126 Stig Larsson .25 .50
127 Sven-Bertil Lindstrom .25 .50
128 Thomas Palm .25 .50
129 Bjorn Palmqvist .25 .50
130 Ulf Rydin .25 .50
131 Ove Svensson .25 .50
132 Per-Allan Wikstrom .25 .50
133 Anders Andren .25 .50
134 Per Lundstrom .25 .50
135 Lennart Andersson .50 1.00
136 Kent Bodin .50 1.00
137 Bjorn Fagerlund .50 1.00
138 Ake Carlsson .25 .50
139 Nils Johansson .25 .50
140 Lars-Goran Nilsson .25 .50
141 Kent Olsson .50 1.00
142 Hans-Ake Rosendahl .25 .50
143 Karl-Johan Sundqvist .25 .50
144 Benny Andersson .25 .50
145 Hasse Andersson .25 .50
146 Kent-Erik Andersson .25 .50
147 Berndt Augustsson .25 .50
148 Kjell Augustsson .25 .50
149 Per-Ole Backman .25 .50
150 Conny Evensson .50 1.00
151 Sten Johansson .25 .50
152 Leif Labraaten .25 .50
153 Sven-Ove Olsson .25 .50
154 Ulf Sterner .25 .50
155 Christer Abrahamsson 1.00 2.00
156 Krister Sterner .50 1.00
157 Thommy Abrahamsson .50 1.00
158 Karl-Gustaf Alander .25 .50
159 Gunnar Andersson .25 .50
160 Roland Bond .25 .50
161 Ake Danielsson .25 .50
162 Ulf Weinstock .25 .50
163 Per-Olov Brasar 1.00 2.00
164 Kjell Brus .25 .50
165 Hans Jax .25 .50
166 Dan Labraaten 1.00 2.00
167 Roger Lindqvist .25 .50
168 Ulf Martensson .25 .50
169 Stig Nordin .25 .50
170 Olle Sjogren .25 .50
171 Ingemar Snis .25 .50
172 Dan Soderstrom .25 .50
173 Bo Theander .30 .75
174 Mats Ahlberg .25 .50
175 Gunnar Backman .25 .50
176 Ivar Larsson .50 1.00
177 Sture Andersson .25 .50
178 Lage Edin .25 .50
179 Kjell-Rune Milton .25 .50
180 Per-Olof Uusitalo .25 .50
181 Ulf Wigren .25 .50
182 Hakan Dahlof .25 .50
183 Anders Hedberg 4.00 8.00
184 Torbjorn Hubinette .25 .50
185 Assar Lundgren .25 .50
186 Per Lundqvist .25 .50
187 Christer Nilsson .25 .50
188 Kenneth Nordenberg .25 .50
189 Anders Nordin .25 .50
190 Hakan Nygren .25 .50
191 Ulf Thors .25 .50
192 Ulf Torstensson .25 .50
193 Lars Ohman .25 .50
194 Tore Ohman .25 .50
195 Tony Esposito 17.50 35.00
196 Bobby Orr 50.00 100.00
197 Jean Beliveau 12.50 35.00
198 Gordie Howe 40.00 75.00
199 Phil Esposito 12.50 35.00
200 Bobby Hull 20.00 40.00
201 Bengt-Ake Gustavsson .50 1.00
202 Lars Gustavsson .50 1.00
203 Tommy Andersson .25 .50
204 Hans-Olov Ernlund .25 .50
205 Tord Johansson .25 .50
206 Lars Mjoberg .25 .50
207 Per-Erik Olsson .25 .50
208 Tord Svensson .25 .50
209 Jan Danielsson .25 .50
210 Tommy Eriksson .50 1.00
211 Gote Hansson .25 .50
212 Hans Hansson .25 .50
213 Sven-Ake Jacobsson .25 .50
214 Mats Lonn .25 .50
215 Borje Marcus .25 .50
216 Lars Munther .25 .50
217 Ulf Nises .25 .50
218 Anders Rosen .25 .50
219 Borje Skogs .50 1.00
220 Kent Sundkvist .50 1.00
221 Mikael Collin .50 1.00
222 Bjorn Jansson .50 1.00
223 Curt Larsson .50 1.00
224 Thommie Bergman 1.50 3.00
225 Arne Carlsson .25 .50
226 Christer Karlsson .25 .50
227 Eilert Maatta .25 .50
228 Jan Schullstrom .25 .50
229 Borje (Poppen) Burlin .25 .50
230 Hans Carlsson .25 .50
231 Tommy Carlsson .25 .50
232 Mats Hysing .25 .50
233 Bertil Jacobsson .25 .50
234 Stig-Goran Johansson .50 1.00
235 Dan Landegren .25 .50
236 Kjell Landstrom .25 .50
237 Soren Maatta .25 .50
238 Nils-Olov Schilstrom .25 .50
239 Dick Yderstrom .25 .50
240 Carl Goran Oberg .25 .50
241 Anders Claesson .50 1.00
242 Kent Othberg .50 1.00
243 Jan Johansson .25 .50
244 Jan-Erik Nilsson .25 .50
245 Stefan Pettersson .25 .50
246 Tord Salomonsson .25 .50
247 Lennart Svedberg .50 1.00
248 Bo Berggren .25 .50
249 Bjorn Broman .25 .50
250 Lennart Broman .25 .50
251 Ove Larsson .25 .50
252 Rolf Larsson .25 .50
253 Orjan Lindstrom .25 .50
254 Arne Lundstrom .25 .50
255 Fhinn Lundstrom .25 .50
256 Ake Lundstrom .25 .50
257 Lennart Norberg .25 .50
258 Hakan Pettersson .25 .50
259 Ake Soderberg .25 .50
260 Olle Ahman .25 .50
261 Christer Andersson .50 1.00
262 Bengt Gustavsson .25 .50
263 Goran Astrom .25 .50
264 Anders Brostrom .25 .50
265 Kenneth Ekman .25 .50
266 Soren Gunnarsson .25 .50
267 Lars-Erik Jacobsson .25 .50
268 Des Moroney .25 .50
269 Borje Maatta .25 .50
270 Tommy Pettersson .25 .50
271 Bengt Alm .25 .50
272 Sven Crabo .25 .50
273 Bengt Eriksson .25 .50
274 Kurt Jakobsson .25 .50
275 Leif Jakobsson .25 .50
276 Lars-Goran Johansson .25 .50
277 Bert Karlsson .25 .50
278 Benny Runesson .25 .50
279 Ake Ryman .25 .50
280 Jan Roger Strand .25 .50
281 Christer Grahn .30 .75
282 Ronny Sandstrom .25 .50
283 John Andersson .25 .50
284 Karl-Olov Eriksson .25 .50
285 Anders Hagstrom .25 .50
286 Ulf Ingvarsson .25 .50
287 Rolf Jager .25 .50
288 Erik Jarvholm .25 .50
289 Bo Westling .25 .50
290 Ulf Barrefjord .25 .50
291 Kent Bjork .25 .50
292 Lars Dahlgren .25 .50
293 Ulf Larsson .25 .50
294 Jan Lundqvist .25 .50
295 Ulf Lundstrom .25 .50
296 Bengt Lovgren .25 .50
297 Leif Martensson .25 .50
298 Lars-Ake Nordin .25 .50
299 Lars Sjostrom .25 .50
300 Kjell Sundstrom .25 .50
301 Ronny Andersson .50 1.00
302 Ingemar Caris .50 1.00
303 Anders Johansson .25 .50
304 Hakan Norstrom .25 .50
305 Jan Olsen .25 .50
306 Lars-Erik Sjoberg .50 1.00
307 Bengt Sjoholm .25 .50
308 Kjell Andersson .25 .50
309 Svante Granholm .25 .50
310 Kjell-Ove Gustavsson .25 .50
311 Henrik Hedlund .25 .50
312 Leif Henriksson .25 .50
313 Lars-Erik Johansson .25 .50
314 Bjorn Lindberg .25 .50
315 Evert Lindstrom .25 .50
316 Willy Lindstrom 1.00 2.00
317 Leif Nilsson .25 .50
318 Kurt Olofsson .25 .50
319 Roger Olsson .25 .50
320 Kjell-Ronnie Pettersson .25 .50
321 Kenneth Holmstedt .50 1.00
322 Lars-Erik Larsson .25 .50
323 Lennart Eriksson .25 .50
324 Lennart Gustavsson .25 .50
325 Jan-Ake Karlsson .25 .50
326 Rolf Karlsson .25 .50
327 Bengt Lundberg .25 .50
328 Anders Thelander .25 .50
329 Kent Bengtsson .25 .50
330 Gunnar Backman .50 1.00
331 Stefan Canderyd .25 .50
332 Curt Edenvik .25 .50
333 Per Edenvik .25 .50
334 Weine Gullberg .25 .50
335 Nils-Arne Hedqvist .25 .50
336 Bengt-Ake Karlsson .25 .50
337 Christer Kihlstrom .25 .50
338 Stig-Olof Persson .25 .50
339 Christer Sjoberg .25 .50
340 Roddy Skyllqvist .25 .50
341 Lars Blomqvist .50 1.00
342 Bjorn Forsberg .50 1.00
343 Anders Hedlund .25 .50
344 Lennart Johansson .25 .50
345 Martin Kruger .25 .50
346 Harry Namd .25 .50
347 Lennart Strohm .25 .50
348 Peter Bejemark .25 .50
349 Bertil Bond .25 .50
350 Nils Carlsson .25 .50
351 Ulf Pilo .25 .50
352 Claes-Ove Fjallby .25 .50
353 Lars Granlund .25 .50
354 Kjell Keijser .25 .50
355 Lennart Lange .25 .50
356 Bo Mellbin .25 .50
357 Lars Starck .25 .50
358 Leif Svensson .25 .50
359 Kjell Ahlen .25 .50
360 Henry Svensson .25 .50
361 Sven-Allan Ellstrom .50 1.00
362 Tommy Eriksson .50 1.00
363 Walter Winsth .50 1.00
364 Hans-Ake Andersson .25 .50
365 Jan Andersson .25 .50
366 Hans Bejbom .25 .50
367 Goran Borell .25 .50
368 Bo Schilstrom .25 .50
369 Bjarne Brostrom .25 .50
370 Kenneth Calen .25 .50
371 Lennart Carlsson .25 .50
372 Mats Davidsson .25 .50
373 Rolf Hansson .25 .50
374 Rune Norrstrom .25 .50
375 Gunther Rauch .25 .50
376 Jan Vestberg .25 .50
377 Bengt Wistling .25 .50
378 Kent Zetterberg .25 .50
379 Goran Akerlund .25 .50
380 Uno Ohrlund .25 .50
381 Goran Hogosta .60 1.50
382 Juha Raninen .50 1.00
383 Bert Backman .25 .50
384 Christer Collin .25 .50
385 Dag Olsson .25 .50
386 Bjorn Resare .25 .50
387 Lars Thoreus .25 .50
388 Stig Andersson .25 .50
389 Borje Engblom .25 .50
390 Christer Englund .25 .50
391 Bo Eriksson .25 .50
392 Mats Eriksson .25 .50
393 Roland Eriksson .25 .50
394 Olle Henriksson .25 .50
395 Yngve Hindrikes .25 .50
396 Kjell Jansson .25 .50
397 Jan Johansson .25 .50
398 Jan Karlsson .25 .50
399 Agne Norberg .25 .50
400 Christian Reuthie .25 .50

1972-73 Swedish Stickers

This 300-sticker set was issued in Sweden by Williams Forlags AB for the 1972-73 season. While the majority of the set is taken up by players from the Swedish Elitserien, there also are stickers featuring stars from Russia, Czechoslovakia, Finland and the NHL. Key stickers include pre-NHL appearances from Anders Hedberg, Borje Salming and Ulf Nilsson. NHL stars such as Bobby Orr, Ken Dryden and Bobby Hull also are featured, along with Soviet greats such as Tretiak and Kharlamov. The card fronts feature a posed color photo, while the backs have the sticker number and player information in Swedish. A book to hold the stickers was available at the time for 3.5 kroner, or about fifty cents. It is filled with stories about the teams, league schedules and photos, along with spaces for the stickers. It is valued now at $25. The prices below are for unused stickers; because it was the habit then to put them in the album, relatively few remain in their original state.

COMPLETE SET (300) 150.00 300.00
1 Christer Abrahamsson 1.00 2.00
2 Leif Holmqvist .50 1.00
3 Tommy Abrahamsson .50 1.00
4 Thommie Bergman 1.00 2.00
5 Bjorn Johansson .25 .50
6 Kjell-Rune Milton .25 .50
7 Borje Salming 5.00 10.00
8 Lars-Erik Sjoberg 1.00 2.00
9 Karl-Johan Sundqvist .25 .50
10 Stig Ostling .25 .50
11 Inge Hammarstrom 1.00 2.00
12 Anders Hedberg 2.50 5.00
13 Stig-Goran Johansson .25 .50
14 Stefan Karlsson .25 .50
15 Hans Lindberg .25 .50
16 Mats Lindh .25 .50
17 Tord Lundstrom .25 .50
18 Lars-Goran Nilsson .25 .50
19 Bjorn Palmqvist .25 .50
20 Hakan Wickberg .25 .50
21 Jiri Holecek .50 1.00
22 Josef Horesovsky .25 .50
23 Frantisek Pospisil .38 .75
24 Jaroslav Holik .25 .50
25 Jiri Holik .38 .75
26 Vaclav Nedomansky 1.00 2.00
27 Vladislav Tretiak 10.00 20.00
28 Gennadi Tsigankov .38 .75
29 Igor Romisjevskij .38 .75
30 Valeri Kharlamov 5.00 10.00
31 Alexander Maltsev 2.50 5.00
32 Vladimir Vikulov .38 .75
33 Jorma Valtonen .38 .75
34 Pekka Marjamaki .25 .50
35 Matti Keinonen .25 .50
36 Veli-Pekka Ketola 1.00 2.00
37 Lauri Mononen .25 .50
38 Lasse Oksanen .25 .50
39 Krister Sterner .50 1.00
40 Sten-Ake Bark .25 .50
41 Jan-Erik Silfverberg .25 .50
42 Steffan Andersson .25 .50
43 Roland Eriksson .25 .50
44 Gunnar Johansson .25 .50
45 Jiri Holecek .50 1.00
46 Thommie Bergman 1.00 2.00
47 Josef Horesovsky .25 .50
48 Vladimir Vikulov .38 .75
49 Alexander Maltsev 2.50 5.00
50 Valeri Kharlamov 5.00 10.00
51 Leif Holmqvist .50 1.00
52 Lars Danielsson .25 .50
53 Ake Fagerstrom .25 .50
54 Per-Arne Hubinette .25 .50
55 Hakan Lindgren .25 .50
56 Bert-Ola Nordlander .25 .50
57 Bo Olofsson .25 .50
58 Soren Sjogren .25 .50
59 Jan Olsson .25 .50
60 Lennart Selinder .25 .50
61 Jan Olof Kroon .25 .50
62 Rolf Edberg .25 .50
63 Ulf Nilsson 2.50 5.00
64 Leif Holmgren .25 .50
65 Jan Ostling .25 .50
66 Christer Grahn .50 1.00
67 Karl-Olov Grahn .50 1.00
68 Anders Hagstrom .25 .50
69 Erik Jarvholm .25 .50
70 Bo Westling .25 .50
71 Ulf Ingvarsson .25 .50
72 Bengt Lovgren .25 .50
73 Kjell Sundstrom .25 .50
74 Kent Bjork .25 .50
75 Ulf Lundstrom .25 .50
76 Mats Lundmark .25 .50
77 Ulf Barrefjord .25 .50
78 Lars Dahlgren .25 .50
79 Olle Nilsson .25 .50
80 Roger Nilsson .25 .50
81 Willie Lofqvist .50 1.00
82 Jan-Erik Silfverberg .25 .50
83 Kjell Johnsson .25 .50
84 Jan-Olof Svensson .25 .50
85 Stig Salming .25 .50
86 Borje Salming 5.00 10.00
87 Stig Ostling .25 .50
88 Tord Lundstrom .25 .50
89 Inge Hammarstrom 1.00 2.00
90 Lars-Goran Nilsson .25 .50
91 Hans Lindberg .25 .50
92 Hakan Wickberg .25 .50
93 Jan-Erik Lyck .25 .50
94 Stefan Karlsson .25 .50
95 Lars Oberg .25 .50
96 Roland Einarsson .50 1.00
97 Billy Sundstrom .25 .50
98 Anders Rylin .25 .50
99 Tomas Carlsson .25 .50
100 Ulf Ojerklint .25 .50
101 L-A Gustavsson .50 1.00
102 Jorgen Palm .25 .50
103 Lars-Ake Lundell .25 .50
104 Ake Eklof .25 .50
105 Bengt-Ake Karlsson .25 .50
106 Bjorn Palmqvist .25 .50
107 Per-Allan Wickstrom .25 .50
108 Sven-Bertil Lindstrom .25 .50
109 Totte Bengtsson .25 .50
110 Stig Larsson .25 .50
111 Ken Dryden 20.00 40.00
112 Jacques Laperriere 1.50 3.00
113 Bobby Orr 37.50 75.00
114 Brad Park 2.50 5.00
115 Phil Esposito 10.00 20.00
116 Rod Gilbert 2.50 5.00
117 Vic Hadfield 1.50 3.00
118 Bobby Hull 15.00 30.00
119 Frank Mahovlich 5.00 10.00
120 Jean Ratelle 2.50 5.00
121 Lennart Andersson .50 1.00
122 Karl-Johan Sundqvist .25 .50
123 Nicke Johansson .25 .50
124 Lars-Goran Nilsson .25 .50
125 Ake Carlsson .25 .50
126 Hans-Ake Rosendahl .25 .50
127 Sten-Ake Dark .25 .50
128 Par Backman .25 .50
129 Leif Labraaten .25 .50
130 Berndt Augustsson .25 .50
131 Uffe Sterner .25 .50
132 Benny Andersson .25 .50
133 Conny Evensson .50 1.00
134 Kjell Augustsson .25 .50
135 Hans Andersson .25 .50
136 Kenneth Holmstedt .50 1.00
137 Lennart Gustavsson .25 .50
138 Lennart Eriksson .25 .50
139 Rolf Carlsson .25 .50
140 Bengt Lundberg .25 .50
141 Jan-Ake Karlsson .25 .50
142 Curt Edenvik .25 .50
143 Per Edenvik .25 .50
144 Weine Gullberg .25 .50
145 Gunnar Backman .50 1.00
146 Roddy Skyllqvist .25 .50
147 Stefan Canderyd .25 .50
148 Christer Kihlstrom .25 .50
149 Nils-Arne Hedqvist .25 .50
150 Stig-Olof Persson .25 .50
151 Christer Abrahamsson 1.00 2.00
152 Thommy Abrahamsson .50 1.00
153 Roland Bond .25 .50
154 Gunnar Andersson .25 .50
155 Ulf Weinstock .25 .50
156 Ake Danielsson .25 .50
157 Peter Gudmundsson .25 .50
158 Olle Sjogren .25 .50
159 Hans Jax .25 .50
160 Mats Ahlberg .25 .50
161 Dan Labraaten 1.00 2.00
162 Ulf Martensson .25 .50
163 Kjell Brus .25 .50
164 Dan Soderstrom .25 .50
165 Per Olof Brasar 1.00 2.00
166 Ivar Larsson .50 1.00
167 Sture Andersson .25 .50
168 Lage Edin .25 .50
169 Kjell Rune Milton .25 .50
170 Ulf Wigren .25 .50
171 Hakan Dahllof .25 .50
172 Anders Hedberg 2.50 5.00
173 Assar Lundgren .25 .50
174 Christer Nilsson .25 .50
175 Anders Nordin .25 .50
176 Hakan Nygren .25 .50
177 Ulf Thors .25 .50
178 Ulf Torstensson .25 .50
179 Lasse Ohman .25 .50
180 Tore Ohman .25 .50
181 Bengt Ake Gustafsson .38 .75
182 Tommy Andersson .25 .50
183 Hans-Olof Ernlund .25 .50
184 Tord Johansson .25 .50
185 Tord Svensson .25 .50
186 Jan Danielsson .25 .50
187 Tommy Eriksson .50 1.00
188 Gote Hansson .25 .50
189 Hans Hansson .25 .50
190 Sven-Ake Jacobsson .25 .50
191 Mats Lonn .25 .50
192 Lars Mjoberg .25 .50
193 Lars Munther .25 .50
194 Ulf Nises .25 .50
195 Borje Skogs .25 .50
196 Roland Lestander .25 .50
197 Bosse Andersson .25 .50
198 Hakan Dahlin .25 .50
199 Martin Johansson .25 .50
200 Anders Lindberg .25 .50
201 Lars-Fredrik Nystrom .25 .50
202 Hans Gunnar Skarin .25 .50
203 Jerry Aberg .25 .50
204 Anders Almqvist .25 .50
205 Christer Johansson .25 .50
206 Per Johansson .25 .50
207 Martin Karlsson .25 .50
208 Lars-Gunnar Lundberg .25 .50
209 Hardy Nilsson .25 .50
210 Kjell-Arne Wikstrom .25 .50
211 Mikael Collin .50 1.00
212 Curt Larsson .50 1.00
213 Arne Carlsson .25 .50
214 Bjorn Johansson .25 .50
215 Nils-Olov Schilstrom .25 .50
216 Jan Schullstrom .25 .50
217 Borje Burlin .25 .50
218 Hans Carlsson .25 .50
219 Mats Hysing .25 .50
220 Bertil Jacobsson .25 .50
221 Stisse Johansson .25 .50
222 Dan Landegren .25 .50
223 Kjell Landstrom .25 .50
224 Dick Yderstrom .25 .50
225 Carl-Goran Oberg .25 .50
226 Christer Sehlstedt .25 .50
227 Tommie Lindgren .25 .50
228 Jan-Erik Nilsson .25 .50
229 Stefan Pettersson .25 .50
230 Tord Nansen .25 .50
231 Bo Berggren .25 .50
232 Bjorn Broman .25 .50
233 Ove Larsson .25 .50
234 Kent Lindgren .25 .50
235 Orjan Lindstrom .25 .50
236 Lennart Norberg .25 .50
237 Arne Lundstrom .25 .50
238 Hakan Pettersson .25 .50
239 Ake Soderberg .25 .50
240 Olle Ahman .25 .50
241 Christer Andersson 1.00 2.00
242 Anders Brostrom .25 .50
243 Kenneth Ekman .25 .50
244 Soren Gunnarsson .25 .50
245 Borje Maatta .25 .50
246 Tommy Pettersson .25 .50
247 Kurt Jakobsson .25 .50
248 Leif Jakobsson .25 .50
249 Lars-Goran Johansson .25 .50
250 Bengt-Goran Karlsson .25 .50
251 Derndt Karlsson .25 .50
252 Tadeusz Niedomyst .25 .50
253 Benny Runesson .25 .50
254 Ake Ryman .25 .50
255 Jan-Roger Strand .25 .50
256 Goran Hogosta .50 1.00
257 Bert Backman .25 .50
258 Christer Collin .25 .50
259 Bo Eriksson .25 .50
260 Hakan Norstrom .25 .50
261 Lars Thoreus .25 .50
262 Stig Andersson .25 .50
263 Mats Eriksson .25 .50
264 Roland Eriksson .25 .50
265 Kjell Fhinn .25 .50
266 Olle Henriksson .25 .50
267 Yngve Hindrikes .25 .50
268 Jan Karlsson .25 .50
269 Kjell Jansson .25 .50
270 Ingemar Snis .25 .50
271 Christer Stahl .25 .50
272 Leif Andersson .25 .50
273 Tommy Eriksson .50 1.00
274 Christer Holmstrom .25 .50
275 Curt Lundmark 1.00 2.00
276 Dennis Pettersson .25 .50
277 Ove Thelin .25 .50
278 Bo Wahlberg .25 .50
279 Gote Gustavsson .25 .50
280 Christer Lindgren .25 .50
281 Kent Persson .25 .50
282 Par Marts .25 .50
283 Ove Stenlund .25 .50
284 Bo Olsson .25 .50
285 Bo Astrom .25 .50
286 Ronny Andersson .50 1.00
287 Roger Bergman .25 .50
288 Thommie Bergman 1.00 2.00
289 Anders Johansson .25 .50
290 Jan Olsen .25 .50

291 Lars Erik Sjoberg	1.00	2.00
292 Kjell Andersson	.25	.50
293 Svante Granholm	.25	.50
294 Henrik Hedlund	.25	.50
295 Leif Henriksson	.25	.50
296 Mats Lindh	.25	.50
297 Evert Lindstrom	.25	.50
298 Willy Lindstrom	1.00	2.00
299 Roger Olsson	.25	.50
300 Kjell-Ronnie Pettersson	.25	.50

1972 Swedish Semic World Championship

Printed in Italy by Semic Press, the 233 cards comprising this set measure 1 7/8" by 2 1/2" and feature posed color player photos on their white-bordered fronts. The white back carries the player's name and text in Swedish. The cards are numbered on the back and arranged by national teams as follows: Soviet Union (1-20), Czechoslovakia (21-41), Sweden (42-70), Finland (71-92), Germany (93-117), United States (118-137), France (138-162), and Canada (163-233).

COMPLETE SET (233)	200.00	400.00
1 Viktor Konovalenko	.38	.75
2 Vitalij Davydov	.38	.75
3 Vladimir Lutjenko	.38	.75
4 Viktor Kuskin	.38	.75
5 Alexander Ragulin	.75	3.00
6 Igor Romitjevskij	.38	.75
7 Gennadij Tsigankov	.38	.75
8 Vjatsjeslav Starsjinov	.75	1.50
9 Evgenij Zimin	.50	1.00
10 Alexander Maltsev	2.50	5.00
11 Anatolij Firsov	1.25	2.00
12 Evgenij Misjakov	.38	.75
13 Boris Michailov	2.00	4.00
14 Juri Ljapkin	.50	1.00
15 Alexander Martinyk	.38	.75
16 Vladimir Petrov	2.00	4.00
17 Valeri Kharlamov	5.00	10.00
18 Vladimir Vikulov	.38	.75
19 Vladimir Sjadrin	.50	1.00
20 Vladislav Tretiak	10.00	20.00
21 Marcel Sakac	.25	.50
22 Jiri Holecek	.50	1.00
23 Josef Horesovsky	.25	.50
24 Oldrich Machac	.25	.50
25 Rudolf Tajcnar	.25	.50
26 Frantisek Panchartek	.25	.50
27 Frantisek Pospisil	.38	.75
28 Jiri Kochta	.25	.50
29 Jan Havel	.25	.50
30 Vladimir Martinec	.25	.50
31 Richard Farda	.25	.50
32 Bohuslav Stastny	.38	.75
33 Vaclav Nedomansky	.75	1.50
34 Josef Cerny	.25	.50
35 Bedrich Brunchk	.25	.50
36 Jan Suchy	.25	.50
37 Eduard Novak	.25	.50
38 Jiri Bubla	.75	1.50
39 Jiri Holik	.38	.75
40 Ivan Hlinka	1.00	2.00
41 Vladimir Bednar	.25	.50
42 Leif Holmqvist	.50	1.00
43 Christer Abrahamsson	1.00	2.00
44 Christer Andersson	.50	1.00
45 Lars-Erik Sjoberg	.75	1.50
46 Lennart Svedberg	.50	1.00
47 Stig-Goran Johansson	.25	.50
48 Bert-Ola Nordlander	.25	.50
49 Thommy Abrahamsson	.50	1.00
50 Arne Carlsson	.25	.50
51 Stefan Karlsson	.25	.50
52 Hakan Wickberg	.25	.50
53 Hakan Nygren	.25	.50
54 Lars-Goran Nilsson	.25	.50
55 Thommie Bergman	1.00	2.00
56 Ulf Sterner	.38	.75
57 Hans Lindberg	.25	.50
58 Tord Lundstrom	.25	.50
59 Gunnar Andersson	.25	.50
60 Bjorn Palmqvist	.25	.50
61 Inge Hammarstrom	1.00	2.00
62 Kjell-Rune Milton	.25	.50
63 Kjell Brus	.25	.50
64 Kenneth Ekman	.25	.50
65 Bengt-Goran Karlsson	.25	.50
66 Hakan Pettersson	.25	.50
67 Dan Labraaten	.75	1.50
68 Dan Soderstrom	.25	.50
69 Anders Hedberg	2.50	5.00
70 Ake Soderberg	.25	.50
71 Urpo Ylonen	.25	.50
72 Ilpo Koskela	.25	.50
73 Seppo Lindstrom	.25	.50
74 Hannu Luojola	.25	.50
75 Pekka Marjamaki	.25	.50
76 Jouko Oystila	.25	.50
77 Heikki Jarn	.25	.50
78 Esa Isaksson	.25	.50
79 Veli-Pekka Ketola	.75	1.50
80 Harri Linnonmaa	.25	.50
81 Erkki Mononen	.25	.50
82 Lauri Mononen	.25	.50
83 Matti Murto	.25	.50
84 Lasse Oksanen	.25	.50
85 Esa Peltonen	.25	.50
86 Seppo Repo	.25	.50
87 Tommi Salmelainen	.25	.50
88 Juhani Tamminen	.25	.50
89 Jorma Vehmanen	.25	.50
90 Jorma Valtonen	.38	.75
91 Matti Keinonen	.25	.50
92 Juha Rantasila	.25	.50
93 Toni Kehle	.25	.50
94 Josef Schramm	.25	.50
95 Walter Stadler	.25	.50
96 Josef Volk	.25	.50
97 Hans Schichtl	.25	.50
98 Erwin Riedmeier	.25	.50
99 Werner Modes	.25	.50
100 Johann Eimannsberger	.25	.50
101 Karlheinz Egger	.25	.50
102 Lorenz Funk, Sr.	.25	.50
103 Klaus Ego	.25	.50
104 Anton Hofherr	.25	.50
105 Otto Schneitberger	.25	.50
106 Heinz Weisenbach	.25	.50
107 Alois Schloder	.25	.50
108 Gustav Hanig	.25	.50
109 Rainer Philipp	.25	.50
110 Bernd Kuhn	.25	.50
111 Paul Langner	.25	.50
112 Franz Hofherr	.25	.50
113 Reinhold Bauer	.25	.50
114 Johann Rotkirch	.25	.50
115 Walter Koberle	.25	.50
116 Rainer Makatsch	.25	.50
117 Carl Wetzel	.38	.75
118 Mike Curran	.38	.75
119 Jim McElmury	.38	.75
120 Bruce Riutta	.38	.75
121 Tom Mellor	.38	.75
122 Don Ross	.38	.75
123 Gary Gambucci	.38	.75
124 Keith Christiansen	.38	.75
125 Len Lilyholm	.38	.75
126 Henry Boucha	.75	3.00
127 Craig Falkman	.38	.75
128 Tim Sheehy	.38	.75
129 Kevin Ahearn	.38	1.00
130 Craig Patrick	1.00	2.00
131 Pete Fichuk	.38	1.00
132 George Konik	.38	1.00
133 Dick McGlynn	.38	1.00
134 Dick Toomey	.38	1.00
135 Paul Schilling	.38	1.00
136 Bob Lindberg	.38	1.00
137 Dick Tomasoni	.38	1.00
138 Nando Mathieu	.25	.50
139 Francis Reinhard	.25	.50
140 Gaston Furrer	.25	.50
141 Bruno Wittwer	.25	.50
142 Andre Berra	.25	.50
143 Hans Keller	.25	.50
144 Peter Luthi	.25	.50
145 Peter Aeschlimann	.25	.50
146 Werner Kuenzi	.25	.50
147 Tony Neininger	.25	.50
148 Jacques Pousaz	.25	.50
149 Roger Chappot	.25	.50
150 Charly Henzen	.25	.50
151 Paul Probst	.25	.50
152 Guy Dubois	.25	.50
153 Rene Squaldo	.25	.50
154 Rene Hueguenin	.25	.50
155 Gaston Pelletier	.25	.50
156 Beat Kaufmann	.25	.50
157 Alfio Molina	.25	.50
158 Gerald Rigolet	.25	.50
159 Harald Jones	.25	.50
160 Gilbert Mathieu	.25	.50
161 Michel Turler	.25	.50
162 Reto Taillens	.25	.50
163 Norm Ullman	1.50	5.00
164 Dave Keon	2.50	10.00
165 Roger Crozier	2.50	5.00
166 Ron Ellis	1.50	5.00
167 Paul Henderson	2.50	10.00
168 Jim Dorey	.50	1.00
169 Jacques Plante	15.00	30.00
170 Jean-Guy Gendron	.50	1.00
171 Gary Smith	1.50	3.00
172 Dennis Hextall	.50	2.00
173 Norm Ferguson	.50	1.00
174 Simon Nolet	.50	1.00
175 Bernie Parent	5.00	10.00
176 Ted Hampson	.50	1.00
177 Earl Ingarfield	.50	1.00
178 Larry Hillman	.50	2.00
179 Gary Dornhoefer	1.00	3.00
180 Gary Croteau	.50	1.00
181 Carol Vadnais	.50	2.00
182 Jim Roberts	.50	2.00
183 Red Berenson	1.50	5.00
184 Phil Esposito	12.50	25.00
185 John McKenzie	1.00	3.00
186 Barclay Plager	1.00	3.00
187 Glenn Hall	7.50	15.00
188 Gerry Cheevers	7.50	15.00
189 Jim McKenny	.50	1.00
190 Gordie Howe	25.00	50.00
191 Garry Unger	1.00	3.00
192 Roy Edwards	1.50	5.00
193 Alex Delvecchio	2.50	5.00
194 Brad Park	2.50	10.00
195 Frank Mahovlich	5.00	10.00
196 Phil Goyette	.50	1.00
197 Don Marshall	.50	1.00
198 Henri Richard	5.00	10.00
199 Claude Larose	.50	1.00
200 Bobby Rousseau	.50	1.00
201 Lorne Worsley	5.00	10.00
202 Gilles Marotte	.75	1.50
203 Bob Pulford	1.50	5.00
204 Yvan Cournoyer	2.50	5.00
205 Eddie Joyal	.50	1.00
206 Ross Lonsberry	.50	1.00
207 Jean Beliveau	10.00	20.00
208 Jacques Lemaire	2.50	5.00
209 Orland Kurtenbach	.75	1.50
210 Andre Boudrias	.50	1.00
211 Jim Neilson	.50	2.00
212 Walter Tkaczuk	1.00	3.00
213 Ed Giacomin	5.00	10.00
214 Jean Ratelle	2.50	5.00
215 Les Binkley	1.50	5.00
216 Jean Pronovost	.50	1.00
217 Bryan Watson	.50	2.00
218 Dean Prentice	.50	1.00
219 Jean-Paul Parise	1.00	3.00
220 Bill Goldsworthy	.75	3.00
221 Wayne Maki	.50	2.00
222 Dale Tallon	.75	3.00
223 Bobby Orr	37.50	75.00
224 Pit Martin	.50	2.00
225 Jacques Laperriere	1.50	3.00
226 Bill Flett	.50	2.00
227 Stan Mikita	7.50	15.00
228 Bobby Hull	15.00	30.00
229 Larry Pleau	.50	2.00
230 Keith Magnuson	1.00	2.00
231 Tony Esposito	7.50	15.00
232 Rogatien Vachon	4.00	10.00
233 Mickey Redmond	7.50	15.00

1973-74 Swedish Stickers

This 243-sticker set was produced in Sweden by Williams Forlags AB. It features players from the top Swedish league, as well as several Russian teams. The set includes such legendary figures as Valeri Kharlamov, Vladislav Tretiak and a rare card of notorious head coach Vselvolod Bobrov. The fronts feature a color player photo, while the backs have sticker number and information in Swedish. There was an album available to store the set; it currently retails for around $20.

COMPLETE SET (243)	100.00	175.00
1 Christer Abrahamsson	1.00	2.00
2 William Lofqvist	.50	1.00
3 Arne Karlsson	.25	.50
4 Lars-Erik Sjoberg	1.00	2.00
5 Bjorn Johansson	.25	.50
6 Thommy Abrahamsson	.50	1.00
7 Borje Salming	5.00	10.00
8 Karl Johan Sundqvist	.25	.50
9 Ulf Sterner	.25	.50
10 Ulf Nilsson	2.50	5.00
11 Kjell-Arne Wickstrom	.25	.50
12 Inge Hammarstrom	2.50	5.00
13 Hakan Wickberg	.25	.50
14 Tord Lundstrom	.25	.50
15 Dan Soderstrom	.25	.50
16 Mats Ahlberg	.50	1.00
17 Anders Hedberg	2.50	5.00
18 Dick Yderstrom	.30	.75
19 Stefan Karlsson	.25	.50
20 Roland Bond	.25	.50
21 Kjell-Rune Milton	.25	.50
22 Willy Lindstrom	.75	1.50
23 Kurt Carlsson	.30	.75
24 Mats Walltin	.25	.50
25 Roland Eriksson	.25	.50
26 Martin Karlsson	.25	.50
27 Jiri Holecek	.50	1.00
28 Josef Horesovsky	.25	.50
29 Oldrich Machac	.25	.50
30 Vladimir Martinec	.50	1.00
31 Vaclav Nedomansky	.75	1.50
32 Jiri Kochta	.25	.50
33 Jorma Waltonen	.50	1.00
34 Heikki Riihiranta	.50	1.00
35 Lauri Mononen	.25	.50
36 Timo Turunen	.25	.50
37 Matti Keinonen	.25	.50
38 Seppo Repo	.25	.50
39 Christer Abrahamsson	.75	1.50
40 Lars Stenvall	.25	.50
41 Per Karlsson	.25	.50
42 Roland Bond	.25	.50
43 Thommy Abrahamsson	.50	1.00
44 Ulf Weinstock	.25	.50
45 Gunnar Andersson	.25	.50
46 Hans Eriksson	.25	.50
47 Peter Gudmundsson	.25	.50
48 Mats Ahlberg	.50	1.00
49 Per-Olov Brasar	.75	1.50
50 Roger Lindqvist	.25	.50
51 Dan Soderstrom	.25	.50
52 Ulf Martensson	.25	.50
53 Kjell Brus	.25	.50
54 Hans Jax	.25	.50
55 Dan Labraaten	.75	1.50
56 Nils-Olov Olsson	.25	.50
57 Stig Nordin	.25	.50
58 Bo Theander	.25	.50
59 Curt Larsson	.50	1.00
60 Mikael Collin	.50	1.00
61 Arne Carlsson	.25	.50
62 Leif Svensson	.25	.50
63 Sverker Torstensson	.25	.50
64 Bjorn Johansson	.25	.50
65 Stisse Johansson	.25	.50
66 Carl-Goran Oberg	.25	.50
67 Mats Hysing	.25	.50
68 Mats Walltin	.25	.50
69 Hans Carlsson	.25	.50
70 Nils-Olov Schilstrom	.25	.50
71 Kjell-Arne Wickstrom	.25	.50
72 Jan Schullstrom	.25	.50
73 Borje Burlin	.25	.50
74 Dick Yderstrom	.30	.75
75 Dan Landegren	.25	.50
76 Kjell Landstrom	.25	.50
77 Vladislav Tretjak	10.00	20.00
78 Alexander Sidelnikov	1.00	2.00
79 Alexander Ragulin	1.25	2.50
80 Vladimir Luttjenko	1.00	2.00
81 Gennadij Tsygankov	.75	1.50
82 Alexander Gusev	.50	1.00
83 Jevgenij Poladiev	.30	.75
84 Jurij Liapkin	.75	1.50
85 Valerij Vasiljev	1.50	3.00
86 Boris Michailov	2.50	5.00
87 Valeri Kharlamov	5.00	10.00
88 Vladimir Petrov	2.50	5.00
89 Alexander Maltsev	2.50	5.00
90 Vladimir Sjadrin	1.25	2.50
91 Alexander Yakusjev	2.50	5.00
92 Alexander Martynjuk	.30	.75
93 Vjateslav Anissin	.50	1.00
94 Jurij Lebedev	1.00	2.00
95 Alexander Bodunov	.50	1.00
96 Alexander Volchkov	1.00	2.00
97 Vsevolod Bobrov	2.00	4.00
98 Konstantin Loktev	.25	.50
99 Anatolij Firsov	1.50	3.00
100 Viktor Kuzkin	.50	1.00
101 Jurij Blochin	.25	.50
102 Vladimir Vikulov	.50	1.00
103 Jurij Blinov	.50	1.00
104 Jevgenij Misjakov	1.00	2.00
105 Vladimir Trunov	.25	.50
106 Sergej Glazov	.25	.50
107 Vladimir Popov	.75	1.50
108 Viktor Zinger	.50	1.00
109 Viktor Krivolapov	.30	.75
110 Jevgenij Kazatjkin	.25	.50
111 Viktor Korotkov	.75	1.50
112 Valentin Markov	.25	.50
113 Alexander Sapjolkin	.25	.50
114 Leonid Borzov	.25	.50
115 Gennadij Krylov	.25	.50
116 Konstantin Klimov	.25	.50
117 Jevgenij Zimin	.50	1.00
118 Vladimir Gurejev	.25	.50
119 Viktor Jaroslavtsev	.25	.50
120 Alexander Pasjkov	.30	.75
121 Vladimir Polupanov	.50	1.00
122 Vitalij Davydov	.75	1.50
123 Michail Alexeenko	.25	.50
124 Alexander Filippov	.50	1.00
125 Valerij Nazarov	.25	.50
126 Vladimir Orlov	.25	.50
127 Stanislav Sjtjegolev	.25	.50
128 Anatolij Bjelonozjkin	.25	.50
129 Vladimir Devjatov	.25	.50
130 Jevgenij Kotlov	.25	.50
131 Anatolij Motovilov	.25	.50
132 Jurij Reps	.25	.50
133 Igor Samotjernov	.25	.50
134 Alexander Sevidov	.25	.50
135 Viktor Sjilov	.25	.50
136 Jurij Tjitjurin	.30	.75
137 Sune Odling	.25	.50
138 Lars-Erik Sjoberg	1.00	2.00
139 Bengt Sjoholm	.25	.50
140 Leif Henriksson	.25	.50
141 Henric Hedlund	.25	.50
142 Roger Olsson	.25	.50
143 Kjell-Rune Milton	.25	.50
144 Kjell-Ronnie Pettersson	.25	.50
145 Svante Granholm	.25	.50
146 Kjell Andersson	.25	.50
147 Lars-Erik Esbjorn	.25	.50
148 Bjorn Lindberg	.25	.50
149 Willy Lindstrom	.75	1.50
150 Evert Lindstrom	.25	.50
151 Lars-Erik Johansson	.25	.50
152 Krister Sterner	.30	.75
153 Mats Lindh	.25	.50
154 Roger Bergman	.25	.50
155 Willie Lofqvist	.50	1.00
156 Jan Olov Svensson	.25	.50
157 Jan Erik Silfverberg	.25	.50
158 Stig Ostling	.50	1.00
159 Kjell Johansson	.25	.50
160 Borje Salming	5.00	10.00
161 Stig Salming	.50	1.00
162 Tord Lundstrom	.25	.50
163 Hakan Wickberg	.25	.50
164 Inge Hammarstrom	2.50	5.00
165 Lars Goran Nilsson	.25	.50
166 Jan Erik Lyck	.25	.50
167 Stefan Karlsson	.25	.50
168 Lennart Lind	.50	1.00
169 Hans Ake Persson	.25	.50
170 Lars Oberg	.25	.50
171 Lars Erik Eriksson	.25	.50
172 Bjorn Fagerlund	.30	.75
173 Nicke Johansson	.25	.50
174 Lars Goran Nilsson	.25	.50
175 Hans Erik Jansson	.25	.50
176 Per Backman	.25	.50
177 Jorgen Palm	.25	.50
178 Conny Evensson	.30	.75
179 Ulf Sterner	.25	.50
180 Sven Ake Rudby	.25	.50
181 Lennart Andersson	.30	.75
182 Kent Erik Andersson	.25	.50
183 Hans Ake Rosendahl	.25	.50
184 Karl Johan Sundqvist	.25	.50
185 Hasse Andersson	.25	.50
186 Benny Andersson	.25	.50
187 Gunnar Johansson	.25	.50
188 Sten Ake Bark	.25	.50
189 Lasse Zetterstrom	.25	.50
190 Leif Holmqvist	.50	1.00
191 Bert Jattne	.50	1.00
192 Lars Danielsson	.50	1.00
193 Hakan Lindgren	.25	.50
194 Ake Fagerstrom	.25	.50
195 Bert-Ola Nordlander	.30	.75
196 Leif Holmgren	.25	.50
197 Soren Sjogren	.25	.50
198 Hans Lindberg	.25	.50
199 Jan-Olov Kroon	.25	.50
200 Rolf Edberg	.25	.50
201 Lennart Selinder	.50	1.00
202 Ulf Nilsson	2.50	5.00
203 Jan Olsson	.25	.50
204 Jan Ostling	.25	.50
205 Christer Lundberg	.25	.50
206 Christer Englund	.25	.50
207 Bo Olofsson	.25	.50
208 Roland Einarsson	.50	1.00
209 Ake Danielsson	.25	.50
210 Billy Sundstrom	.25	.50
211 Thomas Carlsson	.25	.50
212 Stig Larsson	.25	.50
213 Lars Ake Gustavsson	.50	1.00
214 Bjorn Palmqvist	.25	.50
215 Anders Hedberg	2.50	5.00
216 Anders Rylin	.25	.50
217 Sven Bertil Lindstrom	.25	.50
218 Kjell Nilsson	.25	.50
219 Claes Goran Wallin	.25	.50
220 Ake Eklof	.25	.50
221 Peder Nilsson	.30	.75
222 Lars Ake Lundell	.25	.50
223 Bengt Ake Karlsson	.25	.50
224 Ove Svensson	.25	.50
225 Soren Johansson	.25	.50
226 Christer Sehlstedt	.30	.75
227 Lage Edin	.25	.50
228 Tommy Andersson	.25	.50
229 Janerik Nilsson	.25	.50
230 Tommie Lindgren	.25	.50
231 Bo Bergman	.25	.50
232 Lennart Norberg	.25	.50
233 Olle Ahman	.25	.50
234 Arne Lundstrom	.30	.75
235 Kent Lindgren	.25	.50
236 Orjan Lindstrom	.25	.50
237 Kent Othberg	.30	.75
238 Finn Lundstrom	.25	.50
239 Ake Soderberg	.25	.50
240 Jan Kock	.25	.50
241 Ove Larsson	.25	.50
242 Hakan Pettersson	.25	.50
243 Stefan Pettersson	.25	.50

1974-75 Swedish Stickers

This set of 324 stickers commemorates the competitors on the 1974-75 World Championship, along with players from club teams across Europe. The stickers -- which measure approximately 3" by 2" -- feature action photography on the front, with player name and card number along the bottom. The backs have the set logo, a reprise of the card number and encouragement in Swedish to build the entire set. The last six cards were recently identified by Swedish collector Per Vedin.

COMPLETE SET (324)	100.00	175.00
1 Vladislav Tretiak	7.50	15.00
2 Gennadij Tsigannkov	.50	1.00
3 Valerij Vasiljev	1.50	3.00
4 Alexander Gusev	.50	1.00
5 Valeri Kharlamov	3.00	10.00
6 Vladimir Petrov	2.00	4.00
7 Boris Michailov	2.00	4.00
8 Alexander Maltsev	2.00	4.00
9 Alexander Yakusjev	2.00	4.00
10 Jiri Chra	1.50	3.00
11 Jiri Bubla	.50	1.00
12 Milan Kuzela	.25	.50
13 Oldrich Machac	.25	.50
14 Ivan Hlinka	.50	1.00
15 Vaclav Nedomansky	.75	1.50
16 Boshulav Stastny	.75	1.50
17 Vladimir Martinec	.25	.50
18 Richard Farda	.25	.50
19 Curt Larsson	.30	.75
20 Lars-Erik Sjoberg	1.00	2.00
21 Thommy Abrahamsson	.50	1.00
22 Kjell-Rune Milton	.25	.50
23 Anders Hedberg	2.00	4.00
24 Mats Ahlberg	.30	.75
25 Dan Soderstrom	.25	.50
26 Ulf Nilsson	2.00	4.00
27 Per-Olof Brassar	.75	1.50
28 Stig Wetzell	.25	.50
29 Juha Rantasila	.25	.50
30 Heikki Riihiranta	.50	1.00
31 Timo Saari	.25	.50
32 Seppo Repo	.25	.50
33 Esa Peltonen	.25	.50
34 Juhani Tamminen	.50	1.00
35 Matti Murto	.25	.50
36 Harri Linnonmaa	.25	.50
37 Gennadij Lapsjenkov	.50	1.00
38 Pjotr Zjulin	.25	.50
39 Vladimir Merinov	.25	.50
40 Sergej Tyznych	1.00	2.00
41 Valerij Kostin	.25	.50
42 Valerij Nikitin	.50	1.00
43 Sergej Gusev	.50	1.00
44 Valentin Kozin	.25	.50
45 Viktor Liksiutkin	.25	.50
46 Alexander Golikov	.50	1.00
47 Viktor Zhluktov	.50	1.00
48 Anatolij Frolov	.75	1.50
49 Vladimir Golikov	1.00	2.00
50 Nikolaj Epstein	.25	.50
51 Alexander Kasjajev	.25	.50
52 Alexander Sidelnikov	1.00	2.00
53 Valerij Kuzmin	.50	1.00
54 Viktor Kuznetsov	.50	1.00
55 Jurij Terechin	.30	.75
56 Jurij Tjitjurin	.30	.75
57 Jurij Sjatavalov	.30	.75
58 Vjatjeslav Anissin	.30	.75
59 Alexander Bodunov	.50	1.00
60 Jurij Lebedev	.75	1.50
61 Igor Dmitriev	2.00	4.00
62 Konstantin Klimov	.30	.75
63 Sergej Kapustin	.30	.75
64 Vladimir Repnjov	.30	.75
65 Jevgenij Kucharzj	.30	.75
66 Boris Kulagin	1.00	2.00
67 Viktor Afonin	.25	.50
68 Juris Liberts	.30	.75
69 Igor Kobzev	.30	.75
70 Valerij Odintsov	.30	.75
71 Vjatjeslav Nazarov	.50	1.00
72 Andris Hendelis	.30	.75
73 Alexander Sokolovskij	.30	.75
74 Michail Denisov	.30	.75
75 Helmut Balderis	2.00	4.00
76 Vladimir Sorokin	.25	.50
77 Vladimir Sernjajev	.25	.50
78 Viktor Veriznikov	.25	.50
79 Vladimir Markov	.25	.50
80 Viktor Tichonov	2.50	5.00
81 Edgar Rosenberg	.25	.50
82 Alexander Kotomkin	.25	.50
03 Vladimir Astafjev	.50	1.00
84 Alexander Kulikov	.25	.50
85 Sergej Mosjkarov	.25	.50
86 Vjatjeslav Usjmakov	.25	.50
87 Jurij Fjodorov	.50	1.00
88 Victor Dobrochotov	.25	.50
89 Vitalij Krajov	.25	.50
90 Alexej Masjin	.25	.50
91 Vladimir Orlov	.25	.50
92 Vladimir Smagin	.25	.50
93 Alexander Usov	.25	.50
94 Alexander Fedotov	.50	1.00
95 Alexander Prilepskij	.25	.50
96 Alexander Rogov	.25	.50
97 Seppo Ahokainen	.25	.50
98 Lasse Oksanen	.25	.50
99 Jorma Peltonen	.50	1.00
100 Henry Leppa	.25	.50
101 Seppo Suoraniemi	.25	.50
102 Timi Sutinen	.25	.50
103 Jorma Valtonen	.50	1.00
104 Antti Leppanen	.25	.50
105 Pekka Marjamaki	.25	.50
106 Juoko Oystila	.25	.50
107 Seppo Lindstrom	.25	.50
108 Veli-Pekka Ketola	.75	1.50
109 Jiri Holecek	.50	1.00
110 Jiri Kochta	.25	.50
111 Josef Horesovsky	.25	.50
112 Jaroslav Sima	.25	.50
113 Frantisek Vorlicek	.25	.50
114 Vladimir Kostka	.25	.50
115 Jaroslav Holik	.30	.75
116 Jiri Holik	.50	1.00
117 Jan Suchy	.30	.75
118 Josef Augusta,	.25	.50
119 Miroslav Dvorak	.50	1.00
120 Jan Hrbaty	.25	.50
121 AIK	.25	.50
122 If Bjorkloven	.25	.50
123 Brynas IF	.25	.50
124 Djurgardens IF	.25	.50
125 Farjestads BK	.25	.50
126 IF Karlskoga	.25	.50
127 Leksands IF	.25	.50
128 MoDo	.25	.50
129 Mora IK	.25	.50
130 Skelleftea AIK	.25	.50
131 Sodertalje SK	.25	.50
132 Timra IK	.25	.50
133 Tingsryds AIF	.25	.50
134 V. Frolunda IF	.25	.50
135 Vasteras IK	.25	.50
136 Orebro IK	.25	.50
137 Christer Abrahamsson	.75	1.50
138 Christer Andersson	.25	.50
139 Mikael Collin	.50	1.00
140 Bjorn Fagerlund	.25	.50
141 Christer Grahn	.50	1.00
142 Kenneth Holmstedt	.25	.50
143 Goran Hogosta	.50	1.00
144 Bert Jattne	.25	.50
145 Curt Larsson	.30	.75
146 Ivar Larsson	.25	.50
147 Wille Lofqvist	.50	1.00
148 Peder Nilsson	.25	.50
149 Christer Sehlstedt	.25	.50
150 Krister Sterner	.30	.75
151 Christer Stahl	.25	.50
152 Sune Odling	.25	.50
153 Thommy Abrahamsson	.50	1.00
154 Gunnar Andersson	.25	.50
155 Jan Andersson	.25	.50
156 Leif Andersson	.25	.50
157 Sture Andersson	.25	.50
158 Tommy Andersson	.25	.50
159 Sten Ake Bark	.25	.50
160 Roger Bergman	.25	.50
161 Roland Bond	.25	.50
162 Arne Carlsson	.25	.50
163 Thomas Carlsson	.25	.50
164 Lasse Danielsson	.25	.50
165 Ake Danielsson	.25	.50
166 Kenneth Ekman	.25	.50
167 Lars Erik Esbjors	.25	.50
168 Soren Gunnarsson	.25	.50
169 Mats Hysing	.25	.50
170 Bjorn Johansson	.25	.50
171 Martin Johansson	.25	.50
172 Jan Kock	.25	.50
173 Hakan Lindgren	.25	.50
174 Larsake Lundell	.25	.50
175 Mats Lundmark	.25	.50
176 Kjell-Rune Milton	.25	.50
177 Jan Erik Nilsson	.25	.50
178 Lars Goran Nilsson	.25	.50
179 Hakan Nygren	.25	.50
180 Jan Olsson	.25	.50
181 Jorgen Palm	.25	.50
182 Dennis Pettersson	.25	.50
183 Stefan Pettersson	.25	.50
184 Anders Rylin	.25	.50
185 Stig Salming	.30	.75
186 Nils-Olof Schilstrom	.25	.50
187 Jan Erik Silfverberg	.25	.50
188 Lars Erik Sjoberg	1.50	3.00
189 Karl-Johan Sundqvist	.25	.50
190 Jan-Olof Svensson	.25	.50
191 Leif Svensson	.25	.50
192 Tord Svensson	.25	.50
193 Sverker Torstensson	.25	.50
194 Mats Walltin	.25	.50
195 Ulf Weinstock	.25	.50
196 Jan Ove Wiberg	.25	.50
197 Lars Zetterstrom	.25	.50
198 Stig Ostling	.30	.75
199 Hans Andersson	.25	.50
200 Kent-Erik Andersson	.25	.50
201 Kjell Andersson	.25	.50
202 Ulf Barrefjord	.25	.50
203 Kent Bengtsson	.25	.50
204 Bo Berggren	.25	.50
205 Kjell Brus	.25	.50
206 Per-Olof Brasar	.75	1.50
207 Borje Burlin	.25	.50
208 Per Backman	.25	.50
209 Stefan Canderyd	.25	.50
210 Hans Carlsson	.25	.50
211 Hakan Dahlov	.25	.50
212 Rolf Edberg	.25	.50
213 Ake Eklof	.25	.50
214 Roland Eriksson	.25	.50
215 Conny Evensson	.50	1.00
216 Svante Granholm	.25	.50
217 Peter Gudmundsson	.25	.50
218 Hans Hansson	.25	.50
219 Anders Hedberg	2.00	4.00
220 Henric Hedlund	.25	.50
221 Nils Arne Hedqvist	.25	.50
222 Leif Henriksson	.25	.50
223 Leif Holmgren	.25	.50
224 Sven-Ake Jacobsson	.25	.50
225 Hans Jax	.25	.50
226 Christer Johansson	.25	.50
227 Gunnar Johansson	.25	.50
228 Lars Erik Johansson	.25	.50
229 Stig-Goran Johansson	.25	.50
230 Soren Johansson	.25	.50
231 Bengt Goran Karlsson	.25	.50
232 Bengt-Ake Karlsson	.25	.50
233 Martin Karlsson	.25	.50
234 Stefan Karlsson	.25	.50
235 Jan-Olov Kroon	.25	.50
236 Dan Labraaten	.75	1.50
237 Dan Landegren	.25	.50
238 Kjell Landstrom	.25	.50
239 Ove Larsson	.25	.50
240 Stig Larsson	.25	.50
241 Hans Lindberg	.25	.50
242 Mats Lindh	.25	.50
243 Willy Lindstrom	.50	1.00
244 Orjan Lindstrom	.25	.50
245 Christer Lundberg	.25	.50
246 Lars-Gunnar Lundberg	.25	.50-
247 Per Lundqvist	.25	.50
248 Arne Lundstrom	.50	1.00
249 Fhinn Lundstrom	.25	.50
250 Bengt Lovgren	.25	.50
251 Ulf Martensson	.25	.50
252 Par Marts	.25	.50
253 Tadeusz Niedomysl	.25	.50
254 Hardy Nilsson	.25	.50
255 Lars Goran Nilsson	.25	.50
256 Ulf Nilsson	2.00	4.00
257 Anders Nordin	.25	.50
258 Nils-Olof Olsson	.25	.50
259 Bjorn Palmqvist	.25	.50
260 Kent Persson	.25	.50
261 Hakan Pettersson	.25	.50
262 Sven-Ake Rudby	.25	.50
263 Benny Runesson	.25	.50
264 Jan Roger Strand	.25	.50
265 Ake Soderberg	.50	1.00
266 Dan Soderstrom	.25	.50
267 Ulf Torstensson	.25	.50
268 Claes Goran Wallin	.25	.50
269 Hakan Wickberg	.25	.50
270 Kjell Arne Wickstrom	.25	.50
271 Per Allan Wickstrom	.25	.50
272 Dick Yderstrom	.25	.50
273 Mats Ahlberg	.30	.75
274 Olle Ahman	.25	.50
275 Lars Oberg	.25	.50
276 Jan Ostling	.25	.50
277 Akning	.25	.50
278 Akning	.25	.50
279 Akning	.25	.50
280 Skott	.25	.50
281 Skott	.25	.50
282 Skott	.25	.50
283 Puckforing	.25	.50
284 Tekning	.25	.50
285 Malvaktsspel	.50	1.00
286 Malvaktsspel	.50	1.00
287 Forsvarsspel	.25	.50
288 Forsvarsspel	.25	.50
289 Forsvarsspel	.25	.50
290 Forsvarsspel	.25	.50
291 Forsvarsspel	.25	.50
292 Forsvarsspel	.25	.50
293 Forsvarsspel	.25	.50
294 Forsvarsspel	.25	.50
295 Forsvarsspel	.25	.50
296 Forsvarsspel	.25	.50
297 Forsvarsspel	.25	.50
298 Forsvarsspel	.25	.50
299 Forsvarsspel	.25	.50
300 Forsvarsspel	.25	.50
301 Forsvarsspel	.25	.50
302 Forsvarsspel	.25	.50
303 Anfallsspel	.25	.50
304 Anfallsspel	.25	.50
305 Anfallsspel	.25	.50
306 Anfallsspel	.25	.50
307 Anfallsspel	.25	.50
308 Anfallsspel	.25	.50
309 Anfallsspel	.25	.50
310 Anfallsspel	.25	.50
311 Anfallsspel	.25	.50
312 Anfallsspel	.25	.50
313 Inge Hammarstrom	1.00	2.00
314 Borje Salming	3.00	6.00
315 Thommie Bergman	1.25	2.50
316 Leif Holmqvist	.50	1.00
317 Ulf Sterner	.25	.50
318 Tord Lundstrom	.25	.50
319 Tre Kroner puzzle	.25	.50
320 Tre Kroner puzzle	.25	.50
321 Tre Kroner puzzle	.25	.50
322 Tre Kroner puzzle	.25	.50
323 Tre Kroner puzzle	.25	.50
324 Tre Kroner puzzle	.25	.50

1974 Swedish Semic World Championship Stickers

12. Anders Hedberg

This 100-sticker set featuring World Championship players was produced by Semic of Sweden. The stickers measure approximately 2" by 3", and were designed to be placed on one of four team-specific posters. The cards were issued in sheets of two.

COMPLETE SET (100)	40.00	80.00
1 Christer Abrahamsson	.75	1.50
2 William Lofqvist	.50	1.00
3 Arne Carlsson	.25	.50
4 Lars-Erik Sjoberg	1.00	2.00
5 Bjorn Johansson	.25	.50
6 Tommy Abrahamsson	.50	1.00
7 Karl-Johan Sundqvist	.25	.50
8 Ulf Nilsson	2.00	4.00
9 Hakan Wickberg	.25	.50
10 Dan Soderstrom	.25	.50
11 Mats Ahlberg	.30	.75
12 Anders Hedberg	2.00	4.00
13 Dick Yderstrom	.25	.50
14 Stefan Karlsson	.25	.50
15 Roland Bond	.25	.50
16 Kjell-Rune Milton	.25	.50
17 Willy Lindstrom	.50	1.00
18 Mats Waltin	.25	.50
19 Lars-Goran Nilsson	.25	.50
20 Bjorn Palmquist	.25	.50
21 Stig-Goran Johansson	.25	.50
22 Bo Berggren	.25	.50
23 Dan Labraaten	.75	1.50
24 Curt Larsson	.30	.75
25 Mats Lindh	.25	.50
26 Vladislav Tretiak	7.50	15.00
27 Alexander Ragulin	.50	1.00
28 Vladimir Luttjenko	.50	1.00
29 Gennadij Tsygankov	.50	1.00
30 Alexander Gusev	.50	1.00
31 Jevgenij Poladiev	.25	.50
32 Jurij Ljapkin	.50	1.00
33 Boris Michailov	2.00	4.00
34 Valeri Kharlamov	3.00	10.00
35 Vladimir Petrov	2.00	3.00
36 Alexander Maltsev	2.00	4.00
37 Vladimir Sjadrin	.30	.75
38 Alexander Yakusjev	2.00	4.00
39 Alexander Martynjuk	.30	.75
40 Jurij Lebedev	.75	1.50
41 Alexander Bodunov	.50	1.00
42 Anatolij Firsov	.75	1.50
43 Vitalij Davydov	.30	.75
44 Vjateslav Starsjinov	.30	.75
45 Viktor Kuzkin	.25	.50
46 Igor Romitjevskij	.25	.50
47 Jevgenij Zimin	.30	.75
48 Jevgenij Misjakov	.50	1.00
49 Vladimir Vikulov	.30	.75
50 Viktor Konovalenko	.50	1.00
51 Jiri Holecek	.50	1.00
52 Frantisek Pospisil	.30	.75
53 Jiri Bubla	.50	1.00
54 Josef Horesovsky	.25	.50
55 Oldrich Machac	.25	.50
56 Vladimir Martinec	.25	.50
57 Vaclav Nedomansky	.75	1.50
58 Jiri Kochta	.25	.50
59 Milan Novy	.50	1.00
60 Jaroslav Holik	.30	.75
61 Jiri Holik	.50	1.00
62 Jiri Klapac	.25	.50
63 Richard Farda	.30	.75
64 Bohuslav Stastny	.30	.75
65 Jiri Novak	.25	.50
66 Ivan Hlinka	.30	.75
67 Jan Suchy	.30	.75
68 Vladimir Bednar	.25	.50
69 Rudolf Tajcnar	.25	.50
70 Josef Cerny	.25	.50
71 Jan Havel	.30	.75
72 Marcel Sakac	.25	.50
73 Frantisek Pancharek	.25	.50
74 Bedrich Brunchk	.25	.50
75 Edvard Novak	.25	.50
76 Jorma Valtonen	.50	1.00
77 Seppo Lindstrom	.25	.50
78 Pekka Marjamaki	.25	.50
79 Pekka Rautakallio	.75	1.50
80 Heikki Riihiranta	.50	1.00
81 Seppo Suoraniemi	.25	.50
82 Jouko Oystila	.25	.50
83 Veli-Pekka Ketola	.75	1.50
84 Henry Leppa	.25	.50
85 Harri Linnonmaa	.25	.50
86 Matti Murto	.25	.50
87 Lasse Oksanen	.25	.50
88 Esa Peltonen	.25	.50
89 Seppo Repo	.25	.50
90 Raimo Suoniemi	.25	.50
91 Timo Sutinen	.25	.50
92 Juhani Tamminen	.50	1.00
93 Leo Seppanen	.25	.50
94 Hannu Haapalainen	.25	.50
95 Pertti Valkeapaa	.25	.50
96 Sakari Ahlberg	.25	.50
97 Antti Leppanen	.25	.50
98 Kalevi Numminen	.25	.50
99 Lauri Mononen	.25	.50
100 Ilpo Koskela	.30	.75
NNO Valeri Kharlamov poster		
NNO Vaclav Nedomansky poster		
NNO Ulf Nilsson poster		
NNO Timo Sutinen poster		

1981 Swedish Semic Hockey VM Stickers

This 144-sticker set was released in conjunction with the 1981 World Championships. The stickers, which measure 3" by 2 1/8", feature a color photo on the front along with the player name, country and national flag. The backs contain the card number and a remainder to place the stickers in the special set album (which retails now in the $25 range). The set is notable for the inclusion of Glenn Anderson in his RC year, as well as Mats Naslund and Neal Broten prior to their RCs. The set also features members of the American "Miracle On Ice" Olympic team; in some cases, these are the only "legitimate" card-like elements of players such as Mike Eruzione, Buzz Schneider, etc.

COMPLETE SET (144)	50.00	125.00
1 Goran Hogosta	.20	.50
2 Tomas Jonsson	.20	.50
3 Ulf Weinstock	.08	.25
4 Goran Nilsson	.08	.25
5 Jan Eriksson	.08	.25
6 Tommy Samuelsson	.08	.25
7 Mats Waltin	.08	.25
8 Peter Helander	.08	.25
9 Per Lundqvist	.08	.25
10 Conny Silfverberg	.08	.25
11 Mats Naslund	2.00	5.00
12 Lennart Norberg	.08	.25
13 Bengt Lundholm	.40	1.00
14 Leif Holmgren	.08	.25
15 Bo Berglund	.40	1.00
16 Dan Soderstrom	.08	.25
17 Lars Molin	.30	.75
18 Tore Oqvist	.08	.25
19 Ari Hellgren	.08	.25
20 Hannu Lassila	.08	.25
21 Kari Eloranta	.40	1.00
22 Lasse Litma	.08	.25
23 Seppo Suoraniemi	.08	.25
24 Tapio Levo	.20	.50
25 Timo Nummelin	.08	.25
26 Reijo Ruotsalainen	.60	1.50
27 Markku Kiimalainen	.08	.25
28 Mikko Leinonen	.30	.75
29 Reijo Leppanen	.08	.25
30 Hannu Koskinen	.08	.25
31 Timo Susi	.08	.25
32 Jukka Porvari	.08	.25
33 Arto Javanainen	.08	.25
34 Juhanni Tamminen	.40	1.00
35 Pertti Koivulahti	.08	.25
36 Antero Lehtonen	.08	.25
37 Vladislav Tretiak	4.00	10.00
38 Vladimir Mysjkin	.60	1.50
39 Slava Fetisov	2.50	6.00
40 Vladimir Luttjenko	.30	.75
41 Sergei Babinov	.20	.50
42 Vasilij Pervuchin	.30	.75
43 Sergej Starikov	.30	.75
44 Zinetula Biljaletdinov	.30	.75
45 Vladimir Krutov	2.00	5.00
46 Alexander Maltsev	1.25	3.00
47 Jurij Lebedev	.30	.75
48 Viktor Tiumenev	.20	.50
49 Nikolaj Drozdetskij	.08	.25
50 Valeri Kharlamov	2.50	6.00
51 Sergej Makarov	2.00	5.00
52 Vladimir Golikov	.30	.75
53 Alexander Skvortsov	.20	.50
54 Michail Varnakov	.30	.75
55 Jiri Kralik	.20	.50
56 Jaromir Sindel	.60	1.50
57 Miroslav Dvorak	.30	.75
58 Frantisek Kaberle	.20	.50
59 Arnold Kadlec	.20	.50
60 Jan Neliba	.08	.25
61 Radoslav Svoboda	.08	.25
62 Jaroslav Lycka	.08	.25
63 Milan Novy	.40	1.00
64 Jaroslav Pouzar	.40	1.00
65 Miroslav Frycer	.60	1.50
66 Karel Holy	.08	.25
67 Ladislav Svozil	.08	.25
68 Marian Bezak	.08	.25
69 Jindrich Kokrment	.08	.25
70 Jiri Lala	.30	.75
71 Ludos Penicka	.08	.25
72 Ivan Hlinka	.75	2.00
73 Wayne Stephenson	.75	2.00
74 Ron Paterson	.30	.75
75 Warren Anderson	.30	.75
76 Brad Pirie	.30	.75
77 Randy Gregg	.60	1.50
78 Tim Watters	.40	1.00
79 Joe Grant	.30	.75
80 Don Spring	.30	.75
81 Ron Davidson	.30	.75
82 Glenn Anderson	4.00	10.00
83 Kevin Maxwell	.30	.75
84 Jim Nill	.40	1.00
85 John Devaney	.30	.75
86 Paul MacLean	.60	1.50
87 Dan D'Alvise	.30	.75
88 Ken Berry	.30	.75
89 David Hindmarch	.30	.75
90 Kevin Primeau	.40	1.00
91 Steve Janaszak	2.00	5.00
92 Bob Suter	2.00	5.00
93 Ken Morrow	2.00	5.00
94 Mike Ramsey	2.00	5.00
95 Bill Baker	2.00	5.00
96 Dave Christian	2.00	5.00
97 Les Auge	.40	1.00
98 Dave Silk	2.00	5.00
99 Neal Broten	2.00	5.00
100 Mark Johnson	2.00	5.00
101 Steve Christoff	2.00	5.00
102 Mark Pavelich	2.00	5.00
103 Eric Strobel	2.00	5.00
104 Mike Eruzione	10.00	25.00
105 Rob McClanahan	2.00	5.00
106 Buzz Schneider	2.00	5.00
107 Phil Verchota	2.00	5.00
108 John Harrington	2.00	5.00
109 Leif Holmqvist	.40	1.00
110 Kjell Svensson	.30	.75
111 Roland Stoltz	.08	.25
112 Bert-Ola Nordlander	.08	.25
113 Nils Johansson	.08	.25
114 Lennart Svedberg	.20	.50
115 Ulf Sterner	.08	.25
116 Hakan Wickberg	.08	.25
117 Tord Lundstrom	.08	.25
118 Carl-Goran Oberg	.08	.25
119 Eilert Maatta	.08	.25
120 Lars-Goran Nilsson	.08	.25
121 Nils Nilsson	.08	.25
122 Hans Oberg	.08	.25
123 Lars-Erik Lundvall	.08	.25
124 Sven Tumba Johansson	.20	.50
125 Lars Bjorn	.08	.25
126 Ronald Pettersson	.08	.25
127 World Championships 1981	.08	.25
128 Sweden	.08	.25
129 Finland	.08	.25
130 Soviet Union	.08	.25
131 CSSR	.08	.25
132 Canada	.30	.75
133 U.S.A.	.30	.75
134 West Germany	.08	.25
135 Holland	.08	.25
136 Referee's Signs	.08	.25
137 Referee's Signs	.08	.25
138 Referee's Signs	.08	.25
139 Referee's Signs	.08	.25
140 Referee's Signs	.08	.25
141 Referee's Signs	.08	.25
142 Referee's Signs	.08	.25
143 Referee's Signs	.08	.25
144 Referee's Signs	.08	.25

1982 Swedish Semic VM Stickers

This 162-sticker set was released in 1982 to commemorate the World Championships held in Helsinki and Tampere, Finland. The stickers measure 3" by 2 1/8" and feature color photos along with the player's name and emblem (national or NHL) on the front. The backs have the sticker number, along with text in both Finnish and Swedish. The set does not include any North American-born NHLers, but does have several prominent Swedish NHL stars, including Hakan Loob, Mats Naslund, and Kent Nilsson.

COMPLETE SET (162)	24.00	60.00
1 Peter Lindmark	.40	1.00
2 Gote Walitalo	.08	.25
3 Gunnar Leidborg	.08	.25
4 Goran Lindblom	.08	.25
5 Thomas Eriksson	.08	.25
6 Mats Waltin	.08	.25
7 Jan Eriksson	.08	.25
8 Mats Thelin	.30	.75
9 Peter Helander	.08	.25
10 Tommy Samuelsson	.08	.25
11 Bo Ericsson	.08	.25
12 Peter Andersson	.20	.50
13 Mats Naslund	2.00	5.00
14 Ulf Isaksson	.08	.25
15 Patrik Sundstrom	.75	2.00
16 Peter Sundstrom	.60	1.50
17 Thomas Rundqvist	.30	.75
18 Mats Ulander	.08	.25
19 Tommy Morth	.08	.25
20 Ove Olsson	.08	.25
21 Rolf Edberg	.08	.25
22 Hakan Loob	1.50	4.00
23 Leif Holmgren	.40	1.00
24 Jan Erixon	.60	1.50
25 Harald Luckner	.08	.25
26 Hannu Kamppuri	.40	1.00
27 Hannu Issila	.20	.50
28 Kari Heikkila	.08	.25
29 Timo Nummelin	.08	.25
30 Pertti Lehtonen	.08	.25
31 Raimo Hirvonen	.08	.25
32 Seppo Suoraniemi	.08	.25
33 Juha Huikari	.08	.25
34 Hannu Helander	.08	.25
35 Lasse Litma	.08	.25
36 Hakan Hjerpe	.08	.25
37 Kari Jalonen	.20	.50
38 Arto Javanainen	.08	.25
39 Jari Lindgren	.08	.25
40 Markku Kiimalainen	.08	.25
41 Jarmo Makitalo	.08	.25
42 Jorma Sevon	.08	.25
43 Erkki Laine	.08	.25
44 Hannu Koskinen	.08	.25
45 Reijo Leppanen	.08	.25
46 Pekka Arbelius	.08	.25
47 Markku Hakulinen	.08	.25
48 Timo Susi	.08	.25
49 Esa Peltonen	.08	.25
50 Juhani Tamminen	.40	1.00
51 Vladislav Tretiak	4.00	10.00
52 Vladimir Mysjkin	.30	.75
53 Slava Fetisov	2.00	5.00
54 Sergej Babinov	.20	.50
55 Vasilij Pervuchin	.20	.50
56 Valerij Vasiljev	.30	.75
57 Alexei Kasatonov	.75	2.00
58 Zinetula Biljaletdinov	.40	1.00
59 Sergej Starikov	.30	.75
60 Sergej Makarov	1.25	3.00
61 Sergej Sjepelev	.30	.75
62 Vladimir Krutov	1.25	3.00
63 Nikolaj Drozdetskij	.30	.75
64 Viktor Zjluktov	.20	.50
65 Viktor Sjalimov	.20	.50
66 Vladimir Golikov	.20	.50
67 Aleksandr Maltsev	1.00	2.50
68 Andrej Khomutov	.75	2.00
69 Sergej Svetlov	.20	.50
70 Helmut Balderis	.30	.75
71 Sergej Kapustin	.20	.50
72 Vladimir Zubkov	.20	.50
73 Aleksandr Kozjevnikov	.20	.50
74 Jurij Lebedev	.20	.50
75 Nikolaj Makarov	.20	.50
76 Jiri Kralik	.20	.50
77 Karel Lang	.20	.50
78 Jaromir Sindel	.40	1.00
79 Miroslav Horava	.20	.50
80 Milan Chalupa	.20	.50
81 Stanislav Hajdusek	.08	.25
82 Arnold Kadlec	.20	.50
83 Miroslav Dvorak	.20	.50
84 Jan Neliba	.08	.25
85 Petr Misek	.08	.25
86 Eduard Uvira	.08	.25
87 Milan Novy	.20	.50
88 Frantisek Cerny	.20	.50
89 Jiri Lala	.20	.50
90 Jindrich Kokrment	.08	.25
91 Frantisek Cernik	.20	.50
92 Darius Rusnak	.08	.25
93 Dusan Pasek	.20	.50
94 Lubomir Penicka	.08	.25
95 Jaroslav Korbela	.08	.25
96 Peter Ihnacak	.40	1.00
97 Jaroslav Hrdina	.08	.25
98 Igor Liba	.20	.50
99 Peter Slania	.08	.25
100 Vincent Lukac	.08	.25
101 Erich Weishaupt	.20	.50
102 Bernhard Engelbrecht	.20	.50
103 Robert Murray	.20	.50
104 Peter Gailer	.08	.25
105 Udo Kiessling	.20	.50
106 Harold Kreis	.20	.50
107 Joachim Reil	.08	.25
108 Harald Krull	.08	.25
109 Ulrich Egen	.08	.25
110 Marcus Kuhl	.08	.25
111 Peter Schiller	.08	.25
112 Erich Kuhnhackl	.20	.50
113 Holger Meitinger	.08	.25
114 Ernst Hofner	.08	.25
115 Vladimir Vacatko	.08	.25
116 Manfred Wolf	.08	.25
117 Johann Morz	.08	.25
118 Franz Reindl	.08	.25
119 Helmut Steiger	.08	.25
120 Georg Holzmann	.08	.25
121 Roy Roedger	.08	.25
122 Jim Corsi	.40	1.00
123 Nick Sanza	.08	.25
124 Guido Tenisi	8.00	20.00
125 Erwin Kostner	.08	.25
126 Mike Amodeo	.20	.50
127 John Bellio	.08	.25
128 Dave Tomassoni	.08	.25
129 Daniel Pupillo	.08	.25
130 Giulio Francella	.08	.25
131 Fabio Polloni	.08	.25
132 Adolf Insam	.08	.25
133 Patrick Dell'Jannone	.08	.25
134 Rick Bragnalo	.08	.25
135 Michael Mair	.08	.25
136 Alberto DiFazio	.08	.25
137 Cary Farelli	.08	.25
138 Tom Milani	.08	.25
139 Martin Pavlu	.08	.25
140 Bob De Piero	.08	.25
141 Grant Goegan	.08	.25
142 Jerry Ciarcia	.08	.25
143 Borje Salming	2.00	5.00
144 Lars Lindgren	.20	.50
145 Ulf Nilsson	.75	2.00
146 Bengt-Ake Gustavsson	.60	1.50
147 Kent Nilsson	1.50	4.00
148 Thomas Gradin	1.25	3.00
149 Lars Molin	.30	.75
150 Thomas Steen	1.25	3.00
151 Bengt Lundholm	.30	.75
152 Jorgen Pettersson	.30	.75
153 Jukka Porvari	.20	.50
154 Tapio Levo	.20	.50
155 Reijo Ruotsalainen	.30	.75
156 Matti Hagman	.30	.75
157 Risto Siltanen	.30	.75
158 Ilkka Sinisalo	.40	1.00
159 Markus Mattsson	.30	.75
160 Mikko Leinonen	.20	.50
161 Pekka Rautakallio	.40	1.00
162 Veli-Pekka Ketola	.40	1.00

1983-84 Swedish Semic Elitserien

16. Per-Erik Eklund

Card fronts feature action photos from players in the Swedish Elite League. Many players have cards in this set that predate their NHL Rookie Cards, which make for unique and challenging collectibles.

COMPLETE SET (243)	24.00	60.00
1 Gunnar Leidborg	.20	.50
2 Peter Aslin	.40	1.00
3 Mats Thelin	.40	1.00
4 Jan Eriksson	.08	.25
5 Hans Cederholm	.08	.25
6 Bo Ericsson	.08	.25
7 Bjorn Hellman	.08	.25
8 Tomas Nord	.08	.25
9 Anders Wallin	.08	.25
10 Mats Alba	.08	.25
11 Ronny Jansson	.08	.25
12 Roger Lindstrom	.08	.25
13 Mats Hessel	.08	.25
14 Peter Gradin	.08	.25
15 Mats Ulander	.08	.25
16 Per-Erik Eklund	1.25	3.00
17 Ulf Isaksson	.08	.25
18 Rolf Eriksson	.08	.25
19 Michael Wikstrom	.08	.25
20 Leif Holmgren	.08	.25
21 Per Martinelle	.08	.25
22 Tommy Lehmann	.30	.75
23 Hans Norberg	.08	.25
24 Jan Ericsson	.08	.25
25 Per Backman	.08	.25
26 Gote Walitalo	.08	.25
27 Jakob Gustavsson	.08	.25
28 Staffan Andersson	.08	.25
29 Torbjorn Andersson	.08	.25
30 Anders Bostrom	.08	.25
31 Jan Lindholm	.08	.25
32 Ulf Nilsson	2.00	5.00
33 Par Sjolander	.08	.25
34 Lennart Dahlberg	.08	.25
35 Rolf Berglund	.08	.25
36 Patrik Aberg	.08	.25
37 Tom Eklund	.08	.25
38 Stefan Nilsson	.08	.25
39 Matti Pauna	.08	.25
40 Jan Lundstrom	.08	.25
41 Mikael Andersson	1.25	3.00
42 Hans Edlund	.08	.25
43 Jon Lundstrom	.08	.25
44 Tony Lundgren	.08	.25
45 Ulf Wikgren	.08	.25
46 Tomas Hedin	.08	.25
47 Lars-Gunnar Pettersson	.08	.25
48 Peter Edstrom	.08	.25
49 Tore Okvist	.08	.25
50 Tommy Sandlin	.30	.75
51 Lars Eriksson	.08	.25
52 Ake Lilljebjorn	.20	.50
53 Anders Backstrom	.08	.25
54 Goran Grundstrom	.08	.25
55 Jan Kock	.08	.25
56 Gunnar Persson	.08	.25
57 Torbjorn Mattsson	.08	.25
58 Stig Ostling	.08	.25
59 Hans Johansson	.08	.25
60 Robert Nordmark	.40	1.00
61 Mikael Sandstrom	.08	.25
62 Anders Carlsson	.08	.25
63 Christer Andersson	.08	.25
64 Per Hedenstrom	.08	.25
65 Bjorn Akerblom	.08	.25
66 Conny Silfverberg	.08	.25
67 Jonny Stridh	.08	.25
68 Goran Sjoberg	.08	.25
69 Kenneth Andersson	.08	.25
70 Fredrik Lundstrom	.08	.25
71 Henrik Cedergren	.08	.25
72 Tomas Sandstrom	1.25	3.00
73 Anders Huss	.08	.25
74 Stig Salming	.20	.50
75 Rolf Ridderwall	.40	1.00
76 Bo Larsson	.08	.25
77 Mikael Westling	.08	.25
78 Tord Nansen	.08	.25
79 Tommy Albelin	1.25	3.00
80 Orvar Stambert	.08	.25
81 Karl-Erik Lilja	.08	.25
82 Mats Waltin	.08	.25
83 Stefan Perlstrom	.08	.25
84 Michael Thelven	.20	.50
85 Stefan Jansson	.08	.25
86 Jens Ohling	.08	.25
87 Peter Nilsson	.08	.25
88 Hakan Eriksson	.08	.25
89 Jorgen Holmberg	.08	.25
90 Tommy Morth	.08	.25
91 Jan Claesson	.08	.25
92 Per Goransson	.08	.25
93 Martin Linse	.08	.25
94 Bjorn Carlsson	.08	.25
95 Hakan Sodergren	.08	.25
96 Anders Johnsson	.08	.25
97 Jan Viktorsson	.20	.50
98 Jeff Hallegard	.08	.25
99 Leif Boork	.08	.25
100 Hakan Hermansson	.08	.25
101 Thomas Blom	.08	.25
102 Christer Dalgard	.08	.25
103 Tommy Samuelsson	.08	.25
104 Lars-Goran Nilsson	.08	.25
105 Peter Andersson	.40	1.00
106 Mats Lusth	.08	.25
107 Tommy Moller	.08	.25
108 Leif Carlsson	.08	.25
109 Urban Larsson	.08	.25
110 Hakan Nordin	.08	.25
111 Harald Luckner	.08	.25
112 Thomas Rundqvist	.60	1.50
113 Kjell Dahlin	.75	2.00
114 Robin Eriksson	.08	.25
115 Jan Ingman	.08	.25
116 Stefan Persson	.08	.25
117 Peter Berndtsson	.08	.25
118 Anders Steen	.08	.25
119 Claes-Henrik Silliver	.08	.25
120 Magnus Roupe	.40	1.00
121 Jan Wickberg	.08	.25
122 Dan Mohlin	.08	.25
123 Kent Olsson	.08	.25
124 Stefan Lunner	.08	.25
125 Niklas Holmberg	.08	.25
126 Anders Alverud	.08	.25
127 Stefan Svensson	.08	.25
128 Lars Karlsson	.08	.25
129 Ulf Weinstock	.08	.25
130 Kjell Samuelsson	1.25	3.00
131 Magnus Svensson	.40	1.00
132 Ove Pettersson	.08	.25
133 Hans Eriksson	.08	.25
134 Ulf Samuelsson	1.25	3.00
135 Roland Eriksson	.08	.25
136 Kjell Bond	.08	.25
137 Per Nordlinder	.08	.25
138 Ivan Hansen	.08	.25
139 Sivert Andersson	.08	.25
140 Jonas Bergkvist	.40	1.00
141 Per-Olof Carlsson	.08	.25
142 Dan Labraaten	.60	1.50
143 Ulf Skoglund	.08	.25
144 Ove Olsson	.08	.25
145 Mikael Leek	.08	.25
146 Mats Loov	.08	.25
147 Lennart Ahlberg	.08	.25
148 Hardy Astrom	2.00	5.00
149 Anders Bergman	.08	.25
150 Per Forsberg	.08	.25
151 Sture Andersson	.08	.25
152 Mikael Good	.08	.25
153 Jan Nyman	.08	.25
154 Roger Eliasson	.08	.25
155 Jan Karlsson	.08	.25
156 Lennart Jonsson	.08	.25
157 Robert Frestadius	.08	.25
158 Juha Tuohimaa	.08	.25
159 Jerry Lundberg	.08	.25
160 Tommy Sjalin	.08	.25
161 Ulf Norberg	.08	.25
162 Michael Hjalm	.08	.25
163 Per Nilsson	.08	.25
164 Lars Nyberg	.08	.25
165 Ulf Odmark	.08	.25
166 Ingemar Strom	.08	.25
167 Erik Holmberg	.08	.25
168 Lars Bystrom	.08	.25
169 Lars Hellstrom	.08	.25
170 Henry Saleva	.08	.25
171 Hardy Nilsson	.08	.25
172 Mats Abrahamsson	.08	.25
173 Ulf Nilsson	2.00	5.00
174 Jens Johansson	.08	.25
175 Lars Marklund	.08	.25
176 Robert Ohman	.08	.25
177 Goran Lindblom	.08	.25
178 Ola Stenlund	.08	.25
179 Ulf Agren	.08	.25
180 Thomas Ahlen	.08	.25
181 Tomas Jonsson	.75	2.00
182 Mikael Granstedt	.08	.25
183 Mats Lundstrom	.08	.25
184 Per Andersson	.08	.25
185 Johnny Forsman	.10	.25
186 Lars Nystrom	.08	.25
187 Niklas Mannberg	.08	.25
188 Peter Lundmark	.75	2.00
189 Claes Lindblom	.08	.25
190 Leif Hedlund	.08	.25
191 Roland Stoltz	.08	.25
192 Martin Pettersson	.08	.25
193 Jorgen Marklund	.08	.25
194 Mats Lundstrom	.08	.25
195 Tommy Andersson	.08	.25
196 Ake Andersson	.08	.25
197 Lars Fernqvist	.08	.25
198 Anders Eldebrink	.40	1.00
199 Ulf Borg	.08	.25
200 Mats Kihlstrom	.30	.75
201 Bo Andersson	.08	.25
202 Peter Ekroth	.08	.25
203 Jukka Hirsimaki	.08	.25
204 Stefan Jonsson	.08	.25
205 Peter Loob	.20	.50
206 Tomas Jernberg	.08	.25
207 Dan Hermansson	.08	.25
208 Glenn Johansson	.08	.25
209 Leif R. Carlsson	.08	.25
210 Johan Mellstrom	.08	.25
211 Tomas Gustavsson	.08	.25
212 Olof Johansson	.08	.25
213 Peter Wallin	.08	.25
214 Hans Sarkijarvi	.08	.25
215 Reine Karlsson	.08	.25
216 Conny Jansson	.08	.25
217 Jarmo Makitalo	.08	.25
218 Mikael Johansson	.08	.25
219 Timo Lahtinen	.08	.25
220 Goran Nilsson	.08	.25
221 Joakim Hokegard	.08	.25
222 Peter Pettersson	.08	.25
223 Goran Nilsson	.08	.25
224 Jan Carlsson	.08	.25
225 Soren Johansson	.08	.25
226 Thomas Lundin	.08	.25
227 Calle Johansson	.75	2.00
228 Anders Brostrom	.08	.25
229 Stefan Larsson	.08	.25
230 Thomas Karrbrandt	.08	.25
231 Roger Hagglund	.08	.25
232 Christer Kellgren	.08	.25
233 Kent Eriksson	.08	.25
234 Mikael Andersson	1.25	3.00
235 Ove Karlsson	.08	.25
236 Peter Elander	.08	.25
237 Hans Jonsson	.08	.25
238 Hasse Sjoo	.08	.25
239 Ulf Labraaten	.08	.25
240 Jens Hellgren	.08	.25
241 Roger Ahsberg	.08	.25
242 Kurt Carlsson	.08	.25
243 Peter Gustavsson	.08	.25

1983 Swedish Semic VM Stickers

Per-Erik Eklund

COMPLETE SET (162)	40.00	80.00
1 Peter Lindmark	.40	1.00
2 Gote Walitalo	.08	.25
3 Lars Eriksson	.08	.25
4 Roger Hagglund	.08	.25
5 Thomas Eriksson	.30	.75
6 Mats Waltin	.08	.25
7 Jan Eriksson	.08	.25
8 Mats Thelin	.30	.75
9 Michael Thelven	.20	.50
10 Peter Andersson	.40	1.00
11 Bo Ericson	.08	.25
12 Bo Berglund	.20	.50
13 Tomas Sandstrom	1.25	3.00
14 Per-Erik Eklund	.75	2.00
15 Roland Eriksson	.08	.25
16 Peter Sundstrom	.40	1.00
17 Thomas Rundqvist	.60	1.50
18 Mats Ulander	.08	.25
19 Tommy Morth	.08	.25
20 Ove Olsson	.08	.25
21 Håkan Sodergren	.08	.25
22 Håkan Loob	2.00	5.00
23 Leif Holmgren	.08	.25
24 Jan Erixon	.40	1.00
25 Tom Eklund	.08	.25
26 Hannu Kamppuri	.40	1.00
27 Rauli Sohlman	.08	.25
28 Kari Takko	.40	1.00
29 Pekka Rautakallio	.40	1.00
30 Pertti Lehtonen	.08	.25
31 Hannu Haapalainen	.08	.25
32 Markus Lehto	.08	.25
33 Juha Huikari	.08	.25
34 Hannu Helander	.08	.25
35 Lasse Litma	.08	.25
36 Arto Routanen	.08	.25
37 Raimo Summanen	.20	.50
38 Arto Javaninen	.08	.25
39 Jari Lindgren	.08	.25
40 Risto Jalo	.20	.50
41 Petri Skriko	.08	.25
42 Juha Nurmi	.08	.25
43 Erkki Laine	.20	.50
44 Anssi Melametsa	.08	.25
45 Reijo Leppanen	.08	.25
46 Matti Hagman	.40	1.00
47 Kari Makkonen	.08	.25
48 Timo Susi	.08	.25
49 Harri Touhimaa	.08	.25
50 Arto Jokinen	.08	.25
51 Vladislav Tretiak	6.00	15.00
52 Vladimir Mysjkin	.40	1.00
53 Vjatjeslav Fetisov	2.00	5.00
54 Sergej Babinov	.08	.25
55 Vasilij Pervuchin	.30	.75
56 Sergej Gimajev	.08	.25
57 Aleksej Kasatonov	.40	1.00
58 Zinetula Biljaletdinov	.20	.50
59 Sergej Starikov	.08	.25
60 Sergej Makarov	2.00	5.00
61 Sergej Sjepelev	.08	.25
62 Vladimir Krutov	2.00	5.00
63 Nikolaj Drozdetskij	.08	.25
64 Viktor Zjluktov	.08	.25
65 Viktor Sjalimov	.08	.25
66 Vladimir Golikov	.08	.25
67 Aleksandr Maltsev	1.25	3.00
68 Andrej Chomutov	.40	1.00
69 Vjatjeslav Bykov	.30	.75
70 Michail Vasiljev	.08	.25
71 Sergej Kapustin	.20	.50
72 Aleksandr Gerasimov	.08	.25
73 Aleksandr Kozjevnikov	.08	.25
74 Igor Larionov	4.00	10.00
75 Vladimir Zubkov	.08	.25
76 Jiri Kralik	.08	.25
77 Karel Lang	.20	.50
78 Jaromir Sindel	.20	.50
79 Miroslav Horava	.20	.50
80 Milan Chalupa	.20	.50
81 Stanislav Hajdusek	.08	.25
82 Arnold Kadlec	.20	.50
83 Ladislav Kolda	.08	.25
84 Jaroslav Benak	.08	.25
85 Radoslav Svoboda	.08	.25
86 Eduard Uvira	.08	.25
87 Antonin Planovsky	.08	.25
88 Petr Slanina	.08	.25
89 Jiri Lala	.20	.50
90 Jindrich Kokrment	.08	.25
91 Frantisek Cernik	.08	.25
92 Darius Rusnak	.08	.25
93 Dusan Pasek	.30	.75
94 Pavel Richtr	.08	.25
95 Jaroslav Korbela	.08	.25
96 Ivan Dornic	.08	.25
97 Jiri Hrdina	.08	.25
98 Igor Liba	.20	.50
99 Jiri Dudacek	.20	.50
100 Vincent Lukac	.08	.25
101 Erich Weishaupt	.08	.25
102 Bernhard Engelbrecht	.08	.25
103 Karl-Heinz Friesen	.30	.75
104 Ignaz Berndaner	.08	.25
105 Udo Kiessling	.20	.50
106 Harold Kreis	.08	.25
107 Joachim Reil	.08	.25
108 Gerd Truntschka	.20	.50
109 Ulrich Egen	.08	.25
110 Marcus Kuhl	.08	.25
111 Peter Schiller	.08	.25
112 Erich Kühnhackl	.20	.50
113 Holger Meitinger	.08	.25
114 Ernst Hofner	.08	.25
115 Dieter Hegen	.08	.25
116 Manfred Wolf	.08	.25
117 Johann Morz	.08	.25
118 Franz Reindl	.08	.25
119 Helmut Steiger	.08	.25
120 Horst-Peter Kretschmer	.08	.25
121 Roy Roedger	.08	.25
122 Jim Corsi	.08	.25
123 Nick Sanza	.08	.25
124 Guido Tenisi	8.00	20.00
125 Erwin Kostner	.08	.25
126 Mike Amodeo	.20	.50
127 John Bellio	.08	.25
128 Dave Tomassoni	.08	.25
129 Bob Manno	.30	.75
130 Gino Pasqualotto	.08	.25
131 Fabio Polloni	.08	.25
132 Adolf Insam	.08	.25
133 Constant Priondolo	.08	.25
134 Rick Bragnalo	.08	.25
135 Michael Mair	.08	.25
136 Alberto Di Fazio	.08	.25
137 Cary Farelli	.08	.25
138 Tom Milani	.08	.25
139 Martin Pavlu	.08	.25
140 Bob De Piero	.08	.25
141 Grant Goegan	.08	.25
142 Jerry Ciarcia	.08	.25
143 Rene Bielke	.08	.25
144 Ingolf Spantig	.08	.25
145 Frank Braun	.08	.25
146 Joachim Lempio	.08	.25
147 Reinhardt Fengler	.08	.25

148 Dieter Frenzel .08 .25
149 Klaus Schroder .08 .25
150 Dietmar Peters .08 .25
151 Dieter Simon .08 .25
152 Andreas Ludwig .08 .25
153 Detlef Radant .08 .25
154 Friedhelm Bogelsack .08 .25
155 Thomas Graul .08 .25
156 Roland Peters .08 .25
157 Frank Proske .08 .25
158 Fred Bartell .08 .25
159 Harald Kuhnke .08 .25
160 Gerhard Müller .08 .25
161 Harald Bolke .08 .25
162 Dieter Kinzel .08 .25

1984-85 Swedish Semic Elitserien

This 243-sticker set captures the top players in the Swedish Eliteserien. The stickers were produced by Semic Press AB, and measure approximately 3" by 2 1/4". The fronts display a color portrait along with player name, card number and team emblem. The backs have ordering information for the set album (valued at $10) and more stickers.

COMPLETE SET (243) 20.00 50.00
1 Gunnar Leidborg .20 .50
2 Tomas Ostlund .75 2.00
3 Jan Eriksson .08 .25
4 Tomas Nord .08 .25
5 Bjorn Hellman .08 .25
6 Hans Cederholm .08 .25
7 Mats Alba .08 .25
8 Roger Hellgren .08 .25
9 Peter Zetterholm .08 .25
10 Tony Barthelsson .08 .25
11 Roger Lindstrom .08 .25
12 Mats Hessel .08 .25
13 Peter Gradin .08 .25
14 Per-Erik Eklund .75 2.00
15 Ulf Isaksson .08 .25
16 Harri Tiala .08 .25
17 Michael Wikstrom .08 .25
18 Per Backe .08 .25
19 Per Martinelle .08 .25
20 Tommy Lehmann .20 .50
21 Hans Norberg .08 .25
22 Odd Nilsson .08 .25
23 Henrik Cedergren .08 .25
24 Stefan Sandin .08 .25
25 Per Backman .08 .25
26 Gote Walitalo .08 .25
27 Jakob Gustavsson .08 .25
28 Torbjorn Andersson .08 .25
29 Anders Bostrom .08 .25
30 Jan Lindholm .08 .25
31 Lars Karlsson .08 .25
32 Rolf Berglund .08 .25
33 Lennart Dahlberg .08 .25
34 Patric Aberg .08 .25
35 Ulf Nilsson 1.50 4.00
36 Mats Jacobsson .08 .25
37 Michael Hjalm .08 .25
38 Stefan Nilsson .08 .25
39 Matti Pauna .08 .25
40 Jan Lundstrom .08 .25
41 Mikael Andersson .40 1.00
42 Hans Edlund .20 .50
43 Jon Lundstrom .08 .25
44 Tony Lundgren .08 .25
45 Ulf Wikgren .08 .25
46 Thomas Hedin .08 .25
47 Lars-Gunnar Pettersson .08 .25
48 Peter Edstrom .08 .25
49 Tommy Sandlin .20 .50
50 Lars Eriksson .08 .25
51 Ake Lilljebjorn .20 .50
52 Mats Kihlstrom .20 .50
53 Anders Backstrom .08 .25
54 Lars Ivarsson .40 1.00
55 Jan Kock .08 .25
56 Gunnar Persson .08 .25
57 Torbjorn Mattsson .08 .25
58 Per Jarnberg .08 .25
59 Hans Johansson .08 .25
60 Anders Huss .08 .25
61 Per Nilsson .08 .25
62 Owe Eriksson .08 .25
63 Christer Andersson .08 .25
64 Per Hedenstrom .08 .25
65 Jan Larsson .08 .25
66 Conny Silfverberg .08 .25
67 Jonny Stridh .08 .25
68 Erik Holmberg .08 .25
69 Kenneth Andersson .08 .25
70 Fredrik Lundstrom .08 .25
71 Peter Eriksson .08 .25
72 Peter Eriksson .08 .25
73 Stig Salming .20 .50
74 Rolf Ridderwall .40 1.00
75 Mats Ytter .08 .25
76 Michael Thelven .30 .75
77 Stefan Perlstrom .08 .25
78 Tord Nansen .08 .25
79 Tommy Albelin .75 2.00
80 Orvar Stambert .08 .25
81 Karl-Erik Lilja .08 .25
82 Kristian Henriksson .08 .25
83 Arto Blomsten .30 .75
84 Anders Johnsson .08 .25
85 Pontus Molander .08 .25
86 Jens Ohling .08 .25
87 Peter Nilsson .08 .25
88 Hakan Sodergren .08 .25
89 Jorgen Holmberg .08 .25
90 Tommy Morth .08 .25
91 Jan Claesson .08 .25
92 Per Goransson .08 .25
93 Jan Viktorsson .20 .50
94 Bjorn Carlsson .08 .25
95 Erik Ahlstrom .08 .25
96 Peter Schank .08 .25
97 Ake Eksell .08 .25
98 Gunnar Svensson .08 .25
99 Peter Lindmark .08 .25
100 Christer Dalgard .08 .25
101 Hakan Nordin .08 .25
102 Fredrik Olausson 1.25 3.00
103 Tommy Samuelsson .08 .25
104 Anders Svensson .08 .25
105 Peter Andersson .30 .75
106 Mats Lusth .08 .25
107 Tommy Moller .08 .25
108 Leif Carlsson .08 .25
109 Kent-Erik Andersson .08 .25
110 Erkki Laine .08 .25
111 Harald Luckner .08 .25
112 Staffan Lundh .08 .25
113 Kjell Dahlin .75 2.00
114 Dan Mohlin .08 .25
115 Jan Ingman .08 .25
116 Stefan Persson .40 1.00
117 Peter Berndtsson .08 .25
118 Lars Karlsson .08 .25
119 Claes-Henrik Silfver .08 .25
120 Magnus Roupe .30 .75
121 Conny Evensson .30 .75
122 Bo Larsson .08 .25
123 Hans-Goran Elo .08 .25
124 Carsten Bokstrom .08 .25
125 Claes Norstrom .08 .25
126 Alf Tornqvist .08 .25
127 Bruno Ohlzon .08 .25
128 Peter Lindgren .08 .25
129 Christian Due-Boije .20 .50
130 Tony Landeskog .08 .25
131 Tomas Lunden .08 .25
132 Lars Lindskog .08 .25
133 Anders Karlsson .08 .25
134 Morgan Craas .08 .25
135 Ulf Andersson .08 .25
136 Timo Salomaa .08 .25
137 Ulf Radbjer .08 .25
138 Hans Segerberg .08 .25
139 Roger Melin .08 .25
140 Rolf Edberg .08 .25
141 Lasse Bjork .08 .25
142 Robin Eriksson .08 .25
143 Thomas Jagenstedt .08 .25
144 Jan Lindberg .08 .25
145 Bjorn Berggren .08 .25
146 Tommy Nilsson .08 .25
147 Stefan Lunner .08 .25
148 Niklas Holmberg .08 .25
149 Anders Alverud .08 .25
150 Stefan Svensson .08 .25
151 Jussi Lepisto .08 .25
152 Kjell Samuelsson .75 2.00
153 Magnus Svensson .30 .75
154 Ove Pettersson .08 .25
155 Stefan Nilsson .08 .25
156 Jens Christiansson .08 .25
157 Orjan Lindmark .08 .25
158 Tomas Gustafsson .08 .25
159 Jan Segersten .08 .25
160 Jonas Bergqvist .40 1.00
161 Per-Olof Carlsson .08 .25
162 Hannu Oksanen .08 .25
163 Dan Labraaten .60 1.50
164 Ulf Skoglund .08 .25
165 Ove Olsson .08 .25
166 Mats Loov .08 .25
167 Hakan Olsson .08 .25
168 Carl-Erik Larsson .08 .25
169 Dan Soderstrom .08 .25
170 Mats Blomqvist .08 .25
171 Robert Skoog .08 .25
172 Lars Lindgren .08 .25
173 Robert Nordmark .30 .75
174 Kjell-Ake Johansson .08 .25
175 Kari Heikkila .08 .25
176 Torbjorn Wirf .08 .25
177 Lars Modig .08 .25
178 Bo Eriksson .08 .25
179 Roger Ohman .30 .75
180 Mats Ohman .08 .25
181 Matti Ruisma .08 .25
182 Erik Stalnacke .08 .25
183 Jari Lindgren .08 .25
184 Jens Hellgren .08 .25
185 Lars-Goran Niemi .08 .25
186 Tore Okvist .08 .25
187 Ingemar Mikko .08 .25
188 Roger Mikko .08 .25
189 Rolf Karlsson .08 .25
190 Petter Antti .08 .25
191 Johan Stromvall .08 .25
192 Tomas Backstrom .08 .25
193 Jan Nilsson .08 .25
194 Freddy Lindfors .08 .25
195 Mats Abrahamsson .08 .25
196 Ulf Nilsson 1.50 4.00
197 Goran Lindblom .08 .25
198 Thomas Ahlen .08 .25
199 Jens Johansson .08 .25
200 Lars Marklund .08 .25
201 Ola Stenlund .08 .25
202 Ulf Lindblom .08 .25
203 Olle Haggstrom .08 .25
204 Ulf Agren .08 .25
205 Mikael Granstedt .08 .25
206 Hans Nilsson .08 .25
207 Per Andersson .08 .25
208 Jonny Forsman .08 .25
209 Lars Nystrom .08 .25
210 Niklas Mannberg .08 .25
211 Peter Lundmark .40 1.00
212 Claes Lindblom .08 .25
213 Leif Hedlund .08 .25
214 Roland Stoltz .08 .25
215 Martin Pettersson .08 .25
216 Jorgen Marklund .08 .25
217 Mats Lundstrom .08 .25
218 Tommy Andersson .08 .25
219 Hardy Astrom 1.25 3.00
220 Sam Lindstahl .30 .75
221 Jari Luoma .08 .25
222 Anders Eldebrink .30 .75
223 Ulf Borg .08 .25
224 Bo Ericson .08 .25
225 Tomas Jernberg .08 .25
226 Peter Ekroth .08 .25
227 Stefan Jonsson .08 .25
228 Niklas Gallstedt .08 .25
229 Jonas Heed .08 .25
230 Jarmo Makitalo .08 .25
231 Thom Eklund .08 .25
232 Dan Hermansson .08 .25
233 Glenn Johansson .08 .25
234 Leif R. Carlsson .08 .25
235 Johan Mellstrom .08 .25
236 Niclas Lindgren .08 .25
237 Peter Wallin .08 .25
238 Hans Sarkijarvi .08 .25
239 Anders Carlsson .08 .25
240 Reine Karlsson .08 .25
241 Conny Jansson .08 .25
242 Stefan Karlsson .08 .25
243 Timo Lahtinen .08 .25

1985-86 Swedish Panini Stickers

This set of 240 stickers was produced by Panini Italy for distribution in Sweden. The stickers feature the top players of the Swedish elite league and were packaged five per pack. The 2 1/2" by 2" stickers feature a player portrait on the front. An album for housing the stickers also was available; it now trades in the $10 range. North American collectors may not rave about the player selection, but some of Sweden's best are represented including Peter Lindmark, Tomas Rundqvist and Anders Eldebrink. Some sticker are half of a larger image -- these are designated by U (upper), L (lower or left) and R (right).

COMPLETE SET (240) 25.00 60.00
1 AIK Team Emblem .08 .25
2 Per Backman .08 .25
3 Tomas Ostlund .75 2.00
4 Gunnar Leidborg .08 .25
5 Jari Munck .08 .25
6 Jan Eriksson .08 .25
7 Hans Cederholm .08 .25
8 Bjorn Hellman .08 .25
9 Tomas Ahlen .08 .25
10 Roger Hellgren .08 .25
11 Mats Alba .08 .25
12 Roger Lindstrom .08 .25
13 Team Picture Left .08 .25
14 Team Picture Right .08 .25
15 Mats Hessel .08 .25
16 Peter Gradin .08 .25
17 Thomas Bjuhr .08 .25
18 Per Martinelle .08 .25
19 Tommy Lehman .20 .50
20 Thomas Jagenstedt .08 .25
21 Hans Segerberg .08 .25
22 Odd Nilsson .08 .25
23 Bjorkloven Team Picture L .08 .25
24 Bjorkloven Team Picture U .08 .25
25 Jakob Gustavsson .08 .25
26 Gote Walitalo .08 .25
27 Torbjorn Andersson .08 .25
28 Jan Lindholm .08 .25
29 Lars Karlsson .08 .25
30 Calle Johansson .75 2.00
31 Ulf Nilsson 1.25 3.00
32 Rolf Berglund .08 .25
33 Matti Pauna .08 .25
34 Mikael Andersson .75 2.00
35 Tommy Sandlin .08 .25
36 Team Emblem .08 .25
37 Hans Edlund .08 .25
38 Ulf Dahlen 1.25 3.00
39 Mikael Hjalm .08 .25
40 Jon Lundstrom .08 .25
41 Lars-Gunnar Pettersson .08 .25
42 Peter Edstrom .08 .25
43 Tore Oqvist .08 .25
44 Par Edlund .08 .25
45 Brynas Team Emblem .08 .25
46 Stig Salming .08 .25
47 Lars Eriksson .08 .25
48 Ake Lilljebjorn .08 .25
49 Anders Backstrom .08 .25
50 Lars Ivarsson .08 .25
51 Mats Kihlstrom .08 .25
52 Jan Ove Mettavainio .08 .25
53 Gunnar Persson .08 .25
54 Torbjorn Mattsson .08 .25
55 Christer Andersson .08 .25
56 Per Hedenstrom .08 .25
57 Team Picture L .08 .25
58 Team Picture R .08 .25
59 Per Nilsson .08 .25
60 Conny Silfverberg .08 .25
61 Jonny Stridh .08 .25
62 Owe Eriksson .08 .25
63 Kenneth Andersson .08 .25
64 Erik Holmberg .08 .25
65 Joakim Pehrson .08 .25
66 Anders Huss .20 .50
67 Djurgarden Team Picture L .08 .25
68 Djurgarden Team Picture R .08 .25
69 Rolf Ridderwall .40 1.00
70 Mats Ytter .20 .50
71 Orvar Stambert .08 .25
72 Karl-Erik Lilja .08 .25
73 Arto Blomsten .20 .50
74 Stefan Perlstrom .08 .25
75 Peter Lindgren .08 .25
76 Tommy Albelin .30 .75
77 Jens Ohling .08 .25
78 Peter Nilsson .08 .25
79 Gunnar Svenson .08 .25
80 Team Emblem .08 .25
81 Jorgen Holmberg .08 .25
82 Tommy Morth .08 .25
83 Bjorn Carlsson .08 .25
84 Hakan Sodergren .20 .50
85 Anders Johnson .08 .25
86 Mikael Johansson .08 .25
87 Jan Viktorsson .08 .25
88 Erik Ahlstrom .08 .25
89 Farjestad Team Emblem .08 .25
90 Conny Evensson .20 .50
91 Peter Lindmark .60 1.50
92 Christer Dalgard .08 .25
93 Tommy Samuelsson .08 .25
94 Peter Andersson .30 .75
95 Mats Lusth .08 .25
96 Leif Karlsson .08 .25
97 Fredrik Olausson .75 2.00
98 Hakan Nordin .08 .25
99 Harald Luckner .08 .25
100 Tomas Rundqvist .20 .50
101 Team Picture L .08 .25
102 Team Picture R .08 .25
103 Jan Ingman .08 .25
104 Erkki Laine .08 .25
105 Stefan Persson .40 1.00
106 Claes-Henrik Silfver .08 .25
107 Magnus Roupe .30 .75
108 Mikael Holmberg .08 .25
109 Kent-Erik Andersson .08 .25
110 Staffan Lundh .08 .25
111 Kjell Dahlin U .20 .50
112 Kjell Dahlin L .20 .50
113 Kjell Samuelsson U .40 1.00
114 Kjell Samuelsson L .40 1.00
115 Peter Lindmark U .20 .50
116 Peter Lindmark L .20 .50
117 Pelle Lindberg U 4.00 10.00
118 Pelle Lindberg L 4.00 10.00
119 Per-Erik Eklund U .30 .75
120 Per-Erik Eklund L .30 .75
121 Anders Eldebrink L .15 .40
122 Anders Eldebrink R .15 .40
123 Michael Thelven U .15 .40
124 Michael Thelven L .15 .40
125 Dan Labraaten L .20 .50
126 Dan Labraaten R .20 .50
127 Ove Olsson L .08 .25
128 Ove Olsson R .08 .25
129 Kent-E Andersson L .08 .25
130 Kent-E Andersson R .08 .25
131 Leksand Team Emblem .08 .25
132 Dan Soderstrom .08 .25
133 Stefan Lunner .08 .25
134 Peter Aslin .40 1.00
135 Jussi Lepisto .08 .25
136 Magnus Svensson .30 .75
137 Owe Pettersson .08 .25
138 Stefan Nilsson .08 .25
139 Orjan Lindmark .08 .25
140 Tomas Nord .08 .25
141 Robert Burakovsky .20 .50
142 Jan Segersten .08 .25
143 Team Picture L .08 .25
144 Team Picture R .08 .25
145 Jonas Bergkvist .30 .75
146 Per-Olof Carlsson .08 .25
147 Dan Labraaten .40 1.00
148 Ulf Skoglund .08 .25
149 Ove Olsson .08 .25
150 Heinz Ehlers .08 .25
151 Mats Loov .08 .25
152 Jarmo Makitalo .08 .25
153 Lulea Team Picture L .08 .25
154 Lulea Team Picture R .08 .25
155 Mats Blomqvist .08 .25
156 Robert Skoog .08 .25
157 Lars Modig .08 .25
158 Kjell-Ake Johansson .08 .25
159 Bo Eriksson .08 .25
160 Robert Nordmark .20 .50
161 Kari Heikkila .08 .25
162 Lars Lindgren .08 .25
163 Roger Mikko .08 .25
164 Kari Jaako .08 .25
165 Hans Lindberg .08 .25
166 Team Emblem .08 .25
167 Petter Antti .08 .25
168 Johan Stromvall .08 .25
169 Juha Nurmi .08 .25
170 Erik Stalnacke .08 .25
171 Lars Hurtig .08 .25
172 Jari Lindgren .08 .25
173 Jens Hellgren .08 .25
174 Hans Norberg .08 .25
175 HV 71 Team Emblem .08 .25
176 Curt Lundmark .40 1.00
177 Kenneth Johansson .08 .25
178 Tomas Javeblad .08 .25
179 Nils-G Svensson .08 .25
180 Bert-Roland Naslund .08 .25
181 Kevan Beaton .08 .25
182 Jan Hedell .08 .25
183 Fredrik Stillman .15 .40
184 Kari Eloranta .30 .75
185 Klas Heed .08 .25
186 Hans Sallin .08 .25
187 Team Picture L .08 .25
188 Team Picture R .08 .25
189 Ove Tornberg .08 .25
190 Thomas Ljungberg .08 .25
191 Bengt Kinell .08 .25
192 Uno Johansson .08 .25
193 Uno Johansson .08 .25
194 Ivan Hansen .08 .25
195 Thomas Lindster .08 .25
196 Per Martinsson .08 .25
197 MoDo Team Picture L .08 .25
198 MoDo Team Picture R .08 .25
199 Anders Bergman .08 .25
200 Goran Anmark .08 .25
201 Thomas Olofsson .08 .25
202 Jorgen Palm .08 .25
203 Ulf Agren .08 .25
204 Roger Eliasson .08 .25
205 Juha Tuohimaa .08 .25
206 Jan Karlsson .08 .25
207 Lennart Jonsson .08 .25
208 Ulf Norberg .08 .25
209 Hakan Nygren .08 .25
210 Team Emblem .08 .25
211 Hakan Hjerpe .08 .25
212 Anders Wikberg .08 .25
213 P-A Alexandersson .08 .25
214 Ingemar Strom .08 .25
215 Tommy Eriksson .08 .25
216 Lars Molin .20 .50
217 Lars Bystrom .08 .25
218 Pekka Arbelius .08 .25
219 Sodertalje Team Emblem .08 .25
220 Kjell Larsson .08 .25
221 Sam Lindstal .08 .25
222 Hardy Astrom 1.25 3.00
223 Anders Eldebrink .30 .75
224 Niklas Gallstedt .08 .25
225 Jonas Heed .08 .25
226 Peter Ekroth .08 .25
227 Bo Eriksson .08 .25
228 Stefan Jonsson .08 .25
229 Thom Eklund .08 .25
230 Glenn Johansson .08 .25
231 Team Picture L .08 .25
232 Team Picture R .08 .25
233 Leif Carlsson .08 .25
234 Jan Claesson .08 .25
235 Niclas Lindgren .08 .25
236 Peter Wallin .08 .25
237 Hans Sarkijarvi .08 .25
238 Reine Karlsson .08 .25
239 Conny Jansson .08 .25
240 Anders Carlsson .08 .25

1986-87 Swedish Panini Stickers

This 270-sticker set features the top players in Sweden for the '86-87 season. The stickers -- which measure approximately 2 1/2" by 2" -- were produced by Panini in Italy. The fronts feature a portrait along with name and team logo. The backs are numbered and include information about completing the set and the available album (valued at $10). The set is short on recognizable names, but does include early appearances by Ulf Dahlen and Calle Johansson, among others.

COMPLETE SET (270) 20.00 50.00
1 Bjorkloven Team Emblem .08 .25
2 Hans Lindberg .08 .25
3 Gote Walitalo .08 .25
4 Jakob Gustavsson .08 .25
5 Torbjorn Andersson .08 .25
6 Lars Karlsson .08 .25
7 Calle Johansson .40 1.00
8 Rolf Berglund .08 .25
9 Patrik Aberg .08 .25
10 Niclas Holmgren .08 .25
11 Roger Hagglund .08 .25
12 Team Picture Left .08 .25
13 Team Picture Right .08 .25
14 Peter Andersson .30 .75
15 Tore Oqvist .08 .25
16 Johan Tornqvist .08 .25
17 Par Edlund .08 .25
18 Stefan Nilsson .08 .25
19 Matti Pauna .08 .25
20 Lars-Gunnar Pettersson .08 .25
21 Mikael Hjalm .08 .25
22 Hans Edlund .08 .25
23 Peter Sundstrom .40 1.00
24 Jon Lundstrom .08 .25
25 Peter Edstrom .08 .25
26 Mikael Andersson .40 1.00
27 Ulf Dahlen .75 2.00
28 Brynas Team Emblem .08 .25
29 Stig Salming .08 .25
30 Ake Lilljebjorn .08 .25
31 Lars Eriksson .08 .25
32 Christer Lundqvist .08 .25
33 Lars Ivarsson .08 .25
34 Torbjorn Mattsson .08 .25
35 Gunnar Persson .08 .25
36 Anders Backstrom .08 .25
37 Team Picture L .08 .25
38 Team Picture R .08 .25
39 Jan Ove Mettavainio .08 .25
40 Par Djoos .20 .50
41 Tommy Sjodin .40 1.00
42 Conny Silfverberg .08 .25
43 Christer Andersson .08 .25
44 Kenneth Andersson .08 .25
45 Lars Andersson .08 .25
46 Anders Huss .08 .25
47 Joakim Pehrson .08 .25
48 Jonny Stridh .08 .25
49 Patrik Eriksson .08 .25
50 Anders Ivarsson .08 .25
51 Mikael Lindholm .08 .25
52 Jan Larsson .08 .25
53 Peter Eriksson .08 .25
54 Jan Gronberg .08 .25
55 Djurgarden Team Emblem .08 .25
56 Leif Boork .08 .25
57 Rolf Ridderwall .40 1.00
58 Hans-Goran Elo .08 .25
59 Tommy Albelin .40 1.00
60 Orvar Stambert .08 .25
61 Tomas Eriksson .08 .25
62 Stefan Perlstrom .08 .25
63 Arto Blomsten .20 .50
64 Christian Due-Boije .20 .50
65 Kalle Lilja .08 .25
66 Team Picture L .08 .25
67 Team Picture R .08 .25
68 Stefan Jansson .08 .25
69 Hakan Sodergren .08 .25
70 Jens Ohling .08 .25
71 Peter Nilsson .08 .25
72 Tommy Morth .08 .25
73 Bjorn Carlsson .08 .25
74 Per Goransson .08 .25
75 Pontus Molander .08 .25
76 Jeff Hallegard .08 .25
77 Tomaz Eriksson .08 .25
78 Mikael Johansson .08 .25
79 Anders Johnson .08 .25
80 Jan Viktorsson .08 .25
81 Johan Garpenlov .40 1.00
82 Farjestad Team Emblem .08 .25
83 Conny Evensson .20 .50
84 Peter Lindmark .40 1.00
85 Christer Dalgard .08 .25
86 Tommy Samuelsson .08 .25
87 Mats Lusth .08 .25
88 Peter Andersson .08 .25
89 Hakan Nordin .08 .25
90 Leif Carlsson .08 .25
91 Team Picture L .08 .25
92 Team Picture R .08 .25
93 Patrik Lundback .08 .25
94 Anders Berglund .08 .25
95 Roger Johansson .08 .25
96 Thomas Rundqvist .20 .50
97 Harald Luckner .08 .25
98 Erkki Laine .08 .25
99 Jan Ingman .08 .25
100 Staffan Lund .08 .25
101 Claes-Henrik Silfver .08 .25
102 Magnus Roupe .20 .50
103 Stefan Persson .40 1.00
104 Daniel Rydmark .08 .25
105 Bo Svanberg .08 .25
106 Mikael Holmberg .08 .25
107 Thomas Tallberg .08 .25
108 Kjell Augustsson .08 .25
109 HV 71 Team Emblem .08 .25
110 Curt Lundmark .20 .50
111 Thomas Javeblad .08 .25
112 Kenneth Johansson .08 .25
113 Kari Eloranta .30 .75
114 Jan Hedell .08 .25
115 Arto Routanen .08 .25
116 Klas Heed .08 .25
117 Bert-Roland Naslund .08 .25
118 Nils-Gunnar Svensson .08 .25
119 Fredrik Stillman .08 .25
120 Team Picture L .08 .25
121 Team Picture R .08 .25
122 Nicklas Carlsson .08 .25
123 Ivan Hansen .08 .25
124 Thomas Ljungberg .08 .25
125 Peter Eriksson .08 .25
126 Hans Wallin .08 .25
127 Ove Thornberg .08 .25
128 Per Martinsson .08 .25
129 Mats Loov .08 .25
130 Stefan Nilsson .08 .25
131 Peter Eriksson .08 .25
132 Thomas Lindster .08 .25
133 Boo Peterzen .08 .25
134 Stefan Falk .08 .25
135 Torgny Karlsson .08 .25
136 Leksand Team Emblem .08 .25
137 Kalle Alander .08 .25
138 Peter Aslin .30 .75
139 Bengt-Ake Pers .08 .25
140 Magnus Svensson .20 .50
141 Ove Pettersson .08 .25
142 Stefan Nilsson .08 .25
143 Jens Christiansson .08 .25
144 Leif Eriksson .08 .25
145 Team Picture L .08 .25
146 Team Picture R .08 .25
147 Orjan Lindmark .08 .25
148 Thomas Nord .08 .25
149 Peter Imhauser .08 .25
150 Dan Labraaten .40 1.00
151 Ulf Skoglund .08 .25
152 Jarmo Makitalo .08 .25
153 Per-Olof Carlsson .08 .25
154 Ove Olsson .08 .25
155 Heinz Ehlers .08 .25
156 Jonas Bergqvist .20 .50
157 Robert Burakovsky .20 .50
158 Carl-Erik Larsson .08 .25
159 Cenneth Soderlund .08 .25
160 Ola Sundberg .08 .25
161 Ronny Reichenberg .08 .25
162 Hans Jax .08 .25
163 Lulea Team Emblem .08 .25
164 Freddy Lindfors .08 .25
165 Mats Blomqvist .08 .25
166 Robert Skoog .08 .25
167 Robert Nordmark .20 .50
168 Lars Lindgren .08 .25
169 Lars Modig .08 .25
170 Bo Eriksson .08 .25
171 Kjell-Ake Johansson .08 .25
172 Roger Akerstrom .08 .25
173 Juha Tuohimaa .08 .25
174 Team Picture L .08 .25
175 Team Picture R .08 .25
176 Mats Ohman .08 .25
177 Erik Stalnacke .08 .25
178 Juha Nurmi .08 .25
179 Lars-Goran Niemi .08 .25
180 Hans Norberg .08 .25
181 Jari Lindgren .08 .25
182 Roger Mikko .08 .25
183 Lars Hurtig .08 .25
184 Johan Stromvall .08 .25
185 Jens Hellgren .08 .25
186 Kari Jaako .08 .25
187 Stefan Nilsson .08 .25
188 Ulf Taavola .08 .25
189 Tomas Edstrom .08 .25
190 MoDo Team Emblem .08 .25
191 Hakan Nygren .08 .25
192 Anders Bergman .08 .25
193 Fredrik Andersson .08 .25
194 Robert Frestadius .08 .25
195 Jouko Narvanmaa .08 .25
196 Jan Asplund .08 .25
197 Ulf Agren .08 .25
198 Jorgen Palm .08 .25
199 Team Picture L .08 .25
200 Team Picture R .08 .25
201 Per Forsberg .08 .25
202 Jens Johansson .08 .25
203 Hans Lodin .08 .25
204 Lars Molin .08 .25
205 Per-Arne Alexandersson .08 .25
206 Pecka Arbelius .08 .25
207 Per Nilsson .08 .25
208 Anders Wikberg .08 .25
209 Lars Bystrom .08 .25
210 Ulf Odmark .08 .25
211 Robert Tedenby .08 .25
212 Kent Lantz .08 .25
213 Ulf Sandstrom .08 .25
214 Mikael Pettersson .08 .25
215 Peter Smedberg .08 .25
216 Mikael Stahl .08 .25
217 Skelleftea Team Emblem .08 .25
218 Christer Abrahamsson .40 1.00
219 Mats Abrahamsson .08 .25
220 Ulf Nilsson 1.00 2.50
221 Goran Lindblom .08 .25
222 Lars Marklund .08 .25
223 Ola Stenlund .08 .25
224 Serge Roy .20 .50
225 Mikael Lindman .08 .25
226 Robert Larsson .08 .25
227 Stefan Svensson .08 .25
228 Team Picture L .08 .25
229 Team Picture R .08 .25
230 Roland Stoltz .08 .25
231 Martin Pettersson .08 .25
232 Jonny Forsman .08 .25
233 Tomas Hedin .08 .25
234 Mikael Granstedt .08 .25
235 Randy Heath .08 .25
236 Peter Lundmark .30 .75
237 Niklas Mannberg .08 .25
238 Claes Lindblom .20 .50
239 Mats Lundmark .08 .25
240 Jorgen Marklund .08 .25
241 Daniel Pettersson .08 .25
242 Mats Lundstrom .08 .25
243 Hans Hjalmar .08 .25
244 Sodertalje Team Emblem .08 .25
245 Dan Hober .08 .25
246 Sam Lindstahl .08 .25
247 Reino Sundberg .08 .25
248 Anders Eldebrink .20 .50
249 Mats Kihlstrom .08 .25
250 Ulf Borg .08 .25
251 Bo Ericsson .08 .25
252 Peter Ekroth .08 .25
253 Team Picture L .08 .25
254 Team Picture R .08 .25
255 Jonas Heed .08 .25
256 Stefan Jonsson .08 .25
257 Hans Pettersson .08 .25
258 Hans Sarkijarvi .08 .25
259 Thom Eklund .08 .25
260 Glenn Johansson .08 .25
261 Peter Loob .08 .25
262 Niklas Lindgren .08 .25
263 Conny Jansson .08 .25
264 Tomas Jernberg .08 .25
265 Reine Karlsson .08 .25
266 Anders Frykbo .08 .25
267 Jan Loob .08 .25
268 Peter Larsson .08 .25
269 Erik Holmberg .08 .25
270 Jorgen Winborg .08 .25

1987-88 Swedish Panini Stickers

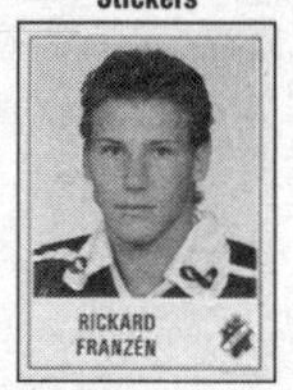

This 270-sticker set features the top players from the Elitserien. The stickers -- which measure approximately 2 1/2" by 2" -- were produced by Panini in Italy. The fronts feature a portrait along with player name and team logo. The backs are numbered and contain information about completing the set and acquiring a collector's album (valued now at about $10).

COMPLETE SET (270) 20.00 50.00
1 AIK Team Emblem .08 .25
2 AIK Team Picture Left .08 .25
3 AIK Team Picture Right .08 .25
4 Lars-Gunnar Jansson .08 .25
5 Ake Liljebjorn .08 .25
6 Thomas Ostlund .40 1.00
7 Jan Eriksson .08 .25
8 Hans Cederholm .08 .25
9 Rickard Franzen .08 .25
10 Thomas Ahlen .08 .25
11 Mats Thelin .20 .50
12 Bjorn Hellman .08 .25
13 Peter Gradin .20 .50
14 Bjorn Carlsson .08 .25
15 Anders Gozzi .08 .25
16 Per Martinelle .08 .25
17 Bo Berglund .20 .50
18 Thomas Gradin .40 1.00
19 Hans Segerberg .08 .25
20 Odd Nilsson .08 .25
21 Mats Hessel .08 .25
22 IF Bjorkloven Team Emblem .08 .25
23 IF Bjorkloven Team Picture Left .08 .25
24 IF Bjorkloven Team Picture Right .08 .25

25 Rolf Jager .08 .25
26 Gote Walitalo .08 .25
27 Staffan Andersson .08 .25
28 Torbjorn Andersson .08 .25
29 Lars Karlsson .08 .25
30 Roger Hagglund .08 .25
31 Rolf Berglund .08 .25
32 Peter Andersson .08 .25
33 Age Ellingsen .08 .25
34 Matti Pauna .08 .25
35 Tore Oqvist .08 .25
36 Mikael Andersson .40 1.00
37 Hans Edlund .08 .25
38 Johan Tornqvist .08 .25
39 Peter Edstrom .08 .25
40 Par Edlund .08 .25
41 Erik Kristiansen .08 .25
42 Ulf Andersson .08 .25
43 Brynas IF Team Emblem .08 .25
44 Brynas IF Team Picture Left .08 .25
45 Brynas IF Team Picture Right .08 .25
46 Tord Lundstrom .08 .25
47 Lars Eriksson .08 .25
48 Michael Sundlov .40 1.00
49 Lars Ivarsson .08 .25
50 Par Djoos .20 .50
51 Jan Ove Mettavainio .08 .25
52 Anders Backstrom .08 .25
53 Gunnar Persson .08 .25
54 Christer Andersson .08 .25
55 Conny Silfverberg .08 .25
56 Jonny Stridh .08 .25
57 Kyosti Karjalainen .20 .50
58 Willy Lindstrom .30 .75
59 Joakim Pehrson .08 .25
60 Patrik Erickson .08 .25
61 Anders Huss .08 .25
62 Peter Eriksson .08 .25
63 Jan Larsson .08 .25
64 Djurgardens IF Team Emblem .08 .25
65 Djurgardens IF .08 .25
Team Picture Left
66 Djurgardens IF .08 .25
Team Picture Right
67 Ingvar Karlsson .08 .25
68 Rolf Ridderwall .40 1.00
69 Hans-Goran Elo .08 .25
70 Orvar Stambert .08 .25
71 Kalle Lilja .08 .25
72 Arto Blomsten .20 .50
73 Stefan Jansson .08 .25
74 Tomas Eriksson .08 .25
75 Christian Due-Boije .20 .50
76 Jens Ohling .08 .25
77 Pontus Molander .08 .25
78 Tommy Morth .08 .25
79 Johan Garpenlov .40 1.00
80 Hakan Sodergren .08 .25
81 Anders Johnson .08 .25
82 Mikael Johansson .08 .25
83 Jan Viktorsson .08 .25
84 Peter Nilsson .08 .25
85 Farjestads BK Team Emblem .08 .25
86 Farjestads BK .08 .25
Team Picture Left
87 Farjestads BK .08 .25
Team Picture Right
88 Per Backman .08 .25
89 Peter Lindmark .40 1.00
90 Christer Dalgard .08 .25
91 Tommy Samuelsson .08 .25
92 Peter Andersson .08 .25
93 Mats Lusth .08 .25
94 Leif Carlsson .08 .25
95 Jesper Duus .08 .25
96 Hakan Nordin .08 .25
97 Thomas Rundqvist .20 .50
98 Staffan Lund .08 .25
99 Harald Luckner .08 .25
100 Erkki Laine .08 .25
101 Stefan Persson .30 .75
102 Bo Svanberg .08 .25
103 Claes-Henrik Silfver .08 .25
104 Mikael Holmberg .08 .25
105 Roger Johansson .08 .25
106 HV 71 Team Emblem .08 .25
107 HV 71 Team Picture Left .08 .25
108 HV 71 Team Picture Right .08 .25
109 Curt Lundmark .40 1.00
110 Kenneth Johansson .08 .25
111 Boo Peterzen .08 .25
112 Arto Routanen .08 .25
113 Jan Hedell .08 .25
114 Fredrik Stillman .08 .25
115 Reijo Ruotsalainen .40 1.00
116 Bert-Roland Naslund .08 .25
117 Peter Eriksson .08 .25
118 Hans Wallin .08 .25
119 Peter Berndtsson .08 .25
120 Mats Loov .08 .25
121 Thomas Lindster .08 .25
122 Peter Eriksson .08 .25
123 Hasse Sjoo .08 .25
124 Stefan Nilsson .08 .25
125 Stefan Falk .08 .25
126 Ove Thornberg .08 .25
127 Wash Out .08 .25
128 Butt-Ending .08 .25
129 Fordrojd Signal .08 .25
130 Hakning .08 .25
131 Charging .08 .25
132 Olampligt Upptradande .08 .25
133 Fasthallning .08 .25
134 Hog Klubba .08 .25
135 Tripping .08 .25
136 Cross Checking .08 .25
137 Armbagstackling .08 .25
138 Icing .08 .25
139 Icing .08 .25
140 Boarding .08 .25
141 Slashing .08 .25
142 Roughing .08 .25
143 Spearing .08 .25
144 Interference .08 .25
145 Leksands IF Team Emblem .08 .25
146 Leksands IF Team Picture Left .08 .25
147 Leksands IF .08 .25
Team Picture Right
148 Christer Abrahamsson .40 1.00
149 Peter Aslin .20 .50
150 Bengt-Ake Pers .08 .25
151 Magnus Svensson .20 .50
152 Stefan Nilsson .08 .25
153 Orjan Lindmark .08 .25
154 Thomas Nord .08 .25
155 Peter Imhauser .08 .25
156 Stefan Larsson .08 .25
157 Robert Burakovsky .20 .50
158 Jonas Bergqvist .20 .50
159 Heinz Ehlers .08 .25
160 Ivan Hansen .08 .25
161 Jarmo Makitalo .08 .25
162 Dan Labraaten .30 .75
163 Per-Olof Carlsson .08 .25
164 Carl-Erik Larsson .08 .25
165 Ulf Skoglund .08 .25
166 Lulea Hockey Team Emblem .08 .25
167 Lulea Hockey .08 .25
Team Picture Left
168 Lulea Hockey .08 .25
Team Picture Right
169 Freddy Lindfors .08 .25
170 Tomas Javeblad .08 .25
171 Robert Skoog .08 .25
172 Juha Tuohimaa .08 .25
173 Bo Eriksson .08 .25
174 Roger Akerstrom .08 .25
175 Lars Lindgren .08 .25
176 Lars Modig .08 .25
177 Erik Stalnacke .08 .25
178 Johan Stromvall .08 .25
179 Juha Nurmi .08 .25
180 Lars-Goran Niemi .08 .25
181 Jari Lindgren .08 .25
182 Lars-Gunnar Pettersson .08 .25
183 Hans Norberg .08 .25
184 Kari Jaako .08 .25
185 Lars Hurtig .08 .25
186 Jens Hellgren .08 .25
187 MoDo Hockey Team Emblem .08 .25
188 MoDo Hockey .08 .25
Team Picture Left
189 MoDo Hockey .08 .25
Team Picture Right
190 Anders Nordin .08 .25
191 Anders Bergman .08 .25
192 Fredrik Andersson .08 .25
193 Hans Lodin .08 .25
194 Jens Johansson .08 .25
195 Juouko Narvanmaa .08 .25
196 Robert Frestadius .08 .25
197 Per Forsberg .08 .25
198 Mikael Hjalm .08 .25
199 Ulf Sandstrom .08 .25
200 Ulf Odmark .08 .25
201 Per Nilsson .08 .25
202 Anders Wikberg .08 .25
203 Lars Molin .20 .50
204 Per-Arne Alexandersson .08 .25
205 Lars Bystrom .08 .25
206 Mikael Stahl .08 .25
207 Ove Pettersson .08 .25
208 Skelleftea Hockey Team .08 .25
Emblem
209 Skelleftea Hockey Team .08 .25
Picture Left
210 Skelleftea Hockey Team .08 .25
Picture Right
211 Tommie Bergman .40 1.00
212 Ulf Nilsson .75 2.00
213 Sam Lindstahl .20 .50
214 Lars Marklund .08 .25
215 Goran Lindblom .08 .25
216 Ola Stenlund .08 .25
217 Stefan Svensson .08 .25
218 Kari Suoraniemi .08 .25
219 Hans Hjalmar .08 .25
220 Mikael Granstedt .08 .25
221 Mats Lundstrom .08 .25
222 Jonny Forsman .08 .25
223 Kari Jalonen .20 .50
224 Claes Lindblom .20 .50
225 Tomas Hedin .08 .25
226 Martin Pettersson .08 .25
227 Jorgen Marklund .08 .25
228 Niklas Mannberg .08 .25
229 Sodertalje SK Team Emblem .08 .25
230 Sodertalje SK .08 .25
Team Picture Left
231 Sodertalje BK .08 .25
Team Picture Right
232 John Pettersson .08 .25
233 Reino Sundberg .08 .25
234 Jari Luoma .08 .25
235 Anders Eldebrink .20 .50
236 Mats Kihlstrom .08 .25
237 Jonas Heed .08 .25
238 Bo Ericsson .08 .25
239 Ulf Borg .08 .25
240 Stefan Jonsson .08 .25
241 Mats Hallin .08 .25
242 Glenn Johansson .08 .25
243 Thomas Ljungberg .08 .25
244 Hans Sarkijarvi .08 .25
245 Thom Eklund .08 .25
246 Peter Larsson .08 .25
247 Conny Jansson .08 .25
248 Niklas Lindgren .08 .25
249 Reine Karlsson .08 .25
250 Vasby IK Team Emblem .08 .25
251 Vasby IK Team Picture Left .08 .25
252 Vasby IK Team Picture Right .08 .25
253 Anders Jacobsen .08 .25
254 Jorgen Larsson .08 .25
255 Stefan Sohlin .08 .25
256 Torbjorn Mattsson .08 .25
257 Hakan Persson .08 .25
258 Kenneth Lindqvist .08 .25
259 Jens Mackegard .08 .25
260 Anders Lindberg .08 .25
261 Mats Edholm .08 .25
262 Mats Poppler .08 .25
263 Claes Gustafsson .08 .25
264 Per Bergman .08 .25
265 Peter Wallen .08 .25
266 Hans-Rickard Andersson .08 .25
267 Arto Heinola .08 .25
268 Mats Lindberg .08 .25
269 Urban Jakobsson .08 .25
270 Stefan Sandin .08 .25

1989-90 Swedish Semic Elitserien Stickers

This 285-sticker set captures the excitement of the Elitserien in thrilling posed color photos. The 3" by 2 1/8" sticker fronts are complemented by player name, sticker number and team emblem. the backs contain an ad for Pripp's Energy drink. The set is notable for the first "card" appearances of Mats Sundin and Nicklas Lidstrom.

COMPLETE SET (285) 20.00 50.00
1 AIK .08 .25
2 Ake Lilljebjorn .08 .25
3 Thomas Ostlund .30 .75
4 Mats Thelin .08 .25
5 Thomas Ahlen .08 .25
6 Petri Liimatainen .08 .25
7 Roger Ohman .08 .25
8 Rikard Franzen .08 .25
9 Stefan Claesson .08 .25
10 Tommy Hedlund .08 .25
11 Stefan Jansson .08 .25
12 Peter Gradin .08 .25
13 Thomas Gradin .20 .50
14 Bo Berglund .08 .25
15 Heinz Ehlers .08 .25
16 Robert Burakovsky .08 .25
17 Alexander Kozjevnikov .08 .25
18 Peter Hammarstrom .08 .25
19 Anders Gozzi .08 .25
20 Thomas Bjuhr .08 .25
21 Patric Englund .08 .25
22 Odd Nilsson .08 .25
23 Mats Lindberg .08 .25
24 Peter Johansson .08 .25
25 Patric Kjellberg .30 .75
26 Brynas IF .08 .25
27 Lars Eriksson .08 .25
28 Michael Sundlov .08 .25
29 Par Djoos .08 .25
30 Tommy Sjodin .08 .25
31 Nikolaj Davydkin .08 .25
32 Niklas Gallstedt .08 .25
33 Mikael Lindman .08 .25
34 Jan-Erik Stormqvist .08 .25
35 Tommy Melkersson .08 .25
36 Mikael Enander .08 .25
37 Anders Huss .08 .25
38 Anders Carlsson .08 .25
39 Willy Lindstrom .20 .50
40 Kyosti Karjalainen .08 .25
41 Jan Larsson .08 .25
42 Patrik Erickson .08 .25
43 Joakim Pehrson .08 .25
44 Johan Brummer .08 .25
45 Peter Eriksson .08 .25
46 Peter Gustafsson .08 .25
47 Tomas Olund .08 .25
48 Magnus Asberg .08 .25
49 Djurgardens IF .08 .25
50 Rolf Ridderwall .20 .50
51 Tommy Soderstrom .60 1.50
52 Thomas Eriksson .08 .25
53 Arto Blomsten .08 .25
54 Orvar Stambert .08 .25
55 Christian Due-Boje .08 .25
56 Kenneth Kennholt .08 .25
57 Mats Waltin .08 .25
58 Karl-Erik Lilja .08 .25
59 Marcus Ragnarsson .20 .50
60 Hakan Sodergren .08 .25
61 Mikael Johansson .08 .25
62 Jens Ohling .08 .25
63 Jan Viktorsson .08 .25
64 Peter Nilsson .08 .25
65 Charles Berglund .08 .25
66 Kent Johansson .08 .25
67 Johan Garpenlov .20 .50
68 Ola Andersson .08 .25
69 Anders Johnson .08 .25
70 Bengt Akerblom .08 .25
71 Ola Josefsson .08 .25
72 Mats Sundin 4.00 10.00
73 Farjestads BK .08 .25
74 Anders Bergman .08 .25
75 Jorgen Ryden .08 .25
76 Tommy Samuelsson .08 .25
77 Fredrik Olausson .30 .75
78 Peter Hasselblad .08 .25
79 Jesper Duus .08 .25
80 Anders Berglund .08 .25
81 Mattias Andersson .08 .25
82 Mattias Olsson .08 .25
83 Greger Artursson .08 .25
84 Jakob Karlsson .08 .25
85 Thomas Rundqvist .08 .25
86 Staffan Lundh .08 .25
87 Jan Ingman .08 .25
88 Kjell Dahlin .08 .25
89 Bengt-Ake Gustafsson .20 .50
90 Magnus Roupe .08 .25
91 Hakan Loob .40 1.00
92 Mikael Holmberg .08 .25
93 Daniel Rydmark .08 .25
94 Lars Karlsson .08 .25
95 Peter Ottosson .08 .25
96 HV 71 .08 .25
97 Kenneth Johansson .08 .25
98 Claes Heljemo .08 .25
99 Lars Ivarsson .08 .25
100 Arto Ruotanen .08 .25
101 Fredrik Stillman .08 .25
102 Klas Heed .08 .25
103 Nils-Gunnar Svensson .08 .25
104 Per Gustafsson .08 .25
105 Tommy Fritz .08 .25
106 Mats Nilsson .08 .25
107 Hasse Sjoo .08 .25
108 Mats Loov .08 .25
109 Ove Thornberg .08 .25
110 Eddy Ericsson .08 .25
111 Ivan Avdejev .08 .25
112 Stefan Persson .20 .50
113 Rick Erdall .08 .25
114 Stefan Nilsson .08 .25
115 Stefan Ornskog .08 .25
116 Patrik Ross .08 .25
117 Stefan Falk .08 .25
118 Claes Roupe .08 .25
119 Peter Ekelund .08 .25
120 Leksands IF .08 .25
121 Peter Aslin .30 .75
122 Olow Sundstrom .08 .25
123 Jonas Leven .08 .25
124 Tomas Jonsson .20 .50
125 Magnus Svensson .08 .25
126 Ricard Persson .20 .50
127 Per Lundell .08 .25
128 Tomas Nord .08 .25
129 Peter Wallin .08 .25
130 Orjan Lindmark .08 .25
131 Henric Bjorkman .08 .25
132 Anders Pettersson .08 .25
133 Per-Olof Carlsson .08 .25
134 Tomas Forslund .20 .50
135 Niklas Eriksson .08 .25
136 Richard Kromm .08 .25
137 Jarmo Makitalo .08 .25
138 Peter Lundmark .30 .75
139 Ronny Reichenberg .08 .25
140 Cenneth Soderlund .08 .25
141 Jens Nielsen .08 .25
142 Marcus Thuresson .08 .25
143 Anders Broms .08 .25
144 Joakim Backlund .08 .25
145 Lulea HF .08 .25
146 Robert Skoog .08 .25
147 Tomas Javeblad .08 .25
148 Lars Modig .08 .25
149 Jan-Ove Mottavainio .08 .25
150 Osmo Soutokorva .08 .25
151 Torbjorn Lindberg .08 .25
152 Timo Jutila .20 .50
153 Roger Akerstrom .08 .25
154 Per Ljusterang .08 .25
155 Tomas Lilja .08 .25
156 Johan Stromvall .08 .25
157 Lars-Gunnar Pettersson .08 .25
158 Lars Hurtig .08 .25
159 Morgan Samuelsson .08 .25
160 Stefan Nilsson .08 .25
161 Vesa Kangas .08 .25
162 Kari Jaako .08 .25
163 Juha Nurmi .20 .50
164 Jens Hellgren .08 .25
165 Tomas Berglund .08 .25
166 Lars Edstrom .08 .25
167 Petter Antti .08 .25
168 MoDo HK .08 .25
169 Fredrik Andersson .08 .25
170 Goran Anmark .08 .25
171 Timo Blomqvist .08 .25
172 Hakan Stromqvist .08 .25
173 Robert Frestadius .08 .25
174 Lars Jansson .08 .25
175 Hans Lodin .08 .25
176 Ove Pettersson .08 .25
177 Tony Olofsson .08 .25
178 Jorgen Eriksson .08 .25
179 Ulf Sandstrom .08 .25
180 Michael Hjalm .08 .25
181 Urban Nordin .08 .25
182 Lars Bystrom .08 .25
183 Jens Ohman .08 .25
184 Ulf Odmark .08 .25
185 Mikael Stahl .08 .25
186 Per Nilsson .08 .25
187 Ingemar Strom .08 .25
188 Kent Lantz .08 .25
189 Kent Norberg .08 .25
190 Patrik Soderholm .08 .25
191 Skelleftea HC .08 .25
192 Sam Lindstahl .08 .25
193 Dick Andersson .08 .25
194 Kari Suoraniemi .08 .25
195 Robert Larsson .08 .25
196 Kari Yli-Maenpaa .08 .25
197 Ola Stenlund .08 .25
198 Tony Barthelson .08 .25
199 Lars Marklund .08 .25
200 Glenn Hedman .08 .25
201 Dick Burlin .08 .25
202 Michael Granstedt .08 .25
203 Pekka Jarvela .08 .25
204 Hans Hjalmar .08 .25
205 Mats Lundstrom .08 .25
206 Martin Pettersson .08 .25
207 Johnny Forsman .08 .25
208 Daniel Pettersson .08 .25
209 Niklas Mannberg .08 .25
210 Niklas Brannstrom .08 .25
211 Jan Johansson .08 .25
212 Jorgen Wannstrom .08 .25
213 Leif Johansson .08 .25
214 Par Mikaelsson .08 .25
215 Fredrik Andersson .08 .25
216 Sodertalje SK .08 .25
217 Reino Sundberg .08 .25
218 Jari Luoma .08 .25
219 Anders Eldebrink .08 .25
220 Mats Kilstrom .08 .25
221 Jonas Heed .08 .25
222 Hans Pettersson .08 .25
223 Jan Bergman .08 .25
224 Thomas Carlsson .08 .25
225 Stefan Jonsson .08 .25
226 Thom Eklund .08 .25
227 Ola Rosander .08 .25
228 Bjorn Carlsson .08 .25
229 Thomas Sjogren .08 .25
230 Thomas Ljungbergh .08 .25
231 Stefan Olsson .08 .25
232 Reine Landgren .08 .25
233 Anders Frykbo .08 .25
234 Conny Jansson .08 .25
235 Peter Larsson .08 .25
236 Tomaz Eriksson .08 .25
237 Erik Holmberg .08 .25
238 Patrik Lindh .08 .25
239 Vasteras IK .08 .25
240 Mats Yter .08 .25
241 Par Hellenberg .08 .25
242 Jan Eriksson .08 .25
243 Peter Popovic .20 .50
244 Tore Lindgren .08 .25
245 Leif Rohlin .20 .50
246 Henrik Andersson .08 .25
247 Nicklas Lidstrom 4.00 10.00
248 Jan Karlsson .08 .25
249 Peter Jacobsson .08 .25
250 Patrik Juhlin .20 .50
251 Goran Sjoberg .08 .25
252 Fredrik Nilsson .08 .25
253 Stefan Hellkvist .08 .25
254 Tomas Strandberg .08 .25
255 Anders Berglund .08 .25
256 Claes Lindblom .08 .25
257 Magnus Wallin .08 .25
258 Bjorn Akerblom .08 .25
259 Joakim Lundholm .08 .25
260 Jorgen Holmberg .08 .25
261 Ronny Hansen .08 .25
262 Misjal Fachrutdinov .30 .75
263 Vastra Frolunda HC .08 .25
264 Hakan Algotsson .30 .75
265 Per Lundbergh .08 .25
266 Jan Karlsson .08 .25
267 Joacim Esbjors .08 .25
268 Leif Carlsson .08 .25
269 Stefan Axelsson .08 .25
270 Peter Ekroth .08 .25
271 Jorgen Palm .08 .25
272 Hakan Nordin .08 .25
273 Stefan Larsson .08 .25
274 Mikael Andersson .20 .50
275 Terho Koskela .08 .25
276 Patrik Carnback .20 .50
277 Serge Boisvert .08 .25
278 Arto Sirvio .08 .25
279 Peter Berndtsson .08 .25
280 Jorgen Pettersson .08 .25
281 Niklas Andersson .08 .25
282 Peter Gustavsson .08 .25
283 Paul Andersson .08 .25
284 Mats Graesen .08 .25
285 Kent Orrgren .08 .25

1989 Swedish Semic World Championship Stickers

This 200-sticker set captures some of the players who have represented their country at the World Championships. The stickers, which came in packs of five, measure 3" by 2 1/8" and feature color photos, along with player name, card number and national flag. The backs contain an ad for Pepsi. The NHL players are pictured in their team sweaters, including stars such as Wayne Gretzky and Patrick Roy. An album to house the set also was available; it retails for about $10.

COMPLETE SET (200) 60.00 125.00
1 Sweden National Emblem .02 .10
2 Tommy Sandlin .08 .25
3 Peter Lindmark .08 .25
4 Rolf Ridderwall .08 .25
5 Tomas Jonsson .08 .25
6 Tommy Albelin .08 .25
7 Mats Kihlstrom .02 .10
8 Tommy Samuelsson .02 .10
9 Anders Eldebrink .05 .15
10 Fredrik Olausson .05 .15
11 Peter Andersson .05 .15
12 Thomas Eriksson .02 .10
13 Thom Eklund .02 .10
14 Bo Berglund .05 .15
15 Thomas Steen .15 .40
16 Ulf Sandstrom .02 .10
17 Jonas Bergkvist .08 .25
18 Thomas Rundqvist .05 .15
19 Per-Erik Eklund .20 .50
20 Bengt-Ake Gustavsson .02 .10
21 Patrik Sundstrom .15 .40
22 Mikael Johansson .05 .15
23 Hakan Sodergren .02 .10
24 Kent Nilsson .20 .50
25 Lars-Gunnar Pettersson .02 .10
26 Finland National Emblem .02 .10
27 Pentti Matikainen .02 .10
28 Jukka Tammi .08 .25
29 Sakari Lindfors .08 .25
30 Reijo Ruotsalainen .08 .25
31 Kari Eloranta .08 .25
32 Timo Blomqvist .08 .25
33 Simo Saarinen .08 .25
34 Hannu Virta .08 .25
35 Jouko Narvanmaa .02 .10
36 Jarmo Kuusisto .02 .10
37 Kari Suoraniemi .02 .10
38 Reijo Mikkolainen .02 .10
39 Raimo Helminen .08 .25
40 Raimo Summanen .08 .25
41 Mikko Makela .08 .25
42 Kari Jalonen .02 .10
43 Kari Laitinen .02 .10
44 Petri Skriko .15 .40
45 Erkki Laine .02 .10
46 Pauli Jarvinen .02 .10
47 Jukka Vilander .02 .10
48 Esa Keskinen .15 .40
49 Ari Vuori .02 .10
50 Mika Nieminen .15 .40
51 Canada National Emblem .08 .25
52 Dave King .08 .25
53 Grant Fuhr .75 2.00
54 Patrick Roy 12.00 30.00
55 Ron Hextall .75 2.00
56 Al MacInnis .60 1.50
57 Ray Bourque 4.00 10.00
58 Scott Stevens .20 .50
59 Paul Coffey 1.25 3.00
60 Zarley Zalapski .15 .40
61 James Patrick .15 .40
62 Kevin Lowe .15 .40
63 Brad McCrimmon .15 .40
64 Mario Lemieux 12.00 30.00
65 Wayne Gretzky 20.00 50.00
66 Denis Savard .30 .75
67 Dale Hawerchuk .40 1.00
68 Luc Robitaille .75 2.00
69 Mark Messier 4.00 10.00
70 Michel Goulet .20 .50
71 Cam Neely 2.00 5.00
72 Steve Yzerman 10.00 25.00
73 Bernie Nicholls .30 .75
74 Joe Nieuwendyk .40 1.00
75 Mike Gartner .40 1.00
76 USSR National Emblem .08 .25
77 Viktor Tichonov .07 .20
78 Jevgenij Belosjekin .20 .50
79 Sergei Mylnikov .20 .50
80 Sergei Golosjumov .08 .25
81 Alexei Kasatonov .20 .50
82 Aleksej Gusarov .08 .25
83 Andrej Smirnov .05 .15
84 Valerij Sirjajev .05 .15
85 Igor Stelnov .05 .15
86 Vladimir Konstantinov 1.25 3.00
87 Slava Fetisov .40 1.00
88 Sergei Jasjin .05 .15
89 Vladimir Krutov .30 .75
90 Igor Larionov .75 2.00
91 Valerij Kamenskij .20 .50
92 Vjatjeslav Bykov .20 .50
93 Andrej Chomutov .20 .50
94 Yuri Khmylev .20 .50
95 Sergei Nemchinov .20 .50
96 Sergei Makarov .40 1.00
97 Igor Jesmantovitj .05 .15
98 Andrei Lomakin .07 .20
99 Anatolij Semjonov .08 .25
100 Aleksandr Tjernych .05 .15
101 West Germany .02 .10
(National Emblem
102 Xaver Unsinn .08 .25
103 Karl Friesen .08 .25
104 Josef Schlickenrieder .02 .10
105 Matthias Hoppe .02 .10
106 Andreas Niederberger .02 .10
107 Udo Kiessling .05 .15
108 Uli Hiemer .05 .15
109 Harold Kreis .05 .15
110 Manfred Schuster .02 .10
111 Jorg Hanft .02 .10
112 Ron Fischer .02 .10
113 Michael Heidt .05 .15
114 Dieter Hegen .05 .15
115 Gerd Truntschka .05 .15
116 Helmut Steiger .02 .10
117 Georg Franz .02 .10
118 Georg Holzmann .02 .10
119 Peter Obresa .02 .10
120 Bernd Truntschka .05 .15
121 Manfred Wolf .02 .10
122 Roy Roedger .02 .10
123 Axel Kammerer .02 .10
124 Peter Draisaitl .07 .20
125 Daniel Held .02 .10
126 Poland National Emblem .02 .10
127 Leszek Lejczyk .07 .20
128 Jerzy Mruk .07 .20
129 Andrezej Hanisz .02 .10
130 Dariusz Wieczorek .02 .10
131 Jacek Zamojski .02 .10
132 Marek Cholewa .02 .10
133 Henryk Gruth .02 .10
134 Robert Szopinski .02 .10
135 Jerzy Potz .02 .10
136 Andrzej Swiatek .02 .10
137 Ludvik Czapka .02 .10
138 Piotr Zdunek .02 .10
139 Jedrzej Kasperczyk .02 .10
140 Krzysztof Podsiadlo .02 .10
141 Miroslaw Copija .02 .10
142 Krzysztof Bujar .02 .10
143 Janusz Adamiec .02 .10
144 Jacek Solinski .02 .10
145 Roman Steblecki .02 .10
146 Adam Fraszko .02 .10
147 Leszek Minge .02 .10
148 Piotr Kwasigroch .02 .10
149 Ireneusz Pacula .02 .10
150 1989 World Championship .02 .10
Emblem
151 USA National Emblem .08 .25
152 Art Berglund .08 .25
153 Tom Barrasso .20 .50
154 John Vanbiesbrouck 1.25 3.00
155 Gary Suter .20 .50
156 Phil Housley .20 .50
157 Chris Chelios 1.25 3.00
158 Mike Ramsey .08 .25
159 Rod Langway .08 .25
160 Mark Howe .15 .40
161 Brian Leetch .75 2.00
162 Al Iafrate .15 .40
163 Jimmy Carson .05 .15
164 Pat LaFontaine .40 1.00
165 Neal Broten .20 .50
166 Dave Christian .15 .40
167 Brett Hull 4.00 10.00
168 Bob Carpenter .08 .25
169 Ed Olczyk .08 .25
170 Joe Mullen .20 .50
171 Bob Brooke .05 .15
172 Brian Lawton .05 .15
173 Craig Janney .20 .50
174 Mark Johnson .08 .25
175 Chris Nilan .08 .25
176 CSSR National Emblem .02 .10
177 Pavel Wohl .08 .25
178 Dominik Hasek 6.00 15.00
179 Jaromir Sindel .08 .25
180 Petr Briza .40 1.00
181 Antonin Stavjana .08 .25
182 Bedrich Scerban .07 .20
183 Petr Slanina .02 .10
184 Frantisek Kucera .07 .20
185 Jergus Baca .05 .15
186 Leo Gudas .05 .15
187 Drahomir Kadlec .05 .15
188 Mojmir Bozik .02 .10
189 Petr Vlk .02 .10
190 Vladimir Ruzicka .08 .25
191 Otakar Janecky .08 .25
192 Jan Vodila .02 .10
193 Jiri Dolezal .02 .10
194 Rostislav Vlach .02 .10
195 Jiri Kucera .07 .20
196 Jiri Sejba .05 .15
197 Oldrich Valek .02 .10
198 Jiri Lala .05 .15
199 Robert Kron .08 .25
200 Petr Rosol .05 .15

1990-91 Swedish Semic Elitserien Stickers

This 294-sticker set features the players of the Swedish Elitserien. The stickers measure 3" by 2 1/8" and utilize posed color player photos on the front, along with sticker number, name and club emblem. The backs feature consumer ads. The set includes the first "card" of players such as Mikael Renberg and Markus Naslund.

COMPLETE SET (294) 16.00 40.00
1 MoDo Hockey Team .02 .10
Team Emblem
2 MoDo Hockey .02 .10
Team Picture
3 Fredrik Andersson .08 .25
4 Goran Anmark .08 .25
5 Ari Salo .02 .10
6 Anders Berglund .02 .10
7 Lars Jansson .02 .10
8 Hans Lodin .02 .10
9 Ove Pettersson .02 .10
10 Jorgen Eriksson .02 .10
11 Tony Olofsson .02 .10
12 Tomas Nanzen .02 .10
13 Michael Hjalm .02 .10
14 Erik Holmberg .02 .10
15 Urban Nordin .02 .10
16 Kent Lantz .02 .10
17 Lars Bystrom .02 .10
18 Jens Ohman .02 .10
19 Ulf Odmark .02 .10
20 Mikael Stahl .02 .10
21 Ingemar Strom .02 .10
22 Tommy Pettersson .02 .10
23 Markus Naslund 2.00 5.00
24 Per Wallin .05 .15
25 Vastra Frolunda HC .02 .10
Team Emblem
26 Vastra Frolunda HC .02 .10
(Team Picture
27 Ako Liilljebjorn .20 .50
28 Hakan Algotsson .20 .50
29 Leif Carlsson .02 .10
30 Jonas Heed .02 .10
31 Hakan Nordin .02 .10
32 Joacim Esbjors .05 .15
33 Stefan Axelsson .15 .40
34 Stefan Larsson .05 .15
35 Jorgen Palm .02 .10
36 Oscar Ackerstrom .02 .10
37 Patrik Carnback .20 .50
38 Mats Lundstrom .02 .10
39 Niklas Andersson .08 .25
40 Serge Boisvert .07 .20
41 Arto Sirvio .02 .10
42 Terho Koskela .02 .10
43 Kari Jaako .02 .10
44 Peter Berndtsson .02 .10
45 Mikael Andersson .08 .25
46 Par Edlund .02 .10
47 Jonas Andersson .02 .10
48 Johan Witehall .20 .50
49 Sodertalje SK .02 .10
Team Emblem
50 Sodertalje SK .02 .10
Team Picture
51 Reino Sundberg .08 .25
52 Jari Luoma .08 .25
53 Mats Kilstrom .02 .10
54 Stefan Jonsson .02 .10
55 Peter Ekroth .02 .10
56 Mats Waltin .02 .10
57 Jan Bergman .02 .10
58 Hans Pettersson .02 .10
59 Stefan Nyman .02 .10
60 Conny Jansson .02 .10
61 Thom Eklund .02 .10
62 Otakar Hascak .07 .20
63 Morgan Samuelsson .05 .15
64 Reine Landgren .02 .10
65 Bjorn Carlsson .02 .10
66 Ola Andersson .02 .10
67 Tomaz Eriksson .02 .10
68 Bert-Olov Karlsson .02 .10
69 Ola Rosander .02 .10
70 Stefan Olsson .02 .10
71 Scott Moore .02 .10
72 Anders Frykbo .02 .10
73 AIK .02 .10
Team Emblem
74 AIK .02 .10
Team Picture
75 Thomas Ustlund .20 .50
76 Sam Lindstahl .08 .25
77 Borje Salming 1.25 3.00
78 Mats Thelin .08 .25
79 Petter Salsten .02 .10

80 Petri Liimatainen .02 .10
81 Rikard Franzen .05 .15
82 Stefan Claesson .02 .10
83 Torbjorn Mattsson .02 .10
84 Daniel Jardemyr .02 .10
85 Robert Burakovsky .07 .20
86 Peter Gradin .02 .10
87 Thomas Bjuhr .02 .10
88 Heinz Ehlers .02 .10
89 Tommy Lehmann .07 .20
90 Peter Hammarstrom .02 .10
91 Patric Kjellberg .40 1.00
92 Patric Englund .02 .10
93 Mats Lindberg .02 .10
94 Peter Johansson .02 .10
95 Kristian Gahn .07 .20
96 Niklas Sundblad .08 .25
97 Erik Andersson .02 .10
98 HV 71 .02 .10
Team Emblem
99 HV 71 .02 .10
Team Picture
100 Peter Aslin .20 .50
101 Kenneth Johansson .08 .25
102 Arto Ruotanen .02 .10
103 Fredrik Stillman .05 .15
104 Lars Ivarsson .02 .10
105 Klas Heed .02 .10
106 Per Gustafsson .20 .50
107 Mathias Svedberg .02 .10
108 Tommy Fritz .02 .10
109 Mats Nilsson .02 .10
110 Peter Eriksson .02 .10
111 Risto Kurkinen .02 .10
112 Thomas Ljungbergh .02 .10
113 Ove Thornberg .02 .10
114 Mats Loov .02 .10
115 Eddy Ericsson .02 .10
116 Stefan Ornskog .08 .25
117 Patrik Ross .02 .10
118 Stefan Persson .08 .25
119 Dennis Strom .02 .10
120 Peter Ekelund .02 .10
121 Jonas Jonsson .02 .10
122 Torbjorn Persson .02 .10
123 Malmo IF .02 .10
(Team Emblem
124 Malmo IF .02 .10
Team Picture
125 Peter Lindmark .20 .50
126 Roger Nordstrom .08 .25
127 Timo Blomqvist .08 .25
128 Peter Andersson .08 .25
129 Mats Lusth .02 .10
130 Johan Salle .02 .10
131 Roger Ohman .05 .15
132 Anders Svensson .02 .10
133 Peter Imhauser .02 .10
134 Johan Norgren .02 .10
135 Raimo Helminen .20 .50
136 Peter Sundstrom .08 .25
137 Mats Hallin .02 .10
138 Matti Pauna .02 .10
139 Patrik Gustavsson .02 .10
140 Hakan Ahlund .02 .10
141 Daniel Rydmark .05 .15
142 Lennart Hermansson .02 .10
143 Carl-Erik Larsson .02 .10
144 Rick Erdall .02 .10
145 Bo Svanberg .02 .10
146 Fredrik Johansson .02 .10
147 Jens Hemstrom .02 .10
148 Vasteras IK .02 .10
Team Emblem
149 Vasteras IK .02 .10
Team Picture
150 Mats Ytter .08 .25
151 Par Hellenberg .08 .25
152 Nicklas Lidstrom 2.00 5.00
153 Leif Rohlin .15 .40
154 Peter Popovic .20 .50
155 Jan Karlsson .02 .10
156 Henrik Andersson .02 .10
157 Tore Lindgren .02 .10
158 Peter Jacobsson .02 .10
159 Pierre Ivarsson .02 .10
160 Jan Eriksson .02 .10
161 Goran Sjoberg .02 .10
162 Misjat Fachrutdinov .05 .15
163 Anders Berglund .02 .10
164 Claes Lindblom .02 .10
165 Jorgen Holmberg .02 .10
166 Stefan Hellkvist .02 .10
167 Tomas Strandberg .02 .10
168 Bjorn Akerblom .02 .10
169 Ronny Hansen .02 .10
170 Fredrik Nilsson .05 .15
171 Patrik Juhlin .20 .50
172 Henrik Nilsson .02 .10
173 Brynas IF .02 .10
Team Emblem
174 Brynas IF .02 .10
Team Picture
175 Michael Sundlov .20 .50
176 Lars Eriksson .08 .25
177 Tommy Sjodin .08 .25
178 Brad Berry .02 .10
179 Niklas Gallstedt .02 .10
180 Mikael Lindman .02 .10
181 Urban Molander .02 .10
182 Jan-Erik Stormqvist .02 .10
183 Stefan Klockare .07 .20
184 Tommy Melkersson .02 .10
185 Anders Carlsson .02 .10
186 Patrik Erickson .02 .10
187 Anders Huss .02 .10
188 Jan Larsson .02 .10
189 Peter Larsson .02 .10
190 Anders Gozzi .05 .15
191 Joakim Pehrson .05 .15
192 Peter Gustafsson .02 .10
193 Peter Eriksson .02 .10
194 Johan Brummer .02 .10
195 Tomas Olund .02 .10
196 Kenneth Andersson .02 .10
197 Leksands IF .02 .10
Team Emblem
198 Leksands IF .02 .10
Team Picture
199 Olow Sundstrom .08 .25
200 Lars-Erik Lord .08 .25
201 Jonas Leven .08 .25
202 Tomas Jonsson .08 .25
203 Ricard Persson .08 .25
204 Per Lundell .02 .10
205 Tomas Nord .02 .10
206 Mattias Andersson .02 .10
207 Henric Bjorkman .02 .10
208 Orjan Lindmark .02 .10
209 Tomas Forslund .08 .25
210 Niklas Eriksson .02 .10
211 Peter Lundmark .05 .15
212 Per-Olof Carlsson .02 .10
213 Marcus Thuresson .02 .10
214 Jens Nielsen .02 .10
215 Cenneth Soderlund .02 .10
216 Markus Akerblom .05 .15
217 Ronny Reichenberg .02 .10
218 Fredrik Olsson .02 .10
219 Niklas Hillblom .02 .10
220 Magnus Gustafsson .02 .10
221 Fredrik Jax .05 .15
222 Lulea HF .02 .10
Team Emblem
223 Lulea HF .02 .10
Team Picture
224 Robert Skoog .08 .25
225 Tomas Javeblad .08 .25
226 Timo Jutila .08 .25
227 Per Ljusterang .02 .10
228 Lars Modig .02 .10
229 Torbjorn Lindberg .02 .10
230 Tomas Lilja .20 .50
231 Osmo Soutokorva .02 .10
232 Jan-Ove Mettavainio .02 .10
233 Roger Akerstrom .02 .10
234 Johan Stromvall .02 .10
235 Ulf Sandstrom .02 .10
236 Lars-Gunnar Pettersson .02 .10
237 Pauli Jarvinen .02 .10
238 Lars Hurtig .02 .10
239 Tomas Berglund .02 .10
240 Stefan Nilsson .02 .10
241 Mikael Renberg .75 2.00
242 Hans Hjalmar .02 .10
243 Jens Hellgren .02 .10
244 Lars Edstrom .02 .10
245 Robert Nordberg .08 .25
246 Farjestads BK .02 .10
Team Emblem
247 Farjestads BK .02 .10
Team Picture
248 Anders Bergman .08 .25
249 Jorgen Ryden .08 .25
250 Patrik Haltia .08 .25
251 Tommy Samuelsson .02 .10
252 Jim Leavins .02 .10
253 Peter Hasselblad .02 .10
254 Jesper Duus .02 .10
255 Mattias Olsson .02 .10
256 Greger Artursson .02 .10
257 Jakob Karlsson .02 .10
258 Thomas Rhodin .02 .10
259 Bengt-Ake Gustafsson .15 .40
260 Hakan Loob .40 1.00
261 Thomas Rundqvist .08 .25
262 Kjell Dahlin .08 .25
263 Magnus Roupe .08 .25
264 Jan Ingman .02 .10
265 Lars Karlsson .02 .10
266 Mikael Holmberg .02 .10
267 Staffan Lundh .02 .10
268 Peter Ottosson .02 .10
269 Jonas Hoglund 1.25 3.00
270 Clas Eriksson .02 .10
271 Djurgardens IF .02 .10
Team Emblem
272 Djurgardens IF .02 .10
Team Picture
273 Tommy Soderstrom .40 1.00
274 Joakim Persson .20 .50
275 Thomas Eriksson .02 .10
276 Arto Blomsten .08 .25
277 Kenneth Kennholt .05 .15
278 Christian Due-Boje .07 .20
279 Orvar Stambert .02 .10
280 Per Nygards .02 .10
281 Marcus Ragnarsson .20 .50
282 Thomas Johansson .02 .10
283 Ronnie Pettersson .02 .10
284 Charles Berglund .02 .10
285 Jan Viktorsson .02 .10
286 Jens Ohling .05 .15
287 Ola Josefsson .02 .10
288 Peter Nilsson .02 .10
289 Andres Johnson .02 .10
290 Hakan Sodergren .02 .10
291 Stefan Gustavson .02 .10
292 Magnus Jansson .02 .10
293 Mikael Johansson .02 .10
294 Johan Lindstedt .02 .10

1991-92 Swedish Semic Elitserien Stickers

This 360-sticker series captures the players of the Swedish Elitserien. The sticker, which measure 3" by 2 1/8", have posed color photos on the front, along with player name, team emblem and sticker number. The backs note the set's sponsor "Cloetta" -- a Swedish confectioner. The set includes early appearances by Mats Sundin, Peter Forsberg and Mikael Renberg. An album was available to house the sticker collection; it is valued at $10.

COMPLETE SET (360) 20.00 50.00
1 AIK .02 .10
Team Emblem
2 Thomas Ostlund .08 .25
3 Sam Lindstahl .08 .25
4 Borje Salming .30 .75
5 Petri Liimatainen .02 .10
6 Mats Thelin .08 .25
7 Rikard Franzen .05 .15
8 Petter Sahlsten .02 .10
9 Daniel Jardemyr .02 .10
10 Thomas Nilsson .02 .10
11 Niclas Havelid .02 .10
12 Mattias Norstrom .08 .25
13 Peter Gradin .02 .10
14 Peter Hammarstrom .02 .10
15 Patrik Erickson .05 .15
16 Thomas Bjuhr .02 .10
17 Thomas Strandberg .02 .10
18 Tommy Lehmann .07 .20
19 Mats Lindberg .02 .10
20 Patric Kjellberg .20 .50
21 Michael Nylander .40 1.00
22 Patric Englund .02 .10
23 Niclas Sundblad .20 .50
24 Kristian Gahn .08 .25
25 Erik Andersson .02 .10
26 Bjorn Ahlstrom .02 .10
27 Brynas .02 .10
Team Emblem
28 Michael Sundlov .08 .25
29 Lars Eriksson .08 .25
30 Lars Karlsson .02 .10
31 Tommy Sjodin .07 .20
32 Nikolaj Davydkin .02 .10
33 Niklas Gallstedt .02 .10
34 Mikael Lindman .02 .10
35 Tommy Melkersson .02 .10
36 Mikael Enander .02 .10
37 Urban Molander .02 .10
38 Stefan Klockare .05 .15
39 Anders Huss .05 .15
40 Mikael Lindholm .02 .10
41 Jan Larsson .02 .10
42 Anders Gozzi .05 .15
43 Peter Larsson .05 .15
44 Thomas Tallberg .05 .15
45 Peter Gustafsson .02 .10
46 Joakim Persson .20 .50
47 Peter Eriksson .02 .10
48 Ove Mohlin .05 .15
49 Jonas Johnsson .02 .10
50 Johan Schillgard .02 .10
51 Andreas Dackell .08 .25
52 Tom Bissett .05 .15
53 Djurgarden .02 .10
Team Emblem
54 Tommy Soderstrom .30 .75
55 Joakim Persson .20 .50
56 Petter Ronnqvist .08 .25
57 Thomas Eriksson .02 .10
58 Kenneth Kennholt .05 .15
59 Arto Blomsten .07 .20
60 Orvar Stambert .02 .10
61 Christian Due-Boje .05 .15
62 Marcus Ragnarsson .20 .50
63 Per Nygards .02 .10
64 Thomas Johansson .02 .10
65 Mikael Johansson .02 .10
66 Charles Berglund .05 .15
67 Jan Viktorsson .05 .15
68 Ola Josefsson .02 .10
69 Jens Ohling .05 .15
70 Magnus Jansson .02 .10
71 Peter Nilsson .02 .10
72 Fredrik Lindquist .08 .25
73 Mariusz Czerkawski .60 1.50
74 Johan Lindstedt .02 .10
75 Stefan Ketola .08 .25
76 Erik Huusko .05 .15
77 Anders Huusko .05 .15
78 Farjestad .02 .10
Team Emblem
79 Anders Bergman .08 .25
80 Jorgen Ryden .08 .25
81 Patrik Haltia .15 .40
82 Tommy Samuelsson .02 .10
83 Per Lundell .02 .10
84 Leif Carlsson .02 .10
85 Jesper Duus .02 .10
86 Mattias Olsson .02 .10
87 Thomas Rhodin .02 .10
88 Jakob Karlsson .02 .10
89 Greger Artursson .02 .10
90 Thomas Rundqvist .05 .15
91 Bengt-Ake Gustafsson .05 .15
92 Hakan Loob .40 1.00
93 Lars Karlsson .02 .10
94 Magnus Roupe .07 .20
95 Kjell Dahlin .08 .25
96 Staffan Lundh .02 .10
97 Peter Ottosson .02 .10
98 Niklas Brannstrom .02 .10
99 Jonas Hoglund .75 2.00
100 Clas Eriksson .02 .10
101 Andreas Johansson .20 .50
102 Mathias Johansson .02 .10
103 HV 71 .02 .10
Team Emblem
104 Peter Aslin .15 .40
105 Boo Ahl .20 .50
106 Stefan Magnusson .02 .10
107 Fredrik Stillman .07 .20
108 Lars Ivarsson .02 .10
109 Klas Heed .02 .10
110 Arto Ruotanen .02 .10
111 Per Gustafsson .02 .10
112 Tommy Fritz .02 .10
113 Mathias Svedberg .02 .10
114 Kristian Pedersen .02 .10
115 Peter Eriksson .02 .10
116 Risto Kurkinen .02 .10
117 Ove Thornberg .02 .10
118 Stefan Ornskog .08 .25
119 Thomas Ljungberg .02 .10
120 Patrik Ross .02 .10
121 Eddy Ericsson .02 .10
122 Dennis Strom .02 .10
123 Torbjorn Persson .02 .10
124 Jonas Jonsson .02 .10
125 Peter Ekelund .02 .10
126 Stefan Falk .08 .25
127 Ronny Nilsson .02 .10
128 Leksand .02 .10
Team Emblem
129 Olow Sundstrom .08 .25
130 Jonas Leven .08 .25
131 Tomas Jonsson .08 .25
132 Ricard Persson .08 .25
133 Magnus Svensson .15 .40
134 Mattias Andersson .02 .10
135 Henric Bjorkman .02 .10
136 Orjan Lindmark .02 .10
137 Orjan Nilsson .02 .10
138 Tomas Ring .02 .10
139 Roger Johansson .02 .10
140 Marcus Thuresson .02 .10
141 Per-Olof Carlsson .02 .10
142 Jens Nielsen .02 .10
143 Cenneth Soderlund .02 .10
144 Markus Akerblom .07 .20
145 Fredrik Jax .07 .20
146 Reine Rauhala .05 .15
147 Niklas Eriksson .02 .10
148 Martin Wiita .02 .10
149 Jonas Bergqvist .07 .20
150 Hannu Jarvenpaa .08 .25
151 Lulea .02 .10
Team Emblem
152 Robert Skoog .08 .25
153 Erik Granqvist .08 .25
154 Timo Jutila .08 .25
155 Tomas Lilja .02 .10
156 Lars Modig .02 .10
157 Per Ljusterang .02 .10
158 Jari Gronstrand .02 .10
159 Torbjorn Lindberg .02 .10
160 Patrik Hoglund .07 .20
161 Petter Nilsson .02 .10
162 Daniel Behm .02 .10
163 Johan Stromvall .02 .10
164 Pauli Jarvinen .02 .10
165 Lars Edstrom .02 .10
166 Lars-Gunnar Pettersson .02 .10
167 Stefan Nilsson .02 .10
168 Lars Hurtig .02 .10
169 Tomas Berglund .02 .10
170 Robert Nordberg .08 .25
171 Mikael Renberg .75 2.00
172 Ulf Sandstrom .02 .10
173 Jens Hellgren .02 .10
174 Mikael Engstrom .02 .10
175 Malmo .02 .10
Team Emblem
176 Peter Lindmark .15 .40
177 Roger Nordstrom .15 .40
178 Johan Mansson .02 .10
179 Timo Blomqvist .15 .40
180 Peter Andersson .08 .25
181 Mats Lusth .02 .10
182 Roger Ohman .02 .10
183 Johan Salle .02 .10
184 Anders Svensson .02 .10
185 Johan Norgren .02 .10
186 Raimo Helminen .15 .40
187 Mats Hallin .08 .25
188 Mats Naslund .40 1.00
189 Robert Burakovsky .08 .25
190 Hakan Ahlund .02 .10
191 Peter Sundstrom .15 .40
192 Daniel Rydmark .07 .20
193 Matti Pauna .02 .10
194 Roger Hansson .02 .10
195 Patrik Gustavsson .02 .10
196 Rick Erdall .02 .10
197 Bo Svanberg .02 .10
198 Jesper Mattsson .20 .50
199 Jonas Hakansson .02 .10
200 MoDo .02 .10
Team Emblem
201 Fredrik Andersson .08 .25
202 Goran Arnmark .08 .25
203 Miroslav Horava .08 .25
204 Hans Lodin .02 .10
205 Lars Jansson .02 .10
206 Jorgen Eriksson .02 .10
207 Anders Berglund .02 .10
208 Osmo Soutokorva .02 .10
209 Tomas Nanzen .02 .10
210 Hans Jonsson .20 .50
211 Fredrik Bergqvist .02 .10
212 Erik Holmberg .02 .10
213 Peter Forsberg 4.00 10.00
214 Markus Naslund 1.25 3.00
215 Magnus Wernblom .02 .10
216 Lars Bystrom .02 .10
217 Kent Lantz .02 .10
218 Per Wallin .07 .20
219 Lennart Henriksson .02 .10
220 Ingemar Strom .02 .10
221 Ulf Odmark .02 .10
222 Jens Ohman .02 .10
223 Tommy Pettersson .02 .10
224 Andreas Salomonsson .05 .15
225 Sodertalje .02 .10
Team Emblem
226 Reino Sundberg .08 .25
227 Stefan Dernestal .08 .25
228 Mats Kihlstrom .02 .10
229 Stefan Jonsson .02 .10
230 Jan Bergman .02 .10
231 Peter Ekroth .02 .10
232 Stefan Nyman .02 .10
233 Thomas Carlsson .02 .10
234 Stefan Claesson .02 .10
235 Oto Hascak .07 .20
236 Morgan Samuelsson .02 .10
237 Tomaz Eriksson .02 .10
238 Thom Eklund .02 .10
239 Conny Jansson .02 .10
240 Bjorn Carlsson .02 .10
241 Scott Moore .02 .10
242 Reine Landgren .02 .10
243 Ola Rosander .02 .10
244 Stefan Olsson .02 .10
245 Anders Frykbo .02 .10
246 Ola Andersson .02 .10
247 Joe Tracy .02 .10
248 Christer Ljungberg .02 .10
249 Patrik Nyberg .02 .10
250 Joakim Skold .02 .10
251 Vasteras .02 .10
Team Emblem
252 Mats Ytter .08 .25
253 Par Hellenberg .08 .25
254 Tommy Salo 1.50 4.00
255 Nicklas Lidstrom 1.50 4.00
256 Robert Nordmark .08 .25
257 Leif Rohlin .15 .40
258 Roger Akerstrom .05 .15
259 Peter Popovic .08 .25
260 Jan Karlsson .02 .10
261 Tore Lindgren .02 .10
262 Peter Jacobsson .02 .10
263 Pierre Ivarsson .02 .10
264 Misjat Fachrutdinov .02 .10
265 Paul Andersson .02 .10
266 Patrik Juhlin .20 .50
267 Henrik Nilsson .02 .10
268 Anders Berglund .02 .10
269 Claes Lindblom .02 .10
270 Jorgen Holmberg .02 .10
271 Stefan Hellkvist .02 .10
272 Fredrik Nilsson .08 .25
273 Johan Brummer .02 .10
274 Micael Karlberg .02 .10
275 Niclas Lundberg .02 .10
276 Vastra Frolunda .02 .10
Team Emblem
277 Ake Lilljebjorn .08 .25
278 Hakan Algotsson .15 .40
279 Hakan Nordin .02 .10
280 Jonas Heed .02 .10
281 Joacim Esbjors .05 .15
282 Stefan Larsson .02 .10
283 Stefan Axelsson .08 .25
284 Oscar Ackestrom .02 .10
285 Jerk Hogstrom .02 .10
286 Patric Aberg .02 .10
287 Patrik Carnback .08 .25
288 Serge Boisvert .08 .25
289 Mats Lundstrom .02 .10
290 Mikael Andersson .20 .50
291 Kari Jaako .02 .10
292 Terho Koskela .02 .10
293 Lars Dahlstrom .02 .10
294 Jerry Persson .02 .10
295 Peter Berndtsson .02 .10
296 Thomas Sjogren .05 .15
297 Par Edlund .02 .10
298 Christian Lechtaler .02 .10
299 Jonas Esbjors .05 .15
300 Dennis Fredriksson .02 .10
301 Mats Hjalmarsson .02 .10
302 Leif Holmgren CO .02 .10
303 Tommy Sandlin CO .02 .10
304 Lars Falk CO .02 .10
305 Harald Luckner CO .02 .10
306 Lars-Erik Lundstrom CO .02 .10
307 Staffan Tholson CO .02 .10
308 Freddy Lindfors CO .02 .10
309 Timo Lahtinen CO .02 .10
310 Jan-Ake Andersson CO .02 .10
311 Claes-Goran Wallin CO .02 .10
312 Mikael Lundstrom CO .02 .10
313 Leif Boork CO .02 .10
314 Thomas Rundqvist .08 .25
315 Hakan Loob .40 1.00
316 Tommy Soderstrom .30 .75
317 Niklas Andersson .08 .25
318 Hakan Loob .40 1.00
319 Tomas Sandstrom .20 .50
320 Rolf Ridderwall .08 .25
321 Thomas Eriksson .02 .10
322 Nicklas Lidstrom 1.50 4.00
323 Mats Sundin 1.50 4.00
324 Thomas Rundqvist .08 .25
325 Hakan Loob .40 1.00
326 Marcus Karlsson .02 .10
327 Anders Eriksson .02 .10
328 Mats Lindgren .20 .50
329 Mikael Hakansson .08 .25
330 Mathias Johansson .02 .10
331 Niclas Sundstrom .40 1.00
332 Jesper Mattsson .20 .50
333 Anders Soderberg .20 .50
334 Swedish IHF Emblem .02 .10
335 1991 World Champions .02 .10
336 Rolf Ridderwall .08 .25
337 Peter Lindmark .15 .40
338 Tommy Soderstrom .30 .75
339 Kjell Samuelsson .08 .25
340 Calle Johansson .20 .50
341 Nicklas Lidstrom 1.50 4.00
342 Tomas Jonsson .08 .25
343 Peter Andersson .08 .25
344 Kenneth Kennholt .05 .15
345 Fredrik Stillman .07 .20
346 Thomas Rundqvist .08 .25
347 Hakan Loob .40 1.00
348 Bengt-Ake Gustafsson .08 .25
349 Mats Naslund .40 1.00
350 Mikael Johansson .02 .10
351 Charles Berglund .05 .15
352 Jan Viktorsson .05 .15
353 Johan Garpenlov .02 .10
354 Anders Carlsson .02 .10
355 Patrik Ericksson .05 .15
356 Jonas Bergqvist .07 .20
357 Mats Sundin 1.50 4.00
358 Per-Erik Eklund .02 .10
359 Conny Evensson .02 .10
360 Curt Lundmark .02 .10

1991 Swedish Semic World Championship Stickers

These hockey stickers, which measure approximately 2 1/8" by 2 7/8", were sold five to a packet. Also an album was available to display all 250 stickers. The fronts display color posed player shots framed by a red inner border studded with yellow miniature stars and a white outer border. The team flag, the player's name, and the sticker number appear in the white border below the picture. The backs were different based on distribution; blank backs were sold in Czechoslovakia; Marabou Chocloate ads were on the backs of cards sold in Finlands and Milky Way ads were on the back of cards sold in Sweden. The stickers are grouped according to country. Teemu Selanne appears in his Rookie Card year.

COMPLETE SET (250) 50.00 125.00
1 Finnish Emblem .02 .10
2 Markus Ketterer .20 .50
3 Sakari Lindfors .08 .25
4 Jukka Tammi .08 .25
5 Timo Jutila .05 .15
6 Hannu Virta .05 .15
7 Simo Saarinen .02 .10
8 Jukka Marttila .02 .10
9 Ville Siren .05 .15
10 Pasi Huura .05 .15
11 Hannu Henriksson .02 .10
12 Arto Ruotanen .02 .10
13 Ari Haanpaa .02 .10
14 Pauli Jarvinen .02 .10
15 Teppo Kivela .02 .10
16 Risto Kurkinen .02 .10
17 Mika Nieminen .05 .15
18 Jari Kurri .40 1.00
19 Esa Keskinen .08 .25
20 Raimo Summanen .02 .10
21 Teemu Selanne 3.00 8.00
22 Jari Torkki .02 .10
23 Hannu Jarvenpaa .05 .15
24 Raimo Helminen .05 .15
25 Timo Peltomaa .05 .15
26 Swedish Emblem .02 .10
27 Peter Lindmark .08 .25
28 Rolf Ridderwall .05 .15
29 Tommy Soderstrom .20 .50
30 Thomas Eriksson .05 .15
31 Nicklas Lidstrom 2.00 5.00
32 Tomas Jonsson .05 .15
33 Tommy Samuelsson .02 .10
34 Fredrik Stillman .05 .15
35 Peter Andersson .05 .15
36 Peter Andersson .05 .15
37 Kenneth Kennholt .05 .15
38 Hakan Loob .08 .25
39 Thomas Rundqvist .05 .15
40 Hakan Ahlund .02 .10
41 Jan Viktorsson .02 .10
42 Charles Berglund .05 .15
43 Mikael Johansson .02 .10
44 Robert Burakovsky .02 .10
45 Bengt-Ake Gustafsson .05 .15
46 Patrik Carnback .02 .10
47 Patrik Erickson .02 .10
48 Anders Carlsson .02 .10
49 Mats Naslund .15 .40
50 Kent Nilsson .15 .40
51 Canadian Emblem .40 1.00
52 Patrick Roy 6.00 15.00
53 Ed Belfour .75 2.00
54 Daniel Berthiaume .05 .15
55 Ray Bourque 2.00 5.00
56 Scott Stevens .30 .75
57 Al MacInnis .60 1.50
58 Paul Coffey .75 2.00
59 Paul Cavallini .05 .15
60 Zarley Zalapski .05 .15
61 Steve Duchesne .05 .15
62 Dave Ellett .05 .15
63 Mark Messier 1.50 4.00
64 Wayne Gretzky 10.00 25.00
65 Steve Yzerman 6.00 15.00
66 Pierre Turgeon .60 1.50
67 Bernie Nicholls .20 .50
68 Cam Neely 1.50 4.00
69 Joe Nieuwendyk .30 .75
70 Luc Robitaille .60 1.50
71 Kevin Dineen .05 .15
72 John Cullen .05 .15
73 Steve Larmer .07 .20
74 Mark Recchi .60 1.50
75 Joe Sakic 2.00 5.00
76 Soviet Emblem .20 .50
77 Arturs Irbe .40 1.00
78 Alexei Marin .02 .10
79 Mikhail Shtalenkov .08 .25
80 Vladimir Malakhov .08 .25
81 Vladimir Konstantinov .40 1.00
82 Igor Kravchuk .05 .15
83 Ilya Byakin .05 .15
84 Dimitri Mironov .07 .20
85 Vladimir Turikov .02 .10
86 Vjatjeslav Uvajev .02 .10
87 Vladimir Fedosov .02 .10
88 Valeri Kamensky .20 .50
89 Pavel Bure 1.50 4.00
90 Vyacheslav Butsayev .05 .15
91 Igor Maslennikov .02 .10
92 Evgeny Davydov .05 .15
93 Andrei Kovalev .02 .10
94 Alexander Semak .05 .15
95 Alexei Zhamnov .15 .40
96 Sergei Nemchinov .05 .15
97 Viktor Gordijuk .02 .10
98 Vyacheslav Kozlov .30 .75
99 Andrei Khomotov .20 .50
100 Vyacheslav Bykov .15 .40
101 Czech Emblem .02 .10
102 Petr Briza .08 .25
103 Dominik Hasek 2.00 5.00
104 Eduard Hartmann .05 .15
105 Bedrich Scerban .05 .15
106 Jiri Slegr .07 .20
107 Josef Reznicek .02 .10
108 Petr Pavlas .02 .10
109 Peter Slanina .02 .10
110 Martin Maskarinec .02 .10
111 Antonin Stavjana .05 .15
112 Stanislav Medrik .02 .10
113 Dusan Pasek .07 .20
114 Jiri Lala .05 .15
115 Darius Rusnak .02 .10
116 Oto Hascak .05 .15
117 Radek Toupal .05 .15
118 Pavel Pycha .02 .10
119 Lubomir Kolnik .02 .10
120 Libor Dolana .02 .10
121 Ladislav Lubina .05 .15
122 Tomas Jelinek .02 .10
123 Petr Vlk .02 .10
124 Vladimir Petrovka .02 .10
125 Richard Zemlicka .05 .15
126 U.S.A. Emblem .20 .50
127 John Vanbiesbrouck .75 2.00
128 Mike Richter .75 2.00
129 Chris Terreri .08 .25
130 Chris Chelios .75 2.00
131 Brian Leetch .40 1.00
132 Gary Suter .07 .20
133 Phil Housley .08 .25
134 Mark Howe .05 .15
135 Al Iafrate .08 .25
136 Kevin Hatcher .08 .25
137 Mathieu Schneider .08 .25
138 Pat LaFontaine .30 .75
139 Darren Turcotte .05 .15
140 Neal Broten .07 .20
141 Mike Modano 1.50 4.00
142 Dave Christian .05 .15
143 Craig Janney .15 .40
144 Brett Hull 1.50 4.00
145 Kevin Stevens .15 .40
146 Joe Mullen .08 .25
147 Tony Granato .07 .20
148 Ed Olczyk .05 .15
149 Jeremy Roenick 1.50 4.00
150 Jimmy Carson .05 .15
151 West German Emblem .02 .10
152 Helmut De Raaf .02 .10
153 Josef Heiss .07 .20
154 Karl Friesen .07 .20
155 Uli Hiemer .05 .15
156 Harold Kreis .02 .10
157 Udo Kiessling .05 .15
158 Michael Schmidt .02 .10
159 Michael Heidt .05 .15
160 Andreas Pokorny .02 .10
161 Bernd Wagner .02 .10
162 Uwe Krupp .08 .25
163 Gerd Truntschka .05 .15
164 Bernd Truntschka .05 .15
165 Thomas Brandl .02 .10
166 Peter Draisaitl .02 .10
167 Andreas Brockmann .02 .10
168 Ulrich Liebsch .02 .10
169 Ralf Hantschke .02 .10
170 Thomas Schinko .02 .10
171 Anton Krinner .02 .10
172 Thomas Werner .02 .10
173 Dieter Hegen .05 .15
174 Helmut Steiger .02 .10
175 Georg Franz .02 .10
176 Swiss Emblem .02 .10
177 Renato Tosio .02 .10
178 Reto Pavoni .05 .15
179 Dino Stecher .02 .10
180 Sven Leuenberger .02 .10
181 Rick Tschumi .02 .10
182 Patrice Brasey .02 .10
183 Didier Massy .02 .10
184 Sandro Bertaggia .02 .10
185 Samuel Balmer .02 .10
186 Martin Rauch .02 .10
187 Marc Leuenberger .02 .10
188 Jorg Eberle .02 .10
189 Fredy Luthi .02 .10
190 Andy Ton .02 .10
191 Raymond Walder .02 .10
192 Manuele Celio .02 .10
193 Roman Wager .02 .10
194 Felix Hollenstein .02 .10
195 Andre Rotheli .02 .10
196 Christian Weber .02 .10
197 Peter Jaks .02 .10
198 Gil Montandon .02 .10
199 Oliver Hoffmann .02 .10
200 Thomas Vrabec .02 .10
201 Teppo Numminen .07 .20
202 Jyrki Lumme .05 .15
203 Esa Tikkanen .15 .40
204 Petri Skriko .05 .15
205 Christian Ruutu .07 .20
206 Ilkka Sinisalo .07 .20
207 Calle Johansson .07 .20
208 Tomas Sandstrom .07 .20
209 Thomas Steen .07 .20
210 Per-Erik Eklund .07 .20
211 Mats Sundin .60 1.50
212 Johan Garpenlov .07 .20
213 Slava Fetisov .40 1.00
214 Alexei Kasatonov .15 .40
215 Mikhail Tatarinov .02 .10
216 Sergei Makarov .20 .50
217 Igor Larionov .40 1.00
218 Alexander Mogilny .60 1.50
219 Sergei Fedorov 1.50 4.00
220 Petr Klima .05 .15
221 David Volek .07 .20
222 Michal Pivonka .08 .25
223 Robert Reichel .08 .25
224 Robert Holik .20 .50
225 Jaromir Jagr 2.00 5.00
226 Urpo Ylonen .02 .10
227 Ilpo Koskela .02 .10
228 Pekka Rautakallio .07 .20
229 Lasse Oksanen .02 .10
230 Veli-Pekka Ketola .07 .20
231 Leif Holmqvist .05 .15
232 Lennart Svedberg .04 .10
233 Sven Tumba Johansson .02 .10
234 Ulf Sterner .02 .10

235 Anders Hedberg .08 .25
236 Ken Dryden 2.00 5.00
237 Bobby Orr 6.00 15.00
238 Gordie Howe 2.00 5.00
239 Bobby Hull 1.25 3.00
240 Phil Esposito 1.50 4.00
241 Vladislav Tretiak 1.50 4.00
242 Alexander Ragulin .08 .25
243 Anatoli Firsov .08 .25
244 Valeri Kharlamov .40 1.00
245 Alexander Maltsev .20 .50
246 Jiri Holecek .07 .20
247 Jan Suchy .02 .10
248 Jozef Golonka .02 .10
249 Vaclav Nedomansky .07 .20
250 Ivan Hlinka .07 .20

1992-93 Swedish Semic Elitserien Stickers

This 356-sticker set covers the Swedish Elitserien. The stickers, which measure 3" by 2 1/8", feature posed color photos and player name on the front. The back has card number, and a cartoon ad for Buster, a sports magazine for Swedish boys. The set is highlighted by the pre-NHL appearances of Peter Forsberg, Mikael Renberg and Tommy Salo, as well as former greats such as Borje Salming and Hakan Loob.

COMPLETE SET (356) 30.00 75.00
1 AIK Team Picture .02 .10
2 AIK Team Picture .02 .10
3 Brynas Team Picture .02 .10
4 Brynas Team Picture .02 .10
5 Djurgarden Team Picture .02 .10
6 Djurgarden Team Picture .02 .10
7 Farjestad Team Picture .02 .10
8 Farjestad Team Picture .02 .10
9 HV 71 Team Picture .02 .10
10 HV 71 Team Picture .02 .10
11 Leksand Team Picture .02 .10
12 Leksand Team Picture .02 .10
13 Lulea Team Picture .02 .10
14 Lulea Team Picture .02 .10
15 Malmo Team Picture .02 .10
16 Malmo Team Picture .02 .10
17 MoDo Team Picture .02 .10
18 MoDo Team Picture .02 .10
19 Rogle Team Picture .02 .10
20 Rogle Team Picture .02 .10
21 Vasteras Team Picture .02 .10
22 Vasteras Team Picture .02 .10
23 Vastra Frolunda Team .02 .10
24 Vastra Frolunda Team .02 .10
25 AIK Team Emblem .02 .10
26 Rolf Ridderwall .08 .25
27 Sam Lindstahl .07 .20
28 Ronnie Karlsson .02 .10
29 Mats Thelin .08 .25
30 Mattias Norstrom .30 .75
31 Dick Tarnstrom .08 .25
32 Petri Liimatainen .02 .10
33 Rikard Franzen .05 .15
34 Daniel Jardemyr .02 .10
35 Niclas Havelid .40 1.00
36 Borje Salming .75 2.00
37 Thomas Bjuhr .02 .10
38 Peter Hammarstrom .02 .10
39 Thomas Strandberg .02 .10
40 Mats Lindberg .02 .10
41 Anders Bjork .02 .10
42 Anders Johnson .02 .10
43 Patrik Erickson .05 .15
44 Torbjorn Ohrlund .02 .10
45 Bjorn Ahlstrom .02 .10
46 Niclas Sundblad .05 .15
47 Patric Englund .02 .10
48 Kristian Gahn .02 .10
49 Morgan Samuelsson .05 .15
50 Brynas Team Emblem .02 .10
51 Michael Sundlov .20 .50
52 Lars Karlsson .08 .25
53 Bedrich Scerban .05 .15
54 Mikael Lindman .02 .10
55 Tommy Melkersson .02 .10
56 Stefan Klockare .05 .15
57 Mikael Enander .02 .10
58 Roger Karlsson .02 .10
59 Niklas Gallstedt .02 .10
60 Christer Olsson .20 .50
61 Anders Carlsson .02 .10
62 Thomas Tallberg .05 .15
63 Tom Bissett .05 .15
64 Andreas Dackell .40 1.00
65 Mikael Wahlberg .02 .10
66 Jan Larsson .02 .10
67 Anders Gozzi .02 .10
68 Ove Molin .02 .10
69 Anders Huss .05 .15
70 Peter Gustafsson .02 .10
71 Jonas Johnsson .02 .10
72 Peter Larsson .02 .10
73 Mikael Lindholm .02 .10
74 Djurgarden Team Emblem .02 .10
75 Thomas Ostlund .20 .50
76 Petter Ronnquist .07 .20
77 Christian Due-Boje .05 .15
78 Arto Blomsten .05 .15
79 Kenneth Kennholt .07 .20
80 Marcus Ragnarsson .20 .50
81 Thomas Johansson .02 .10
82 Joakim Lundberg .02 .10
83 Thomas Eriksson .02 .10
84 Bjorn Nord .08 .25
85 Mikael Magnusson .02 .10
86 Charles Berglund .02 .10
87 Erik Huusko .05 .15
88 Anders Huusko .05 .15
89 Tony Skopac .02 .10
90 Jens Ohling .07 .20
91 Peter Nilsson .02 .10
92 Magnus Jansson .02 .10
93 Kent Nilsson .30 .75
94 Mikael Hakansson .02 .10
95 Ola Josefsson .02 .10
96 Jerry Friman .02 .10
97 Fredrik Lindquist .15 .40
98 Mathias Hallback .02 .10
99 Jan Viktorsson .02 .10
100 Farjestad .02 .10
Team Emblem
101 Anders Bergman .08 .25
102 Jonas Eriksson .07 .20
103 Patrik Haltia .20 .50
104 Tommy Samuelsson .02 .10
105 Jesper Duus .08 .25
106 Leif Carlsson .02 .10
107 Per Lundell .02 .10
108 Jakob Karlsson .02 .10
109 Thomas Rhodin .02 .10
110 Mattias Olsson .02 .10
111 Hakan Loob .40 1.00
112 Thomas Rundqvist .02 .10
113 Andreas Johansson .20 .50
114 Staffan Lundh .02 .10
115 Jonas Hoglund .40 1.00
116 Bengt-Ake Gustafsson .15 .40
117 Mattias Johansson .02 .10
118 Clas Eriksson .02 .10
119 Peter Ottosson .02 .10
120 Niklas Brannstrom .02 .10
121 Lars Karlsson .08 .25
122 Peter Hagstrom .02 .10
123 Kjell Dahlin .15 .40
124 HV 71 .02 .10
Team Emblem
125 Peter Aslin .08 .25
126 Bono Ahl .20 .50
127 Antonin Stavjana .07 .20
128 Klas Heed .02 .10
129 Tommy Fritz .02 .10
130 Kristian Pedersen .02 .10
131 Per Gustafsson .20 .50
132 Mathias Svedberg .02 .10
133 Niclas Rahm .02 .10
134 Martin Danielsson .02 .10
135 Fredrik Stillman .02 .10
136 Lars Ivarsson .02 .10
137 Ove Thornberg .02 .10
138 Peter Ekelund .02 .10
139 Eddy Eriksson .02 .10
140 Stefan Ornskog .07 .20
141 Patrik Ross .02 .10
142 Torbjorn Persson .02 .10
143 Kamil Kastak .07 .20
144 Dennis Strom .02 .10
145 Peter Eriksson .02 .10
146 Magnus Axelsson .02 .10
147 Stefan Falk .07 .20
148 Thomas Ljungberg .02 .10
149 Leksand .02 .10
Team Emblem
150 Ake Lilljebjorn .08 .25
151 Jonas Leven .08 .25
152 Johan Hedberg 1.25 3.00
153 Tomas Jonsson .15 .40
154 Henric Bjorkman .02 .10
155 Mattias Andersson .02 .10
156 Rickard Persson .08 .25
157 Orjan Nilsson .02 .10
158 Magnus Svensson .08 .25
159 Orjan Lindmark .02 .10
160 Jan Huokko .02 .10
161 Reine Rauhala .02 .10
162 Emil Skoglund .02 .10
163 Jens Nielsen .02 .10
164 Marcus Thuresson .02 .10
165 Niklas Eriksson .02 .10
166 Tomas Srsen .05 .15
167 Jonas Bergqvist .08 .25
168 Per-Olof Carlsson .02 .10
169 Markus Akerblom .02 .10
170 Greg Parks .05 .15
171 Mattias Loof .02 .10
172 Cenneth Soderlund .02 .10
173 Jarmo Makitalo .02 .10
174 Lulea .02 .10
Team Emblem
175 Robert Skoog .07 .20
176 Erik Grankvist .07 .20
177 Lars Modig .02 .10
178 Patrik Hoglund .02 .10
179 Niklas Bjornfot .02 .10
180 Torbjorn Lindberg .02 .10
181 Ville Siren .08 .25
182 Petter Nilsson .02 .10
183 Joakim Gunler .02 .10
184 Tomas Lilja .02 .10
185 Stefan Jonsson .02 .10
186 Stefan Nilsson .07 .20
187 Johan Stromvall .02 .10
188 Robert Nordberg .05 .15
189 Tomas Berglund .05 .15
190 Mikael Renberg .75 2.00
191 Lars-Gunnar Pettersson .02 .10
192 Lars Edstrom .02 .10
193 Kyosti Karjalainen .07 .20
194 Lars Hurtig .02 .10
195 Fredrik Oberg .02 .10
196 Mikael Engstrom .02 .10
197 Mika Nieminen .20 .50
198 Malmo .02 .10
Team Emblem
199 Peter Lindmark .20 .50
200 Roger Nordstrom .08 .25
201 Johan Mansson .02 .10
202 Anders Svensson .02 .10
203 Timo Blomqvist .08 .25
204 Johan Norgren .02 .10
205 Mats Lusth .02 .10
206 Peter Hasselblad .02 .10
207 Robert Svehla .20 .50
208 Johan Salle .02 .10
209 Roger Ohman .02 .10
210 Raimo Helminen .20 .50
211 Roger Hansson .07 .20
212 Per Rosenqvist .02 .10
213 Bo Svanberg .02 .10
214 Daniel Rydmark .07 .20
215 Patrik Sylvegard .02 .10
216 Jonas Hakansson .02 .10
217 Jesper Mattsson .20 .50
218 Hakan Ahlund .02 .10
219 Peter Sundstrom .15 .40
220 Mats Naslund .75 2.00
221 Robert Burakovsky .05 .15
222 MoDo .02 .10
Team Emblem
223 Fredrik Andersson .07 .20
224 Anders Nasstrom .07 .20
225 Anders Berglund .02 .10
226 Miroslav Horava .05 .15
227 Hans Lodin .02 .10
228 Lars Jansson .02 .10
229 Jorgen Eriksson .02 .10
230 Anders Eriksson .40 1.00
231 Hans Jonsson .02 .10
232 Tomas Nanzen .02 .10
233 Mattias Timander .20 .50
234 Fredrik Bergqvist .02 .10
235 Magnus Wernblom .07 .20
236 Martin Hostak .05 .15
237 Mikael Pettersson .02 .10
238 Lennart Hermansson .02 .10
239 Tommy Lehmann .07 .20
240 Markus Naslund .40 1.00
241 Ulf Odmark .02 .10
242 Peter Forsberg 6.00 15.00
243 Andreas Salomonsson .02 .10
244 Niklas Sundstrom .40 1.00
245 Lars Bystrom .02 .10
246 Erik Holmberg .02 .10
247 Henrik Gradin .02 .10
248 Rogle .02 .10
Team Emblem
249 Kenneth Johansson .08 .25
250 Billy Nilsson .08 .25
251 Orjan Jacobsson .02 .10
252 Daniel Johansson .02 .10
253 Kenny Jonsson .60 1.50
254 Kari Eloranta .08 .25
255 Kari Suoraniemi .02 .10
256 Hakan Persson .02 .10
257 Rikard Gronborg .02 .10
258 Stefan Nilsson .02 .10
259 Per Ljusterang .02 .10
260 Igor Stelnov .02 .10
261 Peter Lundmark .08 .25
262 Heinz Ehlers .02 .10
263 Michael Hjalm .02 .10
264 Jan Ericson .02 .10
265 Pelle Svensson .02 .10
266 Mats Loov .05 .15
267 Stefan Elvenes .05 .15
268 Roger Elvenes .07 .20
269 Peter Wennberg .02 .10
270 Per Wallin .08 .25
271 Torgny Lowgren .02 .10
272 Jorgen Jonsson .02 .10
273 Vasteras .02 .10
Team Emblem
274 Mats Ytter .08 .25
275 Tommy Salo .75 2.00
276 Erik Bergstrom .02 .10
277 Pierre Ivarsson .02 .10
278 Peter Popovic .20 .50
279 Sergei Fokin .02 .10
280 Edvin Frylen .08 .25
281 Leif Rohlin .15 .40
282 Peter Karlsson .02 .10
283 Peter Jacobsson .02 .10
284 Roger Akerstrom .05 .15
285 Robert Nordmark .07 .20
286 Patrik Juhlin .20 .50
287 Mishat Fahrutdinov .05 .15
288 Henrik Nilsson .02 .10
289 Mikael Pettersson .02 .10
290 Fredrik Nilsson .05 .15
291 Stefan Hellkvist .02 .10
292 Henrik Pettersson .02 .10
293 Micael Karlberg .02 .10
294 Anders Berglund .02 .10
295 Claes Lindblom .05 .15
296 Johan Brummer .02 .10
297 Patrik Ulin .02 .10
298 Paul Andersson .02 .10
299 Vastra Frolunda .02 .10
Team Emblem
300 Hakan Algotsson .20 .50
301 Mikael Sandberg .08 .25
302 Patric Aberg .02 .10
303 Joacim Esbjors .05 .15
304 Oscar Ackestrom .02 .10
305 Jonas Heed .02 .10
306 Stefan Axelsson .08 .25
307 Ronnie Sundin .20 .50
308 Stefan Larsson .02 .10
309 Jonathan Hagrenius .02 .10
310 Serge Boisvert .05 .15
311 Jerry Persson .02 .10
312 Trond Magnussen .02 .10
313 Terho Koskela .02 .10
314 Peter Berndtsson .02 .10
315 Mikael Persson .02 .10
316 Mats Hjalmarsson .02 .10
317 Henrik Lundin .02 .10
318 Jonas Esbjors .02 .10
319 Daniel Alfredsson 1.00 2.50
320 Stefan Ketola .02 .10
321 Lars Dahlstrom .02 .10
322 Par Edlund .02 .10
323 Thomas Sjogren .05 .15
324 Leif Holmgren CO .02 .10
325 Tommy Sandlin CO .02 .10
326 Lars Falk CO .02 .10
327 Harald Luckner CO .02 .10
328 Lars-Erik Lundstrom CO .02 .10
329 Wayne Fleming CO .02 .10
330 Freddy Lindfors CO .02 .10
331 Timo Lahtinen CO .02 .10
332 Kent Forsberg CO .08 .25
333 Christer Abrahamsson CO .08 .25
334 Mikael Lundstrom CO .02 .10
335 Leif Boork CO .02 .10
336 Tommy Sjodin .08 .25
337 Hakan Loob .40 1.00
338 Michael Nylander .40 1.00
339 Michael Nylander .40 1.00
340 Hakan Loob .40 1.00
341 Calle Johansson .20 .50
342 Tommy Sandlin CO .40 1.00
343 Tommy Soderstrom .40 1.00
344 Tommy Sjodin .08 .25
345 Peter Andersson .05 .15
346 Hakan Loob .40 1.00
347 Peter Forsberg 6.00 15.00
348 Mats Sundin 2.00 5.00
349 Jonas Forsberg .20 .50
350 Stefan Bjork .05 .15
351 Edvin Frylen .08 .25
352 Mikael Tjallden .05 .15
353 Johan Davidsson .20 .50
354 Markus Eriksson .05 .15
355 Fredrik Lindh .05 .15
356 Peter Nylander .05 .15

1993-94 Swedish Semic Elitserien

This 320-sticker set was the collectible to own for fans of the Elitserien. This comprehensive issue had a posed player photo and name on the front, with card number and a cartoon ad for the whimsical boy's sports magazine, "Buster" on the back.

COMPLETE SET (320) 24.00 60.00
1 Bjorkloven Team Emblem .02 .10
2 Patrik Hofbauer .02 .10
3 Jorgen Wikstrom .02 .10
4 Mattias Hedlund .02 .10
5 Yuri Kuznetsov .07 .20
6 Ulf Odling .02 .10
7 Jorgen Eriksson .02 .10
8 Jorgen Hermansson .02 .10
9 Peter Andersson .02 .10
10 Joakim Lindgren .02 .10
11 Glenn Hedman .02 .10
12 Roger Kyro .02 .10
13 Niklas Norberg .02 .10
14 Alexander Belyavsky .05 .15
15 Anders Nejdsater .02 .10
16 Stefan Olofsson .02 .10
17 Mikael Andersson .08 .25
18 Ulf Andersson .02 .10
19 Patrik Sundstrom .08 .25
20 Hakan Hermansson .02 .10
21 Micael Karlberg .02 .10
22 Peder Bejegard .02 .10
23 Johan Boman .02 .10
24 Joakim Lindgren .02 .10
25 Brynas Team Emblem .02 .10
26 Michael Sundlov .07 .20
27 Lars Karlsson .07 .20
28 Bedrich Scerban .02 .10
29 Mikael Lindman .02 .10
30 Johan Tornberg .02 .10
31 Tommy Melkersson .02 .10
32 Stefan Klockare .05 .15
33 Mikael Enander .02 .10
34 Mikael Wiklander .02 .10
35 Christer Olsson .08 .25
36 Thomas Tallberg .05 .15
37 Andreas Dackell .40 1.00
38 Mikael Wahlberg .02 .10
39 Anders Gozzi .02 .10
40 Niklas Gallstedt .02 .10
41 Per-Johan Johansson .02 .10
42 Joakim Persson .08 .25
43 Branislav Janos .02 .10
44 Ove Molin .02 .10
45 Anders Huss .02 .10
46 Jonas Johnsson .02 .10
47 Peter Larsson .02 .10
48 Anders Carlsson .02 .10
49 Djurgarden Team Emblem .02 .10
50 Thomas Ostlund .08 .25
51 Petter Ronnquist .05 .15
52 Christian Due-Boje .05 .15
53 Marcus Ragnarsson .20 .50
54 Joakim Musakka .02 .10
55 Thomas Johansson .02 .10
56 Thomas Eriksson .02 .10
57 Bjorn Nord .08 .25
58 Mikael Magnusson .02 .10
59 Robert Nordmark .05 .15
60 Charles Berglund .02 .10
61 Erik Huusko .05 .15
62 Anders Huusko .05 .15
63 Jens Ohling .05 .15
64 Peter Nilsson .02 .10
65 Magnus Jansson .02 .10
66 Mikael Hakansson .02 .10
67 Ola Josefsson .02 .10
68 Jerry Friman .02 .10
69 Mariusz Czerkawski .40 1.00
70 Fredrik Lindquist .07 .20
71 Mattias Hallback .02 .10
72 Patrik Erickson .02 .10
73 Farjestad Team Emblem .02 .10
74 Anders Bergman .08 .25
75 Jonas Eriksson .07 .20
76 Tommy Samuelsson .02 .10
77 Jesper Duus .02 .10
78 Leif Carlsson .02 .10
79 Per Lundell .02 .10
80 Brian Tutt .05 .15
81 Jakob Karlsson .02 .10
82 Thomas Rhodin .05 .15
83 Mattias Olsson .02 .10
84 Hakan Loob .30 .75
85 Andreas Johansson .20 .50
86 Magnus Arvedsson .40 1.00
87 Anders Oberg .02 .10
88 Mattias Johansson .02 .10
89 Mats Lindgren .20 .50
90 Clas Eriksson .02 .10
91 Patrik Degerstedt .02 .10
92 Peter Ottosson .02 .10
93 Niklas Brannstrom .02 .10
94 Lars Karlsson .07 .20
95 Kjell Dahlin .08 .25
96 Jonas Hoglund .40 1.00
97 HV 71 Team Emblem .02 .10
98 Peter Aslin .08 .25
99 Boo Ahl .08 .25
100 Antonin Stavjana .07 .20
101 Kenneth Kennholt .05 .15
102 Hans Abrahamsson .02 .10
103 Andreas Schultz .02 .10
104 Per Gustafsson .08 .25
105 Mathias Svedberg .02 .10
106 Niklas Rahm .02 .10
107 Fredrik Stillman .02 .10
108 Owe Thornberg .02 .10
109 Thomas Gustavsson .02 .10
110 Stefan Ornskog .05 .15
111 Peter Hammarstrom .02 .10
112 Torbjorn Persson .02 .10
113 John Byce .05 .15
114 Peter Eriksson .02 .10
115 Magnus Axelsson .05 .15
116 Stefan Falk .05 .15
117 Patric Kjellberg .07 .20
118 Johan Davidsson .20 .50
119 Thomas Ljungberg .02 .10
120 Patrik Ross .02 .10
121 Leksand Team Emblem .02 .10
122 Johan Hedberg .75 2.00
123 Ake Lilljebjorn .05 .15
124 Tomas Jonsson .08 .25
125 Stefan Bergkvist .05 .15
126 Henric Bjorkman .02 .10
127 Hans Lodin .02 .10
128 Magnus Svensson .05 .15
129 Orjan Lindmark .02 .10
130 Jan Huokko .02 .10
131 Roger Johansson .02 .10
132 Per Widmark .02 .10
133 Marcus Thuresson .02 .10
134 Niklas Eriksson .02 .10
135 Peter Ciavaglia .05 .15
136 Jonas Bergkvist .08 .25
137 Martin Wiita .02 .10
138 Markus Akerblom .02 .10
139 Greg Parks .05 .15
140 Mattias Loof .02 .10
141 Andreas Karlsson .02 .10
142 Markus Eriksson .02 .10
143 Tomas Forslund .08 .25
144 Jarmo Makitalo .02 .10
145 Lulea Team Emblem .02 .10
146 Robert Skoog .05 .15
147 Erik Grankvist .07 .20
148 Lars Modig .02 .10
149 Patrik Hoglund .02 .10
150 Niklas Bjornfot .02 .10
151 Torbjorn Lindberg .02 .10
152 Ville Siren .07 .20
153 Petter Nilsson .02 .10
154 Tomas Lilja .02 .10
155 Stefan Jonsson .02 .10
156 Stefan Nilsson .02 .10
157 Joakim Gunler .02 .10
158 Johan Stromvall .02 .10
159 Kyosti Karjalainen .07 .20
160 Robert Nordberg .02 .10
161 Tomas Berglund .02 .10
162 Lars-Gunnar Pettersson .02 .10
163 Lars Edstrom .02 .10
164 Lars Hurtig .02 .10
165 Fredrik Oberg .02 .10
166 Mikael Engstrom .02 .10
167 Johan Rosen .02 .10
168 Mika Nieminen .08 .25
169 Malmo Team Emblem .02 .10
170 Peter Lindmark .08 .25
171 Roger Nordstrom .05 .15
172 Daniel Granqvist .05 .15
173 Johan Norgren .02 .10
174 Johan Salle .02 .10
175 Petri Liimatainen .02 .10
176 Peter Hasselblad .02 .10
177 Robert Svehla .08 .25
178 Ricard Persson .08 .25
179 Roger Ohman .02 .10
180 Raimo Helminen .08 .25
181 Marcus Magnertoft .02 .10
182 Mattias Bosson .02 .10
183 Roger Hansson .02 .10
184 Bo Svanberg .02 .10
185 Daniel Rydmark .07 .20
186 Patrik Sylvegard .02 .10
187 Jens Hemstrom .02 .10
188 Jesper Mattsson .08 .25
189 Hakan Ahlund .02 .10
190 Peter Sundstrom .08 .25
191 Mats Naslund .40 1.00
192 Mikko Makela .07 .20
193 MoDo Team Emblem .02 .10
194 Henrik Arvsell .02 .10
195 Fredrik Andersson .05 .15
196 Anders Berglund .02 .10
197 Mattias Timander .08 .25
198 Miroslav Horava .05 .15
199 Lars Jansson .02 .10
200 Anders Eriksson .20 .50
201 Hans Jonsson .20 .50
202 Tomas Nanzen .02 .10
203 Fredrik Bergqvist .02 .10
204 Magnus Wernblom .05 .15
205 Anders Soderberg .08 .25
206 Martin Hostak .05 .15
207 Lennart Hermansson .02 .10
208 Ulf Odmark .02 .10
209 Peter Forsberg 4.00 10.00
210 Per Svartvadet .20 .50
211 Andreas Salomonsson .02 .10
212 Niklas Sundstrom .40 1.00
213 Lars Bystrom .02 .10
214 Mats Lundstrom .02 .10
215 Erik Holmberg .02 .10
216 Henrik Gradin .02 .10
217 Rogle Team Emblem .02 .10
218 Kenneth Johansson .07 .20
219 Magnus Swardh .02 .10
220 Daniel Johansson .08 .25
221 Kari Suoraniemi .02 .10
222 Pierre Johnsson .02 .10
223 Kenny Jonsson .40 1.00
224 Per Ljusterang .02 .10
225 Arto Ruotanen .02 .10
226 Daniel Tjarnquist .08 .25
227 Kari Eloranta .05 .15
228 Per Wallin .08 .25
229 Peter Lundmark .05 .15
230 Roger Elvenes .05 .15
231 Michael Hjalm .02 .10
232 Mattias Olvestedt .02 .10
233 Jan Ericsson .02 .10
234 Tomas Srsen .02 .10
235 Pelle Svensson .02 .10
236 Jorgen Jonsson .02 .10
237 Stefan Elvenes .05 .15
238 Fredrik Moller .02 .10
239 Tord Elvenes .02 .10
240 Mats Loov .02 .10
241 Vasteras Team Emblem .02 .10
242 Mats Ytter .07 .20
243 Tommy Salo .40 1.00
244 Sergei Fokin .02 .10
245 Edvin Frylen .07 .20
246 Leif Rohlin .08 .25
247 Peter Karlsson .02 .10
248 Peter Jacobsson .02 .10
249 Thomas Carlsson .02 .10
250 Lars Ivarsson .02 .10
251 Roger Akerstrom .05 .15
252 Patrik Juhlin .08 .25
253 Alexei Salomatin .05 .15
254 Mishat Fahrutdinov .05 .15
255 Henrik Nilsson .02 .10
256 Mikael Pettersson .02 .10
257 Stefan Hellkvist .02 .10
258 Jens Nielsen .02 .10
259 Hans Huczkowski .02 .10
260 Claes Lindblom .02 .10
261 Johan Brummer .02 .10
262 Dejan Kostic .02 .10
263 Paul Andersson .02 .10
264 Henrik Nordfeldt .02 .10
265 V.Frolunda Team Emblem .02 .10
266 Hakan Algotsson .08 .25
267 Mikael Sandberg .07 .20
268 Stefan Nyman .02 .10
269 Joacim Esbjors .05 .15
270 Oscar Ackestrom .02 .10
271 Vladimir Kramskoy .02 .10
272 Richard Sohrman .02 .10
273 Stefan Axelsson .05 .15
274 Ronnie Sundin .08 .25
275 Stefan Larsson .02 .10
276 Thomas Sjogren .02 .10
277 Serge Boisvert .05 .15
278 Jerry Persson .02 .10
279 Terho Koskela .02 .10
280 Peter Strom .02 .10
281 Peter Berndtsson .02 .10
282 Henrik Lundin .02 .10
283 Jonas Esbjors .02 .10
284 Daniel Alfredsson 1.00 2.50
285 Stefan Ketola .02 .10
286 Lars Dahlstrom .02 .10
287 Par Edlund .02 .10
288 Oto Hascak .05 .15
289 Lars-Gunnar Jansson CO .02 .10
290 Tommy Sandlin CO .02 .10
291 Tommy Boustedt CO .02 .10
292 Jorgen Palm CO .02 .10
293 Hakan Nygren CO .02 .10
294 Wayne Fleming CO .02 .10
295 Sakari Pietila CO .02 .10
296 Timo Lahtinen CO .02 .10
297 Kent Forsberg CO .07 .20
298 Christer Abrahamsson CO .08 .25
299 Mikael Lundstrom CO .02 .10
300 Leif Boork CO .02 .10
301 Peter Forsberg 4.00 10.00
302 Peter Forsberg 4.00 10.00
303 Hakan Loob .30 .75
304 Kenny Jonsson .40 1.00
305 Peter Forsberg 4.00 10.00
306 Mats Sundin 1.50 4.00
307 Micheal Sundlov AS .07 .20
308 Roger Akerstrom AS .05 .15
309 Fredrik Stillman AS .02 .10
310 Mikael Renberg AS .40 1.00
311 Peter Forsberg AS 4.00 10.00
312 Ulf Dahlen AS .08 .25
313 Pal Grotnes FS .02 .10
314 Daniel Tjarnquist FS .08 .25
315 Henrik Rehnberg FS .05 .15
316 Mattias Ohlund FS .40 1.00
317 Jan Labraaten FS .08 .25
318 Patrik Wallenberg FS .07 .20
319 Niklas Wallin FS .07 .20
320 Tobias Thermell FS .07 .20

1993 Swedish Semic World Championships Stickers

This 1993 issue of 288-stickers was issued in Sweden to commemorate the 1993 World Championships. The stickers measure 3" by 2 1/8" and feature players from ten nations, mostly in action shots in their national team garb. The NHL players (#169-208) are shown in the club team sweaters. The backs bear the sticker number, as well as player information in Swedish. An album to hold the stickers is valued at about $10.

COMPLETE SET (288) 24.00 60.00
1 Peter Aslin .08 .25
2 Hakan Algotsson .08 .25
3 Kenneth Kennholt .02 .10
4 Arto Blomsten .05 .15
5 Tomas Jonsson .02 .10
6 Fredrik Stillman .02 .10
7 Stefan Larsson .02 .10
8 Peter Popovic .08 .25
9 Hakan Loob .08 .25
10 Thomas Rundqvist .02 .10
11 Patrik Juhlin .08 .25
12 Mikael Renberg .20 .50
13 Peter Forsberg 2.00 5.00
14 Markus Naslund .60 1.50
15 Bengt-Ake Gustafsson .08 .25
16 Jan Larsson .02 .10
17 Fredrik Nilsson .02 .10
18 Roger Hansson .02 .10
19 Tommy Soderstrom .08 .25
20 Anders Eldebrink .05 .15
21 Ulf Samuelsson .08 .25
22 Kjell Samuelsson .08 .25
23 Nicklas Lidstrom 1.25 3.00
24 Tommy Sjodin .05 .15
25 Calle Johansson .08 .25
26 Fredrik Olausson .08 .25
27 Peter Andersson .05 .15
28 Tommy Albelin .05 .15
29 Roger Johansson .05 .15
30 Par Djoos .05 .15
31 Mikael Johansson .02 .10
32 Tomas Sandstrom .08 .25
33 Mats Sundin .60 1.50
34 Ulf Dahlen .08 .25
35 Jan Erixon .05 .15
36 Thomas Steen .08 .25
37 Mikael Andersson .05 .15
38 Johan Garpenlov .08 .25
39 Per-Erik Eklund .08 .25
40 Michael Nylander .08 .25
41 Tomas Forslund .02 .10
42 Patric Kjellberg .20 .50
43 Patrik Carnback .02 .10
44 Niclas Andersson .02 .10
45 Markus Ketterer .08 .25
46 Sakari Lindfors .08 .25
47 Jarmo Myllys .20 .50
48 Peter Ahola .05 .15
49 Mikko Haapakoski .02 .10
50 Kai Harila .02 .10
51 Pasi Huura .05 .15
52 Waltteri Immonen .05 .15
53 Timo Jutila .02 .10
54 Janne Laukkanen .08 .25
55 Harri Laurila .02 .10
56 Jyrki Lumme .08 .25
57 Teppo Numminen .08 .25
58 Sami Nuutinen .02 .10
59 Ville Siren .05 .15
60 Pasi Sormunen .02 .10
61 Mika Stromberg .05 .15
62 Mika Alatalo .20 .50
63 Raimo Helminen .02 .10
64 Pauli Jarvinen .02 .10
65 Jarmo Kekalainen .05 .15
66 Jari Korpisalo .05 .15
67 Jari Kurri .40 1.00
68 Mikko Makela .08 .25
69 Mika Nieminen .08 .25
70 Timo Norppa .02 .10
71 Janne Ojanen .02 .10
72 Timo Peltomaa .02 .10
73 Rauli Raitanen .02 .10
74 Juha Riihijarvi .08 .25
75 Christian Ruuttu .08 .25
76 Timo Saarikoski .02 .10
77 Teemu Selanne 2.00 5.00
78 Jukka Seppo .05 .15
79 Petri Skriko .08 .25
80 Esa Tikkanen .20 .50
81 Pekka Tuomisto .02 .10
82 Petri Varis .08 .25
83 Jarkko Varvio .05 .15
84 Vesa Viitakoski .05 .15
85 Marko Virtanen .02 .10
86 Jali Wahlsten .02 .10
87 Sami Wahlsten .02 .10
88 Pentti Matikainen .02 .10
89 Petr Briza .08 .25
90 Roman Turek .40 1.00
91 Milos Holan .02 .10
92 Drahomir Kadlec .05 .15
93 Bedrich Scerban .05 .15
94 Frantisek Prochazka .02 .10
95 Richard Zemlicka .08 .25
96 Roman Horak .40 1.00
97 Lubos Rob .02 .10
98 Jiri Kucera .05 .15
99 Tomas Kapusta .02 .10
100 Roman Rysanek .02 .10
101 Roman Hamrlik .08 .25
102 Robert Svehla .08 .25
103 Tomas Jelinek .05 .15
104 Petr Klima .08 .25
105 Josef Beranek .07 .20
106 Robert Petrovicky .05 .15
107 Kamil Kastak .05 .15
108 David Volek .05 .15
109 Renato Tosio .02 .10
110 Patrick Schopf .02 .10
111 Samuel Balmer .02 .10
112 Andreas Beutler .02 .10
113 Patrice Brasey .02 .10
114 Rick Tschumi .02 .10
115 Sven Leuenberger .02 .10
116 Sandro Bertaggia .02 .10
117 Patrick Howald .02 .10
118 Andy Ton .02 .10
119 Keith Fair .02 .10
120 Mario Brodmann .02 .10
121 Fredy Luhti .02 .10
122 Jorg Eberle .05 .15
123 Roman Wager .02 .10
124 Manuele Celio .02 .10
125 Christian Weber .02 .10
126 Roger Thony .02 .10
127 Felix Hollenstein .02 .10
128 Gil Montandon .02 .10
129 Nikolai Khabibulin .60 1.50
130 Alexei Chervlakov .02 .10
131 Ilja Biakin .05 .15
132 Dmitri Filimonov .05 .15
133 Alexander Karpovtsev .08 .25
134 Sergei Sorokin .05 .15

135 Andrei Sapozhnikov .02 .10
136 Alexei Yashin .20 .50
137 Alexander Cherbayev .02 .10
138 Konstantin Astrakhantsev .05 .15
139 Sergei Petrenko .05 .15
140 Viktor Kozlov .08 .25
141 Roman Oksyuta .02 .10
142 Vladimir Malakhov .08 .25
143 Andrei Lomakin .05 .15
144 Dimitri Yushkevich .08 .25
145 Igor Korolev .02 .10
146 Darius Kasparaitis .08 .25
147 Vyacheslav Bykov .08 .25
148 Andrei Khomutov .08 .25
149 Helmut De Raaf .02 .10
150 Klaus Merk .08 .25
151 Michael Heidt .08 .25
152 Michael Schmidt .02 .10
153 Uli Hiemer .02 .10
154 Andreas Niederberger .02 .10
155 Rick Amann .02 .10
156 Andreas Brockmann .02 .10
157 Gerd Truntschka .05 .15
158 Dieter Hegen .05 .15
159 Stefan Ustorf .05 .15
160 Georg Holzmann .02 .10
161 Ernst Kopf Jr. .02 .10
162 Bernd Truntschka .05 .15
163 Raimund Hilger .02 .10
164 Wolfgang Kummer .02 .10
165 Georg Franz .02 .10
166 Thomas Brandl .02 .10
167 Michael Rumrich .02 .10
168 Uwe Krupp .08 .25
169 Tom Barrasso .20 .50
170 Mike Richter .60 1.50
171 Brian Leetch .60 1.50
172 Chris Chelios .60 1.50
173 Al Iafrate .08 .25
174 Phil Housley .08 .25
175 Kevin Hatcher .08 .25
176 Gary Suter .08 .25
177 Mathieu Schneider .08 .25
178 Joe Mullen .08 .25
179 Kevin Stevens .08 .25
180 Jeremy Roenick 1.50 4.00
181 Tony Granato .08 .25
182 Mike Modano 1.25 3.00
183 Pat LaFontaine .30 .75
184 Ed Olczyk .05 .15
185 Brett Hull 1.50 4.00
186 Craig Janney .08 .25
187 Jimmy Carson .05 .15
188 Tony Amonte .40 1.00
189 Patrick Roy 5.00 12.00
190 Kirk McLean .20 .50
191 Larry Murphy .20 .50
192 Ray Bourque 2.00 5.00
193 Al MacInnis .60 1.50
194 Steve Duchesne .08 .25
195 Eric Desjardins .20 .50
196 Scott Stevens .30 .75
197 Paul Coffey .60 1.50
198 Mario Lemieux 5.00 12.00
199 Wayne Gretzky 6.00 15.00
200 Rick Tocchet .20 .50
201 Eric Lindros 1.25 3.00
202 Mark Messier 1.25 3.00
203 Steve Yzerman 4.00 10.00
204 Luc Robitaille .60 1.50
205 Mark Recchi .60 1.50
206 Joe Sakic 2.00 5.00
207 Owen Nolan .40 1.00
208 Gary Roberts .20 .50
209 David Delfino .08 .25
210 Mike Rosati .08 .25
211 Robert Oberrauch .02 .10
212 Jim Camazzola .02 .10
213 Bill Stewart .02 .10
214 Mike DeAngelis .02 .10
215 Anthony Circelli .02 .10
216 Georg Comploy .02 .10
217 Frank DiMuzio .02 .10
218 Gates Orlando .05 .15
219 John Vecchiarelli .02 .10
220 Joe Foglietta .02 .10
221 Lucio Topatigh .02 .10
222 Carmine Vani .05 .15
223 Lino DeToni .02 .10
224 Mario Chitarroni .02 .10
225 Bruno Zarrillo .02 .10
226 Maurizio Mansi .02 .10
227 Stefan Figliuzzi .02 .10
228 Santino Pellegrino .02 .10
229 Jim Marthinsen .08 .25
230 Rob Schistad .08 .25
231 Petter Salsten .02 .10
232 Cato Tom Andersen .02 .10
233 Tommy Jakobsen .02 .10
234 Svein E Norstebo .02 .10
235 Jon Magne Karlstad .02 .10
236 Kim Sogaard .02 .10
237 Geir Hoff .02 .10
238 Erik Kristiansen .02 .10
239 Petter Thoresen .02 .10
240 Ole Eskild Dahlstrom .02 .10
241 Espen Knutsen .20 .50
242 Oystein Olsen .02 .10
243 Roy Johansen .02 .10
244 Trond Magnussen .02 .10
245 Arne Billkvam .02 .10
246 Marius Rath .02 .10
247 Tom Erik Olsen .02 .10
248 Morten Finstad .02 .10
249 Petri Ylonen .08 .25
250 Michel Valliere .08 .25
251 Stephane Botteri .02 .10
252 Serge Poudrier .05 .15
253 Eric Durand .02 .10
254 Jean-Philippe Lemoine .05 .15
255 Denis Perez .05 .15
256 Sebastien Marquet .02 .10
257 Michael Babin .02 .10
258 Stephane Barin .02 .10
259 Arnaud Briand .02 .10
260 Yves Crettenand .02 .10
261 Laurent Deschaume .02 .10
262 Roger Dube .02 .10
263 Patrick Dunn .02 .10
264 Franck Pajonkowski .05 .15
265 Pierre Pousse .02 .10
266 Antoine Richer .02 .10
267 Christophe Ville .02 .10
268 Philippe Bozon .40 1.00
269 Brian Stankiewicz .02 .10
270 Claus Dalpiaz .08 .25
271 Michael Shea .08 .25
272 Robin Doyle .02 .10
273 Martin Ulrich .02 .10
274 Martin Krainz .02 .10
275 Erich Solderer .02 .10
276 Michael Guntner .02 .10
277 Friedrich Ganster .02 .10
278 Wayne Groulx .02 .10
279 Dieter Kalt .02 .10
280 Werner Kerth .02 .10
281 Arno Maier .02 .10
282 Richard Nasheim .02 .10
283 Christian Perthaler .02 .10
284 Andreas Puschnig .02 .10
285 Gerhard Puschnik .02 .10
286 Walter Putnik .02 .10
287 Reinhard Lampert .02 .10
288 Mario Schaden .02 .10

1994-95 Swedish Leaf

The 1994-95 Leaf Swedish hockey set consists of 320 standard-size cards that were issued in two series. The fronts feature color action player photos that are full-bleed except on the left, where a team color-coded stripe carries the player's name and his team's name. Leaf's logo in gold-foil appears in one of the corners. The team color-coded backs carry a color player close-up with a short biography, career stats and the team logo. Each series closes with team cards (135-158, 307-318) and checklists (159-160, 319-320).

COMPLETE SET (320) 26.00 65.00
COMPLETE SERIES 1 (1-160) 10.00 25.00
COMPLETE SERIES 2 (161-320) 16.00 40.00
1 Thomas Tallberg .02 .10
2 Hakan Algotsson .08 .25
3 Mikael Magnusson .02 .10
4 Per Lundell .02 .10
5 Kenneth Kennholt .02 .10
6 Jan Huokko .02 .10
7 Petter Nilsson .02 .10
8 Johan Norgren .02 .10
9 Anders Berglund .02 .10
10 Kari Eloranta .07 .20
11 Sam Lindstahl .02 .10
12 Johan Rosen .02 .10
13 Jonas Johnsson .02 .10
14 Erik Huusko .07 .20
15 Thomas Rhodin .02 .10
16 Patric Kjellberg .15 .40
17 Fredrik Andersson .02 .10
18 Stefan Nilsson .02 .10
19 Petri Liimatainen .02 .10
20 Lars Jansson .02 .10
21 Per Wallin .02 .10
22 Mika Nieminen .15 .40
23 Lars Ivarsson .02 .10
24 Ronnie Sundin .15 .40
25 Bedrich Scerban .02 .10
26 Anders Huusko .02 .10
27 Erik Granqvist .02 .10
28 Stefan Ornskog .07 .20
29 Marcus Thuresson .02 .10
30 Johan Stromvall .02 .10
31 Peter Hasselblad .02 .10
32 Anders Eriksson .20 .50
33 Roger Elvenes .02 .10
34 Stefan Larsson .02 .10
35 Alexei Salomatin .02 .10
36 Niclas Havelid .40 1.00
37 Mikael Lindman .02 .10
38 Jens Ohling .02 .10
39 Hakan Loob .30 .75
40 Johan Hedberg .60 1.50
41 Niklas Eriksson .02 .10
42 Robert Nordberg .05 .15
43 Robert Svehla .40 1.00
44 Hans Jonsson .30 .75
45 Thomas Srsen .02 .10
46 Thomas Sjogren .02 .10
47 Mishat Fahrutdinov .02 .10
48 Thomas Strandberg .02 .10
49 Andreas Dackell .30 .75
50 Peter Nilsson .02 .10
51 Andreas Johansson .30 .75
52 Stefan Falk .02 .10
53 Marcus Akerblom .02 .10
54 Peter Aslin .08 .25
55 Ricard Persson .15 .40
56 Tomas Nanzen .02 .10
57 Per-Johan Svensson .02 .10
58 Terho Koskela .02 .10
59 Henrik Nilsson .02 .10
60 Mats Lindberg .02 .10
61 Anders Huss .02 .10
62 Magnus Jansson .02 .10
63 Mats Lindgren .20 .50
64 Thomas Ljungberg .02 .10
65 Tomas Forslund .08 .25
66 Thomas Ostlund .15 .40
67 Raimo Helminen .08 .25
68 Magnus Wernblom .02 .10
69 Jorgen Jonsson .02 .10
70 Peter Berndtsson .02 .10
71 Stefan Hellkvist .02 .10
72 Tommy Lehmann .07 .20
73 Stefan Klockare .02 .10
74 Ola Josefsson .02 .10
75 Peter Lindmark .08 .25
76 Owe Thornberg .02 .10
77 Jarmo Makitalo .02 .10
78 Tomas Berglund .02 .10
79 Bo Svanberg .02 .10
80 Lennart Hermansson .02 .10
81 Stefan Elvenes .02 .10
82 Daniel Alfredsson 1.50 4.00
83 Claes Lindblom .02 .10
84 Bjorn Ahlstrom .02 .10
85 Ove Molin .02 .10
86 Fredrik Lindquist .20 .50
87 Clas Eriksson .02 .10
88 Peter Hammarstrom .02 .10
89 Magnus Swardh .02 .10
90 Lars Hurtig .02 .10
91 Daniel Rydmark .02 .10
92 Lars Bystrom .02 .10
93 Mats Loov .02 .10
94 Lars Dahlstrom .02 .10
95 Johan Brummer .02 .10
96 Patric Englund .02 .10
97 Christer Olsson .15 .40
98 Patrik Erickson .02 .10
99 Peter Ottosson .02 .10
100 Tomas Jonsson .08 .25
101 Lars Modig .02 .10
102 Ake Lilljebjorn .02 .10
103 Patrik Sylvegard .02 .10
104 Daniel Johansson .20 .50
105 Edvin Frylen .08 .25
106 Par Edlund .02 .10
107 Paul Andersson .02 .10
108 Rikard Franzen .02 .10
109 Christian Due-Boje .08 .25
110 Tommy Samuelsson .02 .10
111 Mathias Svedberg .02 .10
112 Hans Lodin .02 .10
113 Jonas Eriksson .08 .25
114 Mikael Engstrom .02 .10
115 Hakan Ahlund .02 .10
116 Kari Suoraniemi .02 .10
117 Peter Jacobsson .02 .10
118 Kristian Gahn .02 .10
119 Tommy Melkersson .02 .10
120 Oscar Ackestrom .02 .10
121 Thomas Johansson .02 .10
122 Jesper Duus .02 .10
123 Hans Abrahamsson .02 .10
124 Orjan Lindmark .02 .10
125 Torbjorn Lindberg .02 .10
126 Michael Sundlov .08 .25
127 Peter Sundstrom .08 .25
128 Pierre Johnsson .02 .10
129 Thomas Carlsson .02 .10
130 Stefan Axelsson .02 .10
131 Robert Nordmark .07 .20
132 Torbjorn Persson .02 .10
133 Bjorn Nord .02 .10
134 Mats Ytter .02 .10
135 AIK .02 .10
Team Statistics
136 Brynas IF .02 .10
Team Statistics
137 Djurgardens IF .02 .10
Team Statistics
138 Vastra Frolunda .02 .10
Team Statistics
139 Farjestad BK .02 .10
Team Statistics
140 HV-71 .02 .10
Team Statistics
141 Leksand IF .02 .10
Team Statistics
142 Lulea HF .02 .10
Team Statistics
143 Malmo IF .02 .10
Team Statistics
144 MoDo Hockey .02 .10
Team Statistics
145 Rogle BK .02 .10
Team Statistics
146 Varsteras IK .02 .10
Team Statistics
147 AIK Logo .02 .10
148 Brynas IF Logo .02 .10
149 Djurgardens IF .02 .10
150 Vastra Frolunda Logo .02 .10
151 Farjestads BK .02 .10
152 HV-71 Logo .02 .10
153 Leksands IF Logo .02 .10
154 Lulea HF .02 .10
155 Malmo IF .02 .10
156 MoDo Hockey .02 .10
157 Rogle BK .02 .10
158 Vasteras IK .02 .10
159 Checklist 1-80 .02 .10
160 Checklist 81-160 .02 .10
161 Kenneth Johansson .08 .25
162 Stefan Jonsson .02 .10
163 Mikael Wahlberg .02 .10
164 Per Djoos .08 .25
165 Andreas Schultz .02 .10
166 Sacha Molin .02 .10
167 Marcus Ramen .02 .10
168 Jergus Baca .02 .10
169 Erik Bergstrom .02 .10
170 Jonas Forsberg .15 .40
171 Olli Kaski .02 .10
172 Morgan Samuelsson .02 .10
173 Anders Burstrom .02 .10
174 Stanislav Meciar .02 .10
175 Leif Rohlin .15 .40
176 Lars Edstrom .02 .10
177 Esa Keskinen .08 .25
178 Daniel Casselstahl .02 .10
179 Mattias Timander .20 .50
180 Peter Nordstrom .02 .10
181 Patric Aberg .02 .10
182 Mikael Enander .02 .10
183 Charles Berglund .08 .25
184 Jonas Andersson-Junkka .15 .40
185 Sergei Fokin .02 .10
186 Boo Ahl .15 .40
187 Jiri Kucera .08 .25
188 Roger Nordstrom .02 .10
189 Peter Forsberg 6.00 15.00
190 Arto Ruotanen .02 .10
191 Mikael Wiklander .02 .10
192 Joakim Persson .08 .25
193 Peter Larsson .02 .10
194 Per Eklund .15 .40
195 Joacim Esbjors .02 .10
196 Magnus Arvedsson .60 1.50
197 Marko Palo .02 .10
198 Mikael Holmberg .02 .10
199 Mikael Renberg .75 2.00
200 Tero Lehtera .15 .40
201 Fredrik Lindh .02 .10
202 Johan Finnstrom .02 .10
203 Peter Popovic .08 .25
204 Tony Barthelson .02 .10
205 Stefan Polla .02 .10
206 Jonas Esbjors .02 .10
207 Roger Hansson .02 .10
208 Mikael Hakansson .02 .10
209 Daniel Tjarnqvist .15 .40
210 Anders Carlsson .08 .25
211 Dick Tarnstrom .15 .40
212 Johan Tornberg .02 .10
213 Joakim Lundberg .02 .10
214 Marko Jantunen .15 .40
215 Patrik Haltia .02 .10
216 Fredrik Stillman .02 .10
217 Andy Schneider .02 .10
218 Thomas Holmstrom ERC 2.00 5.00
219 Jens Hemstrom .02 .10
220 Anders Soderberg .20 .50
221 Peter Lundmark .02 .10
222 Patrik Juhlin .15 .40
223 Anders Gozzi .02 .10
224 Marcus Ragnarsson .30 .75
225 Mattias Olsson .02 .10
226 Andreas Karlsson .20 .50
227 Tomas Lilja .02 .10
228 Stefan Ohman .02 .10
229 Jarmo Kekalainen .08 .25
230 Tony Skopac .02 .10
231 Lars Karlsson .08 .25
232 Mats Sundin 1.00 2.50
233 Peter Strom .02 .10
234 Mattias Johansson .02 .10
235 Johan Lindbom .02 .10
236 Mats Lusth .02 .10
237 Marcus Magnertoft .02 .10
238 Martin Hostak .02 .10
239 Mikael Pettersson .02 .10
240 Johan Akerman .02 .10
241 Mathias Hallback .02 .10
242 Johan Davidsson .20 .50
243 Per-Erik Eklund .15 .40
244 Johan Salle .02 .10
245 Per Svartvadet .20 .50
246 Ville Siren .08 .25
247 Mattias Loof .02 .10
248 Per-Johan Axelsson .60 1.50
249 Peter Gerhardsson .02 .10
250 Jonas Bergqvist .08 .25
251 Per-Johan Johansson .40 1.00
252 Mattias Bosson .02 .10
253 Andreas Olsson .02 .10
254 Patrik Zetterberg .02 .10
255 Michael Johansson .02 .10
256 Stefan Gustavson .02 .10
257 Jerry Persson .02 .10
258 Stefan Nilsson .02 .10
259 Roger Johansson .02 .10
260 Jarmo Myllys .20 .50
261 Kyosti Karjalainen .02 .10
262 Thomas Eriksson .02 .10
263 Michael Hjalm .02 .10
264 Espen Knutsen .40 1.00
265 Andreas Salomonsson .02 .10
266 Patrik Hoglund .02 .10
267 Peter Andersson .02 .10
268 Brett Hauer .08 .25
269 Stefan Ketola .02 .10
270 Patrik Carnback .08 .25
271 Petter Ronnqvist .02 .10
272 Roger Ohman .02 .10
273 Fredrik Modin .75 2.00
274 Alexander Beliavski .02 .10
275 Niklas Brannstrom .02 .10
276 Per Gustafsson .15 .40
277 Nicklas Nordqvist .02 .10
278 Roger Akerstrom .02 .10
279 Jiri Vykoukal .02 .10
280 Jesper Mattsson .15 .40
281 Henrik Nordfeldt .02 .10
282 Joakim Musakka .02 .10
283 Anders Johnson .02 .10
284 Niklas Sundstrom .40 1.00
285 Nicklas Lidstrom 1.00 2.50
286 Tomas Sandstrom .40 1.00
287 Jens Nielsen .02 .10
288 Mattias Ohlund .75 2.00
289 Markus Eriksson .02 .10
290 Mikael Sandberg .08 .25
291 Sergeij Pushkov .02 .10
292 Jonas Hoglund .40 1.00
293 Peter Ekelund .02 .10
294 Fredrik Bergqvist .02 .10
295 Torgny Bendelin .02 .10
296 Tommy Sandlin CO .02 .10
297 Tommy Boustedt CO .02 .10
298 Conny Evensson CO .02 .10
299 Sune Bergman CO .02 .10
300 Wayne Fleming CO .02 .10
301 Lars Bergstrom CO .02 .10
302 Hannu Jortikka CO .02 .10
303 Leif Boork CO .02 .10
304 Christer Abrahamsson CO .08 .25
305 Randy Edmonds CO .02 .10
306 Ulf Labraaten CO .02 .10
307 AIK .02 .10
308 Brynas IF .02 .10
309 Djurgardens IF .02 .10
310 Farjestads BK .02 .10
311 HV 71 .02 .10
312 Leksands IF .02 .10
313 Lulea HF .02 .10
314 Malmo IF .02 .10
315 MoDo .02 .10
316 Rogle BK .02 .10
317 Vasteras IK .02 .10
318 Vastra Frolunda .02 .10
319 Checklist 161-240 .02 .10
320 Checklist 241-320 .02 .10
NNO1 Malmo IF SuperChase 10.00 25.00
NNO2 M.Lindgren SuperChase 6.00 15.00

1994-95 Swedish Leaf Clean Sweepers

This 10-card standard size set highlights 10 of the top goalies in the Swedish Eliteserien. The cards were randomly inserted into series one packs. The fronts have a color photo with the player's name in yellow on a red background at the bottom. The word "Cleansweepers" is at the top in gold-foil as are the words "Elit Set" in the bottom right corner. The backs have player information in green with a blue background. The cards are numbered "X of 10."

COMPLETE SET (10) 10.00 25.00
1 Peter Lindmark 1.25 3.00
2 Michael Sundlov 1.25 3.00
3 Thomas Ostlund 1.25 3.00
4 Jonas Eriksson 1.25 3.00
5 Peter Aslin 1.25 3.00
6 Ake Lilljebjorn 1.25 3.00
7 Johan Hedberg 2.00 5.00
8 Henrik Arvsell 1.25 3.00
9 Frederik Andersson 1.25 3.00
10 Hakan Algotsson 1.25 3.00

1994-95 Swedish Leaf Foreign Affairs

Featuring foreign-born players competing in the Elitserien, this ten-card set was inserted in series two foil packs. The fronts feature a color player cutout superimposed over his country's flag. The words "Foreign Affairs" in foil letters are printed on the bottom, while the player's name and his team's name appear vertically on the right. The backs carry player profile. All information is printed in Swedish.

COMPLETE SET (10) 8.00 20.00
1 Espen Knutsen 2.00 5.00
2 Esa Keskinen .75 2.00
3 Marko Jantunen .75 2.00
4 Jarmo Myllys 1.25 3.00
5 Jiri Kucera .75 2.00
6 Jiri Vykoukal .75 2.00
7 Jarmo Kekalainen .75 2.00
8 Olli Kaski .75 2.00
9 Jergus Baca .75 2.00
10 Tero Lehtera .75 2.00

1994-95 Swedish Leaf Gold Cards

This 24-card standard size set commemorates the members of Sweden's 1994 Olympic gold medal team. The cards were randomly inserted into series one packs. The fronts have a full-color photo ghosted over an image of the gold medal with the player's name at the bottom. The words "Gold Cards" are at the bottom in gold-foil as are the words "Elit Set" in the top right corner. The backs have the player's name and information with a stick figure playing hockey numerous times being the background. The cards are numbered "X of 24."

COMPLETE SET (24) 30.00 75.00
1 Title Card 2.00 5.00
2 Andreas Dackell 1.25 3.00
3 Charles Berglund .75 2.00
4 Christian Due-Boje .75 2.00
5 Daniel Rydmark .75 2.00
6 Fredrik Stillman .75 2.00
7 Hakan Algotsson 1.25 3.00
8 Hakan Loob 1.25 3.00
9 Jonas Bergqvist .75 2.00
10 Jorgen Jonsson .75 2.00
11 Kenny Jonsson 1.25 3.00
12 Leif Rohlin .75 2.00
13 Magnus Svensson .75 2.00
14 Mats Naslund 1.25 3.00
15 Michael Sundlov 1.25 3.00
16 Niklas Eriksson .75 2.00
17 Patric Kjellberg .75 2.00
18 Patrick Juhlin .75 2.00
19 Peter Forsberg 15.00 40.00
20 Roger Hansson .75 2.00
21 Roger Johansson .75 2.00
22 Stefan Ornskog .75 2.00
23 Tomas Jonsson .75 2.00
24 Tommy Salo 2.00 5.00

1994-95 Swedish Leaf Guest Special

Featuring players who joined the Elitserien during the 1994 NHL lockout, this eight card set was inserted in second-series foil packs. The fronts feature a color player action shot. The words "Guest Special" appear in a foil bar above the photo, while the player's name is printed in a foil bar below. The horizontal backs carry a color player cut-out superimposed over a drawing of the world.

COMPLETE SET (8) 16.00 40.00
1 Mats Sundin 4.00 10.00
2 Tomas Sandstrom .75 2.00
3 Peter Forsberg 10.00 25.00
4 Nicklas Lidstrom 4.00 10.00
5 Mikael Renberg 1.25 3.00
6 Roger Johansson .40 1.00
7 Peter Popovic .40 1.00
8 Patrick Juhlin .40 1.00

1994-95 Swedish Leaf NHL Draft

This ten-card standard-size set featuring players drafted by NHL teams in 1994 was inserted in second-series foil packs. The fronts feature a color player action shot. The year 1994 is separated by the NHL draft logo. The backs contain information in Swedish about the player's selection in the 1994 NHL draft.

COMPLETE SET (10) 12.00 30.00
1 Mattias Ohlund 1.50 4.00
2 Johan Davidsson .40 1.00
3 Fredrik Modin 1.50 4.00
4 Johan Finnstrom .40 1.00
5 Edvin Frylen .40 1.00
6 Daniel Alfredsson 3.00 8.00
7 Patrik Haltia 1.25 3.00
8 Peter Strom .40 1.00
9 Thomas Holmstrom 4.00 10.00
10 Dick Tarnstrom .75 2.00

1994-95 Swedish Leaf Playmakers

This six-card standard size set shines the spotlight on five of the top goal scorers in the Swedish Elitserien. The cards were randomly inserted into series one packs. The fronts have a full-color photo with an orange and black background. The words "Play Makers" are on the left side and the words "Elit Set" is in the bottom right corner in gold-foil. The backs have "Play Makers" at the top in silver with an orange background. The player's name and number of assists he had in each of the previous three seasons with a black background. Card #1 is different in that it is a title card and has a picture of all five players in the set. The cards are numbered "X of 6."

COMPLETE SET (6) 2.00 5.00
1 Title Card .75 2.00
2 Stefan Nilsson .40 1.00
3 Mika Nieminen .40 1.00
4 Raimo Helminen .40 1.00
5 Peter Larsson .40 1.00
6 Hakan Loob .75 2.00

1994-95 Swedish Leaf Rookie Rockets

Inserted in second-series foil packs, this 10-card set features rookies in the Swedish league. Borderless horizontal fronts feature a color player cut-out along with "Rookie" in big foil letters. The player's name and his team's name appears in a red bar on the bottom. The horizontal back carry another color player cut-out along with player profile.

COMPLETE SET (10) 8.00 20.00
1 Fredrik Modin 1.25 3.00
2 Jonas Andersson-Junkka .75 2.00
3 Thomas Holmstrom 4.00 10.00
4 Mattias Ohlund 1.25 3.00
5 Per Eklund .40 1.00
6 Daniel Tjarnqvist .40 1.00
7 Joakim Persson .75 2.00
8 Patrik Haltia .75 2.00
9 Andreas Karlsson .40 1.00
10 Stefan Nilsson .40 1.00

1994-95 Swedish Leaf Studio Signatures

This 12-card standard-size set was inserted in second-series foil packs. The fronts feature borderless color studio photos. The player's facsimile autograph in foil letters appears at the bottom. The backs carry a drawing of the player in close-up.

COMPLETE SET (12) 4.00 10.00
1 Rikard Franzen .40 1.00
2 Anders Huss .40 1.00
3 Jens Ohling .40 1.00
4 Tommy Samuelsson .40 1.00
5 Fredrik Stillman .40 1.00
6 Jonas Bergqvist .40 1.00
7 Johan Stromvall .40 1.00
8 Roger Nordstrom .40 1.00
9 Lars Bystrom .40 1.00
10 Roger Elvenes .40 1.00
11 Leif Rohlin .75 2.00
12 Tero Koskela .40 1.00

1994-95 Swedish Leaf Top Guns

This 10-card standard size set consists of some of the top goal scorers in the Swedish Elitserien. The cards were randomly inserted into series one packs. The fronts have a full-color photo with a background that looks like fire works. In one of the top corners the words "Top Gun" are in gold-foil as are the words "Elit Set" in the bottom right corner. The backs have "Top Gun" in red at the top as if it were underneath rippling water. At the bottom is the number of goals they scored each of the previous three seasons. The cards are numbered "X of 10."

COMPLETE SET (10) 4.80 12.00
1 Thomas Srsen .40 1.00
2 Hakan Loob 1.25 3.00
3 Lars Hurtig .40 1.00
4 Stefan Elvenes .40 1.00
5 Jorgen Jonsson .40 1.00
6 Robert Svehla 1.25 3.00
7 Daniel Rydmark .40 1.00
8 Owe Thornberg .40 1.00
9 Patric Kjellberg .75 2.00
10 Mats Loov .40 1.00

1994 Swedish Olympics Lillehammer*

This listing includes only the hockey cards from a larger Swedish issue that was released to commemorate the 1994 Olympic Games, which were held in Lillehammar.

COMPLETE HOCKEY SET (56) 15.00 30.00
273 Ice Hockey Logo .02 .10
274 Russian Team Puzzle .07 .20
275 Russian Team Puzzle .07 .20
276 Russian Team Puzzle .07 .20
277 Russian Team Puzzle .07 .20
278 Russian Team Puzzle .07 .20
279 Russian Team Puzzle .07 .20
280 Konstantin Astrakhantsev .20 .50
281 Viacheslav Bykov .20 .50
282 Sergei Sorokin .20 .50
283 Alexander Smirnov .20 .50
284 Swedish Team Sticker .07 .20
285 Swedish Team Sticker .07 .20
286 Swedish Team Sticker .07 .20
287 Swedish Team Sticker .07 .20
288 Swedish Team Sticker .07 .20
289 Swedish Team Sticker .07 .20
290 Markus Naslund .75 2.00
291 Peter Forsberg 4.00 10.00
292 Mats Sundin 1.50 4.00
293 Mikael Renberg .20 .50
294 Tommy Soderstrom .20 .50
295 Finnish Team Puzzle .07 .20
296 Finnish Team Puzzle .07 .20
297 Finnish Team Puzzle .07 .20
298 Finnish Team Puzzle .07 .20
299 Finnish Team Puzzle .07 .20
300 Finnish Team Puzzle .07 .20
301 Markus Ketterer .20 .50
302 Vesa Viitakoski .07 .20
303 Esa Tikkanen .20 .50
304 Erik Hamalainen .07 .20
305 Norwegian Team Puzzle .07 .20
306 Norwegian Team Puzzle .07 .20
307 Norwegian Team Puzzle .07 .20
308 Norwegian Team Puzzle .07 .20
309 Norwegian Team Puzzle .07 .20
310 Norwegian Team Puzzle .07 .20
311 Jim Marthinsen .20 .50
312 Erik Kristiansen .07 .20
313 Petter Salsten .07 .20
314 Eric Lindros 1.50 4.00
315 Greg Johnson .20 .50
316 Allain Roy .20 .50
317 Hank Lammens .30 .75
318 Leo Gudas .20 .50
319 Petr Briza .30 .75
320 Petr Rosol .20 .50
321 Otakar Janecky .20 .50
322 Mike Richter .75 2.00
323 Brett Hull 2.00 5.00
324 Chris Chelios .75 2.00
325 Pat Lafontaine .75 2.00
326 Claus Dalpiaz .20 .50
327 Stephane Barin .07 .20
328 Gerd Truntschka .07 .20

1995-96 Swedish Leaf

The 1995-96 Leaf Elit set was issued in two series (150 and 160 cards, respectively) and featured the players of Sweden's top league, the Elitserien. The cards feature a full-bleed design, with the player's name ghosted along the bottom. The set was distributed in 8-card packs. The NNO Per-Erik (Pelle) Eklund card was randomly inserted in series 1 packs, while the HV71 card, commemorating the team's 1994-95 championship, could be found in series 2 packs.

COMPLETE SET (310) 16.00 40.00
COMPLETE SERIES 1 (150) 8.00 20.00
COMPLETE SERIES 2 (160) 8.00 20.00
1 Hakan Loob .20 .50
2 AIK .08 .25
3 AIK, Season Stats .05 .15
4 Joakim Persson .08 .25
5 Niclas Havelid .30 .75
6 Tony Barthelson .05 .15
7 Patric Aberg .05 .15
8 Johan Akerman .05 .15
9 Dick Tarnstrom .08 .25
10 Stefan Gustavson .05 .15
11 Anders Gozzi .05 .15
12 Morgan Samuelsson .08 .25
13 Brynas IF .05 .15
14 Brynas, Season Stats .05 .15
15 Michael Sundlov .08 .25
16 Stefan Klockare .08 .25
17 Bedrich Scerban .05 .15
18 Andreas Dackell .30 .75
19 Fredrik Modin .75 2.00
20 Ove Molin .05 .15
21 Mikael Wahlberg .05 .15
22 Thomas Tallberg .05 .15
23 Peter Larsson .05 .15
24 Stefan Ketola .08 .25
25 Djurgardens IF .08 .25
26 Djurgarden, Season Stats .05 .15
27 Jonas Forsberg .15 .40
28 Christian Due-Boje .08 .25
29 Mikael Magnusson .05 .15
30 Thomas Johansson .05 .15
31 Joakim Musakka .05 .15
32 Erik Hussko .08 .25
33 Jens Ohling .05 .15
34 Per Eklund .08 .25
35 Espen Knutsen .40 1.00
36 Patrik Erickson .05 .15
37 Farjestads BK .05 .15
38 Farjestad, Season Stats .05 .15
39 Patrik Haltia .08 .25
40 Sergei Fokin .05 .15
41 Thomas Rhodin .05 .15
42 Stefan Nilsson .05 .15
43 Magnus Arvedsson .30 .75
44 Mattias Johansson .05 .15
45 Clas Eriksson .05 .15
46 Peter Ottosson .05 .15
47 HV 71 .05 .15
48 HV 71, Season Stats .05 .15
49 Boo Ahl .15 .40
50 Kenneth Kennholt .05 .15
51 Hans Abrahamsson .05 .15
52 Peter Hammarstrom .05 .15
53 Johan Davidsson .20 .50
54 Stefan Falk .05 .15
55 Johan Lindbom .05 .15
56 Esa Keskinen .08 .25
57 Stefan Ornskog .08 .25
58 Peter Ekelund .05 .15
59 Leksands IF .05 .15
60 Leksand, Season Stats .05 .15
61 Johan Hedberg 1.50 4.00
62 Tomas Jonsson .08 .25
63 Hans Lodin .05 .15
64 Orjan Lindmark .05 .15

65 Jan Huokko	.05	.15
66 Markus Eriksson	.05	.15
67 Andreas Karlsson	.05	.15
68 Mikael Holmberg	.05	.15
69 Jonas Bergqvist	.08	.25
70 Niklas Eriksson	.05	.15
71 Per-Erik Eklund	.08	.25
72 Lulea HF	.05	.15
73 Lulea, Season Stats	.05	.15
74 Jarmo Myllys	.20	.50
75 Mattias Ohlund	.40	1.00
76 Lars Modig	.05	.15
77 Torbjorn Lindberg	.05	.15
78 Roger Akerstrom	.05	.15
79 Stefan Jonsson	.05	.15
80 Johan Rosen	.05	.15
81 Tomas Berglund	.05	.15
82 Robert Nordberg	.05	.15
83 Jiri Kucera	.08	.25
84 Tomas Holmstrom	.75	2.00
85 Malmo IF	.05	.15
86 Malmo, Season Stats	.05	.15
87 Peter Andersson	.05	.15
88 Roger Ohman	.05	.15
89 Marcus Magnertoft	.05	.15
90 Patrik Sylvegard	.05	.15
91 Hakan Ahlund	.05	.15
92 Jesper Mattsson	.08	.25
93 Roger Hansson	.05	.15
94 Mattias Bosson	.05	.15
95 Bo Svanberg	.05	.15
96 Raimo Helminen	.05	.15
97 MoDo Hockey	.08	.25
98 MoDo, Season Stats	.05	.15
99 Petter Ronnqvist	.08	.25
100 Lars Jansson	.05	.15
101 Mattias Timander	.20	.50
102 Hans Jonsson	.05	.15
103 Anders Soderberg	.15	.40
104 Martin Hostak	.05	.15
105 Kyosti Karjalainen	.08	.25
106 Mikael Hakanson	.05	.15
107 Per Svartvadet	.15	.40
108 Andreas Salomonsson	.40	1.00
109 Lars Bystrom	.05	.15
110 Magnus Wernblom	.05	.15
111 Rogle BK	.05	.15
112 Rogle, Season Stats	.05	.15
113 Magnus Swardh	.08	.25
114 Arto Ruotanen	.05	.15
115 Johan Finnstrom	.08	.25
116 Daniel Tjarnqvist	.20	.50
117 Pierre Johnsson	.05	.15
118 Per Wallin	.08	.25
119 Michael Johansson	.05	.15
120 Per-Johan Svensson	.05	.15
121 Roger Elvenes	.05	.15
122 Mats Loov	.05	.15
123 Michael Hjalm	.08	.25
124 Vasteras IK	.05	.15
125 Vasteras, Season Stats	.05	.15
126 Mats Ytter	.08	.25
127 Erik Bergstrom	.08	.25
128 Lars Ivarsson	.05	.15
129 Mishat Fahrutdinov	.05	.15
130 Claes Lindblom	.05	.15
131 Paul Andersson	.05	.15
132 Henrik Nordfeldt	.05	.15
133 Alexei Salomatin	.05	.15
134 Mikael Pettersson	.05	.15
135 Vastra Frolunda HC	.05	.15
136 Frolunda, Season Stats	.05	.15
137 Hakan Algotsson	.08	.25
138 Jonas Andersson-Junkka	.08	.25
139 Stefan Larsson	.05	.15
140 Par Djoos	.05	.15
141 Ronnie Sundin	.08	.25
142 Par Edlund	.08	.25
143 Peter Berndtsson	.05	.15
144 Joacim Esbjors	.05	.15
145 Alexander Beliavski	.05	.15
146 Jonas Esbjors	.05	.15
147 Marko Jantunen	.08	.25
148 Peter Strom	.05	.15
149 Checklist 1-75	.05	.15
150 Checklist 76-150	.05	.15
151 AIK	.08	.25
152 AIK, Captains	.05	.15
153 Mikael Nilsson	.05	.15
154 Juha Jokiharju	.08	.25
155 Stefan Andersson	.05	.15
156 Thomas Strandberg	.05	.15
157 Mats Lindberg	.05	.15
158 Peter Gerhardsson	.05	.15
159 Tommy Lehmann	.08	.25
160 Tommy Hedlund	.05	.15
161 Peter Wallin	.08	.25
162 Bjorn Ahlstrom	.05	.15
163 Erik Hamalainen	.08	.25
164 Patric Englund	.05	.15
165 Rikard Franzen	.05	.15
166 Brynas IF	.05	.15
167 Brynas, Captains	.05	.15
168 Lars Karlsson	.05	.15
169 Jonas Lofstrom	.05	.15
170 Stefan Polla	.05	.15
171 Mikael Lind	.05	.15
172 Brian Rafalski	.75	2.00
173 Roger Kyro	.05	.15
174 Per-Johan Johansson	.05	.15
175 Greg Parks	.05	.15
176 Per Lofstrom	.05	.15
177 Jonas Johnsson	.05	.15
178 Mikael Lindman	.05	.15
179 Mikael Wiklander	.05	.15
180 Tommy Melkersson	.05	.15
181 Djurgardens IF	.08	.25
182 Djurgarden, Captains	.05	.15
183 Thomas Ostlund	.20	.50
184 Patrik Hofbauer	.05	.15
185 Magnus Jansson	.05	.15
186 Niklas Falk	.05	.15
187 Ola Josefsson	.05	.15
188 Joakim Lundberg	.05	.15
189 Fredrik Lindquist	.15	.40
190 Patrik Kjellberg	.20	.50
191 Jan Viktorsson	.08	.25
192 Bjorn Nord	.05	.15
193 Tommy Jacobsen	.05	.15
194 Anders Huusko	.05	.15
195 Kristofer Ottosson	.05	.15
196 Vastra Frolunda HC	.05	.15
197 Frolunda, Captains	.05	.15
198 Mikael Sandberg	.05	.15
199 Jerry Persson	.05	.15
200 Peter Hogardh	.05	.15
201 Stefan Axelsson	.08	.25
202 Lars Edstrom	.05	.15
203 Lars-Goran Wiklander	.08	.25
204 Per-Johan Axelsson	.40	1.00
205 Henrik Nilsson	.05	.15
206 Petteri Nummelin	.08	.25
207 Christian Ruuttu	.20	.50
208 Oscar Ackestrom	.05	.15
209 Farjestads BK	.05	.15
210 Farjestad, Captains	.05	.15
211 Markus Ketterer	.08	.25
212 Bjorn Eriksson	.05	.15
213 Jonas Hoglund	.40	1.00
214 Peter Nordstrom	.05	.15
215 Jorgen Jonsson	.05	.15
216 Greger Artursson	.05	.15
217 Jesper Duus	.05	.15
218 Roger Johansson	.05	.15
219 Leif Carlsson	.05	.15
220 Per Lundell	.05	.15
221 Vitali Prokhorov	.08	.25
222 HV 71	.05	.15
223 HV 71, Captains	.05	.15
224 Kenneth Johansson	.05	.15
225 Thomas Gustavsson	.05	.15
226 Marcus Thuresson	.05	.15
227 Vesa Salo	.08	.25
228 Kai Nurminen	.20	.50
229 Johan Brummer	.05	.15
230 Daniel Johansson	.08	.25
231 Per Gustafsson	.08	.25
232 Niklas Rahm	.05	.15
233 Leksands IF	.05	.15
234 Leksand, Captains	.05	.15
235 Per-Ragnar Bergkvist	.08	.25
236 Anders Carlsson	.05	.15
237 Micael Karlberg	.05	.15
238 Torgny Lowgren	.05	.15
239 Stefan Hellkvist	.05	.15
240 Markus Akerblom	.05	.15
241 Joakim Lidgren	.05	.15
242 Tomas Forslund	.08	.25
243 Torbjorn Johansson	.05	.15
244 Nicklas Nordqvist	.05	.15
245 Lulea HF	.05	.15
246 Lulea, Captains	.05	.15
247 Erik Grankvist	.05	.15
248 Mikael Lindholm	.05	.15
249 Johan Stromvall	.05	.15
250 Anders Burstrom	.05	.15
251 Lars Hurtig	.05	.15
252 Stefan Nilsson	.05	.15
253 Jan Mertzig	.08	.25
254 Petter Nilsson	.05	.15
255 Malmo IF	.05	.15
256 Malmo IF, Captains	.05	.15
257 Peter Lindmark	.08	.25
258 Roger Nordstrom	.08	.25
259 Andreas Lilja	.05	.15
260 Brian McReynolds	.05	.15
261 Ilja Byakin	.08	.25
262 Robert Burakovsky	.05	.15
263 Mikael Burakovsky	.05	.15
264 Stefan Elvenes	.08	.25
265 Johan Salle	.05	.15
266 Kim Johnsson	.05	.15
267 Peter Hasselblad	.05	.15
268 Marko Palo	.05	.15
269 MoDo Hockey	.08	.25
270 MoDo, Captains	.08	.25
271 Fredrik Andersson	.05	.15
272 Frantisek Kaberle	.08	.25
273 Samuel Pahlsson	.30	.75
274 Jan Larsson	.05	.15
275 Per-Anton Lundstrom	.08	.25
276 Tomas Nansen	.05	.15
277 Marcus Karlsson	.05	.15
278 Jan-Axel Alavaara	.08	.25
279 Kristian Gahn	.08	.25
280 Rogle BK	.05	.15
281 Rogle, Captains	.05	.15
282 Patrik Backlund	.05	.15
283 Peter Lundmark	.05	.15
284 Anders Berglund	.05	.15
285 Harijs Vitolins	.05	.15
286 Jens Nielsen	.05	.15
287 Greg Brown	.08	.25
288 Bjorn Linden	.05	.15
289 Vasteras IK	.05	.15
290 Vasteras, Captains	.05	.15
291 Jakob Karlsson	.05	.15
292 Patrik Zetterberg	.05	.15
293 Mattias Loof	.05	.15
294 Johan Tornberg	.05	.15
295 Andrei Korolev	.05	.15
296 Mattias Olsson	.05	.15
297 Roger Rosen	.05	.15
298 Andrei Lulin	.05	.15
299 Edvin Frylen	.08	.25
300 Mats Lusth	.05	.15
301 Fredrik Oberg	.05	.15
302 Jarmo Myllys AS	.20	.50
303 Tomas Jonsson AS	.08	.25
304 All Stars Andersson	.08	.25
305 Hakan Loob AS	.20	.50
306 Esa Keskinen AS	.08	.25
307 Christian Ruuttu AS	.08	.25
308 Checklist 151-230	.05	.15
309 Checklist 231-310	.05	.15
310 Checklist Insert Cards	.05	.15
NNO Per-Erik Eklund	4.00	10.00
NNO HV71, Svenska Mastare	4.00	10.00

1995-96 Swedish Leaf Champs

Randomly inserted in series 1 packs at a rate of 1:11, this 15-card set celebrates members of Sweden's championship team. The cards are individually serially numbered on the back. It is believed that 1,000 of each were produced.

COMPLETE SET (15)	10.00	25.00
1 Tomas Jonsson	.75	2.00
2 Patrik Kjellberg	1.25	3.00
3 Hakan Loob	1.25	3.00
4 Peter Lindmark	1.25	3.00
5 Anders Carlsson	.75	2.00
6 Raimo Helminen	1.25	3.00
7 Esa Keskinen	.75	2.00
8 Jan Larsson	.75	2.00
9 Roger Johansson	.75	2.00
10 Andreas Dackell	1.25	3.00
11 Stefan Ornskog	.75	2.00
12 Michael Sundlov	1.25	3.00
13 Per-Erik Eklund	.75	2.00
14 Kenneth Kennholt	.75	2.00
15 Jan Viktorsson	.75	2.00

1995-96 Swedish Leaf Face to Face

Randomly inserted in series two packs at a rate of 1:5, this 15-card set features the top two talents on each of the Elitserien teams.

COMPLETE SET (15)	6.00	15.00
1 Morgan Samuelsson Tomas Strandberg	.40	1.00
2 Bedrich Scerban Greg Parks	.40	1.00
3 Erik Huusko Anders Huusko	.40	1.00
4 Stefan Larsson Marko Jantunen	.40	1.00
5 Hakan Loob Roger Johansson	.75	2.00
6 Kenneth Kennholt Per Gustafsson	.40	1.00
7 Stefan Hellkvist Tomas Forslund	.40	1.00
8 Tomas Holmstrom Roger Akerstrom	2.00	5.00
9 Stefan Elvenes Robert Burakovsky	.40	1.00
10 Martin Hostak Mattias Timander	.40	1.00
11 Mats Loov Michael Hjalm	.40	1.00
12 Alexei Salomatin Fredrik Oberg	.40	1.00
13 Patrik Erickson Espen Knutsen	1.25	3.00
14 Peter Andersson Peter Hasselblad	.40	1.00
15 Tomas Jonsson Markus Akerblom	.40	1.00

1995-96 Swedish Leaf Goldies

Randomly inserted in series 1 packs at a rate of 1:14, this 10-card set captures some of the top young scorers in Sweden.

COMPLETE SET (10)	6.00	15.00
1 Morgan Samuelsson	.75	2.00
2 Ove Molin	.75	2.00
3 Fredrik Lindquist	.75	2.00
4 Peter Strom	.75	2.00
5 Mattias Johansson	.75	2.00
6 Stefan Ornskog	.75	2.00
7 Niklas Eriksson	.75	2.00
8 Johan Rosen	.75	2.00
9 Roger Ohman	.75	2.00
10 Anders Soderberg	.75	2.00

1995-96 Swedish Leaf Mega

The fifteen cards in this set were randomly inserted at a rate of 1:20 series 1 packs.

COMPLETE SET (15)	12.00	30.00
1 Michael Sundlov	1.25	3.00
2 Jonas Bergqvist	1.25	3.00
3 Marko Jantunen	.75	2.00
4 Thomas Ostlund	1.25	3.00
5 Tomas Jonsson	.75	2.00
6 Esa Keskinen	.75	2.00
7 Roger Nordstrom	.75	2.00
8 Mattias Ohlund	1.50	4.00
9 Hakan Loob	1.25	3.00
10 Raimo Helminen	.75	2.00
11 Per-Erik Eklund	1.25	3.00
12 Jarmo Myllys	1.50	4.00
13 Rikard Franzen	.75	2.00
14 Christer Olsson	.75	2.00
15 Per Gustafsson	.75	2.00

1995-96 Swedish Leaf Rookies

Randomly inserted in series one packs at a rate of 1:6, this nine card set reveals Leaf's picks as the top frosh in the Elitserien.

COMPLETE SET (9)	6.00	15.00
1 Peter Wallin	.75	2.00
2 Jan-Axel Alavaara	.75	2.00
3 Niklas Falk	.75	2.00
4 Lars-Goran Wiklander	.75	2.00
5 Torbjorn Johansson	.75	2.00
6 Jan Mertzig	.75	2.00
7 Mikael Burakovsky	.75	2.00
8 Marcus Karlsson	.75	2.00
9 Roger Rosen	.75	2.00

1995-96 Swedish Leaf Spidermen

The stingiest netminders in Sweden are the focus of this 14-card set. The cards were randomly inserted at the rate of 1:8 series one packs.

COMPLETE SET (14)	20.00	40.00
1 Joakim Persson	1.25	3.00
2 Michael Sundlov	1.25	3.00
3 Thomas Ostlund	1.50	4.00
4 Hakan Algotsson	1.25	3.00
5 Patrik Haltia	1.25	3.00
6 Boo Ahl	1.50	4.00
7 Johan Hedberg	2.00	5.00
8 Jarmo Myllys	1.50	4.00
9 Jonas Forsberg	1.50	4.00
10 Petter Ronnqvist	1.25	3.00
11 Magnus Swardh	1.25	3.00
12 Mats Ytter	1.25	3.00
13 Mikael Sandberg	1.25	3.00
14 Roger Nordstrom	1.25	3.00

1995-96 Swedish Upper Deck

The 1995-96 Upper Deck Swedish Elit set was issued in one series totaling 260 cards. The set was issued in 10-card packs and features players from the Swedish Elitserien and was endorsed by its Players Association (SICO). The highlight is the subset Where Are They Now? (234-248) which showcases a number of former Swedish stars now in the NHL.

COMPLETE SET (260)	16.00	40.00
1 Joakim Persson	.08	.25
2 Erik Hamalainen	.08	.25
3 Dick Tarnstrom	.08	.25
4 Rikard Franzen	.02	.10
5 Niclas Havelid	.30	.75
6 Tony Barthelson	.02	.10
7 Tommy Hedlund	.02	.10
8 Patric Aberg	.02	.10
9 Stefan Gustavson	.02	.10
10 Anders Gozzi	.02	.10
11 David Engblom	.02	.10
12 Stefan Andersson	.02	.10
13 Tomas Strandberg	.02	.10
14 Mats Lindberg	.02	.10
15 Tommy Lehmann	.08	.25
16 Bjorn Ahlstrom	.02	.10
17 Patrik Englund	.02	.10
18 Morgan Samuelsson	.08	.25
19 Michael Sundlov	.20	.50
20 Bedrich Scerban	.02	.10
21 Mikael Lindman	.02	.10
22 Mikael Wiklander	.02	.10
23 Tommy Melkersson	.02	.10
24 Stefan Klockare	.08	.25
25 Per Lofstrom	.02	.10
26 Jonas Johnsson	.02	.10
27 Roger Kyro	.02	.10
28 Jonas Lofstrom	.02	.10
29 Stefan Ketola	.08	.25
30 Mikael Wahlberg	.02	.10
31 Stefan Polla	.02	.10
32 Greg Parks	.02	.10
33 Ove Molin	.02	.10
34 Peter Larsson	.02	.10
35 Fredrik Modin	.40	1.00
36 Andreas Dackell	.30	.75
37 Thomas Ostlund	.20	.50
38 Tommy Jakobsen	.02	.10
39 Christian Due-Boje	.08	.25
40 Thomas Johansson	.02	.10
41 Joakim Lundberg	.02	.10
42 Bjorn Nord	.02	.10
43 Mikael Magnusson	.02	.10
44 Erik Huusko	.08	.25
45 Anders Huusko	.02	.10
46 Kristofer Ottosson	.02	.10
47 Magnus Jansson	.02	.10
48 Niklas Falk	.08	.25
49 Ola Josefsson	.02	.10
50 Per Eklund	.08	.25
51 Espen Knutsen	.40	1.00
52 Jens Ohling	.02	.10
53 Patric Kjellberg	.30	.75
54 Patrik Erickson	.02	.10
55 Jan Viktorsson	.08	.25
56 Markus Ketterer	.20	.50
57 Jesper Duus	.02	.10
58 Sergei Fokin	.02	.10
59 Per Lundell	.02	.10
60 Thomas Rhodin	.02	.10
61 Henrik Rehnberg	.02	.10
62 Roger Johansson	.02	.10
63 Leif Carlsson	.02	.10
64 Hakan Loob	.20	.50
65 Stefan Nilsson	.02	.10
66 Vitali Prokhorov	.08	.25
67 Magnus Arvedsson	.08	.25
68 Jonas Hoglund	.40	1.00
69 Mathias Johansson	.02	.10
70 Patrik Wallenberg	.02	.10
71 Claes Eriksson	.02	.10
72 Jorgen Jonsson	.02	.10
73 Peter Nordstrom	.02	.10
74 Peter Ottosson	.02	.10
75 Boo Ahl	.15	.40
76 Per Gustafsson	.08	.25
77 Niklas Rahm	.02	.10
78 Hans Abrahamsson	.02	.10
79 Kenneth Kennholt	.02	.10
80 Daniel Johansson	.08	.25
81 Vesa Salo	.08	.25
82 Thomas Gustavsson	.02	.10
83 Stefan Ornskog	.08	.25
84 Stefan Falk	.02	.10
85 Peter Hammarstrom	.02	.10
86 Johan Davidsson	.20	.50
87 Peter Ekelund	.02	.10
88 Johan Lindbom	.02	.10
89 Esa Keskinen	.08	.25
90 Kai Nurminen	.20	.50
91 Magnus Eliasson	.02	.10
92 Marcus Thuresson	.02	.10
93 Johan Brummer	.02	.10
94 Johan Hedberg	.40	1.00
95 Tomas Jonsson	.08	.25
96 Torbjorn Johansson	.02	.10
97 Hans Lodin	.02	.10
98 Orjan Lindmark	.02	.10
99 Jan Huokko	.02	.10
100 Joakim Lidgren	.02	.10
101 Per-Erik Eklund	.08	.25
102 Anders Carlsson	.02	.10
103 Niklas Eriksson	.02	.10
104 Mikael Karlberg	.02	.10
105 Jonas Bergqvist	.08	.25
106 Torgny Lowgren	.02	.10
107 Stefan Hellkvist	.02	.10
108 Markus Akerblom	.02	.10
109 Mikael Holmberg	.02	.10
110 Andreas Karlsson	.02	.10
111 Markus Akerblom	.02	.10
112 Tomas Forslund	.08	.25
113 Jarmo Myllys	.20	.50
114 Lars Modig	.02	.10
115 Patrik Hoglund	.02	.10
116 Torbjorn Lindberg	.02	.10
117 Jan Mertzig	.08	.25
118 Petter Nilsson	.02	.10
119 Mattias Ohlund	.40	1.00
120 Roger Akerstrom	.02	.10
121 Stefan Jonsson	.02	.10
122 Stefan Nilsson	.02	.10
123 Tomas Holmstrom	.75	2.00
124 Mikael Lindholm	.02	.10
125 Johan Stromvall	.02	.10
126 Jiri Kucera	.08	.25
127 Joakim Backlund	.02	.10
128 Robert Nordberg	.02	.10
129 Tomas Berglund	.02	.10
130 Frederik Johansson	.02	.10
131 Lars Hurtig	.02	.10
132 Johan Rosen	.02	.10
133 Roger Nordstrom	.08	.25
134 Kim Johnsson	.40	1.00
135 Peter Hasselblad	.02	.10
136 Ilya Byakin	.08	.25
137 Johan Salle	.02	.10
138 Peter Andersson	.02	.10
139 Roger Ohman	.02	.10
140 Marko Palo	.02	.10
141 Raimo Helminen	.08	.25
142 Mattias Bosson	.02	.10
143 Markus Magnertoft	.02	.10
144 Roger Hansson	.02	.10
145 Bo Svanberg	.02	.10
146 Patrik Sylvegard	.02	.10
147 Brian McReynolds	.02	.10
148 Hakan Ahlund	.02	.10
149 Robert Burakovsky	.02	.10
150 Stefan Elvenes	.08	.25
151 Patrik Boij	.02	.10
152 Petter Ronnqvist	.08	.25
153 Mattias Timander	.20	.50
154 Lars Jansson	.02	.10
155 Frantisek Kaberle	.20	.50
156 Hans Jonsson	.02	.10
157 Tomas Nansen	.02	.10
158 Marcus Karlsson	.02	.10
159 Kristian Gahn	.08	.25
160 Magnus Wernblom	.02	.10
161 Anders Soderberg	.15	.40
162 Martin Hostak	.02	.10
163 Kyosti Karjalainen	.08	.25
164 Mikael Hakanson	.02	.10
165 Jan Larsson	.02	.10
166 Per Svartvadet	.15	.40
167 Andreas Salomonsson	.40	1.00
168 Samuel Pahlsson	.60	1.50
169 Lars Bystrom	.02	.10
170 Magnus Swardh	.08	.25
171 Anders Berglund	.02	.10
172 Pierre Johnsson	.02	.10
173 Johan Finnstrom	.08	.25
174 Arto Ruotanen	.02	.10
175 Daniel Tjarnqvist	.20	.50
176 Greg Brown	.02	.10
177 Per Wallin	.08	.25
178 Peter Lundmark	.02	.10
179 Roger Elvenes	.08	.25
180 Michael Hjalm	.08	.25
181 Jens Hemstrom	.02	.10
182 Pelle Svensson	.02	.10
183 Harijs Vitolins	.02	.10
184 Jens Nielsen	.02	.10
185 Mats Loov	.02	.10
186 Mats Ytter	.08	.25
187 Lars Ivarsson	.02	.10
188 Edvin Frylen	.08	.25
189 Andrei Lyulin	.02	.10
190 Johan Tornberg	.02	.10
191 Mattias Olsson	.02	.10
192 Mats Lusth	.02	.10
193 Fredrik Oberg	.02	.10
194 Alexei Salomatin	.02	.10
195 Mishat Fahrutdinov	.02	.10
196 Mikael Pettersson	.02	.10
197 Andrei Korolev	.02	.10
198 Mattias Loof	.02	.10
199 Claes Lindblom	.02	.10
200 Paul Andersson	.02	.10
201 Roger Rosen	.02	.10
202 Hakan Algotsson	.08	.25
203 Par Djoos	.08	.25
204 Mikael Sandberg	.02	.10
205 Joachim Esbjors	.02	.10
206 Stefan Axelsson	.08	.25
207 Ronnie Sundin	.15	.40
208 Stefan Larsson	.02	.10
209 Petteri Nummelin	.08	.25
210 Christian Ruuttu	.20	.50
211 Marko Jantunen	.08	.25
212 Peter Strom	.02	.10
213 Peter Berndtsson	.02	.10
214 Lars Edstrom	.02	.10
215 Peter Hogardh	.02	.10
216 Par Edlund	.02	.10
217 Lars-Goran Wiklander	.08	.25
218 Henrik Nilsson	.02	.10
219 Rikard Franzen	.02	.10
220 Fredrik Modin	.30	.75
221 Anders Soderberg	.15	.40
222 Per Eklund	.08	.25
223 Hakan Loob	.20	.50
224 Markus Ketterer	.08	.25
225 Esa Keskinen	.08	.25
226 Per Gustafsson	.08	.25
227 Tomas Jonsson	.08	.25
228 Per-Erik Eklund	.08	.25
229 Mattias Ohlund	.40	1.00
230 Jarmo Myllys	.20	.50
231 Peter Andersson	.02	.10
232 Raimo Helminen	.08	.25
233 Christian Ruuttu	.20	.50
234 Peter Forsberg	3.00	8.00
235 Mikael Renberg	.20	.50
236 Mats Sundin	1.00	2.50
237 Michael Nylander	.20	.50
238 Tommy Soderstrom	.20	.50
239 Nicklas Lidstrom	.75	2.00
240 Kenny Jonsson	.30	.75
241 Patrik Carnback	.08	.25
242 Johan Garpenlov	.20	.50
243 Magnus Svensson	.15	.40
244 Patrik Juhlin	.15	.40
245 Markus Naslund	.75	2.00
246 Tommy Salo	.40	1.00
247 Fredrik Olausson	.20	.50
248 Tommy Albelin	.08	.25
249 Rikard Franzen	.02	.10
250 Jonas Johnsson	.02	.10
251 Thomas Ostlund	.20	.50
252 Hakan Loob	.20	.50
253 Per Gustafsson	.08	.25
254 Per-Erik Eklund	.08	.25
255 Tomas Jonsson	.08	.25
256 Mattias Ohlund	.40	1.00
257 Peter Andersson	.02	.10
258 Christian Ruuttu	.20	.50
259 Checklist	.02	.10
260 Checklist	.02	.10

1995-96 Swedish Upper Deck 1st Division Stars

This 20-card insert series, which was included in packs at indeterminate odds (estimated at 1:8) features players from the Swedish First Division, a league one step below the Elitserien.

COMPLETE SET (20)	6.00	15.00
DS1 Anders Huss	.40	1.00
DS2 Igor Vlasov	.40	1.00
DS3 Ulf Sandstrom	.40	1.00
DS4 Hans Huczkowski	.40	1.00
DS5 Johan Ramstedt	.40	1.00
DS6 Anders Eldebrink	.40	1.00
DS7 Niklas Brannstrom	.40	1.00
DS8 Peter Nilsson	.40	1.00
DS9 Sam Lindstahl	.40	1.00
DS10 Tony Skopac	.40	1.00
DS11 Jonas Eriksson	.40	1.00
DS12 Anders Lonn	.40	1.00
DS13 Peter Hagstrom	.40	1.00
DS14 Magnus Roupe	.40	1.00
DS15 Peter Pettersson	.40	1.00
DS16 Peter Eriksson	.40	1.00
DS17 Fredrik Bergqvist	.40	1.00
DS18 Larry Pilut	.40	1.00
DS19 Peter Olsson	.40	1.00
DS20 Staffan Lundh	.40	1.00

1995-96 Swedish Upper Deck Ticket to North America

This 20-card set was randomly inserted in packs at indeterminate odds (estimated at 1:10) and features athletes whose strong play has led to them being selected in the draft and may earn them a shot at the NHL.

COMPLETE SET (20)	12.00	30.00
NA1 Joakim Persson	.75	2.00
NA2 Dick Tarnstrom	.75	2.00
NA3 Andreas Dackell	.75	2.00
NA4 Fredrik Modin	1.25	3.00
NA5 Per Eklund	.40	1.00
NA6 Espen Knutsen	1.25	3.00
NA7 Fredrik Lindquist	.40	1.00
NA8 Jonas Hoglund	.75	2.00
NA9 Jorgen Jonsson	.40	1.00
NA10 Johan Davidsson	.75	2.00
NA11 Per Gustafsson	.40	1.00
NA12 Johan Lindbom	.40	1.00
NA13 Markus Akerblom	.40	1.00
NA14 Jan Huokko	.40	1.00
NA15 Tomas Holmstrom	4.00	10.00
NA16 Mattias Ohlund	1.25	3.00
NA17 Johan Rosen	.40	1.00
NA18 Frantisek Kaberle	.75	2.00
NA19 Mattias Timander	.75	2.00
NA20 Magnus Wernblom	.40	1.00

1995 Swedish Globe World Championships

This 270-card set was produced by Semic Press to commemorate the 1995 World Championships, which were held in Stockholm. The players pictured have represented their countries at some point in international competition, and thus are shown wearing their national team garb. Card fronts feature a variegated yellow-orange border, with the Globe and World Championships logo (VM '95) along the top. Player name and country are listed in a blue bar and in Swedish text, along the bottom. A silver foil Globe '95 icon is set in the lower left corner. Card backs include a small reprise of the front photo, along with personal information, including all statistics from major international tournaments. No card number 85 is in the set - Mike Gartner was misnumbered 86. An NNO two-sided card of Peter Forsberg and Mats Sundin was randomly inserted in packs. It is believed that there are less than 2,000 of these cards in circulation. A special binder was released to store the set; it is valued at $5.

COMPLETE SET (270)	20.00	50.00
1 Tommy Soderstrom	.08	.25
2 Roger Nordstrom	.02	.10
3 Tommy Salo	.40	1.00
4 Hakan Algotsson	.07	.20
5 Thomas Ostlund	.08	.25
7 Ulf Samuelsson	.05	.15
8 Calle Johansson	.07	.20
9 Nicklas Lidstrom	.60	1.50
10 Tommy Albelin	.05	.15
11 Peter Andersson	.02	.10
12 Magnus Svensson	.05	.15
13 Mats Sundin	.40	1.00
14 Tomas Jonsson	.05	.15
15 Kenny Jonsson	.08	.25
16 Tommy Sjodin	.05	.15
17 Fredrik Stillman	.02	.10
18 Marcus Ragnarsson	.08	.25
19 Peter Popovic	.05	.15
20 Arto Blomsten	.02	.10
21 Peter Forsberg	1.25	3.00
22 Roger Johansson	.02	.10
23 Leif Rohlin	.05	.15
24 Bjorn Nord	.02	.10
25 Stefan Larsson	.02	.10
26 Fredrik Olausson	.05	.15
27 Kjell Samuelsson	.05	.15
28 Tomas Sandstrom	.08	.25
29 Mikael Renberg	.08	.25
30 Mikael Johansson	.02	.10
31 Patrik Juhlin	.05	.15
32 Roger Hansson	.02	.10
33 Daniel Rydmark	.05	.15
34 Jonas Bergqvist	.05	.15
35 Michael Nylander	.08	.25
36 Johan Garpenlov	.05	.15
37 Charles Berglund	.02	.10
38 Jorgen Jonsson	.02	.10
39 Stefan Ornskog	.02	.10
40 Thomas Steen	.05	.15
41 Patrik Carnback	.05	.15
42 Mikael Andersson	.05	.15
43 Markus Naslund	.30	.75
44 Andreas Dackell	.08	.25
45 Erik Huusko	.02	.10
46 Tomas Forslund	.05	.15
47 Daniel Alfredsson	.20	.50
48 Ulf Dahlen	.08	.25
49 Anders Huusko	.02	.10
50 Tomas Holmstrom	.40	1.00
51 Niklas Andersson	.02	.10
52 Hakan Loob	.08	.25
53 Per-Erik Eklund	.05	.15
54 Patrik Erickson	.02	.10
55 Jonas Forsberg	.08	.25
56 Daniel Johansson	.05	.15
57 Mattias Ohlund	.08	.25
58 Anders Eriksson	.08	.25
59 Fredrik Modin	.20	.50
60 Niklas Sundstrom	.08	.25
61 Jesper Mattson	.08	.25
62 Johan Davidsson	.08	.25
63 Mats Lindgren	.08	.25
64 Leif Holmqvist	.02	.10
65 Pelle Lindbergh	.40	1.00
66 Lennart Svedberg	.02	.10
67 Borje Salming	.08	.25
68 Sven Tumba Johansson	.02	.10
69 Ulf Sterner	.02	.10
70 Anders Hedberg	.08	.25
71 Kent Nilsson	.08	.25
72 Mats Naslund	.08	.25
73 Patrick Roy	2.50	6.00
74 Ed Belfour	.60	1.50
75 Bill Ranford	.20	.50
76 Paul Coffey	.40	1.00
77 Ray Bourque	.75	2.00
78 Steve Smith	.05	.15
79 Al MacInnis	.30	.75
80 Mark Tinordi	.05	.15
81 Scott Stevens	.08	.25

82 Rob Blake .30 .75
83 Theo Fleury .40 1.00
84 Mark Messier .60 1.50
85 Mike Gartner UER .20 .50
card numbered #86
86 Brendan Shanahan .60 1.50
87 Mario Lemieux 2.50 6.00
88 Eric Lindros 1.25 3.00
89 Steve Yzerman 2.50 6.00
90 Adam Oates .20 .50
91 Paul Kariya 1.50 4.00
92 Rick Tocchet .20 .50
93 Doug Gilmour .40 1.00
94 Luc Robitaille .30 .75
95 Jason Arnott .20 .50
96 Adam Graves .20 .50
97 Petr Nedved .08 .25
98 Mark Recchi .30 .75
99 Wayne Gretzky 3.00 8.00
100 Mike Richter .60 1.50
101 John Vanbiesbrouck .40 1.00
102 Tom Barrasso .08 .25
103 Brian Leetch .30 .75
104 Gary Suter .08 .25
105 Kevin Hatcher .05 .15
106 Phil Housley .08 .25
107 Chris Chelios .40 1.00
108 Eric Weinrich .05 .15
109 Derian Hatcher .08 .25
110 Craig Wolanin .05 .15
111 Mike Modano .60 1.50
112 Joe Mullen .08 .25
113 Joel Otto .08 .25
114 Doug Brown .08 .25
115 Brett Hull .60 1.50
116 Pat LaFontaine .30 .75
117 Jeremy Roenick .60 1.50
118 Craig Janney .08 .25
119 Kevin Miller .05 .15
120 Tony Granato .08 .25
121 Tony Amonte .30 .75
122 Kevin Stevens .08 .25
123 Darren Turcotte .05 .15
124 Scott Young .20 .50
125 Doug Weight .30 .75
126 Phil Bourque .05 .15
127 Markus Ketterer .05 .15
128 Jarmo Myllys .20 .50
129 Jyrki Lumme .08 .25
130 Timo Jutila .05 .15
131 Marko Kiprusoff .05 .15
132 Hannu Virta .05 .15
133 Teppo Numminen .08 .25
134 Janne Laukkanen .08 .25
135 Mika Nieminen .08 .25
136 Janne Ojanen .05 .15
137 Jari Kurri .20 .50
138 Esa Tikkanen .08 .25
139 Saku Koivu .40 1.00
140 Teemu Selanne .75 2.00
141 Raimo Helminen .05 .15
142 Mikko Makela .05 .15
143 Christian Ruuttu .05 .15
144 Esa Keskinen .05 .15
145 Dominik Hasek .60 1.50
146 Petr Briza .08 .25
147 Richard Smehlik .05 .15
148 Leo Gudas .02 .10
149 Roman Hamrlik .08 .25
150 Antonin Stavjana .05 .15
151 Jiri Slegr .05 .15
152 Jiri Vykoukal .05 .15
153 Tomas Jelinek .05 .15
154 Richard Zemlicka .05 .15
155 Robert Lang .08 .25
156 Michal Pivonka .08 .25
157 Jaromir Jagr 1.25 3.00
158 Josef Beranek .05 .15
159 Robert Reichel .05 .15
160 Petr Hrbek .02 .10
161 Jiri Kucera .05 .15
162 Kamil Kastak .02 .10
163 Andrei Trefilov .08 .25
164 Mikhail Shtalenkov .08 .25
165 Sergei Zubov .08 .25
166 Vladimir Malakhov .05 .15
167 Igor Kravchuk .05 .15
168 Alexei Gusarov .05 .15
169 Alexei Zhitnik .08 .25
170 Alexander Smirnov .02 .10
171 Dimitri Yushkevich .08 .25
172 Alexei Yashin .15 .40
173 Alexei Zhamnov .08 .25
174 Pavel Bure .75 2.00
175 Sergei Fedorov .75 2.00
176 Andrei Kovalenko .08 .25
177 Alexei Kovalev .20 .50
178 Andrei Khomutov .05 .15
179 Valeri Kamensky .08 .25
180 Viacheslav Bykov .07 .20
181 Claus Dalpiaz .02 .10
182 Michael Puschacher .05 .15
183 Ken Strong .02 .10
184 Martin Ulrich .02 .10
185 Andreas Puschnik .02 .10
186 Herbert Hohenberger .08 .25
187 Marty Dallmann .02 .10
188 James Burton .02 .10
189 Michael Shea .02 .10
190 Jim Marthinsen .08 .25
191 Orjan Lovdal .02 .10
192 Cato Tom Andersen .02 .10
193 Geir Hoff .02 .10
194 Tommy Jakobsen .02 .10
195 Marius Rath .02 .10
196 Trond Magnussen .02 .10
197 Svein Enok Norstebo .02 .10
198 Espen Knutsen .20 .50
199 Petri Ylonen .05 .15
200 Michel Valliere .02 .10
201 Franck Pajonkowski .05 .15
202 Pierrick Maia .02 .10
203 Christophe Ville .02 .10
204 Serge Poudrier .02 .10
205 Philippe Bozon .05 .15
206 Gerald Guennelon .02 .10
207 Antoine Richer .02 .10
208 Reto Pavoni .05 .15
209 Renato Tosio .05 .15
210 Jorg Eberle .02 .10
211 Fredy Luthi .02 .10
212 Christian Weber .02 .10
213 Sandro Bertaggia .02 .10
214 Patrick Howald .02 .10
215 Gil Montandon .02 .10
216 Rick Tschumi .02 .10
217 Klaus Merk .07 .20
218 Josef Heiss .08 .25
219 Rick Amann .02 .10
220 Michael Rumrich .02 .10
221 Thomas Brandl .02 .10
222 Andreas Niederberger .02 .10
223 Leo Stefan .02 .10
224 Stefan Ustorf .05 .15
225 Dieter Hegen .05 .15
226 Michael Rosati .05 .15
227 Bruno Campese .05 .15
228 Roberto Oberrauch .02 .10
229 Anthony Circelli .02 .10
230 Bill Stewart .02 .10
231 Bruno Zarillo .02 .10
232 Gaetano Orlando .02 .10
233 Stefan Figliuzzi .02 .10
234 Jimmy Camazzola .02 .10
235 Vladislav Tretiak .40 1.00
236 Slava Fetisov .20 .50
237 Alexei Kasatonov .08 .25
238 Sergei Makarov .08 .25
239 Igor Larionov .30 .75
240 Vladimir Krutov .08 .25
241 Valeri Kharlamov .08 .25
242 Vladimir Petrov .05 .15
243 Boris Mikhailov .08 .25
244 Sweden Olympic Gold 94 .08 .25
245 Sweden Olympic Hakan Loob .08 .25
246 Sweden Olympic Gold .08 .25
247 Canada World Champs 94 Team .30 .75
248 Canada Steve Thomas .08 .25
249 Canada Luc Robitaille .20 .50
250 Manon Rheaume 1.25 3.00
251 Sundin and Andersson .20 .50
252 Brolin and Knutsen .08 .25
253 Peter Forsberg Special 1.25 3.00
254 Peter Forsberg Special 1.25 3.00
255 Peter Forsberg Special 1.25 3.00
256 Mats Sundin Special .40 1.00
257 Mats Sundin Special .40 1.00
258 Mats Sundin Special .40 1.00
259 Mikael Renberg Special .08 .25
260 Mikael Renberg Special .08 .25
261 Mikael Renberg Special .08 .25
262 Eric Lindros Special 1.25 3.00
263 Eric Lindros Special 1.25 3.00
264 Eric Lindros Special 1.25 3.00
265 Wayne Gretzky Special 3.00 8.00
266 Wayne Gretzky Special 3.00 8.00
267 Wayne Gretzky Special 3.00 8.00
268 Checklist 1-90 Renberg .08 .25
269 Checklist 91-180 Sundin .40 1.00
270 Checklist 181-270 Forsberg 1.25 3.00
XX Binder 2.00 5.00
NNO Peter Forsberg 10.00 20.00
Mats Sundin

1995 Swedish World Championships Stickers

This set recently was confirmed by collector Per Vedin. We have no pricing information at this point, and thus are listing the set below for checklisting purposes only.

COMPLETE SET (300) 75.00
1 Bill Ranford .02 .10
2 Stephane Fiset .20 .50
3 Steve Duchesne .08 .25
4 Brad Schlegel .02 .10
5 Luke Richardson .02 .10
6 Darryl Sydor .02 .10
7 Yves Racine .02 .10
8 Rob Blake .20 .50
9 Marc Bergevin .02 .10
10 Paul Coffey .60 1.50
11 Jason Arnott .20 .50
12 Geoff Sanderson .20 .50
13 Shayne Corson .20 .50
14 Mike Ricci .20 .50
15 Kelly Buchberger .20 .50
16 Brendan Shanahan .75 2.00
17 Patrick Verbeek .20 .50
18 Nelson Emerson .20 .50
19 Rod Brind'Amour .20 .50
20 Joe Sakic 2.00 5.00
21 Luc Robitaille .60 1.50
22 Stephen Thomas .08 .25
23 Paul Kariya 1.50 4.00
24 Theo Fleury .40 1.00
25 Dave Gagner .20 .50
26 Valeri Ivannikov .02 .10
27 Mikhail Shtalenkov .20 .50
28 Nikolai Tsulygin .02 .10
29 Dmitri Krasotkin .02 .10
30 Morat Davydov .02 .10
31 Andrei Sklopintsev .02 .10
32 Oleg Davydov .02 .10
33 Evgeni Gribko .02 .10
34 Andrei Yakhanov .02 .10
35 Igor Nikulin .02 .10
36 Valeri Kamensky .02 .10
37 Boris Timofeev .02 .10
38 Dmitri Denisov .02 .10
39 Rail Muftiev .02 .10
40 Andrei Tarasenko .02 .10
41 Oleg Belov .02 .10
42 Andrei Kovalenko .02 .10
43 Igor Varitski .02 .10
44 Ravil Yakubov .02 .10
45 Viacheslav Kozlov .20 .50
46 Alexander Vinogradov .02 .10
47 Yuri Tsyplakov .02 .10
48 Stanislav Romanov .02 .10
49 Slava Bykov .08 .25
50 Andrei Khomutov .08 .25
51 Joseph Heiss .08 .25
52 Klaus Merk .08 .25
53 Mirko Lüdemann .02 .10
54 Ulrich Hiemer .02 .10
55 Torsten Kienass .02 .10
56 Jayson Meyer .02 .10
57 Josef Lehner .02 .10
58 Ron Fischer .08 .25
59 Michael Bresagk .02 .10
60 Andreas Niederberger .02 .10
61 Peter Gulda .02 .10
62 Jan Benda .08 .25
63 Thomas Brandl .02 .10
64 Andreas Lupzig .02 .10
65 Michael Rumrich .02 .10
66 Benoit Doucet .08 .25
67 Raimond Hilger .02 .10
68 Georg Franz .02 .10
69 Jorg Handrick .02 .10
70 Dieter Hegen .08 .25
71 Ernst Kopf .02 .10
72 Gunter Oswald .02 .10
73 Georg Holzmann .02 .10
74 Jürgen Rumrich .02 .10
75 Leo Stefan .02 .10
76 Bruno Campese .08 .25
77 Michael Rosati .20 .50
78 Giovanni Marchetti .02 .10
79 Georg Comploj .02 .10
80 Luigi da Corte .02 .10
81 Robert Oberrauch .02 .10
82 Anthony Circelli .02 .10
83 Alex Thaler .02 .10
84 Carlo Lorenzi .02 .10
85 Michael de Angelis .02 .10
86 Emilio Iovio .02 .10
87 Gaetano Orlando .08 .25
88 Lucio Topatigh .02 .10
89 Stefano Figliuzzi .02 .10
90 Bruno Zarrillo .02 .10
91 Mark Montanari .02 .10
92 Armando Chelodi .02 .10
93 Mirko Moroder .02 .10
94 Alex Gschliesser .02 .10
95 Maurizio Mansi .02 .10
96 Petri Ylönen .05 .15
97 Michel Valliere .08 .25
98 Serge Djelloul .02 .10
99 Christophe Moyon .02 .10
100 Gerald Guennelon .02 .10
101 Philippe Lemoine .02 .10
102 Denis Perez .08 .25
103 Serge Poudrier .08 .25
104 Steven Woodburn .02 .10
105 Michael Babin .02 .10
106 Benjamin Agnel .02 .10
107 Stephane Arcangeloni .02 .10
108 Laurent Deschaume .02 .10
109 Pierre Pousse .02 .10
110 Patrick Dunn .02 .10
111 Pierrick Maia .02 .10
112 Philippe Bozon .40 1.00
113 Christian Pouget .02 .10
114 Antoine Richer .02 .10
115 Richard Aimonetto .02 .10
116 Reto Pavoni .02 .10
117 Renato Tosio .02 .10
118 Marco Bayer .02 .10
119 Sandro Bertaggia .02 .10
120 Fredy Bobillier .02 .10
121 Dino Kessler .02 .10
122 Sven Leuenberger .02 .10
123 Martin Steinegger .02 .10
124 Andreas Zehnder .02 .10
125 Misko Antisin .02 .10
126 Gian-Marco Crameri .08 .25
127 Jörg Eberle .08 .25
128 Patrick Fischer .02 .10
129 Patrick Howald .02 .10
130 Marcel Jenni .02 .10
131 Gil Montandon .02 .10
132 Pascal Schaller .02 .10
133 Andy Ton .02 .10
134 Roberto Triulzi .02 .10
135 Theo Wittman .02 .10
136 Roger Nordstrom .02 .10
137 Thomas Ostlund .08 .25
138 Magnus Svensson .02 .10
139 Tommy Sjodin .08 .25
140 Fredrik Stillman .02 .10
141 Tomas Jonsson .02 .10
142 Stefan Larsson .02 .10
143 Leif Rohlin .02 .10
144 Marcus Ragnarsson .02 .10
145 Christer Olsson .02 .10
146 Morgan Samuelsson .02 .10
147 Andreas Dackell .02 .10
148 Jonas Johnsson .02 .10
149 Charles Berglund .02 .10
150 Erik Huusko .02 .10
151 Daniel Rydmark .02 .10
152 Patrik Carnbäck .02 .10
153 Mats Lindgren .02 .10
154 Jonas Bergkvist .02 .10
155 Stefan Ornskog .02 .10
156 Per-Erik Eklund .08 .25
157 Thomas Forslund .02 .10
158 Roger Hansson .02 .10
159 Hakan Ahlund .02 .10
160 Daniel Alfredsson .20 .50
161 Jarmo Myllys .20 .50
162 Jukka Tammi .08 .25
163 Mika Stromberg .08 .25
164 Erik Hamalainen .02 .10
165 Karri Kivi .02 .10
166 Timo Jutila .02 .10
167 Petteri Nummelin .02 .10
168 Hannu Virta .02 .10
169 Marko Kiprusoff .02 .10
170 Waltteri Immonen .08 .25
171 Janne Ojanen .20 .50
172 Esa Keskinen .02 .10
173 Marko Jantunen .02 .10
174 Saku Koivu .40 1.00
175 Marko Palo .02 .10
176 Tero Lehtera .02 .10
177 Mika Alatalo .20 .50
178 Ville Peltonen .02 .10
179 Raimo Helminen .02 .10
180 Petri Varis .08 .25
181 Jokke Heinänen .02 .10
182 Timo Saarikoski .02 .10
183 Sami Kapanen .20 .50
184 Tero Arkiomaa .02 .10
185 Mika Nieminen .08 .25
186 Peter Briza .20 .50
187 Roman Turek .20 .50
188 Milos Holan .08 .25
189 Drahomir Kadlec .08 .25
190 Frantisek Kaberle .02 .10
191 Bedrich Scerban .08 .25
192 Roman Hamrlik .08 .25
193 Jan Vopat .02 .10
194 Antonin Stavjana .02 .10
195 Jiri Vykoukal .02 .10
196 Jiri Veber .02 .10
197 Frantisek Musil .02 .10
198 Richard Zemlicka .08 .25
199 Kamil Kastak .08 .25
200 Jiri Kucera .08 .25
201 Roman Horak .02 .10
202 Martin Rucinsky .08 .25
203 Josef Beranek .08 .25
204 Bobby Holik .08 .25
205 Otakar Janecky .08 .25
206 Jiri Dolezal .02 .10
207 Martin Straka .08 .25
208 Martin Hostak .02 .10
209 Radek Toupal .02 .10
210 Tomas Kapusta .02 .10
211 Guy Hebert .40 1.00
212 Mike Richter .60 1.50
213 Shawn Chambers .02 .10
214 Sean Hill .02 .10
215 Don McSween .02 .10
216 Pat Neaton .02 .10
217 Barry Richter .02 .10
218 Craig Wolanin .02 .10
219 Gary Suter .08 .25
220 Robert Beers .02 .10
221 Brett Hauer .02 .10
222 Peter Ciavaglia .20 .50
223 Phil Bourque .02 .10
224 Shjon Podein .08 .25
225 John Lilley .08 .25
226 Tim Sweeney .08 .25
227 Scott Young .08 .25
228 Craig Janney .08 .25
229 Joe Sacco .08 .25
230 Jeffrey Lazaro .08 .25
231 Doug Weight .40 1.00
232 Thomas Bissett .20 .50
233 James Campbell .02 .10
234 Mark Beaufait .08 .25
235 Peter Ferraro .08 .25
236 Jim Marthinsen .08 .25
237 Robert Schistad .08 .25
238 Jan Roar Fagerli .02 .10
239 Petter Salsten .02 .10
240 Carl Oscar Boe Andersen .02 .10
241 Svein Enok Norstebo .02 .10
242 Tommie Eriksen .02 .10
243 Tom Erik Olsen .02 .10
244 Geir Hoff .02 .10
245 Bjorn Anders Dahl .02 .10
246 Trond Magnussen .02 .10
247 Orjan Lovdahl .02 .10
248 Espen Knutsen .20 .50
249 Rune Gulliksen .02 .10
250 Erik Paulsen .02 .10
251 Sjur Robert Nilsen .02 .10
252 Petter Thoresen .02 .10
253 Rune Fjeldstad .02 .10
254 Erik Tveten .02 .10
255 Henrik Aaby .02 .10
256 Michael Puschacher .02 .10
257 Claus Dalpiaz .08 .25
258 Michael Guntner .02 .10
259 Martin Ulrich .02 .10
260 Peter Kasper .02 .10
261 Engelbert Linder .02 .10
262 Herbert Hohenberger .02 .10
263 Gerhard Unterluggauer .02 .10
264 Martin Krainz .02 .10
265 Helmut Karel .02 .10
266 Werner Kerth .02 .10
267 Dieter Kalt .02 .10
268 Patrick Pilloni .02 .10
269 Mario Schaden .02 .10
270 Wolfgang Kromp .02 .10
271 Gunter Lanzinger .02 .10
272 Manfred Muhr .02 .10
273 Gerald Ressman .02 .10
274 Siegfried Haberl .02 .10
275 Christoph Brandner .02 .10
276 Wayne Gretzky 6.00 15.00
277 Mario Lemieux 5.00 12.00
278 Eric Lindros 1.50 4.00
279 Mark Messier 1.25 3.00
280 Steve Yzerman 4.00 10.00
281 Pavel Bure 1.00 2.50
282 Sergei Fedorov 1.25 3.00
283 Igor Larionov .40 1.00
284 Sergei Makarov .40 1.00
285 Alexander Mogilny .40 1.00
286 Ulf Dahlen .08 .25
287 Peter Forsberg 2.00 5.00
288 Mikael Renberg .20 .50
289 Ulf Samuelsson .08 .25
290 Tomas Sandström .08 .25
291 Thomas Steen .08 .25
292 Mats Sundin .60 1.50
293 Jari Kurri .40 1.00
294 Teemu Selanne 2.00 5.00
295 Esa Tikkanen .20 .50
296 Dominik Hasek 1.25 3.00
297 Jaromir Jagr 1.50 4.00
298 Robert Reichel .02 .10
299 Brett Hull 1.50 4.00
300 Brian Leetch .60 1.50

1996 Swedish Semic Wien

The 1996 Semic Wien set was issued in one series totaling 240 cards to commemorate the 1996 World Championships held in Vienna. The set features players who have competed for their countries in various tournaments, wearing their national team colors. Many top NHLers are featured, including Wayne Gretzky, Eric Lindros and Ray Bourque. The cards were distributed in ten-card packs.

COMPLETE SET (240) 16.00 40.00
1 Jarmo Myllys .08 .25
2 Marko Kiprusoff .05 .15
3 Petteri Nummelin .02 .10
4 Erik Hamalainen .02 .10
5 Timo Jutila .05 .15
6 Janne Niinimaa .08 .25
7 Raimo Summanen .05 .15
8 Janne Ojanen .05 .15
9 Esa Keskinen .05 .15
10 Ari Sulander .08 .25
11 Saku Koivu .20 .50
12 Jukka Tammi .08 .25
13 Marko Palo .02 .10
14 Raimo Helminen .05 .15
15 Antti Tormanen .07 .20
16 Ville Peltonen .08 .25
17 Tero Lehtera .05 .15
18 Mika Stromberg .05 .15
19 Sami Kapanen .15 .40
20 Jere Lehtinen .15 .40
21 Juha Ylonen .07 .20
22 Mika Nieminen .07 .20
23 Hannu Virta .05 .15
24 Jari Kurri .15 .40
25 Christian Ruuttu .05 .15
26 Jyrki Lumme .05 .15
27 Teppo Numminen .08 .25
28 Esa Tikkanen .08 .25
29 Janne Laukkanen .07 .20
30 Aki Berg .08 .25
31 Teemu Selanne .60 1.50
32 Markus Ketterer .08 .25
33 Joni Lehto .02 .10
34 Juha Riihijarvi .08 .25
35 Sakari Lindfors .08 .25
36 Kai Nurminen .08 .25
37 Huey, Dewey, Louie .20 .50
38 Tommy Soderstrom .08 .25
39 Tommy Salo .20 .50
40 Thomas Ostlund .07 .20
41 Boo Ahl .07 .20
42 Calle Johansson .07 .20
43 Tommy Albelin .05 .15
44 Ulf Samuelsson .05 .15
45 Nicklas Lidstrom .40 1.00
46 Magnus Svensson .05 .15
47 Tomas Jonsson .05 .15
48 Tommy Sjodin .05 .15
49 Marcus Ragnarsson .08 .25
50 Christer Olsson .02 .10
51 Rikard Franzen .02 .10
52 Mattias Ohlund .08 .25
53 Kenny Jonsson .08 .25
54 Roger Johansson .02 .10
55 Anders Eriksson .08 .25
56 Mats Sundin .30 .75
57 Peter Forsberg .75 2.00
58 Mikael Renberg .08 .25
59 Tomas Sandstrom .07 .20
60 Ulf Dahlen .05 .15
61 Michael Nylander .05 .15
62 Patrik Juhlin .05 .15
63 Patrik Carnback .05 .15
64 Andreas Johansson .07 .20
65 Mikael Johansson .02 .10
66 Per-Erik Eklund .05 .15
67 Tomas Forslund .05 .15
68 Andreas Dackell .07 .20
69 Per Eklund .05 .15
70 Tomas Holmstrom .20 .50
71 Jonas Bergqvist .05 .15
72 Daniel Alfredsson .15 .40
73 Fredrik Modin .08 .25
74 Magic Moment .40 1.00
75 Ed Belfour .40 1.00
76 Bill Ranford .08 .25
77 Sean Burke .08 .25
78 Ray Bourque .60 1.50
79 Paul Coffey .20 .50
80 Scott Stevens .08 .25
81 Al MacInnis .20 .50
82 Larry Murphy .20 .50
83 Eric Desjardins .08 .25
84 Steve Duchesne .07 .20
85 Mario Lemieux 1.50 4.00
86 Mark Messier .40 1.00
87 Theo Fleury .30 .75
88 Eric Lindros .60 1.50
89 Rick Tocchet .15 .40
90 Brendan Shanahan .40 1.00
91 Claude Lemieux .15 .40
92 Joe Juneau .08 .25
93 Luc Robitaille .30 .75
94 Paul Kariya .75 2.00
95 Joe Sakic .75 2.00
96 Mark Recchi .20 .50
97 Jason Arnott .15 .40
98 Rod Brind'Amour .15 .40
99 Wayne Gretzky 2.00 5.00
100 Adam Oates .20 .50
101 Steve Yzerman 1.50 4.00
102 Roman Turek .20 .50
103 Dominik Hasek .40 1.00
104 Petr Briza .08 .25
105 Antonin Stavjana .05 .15
106 Frantisek Kaberle .07 .20
107 Jiri Vykoukal .05 .15
108 Jan Vopat .07 .20
109 Libor Prochazka .02 .10
110 Petr Kuchyna .05 .15
111 Frantisek Musil .02 .10
112 Leo Gudas .02 .10
113 Jiri Slegr .07 .20
114 Pavel Patera .08 .25
115 Otakar Vejvoda .08 .25
116 Martin Prochazka .08 .25
117 Jiri Kucera .08 .25
118 Pavel Janku .07 .20
119 Roman Meluzin .02 .10
120 Richard Zemlicka .02 .10
121 Martin Hostak .02 .10
122 Jiri Dopita .07 .20
123 Radek Belohlav .07 .20
124 Roman Horak .02 .10
125 Jaromir Jagr .60 1.50
126 Michal Pivonka .08 .25
127 Josef Beranek .05 .15
128 Robert Reichel .08 .25
129 Nikolai Khabibulin .20 .50
130 Sergei Abramov .07 .20
131 Yevgeny Tarasov .02 .10
132 Igor Kravchuk .07 .20
133 Dmitri Mironov .08 .25
134 Alexei Zhitnik .08 .25
135 Vladimir Malakhov .07 .20
136 Sergei Zubov .08 .25
137 Dimitri Yushkevich .08 .25
138 Ilya Byakin .02 .10
139 Alexander Smirnov .02 .10
140 Andrei Skopintsev .02 .10
141 Sergei Fedorov .60 1.50
142 Pavel Bure .75 2.00
143 Alexei Zhamnov .08 .25
144 Andrei Kovalenko .08 .25
145 Igor Korolev .05 .15
146 Slava Kozlov .15 .40
147 Viktor Kozlov .08 .25
148 Alexei Yashin .15 .40
149 Valeri Kamensky .08 .25
150 Stanislav Romanov .02 .10
151 Viacheslav Bykov .07 .20
152 Andrei Khomutov .08 .25
153 Sergei Berezin .15 .40
154 German Titov .08 .25
155 Dmitri Denisov .02 .10
156 John Vanbiesbrouck .20 .50
157 Jim Carey .08 .25
158 Mike Richter .30 .75
159 Chris Chelios .30 .75
160 Brian Leetch .30 .75
161 Phil Housley .08 .25
162 Gary Suter .07 .20
163 Kevin Hatcher .07 .20
164 Brett Hull .40 1.00
165 Pat LaFontaine .15 .40
166 Mike Modano .40 1.00
167 Jeremy Roenick .40 1.00
168 Keith Tkachuk .30 .75
169 Joe Mullen .07 .20
170 Craig Janney .08 .25
171 Joel Otto .07 .20
172 Doug Weight .20 .50
173 Scott Young .08 .25
174 Michael Rosati .05 .15
175 Bruno Campese .05 .15
176 Robert Oberrauch .02 .10
177 Robert Nardella .02 .10
178 Stefano Figliuzzi .02 .10
179 Maurizio Mansi .02 .10
180 Gaetano Orlando .02 .10
181 Mario Chitarroni .02 .10
182 Martin Pavlu .02 .10
183 Petri Ylonen .07 .20
184 Michel Valliere .02 .10
185 Serge Poudrier .02 .10
186 Denis Perez .02 .10
187 Antoine Richer .02 .10
188 Philippe Bozon .05 .15
189 Christian Pouget .02 .10
190 Franck Pajonkowski .05 .15
191 Stephane Barin .02 .10
192 Klaus Merk .07 .20
193 Marc Seliger .05 .15
194 Mirco Ludemann .02 .10
195 Jayson Meyer .02 .10
196 Benoit Doucet .05 .15
197 Thomas Brandl .02 .10
198 Dieter Hegen .02 .10
199 Martin Reichel .02 .10
200 Leo Stefan .02 .10
201 Robert Schistad .02 .10
202 Jim Marthinsen .07 .20
203 Tommy Jakobsen .02 .10
204 Petter Salsten .02 .10
205 Svein Norstebo .02 .10
206 Espen Knutsen .08 .25
207 Trond Magnussen .02 .10
208 Henrik Aaby .02 .10
209 Marius Rath .02 .10
210 Claus Dalpiaz .05 .15
211 Michael Puschacher .02 .10
212 Robin Doyle .02 .10
213 James Burton .02 .10
214 Herbert Hohenberger .02 .10
215 Andreas Pusnik .02 .10
216 Richard Nasheim .02 .10
217 Deiter Kalt .02 .10
218 Werner Kerth .02 .10
219 Eduard Hartmann .05 .15
220 Jaromir Dragan .08 .25
221 Robert Svehla .08 .25
222 Lubomir Sekeras .02 .10
223 Marian Smerciak .02 .10
224 Jergus Baca .02 .10
225 Stanslav Medrik .02 .10
226 Miroslav Marcinko .02 .10
227 Peter Stastny .08 .25
228 Peter Bondra .20 .50
229 Zdeno Ciger .08 .25
230 Jozef Stumpel .08 .25
231 Miroslav Satan .20 .50
232 Lubomir Kolnik .07 .20
233 Robert Petrovicky .05 .15
234 Zigmund Palffy .20 .50
235 Oto Hascak .05 .15
236 Jozef Dano .02 .10
237 Checklist .08 .25
238 Checklist .08 .25
239 Checklist .08 .25
240 Checklist .08 .25
NNO Mikael Renberg 10.00 25.00
Saku Koivu Super Chase

1996 Swedish Semic Wien All-Stars

Randomly inserted in packs at a rate of 1:20, this 6-card, double-sided set acknowledges the first and second team all-stars from the 1995 WC. Both sides share similar designs; the player on the side with the gold foil stars across the top was the first team selection.

COMPLETE SET (6) 3.00 8.00
AS1 Roman Turek .75 2.00
Jarmo Myllys
AS2 Timo Jutila .20 .50
Christer Olsson
AS3 Tommy Sjodin .20 .50
Marko Kiprusoff
AS4 Jere Lehtinen .75 2.00
Sergei Berezin
AS5 Saku Koivu 2.00 5.00
Pelle Eklund
AS6 Ville Peltonen .40 1.00
Andrew McKim

1996 Swedish Semic Wien Coca-Cola Dream Team

This 12-card set was created as a promotion to tie in with both the World Championships and the Semic Wien set. The cards were issued four to a pack at participating Shell gas stations in Sweden with the purchase of a Coca-Cola product. The cards mirror their counterparts in the regular Semic Wien set, save for the numbering and the silver Dream Team icon on the upper corner of each.

COMPLETE SET (12) 20.00 50.00
1 Tommy Soderstrom .75 2.00
2 Boo Ahl .75 2.00
3 Tomas Jonsson .40 1.00
4 Rikard Franzen .40 1.00
5 Mattias Ohlund 1.25 3.00
6 Roger Johansson .40 1.00
7 Mats Sundin 4.00 10.00
8 Peter Forsberg 12.00 30.00
9 Mikael Renberg 1.25 3.00
10 Per-Erik Eklund .40 1.00
11 Andreas Dackell 1.25 3.00
12 Jonas Bergqvist .75 2.00

1996 Swedish Semic Wien Hockey Legends

Randomly inserted in packs at a rate of 1:6, this 18-card set recalls some of the best to lace 'em up on either side of the pond. The card front features a period action photo, with the Hockey Legends logo above in gold foil. The backs display another vintage photo, along with career notes and international play totals. The cards are numbered with an HL prefix.

COMPLETE SET (18) 14.00 35.00
HL1 Ken Dryden 4.00 10.00
HL2 Guy Lafleur 2.00 5.00
HL3 Mike Bossy 1.50 4.00
HL4 Valeri Vasiliev .40 1.00
HL5 Anatoli Firsov .40 1.00
HL6 Alexander Maltsev .75 2.00
HL7 Tony Esposito 2.00 5.00
HL8 Rod Langway .40 1.00
HL9 Bryan Trottier 1.25 3.00
HL10 Lennart Haggroth .40 1.00
HL11 Ulf Nilsson .75 2.00
HL12 Lars-Gunnar Lundberg .40 1.00
HL13 Veli-Pekka Ketola .40 1.00
HL14 Lasse Oksanen .40 1.00
HL15 Pekka Rautakallio .40 1.00
HL16 Jiri Holecek .75 2.00
HL17 Jan Suchy .40 1.00
HL18 Vaclav Nedomansky .75 2.00

1996 Swedish Semic Wien Nordic Stars

Randomly inserted in packs at a rate of 1:48, this 6-card set heaps praise on Scandinavia's best. Card fronts utilize an action photo over a stylized background with an apt description of the player prominently featured. The backs display international totals, with a brief bio in English. The cards are numbered with an NS prefix.

COMPLETE SET (6) 10.00 25.00
NS1 Peter Forsberg 4.00 10.00
NS2 Teemu Selanne 2.50 6.00
NS3 Mats Sundin 2.00 5.00
NS4 Jari Kurri 2.00 5.00
NS5 Nicklas Lidstrom 2.00 5.00
NS6 Esa Tikkanen .75 2.00

1996 Swedish Semic Wien Super Goalies

Randomly inserted in packs at a rate of 1:12, this 9-card set captures the last line of defense of some elite hockey nations. The fronts have an action photo over a ghosted, maskless image. The back has another photo and a brief bio in English. The cards are numbered with an SG prefix out of 9. The key card is a rare shot of Patrick Roy from a Team Canada training camp session.

COMPLETE SET (9) 15.00 30.00
SG1 Dominik Hasek 4.00 8.00
SG2 Ed Belfour 2.00 5.00

SG3 Jarmo Myllys .75 2.00
SG4 Tommy Soderstrom .75 2.00
SG5 Jim Carey .75 2.00
SG6 Roman Turek 1.25 3.00
SG7 Patrick Roy 8.00 20.00
SG8 Markus Ketterer .75 2.00
SG9 Tommy Salo .75 2.00

1997-98 Swedish Alfabilder Autographs

These cards are part of a larger multi-sport set of autographs issued within Sweden. We have listed just the hockey players in the set, below. If anyone has information on other hockey players in this set, or on the set itself, please forward it to hockeymag@beckett.com.

1 Sven Tumba Johansson 8.00 20.00
2 Roland Stoltz 4.00 10.00
3 Eilert Maatta 4.00 10.00
4 Lennart Haggroth 6.00 15.00
5 Nisse Nilsson 4.00 10.00
6 Ulf Sterner 8.00 20.00
7 Leif Holmqvist 8.00 20.00
8 Tord Lundstrom 4.00 10.00
9 Borje Salming 20.00 50.00
10 Anders Hedberg 12.00 30.00
11 Anders Kallur 6.00 15.00
12 Stefan Persson 6.00 15.00
13 Goran Hogosta 4.00 10.00
14 Bengt-Ake Gustafsson 8.00 20.00
15 Mats Naslund 12.00 30.00
16 Kent Nilsson 12.00 30.00
17 Hakan Loob 12.00 30.00
18 Peter Lindmark 10.00 25.00

1997-98 Swedish Collector's Choice

This set was produced by Upper Deck for the Swedish SEL. The cards came in 10-card packs for about $1.50 per pack. It is noteworthy for featuring early cards of Daniel and Henrik Sedin.

COMPLETE SET (225) 10.00 25.00
1 Miikka Kiprusoff 1.25 3.00
2 Karri Kivi .02 .10
3 Erik Hamalainen .07 .20
4 Libor Prochazka .02 .10
5 Dick Tarnstrom .20 .50
6 Niclas Havelid .20 .50
7 Tomas Strandberg .02 .10
8 Stefan Gustavsson .02 .10
9 Anders Gozzi .02 .10
10 Pavel Patera .15 .40
11 David Engblom .02 .10
12 Peter Hammarstrom .02 .10
13 Mats Lindberg .02 .10
14 Fredrik Krekula .02 .10
15 Otakar Vojvoda .02 .10
16 Bjorn Ahlstrom .02 .10
17 Michael Sundlov .08 .25
18 Pär Djoos .02 .10
19 Tommy Melkersson .02 .10
20 Stefan Klockare .02 .10
21 Johan Hansson .02 .10
22 Per Lofstrom .02 .10
23 Tommy Westlund .08 .25
24 Teppo Kivela .02 .10
25 Niclas Wallin .30 .75
26 Roger Kyro .02 .10
27 Ove Molin .02 .10
28 Mikko Luovi .02 .10
29 Evgenij Davydov .02 .10
30 Anders Huss .02 .10
31 Peter Nylander .02 .10
32 Jan Larsson .02 .10
33 Tommy Soderstrom .20 .50
34 Marcus Matthiasson .02 .10
35 Daniel Carlsson .02 .10
36 Ronnie Pettersson .02 .10
37 Kenneth Kennholt .02 .10
38 Bjorn Nord .07 .20
39 Mikael Hakansson .07 .20
40 Daniel Tjarnqvist .20 .50
41 Charles Berglund .02 .10
42 Mikael Johansson .02 .10
43 Marcus Nilsson .20 .50
44 Nichlas Falk .08 .25
45 Fredrik Lindqvist .08 .25
46 Patric Kjellberg .20 .50
47 Patrik Erickson .02 .10
48 Jan Viktorsson .02 .10
49 Niklas Anger .02 .10
50 Boris Rousson .08 .25
51 Peter Jakobsson .02 .10
52 Peter Nordstrom .08 .25
53 Sergei Fokin .02 .10
54 Niklas Sjokvist .02 .10
55 Jaroslav Spacek .08 .25
56 Greger Artursson .02 .10
57 Roger Johansson .02 .10
58 Stefan Nilsson .02 .10
59 Pelle Prestberg .02 .10
60 Kristian Huselius .75 2.00
61 Mathias Johansson .02 .10
62 Trond Magnussen .02 .10
63 Claes Eriksson .02 .10
64 Jorgen Jonsson .15 .40
65 Atle Olsen .02 .10
66 Patrik Wallenberg .02 .10
67 Lars-Goran Wiklander .02 .10
68 Mikael Sandberg .08 .25
69 Christer Olsson .02 .10
70 Joachim Esbjors .02 .10
71 Henrik Nilsson .02 .10
72 Arto Blomsten .02 .10
73 Magnus Johansson .02 .10
74 Stefan Larsson .02 .10
75 Par Edlund .02 .10
76 Marko Jantunen .02 .10
77 Joni Lius .02 .10
78 Patrik Carnback .07 .20
79 Ville Peltonen .20 .50
80 Peter Berndtsson .02 .10
81 Kai Nurminen .07 .20
82 Jonas Esbjors .02 .10
83 Peter Strom .02 .10
84 Kari Takko .08 .25
85 Johan Forsander .08 .25
86 Jouni Loponen .02 .10
87 David Petrasek .02 .10
88 Daniel Johansson .07 .20
89 Fredrik Stillman .02 .10
90 Anatoly Fedotov .02 .10
91 Stefan Ornskog .02 .10
92 Stefan Falk .02 .10
93 Peter Ekelund .02 .10
94 Esa Keskinen .02 .10
95 Patrik Lundback .02 .10
96 Anders Huusko .02 .10
97 Magnus Svensson .02 .10
98 Alexei Salomatin .02 .10
99 Patrik Englund .02 .10
100 Ake Lilljebjorn .08 .25
101 Tomas Jonsson .02 .10
102 Torbjorn Johansson .02 .10
103 Hans Lodin .02 .10
104 Magnus Svensson .02 .10
105 Andreas Karlsson .20 .50
106 Joakim Lidgren .02 .10
107 Fredrik Jonsson .02 .10
108 Per-Erik Eklund .02 .10
109 Anders Carlsson .02 .10
110 Johan Witehall .02 .10
111 Jens Nielsen .02 .10
112 Niklas Eriksson .02 .10
113 Jonas Bergqvist .07 .20
114 Stefan Hellkvist .02 .10
115 Markus Akerblom .07 .20
116 Anders Lonn .02 .10
117 Jarmo Myllys .08 .25
118 Johan Finnstrom .07 .20
119 Sergei Bautin .02 .10
120 Jan Mertzig .07 .20
121 Osmo Soutokorva .02 .10
122 Roger Akerstrom .02 .10
123 Stefan Jonsson .07 .20
124 Stefan Nilsson .02 .10
125 Jonas Ronnqvist .08 .25
126 Joakim Backlund .02 .10
127 Robert Nordberg .02 .10
128 Mikael Lovgren .02 .10
129 Anders Burstrom .02 .10
130 Fredrik Johansson .02 .10
131 Mika Alatalo .20 .50
132 Fredrik Nilsson .20 .50
133 Roger Nordstrom .08 .25
134 Andrew Verner .08 .25
135 Marko Kiprusoff .08 .25
136 Kim Johnsson .02 .10
137 Magnus Nilsson .02 .10
138 Jesper Damgaard .02 .10
139 Marek Malik .07 .20
140 Mats Lusth .02 .10
141 Janne Ojanen .07 .20
142 Mikko Peltola .02 .10
143 Mathias Bosson .02 .10
144 Daniel Rydmark .02 .10
145 Patrik Sylvegard .02 .10
146 Juha Riihijarvi .07 .20
147 Fredrik Oberg .02 .10
148 Mikael Burakovsky .02 .10
149 Peter Ronnqvist .08 .25
150 Pierre Hedin .15 .40
151 Jan-Axel Alavaara .02 .10
152 Frantisek Kaberle .20 .50
153 Hans Jonsson .20 .50
154 Jonas Junkka .07 .20
155 Marcus Karlsson .02 .10
156 Kristian Gahn .08 .25
157 Magnus Wernblom .08 .25
158 Anders Soderberg .08 .25
159 Daniel Sedin 1.25 3.00
160 Henrik Sedin 1.25 3.00
161 Samuel Pahlsson .30 .75
162 Per Svartvadet .15 .40
163 Andreas Salomonsson .02 .10
164 Ravil Yakubov .20 .50
165 David Vyborny .20 .50
166 Magnus Lindqvist .08 .25
167 Anders Eldebrink .02 .10
168 Johan Norgren .02 .10
169 Christian Due-Boje .02 .10
170 Jonas Heed .02 .10
171 Josef Boumedienne .15 .40
172 Marko Virtanen .02 .10
173 Kyosti Karjalainen .02 .10
174 Jorgen Bemstrom .02 .10
175 Joakim Ericsson .02 .10
176 Jens Ohling .02 .10
177 Martin Hostak .02 .10
178 Lars Dahlstrom .08 .25
179 Niklas Brannstrom .02 .10
180 Mikko Makela .02 .10
181 Petr Korinek .02 .10
182 Joakim Persson .08 .25
183 Tobias Lilja .07 .20
184 Edvin Frylen .07 .20
185 Jakob Karlsson .07 .20
186 Johan Tornberg .02 .10
187 Patrik Hoglund .02 .10
188 Mattias Loof .02 .10
189 Mikael Pettersson .02 .10
190 Johan Molin .02 .10
191 Fredrik Eriksson .02 .10
192 Henrik Nordfeldt .02 .10
193 Jonas Olsson .02 .10
194 Roger Jonsson .02 .10
195 Roger Rosen .02 .10
196 Henric Bjorkman .02 .10
197 Harri Sillgren .02 .10
198 Paul Andersson-Everberg .02 .10
199 Tommy Soderstrom .20 .50
200 Stefan Nilsson .02 .10
201 Tomas Jonsson .02 .10
202 Jonas Bergqvist .07 .20
203 Christer Olsson .02 .10
204 Per Svartvadet .15 .40
205 Anders Huss .02 .10
206 Roger Johansson .02 .10
207 Stefan Ornskog .02 .10
208 Anders Eldebrink .02 .10
209 Niclas Havelid .20 .50
210 Charles Berglund .02 .10
211 Kai Nurminen .07 .20
212 Stefan Nilsson .02 .10
213 Per-Erik Eklund .02 .10
214 Janne Ojanen .07 .20
215 Per Svartvadet .15 .40
216 Michael Sundlov .08 .25
217 Roger Johansson .02 .10
218 Stefan Ornskog .02 .10
219 Kyosti Karjalainen .02 .10
220 Roger Rosen .02 .10
221 Jonas Bergqvist .07 .20
222 Esa Keskinen .02 .10
223 Christer Olsson .02 .10
224 Checklist .05
225 Checklist .05

1997-98 Swedish Collector's Choice Crash the Game Exchange

Mirroring the chase program first used in North America, these interactive cards allowed fans a chance to redeem them for specially foiled complete Crash sets. The cards were inserted 1:8 packs.

COMPLETE SET (30) 10.00 25.00
C1 Patric Kjellberg .40 1.00
C2 Mikael Johansson .40 1.00
C3 Daniel Tjarnqvist .40 1.00
C4 Christer Olsson .40 1.00
C5 Ville Peltonen .40 1.00
C6 Kai Nurminen .40 1.00
C7 Stefan Nilsson .40 1.00
C8 Jan Mertzig .40 1.00
C9 Anders Carlsson .40 1.00
C10 Jonas Bergqvist .40 1.00
C11 Magnus Svensson .40 1.00
C12 Janne Ojanen .40 1.00
C13 Marko Kiprusoff .40 1.00
C14 Juha Riihijarvi .40 1.00
C15 Daniel Sedin 2.00 5.00
C16 Henrik Sedin 2.00 5.00
C17 Evgenij Davydov .40 1.00
C18 Anders Huss .40 1.00
C19 Jan Larsson .40 1.00
C20 Roger Johansson .40 1.00
C21 Jorgen Jonsson .40 1.00
C22 Kristian Huselius 1.25 3.00
C23 Stefan Ornskog .40 1.00
C24 Anders Huusko .40 1.00
C25 Esa Keskinen .40 1.00
C26 Joakim Eriksson .40 1.00
C27 Anders Eldebrink .40 1.00
C28 Mikko Makela .40 1.00
C29 Henric Bjorkman .40 1.00
C30 Roger Rosen .40 1.00

1997-98 Swedish Collector's Choice Crash the Game Redemption

These cards were issued in complete set form in exchange for a winning Crash the Game insert card. They feature gold foil fronts, and backs which feature information on the winner.

COMPLETE SET (30) 10.00 20.00
R1 Patric Kjellberg .60 1.50
R2 Mikael Johansson .20 .50
R3 Daniel Tjarnqvist .30 .75
R4 Christer Olsson .20 .50
R5 Ville Peltonen .60 1.50
R6 Kai Nurminen .20 .50
R7 Stefan Nilsson .20 .50
R8 Jan Mertzig .20 .50
R9 Anders Carlsson .20 .50
R10 Jonas Bergqvist .20 .50
R11 Magnus Svensson .20 .50
R12 Janne Ojanen .30 .75
R13 Marko Kiprusoff .60 1.50
R14 Juha Riihijarvi .20 .50
R15 Daniel Sedin 1.50 4.00
R16 Henrik Sedin 1.50 4.00
R17 Evgenij Davydov .20 .50
R18 Anders Huss .20 .50
R19 Jan Larsson .20 .50
R20 Roger Johansson .20 .50
R21 Jorgen Jonsson .30 .75
R22 Kristian Huselius 1.25 3.00
R23 Stefan Ornskog .20 .50
R24 Anders Huusko .20 .50
R25 Esa Keskinen .20 .50
R26 Joakim Eriksson .20 .50
R27 Anders Eldebrink .20 .50
R28 Mikko Makela .20 .50
R29 Henric Bjorkman .20 .50
R30 Roger Rosen .20 .50

1997-98 Swedish Collector's Choice Select

This chase set features elite players from the past and present of the SEL. The cards were inserted 1:8 packs.

COMPLETE SET (15) 40.00 80.00
UD1 Peter Forsberg 12.00 30.00
UD2 Daniel Sedin 4.00 10.00
UD3 Niclas Falk .75 2.00
UD4 Marko Jantunen .40 1.00
UD5 Ville Peltonen 1.25 3.00
UD6 Jorgen Jonsson .75 2.00
UD7 Roger Johansson .40 1.00
UD8 Stefan Ornskog .75 2.00
UD9 Henrik Sedin 4.80 10.00
UD10 Jonas Bergqvist .40 1.00
UD11 Tomas Jonsson .40 1.00
UD12 Stefan Nilsson .40 1.00
UD13 Janne Ojanen .40 1.00
UD14 Magnus Wernblom .40 1.00
UD15 Edvin Frylen .40 1.00
NNO Peter Forsberg Elite 20.00 50.00

1997-98 Swedish Collector's Choice Stick'Ums

These stickers were inserted 1:4 packs and feature top players of the SEL.

COMPLETE SET (15) 4.00 10.00
S1 Miikka Kiprusoff 1.25 3.00
S2 Marcus Nilsson .40 1.00
S3 Christer Olsson .08 .25
S4 Jorgen Jonsson .20 .50
S5 Fredrik Stillman .08 .25
S6 Per-Erik Eklund .20 .50
S7 Jarmo Myllys .20 .50
S8 Daniel Rydmark .08 .25
S9 Henric Bjorkman .08 .25
S10 Henrik Sedin 1.00 2.50
S11 Daniel Sedin 1.00 2.50
S12 Anders Huss .08 .25
S13 Patrik Carnback .08 .25
S14 Daniel Tjarnqvist .20 .50
S15 Jonas Bergqvist .20 .50

1998-99 Swedish UD Choice

This Upper Deck-produced issue features the players of the Swedish Elitserien. The design mimics that of the 1998-99 North American UD Choice set. It is noteworthy for featuring early cards of Daniel and Henrik Sedin, along with Johan Hedberg and Mattias Karlin. The final two cards in the listing are the first-ever memorabilia cards issued in Sweden. Both feature a pair of swatches from the jerseys of the Sedin Twins, but the second also is graced by the autograph of both players on the jersey swatches.

COMPLETE SET (225) 10.00 25.00
1 Jonas Forsberg .08 .25
2 Rikard Franzen .02 .10
3 Mathias Svedberg .02 .10
4 Dick Tarnstrom .20 .50
5 Jan Sandstrom .02 .10
6 Johan Silfwerplatz .02 .10
7 Henrik Tallinder .20 .50
8 Stefan Gustavson .02 .10
9 Kristian Gahn .20 .50
10 Bjorn Ahlstrom .02 .10
11 Peter Hammarstrom .02 .10
12 Anders Gozzi .02 .10
13 Fredrik Krekula .02 .10
14 Erik Norback .02 .10
15 Niklas Anger .20 .50
16 Mats Lindberg .02 .10
17 Jorgen Wikstrom .02 .10
18 Per-Anton Lundstrom .08 .25
19 Mattias Hedlund .02 .10
20 Jorgen Hermansson .02 .10
21 Fredrik Bergqvist .02 .10
22 Joakim Lidgren .02 .10
23 Robert Karlsson .02 .10
24 Christian Lechtaler .02 .10
25 Aleksandrs Beljavskis .02 .10
26 Jens Ohman .02 .10
27 Stefan Ohman .02 .10
28 Martin Wiita .02 .10
29 Johan Ramstedt .08 .25
30 Per Ledin .02 .10
31 Jukka Penttinen .02 .10
32 Aleksandrs Semjonovs .02 .10
33 Johan Holmqvist .60 1.50
34 Tommy Melkersson .02 .10
35 Marko Tuulola .02 .10
36 Johan Hansson .02 .10
37 Par Djoos .02 .10
38 Per Lofstrom .02 .10
39 Niclas Wallin .20 .50
40 Roger Kyro .02 .10
41 Ove Molin .02 .10
42 Stefan Lundqvist .02 .10
43 Peter Nylander .02 .10
44 Jan Larsson .02 .10
45 Teppo Kivela .02 .10
46 Tom Bissett .08 .25
47 Anders Huss .08 .25
48 Mikko Luovi .08 .25
49 Tommy Soderstrom .30 .75
50 Bjorn Nord .08 .25
51 Ronnie Pettersson .02 .10
52 Thomas Johansson .02 .10
53 Daniel Tjarnqvist .20 .50
54 Anders Myrvold .08 .25
55 Mikael Magnusson .02 .10
56 Mikael Johansson .02 .10
57 Nichlas Falk .08 .25
58 Mikael Hakanson .02 .10
59 Charles Berglund .08 .25
60 Lars-Goran Wiklander .02 .10
61 Per Eklund .07 .20
62 Jan Viktorsson .02 .10
63 Patrik Erickson .02 .10
64 Espen Knutsen .40 1.00
65 Jimmie Olvestad .20 .50
66 Mikael Sandberg .02 .10
67 Christer Olsson .02 .10
68 Petter Nilsson .02 .10
69 Magnus Johansson .02 .10
70 Ronnie Sundin .08 .25
71 Radek Hamr .02 .10
72 Stefan Larsson .02 .10
73 Mattias Nilimaa .02 .10
74 Linus Fagemo .02 .10
75 Marko Jantunen .02 .10
76 Patrik Carnback .02 .10
77 Peter Berndtsson .02 .10
78 Mikael Samuelsson .30 .75
79 Peter Strom .02 .10
80 Par Edlund .02 .10
81 Henrik Nilsson .20 .50
82 Jonas Johnsson .02 .10
83 Kimmo Lecklin .02 .10
84 Roger Johansson .02 .10
85 Sergei Fokin .02 .10
86 Greger Artursson .02 .10
87 Jonas Elofsson .20 .50
88 Peter Jakobsson .02 .10
89 Dimitri Erofeev .02 .10
90 Patrik Zetterberg .02 .10
91 Niklas Sjokvist .02 .10
92 Trond Magnussen .02 .10
93 Peter Hagstrom .02 .10
94 Pelle Prestberg .02 .10
95 Mathias Johansson .08 .25
96 Michael Holmqvist .20 .50
97 Clas Eriksson .02 .10
98 Kristian Huselius 1.00 2.50
99 Jorgen Jonsson .20 .50
100 Kari Takko .08 .25
101 David Petrasek .02 .10
102 Daniel Johansson .20 .50
103 Per Gustafsson .02 .10
104 Fredrik Stillman .02 .10
105 Nicklas Rahm .02 .10
106 Mikael Lindman .02 .10
107 Jerry Persson .02 .10
108 Esa Keskinen .02 .10
109 Peter Ekelund .02 .10
110 Antti Tormanen .08 .25
111 Marcus Kristoffersson .20 .50
112 Anders Huusko .02 .10
113 Erik Huusko .02 .10
114 Johan Lindbom .08 .25
115 Jarkko Varvio .02 .10
116 Ulf Dahlen .08 .25
117 Johan Hedberg .40 1.00
118 Jan Huokko .02 .10
119 Torbjorn Johansson .02 .10
120 Hans Lodin .02 .10
121 Nicklas Nordqvist .02 .10
122 Stefan Bergqvist .02 .10
123 Magnus Svensson .02 .10
124 Andreas Karlsson .20 .50
125 Per-Erik Eklund .08 .25
126 Anders Carlsson .02 .10
127 Niklas Eriksson .02 .10
128 Stefan Hellkvist .02 .10
129 Jens Nielsen .02 .10
130 Anders Lonn .02 .10
131 Markus Akerblom .02 .10
132 Mikael Karlberg .02 .10
133 Jarmo Myllys .08 .25
134 Stefan Jonsson .02 .10
135 Osmo Soutokorva .02 .10
136 Johan Finnstrom .02 .10
137 Roger Akerstrom .08 .25
138 Igor Matushkin .02 .10
139 Jonas Ronnqvist .20 .50
140 Thomas Sjogren .02 .10
141 Tomas Berglund .02 .10
142 Mikael Lovgren .02 .10
143 Anders Burstrom .02 .10
144 Jorgen Bemstrom .02 .10
145 Martin Hostak .02 .10
146 Bert-Olav Karlsson .02 .10
147 Lars Edstrom .02 .10
148 Jiri Kucera .02 .10
149 Andrew Verner .08 .25
150 Kim Johnsson .08 .25
151 Kari Harila .02 .10
152 Niclas Havelid .40 1.00
153 Jesper Damgaard .02 .10
154 Johan Tornberg .02 .10
155 Mats Lusth .02 .10
156 Jan Hammar .02 .10
157 Marcus Magnertoft .02 .10
158 Marcus Thuresson .08 .25
159 Magnus Nilsson .02 .10
160 Mikael Lindholm .08 .25
161 Patrik Sylvegard .02 .10
162 Juha Riihijarvi .08 .25
163 Jesper Mattsson .08 .25
164 Niklas Sundblad .02 .10
165 Toivo Suursoo .02 .10
166 Pelle Ronnquist .08 .25
167 Pierre Hedin .02 .10
168 Per Hallberg .02 .10
169 Jan-Axel Alavaara .02 .10
170 Hans Jonsson .20 .50
171 Lars Jansson .02 .10
172 Frantisek Kaberle .20 .50
173 Andreas Salomonsson .08 .25
174 Magnus Wernblom .08 .25
175 Mikael Pettersson .02 .10
176 Per Svartvadet .02 .10
177 Daniel Sedin .75 2.00
178 Henrik Sedin .75 2.00
179 Jan Alinc .02 .10
180 Samuel Pahlsson .40 1.00
181 Anders Soderberg .20 .50
182 Magnus Eriksson .02 .10
183 Andrei Lulin .02 .10
184 Jakob Karlsson .08 .25
185 Patrik Hoglund .02 .10
186 Joakim Lundberg .02 .10
187 Arto Blomsten .02 .10
188 Mattias Loof .02 .10
189 Mikael Pettersson .02 .10
190 Joakim Backlund .02 .10
191 Daniel Rydmark .02 .10
192 Johan Molin .02 .10
193 Paul Andersson-Everberg .02 .10
194 Henrik Nordfeldt .02 .10
195 Jonas Olsson .02 .10
196 Fredrik Oberg .02 .10
197 Roger Rosen .02 .10
198 Roland Stoltz .02 .10
199 Lars Bjorn .02 .10
200 Ulf Sterner .02 .10
201 Leif Holmqvist .08 .25
202 Hans Mild .02 .10
203 Bert-Ola Nordlander .02 .10
204 Eilert Maatta .02 .10
205 Ronald Pettersson .02 .10
206 Tord Lundstrom .02 .10
207 Lennart Svedberg .08 .25
208 Roland Stoltz .02 .10
209 Eilert Maatta .02 .10
210 Lennart Svedberg .08 .25
211 Tord Lundstrom .02 .10
212 Leif Holmqvist .08 .25
213 Magnus Nilsson .20 .50
214 Mikael Holmqvist .20 .50
215 Mattias Karlin .20 .50
216 Pierre Hedin .20 .50
217 Henrik Petre .20 .50
218 Johan Forsander .08 .25
219 Daniel Sedin .75 2.00
220 Henrik Sedin .75 2.00
221 Markus Nilsson .40 1.00
222 Checklist .02 .10
223 Checklist .02 .10
224 Checklist .02 .10
225 Checklist .02 .10
GJ1 D.Sedin/H.Sedin 20.00 50.00
GJA1 D.Sedin/H.Sedin 75.00 200.00

1998-99 Swedish UD Choice Day in the Life

This insert set captures moments in the regular lives of the SEL's biggest stars.

COMPLETE SET (10) 4.00 10.00
1 Rikard Franzen .40 1.00
2 Par Djoos .40 1.00
3 Tommy Soderstrom .75 2.00
4 Pelle Prestberg .40 1.00
5 Esa Keskinen .40 1.00
6 Johan Hedberg .75 2.00
7 Jarmo Myllys .75 2.00
8 Marcus Thuresson .40 1.00
9 Samuel Pahlsson 1.00 2.50
10 Christer Olsson .40 1.00

1999-00 Swedish Upper Deck

This 220-card set captures the heroes of Sweden's Elitserien. The cards were produced by Upper Deck and mirror the UD MVP set produced earlier in the year for NHL fans.

COMPLETE SET (220) 10.00 25.00
1 Mattias Pettersson .07 .20
2 Rikard Franzen .08 .25
3 Mattias Svedberg .07 .20
4 Dick Tarnstrom .30 .75
5 Jan Sandstrom .07 .20
6 Anders Myrvold .08 .25
7 Henrik Tallinder .20 .50
8 Per-Anton Lundstrom .07 .20
9 Kristian Gahn .07 .20
10 Björn Ahlstrom .07 .20
11 Stefan Gustavsson .07 .20
12 Jarkko Varvio .08 .25
13 Fredrik Krekula .07 .20
14 Erik Norback .07 .20
15 Niklas Anger .15 .40
16 Mats Lindberg .07 .20
17 Erik Andersson .07 .20
18 Johan Holmqvist .60 1.50
19 Tommy Sjodin .08 .25
20 Marko Tuulola .07 .20
21 Henrik Petre .15 .40
22 Par Djoos .08 .25
23 Niclas Wallin .40 1.00
24 Roger Kyro .07 .20
25 Ove Molin .07 .20
26 Stefan Lundqvist .07 .20
27 Goran Hermansson .07 .20
28 Jan Larsson .07 .20
29 Daniel Rudslätt .07 .20
30 Tom Bissett .15 .40
31 Kenneth Bergqvist .07 .20
32 Mikko Luovi .07 .20
33 Johan Lindstrom .07 .20
34 Daniel Olsson .07 .20
35 Tommy Soderstrom .20 .50
36 Bjorn Nord .15 .40
37 Niklas Kronwall 1.00 2.50
38 Thomas Johansson .08 .25
39 Daniel Tjarnqvist .20 .50
40 Mikael Magnusson .07 .20
41 Mikael Johansson .07 .20
42 Niklas Falk .15 .40
43 Mikael Hakansson .15 .40
44 Charles Berglund .08 .25
45 Lars-Goran Wiklander .07 .20
46 Per Eklund .08 .25
47 Kristofer Johansson .07 .20
48 Mathias Tjarnqvist .15 .40
49 Espen Knutsen .40 1.00
50 Jimmie Olvestad .20 .50
51 Mikko Konttila .07 .20
52 Vesa Toskala .75 2.00
53 Roger Johansson .07 .20
54 Sergei Fokin .07 .20
55 Greger Artursson .07 .20
56 Jonas Elofsson .15 .40
57 Radek Hamr .07 .20
58 Henrik Rehnberg .07 .20
59 Peter Nordstrom .08 .25
60 Niklas Sjokvist .07 .20
61 Trond Magnussen .07 .20
62 Peter Hagstrom .07 .20
63 Pelle Prestberg .07 .20
64 Mathias Johansson .15 .40
65 Tore Vikingstad .07 .20
66 Clas Eriksson .07 .20
67 Marko Jantunen .07 .20
68 Christian Berglund .20 .50
69 Mario Brunetta .15 .40
70 Petter Nilsson .07 .20
71 Magnus Johansson .07 .20
72 Ronnie Sundin .15 .40
73 Stefan Larsson .07 .20
74 Christian Backman .15 .40
75 Par Edlund .08 .25
76 Reid Simonton .07 .20
77 Kristian Huselius .40 1.00
78 Pasi Saarela .07 .20
79 Juha Ikonen .07 .20
80 Linus Fagemo .07 .20
81 Patrik Carnback .08 .25
82 Peter Berndtsson .07 .20
83 Peter Strom .07 .20
84 Henrik Nilsson .07 .20
85 Jonas Johnsson .07 .20
86 Kari Takko .15 .40
87 David Petrasek .07 .20
88 Joacim Esbjors .07 .20
89 Per Gustafsson .08 .25
90 Jani Nikko .07 .20
91 Mikael Lindman .07 .20
92 Oleg Belov .08 .25
93 Jonas Esbjors .07 .20
94 Jonas Forsander .15 .40
95 Peter Ekelund .07 .20
96 Antti Tormanen .08 .25
97 Anders Lonn .07 .20
98 Gabriel Karlsson .07 .20
99 Johan Hult .07 .20
100 Mattias Remstam .07 .20
101 Daniel Wallin .07 .20
102 Johan Lindbom .07 .20
103 Reinhard Divis .40 1.00
104 Jan Huokko .07 .20
105 Torbjorn Johansson .07 .20
106 Per Lundell .07 .20
107 David Ytfeldt .07 .20
108 Stefan Bergkvist .07 .20
109 Patrik Allvin .07 .20
110 Niklas Persson .07 .20
111 Martin Jansson .07 .20
112 Anders Carlsson .07 .20
113 Niklas Eriksson .07 .20
114 Stefan Hellkvist .07 .20
115 Jens Nielsen .07 .20
116 Morten Green .07 .20
117 Markus Akerblom .07 .20
118 Mikael Karlberg .07 .20
119 Mattias Elm .07 .20
120 Edvin Frylen .07 .20
121 Martin Knold .07 .20
122 Erkki Saramaa .07 .20
123 Nicklas Nordqvist .07 .20
124 Jesper Andersson .07 .20
125 Henrik Andersson .07 .20
126 Henrik Nordfeldt .07 .20
127 Ulf Soderstrom .07 .20
128 Ragnar Karlsson .07 .20
129 Fredrik Elmvall .07 .20
130 Peter Casparsson .07 .20
131 Dennis Ejdeholm .07 .20
132 Mattias Nilimaa .07 .20
133 Mike Helber .07 .20
134 Johan Bylow .07 .20
135 Jarmo Myllys .15 .40
136 Vaclav Burda .07 .20
137 Osmo Soutukorva .07 .20
138 Johan Finnstrom .08 .25
139 Roger Akerstrom .07 .20
140 Torbjorn Lindberg .07 .20
141 Jonas Ronnqvist .40 1.00
142 Jonathan Hedstrom .15 .40
143 Tomas Berglund .07 .20
144 Mikael Lovgren .07 .20
145 Anders Burstrom .07 .20
146 Jörgen Bemstrom .07 .20
147 Martin Hostak .07 .20
148 Hans Huczkowski .07 .20
149 Lars Edstrom .07 .20
150 Jiri Kucera .08 .25
151 Andreas Hadelov .07 .20
152 Johan Tornberg .07 .20
153 Mats Lusth .07 .20
154 Andreas Lilja .07 .20
155 Peter Jakobsson .07 .20
156 Mikael Malmstrom .07 .20
157 Tomas Sandstrom .20 .50
158 Kim Staal .07 .20
159 Jan Hammar .07 .20
160 Marcus Magnertoft .07 .20
161 Marcus Thuresson .07 .20
162 Magnus Nilsson .07 .20
163 Mikael Lindholm .07 .20
164 Juha Riihijarvi .07 .20
165 Jesper Mattsson .08 .25
166 Niklas Sundblad .08 .25
167 Toivo Suursoo .07 .20
168 Tobias Lundstrom .07 .20
169 Pierre Hedin .15 .40
170 Per Hallberg .07 .20
171 Jan-Axel Alavaara .07 .20
172 Jesper Duus .07 .20
173 Francois Bouchard .07 .20
174 Andreas Pihl .07 .20
175 Andreas Salomonsson .30 .75
176 Magnus Wernblom .07 .20
177 Mikael Pettersson .07 .20
178 Mattias Weinhandl .30 .75
179 Daniel Sedin .60 1.50
180 Henrik Sedin .60 1.50
181 Tommy Pettersson .07 .20
182 Samuel Pahlsson .40 1.00
183 Anders Soderberg .15 .40
184 Mattias Karlin .15 .40
185 Magnus Eriksson .07 .20
186 Andrei Lulin .07 .20
187 Denis Chervyakov .07 .20
188 Dimitri Chikin .07 .20
189 Joakim Lundberg .07 .20
190 Henric Bjorkman .07 .20
191 Roger Jonsson .07 .20
192 Peter Nylander .07 .20
193 Mikael Pettersson .07 .20
194 Patrik Zetterberg .07 .20
195 Daniel Rydmark .08 .25
196 Johan Molin .07 .20

197 Paul Andersson-Everberg .07 .20
198 Jonas Finn-Olsson .07 .20
199 Fredrik Oberg .07 .20
200 Roger Rosen .07 .20
201 Henrik Tallinder .15 .40
202 Kenneth Bergqvist .07 .20
203 Mathias Tjarnqvist .15 .40
204 Jimmie Olvestad .30 .75
205 Jonas Elofsson .15 .40
206 Christian Berglund .30 .75
207 Johan Forsander .15 .40
208 David Ytfeldt .07 .20
209 Niklas Persson .07 .20
210 Henrik Andersson .07 .20
211 Jonathan Hedström .20 .50
212 Kim Staal .07 .20
213 Pierre Hedin .15 .40
214 Mattias Weinhandl .30 .75
215 Rikard Ekstrom .07 .20
216 Christian Backman .20 .50
217 Daniel Sedin CL .20 .50
218 Peter Ekelund CL .07 .20
219 Tommy Soderstrom CL .15 .40
220 Henrik Sedin CL .20 .50

1999-00 Swedish Upper Deck Hands of Gold

This set, featuring the top snipers in the Elitserien, was randomly inserted into packs of 1999-2000 UD SHL.

COMPLETE SET (15) 12.00 30.00
1 Mats Lindberg .75 2.00
2 Daniel Sedin 2.00 5.00
3 Jan Larsson 2.00 5.00
4 Per Eklund 1.25 3.00
5 Thomas Johansson .75 2.00
6 Per Eklund 1.25 3.00
7 Peter Ekelund .75 2.00
8 Anders Carlsson .75 2.00
9 Peter Ekelund .75 2.00
10 Jonas Ronnqvist .75 2.00
11 Marcus Thuresson .75 2.00
12 Daniel Sedin 1.25 3.00
13 Henrik Sedin 1.25 3.00
14 Daniel Rydmark .75 2.00
15 Kristian Huselius 2.00 5.00

1999-00 Swedish Upper Deck Lasting Impressions

This insert set features a number of Sweden's top young stars and veterans.

COMPLETE SET (12) 12.00 30.00
1 Rikard Franzen 1.25 3.00
2 Par Djoos 1.25 3.00
3 Charles Berglund 1.25 3.00
4 Roger Johansson 1.25 3.00
5 Kari Takko 1.50 4.00
6 Anders Carlsson 1.25 3.00
7 Mike Helber 1.25 3.00
8 Jiri Kucera 1.25 3.00
9 Juha Riihijarvi 1.25 3.00
10 Samuel Pahlsson 2.00 5.00
11 Magnus Eriksson 1.25 3.00
12 Patrik Carnback 1.25 3.00

1999-00 Swedish Upper Deck PowerDeck

Like the NHL versions that preceded them, these small CD-ROMs offer video action, still shots and statistics when loaded onto your home PC.

COMPLETE SET (2) 3.00 8.00
1 SHL 2.00 5.00
2 Daniel Sedin 2.00 5.00
Henrik Sedin

1999-00 Swedish Upper Deck SHL Signatures

These sweet inserts feature a genuine autograph from a star of the Swedish Elitserien.

COMPLETE SET (20) 70.00 150.00
1 Stefan Gustavsson 2.00 5.00
2 Rikard Franzen 2.00 5.00
3 Johan Holmqvist 6.00 12.00
4 Espen Knutsen 6.00 12.00
5 Peter Nordstrom 2.00 5.00
6 Marko Jantunen 2.00 5.00
7 Kristian Huselius 8.00 20.00
8 Jonas Johnsson 2.00 5.00
9 Per Gustafsson 2.00 5.00
10 Johan Lindbom 4.00 10.00
11 Stefan Hellkvist 2.00 5.00
12 Ulf Soderstrom 2.00 5.00
13 Jarmo Myllys 4.00 10.00
14 Johan Tornberg 2.00 5.00
15 Daniel Sedin 10.00 20.00
16 Henrik Sedin 10.00 20.00
17 Magnus Eriksson 2.00 5.00
18 Tommy Sjodin 2.00 5.00
19 Tommy Soderstrom 4.00 10.00
20 Tomas Sandstrom 4.00 10.00

1999-00 Swedish Upper Deck Snapshots

This insert set features more of the top performers of the SHL.

COMPLETE SET (15) 12.00 30.00
1 Anders Myrvold .75 2.00
2 Johan Holmqvist 1.25 3.00
3 Ove Molin .40 1.00
4 Tommy Soderstrom 1.25 3.00
5 Espen Knutsen 1.50 4.00
6 Peter Nordstrom .40 1.00
7 Per Gustafsson .40 1.00
8 Stefan Bergkvist .40 1.00
9 Mattias Elm .40 1.00
10 Jarmo Myllys 1.50 4.00
11 Tomas Sandstrom 1.50 4.00
12 Magnus Wernblom .40 1.00
13 Mattias Weinhandl 1.50 4.00
14 Denis Chervyakov .40 1.00
15 Kristian Huselius 4.00 10.00

2000-01 Swedish Upper Deck

This set was produced by Upper Deck for distribution in the Swedish market and features the top players of the SHL. The design for the set mimics the one used for 2000-01 UD MVP in North America.

COMPLETE SET (220) 15.00 40.00
1 Tim Thomas .60 1.50
2 Per-Anton Lundstrom .15 .40
3 Dick Tarnstrom .20 .50
4 Rikard Franzen .04 .10
5 Rikard Ekstrom .04 .10
6 Jan Sandstrom .04 .10
7 Stefan Gustavson .04 .10
8 Anders Gozzi .04 .10
9 Stefan Hellkvist .04 .10
10 Mats Lindberg .04 .10
11 Bjorn Danielsson .04 .10
12 Erik Andersson .04 .10
13 Bjorn Ahlstrom .04 .10
14 Kristian Gahn .04 .10
15 Petter Sandstrom .04 .10
16 Mattias Hedlund .04 .10
17 Tommi Hamalainen .04 .10
18 Jorgen Hermansson .04 .10
19 Jesper Jager .04 .10
20 Christian Lechtaler .04 .10
21 Aleksanders Beliavskis .04 .10
22 Johan Ramstedt .04 .10
23 Lars Briell .04 .10
24 Johan Boman .04 .10
25 Aleksanders Semjonovs .04 .10
26 Mathias Bosson .04 .10
27 Niko Halttunen .04 .10
28 Fredrik Nasvall .04 .10
29 Johan Asplund .15 .40
30 Henrik Petre .04 .10
31 Par Djoos .04 .10
32 Tommy Sjodin .04 .10
33 Christer Olsson .04 .10
34 Marko Tuulola .04 .10
35 Johan Molin .04 .10
36 Tony Martensson .04 .10
37 Tom Bissett .15 .40
38 Roger Kyro .04 .10
39 Ove Molin .04 .10
40 Mikko Luovi .04 .10
41 Daniel Rudslatt .04 .10
42 Kenneth Bergqvist .04 .10
43 Jan Larsson .04 .10
44 Mikael Tellqvist .75 2.00
45 Niklas Kronwall 1.00 2.50
46 Francois Bouchard .04 .10
47 Edvin Frylen .04 .10
48 Mikael Magnusson .04 .10
49 Daniel Tjarnqvist .20 .50
50 Charles Berglund .04 .10
51 Kristofer Ottosson .04 .10
52 Kyosti Karjalainen .04 .10
53 Nichlas Falk .04 .10
54 Mathias Tjarnqvist .15 .40
55 Jimmie Olvestad .20 .50
56 Johan Garpenlov .04 .10
57 Andreas Salomonsson .20 .50
58 Mikael Johansson .04 .10
59 Vladimir Orszagh .15 .40
60 Henrik Lundqvist 8.00 20.00
61 Magnus Johansson .04 .10
62 Christian Backman .04 .10
63 Nicklas Rahm .04 .10
64 Ronnie Sundin .04 .10
65 Par Edlund .04 .10
66 Magnus Kahnberg .04 .10
67 Pelle Prestberg .04 .10
68 Patrik Carnback .04 .10
69 Juha Ikonen .04 .10
70 Jari Tolsa .04 .10
71 Kristian Huselius .40 1.00
72 Peter Strom .04 .10
73 Henrik Nilsson .04 .10
74 Jonas Johnsson .04 .10
75 Mikael Andersson .04 .10
76 Magnus Eriksson .04 .10
77 Sergei Fokin .04 .10
78 Jonas Frogren .04 .10
79 Thomas Rhodin .04 .10
80 Greger Artursson .04 .10
81 Radek Hamr .04 .10
82 Roger Johansson .04 .10
83 Marko Jantunen .04 .10
84 Ulf Soderstrom .04 .10
85 Christian Berglund .04 .10
86 Mathias Johansson .04 .10
87 Trond Magnussen .04 .10
88 Peter Nordstrom .15 .40
89 Clas Eriksson .04 .10
90 Jorgen Jonsson .04 .10
91 Marcel Jenni .04 .10
92 Stefan Liv .60 1.50
93 Joacim Esbjors .04 .10
94 Per Gustafsson .04 .10
95 Fredrik Stillman .04 .10
96 Mikael Lindman .04 .10
97 Peter Ottosson .04 .10
98 Oleg Belov .04 .10
99 Peter Ekelund .04 .10
100 Johan Hult .04 .10
101 Johan Lindbom .04 .10
102 Jonas Esbjors .04 .10
103 Johan Forsander .04 .10
104 Mattias Remstam .04 .10
105 Fredrik Oberg .04 .10
106 Reinhard Divis .40 1.00
107 Magnus Svensson .04 .10
108 Jan Huokko .04 .10
109 Stefan Bergkvist .04 .10
110 Lars Jonsson .20 .50
111 Per Lofstrom .04 .10
112 Jens Nielsen .04 .10
113 Niklas Eriksson .04 .10
114 Daniel Widing .04 .10
115 Niklas Persson .04 .10
116 Henrik Nordfeldt .04 .10
117 Tore Vikingstad .15 .40
118 Mikael Karlberg .04 .10
119 Robert Burakovsky .04 .10
120 Jarmo Myllys .20 .50
121 Torbjorn Lindberg .04 .10
122 Petter Nilsson .04 .10
123 Osmo Soutokorva .04 .10
124 Roger Akerstrom .04 .10
125 Johan Finnstrom .04 .10
126 Jiri Kucera .04 .10
127 Jonathan Hedstrom .20 .50
128 Tomas Berglund .04 .10
129 Mikael Renberg .20 .50
130 Anders Burstrom .04 .10
131 Hans Huczkowski .04 .10
132 Martin Hostak .04 .10
133 Lars Edstrom .04 .10
134 Sami Mettovaara .04 .10
135 Andreas Hadelov .04 .10
136 David Petrasek .04 .10
137 Peter Jakobsson .04 .10
138 Joakim Lundberg .04 .10
139 Christian Due-Boje .04 .10
140 Johan Tornberg .04 .10
141 Henrik Malmstrom .04 .10
142 Marcus Thuresson .04 .10
143 Daniel Rydmark .04 .10
144 Juha Riihijarvi .04 .10
145 Jesper Mattsson .04 .10
146 Fredrik Lindquist .04 .10
147 Tomas Sandstrom .04 .10
148 Kim Staal .04 .10
149 Jan Hammar .04 .10
150 Tobias Lundstrom .04 .10
151 Andreas Pihl .04 .10
152 Pierre Hedin .04 .10
153 Jan-Axel Alavaara .04 .10
154 Lars Jansson .04 .10
155 Per Hallberg .04 .10
156 Jesper Duus .04 .10
157 Magnus Wernblom .04 .10
158 Anders Soderberg .15 .40
159 Tommy Pettersson .04 .10
160 Mattias Weinhandl .40 1.00
161 Peter Hogardh .04 .10
162 Patrik Wallenberg .04 .10
163 Jorgen Bemstrom .04 .10
164 Stefan Ohman .04 .10
165 Boo Ahl .15 .40
166 Pasi Petrilainen .15 .40
167 Stefan Klockare .04 .10
168 Daniel Casselstahl .04 .10
169 Marcus Karlsson .04 .10
170 Robert Carlsson .04 .10
171 Per Hallin .04 .10
172 Nik Zupancic .04 .10
173 Timo Peltomaa .04 .10
174 Linus Fagemo .04 .10
175 Henrik Zetterberg ERC 4.00 10.00
176 Mikael Lind .04 .10
177 Anders Huss .04 .10
178 Markus Matthiasson .04 .10
179 Stefan Hellkvist SS .04 .10
180 Kristian Gahn SS .04 .10
181 Bjorn Ahlstrom SS .04 .10
182 Aleksanders Beliavskis SS .04 .10
183 Tom Bissett SS .15 .40
184 Tommy Sjodin SS .04 .10
185 Ove Molin SS .04 .10
186 Mikael Tellqvist SS .75 2.00
187 Mikael Johansson SS .04 .10
188 Vladimir Orszagh SS .15 .40
189 Johan Garpenlov SS .04 .10
190 Christian Berglund SS .04 .10
191 Jorgen Jonsson SS .04 .10
192 Radek Hamr SS .04 .10
193 Kristian Huselius SS .40 1.00
194 Mikael Andersson SS .04 .10
195 Patrik Carnback SS .04 .10
196 Per Gustafsson SS .04 .10
197 Johan Lindbom SS .04 .10
198 Oleg Belov SS .04 .10
199 Robert Burakovsky SS .04 .10
200 Mikael Renberg SS .20 .50
201 Petter Nilsson SS .04 .10
202 Jarmo Myllys SS .20 .50
203 Tomas Sandstrom SS .15 .40
204 Marcus Thuresson SS .04 .10
205 Fredrik Lindquist SS .04 .10
206 Magnus Wernblom SS .04 .10
207 Mattias Weinhandl SS .20 .50
208 Henrik Zetterberg SS 4.00 10.00
209 Mats Lindberg CL .04 .10
210 Jorgen Hermansson CL .04 .10
211 Par Djoos CL .04 .10
212 Jimmie Olvestad CL .15 .40
213 Christian Backman CL .04 .10
214 Radek Hamr CL .04 .10
215 Peter Ekelund CL .04 .10
216 Lars Jonsson CL .20 .50
217 Mikael Renberg CL .20 .50
218 Fredrik Lindqvist CL .04 .10
219 Mattias Weinhandl CL .20 .50
220 Marcus Karlsson CL .04 .10

2000-01 Swedish Upper Deck Game Jerseys

This pair of memorabilia cards featuring Sweden's top young prospects were randomly inserted in packs at a rate of 1:216.

COMPLETE SET (2) 40.00 50.00
DS Daniel Sedin 20.00 30.00
HS Henrik Sedin 20.00 30.00

2000-01 Swedish Upper Deck Masked Men

This set features the top goaltenders in the Swedish Elitserien. The cards were randomly inserted at a rate of 1:24 packs.

COMPLETE SET (7) 20.00 40.00
M1 Tim Thomas 3.00 8.00
M2 Mikael Tellqvist 6.00 15.00
M3 Magnus Eriksson 2.50 6.00
M4 Reinhard Divis 4.00 10.00
M5 Jarmo Myllys 2.50 6.00
M6 Andreas Hadelov 2.00 5.00
M7 Boo Ahl 2.00 5.00

2000-01 Swedish Upper Deck SHL Excellence

This set honors two players on the same team who achieved excellence in the SHL. The cards were inserted 1:24 packs.

COMPLETE SET (5) 15.00 30.00
S1 V.Orszagh/J.Garpenlov 2.00 5.00
S2 C.Berglund/J.Jonsson 2.00 5.00
S3 P.Carnback/K.Huselius 4.00 10.00
S4 M.Renberg/J.Myllys 2.50 6.00
S5 M.Weinhandl/M.Wernblom 3.00 8.00

2000-01 Swedish Upper Deck SHL Signatures

This set of signed cards featuring the top stars of the Swedish Elite League were inserted 1:17 packs. The cards ape the design used earlier in the year in Upper Deck's MVP Pro Sign issue.

COMPLETE SET (42) 225.00 450.00
AB Alexander Beliavski 4.00 10.00
AG Anders Gozzi 4.00 10.00
AH Andreas Hadelov 4.00 10.00
AS Alexander Semjonovs 4.00 10.00
BA Boo Ahl 4.00 10.00
CB Christian Backman 4.00 10.00
CH Christian Berglund 4.00 10.00
DR Daniel Rydmark 4.00 10.00
FL Fredrik Lindquist 4.00 10.00
GA Greger Artursson 4.00 10.00
HZ Henrik Zetterberg 25.00 60.00
JE Jonas Esbjors 4.00 10.00
JG Johan Garpenlov 4.00 10.00
JH Jorgen Hermansson 4.00 10.00
JJ Jorgen Jonsson 4.00 10.00
JL Jan Larsson 4.00 10.00
JN Jens Nielsen 4.00 10.00
JO Jonathan Hedstrom 8.00 20.00
KG Kristian Gahn 4.00 10.00
KH Kristian Huselius 12.50 30.00
MA Mikael Andersson 4.00 10.00
ME Mikael Tellqvist 12.50 30.00
MH Martin Hostak 4.00 10.00
MI Mattias Weinhandl 8.00 20.00
MJ Mikael Johansson 4.00 10.00
ML Mats Lindberg 4.00 10.00
MN Mikael Renberg 8.00 20.00
MR Mattias Remstam 4.00 10.00
MS Magnus Svensson 4.00 10.00
MT Marcus Thuresson 4.00 10.00
MW Magnus Wernblom 4.00 10.00
NK Niklas Kronwall 20.00 50.00
OB Oleg Belov 4.00 10.00
OM Ove Molin 4.00 10.00
PC Patrik Carnback 4.00 10.00
PD Par Djoos 4.00 10.00
PN Petter Nilsson 4.00 10.00
RD Reinhard Divis 10.00 25.00
RJ Roger Johansson 4.00 10.00
SH Stefan Hellkvist 4.00 10.00
TB Tom Bissett 4.00 10.00
TL Tobias Lundstrom 4.00 10.00

2000-01 Swedish Upper Deck Top Draws

This set highlights the most popular players in the SHL. Singles were inserted 1:8 packs.

COMPLETE SET (11) 7.50 15.00
T1 Bjorn Ahlstrom .40 1.00
T2 Ove Molin .40 1.00
T3 Mikael Tellqvist 2.00 5.00
T4 Patrik Carnback .40 1.00
T5 Roger Johansson .40 1.00
T6 Oleg Belov .40 1.00
T7 Jens Nielsen .40 1.00
T8 Jonathan Hedstrom .40 1.00
T9 Fredrik Lindquist .40 1.00
T10 Mattias Weinhandl .75 2.00
T11 Anders Huss .40 1.00

2000-01 Swedish Upper Deck Top Playmakers

This insert set honors athletes who consistently top the SHL scoring charts. Cards were inserted at a rate of 1:24 packs.

COMPLETE SET (8) 15.00 30.00
P1 Mats Lindberg 1.50 4.00
P2 Jan Larsson 1.50 4.00
P3 Mikael Johansson 1.50 4.00
P4 Jonas Johnsson 1.50 4.00
P5 Jorgen Jonsson 1.50 4.00
P6 Martin Hostak 1.50 4.00
P7 Juha Riihijarvi 1.50 4.00
P8 Mattias Weinhandl 2.50 6.00

2001-02 Swedish Alfabilder

COMPLETE SET (18) 10.00 25.00
1 Sven Tumba Johansson .40 1.00
2 Roland Rolle Stoltz .40 1.00
3 Eilert Mattaa .40 1.00
4 Lennart Klimpen Haggroth .40 1.00
5 Nisse Nilsson .40 1.00
6 Ulf Sterner .40 1.00
7 Leif Honken Holmqvist .75 2.00
8 Tord Lundstrom .40 1.00
9 Borje Salming 2.00 5.00
10 Anders Hedberg 1.25 3.00
11 Anders Kallur .75 2.00
12 Stefan Persson .75 2.00
13 Goran Hogosta .40 1.00
14 Bengt-Ake Gustavsson .40 1.00
15 Mats Naslund 1.25 3.00
16 Kent Nilsson 1.25 3.00
17 Hakan Loob 1.25 3.00
18 Peter Lindmark .75 2.00

2001-02 Swedish Brynas Tigers

This set features the Tigers of the Swedish Elite League. The set is postcard-styled and sized, with a posed photo on the front, and a b/w head shot and brief stats on the back.

COMPLETE SET (27) 10.00 25.00
1 Adam Andersson .40 1.00
2 Johan Asplund .80 2.00
3 Kenneth Bergqvist .40 1.00
4 Tom Bissett .60 1.50
5 Bjorn Danielsson .40 1.00
6 Par Djoos .40 1.00
7 Jonas Floberg .40 1.00
8 Kristoffer Jobs .40 1.00
9 Daniel Johansson .40 1.00
10 Roger Kyro .40 1.00
11 Jan Larsson .40 1.00
12 Mikko Luovi .40 1.00
13 Per Mars .40 1.00
14 Tony Martensson .40 1.00
15 Roger Melin .40 1.00
16 Ove Molin .40 1.00
17 Christer Olsson .40 1.00
18 Jussi Pekkala .40 1.00
19 Gunnar Persson .40 1.00
20 Henrik Petre .40 1.00
21 Mattias Pettersson .40 1.00
22 Henrik Rehnberg .40 1.00
23 Daniel Rudslatt .40 1.00
24 Tommy Sjodin .40 1.00
25 Jonas Soling .40 1.00
26 Daniel Wagstrom .40 1.00
27 Team Card .40 1.00

2002-03 Swedish Malmo Red Hawks

1 Joakim Lundberg .40 1.00
2 Johan Bjork .40 1.00
3 Peter Hasselbald .40 1.00
4 Henrik Malmstrom .40 1.00
5 Jan Hammer .40 1.00
6 Marcus Magnertoft .40 1.00
7 Marcus Thuresson .40 1.00
8 Frans Nielsen .40 1.00
9 Daniel Rydmark .40 1.00
10 Juha Riihijarvi .40 1.00
11 Jesper Mattsson .40 1.00
12 David Petrasek .40 1.00
13 Mikael Wahlberg .40 1.00
14 Toivo Suursoo .40 1.00
15 Janne Vas .40 1.00
16 Robert Borgqvist .40 1.00
17 Petri Liimatainen .40 1.00
18 Johan Norgren .40 1.00
19 Andreas Valdix .40 1.00
20 Peter Andersson .40 1.00
21 Roger Ohman .40 1.00

2002-03 Swedish SHL

This set features the top players of the Swedish Elite league.

COMPLETE SET (292) 20.00 50.00
1 Johan Asplund .20 .50
2 Par Djoos .08 .20
3 Tommy Sjodin .08 .20
4 Henrik Rehnberg .08 .20
5 Adam Andersson .08 .20
6 Tony Martensson .08 .20
7 Roger Kyro .08 .20
8 Ove Molin .08 .20
9 Bjorn Danielsson .08 .20
10 Jan Larsson .08 .20
11 Jonas Soling .08 .20
12 Sergei Naumov .20 .50
13 Ronnie Pettersson .08 .20
14 Bjorn Nord .08 .20
15 Mikael Magnusson .08 .20
16 Tomas Strandberg .08 .20
17 Peter Lindelof .08 .20
18 Mikael Johansson .08 .20
19 Christian Eklund .08 .20
20 Johan Forsander .08 .20
21 Mikael Hakanson .08 .20
22 Nils Ekman .20 .50
23 Martin Gerber .40 1.00
24 Mats Trygg .08 .20
25 Jonas Frogren .08 .20
26 Thomas Rhodin .08 .20
27 Greger Artursson .08 .20
28 Marko Jantunen .08 .20
29 Claes Eriksson .08 .20
30 Rickard Wallin .08 .20
31 Marcel Jenni .08 .20
32 Mathias Johansson .08 .20
33 Peter Hammarstrom .08 .20
34 Boo Ahl .20 .50
35 Daniel Ljungqvist .08 .20
36 Per Gustafsson .08 .20
37 Jouni Loponen .08 .20
38 Richard Pavlikovsky .08 .20
39 Peter Ekelund .08 .20
40 Anders Huusko .08 .20
41 Mattias Remstam .08 .20
42 Johan Hult .08 .20
43 Bjorn Melin .08 .20
44 Kalle Sahlstedt .08 .20
45 Fredrik Jensen .08 .20
46 Mathias Ahxner .08 .20
47 Martin Knold .08 .20
48 Christoffer Norgren .08 .20
49 Johan Bulow .08 .20
50 Fredrik Johansson .08 .20
51 Henrik Andersson .08 .20
52 Fredrik Emvall .08 .20
53 Per Eklund .08 .20
54 Stefan Pettersson .08 .20
55 Magnus Gastrin .08 .20
56 Daniel Henriksson .20 .50
57 Jonas Andersson-Junkka .08 .20
58 Jan Sandstrom .08 .20
59 Petter Nilsson .08 .20
60 Roger Akerstrom .08 .20
61 Stefan Nilsson .08 .20
62 Jonathan Hedstrom .08 .20
63 Per Ledin .08 .20
64 Anders Burstrom .08 .20
65 Hans Huczkowski .08 .20
66 Emil Lundberg .08 .20
67 Andreas Hadelov .20 .50
68 Peter Hasselblad .08 .20
69 Peter Andersson .08 .20
70 Roger Ohman .08 .20
71 Henrik Malmstrom .08 .20
72 Marcus Thuresson .08 .20
73 Daniel Rydmark .08 .20
74 Juha Riihijarvi .08 .20
75 Marcus Magnertoft .08 .20
76 Mika Hannula .08 .20
77 Jesper Mattsson .08 .20
78 Peter Hirsch .20 .50
79 Pierre Hedin .08 .20
80 Jan Oberg .08 .20
81 Magnus Wernblom .08 .20
82 Tommy Pettersson .08 .20
83 Peter Hogardh .20 .50
84 Peter Oberg .08 .20
85 Joakim Lindstrom .08 .20
86 Magnus Hedlund .08 .20
87 Mattias Wennerberg .08 .20
88 Stefan Ohman .08 .20
89 Rolf Wanhainen .20 .50
90 Ola Mollerstedt .08 .20
91 Stefan Bernstrom .08 .20
92 Peter Popovic .08 .20
93 Peter Ahola .08 .20
94 Jesper Bjorck .08 .20
95 Jukka Tiilikainen .08 .20
96 Erik Norback .08 .20
97 Juha Lind .20 .50
98 Peter Gerhardsson .08 .20
99 Jorgen Bernstrom .08 .20
100 Fredrik Andersson .08 .20
101 Tommi Rajamaki .08 .20
102 David Halvardsson .08 .20
103 Daniel Casselstahl .08 .20
104 Niklas Nordgren .08 .20
105 Markus Matthiasson .20 .50
106 Robert Carlsson .08 .20
107 Per Hallin .08 .20
108 Henrik Zetterberg 1.00 2.50
109 Mikael Lind .08 .20
110 Ed Ward .08 .20
111 Henrik Lundqvist 2.00 5.00
112 Jan-Axel Alavaara .08 .20
113 Christian Backman .08 .20
114 Ronnie Sundin .08 .20
115 Magnus Kahnberg .08 .20
116 Jens Karlsson .08 .20
117 Juha Ikonen .08 .20
118 Jari Tolsa .08 .20
119 Niklas Andersson .08 .20
120 Jonas Johnsson .08 .20
121 Peter Strom .08 .20
122 Brynas IF Logo .08 .20
123 Djurgardens Logo .08 .20
124 Farjestads Logo .08 .20
125 HV 71 Logo .08 .20
126 Leksands Logo .08 .20
127 Linkopings Logo .08 .20
128 Lulea Logo .08 .20
129 Malmo Logo .08 .20
130 MoDo Logo .08 .20
131 Sodertalje Logo .08 .20
132 Timra Logo .08 .20
133 Vastra Frolunda Logo .08 .20
134 Christer Olsson CL .08 .20
135 Thomas Ostlund CL .08 .20
136 Jorgen Jonsson CL .08 .20
137 Johan Davidsson CL .08 .20
138 Mikael Sandberg CL .15 .40
139 Tomas Berglund CL .08 .20
140 Tomas Sandstrom CL .08 .20
141 Richard Lintner CL .08 .20
142 Peter Larsson CL .08 .20
143 Henrik Zetterberg CL .75 2.00
144 Joel Lundqvist CL .08 .20
145 Jamie Ram .20 .50
146 Daniel Johansson .08 .20
147 Jussi Pekkala .08 .20
148 Veli-Pekka Laitinen .08 .20
149 Kristoffer Jobs .08 .20
150 Jonas Floberg .08 .20
151 Simon Ostlund .08 .20
152 Tommi Miettinen .08 .20
153 Niklas Anger .15 .40
154 Daniel Wagstrom .08 .20
155 Joaquin Gage .15 .40
156 Bjorn Bjurling .08 .20
157 Niklas Kronwall .40 1.00
158 Per-Anton Lundstrom .20 .50
159 Kristofer Ottosson .08 .20
160 Joakim Eriksson .08 .20
161 Daniel Rudslatt .08 .20
162 Nichlas Falk .08 .20
163 Matthias Trattnig .08 .20
164 Fredrik Lindquist .08 .20
165 Johan Lindstrom .08 .20
166 Mikael Gerden .08 .20
167 Sinuhe Wallinheimo .08 .20
168 Per Lundell .08 .20
169 Per Hallberg .08 .20
170 Radek Hamr .08 .20
171 Ulf Soderstrom .08 .20
172 Marius Trygg .08 .20
173 Peter Nordstrom .08 .20
174 Jorgen Jonsson .08 .20
175 Par Backer .08 .20
176 Pelle Prestberg .08 .20
177 Dieter Kalt .08 .20
178 Stefan Liv .60 1.50
179 Mika Niskanen .08 .20
180 Timmy Pettersson .08 .20
181 Daniel Josefsson .08 .20
182 Jani Hassinen .08 .20
183 Sebastian Meijer .08 .20
184 Niklas Brannstrom .08 .20
185 Par Arlbrandt .08 .20
186 Pasi Maattanen .08 .20
187 Johan Davidsson .15 .40
188 Jonas Fransson .08 .20
189 Sean Gauthier .15 .40
190 Christer Olsson .08 .20
191 Niklas Gallstedt .08 .20
192 Hans Lodin .08 .20
193 Per Lofstrom .08 .20
194 Mike Stapleton .08 .20
195 Jens Nielsen .08 .20
196 Niklas Eriksson .08 .20
197 Mikael Karlberg .08 .20
198 Mikael Pettersson .08 .20
Robert Nilsson
199 Tobias Holm .08 .20
200 Niklas Persson .08 .20
201 Goran Hermansson .08 .20
202 Tomas Forslund .08 .20
203 Henrik Nordfeldt .08 .20
204 Johan Rosen .08 .20
205 Joel Davis .08 .20
206 Mikael Sandberg .15 .40
207 Andreas Pihl .08 .20
208 Jan Mertzig .08 .20
209 Thomas Johansson .08 .20
210 Andreas Holmqvist .08 .20
211 Barry Richter .15 .40
212 Stefan Gustavson .08 .20
213 Brian Felsner .15 .40
214 Johan Franzen ERC 1.00 2.50
215 Tim Eriksson .08 .20
216 Mikael Hakanson .08 .20
217 Gusten Tornqvist .08 .20
218 Pavel Skrbek .08 .20
219 Patrik Bjaarnhjelm .08 .20
220 Johan Forsberg .20 .50
221 Fredrik Svensson .08 .20
222 Linus Fagemo .20 .50
223 Patrik Tano .08 .20
224 Kamil Brabenec .08 .20
225 Thomas Berglund .08 .20
226 Jonas Hagerback .08 .20
227 Magnus Nilsson .08 .20
228 Robert Borgqvist .08 .20
229 Joakim Lundberg .08 .20
230 David Petrasek .08 .20
231 Petri Liimatainen .08 .20
232 Johan Norgren .08 .20
233 Jan Hammar .08 .20
234 Frans Nielsen .08 .20

235 Mikael Wahlberg .08 .20
236 Toivo Suursoo .08 .20
237 Juuso Riksman .08 .20
238 Tobias Enstrom .08 .20
239 Jesper Damgaard .08 .20
240 Erik Leverstrom .08 .20
241 Dusan Milo .08 .20
242 Martin Johansson .08 .20
243 Anders Soderberg .15 .40
244 Jonas Almtorp .08 .20
245 Fredrik Warg .08 .20
246 Joakim Lindstrom .08 .20
247 Morten Green .08 .20
248 Miroslav Hlinka .08 .20
249 Magnus Lindquist .08 .20
250 Alexander Blomqvist .08 .20
251 Anders Back .08 .20
252 Leif Rohlin .08 .20
253 Robert Carlsson .08 .20
254 Antti Tormanen .08 .20
255 David Svee .08 .20
256 Gabriel Karlsson .08 .20
257 Mattias Carlsson .08 .20
258 Peter Larsson .08 .20
259 Patrik Zetterberg .08 .20
260 Kristian Gahn .08 .20
261 Kimmo Kapanen .08 .20
262 Martin Lindman .08 .20
263 Kalle Koskinen .08 .20
264 Robert Jindrich .08 .20
265 Par Styf .08 .20
266 Patrik Wallenberg .08 .20
267 Christian Soderstrom .08 .20
268 Henrik Eriksson .08 .20
269 Valeri Krykov .08 .20
270 Toni Koivunen .08 .20
271 Markus Akerblom .08 .20
272 Fredrik Norrena .40 1.00
273 Magnus Johansson .08 .20
274 Kimmo Eronen .08 .20
275 Oscar Ackestrom .08 .20
276 Erik Kakko .08 .20
277 Mattias Luukkonen .08 .20
278 Patrik Carnback .08 .20
279 Alexander Steen ERC 1.50 4.00
280 Joel Lundqvist .08 .20
281 Jonas Esbjors .08 .20
282 Mikael Andersson .08 .20
283 Jamie Ram .20 .50
284 Joaquin Gage .20 .50
285 Sinuhe Wallinheimo .20 .50
286 Stefan Liv .60 1.50
287 Sean Gauthier .15 .40
288 Mikael Sandberg .08 .20
289 Daniel Henriksson .08 .20
290 Andreas Hadelov .08 .20
291 Peter Hirsch .20 .50
292 Magnus Lindquist .08 .20
293 Kimmo Kapanen .08 .20
294 Fredrik Norrena .40 1.00

2002-03 Swedish SHL Dynamic Duos

These cards were randomly inserted at a rate of 1:16 series two packs.

COMPLETE SET (9) 6.00 15.00
1 Par Djoos .75 2.00
Tommy Sjodin
2 Mikael Johansson .75 2.00
Kristofer Ottosson
3 Par Backer .75 2.00
Jorgen Jonsson
4 Lars Jonsson 1.25 3.00
Daniel Widing
5 Petr Nilsson .75 2.00
Stefan Nilsson
6 Mika Hannula .75 2.00
Juha Riihijarvi
7 Juha Lind .75 2.00
Antti Tormanen
8 Markus Matthiasson .75 2.00
Markus Akerblom
9 Joel Lundqvist 2.00 5.00
Alexander Steen

2002-03 Swedish SHL Masks

These cards were randomly inserts in series 2 packs at a rate of 1:32.

COMPLETE SET (9) 25.00 50.00
1 Sinuhe Wallinheimo 3.00 8.00
2 Stefan Liv 4.00 10.00
3 Sean Gauthier 3.00 8.00
4 Mikael Sandberg 3.00 8.00
5 Andreas Hadelov 3.00 8.00
6 Peter Hirsch 3.00 8.00
7 Magnus Lindquist 3.00 8.00
8 Kimmo Kapanen 3.00 8.00
9 Fredrik Norrena 4.00 10.00

2002-03 Swedish SHL Netminders

This set features top Swedish goalies and was inserted 1:8 series one packs.

COMPLETE SET (9) 15.00 20.00
NM1 Martin Gerber 2.00 5.00
NM2 Sergei Naumov 2.00 2.00
NM3 Stefan Liv 2.00 5.00
NM4 Rolf Wanhainen 2.00 2.00
NM5 Peter Hirsch 2.00 2.00
NM6 Daniel Henriksson 2.00 2.00
NM7 Mikael Sandberg 2.00 2.00
NM8 Johan Asplund 2.00 2.00
NM9 Andreas Hadelov 2.00 2.00

2002-03 Swedish SHL Next Generation

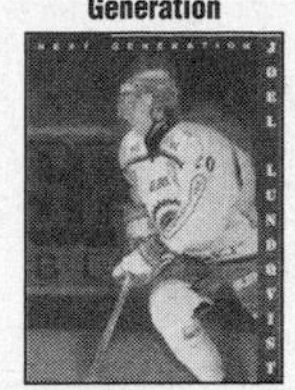

This set features the top young players in the SHL and was inserted 1:16 series one packs.

COMPLETE SET (9) 15.00 30.00
NG1 Joel Lundqvist 1.50 4.00
NG2 Par Backer 1.50 4.00
NG3 Magnus Hedlund 1.50 4.00
NG4 Adam Andersson 1.50 4.00
NG5 Henrik Lundqvist 1.50 4.00
NG6 Joakim Lindstrom 1.50 4.00
NG7 Jonas Johansson 1.50 8.00
NG8 Bjorn Melin 1.50 4.00
NG9 Jens Karlsson 2.00 5.00

2002-03 Swedish SHL Parallel

These cards were issued as random inserts in packs.

*PARALLEL: 2X TO 5X BASIC CARDS

2002-03 Swedish SHL Promos

This 11-card set was created to promote the new series of SHL cards, produced by Sweden's The Card Cabinet. The cards feature different photos and numbering than those of the same players in the base set.

COMPLETE SET (11) 8.00 20.00
TCC1 Tommy Sjodin .40 1.00
TCC2 Christian Eklund .40 1.00
TCC3 Martin Gerber .80 2.00
TCC4 Stefan Liv .80 2.00
TCC5 Per Eklund .40 1.00
TCC6 Jonas Andersson-Junkka .40 1.00
TCC7 Mika Hannula .40 1.00
TCC8 Mattias Weinhandl .80 2.00
TCC9 Peter Popovic .40 1.00
TCC10 Henrik Zetterberg 6.00 15.00
TCC11 Jan-Axel Alavaara .40 1.00

2002-03 Swedish SHL Sharpshooters

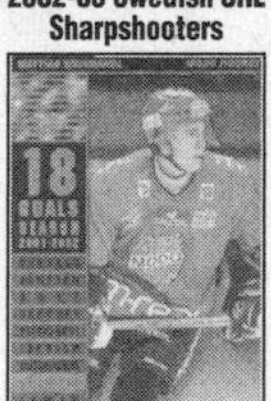

This set features the best snipers in the SHL and was inserted 1:8 series one packs.

COMPLETE SET (9) 20.00 40.00
SS1 Peter Hogardh 1.50 4.00
SS2 Jorgen Jonsson 1.50 4.00
SS3 Dieter Kalt 1.50 4.00
SS4 Per-Age Skroder 2.50 6.00
SS5 Juha Riihijarvi 1.50 4.00
SS6 Peter Larsson 1.50 4.00
SS7 Markus Matthiasson 1.50 4.00
SS8 Mattias Weinhandl 2.50 6.00
SS9 Nils Ekman 2.50 6.00

2002-03 Swedish SHL Signatures

This set features autographs of many of the top stars of the SHL. The cards were inserted 1:32 series one packs.

STATED ODDS 1:32
1 Jonas Soling 4.00 10.00
2 Ove Molin 4.00 10.00
3 Nils Ekman 6.00 15.00
4 Kristofer Ottosson 4.00 10.00
5 Jorgen Jonsson 6.00 15.00
6 Rickard Wallin 6.00 15.00
7 Johan Davidsson 6.00 15.00
8 Mikael Sandberg 6.00 15.00
9 Stefan Nilsson 4.00 10.00
10 Andreas Hadelov 6.00 15.00
11 Jesper Mattsson 4.00 10.00
12 Peter Hogardh 6.00 15.00
13 Rolf Wanhainen 6.00 15.00
14 Juha Lind 6.00 15.00
15 Henrik Zetterberg 30.00 75.00
16 Per Hallin 4.00 10.00
17 Niklas Andersson 4.00 10.00
18 Alexander Steen 15.00 40.00

2002-03 Swedish SHL Signatures Series II

Inserted at a rate of 1:32 series 2 packs. The cards are unnumbered and listed below in checklist order.

STATED ODDS 1:32 SERIES II PACKS
1 Stefan Pettersson 6.00 15.00
2 Daniel Henriksson 6.00 15.00
3 Erik Nordback 6.00 15.00
4 Bjorn Nord 6.00 15.00
5 Ulf Soderstrom 6.00 15.00
6 Stefan Liv 10.00 25.00
7 Mikael Hakansson 6.00 15.00
8 Joel Lundqvist 10.00 25.00
9 Robert Carlsson 6.00 15.00
10 Peter Popovic 6.00 15.00
11 Magnus Wernblom 6.00 15.00
12 Juha Riihijarvi 6.00 15.00
13 Jonathan Hedstrom 8.00 20.00
14 Marcus Thuresson 6.00 15.00
15 Per Eklund 6.00 15.00
16 Antti Tormanen 6.00 15.00
17 Fredrik Lindqvist 6.00 15.00
18 Jens Nielsen 6.00 15.00
19 Sean Gauthier 6.00 15.00
20 Niklas Eriksson 6.00 15.00
21 Leif Rohlin 6.00 15.00
22 Lars Jonsson 8.00 20.00
23 Kalle Sahlstedt SP 15.00 40.00
24 Per-Age Skroder SP 15.00 40.00
25 Dieter Kalt 6.00 15.00
26 Johan Asplund 8.00 20.00

2002-03 Swedish SHL Team Captains

Inserted in series two at a rate of 1:8 packs.

COMPLETE SET (9) 6.00 15.00
1 Jan Larsson .75 2.00
2 Nichlas Falk .75 2.00
3 Jorgen Jonsson .75 2.00
4 Johan Davidsson .75 2.00
5 Christer Olsson .75 2.00
6 Stefan Gustavson .75 2.00
7 Roger Akerstrom .75 2.00
8 Pierre Hedin .75 2.00
9 Peter Popovic .75 2.00

2003-04 Swedish Elite

Sold in two series, with each containing 144 cards.

COMPLETE SET (288) 20.00 40.00
COMMON CARD (1-144) .02 .05
SEMISTARS/GOALIES .08 .20
UNLISTED STARS .20 .50

2003-04 Swedish Elite Enforcers

COMPLETE SET (12) 5.00 10.00
STATED ODDS 1:8 SERIES 2
EF1 Hannes Hyvonen .40 1.00
EF2 Oscar Ackestrom .40 1.00
EF3 Thomas Berglund .40 1.00
EF4 Andreas Pihl .40 1.00
EF5 Joel Lundqvist .75 2.00
EF6 Par Styf .40 1.00
EF7 Bert Robertsson .40 1.00
EF8 Bjorn Nord .40 1.00
EF9 Henrik Nordfeldt .40 1.00
EF10 Christian Sjogren .40 1.00
EF11 Niklas Sundblad .40 1.00
EF12 Magnus Wernblom .40 1.00

2003-04 Swedish Elite Global Impact

COMPLETE SET (12) 6.00 15.00
STATED ODDS 1:8 SERIES 2
GI1 Markus Korhonen .75 2.00
GI2 Richard Lintner .40 1.00
GI3 Tomi Kallio .75 2.00
GI4 Sinuhe Wallinheimo .75 2.00
GI5 Per-age Skroder .40 1.00
GI6 Mike Bales 1.25 3.00
GI7 Brian Felsner 1.00 2.50
GI8 Kamil Brabenec .40 1.00
GI9 Toivo Suursoo .40 1.00
GI10 Jesper Damgaard .40 1.00
GI11 Juha Lind .40 1.00
GI12 Jan Nemecek .40 1.00

2003-04 Swedish Elite Hot Numbers

COMPLETE SET (12) 8.00 20.00
STATED ODDS 1:16 SERIES 2
HN1 Stefan Liv 1.50 4.00
HN2 Robert Nilsson .75 2.00
HN3 Nicklas Falk .40 1.00
HN4 Alexander Steen 3.00 8.00
HN5 Jorgen Jonsson .40 1.00
HN6 Rolf Wanhainen .75 2.00
HN7 Markus Matthiasson .40 1.00
HN8 Thomas Johansson .40 1.00
HN9 Daniel Henriksson .75 2.00
HN10 Mikael Lind .40 1.00
HN11 Petri Liimatainen .40 1.00
HN12 Per Svartvadet .75 2.00

2003-04 Swedish Elite Jerseys

COMPLETE SET (5) 25.00 60.00
1 Kimmo Kapanen 4.00 10.00
2 Sinuhe Wallinheimo 8.00 20.00
3 Daniel Henriksson 4.00 10.00
4 Henrik Lundqvist 8.00 20.00
5 Magnus Johansson 4.00 10.00

2003-04 Swedish Elite Masks

COMPLETE SET (4) 15.00 30.00
1 Sinuhe Wallinheimo 4.00 10.00
2 Stefan Liv 5.00 12.00
3 Andreas Hadelov 4.00 10.00
4 Kimmo Kapanen 4.00 10.00

2003-04 Swedish Elite Masks II

COMPLETE SET (4) 15.00 30.00
STATED ODDS 1:32 SERIES 2
1 Stefan Liv 5.00 12.00
2 Kimmo Kapanen 4.00 10.00
3 Andreas Hadelov 4.00 10.00
4 Sinuhe Wallinheimo 4.00 10.00

2003-04 Swedish Elite Rookies

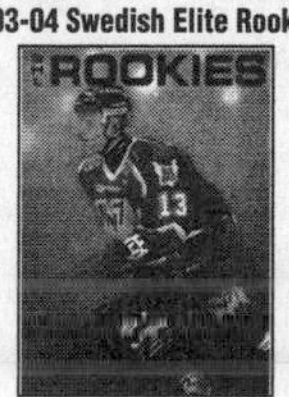

These cards were inserted at a rate of 1:8 packs.

COMPLETE SET (9) 6.00 15.00
STATED ODDS 1:8
1 Adam Andersson .40 1.00
2 Joakim Lundstrom .40 1.00
3 Nicklas Eckerblom .40 1.00
4 Alexander Steen 3.00 8.00
5 Sebastian Meijer .40 1.00
6 Robert Nilsson 1.00 2.50
7 Frans Nielsen 1.00 2.50
8 Tobias Enstrom .40 1.00
9 Joakim Lindstrom .40 1.00

2003-04 Swedish Elite Signatures

These authentic signatures were inserted at a rate of 1:32 Series 1 packs.

COMPLETE SET (16) 50.00 125.00
STATED ODDS 1:32 SERIES 1
1 Antti Tormanen 4.00 10.00
2 Tommy Sjodin 4.00 10.00
3 Joel Lundqvist 8.00 20.00
4 Daniel Henriksson 4.00 10.00
5 Tobias Enstrom 4.00 10.00
6 Jonas Johansson 4.00 10.00
7 Mika Lehtinen 4.00 10.00
8 Tommi Miettinen 4.00 10.00
9 Peter Popovic 4.00 10.00
10 Fredrik Norrena 8.00 20.00
11 Jonas Andersson-Junkka 4.00 10.00
12 Magnus Wernblom 4.00 10.00
13 Niklas Anger 4.00 10.00
14 Patrik Bjaarnhjelm 4.00 10.00
15 Mattias Wennerberg 4.00 10.00
16 Robert Nilsson SP 10.00 25.00

2003-04 Swedish Elite Signatures II

STATED ODDS 1:32 SERIES 2
1 Sinuhe Wallinheimo 6.00 15.00
2 Per Hallberg 4.00 10.00
3 Par Backer 4.00 10.00
4 Jorgen Jonsson 4.00 10.00
5 Par Styf 4.00 10.00
6 Markus Matthiasson 4.00 10.00
7 Kimmo Kapanen 6.00 15.00
8 Niklas Kronwall 15.00 40.00
9 Bjorn Nord 4.00 10.00
10 Daniel Rudslatt 4.00 10.00
11 Per Eklund 4.00 10.00
12 Pasi Maatanen 4.00 10.00
13 Peter Ekelund 4.00 10.00
14 Stefan Liv 12.00 30.00
15 Johan Davidsson SP 20.00 50.00
16 Daniel Rydmark 4.00 10.00
17 Petri Liimatainen 4.00 10.00
18 Andreas Hadelov 6.00 15.00
19 Christer Olsson 4.00 10.00
20 Niklas Eriksson 4.00 10.00
21 Jens Nielsen 4.00 10.00

2003-04 Swedish Elite Stars of the Game

COMPLETE SET (9) 8.00 20.00
STATED ODDS 1:32
1 Kristofer Ottosson 1.25 3.00
2 Niklas Andersson 1.25 3.00
3 Jorgen Jonsson 1.25 3.00
4 Johan Davidsson 1.25 3.00
5 Per Eklund 1.25 3.00
6 Jonas Ronnqvist 1.25 3.00
7 Juha Riihijarvi 1.25 3.00
8 Antti Tormanen 1.25 3.00
9 Niklas Nordgren 1.25 3.00

2003-04 Swedish Elite Zero Hero

COMPLETE SET (9) 15.00 40.00
STATED ODDS 1:16
1 Henrik Lundqvist 5.00 12.00
2 Rolf Wanhainen 2.00 5.00
3 Andreas Hadelov 2.00 5.00
4 Joaquin Gage 2.00 5.00
5 Sinuhe Wallinheimo 2.00 5.00
6 Stefan Liv 2.50 6.00
7 Sean Gauthier 2.00 5.00
8 Juuso Riksman 2.00 5.00
9 Kimmo Kapanen 2.00 5.00

2003-04 Swedish MoDo Postcards

We have confirmed a handful of singles from this set, thanks to collector Vinnie Montalbano. There are very likely many more yet to be confirmed. If you have any other information about this set, please email us at hockeymag@beckett.com.

COMPLETE SET (?)
1 Jonas Almtorp
2 Kari Haakana
3 Andreas Salomonsson
4 Mattias Wennerberg

2004-05 Swedish Alfabilder Alfa Stars

COMPLETE SET (54) 10.00 25.00
1 Johan Hedberg .20 .50
2 Mattias Ohlund .20 .50
3 Kim Johnsson .20 .50
4 Kenny Jonsson .20 .50
5 Nicklas Lidstrom .40 1.00
6 Mikael Renberg .20 .50
7 Stefan Liv .40 1.00
8 Christian Backman .20 .50
9 Magnus Kahnberg .20 .50
10 Andreas Johansson .20 .50
11 Daniel Alfredsson .40 1.00
12 Daniel Sedin .40 1.00
13 Mats Sundin .75 2.00
14 Mattias Norstrom .20 .50
15 Johan Davidsson .20 .50
16 Tomas Holmstrom .40 1.00
17 Marcus Ragnarsson .20 .50
18 Marcus Nilson .20 .50
19 Markus Naslund .75 2.00
20 Henrik Sedin .40 1.00
21 Peter Forsberg 2.00 5.00
22 Per-Johan Axelsson .20 .50
23 Kristian Huselius .20 .50
24 Michael Nylander .20 .50
25 Mattias Weinhandl .20 .50
26 Samuel Pahlsson .20 .50
27 Jorgen Jonsson .20 .50
28 Dick Tarnstrom .20 .50
29 Nils Ekman .20 .50
30 Henrik Lundqvist 3.00 8.00
31 Fredrik Olausson .20 .50
32 Mikael Tellqvist .40 1.00
33 Fredrik Modin .20 .50
34 Niklas Sundstrom .20 .50
35 Tommy Salo .20 .50
36 Daniel Tjarnqvist .20 .50
37 Fredrik Sjostrom .20 .50
38 Robert Nilsson .20 .50
39 Alexander Steen 2.00 5.00
40 Henrik Zetterberg .75 2.00
41 Tomas Sandstrom .20 .50
42 Tomas Jonsson .20 .50
43 Jonas Bergqvist .20 .50
44 Magnus Svensson .20 .50
45 Challe Berglund .20 .50
46 Leif Holmqvist .20 .50
47 Borje Salming .40 1.00
48 Sven Tumba Johansson .20 .50
49 Ulf Sterner .20 .50
50 Anders Kallur .20 .50
51 Mats Naslund .20 .50
52 Hakan Loob .20 .50
53 Kent Nilsson .20 .50
54 Pekka Lindmark .20 .50

2004-05 Swedish Alfabilder Alfa Stars Golden Ice

COMPLETE SET (12) 10.00 25.00
1 Jonas Bergqvist .75 2.00
2 Sven Tumba .75 2.00
3 Hakan Loob .75 2.00
4 Peter Forsberg 4.00 10.00
5 Pekka Lindmark .75 2.00
6 Tomas Jonsson .75 2.00
7 Challe Berglund .75 2.00
8 Tommy Salo .75 2.00
9 Jorgen Jonsson .75 2.00
10 M.Renberg/N.Sundstrom 1.25 3.00
11 M.Norstrom/M.Ohlund 1.25 3.00
12 F.Modin/K.Johnsson 1.25 3.00

2004-05 Swedish Alfabilder Autographs

Random inserts in Swedish product, limited to 200 copies each.

COMPLETE SET (28) 150.00 300.00
101 Markus Naslund 12.00 30.00
102 Henrik Zetterberg 12.00 30.00
103 Peter Forsberg 25.00 60.00
104 Per-Johan Axelsson 3.00 8.00
105 Henrik Sedin 4.00 10.00
106 Mikael Renberg 3.00 8.00
107 Nicklas Lidstrom 12.00 30.00
108 Tomas Sandstrom 4.00 10.00
109 Johan Hedberg 4.00 10.00
110 Tomas Jonsson 3.00 8.00
111 Michael Nylander 4.00 10.00
112 Mikael Tellqvist 10.00 25.00
113 Nils Ekman 4.00 10.00
114 Mattias Ohlund 3.00 8.00
115 Fredrik Modin 3.00 8.00
116 Jonas Bergqvist 3.00 8.00
117 Tommy Salo 4.00 10.00
118 Dick Tarnstrom 3.00 8.00
119 Niklas Sundstrom 3.00 8.00
120 Tomas Holmstrom 8.00 20.00
121 Charles Berglund 3.00 8.00
122 Christian Backman 3.00 8.00
123 Magnus Svensson 3.00 8.00
124 Marcus Nilson 4.00 10.00
125 Samuel Pahlsson 4.00 10.00
126 Daniel Tjarnqvist 3.00 8.00
127 Kristian Huselius 4.00 10.00
128 Mattias Weinhandl 3.00 8.00

2004-05 Swedish Alfabilder Limited Autographs

Parallel to the basic autographs, these cards are limited to just 50 copies.

COMPLETE SET (28) 500.00 700.00
101 Markus Naslund 20.00 50.00
102 Henrik Zetterberg 20.00 50.00
103 Peter Forsberg 75.00 200.00
104 Per-Johan Axelsson 8.00 20.00
105 Henrik Sedin 8.00 20.00
106 Mikael Renberg 8.00 20.00
107 Nicklas Lidstrom 20.00 50.00
108 Tomas Sandstrom 8.00 20.00
109 Johan Hedberg 8.00 20.00
110 Tomas Jonsson 8.00 20.00
111 Michael Nylander 8.00 20.00
112 Mikael Tellqvist 15.00 40.00
113 Nils Ekman 8.00 20.00
114 Mattias Ohlund 8.00 20.00
115 Fredrik Modin 12.00 30.00
116 Jonas Bergqvist 8.00 20.00
117 Tommy Salo 8.00 20.00
118 Dick Tarnstrom 8.00 20.00
119 Niklas Sundstrom 8.00 20.00
120 Tomas Holmstrom 15.00 40.00
121 Charles Berglund 8.00 20.00
122 Christian Backman 8.00 20.00
123 Magnus Svensson 8.00 20.00
124 Marcus Nilson 8.00 20.00
125 Samuel Pahlsson 8.00 20.00
126 Daniel Tjarnqvist 8.00 20.00
127 Kristian Huselius 8.00 20.00
128 Mattias Weinhandl 8.00 20.00

2004-05 Swedish Alfabilder Next In Line

COMPLETE SET (6) 15.00 40.00
1 Leif Holmqvist 2.00 5.00
Tommy Salo
2 Borje Salming 4.00 10.00
Nick Lidstrom
3 Sven Johansson 6.00 15.00
Peter Forsberg
4 Ulf Sterner 4.00 10.00
Henrik Zetterberg
5 Hakan Loob 4.00 10.00
Mats Naslund
6 Kent Nilsson 2.00 5.00
Robert Nilsson

2004-05 Swedish Alfabilder Proof Parallels

COMPLETE SET (54)
3X TO 5X BASE CARD

2004-05 Swedish Djurgardens Postcards

These standard postcard-sized collectibles were issued by the team. All copies we've seen have been signed, so it's likely that's the only way they were made available. It's also likely that more singles exist than listed below. If you have information, contact us at hockeymag@beckett.com.

COMPLETE SET (?)
1 Mariusz Czerkawski .75 2.00
2 Daniel Fernholm .75 2.00
3 Espen Knutsen 1.25 3.00
4 Marcus Kristofferson .75 2.00
5 Staffan Kronwall 1.25 3.00
6 Robert Nilsson 1.25 3.00
7 Jimmie Olvestad .75 2.00
8 Kristofer Ottosson .75 2.00
9 Mika Stromberg .75 2.00
10 Daniel Tjarnqvist .75 2.00

2004-05 Swedish Elitset

COMPLETE SET (288) 15.00 40.00
1 Markus Korhonen .08 .20
2 Daniel Johansson .08 .20
3 Tommy Sjodin .08 .20
4 Daniel Casselstahl .08 .20
5 Henrik Malmstrom .08 .20
6 Jakob Johansson .08 .20
7 Patrik Ronnqvist .08 .20
8 Roger Kyro .08 .20
9 Ove Molin .08 .20
10 Bjorn Danielsson .08 .20
11 Tommi Miettinen .08 .20
12 Bjorn Bjurling .08 .20
13 Staffan Kronwall .08 .20
14 Johnny Oduya .20 .50
15 Daniel Rudslatt .08 .20
16 Nichlas Falk .08 .20
17 Tomas Kollar .08 .20
18 Christian Eklund .08 .20
19 Fredrik Bremberg .08 .20
20 Mikael Johansson .08 .20
21 Marcus Kristoffersson .20 .50
22 Kenneth Bergqvist .08 .20
23 Johan Jonfeldt .08 .20
24 Jan-Axel Alavaara .08 .20
25 Antti-Jussi Niemi .08 .20
26 Ronnie Sundin .08 .20
27 Magnus Kahnberg .08 .20
28 Alexander Steen 1.50 4.00
29 Jari Tolsa .08 .20
30 Jonas Esbjors .08 .20
31 Niklas Andersson .08 .20
32 Peter Strom .08 .20
33 Jonas Johnson .30 .75
34 Jens Karlsson .08 .20
35 Fredrik Eriksson .08 .20
36 Martin Lindman .08 .20
37 Jonas Frogren .08 .20
38 Greger Artursson .08 .20
39 Radek Hamr .08 .20
40 Janne Gronvall .08 .20
41 Hannes Hyvonen .08 .20
42 Peter Nordstrom .08 .20
43 Par Backer .08 .20
44 Marcel Jenni .08 .20
45 Peter Hammarstrom .08 .20
46 Dieter Kalt .08 .20
47 Stefan Liv .40 1.00
48 Fredrik Olausson .08 .20
49 Ola Thorwalls .08 .20
50 Jouni Loponen .08 .20
51 Stefan Hellkvist .08 .20
52 Per-Age Skroder .08 .20
53 Peter Ekelund .08 .20
54 Martin Thornberg .08 .20
55 Anders Huusko .08 .20
56 Kalle Sahlstedt .08 .20
57 Pasi Maattanen .08 .20
58 Mattias Remstam .08 .20
59 Johan Davidsson .08 .20
60 Fredrik Norrena .20 .50
61 Peter Casparsson .08 .20
62 Martin Knold .08 .20
63 Jyrki Valivaara .08 .20
64 Mikko Peltola .08 .20
65 Tim Eriksson .08 .20
66 Fredrik Emvall .08 .20
67 Jussi Tarvainen .08 .20
68 Mikael Hakanson .08 .20
69 Per Eklund .08 .20
70 Gusten Tornqvist .08 .20
71 Jonas Andersson-Junkka .08 .20
72 Jan Sandstrom .08 .20
73 Tuukka Mantyla .08 .20
74 Stefan Nilsson .08 .20
75 Linus Fagemo .08 .20
76 Emil Lundberg .08 .20
77 Thomas Berglund .08 .20
78 Hans Huczkowski .08 .20
79 Per Ledin .08 .20
80 Johan Tellstrom .08 .20
81 Pierre Berggren .08 .20
82 Robert Borgqvist .08 .20
83 David Petrasek .08 .20
84 Magnus Osterby .08 .20
85 Petri Liimatainen .08 .20
86 Johan Norgren .08 .20
87 Peter Andersson .08 .20
88 Marcus Magnertoft .08 .20
89 Frans Nielsen .08 .20
90 Daniel Rydmark .08 .20
91 Mikael Wahlberg .08 .20
92 Kim Staal .08 .20
93 Jan Oberg .08 .20
94 Martin Johansson .08 .20
95 Lars Jansson .08 .20
96 Anders Soderberg .08 .20
97 Tommy Pettersson .08 .20
98 Fredrik Warg .08 .20
99 Magnus Hedlund .08 .20
100 Morten Green .08 .20
101 Magnus Gastrin .08 .20
102 Bengt Hoglund .08 .20
103 Adam Andersson .08 .20
104 Henrik Petre .08 .20
105 Daniel Back .08 .20
106 Hakan Bogg .08 .20
107 Jonas Westerling .08 .20
108 Magnus Sandberg .08 .20
109 Magnus Lindquist .08 .20
110 Bert Robertsson .08 .20
111 Jonathan Ericsson .08 .20
112 Stefan Bernstrom .08 .20
113 Erik Norback .08 .20
114 Joakim Eriksson .08 .20
115 Robert Dome .08 .20
116 Robert Carlsson .08 .20
117 Teemu Riihijarvi .08 .20
118 Gabriel Karlsson .08 .20
119 Jorgen Bemstrom .08 .20
120 Peter Larsson .08 .20
121 Kimmo Kapanen .20 .50
122 Tommi Rajamaki .08 .20
123 Jesper Jager .08 .20
124 Sanny Lindstrom .08 .20
125 Kalle Koskinen .08 .20
126 Par Styf .08 .20
127 Christian Soderstrom .08 .20
128 Niklas Nordgren .08 .20
129 Valeri Krykov .08 .20
130 Per Hallin .08 .20
131 Christian Sjogren .08 .20
132 Fredrik Sundin .08 .20
133 Peter Andersson .08 .20
134 Ove Molin .08 .20
135 Daniel Rydmark .08 .20
136 Johan Davidsson .08 .20
137 Thomas Berglund .08 .20
138 Pelle Prestberg .08 .20
139 Mathias Johansson .08 .20
140 Roger Kyro .08 .20
141 Kristofer Ottosson .08 .20
142 Nichlas Falk .08 .20
143 Dieter Kalt .08 .20
144 Tomi Kallio .20 .50
145 Johan Holmqvist .20 .50
146 Niklas Andersson .08 .20
147 Mikko Kuparinen .08 .20
148 Mattias Karlsson .08 .20
149 Sebastian Sulku .08 .20
150 Jonas Soling .08 .20
151 Nicklas Danielsson .08 .20
152 Andreas Dackell .20 .50
153 Mikko Luovi .08 .20
154 Mikael Lind .08 .20
155 Vesa Viitakoski .08 .20
156 Rolf Wanhainen .08 .20
157 Mika Stromberg .08 .20
158 Daniel Fernholm .08 .20
159 Daniel Tjarnqvist .08 .20
160 Rikard Franzen .08 .20
161 Nils Ekman .20 .50
162 Kristofer Ottosson .08 .20
163 Robert Nilsson .08 .20
164 Johannes Salmonsson .08 .20
165 Marcus Nilson .30 .75
166 Jimmie Olvestad .08 .20
167 Espen Knutsen .30 .75
168 Mariusz Czerkawski .20 .50
169 Henrik Lundqvist 2.00 5.00
170 Tom Koivisto .08 .20
171 Arto Tukio .08 .20
172 Christian Backman .08 .20
173 Peter Hogardh .08 .20
174 Joel Lundqvist .08 .20
175 Loui Eriksson .60 .75
176 Samuel Pahlsson .20 .50
177 Martin Pluss .08 .20
178 Per-Johan Axelsson .20 .50
179 Tomi Kallio .20 .50
180 Daniel Henriksson .20 .50
181 Robin Jonsson .08 .20
182 Per Hallberg .08 .20
183 Mats Trygg .08 .20
184 Pelle Prestberg .08 .20
185 Jesper Mattsson .08 .20
186 Christian Berglund .08 .20
187 Jonas Hoglund .20 .50
188 Mathias Johansson .08 .20
189 Jorgen Jonsson .08 .20
190 Fredrik Eriksson .08 .20
191 Calle Steen .08 .20
192 Boo Ahl .20 .50
193 Daniel Ljungqvist .08 .20
194 Per Gustafsson .08 .20
195 Johan Halvardsson .08 .20
196 Kimmo Peltonen .08 .20
197 Mathias Tjarnqvist .20 .50
198 Andreas Karlsson .08 .20
199 Andreas Jamtin .08 .20
200 Stefan Pettersson .08 .20
201 Daniel Sperrle .08 .20
202 Magnus Johansson .08 .20
203 Henrik Tallinder .20 .50
204 Christoffer Norgren .08 .20
205 Jakob Karlsson .08 .20
206 Johan Franzen .40 1.00
207 Tony Martensson .08 .20
208 Ulf Soderstrom .08 .20
209 Brendan Morrison .20 .50
210 Kristian Huselius .20 .50
211 Mike Knuble .20 .50
212 Johan Lindstrom .08 .20
213 Kristian Antila .08 .20

214 Johan Fransson .20 .50
215 Niclas Wallin .08 .20
216 Roger Akerstrom .08 .20
217 Jaroslav Obsut .08 .20
218 Jonas Ronnqvist .08 .20
219 Thomas Koch .08 .20
220 Justin Williams .20 .50
221 Jonas Nordquist .08 .20
222 Fredrik Hynning .08 .20
223 Karl Fabritius .08 .20
224 Tomas Holmstrom .40 1.00
225 Andreas Hadelov .20 .50
226 Christopher Nilstorp .20 .50
227 Miska Kangasniemi .08 .20
228 Bjorn Melin .08 .20
229 Jan Hammar .08 .20
230 Jason Deleurme .08 .20
231 Carl Soderberg .60 1.50
232 Andreas Valdix .08 .20
233 Mika Hannula .08 .20
234 Peter Hammarstrom .08 .20
235 Markus Matthiasson .08 .20
236 Tommy Salo .20 .50
237 Mattias Timander .08 .20
238 Hans Jonsson .08 .20
239 Tobias Enstrom .08 .20
240 Jesper Damgaard .08 .20
241 Oscar Hedman .08 .20
242 Pierre Hedin .08 .20
243 Daniel Sedin .40 1.00
244 Mattias Weinhandl .20 .50
245 Andreas Salomonsson .20 .50
246 Peter Oberg .08 .20
247 Henrik Sedin .40 1.00
248 Peter Forsberg 1.25 3.00
249 Alexander Steen .75 4.00
250 Per Svartvadet .20 .50
251 Tero Leinonen .08 .20
252 Andreas Lilja .08 .20
253 Marko Kauppinen .08 .20
254 Pavel Skrbek .08 .20
255 Calle Bergstrom .08 .20
256 Peter Nolander .08 .20
257 Jonathan Granstrom .08 .20
258 Marcus Eriksson .08 .20
259 Shawn Horcoff .20 .50
260 Kenneth Bergqvist .08 .20
261 Anders Nilsson .08 .20
262 Martin Jansson .08 .20
263 Mikael Simons .08 .20
264 Peter Nylander .08 .20
265 Rastislav Stana .30 .75
266 Niclas Havelid .08 .20
267 Dick Tarnstrom .20 .50
268 Peter Popovic .08 .20
269 Petri Liimatainen .08 .20
270 Timmy Pettersson .08 .20
271 Jan Huokko .08 .20
272 Anders Burstrom .08 .20
273 Nicklas Bergfors .40 1.00
274 Jonas Andersson .08 .20
275 Peter Ferraro .20 .50
276 Chris Ferraro .20 .50
277 Miikka Kiprusoff .75 2.00
278 Jimmy Danielsson .08 .20
279 Johan Svedberg .08 .20
280 Mats Hansson .08 .20
281 Lars Jonsson .20 .50
282 Teemu Aalto .08 .20
283 Robert Carlsson .08 .20
284 Kristian Gahn .08 .20
285 Yared Hagos .20 .50
286 Henrik Zetterberg .75 2.00
287 Magnus Nilsson .08 .20
288 Jonathan Hedstrom .20 .50

2004-05 Swedish Elitset Dominators

Inserted at a rate of 1:16 series 2 packs.

COMPLETE SET (9) 25.00 50.00
STATED ODDS 1:16 SERIES 2
1 Magnus Kahnberg 1.25 3.00
Pelle Prestberg
Joakim Eriksson
2 Peter Forsberg 6.00 15.00
Henrik Zetterberg
Kristian Huselius
3 Miikka Kiprusoff 6.00 15.00
Tommy Salo
Johan Holmqvist
4 Johan Fransson 4.00 10.00
Alexander Steen
Henrik Lundqvist
5 Brendan Morrison 3.00 8.00
Justin Williams
Shawn Horcoff
6 Henrik Tallinder 3.00 8.00
Tomas Holmstrom
Andreas Lilja
7 Espen Knutsen 1.25 3.00
Martin Pluss
Tomi Kallio
8 Dick Tarnstrom 1.25 3.00
Fredrik Olausson
Daniel Tjarnqvist
9 Henrik Sedin 6.00 15.00
Daniel Sedin
Peter Forsberg

2004-05 Swedish Elitset Forsberg Tribute

Inserted 1:8 series 1 packs.

COMPLETE SET (6) 10.00 25.00
STATED ODDS 1:8
1 Peter Forsberg 2.00 5.00
2 Peter Forsberg 2.00 5.00
3 Peter Forsberg 2.00 5.00
4 Peter Forsberg 2.00 5.00
5 Peter Forsberg 2.00 5.00
6 Peter Forsberg 2.00 5.00

2004-05 Swedish Elitset Future Stars

Inserted 1:8 series 1 packs.

COMPLETE SET (12) 15.00 30.00
STATED ODDS 1:8 SERIES 1
1 Carl Soderberg 1.50 4.00
2 Loui Eriksson 2.00 5.00
3 Linus Videll .75 2.00
4 Johan Fransson 2.00 5.00
5 Robert Nilsson 2.00 5.00
6 Nicklas Danielsson .75 2.00
7 Andreas Valdix .75 2.00
8 Alexander Steen 4.00 10.00
9 Joakim Lundstrom .75 2.00
10 Daniel Fernholm .75 2.00
11 Joakim Lindstrom .75 2.00
12 Mats Hansson .75 2.00

2004-05 Swedish Elitset Gold

3X to 5X BASE CARD VALUE

2004-05 Swedish Elitset High Expectations

Inserted 1:16 in series 1 packs.

COMPLETE SET (10) 10.00 25.00
STATED ODDS 1:16 SERIES 1
1 Jonas Soling .75 2.00
2 Tomas Kollar .75 2.00
3 Henrik Lundqvist 6.00 15.00
4 Mathias Johansson .75 2.00
5 Bjorn Melin .75 2.00
6 Tim Eriksson .75 2.00
7 Jonas Ronnqvist .75 2.00
8 Mattias Wennerberg .75 2.00
9 Peter Popovic .75 2.00
10 Yared Hagos 1.25 3.00

2004-05 Swedish Elitset In The Crease

Inserted 1:32 series 1 packs.

COMPLETE SET (10) 15.00 40.00
STATED ODDS 1:32 SERIES 1
1 Markus Korhonen 1.25 3.00
2 Bjorn Bjurling 1.25 3.00
3 Henrik Lundqvist 10.00 25.00
4 Sinuhe Wallinheimo 1.25 3.00
5 Stefan Liv 2.00 5.00
6 Fredrik Norrena 2.00 5.00
7 Daniel Henriksson 1.25 3.00
8 Andreas Hadelov 1.25 3.00
9 Rolf Wanhainen 1.25 3.00
10 Kimmo Kapanen 1.25 3.00

2004-05 Swedish Elitset Jerseys Series 1

STATED PRINT RUN 35 SETS
1 Markus Korhonen 12.00 30.00
2 Kimmo Kapanen 12.00 30.00
3 Sinuhe Wallinheimo 12.00 30.00
4 Henrik Lundqvist 30.00 75.00
5 Per Gustavsson 12.00 30.00

2004-05 Swedish Elitset Jerseys Series 2

STATED PRINT RUN 35 SETS
AH Andreas Hadelov 12.00 30.00
PP Peter Popovic 12.00 30.00
SL Stefan Liv 20.00 50.00
TJ Thomas Johansson 12.00 30.00

2004-05 Swedish Elitset Limited Signatures

Random inserts in series 2 packs, limited to 50 copies each.

COMPLETE SET (6)
STATED PRINT RUN 50 SETS
INSERTED RANDOMLY SERIES 2
1 Daniel Henriksson 10.00 25.00
2 Jorgen Jonsson 10.00 25.00
3 Per Gustavsson 10.00 25.00
4 Andreas Lilja 10.00 25.00
5 Niclas Havelid 10.00 25.00
6 Jonas Ronnqvist 10.00 25.00

2004-05 Swedish Elitset Masks

Inserted 1:32 series 2 packs.

COMPLETE SET (8) 50.00 100.00
STATED ODDS 1:32 SERIES 2
1 Johan Holmqvist 4.00 10.00
2 Bjorn Bjurling 4.00 10.00
3 Henrik Lundqvist 12.00 30.00
4 Stefan Liv 6.00 15.00
5 Andreas Hadelov 4.00 10.00
6 Gusten Tornqvist 4.00 10.00
7 Rastislav Stana 6.00 15.00
8 Miikka Kiprusoff 12.00 30.00

2004-05 Swedish Elitset Signatures

Inserted 1:32 series 1 packs.

COMPLETE SET (15) 100.00 175.00
STATED ODDS 1:32 SERIES 1
1 Andreas Hadelov 6.00 15.00
2 Andreas Valdix 6.00 15.00
3 Joakim Eriksson 6.00 15.00
4 Rolf Wanhainen 6.00 15.00
5 Jonas Ronnqvist 6.00 15.00
6 Johan Fransson 10.00 25.00
7 Per Svartvadet 6.00 15.00
8 Bjorn Bjurling 6.00 15.00
9 Niklas Falk 6.00 15.00
10 Robert Carlsson 6.00 15.00
11 Yared Hagos 6.00 15.00
12 Joakim Lundstrom 6.00 15.00
13 Mikael Lind 6.00 15.00
14 Pelle Prestberg 6.00 15.00
15 Hannes Hyvonen 6.00 15.00

2004-05 Swedish Elitset Signatures Series A

STATED ODDS 1:32 SERIES 2
1 Frans Nielsen 4.00 10.00
2 Kim Staal 4.00 10.00
3 Per Eklund 4.00 10.00
4 Fredrik Norrena 6.00 15.00
5 Mikko Peltola 4.00 10.00
6 Tim Eriksson 4.00 10.00
7 Roger Akerstrom 4.00 10.00
8 Daniel Henriksson 4.00 10.00
9 Mats Hansson 4.00 10.00
10 Kimmo Kapanen 6.00 15.00
11 Tommi Miettinen 4.00 10.00
12 Bjorn Danielsson 4.00 10.00
13 Marcel Jenni 4.00 10.00
14 Henrik Lundqvist 20.00 50.00
15 Tomi Kallio 4.00 10.00
16 Niklas Andersson 4.00 10.00
17 Antti-Jussi Niemi 4.00 10.00

2004-05 Swedish Elitset Signatures Series B

STATED ODDS 1:32 SERIES 2
1 Andreas Dackell 4.00 10.00
2 Johan Holmqvist 6.00 15.00
3 Daniel Henriksson 4.00 10.00
4 Jonas Hoglund 4.00 10.00
5 Jorgen Jonsson 4.00 10.00
6 Mathias Johansson 4.00 10.00
7 Kimmo Peltonen 4.00 10.00
8 Mathias Tjarnqvist 6.00 15.00
9 Stefan Pettersson 4.00 10.00
10 Andreas Lilja 6.00 15.00
11 Mikael Simons 4.00 10.00
12 Peter Nylander 4.00 10.00
13 Dick Tarnstrom 4.00 10.00
14 Niclas Havelid 6.00 15.00
15 Peter Forsberg 30.00 75.00
16 Tommy Salo 6.00 15.00
17 Tomas Holmstrom 10.00 25.00

2004-05 Swedish HV71 Postcards

We have confirmed a handful of cards from this Swedish issue, thanks to collector Vinnie Montalbano. It's a certainty that others exist. If you know of others, please email hockeymag@beckett.com.

COMPLETE SET (?)
1 Brian Boucher 1.25 3.00
2 Andreas Jamtin .75 2.00
3 Simon Skoog .75 2.00
4 David Fredriksson .75 2.00
5 Fredrik Olausson .75 2.00
6 Per Gustafsson .75 2.00
7 Peter Ekelund .75 2.00
8 Anders Huusko .75 2.00

2004-05 Swedish MoDo Postcards

These 5X7 postcards were issued by the team, apparently in set form. They are unnumbered and feature more than a dozen moonlighting NHLers.

COMPLETE SET (30) 20.00 40.00
1 Peter Forsberg 4.00 10.00
2 Henrik Sedin 2.00 5.00
3 Daniel Sedin 2.00 5.00
4 Mattias Weinhandl .75 2.00
5 Adrian Aucoin .75 2.00
6 Mattias Timander .75 2.00
7 Per Svartvadet .75 2.00
8 Alexander Steen 4.00 10.00
9 Tommy Salo .75 2.00
10 Markus Naslund 2.00 5.00
11 Andreas Salomonsson .75 2.00
12 Frantisek Kaberle .75 2.00
13 Hans Jonsson .40 1.00
14 Joakim Lindstrom .40 1.00
15 Pierre Hedin .40 1.00
16 Dan Hinote .75 2.00
17 Lars Jansson .40 1.00
18 Magnus Gastrin .40 1.00
19 Mattias Hellstrom .40 1.00
20 Tobias Viklund .40 1.00
21 Michael Zajkowski .40 1.00
22 Morten Green .40 1.00
23 Mattias Wennerberg .40 1.00
24 Magnus Hedlund .40 1.00
25 Peter Oberg .40 1.00
26 Fredrik Warg .40 1.00
27 Oscar Hedman .40 1.00
28 Tobias Enstrom .40 1.00
29 Jan Oberg .40 1.00
30 Jesper Damgaard .40 1.00

2004-05 Swedish Pure Skills

COMPLETE SET (144) 20.00 50.00
1 Johan Holmqvist .20 .50
2 Chris Phillips .08 .20
3 Tommy Sjodin .08 .20
4 Andreas Dackell .08 .20
5 Tommi Miettinen .08 .20
6 Ronald Petrovicky .08 .20
7 Mikael Lind .08 .20
8 Jose Theodore 1.25 3.00
9 Daniel Tjarnqvist .08 .20
10 Dan Boyle .08 .20
11 Nils Ekman .08 .20
12 Marcus Nilson .08 .20
13 Espen Knutsen .08 .20
14 Mariusz Czerkawski .08 .20
15 Henrik Lundqvist 1.50 4.00
16 Tom Koivisto .08 .20
17 Sami Salo .08 .20
18 Christian Backman .08 .20
19 Daniel Alfredsson .40 1.00
20 Niklas Andersson .08 .20
21 Samuel Pahlsson .20 .50
22 Martin Pluss .08 .20
23 Jonas Johnson .08 .20
24 Tomi Kallio .08 .20
25 Martin Gerber .30 .75
26 Zdeno Chara .30 .75
27 Sheldon Souray .08 .20
28 Pelle Prestberg .08 .20
29 Christian Berglund .08 .20
30 Jonas Hoglund .08 .20
31 Peter Nordstrom .08 .20
32 Jorgen Jonsson .08 .20
33 Marian Gaborik 1.25 3.00
34 Stefan Liv .40 1.00
35 Anders Eriksson .08 .20
36 Per Gustafsson .08 .20
37 Manny Malhotra .08 .20
38 Andreas Karlsson .08 .20
39 Jonathan Cheechoo .60 1.50
40 Johan Davidsson .08 .20
41 Fredrik Norrena .40 1.00
42 Magnus Johansson .08 .20
43 Thomas Johansson .08 .20
44 Mikko Peltola .08 .20
45 Tony Martensson .08 .20
46 Brendan Morrison .20 .50
47 Michael Knuble .20 .50
48 Kristian Antila .20 .50
49 Niclas Wallin .08 .20
50 Roger Akerstrom .08 .20
51 Jaroslav Obsut .08 .20
52 Jonas Ronnqvist .08 .20
53 Justin Williams .20 .50
54 Per Ledin .08 .20
55 Tomas Holmstrom .40 1.00
56 Andreas Hadelov .20 .50
57 David Petrasek .08 .20
58 Peter Andersson .08 .20
59 Bjorn Melin .08 .20
60 Carl Soderberg .40 1.00
61 Mika Hannula .08 .20
62 Tommy Salo .20 .50
63 Mattias Timander .08 .20
64 Adrian Aucoin .20 .50
65 Daniel Sedin .30 .75
66 Mattias Weinhandl .20 .50
67 Markus Naslund .75 2.00
68 Henrik Sedin .30 .75
69 Peter Forsberg 2.00 5.00
70 Alexander Steen .75 2.00
71 Per Svartvadet .08 .20
72 Dan Hinote .20 .50
73 Tero Leinonen .20 .50
74 Pavel Skrbek .08 .20
75 Daniel Cleary .08 .20
76 Rastislav Pavlikovsky .08 .20
77 Marian Hossa .75 2.00
78 Shawn Horcoff .30 .75
79 Ladislav Nagy .30 .75
80 Marcel Hossa .30 .75
81 Rastislav Stana .30 .75
82 Dick Tarnstrom .20 .50
83 Peter Popovic .08 .20
84 Joakim Eriksson .08 .20
85 Kyle Calder .20 .50
86 Mikael Samuelsson .08 .20
87 Scott Thornton .20 .50
88 Dragan Umicevic .08 .20
89 Miikka Kiprusoff .75 2.00
90 Aki-Petteri Berg .08 .20
91 Teemu Aalto .08 .20
92 Niklas Nordgren .08 .20
93 Yared Hagos .20 .50
94 Henrik Zetterberg .75 2.00
95 Kent Manderville .08 .20
96 Jonathan Hedstrom .20 .50
97 Landon Wilson .20 .50
98 Ladislav Kohn .08 .20
99 Mike Ribeiro .20 .50
100 Tomas Vokoun .75 2.00
101 Marek Zidlicky .20 .50
102 Jere Karalahti .20 .50
103 Jarno Kultanen .08 .20
104 Lasse Pirjeta .20 .50
105 Jarkko Ruutu .20 .50
106 Timo Parssinen .08 .20
107 Brett Harkins .20 .50
108 Mika Noronen .20 .50
109 Josh Holden .20 .50
110 Riku Hahl .20 .50
111 Jani Rita .20 .50
112 Juuso Riksman .08 .20
113 Sami Helenius .08 .20
114 Steve Kariya .40 1.00
115 Patrik Stefan .20 .50
116 Hannes Hyvonen .08 .20
117 Tim Thomas .40 1.00
118 Ossi Vaananen .20 .50
119 Marko Jantunen .08 .20
120 Toni Dahlman .08 .20
121 Glen Metropolit .20 .50
122 Sinuhe Wallinheimo .20 .50
123 Steve Martins .20 .50
124 Jarkko Immonen .20 .50
125 Jody Shelley .40 1.00
126 Niklas Backman 1.00 2.50
127 Janne Niinimaa .20 .50
128 Josef Boumedienne .08 .20
129 Petr Tenkrat .08 .20
130 Michael Nylander .20 .50
131 Dwayne Roloson .75 2.00
132 Erik Hamalainen .08 .20
133 Esa Pirnes .08 .20
134 Pasi Nurminen .08 .20
135 Jarmo Myllys .20 .50
136 Andrew Raycroft 1.00 2.50
137 Ville Nieminen .20 .50
138 Stefan Ohman .08 .20
139 Teemu Lassila .08 .20
140 Craig Rivet .20 .50
141 Saku Koivu .60 1.50
142 Antti Aalto .08 .20
143 Scott Langkow .08 .20
144 Jason Williams .30 .75

2004-05 Swedish Pure Skills Jerseys

Limited to 35 copies each.

COMPLETE SET (4) 30.00 80.00
JR Jarkko Ruutu 10.00 25.00
PS Per Svartvadet 10.00 25.00
TS Tommy Salo 10.00 25.00
VN Ville Nieminen 10.00 25.00

2004-05 Swedish Pure Skills Parallel

Inserted at a rate of 1:4 packs and limited to just 100 copies.

5X to 8X BASE CARD VALUE

2004-05 Swedish Pure Skills Professional Power

COMPLETE SET (25) 30.00 75.00
AB Aki-Petteri Berg .75 2.00
CR Craig Rivet 1.25 3.00
DA Daniel Alfredsson 2.00 5.00
DS Daniel Sedin 1.25 3.00
DT Daniel Tjarnqvist .75 2.00
DT Dick Tarnstrom 1.25 3.00
HS Henrik Sedin 1.25 3.00
HZ Henrik Zetterberg 4.00 10.00
JN Janne Niinimaa .75 2.00
MC Mariusz Czerkawski .75 2.00
MG Marian Gaborik 6.00 15.00
MH Marian Hossa 4.00 10.00
MN Marcus Nilson .75 2.00
MN Michael Nylander 1.25 3.00
MN Markus Naslund 4.00 10.00
MZ Marek Zidlicky .75 2.00
OV Ossi Vaananen .75 2.00
PF Peter Forsberg 10.00 25.00
PS Patrik Stefan .75 2.00
RH Raimo Helminen .75 2.00
SK Saku Koivu 4.00 10.00
SP Samuel Pahlsson .75 2.00
SS Sami Salo .75 2.00
VN Ville Nieminen .75 2.00
ZC Zdeno Chara 1.25 3.00

2004-05 Swedish Pure Skills Signatures Limited

Limited to just 50 copies each.

PRINT RUN 50 SER.#'d SETS 100.00 200.00
1 Andreas Dackell 10.00 25.00
2 Peter Forsberg 50.00 125.00
3 Henrik Zetterberg 20.00 50.00
4 Miikka Kiprusoff 20.00 50.00

2004-05 Swedish Pure Skills The Wall

Inserted at a rate of 1:40.

COMPLETE SET (10) 40.00 100.00
AR Andrew Raycroft 8.00 20.00
FN Fredrik Norrena 2.00 5.00
HL Henrik Lundqvist 8.00 20.00
JT Jose Theodore 10.00 25.00
MG Martin Gerber 4.00 10.00
MK Miikka Kiprusoff 10.00 25.00
MN Mika Noronen 2.00 5.00
NB Niklas Backstrom 4.00 10.00
TS Tommy Salo 2.00 5.00
TT Tim Thomas 6.00 15.00

2005-06 Swedish SHL Elitset

COMPLETE SET (288) 25.00 60.00
1 Johan Holmqvist .40 1.00
2 Niklas Andersson .20 .50
3 Mikko Kuparinen .10 .25
4 Tommy Sjodin .10 .25
5 Sebastian Sulku .10 .25
6 Henrik Malmstrom .10 .25
7 Andreas Dackell .10 .25
8 Ove Molin .10 .25
9 Björn Danielsson .10 .25
10 Tommi Miettinen .10 .25
11 Mikael Lind .10 .25
12 Vesa Viitakoski .10 .25
13 Jose Theodore 1.25 3.00
14 Ronnie Pettersson .10 .25
15 Daniel Tjarnqvist .20 .50
16 Christopher Thorn .10 .25
17 Robert Nilsson .75 2.00
18 Daniel Rudslat .10 .25
19 Nichlas Falk .10 .25
20 Marcus Nilson .20 .50
21 Jimmie Ölvestad .20 .50
22 Patrick Thoresen .40 1.00
23 Tom Koivisto .10 .25
24 Antti-Jussi Niemi .10 .25
25 Sami Salo .10 .25
26 Daniel Alfredsson .75 2.00
27 Magnus Kahnberg .10 .25
28 Peter Hogardh .10 .25
29 Jari Tolsa .10 .25
30 Joel Lundqvist .20 .50
31 Jonas Esbjors .10 .25
32 Niklas Andersson .10 .25
33 Samuel Pahlsson .20 .50
34 Martin Pluss .10 .25
35 Jonas Johnson .10 .25
36 Tomi Kallio .10 .25
37 Martin Gerber .40 1.00
38 Daniel Henriksson .10 .25
39 Robin Jonsson .10 .25
40 Jonas Frogren .10 .25
41 Radek Hamr .10 .25
42 Zdeno Chara .75 2.00
43 Pelle Prestberg .10 .25
44 Jesper Mattsson .10 .25
45 Jonas Hoglund .10 .25
46 Mathias Johansson .10 .25
47 Peter Nordstrom .10 .25
48 Fredrik Eriksson .10 .25
49 Par Backer .10 .25
50 Stefan Liv .40 1.00
51 Anders Eriksson .10 .25
52 Daniel Ljungqvist .10 .25
53 Per Gustafsson .10 .25
54 Simon Skoog .10 .25
55 Ola Svanberg .10 .25
56 Johan Halvardsson .10 .25
57 Anders Huusko .10 .25
58 Andreas Karlsson .10 .25
59 Pasi Maattanen .10 .25
60 Stefan Pettersson .10 .25
61 Johan Davidsson .10 .25
62 Johan Backlund .10 .25
63 Stefan Bemstrom .10 .25
64 Örjan Lindmark .10 .25
65 Jens Bergenstrom .10 .25
66 Niklas Eriksson .10 .25
67 Niklas Persson .10 .25
68 Johan Rosen .10 .25
69 Fredrik Norrena .40 1.00
70 Magnus Johansson .10 .25
71 Thomas Johansson .10 .25
72 Christoffer Norgren .10 .25
73 Jyrki Valivaara .10 .25
74 Mikko Peltola .10 .25
75 Ult Soderstrom .10 .25
76 Johan Andersson .10 .25
77 Tim Eriksson .10 .25
78 Michael Knuble .20 .50
79 Fredrik Emwall .10 .25
80 Jussi Tarvainen .10 .25
81 Mikael Hakanson .10 .25
82 Gusten Tornqvist .10 .25
83 Johan Fransson .10 .25
84 Jan Sandström .10 .25
85 Jaroslav Obsut .10 .25
86 Jonas Ronnqvist .10 .25
87 Thomas Koch .10 .25
88 Emil Lundberg .10 .25
89 Jonas Nordquist .10 .25
90 Fredrik Hynning .10 .25
91 Karl Fabricius .10 .25
92 Michael Zajkowski .10 .25
93 Hans Jonsson .10 .25
94 Tobias Enstrom .10 .25
95 Jesper Damgaard .10 .25
96 Oscar Hedman .10 .25
97 Daniel Sedin .40 1.00
98 Mattias Weinhandl .10 .25
99 Andreas Salomonsson .10 .25
100 Markus Naslund .75 2.00
101 Henrik Sedin .40 1.00
102 Peter Forsberg 2.00 5.00
103 Morten Green .10 .25
104 Per Svartvadet .10 .25
105 Magnus Gastrin .10 .25
106 Calle Bergstrom .10 .25
107 Peter Nolander .10 .25
108 Jonathan Granstrom .10 .25
109 Hakan Bogg .10 .25
110 Shawn Horcoff .40 1.00
111 Jonas Westerling .10 .25
112 Marian Hossa .75 2.00
113 Marcus Eriksson .10 .25
114 Magnus Sandberg .10 .25
115 Kenneth Bergkvist .10 .25
116 Anders Nilsson .10 .25
117 Mikael Simons .10 .25
118 Magnus Lindquist .10 .25
119 Bert Robertsson .10 .25
120 Nicklas Grossman .10 .25
121 Dick Tarnstrom .10 .25
122 Petri Liimatainen .10 .25
123 Timmy Pettersson .10 .25
124 Jan Huokko .10 .25
125 Anders Burstrom .10 .25
126 Robert Carlsson .10 .25
127 Nicklas Bergfors .40 1.00
128 Erik Norback .10 .25
129 Gabriel Karlsson .10 .25
130 Jörgen Bemstrom .10 .25
131 Miikka Kiprusoff 1.25 3.00
132 Johan Svedberg .10 .25
133 Sanny Lindstrom .10 .25
134 Kalle Koskinen .10 .25
135 Mats Hansson .10 .25
136 Teemu Aalto .10 .25
137 Christian Soderstrom .10 .25
138 Robert Carlsson .10 .25
139 Niklas Nordgren .20 .50
140 Per Hallin .10 .25
141 Kristian Gahn .10 .25
142 Henrik Zetterberg .75 2.00
143 Magnus Nilsson .10 .25
144 Jonathan Hedstrom .10 .25
145 Markus Korhonen .10 .25
146 Daniel Johansson .10 .25
147 Martin Öhrstedt .10 .25
148 Jörgen Sundqvist .10 .25
149 Daniel Casselstahl .10 .25
150 Rodrigo Lavins .10 .25
151 Antti Aarnio .10 .25
152 Jonas Almtorp .10 .25
153 Mathias Mansson .10 .25
154 Nicklas Backstrom 4.00 10.00
155 Lars-Erik Spets .10 .25
156 Mikael Wahlberg .10 .25
157 Petter Ronnquist .10 .25
158 Teemu Lassila .10 .25
159 André Mattsson .10 .25
160 Jonas Liwing .10 .25
161 Erik Ryman .10 .25
162 Adam Andersson .10 .25
163 Jesper Bjorck .10 .25
164 Henrik Nordfeldt .10 .25
165 Johan Ejdepvist .10 .25
166 Christofer Lofberg .10 .25
167 Patric Hornqvist .10 .25
168 Fredrik Bremberg .10 .25
169 Marcus Kristofferson .10 .25
170 Per Eklund .10 .25
171 Mikael Sandberg .10 .25
172 Tommy Salo .20 .50
173 Jan-Axel Alavaara .10 .25
174 Arto Tukio .10 .25
175 Richard Demén-Willaume .10 .25
176 Ronnie Sundin .10 .25
177 Johnny Oduya .20 .50
178 Sebastian Karlsson .10 .25
179 Kirill Starkov .10 .25
180 Johan Witehall .10 .25
181 Christopher Heino-Lindberg .10 .25
182 Rami Alanko .10 .25
183 Per Hallberg .10 .25
184 Thomas Rhodin .10 .25
185 Mikael Johansson .10 .25
186 Rickard Wallin .10 .25
187 Jörgen Jonsson .10 .25
188 Fredrik Eriksson .10 .25
189 Johan Olsson .10 .25
190 Emil Kåberg .10 .25
191 Per Ledin .10 .25
192 Erik Ersberg 1.00 2.50
193 Fredrik Olausson .10 .25
194 Lars Jonsson .20 .50
195 Mika Niskanen .10 .25
196 David Petrasek .10 .25
197 Martin Thornberg .10 .25
198 David Fredriksson .10 .25
199 Björn Melin .10 .25
200 Jens Karlsson .10 .25
201 Mattias Remstam .10 .25
202 Mika Hannula .10 .25
203 Tomas Duba .10 .25
204 Elias Granat .10 .25
205 Magnus Osterby .10 .25
206 Yan Golubovsky .10 .25
207 Jan Srdinko .10 .25
208 Patrik Hucko .10 .25
209 Patrik Wallenberg .10 .25
210 Mike Watt .10 .25
211 Sebastian Meijer .10 .25
212 Jesper Ollas .10 .25
213 Niklas Broms .10 .25
214 Magnus Hedlund .10 .25
215 Oscar Steen .10 .25
216 Jimmie Ericsson .10 .25
217 Jukka Tiilikainen .10 .25
218 Jiri Bicek .10 .25
219 Jonas Fransson .10 .25
220 Andreas Pihl .10 .25
221 Mikko Luoma .10 .25
222 Victor Ringberg .10 .25
223 Tony Martensson .10 .25
224 Jonas Soling .10 .25
225 Sami Torkki .10 .25
226 Johan Lindstrom .10 .25
227 Patric Blomdahl .10 .25
228 David Rautio .10 .25
229 Mattias Modig .10 .25
230 Erik Lindberg .10 .25
231 Pekka Saravo .10 .25
232 Pavel Skrbek .10 .25
233 Per Savilahti-Nagander .10 .25
234 Johan Harju .10 .25
235 Mikael Renberg .20 .50
236 Ragnar Karlsson .10 .25
237 Vladimir Machulda .10 .25
238 Lubomir Bartecko .10 .25
239 Magnus Isaksson .10 .25
240 Christopher Königsson .10 .25
241 Karol Krizan .10 .25
242 Mattias Timander .10 .25
243 Vladimir Sicak .10 .25
244 Tobias Viklund .10 .25
245 Mattias Hellstrom .10 .25
246 Pasi Tuominen .10 .25
247 Rastislav Pavlikovsky .10 .25
248 Peter Öberg .10 .25
249 Mikael Pettersson .10 .25
250 Miloslav Horava .10 .25
251 Jan Pardavy .10 .25
252 Daniel Sperrle .10 .25
253 Petri Vehanen .10 .25
254 Peter Smrek .10 .25
255 Atvars Tribuntsovs .10 .25
256 Ross Lupaschuk .10 .25
257 Pierre Johnsson .10 .25
258 Jarno Kultanen .10 .25
259 Thomas Skogs .10 .25
260 Jordan Krestanovich .10 .25
261 Marco Tuokko .10 .25
262 Eric Johansson .10 .25
263 Kalle Kerman .10 .25
264 Peter Fabus .10 .25
265 Teemu Elomo .10 .25
266 Martin Jansson .10 .25
267 Rastislav Stana .20 .50
268 Stanislav Neckar .10 .25
269 Henrik Petre .10 .25
270 Jonathan Ericsson .10 .25
271 Daniel Ljungqvist .10 .25
272 Pasi Petrilainen .10 .25
273 Per-Åke Skroder .10 .25
274 Christoph Brandner .10 .25
275 Anze Kopitar 6.00 15.00
276 Tomas Kollar .10 .25
277 Dragan Umicevic .10 .25
278 Petr Leska .10 .25
279 Johan Asplund .10 .25
280 Mika Oksa .10 .25
281 Par Styf .10 .25
282 Carl-Johan Johansson .10 .25
283 Peter Regin .10 .25
284 Frans Nielsen .40 1.00
285 Mattias Wennerberg .10 .25
286 Peter Strom .10 .25
287 Valeri Krykov .10 .25
288 Fredrik Warg .10 .25

2005-06 Swedish SHL Elitset Autographed Jerseys

These cards are not priced due to lack of market activity.

GWAKO Kristofer Ottosson
GWAMK Marcus Kristoffersson

2005-06 Swedish SHL Elitset Catchers

COMPLETE SET (12) 40.00 80.00
STATED ODDS 1:16 SER. 2 PACKS
1 Johan Holmqvist 3.00 8.00

2 Teemu Lassila 3.00 8.00
3 Tommy Salo 3.00 8.00
4 Daniel Henriksson 3.00 8.00
5 Stefan Liv 4.00 10.00
6 Johan Backlund 3.00 8.00
7 Fredrik Norrena 4.00 10.00
8 David Rautio 3.00 8.00
9 Karol Krizan 3.00 8.00
10 Petri Vehanen 3.00 8.00
11 Rastislav Stana 4.00 10.00
12 Mika Oksa 3.00 8.00

2005-06 Swedish SHL Elitset Catchers Gold

These parallel cards are not priced due to lack of market information.

COMPLETE SET (12)
STATED ODDS 1:120 SER. 2 PACKS

2005-06 Swedish SHL Elitset Gold

COMPLETE SET (288)
NOT PRICED DUE TO SCARCITY

2005-06 Swedish SHL Elitset Icons

COMPLETE SET (9) 15.00 30.00
STATED ODDS 1:32 SER. 2 PACKS
1 Peter Hammarström 2.00 5.00
2 Jörgen Jönsson 2.00 5.00
3 Mathias Johansson 2.00 5.00
4 Thomas Johansson 2.00 5.00
5 Jonas Johnsson 2.00 5.00
6 Kristian Gahn 2.00 5.00
7 Ove Molin 2.00 5.00
8 Per Gustafsson 2.00 5.00
9 Fredrik Bremberg 2.00 5.00

2005-06 Swedish SHL Elitset Playmakers

COMPLETE SET (12) 25.00 60.00
STATED ODSS 1:32 SER. 1 PACKS
1 Mikael Lind 2.00 5.00
2 Marcus Nilson 2.00 5.00
3 Niklas Andersson 2.00 5.00
4 Daniel Alfredsson 4.00 10.00
5 Jörgen Jönsson 2.00 5.00
6 Johan Davidsson 2.00 5.00
7 Brendan Morrison 2.00 5.00
8 Daniel Sedin 3.00 8.00
9 Henrik Sedin 3.00 8.00
10 Marian Hossa 6.00 15.00
11 Scott Thornton 2.00 5.00
12 Henrik Zetterberg 6.00 15.00

2005-06 Swedish SHL Elitset Rookies

COMPLETE SET (9) 12.00 30.00
STATED ODDS 1:32 SER. 2 PACKS
1 Alexander Ribbenstrand 1.50 4.00
2 Anton Axelsson 1.50 4.00
3 Christopher Heino-Lindberg 1.50 4.00
4 Erik Andersson 1.50 4.00
5 Mattias Ritola 1.50 4.00
6 Robin Lindqvist 1.50 4.00
7 Tommy Enström 1.50 4.00
8 Jens Jakobs 1.50 4.00
9 Anton Strålman 2.50 6.00

2005-06 Swedish SHL Elitset Series One Jerseys

COMPLETE SET (4)
STATED PRINT RUN 35 #'d SETS
NOT PRICED DUE TO SCARCITY
1 Stefan Liv
2 Per Svartvadet
3 Thomas Johansson
4 Henrik Lundqvist

2005-06 Swedish SHL Elitset Series One Signatures

COMPLETE SET (15) 100.00 200.00
RANDOM INSERTS IN PACKS
1 Ulf Soderstoöm 6.00 15.00
2 Tim Eriksson 6.00 15.00
3 Petri Liimatainen 6.00 15.00
4 Nicklas Grossman 6.00 15.00
5 Oscar Hedman 6.00 15.00
6 Tobias Viklund 6.00 15.00
7 Johan Davidsson 6.00 15.00
8 Ola Svanberg 6.00 15.00
9 Anders Huusko 6.00 15.00
10 Jonas Hoglund 6.00 15.00
11 Daniel Henriksson 6.00 15.00
12 Johan Fransson 6.00 15.00
13 Karl Fabricius 6.00 15.00
14 Gusten Tornqvist 6.00 15.00
15 Christopher Thorn 6.00 15.00

2005-06 Swedish SHL Elitset Series Two Jerseys

COMPLETE SET (4)
PRINT RUN 35 SER.#'d SETS
NOT PRICED DUE TO SCARCITY
GWFN Fredrik Norrena
GWJD Johan Davidsson
GWJJ Jorgen Jonsson
GWKO Kristofer Ottosson

2005-06 Swedish SHL Elitset Series Two Signatures

The short printed autographs are not priced due to a lack of market activity.

1 Mathias Mansson SP
2 Mikael Wahlberg SP
3 Adam Andersson 6.00 15.00
4 Patrick Thoresen 8.00 20.00
5 Niklas Andersson 6.00 15.00
6 Magnus Kahnberg 6.00 15.00
7 Tomi Kallio 8.00 20.00
8 Mathias Johansson 6.00 15.00
9 Jesper Mattson 6.00 15.00
10 Thomas Rhodin 6.00 15.00
11 Per Gustafsson 6.00 15.00
12 Stefan Liv 10.00 25.00
13 [illegible] 6.00 15.00
14 Tomas Duba 6.00 15.00
15 Orjan Lindmark 6.00 15.00
16 Niklas Persson 6.00 15.00
17 Fredrik Emwall 6.00 15.00
18 Tony Martensson 6.00 15.00
19 Fredrik Norrena 8.00 20.00
20 Lubomir Bartecko 6.00 15.00
21 David Rautio 6.00 15.00
22 Mikael Renberg 10.00 25.00
23 Christoph Brandner 6.00 15.00
24 Anze Kopitar 75.00 125.00
25 Jan Huokko 6.00 15.00
26 Peter Strom 6.00 15.00
27 Christian Soderstrom 6.00 15.00
28 Mattias Wennerberg 6.00 15.00
29 Mats Hansson SP
30 Henrik Lundqvist SP
31 Jöörgen Jonsson SP
32 Joel Lundqvist SP

2005-06 Swedish SHL Elitset Star Potential

COMPLETE SET (18) 15.00 40.00
STATED ODSS 1:8 SER. 1 PACKS
1 Niklas Andersson .75 2.00
2 Nicklas Backstrom 2.50 6.00
3 Robert Nilsson .75 2.00
4 Christopher Thorn 1.50 4.00
5 Loui Eriksson 1.50 4.00
6 Henrik Lundqvist 4.00 10.00
7 Robin Jonsson .75 2.00
8 Ola Svanberg .75 2.00
9 Tony Martensson .75 2.00
10 Johan Fransson .75 2.00
11 Tobias Enstrom .75 2.00
12 Oscar Hedman .75 2.00
13 Jonathan Granstrom .75 2.00
14 Nicklas Bergfors 1.50 4.00
15 Dragan Umisevic .75 2.00
16 Linus Videll .75 2.00
17 Yared Hagos .75 2.00
18 Mats Hansson .75 2.00

2005-06 Swedish SHL Elitset Stoppers

COMPLETE SET (12) 30.00 75.00
STATED ODDS 1:16 SER. 1 PACKS
1 Johan Holmqvist 3.00 8.00
2 Jose Theodore 6.00 15.00
3 Rolf Wanhainen 2.00 5.00
4 Henrik Lundqvist 6.00 15.00
5 Martin Gerber 3.00 8.00
6 Daniel Henriksson 2.00 5.00
7 Stefan Liv 3.00 8.00
8 Fredrik Norrena 3.00 8.00
9 Tommy Salo 2.00 5.00
10 Tero Leinonen 2.00 5.00
11 Rastislav Stana 2.00 5.00
12 Miikka Kiprusoff 6.00 15.00

2005-06 Swedish SHL Elitset Teammates

COMPLETE SET (12) 8.00 20.00
STATED ODDS 1:8 SER. 2 PACKS
1 Andreas Dackell .75 2.00
Mikael Lind
2 Nichlas Falk .75 2.00
Patrick Thoresen
3 Jonas Höglund .75 2.00
Pelle Prestberg
4 Niklas Andersson .75 2.00
Tomi Kallio
5 Johan Davidsson .75 2.00
Mathias Remstam
6 Niklas Person .75 2.00
Patrik Wallenberg
7 Fredrik Emwall .75 2.00
Ulf Södorström
8 Karl Fabricius 1.25 3.00
Mikael Renberg
9 Andreas Salomonsson .75 2.00
Per Svartvadet
10 Anders Nilsson .75 2.00
Kalle Kerman
11 Jörgen Bemström .75 2.00
Timmy Pettersson
12 Robert Carlsson .75 2.00
Valeri Krykov

2006-07 Swedish SHL Elitset

COMPLETE SET (288) 25.00 50.00
1 Johan Holmqvist .40 1.00
2 Daniel Johansson .10 .25
3 Tommy Södin .10 .25
4 Jörgen Sundqvist .10 .25
5 Rodrigo Lavins .10 .25
6 Henrik Malmström .10 .25
7 Jonas Almtorp .10 .25
8 Andreas Dackel .10 .25
9 Mathias Månsson .10 .25
10 Ove Molin .10 .25
11 Lars-Erik Spets .10 .25
12 Mikael Lind .10 .25
13 Petter Rönnquist .10 .25
14 Ronnie Pettersson .10 .25
15 Alexander Ribbenstrand .10 .25
16 Jonas Liwing .10 .25
17 Jesper Björck .10 .25
18 Henrik Nordfeldt .10 .25
19 Johan Eneqvist .10 .25
20 Nichlas Falk .10 .25
21 Christofer Löfberg .10 .25
22 Patric Hörnqvist .10 .25
23 Jimmie Olvestad .10 .25
24 Patrick Thoresen .60 1.50
25 Per Eklund .10 .25
26 Mikael Sandberg .10 .25
27 Tom Koivisto .10 .25
28 Antti-Jussi Niemi .10 .25
29 Arto Tukio .10 .25
30 Richard Demen-Willaume .10 .25
31 Johnny Oduya .30 .75
32 Magnus Kahnberg .10 .25
33 Peter Högardh .10 .25
34 Kirill Starkov .10 .25
35 Joel Lundqvist .60 1.50
36 Jonas Esbjörs .10 .25
37 Niklas Andersson .10 .25
38 Martin Plass .10 .25
39 Tomi Kallio .10 .25
40 Daniel Henriksson .10 .25
41 Rami Alanko .10 .25
42 Robin Jonsson .10 .25
43 Jonas Frögren .10 .25
44 Thomas Rhodin .10 .25
45 Jesper Mattsson .10 .25
46 Jonas Höglund .20 .50
47 Rickard Wallin .10 .25
48 Mathias Johansson .10 .25
49 Peter Nordström .10 .25
50 Jörgen Jönsson .10 .25
51 Per Ledin .10 .25
52 Pelle Prestberg .10 .25
53 Stefan Liv .40 1.00
54 Fredrik Olausson .10 .25
55 Per Gustafsson .10 .25
56 Ola Svanberg .10 .25
57 David Petrasek .10 .25
58 Johan Halvardsson .10 .25
59 Martin Thörnberg .10 .25
60 Erik Andersson .10 .25
61 David Fredriksson .10 .25
62 Andreas Karlsson .10 .25
63 Björn Melin .10 .25
64 Mattias Remstam .10 .25
65 Johan Davidsson .10 .25
66 Stefan Pettersson .10 .25
67 Mika Hannula .10 .25
68 Jonas Fransson .10 .25
69 Mikko Luoma .10 .25
70 Magnus Johansson .10 .25
71 Christoffer Norgren .10 .25
72 Jyrki Välivaara .10 .25
73 Tony Mårtensson .10 .25
74 Jonas Soling .10 .25
75 Ulf Söderström .10 .25
76 Tim Eriksson .10 .25
77 Sami Torkki .10 .25
78 Fredrik Emwall .10 .25
79 Jussi Tarvainen .10 .25
80 Johan Lindström .10 .25
81 Mikael Håkansson .10 .25
82 David Rautio .10 .25
83 Johan Fransson .10 .25
84 Erik Lindberg .10 .25
85 Jan Sandström .10 .25
86 Pekka Saravo .10 .25
87 Thomas Koch .10 .25
88 Emil Lundberg .10 .25
89 Fredrik Hynning .10 .25
90 Mikael Renberg .20 .50
91 Ragnar Karlsson .10 .25
92 Vladimir Machulda .10 .25
93 Lubomir Bartecko .10 .25
94 Robin Lindqvist .10 .25
95 Gustaf Wesslau .10 .25
96 Edvin Frylen .10 .25
97 Jan Öberg .10 .25
98 Juha Riihijärvi .10 .25
99 Mikael Wahlberg .10 .25
100 Robert Tomik .10 .25
101 Markus Matthiasson .10 .25
102 Karol Krizan .10 .25
103 Mattias Timander .10 .25
104 Hans Jonsson .10 .25
105 Tobias Enström .10 .25
106 Jesper Damgaard .10 .25
107 Oscar Hedman .10 .25
108 Tobias Viklund .10 .25
109 Pasi Tuominen .10 .25
110 Morten Green .10 .25
111 Andreas Salomonsson .10 .25
112 Peter Öberg .10 .25
113 Mikael Pettersson .10 .25
114 Per Svartvadet .10 .25
115 Magnus Gästrin .10 .25
116 Petri Vehanen .10 .25
117 Atvars Tribuntsovs .10 .25
118 Jarno Kultanen .10 .25
119 Thomas Skogs .10 .25
120 Calle Bergström .10 .25
121 Eric Johansson .10 .25
122 Kenneth Bergqvist .10 .25
123 Andreas Nilsson .10 .25
124 Teemu Elomo .10 .25
125 Martin Jansson .10 .25
126 Mikael Simons .10 .25
127 Andreas Hadelöv .10 .25
128 Fredrik Bergqvist .10 .25
129 Libor Prochazka .10 .25
130 Johan Ramstedt .10 .25
131 Pontus Petterström .10 .25
132 Daniel Welser .10 .25
133 Brett Harkins .10 .25
134 Johan Asplund .10 .25
135 Anton Strålman .40 1.00
136 Carl-Johan Johansson .10 .25
137 Peter Regin .10 .25
138 Frans Nielsen .40 1.00
139 Per Hallin .10 .25
140 Kristian Gahn .10 .25
141 Magnus Nilsson .10 .25
142 Mattias Wennerberg .10 .25
143 Peter Ström .10 .25
144 Fredrik Warg .10 .25
145 Robert Kristan .10 .25
146 Daniel Sperrle .20 .50
147 Antti Hulkkonen .10 .25
148 Nicholas Angell .10 .25
149 Peter Nolander .10 .25
150 Daniel Casselståhl .10 .25
151 Daniel Hermansson .10 .25
152 Nicklas Bäckström 2.00 5.00
153 Johannes Salmonsson .10 .25
154 Björn Danielsson .10 .25
155 Mads Hansen .10 .25
156 Sebastian Karlsson .10 .25
157 Jiri Bicek .10 .25
158 Daniel Larsson .10 .25
159 Teemu Lassila .20 .50
160 Martin Lindman .10 .25
161 Thomas Johansson .10 .25
162 Timmy Pettersson .10 .25
163 Fredrik Ericson .10 .25
164 Kristofer Ottosson .10 .25
165 Christian Eklund .10 .25
166 Fredrik Bremberg .10 .25
167 Pär Bäcker .10 .25
168 Morten Ask .10 .25
169 Nicklas Danielsson .10 .25
170 Dragan Umicevic .10 .25
171 Tommy Salo .20 .50
172 Jan-Axel Alavaara .10 .25
173 Markus Seikola .10 .25
174 Ronnie Sundin .10 .25
175 Tomi Pettinen .10 .25
176 Jonas Ahnelöv .10 .25
177 Johan Fransson .10 .25
178 Fredrik Johansson .10 .25
179 Karl Fabricius .10 .25
180 Anton Axelsson .10 .25
181 Steve Kariya .40 1.00
182 Johan Ryno .10 .25
183 Christopher Heino-Lindberg .20 .50
184 Atte Pentikäinen .10 .25
185 Janne Niskala .10 .25
186 Esa Pirnes .10 .25
187 Per Åslund .10 .25
188 Emil Kåberg .10 .25
189 Christian Söderström .10 .25
190 Mikael Johansson .10 .25
191 Erik Ersberg .10 .25
192 Scott Langkow .20 .50
193 Johan Åkerman .10 .25
194 Daniel Grillfors .10 .25
195 Pasi Puistola .10 .25
196 Lance Ward .10 .25
197 Erik Andersson .10 .25
198 Andreas Falk .10 .25
199 Jari Kauppila .10 .25
200 Timo Vertala .10 .25
201 Jukka Voutilainen .10 .25
202 Andreas Jämtin .10 .25
203 Roman Cechmanek .20 .50
204 Christopher Kelleher .10 .25
205 Carl Gunnarsson .10 .25
206 Andreas Holmqvist .10 .25
207 Oscar Ackeström .10 .25
208 Joakim Eriksson .10 .25
209 Martin Samuelsson .20 .50
210 Niklas Olausson .10 .25
211 Patric Blomdahl .10 .25
212 Tero Leinonen .10 .25
213 Pavel Skrbek .10 .25
214 Roger Åkerström .10 .25
215 Per Savilahti-Nagander .10 .25
216 Jaroslav Obsut .10 .25
217 Tomas Wallgren .10 .25
218 Martin Chabada .10 .25
219 Jesse Niinimäki .10 .25
220 Anders Burström .10 .25
221 Kalle Kerman .10 .25
222 Johan Harju .10 .25
223 Viktor Lindgren .10 .25
224 Tomas Surovy .20 .50
225 Rastislav Stana .10 .25
226 Patrik Hersley .10 .25
227 Johan Björk .10 .25
228 Ross Lupaschuk .10 .25
229 Simon Skoog .10 .25
230 Andreas Thuresson .10 .25
231 Lasse Pirjetä .10 .25
232 Milan Bartovic .10 .25
233 Nicklas Jadeland .10 .25
234 Marcus Paulsson .10 .25
235 Mikael Johansson .10 .25
236 David Moravec .10 .25
237 Linus Fagemo .10 .25
238 Michal Zajkowski .10 .25
239 Tommy Wargh .10 .25
240 Adam Andersson .10 .25
241 Mattias Hellström .10 .25
242 Per-Åke Skröder .10 .25
243 Oscar Steen .10 .25
244 Niklas Sundström .10 .25
245 Miloslav Horava .10 .25
246 Johan Nilsson .10 .25
247 Robert Döme .10 .25
248 Juha Pitkämäki .10 .25
249 Mikko Rämö .10 .25
250 Tomas Slovak .10 .25
251 Pierre Johnsson .10 .25
252 Antti Bruun .10 .25
253 Mikko Kurvinen .10 .25
254 Miroslav Blatek .10 .25
255 Håkan Bogg .10 .25
256 Anders Bastiansen .10 .25
257 Marco Tuokko .10 .25
258 Ryan Jardine .10 .25
259 Eric Beaudoin .10 .25
260 Pavel Brendl .20 .50
261 Dave Stathos .10 .25
262 Per Helmersson .10 .25
263 Per-Anton Lundström .10 .25
264 Fredrik Lindgren .10 .25
265 Daniel Sondell .10 .25
266 Kari Haakana .10 .25
267 Richard Lintner .10 .25
268 Magnus Wernblom .10 .25
269 Fredrik Krekula .10 .25
270 Jason King .20 .50
271 Jimmie Eriksson .10 .25
272 Anders Söderberg .10 .25
273 Marcus Kristoffersson .10 .25
274 Markku Tähtinen .10 .25
275 Fredrik Öberg .10 .25
276 Johan Backlund .10 .25
277 Sanny Lindström .10 .25
278 Kalle Koskinen .10 .25
279 Kimmo Lotvonen .10 .25
280 Petri Kokko .10 .25
281 Pär Styf .10 .25
282 Oscar Sundh .10 .25
283 Peter Nylander .10 .25
284 Robert Carlsson .10 .25
285 Johan Andersson .10 .25
286 Timo Pärssinen .10 .25
287 Riku Hahl .20 .50
288 Jonathan Hedström .10 .25
NNO Nicklas Backstrom ROY Gold
NNO Nicklas Backstrom ROY Silver

2006-07 Swedish SHL Elitset Goal Patrol

1 Johan Holmqvist 5.00 12.00
2 Markus Korhonen 4.00 10.00
3 Teemu Lassila 4.00 10.00
4 Tommy Salo 4.00 10.00
5 Mikael Sandberg 4.00 10.00
6 Christopher Heino-Lindberg 4.00 10.00
7 Daniel Henriksson 4.00 10.00
8 Stefan Liv 5.00 12.00
9 Tomas Duba 4.00 10.00
10 Jonas Fransson 4.00 10.00
11 Fredrik Norrena 6.00 15.00
12 Mattias Modig 4.00 10.00
13 David Rautio 4.00 10.00
14 Karol Krizan 4.00 10.00
15 Daniel Sperrle 4.00 10.00
16 Petri Vehanen 4.00 10.00
17 Magnus Lindquist 4.00 10.00
18 Mika Oksa 4.00 10.00

2006-07 Swedish SHL Elitset In The Crease

1 Johan Holmqvist 5.00 12.00
2 Teemu Lassila 4.00 10.00
3 Tommy Salo 4.00 10.00
4 Daniel Henriksson 4.00 10.00
5 Stefan Liv 5.00 12.00
6 Fredrik Norrena 6.00 15.00
7 Mattias Modig 4.00 10.00
8 Karol Krizan 4.00 10.00
9 Petri Vehanen 4.00 10.00

2006-07 Swedish SHL Elitset Performers

1 Nicklas Bäckström 6.00 15.00
2 Dragan Umicevic 1.50 4.00
3 Niklas Andersson 1.50 4.00
4 Tomi Kallio 1.50 4.00
5 Mathias Johansson 1.50 4.00
6 Mika Hannula 1.50 4.00
7 Johan Davidsson 1.50 4.00
8 Tony Mårtensson 1.50 4.00
9 Mikael Håkansson 1.50 4.00
10 Mikael Renberg 2.00 5.00
11 Lasse Pirjetä 1.50 4.00
12 Juha Riihijärvi 1.50 4.00
13 Per Svartvadet 1.50 4.00
14 Pavel Brendl 1.50 4.00
15 Magnus Wernblom 1.50 4.00
16 Anders Söderberg 1.50 4.00
17 Timo Pärssinen 1.50 4.00
18 Jonathan Hedström 1.50 4.00

2006-07 Swedish SHL Elitset Playmakers

1 Mikael Lind 1.50 4.00
2 Fredrik Bremberg 1.50 4.00
3 Niklas Andersson 1.50 4.00
4 Joel Lundqvist 2.50 6.00
5 Jörgen Jönsson 1.50 4.00
6 Rickard Wallin 1.50 4.00
7 Andreas Karlsson 1.50 4.00
8 Tony Mårtensson 1.50 4.00
9 Lubomir Bartecko 1.50 4.00
10 Andreas Salomonsson 1.50 4.00
11 Hågan Bogg 1.50 4.00
12 Frans Nielsen 2.50 6.00

2007-08 Swedish Lulea Postcards

COMPLETE SET (21) 15.00 30.00
1 Robin Olsson .75 2.00
2 Mikko Pukka .75 2.00
3 Jan Sandstrom .75 2.00
4 Johan Ejdepalm .75 2.00
5 Tommi Miettinen .75 2.00
6 Pekka Saravo .75 2.00
7 Pavel Skrbek .75 2.00
8 Martin Chabada .75 2.00
9 Cory Larose .75 2.00
10 Anders Burstrom .75 2.00
11 Johan Harju .75 2.00
12 Lubos Bartecko .75 2.00
13 Mats Lavander .75 2.00
14 Robin Lindqvist .75 2.00
15 Viktor Lindgren .75 2.00
16 Linus Omark .75 2.00
17 Mikael Lidhammer .75 2.00
18 Per Savilahti-Nagander .75 2.00
19 Mattias Modig .75 2.00
20 Jaroslav Obsut .75 2.00
21 Gusten Tornqvist .75 2.00

2007-08 Swedish Malmo Red Hawks

COMPLETE SET (23) 15.00 30.00
1 Robin Weihager .75 2.00
2 Johan Bjork .75 2.00
3 Daniel Casselstahl .75 2.00
4 Jonathan Sjolund .75 2.00
5 Jan Oberg .75 2.00
6 Robin Alvarez .75 2.00
7 Kim Johansson .75 2.00
8 Martin Samuelsson .75 2.00
9 Marcus Paulsson .75 2.00
10 Mikael Wahlberg .75 2.00
11 Carl Soderberg 1.25 3.00
12 Emil Lundgren .75 2.00
13 Antti Bruun .75 2.00
14 Jani Hurme 1.25 3.00
15 Jyrki Valivaara .75 2.00
16 Calle Steen .75 2.00
17 Mikko Eloranta .75 2.00
18 Andreas Bystrom .75 2.00
19 Ville Nieminen 1.25 3.00
20 Patrik Lundh .75 2.00
21 Jens Svensson .75 2.00
22 Fredrik Eriksson .75 2.00
23 Tommas Wallgren .75 2.00

2007-08 Swedish SHL Elitset

Issued in two 144-card series.

COMPLETE SET (288) 30.00 60.00
1 Daniel Sperrle .10 .25
2 Daniel Johansson .10 .25
3 Antti Hulkkonen .10 .25
4 Nicholas Angell .10 .25
5 Peter Nolander .10 .25
6 Mathias Månsson .10 .25
7 Daniel Hermansson .10 .25
8 Johannes Salmonsson .10 .25
9 Björn Danielsson .10 .25
10 Mads Hanssen .10 .25
11 Sebastian Karlsson .10 .25
12 Daniel Larsson .10 .25
13 Ronnie Pettersson .10 .25
14 Dennis Persson .10 .25
15 Thomas Johansson .10 .25
16 Jonas Liwing .10 .25
17 Timmy Pettersson .10 .25
18 Fredrik Ericson .10 .25
19 Kristofer Ottosson .10 .25
20 Nichlas Falk .10 .25
21 Jimmie Ölvestad .10 .25
22 Christian Eklund .10 .25
23 Pär Bäcker .10 .25
24 Morten Ask .10 .25
25 Nicklas Danielsson .10 .25
26 Joel Gistedt .20 .50
27 Ronnie Sundin .10 .25
28 Fredrik Johansson .10 .25
29 Karl Fabricius .10 .25
30 Steve Kariya .40 1.00
31 Jonas Esbjörs .10 .25
32 Niklas Andersson .10 .25
33 Martin Plüss .10 .25
34 Johan Ryno .10 .25
35 Tomi Kallio .10 .25
36 Christopher Heino-Lindberg .10 .25
37 Jonas Frögren .10 .25
38 Thomas Rhodin .10 .25
39 Pelle Prestberg .10 .25
40 Jesper Mattsson .10 .25
41 Esa Pirnes .10 .25
42 Jonas Höglund .10 .25
43 Peter Nordström .10 .25
44 Emil Kåberg .10 .25
45 Christian Söderström .10 .25
46 Mathias Johansson .10 .25
47 Mikael Johansson .10 .25
48 Erik Ersberg .10 .25
49 Johan Åkerman .10 .25
50 Per Gustafsson .10 .25
51 Pasi Puistola .10 .25
52 David Petrasek .10 .25
53 Martin Thörnberg .10 .25
54 Andreas Falk .10 .25
55 David Fredriksson .10 .25
56 Jari Kauppila .10 .25
57 Timo Vertala .10 .25
58 Jukka Voutilainen .10 .25
59 Andreas Jämtin .10 .25
60 Johan Davidsson .10 .25
61 Jonas Fransson .10 .25
62 Magnus Johansson .10 .25
63 Tony Mårtensson .10 .25
64 Ulf Söderström .10 .25
65 Joakim Eriksson .10 .25
66 Tim Eriksson .10 .25
67 Niklas Olausson .10 .25
68 Sami Torkki .10 .25
69 Fredrik Emwall .10 .25
70 Johan Lindström .10 .25
71 Mikael Håkansson .10 .25
72 Patric Blomdahl .10 .25
73 Jan Sandström .10 .25
74 Pekka Saravo .10 .25
75 Pavel Skrbek .10 .25
76 Jaroslav Obsut .10 .25
77 Tomas Wallgren .10 .25
78 Martin Chabada .10 .25
79 Jesse Niinimäki .10 .25
80 Andreas Burström .10 .25
81 Kalle Kerman .10 .25
82 Johan Harju .10 .25
83 Robin Lindqvist .10 .25
84 Viktor Lindgren .10 .25
85 Linus Omark .10 .25
86 Karol Krizan .10 .25
87 Mattias Timander .10 .25
88 Hans Jonsson .10 .25
89 Oscar Hedman .10 .25
90 Adam Andersson .10 .25
91 Mattias Hellström .10 .25
92 Per-Åke Skröder .10 .25
93 Andreas Salomonsson .10 .25
94 Peter Öberg .10 .25
95 Mikael Pettersson .10 .25
96 Niklas Sundström .10 .25
97 Miloslav Horava .10 .25
98 Magnus Gästrin .10 .25
99 Juha Pitkämäki .10 .25
100 Pierre Johnsson .10 .25
101 Jarno Kultanen .10 .25
102 Thomas Skogs .10 .25
103 Antti Bruun .10 .25
104 Anders Bastiansen .10 .25
105 Marco Tuokko .10 .25
106 Eric Beaudoin .10 .25
107 Kenneth Bergqvist .10 .25
108 Anders Nilsson .10 .25
109 Teemu Elomo .10 .25
110 Martin Jansson .10 .25
111 Andreas Hadelöv .10 .25
112 Per-Anton Lundström .10 .25
113 Fredrik Lindgren .10 .25
114 Kari Haakana .10 .25
115 Fredrik Krekula .10 .25
116 Johan Ramstedt .10 .25
117 Pontus Pettersson .10 .25
118 Jimmie Eriksson .10 .25
119 Anders Söderberg .10 .25
120 Marcus Kristoffersson .10 .25
121 Fredrik Öberg .10 .25
122 Jhonas Enroth .40 1.00
123 Martin Thelander .10 .25
124 Daniel Josefsson .10 .25
125 Fredric Andersson .10 .25
126 Robert Carlsson .10 .25
127 Jörgen Bemström .10 .25
128 Tony Lagerström .10 .25
129 Ragnar Karlsson .10 .25
130 Tomas Kollar .10 .25
131 Johan Sjödell-Wiklander .10 .25
132 Andrée Persson .10 .25
133 Johan Backlund .10 .25
134 Anton Strålman .75 2.00
135 Sanny Lindström .10 .25
136 Kimmo Lotvonen .10 .25
137 Petri Kokko .10 .25
138 Pär Styf .10 .25
139 Peter Regin .10 .25
140 Johan Andersson .10 .25
141 Björn Svensson .10 .25
142 Timo Pärssinen .10 .25
143 Riku Hahl .10 .50
144 Jonathan Hedström .20 .50
145 Markus Korhonen .10 .25
146 Tommy Sjödin .10 .25
147 Niclas Andersén .10 .25
148 Pavel Brendl .20 .50
149 Andreas Dackell .10 .25
150 Daniel Widing .10 .25
151 Markus Kankaanperä .10 .25
152 Alexander Sundström .10 .25
153 Lars Erik Spets .10 .25
154 Jusso Hietanen .10 .25
155 Ove Molin .10 .25
156 Janne Hauhtonen .10 .25
157 Jörgen Sundqvist .10 .25
158 Daniel Larsson .10 .25
159 David Printz .20 .50
160 Fredrik Bremberg .10 .25
161 Patric Hörnqvist .10 1.00
162 Dick Axelsson .10 .25
163 Andreas Engqvist .10 .25
164 Niklas Anger .10 .25
165 Edvin Frylén .10 .25
166 Oscar Eklund .10 .25
167 Mark Owuya .40 1.00
168 Jiri Marusak .10 .25
169 Ari Ahonen .40 1.00
170 Toni Söderholm .10 .25
171 Jonas Johnson .10 .25
172 Jonas Nordquist .10 .25
173 Philip Larsen .10 .25
174 Fredrik Pettersson .10 .25
175 Magnus Kahnberg .10 .25
176 Antti-Jussi Niemi .10 .25
177 Jonas Ahnelöv .10 .25
178 Andreas Holmqvist .10 .25
179 Johan Andersson .10 .25
180 Tomi Kallio .10 .25
181 Oscar Ackeström .10 .25
182 Michael Holmqvist .10 .25
183 Jonas Gustavsson .10 .25
184 Johan Motin .10 .25
185 Jens Skålberg .10 .25
186 Dominik Granak .10 .25
187 Rickard Wallin .10 .25
188 Per Åslund .10 .25
189 Jörgen Jönsson .10 .25
190 Martin Johansson .10 .25
191 Eero Somervuori .10 .25
192 Fabian Brunnström .10 2.50
193 Dave Cullen .10 .25
194 Stefan Liv .40 1.00
195 Mikko Luoma .10 .25
196 Daniel Grillfors .10 .25
197 Per Ledin .10 .25
198 Stefan Pettersson .10 .25
199 Jan Hrdina .10 .25
200 Jonas Johansson .10 .25
201 Andreas Jämtin .10 .25
202 Lance Ward .10 .25
203 Andreas Falk .10 .25
204 Andreas Andersson .10 .25
205 Rastislav Stana .10 .25
206 Fredrik Emvall .10 .25
207 Daniel Fernholm .10 .25
208 Calle Gunnarsson .10 .25
209 Mattias Weinhandl .10 .50
210 Ville Vahalahti .10 .25
211 Niklas Persson .10 .25
212 Patrik Zackrisson .10 .25
213 Kim Staal .10 .25
214 Tony Mårtensson .10 .25
215 Mattias Carlsson .10 .25
216 Andreas Pihl .10 .25
217 Mattias Modig .10 .25
218 Gusten Törnqvist .10 .25
219 Mikko Pukka .10 .25
220 Jan Sandström .10 .25
221 Jussi Tarvainen .10 .25
222 Tommi Miettinen .10 .25
223 Magnus Isaksson .10 .25
224 Mats Lavander .10 .25
225 Mikael Lidhammar .10 .25
226 Johan Ejdepalm .10 .25
227 Robin Olsson .10 .25
228 Michal Zajkowski .10 .25
229 Per Hållberg .10 .25
230 Victor Hedman .75 2.00
231 Tommy Wargh .10 .25
232 Pierre Hedin .10 .25
233 Magnus Wernblom .10 .25
234 Fredrik Warg .10 .25
235 Per Svartvadet .10 .25
236 Jari Tolsa .10 .25
237 Andreas Molinder .10 .25
238 Oscar Steen .10 .25
239 Lars Johansson .10 .25
240 Marco Tuokko .10 .25
241 Yared Hagos .20 .50
242 Ivan Huml .20 .50
243 Jonathan Granström .10 .25
244 Toni Dahlman .10 .25
245 Håkan Bogg .10 .25
246 Johan Lindström .10 .25
247 Tero Määttä .10 .25
248 Mikko Kurvinen .10 .25
249 Adam Andersson .10 .25
250 Martti Järventie .10 .25
251 Nicklas Dahlberg .10 .25
252 Jan Novak .10 .25
253 Christoffer Norgren .10 .25
254 Tobias Viklund .10 .25
255 Pontus Petterström .10 .25
256 Lee Goren .40 1.00
257 Thomas Larsson .10 .25

258 Mikael Renberg .40 1.00
259 Kimmo Koskenkorva .10 .25
260 Kent McDonnell .20 .50
261 Erik Andersson .10 .25
262 Erik Forssell .10 .25
263 Jimmie Ericsson .10 .25
264 Björn Bjurling .10 .25
265 Linus Klasen .10 .25
266 Stefan Gråhns .10 .25
267 Per Hallin .10 .25
268 Pär Arlbrandt .10 .25
269 Linus Videll .10 .25
270 Petri Pakaslahti .10 .25
271 Martin Cibak .10 .25
272 Jens Olsson .10 .25
273 Kristian Kudroc .10 .25
274 Jarno Kultanen .10 .25
275 Stefan Bernström .10 .25
276 Duane Harmer .10 .25
277 Magnus Åkerlund .10 .25
278 Pär Styf .10 .25
279 Anton Axelsson .10 .25
280 Oscar Sundh .10 .25
281 Jonathan Hedström .10 1.00
282 Erik Andersson .10 .25
283 Mika Pyörälä .10 .25
284 Robert Carlsson .10 .25
285 Robin Jonsson .10 .25
286 Sanny Lindström .10 .25
287 Riku Hahl .10 .25
288 Kalle Koskinen .10 .25

2007-08 Swedish SHL Elitset Complete Players

1 Nicklas Bäckström 4.00 10.00
2 Fredrik Bremberg 1.25 3.00
3 Steve Kariya 1.50 4.00
4 Martin Plüss 1.25 3.00
5 Peter Nordström 1.25 3.00
6 Andreas Jämtin 1.25 3.00
7 Johan Davidsson 1.25 3.00
8 Joakim Eriksson 1.25 3.00
9 Tony Mårtensson 1.25 3.00
10 Jaroslav Obsut 1.25 3.00
11 Tomas Surovy 1.25 3.00
12 Anders Bastiansen 1.25 3.00
13 Robert Döme 1.25 3.00
14 Per Svartvadet 1.25 3.00
15 Jimmie Eriksson 1.25 3.00
16 Linus Videll 1.25 3.00
17 Johan Backlund 1.25 3.00
18 Jonathan Hedström 2.00 5.00

2007-08 Swedish SHL Elitset Double Impact

COMPLETE SET (12) 12.00 30.00
1 Patric Hornqvist 2.00 5.00
Fredrik Bremberg
2 Tommy Sjodin 1.25 3.00
Mathias Mansson
3 Andreas Holmqvist 1.25 3.00
Michael Holmqvist
4 Per-Age Skroder 1.25 3.00
Nicklas Sundstrom
5 Tim Eriksson 1.25 3.00
Fredrik Emwall
6 Eero Somervuori 1.25 3.00
Jorgen Jonsson
7 Linus Omark 1.25 3.00
Johan Harju
8 Toni Dahlman 1.25 3.00
Juha Pitkamaki
9 Mikael Renberg 1.50 4.00
Jimmie Ericsson
10 Jhonas Enroth 2.00 5.00
Linus Klasen
11 Jonathan Hedstrom 2.00 5.00
Riku Hahl
12 Andreas Jamtin 1.25 3.00
Per Ledin

2007-08 Swedish SHL Elitset Double Jerseys

COMPLETE SET (4)
NOT PRICED DUE TO SCARCITY
1 Mikael Renberg
Fredrik Bremberg/20
2 Jorgen Jonsson
Tony Martensson/20
3 Per Svartvadet
Kristofer Ottosson/25
4 Johan Davidsson
Robert Carlsson/25

2007-08 Swedish SHL Elitset Future Watch

COMPLETE SET (12) 20.00 50.00
1 Niclas Andersén 2.50 6.00
2 Dick Axelsson 2.50 6.00
3 Philip Larsen 2.50 6.00
4 Johan Motin 2.50 6.00
5 Fredrik Pettersson 2.50 6.00
6 Patrik Zackrisson 2.50 6.00
7 Mattias Modig 2.50 6.00
8 Victor Hedman 6.00 15.00
9 Alexander Sundström 2.50 6.00
10 Thomas Larsson 2.50 6.00
11 Linus Klasen
12 Tobias Forsberg

2007-08 Swedish SHL Elitset Future Watch Gold

We have no pricing for this parallel. If you have any information, please forward it to hockeymag@beckett.com.

COMPLETE SET (12)
1 Niclas Andersén
2 Dick Axelsson
3 Philip Larsen
4 Johan Motin
5 Fredrik Pettersson
6 Patrik Zackrisson
7 Mattias Modig
8 Victor Hedman
9 Alexander Sundström
10 Thomas Larsson
11 Linus Klasen
12 Tobias Forsberg

2007-08 Swedish SHL Elitset Great Gloves

COMPLETE SET (9) 15.00 40.00
1 Daniel Sperrle 2.50 6.00
2 Daniel Larsson 2.50 6.00
3 Christopher Heino-Lindberg 2.50 6.00
4 Erik Ersberg 2.50 6.00
5 Jonas Fransson 2.50 6.00
6 Karol Krizan 2.50 6.00
7 Juha Pitkämäki 2.50 6.00
8 Andreas Hadelöv 2.50 6.00
9 Johan Backlund 2.50 6.00

2007-08 Swedish SHL Elitset Jersey Autographs

COMPLETE SET (2)
NOT PRICED DUE TO SCARCITY
1 Tony Mårtensson
2 Mikael Renberg

2007-08 Swedish SHL Elitset Jerseys

1 Kristofer Ottosson 10.00 25.00
2 Arto Tukio 10.00 25.00
3 Dennis Persson 10.00 25.00
4 Mathias Johansson 10.00 25.00
5 Stefan Liv 15.00 40.00

2007-08 Swedish SHL Elitset Signatures

1 Jimmie Ölvestad 4.00 10.00
2 Dragan Umicevic 4.00 10.00
3 Peter Nordström 4.00 10.00
4 Tero Leinonen 4.00 10.00
5 Martin Chabada 4.00 10.00
6 Johan Harju 4.00 10.00
7 Rickard Lintner 4.00 10.00
8 Johan Backlund 4.00 10.00
9 Jonathan Hedström 8.00 20.00
10 Riku Hahl 4.00 10.00
11 Timo Pärssinen 4.00 10.00
12 Mikael Johansson 4.00 10.00
13 Esa Pirnes 4.00 10.00
14 Johan Davidsson 4.00 10.00
15 Tony Mårtensson 4.00 10.00
16 Joakim Eriksson 4.00 10.00
17 Karol Krizan 4.00 10.00
18 Juha Pitkämäki 5.00 12.00
19 Mikael Simons 4.00 10.00
20 Tomas Skogs 4.00 10.00
21 Jhonas Enroth 8.00 20.00
22 Johan Sjödell-Wiklander 5.00 12.00
23 Fredrik Sonntag 4.00 10.00
24 Robert Carlsson 4.00 10.00
25 Jimmie Olvestad 4.00 10.00
26 Daniel Larsson 4.00 10.00
27 Patric Hörnqvist 6.00 15.00
28 Nicklas Sundstrom 4.00 10.00
29 Tommy Wargh 4.00 10.00
30 Andreas Falk 4.00 10.00
31 Johan Akerman 4.00 10.00
32 Johan Backlund 4.00 10.00
33 Riku Hahl 6.00 15.00
34 Oscar Sundh 4.00 10.00
35 Timo Pärssinen 4.00 10.00
36 Christian Söderström 4.00 10.00
37 Eric Beaudoin 4.00 10.00
38 Bjorn Danielsson 4.00 10.00
39 Mathias Mansson 4.00 10.00
40 Martin Chabada 4.00 10.00
41 Linus Omark 4.00 10.00
42 Johan Harju 4.00 10.00
43 Johan Ramstedt 4.00 10.00
44 Pontus Pettersson 4.00 10.00
45 Andreas Hadelöv 4.00 10.00
46 Jimmie Eriksson 4.00 10.00

2007-08 Swedish SHL Elitset Signed by the Numbers

We have no pricing for this set. If you have any information, please contact us at hockeymag@beckett.com.

1 Jimmie Olvestad
2 Dragan Umicevic
3 Tero Leinonen
4 Riku Hahl
5 Johan Backlund
6 Mikael Johansson
7 Johan Davidsson
8 Tony Mårtensson
9 Juha Pitkämäki
10 Jimmie Olvestad
11 Fredrik Bremberg
12 Linus Omark
13 Niklas Sundström
14 Johan Backlund

2007-08 Swedish SHL Elitset The Dominators

COMPLETE SET (18) 25.00 50.00
1 Pavel Brendl 2.00 5.00
2 Patric Hörnqvist 2.00 5.00
3 Jimmie Olvestad 1.50 4.00
4 Jonas Nordquist 1.50 4.00
5 Rickard Wallin 1.50 4.00
6 Martin Thornberg 1.50 4.00
7 Jan Hrdina 1.50 4.00
8 Mattias Weinhandl 1.50 4.00
9 Jan Sandström 1.50 4.00
10 Jari Tolsa 1.50 4.00
11 Niklas Sundström 1.50 4.00
12 Juha Pitkämäki 2.00 5.00
13 Fredrik Lindgren 1.50 4.00
14 Sanny Lindström 1.50 4.00
15 Per Hallin 1.50 4.00
16 Riku Hahl 2.00 5.00
17 Esa Pirnes 1.50 4.00
18 Mathias Mansson 1.50 4.00

2007-08 Swedish SHL Elitset The Guardians

COMPLETE SET (12) 30.00 75.00
1 Markus Korhonen 3.00 8.00
2 Daniel Larsson 3.00 8.00
3 Joel Gistedt 3.00 8.00
4 Stefan Liv 3.00 8.00
5 Rastislav Stana 3.00 8.00
6 Mattias Modig 3.00 8.00
7 Karol Krizan 3.00 8.00
8 Juha Pitkämäki 3.00 8.00
9 Jhonas Enroth 3.00 8.00
10 Magnus Akerlund 3.00 8.00
11 Andreas Hadelöv 3.00 8.00
12 Christopher Heino-Lindberg 3.00 8.00

2007-08 Swedish SHL Elitset The Guardians Silver

We have no pricing information on this parallel set. If you can help, drop us a line at hockeymag@beckett.com.

STATED PRINT RUN 35 COPIES
1 Markus Korhonen
2 Daniel Larsson
3 Joel Gistedt
4 Stefan Liv
5 Rastislav Slana
6 Mattias Modig
7 Karol Krizan
8 Juha Pitkämäki
9 Jhonas Enroth
10 Magnus Akerlund
11 Andreas Hadelöv
12 Christopher Heino-Lindberg

2007-08 Swedish SHL Elitset The Specialists

COMPLETE SET (9) 20.00 40.00
1 Karol Krizan 2.00 5.00
2 Juha Pitkämäki 2.50 6.00
3 Janne Niskala 2.00 5.00
4 Johan Åkerman 2.00 5.00
5 Fredrik Bremberg 2.00 5.00
6 Nicklas Bäckström 6.00 15.00
7 Fredrik Emvall 2.00 5.00
8 Tomi Kallio 2.00 5.00
9 Mikael Renberg 2.50 6.00

2007-08 Swedish SHL Elitset The Specialists Gold

We have no pricing data on this parallel set. Can you help? Drop us a line at hockeymag@beckett.com.

1 Karol Krizan
2 Juha Pitkämäki
3 Janne Niskala
4 Johan Åkerman
5 Fredrik Bremberg
6 Nicklas Bäckström
7 Fredrik Emvall
8 Tomi Kallio
9 Mikael Renberg

2007-08 Swedish SHL Elitset Wave of the Future

COMPLETE SET (9) 20.00 50.00
1 Patric Hörnqvist 4.00 10.00
2 Joel Gistedt 2.50 6.00
3 Niklas Olausson 2.50 6.00
4 Linus Omark 2.50 6.00
5 Tommy Warg 2.50 6.00
6 Lars Johansson 2.50 6.00
7 Jhonas Enroth 4.00 10.00
8 Oscar Sundh 2.50 6.00
9 Anton Strålman 5.00 12.00

2009-10 Swedish Upper Deck Victory

COMPLETE SET (250) 75.00 150.00
COMP.SET w/o SPs (200) 30.00 60.00
ROOKIE STATED ODDS 1:4
1 Ryan Getzlaf .60 1.50
2 Scott Niedermayer .25 .60
3 Jean-Sebastien Giguere .40 1.00
4 Corey Perry .40 1.00
5 Chris Pronger .30 .75
6 Bryan Little .40 1.00
7 Ilya Kovalchuk .50 1.25
8 Kari Lehtonen .40 1.00
9 Colby Armstrong .25 .60
10 Todd White .25 .60
11 Slava Kozlov .25 .60
12 Michael Ryder .30 .75
13 David Krejci .30 .75
14 Patrice Bergeron .40 1.00
15 Blake Wheeler .50 1.25
16 Zdeno Chara .25 .60
17 Phil Kessel .40 1.00
18 Tim Thomas .40 1.00
19 Marc Savard .25 .60
20 Clarke MacArthur .25 .60
21 Derek Roy .40 1.00
22 Ryan Miller .40 1.00
23 Drew Stafford .40 1.00
24 Jason Pominville .40 1.00
25 Thomas Vanek .40 1.00
26 David Moss .30 .75
27 Mike Cammalleri .30 .75
28 Jarome Iginla .75 2.00
29 Todd Bertuzzi .40 1.00
30 Dion Phaneuf .60 1.50
31 Miikka Kiprusoff .40 1.00
32 Daymond Langkow .25 .60
33 Rene Bourque .25 .60
34 Olli Jokinen .25 .60
35 Cam Ward .40 1.00
36 Ray Whitney .25 .60
37 Eric Staal .50 1.25
38 Brandon Sutter .40 1.00
39 Rod Brind'Amour .30 .75
40 Tuomo Ruutu .25 .60
41 Patrick Kane .75 2.00
42 Nikolai Khabibulin .40 1.00
43 Martin Havlat .30 .75
44 Jonathan Toews 1.00 2.50
45 Patrick Sharp .30 .75
46 Brian Campbell .30 .75
47 Kris Versteeg .50 1.25
48 John-Michael Liles .30 .75
49 Ryan Smyth .40 1.00
50 T.J. Hensick .25 .60
51 Peter Budaj .40 1.00
52 Milan Hejduk .40 1.00
53 Paul Stastny .40 1.00
54 Wojtek Wolski .25 .60
55 Jakub Voracek .40 1.00
56 Derick Brassard .40 1.00
57 Rick Nash .40 1.00
58 Steve Mason .60 1.50
59 R.J. Umberger .30 .75
60 Kristian Huselius .25 .60
61 Marty Turco .30 .75
62 Brad Richards .30 .75
63 Mike Modano .40 1.00
64 Loui Eriksson .25 .60
65 Brenden Morrow .30 .75
66 Mike Ribeiro .25 .60
67 Fabian Brunnstrom .40 1.00
68 Johan Franzen .25 .60
69 Nicklas Lidstrom .50 1.25
70 Jiri Hudler .25 .60
71 Pavel Datsyuk .40 1.00
72 Ty Conklin .30 .75
73 Marian Hossa .60 1.50
74 Tomas Holmstrom .30 .75
75 Henrik Zetterberg .75 2.00
76 Ales Kotalik .25 .60
77 Andrew Cogliano .50 1.25
78 Ales Hemsky .30 .75
79 Sheldon Souray .25 .60
80 Sam Gagner .50 1.25
81 Shawn Horcoff .25 .60
82 Dustin Penner .25 .60
83 Dwayne Roloson .30 .75
84 Michael Frolik .30 .75
85 Tomas Vokoun .40 1.00
86 Jay Bouwmeester .40 1.00
87 Nathan Horton .25 .60
88 Stephen Weiss .25 .60
89 David Booth .25 .60
90 Anze Kopitar .40 1.00
91 Jack Johnson .30 .75
92 Alexander Frolov .30 .75
93 Drew Doughty .75 2.00
94 Dustin Brown .30 .75
95 Erik Ersberg .30 .75
96 Marian Gaborik .60 1.50
97 Marek Zidlicky .25 .60
98 Mikko Koivu .40 1.00
99 Andrew Brunette .25 .60
100 Niklas Backstrom .40 1.00
101 Antti Miettinen .25 .60
102 Andrei Kostitsyn .30 .75
103 Carey Price 1.00 2.50
104 Saku Koivu .40 1.00
105 Andrei Markov .30 .75
106 Robert Lang .25 .60
107 Alex Tanguay .30 .75
108 Alex Kovalev .40 1.00
109 Max Pacioretty .40 1.00
110 Jason Arnott .25 .60
111 Dan Ellis .25 .60
112 Ryan Suter .25 .60
113 Jean-Pierre Dumont .25 .60
114 Shea Weber .30 .75
115 Martin Erat .40 1.00
116 Martin Brodeur 1.00 2.50
117 Brian Gionta .40 1.00
118 Travis Zajac .25 .60
119 Patrik Elias .30 .75
120 Scott Clemmensen .30 .75
121 Zach Parise .40 1.00
122 Josh Bailey .30 .75
123 Rick DiPietro .40 1.00
124 Doug Weight .25 .60
125 Kyle Okposo .40 1.00
126 Mark Streit .25 .60
127 Henrik Lundqvist .75 2.00
128 Scott Gomez .40 1.00
129 Wade Redden .25 .60
130 Chris Drury .30 .75
131 Marc Staal .50 1.25
132 Nikolai Zherdev .25 .60
133 Markus Naslund .40 1.00
134 Nik Antropov .25 .60
135 Daniel Alfredsson .40 1.00
136 Jason Spezza .50 1.25
137 Filip Kuba .25 .60
138 Antoine Vermette .25 .60
139 Dany Heatley .75 2.00
140 Alex Auld .30 .75
141 Mike Richards .75 2.00
142 Martin Biron .30 .75
143 Mike Knuble .40 1.00
144 Daniel Briere .40 1.00
145 Jeff Carter .40 1.00
146 Scott Hartnell .25 .60
147 Simon Gagne .40 1.00
148 Shane Doan .40 1.00
149 Peter Mueller .50 1.25
150 Mikkel Boedker .30 .75
151 Ilya Bryzgalov .30 .75
152 Kyle Turris .50 1.25
153 Chris Kunitz .40 1.00
154 Bill Guerin .25 .60
155 Petr Sykora .25 .60
156 Marc-Andre Fleury .60 1.50
157 Miroslav Satan .25 .60
158 Evgeni Malkin 1.00 2.50
159 Jordan Staal .50 1.25
160 Sidney Crosby 2.00 5.00
161 Alex Goligoski .30 .75
162 Devin Setoguchi .30 .75
163 Joe Pavelski .25 .60
164 Ryane Clowe .25 .60
165 Evgeni Nabokov .40 1.00
166 Patrick Marleau .40 1.00
167 Dan Boyle .25 .60
168 Joe Thornton .75 2.00
169 Manny Legace .30 .75
170 Paul Kariya .40 1.00
171 Patrik Berglund .75 2.00
172 Keith Tkachuk .30 .75
173 Brad Boyes .30 .75
174 Vincent Lecavalier .50 1.25
175 Vaclav Prospal .25 .60
176 Steven Stamkos 1.00 2.50
177 Martin St. Louis .40 1.00
178 Mike Smith .30 .75
179 Luke Schenn .60 1.50
180 Matt Stajan .30 .75
181 Mikhail Grabovski .30 .75
182 Vesa Toskala .40 1.00
183 Tomas Kaberle .25 .60
184 Alexei Ponikarovsky .25 .60
185 Nikolai Kulemin .30 .75
186 Kevin Bieksa .25 .60
187 Daniel Sedin .50 1.25
188 Henrik Sedin .60 1.50
189 Ryan Kesler .30 .75
190 Roberto Luongo 1.00 2.50
191 Mats Sundin .40 1.00
192 Steve Bernier .25 .60
193 Mike Green .75 2.00
194 Alexander Ovechkin 1.50 4.00
195 Nicklas Backstrom .75 2.00
196 Alexander Semin .40 1.00
197 Simeon Varlamov .75 2.00
198 Sergei Fedorov .75 2.00
199 Sidney Crosby CL 2.00 5.00
200 Alexander Ovechkin CL 1.50 4.00
201 Chris Durno .75 2.00
202 Peter Regin 1.25 3.00
203 Kevin Quick .60 1.50
204 Taylor Chorney 1.00 2.50
205 Mike Santorelli .60 1.50
206 Alexander Sulzer .60 1.50
207 Troy Bodie .75 2.00
208 Matt Beleskey 1.00 2.50
209 Kevin Westgarth .75 2.00
210 John Scott 1.00 2.50
211 Mikael Backlund 1.50 4.00
212 Byron Bitz .75 2.00
213 Matt Pelech 1.00 2.50
214 Tim Wallace .60 1.50
215 Ben Lovejoy 1.50 4.00
216 Riley Armstrong .75 2.00
217 Christian Hanson 1.25 3.00
218 Sean Collins .75 2.00
219 Riku Helenius 1.00 2.50
220 Ville Leino 1.25 3.00
221 Michal Neuvirth 2.50 6.00
222 Artem Anisimov 1.25 3.00
223 Davis Drewiske 1.00 2.50
224 David Schlemko .75 2.00
225 Luca Caputi 1.25 3.00
226 Jakub Petruzalek 1.00 2.50
227 Ryan Vesce .75 2.00
228 Jay Beagle 1.00 2.50
229 Jhonas Enroth 1.25 3.00
230 Brandon Segal .75 2.00
231 Tim Stapleton 1.00 2.50
232 Jesse Joensuu 1.25 3.00
233 John Negrin .75 2.00
234 Grant Lewis .75 2.00
235 Cal O'Reilly 1.00 2.50
236 Brian Salcido .75 2.00
237 Phil Oreskovic 1.00 2.50
238 Kris Chucko .75 2.00
239 Joel Rechlicz 1.00 2.50
240 Andrew MacDonald .75 2.00
241 Antti Niemi 3.00 8.00
242 Ivan Vishnevskiy 1.25 3.00
243 Mike McKenna .75 2.00
244 Spencer Machacek .75 2.00
245 Tom Wandell 3.00 8.00
246 Michael Vernace .75 2.00
247 Yannick Weber 1.25 3.00
248 Matt Hendricks .75 2.00
249 Scott Lehman .60 1.50
250 T.J. Galiardi 1.25 3.00

2009-10 Swedish Upper Deck Victory Svenska Superstjarnor

COMPLETE SET (20) 12.00 30.00
STATED ODDS 1:6
SS1 Henrik Lundqvist 1.50 4.00
SS2 Loui Eriksson .50 1.25
SS3 Alexander Edler .50 1.25
SS4 P.J. Axelsson .75 2.00
SS5 Nicklas Lidstrom 1.00 2.50
SS6 Mattias Ohlund .50 1.25
SS7 Mikael Samuelsson .50 1.25
SS8 Henrik Zetterberg 1.50 4.00
SS9 Michael Nylander .50 1.25
SS10 Niklas Kronwall .60 1.50
SS11 Daniel Alfredsson .75 2.00
SS12 Kim Johnsson .50 1.25
SS13 Mats Sundin .75 2.00
SS14 Tomas Holmstrom .60 1.50
SS15 Fredrik Modin .50 1.25
SS16 Henrik Sedin 1.25 3.00
SS17 Daniel Sedin 1.00 2.50
SS18 Kristian Huselius .50 1.25
SS19 Nicklas Backstrom 1.50 4.00
SS20 Johan Franzen .50 1.25

1993-94 Swiss HNL

This large set, released by Jurg Ochsner and sponsored by Ford and Sport newspaper, appears to include everyone who performed in the Swiss National League in 1992-93. The set is highlighted by bright, team-color coordinated design elements and sharp photography, as well as the presence of several ex-NHLers. The set appears to use three languages on the card fronts, varying as to the main language in the team's home locale. All coaches cards below are marked TR (the abbreviation for the French "traineur"). A limited number of factory sets were available; each was serially numbered out of 3,000 and registered to the person making the purchase. A collectible binder to hold the set is valued at $5.

COMPLETE SET (510) 24.00 60.00
1 Title Card .05 .15
2 Title Card .05 .15
3 Title Card .05 .15
4 EHC-Kloten .05 .15
5 EHC-Kloten .05 .15
6 Conny Evensson CO .07 .20
7 Ernst Bruderer ACO .05 .15
8 Reto Pavoni .20 .50
9 Claudio Bayer .20 .50
10 Martin Bruderer .05 .15
11 Anders Eldebrink .08 .25
12 Marco Kloti .05 .15
13 Marco Knecht .05 .15
14 Martin Kout .05 .15
15 Fausto Mazzoleni .05 .15
16 Daniel Sigg .05 .15
17 Daniel Weber .05 .15
18 Manuele Celio .05 .15
19 Patric Della Rossa .20 .50
20 Michael Diener .05 .15
21 Bruno Erni .05 .15
22 Oliver Hoffmann .05 .15
23 Felix Hollenstein .08 .25
24 Mikael Johansson .08 .25
25 Daniel Knecht .05 .15
26 Roger Meier .05 .15
27 Sacha Ochsner .08 .25
28 Peter Schlagenhauf .05 .15
29 Roman Wager .08 .25
30 HC Fribourg-Gotteron .05 .15
31 HC Fribourg-Gotteron .05 .15
32 Paul-Andre Cadieux CO .05 .15
33 Francois Huppe ACO .05 .15
34 Dino Stecher .20 .50
35 Marc Gygli .20 .50
36 Patrice Brasey .05 .15
37 Fredy Bobillier .05 .15
38 Antoine Descloux .05 .15
39 Christian Hofstetter .05 .15
40 Doug Honegger .05 .15
41 Olivier Keller .05 .15
42 David Leibzig .05 .15
43 Didier Princi .05 .15
44 Joel Aeschlimann .05 .15
45 Christophe Brown .05 .15
46 Slava Bykov .20 .50
47 Stefan Grogg .05 .15
48 Andrej Khomutov .20 .50
49 Marc Leuenberger .05 .15
50 Bruno Maurer .05 .15
51 Frank Monnier .05 .15
52 Alain Reymond .05 .15
53 Mario Rottaris .05 .15
54 Pascal Schaller .05 .15
55 Chad Silver .05 .15
56 SC Bern .05 .15
57 SC Bern .05 .15
58 Hannu Jortikka CO .05 .15
59 Jim Koleff ACO .05 .15
60 Renato Tosio .20 .50
61 Roland Meyer .20 .50
62 Raoul Baumgartner .05 .15
63 Andreas Beutler .05 .15
64 Martin Brich .05 .15
65 Mikko Haapakoski .05 .15
66 Martin Rauch .05 .15
67 Jorg Reber .05 .15
68 Daniel Rutschi .05 .15
69 Gaetan Voisard .08 .25
70 Peter Bartschi .05 .15
71 Michael Buhler .05 .15
72 Rene Friedli .05 .15
73 Regis Fuchs .05 .15
74 Gregor Horak .05 .15
75 Michael Meier .05 .15
76 Gil Montandon .05 .15
77 Dan Quinn .20 .50
78 Harry Rogenmoser .05 .15
79 Roberto Triulzi .05 .15
80 Thomas C. Vrabec .05 .15
81 HC Lugano .05 .15
82 HC Lugano .05 .15
83 John Slettvoll CO .05 .15
84 Bruno Rogger ACO .05 .15
85 Lars Weibel .20 .50
86 Christophe Wahl .20 .50
87 Samuel Balmer .05 .15
88 Sandro Bertaggia .20 .50
89 Per Djoos .08 .25
90 Claudio Ghillioni .05 .15
91 Davide Jelmini .05 .15
92 Sven Leuenberger .05 .15
93 Ruedi Niderost .05 .15
94 Patrick Sutter .05 .15
95 Jean-Jacques Aeschlimann .08 .25
96 Jorg Eberle .08 .25
97 Ruben Fontana .05 .15
98 Axel Heim .05 .15
99 Christian Hofstetter .05 .15
100 Patrick Howald .08 .25
101 Marcel Jenni .05 .15
102 Andreas Keller .05 .15
103 Jan Larsson .05 .15
104 Andre Rotheli .05 .15
105 Matthias Schenkel .05 .15
106 Raymond Walder .05 .15
107 EV Zug .05 .15
108 EV Zug .05 .15
109 Bjorn Kinding CO .05 .15
110 Sean Simpson ACO .05 .15
111 Patrick Schopf .20 .50
112 Tony Koller .20 .50
113 Jakub Horak .05 .15
114 Dino Kessler .08 .25
115 Andre Kunzi .05 .15
116 Thomas Kunzi .05 .15
117 Andreas Ritsch .05 .15
118 Bill Schafhauser .05 .15
119 Pat Schafhauser .05 .15
120 Misko Antisin .08 .25
121 Mario Brodmann .05 .15
122 Tom Fergus .20 .50
123 Andreas Fischer .05 .15
124 Patrick Fischer .05 .15
125 Daniel Giger .05 .15
126 Daniel Meier .05 .15
127 Colin Muller .05 .15
128 Philipp Neuenschwander .05 .15
129 Daniel Schaltegger .05 .15
130 Franz Steffen .05 .15
131 Ken Yaremchuk .20 .50
132 HC Ambri-Piotta .05 .15
133 HC Ambri-Piotta .05 .15
134 Perry Pearn CO .08 .25
135 Dale McCourt ACO .08 .25
136 Markus Bachschmied .20 .50
137 Marco Baron .20 .50
138 Mark Astley .08 .25
139 Brenno Celio .05 .15
140 Filippo Celio .05 .15
141 Ivan Gazzaroli .05 .15
142 Tiziano Gianini .08 .25
143 Blair Muller .05 .15
144 Luigi Riva .05 .15
145 Rick Tschumi .20 .50
146 Nicola Celio .08 .25
147 Keith Fair .05 .15
148 Igor Fedulov .05 .15
149 Mathias Holzer .05 .15
150 Peter Jaks .05 .15
151 Vincent Lechenne .05 .15
152 Juri Leonov .05 .15
153 Petr Malkov .05 .15
154 Markus Studer .05 .15
155 Stefano Togni .05 .15
156 Luca Vigano .05 .15
157 Theo Wittmann .05 .15
158 Zurcher SC .05 .15
159 Zurcher SC .05 .15
160 Arno Del Curto CO .05 .15
161 Ueli Hofmann ACO .05 .15
162 Daniel Riesen .20 .50
163 Rolf Simmen .20 .50
164 Marco Bayer .08 .25
165 Jiri Faic .05 .15
166 Yvan Griga .05 .15
167 Noel Guyaz .05 .15
168 Edgar Salis .05 .15
169 Christian Sigrist .05 .15
170 Bruno Vollmer .05 .15
171 Andreas Zehnder .05 .15
172 Matthias Baechler .05 .15
173 Vjeran Ivankovic .05 .15
174 Peter Kobel .05 .15
175 Ronnie Leuthold .05 .15
176 Claudio Micheli .05 .15
177 Patrizio Morger .05 .15
178 Sergei Priakhin .08 .25
179 Roger Thony .05 .15
180 Andy Ton .05 .15
181 Christian Weber .05 .15
182 Vladimir Yeremin .05 .15
183 Michel Zeiter .05 .15
184 EHC Biel-Bienne .05 .15
185 EHC Biel-Bienne .05 .15
186 Jakob Kolliker CO .05 .15
187 Beat Lautenschlager ACO .05 .15
188 Oliver Anken .20 .50
189 Christian Cretin .20 .50
190 Beat Cattaruzza .05 .15
191 Jean-Michel Clavien .05 .15
192 Sven Dick .05 .15
193 Daniel Dubois .05 .15
194 Leo Gudas .08 .25
195 Bjorn Schneider .05 .15
196 Martin Steinegger .05 .15
197 Gaetan Boucher .05 .15
198 Thomas Burillo .05 .15
199 Reynald De Ritz .05 .15
200 Patrick Glanzmann .05 .15
201 Freddy Luthi .05 .15
202 Beat Nuspliger .05 .15
203 Cyrill Pasche .05 .15
204 Robert Yannick .05 .15
205 Andre Rufener .05 .15
206 Bernhard Schuemperli .08 .25
207 Marc Weber .08 .25
208 Ramil Yuldashev .05 .15
209 HC Davos .05 .15
210 HC Davos .05 .15
211 Mats Waltin CO .05 .15
212 Marcus Theus ACO .05 .15
213 Nando Wieser .20 .50
214 Marino Buriola .20 .50
215 Thomi Derungs .05 .15
216 Andy Egli .05 .15
217 Beat Equilino .05 .15
218 Marc Gianola .05 .15
219 Andrea Haller .05 .15
220 Didier Massy .05 .15
221 Roland Ruedi .05 .15
222 Roger Sigg .05 .15
223 Mica Blaha .08 .25
224 Gian Marco Crameri .05 .15
225 Remo Gross .05 .15
226 Martin Hanggi .05 .15
227 Markus Morf .05 .15
228 Rene Muller .05 .15
229 Andi Naser .05 .15
230 Oliver Roth .05 .15
231 Rato Schneider .05 .15
232 Serge Soguel .05 .15
233 Gilles Thibaudeau .20 .50
234 Steve Tsujiura .08 .25
235 EHC Olten .05 .15
236 EHC Olten .05 .15
237 Dick Decloe CO .05 .15
238 Beat Aebischer .20 .50
239 Sascha Friedli .20 .50
240 Matthias Aregger .05 .15
241 Eric Bourquin .05 .15
242 Fabian Gull .05 .15
243 Urs Hirschi .05 .15
244 Alessandro Reinhart .05 .15
245 Christian Schuster .05 .15
246 Christian Silling .05 .15
247 Richard Stucki .05 .15
248 Adrian Bachofner .05 .15
249 Markus Butler .05 .15
250 Ralph Donghi .05 .15
251 Guido Egli .05 .15
252 Paul Gagne .20 .50
253 Thomas Loosli .05 .15
254 Steve Metzger .05 .15
255 Viktor Muller .05 .15
256 Mike Richard .05 .15
257 Kevin Schlapfer .05 .15
258 Peter Trummer .05 .15
259 Andre Von Rohr .05 .15
260 HC Ajoie .05 .15
261 HC Ajoie .05 .15
262 Michael McNamara CO .05 .15
263 Claude Fugere ACO .05 .15
264 Nicola Fraschina .20 .50
265 Didier Tosi .20 .50
266 Dave Baechler .05 .15
267 Sandro Capaul .05 .15
268 Romain Fleury .05 .15
269 Carl Lapointe .05 .15
270 John Miner .05 .15
271 Daniel Rohrbach .05 .15
272 Ralph Tanner .05 .15

273 Yann Voillat .05 .15
274 Mauro Bornet .05 .15
275 Kalle Furer .05 .15
276 Thomas Griga .05 .15
277 Patrice Heiz .05 .15
278 Willy Kohler .05 .15
279 Daniel Lamminger .05 .15
280 Francois Marquis .05 .15
281 Marco Mozzini .05 .15
282 Giovanni Pestrin .05 .15
283 Ken Priestlay .08 .25
284 Frederic Rothen .05 .15
285 EHC Chur .05 .15
286 EHC Chur .05 .15
287 Bengt Ericsson CO .05 .15
288 Roberto Lavoie ACO .05 .15
289 Peter Martin .20 .50
290 Thomas Liesch .20 .50
291 Marco Capaul .05 .15
292 Marco Gazzola .05 .15
293 Bruno Habisreutinger .05 .15
294 Markus Knobel .05 .15
295 Thomas Locher .05 .15
296 Roger Schnoz .05 .15
297 Roland Simonet .05 .15
298 Ivo Stoffel .05 .15
299 Rene Ackermann .05 .15
300 Patrice Bosch .05 .15
301 Harry Derungs .05 .15
302 Marco Ferrari .05 .15
303 Miguel Fondado .05 .15
304 Claudio Kalser .05 .15
305 Claudio Krattli .05 .15
306 Zbysek Kurylowski .05 .15
307 Andrei Kwartalnov .05 .15
308 Albert Malgin .05 .15
309 Wayne Manley .05 .15
310 Riccardo Signorell .05 .15
311 HC Martigny .05 .15
312 HC Martigny .05 .15
313 Bob Mongrain CO .05 .15
314 Thierry Andrey .20 .50
315 Florian Garnier .20 .50
316 Thierry Evequoz .05 .15
317 Alexandre Formaz .05 .15
318 Tom Jaeggi .05 .15
319 Adrian Jezzone .05 .15
320 Jaques Mauron .05 .15
321 Patrick Neukom .05 .15
322 Brian Rueger .05 .15
323 Patrick Steck .05 .15
324 Steve Aebersold .05 .15
325 Nicolas Baumann .05 .15
326 Alain Bernard .05 .15
327 Jean-Daniel Bonito .05 .15
328 Olivier Ecoeur .05 .15
329 Kelly Glowa .05 .15
330 Thomas Heldner .05 .15
331 Thierry Moret .05 .15
332 Stefan Nussberger .05 .15
333 Petr Rosol .08 .25
334 Gabriel Taccoz .05 .15
335 SC Herisau .05 .15
336 SC Herisau .05 .15
337 Mike McParland CO .05 .15
338 Mark McGregor ACO .05 .15
339 Stephan Mort .20 .50
340 Stefan Allenspach .20 .50
341 Urs Balzarek .05 .15
342 Sascha Bleiker .05 .15
343 Damian Freitag .05 .15
344 Karl Knopf .05 .15
345 Andy Krapf .05 .15
346 Andreas Maag .05 .15
347 Paul Summermatter .05 .15
348 Markus Wetter .05 .15
349 Marco Beer .05 .15
350 Bernhard Blochliger .05 .15
351 Libor Dolana .05 .15
352 Philipp Egli .05 .15
353 Marco Fischer .05 .15
354 Reto Germann .05 .15
355 Urs Hartmann .05 .15
356 Markus Keller .05 .15
357 Trevor Meier .05 .15
358 Roger Nater .05 .15
359 Petr Vlk .08 .25
360 Gerd Zenhausern .05 .15
361 SC Rapperswil-Jona .05 .15
362 SC Rapperswil-Jona .05 .15
363 Pekka Rautakallio CO .20 .50
364 Ueli Scheidegger ACO .05 .15
365 Marius Boesch .05 .15
366 Michael Habig .08 .25
367 Armin Berchtold .05 .15
368 Daniel Bunzli .05 .15
369 Erich Frey .05 .15
370 Patrick Gotz .05 .15
371 Marc Haueter .05 .15
372 Christian Langer .05 .15
373 Markus Naef .05 .15
374 Daniel Aeschbacher .05 .15
375 Ray Allison .05 .15
376 Tom Bissett .20 .50
377 Warren Bruetsch .05 .15
378 Turi Camenzind .05 .15
379 Jean-Noel Honegger .05 .15
380 Roman Kessler .05 .15
381 Hans Kossman .05 .15
382 Marco Seeholzer .05 .15
383 Laurent Stehlin .05 .15
384 Marco Werder .05 .15
385 EHC Bulach .05 .15
386 EHC Bulach .05 .15
387 Lars-Erik Lundstrom CO .05 .15
388 Urs Liljequist ACO .05 .15
389 Ronnie Rueger .20 .50
390 Carlo Buriola .20 .50
391 Rolf Bunter .05 .15
392 David Erny .05 .15
393 Urs Gull .05 .15
394 Thomas Jaggli .05 .15
395 Stefan Meier .05 .15
396 Marco Schellenberg .05 .15
397 Marcel Schonhaar .05 .15
398 Robin Bauer .05 .15
399 Daniele Celio .05 .15
400 Peter Ekelund .05 .15
401 Urs Luthi .05 .15
402 Don McLaren .08 .25
403 Kim Pedersen .05 .15
404 Matthias Pittet .05 .15
405 Ercan Sahin .05 .15
406 Thomas Studer .05 .15
407 Markus Suter .05 .15
408 Martin Caretta .05 .15
409 Mike Tschumi .05 .15
410 Lausanne HC .05 .15
411 Lausanne HC .05 .15
412 Jean Lussier CO .05 .15
413 Beat Kindler .08 .25
414 Michel Pilet .05 .15
415 Urs Burkart .05 .15
416 Jean Gagnon .05 .15
417 Nicolas Goumaz .05 .15
418 Fabian Guignard .05 .15
419 Benedict Sapin .05 .15
420 Raymond Wyssen .05 .15
421 Laurent Bucher .05 .15
422 Olivier Chenuz .05 .15
423 Alain Comte .05 .15
424 Martin Desjardins .05 .15
425 Gaby Epiney .05 .15
426 Stephane Gasser .05 .15
427 Nicolas Gauch .05 .15
428 Gilles Guyaz .05 .15
429 Dan Hodgson .20 .50
430 Maxime Lapointe .05 .15
431 Laurent Pasquini .05 .15
432 Gilles Prince .05 .15
433 Yannick Theler .05 .15
434 HC Thurgau .05 .15
435 HC Thurgau .05 .15
436 Anders Sorensen CO .05 .15
437 Max Baumann .05 .15
438 Martin Studer .20 .50
439 Thomas Berger .20 .50
440 Andy Gasser .05 .15
441 Patrick Henry .05 .15
442 Reto Muller .05 .15
443 Ralph Ott .05 .15
444 Mike Posma .05 .15
445 Hadrian Rosenberg .05 .15
446 Marcel Stocker .05 .15
447 Robert Wiesmann .05 .15
448 Gianni Dalla Vecchia .05 .15
449 Dan Daoust .20 .50
450 Matthias Keller .05 .15
451 Roger Keller .05 .15
452 Peter Kostli .05 .15
453 Bernhard Lauber .05 .15
454 Benjamin Mueller .05 .15
455 Silvio Schai .05 .15
456 Rolf Schrepfer .05 .15
457 Robert Slehofer .05 .15
458 Thomas Steger .05 .15
459 Cuno Weisser .05 .15
460 Grasshoppers-Club Zurich .05 .15
461 Grasshoppers-Club Zurich .05 .15
462 Esa Siren CO .05 .15
463 Bruno Aegerter ACO .05 .15
464 Marcel Kohli .20 .50
465 Olivier Leuenberger .20 .50
466 Giorgio Giacomelli .05 .15
467 Roman Honegger .05 .15
468 Sandro Just .05 .15
469 Mats Lusth .05 .15
470 Marcel Wick .05 .15
471 Lukas Zehnder .05 .15
472 Rolf Ziegler .05 .15
473 Jerry Zuurmond .05 .15
474 Alain Ayer .05 .15
475 Leo Cadisch .05 .15
476 Pascal Fah .05 .15
477 Roman Furrer .05 .15
478 Marco Hagmann .05 .15
479 Peter Hofmann .05 .15
480 Adrian Hotz .05 .15
481 Patrick Looser .05 .15
482 Oliver Muffler .05 .15
483 Keith Osborne .08 .25
484 Thierry Paterlini .05 .15
485 Markus Schellenberg .05 .15
486 HC La Chaux-de-Fonds .05 .15
487 HC LaChaux-de-Fonds .05 .15
488 Ricardo Fuhrer CO .05 .15
489 Jean-Luc Schnegg .08 .25
490 Thierry Loup .08 .25
491 Thierry Baume .05 .15
492 Jean-Luc Christen .05 .15
493 Thierry Murisier .05 .15
494 Danny Ott .05 .15
495 Guido Pfosi .05 .15
496 Rene Raess .05 .15
497 Valeri Shirajev .08 .25
498 Frank Vuillemin .05 .15
499 Marco Dick .05 .15
500 Michael Ferrari .05 .15
501 Olivier Gazzaroli .05 .15
502 Sandy Jeannin .05 .15
503 Lane Lambert .08 .25
504 Guido Laczko .05 .15
505 Boris Leimgruber .05 .15
506 Claude Luthi .05 .15
507 Patrick Oppliger .05 .15
508 Jean-Luc Rod .05 .15
509 Gabriel Rohrbach .05 .15
510 Yvan Zimmermann .05 .15

1995-96 Swiss HNL

This very large set, released by Jurg Ochsner and sponsored by the Swiss Bank Society appears to include everyone who performed in the Swiss national hockey league in 1994-95. They were distributed in 6-card packs for 2 francs. The set is highlighted by marvelous color action photography, a subset of six NNO referee cards, and the inclusion of six NHLers who played in Switzerland during the NHL lockout including Doug Gilmour and Chris Chelios. Of interest is the usage of three languages (French, German and Italian) on the card fronts, which varies by the main language in the team's home locale. Note: the TR suffix in this case is the direct translation of coach (traineur). A collector's album also was available by mail. It is valued at $5.00.

COMPLETE SET (545) 30.00 75.00
1 Kloten .02 .10
2 Kloten .02 .10
3 Alpo Suhonen CO .20 .50
4 Ernst Bruderer ACO .02 .10
5 Matthias Muller .08 .25
6 Reto Pavoni .20 .50
7 Marco Bayer .02 .10
8 Martin Bruderer .02 .10
9 Marco Kloti .02 .10
10 Michael Kress .02 .10
11 Marc Ochsner .02 .10
12 Bjorn Schneider .02 .10
13 Daniel Sigg .02 .10
14 Daniel Weber .02 .10
15 Charles Berglund .02 .10
16 Manuele Celio .02 .10
17 Patrik Della Rossa .02 .10
18 Michael Diener .02 .10
19 Bruno Erni .02 .10
20 Oliver Hoffmann .02 .10
21 Felix Hollenstein .02 .10
22 Mathias Holzer .02 .10
23 Mikael Johansson .02 .10
24 Roger Meier .02 .10
25 Sacha Oscsner .02 .10
26 Frederic Rothen .02 .10
27 Roman Wager .02 .10
28 ZSC .02 .10
29 ZSC .02 .10
30 Larry Huras CO .02 .10
31 Ted Snell ACO .02 .10
32 Thomas Papp .15 .40
33 Dino Stecher .15 .40
34 Patrick Hager .02 .10
35 Martin Kout .02 .10
36 Didier Princi .02 .10
37 Edgar Salis .02 .10
38 Bruno Steck .02 .10
39 Nicholas Steiger .02 .10
40 Andreas Zehnder .02 .10
41 Mario Brodmann .02 .10
42 Marc Fortier .08 .25
43 Nicholas Gauch .02 .10
44 Vjeran Ivankovic .02 .10
45 Sandy Jeannin .02 .10
46 Patrick Lebeau .20 .50
47 Phillipp Luber .02 .10
48 Don McLaren .08 .25
49 Claudio Micheli .02 .10
50 Patrizio Morger .02 .10
51 Marco Seeholzer .02 .10
52 Bruno Vollmer .02 .10
53 Michel Zeiter .02 .10
54 Fribourg .02 .10
55 Fribourg .02 .10
56 Kjell Larsson CO .02 .10
57 Ueli Hofmann ACO .02 .10
58 David Aebischer ERC 15.00 40.00
59 Thomas Berger .15 .40
60 Steve Meuwly .07 .20
61 Johan Bertholet .02 .10
62 Fredy Bobillier .02 .10
63 Patrice Brasey .02 .10
64 Antoine Descloux .02 .10
65 Andy Egli .02 .10
66 Christian Hofstetter .02 .10
67 Olivier Keller .02 .10
68 Andrei Lomakin .08 .25
69 Mark Streit .02 .10
70 Christophe Brown .02 .10
71 Slava Bykov .20 .50
72 Matthias Bachler .02 .10
73 Axel Heim .02 .10
74 Andrei Khomutov .20 .50
75 Marc Leuenberger .02 .10
76 Alfred Luthi .04 .10
77 Daniel Meier .02 .10
78 Mario Rottaris .02 .10
79 Pascal Schaller .02 .10
80 Sacha Schneider .02 .10
81 Joel Aeschlimann .02 .10
82 Bern .02 .10
83 Bern .02 .10
84 Brian Lefley CO .02 .10
85 Ueli Schwarz ACO .02 .10
86 Reto Schurch .15 .40
87 Renato Tosio .15 .40
88 Mikko Haapakoski .02 .10
89 Christian Langer .02 .10
90 Sven Leuenberger .02 .10
91 Phillippe Portner .02 .10
92 Martin Rauch .02 .10
93 Pascal Sommer .02 .10
94 Martin Steinegger .02 .10
95 Gaetan Voisard .02 .10
96 Rene Friedli .02 .10
97 Regis Fuchs .02 .10
98 Patrick Howald .02 .10
99 Andy Keller .02 .10
100 Vincent Lechenne .02 .10
101 Lars Leuenberger .02 .10
102 Trevor Meier .02 .10
103 Gilles Montandon .02 .10
104 Philippe Muller .02 .10
105 Gaetano Orlando .08 .25
106 Roberto Triuizi .02 .10
107 Thomas Vrabec .02 .10
108 Davos .02 .10
109 Davos .02 .10
110 Mats Waltin CO .02 .10
111 Evgeni Popichin ACO .02 .10
112 Ivo Kleeb .15 .40
113 Nando Wiesser .15 .40
114 Samuel Balmer .02 .10
115 Martin Brich .02 .10
116 Beat Equilino .02 .10
117 Ivan Gazzaroli .02 .10
118 Marc Gianola .02 .10
119 Andrea Haeller .02 .10
120 Doug Honegger .02 .10
121 Andrej Kovalev .02 .10
122 Jan Alston .02 .10
123 Gian-Marco Crameri .02 .10
124 Dan Hodgson .20 .50
125 Rene Muller .02 .10
126 Andy Naser .02 .10
127 Oliver Roth .02 .10
128 Ivo Ruthemann .02 .10
129 Reto Stirnimann .02 .10
130 Reto Von Arx .02 .10
131 Christian Weber .02 .10
132 Lugano .02 .10
133 Lugano .02 .10
134 John Slettvoll CO .02 .10
135 Nicola Fraschina .15 .40
136 Lars Weibel .30 .75
137 Sandro Bertaggia .07 .20
138 Francesco Bizzozero .02 .10
139 Michel Kamber .02 .10
140 Ruedi Niderost .02 .10
141 Pat Schafhauser .02 .10
142 Tommy Sjodin .08 .25
143 Patrick Sutter .02 .10
144 Rick Tschumi .02 .10
145 J. Jacques Aeschlimann .02 .10
146 Markus Butler .02 .10
147 Jorg Eberle .02 .10
148 Keith Fair .02 .10
149 Marcel Jenni .02 .10
150 Stephan Lebeau .40 1.00
151 Patrick Looser .02 .10
152 Stefano Togni .02 .10
153 Andy Ton .02 .10
154 Remo Walder .02 .10
155 EVZ .02 .10
156 EVZ .02 .10
157 Jim Koleff CO .02 .10
158 Bob Lesley ACO .02 .10
159 Sacha Friedli .15 .40
160 Patrick Schopf .15 .40
161 Livio Fazio .02 .10
162 Stefan Grauwiler .02 .10
163 Dino Kessler .02 .10
164 Andre Kunzi .02 .10
165 Thomas Kunzi .02 .10
166 Fausto Mazzoleni .02 .10
167 John Miner .02 .10
168 Bill Schafhauser .02 .10
169 Steve Aebersold .02 .10
170 Misko Antisin .02 .10
171 Patrick Fischer .02 .10
172 Daniel Giger .02 .10
173 Mathias Keller .02 .10
174 Marco Koppel .02 .10
175 Colin Muller .02 .10
176 Philipp Neuenschwander .02 .10
177 Andre Rotheli .02 .10
178 Chad Silver .02 .10
179 Franz Steffen .02 .10
180 Ken Yaremchuk .20 .50
181 Ambri Piotta .02 .10
182 Ambri Piotta .02 .10
183 Alexander Yakushev CO .08 .25
184 Petr Malkov ACO .02 .10
185 Markus Bachschmied .15 .40
186 Paolo Della Bella .15 .40
187 Pauli Jaks .20 .50
188 Brenno Celio .02 .10
189 Tiziano Gianini .07 .20
190 Fabian Gull .02 .10
191 Noel Guyaz .02 .10
192 Jakub Horak .02 .10
193 Alessandro Reinhart .02 .10
194 Luigi Riva .02 .10
195 Gianni Sanese .02 .10
196 Oskar Szczepaniec .02 .10
197 Mattia Baldi .02 .10
198 Nicola Celio .02 .10
199 Dmitri Denisov .02 .10
200 Gaby Epiney .02 .10
201 John Fritsche .02 .10
202 Patrick Glanzmann .02 .10
203 Thomas Heldner .02 .10
204 Paolo Imperatori .02 .10
205 Peter Jaks .02 .10
206 Dimitri Kvartalnov .20 .50
207 Omar Tognini .02 .10
208 Nicola Pini .02 .10
209 Luca Vigano .02 .10
210 Theo Wittmann .02 .10
211 Rapperswil .02 .10
212 Rapperswil .02 .10
213 Pekka Rautakallio CO .08 .25
214 Ueli Scheidegger ACO .02 .10
215 Claudio Bayer .15 .40
216 Christian Cretin .15 .40
217 Daniel Bunzli .02 .10
218 Marco Capaul .02 .10
219 Roland Kradolfer .02 .10
220 Blair Muller .02 .10
221 Andreas Ritsch .02 .10
222 Daniel Rutschi .02 .10
223 Roger Sigg .02 .10
224 Adrian Bachofner .02 .10
225 Arthur Camenzind .02 .10
226 Christian Hofstetter .02 .10
227 Michael Meier .02 .10
228 Mike Richard .07 .20
229 Harry Rogenmoser .02 .10
230 Andy Rufener .02 .10
231 Sergio Soguel .02 .10
232 Gilles Thibaudeau .08 .25
233 Roger Thony .02 .10
234 Marc Weber .02 .10
235 Marco Werder .02 .10
236 Lausanne HC .02 .10
237 Jean Lussier CO .02 .10
238 Thierry Andrey .15 .40
239 Beat Kindler .15 .40
240 Jean Gagnon .02 .10
241 Fabian Guignard .02 .10
242 Philippe Marquis .02 .10
243 Stephan Schneider .02 .10
244 Roland Simonet .02 .10
245 Ivo Stoffel .02 .10
246 Marcel Wick .02 .10
247 Raymond Wyssen .02 .10
248 Martin Desjardins .02 .10
249 Maxime Lapointe .02 .10
250 Bruno Maurer .02 .10
251 Frank Monnier .02 .10
252 Cyrill Pasche .02 .10
253 Laurent Pasquini .02 .10
254 Alain Reymond .02 .10
255 Yannick Robert .02 .10
256 Kevin Schlapfer .02 .10
257 Gabriel Taccoz .02 .10
258 Claude Verret .02 .10
259 Gerd Zenhausern .02 .10
260 Biel .02 .10
261 Biel .02 .10
262 Barry Jenkins CO .02 .10
263 Sacha Devaux .15 .40
264 Christoph Wahl .15 .40
265 Beat Cattaruzza .02 .10
266 Sven Dick .02 .10
267 Claudio Ghillioni .02 .10
268 Stefan Lutz .02 .10
269 Guido Pfosi .02 .10
270 Sven Schmid .02 .10
271 Daniel Schneider .02 .10
272 Frank Aeschlimann .02 .10
273 Thomas Burillo .02 .10
274 Stefan Choffat .02 .10
275 Reynald DeRitz .02 .10
276 Marco Dick .02 .10
277 Ralph Donghi .02 .10
278 Stefan Groff .02 .10
279 Andrei Kvartalnov .02 .10
280 Albert Malgin .02 .10
281 Oliver Muller .02 .10
282 Michel Riesen .75 2.00
283 Bernhard Schumperli .08 .25
284 Mike Tschumi .02 .10
285 Grasshoppers .02 .10
286 Grasshoppers .02 .10
287 Bruno Aegerter CO .02 .10
288 Matti Alatalo ACO .02 .10
289 Marcel Kohli .15 .40
290 Stephan Morf .15 .40
291 Michel Faeh .02 .10
292 Marc Haueter .02 .10
293 Roman Honegger .02 .10
294 Arne Ramholt .02 .10
295 Hannu Virta .08 .25
296 Rolf Ziegler .02 .10
297 Jerry Zuurmond .02 .10
298 Alain Ayer .02 .10
299 Andre Baumann .02 .10
300 Warren Bruetsch .02 .10
301 Pascal Faeh .02 .10
302 Roman Furrer .02 .10
303 Marco Hagmann .02 .10
304 Dominik Jenny .02 .10
305 Mika Nieminen .02 .10
306 Fabio Obrist .02 .10
307 Thierry Paterlini .02 .10
308 Marco Schellenberg .02 .10
309 Mathias Schenkel .02 .10
310 Peter Schlagenhauf .02 .10
311 Markus Studer .02 .10
312 Thomas Ziegler .02 .10
313 Thurgau .02 .10
314 Thurgau .02 .10
315 Mike McParland CO .02 .10
316 Fritz Lanz ACO .02 .10
317 Roger Hugentobler .15 .40
318 Peter Martin .15 .40
319 Dominik Schmid .02 .10
320 Andrea Baumgartner .02 .10
321 Nicolas Goumaz .02 .10
322 Martin Granicher .02 .10
323 Ralph Ott .02 .10
324 Henry Patrick .02 .10
325 Mike Posma .02 .10
326 Marcel Schmid .02 .10
327 Robert Wiesmann .02 .10
328 Dan Daoust .20 .50
329 Slaven Imhof .02 .10
330 Roger Keller .02 .10
331 Martin Knopfli .02 .10
332 Guido Laczko .02 .10
333 Bernhard Lauber .02 .10
334 Gery Othman .02 .10
335 Rolf Schrepfer .02 .10
336 Thomas Seitz .02 .10
337 Robert Slehofer .02 .10
338 Rene Stussi .02 .10
339 Cuno Weisser .02 .10
340 Benjamin Winkler .02 .10
341 Langnau .02 .10
342 Langnau .02 .10
343 Paul Andre Cadieux CO .02 .10
344 Jakob Kolliker ACO .02 .10
345 Thomas Dreier .15 .40
346 Toni Koller .15 .40
347 Daniel Aegerter .02 .10
348 Raoul Baumgartner .02 .10
349 Andreas Beutler .02 .10
350 Urs Hirschi .02 .10
351 Stefan Probst .02 .10
352 Raphael Schneider .02 .10
353 Pascal Stoller .02 .10
354 Rolf Badertscher .02 .10
355 Peter Bartschi .02 .10
356 Beat Friedrich .02 .10
357 Walter Gerber .02 .10
358 Kelly Glowa .02 .10
359 Alan Hirschi .02 .10
360 Markus Hirschi .02 .10
361 Gregor Horak .02 .10
362 Lane Lambert .08 .25
363 Beat Nuspliger .02 .10
364 Stefan Tschiemer .02 .10
365 Chaux De Fonds .02 .10
366 Chaux De Fonds .02 .10
367 Riccardo Fuhrer CO .02 .10
368 Roland Meyer .15 .40
369 Jean-Luc Schnegg .15 .40
370 Eric Dourquin .02 .10
371 Daniel Dubois .02 .10
372 Andres Egger .02 .10
373 Daniel Elsener .02 .10
374 Thierry Murisier .02 .10
375 Daniel Ott .02 .10
376 Jorg Reber .02 .10
377 Valeri Chiriaev .02 .10
378 Michele Bizzozero .02 .10
379 Philippe Bozon .40 1.00
380 Jean-Marc Brunner .02 .10
381 Florian Chappot .02 .10
382 Gilles Dubois .02 .10
383 Willy Kohler .02 .10
384 Boris Leimgruber .02 .10
385 Patrick Oppliger .02 .10
386 Benoit Pont .02 .10
387 Laurent Stehlin .02 .10
388 Olivier Wuthrich .02 .10
389 Herisau .02 .10
390 Herisau .02 .10
391 Mark McGregor CO .02 .10
392 Reto Roveda ACO .02 .10
393 Michael Habig .15 .40
394 Ronald Rueger .15 .40
395 Urs Balzarek .02 .10
396 Thomas Derungs .02 .10
397 Damian Freitag .02 .10
398 Roland Habisreutinger .02 .10
399 Marco Knecht .02 .10
400 Karl Knopf .02 .10
401 Andy Maag .02 .10
402 Krister Cantoni .02 .10
403 Rico Enzler .02 .10
404 John Fust .02 .10
405 Remo Gastaldo .02 .10
406 Reto German .02 .10
407 Frank Guay .02 .10
408 Daniel Knecht .02 .10
409 Andy Krapf .02 .10
410 Roger Nater .02 .10
411 Marco Tanner .02 .10
412 Claude Vilgrain .40 1.00
413 Chur .02 .10
414 Chur .02 .10
415 Juri Voshakov CO .02 .10
416 Thomas Liesch .15 .40
417 Reto Zuccolini .15 .40
418 Sacha Bleiker .02 .10
419 Patrick Fischer .02 .10
420 Bruno Habisreutinger .02 .10
421 Jurg Hardegger .02 .10
422 Dominic Meier .02 .10
423 Loris Papa .02 .10
424 Robert Papp .02 .10
425 Valery Belov .02 .10
426 Valery Cherny .02 .10
427 Miguel Fondado .02 .10
428 Oliver Gazzaroli .02 .10
429 Claudio Krattli .02 .10
430 Claudio Peer .02 .10
431 Michael Putzi .02 .10
432 Roger Rieder .02 .10
433 Riccardo Signorell .02 .10
434 Peter Thoma .02 .10
435 Patrick Werthan .02 .10
436 Olten .02 .10
437 Olten .02 .10
438 Milan Mrukvia ACO .02 .10
439 Beat Aebischer .15 .40
440 Thierry Loup .15 .40
441 Ralph Gugelmann .02 .10
442 Roland Ruedi .02 .10
443 Andre Schneeberger .02 .10
444 Richard Stucki .02 .10
445 Thomas Studer .02 .10
446 Ville Siren .08 .25
447 Pius Weber .02 .10
448 Rene Ackermann .02 .10
449 Lars Aebi .02 .10
450 Andreas Fischer .02 .10
451 Marcel Franzi .02 .10
452 Paul Gagne .20 .50
453 Stephane Gasser .02 .10
454 Pirmin Keller .02 .10
455 Claude Luthi .02 .10
456 Patrick Siegwart .02 .10
457 Patrik Traber .02 .10
458 Andre Van Rohr .02 .10
459 HCM .02 .10
460 Kent Ruhnke CO .02 .10
461 Patrick Grand .15 .40
462 Didier Tosi .15 .40
463 Pascal Avanthay .02 .10
464 Bernard Bauer .02 .10
465 Ayocholos Escher .02 .10
466 Thierry Evequoz .02 .10
467 David Jelmini .02 .10
468 Xavier Kappeler .02 .10
469 Patrik Neukom .02 .10
470 Pierre-Alain Ancay .02 .10
471 Florian Andenmatten .02 .10
472 J-Daniel Bonito .02 .10
473 Alain Darbellay .02 .10
474 Olivier Ecoeur .02 .10
475 Igor Fedulov .02 .10
476 Nicolas Gastaldo .02 .10
477 Thierry Moret .02 .10
478 Stephan Nussberger .02 .10
479 Achim Pleschberger .02 .10
480 Petr Rosol .02 .10
481 Fabrizio Silietti .02 .10
482 Yannick Theler .02 .10
483 Geneve .02 .10
484 Geneve .02 .10
485 Francois Huppe CO .02 .10
486 Gary Shennan ACO .02 .10
487 Jean-Philippe Challande .15 .40
488 Jerome Hagmann .15 .40
489 Claude Cienciala .02 .10
490 Chris Felix .02 .10
491 Romain Fleury .02 .10
492 Daniel Herlea .02 .10
493 Camille Meylan .02 .10
494 Toni Nelli .02 .10
495 Christian Corona .02 .10
496 David Leibzig .02 .10
497 Antoine Cloux .02 .10
498 Nicolas Corthay .02 .10
499 Marc Hinni .02 .10
500 Olivier Honsberger .02 .10
501 Gael Kertudo .02 .10
502 Jorg Ledermann .02 .10
503 Andrew McKim .20 .50
504 Benjamin Muller .02 .10
505 Martin Stastny .02 .10
506 Michel Wicky .02 .10
507 Swiss National Team .08 .25
508 C. Weber/J. Eberle .20 .50
509 J.J Aeschlimann/T.Vrabec .08 .25
510 S.Bertaggia/L.Weibel .20 .50
511 Lars Weibel .20 .50
512 Tommy Sjodin .08 .25
513 Andrei Khomutov .20 .50
514 Lars Weibel .20 .50
515 Anders Eldebrink .08 .25
516 Ken Yaremchuk .20 .50
517 Reto Pavoni .20 .50
518 Dino Kessler .02 .10
519 Fausto Mazzoleni .02 .10
520 Andy Ton .02 .10
521 Dan Hodgson .20 .50
522 Roman Wager .02 .10
523 Reto Pavoni .20 .50
524 Reijo Ruotsalainen .20 .50
525 Tommy Sjodin .08 .25
526 Andrei Kvartalnov .02 .10
527 Mikael Johansson .02 .10
528 Ken Yaremchuk .40 1.00
529 Reto Pavoni .20 .50
530 Dino Kessler .02 .10
531 Marco Bayer .02 .10
532 Misko Antisin .02 .10
533 Sacha Ochsner .02 .10
534 Roman Wager .02 .10
535 Reto Pavoni .20 .50
536 Reijo Ruotsalainen .20 .50
537 Andreas Eldebrink .08 .25
538 Ken Yaremchuk .40 1.00
539 Mikael Johansson .02 .10
540 Tom Fergus .40 1.00
541 Dan Quinn .20 .50
542 Valeri Kamenski .40 1.00
543 Phil Housley .40 1.00
544 Chris Chelios 6.00 15.00
545 Doug Gilmour 6.00 15.00
NNO Danny Kurmann .02 .10
NNO Beat Eichmann .02 .10
NNO Roland Stadler .02 .10
NNO Beat Eichmann .02 .10
NNO Reto Bertolotti .02 .10

1996-97 Swiss HNL

This set features the players from both the A and B leagues from Switzerland. We've been unable to identify all of the players completely. If you can provide additional information, please forward it to hockeymag@beckett.com

COMPLETE SET (588) 40.00 80.00
1 EHC Kloten .02 .10
2 Fleming CO .02 .10
3 Schumacher .02 .10
4 Reto Pavoni .02 .10
5 Walter .02 .10
6 Marco Bayer .02 .10
7 Greg Brown .02 .10
8 Martin Bruderer .02 .10
9 Marco Kloti .02 .10
10 Marco Knecht .02 .10
11 Michael Kress .02 .10
12 Bjorn Schneider .02 .10
13 Daniel Weber .02 .10
14 Robin Bauer .02 .10
15 Charles Berglund .02 .10
16 Matthias Bachler .02 .10
17 Manuele Celio .02 .10
18 Patrick Della Rossa .02 .10
19 Jorg Eberle .02 .10
20 Felix Hollenstein .02 .10
21 Mathias Holzer .02 .10
22 Mikael Johansson .02 .10
23 Martin Pluss .02 .10
24 Frederic Rothen .02 .10
25 Roman Wager .02 .10
26 SC Bern .02 .10
27 Chuck Lefley CO .02 .10
28 Schwarz .02 .10
29 Renato Tosio .02 .10
30 Alex Reinhard .02 .10
31 Timo Jutila .02 .10
32 Christian Langer .02 .10
33 Sven Leuenberger .02 .10
34 Martin Rauch .02 .10
35 Ville Siren .02 .10
36 Martin Steinegger .02 .10
37 Gaetan Voisard .02 .10
38 Rene Friedli .02 .10
39 Regis Fuchs .02 .10
40 Patrick Howald .02 .10
41 Vincent Lechenne .02 .10
42 Stefan Moser .02 .10
43 Trevor Meier .02 .10
44 Gil Montandon .02 .10
45 Michael Mouther .02 .10
46 Laurent Muller .02 .10
47 Philppe Mueller .02 .10
48 Gates Orlando .20 .50
49 Thierry Paterlini .02 .10
50 Roberto Triulzi .02 .10
51 EV Zug .02 .10
52 Jim Koleff CO .02 .10
53 Simpson .02 .10
54 Patrick Schopf .02 .10
55 Ronnie Rueger .02 .10
56 Livio Fazio .02 .10
57 Stefan Grauwiler .02 .10
58 Dino Kessler .02 .10
59 Andre Kunzi .02 .10
60 Thomas Kunzi .02 .10
61 John Miner .02 .10
62 Patrick Sutter .02 .10
63 Steve Aebersold .02 .10
64 Misko Antisin .02 .10
65 Patrick Fischer .02 .10
66 Daniel Giger .02 .10
67 Stephen Grogg .02 .10
68 Bill McDougall .02 .10
69 Colin Muller .02 .10

Card	Low	High
70 Phil Neuenschwander	.02	.10
71 Philipp Orlandi	.02	.10
72 Andre Rotheli	.02	.10
73 Chad Silver	.02	.10
74 Franz Steffen	.02	.10
75 Wes Walz	.75	2.00
76 HC Ambri Piotta	.02	.10
77 Alexander Jakushev CO	.20	.50
78 Pauli Jaks	.20	.50
79 Paolo Della Bella	.02	.10
80 Brenno Celio	.02	.10
81 Ivan Gazzaroli	.02	.10
82 Tiziano Gianini	.02	.10
83 Noel Guyaz	.02	.10
84 Jakub Horak	.02	.10
85 Alessandro Reinhart	.02	.10
86 Oskar Szczepaniec	.02	.10
87 Dmitri Tsygurov	.02	.10
88 Mattia Baldi	.02	.10
89 Nicola Celio	.02	.10
90 John Fritsche	.02	.10
91 Patrick Glanzmann	.02	.10
92 Thomas Heldner	.02	.10
93 Peter Jaks	.02	.10
94 Dmitri Kvartalnov	.20	.50
95 Oleg Petrov	.02	.10
96 Omar Tognini	.02	.10
97 Igor Chibirev	.02	.10
98 Luca Vigano	.02	.10
99 Theo Wittmann	.02	.10
100 HC Davos	.02	.10
101 Del Curto CO	.02	.10
102 Evgeni Popichin ACO	.02	.10
103 Nando Wieser	.02	.10
104 Thomas Berger	.02	.10
105 Samuel Balmer	.02	.10
106 Beat Equilino	.02	.10
107 Marc Gianola	.02	.10
108 Malier	.02	.10
109 Valeri Shiryaev	.02	.10
110 Daniel Sigg	.02	.10
111 Mark Streit	.40	1.00
112 Jan Von Arx	.02	.10
113 Dan Hodgson	.02	.10
114 Philipp Luber	.02	.10
115 Rene Mueller	.02	.10
116 Andy Naser	.02	.10
117 Sergei Petrenko	.02	.10
118 Oliver Roth	.02	.10
119 Ivo Ruthemann	.02	.10
120 Mario Schocher	.02	.10
121 Reto Stirnimann	.02	.10
122 Reto Von Arx	.20	.50
123 Christian Weber	.02	.10
124 Ken Yaremchuk	.20	.50
125 SC Rapperswil Jona	.02	.10
126 Pekka Rautakallio CO	.02	.10
127 Ueli Scheidegger	.02	.10
128 Claudio Bayer	.02	.10
129 Remo Wehrli	.02	.10
130 Daniel Buenzli	.02	.10
131 Marko Capaul	.02	.10
132 Kari Martikainen	.02	.10
133 Dominic Meier	.02	.10
134 Blair Muller	.02	.10
135 Mathias Seger	.02	.10
136 Roger Sigg	.02	.10
137 Adrian Bachofner	.02	.10
138 Arthur Camenzind	.02	.10
139 Daniel Bunzli	.02	.10
140 Christian Hofstetter	.02	.10
141 Michel Meier	.02	.10
142 Mike Richard	.02	.10
143 Harry Rogenmoser	.02	.10
144 Sergio Soguel	.02	.10
145 Gilles Thibaudeau	.02	.10
146 Roger Thony	.02	.10
147 Mark Weber	.02	.10
148 Christian Wolhwend	.02	.10
149 HC Lugano	.02	.10
150 Mats Waltin CO	.02	.10
151 Gunnar Leidborg	.02	.10
152 Lars Weibel	.20	.50
153 Davide Gislimberti	.02	.10
154 Sandro Bertaggia	.02	.10
155 Fabian Guignard	.02	.10
156 David Jelmini	.02	.10
157 Rudi Niderost	.02	.10
158 Luigi Riva	.02	.10
159 Tommy Sjodin	.02	.10
160 Rick Tschumi	.02	.10
161 Jerry Zuurmond	.02	.10
162 J.-J. Aeschlimann	.02	.10
163 Markus Butler	.02	.10
164 Gian-Marco Crameri	.02	.10
165 Bruno Erni	.02	.10
166 Keith Fair	.02	.10
167 Marcel Jenni	.02	.10
168 Marcel Franzi	.02	.10
169 Stephan Lebeau	.20	.50
170 Stefano Togni	.02	.10
171 Andy Ton	.02	.10
172 Raymond Walder	.02	.10
173 Marco Werder	.02	.10
174 Michael Nylander	.20	.50
175 Zurcher SC	.02	.10
176 Alpo Suhonen CO	.02	.10
177 Fruliger	.02	.10
178 Thomas Papp	.02	.10
179 M. Muller	.02	.10
180 Patrick Hager	.02	.10
181 Martin Kout	.02	.10
182 Robert Nordmark	.02	.10
183 Didier Princi	.02	.10
184 Edgar Salis	.02	.10
185 Bruno Steck	.02	.10
186 Nicolas Steiger	.02	.10
187 Andreas Zehnder	.02	.10
188 Mario Brodmann	.02	.10
189 Marc Fortier	.02	.10
190 Axel Heim	.02	.10
191 Vjeran Ivankovic	.02	.10
192 Sandy Jeannin	.02	.10
193 Peter Kobel	.02	.10
194 Patrick Lebeau	.20	.50
195 Claudio Micheli	.02	.10
196 Patrizio Morger	.02	.10
197 Bruno Vollmer	.02	.10
198 Michel Zeiter	.02	.10
199 Gerd Zenhausern	.02	.10
200 HC Fribourg	.02	.10
201 Larsson CO	.02	.10
202 Courvoisier	.02	.10
203 Thomas Ostlund	.02	.10
204 Steve Meuwly	.02	.10
205 David Aebischer	4.00	10.00
206 Fredy Bobillier	.02	.10
207 Patrice Brasey	.02	.10
208 Antoine Descloux	.02	.10
209 Andi Egli	.02	.10
210 Christian Hofstetter	.02	.10
211 Olivier Keller	.02	.10
212 Philippe Marquis	.02	.10
213 Marc Werlen	.02	.10
214 Christophe Brown	.02	.10
215 Slava Bykov	.20	.50
216 David Dousse	.02	.10
217 Stefan Choffat	.02	.10
218 Andrei Khomutov	.20	.50
219 Daniel Meier	.02	.10
220 Patrick Oppliger	.02	.10
221 Mario Rottaris	.02	.10
222 Pascal Schaller	.02	.10
223 Didier Schafer	.02	.10
224 Al Raymond	.02	.10
225 HC La Chaux De Fonds	.02	.10
226 Ricardo Fuhrer CO	.02	.10
227 Jean-Luc Schnegg	.02	.10
228 Roland Meyer	.02	.10
229 Eric Bourquin	.02	.10
230 Rob Cowie	.02	.10
231 Daniel Dubois	.02	.10
232 Dan Eisener	.02	.10
233 Thierry Murisier	.02	.10
234 Dany Ott	.02	.10
235 Jorg Reber	.02	.10
236 Pascal Sommer	.02	.10
237 Jan Alston	.40	1.00
238 Florian Andenmatten	.02	.10
239 Loic Burkhalter	.02	.10
240 Christer Cantoni	.02	.10
241 Florian Chappot	.02	.10
242 Michael Diener	.02	.10
243 Gilles Dubois	.02	.10
244 Rob Gaudreau	.02	.10
245 Boris Leimgruber	.02	.10
246 Benoit Pont	.02	.10
247 Bernhard Schumperli	.02	.10
248 Michel Wicky	.02	.10
249 HC Lausanne	.02	.10
250 Johnston	.02	.10
251 Beat Kindler	.02	.10
252 Bernhard Lauber	.02	.10
253 Sebastien De Allegri	.02	.10
254 Thierry Evequoz	.02	.10
255 Nicolas Goumaz	.02	.10
256 Cull	.02	.10
257 Ivo Stoffel	.02	.10
258 Turcotte	.02	.10
259 Philippe Bozon	.40	1.00
260 Johan Bertholet	.02	.10
261 Andre Doll	.02	.10
262 Rolf Ziegler	.02	.10
263 Horvath	.02	.10
264 Bruno Maurer	.02	.10
265 Alfie Michaud	.20	.50
266 Frank Monnier	.02	.10
267 Patrice Pellet	.02	.10
268 Mario Seeholzer	.02	.10
269 Robert Slehofer	.02	.10
270 Laurent Stehlin	.02	.10
271 Grasshoppers	.02	.10
272 Bruno Aegerter	.02	.10
273 Alatalo	.02	.10
274 Marcel Kohli	.02	.10
275 Olivier Wissmann	.02	.10
276 Martin Brich	.02	.10
277 Marc Haueter	.02	.10
278 FahM.	.02	.10
279 Roman Honegger	.02	.10
280 Arne Ramholt	.02	.10
281 Daniel Rutschi	.02	.10
282 Alain Ayer	.02	.10
283 Andre Baumann	.02	.10
284 Warren Brutsch	.02	.10
285 Roman Furrer	.02	.10
286 Marco Hagmann	.02	.10
287 Patrick Looser	.02	.10
288 Lasse Nieminen	.02	.10
289 Andy Rufener	.02	.10
290 Christian Ruuttu	.20	.50
291 Mathias Schenkel	.02	.10
292 Peter Schlagenhauf	.02	.10
293 HC Thurgau	.02	.10
294 Mike McParland	.02	.10
295 Peter Martin	.02	.10
296 Sutter	.02	.10
297 Martin Granicher	.02	.10
298 Henry	.02	.10
299 Ralph Ott	.02	.10
300 Mike Posma	.02	.10
301 Marcel Schmid	.02	.10
302 Christian Schuster	.02	.10
303 Robert Wiesmann	.02	.10
304 Dan Daoust	.02	.10
305 Slaven Imhof	.02	.10
306 Matthias Keller	.02	.10
307 Ronny Keller	.02	.10
308 Guido Laczko	.02	.10
309 Don McLaren	.02	.10
310 Gery Othman	.02	.10
311 Rolf Schrepfer	.02	.10
312 Rene Stussi	.02	.10
313 Cuno Weisser	.02	.10
314 Benjamin Winkler	.02	.10
315 SC Langnau	.02	.10
316 Paul-Andre Cadieux	.02	.10
317 Jakub Kolliker	.02	.10
318 Martin Gerber ERC	4.00	10.00
319 Thomas Dreier	.02	.10
320 Daniel Aegerter	.02	.10
321 Raoul Baumgartner	.02	.10
322 Andreas Beutler	.02	.10
323 Mario Doyon	.02	.10
324 Roland Kradolfer	.02	.10
325 Raphael Schneider	.02	.10
326 Pascal Stoller	.02	.10
327 Rolf Badertscher	.02	.10
328 Bruno Brechbuhl	.02	.10
329 Peter Bartschi	.02	.10
330 Walter Gerber	.02	.10
331 Markus Hirschi	.02	.10
332 Jakub Horak	.02	.10
333 Andreas Keller	.02	.10
334 Beat Nuspliger	.02	.10
335 Greg Parks	.02	.10
336 Kevin Schlapfer	.02	.10
337 Stefan Tschiemer	.02	.10
338 SC Herisau	.02	.10
339 McGregor	.02	.10
340 Markus Bachschmied	.02	.10
341 Schiess	.02	.10
342 Urs Balzarek	.02	.10
343 Damien Freitag	.02	.10
344 Fritz	.02	.10
345 Thomas Jaggli	.02	.10
346 Karl Knopf	.02	.10
347 Andy Krapf	.02	.10
348 Andy Maag	.02	.10
349 Devin Edgerton	.02	.10
350 Rico Enzler	.02	.10
351 John Fust	.02	.10
352 Martin Hanggi	.02	.10
353 Francois Marquis	.02	.10
354 Ludwig Marek	.02	.10
355 Pinelli	.02	.10
356 Ivo Ruthemann	.02	.10
357 Scheiwiller	.02	.10
358 Claude Vilgrain	.40	1.00
359 Sacha Weibel	.02	.10
360 HC Martigny	.02	.10
361 Steve Pochon	.02	.10
362 Patrick Grand	.02	.10
363 Didier Tosi	.02	.10
364 Pascal Avanthay	.02	.10
365 Jean-Michel Clavien	.02	.10
366 Ayocholos Escher	.02	.10
367 Alan Hirschi	.02	.10
368 Patrik Neukom	.02	.10
369 Benedikt Sapin	.02	.10
370 Marc Zurbriggen	.02	.10
371 Jean-Daniel Bonito	.02	.10
372 Igor Fedulov	.02	.10
373 Nicolas Gastaldo	.02	.10
374 Paolo Imperatori	.02	.10
375 Thierry Moret	.02	.10
376 Stephan Nussberger	.02	.10
377 Petr Rosol	.02	.10
378 Fabrizio Silietti	.02	.10
379 Yannick Theler	.02	.10
380 Natal Zurbriggen	.02	.10
381 EHC Biel-Bienne	.02	.10
382 Michael Zettel	.02	.10
383 Christoph Wahl	.02	.10
384 Devaux	.02	.10
385 Sven Dick	.02	.10
386 Romain Fleury	.02	.10
387 Claudio Ghillioni	.02	.10
388 Urs Hirschi	.02	.10
389 Sven Schmid	.02	.10
390 Daniel Schneider	.02	.10
391 Alain Villard	.02	.10
392 Thomas Burillo	.02	.10
393 Reynald De Ritz	.02	.10
394 Marco Dick	.02	.10
395 Paul Gagne	.02	.10
396 Gabriel Taccoz	.02	.10
397 Shawn Heaphy	.02	.10
398 Maxime Lapointe	.02	.10
399 Luthi	.02	.10
400 Serge Meyer	.02	.10
401 Cyrill Pasche	.02	.10
402 Michel Riesen	.20	.50
403 HC Geneve-Servette	.02	.10
404 Huppe	.02	.10
405 Hagmann	.02	.10
406 Michel Pilet	.02	.10
407 Francesco Bizzozero	.02	.10
408 Daniel Herlea	.02	.10
409 Pascal Lamprecht	.02	.10
410 Thevoz	.02	.10
411 Daniel Zieri	.02	.10
412 Christian Serena	.02	.10
413 Nicolas Studer	.02	.10
414 Joel Aeschlimann	.02	.10
415 Antoine Cloux	.02	.10
416 Claude Verret	.02	.10
417 Martin Desjardins	.02	.10
418 Olivier Ecoeur	.02	.10
419 Gaby Epiney	.02	.10
420 Laurent Faller	.02	.10
421 Nicholas Gauch	.02	.10
422 Olivier Honsberger	.02	.10
423 Gael Kertudo	.02	.10
424 Jorg Ledermann	.02	.10
425 EHC Olten	.02	.10
426 Hoffmann	.02	.10
427 Beat Aebischer	.02	.10
428 Thierry Loup	.02	.10
429 Ralph Gugelmann	.02	.10
430 Bruno Habisreutinger	.02	.10
431 Phillippe Portner	.02	.10
432 Gianni Sanese	.02	.10
433 Schonauer	.02	.10
434 Richard Stucki	.02	.10
435 Thomas Studer	.02	.10
436 Dobler	.02	.10
437 Yannick Dube	.02	.10
438 Mario Koppel	.02	.10
439 Luthi	.02	.10
440 Muller	.02	.10
441 Nicola Pini	.02	.10
442 Thomas Seitz	.02	.10
443 Patrick Siegwart	.02	.10
444 Pirmin Keller	.02	.10
445 Andre Von Rohr	.02	.10
446 Andre Von Rohr	.02	.10
447 EHC Chur	.02	.10
448 Voschakov	.02	.10
449 Thomas Liesch	.02	.10
450 Reto Zuccolini	.02	.10
451 Armin Berchtold	.02	.10
452 Sacha Bleiker	.02	.10
453 Sandro Capaul	.02	.10
454 Patrick Fischer	.02	.10
455 Andreas Ritsch	.02	.10
456 Stefan Schneider	.02	.10
457 Roland Simonet	.02	.10
458 Rene Ackermann	.02	.10
459 Andreas Fischer	.02	.10
460 Miguel Fondado	.02	.10
461 Claudio Peer	.02	.10
462 Reto Germann	.02	.10
463 Albert Malgin	.02	.10
464 Roger Rieder	.02	.10
465 Michael Rosenast	.02	.10
466 Riccardo Signorell	.02	.10
467 Harijs Vitolinsh	.02	.10
468 Patrick Werthan	.02	.10
469 Nussle	.02	.10
470 SC Luzern	.02	.10
471 Hansson	.02	.10
472 Beat Lautenschlager	.02	.10
473 Patrice Bosch	.02	.10
474 Rosset	.02	.10
475 Alain Comte	.02	.10
476 Dominik Jenny	.02	.10
477 Samuelsson	.02	.10
478 Ron Stillhardt	.02	.10
479 Marco Tanner	.02	.10
480 Markus Wetter	.02	.10
481 Martin Bahnik	.02	.10
482 Baiada	.02	.10
483 Buchel	.02	.10
484 Marco Fischer	.02	.10
485 P. Giger	.02	.10
486 Daniel Lamminger	.02	.10
487 M. Ledermann	.02	.10
488 Daniel Mares	.02	.10
489 P. Mares	.02	.10
490 Marco Mozzini	.02	.10
491 Mario Schocher	.02	.10
492 Ramil Yuldaschev	.02	.10
493 Ron Stillhardt	.02	.10
494 HC Ajoie	.02	.10
495 Hans Kossmann	.02	.10
496 Christian Cretin	.02	.10
497 Rosado	.02	.10
498 Rapheal Berger	.02	.10
499 Matthias Bachler	.02	.10
500 Erich Frey	.02	.10
501 Heusler	.02	.10
502 M. Reinhard	.02	.10
503 Julien Vauclair ERC	.40	1.00
504 Yann Voillat	.02	.10
505 Patrick Adami	.02	.10
506 Denis Challitoux	.02	.10
507 Guyaz	.02	.10
508 Alexandre Von Arb	.02	.10
509 Holmberg	.02	.10
510 Honegger	.02	.10
511 Herve Meyer	.02	.10
512 Marc Fritsche	.02	.10
513 Migy	.02	.10
514 Giovanni Pestrin	.02	.10
515 Geoffrey Vauclair	.02	.10
516 Reto Pavoni	.02	.10
517 Gaetan Voisard	.02	.10
518 Martin Bruderer	.02	.10
519 Felix Hollenstein	.02	.10
520 Gil Montandon	.02	.10
521 Patrick Howald	.02	.10
522 National Team	.02	.10
523 Schenk	.02	.10
524 Paul-Andre Cadieux	.02	.10
525 Jakub Kolliker	.02	.10
526 Reto Pavoni	.02	.10
527 Pauli Jaks	.20	.50
528 Samuel Balmer	.02	.10
529 Marco Bayer	.02	.10
530 Sandro Bertaggia	.02	.10
531 Martin Bruderer	.02	.10
532 Tiziano Gianini	.02	.10
533 Sven Leuenberger	.02	.10
534 Gaetan Voisard	.02	.10
535 Andreas Zehnder	.02	.10
536 Manuele Celio	.02	.10
537 Nicola Celio	.02	.10
538 Patrick Fischer	.02	.10
539 Felix Hollenstein	.02	.10
540 Peter Jaks	.02	.10
541 Sandy Jeannin	.02	.10
542 Marcel Jenni	.02	.10
543 Harry Rogenmoser	.02	.10
544 Frederic Rothen	.02	.10
545 Reto Von Arx	.20	.50
546 Christian Weber	.02	.10
547 Michel Zeiter	.02	.10
548 SIHL	.02	.10
549 Swiss National Inline Team	.02	.10
550 Alain Wittwer	.02	.10
551 Markus Bachschmied	.02	.10
552 Waber	.02	.10
553 Ochsner	.02	.10
554 Mueller	.02	.10
555 Bauer	.02	.10
556 Ivo Ruthemann	.02	.10
557 Sven Lindemann	.02	.10
558 Alexandre Von Arb	.02	.10
559 Ronnie Rueger	.02	.10
560 Kuendig	.02	.10
561 Klaus	.02	.10
562 Guido Lindemann	.02	.10
563 Rico Enzler	.02	.10
564 Andres Egger	.02	.10
565 Kuendig	.02	.10
566 Wild	.02	.10
567 Johansson	.02	.10
568 Patrick Howald	.02	.10
569 Muller	.02	.10
570 Tschibirev	.02	.10
571 Jan Alston	.40	1.00
572 Mike Richard	.02	.10
573 Stephan Lebeau	.20	.50
574 Marc Fortier	.02	.10
575 Slava Bykov	.20	.50
576 Frank Monnier	.02	.10
577 Patrick Oppliger	.02	.10
578 Lasse Nieminen	.02	.10
579 Dan Daoust	.20	.50
580 Glowa	.02	.10
581 Claude Vilgrain	.40	1.00
582 Petr Rosol	.02	.10
583 Dmitri Kvartalnov	.20	.50
584 Andrew McKim	.20	.50
585 Rene Ackermann	.02	.10
586 Valery Cherny	.02	.10
587 Referees	.02	.10
588 Referees	.02	.10

1998-99 Swiss Power Play Stickers

Card	Low	High
COMPLETE SET (382)	40.00	80.00
1 Team Ambri Left	.07	.20
2 Team Ambri Right	.07	.20
3 Larry Hurras	.07	.20
4 Pauli Jaks	.07	.20
5 Peter Martin	.07	.20
6 Fredy Bobillier	.07	.20
7 Ivan Gazzaroli	.07	.20
8 Tiziano Gianini	.07	.20
9 Giordano Guidotti	.07	.20
10 Leif Rohlin	.07	.20
11 Edgar Salis	.07	.20
12 Bruno Steck	.07	.20
13 Oliver Tschanz	.07	.20
14 Mattia Baldi	.07	.20
15 Krister Cantoni	.07	.20
16 Manuele Celio	.07	.20
17 Nicola Celio	.07	.20
18 Paul DiPietro	.20	.50
19 John Fritsche	.07	.20
20 Vjeran Ivankovic	.07	.20
21 Oleg Petrov	.07	.20
22 Franz Steffen	.07	.20
23 Omar Tognini	.07	.20
24 Theo Wittmann	.07	.20
25 Thomas Ziegler	.07	.20
26 Team Bern Left	.07	.20
27 Team Bern Right	.07	.20
28 Ueli Schwarz	.07	.20
29 Renato Tosio	.07	.20
30 Reto Schurch	.07	.20
31 Alexander Godynyuk	.07	.20
32 Sven Leuenberger	.07	.20
33 Martin Rauch	.07	.20
34 Bjorn Schneider	.07	.20
35 Stefan Schneider	.07	.20
36 Pascal Sommer	.07	.20
37 Martin Steinegger	.07	.20
38 Gregor Thommen	.07	.20
39 Bjorn Christen	.07	.20
40 David Jobin	.07	.20
41 Patrick Howald	.07	.20
42 Boris Leimgruber	.07	.20
43 Lars Leuenberger	.07	.20
44 Dave McLlwain	.07	.20
45 Gil Montandon	.07	.20
46 Daniel Marois	.07	.20
47 Michel Mouther	.07	.20
48 Thierry Paterlini	.07	.20
49 Roberto Triulzi	.07	.20
50 Marc Weber	.07	.20
51 Team Davos Left	.07	.20
52 Team Davos Right	.07	.20
53 Arno Del Curto	.07	.20
54 Stephane Beauregard	.20	.50
55 Marco Wegmuller	.07	.20
56 Beat Equilino	.07	.20
57 Marc Gianola	.07	.20
58 Andrea Haller	.07	.20
59 Michael Kress	.07	.20
60 Pettri Nummelin	.07	.20
61 Mark Streit	.40	1.00
62 Jan Von Arx	.07	.20
63 Andre Baumann	.07	.20
64 Sandy Jeannin	.07	.20
65 Rene Muller	.07	.20
66 Kai Nurminen	.07	.20
67 Peter Kobel	.07	.20
68 Sandro Rizzi	.07	.20
69 Oliver Roth	.07	.20
70 Ivo Ruthemann	.07	.20
71 Mario Schocher	.07	.20
72 Reto Stirnimann	.07	.20
73 Reto Von Arx	.20	.50
74 Beat Helbstab	.07	.20
75 Timo Helbling	.20	.50
76 Team Fribourg Left	.07	.20
77 Team Fribourg Right	.07	.20
78 Andre Peloffy	.07	.20
79 David Aebischer	2.00	5.00
80 Thomas Ostlund	.20	.50
81 Alain Sansonnens	.07	.20
82 Patrice Brasey	.07	.20
83 Antoine Descloux	.07	.20
84 Livio Fazio	.07	.20
85 Romain Fleury	.07	.20
86 Olivier Keller	.07	.20
87 Philippe Marquis	.07	.20
88 Marc Werlen	.07	.20
89 Igor Chibirev	.07	.20
90 Flavien Conne	.07	.20
91 David Dousse	.07	.20
92 Rene Furler	.07	.20
93 Daniel Giger	.07	.20
94 Goran Bezina	.07	.20
95 Philipp Orlandi	.07	.20
96 Mario Rottaris	.07	.20
97 Pascal Schaller	.07	.20
98 Robert Slehofer	.07	.20
99 Pavel Torgajev	.07	.20
100 Gerd Zenhausern	.07	.20
101 Team Kloten Left	.07	.20
102 Team Kloten Right	.07	.20
103 Reto Pavoni	.07	.20
104 Marco Buhrer	.07	.20
105 Samuel Balmer	.07	.20
106 Marco Bayer	.07	.20
107 Martin Bruderer	.07	.20
108 Marco Kloti	.07	.20
109 Beat Meier	.07	.20
110 Tommy Sjodin	.07	.20
111 Daniel Weber	.07	.20
112 Benjamin Winkler	.07	.20
113 Philipp Folghera	.07	.20
114 Thomas Heldner	.07	.20
115 Felix Hollenstein	.07	.20
116 Sven Lindemann	.07	.20
117 Bill McDougall	.07	.20
118 Martin Pluss	.07	.20
119 Frederic Rothen	.07	.20
120 Andy Rufener	.07	.20
121 Matthias Schenkel	.07	.20
122 Rene Stussi	.07	.20
123 Chris Tancill	.07	.20
124 Adrian Wichser	.07	.20
125 Team Langnau Left	.07	.20
126 Team Langnau Right	.07	.20
127 Jakob Kolliker	.07	.20
128 Martin Gerber	2.00	5.00
129 Ivo Kleeb	.07	.20
130 Daniel Aegerter	.07	.20
131 Mario Doyon	.07	.20
132 Marco Knecht	.07	.20
133 Pascal Muller	.07	.20
134 Wesley Snell	.07	.20
135 Oskar Szczepaniec	.07	.20
136 Markus Wuthrich	.07	.20
137 Alexis Vacheron	.07	.20
138 Rolf Bradertscher	.07	.20
139 Peter Bartschi	.07	.20
140 Bruno Brechbuhl	.07	.20
141 Marc Buhlmann	.07	.20
142 Todd Elik	.07	.20
143 Marco Fischer	.07	.20
144 John Fust	.07	.20
145 Andy Keller	.07	.20
146 Michael Liniger	.07	.20
147 Greg Parks	.07	.20
148 Benoit Pont	.07	.20
149 Stefan Tschiemer	.07	.20
150 Team Lugano Left	.07	.20
151 Team Lugano Right	.07	.20
152 Jim Koleff CO	.07	.20
153 Cristobal Huet	6.00	15.00
154 Lars Weibel	.07	.20
155 Peter Andersson	.07	.20
156 Mark Astley	.07	.20
157 Sandro Bertaggia	.07	.20
158 Fabian Guignard	.07	.20
159 Rick Tschumi	.07	.20
160 Julien Vauclair	.20	.50
161 Gaëtan Voisard	.07	.20
162 Rolf Ziegler	.07	.20
163 Jean Jacques Aeschlimann	.07	.20
164 Misko Antisin	.07	.20
165 Gian Marco Crameri	.07	.20
166 Andre Doll	.07	.20
167 Keith Fair	.07	.20
168 Patrick Fischer	.07	.20
169 Regis Fuchs	.07	.20
170 Marcel Jenni	.07	.20
171 Trevor Meier	.07	.20
172 Andy Naser	.07	.20
173 Gaetano Orlando	.20	.50
174 Geoffrey Vauclair	.07	.20
175 Team Rapperswil Left	.07	.20
176 Team Rapperswil Right	.07	.20
177 Mark McGregor	.07	.20
178 Claudio Bayer	.07	.20
179 Remo Wehrli	.07	.20
180 Marco Capaul	.07	.20
181 Christian Langer	.07	.20
182 Dominic Meier	.07	.20
183 Jorg Reber	.07	.20
184 Matthias Seger	.07	.20
185 Daniel Sigg	.07	.20
186 Roger Sigg	.07	.20
187 Adrian Bachofner	.07	.20
188 Markus Butler	.07	.20
189 Rene Friedli	.07	.20
190 Oliver Hoffmann	.07	.20
191 Christian Hofstetter	.07	.20
192 Chris Lindberg	.07	.20
193 Frank Monnier	.07	.20
194 Mark Ouimet	.07	.20
195 Mike Richard	.07	.20
196 Harry Rogenmoser	.07	.20
197 Bernhard Schumperli	.07	.20
198 Ken Yaremchuk	.07	.20
199 Team EVZ Left	.07	.20
200 Team EVZ Right	.07	.20
201 Sean Simpson	.07	.20
202 Ronald Rueger	.07	.20
203 Patrick Schopf	.07	.20
204 Raphaël Berger	.07	.20
205 Matthias Holzer	.07	.20
206 Jakub Horak	.07	.20
207 Dino Kessler	.07	.20
208 Reto Kobach	.07	.20
209 Andre Kunzi	.07	.20
210 Thomas Kunzi	.07	.20
211 Patrick Sutter	.07	.20
212 Christoph Brown	.07	.20
213 Jorg Eberle	.07	.20
214 Devin Edgerton	.07	.20
215 Stefan Grogg	.07	.20
216 Daniel Meier	.07	.20
217 Colin Muller	.07	.20
218 Patrick Oppliger	.07	.20
219 Andre Rotheli	.07	.20
220 Sacha Schneider	.07	.20
221 Kevin Todd	.07	.20
222 Samuel Villiger	.07	.20
223 Wes Walz	.40	1.00
224 Team ZSC Left	.07	.20
225 Team ZSC Right	.07	.20
226 Kent Ruhnke	.07	.20
227 Thomas Papp	.07	.20
228 Ari Sulander	.20	.50
229 Martin Brich	.07	.20
230 Marc Haueter	.07	.20
231 Michel Kamber	.07	.20
232 Martin Kout	.07	.20
233 Kari Martikainen	.07	.20
234 Adrien Plavsic	.07	.20
235 Pascal Stoller	.07	.20
236 Andreas Zehnder	.07	.20
237 Patrik Della Rossa	.07	.20
238 Axel Heim	.07	.20
239 Dan Hodgson	.07	.20
240 Peter Jaks	.07	.20
241 Claudio Micheli	.07	.20
242 Patrizio Morger	.07	.20
243 Laurent Muller	.07	.20
244 Rolf Schrepfer	.07	.20
245 Chad Silver	.07	.20
246 Christian Weber	.07	.20
247 Michel Zeiter	.07	.20
248 National Team Left	.07	.20
249 National Team Right	.07	.20
250 Raphael Kruger	.07	.20
251 David Aebischer	2.00	5.00
252 Misko Antisin	.07	.20
253 Mattia Baldi	.07	.20
254 Gian Marco Crameri	.07	.20
255 Patrick Fischer	.07	.20
256 Peter Jaks	.07	.20
257 Sandy Jeannin	.07	.20
258 Marcel Jenni	.07	.20
259 Dino Kessler	.07	.20
260 Claudio Micheli	.07	.20
261 Reto Pavoni	.07	.20
262 Martin Pluss	.07	.20
263 Martin Rauch	.07	.20
264 Ivo Ruthemann	.07	.20
265 Edgar Salis	.07	.20
266 Matthias Seger	.07	.20
267 Franz Steffen	.07	.20
268 Martin Steinegger	.07	.20
269 Mark Streit	.20	.50
270 Patrick Sutter	.07	.20
271 Reto Von Arx	.20	.50
272 Michel Zeiter	.07	.20
273 Bill Gilligan	.07	.20
274 Marco Buhrer	.07	.20
275 Ralph Bundi	.07	.20
276 Alex Chatelain	.07	.20
277 Bjorn Christen	.07	.20
278 Flavien Conne	.07	.20
279 Patrick Fischer	.07	.20
280 Sven Lindemann	.07	.20
281 Michel Mouther	.07	.20
282 Laurent Muller	.07	.20
283 Marc Reichert	.07	.20
284 Alain Reist	.07	.20
285 Michel Riesen	.20	.50
286 Sandro Rizzi	.07	.20
287 Mario Schocher	.07	.20
288 Rene Stussi	.07	.20
289 Julien Vauclair	.20	.50
290 Jan Von Arx	.07	.20
291 Marc Werlen	.07	.20
292 Adrian Wichser	.07	.20
293 Markus Wuthrich	.07	.20
294 Thomas Ziegler	.07	.20
295 Team Biel Left	.07	.20
296 Team Biel Right	.07	.20
297 Christian Cretin Alain Reist	.07	.20
298 Sven Schmid Paul Gagne	.07	.20
299 Paul-Andre Cadieux	.07	.20
300 Shawn Heaphy Cyrill Pasche	.07	.20
301 Team La Chaux de Fonds Left	.07	.20
302 Team La Chaux de Fonds Right	.07	.20
303 Thomas Berger Valeri Schirjaev	.07	.20
304 Lugio Riva Steve Aebersold	.07	.20
305 Riccardo Fuhrer	.07	.20
306 Stephan Lebeau Stefano Togni	.07	.20
307 Team Chur Left	.07	.20
308 Team Chur Right	.07	.20
309 Thomas Liesch Patrick Fischer	.07	.20
310 Mike Posma Mario Brodmann	.07	.20
311 Mike McParland	.07	.20
312 Harijs Vitolinsh Reymond Walder	.07	.20
313 Team GC Left	.07	.20
314 Team GC Right	.07	.20
315 Olivier Wissmann Arne Ramholt	.07	.20
316 Marco Schellenberg Domenic Amodeo	.07	.20
317 Dave Tietzen	.07	.20
318 Mark Kaufman Riccardo Signorell	.07	.20
319 Team Servette Left	.07	.20
320 Team Servette Right	.07	.20
321 Steve Meuwly David Leibzig	.07	.20
322 Maxime Lapointe Christian Serena	.07	.20
323 Jean Perron CO	.07	.20
324 Mark Jorris Sandy Smith	.07	.20
325 Team Herisau Left	.07	.20
326 Team Herisau Right	.07	.20
327 Fabian Gull Robert Burakowsky	.07	.20
328 Markus Bachschmied Urs Balzarek	.07	.20
329 Evgeny Popichin	.07	.20
330 Alain Fraser Cuno Weisser	.07	.20
331 Team Lausanne Left	.07	.20
332 Team Lausannne Right	.07	.20
333 Beat Kindler Serge Poudrier	.07	.20
334 Andy Krapf Jorg Ledermann	.07	.20
335 Benoit Laporte	.07	.20
336 Slava Bykov Daniel Nakaoka	.07	.20
337 Team Martigny Left	.07	.20
338 Team Martigny Right	.07	.20
339 Didier Tosi	.07	.20

Jean-Michel Clavien
340 Benedict Sapin .07 .20
Jean-Daniel Bonito
341 Petr Rosol .07 .20
342 Nicolas Gastaldo .07 .20
Thierry Moret
343 Team Olten Left .07 .20
344 Team Olten Right .07 .20
345 Beat Aebischer .07 .20
Richard Stucki
346 Igor Boriskov .07 .20
Albert Malgin
347 Markus Graf .07 .20
348 Luca Vigano .07 .20
Andre Von Rohr
349 Team Sierre Left .07 .20
350 Team Sierre Right .07 .20
351 Matthias Lauber .07 .20
Michel Fah
352 Philippe Faust .07 .20
Bruno Erni
353 Christian Wittwer .07 .20
354 Marco Poulsen .07 .20
Gilles Thibaudeau
355 Team Thurgau Left .07 .20
356 Team Thurgau Right .07 .20
357 Marius Bosch .07 .20
Patrick Henry
358 Ralph Ott .07 .20
Scott Beattie
359 Henryk Gruth .07 .20
360 Kevin Miehm .07 .20
Roman Wager
A SEHV / LSHG .07 .20
B HC Ambri Piotta .07 .20
C SC Bern .07 .20
D HC Davos .07 .20
E HC Fribourg Gotteron .07 .20
F EHC Kloten .07 .20
G SC Langnau .07 .20
H HC Lugano .07 .20
I SC Rapperswil-Jona .07 .20
J EV Zug .07 .20
K ZSC Lions .07 .20
L EHC Biel-Bienne .07 .20
M HC La Chaux De Fonds .07 .20
N EHC Chur .07 .20
O Grasshoppers .07 .20
P HC Geneve Servette .07 .20
Q SC Herisau .07 .20
R HC Lausanne .07 .20
S EHC Martigny .07 .20
T EHC Olten .07 .20
U HC Sierre .07 .20
V HC Thurgau .07 .20

1999-00 Swiss Panini Stickers

COMPLETE SET (380) 40.00 80.00
1 Team Ambri Left .07 .20
2 Team Ambri Right .07 .20
3 Larry Huras .07 .20
4 Pauli Jaks .07 .20
5 Peter Martin .07 .20
6 Fredy Bobillier .07 .20
7 Ivan Gazzaroli .07 .20
8 Tiziano Gianini .07 .20
9 John Gobbi .07 .20
10 Thomas Kunzi .07 .20
11 Leif Rohlin .07 .20
12 Bruno Steck .07 .20
13 Krister Cantoni .07 .20
14 Manuele Celio .07 .20
15 Nicola Celio .07 .20
16 Luca Cereda .20 .50
17 Alain Demuth .07 .20
18 Paolo Duca .07 .20
19 John Fritsche .07 .20
20 Ryan Gardner .07 .20
21 Vitaly Lakhmatov .07 .20
22 Stephan Lebeau .20 .50
23 Patrick Lebeau .20 .50
24 Franz Steffen .07 .20
25 Thomas Ziegler .07 .20
26 Team Bern Left .07 .20
27 Team Bern Right .07 .20
28 Pekka Rautakallio CO .07 .20
29 Martin Kilchor .07 .20
30 Renato Tosio .07 .20
31 David Jobin .07 .20
32 Sven Leuenberger .07 .20
33 Petri Liimatainen .07 .20
34 Martin Rauch .07 .20
35 Pascal Sommer .07 .20
36 Martin Steinegger .07 .20
37 Fabian Stephan .07 .20
38 Gregor Thommen .07 .20
39 Alex Chatelain .07 .20
40 Bjorn Christen .07 .20
41 Patrick Howald .07 .20
42 Roland Kaser .07 .20
43 Boris Leimgruber .07 .20
44 Lars Leuenberger .07 .20
45 Dave McLlwain .07 .20
46 Thierry Paterlini .07 .20
47 Jackson Penney .07 .20
48 Marc Reichert .07 .20
49 Ivo Ruthemann .07 .20
50 Marc Weber .07 .20
51 Team Davos Left .07 .20
52 Team Davos Right .07 .20
53 Arno Del Curto .07 .20
54 Petter Ronnqvist .07 .20
55 Marco Wegmuller .07 .20
56 Beat Equilino .07 .20
57 Marc Gianola .07 .20
58 Andreas Haller .07 .20
59 Timo Helbling .20 .50
60 Beat Heldstab .07 .20
61 Petteri Nummelin .07 .20
62 Jan Von Arx .07 .20
63 Andre Baumann .07 .20
64 Patrick Fischer .07 .20
65 Marc Heberlein .07 .20
66 Sandy Jeannin .07 .20
67 Michael Kress .07 .20
68 Fredrik Lindquist .07 .20
69 Rene Muller .07 .20
70 Claudio Neff .07 .20
71 Sandro Rizzi .07 .20
72 Oliver Roth .07 .20
73 Frederic Rothen .07 .20
74 Mario Schocher .07 .20
75 Reto Von Arx .20 .50
76 Team Fribourg Left .07 .20
77 Team Fribourg Right .07 .20
78 Ueli Schwarz .07 .20
79 Thomas Ostlund .20 .50
80 Alain Sansonnens .07 .20
81 Goran Bezina .07 .20
82 Livio Fazio .07 .20
83 Romain Fleury .07 .20
84 Fabian Guignard .07 .20
85 Philippe Marquis .07 .20
86 Mika Stromberg .07 .20
87 Marc Werlen .07 .20
88 Rolf Ziegler .07 .20
89 Robert Burakowski .07 .20
90 Flavien Conne .07 .20
91 Rene Furler .07 .20
92 Daniel Giger .07 .20
93 Gil Montandon .07 .20
94 Colin Muller .07 .20
95 Michael Neininger .07 .20
96 Real Raemy .07 .20
97 Mario Rottaris .07 .20
98 Pascal Schaller .07 .20
99 Robert Slehofer .07 .20
100 Gerd Zenhausern .07 .20
101 Team Kloten Left .07 .20
102 Team Kloten Right .07 .20
103 Vladimir Jursinov CO .07 .20
104 Reto Pavoni .07 .20
105 Samuel Balmer .07 .20
106 Andre Bielmann .07 .20
107 Martin Bruderer .07 .20
108 Martin Hohener .07 .20
109 Marco Kloti .07 .20
110 Arne Ramholt .07 .20
111 Oskar Szczepaniec .07 .20
112 Benjamin Winkler .07 .20
113 Mathias Wuest .07 .20
114 Thomas Heldner .07 .20
115 Felix Hollenstein .07 .20
116 Peter Kobel .07 .20
117 Sven Lindemann .07 .20
118 Andrew McKim .20 .50
119 Andreas Nauser .07 .20
120 Martin Pluss .07 .20
121 Sebastien Reuille .07 .20
122 Andy Rufener .07 .20
123 Matthias Schenkel .07 .20
124 Tomas Strandberg .07 .20
125 Adrian Wichser .07 .20
126 Team Langnau Left .07 .20
127 Team Langnau Right .07 .20
128 Bengt-Ake Gustafsson .07 .20
129 Alfred Bohren .07 .20
130 Martin Gerber 2.00 5.00
131 Adrian Hunziker .07 .20
132 Daniel Aegerter .07 .20
133 Antoine Descloux .07 .20
134 Steve Hirschi .07 .20
135 Erik Kakko .07 .20
136 Pascal Muller .07 .20
137 Markus Wuthrich .07 .20
138 Rolf Badertscher .07 .20
139 Daniel Bieri .07 .20
140 Bruno Brechbuhl .07 .20
141 Marc Buhlmann .07 .20
142 Todd Elik .07 .20
143 John Fust .07 .20
144 Daniel Gauthier .07 .20
145 Bjorn Guazzini .07 .20
146 Matthias Holzer .07 .20
147 Michael Liniger .07 .20
148 Benoit Pont .07 .20
149 Stefan Tschiemer .07 .20
150 Team Lugano Left .07 .20
151 Team Lugano Right .07 .20
152 Jim Koleff CO .07 .20
153 Cristobal Huet 4.00 10.00
154 Lars Weibel .20 .50
155 Peter Andersson .07 .20
156 Mark Astley .07 .20
157 Sandro Bertaggia .07 .20
158 Olivier Keller .07 .20
159 Rick Tschumi .07 .20
160 Julien Vauclair .20 .50
161 Gaëtan Voisard .20 .50
162 J.Jacques Aeschlimann .07 .20
163 Misko Antisin .07 .20
164 Philippe Bozon .40 1.00
165 Gian Marco Crameri .07 .20
166 Andre Doll .07 .20
167 Christian Dube .07 .20
168 Keith Fair .07 .20
169 Igor Fedulov .07 .20
170 Regis Fuchs .07 .20
171 Marcel Jenni .07 .20
172 Trevor Meier .07 .20
173 Andy Naser .07 .20
174 Geoffrey Vauclair .07 .20
175 Team Rapperswil Left .07 .20
176 Team Rapperswil Right .07 .20
177 Evgeny Popichin .07 .20
178 Claudio Bayer .07 .20
179 Remo Wehrli .07 .20
180 Marco Capaul .07 .20
181 Dominic Meier .07 .20
182 Jorg Reber .07 .20
183 Alain Reist .07 .20
184 Daniel Sigg .07 .20
185 Roger Sigg .07 .20
186 Magnus Svensson .07 .20
187 Loic Burkhalter .07 .20
188 Markus Butler .07 .20
189 Rene Friedli .07 .20
190 Sandro Haberlin .07 .20
191 Axel Heim .07 .20
192 Oliver Hoffmann .07 .20
193 Vjeran Ivankovic .07 .20
194 Frank Monnier .07 .20
195 Mark Ouimet .07 .20
196 Mike Richard .07 .20
197 Bernhard Schumperli .07 .20
198 Marcel Sommer .07 .20
199 Paul Ysebaert .07 .20
200 Team EVZ Left .07 .20
201 Team EVZ Right .07 .20
202 Rauno Korpi .07 .20
203 Ronnie Rueger .07 .20
204 Patrick Schopf .07 .20
205 Marco Bayer .07 .20
206 Raphael Berger .07 .20
207 Patrick Fischer .07 .20
208 Jakub Horak .07 .20
209 Dino Kessler .07 .20
210 Reto Kobach .07 .20
211 Andre Kunzi .07 .20
212 Patrick Sutter .07 .20
213 Christophe Brown .07 .20
214 Paul Di Pietro .20 .50
215 Stefan Grogg .07 .20
216 Daniel Meier .07 .20
217 Stefan Niggli .07 .20
218 Patrick Oppliger .07 .20
219 Andre Rotheli .07 .20
220 Sascha Schneider .07 .20
221 Rene Stussi .07 .20
222 Chris Tancill .07 .20
223 Samuel Villiger .07 .20
224 Dave Roberts .07 .20
225 Team ZSC Left .07 .20
226 Team ZSC Right .07 .20
227 Kent Ruhnke .07 .20
228 Thomas Papp .07 .20
229 Ari Sulander .20 .50
230 Ronny Keller .07 .20
231 Martin Kout .07 .20
232 Kari Martikainen .07 .20
233 Adrien Plavsic .07 .20
234 Edgar Salis .07 .20
235 Mathias Seger .07 .20
236 Pascal Stoller .07 .20
237 Andreas Zehnder .07 .20
238 Mattia Baldi .07 .20
239 Robin Bauer .07 .20
240 Patric Della Rossa .07 .20
241 Dan Hodgson .07 .20
242 Peter Jaks .07 .20
243 Claudio Micheli .07 .20
244 Patrizio Morger .07 .20
245 Laurent Muller .07 .20
246 Rolf Schrepfer .07 .20
247 Reto Stirnimann .07 .20
248 Christian Weber .07 .20
249 Michel Zeiter .07 .20
250 Ralph Krueger .07 .20
251 National Team Left .07 .20
252 National Team Right .07 .20
253 David Aebischer 2.00 5.00
254 Pauli Jaks .20 .50
255 Reto Pavoni .07 .20
256 Olivier Keller .07 .20
257 Philippe Marquis .07 .20
258 Ivo Ruthemann .07 .20
259 Mathias Seger .07 .20
260 Martin Steinegger .07 .20
261 Mark Streit .20 .50
262 Patrick Sutter .07 .20
263 Benjamin Winkler .07 .20
264 Mattia Baldi .07 .20
265 Gian Marco Crameri .07 .20
266 Patric Della Rossa .07 .20
267 Patrick Fischer .07 .20
268 Sandy Jeannin .07 .20
269 Marcel Jenni .07 .20
270 Laurent Muller .07 .20
271 Martin Pluss .07 .20
272 Sandro Rizzi .07 .20
273 Geoffrey Vauclair .07 .20
274 Reto Von Arx .20 .50
275 Michel Zeiter .07 .20
276 John Slettvoll .07 .20
277 National U20 TeamLeft .07 .20
278 National U20 Team Right .07 .20
279 Marco Buhrer .07 .20
280 Oliver Wissmann .07 .20
281 Goran Bezina .07 .20
282 David Jobin .07 .20
283 Pascal Muller .07 .20
284 Alain Reist .07 .20
285 Gregor Thommen .07 .20
286 Alex Vacheron .07 .20
287 Julien Vauclair .20 .50
288 Fabio Beccarelli .07 .20
289 Luca Cereda .20 .50
290 Bjorn Christen .07 .20
291 Flavien Conne .07 .20
292 Alain Demuth .07 .20
293 Philipp Folghera .07 .20
294 Roland Kaser .07 .20
295 Cornel Prinz .07 .20
296 Marc Reichert .07 .20
297 Michel Riesen .20 .50
298 Sandro Tschour .07 .20
299 Adrian Wichser .07 .20
300 Team Biel Left .07 .20
301 Team Biel Right .07 .20
302 Paul Gagne .07 .20
303 Sebastien Kohler .07 .20
Sven Schmid
304 Gilles Dubois .07 .20
Michel Mongeau
305 Cyrill Pasche .20 .50
Claude Vilgrain
306 La Chaux De Fonds Left .07 .20
307 La Chaux De Fonds Right .07 .20
308 Jaroslav Jagr .07 .20
309 Thomas Berger .07 .20
Ruedi Niderost
310 Luigi Riva .07 .20
Valeri Shiryayev
311 Steve Aebersold .07 .20
Christian Pouget
312 Team Chur Left .07 .20
313 Team Chur Right .07 .20
314 Mike McParland .07 .20
315 Nando Wieser .07 .20
Matthias Bachler
316 Michael Meier .07 .20
Roger Rieder
317 Sandro Tschour .07 .20
Theo Wittmann
318 Team GC Left .07 .20
319 Team GC Right .07 .20
320 Riccardo Fuhrer .07 .20
321 Oliver Wissmann .07 .20
Pascal Fah
322 David Fehr .07 .20
Oliver Kamber
323 Patrick Looser .07 .20
Riccardo Signorell
324 Team Lausanne Left .07 .20
325 Team Lausanne Right .07 .20
326 Benoit Laporte .07 .20
327 Beat Kindler .07 .20
Slava Bykov
328 Patrick Glove .07 .20
Maxime Lapointe
329 Jorg Ledermann .07 .20
Valentin Wirz
330 Team Olten Left .07 .20
331 Team Olten Right .07 .20
332 Markus Graf .07 .20
333 Beat Aebischer .07 .20
Andy Egli
334 Richard Stucki .07 .20
Evgeny Davydov
335 Michel Mouther .07 .20
Mikhail Volkov
336 Team Servette Left .07 .20
337 Team Servette Right .07 .20
338 Francois Huppe .07 .20
339 David Bochy .07 .20
Christian Serena
340 Sott Beatti .07 .20
Shawn Heaphy
341 Paul Savary .07 .20
Michel Wicky
342 Team Sierre Left .07 .20
343 Team Sierre Right .07 .20
344 Kevin Primeau .07 .20
345 Matthias Lauber .07 .20
Adrian Jezzone
346 Patrick Neukom .07 .20
Phillipp Luber
347 Dimitri Shamolin .07 .20
Gilles Thibaudeau
348 Team Thurgau Left .07 .20
349 Team Thurgau Right .07 .20
350 Robert Wiesmann .07 .20
351 Marco Buhrer .07 .20
Stefan Grauwiler
352 Domenic Amodeo .07 .20
Mathias Keller
353 Patrick Meier .07 .20
Morgan Samuelsson
354 Team Visp Left .07 .20
355 Team Visp Right .07 .20
356 Bruno Zenhausern .07 .20
357 Reiner Karlen .07 .20
Wesley Snell
358 Marc Zurbriggen .07 .20
Franziskus Heinzmann
359 Andy Egli .07 .20
Gabriel Taccoz
A SEHV / LSHG .07 .20
B HC Ambri Piotta .07 .20
C SC Bern .07 .20
D HC Davos .07 .20
E HC Fribourg Gotteron .07 .20
F EHC Kloten .07 .20
G SC Langnau .07 .20
H HC Lugano .07 .20
I SC Rapperswil-Jona .07 .20
J EV Zug .07 .20
K ZSC Lions .07 .20
L EHC Biel-Bienne .07 .20
M HC La Chaux De Fonds .07 .20
N EHC Chur .07 .20
O Grasshoppers .07 .20
P HC Lausanne .07 .20
Q EHC Olten .07 .20
R HC Geneve Servette .07 .20
S HC Sierre .07 .20
T HC Thurgau .07 .20
U Visp .07 .20

2000-01 Swiss Panini Stickers

COMPLETE SET (322) 20.00 50.00
1 Logo Swiss Hockey Federation .08 .20
2 Ambri Team Card .08 .20
3 Ambri Team Card .08 .20
4 Ambri Logo .08 .20
5 Pietre Page .08 .20
6 Pauli Jaks .08 .20
7 Gianluca Mona .08 .20
8 Fredy Bobillier .08 .20
9 Ivan Gazzaroli .08 .20
10 Tiziano Gianini .08 .20
11 Thomas Kunzi .08 .20
12 Leif Rohlin .08 .20
13 Krister Cantoni .08 .20
14 Manuele Celio .08 .20
15 Nicola Celio .08 .20
16 Alain Demuth .08 .20
17 Paolo Duca .08 .20
18 John Fritsche .08 .20
19 Ryan Gardner .08 .20
20 Paolo Imperatori .08 .20
21 Vitaly Lakhmatov .08 .20
22 Stephan Lebeau .08 .20
23 Dan Marois .08 .20
24 Omar Tognini .08 .20
25 Thomas Ziegler .08 .20
26 Logo SCB .08 .20
27 Team Card SCB .08 .20
28 Team Card SCB .08 .20
29 Pekka Rautakallio .08 .20
30 Renato Tosio .08 .20
31 David Jobin .08 .20
32 Marc Leuenberger .08 .20
33 Sven Leuenberger .08 .20
34 Dominic Meier .08 .20
35 Frederik Olausson .08 .20
36 Martin Steinegger .08 .20
37 Fabian Stephan .08 .20
38 Rolf Ziegler .08 .20
39 Alex Chatelain .08 .20
40 Bjorn Christen .08 .20
41 Patrick Howald .08 .20
42 Andreas Johansson .08 .20
43 Patrick Juhlin .08 .20
44 Rolan Kasar .08 .20
45 Boris Leimgruber .08 .20
46 Marc Reichert .08 .20
47 Ivo Ruthemann .08 .20
48 Franz Steffen .08 .20
49 Marc Weber .08 .20
50 La Chaux De Fonds Logo .08 .20
51 Chaux Fonds Team Card .08 .20
52 Chaux Fonds Team Card .08 .20
53 Dan Hober .08 .20
54 Thomas Berger .08 .20
55 Gilles Cattela .08 .20
56 Pascal Avanthay .08 .20
57 Raphael Brusa .08 .20
58 Fabian Guignard .08 .20
59 Ruedi Niderost .08 .20
60 Roger Ohmann .08 .20
61 Valery Schirjaev .08 .20
62 Alexis Vacheron .08 .20
63 Steve Aebersold .08 .20
64 Thomas Derungs .08 .20
65 Claude Luthi .08 .20
66 Fabrice Maillat .08 .20
67 Thibaut Monnet .08 .20
68 Daniel Nakaota .08 .20
69 Stefan Nilsson .08 .20
70 Steve Pochon .08 .20
71 Philippe Halmann .08 .20
72 Julien Turler .08 .20
73 Sami Villiger .08 .20
74 Chur Logo .08 .20
75 Chur Team Card .08 .20
76 Chur Team Card .08 .20
77 Mike McParland .08 .20
78 Marco Buhrer .08 .20
79 Nando Wieser .08 .20
80 Noel Guyaz .08 .20
81 Christian Langer .08 .20
82 Ivo Stoffel .08 .20
83 Pasi Sormunen .08 .20
84 Mika Stromberg .08 .20
85 Matthias Bachler .08 .20
86 Fabio Beccarelli .08 .20
87 Patrick Kruger .08 .20
88 Michael Meier .08 .20
89 Daniel Peer .08 .20
90 Roger Rieder .08 .20
91 Michael Rosenast .08 .20
92 Oliver Roth .08 .20
93 Rene Stussi .08 .20
94 Sandro Tschour .08 .20
95 Harijs Vitolinsh .08 .20
96 Raymond Walder .08 .20
97 Theo Wittmann .08 .20
98 HC Davos Logo .08 .20
99 HC Davos Team Card .08 .20
100 HC Davos Team Card .08 .20
101 Arno Del Curto .08 .20
102 Petter Ronnquist .08 .20
103 Lars Weibel .08 .20
104 Beat Equilino .08 .20
105 Marc Gianola .08 .20
106 Andrea Haller .08 .20
107 Michael Kress .08 .20
108 Kevin Miller .08 .20
109 Ralph Ott .08 .20
110 Jan Von Arx .08 .20
111 Andre Baumann .08 .20
112 Lonny Bohonos .08 .20
113 Pat Falloon .08 .20
114 Patrick Fischer .08 .20
115 Marc Heberlein .08 .20
116 Rene Muller .08 .20
117 Claudio Neff .08 .20
118 Thierry Paterlini .08 .20
119 Sandro Rizzi .08 .20
120 Frederic Rothen .08 .20
121 Mario Schocher .08 .20
122 Gotteron Logo .08 .20
123 Gotteron Team Card .08 .20
124 Gotteron Team Card .08 .20
125 Serge Pelletier .08 .20
126 Thomas Ostlund .20 .50
127 Alain Sansonnens .08 .20
128 Raphael Berger .08 .20
129 Goran Bezina .08 .20
130 Christoph Decurtins .08 .20
131 Antoine Descloux .08 .20
132 Livio Fazio .08 .20
133 Philippe Marquis .08 .20
134 Martin Rauch .08 .20
135 Marc Werlen .08 .20
136 Craig Ferguson .08 .20
137 Lars Leuenberger .08 .20
138 Silvan Lussy .08 .20
139 Gil Montandon .08 .20
140 Michael Mouther .08 .20
141 Mario Rottaris .08 .20
142 Jean Yves Roy .08 .20
143 Pascal Schaller .08 .20
144 Robert Slehofer .08 .20
145 Gerd Zenhausern .08 .20
146 Kloten Logo .08 .20
147 Kloten Team Card .08 .20
148 Kloten Team Card .08 .20
149 Vladimir Yursinov CO .08 .20
150 Reto Pavoni .20 .50
151 Martin Hohener .08 .20
152 Ronny Keller .08 .20
153 Marko Kiprusoff .08 .20
154 Marco Kloti .08 .20
155 Dejan Lozanov .08 .20
156 Oskar Szczepaniec .08 .20
157 Beni Winkler .08 .20
158 Sven Helfenstein .08 .20
159 Felix Hollenstein .08 .20
160 Andy Keller .08 .20
161 Sven Lindemann .08 .20
162 Andreas Nauser .08 .20
163 Fredrik Nilsson .08 .20
164 Martin Pluss .08 .20
165 Sebastian Reuille .08 .20
166 Andy Rufener .08 .20
167 Adi Wichser .08 .20
168 Thomas Widmer .08 .20
169 Mathias Wust .08 .20
170 Langnau Logo .08 .20
171 Langnau Team Card .08 .20
172 Langnau Team Card .08 .20
173 Bengt Ake Gustafsson .08 .20
174 Martin Gerber .75 2.00
175 Martin Zerzuben .08 .20
176 Daniel Aegerter .08 .20
177 Samuel Balmer .08 .20
178 Steve Hirschi .08 .20
179 Erik Kakko .08 .20
180 Pascal Muller .08 .20
181 Pascal Stoller .08 .20
182 Florian Andenmatten .08 .20
183 Rolf Badertscher .08 .20
184 Bruno Brechbuhl .08 .20
185 John Fust .08 .20
186 Daniel Gauthier .08 .20
187 Thomas Heldner .08 .20
188 Matthias Holzer .08 .20
189 Michael Neininger .08 .20
190 Benoit Pont .08 .20
191 Vlastimil Plavucha .08 .20
192 Daniel Steiner .08 .20
193 Stefan Tschiemer .08 .20
194 Lugano Logo .08 .20
195 Lugano Team Card .08 .20
196 Lugano Team Card .08 .20
197 Jim Koleff .08 .20
198 Cristobal Huet .08 5.00
199 Peter Martin .08 .20
200 Peter Andersson .08 .20
201 Mark Astley .08 .20
202 Sandro Bertaggia .08 .20
203 Olivier Keller .08 .20
204 Rick Tschumi .08 .20
205 Gaetan Voisard .08 .20
206 Jean-Jacques Aeschlimann .08 .20
207 Misko Antisin .08 .20
208 Philippe Bozon .40 1.00
209 Flavien Conne .08 .20
210 Christian Dube .08 .20
211 Keith Fair .08 .20
212 Igor Fedulov .08 .20
213 Regis Fuchs .08 .20
214 Sandy Jeannin .08 .20
215 Trevor Meier .08 .20
216 Andy Naser .08 .20
217 Geoffrey Vauclair .08 .20
218 Rapperswil Logo .08 .20
219 Rapperswil Team Card .08 .20
220 Rapperswil Team Card .08 .20
221 Evgeny Popikhin .08 .20
222 Claudio Bayer .08 .20
223 Matthias Lauber .08 .20
224 Marco Capaul .08 .20
225 Jakub Horak .08 .20
226 Kari Martikainen .08 .20
227 Jorg Reber .08 .20
228 Alain Reist .08 .20
229 Roger Sigg .08 .20
230 Loic Burkhalter .08 .20
231 Markus Butler .08 .20
232 Rene Friedli .08 .20
233 Rene Furler .08 .20
234 Dani Giger .08 .20
235 Sandro Haberlin .08 .20
236 Axel Heim .08 .20
237 Philppe Luber .08 .20
238 Dale McTavish .08 .20
239 Patrizio Morger .08 .20
240 Mike Richard .08 .20
241 Bernhard Schumperli .08 .20
242 EVZ Logo .08 .20
243 EVZ Team Card .08 .20
244 EVZ Team Card .08 .20
245 Andre Peloffy .08 .20
246 Ronnie Rueger .08 .20
247 Patrick Schopf .08 .20
248 Marco Bayer .08 .20
249 Ralph Bundi .08 .20
250 Patrick Fischer .08 .20
251 Dino Kessler .08 .20
252 Andre Kunzi .08 .20
253 Reto Kobach .08 .20
254 Patrick Sutter .08 .20
255 Christophe Brown .08 .20
256 Paul Di Pietro .20 .50
257 Todd Elik .08 .20
258 Stefan Grogg .08 .20
259 Vjeran Ivankovic .08 .20
260 Daniel Meier .08 .20
261 Stefan Niggli .08 .20
262 Patrick Oppliger .08 .20
263 Andre Rotheli .08 .20
264 Sascha Schneider .08 .20
265 Chris Tancill .08 .20
266 ZSC Logo .08 .20
267 ZSC Team Card .08 .20
268 ZSC Team Card .08 .20
269 Larry Hurras .08 .20
270 Thomas Papp .08 .20
271 Ari Sulander .20 .50
272 Martin Kout .08 .20
273 Adrien Plavsic .08 .20
274 Edgar Salis .08 .20
275 Mathias Seger .08 .20
276 Bruno Seck .08 .20
277 Andreas Zehnder .08 .20
278 Mattia Baldi .08 .20
279 Gian Marco Crameri .08 .20
280 Patric Della Rossa .08 .20
281 Daniel Hodgson .08 .20
282 Peter Jaks .08 .20
283 Andrew McKim .20 .50
284 Claudio Micheli .08 .20
285 Laurent Muller .08 .20
286 Mark Ouimet .08 .20
287 Rolf Schrepfer .08 .20
288 Reto Stirnimann .08 .20
289 Michel Zeiter .08 .20
290 HC Ajoie Logo .08 .20
291 Yann Voillat .08 .20
292 Chris Belanger .08 .20
293 EHC Basel Logo .08 .20
294 Todd Wetzel .08 .20
295 Patrick Girard .08 .20
296 EHC Biel Logo .08 .20
297 Sven Schmid .08 .20
298 Kevin Schlapfer .08 .20
299 GCK Lions Logo .08 .20
300 Patrick Looser .08 .20
301 Mikko Myllykoski .08 .20
302 HC Geneve Logo .08 .20
303 Patrice Brasey .08 .20
304 Scott Beattie .08 .20
305 SC Herisau Logo .08 .20
306 Andy Karpf .08 .20
307 Patrick Amann .08 .20
308 HC Lausanne Logo .08 .20
309 Beat Kindler .08 .20
310 Serge Poudrier .08 .20
311 EHC Olten Logo .08 .20
312 Beat Aebischer .08 .20
313 Richard Stucki .08 .20
314 HC Sierre Logo .08 .20
315 Jean Michel Clavien .08 .20
316 Gaby Epiney .08 .20
317 HC Thurgau Logo .08 .20
318 Martin Bruderer .08 .20
319 Morgan Samuelsson .08 .20
320 EHC Visp Logo .08 .20
321 Stefan Ketola .08 .20
322 Gabriel Taccoz .08 .20

2000-01 Swiss Panini Stickers National Team Insert

P1 Martin Gerber 1.00 2.50
P2 David Aebischer 1.00 2.50
P3 Reto Pavoni .40 1.00
P4 Patrick Fisher .40 1.00
P5 Olivier Keller .40 1.00
P6 Martin Steinegger .40 1.00
P7 Edgar Salis .40 1.00
P8 Mark Streit .40 1.00
P9 Julien Vauclair .40 1.00
P10 Patrick Sutter .40 1.00
P11 Mathias Seger .40 1.00
P12 Rolf Ziegler .40 1.00
P13 Flavien Conne .40 1.00
P14 Jean-Jaques Aeschlimann .40 1.00
P15 Mattia Baldi .40 1.00
P16 Patric Della Rossa .40 1.00
P17 Marcel Jenni .40 1.00
P18 Gian Marco Crameri .40 1.00
P19 Claudio Micheli .40 1.00
P20 Alain Demuth .40 1.00
P21 Thomas Ziegler .40 1.00
P22 Patrick Fischer .40 1.00
P23 Ivo Ruthemann .40 1.00
P24 Reto Von Arx .40 1.00
P25 Michel Zeiter .40 1.00
P26 Michel Riesen .40 1.00
P27 Sandy Jeannin .40 1.00
P28 Lurent Muller .40 1.00
P29 Martin Pluss .40 1.00
P30 Adi Wichser .40 1.00

2000-01 Swiss Slapshot Mini-Cards

COMPLETE SET (192) 20.00 40.00
LT1 Martin Gerber 2.00 5.00
LT2 Daniel Aegerter .10 .25
LT3 Samuel Balmer .10 .25
LT4 Beat Gerber .10 .25
LT5 Steve Hirschi .10 .25
LT6 Erik Kakko .10 .25
LT7 Pascal Muller .10 .25
LT8 Pascal Stoller .10 .25
LT9 Rolf Badertscher .10 .25
LT10 Bruno Brechbuhl .10 .25
LT11 John Fust .10 .25
LT12 Daniel Gauthier .10 .25
LT13 Thomas Heldner .10 .25
LT14 Matthias Holzer .10 .25
LT15 Vlastimil Plavucha .10 .25
LT16 Benoit Pont .10 .25
RJ1 Claudio Bayer .10 .25
RJ2 Marco Capaul .10 .25
RJ3 Kari Martikainen .10 .25
RJ4 Roger Sigg .10 .25
RJ5 Jorg Reber .10 .25
RJ6 Loic Burkhalter .10 .25
RJ7 Markus Butler .10 .25
RJ8 Rene Friedli .10 .25
RJ9 Rene Furler .10 .25
RJ10 Daniel Giger .10 .25
RJ11 Axel Heim .10 .25
RJ12 Philipp Luber .10 .25
RJ13 Dale McTavish .10 .25
RJ14 Patrizio Morger .10 .25
RJ15 Mike Richard .10 .25
RJ16 Bernhard Schumperli .10 .25
EVZ1 Ronnie Rueger .10 .25
EVZ2 Patrick Schopf .10 .25
EVZ3 Marco Bayer .10 .25
EVZ4 Patrick Fischer .10 .25
EVZ5 Dino Kessler .10 .25
EVZ6 Andre Kunzi .10 .25
EVZ7 Patrick Sutter .10 .25
EVZ8 Paul Di Pietro .20 .50
EVZ9 Todd Elik .20 .50
EVZ10 Stefan Grogg .10 .25
EVZ11 Vjeran Ivankovic .10 .25
EVZ12 Daniel Meier .10 .25
EVZ13 Patrick Oppliger .10 .25
EVZ14 Andre Rotheli .10 .25
EVZ15 Sascha Schneider .10 .25
EVZ16 Chris Tancill .10 .25
HCD1 Lars Weibel .20 .50
HCD2 Beat Equilino .10 .25
HCD3 Marc Gianola .10 .25
HCD4 Andreas Haller .10 .25
HCD5 Ralph Ott .10 .25
HCD6 Jan Von Arx .10 .25
HCD7 Andre Baumann .10 .25

HCD8 Lonny Bohonos .20 .50
HCD9 Patrick Fischer .10 .25
HCD10 Kevin Miller .20 .50
HCD11 Rene Muller .10 .25
HCD12 Thierry Paterlini .10 .25
HCD13 Sandro Rizzi .10 .25
HCD14 Frederic Rothen .10 .25
HCD15 Mario Schocher .10 .25
HCD16 Pat Falloon .20 .50
HCL1 Cristobal Huet 2.00 5.00
HCL2 Peter Anderson .10 .25
HCL3 Igor Fedulov .10 .25
HCL4 Sandro Bertaggia .10 .25
HCL5 Olivier Keller .10 .25
HCL6 Julien Vauclair .10 .25
HCL7 Gaetan Voisard .10 .25
HCL8 J.-Jacques Aeschlimann .10 .25
HCL9 Misko Antisin .10 .25
HCL10 Philippe Bozon .40 1.00
HCL11 Jan-Philippe Cadieux .10 .25
HCL12 Flavien Conne .10 .25
HCL13 Christian Dube .10 .25
HCL14 Regis Fuchs .10 .25
HCL15 Sandy Jeannin .10 .25
HCL16 Keith Fair .10 .25
SCB1 Renato Tosio .10 .25
SCB2 David Jobin .10 .25
SCB3 Sven Leuenberger .10 .25
SCB4 Dominic Meier .10 .25
SCB5 Frederik Olausson .10 .25
SCB6 Martin Steinegger .10 .25
SCB7 Rolf Ziegler .10 .25
SCB8 Bjorn Christen .10 .25
SCB9 Patrick Howald .10 .25
SCB10 Andreas Johansson .10 .25
SCB11 Patrick Juhlin .10 .25
SCB12 Alex Chatelain .10 .25
SCB13 Boris Leimgruber .10 .25
SCB14 Ivo Ruthemann .10 .25
SCB15 Franz Steffen .10 .25
SCB16 Marc Weber .10 .25
EHCC1 Nando Wieser .10 .25
EHCC2 Noel Guyaz .10 .25
EHCC3 Christian Langer .10 .25
EHCC4 Ivo Stoffel .10 .25
EHCC5 Mika Stromberg .10 .25
EHCC6 Pasi Sormunen .10 .25
EHCC7 Matthias Bachler .10 .25
EHCC8 Patrick Kruger .10 .25
EHCC9 Michael Meier .10 .25
EHCC10 Michael Rosenast .10 .25
EHCC11 Oliver Roth .10 .25
EHCC12 Marc Haueter .10 .25
EHCC13 Sandro Tschuor .10 .25
EHCC14 Raymond Walder .10 .25
EHCC15 Theo Wittmann .10 .25
EHCC16 UNKNOWN .10 .25
EHCK1 Reto Pavoni .10 .25
EHCK2 Martin Hohener .10 .25
EHCK3 Marko Kiprusoff .10 .25
EHCK4 Marco Kloti .10 .25
EHCK5 Oskar Szczepaniec .10 .25
EHCK6 UNKNOWN .10 .25
EHCK7 Fredrik Nilsson .10 .25
EHCK8 Sven Helfenstein .10 .25
EHCK9 Felix Hollenstein .10 .25
EHCK10 Andy Keller .10 .25
EHCK11 Sven Lindemann .10 .25
EHCK12 Martin Pluss .10 .25
EHCK13 Sebastien Reuille .10 .25
EHCK14 Andre Rufener .10 .25
EHCK15 Steve Washburn .10 .25
EHCK16 Adrian Wichser .10 .25
HCAP1 Pauli Jaks .10 .25
HCAP2 Fredy Bobillier .10 .25
HCAP3 Ivan Gazzaroli .10 .25
HCAP4 Tiziano Gianini .10 .25
HCAP5 Thomas Kunzi .10 .25
HCAP6 Leif Rohlin .10 .25
HCAP7 Krister Cantoni .10 .25
HCAP8 Manuele Celio .10 .25
HCAP9 Nicola Celio .10 .25
HCAP10 Alain Demuth .10 .25
HCAP11 Paolo Duca .10 .25
HCAP12 John Fritsche .10 .25
HCAP13 Ryan Gardner .10 .25
HCAP14 Paolo Imperatori .10 .25
HCAP15 Stephan Lebeau .20 .50
HCAP16 Daniel Marois .20 .50
HCCF1 Thomas Berger .10 .25
HCCF2 Raphael Brusa .10 .25
HCCF3 Fabian Guignard .10 .25
HCCF4 Valeri Shiryaev .10 .25
HCCF5 Ruedi Niderost .10 .25
HCCF6 Roger Ohmann .10 .25
HCCF7 Alexis Vacheron .10 .25
HCCF8 Steve Aebersold .10 .25
HCCF9 Thomas Derungs .10 .25
HCCF10 Claude Luthi .10 .25
HCCF11 Fabrice Maillat .10 .25
HCCF12 Daniel Nakaoka .10 .25
HCCF13 Stefan Nilsson .10 .25
HCCF14 Julien Turler .10 .25
HCCF15 Samuel Villiger .10 .25
HCCF16 Thibaut Monnet .10 .25
HCFG1 Thomas Ostlund .20 .50
HCFG2 Goran Bezina .10 .25
HCFG3 Antonie Descloux .10 .25
HCFG4 Livio Fazio .10 .25
HCFG5 Philippe Marquis .10 .25
HCFG6 Martin Rauch .10 .25
HCFG7 Marc Werlen .10 .25
HCFG8 Craig Ferguson .10 .25
HCFG9 Lars Leuenberger .10 .25
HCFG10 Gil Montandon .10 .25
HCFG11 Mario Rottaris .10 .25
HCFG12 Jean-Yves Roy .10 .25
HCFG13 Pascal Schaller .10 .25
HCFG14 Robert Slehofer .10 .25
HCFG15 Gerd Zenhäusern .10 .25
HCFG16 Michel Mouther .10 .25
ZSCL1 Ari Sulander .20 .50
ZSCL2 Adrien Plavsic .10 .25
ZSCL3 Edgar Salis .10 .25
ZSCL4 Matthias Seger .10 .25
ZSCL5 Mark Streit .20 .50
ZSCL6 Andreas Zehnder .10 .25
ZSCL7 Mattia Baldi .10 .25
ZSCL8 Gian Marco Crameri .10 .25
ZSCL9 Patric Della Rossa .10 .25
ZSCL10 Dan Hodgson .10 .25
ZSCL11 Peter Jaks .10 .25
ZSCL12 Andrew McKim .20 .50
ZSCL13 Claudio Micheli .10 .25
ZSCL14 Laurent Muller .10 .25
ZSCL15 Rolf Schrepfer .10 .25
ZSCL16 Michel Zeiter .10 .25

2001-02 Swiss EV Zug Postcards

These unnumbered 4X6 postcards were issued by the team and feature stylized action photos.

COMPLETE SET (27) 10.00 25.00
1 Team photo .40 1.00
2 Doug Mason .40 1.00
3 Richmond Gosselin .40 1.00
4 Patrick Schopf .40 1.00
5 Ronnie Rueger .40 1.00
6 Ruedi Niderost .40 1.00
7 Ralf Bundi .40 1.00
8 Patrick Fischer .40 1.00
9 Fabio Schumacher .40 1.00
10 Pascal Muller .40 1.00
11 Arne Ramholt .40 1.00
12 Kevin Gloor .40 1.00
13 Andre Kunzi .40 1.00
14 Reto Kobach .40 1.00
15 Thomas Nussli .40 1.00
16 Stefan Voegele .40 1.00
17 Stefan Niggli .40 1.00
18 Duri Camichel .40 1.00
19 Vjeran Ivankovic .40 1.00
20 Patrick Oppliger .40 1.00
21 Frederic Rothen .40 1.00
22 Stefan Grogg .40 1.00
23 Christoph Brown .40 1.00
24 Chris Tancill .75 2.00
25 Todd Elik .75 2.00
26 Joel Savage .75 2.00
27 Paul DiPietro .75 2.00

2001-02 Swiss HNL

This series features the top players in the Swiss Elite League, one of the top European circuits.

COMPLETE SET (480) 30.00 75.00
1 Larry Huras .10 .25
2 Thomas Papp .10 .25
3 Ari Sulander .40 1.00
4 Martin Kout .10 .25
5 Adrian Plavsic .10 .25
6 Tim Ramholt .60 1.50
7 Edgar Salis .10 .25
8 Mathias Seger .10 .25
9 Bruno Steck .10 .25
10 Mark Streit .10 .25
11 Jan Alston .20 .50
12 Mattia Baldi .10 .25
13 Gian-Marco Crameri .10 .25
14 Patric Della Rossa .10 .25
15 Paolo Duca .10 .25
16 Dan Hodgson .20 .50
17 Peter Jaks .10 .25
18 Claudio Micheli .10 .25
19 Mark Ouimet .20 .50
20 Morgan Samuelsson .10 .25
21 Stefan Schnyder .10 .25
22 Reto Stirnimann .10 .25
23 Petri Varis .20 .50
24 Michel Zeiter .10 .25
25 Zinetoula Bilyaletdinov .10 .25
26 Paolo Della Bella .10 .25
27 Cristobal Huet ERC 1.60 5.00
28 Mark Astley .20 .50
29 Sandro Bertaggia .10 .25
30 Olivier Keller .10 .25
31 Petteri Nummelin .10 .25
32 Patrick Sutter .10 .25
33 Rick Tschumi .10 .25
34 Gaetan Voisard .10 .25
35 Jean-Jacques Aeschlimann .10 .25
36 Jan Cadieux .10 .25
37 Gregory Christen .10 .25
38 Flavien Conne .10 .25
39 Christian Dube .10 .25
40 Keith Fair .10 .25
41 Regis Fuchs .10 .25
42 Ryan Gardner .20 .50
43 Sandy Jeannin .10 .25
44 Mike Maneluk .20 .50
45 Andy Naser .10 .25
46 Andre Rotheli .10 .25
47 Raffaele Sannitz .30 .75
48 Geoffrey Vauclair .10 .25
49 Kloten-Flyers .10 .25
50 Vladimir Jursinov .10 .25
51 Flavio Ludke .10 .25
52 Reto Pavoni .20 .50
53 Severin Blindenbacher .10 .25
54 Manuel Gossweiler .10 .25
55 Fabian Guignard .10 .25
56 Roman Hardmeier .10 .25
57 Martin Hohener .10 .25
58 Ronny Keller .10 .25
59 Chris O'Sullivan .20 .50
60 Gregor Thommen .10 .25
61 Mathias Wust .10 .25
62 Andre Bielmann .10 .25
63 Patrik Bartschi .10 .25
64 Andreas Cellar .10 .25
65 Felix Hollenstein .10 .25
66 Andy Keller .10 .25
67 Dario Kostovic .10 .25
68 Sven Lindemann .10 .25
69 Fredrik Nilsson .10 .25
70 Emanuel Peter .10 .25
71 Martin Pluss .10 .25
72 Kimmo Rintanen .10 .25
73 Adrian Wichser .30 .75
74 Thomas Widmer .10 .25
75 Riccardo Fuhrer .10 .25
76 Marco Buhrer .20 .50
77 Andreas Schweizer .10 .25
78 Rikard Franzen .10 .25
79 David Jobin .10 .25
80 Sven Leuenberger .10 .25
81 Marc Leuenberger .10 .25
82 Dominic Meier .10 .25
83 Martin Steinegger .10 .25
84 Rolf Ziegler .10 .25
85 Derek Armstrong .20 .50
86 Andre Baumann .10 .25
87 Alex Chatelain .10 .25
88 Sven Hellenstein .10 .25
89 Patrik Juhlin .20 .50
90 Laurent Muller .10 .25
91 Philippe Muller .10 .25
92 Marc Reichert .10 .25
93 Ivo Ruthemann .10 .25
94 Rolf Schrepfer .10 .25
95 Franz Steffen .10 .25
96 Fabian Sutter .10 .25
97 Marc Weber .10 .25
98 Arno Del Curto .10 .25
99 Jonas Hiller 1.00 2.50
100 Lars Weibel .20 .50
101 Beat Equilino .10 .25
102 Beat Forster .10 .25
103 Marc Gianola .10 .25
104 Andrea Haller .10 .25
105 Michael Kress .10 .25
106 Ralph Ott .10 .25
107 Jan von Arx .10 .25
108 Benjamin Winkler .10 .25
109 Andres Ambuhl .10 .25
110 Lonny Bohonos .20 .50
111 Andreas Camenzind .10 .25
112 Bjorn Christen .10 .25
113 Patrick Fischer .10 .25
114 Joel Frohlicher .10 .25
115 Stefan Gahler .10 .25
116 Marc Heberlein .10 .25
117 Josef Marha .10 .25
118 Kevin Miller .20 .50
119 Rene Muller .10 .25
120 Sandro Rizzi .10 .25
121 Serge Pelletier .10 .25
122 Matthias Lauber .20 .50
123 Gianluca Mona .20 .50
124 Raphaël Berger .10 .25
125 Antoine Descloux .10 .25
126 Mike Gaul .20 .50
127 Lukas Gerber .10 .25
128 Philippe Marquis .10 .25
129 Martin Rauch .10 .25
130 Marc Werlen .10 .25
131 Craig Ferguson .20 .50
132 Gilbert Flueler .10 .25
133 Christof Hillebrand .10 .25
134 Patrick Howald .10 .25
135 Lars Leuenberger .10 .25
136 Silvan Lussy .10 .25
137 David Maurer .10 .25
138 Thibaut Monnet .10 .25
139 Gil Montandon .10 .25
140 Michel Mouther .10 .25
141 Mario Rottaris .10 .25
142 Jean-Yves Roy .20 .50
143 Robert Slehofer .10 .25
144 Colin Muller .10 .25
145 Evgeni Popichin .10 .25
146 Thomas Berger .20 .50
147 Simon Zuger .20 .50
148 Marco Capaul .10 .25
149 Livio Fazio .10 .25
150 Jakub Horak .10 .25
151 Kari Martikainen .10 .25
152 Alain Reist .10 .25
153 Marc Schefer .10 .25
154 Fabian Stephan .10 .25
155 Markus Butler .10 .25
156 Rene Friedli .10 .25
157 Daniel Giger .10 .25
158 Axel Heim .10 .25
159 Philipp Luber .10 .25
160 Dale McTavish .20 .50
161 Claudio Moggi .10 .25
162 Sandro Moggi .10 .25
163 Patrizio Morger .10 .25
164 Sebastien Reuille .10 .25
165 Mike Richard .10 .25
166 Morgan Samuelsson .10 .25
167 Doug Mason .10 .25
168 Ronnie Rueger .20 .50
169 Patrick Schopf .10 .25
170 Ralf Bundi .10 .25
171 Patrick Fischer .10 .25
172 Reto Kobach .10 .25
173 Andre Kunzi .10 .25
174 Pascal Muller .10 .25
175 Ruedi Niderost .10 .25
176 Arne Ramholt .10 .25
177 Fabio Schumacher .10 .25
178 Christophe Brown .10 .25
179 Duri Camichel .10 .25
180 Paul Di Pietro .20 .50
181 Todd Elik .20 .50
182 Stefan Grogg .10 .25
183 Vjeran Ivankovic .10 .25
184 Stefan Niggli .10 .25
185 Thomas Nussli .10 .25
186 Patrick Oppliger .10 .25
187 Frederic Rothen .10 .25
188 Joel Savage .20 .50
189 Chris Tancill .20 .50
190 Vassily Tikhonov .10 .25
191 Claudio Bayer .20 .50
192 Marco Streit .20 .50
193 Daniel Aegerter .10 .25
194 Samuel Balmer .10 .25
195 Beat Gerber .10 .25
196 Steve Hirschi .10 .25
197 Erik Hamalainen .10 .25
198 Thomas Kunzi .10 .25
199 Pascal Stoller .10 .25
200 Rolf Badertscher .10 .25
201 Brian Bonin .20 .50
202 Bruno Brechbuhl .10 .25
203 John Fust .10 .25
204 Daniel Gauthier .10 .25
205 Thomas Heldner .10 .25
206 Matthias Holzer .10 .25
207 Benjamin Pluss .10 .25
208 Benoit Pont .10 .25
209 Bernhard Schumperli .10 .25
210 Daniel Steiner .10 .25
211 Rostislav Cada .10 .25
212 Lorenzo Barenco .10 .25
213 Pauli Jaks .20 .50
214 Marco Bayer .10 .25
215 Nicola Celio .10 .25
216 Ivan Gazzaroli .10 .25
217 Tiziano Gianini .10 .25
218 John Gobbi .10 .25
219 Andreas Hanni .10 .25
220 Martin Stepanek .10 .25
221 Loïc Burkhalter .10 .25
222 Corsin Camichel .10 .25
223 Krister Cantoni .10 .25
224 Manuele Celio .10 .25
225 Alain Demuth .10 .25
226 John Fritsche .10 .25
227 Paolo Imperatori .10 .25
228 Roland Kaser .10 .25
229 Vitaly Lakhmatov .10 .25
230 Michel Liniger .10 .25
231 Robert Petrovicky .10 .25
232 Omar Tognini .10 .25
233 Tomas Vlasak .10 .25
234 Niklas Wikegard .10 .25
235 Tobias Stephan .80 3.00
236 Nando Wieser .10 .25
237 Rene Back .10 .25
238 Cyrill Geyer .10 .25
239 Noel Guyaz .10 .25
240 Marc Haueter .10 .25
241 Ivo Stoffel .10 .25
242 Mika Stromberg .10 .25
243 Andreas Zehnder .10 .25
244 Fabio Beccarelli .10 .25
245 Matthias Bachler .10 .25
246 Kristian Gahn .10 .25
247 Patrick Kruger .10 .25
248 Michael Meier .10 .25
249 Daniel Peer .10 .25
250 Roger Rieder .10 .25
251 Oliver Roth .10 .25
252 Ivo Simeon .10 .25
253 Rene Stussi .10 .25
254 Sandro Tschuor .10 .25
255 Johan Witehall .10 .25
256 Theo Wittmann .10 .25
257 HC Lausanne .10 .25
258 Mike McParland .10 .25
259 Beat Kindler .20 .50
260 Reto Schurch .20 .50
261 Malik Benturqui .10 .25
262 Michel Kamber .10 .25
263 Dejan Lozanov .10 .25
264 Michel N'Goy .10 .25
265 Serge Poudrier .10 .25
266 Roger Sigg .10 .25
267 Thomas Studer .10 .25
268 Oliver Tschanz .10 .25
269 Florian Andenmatten .10 .25
270 Andrei Bashkirov .20 .50
271 Daniel Bieri .10 .25
272 Thierry Bornand .10 .25
273 Sandro Haberlin .10 .25
274 Oliver Kamber .10 .25
275 Trevor Meier .10 .25
276 Philippe Orlandi .10 .25
277 Dmitri Shamolin .10 .25
278 Samuel Villiger .10 .25
279 Sacha Weibel .20 .50
280 Gerd Zenhausern .10 .25
281 Michel Lussier .10 .25
282 Gilles Cattela .10 .25
283 Thierry Noel .10 .25
284 Oliver Amadio .10 .25
285 Pascal Avanthay .10 .25
286 Nicolas Bernasconi .10 .25
287 Raphaël Brusa .10 .25
288 Valeri Chiriaev .10 .25
289 Marc Tschudy .10 .25
290 Alexis Vacheron .10 .25
291 Steve Aebersold .10 .25
292 Jesse Belanger .20 .50
293 Thomas Deruns .10 .25
294 Jamie Heinrich .10 .25
295 Vincent Lechenne .10 .25
296 Claude Luethi .10 .25
297 Fabrice Maillat .10 .25
298 Daniel Nakaoka .10 .25
299 Michael Neininger .10 .25
300 Philippe Thalmann .10 .25
301 Markus Graf .10 .25
302 Marco Wegmuller .20 .50
303 Martin Zerzuben .10 .25
304 Sven Dick .10 .25
305 Serge Meyer .10 .25
306 Jorg Reber .10 .25
307 Sven Schmid .10 .25
308 Bjorn Schneider .10 .25
309 Pascal Sommer .10 .25
310 Mauro Beccarelli .10 .25
311 Philipp Folghera .10 .25
312 Rene Furler .10 .25
313 Stefan Moser .10 .25
314 Andreas Nauser .10 .25
315 Cyrill Pasche .10 .25
316 Reggie Savage .20 .50
317 Ryan Savoia .20 .50
318 Kevin Schlapfer .10 .25
319 Marco Signer .10 .25
320 Stefan Tschiemer .10 .25
321 Chris McSorley .10 .25
322 David Bochy .10 .25
323 Flavio Streit .10 .25
324 Fredy Bobillier .10 .25
325 Patrice Brasey .10 .25
326 Fabian Gull .10 .25
327 David Leibzig .10 .25
328 Todd Richards .20 .50
329 Nicolas Studer .10 .25
330 Misko Antisin .10 .25
331 Philippe Bozon .40 2.00
332 Igor Fedulov .10 .25
333 Marco Fischer .10 .25
334 Xavier Gattuso .10 .25
335 Maxime Lapointe .10 .25
336 Boris Leimgruber .10 .25
337 Paul Savary .10 .25
338 Didier Schafer .10 .25
339 Pascal Schaller .10 .25
340 Mario Schocher .10 .25
341 Bruno Aegerter .10 .25
342 Rainer Karlen .10 .25
343 Marc Zimmermann .20 .50
344 Beat Heldstab .10 .25
345 Karl Knopf .10 .25
346 Philipp Portner .10 .25
347 Francis Reichmuth .10 .25
348 Marco Schupbach .10 .25
349 Marc Zurbriggen .10 .25
350 Patrick Aeberli .10 .25
351 Sergio Biner .10 .25
352 Marc Buhlmann .10 .25
353 Nicolas Gastaldo .10 .25
354 Stefan Ketola .10 .25
355 Swen Kohler .10 .25
356 Richard Laplante .10 .25
357 Cedric Metrailler .10 .25
358 Detlef Prediger .10 .25
359 Gabriel Taccoz .10 .25
360 Ken Zurfluh .10 .25
361 Arnold Lortscher .10 .25
362 Beat Aebischer .10 .25
363 Rainer Kalin .10 .25
364 Francesco Bizzozero .10 .25
365 Christoph Decurtins .10 .25
366 Mark Emmenegger .10 .25
367 Ruedi Forster .10 .25
368 Jurg Hardegger .10 .25
369 Richard Stucki .10 .25
370 Stefan Wuthrich .10 .25
371 Alain Ayer .10 .25
372 Yanick Dube .10 .25
373 Reto Germann .10 .25
374 Patrick Giroud .10 .25
375 Bjorn Guazzini .10 .25
376 Albert Malgin .10 .25
377 Oliver Muller .10 .25
378 Patrick Siegwart .10 .25
379 Andre von Rohr .10 .25
380 Matti Alatalo .10 .25
381 Christian Weber .10 .25
382 Marc Eichmann .10 .25
383 Matthias Schoder .20 .50
384 Stefan Badrutt .10 .25
385 Chris Belanger .10 .25
386 Thomi Derungs .10 .25
387 Michael Hofer .10 .25
388 Andri Stoffel .10 .25
389 Andreas Furrer .10 .25
390 Lukas Grauwiler .10 .25
391 Rolf Hildebrand .10 .25
392 Alex Krstic .10 .25
393 Patrick Landolt .10 .25
394 Patrick Looser .10 .25
395 Dean Seymour .10 .25
396 Riccardo Signorell .10 .25
397 Pascal Tiegermann .10 .25
398 Thomas Walser .10 .25
399 Simon Wanner .10 .25
400 Merlin Malinowski .10 .25
401 Olivier Gigon .10 .25
402 Sebastien Kohler .20 .50
403 Ludovic Aubry .10 .25
404 Eric Bourquin .10 .25
405 Dany Ott .10 .25
406 Christian Schuster .10 .25
407 Wes Snell .10 .25
408 Markus Wuthrich .10 .25
409 Steven Barras .10 .25
410 Martin Bergeron .10 .25
411 Scott Biser .10 .25
412 Florian Conz .10 .25
413 Real Gerber .10 .25
414 Sacha Gueme .10 .25
415 Shawn Heaphy .10 .25
416 Jerome Kohler .10 .25
417 Jean-Charles Lapaire .10 .25
418 Boe Leslie .10 .25
419 Steve Pochon .10 .25
420 Yann Voillat .10 .25
421 Didier Massy .10 .25
422 Gregory Berclaz .10 .25
423 Roland Meyer .10 .25
424 Johan Bertholet .10 .25
425 Lionel D'Urso .10 .25
426 Cedric Favre .10 .25
427 Jonathan Lussier .10 .25
428 Pietro Ottini .10 .25
429 Emmanuel Tacchini .10 .25
430 Beat Brantschen .10 .25
431 Elvis Clavien .10 .25
432 Gaby Epiney .10 .25
433 Kelly Glowa .10 .25
434 Pietro Juri .10 .25
435 Daniel Mares .10 .25
436 Cedric Melly .10 .25
437 Thierry Metrailler .10 .25
438 Fabrizio Silietti .10 .25
439 Daniel Wobmann .10 .25
440 Raymond Zahnd .10 .25
441 Christian Ruegg .10 .25
442 Mathias Muller .10 .25
443 Pascal Sievert .10 .25
444 Claude Amstutz .10 .25
445 Roland Kradolfer .10 .25
446 Pascal Lamprecht .10 .25
447 Patrick Mader .10 .25
448 Michael Marki .10 .25
449 Alessandro Sellitto .10 .25
450 Daniel Sigg .10 .25
451 Rico Beltrame .10 .25
452 Marius Brugger .10 .25
453 Joel Camenzind .10 .25
454 Michael Diener .10 .25
455 Timmy Hoppe .10 .25
456 Roland Korsch .10 .25
457 Real Raemy .10 .25
458 Marco Seeholzer .10 .25
459 Harijs Vitolinsch .10 .25
460 Jacques Zimmermann .10 .25
461 Beat Lautenschlager .10 .25
462 Davide Gislimberti .10 .25
463 Peter Mettler .20 .50
464 Marc Gautschi .10 .25
465 Zbynek Hybler .10 .25
466 Stephane Julien .10 .25
467 Kim Schedegger .10 .25
468 Olivier Schaublin .10 .25
469 Dominik Z'berg .10 .25
470 Philipp Dornbierer .10 .25
471 Patrick Girod .10 .25
472 Marco Graf .10 .25
473 Andreas Haner .10 .25
474 Michael Murer .10 .25
475 Robert Othmann .10 .25
476 Steve Potvin .10 .25
477 David Raissle .10 .25
478 Jarkko Schaublin .10 .25
479 Lovis Schonenberger .10 .25
480 Marcel Sommer .10 .25

2002-03 Swiss EV Zug Postcards

These unnumbered 4X6 postcards were issued by the team and feature stylized action photos on the front.

COMPLETE SET (26) 10.00 25.00
1 Team photo .40 1.00
2 Doug Mason .40 1.00
3 Chris Tancill .75 2.00
4 Paul DiPietro .75 2.00
5 Richmond Gosselin .40 1.00
6 Patrick Schopf .40 1.00
7 Peter Mettler .40 1.00
8 Ruedi Niderost .40 1.00
9 Ralf Bundi .40 1.00
10 Charles Simard .40 1.00
11 Patrick Fischer .40 1.00
12 Fabio Schumacher .40 1.00
13 Pascal Muller .40 1.00
14 Gaetan Voisard .40 1.00
15 Lovis Schonenberger .40 1.00
16 Stefan Voegele .40 1.00
17 Stefan Niggli .40 1.00
18 Duri Camichel .40 1.00
19 Patrick Oppliger .40 1.00
20 Paolo Duca .40 1.00
21 Andre Rufener .40 1.00
22 Alain Demuth .40 1.00
23 Oliver Kamber .40 1.00
24 Frederic Rothen .40 1.00
25 Joel Savage .75 2.00
26 Chris Armstrong .40 1.00

2002-03 Swiss HNL

This series features the top players in the Swiss Elite League, one of the top European circuits. The set features top prospects Tobias Stephan and Tim Ramholt.

COMPLETE SET (499) 30.00 75.00
1 Lars Weibel .20 .50
2 Andrea Haller .10 .25
3 Jonas Hiller 1.00 2.50
4 Jan von Arx .10 .25
5 Lonny Bohonos .20 .50
6 Marco Gruber .10 .25
7 Marc Gianola .10 .25
8 Josef Marha .10 .25
9 Michel Riesen .80 1.00
10 Reto von Arx .20 .50
11 Ralph Ott .10 .25
12 Ari Sulander .40 1.00
13 Martin Kout .10 .25
14 Edgar Salis .10 .25
15 Andres Ambuhl .10 .25
16 Jan Alston .20 .50
17 Gian-Carlo Hendry .10 .25
18 Peter Jaks .10 .25
19 Patrick Fischer .10 .25
20 Mark Ouimet .20 .50
21 Reto Stirnimann .10 .25
22 Davide Gislimberti .10 .25
23 Marc Heberlein .10 .25
24 Sandro Bertaggia .10 .25
25 Olivier Keller .10 .25
26 Jean-Jacques Aeschlimann .10 .25
27 Thierry Paterlini .10 .25
28 Flavien Conne .10 .25
29 Ryan Gardner .20 .50
30 Corey Millen .10 .25
31 Fabian Sutter .10 .25
32 Andre Rotheli .10 .25
33 Vladimir Jursinov .10 .25
34 Lukas Baumgartner .10 .25
35 Matthias Schoder .20 .50
36 Martin Hohener .10 .25
37 Alain Reist .10 .25
38 Deny Bartschi .10 .25
39 Jakub Horak .10 .25
40 Jaroslav Hlinka .10 .25
41 Sven Lindemann .10 .25
42 Marc Reichert .10 .25
43 Tim Ramholt .40 1.00
44 Thomas Widmer .10 .25
45 Gianluca Mona .20 .50
46 Mike Gaul .20 .50
47 Mark Streit .10 .25
48 Philippe Marquis .10 .25
49 Patrick Howald .10 .25
50 David Maurer .10 .25
51 Patric Della Rossa .10 .25
52 Michel Mouther .10 .25
53 Robert Slehofer .10 .25
54 Pauli Jaks .20 .50
55 Dan Hodgson .20 .50
56 Ivan Gazzaroli .10 .25
57 Martin Rauch .10 .25
58 Loic Burkhalter .10 .25
59 Claudio Micheli .10 .25
60 Nicola Celio .10 .25
61 Paolo Imperatori .10 .25
62 Robert Petrovicky .10 .25
63 Raeto Raffainer .10 .25
64 Doug Mason .10 .25
65 Chris Armstrong .10 .25
66 Ruedi Niderost .10 .25
67 Jim Koleff .10 .25
68 Duri Camichel .10 .25
69 Paolo Duca .10 .25
70 Patrick Oppliger .10 .25
71 Mark Astley .20 .50
72 Joel Savage .20 .50
73 Stefan Voegele .10 .25
74 Marc Eichmann .10 .25
75 Andreas Hanni .10 .25
76 Marc Leuenberger .10 .25
77 Martin Steinegger .10 .25
78 Alex Chatelain .10 .25
79 Patrick Sutter .10 .25
80 Patrik Juhlin .20 .50
81 Laurent Muller .10 .25
82 Rolf Schrepfer .10 .25
83 Krister Cantoni .10 .25
84 Beat Kindler .20 .50
85 Fredy Bobillier .10 .25
86 Serge Poudrier .10 .25
87 Regis Fuchs .10 .25
88 Florian Andenmatten .10 .25
89 Thierry Bornand .10 .25
90 Philippe Orlandi .10 .25
91 Mike Maneluk .20 .50
92 Sacha Weibel .20 .50
93 Kari Eloranta .20 .50
94 Livio Fazio .10 .25
95 Andy Naser .10 .25
96 Kari Martikainen .10 .25
97 Patrick Aeberli .10 .25
98 Axel Heim .10 .25
99 Adrian Wichser .20 .50
100 Patrizio Morger .10 .25
101 Jarno Peltonen .10 .25
102 Thomas Walser .10 .25
103 Tobias Stephan .60 2.00
104 Marco Streit .20 .50
105 Beat Gerber .10 .25
106 Pascal Stoller .10 .25
107 Fabian Guignard .10 .25
108 Bruno Brechbuhl .10 .25
109 Todd Elik .20 .50
110 Benjamin Pluss .10 .25
111 Marco Kloti .10 .25
112 Bernhard Schumperli .10 .25
113 Fabien Hecquet .10 .25
114 Brett Hauer .20 .50
115 Cyrill Buhler .10 .25
116 Wes Snell .10 .25
117 Misko Antisin .10 .25
118 Gian-Marco Crameri .10 .25
119 Andreas Camenzind .10 .25
120 Daniel Meier .10 .25
121 Paul Savary .10 .25
122 Dario Kostovic .10 .25
123 Michel Lussier .10 .25
124 Romano Lemm .10 .25
125 Oliver Amadio .10 .25
126 Dejan Lozanov .10 .25
127 Emanuel Peter .10 .25
128 Steve Aebersold .10 .25
129 Martin Pluss .10 .25
130 Boris Leimgruber .10 .25
131 Daniel Nakaoka .10 .25
132 Roger Rieder .10 .25
133 Julien Turler .10 .25
134 Kimmo Rintanen .10 .25
135 Martin Zerzuben .10 .25
136 Sven Dick .10 .25
137 Colin Muller .10 .25
138 Bjorn Schneider .10 .25
139 Matthias Lauber .20 .50
140 Mauro Beccarelli .10 .25
141 Stefan Moser .10 .25
142 Raphael Berger .10 .25
143 Kevin Schlapfer .10 .25
144 Alain Birbaum .10 .25
145 Thomas Papp .10 .25
146 Michael Hofer .10 .25
147 Lukas Gerber .10 .25
148 Andri Stoffel .10 .25
149 Tiziano Gianini .10 .25
150 Sandro Moggi .10 .25
151 Riccardo Signorell .10 .25
152 Oliver Tschanz .10 .25
153 Simon Wanner .10 .25
154 Craig Ferguson .20 .50
155 Rainer Karlen .10 .25
156 Beat Heldstab .10 .25
157 Vjeran Ivankovic .10 .25
158 Marco Schupbach .10 .25
159 Silvan Lussy .10 .25
160 Michael Gerber .10 .25
161 Cedric Metrailler .10 .25
162 Thibaut Monnet .10 .25
163 Stephane Roy .10 .25
164 Gil Montandon .10 .25
165 Merlin Malinowski .10 .25
166 Olivier Devaux .10 .25
167 Mario Rottaris .10 .25
168 Dany Ott .10 .25
169 Jean-Yves Roy .20 .50
170 Markus Wuthrich .10 .25
171 Florian Conz .10 .25
172 Valentin Wirz .10 .25
173 Jerome Kohler .10 .25
174 Rostislav Cada .10 .25
175 Yann Voillat .10 .25
176 Rainer Kalin .10 .25
177 Simon Zuger .20 .50
178 Jurg Hardegger .10 .25
179 Robin Breitbach .10 .25
180 Richard Stucki .10 .25
181 Reto Germann .10 .25
182 John Gobbi .10 .25
183 Claude Luethi .10 .25
184 Reto Kobach .10 .25
185 Robert Ohmann .10 .25
186 Matthias Muller .10 .25
187 Martin Stepahek .10 .25
188 Pascal Lamprecht .10 .25
189 Alan Tallarini .10 .25
190 Andre Nussbaum .10 .25
191 Michael Diener .10 .25

192 Corsin Camichel .10 .25
193 Timmy Hoppe .10 .25
194 Manuele Celio .10 .25
195 Marco Signer .10 .25
196 Beat Lautenschlager .10 .25
197 John Fritsche .10 .25
198 Marco Knecht .10 .25
199 John Fust .10 .25
200 Alexis Vacheron .10 .25
201 Martin Bergeron .10 .25
202 Vitaly Lakhmatov .10 .25
203 Andreas Haner .10 .25
204 Michel Liniger .10 .25
205 Marco Seeholzer .10 .25
206 Samuel Villiger .10 .25
207 Zdenek Sedlak .10 .25
208 Roland Meyer .10 .25
209 Egor Shastin .10 .25
210 Cedric Favre .10 .25
211 Roland Kradolfer .10 .25
212 Peter Mettler .20 .50
213 Severin Cavegn .10 .25
214 Patrick Schopf .20 .50
215 Antoine Lussier .10 .25
216 Oleg Siritsa .10 .25
217 Patrick Fischer .10 .25
218 Sascha Friedli .10 .25
219 Pascal Muller .10 .25
220 Rolf Diethelm .10 .25
221 Alan Hirschi .10 .25
222 Charles Simard .10 .25
223 Mario Heiniger .10 .25
224 Gaetan Voisard .10 .25
225 Marco Pistolato .10 .25
226 Mischa von Gunten .10 .25
227 Alain Demuth .10 .25
228 Ralph Krueger .10 .25
229 Paul Di Pietro .20 .50
230 Flavien Conne .10 .25
231 Alain Demuth .10 .25
232 Oliver Kamber .10 .25
233 Martin Hohener .10 .25
234 Stefan Niggli .10 .25
235 David Jobin .10 .25
236 Marc Reichert .10 .25
237 Frederic Rothen .10 .25
238 Mathias Seger .10 .25
239 Andre Rufener .10 .25
240 Patrick Sutter .10 .25
241 Winners Pluss .10 .25
242 Lovis Schonenberger .10 .25
243 Lonny Bohonos .20 .50
244 Chris Tancill .20 .50
245 Mike Maneluk .20 .50
246 Martin Pluss .10 .25
247 Kent Ruhnke .10 .25
248 Arno Del Curto .10 .25
249 Marco Buhrer .20 .50
250 Florian Blatter .10 .25
251 Michael Kress .10 .25
252 Rikard Franzen .10 .25
253 Benjamin Winkler .10 .25
254 David Jobin .10 .25
255 Bjorn Christen .10 .25
256 Steivan Hasler .10 .25
257 Sven Leuenberger .10 .25
258 Kevin Miller .20 .50
259 Dominic Meier .10 .25
260 Sandro Rizzi .10 .25
261 Pekka Rautakallio .20 .50
262 Rolf Ziegler .10 .25
263 Rene Back .10 .25
264 Sebastien Bordeleau .20 .50
265 Arne Ramholt .10 .25
266 Mathias Seger .10 .25
267 Christian Dube .10 .25
268 Mattia Baldi .10 .25
269 Sven Helfenstein .10 .25
270 Rolf Hildebrand .10 .25
271 Christian Matte .20 .50
272 Andy Keller .10 .25
273 Derek Plante .20 .50
274 Lars Leuenberger .10 .25
275 Michel Zeiter .10 .25
276 Ronnie Rueger .20 .50
277 Philippe Muller .10 .25
278 Noel Guyaz .10 .25
279 Ivo Ruthemann .10 .25
280 Petteri Nummelin .10 .25
281 Jan Cadieux .10 .25
282 Thomas Ziegler .10 .25
283 Keith Fair .10 .25
284 Mike McParland .10 .25
285 Sandy Jeannin .10 .25
286 Mirko Murovic .20 .50
287 Reto Schurch .20 .50
288 Raffaele Sannitz .20 .50
289 Malik Benturqui .10 .25
290 Flavio Ludke .10 .25
291 Severin Blindenbacher .10 .25
292 Ronny Keller .10 .25
293 Marko Kiprusoff .10 .25
294 Michel N'Goy .10 .25
295 Gregor Thommen .10 .25
296 Patrik Bartschi .10 .25
297 Thomas Studer .10 .25
298 Marc Werlen .10 .25
299 Andrei Bashkirov .20 .50
300 Daniel Bieri .10 .25
301 Mathias Holzer .10 .25
302 Trevor Meier .10 .25
303 Dmitri Shamolin .10 .25
304 Jarrod Skalde .20 .50
305 Michel Wicky .10 .25
306 Gerd Zenhausern .10 .25
307 Thomas Berger .20 .50
308 Marco Capaul .10 .25
309 Cyrill Geyer .10 .25
310 Michel Kamber .10 .25
311 Marc Schefer .10 .25
312 Fabian Stephan .10 .25
313 Markus Butler .10 .25
314 Daniel Giger .10 .25
315 Philipp Luber .10 .25
316 Dale McTavish .20 .50
317 Thomas Nussli .10 .25
318 Mikko Peltola .10 .25
319 Sebastien Reuille .10 .25
320 Niki Siren .10 .25
321 Alfred Bohren .10 .25
322 Claudio Bayer .20 .50
323 Daniel Aegerter .10 .25
324 Samuel Balmer .10 .25
325 Steve Hirschi .10 .25
326 Thomas Kunzi .10 .25
327 Mathias Wust .10 .25
328 Brian Bonin .20 .50
329 Marc Buhlmann .10 .25
330 Mike Craig .20 .50
331 Stefan Grogg .10 .25
332 Thomas Heldner .10 .25
333 Benoit Pont .10 .25
334 Sascha Schneider .10 .25
335 Daniel Steiner .10 .25
336 Chris McSorley .10 .25
337 Reto Pavoni .20 .50
338 Patrice Brasey .10 .25
339 Jamie Heward .20 .50
340 Dino Kessler .10 .25
341 Nicolas Studer .10 .25
342 Pierre-Alain Ancay .10 .25
343 Yvan Benoit .10 .25
344 Philippe Bozon .40 1.00
345 Thomas Derungs .10 .25
346 Igor Fedulov .10 .25
347 Michael Neininger .10 .25
348 Kevin Romy .10 .25
349 Pascal Schaller .10 .25
350 Theo Wittmann .10 .25
351 Florien Bruegger .10 .25
352 Gilles Cattela .10 .25
353 Nicolas Bernasconi .10 .25
354 Valeri Chiriaev .10 .25
355 Jonathan Pan .10 .25
356 Marc Tschudy .10 .25
357 Philippe Fontana .10 .25
358 Jamie Heinrich .10 .25
359 Fabrice Maillat .10 .25
360 Damien Micheli .10 .25
361 Philippe Thalmann .10 .25
362 Omar Tognini .10 .25
363 Bror Hansson .10 .25
364 Simon Rytz .10 .25
365 Fabian Beck .10 .25
366 Chris Belanger .10 .25
367 Serge Meyer .10 .25
368 Jorg Reber .10 .25
369 Remo Altorfer .10 .25
370 Fabio Beccarelli .10 .25
371 Rene Furler .10 .25
372 Vincent Lechenne .10 .25
373 Steve Pochon .10 .25
374 Ryan Savoia .20 .50
375 Christian Weber .10 .25
376 Yves Burlimann .10 .25
377 Marco Baumann .10 .25
378 Andreas Furrer .10 .25
379 Patrick Meichtry .10 .25
380 Daniel Schnyder .10 .25
381 Lukas Grauwiler .10 .25
382 Claudio Moggi .10 .25
383 Andreas Nauser .10 .25
384 Mike Richard .10 .25
385 Pascal Tiegermann .10 .25
386 Petri Varis .20 .50
387 Alexis Weber .10 .25
388 Bruno Aegerter .10 .25
389 Marc Zimmermann .20 .50
390 Stefan Badrutt .10 .25
391 Philipp Portner .10 .25
392 Kim Scheidegger .10 .25
393 Marc Zurbriggen .10 .25
394 Nicolas Gastaldo .10 .25
395 Stefan Gahler .10 .25
396 Stefan Ketola .10 .25
397 Marcel Moser .10 .25
398 Detlef Prediger .10 .25
399 Adrian Witschi .10 .25
400 Ken Zurfluh .10 .25
401 Michael Fluckiger .10 .25
402 Ludovic Aubry .10 .25
403 John Miner .10 .25
404 Jonathan Miner .10 .25
405 Christian Schuster .10 .25
406 Martin Schupbach .10 .25
407 Steven Barras .10 .25
408 Elvis Clavien .10 .25
409 Gilbert Flueler .10 .25
410 Sacha Guerne .10 .25
411 Christoph Lindberg .10 .25
412 Cyrill Pasche .10 .25
413 Arnold Lortscher .10 .25
414 Beat Aebischer .20 .50
415 Francesco Bizzozero .10 .25
416 Ruedi Forster .10 .25
417 Karl Knopf .10 .25
418 Francis Reichmuth .10 .25
419 Stefan Wuthrich .10 .25
420 Martin Gendron .20 .50
421 Kevin Gloor .10 .25
422 Bjorn Guazzini .10 .25
423 Albert Malgin .10 .25
424 Oliver Muller .10 .25
425 Patrick Siegwart .10 .25
426 Christian Ruegg .10 .25
427 Pasqual Sievert .10 .25
428 Christoph Decurtins .10 .25
429 Patrick Mader .10 .25
430 Michael Marki .10 .25
431 Raphael Schoop .10 .25
432 Daniel Sigg .10 .25
433 Philipp Dornbierer .10 .25
434 Curdin Grischott .10 .25
435 Roland Korsch .10 .25
436 Mikko Liukkonen .10 .25
437 Christian Strasser .10 .25
438 Harijs Vitolinsch .10 .25
439 Flavio Streit .10 .25
440 Stephane Julien .10 .25
441 Roland Kaser .10 .25
442 Olivier Schaublin .10 .25
443 Andreas Zehnder .10 .25
444 Rolf Badertscher .10 .25
445 Marco Fischer .10 .25
446 Marco Graf .10 .25
447 Cornel Prinz .10 .25
448 David Raissle .10 .25
449 Marcel Sommer .10 .25
450 Rene Stussi .10 .25
451 Kim Collins .10 .25
452 Thomas Baumle .10 .25
453 Lionel D'Urso .10 .25
454 Philippe Faust .10 .25
455 Fabian Gull .10 .25
456 Terry Hollinger .10 .25
457 Andre Bielmann .10 .25
458 Joel Camenzind .10 .25
459 Derek Cormier .10 .25
460 Maxime Lapointe .10 .25
461 Thierry Metrailler .10 .25
462 Didier Schafer .10 .25
463 Daniel Wobmann .10 .25
464 Ernst Bruderer .10 .25
465 Andreas Schweizer .10 .25
466 Simon Born .10 .25
467 Bernhard Fankhauser .10 .25
468 Marcel Habisreutinger .10 .25
469 Reto Klay .10 .25
470 Lars Sommer .10 .25
471 Eric Lecompte .20 .50
472 Martin Meyer .10 .25
473 Tassilo Schwarz .10 .25
474 Zeno Schwarz .10 .25
475 Martin Wuthrich .10 .25
476 Bruno Zarrillo .20 .50
477 Jean-Jacques Aeschlimann .10 .25
478 Reto von Arx .20 .50
479 Gian-Marco Crameri .10 .25
480 Patric Della Rossa .10 .25
481 Patrick Fischer .10 .25
482 Martin Gerber 4.00 5.00
483 Sandy Jeannin .10 .25
484 Marcel Jenni .10 .25
485 Olivier Keller .10 .25
486 Martin Pluss .10 .25
487 Michel Riesen .80 1.00
488 Ivo Ruthemann .10 .25
489 Martin Steinegger .10 .25
490 Mark Streit .10 .25
491 Lars Weibel .20 .50
492 Rolf Ziegler .10 .25
493 Cristobal Huet .80 3.00
494 Mark Streit .10 .25
495 Charly Oppliger .10 .25
496 Fredy Pargatzi .10 .25
497 Lonny Bohonos .20 .50
498 Patrik Juhlin .20 .50
499 Felix Hollenstein .10 .25

2002-03 Swiss SCL Tigers

COMPLETE SET (7)
1 Johan Fransson .75 2.00
2 Pavel Skrbek .75 2.00
3 Jonas Ronnqvist .75 2.00
4 Magnus Nilsson .75 2.00
5 Gusten Tornqvist .75 2.00
6 Daniel Henriksson .75 2.00
7 Todd Elik .75 2.00

2003-04 Swiss EV Zug Postcards

These unnumbered 4X6 postcards were issued by the team and feature a colour headshot on the front. The two Patrick Fischers are different players with the same name. The Claude Lemieux single was issued as an update later in the season and so the set is considered complete without it.

COMPLETE SET (27) 10.00 25.00
1 Team Photo .40 1.00
2 Silvan Anthamatten .40 1.00
3 Duri Camichel .40 1.00
4 Corsin Casutt .40 1.00
5 Alain Demuth .40 1.00
6 Rafael Diaz .40 1.00
7 Paul Dipietro .40 1.00
8 Thomas Dommen .40 1.00
9 Paolo Duca .40 1.00
10 Livio Fazio .40 1.00
11 Patrick Fischer .40 1.00
12 Patrick Fischer .40 1.00
13 Daniel Giger .40 1.00
14 Andreas Kung .40 1.00
15 Colin Muller .40 1.00
16 Pascal Muller .40 1.00
17 Patrick Oppliger .40 1.00
18 Barry Richter .40 1.00
19 Frederic Rothen .40 1.00
20 Joel Savage .40 1.00
21 Lovis Schonenberger .40 1.00
22 Patrick Schopf .40 1.00
23 Fabio Schumacher .40 1.00
24 Sean Simpson .40 1.00
25 Chris Tancill .40 1.00
26 Michael Tobler .40 1.00
27 Claude Voisard .40 1.00
28 Claude Lemieux 4.00 10.00

2004-05 Swiss Davos Postcards

Cards measure 4X6 and feature a head shot on the front. All cards are autographed except for the group cards. Set is noteworthy for the inclusion of Joe Thornton and Rick Nash.

COMPLETE SET (30) 40.00 80.00
1 Team photo .40 1.00
2 Team history .40 1.00
3 Andres Ambuhl 1.25 3.00
4 Thomas Baumle 1.25 3.00
5 Florian Blatter 1.25 3.00
6 Daniell Boss 1.25 3.00
7 Bjorn Christen 1.25 3.00
8 Franco Collenberg 1.25 3.00
9 Arno Del Curto 1.25 3.00
10 Beat Forster 1.25 3.00
11 Marc Gianola 1.25 3.00
12 Peter Guggisberg 1.25 3.00
13 Niklas Hagman 2.00 5.00
14 Andreas Haller 1.25 3.00
15 Stevan Hasler 1.25 3.00
16 Marc Heberlein 1.25 3.00
17 Jonas Hiller 2.00 5.00
18 Michael Kress 1.25 3.00
19 Josef Marha 1.25 3.00
20 Laurent Muller 1.25 3.00
21 Rick Nash 12.00 30.00
22 Claudio Neff 1.25 3.00
23 Arne Ramholt 1.25 3.00
24 Michel Riesen 1.25 3.00
25 Sandro Rizzi 1.25 3.00
26 Fabian Sutter 1.25 3.00
27 Joe Thornton 15.00 40.00
28 Jan Von Arx 1.25 3.00
29 Reto Von Arx 1.25 3.00
30 Benjamin Winkler 1.25 3.00

2004-05 Swiss EV Zug Postcards

The cards are approximately 4X6. We've seen signed versions of the cards as well, but it's not known whether they were issued that way officially, or signed afterwards.

COMPLETE SET (28) 10.00 25.00
1 Brett Hauer .75 2.00
2 Niko Kapanen .75 2.00
3 Mike Fisher 1.25 3.00
4 Barry Richter .40 1.00
5 Oleg Petrov .40 1.00
6 Lars Weibel .40 1.00
7 Rafael Walter .40 1.00
8 Jan Feldmann .40 1.00
9 Livio Fazio .40 1.00
10 Pascal Muller .40 1.00
11 Rafael Diaz .40 1.00
12 Rene Back .40 1.00
13 Gaetan Voisard .40 1.00
14 Silvan Anthamatten .40 1.00
15 Patric Della Rosa .40 1.00
16 Gian-Marco Crameri .40 1.00
17 Patrick Fisher .40 1.00
18 Duri Camichel .40 1.00
19 Patrick Oppliger .40 1.00
20 Duca Paolo .40 1.00
21 Fabian Schnyder .40 1.00
22 Corsin Casutt .40 1.00
23 Daniel Giger .40 1.00
24 Frederic Rothen .40 1.00
25 Beat Schuler .40 1.00
26 Sean Simpson CO .40 1.00
27 Colin Muller ACO .40 1.00
28 Team Photo .40 1.00

2004-05 Swiss Lausanne HC Postcards

Standard postcard-sized collectibles were sold by the team in set form. The series in noteworthy for the inclusion of reigning NHL scoring champ Martin St. Louis. The cards are unnumbered. Checklist courtesy of collector Vincent Montalbano.

COMPLETE SET (25) 25.00
1 Pascal Schaller .40 1.00
2 Robert Stehofer .40 1.00
3 Alain Reist .40 1.00
4 Bruno Steck .40 1.00
5 Andy Roach .75 2.00
6 Thomas Berger .40 1.00
7 Patrick Boileau .75 2.00
8 Florian Andenmatten .40 1.00
9 Sunshine Romerio .40 1.00
10 Julien Turler .40 1.00
11 Gerd Zenhausern .40 1.00
12 Loic Merz .40 1.00
13 Martin St. Louis 4.00 10.00
14 Christophe Brown .40 1.00
15 Michael Ngoy .40 1.00
16 Mathias Holzer .40 1.00
17 Laurent Emery .40 1.00
18 Florian Conz .40 1.00
19 Marko Tuomainen .40 1.00
20 Michael Kamber .40 1.00
21 Lovis Schonenberger .40 1.00
22 Sacha Weibel .40 1.00
23 Eric Landry .40 1.00
24 Bill Stewart CO .10 .25
25 Gary Sheehan ACO .10 .25

2007-08 Swiss HC Lugano

COMPLETE SET (27) 15.00 30.00
1 Krister Cantoni .60 1.50
2 Alessandro Chiesa .60 1.50
3 Flavien Conne .60 1.50
4 Fabrizio Conte .60 1.50
5 Andreas Hanni .60 1.50
6 Timo Helbling .60 1.50
7 Jukka Hentunen .60 1.50
8 Steve Hirschi .60 1.50
9 Sandy Jeannin .60 1.50
10 Mike Knoepfli .60 1.50
11 Dario Kostovic .60 1.50
12 Marty Murray .60 1.50
13 Andy Naser .60 1.50
14 Thierry Paterlini .60 1.50
15 Kevin Romy .60 1.50
16 Raffaele Sannitz .60 1.50
17 Yannick Tremblay .60 1.50
18 Julien Vauclair .60 1.50
19 Tristan Vauclair .60 1.50
20 Raffael Walter .60 1.50
21 Landon Wilson .60 1.50
22 Valentin Wirz .60 1.50
23 Simon Zuger .60 1.50
24 Ivano Zanatta HC .10 .25
25 Diego Scandella AC .10 .25
26 Dusan Sidor .60 1.50
27 Tiziano Muzio .60 1.50

1954 UK A and BC Chewing Gum

The cards listed below were part of a multi-sport set issued in England, possibly with packs of A and BC Chewing Gum. They feature b&w headshots and blank backs. The players appear to be from an early English league. It's quite possible that other hockey players were featured. If you can address this checklist, please contact us at hockeymag@beckett.com.

COMPLETE SET (?)
35 Chick Zamick 8.00 20.00
36 Cliff Ryan 8.00 20.00
37 Sonny Rost 8.00 20.00
38 Malcolm Davidson 8.00 20.00
39 Ray Gariepy 12.00 30.00
40 George Beach 8.00 20.00
41 Lefty Wilmot 8.00 20.00
74 Bill Johnson 8.00 20.00
75 Joe Shack 8.00 20.00
76 Tony Licari 8.00 20.00

1998-99 UK Basingstoke Bison

This set features the Bison of the British Hockey League. The set was produced by Armchair Sports, an English card shop, and was sold by that store and the team. The print run has been confirmed at 200 sets.

COMPLETE SET (24) 4.00 10.00
1 Rick Strachan .25 .60
2 Joe Baird .25 .60
3 Chris Crombie .25 .60
4 Steve Smillie .25 .60
5 Chris Bailey .25 .60
6 Bjarne Levison .25 .60
7 Mike Ellis .25 .60
8 Chris Chard .25 .60
9 Anthony Page .25 .60
10 Adam Cathcart .25 .60
11 Rick Fera .25 .60
12 Gary Clark .25 .60
13 Tony Redmond .25 .60
14 Alec Field .25 .60
15 Hakan Klys .25 .60
16 Mitch Grant .25 .60
17 Jake Armstrong .25 .60
18 Don Depoe CO .02 .10
19 Garlunkel's MASCOT .02 .10
20 The Puck .02 .10
21 The Goal .02 .10
22 Penalty Shots .02 .10
23 Team CL .02 .10
NNO Competition .02 .10

1999-00 UK Basingstoke Bison

This set features the Bison of Britain's top hockey league. The set was produced by Armchair Sports, a card shop in the UK, and was sold by the team at home games. The print run has been confirmed at 200 sets.

COMPLETE SET (22) 4.00 10.00
1 Rick Strachan .20 .50
2 Dru Burgess .20 .50
3 Danny Meyers .20 .50
4 Gary Clark .20 .50
5 Peter Romeo .20 .50
6 Mike Ellis .20 .50
7 Joey Baird .20 .50
8 Charlie Colon .20 .50
9 Wayne Crawford .20 .50
10 Alec Field .20 .50
11 Tony Redmond .20 .50
12 Mitch Grant .20 .50
13 Duncan Paterson .20 .50
14 Dwayne Newman .20 .50
15 Mark Barrow .20 .50
16 Adam Greener .20 .50
17 Face Off .08 .25
18 Goal Mouth Scramble .08 .25
19 Joe Watkins .20 .50
20 Michael Knights .20 .50
21 Jeff Daniels .20 .50
22 Team CL .02 .10

2003-04 UK Basingstoke Bison

COMPLETE SET (21) 4.00 10.00
1 Curtis Cruickshank .30 .75
2 Dean Skinns .30 .75
3 David Geris .30 .75
4 James Hutchinson .20 .50
5 Phil Roy .20 .50
6 Doug Schueller .20 .50
7 Kim Vahanen .20 .50
8 Joe Ciccarello .20 .50
9 Martin Filip .20 .50
10 Richard Hargreaves .20 .50
11 Darren Hurley .20 .50
12 Jaromir Kverka .20 .50
13 Steve Moria .20 .50
14 Blake Sorensen .20 .50
15 Shaun Thompson .20 .50
16 Nicky Watt .30 .75
17 Christian Wirtauer .20 .50
18 Chris Slater .20 .50
19 Luc Chabot .20 .50
20 Matt Reid .20 .50
21 Checklist .01 .01

2001-02 UK Belfast Giants

This 35-card set featured the Belfast Giants of the British Ice Hockey Superleague for the seasons of 2001-02 and 2002-03. Please note that card #13 was not produced. This set was produced by Armchair Sports in England.

COMPLETE SET (35) 8.00 20.00
1 Mike Bales .40 1.00
2 Terran Sandwith .30 .75
3 Dave Whistle CO .04 .10
4 Shane Johnson .30 .75
5 Colin Ward .30 .75
6 Kevin Riehl .30 .75
7 Rob Stewart .30 .75
8 Jason Ruff .30 .75
9 Sean Berens .30 .75
10 Jeff Hoad .30 .75
11 David Matsos .30 .75
12 Curtis Bowen .30 .75
14 Chad Allan .30 .75
15 Rod Stevens .30 .75
16 Paxton Schulte .40 1.00
17 Jason Bowen .40 1.00
18 Mark Cavallin .30 .75
19 Todd Kelman .30 .75
20 Checklist .01
21 Tom Blatchford TR .04 .10
22 Redemption Card .01
23 Shayne Toporowski .40 1.00
24 Derek Wilkinson .30 .75
25 Paul Ferone .30 .75
26 Todd Goodwin .30 .75
27 Kory Karlander .30 .75
28 Doug Searle .30 .75
29 Jerry Keefe .30 .75
30 Jason Wright .30 .75
31 Steve Roberts .30 .75
32 Mark Cavallin .30 .75
33 Mike Bales NM .40 1.00
34 Front Office .04 .10
35 Checklist .01

2003-04 UK Belfast Giants

Unnumbered cards, listed in alphabetical order.

COMPLETE SET (19) 5.00 10.00
1 Sean Berens .20 .50
2 Curt Bowen .30 .75
3 Jason Bowen .20 .50
4 Mark Finney .20 .50
5 Leigh Jamieson .20 .50
6 Shane Johnson .20 .50
7 Todd Kelman .20 .50
8 Brad Kenny .20 .50
9 Gareth Martin .20 .50
10 Chris McGimpsey .30 .75
11 Mark Morrison .20 .50
12 Jason Ruff .20 .50
13 Colin Ryder .30 .75
14 Paul Sample .20 .50
15 Paxton Schulte .20 .50
16 Rob Stewart .20 .50
17 Grant Taylor .20 .50
18 Graeme Walton .20 .50
19 Colin Ward .20 .50

2004-05 UK Brent Bobyck Testimonial

COMPLETE SET (12) 2.00 5.00
COMMON CARD (1-12)
1 Brent Bobyck 1994-95 .20 .50
2 Brent Bobyck 1995-96 .20 .50
3 Brent Bobyck 1996-97 .20 .50
4 Brent Bobyck 1997-98 .20 .50
5 Brent Bobyck 1998-99 .20 .50
6 Brent Bobyck 1999-00 .20 .50
7 Brent Bobyck 2000-01 .20 .50
8 Brent Bobyck 2001-02 .20 .50
9 Brent Bobyck 2002-03 .20 .50
10 Brent Bobyck 2003-04 .20 .50
11 Brent Bobyck 2004-05 .20 .50
12 Brent Bobyck CL .02 .10

2000-01 UK Cardiff Devils

This set features the Devils of the British league. It is believed that this is an incomplete checklist and so is not priced in set form. If you know of additional singles, please contact us at hockeymag@beckett.com.

COMPLETE SET (14)
1 Derek Herlofsky .20 .50
2 Alan Schuler .20 .50
3 Vezio Sacratini .20 .50
4 Clayton Norris .20 .50
5 Rick Strachan .20 .50
6 John Parco .20 .50
7 Kip Noble .20 .50
8 Steve Thornton .20 .50
9 Dennis Chasse .20 .50
10 Mike Ware .20 .50
11 Steve Moria .20 .50
12 Frank Evans .20 .50
13 Jonathan Phillips .20 .50
14 Ian McIntyre .20 .50

2001-02 UK Cardiff Devils

This set was produced by Armchair Sports in England.

COMPLETE SET (19) 5.00 10.00
1 Clayton Norris .30 .75
2 Rick Strachan .20 .50
3 Alan Schuler .20 .50
4 Kim Ahlroos .20 .50
5 John Parco .20 .50
6 Frank Evans .20 .50
7 Denis Chasse .40 1.00
8 Steve Thornton .30 .75
9 Dwight Parrish .20 .50
10 Steve Moria .20 .50
11 Jonathan Phillips .20 .50
12 Ian McIntyre .20 .50
13 Ivan Matulik .20 .50
14 Mike Ware .30 .75
15 Vezio Sacratini .20 .50
16 Steve Lyle .30 .75
17 Derek Herlofsky .40 1.00
18 Kip Noble .20 .50
19 Checklist .02 .10

2002-03 UK Cardiff Devils

This 19-card set featured the Cardiff Devils of the British Ice Hockey Superleague. Each card was numbered at the bottom of the card back. This set was available during home games.

COMPLETE SET (19) 5.00 10.00
1 Clayton Norris .20 .50
2 Rick Strachan .20 .50
3 Alan Schuler .20 .50
4 Kim Ahlroos .20 .50
5 John Parco .20 .50
6 Frank Evans .20 .50
7 Denis Chasse .40 1.00
8 Steve Thornton .30 .75
9 Dwight Parrish .20 .50
10 Steve Moria .20 .50
11 Jonathan Phillips .20 .50
12 Ian McIntyre .20 .50
13 Ivan Matulik .20 .50
14 Mike Ware .30 .75
15 Vezio Sacratini .20 .50
16 Stevie Lyle .30 .75
17 Derek Herlofsky .30 .75
18 Kip Noble .20 .50
19 Checklist .01 .01

2003-04 UK Cardiff Devils

COMPLETE SET (21) 5.00 10.00
1 Jason Cugnet .30 .75
2 Jeff Burgoyne .20 .50
3 Matt Myers .20 .50
4 Jason Stone .20 .50
5 David James .20 .50
6 Phil Manny .20 .50
7 Russ Romaniuk .40 1.00
8 Phil Hill .20 .50
9 Jonathan Phillips .20 .50
10 Jeff Brown .20 .50
11 Ivan Matulik .20 .50
12 Ed Patterson .20 .50
13 Mike Ware .30 .75
14 Vezio Sacratini .20 .50
15 Neil Francis .20 .50
16 James Manson .20 .50
17 Jason Becker .20 .50
18 Dennis Maxwell .20 .50
19 Doug McEwen .20 .50
20 Dave Whistle CO .02 .10
21 Checklist .01 .01

2002-03 UK Coventry Blaze

This 24-card set featured the Coventry Blaze of the Findus British National League. They were available at home games. Cards were unnumbered and are listed below in checklist order.

COMPLETE SET (24) 5.00 12.00
1 Greg Rockman .20 .50
2 Jody Lehman .20 .50
3 Steve Carpenter .20 .50
4 Alan Levers .20 .50
5 James Pease .20 .50
6 Andreas Moborg .20 .50
7 Mathias Soderstrom .20 .50
8 Adam Radmall .20 .50
9 Ron Shudra .30 .75
10 Shaun Johnson .20 .50
11 Steve Chartrand .20 .50
12 Kurt Irvine .20 .50
13 Russ Cowley .20 .50
14 Tom Watkins .20 .50
15 Ashley Tait .30 .75
16 Gareth Owens .20 .50
17 Joel Poirier .30 .75
18 Hilton Ruggles .20 .50
19 Lee Richardson .20 .50
20 Michael Tasker .20 .50
21 Paul Thompson CO .02 .10
22 Steve Small .02 .10
Phil Hadley
John Crook
23 Blaze Dancers .20 .50
24 Checklist .01 .01

2003-04 UK Coventry Blaze

COMPLETE SET (18) 5.00 12.00
1 Alan Levers .25 .60
2 Mathias Soderstrom .25 .60
3 Steve Carpenter .30 .75
4 Jody Lehman .25 .60

5 Steve O'Brien .25 .60
6 Steve Gallace .25 .60
7 Adam Radmall .25 .60
8 Shaun Johnson .25 .60
9 Graham Schlender .25 .60
10 Steve Chartrand .25 .60
11 Russ Cowley .25 .60
12 Tom Watkins .25 .60
13 Ashley Tait .30 .75
14 Gareth Owen .25 .60
15 Joel Poirier .30 .75
16 Hilton Ruggles .25 .60
17 Lee Richardson .25 .60
18 Michael Tasker .25 .60

2003-04 UK Coventry Blaze Calendars

COMPLETE SET (12) 5.00 10.00
1 Mathias Soderstrom .40 1.00
2 Ashley Tait .40 1.00
3 Steve Carpenter .40 1.00
4 Steve Chartrand .40 1.00
Shaun Johnson
5 Russ Cowley .40 1.00
Tom Watkins
6 Graham Schlender .40 1.00
7 Jody Lehman .40 1.00
8 Michael Tasker .40 1.00
Hilton Ruggles
9 Lee Richardson .40 1.00
Alan Levers
10 Joel Poirier .40 1.00
11 Garth Owen .40 1.00
Adam Radmall
12 Steve Gallace .40 1.00
Steve O'Brien

2003-04 UK Coventry Blaze History

COMPLETE SET (18) 5.00 10.00
1 Steve Chartrand .20 .50
2 Kurt Irvine .20 .50
3 Mathias Soderstrom .20 .50
4 Michael Tasker .20 .50
5 A.J. Kelham .20 .50
6 Hilton Ruggles .20 .50
7 Luc Chabot .20 .50
8 Paul Thompson .20 .50
9 Steve Carpenter .30 .75
10 Shaun Johnson .20 .50
11 Andrew McNiven .20 .50
12 Jody Lehman .30 .75
13 Justin George .20 .50
14 Claude Dumas .20 .50
15 Craig Chapman .20 .50
16 Stephen Cooper .30 .75
17 Mike Shewan .20 .50
18 Ron Shudra .30 .75

2004-05 UK Coventry Blaze

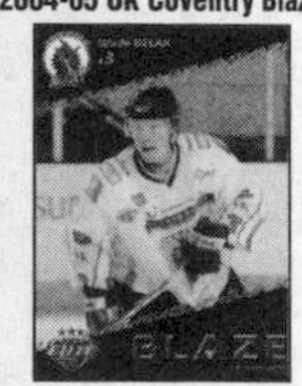

Produced by Cardtraders.co.UK.

COMPLETE SET (25) 5.00 10.00
1 Wade Belak .30 .75
2 Adam Brittle .20 .50
3 Adam Calder .20 .50
4 Tom Carlon .20 .50
5 Dan Carlson .20 .50
6 Luc Chabot ACO .02 .10
7 Russ Cowley .20 .50
8 Jody Lehman .20 .50
9 Neal Martin .20 .50
10 Chris McNamara .20 .50
11 Pavol Mihalik .20 .50
12 Andre Payette .20 .50
13 James Pease .20 .50
14 Joel Poirier .20 .50
15 Graham Schlender .20 .50
16 Doug Schueller .20 .50
17 Dan Shea .20 .50
18 Ashley Tait .30 .75
19 Paul Thompson CO .02 .10
20 Michal Vrabel .20 .50
21 Tom Watkins .20 .50
22 Nathanael Williams .20 .50
23 S.Small/A.Henry .20 .50
24 A.Buxton/M.Cowley .20 .50
25 Kix Kat MASCOT .01 .01

2004-05 UK Coventry Blaze Champions

COMPLETE SET (20) 5.00 10.00
1 Jody Lehman .30 .75
2 Dan Shea .20 .50
3 Wade Belak .40 1.00
4 Neal Martin .20 .50
5 Doug Schueller .20 .50
6 Pavol Mihalik .20 .50
7 Jozef Lukac .20 .50
8 James Pease .20 .50
9 Andre Payette .20 .50
10 Dan Carlson .20 .50
11 Graham Schlender .20 .50
12 Adam Calder .20 .50
13 Ashley Tait .30 .75
14 Joel Poirier .20 .50
15 Russ Cowley .20 .50
16 Chris McNamara .20 .50
17 Nathanael Williams .20 .50
18 Tom Watkins .20 .50
19 Card List .01 .05
20 Paul Thompson .20 .50

2006-07 UK Coventry Blaze

COMPLETE SET (20) 8.00 15.00
1 Neal Martin .30 .75
2 Joe Henry .30 .75
3 Reid Simonton .30 .75
4 Samy Nasreddine .30 .75
5 Tom Pease .30 .75
6 Barrie Moore .30 .75
7 Tom Watkins .30 .75
8 Ashley Tait .30 .75
9 James Pease .30 .75
10 Tom Carlon .30 .75
11 Adam Calder .30 .75
12 Dan Carlson .30 .75
13 Steve Fone .30 .75
14 Gareth Owen .30 .75
15 Trevor Koenig .30 .75
16 Danny Stewart .30 .75
17 Michael Wales .30 .75
18 Rumun Ndur .30 .75
19 Sylvain Cloutier .30 .75
20 Paul Thompson .30 .75

2007-08 UK Coventry Blaze

COMPLETE SET (43) 15.00 25.00
1 Hayden Laverick .30 .75
2 James Archer .30 .75
3 Josh Bruce .30 .75
4 Neal Martin .30 .75
5 Joe Henry .30 .75
6 Ryan Selwood .30 .75
7 James Cooke .30 .75
8 Tom Ledgard .30 .75
9 Scott Murray .30 .75
10 Ian Hunt .30 .75
11 Jonathan Weaver .30 .75
12 Russell Cowley .30 .75
13 Barrie Moore .30 .75
14 Tom Watkins .30 .75
15 James Pease .30 .75
16 Luke Curtis .30 .75
17 Chris Wilcox .30 .75
18 Adam Calder .30 .75
19 Dan Carlson .30 .75
20 Kieran Papps .30 .75
21 Steve Fone .30 .75
22 Stuart Dayton .30 .75
23 Dan Shea .30 .75
24 Trevor Koenig .30 .75
25 Aram Todd .30 .75
26 Danny Stewart .30 .75
27 Ollie Nabbs .30 .75
28 KC Timmons .30 .75
29 Matt Halford .30 .75
30 Tom Pease .30 .75
31 Scott Mulholland .30 .75
32 Rumun Ndur .30 .75
33 Tom Hooper .30 .75
34 Matt Soderstrom .30 .75
35 Michael Tasker .30 .75
36 Sylvain Cloutier .30 .75
37 Daniel Burgess .30 .75
38 Curtis Huppe .30 .75
39 David Vychodil .30 .75
40 Paul Thompson HC .02 .10
41 Luc Chabot AC .02 .10
42 Joel Poirier HC .02 .10
43 Reg Wilcox AC .02 .10

2001-02 UK Dundee Stars

This set was produced by Armchair Sports in England.

COMPLETE SET (18) 5.00 10.00
1 Checklist .02 .10
2 Nate Leslie .25 .60
3 Scott Young .25 .60
4 Tony Hand .30 .75
5 Paul Berrington .25 .60
6 Gary Dowd .25 .60
7 Teeder Wynne .25 .60
8 Mikko Inkinen .25 .60
9 Andrew Finlay .25 .60
10 Jan Mikel .25 .60
11 Craig Nelson .25 .60
12 Dominic Hopkins .25 .60
13 Stewart Rugg .25 .60
14 Patrick Lochi .25 .60
15 Stephen Murphy .25 .60
16 Slava Koulikov .25 .60
17 Martin Wilta .25 .60
18 Scott Kirton .25 .60

2002-03 UK Dundee Stars

This 18-card set was produced by cardtraders.co.uk to commerorate the champions of the 2001-02 British National League, the Dundee Stars. The sets were limited to a production run of 495 total.

COMPLETE SET (18) 5.00 10.00
1 Checklist .01
2 Nate Leslie .25 .60
3 Scott Young .25 .60
4 Tony Hand .30 .75
5 Paul Berrington .25 .60
6 Gary Dowd .25 .60
7 Teeder Wynne .25 .60
8 Mikko Inkinen .25 .60
9 Andy Finlay .25 .60
10 Jan Mikel .25 .60
11 Craig Nelson .25 .60
12 Dominic Hopkins .25 .60
13 Stewart Rugg .25 .60
14 Patric Lochi .25 .60
15 Stephen Murphy .25 .60
16 Viatcheslav Koulikov .25 .60
17 Martin Wilta .25 .60
18 Scott Kirton .25 .60

2004-05 UK Edinburgh Capitals

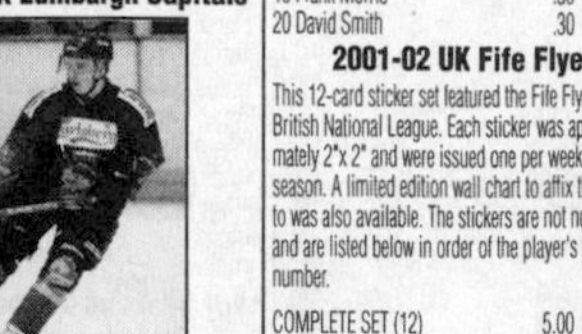

Produced by Cardtraders.co.UK.

COMPLETE SET (18) 5.00 12.00
1 Jan Krajicek .30 .75
2 Mindraugas Kieras .40 1.00
3 Laurie Dunbar .30 .75
4 Steven Francey .30 .75
5 Marty Johnston .30 .75
6 Craig Wilson .30 .75
7 David Beatson .30 .75
8 Ross Hay .30 .75
9 Steven Lynch .30 .75
10 Daniel McIntyre .30 .75
11 Neil Hay .30 .75
12 Martin Cingel .30 .75
13 Dino Bauba .30 .75
14 David Trofimenkoff .40 1.00
15 Rastislav Bohme .30 .75
16 Miroslav Droppa .30 .75
17 Ryan Ford .40 1.00
18 Checklist .02 .10

2007-08 UK Edinburgh Capitals

COMPLETE SET (19) 7.00 15.00
1 Kyle Horne .40 1.00
2 Mark Garside .40 1.00
3 Jordan Steele .40 1.00
4 Ryan Crane .40 1.00
5 Colin Hemingway .40 1.00
6 Mark Wires .40 1.00
7 Neil Hay .40 1.00
8 Ross Dalgleish .40 1.00
9 Mike Stutzel .40 1.00
10 Adam Stefishen .40 1.00
11 Doug Christiansen .40 1.00
12 Martin Cingel .40 1.00
13 Dino Bauba .40 1.00
14 Mark Paterson .40 1.00
15 Iain Bowie .40 1.00
16 J.F. Perras .40 1.00
17 Ryan Ford .40 1.00
18 Patrik Luza .40 1.00
19 Ben O'Connor .40 1.00

2004-05 UK EIHL All-Stars

COMPLETE SET (18) 5.00 12.00
1 Jody Lehman .30 .75
2 Wade Belak .40 1.00
3 Neal Martin .20 .50
4 Tony Hand .40 1.00
5 Adam Calder .20 .50
6 Jon Cullen .20 .50
7 Martin Klempa .20 .50
8 Rob Davison .40 1.00
9 Dion Darling .20 .50
10 Dan Carlson .20 .50
11 George Awarda .20 .50
12 Vezio Sacratini .20 .50
13 Curtis Cruickshank .30 .75
14 Eric Cairns .40 1.00
15 Nick Boynton .40 1.00
16 Shawn Maltby .40 1.00
17 David Clarke .20 .50
18 Scott Nichol .40 1.00

1996-97 UK Fife Flyers

This set features the Flyers of Britain's top league. It was produced by the team and sold at home games.

COMPLETE SET (20) 5.00 12.00
1 Gavin Fleming .30 .75
2 John Reid .30 .75
3 Russ Parent .30 .75
4 Derek E. King .30 .75
5 Colin Grubb .30 .75
6 Colin Hamilton .30 .75
7 Andy Finlay .30 .75
8 Richard Dingwall .30 .75
9 Andy Samuel .30 .75
10 Wayne Maxwell .30 .75
11 Craig Wilson .30 .75
12 Daryl Venters .30 .75
13 Gordon Latto .30 .75
14 Richard Danskin .30 .75
15 Martin McKay .30 .75
16 Kyle Horne .30 .75
17 Mark Morrison CO .20 .50
18 Frank Morris .30 .75
19 Steven E. King .30 .75
20 Lee Mercer .30 .75

1997-98 UK Fife Flyers

This set features the Flyers of the British Ice Hockey League. The sets were sold by the team at its souvenir stands on game nights.

COMPLETE SET (20) 4.80 12.00
1 Team Photo .20 .50
2 Bernie McCrone .30 .75
3 Wayne Maxwell .30 .75
4 Derek E. King .30 .75
5 Mark Slater .30 .75
6 Bill Moody .30 .75
7 Lee Cowmedow .30 .75
8 Richard Charles .30 .75
9 Andy Finlay .30 .75
10 Daryl Venters .30 .75
11 Steven E. King .30 .75
12 Andy Samuel .30 .75
13 Gordon Latto .30 .75
14 Mark Morrison CO .20 .50
15 John Haig .30 .75
16 Lee Mercer .30 .75
17 Gary Wishart .30 .75
18 Colin Hamilton .30 .75
19 Frank Morris .30 .75
20 David Smith .30 .75

2001-02 UK Fife Flyers

This 12-card sticker set featured the Fife Flyers of the British National League. Each sticker was approximately 2"x 2" and were issued one per week during the season. A limited edition wall chart to affix the stickers to was also available. The stickers are not numbered and are listed below in order of the player's jersey number.

COMPLETE SET (12) 5.00 10.00
1 Shawn Silver .40 1.00
2 Derek King .40 1.00
3 Kyle Horner .40 1.00
4 Todd Dutiaume .40 1.00
5 Steven King .40 1.00
6 Mark Morrison .40 1.00
7 Mark Dutiaume .40 1.00
8 Gary Wishart .40 1.00
9 Iain Robertson .40 1.00
10 Karry Biette .40 1.00
11 Russell Monteith .40 1.00
12 Frank Morris .40 1.00

1994-95 UK Guildford Flames

This set features the Flames of the British Hockey League. The set was produced by Armchair Sports, an English card shop, and was sold by that store and the team on game nights.

COMPLETE SET (25) 4.00 10.00
1 Ben Challice .20 .50
2 Wayne Trunchion .20 .50
3 Terry Kurtenbach .20 .50
4 Fred Perlini .20 .50
5 Andy Sparks .20 .50
6 Rob Friesen .20 .50
7 Drew Chapman .20 .50
8 Kevin Parish .20 .50
9 John Noctor .20 .50
10 Ron Charbonneau GM .02 .10
11 Peter Morley .20 .50
12 Andy Allan .20 .50
13 Ryan Campbell .20 .50
14 Ronnie Evans-Harvey .20 .50
15 Paul Thompson .20 .50
16 Bill Rawles .20 .50
17 Nicky Landoli .20 .50
18 Elliott Andrews .20 .50
19 Dean Russell-Samways .20 .50
20 Home Kit .02 .10
21 Away Kit .02 .10
22 5 Imports .20 .50
23 3 Letters .02 .10
24 Spectrum .02 .10
25 Checklist .02 .10

1995-96 UK Guildford Flames

This set features the Flames of the British Hockey League. The set was produced by Armchair Sports, an English card shop, and was sold by that store and the team on game nights.

COMPLETE SET (30) 6.00 15.00
1 Dave Gregory .20 .50
2 Wayne Trunchion .20 .50
3 Andy Allan .20 .50
4 Terry Kurtenbach .20 .50
5 Ryan Campbell .20 .50
6 Fred Perlini .20 .50
7 Ronnie Evans-Harvey .20 .50
8 Andy Sparks .20 .50
9 Paul Thompson .20 .50
10 Nick Rothwell .20 .50
11 Drew Chapman .20 .50
12 Troy Kennedy .20 .50
13 Barrie Aisbitt .20 .50
14 Elliott Andrews .20 .50
15 Darrin Zinger .20 .50
16 Dean Russell-Samways .20 .50
17 Dave Graham .20 .50
18 Ivan Brown .20 .50
19 Home Kit .20 .50
20 Away Kit .20 .50
21 Spectrum .20 .50
22 Checklist .20 .50
23 Home Action .20 .50
24 Away Action .20 .50
25 P.C. Jim Bennett .20 .50
26 Terry Kurtenbach GOLD .20 .50
27 Paul Thompson GOLD .20 .50
28 Fred Perlini GOLD .20 .50
29 Future GOLD .20 .50
30 Celebration GOLD .20 .50

1996-97 UK Guildford Flames

This set features the Flames of the British Hockey League. The set was produced by Armchair Sports, an English card shop, and was sold by that store and the team on game nights.

COMPLETE SET (30) 5.00 12.00
1 John Wolfe .20 .50
2 Rob Lamey .20 .50
3 Wayne Crawford .20 .50
4 Terry Kurtenbach .20 .50
5 Ryan Campbell .20 .50
6 Fred Parlini .20 .50
7 Paul Thompson .20 .50
8 Mike Bettens .20 .50
9 Mark Finney .20 .50
10 Ryan Ferster .20 .50
11 Nick Cross .20 .50
12 Damian Smith .20 .50
13 Mike Mowbray .20 .50
14 Elliott Andrews .20 .50
15 Darrin Zinger .20 .50
16 Brad Kirkwood .20 .50
17 Derek DeCosty .20 .50
18 Mark Hazelhurst .20 .50
19 Lee Saunders .20 .50
20 Barrie Aisbitt .20 .50
21 Paul McCallion .20 .50
22 Valeri Vasie .20 .50
23 Goalies .20 .50
24 Capt. & Ast.Capt. .20 .50
25 Celebration .08 .25
26 Pep Talk .08 .25
27 Home Kit .08 .25
28 Away Kit .08 .25
29 Spectrum .08 .25
30 Training Staff .08 .25

1997-98 UK Guildford Flames

This set features the Flames of the British Hockey League. The set was produced by Armchair Sports, an English card shop, and was sold by that store and the team on game nights.

COMPLETE SET (30) 4.80 12.00
1 Peter Morley .20 .50
2 Rob Lamey .30 .75
3 Andrew Hannah .30 .75
4 Joe Johnson .30 .75
5 Terry Kurtenbach .30 .75
6 Ryan Campbell .20 .50
7 Scott Adair .20 .50
8 Paul Thompson .20 .50
9 Ricky Plant .20 .50
10 Pete Kasowski .20 .50
11 Andrew Einhorn .20 .50
12 Bobby Brown .20 .50
13 Anthony Page .20 .50
14 Nick Rothwell .20 .50
15 Mike Harding .20 .50
16 Darrin Zinger .30 .75
17 Jamie Organ .20 .50
18 Barcley Pearce .20 .50
19 Simon Smith .20 .50
20 Russ Plant .20 .50
21 Stan Marple CO .02 .10
22 Home Kit .02 .10
23 Away Kit .02 .10
24 Dressing Room .02 .10
25 Capt. & Ast. Capt. .20 .50
26 Celebration .02 .10
27 Checklist .02 .10
28 Spectrum .02 .10
29 Sizzler .02 .10
30 Training Staff .02 .10

1998-99 UK Guildford Flames

This set features the Flames of the British Hockey League. The set was produced by Armchair Sports, an English card shop, and was sold by that store and the team on game nights.

COMPLETE SET (30) 4.00 10.00
1 Team CL .02 .10
2 Ryan Campbell .20 .50
3 Robin Davison .20 .50
4 Derek DeCosty .20 .50
5 Dominic Hopkins .20 .50
6 Simon Howard .20 .50
7 Kirk Humphreys .20 .50
8 Andy Johnston .20 .50
9 Rob Johnston .20 .50
10 Peter Kasowski .20 .50
11 Terry Kurtenbach .20 .50
12 Rob Lamey .20 .50
13 Adrian Lomonaco .20 .50
14 Sam Mager .20 .50
15 Stan Marple CO .02 .10
16 Brian Mason .20 .50
17 Peter Morley .20 .50
18 Jamey Organ .20 .50
19 Barcley Pearce .20 .50
20 Andy Pickles .20 .50
21 Greg Randall .20 .50
22 Sizzler MASCOT .02 .10
23 Simon Smith .20 .50
24 Scott Stephenson .20 .50
25 Paul Thompson .20 .50
26 Captain & Assistants .02 .10
27 GB Uniform .02 .10
28 Trophies .02 .10
29 Home Kit .02 .10
30 Away Kit .02 .10

1999-00 UK Guildford Flames

This set features the Flames of the British Hockey League. The set was produced by Armchair Sports, an English card shop, and was sold by that store and the team on game nights.

COMPLETE SET (30) 4.00 10.00
1 Team CL .02 .10
2 Biette, Crombie, Dixon .20 .50
3 Team Photo (home) .20 .50
4 Team Photo (away) .20 .50
5 Celebration .02 .10
6 Karry Biette .20 .50
7 Tom Brown .20 .50
8 Ryan Campbell .20 .50
9 Gary Clark .20 .50
10 Chris Crombie .20 .50
11 Derek Decosty .20 .50
12 Paul Dixon .20 .50
13 GB Uniform .02 .10
14 Patrick Flanagan .20 .50
15 Dominic Hopkins .20 .50
16 Simon Howard .20 .50
17 Adrian Jenkinson TR .02 .10
18 Peter Kasowski .20 .50
19 Grant King .20 .50
20 Rob Lamey .20 .50
21 James Manson .20 .50
22 Stan Marple CO .02 .10
23 Stan Marple CO .02 .10
24 Jamey Organ .20 .50
25 Barcley Pearce .20 .50
26 Rick Plant .20 .50
27 Russ Plant .20 .50
28 Sizzlers MASCOT .02 .10
29 Jamie Thompson .20 .50
30 Mike Urquhart ACO .02 .10

2000-01 UK Guildford Flames

This set features the Bison of the British Hockey League. The set was produced by Armchair Sports, an English card shop, and was sold by that store and the team.

COMPLETE SET (30) 4.00 10.00
1 Karry Biette .14 .35
2 Tom Brown .14 .35
3 Ryan Campbell .14 .35
4 Scott Campbell .14 .35
5 Wayne Crawford .14 .35
6 Chris Crombie .14 .35
7 Derek DeCosty .14 .35
8 Paul Dixon .14 .35
9 John Haig .14 .35
10 Adrian Jenkinson TR .10 .25
11 Jason Jennings .14 .35
12 Grant King .14 .35
13 Rob Lamey .14 .35
14 Stan Marple CO .10 .25
15 Stan Marple CO .10 .25
16 Mark McArthur .20 .50
17 Tyrone Miller .14 .35
18 Jason Moses .14 .35
19 Barcley Pearce .14 .35
20 Ricky Plant .14 .35
21 Sizzler MASCOT .10 .25
22 Jason Stone .14 .35
23 David Smith .14 .35
24 Mike Urquhart .14 .35
25 Team Photo (home) .14 .35
26 Team Photo (away) .14 .35
27 Captain & Assistants .14 .35
28 Home Grown .14 .35
29 Celebration .10 .25
30 Logo Card .10 .25

2001-02 UK Guildford Flames

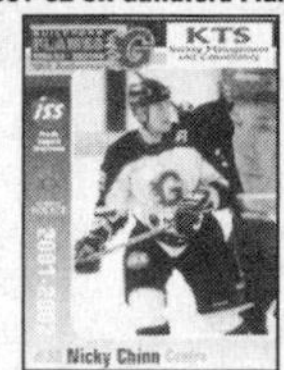

This team set was produced to honor Guildford's tenth anniversary season. The set was co-sponsored by the Surrey Police Department and was available at Flames' home games. The cards were unnumbered and are listed below in checklist order.

COMPLETE SET (30) 5.00 12.00
1 Checklist .04 .10
2 Mark McArthur .30 .75
3 Michael Plenty .20 .50
4 Stan Marple .20 .50
5 Regan Stocco .20 .50
6 Derek DeCosty .20 .50
7 Todd Wetzel .20 .50
8 Ricky Plant .20 .50
9 John Haig .20 .50
10 Tony Redmond .20 .50
11 Paul Dixon .20 .50
12 Grant King .30 .75
13 Greg Burke .20 .50
14 Scott Campbell .20 .50
15 Nicky Chinn .30 .75
16 Mark Galazzi .20 .50
17 David Smith .20 .50
18 Jason Dailey .20 .50
19 Michael Timms .20 .50
20 Mikko Koivunoro .20 .50
21 Stan Marple HCO .04 .10
22 Mike Urquhart ACO .04 .10
23 Adrian Jenkinson TR .04 .10
24 Paul Dixon .20 .50
Derek DeCosty
Nicky Chinn
25 Team Photo Home .20 .50
26 Team Photo Away .20 .50
27 Sizzler MASCOT .04 .10
28 Jason Dailey .20 .50
Celebration
29 Trophies .04 .10
30 Mark McArthur .20 .50
Grant King

2002-03 UK Guildford Flames

This 30-card set featured players from the Guildford Flames of the British National League. The cards were available at home games. The cards were not numbered and were listed below in checklist order.

COMPLETE SET (30) 5.00 12.00
1 Ian Herbers .20 .50
2 Stan Marple HCO .20 .50
3 David Clarke .20 .50
4 Derek DeCosty .20 .50
5 Craig Lyons .20 .50
6 Ricky Plant .20 .50
7 Tony Redmond .20 .50
8 Paul Dixon .20 .50
9 Jason Lafreniere .30 .75
10 Jason Bowen .20 .50
11 Grant King .20 .50
12 Mike Torchia .30 .75
13 Corey Lyons .20 .50
14 Nicky Chinn .30 .75
15 Jeff White .20 .50
16 Mark Galazzi .20 .50
17 Ricky Skene .20 .50
18 Mike Urquhart ACO .02 .10
19 Stan Marple HCO .02 .10
20 Adrian Jenkinson TR .02 .10
21 Paul Dixon .20 .50
Corey Lyons
Jason Lafreniere
22 Team Photo .20 .50
Home
23 Team Photo .20 .50
Away
24 Team Photo .20 .50
Alternate
25 Sizzler MASCOT .02 .10
26 Grant King .30 .75
Mike Torchia
27 Ricky Plant GB .20 .50
28 David Clarke GB .20 .50
29 Andy Sparks .20 .50
Fred Perlini
Ryan Campbell
Retired Numbers
30 Checklist .01 .01

2003-04 UK Guildford Flames

COMPLETE SET (30) 5.00 12.00
1 Header Card .02 .10
2 Peter Michnac .20 .50
3 Stan Marple .20 .50
4 Marian Smerciak .20 .50
5 Neil Liddiard .20 .50
6 Ryan Vince .20 .50
7 Ricky Plant .30 .75
8 Michael Timms .20 .50
9 Tony Redmond .20 .50
10 Milos Melicherik .20 .50
11 Paul Dixon .20 .50
12 Rastislav Palov .20 .50
13 Jozef Kohut .20 .50
14 Joe Dollin .20 .50
15 Stevie Lyle .40 1.00
16 Peter Konder .20 .50
17 Mark Galazzi .20 .50
18 Nick Cross .20 .50
19 Paul Dixon ACO .02 .10
20 Stan Marple HCO .02 .10
21 Dave Wiggins AM .02 .10
22 Captains & Assistants .20 .50
23 Home Kit .02 .10
24 Away Kit .02 .10
25 Mascot .02 .10
26 Action Card .02 .10
27 Flames Goalies .30 .75
28 Flames Eastern Europeans .20 .50
29 British Line .30 .75
30 Ricky Plant .20 .50
Leading British Points

2004-05 UK Guildford Flames

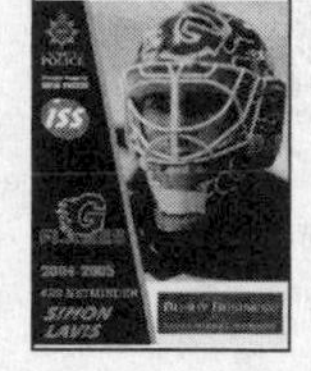

Produced by the team and available through the team's store and Armchair Sports.

COMPLETE SET (30) 5.00 12.00
1 Guildford Flames .02 .10
2 Peter Michnac .20 .50
3 Neil Liddiard .20 .50
4 Marian Smerciak .20 .50
5 David Savage .20 .50
6 Jason Reilly .20 .50
7 Stuart Potts .20 .50
8 Adam Walker .20 .50
9 Milos Melicherik .20 .50
10 Paul Dixon .20 .50
11 Andrew Hemmings .20 .50
12 Rastislav Palov .20 .50
13 Dusan Pohorelec .20 .50
14 Jozef Kohut .20 .50
15 Simon Lavis .20 .50
16 Miroslav Bielik .20 .50
17 Tom Annetts .20 .50
18 Peter Konder .20 .50
19 Nick Cross .20 .50
20 Paul Dixon .20 .50
21 Stan Marple CO .02 .10
22 Dave Wiggin ACO .02 .10
23 Captains and Assistants .20 .50
24 Home Jersey Team Photo .02 .10
25 Away Jersey Team Photo .02 .10
26 Sizzler MASCOT .01 .01
27 Celebration .02 .10
28 Netminders .30 .75
29 Playoff Trophy .01 .01
30 Terry Kurtenbach JSY RET .20 .50

2006-07 UK Guildford Flames

COMPLETE SET (24) 8.00 15.00
1 Neil Liddiard .25 .60
2 Marian Smerciak .25 .60
3 David Savage .25 .60
4 Ben Johnson .25 .60
5 Rob Lamey .25 .60
6 Stuart Potts .25 .60
7 Andrew Hemmings .25 .60
8 Rick Plant .25 .60
9 Robert Young .25 .60
10 Ben Duggan .25 .60
11 Milos Melicherik .25 .60
12 Paul Dixon .25 .60
13 Vaclav Zavoral .25 .60
14 Simon James .25 .60
15 Joe Watkins .40 1.00
16 Tom Annetts .40 1.00
17 Chris Wiggins .25 .60
18 Ben Austin .25 .60
19 Jozef Kohut .25 .60
20 Adam Hyman .25 .60
21 Rick Skene .25 .60
22 Ollie Bronniman .25 .60
23 Stan Marple .25 .60
24 Paul Dixon .25 .60

2007-08 UK Guildford Flames

COMPLETE SET (22) 7.00 15.00
1 Neil Liddiard .30 .75
2 David Savage .30 .75
3 Ben Johnson .30 .75
4 Rob Lamey .30 .75
5 Stuart Potts .30 .75
6 Rick Plant .30 .75

7 Ben Duggan .30 .75
8 Terry Miles .30 .75
9 Milos Melicherik .30 .75
10 Paul Dixon .30 .75
11 Vaclav Zavoral .30 .75
12 Dominic Hopkins .30 .75
13 Joe Watkins .60 1.50
14 Alexander Mettam .30 .75
15 Lukas Smital .30 .75
16 Ben Austin .30 .75
17 Jozef Kohut .30 .75
18 Nick Cross .30 .75
19 Rick Skene .30 .75
20 Taras Foremsky .30 .75
21 Ollie Bronnimann .30 .75
22 Paul Dixon HC .10 .25

1999-00 UK Hull Thunder

This set features the Thunder of the British league. The set was produced by card shop Armchair Sports and was sold at the store and at home games. The print run has been confirmed at 500 sets.

COMPLETE SET (20) 4.00 10.00
1 Team CL .02 .10
2 Don Depoe CO .08 .25
3 Ian Defty .20 .50
4 Simon Greaves .20 .50
5 Mark Florence .20 .50
6 Dan Carney .20 .50
7 Stephen Johnson .20 .50
8 Anthony Johnson .20 .50
9 Scott Stephenson .20 .50
10 Tam Watkins .20 .50
11 Paul Thompson .20 .50
12 Jason Tatarnic .20 .50
13 Mark Pallister .20 .50
14 Ron Shudra .20 .50
15 Pasi Raitanen .30 .75
16 Steve Morden .20 .50
17 Slava Koulikov .20 .50
18 Steve Brown .20 .50
19 Chris Douglas .20 .50
20 Chris Bailey .20 .50

2001-02 UK Hull Thunder

Produced and sold by Armchair Sports, a British card shop, this 25-card set was sold at that shop and also at Thunder home games. The total print run has been confirmed at only just sets.

COMPLETE SET (25) 4.00 10.00
1 Checklist .04 .10
2 Mike Bishop CO .04 .10
3 Stephen Foster .20 .50
4 Andy Moffat .20 .50
5 Mike Bishop .20 .50
6 Corey Lyons .20 .50
7 Andy Munroe .20 .50
8 Mark Florence .20 .50
9 Stephen Johnson .20 .50
10 Anthony Johnson .20 .50
11 Anthony Payne .20 .50
12 Ryan Lake .20 .50
13 Karl Hopper UER .20 .50
14 Michael Bowman .20 .50
15 Stephen Wallace .20 .50
16 Ian Defty .20 .50
17 Oleg Synkov .20 .50
18 Steve Smillie .20 .50
19 Rob McCaig .20 .50
20 Darren Houghton .20 .50
21 Daryl Lavoie .20 .50
22 Eric Lavigne .20 .50
23 Mike O'Connor GM .04 .10
24 Jerry Ward ACO .04 .10
25 Vanessa Brown TR .04 .10

2002-03 UK Hull Thunder

This 25-card set featured the Hull Thunder of the British National League. This set was produced by Armchair Sports and was available through them or the club shops on game nights.

COMPLETE SET (25) 5.00 12.00
1 Checklist .01 .01
2 Mike Bishop HCO .02 .10
3 Stephen Foster .20 .50
4 Keith Leyland .20 .50
5 Anthony Payne .20 .50
6 Scott Young .20 .50
7 Nathan Hunt .20 .50
8 Paul Ferone .20 .50
9 Andy Munroe .20 .50
10 Mark Florence .20 .50
11 Paul Wallace .20 .50
12 Mike Morin .20 .50
13 Ryan Lake .20 .50
14 Karl Hopper .20 .50
15 Mark Bultje .20 .50
16 Jonathan Weaver .20 .50
17 Steve Smillie .20 .50
18 Dominic Parlatore .20 .50
19 Dan Currie .30 .75
20 Sam Roberts .20 .50
21 Eoin McInerney .40 1.00
22 Marc West .20 .50
23 Mike Bishop .20 .50
24 Eric Lavigne .30 .75
25 Mike O'Connor GM .02 .10

1993-94 UK Humberside Hawks

This postcard set commemorates a now-defunct club in the British Ice Hockey League. The set was sponsored by BAE Aerospace and was given away during the season on game nights.

COMPLETE SET (18) 6.00 15.00
1 Kenny Johnson .40 1.00
2 Gavin De Jonge .40 1.00
3 Chris Hobson .40 1.00
4 Mike Bishop .40 1.00
6 Paul Simpson .40 1.00
7 Stewart Carvil .40 1.00
8 Shaun Johnson .40 1.00
9 Arren Burn .40 1.00
10 Stephen Johnson .40 1.00
12 Anthony Johnson .40 1.00
15 Anthony Payne .40 1.00
16 Andy Giles .40 1.00
17 Mike O'Conner .40 1.00
19 Andy Steel .40 1.00
20 Frank Killen .40 1.00
21 Dan Dorian .40 1.00
23 Alexander Koulikov .40 1.00
NNO Peter Johnson CO .40 1.00

1994-95 UK Humberside Hawks

This postcard set commemorates a now-defunct club in the British Ice Hockey League. The set was sponsored by BAE Aerospace and was given away during the season on game nights.

COMPLETE SET (20) 8.00 20.00
2 Malcolm Bell .40 1.00
4 Mike Bishop .40 1.00
5 Scott Young .40 1.00
6 Paul Simpson .40 1.00
8 Shaun Johnson .40 1.00
9 Wayne Anchikoski .60 1.50
10 Stephen Johnson .40 1.00
12 Anthony Johnson .40 1.00
14 Tony Saxby .40 1.00
15 Darcy Cahill .40 1.00
16 Chris Hobson .40 1.00
17 Danny Parkin .40 1.00
19 Scott Morrison .40 1.00
20 Danny Thompson .40 1.00
21 Paul Cast .40 1.00
22 Andy Port .40 1.00
23 Dominik Love .40 1.00
NNO Peter Johnson CO .20 .50
NNO Gavin De Jonge .40 1.00
NNO David Standling .40 1.00

2002-03 UK Ivan Matulik Testimonial

Set features prominent UK star Ivan Matulik, with one card for each season he played in England.

COMPLETE SET (12) 2.00 5.00
1 Header .20 .50
2 Sheffield Steelers .20 .50
3 Murrayfield Racers .20 .50
4 Cardiff Devils .20 .50
5 Cardiff Devils .20 .50
6 Cardiff Devils .20 .50
7 Cardiff Devils .20 .50
8 Cardiff Devils .20 .50
9 Cardiff Devils .20 .50
10 Manchester Storm .20 .50
11 Manchester Storm .20 .50
12 Cardiff Devils .20 .50

1998-99 UK Kingston Hawks

This set features the Hawks of the British league. The set was produced by Armchair Sports, a local card shop, and sold at that store and at home games. The print run has been confirmed at 500 sets.

COMPLETE SET (25) 4.00 10.00
1 Dale Lambert CO .15 .40
2 Ian Defty .15 .40
3 Mikko Pynnonen .20 .50
4 Simon Greaves .15 .40
5 Kelly Reed .15 .40
6 Dominic Love .20 .50
7 Bjorn Widmark .20 .50
8 Steve Nemeth .20 .50
9 Christer Widmark .20 .50
10 Stephen Johnson .15 .40
11 Mark Florence .15 .40
12 Anthony Payne .15 .40
13 Chris Hobson .15 .40
14 Mark McCoy .20 .50
15 Andy Steel .15 .40
16 Paddy O'Conner .15 .40
17 Ashley Tait .15 .40
18 Matt Staunton .15 .40
19 Pasi Raitanen .20 .50
20 Jason Coles .15 .40
21 Simon Leach .15 .40
22 Lucas Miller .15 .40
23 Michael Tasker .15 .40
24 Keith Milhench GM .02 .10
25 Team CL .02 .10

1997-98 UK Kingston Hawks Stickers

Produced by the team owner, this 20-sticker set came with a wall chart and the stickers could be bought as a set or singles.

COMPLETE SET (20) 4.80 12.00
1 Keith Milhench CO .08 .25
2 Bobby McEwen ACO .08 .25
3 Malcolm Bell .30 .75
4 Michael Knights .30 .75
5 Paul Simpson .30 .75
6 Kelly Reid .30 .75
7 Dominic Love .30 .75
8 Phil Brook .30 .75
9 Anthony Payne .30 .75
10 Chris Hobson .30 .75
11 Steve Smillie .30 .75
12 Andy Steel .30 .75
13 Ashley Tait .30 .75
14 Slava Koulikov .30 .75
15 Norman Pinnington .30 .75
16 Tony McAleavy .30 .75
17 Pasi Raitinen .30 .75
18 The Kingston Kid .08 .25
19 Ian Dolty .30 .75
20 Michael Tasker .30 .75

2000-01 UK Kudos ISL

COMPLETE SET (169) 12.00 30.00
1 Ice Hockey Superleague .10 .30
2 Jim Lynch .10 .30
3 Paul Heavey .10 .30
4 Philippe Derouville .10 .30
5 Colin Ryder .10 .30
6 Trevor Doyle .10 .30
7 Derek Eberle .10 .30
8 Anders Hillstorm .10 .30
9 Jan Mikel .10 .30
10 Johan Silfwerplatz .10 .30
11 Scott Young .10 .30
12 Dainius Bauyba .10 .30
13 Cam Bristow .10 .30
14 Shawn Bryam .10 .30
15 Ed Courtenay .10 .30
16 Tony Hand .10 .30
17 Rhett Gordon .10 .30
18 Mike Harding .10 .30
19 Mark Montanari .10 .30
20 Jonathon Weaver .10 .30
21 Teeder Wynne .10 .30
22 Dave Whistle .10 .30
23 Mark Cavallin .10 .30
24 Todd Kelman .10 .30
25 Kevin Riehl .10 .30
26 Paxton Schulte .10 .30
27 Colin Ward .10 .30
28 Jeff Hoad .10 .30
29 Shane Johnson .10 .30
30 Enio Sacilotto .10 .30
31 Brian Greer .10 .30
32 Joe Watkins .10 .30
33 Matej Bukna .10 .30
34 Jimmy Drolet .10 .30
35 Jason Mansoff .10 .30
36 Mark Matier .10 .30
37 Steve O'Rourke .10 .30
38 Reid Simonton .10 .30
39 Brent Bobyck .10 .30
40 Chris Brant .10 .30
41 Mark Bultje .10 .30
42 Joe Cardarelli .10 .30
43 Dan Ceman .10 .30
44 Joe Ciccarello .10 .30
45 Darren Hurley .10 .30
46 Blaxe Knox .10 .30
47 Stephane Roy .10 .30
48 Bard Wingfield .10 .30
49 Doug McCarthy .10 .30
50 Troy Walkington .10 .30
51 Stevie Lyle .10 .30
52 Derek Herlofsky .10 .30
53 Frank Evans .10 .30
54 Kip Noble .10 .30
55 Claton Norris .10 .30
56 Dwight Parrish .10 .30
57 Alan Schuler .10 .30
58 Rick Strachan .10 .30
59 Denis Chasse .10 .30
60 James Hanlon .10 .30
61 Rick Kowalsky .10 .30
62 Ivan Matulik .10 .30
63 Ian Macintyre .10 .30
64 Steve Moria .10 .30
65 John Parco .10 .30
66 Vezio Sacratini .10 .30
67 Steve Thornton .10 .30
68 Mike Ware .10 .30
69 Chris McSorley .10 .30
70 Trevor Robins .10 .30
71 Shawn Silver .10 .30
72 Rich Bronilla .10 .30
73 Martin Neal .10 .30
74 Randy Perry .10 .30
75 Mikael Tjallden .10 .30
76 Nicky Chinn .10 .30
77 Pat Ferschweiler .10 .30
78 Claude Jutras .10 .30
79 Mikko Koivynoro .10 .30
80 Mark Kolesar .10 .30
81 Jay Neal .10 .30
82 Ryan Richardson .10 .30
83 Paul Rushforth .10 .30
84 David Vallieres .10 .30
85 Darby Walker .10 .30
86 Brendan Yarema .10 .30
87 Terry Cristensen .10 .30
88 Daryl Lipsey .10 .30
89 Frank Pietrangelo .10 .30
90 Dave Trofimenkoff .10 .30
91 Curtis Bowen .10 .30
92 Matt Eldred .10 .30
93 Perry Johnson .10 .30
94 Troy Neumeier .10 .30
95 Rob Robinson .10 .30
96 Blair Scott .10 .30
97 Pierre Allard .10 .30
98 Kevin Brown .10 .30
99 Greg Bullock .10 .30
100 Doug Doull .10 .30
101 Marty Flichel .10 .30
102 Trevor Gallant .10 .30
103 Jason Glover .10 .30
104 Mike Morin .10 .30
105 Corey Spring .10 .30
106 Shyne Stevenson .10 .30
107 Rob Trumbly .10 .30
108 Jukka Jalonen .10 .30
109 Jimmy Hibbert .10 .30
110 Tommi Satosaari .10 .30
111 Craig Binns .10 .30
112 Santeri Immonen .10 .30
113 Arttu Kayhko .10 .30
114 Miroslav Mosnar .10 .30
115 Darren Mcausland .10 .30
116 Rob Wilson .10 .30
117 Tero Arkiomaa .10 .30
118 Louis Bedard .10 .30
119 Tomas Kupka .10 .30
120 Matt Oates .10 .30
121 Joel Poirier .10 .30
122 Timo Salonen .10 .30
123 Tommi Siva .10 .30
124 Alex Dampier .10 .30
125 Edin McInerney .10 .30
126 Willis Jordan .10 .30
127 Greg Burke .10 .30
128 Ryan Gillis .10 .30
129 Eric Lavigne .10 .30
130 Daryl Lavoie .10 .30
131 Jim Paek .10 .30
132 Duncan Paterson .10 .30
133 Pierre Claude Drouin .10 .30
134 Graham Garden .10 .30
135 Greg Hadden .10 .30
136 Jamie Leach .10 .30
137 Daryl Moxam .10 .30
138 Barry Nieckar .10 .30
139 David Struch .10 .30
140 Ashley Tait .10 .30
141 Randall Weber .10 .30
142 Mike Blaisdell .10 .30
143 Mike O'Neill .10 .30
144 Steve Carpenter .10 .30
145 Shayne McCosh .10 .30
146 Jeff Sebastian .10 .30
147 Kayle Short .10 .30
148 Adam Smith .10 .30
149 Dennis Vial .10 .30
150 Scott Allison .10 .30
151 Paul Beraldo .10 .30
152 Rick Brebant .10 .30
153 Dale Craigwell .10 .30
154 David Longstaff .10 .30
155 Scott Metcalfe .10 .30
156 Warren Norris .10 .30
157 Steve Roberts .10 .30
158 Kent Simpson .10 .30
159 Jason Weaver .10 .30
160 Brent Bobyck .10 .30
161 Ayr Scottish Eagles .02 .10
162 Belfast Giants .02 .10
163 Bracknell Bees .02 .10
164 Bt Cardif Devils .02 .10
165 London Knights .02 .10
166 Manchester Storm .02 .10
167 Newcastle Jesters .02 .10
168 Nottingham Panthers .02 .10
169 Sheffield Steelers .02 .10

1999-00 UK London Knights

This postcard sized set features the Knights of the top British league. The set was produced by Armchair Sports and sold by that card shop, as well as by the team at home games.

COMPLETE SET (17) 3.60 9.00
1 Tom Ashe .20 .50
2 Mark Bultje .20 .50
3 John Byce .30 .75
4 Scott Campbell .20 .50
5 Mark Cavallin .30 .75
6 Ryan Duthie .20 .50
7 Jeff Hoad .20 .50
8 Marc Hussey .30 .75
9 Guy Leveque .20 .50
10 Neal Martin .20 .50
11 Chris McSorley CO .20 .50
12 Tim Murray .20 .50
13 Scott Rex CO .08 .25
14 Paul Rushforth .20 .50
15 Claudio Scremin .30 .75
16 Mike Ware .30 .75
17 Todd Wetzel .20 .50

2001-02 UK London Knights

This set was produced by Armchair Sports in England.

COMPLETE SET (28) 5.00 12.00
1 Logo and Checklist .02 .10
2 Doug Serle .20 .50
3 Gerald Adams .20 .50
4 Kim Ahlroos .20 .50
5 Sean Blanchard .20 .50
6 Trevor Roenick .30 .75
7 David Struch .20 .50
8 Dave Clark .20 .50
9 Nathan Leslie .20 .50
10 Maurizio Mansi .20 .50
11 Steve Thornton .20 .50
12 Mark Kolesar .20 .50
14 Mike Barrie .20 .50
15 Greg Burke .20 .50
16 Bob Leslie HCO .02 .10
17 Ian McIntyre .20 .50
18 Ritchie Bronilla .20 .50
19 Vezio Sacratini .20 .50
20 Trevor Robins .20 .50
21 Jason Ellery EQM .02 .10
22 Mike Ware .20 .50
23 Rob Donovan .20 .50
24 David Trofimenkoff .20 .50
25 Dominic Amodeo .30 .75
26 Scott Bailey .30 .75
27 Paul Rushforth .20 .50
28 Mighty Knight MASCOT .02 .10
29 Dave Struch .20 .50
Mark Kolesar
30 Vez .20 .50
Mo
Dom
31 London Knights Logo .02 .10
32 Mark Kolesar .20 .50
Mike Barrie
33 Rob Donovan .20 .50
Mo Mansi
34 Ian McIntyre .20 .50
Dave Trofimenkoff
35 Mo Mansi .20 .50
Sue Chetham

2002-03 UK London Knights

This set was produced by Armchair Sports in England.

COMPLETE SET (24) 5.00 10.00
1 Checklist .01 .01
2 Ake Lilljebjorn .20 .50
3 Gerald Adams .20 .50
4 Kim Ahlroos .20 .50
5 Nathan Leslie .20 .50
6 Moe Mansi .20 .50
7 Mark Kolesar .30 .75
8 A.J. Kelham .20 .50
9 Jeff Hoad .20 .50
10 Chris Slater .20 .50
11 Ian McIntyre .20 .50
12 Greg Burke .20 .50
13 Steve Aronson .20 .50
14 Rich Bronilla .20 .50
15 Vezio Sacratini .20 .50
16 Dave Trofimenkoff .30 .75
17 Paul Rushforth .20 .50
18 Sean Blanchard .30 .75
19 Dennis Maxwell .30 .75
20 Ed Patterson .30 .75
21 Bob Leslie CO .02 .10
22 Mighty Knight .02 .10
23 Jim Brithen CO .02 .10
24 Jason Ellery EQM .02 .10

2003-04 UK London Racers

COMPLETE SET (20) 5.00 10.00
1 Chris Bailey .20 .50
2 Noel Burkitt .20 .50
3 Nick Burton .20 .50
4 Lukas Filip .20 .50
5 Kalle Konsti .20 .50
6 Zoran Kozic .20 .50
7 Evan Lindsay .30 .75
8 Marc Long .20 .50
9 Mike McKinnon .20 .50
10 Brian McLaughlin .20 .50
11 Sean Murdoch .20 .50
12 Mojmir Musil .20 .50
13 Oscar MASCOT .01 .01
14 Jason Robinson .20 .50
15 Mark Scott .20 .50
16 Jani Tuominen .20 .50
17 Warren Tait .20 .50
18 Matt Van der Velden .30 .75
19 Erik Zachrisson .20 .50

2004-05 UK London Racers

According to minor league expert Ralph Slate, there were just 50 copies produced of this set. As a result, you'll no doubt understand why we have no pricing information for this series.

COMPLETE SET (18)
1 Scott Nichol
2 Eric Cairns
3 Jeremy Cornish
4 Dennis Maxwell
5 Denis Ladouceur
6 Joe Watkins
7 Mark Gouett
8 Jim Vickers
9 Ian McIntyre
10 Jason Robinson
11 Steve Moria
12 Joe Ciccarello
13 Mark Thomas
14 Jason Hewitt
15 Adam Dopson
16 Mark Foord
17 Richard Hargreaves
18 J.J. McGrath

2004-05 UK London Racers Playoffs

COMPLETE SET (18) 6.00 15.00
1 Eric Cairns .60 1.50
2 Joe Ciccarello .30 .75
3 Jeremy Cornish .30 .75
4 Adam Dobson .40 1.00
5 Matt Foord .30 .75
6 Mark Gouett .30 .75
7 Richard Hargreaves .30 .75
8 Jason Hewitt .30 .75
9 Denis Ladouceur .30 .75
10 Dennis Maxwell .30 .75
11 J.J. McGrath .30 .75
12 Ian McIntyre .30 .75
13 Steve Moria .30 .75
14 Scott Nichol .60 1.50
15 Jason Robinson .30 .75
16 Mark Thomas .30 .75
17 Jim Vickers .30 .75
18 Joe Watkins .30 .75

2003-04 UK Manchester Phoenix

COMPLETE SET (22) 5.00 10.00
1 Jayme Platt .30 .75
2 Rick Brebant .20 .50
3 Dave Clancy .30 .75
4 Dwight Parrish .20 .50
5 Mike Lankshear .20 .50
6 Mark Thomas .20 .50
7 Carl Greenhous .20 .50
8 Mark Bultje .20 .50
9 David Kozier .20 .50
10 Mike Morin .20 .50
11 Petteri Lotila .20 .50
12 Chad Brandimore .20 .50
13 George Awada .20 .50
14 Marc Lovell .20 .50
15 Jason Hewitt .20 .50
16 Aaron Davies .20 .50
17 Darcy Anderson .20 .50
18 Mika Skytta .20 .50
19 Jeff Sebastian .20 .50
20 Nick Poole .20 .50
21 Manace MASCOT .02 .10
NNO Checklist .01 .01
NNO Checklist .01 .01

2001-02 UK Manchester Storm

Produced by Cardtraders.com, this 24-card set was available at Storm home games. The production run was limited to just 495 sets. Card #13 was not printed for superstitious reasons. Card #24 card was redeemable for a limited edition 12"x12" team card that was individually serial-numbered to 125.

COMPLETE SET (24) 4.80 12.00
1 Paul Ferone .20 .50
2 Dan Preston .20 .50
3 Trevor Gallant .20 .50
4 Mike Morin .20 .50
5 Dwight Parrish .20 .50
6 Mark Bultje .20 .50
7 Joe Busillo .20 .50
8 Ivan Matulik .20 .50
9 Pierre Allard .20 .50
10 Russ Romaniuk .20 .50
11 Joe Cardarelli .20 .50
12 Stevie Lyle .30 .75
14 Mike Torchia .40 1.00
15 Kayle Short .20 .50
16 Justin Hocking .30 .75
17 Kris Miller .20 .50
18 Russ Richardson .20 .50
19 Daryl Lipsey HCO .04 .10
20 Mike Torchia .30 .75
21 Stevie Lyle .30 .75
22 Lightning Jack MASCOT .04 .10
23 Rob Wilson .04 .10
24 Redemption Card .04 .10
25 Checklist .04 .10

2001-02 UK Manchester Storm Retro

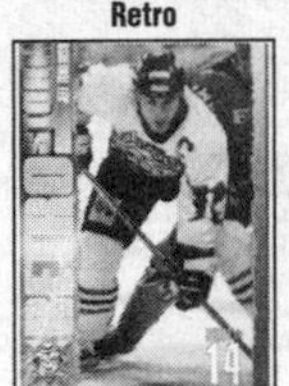

This 21-card set featured some of the most popular players from the history of the Manchester Storm of the British Ice Hockey Superleague. Cards are not numbered and are listed below by jersey number.

COMPLETE SET (21) 5.00 10.00
1 Dale Jago .20 .50
2 Craig Woodcroft .20 .50
3 Trevor Gallant .20 .50
4 Kelly Askew .20 .50
5 Jeff Tomlinson .20 .50
6 Daryl Lipsey .20 .50
7 Mike Morin .20 .50
8 Shawn Byram .20 .50
9 Pierre Allard .20 .50
10 Mark Bernard .20 .50
11 John Finnie .20 .50
12 Blair Scott .20 .50
13 Hilton Ruggles .20 .50
14 David Trofimenkoff .20 .50
15 Jim Hrivnak .30 .75
16 Frank Pietrangelo .30 .75
17 Brad Rubachuk .20 .50
18 Stefan Ketola .20 .50
19 Jeff Jablonski .20 .50
20 Kris Miller .20 .50
21 Logo Card .01 .01

2002-03 UK Manchester Storm

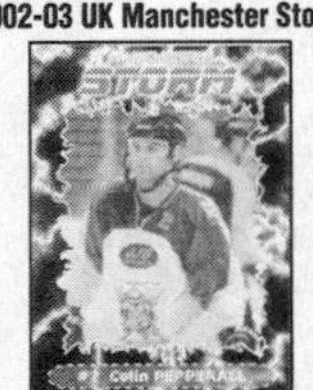

This set was produced by Armchair Sports in England.

COMPLETE SET (21) 5.00 10.00
1 Colin Pepperall .20 .50
2 Dan Preston .20 .50
3 Shawn Maltby .20 .50
4 Geoff Peters .20 .50
5 Mike Perna .20 .50
6 Pasi Nielikainen .20 .50
7 Dwight Parrish .20 .50
8 Mark Bultje .20 .50
9 Rob Wilson .20 .50
10 Ivan Matulik .20 .50
11 Pierre Allard .20 .50
12 David Longstaff .20 .50
13 Ryan Stewart .20 .50
14 Joe Cardarelli .20 .50
15 Stevie Lyle .30 .75
16 Mike Torchia .30 .75
17 Dan Hodge .20 .50
18 Daryl Lipsey HCO .02 .10
19 Mike Torchia .30 .75
20 Stevie Lyle .30 .75
21 Checklist .01 .01

2004-05 UK Milton Keynes Lightning

The Lightning play in the English Premier Ice Hockey League. Reportedly just 200 sets were produced, but some of those were apparently broken by the team in order to sell some cards individually. We have not confirmed any sales of these sets or singles and thus are leaving the set unpriced for now.

COMPLETE SET (20)
1 Checklist
2 Steve Carpenter
3 Michael Wales
4 Phil Wooderson
5 Bari McKenzie
6 Gary Clarke
7 Kurt Irvine
8 Dean Campbell
9 Adam Carr
10 Jamie Randall
11 Chris McEwen
12 Dwayne Newman
13 Mikko Skinnari
14 Allen Sutton
15 Matt Van der Velden
16 Greg Randall
17 Simon Howard
18 Ross Bowers
19 Nick Poole
20 David Coffey
Tom Ledgard

2000-01 UK Nottingham Panthers

This set features the Panthers of Britain's top hockey league. The cards were produced by Cardtraders.com, and available from the team on game nights. Card #13 does not exist due to superstitious reasons.

COMPLETE SET (30) 4.80 12.00
1 Checklist .04 .10
2 Jordan Willis .30 .75
3 Paul Moran .16 .40
4 Duncan Paterson .16 .40
5 Kevin Hoffman .16 .40
6 David Struch .16 .40
7 Randall Weber .16 .40
8 Greg Hadden .16 .40
9 Daryl Lavoie .16 .40
10 P.C. Drouin .20 .50
11 Marc Levers .16 .40
12 Darryl Moxam .20 .50
14 Greg Burke .16 .40
15 Ashley Tait .16 .40
16 Ryan Gillis .16 .40
17 Jim Paek .20 .50
18 Chris Baxter .16 .40
19 Jamie Leach .30 .75
20 Eoin McInerney .30 .75
21 Robert Nordmark .16 .40
22 Graham Garden .16 .40
23 Casson Masters .16 .40
24 Barry Nieckar .20 .50
25 Eric Lavigne .20 .50
27 Peter Woods CO .04 .10
28 Redemption Voucher .01
29 Alex Dampier DOH .04 .10
30 Gary Moran GM .04 .10
31 Team Photo .16 .40
32 Player Awards .16 .40
NA Robert Nordmark .16 .40

2001-02 UK Nottingham Panthers

Produced by Cardtraders.com, this 28-card set was available at Panthers home games. The production run was limited to just 495 sets, and each card states that on the card back. Card #13 was not printed for superstitious reasons.

COMPLETE SET (28) 4.80 12.00
1 Team Logo .04 .10
2 Brent Pope .20 .50
3 Clayton Norris .20 .50
4 Patrick Wallenberg .20 .50
5 Randall Weber .20 .50
6 Greg Hadden .20 .50
7 Frank Evans .20 .50
8 Claude Savoie .20 .50
9 P.C. Drouin .30 .75
10 Steve Moira .20 .50
11 Ashley Tait .30 .75
12 Paul Adey CO .04 .10
14 Jimmy Drolet .30 .75
15 Danny Lorenz .30 .75
16 Joel Poirier .20 .50
17 Paul Moran .20 .50
18 Barry Nieckar .30 .75
19 Darren Maloney .20 .50
20 Calle Carlsson .20 .50
21 Pasi Hakkinen .20 .50
22 A.J. Kelham .20 .50
23 Alex Dampier CO .04 .10
24 Lee Jinman .30 .75
25 Gary Moran GM .04 .10
26 Paws MASCOT .04 .10
27 Equipment Managers .04 .10
28 Trainers .04 .10
29 Head Office .04 .10
30 Christian Sjogren .20 .50
31 Jim Paek .20 .50
32 Danny Lorenz .20 .50

2002-03 UK Nottingham Panthers

Produced by cardtraders.uk, this 22-card set featured the Nottingham Panthers of the British Ice Hockey Superleague. The cards are unnumbered and are listed below in checklist order.

COMPLETE SET (22) 4.00 10.00
1 Mika Pietila .20 .50
2 Jim Paek .20 .50
3 Marc Hussey .20 .50
4 Eric Charron .20 .50
5 Greg Hadden .20 .50

6 Dody Wood .30 .75
7 Briane Thompson .20 .50
8 Jason Elders .20 .50
9 Kristian Taubert .20 .50
10 Scott Allison .20 .50
11 Mark Cadotte .20 .50
12 Petter Sandstrom .20 .50
13 John Purves .30 .75
14 Paul Moran .20 .50
15 Barry Nieckar .30 .75
16 Jason Clarke .20 .50
17 Lee Jinman .30 .75
18 Paul Adey .20 .50
19 Mascot .02 .10
20 Gary Moran GM .02 .10
21 Checklist .02 .10
22 Front Office .02 .10

2003-04 UK Nottingham Panthers

COMPLETE SET (18) 5.00 10.00
1 Niklas Sundberg .30 .75
2 David Clarke .20 .50
3 Kim Ahlroos .20 .50
4 James Morgan .20 .50
5 David Struch .20 .50
6 Robert Stancok .20 .50
7 Briane Thompson .20 .50
8 Marc Levers .20 .50
9 Kristian Taubert .20 .50
10 Mikko Koivunoro .20 .50
11 Geoff Woolhouse .30 .75
12 Joel Salonen .20 .50
13 Mark Cadotte .30 .75
14 Paul Moran .20 .50
15 Daniel Scott .20 .50
16 Calle Carlsson .20 .50
17 John Craighead .30 .75
18 Paul Addey CO .02 .10

2004-05 UK Nottingham Panthers

Produced by the team and sold in the club shop.

COMPLETE SET (20) 5.00 10.00
1 Paul Adey CO .02 .10
2 Kim Ahlroos .20 .50
3 Calle Carlsson .20 .50
4 David Clarke .20 .50
5 Mark Codotte .20 .75
6 John Craighead .20 .50
7 Curtis Cruickshank .20 .50
8 Marek Ivan .20 .50
9 Konstantin Kalmikov .20 .50
10 Jan Krulis .20 .50
11 Jan Magdosko .20 .50
12 Steve McKenna .40 1.00
13 Gary Moran GM .02 .10
14 Paul Moran .20 .50
15 Matt Myers .20 .50
16 Scott Ricci .20 .50
17 Daniel Scott .20 .50
18 Roman Tvrdon .20 .50
19 Richard Wojciak .20 .50
20 Geoff Woolhouse .20 .50

2006-07 UK Nottingham Panthers

COMPLETE SET (20) 8.00 15.00
1 Joe Cardarelli .30 .75
2 David Clarke .30 .75
3 James Cooke .30 .75
4 James Ferrara .30 .75
5 Jan Krajicek .30 .75
6 Sean McAslan .30 .75
7 Danny Meyers .30 .75
8 Paul Moran .30 .75
9 Matt Myers .30 .75
10 James Neil .30 .75
11 Corey Neilson .30 .75
12 Matus Petricko .30 .75
13 Mike Rees .30 .75
14 Rastislav Rovnianek .30 .75
15 Ryan Shmyr .30 .75
16 Steve Simoes .30 .75
17 Rod Stevens .30 .75
18 Geoff Woolhouse .60 1.50
19 Mike Ellis CO .02 .10
20 Calle Carlsson ACO .02 .10

2007-08 UK Nottingham Panthers

COMPLETE SET (19) 7.00 15.00
1 Tom Askey .40 1.00
2 Geoff Woolhouse .40 1.00
3 Patrik Wallenberg .30 .75
4 Matt Myers .30 .75
5 Jon Coleman .30 .75
6 James Neil .30 .75
7 Robert Stancok .30 .75
8 Johan Molin .30 .75
9 Marc Levers .30 .75
10 James Ferrara .30 .75
11 Danny Meyers .30 .75
12 Mark Richardson .30 .75
13 Kevin Bergin .30 .75
14 Ryan Shmyr .30 .75
15 Eric Nelson .30 .75
16 Steve Pelletier .30 .75
17 Sean McAslan .30 .75
18 Corey Neilson .30 .75
19 Mike Ellis .30 .75

2002-03 UK Peterborough Phantoms

This set was produced by Armchair Sports in England.

COMPLETE SET (18) 5.00 10.00
1 Luc Chabot .30 .75
2 James Moore .25 .60
3 David Whitwell .25 .60
4 Craig Britton .25 .60
5 Jon Fone .25 .60
6 Pete Morley .25 .60
7 Jessie Hammill .25 .60
8 Jason Buckman .25 .60
9 Lewis Buckman .25 .60
10 Russell Coleman .25 .60
11 Duncan Cook .25 .60
12 Darren Cotton .25 .60
13 Jon Cotton .25 .60
14 James Ellwood .25 .60
15 Grant Hendry .25 .60
16 Doug McEwen .25 .60
17 Shaun Yardley .25 .60
18 Checklist .01 .01

2004-05 UK Ron Shudra Testimonial

COMPLETE SET (16) 3.00 8.00
1 Ron Shudra 1990-91 .20 .50
2 Ron Shudra 1991-92 .20 .50
3 Ron Shudra 1992-93 .20 .50
4 Ron Shudra 1993-94 .20 .50
5 Ron Shudra 1994-95 .20 .50
6 Ron Shudra 1995-96 .20 .50
7 Ron Shudra 1996-97 .20 .50
8 Ron Shudra 1997-98 .20 .50
9 Ron Shudra 1998-99 .20 .50
10 Ron Shudra 1999-00 .20 .50
11 Ron Shudra 2000-01 .20 .50
12 Ron Shudra 2001-02 .20 .50
13 Ron Shudra 2002-03 .20 .50
14 Ron Shudra 2003-04 .20 .50
15 Ron Shudra 2004-05 .20 .50
16 Ron Shudra CL .20 .50

2000-01 UK Sekonda Superleague

This 206-card set produced by Kudos featured the players of the British Superleague. The cards were unnumbered, and so are listed in team set order below. The last 36 cards of the set were available as an update set to the original 170-card base set. Cards were available at most Superleague venues in 5-card cello packs or as team sets or the complete league set.

COMPLETE SET (170) 20.00 50.00
COMPLETE UPDATE SET (36) 4.00 10.00
1 Ice Hockey Superleague .10 .25
2 Jim Lynch CO .10 .25
3 Paul Heavey ACO .10 .25
4 Philippe DeRouville .40 1.00
5 Colin Ryder .30 .75
6 Trevor Doyle .20 .50
7 Derek Eberle .20 .50
8 Anders Hillstrom .20 .50
9 Jan Mikel .20 .50
10 Johan Silfwerplatz .20 .50
11 Scott Young .20 .50
12 Dainius Bauyba .20 .50
13 Cam Bristow .20 .50
14 Shawn Byram .20 .50
15 Ed Courtenay .30 .75
16 Tony Hand .30 .75
17 Rhett Gordon .20 .50
18 Mike Harding .20 .50
19 Mark Montanari .20 .50
20 Jonathan Weaver .20 .50
21 Teeder Wynne .20 .50
22 David Whistle CO .10 .25
23 Mark Cavallin .20 .50
24 Todd Kelman .20 .50
25 Kevin Riehl .20 .50
26 Paxton Schulte .20 .50
27 Colin Ward .20 .50
28 Jeff Hoad .20 .50
29 Shane Johnson .20 .50
30 Enio Sacilotto CO .10 .25
31 Brian Greer .20 .50
32 Joe Watkins .20 .50
33 Matej Bukna .20 .50
34 Jimmy Drolet .20 .50
35 Jason Mansoff .20 .50
36 Mark Matier .20 .50
37 Steve O'Rourke .20 .50
38 Reid Simonton .20 .50
39 Brent Bobyck .20 .50
40 Chris Brant .20 .50
41 Mark Bultje .20 .50
42 Joe Cardarelli .20 .50
43 Dan Ceman .20 .50
44 Joe Ciccarello .20 .50
45 Darren Hurley .20 .50
46 Blake Knox .20 .50
47 Stephane Roy .20 .50
48 Brad Wingfield .20 .50
49 Doug McCarthy CO .10 .25
50 Troy Walkington CO .10 .25
51 Stevie Lyle .80 2.00
52 Derek Herlofsky .40 1.00
53 Frank Evans .20 .50
54 Kip Noble .20 .50
55 Clayton Norris .10 .25
56 Dwight Parrish .20 .50
57 Alan Schuler .20 .50
58 Rick Strachan .20 .50
59 Denis Chasse .20 .50
60 James Hanlon .20 .50
61 Rick Kowalsky .20 .50
62 Ivan Matulik .20 .50
63 Ian McIntyre .20 .50
64 Steve Moria .20 .50
65 John Parco .20 .50
66 Vezio Sacratini .20 .50
67 Steve Thornton .20 .50
68 Mike Ware .20 .50
69 Chris McSorley CO .20 .50
70 Trevor Robins .20 .50
71 Shawn Silver .20 .50
72 Rich Bronilla .20 .50
73 Neal Martin .20 .50
74 Randy Perry .20 .50
75 Mikael Tjallden .20 .50
76 Nicky Chinn .30 .75
77 Pat Ferschweiler .20 .50
78 Claude Jutras .20 .50
79 Mikko Koivunoro .20 .50
80 Mark Kolesar .20 .50
81 Jay Neal .20 .50
82 Bryan Richardson .20 .50
83 Paul Rushforth .20 .50
84 David Vallieres .20 .50
85 Darby Walker .20 .50
86 Brendan Yarema .20 .50
87 Terry Cristensen CO .10 .25
88 Daryl Lipsey ACO .10 .25
89 Frank Pietrangelo .40 1.00
90 Dave Trofimenkoff .40 1.00
91 Curtis Bowen .20 .50
92 Matt Eldred .20 .50
93 Perry Johnson .20 .50
94 Troy Neumeier .20 .50
95 Rob Robinson .20 .50
96 Blair Scott .20 .50
97 Pierre Allard .20 .50
98 Kevin Brown .20 .50
99 Greg Bullock .20 .50
100 Doug Doull .20 .50
101 Marty Flichel .20 .50
102 Trevor Gallant .10 .25
103 Jason Glover .20 .50
104 Mike Morin .20 .50
105 Corey Spring .20 .50
106 Shayne Stevenson .20 .50
107 Rob Trumbley .20 .50
108 Jukka Jalonen CO .10 .25
109 Jim Hibbert .20 .50
110 Tommi Satosaari .20 .50
111 Craig Binns .20 .50
112 Santeri Immonen .20 .50
113 Arttu Kaykho .20 .50
114 Miroslav Mosnar .20 .50
115 Darren McAusland .20 .50
116 Rob Wilson .20 .50
117 Tero Arkiomaa .20 .50
118 Louis Bedard .20 .50
119 Tomas Kupka .20 .50
120 Matt Oates .20 .50
121 Joel Poirer .20 .50
122 Timo Salonen .20 .50
123 Tommi Sova .20 .50
124 Alex Dampier CO .10 .25
125 Eoin McInerney .40 1.00
126 Jordan Willis .40 1.00
127 Greg Burke .20 .50
128 Ryan Gillis .20 .50
129 Eric Lavigne .20 .50
130 Daryl Lavoie .20 .50
131 Jim Paek .20 .50
132 Duncan Paterson .20 .50
133 P.C. Drouin .20 .50
134 Graham Garden .20 .50
135 Greg Hadden .20 .50
136 Jamie Leach .20 .50
137 Daryl Moxam .20 .50
138 Barry Nieckar .20 .50
139 David Struch .20 .50
140 Ashley Tait .20 .50
141 Randall Weber .20 .50
142 Mike Blaisdell CO .20 .50
143 Mike O'Neill .40 1.00
144 Steve Carpenter .20 .50
145 Shayne McCosh .20 .50
146 Jeff Sebastian .20 .50
147 Kayle Short .20 .50
148 Adam Smith .20 .50
149 Dennis Vial .40 1.00
150 Scott Allison .20 .50
151 Paul Beraldo .20 .50
152 Rick Brebant .20 .50
153 Dale Craigwell .20 .50
154 David Longstaff .20 .50
155 Scott Metcalfe .20 .50
156 Warren Norris .20 .50
157 Steve Roberts .20 .50
158 Kent Simpson .20 .50
159 Jason Weaver .20 .50
160 Brent Bobyck .20 .50
161 Ayr Eagles .10 .25
162 Belfast Giants .10 .25
163 Bracknell Bees .10 .25
164 Cardiff Devils .10 .25
165 London Knights .10 .25
166 Manchester Storm .10 .25
167 Newcastle Jesters .10 .25
168 Nottingham Panthers .10 .25
169 Sheffield Steelers .10 .25
170 Lucky Card .40 1.00
171 Tony Hand .20 .50
172 Jason Bowen .10 .25
173 Paul Ferone .10 .25
174 Todd Goodwin .10 .25
175 Kory Karlander .10 .25
176 Jerry Keefe .10 .25
177 Steve Roberts .10 .25
178 Doug Searle .10 .25
179 Rod Stevens .10 .25
180 Rob Stewart .10 .25
181 Derek Wilkinson .40 1.00
182 Jason Wright .10 .25
183 Bob Maudie .10 .25
184 Jason Heywood .10 .25
185 Frank Defrenza .10 .25
186 J-F Tremblay .10 .25
187 Kim Ahlroos .10 .25
188 Aaron Boh .20 .50
189 Terry Marchant .10 .25
190 Grant Richison .10 .25
191 Mikael Tjallden .10 .25
192 Brendan Yarema .20 .50
193 Brent Bobyck .10 .25
194 Pat Mazzoli .10 .25
195 Barrie Moore .10 .25
196 Eric Fenton .20 .50
197 Daniel Lacroix .20 .50
198 Chris Baxter .10 .25
199 Casson Masters .10 .25
200 Robert Nordmark .10 .25
201 Paul Adey .10 .25
202 Kent Simpson .10 .25
203 Mike Torchia .40 1.00
204 Checklist .04 .10
205 Checklist .04 .10
206 Checklist .04 .10

1993-94 UK Sheffield Steelers

This 19-card set was produced as part of a Drugs Freeze program and originally came with a collector's album.

COMPLETE SET (19) 4.00 10.00
1 Andy Havenhand .20 .50
2 Alan Hague .20 .50
3 Tim Cranston .20 .50
4 Neil Abel .20 .50
5 Scott Neil .20 .50
6 Steve Nemeth .20 .50
7 Tommy Plommer .20 .50
8 Ivan Matulik .20 .50
9 Danny Boome .20 .50
10 Mark Wright .20 .50
11 Chris Kelland .20 .50
12 Les Millie .20 .50
13 Selmar Odeline .20 .50
14 Ron Shudra .20 .50
15 Martin McKay .20 .50
16 Dampier w/Tuyl .20 .50
17 Netminders .30 .75
18 Team Photo .30 .75
19 Sheffield Scimitars .20 .50

1994-95 UK Sheffield Steelers

This set features the Steelers of the British league. The cards are regulation size and were sold by the team at home games as part of a Drugs Freeze program.

COMPLETE SET (25) 4.00 10.00
1 Alex Dampier MGR .08 .25
2 Clyde Tuyl CO .08 .25
3 Paul Jackson .30 .75
4 Scott Neil .20 .50
5 Team Photo .20 .50
6 Ron Handy .20 .50
7 Patrick O'Conner .20 .50
8 Dean Smith .20 .50
9 Mike O'Conner .20 .50
10 Backroom Staff .08 .25
11 Tim Cranston .20 .50
12 Les Millie .20 .50
13 Alan Hague .20 .50
14 Perry Doyle .20 .50
15 Ron Shudra .20 .50
16 Mark Wright .20 .50
17 Tommy Plommer .20 .50
18 Scott Heaton .20 .50
19 Neil Abel .20 .50
20 Steeler Dan .08 .25
21 Rob Wilson .20 .50
22 Chris Kelland .20 .50
23 Andy Havenhand .20 .50
24 Martin McKay .20 .50
25 Steve Nemeth .30 .75

1995-96 UK Sheffield Steelers

This set features the Steelers of the British league. This 24-card set was produced as part of a Drugs Freeze program and originally came with a collector's album.

COMPLETE SET (24) 4.00 10.00
1 Martin McKay .15 .40
2 Ron Shudra .15 .40
3 Ken Priestlay .20 .50
4 Steve Nemeth .20 .50
5 Tommy Plommer .15 .40
6 Nicky Chinn .40 1.00
7 Tony Hand .40 1.00
8 Mike O'Conner .15 .40
9 Mark Wright .15 .40
10 Chris Kelland .15 .40
11 Andre Malo .15 .40
12 Les Millie .15 .40
13 Sheffield Arena .08 .25
14 Team Photo .15 .40
15 Scott Heaton .15 .40
16 Tim Cranston .15 .40
17 Neil Abel .15 .40
18 Scott Neil .15 .40
19 Perry Doyle .15 .40
20 Backroom Staff .08 .25
21 Alex Dampier MGR .08 .25
22 Clyde Tuyl CO .08 .25
23 The Silverware .08 .25
24 Steeler Foggy Dan .08 .25

1997-98 UK Sheffield Steelers

This set features the Steelers of the British Ice Hockey League. This 25-card set was produced as part of a Drugs Freeze program and originally came with a collector's album. The sets were available on game nights.

COMPLETE SET (25) 4.80 12.00
1 James Hibbert .20 .50
2 Tim Cranston .20 .50
3 Rob Wilson .20 .50
4 Ken Priestlay .20 .50
5 Tommy Plommer .20 .50
6 Frank Kovacs .20 .50
7 Nicky Chinn .30 .75
8 David Longstaff .20 .50
9 Tony Hand .30 .75
10 Dion Del Monte .20 .50
11 Scott Allison .20 .50
12 Chris Kelland .20 .50
13 Sheffield Arena .08 .25
14 Team Photo .08 .25
15 Andre Malo .20 .50
16 Jamie Van Der Horst .20 .50
17 Andre Malo .20 .50
18 Mike Ware .20 .50
19 Ron Shudra .20 .50
20 Ed Courteney .30 .75
21 Piero Greco .20 .50
22 Corey Beaulieu .20 .50
23 Steeler Foggy Dan .08 .25
24 Alex Dampier MGR .08 .25
25 Clyde Tuyl CO .08 .25

1999-00 UK Sheffield Steelers

This postcard size set features the Steelers of the top British league. The cards were produced by Armchair Sports, a British card shop, and sold there and by the team.

COMPLETE SET (22) 4.80 12.00
1 Mike Blaisdell CO .20 .50
2 Dan Ceman .30 .75
3 Greg Clancy .20 .50
4 Ed Courtenay .40 1.00
5 Dale Craigwell .40 1.00
6 Matt Hoffman .20 .50
7 Dale Junkin .20 .50
8 Derek Laxdal .30 .75
9 David Longstaff .20 .50
10 Andre Malo .20 .50
11 Mark Matier .20 .50
12 Shayne McCosh .20 .50
13 Don McKee CO .02 .10
14 Kip Noble .20 .50
15 Thomas Plommer .20 .50
16 Kayle Short .20 .50
17 Shawn Silver .20 .50
18 Grant Sjerven .20 .50
19 Dennis Vial .40 1.00
20 Jason Weaver .20 .50
21 Rob Wilson .20 .50
22 Teeder Wynne .20 .50

2000-01 UK Sheffield Steelers

This set features the Steelers of the British Sekonda league, the top division in the UK. The cards were sold in set form by the team.

COMPLETE SET (27) 4.00 10.00
1 Logo Card .10 .25
2 Champions .14 .35
3 Team Photo .14 .35
4 Paul Adey .14 .35
5 Scott Allison .14 .35
6 Andy & Paul .04 .10
7 Paul Beraldo .20 .50
8 Mike Blaisdell .20 .50
9 Brent Bobyck .14 .35
10 Rick Brebant .14 .35
11 Steve Carpenter .14 .35
12 Dale Craigwell .30 .75
13 Steeler Dan MASCOT .10 .25
14 David Longstaff .14 .35
15 Shayne McCosh .20 .50
16 Scott Metcalfe .20 .50
17 Warren Norris .14 .35
18 Mike O'Neill .30 .75
19 Steve Roberts .14 .35
20 Jeff Sebastian .14 .35
21 Kayle Short .14 .35
22 David Simms CO .10 .25
23 Kent Simpson .14 .35
24 Adam Smith .14 .35
25 Mike Torchia .40 1.00
26 Dennis Vial .20 .50
27 Jason Weaver .14 .35

2000-01 UK Sheffield Steelers Centurions

Produced by Cardtraders.com, this 18- card set celebrates the players who have represented Sheffield in more than 100 games. The set was sold on game nights and was also available through Armchair Sports.

COMPLETE SET (18) 4.00 10.00
1 Ed Courtenay .40 1.00
2 Tommy Plommer .20 .50
3 David Longstaff .20 .50
4 Rob Wilson .20 .50
5 Ron Shudra .20 .50
6 Tim Cranston .20 .50
7 Chris Kelland .20 .50
8 Andre Malo .20 .50
9 Ken Priestlay .30 .75
10 Scott Neil .30 .75
11 Tony Hand .40 1.00
12 Kayle Short .20 .50
13 Mike O'Connor .20 .50
14 Scott Allison .20 .50
15 Neil Abel .20 .50
16 Steve Nemeth .20 .50
17 Checklist .04 .10
18 Ron Shudra .20 .50
Player of the Decade

2001-02 UK Sheffield Steelers

COMPLETE SET (19) 5.00 10.00
1 Scott Allison .20 .50
2 Ryan Bach .30 .75
3 Cal Benazic .20 .50
4 Mike Blaisdell CO .20 .50
5 Brent Bobyck .20 .50
6 Chris Brant .20 .50
7 Rick Brebant .20 .50
8 Jeff Brown .20 .50
9 Mark Dutiaume .20 .50
10 Paul Kruse .30 .75
11 Mark Laniel .20 .50
12 Brad Lauer .20 .50
13 Peter Leboutillier .30 .75
14 Chris Lipsett .20 .50
15 Jason Mansoff .20 .50
16 Bob Maudie .20 .50
17 Kevin Miehm .20 .50
18 Jeff Sebastian .20 .50
19 Ron Shudra .20 .50

2002-03 UK Sheffield Steelers

COMPLETE SET (19) 5.00 10.00
1 Mike Blaisdell CO .20 .50
2 Brent Bobyck .20 .50
3 Rick Brebant .20 .50
4 Jeff Brown .20 .50
5 Calle Carlsson .20 .50
6 Dion Darling .20 .50
7 Mark Dutiaume .20 .50
8 Iain Fraser .20 .50
9 Rhett Gordon .20 .50
10 Joel Laing .30 .75
11 Marc Laniel .20 .50
12 Scott Levins .20 .50
13 Mike Morin .20 .50
14 Warren Norris .20 .50
15 Trevor Prior .20 .50
16 Jason Sessa .30 .75
17 Kent Simpson .30 .75
18 Chris Szysky .20 .50
19 Timo Willman .20 .50

2003-04 UK Sheffield Steelers

COMPLETE SET (21) 5.00 10.00
1 Gerald Adams .20 .50
2 Erik Anderson .20 .50
3 Mike Blaisdell CO .20 .50
4 Ben Bliss .20 .50
5 Brent Bobyck .20 .50
6 Kevin Bolibruck .20 .50
7 Christian Bronsard .30 .75
8 Dion Darling .20 .50
9 Kirk DeWaele .20 .50
10 Rob Dopson .30 .75
11 Steve Duncombe .20 .50
12 Mark Dutiaume .20 .50
13 Steve Ellis .20 .50
14 Gavin Farrand .20 .50
15 Joel Irving .20 .50
16 Ryan Lake .20 .50
17 David Lawrence .30 .75
18 Marc Lefebvre .20 .50
19 Mike Peron .20 .50
20 Pasi Raitanan UER .30 .75
21 Ron Shudra .30 .75

2003-04 UK Sheffield Steelers Stickers

COMPLETE SET (18) 7.00
1 Mark Dutiaume .20 .50
2 Gavin Farrand .20 .50
3 Mike Peron .20 .50
4 Ryan Lake .20 .50
5 Dion Darling .20 .50
6 Davey Lawrence .20 .50
7 Rob Dopson .30 .75
8 Steve Ellis .20 .50
9 Ron Shudra .30 .75
10 Brent Bobyck .20 .50
11 Erik Anderson .20 .50
12 Kirk DeWaele .20 .50
13 Joel Irving .20 .50
14 Steve Duncombe .20 .50
15 Dan Hughes .20 .50
16 Marc Lefebvre .30 .75
17 Ben Bliss .20 .50
18 Gerald Adams .20 .50

2004-05 UK Sheffield Steelers

COMPLETE SET (20) 5.00 10.00
1 Jayme Platt .20 .50
2 David Lawrence .20 .50
3 Daryl Andrews .20 .50
4 Gerad Adams .20 .50
5 Steve Duncombe .20 .50
6 Ron Shudra .30 .75
7 Dion Darling .30 .75
8 David Cousineau .20 .50
9 Marc Lefebvre .30 .75
10 Mike Peron .20 .50
11 Mark Dutiaume .30 .75
12 Rob Stewart .20 .50
13 Erik Anderson .20 .50
14 Gavin Ferrand .20 .50
15 Joe Ciccarello .20 .50
16 Ben Bliss .20 .50
17 Paul Sample .20 .50
18 Jeff Christian .20 .50
19 Brent Bobyck .20 .50
20 Checklist .01 .01

1994-95 UK Solihul Barons

This set features the Barons of the British league. Any additional information can be forwarded to hockeymag@beckett.com.

COMPLETE SET (15) 5.00 10.00
1 Jake Armstrong .30 .75
2 Stephen Doyle .30 .75
3 Paul Frankum .30 .75
4 Justin George .30 .75
5 Andy Havenhand .30 .75
6 Nick Henry .30 .75
7 Richard Hillas .30 .75
8 Phil Lee .30 .75
9 Declan McNaughton .30 .75
10 Joel Pickering .30 .75
11 Dan Prachar .30 .75
12 Gareth Roddis .30 .75
13 Jamie Van der Horst .30 .75
14 Dave Wilkie .30 .75
15 Liam Young .30 .75

1995-96 UK Solihull Barons

This set features the Barons of the British league. Little is known about this set beyond the confirmed checklist. Additional information can be forwarded to hockeymag@beckett.com.

COMPLETE SET (13) 2.00 5.00
1 Jamie Van Der Horst .20 .50
2 Nick Henry .20 .50
3 Gareth Roddis .20 .50
4 Jake Armstrong .20 .50
5 Andy Havenhand .20 .50
6 Paul Frankum .20 .50
7 David Wilkie .20 .50
8 Phil Lee .20 .50
9 Dan Pracher .20 .50
10 Alan Hague .20 .50
11 Justin George .20 .50
12 Liam Young .20 .50
13 Stephen Doyle .20 .50

2004-05 UK Steven Carpenter Testimonial

COMPLETE SET (10) 2.00 5.00
1 Steven Carpenter 1996-97 .20 .50
2 Steven Carpenter 1997-98 .20 .50
3 Steven Carpenter 1998-99 .20 .50
4 Steven Carpenter 1999-00 .20 .50
5 Steven Carpenter 2000-01 .20 .50
6 Steven Carpenter 2001-02 .20 .50
7 Steven Carpenter 2002-03 .20 .50
8 Steven Carpenter 2003-04 .20 .50
9 Steven Carpenter 2004-05 .20 .50
10 Steven Carpenter CL .20 .50

2004-05 UK Thommo's Top 10

COMPLETE SET (10) 5.00 10.00
1 Greg Hadden .40 1.00
2 Tony Hand .60 1.50
3 Claudio Scremin .40 1.00
4 Rick Brebant .40 1.00
5 Mike Blaisdell .40 1.00
6 Joel Laing .40 1.00
7 Darryl Olsen .40 1.00
8 Marty Dallman .40 1.00
9 Dennis Vial .60 1.50
10 Patrice Lefebvre .60 1.50

2004-05 UK U-20 Team

COMPLETE SET (23) 5.00 10.00
1 David Lawrence .20 .50
2 Kevin Phillips .20 .50
3 Simon Butterworth .20 .50
4 Shaun Thompson .20 .50
5 Kurt Reynolds .20 .50
6 Shane Moore .20 .50
7 Steven Duncombe .20 .50
8 Leigh Jamieson .20 .50
9 Adam Brittle .20 .50
10 Chad Reekie .20 .50
11 Chace Ferrand .20 .50
12 David Phillips .20 .50
13 Bari McKenzie .20 .50
14 Lee Mitchell .20 .50
15 Tom Carlon .20 .50
16 Mark Richardson .20 .50
17 Adam Walker .20 .50
18 Euan Forsyth .20 .50
19 Andrew Thornton .20 .50
20 Luke Boothroyd .20 .50
21 Lewis Day .20 .50
22 Geoffrey Woolhouse .20 .50
23 Checklist .01 .01

1998-99 Abilene Aviators

This set features the Aviators of the WPHL. The set was issued as a promotional giveaway in set form. The Don Margettie card was issued separately at another promotional event and is not part of the complete set proper. The cards are unnumbered and are listed alphabetically.

COMPLETE SET (21) 8.00 20.00
1 Erik Noack .40 1.00
2 Jeff Triano CO .20 .50
3 Don Margettie .40 1.00
4 Tony Martino .40 1.00
5 Mathieu Raby .60 1.50
6 Derek Booth .40 1.00
7 Mario Dumoulin .40 1.00
8 Charlie Lawson .40 1.00
9 Jean-Francois Gregoire .40 1.00
10 Craig Perrett .40 1.00
11 Eric Naud .60 1.50
12 Stephane Roy .40 1.00
13 Charles Poulin .40 1.00
14 Jayson Brunette .40 1.00
15 Stephen Maltby .40 1.00
16 Terho Koskela .40 1.00
17 Francois Archambault .40 1.00
18 Marty Dallman .40 1.00
19 Mario Cormier .40 1.00
20 Eric Brule .40 1.00
21 Don Margettie PROMO 2.00 5.00

1995-96 Adirondack Red Wings

This 25-card set produced by Split Second features the Adirondack Red Wings of the AHL. The sets were available at games and by mail. The cards feature a glossy action photo along with team and manufacturer logos on the front. The cards are unnumbered and listed below in alphabetical order.

COMPLETE SET (25) 4.80 12.00
1 Jeff Bloemberg .15 .40
2 Curtis Bowen .15 .40
3 Dave Chyzowski .15 .40

4 Sylvain Cloutier .15 .40
5 Ryan Duthie .15 .40
6 Anders Eriksson .20 .50
7 Yan Golubovski .30 .75
8 Ben Hankinson .15 .40
9 Kevin Hodson .40 1.00
10 Scott Hollis .15 .40
11 Mike Knuble .40 1.00
12 Jason MacDonald .20 .50
13 Mark Major .15 .40
14 Norm Maracle .40 1.00
15 Kurt Miller .15 .40
16 Mike Needham .15 .40
17 Troy Neumeier .15 .40
18 Mark Ouimet .15 .40
19 Jamie Pushor .20 .50
20 Stacy Roest .40 1.00
21 Brandon Smith .20 .50
22 Kerry Toporowski .15 .40
23 Wes Walz .40 1.00
24 Aaron Ward .30 .75
25 Hockeye MASCOT .02 .10

1999-00 Adirondack IceHawks

This set features the IceHawks of the UHL. The cards were produced by Blue Line Sports and were sold at home games.

COMPLETE SET (25) 4.00 10.00
1 Header/Checklist .08 .25
2 Stephan Brochu .20 .50
3 Eric Boyte .20 .50
4 David Dartsch .20 .50
5 John Batten .20 .50
6 Larry Empey .20 .50
7 Chris Ross .20 .50
8 Trent Schachle .20 .50
9 Checklist .08 .25
10 Shawn Yakimishyn .20 .50
11 Francois Sasseville .20 .50
12 Guillaume Rodrigue .20 .50
13 Trevor Jobe .20 .50
14 Tony Cimellaro .20 .50
15 Cameron MacDonald .20 .50
16 Bobby Cunningham .20 .50
17 Checklist .08 .25
18 Alexei Deev .20 .50
19 Wade Welte .20 .50
20 Alexei Yegorov .30 .75
21 Chad Ford .20 .50
22 Jack Greig .20 .50
23 Ben Metzger .20 .50
24 Robbie Nichols .20 .50
25 Hawkeye .08 .25

1999-00 AHL All-Stars

This 12-card set showcases the 2000 AHL All-Stars with full-color action photos. The cards were available at the rink the day of the AS Game. The cards are not numbered and are listed below alphabetically.

COMPLETE SET (12) 8.00 20.00
1 Martin Brochu .60 1.50
2 Craig Ferguson .40 1.00
3 Peter Ferraro .40 1.00
4 Michael Gaul .40 1.00
5 Miikka Kiprusoff 2.00 5.00
6 Christian Matte .60 1.50
7 Chris O'Sullivan .40 1.00
8 Martin St. Louis 2.00 5.00
9 Brad Tiley .40 1.00
10 Daniel Trebil .40 1.00
11 Alexandre Volchkov .40 1.00
12 Bob Wren .40 1.00

2004-05 AHL All-Stars

COMPLETE SET (49) 10.00 20.00
1 Keith Ballard .10 .25
2 Nolan Baumgartner .10 .25
3 Sean Bergenheim .10 .25
4 Patrice Bergeron 1.25 3.00
5 Brandon Bochenski .30 .75
6 Rene Bourque .20 .50
7 Jay Bouwmeester .40 1.00
8 Dustin Brown .40 1.00
9 Mike Cammalleri .40 1.00
10 Craig Darby .10 .25
11 Christian Ehrhoff .10 .25
12 Steve Eminger .10 .25
13 Simon Gamache .20 .50
14 Mathieu Garon .30 .75
15 Denis Grebeshkov .10 .25
16 Dan Hamhuis .10 .25
17 Andy Hilbert .10 .25
18 Michael Holmqvist .10 .25
19 Andrew Hutchinson .10 .25
20 Ryan Kesler .10 .25
21 Jason King .10 .25
22 Chuck Kobasew .30 .75
23 Mikko Koivu .40 1.00
24 Niklas Kronwall .30 .75
25 Jason Labarbera .20 .50
26 Kari Lehtonen 1.25 3.00
27 Joey MacDonald .20 .50
28 Ryan Miller .60 1.50
29 Antero Niittymaki .40 1.00
30 Lawrence Nycholat .10 .25
31 Michel Ouellet .10 .25
32 Zach Parise 1.25 3.00
33 Eric Perrin .10 .25
34 Joni Pitkanen .20 .50
35 Tomas Plekanec .20 .50
36 Brian Pothier .10 .25
37 Travis Roche .10 .25
38 Tony Salmelainen .10 .25
39 Patrick Sharp .10 .25
40 Jason Spezza .75 2.00
41 Eric Staal .60 1.50
42 Alexander Svitov .10 .25
43 Brad Tiley .10 .25
44 Anton Volchenkov .10 .25
45 Kyle Wellwood .30 .75
46 Dennis Wideman .10 .25
47 Finland Representatives .20 .50
48 Manchester Monarchs .10 .25
49 Checklist .01 .01

2002-03 AHL Top Prospects

This series was produced by Choice Marketing in conjunction with the PHPA and the AHL. The set was sold online and at rinks around the league. The set features a number of top prospects on their first pro cards.

COMPLETE SET (45) 8.00 20.00
1 Ramzi Abid .10 .25
2 Alex Auld .30 .75
3 Jared Aulin .20 .50
4 Jason Bacashihua .20 .50
5 Kris Beech .10 .25
6 Brad Boyes .30 .75
7 Scott Clemmensen .20 .50
8 Ty Conklin .20 .50
9 Niko Dimitrakos .10 .25
10 Rick DiPietro .60 1.50
11 Micki Dupont .10 .25
12 Ray Emery .40 1.00
13 Shane Endicott .10 .25
14 Garnet Exelby .20 .50
15 Jim Fahey .10 .25
16 Ron Hainsey .20 .50
17 Darren Haydar .20 .50
18 Jonathan Hedstrom .10 .25
19 Jeff Heerema .10 .25
20 Andy Hilbert .10 .25
21 Trent Hunter .20 .50
22 Mike Komisarek .20 .50
23 Tomas Kopecky .20 .50
24 Pascal Leclaire .40 1.00
25 Guillaume Lefebvre .10 .25
26 Michael Leighton .20 .50
27 Roman Lyashenko .10 .25
28 Tomas Malec .10 .25
29 Ryan Miller .75 2.00
30 Shaone Morrisonn .20 .50
31 Filip Novak .10 .25
32 Steve Ott .40 1.00
33 Maxime Ouellet .20 .50
34 Justin Papineau .10 .25
35 John Pohl .10 .25
36 Brandon Reid .10 .25
37 Jani Rita .10 .25
38 Phillippe Sauve .20 .50
39 Jason Spezza 1.25 3.00
40 Charlie Stephens .10 .25
41 Jeff Taffe .10 .25
42 J.P. Vigier .10 .25
43 Kyle Wanvig .10 .25
44 Duvie Westcott .10 .25
45 Tomas Zizka .10 .25

2003-04 AHL Top Prospects

This series was produced by Choice Marketing and sold in complete set form at AHL rinks.

COMPLETE SET (46) 6.00 15.00
1 Anton Babchuk .10 .25
2 Jason Bacashihua .20 .50
3 Ryan Bayda .10 .25
4 Brad Boyes .20 .50
5 Ilja Bryzgalov .20 .50
6 Peter Budaj .20 .50
7 Carlo Colaiacovo .10 .25
8 Ray Emery .40 1.00
9 Kurtis Foster .10 .25
10 Denis Grebeshkov .10 .25
11 Chris Higgins .40 1.00
12 Jiri Hudler .40 1.00
13 Ryan Kesler .10 .25
14 Mike Komisarek .10 .25
15 Lukas Krajicek .10 .25
16 Niklas Kronwall .30 .75
17 Brooks Laich .10 .25
18 Pascal Leclaire .20 .50
19 Kari Lehtonen .75 2.00
20 David LeNeveu .20 .50
21 Ross Lupaschuk .10 .25
22 Justin Mapletoft .10 .25
23 Jay McClement .10 .25
24 Ryan Miller .40 1.00
25 Shaone Morrisonn .10 .25
26 Maxime Ouellet .20 .50
27 Johnny Pohl .20 .50
28 Jason Pominville .40 1.00
29 Mark Popovic .10 .25
30 Jani Rita .10 .25
31 Derek Roy .40 1.00
32 Patrick Sharp .10 .25
33 Charlie Stephens .10 .25
34 Alexander Suglobov .10 .25
35 Tomas Surovy .10 .25
36 Jeff Taffe .10 .25
37 Petr Taticek .10 .25
38 Hannu Toivonen .40 1.00
39 Fedor Tjutin .10 .25
40 Scott Upshall .20 .50
41 Stephane Veilleux .10 .25
42 Kyle Wanvig .10 .25
43 Stephen Weiss .20 .50
44 Kyle Wellwood .40 1.00
45 Jeff Woywitka .10 .25
NNO Checklist .01 .01

2004-05 AHL Top Prospects

COMPLETE SET (61) 10.00 25.00
1 Zach Parise 1.00 2.50
2 Alexander Suglobov .10 .25
3 Jason Spezza .60 1.50
4 Antoine Vermette .20 .50
5 Anton Volchenkov .10 .25
6 Sean Bergenheim .10 .25
7 Karl Lehtonen 1.00 2.50
8 Karl Stewart .10 .25
9 Joffrey Lupul .30 .75
10 Stanislav Chistov .10 .25
11 Marcel Goc .10 .25
12 Brad Winchester .10 .25
13 Doug Lynch .10 .25
14 Niklas Kronwall .30 .75
15 Nathan Robinson .10 .25
16 Tomas Plekanec .20 .50
17 Trevor Daley .10 .25
18 Jozef Balej .10 .25
19 Jason Labarbera .20 .50
20 Peter Budaj .20 .50
21 Pierre-Marc Bouchard .30 .75
22 Brent Burns .20 .50
23 Mikko Koivu .40 1.00
24 Eric Staal .60 1.50
25 Chuck Kobasew .20 .50
26 Brent Krahn .20 .50
27 Yanick Lehoux .10 .25
28 Mike Cammalleri .40 1.00
29 Dustin Brown .20 .50
30 Denis Grebeshkov .10 .25
31 Jason King .10 .25
32 Ryan Kesler .10 .25
33 Timofei Shishkanov .10 .25
34 Scottie Upshall .20 .50
35 Jordin Tootoo .40 1.00
36 Mikhail Yakubov .10 .25
37 Anton Babchuk .10 .25
38 R.J. Umberger .20 .50
39 Joni Pitkanen .20 .50
40 Antero Niittymaki .40 1.00
41 Steve Eminger .10 .25
42 Jakub Klepis .10 .25
43 Patrice Bergeron 1.00 2.50
44 Hannu Toivonen .40 1.00
45 Derek Roy .20 .50
46 Thomas Vanek 1.00 2.50
47 Stephen Weiss .20 .50
48 Jay Bouwmeester .30 .75
49 Nathan Horton .30 .75
50 Adam Henrich .10 .25
51 Kyle Wellwood .30 .75
52 Matthew Stajan .30 .75
53 Carlo Colaiacovo .20 .50
54 Alexander Svitov .10 .25
55 David LeNeveu .20 .50
56 Michel Ouellet .10 .25
57 Ryan Whitney .30 .75
58 Marc-Andre Fleury .60 1.50
59 Mike Glumac .10 .25
60 Peter Sejna .10 .25
NNO Checklist .01 .01

2005-06 AHL All-Stars

COMPLETE SET (45) 10.00 25.00
1 Keith Aucoin .20 .50
2 Sven Butenschon .20 .50
3 Braydon Coburn .20 .50
4 Yann Danis .40 1.00
5 Andy Delmore .20 .50
6 Eric Fehr .20 .50
7 Valtteri Filppula .40 1.00
8 Wade Flaherty .40 1.00
9 Bruno Gervais .20 .50
10 Denis Grebeshkov .20 .50
11 Denis Hamel .20 .50
12 Mark Hartigan .20 .50
13 Eric Healey .20 .50
14 Jiri Hudler .40 1.00
15 Vitaly Kolesnik .40 1.00
16 Kirby Law .20 .50
17 Junior Lessard .40 1.00
18 Corey Locke .20 .50
19 Donald MacLean .20 .50
20 Al Montoya .75 2.00
21 Mike Mottau .20 .50
22 Curtis Murphy .20 .50
23 Filip Novak .20 .50
24 Lawrence Nycholat .20 .50
25 Patrick O'Sullivan .40 1.00
26 Nathan Paetsch .20 .50
27 Libor Pivko .20 .50
28 Thomas Pock .20 .50
29 Johnny Pohl .20 .50
30 Richie Regehr .20 .50
31 Pekka Rinne .40 1.00
32 Pat Rissmiller .20 .50
33 Jimmy Roy .20 .50
34 Dany Sabourin .40 1.00
35 Ryan Shannon .20 .50
36 John Slaney .20 .50
37 Martin St. Pierre .20 .50
38 Alexander Suglobov .20 .50
39 Jeff Tambellini .20 .50
40 Layne Ulmer .20 .50
41 Ryan Vesce .20 .50
42 Noah Welch .20 .50
43 Erik Westrum .40 1.00
44 AHL All-Stars .20 .50
NNO Checklist .01 .01

2005-06 AHL Top Prospects

COMPLETE SET (50) 15.00 25.00
1 Nicklas Bergfors .20 .50
2 Steve Bernier .40 1.00
3 Kevin Bieksa .20 .50
4 Chris Bourque .40 1.00
5 Alexandre Burrows .20 .50
6 Braydon Coburn .20 .50
7 Jeremy Colliton .20 .50
8 Ryan Craig .20 .50
9 Yann Danis .40 1.00
10 Nigel Dawes .20 .50
11 Patrick Eaves .40 1.00
12 Dan Ellis .40 1.00
13 Eric Fehr .20 .50
14 Valtteri Filppula .40 1.00
15 Tomas Fleischmann .20 .50
16 Bruno Gervais .20 .50
17 Mike Glumac .20 .50
18 Josh Harding .40 1.00
19 Jim Howard .40 1.00
20 Jean-Francois Jacques .20 .50
21 Matt Jones .20 .50
22 Vitaly Kolesnik .40 1.00
23 Staffan Kronwall .20 .50
24 Ryan Lannon .20 .50
25 Al Montoya .75 2.00
26 Eric Nystrom .20 .50
27 Patrick O'Sullivan .40 1.00
28 Nathan Paetsch .20 .50
29 Dustin Penner .40 1.00
30 Alexandre Picard .20 .50
31 Libor Pivko .20 .50
32 Geoff Platt .20 .50
33 Konstantin Pushkarev .20 .50
34 Tyler Redenbach .20 .50
35 Pekka Rinne .40 1.00
36 Peter Sejna .20 .50
37 Ryan Shannon .20 .50
38 Brian Sipotz .20 .50
39 Martin St. Pierre .20 .50
40 Yan Stastny .20 .50
41 Barry Tallackson .20 .50
42 Jeff Tambellini .20 .50
43 Chris Thorburn .20 .50
44 Lauri Tukonen .20 .50
45 Ryan Vesce .20 .50
46 Roman Voloshenko .20 .50
47 Ben Walter .20 .50
48 Noah Welch .20 .50
49 Jeremy Williams .40 1.00
50 Checklist .01 .01

2006-07 AHL Top Prospects

1 Kyle Cumiskey .20 .50
2 Justin Peters .20 .50
3 Andrew Ebbett .20 .50
4 Josh Hennessy .30 .75
5 Jeff Tambellini .20 .50
6 Robert Nilsson .20 .50
7 Blake Comeau .20 .50
8 Brett Sterling .30 .75
9 Nathan Oystrick .20 .50
10 Boris Valabik .20 .50
11 Jonathan Ericsson .20 .50
12 Jimmy Howard .40 1.00
13 Jaroslav Halak .75 2.00
14 Ryan Callahan .20 .50
15 Daniel Girardi .30 .75
16 Jeff Schultz .20 .50
17 Benoit Pouliot .40 1.00
18 Joel Lundqvist .40 1.00
19 Vojtech Polak .20 .50
20 Andy Greene .20 .50
21 Matt Moulson .20 .50
22 Peter Harrold .20 .50
23 Colby Genoway .20 .50
24 Alex Edler .30 .75
25 Rich Peverley .20 .50
26 Cal O'Reilly .20 .50
27 Troy Brouwer .30 .75
28 Dustin Byfuglien .20 .50
29 Corey Crawford .30 .75
30 Dustin Boyd .30 .75
31 Curtis McElhinney .20 .50
32 Roman Polak .20 .50
33 Marek Schwarz .40 1.00
34 Stefan Ruzicka .20 .50
35 Ryan Shannon .20 .50
36 David Krejci .30 .75
37 Matt Lashoff .30 .75
38 Clarke MacArthur .20 .50
39 Drew Stafford .75 2.00
40 Bill Thomas .20 .50
41 Blair Jones .20 .50
42 Karri Ramo .30 .75
43 Tomas Popperle .20 .50
44 Colin Murphy .20 .50
45 Justin Pogge .75 2.00
46 Jon Filewich .20 .50
47 Rob Schremp .60 1.50
48 Jeff Drouin-Deslauriers .30 .75
49 Joe Pavelski .40 1.00
50 Thomas Greiss .30 .75

2007-08 AHL Top Prospects

COMPLETE SET (50) 12.00 20.00
1 Bobby Hughes .20 .50
2 Brian Lee .20 .50
3 Nick Foligno .20 .50
4 Frans Nielsen .20 .50
5 Blake Comeau .20 .50
6 Brett Sterling .20 .50
7 Ondrej Pavelec .30 .75
8 Jonathan Ericsson .40 1.00
9 Jakub Kindl .20 .50
10 Sergei Kostitsyn .40 1.00
11 Ryan O'Byrne .20 .50
12 Greg Moore .20 .50
13 Brodie Dupont .20 .50
14 Kyle Wilson .20 .50
15 Daren Machesney .20 .50
16 Petr Kalus .20 .50
17 Cal Clutterbuck .20 .50
18 Mark Fistric .20 .50
19 T.J. Hensick .20 .50
20 Chris Stewart .20 .50
21 Mark Fraser .20 .50
22 Teddy Purcell .30 .75
23 Brian Boyle .60 1.50
24 Luc Bourdon .30 .75
25 Michael Grabner .20 .50
26 Cal O'Reilly .20 .50
27 Cody Franson .20 .50
28 Vladimir Mihalik .20 .50
29 Roman Polak .20 .50
30 Marek Schwarz .30 .75
31 Jonathan Matsumoto .20 .50
32 Ryan Parent .30 .75
33 Bobby Ryan .30 .75
34 Brian Salcido .20 .50
35 Matt Hunwick .20 .50
36 Tuukka Rask .30 .75
37 Kris Chucko .20 .50
38 Matt Pelech .20 .50
39 Stefan Meyer .20 .50
40 Marek Zagrapan .20 .50
41 Cam Barker .20 .50
42 Jack Skille .20 .50
43 Keith Yandle .20 .50
44 Colin McDonald .20 .50
45 Marc Pouliot .20 .50
46 Derick Brassard .20 .50
47 Justin Pogge .40 1.00
48 Kristopher Letang .20 .50
49 Mike Iggulden .20 .50
50 Lukas Kaspar .20 .50

1995-96 AHCA

This 10-card set was produced by the American Hockey Coaches Association for the College Hockey Centennial and features black-and-white photos in a tan border. The backs carry information about the events pictured on the front, which all are key in the history of the development of hockey in the United States.

COMPLETE SET (10) 2.00 5.00
1 The Pioneers .20 .50
2 The Inspiration .40 1.00
Hobey Baker
3 The Personalities .20 .50
John Mariucci
4 The Champions .20 .50
Michigan
5 The Colleges .20 .50
Edward Jeremiah
6 The Coaches .20 .50
Ron Mason
7 The Records .20 .50
1970 Cornell squad
8 The Moments .20 .50
Dean Talafous
9 The Traditions .20 .50
1978 Boston University Champions
10 The Future .40 1.00
Cammi Granato

1991-92 Air Canada SJHL

This 250-card standard-size set features players in the Saskatchewan Junior Hockey League. The set included an entry form for a contest sponsored by Air Canada and Old Dutch, which entitled the winner to a trip for two to anywhere in North America. The cards features posed color player photos with team color-coded shadow borders. The pictures are set on thin, white card stock with the team name in a yellow bar at the top. The player's name appears in the white margin at the bottom. The backs are white and carry biographical information and a player profile. The cards are numbered on the back and were issued in five series denoted by the letters A, B, C, D, and E as card number prefixes.

COMPLETE SET (250) 14.00 35.00
A1 Dean Normand .10 .30
A2 Dan Meyers .08 .25
A3 Tyson Balog .07 .20
A4 Tyler McMillan .07 .20
A5 Jason Selkirk .07 .20
A6 Bryce Bohun .07 .20
A7 Blaire Hornung .07 .20
A8 Craig McKechnie .07 .20
A9 Rejean Stringer .07 .20
A10 Corri Moffat .07 .20
A11 Dion Johnson .07 .20
A12 Rod Krushel .07 .20
A13 Mike Langen .07 .20
A14 Jeff Hassman .07 .20
A15 Dean Moore .07 .20
A16 Trevor Wathen .07 .20
A17 Curtis Knight .07 .20
A18 Chris Morgan .07 .20
A19 Trevor Thurstan .07 .20
A20 Wayne Filipenko .07 .20
A21 Jason Feiffer .07 .20
A22 Layne Douglas .07 .20
A23 Dave Gardner .07 .20
A24 Ryan Sandholm .07 .20
A25 Corey McKee .07 .20
A26 Trevor Schmiess .07 .20
A27 Todd Hollinger .20 .50
A28 Jay Dunn .07 .20
A29 Jamie Ling .10 .30
A30 Todd Small .07 .20
A31 Barret Kropf .07 .20
A32 Dean Gerard .07 .20
A33 Christian Dutil .20 .50
A34 Tyler Scheidt .07 .20
Aaron Campbell
A35 Dean Sideroff .07 .20
A36 Dan Dufresne .07 .20
A37 Cam Yager .07 .20
A38 Richard Nagy .08 .25
A39 Aaron Cain .20 .50
A40 Rob Beck .07 .20
A41 Blair Wagar .07 .20
A42 Kim Maier .07 .20
A43 Brent Hoiness .07 .20
A44 Troy Edwards .07 .20
A45 Evan Anderson .07 .20
A46 Carlin Nordstrom .07 .20
A47 Dean Seymour .07 .20
A48 Scott Wotton .10 .30
A49 Curtis Joseph 4.00 10.00
SJHL All Star
B1 Richard Boscher .07 .20
B2 James Schaeffler .07 .20
B3 Wes Rommel .07 .20
B4 Corey Thompson .07 .20
B5 Rob Phillips .10 .30
B6 Jim McLean .07 .20
B7 Trevor Warrener .20 .50
B8 Peter Boake .07 .20
B9 Kevin Riffel .07 .20
B10 Tom Perry .07 .20
B11 Mark Baird .07 .20
B12 Stacy Prevost .07 .20
B13 Taras Lendzyk .07 .20
B14 Shawn Reis .07 .20
B15 Shawn Thompson .07 .20
B16 Curtis Kleisinger .07 .20
B17 Kent Rogers .07 .20
B18 Scott Christion .10 .30
B19 Gerald Tallaire .07 .20
B20 Kelly Hollingshead .10 .30
B21 Mike Savard .10 .30
B22 Darren Maloney .07 .20
B23 Jason Hynd .07 .20
B24 Scott Stewart .07 .20
B25 Scott Beattie .10 .30
SJHL All Star
B26 Dave McAmmond .07 .20
B27 Myles Gibb .07 .20
B28 Ryan Bach .20 .50
B29 Martin Smith .07 .20
B30 Leigh Brookbank .07 .20
B31 Todd Markus .07 .20
B32 The Boys From PA .10 .30
Dean Gerard
Darryn Listwan
Scott Rogers
Brad Federenko
Derek Simonson
Jeff Greenwood
B33 Randy Muise .07 .20
B34 George Gervais .07 .20
B35 Keith Harris .07 .20
B36 Jamie Stelmak .07 .20
B37 Bart Vanstaalduinen .07 .20
B38 Scott Murray .07 .20
B39 Danny Galarneau .07 .20
B40 Keith Murphy .07 .20
B41 Jeff Kungle .10 .30
B42 Michel Cook .07 .20
B43 Daryl Krauss .07 .20
B44 Derek Wynne .07 .20
B45 Dereck Crimin .07 .20
B46 Jason Brown .07 .20
B47 Bruce Matatall .07 .20
B48 Chris Hatch .07 .20
B49 Kurtise Souchotte .07 .20
B50 Michael Brennan .07 .20
B51 Orrin Hergott .07 .20
C1 Craig Matatall .07 .20
C2 Brad Prefontaine .07 .20
C3 Mike Evans .07 .20
C4 Jody Reiter .07 .20
C5 Jeremy Mylymok .07 .20
C6 Dave Doucet .10 .30
C7 Randy Kerr .07 .20
C8 Gordon McCann .07 .20
C9 Quinn Fair .07 .20
C10 Kyle Niemegeers .07 .20
C11 Ryan Smith .10 .30
C12 Mike Hillock .07 .20
C13 Vern Anderson .07 .20
C14 Trent Hamm .07 .20
C15 Curtis Folkett ACO .07 .20
C16 Warren Pickford .07 .20
C17 Craig Volstad .07 .20
C18 Sean Tallaire .10 .30
C19 Jason Yaganiski .07 .20
C20 Jim McLarty .07 .20
C21 Jamie Byfuglien .07 .20
C22 Terry Metro .07 .20
C23 Todd Kozak .07 .20
C24 Jeff Huckle .07 .20
C25 Darren McLean .07 .20
C26 Bret Mohninger .07 .20
C27 Tim Slukynsky .07 .20
C28 Roman Mrhalek .07 .20
C29 Joel Martinson .07 .20
C30 Ron Patterson .07 .20
C31 Mark Gorgi .07 .20
C32 Tom Thomson .07 .20
C33 Greg Wahl .07 .20
C34 Craig Perrett .07 .20
C35 Mike Harder .07 .20
C36 Jeff Cole .07 .20
C37 Justin Christoffer .07 .20
C38 Nolan Weir .07 .20
C39 Jeff Knight .07 .20
C40 Lyle Vaughan .07 .20
C41 Scott Bellefontaine .07 .20
C42 Trevor Mathias .07 .20
C43 Chris Schinkel .10 .30
C44 Scott Rogers .08 .25
C45 Shane Holunga .07 .20
C46 Dwayne Rhinehart .07 .20
C47 Eddy Marchant .07 .20
C48 Travis Smith .07 .20
C49 Not Known .07 .20
C50 Mike Hidlebaugh .07 .20
D1 Darcy Herlick .07 .20
D2 Joel Appleton .07 .20
D3 Bobby Standish .07 .20
D4 Kory Karlander .10 .30
D5 Brett Kinaschuk .07 .20
D6 Kevin Messer .07 .20
D7 Jason Martin .07 .20
D8 Devin Zimmer .07 .20
D9 David Foster .07 .20
D10 Bob Schwark .07 .20
D11 Ted Grayling .07 .20
D12 Travis Vantighem .10 .30
D13 Darren Houghton .07 .20
D14 Wade Welte .07 .20
D15 1991 NB All Stars .20 .50
Martin Smith
Ron Gunville
Derek Knorr
Geoff McMaster
Trevor Converse
D16 Kevin Powell .07 .20
D17 Returning Hounds .07 .20
Dave Lovesin
Bernie Adlys
Bart Vanstaalduinen
Scott Christion
Bob MacIntosh
Rice Thompson
Adam Thompson
D18 Dennis Budeau .07 .20
D19 Darren Opp .07 .20
D20 Jeff Greenwood .07 .20
D21 Mark Daniels .20 .50
D22 Todd Murphy .07 .20
D23 Scott Weaver .07 .20
D24 Robby Bear .07 .20
D25 Nigel Werenka .10 .30
D26 Sean Timmins .07 .20
D27 Ken Malenfant .07 .20
D28 Greg Taylor .07 .20
D29 Sheldon Bylsma .07 .20
D30 Clint Hooge .07 .20
D31 Bob McIntosh .07 .20
D32 Dave Lovsin .07 .20
D33 Jeremy Mathies .07 .20
D34 Blaine Fomradas .07 .20
D35 Cory Borys .07 .20
D36 Brad Purdie .07 .20
D37 J. Sotropa .07 .20
D38 Duane Vardale .07 .20
D39 Jim Nellis .07 .20
D40 Brent Sheppard .07 .20
D41 Cam Bristow .07 .20
D42 Steven Brent .07 .20
D43 Mike Matteucci .07 .20
D44 Bryan Cossette .07 .20
D45 Tyler Kuhn .07 .20
D46 Dave Debusschere .07 .20
D47 Darryl Dickson .07 .20
D48 Derek Meikle .07 .20
D49 Parris Duffus .20 .50
Ex SJHLer
D50 Lance Wakefield .10 .30
E1 Brooke Battersby .07 .20
E2 Jay Dobrescu .07 .20
E3 Blair Allison .07 .20
E4 Shane Johnson .07 .20
E5 Carson Cardinal .07 .20
E6 Dean Pooyak .07 .20
E7 Mark Loeppky .07 .20
E8 Travis Cheyne .07 .20
E9 Karl Johnson .07 .20
E10 Jason Ahenakew .07 .20
E11 Darren Schmidt .10 .30
E12 Larry Empey .07 .20
E13 Colin Froese .07 .20
E14 Darryn Listwan .07 .20
E15 Todd MacMillan .07 .20
E16 Ken Ruddock .07 .20
E17 Derek Simonson .07 .20
E18 Lyle Ehrmantraut .07 .20
E19 Jody Weller .07 .20
E20 Danny Dennis .07 .20
E21 Trent Harper .07 .20
E22 Jason Prokopetz .10 .30
E23 Tom Thomson .07 .20
E24 Trent Dumaine .07 .20
E25 Mike Wevers .07 .20
E26 Darren Duncalfe .07 .20
E27 Regan Simpson .07 .20
E28 Jeff Bloski .07 .20
E29 Blake Sutton .07 .20
E30 Darcy Blair .10 .30
E31 Marty Craigdallie .07 .20
E32 Jason Krug .07 .20
E33 Mark Hansen .07 .20
E34 Bernie Adlys .07 .20
E35 Brett Colborne .07 .20
E36 Tony Bergin .07 .20
E37 Ian Adamson .07 .20
E38 Darren MacMillan .07 .20
E39 Rob Neighbour .07 .20
E40 Jeff Lawson .07 .20
E41 Derrick Brucks .07 .20
E42 Todd Schoenroth .07 .20
E43 Jody Forseth .07 .20
E44 Derek Beuselinck .07 .20
E45 Clint Wensley .07 .20
E46 Darren Donald .07 .20
E47 Shane Stangby .07 .20
E48 Jamie Dunn .07 .20
E49 Steve Sabo .07 .20
E50 Anthony Toth .07 .20

1991-92 Air Canada SJHL All-Stars

This 50-card standard-size set features Saskatchewan Junior Hockey League All-Stars. The set included an entry form for a contest sponsored by Air Canada and Old Dutch, which entitled the winner to a trip for two to anywhere in North America. The cards feature posed color player photos with yellow shadow borders. The pictures are set against a white card face accented with an screened pale purple star pattern. The words "All Star" appear in red within a yellow and black striped bar at the top, while the player's name is printed below the photo. The backs carry the player's name, biographical information, and a player profile.

COMPLETE SET (50) 4.80 12.00
1 Jeff Kungle .15 .40
2 Jay Dunn .00 .25
3 Kevin Dickie .08 .25
4 Martin Smith .08 .25
5 Jeff Cole .08 .25
6 Trent Hamm .08 .25
7 Kent Rogers .08 .25
8 Dean Gerard .08 .25
9 Jim McLarty .08 .25
10 Malcolm Kostuchenko .08 .25
11 Mark Scollan .08 .25
12 Brad Federenko .20 .50
13 Rob Beck .08 .25
14 Bryce Bohun .08 .25
15 Kory Karlander .15 .40
16 Scott Christion .15 .40
17 Tyler Kuhn .08 .25
18 Corri Moffatt .08 .25
19 Layne Douglas .08 .25
20 Shane Holunga .08 .25
21 Mike Matteucci .08 .25
22 Bart Vanstaalduinen .08 .25
23 Brad McEwen .08 .25
24 Kim Maier .08 .25
25 Jamie Ling .20 .50
26 Dean Seymour .08 .25
27 Derek Crimin .08 .25
28 Evan Anderson .08 .25
29 Craig Matatall .08 .25
30 Keith Murphy .08 .25
31 Jason Feiffer .08 .25
32 Michel Cook .08 .25
33 Rod Krushel .08 .25
34 Tyler Rice .15 .40
35 Gerald Tallaire .20 .50
36 Richard Nagy .08 .25
37 Taras Lendzyk .08 .25
38 Jeff Knight .08 .25
39 Darren Opp .08 .25
40 Dwayne Rhinehart .08 .25
41 Minot Americans .08 .25
Layne Douglas

Derek Crimin
42 Scott Bellefontaine .08 .25
43 Darren Maloney .08 .25
44 North Division .20 .50
All-Star Team
Team Photo
45 Yorkton Terriers .20 .50
All Stars
Michel Cook
Dean Seymour
Scott Bellefontaine
46 Melville Millionaires .20 .50
All Stars
Team Photo
47 Best 1992 All-Stars .20 .50
Kevin Dickie CO
Mike Matteucci
Kory Karlander
Kim Maier
Darren Opp
Richard Nagy
Mark Scollan
48 Estevan Bruins .20 .50
All Stars
Gerald Tallaire
Kim Maier
Mike Matteucci
Evan Anderson
49 Notre Dame Hounds .20 .50
All Stars
Tyler Rice
Scott Christion
Bart Van Staalduinen
Jamie Ling
Craig Matatall
50 Bob Robson CO .08 .25

2003-04 Alaska Aces

Produced by RBI Sports and sold at the team's rink.

COMPLETE SET (16) 10.00 20.00
1 Jordan Cameron .50 1.25
2 Kimbi Daniels .50 1.25
3 Bret DeCecco .50 1.25
4 Wes Dorey .50 1.25
5 Jonathan Gauthier .50 1.25
6 Malcolm Hutt .50 1.25
7 Mike Jones .50 1.25
8 Charles Linglet .50 1.25
9 Chris Lipsett .50 1.25
10 Lance Mayes .75 2.00
11 Keith McCambridge .50 1.25
12 Ryan Moren .50 1.25
13 Dan Murphy .75 2.00
14 Shane Palahicky .50 1.25
15 Garrett Prosofsky .50 1.25
16 Mark Smith .50 1.25

1995-96 Alaska Gold Kings

This 19-card set of the Alaska Gold Kings appears to be the first set produced for a club in the West Coast Hockey League. The set was manufactured and distributed by Jessen Associates. The fronts feature action color photos, complemented by the player's name, number and position, the team logo and the league name. The backs contain biographical and statistical data. The set is unnumbered, and listed in alphabetical order.

COMPLETE SET (19) 3.60 9.00
1 Title Card .08 .25
2 Derby Bognar .20 .50
3 Geoff Bumstead .30 .75
4 Chris Cahill .20 .50
5 Warren Carter .20 .50
6 John Haddad .20 .50
7 Todd Henderson .20 .50
8 Wade Klippenstein .20 .50
9 Matt Koleski .20 .50
10 Donald Lester .20 .50
11 Derek Linnell .20 .50
12 Jamie Loewen .20 .50
13 Travis MacMillan .20 .50
14 Kirk Patton .20 .50
15 Guy Prince .20 .50
16 Rob Proffitt .20 .50
17 Ryan Reynard .20 .50
18 Wayne Sawchuk CO .02 .10
19 Shawn Ulrich .30 .75

1996-97 Alaska Gold Kings

This 14-card set of "Alaska's 1st Professional Hockey Team" features the Gold Kings of the West Coast Hockey League. The set was produced by Split Second, using unusually heavy card stock, and features grainy action photos on the front, along with the player's name and jersey number, and the team logo. The backs all include the team logo, as well as those of sponsors Coca-Cola of Fairbanks, Winchell's, Club Golf and Twisted Stitches. No player info is included. The cards are unnumbered, and are listed below alphabetically.

COMPLETE SET (14) 3.00 8.00
1 Mark Costea .30 .75
2 Shane Fisher .30 .75
3 Colin Foley .30 .75
4 Chris French .30 .75
5 Yoshifumi Fujitsawa .30 .75
6 Todd Henderson .30 .75
7 Kelly Hrycun .30 .75
8 Shawn Lofroth .30 .75
9 Brad McCaughey CO .02 .10
10 Billy McGuigan .30 .75
11 Jay Murphy .30 .75
12 Sergei Olympiev .30 .75
13 Orion The Lion .02 .10
Mascot
14 Shawn Ulrich .30 .75

1996-97 Albany River Rats

This set features the River Rats of the AHL. The set was produced by Split Second and sold by the team at the rink for $5.

COMPLETE SET (26) 6.00 15.00
1 Eric Bertrand .20 .50
2 Brad Bombardir .20 .50
3 Steve Brule .20 .50
4 Mike Dunham .40 1.00
5 Patrik Elias .75 2.00
6 Bryan Helmer .20 .50
7 Bobby House .20 .50
8 Geordie Kinnear .20 .50
9 Chris McAlpine .20 .50
10 Krzysztof Oliwa .40 1.00
11 Jay Pandolfo .40 1.00
12 Denis Pederson .30 .75
13 Pascal Rheaume .30 .75
14 Vadim Sharifijanov .30 .75
15 Richard Shulmistra .30 .75
16 Peter Sidorkiewicz .30 .75
17 Zdenek Skorepa .20 .50
18 Sheldon Souray .20 .50
19 Mark Strobel .20 .50
20 Steve Sullivan .40 1.00
21 Sergei Vyshedkevich .20 .50
22 John Cunniff CO .02 .10
23 Dennis Gendron CO .02 .10
24 Rowdy MASCOT .02 .10
25 AHL Web Site .01
26 PHPA Web Site .01

1997-98 Albany River Rats

This set features the River Rats of the AHL. The set was produced by SplitSecond and was sold by the team at home games.

COMPLETE SET (26) 6.00 15.00
1 Eric Bertrand .15 .40
2 Jiri Bicek .40 1.00
3 Steve Brule .15 .40
4 Bryan Helmer .15 .40
5 Bobby House .15 .40
6 Geordie Kinnear .20 .50
7 Sasha Lakovic .20 .50
8 Judd Lambert .20 .50
9 John Madden .75 2.00
10 Brendan Morrison .75 2.00
11 Jay Pandolfo .20 .50
12 Richard Rochefort .15 .40
13 Vadim Sharifijanov .20 .50
14 Peter Sidorkiewicz .20 .50
15 Zdenek Skorepa .15 .40
16 Rob Skrlac .15 .40
17 Ken Sutton .15 .40
18 Paul Traynor .15 .40
19 Sergei Vyshedkevich .20 .50
20 Colin White .30 .75
21 Jeff Williams .15 .40
22 Peter Zezel .30 .75
23 John Cunniff CO .08 .25
24 Dennis Gendron CO .08 .25
25 PHPA Web Site .01
26 AHL Web Site .01

1998-99 Albany River Rats

This set features the River Rats of the AHL. The set was produced by SplitSecond and was sold by the team at its souvenir stands.

COMPLETE SET (25) 4.80 12.00
1 Eric Bertrand .15 .40
2 Jiri Bicek .30 .75
3 Steve Brule .20 .50
4 Mike Buzak .15 .40
5 David Cunniff .15 .40
6 Pierre Dagenais .30 .75
7 Josh DeWolf .15 .40
8 Sascha Goc .20 .50
9 Frederic Henry .15 .40
10 Geordie Kinnear .20 .50
11 John Madden .75 2.00
12 Rob Pattison .15 .40
13 Henrik Rehnberg .15 .40
14 Richard Rochefort .15 .40
15 Alexander Semak .15 .40
16 Rob Skrlac .15 .40
17 Ken Sutton .15 .40
18 Chris Thompson .15 .40
19 Sergei Vyshedkevich .15 .40
20 Colin White .30 .75
21 Jeff Williams .15 .40
22 Red Gendron CO .02 .10
23 John Cunniff CO .02 .10
24 Rowdy MASCOT .02 .10
25 AHL Web Site .01

1999-00 Albany River Rats

This 26-card set showcases the AHL River Rats, and was sold by the team at its souvenir shop. The cards are not numbered so they are listed alphabetically.

COMPLETE SET (26) 4.80 12.00
1 George Awada .15 .40
2 Jiri Bicek .30 .75
3 Steve Brule .20 .50
4 Bobby Carpenter ACO .20 .50
5 Sylvain Cloutier .15 .40
6 David Cunniff .15 .40
7 John Cunniff CO .15 .40
8 Pierre Dagenais .30 .75
9 Jean-Francois Damphousse .60 1.50
10 Josh DeWolf .15 .40
11 Dennis Gendron ACO .15 .40
12 Sascha Goc .30 .75
13 Stanislav Gron .40 1.00
14 Frederic Henry .30 .75
15 Steve Kelly .20 .50
16 Andre Lakos .15 .40
17 Sasha Lakovic .20 .50
18 Carlyle Lewis .15 .40
19 David Maley .15 .40
20 Willie Mitchell .15 .40
21 Richard Rochefort .15 .40
22 Rob Skrlac .15 .40
23 Ken Sutton .15 .40
24 Rowdy MASCOT .02 .10
25 Colin White .30 .75
26 Jeff Williams .15 .40

2000-01 Albany River Rats

This set features the River Rats of the AHL and was produced by Choice Marketing. The cards were sold in set form by the team at its souvenir stands.

COMPLETE SET (27) 4.00 10.00
1 Daryl Andrews .14 .35
2 Jiri Bicek .30 .75
3 Max Birbraer .20 .50
4 Josef Boumedienne .14 .35
5 Sylvain Cloutier .14 .35
6 Mike Commodore .20 .50
7 Pierre Dagenais .30 .75
8 Chris Ferraro .14 .35
9 Sascha Goc .20 .50
10 Stanislav Gron .40 1.00
11 Mike Jefferson .20 .50
12 Andre Lakos .14 .35
13 Jason Lehoux .14 .35
14 Carlyle Lewis .14 .35
15 Willie Mitchell .20 .50
16 Lucas Nehrling .14 .35
17 Henrik Rehnberg .14 .35
18 Richard Rochefort .14 .35
19 Michael Rupp .40 1.00
20 Rob Skrlac .14 .35
21 Ed Ward .14 .35
22 Jean-Francois Damphousse .30 .75
23 Frederic Henry .20 .50
24 John Cunniff CO .04 .10
25 Bobby Carpenter ACO .10 .25
26 Alex Zinevych .14 .35
27 Team CL .04 .10

2001-02 Albany River Rats

This set features the River Rats of the AHL. The cards were produced by Choice Marketing and sold at home games.

COMPLETE SET (28) 6.00 12.00
1 Checklist .04 .10
2 Sylvain Cloutier .10 .25
3 Jean-Francois Damphousse .20 .50
4 Mike Commodore .10 .25
5 Daryl Andrews .10 .25
6 Andre Lakos .10 .25
7 Mikko Jokela .20 .50
8 Joel Dezainde .10 .25
9 Jiri Bicek .20 .75
10 Stanislav Gron .30 .75
11 Brian Gionta .40 1.00
12 Richard Rochefort .10 .25
13 Michael Rupp .20 .75
14 Ted Drury .10 .25
15 Max Birbraer .20 .50
16 Christian Berglund .10 .25
17 Scott Cameron .10 .25
18 Jason Lehoux .10 .25
19 Brett Clouthier .10 .25
20 Bruce Gardiner .10 .25
21 Stephen Guolla .20 .50
22 Victor Uchevatov .10 .25
23 Joel Bouchard .10 .25
24 Ari Ahonen 2.00 3.00
25 Scott Clemmensen .80 1.00
26 Bob Carpenter CO .04 .10
27 Geordie Kinnear ACO .04 .10
28 Rowdy .10

2002-03 Albany River Rats

This set was produced by Choice Marketing and sold at home games.

COMPLETE SET (28) 5.00 12.00
1 Ari Ahonen .40 1.00
2 Alex Brooks .20 .50
3 Brett Clouthier .20 .50
4 Christian Berglund .20 .50
5 Craig Darby .20 .50
6 Chris Hartsburg .20 .50
7 Daryl Andrews .20 .50
8 David Roche .20 .50
9 Eric Johansson .20 .50
10 Jiri Bicek .20 .50
11 Joe Hulbig .20 .50
12 Jason Lehoux .20 .50
13 Krisjanis Redlihs .20 .50
14 Ken Sutton .20 .50
15 Max Birbraer .40 1.00
16 Mikko Jokela .20 .50
17 Mike Matteucci .20 .50
18 Michael Rupp .40 1.00
19 Ray Giroux .20 .50
20 Rob Skrlac .20 .50
21 Scott Cameron .20 .50
22 Scott Clemmensen .40 1.00
23 Victor Uchevatov .20 .50
24 Greg Crozier .20 .50
25 Dennis Gendron HCO .02 .10
26 Geordie Kinnear ACO .02 .10
27 Gates Orlando ACO .02 .10
NNO Checklist .01 .01

2002-03 Albany River Rats AAP

This set was issued as a promotional giveaway at a late-season game. The card backs all feature an ad for Advance Auto Parts. The cards are unnumbered and so are listed below in alphabetical order.

COMPLETE SET (25) 10.00 20.00
1 Checklist card .01 .01
2 Ari Ahonen .50 1.25
3 Daryl Andrews .40 1.00
4 Max Birbraer .50 1.25
5 Alex Brooks .40 1.00
6 Scott Cameron .40 1.00
7 Scott Clemmensen .50 1.25
8 Brett Clouthier .40 1.00
9 Greg Crozier .40 1.00
10 Craig Darby .40 1.00
11 Ray Giroux .40 1.00
12 Red Gendron CO .02 .10
13 Chris Hartsburg .40 1.00
14 Joe Hulbig .40 1.00
15 Eric Johansson .40 1.00
16 Mikko Jokela .40 1.00
17 Jason Lehoux .40 1.00
18 Mike Matteucci .40 1.00
19 Krisjanis Redlihs .40 1.00
20 Dave Roche .40 1.00
21 Rowdy MASCOT .02 .10
22 Michael Rupp .50 1.25
23 Rob Skrlac .40 1.00
24 Ken Sutton .40 1.00
25 Victor Uchevatov .40 1.00

2003-04 Albany River Rats

This set was produced by Choice Marketing and sold at home games.

COMPLETE SET (30) 5.00 12.00
1 Checklist .01 .01
2 Ari Ahonen .30 .75
3 Maxim Balmochnykh .15 .40
4 Jiri Bicek .15 .40
5 Alex Brooks .15 .40
6 Scott Clemmensen .30 .75
7 Brett Clouthier .15 .40
8 Greg Crozier .15 .40
9 Craig Darby .15 .40
10 Matt DeMarchi .15 .40
11 Adrian Foster .15 .40
12 Ray Giroux .15 .40
13 Tyler Hanchuck .15 .40
14 Chris Hartsburg .15 .40
15 Joe Hulbig .15 .40
16 Eric Johansson .15 .40
17 Steve Kariya .60 1.50
18 Matus Kostur .15 .40
19 Mike Matteucci .15 .40
20 Ryan Murphy .15 .40
21 Ahren Nittel .30 .75
22 Tuomas Pihlman .30 .75
23 Ilkka Pikkarainen .15 .40
24 Krisjanis Redlihs .15 .40
25 Rob Skrlac .15 .40
26 Alexander Suglobov .15 .40
27 Victor Uchevatov .15 .40
28 Dennis Gendron CO .02 .10
29 Gates Orlando ACO .02 .10
30 Geordie Kinnear ACO .02 .10

2003-04 Albany River Rats Kinko's

COMPLETE SET (25) 15.00 30.00
1 Ari Ahonen .60 1.50
2 Maxim Balmochnykh .40 1.00
3 Jiri Bicek .40 1.00
4 Alex Brooks .40 1.00
5 Scott Clemmensen .60 1.50
6 Brett Clouthier .40 1.00
7 Greg Crozier .40 1.00
8 Craig Darby .40 1.00
9 Matt DeMarchi .40 1.00
10 Adrian Foster .40 1.00
11 Ray Giroux .40 1.00
12 Tyler Hanchuck .40 1.00
13 Chris Hartsburg .40 1.00
14 Joe Hulbig .40 1.00
15 Eric Johansson .40 1.00
16 Steve Kariya 1.25 3.00
17 Matus Kostur .40 1.00
18 Mike Matteucci .40 1.00
19 Ryan Murphy .40 1.00
20 Ahren Nittel .75 2.00
21 Tuomas Pihlman .40 1.00
22 Ilkka Pikkarainen .40 1.00
23 Krisjanis Redlihs .40 1.00
24 Rob Skrlac .40 1.00
25 Alexander Suglobov .40 1.00
26 Victor Uchevatov .40 1.00

2004-05 Albany River Rats

COMPLETE SET (25) 6.00 15.00
1 Ari Ahonen .30 .75
2 Bobby Allen .15 .40
3 Alex Brooks .15 .40
4 Scott Clemmensen .30 .75
5 Brett Clouthier .15 .40
6 Matt DeMarchi .15 .40
7 Adrian Foster .15 .40
8 David Hale .40 1.00
9 Cam Janssen .40 1.00
10 Eric Johansson .15 .40
11 Teemu Kesa .15 .40
12 Ivan Khomutov .15 .40
13 Dean McAmmond .15 .40
14 Ryan Murphy .15 .40
15 Ahren Nittel .30 .75
16 Zach Parise 2.00 5.00
17 Tuomas Pihlman .15 .40
18 Ilkka Pikkarainen .15 .40
19 Krisjanis Redlihs .15 .40
20 Pascal Rheaume .15 .40
21 Ray Schultz .15 .40
22 Rob Skrlac .15 .40
23 Aaron Voros .15 .40
24 Aleksander Suglobov .15 .40
25 Robbie Ftorek CO .02 .10

2005-06 Albany River Rats

COMPLETE SET (28) 6.00 15.00
1 Ari Ahonen .40 1.00
2 Bobby Allen .20 .50
3 Nicklas Bergfors .20 .50
4 Alex Brooks .20 .50
5 Ben Carpentier .20 .50
6 David Clarkson .20 .50
7 Matt DeMarchi .20 .50
8 Frank Doyle .40 1.00
9 Adrian Foster .20 .50
10 David Hale .20 .50
11 Cam Janssen .40 1.00
12 Teemu Kesa .20 .50
13 Ivan Khomutov .20 .50
14 Bryan Miller .20 .50
15 Ryan Murphy .20 .50
16 Ahren Nittel .40 1.00
17 Tuomas Pihlman .20 .50
18 Ilkka Pikkarainen .20 .50
19 Krisjanis Redlihs .20 .50
20 Pascal Rheaume .20 .50
21 Jason Ryznar .20 .50
22 Ray Schultz .20 .50
23 Mike Sgroi .20 .50
24 Aleksander Suglobov .20 .50
25 Barry Tallackson .40 1.00
26 Aaron Voros .20 .50
27 Petr Vrana .20 .50
28 Robbie Ftorek .02 .10

2006-07 Albany River Rats

COMPLETE SET (27) 5.00 12.00
1 Kevin Estrada .20 .50
2 Keith Aucoin .20 .50
3 Ryan Bayda .20 .50
4 Joe Barnes .20 .50
5 Jesse Boulerice .20 .50
6 Johnny Boychuck .20 .50
7 Tim Conboy .20 .50
8 Kyle Cumiskey .20 .50
9 Dan DaSilva .20 .50
10 Pat Dwyer .20 .50
11 Jeff Finger .20 .50
12 Dave Gove .20 .50
13 Ben Guite .20 .50
14 Scott Kelman .20 .50
15 Mitch Love .20 .50
16 Cody McLeod .20 .50
17 Matt Murley .20 .50
18 Justin Peters .30 .75
19 Jakub Petruzalek .20 .50
20 Peter Tsimikalis .20 .50
21 Tyler Weiman .30 .75
22 Shane Willis .20 .50
23 Brett Carson .20 .50
24 Tom Rowe HC .02 .10
25 Joe Sacco CO .02 .10
NNO Rowdy MASCOT .02 .10
NNO Checklist .01 .01

1999-00 Alexandria Warthogs

This set features the Warthogs of the WPHL. The singles were handed out one per home game throughout the season. The card of Jason Leveille was not widely distributed to the public because of an early season trade. A few copies, however, have made their way onto the secondary market.

COMPLETE SET (23) 20.00 50.00
1 Mark Biesenthal .75 2.00
2 Jeff Blair .75 2.00
3 Jason Desloover .75 2.00
4 Josh Dobbyn .75 2.00
5 Valeri Ermolov .75 2.00
6 Dion Hagan .75 2.00
7 Daniel Korber .75 2.00
8 Chris Low .75 2.00
9 Jay Mazur .75 2.00
10 Jim Mroz .75 2.00
11 Matt Osiecki .75 2.00
12 Chris Peach .75 2.00
13 Marc Pethke .75 2.00
14 Robert Plante .75 2.00
15 Regan Stocco .75 2.00
16 Matt Turek .75 2.00
17 Colby Van Tassel .75 2.00
18 Miles Van Tassel .75 2.00
19 Mike Zruna CO .40 1.00
20 Jason Leveille 4.00 10.00
21 Marcus Adolfsson .75 2.00
22 Bill Weir .75 2.00
23 Chad Wilchynski .75 2.00

1998-99 Amarillo Rattlers

This 21-card set was a promotional giveaway that was handed out over five Rattlers home games.

COMPLETE SET (21) 10.00 25.00
1 Matt Brenner .60 1.50
2 Chris Brooks .60 1.50
3 Stephen Douglas .60 1.50
4 Steve Ferranti .60 1.50
5 Bob Gohde .60 1.50
6 Brad Haelzle .60 1.50
7 Derek Innanen .60 1.50
8 Trevor Janicki .60 1.50
9 Brendan Kenny .60 1.50
10 Todd Laurin .60 1.50
11 Adam Lord .60 1.50
12 Cal McGowan .75 2.00
13 Jim McLean .60 1.50
14 David Rattray .60 1.50
15 Jaynen Rissling .60 1.50
16 Per Schlyter .60 1.50
17 Scott W. Stevens .60 1.50
18 Neil Gondek ACO .08 .25
19 Ken Karpuk CO .08 .25
20 Amarillo Rattlers .08 .25
21 Greg Sieg TR .08 .25

2000-01 Amarillo Rattlers

This set features the Rattlers of the WPHL. It is believed that the set was a promotional giveaway, but that cannot be confirmed.

COMPLETE SET (20) 8.00 20.00
1 Eric Andersen .40 1.00
2 Chris Bell .40 1.00
3 Rodney Bowers .40 1.00
4 Jeff Cheeseman .40 1.00
5 Marc Dupuis .40 1.00
6 Larry Empey .40 1.00
7 Vincent Grant .40 1.00
8 Brad Haelzle .40 1.00
9 Toby Harris .40 1.00
10 Robert Holsinger .75 2.00
11 Todd MacDonald .75 2.00
12 Jeff Mancini .40 1.00
13 Jodi Murphy .75 2.00
14 Billy Newson .40 1.00
15 Jay Pecora .40 1.00
16 Doug Shepherd .40 1.00
17 Tony White .40 1.00
18 Chad Wilchynski .40 1.00
19 Kevin Abrams CO .08 .25
20 Team Card .08 .25

1993-94 Amos Les Forestiers

This 26-card standard-size set features Les Forestiers, a Midget AAA team in the province of Quebec. Les Forestiers is one of ten teams in the province from which the junior teams pick their players. The production run was reportedly 505 sets, including 60 autographed sets randomly placed in the lot. On a white card face, the fronts display posed color player photos framed by blue on the left and top and by magenta on the right and bottom. Player identification is printed in the top border, and the team name is printed in the left border. The backs present biographical and trivia information. The set includes 1995 NHL first rounder, Martin Biron.

COMPLETE SET (26) 14.00 35.00
1 Jean-Francois Belley .40 1.00
2 Carl Benoit .40 1.00
3 Martin Biron 6.00 15.00
4 David Bolduc .40 1.00
5 Martin Bradette .40 1.00
6 Dave Fontaine .40 1.00
7 Paul-Sebastien Gagnon .40 1.00
8 Eric Germain .40 1.00
9 Eric Houle .40 1.00
10 Jacques Larrivee ACO .08 .25
11 Yannick Lavoie .40 1.00
12 Mathieu Letourneau .40 1.00
13 Vincent Levasseur .40 1.00
14 Jonathan Levesque .40 1.00
15 Eric Naud .40 1.00
16 Christian Neveu .40 1.00
17 Patrick Pelchat .40 1.00
18 John Pyliotis .40 1.00
19 Luc St-Germain .40 1.00
20 Frederick Servant .40 1.00
21 Philippe Tremblay .40 1.00
22 Serge Trepanier CO .08 .25
23 Dany Villeneuve .40 1.00
24 Les Veterans .40 1.00
Christian Neveu
Mathieu Letourneau
25 Team Photo/CL .40 1.00
26 Title card .08 .25

1992-93 Anaheim Bullfrogs RHI

This set features the Bullfrogs of Roller Hockey International. The set was sold by the team at home games.

COMPLETE SET (20) 4.00 10.00
1 Header Card .02 .10
2 Maury Silver .20 .50
3 Stuart Silver .20 .50
4 Marc Lyons .20 .50
5 Kevin Kerr .20 .50
6 Grant Sonier ACO .08 .25
7 Barry Potomski .30 .75
8 Bob McKillop .20 .50
9 Rob Laurie .30 .75
10 Bill Horn .20 .50
11 Savo Mitrovic .20 .50
12 Chris McSorley CO .20 .50
13 Victor Gervais .30 .75
14 Darren Perkins .20 .50
15 Christian LaLonde .20 .50
16 Joe Cook .20 .50
17 Ken Murchison .20 .50
18 Brad McCaghey .20 .50
19 Devin Edgerton .20 .50
20 Mike Butters .20 .50

1993-94 Anaheim Bullfrogs RHI

This 21-piece set commemorates one of the most successful teams in the brief-lived Roller Hockey International. Along with traditional cards, each set also came with a POG slammer. The cards are unnumbered, and so are listed below alphabetically

COMPLETE SET (21) 3.20 10.00
1 Shayne Arsenault .20 .50
2 Steve Beadle .20 .50
3 Jim Brown .20 .50
4 Joe Cook .20 .50
5 Victor Gervais .20 .50
6 Chris Gordon .20 .50
7 Kevin Kerr .30 .75
8 Yuri Krivokhija .20 .50
9 Christian Lalonde .20 .50
10 Darren Langdon .30 .75
11 Rob Laurie .30 .75
12 Brad McCaughey .20 .50
13 Bobby McKillop .30 .75
14 Savo Mitrovic .20 .50
15 Ken Murchison .20 .50
16 Darren Perkins .20 .50
17 Grant Sonier CO .08 .25
NNO 1993 RHI World Champions .20 .50
NNO Medallion Slammer .20 .50
NNO Header .02 .10
NNO The Mask .30 .75

1994-95 Anaheim Bullfrogs RHI

This set features the Bullfrogs of Roller Hockey Intl. The 20-card set was sold by the team at home games. Because the singles are not numbered, the players appear alphabetically.

COMPLETE SET (20) 3.60 10.00
1 Darren Banks .30 .75
2 Jared Bednar .20 .50
3 Steve Cadieux .20 .50
4 Joe Cook .20 .50
5 Mark Deazeley .20 .50
6 Victor Gervais .30 .75
7 Chris Gordon .20 .50
8 Fredrik Jax .20 .50
9 Rick Judson .20 .50
10 Rob Laurie .20 .50
11 BJ MacPherson .20 .50
12 Brad McCaughey .20 .50
13 Savo Mitrovic .20 .50
14 Marc Ouimet .30 .75
15 Darren Perkins .20 .50
16 Daniel Shank .30 .75
17 Grant Sonier CO .02 .10
18 Brad Tiley .20 .50
19 Todd Wetzel .20 .50
20 Header/Checklist .01 .01

1995-96 Anaheim Bullfrogs RHI

Little is known about this set beyond the confirmed checklist. Any additional information can be forwarded to hockeymag@beckett.com.

COMPLETE SET (20) 3.00 8.00
1 Checklist .02 .10
2 Grant Sonier CO .02 .10
3 Brad McCaughey ACO .02 .10
4 Victor Gervais .15 .40
5 Darren Perkins .15 .40
6 Savo Mitrovic .15 .40
7 Joe Cook .15 .40
8 Todd Wetzel .15 .40
9 Scott Bell .15 .40
10 Rick Judson .15 .40
11 BJ MacPherson .15 .40
12 Rob Laurie .15 .40
13 Darren Banks .20 .50
14 Sean O'Brien .15 .40
15 Jakub Ficenec .15 .40
16 Mark Stitt .15 .40
17 Glenn Stewart .15 .40
18 Mark DeSantis .15 .40
19 Tom Menicci .15 .40
20 Eric Raymond .15 .40

1996-97 Anaheim Bullfrogs RHI

This 21-card set was available late in the season, and could only be purchased at games. The cards are unnumbered, and are listed below in the order they were packaged. They were produced by Star Images Assoc.

COMPLETE SET (21) 3.60 9.00
1 Bullfrogs Logo .02 .10
2 Zeus Mascot .02 .10
3 Rob Laurie .20 .50
4 Victor Gervais .20 .50
5 Doug McCarthy .20 .50
6 Kurt Seher .20 .50
7 Marty Yewchuk .20 .50
8 David Goverde .25 .60
9 BJ MacPherson .02 .10
10 Rick Judson .25 .60
11 Jakub Ficenec .20 .50
12 Tom Menicci .20 .50
13 Glenn Stewart .20 .50
14 Mark Stitt .20 .50
15 Jim Bermingham .20 .50
16 Todd Wetzel .20 .50
17 Joe Cook .20 .50
18 Ray Edwards .20 .50
19 Chris Newans .20 .50
20 Darren Perkins .20 .50
21 Brad McCaughey CO .02 .10

1994-95 Anchorage Aces

This set features the Aces of the WCHL. Little is known about this set beyond the checklist, which was provided by Ralph Slate of www.hockeydb.com. Any additional information can be forwarded to hockeymag@beckett.com.

COMPLETE SET (27) 4.80 12.00
1 Kevin Fitzgerald .20 .50
2 Tony Link .20 .50
3 Zack Westin .20 .50
4 Kory Wright .20 .50
5 Kord Cernich .20 .50
6 Darrin Semeniuk .20 .50
7 Brian Kraft .20 .50
8 Raymond Blackadar .20 .50
9 Jim Tobin .20 .50
10 Tracy Link .20 .50
11 Michael Warde .20 .50
12 Garvin Federenko .20 .50
13 Jim Mayes .20 .50
14 Vern Hickel .20 .50
15 Derek Donald .20 .50
16 Brian Majeske .20 .50
17 Chad Meyhoff .20 .50
18 Doug Spooner .20 .50
19 Maurice Hall .20 .50
20 Pete McEnaney .20 .50
21 Keith Street .20 .50
22 Georg Thiele .20 .50
23 Tim Molle .20 .50
24 Brian Bethard .20 .50
25 Dean Trboyevich .20 .50
26 Logo Card .04 .10
27 Team Photo/Checklist .20 .50

1996-97 Anchorage Aces

This 16-card set was produced as a promotional giveaway for the Anchorage Aces of the WCHL. The fronts feature posed photos with the players blatantly shilling for the Subway chain; that company's logo is prominently displayed in the lower left corner, along with those of the local FOX TV outlet and KWHL radio. The backs feature sketchy bio information. As the cards are unnumbered, they are listed below in alphabetical order.

COMPLETE SET (16) 3.00 8.00
1 Alaska's Morning Show .02 .10
2 Derek Donald .30 .75
3 Kiddie Fox .02 .10
4 Dean Larson .30 .75
5 Steve MacSwain .30 .75
6 Mark The Hitman .02 .10
7 J.J. Michaels .30 .75
8 Black Mike .02 .10
9 Craig Mittleholt .30 .75
10 Chris Newans .30 .75
11 Frank Ouellette .30 .75
12 Chad Richard .30 .75
13 Sean Rowe .30 .75
14 Keith Street .30 .75
15 Dean Trboyevich .30 .75
16 Free Q-Zar Game Card .01

1997-98 Anchorage Aces

This set features the Aces of the WCHL. The set was produced by the team and sold at home games.

COMPLETE SET (25) 3.60 9.00
1 Title Card .02 .10
2 Walt Poddubny CO .20 .50
3 Kenny Huizenga .20 .50
4 Kord Cernich .20 .50
5 Bobby Cunningham .20 .50

6 Derek Donald	.20	.50
7 Dallas Ferguson	.20	.50
8 Derek Gauthier	.20	.50
9 Jason Gibson	.20	.50
10 Marc LaForge	.20	.50
11 Dean Larson	.20	.50
12 Dave Latta	.20	.50
13 Steve MacSwain	.20	.50
14 Chris Newans	.20	.50
15 Hayden O'Rear	.20	.50
16 Brian Renfrew	.20	.50
17 Sean Rowe	.20	.50
18 Jason Shmyr	.20	.50
19 Keith Street	.20	.50
20 Sergei Tkachenko	.20	.50
21 George Wilcox	.20	.50
22 Paul Williams	.20	.50
23 Mascot	.02	.10
24 Mascot	.02	.10
25 Mascot	.02	.10

1998-99 Anchorage Aces

This set features the Aces of the WHL. The cards measure 2 1/2 by 3 1/2 and feature a full-bleed color photo on the front. The team logo is blown up in the lower left corner. The backs feature stats over a ghosted player head shot.

COMPLETE SET (26)	4.00	10.00
1 Checklist/Team Photo	.20	.50
2 Dean Trboyevich	.20	.50
3 Kevin Epp	.20	.50
4 Hayden O'Rear	.20	.50
5 Richard Peacock	.20	.50
6 Sean Rowe	.20	.50
7 Boomer Mascot	.02	.10
8 George Wilcox	.20	.50
9 Sergei Tkachenko	.20	.50
10 Frank Jury TR	.02	.10
11 Walt Poddubny HCO	.20	.50
12 Kent Baumbach	.20	.50
13 Wade Brookbank	.20	.50
14 Keith Street	.20	.50
15 Bob Cunningham	.20	.50
16 Kord Cernich	.20	.50
17 Paul Williams	.20	.50
18 Evgeny Kourilin	.20	.50
19 Jason Gibson	.20	.50
20 Steve MacSwain	.20	.50
21 Dean Larson	.20	.50
22 Dallas Ferguson	.20	.50
23 Derek Gauthier	.20	.50
24 Yvan Corbin	.20	.50
25 Sponsor Card	.02	.10
26 Fred Rannard BR	.02	.10

1999-00 Anchorage Aces

This set features the Aces of the WCHL. The card fronts feature a full-bleed color photo, along with the logos of sponsors Subway and Wideo City. The backs contain a b/w head shot and stats from the previous season.

COMPLETE SET (28)	4.00	10.00
1 Bob Wilkie HCO	.08	.25
2 Fred Rannard	.20	.50
3 Paul Williams	.20	.50
4 Steve MacSwain	.20	.50
5 Marc Charbonneau	.20	.50
6 Chad Power	.20	.50
7 Brian Elder	.20	.50
8 Tim Lozinik	.20	.60
9 Sponsor Card		.01
10 Sponsor Card		.01
11 Kord Cernich	.20	.50
12 George Wilcox	.20	.50
13 Keith Street	.20	.50
14 Derek Gauthier	.20	.50
15 Ruslan Batyrshin	.30	.75
16 Sean Rowe	.20	.50
17 Dean Larson	.20	.50
18 Team Photo	.20	.50
19 Sponsor Card		.01
20 Sponsor Card		.01
21 Walt Poddubny HCO	.20	.50
22 Dallas Ferguson	.20	.50
23 Chad Richard	.20	.50
24 Denis Pigolitsyn	.20	.50
25 Clayton Read	.20	.50
26 Marc Delmore	.20	.50
27 Lada Hampeis	.20	.50
28 Sponsor Card		.01

2001-02 Anchorage Aces

This set features the Aces of the WCHL. The set was given away at a home game late in the season.

COMPLETE SET (22)	8.00	20.00
1 Shane Calder	.40	1.00
2 Bob Cunningham	.40	1.00
3 Kimbi Daniels	.40	1.00
4 Simon Duplessis	.40	1.00
5 Yuri Krivokhija	.40	1.00
6 Brian LaFleur	.40	1.00
7 Dean Larson	.40	1.00
8 Michael Marostega	.40	1.00
9 Jamie McCaig	.40	1.50
10 Chris Newans	.40	1.00
11 Denis Pigolitsin	.40	1.00
12 Tobin Praznik	.40	1.00
13 Chad Richard	.40	1.50
14 Olie Sundstrom	.60	1.50
15 Paul Williams	.40	1.00
16 J.J. Wrobel	.40	1.00
17 Jami Yoder	.40	1.00
18 B.J. Young	.40	1.00
19 Walt Poddubny CO	.10	.25
20 Boomer MASCOT	.04	.10
21 ACS Wireless		.01
22 Team Photo	.20	.50

1990-91 Arizona Icecats

Produced by the Ninth Inning, this 16-card standard-size set features members of the Arizona Icecats. Production was reportedly limited to 2,150 sets, obtainable either at the Tucson Convention Center Ice Arena on game days or at the Ninth Inning (a card shop). The front features a posed color photo of the player, with thin black border on white card stock. The upper left and lower right hand corners of the picture are cut out, with the year and the team logo inserted in these spaces respectively. The back presents biographical information in a black box. Although the individual cards are unnumbered, they are checklisted below according to the numbering assigned to them on the checklist card.

COMPLETE SET (16)	3.00	8.00
1 Leo Golembiewski CO	.30	.75
2 Icecat Leaders	.40	1.00
Kevin Sheehan		
John Allen		
Leo Golembiewski CO		
Kelly Walker		
John Wegener		
3 John Allen	.30	.75
4 Don Carlson	.20	.50
5 Dan Divjak	.30	.75
6 Frank DeMaio	.20	.50
7 Jeremy Goltz	.30	.75
8 Aaron Joffe	.20	.50
9 Dan O'Day	.20	.50
10 Dan Olberg	.20	.50
11 Cory Oleson	.30	.75
12 Kevin Sheehan	.30	.75
13 Dean Sives	.20	.50
14 Kelly Walker	.30	.75
15 John Wegener	.30	.75
16 Logo Card/Checklist	.20	.50

1991-92 Arizona Icecats

This 20-card standard-size set features members of the Arizona Icecats. The front features a posed color photo of the player, with thin blue border and a blue shadow-border on white card stock. The player's name appears in the bottom shadow- border. The back presents biographical information and statistics in a black shadow-bordered box. Though the individual cards are unnumbered, they are checklisted below according to the numbering assigned to them on the checklist card.

COMPLETE SET (20)	4.00	10.00
1 Leo Golembiewski CO	.08	.25
2 Don Carlson	.20	.50
3 Kelly Walker	.30	.75
4 Cory Oleson	.30	.75
5 Drew Sibr	.20	.50
6 Dan Divjak	.30	.75
7 Jeremy Goltz	.20	.50
8 Aaron Joffe	.20	.50
9 Tommy Smith	.20	.50
10 Dan Anderson	.20	.50
11 Dean Sives	.20	.50
12 Steve Hutchings	.20	.50
13 Shane Fausel	.20	.50
14 Greg Mitchell	.20	.50
15 Ricky Pope	.20	.50
16 Nate Soules	.20	.50
17 Flavio Gentile	.20	.50
18 Icecats Leaders	.20	.50
Leo Golembiewski CO		
Kelly Walker		
Cory Oleson		
Jeremy Goltz		
Dan Divjak		
19 Glenn Hall	1.00	2.50
Honorary Captain		
20 Logo Card/Checklist	.08	.25

1992-93 Arizona Icecats

This 16-card standard-size set features the Arizona Icecats hockey team. The fronts display a posed color player photo with multiple blue drop borders. The player's name appears in a royal blue stripe across the bottom of the picture. The backs carry biographical information and statistics in a black shadow-bordered box. Though the individual cards are unnumbered, they are checklisted below according to the numbering assigned to them on the checklist card.

COMPLETE SET (20)	3.00	8.00
1 Leo Golembiewski CO	.08	.25
2 Kelly Walker	.25	.60
3 Cory Oleson	.25	.60
4 Tommy Smith	.20	.50
5 John Allen	.20	.50
6 Dan Anderson	.20	.50
7 Aaron Joffe	.20	.50
8 Dan Divjak	.25	.60
9 Jeremy Goltz	.20	.50
10 Steve Hutchings	.20	.50
11 Greg Mitchell	.20	.50
12 Ricky Pope	.20	.50
13 Nate Soules	.20	.50
14 Matt Glines	.20	.50
15 Mark Thawley	.20	.50
16 Andie Zafrani	.20	.50
17 Chris Noga	.20	.50
18 Jim Kolbe	.08	.25
Honorary Captain		
19 Coach and Top Gun Line	.30	.75
Cory Oleson		
Leo Golembiewski CO		
Kelly Walker		
Tommy Smith		
John Allen		
Dan Anderson		
20 Logo Card/Checklist	.08	.25

1993-94 Arizona Icecats

Yet another set issued by the most hobby-friendly club hockey team in the United States. This year's celebrity captain is that exemplary American, Oliver North. The set was sold by the team to raise money for the program.

COMPLETE SET (20)	3.00	8.00
1 Header Card	.08	.25
2 Leo Golembiewski CO	.08	.25
3 Greg Mitchell	.20	.50
4 Ricky Pope	.20	.50
5 Dan Divjak	.25	.60
6 Brian Consolino	.20	.50
7 Papa Bear	.20	.50
8 Steve Hutchings	.20	.50
9 Joel Nusbaum	.20	.50
10 Sam Battaglia	.20	.50
11 Kiva Gippo	.20	.50
12 Jeremy Goltz	.20	.50
13 Peter Scott	.20	.50
14 Kevin Oztekin	.20	.50
15 Nate Soules	.20	.50
16 Chris Noga	.20	.50
17 Dennis Hands	.20	.50
18 Mark Thawley	.20	.50
19 Leader Card	.08	.25
20 Oliver North	.30	.75

1994-95 Arizona Icecats

This low-tech set features the Icecats of the NCAA. The fronts offer a posed on-ice photo, taken in front of a bad backdrop. The backs feature 1993-94 stats and a pre-printed autograph.

COMPLETE SET (24)	10.00	25.00
1 Title Card/CL	.02	.10
2 Leo Golembiewski CO	.40	1.00
3 Steve Hutchings	.40	1.00
4 Nate Soules	.40	1.00
5 Chris Noga	.40	1.00
6 Kevin Oztekin	.40	1.00
7 Greg Mitchell	.40	1.00
8 Ricky Pope	.40	1.00
9 Brian Consolino	.40	1.00
10 John Muntz	.40	1.00
11 Joel Nusbaum	.40	1.00
12 Sam Battaglia	.40	1.00
13 Kiva Gippo	.40	1.00
14 Peter Scott	.40	1.00
15 Dennis Hands	.60	1.50
16 Mark Thawley	.40	1.00
17 Ryan Rockabrand	.40	1.00
18 Joe Joyce	.40	1.00
19 Jeremy Walters	.40	1.00
20 Ethan Kaulas	.40	1.00
21 Reg Kerr		
Glen Hall	.75	2.00
22 Leo Golembiewski		
Keith Magnuson	.40	1.00
23 Stan Mikita		
Glen Hall		
Keith Magnuson		
Al Secord	2.00	5.00
24 Madhouse on Main Street	.02	.10

1995-96 Arizona Icecats

This set features the Icecats of the ACHA. The cards feature a posed photo on the front, framed by a purple border. The sparse backs offer peronsal data and stats.

COMPLETE SET (23)		25.00
1 Title Card/CL		.01
2 Leo Golembiewski CO	.02	.10
3 Chris Noga	.40	1.00
4 John Muntz	.40	1.00
5 Kevin Oztekin	.40	1.00
6 Mark Thawley	.40	1.00
7 Sam Battaglia	.40	1.00
8 Peter Scott	.40	1.00
9 Joel Nusbaum	.40	1.00
10 Ryan Rockabrand	.40	1.00
11 Andy Knick	.40	1.00
12 Brian Meehan	.40	1.00
13 Bob Majka	.40	1.00
14 Ben Ruston	.40	1.00
15 Jeff Rice	.40	1.00
16 Brian Consolino	.40	1.00
17 Bryan Fork	.40	1.00
18 Joel Hilshey	.50	1.25
19 Joe Joyce	.40	1.00
20 Jeremy Goltz ACO	.02	.10
21 Icecat Leaders	.02	.10
22 Scotty Bowman	2.00	5.00
23 Scotty Bowman Hon Capt.	2.00	5.00

1996-97 Arizona Icecats

This set features the Icecats of the ACHA. The cards are standard-sized and feature a posed shot framed by a thick red border. The sparse backs list personal data and last season's stats.

COMPLETE SET (25)	4.00	25.00
1 Title Card/CL		.01
2 Leo Golembiewski HCO	.02	.10
3 Kevin Baskel	.40	1.00
4 Sam Battaglia	.40	1.00
5 Brian Consolino	.40	1.00
6 Josh Flett	.40	1.00
7 Eric Holton	.40	1.00
8 Paul Juran	.40	1.00
9 Andy Knick	.40	1.00
10 Eliot Komar	.40	1.00
11 Beau Lemire	.50	1.25
12 Joe McCaffrey	.40	1.00
13 Brian Meehan	.40	1.00
14 Joel Nusbaum	.40	1.00
15 Ace Pascual	.40	1.00
16 Rob Poupard	.40	1.00
17 Ben Ruston	.40	1.00
18 Peter Scott	.40	1.00
19 Mike Tesi	.40	1.00
20 Tom Thompson	.40	1.00
21 Dave Weiss	.40	1.00
22 Bob Majka	.40	1.00
23 Leo Golembiewski HCO	.02	.10
24 Jeremy Goltz ACO	.02	.10
25 Stan Mikita Hon Capt.	2.00	5.00

1997-98 Arizona Icecats

This set features the Icecats of the ACHA. The cards feature a posed color photo framed by a thick white border. Card numbers are found on the front, lower right. The sparse backs list player personal data.

COMPLETE SET (26)	10.00	25.00
1 Title Card/CL		.01
2 Leo Golembiewski HCO	.02	.10
3 Benedictine HOF		.01
4 Kevin Baskel	.40	1.00
5 Jordan Bolton	.60	1.50
6 Tyler Brush	.40	1.00
7 Ed Carfora	.40	1.00
8 Paul Dorn	.40	1.00
9 Chad Dyjak	.40	1.00
10 Rodney Glassman	.40	1.00
11 Mike Graves	.40	1.00
12 Marc Harris	.40	1.00
13 Joe McCaffrey	.40	1.00
14 Charles McCarty	.40	1.00
15 Bob Majka	.40	1.00
16 Brian Meehan	.40	1.00
17 Ace Pascual	.40	1.00
18 Joe Peplinski	.60	1.50
19 Ben Ruston	.40	1.00
20 Mike Tesi	.40	1.00
21 Tom Thompson	.40	1.00
22 Kory Wagstaff	.40	1.00
23 Max Wilkie	.40	1.00
24 Jim Wilkey	.40	1.00
25 Jeremy Goltz ACO	.02	.10
26 Rex Allen, Jr. Hon Capt.	.40	1.00

1998-99 Arizona Icecats

COMPLETE SET (27)	10.00	25.00
1 Tyler Brush	.40	1.00
2 Ed Carfora	.40	1.00
3 Quinn Carter	.40	1.00
4 Hunter Cherenack	.40	1.00
5 Paul Dorn	.40	1.00
6 Andrew Edwards	.40	1.00
7 Rodney Glassman	.40	1.00
8 Leo Golembiewski CO	.02	.10
9 Jeremy Goltz ACO	.02	.10
10 Mike Graves	.40	1.00
11 Marc Harris	.40	1.00
12 Bobby Hull HON CPT	2.00	5.00
13 Pavel Jandura	.40	1.00
14 Bob Majka	.40	1.00
15 Joe McCaffrey	.40	1.00
16 Kyle McNeilance	.40	1.00
17 Brian Meehan	.40	1.00
18 Kevin Meehan	.40	1.00
19 Mark Meister	.40	1.00
20 Eugene Mesh	.40	1.00
21 Jason Morgan	.40	1.00
22 Kyle Neary	.40	1.00
23 Jason Royce	.40	1.00
24 Mike Tesi	.40	1.00
25 Tom Thompson	.40	1.00
26 Team Leaders	.40	1.00
27 Checklist	.02	.10

1999-00 Arizona Icecats

COMPLETE SET (28)	8.00	20.00
1 Tyler Brush	.40	1.00
2 Ed Carfora	.40	1.00
3 Hunter Cherenack	.40	1.00
4 Paul Dorn	.40	1.00
5 Andrew Edwards	.40	1.00
6 Dave Galardini	.40	1.00
7 Leo Golembiewski CO	.02	.10
8 Jeremy Goltz ACO	.02	.10
9 Mike Graves	.40	1.00
10 Marc Harris	.40	1.00
11 Chase Hoyt	.40	1.00
12 Pavel Jandura	.40	1.00
13 Dave Loftus	.40	1.00
14 Bob Majka	.40	1.00
15 Joe McCaffrey	.40	1.00
16 Kyle McNeilance	.40	1.00
17 Brian Meehan	.40	1.00
18 Kevin Meehan	.40	1.00
19 Mark Meister	.40	1.00
20 Jason Morgan	.40	1.00
21 Kyle Neary	.40	1.00
22 Ryan Roth	.40	1.00
23 Jason Royce	.40	1.00
24 Sgt. Slaughter HON CPT	.75	2.00
25 Tom Thompson	.40	1.00
26 Team Leaders	.40	1.00
27 L. Golembiewski Golf Classic	.02	.10
28 Checklist	.02	.10

2000-01 Arizona Icecats

COMPLETE SET (30)	8.00	20.00
1 Header/Checklist	.02	.10
2 Joe Roysen	.30	.75
3 Tyler Brush	.40	1.00
4 Ed Carfora	.40	1.00
5 Paul Dorn	.40	1.00
6 Andrew Edwards	.40	1.00
7 Andrew Fredericks	.40	1.00
8 Dave Galardini	.40	1.00
9 Mike Graves	.40	1.00
10 Marc Harris	.40	1.00
11 Pavel Jandura	.40	1.00
12 Braden Koprivica	.40	1.00
13 Wes Krisay	.40	1.00
14 Dave Loftus	.40	1.00
15 Kyle McNeilance	.40	1.00
16 Kevin Meehan	.40	1.00
17 Jason Morgan	.40	1.00
18 Kyle Neary	.40	1.00
19 Bill Pardue	.40	1.00
20 Jason Royce	.40	1.00
21 John Saunders	.40	1.00
22 Stefan Thomasson	.40	1.00
23 Bill Veasey	.40	1.00
24 Tom Wood	.40	1.00
25 Leo Golembiewski CO	.02	.10
26 Brian Meehan ACO	.02	.10
27 Bob Leoni ACO	.02	.10
28 Team Leaders	.20	.50
29 Golf Classic	.02	.10
30 Joe Cristiani HON CAPT	.02	.10

2001-02 Arizona Icecats

COMPLETE SET (26)	8.00	20.00
1 Bryan Aronchick	.40	1.00
2 Shaun Brooks	.40	1.00
3 Papa Joe Chevalier HON CPT	.20	.50
4 Andrew Fredericks	.40	1.00
5 Dave Galardini	.40	1.00
6 Leo Golembiewski CO	.02	.10
7 Pavel Jandura	.40	1.00
8 Matt Johnson	.40	1.00
9 Braden Koprivica	.40	1.00
10 Wes Krisay	.40	1.00
11 Dave Loftus	.40	1.00
12 Brian Meehan ACO	.02	.10
13 Kevin Meehan	.40	1.00
15 Mickey Meehan	.40	1.00
16 Matt Naylor	.40	1.00
17 Kyle Neary	.40	1.00
18 Bill Pardue	.40	1.00
19 John Saunders	.40	1.00
20 Mike Smith	.40	1.00
21 Tom Wolf	.40	1.00
22 Tom Wood	.40	1.00
23 Nick Woods	.40	1.00
24 Jerald Zivic	.40	1.00
25 Team Leaders	.20	.50
26 Checklist	.02	.10

2002-03 Arizona Icecats

COMPLETE SET (32)	10.00	25.00
1 Bryan Aronchick	.40	1.00
2 Matt Baumann	.40	1.00
3 Shaun Brooks	.40	1.00
4 Banks Concepcion	.40	1.00
5 Cole Dunlop	.40	1.00
6 Andrew Fredericks	.40	1.00
7 Justin Guerra	.40	1.00
8 Don Holtz	.40	1.00
9 Matt Johnson	.40	1.00
10 Rick Karasch	.40	1.00
11 Braden Koprivica	.40	1.00
12 Wes Krisay	.40	1.00
13 Dave Loftus	.40	1.00
14 Mickey Meehan	.40	1.00
15 Keith Mitchell	.40	1.00
16 Matt Muller	.40	1.00
17 Matt Naylor	.40	1.00
18 Eric Ormson	.40	1.00
19 Bill Pardue	.40	1.00
20 Mike Pelletier	.40	1.00
21 Brian Pollock	.40	1.00
22 Mike Smith	.40	1.00
23 Dan Whitlock	.40	1.00
24 Drew Williamson	.40	1.00
25 Tim Wochok	.40	1.00
26 Nick Woods	.40	1.00
27 Leo Golembiewski CO	.02	.10
28 Brian Meehan ACO	.02	.10
29 Team Leaders	.20	.50
30 Dwain Pipe MASCOT	.02	.10
31 Don Rickles HON CPT	.40	1.00
32 Checklist	.02	.10

2003-04 Arizona Icecats

COMPLETE SET (31)	8.00	20.00
1 Bryan Aronchick	.40	1.00
2 Shaun Brooks	.40	1.00
3 Anthony Capone	.40	1.00
4 Banks Concepion	.40	1.00
5 Kevin Conners	.40	1.00
6 Dave Cwik	.40	1.00
7 Cole Dunlop	.40	1.00
8 Andrew Fredericks	.40	1.00
9 Don Holtz	.40	1.00
10 Rick Karasch	.40	1.00
11 Jerod Keene	.40	1.00
12 Eric Kowalek	.40	1.00
13 Casey Leyva	.40	1.00
14 Bryan Meagher	.40	1.00
15 Mickey Meehan	.40	1.00
16 Jeff Merritt	.40	1.00
17 Keith Mitchell	.40	1.00
18 Josh Parry	.40	1.00
19 D.J Pelletier	.40	1.00
20 Brian Pollock	.40	1.00
21 Mike Smith	.40	1.00
22 Dan Whitlock	.40	1.00
23 Drew Williamson	.40	1.00
24 Tim Wochok	.40	1.00
25 Leo Golembiewski CO	.02	.10
26 Brian Meehan ACO	.02	.10
27 Team Leaders	.20	.50
28 Dwain Pipe MASCOT	.02	.10
29 Don Rickles	.40	1.00
30 John McCain HON CPT	.40	1.00
31 Header Card	.02	.10

2004-05 Arizona Icecats

COMPLETE SET (34)	6.00	15.00
1 Bryan Aronchick	.30	.75
2 Anthony Capone	.30	.75
3 Cole Dunlop	.30	.75
4 Luke Edwall	.30	.75
5 Leo Golembiewski CO	.02	.10
6 Don Holtz	.30	.75
7 Craig Irwin	.30	.75
8 Eric Kowalek	.30	.75
9 Dave Lawrence	.30	.75
10 Casey Leyva	.30	.75
11 Scott Marshall	.30	.75
12 Brian Meehan ACO	.02	.10
13 Mickey Meehan	.30	.75
14 Keith Mitchell	.30	.75
15 Josh Parry	.30	.75
16 D.J. Pelletier	.30	.75
17 Mike Pelletier	.30	.75
18 Mark Perzi	.30	.75
19 Jay Punsky	.30	.75
20 Max Sliwinski	.30	.75
21 Mike Smith	.30	.75
22 Doug Wilson	.30	.75
23 Tim Wochok	.30	.75
24 Jerald Zivic	.30	.75
25 Team Leaders	.20	.50
26 Equipment Managers	.02	.10
27 Sgt. Slaughter	.40	1.00
28 L. Gombiewski Celebrity Golf	.02	.10
29 Dwain Pipe MASCOT	.02	.10
30 Sons of the Pioneers	.02	.10
31 Team Picture	.20	.50
32 Sen. John McCain	.40	1.00
33 Willie Nelson HON CPT	.40	1.00
34 Header Card	.02	.10

2002-03 Arkansas Riverblades

COMPLETE SET (24)	10.00	25.00
1 Jason Bermingham	.40	1.00
2 Mike Cirillo	.40	1.00
3 Ryan Coole	.40	1.00
4 Aaron Davis	.40	1.00
5 Scott Fankhouser	.75	2.00
6 Ernie Hartlieb	.40	1.00
7 Maxim Linnik	.40	1.00
8 Eric Long	.40	1.00
9 Terry Marchant	.40	1.00
10 Matt Pagnutti	.40	1.00
11 Samuel Paquet	.40	1.00
12 Mike Renzi	.40	1.00
13 Jason Saal	.75	2.00
14 Mike Sandbeck	.40	1.00
15 Mark Scott	.40	1.00
16 Bud Smith	.40	1.00
17 Jimi St. John	.40	1.00
18 Dean Stock	.40	1.00
19 Dean Stork	.40	1.00
20 Garry Toor	.40	1.00
21 Damon Whitton	.40	1.00
22 Chris Cichocki HCO	.10	.25
23 RiverBabes	.40	1.00
24 Rocky Bear-Boa Mascot	.02	.10

1999-00 Asheville Smoke

This set was given out in three series at home games. The cards feature jersey numbers on the back, but are listed below in alphabetical order because of duplicate and skipped numbers.

COMPLETE SET (27)	30.00	75.00
1 Checklist	.08	.25
2 Francois Bourdeau	1.25	3.00
3 Dan Brenzavich	1.25	3.00
4 Peter Cermak	1.25	3.00
5 Frank DeFrenza	1.25	3.00
6 Paul Giblin	1.25	3.00
7 Brent Gretzky	2.00	5.00
8 Francois Leroux	1.25	3.00
9 Dan McIntyre	1.25	3.00
10 Rob Milliken	1.25	3.00
11 Hayden O'Rear	1.25	3.00
12 Vaclav Pazourek	1.25	3.00
13 Cory Peterson	1.25	3.00
14 Jon Pirrong	2.00	5.00
15 Ken Plaquin	1.25	3.00
16 Ryan Prentice	1.25	3.00
17 Josh Tymchak	1.25	3.00
18 Shawn Ulrich	1.25	3.00
19 Lindsay Vallis	1.25	3.00
20 Richie Walcott	1.25	3.00
21 Bruce Watson	1.25	3.00
22 Cory Peterson	1.25	3.00
Josh Tymchak		
Bruce Watson		
23 Keith Gretzky HCO	1.25	3.00
24 Aaron Fackler EM	.08	.25
25 Smoky Mascot	.08	.25
26 Sponsor Card		.01
27 Team Photo	.40	1.00

2000-01 Asheville Smoke

This set features the Smoke of the UHL. The set was produced by Roox, and was distributed as a promotional giveaway over the course of three home games.

COMPLETE SET (27)	7.20	18.00
1 Ryan Alkia	.30	.75
2 Brent Belecki	.30	.75
3 Blue Bennefield	.30	.75
4 Derek Crimin	.30	.75
5 Alexandre Fomitchev	.40	1.00
6 John Hewitt	.30	.75
7 Olaf Kjenstad	.40	1.00
8 Dominic Maltais	.40	1.00
9 Tyler Prosofsky	.30	.75
10 Bobby Rapoza	.30	.75
11 Bogdan Rudenko	.30	.75
12 J.C. Ruid	.30	.75
13 Lee Svangstu	.30	.75
14 Shawn Ulrich	.30	.75
15 Pat Bingham CO	.20	.50
16 Smoky MASCOT	.04	.10
17 Ingles Zamboni SPONSOR	.04	.10
18 Manager TR	.04	.10
19 Tom Wilson	.30	.75
20 Brett Colborne	.30	.75
21 Robert Marshall	.30	.75
22 Alex Dumas	.30	.75
23 Vitali Andreev	.30	.75
24 Evan Lindsay	.40	1.00
25 Bruce Watson	.40	1.00
26 Asheville Smoke	.04	.10
27 He Shoots Team Card	.10	.25

2001-02 Asheville Smoke

This set features the Smoke of the UHL. The cards were issued as a promotional giveaway, apparently at three different home games. Any additional information on this set can be forwarded to hockeymag@beckett.com.

COMPLETE SET (24)	8.00	20.00
1 Team Photo	.20	.50
2 Kris Mallette	.40	1.50
3 Tyler McMillan	.40	1.00
4 Mike Payne	.40	1.00
5 Chad Wagner	.40	1.50
6 Forrest Gore	.40	1.00
7 Tom Wilson	.40	1.00
8 Todd Bisson	.40	1.00
9 Geoff Derouin	.40	1.50
10 Bobby Rapoza	.40	1.00
11 Kamil Kuriplach	.40	1.00
12 Todd MacIsaac	.40	1.00
13 Sean Fitzgerald	.40	1.00
14 Samuel Paquet	.40	1.00
15 Kris Schultz	.40	1.00
16 Bob Dalessio EQMG	.04	.10
17 Smoky MASCOT	.04	.10
18 Curtis Menzul	.40	1.00
19 Cory Peterson	.40	1.00
20 Jean-Francois Dufour	.40	1.00
21 Jeff Petruic	.40	1.00
22 J.C. Ruid	.40	1.00
23 Blaine Russell	.40	1.50
24 Shawn Ulrich CO	.04	.10

1992-93 Atlanta Knights

Released by the team, this 24-card set features the 1992-93 Atlanta Knights. Base cards feature full color action photography and white borders. The set's print run was limited to 5000, and they were sold at the Omni Arena during the season for $5. This set is not numbered so it appears in packing order.

COMPLETE SET (24)	4.80	12.00
1 Header Card	.02	.10
2 Manon Rheaume	2.00	5.00
3 Jeff Buchanan	.08	.25
4 Matt Hervey	.08	.25
5 Rick Lanz	.08	.25
6 Colin Miller	.08	.25
7 Keith Osborne	.08	.25
8 Jason Lafreniere	.08	.25
9 Jock Callander	.40	1.00
10 Brent Gretzky	.20	.50
11 Steve Maltais	.40	1.00
12 Serguei Ossipov	.08	.25
13 Shayne Stevenson	.20	.50
14 Scott Boston	.08	.25
15 Jean Blouin	.08	.25
16 Shawn Rivers	.20	.50
17 Dan Vincelette	.08	.25
18 Chris Lipuma	.08	.25
19 Don Burke	.08	.25
20 Christian Campeau	.08	.25
21 Tim Bergland	.08	.25
22 J.C. Bergeron	.20	.50
23 David Littman	.20	.50
24 Gene Ubriaco HCO	.02	.10

1993-94 Atlanta Knights

Released by the team, this 24-card set features the 1992-93 Atlanta Knights. Base cards feature full color action photography and white borders. Set print run was limited to 5000, and were sold at the Omni Arena during the season for $5.00.

COMPLETE SET (24)	6.00	15.00
1 Mike Greenlay	.20	.50
2 Jeff Buchanan	.15	.40
3 Eric Charron	.15	.40
4 Colin Miller	.15	.40
5 Brent Gretzky	.30	.75
6 Steve LaRouche	.15	.40
7 Marc Tardif	.20	.50
8 Jeff Madill	.15	.40
9 Devin Edgerton	.15	.40
10 Bill McDougall	.15	.40
11 Jason Ruff	.15	.40
12 Eric Dubois	.15	.40
13 Martin Tanguay	.15	.40
14 Stan Drulia	.30	.75
15 Normand Rochefort	.15	.40
16 Shawn Rivers	.20	.50
17 Chris Lipuma	.15	.40
18 Cory Cross	.15	.40
19 Christian Campeau	.15	.40
20 Tim Bergland	.15	.40
21 J.C. Bergeron	.20	.50
22 Manon Rheaume	2.50	6.00
23 Gene Ubriaco HCO	.02	.10
CL Header Card	.02	.10

1994-95 Atlanta Knights

Released by the team, this 24-card set features the 1992-93 Atlanta Knights. Base cards feature full color action photography and white borders. Set print run was limited to 5000, and were sold at the Omni Arena during the season for $5.00. This set is not numbered so it appears in packing order

COMPLETE SET (27)	3.20	10.00
1 Header Card	.02	.10
2 Mike Greenlay	.30	.75
3 Chris Nelson	.15	.40
4 Dorok Mayor	.16	.40
5 Drew Bannister	.15	.40
6 Allen Pedersen	.15	.40
7 Colin Miller	.15	.40
8 Brent Gretzky	.30	.75
9 Peter Ferraro	.15	.40
10 Devin Edgerton	.15	.40
11 Chris Ferraro	.30	.75
12 Jason Ruff	.15	.40
13 Eric Dubois	.15	.40
14 Stan Drulia	.30	.75
15 Allen Egeland	.15	.40
16 Aaron Gavey	.15	.40
17 Yves Heroux	.15	.40
18 Brian Straub	.15	.40
19 Jeff Toms	.15	.40
20 Chris Lipuma	.15	.40
21 Cory Cross	.15	.40
22 Christian Campeau	.15	.40
23 Derek Wilkinson	.30	.75
24 Brantt Myhres	.30	.75
25 John Paris Jr. HCO	.02	.10
26 Scott Gordon ACO	.02	.10
27 Sir Hat Trick Mascot	.02	.10

1995-96 Atlanta Knights

This set features the Knights of the IHL. The set was produced by Edge Ice.

COMPLETE SET (25)	4.80	12.00
1 Drew Bannister	.20	.50
2 Doug Barrault	.20	.50
3 Corey Beaulieu	.20	.50
4 Ryan Brown	.20	.50
5 Christian Campeau	.20	.50
6 Stan Drulia	.30	.75
7 Eric Dubois	.20	.50
8 Allan Egeland	.20	.50
9 Brantt Myhres	.30	.75
10 Mark Greig	.20	.50
11 Bob Halkidis	.20	.50
12 Alexandre LaPorte	.20	.50
13 Chris LiPuma	.20	.50
14 Tyler Moss	.30	.75
15 Brent Peterson	.20	.50
16 Adrien Plavsic	.20	.50
17 Jason Ruff	.20	.50
18 Reggie Savage	.20	.50
19 Corey Spring	.20	.50
20 Jeff Toms	.20	.50
21 Derek Wilkinson	.30	.75
22 John Paris CO	.08	.25
23 Scott Gordon CO	.08	.25
24 Kurt Harvey TR	.02	.10
25 Sir Hat Trick MAS	.02	.10

2001-02 Atlantic City Boardwalk Bullies

These cards were handed out by the team at home games and player appearances. They appear to be hand cut and, therefore are varying sizes. The checklist may be incomplete.

COMPLETE SET (26) 10.00 20.00
1 Checklist .01 .01
2 Shane Belter .40 1.00
3 John Campbell .40 1.00
4 J.F. Caudron .40 1.00
5 Vratislav Cech .40 1.00
6 Kevin Colley .40 1.00
7 Sasha Cucuz .40 1.00
8 Luke Curtin .40 1.00
9 Shawn Degagne .60 1.50
10 Keith Dupee .40 1.00
11 Kirk Furey .40 1.00
12 Tyler Johnston .40 1.00
13 Jerry Keele .40 1.00
14 Daniel Lacroix .40 1.00
15 Mark Loeding .40 1.00
16 Scott Matzka .40 1.00
17 Jamie O'Leary .40 1.00
18 Stefan Rivard .60 1.50
19 Rob Stanfield .40 1.00
20 Scott Stirling .60 1.50
21 Ian Walterson .40 1.00
22 Mike Haviland HCO .02 .10
23 Leigh Mendelson ACO .02 .10
24 Rick Bronwell EQM .02 .10
25 Woolly MASCOT .02 .10
26 Damien Hess TR .02 .10

2002-03 Atlantic City Boardwalk Bullies

It is believed these cards were handed out as singles by the team at home games and at public appearances. The checklist below may not be complete. Please forward any additional info to hockeymag@beckett.com.

COMPLETE SET (25) 10.00 20.00
1 Rick Bronwell EQM .02 .10
2 J. F. Caudron .40 1.00
3 Steve Cheredaryk .40 1.00
4 Kevin Colley .60 1.50
5 Luke Curtin .40 1.00
6 Kirk Furey .40 1.00
7 Jade Galbraith .75 2.00
8 Jerry Galway .40 1.00
9 Mike Haviland HCO .02 .10
10 Jimmy Henkel .40 1.00
11 Damien Hess TR .02 .10
12 Mark Loeding .40 1.00
13 Shawn Maltby .60 1.50
14 Scott Matzka .40 1.00
15 Leigh Mendelson ACO .02 .10
16 Ryan Mougenel .40 1.00
17 Steve Munn .40 1.00
18 Mike Nicholishen .40 1.00
19 Stefan Rivard .40 1.00
20 Paul Spadafora .40 1.00
21 Scott Stirling .60 1.50
22 Ian Walterson .40 1.00
23 Matthew Yeats .60 1.50
24 Wooly MASCOT .02 .10
25 Checklist .01 .01

2003-04 Atlantic City Boardwalk Bullies

Little is known about this set, beyond the checklist information provided by the great Ralph Slate.

COMPLETE SET (30) 10.00 25.00
1 Bujar Amidovski .75 2.00
2 Jon Cullen .40 1.00
3 Luke Curtin .40 1.00
4 Chad Dameworth .40 1.00
5 Danny Eberly .40 1.00
6 Brian Fahey .40 1.00
7 Aaron Foster .40 1.00
8 Kirk Furey .40 1.00
9 Jim Henkel .40 1.00
10 Scott Horvath .40 1.00
11 Matt Hubbauer .40 1.00
12 Jim Leger .40 1.00
13 John Longo .40 1.00
14 Preston Mizzi .40 1.00
15 Jake Moreland .40 1.00
16 Steve Munn .40 1.00
17 Sam Paolini .40 1.00
18 Joshua Prudden .40 1.00
19 Dave Reid .40 1.00
20 Stefan Rivard .40 1.00
21 John Sabo .40 1.00
22 Pierre-Luc Sleigher .40 1.00
23 Marc St. Jean .40 1.00
24 Scott Stirling .40 1.00
25 Ian Walterson .40 1.00
26 Kam White .40 1.00
27 Mike Haviland HCO .02 .10
28 Matt Thomas ACO .02 .10
29 Mascot .02 .10
30 Checklist .01 .01

2003-04 Atlantic City Boardwalk Bullies RBI Sports

This team set was sold at home games.

COMPLETE SET (16) 3.00 8.00
17 Jon Cullen .20 .50
18 Luke Curtin .20 .50
19 Danny Eberly .20 .50
20 Brian Fahey .20 .50
21 Aaron Foster .20 .50
22 Scott Horvath .20 .50
23 Jake Moreland .20 .50
24 Steve Munn .20 .50
25 Sam Paolini .20 .50
26 Joshua Prudden .20 .50
27 Dave Reid .20 .50
28 Stefan Rivard .20 .50
29 Pierre-Luc Sleigher .20 .50
30 Scott Stirling .20 .50
31 Ian Walterson .20 .50
32 Kam White .20 .50

2004-05 Atlantic City Boardwalk Bullies

These cards were given away over the course of the season. It's believed the checklist is complete, and the card numbering may be inaccurate. If you know of other cards, please email us at hockeymag@beckett.com.

COMPLETE SET (30) 10.00 25.00
1 Dave Reid .40 1.00
2 Ian Walterson .40 1.00
3 Fraser Clair .40 1.00
4 Brad Both .40 1.00
5 Colin Shields .40 1.00
6 Scott Horvath .40 1.00
7 Kelsey Muench .40 1.00
8 Derek Edwardson .40 1.00
9 Jason Notermann .40 1.00
10 Dustan Heintz .40 1.00
11 Tom Reimann .40 1.00
12 Paul Caponigri .40 1.00
13 Luke Curtin .40 1.00
14 Eric Nelson .40 1.00
15 Trevor Koenig .60 1.50
16 Brian Maddox TR .02 .10
17 Matt Thomas CO .02 .10
18 Mark French ACO .02 .10
19 Chris Burke EQM .02 .10
20 Brian Fahey .40 1.00
21 Vincent Macri .40 1.00
22 Jake Moreland .60 1.50
23 Dan Peters .40 1.00
24 Brett Peterson .40 1.00
25 Peter Bournazakis .40 1.00
26 Shawn Mather .40 1.00
27 Brett Nowak .40 1.00
28 Jean-Francois Plourde .40 1.00
29 Ryan Reid .40 1.00
30 Woolly MASCOT .02 .10

2004-05 Atlantic City Boardwalk Bullies Kinko's

COMPLETE SET (30) 10.00 25.00
1 Kelly Cup CL .02 .10
2 Jake Moreland .40 1.00
3 Bujar Amidovski .75 2.00
4 Steve Munn .40 1.00
5 Brian Fahey .40 1.00
6 Kam White .40 1.00
7 Dave Reid .40 1.00
8 Ian Walterson .40 1.00
9 Pierre-Luc Sleigher .40 1.00
10 Danny Eberly .40 1.00
11 Jim Henkel .40 1.00
12 Scott Horvath .40 1.00
13 Sam Paolini .40 1.00
14 John Sabo .40 1.00
15 Josh Prudden .40 1.00
16 John Longo .40 1.00
17 Matt Hubbauer .40 1.00
18 Marc St.Jean .40 1.00
19 Stefan Rivard .40 1.00
20 Chad Dameworth .40 1.00
21 Preston Mizzi .40 1.00
22 Jim Leger .40 1.00
23 Kirk Furey .40 1.00
24 Aaron Foster .40 1.00
25 Luke Curtin .40 1.00
26 Jon Cullan .40 1.00
27 Scott Stirling .40 1.00
28 Mike Haviland .40 1.00
29 Matt Thomas .40 1.00
30 Wooly .02 .10

2001-02 Augusta Lynx

This set features the Lynx of the ECHL. The cards were given away at eight different games, one per night.

COMPLETE SET (8) 6.00 15.00
1 Patrick Yetman .80 2.00
2 Scott Morrow .80 2.00
3 Cris Classen .80 2.00
4 Tyler Willis 1.20 3.00
5 Jeff Bes 1.20 3.00
6 Wes Swinson .80 2.00
7 Guy Larose .80 2.00
8 John Whitwell .80 2.00

2002-03 Augusta Lynx

COMPLETE SET (18) 10.00 20.00
61 Ryan Crane .40 1.00
62 Curtis Cruickshank .60 1.50
63 Tom Draper .60 1.50
64 Chris Gustafson .40 1.00
65 Tyson Holly .40 1.00
66 Andrew Ianiero .40 1.00
67 Martin Lapointe .40 1.00
68 Ryan Lauzon .40 1.00
69 Jay Leach .60 1.50
70 Mike Legg .40 1.00
71 Vince Malts .40 1.00
72 Brad Ralph .40 1.00
73 Philippe Roy .40 1.00
74 Josh St. Louis .40 1.00
75 Jim Shepherd .40 1.00
76 Chris Thompson .40 1.00
77 Mark Thompson .40 1.00
78 Andrew Williamson .40 1.00

2003-04 Augusta Lynx

This set was sold by the team at home games. The odd numbering reflects this portion of the entire league run produced by RBI Sports. Production supposedly was limited to 250 sets.

COMPLETE SET (16) 10.00 25.00
33 Todd Bennett .60 1.50
34 Scott Corbett .60 1.50
35 John Cronin .60 1.50
36 Brandon Doria .60 1.50
37 Matt Dzieduszycki .60 1.50
38 Paul Elliott .60 1.50
39 Jonathan Gagnon .60 1.50
40 Louis Goulet .60 1.50
41 Nick Greenough .60 1.50
42 Peter Hamerlik .75 2.00
43 Greg Jacina .60 1.50
44 Scott Kelman .60 1.50
45 Robert Liscak .60 1.50
46 Gregg Naumenko .75 2.00
47 Treavor Peterson .60 1.50
48 Shawn Weiman .60 1.50

2006-07 Augusta Lynx

COMPLETE SET (21) 15.00 30.00
1 Garrett Bembridge .75 2.00
2 Sean Blanchard .60 1.50
3 Mike Erickson .60 1.50
4 Louis Goulet .60 1.50
5 Shane Hynes .60 1.50
6 Jamie Johnson .60 1.50
7 Jason Kostadine .60 1.50
8 Nick Kuiper .60 1.50
9 Ryan Lang .60 1.50
10 Eric Lundberg .60 1.50
11 Roman Marakhovski .60 1.50
12 Nathan Marsters 1.25 3.00
13 David McKee 1.25 3.00
14 Brian Passmore .75 2.00
15 Joe Pereira .60 1.50
16 Jason Platt .60 1.50
17 Nathan Saunders .60 1.50
18 Ken Scuderi .60 1.50
19 Aaron Slattengren .60 1.50
20 Dirk Southern .60 1.50
21 Weston Tardy .60 1.50

1997-98 Austin Ice Bats

This 24-card set featuring the Ice Bats of the WPHL was sold at the final home game and during the playoffs.

COMPLETE SET (24) 5.00 10.00
1 Ryan Anderson .20 .50
2 Chad Erickson .30 .75
3 Tim Findlay .30 .75
4 Todd Harris .20 .50
5 Rob Hartnell .20 .50
6 Chris Haskett .20 .50
7 Kyle Haviland .20 .50
8 Mike Jackson .20 .50
9 Jeff Kungle .20 .50
10 Darrin MacKay .20 .50
11 Dean Mando .20 .50
12 Keith Moran .20 .50
13 Ryan Pawluk .20 .50
14 Derek Riley .20 .50
15 Jason Rose .20 .50
16 Andy Ross .20 .50
17 Brett Seguin .20 .50
18 Christian Soucy .30 .75
19 Jeremy Thompson .20 .50
20 Richard Uniacke .20 .50
21 Joe Van Volsen .20 .50
22 Paul Lawless CO .08 .25
23 Fang Mascot .02 .10
24 Ice Bats Hummer PROMO .02 .10

1999-00 Austin Ice Bats

This set features the Ice Bats of the WPHL. The cards were handed out as promotional giveaways at two home games. There were two cards (Nos. 29 & 30) that were only given out at Lowe's Home Improvement when a redemption card from the set was turned in.

COMPLETE SET (34) 12.00 30.00
1 Andy Ross .40 1.00
2 Shawn Legault .40 1.00
3 Craig Stahl .40 1.00
4 Ryan Pisiak .40 1.00
5 David Moore .40 1.00
6 David Brosseau .40 1.00
7 Jeff Greenlaw .40 1.00
8 Jeff Kungle .40 1.00
9 Bryan McMullen .40 1.00
10 Dan Price .40 1.00
11 Brent Hughes CO .08 .25
12 Glen Norman .40 1.00
13 Clint Shuman TR .08 .25
14 The IceBatmobile .08 .25
15 Rob Laurie .60 1.50
16 Brent Currie .40 1.00
17 Stu Kulak .40 1.00
18 Kelly Smart .40 1.00
19 Jim Shepherd .40 1.00
20 Ryan Anderson .40 1.00
21 Laird Lidster .40 1.00
22 Matt Sharuga .40 1.00
23 Derek Nicolson .40 1.00
24 Ryan Brindley .40 1.00
25 Tyler Perry .40 1.00
26 Fang MAS .08 .25
27 Ken McRae CO .08 .25
28 Gunner Garrett TR .08 .25
29 Ryan Pisiak 1.25 3.00
30 Ryan Anderson 1.25 3.00
31 Shawn Legault .40 1.00
32 Ryan Anderson .40 1.00
33 David Moore .40 1.00
34 Andy Ross .40 1.00

2000-01 Austin Ice Bats

This set features the Ice Bats of the WPHL. The set was released as a promotional giveaway, and was handed out over the course of two home games. Cards # 29 and 30 were redemption cards that could be acquired at a local hardware store.

COMPLETE SET (30) 8.00 30.00
1 Ryan Anderson .30 1.00
2 David Brosseau .30 1.00
3 Bobby Brown .30 1.00
4 Jonathan Forest .30 1.00
5 Mike Gaffney .40 1.50
6 Jeff Greenlaw .30 1.00
7 Daniel Kletke .30 1.00
8 Jeff Kungle .30 1.00
9 Eric Landry .40 1.50
10 Roger Lewis .30 1.00
11 Josh Maser .30 1.00
12 Bryan McMullen .30 1.00
13 Derek Nicolson .30 1.00
14 Erik Noack .30 1.00
15 Keith O'Brien .30 1.00
16 Tyler Perry .30 1.00
17 Philippe Plante .30 1.00
18 Dan Price .30 1.00
19 Brett Seguin .40 1.50
20 Kelly Smart .30 1.00
21 Troy Stonier .30 1.00
22 Daniel Tetrault .30 1.00
23 Brent Hughes CO .20 .50
24 Ken McRae CO .20 .50
25 Clint Shuman TR .10 .10
26 CC Comedy Club .01 .02
27 Hooters Hot Shot .20 .50
28 Fang MASCOT .04 .10
29 Redemption .04 .10
29R Spike & Fang MASCOTS .40 3.00
30 Redemption .04 .10
30R Ice Bats All Stars .80 3.00

2001-02 Austin Ice Bats

This set features the Ice Bats of the WPHL. The set was handed out to fans at a single home game early in 2002.

COMPLETE SET (25) 8.00 20.00
1 Ryan Anderson .40 1.00
2 Bobby Brown .40 1.00
3 Patrick Brownlee .40 1.00
4 Jeff Greenlaw .40 1.00
5 Ian LaRocque .40 1.00
6 Eric Labelle .40 1.00
7 Tab Lardner .40 1.00
8 Darryl McArthur .60 1.50
9 Dan McIntyre .40 1.00
10 Bryan McMullen .40 1.00
11 Dominic Periard .40 1.00
12 Ryan Pisiak .40 1.00
13 Dan Price .40 1.00
14 Brett Seguin .40 1.00
15 Kelly Smart .40 1.00
16 Gerald Tallaire .60 1.50
17 Daniel Tetrault .60 1.50
18 Greg Willers .40 1.00
19 Jeff Worlton .40 1.00
20 Brent Hughes CO .10 .25
21 Ken McRae ACO .10 .25
22 Fang MASCOT .04 .10
23 Glen Norman DB .04 .10
24 Clint Shuman TR .04 .10
24 Gunner Garrett EQMG .04 .10
25 Hootie Celebrates .04 .10

2002-03 Austin Ice Bats

COMPLETE SET (24) 10.00 20.00
1 Matt Barnes .60 1.50
2 Peter Brady .60 1.50
3 Patrick Brownlee .40 1.00
4 Mike Gaffney .40 1.00
5 Jeff Greenlaw .40 1.00
6 Doug Johnson .40 1.00
7 Tab Lardner .40 1.00
8 Shawn Legault .60 1.50
9 Darryl McArthur .40 1.00
10 Scott McCallum .40 1.00
11 Mike Olynyk .40 1.00
12 Randy Ponte .40 1.00
13 Dan Price .40 1.00
14 Mike Rees .40 1.00
15 Brett Seguin .40 1.00
16 Matt Sharuga .40 1.00
17 Kelly Smart .40 1.00
18 Gerald Tallaire .40 1.00
19 Brent Hughes HCO .10 .25
20 Jeff Kungle ACO .10 .25
21 Gunner Garrett EQM .02 .10
22 Fang Mascot .02 .10
23 Fang's Gang .02 .10
24 Clint Shuman TR .02 .10

2003-04 Austin Ice Bats

This set was issued as a promotional giveaway and split over two home games, making it difficult to complete. The cards are unnumbered and listed below in alphabetical order.

COMPLETE SET (24) 15.00 30.00
1 Peter Brady .60 1.50
2 Patrick Brownlee .60 1.50
3 Brandon Carper .60 1.50
4 Shawn Conschafter .60 1.50
5 Jonathan Forest .60 1.50
6 Brent Hughes .60 1.50
7 Tab Lardner .60 1.50
8 Shawn Legault .75 2.00
9 Chris Legg .60 1.50
10 Darryl McArthur .75 2.00
11 Scott McCallum .60 1.50
12 Mike Olynyk .60 1.50
13 Brett Seguin .60 1.50
14 Kelly Smart .60 1.50
15 Josh St. Louis .60 1.50
16 Derek Stone .60 1.50
17 Gerald Tallaire .60 1.50
18 Daniel Tetrault .60 1.50
19 Clint Way .60 1.50
20 Jeff Greenlaw HCO .10 .25
21 Gunner Garrett EQM .02 .10
22 Cheerleaders .10 .25
23 Mascot .02 .10
24 Clint Shuman TR .02 .10

2004-05 Austin Ice Bats

Issued as a stadium giveaway in two parts.

COMPLETE SET (23) 15.00 30.00
1 Peter-Emmanuel Brady .75 2.00
2 Brian Pasko .60 1.50
3 Kelly Smart .60 1.50
4 Ryan Leasa .60 1.50
5 Kris Knoblauch .60 1.50
6 Chris Richards .60 1.50
7 Dallas Anderson 1.25 3.00
8 John McNabb .75 2.00
9 Mike Olynyk .75 2.00
10 Sponsor Card .01 .01
11 Clint Shuman TR .02 .10
12 Fang MASCOT .02 .10
13 Matt Barnes 1.25 2.00
14 Benoit Genesse .60 1.50
15 Jonathan Jolette .60 1.50
16 Jeff Neufeld .60 1.50
17 Jared Dumba .60 1.50
18 Mike Mohr .60 1.50
19 Arturs Kupaks .60 1.50
20 Vinnie Jonasson .60 1.50
21 Greg Gatto CO .02 .10
22 Gunner Garrett EQM .02 .10
23 Bat Girls .20 .50

2006-07 Austin Ice Bats

Set was issued in two, 12-card perforated sheets. The cards are oversized.

1 Miguel Beaudry .60 1.50
2 Adam Holmgren .60 1.50
3 Chad McIver .60 1.50
4 Chris Murphy .60 1.50
5 Chris Ovington .60 1.50
6 Tony Quesada .60 1.50
7 John Ronan .60 1.50
8 Ray Smegal .60 1.50
9 Julian Smith .60 1.50
10 Mike Tucciarone .60 1.50
11 Terry Virtue .60 1.50
12 Logo Card .10 .25
13 Jordan Biachin .75 2.00
14 Kevin Couture .60 1.50
15 Aaron Davis .60 1.50
16 Britt Dougherty .60 1.50
17 Jason Kenyon .60 1.50
18 Henry Kuster .60 1.50
19 John McNabb .60 1.50
20 J.F. Picard .60 1.50
21 Mike Possin .60 1.50
22 Aaron Wilson .60 1.50
23 Fang MASCOT .10 .25
24 Logo Card .10 .25

1999-00 Baie-Comeau Drakkar

This set features the Drakkar of the QMJHL. The set was produced by card store CTM Ste-Foy and was sold at that shop and at home games.

COMPLETE SET (28) 4.00 10.00
1 Daniel Bergeron .15 .40
2 Jerome Bergeron .15 .40
3 Eric Bleau .15 .40
4 Marco Charpentier .15 .40
5 Jean-Philippe Chartier .30 .75
6 Serge Crochetiere .15 .40
7 Sylvain Deschatelets .15 .40
8 Kevin Deslauriers .15 .40
9 Maxime Fortunus .15 .40
10 Jonathan Gautier .15 .40
11 Duilio Grande .15 .40
12 Evgeny Gusakov .15 .40
13 Paul Lavoie .15 .40
14 Robin Leblanc .15 .40
15 Yannick Lehoux .30 .75
16 Charles Linglet .15 .40
17 Andre Mercure .15 .40
18 Chris Page .15 .40
19 Dominic Periard .15 .40
20 Jerome Petit .15 .40
21 Ghyslain Rousseau .30 .75
22 Bruno St. Jacques .30 .75
23 Eric Tremblay .15 .40
24 Guy Turmel .15 .40
25 Patrick Daviault CO .02 .10
26 Richard Martel CO .02 .10
27 Michel Larocque TR .02 .10
28 Brian St.Louis TR .02 .10

2000-01 Baie-Comeau Drakkar

This set features the Drakkar of the QMJHL. The set was produced by CTM-Ste-Foy and was sold through that shop and at home games.

COMPLETE SET (26) 3.60 9.00
1 Jonathan Walsh .14 .35
2 Joel Perrault .14 .35
3 Pierre-Andre Leblanc .14 .35
4 Dominic Periard .14 .35
5 Maxime Fortunus .14 .35
6 Pascal Pelletier .14 .35
7 Robin Leblanc .14 .35
8 Luis Tremblay .14 .35
9 Thierry Douville .14 .35
10 Marco Charpentier .14 .35
11 Premysl Duben .14 .35
12 Yanick Lehoux .40 1.00
13 Duilio Grande .14 .35
14 Kevin Deslauriers .14 .35
15 Matthew Hyde .14 .35
16 Guy Turmel .14 .35
17 Evgeny Gusakov .14 .35
18 Ghyslain Rousseau .20 .50
19 David St. Germain .20 .50
20 Jonathan Jolette .14 .35
21 Martin Mandeville .14 .35
22 Daniel Bergeron .14 .35
23 Charles Linglet .14 .35
24 Jonathan Gautier .14 .35
25 Richard Martel CO CL .04 .10
NNO Snorri MASCOT .04 .10

2000-01 Baie-Comeau Drakkar Signed

This set is exactly the same as the base Drakkar set from this season, save that every card has been hand signed by the player pictured. Each card also is serial numbered out of just 100.

COMPLETE SET (26) 20.00 50.00
1 Jonathan Walsh .80 2.00
2 Joel Perrault .80 2.00
3 Pierre-Andre Leblanc .80 2.00
4 Dominic Periard .80 2.00
5 Maxime Fortunus .80 2.00
6 Pascal Pelletier .80 2.00
7 Robin Leblanc .80 2.00
8 Luis Tremblay .80 2.00
9 Thierry Douville .80 2.00
10 Marco Charpentier .80 2.00
11 Premysl Duben .80 2.00
12 Yanick Lehoux 2.00 5.00
13 Duilio Grande .80 2.00
14 Kevin Deslauriers .80 2.00
15 Matthew Hyde .80 2.00
16 Guy Turmel .80 2.00
17 Evgeny Gusakov .80 2.00
18 Ghyslain Rousseau 2.00 5.00
19 David St. Germain 2.00 5.00
20 Jonathan Jolette .80 2.00
21 Martin Mandeville .80 2.00
22 Daniel Bergeron .80 2.00
23 Charles Linglet .80 2.00
24 Jonathan Gautier .80 2.00
25 Richard Martel CO CL .04 .10
NNO Snorri MASCOT .04 .10

2001-02 Baie-Comeau Drakkar

This set features les Drakkar of the QMJHL. The set was produced by well-known card shop CTM Ste-Foy, and was sold at the team's home games. It was reported that less than 1,000 sets were produced.

COMPLETE SET (25) 4.80 12.00
1 Joel Perrault .20 .50
2 Louis-Philippe Martin .20 .50
3 Jonathan Lachance .20 .50
4 Maxime Fortunus .20 .50
5 Pascal Pelletier .20 .50
6 Robin Leblanc .20 .50
7 Luis Tremblay .20 .50
8 Thierry Douville .20 .50
9 Martin Kuna .20 .50
10 Yanick Lehoux .30 .75
11 Duilio Grande .20 .50
12 Kevin Deslauriers .20 .50
13 Matthew Hyde .20 .50
14 Jean Junior Morin .20 .50
15 Ghyslain Rousseau .20 .75
16 Jonathan Dupras .20 .50
17 Caleb Moffat .20 .50
18 Marc-Andre Roy .20 .50
19 Martin Mandeville .20 .50
20 Daniel Bergeron .20 .75
21 Charles Linglet .20 .50
22 Jean-Francois Savage .20 .50
23 Benoit Mondou .20 .75
24 Jean-Francois Jacques .20 .50
NNO Richard Martel CO/CL .04 .10

2002-03 Baie Comeau Drakkar

COMPLETE SET (26) 5.00 12.00
1 Maxime Belanger .20 .50
2 Joel Perrault .30 .75
3 Alexandre Lamarche .20 .50
4 Jean-Philippe Gauthier .20 .50
5 Louis-Philippe Martin .20 .50
6 Maxime Fortunus .20 .50
7 Pascal Pelletier .20 .50
8 Robin Leblanc .20 .50
9 Luis Tremblay .20 .50
10 Thierry Douville .20 .50
11 Jimmy Arsenault .20 .50
12 Travis Antler .20 .50
13 Kevin Deslauriers .20 .50
14 Patrick Lepage .30 .75
15 Sebastien Leonard .20 .50
16 Philip Lacroix .30 .75
17 Michel Bergevin-Robinson .30 .75
18 Caleb Moffat .20 .50
19 Marc-Andre Roy .20 .50
20 Patrick Thoresen .40 1.00
21 Martin Mandeville .20 .50
22 Charles Linglet .20 .50
23 Benoit Mondou .30 .75
24 Jean-Francois Jacques .20 .50
25 Richard Martel CO/CL .01 .01
26 Snorri MASCOT .01 .01

2003-04 Baie Comeau Drakkar

This set was produced by CTM Sports and sold at home games.

COMPLETE SET (27) 5.00 12.00
1 Ryan-James Hand .20 .50
2 Patrick Simaro .20 .50
3 Ryan Lehr .20 .50
4 Maxime Belanger .20 .50
5 Martin Krayzel .20 .50
6 Alexandre Blais .20 .50
7 Jonathan Duchesneau .20 .50
8 Alexandre Lamarche Froelich .20 .50
9 Maxime Fortunas .20 .50
10 Robin Leblanc .20 .50
11 Luis Tremblay .20 .50
12 Frederic Gariepy .20 .50
13 Vitaly Lanochkin .20 .50
14 Olivier Furlong .20 .50
15 Simon Lepage .20 .50
16 Loic Lacasse .30 .75
17 Patrick Laurin .20 .50
18 Julien Walsh .30 .75
19 Pierre-Luc Leblond-Letourneau .20 .50
20 Martin Mandeville .20 .50
21 Nicolas Robillard .20 .50
22 Petr Preucil .20 .50
23 Philippe Cote .20 .50
24 Jean-Francois Jacques .30 .75
25 Alexandre Dulac Lemelin .20 .50
26 Maxime Fortunas TL .20 .50
27 Jean-Francois Jacques TL .30 .75

2004-05 Baie-Comeau Drakkar

A total of 350 team sets were produced.

COMPLETE SET (24) 10.00
1 Alexandre Blais .50
2 Alexandre Dulac-Lemelin .50
3 Alexandre Picard-Hooper .50
4 Banjamin Breault .50
5 Erick Lajoie .50
6 Francois Bouchard .50
7 Jean-Francois Jacques .50
8 Joakim Jensen .50
9 Jonathan Duchesneau .50
10 Loic Lacasse .75
11 Martin Aubin .50
12 Martin Mandeville .50
13 Mathieu Gravel .50
14 Maxime Belanger .50
15 Michael Dupont .75
16 Nicolas Robillard .50
17 Patrick Simard .50
18 Philippe Cote .50
19 Pierre-Luc Leblond-Letourneau .50
20 Ryan Lehr .50
21 Ryan-James Hand .50
22 Sebastien Blouin .50
23 Tomas Fendek .50
24 Vitaly Lanochkin .50

2005-06 Baie-Comeau Drakkar

COMPLETE SET (22) 5.00 10.00
1 Benjamin Breault .20 .50
2 Charles-Antoine Messier .20 .50
3 Patrick Simard .20 .50
4 Ryan Lehr .20 .50
5 Tomas Fendek .20 .50
6 Alexandre Blais .20 .50
7 Jonathan Duchesneau .20 .50
8 Christian Landry .20 .50
9 Francois Chabot .20 .50
10 Alexandre Picard-Hooper .20 .50
11 Francois Bouchard .20 .50
12 Jean-Sebastien Hogg .20 .50
13 Adam Bourque-Leblanc .20 .50
14 Joakim Jensen .20 .50
15 Alexandre Dulac-Lemelin .20 .50
16 Maxime D. Ouimet .20 .50
17 Oliver Donais .20 .50
18 Samuel Beland .20 .50
19 Francois Filion .20 .50
20 Loic Lacasse .20 .50
21 Michael Dupont .20 .50
22 Martin Aubin .20 .50

1998-99 Bakersfield Condors

This set features the Condors of the WCHL. The cards measure 2 5/8 by 3 5/8 and feature a full-bleed color photo on the front. The backs feature player stats and the logo of sponsor KRAB radio

COMPLETE SET (24) 4.00 10.00
1 Jamie Adams .30 .75
2 Kevin Barrett .30 .75
3 Brady Blain .30 .75
4 Marc Boxer .30 .75
5 Steve Chelios .40 1.00
6 Jamie Cooke .30 .75
7 Steve Dowhy .30 .75
8 Brad Guzda .30 .75
9 Nick Hriczov .30 .75
10 Kelly Hrycun .30 .75
11 Marcel Kuris .30 .75
12 Dan Marcotte .30 .75
13 Brian McCarthy .30 .75
14 Glen Mears .30 .75
15 Al Murphy .30 .75
16 Jay Neal .30 .75
17 Zbynek Neckar .30 .75
18 Dan Reja .30 .75
19 Stephane St. Amour .40 1.00
20 Briane Thompson .30 .75
21 Peter Zurba .30 .75
22 Bakersfield Centennial Arena .02 .10
23 Kevin MacDonald HCO .02 .10
24 Colonel Claw'd Mascot .02 .10

1999-00 Bakersfield Condors

This set features the Condors of the WCHL. The set was issued as a promotional giveaway at a home game midway through the season. It was later offered for sale at home games and by mail order.

COMPLETE SET (24) 8.00 20.00
1 Cory Banika .40 1.00
2 Philippe Bergeron .40 1.00
3 Kevin Boyd .40 1.00
4 Jamie Cooke .40 1.00
5 Dan Currie .60 1.50
6 Chris Dearden .40 1.00
7 Steve Dowhy .40 1.00
8 Chris Droeske .40 1.00
9 Brad Guzda .40 1.00
10 Paul McInnis .40 1.00
11 Glen Mears .40 1.00
12 Zbynek Neckar .40 1.00
13 Jani Ojala .40 1.00
14 Brad Phillips .40 1.00
15 Clark Polglase .40 1.00
16 Jason Reesor .40 1.00
17 Paul Rosebush .40 1.00
18 Briane Thompson .40 1.00
19 Rhett Trombley .40 1.00
20 Paul Willett .40 1.00
21 Kevin MacDonald CO .08 .25
22 Bakersfield Centennial .08 .25
23 Colonel Claw'd MAS .08 .25
24 Michael Ropchan TR .08 .25

2000-01 Bakersfield Condors

This set features the Condors of the WCHL. The set was issued as a promotional giveaway at a game midway through the season. The cards are unnumbered and are listed below alphabetically.

COMPLETE SET (24) 8.00 20.00
1 Trevor Amundrud .30 .75
2 Cory Banika .30 .75
3 Karel Betik .60 1.50
4 Kevin Boyd .30 .75
5 Jamie Cooke .30 .75
6 Dan Currie .60 1.50
7 Jean-Paul Davis .30 .75
8 Chris Dearden .30 .75
9 Quinn Fair .30 .75
10 Ben Gustavson .30 .75
11 Denis Ivanov .30 .75
12 Bryan Lachance .30 .75
13 Peter MacKellar .30 .75
14 Craig Martin .40 1.00
15 Glen Mears .30 .75
16 Pavel Mikulchik .30 .75
17 Matt Mullin .60 1.50
18 Jason Reesor .30 .75

19 Paul Rosebush .30 .75
20 Paul Willett .60 1.50
21 Paul Willett MVP .60 1.50
22 Kevin MacDonald CO .10 .25
23 Centenial Gardens ARENA .10 .25
24 Colonel/Cal MASCOTS .10 .25

2001-02 Bakersfield Condors

COMPLETE SET (24) 10.00 20.00
1 Ken Baker .40 1.00
2 Peter Brearley .40 1.00
3 Luciano Caravaggio .40 1.00
4 Jamie Cooke .40 1.00
5 Mark Edmundson .40 1.00
6 Todd Esselmont .40 1.00
7 Quinn Fair .40 1.00
8 Chris Felix .40 1.00
9 Jason Firth .40 1.00
10 Jeff Goldie .40 1.00
11 Ryan Hartung .40 1.00
12 Scott Hay .60 1.50
13 Sasha Lakovic .60 1.50
14 Josh Maser .40 1.00
15 Glen Mears .40 1.00
16 David Milek .40 1.00
17 Jason Ralph .40 1.00
18 Paul Rosebush .40 1.00
19 John Vary .40 1.00
20 Paul Willett .40 1.00
21 Paul Kelly HCO .02 .10
22 Condors in the Community .02 .10
23 Baby Cal MASCOT .02 .10
24 Colonel Claw MASCOT .02 .10

2002-03 Bakersfield Condors

COMPLETE SET (24) 10.00 20.00
1 Nate Anderson .40 1.00
2 David Bell .40 1.00
3 Shawn Byram .40 1.00
4 Jamie Cooke .40 1.00
5 Danielle Dube .40 1.00
6 Guy Dupuis .40 1.00
7 Quinn Fair .40 1.00
8 Jeff Goldie .40 1.00
9 Jason Jackman .40 1.00
10 Denis Ladouceur .40 1.00
11 Jonas Lennartsson .40 1.00
12 Christoffer Norgren .40 1.00
13 Jason Ralph .40 1.00
14 Jordan Roach .40 1.00
15 Paul Rosebush .40 1.00
16 Christian Skoryna .40 1.00
17 Jonathan Sorg .40 1.00
18 Kevin St. Pierre .60 1.50
19 Paul Willett .40 1.00
20 J.J. Wrobel .40 1.00
21 Paul Kelly HCO .10 .25
22 Martin Raymond ACO .10 .25
23 Colonel Claw'd/Baby Cal .02 .10

2003-04 Bakersfield Condors

The 25-card main set was issued as a promotional giveaway. No production run was announced.

COMPLETE SET (25) 10.00 25.00
1 Todd Alexander .40 1.00
2 Johan Astrom .40 1.00
3 Jamie Cooke .40 1.00
4 Paul Kelly CO .10 .25
5 Martin Raymond ACO .10 .25
6 Andrew Ianiero .40 1.00
7 Jason Jackman .40 1.00
8 Peter Hirsch .40 1.00
9 Devin Francon .40 1.00
10 Paul Rosebush .40 1.00
11 Kevin Riehl .40 1.00
12 Mascot .02 .10
13 Vince Malts .40 1.00
14 Quinn Fair .40 1.00
15 Jimmy Drolet .40 1.00
16 Glen Mears .40 1.00
17 Jon Mirasty .40 1.00
18 Darren Shakotko .40 1.00
19 Jani Virtanen .40 1.00
20 Joe Watkins .60 1.50
21 Paul Willett .40 1.00
22 Randy Perry .40 1.00
23 Jason Ralph .40 1.00
24 Denis Ladouceur .40 1.00
25 Jonas Lennartsson .40 1.00

2004-05 Bakersfield Condors

COMPLETE SET (24) 15.00 30.00
1 Ryan Coole .40 1.00
2 Guy Dupuis .40 1.00
3 Yutaka Fukufuji 4.00 10.00
4 Ryan Gillis .40 1.00
5 Ty Hennes .40 1.00
6 Mike Hofstrand .40 1.00
7 Connor James .40 1.00
8 David Kudelka .40 1.00
9 Ashlee Langdone .40 1.00
10 Tony Lawrence .40 1.00
11 Brett Lutes .40 1.00
12 Brad Mehalko .40 1.00
13 Dylan Mills .40 1.00
14 Lars Peder Nagel .40 1.00
15 Paul Rosebush .40 1.00
16 Vlad Serov .40 1.00
17 Dennis Shiryaev .40 1.00
18 Kevin St. Jacques .40 1.00
19 Luis Tremblay .40 1.00
20 Chris Twerdun .40 1.00
21 Jason Wolfe .60 1.50
22 Marty Raymond CO .02 .10
23 Paul Willet ACO .02 .10
24 Mascots .02 .10

2005-06 Bakersfield Condors

COMPLETE SET (23) 8.00 20.00
1 Marty Raymond .40 1.00
2 Kevin Kotyluk .40 1.00
3 Brian Collins .40 1.00
4 Scott Balan .40 1.00
5 Paul Rosebush .40 1.00
6 Reagan Leslie .40 1.00
7 Scott Basiuk .40 1.00
8 Alexandre Bolduc .40 1.00
9 Nick Economakos .40 1.00
10 Oriel McHugh .40 1.00
11 Dennis Shiryaev .40 1.00
12 Kevin St.Jacques .40 1.00
13 Ryan Munce .40 1.00
14 Mike Hofstrand .40 1.00
15 Dave Bonk .40 1.00
16 Scott Borders .40 1.00
17 Andrew Ianiero .40 1.00
18 Eric Neilson .40 1.00
19 Kevin Truelson .40 1.00
20 Sean Venedam .40 1.00
21 Mark Pederson .40 1.00
22 Joel Irving .40 1.00
23 Mathieu Brunelle .40 1.00

2006-07 Bakersfield Condors

1 Sean Venedam .40 1.00
2 Rane Carnegie .60 1.50
3 Steve Rodberg .40 1.00
4 Brett Lutes .40 1.00
5 Coaches .10 .25
6 Kevin Truelson .40 1.00
7 David Kudelka .40 1.00
8 Andrew Oke .40 1.00
9 Andrew Ianiero .40 1.00
10 Alex Kim .40 1.00
11 Danny Taylor .40 1.00
12 Scott Borders .40 1.00
13 Mike Hofstrand .40 1.00
14 Josh Libenow .40 1.00
15 Alexandre Bolduc .40 1.00
16 Alec Rogosheske .40 1.00
17 Tyler Scott .40 1.00
18 Tyler Liebel .40 1.00
19 Jamie Hodson .75 2.00
20 Kevin St. Jacques .40 1.00
21 Scotty Balan .40 1.00
22 Kevin Asselin .40 1.00
23 Todd Griffith .40 1.00
24 Reagan Leslie .40 1.00

1997-98 Bakersfield Fog

Little is known about this set, though it is believed that it was sold by the team throughout the season. Any additional information can be forwarded to hockeymag@beckett.com.

COMPLETE SET (24) 12.00
1 John Devereaux .25 .60
2 Steve Dowhy .25 .60
3 Igor Galkin .40 1.00
4 Jeff Gorman .25 .60
5 Kelly Hrycun .25 .60
6 Jeff Jubenville .25 .60
7 Don Lester .25 .60
8 Brian McCarthy .25 .60
9 Glen Mears .25 .60
10 Rob Milliken .40 1.00
11 Jodi Murphy .40 1.00
12 Jay Neal .25 .60
13 Jeff Pierce .25 .60
14 Andrew Plumb .25 .60
15 Iannique Renaud .25 .60
16 Eddy Skazyk .40 1.00
17 Lindsay Vallis .25 .60
18 Wade Welte .40 1.00
19 Jason White .25 .60
20 Keith Gretzky HCO .20 .50
21 Tule Fog Mascot .02 .10
22 Bakersfield Arena .02 .10
23 Sponsor Card .04 .01
24 Dick Earle TR .02 .10

1991-92 Baltimore Skipjacks

This 15-card set was issued as a promotional giveaway in 3-card perforated strips. The set commemorated the team's 10th anniversary and was sponsored by Wendy's and Coca-Cola. The cards are numbered card "xx" of 15.

COMPLETE SET (15) 8.00 20.00
1 Tim Taylor .40 1.00
2 Brent Hughes .30 .75
3 Trevor Halverson .30 .75
4 Bobby Reynolds .30 .75
5 Ken Lovsin .30 .75
6 Olaf Kolzig 4.00 10.00
7 Reggie Savage .30 .75
8 Jim Mathieson .40 1.00
9 Todd Hlushko .40 1.00
10 Mark Ferner .30 .75
11 John Purves .30 .75
12 Steve Seftel .30 .75
13 Craig Duncanson .30 .75
14 Simon Wheeldon .40 1.00
15 Bob Babcock .30 .75

1995-96 Barrie Colts

This set features the expansion Colts of the OHL. These attractive cards feature full-bleed photos on the front, along with a dynamic chartreuse design element along the right side. The back's feature a head shot and commentary from coach Bert Templeton. The set was sold by the team at home games and is noteworthy for the inclusion of future NHLers Dan Tkaczuk, Jan Bulis and Jeff Cowan.

COMPLETE SET (28) 4.80 12.00
1 Mauricio Alvarez .20 .50
2 Brian Barker .20 .50
3 Brock Boucher .20 .50
4 Jan Bulis .30 .75
5 Jason Cannon .20 .50
6 Jeff Cowan .30 .75
7 Shane Delaronde .30 .75
8 Robert DuBois .20 .50
9 Shawn Frappier .20 .50
10 Chris George .20 .50
11 In Action .02 .10
12 In Action .02 .10
13 In Action .02 .10
14 In Action .02 .10
15 Gerry Lanigan .20 .50
16 Quade Lightbody .20 .50
17 Jeremy Miculinic .20 .50
18 Andrew Morrison .20 .50
19 Luch Nasato .30 .75
20 Bert Templeton CO .08 .25
21 Jeff Tetzlaff .20 .50
22 Chris Thompson .30 .75
23 Justin Robinson .20 .50
24 Daniel Tkaczuk .30 .75
25 Alexander Volchkov .20 .50
26 Caleb Ward .20 .50
27 Mike White .20 .50
28 Darrell Woodley .20 .50

1996-97 Barrie Colts

This set was produced and sold by the team at home games. It is notable for featuring future NHLers Martin Skoula, Brian Finley and Daniel Tkaczuk. The cards are unnumbered, and so are unnumbered and checklisted below in alphabetical order.

COMPLETE SET (30) 6.00 15.00
1 Brian Barker .20 .50
2 Brock Boucher .20 .50
3 Casey Burnette .20 .50
4 Michael Christian .20 .50
5 Keith Delaney .20 .50
6 Adam Deleeuw .20 .50
7 Chris Feil .20 .50
8 Brian Finley .40 1.00
9 Michael Henrich .30 .75
10 John Hultberg .20 .50
11 Richard Kazda .20 .50
12 Darren Keily TR .02 .10
13 Cody Leibel .20 .50
14 Mihajlo Martinovich .20 .50
15 Kevin McClelland ACO .02 .10
16 Walker McDonald .20 .50
17 Jeff McKercher .20 .50
18 Luch Nasato .25 .60
19 Ryan O'Keefe .20 .50
20 Jason Pinizzotto .20 .50
21 Ryan Shaver .20 .50
22 Martin Skoula .40 1.00
23 Nick Smith .20 .50
24 Brandon Sugden .25 .60
25 Bert Templeton CO .20 .50
26 Jeff Tetzlaff .20 .50
27 Daniel Tkaczuk .30 .75
28 Charlie Horse(Mascot) .02 .10
29 Barrie Colts Team Picture .20 .50
30 Checklist .02 .10

1997-98 Barrie Colts

This attractive set was produced by the team and sold at home games. The set is unnumbered and checklisted below in alphabetical order.

COMPLETE SET (27) 4.80 10.00
1 Brian Barker .15 .40
2 Brock Boucher .15 .40
3 Jan Bulis .30 .75
4 Casey Burnette .15 .40
5 Jason Cannon .15 .40
6 Keith Delaney .15 .40
7 Chris George .15 .40
8 Nick Grady .15 .40
9 Mike Henrich .30 .75
10 John Hultberg .20 .50
11 Marcel Kars .15 .40
12 Darren Keily TR .02 .10
13 Gerry Lanigan .15 .40
14 Kevin McClelland .02 .10
15 Walker McDonald .15 .40
16 Jeff McKercher .15 .40
17 Brad Morgan .15 .40
18 Luch Nasato .30 .75
19 Corey Neilson .15 .40
20 Nick Smith .15 .40
21 Bert Templeton CO .15 .40
22 Jeff Tetzlaff .15 .40
23 Chris Thompson .15 .40
24 Daniel Tkaczuk .30 .75
25 Alexandre Volchkov .20 .50
26 Darrell Woodley .15 .40
27 Charlie Horse MAS .02 .10

1998-99 Barrie Colts

Released by the Colts in conjunction with Coca-Cola, this 25-card set pictures the 1998-99 Barrie Colts. Base cards feature full color action photography, white borders, and a blue nameplate along with the Coca-Cola logo along the bottom of the card.

COMPLETE SET (25) 7.20 15.00
1 Ryan O'Keefe .20 .50
2 Andre Lakos .20 .50
3 Shawn Cation .20 .50
4 Ed Hill .20 .50
5 Joel Dezainde .20 .50
6 Daniel Tkaczuk .30 .75
7 Martin Skoula .30 .75
8 Jerry Connell .20 .50
9 Tim Verbeek .20 .50
10 Rick Hwodeky .20 .50
11 Scott Cameron .30 .75
12 Ryan Barnes .20 .50
13 Sheldon Keefe .30 .75
14 Jeff Tetzlaff .20 .50
15 Chris Feil .20 .50
16 Michael Henrich .30 .75
17 Mike Christian .20 .50
18 Nick Smith .20 .50
19 Mike Jefferson .40 1.00
20 Denis Shvidki .30 .75
21 Brian Finley .30 .75
22 Ben Vanderklok .20 .50
23 Bert Templeton HCO .02 .10
24 Darren Keily TR .02 .10
Gary Scott TR
25 Charlie Horse MASCOT .02 .10

2000-01 Barrie Colts

This set features the Colts of the OHL. The set was sponsored by the Colts and Cops foundation and was distributed by the team's booster club at home games.

COMPLETE SET (24) 4.00 10.00
1 Frantisek Bakrlik .14 .35
2 Tim Branham .20 .50
3 Jordan Brenner .14 .35
4 Dean Byvelds .14 .35
5 David Chant .40 1.00
6 Fraser Clair .14 .35
7 Mike D'Alessandro .30 .75
8 Blaine Down .14 .35
9 Matt Dzieduszycki .14 .35
10 Shayne Fryia .14 .35
11 Matt Grennier .14 .35
12 Bryan Hayes .14 .35
13 Tyler Hanchuck .20 .50
14 Mike Henderson .14 .35
15 Ed Hill .20 .35
16 Charlie Horse Mascot/CL .10 .10
17 Gregg Mizzi .14 .35
18 Stephen Morris .14 .35
19 Jan Platil .14 .35
20 Neil Posillico .14 .35
21 Aaron Power .14 .35
22 Erik Reitz .14 .35
23 Bud Stefanski CO .10 .10
24 Brent Sullivan .14 .35
25 Joey Tenute .14 .35

2001-02 Barrie Colts

This set is unnumbered and is listed below in the order it appears on the checklist.

COMPLETE SET (23) 5.00 10.00
1 David Chant .40 1.00
2 Ryan Stokes .20 .50
3 Rick Arnaldo .20 .50
4 Eric Reitz .30 .75
5 Aaron Powers .20 .50
6 Steven Morris .20 .50
7 Blaine Down .20 .50
8 Joey Tenute .20 .50
9 Nick Lees .20 .50
10 Tyler Hanchuck .20 .50
11 B.J. Crombeen .20 .50
12 Andrew Shennan .20 .50
13 Jeremy Swanson .20 .50
14 Simon Barq .20 .50
15 Frantisek Bakrlik .20 .50
16 Daniel Girardi .20 .50
17 Kevin Ambroski .20 .50
18 Steve Farquharson .20 .50
19 Jan Platil .20 .50
20 Shayne Fria .20 .50
21 Fraser Clair .20 .50
22 Mascot .02 .10
23 Arena Card .02 .10

2002-03 Barrie Colts

COMPLETE SET (24) 5.00 10.00
1 Evan Brophey .20 .50
2 Justin DaCosta .20 .50
3 Andrew Shennan .20 .50
4 Zach Tranmer .20 .50
5 Michael Tuomi .20 .50
6 Simon Barg .20 .50
7 Ryan Sharp .20 .50
8 Nick Lees .20 .50
9 Hunter Tremblay .20 .50
10 Riley Moher .20 .50
11 Eric Himelfarb .30 .75
12 Mark Langdon .20 .50
13 Luc Chiasson .20 .50
14 Jeremy Swanson .20 .50
15 Kenny Jung .20 .50
16 Tyler Lawson .20 .50
17 Daniel Girardi .20 .50
18 Michael Ouzas .30 .75
19 Paulo Colaiacovo .40 1.00
20 B.J. Crombeen .20 .50
21 Dan Speer .20 .50
22 Jan Platil .20 .50
23 Mascot .02 .10
24 Barrie Molson Centre .02 .10

2003-04 Barrie Colts

Cards are listed according to the order they appear on the checklist card.

COMPLETE SET (24) 6.00 15.00
1 Thomas Lee .30 .75
2 Steve Spade .30 .75
3 Evan Brophey .30 .75
4 Ryan Hamilton .30 .75
5 Andrew Shennan .30 .75
6 Chad Thompson .30 .75
7 Chris Morrison .30 .75
8 Chad Robinson .30 .75
9 Hunter Tremblay .30 .75
10 Bryan Little 1.50 4.00
11 Scott Hotham .40 1.00
12 Mark Langdon .30 .75
13 Jeremy Swanson .30 .75
14 Michael Root .30 .75
15 Travis Fuller .30 .75
16 Paolo Colaiacovo .60 1.50
17 Lukas Bolf .30 .75
18 B.J. Crombeen .30 .75
19 Georgy Ryazantsev .30 .75
20 Dan Speer .30 .75
21 Cory Stillman .30 .75
22 Andrew Dennis .30 .75
23 Mascot/Checklist .02 .10
24 Barrie Molson Centre .02 .10

2004-05 Barrie Colts

Unnumbered cards, listed below in checklist order.

COMPLETE SET (25) 5.00 10.00
1 Jeff Weber .20 .50
2 Nathan Martine .20 .50
3 Michael Lombardi .20 .50
4 Nicholas Plastino .20 .50
5 Ryan Hamilton .20 .50
6 Andrew Shennan .20 .50
7 Dan Speer .20 .50
8 Mike Roelofsen .20 .50
9 Chris Morrison .20 .50
10 Chad Robinson .20 .50
11 Hunter Tremblay .20 .50
12 Bryan Little .40 1.00
13 Scott Hotham .20 .50
14 Aaron Lewicki .20 .50
15 Michael Root .20 .50
16 Travis Fuller .20 .50
17 Michael Birner .20 .50
18 Francois Thuot .20 .50
19 Lukas Bolf .20 .50
20 B.J. Crombeen .30 .75
21 Andrew Marshall .20 .50
22 Jordan Shine .20 .50
23 Andrew Hotham .20 .50
24 Andrew Dennis .20 .50
25 Mascot/Checklist .02 .10

2004-05 Barrie Colts 10th Anniversary

COMPLETE SET (25) 5.00 12.00
1 Daniel Tkaczuk .20 .50
2 Bryan Little .40 1.00
3 Michael Henrich .20 .50
4 Martin Skoula .20 .50
5 Blaine Down .20 .50
6 Jan Bulis .20 .50
7 Erik Reitz .30 .75
8 Jeremy Swanson .20 .50
9 Luch Nasato .20 .50
10 B.J. Crombeen .30 .75
11 Jan Platil .20 .50
12 Denis Shvidki .20 .50
13 Joey Tenute .20 .50
14 Aaron Power .20 .50
15 Alexander Volchkov .20 .50
16 Mark Langdon .20 .50
17 Fraser Clair .20 .50
18 Nick Lees .20 .50
19 Cory Stillman .20 .50
20 Jeff Tetzlaff .20 .50
21 Tim Verbeek .20 .50
22 Matt Dzieduszycki .20 .50
23 Paulo Colaiacovo .30 .75
24 David Chant .30 .75
25 Brian Finley .30 .75

2006-07 Barrie Colts

1 Andrew Perugini .30 .75
2 Michael Hutchinson .30 .75
3 Kyle Van De Bospoort .20 .50
4 Brian Lashoff .20 .50
5 Thomas Marcinko .30 .75
6 Nicolas Plastino .20 .50
7 Shawn Franck .20 .50
8 Alex Hutchings .20 .50
9 Hunter Tremblay .20 .50
10 Bryan Little .60 1.50
11 Stefan Della Rovere .30 .75
12 Richard Clune .20 .50
13 Ryan Bellows .20 .50
14 Mike Webber .20 .50
15 Chris Purves .20 .50
16 Tyson Aitcheson .20 .50
17 Matthew Bragg .20 .50
18 Kris Sparre .20 .50
19 Ryan Gottschalk .20 .50
20 Andrew Marshall .20 .50
21 Cort McGillis .20 .50
22 Vladimir Nikiforov .20 .50
23 George Lovatsis .20 .50
24 Joe Pleckaitis .20 .50
25 Michael Lombardi .20 .50
26 T.J. Baltani .30 .75
27 Checklist .02 .10
LE2 Andrew Perugini 2.00 5.00

1951-52 Bas Du Fleuve

This set features top players from the Quebec Senior League. The cards are similar in size to the Parkhurst set that was released this season. The key card in the set pictures Denis Brodeur.

COMPLETE SET (58) 350.00 700.00
1 Gordon Poirier 12.50 25.00
2 Denis Brodeur 25.00 50.00
3 Conrad Poitras 7.50 15.00
4 Clement Tremblay 7.50 15.00
5 Raymond Leduc 7.50 15.00
6 Jacques Armstrong 7.50 15.00
7 Joe Schmidt 7.50 15.00
8 Gilles Laroche 7.50 15.00
9 Frank Pearce 7.50 15.00
10 Wayne Stephenson 7.50 15.00
11 Guy Lapointe 7.50 15.00
12 Guy Delisle 7.50 15.00
13 Ossie Carnegie 10.00 20.00
14 Gilbert Girouard 7.50 15.00
15 Jean-Paul Vandal 7.50 15.00
16 Guy Lalonde 7.50 15.00
17 Roland Bilodeau 7.50 15.00
18 Gaetan Laliberte 7.50 15.00
19 Maurice Benoit 7.50 15.00
20 Thomas McDougall 7.50 15.00
21 Roger Guay 7.50 15.00
22 Bob Brault 7.50 15.00
23 Edouard Theberge 7.50 15.00
24 Paul Lessard 7.50 15.00
25 Lucien Gilbert 7.50 15.00
26 Real Lafreniere 7.50 15.00
27 Ronald Limoges 7.50 15.00
28 Roger Ste. Marie 7.50 15.00
29 Arthur Leyte 7.50 15.00
30 Magella Laforest 7.50 15.00
31 Bill Leblanc 7.50 15.00
32 Pius Gaudet 7.50 15.00
33 Jean-Roch Bellavance 7.50 15.00
34 Gerard Lachance 7.50 15.00
35 Marcel St. Pierre 7.50 15.00
36 Pierre Brillant 7.50 15.00
37 Paul Provost 7.50 15.00
38 Maurice Lamirande 7.50 15.00
39 Roger Hayfield 7.50 15.00
40 Normand Bellavance 7.50 15.00
41 Marcel Houde 7.50 15.00
42 Dan Janelle 7.50 15.00
43 Roland Rossignol 7.50 15.00
44 Roger Gagne 7.50 15.00
45 Jacques Monette 7.50 15.00
46 Bernie Bernaquez 7.50 15.00
47 Paul Gagnon 7.50 15.00
48 Jean-Marie Fillion 7.50 15.00
49 Bert Scullion 7.50 15.00
50 Don Bellringer 7.50 15.00
51 Frank Cote 7.50 15.00
52 Eddy Bolan 7.50 15.00
53 Maurice Parr 7.50 15.00
54 Many McIntyre 7.50 15.00
55 Roger Jodoin 7.50 15.00
56 Mario Senecal 7.50 15.00
57 Denis Fillion 7.50 15.00
58 Marcel Fillion 12.50 25.00

1952-53 Bas Du Fleuve

This set features players from the Quebec Senior League. The cards are similar in size to the 1951-52 Parkhurst set. Noteworthy players include Denis Brodeur (father of Martin and former Canadian Olympic goalie) and Marcel Paille.

COMPLETE SET (65) 400.00 800.00
1 Roger Gagner 12.50 25.00
2 Martial Pruneau 7.50 15.00
3 Fernand Gladu 7.50 15.00
4 Joseph Lacoursiere 7.50 15.00
5 Maurice Lamirande 7.50 15.00
6 Denis Smith 7.50 15.00
7 Real Jacques 7.50 15.00
8 Roland Landry 7.50 15.00
9 Dan Janelle 7.50 15.00
10 Pete Gaudette 7.50 15.00
11 Normand Bellavance 7.50 15.00
12 Roger Hayfield 7.50 15.00
13 Bill LeBlanc 7.50 15.00
14 Victor Corbin 7.50 15.00
15 Gerard Lachance 7.50 15.00
16 Guy Labrie 7.50 15.00
17 Denis Brodeur 15.00 30.00
18 Gerard Paquin 7.50 15.00
19 Irene St. Hilaire 10.00 20.00
20 Guy Gervais 7.50 15.00
21 Marcel Benoit 7.50 15.00
22 Roger Dumas 7.50 15.00
23 Gaston Gervais 7.50 15.00
24 Maurice St. Jean 7.50 15.00
25 Frank Pearce 7.50 15.00
26 Fernand Bernaquez 7.50 15.00
27 Henri-Paul Gagnon 7.50 15.00
28 Jean-Jacques Pichette 7.50 15.00
29 Jim Hayes 7.50 15.00
30 Fernand Rancourt 7.50 15.00
31 Nils Tremblay 7.50 15.00
32 Clement Tremblay 7.50 15.00
33 Jacques Lalancette 7.50 15.00
34 Marcel Fillion 10.00 20.00
35 Jacques Monette 7.50 15.00
36 Frank Cote 7.50 15.00
37 Bernie Lemonde 7.50 15.00
38 Guildor Levesque 7.50 15.00
39 Hector Legris 7.50 15.00
40 Jacques Gagnon 7.50 15.00
41 Donat Deschesnes 7.50 15.00
42 Bertrand LePage 7.50 15.00
43 Paul Lavoie 7.50 15.00
44 Denis Fillion 7.50 15.00
45 Floyd Crawford 12.50 25.00
46 Paul Duchesne 7.50 15.00
47 Rene Pronovost 7.50 15.00
48 Roger Jodoin 7.50 15.00
49 Mario Senecal 7.50 15.00
50 Garry Plamondon 12.50 25.00
51 Marcel Paille 7.50 15.00
52 Rene Pepin 7.50 15.00
53 Gilles Desrosiers 7.50 15.00
54 Edgard Gendron 7.50 15.00
55 Ronald Limoges 7.50 15.00
56 Roland Bilodeau 7.50 15.00
57 Leon Bouchard 7.50 15.00
58 Bob Leger 7.50 15.00
59 Conrad L'Heureux 7.50 15.00
60 Raymond Leduc 7.50 15.00
61 Bob Brault 7.50 15.00
62 Roger Ste. Marie 7.50 15.00
63 Real Lafreniere 7.50 15.00
64 Lucien Gilbert 7.50 15.00
65 Louis Desrosiers 12.50 25.00

1998-99 Baton Rouge Kingfish

This set features the Kingfish of the ECHL. The set was issued in five strips, each containing five cards, as a promotional giveaway at a home game.

COMPLETE SET (25) 8.00 20.00
1 Brett Abrahamson .40 1.00
2 Chris Aldous .40 1.00
3 Cam Brown .40 1.00
4 Jason Byrnes .40 1.00
5 Paul Croteau .40 1.00
6 Luke Curtin .40 1.00
7 Allan Hitchen .40 1.00
8 Scott Humeniuk .40 1.00
9 Trevor Jobe .40 1.00
10 Billy-Jay Johnston .40 1.00
11 Mike Josephson .40 1.00
12 Martin Laroche .40 1.00
13 Michel Massie .40 1.00
14 Eric Montreuil .40 1.00
15 Jon Rempel .40 1.00
16 Bryan Richardson .40 1.00
17 Dan Shermerhorn .40 1.00
18 Bob Westerby .40 1.00
19 Jordan Willis .60 1.50
20 Barry Smith CO .08 .25
21 Ron Hansis GM .02 .10
22 Bob McGill CO .08 .25
23 Huey P. Kingfish MAS .08 .25
24 Pat Loughlin TR .02 .10
25 Chris Kenyon .40 1.00

1998-99 BC Icemen

This set features the BC Icemen of the United Hockey League. Little else is known about this set at this time. Any additional information can be forwarded to hockeymag@beckett.com.

COMPLETE SET (22) 4.80 12.00
1 Mark Dutiaume .30 .75
2 Pete Vandermeer .20 .50
3 Patrice Robitaille .20 .50
4 Ales Dvorak .20 .50
5 Shane Dow .20 .50
6 Scott Ricci .20 .50
7 Doug Johnson .20 .50
8 Justin Kearns .30 .75
9 Justin Plamondon .30 .75
10 Jarno Mensonen .20 .50
11 Jamie Bird .20 .50
12 Greg Pajor .20 .50
13 Derek Knorr .20 .50
14 Chris Kavanagh .20 .50
15 Dallas Mann .20 .50
16 Jon Hillebrandt .30 .75
17 Dieter Kochan .75 2.00
18 Brad Jones HCO .08 .25
19 Brian Waselko TR .08 .25
20 Mike Thornton BR .08 .25
21 Phamtom Mascot .08 .25
22 Bamboni Mascot .08 .25

1998-99 BC Icemen II

This set is numbered out of 25 and features the Iceman of the United Hockey League. It is believed that this set was offered as a promotional giveaway at a late-season home game.

COMPLETE SET (27) 8.00 20.00
1 Ales Dvorak .30 .75
2 Shane Dow .30 .75
3 Scott Ricci .30 .75
4 Pete Vandermeer .30 .75
5 Doug Johnson .30 .75
6 Mark Dutiaume .60 1.50
7 Justin Kearns .30 .75
8 Patrice Robitaille .30 .75
9 Justin Plamondon .40 1.00
10 Chris Greenville .30 .75
11 Jarno Mensonen .30 .75
12 Jamie Bird .30 .75
13 Greg Pajor .30 .75
14 Dmitri Deryabin .30 .75
15 Derek Knorr .30 .75
16 Peter Cermak .30 .75
17 Chris Kavanagh .30 .75
18 Jon Hillebrandt .75 2.00
19 Dieter Kochan 1.50 4.00
20 Brad Jones HCO .20 .50
21 Brian Wesiko TR .08 .25
22 Dallas Mann .30 .75
23 Mike Thornton BR .08 .25
24 Phamton Mascot .08 .25
25 Bamboni Mascot .08 .25
NNO Checklist .08 .25
NNO UHL Website .02 .10

2001-02 BC Icemen

This set features the Icemen of the UHL. The set was issued as a promotional giveaway at a last-season home game. The cards are unnumbered and are listed below in alphabetical order.

COMPLETE SET (29) 8.00 20.00
1 Chris Allen .30 .75
2 Eric Andersen .30 .75
3 Alex Andreyev .30 .75
4 Keith Aucoin .30 .75
5 Martin Belanger .30 .75
6 Karel Betik .40 1.00
7 Glendon Cominetti .30 .75
8 Ross Dufresne .30 .75
9 R.J. Gates .30 .75
10 Chris Grenville .30 .75
11 Eric Heffler .30 .75
12 David Jesiolowski .40 1.00
13 Marc Lauzon .30 .75
14 Jim Nagle .30 .75
15 Ryan Pepperall .30 .75
16 Larry Pierce .30 .75
17 Justin Plamondon .30 .75
18 Sean Rowe .60 1.50
19 Erasmo Saltarelli .30 .75
20 Bryan Schoen .40 1.00
21 Trevor Shoaf .30 .75
22 Marc Tropper .30 .75
23 Rob Voltera .30 .75
24 Derek Wood .30 .75
25 Brad Jones CO .10 .25
26 Pedro Trindade MGR .04 .10
27 Bamboni MASCOT .10 .25
28 Phantom MASCOT .10 .25
29 Jason Weinstein PR .04 .10

1983-84 Belleville Bulls

This 30-card police set measures approximately 2 5/8" by 4 1/8" and was sponsored by the Board of Commissioners of Police and other local organizations. The fronts feature posed color player photos with white borders. The player's name and position appear at the bottom. The backs carry P.L.A.Y. (Police, Laws and Youth) Card Tips from The Bulls which consist of a hockey term and relate it to everyday life.

COMPLETE SET (30) 28.00 80.00
1 Belleville Bulls Logo .10 .01
2 Quinte Sports Centre .10 .01
3 Dan Quinn .75 2.00
4 Dave MacLean .20 .50
5 Scott Gardiner .20 .50
6 Mike Knuude .20 .50
7 Brian Martin .20 .50
8 R. Vaughan OWN .08 .25
9 John McDonald .30 .75
10 Brian Small .20 .50
11 Mike Savage .20 .50
12 Dunc MacIntyre .20 .50
13 Charlie Moore .20 .50
14 Jim Andanoff .20 .50
15 Mario Martini .20 .50
16 Rick Adolfi .20 .50
17 Mike Vellucci .20 .50
18 Scott McMichel .20 .50
19 Ali Butorac .20 .50
20 Al Iafrate 1.25 3.00
21 Rob Crocock .20 .50
22 Craig Coxe .60 1.50
23 Grant Robertson .20 .50
24 Craig Billington 1.25 3.00
25 Darren Gani .20 .50
26 Tim Bean .20 .50
27 Wayne Gretzky 30.00 75.00
28 Russ Soule TR .08 .25
29 Larry Mavety CO/GM .08 .25
30 Team Photo .20 .50

1984-85 Belleville Bulls

This 31-card police set measures approximately 2 5/8" by 4 1/8" and was sponsored by the City of Belleville Police Force and other local organizations. The fronts feature posed color player photos with white borders. The player's name, position, and the season (1984-85) appear at the bottom. The backs carry P.L.A.Y. (Police, Laws and Youth) Card Tips from The Bulls which explain a hockey term and relate it to everyday life.

COMPLETE SET (31) 6.00 15.00
1 Team photo .20 .50
2 R. Vaughan OWN .02 .10
3 Larry Mavety CO/MG .02 .10
4 Dunc MacIntyre .20 .50
5 Belleville Bulls Logo .02 .10
6 Mike Knuude .20 .50
7 John Purves .40 1.00
8 Charlie Moore .20 .50
9 Stan Drulia .40 1.00
10 Craig Billington .75 2.00
11 Dave MacLean .20 .50
12 Darren Moxam .20 .50
13 Shane Doyle .20 .50
14 Larry VanHerzele .20 .50
15 Tim Bean .20 .50
16 Kent Brimmer .20 .50
17 Angelo Catenaro .20 .50
18 Steve Linesman .20 .50
19 Grant Robertson .20 .50
20 John Reid .20 .50
21 Dean Whyte .20 .50
22 Darren Gani .20 .50
23 Roger Robertson .20 .50
24 Gary Callaghan .20 .50
25 John Tamer .20 .50
26 Todd Hawkins .20 .50
27 Jim Andanoff .20 .50
28 Chris Rutledge TR .02 .10
29 Matt Taylor .20 .50
30 Mike Hartman .40 1.00
NNO Title Card .10 .01

2000-01 Belleville Bulls

This set features the Bulls of the OHL. The cards were produced by the team and sold at home games. The cards are instantly recognizable by virtue of having three colour headshots on the back.

COMPLETE SET (29) 4.80 15.00
1 Team Photo .10 .25
2 Paulo Colaiacovo .40 1.00
3 Nick Policelli .20 .50
4 Matt Coughlin .20 .50
5 Mike Jacobsen .20 .50
6 Malcolm Hutt .20 .50
7 Cody McCormick .20 .50
8 Mike Renzi .20 .50
9 Andrew Brown .20 .50
10 Andre Deveaux .20 .50
11 Matt Stajan .20 1.50
12 Alex White .20 .50
13 David Silverstone .20 .50
14 Randy Rowe .20 .50
15 Brad Efthimiou .20 .50
16 Dan Growden .20 .50
17 Adam Paiement .20 .50
18 Jan Chovan .30 .75
19 Branko Radivojevic .40 1.50
20 David Cornacchia .20 .50
21 Rob Dmytruk .20 .50
22 Nate Robinson .20 .50
23 Kyle Wellwood 1.00 2.50
24 In Action .08 .20
25 In Action .08 .20
26 In Action .08 .20
27 Jim Hulton CO .04 .10
28 Fan Pictures .01
29 Directory .01

2001-02 Belleville Bulls

This set features the Bulls of the OHL. The cards are slightly oversized, and were issued by the team. As they are unnumbered, they are listed below in alphabetical order.

COMPLETE SET (29) 4.80 12.00
1 Title card .04 .11
2 James Boyd ACO .04 .11
3 Andrew Brown .20 .50
4 Rane Carnegie .20 .50
5 Jan Chovan .31 .78
6 Paulo Colaiacovo .31 .78
7 Matt Coughlin .20 .50
8 Andre Deveaux .20 .50
9 Jake Gilmour .20 .50
10 Dan Growden .20 .50
11 Jim Hulton CO .20 .50
12 Malcolm Hutt .20 .50
13 Michael Knight .20 .50
14 Neill MacInnis .20 .50
15 Oliver Maron .20 .50
16 Cody McCormick .20 .50
17 Adam Paiement .20 .50
18 Marc Rancourt .20 .50
19 Michael Renzi .20 .50
20 Nathan Robinson .40 1.00
21 David Silverstone .20 .50
22 Matt Stajan .20 .50
23 Adam Sturgeon .20 .50
24 Kyle Wellwood .75 2.00
25 Alex White .20 .50
26 Celebration card .04 .11
27 Celebration card .04 .11
28 Michael Renzi .40 1.00
Matt Coughlin
Cody McCormick
Kyle Wellwood
29 Bullie Mascot .04 .11

2001-02 Belleville Bulls Update

This set features the Bulls of the OHL. The set was created late in the season simply to take advantage of the presence of hobby favorite Jason Spezza, who was traded to the Bulls from Windsor halfway through the season. The design is the same as that used for the main set issued earlier that season, but these cards are regulation sized. It is believed that as few as 500 of these sets were produced. The cards are unnumbered, so are listed below in alphabetical order.

COMPLETE SET (9) 4.00 10.00
1 David Clarkson .10 .25
2 Steve Cooke .10 .25
3 Michael Mole .40 1.00
4 Neil Smith .10 .25
5 Jason Spezza 1.20 3.00
6 Jason Spezza 1.20 3.00
7 Jason Spezza 1.20 3.00
8 Glenn Ridler .10 .25
9 Lubos Velebny .10 .25

2002-03 Belleville Bulls

COMPLETE SET (30) 6.00 15.00
1 Blake Allan .20 .50
2 Andrew Brown .20 .50
3 Rane Carnegie .20 .50
4 Steve Cooke .20 .50
5 Andre Deveaux .20 .50
6 Jake Gilmour .20 .50
7 Todd Griffith .20 .50
8 Malcolm Hutt .20 .50
9 Mike Knight .20 .50
10 Josh Manning .20 .50
11 Oliver Maron .20 .50
12 Cody McCormick .30 .75
13 Michael Mole .30 .75
14 Adam Paiment .20 .50
15 Marc Rancourt .20 .50
16 Neil Smith .20 .50
17 Matt Stajan .60 1.50
18 Ivan Svarny .20 .50
19 Cody Thornton .20 .50
20 Eric Tobia .30 .75
21 Darcy Tuplin .20 .50
22 Patrick Turcotte .20 .50
23 Jordon Watson .20 .50
24 Coaches .02 .10
25 Michael Mole .30 .75
Eric Tobia
26 Matt Stajan .60 1.50
27 Andre Deveaux .20 .50
28 Rookies .20 .50
29 Defencemen .02 .10
30 Team Captains .02 .10

2003-04 Belleville Bulls

Created by Extreme Sportscards, this 22-card set was sold a home games and by Cartes Timbres Ste-Foy. Cards are unnumbered and are listed below by jersey number.

COMPLETE SET (22) 5.00 10.00
1 Rane Carnegie .20 .50
2 Cody Thornton .20 .50
3 Matt Kelly .20 .50
4 Dan Rogers .20 .50
5 Marc Rancourt .20 .50
6 Eric Tobia .30 .75
7 Ryan Berard .20 .50
8 Josh Francis .20 .50
9 Andrew Brown .20 .50
10 Michael Knight .20 .50
11 Aaron Lewicki .20 .50
12 Geoff Patton .20 .50
13 Jake Gilmour .20 .50
14 Ivan Svarny .20 .50
15 Todd Griffith .20 .50
16 David Edgeworth .20 .50
17 Josh Manning .20 .50
18 Milan Hluchy .20 .50
19 Mike Roelofsen .20 .50
20 Shaun Clinton .20 .50
21 Andrew Brown TL .20 .50
22 Rane Carnegie TL .20 .50

2004-05 Belleville Bulls

A total of 400 team sets were produced.

COMPLETE SET (24) 5.00 12.00
1 Andrew Maksym .20 .50
2 Bobby Davey .20 .50
3 Cody Thornton .20 .50
4 Connor Cameron .20 .50
5 Jeff Leavitt .20 .50
6 Eric Tobia .20 .50
7 Evan Brophey .20 .50
8 Geoff Killing .20 .50
9 John Hughes .20 .50
10 Kevin Lalande .20 .50
11 Kyle Sonnenberg .20 .50
12 Lubomir Stach .20 .50
13 Mark Rancourt .20 .50
14 Marc Johnson .20 .50
15 Martin Novak .20 .50
16 Matt Beleskey .20 .50
17 Matt Kelly .20 .50
18 Pat Sutton .20 .50
19 Ryan Berard .20 .50
20 Ryan Roraback .20 .50
21 Scott Baker .20 .50
22 Shawn Matthias .40 1.00
23 Steve Spade .20 .50
NNO Marc Rancourt CAP .75 2.00

2005-06 Belleville Bulls

COMPLETE SET (24) 8.00 15.00
1 Matt Beleskey .30 .75
2 Ryan Roraback .30 .75
3 Sebastian Dahm .30 .75
4 Kyle Jukosky .30 .75
5 Matt Smyth .30 .75
6 P.K. Subban 2.00 5.00
7 Michael Neal .30 .75
8 Scott Baker .30 .75
9 Bryan Cameron .30 .75
10 Bobby Davey .30 .75
11 Bud Kelly .30 .75
12 Geoff Killing .30 .75
13 Nicholas Pageau .30 .75
14 John Hughes .30 .75
15 Bryan Cameron .30 .75
16 Steve Spade .30 .75
17 Kevin Lalande .30 .75
18 Ryan Berard .30 .75
19 Andrew Maksym .30 .75
20 Jeff Leavitt .30 .75
21 Shawn Matthias .40 1.00
22 Cory Tanaka .30 .75
23 Andrew Gibbons .30 .75
24 Andrew Self .30 .75

2006-07 Belleville Bulls

COMPLETE SET (23) 5.00 12.00
1 Matt Pelech .20 .50
2 Bryan Cameron .20 .50
3 Matt Beleskey .20 .50
4 Stephen Blunden .20 .50
5 Erik Caladi .20 .50
6 Tyler Donati .20 .50
7 Andrew Gibbons .20 .50
8 Jeff Leavitt .20 .50
9 Shawn Matthias .20 .50
10 Michael Neal .20 .50
11 Aaron Snow .20 .50
12 Cory Tanaka .20 .50
13 Eric Tangradi .20 .50
14 Matthew Tipoff .20 .50
15 Paul Cianfrini .20 .50
16 Geoff Killing .20 .50
17 Shawn Lalonde .20 .50
18 Nicholas Pageau .20 .50
19 P.K. Subban 1.00 2.50
20 Steven Whitely .20 .50
21 Kevin Lalande .20 .50
22 Mike Murphy .20 .50
LE2 Shawn Matthias 1.00 2.50

1981-82 Billings Bighorns

We've confirmed one single from this early WHL set to date and it is believed that many others exist as well, possibly including former first overall pick Gord Kluzak. Any additional information can be forwarded to hockeymag@beckett.com.

NNO Harry Mahood 4.00 10.00

1992-93 Binghamton Rangers

Issued by the team, these cards are printed on thin card stock. The cards themselves are not numbered, but numbers are assigned to each on the checklist card. The front is a full bleed photo with the player name appearing only on the back.

COMPLETE SET (24) 4.00 10.00
1 Team Card .15 .40
2 Mike Hurlbut .15 .40
3 Michael Stewart .15 .40
4 Craig Duncanson .15 .40
5 Rick Bennett .15 .40
6 Dave Thomlinson .15 .40
7 Mike Stevens .15 .40
8 Rob Kenny .15 .40
9 Chris Cichocki .15 .40
10 Sergei Zubov .40 1.00
11 Don Biggs .15 .40
12 Joby Messier .15 .40
13 Steven King .15 .40
14 Dave Archibald .15 .40
15 Brian McReynolds .15 .40
16 Dave Marcinyshyn .15 .40
17 Jean-Yves Roy .15 .40
18 Peter Fiorentino .15 .40
19 Daniel Lacroix .15 .40
20 Per Djoos .15 .40
21 Boris Rousson .30 .75
22 Corey Hirsch .30 .75
23 Rockey Ranger .08 .25
Mascot
24 Ranger Victory .15 .40

1994-95 Binghamton Rangers

This 22-card standard-size set was manufactured and distributed by Jessen Associates, Inc. for Classic. The fronts display color action player photos with a dark blue marbleized inner border and a black outer border. The player's name, jersey number, and position appear in the teal border on the right edge. Inside a black border on a marbleized background, the backs present biography, statistics, and sponsor logos. The cards are unnumbered and checklisted below in alphabetical order.

COMPLETE SET (22) 4.00 10.00
1 Eric Cairns .30 .75
2 Craig Duncanson .15 .40
3 Peter Fiorentino .15 .40
4 Ken Gernander .15 .40
5 Jim Hiller .15 .40
6 Corey Hirsch .30 .75
7 Rob Kenny .15 .40
8 Andrei Kudinov .15 .40
9 Darren Langdon .30 .75
10 Scott Malone .15 .40
11 Shawn McCosh .15 .40
12 Mike McLaughlin .15 .40
13 Joby Messier .15 .40
14 Jeff Nielsen .15 .40
15 Mattias Norstrom .30 .75
16 Jamie Ram .30 .75
17 Barry Richter .20 .50
18 Jean-Yves Roy .15 .40
19 Brad Rubachuk .15 .40
20 Dave Smith .15 .40
21 Dmitri Starostenko .15 .40
22 Michael Stewart .15 .40
23 Darcy Werenka .15 .40

1995-96 Binghamton Rangers

This 25-card set of the AHL Binghamton Rangers was manufactured and distributed by SplitSecond. The fronts feature color action player photos, while the backs carry player information. The cards are unnumbered and checklisted below in alphabetical order.

COMPLETE SET (25) 4.00 10.00
1 Sylvain Blouin .20 .50
2 George Burnett CO .02 .10
3 Mike Busniuk ACO .02 .10
4 Eric Cairns .30 .75
5 Chris Ferraro .30 .75
6 Peter Ferraro .40 1.00
7 Maxim Galanov .20 .50
8 Ken Gernander .20 .50
9 Brad Jones .15 .40
10 Pavel Komarov .15 .40
11 Andrei Kudinov .15 .40
12 Daniel Lacroix .20 .50
13 Steve Larouche .20 .50
14 Jon Hillebrandt .20 .50
15 Scott Malone .15 .40
16 Cal McGowan .15 .40
17 Jeff Nielsen .15 .40
18 Jamie Ram .20 .50
19 Shawn Reid .15 .40
20 Barry Richter .20 .50
21 Andy Silverman .15 .40
22 Lee Sorochan .20 .50
23 Dmitri Starostenko .15 .40
24 Ryan Vandenbussche .30 .75
25 Rick Willis .15 .40

1996-97 Binghamton Rangers

This 24-card set features the Binghamton Rangers of the AHL. The cards were produced by SplitSecond and distributed by the team. The cards feature an action photo on the front, along with player name, number and team logo. The backs feature limited stats. The unnumbered cards are listed below alphabetically.

COMPLETE SET (24) 4.00 10.00
1 Micah Aivazoff .20 .50
2 Sylvain Blouin .15 .40
3 George Burnett CO .02 .10
4 Mike Busniuk ACO .02 .10
5 Ed Campbell .15 .40
6 Dan Cloutier 1.00 2.50
7 Chris Ferraro .20 .50
8 Peter Ferraro .20 .50
9 Peter Fiorentino .15 .40
10 Eric Flinton .15 .40
11 Maxim Golanov .15 .40
12 Ken Gernander .15 .40
13 Mike Martin .15 .40
14 Bob Maudie .15 .40
15 Jeff Nielsen .15 .40
16 Rocky Raccoon .02 .10
17 Ken Shepard .15 .40
18 Andy Silverman .15 .40
19 Adam Smith .15 .40
20 Lee Sorochan .20 .50
21 Ryan VandenBussche .30 .75
22 Vladimir Vorobiev .15 .40
23 Rick Willis .15 .40
24 AHL Hockey Card .01

2003-04 Binghamton Senators

This set was sold by the team at home games.

COMPLETE SET (24) 6.00 15.00
1 Steve Bancroft .20 .50
2 Dennis Bonvie .40 1.00
3 Daniel Corso .20 .50
4 Ray Emery .40 1.00
5 Alexandre Giroux .20 .50
6 Denis Hamel .40 1.00
7 Andy Hedlund .20 .50
8 Jody Hull .20 .50
9 David Hymovitz .20 .50
10 Chris Kelly .40 1.00
11 Brooks Laich .20 .50
12 Josh Langfeld .20 .50
13 Chris Leinweber .20 .50
14 Brian McGrattan .40 1.00
15 Serge Payer .20 .50
16 Jan Platil .20 .50
17 Christoph Schubert .20 .50
18 Peter Smrek .20 .50
19 Billy Thompson .40 1.00
20 Tony Tuzzolino .20 .50
21 Julien Vauclair .20 .50
22 Antoine Vermette .40 1.00
23 Greg Watson .20 .50
24 Mascot .02 .10

2003-04 Binghamton Senators Postcards

According to minor league expert Ralph Slate, these cards were issued as a promotional giveaway. A single card was given out each week that a fan bought a newspaper at a Quickway gas station. The cards are numbered on the front, card x of 12, and a bonus 13th card exists of the mascot.

COMPLETE SET (13) 15.00 30.00
1 Chris Kelly 1.25 3.00
2 Josh Langfeld .75 2.00
3 Julien Vauclair .75 2.00
4 Daniel Corso .75 2.00
5 Dennis Bonvie 1.25 3.00
6 David Hymovitz .75 2.00
7 Brooks Laich .75 2.00
8 Brian McGrattan 1.25 3.00
9 Alexandre Giroux .75 2.00
10 Denis Hamel 1.25 3.00
11 Antoine Vermette 1.25 3.00
12 Ray Emery 1.50 4.00
NNO Mascot .75 2.00

2004-05 Binghamton Senators

COMPLETE SET (26) 6.00 15.00
1 Brandon Bochenski .30 .75
2 Danny Bois .20 .50
3 Ray Emery .40 1.00
4 Jesse Fibiger .20 .50
5 Denis Hamel .40 1.00
6 Andy Hedlund .20 .50
7 Pat Kavanagh .20 .50
8 Chris Kelly .30 .75
9 Neil Komadoski .20 .50
10 Josh Langfeld .20 .50
11 Brian McGrattan .40 1.00
12 Arpad Mihaly .20 .50
13 Jan Platil .20 .50
14 Brian Pothier .20 .50
15 Grant Potulny .20 .50
16 Christoph Schubert .20 .50
17 Jason Spezza .50 2.00
18 Charlie Stephens .20 .50
19 Billy Thompson .30 .75
20 Antoine Vermette .30 .75
21 Anton Volchenkov .20 .50
22 Greg Watson .20 .50
23 David Cameron CO .02 .10
24 John Paddock CO .02 .10
25 Mike Busniuk ACO .02 .10
26 Max MASCOT .02 .10

2004-05 Binghamton Senators Hess

Given away one at a time at local gas stations with the purchase of a newspaper. They measure approximately 3 7/8 by 4 7/8.

COMPLETE SET (14) 20.00 35.00
1 Chris Kelly 1.25 3.00
2 Denis Hamel 1.50 4.00
3 Brian Pothier .75 2.00
4 Christoph Schubert .75 2.00
5 Pat Kavanagh .75 2.00
6 Antoine Vermette 1.25 3.00
7 Brandon Bochenski 1.25 3.00
8 Andy Hedlund .75 2.00
9 Brian McGrattan 1.25 3.00
10 Josh Langfeld .75 2.00
11 Anton Volchenkov .75 2.00
12 Jason Spezza 5.00 10.00
13 Ray Emery 1.50 4.00
NNO Cover card .10 .25

2005-06 Binghamton Senators

COMPLETE SET (22) 10.00 25.00
1 Denis Hamel .75 2.00
2 Danny Bois .40 1.00
3 Jeff Heerema .40 1.00
4 Unknown
5 Jan Platil .40 1.00
6 Charlie Stephens .40 1.00
7 Steve Martins .40 1.00
8 Brad Norton .40 1.00
9 Filip Novak .40 1.00
10 Billy Thompson .75 2.00
11 Grant Potulny .40 1.00
12 Patrick Eaves 1.25 3.00
13 Brett Clouthier .40 1.00
14 Tomas Malec .40 1.00
15 Kelly Guard .75 2.00
16 Neil Petruic .40 1.00
17 Brandon Bochenski .75 2.00
18 Brennan Evans .40 1.00
19 Gregg Johnson .40 1.00
20 Jeff Glass .75 2.00
21 Lance Ward .40 1.00
22 Sponsor Card .02 .10
23 Joe Cullen
24 Neil Komadoski
25 Billy Thompson
26 Greg Watson
27 Max The Mascot
28 Dave Cameron
29 Mike Busniuk
30 Domenic Nicoletta
31 Tom Severance

2005-06 Binghamton Senators Quickway

COMPLETE SET (22) 10.00 25.00
1 Denis Hamel .40 1.00
2 Danny Bois .40 1.00
3 Jeff Heerema .40 1.00
4 Joe Cullen .40 1.00
5 Jan Platil .40 1.00
6 Charlie Stephens .40 1.00
7 Steve Martins .40 1.00
8 Brad Norton .40 1.00
9 Filip Novak .40 1.00
10 Billy Thompson .75 2.00
11 Grant Potulny .40 1.00
12 Patrick Eaves 1.25 3.00
13 Brett Clouthier .40 1.00
14 Tomas Malec .40 1.00
15 Kelly Guard .75 2.00
16 Neil Petruic .40 1.00
17 Brandon Bochenski .75 2.00
18 Brennan Evans .40 1.00
19 Gregg Johnson .40 1.00
20 Jeff Glass .75 2.00
21 Lance Ward .40 1.00

2006-07 Binghamton Senators

1 Jamie Allison .30 .75
2 Michal Barinka .30 .75
3 Danny Bois .30 .75
4 Charlie Cook .30 .75
5 Andrew Ebbett .30 .75
6 Chanse Fitzpatrick .30 .75
7 Jeff Glass .60 1.50
8 Kelly Guard .60 1.50
9 Andy Hedlund .30 .75
10 Jeff Heerema .30 .75
11 Josh Hennessy .60 1.50
12 Neil Komadoski .30 .75
13 Arttu Luttinen .30 .75
14 Tomas Malec .30 .75
15 Brian Maloney .30 .75
16 Serge Payer .30 .75
17 Cory Pecker .30 .75
18 Neil Petruic .30 .75
19 Grant Potulny .30 .75
20 Bobby Robins .30 .75
21 Ryan Vesce .30 .75
22 Mike Busniuk .30 .75
23 Dave Cameron CO .10 .25
24 Dom Nicoletta TR .02 .10
25 Tom Severance EQ .02 .10
26 Grady Whittenburg ANN .02 .10
27 Maximus MASCOT .02 .10

2006-07 Binghamton Senators 5th Anniversary

COMPLETE SET (35) 10.00 25.00
1 Steve Bancroft .30 .75
2 Cody Bass .30 .75
3 Brandon Bochenski .60 1.50
4 Danny Bois .30 .75
5 Dennis Bonvie .60 1.50
6 Patrick Eaves .60 1.50
7 Ray Emery .60 1.50
8 Alexandre Giroux .30 .75
9 Jeff Glass .40 1.00
10 Kelly Guard .40 1.00
11 Denis Hamel .40 1.00
12 Andy Hedlund .30 .75
13 Jeff Heerema .30 .75
14 David Hymovitz .30 .75
15 Chris Kelly .30 .75
16 Josh Langfeld .30 .75
17 Steve Martins .30 .75
18 Brian McGrattan .60 1.50
19 Joe Murphy .30 .75
20 Filip Novak .30 .75
21 Serge Payer .30 .75
22 Cory Pecker .30 .75
23 Jan Platil .30 .75
24 Brian Pothier .30 .75
25 Grant Potulny .30 .75
26 Bobby Robins .30 .75
27 Christoph Schubert .30 .75
28 Brad Smyth .30 .75
29 Jason Spezza .75 2.00
30 Charlie Stephens .30 .75
31 Billy Thompson .30 .75
32 Julien Vauclair .30 .75
33 Antoine Vermette .40 1.00
34 Anton Volchenkov .40 1.00
35 Max MASCOT .02 .10

2007-08 Binghamton Senators

COMPLETE SET (30) 10.00 20.00
1 Greg Amadio .30 .75
2 Cody Bass .30 .75
3 Danny Bois .30 .75
4 Matt Carkner .30 .75
5 Niko Dimitrakos .30 .75
6 Tyler Donati .30 .75
7 Brian Elliott .40 1.00
8 Ray Emery .40 1.00
9 Nick Foligno .40 1.00
10 Jeff Glass .40 1.00
11 Denis Hamel .30 .75
12 Josh Hennessy .30 .75
13 Matt Kinch .30 .75
14 Tomas Kudelka .30 .75
15 Brian Lee .60 1.50
16 Justin Mapletoft .30 .75
17 Greg Mauldin .30 .75
18 Scott May .30 .75
19 Alexander Nikulin .30 .75
20 Lawrence Nycholat .30 .75
21 Derek Smith .30 .75
22 Geoff Waugh .30 .75
23 Shawn Weller .40 1.00
24 Jeremy Yablonski .40 1.00
25 Ilya Zubov .40 1.00
26 Cory Clouston HC .02 .10
27 Mike Busniuk AC .02 .10
28 Tom Severance EQ .02 .10
29 Domenic Nicoletta TR .02 .10
NNO Max MASCOT/Checklist .02 .10

1992-93 Birmingham Bulls

The cards are larger than the standard size, and are numbered on the back. The set is sponsored by Fox-21, Coca-Cola and radio station WJOX-FM.

COMPLETE SET (23) 3.00 8.00
1 Logo Card .02 .10
2 Jim Larkin .15 .40
3 Brett Barnett .15 .40
4 Joe Flanagan .15 .40
5 Butch Kaebel .15 .40
6 Scott Matusovich .15 .40
7 Chuck Hughes .15 .40
8 Dave Craievich .15 .40
9 Alexander Khavanov .15 .40
10 Paul Marshall .15 .40
11 Jim Peters .15 .40
12 Chris Marshall .15 .40
13 Jerome Bechard .15 .40
14 Jean-Alain Schneider .15 .40
15 Kevin Kerr .15 .40
16 Rob Krauss .15 .40
17 Greg Burke .15 .40
18 Mark Romaine .15 .40
19 Bruce Garber CO .02 .10
20 Phil Roberto ACO .08 .25
21 Dave Cavaliere TR .02 .10
22 Tim Woodburn ANN .02 .10
NNO Team Logo/ CL .02 .10

1993-94 Birmingham Bulls

Sponsored by Coca-Cola, Fox 21 TV and WJOX AM 690, this 23-card set measures approximately 2 5/8" by 3 5/8" and features the 1993-94 Birmingham Bulls of the East Coast Hockey League. On a white card face, the fronts have posed color player photos. The team name and logo are printed above the photo, while the player's name, his position and sponsor logos appear below the picture. The horizontal backs carry player biography, profile and sponsor logos.

COMPLETE SET (23) 4.00 10.00
1 Logo Card .02 .10
2 Jim Larkin .20 .50
3 Brett Barnett .20 .50
4 Joe Flanagan .20 .50
5 Butch Kaebel .20 .50
6 Scott Matusovich .20 .50
7 Chuck E. Hughes .20 .50
8 Dave Craievich .20 .50
9 Alexander Khavanov .75 2.00
10 Paul Marshall .20 .50
11 Jim Peters .20 .50
12 Chris Marshall .20 .50
13 Jerome Bechard .20 .50
14 Jean-Alain Schneider .20 .50
15 Kevin Kerr .20 .50
16 Rob Krauss .20 .50
17 Greg Burke .20 .50
18 Mark Romaine .20 .50
19 Bruce Garber CO .02 .10
20 Phil Roberto ACO .02 .10
21 Dave Cavaliere TR .02 .10
22 Tim Woodburn ANN .02 .10
NNO Title Card CL .02 .10

1993-94 Birmingham Bulls Birmingham News

This set features the Bulls of the ECHL. It is believed that these were offered as a promotional giveaway. Unlike the other issue available this season, the cards feature an image of the Birmingham News on the front and back.

COMPLETE SET (27) 4.80 12.00
1 Phil Roberto CO .07 .20
2 Phil Roberto CO .07 .20
3 Jerome Bechard .20 .50
4 Marc Beran .20 .50
5 Dave Craievich .20 .50
6 Murray Duval .20 .50
7 Dan Fournel .30 .75
8 Jon Duval .20 .50
9 Joe Flanagan .20 .50
10 Todd Harris .20 .50
11 Bill Kovacs .20 .50
12 Jim Larkin .20 .50
13 Paul Marshall .20 .50
14 Jim Mill .30 .75
15 Brad Mullahy .20 .50
16 Tom Neziol .20 .50
17 Darcy Norton .20 .50
18 Jay Schiavo .20 .50
19 J.A. Schneider .20 .50
20 Brad Smyth .30 .75
21 Rick Girhiny .20 .50
22 Sandy Galuppo .20 .50
23 Jamie Linden .30 .75
24 Ed Krayer ACO .02 .10
25 Joel Stern ANN .02 .10
26 Mark Mills EQM .02 .10
27 Header Card/CL .02 .10

1994-95 Birmingham Bulls

Sponsored by Chevron, WBMG 45, and The New Mix 94.5 FM, this 22-card set measures approximately 2 3/4" by 3 3/4" and features the 1994-95 Birmingham Bulls of the ECHL. On a white card face, the fronts have posed color player photos. The cards are unnumbered and checklisted below in alphabetical order.

COMPLETE SET (22) 3.00 8.00
1 Greg Bailey .15 .40
2 Norm Bazin .15 .40
3 Jerome Bechard .15 .40
4 Dave Boyd .15 .40
5 David Craievich .15 .40

6 Rob Donovan .15 .40
7 Jon Duval .15 .40
8 Sandy Galuppo .20 .50
9 Todd Harris .15 .40
10 Ian Hebert .15 .40
11 Craig Johnson .15 .40
12 John Joyce .15 .40
13 Chris Kerber ANN .02 .10
14 Olaf Kjenstad .20 .50
15 Mike Krassner EQMG .02 .10
16 Jim Larkin .15 .40
17 Craig Lutes .15 .40
18 Mark Michaud .15 .40
19 Jean-Marc Plante .15 .40
20 Phil Roberto CO .15 .40
21 Brad Smyth .15 .40
22 Title Card CL .02 .10

1995-96 Birmingham Bulls

This odd-sized (2 3/4" by 3 3/4") 29-card set features the Birmingham Bulls of the ECHL. The cards feature an action shot along with the team logo and player name on the front. The unnumbered backs contain player stats and sponsor logos. The set also contains a 6-card subset of WJOX DJs. The set was available through the team; apparently, no mail order was available.

COMPLETE SET (29) 4.00 10.00
1 Toro the Bull .02 .10
2 Phil Roberto CO .08 .25
3 Lance Brady .20 .50
4 Jeff Wells .20 .50
5 Brad Prefontaine .20 .50
6 Mark Raiter .20 .50
7 Rob Donovan .20 .50
8 Chris Grenville .20 .50
9 Colin Gregor .20 .50
10 Mike Latendresse .30 .75
11 John Morabito .20 .50
12 Brendan Creagh .20 .50
13 Chris Bergeron .20 .50
14 Jerome Bechard .20 .50
15 Craig Lutes .20 .50
16 Ian Hebert .20 .50
17 John Joyce .20 .50
18 Jeff Callinan .20 .50
19 Jason Dexter .20 .50
20 Olaf Kjenstad .20 .50
21 Chad Erickson .30 .75
22 Ray Pack EQMG .02 .10
23 Chris Kerber ANN .02 .10
24 M.Coulter/S.Griffi DJs .02 .10
25 Doug Laxton DJ .02 .10
26 Randy Armstrong DJ .02 .10
27 Lee Davis DJ .02 .10
28 Herb Winches DJ .02 .10
29 Ben Cook DJ .02 .10

1982-83 Birmingham South Stars

This set is believed to have been issued in the form of perforated program pull-outs. It is not known if this checklist is complete.

COMPLETE SET (16) 24.00 60.00
1 Frank Beaton 1.25 3.00
2 Bob Bergloff 1.25 3.00
3 Bob Boileau 1.25 3.00
4 Rollie Boutin 1.25 3.00
5 Murray Brumwell 1.25 3.00
6 Steve Carlson 8.00 20.00
7 Dave Debol .75 2.00
8 Jim Dobson .75 2.00
9 Dave Richter 1.25 3.00
10 Keith Hanson .75 2.00
11 Peter Hayek .75 2.00
12 Glenn Hicks .75 2.00
13 Craig Homola .75 2.00
14 Wes Jarvis 1.25 3.00
15 Warren Young 2.00 5.00
16 Markus Mattsson 1.25 3.00

2006-07 Bloomington PrairieThunder

COMPLETE SET (24) 8.00 15.00
1 Mike Adamek .30 .75
2 Trevor Baker .30 .75
3 Jon Booras .30 .75
4 Jarad Bourassa .30 .75
5 Steffan Braunlich .30 .75
6 John Spoltore .30 .75
7 Mike Zbriger .30 .75
8 B.J. Gaustad .30 .75
9 Ryan Gillis .30 .75
10 Alex Goupil .30 .75
11 Dion Hyman .30 .75
12 Andrew Lackner .30 .75
13 Andre Niec .30 .75
14 Jason Payne .30 .75
15 Mark Phenow .30 .75
16 Tyler Rennette .30 .75
17 Jeff Reynaert .30 .75
18 Shawn Roed .30 .75
19 Tim Schneider .30 .75
20 Chip MASCOT .02 .10
21 Brad Thompson .30 .75
22 Derek Booth CO .10 .25
23 Clay Roffer EQ MGR .02 .10
24 Chris Walter TR .02 .10

2001-02 Bossier-Shreveport Mudbugs

This set features the Mudbugs of the WPHL. The set was sold by the team at home games. The cards are unnumbered, so they are listed in alphabetical order.

COMPLETE SET (24) 4.00 10.00
1 Tony Bergin .20 .50
2 Trevor Buchanah .20 .50
3 Jason Campbell .20 .50
4 Bob Case TR .04 .11
5 Greg Foster .20 .50
6 Tim Hill .20 .50
7 Mike Johnson .20 .50
8 Derek Kups .20 .50
9 Bill Lang .20 .50
10 Chad Lang .31 .78
11 Dave Lemay .20 .50
12 Forbes MacPherson .20 .50
13 David Mills .20 .50
14 Scott Muscutt CO .04 .11
15 Pat Powers .20 .50
16 Ryan Rintoul .20 .50
17 Mark Rupnow .20 .50
18 Corey Smith .20 .50
19 Jim Sprott .20 .50
20 Brandon Walker BR .04 .11
21 Billy Welker EQMG .04 .11
22 Dan Wildfong .20 .50
23 Clawed MASCOT .04 .11
24 Team Photo .10 .25

2002-03 Bossier-Shreveport Mudbugs

COMPLETE SET (24) 6.00 15.00
1 Jason Basile .30 .75
2 Tony Bergin .30 .75
3 Chris Brassard .30 .75
4 Trevor Buchanan .30 .75
5 Dru Burgess .30 .75
6 Jason Campbell .30 .75
7 Ken Carroll .30 .75
8 Chris Chelios .30 .75
9 Jonathan Forest .30 .75
10 Jeff Glowa .30 .75
11 Willie Hubloo .30 .75
12 Forbes MacPherson .30 .75
13 Craig Minard .30 .75
14 David Oliver .30 .75
15 Mark Rupnow .30 .75
16 Jim Sprott .30 .75
17 Chad Spurr .30 .75
18 Luc Theoret .30 .75
19 Dan Wildfong .30 .75
20 Scott Muscutt CO .02 .10
21 Billy Welker EQM .02 .10
21 George Bullock Jr. TR .02 .10
23 Team Photo .20 .50
24 Steve Mears ANN .02 .10

2003-04 Bossier-Shreveport Mudbugs

COMPLETE SET (25) 6.00 15.00
1 Jason Basile .30 1.00
2 Travis Bell .30 .75
3 Jeff Blair .30 .75
4 Wes Blevins .30 .75
5 Chris Brassard .30 .75
6 Trevor Buchanan .30 .75
7 Jason Campbell .30 .75
8 Ken Carroll .30 .75
9 Colin Kendall .30 .75
10 Quade Lightbody .40 1.00
11 Forbes MacPherson .30 .75
12 Ryan Manitowich .30 .75
13 Craig Minard .40 1.00
14 David Oliver .30 .75
15 Craig Soke .30 .75
16 Jim Sprott .30 .75
17 Chad Spurr .30 .75
18 Dan Wildfong .30 .75
19 Scott Muscutt CO .02 .10
20 John Madden OWN .02 .10
21 George Bullock Jr. TR .02 .10
22 Billy Welker EQM .02 .10
23 Mascot .02 .10
24 Team photo .20 .50
25 Steve Mears ANN .02 .10

2005-06 Bossier-Shreveport Mudbugs

COMPLETE SET (26) 6.00 15.00
1 Jason Basile .30 .75
2 Chris Brassard .30 .75
3 David Cacciola .30 .75
4 Jason Campbell .30 .75
5 Ken Carroll .30 .75
6 Jeremy Downs .30 .75
7 Chad Kemp .30 .75
8 Quade Lightbody .40 1.00
9 Dale Lupul .30 .75
10 Ryan Manitowich .30 .75
11 Blair Manning .30 .75
12 Craig Minard .30 .75
13 Shane Palahicky .30 .75
14 Chris Shaw .30 .75
15 Scott Sheppard .30 .75
16 Brett Smith .30 .75
17 Chad Spurr .30 .75
18 Martin Stuchlik .30 .75
19 Milan Vodrazka .30 .75
20 Dan Wildfong .30 .75
21 Scott Muscutt HC .02 .10
22 Trevor Buchanan AC .02 .10
23 Billy Welker EM .02 .10
24 Clawed & Lil' Bugger MASCOTS .02 .10
25 George Bullock Jr. TR .02 .10
26 Steve Mears ANNCR .02 .10

2003-04 Boston College Eagles

This set was issued as a promotional giveaway at a home game. It comes in a perforated strip and features the Eagles' six graduating seniors and a team photo.

COMPLETE SET (7) 5.00 10.00
1 Ben Eaves .75 2.00
2 Tony Voce .75 2.00
3 Brett Peterson .75 2.00
4 Ty Hennes .75 2.00
5 J.D. Forrest .75 2.00
6 Justin Dziama .75 2.00
7 Team Photo .40 1.00

2003-04 Boston University Terriers

This set was issued as a promotional giveaway at a late-season home game.

COMPLETE SET (27) 25.00
1 Mark Mullen 1.00
2 Stephen Siwiec 1.00
3 Gregg Johnson 1.00
4 John Laliberte 1.00
5 Thomas Morrow 1.00
6 Jack Parker HCO 1.00
7 Stephen Greeley 1.00
8 Brian McConnell 1.00
9 E.J. Solimine 1.00
10 Sean Fields 1.00
11 Bryan Miller 1.00
12 Jakabs Redlihs 1.00
13 Kevin Schaeffer 1.00
14 Brad Zancanaro 1.00
15 Sean Sullivan 1.00
16 Ryan Whitney 3.00
17 David Van Der Gulik 1.00
18 Eric Thomassian 1.00
19 Ken Roche 1.00
20 David Klema 1.00
21 Dan Spang 1.00
22 Ken Magowan 1.00
23 Matt Radoslovich 1.00
24 Harry Agganis Arena .10
25 John Curry 1.00
26 Frantisek Skladany 1.50
27 Mascot .10

2003-04 Bowling Green Falcons

This 18-card set was issued in two series of 9 cards each. Cards in each series were issued on perforated sheets and feature current and former players. Series 1 9cards 1-9) were limited to 2000 sheets while Series 2 was limited to 1000. Both sets were sponsored by the Sentinel Tribune.

COMPLETE SET (18) 35.00
1 Brian Holzinger 2.00
2 Brian Escobedo 1.00
3 Alex Rogosheske 1.00
4 George McPhee 1.00
5 Garry Galley 2.00
6 D'Arcy McConvey 1.00
7 Rob Blake 5.00
8 Mark Wires 1.00
9 Jordan Sigalet 10.00
10 Steve Brudzewski 2.00
11 Erik Eaton 2.00
12 Dan Kane 2.00
13 Gary Kruzich 2.00
14 Dave Ellet 2.00
15 Kevin Bieksa 2.00
16 Ryan Minnabarriet 2.00
17 Gino Cavallini 2.00
18 John Samanski 2.00

1999-00 Brampton Battalion

This set pictures the second-year Brampton Battalions of the Ontario Hockey League. The set was available at the team's rink, and through the mail from sponsor Frozen Pond, a Toronto-based memorabilia dealer. The set is highlighted by 2000 NHL Entry Draft first rounders Raffi Torres and Rostislav Klesla. It also includes a card of 2001 second overall pick Jason Spezza, who played with the team during its inaugural season of 1998-99.

COMPLETE SET (27) 10.00 25.00
1 Header Card .02 .10
2 Team Photo .08 .25
3 David Chant .60 1.50
4 Scott Della Vedova .08 .25
5 Tyler Hanchuck .08 .25
6 Jason Maleyko .08 .25
7 Paul Flache .08 .25
8 Cam McLaughlin .08 .25
9 Rostislav Klesla .60 1.50
10 Brad Woods .08 .25
11 Raffi Torres .75 2.00
12 Matt Reynolds .08 .25
13 Chris Rowan .08 .25
14 Lukas Havel .08 .25
15 Mike Rice .08 .25
16 Tyler Dukelow .08 .25
17 Jay McClement .20 .50
18 Matt Grennier .08 .25
19 Kurt MacSweyn .08 .25
21 Aaron Van Leusen .08 .25
21 Chris Cook .08 .25
22 Jay Harrison .40 1.00
23 Richard Kearns .08 .25
24 Jeff Bateman .20 .50
25 Scott Thompson .08 .25
26 Blair McLaughlin .08 .25
27 Jason Spezza 4.00 10.00
28 Stan Butler CO .08 .25
29 Bobby Jones .08 .25
30 Raffi Torres .75 2.00
31 Jason Maleyko .08 .25
32 Inaugural Season .02 .10

2000-01 Brampton Battalion

COMPLETE SET (32) 6.00 15.00
1 Logo .02 .10
2 Team Picture .02 .10
3 2001 WJC Banner .02 .10
4 Brian Finley .30 .75
5 •Travis Parent .20 .50
6 Jason Maleyko .20 .50
7 Paul Flache .20 .50
8 Corey LeClair .20 .50
9 Rostislav Klesla .60 1.50
10 Adam Henrich .20 .50
11 Raffi Torres .60 1.50
12 Chris Clayton .20 .50
13 Chris Rowan .20 .50
14 Lukas Havel .20 .50
15 Jonah Leroux .20 .50
16 Jay McClement .20 .50
17 Kurt MacSweyn .20 .50
18 Aaron Van Leusen .20 .50
19 Jay Harrison .30 .75
20 Ryan Bowness .20 .50
21 Jeff Bateman .20 .50
22 Scott Thompson .20 .50
23 Alex MacDonell .20 .50
24 Anthony Marshall .20 .50
25 Brad Topping .20 .50
26 Stan Butler HCO .02 .10
27 Derrick Smith ACO .02 .10
28 Rostislav Klesla .60 1.50
All-Star
29 Raffi Torres .60 1.50
All-Star
30 Jay Harrison .30 .75
1998 First Round
31 Jay McClement .20 .50
1999 First Round
32 Adam Henrich .20 .50
2000 First Round

2003-04 Brampton Batallion

The Kreps card was randomly inserted among the team sets.

COMPLETE SET (24) 12.00
1 Ryan Bowness .50
2 Chris Clayton .50
3 Kevin Couture .75
4 Nick Duff .50
5 Jamie Fraser .50
6 Tyler Harrison .50
7 Robert Heickert .50
8 Adam Henrich .50
9 Kamil Kreps 1.50
10 Aaron Lobb .50
11 Martin Lojek .50
12 Howie Martin .50
13 Eliott McCormick .50
14 Brock McPherson .50
15 Geordie Michie .50
16 Phil Oreskovic .50
17 Ryan Oulahen .50
18 Erik Schwanz .50
19 John Seymour .50
20 Stuart Simmons .50
21 Rob Smith .50
22 Patrick Sweeney .50
23 Brad Topping .75
24 Wojtek Wolski 1.50
NNO Kamil Kreps LTD

2004-05 Brampton Battalion

A total of 300 team sets were produced.

COMPLETE SET (25) 12.00
1 Wojtek Wolski 1.50
2 Daren Machesney .50
3 Kevin Couture .50
4 Michael Vernace .50
5 Stuart Simmons .50
6 Phil Oreskovic .75
7 Nick Duff .50
8 Martin Lojek .50
9 Tomas Strycnl .50
10 Danny McDonald .50
11 Aaron Snow .50
12 Brock McPherson .50
13 John de Gray .50
14 Howie Martin .50
15 Luke Lynes .50
16 Graham McNabb .50
17 Luch Aquino .50
18 John Seymour .50
19 Patrick Sweeney .50
20 Tyler Harrison .50
21 J.F. Houle .50
22 Scott Boomsma .50
23 Jason Cassidy .50
24 Ryan Oulahen .50
25 Kyle Sonnenberg .50

2005-06 Brampton Battalion

COMPLETE SET (25) 5.00 12.00
1 Wojtek Wolski .60 1.50
2 Phil Oreskovic .20 .50
3 Nick Duff .20 .50
4 John de Gray .20 .50
5 Daren Machesney .20 .50
6 Bryan Pitton .20 .50
7 Michael Vernace .20 .50
8 Tomas Strycnl .20 .50
9 Stephane Chabot .20 .50
10 Aaron Snow .20 .50
11 Matt Smyth .20 .50
12 Howie Martin .20 .50
13 Luke Lynes .20 .50
14 Graham McNabb .20 .50
15 Justin Levac .20 .50
16 Luch Aquino .20 .50
17 John Seymour .20 .50
18 Nolan Waker .20 .50
19 Taylor Raszka .20 .50
20 Cody Smith .20 .50
21 Jason Cassidy .20 .50
22 Michal Kljna .20 .50
23 Kyle Sonnenburg .20 .50
24 Corey George .20 .50
25 Brock McPherson .20 .50

2006-07 Brampton Battalion

1 Sarge's Checklist .02 .10
2 Patrick Killeen .30 .75
3 Bryan Pitton .30 .75
4 Ken Peroff .30 .75
5 Dalyn Flatt .30 .75
6 Brad Albert .30 .75
7 Tomas Strycnl .30 .75
8 Stephane Chabot .30 .75
9 John De Gray .30 .75
10 Kyle Sonnenburg .30 .75
11 Conor O'Donnell .30 .75
12 Matt Smyth .30 .75
13 Thomas Stajan .30 .75
14 Luke Lynes .30 .75
15 Graham McNabb .30 .75
16 Jason Dale .30 .75
17 Justin Levac .30 .75
18 Cody Hodgson .30 .75
19 John Seymour .30 .75
20 Mike Lomas .30 .75
21 John Hughes .30 .75
22 Kyle Decoste .30 .75
23 Michal Klejna .30 .75

1982-83 Brandon Wheat Kings

This 24-card set measures approximately 2 1/4" by 4" and features posed color player photos with thin yellow borders on a white card face. The player's name appears on the picture at the bottom. The backs carry P.L.A.Y. (Police, Laws and Youth) Tips From The Kings, which consist of a hockey term and relates it to a real life situation. Sponsor logos appear on the lower portion of the back.

COMPLETE SET (24) 12.00 30.00
1 Wheat Kings Logo .20 .50
2 Kevin Pylypow .30 .75
3 Dean Kennedy .40 1.00
4 Sonny Sodke .30 .75
5 Darren Schmidt .30 .75
6 Cam Plante .30 .75
7 Sid Cranston .30 .75
8 Bruce Thomson .30 .75
9 Dave McDowall CO .20 .50
10 Bill Vince .30 .75
11 Kelly Glowa .30 .75
12 Tom McMurchy .30 .75
13 Ed Palichuk .30 .75
14 Roy Caswell .30 .75
15 Allan Tarasuk .30 .75
16 Brent Jessiman .30 .75
17 Randy Slawson .30 .75
18 Gord Smith .30 .75
19 Mike Sturgeon .30 .75
20 Larry Bumstead .30 .75
21 Kirk Blomquist .30 .75
22 Ron Loustel .30 .75
23 Ron Hextall 6.00 15.00
24 Brandon Police Logo .08 .25

1983-84 Brandon Wheat Kings

This 24-card set measures approximately 2 1/4" by 4" and features color posed action player photos with thin yellow borders on a white card face. The player's name is printed on the picture at the bottom. The backs carry P.L.A.Y. (Police, Laws and Youth) Tips From The Kings. Sponsor logos appear in the lower portion of the card.

COMPLETE SET (24) 10.00 25.00
1 Bryan Wells .20 .50
2 Jim Agnew .40 1.00
3 Gord Paddock .20 .50
4 John Dzikowski .20 .50
5 Kelly Kozack .20 .50
6 Byron Lomow .20 .50
7 Pat Loyer .20 .50
8 Rob Ordman .20 .50
9 Brad Wells .20 .50
10 Dave Thomlinson .30 .75
11 Cam Plante .20 .50
12 Jay Palmer .30 .75
13 Boyd Lomow .20 .50
14 Brent Jessiman .20 .50
15 Paul More .20 .50
16 Stacy Pritt .20 .50
17 Brandon City Police .08 .25
18 Jack Sangster CO .20 .50
19 Derek Laxdal .30 .75
20 Ray Ferraro 2.00 5.00
21 Allan Tarasuk .20 .50
22 Randy Cameron .20 .50
23 Dave Curry .20 .50
24 Ron Hextall 4.00 10.00

1984-85 Brandon Wheat Kings

This 24-card set measures approximately 2 1/4" by 4" and features color posed action player photos with thin yellow borders on a white card face. The player's name is printed on the picture at the bottom. The backs carry P.L.A.Y. (Police, Laws and Youth) Tips From The Kings. Sponsor logos appear on the lower portion of the card.

COMPLETE SET (24) 4.80 12.00
1 Garnet Kazuik .20 .50
2 Brent Mireau .20 .50
3 Byron Lomow .20 .50
4 Dean Shaw .20 .50
5 Dean Sexsmith .20 .50
6 Brad Mueller .20 .50
7 John Dzikowski .20 .50
8 Artie Feher .20 .50
9 Pat Loyer .20 .50
10 Murray Rice .20 .50
11 Derek Laxdal .30 .75
12 Perry Fafard .20 .50
13 Lee Trim .20 .50
14 Dan Hart .20 .50
15 Trent Ciprick .20 .50
16 Jeff Waver .20 .50
17 Brandon City Police .20 .50
18 Jack Sangster CO .08 .25
19 Darwin McPherson .20 .50
20 Pokey Reddick .75 2.00
21 Boyd Lomow .20 .50
22 Dave Thomlinson .30 .75
23 Paul More .20 .50
24 Brent Severyn .40 1.00

1985-86 Brandon Wheat Kings

This 24-card set measures approximately 2 1/4" by 4" and features color posed action player photos with thin yellow borders on a white card face. The player's name is printed on the picture at the bottom. The backs carry P.L.A.Y. (Police, Laws and Youth) Tips From The Kings. Sponsor logos appear in the lower portion of the card.

COMPLETE SET (24) 4.80 12.00
1 Kelly Hitchins .20 .50
2 Brent Mireau .20 .50
3 Byron Lomow .20 .50
4 Bob Heeney .20 .50
5 Dean Sexsmith .20 .50
6 Dave Curry .20 .50
7 John Dzikowski .20 .50
8 Artie Feher .20 .50
9 Kevin Mayo .20 .50
10 Murray Rice .20 .50
11 Derek Laxdal .40 1.00
12 Al Cherniwchan .20 .50
13 Lee Trim .20 .50
14 Terry Yake .40 1.00
15 Trent Ciprick .20 .50
16 Jeff Waver .20 .50
17 Team Photo .20 .50
18 Jack Sangster CO .20 .50
19 Mike Morin .20 .50
20 Jason Phillips .20 .50
21 Rod Williams .20 .50
22 Dave Thomlinson .40 1.00
23 Shane Eirickson .20 .50
24 Randy Hoffart .20 .50

1988-89 Brandon Wheat Kings

This 24-card set measures approximately 2 1/4" by 4" and features posed, color player photos with a thin yellow border stripe against a white card face. The backs carry P.L.A.Y. (Police, Laws and Youth) Tips from the Kings and sponsor logos.

COMPLETE SET (24) 6.00 15.00
1 Kevin Cheveldayoff .20 .50
2 Bob Woods .20 .50
3 Dwayne Newman .20 .50
4 Mike Vandenberghe .20 .50
5 Brad Woods .20 .50
6 Gary Audette .20 .50
7 Mark Bassen .20 .50
8 Troy Frederick .20 .50
9 Troy Kennedy .20 .50
10 Barry Dreger .20 .50
11 Bill Whistle .20 .50
12 Jeff Odgers .40 1.00
13 Sheldon Kowalchuk .20 .50
14 Chris Robertson .20 .50
15 Don Laurin .20 .50
16 Curtis Folkett .20 .50
17 Team Photo .20 .50
18 Kelly McCrimmon ACO .20 .50
19 Doug Sauter CO .20 .50
20 Kelly Hitchins .20 .50
21 Trevor Kidd 1.25 3.00
22 Pryce Wood .20 .50
23 Cam Brown .20 .50
24 Greg Hutchings .20 .50

1989-90 Brandon Wheat Kings

This 24-card P.L.A.Y. (Police, Laws and Youth) set measures approximately 2 1/4" by 4". The fronts display color posed action photos inside of yellowish-orange borders. The player's name is printed in black across the bottom of the picture. In addition to sponsor logos, the backs carry "P.L.A.Y. Tips from the Kings" in the form of safety messages.

COMPLETE SET (24) 4.80 12.00
1 Trevor Kidd 1.25 3.00
2 Troy Frederick .20 .50
3 Kelly Thiessen .30 .75
4 Pryce Wood .20 .50
5 Mike Vandenberghe .20 .50
6 Chris Constant .20 .50
7 Hardy Sauter .20 .50
8 Cam Brown .20 .50
9 Bart Cote .20 .50
10 Jeff Hoad .20 .50
11 Kevin Robertson .20 .50
12 Dwayne Newman .20 .50
13 Calvin Flint .20 .50
14 Glen Webster .20 .50
15 Greg Hutchings .30 .75
16 Rob Puchniak .20 .50
17 Gary Audette .20 .50
18 Kevin Schmalz .20 .50
19 Dwayne Gylywoychuk .20 .50
20 Jeff Odgers .30 .75
21 Brian Purdy .20 .50
22 Merv Priest .20 .50
23 Doug Sauter CO .08 .25
24 Team Photo .20 .50

1990-91 Brandon Wheat Kings

This 24-card set measures approximately 2 1/4" by 4". The fronts feature posed color player photos with thin orange borders. The player's name appears on the picture at the bottom, while his uniform number and position are printed in the upper corners. On a white background, the backs carry P.L.A.Y. (Police, Laws and Youth) "Tips From The Kings". Sponsor logos and room for an autograph appear on the lower portion.

COMPLETE SET (24) 5.60 14.00
1 Jeff Hoad .20 .50
2 Merv Priest .20 .50
3 Mike Vandenberghe .20 .50
4 Bart Cole .20 .50
5 Hardy Sauter .20 .50
6 Mark Johnston ACO .08 .25
7 Kelly McCrimmon CO .08 .25
8 Team Photo .20 .50
9 Kevin Robertson .20 .50
10 Glen Webster .20 .50
11 Greg Hutchings .20 .50
12 Dan Kopec .20 .50
13 Dwayne Gylywoychuk .20 .50
14 Brian Purdy .20 .50
15 Trevor Kidd 1.25 3.00
16 Johan Skillgard .20 .50
17 Stu Scantlebury .20 .50
18 Byron Penstock .20 .50
19 Rob Puchniak .20 .50
20 Gary Audette .20 .50
21 Calvin Flint .20 .50
22 Jason White .20 .50
23 Chris Constant .20 .50
24 Glen Gulutzan .20 .50

1992-93 Brandon Wheat Kings

These 24 standard-size cards feature color player action shots on their fronts. Each picture is trimmed in white and has its corners blacked out, giving the impression of a mounted photograph. The cards are unnumbered and checklisted below in alphabetical order.

COMPLETE SET (24) 4.00 10.00
1 Aris Brimanis .15 .40
2 Colin Cloutier .20 .50
3 Chris Dingman .30 .75
4 Mike Dubinsky .20 .50
5 Todd Dutiaume .15 .40
6 Mark Franks .15 .40
7 Craig Geekie .15 .40
8 Dwayne Gylywoychuk .15 .40
9 Scott Hlady .15 .40
10 Jeff Hoad .15 .40
11 Bobby House .15 .40
12 Chris Johnston .15 .40
13 Mark Kolesar .20 .50
14 Scott Laluk .15 .40
15 Mike Maneluk .20 .50
16 Sean McFatridge .15 .40
17 Marty Murray .30 .75
18 Byron Penstock .20 .50
19 Darren Ritchie .15 .40
20 Trevor Robins .20 .50
21 Ryan Smith .15 .40
22 Jeff Staples .15 .40
23 Darcy Werenka .20 .50
24 Willie MASCOT .02 .10

1993-94 Brandon Wheat Kings

This set features the Wheat Kings of the WHL. The cards feature an action photo on the front, framed by black and gold borders. The cards were sold at home games.

COMPLETE SET (24) 6.00 15.00
1 Byron Penstock .30 .75
2 Craig Hordal .30 .75
3 Jeff Staples .20 .50
4 Scott Laluk .20 .50
5 Wade Redden .75 2.00
6 Justin Kurtz .30 .75
7 Sven Butenschon .20 .50
8 Adam Magarrell .20 .50
9 Dwayne Gylywoychuk .20 .50
10 Scott Hlady .20 .50
11 Joel Korenko .20 .50
12 Chris Johnston .20 .50
13 Bobby Brown .20 .50
14 Mark Kolesar .20 .50
15 Chris Low .20 .50
16 Dean Kletzel .20 .50
17 Darren Ritchie .20 .50
18 Mark Dutiaume .20 .50
19 Mike Dubinsky .20 .50
20 Chris Dingman .30 .75
21 Mike Maneluk .30 .75
22 Colin Cloutier .20 .50
23 Paul Bailley .20 .50
24 Marty Murray .30 .75

1994-95 Brandon Wheat Kings

This set features the Wheat Kings of the WHL and was sponsored by 7-Eleven and CKX Radio and was printed by Leech Printing. The set is not numbered and so is listed alphabetically.

COMPELTE SET (24) 6.00 15.00
1 Bobby Brown .20 .50
2 Sven Butenschon .20 .50
3 Colin Cloutier .20 .50
4 Chris Dingman .30 .75
5 Mike Dubinsky .20 .50
6 Mark Dutiaume .20 .50
7 Brian Elder .20 .50
8 Dean Kletzel .20 .50
9 Joel Korenko .20 .50
10 Justin Kurtz .30 .75
11 Scott Laluk .20 .50
12 Chris Low .20 .50
13 Adam Magarrell .20 .50
14 Marty Murray .20 .50
15 Byron Penstock .20 .50
16 Kevin Pozzo .20 .50
17 Wade Redden .75 2.00
18 Darren Ritchie .20 .50
19 Peter Schaefer .30 .75
20 Kelly Smart .20 .50
21 Jeff Staples .20 .50
22 Oleg Tverdovsky .40 1.00
23 Darren Van Oene .20 .50
24 Ian Walterson .20 .50

1995-96 Brandon Wheat Kings

This set was sponsored by 7-11 and was printed by Leech Printing. It is believed that it was sold in set-form by the team. The set is not numbered so the checklist appears below in alphabetical order.

COMPLETE SET (24) 6.00 15.00
1 Bobby Brown .20 .50
2 Sven Butenschon .20 .50
3 Stefan Cherneski .20 .50
4 Cory Cyrenne .30 .75
5 David Draguzas .20 .50
6 Chris Dingman .30 .75
7 Mark Dutiaume .20 .50
8 Brian Elder .20 .50
9 Burke Henry .20 .50
10 Vincent Jonasson .20 .50
11 Dean Kletzel .20 .50
12 Justin Kurtz .30 .75
13 Mike LeClerc .40 1.00
14 Andrei Lupandin .20 .50
15 Wade Redden .75 2.00
16 Ryan Robson .20 .50
17 Peter Schaefer .30 .75
18 Jason Skilnick .20 .50
19 Kelly Smart .20 .50
20 Daryl Stockham .20 .50

21 Jeff Temple .20 .50
22 Daniel Tetrault .20 .50
23 Gerhard Unterluggauer .20 .50
24 Darren Van Oene .30 .75

1996-97 Brandon Wheat Kings

COMPLETE SET (24) 7.00 12.00
1 Les Borsheim .20 .50
2 Daniel Tetrault .20 .50
3 Burke Henry .40 1.00
4 Darryl Stockham .20 .50
5 Gerhard Unterluggauer .20 .50
6 Josh Woitas .20 .50
7 Mark Dutiaume .20 .50
8 Johnathan Aitken .30 .75
9 Dorian Anneck .20 .50
10 Brian Elder .20 .50
11 Andreii Lupandin .20 .50
12 Brad Twordik .20 .50
13 Jeff Katcher .20 .50
14 Kelly Smart .20 .50
15 Peter Schaefer .40 1.00
16 Ryan Robson .20 .50
17 Cory Cyrenne .40 1.00
18 Jason Boyd .20 .50
19 Darren Van Oene .20 .50
20 Stefan Cherneski .20 .50
21 Aaron Goldade .20 .50
22 Justin Kurtz .20 .50
23 David Haun .20 .50
24 Bobby Leavins .20 .50

1997-98 Brandon Wheat Kings

This set features the Wheat Kings of the WHL. The set is sponsored by McDonald's and P.L.A.Y. The cards are unnumbered, so are listed in alphabetical order.

COMPLETE SET (26) 6.00 15.00
1 Alex Argyriou .20 .50
2 Johnathan Aitken .20 .50
3 Les Borsheim .20 .50
4 Stefan Cherneski .20 .50
5 Jomar Cruz .30 .75
6 Cory Cyrenne .30 .75
7 Brett Girard .20 .50
8 Aaron Goldade .20 .50
9 Bevin Guenther .20 .50
10 David Haun .20 .50
11 Burke Henry .20 .50
12 Jamie Hodson .40 1.00
13 Andrew Kaminsky .20 .50
14 Kirby Law .40 1.00
15 Bobby Leavins .20 .50
16 Andrei Lupandin .20 .50
17 Scott McCallum .20 .50
18 Brooks Paisley .20 .50
19 Randy Ponte .20 .50
20 Ryan Robson .20 .50
21 Wade Skolney .20 .50
22 Kelly Smart .20 .50
23 Daniel Tetrault .30 .75
24 Brent Twordik .20 .50
25 Darren Van Oene .20 .50
26 Josh Woitas .20 .50

1998-99 Brandon Wheat Kings

This set features the Wheat Kings of the WHL. The set was sold by the team at home games and was sponsored by McDonald's. The cards are unnumbered, and so are listed below alphabetically.

COMPLETE SET (24) 4.80 12.00
1 Alex Argyriou .20 .50
2 Ryan Craig .20 .50
3 Jomar Cruz .30 .75
4 Jan Fadrny .20 .50
5 Brett Girard .20 .50
6 Aaron Goldade .20 .50
7 Burke Henry .20 .50
8 Jamie Hodson .30 .75
9 Ryan Johnston .20 .50
10 J.D. Kehler .20 .50
11 Petr Kudrna .20 .50
12 Andrew Kaminsky .20 .50
13 Andrei Lupandin .20 .50
14 Scott McCallum .20 .50
15 Richard Mueller .20 .50
16 Randy Ponte .20 .50
17 Ryan Robson .20 .50
18 Wade Skolney .20 .50
19 Daniel Tetrault .20 .50
20 Brett Thurston .20 .50
21 Brad Twordik .20 .50
22 Cory Unser .20 .50
23 Mike Wirll .20 .50
24 Justin Yeoman .20 .50

1999-00 Brandon Wheat Kings

This set features the Wheaties of the WHL. The set was sold by the team at home games. The cards are unnumbered, so are listed below alphabetically.

COMPLETE SET (24) 6.00 25.00
1 Mark Ardelan .20 .50
2 Milan Bartovic .20 .50
3 Les Borsheim .20 .50
4 Ryan Craig .20 .50
5 Brett Dickie .20 .50
6 Ryan Diduck .20 .50
7 Jan Fadrny .20 .50
8 Brett Girard .20 .50
9 Aaron Goldade .20 .50
10 Kevin Harris .20 .50
11 Jamie Hodson .30 .75
12 J.D. Kehler .20 .50
13 Colin McRae .20 .50
14 Robert McVicar .30 .75
15 Richard Mueller .20 .50
16 Randy Ponte .20 .50
17 Bart Rushmer .20 .50
18 Wade Skolney .20 .50
19 Daniel Tetrault .20 .50
20 Brett Thurston .20 .50
21 Jordin Tootoo 6.00 15.00
22 Brad Twordik .20 .50
23 Cory Unser .20 .50
24 Mike Wirll .20 .50

2000-01 Brandon Wheat Kings

COMPLETE SET (24) 10.00 25.00
1 Jordin Tootoo 4.00 10.00
2 Jamie Hodson .30 .75
3 Mark Ardelan .20 .50
4 Reagan Leslie .20 .50
5 Brett Thurston .20 .50
6 Travis Young .20 .50
7 Brett Dickie .20 .50
8 Richard Mueller .20 .50
9 Nolan Yonkman .30 .75
10 Brett Girard .20 .50
11 James Marquis .20 .50
12 Colin McRae .20 .50
13 Aaron Goldade .20 .50
14 Milan Bartovic .20 .50
15 J.D. Kehler .20 .50
16 Lance Monych .40 1.00
17 Tim Konsorada .20 .50
18 Caine Pearpoint .20 .50
19 Ryan Craig 1.25 3.00
20 Randy Ponte .40 1.00
21 Kevin Harris .20 .50
22 Wade Skolney .20 .50
23 Jiri Jakes .20 .50
24 Robert McVicar .30 .75

2001-02 Brandon Wheat Kings

This set features the Wheaties of the WHL. The set was produced by the team and sponsored by McDonald's and was offered for sale at the team's souvenir shop. The cards are black bordered, and so are highly condition sensitive. As they are unnumbered, they are listed below alphabetically.

COMPLETE SET (24) 25.00
1 Andre Blanchette .20 .50
2 Dustin Bru .20 .50
3 Ryan Craig .20 .50
4 Brett Dickie .20 .50
5 Travis Eagles .20 .50
6 Eric Fehr .20 .50
7 Adrian Foster .40 1.00
8 Josh Garbutt .31 .78
9 Kevin Harris .20 .50
10 Jiri Jakes .31 .78
11 Tim Konsorada .20 .50
12 Reagan Leslie .20 .50
13 Geoff McIntosh .20 .50
14 Colin McRae .20 .50
15 Robert McVicar .20 .50
16 Lance Monych .20 .50
17 Caine Pearpoint .20 .50
18 Randy Ponte .40 1.00
19 Wade Skolney .20 .50
20 Ryan Stone .20 .50
21 Brett Thurston .20 .50
22 Jordin Tootoo .80 2.00
23 Willie MASCOT .04 .11
24 Travis Young .20 .50

2002-03 Brandon Wheat Kings

This 23-card set was sold at home games. An early card of Jordin Tootoo highlights this set.

COMPLETE SET (23) 25.00
1 Jonathan Webb .50
2 Roagan Loslie .50
3 Brett Thurston .50
4 Bryan Nathe .50
5 Brett Dickie .50
6 Josh Garbutt .50
7 Andre Blanchette .50
8 Richard Jasovsky .50
9 Tyler Dyck .50
10 Dorok Woronka .50
11 Teegan Moore .50
12 Eric Fehr 3.00
13 Ryan Stone .50
14 Lance Monych .50
15 Tim Konsorada .50
16 Rick Kozak .50
17 Jordin Tootoo 10.00
18 Greg Watson 1.00
19 Ryan Craig .50
20 Ole-Kristian Tollefson .50
21 Jeff Topilko .50
22 Geoff McIntosh .75
23 Robert McVicar .75

2003-04 Brandon Wheat Kings

COMPLETE SET (24) 6.00 15.00
1 Josh Harding 1.25 3.00
2 Tyler Boldt .20 .50
3 Stephan Lenoski .20 .50
4 Erik Christensen .40 1.00
5 Lance Monych .40 1.00
6 Mark Derlago .20 .50
7 Corey Courchene .20 .50
8 Richard Jasovsky .20 .50
9 Tim Konsorada .20 .50
10 Codey Burki .20 .50
11 Teegan Moore .20 .50
12 Ryan Stone .40 1.00
13 Reagan Leslie .20 .50
14 Ole-Kristian Tollefsen .40 1.00
15 Steven Later .20 .50
16 Eric Fehr .75 2.00
17 Andre Blanchette .20 .50
18 Jeff Topilko .20 .50
19 Mark Louis .20 .50
20 Mark Shefchyk .20 .50
21 Jonathan Webb .20 .50
22 Tyler Dyck .20 .50
23 Derek LeBlanc .20 .50
24 Mike Nichol .20 .50

2004-05 Brandon Wheat Kings

COMPLETE SET (24) 20.00
1 Mike Nichol .75
2 Jonathan Webb .75
3 Corey Courchene .75
4 Mike Cann .75
5 Theran Yeo .75
6 Steven Later .75
7 Daryl Boyle .75
8 Cole Hunter .75
9 Sami Sandell .75
10 Tyler Strautman .75
11 Eric Fehr 2.00
12 Teegan Moore .75
13 Ryan Stone 1.50
14 Lance Monych 1.00
15 Tim Konsorada 1.00
16 Jakub Sindel .75
17 Riley Day .75
18 Codey Burki .75
19 Derek LeBlanc .75
20 Ryan Reaves .75
21 Jeff Topilko .75
22 Mark Louis .75
23 Stephan Lenoski .75
24 Tyler Plante .75

2005-06 Brandon Wheat Kings

COMPLETE SET (24) 10.00 18.00
1 Keith Aulie .30 .75
2 Daryl Boyle .30 .75
3 Codey Burki .30 .75
4 Andrew Clark .30 .75
5 Corey Courchene .30 .75
6 Riley Day .30 .75
7 Mark Derlago .30 .75
8 Tyler Dittmer .30 .75
9 Chad Erb .30 .75
10 Matt Hallick .30 .75
11 Cole Hunter .30 .75
12 Kurt Jory .30 .75
13 Bryan Kauk .30 .75
14 Dustin Kohn .30 .75
15 Stephan Lenoski .30 .75
16 Mark Louis .30 .75
17 Teegan Moore .30 .75
18 Tyler Plante .30 .75
19 Ryan Reaves .30 .75
20 Sami Sandell .30 .75
21 Tyler Strautman .30 .75
22 Jeff Topilko .30 .75
23 John Wikner .30 .75
24 Theran Yeo .30 .75

1983-84 Brantford Alexanders

This 30-card set measures approximately 2 3/4" by 3 1/2". The fronts feature posed color player photos inside a thin black picture frame and white outer borders. The player's name appears on the picture at the bottom. On a white background, the backs carry the player's name, number, and a short biography in the upper portion; P.L.A.Y. (Police, Laws and Youth) "Tips From The Alexanders And The Brantford and Area Police" in the middle; and sponsor logos in the lower portion.

COMPLETE SET (30) 12.00 30.00
1 Ken Gratton ACO .20 .50
2 Shayne Corson 2.00 5.00
3 Bob Probert 3.00 8.00
4 Bruce Bell .60 1.50
5 Warren Bechard ACO .20 .50
6 Jason Lafreniere .40 1.00
7 Rob Moffat .30 .75
8 Jack Calbeck PR .20 .50
9 Marc West .30 .75
10 Larry Van Herzele .30 .75
11 Doug Stewart .30 .75
12 Brian MacDonald .30 .75
13 Dave Draper CO/GM .20 .50
14 Jeff Jackson .60 1.50
15 Steve Linseman .30 .75
16 Steve Short .30 .75
17 Allan Bester .75 2.00
18 John Weir COP .20 .50
19 Chris Pusey .30 .75
20 Mike Millar .30 .75
21 Chris Glover .30 .75
22 Bob Pierson .30 .75
23 Phil Priddle .30 .75
24 Grant Anderson .30 .75
25 Ken Gagner .30 .75
26 Andy Alway TR .20 .50
27 Todd Francis .30 .75
28 John Meulenbroeks .30 .75
29 Mike Chettleburgh .30 .75
30 Bill Dynes TR .20 .50

1994-95 Brantford Smoke

Sponsored by Calbeck's Sports Centre and Davis Fuels, and printed by Slapshot Images Ltd., this 26-card set features the 1994-95 Brantford Smoke of the Colonial Hockey League.

COMPLETE SET (26) 3.00 8.00
1 Checklist .02 .10
2 Bob Delorimiere .15 .40
3 Todd Francis .15 .40
4 Pete Liptrott .15 .40
5 Lorne Knauft .15 .40
6 Paul Polillo .15 .40
7 Rob Arabski .15 .40
8 Derek Gauthier .15 .40
9 Joe Simon .15 .40
10 Brad Barton .15 .40
11 Terry Chitaroni .20 .50
12 Paul Mitton .15 .40
13 Wayne MacPhee .15 .40
14 Brian Blad .20 .50
15 John Laan .15 .40
16 Shane MacEachern .15 .40
17 Wayne Muir .15 .40
18 Ted Miskolczi .15 .40
19 Marc Delorme .15 .40
20 Mike Speer .15 .40
21 Bob Baird TR .02 .10
Ken Crabb TR
22 Ken Gratton CO .02 .10
23 Team Photo .20 .50
24 Craig Newton .02 .10
25 Joe Lowes .02 .10
NNO Ad Card .02 .10

2003-04 Bridgeport Sound Tigers

This set was issued as a promotional giveaway at several home games. The cards were issued in perforated strips, with one strip specific per game. The cards are numbered, but numbers 1-8 are repeated twice.

COMPLETE SET (20) 40.00
1A Wade Dubielewicz 5.00
1B Ryan Kraft 1.50
2A Ben Guite 1.50
2B Kevin Colley 1.50
3A Cole Jarrett 1.50
3B Rob Collins 1.50
4A Alan Letang 1.50
4B Jeff Hamilton 1.50
5A Dieter Kochan 5.00
5B Cail MacLean 1.50
6A Eric Manlow 1.50
6B Justin Mapletoft 3.00
7A Graham Belak 1.50
7B Alain Nasreddine 1.50
8A Martin Kariya 10.00
8B Tomi Pettinen 1.50
9 Brandon Smith 1.50
10 Derek Bekar 1.50
11 Blaine Down 1.50
12 Jody Robinson 1.50

1991-92 British Columbia JHL

This 172-card standard-size set features players of the British Columbia Junior Hockey League. The card design features action and posed color player photos. A border design that frames the picture is royal blue at the bottom and fades to pale blue and white at the top. Overlapping this frame at the top is a bar with a blue speckled pattern, which contains the player's name, team name, or card title. The team logo appears within a royal blue circle that is superimposed over the lower right corner of the picture. The backs carry a black-and-white close-up, statistics, and biographical information. Topical subsets featured are Stars of the Future (81, 91, 93, 106, 146-147, 164, 166, 168-169), Coastal All-Stars (151-154, 163), and Interior All-Stars (155-162). The cards are numbered on the back and checklisted below according to teams as follows: Vernon Lakers (1-17, 23-25), Kelowna Spartans (18-22, 26-41), Nanaimo Clippers (42-62, 79-80, 153), Merritt Centennials (63-78, 82, 107), Chilliwack Chiefs (81, 127-145), Surrey Eagles (83, 106, 108-117, 119-126), and Penticton Panthers (85-105, 118, 147).

COMPLETE SET (173) 40.00 100.00
1 Vernon Lakers .08 .25
Team Photo
2 Scott Longstaff .05 .15
3 Rick Crowe .05 .15
4 Sheldon Wolitski .05 .15
5 Kevan Rilcof .05 .15
6 Greg Buchanan .05 .15
7 Vernon Lakers .05 .15
Executives
8 Murray Caton .05 .15
9 Adrian Bubola .05 .15
10 Troy Becker .05 .15
11 Shawn Potyok .05 .15
12 John Morabito .05 .15
13 Peter Zurba .05 .15
14 Chad Schraeder .05 .15
15 Shawn Bourgeois .05 .15
16 Michal Sup .05 .15
17 Rick Eremenko .05 .15
18 David Lemanowicz .05 .15
19 Daniel Blasko .05 .15
20 Gary Audette .20 .50
21 Graham Harder .05 .15
22 Ryan Nessman .05 .15
23 Jason Switzer .05 .15
24 Roland Ramoser .05 .15
25 Dusty McLellan .05 .15
26 Dustin Green .05 .15
27 Steve Roberts .05 .15
28 Jason Lowe .05 .15
29 Brad Knight .05 .15
30 Pavel Suchanek .05 .15
31 Ken Crockett .05 .15
32 Adam Smith .08 .25
33 Glen Pullishy .05 .15
34 Mike Zambon .05 .15
35 Scott Chartier .08 .25
36 Donny Hearn .05 .15
37 Jeff Denham .05 .15
38 Jamie Marriott .05 .15
39 Silverio Mirao .05 .15
40 Darren Tymchyshyn .05 .15
41 Mark Basanta .05 .15
42 Trevor Prest .05 .15
43 Jim Lessard .05 .15
44 Jade Kersey .05 .15
45 Geordie Young .05 .15
46 Darren Holmes .05 .15
47 Wade Dayley .05 .15
48 Dan Murphy .05 .15
49 Paul Taylor .05 .15
50 Sjon Wynia .05 .15
51 Ryan Loxam .05 .15
52 Andy Faulkner .05 .15
53 Scott Kowalski .05 .15
54 Mickey McGuire .05 .15
55 Jason Disiewich .05 .15
56 Jim Ingram .05 .15
57 Ryan Keller .05 .15
58 Brian Schiebel .05 .15
59 Shawn York .05 .15
60 Sean Krause .05 .15
61 Casey Hungle .05 .15
62 Chris Jones .05 .15
63 Doug Stewart .05 .15
64 Jason Sirota .08 .25
65 Dave Dunnigan .05 .15
66 Aaron Hoffman .05 .15
67 Jason Timewell .05 .15
68 Pat Meehan .05 .15
69 Mike Leduc .05 .15
70 Brad Koopmans .05 .15
71 Guy Prince .05 .15
72 Dorel Gecse .05 .15
73 Scott Salmond .05 .15
74 Brian Zakall .05 .15
75 Mike Josephson .05 .15
76 Derek Harper .05 .15
77 John Graham .05 .15
78 Dan Morrissey .08 .25
79 Glenn Calder .05 .15
80 Jason Northard .05 .15
81 Chris Kerr .05 .15
82 Bill Muckalt .40 1.00
83 Greg Hunt .05 .15
84 Paul Kariya 10.00 25.00
1990-91 All-Star Team
85 Dean Rowland .05 .15
86 Paul Kariya 10.00 25.00
(Skating)
87 David Kilduff .05 .15
88 Jeff Tory .05 .15
89 Mike Newman. .05 .15
90 Tyler Boucher .05 .15
91 Paul Kariya 10.00 25.00
(Skating with stick)
92 Phil Valk .05 .15
93 Paul Kariya 10.00 25.00
(Passing)
94 Bob Lewis .05 .15
95 Steve Williams .05 .15
96 James Pelzer .05 .15
97 Shawn Carter .05 .15
98 Ryan Erasmas .08 .25
99 John Dehart .05 .15
100 David Green .05 .15
101 Derek Gecse .05 .15
102 Brian Barnes .05 .15
103 Jason Given .05 .15
104 Jason Podollan .20 .50
105 Brian Veale .05 .15
106 Rob Tallas .30 .75
107 Bob McBurnie .05 .15
108 Paul McMillan .05 .15
109 Ryan Donovan .05 .15
110 Kevin Robertson .05 .15
111 Milt Mastad .08 .25
112 Kees Roodbol .05 .15
113 Carey Causey .05 .15
114 Patrick O'Flaherty .05 .15
115 Chad Vestergaard .05 .15
116 Tyler Quiring .08 .25
117 Loui Mellios .05 .15
118 Bob Bell .05 .15
119 Rob Tallas .30 .75
120 Clint MacDonald .05 .15
121 Bart Taylor .05 .15
122 Mark Basanta .05 .15
123 Don McCusker .05 .15
124 Jason Howse .05 .15
125 Mike McKinlay .05 .15
126 Trevor Pennock .05 .15
127 Dean Shmyr .08 .25
128 Chris Kerr .05 .15
129 Erin Thornton .05 .15
130 Dennis Archibald .05 .15
131 Brian McDonald .05 .15
132 Bob Quinnell .05 .15
133 Clint Black .05 .15
134 Jason Peters .05 .15
135 Doug Ast .05 .15
136 Jason Bilous .08 .25
137 Lee Schill .05 .15
138 Jason Sanford .05 .15
139 Jeff Hokanson .05 .15
140 Marc Gagnon .05 .15
141 Gunnar Henrikson .05 .15
142 Jamie Lund .05 .15
143 Jason White .05 .15
144 Jag Bal .05 .15
145 Brad Loring .05 .15
146 Marc Gagnon .05 .15
147 Brian Veale .05 .15
148 Checklist 1 .05 .15
149 Checklist 2 .05 .15
150 The Centennial Cup .08 .25
151 Brian Law .05 .15
152 Al Radke .05 .15
153 Andy Faulkner .08 .25
Jason Disiewich
Darren Holmes
Casey Hungle
Chris Jones
154 1982 Coastal Division .08 .25
Team Photo
155 Dusty McLellan .08 .25
Roland Ramoser
Rick Eremenko
Sheldon Wolitski
Shawn Potyok
Scott Longstaff
156 Hendrikson .08 .25
Anchikoski
Marc Gagnon
Jason White
157 John Graham .08 .25
Dave Dunnigan
158 Scott Chartier .08 .25
Mike Zambon
Paul Taylor
Jason Lowe
159 Jeff Tory .08 .25
Tyler Boucher
David Kilduff
Lee Davidson
John Dehart
Burns
160 Didmon .08 .25
Bentham
Marsh
Walsh
161 Lipsett .08 .25
McNeill
Klyn
Edgington
162 1991 Interior .08 .25
All-Stars Team
Photo
163 Johnson .08 .25
Meek
Welker
Fitzpatrick
Collins
Sofikitas
Hutson
Herman
164 John Dehart .05 .15
165 John Craighead .08 .25
166 Mike Josephson .05 .15
167 Wayne Anchikoski .20 .50
168 Paul Kariya 10.00 25.00
(Stars of the Future
on the front)
169 Jim Lessard .05 .15
170 Tommi Virkgunen .05 .15
NNO Wayne Anchikoski .20 .50
NNO John Craighead .08 .25
NNO Tommi Virkgunen .08 .25

1992-93 British Columbia JHL

This 246-card standard-size set showcases players in the British Columbia Junior Hockey League. The cards feature color, action player photos with white borders. The player's name and position appear at the top. The team name is at the bottom. The backs carry the team logo in orange and black, statistics, and biographical information. The cards are numbered on the back and are in team order as follows: Bellingham Ice Hawks (1-23), Chilliwack Chiefs (24-45), Kelowna Spartans (46-70), Merritt Centennials (71-92), Nanaimo Clippers (93-116, 240), Penticton Panthers (117-140), Powell River Paper Kings (141-163, 245), Surrey Eagles (164-188), Vernon Lakers (189-211), and Victoria Warriors (212-233). The set closes with an Alumni of the BCJHL subset (234-239, 241) and other miscellaneous cards (242-246).

COMPLETE SET (246) 10.00 50.00
1 Tom Wittenberg .08 .25
2 Kendel Kelly .08 .25
3 Gus Rettschlag .08 .25
4 Don Barr .08 .25
5 Dave Kirkpatrick .08 .25
6 Josh Flett .08 .25
7 Paul McKenna .08 .25
8 Brad Wingfield .08 .25
9 Derek Gesce .08 .25
10 Garry Gulash .08 .25
11 Tim Bell .08 .25
12 Dean Stork .08 .25
13 Wes Reusse .08 .25
14 Jason Peipmann .08 .25
15 Tyler Johnston .08 .25
16 Jason Delesoy .08 .25
17 The Ice Man .02 .10
18 Don Barr .08 .25
19 Brad Swain .08 .25
20 Wes Rudy .08 .25
21 Michael Sigouin .08 .25
22 Kevan Rilcof .08 .25
23 Brian Preston .08 .25
24 Doug Ast .08 .25
25 Knut Engqvist .08 .25
26 Zac George .08 .25
27 Clint Black .08 .25
28 Cameron Campbell .08 .25
29 Dan Davies .08 .25
30 Bryce Munro .08 .25
31 Ryan Dayman .08 .25
32 Kevin Kimura .08 .25
33 Paul Nicolls .08 .25
34 Thomas Kraft .08 .25
35 Erin Thornton .08 .25
36 Brad Loring .08 .25
37 Jag Bal .08 .25
38 Jeff Grabinsky .08 .25
39 Johan Ahrgren .08 .25
40 The Lethal Weapon .08 .25
41 Two Unidentified .08 .25
Players
42 Judd Lambert .08 .25
43 Brian Schiebel .08 .25
44 Dennis Archibald .08 .25
45 David Longbroek .08 .25
46 Silverio Mirao .08 .25
47 Jason Haakstad .08 .25
48 Lee Grant .08 .25
49 Ryan Esselmont .08 .25
50 Steve Roberts .08 .25
51 Curtis Fry .08 .25
52 David Dollard .08 .25
53 Diano Zol .08 .25
54 Bob Needham .08 .25
55 Dustin Green .08 .25
56 Darren Tymchyshyn .08 .25
57 Peter Arvanitis .08 .25
58 Don Hearn .08 .25
59 Title Card .10 .01
(Unnumbered)
60 Martin Masa .08 .25
61 Steffon Walby .20 .50
62 Joel Irwin .08 .25
63 Brent Bradford .08 .25
64 Dieter Kochan 2.00 5.00
65 Brendan Kenny .08 .25
66 Marty Craigdallie .08 .25
67 Graeme Harder .08 .25
68 Pavel Suchanek .08 .25
69 Shane Johnson .08 .25
70 Burt Henderson .08 .25
71 Tyler Willis .08 .25
72 Mike Olaski .08 .25
73 David Green .08 .25
74 Tom Mix .08 .25
75 Walter(Guy) Prince .08 .25
76 Joseph Rybar .40 1.00
77 Bill Muckalt .75 2.00
78 Jason Mansoff .08 .25
79 Duane Puga .08 .25
80 Aaron Hoffman .08 .25
81 Dan Blasko .08 .25
82 Rob Szatmary .08 .25
83 Mike Minnis .08 .25
84 Pat Meehan .08 .25
85 Andre Robichaud .08 .25
86 The Terminator .02 .10
87 Derrek Harper .08 .25
88 Dan Morrissey .08 .25
89 Joey Kennedy .08 .25
90 Derrek Harper .08 .25
91 Lawrence Klyne .08 .25
92 Ryan Beamin .08 .25
93 Sjon Wynia .08 .25
94 Jason Disiewich .08 .25
95 Jason Sanford .08 .25
96 Casey Hungle .08 .25
97 Brent Murcheson .08 .25
98 Glenn Calder .08 .25
99 Jade Kersey .08 .25
100 Shawn York .08 .25
101 Bob Quinnell .08 .25
102 Geordie Dunstan .08 .25
103 Cory Crowther .08 .25
104 Jason Hodson .08 .25
105 Chris Jones .08 .25
106 Cory Green .08 .25
107 Chris Buie .08 .25
108 Shaun Peet .08 .25
109 Jason Wood .08 .25
110 Dan Murphy .08 .25
111 Jason Disiewich .08 .25
112 Cory Dayley .08 .25
113 Brian Veale .08 .25
114 Jason Northard .08 .25
115 Phil Valk .08 .25
116 Wade Dayley .08 .25
117 Brendan Morrison 4.00 10.00
118 Marcel Sakac .08 .25
119 Tyler Boucher .08 .25
120 Ray Guze .08 .25
121 Brian Barnes .08 .25
122 Jason Given .08 .25
123 Michael Dairon .08 .25
124 Mike Newman .08 .25
125 Craig Fletcher .08 .25
126 Ty Davidson .08 .25
127 Miki Antonik .08 .25
128 Rob Pennoyer .08 .25
129 Dave Whitworth .08 .25
130 Steve Williams .08 .25
131 Robbie Trampuh .08 .25
132 Mark Filipenko .08 .25
133 Clint MacDonald .08 .25
134 Colin Ryder .08 .25
135 David Kilduff .08 .25
136 Mickey McGuire .08 .25
137 Randy Polacik .08 .25
138 Jeff Tory .08 .25
139 Chris Buckman .08 .25
140 Bill Moody .08 .25
141 Rick McLarren .08 .25
142 The Phantom .02 .10
143 Jason Zaichkowski .08 .25
144 Tony Hrycuik .08 .25
145 Cameron Knox .08 .25
146 Mike Warriner .08 .25
147 Robb Gordon .08 .25
148 Mike Pawluk .08 .25
149 Tim Harris .08 .25
150 Mike Bzdel .08 .25
151 Chad Wilson .08 .25
152 Andrew Plumb .08 .25
153 Andy MacIntosh .08 .25
154 Stefan Brannare .08 .25
155 Matt Sharrers .08 .25
156 Brent Berry .08 .25
157 Ryan Douglas .08 .25
158 Heath Dennison .08 .25
159 Chad Vizzutti .08 .25
160 Adam Lord .08 .25
161 Brad Klyn .08 .25
162 Andrew Young .08 .25
163 Casey Lemanski .08 .25
164 Mike McKinlay .08 .25

165 Derek Robinson .08 .25
166 Kees Roodbol .08 .25
167 Scott Boucher .08 .25
168 Shawn Gervais .08 .25
169 Ryan Schaffer .08 .25
170 Kevin Robertson .08 .25
171 Ryan Donovan .08 .25
172 Bart Taylor .08 .25
173 Greg Hunt .08 .25
174 Darcy George .08 .25
175 Shane Tidsbury .08 .25
176 Rob Smillie .08 .25
177 Chad Vestergaard .08 .25
178 Al Kinisky .08 .25
179 Patrick O'Flaherty .08 .25
180 Loui Mellios .08 .25
181 Lorin Murdock .08 .25
(Unnumbered)
182 Jason Genik .08 .25
183 Rob Herrington .08 .25
184 Loui Mellios .08 .25
185 Cal Benazic .08 .25
186 Richard Kraus .08 .25
187 Geoff White .08 .25
188 Kirk Buchanan .08 .25
189 Peter Zurba .08 .25
190 John Morabito .08 .25
191 Corey Kruchkowski .08 .25
192 Spencer Ward .08 .25
193 Danny Shermerhorn .08 .25
194 Mark Davies .08 .25
195 Jason Rushton .08 .25
196 Chad Buckle .08 .25
197 Serge Beauchesne .08 .25
198 Todd Kelman .08 .25
199 Jason Switzer .08 .25
200 Eon MacFarlane .08 .25
201 Terry Ryan .20 .50
202 Shawn Bourgeois .08 .25
203 Chad Schraeder .08 .25
204 Dusty McLellan .08 .25
205 The Predator .08 .25
206 Danny Shermerhorn .08 .25
207 Chris Godard .08 .25
208 Jason Chipman .08 .25
209 Christian Twomey .08 .25
210 Ryan Loxam .08 .25
211 Greg Buchanan .08 .25
212 Kees Roodbol .08 .25
213 Ryan Keller .08 .25
214 Kevin Paschal .08 .25
215 David Hebky .08 .25
216 Vince Devlin .08 .25
217 Mike Cole .08 .25
218 Daljit Takhar .08 .25
219 Scott Hall .08 .25
220 Derek Lawrence .08 .25
221 Mark Basanta .08 .25
222 Jan Kloboucek .08 .25
223 Randy Barker .08 .25
224 Kris Gailloux .08 .25
225 Tyson Scheuer .08 .25
226 Brent Wormald .08 .25
227 Vince Devlin .08 .25
228 Gus Miller .08 .25
229 Todd McKave .08 .25
230 Lawrence Oliver .08 .25
231 Scott Garvin .08 .25
232 Rob Millikon .08 .25
233 Roman Kobrc .08 .25
234 Dan Skene .08 .25
235 Blair Marsh .08 .25
236 Maco Balkovec .08 .25
237 Scott Kirton .08 .25
238 Blaine Moore .08 .25
239 Nigel Creightney .08 .25
240 Bill Zapt .08 .25
241 Jason Elders .08 .25
242 BCJHL Officials .02 .10
(Unidentified Referee)
243 Masks of the BCJHL .40 1.00
The Black Panther
244 Masks of the BCJHL .40 1.00
The Puck Pirate
(Unnumbered)
245 Mike Pawluk .08 .25
BCJHL MVP
246 Steffon Walby .20 .50
Captains of the BCJHL

1987-88 Brockville Braves

This 25-card set is printed on thin card stock, measures 2 5/8" by 3 5/8", and features posed color player photos with red studio backgrounds. The pictures are set on a white card face and show the player's name, position, and season in the white margin below the photo.

COMPLETE SET (25) 4.00 10.00
1 Title Card .08 .25
2 Steve Harper TR .08 .25
3 Peter Kelly TR .08 .25
4 Mac MacLean CO/MG .08 .25
5 Mike McCourt .20 .50
6 Paul MacLean .20 .50
7 Mark Michaud .20 .50
8 Alain Marchessault .20 .50
9 Tom Roman .20 .50
10 Darren Burns .20 .50
11 Scott Halpenny .20 .50
12 Ray Gallagher .20 .50
13 Bob Lindsay .20 .50
14 Brett Harkins .40 1.00
15 Dave Hyrsky .20 .50
16 Richard Marchessault .20 .50
17 Scott Boston .20 .50
18 Steve Hogg .30 .75
19 Chris Webster .20 .50
20 Stuart Birnie .20 .50
21 Brett Dunk .20 .50
22 Charles Cusson .20 .50
23 Pat Gooley .20 .50
24 Andy Rodman .20 .50
25 Peter Radlein .20 .50

1988-89 Brockville Braves

This 25-card set is printed on thin card stock, measures 2 5/8" by 3 5/8", and features posed color player photos with pale blue studio backgrounds. The pictures are set on a white card face and show the player's name, position, and season in the white margin below the photo.

COMPLETE SET (25) 4.00 10.00
1 Ray Gallagher .20 .50
2 Peter Kelly TR .08 .25
3 Steve Harper TR .08 .25
4 Winston Jones ACO .08 .25
5 Mac MacLean CO/GM .08 .25
6 Kevin Doherty .20 .50
7 Stuart Birnie .20 .50
8 Charles Cusson .20 .50
9 Paul MacLean .20 .50
10 Bob Lindsay .20 .50
11 Darren Burns .20 .50
12 Rick Pracey .30 .75
13 Mike Malloy .20 .50
14 Dave Hyrsky .20 .50
15 Rob Percival .20 .50
16 Jarrett Eligh .20 .50
17 Pat Gooley .20 .50
18 Michael Bracco .30 .75
19 Ken Crook .20 .50
20 Brad Osborne .20 .50
21 Todd Reynolds .20 .50
22 Mike McCourt .20 .50
23 Chris Webster .20 .50
24 Kevin Lune .20 .50
25 Title Card .20 .50

1951-52 Buffalo Bison

This set features the Bison of the AHL. Little is known about this set, but it is believed to be oversized and distributed in set form by the team.

COMPLETE SET (19) 50.00 100.00
1 Team Photo 5.00 10.00
2 Don Ashbee 5.00 10.00
3 Frankie Christy 2.50 5.00
4 Gerry Couture 4.00 8.00
5 Lou Crowdis 2.50 5.00
6 Harry Dick 2.50 5.00
7 Lloyd Finkbeiner 2.50 5.00
8 Ab Demarco 5.00 10.00
9 Leroy Goldsworthy 2.50 5.00
10 Les Hickey 5.00 10.00
11 Vern Kaiser 2.50 5.00
12 Sam Lavitt 2.50 5.00
13 Stan Long 2.50 5.00
14 Cal Mackay 5.00 10.00
15 Ed Mazur 2.50 5.00
16 Sid McNabney 2.50 5.00
17 George Pargeter 2.50 5.00
18 Gordie Pennell 2.50 5.00
19 Grant Warwick 2.50 5.00

1995 Buffalo Stampedes RHI

This standard size, team issued set, features color borderless fronts with players name and "1994 World Champions" in gold along the left side of the card. Backs are grey and black on a white background and feature biographical information along with 1994 statistics. The set came boxed and was available at home games. Cards are unnumbered and checklisted below by jersey number, each of which is prominently displayed on the card back.

COMPLETE SET (21) 4.00 10.00
14 John Hendry .20 .50
16 Tom Nemeth .30 .75
19 John Vechiarelli IA .30 .75
19 John Vechiarelli .30 .75
20 Len Soccio .20 .50
24 Chris Bergeron .20 .50
32 Mark Major .20 .50
34 Jason Cirone .20 .50
36 Nick Vitucci .30 .75
37 Dave Lemay .20 .50
43 John Blessman .20 .50
44 Jay Neal .20 .50
61 Craig Martin .20 .50
72 Rick Corriveau .20 .50
94 Alex Hicks .30 .75
NNO1 Header Card .02 .10
NNO2 Title Card .02 .10
NNO3 Team Photo .02 .10
NNO4 Jerry Buchwald .02 .10
NNO5 Stampede Cheerleaders .20 .50
NNO6 Claude the Trumpeter .08 .25

1998-99 Calgary Hitmen

This 26-card set was sold by the team in set form. It features early cards of several top prospects including Pavel Brendl, Jordan Krestanovich and Kris Beech.

COMPLETE SET (26) 8.00 20.00
1 Matt Kinch .30 .75
2 Ryan Shannon .20 .50
3 Jeff Feniak .20 .50
4 Kenton Smith .30 .75
5 Rod Sarich .20 .50
6 Pavel Brendl .60 1.50
7 Chris Nielsen .30 .75
8 Sean McAslan .20 .50
9 Jordan Krestanovich .60 1.50
10 Michael Bubnick .20 .50
11 Kris Beech .75 2.00
12 Ryan Geremia .20 .50
13 Wade Davis .20 .50
14 Brad Moran .30 .75
15 Lyle Steenbergen .20 .50
16 Curtis Rich .20 .50
17 Ryan Andres .20 .50
18 Brent Dodginghorse .20 .50
19 Jerred Smithson .20 .50
20 Peter Bergman .20 .50
21 Alexandre Fomitchev .30 .75
22 Eric Clark .20 .50
23 Donald Choukalos .30 .75
24 Dean Clark HCO .02 .10
25 Jeff Maher ACO .02 .10
26 Vulk MASCOT .02 .10

1998-99 Calgary Hitmen Autographs

This 26-card set resembles the regular set in every way other than carrying player autographs. Please note that Alexandre Fomitchev did not sign any of his cards though the sets were sold including that card in unsigned form.

COMPLETE SET (26) 40.00 80.00
1 Matt Kinch 1.25 3.00
2 Ryan Shannon 5.00 12.00
3 Jeff Feniak 1.25 3.00
4 Kenton Smith 1.25 3.00
5 Rod Sarich 1.25 3.00
6 Pavel Brendl 4.00 10.00
7 Chris Nielsen 1.25 3.00
8 Sean McAslan 1.25 3.00
9 Jordan Krestanovich 4.00 10.00
10 Michael Bubnick 1.25 3.00
11 Kris Beech 4.00 10.00
12 Ryan Geremia 1.25 3.00
13 Wade Davis 1.25 3.00
14 Brad Moran 1.25 3.00
15 Lyle Steenbergen 1.25 3.00
16 Curtis Rich 1.25 3.00
17 Ryan Andres 1.25 3.00
18 Brent Dodginghorse 1.25 3.00
19 Jerred Smithson 1.25 3.00
20 Peter Bergman 1.25 3.00
21 Alexandre Fomitchev .20 .50
UNSIGNED
22 Eric Clark 1.25 3.00
23 Donald Choukalos 1.25 3.00
24 Dean Clark HCO 2.00 5.00
25 Jeff Maher ACO 1.25 3.00
26 Vulk MASCOT .20 .50

1999-00 Calgary Hitmen

This team-issued set features the WHL's Hitmen. It was sold by the team at the rink and through its web site. The set is notable for featuring several first rounders, including Pavel Brendl, Kris Beech and Brent Krahn.

COMPLETE SET (26) 6.00 10.00
1 Kris Beech .40 1.00
2 Pavel Brendl .30 .75
3 Michael Bubnick .08 .25
4 Jared Carli .08 .25
5 Dean Clark CO .02 .10
6 Eric Clark .08 .25
7 Sean Connors .08 .25
8 Wade Davis .08 .25
9 Jeff Feniak .08 .25
10 Owen Fussey .08 .25
11 Robin Gomez .20 .50
12 Matt Kinch .30 .75
13 Brent Krahn .60 1.50
14 Jordan Krestanovich .40 1.00
15 Anders Lovdahl .15 .40
16 Jeff Maher ACO .08 .25
17 Sean McAslan .08 .25
18 Brad Moran .20 .50
19 Chris Nielsen .08 .25
20 Shaun Norrie .08 .25
21 Rod Sarich .08 .25
22 Brandon Segal .08 .25
23 Kenton Smith .15 .40
24 Jerred Smithson .08 .25
25 Vulk Mascot .02 .10
26 Calgary Herald .01
27 Playstation Coupon .01

1999-00 Calgary Hitmen Autographs

This 27-card set features the 1999-00 Calgary Hitmen of the Western Hockey League in an autographed parallel version of the main release. All players except Eric Clark and Jeff Feniak signed their cards, as the two players were dealt before the set was released. These cards are marked below as DNS. Cards are not numbered, so they appear alphabetically.

COMPLETE SET (27) 40.00 100.00
1 Kris Beech 4.00 10.00
2 Pavel Brendl 3.00 8.00
3 Michael Bubnick 1.25 3.00
4 Jared Carli 1.25 3.00
5 Dean Clark CO 1.25 3.00
6 Eric Clark DNS .08 .25
7 Sean Connors 1.25 3.00
8 Wade Davis 1.25 3.00
9 Jeff Feniak DNS .08 .25
10 Owen Fussey 1.25 3.00
11 Robin Gomez 2.00 5.00
12 Matt Kinch 3.00 8.00
13 Brent Krahn 4.00 10.00
14 Jordan Krestanovich 4.00 10.00
15 Anders Lovdahl 2.00 5.00
16 Jeff Maher ACO 1.25 3.00
17 Sean McAslan 1.25 3.00
18 Brad Moran 3.00 8.00
19 Chris Nielsen 3.00 8.00
20 Shaun Norrie 1.25 3.00
21 Rod Sarich 1.25 3.00
22 Brandon Segal 1.25 3.00
23 Kenton Smith 2.00 5.00
24 Jerred Smithson 1.25 3.00
25 Vulk Mascot .40 1.00
26 Calgary Herald .01
27 Playstation Coupon .01

2000-01 Calgary Hitmen

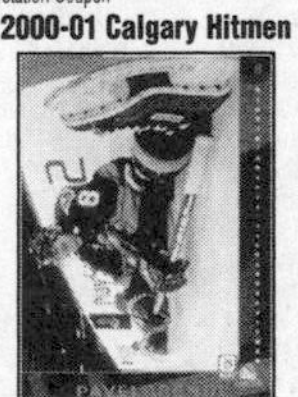

This set features the Hitmen of the WHL. The set was produced by the team, and sold at its souvenir stands at home games.

COMPLETE SET (28) 6.00 15.00
1 Toni Bader .20 .50
2 Kris Beech .40 1.00
3 Brady Block .20 .50
4 John Boychuk .40 1.00
5 Adam Breitkreuz .20 .50
6 Pavel Brendl .60 1.00
7 Michael Bubnick .20 .50
8 Jared Carli .20 .50
9 Dean Clark CO .10 .25
10 Wade Davis .20 .50
11 Mike Egener .20 .50
12 Dan Ehrman .20 .50
13 Owen Fussey .20 .50
14 Robin Gomez .20 .50
15 Matt Kinch .20 .50
16 Brent Krahn .40 1.00
17 Jordan Krestanovich .20 .50
18 Jeff Maher CO .10 .25
19 Sean McAslan .20 .50
20 Shaun Norrie .20 .50
21 Rod Sarich .20 .50
22 Brandon Segal .20 .50
23 Shaun Sutter .20 .50
24 David Vrbata .20 .50
25 The Vulk MASCOT .04 .10
26 Chad Wolkowski .20 .50
27 Calgary Herald .01
28 Toys R Us .01

2001-02 Calgary Hitmen

This set features the Hitmen of the WHL. The set was sold by the team at its souvenir stands. The set is noteworthy for including the first card of 2002 first-rounder Fredrik Sjostrom.

COMPLETE SET (26) 4.80 12.00
1 Paul Albers .20 .50
2 Kyle Annesley .20 .50
3 Tyler Beechey .30 .75
4 Johnny Boychuk .40 1.00
5 Adam Breitkreuz .20 .50
6 Michael Bubnick .20 .50
7 Jared Carli .20 .50
8 Wade Davis .20 .50
9 Mike Egener .20 .50
10 Dan Ehrman .20 .50
11 Owen Fussey .30 .75
12 Richard Kromm CO .04 .10
13 Sebastien LaPlante .20 .50
14 Jeff Maher ACO .04 .10
15 Ryan Martin .30 .75
16 Lance Morrison .20 .50
17 Ryan Papaioannou .20 .50
18 Wes Rypien .20 .50
19 Rod Sarich .20 .50
20 Brandon Segal .30 .75
21 Dennis Sergeyev .20 .50
22 Mark Shefchyk .20 .50
23 Fredrik Sjostrom .80 2.00
24 Rob Smith .20 .50
25 The Vulk MASCOT .01
26 Chad Wolkowski .20 .50

2001-02 Calgary Hitmen Autographed

This set features the Hitmen of the WHL. The set was sold in autographed form at team souvenir stands. Unfortunately, the card of team mascot The Vulk is not autographed. The cards are unnumbered, and so are listed below in alphabetical order.

COMPLETE SET (26) 20.00 50.00
1 Paul Albers .80 2.00
2 Kyle Annesley .80 2.00
3 Tyler Beechey 1.20 3.00
4 Johnny Boychuk 1.60 5.00
5 Adam Breitkreuz .80 2.00
6 Michael Bubnick .80 2.00
7 Jared Carli .80 2.00
8 Wade Davis .80 2.00
9 Mike Egener .80 2.00
10 Dan Ehrman .80 2.00
11 Owen Fussey .80 2.00
12 Richard Kromm CO .40 1.00
13 Sebastien LaPlante .80 2.00
14 Jeff Maher ACO .40 1.00
15 Ryan Martin 1.20 3.00
16 Lance Morrison .80 2.00
17 Ryan Papaioannou .80 2.00
18 Wes Rypien .80 2.00
19 Rod Sarich .80 2.00
20 Brandon Segal 1.20 3.00
21 Dennis Sergeyev .80 2.00
22 Mark Shefchyk .80 2.00
23 Fredrik Sjostrom 4.00 10.00
24 Rob Smith .80 2.00
25 The Vulk MASCOT .01
26 Chad Wolkowski .80 2.00

2002-03 Calgary Hitmen

COMPLETE SET (26) 8.00 18.00
1 Lance Morrison .20 .50
2 Michael Bubnick .20 .50
3 Cary Gladue .20 .50
4 Kris Deines .20 .50
5 Kyle Annesley .20 .50
6 Rob Smith .20 .50
7 Mark Shefchyk .20 .50
8 Bruno Campese ACO .02 .10
9 Richard Kromm HCO .02 .10
10 Mascot .02 .10
11 Fredrik Sjostrom .40 1.00
12 Wade Davis .20 .50
13 Paul Albers .20 .50
14 Patrick Wellar .20 .50
15 Marc Lesage .20 .50
16 Aaron Boogaard .20 .50
17 Jiri Cetkovsky .20 .50
18 Brandon Segal .20 .50
19 Owen Fussey .20 .50
20 Tyler Feakes .20 .50
21 Andy Rogers .20 .50
22 Steven Covington .20 .50
23 Johnny Boychuk .40 1.00
24 Michael Egener .40 1.00
25 Brent Krahn .40 1.00
26 Ryan Getzlaf 2.00 5.00

2003-04 Calgary Hitmen

COMPLETE SET (21) 6.00 15.00
1 Scott Bowles .30 .75
2 Brett Carson .20 .50
3 Dmitri Chupilkin .20 .50
4 Steve Covington .20 .50
5 Kris Deines .20 .50
6 Mike Egener .30 .75
7 Gerry Festa .30 .75
8 Paul Gentile .20 .50
9 Ryan Getzlaf 1.00 2.50
10 Dustin Kohn .20 .50
11 Andrew Ladd .75 2.00
12 Shaun Landolt .20 .50
13 Riley Merkley .20 .50
14 Andy Rogers .20 .50
15 Mark Rooneem .20 .50
16 Jeff Schultz .20 .50
17 Brandon Segal .20 .50
18 Tomas Troliga .20 .50
19 Patrick Wellar .20 .50
20 Darryl Yacboski .20 .50
21 Lee Zalasky .20 .50

2004-05 Calgary Hitmen

COMPLETE SET (25) 15.00 25.00
1 Karl Alzner .60 1.50
2 Brett Carlson .30 .75
3 Steven Covington .30 .75
4 Keegan Dansereau .30 .75
5 Brodie Dupont .30 .75
6 Ryan Getzlaf .60 2.00
7 Tyler Harder .30 .75
8 Dustin Kohn .30 .75
9 Andrew Ladd .60 1.50
10 Shaun Landolt .30 .75
11 Tyrel Lucas .30 .75
12 Riley Merkley .30 .75
13 Darryl Musialuk .30 .75
14 Brett O'Malley .30 .75
15 Justin Pogge 2.00 5.00
16 Konstantin Pushkarev .40 1.00
17 Isaac Reid .30 .75
18 Jeff Schultz .40 1.00
19 Daniel Spence .30 .75
20 Ryan White .30 .75
21 Darryl Yacboski .30 .75
22 Dylan Yeo .30 .75
23 Dean Evason .02 .10
Kelly Kisio CO
24 Blaine Forsythe ACO .02 .10
Farley MASCOT
25 Ryan Getzlaf/Calgary Herald .60 1.50

2005-06 Calgary Hitmen

COMPLETE SET (28) 8.00 15.00
1 Karl Alzner .40 1.00
2 Brett Carson .30 .75
3 Steve Covington .30 .75
4 Keegan Dansereau .30 .75
5 Kris Deines .30 .75
6 Brodie Dupont .30 .75
7 Curtis Kelner .30 .75
8 Derek LeBlanc .30 .75
9 Ryan Letts .30 .75
10 Craig Lineker .30 .75
11 Carson McMillan .30 .75
12 Riley Merkley .30 .75
13 Shaden Moore .30 .75
14 Fredrik Pettersson .30 .75
15 Alexandre Plante .30 .75
16 Justin Pogge 1.25 3.00
17 Mike Reich .30 .75
18 Jeff Schultz .30 .75
19 Brett Sonne .40 1.00
20 Daniel Spence .30 .75
21 Lukas Vantuch .40 1.00
22 Ryan White .40 1.00
23 Dylan Yeo .30 .75
24 Kelly Kisio CO .10 .25
25 Blaine Forsythe ACO .10 .25
26 Dave Lowry ACO .10 .25
27 Farley the Fox MASCOT .10 .25
28 SPONSORS .01 .01

2007-08 Calgary Oval X-Treme

1 Lyndsay Baird .20 .50
2 Kelly Bechard .40 1.00
3 Delaney Collins .40 1.00
4 Meghan Corbett .20 .50
5 Gillian Ferrari .40 1.00
6 Kaley Hall .20 .50
7 Gina Kingsbury .40 1.00
8 Carla MacLeod .40 1.00
9 Stephanie Ramsay .20 .50
10 Rebecca Russell .20 .50
11 Colleen Sostorics .40 1.00
12 Laura St. Croix .20 .50
13 Amanda Tapp .20 .50
14 Meagan Walton .20 .50
15 Linuo Wang .20 .50
16 Samantha Watt .20 .50
17 Hayley Wickenheiser 1.00 2.50
18 Shi Yao .20 .50
19 Team Card .10 .25

2003-04 Camrose Kodiaks

Team-issued set from the Tier 2 BCJHL. The cards are not numbered. Checklist courtesy of collector Vinnie Montalbano.

COMPLETE SET (25) 6.00 15.00
1 Dan Bertram .40 1.00
2 Steve Bounds .30 .75
3 MacGregor Sharp .30 .75
4 Jared Veuger .30 .75
5 Jody Pederson .30 .75
6 Matt McKnight .30 .75
7 Travis Friedley .30 .75
8 Kyle Smith .30 .75
9 Rob MacIntyre .30 .75
10 Owen Langis .30 .75
11 Mason Raymond .30 .75
12 Ryan Muspratt .30 .75
13 Ryan Antoniuk .30 .75
14 Chance Olsen .30 .75
15 Logan Gorsalitz .30 .75
16 Ryan Armstrong .30 .75
17 Lee Jubinville .30 .75
18 Justin Taylor .30 .75
19 Chris Wanchulak .30 .75
20 Justin Blacklock .30 .75
21 Todd Steil .30 .75
22 Bob Graham .30 .75
23 David Thompson .30 .75
24 Ryan Muth .30 .75
25 Coaches .02 .10

2004-05 Camrose Kodiaks

The Kodiaks are a Tier 2 Alberta Junior Hockey League squad. This set may not be complete. Additional information can be forwarded to hockeymag@beckett.com.

COMPLETE SET (16?)
1 Jody Pederson 1.00
2 Kirk Irving 1.00
3 Clark Thompson 1.00
4 Ryan Mayko 1.00
5 Logan Gorsalitz 1.00
6 Lee Jubinville 1.00
7 Todd Steil 1.00
8 Derek Wolbeck 1.00
9 Kyle Parkes 1.00
10 MacGregor Sharp 1.00
11 Chance Olsen 1.00
12 David Thompson 1.00
13 Mason Raymond 1.00
14 A.J. Nelson 1.00
15 Jason Roberts 1.00
16 Travis Friedley 1.00

2007-08 Camrose Kodiaks

1 David Anderson .30 .75
2 Jeremy Beirnes SP .30 .75
3 Scott Buchanan .30 .75
4 Nick Chartier .30 .75
5 Owen Chatwin .30 .75
6 Joe Colborne .75 2.00
7 Mike Connolly .30 .75
8 Nigel Dube .30 .75
9 Colin Dueck .30 .75
10 Wyatt Hamilton .30 .75
11 Jordan Heck .30 .75
12 Andre Hormen SP .30 .75
13 David Jacobsen .30 .75
14 Clayton Jardine .30 .75
15 Mathieu Larochelle .30 .75
16 Alex Macleod SP .30 .75
17 Andrew MacWilliam .30 .75
18 Kyle Miller .30 .75
19 Dylan Olsen .30 .75
20 Shawn Ostrow .30 .75
21 Geoff Peet .30 .75
22 Dean Petiot .30 .75
23 Karl Stollery .30 .75
24 Jesse Todd .30 .75
25 Alien York .30 .75

1994-95 Cape Breton Oilers

This 23-card standard-size set was manufactured and distributed by Jessen Associates, Inc. for Classic. The cards are unnumbered and checklisted below in alphabetical order.

COMPLETE SET (23) 4.80 12.00
1 Scott Allison .15 .40
2 Martin Bakula .15 .40
3 Ladislav Benysek .15 .40
4 Dennis Bonvie .30 .75
5 Jozef Cierny .15 .40
6 Duane Dennis .15 .40
7 Greg DeVries .30 .75
8 Joaquin Gage .30 .75
9 Ian Herbers .15 .40
10 Ralph Intranuovo .15 .40
11 Claude Jutras .15 .40
12 Marc LaForge .15 .40
13 Todd Marchant .40 1.00
14 Darcy Martini .15 .40
15 Roman Oksiuta .15 .40
16 David Oliver .30 .75
17 Steve Passmore .40 1.00
18 Nick Stajduhar .15 .40
19 John Van Kessel .15 .40
20 David Vyborny .15 .40
21 Peter White .15 .40
22 Tyler Wright .30 .75
23 Brad Zavisha .15 .40

2001-02 Cape Breton Screaming Eagles

This set features the Screaming Eagles of the QMJHL. The set was produced by CTM Ste-Foy and was sold at Eagles home games. It was reported that less than 1,000 sets were produced.

COMPLETE SET (23) 6.00 15.00
1 Steve Villeneuve .20 .50
2 Maxime Lessard .20 .50
3 Pierre-Luc Laprise .20 .50
4 David Cloutier .20 .50
5 Stuart MacRae .20 .50
6 Dominic Noel .20 .50
7 Jean-Philippe Cote .20 .50
8 Martin Kasik .20 .50
9 Steve Dixon .30 .75
10 Marc-Olivier Vary .20 .50
11 Justin Hawco .20 .50
12 Pierre-Luc Emond .20 .50
13 Guillaume Demers .20 .50
14 Rodrigue Boucher .20 .50
15 George Davis .20 .50
16 Andre Martineau .20 .50
17 Carl McLean .20 .50
18 Pascal Morency .20 .50
19 Mathieu Dumas .20 .50
20 Jean-Francois Dufort .20 .50
21 Marc-Andre Fleury 2.00 5.00
22 Jasen Awalt .20 .50
23 Kevin Asselin .20 .50

2002-03 Cape Breton Screaming Eagles

The cards are not numbered are are listed below in the order they appear on the checklist card.

COMPLETE SET (25) 6.00 15.00
1 Marc-Andre Fleury 1.25 3.00
2 Martin Houle .60 1.50
3 Maxime Lessard .15 .40
4 Nathan Veinot .30 .75
5 Maxime Robert .15 .40
6 Jean-Claude Sawyer .15 .40
7 Vincent Zaore-Vanie .15 .40
8 Stephen Dixon .30 .75
9 Martin Slovak .15 .40
10 Joel Maas .15 .40
11 Pierre-Luc Emond .15 .40
12 Guillaume Demers .15 .40
13 Gregory Hoffe .15 .40
14 Jonathan Labelle .15 .40
15 Kevin Asselin .15 .40
16 Jared Vokey .15 .40
17 Michel Charette .15 .40
18 Samuel Beland .15 .40
19 Jean-Francois Dufort .30 .75
20 Patrick Gilbert .15 .40
21 Martin Trempe .15 .40
22 Steeve Villeneuve .15 .40
23 Stuart McRae .15 .40
24 Jean-Philippe Cote .15 .40
25 George Davis .15 .40
26 Marc-Andre Fleury CL 1.25 3.00

2003-04 Cape Breton Screaming Eagles

COMPLETE SET (24) 6.00 15.00
2 Adam Pardy .20 .50
4 Steve Villeneuve .20 .50
6 Tim Ramholt .20 .50
8 Nathan Veinot .20 .50
11 Francois-Pierre Guenette .20 .50
12 Jean-Claude Sawyer .20 .50
13 Vincent Zaore-Vanie .20 .50
14 Stephen Dixon .30 .75
15 Alexandre Picard .40 1.00
18 Guillaume Demers .20 .50
19 Gregory Hoffe .20 .50
20 Neil Smith .20 .50
21 Michael Tessier .20 .50
22 Kevin Asselin .20 .50
23 Jean-Francois Cyr .20 .50
24 Charles Fontaine .20 .50
26 Samuel Beland .20 .50
27 Philippe Bertrand .20 .50
28 Vincent Lambert .20 .50
29 Marc-Andre Fleury 1.25 3.00
30 Francois Proteau .30 .75
31 Martin Houle .40 1.00
41 Marc-Andre Bernier .40 1.00
84 Nicolas Corbeil .30 .75

2004-05 Cape Breton Screaming Eagles

A total of 750 team sets were produced.

COMPLETE SET (23) 5.00 12.00
1 Martin Houle .40 1.00
2 Kevin Asselin .20 .50
3 Stephen Dixon .30 .75
4 Samuel Beland .20 .50
5 Philippe Bertrand .20 .50
6 Chris Culligan .20 .50
7 Guillaume Demers .20 .50
8 Charles Fontaine .20 .50
9 Luke Gallant .20 .50
10 Vladimir Kubus .20 .50
11 Vincent Lambert .20 .50
12 Brandon MacDonald .20 .50
13 Dean Ouellet .20 .50
14 Adam Pardy .20 .50
15 Leonard Puterman .20 .50

16 Jean-Claude Sawyer .20 .50
17 James Sheppard .60 1.50
18 Neil Smith .20 .50
19 Francois Theriault .20 .50
20 David Victor .20 .50
21 Tyler Whitehead .20 .50
22 Vincent Zaore .20 .50
23 David Davenport .20 .50

2005-06 Cape Breton Screaming Eagles

COMPLETE SET (25) 5.00 12.00
1 James Sheppard .50 1.25
2 Ondrej Pavelec .30 .75
3 Jason Swit .20 .50
4 David Victor .20 .50
5 Darrell Simich .20 .50
6 Chris Culligan .20 .50
7 Robert Slaney .20 .50
8 Dean Ouellet .20 .50
9 Vladimir Kubus .20 .50
10 Brad Gallant .20 .50
11 Jean-Claude Sawyer .20 .50
12 Francois Gauthier .20 .50
13 Philippe Bertrand .20 .50
14 Scott Brannon .20 .50
15 Etienne Breton .20 .50
16 Jeff Grenier .20 .50
17 Brendon MacDonald .20 .50
18 Kevin Asselin .20 .50
19 Francois Theriault .20 .50
20 Charles Fontaine .20 .50
21 Vincent Zaore .20 .50
22 David Davenport .20 .50
23 Paul McIlveen .20 .50
24 Cam Fergus .20 .50
25 Alexandre Blais .20 .50

2006-07 Cape Breton Screaming Eagles

COMPLETE SET (25) 8.00 15.00
1 James Sheppard .60 1.50
2 Étienne Breton .30 .75
3 Jason Swit .30 .75
4 Daniel Fazzalari .30 .75
5 Chris Culligan .30 .75
6 Robert Sanley .30 .75
7 Dean Ouellet .30 .75
8 Scott Brannon .30 .75
9 Brad Gallant .30 .75
10 Jean-Claude Sawyer .30 .75
11 Cam Fergus .30 .75
12 Jean-Christophe Gauthier .30 .75
13 Oskars Bartulis .30 .75
14 Alexandre Quesnel .30 .75
15 François Gauthier .30 .75
16 Stephen Ceccanese .30 .75
17 Brendon Macdonald .30 .75
18 Charlie Pens .30 .75
19 Mark Barberio .30 .75
20 Mickey Macdonald .30 .75
21 Nick Macneil .30 .75
22 Paul McIlveen .30 .75
23 Ondrej Pavelec .40 1.00
24 David Davenport .30 .75
25 Screech MASCOT .02 .10

2003-04 Cape Fear Fire Antz

This set features the fearsome Fire Antz of the SEHL. According to minor league expert Ralph Slate, the cards seem to have been put together by hand, with two matte photo pieces of paper glued together.

COMPLETE SET (17) 15.00 30.00
1 David Bagley .75 2.00
2 Mike Bournazakis .75 2.00
3 Kevin Fines .75 2.00
4 Ryan Kiley .75 2.00
5 Matt Kohansky .75 2.00
6 Dave Leger .75 2.00
7 Mike Maurice .75 2.00
8 Darren McLean .75 2.00
9 Chris Migliore .75 2.00
10 Marc Milburn .75 2.00
11 Glenn Ridler 1.00 2.50
12 Tim Rink .75 2.00
13 Matt Shannon .75 2.00
14 Aaron Shrieves .75 2.00
15 Rob Vessio .75 2.00
16 Scott Young .75 2.00
17 Scott Rex CO .25

1996-97 Carolina Monarchs

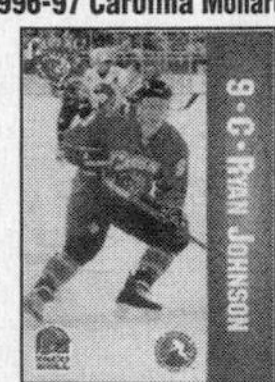

This 30-card set was released by Multi-Ad services and sponsored by Taco Bell, whose logo appears on the front of the card. This set is not numbered so the cards appear alphabetically.

COMPLETE SET (30) 4.80 12.00
1 Checklist .02 .10
2 Chris Armstrong .15 .40
3 Drake Berehowsky .30 .75
4 Ashley Buckberger .15 .40
5 Chad Cabana .15 .40
6 Jon Christiano ACO .15 .40
7 Gilbert Dionne .30 .75
8 Trevor Doyle .15 .40
9 Ivan Droppa .15 .40
10 Craig Ferguson .20 .50
11 Craig Fisher .15 .40
12 Bob Halkidis .15 .40
13 Ryan Johnson .15 .40
14 Richard Kromm HCO .02 .10
15 Filip Kuba .15 .40
16 David Lemanowicz .08 .25
17 Craig Martin .20 .50
18 Eric Montreuil .15 .40
19 David Nemirovsky .15 .40
20 Jason Podollan .15 .40
21 Gaetan Poirier .15 .40
22 Garin Smith .15 .40
23 Geoff Smith .15 .40
24 Herbert Vasiljevs .15 .40
25 Steve Washburn .20 .50
26 Kevin Weekes .40 1.00
27 Dean Aayonce .15 .40
28 Monty MASCOT .02 .10
29 Prospect Card .15 .40
30 PHPA Web Site .01

2006-07 Cedar Rapids RoughRiders

COMPLETE SET (25) 10.00 20.00
1 Richard Bachman .40 1.00
2 Robin Bergman .40 1.00
3 David Boehm .40 1.00
4 Aaron Bogosian .40 1.00
5 Rob Bordson .40 1.00
6 Pat Cannone .40 1.00
7 Jacob Cepis .40 1.00
8 Brett Dickinson .40 1.00
9 Doug Jones .40 1.00
10 Sergei Kolosov .40 1.00
11 Scott Mathis .40 1.00
12 Kent Patterson .40 1.00
13 Mike Seidel .40 1.00
14 Ian Slater .40 1.00
15 Tomi Stahlhammer .40 1.00
16 Evan Stephens .40 1.00
17 Tyler Thompson .40 1.00
18 Matt Tomassoni .40 1.00
19 Kevin Wehrs .40 1.00
20 Casey Wellman .40 1.00
21 Scott Wietecha .40 1.00
22 Tommy Wingels .40 1.00
23 Mark Carlson CO .10 .25
24 Joe Exter ACO .10 .25
25 Ricochet MASCOT .02 .10

1994-95 Central Hockey League

This 127-card standard-size set features the seven teams of the Central Hockey League. Reportedly only 13,000 of each card were produced. The cards were available in pack form only, either at team rinks or from the league for 3.00 by mail. The fronts feature borderless color action player photos except on the left, where a gray bar edges the picture and carries the CHL logo, the player's name and number, and the team logo. On a white background with light gray team logos, the horizontal backs carry a short player biography, profile and stats. The cards are unnumbered, grouped alphabetically within teams and checklisted below alphabetically according to teams as follows: Dallas Freeze (1-18), Ft. Worth Fire (19-36), Memphis Riverkings (37-54), Oklahoma City Blazers (55-72), San Antonio Iguanas (73-90), Tulsa Oilers (91-108), and Wichita Thunder (109-126).

COMPLETE SET (127) 16.00 40.00
1 Jamie Adams .15 .40
2 Wayne Anchikoski .20 .50
3 Jeff Beaudin .15 .40
4 Troy Binnie .20 .50
5 Don Burke .15 .40
6 Derek Crawford .15 .40
7 Ray Desouza .15 .40
8 Ron Flockhart CO .15 .40
9 Jon Gustafson .20 .50
10 Jason Heiland .15 .40
11 James Jensen .15 .40
12 Frank LaScala .15 .40
13 Ryan Leschasin .15 .40
14 Rob Madia .15 .40
15 Rob McCaig .15 .40
16 Jim McGeough .20 .50
17 Doug Roberts .15 .40
18 Jason Taylor .15 .40
19 Scott Allen .15 .40
20 Bruce Bell .20 .50
21 Francois Bourdeau .15 .40
22 Troy Frederick .15 .40
23 Steve Harrison CO .15 .40
24 Alex Kholomeyev .20 .50
25 Dominic Maltais .20 .50
26 Martin Masa .20 .50
27 Jeff Massey .15 .40
28 Mike McCormick .15 .40
29 Pat McGarry .20 .50
30 Dwight Mullins .15 .40
31 Eric Ricard .15 .40
32 Sean Rowe .15 .40
33 Bryan Schoen .15 .40
34 Darren Srochenski .15 .40
35 Andy Stewart .15 .40
36 Stephen Tepper .15 .40
37 Denis Beauchamp .15 .40
38 Herb Boxer CO .15 .40
39 Nicolas Brousseau .15 .40
40 Scott Brower .20 .50
41 Dan Brown .15 .40
42 Brian Cook .15 .40
43 Brent Fleetwood .15 .40
44 Francois Gagon .15 .40
45 Dominic Grand-Maison .15 .40
46 Kyle Haviland .15 .40
47 Jamie Hearn .15 .40
48 Mike Jackson .20 .50
49 Paul Krake .20 .50
50 Layne LeBel .15 .40
51 Steve Magnusson .15 .40
52 Mark McGinn .15 .40
53 Darren Miciak .15 .40
54 Bobby Wallwork .20 .50
55 Ron Aubrey .20 .50
56 Joe Burton .20 .50
57 George Dupont .20 .50
58 Tom Gomes .15 .40
59 Sean Gorman .15 .40
60 Viktor Ignatjev .20 .50
61 Chris Laganas .15 .40
62 Michael McEwen CO .20 .50
63 Chris McMurtry .15 .40
64 Derry Menard .15 .40
65 Sergei Naumov .20 .50
66 Trent Pankewicz .15 .40
67 Alan Perry .30 .75
68 Eric Plante .15 .40
69 Dave Slifka .15 .40
70 Steve Simoni .15 .40
71 Michel St. Jacques .15 .40
72 Tom Thornbury .15 .40
73 Trevor Buchanan .15 .40
74 Link Gaetz .30 .75
75 Sean Goldsworthy .15 .40
76 Fred Goltz .15 .40
77 Sheldon Gorski .15 .40
78 Ross Harris .15 .40
79 Dale Henry .20 .50
80 Paul Jackson .30 .75
81 Scot Kelsey .15 .40
82 John Klaers .15 .40
83 Stu Kulak .20 .50
84 Ken Plaquin .15 .40
85 Brian Shantz .20 .50
86 Dean Shmyr .20 .50
87 Adam Thompson .15 .40
88 John Torchetti .15 .40
89 Ken Venis .15 .40
90 Mike Williams .15 .40
91 Colin Baustad .15 .40
92 Luc Beausoleil .20 .50
93 Mike Berger .15 .40
94 Shawn Cavallin .15 .40
95 Shaun Clouston .15 .40
96 Michel Couvrette .15 .40
97 Taylor Hall .15 .40
98 Ryan Harrison .15 .40
99 Sasha Lakovic .30 .75
100 Chuck Loreto .15 .40
101 Tony Martino .20 .50
102 David Moore .15 .40
103 Sylvain Naud .20 .50
104 Dan O'Rourke .15 .40
105 Jody Praznik .15 .40
106 Andy Ross .15 .40
107 Mike Shea .15 .40
108 Garry Unger CO .30 .75
109 Bob Berg .15 .40
110 John DePourcq .20 .50
111 Dave Doucette .20 .50
112 Ron Handy .20 .50
113 Mark Hilton .15 .40
114 Darcy Kaminski .15 .40
115 Mark Karpen .15 .40
116 Jim Latos .15 .40
117 George Maneluk .20 .50
118 Greg Neish .15 .40
119 Brent Sapergia .30 .75
120 Doug Shedden CO .20 .50
121 Greg Smith .15 .40
122 Conrade Thomas .15 .40
123 John Vary .15 .40
124 Rob Weingartner .15 .40
125 Bryan Wells .15 .40
126 Jack Williams .15 .40
127 Title Card CL .15 .40

1995-96 Central Hockey League

This set features the players of the Central Hockey League. The cards feature action photography on the front ensconced in a gray marble border, highlighted by the team logo in the top left corner. The backs contain another photo, and player information. The cards are unnumbered, so they are listed alphabetically by team, and then by name. They were available in packs at CHL games.

COMPLETE SET (90) 14.00 35.00
1 Scott Allen .15 .40
2 Trevor Burgess .15 .40
3 Brian Caruso .15 .40
4 Trevor Converse .15 .40
5 Steve Dykstra .30 .75
6 Troy Frederick .15 .40
7 Phil Groeneveld .15 .40
8 Mark Hilton .20 .50
9 Jeff Massey .15 .40
10 Dennis Miller .15 .40
11 Dwight Mullins .15 .40
12 Steve Plouffe .30 .75
13 Vern Ray .15 .40
14 Kyle Reeves .30 .75
15 Troy Stephens .15 .40
16 Sean Whyte .20 .50
17 Scorch .02 .10
18 Bill McDonald .15 .40
19 Scott Brower .20 .50
20 Dan Brown .15 .40
21 Jamie Cooke .15 .40
22 Kevin Evans .15 .40
23 Brent Fleetwood .15 .40
24 Ron Fogarty .15 .40
25 Trent Gleason .15 .40
26 Derek Grant .15 .40
27 Mike Jackson .30 .75
28 Scot Kelsey .15 .40
29 Steve Magnusson .15 .40
30 Carl Menard .30 .75
31 Chris Morque .15 .40
32 Rick Robus .15 .40
33 Andy Ross .15 .40
34 Stephane Roy .15 .40
35 Doug Stromback .15 .40
36 Herb Boxer .15 .40
37 Kevin Barrett .15 .40
38 Carl Boudreau .30 .75
39 Joe Burton .15 .40
40 George Dupont .15 .40
41 Dominic Fafard .15 .40
42 Jean-Ian Filiatrault .20 .50
43 Tom Gomes .15 .40
44 Todd Harris .15 .40
45 Mervin Kopeck .15 .40
46 Doug Lawrence .30 .75
47 Kevin Lune .15 .40
48 Steve Moore .15 .40
49 Simon Olivier .15 .40
50 Darren Pengelly .20 .50
51 Steve Simoni .15 .40
52 Barkley Swenson .15 .40
53 Serge Tkachenko .20 .50
54 Doug Sauter .15 .40
55 Colin Baustad .15 .40
56 Mike Berger .15 .40
57 Mike Chase .15 .40
58 Trevor Ellerman .15 .40
59 Bryan Forslund .15 .40
60 Taylor Hall .15 .40
61 Craig Hamelin .15 .40
62 Ryan Harrison .15 .40
63 John Laan .15 .40
64 Glen Lang .15 .40
65 Dave Larouche .15 .40
66 Tony Martino .30 .75
67 Sylvain Naud .30 .75
68 Jim Peters .15 .40
69 Cory Peterson .15 .40
70 Chris Robertson .15 .40
71 Kyuin Shim .15 .40
72 Garry Unger .30 .75
73 Clint Black .15 .40
74 Mike Chighisola .15 .40
75 Leonard Devuono .15 .40
76 Ty Eigner .30 .75
77 Anton Fedorov .20 .50
78 Paul Krake .30 .75
79 Antonin Necas .15 .40
80 Ryan Pisiak .15 .40
81 Richard Roesler .15 .40
82 Jason Rushton .15 .40
83 Art Saran .15 .40
84 Stefan Simoes .15 .40
85 Greg Smith .15 .40
86 Dale Turnbull .15 .40
87 Rob Weingartner .15 .40
88 Bryan Wells .15 .40
89 Jack Williams .15 .40
90 Don Jackson .30 .75

1997-98 Central Texas Stampede

Little is known about this set other than the confirmed checklist. Additional information can be forwarded to hockeymag@beckett.com.

COMPLETE SET (20) 3.60 9.00
1 Matt Brenner .20 .50
2 Mike Dick .20 .50
3 Darren Duncalfe .20 .50
4 Larry Dyck .20 .50
5 Dwayne Gylywoychuk .20 .50
6 Ricky Jacob .20 .50
7 Peter Jas .20 .50
8 Dean Kolstad .30 .75
9 Jacques Mailhot .30 .75
10 Don McGrath .20 .50
11 Derek Nicolson .20 .50
12 Jeff Rask .20 .50
13 Layne Roland .20 .50
14 Alex Rummo .20 .50
15 Doug Smith .20 .50
16 Greg Smith .20 .50
17 Joe Tassone .20 .50
18 Jason Taylor .20 .50
19 Peter Zurba .20 .50
20 Wild Thing Mascot .02 .10

1996-97 Charlotte Checkers

This set was only available at the bakery department of a Charlotte Super Shop & Save grocery store, and thus is extremely difficult to find in the secondary market.

COMPLETE SET (20) 14.00 35.00
1 J.F. Aube .75 2.00
2 Eric Boulton 2.00 5.00
3 David Brosseau .75 2.00
4 Jeff Connolly .75 2.00
5 Kimbi Daniels .75 2.00
6 Mickey Elick .75 2.00
7 Eric Fenton .75 2.00
8 Mick Kempffer .75 2.00
9 Jay Kenney .75 2.00
10 Scott Kirton .75 2.00
11 Darcy Mitani .75 2.00
12 Darryl Noren .75 2.00
13 Kevin Rappana .75 2.00
14 Matt Robbins .75 2.00
15 Evgeni Ryabchikov .75 2.00
16 Kurt Seher .75 2.00
17 Nick Vitucci 1.25 3.00
18 Shawn Wheeler .75 2.00
19 John Marks HCO .20 .50
20 Chubby Checker Mascot .02 .10

1997-98 Charlotte Checkers

This 26-card set was given away by both the bakery of a Charlotte Hannaford grocery store and sold by the team. Note: three versions of card #25 exist.

COMPLETE SET (28) 15.00 30.00
1 Matt Alvey .40 1.00
2 Eric Boulton 1.25 3.00
3 David Brosseau .40 1.00
4 Paxton Schafer .60 1.50
5 Kurt Seher .40 1.00
6 Stephane Soulliere .40 1.00
7 Derek Crimin .40 1.00
8 Eric Flinton .40 1.00
9 Justin Gould .40 1.00
10 Jason Kelly .40 1.00
11 Mike Hartman .40 1.00
12 Jeff Heil .40 1.00
13 Jay Kenney .40 1.00
14 Milt Mastad .40 1.00
15 Dean Moore .40 1.00
16 Darryl Noren .40 1.00
17 Dale Purinton 1.25 3.00
18 Andre Roy 1.25 3.00
19 P.C. Drouin .60 1.50
20 Bill McCauley .40 1.00
21 Shawn Wheeler ACO .02 .10
22 John Marks HCO .02 .10
23 Chubby Checker Mascot .02 .10
24 Checklist .01
25 Darryl Noren CAP .60 1.50
25 Cric Flinton CAP .60 1.50
25 Kurt Seher CAP .60 1.50
26 PHPA Web Site .01

1998-99 Charlotte Checkers

This set was issued as a promotional giveaway through a local grocery store named Hannaford's. As such, it is extremely difficult to find on the secondary market.

COMPLETE SET (24) 10.00 25.00
1 J.F. Aube .60 1.50
2 Shannon Basaraba .40 1.00
3 Doug Battaglia .40 1.00
4 David Brosseau .40 1.00
5 Tom Brown .40 1.00
6 Pat Brownlee .40 1.00
7 Brooke Chateau .40 1.00
8 Jeff Heil .40 1.00
9 Boyd Kane .60 1.50
10 Kevin Kreutzer .40 1.00
11 Darryl Noren .60 1.50
12 Jason Norrie .40 1.00
13 Nikolai Pronin .40 1.00
14 Kurt Seher .60 1.50
15 Bob Sheehan .40 1.00
16 Ryan Sittler .40 1.00
17 Martin Sychra .40 1.00
18 Dean Zayonce .40 1.00
19 Shawn Wheeler CO .08 .25
20 Chubby Checker .08 .25
21 The Captains .40 1.00
22 Doug Battaglia
Pat Brownlee
23 J.F. Aube .40 1.00
Bob Sheehan
24 Checklist .02 .10

1999-00 Charlotte Checkers

This set features the Checkers of the ECHL. The cards were produced by Roox, and handed out as promotional giveaways over the course of several home games.

COMPLETE SET (38) 8.00 20.00
1 Jason Dailey .20 .50
2 Brooke Chateau .20 .50
3 Rocky Welsing .20 .50
4 Kurt Seher .20 .50
5 Kevin Hilton .20 .50
6 Reggie Brezeault .20 .50
7 Lee Hamilton .20 .50
8 Dave Risk .20 .50
9 Taras Lendzyk .20 .50
10 Kurt Mallett .20 .50
11 Tyler Deis .20 .50
12 Mike Rucinski .30 .75
13 Derek Wilkinson .40 1.00
14 Richard Scott .40 1.00
15 David Beauregard .30 .75
16 Mike Jaros .20 .50
17 Darryl Noren .20 .50
18 Marc Tropper .20 .50
19 Scott Bailey .40 1.00
20 Jeff Brown .20 .50
21 Boyd Kane .40 1.00
22 Chubby Checker MASCOT .02 .10
23 The Carolina Cup .02 .10
24 Marc Tropper .30 .75
24 Brooke Chateau .20 .50
25 Mark Burgess TR .02 .10
26 Don MacAdam CO .02 .10
27 Scott Bailey .40 1.00
28 Dean Mando .30 .75
29 Kevin Pozzo .20 .50
30 Martin Cerven .20 .50
31 Marc Tropper AS .30 .75
32 Scott Bailey .40 1.00
33 Mike Rucinski .40 1.00
34 David Beauregard .30 .75
34 Tyler Deis .20 .50
35 Darryl Noren .20 .50
36 Checklist .04 .10

2000-01 Charlotte Checkers

This set features the Checkers of the ECHL. It is believed that it was issued as a promotional giveaway over two home games, then later sold by the team at its souvenir stands.

COMPLETE SET (36) 10.00 25.00
1 Jason Labarbera .60 1.50
2 Scott Bailey .40 1.00
3 Scott King .40 1.00
4 Marc Tropper .30 .75
5 Boyd Kane .30 .75
6 Justin Harney .30 .75
7 Kurt Seher .30 .75
8 Brad Mehalko .30 .75
9 Kevin Hilton .30 .75
10 Mathieu Benoit .30 .75
11 David Oliver .30 .75
12 Lee Hamilton .30 .75
13 Wes Jarvis .30 .75
14 Josh MacNevin .30 .75
15 Kevin Pozzo .30 .75
16 Don MacAdam HCO .08 .25
17 Dave Baseggio CO .08 .25
18 Chubby Checker MASCOT .08 .25
19 Paul Giblin .30 .75
20 Tyler Deis .30 .75
21 Mark Spence .30 .75
22 Bob MacIsaac .30 .75
23 Steve Duke .30 .75
24 Andre Signoretti .30 .75
25 Brandon Dietrich .30 .75
26 Mike Derecola .30 .75
27 Chris Plumhoff .30 .75
28 Chubby Checker MASCOT .08 .25
29 Richard Scott .40 1.00
30 Vitali Yeremeyev .60 1.50
31 Benjamin Carpentier .30 .75
32 Francois Fortier .30 .75
33 Scott Wray .30 .75
34 Mark Moore .30 .75
35 Bryce Wandler .30 .75
36 Checklist .08 .10

2002-03 Charlotte Checkers

COMPLETE SET (18) 20.00
79 Nicholas Bilotto 1.00
80 Kevin Caulfield 1.00
81 Brandon Cullen 1.50
82 Allan Egeland 1.00
83 David Evans 1.00
84 David Inman 1.00
85 Dusty Jamieson 1.00
86 Vince Malts 1.00
87 Walker McDonald 1.00
88 Konrad McKay 1.50
89 Scott Meyer 1.50
90 Eduard Pershin 1.00
91 Kurt Seher 1.00
92 Takahito Suzuki 1.50
94 Craig Weller 1.00
95 Chad Wilchynski 1.00
96 Colin Zulianello 1.00

2003-04 Charlotte Checkers

This set was produced by RBI Sports. The numbering below reflects the entire print run of the RBI ECHL set. It has been reported that just 250 copies of this set were produced.

COMPLETE SET (16) 15.00
65 Nicholas Bilotto 1.00
66 Kevin Caulfield 1.00
67 Doug Christiansen 1.00
68 Ryan Cuthbert 1.00
69 Allan Egeland 1.00
70 Blaz Emersic 1.00
71 Kengo Ito 1.00
72 Steven MacIntyre 1.00
73 Konrad McKay 1.00
74 Scott Meyer 1.50
75 Daisuke Obara 1.00
76 Rory Rawlyk 1.00
77 David St. Germain 1.50
78 Marc St. Jean 1.00
79 Jeff State 1.00
80 Mike Wirll 1.00

2002-03 Chicago Steel

This set features the Steel of the USHL.

COMPLETE SET (24) 20.00
1 Bill Bagron 1.00
2 Jordan Black 1.00
3 Dan Charleston 1.00
4 Adam D'Alba 1.50
5 Jeff Dunne 1.00
6 Josh Elzinga 1.00
7 Rene Gauthier 1.00
8 Ben Geelan 1.00
9 Brady Greco 1.50
10 Michael Grenzy 1.00
11 Eric Helstedt 1.00
12 Mike Kennedy 1.00
13 Vojtech Kloz 1.00
14 Justin Lewandowski 1.00
15 Travis Moran 1.00
16 Joseph Pearce 2.50
17 Topher Scott 1.00
18 Eric Slais 1.00
19 Chad Solberg 1.00
20 Alex Spezia 1.00
21 Lee Sweatt 1.00
22 Blake Williams 1.00
23 A.J. Toews CO .10
24 Rusty Steel MASCOT .10

2003-04 Chicago Steel

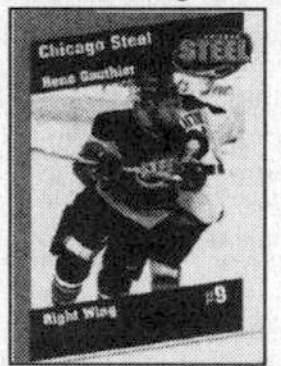

This set features the Steel of the USHL. Little is known about the set beyond the checklist info.

COMPLETE SET (18) 18.00
1 Matt McIlvane 1.50
2 Dan Marziani 1.00
3 Shane Connelly 1.50
4 Mike Van Wagner 1.00
5 Jay Sprague 1.00
6 Matt Clackson 1.00
7 Justin Lewandowski 1.00
8 Kevin Roeder 1.00
9 David Marshall 1.00
10 Chris Walsh 1.00
11 Jeff Dunne 1.00
12 Eric Lampe 1.00
13 Ryan Kim 1.00
14 John Kearns 1.00
15 Ryan Hawkins 1.00
16 T.J. Fox 1.00
17 Alex Spezia 1.00
18 Rene Gauthier 1.00
19 Rusty Steel MASCOT .10

2004-05 Chicago Steel

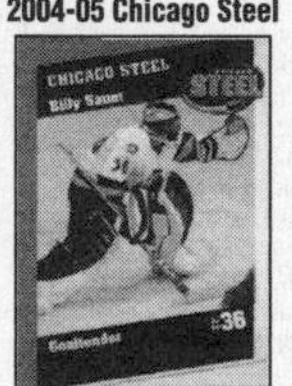

We have confirmed a handful of cards from this USHL set. If you have additional information, please contact us at hockeymag@beckett.com.

COMPLETE SET (?)
1 Nathan Perkovich 1.00
2 T.J. Fox 1.00
3 Kevin Swallow 1.00
4 Eric Slais 1.00
5 Billy Sauer 1.00
6 Shane Connelly 1.00
7 Chris Clackson 1.00
8 Sami Liimainen 1.00
9 Ryan Oldis 1.00
10 Joe Loprieno 1.00

1998-99 Chicago Wolves

This set features the Wolves of the IHL. The set was handed out at a game in March as a promotional item.

COMPLETE SET (25) 8.00 20.00
1 Brent Gretzky .40 1.00
2 Dan Plante .30 .75
3 Tim Bergland .30 .75
4 Steve Maltais .75 2.00
5 Steve Gosselin .40 1.00
6 Scott Pearson .30 .75
7 Niklas Andersson .40 1.00
8 Chris LiPuma .30 .75
9 Pat Jablonski .40 1.00
10 Skates MASCOT .02 .10
11 Tim Breslin .30 .75
12 Chris Marinucci .30 .75
13 Steve Larouche .30 .75
14 Wendell Young .75 2.00
15 Glen Featherstone .30 .75
16 Bob Nardella .30 .75
17 Guy Larose .30 .75
18 Dennis Vial .40 1.00
19 Kevin Dahl .30 .75
20 Jeremy Mylymok .30 .75
21 Paul Koch .30 .75
22 Tom Tilley .30 .75
23 John Anderson HCO .20 .50
24 Kevin Miller .40 1.00
25 PHPA Web Site .01

1998-99 Chicago Wolves Turner Cup

This 24-card set was handed out at two separate games. It showcases players from the Turner Cup Championship team of 1997-98, although it was released in the 1998-99 season. Note: there at two different versions of card #3.

COMPLETE SET (25) 10.00 25.00
1 Wendell Young .75 2.00
2 John Anderson .20 .50
3 Dave Craievich .20 .50
3 Ray LeBlanc 1.25 3.00
4 Paul Koch .20 .50
5 Kevin Dahl .20 .50
6 Jeremy Mylymok .20 .50
7 Bob Nardella .20 .50
8 Marc Rodgers 1.25 3.00
9 Marc Potvin .75 2.00
10 Steve Larouche .40 1.00
11 Steve Maltais 1.25 3.00
12 Doug Barrault .20 .50
13 Jamie Baker .20 .50
14 Chris Marinucci .20 .50
15 Tim Breslin .20 .50
16 Dennis Vial 1.25 3.00
17 Tom Tilley .20 .50
18 Scott Pearson .20 .50
19 Steve Martins .30 .75
20 Matt Martin .20 .50
21 Tim Bergland .20 .50
22 Alexander Semak .40 1.00
23 Ravil Gusmanov .20 .50
24 Stephane Beauregard .75 2.00

1999-00 Chicago Wolves

This set features the Wolves of the IHL. The set was issued as a promotional giveaway and was limited to 5,000 total sets.

COMPLETE SET (25) 8.00 20.00
1 Header Card/PHPA .01
2 Wendell Young .75 2.00
3 Kevin Dahl .30 .75
4 Dallas Eakins .30 .75
5 Bob Nardella .30 .75
6 Niklas Andersson .30 .75
7 Steve Larouche .75 2.00
8 Steve Maltais .75 2.00
9 Chris Marinucci .30 .75
10 Brian Noonan .40 1.00
11 Guy Larose .30 .75
12 Sean Berens .30 .75
13 Glen Featherstone .30 .75
14 Tom Tilley .30 .75
15 Scott Pearson .30 .75
16 Greg Andrusak .30 .75
17 Dean Malkoc .30 .75
18 David Mackey .30 .75
19 Dan Plante .30 .75
20 Chris LiPuma .30 .75
21 Andrei Trefilov .40 1.00
22 Daniel Lacroix .30 .75
23 John Anderson CO .08 .25
24 Marty Howe CO .20 .50
25 Skates MASCOT .08 .25

2000-01 Chicago Wolves

This set features the Wolves of the IHL. The set is noteworthy for the inclusion of Rick DiPietro, the first overall pick of the 2000 NHL Entry Draft. It is oversized, and is believed to have been handed out at a home game in February, 2001.

COMPLETE SET (25) 10.00 25.00
1 John Anderson .20 .50
2 Niklas Anderson .20 .50
3 Jesse Belanger .40 1.00
4 Rob Brown .40 1.00
5 Kevin Dahl .20 .50
6 Rick DiPietro 4.00 10.00
7 Ted Drury .20 .50
8 Dallas Eakins .20 .50
9 Glen Featherstone .20 .50
10 Eric Houde .20 .50
11 Paul Kruse .20 .50
12 Guy Larose .20 .50
13 Steve Larouche .40 1.00
14 Mark Lawrence .30 .75
15 Chris LiPuma .20 .50
16 Steve Maltais .80 2.00
17 Dean Melanson .20 .50
18 Bob Nardella .30 .75
19 Brian Noonan .40 1.00
20 Robert Petrovicky .30 .75
21 Dan Plante .20 .50
22 Tom Tilley .40 1.00
23 Wendell Young .40 1.00
24 Chicago Wolves .20 .25

25 Skates MASCOT .10 .25
NNO Header Card .02 .10

2001-02 Chicago Wolves

This set features the Wolves of the AHL. It was issued as a promotional giveaway at a game in March 2002. The set is slightly oversized. Since the cards are unnumbered, they are listed below in alphabetical order.

COMPLETE SET (25) 9.78 25.00
1 Bryan Adams .30 .75
2 Zdenek Blatny .40 1.00
3 Rob Brown .40 1.00
4 Frederic Cassivi .40 1.00
5 Jeff Dessner .30 .75
6 Dallas Eakins .30 .75
7 Garnet Exelby .40 1.50
8 Kurtis Foster .30 .75
9 Darcy Hordichuk .80 2.00
10 Derek MacKenzie .30 .75
11 Steve Maltais .40 1.00
12 Norm Maracle .40 1.00
13 Bob Nardella .30 .75
14 Pasi Nurminen 1.20 3.00
15 Kamil Piros .60 1.00
16 Dan Plante .30 .75
17 Brian Pothier .40 1.00
18 Luke Sellars .30 .75
19 Ben Simon .30 .75
20 Jarrod Skalde .40 1.00
21 Dan Snyder .40 1.00
22 Brad Tapper .40 1.00
23 J.P. Vigier .40 1.00
24 Mike Weaver .40 1.00
25 Skates MASCOT .10 .25

2002-03 Chicago Wolves

This set was issued as a promotional giveaway at a late-season home game. The cards are unnumbered and are listed below in alphabetical order.

COMPLETE SET (25) 35.00
1 John Anderson CO .25
2 Zdenek Blatny 1.50
3 Rob Brown 1.00
4 Frederic Cassivi 1.50
5 Joey DiPenta 3.00
6 Dallas Eakins 1.00
7 Garnet Exelby 3.00
8 Jeff Farkas 1.00
9 Kurtis Foster 1.00
10 Simon Gamache 3.00
11 Mark Hartigan 1.00
12 Milan Hnilicka 3.00
13 Andreas Karlsson 1.00
14 Francis Lessard 1.00
15 Derek MacKenzie 1.00
16 Steve Maltais 3.00
17 Norm Maracle 3.00
18 Kamil Piros 2.00
19 Kirill Safronov 1.00
20 Luke Sellars 1.00
21 Ben Simon 1.00
22 Skates MASCOT .10
23 Ryan Tobler 1.00
24 Libor Ustrnul 1.00
25 J.P. Vigier 2.00

2003-04 Chicago Wolves

COMPLETE SET (25) 15.00 30.00
1 Stephen Baby .40 1.00
2 Zdenek Blatny .40 1.00
3 Jim Campbell .40 1.00
4 Frederic Cassivi .60 1.50
5 Daniel Corso .40 1.00
6 Joe DiPenta .60 1.50
7 Kurtis Foster .40 1.00
8 Michael Garnett .60 1.50
9 Greg Hawgood .40 1.00
10 Eric Healey .40 1.00
11 Shawn Heins .40 1.00
12 Kari Lehtonen 2.00 5.00
13 Derek MacKenzie .40 1.00
14 Brian Maloney .40 1.00
15 Steve Maltais .60 1.50
16 Kamil Piros .40 1.00
17 Tommi Santala .40 1.00
18 Luke Sellars .40 1.00
19 Karl Stewart .40 1.00
20 Brian Swanson .40 1.00
21 Libor Ustrnul .40 1.00
22 Mike Weaver .40 1.00
23 Brendan Yarema .40 1.00
24 John Anderson HCO .10 .25
25 Mascot .02 .10

2004-05 Chicago Wolves

COMPLETE SET (25) 40.00 75.00
1 Kari Lehtonen 5.00 10.00
2 Brad Larsen 1.00 2.50
3 Travis Roche 1.00 2.50
4 Michael Garnett 1.25 3.00
5 Greg Hawgood 1.00 2.50
6 Joe Corvo 1.00 2.50
7 Libor Ustrnul 1.00 2.50
8 Paul Flache 1.00 2.50
9 Colin Stuart 1.00 2.50
10 Kyle Rossiter 1.00 2.50
11 Brian Maloney 1.00 2.50
12 J.P. Vigier 1.50 4.00
13 Ben Simon 1.00 2.50
14 Brian Sipotz 1.00 2.50
15 Tim Wedderburn 1.00 2.50
16 Lonny Bohonos 1.50 4.00
17 Cory Larose 1.00 2.50
18 Kip Brennan 1.50 4.00
19 Stephen Baby 1.00 2.50
20 Kevin Doell 1.00 2.50
21 Karl Stewart 1.00 2.50
22 Steve Maltais 2.00 5.00
23 Derek MacKenzie 1.00 2.50
24 Tommi Santala 1.00 2.50
25 Skates MASCOT .40 1.00

2005-06 Chicago Wolves

COMPLETE SET (25) 10.00 25.00
1 Ramzi Abid .40 1.00
2 Stephen Baby .40 1.00
3 Scott Barney .40 1.00
4 Braydon Coburn .75 2.00
5 Kevin Doell .40 1.00
6 Pat Dwyer .40 1.00
7 Michael Garnett .75 2.00
8 Tomas Kloucek .40 1.00
9 Francis Lessard .40 1.00
10 Derek MacKenzie .40 1.00
11 Brian Maloney .40 1.00
12 Kip Miller .40 1.00
13 Justin Morrison .40 1.00
14 Nick Naumenko .40 1.00
15 Mark Popovic .40 1.00
16 Travis Roche .40 1.00
17 Jared Ross .40 1.00
18 Brian Sipotz .40 1.00
19 Karl Stewart .40 1.00
20 Colin Stuart .40 1.00
21 Tuomas Tarkki .40 1.00
22 Billy Tibbetts .40 1.00
23 Tim Wedderburn .40 1.00
24 John Anderson HC .02 .10
25 Skates MASCOT .02 .10

2007-08 Chicago Wolves

COMPLETE SET (27) 6.00 15.00
1 Joey Crabb .30 .75
2 Guillaume Desbiens .30 .75
3 Andre Deveaux .30 .75
4 Kevin Doell .30 .75
5 Brian Fahey .30 .75
6 Collton Fretter .30 .75
7 Robert Gherson .30 .75
8 Alexandre Giroux .30 .75
9 Darren Haydar .30 .75
10 Jason Krog .30 .75
11 Joel Kwiatkowski .30 .75
12 Jordan LaVallee .30 .75
13 Scott Lehman .30 .75
14 Grant Lewis .30 .75
15 Bryan Little .30 .75
16 Steve Martins .30 .75
17 Nathan Oystrick .30 .75
18 Chad Painchaud .30 .75
19 Ondrej Pavelec .75 2.00
20 Karel Pilar .30 .75
21 Jesse Schultz .30 .75
22 Brian Sipotz .30 .75
23 Brett Sterling .30 .75
24 Colin Stuart .30 .75
25 Boris Valabik .30 .75
26 John Anderson HC .30 .75
27 Skates MASCOT .30 .75

1984-85 Chicoutimi Sagueneens

This 24-card set sponsored by Mike's restaurants measures approximately 8 1/2" by 11" and features black-and-white player photos in a white-black-white-red frame. The complete set was issued in a protective folder. This folder is valued at $1. The card backs are blank. The cards are unnumbered and checklisted below in alphabetical order.

COMPLETE SET (24) 16.00 40.00
1 Mario Barbe .40 1.00
2 Mario Bazinet .40 1.00
3 Daniel Bedard .40 1.00
Michel Boivin
Guy Byatt
Jean-Marc Couture
Patrice Gosselin
Jean-Yves Laberge
Germain Munger
Reginald Riverin
4 Daniel Berthiaume 1.25 3.00
5 Francois Breault .60 1.50
6 Gregg Choules .40 1.00
7 Christian Duperron .40 1.00
8 Luc Dufour .40 1.00
9 Luc Duval .40 1.00
10 Patrick Emond .40 1.00
11 Marc Fortier .60 1.50
12 Steven Gauthier .40 1.00
13 Yves Heroux .60 1.50
14 Daniel Jomphe .40 1.00
15 Gilles Laberge .40 1.00
16 Claude Lajoie .40 1.00
17 Serge Lauzon .40 1.00
18 Roch Marinier .60 1.50
19 Pierre Millier .40 1.00
20 Marc Morin .40 1.00
21 Scott Rettew .40 1.00
22 Jean-Marc Richard .40 1.00
23 Stephane Richer 5.00 12.00
24 Pierre Sevigny .40 1.00

2000-01 Chicoutimi Sagueneens

This set features the Sagueneens of the QMJHL. It was produced by CTM-Ste-Foy, and was sold by that company, as well as by the team at home games.

COMPLETE SET (23) 4.80 15.00
1 Olivier Dannel .20 .50
2 Alex Turcotte .20 .50
3 Mathieu Betournay .20 .50
4 Michel Finn .20 .50
5 Eric Betournay .20 .50
6 Jonathan Francoeur .20 .50
7 Sebastien Laprise .20 .50
8 Sylvain Watt .20 .50
9 Sebastien Lucier .20 .50
10 Stanislav Hudec .20 .50
11 Christian Larrivee .20 .50
12 Francois Caron .20 .50
13 Eric Beaudin .20 .50
14 Alain Chenard .20 .50
15 Karl St-Pierre .20 .50
16 Michael Parent .20 .50
17 David Ouellet Beaudry .20 .50
18 Jean-Francois Demers .20 .50
19 Dave Verville .30 .75
20 Guillaume Karrer .20 .50
21 Martin Beauchesne .20 .50
22 Jean-Micheal Martin .20 .50
23 Pierre-Marc Bouchard 2.00 5.00

2000-01 Chicoutimi Sagueneens Signed

This set is exactly the same as the base Sagueneens set from this season, save that every card has been hand signed by the player pictured. Each card also is serial numbered out of just 100.

COMPLETE SET (23) 18.00 50.00
1 Olivier Dannel .80 2.00
2 Alex Turcotte .80 2.00
3 Mathieu Betournay .80 2.00
4 Michel Finn .80 2.00
5 Eric Betournay .80 2.00
6 Jonathan Francoeur .80 2.00
7 Sebastien Laprise .80 2.00
8 Sylvain Watt .80 2.00
9 Sebastien Lucier .80 2.00
10 Stanislav Hudec .80 2.00
11 Christian Larrivee .80 2.00
12 Francois Caron .80 2.00
13 Eric Beaudin .80 2.00
14 Alain Chenard .80 2.00
15 Karl St-Pierre .80 2.00
16 Michael Parent .80 2.00
17 David Ouellet Beaudry .80 2.00
18 Jean-Francois Demers .80 2.00
19 Dave Verville 2.00 5.00
20 Guillaume Karrer .80 2.00
21 Martin Beauchesne .80 2.00
22 Jean-Micheal Martin .80 2.00
23 Pierre-Marc Bouchard 10.00 25.00

2001-02 Chicoutimi Sagueneens

COMPLETE SET (23) 15.00
1 Team Card .01
2 Sebastien Lucier .50
3 Eric Betournay .50
4 Pierre-Alexandre Parenteau .75
5 Stanislav Hudec .50
6 Christian Larrivee .50
7 Patrick Tessier .50
8 Pierre-Luc Briere .50
9 Yvan Busque .50
10 Alexandre Blackburn .75
11 Jean-Francois Demers .50
12 Eric Tetrault .50
13 Jeff Drouin Deslauriers 1.50
14 Eric Borbeau .50
15 Michael Lanthier .50
16 Nicolas Marcotte .50
17 Hugues Verpaelst .50
18 Francis Lemieux .50
19 Jean-Vincent Lachance .50
20 Martin Chabot .50
21 Rosario Ruggeri .50
22 Bruno Champagne .50
23 Pierre-Marc Bouchard 3.00

2004-05 Chicoutimi Sagueneens

A total of 1,100 team sets were produced.

COMPLETE SET (24) 12.00
1 Alexandre Lamarche .50
2 Alexandre Vincent .50
3 Bernard Elhokayen .50
4 Brandon Verge .50
5 Brent Macsween .50
6 David Deshamais .50
7 Francis Lamiaux .50
8 Francis Verreault .50
9 Gabriel Houde-Brisson .50
10 Guillaume Lepine .50
11 Julien Brouillette .50
12 Louis-Etienne Leblanc .50
13 Marc-Andre Roy .50
14 Marek Zagrapan 1.50
15 Mathieu Bolduc .50
16 Romy Elayoubi .75
17 Stanislav Lascek .50
18 Maxime Boisclair 1.00
19 Nicolas Blanchard .50
20 Nicolas Marcotte .50
21 Ryan Spaulding .50
22 Shayne Tremblay .50
23 Travis Coles .50
24 Yan Gaudette .50

2005-06 Chicoutimi Sagueneens

COMPLETE SET (31) 6.00 15.00
1 David Deshamais .20 .50
2 Stanislav Lascek .20 .50
3 Marek Zagrapan .40 1.00
4 Nicolas Blanchard .20 .50
5 Maxime Boisclair .40 1.00
6 Francis Verreault .20 .50
7 Shayne Tremblay .20 .50
8 Sylvain Michaud .20 .50
9 Alexandre Vincent .20 .50
10 Julien Brouillette .20 .50
11 Geoff Oliver .20 .50
12 Gabriel Carle .20 .50
13 Marc Myre .20 .50
14 Pierre-Luc Huot .20 .50
15 Maxime Tanguay .20 .50
16 Mathieu Bolduc .20 .50
17 Louis-Etienne Leblanc .20 .50
18 Jean-Claude Milot .20 .50
19 Brent MacSween .20 .50
20 Guillaume Lepine .20 .50
21 Oliver Lajeunesse .20 .50
22 Bruno-Pierre Gosselin .20 .50
23 Matthew Block .20 .50
24 Ryan Lehr .20 .50
25 Patrick Coulombe .20 .50
26 Jean-Sebastien Adam .20 .50
27 Gabriel Boies .20 .50
28 Nicolas Lafontaine .20 .50
29 Benoit Piche .20 .50
30 Jean-Sebastien Cote .20 .50
31 Sago MASCOT .02 .10

2006-07 Chicoutimi Sagueneens

COMPLETE SET (23) 8.00 15.00
1 David Deshamais .30 .75
2 Luc-Oliver Blain .30 .75
3 Nicolas Blanchard .30 .75
4 Mathieu Bolduc .30 .75
5 Julien Brouillette .30 .75
6 Patrick Campbell .30 .75
7 Francois Chabot .30 .75
8 Joel Champagne .30 .75
9 Derek Famulare .30 .75
10 Christopher Guay .30 .75
11 Alexandre Imbeault .30 .75
12 Dominic Jalbert .30 .75
13 Marc-Andre Julien .30 .75
14 Francois Levesque .30 .75
15 Jurai Mikus .30 .75
16 Bobby Nadeau .40 1.00
17 Olivier Painchaud .30 .75
18 Maxime Provencher .30 .75
19 Antoine Roussel .30 .75
20 Tommy Tremblay .30 .75
21 Kirill Tulupov .30 .75
22 Francois Verreault-Paul .30 .75
23 Joel Rechlicz .30 .75

2006-07 Chilliwack Bruins

COMPLETE SET (25) 15.00 25.00
1 Alex Archibald .60 1.50
2 Matt Esposito .60 1.50
3 Kevin Boutilier .40 1.00
4 Dylan Chapman .40 1.00
5 Cody Hobbs .40 1.00
6 Nick Holden .40 1.00
7 Craig Lineker .40 1.00
8 Scott Maetche .40 1.00
9 Cam Stevens .40 1.00
10 Matt McCue .40 1.00
11 Josh Aspenlind .40 1.00
12 Patrick Bhungal .40 1.00
13 Donnie Glennie .40 1.00
14 Colton Graf .40 1.00
15 Aki Kangasmaki .40 1.00
16 Colby Kulharek .40 1.00
17 Matt Meropoulis .40 1.00
18 Dillon Johnstone .40 1.00
19 Oscar Moller .75 2.00
20 Special Edition Oscar Moller .75 2.00
21 Ken Petkau .40 1.00
22 Mark Santorelli .40 1.00
23 Cody Smuk .40 1.00
24 Mike Proudley .40 1.00
25 Bruiser MASCOT CL .02 .10

1990-91 Cincinnati Cyclones

This 23-card set of the Cincinnati Cyclones of the ECHL was produced by 7th Inning Sketch. for distribution by the team. The cards are numbered 19-41 presumably because the company produced card sets for many ECHL teams this year.

COMPLETE SET (23) 3.00 8.00
19 Steve McGrinder .15 .40
20 Steve Shaunessy .15 .40
21 Jay Rose .15 .40
22 Don Gagne .15 .40
23 Mike Williams .15 .40
24 Mike Chighisola .15 .40
25 Daryl Harpe .15 .40
26 Steve Cadieux .15 .40
27 Jeff Salzbrunn .15 .40
28 Rob Gador .15 .40
29 Chris Marshall .15 .40
30 Doug Melnyk .15 .40
31 Mark Turner .15 .40
32 Kevin Kerr .15 .40
33 Rob Krauss .15 .40
34 Mark Marentette .15 .40
35 Jamie Kompon .15 .40
36 Tom Neziol .15 .40
37 John Fletcher .15 .40
38 Dennis Desrosiers CO .08 .25
39 Todd Harrison TR .08 .25
40 Terry Ficorelli .15 .40
41 Craig Daly .15 .40

1991-92 Cincinnati Cyclones

The 1991-92 Cincinnati Cyclones of the East Coast Hockey League are represented in this 25-card set, which was sponsored by Cincinnati Bell Telephone and 19 XIX Fox. The cards measure 2 3/8" by 3 1/2" and feature posed color action shots enclosed by a white border. The team logo and year appear across the top of the card face, with the team name in silver outlined in red. The white front bottom portion of the card carries player information, the 19XIX Fox logo, and the Cincinnati Bell Telephone logo. Horizontally oriented backs carry biography and statistics in a white box surrounded by a gray border. The cards are unnumbered and checklisted below in alphabetical order.

COMPLETE SET (25) 3.00 8.00
1 Dan Beaudette .20 .50
2 Steve Benoit TR .02 .10
3 Steve Cadieux .15 .40
4 Craig Charron .15 .40
5 David Craievich .15 .40
6 Doug Dadswell .20 .50
7 Dennis Desrosiers CO .02 .10
8 Terry Ficorelli ANN .02 .10
9 Jeff Hogden .15 .40
10 Kevin Kerr .15 .40
11 Jaan Luik .15 .40
12 Scott Luik .15 .40
13 Chris Marshall .15 .40
14 Daryn McBride .15 .40
15 Doug Melnyk .15 .40
16 David Moore .15 .40
17 Tom Neziol .15 .40
18 Mark Romaine .15 .40
19 Jay Rose .15 .40
20 Martin St. Amour .20 .50
21 Kevin Scott .15 .40
22 Peter Schure .15 .40
23 Steve Shaunessy .15 .40
24 Blaine Stoughton CO .20 .50
25 Bobby Wallwork .15 .40

1992-93 Cincinnati Cyclones

These standard-sized cards were released in set form and sold by the team. The set includes the logo of sponsor, Bell.

COMPLETE SET (30) 3.00 8.00
1 Bill Armstrong .10 .30
2 Ralph Barahona .15 .40
3 Mike Bodnarchuk .15 .40
4 Craig Charron .15 .40
5 Todd Copeland .15 .40
6 Doug Dadswell .30 .75
7 Mike Dagenais .15 .40
8 Kevin Dean .15 .40
9 Chad Erickson .30 .75
10 Todd Flichel .15 .40
11 Alan Hepple .10 .30
12 Dennis Holland .15 .40
13 Sergei Kharin .15 .40
14 David Latta .15 .40
15 Jeff Madill .15 .40
16 Jon Morris .15 .40
17 Dean Morton .15 .40
18 Chris Nelson .15 .40
19 Darcy Norton .15 .40
20 Howie Rosenblatt .20 .50
21 Scott Shaunessy .15 .40
22 Mario Thyer .15 .40
23 Al Tuer .10 .30
24 Dennis Desrosiers HCO .02 .10
25 Blaine Stoughton ACO .20 .50
26 Alex Ochoa TR .10 .30
27 Mr. Cyclone Mascot .02 .10
28 Steve Benoit EM .02 .10
29 Terry Ficorelli ANN .15 .40
30 Wildman Walker ANN .08 .25

1993-94 Cincinnati Cyclones

Little is known about this set beyond the confirmed checklist. Anyone with additional information should write hockeymag@beckett.com.

COMPLETE SET (32) 4.00 10.00
1 Doug Barrault .15 .40
2 Len Barrie .30 .75
3 Don Biggs .15 .40
4 Chris Cichocki .10 .30
5 Jason Cirone .15 .40
6 Dallas Eakins .20 .50
7 Daniel Gauthier .15 .40
8 Jeff Greenlaw .15 .40
9 Rick Hayward .15 .40
10 Gord Hynes .15 .40
11 Ian Kidd .15 .40
12 Marc LaBelle .15 .40
13 Paul Lawless .15 .40
14 Jamie Leach .15 .40
15 Patrick Lebeau .20 .50
16 Ray LeBlanc .30 .75
17 Jamie Linden .15 .40
18 Jaroslav Nedved .15 .40
19 Darcy Norton .15 .40
20 Pokey Reddick .30 .75
21 Stephane Richer .15 .40
22 Jeff Serowik .15 .40
23 Scott Shaunessy .15 .40
24 Brad Smyth .10 .30
25 Dennis Desrosiers HCO .02 .10
26 Richard Kromm ACO .02 .10
27 Wildman Walker ANN .02 .10
28 Mr. Cyclone Mascot .02 .10
29 Mike Spilman TR .02 .10
30 Steve Benoit EQM .02 .10
31 Terry Ficorelli ANN .02 .10
NNO Header/Checklist .02 .10

1995-96 Cincinnati Cyclones

The set features the Cyclones of the IHL. The set was produced by Edge Ice and was sold by the team at its souvenir stands.

COMPLETE SET (25) 4.00 10.00
1 Don Biggs .20 .50
2 Frederic Chabot .40 1.00
3 Chris Cichocki .20 .50
4 Chris Dahlquist .20 .50
5 Dale DeGray .20 .50
6 Brian Dobbin .20 .50
7 Len Esau .20 .50
8 Jeff Greenlaw .20 .50
9 Todd Hawkins .20 .50
10 Duane Joyce .20 .50
11 Chris Kontos .30 .75
12 Marc LaBelle .20 .50
13 Paul Lawless .30 .75
14 Danny Lorenz .30 .75
15 Doug MacDonald .20 .50
16 Dave Marcinyshyn .20 .50
17 Scott Thomas .20 .50
18 Dave Tomlinson .20 .50
19 Jeff Wells .20 .50
20 Bob Wilkie .20 .50
21 Nick Kenney TR .02 .10
22 Mark Mills TR .02 .10
23 Al Hill CO .02 .10
24 Ron Smith CO .02 .10
25 Snowbird MAS .02 .10

1996-97 Cincinnati Cyclones

This 25-card set was produced by Split Second and was sponsored by WGRR radio and WCPD TV. The unnumbered cards feature an action photo on the front, and stats package on the back. They are numbered below according to their sweater numbers, which are prominently featured on the backs.

COMPLETE SET (25) 4.00 10.00
1 Todd MacDonald .30 .75
3 Duane Joyce .20 .50
4 Ted Crowley .20 .50
5 Jeff Wells .20 .50
6 Myles O'Connor .20 .50
12 Todd Hawkins .20 .50
13 Paul Lawless .20 .50
17 Mike Casselman .20 .50
19 Scott Thomas .30 .75
22 Don Biggs .20 .50
24 Tony Horacek .20 .50
26 Marc Laniel .20 .50
27 Dave Marcinyshyn .20 .50
28 Scott Morrow .20 .50
29 Jeff Greenlaw .20 .50
31 Geoff Sarjeant .30 .75
33 Chris Cichocki .20 .50
37 Eric Dandenault .20 .50
44 Doug MacDonald .20 .50
51 Dale DeGray .20 .50
NNO Nick Kenney TR .02 .10
NNO Snowbird (Mascot) .02 .10
NNO Ron Smith CO .02 .10
NNO Mark Mills EQMG .02 .10
NNO Al Hill ACO .02 .10

1997-98 Cincinnati Cyclones

This set features the Cyclones of the IHL. The cards were sponsored by Cincinnati Bell, and were issued as promotional giveaways.

COMPLETE SET (24) 4.80 12.00
1 Don Biggs .30 .75
2 Paul Broten .20 .50
3 Mike Casselman .20 .50
4 Eric Dandenault .20 .50
5 Gilbert Dionne .30 .75
6 Jeff Greenlaw .20 .50
7 Todd Hawkins .20 .50
8 Burt Henderson .20 .50
9 Steven King .20 .50
10 Marc LaBelle .20 .50
11 Doug MacDonald .20 .50
12 Todd MacDonald .20 .50
13 Pat MacLeod .20 .50
14 Scott Morrow .20 .50
15 Geoff Sarjeant .30 .75
16 Todd Simon .30 .75
17 Jeff Sirkka .20 .50
18 Jeff Wells .20 .50
19 David Williams .20 .50
20 Ron Smith CO .08 .25
21 Chris Cichocki CO .08 .25
22 Snowbird MAS .02 .10
23 Nick Kenney TR .02 .10
24 Mark Mills TR .02 .10

1998-99 Cincinnati Cyclones

Card fronts feature full color photos along with team name and position. Backs feature 1997-98 statistics and biographical information. Cards are unnumbered and checklisted below in alphabetical order.

COMPLETE SET (30) 6.00 10.00
1 Kaspars Astashenko .20 .50
2 Frederic Cassivi .30 .75
3 Phil Crowe .15 .40
4 Eric Dandenault .15 .40
5 Gilbert Dionne .30 .75
6 Todd Hawkins .15 .40
7 Jani Hurme .75 2.00
8 Burt Henderson .15 .40
9 Chris Joseph .15 .40
10 Ole Kjenstad .15 .40
11 Fred Knipscheer .15 .40
12 Doug Macdonald .15 .40
13 Pat Macleod .15 .40
14 Scott Morrow .15 .40
15 Tom Nemeth .15 .40
16 Kirk Nielsen .15 .40
17 Ed Patterson .15 .40
18 Rastislav Pavlikovsky .15 .40
19 Jeff Shevalier .15 .40
20 Todd Simon .15 .40
21 Geoff Smith .15 .40
22 Jeff Wells .15 .40
23 Snowbird Mascot .02 .10
24 Nick Kenney TR .02 .10
25 Mark Mills EQ .02 .10
26 Scott Macpherson ACO .02 .10
27 Chris Cichocki ACO .02 .10
28 Ron Smith CO .02 .10
29 Team Card .02 .10
30 Logo Card .04 .01

1998-99 Cincinnati Cyclones 2

This set features the Cyclones of the IHL. The set was issued as a promotional giveaway and was sponsored by Bell Telephone.

COMPLETE SET (30) 10.00 25.00
1 Todd Hawkins .40 1.00
2 Kirk Nielsen .40 1.00
3 Ed Patterson .40 1.00
4 Fred Knipscheer .40 1.00
5 Doug Macdonald .40 1.00
6 Todd Simon .40 1.00
7 Phil Crowe .40 1.00
8 Gilbert Dionne .40 1.00
9 Scott Morrow .40 1.00
10 Rastislav Pavlikovsky .40 1.00
11 Jeff Shevalier .40 1.00
12 Kaspars Astashenko .40 1.00
13 Eric Dandenault .40 1.00
14 Burt Henderson .40 1.00
15 Chris Joseph .40 1.00
16 Pat MacLeod .40 1.00
17 Geoff Smith .40 1.00
18 Jeff Wells .40 1.00
19 Frederic Cassivi .75 2.00
20 Jani Hurme .75 2.00
21 Tom Nemeth .40 1.00
22 Olaf Kjenstad .40 1.00
23 Team Photo Card .20 .50
24 Ron Smith CO .20 .50
25 Chris Cichocki CO .20 .50
26 Scott MacPherson CO .20 .50
27 Mark Mills EM .20 .50
28 Nick Kenney TR .02 .10
29 Snowbird MASCOT .02 .10
30 PHPA Card .01 .05

1999-00 Cincinnati Cyclones

This team set of the Cincinnati Cyclones of the IHL was sponsored by Cincinnati Bell. The cards show a color action photo of each player on front and individual stats on the card backs. The cards are not numbered and are listed below alphabetically.

COMPLETE SET (27) 4.80 10.00
1 Team Logo .08 .25
2 Craig Adams .20 .50
3 Steve Bancroft .20 .50
4 Eric Dandenault .20 .50
5 Gilbert Dionne .30 .75
6 Gilbert Dionne MVP .30 .75
7 Mark Fitzpatrick .30 .75
8 Len Esau .20 .50
9 Todd Hawkins .20 .50
10 David Karpa .20 .50
11 Greg Koehler .20 .50
12 Greg Kuznik .20 .50
13 Craig McDonald .30 .75
14 Pat McLeod .20 .50
15 Ian McNeil .20 .50
16 Randy Petruk .30 .75
17 Mike Rucinski .20 .50
18 Todd Simon .30 .75
19 Nikos Tselios .30 .75
20 Stefan Ustorf .30 .75
21 Shane Willis .40 1.00
22 Chris Cichocki CO .08 .25
23 Nick Kenney TR .02 .10
24 Mark Mills EM .02 .10
25 Ron Smith HCO .02 .10
26 Snowbird MASCOT .02 .10
27 PHPA Logo .01

2000-01 Cincinnati Cyclones

This set features the Cyclones of the IHL. The cards were produced by Multi-Ad Sports, and were issued as a promotional giveaway.

COMPLETE SET (30) 10.00 20.00
1 Nikos Tselios .40 .75
2 Jeremiah McCarthy .30 .50
3 Greg Kuznik .30 .75
4 Byron Ritchie .40 1.00
5 Craig MacDonald .30 .75
6 Greg Koehler .20 .50
7 Stefan Ustorf .30 .50
8 Jeff Heerema .40 1.00
9 Mike Rucinski .40 1.00
10 Ian MacNeil .20 .50
11 Gilbert Dionne .40 1.00
12 Erik Cole 1.50 4.00
13 Reggie Berg .30 .50
14 Jon Rohloff .20 .50
15 Len Esau .20 .50
16 Brian Felsner .30 .75
17 Brad DeFauw .20 .50
18 Harlan Pratt .20 .50
19 Jaroslav Svoboda .75 1.00
20 Jean-Marc Pelletier .40 1.00
21 Corey Hirsch .30 .75
22 Marc Magliarditi .30 .75
23 Ron Smith CO .10 .25
24 Mark Mills EM .04 .10
25 Nick Kenney TR .04 .10
26 Snowbird MASCOT .04 .10
27 GMC Zamboni SPONSOR .01
28 Team Photo .20 .25
29 The Firstar Center .01
30 PHPA Web Site .01

1998-99 Cincinnati Mighty Ducks

This 29-card set was handed out at a game in February. It is not thought that it was available through any other channels, and therefore is quite difficult to acquire.

COMPLETE SET (29) 8.00 20.00
1 Buster MASCOT .08 .25
2 Marc Andreozzi TR .02 .10
3 Gary Linquist EM .02 .10
4 John Walton .30 .75
5 Ed Johnstone ACO .08 .25
6 Moe Mantha HCO .08 .25
7 Frank Banham .40 1.00
8 Mike LeClerc 1.25 3.00
9 Byron Briske .30 .75
10 Eric Lecompte .30 .75
11 Terran Sandwith .30 .75
12 Jamie Ram .40 1.00
13 Craig Reichert .30 .75
14 Joel Kwiatkowski .30 .75
15 Mike Crowley .40 1.00
16 Matt Leon .30 .75
17 Jeremy Stevenson .30 .75
18 Dan Trebil .30 .75
19 Bob Wren .30 .75
20 Lloyd Shaw .30 .75
21 Igor Nikulin .30 .75
22 Jeff Winter .30 .75
23 Tony Mohagen .30 .75
24 Tony Tuzzolino .30 .75
25 Peter LeBoutillier .30 .75
26 Tom Askey .60 1.50
27 Marc Chouinard .40 1.00
28 Scott Ferguson .30 .75
29 PHPA Web Site .04 .01

1999-00 Cincinnati Mighty Ducks

This set features the Mighty Ducks of the AHL. The set was issued as a promotional giveaway at a home game during March of 2000.

COMPLETE SET (32) 12.00 30.00
1 Parent Clubs .08 .25
2 Moe Mantha CO .08 .25
3 Jason Payne .30 .75

4 Jeff Nielsen ALUM	.30	.75
5 Antti Aalto ALUM	.40	1.00
6 Ruslan Salei ALUM	.30	.75
7 Joel Kwiatkowski	.30	.75
8 Aren Miller	.40	1.00
9 Dan Trebil	.30	.75
10 Rastislav Pavlikovsky	.30	.75
11 Frank Banham	.40	1.00
12 Scott Ferguson	.30	.75
13 Maxim Balmochnykh	.60	1.50
14 Darryl Laplante	.60	1.50
15 Johan Davidsson	.60	1.50
16 Peter Leboutillier	.30	.75
17 Jesse Wallin	.40	1.00
18 Alexandre Jacques	.30	.75
19 B.J. Young	.30	.75
20 Ed Johnstone CO	.08	.25
21 Ryan Hoople	.30	.75
22 Matt Cullen ALUM	.75	2.00
22 Pavel Trnka ALUM	.30	.75
22 Mike LeClerc	.75	2.00
23 Buster MASCOT	.08	.25
24 Jeremy Stevenson	.30	.75
25 Jay Legault	.30	.75
26 Marc Chouinard	.40	1.00
27 Torrey DiRoberto	.40	1.00
28 Maxim Kuznetsov	.40	1.00
29 Shane Hnidy	.30	.75
30 Vitali Vishnevsky	.40	1.00
31 Bob Wren	.30	.75
32 Gregg Naumenko	.60	1.50

2001-02 Cincinnati Mighty Ducks

This set features the Mighty Ducks of the AHL. The cards were issued as a promotional giveaway at a home game late in the season. As the cards are unnumbered, they are listed below in alphabetical order.

COMPLETE SET (28)	10.00	25.00
1 Sean Avery	1.00	2.50
2 Maxim Balmochnykh	.40	1.00
3 Drew Bannister	.30	.75
4 Ryan Barnes	.30	.75
5 Travis Brigley	.30	.75
6 Aris Brimanis	.30	.75
7 Steve Brule	.30	.75
8 Ilja Bryzgalov	1.00	2.50
9 Garrett Burnett	.40	1.00
10 Yuri Butsayev	.30	.75
11 Josh DeWolf	.30	.75
12 Jason Elliott	.60	1.50
13 Ryan Gaucher	.30	.75
14 Andy McDonald	1.00	2.50
15 Antti-Jussi Niemi	.40	1.00
16 Timo Parssinen	.40	1.00
17 Peter Podhradsky	.30	.75
18 Bruce Richardson	.30	.75
19 Bert Robertsson	.30	.75
20 David Roche	.30	.75
21 Jonas Ronnqvist	.40	1.00
22 Jarrett Smith	.30	.75
23 Brian White	.30	.75
24 Jason Williams	.40	1.00
25 Dwayne Zinger	.30	.75
26 Mike Babcock CO	.10	.25
27 Kevin Kaminski ACO	.10	.25
28 Buster the Duck MASCOT	.02	.10

2002-03 Cincinnati Mighty Ducks

This set was given away over the course of two home games, Dec. 14, 2002 and March 23, 2003. The cards are unnumbered and listed below by series in alphabetical order.

COMPLETE SET (28)	15.00	30.00
A1 Mike Commodore	1.25	3.00
A2 Samuel Pahlsson	.75	2.00
A3 Jean-Francois Damphousse	.75	2.00
A4 Todd Reirden	.40	1.00
A5 Jonathan Hedstrom	.75	2.00
A6 Chris O'Sullivan	.40	1.00
A7 Jarrett Smith	.40	1.00
A8 Travis Brigley	.40	1.00
A9 Brian Gornick	.40	1.00
A10 Tony Martensson	.40	1.00
A11 Cory Pecker	.75	2.00
A12 Nick Smith	.40	1.00
A13 Cam Severson	1.25	3.00
A14 Pete Podrasky	.40	1.00
B1 Ilja Bryzgalov	1.25	3.00
B2 Darryl Williams ACO	.20	.50
B3 Brad Shaw CO	.20	.50
B4 Buster MASCOT	.02	.10
B5 Puck Boy	.02	.10
B6 Jan Tabacek	.40	1.00
B7 Mark Popovic	.75	2.00
B8 Rob Valicevic	.40	1.00
B9 Ben Guite	.75	2.00
B10 Francis Belanger	.40	1.00
B11 Team Photo	.40	1.00
B12 Josh DeWolf	.40	1.00
B13 Jason Krog	.75	2.00
B14 Alexei Smirnov	.40	1.00

2003-04 Cincinnati Mighty Ducks

It's thought that these were issued as promotional giveaways at two Ducks home games. Anyone with additional information, please contact us at hockeymag@beckett.com.

COMPLETE SET (28)	10.00	25.00
A1 Keith Aucoin	.40	1.00
A2 Eddie Ferhi	.40	1.00
A3 Mike Mottau	.40	1.00
A4 Pierre-Alexander Parenteau	.40	1.00
A5 Cory Pecker	.40	1.00
A6 Mark Popovic	.40	1.00
A7 Todd Reirden	.40	1.00
A8 Andy Reierson	.40	1.00
A9 Cam Severson	.40	1.00
A10 Alexei Smirnov	.40	1.00
A11 Nick Smith	.40	1.00
A12 Joel Stepp	.40	1.00
A13 Darryl Williams ACO	.10	.25
A14 Puck Boy	.10	.25
B1 Juha Alen	.40	1.00
B2 Chris Armstrong	.40	1.00
B3 Sheldon Brookbank	.40	1.00
B4 Ilja Bryzgalov	.75	2.00
B5 Brian Gornick	.40	1.00
B6 Casey Hankinson	.40	1.00
B7 Mikael Holmqvist		1.00
B8 Chris Kunitz	1.00	2.50
B9 Tony Martensson	.40	1.00
B10 Shane O'Brien	.75	2.00
B11 Joel Perrault	.40	1.00
B12 Igor Pohanka	.40	1.00
B13 Brad Shaw CO	.10	.25
B14 Mascot	.02	.10

2004-05 Cincinnati Mighty Ducks

This set was produced by Choice Marketing and given away in two parts at different Mighty Ducks home games.

COMPLETE SET (30)	15.00	30.00
1 Brad Shaw CO	.20	.50
2 Dan Bylsma ACO	.20	.50
3 Aaron Rome	.75	2.00
4 Juha Alen	.40	1.00
5 Kurtis Foster	.40	1.00
6 Shane O'Brien	.75	2.00
7 Mark Popovic	.40	1.00
8 Tim Brent	.40	1.00
9 Buster MASCOT	.02	.10
10 Joel Perrault	.40	1.00
11 Zenon Konopka	.40	1.00
12 Igor Pohanka	.40	1.00
13 Sean O'Connor	.40	1.00
14 Chris Kunitz	.75	2.00
15 Joffrey Lupul	1.50	4.00
16 Joel Stepp	.40	1.00
17 Sheldon Brookbank	.40	1.00
18 Michael Holmqvist	.40	1.00
19 Cory Pecker	.40	1.00
20 Curtis Glencross	.40	1.00
21 Sponsor card	.02	.10
22 Alexei Smirnov	.40	1.00
23 Stanislav Chistov	.75	2.00
24 Dustin Penner	1.50	4.00
25 Pierre Parenteau	.40	1.00
26 Checklist	.02	.10
27 Tomas Malec	.40	1.00
28 Eddie Ferhi	.40	1.00
29 Ilja Bryzgalov	.75	2.00
30 Frederic Cassivi	.75	2.00

1992-93 Clarkson Knights

Issued in 1993 at the end of the hockey season, this 24-card standard-size set features the Clarkson Knights of the ECAC (Eastern Collegiate Athletic Conference). The cards feature on-ice player action and posed photos on the fronts. The pictures are on a white card face with the Clarkson hockey logo and name at the top and the player's name and position at the bottom. The horizontal backs carry biography, statistics for the 1991-92 and 1992-93 seasons, and career summary. The Clarkson hockey logo appears in the lower right. The cards are unnumbered and checklisted below in alphabetical order.

COMPLETE SET (24)	4.80	12.00
1 Josh Bartell	.15	.40
2 Hugo Belanger	.20	.50
3 Craig Conroy	.60	1.50
4 Jason Currie	.15	.40
5 Steve Dubinsky	.20	.50
6 Shawn Fotheringham	.15	.40
7 Dave Green	.15	.40
8 Ed Henrich	.15	.40
9 Chris Lipsett	.15	.40
10 Todd Marchant	.75	2.00
11 Brian Mueller	.20	.50
12 Kevin Murphy	.15	.40
13 Martin d'Orsonnens	.15	.40
14 Steve Palmer	.15	.40
15 Patrice Robitaille	.15	.40
16 Chris Rogles	.20	.50
17 Jerry Rosenheck	.15	.40
18 Chris de Ruiter	.15	.40
19 Guy Sanderson	.15	.40
20 David Seitz	.15	.40
21 Mikko Tavi	.15	.40
22 Patrick Theriault	.15	.40
23 Marko Tuomainen	.20	.50
24 Men's Hockey 1992-93 Martin d'Orsonnens Steve Dubinsky	.15	.40

1951-52 Cleveland Barons

This set was issued as a photo pack. The cards are printed on thin card stock, and measure 9 X 6 inches. The last card, Joe Lund, may be from the previous year's set, as he did not play for Cleveland in 1951-52.

COMPLETE SET (20)	75.00	150.00
1 Bun Cook CO	5.00	10.00
2 Fred Shero	10.00	20.00
3 Ed Reigle	3.00	6.00
4 Ike Hildebrand	3.00	6.00
5 Eddie Olson	3.00	6.00
6 Jerry Reid	3.00	6.00
7 Fred Thurier	3.00	6.00
8 Steve Wochy	3.00	6.00
9 Joe Carveth	4.00	8.00
10 Tom Williams	5.00	10.00
11 Johnny Bower	25.00	50.00
12 Jack Gordon	4.00	8.00
13 Ken Schultz	3.00	6.00
14 Fern Perreault	3.00	6.00
15 Ray Ceresino	3.00	6.00
16 Bob Bailey	3.00	6.00
17 Bob Chrystal	4.00	8.00
18 Phil Samis	3.00	6.00
19 Paul Gladu	3.00	6.00
20 Joe Lund	3.00	6.00

1960-61 Cleveland Barons

This 19-card set of oversized cards measures approximately 6 3/4" by 5 3/8". The set commemorates the Cleveland Barons 1959-60 season which ended with the team in fourth place after elimination in the Calder Cup Playoffs. The white-bordered fronts display action, black-and-white player photos. A facsimile autograph is printed near the bottom of the photo on all the cards except the team photo card. The backs are blank. Since the cards are unnumbered, they are checklisted below alphabetically.

COMPLETE SET (19)	60.00	120.00
1 Ron Attwell	3.00	6.00
2 Les Binkley	5.00	10.00
3 Bill Dineen	4.00	8.00
4 John Ferguson	10.00	20.00
5 Cal Gardner	4.00	8.00
6 Fred Glover	4.00	8.00
7 Jack Gordon	4.00	8.00
8 Aldo Guidolin	4.00	8.00
9 Greg Hicks	3.00	6.00
10 Wayne Larkin	3.00	6.00
11 Moe Mantha	4.00	8.00
12 Gil Mayer	3.00	6.00
13 Eddie Mazur	3.00	6.00
14 Jim Mikol	3.00	6.00
15 Bill Needham	3.00	6.00
16 Cal Stearns	3.00	6.00
17 Bill Sutherland	4.00	8.00
18 Tom Williams	4.00	8.00
19 Team Photo	5.00	10.00

1992-93 Cleveland Lumberjacks

Issued to commemorate the Lumberjacks' first season in Cleveland, these 25 cards feature on their fronts red-trimmed and white-bordered color player action shots and measure 2 3/8" by 3 1/2". The player's name, uniform number and position appear beneath the photo in the lower white margin. The team logo and season are displayed in the margin above the photo. The logos for the two sponsors, WKNR radio and Rusterminator, rest at the bottom. The horizontal backs display the player's name, uniform number, position, biography and stats within the central white rectangle. In the wide gray border, the logos for the team and the sponsors round out the card.

COMPLETE SET (25)	4.00	10.00
1 Title Card	.02	.10
2 Larry Gordon GM	.02	.10
3 Paul Laus	.30	.75
4 Travis Thiessen	.20	.50
5 Phil Russell CO	.20	.50
6 Gilbert Delorme ACO	.20	.50
7 Jamie Heward	.20	.50
8 Greg Andrusak	.20	.50
9 David Quinn	.20	.50
10 Perry Ganchar	.20	.50
11 George Zajankala UER (Birthplace misspelled Revelstroke on back)	.20	.50
12 Todd Nelson	.20	.50
13 Dave Michayluk	.20	.50
14 Bruce Racine	.25	.60
15 Rob Dopson	.25	.60
16 Bert Godin TR	.02	.10
17 Ed Patterson	.25	.60
18 Justin Duberman	.20	.50
19 Sandy Smith	.20	.50
20 Jason Smart	.20	.50
21 Ken Priestlay	.20	.50
22 Daniel Gauthier	.20	.50
23 Robert Melanson	.20	.50
24 Mark Major	.20	.50
25 Paul Dyck	.20	.50

1993-94 Cleveland Lumberjacks

These 24 black-bordered cards feature the 1993-94 Cleveland Lumberjacks of the IHL (International Hockey League). The cards measure approximately 2 3/8" by 3 1/2" and display on their fronts color player action shots framed by red lines. The player's name, uniform number, and position are shown in white lettering in the black margin below the photo. The logos for sponsors WKNR SportsRadio and RusTerminator Electronic Rust Control rest at the bottom. The gray and white horizontal back carries the player's uniform number, name, position, biography, and statistics.

COMPLETE SET (24)	4.00	10.00
1 Title Card	.08	.25
2 Rick Paterson CO	.08	.25
3 Gilbert Delorme ACO	.08	.25
4 Paul Dyck	.30	.75
5 Travis Thiessen	.20	.50
6 Mike Dagenais	.20	.50
7 Chris Tamer	.20	.50
8 Greg Andrusak	.20	.50
9 Todd Hawkins	.20	.50
10 Jamie Black	.20	.50
11 Justin Duberman	.20	.50
13 Jock Callander UER (Misspelled Jack on front)	.30	.75
14 Leonid Toropchenko	.20	.50
15 Victor Gervais	.20	.50
16 Perry Ganchar	.20	.50
17 Ed Patterson	.20	.50
18 Ladislav Karabin	.20	.50
19 Dave Michayluk	.20	.50
20 Jamie Heward	.20	.50
21 Pat Neaton	.20	.50
22 Rob Dopson	.30	.75
23 Steve Bancroft	.20	.50
24 Olie Sundstrom	.20	.50
25 Grant Block	.20	.50

1993-94 Cleveland Lumberjacks Postcards

These 21 black-bordered cards feature the 1993-94 Cleveland Lumberjacks of the IHL (International Hockey League). The white-bordered postcards measure approximately 3 1/2" by 5 1/2" and display on their fronts color player action shots. The player's name, uniform number, position, and biography are shown in yellow lettering within a black rectangle beneath the picture. Sponsor logos for WMMS Radio and The Peak (a sports medicine and injury rehab facility) also appear on the front. The white horizontal back carries a tip on how to treat a minor muscle sprain. The cards are unnumbered and checklisted below in alphabetical order.

COMPLETE SET (22)	4.00	10.00
1 Greg Andrusak	.20	.50
2 Steve Bancroft	.20	.50
3 Jamie Black	.20	.50
4 Grant Block	.20	.50
5 Jock Callander	.30	.75
6 Mike Dagenais	.20	.50
7 Gilbert Delorme ACO	.08	.25
8 Rob Dopson	.30	.75
9 Justin Duberman	.20	.50
10 Paul Dyck	.30	.75
11 Perry Ganchar	.20	.50
12 Todd Hawkins	.20	.50
13 Jamie Heward	.20	.50
14 Ladislav Karabin	.20	.50
15 Dave Michayluk	.20	.50
16 Pat Neaton	.20	.50
17 Rick Paterson CO	.08	.25
18 Ed Patterson	.20	.50
19 Olie Sundstrom	.20	.50
20 Chris Tamer	.20	.50
21 Travis Thiessen	.20	.50
22 Leonid Toropchenko	.20	.50

1994-95 Cleveland Lumberjacks

This set was a game-night giveaway and features many cards that are identical in appearance to those in the 1993-94 issue. The set is unnumbered.

COMPLETE SET (25)	4.80	12.00
1 Rick Paterson HCO	.08	.25
2 Philippe DeRouville	.30	.75
3 Paul Dyck	.25	.60
4 Rick Hayward	.20	.50
5 Mike Dagenais	.20	.50
6 Chris Tamer	.30	.75
7 Len Barrie	.30	.75
8 Eric Murano	.20	.50
9 Brad Lauer	.20	.50
10 Ian Moran	.20	.50
11 Brian Farrell	.20	.50
12 Jock Callander	.30	.75
13 Jeff Christian	.20	.50
14 Larry DePalma	.20	.50
15 Joe Dziedzic	.20	.50
16 Victor Gervais	.20	.50
17 Dominic Pittis	.20	.50
18 Perry Ganchar	.20	.50
19 Ed Patterson	.30	.75
20 Ladislav Karabin	.20	.50
21 Dave Michayluk ACO	.20	.50
22 Michal Straka	.20	.50
23 Corey Beaulieu	.20	.50
24 Olie Sundstrom	.25	.60
25 Dale DeGray	.20	.50

1995-96 Cleveland Lumberjacks

This 24-card set of the Cleveland Lumberjacks was produced by SplitSecond for Collector's Edge. The set is sponsored by Huntington Banks and WKNR Radio. It features color player portraits on the fronts with player information and statistics on the backs. The cards are unnumbered and checklisted below in alphabetical order.

COMPLETE SET (24)	4.80	12.00
1 Peter Allen	.15	.40
2 Bill Armstrong	.15	.40
3 Len Barrie	.30	.75
4 Dave Baseggio	.15	.40
5 Oleg Belov	.15	.40
6 Drake Berehowsky	.15	.40
7 Stefan Bergkvist	.15	.40
8 Jock Callander	.30	.75
9 Jeff Christian	.15	.40
10 Philippe DeRouville	.30	.75
11 Rusty Fitzgerald	.15	.40
12 Corey Foster	.15	.40
13 Perry Ganchar ACO	.02	.10
14 Victor Gervais	.15	.40
15 Rick Hayward	.15	.40
16 Patrick Lalime	1.25	3.00
17 Brad Lauer	.15	.40
18 Dave McLlwain	.20	.50
19 Dave Michayluk	.15	.40
20 Mark Osborne	.15	.40
21 Rick Paterson CO	.02	.10
22 Dominic Pittis	.15	.40
23 Ryan Savoia	.15	.40
24 Mike Stevens	.15	.40
25 Title Card	.02	.10

1996-97 Cleveland Lumberjacks

This postcard set was sponsored by the Peak at Marymount, and was a game-night giveaway. Cards are checklisted below in alphabetical order.

COMPLETE SET (25)	10.00	20.00
1 Peter Allen	.30	.75
2 Bill Armstrong	.30	.75
3 Serge Aubin	.40	1.00
4 Brian Bonin	.40	1.00
5 Sven Butenschon	.30	.75
6 Buzz MASCOT	.08	.25
7 Jock Callendar	.75	2.00
8 Jeff Christian	.30	.75
9 Rusty Fitzgerald	.30	.75
10 Corey Foster	.30	.75
11 Rick Hayward	.30	.75
12 Jan Hrdina	.40	1.00
13 Petr Klima	.40	1.00
14 Lane Lambert	.30	.75
15 Brad Lauer	.30	.75
16 Dave McLlwain	.40	1.00
17 Dave Michayluk	.40	1.00
18 Ian Moran	.40	1.00
19 Mark Osborne	.30	.75
20 Jim Paek	.30	.75
21 Richard Park	.30	.75
22 Rick Paterson CO	.08	.25
23 Ed Patterson	.30	.75
24 Mike Tamburro	.30	.75
25 Derek Wilkinson	.30	.75

1996-97 Cleveland Lumberjacks Multi-Ad

This set features the Lumberjacks of the IHL. The set was sponsored by Mult-Ad Services and was sold by the team at it souvenir stands.

COMPLETE SET (30)	6.00	15.00
1 Checklist	.02	.10
2 Peter Allen	.15	.40
3 Bill Armstrong	.15	.40
4 Serge Aubin	.40	1.00
5 Stefan Bergkvist	.15	.40
6 Brian Bonin	.20	.50
7 Sven Butenschon	.15	.40
8 Jock Callander	.30	.75
9 Jeff Christian	.15	.40
10 Rusty Fitzgerald	.15	.40
11 Corey Foster	.15	.40
12 Perry Ganchar CO	.02	.10
13 Rick Hayward	.15	.40
14 Jan Hrdina	.40	1.00
15 Patrick Lalime	1.25	3.00
16 Lane Lambert	.15	.40
17 Brad Lauer	.15	.40
18 Dave McLlwain	.30	.75
19 Dave Michayluk	.30	.75
20 Ian Moran	.20	.50
21 Mark Osborne	.15	.40
22 Jim Paek	.15	.40
23 Richard Park	.15	.40
24 Rick Paterson CO	.02	.10
25 Ed Patterson	.15	.40
26 Mike Tamburro	.15	.40
27 Derek Wilkinson	.20	.50
28 Buzz MAS	.02	.10
29 Heritage Night	.02	.10
30 Logo Card	.02	.10

1997-98 Cleveland Lumberjacks

This standard-sized set was distributed by the team and sold at home games.

COMPLETE SET (30)	4.00	20.00
1 Team Photo	.02	.10
2 Perry Ganchar HCO	.02	.10
3 Mark Osborne ACO	.02	.10
4 Dave Baseggio	.10	.30
5 Stefan Bergkvist	.10	.30
6 Jock Callander	.40	1.00
7 Mark Cornforth	.10	.30
8 John Craighead	.10	.30
9 Joe Dziedzic	.20	.50
10 Vadim Epantchinsev	.10	.30
11 Rusty Fitzgerald	.10	.30
12 Brett Harkins	.10	.30
13 Rick Hayward	.20	.50
14 Pat Jablonski	.40	1.00
15 Alexei Krivchenkov	.10	.30
16 Lane Lambert	.10	.30
17 Brad Lauer	.10	.30
18 Chris Longo	.10	.30
19 Jason McBain	.10	.30
20 Ryan Mougenel	.10	.30
21 Jim Paek	.10	.30
22 Rob Pearson	.10	.30
23 Eric Perrin	.75	2.00
24 Martin St. Louis	2.00	5.00
25 Mike Tamburro	.10	.30
26 Darren Wetherill	.10	.30
27 Derek Wilkinson	.40	1.00
28 Martin St. Louis Eric Perrin	2.00	5.00
29 Buzz Mascot	.02	.10
30 PHPA Web site	.04	.01

1997-98 Cleveland Lumberjacks Postcards

This set features the Lumberjacks of the AHL. The postcard-sized set was given away as a promotional item at a home game.

COMPLETE SET (25)	7.20	30.00
1 Perry Ganchar HCO	.08	.25
2 Mark Osborne ACO	.08	.25
3 Darren Wetherill	.30	.75
4 Rick Hayward	.30	.75
5 Jim Paek	.30	.75
6 Dave Baseggio	.30	.75
7 Martin St. Louis	4.00	10.00
8 John Craighead	.30	.75
9 Eric Perrin	1.50	4.00
10 Rusty Fitzgerald	.30	.75
11 Chris Longo	.30	.75
12 Jock Callander	.75	2.00
13 Joe Dziedzic	.30	.75
14 Lane Lambert	.30	.75
15 Mark Cornforth	.30	.75
16 Vadim Epantchisev	.30	.75
17 Rob Pearson	.30	.75
18 Jason McBain	.30	.75
19 Alexei Krivchenkov	.30	.75
20 Derek Wilkinson	.40	1.00
21 Brad Lauer	.30	.75
22 Stefan Bergkvist	.30	.75
23 Brett Harkins	.30	.75
24 Mike Tamburro	.30	.75
25 Buzz Mascot	.08	.25

1998-99 Cleveland Lumberjacks

This set was sponsored by The Peak at Marymount, and was initially a game-night giveaway. It later was sold through the team's concession stands.

COMPLETE SET (24)	4.80	12.00
1 Header Card	.04	.01
2 Perry Ganchar HCO	.02	.10
3 Dave Baseggio	.20	.50
4 Jesse Belanger	.20	.50
5 Karel Betik	.20	.50
6 Zac Bierk	.75	2.00
7 Jason Bonsignore	.20	.50
8 Jock Callander	.40	1.00
9 John Cullen	.40	1.00
10 Xavier Delisle	.20	.50
11 Brett Harkins	.20	.50
12 Lane Lambert	.20	.50
13 Mario Larocque	.20	.50
14 Eric Lavigne	.15	.40
15 Chris Longo	.20	.50
16 Jim Paek	.20	.50
17 Eduard Pershin	.15	.40
18 Brent Peterson	.20	.50
19 Jason Ruff	.20	.50
20 Corey Schwab	.30	.75
21 Andrei Skopintsev	.20	.50
22 Corey Spring	.15	.40
23 Derek Wilkinson	.30	.75
24 Buzz MASCOT	.02	.10

1999-00 Cleveland Lumberjacks

This 24-card set pictures the 1999-00 Cleveland Lumberjacks. Cards feature full-color player photos on a non-glossy card stock. Since no number appears, cards are listed alphabetically. It is thought that this set might have been a promotional giveaway.

COMPLETE SET (24)	4.80	12.00
1 Radim Bicanek	.08	.25
2 Buzz Mascot	.02	.10
3 Kyle Calder	.75	2.00
4 Jock Callander	.40	1.00
5 Jeff Christian	.08	.25
6 Ted Crowley	.08	.25
7 Casey Hankinson	.08	.25
8 Brett Harkins	.08	.25
9 Chris Herperger	.08	.25
10 Ty Jones	.20	.50
11 Marc Lamothe	.20	.50
12 Eric Lavigne	.08	.25
13 Chris Longo	.08	.25
14 Evgeni Nabokov	2.00	5.00
15 Jim Paek	.08	.25
16 Jeff Paul	.08	.25
17 Nathan Perrott	.30	.75
18 Geoff Peters	.08	.25
19 Todd Rohloff	.08	.25
20 Remi Royer	.20	.50
21 Reid Simpson	.20	.50
22 Dmitri Tolkunov	.20	.50
23 Todd White	.20	.50
24 Header Card		.01

2000-01 Cleveland Lumberjacks

This set features the Lumberjacks of the IHL. It is believed that the set was issued as a promotional giveaway in January of 2001.

COMPLETE SET (25)	8.00	20.00
1 Christian Matte	.40	1.00
2 Brian Bonin	.40	1.00
3 Mike Matteucci	.40	1.00
4 Eric Charron	.30	.75
5 Nick Naumenko	.30	.75
6 Brett McLean	.30	.75
7 Pavel Patera	.40	.75
8 Chris Longo	.40	.75
9 Ian Herbers	.40	1.00
10 Pascal Dupuis	.30	.75
11 Kai Nurminen	.40	1.00
12 David Brumby	.30	.75
13 Zac Bierk	.60	2.00
14 Jonathon Shockey	.30	.75
15 Darryl Laplante	.40	1.00
16 J.J. Daigneault	.30	.75
17 Garrett Burnett	.30	.75
18 Chris Armstrong	.30	.75
19 Richard Park	.40	1.00
20 Todd McLellan CO	.20	.50
21 Jock Callander CO	.40	1.00
22 Ray Schultz	.30	.75
23 Steve Aronson	.40	1.00
24 Derek Gustafson	.60	1.50
25 Buzz MASCOT	.10	.25

2001-02 Cleveland Barons

This set features the Barons of the AHL. The set was issued as a promotional giveaway, half at a time at two different home games. The cards are unnumbered and are listed in alphabetical order.

COMPLETE SET (24)	9.78	25.00
1 Steve Bancroft	.40	.75
2 Matt Carkner	.31	.75
3 Jonathan Cheechoo	1.20	5.00
4 Adam Colagiacomo	.40	1.00
5 Mike Craig	.31	.75
6 Rob Davison	.31	.75
7 Jesse Fibiger	.31	.75
8 Hannes Hyvonen	.40	.75
9 Jeff Jillson	.80	2.00
10 Seamus Kotyk	.62	2.00
11 Ryan Kraft	.31	.75
12 Eric Laplante	.31	.75
13 Lynn Loyns	.31	1.00
14 Andy Lundbohm	.31	.75
15 Graig Mischler	.31	.75
16 Robert Mulick	.31	.75
17 Adam Nittel	.80	1.00
18 Joel Prpic	.31	.75
19 Brandon Smith	.40	.75
20 Vesa Toskala	1.20	3.00
21 Chad Wiseman	.31	.75
22 Miroslav Zalesak	.31	.75
23 Roy Sommer CO	.10	.25
24 Nick Fotiu ACO	.10	.25

2002-03 Cleveland Barons

The cards are unnumbered and listed below in alphabetical order.

COMPLETE SET (24)	10.00	25.00
1 Matt Carkner	.40	1.00
2 David Cloutier	.40	1.00
3 David Cunniff ACO	.02	.10
4 Rob Davison	.40	1.00
5 Niko Dimitrakos	.60	1.50
6 Jesse Fibiger	.40	1.00
7 Tavis Hansen	.40	1.00
8 John Jakopin	.40	1.00
9 Seamus Kotyk	.60	1.50
10 Ryan Kraft	.40	1.00
11 Eric Laplante	.40	1.00
12 Willie Levesque	.40	1.00
13 Lynn Loyns	.40	1.00
14 Keith McCambridge	.40	1.00
15 Graig Mischler	.40	1.00
16 Yuri Moscevsky	.40	1.00
17 Robert Mulick	.40	1.00
18 Jeff Nelson	.40	1.00
19 Pat Rissmiller	.40	1.00
20 Roy Sommer CO	.02	.10
21 Scott Thomas	.40	1.00
22 Vesa Toskala	1.25	3.00
23 Chad Wiseman	.40	1.00
24 Miroslav Zalesak	.40	1.00

2003-04 Cleveland Barons

COMPLETE SET (25)	5.00	12.00
1 Brad Boyes	.40	1.00
2 Matt Carkner	.20	.50
3 David Cloutier	.20	.50
4 Ryan Clowe	.20	.50
5 Jon DiSalvatore	.20	.50
6 Niko Dimitrakos	.30	.75
7 Christian Ehrhoff	.30	.75
8 Jesse Fibiger	.20	.50
9 Marcel Goc	.40	1.00
10 Tavis Hansen	.20	.50
11 Todd Harvey	.30	.75
12 Seamus Kotyk	.30	.75
13 Lynn Loyns	.20	.50
14 Yuri Moscevsky	.20	.50
15 Robert Mulick	.20	.50
16 Doug Murray	.20	.50
17 Dmitri Patzold	.40	1.00
18 Tomas Plihal	.20	.50
19 Pat Rissmiller	.20	.50
20 Grant Stevenson	.20	.50
21 Craig Valette	.20	.50
22 Miroslav Zalesak	.20	.50
23 Roy Sommer HCO	.02	.10
24 David Cunniff ACO	.02	.10
25 Mascot	.02	.10

2004-05 Cleveland Barons

COMPLETE SET (27)	6.00	15.00
1 Riley Armstrong	.20	.50
2 Nick Bootland	.30	.75
3 Matt Carkner	.30	.75
4 Ryan Clowe	.40	1.00
5 Tim Conboy	.20	.50
6 Scott Dobben	.20	.50
7 Christian Ehrhoff	.30	.75
8 Jim Fahey	.20	.50
9 Aaron Gill	.20	.50
10 Marcel Goc	.40	1.00
11 Josh Gorges	.30	.75
12 Mike Hoffman	.20	.50
13 Shane Joseph	.20	.50
14 Greg Labenski	.20	.50
15 Doug Murray	.20	.50
16 Glenn Olson	.20	.50
17 Dimitri Patzold	.30	.75
18 Tomas Plihal	.20	.50
19 Josh Prudden	.20	.50
20 Patrick Rissmiller	.20	.50
21 Nolan Schaefer	.30	.75
22 Garrett Stafford	.20	.50
23 Grant Stevenson	.20	.50
24 Craig Valette	.20	.50
25 Roy Sommer CO	.02	.10
26 David Cunniff ACO	.02	.10
27 Slapshark MASCOT	.02	.10

2005-06 Cleveland Barons

COMPLETE SET (28)	8.00	15.00
1 Riley Armstrong	.20	.50
2 Steve Bernier	.75	2.00
3 Matt Carkner	.20	.50
4 Tom Cavanagh	.20	.50
5 Ryan Clowe	.30	.75
6 Tim Conboy	.20	.50
7 Ray DiLauro	.20	.50
8 Josh Gorges	.20	.50
9 Josh Hennessy	.20	.50
10 Jamie Holden	.20	.50
11 Mike Iggulden	.20	.50
12 Shane Joseph	.20	.50
13 Lukas Kaspar	.20	.50
14 Doug Murray	.30	.75
15 Glenn Olson	.20	.50
16 Dmitri Patzold	.40	1.00
17 Tomas Plihal	.20	.50
18 Joshua Prudden	.20	.50
19 Pat Rissmiller	.20	.50
20 Nolan Schaefer	.40	1.00
21 Garrett Stafford	.20	.50
22 Brad Staubitz	.20	.50
23 Grant Stevenson	.20	.50
24 Jonathan Tremblay	.20	.50

25 Craig Valette .20 .50
26 Roy Sommer HC .02 .10
27 David Cunniff AC .02 .10
28 Jock Callander .02 .10

1998-99 Colorado Gold Kings

This set was handed out at a home game. Sets that weren't given away were later sold by the team at its souvenir shop.

COMPLETE SET (24) 10.00
1 Nicholas Chabot .20 .50
2 Trevor Converse .20 .50
3 R.J. Enga .20 .50
4 Anton Federov .20 .50
5 Wade Fennig .20 .50
6 Mark Fox .20 .50
7 Jeff Grabinsky .20 .50
8 Shawn Harris .20 .50
9 Don Lester .20 .50
10 Kirk Llano .20 .50
11 Craig Lyons .20 .50
12 Rob McCaig .20 .50
13 Rusty McKie .20 .50
14 Kevin McKinnon .20 .50
15 Bryan McMullen .20 .50
16 Chad Penney .20 .50
17 Tom Perry .20 .50
18 Bob Revermann .20 .50
19 Bogdan Rudenko .20 .50
20 Jason Simon .20 .50
21 Jeff Sirkka .20 .50
22 Brad Toporowski .20 .50
23 Kirk Tomlinson CO .08 .25
24 King Midas Mascot .02 .10

1998-99 Colorado Gold Kings Postcards

This 5x7 set was issued with blank backs and is not numbered. It is believed they were used at player signings and were never issued in team set form, making a complete set quite difficult to compile.

COMPLETE SET (22) 25.00
1 Jason Simon .60 1.50
2 Brad Toporowski .60 1.50
3 Tom Perry .60 1.50
4 Jeff Sirkka .60 1.50
5 Chad Penney .60 1.50
6 Bryan McMullen .60 1.50
7 Bogdan Rudenko .60 1.50
8 Kevin McKinnon .60 1.50
9 Bob Revermann .60 1.50
10 Craig Lyons .60 1.50
11 Kirk Tomlinson HCO .60 1.50
12 Trevor Converse .60 1.50
13 Jeff Grabinsky .60 1.50
14 R.J. Enga .60 1.50
15 Shawn Harris .60 1.50
16 Anton Fedorov .60 1.50
17 Hakan Jansson .60 1.50
18 Wade Fenning .60 1.50
19 Don Lester .60 1.50
20 Mark Fox .60 1.50
21 Kirk Llano .60 1.50
22 McDonald's Coupon .01

1999-00 Colorado Gold Kings Taco Bell

This set features the Gold Kings of the WCHL. The set was sponsored by Taco Bell and sold by the team at home games.

COMPLETE SET (26) 4.80 12.00
1 Travis Thiessen .20 .50
2 R.J. Enga .20 .50
3 Tom Perry .20 .50
4 Corey Lyons .20 .50
5 Bogdan Rudenko .20 .50
6 Don Lester CO .08 .25
7 Stephane Madore .20 .50
8 Steve Dowhy .20 .50
9 Greg Eisler .20 .50
10 Jean-Francois Picard .20 .50
11 King Midas MAS .08 .25
12 Steve Vezina .30 .75
13 Kevin McKinnon .20 .50
14 Craig Lyons .20 .50
15 Aaron Schweitzer .20 .50
16 Carl LeBlanc .20 .50
17 Daniel Olers .20 .50
18 Dean Ewen .20 .50
19 Frederik Beaubien .30 .75
20 Kirk Tomlinson .20 .50
21 Wade Fennig .20 .50
22 Kristoffer Eriksson .20 .50
23 Rob McCaig .20 .50
24 Greg Gatto .20 .50
25 Colorado Gold Kings .08 .25
26 Taco Bell Logo .01

1999-00 Colorado Gold Kings Wendy's

This set features the Gold Kings of the WCHL. The set features postcard-sized photos and a Wendy's ad on the back of each. The set was sold by the team at home games.

COMPLETE SET (22) 4.00 10.00
1 Jean-Francois Picard .20 .50
2 Corey Lyons .20 .50
3 Eric Long .20 .50
4 Wade Fennig .20 .50
5 R.J. Enga .20 .50
6 Travis Thiessen .20 .50
7 Daniel Olers .20 .50
8 Carl LeBlanc .20 .50
9 Greg Eisler .20 .50
10 Kevin McKinnon .20 .50
11 Dean Ewen .20 .50
12 Stephane Madore .20 .50
13 Darcy Anderson .20 .50
14 Tom Perry .20 .50
15 Rob McCaig .20 .50
16 Bogdan Rudenko .20 .50
17 Steve Vezina .30 .75
18 Aaron Schweitzer .20 .50
19 Craig Lyons .20 .50
20 Kirk Tomlinson CO .20 .50
21 Don Lester CO .08 .25
22 King Midas MAS .08 .25

2001-02 Colorado Gold Kings

COMPLETE SET (22) 10.00
1 Dwayne Blais .50
2 Aaron Boh .50
3 Zac Boyer .50
4 Chad Cabana .50
5 Colin Chaulk .50
6 Kirk Daubenspeck .75
7 R.J. Enga .50
8 Mike Garrow .50
9 Mark Gowan .50
10 Brent Henley .50
11 Darcy Johnson .50
12 Jason Knox .50
13 Cam Kryway .50
14 Craig Lyons .50
15 Mike Nicholishen .50
16 Tom Perry .50
17 Greg Schmidt .50
18 Juraj Slovak .50
19 Travis Thiessen .50
20 Allen Pedersen HCO .10
21 Kevin McKinnon ACO .10
22 Mascot .10

2003-04 Colorado Eagles

COMPLETE SET (25) 8.00 20.00
1 Lee Arnold .40 1.00
2 Ryan Bach .40 1.00
3 Gian Baldrica .40 1.00
4 Daniel Bohac .40 1.00
5 Igor Bonderev .40 1.00
6 Jesse Cook .40 1.00
7 Phil Crowe .60 1.50
8 Fraser Filipic .40 1.00
9 Aaron Grosul .40 1.00
10 Cam Kuzyk .40 1.00
11 Mike McGhan .40 1.00
12 Riley Nelson .40 1.00
13 Greg Pankewicz .40 1.00
14 Brad Patterson .40 1.00
15 Lee Ruff .40 1.00
16 Scott Swanson .40 1.00
17 Brent Thompson .60 1.50
18 Ryan Tobler .60 1.50
19 Brad Williamson .40 1.00
20 Karlis Zirnis .40 1.00
21 Chris Stewart CO .02 .10
22 Ralph Backstrom GM .02 .10
23 Mascot .02 .10
24 Team Photo .02 .10
25 Staff .02 .10

2004-05 Colorado Eagles

COMPLETE SET (24) 16.00
1 Team Card .10
2 Ralph Backstrom .10
3 Paulo Colaiacovo 1.00
4 Jesse Cook .75
5 Matt Desrosiers .75
6 Fraser Filipic .75
7 Aaron Grosul .75
8 Chris Hartsburg .75
9 Mike Lephart .75
10 Kris Mallette .75
11 Kevin Marsh .75
12 Kevin McDonald .75
13 Riley Nelson .75
14 Greg Pankewicz .75
15 Sean Robertson .75
16 Lee Ruff .75
17 Chris Stewart CO .75
18 David Svagrovsky .75
19 Ryan Tobler .75
20 Tyler Weiman .75
21 Brad Williamson .75
22 Karlis Zirnis .75
23 Slapshot MASCOT .10
24 Team Staff .10

2005-06 Colorado Eagles

COMPLETE SET (26) 8.00 20.00
1 Erik Adams .40 1.00
2 Lee Arnold .40 1.00
3 Jeff Blair .40 1.00
4 Les Borsheim .40 1.00
5 Paulo Colaiacovo .60 1.50
6 Matt Desrosiers .40 1.00
7 Fraser Filipic .40 1.00
8 Aaron Grosul .40 1.00
9 Chris Hartsburg .40 1.00
10 Garrett Larson .40 1.00
11 Jason Lundmark .40 1.00
12 Ed McGrane .40 1.00
13 Riley Nelson .40 1.00
14 Greg Pankewicz .40 1.00
15 Nick Parillo .40 1.00
16 Scott Polaski .40 1.00
17 Sean Robertson .40 1.00
18 Ryan Tobler .40 1.00
19 Brad Williamson .40 1.00
20 Chris Stewart CO .02 .10
21 Phil Crowe AC .02 .10
22 Ralph Backstrom PRES/GM .10 .25
23 Team Staff .02 .10
24 Eagles Chicks DANCERS .40 1.00
25 Slapshot MASCOT .02 .10
26 Colorado Eagles .20 .50

2006-07 Colorado Eagles•

COMPLETE SET (31) 8.00 15.00
1 Team Card .10 .25
2 Erik Adams .30 .75
3 Lee Arnold .30 .75
4 Jay Birnie .30 .75
5 Tim Boron .30 .75
6 Les Borsheim .30 .75
7 Paulo Colaiacovo .40 1.00
8 Marco Emond .30 .75
9 Fraser Filipic .30 .75
10 Steve Haddon .30 .75
11 Chris Hartsburg .30 .75
12 Brent Hughes .30 .75
13 Seth Leonard .30 .75
14 Ed McGrane .30 .75
15 Riley Nelson .30 .75
16 Greg Pankewicz .30 .75
17 Scott Polaski .30 .75
18 Sean Robertson .30 .75
19 Aaron Schneekloth .30 .75
20 Craig Strain .30 .75
21 Ryan Tobler .30 .75
22 Brad Williamson .30 .75
23 Slapshot MASCOT .10
24 Chris Stewart CO .10 .25
25 Phil Crowe ACO .10 .25
26 Ryan Bach ACO .10 .25
27 Ralph Backstrom PRES .10 .25
28 Tony Deynzer EQ MGR .10
29 Chris Porowski TR .10
30 Tori Holt ANN .02 .10
31 Eagles Chicks DANCERS .20 .50

2007-08 Colorado Eagles

COMPLETE SET (30) 6.00 15.00
1 Team Picture .30 .75
2 Erik Adams .30 .75
3 Jason Beatty .30 .75
4 Jay Birnie .30 .75
5 Les Borsheim .30 .75
6 Bryan Bridges .30 .75
7 Fraser Filipic .30 .75
8 Steve Haddon .30 .75
9 Chris Hartsburg .30 .75
10 Dave Iannazzo .30 .75
11 Sebastien Laplante .30 .75
12 Seth Leonard .30 .75
13 Ed McGrane .30 .75
14 Riley Nelson .30 .75
15 Greg Pankewicz .30 .75
16 Scott Polaski .30 .75
17 Aaron Schneekloth .30 .75
18 Brett Thurston .30 .75
19 Ryan Tobler .30 .75
20 Kris Wiebe .30 .75
21 Brad Williamson .30 .75
22 Chris Stewart HC .30 .75
23 Ryan Bach AC .30 .75
24 Tony Deynzer EQ .30 .75
25 Chris Porowski .30 .75
26 Ralph Backstrom .30 .75
27 Phil Crowe .30 .75
28 Tori Holt .30 .75
29 Eagles Chicks .20 .50
30 Slapshot MASCOT .20 .50

2002-03 Columbia Inferno

COMPLETE SET (18) 25.00
97 Josh Blackburn 2.00
98 Paul Cabana 1.25
99 Robin Carruthers 1.25
100 Trevor Demmans 1.25
101 Regan Darby 1.25
102 Corey Hessler 1.25
103 Eric Labelle 2.00
104 Denis Martynyuk 1.25
105 Barrie Moore 1.25
106 Justin Morrison 1.25
107 Sean Owens 1.25
108 Chris Pittman 1.25
109 Tim Smith 1.25
110 Chris St. Croix 1.25
111 Rejean Stringer 1.25
112 Matt Ulwelling 1.25
113 Dennis Vial 3.00
114 Shawn Wansborough 1.25

2003-04 Columbia Inferno

This set was sold by the team at home games. The numbering reflects this set as part of the entire run of RBI Sports series this year. The production run was reported to be 250 sets.

COMPLETE SET (16) 25.00
97 Greg Amadio 1.50
98 Josh Blackburn 2.00
99 Alexandre Burrows 1.50
100 Paul Cabana 1.50
101 Robin Carruthers 1.50
102 Derek Eastman 1.50
103 Terry Harrison 1.50
104 Corey Hessler 1.50
105 Eric Labelle 1.50
106 Robert McVicar 2.00
107 Barrie Moore 1.50
108 Brandon Nolan 1.50
109 Chris Pittman 1.50
110 Tim Smith 2.00
111 Chris St. Croix 1.50
112 Dennis Vial 2.00

2003-04 Columbia Inferno Update

Produced by RBI Sports as a late season update, this was limited to 250 sets.

COMPLETE SET (6) 5.00
50 Mike Hanson 1.00
51 Sean Owens 1.00
52 Mike Roemensky 1.00
53 Marc-Andre Roy 1.00
54 Jesse Schultz 1.00
55 Matt Ulwelling 1.00

1966-67 Columbus Checkers

This 16-card set measures 4 x 7 1/4" and features a black and white photo on the front along with players name at the bottom. Backs are blank. Cards are unnumbered and checklisted below alphabetically.

COMPLETE SET (16) 35.00 70.00
1 John Bailey 2.50 5.00
2 Moe Bartoli 2.50 5.00
3 Kerry Bond 2.50 5.00
4 Andre Daoust 2.50 5.00
5 Bert Fizzell 2.50 5.00
6 Marcel Goudreau 2.50 5.00
7 Jim Graham 2.50 5.00
8 Paul Jackson 2.50 5.00
9 Ken Laidlaw 2.50 5.00
10 Noel Lirette 2.50 5.00
11 Gary Longman 2.50 5.00
12 Garry Macmillan 2.50 5.00
13 Gary Mork 2.50 5.00
14 Matt Thorpe 2.50 5.00
15 Jack Turner 2.50 5.00
16 Alton White 2.50 5.00

1967-68 Columbus Checkers

Little is known about this early team-issued photo set from the Checkers of the IHL. It is believed they were issued as a promotional item in response to mailed-in requests from fans. Any further information can be forwarded to hockeymag@beckett.com.

COMPLETE SET (16) 37.50 75.00
1 Team Photo 2.50 5.00
2 Moe Bartoli 2.50 10.00
3 Bill Bond 2.50 5.00
4 Serge Boudreault 2.50 5.00
5 Gord Dibley 2.50 10.00
6 Bert Fizzell 2.50 5.00
7 Chuck Kelly 2.50 5.00
8 Ken Saunders 2.50 5.00
9 Nelson Leclair 2.50 5.00
10 Real Paquette 2.50 5.00
11 Dick Proceviat 2.50 5.00
12 Hartley Estabrooks 2.50 5.00
13 Ken Sutyla 2.50 5.00
14 Nelson Tremblay 2.50 5.00
15 Jack Turner 2.50 5.00
16 Al White 2.50 5.00

1997-98 Columbus Cottonmouths

This 24-card set was handed out over the span of five games, and thus is extremely difficult to find in complete form.

COMPLETE SET (24) 8.00 20.00
1 Jerome Bechard .40 1.00
2 Chris Bergeron .40 1.00
3 Claude Fillion .40 1.00
4 Eric Germain .40 1.00
5 Brian Idalski .40 1.00
6 Mick Kempffer .40 1.00
7 Olaf Kjenstadt .40 1.00
8 Doug Mann .40 1.00
9 Grady Manson .40 1.00
10 Derek Marchand .40 1.00
11 Bobby Marshall .40 1.00
12 Randy Murphy .40 1.00
13 Frankie Ouellette .60 1.50
14 Kevin Plager .40 1.00
15 Brad Prefontaine .40 1.00
16 Marcel Richard .40 1.00
17 John Sincinski .40 1.00
18 Greg Taylor .40 1.00
19 David Wainwright .40 1.00
20 Tom Wilson .40 1.00
21 Phil Roberto GM .08 .25
22 Bruce Garber HCO .08 .25
23 Charles B. Morrow .08 .25
24 Pete Carson .40 1.00

1998-99 Columbus Cottonmouths

This 24-card set was handed out at a home game in March of that season, and was later sold for at the team's souvenir stands for $5 per set.

COMPLETE SET (24) 3.60 9.00
1 Jerome Bechard .20 .50
2 Dan Brown .20 .50
3 Derek Crimin .20 .50
4 Claude Fillion .20 .50
5 Brian Idalski .20 .50
6 Mick Kempffer .20 .50
7 Grady Manson .20 .50
8 Roman Markhovski .20 .50
9 Mike Martens .20 .50
10 David Neilson .20 .50
11 Frankie Ouellette .20 .50
12 Kevin Plager .20 .50
13 Brad Prefontaine .20 .50
14 Marcel Richard .20 .50
15 Corwin Saurdiff .20 .50
16 Jean-Alain Schneider .20 .50
17 Robbie Sinclair .20 .50
18 Thomas Stewart .20 .50
19 Tom Wilson .20 .50
20 Derek Marchand ACO .02 .10
21 Phil Roberto GM .02 .10
22 Bruce Garber HCO .02 .10
23 Pete Carson HTR .02 .10
24 Martha Morrow .20 .50

1999-00 Columbus Cottonmouths

This set features the Cottonmouths of the CHL. The set was handed out as a promotional giveaway at home games, with one five-card strip being issued at each game. The complete set was later sold by the team for $5.

COMPLETE SET (28) 4.80 12.00
1 Aaron Vickar .20 .50
2 Kamil Kuriplach .20 .50
3 Mick Kempffer .20 .50
4 Kevin Plager .20 .50
5 Martha Morrow OWN .08 .25
6 Derek Crimin .20 .50
7 Jason Given .20 .50
8 Marcel Richard .20 .50
9 Ryan Aikia .20 .50
10 Phil Roberto GM .08 .25
11 Jerome Bechard .20 .50
12 Doug Mann .20 .50
13 Mark Martins .20 .50
14 Tommi Santala .30 .75
15 Bruce Garber HCO .08 .25
16 Mark Scott .20 .50
17 Kelly Van Hiltgen .20 .50
18 Frankie Ouellette .30 .75
19 Jaroslav Kerestes .20 .50
20 Brian Idalski ACO .08 .25
21 Per Fernhall .20 .50
22 Jackson Hegland .20 .50
23 Robert Frid .20 .50
24 Olaf Kjenstad .30 .75
25 Randy Scrimshire EQM .08 .25
26 Brodie Coffin .20 .50
27 Andy Powers .20 .50
28 Tonda Jackson AGM .08 .25

2000-01 Columbus Cottonmouths

This set features the Cottonmouths of the CHL. The cards were issued as giveaways over the course of five home dates, in the form of five-card perforated strips.

COMPLETE SET (25) 8.00 20.00
1 Jerome Bechard .40 1.00
2 Ryan Brown .40 1.00
3 Kris Cantu .40 1.00
4 Mick Kempffer .40 1.00
5 Jaroslav Kerestes .40 1.00
6 Doug Mann .40 1.00
7 Bobby Marshall .40 1.00
8 Mike Martens .40 1.00
9 Martin Menard .40 1.00
10 Riley Nelson .40 1.00
11 Frankie Ouellette .40 1.00
12 Daniel Payette .40 1.00
13 Andy Powers .40 1.00
14 Greg Quebec .40 1.00
15 Blaine Russell .40 1.00
16 Drew Schoneck .40 1.00
17 Kris Schultz .40 1.00
18 Rob Schweyer .40 1.00
19 Blake Sheane .40 1.00
20 Craig Stahl .40 1.00
21 Bruce Garber CO .10 .25
22 Phil Roberto GM .10 .25
23 Randy Scrimpshire EM .10 .25
24 Boomer MASCOT .10 .25
25 Teri LaSalle TR .10 .25

2002-03 Columbus Cottonmouths

COMPLETE SET (24) 20.00
1 Jerome Bechard 1.00
2 Phil Cole 1.00
3 Randy Copley 1.50
4 Brent Cullaton 1.00
5 Mitch Fritz 1.00
6 Chad Hamilton 1.00
7 J.J. Hunter 1.00
8 Matus Kostur 1.50
9 Mike Lee 1.50
10 Carlyle Lewis 1.50
11 Andrew Long 1.00
12 Sean McAslan 1.00
13 Darren McAusland 1.00
14 John Morlang 1.00
15 Mike Morrison 1.50
16 Ryan Risidore 1.00
17 Bart Rushmer 1.00
18 Darren Tiemstra 1.00
19 Jeff Zehr 1.50
20 Phil Roberto GM/CO .25
21 Larry Kish ACO .25
22 Randy Scrimpshire EQM .25
23 Boomer Mascot .10
24 Owners .01

2003-04 Columbus Cottonmouths

This set was issued as a promotional giveaway over two home games. The cards were issued in perforated sheet form.

COMPLETE SET (30) 15.00 30.00
1 Salvador Diaz-Verson OWN .02 .10
2 Shelby Amos OWN .02 .10
3 Brian Curran CO .02 .10
4 Jerome Bechard ACO .02 .10
5 Heath Kaufman EQM .02 .10
6 Jason Stevens TR .02 .10
7 Rumun Ndur .75 2.00
8 Jason Tapp .75 2.00
9 Mitch Fritz .75 2.00
10 Marc-Andre Thinel .75 2.00
11 Ryan Davis .40 1.00
12 Joel Martin .75 2.00
13 Olivier Michaud .60 1.50
14 Tomas Micka .40 1.00
15 Mascot .02 .10
16 Brad Voth .40 1.00
17 Colin Pepperall .40 1.00
18 Dan Tudin .40 1.00
19 Matt Shasby .40 1.00
20 Mathieu Roy .75 2.00
21 Carlyle Lewis .40 1.00
22 John Morlang .40 1.00
23 Kenton Smith .40 1.00
24 Peter Hogan .40 1.00
25 Ryan Risidore .40 1.00
26 Christian Larrivee .75 2.00
27 Dan Tessier .75 2.00
28 Jean-Francois Plourde .40 1.00
29 Ray DiLauro .40 1.00
30 Matus Kostur .75 2.00

2004-05 Columbus Cottonmouths

Very little is known about this set featuring the Cottonmouths of the SPHL and no pricing is available. Please forward any additional info to hockeymag@beckett.com.

COMPLETE SET (?)
1 Terry Friesen
2 Mick Kempffer
3 Joel Pullman
4 Chris Rook
5 Chad Rycroft
6 Brent Toews
7 Orrin Hergott
8 Tylor Keller
9 Ryan Haggerty
10 Tom McMonagle
11 Colby Will
12 Lorne Misita
13 Matt Mathias
14 Ryan Rulz
15 Craig Stahl
16 Ryan Aikia
17 Brock Johnson
18 Tim Green
19 Daryl Moor
20 Doug Mann
21 Jim Underwood
22 Jerome Bechard CO
23 Michael Slayton EQM
24 Jason Stevens TR

2003-04 Columbus Stars

This set features the Stars of the UHL. The set is labeled as a "youth season pass" on the front. The names of the players are not listed, but they can be identified by their jersey numbers. The back of each card lists the Stars schedule. Since the team folded midway through the season, only a handful of these cards were given out. Due to lack of market activity, we are unable to price these cards.

COMPLETE SET (5)
1 Tom Nemeth
2 Eric Naud
3 Greg Hewitt
4 Scott Levins
5 Chris Taliercio

2000-01 Connecticut Huskies

This set features the Huskies of the NCAA. It is believed that it was issued as a promotional giveaway as are all NCAA issues, but that has not been confirmed. The cards are printed on heavier card stock than usual and feature a swirling blue design along the bottom front.

COMPLETE SET (18) 15.00 30.00
1 Mike Anderson .75 2.00
2 Bret Bostock .75 2.00
3 Mike Boylan .75 2.00
4 Scott Brown .75 2.00
5 Ron D'Angelo .75 2.00
6 Eric Goclowski .75 2.00
7 Michael Goldkind .75 2.00
8 Matt Herhal .75 2.00
9 Anders Johnson .75 2.00
10 Kurt Kamienski .75 2.00
11 Trent Landry .75 2.00
12 Ciro Longobardi .75 2.00
13 Charles Ridolf .75 2.00
14 Evan Schwarz .75 2.00
15 Travis Wood .75 2.00
16 Bruce Marshall CO .20 .50
17 UCONN Huskies .20 .50
18 UCONN SCHEDULE .04 .10

1992-93 Cornell Big Red

This set features Cornell of the NCAA and is believed to be a promotional giveaway. The cards measure an oversized 2 3/4 by 3 3/4. They feature a posed color photo on the front with a white border and the words Cornell Hockey 92 93 on the front. The cards are listed below in alphabetical order.

COMPLETE SET (30) 6.00 15.00
1 Andrew Bandurski .40 1.00
2 Etienne Belzile .20 .50
3 Geoff Bumstead .30 .75
4 Brad Chartrand .20 .50
5 Rick Davis .20 .50
6 John DeHart .20 .50
7 Andre Doll .20 .50
8 P.C. Drouin .40 1.00
9 Dan Dufresne .20 .50
10 Blair Ettles .20 .50
11 Christian Felli .20 .50
12 Russ Hammond .20 .50
13 Shaun Hannah .20 .50
14 Steve Hayden .20 .50
15 Bill Holowatiuk .20 .50
16 Ryan Hughes .20 .50
17 Jake Karam .20 .50
18 Jiri Kloboucek .20 .50
19 Geoff Lopatka .20 .50
20 Joel McArter .20 .50
21 Tyler McManus .20 .50
22 Devon Nilson .20 .50
23 Geoff Raynak .20 .50
24 Mike Sancimino .40 1.00
25 Mark Scollan .20 .50
26 Tim Shean .20 .50
27 Greg Swenson .20 .50
28 Alex Vershinin .20 .50
29 Jason Vogel .20 .50
30 Mark Taylor ACO .02 .10

1993-94 Cornell Big Red

As typically is the case with NCAA sets, this series was issued as a promotional giveaway. The cards are unnumbered, so the set is checklisted below in alphabetical order.

COMPLETE SET (30) 4.80 12.00
1 Vincent Auger .15 .40
2 Andrew Bandurski .15 .40
3 Geoff Bumstead .15 .40
4 Brad Chartrand .15 .40
5 Matt Cooney .15 .40
6 John DeHart .15 .40
7 Andre Doll .15 .40
8 Dan Dufresne .15 .40
9 Blair Ettles .15 .40
10 Christian Felli .15 .40
11 Tony Fergin .15 .40
12 Shaun Hannah .15 .40
13 Bill Holowatiuk .15 .40
14 Jake Karam .15 .40
15 Jason Kendall .15 .40
16 Jiri Kloboucek .15 .40
17 Geoff Lopatka .15 .40
18 Joel McArter .15 .40
19 Tyler McManus .15 .40
20 Jamie Papp .15 .40
21 Mike Sancimino .15 .40
22 Mark Scollan .15 .40
23 Tim Shean .15 .40
24 Eddy Skazyk .15 .40
25 Alex Vershinin .15 .40
26 Jason Weber .15 .40
27 Steve Wilson .15 .40
28 Chad Wilson .15 .40
29 Jason Zubkus .15 .40
30 Mark Taylor ACO .02 .10

1991-92 Cornwall Royals

This 28-card set measures approximately 2 5/8" by 3 3/4". The fronts feature borderless posed color player photos. The player's name appears in the left upper corner, while the team logo is in the right upper corner. The Religious Hospitallers Of St. Joseph Health Centre Of Cornwall logo is printed in a white bar under the photo. On a white background, the backs carry "Royals Against Illegal Drug Tips from Cornwall Police Service" in the upper portion and sponsor logos below.

COMPLETE SET (28) 4.00 10.00
1 Jason Meloche .15 .40
2 Mark Desantis .15 .40
3 Richard Raymond .15 .40
4 Gord Pell .15 .40
5 Dave Lemay .15 .40
6 John Lovell CO .02 .10
7 Ryan Vandenbussche .40 1.00
8 David Babcock .15 .40
9 Sam Oliveira .15 .40
10 Jeremy Stevenson .20 .50
11 Todd Walker .15 .40
12 Jean-Alain Schneider .15 .40
13 Ilpo Kauhanen .20 .50
14 Guy Leveque .20 .50
15 Shayne Gaffar .15 .40
16 Rival Fullum .15 .40
17 Mike Prokopec .20 .50
18 Nathan Lafayette .20 .50
19 Larry Courville .20 .50
20 Chris Clancy .15 .40
21 Tom Nemeth .20 .50
22 Jeff Reid .15 .40
23 Paul Andrea .15 .40
24 John Slaney .40 1.00
25 Alan Letang .15 .40
26 Rob Dykeman .20 .50
27 Paul Fixter CO .02 .10
Brian O'Leary CO
28 Chief of Police .02 .10

1999-00 Cornwall Colts

This set features the Colts of the COHL, a tier 2 junior league. The listing below is NOT complete. Any additional information can be forwarded to hockeymag@beckett.com.

COMPLETE SET (?)
1 Travis Albers
2 Joel Bergeron
3 Matt Collins
4 Jeff Legue
5 Kacey McDonell
6 Luc Paquin

2003-04 Cornwall Colts

The Colts play in the Central Junior Hockey League in Ontario, a Tier 2 circuit. Only two cards are confirmed to exist for this set so far. Information on others can be sent to hockeymag@beckett.com.

COMPLETE SET (?)
1 Aaron Bogosian 1.00
2 Sean Flanagan 1.00

1999-00 Corpus Christi IceRays

This set features the IceRays of the WPHL. The set was produced by Grandstand and issued in two series. The second series was issued during the playoffs, so these contain complete 1999-2000 stats. The cards are unnumbered, and so are listed in alphabetical order.

COMPLETE SET (46) 8.00 20.00
1 Tyler Boucher .20 .50
2 Geoff Bumstead .30 .75
3 Paul Doherty .20 .50
4 Pat Dunn .20 .50
5 Jason Genik .20 .50
6 Regan Harper .20 .50
7 Brent Hoiness .20 .50
8 Trevor Janicki .20 .50
9 Cory Johnson .20 .50
10 Alex Kholomeyev .30 .75
11 Roger Lewis .20 .50
12 Dustin McArthur .20 .50
13 Darryl Olsen .20 .50
14 Jody Praznik .20 .50
15 Tobin Praznik .20 .50
16 Bob Quinnell .20 .50

17 Chris Robertson .20 .50
18 Layne Roland .20 .50
19 Andy Ross .20 .50
20 Dennis Shiryaev .20 .50
21 Eddy Skazyk .20 .50
22 Mike Tomlinson .20 .50
23 Phil Valk .20 .50
24 Quinten Van Horlick .20 .50
25 Mike Vandenberghe .20 .50
26 Kurt Wickenheiser .20 .50
27 Brad Wingfield .20 .50
28 Taylor Hall CO .20 .50
29 Jody Praznik .20 .50
30 Scott Brower .20 .50
31 Geoff Bumstead AS .30 .75
32 Tobin Praznik .20 .50
32 Jody Praznik .20 .50
33 Brad Wingfield .08 .25
33 Geoff Bumstead .30 .75
34 Geoff Bumstead .30 .75
34 Tobin Praznik .08 .25
34 Kurt Wickenheiser .20 .50
35 Radio Celebrities .04 .01
36 Home Opener .02 .10
37 Corpus Christi Icegirls .30 .75
38 Party Patrol .02 .10
39 SugarRay MASCOT .08 .25
40 Corpus Christi IceRays .20 .50
41 Best Fans in the WPHL .02 .10
42 ValueBank Texas .04 .01

1992-93 Dallas Freeze

This 20-card standard-size set features the Dallas Freeze of the Central Hockey League. White-bordered color player photos adorn the fronts of these cards. The Freeze logo appears on both sides of the card. In the border beneath the photo are the player's name and position. The cards are unnumbered and checklisted below in alphabetical order.

COMPLETE SET (20) 3.00 8.00
1 Wayne Anchikoski .20 .50
2 Gary Audette .20 .50
3 Jeff Beaudin .20 .50
4 Troy Binnie .20 .50
5 Brian Bruininks .20 .50
6 Derek Crawford .20 .50
7 Dave Doucette .20 .50
8 Don Dwyer .20 .50
9 Joe Eagan .20 .50
10 Ron Flockhart CO .30 .75
11 Frank Lascala .20 .50
12 Robert Lewis .20 .50
13 Joey Mittelsteadt .20 .50
14 Rico Rossi .20 .50
15 Dean Shmyr .20 .50
16 Doug Sinclair .20 .50
17 Greg Smith .20 .50
18 Jason Taylor .20 .50
19 Mike Zanier .30 .75
20 Team Photo .20 .50

1993-94 Dallas Freeze

These oddly shaped round cards are approximately the size of a hockey puck. They came in a plastic container with the team logo on the front and were available from the team's booster club at home games.

COMPLETE SET (18) 2.50 6.00
1 Wayne Anchikoski .20 .50
2 Jeff Beaudin .15 .40
3 Troy Binnie .20 .50
4 Brian Bruininks .15 .40
5 Derek Crawford .20 .50
6 Dave Doucette .20 .50
7 Don Dwyer .15 .40
8 Mark Holick .15 .40
9 Randy Jaycock .15 .40
10 Frank LaScala .15 .40
11 Robert Lewis .15 .40
12 Joey McTamney .15 .40
13 Joey Mittelsteadt .15 .40
14 Dean Shmyr .15 .40
15 Greg Smith .15 .40
16 Jason Taylor .15 .40
17 Jason White .15 .40
18 Ron Flockhart CO .20 .50

2005-06 Danbury Trashers

COMPLETE SET 5.00 12.00
1 Alex Goupil .20 .50
2 Donny Glover .20 .50
3 Eric Lind .20 .50
4 Drew Omicioli .20 .50
5 Danny Stewart .20 .50
6 Sergei Durden .20 .50
7 David Beauregard .20 .50
8 Frederic Belanger .20 .50
9 Jayme Platt .20 .50
10 Regan Kelly .20 .50
11 Sylvain Daigle .20 .50
12 Dave MacIsaac .20 .50
13 Mike Omicioli .20 .50
14 Luke Sellers .20 .50
15 Troy Smith .20 .50
16 Mario Larocque .20 .50
17 2005-06 UHL All-Stars .20 .50
18 Ryan Barnes .20 .50
19 Ed Campbell .20 .50
20 Jamie Thompson .20 .50
21 Jean-Michel Daoust .20 .50
22 Brad Wingfield .20 .50
23 Shawn Collymore .20 .50
24 Jeff Daw .20 .50
25 David Hymovitz .20 .50
26 Paul Gillis CO .02 .10
27 Paul Sacco .02 .10
28 A.J. Galante OWN .02 .10
29 Scrappy MASCOT .02 .10

1992-93 Dayton Bombers

This set features the Bombers of the ECHL. Just 2,500 sets were produced, with 2,300 given away as a game-night promotion and the remaining 200 sold for $5. The cards are unnumbered and checklisted below in alphabetical order.

COMPLETE SET (24) 4.00 10.00
1 John Beaulieu DJ .02 .10
2 Steve Bogoyevac .20 .50
3 Christopher DJ .02 .10
4 Darren Colbourne .20 .50
5 Derek Crawford .20 .50
6 Dan-O DJ .02 .10
7 Derek Donald .20 .50
8 Ray Edwards .20 .50
9 Doug Evans .20 .50
10 Sandy Galuppo .30 .75
11 Shayne Green .20 .50
12 Rod Houk .20 .50
13 Peter Kasowski .20 .50
14 Steve Kerrigan .20 .50
15 Frank Kovacs .20 .50
16 Darren Langdon .30 .75
17 Denis Larocque .20 .50
18 Darwin McPherson .20 .50
19 Tom Nemeth .20 .50
20 Claude Noel CO .02 .10
21 Tony Peters .20 .50
22 Marshall Phillips .20 .50
23 Mike Reier .20 .50
24 Steve Wilson .20 .50

1993-94 Dayton Bombers

This set features the Bombers of the ECHL. 2,500 sets were produced and given away as a game-night promotion. Cards 19-28 feature radio disc jockeys.

COMPLETE SET (28) 3.00 8.00
1 Title Card CL .02 .10
2 Jeff Levy .15 .40
3 Steve Wilson .15 .40
4 Jason Downey .15 .40
5 Jim Peters .15 .40
6 Ondrej Kriz .15 .40
7 Steve Bogoyevac .15 .40
8 Jason Disiewich .15 .40
9 Marc Savard .15 .40
10 Dan O'Shea .15 .40
11 Tom Nemeth .15 .40
12 Guy Prince .15 .40
13 Ray Edwards .15 .40
14 Sergei Kharin .15 .40
15 Derek Donald .15 .40
16 Darwin McPherson .15 .40
17 Jeff Stolp .15 .40
18 Adam Bomber (Mascot) .02 .10
19 Kim .02 .10
20 Robby .02 .10
21 Lisa .02 .10
22 Marshall Phillips .15 .40
23 Dan-O .02 .10
24 John(B-Man) Beaulieu .02 .10
25 Christopher .02 .10
26 Steve Kerrigan .15 .40
27 Tony Peters .15 .40
28 Shaun Higgins .02 .10
Major Dick Hale

1994-95 Dayton Bombers

This set features the Bombers of the ECHL. 5,000 sets were produced, 1,500 of which were given away as a game night promotion.

COMPLETE SET (24) 3.00 8.00
1 Title Card CL .02 .10
2 Paul Taylor .15 .40
3 Steve Wilson .15 .40
4 Jason Downey .15 .40
5 Craig Charron .15 .40
6 Jim Lessard .15 .40
7 Karson Kaebel .15 .40
8 Jamie Steer .15 .40
9 Rob Hartnell .15 .40
10 Mike Doers .15 .40
11 Sean Gagnon .20 .50
12 Kevin Brown .15 .40
13 John Brill .15 .40
14 Dean Fedorchuk .15 .40
15 Tony Gruba .15 .40
16 Steve Lingren .15 .40
17 Brandon Smith .15 .40
18 Jeff Stolp .20 .50
19 Mike Vandenberghe .15 .40
20 Jim Playfair .15 .40
21 Goal Celebration .15 .40
22 Jamie Steer AS .15 .40
23 Steve Wilson AW .15 .40
24 Jeff Stolp AW .20 .50

1995-96 Dayton Bombers

This set features the Bombers of the ECHL. The cards are oversized (5 by 7 inches). The cards were limited in production to 500 copies each. One card was given away during each of 32 home games (3 games did not feature a card) inside the official game program. Purchase of a program was required to obtain a card.

COMPLETE SET (32) 10.00 25.00
1 Jim Playfair CO .30 .75
2 Sean Ortiz .30 .75
3 Derek Herlofsky .60 1.50
4 Paul Andrea .30 .75
5 Nick Poole .30 .75
6 Steve Lingren .40 1.00
7 Kevin Brown .30 .75
8 Jason Downey .30 .75
9 Sergei Kharin .40 1.00
10 Matt McElwee .30 .75
11 Mike Naylor .30 .75
12 Ted Russell .30 .75
13 Colin Miller .40 1.00
14 Brent Brekke .30 .75
15 John Brill .30 .75
16 Mike Murray .30 .75
17 Sean Gagnon .60 1.50
18 Brian Renfrew .40 1.00
19 Rob Peters .30 .75
20 Jeff Petruic .30 .75
21 Steve Roberts .30 .75
22 George Zajankala .30 .75
23 Adam Bomber MASCOT .30 .75
24 Steve Lingren AS .30 .75
25 Jim Playfair CO AS .30 .75
26 Jerry Buckley .40 1.00
27 Jeremy Stasiuk .30 .75
28 Greg Burke .30 .75
29 Chris Johnston .30 .75
30 Dwayne Gylywoychuk .30 .75
P1 Sean Gagnon .75 2.00
P2 Sergei Kharin .75 2.00

1996-97 Dayton Bombers

This set features the Bombers of the ECHL. The cards were issued as a promotional item within copies of the official game program. They were issued in 2-card strips, with the cards separated by a thin ad for sponsor WTUE radio. One strip was inserted during each of 12 home games over the course of the season. Purchase of the program was required to obtain the cards. The cards themselves were printed on thin stock, with color photos surrounded by a red border. Production was limited to 500 copies of each strip.

COMPLETE SET (24) 10.00 25.00
1 Steve Roberts .40 1.00
2 Chris Sullivan .40 1.00
3 Steve Lingren .40 1.00
4 Jordan Shields .40 1.00
5 Ildar Yubin .40 1.00
6 Dwight Parrish .40 1.00
7 Brian Ridolfi .40 1.00
8 Jordan Willis .75 2.00
9 Dale Hooper .40 1.00
10 Will Clarke .40 1.00
11 Tavis Morrison .40 1.00
12 Trent Schachle .40 1.00
13 John Emmons .60 1.50
14 Sam McKenney .40 1.00
15 Bryan Richardson .40 1.00
16 Ryan Gillis .40 1.00
17 Marty Flichel .60 1.50
18 Jason Downey .40 1.00
19 Troy Christensen .40 1.00
20 Derek Herlofsky .75 2.00
21 Sal Manganaro .40 1.00
22 Tom Nemeth .60 1.50
23 Evgeny Ryabchikov .75 2.00
24 Colin Miller .40 1.00

1998-99 Dayton Bombers

This set was handed out at a game late in the season, making it very difficult to acquire on the secondary market. Any additional information about the set can be forwarded to hockeymag@beckett.com.

COMPLETE SET (25) 4.80 12.00
1 Frederic Bouchard .30 .75
2 Bobby Brown .20 .50
3 Norman Dezainde .20 .50
4 Travis Dillabough .20 .50
5 Ryan Furness .20 .50
6 Dan Hendrickson .20 .50
7 Trevor Koenig .20 .50
8 Justin Krall .20 .50
9 Aaron Kriss .20 .50
10 Jamie Ling .40 1.00
11 Jim Logan .20 .50
12 Colin Miller .20 .50
13 Tom Nemeth .30 .75
14 Brian Regan .20 .50
15 Brian Ridolfi .20 .50
16 Brian Secord .20 .50
17 Chris Wismer .20 .50
18 John Beaulieu ANN .02 .10
19 Dale Coulthard EQM .02 .10
20 Greg Ireland HCO .02 .10
21 Buddy Mascot .02 .10
22 Kerrigan & Christopher .02 .10
23 Team Photo .20 .50
24 Larry Thornton TR .02 .10
25 Lee Stieg .20 .50

1998-99 Dayton Bombers EBK

This 21-card set was different than the giveaway set from the same year, and was sold at games late in the season.

COMPLETE SET (21) 3.00 8.00
1 Frederic Bouchard .20 .50
2 Aaron Kriss .15 .40
3 Brian Secord .15 .40
4 Colin Miller .15 .40
5 Jamie Ling .30 .75
6 Bobby Brown .15 .40
7 Tom Nemeth .20 .50
8 Brian Ridolfi .15 .40
9 Travis Dillabough .15 .40
10 Justin Krall .15 .40
11 Dan Hendrickson .15 .40
12 Ed Gingher ACO .02 .10
13 Brian Regan .15 .40
14 Trevor Koenig .15 .40
15 Greg Ireland HCO .02 .10
16 Colin Miller .02 .10
Tom Nemeth ACO
17 Bucky Mascot .02 .10
18 Brandon Sugden .20 .50
19 Norman Dezainde .20 .50
20 Kiley Hill .15 .40
NNO Checklist .02 .10

1996-97 Dayton Ice Bandits

This set features the Ice Bandits of the ECHL. The set was initially given away as a promotional item, with remaining copies sold by the team at last-season home games.

COMPLETE SET (29) 4.00 10.00
1 Checklist .02 .10
2 Jesse Austin .20 .50
3 Mike Bajurny .20 .50
4 Dan Belisle HCO .02 .10
5 Dan Carter .20 .50
6 Cosmo Clarke .20 .50
7 Bob Clouston .20 .50
8 Tom Colasanto .20 .50
9 Brad Cook .20 .50
10 Richard Fatrola .20 .50
11 Jack Greig .20 .50
12 Kelly Melton .20 .50
13 Andrew Plumb .20 .50
14 Brian Renfrew .20 .50
15 Bobby Rapoza .20 .50
16 Jacque Rodrigue .20 .50
17 Fred Scott .20 .50
18 Troy Stevens .20 .50
19 Larry Thornton TR .02 .10
20 Mike Thornton .20 .50
21 Scott Vettraino .20 .50
22 Marty Wells .20 .50
23 Kevin Young .20 .50
24 The Phantom Mascot .02 .10
25 The Famous Chicken .02 .10
26 WTUE Employees .02 .10
27 WTUE Employees .02 .10
28 WTUE Employees .02 .10
29 WTUE Employees .02 .10

1996-97 Denver University Pioneers

This 10-card set features color action photos on the front and a team schedule on the back. It was issued as a game-night giveaway.

COMPLETE SET (10) 3.00 8.00
1 Travis Smith .40 1.00
2 Jim Mullin .30 .75
3 Mike Corbett .30 .75
4 Petri Gunther .30 .75
5 Garrett Buzan .30 .75
6 Antti Laaksonen .40 1.00
7 Charlie Host .30 .75
8 Erik Andersson .30 .75
9 Warren Smith .30 .75
10 Anders Bjork .30 .75

1999-00 Des Moines Buccaneers

This set features the Buccaneers of the USHL. The set was produced by Roox and sold by the team at home games.

COMPLETE SET (24) 4.00 12.00
1 Dominic Torretti .20 .50
2 Felipe Larranaga .20 .50
3 Paul Baumgartner .20 .50
4 Nathan Berry .20 .50
5 Matt Weber .20 .50
6 Troy Riddle .20 .50
7 Nick Dimella .20 .50
8 Jesse Lane .20 .50
9 Peter Sejna .75 2.00
10 Landon Bathe .20 .50
11 Travis Doan .20 .50
12 Mark Murphy .20 .50
13 Rob Novak .20 .50
14 Alex Kim .20 .50
15 Wade Chiodo .20 .50
16 Jerrid Reinholz .20 .50
17 Miroslav Durak .20 .50
18 Ryan Kirchhoff .20 .50
19 Mark Mullen .20 .50
20 Ryan Bennett .20 .50
21 Jeff Ronkoske .20 .50
22 Mike Mantua .20 .50
23 Paul Morrissey .20 .50
24 Winger MASCOT .02 .10

2007-08 Des Moines Buccaneers

COMPLETE SET (26) 5.00 12.00
1 Nielsson Arcibal .30 .75
2 Josh Balch .30 .75
3 Fredrik Bergman .30 .75
4 Brett Bruneteau .30 .75
5 Greg Burgdoerfer .30 .75
6 Rocco Carzo .30 .75
7 Alexander Denezhkin .30 .75
8 Nate Dewhurst .30 .75
9 Michael Dorr .30 .75
10 Derek Elliott .30 .75
11 Austin Handley .30 .75
12 Keith Kinkaid .30 .75
13 Chris Knowlton .30 .75
14 Cullen Lundholm .30 .75
15 J.P. Maley .30 .75
16 Taylor Matson .30 .75
17 Ryan McKiernan .30 .75
18 Andrew Panzarella .30 .75
19 Bobby Reiners .30 .75
20 Rody Selk .30 .75
21 Brad Walch .30 .75
22 Ryan Walters .30 .75
23 Matt White .30 .75
25 Todd Knott AC .30 .75
26 Rick Comley HC .30 .75
27 Bucky MASCOT .15 .40

1993-94 Detroit Jr. Red Wings

Sponsored by Compuware and printed by Slapshot Images Ltd., this standard size 26-card set features the 1993-94 Detroit Jr. Red Wings. On a geometrical red and white background, the fronts feature color action player photos with thin black borders.

COMPLETE SET (26) 4.00 10.00
1 Todd Harvey .40 1.00
2 Jason Saal .20 .50
3 Aaron Ellis .15 .40
4 Chris Mailloux .15 .40
5 Robin Lacour .15 .40
6 Mike Rucinski .15 .40
7 Eric Cairns .20 .50
8 Matt Ball .15 .40
9 Dale Junkin .15 .40
10 Bill McCauley .15 .40
11 Jeremy Meehan .15 .40
12 Mike Harding .15 .40
13 Brad Cook .15 .40
14 Jeff Mitchell .15 .40
15 Jamie Allison .15 .40
16 Dan Pawlaczyk .15 .40
17 Kevin Brown .15 .40
18 Duane Harmer .15 .40
19 Gerry Skrypec .15 .40
20 Shayne McCosh .15 .40
21 Sean Haggerty .15 .40
22 Nic Beaudoin .15 .40
23 Paul Maurice CO .20 .50
24 Pete DeBoer ACO .20 .50
25 Bob Wren .15 .40
NNO Slapshot Ad Card .01

1994-95 Detroit Jr. Red Wings

Sponsored by Compuware and printed by Slapshot Images Ltd., this 25-card set features the 1994-95 Detroit Jr. Red Wings. On a red and gray background, the fronts feature color action player photos with thin black borders.

COMPLETE SET (25) 4.00 10.00
1 Team Photo CL .15 .40
2 Darryl Foster .15 .40
3 Quade Lightbody .15 .40
4 Ryan MacDonald .15 .40
5 Mike Rucinski .15 .40
6 Murray Sheehan .15 .40
7 Matt Ball .15 .40
8 Gerry Lanigan .15 .40
9 Mike Morrone .15 .40
10 Tom Buckley .15 .40
11 Eric Manlow .30 .75
12 Bill McCauley .15 .40
13 Andrew Taylor .15 .40
14 Scott Blair .15 .40
15 Jeff Mitchell .15 .40
16 Jason Saal .25 .60
17 Jamie Allison .20 .50
18 Bryan Berard .40 1.00
19 Dan Pawlaczyk .15 .40
20 Milan Kostolny .15 .40
21 Duane Harmer .15 .40
22 Shayne McCosh .15 .40
23 Sean Haggerty .15 .40
24 Nic Beaudoin .15 .40
25 Paul Maurice CO/GM .15 .40

1994-95 Detroit Vipers Pogs

This set was handed out at a Vipers game. It was released in the form of a 6-inch circular disk which contains 5 player Pogs and one team logo Pog.

COMPLETE SET (6) .75 2.00
1 John Craighead .20 .50
2 Peter Ciavaglia .20 .50
3 Brad Tiley .20 .50
4 Al Conroy .20 .50
5 Daniel Shank .20 .50
6 Logo Pog .20 .50

1996-97 Detroit Vipers

This odd-sized set commemorates the Detroit Vipers of the IHL. The set was produced by the club as a game-night premium. The cards were issued one per night at twenty different home games, beginning January 3, 1997 and ending April 13. The giveaway dates for each card can be found on the backs of the cards, along with a mugshot, player nickname and biographical data. The fronts feature an action photo, a reproduction of the player's autograph, and the logo of sponsor Ameritech. The unnumbered cards are listed below alphabetically. The set is noteworthy for the inclusion of 1997 draft pick Sergei Samsonov.

COMPLETE SET (20) 30.00 75.00
1 Darren Banks .75 2.00
2 Peter Ciavaglia .75 2.00
3 Yvon Corriveau .75 2.00
4 Phil Crowe .60 1.50
5 Mike Donnelly .75 2.00
6 Stan Drulia 1.25 3.00
7 Len Esau .75 2.00
8 Ian Herbers .60 1.50
9 Bobby Jay .60 1.50
10 Dan Kesa .60 1.50
11 Rich Parent 1.25 3.00
12 Jeff Parrott .60 1.50
13 Wayne Presley .60 1.50
14 Jeff Reese 1.25 3.00
15 Sergei Samsonov 15.00 40.00
16 Brad Shaw 1.25 3.00
17 Todd Simon .75 2.00
18 Patrice Tardif .75 2.00
19 Phil Von Steffenelli .60 1.50
20 Steve Walker .60 1.50

1997-98 Detroit Vipers

The cards in this oversized set was handed out by the team over the course of twenty different games and is nearly impossible in complete set form.

COMPLETE SET (20) 16.00 30.00
1 Peter Ciavaglia .75 2.00
2 Phil Crowe .40 1.00
3 Dan Kesa .40 1.00
4 Stan Drulia .75 2.00
5 Bob Jay .40 1.00
6 Ian Herbers .40 1.00
7 Brad Shaw .75 2.00
8 Steve Walker .75 2.00
9 Trent McCleary .40 1.00
10 Scott Thomas .75 2.00
11 Johan Hedberg 2.00 5.00
12 Jimmy Carson .75 2.00
13 Clayton Beddoes .40 1.00
14 Tim Murray .40 1.00
15 John Gruden .40 1.00
16 Jeff Reese .75 2.00
17 Keith Aldridge .40 1.00
18 Brent Fedyk .40 1.00
19 Darren Banks .75 2.00
20 Vipe-Bear Mascot .40 1.00

1998-99 Detroit Vipers

This set was produced by EBK Sports and was sold through its Web site, as well as at Vipers home games. Cards were numbered "XX of 27" on the card backs.

COMPLETE SET (26) 6.00 15.00
1 Keith Aldridge .20 .50
2 Brad Shaw .40 1.00
3 Tim Murray .15 .40
4 Brian Felsner .15 .40
5 Peter Ciavaglia .30 .75
6 Andy Bezeau .15 .40
7 Mike Gaffney .15 .40
8 Phil Crowe .15 .40
9 John Emmons .15 .40
10 Kory Karlander .15 .40
11 Mike Prokopec .15 .40
12 Stan Drulia .40 1.00
13 Bob Jay .20 .50
14 Darren Banks .20 .50
15 Jeff Whittle .15 .40
16 Steve Walker .15 .40
17 Ian Herbers .15 .40
18 Jani Hurme 1.50 4.00
19 John Gruden .15 .40
20 Kevin Weekes .75 2.00
21 Vipe-Bear Mascot .02 .10
22 Steve Ludzik HCO .02 .10
23 John Blum ACO .02 .10
24 Dave Boyer TR .02 .10
25 Mike Astalos EOM .02 .10
26 Checklist .02 .10
27 IHL/PHPA

1998-99 Detroit Vipers Freschetta

This set was issued as a giveaway late in the season in four different four-card strips. Each strip featured a different color background, and the four colors used are green (cards 1-4), yellow (cards 5-8), red (cards 9-12), and purple (cards 13-16). The cards were unnumbered.

COMPLETE SET (16) 12.00 30.00
1 Kevin Weekes 1.50 4.00
2 Peter Ciavaglia .75 2.00
3 Bob Jay .60 1.50
4 Keith Aldridge .60 1.50
5 Andy Bezeau .60 1.50
6 Stan Drulia 1.25 3.00
7 Ian Herbers .60 1.50
8 John Emmons .60 1.50
9 Mike Prokopec .60 1.50
10 Tim Murray .60 1.50
11 Brad Shaw 1.25 3.00
12 Steve Walker .60 1.50
13 John Gruden .60 1.50
14 Darren Banks .75 2.00
15 Brian Felsner .60 1.50
16 Geoff Sarjeant .75 2.00

1999-00 Detroit Vipers

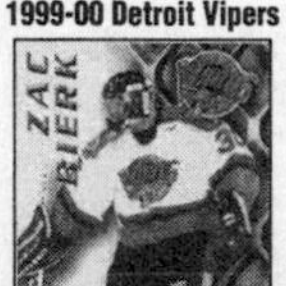

Given out by the team over the span of 15 home games, this 15-card set features the 1999-2000 Detroit Vipers. The set is listed in the order that the players were given away. The dates are as follows: Jan. 15, Jan. 21, Jan. 22, Jan. 25, Jan. 27, Feb. 1, Feb. 6, Feb. 8, Feb. 15, Feb. 22, Feb. 24, Feb. 27, Mar. 12, Mar. 16, and Mar. 28.

COMPLETE SET (15) 14.00 35.00
1 Andy Bezeau 1.25 3.00
2 Nils Ekman 1.25 3.00
3 Mario Larocque 1.25 3.00
4 Steve Walker .75 2.00
5 Matt Elich 1.25 3.00
6 Jeff Shevalier .75 2.00
7 Peter Ciavaglia 1.25 3.00
8 Alek Stojanov .75 2.00
9 Dave Baseggio .75 2.00
10 Zac Bierk 1.50 4.00
11 Kyle Kos .75 2.00
12 Tim Thomas 1.50 4.00
13 Dale Rominski .75 2.00
14 Kyle Freadrich .75 2.00
15 Samuel St. Pierre .75 2.00

1999-00 Detroit Vipers Kid's Club

This 9-card set was given out free to members of the Detroit Vipers Kids Club. The set was issued as one three-by-three, 9-card panel, with perforations to allow the cards to be torn off. The set was sponsored by Keebler and Meijer. The cards are unnumbered and are standard-size. The fronts are full color with green borders. The backs are white with dark purple printing, containing player statistics. The final card in the set was intended to be a "membership card" for the Detroit Vipers Kids Club, containing a blank "name" spot on the card's front.

COMPLETE SET (9) 10.00 25.00
1 Team Logo Card .40 1.00
2 Peter Ciavaglia 2.00 5.00
3 Andy Bezeau 2.00 5.00
4 Stan Drulia 2.00 5.00
5 Steve Walker 2.00 5.00
6 Ian Herbers 2.00 5.00
7 Paulin Bordeleau HCO 2.00 5.00
8 Vipe-Bear Mascot .40 1.00
9 Kid's Club Membership Card .40 1.00

1996-97 Detroit Whalers

This 25-card set was produced by the team and available for sale at games and by mail order for $5. The standard-size cards feature a color action photo with a sea foam green border. The backs contain a headshot, bio and stats.

COMPLETE SET (25) 4.00 10.00
1 Jessie Boulerice .30 .75
2 Mark Cadotte .20 .50
3 Chad Cavanagh .15 .40
4 Harold Druken .40 1.00
5 Steve Dumonski .20 .50
6 Robert Esche .75 2.00
7 Sergei Fedotov .20 .50
8 Randy Fitzgerald .20 .50
9 Eric Gooldy .15 .40
10 Kevin Holdridge .15 .40
11 John Paul Luciuk .15 .40
12 Mike Morrone .15 .40
13 Pat Parthenais .20 .50
14 Julian Smith .15 .40
15 Troy Smith .15 .40
16 Andrew Taylor .15 .40
17 Anthony Terzo .15 .40
18 Jan Vodrazka .15 .40
19 Steve Wasylko .20 .50
20 Nathan West .15 .40
21 Peter DeBoer CO .08 .25
22 Luc Rioux .15 .40
23 Slapshot MASCOT .01
24 Checklist .01
25 Discount Card .01

1993-94 Drummondville Voltigeurs

This set features the Voltigeurs of the QMJHL. The set was printed by Slapshot Images and was sold at home games.

COMPLETE SET (28) 3.00 8.00
1 Title Card .02 .10
Checklist
2 Stephane Routhier .15 .40
3 Yannick Gagnon .15 .40
4 Sebastien Bely .15 .40
5 Martin Latulippe .15 .40
6 Nicolas Savage .15 .40
7 Sylvain Ducharme .15 .40
8 Yan St. Pierre .15 .40
9 Emmanuel Labranche .15 .40
10 Ian Laperriere .30 .75
11 Louis Bernard .15 .40
12 Stephane St. Amour .15 .40
13 Vincent Tremblay .15 .40
14 Denis Gauthier Jr. .30 .75
15 Eric Plante .15 .40
16 Christian Marcoux .15 .40
17 Patrice Charbonneau .15 .40
18 Raymond Delarosbil .15 .40
19 Patrick Livernoche .15 .40
20 Luc Decelles .15 .40
21 Francois Sasseville .15 .40
22 Steve Tardif .15 .40
23 Mathieu Sunderland .15 .40
24 Alexandre Duchesne .15 .40
25 Jean Hamel CO GM .02 .10
26 Mario Carrier ACO .02 .10
27 Me Andre Lepage TR .02 .10
28 Slapshot Ad Card .02 .10

2001-02 Drummondville Voltigeurs

This set features the Voltigeurs of the QMJHL. The set was produced by CTM Ste-Foy, and was sold at that shop as well as at home games. The production run is believed to be fewer than 1,000 sets.

COMPLETE SET (23) 4.00 10.00
1 Jean-Francois Racine .31 .78
2 Patrick Turbide .20 .50
3 Evgueni Nourislamov .20 .50
4 Jean-Philippe Glaude .20 .50
5 Thierry Kaszap .20 .50
6 Eric Jean .20 .50
7 Louis-Philippe Lessard .20 .50
8 Andre Vincent .20 .50
9 Steve Proulx .20 .50
10 Oliver Proulx .20 .50
11 Martin Autotte .20 .50
12 Yanick Riendeau .20 .50
13 Michael Stacey .20 .50
14 Frederic Faucher .20 .50
15 Benoit Paris .20 .50
16 Vincent Tougas .20 .50
17 Kirill Alexeev .20 .50
18 Jean-Francois Cyr .20 .50
19 Carl Zacharie .20 .50
20 Kevin Rainville .20 .50
21 Sylvain Michaud .20 .50
22 Maxime Bouchard .20 .50
NNO Title Card/CL .04 .11

2002-03 Drummondville Voltigeurs

COMPLETE SET (25) 12.00
1 Francis Breault CO .10
2 Evgueni Nourislamov .50
3 Todd Paul .50
4 Andre Joaniss .50
5 Jules Melanson .50
6 Andre Vincent .50
7 Dominic Fisel .50
8 Kevin Lacombe .50
9 Alexandre Demers .50
10 Laurent Lanoie .50
11 Yannick Riendeau .50
12 Patrick Levesque .50
13 Sebastien Laprise .50
14 Benoit Duhamel .50
15 Jonathan Dick .50
16 Kevin Mailhiot .50
17 Jason D'Ascanio .50
18 Thomas Bellemare .50
19 Samuel Villeneuve .50
20 Kevin Duchaine .50
21 Eric Dagenais .50
22 Sylvain Michaud 1.00
23 Pierre Olivier Girouard .75
24 Pier Olivier Begin .75
25 Checklist/Logo .01

2003-04 Drummondville Voltigeurs

COMPLETE SET (22) 6.00 15.00
1 Thomas Bellemare .20 .50
2 David Bouchard .20 .50
3 Maxim Chamberland .20 .50
4 Michel Charrette .20 .50

5 Alexandre Demers .20 .50
6 Keven Gagne .20 .50
7 Samuel Gibbons .20 .50
8 Gabriel Houde-Brisson .20 .50
9 Andre Joanisse .20 .50
10 Kevin Lacombe .20 .50
11 Guillaume Latendresse 2.00 5.00
12 Kevin Mailhiot .20 .50
13 Louis-Philippe Martin .20 .50
14 Jamie McCabe .20 .50
15 Jules Melanson .20 .50
16 Sylvain Michaud .30 .75
17 Pierre Morvan .20 .50
18 Ervins Mustukovs .30 .75
19 Jean-Francois Parent .20 .50
20 Yannick Riendeau .20 .50
21 Frederic St. Denis .20 .50
22 Andre Vincent .20 .50

2004-05 Drummondville Voltigeurs

A total of 330 sets were produced. The NNO cards do not appear in every sealed team bag.

COMPLETE SET (30) 6.00 20.00
1 Guillaume Latendresse .75 2.00
2 Philippe Roberge .20 .50
3 Pier-Olivier Pelletier .60 1.50
4 Derick Brassard 1.25 3.00
5 Chaz Johnson .20 .50
6 Henrick Lavoie .20 .50
7 Mathieu Ste-Marie .20 .50
8 Alexandre Demers .20 .50
9 Keven Gagne .20 .50
10 Andre Vincent .20 .50
11 Frederic St-Denis .20 .50
12 Andre Joanisse .20 .50
13 Louis-Philippe Martin .20 .50
14 Dave Bouchard .20 .50
15 Jules Melanson .20 .50
16 Steve Cacciotti .20 .50
19 Romy Elayoubi .20 .50
20 Cedric Archambault .20 .50
21 Maxime Frechette .20 .50
22 Julien Beaulieu .20 .50
23 Maxime Aubut .20 .50
24 Jean-Philippe Cote .20 .50
25 Maxim Chamberland .20 .50
26 Kevin Mailhiot .20 .50
27 Gaby Roch .20 .50
28 Simon Archambault .20 .50
29 Sylvain Michaud .40 1.00
30 Jesse Arko .20 .50
NNO Derick Brassard 2.00 5.00
NNO Pier-Olivier Pelletier 2.00 5.00

2005-06 Drummondville Voltigeurs

COMPLETE SET (33) 6.00 15.00
1 Guillaume Latendresse .60 1.50
2 Derick Brassard .60 1.50
3 Pier-Olivier Pelletier .30 .75
4 Pierre-Alexandre Marion .15 .40
5 Jules Melanson .15 .40
6 Kevin Mailhiot .15 .40
7 Maxim Mallette .15 .40
8 Joey Pell .15 .40
9 Andre Joanisse .15 .40
10 Maxime Frechette .15 .40
11 Tomas Zohorna .15 .40
12 Dave Bouchard .15 .40
13 Nicolas Sigouin .15 .40
14 Steven Cacciotti .15 .40
15 Tomas Svoboda .15 .40
16 Gaby Roch .15 .40
17 Alexandre Demers .15 .40
18 Frederic St-Denis .15 .40
19 Vincent Beaulieu .15 .40
20 Keven Gagne .15 .40
21 Maxime Aubut .15 .40
22 Paul Yovanic .15 .40
23 Olivier Fortier .15 .40
24 Tirobut .02 .10
25 Bryan Wilson .15 .40
26 Olivier Legault .15 .40
27 Yanick Charron .15 .40
28 Nicolas D'Aoust .15 .40
29 Simon Bouchard .15 .40
30 Olivier Donovan .15 .40
31 Loic Lacasse .30 .75
32 Francis Charette .15 .40
33 Jean-Michel Bolduc .15 .40

2006-07 Drummondville Voltigeurs

COMPLETE SET (26) 8.00 15.00
1 Derick Brassard .75 2.00
2 Bryan Wilson .20 .50
3 Mackenzie Micks .20 .50
4 Drew Paris .20 .50
5 Simon Bouchard .20 .50
6 Benoit Levesque .20 .50
7 Jonathan Duchesneau .20 .50
8 Tomas Zohorna .20 .50
9 Eric Campeau-Charron .20 .50
10 Steven Cacciotti .20 .50
11 Olivier Jannard .20 .50
12 Corey Garland .20 .50
13 Tomas Svoboda .20 .50
14 Gaby Roch .20 .50
15 Alexandre Demers .20 .50
16 Frederic St. Denis .20 .50
17 Stephen Valente .20 .50
18 Sebastien Bernier .20 .50
19 Etienne Bellavance-Martin .20 .50
20 Marc-Olivier Vachon .20 .50
21 Scott Howes .20 .50
22 Maxime Frechette .20 .50
23 Francis Charette .20 .50
24 Pier-Olivier Pelletier .30 .75
25 Maxime Gougeon .30 .75
26 Pierre-Alexandre Marion .20 .50

1994-95 Dubuque Fighting Saints

This 29-card set measures the standard size. The fronts feature color action player photos with the player's name, jersey number, and team logo at the bottom. The team name runs down the left side of the front. The backs carry a black-and-white player portrait, the player's name, jersey number, biographical information, statistics, career summary, and team logo. The cards are unnumbered and checklisted below in alphabetical order.

COMPLETE SET (29) 4.00 10.00
1 Title Card .02 .10
Season schedule
2 Chris Addesa .20 .50
3 Matt Addesa .20 .50
4 Mark Allegrezza .15 .40
5 Todd Barclay .15 .40
6 Jay Boxer ACO .02 .10
7 Geoff Collard .15 .40
8 John Dwyer .15 .40
9 Jayme Filipowicz .20 .50
10 Zach Ham .15 .40
11 Mike Herrera .15 .40
12 Roger Holeczy .15 .40
13 Steve Holeczy .15 .40
14 John Hultberg .30 .75
15 Ryan Karasek .15 .40
16 Mike Kramer TR .02 .10
17 Chris Masters .15 .40
18 A.J. Melanson .15 .40
19 Mike Minichiello .15 .40
20 Berk Nelson .15 .40
21 Nik Patronas .15 .40
22 Andy Powers .15 .40
23 Matt Romaniski .15 .40
24 Tom Ryles .15 .40
25 John Sadowski .15 .40
26 Chris Showalter .15 .40
27 Dan Stepanek .15 .40
28 Trevor Tallackson .15 .40
29 Troy Ward GM/CO .02 .10

1997-98 Dubuque Fighting Saints

This set features the Fighting Saints of the USHL. The set was produced by the team and sold at home games. Card No. 30 was recently confirmed to be Josh Blackburn. Thanks to collector Joseph Bonnett for this information.

COMPLETE SET (30) 4.00 10.00
1 Dubuque Fighting Saints .15 .40
2 Justin Aufmann .15 .40
3 Travis Rotariu .15 .40
4 Marty Rychley .15 .40
5 Mario LeBlanc .15 .40
6 David Patch .15 .40
7 Evan Stensrud .15 .40
8 Josh Kern .15 .40
9 Christian Fletcher .15 .40
10 Scott Deopere .15 .40
11 Jeff Tarala .15 .40
12 Phil Lewandowski .15 .40
13 Joe Dudek .15 .40
14 Trent Landry .15 .40
15 Tom Rouleau .15 .40
16 Kris Harris .15 .40
17 Anders Johnson .15 .40
18 Matt Herhal .15 .40
19 Josh Myers .15 .40
20 David Brien .15 .40
21 Carl Hanson .15 .40
22 Scott Brown .15 .40
23 Adam Pobiak .15 .40
24 Todd Sanden CO .02 .10
25 Tom Hasenzahl CO .02 .10
26 Corey Courtney TR .02 .10
27 Sebastian St. Bernard MAS .02 .10
28 USHL Team Directory .02 .10
29 Schedule .02 .10
30 Josh Blackburn .30 .75

1998-99 ECHL All-Star Northern Conference

Released by EBK Sports, this 21-card set was available for sale at the 1999 ECHL All-Star Game. It was later available for purchase through the PHPA web site.

COMPLETE SET (21) 15.00 40.00
1 Tom O'Connor .75 2.00
2 Duane Harmer 1.25 3.00
3 Jamie Ling 1.25 3.00
4 Darren Maloney .75 2.00
5 Bret Meyers .75 2.00
6 Jim Bermingham 1.25 3.00
7 Jamie Thompson .75 2.00
8 Andrew Williamson .75 2.00
9 Marc Tropper .75 2.00
10 Bobby Brown .75 2.00
11 Jakub Ficenec 1.25 3.00
12 Arturs Kupaks 1.25 3.00
13 Dru Burgess .75 2.00
14 Dan Ceman .75 2.00
15 Ryan Kraft 1.25 3.00
16 Joe Blaznek .75 2.00
17 Casey Kesselring .75 2.00
18 Matt Mullen 1.25 3.00
19 Maxime Gingras 1.50 4.00
20 Karl Infanger .75 2.00
21 Checklist .02 .10

1998-99 ECHL All-Star Southern Conference

Released by EBK Sports, this 21-card set was available for purchase at the All-Star Game, then later through the PHPA web site.

COMPLETE SET (21) 15.00 40.00
1 Jaroslav Obsut 1.25 3.00
2 Terry Lindgren .75 2.00
3 Kelly Hurd .75 2.00
4 Dana Mulvihill .75 2.00
5 Jonas Soling .75 2.00
6 Jamey Hicks .75 2.00
7 Patrick Rochon .75 2.00
8 John Varga 1.25 3.00
9 Dave Seitz .75 2.00
10 Jason Elders .75 2.00
11 Cail MacLean .75 2.00
12 Allan Sirois .75 2.00
13 Shane Calder .75 2.00
14 Chris Valicevic 1.25 3.00
15 J.F. Aube .75 2.00
16 Luke Curtin .75 2.00
17 Jan Kobezda .75 2.00
18 Bujar Amidovski 1.50 4.00
19 Chris Hynnes .75 2.00
20 Chris Wickenheiser 1.50 4.00
21 Checklist .02 .10

1999-00 ECHL All-Star Northern Conference

Released by EBK Sports, this 22-card set was available for purchase through the PHPA web site and at the rink during the 2000 ECHL All-Star Game.

COMPLETE SET (22) 8.00 20.00
1 Alexei Krovopuskov .30 .75
2 Andrew Williamson .30 .75
3 Blaine Fitzpatrick .30 .75
4 Bujar Amidovski .75 2.00
5 Calvin Elfring .30 .75
6 Chad Ackerman .30 .75
7 Chris Gignac .30 .75
8 Curtis Wilgosh .30 .75
9 Derek Walser .30 .75
10 Duane Harmer .30 .75
11 Jamie Ling .30 .75
12 Jan Lasak 1.00 2.50
13 Jason Lawmaster .30 .75
14 Jeff Mitchell .30 .75
15 Joel Irving .30 .75
16 Marc Tropper .30 .75
17 Mark Murphy .30 .75
18 Mike Perna .30 .75
19 Peter Vandermeer .75 2.00
20 Ryan Kraft .75 2.00
21 Sean Matile .30 .75
22 EBK Sports .01

1999-00 ECHL All-Star Southern Conference

Released by EBK Sports, this 22-card set was available for purchase through the PHPA web site and at the rink during the 2000 ECHL All-Star Game.

COMPLETE SET (22) 8.00 20.00
1 Bobby Stewart .30 .75
2 Brad Dexter .30 .75
3 Buddy Smith .30 .75
4 Chris Valicevic .75 2.00
5 Dany Bousquet .40 1.00
6 David Brumby .30 .75
7 Eric Naud .30 .75
8 Greg Schmidt .30 .75
9 Jeff Lazaro .30 .75
10 Jeff Maund .75 2.00
11 John McNabb .30 .75
12 John Spoltore .75 2.00
13 Kelly Perrault .30 .75
14 Luke Curtin .30 .75
15 Marc Magliarditi .75 2.00
16 Neil Fewster .30 .75
17 Sean Venedam .60 1.50
18 Steve O'Brien .30 .75
19 Wes Mason .30 .75
20 Ryan Gaucher .30 .75
21 Olivier Morin .30 .75
22 EBK Sports .01

2002-03 ECHL All-Star Northern

COMPLETE SET (20) 20.00
19 Kevin Colley 1.00
20 Pierre-Luc Courchesne 1.00
21 Ryan Gaucher 1.00
22 Jim Henkel 1.00
23 Jamie Herrington 1.00
24 Andrew Ianiero 1.00
25 Jason Jaffray 1.00
26 Zenon Konopka 1.00
27 Dan Lombard 1.00
28 Brian McCullough 1.00
29 Chris McNamara 1.00
30 Nick Parillo 1.00
31 Geno Parrish 1.00
32 Tyler Rennette 1.00
33 Brad Rooney 1.00
34 Mike Smith 1.00
35 Scott Stirling 1.00
36 Takahito Suzuki 1.00
37 Simon Tremblay 1.00
39 Jonathan Zion 1.00
39 Dustin Wood 1.00

2002-03 ECHL All-Star Southern

COMPLETE SET (21) 20.00
40 Jim Baxter 1.00
41 Kent Davyduke 1.00
42 Mike Glumac 1.00
43 Joe Guenther 1.00
44 Adam Hauser 2.00
45 Corey Hessler 1.00
46 J.J. Hunter 1.00
47 Marty Johnston 1.00
48 Judd Medak 1.00
49 Laurent Meunier 1.00
50 Justin Morrison 1.00
51 Ryan O'Keefe 1.00
52 Rod Sarich 1.00
53 Aaron Schneekloth 1.00
54 Bud Smith 1.00
55 Rejean Stringer 1.00
56 Matt Underhill 1.50
57 Steffon Walby 1.00
58 Brad Williamson 1.00
59 Patrick Yetman 1.00
60 Rob Zepp 2.00

2002-03 ECHL Update

COMPLETE SET (27) 20.00
U1 Rick Adduono HCO .25
U2 Derrick Byfuglien 1.00
U3 Sebastien Centomo 3.00
U4 Jason Christie HCO .25
U5 Pierre-Luc Courchesne 1.00
U6 Kent Davyduke 1.00
U7 Gord Dineen HCO .25
U8 Gerry Fleming HCO .50
U9 Joe Guenther 1.00
U10 Adam Hauser 1.50
U11 Jamie Hodson 1.50
U12 Zenon Konopka 1.50
U13 David Lohrei HCO .25
U14 Don MacAdam HCO .25
U15 Chris McNamara 1.00
U16 John Marks HCO .25
U17 Ryan O'Keefe 1.00
U18 Mike Oliveira 1.00
U19 Davis Payne HCO .50
U20 Bryan Richardson 1.00
U21 Rod Sarich 1.00
U22 Bud Smith 1.00
U23 Niklas Sundberg 1.00
U24 Mark Turner 1.00
U25 Scott White HCO .25
U26 Dustin Wood 1.00
U27 Patrick Yetman 1.00

2003-04 ECHL All-Stars

This was actually issued as two separate team-bagged sets, one for the East and one for the West, but it is combined here. The numbering reflects that this as part of the full season's run of ECHL products released by RBI Sports.

COMPLETE SET (42) 50.00 100.00
241 Morten Ask 3.00
242 Alexandre Burrows 3.00
243 Cory Campbell 3.00
244 Brian Fahey 3.00
245 Chris Houle 2.00
246 Jason Jaffray 2.00
247 Dusty Jamieson 3.00
248 Nate Kiser 2.00
249 Shawn Limpright 2.00
250 Chris Lynch 2.00
251 Jason Maleyko 3.00
252 David Masse 2.00
253 Brian McCullough 2.00
254 Mark McRae 2.00
255 Jason Nolermann 2.00
256 Sam Paolini 2.00
257 Tom Reimann 2.00
258 Randy Rowe 2.00
259 Kevin Spiewak 2.00
260 Scott Stirling 2.00
261 Jonathan Zion 2.00
262 Greg Barber 2.00
263 Greg Chambers 2.00
264 Frederic Cloutier 3.00
265 David Cornacchia 2.00
266 David Cousineau 2.00
267 Dan Ellis 5.00
268 Nick Ganga 2.00
269 Michael Garnett 4.00
270 Brent Gauvreau 2.00
271 Andrew Ianiero 2.00
272 Greg Jacina 3.00
273 Justin Kelly 2.00
274 Charles Linglet 2.00
275 Troy Milam 2.00
276 Corey Neilson 2.00
277 Jean-Francois Plourde 2.00
278 John Snowden 2.00
279 Ben Storey 2.00
280 Joe Talbot 2.00
281 Kevin Truelson 2.00
282 Steffon Walby 3.00

2003-04 ECHL Update RBI Sports

It's believed these cards were issued late in the season and limited to just 250 copies each, in three sets (A, B and C). Little else is known about their distribution.

COMPLETE SET (48) 60.00
49 Joe Talbot 1.00
56 Todd Alexander 1.00
57 Shane Bendera 2.00
58 Jon Mirasty 1.00
59 Joe Watkins 2.00
60 Lucas Lawson 1.00
61 Brett Clouthier 2.00
62 Phil Cole 1.00
63 Tyler Masters 1.00
64 Doug Teskey 1.00
113 Kristian Antila 2.00
114 Matus Kostur 2.00
115 Christian Larrivee 1.00
116 Olivier Michaud 4.00
117 Tomas Micka 1.00
118 Matt Shasby 1.00
119 Marc-Andre Thinel 2.00
120 Sean Connolly 1.00
121 Riley Cote 1.00
122 Jason Crain 1.00
123 Miguel Delisle 1.00
124 Janne Jokila 1.00
125 Andrew Penner 2.00
126 Olivier Proulx 1.00
127 Nicolas Corbeil 1.00
128 Daniel Boisclair 2.00
129 Mark Concannon 1.00
130 Brian Passmore 1.00
131 Michel Robinson 1.00
132 Russell Spence 1.00
133 Anthony Aquino 2.00
134 Wes Fox 1.00
135 Phil Lewandowski 1.00
136 Trevor Prior 2.00
137 Dan Ellis 4.00
138 Armands Berzins 1.00
139 Maxime Fortunus 1.00
140 Derek Gustafson 2.00
141 Jamie Johnson 1.00
142 Ed McGrane 1.00
143 Jean-Francois Soucy 2.00
144 Jeremy Van Hoof 1.00
283 Dustin Johner 1.00
284 Paul Ballantyne 1.00
285 Scott Kabotoff 1.00
286 Joe Exter 4.00
287 Tyler MacKay 1.00
288 Patrick Couture 2.00

1997-98 El Paso Buzzards

Little is known about this set beyond the confirmed checklist. Additional information can be forwarded to hockeymag@beckett.com.

COMPLETE SET (32) 4.00 10.00
1 Jamie Thompson .20 .50
2 Brent Scott .20 .50
3 Mark Sakala .20 .50
4 Jason Rose .20 .50
5 Corri Moffat .20 .50
6 Chris MacKenzie .20 .50
7 Trent Eigner .20 .50
8 Rusty McKie .30 .75
9 Jason Welch .20 .50
10 Martin Balleux .20 .50
11 Corey Heon .20 .50
12 Derek Riley .30 .75
13 Chris Gordon .20 .50
14 Bill Trew .20 .50
15 Jason Carey .20 .50
16 Sandy Lamarre .20 .50
17 Dan Carter .20 .50
18 Robert Haddock .20 .50
19 Mark Hilton .20 .50
20 Todd Brost CO .02 .10
21 Swoop Mascot .02 .10
22 Teresa Fernandez RG .02 .10
23 Greg Sieg TR .02 .10
24 KLAQ Morning Show .02 .10
25 KISS Morning Show .02 .10
26 KROD Morning Show .02 .10
27 Paul Strelzin ANNC .02 .10
28 DJ Card .02 .10
29 TV-7 Anchors .02 .10
30 TV-7 Sports Team .02 .10
31 DJ Card .02 .10
32 TV-7 Reporters .02 .10

1998-99 El Paso Buzzards

This set features the Buzzards of the WPHL. It was produced by the team and was sold at home games. The cards are not numbered, but are ordered by the listing on the checklist card.

COMPLETE SET (28) 20.00 40.00
1 Trent Eigner 1.25 3.00
2 Chris Gordon .75 2.00
3 Robert Haddock .75 2.00
4 Corey Heon .75 2.00
5 Alex Herbison .75 2.00
6 Bill Trew .75 2.00
7 Jeremy Vanin .75 2.00
8 Jason Welch .75 2.00
9 Deuce Wynes .75 2.00
10 Todd Brost CO .40 1.00
11 Steve Pottie .75 2.00
12 Mike Rees .75 2.00
13 Iannique Renaud .75 2.00
14 Jason Rushton .75 2.00
15 Blake Sheane .75 2.00
16 Mark Costea .75 2.00
17 Sandy Lamarre .75 2.00
18 Marc Labelle .75 2.00
19 Corri Moffat .75 2.00
20 Eric Peterson .75 2.00
21 McArthur/Palka .75 2.00
22 Warner/Casas .75 2.00
23 The Mike & Grace Show .02 .10
24 Cruz/Adams/Keith/Steele .02 .10
25 Garcia/Medina/Kaplowitz .02 .10
26 Dodson/Romano .02 .10
27 Paul Strelzin ANN .02 .10
28 Checklist .02 .10

2001-02 El Paso Buzzards

COMPLETE SET (20) 20.00
1 Trent Eigner 1.00
2 Van Burgess 1.00
3 Clint Collins 1.00
4 Rhett Dudley 1.00
5 Kelly Riou 1.00
6 Chris Zaleski 1.00
7 Jeremy Vanin 1.00
8 Derrell Upton 1.00
9 Mike Rees 1.00
10 Justin Van Parys 1.00
11 Trevor Hammer 1.00
12 Jason Tessier 1.00
13 Dory Tisdale 1.00
14 Rob Laurie 1.50
15 Troy Linna 1.00
16 Jeff Levy 1.00
17 Aaron Phillips 1.00
18 Kory Baker 1.00
19 Corey Waring 1.00
20 John Hanson 1.00

2002-03 El Paso Buzzards

This checklist is NOT complete. If you have any information about this set or the cards in it, please email hockeymag@beckett.com.

1 Jeff Levy .30 .75
2 Rhett Dudley .30 .75
3 Chris Zaleski .30 .75
4 John Hanson .30 .75
5 Aaron Phillips .30 .75
6 Rob Laurie .30 .75
7 Kory Baker .30 .75

2003-04 Elmira Jackals

COMPLETE SET (25) 12.00
1 Peter Aubry .75
2 Cal Benazic .50
3 J.F. Boutin .50
4 Trevor Burgess .50
5 Tom Clayton .50
6 Carl Drakensjo .50
7 Nathan Gillies .50
8 Dean Jackson .50
9 Greg Koehler .50
Mike Thompson .50
10 Ed Lowe .50
11 Kris Mallette .75
12 Ryan McIntosh .75
13 Randy Murphy .50
14 Geoff O'Leary .50
15 Matt Osborne .50
16 Neil Posillico .50
17 Michael Prochazka .50
18 Trevor Segstro .50
19 James Sheehan .50
20 Don Smith .50
21 Jamie Thompson .50
23 Todd Brost HCO .20
24 Spud Hamilton EQM .10
25 Brandon Dionne TR .10
26 Team Photo .50

2003-04 Erie Otters

COMPLETE SET (24) 6.00 15.00
1 Derrick Bagshaw .20 .50
2 Michael Blunden .40 1.00
3 Brad Bonello .20 .50
4 Chris Campoli .30 .75
5 Sean Courtney .20 .50
6 Josh Disher .30 .75
7 Tomas Galasek .20 .50
8 Bryan Hamm .20 .50
9 Jacob Heller .20 .50
10 David Herring .20 .50
11 Rob Hisey .20 .50
12 Alex Karaulchuk .20 .50
13 Brian Lee .20 .50
14 Chad Loikets .20 .50
15 Matthew Lynn .20 .50
16 Mike Melinko .20 .50
17 Derek Merlini .20 .50
18 Sean O'Connor .20 .50
19 Ryan O'Marra .40 1.00
20 Josh Patterson .20 .50
21 Geoff Platt .40 1.00
22 Vince Scott .20 .50
23 Jhase Sniderman .30 .75
24 Jason Speight .20 .50

2004-05 Erie Otters

A total of 700 team sets were produced. The NNO cards are randomly inserted.

COMPLETE SET (25) 5.00 12.00
1 Michael Blunden .30 .75
2 Tomas Galasek .20 .50
3 Derek Merlini .20 .50
4 Brett MacLean .20 .50
5 Jhase Sniderman .30 .75
6 Geoff Platt .30 .75
7 Chris Greene .20 .50
8 Sean O'Connor .20 .50
9 Vince Scott .20 .50
10 Jake Heller .20 .50
11 Derrick Bagshaw .20 .50
12 Andrew Hotham .20 .50
13 Brian Lee .20 .50
14 Chad Loikets .20 .50
15 Peter Sergeant .20 .50
16 Josh Kidd .20 .50
17 Ryan O'Marra .40 1.00
18 Eric Regan .20 .50
19 Andrew Shennan .20 .50
20 Jason Speight .20 .50
21 Josh Disher .30 .75
22 David Herring .20 .50
23 Dave MacQueen CO .02 .10
24 Peter Sidorkiewicz ACO .20 .25
25 Shooter MASCOT .02 .10
NNO Ryan O'Marra LTD 2.00 5.00
NNO Geoff Platt LTD 1.50 4.00

2005-06 Erie Otters

COMPLETE SET (23) 5.00 12.00
1 Ryan O'Marra .40 1.00
2 Derrick Bagshaw .20 .50
3 Michael Blunden .40 1.00
4 Chris Greene .20 .50
5 Justin Hodgman .20 .50
6 Patrick Lee .20 .50
7 Jordan Nolan .20 .50
8 Sean O'Connor .20 .50
9 Vince Scott .20 .50
10 Christian Seest Olsen .20 .50
11 Nick Palmieri .20 .50
12 Anthony Peluso .20 .50
13 Josh Vatri .20 .50
14 Jake Heller .20 .50
15 Andrew Hotham .20 .50
16 Josh Kidd .20 .50
17 Chad Loikets .20 .50
18 Josh Disher .20 .50
19 Ryan Ludzik .20 .50
20 Adam Berti .20 .50
21 Bret Nasby .20 .50
22 Jonathan Hull .20 .50
23 Tyler McKinley .20 .50

2006-07 Erie Otters

COMPLETE SET (24) 8.00 15.00
1 Nick Palmieri .20 .50
2 Sean O'Connor .20 .50
3 Patrick Lee .20 .50
4 Derrick Bagshaw .20 .50
5 Mitchell Forbes .20 .50
6 Stanislav Polodna .20 .50
7 Luke Gazdic .20 .50
8 Justin Hodgman .20 .50
9 Josh Vatri .20 .50
10 Shayne Taylor .20 .50
11 Kelly Geoffrey .20 .50
12 Kyle Ramsay .20 .50
13 Zack Torquato .60 1.50
14 Ronny Rogers .20 .50
15 Josh Kidd .20 .50
16 Mitch Gaulton .20 .50
17 Andrew Hotham .20 .50
18 Anthony Peluso .20 .50
19 Brian Shaw .20 .50
20 Michael Liambas .20 .50
21 Ryan Henry .20 .50
22 Jonathan Laniel .40 1.00
23 Justin Garay .40 1.00
24 Ryan Ludzik .40 1.00

1994-95 Erie Panthers

Produced by CJ Sports, this 20-card standard-size set features the Erie Panthers of the East Coast Hockey League. The fronts display color action player photos with gray borders. The player's name, position, and sponsor's name are below. The team name and logo appear at the top. The backs are white, grey, and black with player biography and statistics.

COMPLETE SET (20) 3.00 8.00
1 Title Card .02 .10
2 Ron Hansis CO .02 .10
3 Barry Smith ACO .02 .10
4 Patrick Laughlin TR .02 .10
5 Larry Empey .20 .50
6 Vassili Demin .20 .50
7 Sergei Stas .20 .50
8 Brad Harrison .20 .50
9 Cam Brown .20 .50
10 Kevin McKinnon .20 .50
11 Andrei Kozlov .20 .50
12 Chris Tschupp .20 .50
13 Jason Smith .20 .50
14 Justin Peca .20 .50
15 Francis Ouellette .20 .50
16 Vern Guetens .30 .75
17 Scott Burfoot .30 .75
18 Vyacheslav Polikarkin .20 .50
19 Stephane Charbonneau .20 .50
20 Ian Decorby .20 .50

2003-04 Everett Silvertips

COMPLETE SET (28) 5.00 12.00
1 Checklist .01 .01
2 Bryan Nathe .20 .50
3 Marc Desloges .20 .50
4 Jovan Matic .20 .50
5 Mike Wall .30 .75
6 Michael Wuchterl .20 .50
7 Mark Kress .20 .50
8 Devin Wilson .20 .50
9 Martin Ruzicka .20 .50
10 Curtis Billsten .20 .50
11 Barry Horman .20 .50
12 Shaun Heshka .20 .50
13 Jeff Schmidt .20 .50
14 Cody Thoring .20 .50
15 Ryan Blatchford .20 .50
16 Torrie Wheat .20 .50
17 Mitch Love .20 .50
18 Devin Welsh .20 .50
19 Riley Armstrong .20 .50
20 Tyler Dietrich .20 .50
21 John Dahl .20 .50
22 Jeff Harvey .30 .75
23 Ivan Baranka .20 .50
24 Chad Bassen .20 .50
25 Doug Soetaert GM .02 .10
26 Kevin Constantine CO .02 .10
27 John Becanic ACO .02 .10
28 Jay Varady ACO .02 .10

2004-05 Everett Silvertips

COMPLETE SET (?) 10.00 20.00
1 Header Card .02 .10
2 Tyler Dietrich .20 .50
3 Alex Leavitt .20 .50
4 Mitch Love .20 .50
5 Doug Soetaert .02 .10
6 Mike Wuchterl .20 .50
7 Cody Thoring .20 .50
8 Karel Hromas .20 .50
9 Ryan Blatchford .20 .50
10 Zach Sim .20 .50
11 Mark Kress .20 .50
12 Brennan Zasitko .20 .50
13 Torrie Wheat .20 .50
14 Michael Wall .40 1.00
15 Graham Potuer .20 .50
16 Matt Sawa .20 .50
17 Randy King .20 .50
18 Leland Irving 1.25 3.00
19 Shaun Heshka .20 .50
20 Jonathan Harty .20 .50
21 Zach Hamill 1.25 3.00
22 Taylor Ellington .20 .50
23 Jeremy Creurer .20 .50
24 Brady Calla .30 .75
25 Curtis Billsten .20 .50
26 Ivan Baranka .20 .50
27 Kyle Annesley .20 .50
28 Jay Varady .20 .50
29 John Becanic .20 .50
30 Kevin Constantine .02 .10

2005-06 Everett Silvertips

COMPLETE SET (30) 10.00 20.00
1 Damir Alic .30 .75
2 Brady Calla .30 .75
3 Zack Dailey .30 .75
4 Eric Doyle .30 .75
5 Taylor Ellington .30 .75
6 Matt Esposito .30 .75
7 Undrej Fiala .40 1.00
8 Jason Fransoo .30 .75
9 Zach Hamill .75 2.00
10 Shane Harper .30 .75

11 Jonathon Harty .30 .75
12 Shaun Heshka .30 .75
13 Karel Hromas .30 .75
14 Leland Irving .75 2.00
15 Mark Kress .30 .75
16 John Lammers .30 .75
17 Jonathan Millhouse .30 .75
18 Peter Mueller 2.00 5.00
19 Graham Potuer .30 .75
20 Ryan Sawka .30 .75
21 Zach Sim .30 .75
22 Jesse Smyke .30 .75
23 Brennan Sonne .30 .75
24 Cody Thoring .30 .75
25 Torrie Wheat .30 .75
26 Kevin Constantine HC .02 .10
27 John Becanic AC .02 .10
28 Jay Varady AC .02 .10
29 Scott Scoville DPP .02 .10
30 Zoran Rajcic DO .02 .10

2005 Extreme Top Prospects Signature Edition

This 30-card set was sold only in set form and was limited to just 400 sets. Each card carried a certified player autograph. The Sidney Crosby stick/auto card was inserted in one out of 4 sets and was limited to 150 copies though only 100 copies were used in the sets. The other 50 cards were given to Crosby. Please note that there are two cards numbered S7 and that card S26 does not exist.

S1 Sidney Crosby/300 150.00 250.00
S2 Alex Bourret 6.00 15.00
S3 Guillaume Latendresse 12.00 30.00
S4 Marc-Antoine Pouliot 10.00 25.00
S5 Jean-Francois Jacques 6.00 15.00
S6 David Krejci 6.00 15.00
S7 Daren Machesney 6.00 15.00
S7 Corey Perry 12.50 30.00
S8 Rob Schremp 10.00 25.00
S9 Danny Syvret 6.00 15.00
S10 Petr Vrana 6.00 15.00
S11 Derick Brassard 10.00 25.00
S12 Stephen Dixon 6.00 15.00
S13 James Sheppard 8.00 20.00
S14 Marc Staal 8.00 20.00
S15 Benoit Pouliot 8.00 20.00
S16 Anthony Stewart 6.00 15.00
S17 Michael Ouzas 6.00 15.00
S18 Patrick O'Sullivan 8.00 20.00
S19 Lukas Kaspar 6.00 15.00
S20 Bobby Ryan 10.00 25.00
S21 Stanislav Lascek 6.00 15.00
S22 Marek Zagrapan 6.00 15.00
S23 Josh Hennessy 6.00 15.00
S24 Alexander Radulov 10.00 25.00
S25 Julien Ellis-Plante 8.00 20.00
S27 Wojtek Wolski 10.00 25.00
S28 Michael Richards 10.00 25.00
S29 Boris Valabik 6.00 15.00
S30 Ryan O'Marra 6.00 15.00
SS1 Sidney Crosby Stick AU/100 300.00 500.00

1998-99 Fayetteville Force

Little is known about this Central Hockey League team set beyond the confirmed checklist. Any additional information can be forwarded to hockeymag@beckett.com.

COMPLETE SET (18) 3.60 9.00
1 David Lohrei HCO .20 .50
2 Darren McLean .20 .50
3 Rod Butler .20 .50
4 Steven Toll .20 .50
5 Justin Tomberlin .20 .50
6 Alexandr Chunchukov .20 .50
7 Casey Hungle .20 .50
8 Jason Wright .20 .50
9 Roddy MacCormick .20 .50
10 Lon Hovland .20 .50
11 Chris Bernard .20 .50
12 Dan Dennis .20 .50
13 Chris Ford .20 .50
14 Ryan Guzior .20 .50
15 Chad Remackel .20 .50
16 Colin Muldoon .20 .50
17 Stephen Sangermano .20 .50
18 Tim Hill .20 .50

2006-07 Fayetteville FireAntz

COMPLETE SET (21) 20.00 40.00
1 Mike Clarke .75 2.00
2 Chad Collins• 1.25 3.00
3 Bryan Dobek .75 2.00
4 Chris Furguson .75 2.00
5 Gavin Hodgson .75 2.00
6 Garrett Kindred• 1.25 3.00
7 Nick Kormanyos .75 2.00
8 John Marks HC .20 .50
9 Rob Manchoff CO .20 .50
10 Adam Meyer .75 2.00
11 Marc Norrington .75 2.00
12 Josh Piro .75 2.00
13 Jarrett Robertson .75 2.00
14 Dylan Row .75 2.00
15 Pekka Saittakari .75 2.00
16 Rob Sich .75 2.00
17 B.J. Stephens .75 2.00
18 Josh Tataryn .75 2.00
19 Tim Velemirovich .75 2.00
20 Josh Welter .75 2.00
21 Chad Wilcox .75 2.00

1991-92 Ferris State Bulldogs

This 30-card standard-size set features the 1991-92 Ferris State Bulldogs. The cards were available in the Ferris State University Pro Shop at the arena. The cards are unnumbered and checklisted below in alphabetical order.

COMPLETE SET (30) 4.00 10.00
1 Aaron Asp .20 .50
2 Seth Appert .20 .50
3 J.J. Bamberger .20 .50
4 Kevin Beals ACO .02 .10
5 Scot Bell .20 .50
6 Brad Burnham .20 .50
7 Dan Chaput .20 .50
8 Tim Christian .20 .50
9 Bob Daniels .20 .50
10 Colin Dodunski .20 .50
11 Mick Dolan .20 .50
12 John Duff .20 .50
13 Daryl Filipek .20 .50
14 John Gruden .20 .50
15 Luke Harvey .20 .50
16 Jeff Jestadt .20 .50
17 Dave Karpa .30 .75
18 Gary Kitching .20 .50
19 Mike Kolenda .20 .50
20 Craig Lisko .20 .50
21 Mike May .20 .50
22 Pat Mazzoli .20 .50
23 Robb McIntyre .20 .50
24 Kevin Moore .20 .50
25 Greg Paine .20 .50
26 Dwight Parrish .20 .50
27 Val Passarelli .20 .50
28 Keith Sergott .20 .50
29 Doug Smith .20 .50
30 The Bulldog MASCOT .02 .10

1992-93 Ferris State Bulldogs

This set features the Bulldogs of the NCAA. The cards were issued as a giveaway and are unnumbered, so are listed below in alphabetical order.

COMPLETE SET (30) 8.00 20.00
1 Seth Appert .30 .75
2 Aaron Asp .30 .75
3 J.J. Bamberger .30 .75
4 Kevin Beals .30 .75
5 Scott Bell .30 .75
6 Brad Burnham .30 .75
7 Daniel Chaput .30 .75
8 Tim Christian .30 .75
9 Bob Daniels CO .08 .25
10 Colin Dodunski .30 .75
11 Mick Dolan .30 .75
12 John Duff .30 .75
13 Daryl Filipek .30 .75
14 John Gruden .40 1.00
15 Luke Harvey .30 .75
16 Jeff Jestadt .30 .75
17 Dave Karpa .40 1.00
18 Gary Kitching .30 .75
19 Mike Kolenda .30 .75
20 Craig Lisko .30 .75
21 Mike May .30 .75
22 Pat Mazzoli .30 .75
23 Robb McIntyre .30 .75
24 Kevin Moore .30 .75
25 Greg Paine .30 .75
26 Dwight Parrish .30 .75
27 Val Passarelli .40 1.00
28 Keith Sergott .30 .75
29 Doug Smith .30 .75
30 The Bulldog MASCOT .02 .10

1993-94 Flint Generals

This set of 20 cards features the Flint Generals of the Colonial Hockey League. It was produced for team distribution by Rising Star Sport Promotions. The fronts feature a posed photo, along with league logo and player information. The backs contain a smattering of biographical data and career numbers. The set is unnumbered.

COMPLETE SET (20) 40.00 75.00
1 Header Card .40 1.00
2 Brent Stickney 1.50 4.00
3 Brett Strot 1.50 4.00
4 Brian Sakic 2.00 5.00
5 Chris O'Rourke 1.50 4.00
6 Dan Elsener 1.50 4.00
7 Darcy Austin 1.50 4.00
8 Dominic Niro 1.50 4.00
9 Jim Duhart 1.50 4.00
10 John Heasty 1.50 4.00
11 Keith Whitmore 1.50 4.00
12 Ken Spangler 1.50 4.00
13 Kevin Kerr 1.50 4.00
14 Larry Bernard 1.50 4.00
15 Lorne Knauft 1.50 4.00
16 Marc Vachon 1.50 4.00
17 Mark Gowens 2.00 5.00
18 Peter Horachek 1.50 4.00
19 Stephane Brochu 1.50 4.00
20 Todd Humphrey 2.00 5.00

1994-95 Flint Generals

This 24-card set of the Flint Generals of the Colonial Hockey League was produced by and distributed through the team. The set's familiar look comes from its homage to the lamentable 1991-92 Pro Set issue. The card backs also ape the design, although they are in black and white, containing another photo and player stats.

COMPLETE SET (24) 20.00 50.00
1 Kevin Barrett .75 2.00
2 Larry Bernard .75 2.00
3 Ken Blum .75 2.00
4 Stephane Brochu .75 2.00
5 Keith Carney .75 2.00
6 Ryan Douglas .75 2.00
7 Jim Duhart .75 2.00
8 Ray Gallagher .75 2.00
9 Mark Gowens .75 2.00
10 Peter Horachek .75 2.00
11 Todd Humphrey .75 2.00
12 Fredrik Jax 1.00 2.50
13 Doug Jones .75 2.00
14 Kevin Kerr 1.00 2.50
15 Petr Leska 1.00 2.50
16 Stan Matwijiw 1.25 3.00
17 Glen Mears .75 2.00
18 Kyle Reeves 1.00 2.50
19 Brian Sakic 1.00 2.50
20 Stefan Simoes .75 2.00
21 Ken Spangler .75 2.00
22 Keith Whitmore .75 2.00
23 Jeff Whittle .75 2.00
24 Team Photo .75 2.00

1995-96 Flint Generals

This 25-card set features the Flint Generals of the CHL. The set was produced by, and available only through, the team's booster club. The fronts feature an action photo and team and booster club logos. The back includes another photo, player stats and a brief bio.

COMPLETE SET (25) 4.80 12.00
1 Erin Whitten 1.00 2.50
2 Kevin Kerr .30 .75
3 Sverre Sears .15 .40
4 Scott Burfoot .20 .50
5 John Batten .15 .40
6 Chad Grills .15 .40
7 Lady Generals .30 .75
8 General Rally MASCOT .02 .10
9 Rob Nichols GM/CO .02 .10
10 Mikhail Nemirovsky .15 .40
11 Robin Bouchard .15 .40
12 Dominic Grandmaison .15 .40
13 Andrei Mezin .30 .75
14 Steve Beadle .15 .40
15 Darryl Lafrance .15 .40
16 Chris Gotziaman .15 .40
17 Gerry St. Cyr .30 .75
18 Derek Knorr .15 .40
19 Chris Gordon .20 .50
20 Brett MacDonald .15 .40
21 Brian Sakic .20 .50
22 Jamie Hearn .15 .40
23 Jeff Whittle .15 .40
24 Stephane Brochu .15 .40
25 Jim Duhart .15 .40

1996-97 Flint Generals

This 28-card set was issued as a promotional giveaway over the span of several games. This set is not numbered so the cards appear in alphabetical order.

COMPLETE SET (28) 10.00 25.00
1 Steve Beadle .40 1.00
2 Pascal Belanger .40 1.00
3 Robin Bouchard .40 1.00
4 Stephane Brochu .40 1.00
5 Neil Eisenhut .40 1.00
6 Nick Forbes .40 1.00
7 Igor Galkin .40 1.00
8 Jason Glover .40 1.00
9 Chad Grills .40 1.00
10 John Heasty .40 1.00
11 Kevin Kerr .40 1.00
12 Lorne Knauft .40 1.00
13 Brett MacDonald .40 1.00
14 Andrei Mezin .60 1.50
15 Jason Payne .40 1.00
16 Jason Ralph .40 1.00
17 Dmitri Rodine .40 1.00
18 Zdenek Sikl .40 1.00
19 Ken Spangler .40 1.00
20 Matt Weder .40 1.00
21 Jeff Whittle .40 1.00
22 Ross Wilson .40 1.00
23 Rob Nichols HCO .20 .50
24 Karl Lawson .40 1.00
25 General Rally Mascot .20 .50
26 1996 Colonial Cup Champs .40 1.00
27 1996 Tarry Cup Champs .40 1.00
28 Checklist .20 .50

1997-98 Flint Generals

This set features the Generals of the UHL. The cards were issued as promotional giveaways in 10-card packs at three different games.

COMPLETE SET (30) 12.00 30.00
1 Steve Beadle .40 1.00
2 Stephane Brochu .60 1.50
3 Ian Crockford .40 1.00
4 Nick Forbes .40 1.00
5 Mark Giannetti .40 1.00
6 Jason Glover .40 1.00
7 Chad Grills .40 1.00
8 John Heasty .40 1.00
9 Raitis Ivanans .40 1.00
10 Kevin Kerr .60 1.50
11 Lorne Knauft .40 1.00
12 Ray LeBlanc .75 2.00
13 Brett MacDonald .40 1.00
14 Bryan McMullen .40 1.00
15 Andrei Mezin .75 2.00
16 Matt Mullin .60 1.50
17 Dmitri Rodine .40 1.00
18 Brian Sakic .60 1.50
19 Jeremy Sladovnik .40 1.00
20 Ken Spangler .40 1.00
21 Kahlil Thomas .40 1.00
22 Jeff Whittle .40 1.00
23 Ross Wilson .40 1.00
24 Rob Nichols CO .08 .25
25 General Rally MASCOT .08 .25
26 Mike Zanzarella TR .08 .25
27 Robert Roe STAFF .08 .25
28 Pam The Prize Lady .20 .50
29 Lady Generals .40 1.00
30 Flint Generals .40 1.00

1997-98 Flint Generals EBK

This set features the Generals of the UHL. The set was produced by ebk Sports and was sold by the team at home playoff games.

COMPLETE SET (23) 4.00 10.00
1 Checklist .02 .10
2 Kahlil Thomas .20 .50
3 Ken Spangler .20 .50
4 Stephane Brochu .30 .75
5 Lorne Knauft .20 .50
6 Janis Tomans .20 .50
7 Nick Forbes .20 .50
8 Trevor Jobe .20 .50
9 John Heasty .30 .75
10 Brian Sakic .30 .75
11 Kevin Kerr .30 .75
12 Chad Grills .20 .50
13 UHL All-Stars .20 .50
14 Jeremy Sladovnik .20 .50
15 Jeff Whittle .20 .50
16 Jason Glover .20 .50
17 Steve Beadle .20 .50
18 Bryan McMullen .20 .50
19 Emmanuel Labranche .20 .50
20 Brett MacDonald .20 .50
21 John Batten .20 .50
22 Ross Wilson .20 .50
23 Rob Nichols CO .08 .25

1998-99 Flint Generals

This set features the Generals of the UHL. The cards were issued in packs as a promotional giveaway at one home game. Reports conflict as to whether the packs contained four, six or eight cards. Anyone with additional information can forward it to hockeymag@beckett.com.

COMPLETE SET (22) 8.00 20.00
1 Logo Card .02 .10
2 Chad Grills .40 1.00
3 Jason Payne .40 1.00
4 Jeremy Sladovnik .40 1.00
5 Stephane Brochu .40 1.00
6 Jeff Whittle .40 1.00
7 Rob Nichols CO .08 .25
8 Brian Sakic .60 1.50
9 Checklist .02 .10
10 Nick Forbes .40 1.00
11 Mike Bondy .40 1.00
12 Peter Ambroziak .40 1.00
13 Luch Nasato .60 1.50
14 Mikhail Nemirovsky .40 1.00
15 Bobby Reynolds .40 1.00
16 Generals Staff .02 .10
17 Lorne Knauft .40 1.00
18 Rob Laurie .60 1.50
19 Ross Wilson .40 1.00
20 Jason Glover .40 1.00
21 Brett MacDonald .40 1.00
22 Kahlil Thomas .40 1.00

2001-02 Flint Generals

COMPLETE SET (24) 20.00
1 Joey Bastien 1.00
2 Sylvain Dufresne 1.00
3 Jim Duhart 1.00
4 Stu Dunn 1.50
5 Tim Findlay 1.00
6 Dale Greenwood 1.00
7 Igor Galkin 1.00
8 Lee Jelenic 1.00
9 Lorne Knauft 1.00
10 Corey Laniuk 1.00
11 Tom McKinnon 1.50
12 Frankie Nault 1.00
13 Eric Perricone 1.00
14 Jean-Francois Picard 1.00
15 Bobby Reynolds 1.00
16 Gary Roach 1.00
17 Mike Rutter 1.00
18 Jordan Trew 1.00
19 Mike Varhaug 1.50
20 Martin Woods 1.00
21 Vaclav Zavoral 1.00
22 Kirk Tomlinson HCO .50
23 General Rally MASCOT .10
24 The Lady Generals .10

2007-08 Flint Generals

COMPLETE SET (21) 5.00 12.00
1 Team Checklist .15 .40
2 Jaroslav Cesky .30 .75
3 Eric Marvin .30 .75
4 Martin Ondrej .30 .75
5 Michel Beausoleil .30 .75
6 Greg Bullock .30 .75
7 Jared Dumba .30 .75
8 Brock Wilson .30 .75
9 Kris Mallette .30 .75
10 John DiPace .30 .75
11 Shaun Fisher .30 .75
12 Darren McCarty .30 .75
13 Ryan Jorde .30 .75
14 Josef Fojtik .30 .75
15 Mike Kinnie .30 .75
16 Jordan Fox .30 .75
17 Chad Alban .30 .75
18 Mike Alexiou .30 .75
19 Jonathan Duchesneau .30 .75
20 Nick Tuzzolino .30 .75
21 Justin Depretis .30 .75

1987-88 Flint Spirits

This 20-card standard-size set features white-bordered posed color player photos. The team name and the player's name edge the picture on the left and lower edges respectively. Team logos in the bottom border round out the front. The horizontal backs carry biography, player profile, and statistics.

COMPLETE SET (20) 4.80 12.00
1 Mario Chitaroni .20 .50
2 John Cullen .40 1.00
3 Bob Fleming .20 .50
4 Keith Gretzky .40 1.00
5 Todd Hawkins .20 .50
6 Mike Hoffman .20 .50
7 Curtis Hunt .20 .50
8 Dwaine Hutton .20 .50
9 Trent Kaese .20 .50
10 Tom Karalis .20 .50
11 Ray LeBlanc .40 1.00
12 Darren Lowe .20 .50
13 Brett MacDonald .20 .50
14 Chris McSorley .40 1.00
15 Mike Mersch .20 .50
16 Victor Posa .20 .50
17 Kevin Schamehorn .20 .50
18 Ron Stern .40 1.00
19 Don Waddell .20 .50
20 Dan Woodley .20 .50

1988-89 Flint Spirits

This 22-card standard-size set features posed color player photos. The pictures are set at an angle on the card with green borders on the top and bottom. The player's name appears in the lower green border, while the team appears above. A thin blue line borders the front. The horizontal backs carry the player's name, biographical information, statistics, and career highlights. The cards are unnumbered and checklisted below in alphabetical order.

COMPLETE SET (22) 4.00 10.00
1 Dean Anderson .20 .50
2 Rob Bryden .20 .50
3 John Devereaux .20 .50
4 Stephane Giguere .20 .50
5 Steve Harrison .20 .50
6 Yves Heroux .30 .75
7 Mike Hoffman .20 .50
8 Peter Horachek .20 .50
9 Guy Jacob .20 .50
10 Bob Kennedy .20 .50
11 Gary Kruzich .20 .50
12 Lonnie Loach .40 1.00
13 Brett MacDonald .20 .50
14 Mike MacWilliam .20 .50
15 Moe Mansi .20 .50
16 Mike Mersch .20 .50
17 Michel Mongeau .40 1.00
18 Ken Spangler .20 .50
19 Three Amigos .30 .75
Steve Harrison
Mike Mersch
Mike Hoffman
20 Mark Vichorek .20 .50
21 Troy Vollhoffer .20 .50
22 Don Waddell GM .20 .50

2003-04 Florence Pride

COMPLETE SET (16) 15.00
145 Jack Baker 1.00
146 Craig Brunel 1.00
147 Adam Elzinga 1.00
148 Ryan Gaucher 1.00
149 Wes Goldie 1.00
150 Vladimir Gusev 1.00
151 Kyle Kidney 1.00
152 Dan Lombard 1.00
153 Mark McRae 1.00
154 Matt Reid 1.00
155 Bobby Russell 1.00
156 Allan Sirois 1.00
157 Jeff Szwez 1.00
158 Shaun Sutter 1.00
159 Mike Torney 1.00
160 Matt Underhill 1.50

1998-99 Florida Everblades

Little is known about this East Coast League team set beyond the confirmed checklist. Any additional information can be forwarded to hockeymag@beckett.com.

COMPLETE SET (27) 7.20 50.00
1 Brett Bruininks .75 2.00
2 Matt Brush .75 2.00
3 Nick Checco .75 2.00
4 Matt Demarski .75 2.00
5 Sergei Fedotov .75 2.00
6 Tim Ferguson .75 2.00
7 Bob Ferguson CO .02 .10
8 Hugh Hamilton .75 2.00
9 Mike Jickling .75 2.00
10 Gary Koehler .75 2.00
11 Greg Kuznik .75 2.00
12 Dane Litke .75 2.00
13 Marc Magliarditi 2.00 5.00
14 Kevin McDonald .75 2.00
15 Pat Mikesch .75 2.00
16 P.K. O'Handley ACO .02 .10
17 Josh Penn EQ .02 .10
18 Randy Petruk 2.00 5.00
19 Jason Prokopetz .75 2.00
20 Dan Keimann .75 2.00
21 Eric Ricard .75 2.00
22 Eric Rud .75 2.00
23 Steve Tardif .75 2.00
24 Andrew Taylor .75 2.00
25 Todd Wisocki .75 2.00
26 Mascot .02 .10
27 Title Card .02 .10

1999-00 Florida Everblades

This set features the Everblades of the ECHL. The set was produced by Roox and handed out as a promotional giveaway at a late-season home game.

COMPLETE SET (26) 8.00 20.00
1 Jeff Maund .60 1.50
2 Hugh Hamilton .30 .75
3 Greg Kuznik .30 .75
4 Dane Litke .30 .75
5 Peter Kasper .30 .75
6 Tim Ferguson .30 .75
7 Brent Cullaton .30 .75
8 Reggie Berg .40 1.00
9 Steve Moffatt .30 .75
10 Tom Buckley .30 .75
11 Eric Rud .30 .75
12 Jason Prokopetz .30 .75
13 Terry Lindgren .40 1.00
14 Matt Demarski .30 .75
15 Marc Magliarditi .60 1.50
16 Ty Jones .40 1.00
17 Harlan Pratt .30 .75
18 John Varga .40 1.00
19 Joe Cardarelli .30 .75
20 Steve Tardif .30 .75
21 Andy MacIntyre .30 .75
22 Jason Morgan .30 .75
23 Bob Ferguson CO .08 .25
24 P.K. O'Handley CO .08 .25
25 Swampy MAS .08 .25
26 Celluar One .02 .10

2000-01 Florida Everblades

This set features the Everblades of the ECHL. The set was produced by Roox as a promotional giveaway.

COMPLETE SET (26) 8.00 20.00
1 Bujar Amidovski .80 2.00
2 Reggie Berg .40 1.00
3 Sean Blanchard .40 1.00
4 Tom Buckley .40 1.00
5 Sandy Cohen .40 1.00
6 Randy Copley .40 1.00
7 Matt Demarski .30 .75
8 Bob Ferguson CO .20 .50
9 Hugh Hamilton .30 .75
10 Devin Hartnell .30 .75
11 Darrell Hay .40 1.00
12 Pete Hogan .30 .75
13 John Jennings EM .10 .25
14 Mike Jickling .30 .75
15 Terry Lindgren .40 1.00
16 Andy MacIntyre .30 .75
17 Marc Magliarditi .60 1.50
18 Brent McDonald .30 .75
19 Jason Metcalfe .30 .75
20 Jason Morgan .30 .75
21 P.K. O'Handley CO .20 .50
22 Brent Pope .30 .75
23 Swampee MASCOT .20 .50
24 David Vallieres .30 .75
25 Todd Wisocki TR .10 .25
26 TTI Computers .01

2001-02 Florida Everblades

This set features the Everblades of the ECHL. The cards were produced by Choice Marketing and were issued as a giveaway. A total of 2,000 sets were produced. Each set also includes the ultimate whip, a card promoting a Pikachu cartoon.

COMPLETE SET (21) 8.00 20.00
1 Checklist .20 .50
2 Gerry Fleming CO .20 .50
3 P.K. O'Handley ACO .20 .50
4 Vince Williams .40 1.00
5 Terry Lindgren .62 1.56
6 Duane Harmer .40 1.00
7 Andrew Long .40 1.00
8 Reggie Berg .40 1.00
9 Brent McDonald .40 1.00
10 Tom Buckley .40 1.00
11 Briane Thompson .40 1.00
12 Mike Cirillo .40 1.00
13 Don Smith .40 1.00
14 Joe Blaznek .40 1.00
15 Peter Reynolds .40 1.00
16 Paul Spadafora .62 1.56
17 Keith Anderson .40 1.00
18 Shaun Fisher .40 1.00
19 Randy Petruk .62 1.56
20 Ryan Murphy .40 1.00
21 Swampee .20 .50

2002-03 Florida Everblades

This set was produced by Choice Marketing and given away at a home game.

COMPLETE SET (26) 25.00
1 Keith Anderson 1.00
2 George Awada 1.00
3 Anthony Battaglia 1.00
4 Joe Blaznek 1.00
5 Kevin Brown 1.00
6 Tom Buckley 1.00
7 Sean Curry 1.00
8 Brian Goudie 1.00
9 Duane Harmer 1.00
10 Ed Hill 1.00
11 Marty Johnston 1.00
12 Cam McCormick 1.50
13 Laurent Meunier 1.00
14 Ryan Murphy 1.00
15 Tom Nelson 1.00
16 Peter Reynolds 1.00
17 Lee Ruff 1.00
18 Don Smith 1.00
19 Ryan Stewart 1.00
20 Jimmy Verdule 2.00
21 Jon Insana 1.00
22 Rob Zepp 2.00
23 Gerry Fleming CO .10
24 Terry Lindgren ACO .10
25 Swampee MASCOT .10
26 Checklist .10

2002-03 Florida Everblades RBI

COMPLETE SET (18) 20.00
115 Keith Anderson 1.00
116 George Awada 1.00
117 Anthony Battaglia 1.00
118 Joe Blaznek 1.00
119 Tom Buckley 1.00
120 Brian Goudie 1.00
121 Duane Harmer 1.00
122 Marty Johnston 1.00
123 Cam McCormick 1.50
124 Brent McDonald 1.00
125 Laurent Meunier 1.00
126 Ryan Murphy 1.00
127 Tom Nelson 1.00
128 Jared Newman 1.00
129 Peter Reynolds 1.00
130 Don Smith 1.00
131 Jimmy Verdule 2.00
132 Rob Zepp 2.00

2003-04 Florida Everblades

This set was issued by Choice Marketing and given away at one home game.

COMPLETE SET (25) 8.00 20.00
1 Keith Anderson .40 1.00
2 Reggie Berg .40 1.00
3 Jim Brown .40 1.00
4 Brandon Coalter .40 1.00
5 Paul Esdale .40 1.00
6 Gerry Fleming CO .07 .20
7 Ian Forbes .40 1.00
8 Chris Heisten .40 1.00
9 Tom Buckley .40 1.00
10 Jon Insana .40 1.00
11 Chad Larose .40 1.00
12 Jay Legault .40 1.00
13 Terry Lindgren ACO .07 .20
14 Tim O'Connell .40 1.00
15 Jeff Maund .60 1.50
16 Brian McCullough .40 1.00
17 Brent McDonald .40 1.00
18 Jared Newman .40 1.00
19 Matt Pagnutti .40 1.00
20 Paul Vincent .40 1.00
21 Gray Shaneberger .40 1.00
22 Mascot .07 .20
23 Chris Thompson .40 1.00
24 Ryan Van Buskirk .40 1.00
25 Rob Zepp .75 2.00

2003-04 Florida Everblades RBI Sports

This set was issued by RBI Sports, and is limited to just 250 copies. The numbering sequence continues across all RBI Sports sets issued this season.

COMPLETE SET (16) 18.00
161 Reggie Berg 1.00
162 Brandon Coalter 1.00
163 Paul Esdale 1.00
164 Kevin Holdridge 1.00
165 Jon Insana 1.00
166 Chad Larose 1.00
167 Carl Mallette 1.25
168 Jeff Maund 1.50
169 Brian McCullough 1.00
170 Jared Newman 1.00
171 Stuart Pietersma 1.00
172 Peter Reynolds 1.00
173 Gray Shaneberger 1.00
174 Damian Surma 1.25
175 Ryan Van Buskirk 1.00
176 Rob Zepp 2.00

2004-05 Florida Everblades

COMPLETE SET (30) 20.00
1 Tyler MacKay .75
2 Jared Newman .75
3 Matt Pagnutti .75
4 Shane Hnidy .75
5 Simon Tremblay .75
6 Reggie Berg .75
7 Brent MacDonald .75
8 Steve Saviano .75
9 Ryan Brindley .75
10 Tim Branham .75
11 Brandon Coalter .75
12 Matt Hendricks .75
13 David Lundbohm .75
14 Tim O'Connell .75
15 Bryce Charpentier .75
16 Kris Vernarsky 1.00
17 Brad Church .75
18 Greg Hornby .75
19 Keith Anderson .75
20 Damian Surma .75
21 Rob Zepp 1.00
22 Craig Kowalski .75
23 Chris Lee .75
24 Jason Nobili .75
25 Gerry Fleming .10
26 Todd Wisocki .10
27 John Jennings .10
28 Swampee MASCOT .10
29 Sponsor card .01
30 Checklist .01

2005-06 Florida Everblades

COMPLETE SET (25) 6.00 15.00
1 Jonathan Lehun .30 .75
2 Martin Tuma .30 .75
3 Paul Cabana .30 .75
4 Reggie Berg .30 .75
5 Swampee MASCOT .02 .10
6 Phil Aucoin .30 .75
7 Brandon Coalter .30 .75
8 Ernie Hartlieb .30 .75
9 Phil Osaer .40 1.00
10 Steve Saviano .30 .75
11 Ryan Brindley .30 .75
12 Bryce Charpentier .30 .75
13 Craig Kowalski .30 .75
14 Daniel Sisca .30 .75
15 Anders Strome .30 .75
16 Sean Stefanski .30 .75
17 Corey Neilson .30 .75
18 Grant McNeill .30 .75
19 Chris Lee .30 .75
20 Kevin Bergin .30 .75
21 John Adams .30 .75
22 Vince Bellissimo .30 .75
23 John Ronan .30 .75
24 Jeremy Swanson .30 .75
25 Gerry Fleming HC .02 .10

1990-91 Fort Saskatchewan Traders

This sheet contains 24 standard-size cards. Each card contains a color action player photo with his jersey number and name at the top on a white background. Above this are listed the player's position with the team name and years. At the lower right are the words "Next Generation Sport Cards." Each photo is framed by a thin red line and white border. The cards are unnumbered and checklisted below in alphabetical order.

COMPLETE SET (24) 2.50 6.00
1 Michael Buzak .15 .40
2 Wade Fennig .15 .40
3 Mark Goodkey .15 .40
4 Richard Groten .15 .40
5 Brett Gullion .15 .40
6 Keith Hill .15 .40
7 Justin Hocking .30 .75
8 Ian Kallay .15 .40
9 Scott Lindsay .15 .40
10 Faron Luchkow .15 .40
11 Wayne MacDonald .15 .40
12 Ted Oloriz .15 .40
13 Jason Plandowski .15 .40
14 Dory Reich .15 .40

15 Shawn Reich .15 .40
16 Darren Smith .15 .40
17 Mark Souch .15 .40
18 Bryan Stewart .15 .40
19 Paul Strand .15 .40
20 Tim Wiwchar .15 .40
21 Paul Wozney .15 .40
22 Allen Young .15 .40
23 Jason Yuzda .15 .40
24 Team Photo .20 .50

1993-94 Fort Wayne Komets

Cards are unnumbered and are listed below in alphabetical order.

COMPLETE SET (27) 6.00 15.00
1 Ian Boyce .30 .75
2 Colin Chin .30 .75
3 Lee Davidson .30 .75
4 Guy Dupuis .30 .75
5 Steve Fletcher .75 2.00
6 Sean Gauthier .30 .75
7 Darryl Gilmour .40 1.00
8 Kelly Hurd .30 .75
9 Carey Lucyk .30 .75
10 Kevin MacDonald .30 .75
11 Igor Malykhin .30 .75
12 Brian McKee .30 .75
13 Mitch Messier .40 1.00
14 Max Middendorf .40 1.00
15 John Purves .40 1.00
16 Grant Richison .30 .75
17 Darin Smith .30 .75
18 Dave Smith .30 .75
19 Shayne Stevenson .30 .75
20 David Tretowicz .30 .75
21 Vladimir Tsyplakov .30 .75
22 Doug Wickenheiser .40 1.00
23 Bruce Boudreau CO .20 .50
24 Derek Ray ACO .20 .50
25 Joe Franke TR .20 .50
26 Galen Head EQM .20 .50
27 Team Photo .20 .50

1995-96 Fort Wayne Komets

This set features the Komets of the IHL. The set was produced by Edge Ice and sold at the team's souvenir stands.

COMPLETE SET (25) 4.80 12.00
1 Andy Bezeau .20 .50
2 Colin Chin .20 .50
3 Shawn Cronin .20 .50
4 Guy Dupuis .20 .50
5 Pat Elynuik .20 .50
6 Bob Essensa .30 .75
7 Shawn Evans .20 .50
8 Steven Fletcher .20 .50
9 Peter Ing .20 .50
10 Andrew McBain .20 .50
11 Mitch Messier .20 .50
12 Rob Murphy .20 .50
13 Alex Nikolic .20 .50
14 Grant Richison .20 .50
15 Jeff Rohlicek .20 .50
16 Konstantin Shafronov .20 .50
17 Darin Smith .20 .50
18 Sergei Stas .20 .50
19 Brian Straub .20 .50
20 Chris Tok .20 .50
21 Paul Willett .20 .50
22 Kevin Wortman .20 .50
23 Oleg Yashin .20 .50
24 Derek Ray CO .08 .25
25 Icy MAS .02 .10

1997-98 Fort Wayne Komets

Little is known about this set beyond the confirmed checklist. Additional information can be forwarded to hockeymag@beckett.com.

COMPLETE SET (21) 4.00 10.00
1 Guy Dupuis .20 .50
2 Ian Boyce .20 .50
3 Lee Davidson .20 .50
4 Bruce Racine .30 .75
5 Dan Currie .20 .50
6 Robin Bawa .20 .50
7 Tom Nemeth .20 .50
8 Ed Campbell .20 .50
9 Vyacheslav Butsayev .20 .50
10 Steffon Walby .20 .50
11 Derek Eberle .20 .50
12 Chris Armstrong .20 .50
13 Norm Batherson .20 .50
14 Konstantin Shafronov .20 .50
15 Tom Pederson .20 .50
16 Andrei Bashkirov .20 .50
17 Carlin Nordstrom .20 .50
18 Trevor Doyle .20 .50
19 Eric Boguniecki .30 .75
20 Kevin Weekes .60 1.50
21 Icy D. Eagle Mascot .02 .10

1998-99 Fort Wayne Komets

Little is known about this team set beyond the confirmed checklist. Any additional information can be forwarded to hockeymag@beckett.com.

COMPLETE SET (29) 4.00 10.00
1 Ed Campbell .15 .40
2 Vyacheslav Butsayev .20 .50
3 Ian Boyce .15 .40
4 Eric Boguniecki .20 .50
5 Robin Bawa .15 .40
6 Gerard Gallant ACO .15 .40
7 Icy D. Eagle Mascot .02 .10
8 Guy Dupuis .15 .40
9 Dion Darling .15 .40
10 Bob Chase .15 .40
11 Brad Purdie .15 .40
12 Andrei Petrakov .15 .40
13 David Nemirovsky .20 .50
14 Mike Martin .15 .40
15 Tero Lehtera .20 .50
16 Oleg Shargorodsky .15 .40
17 Shawn Ulmer .20 .50
18 Andre Roy .20 .50
19 Eldon Reddick .20 .50
20 Bruce Racine .20 .50
21 Memorial Coliseum .02 .10
22 Derek Wood .15 .40
23 Lee Sorochan .20 .50
24 Grant Sonier HCO .02 .10
25 Checklist .02 .10
26 Shawn Penn .15 .40
27 PHPA Web Site .01
28 IHL Web Site .01
29 Andrei Bashkirov .15 .40

1999-00 Fort Wayne Komets Points Leaders

This set was produced by the Komets of the UHL to honor their all-time leading scorers. However, since this was their first season in the league, the players pictured performed for the team during its IHL days. The cards are believed to have been issued as a promotional giveaway, but this has not been confirmed.

COMPLETE SET (16) 6.00 15.00
1 Header Card .02 .10
2 Len Thornson .40 1.00
3 Eddie Long .40 1.00
4 Terry McDougall .40 1.00
5 Colin Chin .40 1.00
6 John Goodwin .40 1.00
7 Reg Primeau .40 1.00
8 Merv Dubchek .40 1.00
9 Barry Scully .40 1.00
10 Rob Laird .40 1.00
11 Jim Burton .60 1.50
12 Lionel Repka .40 1.00
13 Norman Waslowski .40 1.00
14 Ron Leef .40 1.00
15 Bobby Rivard .40 1.00
16 Dale Baldwin .40 1.00

1999-00 Fort Wayne Komets Penalty Leaders

This set was produced by the Komets of the UHL to honor their all-time leading pugilists. However, since this was their first season in the league, the players pictured performed for the team during its IHL days. The cards are believed to have been issued as a promotional giveaway, but this has not been confirmed.

COMPLETE SET (16) 8.00 35.00
1 Header Card .02 .10
2 Steven Fletcher 1.25 3.00
3 Dale Baldwin .75 2.00
4 Cal Purinton 1.25 3.00
5 Rob Laird .75 2.00
6 Dave Norris .75 2.00
7 Robin Bawa 1.25 3.00
8 Terry Pembroke .75 2.00
9 Andy Bezeau 1.25 3.00
10 Eddie Long .75 2.00
11 Craig Channell .75 2.00
12 Steve Salvucci .75 2.00
13 Carey Lucyk .75 2.00
14 Lionel Repka .75 2.00
15 Scott Gruhl 1.25 3.00
16 Guy Dupuis .75 2.00

2000-01 Fort Wayne Komets

This set was produced by the team and sold at home games throughout the season. The cards are unnumbered, and are listed below in alphabetical order.

COMPLETE SET (24) 4.80 12.00
1 Frederic Bouchard .20 .50
2 Dave Butler .20 .50
3 Keli Corpse .30 .75
4 Derek Gauthier .30 .75
5 Jason Goulet .20 .50
6 Brent Gretzky .30 .75
7 Kelly Hurd .20 .50
8 Rick Judson .20 .50
9 Dave Lemay .20 .50
10 Jim Logan .20 .50
11 Igor Malykhin .20 .50
12 Darren Martens .20 .50
13 Mike McKay .20 .50
14 Geno Parrish .20 .50
15 Kevin Popp .20 .50
16 Sergei Radchenko .20 .50
17 Gary Ricciardi .20 .50
18 Dan Ronan .20 .50
19 Konstantin Simchuk .20 .50
20 Fred Slukynsky .20 .50
21 Doug Teskey .20 .50
22 Brad Twordik .20 .50
23 Greg Puhalski CO .10 .25
24 Ice Eagle MASCOT .04 .10

2000-01 Fort Wayne Komets Shoe Carnival

This set features the Komets of the UHL. The set was a promotional giveaway, sponsored by a local shoe store. The cards were released in five-card strips, featuring four players and a store coupon.

COMPLETE SET (16) 6.00 15.00
1 Rhett Trombley .40 1.00
2 Gary Ricciardi .40 1.00
3 Jason Goulet .40 1.00
4 Rick Judson .40 1.00
5 Igor Malykhin .40 1.00
6 Doug Teskey .40 1.00
7 Kelly Hurd .40 1.00
8 Mike McKay .40 1.00
9 Brent Gretzky .80 2.00
10 Geno Parrish .40 1.00
11 Dave Lemay .40 1.00
12 Jim Logan .40 1.00
13 Frederic Bouchard .40 1.00
14 Brad Twordik .40 1.00
15 Dan Ronan .40 1.00
16 Derek Gauthier .40 1.00

2001-02 Fort Wayne Komets

This set features the Komets of the UHL. It was produced by Choice Marketing and was sold by the team at it souvenir shop. The production was announced at 1,000 sets.

COMPLETE SET (22) 4.00 10.00
1 Doug Teskey .20 .50
2 Igor Bondarev .20 .50
3 Frederic Bouchard .31 .78
4 Christian Bragnalo .20 .50
5 Derek Gauthier .31 .78
6 Dustin Virag .20 .50
7 Chad Grills .20 .50
8 Kevin Holliday .20 .50
9 Icy D. Eagle Mascot .04 .11
10 Erik Landman .20 .50
11 Jim Logan .20 .50
12 Michael Massie .20 .50
13 David Mayes .20 .50
14 Mike McKay .20 .50
15 Kelly Miller .31 .78
16 Martin Fillion .20 .50
17 Kevin Schmidt .20 .50
18 Ryan Severson .20 .50
19 Matt Swain .20 .50
20 Kevin Bertram .20 .50
21 Steven Desjardins .20 .50
22 Brent Gretzky CO .31 .78

2001-02 Fort Wayne Komets Shoe Carnival

The set of the UHL's Fort Wayne franchise features players from both the current Komets team and former greats. The set was issued as a promotional giveaway, with four cards handed out per night at four different games.

COMPLETE SET (16) 6.00 15.00
1 Dustin Virag .40 1.00
2 Reg Primeau .40 1.00
3 Kevin Holliday .40 1.00
4 Steven Fletcher .80 2.00
5 Brent Gretzky .40 1.00
6 Len Thornson .40 1.00
7 Derek Gauthier .40 1.00
8 Robin Bawa .40 1.00
9 Frederic Bouchard .40 1.00
10 Lionel Repka .40 1.00
11 Michel Masse .40 1.00
12 Eddie Long .40 1.00
13 Doug Teskey .40 1.00
14 Chuck Adamson .40 1.00
15 Jim Logan .40 1.00
16 Ian Boyce .40 1.00

2002-03 Fort Wayne Komets

COMPLETE SET (25) 10.00
1 Marc Barlow .50
2 David Beauregard .50
3 Kevin Bertram .50
4 Ken Boone .50
5 Colin Chaulk .50
6 Parris Duffus .75
7 Joe Franke .50
8 Kevin Kotyluk .75
9 Tom Lawson .75
10 Adam Lewis .75
11 Michel Massie .50
12 Troy Neumeier .50
13 Jake Ortmeyer .50
14 Kelly Perrault .50
15 Eldon Reddick .75
16 Kevin Schmidt .50
17 Jason Selleke .50
18 Ryan Severson .50
19 Bart Stevens .50
20 Bobby Stewart .50
21 Sean Venedam .50
22 Dustin Virag .50
23 Icy D. Eagle MASCOT .01
24 Greg Puhalski HCO .10
NNO Checklist .01

2002-03 Fort Wayne Komets Shoe Carnival

COMPLETE SET (16) 30.00
1 Kelly Perrault 2.00
2 David Beauregard 2.00
3 Jake Ortmeyer 2.00
4 Michel Massie 2.00
5 Tom Lawson 2.00
6 Bobby Stewart 2.00
7 Ryan Severson 2.00
8 Eldon Reddick 3.00
9 Sean Venedam 2.00
10 Kevin Bertram 2.00
11 Marc Barlow 2.00
12 Dustin Virag 2.00
13 Icy D. Eagle MASCOT .10
14 Kevin Schmidt 2.00
15 Colin Chaulk 2.00
16 Adam Lewis 2.00

2003-04 Fort Wayne Komets

This series was produced by Choice Marketing and sold at home games.

COMPLETE SET (23) 10.00
1 Bobby Stewart .50
2 Colin Chaulk .50
3 David Beauregard .50
4 Sean Venedam .50
5 Dan Stewart .50
6 Ryan Severson .50
7 Michel Massie .50
8 Dustin Virag .50
9 Kevin Kotyluk .75
10 Adam Lewis .50
11 Dan Price .50
12 Mascot .10
13 Andy Townsend .50
14 Kevin Schmidt .50
15 Mark Cole .50
16 Mike Perna .50
17 Kelly Perrault .50
18 Kevin Bertram .50
19 Troy Neumeier .50
20 Kelly Shields .75
21 Kevin St. Pierre .75
22 Ryan Coole .50
23 Steve Rodberg .50

2003-04 Fort Wayne Komets 2003 Champions

COMPLETE SET (21) 8.00
1 Colin Chaulk .50
2 Kelly Perrault .50
3 Dustin Virag .50
4 Sean Venedam .50
5 Tom Lawson .50
6 Colin Chaulk .50
7 Tom Lawson .50
8 Parading the Cup .20
9 Dustin Virag .50
10 Kevin Bertram .50
11 Greg Puhalski HCO .20
12 Kelly Perrault .50
13 Dustin Virag .50
14 Michel Massie .50
15 Marc Barlow .50
16 Tom Lawson .50
17 Team Photo .50
17 Komets Fans .10
18 Kelly Perrault .50
19 Kevin Kotyluk .75
20 Sponsor .01

2003-04 Fort Wayne Komets Shoe Carnival

These were issued as a promotional giveaway over the course of four home games. The cards came in four-card perforated strips.

COMPLETE SET (16) 15.00
1 Kelly Perrault 1.00
2 Kevin Schmidt 1.00
3 Kevin Bertram 1.00
4 Adam Lewis 1.00
5 Troy Neumeier 1.00
6 Colin Chaulk 1.00
7 Kevin Kotyluk 1.50
8 Bobby Stewart 1.00
9 Kevin St. Pierre 1.50
10 David Beauregard 1.00
11 Michel Massie 1.00
12 Sean Venedam 1.00
13 Dan Price 1.00
14 Dan Stewart 1.00
15 Ryan Severson 1.00
16 Dustin Virag 1.00

2004-05 Fort Wayne Komets

This set was produced by Choice Marketing and sold at the pro shop.

COMPLETE SET (22) 10.00
1 Colin Chaulk 1.00
2 P.C. Drouin .75
3 Jonathan Goodwin .50
4 Chris Grenville .50
5 Rob Guinn .50
6 David Hukalo .50
7 Jason Kean .50
8 Shane Kenny .50
9 Tyler Masters .75
10 Tom Nelson .50
11 Tom Nemeth .50
12 Troy Nuemeier .50
13 Steve Rodberg .50
14 Kevin St. Pierre .75
15 Danny Stewart .50
16 Andy Townsend .50
17 Sean Venedam .50
18 Dustin Virag .50
19 Jeff Worlton .50
20 Team Checklist .01
21 Mascot .10
22 Sponsor Card .01

2004-05 Fort Wayne Komets Shoe Carnival

This set was issued as a promotional giveaway at a home game.

COMPLETE SET (16) 25.00
1 Colin Chaulk 3.00
2 P.C. Drouin 2.00
3 Jonathan Goodwin 1.50
4 Chris Grenville 1.50
5 Rob Guinn 1.50
6 Jason Kean 1.50
7 Shane Kenny 1.50
8 Tim Krueckl 1.50
9 Corey Lucas 1.50
10 Tyler Masters 2.00
11 Troy Neumeier 1.50
12 Kevin St. Pierre 2.00
13 Dan Stewart 1.50
14 Sean Venedam 2.00
15 Dustin Virag 1.50
16 Jeff Worlton 1.50

2005-06 Fort Wayne Komets Choice

COMPLETE SET (25) 10.00
1 Kevin St. Pierre .20 .50
2 Jeff Worlton .20 .50
3 Jonathan Goodwin .20 .50
4 David Hukalo .20 .50
5 David Frawley .20 .50
6 David Carpentier .20 .50
7 Andrew Luciuk .20 .50
8 Brent Rumble .20 .50
9 Matt Hunter .20 .50
10 Kelly Miller .20 .50
11 Garrett Summerfield .20 .50
12 P.C. Drouin .20 .50
13 Unknown
14 Lance Galbraith .20 .50
15 Mark Smith .20 .50
16 Kevin Kurk .20 .50
17 Guy Dupuis .20 .50
18 Jason Kean .20 .50
19 John Jarram .20 .50
20 A.J. Bozoian .20 .50
21 Rob Guinn .20 .50
22 Mark Lindsay .20 .50
23 Troy Neumeier .20 .50
24 Ryan Jorde .20 .50
25 Icy D. Eagle MASCOT .02 .10

2005-06 Fort Wayne Komets Sprint

COMPLETE SET (16) 20.00
1 A.J. Bozoian .60 1.50
2 David Carpentier .60 1.50
3 Colin Chaulk .60 1.50
4 P.C. Drouin .60 1.50
5 Guy Dupuis .60 1.50
6 Lance Galbraith .60 1.50
7 Lance Galbraith .60 1.50
8 Jonathan Goodwin .60 1.50
9 Rob Guinn .60 1.50
10 David Hukalo .60 1.50
11 John Jarram .60 1.50
12 Ryan Jorde .60 1.50
13 Mark Lindsay .60 1.50
14 Troy Neumeier .60 1.50
15 Brent Rumble .60 1.50
16 Kevin St. Pierre .60 1.50

2006-07 Fort Wayne Komets

COMPLETE SET (24) 10.00 20.00
1 A.J. Bozoian .40 1.00
2 Mike Dombkiewicz .40 1.00
3 Guy Dupuis .40 1.00
4 Martin Gascon .40 1.00
5 Daniel Goneau .40 1.00
6 Jonathan Goodwin .40 1.00
7 Kevin Hansen .40 1.00
8 Jani Honkanen .40 1.00
9 David Hukalo .40 1.00
10 Arthur Kiyaga .40 1.00
11 Jean-Francois Labarre .40 1.00
12 Mario Larocque .75 2.00
13 Dan McWhinney .60 1.50
14 Pascal Morency .40 1.00
15 Bruce Richardson .40 1.00
16 Bogdan Rudenko .40 1.00
17 J.C. Ruid .40 1.00
18 Kevin St. Pierre .60 1.50
19 Matt Syroczynski .40 1.00
20 Brent Henley .40 1.00
21 K.J. Voorhees .40 1.00
22 Pat Bingham .40 1.00
23 Icy D. Eagle MASCOT .02 .10
24 Nesquik SPONSOR .01 .01

1997-98 Fort Worth Brahmas

This 21-card set was sold at home games for $4. The cards do not bear numbers, so they are listed alphabetically.

COMPLETE SET (21) 4.00 10.00
1 Chris Albert .20 .50
2 Steve Carter .20 .50
3 Brian Caruso .20 .50
4 Cosmo DuPaul .20 .50
5 David Graff .20 .50
6 Craig Hayden .20 .50
7 Murray Hogg .20 .50
8 Alex Kholomeyev .30 .75
9 Stephane Larocque .30 .75
10 Rob Laurie .30 .75
11 Mike McCormick .20 .50
12 Nolan McDonald .20 .50
13 Terry Menard .30 .75
14 Max Middendorf .20 .50
15 Mark O'Donnell .20 .50
16 Adam Robbins .20 .50
17 Todd St. Louis .20 .50
18 Mark Strohack .20 .50
19 Gatis Tseplis .20 .50
20 Dwight Mullins ACO .02 .10
21 Bill McDonald CO .02 .10

1998-99 Fort Worth Brahmas

This 20-card set was handed out at a home game and is extremely scarce on the secondary market.

COMPLETE SET (20) 8.00 20.00
1 Terry Menard CO .20 .50
2 Steve Plouffe .60 1.50
3 Tim Green .40 1.00
4 Scott Shaunessy .40 1.00
5 Jim Dinneen .40 1.00
6 Martin Machacek .40 1.00
7 Francois Albert .40 1.00
8 Sean Brady .40 1.00
9 Murray Hogg .40 1.00
10 Ryan Black .40 1.00
11 Mark Strohack .40 1.00
12 Richie Walcott .40 1.00
13 Stephane Larocque .60 1.50
14 Barry Cummins .40 1.00
15 Phil Miaskowski .40 1.00
16 Martin Lamarche .40 1.00
17 Cosmo Dupaul .40 1.00
18 Jon Olofson .60 1.50
19 Craig Hayden .60 1.50
20 Steve Carter .40 1.00

1999-00 Fort Worth Brahmas

This 20-card set features the 1999-00 Fort Worth Brahmas on extra glossy card stock. In the upper left hand corner of each card appears "The Hockey Store" logo from a shop in Arlington, Texas. Cards are not numbered so they appear alphabetically. It is believed that they were issued as a promotional giveaway.

COMPLETE SET (20) 4.00 40.00
1 Louis Bernard .75 2.00
2 Bruiser MASCOT .02 .10
3 Jason Disher .75 2.00
4 Cosmo Dupaul .75 2.00
5 Cory Evans .75 2.00
6 Ross Harris .75 2.00
7 Murray Hogg .75 2.00
8 Alex Kholomeyev .75 2.00
9 Derek Kups .75 2.00
10 Martin Lamarche .75 2.00
11 Stephane Larocque .75 2.00
12 Terry Menard CO .20 .50
13 Jon Olofson 1.25 3.00
14 Steve Plouffe 2.00 5.00
15 Bobby Pochyly .75 2.00
16 Al Rooney .75 2.00
17 Mike Sanderson .75 2.00
18 Dennis Shiryaev .75 2.00
19 Mike Tilson .75 2.00
20 Gatis Tseplis .75 2.00

2000-01 Fort Worth Brahmas

This set features the Brahmas of the WPHL. The set was issued as a promotional giveaway in the form of a pair of unperforated nine-card sheets. The cards are not numbered so they appear below in alphabetical order.

COMPLETE SET (18) 4.80 12.00
1 Clint Cabana .30 .75
2 Justin Cardwell .30 .75
3 Jason Carey .30 .75
4 Steve Dowhy .30 .75
5 Ben Gorewich .30 .75
6 Jake Harney .30 .75
7 Ross Harris .30 1.00
8 Casey Hungle .30 .75
9 Craig Johnson .30 .75
10 Todd Lalonde CO .08 .25
11 Rob Laurie .30 1.00
12 Jason Pain .30 .75
13 Mike Rusk .30 .75
14 Ryan Shannon .30 .75
15 Mike Tilson .30 .75
16 Daniel Villeneuve .30 .75
17 Chad Woollard .30 .75
18 Mark Zacharias .30 .75

2001-02 Fort Worth Brahmas

This set features the Brahmas of the WPHL. The set was handed out at a game early in the season. Because the cards are unnumbered, they are listed below in alphabetical order.

COMPLETE SET (20) 8.00 20.00
1 Brady Austin .40 1.00
2 Jeff Bateman .62 1.56
3 Dave Bourque .40 1.00
4 Justin Cardwell .40 1.00
5 Jason Clarke .40 1.00
6 Kory Cooper .40 1.00
7 Dave Csumrik .40 1.00
8 Adam Davis .40 1.00
9 Sean Hughes .40 1.00
10 Craig Johnson .40 1.00
11 Chris Johnston .40 1.00
12 Cody Leibel .40 1.00
13 Todd Lalonde CO .20 .50
14 Cam MacDonald .40 1.00
15 Mike Tilson .62 1.56
16 Joe Van Volsen .62 1.56
17 Daniel Villeneuve .40 1.00
18 Chad Woollard .40 1.00
19 Scott Wray .40 1.00
20 Bruiser MASCOT .04 .11

2002-03 Fort Worth Brahmas

This set was issued as a promotional giveaway in two 10-card subsets at home games. The cards were printed on thin paper stock and are listed below in alphabetical order. Thanks to Ralph Slate for this checklist.

COMPLETE SET (20) 20.00
1 Adam Davis 1.00
2 Jason Fricker 1.50
3 David Fry 1.00
4 Rob Giffin 1.00
5 Chad Grills 1.00
6 Sean Hughes 1.00
7 Lee Jacobson 1.50
8 Lloyd Marks 1.00
9 Mike McKinnon 1.00
10 Jim Midgley 1.00
11 John Murphy 2.00
12 Jason Reesor 1.00
13 Mike Rusk 1.00
14 Joe Van Volsen 1.00
15 T.J. Warkus 1.00
16 Jeff Washbrook 1.00
17 Justin Williams 1.00
18 Chad Woollard 1.00
19 Bill Inglis CO .10
20 Bruiser MASCOT .10

2003-04 Fort Worth Brahmas

This set was issued as a promotional giveaway over the course of two home games.

COMPLETE SET (20) 20.00
1 Gary Baronick 1.00
2 Joey Bastien 1.00
3 Aaron Davis 1.00
4 Adam Davis 1.00
5 Scott English 1.50
6 Taras Foremsky 1.00
7 Chad Grills 1.00
8 Jan Jas 1.00
9 Jay McGee 1.00
10 Tyler Nilsson 1.50
11 Jason Reesor 1.00
12 Erasmo Saltarelli 1.50
13 Jeff Scharf 1.00
14 Peter Trumbley 1.00
15 Derrell Upton 1.00
16 Jeremy Vanin 1.00
17 Justin Williams 1.00
18 Chad Woollard 1.00
19 Al Sims HCO .20
20 Mascot .10

2004-05 Fort Worth Brahmas

Set was issued as a giveaway at two home games, 10 cards at a time.

COMPLETE SET (20) 30.00
1 Jay Banach 1.50
2 Brian Basner 2.50
3 Brandon Carper 1.50
4 Dave Csumrik 1.50
5 Aaron Davis 1.50
6 Adam Davis 1.50
7A Mark Hynes ERR (Adam Davis back) 1.50
7B Mark Hynes COR 1.50
8A Jan Jas ERR (Mark Hynes back) 1.50
8B Jan Jas COR 1.50
9 Brad Lukowich 2.00
10 Bryan Lundbohm 1.50
11 Dan Murphy 2.00
12 Sheldon Nedjelski 1.50
13 Martin Paquet 1.50
14 Larry Sterling 2.00
15 Nick Udovicic 1.50
16 Derrell Upton 1.50
17 Jorin Welsh 1.50
18 Chad Woollard 1.50
19 Al Sims CO .50
20 Bruiser MASCOT .10

1992-93 Fort Worth Fire

Sponsored by Whataburger, this 18-card set was issued as a cut set and also as a sheet. The sheet was rimmed on the left and right sides by a row of coupons redeemable at Whataburger. Card strips featuring three player cards sandwiched between two coupons were also produced. The cards measure the standard size and feature posed, color player photos with either a peach or a white studio background on white card stock. The picture is set off-center on a white area framed by a thin black line and shadow-bordered. The player's name and uniform number are printed above the photo, while "Whataburger" is printed in burnt orange below. The backs carry biographical information and career highlights. The cards are unnumbered and checklisted below in alphabetical order.

COMPLETE SET (18) 4.00 10.00
1 Ron Aubrey .20 .50
2 Roch Belley .40 1.00
3 Jason Brousseau .20 .50
4 Eric Brule .20 .50
5 Todd Drevitch .20 .50
6 Trevor Duhaime .20 .50
7 Steve Harrison ACO .08 .25
8 Ernest Hornak .20 .50
9 Alex Kholomeyev .30 .75
10 Curt Krolak .20 .50
11 Ryan Leschasin .20 .50
12 Peter Mahovlich CO .75 2.00
13 Mike McCormick .20 .50
14 Mike O'Hara .20 .50
15 Pat Penner .20 .50
16 Paolo Racicot .20 .50
17 Dan Rolfe .20 .50
18 Mike Sanderson .20 .50

1993-94 Fort Worth Fire

This 18-card set is similar in design to the Dallas Freeze issue of this year. The round cards are approximately the size of a hockey puck and came packaged in a plastic container with the team logo on the front. The sets were sold by the team's booster club at home games, and may have been made available through the mail.

COMPLETE SET (18) 2.40 75.00
1 Ron Aubrey 2.00 5.00
2 Derby Bognar 2.00 5.00
3 Reggie Brezeault 2.00 5.00
4 Jason Brousseau 2.00 5.00
5 Ty Eigner 2.00 5.00
6 Todd Huyber 2.00 5.00
7 Chris Jensen 2.00 5.00
8 Chad Johnson 2.00 5.00
9 Ryan Leschasin 2.00 5.00
10 Dominic Maltais 2.00 5.00
11 Mike McCormick 2.00 5.00
12 Patrick McGarry 2.00 5.00
13 Mike O'Hara 2.00 5.00
14 Sean Rowe 2.00 5.00
15 Mike Sanderson 2.50 6.00
16 Rob Striar 2.00 5.00
17 Scott Zygulski 2.00 5.00
18 Steve Harrison CO .75 2.00

1995-96 Fort Worth Fire

This 18-card team set features the Fort Worth Fire of the Central Hockey League. The set apparently was distributed by the booster club. In an unusual twist, the cards were not sold in team sets; instead, a 9-card assortment could be had for $3. Usually, it took three packs to assemble a complete set. The cards feature an action photo on the front, along with player bio and 1994-95 stats on the back.

COMPLETE SET (18) 4.00 10.00
1 Team Photo .30 .75
2 Bill McDonald CO .08 .25
3 Phil Groeneveld .20 .50
4 Vern Ray .20 .50
5 Steve Dykstra .30 .75
6 Trevor Burgess .20 .50
7 Scott Allen .20 .50
8 Sean Whyte .20 .50
9 Troy Frederick .20 .50
10 Troy Stephens .20 .50
11 Jeff Massey .20 .50
12 Dwight Mullins .20 .50
13 Kyle Reeves .40 1.00
14 Mike Gruttaduria .20 .50
15 Mark Hilton .20 .50
16 Brian Caruso .20 .50
17 Dennis Miller .20 .50
18 Steve Plouffe .30 .75

1996-97 Fort Worth Fire

This 18-card set features the CHL champion Fort Worth Fire. It was produced by the team and sold at the rink. The cards feature action photography surrounded by a condition sensitive black border. The player's name and number appear as well. The black and white back contains a player profile, but no numbering, hence the alphabetical listing below.

COMPLETE SET (18) 3.00 8.00
1 Malcolm Cameron .20 .50
2 Steve Carter .20 .50
3 Mike Sanderson .20 .50
4 Stephane Larocque .20 .50
5 Murray Hogg .20 .50
6 Bob Delorimiere .30 .75
7 Steve Plouffe .40 1.00
8 Glenn Painter .20 .50
9 Mark Strohack .20 .50
10 Brian Caruso .20 .50
11 Dwight Mullins .20 .50
12 Terry Menard .20 .50
13 Vern Ray .20 .50
14 Adam Robbins .20 .50
15 Mark O'Donnell .20 .50

16 Mike McCourt .20 .50
17 Ryan Black .20 .50
18 Bill McDonald CO .02 .10

1981-82 Fredericton Express

This 26-card set was issued by the team and endorsed by the Fredericton City Police, R.C.M.P., New Brunswick Highway Patrol, and New Brunswick Police Commission. The cards measure approximately 2 1/2" by 3 3/4" with a white border on the front. The fronts also carry a posed color player photo with the player's name printed below. The cards are numbered on the back.

COMPLETE SET (26) 8.00 20.00
1 Team Photo .20 .50
2 B.J. MacDonald .30 .75
3 Sylvain Cote .20 .50
4 Michel Bolduc .20 .50
5 Gary Lupul .20 .50
6 Clint Malarchuk .75 2.00
7 Tony Currie .20 .50
8 Tim Tookey .20 .50
9 Anders Eldebrink .40 1.00
10 Basil McRae .75 2.00
11 Kelly Elcombe .20 .50
12 Jacques Demers 1.25 3.00
13 Frank Caprice .40 1.00
14 Terry Johnson .20 .50
15 Grant Martin .20 .50
16 Andre Chartrain .20 .50
17 Marc Crawford 1.25 3.00
18 Gaston Therrien .20 .50
19 Andy Schliebener .20 .50
20 Christian Tanguay .20 .50
21 Art Rutland .20 .50
22 Jean MarcGaulin .20 .50
23 Neil Belland .20 .50
24 Andre Cote .20 .50
25 Jim MacRae .20 .50
26 Scott Beckingham .08 .25
Marty Flynn

1982-83 Fredericton Express

Sponsored by CFNB and Pepsi, this 26-card set measures approximately 2 1/2" by 3 3/4" and features posed, color player photos with white borders. The player's name and sponsor logos appear in the lower white margin.

COMPLETE SET (26) 8.00 20.00
1 Team Photo .40 1.00
2 B.J. MacDonald .30 .75
3 Sylvain Cote .30 .75
4 Michel Bolduc .20 .50
5 Gary Lupul .20 .50
6 Clint Malarchuk .75 2.00
7 Tony Currie .20 .50
8 Tim Tookey .20 .50
9 Anders Eldebrink .20 .50
10 Basil McRae 1.25 3.00
11 Kelly Elcombe .20 .50
12 Jacques Demers .75 2.00
13 Frank Caprice .60 1.50
14 Terry Johnson .20 .50
15 Grant Martin .20 .50
16 Andre Chartrain .20 .50
17 Marc Crawford .75 2.00
18 Gaston Therrien .20 .50
19 Andy Schliebener .20 .50
20 Christian Tanguay .20 .50
21 Art Rutland .20 .50
22 Jean-Marc Gaulin .20 .50
23 Neil Belland .20 .50
24 Andre Cote .20 .50
25 Jim MacRae .20 .50
26 Scott Beckingham TR .08 .25
and Marty Flynn TR

1983-84 Fredericton Express

This 27-card set measures 2 1/2" by 3 3/4" and features posed action color player photos with white borders. The player's name, position, and NHL affiliation appear below the picture in the white margin. The horizontal backs are white and carry Police and Express Tips in French and English.

COMPLETE SET (27) 6.00 15.00
1 Team Photo .40 1.00
2 Frank Caprice .60 1.50
3 Michel Dufour .30 .75
4 Brian Ford .30 .75
5 Jean-Marc Lanthier .20 .50
6 Jim Dobson .20 .50
7 Mike Hough .40 1.00
8 Rick Lapointe .30 .75
9 Michel Bolduc .20 .50
10 Christian Tanguay .20 .50
11 Tony Currie .20 .50
12 Moe Lemay .40 1.00
13 Bruce Holloway .20 .50
14 Neil Belland .20 .50
15 Richard Turmel .20 .50
16 Claude Julien .30 .75
17 Andre Chartrain .20 .50
18 Grant Martin .20 .50
19 Rejean Vignola .20 .50
20 Andre Cote .20 .50
21 Jean-Marc Gaulin .20 .50
22 Andy Schliebener .20 .50
23 Stu Kulak .30 .75
24 Mike Eagles .60 1.50
25 Earl Jessiman CO/GM .08 .25
26 Marty Flynn TR .08 .25
Scott Beckingham TR
NNO Checklist .20 .50

1984-85 Fredericton Express

This 28-card set measures approximately 2 1/2" by 3 3/4" and features posed color player photos against a white card face. The player's name, biography, position, and NHL affiliation appear in black print below the picture. Sponsor logos are in the lower corners. The horizontal backs are white and carry Police and Express Tips in French and English.

COMPLETE SET (28) 6.00 15.00
1 Dave Morrison .20 .50
2 Dave Shaw .40 1.00
3 Bruce Holloway .20 .50
4 Roger Haegglund .20 .50
5 Neil Belland .20 .50
6 Gord Donnelly .40 1.00
7 David Bruce .20 .50
8 Claude Julien .20 .50
9 Dan Wood .20 .50
10 Clint Malarchuk .75 2.00
11 Jere Gillis .20 .50
12 Mike Hough .40 1.00
13 Michel Bolduc .20 .50
14 Peter Loob .20 .50
15 Steve Driscoll .20 .50
16 Newell Brown .20 .50
17 Jim Dobson .20 .50
18 Wendell Young .75 2.00
19 Mark Kumpel .30 .75
20 Mike Eagles .40 1.00
21 Tom Thornbury .20 .50
22 Grant Martin .20 .50
23 Marc Crawford .40 1.00
24 Andy Schliebener .20 .50
25 Earl Jessiman CO/GM .08 .25
26 Yvon Vautour .20 .50
27 Craig Coxe .40 1.00
28 Blake Wesley .20 .50

1985-86 Fredericton Express

This 28-card set measures 2 1/2" by 3 3/4" and features posed color player photos against a white card face. The player's name, biography, position, and NHL affiliation appear in black print below the picture. Sponsor logos are in the lower corners. The horizontal backs are white and carry Police and Express Tips in French and English.

COMPLETE SET (28) 4.80 12.00
1 Scott Tottle .20 .50
2 David Bruce .20 .50
3 Team Photo .30 .75
4 Marc Crawford .40 1.00
5 Mike Stevens .20 .50
6 Gary Lupul .20 .50
7 Alain Lemieux .30 .75
8 Mike Hough .40 1.00
9 Tony Currie .20 .50
10 Dunc MacIntyre .20 .50
11 Jere Gillis .20 .50
12 Wendell Young .60 1.50
13 Jean-Marc Lanthier .20 .50
14 Ken Quinney .30 .75
15 Claude Julien .30 .75
16 Michel Petit .40 1.00
17 Luc Guenette .20 .50
18 Andy Schliebener .20 .50
19 Mark Kirton .20 .50
20 Gord Donnelly .30 .75
21 Tom Karalis .20 .50
22 Daniel Poudrier .20 .50
23 Neil Belland .20 .50
24 Dale Dunbar .20 .50
25 Marty Flynn TR .08 .25
Scott Beckingham TR
26 Jean-Marc Gaulin .20 .50
27 Al MacAdam .30 .75
28 Andre Savard CO/GM .20 .50

1986-87 Fredericton Express

This 26-card set measures 2 1/2" by 3 3/4" and features posed color player photos against a white card face. The player's name, biography, position, statistics, and NHL affiliation appear in black print below the picture. Sponsor logos are in the lower corners. The horizontal backs are white and carry public service messages in French and English. The cards are unnumbered and checklisted below in alphabetical order.

COMPLETE SET (26) 4.00 10.00
1 Jim Agnew .20 .50
2 Brian Bertuzzi .20 .50
3 David Bruce .20 .50
4 Frank Caprice .30 .75
5 Marc Crawford .30 .75
6 Steven Finn .30 .75
7 Marty Flynn TR .08 .25
Scott Beckingham TR
8 Jean-Marc Gaulin .20 .50
9 Scott Gordon .30 .75
10 Taylor Hall .20 .50
11 Yves Heroux .20 .50
12 Mike Hough .30 .75
13 Tom Karalis .20 .50
14 Mark Kirton .20 .50
15 Jean-Marc Lanthier .20 .50
16 Jean LeBlanc .20 .50
17 Brett MacDonald .20 .50
18 Duncan MacIntyre .20 .50
19 Greg Malone .20 .50
20 Terry Perkins .20 .50
21 Daniel Poudrier .20 .50
22 Jeff Rohlicek .20 .50
23 Andre Savard CO .20 .50
24 Mike Stevens .20 .50
25 Trevor Stienburg .20 .50
26 Team Photo .30 .75

1992-93 Fredericton Canadiens

Printed on thin card stock, these 28 standard-size cards feature borderless color player action photos on the fronts. Each has the player's name and uniform number printed near the bottom and carries the Professional Hockey Player's Association logo. The white horizontal back displays a black-and-white posed player head shot in the upper left. The player's name, uniform number, and biography appear in a rectangle in the upper right, along with the Canadiens and Stay in School logos. A stat table is placed beneath, and the Pepsi, Village, and Ben's logos at the bottom round out the card. The cards are unnumbered and checklisted below in alphabetical order.

COMPLETE SET (28) 4.80 12.00
1 Jesse Belanger .30 .75
2 Paulin Bordeleau CO .20 .50
3 Donald Brashear .30 .75
4 Patrik Carnback .20 .50
5 Eric Charron .20 .50
6 Frederic Chabot .40 1.00
7 Alain Cote .20 .50
8 Paul DiPietro .30 .75
9 Craig Ferguson .20 .50
10 Gerry Fleming .20 .50
11 Luc Gauthier .20 .50
12 Robert Guillet .20 .50
13 Patric Kjellberg .30 .75
14 Les Kuntar .30 .75
15 Ryan Kuwabara .20 .50
16 Patrick Langlois TR .02 .10
17 Steve Larouche .20 .50
18 Jacques Parent TR .02 .10
19 Charles Poulin .20 .50
20 Oleg Petrov .20 .50
21 Yves Sarault .20 .50
22 Pierre Sevigny .20 .50
23 Darcy Simon .20 .50
24 Turner Stevenson .30 .75
25 Tricolo (Mascot) .02 .10
26 Lindsay Vallis .20 .50
27 Steve Veilleux .20 .50
28 Title card .08 .25

1993-94 Fredericton Canadiens

Printed on thin card stock, this 29-card standard-size features 1993-94 Fredericton Canadiens of the AHL. The fronts display color action player photos framed by red borders. The player's name and number are printed in the border beneath the picture. The horizontal backs carry a black-and-white close-up photo, biography, statistics, and sponsor logos (Ben's Bakery, Village, and Pepsi). The cards are unnumbered and checklisted below in alphabetical order.

COMPLETE SET (29) 4.80 12.00
1 Brent Bilodeau .20 .50
2 Paulin Bordeleau CO .08 .25
3 Donald Brashear .30 .75
4 Martin Brochu .40 1.00
5 Craig Darby .20 .50
6 Kevin Darby .20 .50
7 Mario Doyon .20 .50
8 Craig Ferguson .20 .50
9 Craig Fiander .20 .50
10 Gerry Fleming .20 .50
11 Luc Gauthier ACO .02 .10
12 Robert Guillet .20 .50
13 Les Kuntar .25 .60
14 Ryan Kuwabara .20 .50
15 Patrick Langlois .20 .50
16 Marc Laniel .20 .50
17 Christian Lariviere .20 .50
18 Kevin O'Sullivan .20 .50
19 Denis Ouellete .20 .50
20 Jacques Parent THER .02 .10
21 Oleg Petrov .30 .75
22 Charles Poulin .20 .50
23 Christian Proulx .20 .50
24 Tony Prpic .20 .50
25 Yves Sarault .20 .50
26 Turner Stevenson .30 .75
27 Tricolo (Mascot) .02 .10
28 Lindsay Vallis .20 .50
29 Title Card .02 .10

1994-95 Fredericton Canadiens

Printed on thin card stock, this 30-card standard-size set features the 1994-95 Fredericton Canadiens of the AHL. The fronts display borderless color action photos. The player's number and position, as well as his name, are printed vertically down the left and right sides respectively. The cards are unnumbered and checklisted below in alphabetical order.

COMPLETE SET (30) 4.80 12.00
1 Louis Bernard .15 .40
2 Brent Bilodeau .20 .50
3 Paulin Bordeleau CO .15 .40
4 Donald Brashear .40 1.00
5 Martin Brochu .40 1.00
6 Valeri Bure .60 1.50
7 Jim Campbell .20 .50
8 Paul Chagnon .15 .40
9 Craig Conroy .30 .75
10 Craig Darby .20 .50
11 Dion Darling .15 .40
12 Craig Ferguson .15 .40
13 Scott Fraser .15 .40
14 Luc Gauthier ACO .02 .10
15 Patrick Labrecque .20 .50
16 Marc Lamothe .30 .75
17 Patrick Langlois .15 .40
18 Brad Layzelle .15 .40
19 Derek Maguire .15 .40
20 Chris Murray .20 .50
21 Kevin O'Sullivan .15 .40
22 Jacques Parent THER .02 .10
23 Christian Proulx .15 .40
24 Craig Rivet .20 .50
25 Yves Sarault .15 .40
26 Turner Stevenson .20 .50
27 Martin Sychra .15 .40
28 Tim Tisdale .15 .40
29 Tricolo (Mascot) .02 .10
30 David Wilkie .15 .40

1995-96 Fredericton Canadiens

This 29-card set features color action player photos of the Fredericton Canadiens of the AHL. The backs carry biographical information and player statistics. The cards are unnumbered and checklisted below in alphabetical order.

COMPLETE SET (29) 4.80 12.00
1 Louis Bernard .15 .40
2 Paulin Bordeleau CO .08 .25
3 Sebastien Bordeleau .20 .50
4 Martin Brochu .40 1.00
5 Jim Campbell .20 .50
6 Paul Chagnon .15 .40
7 Craig Conroy .30 .75
8 Keli Corpse .15 .40
9 Dion Darling .15 .40
10 Rory Fitzpatrick .15 .40
11 Scott Fraser .15 .40
12 Gaston Gingras .20 .50
13 David Grenier .15 .40
14 Harold Hersh .20 .50
15 Patrick Labrecque .30 .75
16 Marc Lamothe .30 .75
17 Patrick Langlois .15 .40
18 Alan Letang .20 .50
19 Alexei Lojkin .15 .40
20 Xavier Majic .15 .40
21 Chris Murray .20 .50
22 Jacques Parent .02 .10
23 Craig Rivet .20 .50
24 Mario Roberge .15 .40
25 Pierre Sevigny .20 .50
26 Tricolo (Mascot) .02 .10
27 Darcy Tucker .40 1.00
28 Adam Wiesel .15 .40
29 Luc Gauthier ACO .02 .10

1996-97 Fredericton Canadiens

This set features the Canadiens of the AHL. The set was produced by the team and sold at home games, and is notable for containing one of the earliest and toughest issues of Jose Theodore.

COMPLETE SET (30) 40.00 80.00
1 Sebastien Bordeleau .15 .40
2 Brad Brown .40 1.00
3 Earl Cronan .15 .40
4 Dion Darling .15 .40
5 Jimmy Drolet .15 .40
6 Gerry Fleming .40 1.00
7 Scott Fraser .15 .40
8 Francois Groleau .15 .40
9 Miloslav Guren .15 .40
10 Harold Hersh .40 1.00
11 Eric Houde .15 .40
12 Alan Letang .15 .40
13 David Ling .20 .50
14 Alexei Lojkin .15 .40
15 Boyd Olson .15 .40
16 Tony Prpic .15 .40
17 Jesse Rezansoff .15 .40
18 Craig Rivet .40 1.00
19 Pierre Sevigny .20 .50
20 Todd Sparks .15 .40
21 Jose Theodore 20.00 50.00
22 Tomas Vokoun 8.00 20.00
23 Adam Wiesel .15 .40
24 Paulin Bordeleau CO .02 .10
25 Luc Gauthier CO .02 .10
26 Patrick Langlois TR .02 .10
27 Paul Chagnon TR .02 .10
28 Jacques Parent TR .02 .10
29 Tricolo MAS .02 .10
30 Jolly Rancher .01

2000-01 Fresno Falcons

This set features the Falcons of the WCHL. It is believed that the set was a promotional giveaway sponsored by Carl's Jr. restaurants, but that has not been confirmed. The cards are unnumbered, however, and are listed below in alphabetical order.

COMPLETE SET (30) 8.00 20.00
1 Chris Albert .30 .75
2 Matt Alvey .40 1.00
3 Brad Both .30 .75
4 Brodie Coffin .30 .75
5 Kirk DeWaele .30 .75
6 Sheldon Flaman .40 1.00
7 Terry Friesen .40 1.00
8 Glen Gulutzan .30 .75
9 Don Malko .30 .75
10 Mike Mathers .30 .75
11 Mike McCourt .30 .75
12 David Mitchell .30 .75
13 Kory Mullin .40 1.00
14 Cory Murphy .30 .75
15 Kris Porter .30 .75
16 Chris Skoryna .30 .75
17 Adrian Smith .40 1.00
18 Greg Spenrath .30 .75
19 Rejean Stringer .30 .75
20 Darren Wetherill .30 .75
21 Terry Friesen SO .40 1.00
22 Blaine Moore CO .10 .25
23 Freddie Falcon MASCOT .04 .10
24 Mike Carey TR .04 .10
25 Fresno Falcons Celebration .20 .50
26 TV-47 ANCHORS .01 .05
27 Star-101 DJ's SPONSOR .01 .05
28 Mark Kuntz EM .04 .10
29 Brian Clark .30 .75
30 Team Photo .20 .50

2001-02 Fresno Falcons

This set features the Falcons of the WCHL. It was issued as a promotional giveaway at one home game in March, 2002.

COMPLETE SET (30) 8.00 20.00
1 Brad Both .40 1.00
2 Brodie Coffin .40 1.00
3 Kirk DeWaele .40 1.00
4 Joe Frederick .40 1.00
5 Terry Friesen .62 1.56
6 Glen Gulutzan .40 1.00
7 Dale Junkin .40 1.00
8 Dan Kerluke .40 1.00
9 Mike Mathers .40 1.00
10 Mike McCourt .40 1.00
11 David Mitchell .40 1.00
12 Kory Mullin .40 1.00
13 Cory Murphy .40 1.00
14 Kris Porter .40 1.00
15 Chris Skoryna .40 1.00
16 Adrian Smith .20 .50
17 Greg Spenrath .40 1.00
18 Ryan Tocher .40 1.00
19 Alex Todd .40 1.00
20 Jason Weaver .40 1.00
21 Darren Wetherill .40 1.00
22 Blaine Moore CO .10 .25
23 Game Winner Action Photo .10 .25
24 Mike Carey TR .10
25 Mark Kuntz EQMG .10
26 Freddie Falcon MASCOT .10
27 Team Photo .20 .50
28 Carls Jr. .01 .01
29 Fresno Bee .01 .01
30 KRZR 103.7 .01 .01

2002-03 Fresno Falcons

COMPLETE SET (25) 20.00
1 Checklist .01
2 Kevin Haupt 1.00
3 Chris Kenady 1.00
4 Cory Murphy 1.00
5 Mike Mathers 1.00
6 Alex Todd 1.00
7 Brad Both 1.50
8 Steve Lowe 1.00
9 Scott Borders 1.00
10 Jordan Landry 1.00
11 Colin Embley 1.00
12 Glen Gulutzan 1.00
13 Kirk DeWaele 1.00
14 Jason Weaver 1.00
15 Drew Schoneck 1.50
16 Mark Gowan 1.50
17 Terry Friesen 1.50
18 Joe Frederick 1.00
19 Kayle Short 1.00
20 Jason McBain 1.00
21 Kris Porter 1.00
22 Blaine Moore HCO .10
23 Greg Spenrath ACO .10
24 Happy Star .01
25 KRZR-103.7 .01

2003-04 Fresno Falcons

This set was produced by Choice Marketing and sold at home games.

COMPLETE SET (25) 10.00
1 Scott Borders .50
2 Mike Brusseau .75
3 Blair Clarance .50
4 Terry Friesen .75
5 Nathan Horne .50
6 Mark Jackson .50
7 Michael Kiesman .50
8 Jordan Landry .50
9 Mike Mathers .50
10 Blaine Moore CO .50
11 Kory Mullin .50
12 Dominic Periard .50
13 Kris Porter .50
14 Boris Protsenko .50
15 Riku Rahikainen .50
16 Tapio Sammalkangas .50
17 Mike Sandbeck .50
18 Nolan Schaefer .75
19 Drew Schoneck .50
20 Greg Spenrath CO .50
21 Adam Stefishen .50
22 Kevin Truelson .50
23 Jason Weaver .50
24 John Wroblewski .50
25 Mascot .10
NNO Checklist .01

2004-05 Fresno Falcons

COMPLETE SET (TBD) 25.00
1 David Brisson 1.00
2 Clint Cabana 1.00
3 John Dahl 1.00
4 Thierry Douville 1.00
5 Lanny Gare 1.00
6 Shawn Heaphy 1.00
7 Brett Jaeger 2.00
8 Tomas Jasko 1.00
9 Mike Kiesman 1.00
10 Derek Krestanovich 1.00
11 Simon Lajeunesse 2.00
12 Jim Lorentz 1.00
13 Matt O'Dette 1.00
14 Wes Rypien 1.00
15 Curtis Sheptak 1.00
16 Charles Simard 1.00
17 Greg Spenrath 1.00
18 Shaun Sutter 1.00
19 Dan Tessier 1.00
20 Kevin Truelson 1.00
21 Dustin VanBallegooie 1.00
22 Jason Weaver 1.00
23 John Wroblewski 1.00

2005-06 Fresno Falcons

COMPLETE SET (25) 20.00

2003-04 Gatineau Olympiques

COMPLETE SET (27) 12.00
1 Gabriel Bouthillette .75
2 Scott Brophy .50
3 Bruno Champagne .50
4 Yanick Charron .50
5 Dominic D'Amour .50
6 Jean-Michel Daoust .50
7 Philippe Dupuis .50
8 Vincent Duriau .50
9 Guillaume Fournier .50
10 Martin Frechette .50
11 Nick Fugere .50
12 Derrick Kent .50
13 Olivier Labelle .50
14 Guillaume Labrecque .50
15 Christian Laroche .50
16 Doug O'Brien .50
17 Keven Petit .50
18 Petr Pohl .50
19 Nicolas Ranger .50
20 Maxime Robert .50
21 Sam Roberts .50
22 Maxime Rousseau .50
23 Maxime Talbot .50
24 David Tremblay .50
25 Martin Vagner .50
26 Francis Wathier .50
27 Lance Woodman .50

2004-05 Gatineau Olympiques

A total of 300 team sets were produced.

COMPLETE SET (24) 12.00
1 David Tremblay .75
2 Martin Frechette .50
3 Sam Roberts .50
4 Scott Brophy .50
5 Olivier Laliberte .50
6 Francis Wathier .50
7 Nicolas Ranger .50
8 Keven Petit .50
9 Jonathan Carrier .50
10 Nick Fugere .50
11 Olivier Labelle .50
12 Maxime Rousseau .50
13 Pierre-Luc Lessard .50
14 Brett Morrison .50
15 David Krejci 1.00
16 Petr Pohl .50
17 Ryan Graham .50
18 Guillaume Labrecque .50
19 Cam Fergus .50
20 Dave Starenky .50
21 Bryan Wilson .50
22 Geoffrey Walker .50
23 Francis Gagnon .50
24 Luke Pelham .50

2005-06 Gatineau Olympiques

COMPLETE SET (28) 5.00 12.00
1 David Tremblay .20 .50
2 Olivier Laliberte .20 .50
3 Guillaume Labrecque .20 .50
4 Nick Fugere .20 .50
5 Keven Petit .20 .50
6 Maxime Rousseau .20 .50
7 Claude Giroux .20 .50
8 David Krejci .40 1.00
9 Bryan Wilson .20 .50
10 Martin Frechette .20 .50
11 Jonathan Carrier .20 .50
12 Pierre-Luc Lessard .20 .50
13 Brad Tesink .20 .50
14 Michael Stinziani .20 .50
15 Colin Escott .20 .50
16 Benoit Gervais .20 .50
17 Maxime Malette .20 .50
18 Michel Champagne .20 .50
19 Maxime Langelier-Parent .20 .50
20 Brett Morrison .20 .50
21 Mathieu Curadeau .20 .50
22 Alexandre Boivin .20 .50
23 Bryan Main .20 .50
24 Darryl Smith .20 .50
25 Antonin Manavian .20 .50
26 Matthew Pistilli .20 .50
27 Philippe Cote .20 .50
28 Mascot .02 .10

2006-07 Gatineau Olympiques

COMPLETE SET (28) 8.00 15.00
1 Martin Frechette .20 .50
2 Olivier Laliberte .30 .75
3 Maxime Mallette .20 .50
4 Jonathan Carrier .20 .50
5 Viatcheslav Trukhno .20 .50
6 Steven Delisle .20 .50
7 Daniel Sauve .20 .50
8 Brad Tesink .20 .50
9 Keven Petit .20 .50
10 Brett Morrison .20 .50
11 Jean-Philipp Chabot .20 .50
12 Alexandre Boivin .20 .50
13 Claude Giroux .40 1.00
14 Bryan Main .20 .50
15 Paul Byron .20 .50
16 Benoit Gervais .20 .50
17 Matthew Pistilli .20 .50
18 Darryl Smith .20 .50
19 Travis Stacey .20 .50
20 Michael Stinziani .20 .50
21 Pierre-Marc Guilbault .20 .50
22 Alexandre Touchette .20 .50
23 Ken Dufresne .20 .50
24 Dave Bertrand-Duclos .20 .50
25 Chad Loikets .20 .50
26 David Kveton .20 .50
27 Ryan Mior .30 .75
28 Tyler Pugh .20 .50

1977-78 Granby Vics

This odd-sized (3 1/2 X7") black and white set features the Granby Vics of the LMJHQ. The card fronts are in a horizontal format, with the left half of the card containing a player photo, and the right featuring a player bio and an ad from a local business. The backs are blank and the cards are unnumbered. They are presented below alphabetically.

COMPLETE SET (20) 17.50 35.00
1 Mario Beauregard 1.00 2.00
2 Luc Breton 1.00 2.00
3 Daniel Caron 1.50 3.00
4 Mario Casavant 1.00 2.00
5 Marc Courtemanche 1.00 2.00
6 Yves Courtemanche 1.00 2.00
7 Sylvain d'Amour 1.00 2.00
8 Rene Delorme 1.00 2.00
9 Denis Dumas Jr. 1.00 2.00
10 Pierre Grondin 1.00 2.00
11 Andre Hebert 1.00 2.00
12 Marcel Lachance 1.00 2.00
13 Andre Lemieux 1.00 2.00
14 Pierre Lepage 1.00 2.00
15 Daniel Menard 1.00 2.00
16 Jacques Pomerleau 1.00 2.00
17 Mario Roy 1.00 2.00
18 Alain Tetrault 1.00 2.00
19 Paul Thibert 1.00 2.00
20 Luc Turgeon 1.00 2.00

1996-97 Grand Rapids Griffins

This odd-sized set (2 3/4" by 4") was produced by Meijer Exhibit Graphic Design and sponsored by Kodak and Jim Hill Photography. The set was released in five series of five cards each (plus one title card per series) over the course of the club's inaugural season. As the cards are unnumbered, they are listed below in alphabetical order.

COMPLETE SET (30) 20.00 50.00
1 Kevyn Adams 1.25 3.00
2 Dave Allison CO .40 1.00
3 Danton Cole .75 2.00
4 Keli Corpse .75 2.00
5 Pavol Demitra 4.00 10.00
6 Griff .20 .50
Mascot
7 Ben Hankinson .75 2.00
8 Stanislav Jasecko .75 2.00
10 Sean McCann .75 2.00
11 Cory Johnson .75 2.00
12 Jamie Linden .75 2.00
13 Don McSween .75 2.00
14 Tyler Moss 1.50 4.00
15 Jeff Nelson .75 2.00
16 Todd Nelson .75 2.00
17 Michel Picard .75 2.00
18 Bruce Ramsay .75 2.00
19 Pokey Reddick 1.50 4.00
20 Chad Remackel .75 2.00
21 Travis Richards .75 2.00
22 Matt Ruchty .75 2.00
23 Darcy Simon .75 2.00
24 1996 Inaugural Face-Off .20 .50
25 1996/97 Inaugural Team .75 2.00
26 Van Andel Arena .20 .50
NNO Title card 1 .07 .20
NNO Title card 2 .07 .20
NNO Title card 3 .07 .20
NNO Title card 4 .07 .20
NNO Title card 5 .07 .20

1997-98 Grand Rapids Griffins

Little is known about this set beyond the confirmed checklist. Additional information can be forwarded to hockeymag@beckett.com.

COMPLETE SET (24) 4.00 10.00
1 Michel Picard .30 .75
2 Tom Ashe .20 .50
3 Greg Clancy .20 .50
4 Danton Cole .20 .50
5 Ian Gordon .20 .50
6 Mark Greig .20 .50
7 Shane Hnidy .30 .75
8 Kerry Huffman .20 .50
9 Glen Metropolit .40 1.00
10 Todd Nelson .20 .50
11 Ed Patterson .20 .50
12 Bruce Ramsay .20 .50
13 Eldon Reddick .30 .75
14 Travis Richards .20 .50
15 Matt Ruchty .20 .50
16 Darcy Simon .20 .50
17 Brian Sullivan .20 .50
18 Sean Tallaire .20 .50
19 Dean Trboyevich .20 .50
20 Jason Weaver .20 .50
21 Dave Allison HCO .02 .10
22 Curtis Hunt ACO .02 .10
23 Griff Mascot .02 .10
24 PHPA Web Site .01

1998-99 Grand Rapids Griffins

Little is known about this IHL team set other than the confirmed checklist. It is believed, however, to be an oversized issue. Any additional information can be forwarded to hockeymag@beckett.com

COMPLETE SET (25) 4.80 12.00
1 Tom Ashe .20 .50
2 Jared Bednar .20 .50
3 Radim Bicanek .30 .75
4 Anders Bjork .20 .50
5 Aris Brimanis .20 .50
6 Danton Cole .20 .50
7 Jed Fiebelkorn .20 .50
8 Ian Gordon .20 .50
9 Todd Hlushko .20 .50
10 Kerry Huffman .20 .50
11 Neil Little .75 2.00
12 Glen Metropolit .40 1.00
13 Vaclav Nedomansky .20 .50
14 Robert Petrovicky .30 .75
15 Bruce Ramsay .20 .50
16 Travis Richards .20 .50
17 Gaetan Royer .20 .50
18 Darren Rumble .20 .50
19 Maxim Spiridonov .20 .50
20 Andrei Vasilyev .20 .50
21 Curtis Hunt ACO .02 .10
22 Guy Charron HCO .02 .10
23 Griff Mascot .02 .10
24 The Zone .01
25 PHPA Web Site .01

1999-00 Grand Rapids Griffins

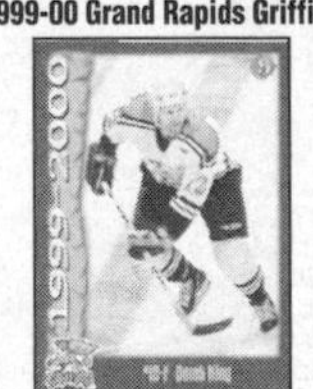

This set features the Griffins of the IHL. The cards were produced by SplitSecond and were sold by the team at its souvenir stands.

COMPLETE SET (25) 6.00 15.00
1 Viachaslav Butsayev .20 .50
2 Guy Charron CO .08 .25
3 Ivan Ciernik .20 .50
4 Danton Cole CO .08 .25
5 John Emmons .20 .50
6 Mike Fountain .30 .75
7 Rick Goldman .20 .50
8 Konstantin Gorovikov .20 .50
9 John Gruden .20 .50
10 Curtis Hunt CO .08 .25
11 Jani Hurme 1.25 3.00
12 Derek King .20 .50
13 Kevin Miller .20 .50
14 Chris Neil .40 1.00
15 Todd Nelson .20 .50
16 Ed Patterson .20 .50
17 Michel Picard .20 .50
18 Phillippe Plante .20 .50
19 Karel Rachunek .30 .75
20 Travis Richards .20 .50
21 Yves Sarault .20 .50
22 Petr Schastlivy .60 1.50
23 Andrei Sryubko .20 .50
24 Chris Szysky .20 .50
25 Dave Van Drunen .20 .50

2000-01 Grand Rapids Griffins

This set features the Griffins of the IHL. The cards were produced by SplitSecond and were sold by the team at home games.

COMPLETE SET (25) 4.00 10.00
1 Keith Aldridge .14 .35
2 Sean Berens .14 .35
3 Vyacheslav Butsayev .14 .35
4 Mathieu Chouinard .40 1.00
5 Ivan Ciernik .14 .35
6 Ilja Demidov .14 .35
7 Mike Fountain .20 .50
8 Sean Gagnon .14 .35
9 Konstantin Gorovikov .14 .35
10 John Gruden .14 .35
11 Derek King .20 .50
12 Joel Kwiatkowski .14 .35
13 Marty McSorley .40 1.00
14 Kip Miller .20 .50
15 Chris Neil .40 1.00
16 David Oliver .14 .35
17 Ed Patterson .14 .35
18 Travis Richards .14 .35
19 David Roberts .14 .35
20 Petr Schastlivy .40 1.00
21 Chris Szysky .14 .35
22 Todd White .20 .50
23 Bruce Cassidy CO .10 .25
24 Danton Cole CO .10 .25
25 Griff MASCOT .04 .10

2001-02 Grand Rapids Griffins

This set features the Griffins of the AHL. The cards were created by Choice Marketing and were issued both as a promotional giveaway, and later were sold at the team's store. A total of 5,000 sets were produced.

COMPLETE SET (24) 4.80 12.00
1 Julien Vauclair .20 .50
2 John Gruden .20 .50
3 Wade Brookbank .20 .50
4 Kip Miller .20 .50
5 Alexandre Giroux .20 .50
6 Hugo Boisvert .20 .50
7 James Black .20 .50
8 Steve Martins .20 .50
9 David Hymovitz .20 .50
10 Chris Szysky .20 .50
11 Petr Schastlivy .40 1.00
12 Jeff Ulmer .20 .50
13 Josh Langfeld .20 .50
14 Chris Kelly .20 .50
15 Joe Murphy .20 .50
16 Travis Richards .20 .50
17 Martin Prusek .62 1.56
18 Chris Bala .20 .50
19 Dave Van Drunen .20 .50
20 Jason Doig .20 .50
21 Joel Kwiatkowski .20 .50
22 Mathieu Chouinard .62 1.56
23 Toni Dahlman .20 .50
24 Bruce Cassidy CO .04 .11
25 Gene Reilly ACO .04 .11
26 Griff MASCOT .04 .11

2002-03 Grand Rapids Griffins

This series was produced by Choice Marketing and, reportedly, was subject to a very odd distribution in which part of this set was given away as a game night promotion and the remaining cards were sold at the team's pro shop. The full set was never sold as a single unit. If anyone knows exactly how these were broken up, please write us at hockeymag@beckett.com.

COMPLETE SET (27) 5.00 12.00
1 Bryan Adams .30 .75
2 Sean Avery .75 2.00
3 Paul Ballantyne .30 .75
4 Ryan Barnes .30 .75
5 Gregor Baumgartner .30 .75
6 Patrick Boileau .30 .75
7 Hugo Boisvert .30 .75
8 Sheldon Brookbank .30 .75
9 Ed Campbell .30 .75
10 Danton Cole CO .02 .10
11 Rob Collins .30 .75
12 Nick Greenough .30 .75
13 Griff MASCOT .02 .10
14 Danny Groulx .30 .75
15 Derek King .30 .75
16 Tomas Kopecky .30 .75
17 Marc Lamothe .30 .75
18 Joey MacDonald .30 .75
19 Mark Mowers .30 .75
20 Todd Nelson .30 .75
21 Michel Picard .30 .75
22 Travis Richards .30 .75
23 Nathan Robinson .30 .75
24 Stacy Roest .30 .75
25 Tim Skarperud .30 .75
26 Dave Van Drunen .30 .75
27 Shoe Carnival Ad .01 .05

2003-04 Grand Rapids Griffins

This set was issued as a promotional giveaway over the course of several home games. As a result, it is very difficult to find in complete set form. We've recently confirmed five additional cards in the checklist. Thanks to collector Dale Spengler.

COMPLETE SET (29) 20.00 30.40
1 Ryan Barnes .60 1.50
2 Hugo Boisvert .60 1.50
3 Darryl Bootland .75 2.00
4 David Brisson .60 1.50
5 Matt Ellis .60 1.50
6 Danny Groulx .60 1.50
7 Jiri Hudler 2.00 5.00
8 Derek King .60 1.50
9 Tomas Kopecky 1.25 3.00
10 Niklas Kronwall 2.00 5.00
11 Marc Lamothe .75 2.00
12 Joey MacDonald 1.25 3.00
13 Kevin Miller .75 2.00
14 Mark Mowers .75 2.00
15 Anders Myrvold .60 1.50
16 Michel Picard .60 1.50
17 Travis Richards .60 1.50
18 Nathan Robinson .75 2.00
19 Aaron Schneekloth .60 1.50
20 Tim Skarperud .60 1.50
21 David Van Drunen .60 1.50
22 Danton Cole CO .10 .25
23 Greg Ireland ACO .02 .10
24 Brad Thompson EQM .02 .10
25 Jiri Hudler 2.00 5.00
26 Kory Karlander .60 1.50
27 Jeff Nelson .60 1.50
28 Rob Snitzer TR .02 .10
29 Shoe Carnival Ad .02 .10

2004-05 Green Bay Gamblers

This set of the USHL Gamblers is noteworthy for including the first card of the fifth overall pick from 2003, Blake Wheeler.

COMPLETE SET (28) 25.00
1 Jeff Carlson 1.00
2 Corey Couturier 1.00
3 Derek Danowski 1.00
4 Jeremy Dehner 1.00
5 Spencer Dillon 1.00
6 Justin Johnson 1.00
7 Carl Lackey ACO .10
8 Tyler Lehrke 1.00
9 Joe Long 1.00
10 Mark Magnowski 1.00
11 Mark Mazzoleni CO .10
12 Andrew Meyer 1.00
13 Brad Miller 1.00
14 Ryan Peterson 1.00
15 Garren Reisweber 1.00
16 Daniel Rosen 1.00
17 Billy Smith 1.00
18 Chris Stansik 1.00
19 Mark Stockdale 1.00
20 Luke Strand ACO .10
21 Dan Sturges 1.00
22 Garrett Suter 1.00
23 Blake Wheeler 3.00
24 Michael Zacharias 1.00
25 Suter/Dehner/Sturges 1.00
26 Missconducts 1.00
27 Mask Card 1.00
28 Mini Plan .01

1991-92 Greensboro Monarchs

This set features the Monarchs of the ECHL. The cards feature borderless, posed and action color player photos. The player's name and position appear on a mustard-colored hockey stick design at the bottom. The backs are subdivided by a red stripe and carry a close-up picture with biographical information above the stripe, and statistics and career highlights below it. The cards are unnumbered and checklisted below in alphabetical order.

COMPLETE SET (19) 3.00 8.00
1 Rob Bateman .25 .60
2 Phil Berger .20 .50
3 Mike Butters .20 .50
4 John Devereaux .20 .50
5 Eric Dubois .20 .50
6 Todd Gordon .20 .50
7 Chris Laganas .20 .50
8 Eric LeMarque .20 .50
9 Timo Makela .20 .50
10 Greg Menges .20 .50
11 Daryl Noren .20 .50
12 Peter Sentner .20 .50
13 Boyd Sutton .20 .50
14 Nick Vitucci .25 .60
15 Shawn Wheeler .20 .50
16 Scott White .20 .50
17 Chris Wolanin .20 .50
18 Dean Zayonce .20 .50
19 Team Photo .20 .50
(Photo of Jeff Brubaker CO on back)

1992-93 Greensboro Monarchs

Sponsored by RBI Sports Cards Inc., this 19-card standard-size set features full-bleed, color, action player photos. The player's name and position appear in a blue and red stripe near the bottom. The backs display a close-up picture alongside biographical information. A red stripe below the photo divides the card in half and serves as a heading for statistics. A player profile appears below the statistics.

COMPLETE SET (19) 3.00 8.00
1 Team Photo .30 .75
2 Chris Wolanin .20 .50
3 Bill Horn .20 .50
4 Brock Woods .20 .50
5 Phil Berger .20 .50
6 Dan Bylsma .20 .50
7 Davis Payne .30 .75
8 Wayne Muir .20 .50
9 Andrei Iakovenko .20 .50
10 Roger Larche .20 .50
11 Jamie Nicolls .20 .50
12 Darryl Noren .20 .50
13 Todd Gordon .20 .50
14 Claude Maillet .20 .50
15 Dave Burke .20 .50
16 Jamie Steer .25 .60
17 Greg Capson .20 .50
18 Chris Lappin .20 .50
19 Greg Menges .20 .50

1993-94 Greensboro Monarchs

This 16-card set of the Greensboro Monarchs of the ECHL was produced by RBI Sportscards. It is similar in design to the Raleigh Icecaps issue from the same year. The cards feature an action photo on the front, while the backs include career stats.

COMPLETE SET (16) 2.00 5.00
1 Phil Berger .20 .50
2 Trevor Burgess .15 .40
3 Dan Bylsma .20 .50
4 Greg Capson .15 .40
5 Brendan Creagh .15 .40
6 Dan Gravelle .15 .40
7 Sebastien LaPlante .15 .40
8 Savo Mitrovic .15 .40
9 Tom Newman .15 .40
10 Jamie Nicolls .15 .40
11 Davis Payne .20 .50
12 Stig Salomonsson .15 .40
13 Sverre Sears .15 .40
14 Chris Valicevic .15 .40
15 John Young .15 .40
16 Dean Zayonce .15 .40

1994-95 Greensboro Monarchs

This 20-card set of the Greensboro Monarchs of the ECHL was again produced by RBI Sportscards. This year's set mimics the design used by Pinnacle in 1993-94, although the photography lacks somewhat in the area of clarity. The backs are numbered, and contain stats for 1993-94. The sets apparently were not sold by the team; speculation suggests the booster club was in charge of distribution.

COMPLETE SET (20) 4.00 10.00
1 Dean Zayonce .20 .50
2 Jeremy Stevenson .20 .50
3 Glenn Stewart .20 .50
4 Peter Skudra .40 1.00
5 Chad Seibel .20 .50
6 Sverre Sears .20 .50
7 Howie Rosenblatt .40 1.00
8 Hugo Proulx .20 .50
9 Davis Payne .20 .50
10 Ron Pasco .20 .50
11 Monte MASCOT .02 .10
12 Scott McKay .20 .50
13 Arturs Kupaks .20 .50
14 Bill Horn .20 .50
15 Dwayne Gylywoychuk .20 .50
16 Jeff Gabriel .20 .50
17 Doug Evans .20 .50
18 Mark DeSantis .20 .60
19 Brendan Creagh .20 .50
20 Phil Berger .20 .50

1999-00 Greensboro Generals

This set features the Generals of the ECHL. The cards were produced by the team and sold at the souvenir stands.

COMPLETE SET (26) 4.00 10.00
1 Ian Walterson .15 .40
2 Clay Awe .15 .40
3 Sal Manganaro .15 .40
4 Oleg Timchenko .15 .40
5 David Whitworth .15 .40
6 T.J. Tanberg .15 .40
7 Keith O'Connell .15 .40
8 Tracy Egeland .15 .40
9 Igor Boiko .15 .40
10 Martin Galik .15 .40
11 Dean Shmyr .15 .40
12 Juraj Slovak .15 .40
13 Aniket Dhadphale .15 .40
14 Dean Zayonce .15 .40
15 Alexei Krovopuskov .15 .40
16 Van Burgess .15 .40
17 Matt Eisler .15 .40
18 Justin Cardwell .15 .40
19 Joel Irwin .15 .40
20 Wes Swinson .15 .40
21 Francis Larivee .30 .75
22 40th Anniversary Puck Drop .15 .40
23 Group Celebrates .15 .40
24 Settling Differences .75 2.00
25 Bill Flynn .15 .40
26 Greensboro Generals CL .08 .25

2001-02 Greensboro Generals

This set features the Generals of the ECHL. The sets were only available to members of the Generals' Kids Club. Reportedly, just 250 sets were made, making it one of the toughest minor league sets ever issued.

COMPLETE SET (20) 16.00 40.00
1 Daniel Passero .80 2.00
2 Rob Sandrock 1.20 3.00
3 Sal Manganaro .80 2.00
4 Vladislav Serov .80 2.00
5 Jarrett Thompson .80 2.00
6 Ryan Kummu .80 2.00
7 David Whitworth .80 2.00
8 Brian Loney .80 2.00
9 Chris Bell .80 2.00
10 Casey Kesselring .80 2.00
11 Shaun Peet .80 2.00
12 Jason Metcalfe .80 2.00
13 Chris Brassard .80 2.00
14 Dion Lassu .80 2.00
15 Jason Robinson .80 2.00
16 Jonathan Forest .80 2.00
17 Craig Stahl .80 2.00
18 Bujar Amidovski 1.20 3.00
19 Graeme Townshend CO .40 1.00
20 Sarge MASCOT .40 1.00

2002-03 Greensboro Generals RBI

COMPLETE SET (18) 15.00
1 Rod Aldoff 1.00
2 Chris Allen 1.00
3 Alex Andreyev 1.00
4 Chris Bell 1.00
5 Daniel Berthiaume 1.50
6 Shane Campbell 1.00
7 Matt Chandler 1.00
8 Kurt Drummond 1.00
9 Sam Ftorek 1.00
10 Pete Gardiner 1.00
11 Kevin Grimes 1.00
12 Olaf Kjenstad 1.00
13 Roman Marakhovski 1.00
14 Jay Murphy 1.00
15 Geno Parrish 1.00
16 Juraj Slovak 1.00
17 Matt Turek 1.00
18 David Whitworth 1.00

2003-04 Greensboro Generals

COMPLETE SET (16) 15.00
177 Alex Andreyev 1.00
178 Mike Bayrack 1.00
179 Daniel Berthiaume 1.50
180 Matt Chandler 1.00
181 Kurt Drummond 1.00
182 Matt Elich 1.00
183 Eric Fortier 1.00
184 Pete Gardiner 1.00
185 Joe Gerbe 1.00
186 Kevin Grimes 1.00
187 Jamie Hodson 1.50
188 Geno Parrish 1.00
189 Tom Reimann 1.00
190 Dean Shmyr 1.00
191 Matt Turek 1.00
192 Mark Turner 1.00

2001-02 Greenville Grrrowl

This set features the terribly named Grrrowl of the ECHL. The set was handed out as a promotional giveaway at a game in February, 2002. The cards are unnumbered, but they are numbered on a checklist card. The listing below mirrors that checklist.

COMPLETE SET (24) 9.78 24.44
1 John Marks CO .20 .50
2 Nick Vitucci ACO .20 .50
3 Eric Lind .40 1.00
4 Judd Stauss .40 1.00
5 Eric Van Acker .40 1.00
6 Roger Trudeau .40 1.00
7 Jason Windle .40 1.00
8 Sean Venedam .80 2.00
9 Jay Langager .40 1.00
10 Steve Rymsha .40 1.00
11 Jonathan Roy .80 2.00
12 Colin Pepperall .40 1.00
13 Kevin Bergin .40 1.00
14 David Bell .40 1.00
15 Damon Whitten .40 1.00
16 Ryan Stewart .40 1.00
17 Martin Masa .40 1.00
18 David Kaczowka .40 1.00
19 Simon Gamache .80 2.00
20 Tyrone Garner .80 2.00
21 Jayme Platt .40 1.00
22 Chad Nelson .40 1.00
23 Grrruff MASCOT .10 .25
24 Greenville Grrrowl CL .10 .25

2002-03 Greenville Grrrowl

COMPLETE SET (23) 20.00
1 Michael Garnett 2.00
2 Paul Flache 1.00
3 Rico Fatticci 1.00
4 Matt Demarski 1.00
5 Tyler Deis 1.00
6 Alexandre Burrows 1.00
7 Josh Legge 1.00
8 David Kaczowka 1.00
9 Mike Henderson 1.00
10 Grrruff MASCOT .10
11 Mark Gouett 1.00
12 Jonathan Gauthier 1.00
13 Judd Medak 1.00
14 Dan McIntyre 1.00
15 Martin Masa 1.00
16 John Marks HCO .10
17 Chris Lynch 1.00
18 Eric Lind 1.00
19 Krzysztof Wieckowski 1.00
20 Nick Vitucci ACO .10
21 Eric Van Acker 1.00
22 John Nail 1.00
23 Checklist .01

2003-04 Greenville Grrrowl

We've recently confirmed the existence of a 24th card in the set of John Nail. Thanks to collector Dale Spengler.

COMPLETE SET (24) 25.00
1 Stacey Bauman 1.00
2 Daniel Boisclair 3.00
3 Steve Burgess 1.00
4 Michael Chin 1.00
5 Bob Cunningham 1.00
6 Randy Dagenais 1.00
7 Robin Delacoure 1.00
8 Matt Demarski 1.00
9 Mike Henderson 1.00
10 Troy Ilijow 1.00
11 Han-Sung Kim 2.00
12 Scott Kirton 1.00
13 Jeremy Kyte 1.00
14 Bryan Lachapelle 1.00
15 David Lizotte 1.00
16 Jason Metcalfe 1.00
17 Mike Nelson 1.00
18 Michel Robinson 2.00
19 Russell Spence 1.00
20 Ryan Stewart 1.00
21 Jonathan Zion 1.50
22 John Marks CO .10
23 Team Photo .10
24 John Nail

1993-94 Guelph Storm

Sponsored by Domino's Pizza and printed by Slapshot Images Ltd., this standard size 31-card set features the 1993-94 Guelph Storm. On a geometrical blue and grey background, the fronts feature color action player photos with thin black borders. The player's name, position and team name, as well as the producer's logo, appear on the front.

COMPLETE SET (31) 4.80 12.00
1 Title Card .15 .40
2 Jeff O'Neill .60 1.50
3 Mark McArthur .20 .50
4 Kayle Short .15 .40
5 Ryan Risidore .15 .40
6 Mike Rusk .15 .40
7 Regan Stocco .15 .40
8 Duane Harmer .15 .40
9 Sylvain Cloutier .15 .40
10 Eric Landry .15 .40
11 Jamie Wright .20 .50
12 Todd Norman .15 .40
13 Mike Pittman .15 .40
14 Ken Belanger .30 .75
15 Viktor Reuta .15 .40
16 Mike Prokopec .15 .40
17 Jeff Williams .20 .50
18 Chris Skoryna .15 .40
19 Stephane Lefebvre .15 .40
20 Jeff Cowan .20 .50
21 Murray Hogg .15 .40
22 Andy Adams .15 .40
23 Todd Bertuzzi 1.25 3.00
24 Grant Pritchett .15 .40
25 Rumun Ndur .20 .50
26 Jeff O'Neill .60 1.50
27 Paul Brydges ACO .02 .10
28 John Lovell CO .02 .10
29 Team Photo/CL .15 .40
30 Domino's Pizza .02 .10
NNO Slapshot Ad Card .02 .10

1994-95 Guelph Storm

Sponsored by Domino's Pizza and Burger King, and printed by Slapshot Images Inc., this 31-card standard-size set features the Storm of the OHL. The cards were sold in set form at the team's rink.

COMPLETE SET (31) 5.60 10.00
1 Team Photo/CL .15 .40
2 Mark McArthur .20 .50
3 Andy Adams .15 .40
4 Bryan McKinney .15 .40
5 Ryan Risidore .20 .50
6 Joel Cort .15 .40
7 Chris Hajt .20 .50
8 Regan Stocco .15 .40
9 Dwayne Hay .20 .50
10 Andrew Clark .15 .40
11 Neil Fewster .15 .40
12 Jamie Wright .20 .50
13 Jason Jackman .15 .40
14 Pat Barton .15 .40
15 Tom Johnson .15 .40
16 Brian Wesenberg .20 .50
17 Mike Pittman .15 .40
18 Jeff Williams .15 .40
19 Todd Norman .20 .50
20 Mike Rusk .15 .40
21 David Lylyk .15 .40
22 Todd Bertuzzi .75 2.00
23 Jeff Cowan .20 .50
24 Rumun Ndur .20 .50
25 Jeff O'Neill .40 1.00
26 Andrew Long .15 .40
27 Craig Hartsburg CO .20 .50
28 Paul Brydges ACO .02 .10
29 Sponsor Card .01
30 Sponsor Card .01
NNO Ad Card .01

1995-96 Guelph Storm

This extremely attractive set was produced by Axiom Communications for distribution by the Storm at the club's pro shop. The set commemorates the team's fifth anniversary, and features strong action photography along with a dazzling design element along the right border. The back features a color mug shot, personal information and logos of sponsors.

COMPLETE SET (30) 4.00 10.00
1 Checklist .15 .40
2 Andrew Clark .15 .40
3 Dwayne Hay .20 .50
4 Jason Jackman .15 .40
5 Burger King Ad .01
6 Nick Bootland .15 .40
7 Andrew Long .15 .40
8 Todd Norman .20 .50
9 Michael Pittman .15 .40
10 Herbert Vasilijevs .20 .50
11 Jeff Williams .15 .40
12 Joel Cort .20 .50
13 Chris Hajt .20 .50
14 Brian Willsie .20 .50
15 Brian Wesenberg .20 .50
16 Mike Lankshear .15 .40
17 Darryl McArthur .15 .40
18 Bryan McKinney .15 .40
19 Regan Stocco .15 .40
20 Ryan Risidore .20 .50
21 Mike Vellinga .15 .40
22 Dan Cloutier .40 1.00
23 Bryan McMullen .20 .50
24 Brett Thompson .20 .50
25 Ryan Robichaud .15 .40
26 Kid's Club .01
27 Jamie Wright .20 .50
28 Guelph Police .01
29 Mike Galati .15 .40
30 Domino's Pizza Ad .01

1996-97 Guelph Storm

This 36-card set continues the tradition of high-quality sets from the Storm. The heavy-stock cards feature action photography on the front, along with player name and number and team logo. The backs include a mug shot and personal information and a safety tip, but no playing stats. The set is noteworthy for the inclusion of Manny Malhotra, expected to be a high pick in 1998.

COMPLETE SET (36) 4.80 12.00
1 Checklist .02 .10
2 Brett Thompson .15 .40
3 David MacDonald .15 .40
4 John Zubyck .15 .40
5 Denis Ivanov .15 .40
6 Joel Cort .15 .40
7 Chris Hajt .20 .50
8 Manny Malhotra .30 .75
9 Mike Dombkiewicz .15 .40
10 Ryan Robichaud .15 .40
11 Kent McDonell .20 .50
12 Joe Gerbe .15 .40
13 Mike Christian .15 .40
14 Brian Wesenberg .15 .40
15 Todd Norman .20 .50
16 Darryl McArthur .15 .40
17 Richard Irwin .15 .40
18 Brian Willsie .15 .40
19 Mike Vellinga .15 .40
20 Jason Jackman .15 .40
21 Chris Madden .30 .75
22 Dwayne Hay .20 .50
23 Joey Bartley .15 .40
24 Mike Lankshear .20 .50
25 Andrew Long .15 .40
26 Matt Bell .15 .40
27 Nick Bootland .20 .50
28 E.J. McGuire .02 .10
29 Rick Allain .02 .10
30 Burger King Ad .01
31 Burger King Kid's Club .01
32 Guelph Police .15 .40
with Malhotra and Norman
33 Domino's Pizza Ad .01
34 Domino's Pizza Ad .01
35 Chris Hajt/Dwayne Hay .15 .40
36 96-97 Team Picture .15 .40

1996-97 Guelph Storm Premier Collection

This odd-sized (4" X 6") collection was issued by the club along with game programs. The set is noteworthy for its outstanding photography and imaginative posing of the subjects; most appear out of hockey garb and in more expressive outfits and poses.

COMPLETE SET (12) 4.80 10.00
1 Todd Norman .40 1.00
2 Brian Wesenberg .40 1.00
3 Mike Vellinga .40 1.00
4 Brett Thompson .40 1.00
5 Joel Cort .40 1.00
6 Jason Jackman .40 1.00
7 Brian Willsie .40 1.00
8 Mike Lankshear .40 1.00
9 Dwayne Hay .40 1.00
10 Manny Malhotra .75 2.00
11 Chris Hajt .40 1.00
12 Nick Bootland .40 1.00

1997-98 Guelph Storm

Card fronts feature a black and white action photo, with players name and number on the bottom. Card backs feature biographical information and are numbered xx/34. Backs also feature sponsor logos and safety tips.

COMPLETE SET (34) 4.80 12.00
1 Header Card .02 .10
2 Chris Thompson .15 .40
3 Daniel Jacques .15 .40
4 Chris Madden .30 .75
5 Kevin Mitchell .15 .40
6 Joey Bartley .15 .40
7 Chris Hajt .20 .50
8 Manny Malhotra .30 .75
9 Mike Dombkiewicz .15 .40
10 Ian Forbes .15 .40
11 Joe Gerbe .15 .40
12 Mike Vellinga .15 .40
13 Lindsay Plunkett .15 .40
14 Kent McDonell .15 .40
15 Matt Lahey .15 .40
16 Bohuslav Subr .15 .40
17 Bob Crummer .15 .40
18 Andrew Long .15 .40
19 Brian McGrattan .15 .40
20 Darryl McArthur .30 .75
21 Brian Willsie .20 .50
22 John Zubyck .15 .40
23 Dusty Jamieson .30 .75
24 Eric Beaudoin .15 .40
25 Jason Jackman .15 .40
26 Nick Bootland .15 .40
27 George Burnett CO .15 .40
28 Rick Allain ACO .02 .10
29 Spyke .02 .10
30 Guelph Police .02 .10
31 Burger King .01
32 Burger King .01
33 Domino's .01
34 Domino's .01

1998-99 Guelph Storm

This set features the Storm of the OHL. The cards feature an action shot on the front, along with a full-color back. The cards were produced by the team and sold at home games.

COMPLETE SET (36) 4.80 12.00
1 Title Card/CL .02 .01
2 Mike D'Alessandro .30 .75
3 Chris Madden .40 1.00
4 Kevin Mitchell .20 .50
5 Jean Sebastien Larocque .20 .50
6 Kevin Dallman .30 .75
7 Matt Rock .20 .50
8 Ian Forbes .20 .50
9 Joe Gerbe .20 .50
10 Bo Subr .30 .75
11 Lindsay Plunkett .20 .50
12 Kent McDonell .20 .50
13 Garrett McAiney .20 .50
14 Nathan Herrington .20 .50
15 Bob Crummer .20 .50
16 Charlie Stephens .30 .75
17 Darryl Knight .20 .50
18 Darryl McArthur .30 .75
19 Ryan Davis .20 .50
20 Joey Bartley .20 .50
21 Frank Jolette .20 .50
22 Eric Beaudoin .20 .50
23 Lucas Nehrling .20 .50
24 Geoff Ward ACO .02 .10
25 Bart Crashley ACO .02 .10
26 Shane Mabey TR .02 .10
27 Russ Hammond ATR .02 .10
28 Spyke MASCOT .02 .10
29 Guelph Police .01
30 1997-98 OHL Champs .02 .10
31 Robertson Cup .02 .10
32 Memorial Cup AS .08 .25
33 Burger King Ad .01
34 Burger King Ad .01
35 Domino's Ad .01
36 Domino's Ad .01

1999-00 Guelph Storm

Released in conjunction with Burger King and Domino's, this 36-card set features the 1999-00 Guelph Storm. Cards are black bordered and contain full color action photography. The last four cards of the set are coupons for Burger King and Domino's.

COMPLETE SET (36) 4.00 10.00
1 Header Card/CL .02 .10
2 Craig Andersson .60 1.50
3 Chris Madden .40 1.00
4 Kevin Mitchell .15 .40
5 Kevin Dallman .15 .40
6 Matt Rock .15 .40
7 Jon Hedberg .15 .40
8 Radek Matalik .15 .40
9 Joe Gerbe .15 .40
10 Bo Suba .15 .40
11 Lindsay Plunkett .15 .40
12 Kent McDonell .30 .75
13 Peter Flache .15 .40
14 Charlie Stephens .30 .75
15 Colt King .30 .75
16 Nick Jones .15 .40
17 Brent Kelly .15 .40
18 Jon Peters .15 .40
19 Derek Hennessey .15 .40
20 Andrew Brown .15 .40
21 Aran Myers .15 .40
22 Matt House .15 .40
23 Eric Beaudoin .15 .40
24 Ian Forbes .15 .40
25 Morgan McCormick .15 .40
26 Paul Gillis .15 .40
27 Bart Crashley .15 .40
28 Shane Mabey .15 .40
29 Russ Hammond .15 .40
30 Spyke Mascot .02 .10
31 Team Photo .15 .40
32 Guelph Police .02 .10
33 Burger King Coupon .01
34 Burger King Coupon .01
35 Domino's Coupon .01
36 Domino's Coupon .01

2000-01 Guelph Storm

We have confirmed this handful of cards to exist, thanks to collector Vinnie Montalbano. If you know of others, please contact us via hockeymag@beckett.com.

COMPLETE SET (?)
1 Craig Anderson .40
2 Andrew Archer .40
3 Dustin Brown .40
4 Kevin Dallman .40

2001-02 Guelph Storm

COMPLETE SET (35) 20.00
1 Fedor Tyutin .40 1.00
2 Frank Burgio .20 .50
3 Kevin Dallman .30 .75
4 Leonid Zvachkin .20 .50
5 Tim Branham .20 .50
6 George Bradley .20 .50
7 Martin St. Pierre .20 .50
8 Malcolm MacMillan .20 .50
9 Michael Krelove .20 .50
10 Colin Power .20 .50
11 Aaron Lobb .20 .50
12 Daniel Paille .75 2.00
13 Alex Butkus .20 .50
14 Ryan Thompson .20 .50
15 Luc Chiasson .20 .50
16 Derek Hennessey .20 .50
17 Evan Kotsopoulos .20 .50
18 Matt Puntureri .20 .50
19 Andrew Archer .20 .50
20 Morgan McCormick .20 .50
21 Chris Beckford-Tseu 1.25 3.00
22 Andrew Penner .30 .75

23 Dustin Brown 1.50 4.00
24 Dwight LaBrosse .20 .50
25 Jeff Jackson CO .08 .20
26 Shawn Camp ACO .20 .50
27 Spyke MASCOT .02 .10
28 Shane Mabey TR .20 .50
29 Russ Hammond ATR .20 .50
30 Police Services .02 .10
31 Dominos .02 .10
32 Guelph Dominators .02 .10
33 Guelph Dominators .02 .10
34 M&T Printing Group .02 .10
35 Checklist .02 .10

2001-02 Guelph Storm Memorial Cup

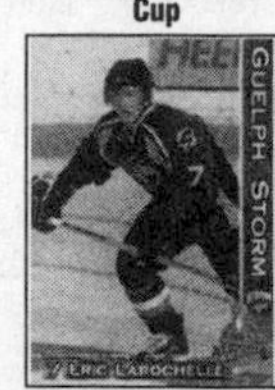

Very similar to other Guelph set of this season, save for the addition of the Memorial Cup logo and a few other small changes in content.

COMPLETE SET (35) 8.00 20.00
1 Fedor Tjutin .60 1.50
2 Kevin Dallman .60 1.50
3 Leonid Zvachkin .30 .75
4 Tim Branham .30 .75
5 Eric Larochelle .30 .75
6 George Bradley .30 .75
7 Martin St. Pierre .30 .75
8 Malcolm MacMillan .30 .75
9 Michael Krelove .30 .75
10 Colin Power .30 .75
11 Aaron Lobb .30 .75
12 Daniel Paille 1.00 2.50
13 Alex Butkus .30 .75
14 Ryan Thompson .30 .75
15 Luc Chiasson .30 .75
16 Derek Hennessey .30 .75
17 Lou Dickenson .30 .75
18 Matt Puntureri .30 .75
19 Scott Rozendal .30 .75
20 Andrew Archer .30 .75
21 Morgan McCormick .30 .75
22 Andrew Penner .40 1.00
23 Dustin Brown 1.50 4.00
24 Dwight LaBrosse .30 .75
25 Jeff Jackson CO .02 .10
26 Shawn Camp ACO .02 .10
27 Spyke MASCOT .02 .10
28 Shane Mabey TR .02 .10
29 Russ Hammond ATR .02 .10
30 Sponsor .02 .10
31 Memorial Cup Card .02 .10
32 Team Photo .02 .10
33 Community .02 .10
34 Community .02 .10
35 Checklist .02 .10

2002-03 Guelph Storm

COMPLETE SET (36) 6.00 15.00
1 Andrew Penner .30 .75
2 Martin St. Pierre .20 .50
3 Andrew Archer .20 .50
4 Ryan Thompson .20 .50
5 Daniel Paille .60 1.50
6 Adam Dennis .30 .75
7 Dustin Brown .60 1.50
8 Eric Larochelle .20 .50
9 George Bradley .20 .50
10 Corey LeClair .20 .50
11 Geoff Patton .20 .50
12 Lou Dickenson .20 .50
13 Matt Ryan .20 .50
14 Colin Power .20 .50
15 Ryan Garlock .40 1.00
16 Steve Zmudczynski .20 .50
17 Leonid Zvachkin .20 .50
18 Brett Trudell .20 .50
19 Michael Okrzesik .20 .50
20 Ryan Callahan .40 1.00
21 Emil Bucic .20 .50
22 Aaron Lobb .20 .50
23 Tyler Haskins .20 .50
24 Malcolm MacMillan .20 .50
25 Matt Puntureri .20 .50
26 Jeff Jackson CO .02 .10
27 Shawn Camp ACO .02 .10
28 Jason Brooks ACO .02 .10
29 Shawn Mabey AT .02 .10
30 Russ Hammond ATR .02 .10
31 Spyke MASCOT .02 .10
32 Ad card .01 .01
33 Junior Storm .01 .01
34 Home Ice .01 .01
35 Guelph Police .01 .01
36 Team Photo/CL .02 .10

2003-04 Guelph Storm

COMPLETE SET (30) 6.00 15.00
1 Header Card .02 .10
2 Danny Taylor .20 .50
3 Mick Okrzesik .20 .50
4 Dan Girardi .40 1.00
5 Kevin Klein .40 1.00
6 Ryan Parent .75 2.00
7 George Bradley .20 .50
8 Marty St. Pierre .20 .50
9 Niko Tuomi .20 .50
10 Mark Lytwyn .20 .50
11 Nathan Spaling .20 .50
12 Steve Zmudczynski .20 .50
13 Dan Paille .40 1.00
14 Brett Trudell .20 .50
15 Shane Hart .20 .50
16 Ryan Garlock .40 1.00
17 Ryan Card .20 .50
18 Matt Ryan .20 .50
19 Ryan Callahan .30 .75
20 Kyle Spurr .20 .50
21 Adam Dennis .40 1.00
22 Jakub Koreis .40 1.00
23 Dustin Brown .40 1.00
24 Shawn Camp CO .02 .10
25 Jason Brooks ACO .02 .10
26 Paul Brydges ACO .02 .10
27 Sponsor Card .02 .10
28 Sponsor Card .02 .10
29 Guelph Police .02 .10
30 Team Photo/CL .02 .10

2004-05 Guelph Storm

COMPLETE SET (31) 8.00 20.00
1 Danny Taylor .30 .75
2 Michael Caruso .30 .75
3 Shawn Haviland .30 .75
4 Michael Okrzesik .30 .75
5 Daniel Girardi .40 1.00
6 Josh Godfrey .30 .75
7 Ryan Parent .40 1.00
8 Brent Mackie .30 .75
9 Andy Hyvarinen .30 .75
10 Jaromir Florian .30 .75
11 Mark Versteeg-Lytwyn .40 1.00
12 Mark O'Leary .40 1.00
13 Steve Zmudczynski .30 .75
14 Scot Zimmerman .30 .75
15 Ryan Kitchen .30 .75
16 Mike McLean .30 .75
17 Kyle Paige .30 .75
18 Matt Lyall .30 .75
19 Matt D'Agostini .30 .75
20 Ryan Card .30 .75
21 Darryl Smith .30 .75
22 Ryan Callahan .40 1.00
23 Kyle Spurr .30 .75
24 Tyler Doig .30 .75
25 Adam Dennis .40 1.00
26 Dave Barr CO .02 .10
27 Jason Brooks ACO .02 .10
28 Trent Cull ACO .02 .10
29 Spyke MASCOT .02 .10
30 Team Photo/CL .02 .10
31 Guelph Police .01 .01

2005-06 Guelph Storm

COMPLETE SET (32) 10.00 25.00
A01 Josh Godfrey .40 1.00
A02 Jamie Arniel .40 1.00
A03 Mark O'Leary .40 1.00
A04 Tyler Doig .40 1.00
A05 Ryan MacDonald .40 1.00
A06 Jason Brooks ACO .02 .10
A07 Guelph Police .01 .01
A08 Guelph Storm CL1 .02 .10
B01 Ryan Pottruff .40 1.00
B02 Ryan Parent 1.00 2.50
B03 Andy Hyvarinen .40 1.00
B04 Kelsey Wilson .40 1.00
B05 Matt D'Agostini .40 1.00
B06 Domino's Pizza SPONSOR .01 .01
B07 Dave Barr CO .02 .10
B08 Guelph Storm CL2 .02 .10
C01 Michael Caruso .40 1.00
C02 Drew Doughty 1.50 4.00
C03 Brandon Biggers .40 1.00
C04 Leigh Salters .40 1.00
C05 Rafael Rotter .40 1.00
C06 M&T Printing SPONSOR .01 .01
C07 Trent Cull ACO .02 .10
C08 Guelph Storm CL3 .02 .10
D01 Shawn Haviland .40 1.00
D02 Kyle Wharton .40 1.00
D03 Jason Pitton .40 1.00
D04 Mike McLean .40 1.00
D05 Harry Young .40 1.00
D06 Ryan Callahan .75 2.00
D07 Jason Guy .40 1.00
D08 Guelph Storm CL4 .02 .10

2006-07 Guelph Storm

COMPLETE SET (25) 8.00 15.00
1 Thomas McCollum .40 1.00
2 Ryan Pottruff .20 .50
3 Joe Underwood .20 .50
4 Brandon Buck .20 .50
5 Drew Doughty 1.25 3.00
6 Matt Kennedy .20 .50
7 Leigh Salters .20 .50
8 Anthony Nigro .20 .50
9 Jeff Hayes .20 .50
10 Tyler Melancon .20 .50
11 Tyler Doig .20 .50
12 Mike McLean .20 .50
13 Patrick Moran .20 .50
14 Anton Hedman .20 .50
15 Luke Pither .20 .50
16 Grant McGee .20 .50
17 Rafael Rotter .20 .50
18 Tim Priamo .20 .50
19 Jamie Arniel .20 .50
20 Ryan Parent .60 1.50
21 Corey Syvret .20 .50
22 Michael Caruso .20 .50
23 Cody St Jacques .20 .50
24 Dave Barr CO .10 .25
25 Rusty Hammond TR .02 .10

2003-04 Gwinnett Gladiators

This set was sponsored by the Gwinnett Daily Post and was issued as a promotional giveaway at a home game. The oversized cards were issued on a perforated sheet.

COMPLETE SET (36) 30.00
1 Checklist .10
2 Kevin Doell 1.00
3 Brad Peddle 1.00
4 Brandon Dietrich 1.00
5 Chris Durno 1.00
6 Rick Emmett 1.00
7 Anthony Aquino 1.50
8 Steve Slonina 1.00
9 Cam Brown 1.00
10 Wes Fox 1.00
11 Mike Buckley 1.50
12 Paul Flache 1.00
13 Joe Bourne 1.00
14 Blue Bennefield 1.50
15 Michael Garnett 1.50
16 Evan Nielsen 1.00
17 Jim Jackson 1.00
18 Troy Milam 1.00
19 Adam Munro 1.50
20 Kris Goodjohn 1.00
21 Mike Vigilante 1.00
22 Phil Lewandowski 1.00
23 J.P. O'Connor 1.00
24 Jeff Pyle CO .25
25 Megan Guthrie TR .25
26 Patrick Houlihan EQM .25
27 Steve Chapman GM .25
28 Dustin Bixby ANN .25
29 Celebration Photo .50
30 Mascot .25
31 Gladiators first ever goal .50
32 Gladiators win first game .50
33 Opening Night .50
34 Scramble in the crease .50
35 Team Photo .50
36 The Zamboni .25

2003-04 Gwinnett Gladiators RBI Sports

This set was produced by RBI Sports, with a print run of 250 sets. The numbering sequence reflects the entire print run of RBI sets this season.

COMPLETE SET (16) 15.00
193 Blue Bennefield 1.50
194 Joe Bourne 1.00
195 Cam Brown 1.00
196 Brandon Dietrich 1.00
197 Kevin Doell 1.00
198 Chris Durno 1.00
199 Rick Emmett 1.00
200 Paul Flache 1.00
201 Michael Garnett 1.50
202 Kris Goodjohn 1.00
203 Jim Jackson 1.00
204 Troy Milam 1.00
205 Adam Munro 1.50
206 Evan Nielsen 1.00
207 Steve Slonina 1.00
208 Mike Vigilante 1.00

2004-05 Gwinnett Gladiators

COMPLETE SET (30) 8.00 20.00
1 T.J. Aceti .60 1.50
2 Adam Berkhoel .75 2.00
3 Dustin Bixby .30 .75
4 Joe Bourne .30 .75
5 Cam Brown .30 .75
6 Jeff Campbell .30 .75
7 Steve Champman GM .02 .10
8 Chris Durno .30 .75
9 Rick Emmett .30 .75
10 Brett Engelhardt .30 .75
11 Sean Fields .30 .75
12 Peter Flache .30 .75
13 Kris Goodjohn .30 .75
14 Megan Guthrie TR .02 .10
15 Patrick Houlihan EQMG .02 .10
16 Jim Jackson .30 .75
17 Lane Manson .30 .75
18 Dave McCullough .30 .75
19 Dr. Brian Morgan .02 .10
20 Chris Peterson .30 .75
21 Jeff Pyle CO .02 .10
22 Brad Schell .30 .75
23 Adam Smyth .30 .75
24 Mike Stathopoulos .30 .75
25 Kevin Truelson .30 .75
26 Ryan Van Buskirk .30 .75
27 Mike Vigilante .30 .75
28 Maximus MASCOT .02 .10
29 Team Picture .02 .10
30 Checklist .02 .10

1989-90 Halifax Citadels

This 26-card set measures approximately 2" by 4 1/4". The fronts feature full-bleed posed action color photos, except at the top where a gray stripe displays the logos of the Farmers Co-Operative Dairy Limited and 92/CJCH. The team logo in the form of a red star appears in the lower right corner, with the player's name in a blue bar that is printed over the team logo. The cards are unnumbered and checklisted below in alphabetical order.

COMPLETE SET (26) 4.80 12.00
1 Joel Baillargeon .20 .50
2 Jamie Baker .25 .60
3 Mario Brunetta .30 .75
4 Gerald Bzdel .20 .50
5 David Espe .20 .50
6 Bryan Fogarty .20 .50
7 Robbie Florek GM .20 .50
8 Scott Gordon .30 .75
9 Dean Hopkins .20 .50
10 Miroslav Ihnacak .20 .50
11 Claude Julien .20 .50
12 Kevin Kaminski .30 .75
13 Claude Lapointe .30 .75
14 Chris McQuaid EQ/MG .08 .25
Brent Smith TR
15 Max Middendorf .20 .50
16 Stephane Morin .30 .75
17 Dave Pichette .20 .50
18 Ken Quinney .20 .50
19 Jean-Marc Richard .20 .50
20 Jean Marc Routhier .20 .50
21 Jaroslav Sevcik .20 .50
22 Brent Severyn .30 .75
23 Greg Smyth .20 .50
24 Trevor Steinburg .20 .50
25 Mark Vermette .20 .50
26 Ladislav Tresl .20 .50

1990-91 Halifax Citadels

This 28-card set measures approximately 2 3/4" by 4 1/4" and features color, posed-action player photos with white borders. The Farmers Co-Operative Dairy Limited and the 92/CJCH logo appear in the top border. The cards are unnumbered and checklisted below in alphabetical order.

COMPLETE SET (28) 4.80 12.00
1 Jamie Baker .20 .50
2 Mike Bishop .15 .40
3 Gerald Bzdel .15 .40
4 Daniel Dore .15 .40
5 Mario Doyon .15 .40
6 Dave Espe .15 .40
7 Stephane Fiset 1.25 3.00
8 Scott Gordon .30 .75
9 Stephane Guerard .15 .40
10 Dean Hopkins ACO .08 .25
11 Miroslav Ihnacak .20 .50
12 Jeff Jackson .20 .50
13 Clement Jodoin CO/MG .08 .25
14 Claude Lapointe .20 .50
15 Dave Latta .15 .40
16 Chris McQuaid EQ MG .08 .25
17 Kip Miller .20 .50
18 Stephane Morin .20 .50
19 Ken Quinney .15 .40
20 Jean-Marc Richard .15 .40
21 Serge Roberge .15 .40
22 Jaroslav Sevcik .15 .40
23 Brent Severyn .30 .75
24 Mike Shuman TR .08 .25
25 Greg Smyth .15 .40
26 Jim Sprott .15 .40
27 Trevor Stienburg .15 .40
28 Mark Vermette .15 .40

1995-96 Halifax Mooseheads

This set features the Mooseheads of the QMJHL. The set was produced by the team, and sold at its souvenir stands.

COMPLETE SET (25) 8.00 25.00
1 Harlin Hayes .20 .50
2 Jean-Sebastien Giguere 4.00 10.00
3 Patrick Lafleur .20 .50
4 Jamie Brown .20 .50
5 Elias Abrahamsson .20 .50
6 Didier Tremblay .20 .50
7 Chris Halverson .20 .50
8 Chris Peyton .20 .50
9 Frederic Belanger .20 .50
10 Joel Theriault .20 .50
11 Mark Lynk .20 .50
12 Derrick Pyke .20 .50
13 Steve Mongrain .20 .50
14 David Carson .20 .50
15 Jody Shelley 2.00 5.00
16 Daniel Payette .20 .50
17 Brian Surette .20 .50
18 Etienne Drapeau .30 .75
19 Billy Manley .20 .50
20 Jan Melichercik .20 .50
21 Nicolas Maheux .20 .50
22 Eric Houde .30 .75
23 Shawn MacKenzie CO .08 .25
24 Clement Jodoin CO .08 .25
25 Chris McQuaid TR .02 .10

1996-97 Halifax Mooseheads I

Series one pictures the team in their home uniforms. It was sold in team-set form early in the season.

COMPLETE SET (27) 12.00 30.00
1 Elias Abrahamsson .30 .75
2 Frederic Belanger .20 .50
3 Martin Bilodeau .20 .50
4 Jamie Brown .20 .50
5 Marc Chouinard .40 1.00
6 Benoit Dusablon .60 1.50
7 Jean-Sebastien Giguere 2.50 6.00
8 Andrew Gilby .20 .50
9 Alex Johnstone .20 .50
10 Eric Laplante .30 .75
11 Jean-Simon Lemay .20 .50
12 Mark Lynk .20 .50
13 Billy Manley .20 .50
14 Alexander Mathieu .20 .50
15 Todd Row .20 .50
16 Ryan Rowell .20 .50
17 Francois Sasseville .20 .50
18 Jody Shelley 1.50 4.00
19 Jeffrey Sullivan .20 .50
20 Alex Tanguay 4.00 10.00
21 Didier Tremblay .30 .75
22 Jason Troini .30 .75
23 Clark Udle .20 .50
24 Clement Jodoin HCO .02 .10
25 Shawn MacKenzie ACO .02 .10
26 Chris McQuaid TR .02 .10
27 Team Photo .20 .50

1996-97 Halifax Mooseheads II

Series 2 features the team in their away uniforms. According to various reports, it was issued later in the season and is considered slightly tougher to acquire.

COMPLETE SET (27) 14.22 35.56
1 Elias Abrahamsson .40 1.00
2 Frederic Belanger .30 .75
3 Martin Bilodeau .30 .75
4 Jamie Brown .30 .75
5 Marc Chouinard .50 1.25
6 Benoit Dusablon .75 2.00
7 Jean-Sebastien Giguere 4.00 10.00
8 Andrew Gilby .30 .75
9 Alex Johnstone .30 .75
10 Eric Laplante .40 1.00
11 Jean-Simon Lemay .30 .75
12 Mark Lynk .30 .75
13 Billy Manley .30 .75
14 Alexander Mathieu .30 .75
15 Todd Row .30 .75
16 Ryan Rowell .30 .75
17 Francois Sasseville .30 .75
18 Jody Shelley 2.00 5.00
19 Jeffrey Sullivan .30 .75
20 Alex Tanguay 5.00 12.00
21 Didier Tremblay .40 1.00
22 Jason Troini .30 .75
23 Clark Udle .30 .75
24 Clement Jodoin HCO .02 .10
25 Shawn MacKenzie ACO .02 .10
26 Chris McQuaid TR .02 .10
27 Team Photo .20 .50

1997-98 Halifax Mooseheads I

As with the previous year's set, Series 1 features the team in their home uniforms. The series was sold by the team at home games.

COMPLETE SET (27) 8.00 20.00
1 Frederic Belanger .20 .50
2 Martin Bilodeau .20 .50
3 Marc-Andre Binette .20 .50
4 Alexandre Couture .20 .50
5 Andrew Gilby .20 .50
6 Alex Johnstone .20 .50
7 Eric Laplante .30 .75
8 P.J. Lynch .20 .50
9 Mark Lynk .20 .50
10 Joey MacDonald .30 .75
11 Ali MacEachern .20 .50
12 Billy Manley .20 .50
13 Alexander Mathieu .20 .50
14 Steve Mongrain .20 .50
15 Ryan Power .20 .50
16 Brandon Reid 1.25 3.00
17 Todd Row .20 .50
18 Dean Stock .20 .50
19 Jeffrey Sullivan .20 .50
20 Alex Tanguay 3.00 8.00
21 Didier Tremblay .30 .75
22 Jason Troini .30 .75
23 Dwight Wolfe .20 .50
24 Danny Grant HCO .20 .50
25 Shawn MacKenzie ACO .02 .10
26 Chris McQuaid TR .02 .10
27 Team Photo .20 .50

1997-98 Halifax Mooseheads II

Series 2 is unnumbered and listed alphabetically. The set features several players who were acquired by the team after the release of Series 1. It also was printed in lesser quantities than the first series.

COMPLETE SET (27) 30.00
1 Checklist .02 .10
2 Frederic Belanger .30 .75
3 Martin Bilodeau .30 .75
4 Marc-Andre Binette .30 .75
5 Alexandre Couture .30 .75
6 Mauro DiPaolo .30 .75
7 Alex Johnstone .30 .75
8 P.J. Lynch .30 .75
9 Joey MacDonald .40 1.00
10 Ali MacEachern .30 .75
11 Boris Majesky .30 .75
12 Billy Manley .30 .75
13 Alexander Mathieu .30 .75
14 Ryan Power .30 .75
15 Stephen Quirk .30 .75
16 Brandon Reid 1.50 4.00
17 A.J.Rivers .30 .75
18 Dean Stock .30 .75
19 Jeffrey Sullivan .30 .75
20 Alex Tanguay 4.00 10.00
21 Jason Troini .30 .75
22 Andrew Warr .30 .75
23 Dwight Wolfe .30 .75
24 Shawn MacKenzie ACO .02 .10
25 Danny Grant HCO .30 .75
26 Hal Mascot .02 .10
27 Alex Tanguay CAN 4.00 10.00
28 Chris McQuad TR .02 .10

1998-99 Halifax Mooseheads

COMPLETE SET (23) 12.00 20.00
1 Alexei Volkov .30 .75
2 Pascal Leclaire .75 2.00
3 Mathieu Paul .20 .50
4 Samuel Seguin .20 .50
5 Billy Manley .20 .50
6 Ladislav Nagy 1.25 3.00
7 Alex Tanguay 1.25 3.00
8 Mike Bray .20 .50
9 Carlyle Lewis .20 .50
10 Frederic Belanger .20 .50
11 David McCutcheon .20 .50
12 Jeff Sullivan .20 .50
13 Alexandre Mathieu .20 .50
14 Jason Troini .20 .50
15 Alex Johnstone .20 .50
16 Ali MacEachern .20 .50
17 Brandon Benedict .20 .50
18 Tyler Reid .20 .50
19 Jasmin Gelinas .20 .50
20 P.J. Lynch .20 .50
21 Mauro DiPaolo .20 .50
22 Brandon Reid .60 1.50
23 Marc-Andre Binette .20 .50
24 Jeff Towriss .20 .50
25 Rocco Anoia .20 .50
26 Daniel Villeneuve .20 .50
27 Alex Tanguay CL .75 2.00

1998-99 Halifax Mooseheads Second Edition

COMPLETE SET (27) 8.00 20.00
1 Tyler Reid .20 .50
2 Jasmin Gelinas .20 .50
3 Hal MASCOT .02 .10
4 Brandon Reid .40 1.00
5 Jeff Sullivan .20 .50
6 Alex Johnstone .20 .50
7 P.J. Lynch .20 .50
8 Mauro Dipaolo .20 .50
9 Marc-andre Binette .20 .50
10 Carlyle Lewis .20 .50
11 David McCutcheon .20 .50
12 Mike Bray .20 .50
13 Samuel Seguin .20 .50
14 Brandon Benedict .20 .50
15 Jason Troini .20 .50
16 Ali MacEachern .20 .50
17 Mathieu Paul .20 .50
18 Alexei Volkov .30 .75
19 Billy Manley .20 .50
20 Frederic Belanger .20 .50
21 Alex Tanguay 1.25 3.00
22 Pascal Leclaire .75 2.00
23 Ladislav Nagy 1.25 3.00
24 Alexandre Mathieu .30 .75
25 World Junior .40 1.00
26 Halifax Radio Team .02 .10
27 Team Card .02 .10

1999-00 Halifax Mooseheads

This 29-card set features the 1999-00 Halifax Mooseheads. Card fronts have white borders, and along the left side, a green status bar containing the player's name fades into a full color action photo. These cards are not numbered, therefore appear in order by the included checklist card.

COMPLETE SET (29) 7.20 18.00
1 Alexei Volkov .40 1.00
2 Pascal Leclaire 2.00 5.00
3 Carlos Sayde .08 .25
4 Joey Dipenta 1.25 3.00
5 Joe Groleau .08 .25
6 Jonathan Boone .08 .25
7 Nick Greenough .08 .25
8 Jason King .08 .25
9 Shawn Lewis .08 .25
10 Ramzi Abid .40 1.00
11 Jonathan St. Louis .08 .25
12 Darrell Jarrett .08 .25
13 Ryan Flinn .60 1.50
14 Robbie Sutherland .08 .25
15 Ali MacEachern .08 .25
16 Brandon Benedict .08 .25
17 Jules-Edy Laraque .40 1.00
18 Jasmin Gelinas .08 .25
19 Hugo Lehoux .08 .25
20 Gary Zinck .08 .25
21 Brandon Reid .75 2.00
22 Benoit Dusablon .40 1.00
23 Hal MASCOT .02 .10
24 Team Photo .08 .25
25 Cover Card 1 .02 .10
26 Cover Card 2 .02 .10
27 Cover Card 3 .02 .10
28 Cover Card 4 .02 .10
29 Cover Card 5 .02 .10

2000-01 Halifax Mooseheads

This attractive set features the Mooseheads of the QMJHL. The set was produced and sold by the team at its souvenir stands. The cards were sponsored by Sobey's and are unnumbered, therefore they are listed below in alphabetical order.

COMPLETE SET (26) 4.80 12.00
1 Brandon Benedict .15 .40
2 Jonathan Boone .15 .40
3 Michael Couch .15 .40
4 Dany Dallaire .30 .75
5 Bruce Gillis .15 .40
6 Nick Greenough .15 .40
7 Milan Jurcina .40 1.00
8 Derrick Kent .15 .40
9 Jason King .15 .40
10 Sergei Klyazmin .30 .75
11 Sebastien Laprise .15 .40
12 Jules-Edy Laraque .30 .75
13 Pascal Leclaire 1.25 3.00
14 Hugo Lehoux .15 .40
15 Ali MacEachern .15 .40
16 A.J. Maclean .15 .40
17 Ryan MacPherson .15 .40
18 Louis Mandeville .15 .40
19 Conor McGuire .15 .40
20 Jules Saulnier .15 .40
21 Giulio Scandella .15 .40
22 Robbie Sutherland .15 .40
23 Randy Upshall .15 .40
24 Ryan White .15 .40
25 Gary Zinck .15 .40
26 Team CL .01 .05

2001-02 Halifax Mooseheads

COMPLETE SET (26) 18.00
1 Dany Dallaire 1.00
2 Jonathan Boutin .75
3 Milan Jurcina 1.00
4 Bobby Clarke .75
5 Sergei Klyazmin .75
6 Francois-Pierre Guenette .75
7 A.J. MacLean .75
8 Bruce Gillis .75
9 Jason King 1.25
10 Derrick Kent .75
11 Giulio Scandella .75
12 Jean-Francois Cyr .75
13 Michael Couch .75
14 Robbie Sutherland .75
15 Ryan White .75
16 Randy Upshall .75
17 Patrick Gilbert .75
18 Brandon Benedict .75
19 Marc-Andre Bernier 1.00
20 Louis-Philippe Lessard .75
21 Alexandre Picard .75
22 Louis Mandeville .75
23 Action Shot 1 .25
24 Action Shot 2 .25
25 Action Shot 3 .25
26 Checklist .01

2002-03 Halifax Mooseheads

This set was issued by the Halifax Mooseheads of the QMJHL. The set is unnumbered and listed below in checklist order.

COMPLETE SET (22) 5.00 10.00
1 Checklist .01
2 Guillaume Lavallee .50
3 Jonathan Boutin .50
4 Milan Jurcina 1.00
5 Stuart McRae .50
6 Francois-Pierre Guenette .50
7 A.J. MacLean .50
8 Kyle Doucet .50
9 Thatcher Bell .50
10 Derrick Kent .50
11 Petr Vrana 1.50
12 Frederik Cabana .50
13 Jean-Francois Cyr .50
14 Jordie Preston .50
15 George Davis .50
16 Randy Upshall .50
17 Brandon Benedict .50
18 Marc-Andre Bernier 1.00
19 Colby MacIntyre .50
20 Jimmy Sharrow .50
21 Alexandre Picard 2.00
22 Steve Villeneuve .50

2003-04 Halifax Mooseheads

COMPLETE SET (26) 15.00
1 Jimmy Sharrow .75
2 Bobby Clarke .50
3 James Pouliot .50
4 Justin Munden .50
5 Evan Jones .50
6 Daniel Sparre .50
7 Petr Vrana 1.00
8 George Davis .50
9 Frederik Cabana .50
10 Jared Vokey .50
11 Jan Steber .50
12 Justin Saulnier .50
13 Jason Churchill .75
14 Ryan Moore .50
15 Randy Upshall .50
16 Sebastien Nolet .75
17 Federick Sonier .50
18 Jean-Francois Brault .50
19 Colby MacIntyre .50
20 Franklin MacDonald .50
21 David Brine .50
22 Pierre-Olivier Beaulieu .50
23 Luciano Lomanno .50
24 Kenzie Sheppard .50
NNO Petr Vrana TL 1.00
NNO Jimmy Sharrow TL .75

2004-05 Halifax Mooseheads

A total of 900 team sets were produced. There is a variation of card #4. The first version featured David Brine with a full cage and a different sweater number. The card was pulled and replaced with an updated photo. A few of the original version made their way into packs, although these all are found with a large black X over the image.

COMPLETE SET (26) 15.00
1 Alexandre Picard 1.00
2 Bryce Swan .50
3 Daniel Sparre .50
4A David Brine 20.00
full cage, X
4B David Brine .50
common version
5 Francois-Pierre Guenette .50
6 Franklin MacDonald .50
7 Frederik Cabana .50
8 James Pouliot .50
9 Jan Steber .50
10 Jason Churchill 1.00
11 Jean-Francois Brault .50
12 Jeff MacAuley .50
13 Jimmy Sharrow .50
14 Ryan Moore .50
15 Justin Saulnier .50
16 Kenzie Sheppard .50
17 Kevin Cormier .50
18 Luciano Lomanno .50
19 Marc-Andre Bernier 1.00
20 Petr Vrana 1.00
21 Pierre-Olivier Beaulieu .50
22 Rane Carnegie .75
23 Roger Kennedy 1.00

24 Ryan Hillier .50
25 Austin Corredato .50
26 Jeremy Duchesne 1.00

2005-06 Halifax Mooseheads

COMPLETE SET (25) 8.00 20.00
1 Jeremy Duchesne .30 .75
2 Roger Kennedy .30 .75
3 Andrew Bodnarchuk .60 1.50
4 Jiri Suchy .30 .75
5 Luciano Lomanno .30 .75
6 Rane Carnegie .30 .75
7 James Pouliot .30 .75
8 Garrett Peters .30 .75
9 Kirk Forrest .30 .75
10 Bryce Swan .30 .75
11 Ryan Hillier .30 .75
12 Justin Saulnier .30 .75
13 Philippe Poirier .30 .75
14 Logan MacMillan .30 .75
15 Daniel Smith .30 .75
16 Ben Macaskill .30 .75
17 Kevin Cormier .30 .75
18 Brent Lynch .30 .75
19 Justin Pender .30 .75
20 Jean-Francois Brault .30 .75
21 Mikhail Aseev .30 .75
22 Franklin MacDonald .30 .75
23 David Brine .30 .75
24 Yuri Cheremetiev .30 .75
25 Frederik Cabana .30 .75

2006-07 Halifax Mooseheads

COMPLETE SET (21) 10.00 18.00
1 Jeremy Duchesne .40 1.00
2 Andrew Bodnarchuk .40 1.00
3 Roger Kennedy .40 1.00
4 Jiri Suchy .30 .75
5 Luciano Lomanno .30 .75
6 Ryan Seymour .30 .75
7 James Pouliot .30 .75
8 Garrett Peters .30 .75
9 Logan Macmillan .30 .75
10 Benjamin Chaisson .30 .75
11 Daniel Smith .30 .75
12 Bryce Swan .30 .75
13 Ryan Hillier .30 .75
14 Jakub Voracek 1.25 3.00
15 Andrew White .30 .75
16 Justin Pender .30 .75
17 Ben Macaskill .30 .75
18 Gabriel O'Connor .30 .75
19 Colby Pridham .30 .75
20 Yuri Cheremetiev .30 .75
21 Eric Louis-Seize .30 .75

1975-76 Hamilton Fincups

This 18-card standard-size set features sepia-tone player portraits. The player's name and position are printed in the lower border, which is also sepia-tone. The team name is superimposed over the picture at the bottom center. The backs are blank and grayish in color. The cards are unnumbered and checklisted below in alphabetical order.

COMPLETE SET (18) 15.00 30.00
1 Jack Anderson .75 1.50
2 Mike Clarke .75 1.50
3 Greg Clause .75 1.50
4 Joe Contini .75 1.50
5 Mike Fedorko .75 1.50
6 Paul Foley .75 1.50
7 Greg Hickey .75 1.50
8 Tony Horvath .75 1.50
9 Mike Keating .75 1.50
10 Archie King .75 1.50
11 Ted Long .75 1.50
12 Dale McCourt 2.50 5.00
13 Dave Norris .75 1.50
14 Greg Redquest .75 1.50
15 Glen Richardson .75 1.50
16 Ron Roscoe .75 1.50
17 Ric Seiling 1.25 2.50
18 Danny Shearer .75 1.50

1999-00 Hamilton Bulldogs

This set features the Bulldogs of the AHL. The cards were produced by SplitSecond and were sold at home games and by mail order.

COMPLETE SET (25) 4.00 10.00
1 Mike Minard .30 .75
2 Chris Hajt .15 .40
3 Brad Norton .15 .40
4 Walt Kyle CO .08 .25
5 Eric Houde .15 .40
6 Kevin Bolibruck .15 .40
7 Daniel Cleary .20 .50
8 Vladimir Vorobiev .20 .50
9 Dan LaCouture .20 .50
10 Brian Swanson .20 .50
11 Martin Laitre .15 .40
12 Peter Sarno .40 1.00
13 Alex Zhurik .15 .40
14 Chad Hinz .15 .40
15 Kevin Brown .15 .40
16 Matthieu Descoteaux .15 .40
17 Jason Chimera .40 1.00
18 Alex Henry .30 .75
19 Sean Selmser .20 .50
20 Ryan Risidore .15 .40
21 Michel Riesen .30 .75
22 Sergei Yerkovich .15 .40
23 Elias Abrahamsson .15 .40
24 Eric Heffler .15 .40
25 Bruiser MASCOT .08 .25

2000-01 Hamilton Bulldogs

This set features the Bulldogs of the AHL. The set was produced by the team and sold at its souvenir stands late in the season.

COMPLETE SET (28) 5.00 12.00
1 Chris Madden .30 .75
2 Terran Sandwith .15 .40
3 Ryan Risidore .15 .40
4 Kurt Drummond .15 .40
5 Chris Hajt .15 .40
6 Brad Norton .15 .40
7 Maxim Spiridonov .15 .40
8 Patrick Cote .30 .75
9 Alex Henry .30 .75
10 Paul Healey .15 .40
11 Jason Chimera .40 1.00
12 Peter Sarno .30 .75
13 Brian Urick .15 .40
14 Michael Henrich .30 .75
15 Brian Swanson .20 .50
16 Martin Laitre .15 .40
17 Chris Albert .15 .40
18 Fernando Pisani .40 1.00
19 Lloyd Shaw .15 .40
20 Scott Ferguson .15 .40
21 Michel Riesen .20 .50
22 Alain Nasreddine .20 .50
23 Chad Hinz .15 .40
24 Joaquin Gage .30 .75
25 Claude Julien CO .10 .25
26 Morey Gare CO .10 .25
27 Bruiser MASCOT .04 .10
28 Team CL .01 .05

2001-02 Hamilton Bulldogs

This set features the Bulldogs of the AHL. It was created by the well-known card shop CTM Ste-Foy, and was sold at that store, as well as by the team. Less than 1,000 sets were reportedly produced.

COMPLETE SET (26) 4.80 12.00
1 Ales Pisa .20 .50
2 Chris Hajt .20 .50
3 Alex Henry .31 .78
4 Jan Horacek .20 .50
5 Kevin Brown .20 .50
6 Jason Chimera .40 1.00
7 Peter Sarno .20 .50
8 Craig Reichert .20 .50
9 Greg Leeb .20 .50
10 Marc-Andre Bergeron .20 .50
11 Brian Swanson .20 .50
12 Jani Rita .40 1.00
13 Fernando Pisani .20 .50
14 Michael Henrich .20 .50
15 Sean Selmser .20 .50
16 Ty Conklin .40 1.00
17 Alain Nasreddine .20 .50
18 Alexei Semenov .31 .78
19 Adam Dewan .20 .50
20 Marc Lamothe .31 .78
21 Sven Butenschon .20 .50
22 Chad Hinz .20 .50
23 Claude Julien CO .04 .11
24 Geoff Ward ACO .04 .11
25 Bruiser Mascot .04 .11
NNO Title Card/CL .04 .11

2002-03 Hamilton Bulldogs

COMPLETE SET (28) 8.00 20.00
1 Bobby Allen .20 .50
2 Ben Carpentier .20 .50
3 Ron Hainsey .40 1.00
4 Tony Salmelainen .20 .50
5 Chad Hinz .20 .50
6 Nate DiCasmirro .20 .50
7 Tomas Plekanec .40 1.00
8 Jason Ward .30 .75
9 Jarret Stoll .40 1.00
10 Matt O'Dette .20 .50
11 Marc-Andre Bergeron .20 .50
12 Jani Rita .30 .75
13 Francois Beauchemin .40 1.00
14 Fernando Pisani .30 .75
15 Michael Ryder 1.25 3.00
16 Michael Henrich .20 .50
17 Ty Conklin .30 .75
18 Eric Fichaud .30 .75
19 Alexei Semenov .20 .50
20 Adam Dewan .20 .50
21 Mathieu Garon .40 1.00
22 Benoit Gratton .20 .50
23 Francois Bouillon .30 .75
24 Mike Komisarek .30 .75
25 Jozef Balej .40 1.00
26 Marcel Hossa .40 1.00
27 Bruiser MASCOT .02 .10
28 Checklist .01 .01

2004-05 Hamilton Bulldogs

COMPLETE SET (30) 20.00
1 Andrew Archer .50
2 Ben Carpentier .50
3 JP Cote .50
4 Trevor Daley .50
5 Yann Danis 1.50
6 Benoit Dusablon .50
7 Dan Ellis 1.50
8 Jonathan Ferland .50
9 Dan Focht .50
10 Ron Hainsey 1.00
11 Chris Higgins 1.00
12 Raitis Ivanans .50
13 Dan Jancevski .50
14 Doug Jarvis CO .10
15 Andrei Kostitsyn 2.50
16 Michael Lambert .50
17 Christian Larrivee .50
18 Corey Locke .50
19 Antti Miettinen 1.00
20 Duncan Milroy .50
21 Gavin Morgan .50
22 Steve Ott 1.50
23 Tomas Plekanec 1.00
24 Philippe Plante .50
25 James Sanford .50
26 Matt Shasby .50
27 Marc-Andre Thinel .75
28 Jason Ward .75
29 Ron Wilson ACO .10
30 Bruiser MASCOT .10

2005-06 Hamilton Bulldogs

COMPLETE SET 6.00 15.00
1 Jonathan Aitken .20 .50
2 Andrew Archer .20 .50
3 Ryan Barnes .20 .50
4 Andre Benoit .20 .50
5 Jean-Philippe Cote .20 .50
6 Yann Danis .40 1.00
7 Jeff Drouin-Deslauriers .40 1.00
8 Jonathan Ferland .20 .50
9 Ron Hainsey .20 .50
10 Raitis Ivanans .40 1.00
11 Jean-Francois Jacques .20 .50
12 Andrei Kostitsyn .40 1.00
13 Michael Lambert .20 .50
14 Maxim Lapierre .20 .50
15 Francis Lemieux .20 .50
16 Corey Locke .20 .50
17 Olivier Michaud .40 1.00
18 Duncan Milroy .20 .50
19 Garth Murray .20 .50
20 Jeff Paul .20 .50
21 Marc-Antoine Pouliot .40 1.00
22 Mathieu Roy .75 2.00
23 James Sanford .20 .50
24 Dan Smith .20 .50
25 Danny Syvret .20 .50
26 Peter Vandermeer .40 1.00
27 Brad Winchester .20 .50
28 Don Lever .02 .10
29 Ron Wilson .02 .10
30 Bruiser .02 .10

2006-07 Hamilton Bulldogs

COMPLETE SET (26) 8.00 15.00
1 Andrew Archer .20 .50
2 Mathieu Aubin .20 .50
3 Ajay Baines .20 .50
4 Andre Benoit .20 .50
5 Kyle Chipchura .30 .75
6 Jean-Philippe Cote .20 .50
7 Matt D'Agostini .20 .50
8 Yann Danis .30 .75
9 Eric Manlow .20 .50
10 Jonathan Ferland .20 .50
11 Jon Gleed .20 .50
12 Mikhail Grabovsky .20 .50
13 Danny Groulx .20 .50
14 Jaroslav Halak .75 2.00
15 Dan Jancevski .20 .50
16 Andrei Kostitsyn .40 1.00
17 Michael Lambert .20 .50
18 Maxim Lapierre .30 .75
19 Francis Lemieux .20 .50
20 Corey Locke .20 .50
21 Duncan Milroy .20 .50
22 Ryan O'Byrne .20 .50
23 Mathieu Roy .40 1.00
24 Zach Stortini .40 1.00
25 Patrick Traverse .20 .50
26 Cory Urquhart .20 .50

1992-93 Hamilton Canucks

Created by Diamond Memories Sportscards to commemorate the Canucks' inaugural season, these 30 standard-size cards feature black-bordered color player action photos on the fronts. The cards are unnumbered and checklisted below in alphabetical order.

COMPLETE SET (30) 4.00 10.00
1 Shawn Antoski .30 .75
2 Robin Bawa .15 .40
3 Jamie Carlson TR .02 .10
4 Jassen Cullimore .20 .50
5 Alain Deeks .15 .40
6 Neil Eisenhut .15 .40
7 Mike Fountain .30 .75
8 Troy Gamble .30 .75
9 Jason Herter .15 .40
10 Pat Hickey PR .02 .10
11 Dane Jackson .15 .40
12 Dan Kesa .15 .40
13 Jeff Lumby ANN .02 .10
14 Mario Marois UER .20 .50
(Last name misspelled
Marios on front)
15 Bob Mason .30 .75
16 Mike Maurice .15 .40
17 Jay Mazur .15 .40
18 Jack McIlhargey CO .02 .10
19 Sandy Moger .30 .75
20 Stephane Morin .15 .40
21 Eric Murano .15 .40
22 Troy Neumeier .15 .40
23 Matt Nowsom CM .02 .10
24 Libor Polasek .15 .40
25 Phil von Stefenelli .15 .40
26 Doug Torrel .15 .40
27 Doug Trefiak TR .02 .10
28 Rick Vaive CO .15 .40
29 Opening Night .15 .40
Puck-Drop
Mario Marois
Pat Hickey PR
AHL President
30 Team Photo .20 .50
(Checklist)

1961-62 Hamilton Red Wings

This oversized set features members of the top farm team of the Red Wings. They were sold as a set by the team.

COMPLETE SET (21) 37.50 75.00
1 Bud Blom 1.50 3.00
2 Eddie Bush 2.00 4.00
3 Bob Dean 1.50 3.00
4 John Gofton 1.50 3.00
5 Bob Hamilton 1.50 3.00
6 Bob Hamilton 1.50 3.00
7 Ron Harris 2.00 4.00
8 Earl Heiskala 2.00 4.00
9 Paul Henderson 7.50 15.00
10 Roger Lafreniere 1.50 3.00
11 Lowell Macdonald 4.00 8.00
12 Pit Martin 5.00 10.00
13 Jim Mclellan 1.50 3.00
14 Harvey Meisenheimer 1.50 3.00
15 Howie Menard 1.50 3.00
16 Wayne Rivers 4.00 8.00
17 Jim Peters 2.00 4.00
18 Bob Wall 1.50 3.00
19 Jack Wildfong 1.50 3.00
20 Terry Urkewicz 1.50 3.00
21 Larry Zilliotto 1.50 3.00

1989-90 Hampton Roads Admirals

This 21-card set of the Hampton Roads Admirals of the ECHL features color photos on the front. The cards are unnumbered, and are listed below in alphabetical order. We've recently learned that 19 of the 21 cards have variations, ie, one version showing a head shot, the other an action shot. We've listed them with letter suffixes detailing action (A) or head shot (H). A complete set includes only one version or ther other. We cannot say which (if either) is more scarce, so we are showing no price difference between the two versions for the time being. The set, which last year was valued at $10, was the subject of fierce bidding wars each time it appeared on eBay in 2005 and earned one of the greatest value jumps in recent memory.

COMPLETE SET (21) 4.00 400.00
1A Mike Black 8.00 20.00
1H Mike Black 8.00 20.00
2 John Brophy CO 10.00 25.00
3A David Buckley 8.00 20.00
3H David Buckley 8.00 20.00
4A Pat Cavanagh 8.00 20.00
4H Pat Cavanagh 8.00 20.00
5A Mike Flanagan 8.00 20.00
5H Mike Flanagan 8.00 20.00
6A Frank Furlan 8.00 20.00
6H Frank Furlan 8.00 20.00
7A Don Gagne 8.00 20.00
7H Don Gagne 8.00 20.00
8A Steve Greenberg 8.00 20.00
8H Steve Greenberg 8.00 20.00
9A Murray Hood 8.00 20.00
9H Murray Hood 8.00 20.00
10A Trevor Jobe 8.00 20.00
10H Trevor Jobe 8.00 20.00
11A Trevor Kruger 8.00 20.00
11H Trevor Kruger 8.00 20.00
12A Chris Lukey 8.00 20.00
12H Chris Lukey 8.00 20.00
13A Brian Martin 8.00 20.00
13H Brian Martin 8.00 20.00
14A Dennis McEwen 8.00 20.00
14H Dennis McEwen 8.00 20.00
15A Bobby McGrath 8.00 20.00
15H Bobby McGrath 8.00 20.00
16A Darren Miciak 8.00 20.00
16H Darren Miciak 8.00 20.00
17A Al Murphy 8.00 20.00
17H Al Murphy 8.00 20.00
18A Jody Praznik 8.00 20.00
18H Jody Praznik 8.00 20.00
19A Alain Raymond 8.00 20.00
19H Alain Raymond 8.00 20.00
20A Wayne Stripp 8.00 20.00
20H Wayne Stripp 8.00 20.00
21 Scott Taylor 8.00 20.00

1990-91 Hampton Roads Admirals

This 20-card was issued by the Hampton Roads Admirals of the ECHL. They feature color action photography on the front, along with another photo and statistical information on the back. The numbering of the set is a mystery, as it clearly carries on from another issue. Interestingly, the previous year's Admirals set is unnumbered. The set, therefore, may be numbered consecutively with other ECHL issues from the same season.

COMPLETE SET (20) 3.00 8.00
41 Scott King .20 .50
42 Greg Bignell .15 .40
43 David Buckley .15 .40
44 Jody Praznik .15 .40
45 John East .15 .40
46 Steve Greenberg .15 .40
47 Darcy Kaminski .15 .40
48 Glen Kehrer .15 .40
49 Murray Hood .15 .40
50 Dennis McEwen .15 .40
51 Billy Nolan .15 .40
52 Bill Thomas .15 .40
53 Pat Cavanagh .15 .40
54 Cory Banika .20 .50
55 Al Murphy .15 .40
56 Harry Mews .15 .40
57 Mark Bernard .15 .40
58 Brian Martin .15 .40
59 Curt Brackenbury ACO .08 .25
60 John Brophy CO .15 .40

1991-92 Hampton Roads Admirals

This 20-card set was produced by the team and available at the rink. The cards feature action photos on the front, with stats and bio on the back. This set, which features an early pro card of Olaf Kolzig, is unnumbered, and listed below alphabetically.

COMPLETE SET (20) 4.00 50.00
1 Mark Bernard 1.25 3.00
2 Mike Chighisola .75 2.00
3 John East .75 2.00
4 Victor Gervais .75 2.00
5 Murray Hood .75 2.00
6 Scott Johnson .75 2.00
7 Olaf Kolzig 6.00 15.00
8 Paul Krepelka .75 2.00
9 Al MacIsaac .75 2.00
10 Brian Martin .75 2.00
11 Dennis McEwen .75 2.00
12 Dave Morissette .75 2.00
13 Billy Nolan .75 2.00
14 Randy Pearce .75 2.00
15 Steve Poapst 1.25 3.00
16 Pete Siciliano .75 2.00
17 Shawn Snesar .75 2.00
18 Keith Whitmore .75 2.00
19 John Brophy CO .40 1.00
20 Darcy Kaminski ACO .02 .10

1992-93 Hampton Roads Admirals

This set is unnumbered and was sponsored by Ward's Corner Sporting Goods, Ogden Services, and radio station WCMS. The set is listed by the order of the player's jersey number, which is listed on the back.

COMPLETE SET (20) 3.00 8.00
1 Shawn Snesar .20 .50
2 Paul Krepelka .20 .50
3 Claude Barthe .20 .50
4 Steve Poapst .30 .75
5 Kelly Sorenson .20 .50
6 Trevor Duhaime .20 .50
7 Steve Mirabile .20 .50
8 Kurt Kabat .20 .50
9 Victor Gervais .25 .60
10 Jason Rathbone .20 .50
11 Rod Taylor .20 .50
12 Al MacIsaac CO .08 .25
13 Brian Martin .20 .50
14 Dave Morissette .20 .50
15 Harry Mews .20 .50
16 Mark Bernard .20 .50
17 Nick Vitucci .30 .75
18 Steve Martell .20 .50
19 Chris Scarlata TR .02 .10
20 John Brophy CO .20 .50

1993-94 Hampton Roads Admirals

This set features the Admirals of the ECHL. The set was sponsored by Ward's Corner Sporting Goods, Ogden Services and radio station WCMS. The set is nearly identical in design to the previous year's set. The cards are unnumbered, and so they are listed alphabetically.

COMPLETE SET (20) 3.00 8.00
1 John Brophy CO .20 .50
2 Rick Burrill TR .02 .10
3 Daniel Chaput .20 .50
4 Brendan Curley .20 .50
5 Victor Gervais .20 .50
6 Brian Goudie .20 .50
7 Shamus Gregga .20 .50
8 Jason MacIntyre .20 .50
9 Al MacIsaac ACO .02 .10
10 Kevin Malgunas .20 .50
11 Dennis McEwen .20 .50
12 Mark Michaud .20 .50
13 Ron Pascucci .20 .50
14 Darren Perkins .20 .50
15 Steven Perkovic .20 .50
16 Shawn Snesar .20 .50
17 Kelly Sorenson .20 .50
18 Rod Taylor .20 .50
19 Richie Walcott .20 .50
20 Shawn Wheeler .20 .50

1994-95 Hampton Roads Admirals

This 23-card set measures the standard size. On a white card face, the fronts feature color action player photos with a simulated blue marble frame and a thin yellow, inner border. The player's name appears inside a hockey stick on the bottom of the photo, with the team logo next to it.

COMPLETE SET (23) 4.80 12.00
1 John Brophy CO .20 .50
2 Al MacIsaac ACO .02 .10
3 Patrick Lalime 2.00 5.00
4 Colin Gregor .15 .40
5 Ron Pascucci .15 .40
6 John Porco .15 .40
7 Trevor Halverson .20 .50
8 Rod Taylor .15 .40
9 Brian Goudie .15 .40
10 Chris Phelps .15 .40
11 Tom Menicci .15 .40
12 Anthony MacAulay .15 .40
13 Rick Kowalsky .15 .40
14 Dennis McEwen .15 .40
15 Kelly Sorenson .15 .40
16 Brendan Curley .15 .40
17 Jason MacIntyre .15 .40
18 Jim Brown .15 .40
19 Matt Mallgrave .15 .40
20 Ron Majic .15 .40
21 Corwin Saurdiff .15 .40
22 Rick Burrill TR .02 .10
23 Team Photo CL .15 .40
NNO Logo Card .02 .10

1995-96 Hampton Roads Admirals

This 25-card set showcases the Hampton Roads Admirals of the ECHL. The set was produced by Q-Cards, and distributed by Ward's Corner Sporting Goods; it may also have been sold through the team at games. The set features action photography on the front and an expanded player information section on the numbered back.

COMPLETE SET (25) 4.00 10.00
1 Team Photo .15 .40
2 John Brophy CO .15 .40
3 Al MacIsaac ACO .02 .10
4 Darryl Paquette .20 .50
5 Mark Bernard .15 .40
6 Ron Pascucci .15 .40
7 Dominic Maltais .15 .40
8 Jason MacIntyre .15 .40
9 Serge Aubin .40 1.00
10 Rick Kowalsky .08 .25
11 Claude Fillion .20 .50
12 Rod Taylor .15 .40
13 Alexei Krivchenkov .15 .40
14 David St. Pierre .15 .40
15 Steve Richards .15 .40
16 Trevor Halverson .30 .75
17 Chris Phelps .15 .40
18 Jeff Kostuch .15 .40
19 Sean Selmser .30 .75
20 Aaron Downey .40 1.00
21 Bob Woods .15 .40
22 Sergei Voronov .15 .40
23 Corwin Saurdiff .20 .50
24 Rick Burrell TR .02 .10
25 Gary Mansfield EQMG .02 .10

1997-98 Hampton Roads Admirals

This 24-card set was produced by a former player with the Ads and was handed out as a promotional giveaway at a home game.

COMPLETE SET (24) 7.20 18.00
1 Chad Ackerman .30 .75
2 Alexander Alexeev .30 .75
3 Rob Bonneau .30 .75
4 Dan Carney .30 .75
5 Dan Ceman .40 1.00
6 Sebastien Charpentier .40 1.00
7 Marty Clapton .30 .75
8 Victor Gervais .30 .75
9 Alexander Kharlamov .40 1.00
10 Rick Kowalsky .30 .75
11 Mike Larkin .30 .75
12 Bill Lincoln .30 .75
13 Ron Majic .30 .75
14 Jason Mansoff .30 .75
15 Chris Phelps .30 .75
16 Joel Poirier .30 .75
17 Jason Saal .60 1.50
18 Kayle Short .30 .75
19 Rod Taylor .30 .75
20 Joel Theriault .30 .75
21 Yuri Yuresko .30 .75
22 John Brophy HCO .20 .50
23 Al MacIsaac ACO .02 .10
24 Trainers .02 .10

1996-97 Hampton Roads Admirals

This 25-card set of the Hampton Roads Admirals of the ECHL was produced by Blueline Communications, and sponsored by Kline Chevrolet and The Score, 1310 AM. The cards feature action photos on the front, along with the player name. The backs include statistical and biographical data.

COMPLETE SET (25) 4.00 10.00
HRA1 Darryl Paquette .20 .50
HRA2 Mike Larkin .15 .40
HRA3 Chris Phelps .15 .40
HRA4 Alex Alexeev .15 .40
HRA5 Joel Theriault .15 .40
HRA6 Neal Martin .15 .40
HRA7 Ryan Mulhern .15 .40
HRA8 Darryl Shedden .15 .40
HRA9 Victor Gervais .15 .40
HRA10 Rod Taylor .15 .40
HRA11 Andy Weidenbach .15 .40
HRA12 Alain Savage .15 .40
HRA13 Randy Pearce .15 .40
HRA14 Chad Ackerman .15 .40
HRA15 Alexei Krivchenkov .15 .40
HRA16 Rick Kowalsky .15 .40
HRA17 Dominic Maltais .15 .40
HRA18 Joel Poirier .20 .50
HRA19 Marc Seliger .30 .75
HRA20 Aaron Downey .30 .75
HRA21 John Brophy CO .20 .50
HRA22 Al MacIsaac ACO .02 .10
HRA23 G.Mansfield EQMG .02 .10
K.Bender TR
HRA24 Salty (Mascot) .02 .10
NNO Team Photo .15 .40

1998-99 Hampton Roads Admirals

This 26-card set was handed out as a promotional giveaway at an Admirals game. Little else is known about the set, other than a confirmation that two versions of card #25 were released.

COMPLETE SET (26) 6.00 15.00
1 Mascot/Checklist .08 .25
2 John Brophy .20 .50
3 Al MacIsaac ACO .08 .25
4 Chris Phelps .20 .50
5 Trevor Johnson .20 .50
6 Jami Yoder .20 .50
7 Joel Poirier .30 .75
8 Alexander Kharlamov .30 .75
9 Bobby Russell .20 .50
10 Trever Fraser .20 .50
11 Jason Deleurme .20 .50
12 Henry Higdon .20 .50
13 Rod Taylor .20 .50
14 Jeff Corbett .20 .50
15 Derek Ernest .20 .50
16 Charlie Retter .20 .50
17 Chad Ackerman .20 .50
18 Boris Zelenko .20 .50
19 Dan Ceman .30 .75
20 Marty Clapton .20 .50
21 Milt Mastad .20 .50
22 Dominic Maltais .30 .75
23 Stephen Valiquette .75 2.00
24 Jason Saal .40 1.00
25 Scott Boggs EM .08 .25
25 Stu Bender TR .08 .25

1998-99 Hampton Roads Admirals 10th Anniversary

This 30-card set was handed out at a game in December, and features alumni of the Admirals, including several prominent NHLers. Because of the unique distribution method, the cards are quite scarce.

COMPLETE SET (30) 10.00 25.00
1 John Brophy HCO .20 .50
2 Rod Taylor .20 .50
3 Victor Gervais .20 .50
4 Brian Martin .20 .50
5 Dennis McEwen .20 .50
6 Chris Phelps .20 .50
7 Randy Pearce .20 .50
8 Murray Hood .20 .50
9 Olaf Kolzig 2.00 5.00
10 Kelly Sorenson .20 .50
11 Mark Bernard .20 .50
12 Andrew Brunette .40 1.00
13 Trevor Halverson .20 .50
14 Rick Kowalsky .20 .50
15 Aaron Downey .75 2.00
16 Patrick Lalime 1.50 4.00
17 Steve Poapst .30 .75
18 Alexander Alexeev .20 .50
19 Harry Mews .20 .50
20 Al MacIsaac .20 .50
21 John Parco .20 .50
22 Kent Hawley .20 .50
23 Dave Flanagan .20 .50
24 Billy Nolan .20 .50
25 Brendan Curley .20 .50
26 Ron Pascucci .20 .50
27 Mark Michaud .20 .50
28 Shawn Snesar .20 .50
29 Byron Dafoe 1.25 3.00
30 Sebastien Charpentier .40 1.00

1999-00 Hampton Roads Admirals

This set features the Admirals of the ECHL. The set was produced by Q-Cards and issued as a promotional giveaway at a home game, and later at Ragazzi's, a local restaurant.

COMPLETE SET (25) 8.00 20.00
1 Chad Ackerman .30 .75
2 Gerad Adams .30 .75
3 Louis Bedard .40 1.00
4 Brad Church .40 1.00
5 Marty Clapton .30 .75
6 Curtis Cruickshank .40 1.00
7 Derek Ernest .30 .75
8 Ryan Gillis .30 .75
9 Trevor Johnson .30 .75
10 Rick Kowalsky .30 .75
11 Jan Lasak 1.25 3.00
12 Dominic Maltais .40 1.00
13 Mike Omicioli .30 .75
14 John Parco .30 .75
15 Dwight Parrish .30 .75
16 Colin Pepperall .30 .75
17 Richard Pitirri .30 .75
18 Bobby Russell .30 .75
19 Mike Siklenka .30 .75
20 Dean Stork .30 .75
21 Rod Taylor .30 .75
22 John Brophy CO .08 .25
23 Al MacIsaac CO .08 .25
24 Stu Bender/Scott Boggs TR .08 .25
NNO Checklist .08 .25

1997-98 Hartford Wolf Pack

This set features the Wolf Pack of the AHL. The singles are postcard-sized, and were issued only to members of the team's Kid's Club.

COMPLETE SET (29) 12.00 35.00
1 Derek Armstrong .40 1.00
2 Sylvain Blouin .60 1.50
3 Eric Cairns .60 1.50
4 Dan Cloutier 1.50 4.00
5 Christian Dube .40 1.00
6 Peter Ferraro .60 1.50
7 Maxim Galanov .40 1.00
8 Ken Gernander .40 1.00
9 Daniel Goneau .40 1.00
10 Todd Hall .40 1.00
11 Johan Lindbom .40 1.00
12 Mike Martin .40 1.00
13 Jason Muzzatti .60 1.50
14 Dale Purinton .75 2.00
15 Marc Savard .75 2.00
16 Pierre Sevigny .40 1.00
17 Adam Smith .40 1.00
18 Geoff Smith .40 1.00
19 Brad Smyth .40 1.00
20 Lee Sorochan .40 1.00
21 Robb Stauber .60 1.50
22 P.J. Stock 1.50 4.00
23 Ronnie Sundin .40 1.00
24 Tim Sweeney .40 1.00
25 Brent Thompson .40 1.00
26 Ryan VandenBussche .75 2.00
27 Vladimir Vorobiev .40 1.00
28 Chris Winnes .40 1.00
29 Sonar MASCOT .08 .25

1998-99 Hartford Wolf Pack

This set features the Wolf Pack of the AHL. The set was given only to members of the team's Kid's Club. The cards bear the logos of Brigham's Ice Cream.

COMPLETE SET (28) 14.00 35.00
1 Derek Armstrong .40 1.00
2 Jeff Brown .40 1.00
3 Ed Campbell .40 1.00
4 Ben Carpentier .40 1.00
5 Christian Dube .40 1.00
6 Bob Errey .40 1.00
7 Jeff Finley .40 1.00
8 Ken Gernander .40 1.00
9 Daniel Goneau .40 1.00
10 Todd Hall .40 1.00

11 Boyd Kane .75 2.00
12 Jean-Francois Labbe .75 2.00
13 Mike Martin .40 1.00
14 Dale Purinton .60 1.50
15 Ryan Risidore .40 1.00
16 Marc Savard .75 2.00
17 Adam Smith .40 1.00
18 Lee Sorochan .60 1.50
19 P.J. Stock 3.00 8.00
20 Brent Thompson .40 1.00
21 Alexei Vasiliev .40 1.00
22 Vladimir Vorobiev .40 1.00
23 Kay Whitmore .60 1.50
24 Chris Winnes .40 1.00
25 Johan Witehall .40 1.00
26 Sonar MASCOT .08 .25
27 Rich Brennan .40 1.00
28 Stefan Cherneski .40 1.00

1999-00 Hartford Wolf Pack

This set features the Wolf Pack of the AHL. These cards were handed out to members of the team's Kid's Club at a special practice. The cards are blank-backed and unnumbered, and therefore are listed in alphabetical order.

COMPLETE SET (23) 12.00 30.00
1 Derek Armstrong .40 1.00
2 Drew Bannister .40 1.00
3 Ben Carpentier .40 1.00
4 Stefan Cherneski .40 1.00
5 Jason Doig .60 1.50
6 Francois Fortier .40 1.00
7 Ken Gernander .40 1.00
8 Daniel Goneau .40 1.00
9 Todd Hall .40 1.00
10 Mike Harder .40 1.00
11 Burke Henry .40 1.00
12 Milan Hnilicka 1.50 4.00
13 Chris Kenady .40 1.00
14 Tomas Kloucek .75 2.00
15 Alexander Korobolin .40 1.00
16 Jean-Francois Labbe .75 2.00
17 Dale Purinton .75 2.00
18 Brad Smyth .60 1.50
19 P.J. Stock 1.25 3.00
20 Tony Tuzzolino .60 1.50
21 Alexei Vasiliev .40 1.00
22 Terry Virtue .60 1.50
23 Johan Witehall .60 1.50

2000-01 Hartford Wolf Pack

This set features the Wolf Pack of the AHL. The set was a very tough giveaway item, available only to members of the team's youth fan club. The cards are unnumbered and blank-backed. Three of the cards (Grosek, Labarbera and Mehalko) do not feature names on the front.

COMPLETE SET (29) 10.00 25.00
1 Derek Armstrong .30 .75
2 Drew Bannister .30 .75
3 Ryan Bast .30 .75
4 Ben Carpentier .30 .75
5 Jason Dawe .30 .75
6 Brandon Dietrich .30 .75
7 Jason Doig .30 .75
8 Dave Duerden .30 .75
9 Ken Gernander .30 .75
10 Michal Grosek .30 1.00
11 Todd Hall .30 .75
12 Burke Henry .30 .75
13 Johan Holmqvist .80 2.00
14 Boyd Kane .30 .75
15 Chris Kenady .30 .75
16 Tomas Kloucek .80 2.00
17 Jason Labarbera .80 2.00
18 Manny Malhotra .60 1.00
19 Brad Mehalko .30 .75
20 Mike Mottau .60 1.50
21 Dale Purinton .40 1.00
22 Bert Robertsson .30 .75
23 Richard Scott .40 1.00
24 Brad Smyth .30 .75
25 Tony Tuzzolino .30 .75
26 Jeff Ulmer .30 .75
27 Terry Virtue .40 1.00
28 Vitali Yeremeyev .60 1.50
29 Sonar MASCOT .10 .25

2001-02 Hartford Wolf Pack

This set features the Wolf Pack of the AHL. These very scarce cards were available only to members of the Wolf Pack Kids Club. The cards are blank backed and unnumbered, so they are listed below in alphabetical order. Minor league expert Ralph Slate reports that Igor Ulanov's card was most likely a late addition, as it is printed on thinner card stock than the rest of the set.

COMPLETE SET (26) 19.56 48.89
1 Benoit Dusablon .80 2.00
2 Jason Dawe .80 2.00
3 Rico Fata .80 2.00
4 Sean Gagnon .80 2.00
5 Ken Gernander .40 1.00
6 Christian Gosselin .40 1.00
7 Michal Grosek .40 1.00
8 Barrett Heisten .80 2.00
9 Johan Holmqvist .80 2.00
10 Wes Jarvis .40 1.00
11 Boyd Kane .80 2.00
12 Matt Kinch .40 1.00
13 Jason Labarbera .80 2.00
14 Jamie Lundmark 4.00 10.00
15 Dave MacIsaac .40 1.00
16 Brad Mehalko .40 1.00
17 Scott Meyer .40 1.00
18 Mike Mottau 1.20 3.00
19 Cam Severson .40 1.00
20 Peter Smrek .80 2.00
21 Brad Smyth .40 1.00
22 Chris St. Croix .40 1.00
23 John Tripp .40 1.00
24 Igor Ulanov 4.00 10.00
25 Terry Virtue .80 2.00
26 Sonar MASCOT .20 .50

2002-03 Hartford Wolf Pack

COMPLETE SET (30) 12.00 30.00
1 Bobby Andrews .40 1.00
2 Dean Arsene .40 1.00
3 Patrick Aufiero .40 1.00
4 Ryan Bast .40 1.00
5 Garrett Burnett .40 1.00
6 Ted Donato .40 1.00
7 Benoit Dusablon .75 2.00
8 Nils Ekman .40 1.00
9 Ken Gernander .40 1.00
10 Johan Holmqvist .75 2.00
11 Dave Karpa .40 1.00
12 Matt Kinch .40 1.00
13 Jason Labarbera .75 2.00
14 Bryce Lampman .40 1.00
15 Cory Larose .40 1.00
16 Janne Laukkanen .40 1.00
17 Roman Lyashenko .40 1.00
18 Garth Murray .40 1.00
19 Chris Pittman .40 1.00
20 Richard Scott .40 1.00
21 Billy Tibbetts 1.25 3.00
22 John Tripp .40 1.00
23 Layne Ulmer .40 1.00
24 Dixon Ward .40 1.00
25 Mike Wilson .40 1.00
26 Patrick Yetman .40 1.00
27 Damon Scott ANN .02 .10
28 Nick Fotiu ACO .20 .50
29 Ryan McGill HCO .20 .50
30 Sonar Mascot .02 .10

2003-04 Hartford Wolf Pack

This set was made available to members of the Wolf Pack Kids Club, according to minor league maven Ralph Slate. The cards are oversized, unnumbered, and are listed below in alphabetical order. The card of Jamie Pushor was most likely a late addition, since it is printed on larger card stock than the rest of the set. It was not included in every set distributed by the team and therefore is considered a short print.

COMPLETE SET (27) 50.00
1 Bobby Andrews 1.00
2 Brandon Cullen 1.00
3 Ryan Cuthbert 1.00
4 Benoit Dusablon 2.00
5 Jayme Filipovicz 1.00
6 Ken Gernander 1.00
7 Paul Healey 1.00
8 Jeff Heerema 2.00
9 John Jakopin 1.00
10 Matt Kinch 1.00
11 Jason Labarbera 3.00
12 Bryce Lampman 1.00
13 Cory Larose 1.00
14 Lucas Lawson 1.00
15 Jason MacDonald 1.00
16 Dominic Moore SP 10.00
17 Garth Murray 1.50
18 Lawrence Nycholat 1.00
19 Phil Osaer 1.00
20 Jamie Pushor SP 10.00
21 Richard Scott 2.00
22 Juris Stals 1.00
23 Jeff State 1.00
24 Fedor Tjutin 3.00
25 Layne Ulmer 1.50
26 Craig Weller 1.00
27 Chad Wiseman 1.00

2004-05 Hartford Wolf Pack

Available only to member's of the team's Kid's Club.

COMPLETE SET (26) 60.00
1 Jozef Balej 3.00
2 Blair Betts 2.00
3 Ken Gernander 2.00
4 Trevor Gillies 3.00
5 Alexandre Giroux 3.00
6 Martin Grenier 2.00
7 Jeff Hamilton 2.00
8 Dwight Helminen 2.00
9 Ryan Hollweg 3.00
10 Jason Labarbera 3.00
11 Bryce Lampman 2.00
12 Lucas Lofton 2.00
13 Dave Liffiton 2.00
14 Jamie Lundmark 3.00
15 Steven MacIntyre 2.00
16 Jeff MacMillan 2.00
17 Dominic Moore 2.00
18 Garth Murray 2.00
19 Lawrence Nycholat 2.00
20 Jed Ortmeyer 3.00
21 Thomas Pock 3.00
22 Jake Taylor 2.00
23 Layne Ulmer 2.00
24 Stephen Valiquette 3.00
25 Craig Weller 2.00
26 Chad Wiseman 2.00

2005-06 Hartford Wolf Pack

COMPLETE SET (28) 15.00 30.00
1 Ivan Baranka .40 1.00
2 Nigel Dawes .75 2.00
3 Lee Falardeau .40 1.00
4 Fedor Fedorov .40 1.00
5 Colby Genoway .40 1.00
6 Robert Gherson .40 1.00
7 Daniel Girardi .75 2.00
8 Alexandre Giroux .40 1.00
9 Bruce Graham .40 1.00
10 Martin Grenier .40 1.00
11 Dwight Helminen .40 1.00
12 Jarkko Immonen .40 1.00
13 Hugh Jessiman .40 1.00
14 Bryce Lampman .40 1.00
15 Dave Liffiton .40 1.00
16 Al Montoya .50 4.00
17 Thomas Pock .40 1.00
18 Dale Purinton .75 2.00
19 Joe Rullier .40 1.00
20 Martin Sonnenberg .40 1.00
21 Daniel Sparre .40 1.00
22 Jake Taylor .40 1.00
23 Craig Weller .40 1.00
24 Chad Wiseman .40 1.00
25 Jim Schoenfeld HC .02 .10
26 Ken Gernander AC .02 .10
27 Ulf Samuelsson AC .02 .10
28 Sonar & Torpedo MASCOTS .01 .01

2006-07 Hartford Wolf Pack

COMPLETE SET (28) 25.00 50.00
1 Ryan Constant .60 1.50
2 Hugh Jessiman .60 1.50
3 Mark Lee .60 1.50
4 Bryce Lampman .60 1.50
5 Corey Potter .60 1.50
6 Bruce Graham .60 1.50
7 Zdenek Bahensky .60 1.50
8 Lee Falardeau .60 1.50
9 Daniel Girardi 1.25 3.00
10 Darius Kasparaitis .60 1.50
11 Steve Valiquette .75 2.00
12 Brad Isbister .60 1.50
13 Jarkko Immonen 1.25 3.00
14 Marvin Degon .60 1.50
15 Lauri Korpikoski 1.25 3.00
16 Jake Taylor .60 1.50
17 Nigel Dawes 1.25 3.00
18 Dale Purinton .60 1.50
19 Dane Byers 1.25 3.00
20 Dwight Helminen .60 1.50
21 Greg Moore .60 1.50
22 Martin Richter .60 1.50
23 Craig Weller .60 1.50
24 Ryan Callahan 1.25 3.00
25 Dave Liffiton .60 1.50
26 Al Montoya 1.25 3.00
27 Francis Lessard .60 1.50
28 Brandon Dubinsky .60 1.50

1992-93 Harvard Crimson

As with most NCAA sets, this product is believed to be a promotional giveaway of some kind. The cards are unnumbered and checklisted below in alphabetical order.

COMPLETE SET (31) 8.00 20.00
1 Brian Adams .30 .75
2 Chris Baird .30 .75
3 Lou Body .30 .75
4 Michel Breistroff .30 .75
5 Perry Cohagen .30 .75
6 Ben Coughlin .30 .75
7 Ted Drury .40 1.00
8 Brian Farell .30 .75
9 Steven Flomenhoft .30 .75
10 Eric Grahling .30 .75
11 Cory Gustafson .30 .75
12 Kevin Hampe ACO .02 .10
13 Steve Hermsdorf .30 .75
14 Tom Holmes .30 .75
15 Aaron Israel .30 .75
16 Jason Karmanos .30 .75
17 Ian Kennish .30 .75
18 Brad Konik .30 .75
19 Bryan Lonsinger .30 .75
20 Derek Maguire .40 1.00
21 Matt Mallgrave .30 .75
22 Geb Marett .30 .75
23 Steve Martins .40 1.00
24 Sean McCann .30 .75
25 Peter McLaughlin .30 .75
26 Keith McLean .30 .75
27 Kirk Nielsen .40 1.00
28 Jerry Pawloski ACO .02 .10
29 Ronn Tomassoni CO .02 .10
30 Tripp Tracy .60 1.50
31 Header Card .02 .10

1994-95 Hershey Bears

This 24-card set was handed out at the Bears charity carnival. The cards are blank-backed so they are listed in alphabetical order.

COMPLETE SET (24) 8.00 20.00
1 Vladislav Boulin .40 1.00
2 Aris Brimanis .40 1.00
3 Bruce Coles .40 1.00
4 Yanick Dupre .40 1.00
5 Tracy Egeland .40 1.00
6 Andre Faust .40 1.00
7 Jeff Finley .40 1.00
8 Milos Holan .40 1.00
9 Paul Jerrard .40 1.00
10 Dan Kordic .40 1.00
11 Les Kuntar .60 1.50
12 Mitch Lamoureux .60 1.50
13 Neil Little 1.25 3.00
14 Mike McHugh .40 1.00
15 Clayton Norris .40 1.00
16 Vaclav Prospal .75 2.00
17 Terran Sandwith .40 1.00
18 Ryan Sittler .40 1.00
19 Bob Wilkie .40 1.00
20 Chris Winnes .40 1.00
21 Mike Stothers ACO .02 .10
22 Brad Dibeler ATR .02 .10
23 Jay Leach HCO .02 .10

1998-99 Hershey Bears

This 40-card set was sponsored by the Lebanon Daily News and features players from the 1998-99 Hershey Bears as well as several cards of past players and teams from this AHL franchise. The team photos carry player checklists on the back of each card.

COMPLETE SET (40) 12.00 30.00
1 Evgeny Lazarev .30 .75
(Mitch Lamoureux
2 Marc Denis 1.50 4.00
3 Jeff Buchanan .15 .40
4 Ted Crowley .15 .40
5 Yuri Babenko .15 .40
6 Evgeny Lazarev .30 .75
7 Scott Parker 1.25 3.00
8 Mike Foligno CO .20 .50
9 Rob Shearer .20 .50
10 Brad Larsen .15 .40
11 1946-47 Team Photo .20 .50
12 Rick Berry .20 .50
13 Troy Crowder .15 .40
14 Dan Hinote .40 1.00
15 Serge Aubin .40 1.00
16 1957-58 Team Photo .20 .50
17 1958-89 Team Photo .20 .50
18 1968-69 Team Photo .20 .50
19 David Aebischer 2.00 5.00
20 Mitch Lamoureux .30 .75
21 Christian Matte .20 .50
22 Dan Smith .15 .40
23 Jay Wells CO .15 .40
24 1973-74 Team Photo .15 .40
25 Ville Nieminen .75 2.00
26 Nick Bootland .15 .40
27 1979-80 Team Photo .20 .50
28 Bruce Richardson .15 .40
29 Brian Willsie .15 .40
30 Hershey Park Arena .08 .25
31 Brian White .15 .40
32 1980-81 Team Photo .20 .50
33 1987-88 Team Photo .20 .50
34 Dan Stuck TR .08 .25
35 1996-97 Team Photo .20 .50
36 Frank Mathers .20 .50
37 Arnie Kullman .15 .40
38 Mike Nykoluk .15 .40
39 Tim Tookey .30 .75
40 Team Logo .08 .25

2000-01 Hershey Bears

This set features the Bears of the AHL. This set was produced as a giveaway with the purchase of a local newspaper. Collectors buying a paper at the game would get one card, making a complete set very difficult to piece together.

COMPLETE SET (20) 5.00 25.00
1 Yuri Babenko .20 1.00
2 Rick Berry .20 1.50
3 Nick Bootland .20 1.00
4 Frederic Cassivi .30 2.00
5 Mike Craig .20 1.00
6 Kelly Fairchild .20 1.00
7 Brad Larsen .20 1.00
8 Yevgeny Lazarev .20 1.50
9 Stewart Malgunas .20 1.00
10 Ville Nieminen .60 3.00
11 Joel Prpic .20 1.00
12 Alex Ryazantsev .30 1.50
13 Philippe Sauve .40 4.00
14 Matthew Scorsune .20 1.00
15 Rob Shearer .20 1.50
16 Dan Smith .20 1.00
17 Ben Storey .20 1.00
18 K.C. Timmons .20 1.00
19 Steffon Walby .20 1.00
20 Brian White .20 1.00

2001-02 Hershey Bears

This set features the Bears of the AHL. The cards were issued singly as a promotional giveaway with the purchase of a Hershey Patriot News newspaper at each home game. The last eight cards were apparently issued as an update set. The series is very difficult to complete due to this distribution. Although the player's jersey number appears on the front and back, the cards are considered unnumbered, and thus are listed in alphabetical order.

COMPLETE SET (28) 20.00 40.00
1 Yuri Babenko .60 1.50
2 Frederic Cassivi .60 1.50
3 Mike Cirillo .60 1.50
4 Coco MASCOT .10 .25
5 Larry Courville .60 1.50
6 Jeff Daw .60 1.50
7 Kelly Fairchild .60 1.50
8 Paul Fixter ACO .10 .25
9 Mike Foligno CO .10 .25
10 Riku Hahl .75 2.00
11 Matt Herr .60 1.50
12 Jordan Krestanovich .60 1.50
13 Mikhail Kuleshov .60 1.50
14 Yevgeny Lazarev .60 1.50
15 Dave MacIsaac .60 1.50
16 Steve Moore .60 1.50
17 Bryan Muir .60 1.50
18 Vaclav Nedorost .60 1.50
19 Brad Norton .60 1.50
20 Jaroslav Obsut .60 1.50
21 Jeff Paul .60 1.50
22 Alex Riazantsev .60 1.50
23 Phil Sauve .75 2.00
24 Matt Scorsune .60 1.50
25 Brent Thompson .60 1.50
26 Rocky Thompson .60 1.50
27 K.C. Timmons .60 1.50
28 Radim Vrbata .75 2.00

2002-03 Hershey Bears

COMPLETE SET (30) 30.00
1 Eric Bertrand 1.00
2 Nick Bootland 1.00
3 Steve Brule 1.00
4 Peter Budaj 2.00
5 Marc Busenburg 1.00
6 Brett Clark 1.00
7 Dale Clarke 1.00
8 Pierre-Luc Emond 1.00
9 Mark Freer 1.00
10 Riku Hahl 2.00
11 Jordan Krestanovich 1.00
12 Mikhail Kuleshov 1.00
13 Cail MacLean 1.00
14 Steve Moore 1.00
15 Bryan Muir 1.00
16 Jeff Paul 1.00
17 Alexander Ryazantsev 1.00
18 Philippe Sauve 3.00
19 Agris Saviels 1.00
20 Charlie Stephens 1.00
21 Marek Svatos 3.00
22 Brent Thompson 1.00
23 K.C.Timmons 1.00
24 Rob Voltera 1.00
25 Tim Wedderburn 1.00
26 Brian Willsie 1.00
27 Mike Foligno HCO .25
28 Paul Fixter ACO .25
29 Coco Mascot .10
30 Giant Center Arena .10

2003-04 Hershey Bears

This set was produced by Choice Marketing and sold as a set at home games.

COMPLETE SET (24) 10.00
1 Peter Budaj .75
2 Jeff Finger .50
3 D.J. Smith .50
4 Brett Clark .50
5 Tomas Slovak .50
6 Pascal Trepanier .50
7 Jordan Krestanovich .50
8 Gavin Morgan .50
9 Eric Perrin 1.00
10 Ryan Craig .50
11 Mikhail Kuleshov .50
12 Shane Willis .50
13 Rob Voltera .50
14 Steve Brule .50
15 Bruce Richardson .50
16 Sheldon Keefe .50
17 Agris Saviels .50
18 Charlie Stephens .50
19 Marc Busenburg .50
20 Mark Jerant .50
21 Evgeny Artyukhin .50
22 Tom Lawson .50
23 Paul Fixter HCO .10
24 Paul Jerrard ACO .10

2003-04 Hershey Bears Patriot News

Singles from this set could be acquired only with the purchase of a Patriot News newspaper at select home games, making these cards, and this set, one of the season's toughest to acquire.

COMPLETE SET (30) 40.00
1 Evgeny Artyukhin 1.50
2 Dennis Bonvie 2.00
3 Steve Brule 1.50
4 Peter Budaj 2.00
5 Marc Busenburg 1.50
6 Brett Clark 1.50
7 Ryan Craig 1.50
8 Jeff Finger 1.50
9 Mark Jerant 1.50
10 Sheldon Keefe 1.50
11 Jordan Krestanovich 1.50
12 Mikhail Kuleshov 1.50
13 Brad Larsen 1.50
14 Tom Lawson 2.00
15 Steve Moore 1.50
16 Gavin Morgan 1.50
17 Eric Perrin 3.00
18 Bruce Richardson 1.50
19 Darren Rumble 1.50
20 Agris Saviels 1.50
21 Tomas Slovak 1.50
22 D.J. Smith 1.50
23 Charlie Stephens 1.50
24 Pascal Trepanier 1.50
25 Mikko Viitanen 1.50
26 Rob Voltera 1.50
27 Shane Willis 1.50
28 Paul Fixter HCO .25
29 Paul Jerrard ACO .25
30 Mascot .25

2004-05 Hershey Bears Patriot News

Cards were available individually with the purchase of a Patriot News newspaper.

COMPLETE SET (31) 40.00
1 Dean Arsene 1.00
2 Chris Bala 1.00
3 Greg Barber 1.00
4 Dennis Bonvie 4.00
5 Johnny Boychuk 1.00
6 Peter Budaj 2.00
7 Brett Clark 1.00
8 Carl Corrazzini 2.00
9 Mathieu Darche 2.00
10 Jeff Finger 1.00
11 Paul Fixter CO .50
12 Martin Hlinka 1.00
13 Paul Jerrard ACO .50
14 Sergei Klyazmin 1.00
15 Tom Lawson 2.00
16 David Masse 1.00
17 Frank Mathers 2.00
18 Frank Mathers 2.00
19 Cody McCormick 2.00
20 Cail MacLean 1.00
21 Eric Perrin 3.00
22 Tom Lawson 1.00
23 Agris Saviels 1.00
24 Frantisek Skladany 1.00
25 Mike Souza 1.00
26 Ryan Steeves 1.00
27 Marek Svatos 3.00
28 Jeff Ulmer 1.00
29 Mikko Viitanen 2.00
30 Martin Wilde 2.00
31 Coco MASCOT .10

2005-06 Hershey Bears

COMPLETE SET (28) 8.00 20.00
1 Dean Arsene .30 .75
2 Jared Aulin .30 .75
3 Chris Bourque .60 1.50
4 Frederic Cassivi .60 1.50
5 Jakub Cutta .30 .75
6 Eric Fehr .30 .75
7 Tomas Fleischmann .30 .75
8 Owen Fussey .30 .75
9 Mike Green .30 .75
10 Jonas Johansson .30 .75
11 Boyd Kane .30 .75
12 Jakub Klepis .30 .75
13 Graham Mink .60 1.50
14 Lawrence Nycholat .30 .75
15 Dave Steckel .30 .75
16 Joey Tenute .30 .75
17 Martin Wilde .30 .75
18 Bruce Boudreau HC .02 .10
19 Bob Woods AC .02 .10
20 Coco the Bear MASCOT .02 .10
21 Kirk Daubenspeck .40 1.00
22 Deryk Engelland .30 .75
23 Colin Forbes .30 .75
24 J.F. Fortin .30 .75
25 Brooks Laich .30 .75
26 Louis Robitaille .75 2.00
27 Mark Wotton .30 .75
28 Dwayne Zinger .30 .75

1995-96 Houston Aeros

This set features the Aeros of the IHL. The cards were produced by Edge Ice and sold at the team's souvenir stands.

COMPLETE SET (25) 4.80 12.00
1 Scott Arniel .30 .75
2 Al Conroy .20 .50
3 Paul DiPietro .20 .50
4 Gord Donnelly .20 .50
5 Rob Dopson .30 .75
6 Mark Freer .20 .50
7 Troy Gamble .30 .75
8 Kevin Grant .20 .50
9 Curtis Hunt .20 .50
10 Steve Jaques .20 .50
11 Gord Kruppke .20 .50
12 Mark Lamb .30 .75
13 Marc Laniel .30 .75
14 Kevin Malgunas .20 .50
15 Mike Maurice .20 .50
16 Scott McCrory .20 .50
17 Myles O'Connor .20 .50
18 Jim Paek .20 .50
19 Vadim Slivchenko .20 .50
20 Graeme Townshend .20 .50
21 Sylvain Turgeon .20 .50
22 Carl Valimont .20 .50
23 Mike Yeo .20 .50
24 Dave Tippett .20 .50
25 Terry Ruskowski CO .20 .50

1999-00 Houston Aeros

Created by ebk Sports, this standard size set was created specifically for the 2000 IHL All-Star Game, which featured the defending Turner Cup champion Aeros against the best players from the rest of the league. The set was sold at the Aeros home rink, although production problems delayed its release. The set features color action photos on a plastic-type stock. The cards are prone to poor centering and cutting.

COMPLETE SET (29) 10.00 25.00
1 Paul Dyck .40 1.00
2 Marty Wilford .40 1.00
3 Matt Swanson .40 1.00
4 Mark Lamb .60 1.50
5 Jeff Daw .40 1.00
6 Brian Wiseman .60 1.50
7 Lane Lambert .60 1.50
8 Brian Felsner .40 1.00
9 Terry Marchant .40 1.00
10 Lee Jinman .40 1.00
11 Rudy Poeschek .60 1.50
12 David Oliver .40 1.00
13 Brad Williamson .40 1.00
14 Mark Major .40 1.00
15 David Wilkie .40 1.00
16 Maxime Gingras .75 2.00
17 Greg Pankewicz .40 1.00
18 Gregg Walters .40 1.00
19 Sandy Moger .60 1.50
20 Frederic Chabot 1.25 3.00
21 Ron Low CO .40 1.00
22 Dave Barr ACO .20 .50
25 Mascot .08 .25
NNO Jerry Meins TR .02 .10
NNO Header Card .02 .10
NNO Steve Sumner EQ .02 .10
NNO Checklist .08 .25

2003-04 Houston Aeros

COMPLETE SET (20) 10.00
1 Chris Bala .50
2 Jason Beckett .50
3 Dan Cavanaugh .50
4 Marc Cavosie .50
5 Mark Cullen .50
6 Josh DeWolf .50
7 Chris Dyment .50
8 Matthew Foy .50
9 Mika Hannula .50
10 Chris Heid .50
11 Jeff Hoggan .50
12 Johan Holmqvist .75
13 Jason Marshall .50
14 Zbynek Michalek .50
15 Kevin Mitchell .50
16 Bill Muckalt .50
17 Eric Reitz .50
18 Stephane Veilleux .50
19 Rickard Wallin .50
20 Kyle Wanvig .50

2004-05 Houston Aeros

This set was handed out in 10-card increments at two different Aeros home games. The cards are unnumbered and so are listed below in alphabetical order.

COMPLETE SET (20) 30.00
1 Derek Boogaard 2.00
2 Pierre-Marc Bouchard 3.00
3 Brent Burns 3.00
4 Dan Cavanaugh 1.00
5 Mark Cullen 1.00
6 John Erskine 1.50
7 Matt Foy 1.00
8 Ray Giroux 1.00
9 Josh Harding 3.00
10 Mikko Koivu 3.00
11 Kirby Law 1.00
12 Junior Lessard 2.00
13 Zbynek Michalek 1.00
14 Todd Reirden 1.00
15 Eric Reitz 1.00
16 Mike Smith 2.00
17 Patrick Traverse 2.00
18 Stephane Veilleux 1.00
19 Rickard Wallin 1.00
20 Kyle Wanvig 1.00

2006-07 Houston Aeros Retro•

COMPLETE SET (10) 5.00 10.00
1 Frederic Chabot .75 2.00
2 Mark Freer .30 .75
3 Cam Stewart .30 .75
4 Brian Wiseman .30 .75
5 Derek Boogaard 1.25 3.00
6 Jeff Christian .30 .75
7 Manny Fernandez .40 1.00
8 Curtis Murphy .30 .75
9 Todd McLellan .30 .75
10 Dave Tippett CO .30 .75

1987-88 Hull Olympiques

This set features a rare card of Wayne Gretzky, who was pictured as a result of buying the team.

COMPLETE SET (24) 80.00
1 Header Card .08 .25
2 Joe Aloi .40 1.00
3 Joel Blain .40 1.00
4 Christian Breton .40 1.00
5 Benoit Brunet .75 2.00
6 Guy Dupuis .40 1.00
7 Martin Gelinas 1.25 3.00
8 Jason Glickman .75 2.00
9 Wayne Gretzky OWN 25.00 60.00
10 Herbert Hohenberger .75 2.00
11 Ken MacDermid .40 1.00
12 Craig Martin .75 2.00
13 Mark McLane .40 1.00
14 Stephane Matteau .75 2.00
15 Kelly Nester .40 1.00
16 Marc Saumier .40 1.00
17 Claude-Charles Sauriol .40 1.00
18 Daniel Shank 1.25 3.00
19 Joe Suk .40 1.00
20 Alain Vigneault .40 1.00
21 George Wilcox .40 1.00
22 Team Card .20 .50
23 Team Card .20 .50
24 Team Card .20 .50

1999-00 Hull Olympiques

Released by Hull Olympiques in conjunction with the Banque Nationale, this 24-card set features the 1999-00 team. Base cards have gray borders, feature full-color photos, and have both the team logo and the Banque Nationale logo on the card front.

COMPLETE SET (24) 4.80 12.00
1 Erich Paroshy .15 .40
2 Andrew Carver .15 .40
3 Bobby Clarke .15 .40
4 Donald Johnstone .15 .40
5 Bruno Lemire .15 .40
6 Derrick Martin .15 .40
7 Alexandre Giroux .30 .75
8 Dustin Russell .15 .40
9 Daniel Hudgin .15 .40
10 Roberto Bissonnette .15 .40
11 Daniel Clermont .15 .40
12 Radim Vrbata .40 1.00
13 Mario Joly .15 .40
14 Jason Lehoux .15 .40
15 Brock Boucher .15 .40
16 Philippe Lacasse .15 .40
17 Paul Spadafora .15 .40
18 Ryan Lauzon .15 .40
19 Michael Ryder 1.25 3.00
20 Adam Rivet .15 .40
21 Patrick Lafreniere .15 .40
22 Eric Lafrance .20 .50
23 Philippe Sauve .40 1.00
24 Team Photo/CL .15 .40
NNO Luc Robitaille .60 1.50

1999-00 Hull Olympiques Signed

This 24-card set parallels the base Hull Olympiques set in an autographed version. The cards are signed on the front in a ghosted area of the photo, while the backs are serial numbered out of 100. The Luc Robitaille card in the set is limited to 100 copies, but it is not signed.

COMPLETE SET (24) 32.00 80.00
1 Erich Paroshy .75 2.00
2 Andrew Carver .75 2.00
3 Bobby Clarke .75 2.00
4 Donald Johnstone .75 2.00
5 Bruno Lemire .75 2.00
6 Derrick Martin .75 2.00
7 Alexandre Giroux 2.00 5.00
8 Dustin Russell .75 2.00
9 Daniel Hudgin .75 2.00
10 Roberto Bissonnette .75 2.00
11 Daniel Clermont .75 2.00
12 Radim Vrbata 6.00 15.00
13 Mario Joly .75 2.00
14 Jason Lehoux .75 2.00

15 Brock Boucher .75 2.00
16 Philippe Lacasse .75 2.00
17 Paul Spadafora .75 2.00
18 Ryan Lauzon .75 2.00
19 Michael Ryder 15.00 30.00
20 Adam Rivet .75 2.00
21 Patrick Lafreniere .75 2.00
22 Eric Lafrance 1.25 3.00
23 Philippe Sauve 6.00 15.00
24 Team Photo/CL .08 .25
NNO Luc Robitaille 6.00 15.00

2000-01 Hull Olympiques

This set features the Olympiques of the QMJHL. The set was produced by CTM-Ste-Foy and was sold by that card shop, as well as by the team at home games.

COMPLETE SET (24) 6.00 20.00
1 Chris Moher .20 .50
2 Andrew Carver .20 .50
3 Bobby Clarke .20 .50
4 Doug O'Brien .20 .50
5 Bruno Lemire .20 .50
6 John Cilladi .20 .50
7 Derrick Martin .20 .50
8 Roberto Bissonnette .20 .50
9 Ales Hemsky 4.00 10.00
10 Phillippe Chainlere .20 .50
11 Jonathan Labelle .20 .50
12 Mario Joly .20 .50
13 Jason Kostadine .20 .50
14 Carl Rochon .20 .50
15 Philippe Lacasse .20 .50
16 Maxime Talbot .75 2.00
17 Jean-Michel Daoust .20 .50
18 Brent G. Roach .20 .50
19 Dale Sullivan .20 .50
20 Adam Rivet .30 .75
21 Eric Lafrance .20 .50
22 Olivier Dannel .30 .75
23 Ian Courville .20 .50
NNO Team CL .01 .05

2000-01 Hull Olympiques Signed

This set is exactly the same as the base Olympiques set from this season, save that every card has been hand signed by the player pictured. Each card also is serial numbered out of just 100. The team CL is not signed.

COMPLETE SET (24) 24.00 60.00
1 Chris Moher .80 2.00
2 Andrew Carver .80 2.00
3 Bobby Clarke .80 2.00
4 Doug O'Brien .80 2.00
5 Bruno Lemire .80 2.00
6 John Cilladi .80 2.00
7 Derrick Martin 1.20 3.00
8 Roberto Bissonnette .80 2.00
9 Ales Hemsky 6.00 30.00
10 Phillippe Chainlere .80 2.00
11 Jonathan Labelle .80 2.00
12 Mario Joly .80 2.00
13 Jason Kostadine .80 2.00
14 Carle Rochon .80 2.00
15 Philippe Lacasse .80 2.00
16 Maxime Talbot .80 2.00
17 Jean-Michel Daoust .80 2.00
18 Brent G. Roach .80 2.00
19 Dale Sullivan .80 2.00
20 Adam Rivet 2.00 5.00
21 Eric Lafrance .80 2.00
22 Olivier Dannel 2.00 5.00
23 Ian Courville .80 2.00
NNO Team CL .10 .25

2001-02 Hull Olympiques

This set features the Olympiques of the QMJHL. The set was produced by CTM Ste-Foy and was sold at Olympiques home games. There were 1,000 copies produced of this set.

COMPLETE SET (23) 4.80 12.00
1 Chris Moher .20 .50
2 Bryan Riddell .20 .50
3 Charles Fontaine .20 .50
4 Dominic D'Amour .20 .50
5 Doug O'Brien .20 .50
6 Francis Wathier .20 .50
7 Derrick Martin .20 .50
8 Phillippe Dupuis .20 .50
9 Scott Gibson .20 .50
10 Ales Hemsky .80 5.00
11 Nick Fugere .20 .50
12 Jonathan Labelle .20 .50
13 Martin Vagner .40 1.00
14 Jason Kostadine .20 .50
15 Jesse Lane .31 .75
16 Philippe Lacasse .20 .50
17 Brent Roach .20 .50
18 Maxime Talbot .20 .50
19 Jean-Michel Daoust .20 .50
20 Dale Sullivan .20 .50
21 Eric Lafrance .31 .75
22 Michael Dilorenzo .31 .75
23 Jean-Junior Morin .20 .50

2002-03 Hull Olympiques

COMPLETE SET (24) 12.00
1 Christopher Pottie .50
2 Jeff Smith .50
3 Charles Fontaine .50
4 Dominic D'Amour .50
5 Doug O'Brien .50
6 Sam Roberts .50
7 Francis Wathier .50
8 Jonathan Bellemare .50
9 Phillippe Dupuis .50
10 Guillaume Labrecque .50
11 Nick Fugere .50
12 Olivier Labelle .50
13 Martin Vagner .75
14 Renaud des Alliers .50
15 Andrew Hayes .50
16 Brent Roach .50
17 Maxime Talbot .50
18 Jean Michel Daoust .50
19 Dale Sullivan .50
20 Mathieu Brunelle .50
21 Eric Lafrance .75
22 David Tremblay .75
23 Tyler Reid .50
24 Checklist/Logo .10

2003 Hull Olympiques Memorial Cup

COMPLETE SET (20) 15.00
1 Jonathan Bellemare .75
2 Mathieu Brunelle .75
3 Dominic D'Amour .75
4 Jean-Michel D'Aoust .75
5 Renaud DesAlliers .75
6 Philippe Dupuis .75
7 Nick Fugere .75
8 Olivier Labelle .75
9 Guillaume Labrecque .75
10 Eric Lafrance 1.00
11 Doug O'Brien .75
12 Tyler Reid .75
13 Sam Roberts .75
14 Brent Roach .75
15 Jeff Smith .75
16 Dale Sullivan .75
17 Maxime Talbot .75
18 David Tremblay 1.00
19 Martin Vagner 1.00
20 Francis Wathier .75

1993-94 Huntington Blizzard

Sponsored by WCHS-TV8, this 27-card standard-size set commemorates the 1993-94 inaugural season of the Huntington Blizzard (ECHL). Just 2,500 sets were produced and each was hand-numbered "X of 2,500" on the title card. One thousand sets were given away on trading card night, with the rest being sold at the souvenir shops in the arena. The fronts feature borderless color action and posed player photos. The player's name and the team logo appear on the front. The cards are unnumbered and checklisted below in alphabetical order.

COMPLETE SET (27) 3.00 8.00
1 Ray Alcindor .15 .40
2 Shayne Antoski .15 .40
3 Greg Bailey .15 .40
4 Jared Bednar .15 .40
5 Andy Borggaard .15 .40
6 Malcolm Cameron .15 .40
7 Dave Dimitri .15 .40
8 Mark Franks .15 .40
9 Ray Gallagher .15 .40
10 Murray Garbutt .15 .40
11 Brad Harrison .15 .40
12 Henry's Blizzard Babes .20 .50
13 Todd Huyber .15 .40
14 Klondike MASCOT .02 .10
15 Ron Majic .15 .40
16 Bob May .15 .40
17 Jim Mill .15 .40
18 Jim Mirabello ANN .02 .10
19 Dan Persigehl ANN .02 .10
20 Paul Pickard CO .02 .10
21 Scott Roberts TV .02 .10
22 Greg Scott .15 .40
23 Geoff Simpson .15 .40
24 Doug Stromback .15 .40
25 Dave Weekley TV .02 .10
26 Misty Zambito .20 .50
27 Title Card .04 .01

1994-95 Huntington Blizzard

This set features the Blizzard of the ECHL. Approximately 3,000 sets were produced; 1,000 were given away on trading card night, while the others were sold at the souvenir shops in the arena.

COMPLETE SET (32) 4.00 10.00
1 Title Card CL .02 .10
2 Steve Barnes .20 .50
3 Jared Bednar .20 .50
4 Jim Bermingham .20 .50
5 Todd Brost .30 .75
6 Alan Brown .20 .50
7 Ray Edwards .20 .50
8 Trent Eigner .20 .50
9 Dan Fournel .20 .50
10 Mark Franks .20 .50
11 Gord Frantti .20 .50
12 Chris Gordon .20 .50
13 Kelly Harper .20 .50
14 J.C. Ihrig TR/EQMG .02 .10
15 Mitch Kean .20 .50
16 Jeff Levy .20 .50
17 Chris Morque .20 .50
18 Derek Schooley .20 .50
19 Jim Solly .20 .50
20 Mike Stone .20 .50
21 Jason Weinrich .20 .50
22 Mark Woolf .20 .50
23 Paul Pickard CO .02 .10
24 Klondike MASCOT .02 .10
25 Blizzard Babes .30 .75
26 Jim Mirabello ANN .02 .10
27 Dan Persigehl ANN .02 .10
28 Spare DJs .02 .10
29 Spare DJs .02 .10
30 Spare DJs .02 .10
31 TV Anchors .02 .10
32 Title Card .04 .01

1998-99 Huntington Blizzard

Little is known about this ECHL team set beyond the confirmed checklist. Any additional information can be forwarded to hockeymag@beckett.com.

COMPLETE SET (27) 3.20 50.00
1 Bill Baaki .75 2.00
2 Mike Perna .75 2.00
3 Chad Lang 1.50 4.00
4 Jamie Sokolsky .75 2.00
5 D.J. Harding .75 2.00
6 Jan Slavik .75 2.00
7 Karson Kaebel 1.50 4.00
8 Jason Bermingham .75 2.00
9 Kelly Harper .75 2.00
10 Derek Smith .75 2.00
11 Jim Bermingham 1.50 4.00
12 Tracy Egeland .75 2.00
13 Brodie Coffin 1.50 4.00
14 Rob Stanfield .75 2.00
15 Kevin Paden .75 2.00
16 Mike Schultz .75 2.00
17 Rich Bronilla .75 2.00
18 Jake Deadmarsh 1.50 4.00
19 Butch Kaebel .75 2.00
20 Blaine Russell .75 2.00
21 Ray Edwards HCO .02 .10
22 Chris Plumhoff EM .02 .10
23 Dave Allen .02 .10
24 Klondike Mascot .02 .10
25 Checklist .02 .10
26 Blizzard Pro Shop .04 .01
27 PHPA/ECHL .04 .01

1999-00 Huntington Blizzard

This set features the Blizzard of the ECHL. The set was produced by Roox and sold by the team at home games.

COMPLETE SET (24) 3.20 50.00
1 Anthony Cappelletti 1.25 3.00
2 Mike Perna 1.25 3.00
3 Jamie Pegg 1.25 3.00
4 Jamie Sokolsky 1.25 3.00
5 Andrew Pearsall 1.25 3.00
6 Jason Bermingham 1.25 3.00
7 Peter Brearley 1.25 3.00
8 Jim Bermingham 1.25 3.00
9 Jim Moss 1.25 3.00
10 Bill Baaki 1.25 3.00
11 Anthony Terzo 1.25 3.00
12 David Oliver 1.25 3.00
13 Keith Cassidy 1.25 3.00
14 Mark Spence 1.25 3.00
15 Ryan Hoople 1.50 4.00
16 Butch Kaebel 1.25 3.00
17 Blaine Russell 1.50 4.00
18 WRVC AM930 .02 .10
19 Huntington Blizzard .15 .40
20 Klondike MAS .02 .10
21 Ray Edwards CO .02 .10
22 Dave Allen .02 .10
23 Kelly Harper .02 .10
24 Curtis Bois .02 .10

1998-99 Huntsville Channel Cats

This 22-card set was given out an early season game. The set contains a message card from the president of the Channel Cats that is dated December 25, 1998.

COMPLETE SET (22) 6.00 15.00
1 Chris Stewart HCO .02 .10
2 John Gibson .40 1.00
3 Igor Bonderev .40 1.00
4 Jonathan Dubois .40 1.00
5 Phil Daigle .40 1.00
6 Pat Bingham ACO .02 .10
7 Mike Degurse .40 1.00
8 Ryan Wood .40 1.00
9 Tyler Quiring .40 1.00
10 Greg Lakovic .40 1.00
11 Wade Gibson .40 1.00
12 Josh Erdman .40 1.00
13 Ken Richardson .40 1.00
14 Todd Dougherty .40 1.00
15 Finnley Mascot .02 .10
16 Clint Collins .40 1.00
17 Mike Gamble .40 1.00
18 Mike Vachon .40 1.00
19 Chris George .40 1.00
20 Derek Puppa .40 1.00
21 Schedule Card .02 .10
22 Message Card .02 .10

2003-04 Huntsville Channel Cats

COMPLETE SET (18) 12.00
1 Claude Amstutz .75
2 Joel Bresciani .75
3 Dan Buccella .75
4 Dave Cadarette .75
5 Matt Carmichael 1.00
6 Allan Carr .75
7 Jason Deguehery .75
8 Mike Degurse 1.00
9 Scott Graham 1.00
10 Daniel Kletko .75
11 Shawn Martin .75
12 Jessi Otis .75
13 James Patterson .75
14 Luke Phillips .75
15 Greg Snitowsky .75
16 Joe Urbanik .75
17 John Gibson CO .25
18 Finnley MASCOT .10

2004-05 Huntsville Havoc

Features the Havoc of the SPHL. Was issued as a give-away at the last home game of the season.

COMPLETE SET (27) 20.00
1 Chaos MASCOT .10
2 John Gibson CO .10
3 Adam MacLean 1.50
4 Steve Howard 1.00
5 Jason Deguehery 1.50
6 Tim Plett 1.00
7 Aaron Lewis 1.00
8 Jeremy Law 1.00
9 Jeff Dams 1.00
10 Brandon Doria 1.00
11 James Patterson 1.00
12 Josh Liebenow 1.00
13 Brad McDonald 1.00
14 Mark Cole 1.00
15 Jason Simon 1.00
16 Doug Merrill 1.00
17 Matt Carmichael 2.00
18 Mike Degurse 1.00
19 Derek McKinlay 1.00
20 Luke Phillips 1.00
21 Dan Bucella 1.00
22 DeWayne Manning TR .10
23 Chad Daniels TR .10
24 John Markushewski DR .10
25 Brian Carter DR .10
26 John Greco DR .10
27 Stanton Davis DR .10

1997-98 Idaho Steelheads

Little is known about this set. It is believed that it was issued as a promotional giveaway at one home game, which would explain its scarcity on the secondary market.

COMPLETE SET (22) 30.00
1 Rob Dumas .60 1.50
2 Frederik Beaubien .75 2.00
3 Patrick Moreau .60 1.50
4 Bill McGuigan .60 1.50
5 Alain Savage .60 1.50
6 Mario Therrien .60 1.50
7 Kevin Deschambeault .60 1.50
8 Sean Farmer .60 1.50
9 Scott Davis .60 1.50
10 Lee Svangstu .60 1.50
11 Troy Edwards .60 1.50
12 Andreas Sjolund .60 1.50
13 Pat O'Connell .60 1.50
14 Patrick Gallagher .60 1.50
15 Sam Fields .60 1.50
16 Marco Pietroniro .60 1.50
17 Dmitri Leonov .75 2.00
18 Jamie Cooke .60 1.50
19 Todd Dougherty .60 1.50
20 Carl Menard .60 1.50
21 Bart Hull .75 2.00
22 Dave Langevin HCO .60 1.50

1998-99 Idaho Steelheads

This set features the Steelheads of the WCHL. It was issued as a promotional giveaway at a late-season home game.

COMPLETE SET (23) 10.00 25.00
1 Alex Alepin .40 1.00
2 Frederik Beaubien .60 1.50
3 Francois Bourdeau .40 1.00
4 Scott Davis .40 1.00
5 Rob Dumas .40 1.00
6 Troy Edwards .40 1.00
7 Christian Friberg .40 1.00
8 Marc Genest .40 1.00
9 Cal Ingraham .75 2.00
10 Jason Lammers .40 1.00
11 Dmitri Leonov .60 1.50
12 Sebastian Parent .40 1.00
13 Marco Pietroniro .40 1.00
14 Tony Prpic .40 1.00
15 Bryan Randall .40 1.00
16 Alain Savage .40 1.00
17 Jonathon Shockey .40 1.00
18 Andreas Sjolund .40 1.00
19 Mario Thierren .40 1.00
20 Jeff Trigg .40 1.00
21 All-Star Trio .60 1.50
22 Clint Malarchuk HCO .60 1.50
23 Bonk Mascot .08 .25

1999-00 Idaho Steelheads

This set features the Steelheads of the WCHL. The cards were first issued as a promotional giveaway. Later, remaining copies were sold by the team.

COMPLETE SET (22) 4.00 10.00
1 Cal Ingraham .30 .75
2 Nicolas Chabot .30 .75
3 Troy Edwards .20 .50
4 Todd Robinson .20 .50
5 Dan Marcotte .20 .50
6 Bryan Randall .20 .50
7 Tom Menicci .20 .50
8 Roy Mitchell .20 .50
9 Scott Davis .20 .50
10 Andrei Lupandin .20 .50
11 Gavin Morgan .20 .50
12 Jeff Petruic .20 .50
13 Clint Malarchuk CO .20 .50
14 Marc Genest .20 .50
15 Darcy Loewen .20 .50
16 Rob Dumas .20 .50
17 Rob Hartnell .20 .50
18 Ryan Johnston .20 .50
19 Matt Garver .20 .50
20 Andreas Sjolund .30 .75
21 Kory Cooper .30 .75
22 Bonk MAS .08 .25

2000-01 Idaho Steelheads

This set features the Steelheads of the WCHL. The cards were produced by Grandstand and issued in five-card strips at five separate home games. The strips are not perforated, making it difficult to acquire cards in single form.

COMPLETE SET (25) 6.00 20.00
1 Chad Alban .40 1.00
2 Colin Anderson .24 .75
3 Adam Borzecki .24 .75
4 Scott Burt .24 .75
5 Rob Concannon .24 .75
6 Thom Cullen .24 .75
7 Bobby Hayes .24 .75
8 Cal Ingraham .40 1.50
9 Kevin Knopp .24 .75
10 Arturs Kupaks .24 .75
11 Mike Legg .24 .75
12 Darcy Loewen .24 .75
13 Matt Martin .24 .75
14 Roy Mitchell .24 .75
15 Jeremy Mylymok .40 1.00
16 Vladimir Nemec .24 .75
17 Barry Potomski .40 1.50
18 Eric Rud .24 .75
19 Dan Shermerhorn .24 .75
20 Kendall Sidoruk .24 .75
21 Shawn Wansborough .24 .75
22 Cal Ingraham AS .40 1.00
23 Jeremy Mylymok AS .40 1.00
24 Todd Hine TR .04 .10
25 Khris Bestel EQM .04 .10

2001-02 Idaho Steelheads

COMPLETE SET (24) 25.00
1 Blair Allison 1.50
2 Scott Burt 1.00
3 Adam Copeland 1.00
4 Jason Cugnet 1.50
5 Thom Cullen 1.00
6 Wes Dorey 1.00
7 Cal Ingraham 1.50
8 Dan Kerluke 1.00
9 Jeremy Mylymok 1.00
10 Matt Oates 1.00
11 Zdenek Ondrej 1.00
12 Derek Paget 1.00
13 Eric Rud 1.00
14 Terry Ryan 1.00
15 Dan Shermerhorn 1.00
16 Jeff Shevalier 1.00
17 Kevin Smyth 1.00
18 Bobby Stewart 1.00
19 Petr Suchanek 1.00
20 Scott Swanson 1.00
21 Garry Toor 1.00
22 Jeremy Yablonski 1.50
23 Edgars Zalfkovskis 1.00
24 John Oliver HCO .25

2004-05 Idaho Steelheads

This ECHL set was originally offered as a game-night giveaway, but the team later sold the remaining few sets for $5 at its pro shop.

COMPLETE SET (27) 15.00
1 Mascot .10
2 John Oliver CO .10
3 Blair Allison ACO .10
4 Frank Doyle 1.00
5 Jeremy Mylymok .50
6 Petr Suchanek .50
7 Billy Tibbetts 1.50
8 Ben Keup .50
9 Scott Burt .50
10 Darren McLachlan 1.00
11 Jim Leger .50
12 Dan Vandermeer .50
13 David Morrisett 1.00
14 Frank Lukes .50
15 Jonathan Zion .50
16 Bobby Russell .50
17 Peter Metcalf .50
18 Warren Peters .50
19 Matt Elich .50
20 Landon Bathe .50
21 Colin Zulianello 1.00
22 Tim Verbeek .50
23 Brett Draney .50
24 David Corracchia .50
25 Darrell Hay .50
26 Marty Flichel .50
27 Lance Galbraith 1.00

2005-06 Idaho Steelheads

COMPLETE SET (26) 10.00 25.00
1 David Bararuk .60 1.50
2 Garrett Bembridge .60 1.50
3 Jarad Bourassa .40 1.00
4 Scott Burt .40 1.00
5 Justin Cox .40 1.00
6 Brian Fahey .40 1.00
7 Marty Flichel .40 1.00
8 Blake Forsyth .40 1.00
9 Mike Gabinet .40 1.00
10 Kevin Gardner .40 1.00
11 Dan Hacker .40 1.00
12 Jim Hakewill .40 1.00
13 Greg Hornby .40 1.00
14 Kurt MacSweyn .40 1.00
15 D'Arcy McConvey .40 1.00
16 Tyrell Moulton .40 1.00
17 Jeremy Mylymok .60 1.50
18 Matt Reid .40 1.00
19 Steve Silverthorn .40 1.00
20 Mike Stutzel .40 1.00
21 Brad Thompson .40 1.00
22 Janos Vas .40 1.00
23 Matthew Yeats .40 1.00
24 Jonathan Zion .40 1.00
25 Derek Laxdal HC .02 .10
26 Bonk MASCOT .02 .10

2006-07 Idaho Steelheads

COMPLETE SET (27) 10.00 20.00
1 Idaho Steelheads .02 .10
2 Kyle Bruce .40 1.00
3 Scott Burt .40 1.00
4 Taggart Desmet .40 1.00
5 Marty Flichel .40 1.00
6 Lance Galbraith .75 2.00
7 Charlie Johnson .40 1.00
8 D'Arcy McConvey .40 1.00
9 Tuomas Mikkonen .40 1.00
10 Derek Nesbitt .40 1.00
11 Greg Rallo .40 1.00
12 Francis Wathier .40 1.00
13 Jeremy Yablonski .75 2.00
14 Cody Blanshan .40 1.00
15 Blake Forsyth .40 1.00
16 Mike Gabinet .40 1.00
17 Darrell Hay .40 1.00
18 Jared Nightingale .40 1.00
19 Colin Peters .40 1.00
20 Kory Scoran .40 1.00
21 Travis Wight .40 1.00
22 John Daigneau .60 1.50
23 Steve Silverthorn .40 1.00
24 Derek Laxdal CO .10 .25
25 Khris Bestel EQ MGR .02 .10
26 Dennis Brogna TR .02 .10
27 Blue MASCOT .02 .10

1998-99 IHL All-Star Eastern Conference

Released by EBK Sports, this 25-card set was available for purchase at the 1999 IHL All-Star Game, then later through the PHPA web site.

COMPLETE SET (25) 14.00 35.00
1 Guy Dupuis .20 .50
2 Viachestav Butsayev .20 .50
3 Zac Bierk .40 1.00
4 Brian Noonan .20 .50
5 Dave Hymovitz .20 .50
6 Marty Turco 8.00 20.00
7 Jon Sim .60 1.50
8 Brad Shaw .75 2.00
9 Pat Neaton .20 .50
10 Peter Ciavaglia .40 1.00
11 Mike Prokopec .20 .50
12 Stan Drulia .40 1.00
13 Steve Walker .75 2.00
14 Todd Richards .20 .50
15 Maxim Spiridonov .20 .50
16 Robert Petrovicky .20 .50
17 Curtis Murphy .20 .50
18 Mark Beaufait .40 1.00
19 Gilbert Dionne .40 1.00
20 Brad Lukowich .40 1.00
21 Bruce Cassidy ACO .08 .25
22 Steve Ludzik HCO .20 .50
23 Keith Aldridge .30 .75
24 IHL Logo .02 .10
25 Checklist .02 .10

1998-99 IHL All-Star Western Conference

Released by EBK Sports, this 24-card set was available for purchase at the 1999 IHL All-Star Game, then later through the PHPA web site.

COMPLETE SET (24) 8.00 20.00
1 Richard Shulmistra .40 1.00
2 Brett Hauer .20 .50
3 Bill Bowler .60 1.50
4 Pat Jablonski .60 1.50
5 Niklas Andersson .20 .50
6 Steve Maltais .75 2.00
7 Tom Tilley .20 .50
8 Dan Ratushny .20 .50
9 Andy Roach .20 .50
10 Rob Valicevic .75 2.00
11 Jeff Tory .20 .50
12 Patrik Augusta .20 .50
13 Kimmo Timonen .75 2.00
14 Mark Mowers .60 1.50
15 Patrice Lefebvre .60 1.50
16 Cam Stewart .20 .50
17 Brian Wiseman .40 1.00
18 Greg Hawgood .40 1.00
19 John Purves .75 2.00
20 Scott Thomas .75 2.00
21 Randy Carlyle ACO .08 .25
22 Dave Tippett HCO .08 .25
23 IHL Logo .02 .10
24 Checklist .02 .10

1999-00 IHL All-Stars

The set was created by ebk Sports to commemorate the members of the 2000 IHL All-Star team. In an unusual scenario, the game pitted the league champion Houston Aeros against the best players from the rest of the IHL. The set was sold only at the Compaq Center in Houston. Production problems led to many cards being off-centered or poorly cut.

COMPLETE SET (24) 16.00 50.00
1 Mike Crowley .75 2.00
2 Nils Ekman .60 1.50
3 Rich Parent .75 2.00
4 Shane Willis 1.25 3.00
5 John Purves .75 2.00
6 Kevin Miller .75 2.00
7 Mike Prokopec .40 1.00
8 Petr Schastlivy 1.25 3.00
9 Marty Turco 10.00 25.00
10 Stewart Malgunas .40 1.00
11 Curtis Murphy .40 1.00
12 Todd White .60 1.50
13 Brett Hauer .40 1.00
14 David Gosselin .40 1.00
15 David Ling .60 1.50
16 Gilbert Dionne .75 2.00
17 Jeff Sharples .40 1.00
18 John Gruden .40 1.00
19 Jarrod Skalde .75 2.00
20 Steve Maltais .75 2.00
21 Bob Bourne ACO .40 1.00
22 Al Sims CO .40 1.00
NNO Checklist Card .08 .25
NNO Header Card .08 .25

1981-82 Indianapolis Checkers

Sponsored by Pizza Hut, this 20-card standard-size set features the Indianapolis Checkers of the CHL. The cards were available singly at Pizza Hut restaurants and Checkers games on alternate weeks. On a blue background, the fronts have color action player photos with thin white borders. The team name appears above the photo in an orange border that extends down the right side. The player's name, position, and number are printed above the photo. The cards are unnumbered and checklisted below in alphabetical order.

COMPLETE SET (20) 12.00 30.00
1 Bruce Andres .40 1.00
2 Frank Beaton .40 1.00
3 Kelly Davis .40 1.00
4 Kevin Devine .40 1.00
5 Glen Duncan .40 1.00
6 Mats Hallin .60 1.50
7 Neil Hawryliw .40 1.00
8 Bob Holland .40 1.00
9 Mike Hordy .40 1.00
10 Kelly Hrudey 4.00 10.00
11 Randy Johnston .40 1.00
12 Red Laurence .40 1.00
13 Tim Lockridge .40 1.00
14 Garth MacGuigan .40 1.00
15 John Marks .60 1.50
16 Darcey Regier .75 2.00
17 Charlie Skjodt .40 1.00
18 Lorne Stamler .40 1.00
19 Steve Stoyanovich .40 1.00
20 Monty Trottier .40 1.00

1982-83 Indianapolis Checkers

Sponsored by Pizza Hut, this 21-card standard-size set features the Indianapolis Checkers of the CHL. The cards were available singly at Pizza Hut restaurants and Checkers games on alternate weeks. On a red-orange background, the fronts have color action player photos with thin white borders. The team name appears above the photo in an orange border that extends down the right side. The player's name, position, and number are printed above the photo. The cards are unnumbered and checklisted below in alphabetical order.

COMPLETE SET (21) 16.00 40.00
1 Kelly Davis .40 1.00
2 Kevin Devine .40 1.00
3 Gord Dineen .60 1.50
4 Glen Duncan .40 1.00
5 Greg Gilbert .75 2.00
6 Mike Gredder .40 1.00
7 Mats Hallin .75 2.00
8 Dave Hanson 4.00 10.00
9 Rob Holland .40 1.00
10 Scott Howson .40 1.00
11 Kelly Hrudey 3.00 8.00
12 Randy Johnston .40 1.00
13 Red Laurence .40 1.00
14 Tim Lockridge .40 1.00
15 Garth MacGuigan .40 1.00
16 Darcey Regier .60 1.50
17 Dan Revell .40 1.00
18 Dave Simpson .40 1.00
19 Lorne Stamler .40 1.00
20 Steve Stoyanovich .40 1.00
21 Monty Trottier .40 1.00

1992-93 Indianapolis Ice

This 26-card set measures the standard size. On a light blue background, the fronts feature posed, color action photos with a thin red border. The team logo appears on the bottom left side, while the player's number, name and position appear in black letters on the right side. The cards are unnumbered and checklisted below in alphabetical order.

COMPLETE SET (26) 4.00 10.00
1 Alexandr Andrievski .15 .40
2 Steve Bancroft .15 .40
3 Zac Boyer .15 .40
4 Rod Buskas .20 .50
5 Shawn Byram .15 .40
6 Joe Cleary .15 .40
7 Rob Conn .15 .40
8 Joe Crowley .15 .40
9 Trevor Dam .15 .40
10 Ivan Droppa .15 .40
11 Tracy Egeland .15 .40
12 Dave Hakstol .15 .40
13 Kevin Hodson .30 .75
14 Tony Horacek .15 .40
15 Tony Hrkac .30 .75
16 Sergei Krivokrasov .30 .75
17 Brad Lauer .20 .50
18 Ray LeBlanc .30 .75
19 Owen Lessard .15 .40
20 Jim Playfair ACO .02 .10
John Marks CO
21 Kevin St. Jacques .15 .40
22 Michael Speer .15 .40
23 Milan Tichy .15 .40
24 Kerry Toporowski .15 .40
25 Sean Williams .15 .40
26 Craig Woodcroft .15 .40

1993-94 Indianapolis Ice

Set was produced by MJ's Collectibles and features cards that are slightly narrower than standard size. Thanks to Dale Spengler for the complete checklist.

COMPLETE SET (25) 6.00 15.00
1 Hugo Belanger .30 .75
2 Zac Boyer .30 .75
3 Shawn Byram .30 .75
4 Rob Cimetta .30 .75
5 Rob Conn .30 .75
6 Joe Crowley .30 .75
7 Ivan Droppa .30 .75
8 Steve Dubinsky .30 .75
9 Karl Dykhuis .30 .75
10 Dino Grossi .30 .75
11 Dave Hakstol .30 .75
13 Bobby House .30 .75
14 Tony Horacek .30 .75
15 Bob Kellogg .30 .75
16 Jeff Ricciardi .30 .75
17 Sergei Krivokrasov .30 .75
18 Chris Rogles .60 1.50
19 Kevin St. Jacques .30 .75
20 Christian Soucy .60 1.50
21 Michael Speer .30 .75
21 Yves Heroux .30 .75
22 Kerry Toporowski .60 1.50
23 Duane Sutter CO .40 1.00
24 Gene Pattel TR .02 .10
25 Polar Bear MASCOT .02 .10

1994-95 Indianapolis Ice

Manufactured and distributed by Jessen Associates, Inc. for Classic, this 26-card standard-size set features the Ice of the IHL. Sets were sold by the team at home games. The cards are unnumbered and checklisted below in alphabetical order.

COMPLETE SET (26) 4.00 10.00
1 Hugo Belanger .15 .40
2 Bruce Cassidy .15 .40
3 Rob Conn .20 .50
4 Ivan Droppa .15 .40
5 Steve Dubinsky .20 .50
6 Karl Dykhuis .20 .50
7 Craig Fisher .15 .40
8 Daniel Gauthier .15 .40
9 Tony Horacek .15 .40
10 Bobby House .15 .40
11 Bob Kellogg .15 .40
12 Sergei Klimovich .15 .40
13 Sergei Krivokrasov .30 .75
14 Andy MacIntyre .15 .40
15 Dean Malkoc .20 .50
16 Matt Oates .15 .40
17 Mike Pomichter .15 .40
18 Mike Prokopec .15 .40
19 Jeff Ricciardi .15 .40
20 Chris Rogles .30 .75
21 Bogdan Savenko .15 .40
22 Jeff Shantz .30 .75
23 Christian Soucy .30 .75
24 Duane Sutter CO .20 .50
25 Travis Thiessen .15 .40
26 Team Photo .15 .40

1995-96 Indianapolis Ice

This 23-card set was produced by SplitSecond for Collector's Edge. The cards featured the standard design element for that season, with the color schemes adapted for that of the team. As they are unnumbered, the cards are listed below alphabetically.

COMPLETE SET (23) 4.00 10.00
1 Bill Armstrong .15 .40
2 James Black .15 .40
3 Jeff Buchanan .15 .40
4 Bruce Cassidy .15 .40
5 Ivan Droppa .15 .40
6 Steve Dubinsky .15 .40
7 Dmitri Filimonov .15 .40
8 Daniel Gauthier .15 .40
9 Ryan Huska .15 .40
10 Sergei Klimovich .15 .40
11 Eric Lecompte .20 .50
12 Andy MacIntyre .15 .40
13 Eric Manlow .15 .40
14 Steve McLaren .15 .40
15 Kip Miller .30 .75
16 Ethan Moreau .30 .75
17 Mike Prokopec .20 .50
18 Andre Racicot .30 .75
19 Jeff Serowik .20 .50
20 Christian Soucy .30 .75
21 Jimmy Waite .30 .75
22 Brad Werenka .20 .50
23 Bob Ferguson .15 .40

1997-98 Indianapolis Ice

Little is known about this set beyond the confirmed checklist. Additional information can be forwarded to hockeymag@beckett.com.

COMPLETE SET (30) 6.00 15.00
1 Bob Ferguson HCO .02 .10
2 Chris Mizer HTR .02 .10
3 Jim Stuckey EM .02 .10
4 Kory Cooper .20 .50
5 Kirk Daubenspeck .30 .75
6 Glen Featherstone .20 .50
7 Brian Felsner .20 .50
8 Martin Gendron .20 .50
9 Jani Hurme 1.25 3.00
10 Ryan Huska .20 .50
11 Marc Hussey .20 .50
12 David Hymovitz .20 .50
13 Marc Lamothe .40 1.00
14 Eric Lecompte .20 .50
15 Eric Manlow .20 .50
16 Steve McLaren .20 .50
17 Kevin Miller .20 .50
18 Craig Mills .20 .50
19 Frank Musil .20 .50
20 Dmitri Nabokov .20 .50
21 Alain Nasreddine .20 .50
22 Ryan Risidore .20 .50
23 Michal Sykora .20 .50
24 Steve Tardif .20 .50
25 Alfie Turcotte .20 .50
26 Petri Varis .20 .50
27 Todd White .20 .50
28 Marty Wilford .20 .50
29 M.J.'s Collectibles .20 .50
30 PHPA Web Site .02 .10

1998-99 Indianapolis Ice

Little is known about this set beyond the confirmed checklist. Any additional information can be forwarded to hockeymag@beckett.com.

COMPLETE SET (29) 4.00 10.00
1 Brian Noonan .20 .50
2 Matt Cooney .15 .40
3 Ryan VandenBussche .30 .75
4 Marty Wilford .15 .40
5 Nathan Perrott .40 1.00
6 Mike Vukonich .15 .40
7 Remi Royer .20 .50
8 Marc Dupuis .15 .40
9 Mike Hall .15 .40
10 Sylvain Cloutier .15 .40
11 Andrei Trefilov .20 .50
12 Andrei Kozyrev .15 .40
13 Chris Herperger .15 .40
14 Marc Lamothe .30 .75
15 Erik Andersson .15 .40
16 Bryan Fogarty .15 .40
17 Slapshot MASCOT .02 .10
18 Bob Lachance .15 .40
19 Kirk Daubenspeck .30 .75
20 Barrie Moore .15 .40
21 Bruce Cassidy HCO .02 .10
22 David Hymovitz .15 .40
23 Justin Hocking .15 .40
24 King Team .01
25 Dale DeGray .15 .40
26 Jeff Paul .15 .40
27 IHL Web Site .01
28 MJ Collectibles .01
29 PHPA Web Site .01

1999-00 Indianapolis Ice

This set features the Ice of the CHL. The set was produced by Roox and sold by the team at home games.

COMPLETE SET (21) 90.00 150.00
1 Mike Berger 3.00 8.00
2 Ken Boone 4.00 10.00
3 Jason Carriere 3.00 8.00
4 Yvan Corbin 3.00 8.00
5 Dan Cousineau 3.00 8.00
6 Robert Davidson 3.00 8.00
7 Jay Hern 3.00 8.00
8 Peter Jas 3.00 8.00
9 Bernie John 3.00 8.00
10 Lubos Krajcovic 3.00 8.00
11 Eric Landry 3.00 8.00
12 Chris MacKenzie 3.00 8.00
13 Jason Mansoff 3.00 8.00
14 Jamie Morris 4.00 10.00
15 Sebastian Pajerski 3.00 8.00
16 Tom Stewart 3.00 8.00
17 Benoit Thibert 4.00 10.00
18 Steven Toll 3.00 8.00
19 M.J. Collectibles .40 1.00
20 Rod Davidson CO 2.00 5.00
21 Joe Trotta CO 2.00 5.00
22 Slapshot MAS 2.00 5.00

2000-01 Indianapolis Ice

This set features the Ice of the CHL. The cards were sold in team set form at the rink and at a shop called MJ's Collectibles. The latter version actually included an extra card, which featured a swatch of Yvan Corbin's jersey.

COMPLETE SET (23) 4.00 10.00
COMPLETE MJ SET (24) 8.00 20.00
1 Ryan Aho .20 .50
2 Dan Back .20 .50
3 Ken Boone .20 .50
4 Brandon Christian .20 .50
5 Yvan Corbin .20 .50
5GJ Yvan Corbin 4.00 10.00
6 Dan Cousineau .20 .50
7 Robert Davidson .20 .50
8 Casey Harris .20 .50
9 Jan Jas .20 .50
10 Peter Jas .20 .50
11 David Jesiolowski .20 .50
12 Bernie John .20 .50
13 Lubos Krajcovic .20 .50
14 Marc Laforge .20 .50
15 Chris MacKenzie .20 .50
16 Aigars Mironovics .20 .50
17 Jamie Morris .20 .50
18 Chris Richards .20 .50
19 Kevin Schmidt .20 .50
20 Jason Selleke .20 .50
21 Rod Davidson CO .10 .25
22 Slapshot MASCOT .04 .10
23 MJ's Collectibles .04 .10

2001-02 Indianapolis Ice

This set features the Ice of the UHL. The set was sold at home games as a 22-card version, at and MJ's Collectibles, which sold a 23-card version featuring a game jersey card of Bernie John. The latter set is priced below. The cards are unnumbered and are listed in alphabetical order.

COMPLETE SET (23) 8.00 20.00
1 Ryan Aikia .20 .50
2 Mike Berger ACO .04 .11
3 Peter Bournazakis .20 .50
4 Dan Cousineau .20 .50
5 Robert Davidson .20 .50
6 Rod Davidson CO .04 .11
7 Charlie Elezi .20 .50
8 Chris George .20 .50
9 Casey Harris .20 .50
10 Jay Hern .20 .50
11 Bernie John .20 .50
12 Bernie John GJ 4.00 10.00
13 Justin Kearns .31 .78
14 Chris MacKenzie .20 .50
15 Don Malko .20 .50
16 Jamie Morris .20 .50
17 Kevin Popp .20 .50
18 Jason Selleke .20 .50
19 Jonathan Sorg .20 .50
20 Dylan Taylor .20 .50
21 J.C. Wells .20 .50
22 Slapshot MASCOT .10 .25
23 MJs Collectibles .01 .02

2002-03 Indianapolis Ice

COMPLETE SET (23) 10.00
1 Ryan Aikia .50
2 Jason Baird .50
3 Ryan Carter .50
4 Bryce Classen .50
5 Jared Dumba .50
6 Nate Elliott .50
7 Randy Holmes .50
8 Bernie John .50
9 Justin Kearns .75
10 Scott Lewis .50
11 Etienne Morin .50
12 Jamie Morris .50
13 Greg Olsen .50
14 Byron Pool .50
15 Kevin Popp .50
16 Shawn Silver .75
17 Kevin St. Jacques .50
18 Kevin St. Jacques .50
19 Andrew Taylor .50
20 Ken McRae CO .10
21 Darrin Flinchem EQM .10
22 Mascot .10
23 Todd Champlin TR .10

2003-04 Indianapolis Ice

COMPLETE SET (24) 10.00
1 Ryan Aikia .50
2 Jason Baird .50
3 Ken Boone .50
4 Ryan Carter .50
5 Philippe Choiniere .50
6 Mario Doyon .50
7 Jared Dumba .50
8 Nate Elliott .50
9 Dave Gilmore .50
10 Joe Guenther .50
11 Russ Guzior .50
12 Bernie John .50
13 Steve Lecuyer .50
14 Chad McIver .50
15 Adam Redmond .50
16 Remi Royer .50
17 Jeff Sanger .75
18 Jason Selleke .50
19 Mike Zeibaq .50
20 Brent Zelenewich .75
21 Ken McRae CO .25
22 Darren Flinchem EQM .10
23 Mascot .10
24 Marc Schlichtenmyer TR .10

2006-07 Iowa Stars

COMPLETE SET (27) 8.00 15.00
1 Greg Amadio .20 .50
2 Mark Ardelan .20 .50
3 Krys Barch .30 .75
4 Chris Conner .40 1.00
5 Dan Ellis .30 .75
6 Loui Eriksson .60 1.50
7 Mark Fistric .30 .75
8 Mike Green .20 .50
9 Nicklas Grossman .20 .50
10 Dan Hacker .20 .50
11 Yared Hagos .20 .50
12 Marius Holtet .20 .50
13 John Lammers .20 .50
14 Junior Lessard .40 1.00
15 Joel Lundqvist .40 1.00
16 Matt Nickerson .40 1.00
17 Toby Petersen .20 .50
18 Vojtech Polak .20 .50
19 Mario Scalzo .20 .50
20 Marty Sertich .40 1.00
21 Tobias Stephan .40 1.00
22 Janos Vas .20 .50
23 Francis Wathier .20 .50
24 Marty Wilford .20 .50
25 Dave Allison CO .02 .10
26 Paul Jerrard ACO .02 .10
27 Shooter MASCOT .02 .10

2000-01 Jackson Bandits

This set features the Bandits of the ECHL. The set was sold at home games late in the 2000-01 season. The singles are over-sized and numbered on the back.

COMPLETE SET (25) 4.80 12.00
1 Mike Tamburro .20 .50
2 Jeff Helperl .20 .50
3 Derek Gustafson .30 .75
4 Randy Fitzgerald .20 .50
5 Milt Mastad .20 .50
6 Jonathon Shockey .20 .50
7 Chris Wismer .20 .50
8 J.P. O'Connor .20 .50
9 Bobby Russell .20 .50
10 Cory Larose .20 .50
11 Brendan Walsh .20 .50
12 Ryan Mougenel .20 .50
13 Chris Peyton .20 .50
14 Brian Callahan .20 .50
15 Jim Bermingham .20 .50
16 Dan Carney .20 .50
17 Dave Stewart .20 .50
18 Brad Peddle .20 .50
19 Denny Felsner .30 .75
20 Steve Wilson .20 .50
21 Quintin Laing .20 .50
22 J.P. Tessier .20 .50
23 Lee Jinman .30 .75
24 Derek Clancey .20 .50
25 Tim Green .20 .50

2000-01 Jackson Bandits Promos

This set features the Bandits of the ECHL. The cards were issued prior to the main set (which is listed below) as a test of the popularity of trading cards as a promotional item. Apparently, the test went well. Any further info on this set can be forwarded to hockeymag@beckett.com.

COMPLETE SET (8) 3.20 8.00
1 David Brumby .40 1.00
2 Derek Gustafson .60 1.50
3 Denny Felsner .60 1.50
4 Brian Callahan .40 1.00
5 Bobby Russell .40 1.00
6 Dave Stewart .40 1.00
7 Mike Tamburro .40 1.00
8 Brendan Walsh .60 1.50

1999-00 Jacksonville Lizard Kings

This set features the Lizard Kings of the ECHL. This set was handed out as a promotional giveaway at a home game early in the season. It is believed that an update set was issued later in the year. Any information on this set can be forwarded to hockeymag@beckett.com.

COMPLETE SET (15) 4.80 12.00
1 Jean-Philippe Soucy .40 1.00
2 Alex Podalinski .30 .75
3 Rich Bronilla .30 .75
4 Brad Federenko .30 .75
5 Dan Reja .40 1.00
6 Ray LeBlanc .60 1.50
7 Mark Giannetti .30 .75
8 Patrick Gingras .30 .75
9 Derek Eberle .40 1.00
10 Eric Naud .40 1.00
11 Bryan Forslund .30 .75
12 Ryan Cirillo .30 .75
13 Lenny the Lizard MAS .20 .50
14 Alain Lemieux CO .20 .50
15 Jacksonville Lizard Kings .20 .50

1989-90 Johnstown Chiefs

This 18-card set of the Johnstown Chiefs of the ECHL was produced by Big League Cards. The set is believed to have been issued by the team, but that is not a certainty. The set's numbering begins with 19, leading to speculation that a 1988-89 set exists as well. The fronts feature a posed photo, with the player seated beside a prominent logo of sponsor Sheetz convenience store.

COMPLETE SET (18) 6.00 50.00
19 Rick Burchill 1.25 3.00
20 Bob Goulet .75 2.00
21 John Messuri .75 2.00
22 Darren Servatius .75 2.00
23 Rick Boyd .75 2.00
24 Bob Kennedy .75 2.00
25 Mike Rossetti .75 2.00
26 Dan Williams .75 2.00
27 Mark Bogoslowski .75 2.00
28 Dean Hall .75 2.00
29 Mitch Molloy .75 2.00
30 Darren Schwartz 1.25 3.00
31 Doug Weiss .75 2.00
32 Marc Vachon .75 2.00
33 Mike Jeffrey 1.25 3.00
34 Frank Dell ANN .08 .25
35 Sean Finn .75 2.00
36 Steve Carlson CO 6.00 15.00

1991-92 Johnstown Chiefs

This 20-card set features the Johnstown Chiefs of the ECHL. The set was sponsored by Ponderosa Steakhouse and KB Card Company and likely was sold by the team at home games. The fronts feature a posed photo along with team and sponsor logos.

COMPLETE SET (20) 4.00 10.00
1 Steve Carlson CO .75 2.00
2 Dana Heinze TR .02 .10
3 John Fletcher .20 .50
4 Mark Krys .20 .50
5 Doug Sinclair .20 .50
6 Bruce Coles .20 .50
7 Doug Weiss .20 .50
8 Dave MacIntyre .20 .50
9 Bob Woods .20 .50
10 Mike Roberts .20 .50
11 Jeff Beaudin .20 .50
12 Brian Ferreira .20 .50
13 Christian Lariviere .20 .50
14 Ted Miskolczi .20 .50
15 Rob Hrytsak .20 .50
16 Mark Green .20 .50
17 Matt Glennon .20 .50
18 Mike Rossetti .30 .75
19 Stan Reddick .30 .75
20 Perry Florio .20 .50

1993-94 Johnstown Chiefs

This 22-card set features the Johnstown Chiefs of the ECHL. The set was sponsored by Ponderosa Steakhouse and KB Card Company and likely was sold by the team at home games. The fronts feature a posed photo along with team and sponsor logos.

COMPLETE SET (22) 3.00 8.00
1 John Bradley .15 .40
2 Campbell Blair .15 .40
3 Francois Bourdeau .15 .40
4 Bob Woods .15 .40
5 Ted Dent .15 .40
6 Matt Hoffman .15 .40
7 Gord Christian .15 .40
8 Tim Hanus .15 .40
9 Phil Soukoroff .15 .40
10 Jason Jennings .15 .40
11 Dusty McLellan .15 .40
12 Dennis Purdie .20 .50
13 Chuck Wiegand .15 .40
14 Jamie Adams .15 .40
15 Jan Beran .15 .40
16 Rob Laurie .20 .50
17 Cory Banika .15 .40
18 Perry Florio .15 .40
19 Rob Leask .15 .40
20 Ed Johnstone CO .08 .25
21 John Daley GM .02 .10
22 Matt Koeck TR .02 .10
NNO Header Card .02 .10

1994-95 Johnstown Chiefs

This 24-card set features the Johnstown Chiefs of the ECHL. The set was likely sold by the team at home games. The fronts feature a posed photo along with team and sponsor logos.

COMPLETE SET (24) 3.00 8.00
1 Cover Card CL .02 .10
2 Jason Brousseau .15 .40
3 Brandon Christian .15 .40
4 Gord Christian .15 .40
5 Bruce Coles .15 .40
6 Ted Dent .15 .40
7 Martin D'Orsonnens .15 .40
8 Perry Florio .15 .40
9 Rod Hinks .15 .40
10 Matt Hoffman .15 .40
11 Aaron Israel .15 .40
12 Jason Jennings .15 .40
13 Rob Laurie .15 .40
14 Rob Leask .15 .40
15 Dennis Purdie .40 1.00
16 Kevin Quinn .15 .40
17 Jason Richard .15 .40
18 Dan Sawyer .15 .40
19 Ben Wyzansky .15 .40
20 Matt Yingst .15 .40
21 Training Staff .02 .10
22 Ed Johnstone CO .02 .10
23 WMTZ-FM Personalities .02 .10
24 WMTZ-FM Personalities .02 .10

1996-97 Johnstown Chiefs

This set was produced by Big League Sports and sponsored by Burger King. The set could only be acquired through the team's Kids Club. Note: There are two versions of card #26, both of which are short printed.

COMPLETE SET (31) 10.00 40.00
1 Greg Callahan .75 2.00
2 Brandon Christian .75 2.00
3 Alexsandr Chunchukov .75 2.00
4 Trevor Converse .75 2.00
5 Chad Dameworth .75 2.00
6 Carl Fleury 1.25 3.00
7 Dan Harrison .75 2.00
8 Jim Krayer .75 2.00
9 Denis Lamoureux .75 2.00
10 Kelly Leroux .75 2.00
11 Martin Masa .75 2.00
12 Klemen Mohoric .75 2.00
13 Sean Perry .75 2.00
14 Ryan Petz .75 2.00
15 Dan Reimann .75 2.00
16 Beau Riedel .75 2.00
17 Ted Russell .75 2.00
18 Ryan Savoia .75 2.00
19 Marc Siegel .75 2.00
20 Lukas Smital .75 2.00
21 Olie Sundstrom .75 2.00
22 Kam White .75 2.00
23 Martin Woods .75 2.00
24 Nick Fotiu HCO .40 1.00
25 Scott Allen ACO .02 .10
26 Dana Heinze TR .08 .25
26 Mic Midderhoff EM .08 .25
27 Chief's Office Staff .08 .25
28 The Iron Dog Mascot .08 .25
29 Home Schedule .08 .25
30 Logo Card .02 .10

1997-98 Johnstown Chiefs

This set features the Chiefs of the ECHL. The cards were issued primarily to members of the team's kid's club. It is believed that local police officers may also have given singles away to local children through other venues. Anyone with additional information may forward it to hockeymag@beckett.com.

COMPLETE SET (29) 6.00 75.00
1 Schedule Card .02 .10
2 Logo Card .02 .10
3 10th Anniversary Logo Card .02 .10
4 The Iron Dog Mascot .02 .10
5 Staff .02 .10
6 Scott Allen ACO .02 .10
7 Nick Fotiu HCO .75 2.00
8 Martin Masa 1.50 4.00
9 Harold Hersh 1.50 4.00
10 Lukas Smital 1.50 4.00
11 Steve Plouffe 4.00 10.00
12 Jonathan Sorg 1.00 2.50
13 Dan Harrison 1.00 2.50
14 Carl Fleury 4.00 10.00
15 Martin Woods 1.00 2.50
16 Mark Yannetti 1.00 2.50
17 Garrett Burnett 1.00 2.50
18 Greg Callahan 1.00 2.50
19 Ivo Jan 1.00 2.50
20 Kelly Leroux 1.00 2.50
21 Brian Scott 1.00 2.50
22 Scott Stephens 1.00 2.50
23 Marcus Draxler 1.00 2.50
24 Brian Callahan 1.00 2.50
25 Francois Archambault 1.00 2.50
26 Dan Dennis 1.00 2.50
27 Reg Cardinal 1.00 2.50
28 Ian Smith 1.00 2.50
29 Yuri Krivokhija 1.00 2.50

1998-99 Johnstown Chiefs

This set was produced by Big League Sports and, like other Johnstown sets, could only be acquired through the Chiefs' Kid's Club.

COMPLETE SET (23) 8.00 20.00
1 Schedule Card .02 .10
2 Logo Card .02 .10
3 Iron Dog Mascot .02 .10
4 Scott Allen HCO .02 .10
5 Galen Head ACO .02 .10
6 Training Staff .02 .10
7 Office Staff .02 .10
8 Etienne Drapeau .40 1.00
9 Jody Shelley 2.00 5.00
10 Jeremy Thompson .40 1.00
11 Carl Fleury .60 1.50
12 Lukas Smital .40 1.00
13 Jonathan Sorg .40 1.00
14 Matt Eisler .40 1.00
15 Martin Masa .40 1.00
16 Shawn Frappier .40 1.00
17 E.J. Bradley .40 1.00
18 Joel Irving .40 1.00
19 Pavel Nestak .40 1.00
20 Kent Simpson .40 1.00
21 Steve Duke .40 1.00
22 Brad Englehart .40 1.00
23 Eric Normandin .40 1.00

1999-00 Johnstown Chiefs

This set features the Chiefs of the ECHL. The cards were issued as promotional giveaways. Police officers attended each game and handed out cards to children, one per night, making the set very difficult to complete.

COMPLETE SET (28) 10.00 25.00
1 Johnstown Chiefs Schedule .08 .25
2 Johnstown Chiefs .40 1.00
3 Iron Dog MASCOT .08 .25
4 Staff Card .08 .25
5 Scott Allen HCO .08 .25
6 Jason Spence .40 1.00
7 Ryan Chaytors .40 1.00
8 Jeffrey Sullivan .40 1.00
9 Andrew Dale .40 1.00
10 Derrick Walser .40 1.00
11 Dmitri Tarabrin .40 1.00
12 Carl Fleury .60 1.50
13 Joel Irving .40 1.00
14 Shawn Frappier .40 1.00
15 John Tripp .40 1.00
16 Chuck Mindel .40 1.00
17 Andrew Clark .40 1.00
18 Jody Shelley 2.00 5.00
19 Brent Bilodeau .40 1.00
20 Mike Vellinga .40 1.00
21 E.J. Bradley .40 1.00
22 Bryan McKinney .40 1.00
23 Mike Thompson .40 1.00
24 Frederic Deschenes .60 1.50
25 Kevin Kellett .40 1.00
26 Tyrone Garner .60 1.50
27 Training Staff .08 .25
28 Frank Cislo DRVR .08 .25

2000-01 Johnstown Chiefs

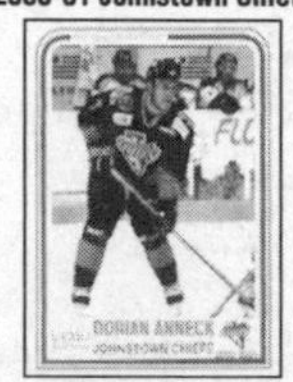

This set features the Chiefs of the ECHL The singles were handed out a designated games, one card at a time, to members of the kid's club, making the complete set very difficult to acquire.

COMPLETE SET (28) 12.00 30.00
1 Schedule Card .04 .10
2 Johnstown Chiefs .40 1.00
3 Scott Allen HCO .10 .25
4 Galen Head ACO .10 .25
5 Toby O'Brien .60 1.50
6 Training Staff .04 .10
7 Radio Guys .04 .10
8 Frank Cislo DRVR .04 .10
9 Front Office Staff .04 .10
10 Iron Dog MASCOT .04 .10
11 Frederic Deschenes .80 2.00
12 Dorian Anneck .60 1.50
13 Maxim Potapov .60 1.50
14 Eric Schneider .60 1.50
15 Jason Spence .60 1.50
16 Michael Kiesman .60 1.50
17 Mikko Kuparinen .80 2.00
18 Brent Bilodeau .80 2.00
19 Mike Vellinga .60 1.50
20 Jeffrey Sullivan .60 1.50
21 Andrew Clark .60 1.50
22 Jan Sulc .60 1.50
23 Dany Sabourin .80 2.00
24 Ryan Tocher .60 1.50
25 Dmitri Tarabrin .60 1.50
26 Mike Rodrigues .60 1.50
27 Mark Thompson .60 1.50
28 Andrew Dale .60 1.50

2001-02 Johnstown Chiefs

This set features the Chiefs of the ECHL. The cards were given away to members of the Chiefs' Kids Club at a rate of one card per game over the course of the season. According to minor league expert Ralph Slate, the card fronts can be misleading. Cards No. 1-10 have no season listed, cards No. 11-15 mistakenly read 2000-01, while cards No. 16-29 read 2001-02. Because of the nature of the distribution, this set is extremely difficult to compile.

COMPLETE SET (29) 19.56 50.00
1 Header Card .02 .10
2 Home Schedule .20 .50
3 Toby & James PRES/GM .20 .50
4 Brent Bilodeau 1.20 3.00
5 Jeffrey Sullivan .80 2.00
6 Kevin Baker .80 2.00
7 Dan Carlson .80 2.00
8 Kevin Clauson .80 2.00
9 Frank Cislo DR .20 .50
10 Staff .20 .50
11 Jim Leger .80 2.00
12 Dany Sabourin 1.20 3.00
13 Lukas Smital .80 2.00
14 J.F. Boutin .80 2.00
15 David Gove 1.20 3.00
16 Frederic Deschenes 1.20 3.00
17 Jason Spence .80 2.00
18 Andrew Clark 1.20 3.00
19 Blair Stayzer 1.20 3.00
20 Mike Rodrigues .80 2.00
21 Philippe Roy .80 2.00
22 Eric Schneider .80 2.00
23 Jim Shepherd .80 2.00
24 Ryan Townsend .80 2.00
25 Chad Onufrechuk .80 2.00
26 Vladimir Nemec .80 2.00
27 Mark White .80 2.00
28 Training Staff .20 .50
29 Mascots .20 .50

2002-03 Johnstown Chiefs

Listed below in alphabetical order.

COMPLETE SET (23) 20.00 40.00
1 Peter Aubry .75 2.00
2 Brent Bilodeau 1.00 2.50
3 J.F. Boutin .75 2.00
4 Pierre-Luc Courchesne .75 2.00
5 Andy Doktorchik .75 2.00
6 Dominic Forget .75 2.00
7 Steve Hildenbrand .75 2.00
8 Jay Langager .75 2.00
9 Jim Leger .75 2.00
10 Vladimir Nemec .75 2.00
11 Toby O'Brien .75 2.00
12 Mike Rodrigues .75 2.00
13 Philippe Roy .75 2.00
14 Mark Scally .75 2.00
15 Lukas Smital .75 2.00
16 Jason Spence .75 2.00
17 Sam St. Pierre .75 2.00
18 Jeff Sullivan .75 2.00
19 Dmitri Tarabrin .75 2.00
20 Ryan Townsend .75 2.00
21 Anniversary Logo .02 .10
22 Mascots .10 .25
23 Training Staff .02 .10

2003-04 Johnstown Chiefs

This set was produced by Big League Cards to be given away to members of the team's kids club. Because they were issued one card per game over the course of the season, it is an incredibly difficult set to complete. It's possible the checklist below is not complete. Please forward additional information to hockeymag@beckett.com. As we have no market information, the cards cannot be priced.

COMPLETE SET (19)
1 Brent Bilodeau
2 Jeffrey Sullivan
3 Dmitri Tarabrin
4 Dominic Forget
5 Ian Manzano
6 Steve Hildenbrand
7 Jay Langager
8 Shawn Mather
9 Josh Piro
10 Cory Campbell
11 Dan Growden
12 Mike James
13 Pierre-Luc Courchesne
14 David Currie
15 Jason Notermann
16 Chad Cavanagh
17 Richard Paul
18 Larry Courville
19 Brent Kelly

2003-04 Johnstown Chiefs RBI Sports

This set was produced by RBI Sports and was limited to 250 copies. The numbering sequence reflects the entire run of RBI series that season.

COMPLETE SET (16) 15.00
209 Brent Bilodeau 1.00
210 Chad Cavanagh 1.00
211 Pierre-Luc Courchesne 1.00
212 Larry Courville 1.00
213 David Currie 1.50
214 Dominic Forget 1.00
215 Steve Hildenbrand 1.00
216 Mike James 1.00
217 Brent Kelly 1.00
218 Jay Langager 1.00
219 Chris Leinweber 1.00
220 Ian Manzano 1.00
221 Shawn Mather 1.00
222 Jason Notermann 1.00
223 Dmitri Patzold 1.50
224 Dmitri Tarabrin 1.00

2004-05 Johnstown Chiefs

An album to store these cards was also produced.

COMPLETE SET (21) 15.00
1 Brent Bilodeau 1.00
2 David Bowman .75
3 David Cann 1.00
4 Chad Cavanagh .75
5 P.L. Courchesne .75
6 David Currie 1.00
7 Jean Desrochers .75
8 Steve Hildenbrand .75
9 Mike James 1.50
10 Brent Kelly .75
11 Chris Leinweber .75
12 Ian Manzano .75
13 Shawn Mather .75
14 Dennis Packard .75
15 Matt J. Reid .75
16 Jeff Sullivan .75
17 Joe Tallari .75
18 Dmitri Tarabrin .75
19 Johnathan Tremblay .75
20 Jeremy Van Hoof .75
21 Toby O'Brien CO .10

2005-06 Johnstown Chiefs

COMPLETE SET (20) 6.00 15.00
1 Doug Andress .30 .75
2 J.B. Bittner .30 .75
3 Jonathan Boutin .30 .75
4 Morgan Cey .30 .75
5 Steve Cygan .30 .75
6 Jean Desrochers .30 .75
7 Gerard Dicaire .30 .75
8 Mike Egener .30 .75
9 Brandon Elliott .30 .75
10 Brady Greco .30 .75
11 Adam Henrich .30 .75
12 Justin Kelly .30 .75
13 Ian Manzano .30 .75
14 Brett Peterson .30 .75
15 Randy Rowe .30 .75

16 Jason Spence	.30	.75
17 Joe Tallari	.30	.75
18 Dmitri Tarabrin	.30	.75
19 John Toffey	.30	.75
20 Ben Wallace	.30	.75

1971-72 Johnstown Jets Acme

This set features the Jets of the EHL. The oversized cards measure 3.5" x 5" and feature black and white photos. The cards are blank backed and unnumbered, and so are listed below in alphabetical order.

COMPLETE SET (16)	40.00	80.00
1 Dave Birch	2.00	5.00
2 Vern Campigatto	2.00	5.00
3 Len Cunning	2.00	5.00
4 Guy Delparte	2.00	5.00
5 Wynne Dempster	2.00	5.00
6 Ron Docken	2.00	5.00
7 Galen Head	2.00	5.00
8 Eddie Kachur	2.00	5.00
9 Reg Kent(Taschuk)	2.00	5.00
10 Jerry MacDonald	2.00	5.00
11 Gene Peacosh	2.50	6.00
12 Dick Roberge	2.00	5.00
13 Jim Trewin	2.00	5.00
14 Brian Vescio	2.00	5.00
15 Bob Vroman	2.50	6.00
16 Gary Wood	2.00	5.00

1972-73 Johnstown Jets

This set features the Jets of the EHL. The cards reportedly were included as a premium in game day programs and measure an oversized 3 1/2 by 5 inches. The photos on the front are black and white, while the backs are blank.

COMPLETE SET (18)	50.00	100.00
1 Ron Docken	2.50	6.00
2 Brian Coughlin	2.00	5.00
3 Tony McCarthy	2.00	5.00
4 Tom Steeves	2.00	5.00
5 Kevin Collins	2.00	5.00
6 Jerry MacDonald	2.00	5.00
7 Wynne Dempster	2.00	5.00
8 Ted Lanyon	2.00	5.00
9 Brian Vescio	2.00	5.00
10 Dennis Erickson	2.50	6.00
11 Vern Campigatto	2.00	5.00
12 Gary Wood	2.00	5.00
13 Dave Birch	2.00	5.00
14 Galen Head	2.50	6.00
15 Reg Kent(Taschuk)	2.00	5.00
16 Tom McVie	2.50	6.00
17 Bill McEwan	2.00	5.00
18 Doug Anderson	2.00	5.00

1952-53 Juniors Blue Tint

The 1952-53 Junior set contains 182 cards measuring approximately 2" by 3". The cards have a blue tint and are numbered on the back. It is not known at this time who sponsored this set. Key cards in this set are "Pre-Rookie Cards" of Al Arbour, Don Cherry, Charlie Hodge, John Muckler, Henri Richard, and Harry Sinden.

COMPLETE SET (182)	1250.00	2500.00
1 Dennis Riggin	7.50	15.00
2 Joe Zorica	5.00	10.00
3 Larry Hillman	10.00	20.00
4 Edward(Ted) Reid	5.00	10.00
5 Al Arbour	37.50	75.00
6 Marlin McAlendin	5.00	10.00
7 Ross Graham	5.00	10.00
8 Cumming Burton	5.00	10.00
9 Ed Palamar	5.00	10.00
10 Elmer Skov	6.00	12.00
11 Eddie Louttit	5.00	10.00
12 Gerry Price	5.00	10.00
13 Lou Dietrich	5.00	10.00
14 Gaston Marcotte	5.00	10.00
15 Bob Brown	5.00	10.00
16 Archie Burton	5.00	10.00
17 Marv Edwards	17.50	35.00
18 Norman Defelice	6.00	12.00
19 Pete Kamula	5.00	10.00
20 Charles Marshall	5.00	10.00
21 Alex Leslie	5.00	10.00
22 Mingy Roberts	5.00	10.00
23 Danny Poliziani	5.00	10.00
24 Allen Kellogg	5.00	10.00
25 Brian Cullen	17.50	35.00
26 Ken Schinkel	6.00	12.00
27 W. Hass	5.00	10.00
28 Don Nash	5.00	10.00
29 Robert Maxwell	5.00	10.00
30 Eddie Mateka	5.00	10.00
31 Joe Kastelic	5.00	10.00
32 Hank Ciesla	6.00	12.00
33 Hugh Barlow	5.00	10.00
34 Claude Roy	5.00	10.00
35 Jean-Guy Gamache	5.00	10.00
36 Leon Michelin	5.00	10.00
37 Gerard Bergeron	5.00	10.00
38 Herve Lalonde	5.00	10.00
39 J.M. Cossette	5.00	10.00
40 Jean-Guy Gendron	10.00	20.00
41 Gamill Bedard	5.00	10.00
42 Alfred Soucy	5.00	10.00
43 Jean Leclerc	5.00	10.00
44 Raymond St.Cyr	6.00	12.00
45 Lester Lahaye	5.00	10.00
46 Yvan Houle	5.00	10.00
47 Louis Desrosiers	5.00	10.00
48 Douglas Lessor	5.00	10.00
49 Irvin Scott	5.00	10.00
50 Danny Blair	5.00	10.00
51 Jim Connelly	6.00	12.00
52 William Chalmers	5.00	10.00
53 Frank Bettiol	5.00	10.00
54 James Holmes	5.00	10.00
55 Birley Dimme	5.00	10.00
56 Donald Beattie	5.00	10.00
57 Terrance Chattington	5.00	10.00
58 Bruce Wallace	5.00	10.00
59 William McCreary	6.00	12.00
60 Fred Brady	5.00	10.00
61 Ronald Murphy	6.00	12.00
62 Lavi Purola	5.00	10.00
63 George Whyte	5.00	10.00
64 Marcel Paille	25.00	50.00
65 Maurice Collins	5.00	10.00
66 Gerard(Butch) Houle	6.00	12.00
67 Gilles Laperriere	5.00	10.00
68 Robert Chevalier	5.00	10.00
69 Bertrand Lepage	5.00	10.00
70 Michel Labadie	5.00	10.00
71 Gabriel Alain	5.00	10.00
72 Jean-Jacques Pichette	6.00	12.00
73A Camille Henry (Citadelles)	12.50	25.00
73B Camille Henry (New York)	100.00	200.00
74 Jean-Guy Gignac	5.00	10.00
75 Leo Amadio	6.00	12.00
76 Gilles Thibault	6.00	12.00
77 Gaston Pelletier	6.00	12.00
78 Adolph Kukulowicz	6.00	12.00
79 Roland Leclerc	5.00	10.00
80 Phil Watson CO	20.00	40.00
81 Raymond Cyr	6.00	12.00
82 Jacques Marcotte	5.00	10.00
83 Floyd (Bud) Hillman	6.00	12.00
84 Bob Attersley	5.00	10.00
85 Harry Sinden	37.50	75.00
86 Stan Parker	5.00	10.00
87 Bob Mader	5.00	10.00
88 Roger Maisonneuve	5.00	10.00
89 Phil Chapman	5.00	10.00
90 Don McIntosh	5.00	10.00
91 Jack Armstrong	5.00	10.00
92 Carlo Montemurro	5.00	10.00
93 Ken Courtney	5.00	10.00
94 Bill Stewart	6.00	12.00
95 Gerald Casey	5.00	10.00
96 Fred Etcher	5.00	10.00
97 Orrin Carver	5.00	10.00
98 Ralph Willis	5.00	10.00
99 Kenneth Robertson	5.00	10.00
100 Don Cherry	175.00	350.00
101 Fred Pletsch	5.00	10.00
102 Larry Thibault	5.00	10.00
103 James Robertson	5.00	10.00
104 Orval Tessier	10.00	20.00
105 Jack Higgins	5.00	10.00
106 Robert White	5.00	10.00
107 Doug Mohns	17.50	35.00
108 William Sexton	5.00	10.00
109 John Martan	5.00	10.00
110 Tony Poeta	6.00	12.00
111 Don McKenney	10.00	20.00
112 Bill Harrington	5.00	10.00
113 Allen (Skip) Peal	5.00	10.00
114 John Ford	5.00	10.00
115 Kenneth Collins	6.00	12.00
116 Marc Boileau	6.00	12.00
117 Doug Vaughan	5.00	10.00
118 Gilles Boisvert	5.00	10.00
119 Buddy Horne	5.00	10.00
120 Graham Joyce	5.00	10.00
121 Gary Collins	5.00	10.00
122 Roy Greenan	5.00	10.00
123 Beryl Klynck	5.00	10.00
124 Grieg Hicks	5.00	10.00
125 Jack (Red) Novak	5.00	10.00
126 Ken Tennant	5.00	10.00
127 Glen Cressman	5.00	10.00
128 Curly Davies	5.00	10.00
129 Charlie Hodge	37.50	75.00
130 Bob McCord	6.00	12.00
131 Gordie Hollinworth	5.00	10.00
132 Ronald Pilon	5.00	10.00
133 Brian Mackay	5.00	10.00
134 Yvon Chasle	5.00	10.00
135 Denis Boucher	6.00	12.00
136 Claude Boileau	5.00	10.00
137 Claude Vinet	5.00	10.00
138 Claude Provost	20.00	40.00
139 Henri Richard	137.50	275.00
140 Les Lilley	5.00	10.00
141 Phil Goyette	17.50	35.00
142 Guy Rousseau	5.00	10.00
143 Paul Knox	5.00	10.00
144 Bill Lee	5.00	10.00
145 Tod Topazzini	6.00	12.00
146 Marc Reaume	6.00	12.00
147 Bill Dineen	17.50	35.00
148 Ed Plata	5.00	10.00
149 Noel Price	6.00	12.00
150 Mike Ratchford	5.00	10.00
151 Jim Logan	5.00	10.00
152 Art Clune	5.00	10.00
153 Jerry MacNamara	5.00	10.00
154 Jack Caffery	6.00	12.00
155 Les Duff	5.00	10.00
156 Murray Costello	6.00	12.00
157 Ed Chadwick	40.00	80.00
158 Mike Desilets	5.00	10.00
159 Ross Watson	5.00	10.00
160 Roger Landry	5.00	10.00
161 Terry O'Connor	5.00	10.00
162 Ovila Gagnon	5.00	10.00
163 Dave Broadbelt	5.00	10.00
164 Sandy Morrisson	5.00	10.00
165 John MacGillvray	5.00	10.00
166 Claude Beaupre	5.00	10.00
167 Eddie Eustache	5.00	10.00
168 Stan Rodek	5.00	10.00
169 Maurice Mantha	6.00	12.00
170 Hector Lalande	6.00	12.00
171 Bob Wilson	5.00	10.00
172 Frank Bonello	5.00	10.00
173 Peter Kowalchuch	5.00	10.00
174 Les Binkley	25.00	50.00
175 John Muckler	20.00	40.00
176 Ken Wharram	17.50	35.00
177 John Sleaver	5.00	10.00
178 Ralph Markarian	5.00	10.00
179 Ken McMeekin	5.00	10.00
180 Don Doomer	5.00	10.00
181 Kenneth (Red) Crawford	5.00	10.00
182 Jim McBurney	7.50	15.00

2001-02 Kalamazoo K-Wings

This set features the K-Wings of the UHL. It was produced by Choice Marketing and sold at the team's souvenir stands.

COMPLETE SET (24)	4.00	10.00
1 Andrew Huggett	.20	.50
2 Michael Goldkind	.20	.50
3 Sergei Deshevyy	.20	.50
4 Randy Holmes	.20	.50
5 Michael Ford	.20	.50
6 Jeff Scharf	.20	.50
7 Mathieu Paul	.20	.50
8 Jim Brown	.20	.50
9 Darcy Anderson	.20	.50
10 Harry Schwefel	.20	.50
11 Greg Dupre	.20	.50
12 Benoit Beausoleil	.20	.50
13 Craig Paterson	.20	.50
14 Jeff Foster	.20	.50
15 Mark Lawrence	.31	.78
16 Steve Moore	.20	.50
17 Tim Knudsen	.31	.78
18 Scott Langkow	.31	.78
19 Brad Cook	.20	.50
20 Sandy Lamarre	.20	.50
21 Ted Laviolette	.20	.50
22 Dennis Desrosiers CO	.04	.11
23 Scott Allison TR	.04	.11
24 Slappy MASCOT	.04	.11
NNO Team CL	.04	.11

1977-78 Kalamazoo Wings

These standard size cards, sponsored by ISB bank, feature black and white photos with a white border. Backs feature players name, position, and card number.

COMPLETE (15)	15.00	30.00
1 George Klsons	1.00	2.00
2 Ron Wilson	1.00	2.00
3 Bob Lemieux	1.00	2.00
4 Len Ircandia	1.00	2.00
5 Ron Kennedy	1.00	2.00
6 Daniel Poulin	1.00	2.00
7 Terry Evans	1.00	2.00
8 Yvon Douris	1.00	2.00
9 Tom Milani	1.00	2.00
10 Mike Wanchuk	1.00	2.00
11 Steve Lee	1.00	2.00
12 Yves Guilmette	1.00	2.00
13 Al Genovy	1.00	2.00
15 Jim Baxter	1.00	2.00
18 Alvin White	1.00	2.00

2002-03 Kalamazoo Wings

COMPLETE SET (29)	20.00
1 Checklist	.10
2 Kirill Alexeev	1.00
3 Tyson Turgeon	1.00
4 Eric Lawson	1.00
5 Quade Lightbody	1.00
6 Herman Hultgren	1.00
7 Bryan Farquhar	1.00
8 Mike Ford	1.00
9 Peter Roed	1.00
10 Joe Pecoraro	1.00
11 Jordan Trew	1.00
12 Glendon Cominetti	1.00
13 Pete Pierman	1.00
14 Kurt Miller	1.00
15 Mark Phenow	1.00
16 Craig Bilick	1.00
17 Mark Lawrence	1.00
18 Justin Cardwell	1.00
19 Richard Keyes	1.00
20 Chad Dameworth	1.00
21 Chad Alban	1.50
22 Brian Rogers	1.00
23 Jeff Reynaert	1.00
24 Mark Kaufman CO	.10
25 Mike Modugno ANN	.10
26 Scott Allison TR	.10
27 Slappy Mascot	.10
28 Shoe Carnival	.01
29 Burger King	.01

2003-04 Kalamazoo Wings

COMPLETE SET (32)	4.00	10.00
1 Checklist	.01	.05
2 Mark Reeds CO	.02	.10
3 Mark Vilneff	.15	.40
4 Guy Dupuis	.15	.40
5 Tyson Turgeon	.15	.40
6 Jim Dube	.15	.40
7 Kevin Caudill	.15	.40
8 Daniel Carriere	.15	.40
9 Steve Doherty	.15	.40
10 Tyler Willis	.30	.75
11 Jeff Turner	.15	.40
12 Kurt Miller	.15	.40
13 Marty Flichel	.15	.40
14 Tim Turner	.15	.40
15 David Hukalo	.15	.40
16 Yannick Carpentier	.15	.40
17 Pat O'Leary	.15	.40
18 Josh Akright	.15	.40
19 Andrew Luciuk	.15	.40
20 Dan Watson	.15	.40
21 Chad Alban	.30	.75
22 Brock McGillis	.30	.75
23 Brent Rumble	.15	.40
24 Nick Bootland	.30	.75
25 Joe Ritson	.15	.40
26 Team Staff	.02	.10
27 Mike Modugno ANN	.02	.10
28 Mascot	.02	.10
29 Ad Card	.01	.05
30 Ad Card	.01	.05
31 Ad Card	.01	.05
32 Ad Card	.01	.05

2004-05 Kalamazoo Wings

COMPLETE SET (30)	5.00	12.00
1 Checklist	.02	.10
2 Mark Reeds CO	.02	.10
3 Josh Elzinga	.20	.50
4 Mark Vilneff	.20	.50
5 Kevin Hoildge	.20	.50
6 Tyson Turgeon	.20	.50
7 Shaun Fisher	.20	.50
8 Daniel Carriere	.20	.50
9 Greg Labenski	.20	.50
10 Tyler Willis	.20	.50
11 Tom Ditzer	.20	.50
12 Steve Doherty	.20	.50
13 Tim Turner	.20	.50
14 Matt Noga	.20	.50
15 Tim Krueckl	.20	.50
16 Yannick Carpentier	.20	.50
17 Ryan Crane	.20	.50
18 Gray Shaneberger	.20	.50
19 Andrew Luciuk	.20	.50
20 Sean Starke	.20	.50
21 Kevin Kotyluk	.20	.50
22 Chad Alban	.40	1.00
23 Joel Martin	.20	.50
24 Mike Manley	.20	.50
25 Daniel Carriere AS Greg Labenski AS	.20	.50
26 Trainers	.02	.10
27 Slappy MASCOT	.02	.10
28 Announcer	.02	.10
29 Rocker Morning Show	.02	.10
30 WKFR Morning Show	.02	.10

2005-06 Kalamazoo Wings

COMPLETE SET (30)	8.00	20.00
1 Kalamazoo Wings CL	.02	.10
2 Mark Reeds HC	.02	.10
3 Josh Elzinga	.40	1.00
4 Mark Vilneff	.40	1.00
5 Mike Dombkiewicz	.40	1.00
6 Jason Deitsch	.40	1.00
7 Daniel Carriere	.40	1.00
8 Tyler Willis	.40	1.00
9 Damian Surma	.40	1.00
10 Tim Turner	.40	1.00
11 Lucas Drake	.40	1.00
12 Tyler Rennette	.40	1.00
13 Dustin Virag	.40	1.00
14 Adam Elzinga	.40	1.00
15 Lee Ruff	.40	1.00
16 Brad Church	.40	1.00
17 Greg Labenski	.40	1.00
18 Kory Karlander	.40	1.00
19 Jeff Reynaert	.40	1.00
20 Mike Manley	.40	1.00
21 Joel Martin	.40	1.00
22 Nick Bootland	.40	1.00
23 K-Wings Alumni	.40	1.00
24 Mike Plandowski TR	.02	.10
25 Eric Bechtol FOM	.02	.10
26 Slappy MASCOT	.02	.10
27 Mike Modugno ANN	.02	.10
28 The Rocker Morning Show	.02	.10
29 The KFR Morning Show	.02	.10
30 Scoopie MASCOT	.02	.10

1984-85 Kamloops Blazers

This set features color action photos on the front along with team name, position, and number. Backs feature safety tips and sponsor logos. Cards are unnumbered and checklisted below in alphabetical order.

COMPLETE SET (24)	8.00	20.00
1 Will Anderson	.30	.75
2 Brian Benning	.30	.75
3 Brian Bertuzzi	.30	.75
4 Rob Brown	.60	1.50
5 Todd Carnelley	.30	.75
6 Dean Clark	.40	1.00
7 Rob Dimaio	.75	2.00
8 Greg Evtushevski	.30	.75
9 Mark Fernor	.30	.75
10 Greg Hawgood	.60	1.50
11 Ken Hitchcock CO	.75	2.00
12 Mark Kachowski	.30	.75
13 Bob Labrier ACO	.08	.25
14 Pat Mangold	.30	.75
15 Gord Mark	.30	.75
16 Len Mark	.30	.75
17 Rob McKinley	.40	1.00
18 Mike Nottingham	.30	.75
19 Neil Pilon	.30	.75
20 Rudy Poeschek	.75	2.00
21 Daryl Reaugh	.75	2.00
22 Ryan Stewart	.30	.75
23 Mark Thietke	.30	.75
24 Gord Walker	.30	.75

1985-86 Kamloops Blazers

This standard size set features full color fronts along with sponsor logs and hockey tips on the backs. Cards are unnumbered and checklisted below in alphabetical order.

COMPLETE SET (26)	8.00	40.00
1 Robin Bawa	.75	2.00
2 Craig Berube	2.00	5.00
3 Pat Bingham	.40	1.00
4 Rob Brown	.75	2.00
5 Todd Carnelly	.40	1.00
6 Randy Hansch	.75	2.00
7 Greg Hawgood	.75	2.00
8 Ken Hitchcock CO	2.00	5.00
9 Mark Kachowski	.40	1.00
10 Troy Kennedy	.40	1.00
11 R.T. Labrier ACO	.07	.20
12 Dave Marcinyshyn	.40	1.00
13 Len Mark	.40	1.00
14 Rob McKinley	.40	1.00
15 Ken Morrison	.40	1.00
16 Pat Nogier	.40	1.00
17 Mike Nottingham	.40	1.00
18 Doug Pickell	.40	1.00
19 Rudy Poeschek	2.00	5.00
20 Mike Ragot	.40	1.00
21 Don Schmidt	.40	1.00
22 Ron Shudra	.40	1.00
23 Peter Soberlak	.40	1.00
24 Lonnie Spink	.40	1.00
25 Chris Tarnowski	.40	1.00
26 Greg Wallace TR	.07	.20

1986-87 Kamloops Blazers

This 24-card sheet was issued in nine four-card sheets. Six of the panels feature two cards and an advertisement, while the other three panels feature four cards per panel. The sheets are perforated vertically but not horizontally, which produces two-card stripes. If cut, the cards would measure the standard size. On a white card face, the fronts display posed action photos inside a bright blue border. The cards are unnumbered and checklisted below in alphabetical order.

COMPLETE SET (24)	12.00	30.00
1 Warren Babe	.20	.50
2 Robin Bawa	.20	.50
3 Rob Brown	.60	1.50
4 Dean Cook	.40	1.00
5 Scott Daniels	.20	.50
6 Mario Desjardines	.20	.50
7 Bill Harrington	.20	.50
8 Greg Hawgood	.40	1.00
9 Serge Lajoie	.20	.50
10 Dave Marcinyshyn	.20	.50
11 Len Mark	.20	.50
12 Rob McKinley	.40	1.00
13 Casey McMillan	.20	.50
14 Darcy Norton	.20	.50
15 Kelly Para	.20	.50
16 Doug Pickell	.20	.50
17 Rudy Poeschek	.60	1.50
18 Mark Recchi	6.00	15.00
19 Don Schmidt	.20	.50
20 Ron Shudra	.20	.50
21 Chris Tarnowski	.20	.50
22 Steve Wienke	.20	.50
23 Rich Wiest	.20	.50
24 Team Photo	.20	.50

1987-88 Kamloops Blazers

This 24-card set was issued in three-card perforated strips each consisting of two player cards and one advertisement or coupon card. (As listed below, two of these advertisement cards display team logos on the front). The strips measure 7 1/2" by 3 1/2", and if cut, the individual cards would measure the standard size. The front features a color posed-action player photo with thin blue borders on a white card face. The cards are unnumbered and checklisted below in alphabetical order.

COMPLETE SET (24)	12.00	30.00
1 Warren Babe	.30	.75
2 Paul Checknita	.30	.75
3 Dave Chyzowski	.40	1.00
4 Dean Cook	.40	1.00
5 Greg Davies	.30	.75
6 Kim Deck	.30	.75
7 Todd Decker	.30	.75
8 Bill Harrington	.30	.75
9 Phil Huber	.30	.75
10 Steve Kloepzig	.30	.75
11 Willie MacDonald	.40	1.00
12 Pat MacLeod	.30	.75
13 Glenn Mulvenna	.40	1.00
14 Mike Needham	.30	.75
15 Darcy Norton	.30	.75
16 Devon Oleniuk	.30	.75
17 Doug Pickell	.30	.75
18 Garth Premak	.30	.75
19 Mark Recchi	6.00	15.00
20 Don Schmidt	.30	.75
21 Alec Shello	.30	.75
22 Team Photo	.20	.50
23 Logo Card	.08	.25
24 Logo Card	.08	.25

1988-89 Kamloops Blazers

This 36-card set was issued in three-card perforated strips that measure approximately 7 1/2" by 3 1/2". After perforation, the individual cards measure approximately 2 1/2" by 3 1/2". One of the cards on each three-card strip has the Kamloops logo in blue and orange on the front and the back contains a coupon. The regular player cards have white borders with an inner royal blue line surrounding a posed player photo. The cards are unnumbered and are checklisted below in alphabetical order.

COMPLETE SET (36)	7.20	18.00
COMMON AD CARD (25-36)	.02	.10
1 Cory Anderson	.20	.50
2 Pat Bingham	.20	.50
3 Ed Bertuzzi	.20	.50
4 Zac Boyer	.20	.50
5 Trevor Buchanan	.20	.50
6 Dave Chyzowski	.20	.50
7 Dean Cook	.30	.75
8 Cory Crichton	.20	.50
9 Kim Deck	.20	.50
10 Ryan Harrison	.20	.50
11 Brad Heschuk	.20	.50
12 Corey Hirsch	1.25	3.00
13 Phil Huber	.20	.50
14 Len Jorgenson	.20	.50
15 Paul Kruse	.30	.75
16 Dave Linford	.20	.50
17 Pat MacLeod	.20	.50
18 Darwin McClelland	.20	.50
19 Cal McGowan	.20	.50
20 Mike Needham	.20	.50
21 Don Schmidt	.20	.50
22 Brian Shantz	.20	.50
23 Darryl Sydor	1.25	3.00
24 Steve Yule	.20	.50
25 Hasty Market Ad		.01
26 McDonalds Ad		.01
27 Mr. Mike's Ad		.01
28 Yellow Submarine Ad		.01
29 Blazers Logo	.02	.10
30 Blazers Logo	.02	.10
31 Blazers Logo	.02	.10
32 Blazers Logo	.02	.10
33 Blazers Logo	.02	.10
34 Blazers Logo	.02	.10
35 Blazers Logo	.02	.10
36 Blazers Logo	.02	.10

1989-90 Kamloops Blazers

This 24-card set is believed to have been released in three-card panel form, as were previous Blazers issues. It is noteworthy for featuring the first card of All-Star defender Scott Niedermayer.

COMPLETE SET (24)	6.00	15.00
1 Len Barrie	.20	.50
2 Craig Bonner	.20	.50
3 Jarrett Bousquet	.20	.50
4 Zac Boyer	.25	.60
5 Murray Duval	.20	.50
6 Shea Esselmont	.20	.50
7 Todd Esselmont	.20	.50
8 Todd Harris	.20	.50
9 Corey Hirsch	.60	1.50
10 Phil Huber	.20	.50
11 Lance Johnson	.20	.50
12 Paul Kruse	.25	.60
13 Dean Malkoc	.20	.50
14 Dale Mason	.20	.50
15 Cal McGowan	.20	.50
16 Joey Mittelsteadt	.20	.50
17 Mike Needham	.25	.60
18 Scott Niedermayer	1.50	4.00
19 Brian Shantz	.20	.50
20 Trevor Sim	.20	.50
21 Darryl Sydor	.75	2.00
22 Jeff Waatchorn	.20	.50
23 Clayton Young	.20	.50
24 Steve Yule	.20	.50

1993-94 Kamloops Blazers

This 24-card set was issued on three-card perforated strips each consisting of two player cards and one advertisement or coupon card. The strips measure 7 1/2" by 3 1/2", and if cut, the individual cards would measure the standard size. The fronts feature a color posed-action player photo with thin blue borders on a white background. The cards are unnumbered and checklisted below in alphabetical order.

COMPLETE SET (24)	12.00	35.00
1 Nolan Baumgartner	.30	.75
2 Rod Branch	.20	.50
3 Jarrett Deuling	.20	.50
4 Shane Doan	2.00	5.00
5 Hnat Domenichelli	.30	.75
6 Scott Ferguson	.20	.50
7 Greg Hart	.20	.50
8 Jason Holland	.20	.50
9 Ryan Huska	.20	.50
10 Jarome Iginla	6.00	15.00
11 Mike Josephson	.20	.50
12 Aaron Keller	.20	.50
13 Mike Krooshoop	.20	.50
14 Scott Loucks	.20	.50
15 Brad Lukowich	.40	1.00
16 Bob Maudie	.20	.50
17 Chris Murray	.20	.50
18 Tyson Nash	1.25	3.00
19 Steve Passmore	.60	1.50
20 Rod Stevens	.20	.50
21 Jason Strudwick	.30	.75
22 Darcy Tucker	1.50	4.00
23 Bob Westerby	.20	.50
24 David Wilkie	.20	.50

1994-95 Kamloops Blazers

This set features the Blazers of the WHL. It is believed that it was issued as a promotional giveaway.

COMPLETE SET (24)	12.00	30.00
1 Darcy Tucker	.75	2.00
2 Jarome Iginla	4.00	10.00
3 Nolan Baumgartner	.40	1.00
4 Jeff Oldenborger	.20	.50
5 Ivan Vologjaninov	.20	.50
6 Shawn McNeil	.20	.50
7 Donnie Kinney	.20	.50
8 Bob Maudie	.20	.50
9 Jason Holland	.20	.50
10 Greg Hart	.20	.50
11 Shane Doan	1.25	3.00
12 Brad Lukowich	.40	1.00
13 Randy Petruk	.40	1.00
14 Jason Strudwick	.40	1.00
15 Jeff Ainsworth	.20	.50
16 Aaron Keller	.20	.50
17 Rod Branch	.20	.50
18 Bob Westerby	.20	.50
19 Tyson Nash	1.25	3.00
20 Hnat Domenichelli	.40	1.00
21 Ryan Huska	.20	.50
22 Jeff Henkelman	.20	.50
23 Cam Severson	.20	.50
24 Kamloops Arena	.04	.10

1995-96 Kamloops Blazers

This set features the Blazers of the WHL. Although the checklist is confirmed, little else is known about the distribution of this set. Additional information can be forwarded to hockeymag@beckett.com.

COMPLETE SET (31)	8.00	20.00
1 Jarome Iginla	2.00	5.00
2 Nolan Baumgartner	.20	.50
3 Jake Deadmarsh	.20	.50
4 Scott Reid	.20	.50
5 Randy Petruk	.30	.75
6 Brad Lukowich	.40	1.00
7 Shawn McNeil	.30	.75
8 Ed Dempsey CO	.08	.25
9 Peter Bergman	.20	.50
10 Greg Hart	.20	.50
11 Hnat Domenichelli	.40	1.00
12 Al Glendenning CO	.08	.25
13 Digger MAS	.02	.10
14 Rob Skrlac	.20	.50
15 Donnie Kinney	.20	.50
16 Chris St. Croix	.20	.50
17 Jeff Oldenborger	.20	.50
18 Steve Albrecht	.20	.50
19 Bob Maudie	.20	.50
20 Blair Rota	.20	.50
21 Brian Henderson CO	.08	.25
22 Aaron Keller	.20	.50
23 Ryan Rishaug	.20	.50
24 Steve Gainey	.40	1.00
25 Jeff Ainsworth	.20	.50
26 Ajay Baines	.20	.50
27 Jordan Landry	.20	.50
28 Jason Holland	.20	.50
29 Kamloops Arena	.08	.25
30 Cadrin Smart	.20	.50
31 Konrad Brand	.20	.50

1996-97 Kamloops Blazers

This 28-card set was distributed in 3-panel strips, each of which contained two player cards and one ad card for a local business. When separated the cards are standard size and feature color photos with player name, number and position at the top, while the bottom left corner is dominated by a flame-like element and an icon identifying the set as the '96-97 Limited Edition. The cards are unnumbered and are listed below in alphabetical order.

COMPLETE SET (28)	8.00	20.00
1 Jeff Ainsworth	.30	.75
2 Steve Albrecht	.30	.75
3 Nils Antons	.30	.75
4 Ajay Baines	.30	.75
5 Konrad Brand	.30	.75
6 Wade Burt	.30	.75
7 Jake Deadmarsh	.30	.75
8 Ed Dempsey CO	.08	.25
9 Digger MAS	.02	.10
10 Micki DuPont	.40	1.00
11 Steve Gainey	.40	1.00
12 Jonathan Hobson	.30	.75
13 Drew Kehler	.30	.75
14 Donnie Kinney	.30	.75
15 Alan Manness	.30	.75
16 Shawn McNeil	.30	.75
17 Randy Petruk	.40	1.00
18 Clayton Pool	.40	1.00
19 Gennady Razin	.30	.75
20 Robyn Regehr	.60	1.50
21 Blair Rota	.30	.75
22 Thomas Scantlebury	.30	.75
23 Steve Shrum	.30	.75
24 Rob Skrlac	.30	.75
25 Darcy Smith	.30	.75
26 Chris St. Croix	.30	.75
27 Spike Wallace	.08	.25
28 Darren Wright	.30	.75

1998-99 Kamloops Blazers

These cards are unnumbered and so are listed below in alphabetical order.

COMPLETE SET (24)	12.00	20.00
1 Jared Aulin	.40	1.00
2 Ajay Baines	.40	1.00
3 Anton Borodkin	.30	.75
4 Mike Brown	.30	.75
5 Paul Deniset	.30	.75
6 Adam Dombrowski	.30	.75
7 Brett Draney	.30	.75
8 Micki Dupont	.40	1.00
9 Kenric Exner	.40	1.00
10 Jordon Flodell	.30	.75
11 Steve Gainey	.40	1.00
12 Aaron Gionet	.30	.75
13 Gable Gross	.30	.75
14 Jonathan Hobson	.30	.75
15 Donnie Kinney	.30	.75
16 David Klatt	.30	.75
17 Kevin MacKie	.30	.75
18 Alan Manness	.30	.75
19 Konstantin Panov	.30	.75
20 Robyn Regehr	.75	2.00
21 Steve Shrum	.30	.75
22 Chris St. Croix	.30	.75
23 Chad Starling	.30	.75
24 Ryan Thorpe	.30	.75

1999-00 Kamloops Blazers

This set features the Blazers of the WHL. The set was produced by the team and sold at its souvenir stands. The cards are unnumbered, so are listed below alphabetically.

COMPLETE SET (24)	6.00	15.00
1 Jared Aulin	.75	2.00
2 Jason Bone	.30	.75
3 Anton Borodkin	.20	.50
4 Erik Christensen	.20	.50
5 Paul Deniset	.20	.50
6 Blaine Depper	.20	.50
7 Brett Draney	.20	.50
8 Micki DuPont	.40	1.00
9 Aaron Gionet	.30	.75
10 Gable Gross	.20	.50
11 Jonathan Hobson	.20	.50
12 Kyle Ladobruk	.20	.50
13 Kevin Mackie	.20	.50
14 Grant McCune	.30	.75
15 Shaone Morrisonn	.60	1.50
16 Mike Munro	.20	.50
17 Konstantin Panov	.30	.75
18 Davis Parley	.30	.75
19 Mark Rooneem	.20	.50
20 Chad Schockenmaier	.20	.50
21 Steve Shrum	.20	.50
22 Chad Starling	.20	.50
23 Jordan Walker	.20	.50
24 Digger MASCOT	.08	.25

2000-01 Kamloops Blazers

COMPLETE SET (24)	6.00	15.00
1 Jared Aulin	.20	.50
2 Steve Belanger	.40	1.00
3 Tyler Boldt	.20	.50
4 Josh Bonar	.20	.50
5 Pat Brandreth	.20	.50
6 Erik Christensen	.40	1.00
7 Paul Elliott	.20	.50
8 Aaron Gionet	.40	1.00
9 Gable Gross	.20	.50
10 Jonathan Hobson	.20	.50
11 Nikita Korovkin	.20	.50
12 Derek Krestanovich	.20	.50
13 Kyle Ladobruk	.20	.50
14 Jarret Lukin	.20	.50
15 Shaone Morrisonn	.40	1.00
16 Colton Orr	1.25	3.00
17 Konstantin Panov	.20	.50

18 Davis Parley .40 1.00
19 Mark Rooneem .20 .50
20 Chad Shockenmaier .20 .50
21 Conlan Seder .20 .50
22 Tyler Sloan .20 .50
23 Scottie Upshall .75 2.00
24 Digger MASCOT .02 .10

2002-03 Kamloops Blazers

Based on previous Kamloops issues, it's possible this checklist is NOT complete. If you know of other cards in the series, please contact us at hockeymag@beckett.com.

COMPLETE SET (19?)
1 The Coaches .02 .10
2 Mascot .02 .10
3 Devan Dubnyk 1.25 3.00
4 Paul Brown .30 .75
5 Wade Davis .30 .75
6 Reid Jorgensen .30 .75
7 Jason Lloyd .30 .75
8 Moises Gutierrez .30 .75
9 Cam Cunning .30 .75
10 Grant Jacobsen .30 .75
11 Josh Morrow .30 .75
12 Davis Parley .60 1.50
13 Jonas Johansson .60 1.50
14 Nikita Korovkin .30 .75
15 Tyler Boldt .30 .75
16 Scottie Upshall .60 1.50
17 Erik Christensen .60 1.50
18 Aaron Gionet .30 .75
19 Kris Hogg .30 .75

2003-04 Kamloops Blazers

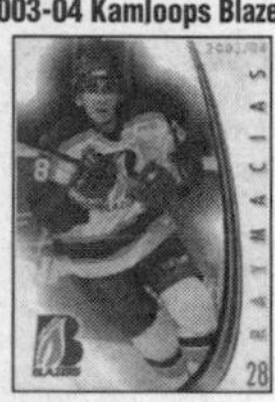

COMPLETE SET (24) 8.00 20.00
1 Geoff McIntosh .30 .75
2 Roman Tesliuk .30 .75
3 Kalvin Sagert .30 .75
4 Max Gordichuk .30 .75
5 Josh Garbutt .30 .75
6 Grant Jacobsen .30 .75
7 Jonas Johansson .60 1.50
8 Nathan Grochmal .30 .75
9 Cam Cunning .30 .75
10 Kris Hogg .30 .75
11 Kyle Sheen .30 .75
12 Brock Nixon .30 .75
13 Rick Kozak .30 .75
14 Paul Brown .40 1.00
15 Conlan Seder .30 .75
16 Codey Becker .30 .75
17 Ryan Bender .30 .75
18 Ray Macias .30 .75
19 Moises Gutierrez .30 .75
20 Devan Dubnyk 1.00 2.50
21 Jarret Lukin .30 .75
22 Reid Jorgensen .30 .75
23 Derek Werenka .30 .75
24 Checklist .02 .10

2004-05 Kamloops Blazers

We have confirmed only a handful of cards from this set. It was issued in 12 strips of three, and contains 36 cards. If you have additional information, please contact us at hockeymag@beckett.com.

COMPLETE SET (36)
1 Checklist
2 Bryan Kauk
3 Reid Jorgensen
4 Devan Dubnyk
5 Ray Macias
6 Adam Chorneyko

2005-06 Kamloops Blazers

COMPLETE SET (25) 6.00 15.00
1 Checklist .02 .10
2 Michael Maniago .30 .75
3 Roman Tesliuk .30 .75
4 Garrett Thiessen .30 .75
5 Keaton Ellerby .30 .75
6 Ryan White .40 1.00
7 Victor Bartley .30 .75
8 Ashton Rome .40 1.00
9 Janick Steinmann .30 .75
10 C.J. Stretch .30 .75
11 Travis Dunstall .30 .75
12 Scott Skrudland .30 .75
13 T.J. Mulock .30 .75
14 Brady Mason .30 .75
15 Brock Nixon .30 .75
16 Matt Kassian .30 .75
17 Kevin Hayman .30 .75
18 Terrance Delaronde .30 .75
19 Ryan Bender .30 .75
20 Ray Macias .30 .75
21 Moises Gutierrez .30 .75
22 Devan Dubnyk .60 1.50
23 Joel Eisenkirch .30 .75
24 Reid Jorgensen .30 .75
25 911 Digger MASCOT .02 .10

2006-07 Kamloops Blazers

COMPLETE SET (25) 10.00 18.00
1 Victor Bartley .30 .75
2 Ryan Bender .30 .75
3 Dustin Butler .40 1.00
4 Terrance Delaronde .30 .75
5 Brenden Dowd .30 .75
6 Travis Dunstall .30 .75
7 Keaton Ellerby .50 1.25
8 Dalyn Flette .40 1.00
9 Sasha Golin .30 .75
10 Mark Hall .30 .75
11 Reid Jorgensen .30 .75
12 Matt Kassian .30 .75
13 Kevin Kraus .30 .75
14 Raymond Macias .30 .75
15 Brady Mason .30 .75
16 Brock Nixon .30 .75
17 Juuso Puustinen .30 .75
18 Alex Rodgers .30 .75
19 Ivan Rohac .30 .75
20 Jordan Rowley .30 .75
21 Tyler Shattock .30 .75
22 C.J. Stretch .30 .75
23 Ryan White .30 .75
24 Kamloops Blazers CL .01 .05
25 Digger MASCOT .02 .10

2007-08 Kamloops Blazers

COMPLETE SET (25) 5.00 12.00
1 Kurt Torbohm .25 .60
2 Spencer Fraipont .25 .60
3 Ivan Rohac .25 .60
4 Mark Hall .25 .60
5 Brady Calla .25 .60
6 CJ Stretch .25 .60
7 Scott Wasden .25 .60
8 Kenton Dulle .25 .60
9 Tyler Shattock .25 .60
10 Juuso Puustinen .25 .60
11 Matt Wray .25 .60
12 Devon Kalinski .25 .60
13 Jimmy Bubnick .25 .60
14 Alex Rodgers .25 .60
15 Sasha Golin .25 .60
16 Jordan Rowley .25 .60
17 Darcy Huisman .25 .60
18 Nick Ross .25 .60
19 Mark Schneider .25 .60
20 James Priestner .25 .60
21 Justin Leclerc .25 .60
22 Mike Gauthier .25 .60
23 Shayne Wiebe .25 .60
24 Digger .15 .40
25 Kamloops Blazers Checklist .15 .40

1990-91 Kansas City Blades

This 20-card standard-size set features posed, color player photos on a black card face. The pictures are bordered on three sides by a red design similar to a shadow border. Player information appears below the photo in the red border. The year and team name are printed at the upper left corner.

COMPLETE SET (20) 4.00 10.00
1 Claudio Scremin .20 .50
2 Jeff Odgers .30 .75
3 Wade Flaherty .30 .75
4 Rick Barkovich .20 .50
5 Ron Handy .20 .50
6 Kevin Sullivan .20 .50
7 Randy Exelby .30 .75
8 Darin Smith .20 .50
9 Stu Kulak .20 .50
10 Andrew Akervik .20 .50
11 Scott White .20 .50
12 Claude Julien .20 .50
13 Mike Hiltner .20 .50
14 Michael Colman .20 .50
15 Kurt Semandel .20 .50
16 Mike Keller .20 .50
17 Mark Karpen .20 .50
18 Lee Giffin .20 .50
19 Cam Plante .20 .50
20 Jim Latos .30 .75

1991-92 Kansas City Blades

This set features the Blades of the IHL. It is believed the set was sold by the team at its souvenir stands. The set is noteworthy as Kansas City won the Turner Cup that year. It also features an early card goaltender Arturs Irbe, who in 1991-92 was an IHL First Team All-Star. The checklist was provided by collector Jeff Barak.

COMPLETE SET (20) 4.80 12.00
1 Pat McLeod .20 .50
2 Rick Lessard .20 .50
3 Duane Joyce .20 .50
4 David Williams .20 .50
5 Arturs Irbe 1.25 3.00
6 Murray Garbutt .20 .50
7 Gary Emmons .20 .50
8 Jeff Madill .20 .50
9 Ron Handy .20 .50
10 Peter Lappin .20 .50
11 Mike Colman .20 .50
12 Ed Courtenay .20 .50
13 Mikhail Kravets .20 .50
14 Claudio Scremin .20 .50
15 Dale Craigwell .20 .50
16 Wade Flaherty .30 .75
17 Kevin Evans .20 .50
18 Larry DePalma .20 .50
19 Dean Kolstad .20 .50
20 Gord Frantti .20 .50

1992-93 Kansas City Blades

Little is known about this set beyond confirmation of the checklist and some recent sales. Any additional information should be forwarded to hockeymag@beckett.com.

COMPLETE SET (20) 4.00 10.00
1 Wade Flaherty .30 .75
2 David Williams .20 .50
3 Duane Joyce .20 .50
4 Jeff Sharples .20 .50
5 Victor Ignatjev .20 .50
6 Jeff McLean .20 .50
7 Brian Lawton .20 .50
8 Troy Frederick .20 .50
9 Jaroslav Otevrel .20 .50
10 Gary Emmons .20 .50
11 Dody Wood .20 .50
12 Ed Courtenay .20 .50
13 Mark Beaufait .20 .50
14 J.F. Quintin .20 .50
15 Dale Craigwell .20 .50
16 Mikhail Kravets .20 .50
17 John Weisbrod .20 .50
18 Mike Colman .20 .50
19 Claudio Scremin .20 .50
20 Dean Kolstad .20 .50

1993-94 Kansas City Blades

Little is known about this set beyond the confirmed checklist. Any additional information should be forwarded to hockeymag@beckett.com.

COMPLETE SET (20) 4.00 10.00
1 Duane Joyce .20 .50
2 Sean Gorman .20 .50
3 Victor Ignatjev .20 .50
4 Jeff McLean .20 .50
5 Kip Miller .30 .75
6 Jaroslav Otevrel .20 .50
7 David Bruce .20 .50
8 Gary Emmons .20 .50
9 Dody Wood .20 .50
10 Lee Leslie .20 .50
11 Alexander Cherbayev .20 .50
12 J.F. Quintin .20 .50
13 Ed Courtenay .20 .50
14 Andrei Nazarov .30 .75
15 Mikhail Kravets .20 .50
16 Mike Colman .20 .50
17 Vlastimil Kroupa .20 .50
18 Andrei Buschan .20 .50
19 Trevor Robins .20 .50
20 Wade Flaherty .30 .75

1994-95 Kansas City Blades

This set features the Blades of the IHL. Beyond the confirmed checklist, we don't have too many details to offer. Anyone up on this set is encouraged to contact us.

COMPLETE SET (20) 4.00 10.00
1 Duane Joyce .20 .50
2 Ken Hammond .20 .50
3 Michal Sykora .20 .50
4 Kevin Wortman .20 .50
5 Andrei Buschan .20 .50
6 Chris Tancill .20 .50
7 Ken Hodge .20 .50
8 David Bruce .20 .50
9 Jan Caloun .30 .75
10 Gary Emmons .20 .50
11 Dody Wood .20 .50
12 Lee Leslie .20 .50
13 Alexander Cherbayev .20 .50
14 J.F. Quintin .20 .50
15 Claudio Scremin .20 .50
16 Dean Grillo .20 .50
17 Andrei Nazarov .30 .75
18 Todd Holt .20 .50
19 Vlastimil Kroupa .20 .50
20 Trevor Robins .20 .50

1995-96 Kansas City Blades

Little is known about this set beyond the confirmed checklist. Additional information should be forwarded to hockeymag@beckett.com.

COMPLETE SET (25) 4.00 10.00
1 Larry Dyck .15 .40
2 Paul Dyck .15 .40
3 Jeff Batters .15 .40
4 David Bruce .15 .40
5 Jan Caloun .30 .75
6 Alexander Cherbayev .20 .50
7 Gary Emmons .15 .40
8 Dean Ewens .15 .40
9 Pat Ferschweiler .15 .40
10 Dean Grillo .15 .40
11 Ken Hammond .15 .40
12 Alexander Osadchy .15 .40
13 Jeff McLean .15 .40
14 Fredrik Nilsson .20 .50
15 Fredrik Oduya .15 .40
16 J.F. Quintin .15 .40
17 Geoff Sarjeant .20 .50
18 Claudio Scremin .15 .40
19 Chris Tancill .20 .50
20 Alexi Yegorov .20 .50
21 Viktor Kozlov .40 1.00
22 Sergei Bautin .15 .40
23 Vasily Tikhonov HCO .02 .10
24 Drew Remenda ACO .02 .10
25 Chilly MASCOT .02 .10

1996-97 Kansas City Blades

Little is known about this set beyond confirmation of the checklist. Additional information can be forwarded to hockeymag@beckett.com.

COMPLETE SET (25) 4.80 12.00
1 Ian Boyce .20 .50
2 David Bruce .30 .75
3 Jason Cirone .20 .50
4 Dale Craigwell .30 .75
5 Brent Cullaton .20 .50
6 Philippe DeRouville .30 .75
7 Larry Dyck .20 .50
8 Paul Dyck .20 .50
9 Gary Emmons .20 .50
10 Dean Ewen .20 .50
11 Bryan Fogarty .20 .50
12 Jason Herter .20 .50
13 Jim Kyte .20 .50
14 Jeff Madill .20 .50
15 Jeff McLean .20 .50
16 John Purves .30 .75
17 J.F. Quintin .20 .50
18 Normand Rochefort .20 .50
19 Claudio Scremin .20 .50
20 Brian Stacey .20 .50
21 Dean Sylvester .30 .75
22 Don Jackson HCO .02 .10
23 Lucien DeBlois ACO .20 .50
24 KC Blades .02 .10
25 PHPA Web Site .02 .10

1997-98 Kansas City Blades Magnets

These magnets were released as promotional giveaways over a series of five games.

COMPLETE SET (5) 4.00 10.00
1 Claudio Scremin .75 2.00
2 Gary Emmons .75 2.00
3 David Bruce .75 2.00
4 Jan Caloun .75 2.00
5 Dean Grillo .75 2.00

1998-99 Kansas City Blades

Little is known about this set beyond the checklist. Any additional information can be forwarded to hockeymag@beckett.com.

COMPLETE SET (30) 6.00 15.00
1 Title Card .02 .10
2 Brian Leitza .20 .50
3 Dan Ratushny .20 .50
4 Trevor Sherban .20 .50
5 Eric Rud .20 .50
6 Tuomas Gronman .20 .50
7 Eric Perrin .20 .50
8 Brendan Yarema .20 .50
9 Brian Bonin .20 .50
10 Pat Ferschweiler .20 .50
11 Dody Wood .40 1.00
12 David Ling .40 1.00
13 Rocky Weising .20 .50
14 Jean-Guy Trudel .30 .75
15 Vlastimil Kroupa .20 .50
16 Steven Low .20 .50
17 Ryan Mulhern .20 .50
18 Brent Bilodeau .20 .50
19 Grant Richison .20 .50
20 Dave Chyzowski .20 .50
21 David Vallieres .20 .50
22 Patrick Lalime .75 2.00
23 Jean Sebastien Aubin .75 2.00
24 Jason Cirone .20 .50
25 Paul MacLean CO .02 .10
26 Gary Emmons ACO .02 .10
27 John Doolan EQ .02 .10
28 Jeff Kreuser TR .02 .10
29 Scrapper Mascot .02 .10
30 Logo Card .02 .10

1999-00 Kansas City Blades

These two oversized cards are likely part of a larger set offered to fans at public autograph signing sessions. Information on others can be forwarded to hockeymag@beckett.com.

COMPLETE SET (2) .75 2.00
1 Gary Emmons .40 1.00
2 Wade Flaherty .40 1.00

1999-00 Kansas City Blades Supercuts

This 29-card set was sponsored by Supercuts and featured an action photo of each player with a small bio on back of each card. The cards are not numbered and are listed below in alphabetical order. It is believed that the cards were offered as a promotional giveaway.

COMPLETE SET 6.00 15.00
1 Tom Askey .40 1.00
2 Joe Blaznek .20 .50
3 Aris Brimanis .20 .50
4 Dave Chyzowski .20 .50
5 Jason Cirone .20 .50
6 Pat Ferschweiler .20 .50
7 Forrest Gore .20 .50
8 Sean Haggerty .20 .50
9 David Ling .40 1.00
10 Steve Lingren .20 .50
11 Tyler Moss .40 1.00
12 Nick Naumenko .20 .50
13 Eric Perrin .20 .50
14 Michal Pivonka .40 1.00
15 Bruce Racine .40 1.00
16 Grant Richison .20 .50
17 Jon Rohloff .20 .50
18 Ray Schultz .20 .50
19 David Valliers .20 .50
20 Jan Vodrazka .20 .50
21 Dody Wood .40 1.00
22 Brendan Yarema .20 .50
23 Scrapper MASCOT .08 .25
24 Jeff Kreuser TR .08 .25
25 John Doolan MGR .08 .25
26 Gary Emmons CO .08 .25
27 Paul MacLean HCO .08 .25
28 PHPA Logo .01
29 Supercuts Coupon .01

2000-01 Kansas City Blades

This set features the Blades of the IHL. The set was issued as a promotional giveaway early in the season and was sponsored by Dick's Sporting Goods.

COMPLETE SET (27) 6.00 15.00
1 Ryan Bonni .30 .75
2 Jan Vodrazka .20 .50
3 Bryan Allen .30 .75
4 Zenith Komarniski .20 .50
5 Sean Tallaire .20 .50
6 Ryan Ready .20 .50
7 Regan Darby .20 .50
8 Dody Wood .20 .50
9 Harold Druken .40 1.00
10 Darrell Hay .20 .50
11 Vadim Sharifijanov .30 .75
12 Steve Lingren .20 .50
13 Josh Holden .40 1.00
14 Mike Brown .30 .75
15 Jeff Scissons .20 .50
16 Jarkko Ruutu .30 .75
17 Pat Kavanagh .20 .50
18 Brad Leeb .20 .50
19 Bryan Helmer .20 .50
20 Artem Chubarov .30 .50
21 Corey Schwab .30 .75
22 Alfie Michaud .30 .75
23 Stan Smyl CO .20 .50
24 Barry Smith CO .10 .25
25 Ryno SPONSOR .01
26 Dick's SPONSOR .01
27 PHPA SPONSOR .01

1998-99 Kelowna Rockets

This 28-card set features the Kelowna Rockets of the Western Hockey League. Among the players featured are 2001 first-round pick Kiel McLeod and San Jose Sharks defender Scott Hannan.

COMPLETE SET (28) 6.00 15.00
1 Ryan Cuthbert .20 .50
2 Jan Dusanek .20 .50
3 B.J. Fehr .20 .50
4 Vernon Fiddler .30 .75
5 Mitch Fritz .20 .50
6 Carsen Germyn .20 .50
7 Scott Hannan .40 1.00
8 Bruce Harrison .20 .50
9 Trevor Hitchings .20 .50
10 J.J. Hunter .20 .50
11 Justin Jack .20 .50
12 Clint Keichinger .20 .50
13 Kevin Korol .20 .50
14 Corey Koski .20 .50
15 Quintin Laing .20 .50
16 Lindsey Materi .20 .50
17 Rory McDade .20 .50
18 Brett McLean .30 .75
19 Gavin McLeod .20 .50
20 Kiel McLeod .40 1.00
21 Lubomir Pistek .20 .50
22 Robby Sandrock .20 .50
23 David Selthun .20 .50
24 Joe Suderman .20 .50
25 Kevin Swanson .20 .50
26 Ryan Wade .20 .50
27 Nolan Yonkman .30 .75
28 Rocky Racoon MASCOT .02 .10

2000-01 Kelowna Rockets

This set features the Rockets of the WHL. It was originally issued in the form of two-card perforated strips as a promotional giveaway. The cards are unnumbered, and so are listed alphabetically.

COMPLETE SET (22) 6.00 15.00
1 Kiel McLeod .40 1.00
2 Rory McDade .30 .75
3 Tomas Oravec .30 .75
4 Carsen Germyn .40 1.00
5 Chris Di Ubaldo .30 .75
6 Ryan Cuthbert .30 .75
7 Randall Gelech .30 .75
8 Blaine Depper .30 .75
9 Gavin McLeod .30 .75
10 Bart Rushmer .30 .75
11 Tyler Mosienko .30 .75
12 Josh Gorges .30 .75
13 Jason Stone .30 .75
14 Brett Palin .30 .75
15 Richie Regehr .40 1.00
16 David Selthun .30 .75
17 Seth Leonard .30 .75
18 Jan Fadrny .30 .75
19 Joe Suderman .30 .75
20 Kevin Swanson .30 .75
21 Rocky Raccoon MASCOT .02 .10
22 Marc Habscheid CO .10 .25
23 Paul Hurd .20 .50
24 Cam Paddock .20 .50
25 Richard Kelly .20 .50
26 Travis Moen .40 1.00

2001-02 Kelowna Rockets

The cards were issued as a promotional giveaway. As they are unnumbered, they are listed in alphabetical order.

COMPLETE SET (28) 20.00
1 Shane Bendera 1.00
2 Jeff Coulter .75
3 Ryan Cuthbert .75
4 Jesse Ferguson .75
5 Randall Gelech .75
6 Josh Gorges 1.00
7 Richard Kelly .75
8 Chuck Kobasew 1.25 3.00
9 Seth Leonard .75
10 Josh Lepp .75
11 Nick Marach .75
12 Ryan Mayko .75
13 Kiel McLeod 1.00
14 Travis Moen 1.00
15 Tyler Mosienko .75
16 Tomas Oravec .75
17 Cam Paddock .75
18 Brett Palin .75
19 Bart Rushmer .75
20 Tomas Slovak .75
21 Stephen Sunderman .75
22 Kevin Young .75
23 Marc Habscheid HCO .20
24 Larry Keating ACO .10
25 Jeff Truitt ACO .10
26 Scott Hoyer TR .10
27 Regan Bartel PA .10
28 Mascot .10

2002-03 Kelowna Rockets

COMPLETE SET (28) 15.00
1 Josh Lepp .75
2 Cam Paddock .50
3 Kiel McLeod 1.00
4 Joel Henituik .50
5 Brett Palin .50
6 Richard Kelly .50
7 Stephen Sunderman .50
8 Tyler Spurgeon .50
9 Joni Lindolf .50
10 Darren Deschamps .50
11 Shea Weber 2.00
12 Randall Gelech .50
13 David Jacobson .50
14 Jesse Schultz .50
15 Blake Comeau .50
16 Ryan Mayko .50
17 Mike Card .50
18 Josh Gorges 1.00
19 Tomas Slovak .50
20 Kelly Guard 1.00
21 Troy Bodie .50
22 Ryan Cuthbert .50
23 Tyler Mosienko .50
24 Mark Olafson .50
25 Nick Tarnasky .50
26 Marc Habscheid HCO .10
27 Jeff Truitt ACO .10
28 Mascot .10

2003 Kelowna Rockets Memorial Cup

Cards are unnumbered and listed below in alphabetical order.

COMPLETE SET (20) 15.00
1 Troy Brodie .75
2 Mike Card .75
3 Blake Comeau .75
4 Ryan Cuthbert .75
5 Simon Ferguson .75
6 Randall Gelech .75
7 Josh Gorges 1.00
8 Kelly Guard 1.50
9 Duncan Keith .75
10 Josh Lepp 1.00
11 Joni Lindolf .75
12 Kiel McLeod 1.00
13 Tyler Mosienko .75
14 Mark Olafson .75
15 Cam Paddock .75
16 Brett Palin .75
17 Jesse Schultz 1.00
18 Tomas Slovak 1.00
19 Tyler Spurgeon 1.00
20 Shea Weber .75

2003-04 Kelowna Rockets

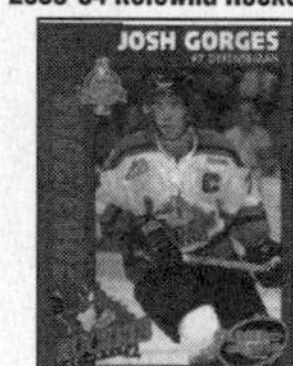

COMPLETE SET (28) 10.00 25.00
1 Michael Blanar .40 1.00
2 Troy Bodie .40 1.00
3 Mike Card .40 1.00
4 Blake Comeau .75 2.00
5 Kyle Cumiskey .40 1.00
6 Darren Deschamps .40 1.00
7 Simon Ferguson .40 1.00
8 Randall Gelech .40 1.00
9 Josh Gorges .75 2.00
10 Kelly Guard .75 2.00
11 Brent Howarth .40 1.00
12 Justin Keller .40 1.00
13 Joni Lindlof .40 1.00
14 Tyler Mosienko .40 1.00
15 Mark Olafson .40 1.00
16 Cam Paddock .40 1.00
17 Brett Palin .40 1.00
18 Chris Ray .40 1.00
19 Kevin Reinholt .40 1.00
20 Tyler Spurgeon .40 1.00
21 Nolan Waker .40 1.00
22 Shea Weber 1.25 3.00
23 Derek Yeomans .40 1.00
24 Marc Habscheid CO .02 .10
25 Jeff Truitt ACO .02 .10
26 Regan Bartel ANN .02 .10
27 Scott Hoyer TR .02 .10
28 Rocky Raccoon MASCOT .02 .10

2004-05 Kelowna Rockets

COMPLETE SET (28) 8.00 20.00
1 Troy Bodie .30 .75
2 Shea Weber 1.25 3.00
3 Justin Keller .30 .75
4 Craig Cuthbert .30 .75
5 Darren Deschamps .30 .75
6 Kristofer Westblom .30 .75
7 Brett Palin .30 .75
8 Kyle Cumiskey .30 .75
9 Chris Ray .30 .75
10 Lauris Darzins .30 .75
11 Rockey Raccoon .02 .10
12 Jeff Truitt .30 .75
13 Colin Joe .30 .75
14 Tyler Mosienko .30 .75
15 Blake Comeau .50 1.25
16 Tyler Spurgeon .30 .75
17 Derek Yeomans .30 .75
18 Ryan Huska .30 .75
19 Scott Hoyer .30 .75
20 Regan Bartel .30 .75
21 Gary Sylvester .30 .75
22 Troy Ofukany .30 .75
23 Kirt Hill .30 .75
24 Brent Howarth .30 .75
25 Clayton Bauer .30 .75
26 Michal Blanar .30 .75
27 Mike Card .30 .75
28 Kevin Reinholt .30 .75

2005-06 Kelowna Rockets

COMPLETE SET (28) 8.00 20.00
1 Cody Almond .30 .75
2 Josiah Anderson .30 .75
3 Clayton Bauer .30 .75
4 Troy Bodie .30 .75
5 Mike Card .30 .75
6 Blake Comeau .60 1.50
7 Liam Couture .30 .75
8 Kyle Cumiskey .30 .75
9 Craig Cuthbert .30 .75
10 Lauris Darzins .30 .75
11 Tysen Dowzak .30 .75
12 Alexander Edler .30 .75
13 Kirt Hill .30 .75
14 Brent Howarth .30 .75
15 Colin Joe .30 .75
16 Justin Keller .30 .75
17 Colin Long .30 .75
18 Myles MacRae .30 .75
19 Troy Ofukany .30 .75
20 Chris Ray .30 .75
21 Kevin Reinholt .30 .75
22 Rob Roteliuk .30 .75
23 Luke Schenn .30 .75
24 Tyler Spurgeon .30 .75
25 Kristofer Westblom .30 .75
26 Derek Yeomans .30 .75
27 Jeff Truitt HC .02 .10
28 Rocky Raccoon MASCOT .02 .10

1984-85 Kelowna Wings

This 56-card safety standard-size set was sponsored by A and W, Pizza Patio, CKIQ (a radio station), and the Kelowna Wings. The cards feature black-and-white posed and action player photos. The words "Kelowna Wings 1984-85" are at the top of card numbers 2-22, while the words "Junior Hockey Grads" appear at the top of card numbers 1 and 23-56. The player's name, position, and the card number are at the bottom. The cards are numbered on the front in the lower right corner.

COMPLETE SET (56) 32.00 80.00
1 Checklist .20 .50
2 Darcy Wakaluk .60 1.50
3 Stacey Nickel .20 .50
4 Jeff Sharples .30 .75
5 Greg Zuk .20 .50
6 Daryn Sivertson .20 .50
7 Randy Cameron .20 .50
8 Mark Fioretti .20 .50
9 Ron Viglasi .20 .50
10 Ian Herbers .20 .50
11 Mike Wegleitner .20 .50
12 Terry Zaporzan .20 .50
13 Dwaine Hutton .20 .50
14 Rod Williams .20 .50
15 Jeff Rohlicek .20 .50
16 Brent Gilchrist .60 1.50
17 Rocky Dundas .20 .50
18 Grant Delcourt .20 .50
19 Cam Laroruk .20 .50
20 Tony Horacek .20 .50
21 Mark Wingerter .20 .50
22 Mick Vukota .20 .50
23 Danny Gare .60 1.50
24 Rich Sutter .40 1.00
25 Alfie Turcotte .20 .50
26 Bryan Trottier 4.00 10.00
27 Bill Derlago .40 1.00
28 Stan Smyl .75 2.00
29 Brent Sutter .75 2.00
30 Mel Bridgman .40 1.00
31 Paul Cyr .30 .75
32 Gary Lupul .20 .50
33 Ray Neufeld .30 .75
34 Brian Propp .75 2.00
35 Bob Nystrom .75 2.00
36 Ryan Walter .40 1.00
37 Russ Courtnall .75 2.00
38 Larry Playfair .20 .50
39 Ron Delorme .20 .50
40 Ron Sutter .40 1.00
41 Bobby Clarke 4.00 10.00
42 Bob Bourne .40 1.00
43 Cam Neely 15.00 40.00
44 Murray Craven .40 1.00
45 Clark Gillies 1.25 3.00
46 Ron Flockhart .40 1.00
47 Harold Snepsts 1.25 3.00
48 Duane Sutter .40 1.00
49 Garth Butcher .40 1.00
50 Bill Hajt .20 .50
51 Jim Benning .20 .50
52 Ray Allison .20 .50
53 Ken Wregget .75 2.00
54 Phil Russell .30 .75
55 Brad McCrimmon .60 1.50
56 Dan Hodgson .20 .50

1996-97 Kentucky Thoroughblades

This set was sold at the Kentucky team store, and featured an SRP of $3.00. Set features color action photos on the front, with statistics and biographical information on the back.

COMPLETE SET (26) 4.80 12.00
1 Ken Belanger .30 .75
2 Alexandre Boikov .20 .50
3 Jan Caloun .30 .75

4 Denis Chervyakov .20 .50
5 Jarrett Deuling .20 .50
6 Iain Fraser .20 .50
7 Dean Grillo .20 .50
8 Steve Guolla .30 .75
9 Sean Haggerty .20 .50
10 Jason Holland .20 .50
11 Lance Leslie .20 .50
12 Chris Lipuma .20 .50
13 Pat Mikesch .20 .50
14 Fredrik Oduya .20 .50
15 Jamie Ram .30 .75
16 Chris Tancill .30 .75
17 Jason Strudwick .30 .75
18 Steve Webb .30 .75
19 Jason Widmer .20 .50
20 Jim Wiley .20 .50
21 Alexei Yegorov .30 .75
NNO Ad Card-In Your Face .01
NNO Ad Card-PHPA .01
NNO Lucky the Mascot .02 .10
NNO Rupp Arena .02 .10
NNO Team Photo .08 .25

1997-98 Kentucky Thoroughblades

Little is known about this set beyond the confirmed checklist. Additional information can be forwarded to hockeymag@beckett.com.

COMPLETE SET (25) 8.00 20.00
1 Team Photo .02 .10
2 Peter Allen .20 .50
3 Niklas Andersson .20 .50
4 Alexandre Boikov .20 .50
5 Zdeno Chara 1.25 3.00
6 Steve Guolla .25 .60
7 Sean Haggerty .20 .50
8 Jason Holland .20 .50
9 Alexander Korolyuk .30 .75
10 Evgeni Nabokov 4.00 10.00
11 Fredrik Oduya .20 .50
12 Chad Penney .20 .50
13 Jamie Ram .30 .75
14 Peter Roed .20 .50
15 Jason Strudwick .20 .50
16 Tony Tuzzolino .30 .75
17 Steve Webb .30 .75
18 Jason Widmer .20 .50
19 Brendan Yarema .20 .50
20 Alexei Yegorov .25 .60
21 Andrei Zyuzin .30 .75
22 Jim Wiley HCO .02 .10
23 Lucky Mascot .02 .10
24 PHPA Web Site .01
25 AHL Web Site .01

1998-99 Kentucky Thoroughblades

This 25-card set was released after the regular season had ended. It was produced by Split Second. All cards are unnumbered, and are listed in alphabetical order.

COMPLETE SET (25) 8.00 20.00
1 Peter Allen .15 .40
2 Eric Boulton .75 2.00
3 Dan Boyle .30 .75
4 Matt Bradley .20 .50
5 Mike Craig .15 .40
6 Jarrett Deuling .15 .40
7 Curtis Doell .15 .40
8 Dave Duerden .15 .40
9 Sean Gauthier .15 .40
10 Christian Gosselin .15 .40
11 Steve Guolla .20 .50
12 Harold Hersh .20 .50
13 Alexander Korolyuk .20 .50
14 Filip Kuba .20 .50
15 Steve Lingren .15 .40
16 Andy MacIntyre .10 .30
17 Evgeni Nabokov 4.00 10.00
Nickname John on card front
18 Jarrod Skalde .30 .75
19 Mark Smith .60 1.50
20 Herbert Vasilijevs .15 .40
21 Eric Veilleux .15 .40
22 Andrei Zyuzin .30 .75
23 Roy Sommer HCO .02 .10
24 Lucky Mascot .02 .10
25 AHL Web Site .01

1999-00 Kentucky Thoroughblades

This set features the Thoroughblades of the AHL. The slightly oversized set was produced by the team and sold at home games.

COMPLETE SET (25) 8.00 20.00
1 Kentucky Thoroughblades .08 .25
2 Coaching Staff .08 .25
3 Chris Armstrong .20 .50
4 Matt Bradley .20 .50
5 Garrett Burnett .20 .50
6 Adam Colagiacomo .30 .75
7 Jon Coleman .20 .50
8 Larry Courville .20 .50
9 Mike Craig .20 .50
10 Jarrett Deuling .20 .50
11 Doug Friedman .20 .50
12 Christian Gosselin .20 .50
13 Scott Hannan .30 .75
14 Johan Hedberg 2.00 5.00
15 Shawn Heins .30 .75
16 Robert Jindrich .30 .75
17 Miikka Kiprusoff 2.00 5.00
18 Eric Landry .20 .50
19 Chris Lipsett .20 .50
20 Andy Lundbohm .20 .50
21 Robert Mulick .20 .50
22 Adam Nittel .40 1.00
23 Peter Roed .20 .50
24 Mark Smith .30 .75
25 Lucky MASCOT .08 .25

2000-01 Kentucky Thoroughblades

This set features the Thoroughblades of the AHL. It is believed that the set was sold by the team, but this is not confirmed. It's also believed that the final five cards were available as redemptions at an area business, which accounts for their scarcity. Any additional information can be forwarded to hockeymag@beckett.com.

COMPLETE SET (30) 30.00 80.00
1 Greg Andrusak .14 .35
2 Steve Bancroft .14 .35
3 Zoltan Batovsky .14 .35
4 Matt Bradley .14 .35
5 Jonathan Cheechoo 4.00 10.00
6 Adam Colagiacomo .20 .50
7 Larry Courville .20 .50
8 Rob Davison .20 .50
9 Jarrett Deuling .14 .35
10 Christian Gosselin .14 .35
11 Robert Jindrich .20 .50
12 Miikka Kiprusoff 4.00 10.00
13 Ryan Kraft .14 .50
14 Eric Laplante .14 .35
15 Chris Lipsett .14 .35
16 Andy Lundbohm .14 .35
17 Dave MacIsaac .14 .35
18 Jim Montgomery .20 .50
19 Robert Mulick .14 .35
20 Adam Nittel .40 1.00
21 Mikael Samuelsson .20 .50
22 Mark Smith .30 .75
23 Vesa Toskala 2.00 5.00
24 Miroslav Zalesak .10 .25
25 Roy Sommer CO .10 .25
Nick Fotiu CO
L1 Kentucky Thoroughblades .40 1.00
P1 Adam Nittel 1.00 2.50
P2 Jonathan Cheechoo 10.00 25.00
SP1 Ryan Kraft .60 2.00
SP2 Evgeni Nabokov 10.00 25.00

1981-82 Kingston Canadians

This 25-card set measures approximately 2 5/8" by 4" and features posed, color player photos on thin white card stock. The player's name, position, and the team logo are printed in black below the picture.

COMPLETE SET (25) 12.00 30.00
1 Canadians Logo .20 .50
2 Scott MacLellan .20 .50
3 Dave Courtemanche .20 .50
4 Mark Reade .20 .50
5 Shawn Babcock .20 .50
6 Phil Bourque .40 1.00
7 Ian MacInnis .20 .50
8 Neil Trineer .20 .50
9 Syl Grandmaitre .20 .50
10 Carmine Vani .30 .75
11 Chuck Brimmer .20 .50
12 Mike Linseman .20 .50
13 Steve Seguin .20 .50
14 Dan Wood .20 .50
15 Kirk Muller 6.00 15.00
16 Jim Aldred .20 .50
17 Rick Wilson .60 1.50
18 Mike Siltala .20 .50
19 Howie Scruton .20 .50
20 Mike Stothers .40 1.00
21 Dennis Smith .20 .50
22 Steve Richey .20 .50
23 Mike Moffat .75 2.00
24 Jim Morrison CO/MG .20 .50
25 Randy Plumb .20 .50

1982-83 Kingston Canadians

This 27-card set measures approximately 2 5/8" by 4 1/8" and features posed action, color player photos with white borders on thin card stock. The player's name, position, and year of issue appear below the picture between the team logo and the Kingston Police Force insignia.

COMPLETE SET (27) 6.00 15.00
1 Jim Morrison MG .08 .25
2 Dennis Smith .30 .75
3 Curtis Collin .30 .75
4 Joel Brown .30 .75
5 Ron Handy .30 .75
6 Carmine Vani .30 .75
7 Al Andrews .40 1.00
8 Mike Siltala .30 .75
9 Syl Grandmaitre .30 .75
10 Steve Seguin .30 .75
11 Brian Dobbin .40 1.00
12 Mark Reade .30 .75
13 John Kemp .40 1.00
14 Dan Mahon .30 .75
15 Keith Knight .30 .75
16 Ron Sanko .30 .75
17 John Landry .30 .75
18 Chris Brant .30 .75
19 Dave Simurda .30 .75
20 Mike Lafoy .30 .75
21 Scott MacLellan .30 .75
22 Brad Walcot .30 .75
23 Steve Richey .30 .75
24 Rod Graham CO .08 .25
25 Ben Levesque .30 .75
26 Canadians Logo .08 .25
27 International Hockey .20 .50
Hall of Fame

1983-84 Kingston Canadians

This 30-card set measures slightly larger than standard at 2 5/8" by 3 5/8" and features posed color player photos with white borders on thin card stock. The player's name, position, and year appears below the picture between the Canadians logo and the Kingston Police Force insignia.

COMPLETE SET (30) 6.00 15.00
1 Checklist .08 .25
2 Dennis Smith .20 .50
3 Ben Levesque .20 .50
4 Const. Arie Moraal .08 .25
5 Tom Allen .20 .50
6 Mike Plesh .20 .50
7 Roger Belanger .20 .50
8 Jeff Chychrun .40 1.00
9 Mike King .20 .50
10 Scott Metcalfe .30 .75
11 David Lundmark .20 .50
12 Tim Salmon .20 .50
13 Ted Linesman .20 .50
14 Chris Clifford .30 .75
15 Todd Elik .40 1.00
16 Kevin Conway .20 .50
17 Barry Burkholder .20 .50
18 Joel Brown .20 .50
19 Steve King .20 .50
20 Craig Kales .20 .50
21 John Humphries TR .08 .25
22 David James .20 .50
23 Dave Simurda .20 .50
24 Allen Bishop .20 .50
25 Jeff Hogg .30 .75
26 Rick Cornacchia CO .30 .75
27 Ken Slater DPP .08 .25
28 Const. Bill Dextater .08 .25
29 Canadians Crest .08 .25
30 IHHOF logo .08 .25

1984-85 Kingston Canadians

This 30-card features the Canadians of the OHL. It measures 2 5/8" by 3 5/8" and features color, posed action player photos with white borders. The player's name, position, and year appear at the bottom.

COMPLETE SET (30) 6.00 15.00
1 Kingston Police Crest .08 .25
2 Rick Cornacchia CO .20 .50
3 Const. Arie Moraal .08 .25
4 Ken Slater DPP .08 .25
5 Kingston Crest .08 .25
6 Scott Metcalfe .30 .75
7 Chris Clifford .30 .75
8 Todd Elik .30 .75
9 Len Spratt .30 .75
10 Mike Plesh .20 .50
11 Marc Lyons .20 .50
12 Barry Burkholder .20 .50
13 Rick Fera .20 .50
14 David Hoover .20 .50
15 Andy Rivers .20 .50
16 Marc Laforge .30 .75
17 Peter Viscovich .20 .50
18 Jeff Chychrun .30 .75
19 Wayne Erskine .20 .50
20 Todd Clarke .20 .50
21 Darren Wright .20 .50
22 Tony Rocca .20 .50
23 Brian Verbeek .20 .50
24 Herb Raglan .30 .75
25 Daril Holmes .20 .50
26 Len Coyle TR .08 .25
27 Ted Linesman .20 .50
28 IHHOF logo .08 .25
29 Troy MacNevin .20 .50
30 Peter Campbell TR .08 .25

1985-86 Kingston Canadians

This 30-card measures approximately 2 5/8" by 3 5/8" and features color, posed action player photos with white borders. The player's name and position appear at the bottom.

COMPLETE SET (30) 4.80 12.00
1 Kingston Police Crest .08 .25
2 Dale Sandles ACO .08 .25
3 Const. Arie Moraal .08 .25
4 Fred O'Donnell GM/CO .08 .25
5 Kingston Crest .08 .25
6 Scott Metcalfe .20 .50
7 Chris Clifford .30 .75
8 Steve Seftel .20 .50
9 Andy Pearson .20 .50
10 Jeff Cornelius .20 .50
11 Marc Lyons .20 .50
12 Barry Burkholder .20 .50
13 Bryan Fogarty .30 .75
14 Jeff Sirkka .20 .50
15 Scott Pearson .30 .75
16 Marc Laforge .20 .50
17 Peter Viscovich .20 .50
18 Jeff Chychrun UER .30 .75
(Name misspelled Chycren)
19 Wayne Erskine .20 .50
20 Todd Clarke .20 .50
21 Darren Wright .20 .50
22 Mike Maurice .20 .50
23 Brian Verbeek .20 .50
24 Mike Fiset .20 .50
25 Daril Holmes .20 .50
26 Len Coyle TR .08 .25
27 Ted Linesman .20 .50
28 IHHOF logo .08 .25
29 Troy MacNevin .20 .50
30 Peter Campbell TR .08 .25

1986-87 Kingston Canadians

This 30-card set measures approximately 2 5/8" by 3 5/8" and features color, posed player portraits with blue studio backgrounds set on a white card face. The player's name, position, and year appear at the bottom.

COMPLETE SET (30) 4.00 10.00
1 Kingston Crest .08 .25
2 Fred O'Donnell GM/CO .02 .10
3 Arie Moraal COP .02 .10
4 Dale Sandles CO .02 .10
5 Kingston Police Crest .02 .10
6 Brian Tessier .30 .75
7 Franco Giammarco .30 .75
8 Peter Liptrott .20 .50
9 Chris Clifford .30 .75
10 Scott Metcalfe .20 .50
11 Scott Pearson .30 .75
12 Bryan Fogarty .30 .75
13 Daril Holmes .20 .50
14 Andy Rivers .20 .50
15 Troy MacNevin .20 .50
16 Marc Laforge .20 .50
17 Wayne Erskine .20 .50
18 Peter Viskovich .20 .50
19 Mike Maurice .20 .50
20 Steve Seftel .20 .50
21 Chad Badaway .20 .50
22 Marc Lyons .20 .50
23 Jeff Sirkka .20 .50
24 Mike Fiset .20 .50
25 John Battice .20 .50
26 Len Coyle TR .02 .10
27 Sloan Torti .20 .50
28 Alain Laforge .20 .50
29 Ted Linesman .20 .50
30 Peter Campbell TR .02 .10

1987-88 Kingston Canadians

This 30-card P.L.A.Y. (Police, Laws and Youth) set measures approximately 2 3/4" by 3 5/8" and features color player portraits with blue studio backgrounds. The fronts are accented by white borders.

COMPLETE SET (30) 4.80 12.00
1 Arie Moraal COP .02 .10
2 Gord Wood GM .02 .10
3 Kingston Police Crest .08 .25
4 Jacques Tremblay CO .08 .25
5 Rhonda Sheridan PR .02 .10
6 Jeff Wilson .30 .75
7 Franco Giammarco .30 .75
8 Peter Liptrott .20 .50
9 David Weiss .30 .75
10 Joel Morin .20 .50
11 Mark Turner .20 .50
12 Jeff Sirkka .20 .50
13 James Henckle .20 .50
14 Mike Bodnarchuk .20 .50
15 Mike Cavanaugh .20 .50
16 Darcy Cahill .20 .50
17 Kevin Falesy .20 .50
18 Dean Pella .20 .50
19 Brad Gratton .20 .50
20 Steve Seftel .20 .50
21 Bryan Fogarty .20 .50
22 Scott Pearson .20 .50
23 Tyler Pella .20 .50
24 Mike Fiset .20 .50
25 John Battice .20 .50
26 Len Coyle TR .02 .10
27 Geoff Schneider .20 .50
28 Chris Lukey .20 .50
29 Trevor Smith .20 .50
30 Peter Campbell TR .02 .10

1993-94 Kingston Frontenacs

Printed by Slapshot Images Ltd., this standard size 25-card set features the 1993-94 Kingston Frontenacs. On a team color-coded background with black stripes, the fronts feature color action player photos with thin black borders. The team name is printed diagonally in the upper left corner of the photo, while the player's name and number appear in a yellow bar in the bottom edge of the photo.

COMPLETE SET (25) 4.00 10.00
1 Greg Lovell .15 .40
2 Marc Lamothe .15 .40
3 Tyler Moss .20 .50
4 Marc Moro .15 .40
5 Trevor Doyle .15 .40
6 Jeff Dacosta .15 .40
7 Gord Walsh .15 .40
8 Brian Scott .15 .40
9 Jason Disher .15 .40
10 Alexander Zhurik .15 .40
11 Ken Boone .15 .40
12 Cail MacLean .15 .40
13 Bill Maranduik .15 .40
14 Martin Sychra .15 .40
15 Duncan Fader .15 .40
16 David Ling .30 .75
17 Chad Kilger .30 .75
18 Greg Kraemer .15 .40
19 Trent Cull .15 .40
20 Steve Parson .15 .40
21 Craig Rivet .15 .40
22 Keli Corpse .15 .40
23 Brett Lindros .30 .75
24 David Allison CO .02 .10
Michael Allison ACO
NNO Slapshot Ad Card .02 .10

1998-99 Kingston Frontenacs

The set features the Frontenacs of the OHL. Sponsored by the Community Sport and Activity News, this team-issued set features color action photos on the front of each card with a headshot and stats of each player on the back. The cards are unnumbered, so they are listed alphabetically.

COMPLETE SET (25) 4.80 12.00
1 Eric Braff .20 .50
2 Brett Clouthier .20 .50
3 Curtis Cruickshank .20 .50
4 Matt Elich .30 .75
5 Aaron Fransen .20 .50
6 Sean Griffin .20 .50
7 Kevin Grimes .20 .50
8 Andrew Ianiero .20 .50
9 Chad Lynch .20 .50
10 D.J. Maracle .20 .50
11 Larry Mavety HCO .08 .25
12 Morgan McCormick .20 .50
13 Walker McDonald .20 .50
14 Matt Price .20 .50
15 Mike Oliveira .20 .50
16 Brett Ormond .20 .50
17 Ryan Rivard .20 .50
18 Jonathan Schill .20 .50
19 Colin Scotland .20 .50
20 Nathan Tennant .20 .50
21 Darryl Thomson .20 .50
22 Ian Turner .20 .50
23 Jamie Young .20 .50
24 Mike Zigomanis .40 1.00
25 Checklist .02 .10

1999-00 Kingston Frontenacs

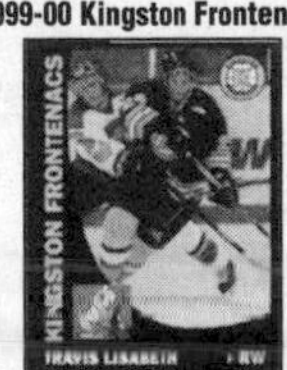

This set features the Frontenacs of the OHL. The slightly oversized cards were produced by the team and sold at home games. The set is noteworthy for an early appearance of goalie Andrew Raycroft and forwards Cory Stillman and Mike Zigomanis.

COMPLETE SET (23) 6.00 15.00
1 Checklist .02 .10
2 Sean Avery .60 1.50
3 Eric Braff .20 .50
4 Brett Clouthier .30 .75
5 Chris Cook .20 .50
6 Sean Griffin .20 .50
7 Brad Horan .20 .50
8 Andrew Ianiero .20 .50
9 Matt Junkins .20 .50
10 Darryl Knight .20 .50
11 Travis Lisabeth .20 .50
12 Doug MacIver .20 .50
13 Shaun Peet .20 .50
14 Jason Polera .20 .50
15 Andrew Raycroft 1.00 2.50
16 Johnathan Schill .20 .50
17 J-F Seguin .20 .50
18 Tomas Skvaridlo .20 .50
19 Mike Smith .20 .50
20 Cory Stillman .40 1.00
21 Nathan Tennant .30 .75
22 Darryl Thomson .20 .50
23 Michael Zigomanis .40 1.00

2000-01 Kingston Frontenacs

This set features the Frontenacs of the OHL. The set was produced by the team and sold at its souvenir stands. The cards are unnumbered, and so are listed below in alphabetical order.

COMPLETE SET (23) 4.80 10.00
1 Eric Braff .15 .40
2 Derek Campbell .15 .40
3 Brett Clouthier .30 .75
4 Chris Cook .15 .40
5 Count Frontenac MASCOT .04 .10
6 Peter Hamerlik .40 1.00
7 Brad Horan .15 .40
8 Andrew Ianiero .15 .40
9 Travis Lisabeth .15 .40
10 Doug MacIver .15 .40
11 The Coaches .04 .10
12 Justin McCutcheon .15 .40
13 Sean McMorrow .20 .50
14 Shane O'Brien .60 1.50
15 Glenn Ridler .30 .75
16 Corey Sabourin .15 .40
17 J.F. Seguin .15 .40
18 Tomas Skvaridlo .15 .40
19 Cory Stillman .30 .75
20 Nathan Tennant .15 .40
21 Darryl Thomson .15 .40
22 Brody Todd .15 .40
23 Mike Zigomanis .40 1.00
NNO Coca Cola .01 .05
NNO Title Card .01 .05

2001-02 Kingston Frontenacs

This set features the Frontenacs of the OHL. The cards were sold by the team at its souvenir stands.

COMPLETE SET (25) 4.80 14.00
1 Header Card .04 .10
2 Chris Cook .20 .50
3 Lou Dickenson .30 .75
4 Josh Gratton .20 .50
5 Peter Hamerlik .40 1.00
6 Chris Hardill .20 .50
7 Brad Horan .20 .50
8 Andrew Ianiero .30 .75
9 Drew Kivell .20 .50
10 Sean Langdon .20 .50
11 Doug MacIver .20 .50
12 Brandon McBride .20 .50
13 Justin McCutcheon .20 .50
14 Kyle Neufeld .20 .50
15 Shane O'Brien .20 .50
16 Scott Sheppard .20 .50
17 Mike Smith .20 .50
18 Sean Stefanski .20 .50
19 Anthony Stewart .20 3.00
20 Cory Stillman .30 .75
21 Justin Suda .20 .50
22 Nathan Tennant .30 .75
23 Ed Van Herpt .20 .50
24 Nick Van Herpt .20 .50
25 Coca-Cola Ad .01

2002-03 Kingston Frontenacs

COMPLETE SET (25) 12.00
1 Header Card .01
2 Chris Cook .50
3 Austin Corredato .50
4 Miguel Delisle .50
5 Drew Fata .50
6 Peter Hamerlik .75
7 Brad Horan .50
8 Bill Kinkel .50
9 Drew Kivell .50
10 Dwight LaBrosse .50
11 Scott Maher .50
12 Brandon McBride .50
13 Justin McCutcheon .50
14 Danny McDonald .50
15 Clay McFadden .50
16 Richard Power .50
17 Bryan Rodney .50
18 Ryan Stephenson .50
19 Anthony Stewart 2.00
20 Cory Stillman .50
21 Justin Suda .50
22 Dan Turple .50
23 Nick Van Herpt .50
24 The Count MASCOT .10
25 Ad card .01

2004-05 Kingston Frontenacs

A total of 500 team sets were produced.

COMPLETE SET (24) 12.00
1 Evan Kotsopoulos .50
2 Anthony Stewart 1.00
3 Bobby Bolt .50
4 Chris Stewart .50
5 Dayne Davis .50
6 David Edgeworth .50
7 Cory Emmerton .50
8 Shawn Futers .50
9 Todd Griffith .50
10 Bobby Hughes .50
11 Michael Kolarz .50
12 Derek Lyons .50
13 Phil Mangan .50
14 Adam Nemeth .50
15 Chris Petrow .50
16 Blake Pronk .50
17 Dany Revelle .50
18 Ben Shutron .50
19 Radek Smolenak .40 1.00
20 Justin Suda .50
21 Justin Wallingford .50
22 Tony Rizzi .50
23 Greg Williams .50
24 Brady Morrison .50

2005-06 Kingston Frontenacs

COMPLETE SET (23) 8.00 20.00
1 Cory Emmerton .60 1.50
2 Chris Stewart .60 1.50
3 Ben Shutron .30 .75
4 Shawn Connors .30 .75
5 Adam Nemeth .30 .75
6 Matt Reis .30 .75
7 Blake Pronk .30 .75
8 Radek Smolenak .60 1.50
9 Luke Pither .30 .75
10 Andrew Kizito .30 .75
11 Tony Rizzi .30 .75
12 Andrew Wilson .30 .75
13 Bobby Hughes .30 .75
14 Justin Wallingford .30 .75
15 Todd Griffith .30 .75
16 Michael Kolarz .30 .75
17 Bobby Bolt .30 .75
18 Connor Cameron .30 .75
19 Mike Looby .30 .75
20 Peder Skinner .30 .75
21 J.F. Houle .30 .75
22 Danny Taylor .40 1.00
23 Daryl Borden .40 1.00

2006-07 Kingston Frontenacs

COMPLETE SET (23) 8.00 15.00
1 Chris Stewart .40 1.00
2 Kyle Bochek .30 .75
3 Bobby Mignardi .30 .75
4 Nathan Moon .30 .75
5 Peder Skinner .30 .75
6 Matt Auffrey .30 .75
7 Matthew Kang .30 .75
8 Bobby Nyholm .30 .75
9 Jesse Biduke .30 .75
10 Bobby Hughes .30 .75
11 Josh Brittain .30 .75
12 Bobby Bolt .30 .75
13 Cory Emmerton .40 1.00
14 Peter Stevens .30 .75
15 Michael Kolarz .30 .75
16 Ben Shutron .40 1.00
17 Kevin Mole .40 1.00
18 Adam Nemeth .30 .75
19 Jonathan Sciacca .30 .75
20 Andrew Kizito .30 .75
21 Justin Wallingford .30 .75
22 Daryl Borden .30 .75
23 Jason Guy .30 .75

1982-83 Kitchener Rangers

This 30-card set measures approximately 2 3/4" by 3 1/2" and features posed action color player photos with black inner borders and white outer borders.

COMPLETE SET (30) 16.00 40.00
1 Waterloo Regional .08 .25
Police Crest
2 Harold Basse .08 .25
Chief of Police
3 Sponsors' Card .08 .25
4 Joe Crozier GM/CO .20 .50
5 Checklist .08 .25
6 Kerry Kerch .30 .75
7 Tom St. James .20 .50
8 Wendell Young .75 2.00
9 David Shaw .60 1.50
10 Darryl Boudreau .20 .50
11 David Bruce .40 1.00
12 Wayne Presley .60 1.50
13 Garnet McKechney .20 .50
14 Kevin Petendra .20 .50
15 Brian Wilks .20 .50
16 Jim Quinn .20 .50
17 Al MacInnis 8.00 20.00
18 Dave Nicholls .20 .50
19 Mike Eagles .60 1.50
20 Mike Hough .60 1.50
21 Greg Puhalski .20 .50
22 Darren Wright .20 .50
23 Todd Steffen .20 .50
24 John Tucker .60 1.50
25 Kent Paynter .20 .50
26 Andy O'Brien .20 .50
27 Les Bradley TR .08 .25
28 Scott Biggs .20 .50
29 Chris Martin TR .08 .25
30 Dave Webster .20 .50

1983-84 Kitchener Rangers

The Kitchener Rangers of the OHL are featured in this 30 card P.L.A.Y. (Police, Law and Youth) set, which was sponsored by the Waterloo Regional Police in conjunction with several company sponsors. The cards measure approximately 2 3/4" by 3 1/2" and are printed on thin card stock. The fronts feature color photos with the players posed in action stances. The photos are framed by black and white borders, and a facsimile autograph is inscribed across the bottom of the picture.

COMPLETE SET (30) 6.00 15.00
1 Joe Mantione .40 1.00
2 Jim Quinn .20 .50
3 Kitchener Rangers logo .08 .25
Checklist
4 Rob MacInnis .20 .50
5 Louie Berardicurti .20 .50
6 Neil Sandilands .20 .50
7 Darren Wright .20 .50
8 Tom Barrett CO/GM .08 .25
9 Brian Wilks .20 .50
10 Garnet McKechney .20 .50
11 David Bruce .40 1.00
12 Kent Paynter .20 .50
13 Sponsor's card .08 .25
P.L.A.Y. Rules
14 Scott Kerr .20 .50
15 Greg Puhalski .20 .50
16 Wayne Presley .40 1.00
17 Carmine Vani .20 .50
18 Shawn Burr .75 2.00
19 Dave Latta .30 .75
20 John Tucker .60 1.50
21 Mike Stevens .20 .50
22 Harold Basse .08 .25
Chief of Police
23 Waterloo Regional .08 .25
Police
24 Peter Bakovic .20 .50
25 Brian Ross .20 .50
26 Brad Balshin .20 .50
27 David Shaw .40 1.00
28 Chris Trainer TR .08 .25
29 Les Bradley TR .08 .25
30 Ray LeBlanc .75 2.00

1984-85 Kitchener Rangers

The Kitchener Rangers of the OHL are featured in this 30-card P.L.A.Y. (Police, Law and Youth) set, which was sponsored by the Waterloo Regional Police in conjunction with several company sponsors. The cards measure approximately 2 3/4" by 3 1/2" and are printed on thin card stock. The fronts feature color photos with the players posed in action stances. The photos are framed by black and white borders, and a facsimile autograph is inscribed across the bottom of the picture.

COMPLETE SET (30) 4.80 12.00
1 Waterloo Regional .08 .25
Police Crest
2 Harold Basse .08 .25
Chief of Police
3 Garnet McKechney .20 .50
4 Tom Barrett GM/CO .08 .25
5 Kitchener Rangers logo .08 .25
Checklist
6 Mike Bishop .30 .75
7 Craig Wolanin .40 1.00
8 Steve Marcolini .20 .50
9 Peter Langlois .20 .50
10 Dave Weiss .30 .75
11 Ken Alexander .20 .50
12 Ian Pound .20 .50
13 Doug Stromback .20 .50
14 Joel Brown .30 .75
15 Brian Wilks .20 .50
16 Robin Rubic .20 .50
17 Kent Paynter .20 .50
18 Jon Helinski .20 .50
19 Greg Puhalski .20 .50
20 Wayne Presley .40 1.00
21 Dave McLlwain .40 1.00
22 Shawn Burr .40 1.00
23 Dave Latta .25 .60
24 John Keller .20 .50
25 Mike Stevens .20 .50
26 Sponsors' Card .08 .25
27 Richard Adolfi .20 .50
28 Grant Sanders .20 .50
29 Les Bradley TR .08 .25
30 Sponsors' Card .08 .25

1985-86 Kitchener Rangers

This 30-card set measures approximately 2 3/4" by 3 1/2" and is printed on thin card stock. The fronts feature color, posed player photos with thin black borders on a white card face. A facsimile autograph is inscribed across the picture. The cards are numbered on the front and back.

COMPLETE SET (30) 4.80 12.00
1 Waterloo Regional .08 .25
Police Crest
2 Harold Basse .08 .25
Chief of Police
3 Sponsors' Card .08 .25
4 Tom Barrett GM/CO .08 .25
5 Kitchener Rangers logo .20 .50
Checklist
6 Dave Weiss .30 .75
7 Steve Marcolini .20 .50
8 Kevin Gant .20 .50
9 Ken Alexander .20 .50
10 Mike Volpe .30 .75
11 Ian Pound .20 .50
12 Brett MacDonald .20 .50
13 Scott Taylor .20 .50
14 Greg Hankkio .20 .50
15 Mike Morrison .20 .50
16 Mike Wolak .20 .50
17 Craig Booker .20 .50
18 Jeff Noble .20 .50
19 Shawn Tyers .20 .50
20 Peter Lisy .20 .50
21 Shawn Burr .40 1.00
22 David Latta .20 .50
23 Ron Sanko .20 .50
24 Doug Jones .20 .50
25 Paul Penelton .20 .50
26 Blair MacPherson .20 .50
27 Richard Hawkins .20 .50
28 Brad Sparkes .20 .50
29 Ron Goodall .20 .50
30 Kevin Duguay TR .20 .50

1986-87 Kitchener Rangers

The Kitchener Rangers of the OHL are featured in this 30-card P.L.A.Y. (Police, Law and Youth) set, which was sponsored by the Waterloo Regional Police in conjunction with several corporate sponsors. The cards measure approximately 2 3/4" by 3 1/2" and are printed on thin card stock. The fronts feature color photos with the players posed in action stances. The photos are framed by black and white borders. The player's name appears in the lower right corner. The cards are numbered on both sides.

COMPLETE SET (30) 4.00 10.00
1 Waterloo Police Crest .02 .10
2 Harold Basse COP .02 .10
3 Sponsor's Card .02 .10
4 Tom Barrett GM/CO .02 .10
5 Checklist .08 .25
6 Dave Weiss .30 .75
7 Darren Rumble .20 .50
8 Kevin Grant .20 .50
9 Len Fawcett .20 .50
10 Darren Beals .30 .75
11 Ed Kister .20 .50
12 Scott Taylor .20 .50
13 Darren Moxam .20 .50
14 Paul Epoch .20 .50
15 Richard Borgo .20 .50
16 Allan Lake .20 .50
17 Jeff Noble .20 .50
18 Mark Montanari .20 .50
19 Jim Hulton .20 .50
20 Kelly Cain .20 .50
21 Craig Booker .20 .50
22 David Latta .20 .50
23 Doug Jones .20 .50
24 Gary Callahan .20 .50
25 Bruno Lapensee .20 .50
26 Scott Montgomery TR .02 .10
27 Ron Goodall .20 .50
28 Discount Card .02 .10
29 Steve Ewing .20 .50
30 Joe McDonnell ACO .08 .25

1987-88 Kitchener Rangers

This 30-card set measures approximately 2 3/4" by 3 1/2" and was sponsored by Waterloo Region Optimist Clubs. The cards, which are printed on thin card stock, feature color posed action player photos with white borders. The card number, the player's name, and the season year appear in black print across the bottom of the photo The cards are numbered on both sides.

COMPLETE SET (30) 4.00 10.00
1 Waterloo Regional Police Crest .02 .10
2 Harold Basse Chief of Police .02 .10
3 Children's Bonus Card .02 .10
4 Joe McDonnell GM/CO .02 .10
5 Kitchener Ranger logo Checklist .08 .25
6 Gus Morschauser .30 .75
7 Rick Allain .20 .50
8 Kevin Grant .20 .50
9 Rob Thiel .20 .50
10 Darren Beals .30 .75
11 Cory Keenan .20 .50
12 Rival Fullum .20 .50
13 Tony Crisp .20 .50
14 Tyler Ertel .20 .50
15 Richard Borgo .20 .50
16 Steven Rice .20 .50
17 Rob Sangster .20 .50
18 Jeff Noble .20 .50
19 Mark Montanari .20 .50
20 Jim Hulton .20 .50
21 Craig Booker .20 .50
22 Doug Jones .20 .50
23 Randy Pearce .20 .50
24 Darren Rumble .20 .50
25 Joe Ranger .20 .50
26 Optimist's Sponsor Card (A-K) .02 .10
27 Ron Goodall .20 .50
28 Allan Lake .20 .50
29 Scott Montgomery TR .02 .10
30 Optimist's Sponsor Card (L-W) .02 .10

1988-89 Kitchener Rangers

The Kitchener Rangers of the OHL are featured in this 30-card P.L.A.Y. (Police, Law and Youth) set, which was sponsored by the Waterloo Regional Police in conjunction with several Optimist Clubs. The cards measure approximately 2 3/4" by 3 1/2" and are printed on thin card stock. The fronts feature color photos with the players posed in action stances. The photos are framed by black and white borders. The cards are numbered on both sides.

COMPLETE SET (30) 4.00 10.00
1 Waterloo Regional Police Crest .02 .10
2 Harold Basse Chief of Police .02 .10
3 Children's Bonus Card .02 .10
4 Joe McDonnell GM/CO .02 .10
5 Kitchener Rangers logo Checklist .20 .50
6 Mike Torchia .30 .75
7 Rick Allain .20 .50
8 John Uniac .20 .50
9 Rob Thiel .20 .50
10 Gus Morschauser .30 .75
11 Cory Keenan .20 .50
12 Rival Fullum .20 .50
13 Jason Firth .20 .50
14 Joey St. Aubin .20 .50
15 Richard Borgo .20 .50
16 Steven Rice .20 .50
17 Rob Sangster .20 .50
18 Gilbert Dionne .30 .75
19 Mark Montanari .20 .50
20 Shayne Stevenson .30 .75
21 Pierre Gagnon .20 .50
22 Kirk Tomlinson .20 .50
23 Randy Pearce .20 .50
24 Brad Barton .20 .50
25 Chris LiPuma .20 .50
26 Optimist's Sponsor's Card (A-K) .02 .10
27 Steve Herniman .20 .50
28 Darren Rumble .20 .50
29 Rick Chambers TR .02 .10
30 Optimist's Sponsor's Card (L-W) .02 .10

1989-90 Kitchener Rangers

The Kitchener Rangers of the OHL are featured in this 30-card P.L.A.Y. (Police, Law and Youth) set, which was sponsored by the Waterloo Regional Police in conjunction with several area Optimist Clubs. The cards measure approximately 2 3/4" by 3 1/2" and are printed on thin card stock. The fronts feature posed color player photos inside a black picture frame and white outer borders. Most cards are numbered on both sides.

COMPLETE SET (30) 4.80 12.00
1 Waterloo Police Crest .02 .10
2 Harold Basse COP .02 .10
3 Children's Bonus Card .02 .10
4 Joe McDonnell GM/CO .02 .10
5 Logo/Checklist .08 .25
6 Mike Torchia .30 .75
7 Rick Allain .20 .50
8 John Uniac .20 .50
9 Jack Williams .20 .50
10 Dave Schill .30 .75
11 John Copley .20 .50
12 Cory Keenan .20 .50
13 Rival Fullum .20 .50
14 Jason Firth .20 .50
15 Joey St. Aubin .20 .50
16 Richard Borgo .20 .50
17 Steven Rice .20 .50
18 Rob Sangster .20 .50
19 Gilbert Dionne .30 .75
20 Jamie Israel .20 .50
21 Shayne Stevenson .30 .75
22 Gib Tucker .20 .50
23 Randy Pearce .20 .50
24 Brad Barton .20 .50
25 Chris Li Puma .20 .50
26 Optimist's Sponsors' Card (A-L) .02 .10
27 Kevin Falesy .20 .50
28 Steve Smith .20 .50
29 Rick Chambers TR .02 .10
30 Optimist's Sponsors' Card (M-W) .02 .10

1990-91 Kitchener Rangers

The Kitchener Rangers of the OHL are featured in this 30-card P.L.A.Y. (Police, Law and Youth) set, which was sponsored by the Waterloo Regional Police in conjunction with several area Optimist Clubs. The cards measure approximately 2 3/4" by 3 1/2" and are printed on thin card stock. The fronts feature color photos with the players posed in action stances. The photos are framed by red and black borders The cards are numbered on both sides.

COMPLETE SET (30) 3.00 8.00
1 Waterloo Regional Police Crest .02 .10
2 Harold Basse Chief of Police .02 .10
3 Joe McDonnell GM/CO .02 .10
4 Rick Chambers TR .02 .10
5 Kitchener Rangers logo Checklist .08 .25
6 Mike Torchia .20 .50
7 Len DeVuono .10 .30
8 John Uniac .10 .30
9 Steve Smith .10 .30
10 Rob Stopar .10 .30
11 Tony McCabe .10 .30
12 Jason Firth .10 .30
13 Joey St. Aubin .10 .30
14 Richard Borgo .10 .30
15 Norm Dezainde .10 .30
16 Jeff Szeryk .10 .30
17 Derek Gauthier .10 .30
18 Jamie Israel .10 .30
19 Shayne McCosh .10 .30
20 Gib Tucker .10 .30
21 Paul McCallion .10 .30
22 Mike Allen .10 .30
23 Brad Barton .10 .30
24 Chris LiPuma .15 .40
25 Justin Cullen .10 .30
26 Optimist's Sponsor's Card (A-K) .02 .10
27 Rod Saarinen .10 .30
28 Jack Williams .10 .30
29 Steven Rice .20 .50
30 Optimist's Sponsor's Card (K-W) .02 .10

1993-94 Kitchener Rangers

Sponsored by Domino's Pizza and printed by Slapshot Images Ltd., this standard size 31-card set features the Kitchener Rangers of the OHL. On a geometrical blue and red background, the fronts feature color action player photos with thin grey borders. The player's name, position and team name, as well as the producer's logo, appear on the front.

COMPLETE SET (31) 3.60 9.00
1 Eric Manlow Jason Gladney Tim Spitig Checklist .15 .40
2 David Belitski .20 .50
3 Darryl Whyte .20 .50
4 Greg McLean .15 .40
5 Jason Hughes .15 .40
6 Gord Dickie .15 .40
7 Travis Riggin .15 .40
8 Norm Dezainde .15 .40
9 Tim Spitzig .15 .40
10 Trevor Gallant .15 .40
11 Chris Pittman .15 .40
12 Ryan Pawluk UER (Name misspelled Pawluck on back) .15 .40
13 Jason Morgan .15 .40
14 James Boyd .15 .40
15 Todd Warriner .30 .75
16 Mark Donahue .15 .40
17 Peter Brearley .15 .40
18 Andrew Taylor .15 .40
19 Jason Gladney .15 .40
20 Wes Swinson .15 .40
21 Matt O'Dette .15 .40
22 Darren Schmidt .15 .40
23 Jason Johnson .15 .40
24 Eric Manlow .15 .40
25 Jeff Lillie .15 .40
26 Sergei Olympiev .15 .40
27 Joe McDonnell CO .02 .10
28 Rick Chambers TR .02 .10
29 Andrew Taylor Travis Riggin David Belitski Top Prospects .15 .40
30 Sponsor Card Domino's Pizza .04 .01
NNO Slapshot Ad Card .04 .01

1994-95 Kitchener Rangers

Sponsored by Domino's Pizza and printed by Slapshot Images Ltd., this 31-card set features the Rangers of the OHL. The sets were sold by the team at home games.

COMPLETE SET (31) 3.00 8.00
1 Checklist .02 .10
2 David Belitski .20 .50
3 Darryl Whyte .20 .50
4 Daniel Godbout .15 .40
5 Greg McLean .15 .40
6 Jason Hughes .15 .40
7 Jason Byrnes .15 .40
8 Paul Traynor .15 .40
9 Travis Riggin .15 .40
10 Tim Spitzig .15 .40
11 Trevor Gallant .15 .40
12 Chris Pittman .20 .50
13 Rick Emmett .15 .40
14 Jason Morgan .15 .40
15 Luch Nasato .30 .75
16 Ryan Pepperall .20 .50
17 Keith Welsh .15 .40
18 Bill McGuigen .15 .40
19 Chris Brassard .15 .40
20 Andrew Taylor .15 .40
21 Rob Deciantis .15 .40
22 Wes Swinson .20 .50
23 Lucas Miller .15 .40
24 Sergei Olympiev .15 .40
25 Rob Maric .15 .40
26 Eric Manlow .20 .50
27 Geoff Ward CO .02 .10
28 Bob Ertel GM .02 .10
29 Rick Chambers TR Dave Nicholls TR .02 .10
30 Sponsor Card Domino's Pizza .04 .01
NNO Ad Card .04 .01

1994-95 Kitchener Rangers Update

This update set has the same design as the 1994-95 Kitchener Rangers set and features players that were traded to the Rangers during the 1994-95 season. It was sold separately and also included a Slapshot ad card with a 1995 calendar on the back. The numbering is a continuation of the regular set.

COMPLETE SET (7) .75 2.00
31 Brian Scott .20 .50
32 Robin LaCour .15 .40
33 Jim Ensom .20 .50
34 Dylan Seca .15 .40
35 Garrett Burnett .15 .40
NNO Craig Bignell ACO Mike Wright ACO .15 .40
NNO Ad Card .01

1996-97 Kitchener Rangers

This set was sold by the team at home games. The cards are unnumbered and so are listed in alphabetical order.

COMPLETE SET (30) 4.00 15.00
1 Jeff Ambrosio .20 .50
2 David Belitski .40 1.00
3 Jason Byrnes .20 .50
4 Peter Bureaux .20 .50
5 Vratislav Cech .20 .50
6 Rob DeCiantis .20 .50
7 Shawn Degagne .20 .50
8 Boyd Devereaux .60 1.50
9 Boyd Devereaux .60 1.50
10 Bryan Duce .20 .50
11 Michal Dvorak .20 .50
12 Darcy Harris .20 .50
13 Bryan Hayton ACO .02 .10
14 Wes Jarvis .20 .50
15 Dan Lebold TR .02 .10
16 Adam Lewis .20 .50
17 Rob Marc .20 .50
18 Mark McMahon .20 .50
19 Ryan Milanovic .30 .75
20 Ryan Mougenel .20 .50
21 Serge Payer .20 .50
22 Ryan Pepperall .20 .50
23 Alan Rourke .20 .50
24 Rob Stanfield .20 .50
25 Paul Traynor .20 .50
26 Tim Verbeek .20 .50
27 Geoff Ward CO .02 .10
28 Keith Welsh .20 .50
29 Header Card .02 .10
30 Checklist .02 .10

1999-00 Kitchener Rangers

This 30-card set features the 1999-00 Kitchener Rangers. Base cards have white and gray borders with a red nameplate along the right side of the card. The set was sold by the team at its souvenir stands.

COMPLETE SET (30) 4.00 10.00
1 John Eminger .15 .40
2 Matt Armstrong .15 .40
3 Serge Payer .20 .50
4 Steve Eminger .60 1.50
5 Andrew Peters .40 1.00
6 Mike Amodeo .15 .40
7 Bill Browne .15 .40
8 Maxim Sharifijanov .20 .50
9 Tex Mascot .02 .10
10 Dan Lebold .15 .40
11 Michael Wehrstedt .15 .40
12 Jeff Snyder .15 .40
13 Ryan Held .20 .50
14 John Dunphy .15 .40
15 Ruslan Akhmadulin .15 .40
16 Bobby Naylor .15 .40
17 Jimmy Gagnon .15 .40
18 Brandon Merli .15 .40
19 Chris Brannen .15 .40
20 Alan Rourke .15 .40
21 Sean McMorrow .30 .75
22 Mike Mazzuca .15 .40
23 Reg Bourcier .20 .50
24 Scott Dickie .20 .50
25 Kevin Bloch .15 .40
26 Jeff McGee .15 .40
27 Derek Roy .75 2.00
28 Header Card/CL .01
29 Kinsmen Club .01
30 Kinsmen Club .01

2000-01 Kitchener Rangers

This set features the Rangers of the OHL. The set was produced by the team and sold at its souvenir stands during home games. The cards are unnumbered, so are listed in alphabetical order.

COMPLETE SET (30) 4.80 10.00
1 Team CL .16 .01
2 Matt Armstrong .16 .40
3 Josh Bennett .16 .40
4 Andre Benoit .16 .40
5 Vasily Bizyayev .16 .40
6 Kevin Bloch CO .04 .10
7 Chris Brannen .16 .40
8 Chris Cava .20 .50
9 Travis Chapman .16 .40
10 Scott Dickie .30 .75
11 John Dunphy .16 .40
12 Steve Eminger .60 1.00
13 Jimmy Gagnon .16 .40
14 Mike Hough .20 .50
15 Jeff Johnston .30 .75
16 Brad Larter .16 .40
17 Dan Lebold TR .04 .10
18 Jamie Minchella .16 .40
19 Steve Richards .16 .40
20 Matt Rock .16 .40
21 Derek Roy .40 1.50
22 Derrick Shultz .30 .75
23 Scott Sheppard .16 .40
24 Sam Skwarchuk .16 .40
25 Marcus Smith .16 .40
26 Jeff Snyder CO .04 .10
27 Tex MASCOT .04 .10
28 Brock Yates .16 .40
29 Kinsmen Club .01
30 Kinsmen Club 2 .01

2001-02 Kitchener Rangers

COMPLETE SET (22) 12.00
1 Scott Dickie .75
2 Nick Policelli .50
3 Thomas Harrison .50
4 Ryan Ramsay .50
5 Steve Eminger .75
6 Peter Kanko 1.00
7 Mike Amodeo .50
8 Matt Grennier .50
9 Derek Roy .75
10 Andre Benoit .50
11 Mike Richards 1.50
12 Petr Hemsky .50
13 John Osborne .50
14 Rafal Martynowski .50
15 Marcus Smith .50
16 T.J. Eason .50
17 Adam Keefe .50
18 Matt Harpwood .50
19 Bill Kinkel .50
20 Jeff Szwez .50
21 Chad McCaffrey .50
22 Checklist .01

2002-03 Kitchener Rangers

COMPLETE SET(19) 12.00
1 Andre Benoit .50
2 Jesse Boucher .50
3 Greg Campbell 1.00
4 David Clarkson .50
5 Carlo DiRienzo .50
6 Scott Dickie .75
7 T.J. Eason .50
8 Steve Eminger 1.00
9 Matt Grennier .50
10 George Halkidis .50
11 Peter Kanko 1.00
12 Adam Keefe .50
13 Rafal Martynowski .50
14 Chad McCaffrey .50
15 Evan McGrath .50
16 Nathan O'Nabigon .50
17 Mike Richards 1.50
18 Derek Roy 1.00
19 Marcus Smith .50

2002-03 Kitchener Rangers Postcards

These five singles were recently confirmed. If you have any additional information about this set, please contact us at hockeymag@beckett.com.

COMPLETE SET (?)
1 Steve Eminger .75 2.00
2 Petr Kanko .75 2.00
3 Michael Richards .75 2.00
4 Derek Roy .75 2.00
5 Evan McGrath .75 2.00

2003-04 Kitchener Rangers

COMPLETE SET (24) 12.00
1 Andre Benoit .50
2 Jesse Boucher .50
3 Mike Chmielewski .50
4 David Clarkson .50
5 Patrick Davis .50
6 Carlo DiRienzo .75
7 Nick Duff .50
8 Cam Fergus .50
9 Peter Franchin .50
10 Chris Gravelding .50
11 Thomas Harrison .50
12 Devereaux Heshmatpour .50
13 Petr Kanko .75
14 Adam Keefe .50
15 Tyson Kellerman .50
16 Matt Lashoff .75
17 Rafal Martynowski .50
18 Paul McFarland .50
19 Evan McGrath .50
20 Nathan O'Nabigon .50
21 Anthony Pototschnik .50
22 Mike Richards 1.00
23 Marcus Smith .50
24 Boris Valabik .75

2003 Kitchener Rangers Memorial Cup

Cards are unnumbered and are listed below in alphabetical order.

COMPLETE SET (19) 18.00
1 Andre Benoit .75
2 Jesse Boucher .75
3 Gregory Campbell 1.50
4 David Clarkson .75
5 Scott Dickie 1.00
6 Carlo Dirienzo 1.00
7 T.J. Eason .75
8 Steve Eminger 1.50
9 Matt Grenier .75
10 George Halkidis .75
11 Petr Kanko 1.50
12 Adam Keefe .75
13 Rafal Martynowski .75
14 Chad McCaffrey .75
15 Evan McGrath .75
16 Nathan O'Nabigon .75
17 Michael Richards 2.00
18 Derek Roy 1.00
19 Marcus Smith .75

2004-05 Kitchener Rangers

A total of 600 team sets were produced.

COMPLETE SET (24) 15.00
2 Andre Benoit .50
2 Michael Richards 1.50
3 Boris Valabik .75
4 Mark Packwood .50
5 Craig Voakes .50
6 Dan Turple .50
7 Dan Gyenes .50
8 David Clarkson .50
9 Eric Pfligler .50
10 Evan McGrath 1.00
11 Jack Combs .50
12 Jakub Kindl .75
13 Joe McCann .50
14 Justin Azevedo .50
15 Justin Piquette .50
16 Kevin Henderson .50
17 Mark Fraser .50
18 Matt Lashoff 1.00
19 Matt Pepe .50
20 Adam Keefe .50
21 Michael Duco .50
22 Myles Applebaum .50
23 Patrick Davis .50
24 Paul McFarland .50

2005-06 Kitchener Rangers

COMPLETE SET (27) 8.00 15.00
1 Dan Turple 1.00
2 Julien Machabee .75
3 Mark Packwood 1.00
4 Matt Lashoff 1.00
5 Patrick Davis .75
6 Justin Azevedo .75
7 Evan McGrath 1.00
8 Sean Smyth .75
9 Dan Gyenes .75
10 Boris Valabik 1.00
11 Kevin Henderson .75
12 Matt Thomson .75
13 Mark Fraser .75
14 Jakub Kindl .75
15 Nick Spaling .75
16 Mike Duco .75
17 Yves Bastien .75
18 Matt Pepe .75
19 Craig Voakes .75
20 Michael Pelech .75
21 Jean-Michel Rizk .75
22 Ryan Donally .75
23 Myles Applebaum .75
24 Matt Auffrey .75
25 Cory Konecny .75
26 David Lomas .75
27 Victor Oreskovich .75

2006-07 Kitchener Rangers

COMPLETE SET (25) 8.00 15.00
1 Jakub Kindl .30 .75
2 Steve Tarasuk .30 .75
3 Nick Spaling .30 .75
4 Scott Timmins .30 .75
5 Mike Duco .30 .75
6 Justin Azevedo .30 .75
7 Yves Bastien .30 .75
8 Mike Mascioli .30 .75
9 Matt Halischuk .30 .75
10 Nazem Kadri .30 .75
11 Matt Pepe .30 .75
12 Robert Bortuzzo .30 .75
13 Dan Gyenes .30 .75
14 Denver Manderson .30 .75
15 Mark Packwood .40 1.00
16 John Murray .40 1.00
17 Jean-Michel Rizk .30 .75
18 Adam Zamec .30 .75
19 Kevin Henderson .30 .75
20 Victor Oreskovich .30 .75
21 Yannick Weber .30 .75
22 Brian Soso .30 .75
23 Phil Varone .30 .75
24 Dan Kelly .30 .75
LE1 Justin Azevedo 1.25 3.00

2007-08 Kitchener Rangers

COMPLETE SET (24) 5.00 12.00
1 Josh Unice .25 .60
2 Mavric Parks .25 .60
3 Alex Dzielski .25 .60
4 Yannick Weber .25 .60
5 Steve Jensen .25 .60
6 Phil Varone .25 .60
7 Dan Kelly .25 .60
8 Steve Tarasuk .25 .60
9 Nick Spaling .25 .60
10 Myles Barbieri .25 .60
11 Scott Timmins .25 .60
12 Mike Duco .25 .60
13 Justin Azevedo .25 .60
14 Mike Mascioli .25 .60
15 Matt Halischuk .25 .60
16 Nazem Kadri .25 .60
17 Matt Pepe .25 .60
18 Robert Bortuzzo .25 .60
19 Brandon Mashinter .25 .60
20 Spencer Anderson .25 .60
21 T.J. Battani .25 .60
22 Doug Clarkson .25 .60
23 Alexei Dostoinov .25 .60
24 Mikkel Boedker .25 .60

1990-91 Knoxville Cherokees

This 19-card set of the Knoxville Cherokees of the ECHL was produced by 7th Inning Sketch, and offered for sale by the team at home games. Interestingly, the set is numbered 101-119, suggesting it is the continuation of a larger (all ECHL?) set. The fronts feature a posed shot, while the backs offer limited player information and logos for the club and the Knoxville News-Sentinel.

COMPLETE SET (19) 3.60 9.00
101 David Williams .25 .60
102 Paul Laus .40 1.00
103 Don Jackson CO .08 .25
104 Steve Ryding .20 .50
105 Jeff Lindsay .20 .50
106 Daniel Gauthier .25 .60
107 Stan Drulia .25 .60
108 Mike Murray .20 .50
109 Tom Sasso .20 .50
110 Butch Kaebel .20 .50
111 Don McClennan .20 .50
112 Jamie Hanlon .20 .50
113 Troy Mick .20 .50
114 Brett Strot .20 .50
115 Dean Anderson .20 .50
116 Quinton Brickley .20 .50
117 Greg Batters .20 .50
118 Alex Daviault .20 .50
119 Mike Greenlay .30 .75

1991-92 Knoxville Cherokees

This 20-card set of the ECHL's Knoxville Cherokees was sponsored by the News-Sentinel, and offered for sale by the team at home games. The cards feature posed shots on the front; the unnumbered backs include vital statistics and a brief career history.

COMPLETE SET (20) 3.60 9.00
1 Bill Nyrop CO .20 .50
2 Galen Head TR .02 .10
3 Mike Greenlay .30 .75
4 Karl Clauss .30 .75
5 Steve Ryding .20 .50
6 Mike Gober .20 .50
7 Chad Thompson .20 .50
8 Trevor Forsythe .20 .50
9 Greg Pankewicz .20 .50
10 David Shute .20 .50
11 Jamie Dabanovich .20 .50
12 Shawn Lillie .20 .50
13 Joel Gardner .20 .50
14 Roman Hubalek .20 .50
15 Bruno Villeneuve .20 .50
16 Troy Mick .20 .50
17 Dean McDonald .20 .50
18 Brett Lawrence .20 .50
19 Dean Anderson .20 .50
20 Robert Melanson .20 .50

1993-94 Knoxville Cherokees

This 20-card standard-size set features the Knoxville Cherokees. On a black background with white borders, the fronts have color action and posed player photos with thin teal borders. The team name appears above the photo, while the player's name, position, and the team logo are under the photo. The cards are unnumbered and checklisted below in alphabetical order.

COMPLETE SET (20) 6.00 15.00
1 Scott Boston .15 .40
2 Cory Cadden .15 .40
3 Tim Chase .15 .40
4 Steven Flomenhoft .15 .40
5 Scott Gordon .20 .50
6 Jon Larson .15 .40
7 Carl LeBlanc .15 .40
8 Kim Maier .15 .40
9 Wes McCauley .15 .40
10 Scott Metcalfe .15 .40
11 Mike Murray .15 .40
12 Hayden O'Rear .15 .40
13 Jeff Reid .15 .40
14 Manon Rheaume 3.00 8.00
15 Marc Rodgers .15 .40
16 Doug Searle .15 .40
17 Barry Smith CO .08 .25
18 Martin Tanguay .15 .40
19 Nicholas Vachon .20 .50
20 Bruno Villeneuve .15 .40

1994-95 Knoxville Cherokees

This 24-card set of the Knoxville Cherokees of the ECHL was issued by the team and available at home games.

COMPLETE SET (24) 3.00 8.00
1 Checklist .02 .10
2 Barry Smith CO .08 .25
3 Aaron Fackler TR .02 .10
4 Andy Davis ANN .02 .10
5 Stephane Menard .15 .40
6 Doug Searle .15 .40
7 Hayden O'Rear .15 .40
8 Sean Brown .15 .40
9 Mike Murray .15 .40
10 Jon Jenkins .15 .40
11 Sean Pronger .30 .75
12 Steven Flomenhoft .15 .40
13 David Neilson .15 .40
14 Jack Callahan .15 .40
15 Carl LeBlanc .15 .40
16 Alain Deeks .20 .50
17 George Zajankala .15 .40
18 Chris Fess .15 .40
19 Michel Gaul .15 .40
20 Pat Murray .15 .40
21 Robb McIntyre .15 .40
22 Vaclav Nedomansky, Jr .15 .40
23 Cory Cadden .15 .40
24 Michael Burman .15 .40

1996-97 Knoxville Cherokees

The 22-card base set was sold in team set form at home games. Cards numbered P1 and P2 were available one night-only giveaways at two Cherokee home games. The designs are the same as those of the base set. Because of the unique distribution of these two cards, they are not considered part of the complete set.

COMPLETE SET (20) 4.00 10.00
1 Knoxville Cherokees .20 .50
2 Barry Smith HCO .20 .50
3 Sean Halifax .20 .50
4 Daniel Chaput .20 .50
5 Jamie Bird .20 .50
6 Matt Turek .20 .50
7 Chris Fees .20 .50
8 Kelly Hollingshead .20 .50
9 Darren Johnson .20 .50
10 Vaclav Nedomansky .20 .50
11 Kent Fearns .20 .50
12 Martin Tanguay .20 .50
13 Wayne Anchikoski .20 .50
14 Jim Brown .20 .50
15 Garrett Burnett .40 1.00
16 Stephane Soulliere .20 .50
17 Dean Moore .20 .50
18 David Neilson .20 .50
19 Mike Vandenberghe .20 .50
20 Brad Guzda .40 1.00
21 Olaf Kjenstad .20 .50
22 PHPA Web Site .02 .10
P1 Brad Guzda LL 2.00 5.00
P2 Jim Brown LL 2.00 5.00

2004-05 Knoxville Ice Bears

Little is known about this set beyond the checklist, therefore it is not priced. Additional info can be forwarded to hockeymag@beckett.com.

COMPLETE SET (24)
1 K.C. Caudill
2 Chris Bodnar
3 Kevin Swider

4 Todd MacIsaac
5 Marcus Forsberg
6 Civic Colisseum
7 Chilly MASCOT
8 TCS card
9 Doug Serle
10 Craig Desjarlais
11 Mike Cragen
12 Darren Caine
13 Curtis Menzul
14 Terry Dunbar
15 Free Kid's Ticket
16 David Bagley
17 Matt Moore
18 Jeff Hansen
19 James Ronayne
20 Miss Icebear
21 Liam McCarthy
22 Jim Bermingham
23 Rob Miller
24 K.J. Voorhees

2005-06 Knoxville Ice Bears

COMPLETE SET (24) 6.00 15.00
1 Jason Bermingham .30 .75
2 Patrick Carriere .30 .75
3 Kevin Caudill .30 .75
4 Mike Craigen .30 .75
5 Nathan Daly .30 .75
6 Marcus Forsberg .30 .75
7 Aaron Lewis .30 .75
8 Ben Manny .30 .75
9 Liam McCarthy .30 .75
10 Curtis Menzul .30 .75
11 Rob Miller .30 .75
12 Matt Moore .30 .75
13 Ryan Person .30 .75
14 Bob Rangus .30 .75
15 Jamie Ronayne .30 .75
16 Doug Searle .30 .75
17 Kevin Swider .30 .75
18 K.J. Voorhees .30 .75
19 Jim Bermingham HC .02 .10
20 Dance Team .02 .10
21 Drew Kitts EM .02 .10
22 Chilly MASCOT .02 .10
23 Tim Douglas TP .02 .10
24 Knoxville Ice Bears .20 .50

1999-00 Knoxville Speed

This set features the Speed of the UHL. The cards were issued as a promotional giveaway, with the first 15 cards going on one night, followed by a second set of 15 (a sponsor card was doubled up).

COMPLETE SET (29) 6.00 15.00
1 Sponsor Card .01
2 Sponsor Card .01
3 Bradley Denis .30 .75
4 Hockey History .01
5 UHL History .01
6 Trevor Jobe .40 1.00
7 Cam Law .30 .75
8 Rusty McKie .40 1.00
9 Eric Mohntreuil .30 .75
10 Mike Murray .30 .75
11 Dan Myre .30 .75
12 Sergei Radchenko .30 .75
13 Bill Russell .30 .75
14 Eric Schneider .30 .75
15 Mike Schultz .30 .75
16 Doug Searle .30 .75
17 Jordan Shaw .30 .75
18 Konstantin Simchuk .40 1.00
19 Jeff Suggitt .30 .75
20 Jeremy Thompson .30 .75
21 Andrew Tortorella .30 .75
22 Dmitry Ustyuzhanin .30 .75
23 Team on the Bench .20 .50
24 Mike Wilhelm EM .02 .10
25 Terry Ruskowski CO .20 .50
26 Tim Douglas TR .02 .10
27 Hersheys/Pilot .01
28 Hersheys/Pilot .01
29 Eyewitness Sports .01

2000-01 Knoxville Speed

This set features the Speed of the UHL. The set was released as a promotional giveaway, with a different mixture of cards being given away at various home games to allow collectors to trade amongst themselves to complete sets.

COMPLETE SET (29) 10.00 30.00
1 Alex Alepin .30 1.00
2 Bradley Denis .60 1.50
3 Craig Desjarlais .60 1.50
4 Brad Guzda .40 1.50
5 Tom Lawson .30 1.00
6 David Mayes .30 1.00
7 Alain Savage .30 1.00
8 Mike Schultz .30 1.00
9 Dean Shmyr .40 1.50
10 Mike Vandenberghe .30 1.00
11 Mike Wilhelm EM .04 .10
12 Nick Paranjape (Fox 43) .04 .10
13 Brad Domonsky .80 2.00
14 Dmitry Ustyuzhanin .30 1.00
15 Yannick Latour .30 1.00
16 Sergei Petrov .60 1.50
17 Iannique Renaud .30 1.00
18 Mikko Sivonen .40 1.50
19 Mike Henderson .80 2.00
20 Geno Parrish .30 1.00
21 Andrew Tortorella .60 1.50
22 Mark Karpen .30 1.00
23 Dan Myre .30 1.00
24 Mike Murray .30 1.00
25 Mike Green .30 1.00
26 Oleg Kuzmin .30 1.00
27 Terry Ruskowski CO .20 .50
28 Tim Douglas TR .04 .10
29 JBG SPONSOR .04 .10

1998-99 Kootenay Ice

This set features the Ice of the WHL. Each card measures approximately 3" x 6" and is unnumbered. The cards were sold by the team at home games.

COMPLETE SET (24) 18.00
1 Clayton Pool .20 .50
2 Scott Roles .20 .50
3 Dean Arsene .20 .50
4 Jesse Ferguson .20 .50
5 Dion Lassu .20 .50
6 Mark Thompson .20 .50
7 Steve McCarthy .75 2.00
8 Rod Leroux .20 .50
9 Mike Green .20 .50
10 Wade Burt .20 .50
11 Nick Marach .20 .50
12 Jaroslav Svoboda .40 1.00
13 Trevor Wasyluk .40 1.00
14 Jarret Stoll 1.25 3.00
15 Jason Jaffray .20 .50
16 Trevor Johnson .20 .50
17 Kyle Wanvig .75 2.00
18 Tyler Beechey .20 .50
19 Stanislav Gron .40 1.00
20 Colin Sinclair .20 .50
21 Jeremy Yablonski .20 .50
22 Graham Belak .20 .50
23 B.J. Boxma .20 .50
24 Brad Tutschek .20 .50

2000-01 Kootenay Ice

This set features the Ice of the WHL. The cards are oversized by about 1/2 inch in height and width, and were sold by the team at home games. The cards are unnumbered, so are listed below in alphabetical order.

COMPLETE SET (24) 8.00 20.00
1 Dean Arsene .20 .50
2 Tyler Beechey .20 .50
3 Dan Blackburn .75 2.00
4 Zdenek Blatny .40 1.00
5 Eric Bowen .20 .50
6 Bret DeCecco .40 1.00
7 Brennan Evans .20 .50
8 Cole Fischer .20 .50
9 Richard Hamula .20 .50
10 Jeff Harvey .20 .50
11 Pat Iannone .20 .50
12 Jason Jaffray .20 .50
13 Trevor Johnson .20 .50
14 Mike Lee .20 .50
15 Steve Makway .20 .50
16 Lance Morrison .20 .50
17 Aaron Rome .20 .50
18 Mascot Shivers .04 .10
19 Colin Sinclair .20 .50
20 Jarret Stoll 1.25 3.00
21 Marek Svatos 2.00 5.00
22 Adam Taylor .20 .50
23 Andy Thompson .20 .50
24 Craig Weller .20 .50

2002-03 Kootenay Ice

We have confirmed a handful of singles from this set, thanks to collector Vinnie Montalbano. If you have any other information about this set, please email us at hockeymag@beckett.com.

COMPLETE SET (?)
1 Gerard Dicaire .30 .75
2 Duncan Milroy .30 .75
3 Tomas Plihal .30 .75
4 Adam Taylor .30 .75

2003-04 Kootenay Ice

COMPLETE SET (25) 8.00 20.00
1 Taylor Dakers .30 .75
2 Jeff Glass 2.00 5.00
3 Derek Price .30 .75
4 Donny Lloyd .30 .75
5 James Cherewyk .30 .75
6 Brad Zanon .30 .75
7 Brad Cole .30 .75
8 Travis Featherstone .30 .75
9 Nigel Dawes .75 2.00
10 Mike Boxma .30 .75
11 Glenn Olson .30 .75
12 Josh Morrow .30 .75
13 Adam Taylor .30 .75
14 Igor Agarunov .30 .75
15 Adam Cracknell .30 .75
16 Jeremy Schenderling .30 .75
17 Dale Mahovsky .30 .75
18 Ryan Russell .30 .75
19 Aaron Bader .30 .75
20 Sean Affleck .30 .75
21 Martin Sagat .30 .75
22 Brett Sutter .60 1.50
23 Checklist .02 .10
24 Shivers MASCOT .02 .10
25 Sponsor .02 .10

2004-05 Kootenay Ice

COMPLETE SET (25) 20.00
1 Laine Allen .75
2 Andy Bossence .75
3 Michael Busto .75
4 James Cherewyk .75
5 Brad Cole .75
6 Adam Cracknell .75
7 Steven DaSilva .75
8 Taylor Dakers .75
9 Nigel Dawes 1.50
10 Joshua Fauth .75
11 Jeff Glass 3.00
12 Chad Greenan .75
13 Casey Lee .75
14 Dale Mahovsky .75
15 Ben Maxwell .75
16 Roman Polak .75
17 Derek Price .75
18 Ryan Russell .75
19 Martin Sagat .75
20 Josh Saywell .75
21 Brett Sutter 1.00
22 Adam Taylor .75
23 Devin Welsh .75
24 Commitment .10
25 Sponsor Card .01

2005-06 Kootenay Ice

COMPLETE SET (25) 15.00
1 Andrew Bailey .30 .75
2 Curtis Billsten .30 .75
3 Lukas Bohunicky .30 .75
4 Michael Busto .30 .75
5 Adam Cracknell .30 .75
6 Steven DaSilva .30 .75
7 Taylor Dakers .30 .75
8 Dalyn Flatt .30 .75
9 Trent Fussi .30 .75
10 Chad Greenan .30 .75
11 Paul Kurceba .30 .75
12 Kris Lazaruk .30 .75
13 Casey Lee .30 .75
14 Paul MacDonald .30 .75
15 Dale Mahovsky .30 .75
16 Ben Maxwell .30 .75
17 John Negrin .30 .75
18 Michal Psurny .30 .75
19 Ryan Russell .30 .75
20 Dustin Sylvester .30 .75
21 Devin Welsh .30 .75
22 Luke Wiens .30 .75
23 Shivers MASCOT .02 .10
24 Concord Pacific SPONSOR .01 .01
25 Kootenay Ice

1991-92 Lake Superior State Lakers

This set features the Lakers of the NCAA. The cards are unnumbered and so are listed in alphabetical order.

COMPLETE SET (28) 20.00
1 1991 CCHA Champs .08 .25
2 Dan Angelelli .30 .75
3 Mark Astley .30 .75
4 Mike Bachusz .30 .75
5 Steve Barnes .30 .75
6 Clayton Beddoes .30 .75
7 Paul Constantin .30 .75
8 Vincent Faucher .30 .75
9 David Gartshore .30 .75
10 Tim Hanley .30 .75
11 John Hendry .30 .75
12 Dean Hulett .30 .75
13 Jeff Jackson CO .20 .50
14 Blaine Lacher .40 1.00
15 Darrin Madeley .40 1.00
16 Kurt Miller .30 .75
17 Sandy Moger .40 1.00
18 Mike Morin .30 .75
19 Jay Ness .30 .75
20 Jim Peters .30 .75
21 Brian Rolston .75 2.00
22 Michael Smith .30 .75
23 Wayne Strachan .30 .75
24 Jason Trzcinski .30 .75
25 Rob Valicevic .60 1.50
26 Darren Wetherill .30 .75
27 Brad Willner .30 .75
28 Jason Welch .30 .75

1992-93 Lake Superior State Lakers

This 33-card standard-size set features the 1992 NCAA Champion Lake Superior State Lakers. The cards feature color, action player photos with gradated blue borders. The player's name and the Lakers logo appears below the picture. The backs carry black-and-white close-up photos along with biographical information, quick facts, and statistics. The cards are unnumbered and checklisted below in alphabetical order.

COMPLETE SET (33) 6.00 15.00
1 Team Photo .20 .50
1992 NCAA Champions
2 Team Photo .20 .50
1992 CCHA Champions
3 Keith Aldridge .20 .50
4 Dan Angelelli .15 .40
5 Mark Astley .20 .50
6 Mike Bachusz .15 .40
7 Steven Barnes .15 .40
8 Clayton Beddoes .15 .40
9 David Gartshore .15 .40
10 Tim Hanley .15 .40
11 Matt Hansen .15 .40
12 John Hendry .15 .40
13 Dean Hulett .15 .40
14 Jeff Jackson .20 .50
15 Blaine Lacher .40 1.00
16 Darrin Madeley .20 .50
17 Mike Matteucci .15 .40
18 Scott McCabe .15 .40
19 Kurt Miller .15 .40
20 Mike Morin .15 .40
21 Jay Ness .15 .40
22 Gino Pulente .15 .40
23 Brian Rolston .75 2.00
24 Paul Sass .15 .40
25 Michael Smith .15 .40
26 Wayne Strachan .15 .40
27 Sean Tallaire .15 .40
28 Adam Thompson .15 .40
29 Jason Trzcinski .15 .40
30 Rob Valicevic .60 1.50
31 Jason Welch .15 .40
32 Darren Wetherill .15 .40
33 Brad Willner .15 .40

2004-05 Lakehead University Thunderwolves

These cards, featuring the CIAU Thunderwolves, were available individually from Quality Markets, making the sets extremely difficult to piece together. The set features Drew Kivell, who appeared in the TV show Making The Cut.

COMPLETE SET (27) 20.00
1 Joel Scherban .75
2 Chris Shaffer .75
3 Jeff Richards .75
4 Erik Lodge .75
5 Murray Magill .75
6 Jason Lange .75
7 Robert Hillier .75
8 Francis Walker .75
9 Andrew Brown .75
10 Kris Callaway .75
11 Jouni Kuokkanen .75
12 Leon Cooper .75
13 Hugo Lehoux .75
14 Michael Wehrstedt .75
15 Mike Self .75
16 Austin Wycisk .75
17 Steve Rawski .75
18 Grant McCune .75
19 Sean Stefanski .75
20 Drew Kivell .75
21 Jesse Baraniuk .75
22 Dene Poulin .75
23 Tobias Whelan .75
24 Chris Whitley .75
25 Peter Cava 1.00
26 Mark Robinson .75
27 Brad Priestlay .75

1993-94 Lakeland Ice Warriors

This set consists of player photos with photocopied biographies glued to the backs. There are variations of several players in this set.

COMPLETE SET (25) 25.00
1 Lakeland Ice Warriors .75 2.00
2 Chief Mascot .40 1.00
3 Chris Babkirk .40 1.00
4 Chris Baxter .40 1.00
5 Pat Bingham .40 1.00
6 Ian Collins .40 1.00
7 Ian Collins .40 1.00
8 Eric Daoust .40 1.00
9 Eric Daoust .40 1.00
10 Derek Edgerly .40 1.00
11 Andrew Ernst .40 1.00
12 John Finnie .40 1.00
13 John Finnie .40 1.00
14 Sean Gabriele .40 1.00
15 John Grand .40 1.00
16 Manny Hawkins .40 1.00
17 Jules Jardine .40 1.00
18 John Labenski .40 1.00
19 Francois Michaud .40 1.00
20 Bob Nicholls .40 1.00
21 Ed Sabo .40 1.00
22 Brent Selman .40 1.00
23 Gary Thomas .40 1.00
24 Dean Turgeon .40 1.00
25 Dave Wright .40 1.00

2004-05 Langley Hornets

This set features the Hornets of the BCJHL. The cards feature an Upper Deck logo as they were produced by the company's personalized card division.

COMPLETE SET (22) 25.00
1 Matt Allen 1.00
2 Aaron Berman 1.00
3 Justin Binab 1.00
4 Tyler Boice 1.00
5 Marcel Bruinsma 1.00
6 Gary Butler 1.00
7 Tyson Chernask 1.00
8 Steve Christie 2.00
9 Tyson Daniels 1.50
10 Gord Edmondson 1.00
11 Brian Harris 1.00
12 Steve Matic 1.00
13 Taylor Moore 2.00
14 Robert Pritchard 1.00
15 Graham Sheppard 1.00
16 Luke Shier 2.00
17 Justin Taylor 1.00
18 Chris Vassos 1.00
19 Nathan Westover 1.00
20 Mike Wilson 1.00
21 Jason Wright 1.00
22 Robert Pritchard#)Brian Harris AS 1.00

2003-04 Laredo Bucks

According to minor league afficionado Ralph Slate, this set was released by the team's booster club, which limited production to just 200 sets and charged a whopping $50 a set to raise funds.

COMPLETE SET (23) 60.00
1 Mike Amodeo 4.00
2 Jeff Bes 3.00
3 Max Birbraer 4.00
4 Brent Cullaton 3.00
5 Jean-Francois David 3.00
6 Serge Dube 3.00
7 Marco Emond 4.00
8 Chris Grenville 3.00
9 David Guerrera 4.00
10 James Hiebert 3.00
11 Dion Hyman 3.00
12 Mark Matier 3.00
13 Bobby-Chad Mitchell 3.00
14 Patrik Nilson 3.00
15 Adam Paiement 3.00
16 Gabriel Proulx 3.00
17 Steve Simoes 3.00
18 Jason Spence 3.00
19 Mike Vellinga 3.00
20 Steve Weidlich 3.00
21 Terry Ruskowski CO 1.00
22 Derek Craft EQM .50
23 Bobby Moore TR .50

1998-99 Las Vegas Coyotes RHI

This 20-card set was handed out as a promotional giveaway at a home game in late July of that season. The cards are not numbered, so they are listed in alphabetical order.

COMPLETE SET (20) 3.00 8.00
1 Konstantin Simchuk .20 .50
2 Jay Neal .20 .50
3 Mike Ciolli .20 .50
4 Jakub Ficenec .20 .50
5 Blake Knox .20 .50
6 Darren Meek .20 .50
7 Mike Jorgensen .20 .50
8 Kirk Llano .20 .50
9 Jamie Cooke .20 .50
10 Tom Perry .20 .50
11 Don Parsons .20 .50
12 Rich Bronilla .20 .50
13 Gerry St. Cyr .30 .75
14 Brad Guzda .20 .50
15 Rob Pallin .20 .50
16 Dan Reja .20 .50
17 Chris McSorley CO .20 .50
18 Howl N. Coyote Mascot .02 .10
19 KOMP Morning Crew .02 .10
20 1999 Las Vegas Coyotes .02 .10

1993-94 Las Vegas Thunder

Sponsored by Saturn, bc and More, and KVBC (Channel 3), this 32-card standard-size set features the 1993-94 Las Vegas Thunder of the IHL. On a black card face, the fronts have posed color player photos with thin white borders. The player's name and number appear under the picture. The team and sponsor logos are printed in the four corners. The cards are unnumbered and checklisted below in alphabetical order. This set may also have been issued as a perforated sheet.

COMPLETE SET (32) 3.00 8.00
1 Brent Ashton .15 .40
2 Boom Boom (Mascot) .02 .10
3 Bob Bourne CO .15 .40
4 Rod Buskas .08 .25
5 Lyndon Byers .30 .75
6 Rich Campbell TR .02 .10
7 Colin Cowherd ANN .02 .10
8 Butch Goring CO .15 .40
9 Steve Gotaas .08 .25
10 Marc Habscheid .08 .25
11 Brett Hauer .08 .25
12 Shawn Heaphy .08 .25
13 Scott Hollis .08 .25
14 Peter Ing .20 .50
15 Steve Jaques .08 .25
16 Bob Joyce .08 .25
17 Jim Kyte .08 .25
18 Patrice Lefebvre .30 .75
19 Clint Malarchuk .20 .50
20 Ken Quinney .08 .25
21 Jean-Marc Richard .08 .25
22 Todd Richards .08 .25
23 Marc Rodgers .08 .25
24 Jeff Sharples .08 .25
25 Randy Smith .08 .25
26 Greg Spenrath .08 .25
27 Bob Strumm GM .02 .10
28 Kirk Tomlinson .08 .25
29 Kerry Toporowski .15 .40
30 Mark Vermette .08 .25
31 Steve Wissman EQMG .02 .10
32 Title Card .02 .10

1994-95 Las Vegas Thunder

This 29-card standard-size set was manufactured and distributed by Jessen Associates, Inc. for Classic. The fronts display color action player photos with a teal marbleized inner border and a black outer border. The player's name, jersey number, and position appear in the teal border on the right edge. The cards are unnumbered and checklisted below in alphabetical order.

COMPLETE SET (29) 4.80 12.00
1 James Black .08 .25
2 Radek Bonk .40 1.00
3 Boom Boom MASCOT .02 .10
4 Rich Campbell TR .02 .10
5 Frank Evans .08 .25
6 Marc Habscheid .20 .50
7 Alex Hicks .20 .50
8 Bob Joyce .20 .50
9 Jim Kyte .08 .25
10 Lark and Craig, DJs .02 .10
11 Patrice Lefebvre .40 1.00
12 Darcy Loewen .20 .50
13 Sal Lombardi EQMG .02 .10
14 Clint Malarchuk .20 .50
15 Andrew McBain .20 .50
16 Chris McSorley CO .20 .50
17 David Neilson .08 .25
18 Jerry Olenyn .08 .25
19 Ken Quinney .20 .50
20 Pokey Reddick .20 .50
21 Jeff Reid .08 .25
22 Manon Rheaume 2.00 5.00
23 Jean-Marc Richard .20 .50
24 Todd Richards .08 .25
25 Marc Rodgers .08 .25
26 Jeff Sharples .08 .25
27 Jarrod Skalde .20 .50
28 Bob Strumm GM/CO .02 .10
29 Kerry Toporowski .20 .50

1995-96 Las Vegas Thunder

This 26-card set of the Las Vegas Thunder of the IHL was produced by Split Second for Collector's Edge Ice. The set was available through the team at home games and by mail. The cards are unnumbered, so are listed alphabetically. The set is notable for containing 1996 Anaheim first rounder Ruslan Salei, as well as bright NHL prospect Bill Bowler.

COMPLETE SET (26) 4.80 12.00
1 Bill Bowler .30 .75
2 Peter Fiorentino .15 .40
3 Greg Hawgood .30 .75
4 Sasha Lakovic .15 .40
5 Patrice Lefebvre .40 1.00
6 Darcy Loewen .15 .40
7 Gord Marx .15 .40
8 Blaine Moore .15 .40
9 Vaclav Nedomansky, Jr .15 .40
10 Pokey Reddick .30 .75
11 Jeff Ricciardi .15 .40
12 Jean-Marc Richard .15 .40
13 Marc Rodgers .40 1.00
14 Chris Rogles .30 .75
15 Ken Quinney .20 .50
16 Ruslan Salei .20 .50
17 Jeff Sharples .20 .50
18 Daniel Shank .20 .50
19 Todd Simon .20 .50
20 Rhett Trombley .15 .40
21 Vladimir Tsyplakov .20 .50
22 Sergei Zholtok .30 .75
23 Chris McSorley CO .08 .25
24 Clint Malarchuk AGM .20 .50
25 Bob Strumm GM .02 .10
26 BoomBoom .02 .10

1996-97 Las Vegas Thunder

This 24-card set of the Las Vegas Thunder of the IHL was produced by Multi-Ad Services and sponsored by Heineken and U.S. Home, among others. The cards were sold by the team at the rink or through the mail. The cards are unnumbered, and are listed below alphabetically.

COMPLETE SET (24) 4.80 12.00
1 Egor Bashkatov .20 .50
2 Boom Boom (Mascot) .02 .10
3 Kevin Dahl .20 .50
4 Chris Dahlquist .20 .50
5 Pavol Demitra .60 1.50
6 Parris Duffus .30 .75
7 Martin Gendron .20 .50
8 Brent Gretzky .20 .50
9 Kerry Huffman .20 .50
10 Igor Karpenko .30 .75
11 Don Larner .20 .50
12 Patrice Lefebvre .40 1.00
13 Darcy Loewen .20 .50
14 Clint Malarchuk AGM .20 .50
15 Chris McSorley CO .02 .10
16 Blaine Moore .20 .50
17 Ken Quinney .30 .75
18 Jeff Serowik .20 .50
19 Jason Simon .20 .50
20 Bob Strumm GM .02 .10
21 Rhett Trombley .20 .50
22 Sergei Yerkovich .20 .50
23 Sergei Zholtok .30 .75
24 Logo Card .02 .10

1997-98 Las Vegas Thunder

This set features the Thunder of the IHL and was sold by the team at home games. The cards are standard-sized and are numbered on the back.

COMPLETE SET (28) 4.80 12.00
1 Ken Quinney .30 .75
2 Manny Legace .60 1.50
3 Jesse Belanger .20 .50
4 Joe Day .20 .50
5 Darcy Loewen .20 .50
6 Trevor Roenick .20 .50
7 Steve Bancroft .20 .50
8 Thom Cullen .20 .50
9 John Slaney .20 .50
10 Sergei Yerkovich .20 .50
11 Bob Strumm GM .02 .10
12 Chris McSorley HCO .08 .25
13 Doug Tretiak EQM .02 .10
14 KKLZ .02 .10
15 Patrice Lefebvre .40 1.00
16 Tim Cheveldae .40 1.00
17 Jeff Christian .20 .50
18 Sergei Klimovich .20 .50
19 Rob Pattison .20 .50
20 Dan Shermerhorn .20 .50
21 Ilya Byakin .20 .50
22 Justin Kurtz .20 .50
23 Radoslav Suchy .20 .50
24 Boom Boom MASCOT .02 .10
25 Clint Malarchuk AGM .20 .50
26 Van Parfet TR .02 .10
27 Dave McCann TV .02 .10
28 PHPA Web Site .04 .01

1998-99 Las Vegas Thunder

Little is known about this set beyond the confirmed checklist. Any additional information can be forwarded to hockeymag@beckett.com.

COMPLETE SET (30) 4.00 10.00
1 Drew Bannister .15 .40
2 Sean Berens .15 .40
3 Dampy Brar .15 .40
4 Dean Ewen .15 .40
5 Petr Franek .15 .40
6 Brad Guzda .15 .40
7 Sami Helenius .30 .75
8 Bryan Helmer .20 .50
9 Scott Hollis .15 .40
10 Kevin Kaminski .30 .75
11 Patrice Lefebvre .30 .75
12 Jason McBain .15 .40
13 Taj Melson .15 .40
14 Brad Miller .15 .40
15 Nick Naumenko .20 .50
16 Petr Nedved .30 .75
17 Trevor Roenick .20 .50
18 Russ Romaniuk .20 .50
19 Konstantin Simchuk .15 .40
20 Andrei Sryubko .15 .40
21 Stefan Ustorf .20 .50
22 Shawn Wansborough .15 .40
23 Mike Wilson .15 .40
24 Bob Strumm GM .02 .10
25 Bob Bourne CO .02 .10
26 Rod Buskas ACO .02 .10
27 Van Parfet TR .02 .10
28 Bubba Kennedy .02 .10
Richard Krouse EQ
29 BoomBoom Mascot .02 .10
30 Logo Card .02 .10

2003-04 Las Vegas Wranglers

COMPLETE SET (24) 10.00
1 Jeff Attard .50
2 Blaine Bablitz .50
3 Cam Bristow .50
4 Ryan Christie .50
5 David Cousineau .50
6 Greg Day .50
7 Deryk Engelland .50
8 Justin Kelly .50
9 Chris Kenady .50
10 Brent Krahn 1.00
11 Marc Magliarditi .75
12 Jason McBain .50
13 Mike McBain .50
14 Tom Nelson .50
15 Kevin O'Flaherty .50
16 Eric Schneider .50
17 Jonathon Shockey .50
18 Kayle Short .50
19 Riku Varjamo .50
20 Chris Wheaton .50
21 Doug Wright .50
22 Glen Gulutzan GM/CO .10
23 Mascot .10
24 Checklist .01

2003-04 Las Vegas Wranglers RBI

This set was produced by RBI Sports and was limited to 250 copies. The set numbering reflects the entire run of RBI sets that season.

COMPLETE SET (16) 15.00
225 Jeff Attard 1.00
226 Cam Bristow 1.00
227 Ryan Christie 1.00
228 David Cousineau 1.00
229 Greg Day 1.00
230 Deryk Engelland 1.00
231 Chris Kenady 1.00
232 Brent Krahn 2.00
233 Marc Magliarditi 1.50
234 Jason McBain 1.00
235 Mike McBain 1.00
236 Tom Nelson 1.00
237 Kevin O'Flaherty 1.00
238 Eric Schneider 1.00
239 Jonathon Shockey 1.00
240 Doug Wright 1.00

2004-05 Las Vegas Wranglers

COMPLETE SET (24) 20.00
1 Mike McBain 1.00
2 Jon Krall 1.00
3 Deryk Engelland 1.00
4 Jason McBain 1.00
5 Dustin Johner 1.00
6 Christian Chartier 1.00
7 Chris Stanley 1.00
8 Adam Huxley 1.00
9 Dana Lattery 1.00
10 Dan Tudin 1.00
11 Jeff Attard 1.00
12 Marc Magliarditi 1.50
13 Hegan Darby 1.00
14 Shawn Limpright 1.00
15 Darren Lynch 1.00
16 Doug Wright 1.00
17 Jason Spence 1.00
18 Sebastien Centomo 2.00
19 Ryan Gaucher 1.00
20 Glen Gulutzan CO .10
21 Drew Schoneck ACO .10
22 Joe Frederick ACO .10
23 Jeff Sharples ACO .10
24 The Duke MASCOT .10

2005-06 Las Vegas Wranglers

COMPLETE SET (25) 15.00
1 Todd Alexander .30 .75
2 Nick Anderson .30 .75
3 Thomas Bellemare .30 .75
4 Christian Chartier .30 .75
5 Steven Crampton .30 .75
6 Matt Dzieduszycki .30 .75
7 Derek Edwardson .30 .75
8 Lee Green .30 .75
9 Tim Hambly .30 .75
10 Shawn Limpright .30 .75
11 Darren Lynch .30 .75
12 Marc Magliarditi .40 1.00
13 Mike McBain .30 .75
14 Mike McKenna .30 .75
15 Chris Neiszner .30 .75
16 Sean O'Connor .30 .75
17 Adam Pardy .30 .75
18 Marco Peluso .30 .75
19 Scott Schoneck .30 .75
20 Tyler Sloan .30 .75
21 Chris Stanley .30 .75
22 Dan Tudin .30 .75
23 Glen Gulutzan CO .02 .10
24 Brent Bilodeau ACO .02 .10
25 The Duke MASCOT .02 .10

2006-07 Las Vegas Wranglers

COMPLETE SET (25)	10.00	20.00
1 Nick Anderson	.30	.75
2 Ryan Bonni	.30	.75
3 Adam Cracknell	.30	.75
4 Steve Crampton	.60	1.50
5 Kelly Czuy	.30	.75
6 Ryan Donally	.30	.75
7 Derek Edwardson	.30	.75
8 Jason Jozsa	.30	.75
9 Jason Krischuk	.30	.75
10 Shawn Limpright	.30	.75
11 Marc Magliarditi	.60	1.50
12 Mike McBain	.30	.75
13 Mike McKenna	.30	.75
14 Arpad Mihaly	.30	.75
15 Tyler Mosienko	.30	.75
16 Kevin Nastiuk	.60	1.50
17 Chris Neiszner	.30	.75
18 Marco Peluso	.30	.75
19 Aaron Power	.30	.75
20 Scott Schoneck	.30	.75
21 Aki Seitsonen	.30	.75
22 Joe Tallari	.30	.75
23 Bryce Thoma	.30	.75
24 Brent Bilodeau ACO	.10	.25
25 Glen Gulutzan CO	.10	.25

1951-52 Laval Dairy Lac St. Jean

The 1951-52 Laval Dairy Lac St. Jean set includes 59 green-and-white tinted cards measuring approximately 1 3/4" by 2 1/2". The backs are blank. The cards are numbered on the front.

COMPLETE SET (59)	750.00	1500.00
1 Eddy Daoust	25.00	50.00
2 Guy Gareau	20.00	40.00
3 Gilles Desrosiers	20.00	40.00
4 Robert Desbiens	20.00	40.00
5 James Hayes	20.00	40.00
6 Paul Gagnon	20.00	40.00
7 Gerry Perreault	20.00	40.00
8 Marcel Dufour	20.00	40.00
9 Armand Bourdon	20.00	40.00
10 Jean-Marc Pichette	25.00	50.00
11 Gerry Gagnon	20.00	40.00
12 Jules Racette	20.00	40.00
13 Real Marcotte	20.00	40.00
14 Gerry Theberge	20.00	40.00
15 Rene Harvey	20.00	40.00
16 Joseph Lacoursiere	20.00	40.00
17 Fernand Benaquez	20.00	40.00
18 Andre Boisvert	20.00	40.00
19 Claude Chretien	20.00	40.00
20 Norbert Clark	20.00	40.00
21 Sylvio Lambert	20.00	40.00
22 Lucien Roy	20.00	40.00
23 Gerard Audet	20.00	40.00
24 Jacques Lalancette	20.00	40.00
25 Maurice St.Jean	20.00	40.00
26 Camille Lupien	20.00	40.00
27 Rodrigue Pelchat	20.00	40.00
28 Conrad L'Heureux	20.00	40.00
29 Paul Tremblay	20.00	40.00
30 Robert Vincent	20.00	40.00
31 Charles Lamirande	20.00	40.00
32 Leon Gaudreault	20.00	40.00
33 Maurice Thiffault	20.00	40.00
34 Marc-Aurele Tremblay	20.00	40.00
35 Rene Pronovost	20.00	40.00
36 Victor Corbin	20.00	40.00
37 Tiny Tamminen	25.00	50.00
38 Guildor Levesque	20.00	40.00
39 Gaston Lamirande	20.00	40.00
40 Guy Gervais	20.00	40.00
41 Rayner Makila	25.00	50.00
42 Jules Tremblay	20.00	40.00
43 Roland Girard	20.00	40.00
44 Germain Bergeron	20.00	40.00
45 Paul Duchesne	20.00	40.00
46 Roger Beaudoin	20.00	40.00
47 Georges Archibal	20.00	40.00
48 Claude Basque	20.00	40.00
49 Roger Sarda	20.00	40.00
50 Edgard Gendron	20.00	40.00
51 Gaston Labossiere	20.00	40.00
52 Roland Clantara	20.00	40.00
53 Florian Gravel	20.00	40.00
54 Jean-Guy Thompson	20.00	40.00
55 Yvan Forton	20.00	40.00
56 Yves Laporte	20.00	40.00
57 Claude Germain	20.00	40.00
58 Gerry Brunet	20.00	40.00
59 Maurice Courteau	25.00	50.00

1951-52 Laval Dairy QSHL

The 1951-52 Laval Dairy QSHL set includes 109 black and white blank-back cards measuring approximately 1 3/4" by 2 1/2". These cards were issued in the province of Quebec and the Ottawa region. The cards are numbered and dated on the front. Key cards in this set are "Pre-Rookie Cards" of Jean Beliveau and Jacques Plante. The card numbering is organized by team as follows: Aces de Quebec (1-18 and 37), Chicoutimi (19-36), Sherbrooke (38-51), Shawinigan Falls (52-67), Valleyfield (68-84), Royals de Montreal (85-100), and Ottawa (101-109).

COMPLETE SET (109)	1000.00	2000.00
1 Jean Beliveau	375.00	750.00
2 Jean Marois	5.00	10.00
3 Joe Crozier	12.50	25.00
4 Jack Gelineau	5.00	10.00
5 Murdo McKay	6.00	12.00
6 Arthur Leyte	5.00	10.00
7 W.(Bill) Leblanc	5.00	10.00
8 Robert Hayes	5.00	10.00
9 Yogi Kraiger	6.00	12.00
10 Frank King	5.00	10.00
11 Ludger Tremblay	6.00	12.00
12 Jackie Leclair	20.00	40.00
13 Martial Pruneau	5.00	10.00
14 Armand Gaudreault	5.00	10.00
15 Marcel Bonin	20.00	40.00
16 Herbie Carnegie	37.50	75.00
17 Claude Robert	5.00	10.00
18 Phil Renaud	5.00	10.00
19 Roland Hebert	5.00	10.00
20 Donat Duschene	5.00	10.00
21 Jacques Gagnon	5.00	10.00
22 Normand Dussault	6.00	12.00
23 Stan Smrke	10.00	20.00
24 Louis Smrke	6.00	12.00
25 Floyd Crawford	5.00	10.00
26 Germain Leger	5.00	10.00
27 Delphis Franche	5.00	10.00
28 Dick Wray	5.00	10.00
29 Guildor Levesque	7.50	15.00
30 Georges Roy	5.00	10.00
31 J.P. Lamirande	5.00	10.00
32 Gerard Glaude	5.00	10.00
33 Marcel Pelletier	10.00	20.00
34 Pete Tkachuck	5.00	10.00
35 Sherman White	5.00	10.00
36 Jimmy Moore	5.00	10.00
37 Punch Imlach	50.00	100.00
38 Alex Sandalax	5.00	10.00
39 William Kyle	5.00	10.00
40 Kenneth Biggs	5.00	10.00
41 Peter Wright	5.00	10.00
42 Rene Pepin	5.00	10.00
43 Tod Campeau	6.00	12.00
44 John Smith	5.00	10.00
45 Thomas McDougall	5.00	10.00
46 Jos. Lepine	5.00	10.00
47 Guy Labrie	5.00	10.00
48 Roger Bessette	5.00	10.00
49 Yvan Dugre	6.00	12.00
50 James Planche	5.00	10.00
51 Nils Tremblay	5.00	10.00
52 Bill MacDonagh	5.00	10.00
53 Georges Ouellet	5.00	10.00
54 Billy Arcand	5.00	10.00
55 Johnny Mahaffy	6.00	12.00
56 Bucky Buchanan	10.00	20.00
57 Al Miller	5.00	10.00
58 Don Penniston	5.00	10.00
59 Spike Laliberte	5.00	10.00
60 Ernie Oakley	5.00	10.00
61 Jack Bownass	5.00	10.00
62 Ted Hodgson	5.00	10.00
63 Lyall Wiseman	5.00	10.00
64 Erwin Grosse	5.00	10.00
65 Mel Read	5.00	10.00
66 Lloyd Henchberger	5.00	10.00
67 Jack Taylor	5.00	10.00
68 Marcel Bessette	5.00	10.00
69 Jack Schmidt	5.00	10.00
70 Paul Saindon	5.00	10.00
71 J.P. Bisaillon	5.00	10.00
72 Eddie Redmond	5.00	10.00
73 Larry Kwong	10.00	20.00
74 Andre Corriveau	5.00	10.00
75 Kitoute Joanette	5.00	10.00
76 Toe Blake	75.00	150.00
77 Georges Bougie	5.00	10.00
78 Jack Irvine	5.00	10.00
79 Paul Larivee	5.00	10.00
80 Paul Leclerc	5.00	10.00
81 Bertrand Bourassa	5.00	10.00
82 Jacques Deslauriers	5.00	10.00
83 Bingo Ernst	5.00	10.00
84 Gaston Gervais	5.00	10.00
85 Gerry Plamondon	6.00	12.00
86 Glen Harmon	5.00	10.00
87 Bob Friday	5.00	10.00
88 Rolland Rousseau	5.00	10.00
89 Billy Goold	5.00	10.00
90 Lloyd Finkbeiner	5.00	10.00
91 Cliff Malone	5.00	10.00
92 Jacques Plante	375.00	750.00
93 Gerard Desaulniers	6.00	12.00
94 Arthur Rose	5.00	10.00
95 Jacques Locas	5.00	10.00
96 Walter Clune	5.00	10.00
97 Louis Denis	5.00	10.00
98 Fernand Perreault	5.00	10.00
99 Douglas McNeil	6.00	12.00
100 Les Douglas	5.00	10.00
101 Howard Riopelle	10.00	20.00
102 Vic Grigg	5.00	10.00
103 Bobby Roberts	5.00	10.00
104 Legs Fraser	5.00	10.00
105 Butch Stahan	5.00	10.00
106 Fritz Frazer	5.00	10.00
107 Bill Robinson	5.00	10.00
108 Eddie Emberg	5.00	10.00
109 Leo Gravelle	12.50	25.00

1951-52 Laval Dairy Subset

The 1951-52 Laval Dairy Subset includes 66 skip-numbered black and white blank-back cards measuring approximately 1 3/4" by 2 1/2". Apparently, this set was intended to update the QSHL set and was issued after the QSHL set perhaps even as late as the 1952-53 season. The card numbering is organized by team as follows: Aces de Quebec (7-15 and 117), Chicoutimi (25-38), Sherbrooke (39-57), Shawinigan Falls (59-67, 89-90, 94-95, 115, 118, and 120), Valleyfield (68-84 and 116), Royals de Montreal (85-86, 92-93, and 96-97), and Ottawa (98-114, 119, and 121).

COMPLETE SET (66)	750.00	1500.00
4 Jack Gelineau SP	25.00	50.00
7 Al Miller	10.00	20.00
8 Walter Pawlyshyn	10.00	20.00
9 Yogi Kraiger SP	25.00	50.00
10 Al Baccari	10.00	20.00
12 Denis Smith	10.00	20.00
13 Pierre Brillant	10.00	20.00
14 Frank Mario	10.00	20.00
15 Danny Nixon	10.00	20.00
25 Leon Bouchard	10.00	20.00
26 Pete Taillefer	10.00	20.00
29 Bucky Buchanan	12.50	25.00
36 Marius Groleau	10.00	20.00
38 Fernand Perreault	10.00	20.00
39 Robert Drainville	10.00	20.00
40 Ronnie Matthews	10.00	20.00
44 Roger Roberge	10.00	20.00
46 Pete Wywrot	10.00	20.00
50 Gilles Dube	10.00	20.00
51 Nils Tremblay SP	25.00	50.00
52 Bob Pepin	10.00	20.00
53 Dewar Thompson	10.00	20.00
55 Irene St.Hilaire	10.00	20.00
56 Martial Pruneau	10.00	20.00
57 Jacques Locas	10.00	20.00
59 Nelson Podolsky	10.00	20.00
60 Bert Giesebrecht	10.00	20.00
61 Steve Brklaicich	10.00	20.00
65 Jack Hamilton	10.00	20.00
66 Dave Gatherum	10.00	20.00
67 Jean-Marie Plante	10.00	20.00
68 Gordie Haworth	12.50	25.00
69 Jack Schmidt SP	25.00	50.00
70 Bruce Cline	12.50	25.00
72 Phil Vitale	10.00	20.00
81 Carl Smelle	10.00	20.00
84 Tom Smelle	10.00	20.00
85 Gerry Plamondon	12.50	25.00
86 Glen Harmon	10.00	20.00
89 Frank Bathgate	10.00	20.00
90 Bernie Lemonde	10.00	20.00
92 Jacques Plante	375.00	750.00
93 Gerard Desaulniers	10.00	20.00
94 J.C. Lebrun	10.00	20.00
95 Bob Leger	10.00	20.00
96 Walter Clune	10.00	20.00
97 Louis Denis	10.00	20.00
98 Jackie Leclair	15.00	30.00
99 John Arundel	10.00	20.00
100 Leslie(Les) Douglas	10.00	20.00
103 Bobby Robertson	10.00	20.00
104 Ray Fredericks	10.00	20.00
106 Emile Dagenais	10.00	20.00
108 Al Kuntz	10.00	20.00
110 Red Johnson	10.00	20.00
111 John O'Flaherty	10.00	20.00
112 Jack Giesebrecht	12.50	25.00
113 Bill Richardson	10.00	20.00
114 Bep Guidolin	20.00	40.00
115 Roger Bedard	10.00	20.00
116 Renald Lacroix	10.00	20.00
117 Gordie Hudson	10.00	20.00
118 Dick Wray	10.00	20.00
119 Ronnie Hurst	10.00	20.00
120 Eddie Joss	10.00	20.00
121 Lyall Wiseman	10.00	20.00

1988-89 Lethbridge Hurricanes

This 24-card set was issued in 12 strips of three perforated cards with the third card on each strip being an ad or coupon card. The strips measure approximately 7 1/2" by 3 1/2". The fronts feature color posed player photos with a heavy black line framing the edge of the card leaving white space between the line and the picture. The team name, player's name, jersey number, and position appear in the white margin at the bottom. The cards are unnumbered and checklisted below in alphabetical order.

COMPLETE SET (24)	4.80	12.00
1 Mark Bassen	.20	.50
2 Pete Berthelsen	.20	.50
3 Bryan Bosch	.20	.50
4 Paul Checknita	.20	.50
5 Kelly Ens	.20	.50
6 Jeff Ferguson	.30	.75
7 Scott Fukami	.20	.50
8 Colin Gregor	.20	.50
9 Mark Greig	.30	.75
10 Rob Hale	.20	.50
11 Ted Hutchings	.20	.50
12 Dusty Imoo	.30	.75
13 Ivan Jessey	.20	.50
14 Mark Kuntz	.20	.50
15 Corey Lyons	.20	.50
16 Shane Mazutinec	.20	.50
17 Casey McMillan	.20	.50
18 Pat Pylypuik	.20	.50
19 Brad Rubachuk	.20	.50
20 Jason Ruff	.30	.75
21 Chad Seibel	.20	.50
22 Wes Walz	.60	1.50
23 Jim Wheatcroft	.20	.50
24 Team Picture	.20	.50

1989-90 Lethbridge Hurricanes

Showing signs of perforation, this 24-card set was issued in strips of several cards each. The cards measure the standard size when separated and feature posed, color player photos. The photos are set on a white card face with a heavy black line framing the edge of the card, leaving white space between the line and the picture. The player's name, jersey number, and position appear in the white margin at the bottom. The backs carry "Tips from the Hurricanes," which are hockey tips and public service messages. The cards are unnumbered and checklisted below in alphabetical order.

COMPLETE SET (24)	8.00	20.00
1 Doug Barrault	.30	.75
2 Peter Berthelsen	.30	.75
3 Bryan Bosch	.30	.75
4 Kelly Ens	.30	.75
5 Mark Greig	.30	.75
6 Ron Gunville	.30	.75
7 Rob Hale	.30	.75
8 Neil Hawryluk	.30	.75
9 David Holzer	.30	.75
10 Dusty Imoo	.60	1.50
11 Darcy Kaminski ACO	.08	.25
12 Bob Loucks CO	.08	.25
13 Corey Lyons	.30	.75
14 Duane Maruschak	.30	.75
15 Jamie McLennan	1.25	3.00
16 Shane Peacock	.30	.75
17 Pat Pylypuik	.30	.75
18 Gary Reilly	.30	.75
19 Brad Rubachuk	.30	.75
20 Jason Ruff	.30	.75
21 Kevin St. Jacques	.30	.75
22 Wes Walz	.60	1.50
23 Darcy Werenka	.40	1.00
24 Brad Zimmer	.30	.75

1993-94 Lethbridge Hurricanes

This 24-card set was issued on three-card perforated strips each consisting of two player cards and one advertisement or coupon card. The strips measure 7 1/2" by 3 1/2", and if cut, the individual cards would measure the standard size. The fronts of each card feature a color posed player photo with thin red borders on a white background. The cards are unnumbered and checklisted below in alphabetical order.

COMPLETE SET (24)	4.80	12.00
1 Rob Daum CO	.08	.25
2 Kirk DeWaele	.20	.50
3 Derek Diener	.20	.50
4 Scott Grieco	.20	.50
5 David Jesiolowski	.20	.50
6 Todd MacIsaac	.20	.50
7 Stan Matwijiw	.40	1.00
8 Larry McMorran	.20	.50
9 Brad Mehalko	.20	.50
10 Shane Peacock	.20	.50
11 Randy Perry	.20	.50
12 Domenic Pittis	.30	.75
12 Byron Ritchie	.25	.60
14 Bryce Salvador	.40	1.00
15 Ryan Smith	.20	.50
16 Lee Sorochan	.30	.75
17 Mark Szoke	.20	.50
18 Scott Townsend	.20	.50
19 David Trofimenkoff	.20	.50
20 Twister (Mascot)	.02	.10
21 Ivan Vologjaninov	.20	.50
22 Jason Widmer	.20	.50
23 Derek Wood	.20	.50
24 Aaron Zarowny	.20	.50

1995-96 Lethbridge Hurricanes

This 25-card set was issued on three-card perforated strips measuring approximately 7 1/2" by 3 1/2". Each strip consists of two player cards and one advertisement card. The cards include player jersey numbers on the front, but are checklisted below alphabetically.

COMPLETE SET (25)	8.00	20.00
1 Mike Bayrack	.40	1.00
2 John Bradley	.40	1.00
3 Travis Brigley	.40	1.00
4 David Brumby	.40	1.00
5 Derek Diener	.40	1.00
6 Scott Grieco	.40	1.00
7 Lee Hamilton	.40	1.00
8 Trevor Hanas	.40	1.00
9 Ryan Hoople	.40	1.00
10 Mike Josephson	.40	1.00
11 Kirby Law	.40	1.00
12 Bryan Maxwell CO	.02	.10
13 Doyle McMorris	.40	1.00
14 Brad Mehalko	.40	1.00
15 Dennis Mullen	.40	1.00
16 Jiri Novotny	.40	1.00
17 Mike O'Grady	.40	1.00
18 Randy Perry	.40	1.00
19 Byron Ritchie	.40	1.00
20 Bryce Salvador	.60	1.50
21 Darren Shakotko	.40	1.00
22 Mark Smith	.40	1.00
23 Dave Taylor	.40	1.00
24 Luc Theoret	.40	1.00
25 Windy MASCOT	.02	.10

1996-97 Lethbridge Hurricanes

This 24-card set features color player photos with the club's nickname serving as a design element along the right border. The player's name and number, along with the team's anniversary logo also are featured. The unnumbered cards are checklisted below alphabetically.

COMPLETE SET (24)	4.80	12.00
1 Travis Brigley	.20	.50
2 David Cameron	.20	.50
3 Matt Demarski	.20	.50
4 Paul Elliott	.20	.50
5 Jason Hegberg	.20	.50
6 Martin Hohenberger	.20	.50
7 Ryan Hoople	.20	.50
8 Mark Ivan	.20	.50
9 Mike Josephson	.20	.50
10 Kirby Law	.30	.75
11 Mike O'Grady	.20	.50
12 Dale Purinton	.75	2.00
13 Byron Ritchie	.30	.75
14 Bryce Salvador	.30	.75
15 Richard Seeley	.20	.50
16 Cam Severson	.20	.50
17 Darren Shakotko	.20	.50
18 Wes Schneider	.20	.50
19 Parry Shockey CO Bryan Maxwell GM	.08	.25
20 Mark Smith	.20	.50
21 Dave Taylor	.20	.50
22 Luc Theoret	.20	.50
23 Evgeni Tsybouk	.25	.60
24 Shane Yellowhorn	.20	.50

1997-98 Lethbridge Hurricanes

This set features the Hurricanes of the WHL. Little else is known about this set beyond the confirmed checklist. Additional information can be forwarded to hockeymag@beckett.com.

COMPLETE SET (25)	4.80	12.00
1 Derrick Atkinson	.20	.50
2 Brady Block	.20	.50
3 Scott Borders	.20	.50
4 Jeff Church	.20	.50
5 Jason Hegberg	.20	.50
6 Derek Holland	.20	.50
7 Curtis Huppe	.20	.50
8 Dustin Kazak	.20	.50
9 Chad Kletzel	.20	.50
10 Vladislav Klochkov	.20	.50
11 Charlie Mattersdorfer	.20	.50
12 Jason McLean	.20	.50
13 Sean Robertson	.20	.50
14 Bart Rushmer	.20	.50
15 Thomas Scantlebury	.20	.50
16 Darren Shakotko	.20	.50
17 Mark Smith	.40	1.00
18 Shaun Sutter	.40	1.00
19 Luc Theoret	.20	.50
20 Kaleb Toth	.20	.50
21 Evgeni Tsybouk	.30	.75
22 Mike Varhaug	.20	.50
23 Trevor Wasyluk	.20	.50
24 Shane Willis	.40	1.00
25 Lethbridge Power	.02	.10

1999-00 Lethbridge Hurricanes

This set features the Hurricanes of the WHL. The set was produced by the team and sold at home games. The cards are unnumbered, and thus are listed alphabetically.

COMPLETE SET (25)	4.80	12.00
1 Derek Atkinson	.20	.50
2 Brian Ballman	.20	.50
3 Nathan Barrett	.20	.50
4 Brady Block	.30	.75
5 Scott Borders	.20	.50
6 Phil Cole	.20	.50
7 Radek Duda	.30	.75
8 Simon Ferguson	.20	.50
9 Jordon Flodell	.20	.50
10 Eric Godard	.30	.75
11 Jason Hegberg	.20	.50
12 Brandon Janes	.20	.50
13 Ryan Jorde	.20	.50
14 Dustin Kazak	.20	.50
15 Angel Krstev	.20	.50
16 Petr Kudrna	.20	.50
17 Darren Lynch	.20	.50
18 Warren McCutheon	.20	.50
19 Justin Ossachuk	.20	.50
20 Derek Parker	.20	.50
21 Brian Patterson	.20	.50
22 Derrick Ruck	.20	.50
23 Thomas Scantlebury	.20	.50
24 Eric Sonnenberg	.20	.50
25 Chad Yaremko	.20	.50

2000-01 Lethbridge Hurricanes

This set features the Hurricanes of the WHL. The set was produced by the team and sold at home games.

COMPLETE SET (25)	4.80	40.00
1 Brian Ballman	.20	1.50
2 Nathan Barrett	.40	5.00
3 Scott Borders	.20	1.50
4 Phil Cole	.20	1.50
5 Simon Ferguson	.20	1.50
6 Matt Fetzner	.20	1.50
7 Mark Forth	.20	1.50
8 Tim Green	.20	1.50
9 Matt Jacques	.20	1.50
10 Adam Johnson	.20	1.50
11 Andrew Jungwirth	.20	1.50
12 Tomas Kopecky	.30	5.00
13 Ryley Layden	.20	1.50
14 Darren Lynch	.20	1.50
15 Joel Martin	.30	2.00
16 Warren McCutcheon	.20	1.50
17 Brett O'Malley	.20	1.50
18 Brian Patterson	.20	1.50
19 Martin Podlesak	.30	2.00
20 Derek Ruck	.20	1.50
21 Thomas Scantlebury	.20	1.50
22 Blake Ward	.30	2.00
23 Twister MASCOT	.04	.10
24 Header Card	.04	.01
25 Sponsor Card		.01

2001-02 Lethbridge Hurricanes

COMPLETE SET (23)		12.00
1 Matthew Berger		.50
2 Simon Ferguson		.50
3 Stewart Thiessen		.50
4 Tim Green		.50
5 Braden Appleby		.50
6 Tomas Kopecky		.75
7 Paul McBrien		.50
8 Nathan Barrett		.75
9 Martin Podlesak		.50
10 Kris Callaway		.50
11 Brian Patterson		.50
12 Ryley Layden		.50
13 D.J. King		.50
14 Logan Koopmans		.75
15 Brett O'Malley		.50
16 Scott Borders		.50
17 David Selthun		.50
18 Clay Plume		.50
19 Blake Ward		.50
20 Brent Seabrook		.50
21 Jeremy Jackson		.50
22 Nick Chibi		.50
23 Tyrell Moulton		.50

2003-04 Lethbridge Hurricanes

We have confirmed a handful of singles from this set, thanks to collector Vinnie Montalbano. If you have any other information about this set, please email us at hockeymag@beckett.com.

COMPLETE SET (?)		
1 Joel Andresen		
2 John Lammers		
3 Jake Riddle		
4 Brent Seabrook		
5 Nick Tarnasky		
6 Kris Versteeg	2.00	5.00

2004-05 Lethbridge Hurricanes

Cards are not numbered.

COMPLETE SET (24)		25.00
1 Mark Ashton		1.00
2 Shawn Mezei		1.00
3 Brennan Chapman		1.00
4 Brent Seabrook		1.00
5 Tyler Redenbach		1.00
6 Kris Versteeg	2.00	5.00
7 Mark Olafson		1.00
8 John Lammers		1.00
9 Martin Ruzicka		1.00
10 Colton Yellow Horn		1.50
11 Kyle Pess		1.00
12 Michael Kaye		1.00
13 Kenny Petkau		1.00
14 Jon Filewich		1.00
15 Chase Hentuik		1.00
16 Neil Rodman		1.00
17 Rob Klinkhammer		1.00
18 Michal Gulasi		1.00
19 Mike Ulrich		1.00
20 Lenny Thunderchild		1.00
21 Jesse Dudas		1.00
22 Aaron Sorochan		1.50
23 Scott Bolland		1.50
24 MASCOT		.10

2005-06 Lethbridge Hurricanes

COMPLETE SET (24)	8.00	20.00
1 Mark Ashton	.40	1.00
2 Andrew Bentz	.40	1.00
3 Zach Boychuk	.40	1.00
4 Ryan Bryce	.40	1.00
5 Mike Cann	.40	1.00
6 Jacob Dietrich	.40	1.00
7 Mitch Fadden	.40	1.00
8 Tayfar Farmanara	.40	1.00
9 Kris Hogg	.40	1.00
10 Michael Kaye	.40	1.00
11 Ryan Kerr	.40	1.00
12 Dwight King	.40	1.00
13 Randy King	.40	1.00
14 Tomas Kudelka	.40	1.00
15 Justin Leclerc	.40	1.00
16 Gavin McHale	.40	1.00
17 Mark Olafson	.40	1.00
18 Isaac Reid	.40	1.00
19 Brad Riege	.40	1.00
20 Roman Wick	.40	1.00
21 Ben Wright	.40	1.00
22 Michael Wuchterl	.40	1.00
23 Colton Yellowhorn	.75	2.00
24 Twister MASCOT	.02	.10

2003-04 Lewiston Maineiacs

COMPLETE SET (28)	12.00	20.00
1 Mathieu Aubin	.30	.75
2 Gabriel Balasescu	.30	.75
3 Vladislav Balaz	.30	.75
4 Alex Bourret	.60	1.50
5 Marc-Andre Cliché	.60	1.50
6 Nicolas Cowan	.30	.75
7 Matthew Davis	.30	.75
8 Chad Denny	.30	.75
9 Pierre-Luc Faubert	.30	.75
10 Karl Fournier	.30	.75
11 Bobby Gates	.30	.75
12 Olivier Legault	.30	.75
13 Travis Mealey	.30	.75
14 Ryan Murphy	.30	.75
15 Jonathan Paiement	.30	.75
16 Alexandre Picard	.75	2.00
17 Brandon Roach	.30	.75
18 Maxime Robert	.30	.75
19 Richard Stehlik	.30	.75
20 Francis Trudel	.30	.75
21 Kevin Turgeon	.30	.75
22 Brandon Verge	.30	.75
23 Sheldon Wenzel	.30	.75
24 Mario Durocher CO	.02	.10
25 Jeff Guay ACO	.02	.10
26 Ed Harding ACO	.02	.10
27 Lewy MASCOT	.02	.10
28 Team Photo/CL	.10	.25

2002-03 Lexington Men O'War

COMPLETE SET (26)	20.00
1 Team Photo	.50
2 Jim Wiley	.75
3 Justin Van Parys	.75
4 Mike Smith	.75
5 Marc-Andre Thinel	.75
6 Jared Smyth	.75
7 Jesse Cook	.75
8 Ben Storey	.75
9 Mark Smith	1.50
10 Dan Murphy	1.50
11 Daryl Moor	.75
12 Alexander Mathieu	.75
13 Dominic Periard	.75
14 Chris Dirkes	.75
15 Van Burgess	.75
16 Fraser Clair	.75
17 Terry Craven	.75
18 Brett Draney	.75
19 Joe Vandermeer	.75
20 Aaron Miskovich	.75
21 Jay Banach	.75
22 Ryan Fultz	.75
23 Mike Sgroi	.75
24 Josh Mizerek	.75
25 Kevin Knopp	.75
26 Mow MASCOT	.10

2000-01 Lincoln Stars

This set featured the Lincoln Stars of the USHL. Cards are numbered XX of 28 on the card backs.

COMPLETE SET (28)	
1 Nick Fouts	.75
2 Ken Scruderi	.40
3 Tom Watkins	.40
4 Andy Schneider	.40
5 Matt Wavra	.40
6 Chris Fournier	.40
7 Mike Fournier	.40
8 John Snowden	.40
9 Nick Fuher	.40
10 Preston Callander	.40
11 Bobby John Byluglien	.40
12 Josh Magnuson	.40
13 Brandon Polich	.40
14 Chad Hontvet	.40
15 Billy Hengen	.40
16 Ryan Young	.40
17 Matthew Trojovsky	.40
18 Lee Marvin	.40
19 Brandon Bochenski	.40
20 Trevor Frischmon	.40
21 Marco Peluso	.40
22 Jake Brandt	.75
23 Justin Johnson	.75
24 Beau Fritz	.75
25 Steve Johnson HCO	.10
26 Steve Ross ACO	.10
27 Corey Courtney TR	.10
28 Mascot	.10

2001-02 Lincoln Stars

This 28-card set features the Lincoln Stars of the USHL.

COMPLETE SET (28)	12.00
1 Ben Assenmacher	.50
2 David Backes	.50
3 Josh Budish	.50
4 Jamie Dowhatko	.50
5 Mike Eickman	.50
6 Luke Erickson	.50
7 Matt Erickson	.50
8 Mike Fournier	.50
9 Trevor Frischmon	.50
10 Beau Fritz	.75
11 Ethan Graham	.50
12 Billy Hengen	.50
13 Chad Hontvet	.50
14 Dan Irmen	.50
15 Patrick Knutson	.50
16 Philippe Lamoureux	.75
17 Lee Marvin	.50
18 T.J. McElroy	.50
19 Ryan Potulny	.50
20 John Snowden	.50
21 Dirk Southern	.50
22 Ryan Swanson	.50
23 Matt Wavra	.50
24 Nate Ziegelmann	.75
25 Steve Johnson HCO	.10
26 Mark Pivetz ACO	.10
27 Corey Courtney TR	.10
28 Mascot	.10

2002-03 Lincoln Stars

This series was issued in two parts. Cards 31-48 were issued as a supplemental set.

COMPLETE SET (48)	20.00
1 Philippe Lamoureux	.50
2 Ethan Graham	.50
3 David Backes	.50
4 Mike Eickman	.50
5 Chris Porter	.50
6 Ryan Potulny	.50
7 Danny Irmen	.50
8 Mike Fournier	.50
9 Tyler Magura	.50
10 John Snowden	.50
11 Ben Gordon	.50
12 Jamison Orr	.50
13 Mick Berge	.50
14 Mike Nesdill	.50
15 Brent Borgen	.50
16 Matt Hayek	.50
17 David Carlisle	.50
18 Luke Erickson	.50
19 Jesse Lindenberg	.50
20 Keith Rodger	.50
21 Robbie Bina	.50
22 Joel Gasper	.50
23 Ross Cherry	.50
24 Nate Ziegelmann	.50
25 Steve Johnson	.50
26 Mark Pivetz	.50
27 Rob Facca	.50
28 Corey Courtney	.50
29 Starzan MASCOT	.10
30 Checklist	.01
31 Mark Schwamberger	.50
32 Jeff McFarland	.50
33 Per Mars	.50
34 David Backes AS	.50
35 Chris Porter AS	.50
36 Ryan Potulny AS	.50
37 Dan Irmen AS	.50
38 John Snowden AS	.50
39 Nate Ziegelmann AS	.50
40 Philippe Lamoureux	.50
41 Ethan Graham	.50
42 David Backes	.50
43 Mike Eickman	.50
44 Ryan Potulny	.50
45 Dan Irmen	.50
46 John Snowden	.50
47 Nate Ziegelmann	.50
48 Update Checklist	.10

2003-04 Lincoln Stars

COMPLETE SET (29)	12.00
1 Philippe Lamoureux	.50
2 Morgan Simonson	.50
3 Kaj Kallarsson	.50
4 Jared Boll	.50
5 Evan Rankin	.50
6 Nick Tuzzolino	.50
7 Garrett Raboin	.50
8 Tyler Magura	.50
9 Ben Gordon	.50
10 Mick Berge	.50
11 Michael Nesdill	.50
12 Brent Borgen	.50
13 Alexcei McAvoy	.50
14 Matt Hayek	.50
15 David Carlisle	.50
16 Andrew Guyer	.50
17 Jesse Lindenberg	.50
18 Chris Tarkir	.50
19 Keith Rodger	.50
20 Adam Bartholomay	.50

21 Michael Waidlich .50
22 Dan Comrie .50
23 Aaron Walski .50
24 Aaron McCloy .50
25 Steve Johnson CO .10
26 Rob Facca ACO .10
27 Corey Courtney TR .01
28 Mascot .10
29 Checklist .01

2003-04 Lincoln Stars Update

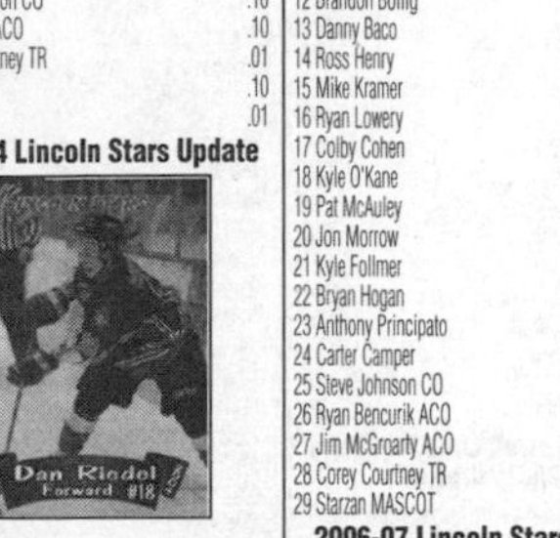

COMPLETE SET (18) 3.00 8.00
30 Checklist .02 .10
31 John Vadnais .20 .50
32 Dan Riedel .20 .50
33 Derek Whitmore .20 .50
34 Jered Bye .20 .50
35 Chris Robinson .20 .50
36 John Swanson .20 .50
37 Matt Weir .20 .50
38 Checklist .02 .10
39 Philippe Lamoureux/Tyler Magura .20 .50
40 Ben Gordon/Mick Berge .20 .50
41 Mike Nesdill/Brent Borgen .20 .50
42 Matt Hayek/David Carlisle .20 .50
43 Philippe Lamoureux RB .20 .50
44 Philippe Lamoureux AS .20 .50
45 Evan Rankin AS .20 .50
46 Nick Tuzzolino AS .20 .50
47 David Carlisle AS .20 .50

2004-05 Lincoln Stars

This USHL set was sold at home games. Reportedly, there were certified autographs included in some sets. We have yet to confirm their existence. If you can help, write us at hockeymag@beckett.com.

COMPLETE SET (30) 12.00
1 Jordan Pearce 1.00
2 Brian Bina .50
3 John Vadnais .50
4 Jared Boll 1.00
5 Dillon Duncan .50
6 Dan Riedel .50
7 Garrett Raboin .50
8 Erik Condra .50
9 Eli Vlaisavljevich .50
10 J.J. Koehler .50
11 Ryan Hohl .50
12 Shawn Gawrys .50
13 Chris Nugent .50
14 David Carlisle .50
15 Mike Kramer .50
16 Mick Berge .50
17 Tom Sawatske .50
18 Brock Trotter .50
19 Chris Robinson .50
20 John Swanson .50
21 Steve Jakiel .50
22 Patrik Valcak .50
23 Linus Klasen .50
24 Steve Johnson CO .10
25 Ryan Bencurik ACO .10
26 Derek Reynolds ACO .10
27 Corey Courtney TR .10
28 Starzan MASCOT .10
29 Checklist .01
30 contest card

2004-05 Lincoln Stars Update

Issued on Feb. 21, 2005 as an update to the team set issued earlier in the season. It has been reported that just 350 copies of the Update series were produced. The set is noteworthy for the inclusion of Brian Lee, the ninth overall pick in 2005.

COMPLETE SET (18) 12.00
31 Brian Lee 4.00
32 Kyle Hardwick .50
33 Chris Vande Velde 1.00
34 Russ Sinkewich .50
35 Ryan Salvis .50
36 Chris Murphy .50
37 Ryan Kelly .50
38 Taylor Raszka .50
39 Jared Boll 1.00
40 Dan Riedel .50
41 Garrett Raboin .50
42 David Carlisle .50
43 Mick Berge .50
44 Chris Robinson .50
45 Jordan Pearce AS 1.00
46 Jared Boll AS 1.00
47 Dan Riedel AS .50
48 Tom Sawatske AS .50

2006-07 Lincoln Stars

COMPLETE SET (29) 10.00 18.00
1 Lincoln Stars .10 .25
2 David Brack .30 .75
3 Chad Langlais .30 .75
4 Rick Carden .30 .75
5 Eric Lake .30 .75
6 Chris Stansik .30 .75
7 Jared Brown .30 .75
8 Matt Bartkowski .30 .75
9 Stephen Schultz .30 .75
10 Ryan Ruikka .30 .75
11 Jason Gregoire .40 1.00
12 Brandon Bollig .30 .75
13 Danny Baco .30 .75
14 Ross Henry .30 .75
15 Mike Kramer .30 .75
16 Ryan Lowery .30 .75
17 Colby Cohen .30 .75
18 Kyle O'Kane .30 .75
19 Pat McAuley .30 .75
20 Jon Morrow .40 1.00
21 Kyle Follmer .30 .75
22 Bryan Hogan .40 1.00
23 Anthony Principato .30 .75
24 Carter Camper .30 .75
25 Steve Johnson CO .10 .25
26 Ryan Bencurik ACO .02 .10
27 Jim McGroarty ACO .02 .10
28 Corey Courtney TR .02 .10
29 Starzan MASCOT .02 .10

2006-07 Lincoln Stars Traded

COMPLETE SET (18) 5.00 12.00
1T Checklist .02 .10
2T Patrick Johnson .30 .75
3T Joey Miller .30 .75
4T J.J Crew .30 .75
5T Mike Hull .30 .75
6T Dan Lawson .30 .75
7T Bryce Christianson .30 .75
8T Chad Langlais .30 .75
9T Chris Stansik .30 .75
10T Jared Brown .30 .75
11T Brandon Bollig .30 .75
12T Danny Baco .30 .75
13T Mike Kramer .30 .75
14T Bryan Hogan .30 .75
15T Chad Langlais .30 .75
16T Stephen Schultz .30 .75
17T Colby Cohen .30 .75
18T Carter Camper .40 1.00

2006-07 Lincoln Stars Upper Deck Signature Series

Each card is signed and serial numbered out of 9, except for the cards of O'Kane and McAuley, who were traded prior to the cards being issued.

1 Danny Baco 20.00 50.00
2 Matt Bartowski 20.00 50.00
3 Brandon Bollig 25.00 60.00
4 David Brack 20.00 50.00
5 Jared Brown 20.00 50.00
6 Carter Camper 20.00 50.00
7 Rick Carden 20.00 50.00
8 Bryce Christianson 20.00 50.00
9 Colby Cohen 20.00 50.00
10 J.J. Crew 20.00 50.00
11 Kyle Follmer 20.00 50.00
12 Jason Gregoire 25.00 60.00
13 Ross Henry 20.00 50.00
14 Bryan Hogan 25.00 60.00
15 Mike Hull 20.00 50.00
16 Patrick Johnson 20.00 50.00
17 Mike Kramer 20.00 50.00
18 Eric Lake 20.00 50.00
19 Chad Langlais 20.00 50.00
20 Dan Lawson 20.00 50.00
21 Pat McAuley 4.00 10.00
22 Joey Miller 20.00 50.00
23 Kyle O'Kane 4.00 10.00
24 Stephen Schultz 20.00 50.00
25 Chris Stansik 20.00 50.00

2007-08 Lincoln Stars

COMPLETE SET (57) 10.00 25.00
1 Kevin Murdock .25 .60
2 Mike Dalhuisen .25 .60
3 Jake Newton .25 .60
4 Dennis Brown .25 .60
5 Michael Sdao .25 .60
6 Rick Carden .25 .60
7 Mike Henderson .25 .60
8 Kyle Follmer .25 .60
9 Jared Festler .25 .60
10 Matt Bartkowski .25 .60
11 Ryan Kretzer .25 .60
12 Kyle Verbeek .25 .60
13 Jason Gregoire .25 .60
14 Brandon Bollig .25 .60
15 Danny Baco .25 .60
16 Ross Henry .25 .60
17 P.J. Tatum .25 .60
18 Travis Erstad .25 .60
19 J.J. Crew .25 .60
20 Kyle Delaurell .25 .60
21 Tyler Brickler .25 .60
22 Tyler Kieffer .25 .60
23 Nick Hopper .25 .60
24 Jimmy McGroarty .25 .60
25 Nick Fuher .25 .60
26 Nick Fouts .25 .60
27 Corey Courtney .25 .60
28 I.C. Starz (Mascot) .15 .40
29 Lincoln Stars CL .15 .40
30 Checklist .15 .40
31 Kevin Murdock .25 .60
32 Mike Dalhuisen .25 .60
33 Lyon Messier .25 .60
34 Jake Newton .25 .60
35 Taylor Kuypers .25 .60
36 Michael Sdao .25 .60
37 Rick Carden .25 .60
38 Kyle Follmer .25 .60
39 Jared Festler .25 .60
40 Matt Bartkowski .25 .60
41 Ryan Kretzer .25 .60
42 Jimmy Hayes .25 .60
43 Jason Gregoire .25 .60
44 Brandon Bollig .25 .60
45 Danny Baco .25 .60
46 Ross Henry .25 .60
47 Chris Forfar .25 .60
48 Travis Erstad .25 .60
49 J.J Crew .25 .60
50 Eric Meland .25 .60
51 Josh Myers .25 .60
52 Tyler Brickler .25 .60
53 David Reekie .25 .60
54 Jared Festler .25 .60
55 Matt Bartkowski .25 .60
56 Jason Gregoire .25 .60
57 Ross Henry .25 .60

1985-86 London Knights

The London Knights of the OHL are featured in this 30-card P.L.A.Y. (Police, Law and Youth) set, which was sponsored by the London Crime Prevention Committee in conjunction with area businesses. The cards measure approximately 2 3/4" by 3 1/2" and are printed on thin card stock. The fronts feature color photos with the players posed in action stances. A facsimile autograph is inscribed at the bottom of the picture.

COMPLETE SET (30) 20.00 50.00
1 LaVerne Shipley CoP .08 .25
2 Joe Ranger .20 .50
3 Kellogg's Ad CL .08 .25
4 Don Boyd GM/CO .08 .25
5 Harry E. Sparling COP .08 .25
6 Murray Nystrom .20 .50
7 Bob Halkidis .30 .75
8 Morgan Watts .20 .50
9 Brendan Shanahan 15.00 40.00
10 Brian Dobbin .30 .75
11 Ed Kister .20 .50
12 Darin Smith .20 .50
13 Greg Puhalski .20 .50
14 Dave Haas .20 .50
15 Pete McLeod .20 .50
16 Frank Tremblay .20 .50
17 Matthew Smyth .20 .50
18 Glen Leslie .20 .50
19 Mike Zombo .20 .50
20 Jamie Groke .20 .50
21 Brad Schlegel .30 .75
22 Kelly Cain .20 .50
23 Tom Allen .20 .50
24 Rod Gerow .20 .50
25 Pat Vachon .20 .50
26 Paul Cook ACO .08 .25
27 Jeff Reese .60 1.50
28 Fred Kean PR .08 .25
29 Scott Cumming .30 .75
30 John Williams ACO .08 .25

1986-87 London Knights

The London Knights of the OHL are featured in this 30-card P.L.A.Y. (Police, Law and Youth) set, which was sponsored by the London Crime Prevention Committee in conjunction with area businesses. The cards measure approximately 2 3/4" by 3 1/2" and are printed on thin card stock. The fronts feature color photos with the players posed in action stances. The set is noteworthy for featuring a card of Brendan Shanahan issued prior to his RC.

COMPLETE SET (30) 14.00 35.00
1 LaVerne Shipley CoP .08 .25
2 Tom Gosnell Mayor .08 .25
3 Kellogg's Ad CL .08 .25
4 Wayne Maxner CO/GM .20 .50
5 Harry E. Sparling COP .08 .25
6 Brendan Shanahan 10.00 25.00
7 Pat Vachon .20 .50
8 Brad Schlegel .20 .50
9 Barry Earhart .20 .50
10 Jean Marc MacKenzie .20 .50
11 Jason Simon .20 .50
12 Jim Sprott .20 .50
13 Bill Long VP .08 .25
14 Murray Nystrom .20 .50
15 Shayne Stevenson .30 .75
16 Don Martin .20 .50
17 Ian Pound .20 .50
18 Peter Lisy .20 .50
19 Steve Marcolini .20 .50
20 Craig Majaury .20 .50
21 Trevor Dam .20 .50
22 Dave Akey .20 .50
23 Dennis McEwen .20 .50
24 Shane Whelan .20 .50
25 Greg Hankkio .20 .50
26 Pat Kelly TR .08 .25
27 Stephen Titus .30 .75
28 Fred Kean PR .08 .25
29 Chris Somers .30 .75
30 Gord Clark MD .08 .25

1993-94 London Knights

This standard size set was issued at home games during the 1993-94 season. Card fronts feature posed, color photos. Card backs feature statistics and biographical information. Cards are unnumbered and checklisted below alphabetically.

COMPLETE SET (29) 4.80 12.00
1 Jason Allison 2.00 5.00
2 Ryan Appel .15 .40
3 Tim Bacik .08 .25
4 Ryan Black .08 .25
5 Chris Brassard .08 .25
6 Ryan Burgoyne .08 .25
7 Brodie Coffin .08 .25
8 Rob Frid .08 .25
9 David Gilmore .08 .25
10 Roy Gray .08 .25
11 John Guirestante .08 .25
12 Brent Holdsworth .08 .25
13 Don Margettie .08 .25
14 Dan Reja .08 .25
15 Daryl Rivers .08 .25
16 Gord Ross .08 .25
17 Kevin Slota .08 .25
18 Brian Stacey .08 .25
19 Nick Stajduhar .08 .25
20 Bill Tibbetts .40 1.00
21 Ben Walker .08 .25
22 Jordan Willis .15 .40
23 Chris Zanutto .08 .25
24 Knights Top Picks .08 .25
Ryan Appel
Ben Walker
Den Reja
Roy Gray
25 Knights Future Stars .40 1.00
Nick Stajduhar
Jason Allison
John Guirestante
Ryan Black
Jordan Willis
26 Gary Agnew CO .02 .10
27 Steve Stoyanovich ACO .02 .10
Tom Hedican CO
28 Murray Nystrom ACO .02 .10
29 Title Card .02 .10

2000-01 London Knights

This series features a 27-card main set and an eight-card "update." The series also features the first junior cards of Rick Nash.

COMPLETE SET (35) 25.00 50.00
1 Mark Hunter/Dale Hunter .20 .50
2 Bobby Turner .20 .50
3 Matt Cooper .20 .50
4 Aaron Lobb .20 .50
5 Lou Dickenson .20 .50
6 Lindsay Hofford ACO .02 .10
7 Kyle Neufeld .20 .50
8 Petr Hemsky .20 .50
9 Rick Nash 8.00 20.00
10 Brent Varty .20 .50
11 Danny Bois .30 .75
12 Joel Scherban .20 .50
13 Brian Dobbin .20 .50
14 Aaron Molnar .30 .75
15 Mike Clarke .20 .50
16 Ian Turner .20 .50
17 John Eminger .20 .50
18 Dan Jancevski .40 1.00
19 Jason Davies .20 .50
20 Logan Hunter .40 1.00
21 Checklist card .01 .01
22 Don Brankley TR .01 .01
23 Josh Chambers .20 .50
24 Chris Kelly .20 .50
25 Matt Albiani .20 .50
26 Matt Junkins .20 .50
27 Mike Stathopoulos .20 .50
U1 Chris Kelly .40 1.00
U2 Mark Hunter ACO .10 .25
U3 Dan Jancevski .40 1.00
U4 Logan Hunter .40 1.00
U5 Dale Hunter CO .20 .50
U6 Danny Bois .40 1.00
U7 Scorch MASCOT .02 .10
U8 Rick Nash 10.00 25.00

2001-02 London Knights

This set features the Knights of the OHL. The set was produced by the team and was sold at its souvenir stands. It's believed that 1,000 total sets were produced. The set is noteworthy for the inclusion of a card of Rick Nash, the first-overall pick in 2002, and Dale Hunter, owner of the Knights.

COMPLETE SET (30) 12.00 25.00
1 Title Card/CL .04 .10
2 Sean Dixon .20 .50
3 Dennis Wideman .30 .75
4 Patrick Barbieri .20 .50
5 Bryan Thompson .20 .50
6 Chris Bain .20 .50
7 Mike Stathopoulos .20 .50
8 Danny Bois .20 .50
9 Matt Iannetta .20 .50
10 Charlie Stephens .20 .50
11 Dylan Hunter .20 .50
12 Logan Hunter .20 .50
13 Sean McMorrow .20 .50
14 Chad Thompson .20 .50
15 Rick Steadman .20 .50
16 Matt Junkins .20 .50
17 Dan Buccella .20 .50
18 Rick Nash 6.00 15.00
19 Robbie Colangelo .20 .50
20 Matt Ioriani .20 .50
21 Ian Turner .20 .50
22 Corey Perry 1.50 4.00
23 Jan Chovan .30 .75
24 Matt Weir .20 .50
25 Alex White .20 .50
26 Jacques Beaulieu ACO .04 .10
27 Lindsay Hofford ACO .04 .10
28 Dale Hunter CO .20 .50
29 Don Brankley TR .01 .05
NNO Mission Hockey AD .01 .01

2002-03 London Knights

COMPLETE CHECKLIST 8.00 20.00
1 Team Picture/CL .02 .10
2 Dennis Wideman .30 .75
3 Logan Hunter .30 .75
4 Corey Perry .75 2.00
5 Mike Stathopoulos .20 .50
6 Danny Bois .30 .75
7 Ryan Hare .20 .50
8 Dylan Hunter .40 1.00
9 Rick Steadman .20 .50
10 Matt Weir .20 .50
11 David Bolland .75 2.00
12 Kyle Piwowarczyk .20 .50
13 Brandon Prust .30 .75
14 Chris Bain .20 .50
15 Adam Nemeth .20 .50
16 Zach Trammer .20 .50
17 Danny Syvret .30 .75
18 Jimmy Ball .20 .50
19 Kyle Quincey .40 1.00
20 Marc Methot .30 .75
21 Gerald Coleman .40 1.00
22 Chris Houle .20 .50
23 Jayme Helmer .20 .50
24 Robbie Drummond .20 .50
25 Tomas Linhart .20 .50
26 Matt Ioriani .20 .50
27 Dale Hunter CO .20 .50
28 Don Brankley TR .01 .01
29 Jacques Beaulieu ACO .02 .10
30 Opening Night .02 .10

2003-04 London Knights

This 26-card set was sponsored by Remax and created by Extreme Sports cards. The set was sold at home games. The Perry team leader card at the end of the checklist is not considered part of the set and the set is complete without it.

COMPLETE SET (26) 10.00 20.00
1 Rob Schremp 1.25 3.00
2 Corey Perry .60 1.50
3 Adam Nemeth .30 .75
4 Danny Syvret .30 .75
5 Ivan Khomutov .20 .50
6 Jacques Beaulieu ACO .02 .10
7 Don Brankley TR .01 .01
8 Trevor Kell .20 .50
9 Dennis Wideman .30 .75
10 Marc Methot .20 .50
11 Vadim Karaga .20 .50
12 Scott Sheppard .20 .50
13 Dale Hunter CO .20 .50
14 Logan Hunter .30 .75
15 Rick Steadman .20 .50
16 Ryan MacDonald .40 1.00
17 Danny Bois .20 .50
18 David Bolland .40 1.00
19 Tommy Mannino .20 .50
20 Gerald Coleman .40 1.00
21 Dylan Hunter .40 1.00
22 Josh Beaulieu .20 .50
23 Robbie Drummond .20 .50
24 Ryan Pottruff .20 .50
25 Brandon Prust .30 .75
26 Danny Richmond .40 1.00
27 Corey Perry TL 2.50 6.00

2004-05 London Knights

Note: there is no card #24. Two cards bear the #25. A total of 2,600 team sets were produced.

COMPLETE SET (26) 15.00
1 Ryan MacDonald .75
2 Rick Steadman .50
3 Steve Ferry .50
4 Rob Schremp 1.00
5 Trevor Kell .50
6 Robbie Drummond .50
7 Bryan Rodney .50
8 Brandon Prust .50
9 Corey Perry 2.00
10 Frank Rediker .50
11 Danny Syvret .75
12 Gerald Coleman .75
13 David Bolland 1.00
14 Josh Beaulieu .50
15 Dylan Hunter 1.00
16 Drew Larman .50
17 Jordan Foreman .50
18 Ryan Pottruff .50
19 Kelly Thomson .50
20 Shawn Futers .50
21 Marc Methot .75
22 Jeff Whitfield .50
23 Dale Hunter CO .50
25 Don Brankley TR .01
25 Jacques Beaulieu ACO .10
NNO Re/Max Sponsor Card .01

2005-06 London Knights

COMPLETE SET (26) 5.00 12.00
1 Rob Schremp .60 1.50
2 Dylan Hunter .40 1.00
3 Trevor Kell .20 .50
4 Kris Belan .20 .50
5 Matt Clarke .20 .50
6 Jamie Vanderveeken .20 .50
7 Sergei Kostitsyn .40 1.00
8 Jordan Foreman .20 .50
9 Adam Perry .20 .50
10 David Bolland .40 1.00
11 Frank Rediker .20 .50
12 Matt McCready .20 .50
13 Scott Aarssen .20 .50
14 Steve Ferry .20 .50
15 Robbie Drummond .20 .50
16 Andrew Wilkins .20 .50
17 Ryan Martinelli .20 .50
18 Corey Syvret .20 .50
19 Josh Beaulieu .20 .50
20 Adam Dennis .40 1.00
21 Steve Mason .60 1.50
22 Dale Hunter CO .02 .10
23 Jacques Beaulieu ACO .02 .10
24 Jeff Perry ACO .02 .10
25 Don Brankley WATERBOY .01 .01
26 Chris Maton .02 .10

2006-07 London Knights

COMPLETE SET (26) 12.00 20.00
1 Sam Gagner 1.25 4.00
2 Patrick Kane 4.00 10.00
3 Steve Mason .40 1.00
4 Todd Perry .30 .75
5 Kevin Bodker .20 .50
6 Scott Aarssen .20 .50
7 David Jarram .20 .50
8 Josh Beaulieu .20 .50
9 Matt Clarke .20 .50
10 Philip Mcrae .20 .50
11 Robbie Drummond .20 .50
12 Tony Dehart .20 .50
13 Sergei Kostitsyn .40 1.00
14 Andrew Wilkins .20 .50
15 Ryan Martinelli .20 .50
16 Jordan Shine .20 .50
17 Adam Hasani .20 .50
18 Stephane Cesar .20 .50
19 Luke Vanmoerkerke .20 .50
20 David Meckler .20 .50
21 Jordan Foreman .20 .50
22 Corey Syvret .20 .50
23 Adam Perry .20 .50
24 Dale Hunter .20 .50
25 Dave Gagner .20 .50
26 Todd Bidner .10 .25

2007-08 London Knights

COMPLETE SET (26) 5.00 12.00
1 Steve Mason .25 .60
2 Stephen Heming .25 .60
3 Michael Zador .25 .60
4 Scott Aarssen .25 .60
5 Matt Ashmann .25 .60
6 Jadran Beljo .25 .60
7 Matt Clarke .25 .60
8 Tucker Hunter .25 .60
9 Garett Hunter .25 .60
10 Tony DeHart .25 .60
11 Kevin Montgomery .25 .60
12 Vladimir Roth .25 .60
13 Andrew Wilkins .25 .60
14 Kale Kerbashian .25 .60
15 Jordan Shine .25 .60
16 Patrick Maroon .25 .60
17 Akim Aliu .25 .60
18 Adam Perry .25 .60
19 Philip McRae .25 .60
20 Tony Romano .25 .60
21 Justin Taylor .25 .60
22 Sean O'Connor .25 .60
23 Dale Hunter .25 .60
24 Dave Gagne .25 .60
25 Pat Curcio .25 .60
26 Don Brankley .25 .60

1997-98 Long Beach Ice Dogs

Little is known about this set beyond the confirmed checklist. Additional information can be forwarded to hockeymag@beckett.com.

COMPLETE SET (20) 4.00 10.00
1 Doug Ast .20 .50
2 Patrik Augusta .20 .50
3 Collin Bauer .20 .50
4 Mike Buzak .20 .50
5 John Byce .20 .50
6 Brian Chapman .20 .50
7 Mark Ferner .20 .50
8 Victor Ignatjev .20 .50
9 Rob Konny .20 .50
10 Dan Lambert .40 1.00
11 Mike Matteucci .20 .50
12 Joby Messier .20 .50
13 Stephane Morin .20 .50
14 Shawn Penn .20 .50
15 Russ Romaniuk .20 .50
16 Nicholas Vachon .20 .50
17 Andrei Vasilyev .20 .50
18 Kay Whitmore .40 1.00
19 Darryl Williams .20 .50
20 Spike MASCOT .02 .10

1998-99 Long Beach Ice Dogs

Little is known about this set beyond the confirmed checklist. Any additional information can be forwarded to hockeymag@beckett.com.

COMPLETE SET (20) 6.00 15.00
1 Doug Ast .20 .50
2 Patrik Augusta .20 .50
3 John Byce .20 .50
4 Dan Bylsma .20 .50
5 Mark Ferner .20 .50
6 Mike Jickling .20 .50
7 Frederick Jobin .20 .50
8 Claude Jutras .20 .50
9 Dan Lambert .30 .75
10 Manny Legace .60 1.50
11 Jocelyn Lemieux .20 .50
12 Mike Matteucci .20 .50
13 Sacha Molin .20 .50
14 Jan Nemecek .20 .50
15 Andy Roach .20 .50
16 Pavel Rosa .20 .50
17 Patrik Stefan 2.00 5.00
18 Darryl Williams .20 .50
19 John Van Boxmeer HCO .08 .25
20 Spike MASCOT .02 .10

1998-99 Long Beach Ice Dogs Promo

This single card of 1999 first-overall pick Patrik Stefan was given out to fans who attended a Long Beach Ice Dogs game during the 1998-99 season. The card was sponsored by Ice Breakers gum and was licensed by the Ice Dogs and the IHL.

NNO Patrik Stefan 2.00 5.00

1999-00 Long Beach Ice Dogs

This 10-card set was given away one card per home game during the 1999-2000 season. As such, complete sets are nearly impossible to find.

COMPLETE SET (10) 6.00 15.00
1 Rene Chapdelaine .75 2.00
2 Pavel Rosa .75 2.00
3 Mike Crowley .75 2.00
4 Mike O'Neill .75 2.00
5 Len Barrie .75 2.00
6 Mike Matteucci .40 1.00
7 Scott Thomas .75 2.00
8 Doug Ast .40 1.00
9 Spike Mascot .40 1.00
10 John Van Boxmeer HCO .40 1.00

1994-95 Los Angeles Blades RHI

This set features the Blades of Roller Hockey International. The cards were sold in set form by the team at home games.

COMPLETE SET (20) 3.00 8.00
1 Checklist .02 .10
2 Chris Nelson .20 .50
3 Mike Burman .20 .50
4 Steve Wilson .20 .50
5 Vaclav Nedomansky, Jr. .20 .50
6 Rob Hartnell .20 .50
7 Kraig Nienhuis .30 .75
8 Eric LeMarque .20 .50
9 Peter Kasowski .20 .50
10 Brett Kurtz .20 .50
11 Terran Sandwith .20 .50
12 Brad Sholl .20 .50
13 Mike Doers .20 .50
14 Steve Bogoyevac .20 .50
15 Sean Gauthier .20 .50
16 Eric Lavigne .20 .50
17 Mike Callahan .20 .50
18 Bobby Hull Jr. CO .20 .50
19 Jeanie Buss .02 .10
20 Los Angeles Blades Logo .02 .10

1995-96 Louisiana Ice Gators

This 21-card set of the Louisiana Ice Gators of the ECHL features borderless color player photos with the player's name, position, and jersey number printed in a green bar across the bottom. The backs carry player information. The cards are unnumbered and checklisted below in alphabetical order. This is the first of two sets released by the Ice Gators in 1995-96, their inaugural season.

COMPLETE SET (21) 4.80 12.00
1 Bob Berg .20 .50
2 John Depourcq .20 .50
3 Wade Fournier .20 .50
4 Fred Goltz .20 .50
5 Ron Handy .20 .50
6 Mike Heany .20 .50
7 Dean Hulett .20 .50
8 Jim Latos .20 .50
9 George Maneluk .30 .75
10 Rob McCaig .20 .50
11 Jason McQuat .20 .50
12 Rod Pasma .30 .75
13 Sean Rowe .20 .50
14 Bryan Schoen .30 .75
15 Darryl Shedden .20 .50
16 Doug Shedden CO .20 .50
17 Fred Spoltore .20 .50
18 Chris Valicevic .20 .50
19 Rob Valicevic .75 2.00
20 John Vary .20 .50
21 Marty Yewchuk .20 .50

1995-96 Louisiana Ice Gators Playoffs

This 21-card set features borderless color player photos with the player's name and jersey number printed in a black bar across the bottom. The backs carry player information. A note on the card back reveals no more than 2,500 sets were produced. The cards are unnumbered and checklisted below in alphabetical order.

COMPLETE SET (21) 4.00 10.00
1 Bob Berg .20 .50
2 Aaron Boh .20 .50
3 Eric Cloutier .20 .50
4 John DePourcq .20 .50
5 Wade Fournier .20 .50
6 Ron Handy .25 .60
7 Mike Heaney .20 .50
8 Dean Hulett .20 .50
9 Jim Latos .20 .50
10 George Maneluk .25 .60
11 Rob McCaig .20 .50
12 Jason McQuat .20 .50
13 Chad Nelson .20 .50
14 Dan O'Rourke .20 .50
15 Rod Pasma .30 .75
16 Darryl Shedden .20 .50
17 Doug Shedden CO .25 .60
18 John Spoltore .25 .60
19 Chuck Thuss .25 .60
20 Rob Valicevic .40 1.00
Chris Valicevic
21 John Vary .20 .50

1995 Louisiana Ice Gators Glossy

We have confirmed the existence of five cards in what might be a larger series of Ice Gators cards. These singles have a laminated finish, unlike the larger base set of Ice Gators cards this season. The cards are unnumbered and listed below in alphabetical order. If you have additional information, please contact us at hockeymag@beckett.com

COMPLETE SET (?)
1 Aaron Boh 4.00 10.00
2 Eric Cloutier 4.00 10.00
3 Chad Nelson 4.00 10.00
4 Dan O'Rourke 4.00 10.00
5 Chuck Thuss 5.00 12.00

1996-97 Louisiana Ice Gators

This set features the Ice Gators of the ECHL. It is believed that this set was issued by the team early in the season. Any additional information can be forwarded to hockeymag@beckett.com.

COMPLETE SET (23) 4.80 12.00
1 Dujar Amidovski .40 1.00
2 Doug Bonner .30 .75
3 Eric Cloutier .20 .50
4 Mark DeSantis .20 .50
5 Louis Dumont .20 .50

6 Blair Manning .20 .50
7 Roger Maxwell .20 .50
8 Jason McQuat .20 .50
9 Stan Melanson .20 .50
10 Jay Murphy .20 .50
11 Michael Murray .20 .50
12 Matt Pagnutti .20 .50
13 Don Parsons .20 .50
14 Team Photo .20 .50
15 Gary Roach .20 .50
16 Ryan Shanahan .20 .50
17 John Spoltore .30 .75
18 Chris Valicevic .30 .75
19 John Varga .30 .75
20 Rob Weingartner .20 .50
21 Billy Thurlow/Bruce Livin .20 .50
22 Doug Shedden HCO .08 .25
23 Alphonse MAS .02 .10

1996-97 Louisiana Ice Gators II

This set was issued by the team later in the season (or during the playoffs) and includes players acquired through the course of the season.

COMPLETE SET (22) 4.00 10.00
1 Aaron Boh .20 .50
2 John DePourcq .20 .50
3 Mark Delmore .20 .50
4 Louis Dumont .20 .50
5 Ron Handy .20 .50
6 Mikhail Kravets .20 .50
7 James Latos .20 .50
8 Rob McCaig .20 .50
9 Jason McQuat .20 .50
10 Stan Melanson .20 .50
11 Joey Mittelsteadt .30 .75
12 Chad Nelson .20 .50
13 Dan O'Rourke .20 .50
14 Ken Ruddick .20 .50
15 Dean Seymour .20 .50
16 Ryan Shanahan .20 .50
17 Darryl Shedden .20 .50
18 Sergei Tkachenko .20 .50
19 Chris Valicevic .30 .75
20 Rob Weingartner .20 .50
21 Jack Williams .20 .50
22 Doug Shedden HCO .08 .25

1997-98 Louisiana Ice Gators

This set features the Ice Gators of the ECHL. Little is known about this set beyond the confirmed checklist. Additional information can be forwarded to hockeymag@beckett.com.

COMPLETE SET (22) 4.00 10.00
1 Louis Dumont .20 .50
2 Jason McQuat .20 .50
3 Alphonse MAS .02 .10
4 Matt Pagnutti .20 .50
5 Richard Smit .20 .50
6 John Varga .30 .75
7 Jay Murphy .20 .50
8 Darrel Woodley .20 .50
9 Scott McKay .20 .50
10 Jack Williams .20 .50
11 Stan Melanson .20 .50
12 Brad Toporowski .20 .50
13 John Jennings EM .02 .10
14 Eric Cloutier .20 .50
15 Ryan Pisiak .20 .50
16 John Spoltore .30 .75
17 Mikhail Kravets .20 .50
18 Paul Rushforth .20 .50
19 Doug Bonner .30 .75
20 Chad Nelson .20 .50
21 Doug Shedden HCO .08 .25
22 Don Parsons .20 .50

1998-99 Louisiana Ice Gators

This set features the Ice Gators of the ECHL. The set was produced by Starz Cards and was sold by the team at home games.

COMPLETE SET (26) 4.00 10.00
1 Mascot .15 .40
2 Bujar Amidovski .30 .75
3 Doug Bonner .30 .75
4 Eric Cloutier .15 .40
5 Mark Desantis .15 .40
6 Louis Dumont .15 .40
7 Blair Manning .15 .40
8 Roger Maxwell .15 .40
9 Jason McQuat .15 .40
10 Stan Melanson .15 .40
11 Jay Murphy .30 .75
12 Mike P. Murray .20 .50
13 Matthew Pagnutti .15 .40
14 Don Parsons .15 .40
15 Gary Roach .15 .40
16 Ryan Shanahan .30 .75
17 Doug Shedden CO .15 .40
18 John Spoltore .02 .10
19 Billy Thurlow .30 .75
Bruce Livin CO
20 Chris Valicevic .30 .75
21 John Varga .30 .75
22 Rob Weingartner .15 .40
23 Team Card .02 .10

1999-00 Louisiana Ice Gators

This set features the Ice Gators of the ECHL. The set was produced by Roox, and sold by the team at home games. The numbering system of the set is less than ideal, as there are two versions of both card No. 1 and 2. It is believed that cards No 21-23 also exist, but they have not yet been confirmed. Anyone with additional information should contact hockeymag@beckett.com.

COMPLETE SET (25) 4.80 12.00
1 Vaclav Nedomansky .20 .50
1 Sean Gauthier .20 .50
2 Mike Oliveira .20 .50
2 Michael Murray .20 .50
3 Matt Pagnutti .20 .50
4 Jesse Rezansoff .20 .50
5 Mike Kucsulain .20 .50
6 Stan Melanson .20 .50
7 Shawn McNeil .20 .50
8 Ryan Shanahan .20 .50
9 John DePourcq .30 .75
10 Hugo Marchand .20 .50
11 Corey Neilson .20 .50
12 Chris Bogas .20 .50
13 Jason McQuat .30 .75
14 John Spoltore .30 .75
15 Dave Arsenault .20 .50
16 Chris Valicevic .30 .75
17 Jason Sessa .20 .50
18 Mark Cadotte .20 .50
19 Jay Murphy .20 .50
20 John Jennings TR .02 .10
24 Dennis Holland CO .02 .10
25 Don Murdoch CO .02 .10
26 Claw'd MAS .08 .25

2000-01 Louisiana Ice Gators

This set features the Ice Gators of the ECHL. The set was sponsored by the Tamahka Trails Golf Club and was sold by the team at its souvenir stands.

COMPLETE SET (25) 4.00 10.00
1 Stan Melanson .16 .40
2 Jay Murphy .16 .40
3 Nathan Borega .16 .40
4 Shawn McNeil .16 .40
5 Ryan Shanahan .16 .40
6 Roman Marakhovski .16 .40
7 Mike Kucsulain .16 .40
8 Dalen Hrooshkin .16 .40
9 Kevin Karlander .16 .40
10 Corey Neilson .16 .40
11 Bruce Richardson .16 .40
12 Jason Saal .30 .75
13 Michael Murray .16 .40
14 Jason McQuat .16 .40
15 John Spoltore .30 .75
16 Mike Valley .16 .40
17 Magnus Nilsson .30 .75
18 Dan Tessier .30 .75
19 Matt Pagnutti .16 .40
20 Roger Maxwell .16 .40
21 Dave Farrish HCO .10 .25
22 John DePourcq ACO .10 .25
23 Johnny Gomez TR .04 .10
24 Greg Sieg EM .04 .10
25 Andy Davis DOB .04 .10

2001-02 Louisiana Ice Gators

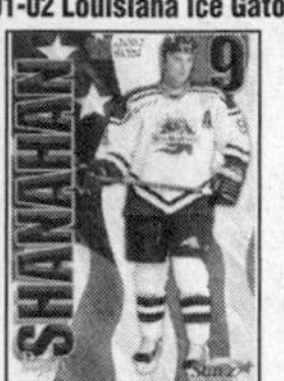

This set features the Ice Gators of the ECHL. The set was produced by Starz Sports and was sold by the team at home games.

COMPLETE SET (26) 4.00 10.00
1 Header Card .04 .10
2 Steve Aronson .20 .50
3 Frederic Cloutier .20 .50
4 Cory Cyrenne .30 .75
5 Andy Davis DBR .04 .10
6 John DePourcq ACO .04 .10
7 Dave Farrish CO .10 .25
8 Dominic Forget .30 .75
9 Russell Hewson .20 .50
10 Konstantin Kalmikov .30 .75
11 Branislav Kvetan .20 .50
12 Greg Labenski .20 .50
13 Marc Magliarditi .30 .75
14 Ryan Marsh .20 .50
15 Shawn McNeil .20 .50
16 Kevin Mitchell .20 .50
17 Jay Murphy .20 .50
18 Corey Neilson .20 .50
19 Dennis Shiryaev .20 .50
20 Randy Perry .20 .50
21 Nathan Rempel .20 .50
22 Ryan Shanahan .20 .50
23 Ricky Casataneda TR .04 .10
Greg Sieg EQMG
24 Chris Valicevic .30 .75
25 Alphonse MASCOT .04 .10

2002-03 Louisiana Ice Gators

COMPLETE SET (25) 12.00
1 Header Card .10
2 Semir Ben-Amor .50
3 Cal Benazic .50
4 Bobby Brown .50
5 Frederic Cloutier .75
6 Kenny Corupe .50
7 John DePourcq .10
8 Daniel Goneau .75
9 Kyle Kettles .50
10 Branislav Kvetan .50
11 Louis Mass .50
12 Shawn McNeil .50
13 Kevin Mitchell .50
14 J.P. Morin .50
15 Nathan Rempel .50
16 Bruce Richardson .50
17 Rod Sarich .50
18 Dennis Shiryaev .50
19 Shawn Skiehar .50
20 Chris Taliercio .50
21 Tony Tuzzolino .50
22 Jeff Worlton .50
23 Dave Farrish HCO .10
24 Andy Davis ANN .10
25 Greg Sieg EQM .10

2003-04 Louisiana Ice Gators

COMPLETE SET (25) 12.00
1 Armands Berzins .50
2 Bobby Brown .50
3 Frederic Cloutier .75
4 Kenny Corupe .50
5 Maxime Fortunus .50
6 Derek Gustafson .75
7 Jason Hamilton .50
8 Brian Herbert .50
9 Jamie Johnson .50
10 Konstantin Kalmikov .50
11 Ben Kilgour .50
12 Martin Masa .50
13 Milt Mastad .50
14 Alex Materukhin .50
15 Ed McGrane .50
16 Kevin Mitchell .50
17 Josh Mizerek .50
18 Rod Sarich .50
19 Dennis Shiryaev .75
20 Ben Storey .50
21 Jim Vickers .50
22 Dave Farrish CO .10
23 Team Photo .50
24 Checklist .01
25 Mascot .01

2004-05 Louisiana Ice Gators

COMPLETE SET (26) 15.00
1 David Bararuk 2.00
2 Josh Barker 1.00
3 Ricky Castaneda TR .10
4 Randy Dagenais .75
5 John Evangelista .75
6 Maxime Fortunus 1.00
7 Jody Green EQMG .10
8 Todd Gordon CO .10
9 Kyle Kettles .75
10 Roger Leonard .75
11 Doug Maciver .75
12 Nathan Marsters .75
13 Wes Mason .75
14 Alex Materukhin .75
15 Mike Omicioli .75
16 Jake Ortmeyer 1.00
17 Pascal Pelletier .75
18 Bryan Perez .75
19 Mark Rooneem .75
20 Shawn Skiehar .75
21 Troy Smith .75
22 Chris Thompson .75
23 Gator Girls .25
24 Gator Girls .25
25 Mascots .01
26 Announcers .01

1999-00 Louisville Panthers

This set features the Panthers of the AHL. The cards were produced by Roox and issued as a promotional giveaway at a late-season home game.

COMPLETE SET (33) 8.00 20.00
1 Craig Ferguson .30 .75
2 Brent Thompson .30 .75
3 Craig Reichert .30 .75
4 Eric Boguniecki .60 1.50
5 Dan Boyle .40 1.00
6 Ivan Novoseltsev .40 1.00
7 Dave Duerden .30 .75
8 Curtis Doell .30 .75
9 Sean Gauthier .40 1.00
10 Peter Ratchuk .30 .75
11 John Jakopin .30 .75
12 Marcus Nilson .40 1.00
13 Paws MASCOT .08 .25
14 Chris Wells .30 .75
15 Kirby Law .40 1.00
16 Chris Allen .30 .75
17 Chad Cabana .30 .75
18 Richard Shulmistra .40 1.00
19 Dwayne Hay .30 .75
20 Joey Tetarenko .60 1.50
21 Paul Brousseau .30 .75
22 Nick Smith .40 1.00
23 Brad Ference .40 1.00
24 Lance Ward .30 .75
25 Jeff Ware .30 .75
26 Paul Harvey .08 .25
27 Andrew Long .30 .75
28 Joe Paterson CO .08 .25
29 Gerard Gallant CO .08 .25
30 Tamer Afr PRES .08 .25
31 Chuck Fletcher GM .08 .25
32 UPS Zamboni .08 .25
33 Indiana Casino Zamboni .08 .25

2000-01 Louisville Panthers

This set features the Panthers of the AHL. The cards were issued as promotional giveaways at two separate games, in two sets of 12-cards apiece.

COMPLETE SET (24) 7.20 18.00
1 Team CL .10 .01
2 Brent Thompson .40 1.00
3 Paul Brousseau .30 .75
4 David Emma .30 .75
5 Joey Tetarenko .40 1.00
6 Peter Ratchuk .40 .75
7 Dave Duerden .30 .75
8 Sean Gauthier .30 .75
9 Kyle Rossiter .30 .75
10 Rocky Thompson .30 .75
11 Denis Shvidki .60 1.00
12 Brad Ference .40 1.00
13 Joe Paterson CO .20 .50
14 Gord Dineen ACO .20 .50
15 Travis Brigley .40 1.00
16 Ryan Bach .40 1.00
17 Andrei Podkonicky .40 .75
18 Mike Harder .40 1.00
19 Evgeny Korolev .30 .75
20 Eric Godard .30 .75
21 Mike Cirillo .30 .75
22 Eric Beaudoin .30 .75
23 Paul Harvey .30 .75
24 Paws Mascot .10 .25

1996-97 Louisville Riverfrogs

This 30-card set of the Louisville Riverfrogs of the ECHL was sponsored by Winn-Dixie, Surge and Fox 41. The cards feature action photography on the front, with '95-96 stats on the back. The cards were sold by the club at the rink and through the mail.

COMPLETE SET (30) 4.00 20.00
1 Checklist .02 .10
2 Sandy Allan .60 1.50
3 Gino Santerre .30 .75
4 Pete Liptrott .30 .75
5 Jason Hanchuk .30 .75
6 Adam Young .30 .75
7 Dan Reja .30 .75
8 Terry Lindgren .30 .75
9 Sheldon Gorski .30 .75
10 Jeff Kostuch .30 .75
11 Randy Stevens .30 .75
12 Chris Rowland .30 .75
13 Chris DeProfio .30 .75
14 Mike Sancimino .30 .75
15 Dean Seymour .30 .75
16 Stephane Madore .30 .75
17 Chet Cullic .30 .75
18 Tim Chase .30 .75
19 Jack Kowal .30 .75
20 Tom MacDonald .30 .75
21 Jimmy Provencher .30 .75
22 Lance Leslie .30 .75
23 Warren Young CO .08 .25
24 R.J. Romero TR .02 .10
25 Mark Shepherd EQMG .02 .10
26 David Wilson ANN .02 .10
27 Rowdy the Riverfrog .02 .10
28 Sandy Allan AS .60 1.50
29 Warren Young CO .08 .25
Brett Young
30 Team Photo .30 .75

1997-98 Louisville Riverfrogs

Little is known about this set beyond the confirmed checklist. Additional information can be forwarded to hockeymag@beckett.com.

COMPLETE SET (29) 4.00 10.00
1 Title Card .02 .10
2 Craig Nelson .15 .40
3 P.J. Lepler .15 .40
4 Jason Pain .15 .40
5 Terry Lindgren .15 .40
6 Michael Flynn .15 .40
7 Sheldon Gorski .15 .40
8 Jeff Kostuch .15 .40
9 Steve Ferranti .15 .40
10 Bob Gohde .15 .40
11 Marko Makinen .15 .40
12 Mike Sancimino .15 .40
13 Tobias Ablad .15 .40
14 Jeff Kiesch .15 .40
15 Stephane Madore .15 .40
16 Chris DeProfio .15 .40
17 Danny Reja .15 .40
18 Jack Kowal .15 .40
19 Dan Reimann .15 .40
20 Rob Frid .15 .40
21 Deiter Kochan .60 1.50
22 Lance Leslie .15 .40
23 Warren Young CO .15 .40
24 R.J. Romeiro TR .02 .10
25 Mark Miller EQ .02 .10
26 Matt Gorsky BR .02 .10
27 Rowdy Mascot .02 .10
28 Sheldon Gorski .15 .40
29 Team Photo .15 .40

1999-00 Lowell Lock Monsters

This set features the Lock Monsters of the AHL. This set was issued in the form of a perforated album, with four pages of cards. The album/set was issued as a promotional giveaway at a game in Feb. 2000.

COMPLETE SET (27) 6.00 15.00
1 Ray Giroux .30 .75
2 Dave MacIsaac .20 .50
3 Richard Seeley .20 .50
4 Nathan LaFayette .20 .50
5 Rich Brennan .30 .75
6 Petr Mika .20 .50
7 Donald MacLean .20 .50
8 Cody Bowtell .20 .50
9 Vladimir Chebaturkin .20 .50
10 David Hymovitz .20 .50
11 Sean Blanchard .20 .50
12 Eric Belanger .20 .50
13 Dmitri Nabokov .20 .50
14 Vladimir Orszagh .40 1.00
15 Greg Phillips .20 .50
16 Jason Krog .40 1.00
17 Eric Brewer .75 2.00
18 Travis Scott .40 1.00
19 Evgeny Korolev .20 .50
20 Stephen Valiquette .60 1.50
21 Jason Podollan .20 .50
22 Jack Baldwin .20 .50
23 Lowell Lock Monsters .08 .25
24 Louie MASCOT .02 .10
25 Bruce Boudreau CO .08 .25
26 Steve Stirling CO .08 .25
27 Tom Rowe GM .08 .25

2000-01 Lowell Lock Monsters

This set features the Lock Monsters of the AHL. The cards were issued as a promotional giveaway in the form of an album with perforatable images. They were distributed at a game in December, 2000.

COMPLETE SET (30) 7.20 20.00
1 Joe Corvo .30 .75
2 Andreas Lilja .30 .75
3 Joe Rullier .30 .75
4 Jeff Daw .20 .50
5 Petr Mika .30 .75
6 Rich Brennan .20 .50
7 Brad Chartrand .20 .50
8 Marko Tuomainen .30 .75
9 Eric Veilleux .20 .50
10 Eric Belanger .40 1.00
11 Peter Leboutillier .20 .50
12 David Hymovitz .20 .50
13 Juraj Kolnik .40 1.00
14 Chris Schmidt .20 .50
15 Kevin Baker .20 .50
16 Steve Passmore .40 1.00
17 Richard Seeley .20 .50
18 Jason Krog .30 1.00
19 Travis Scott .30 1.00
20 Marcel Cousineau .30 1.00
21 Nate Miller .20 .50
22 Branislav Mezei .40 1.00
23 Mathieu Biron .30 .75
24 Kip Brennan .40 1.00
25 Greg Phillips .20 .50
26 Louie MAS .04 .10
27 Mike Pudlick .20 .50
28 Bruce Boudreau CO .10 .25
29 Steve Stirling CO .10 .25
30 Tom Rowe GM .04 .10

2002-03 Lowell Lock Monsters

COMPLETE SET (25) 20.00
1 Igor Knyazev 1.00
2 Nikos Tselios 1.00
3 Sean Curry 1.00
4 Ed Hill 1.00
5 Mike Zigomanis 1.00
6 Ryan Bayda 1.00
7 Craig MacDonald 1.00
8 Jeff Daw 1.00
9 Steve Halko 1.00
10 Jeff Heerema 1.00
11 Brent McDonald 1.00
12 Mike Watt 1.00
13 Tomas Kurka 1.00
14 Damian Surma 1.00
15 Kaspars Astashenko 1.00
16 Greg Kuznik 1.00
17 Tommy Westlund 1.00
18 Randy Petruk 1.50
19 Brett Lysak 1.00
20 Ryan Bast 1.00
21 Jean-Marc Pelletier 1.50
22 Brad DeFauw 1.00
23 Tomas Malec 1.00
24 Lowell Lock Monsters AU .10
25 Lowell Lock Monsters AU .10

2003-04 Lowell Lock Monsters

This set was produced by Choice Marketing and sold at home games.

COMPLETE SET (25) 10.00
1 Alan Rourke .40
2 Brad DeFauw .40
3 Brad Fast .40
4 Brennan Evans .40
5 Brent Krahn .75
6 Brett Lysak .40
7 Damian Surma .40
8 Dany Sabourin .75
9 Dan Sullivan .40
10 Jason Morgan .40
11 Jesse Wallin .40
12 Joey Tetarenko .40
13 Josh Green .40
14 Martin Sonnenberg .40
15 Matt Davidson .40
16 Mike Commodore .40
17 Mike Zigomanis .40
18 Patrick DesRochers .75
19 Pavel Brendl .40
20 Robert Dome .40
21 Ryan Bayda .40
22 Sean Curry .40
23 Tomas Kurka .40
24 Tomas Malec .40
25 Checklist .01

2003-04 Lowell Lock Monsters Photo Album

This was issued as a promotional item in Nov. 2003. The cards came in a perforated album format.

COMPLETE SET (25) 20.00
1 Mike Commodore .75
2 Jesse Wallin .75
3 Sean Curry .75
4 Ryan Bayda .75
5 Jason Morgan .75
6 Mike Zigomanis .75
7 Tomas Kurka .75
8 Damian Surma .75
9 Brad Fast .75
10 Martin Sonnenberg .75
11 Allan Rourke .75
12 Josh Green .75
13 Autograph Card .01
14 Dan Sullivan .75
15 Brett Lysak .75
16 Joey Tetarenko 1.00
17 Robert Dome .75
18 Brad DeFauw .75
19 Pavel Brendl .75
20 Matt Davidson .75
21 Brennan Evans .75
22 Tomas Malec .75
23 Autograph Card .01
24 Dany Sabourin 1.50
25 Patrick DesRochers 1.50

2004-05 Lowell Lock Monsters

COMPLETE SET (24) 15.00
1 Ryan Bayda .50
2 Mike Commodore .50
3 Sean Curry .50
4 Gordie Dwyer 1.00
5 Brennan Evans .50
6 Brad Fast .75
7 Colin Forbes .50
8 Carsen Germyn .50
9 Mark Giordano .50
10 Jim Henkel .50
11 Chuck Kobasew 1.00
12 Brent Krahn 1.00
13 Chad Larose .50
14 Lynn Loyns .50
15 Craig MacDonald .50
16 Brantt Myhres 1.50
17 Richie Regehr .50
18 Danny Richmond .50
19 Allan Rourke .50
20 Eric Staal 2.00
21 Bruno St. Jacques 1.00
22 Justin Taylor .50
23 Cam Ward .40 1.00
24 Mike Zigomanis .50

2004-05 Lowell Lock Monsters Photo Album

This set was issued as a game night giveaway in January of 2005. The cards were distributed in an album format with perforations.

COMPLETE SET (25) 30.00
1 Ryan Bayda 1.00
2 Mike Commodore 1.00
3 Sean Curry 1.00
4 Gordie Dwyer 2.00
5 Brennan Evans 1.00
6 Brad Fast 1.50
7 Colin Forbes 1.00
8 Carsen Germyn 1.00
9 Mark Giordano 1.00
10 Jim Henkel 1.00
11 Chuck Kobasew 2.00
12 Brent Krahn 2.00
13 Chad Larose 1.00
14 Lynn Loyns 1.00
15 Craig MacDonald 1.00
16 Brantt Myhres 3.00
17 Richie Regehr 1.00
18 Danny Richmond 1.00
19 Allan Rourke 1.00
20 Bruno St. Jacques 1.00
21 Eric Staal 4.00
22 Justin Taylor 1.00
23 Cam Ward 2.00
24 Mike Zigomanis 1.00
25 Logo Card .01

2000-01 Lubbock Cotton Kings

This set features the Cotton Kings of the WPHL. It was produced by the team and sold at its souvenir stands.

COMPLETE SET (20) 4.00 10.00
1 Kyle Reeves .30 .75
2 Tracy Egeland .20 .50
3 Jan Melichercik .20 .50
4 Peter Cava .20 .50
5 Dave MacIntyre .20 .50
6 Patrick Brownlee .20 .50
7 Chris Rowland .20 .50
8 Bill McDonald HCO .10 .25
9 Neil Savary .30 .75
10 Lance Leslie .20 .50
11 Mike Hiebert .20 .50
12 Ryan Shmyr .20 .50
13 Brandon Carper .20 .50
14 Trevor Burgess .20 .50
15 Tom Menicci .20 .50
16 Derek Holland .20 .50
17 Walker McDonald .20 .50
18 Cosmo DuPaul .30 .75
19 Adam Robbins .20 .50
20 Lubbock Cotton Kings .20 .25

2003-04 Lubbock Cotton Kings

This set was produced by Choice Marketing and sold at home games.

COMPLETE SET (20) 8.00
1 Checklist .01
2 Craig Binns .50
3 Steve Birch .50
4 Joe Blaznek .50
5 Mike Brusseau .75
6 Jeff Dewar .50
7 Chris Duggan .50
8 Kevin Fines .75
9 Paul Fioroni .50
10 Derek Holland .50
11 Jean-Francois Labarre .50
12 Dave MacIntyre .50
13 Jan Melichercik .50
14 Mathieu Paul .50
15 Sebastien Roy .50
16 Jim Shepherd .50
17 Jeremy Symington .75
18 Rob Vessio .50
19 Kirk Tomlinson HCO .10
20 Mascot .10
NNO Sponsor .01
NNO Sponsor .01

2002-03 Macon Trax

This set features the Trax of the Atlantic Coast league. It was sponsored by Applebees and sold at home games.

COMPLETE SET (20) 8.00
1 Corey Smith .50
2 Dan Welch .50
3 David Deeves .50
4 Landon Bathe .50
5 Tom Stewart .50
6 Corey Lucas .50
7 Rick Emmett .50
8 Jeremy Kyle .50
9 Brad Rice .50
10 Nolan Weir .50
11 Brad Bourhis .50
12 Stephane Desjardins .50
13 Luke Murphy .50
14 Steve Howard .50
15 Geoff Faulkner .50
16 Dennis Brogna TR .10
17 Brian Curran HCO .10
18 Dave Monteiro ACO .10
19 Todd MacGowan EM .10
20 Mascot .10
NNO Checklist .10

1997-98 Macon Whoopee

This 18-card set was produced and sold by the Macon Whoopee Booster Club at home games for $10 each. This set was also available in an autographed version and in uncut sheets.

COMPLETE SET (18) 3.60 9.00
1 Steve Vezina .30 .75
2 Martin Belanger .20 .50
3 John Paris HCO .02 .10
4 Sebastien Parent .20 .50
5 Gary Golczewski .20 .50
6 Jocelyn Langlois .20 .50
7 Joe Letendre .20 .50
8 Martin LaChaine .20 .50
9 Todd MacIsaac .20 .50
10 Patrice Charbonneau .30 .75
11 Marc Genest .20 .50
12 Claude Fillion .20 .50
13 Craig Willard .20 .50
14 Raymond Delarosbil .20 .50
15 Francois Leroux .20 .50
16 Trent Cavicchi .20 .50
17 Alexei Deev .30 .75
18 Alain Cote .20 .50

1997-98 Macon Whoopee Autographs

This 18-card set is the same as the base 1997-98 Macon Whoopee set, but with each card autographed. Autographed uncut sheets were available also. This set was originally sold at the arena for $20.

COMPLETE SET (18) 14.00 35.00
1 Steve Vezina 1.50 4.00
2 Martin Belanger .75 2.00
3 John Paris HCO .75 2.00
4 Sebastien Parent 1.50 4.00
5 Gary Golczewski .75 2.00
6 Jocelyn Langlois .75 2.00
7 Joe Letendre .75 2.00
8 Martin LaChaine .75 2.00
9 Todd MacIsaac .75 2.00
10 Patrice Charbonneau 1.25 3.00
11 Marc Genest .75 2.00
12 Claude Fillion .75 2.00
13 Craig Willard .75 2.00
14 Raymond Delarosbil .75 2.00
15 Francois Leroux .75 2.00
16 Trent Cavicchi .75 2.00
17 Alexei Deev 1.25 3.00
18 Alain Cote .75 2.00

2001-02 Macon Whoopee

This set features the Whoopee of the CHL. The set was produced by Choice Marketing and was issued by the team as a promotional giveaway. The production was limited to 1,000 copies.

COMPLETE SET (21) 8.00 20.00
1 Checklist .40 1.00
2 Andrew Allen .80 2.00
3 Krikor Arman .40 1.00
4 Nic Beaudoin .40 1.00
5 David Brosseau .40 1.00
6 Travis Dillabough .40 1.00
7 Gord Dineen CO .40 1.00
8 Rick Emmett .40 1.00
9 Paul Giblin .40 1.00
10 Mike Green .40 1.00
11 Mike Josetowicz .40 1.00
12 Chris Madden .80 2.00
13 Milt Mastad .40 1.00
14 Luke Murphy .40 1.00
15 Johan Olsson .40 1.00
16 Michel Periard .40 1.00
17 Doug Schueller .40 1.00
18 Kris Waltze .60 1.50
19 Alex Zinevych .40 1.00
20 Casey Kesselring .40 1.00
21 Header Card/CL .04 .10

1995-96 Madison Monsters

This 24-card set features the Madison Monsters of the Colonial Hockey League and was sponsored by Z-104 and Electrolarm. The cards, which apparently were a game night giveaway, feature a color shot on the front, along with the player name and team logo. The backs feature one of the most comprehensive player information packages ever seen on cardboard, including career stats and personal biography. The cards are unnumbered.

COMPLETE SET (24) 8.00 25.00
1 Duane Derksen .75 2.00
2 Brian Downey .40 1.00
3 Dmitri Alekhin .40 1.00
4 Monster MASCOT .02 .10
5 Sean Wilmert .40 1.00
6 Corey Grassel .40 1.00
7 Dan Ruoho .40 1.00
8 Billy Brown TR .02 .10
9 Kent Hawley .40 1.00
10 Dan Laughlin .40 1.00
11 Vyacheslav Polikarkin .40 1.00
12 Todd Dvorak .40 1.00
13 Brian Idalski .40 1.00
14 Gunnar Kroseberg .40 1.00
15 Brett Larson .40 1.00
16 Paul Clatney .40 1.00
17 Matt Loen .40 1.00
18 Stanislav Tkach .60 1.50
19 Glenn Painter .40 1.00
20 Joe Bonvie .60 1.50
21 Mark Johnson CO .60 1.50
22 Justin Morrison .60 1.50
23 Marcel Richard .60 1.50
24 Sponsor card .01 .05

1996-97 Madison Monsters

This 24-card set was given away over the course of four card nights, and was sold later in the season. The cards are not numbered and so they are listed in the order in which they were distributed.

COMPLETE SET (24) 8.00 20.00
1 Electroalarm Services .02 .10
2 Dave Schultz HCO .60 1.50

3 Kent Hawley .40 1.00
4 Alexander Galchenyuk .40 1.00
5 Jeremie Legault .40 1.00
6 Randy Holmes .40 1.00
7 Fran Reed .40 1.00
8 Chris Markstrom .40 1.00
9 Team Photo .40 1.00
10 Duane Derksen .60 1.50
11 Brian Downey .40 1.00
12 Matt Loen .40 1.00
13 Justin Morrison .40 1.00
14 Dave Rowe .40 1.00
15 Colby Van Tassel .40 1.00
16 Dan Ruoho .40 1.00
17 ElectroAlarm Security Sys .02 .10
18 Brian Idalski .40 1.00
19 Brian LaVack .40 1.00
20 Todd Passini .40 1.00
21 Stas Tkatch .40 1.00
22 Joakin Wiberg .40 1.00
23 Jeff Winter .40 1.00
24 Jose Ortiz TR .20 .50

1998-99 Madison Monsters

This set features the Monsters of the UHL. The cards were produced by Roox, and intended as a season-long promotional giveaway. Apparently there was a problem at some point and the promotion was cancelled after the distribution of just 16 cards. If anyone knows of any other cards in this set, please write hockeymag@beckett.com.

COMPLETE SET (16) 8.00 20.00
1 Kent Hawley CO .08 .25
2 Andrew Wilhelm OWN .08 .25
3 Dana Doll TR .08 .25
4 Jason Disher .60 1.50
5 Kelly Stephens .60 1.50
6 Derek Beuselinck .60 1.50
7 Cory Holland .60 1.50
8 Mike Maurice .60 1.50
9 Luke Strand .60 1.50
10 Brian Downey .60 1.50
11 David Fletcher .60 1.50
12 Andy Faulkner .60 1.50
13 Jim Duhart .60 1.50
14 Jay Wilson .60 1.50
15 Ed Corwin .60 1.50
16 Monster Madness .40 1.00

1992-93 Maine Black Bears

This set features the Black Bears of the NCAA. The set was issued as two series (1-16 and 17-36). This set includes one of the first cards of NHL superstar Paul Kariya.

COMPLETE SET (36) 20.00 50.00
1 Title Card .10 .01
2 Mike Dunham 1.25 3.00
3 Andy Silverman .20 .50
4 Matt Martin .20 .50
5 Chris Imes .20 .50
6 Jason Weinrich .20 .50
7 Scott Pellerin .30 .75
8 Dan Murphy .20 .50
9 Dave LaCouture .20 .50
10 Patrice Tardif .40 1.00
11 Eric Fenton .20 .50
12 Jim Montgomery .40 1.00
13 Kent Salfi .20 .50
14 Jean-Yves Roy .40 1.00
15 Garth Snow .40 1.00
16 Cal Ingraham .40 1.00
17 Title Card .10 .01
18 Mike Dunham 1.25 3.00
19 Chris Imes .20 .50
20 Paul Kariya 15.00 40.00
21 Mike Latendresse .20 .50
22 Dan Murphy .20 .50
23 Dave MacIsaac .20 .50
24 Dave LaCouture .20 .50
25 Chris Ferraro .40 1.00
26 Peter Ferraro .40 1.00
27 Jim Montgomery .40 1.00
28 Brad Purdie .20 .50
29 Lee Saunders .20 .50
30 Justin Tomberlin .20 .50
31 Chuck Texeira .20 .50
32 Martin Mercier .20 .50
33 Garth Snow .40 1.00
34 Cal Ingraham .40 1.00
35 Greg Hirsch .20 .50
36 Jamie Thompson .20 .50

1993-94 Maine Black Bears

Measuring the standard size, this 26-card set features the Maine Black Bears. The fronts feature color action player photos with light blue, dark blue, and white borders. A black stripe near the bottom carries the player's name and position in white print. The team logo is superimposed on the picture. The backs carry biographical information, career highlights, and statistics along with a small black-and-white player headshot. The numbering continues where the previous year's numbering left off.

COMPLETE SET (25) 24.00 60.00
37 Paul Kariya 4.00 10.00
Leo Wlasow
Title Card
38 Andy Silverman .20 .50
39 Jason Weinrich .20 .50
40 Jason Mansoff .20 .50
41 Paul Kariya 8.00 20.00
42 Mike Latendresse .20 .50
43 Barry Clukey .20 .50
44 Wayne Conlan .20 .50
45 Dave MacIsaac .20 .50
46 Patrice Tardif .30 .75
47 Brad Purdie .20 .50
48 Dan Shermerhorn .20 .50
49 Lee Saunders .20 .50
50 Justin Tomberlin .20 .50
51 Chuck Texeira .20 .50
52 Tim Lovell .20 .50
53 Cal Ingraham .20 .50
54 Leo Wlasow .20 .50
55 Blair Allison .20 .50
56 Blair Marsh .20 .50
57 Marcel Pineau .20 .50
58 Trevor Roenick .20 .50
59 Reg Cardinal .20 .50
60 Paul Kariya 8.00 20.00
61 Jim Montgomery 4.00 10.00
Paul Kariya
Division I Champions

2004-05 Maine Black Bears

Issued as a promotional giveaway.

COMPLETE SET (32) 50.00
1 Mike Lundin 2.00
2 Tom Zabkowicz 2.00
3 Steve Mullin 2.00
4 Travis Wight 2.00
5 Troy Barnes 2.00
6 Matt Deschamps 2.00
7 John Ronan 2.00
8 Michel Leveille 2.00
9 Keith Johnson 2.00
10 Keenan Hopson 2.00
11 Billy Ryan 2.00
12 Greg Moore 2.00
13 Robert Bellamy 2.00
14 Ben Murphy 2.00
15 Josh Soares 2.00
16 Tim Maxwell 2.00
17 Mike Hamilton 2.00
18 Jon Jankus 2.00
19 Wes Clark 2.00
20 Travis Ramsey 2.00
21 Derek Damon 2.00
22 Brent Shepheard 2.00
23 Matt Lundin 2.00
24 Jimmy Howard 3.00
25 Matt Greyeyes 2.00
26 Ryan Shelley 2.00
27 Bret Tyler 2.00
28 Jeff Mushaluk 2.00
29 Staff .10
30 Erik Soltys ACO .10
31 Tim Whitehead CO .10
32 Team Picture .50

2005-06 Maine Black Bears

COMPLETE SET (32) 10.00 25.00
1 Rob Bellamy .75
2 Ben Bishop 2.00
3 Wes Clark .75
4 Derek Damon .75
5 Simon Danis-Pepin 2.00
6 Matt Duffy .75
7 Chris Hahn .75
8 Mike Hamilton .75
9 John Hopson .75
10 Keenan Hopson .75
11 Jon Jankus .75
12 Keith Johnson .75
13 Vince Laise .75
14 Michel Leveille .75
15 Matt Lundin 1.50
16 Mike Lundin .75
17 Jeff Marshall .75
18 Greg Moore .75
19 Steve Mullin .75
20 Brian Plaszcz .75
21 Travis Ramsey .75
22 Billy Ryan .75
23 Ryan Shelley .75
24 Brent Shepheard .75
25 Josh Soares .75
26 Bret Tyler .75
27 Travis Wight .75
28 Tim Whitehead HC .25
29 Campbell Blair AC .25
30 Dan Kerluke AC .25
31 Grant Standbrook AC .25
32 Maine Black Bears .50

2007-08 Maine Black Bears

COMPLETE SET (32) 6.00 15.00
1 Mike Banwell .25 .60
2 Rob Bellamy .25 .60
3 Glenn Belmore .25 .60
4 Ben Bishop .25 .60
5 Nolan Boike .25 .60
6 Brett Carriere .25 .60
7 Wes Clark .25 .60
8 Simon Danis-Pepin .25 .60
9 David de Kastrozza .25 .60
10 Robby Dee .25 .60
11 Jeff Dimmen .25 .60
12 Matt Duffy .25 .60
13 Shane Foley .25 .60
14 Chris Hahn .25 .60
15 Keenan Hopson .25 .60
16 Tanner House .25 .60
17 Vince Laise .25 .60
18 Jeff Marshall .25 .60
19 Keif Orsini .25 .60
20 Nick Payson .25 .60
21 Travis Ramsey .25 .60
22 Lem Randall .25 .60
23 Billy Ryan .25 .60
24 Kevin Swallow .25 .60
25 Andrew Sweetland .25 .60
26 Bret Tyler .25 .60
27 Josh Van Dyk .25 .60
28 Dave Wilson .25 .60
29 Tim Whitehead HC .15 .40
30 Guy Perron AHC .15 .40
31 Dan Kerluke AC .10 .25
32 Grant Standbrook AC .10 .25

2001-02 Manchester Monarchs

This set features the Monarchs of the AHL. The set was released in two series of 15 cards each and was sold at the team's souvenir stands. Each series was limited to 1,000 copies. As the cards from both series are numbered 1-15, we have added an A and B suffix to differentiate between them.

COMPLETE SET (30) 8.00 20.00
1A Randy Robitaille .24 .60
1B Dane Jackson .24 .60
2A Derek Bekar .24 .60
2B Travis Scott .30 .75
3A Brad Chartrand .24 .60
3B Ted Donato .24 .60
4A Nate Miller .24 .60
4B Joe Rullier .24 .60
5A Andre Payette .24 .60
5B Rich Brennan .24 .60
6A Brett Hauer .24 .60
6B Eric Healey .24 .60
7A Chris Schmidt .24 .60
7B Jason Holland .24 .60
8A Mike Pudlick .24 .60
8B Richard Seeley .24 .60
9A Kip Brennan .30 .75
9B Jaroslav Bednar .40 1.00
10A Tomas Zizka .24 .60
10B Ryan Flinn .60 1.50
11A Jerred Smithson .24 .60
11B Rob Valicevic .60 1.50
12A Joe Corvo .24 .60
12B Steve Kelly .24 .60
13A Stephane Fiset .60 1.50
13B Dan Riva .24 .60
14A Marcel Cousineau .30 .75
14B Scott Thomas .24 .60
15A Bruce Boudreau CO .04 .10
15B Maximillian MASCOT .04 .10

2002-03 Manchester Monarchs

COMPLETE SET (30) 18.00
1 Chris Aldous .50
2 Scott Barney .50
3 Bruce Boudreau HCO .10
4 Kip Brennan .50
5 Mike Cammalleri 2.00
6 Joe Corvo .50
7 Eric Healey .50
8 Steve Heinze .50
9 Dane Jackson .50
10 Steve Kelly .75
11 Yanick Lehoux .50
12 Mike Pudlick .50
13 Joe Rullier .50
14 Travis Scott .75
15 Richard Seeley .50
16 Derek Armstrong .50
17 Jared Aulin 1.50
18 Derek Bekar .50
19 Chris Bogas .50
20 Ryan Flinn 1.00
21 Jeff Giuliano .50
22 Jason Holland .50
23 Cristobal Huet 2.00
24 Maximillian MASCOT .10
25 Dan Riva .50
26 Pavel Rosa .50
27 Chris Schmidt .50
28 Jerred Smithson .50
29 Mat Snesrud .50
30 Tomas Zizka .75

2003-04 Manchester Monarchs

This set was produced by Choice Marketing and sold at home games.

COMPLETE SET (25) 10.00
1 Scott Barney .50
2 Noah Clarke .75
3 Ryan Flinn .75
4 Jeff Giuliano .50
5 Denis Grebeshkov .50
6 Adam Hauser .75
7 Leon Hayward .50
8 Steve Kelly .50
9 Yanick Lehoux .50
10 Bryan Muir .50
11 Doug Nolan .50
12 George Parros .50
13 Pavel Rosa .50
14 Joe Rullier .50
15 Chris Schmidt .50
16 Richard Seeley .50
17 Jerred Smithson .50
18 John Tripp .50
19 Dan Welch .50
20 Tomas Zizka .50
21 Mascot .10
22 Bruce Boudreau HCO .10
23 Jim Hughes ACO .10
24 Verizon Wireless Arena .01
25 Checklist .01

2003-04 Manchester Monarchs Team Issue

This set was given away at a game in Jan. 2004. The set was sponsored by the New Hampshire Tobacco Prevention/Control program. The cards are unnumbered and are listed below in alphabetical order.

COMPLETE SET (20) 20.00
1 Scott Barney 1.00
2 Mathieu Chouinard 1.50
3 Noah Clarke 1.50
4 Ryan Flinn 1.50
5 Jeff Giuliano 1.00
6 Denis Grebeshkov 1.00
7 Milan Hnilicka 1.50
8 Steve Kelly 1.00
9 Yanick Lehoux 1.00
10 Bryan Muir 1.00
11 Doug Nolan 1.00
12 George Parros 1.00
13 Pavel Rosa 1.00
14 Joe Rullier 1.00
15 Chris Schmidt 1.00
16 Richard Seeley 1.00
17 Jerred Smithson 1.00
18 John Tripp 1.00
19 Dan Welch 1.00
20 Tomas Zizka 1.00

2004-05 Manchester Monarchs

Produced by Choice Marketing.

COMPLETE SET (26) 15.00
1 Adam Hauser 1.00
2 Brad Smyth 1.00
3 Chris Schmidt .40
4 Dan Welch .40
5 Dave Steckel .75
6 Denis Grebeshkov .40
7 Doug Nolan .40
8 Dustin Brown 1.00
9 George Parros .40
10 Greg Hogeboom .40
11 Jeff Giuliano .40
12 Joe Rullier .75
13 Mathieu Garon 1.50
14 Matt Ryan .40
15 Michael Cammalleri 1.00
16 Mike Weaver .40
17 Noah Clarke 1.00
18 Petr Kanko 1.00
19 Ryan Flinn 1.00
20 Scott Barney .40
21 Tim Gleason .75
22 Tom Kostopoulos .75
23 Troy Milam .40
24 Yanick Lehoux .75
25 Maximillian MASCOT .01
NNO Checklist .10

2004-05 Manchester Monarchs Tobacco

These cards were issued as a promotional giveaway.

COMPLETE SET (25) 30.00
1 Mathieu Garon 3.00
2 Adam Hauser 2.00
3 Brad Smyth 2.00
4 Chris Schmidt .75
5 Dan Welch .75
6 Dave Steckel 1.50
7 Denis Grebeshkov .75
8 Doug Nolan .75
9 Dustin Brown 2.00
10 George Parros .75
11 Greg Hogeboom .75
12 Jeff Giuliano .75
13 Joe Rullier 1.50
14 Matt Ryan .75
15 Mike Cammalleri 2.00
16 Mike Weaver .75
17 Noah Clarke 2.00
18 Petr Kanko 2.00
19 Ryan Flinn 2.00
20 Scott Barney .75
21 Tim Gleason 1.50
22 Tom Kostopoulos 1.50
23 Troy Milam .75
24 Yanick Lehoux 1.50
25 Mascot .10

2005-06 Manchester Monarchs

This set was issued in two series. The fist series included (1-24), while series 2 had (25-48).

COMPLETE SET (48) 30.00
COMPLETE SER. 1 (24) 15.00
COMPLETE SER. 2 (24)
1 Barry Brust .40 1.00
2 Noah Clarke .25 .60
3 Brad Fast .25 .60
4 Ryan Flinn .40 1.00
5 Jeff Giuliano .25 .60
6 Denis Grebeshkov .25 .60
7 Adam Hauser .40 1.00
8 Connor James .25 .60
9 Petr Kanko .25 .60
10 Joey Mormina .25 .60
11 Ryan Murphy .25 .60
12 Doug Nolan .25 .60
13 Richard Petiot .25 .60
14 Konstantin Pushkarev .25 .60
15 Dany Roussin .25 .60
16 Matt Ryan .25 .60
17 Richard Seeley .25 .60
18 Brad Smyth .25 .60
19 Jeff Tambellini .40 1.00
20 Lauri Tukonen .60 1.50
21 Marty Wilford .40 1.00
22 Derek Clancey AC .02 .10
23 Jim Hughes HC .02 .10
24 Maximillian MASCOT .10 .25
25 Brendan Bernakevitch .25 .60
26 Dustin Brown .40 1.00
27 Michael Cammalleri .40 1.00
28 Noah Clarke .25 .60
29 Ryan Flinn .40 1.00
30 Yutaka Fukufuji 1.25 3.00
31 Mathieu Garon .40 1.00
32 Jeff Giuliano .25 .60
33 Tim Gleason .25 .60
34 Denis Grebeshkov .25 .60
35 Adam Hauser .40 1.00
36 Greg Hogeboom .25 .60
37 Connor James .25 .60
38 Petr Kanko .25 .60
39 Tom Kostopoulos .25 .60
40 Yanick Lehoux .25 .60
41 George Parros .60 1.50
42 Richard Petiot .25 .60
43 Reagan Rome .25 .60
44 Dany Roussin .25 .60
45 Matt Ryan .25 .60
46 Jeff Tambellini .40 1.00
47 Mike Weaver .25 .60
48 Eric Werner .25 .60

2006-07 Manchester Monarchs

COMPLETE SET (24) 7.00 12.00
1 Barry Brust .30 .75
2 Brendan Buckley .20 .50
3 Bryan Schmidt .20 .50
4 Dany Roussin .30 .75
5 Doug Nolan .20 .50
6 Eric Werner .20 .50
7 Jason Labarbera .30 .75
8 Jeff Giuliano .30 .75
9 Joey Mormina .20 .50
10 John Zeiler .20 .50
11 Konstantin Pushkarev .20 .50
12 Lauri Tukonen .40 1.00
13 Matt Moulson .20 .50
14 Matt Ryan .20 .50
15 Ned Lukacevic .20 .50
16 Noah Clarke .20 .50
17 Peter Harrold .20 .50
18 Petr Kanko .20 .50
19 Ryan Murphy .20 .50
20 Shay Stephenson .20 .50
21 Tim Jackman .20 .50
22 Mark Morris CO .02 .10
23 Scott Pellerin ACO .02 .10
24 Max MASCOT .02 .10

1992-93 Manitoba Junior League

We have confirmed the existence of one card in this series. If you have any information about the rest of the checklist, please email us at hockeymag@beckett.com.

COMPLETE SET (?)
181 Dane Litke

1997-98 Manitoba Moose

These oversized cards were inserted in game programs in two series. Cards 7 and 8 in each series were only available at Grapes Leon's Centre with any kid's menu purchase.

COMPLETE SET (16) 40.00
A1 Ralph Intranuovo .75 2.00
A2 Russ Romaniuk .75 2.00
A3 Randy Gilhen .75 2.00
A4 Dave Thomlinson .75 2.00
A5 Fred Brathwaite 2.00 5.00
A6 Mick E. Moose Mascot .40 1.00
A7 Scott Arniel 2.00 5.00
A8 Randy Carlyle HCO 2.00 5.00
B1 Brian Chapman .75 2.00
B2 Radim Bicanek .75 2.00
B3 Michael Stewart .75 2.00
B4 Jason Christie .75 2.00
B5 Greg Pankewicz .75 2.00
B6 Brad Purdie .75 2.00
B7 Kent Fearns 2.00 5.00
B8 Mike Ruark 2.00 5.00

1998-99 Manitoba Moose

This oversized set was issued in two series, with each card inserted into various game programs. The series are numbered C and D which continues the numbering from the previous season. Cards 7 and 8 in each series are much tougher as they were only available at Grapes Leon's Centre with a food purchase.

COMPLETE SET (16) 16.00 40.00
C1 Scott Arniel 1.25 3.00
C2 Bill Bowler 1.25 3.00
C3 Kent Fearns .75 2.00
C4 Brett Hauer .75 2.00
C5 Ralph Intranuovo .75 2.00
C6 Mike Ruark .75 2.00
C7 Michael Stewart 2.00 5.00
C8 Scott Thomas 2.00 5.00
D1 Jason MacDonald 1.25 3.00
D2 Christian Bronsard 1.25 3.00
D3 Jeff Parrott .75 2.00
D4 Brian Chapman .75 2.00
D5 Richard Shulmistra 1.25 3.00
D6 Jimmy Roy .75 2.00
D7 Rhett Gordon 2.00 5.00
D8 Patrice Tardif 2.00 5.00

1999-00 Manitoba Moose

Released in conjunction with Grapes, Husky, and Mohawk, this 22-card set pictures the 1999-00 Manitoba Moose. Each card measures 6.25x9.5" and comes complete with two perforated coupons on the bottom.

COMPLETE SET (22) 10.00 25.00
1 Manny Legace 1.25 3.00
2 Michael Stewart .40 1.00
3 Vladislav Serov .40 1.00
4 Lonny Bohonos .75 2.00
5 Mike Prokopec .75 2.00
6 Jeff Parrott .40 1.00
7 Bill Bowler .75 2.00
8 Mike Ruark .40 1.00
9 Eric Veilleux .40 1.00
10 Brett Hauer .40 1.00
11 Jason Elliott .75 2.00
12 Cory Cyrenne .60 1.50
13 Justin Kurtz .40 1.00
14 Patrice Tardif .75 2.00
15 Jimmy Roy .40 1.00
16 Jason MacDonald .40 1.00
17 Larry Shapley .40 1.00
18 Brian Chapman .40 1.00
19 Marc Rodgers .75 2.00
20 Jim Montgomery .40 1.00
21 M2K Header Card .20 .50
22 Checklist .20 .50

2000-01 Manitoba Moose

This set features the Moose of the IHL. The set was oversized and was sold by the team at home games and through its Web site. The set is noteworthy for the card of Johan Hedberg, who became a huge hobby star after being acquired by the Penguins during this season.

COMPLETE SET 6.00 12.00
1 Mel Angelstad .30 .75
2 Doug Ast .20 .50
3 Cal Benazic .20 .50
4 Philippe Boucher .20 .50
5 Steve Brule .20 .50
6 Brian Chapman .20 .50
7 Dion Darling .20 .50
8 Bobby Dollas .20 .50
9 Rusty Fitzgerald .20 .50
10 Daniel Goneau .20 .50
11 Brett Hauer .20 .50
12 Johan Hedberg 2.00 3.00
13 Dan Kesa .20 .50
14 Justin Kurtz .20 .75
15 Dmitri Leonov .20 .50
16 John MacLean .30 .75
17 Sean Pronger .20 .50
18 Bruce Richardson .20 .50
19 Jimmy Roy .20 .75
20 Mike Ruark .20 .50
21 Scott Thomas .20 .50
22 Ken Wregget .30 .75
23 Mick E. Moose MASCOT .02 .10

2001-02 Manitoba Moose

This set features the Moose of the AHL. The set was sold by the team at its souvenir stand for $15. The cards are slightly oversized. Since they are unnumbered, the cards are listed alphabetically.

COMPLETE SET (23) 6.00 15.00
1 Header Card .04 .10
2 Bryan Allen .30 .75
3 Ryan Bonni .30 .75
4 Brian Chapman .30 .75
5 Artem Chubarov .30 .75
6 Jason Cipolla .30 .75
7 Regan Darby .30 .75
8 Fedor Fedorov .30 .75
9 Darrell Hay .30 .75
10 Bryan Helmer .30 .75
11 Josh Holden .75
12 Steve Kariya .40 1.00
13 Pat Kavanagh .30 .75
14 Zenith Komarniski .30 .75
15 Justin Kurtz .30 .75
16 Brad Leeb .30 .75
17 Alfie Michaud .40 1.00
18 Justin Morrison .30 .75
19 Ryan Ready .30 .75
20 Brandon Reid .40 1.00
21 Jimmy Roy .30 .75
22 Andre Savage .30 .75
23 Mick E. Moose MASCOT .10 .25

2002-03 Manitoba Moose

COMPLETE SET (26) 15.00
1 Header Card .10
2 Mick E. Moose Mascot .10
3 Zenith Komarniski .50
4 Bryan Helmer .50
5 Ryan Ready .50
6 Steve Kariya 1.50
7 Nolan Baumgartner .50
8 Regan Darby .50
9 Jimmy Roy .50
10 Fedor Fedorov 1.00
11 Jaroslav Obsut .50
12 Jason King .50
13 Darrell Hay .50
14 Tyler Moss .75
15 Herbert Vasiljevs .50
16 Nathan Smith .50
17 Alex Auld 1.00
18 Bryan Allen .50
19 Brandon Reid 1.50
20 Jason Goulet .50
21 Justin Kurtz .50
22 Brian Chapman .50
23 Pat Kavanagh .50
24 Rene Vydareny .50
25 Tyler Bouck .50
26 Jason Shmyr .50

2003-04 Manitoba Moose

This set was sold by the team at home games.

COMPLETE SET (24) 15.00
1 Checklist .01
2 Autograph Card .01
3 Mascot .10
4 Tomas Mojzis .60
5 Mikko Jokela .60
6 Nolan Baumgartner .60
7 Chris Nielsen .60
8 Tyler Bouck .60
9 Nathan Smith .60
10 Ryan Ready .60
11 Pat Kavanagh .60
12 Ryan Kesler 2.00
13 Sean Pronger .60
14 Rene Vydareny .60
15 Jimmy Roy .60
16 Justin Morrison .60
17 Martin Grenier .60
18 Tyler Moss 1.00
19 Alex Auld 1.00
20 Dallas Eakins .60
21 Jaroslav Obsut .60
22 Kirill Koltsov .60
23 Brandon Reid 1.00
24 Fedor Fedorov 1.00

2004-05 Manitoba Moose

COMPLETE SET (24) 20.00
1 Kevin Bieksa 1.00
2 Tomas Mojzis 1.00
3 Joey DiPenta 1.50
4 Kent Huskins 1.00
5 Nolan Baumgartner 1.00
6 Justin Morrison 1.00
7 Jeff Heerema 1.00
8 Ryan Kesler 1.50
9 Peter Sarno 1.50
10 Nathan Smith 1.00
11 Jimmy Roy 1.00
12 Jesse Schultz 1.00
13 Brandon Nolan 1.00
14 Jason King 1.50
15 Wade Flaherty 1.50
16 Alex Auld 1.50
17 Josh Green 1.00
18 Lee Goren 1.50
19 Wade Brookbank 1.00
20 Johnathan Aitken 1.00
21 Autograph Card .01
22 MTS Centre 1st Goal .10
23 Inaugural Season .10
24 Mick E. Moose MASCOT .10

2005-06 Manitoba Moose

COMPLETE SET (27) 12.00
1 Jozef Balej .20 .50
2 Ryan Bayda .20 .50
3 Kevin Bieksa .20 .50
4 Mike Brown .20 .50
5 Alexandre Burrows .30 .75
6 Sven Butenschon .20 .50
7 Craig Darby .20 .50
8 Wade Flaherty .40 1.00
9 Maxime Fortunus .20 .50
10 Josh Green .20 .50
11 Jason Jaffray .20 .50
12 Mike Keane .20 .50
13 Nathan McIver .20 .50
14 Tomas Mojzis .20 .50
15 Yuri Moscevsky .20 .50
16 Maxime Ouellet .40 1.00
17 Jimmy Roy .20 .50
18 Prestin Ryan .20 .50
19 Rick Rypien .20 .50
20 Jesse Schultz .40 1.00
21 Brett Skinner .20 .50
22 Nathan Smith .20 .50
23 AHL All-Star Classic .02 .10
24 Autograph Card .02 .10
25 The Home of Hockey .02 .10
26 Manitoba Moose CL .02 .10
27 Mick E. Moose MASCOT .02 .10

2006-07 Manitoba Moose

COMPLETE SET (27) 12.00 20.00
1 Mick E. Moose MASCOT .10 .25
2 Drew McIntyre .40 1.00
3 Alexander Edler .30 .75
4 Prestin Ryan .30 .75
5 Joe Rullier .30 .75
6 Nathan McIver .30 .75
7 Brandon Reid .40 1.00
8 Mike Keane .30 .75
9 Mike Brown .30 .75
10 Jason Jaffray .30 .75
11 Jannik Hansen .60 1.50
12 J.J. Hunter .30 .75
13 Nathan Smith .30 .75
14 Brad Moran .30 .75
15 Jesse Schultz .30 .75
16 Dustin Wood .30 .75
17 Adam Keefe .30 .75
18 Maxime Fortunus .30 .75
19 Marc-Andre Bernier .30 .75
20 Tyler Bouck .30 .75
21 Wade Flaherty .40 1.00
22 Julien Ellis .40 1.00
23 Lee Goren .40 1.00
24 Yannick Tremblay .30 .75
25 Patrick Coulombe .30 .75
26 Shaun Heshka .30 .75
27 Alexandre Bolduc .30 .75

2007-08 Manitoba Moose

COMPLETE SET (29) 6.00 15.00
1 Mike E. Moose MASCOT .15 .40
2 Drew MacIntyre .50 1.25
3 Luc Bourdon .50 1.25
4 Mason Raymond .50 1.25
5 Nathan McIver .20 .50
6 Jozef Balej .20 .50
7 Rick Rypien .20 .50
8 Mike Keane .20 .50
9 Mike Brown .20 .50
10 Jason Jaffray .20 .50
11 Jannik Hansen .50 1.25
12 Zack Fitzgerald .20 .50
13 Greg Classen .20 .50
14 Brad Moran .20 .50
15 Ryan Shannon .20 .50
16 Juraj Simek .20 .50
17 Shaun Heshka .20 .50
18 Maxime Fortunus .20 .50
19 Colby Genoway .20 .50
20 Pierre-Cedric Labrie .20 .50
21 Cory Schneider .50 1.25
22 Michael Grabner .20 .50
23 Jimmy Sharrow .20 .50
24 Danny Groulx .20 .50
25 Alexandre Bolduc .20 .50
26 Team Checklist .10 .25
27 Scott Arniel HC .15 .40
28 Brad Berry AC .10 .25
29 Autograph Card .10 .25

1982-83 Medicine Hat Tigers

These 21 blank-backed cards measure approximately 3" by 4" and feature white-bordered, black-and-white posed studio head shots of the WHL Tigers on the left halves of the cards. The player's name, jersey number and biography, along with a space for an autograph, appear on the right half. The cards are unnumbered and checklisted below in alphabetical order.

COMPLETE SET (21)	8.00	20.00
1 Al Conroy	.60	1.50
2 Murray Craven	.75	2.00
3 Mark Frank	.40	1.00
4 Kevan Guy	.40	1.00
5 Jim Hougen	.40	1.00
6 Ken Jorgenson	.40	1.00
7 Matt Kabayama	.40	1.00
8 Brent Kisilivich	.40	1.00
9 Mark Lamb	1.25	3.00
10 Mike Lay	.40	1.00
11 Dean McArthur	.40	1.00
12 Brent Meckling	.40	1.00
13 Shawn Nagurny	.40	1.00
14 Kodie Nelson	.40	1.00
15 Al Pedersen	.60	1.50
16 Todd Pederson	.40	1.00
17 Jay Reid	.40	1.00
18 Gord Shmyrko	.40	1.00
19 Brent Steblyk	.40	1.00
20 Rocky Trottier	.40	1.00
21 Dan Turner	.40	1.00

1983-84 Medicine Hat Tigers

This 23-card P.L.A.Y. (Police, Laws and Youth) set measures approximately 2 3/4" by 5" and features color player portraits with a wide white bottom border. The border contains the player's jersey number and name. The team logo is also printed in this area. The backs carry sponsor logos and public service "Tips From The Tigers."

COMPLETE SET (23)	12.00	40.00
1 Murray Craven	.75	2.00
2 Shane Churla	2.00	5.00
3 Don Herczeg	.60	1.50
4 Gary Johnson	.60	1.50
5 Brent Kisilivich	.60	1.50
6 Blair MacGregor	.60	1.50
7 Terry Knight	.60	1.50
8 Mark Lamb	1.25	3.00
9 Al Pedersen	.75	2.00
10 Trevor Semeniuk	.60	1.50
11 Dan Turner	.60	1.50
12 Brent Steblyk	.60	1.50
13 Rocky Trottier	.75	2.00
14 Kevan Guy	.75	2.00
15 Bobby Bassen	.75	2.00
16 Brent Meckling	.60	1.50
17 Matt Kabayama	.60	1.50
18 Gord Hynes	.75	2.00
19 Daryl Henry	.60	1.50
20 Jim Kambeitz	.60	1.50
21 Mike Lay	.75	2.00
22 Gord Shmyrko	.60	1.50
23 Al Conroy	.75	2.00

1985-86 Medicine Hat Tigers

This 24-card set measures approximately 2 1/4" by 4" and features posed, color player photos on white card stock. The player's name and the team logo are printed in the larger white margin at the bottom. The player's jersey number and position are printed on the picture in the upper corners. A thin red line encloses the picture, player's name, and logo. The backs display P.L.A.Y. (Police, Laws, and Youth) tips and sponsor logos.

COMPLETE SET (24)	8.00	20.00
1 Mike Claringbull	.30	.75
2 Doug Houda	.40	1.00
3 Mark Kuntz	.30	.75
4 Guy Phillips	.30	.75
5 Rob DiMaio	.75	2.00
6 Al Conroy	.40	1.00
7 Craig Berube	.75	2.00
8 Doug Sauter CO	.20	.50
9 Dean Chynoweth	.40	1.00
10 Scott McCrady	.30	.75
11 Neil Brady	.30	.75
12 Dale Kushner	.30	.75
13 Jeff Wenaas	.30	.75
14 Wayne Hynes	.30	.75
15 Troy Gamble	.75	2.00
16 Bryan Maxwell ACO	.20	.50
17 Gord Hynes	.30	.75
18 Wayne McBean	.40	1.00
19 Mark Pederson	.40	1.00
20 Darren Cota	.30	.75
21 Randy Siska	.30	.75
22 Dave Mackey	.30	.75
23 Mark Fitzpatrick	1.25	3.00
24 Doug Ball TR	.08	.25

1995-96 Medicine Hat Tigers

This 21-card set features color player photos of the Medicine Hat Tigers of the WHL and was sponsored by Pizza Hut. The black front border is highly susceptible to dings, and thus the set is considered condition sensitive. Although the cards feature player jersey numbers on the fronts, they are unnumbered, and thus the set is checklisted below in alphabetical order.

COMPLETE SET (21)	6.00	15.00
1 Johnathan Aitken	.30	.75
2 Brady Austin	.30	.75
3 Cal Benazic	.30	.75
4 Scott Buhler	.30	.75
5 Clint Cabana	.30	.75
6 Mike Eley	.30	.75
7 Josh Green	.40	1.00
8 Curtis Huppe	.30	.75
9 Henry Kuster	.30	.75
10 Aaron Millar	.30	.75
11 Mark Polak	.30	.75
12 Bryan Randall	.30	.75
13 Chad Reich	.30	.75
14 Kyle Ronan	.30	.75
15 Rroary MASCOT	.02	.10
16 Blair St. Martin	.30	.75
17 Paxton Schafer	.30	.75
18 Derek Senkow	.30	.75
19 Darcy Smith	.30	.75
20 Rocky Thompson	.40	1.00
21 Trevor Wasyluk	.40	1.00

1996-97 Medicine Hat Tigers

This 25-card set features posed color player photos surrounded by an orange/yellow border. The player's name, number and position are listed along the left border, while the logos of the team and Canadian Tire can be found along the bottom. The top reads "Medicine Hat News Collector's Edition", leading to speculation that the set was issued as a premium either through the paper, or at a game night sponsored by the paper. The backs contain a large Canadian Tire logo, along with biographical info for the player. The cards are unnumbered, and are checklisted below in alphabetical order.

COMPLETE SET (25)	6.00	15.00
1 Berkeley Buchko	.30	.75
2 Scott Buhler	.30	.75
3 Jason Chimera	.60	1.50
4 Michael Dyck ACO	.02	.10
5 Mike Eley	.30	.75
6 Josh Green	.30	.75
7 Derek Holland	.30	.75
8 Curtis Huppe	.30	.75
9 Henry Kuster	.30	.75
10 Kurt Lackten CO	.02	.10
11 Kevin McDonald	.30	.75
12 Aaron Millar	.30	.75
13 Doug Mosher GM	.02	.10
14 Jaroslav Obsut	.30	.75
15 Colin O'Hara	.30	.75
16 Mark Polak	.30	.75
17 Rroary MASCOT	.02	.10
18 Blair St. Martin	.30	.75
19 Rob Sandrock	.30	.75
20 Dustin Schwartz	.30	.75
21 Lee Svangstu	.30	.75
22 Jeff Temple	.30	.75
23 Rocky Thompson	.30	.75
24 Trevor Wasyluk	.30	.75
25 Chad Wilchynski	.30	.75

1997-98 Medicine Hat Tigers

This set features the Tigers of the WHL. The set was sponsored by the Medicine Hat News and was sold at home games. The cards are unnumbered, and so are listed below in alphabetical order.

COMPLETE SET (25)	4.80	12.00
1 Steve Albrecht	.20	.50
2 James Boyd	.20	.50
3 Konrad Brand	.20	.50
4 Berkeley Buchko	.20	.50
5 Scott Buhler	.40	1.00
6 Rick Carriere CO	.04	.10
7 Jason Chimera	.75	2.00
8 Randall Dyck	.20	.50
9 Shaun Hill	.20	.50
10 Derek Holland	.20	.50
11 Henry Kuster	.20	.50
12 Kevin McDonald	.20	.50
13 Aaron Millar	.20	.50
14 Derek Rupprecht	.20	.50
15 Rob Sandrock	.20	.50
16 Brett Scheffelmaier	.30	.75
17 Justin Schwartz	.20	.50
18 Blair Simpson	.20	.50
19 Blair St. Martin	.20	.50
20 Jeff Temple	.20	.50
21 Brad Voth	.20	.50
22 Trevor Wasyluk	.20	.50
23 Travis Willie	.20	.50
24 Randy Wong ACO	.02	.10
25 Rroary MASCOT	.02	.10

1998-99 Medicine Hat Tigers

This set features the Tigers of the WHL. The set was sponsored by the Medicine Hat News and was sold at home games. The cards are unnumbered, and so are listed below in alphabetical order.

COMPLETE SET (25)	4.80	12.00
1 Brady Austin	.20	.50
2 James Boyd	.20	.50
3 Konrad Brand	.20	.50
4 Berkeley Buchko	.20	.50
5 Scott Buhler	.30	.75
6 Rick Carriere CO	.02	.10
7 Jason Chimera	.60	1.50
8 Martin Cibak	.40	1.00
9 Frazer Donahue	.20	.50
10 Paul Elliott	.20	.50
11 Kris Graf	.20	.50
12 Shaun Hill	.20	.50
13 Denny Johnston	.20	.50
14 Tyson Kentel	.20	.50
15 Cody Lyseng	.20	.50
16 Aaron Millar	.20	.50
17 Derek Rupprecht	.20	.50
18 Brett Scheffelmaier	.30	.75
19 Justin Schwartz	.30	.75
20 Blair Simpson	.20	.50
21 Ben Thompson	.20	.50
22 Brad Voth	.20	.50
23 Kevin Young	.20	.50
24 Randy Wong ACO	.02	.10
25 Rroary MASCOT	.02	.10

1999-00 Medicine Hat Tigers

This set was produced on very thin card stock and is highly susceptible to damage. The cards were sold by the team at its souvenir stands. The set is noteworthy for featuring the first card of 2002 first-rounder Jay Bouwmeester.

COMPLETE SET (25)	10.00	25.00
1 Header Card	.02	.10
2 Chris Ferguson	.20	.50
3 Jay Bouwmeester	6.00	15.00
4 Josh Morrow	.20	.50
5 Paul Elliott	.20	.50
6 Tyson Mulock	.20	.50
7 Kevin Labbe	.20	.50
8 Ryan Hollweg	.30	.75
9 Berkeley Buchko	.20	.50
10 Chris St. Jacques	.20	.50
11 Cody Jensen	.20	.50
12 Ben Thompson	.20	.50
13 Brad Voth	.20	.50
14 Martin Cibak	.20	.50
15 Denny Johnston	.20	.50
16 Konrad Brand	.20	.50
17 Shaun Sutter	.30	.75
18 Ken Davis	.20	.50
19 Ryan Kinasewich	.20	.50
20 Brett Scheffelmaier	.30	.75
21 Justin Taylor	.20	.50
22 Vladimir Sicak	.20	.50
23 Ben McMullin	.30	.75
24 Kyle Kettles	.30	.75
25 Josh Maser	.20	.50
26 Martin Cibak	.20	.50
27 Brett Scheffelmaier	.20	.50
28 Justin Taylor	.20	.50
29 Vladimir Sicak	.20	.50
30 Ben McMullin	.20	.50
31 Kyle Kettles	.20	.50
32 Jash Maser	.20	.50

2000-01 Medicine Hat Tigers

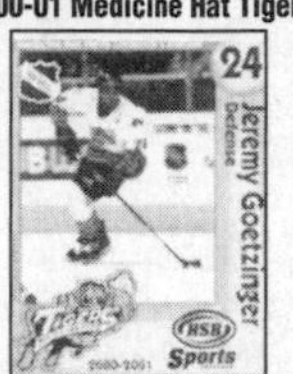

This set features the Tigers of the WHL. The set was sold by the team at its souvenir stands. The cards are unnumbered and is listed below alphabetically. The set features an early card of top prospect Jay Bouwmeester.

COMPLETE SET (26)	8.00	25.00
1 Jay Bouwmeester	4.00	8.00
2 Ryan Chieduch	.16	.40
3 Petr Chvojka	.16	.40
4 Ken Davis	.16	.40
5 Brett Dranoy	.10	.40
6 Bryan Ellerman ACO	.04	.10
7 B.J. Fehr	.16	.40
8 Vernon Fiddler	.16	.40
9 Jeremy Goetzinger	.16	.40
10 Ryan Hollweg	.30	.75
11 Denny Johnston	.16	.40
12 Kyle Kettles	.16	.40
13 Ryan Kinasewich	.16	.40
14 Bob Loucks HCO	.04	.10
15 Joffrey Lupul	2.00	10.00
16 Ben McMullin	.20	.50
17 Josh Morrow	.16	.40
18 Tyson Mulock	.16	.40
19 Ryan Olynyk	.16	.40
20 Brett Scheffelmaier	.30	.75
21 Chris St. Jacques	.16	.40
22 Ben Thompson	.16	.40
23 David Ullmann	.16	.40
24 Brad Voth	.16	.40
25 Randy Wong ACO	.04	.10
26 Mascot	.04	.10

2002-03 Medicine Hat Tigers

These cards are unnumbered and are listed below in alphabetical order.

COMPLETE SET (25)	8.00	20.00
1 Curtis Austring	.20	.50
2 Cam Barker	.60	1.50
3 Chad Bassen	.20	.50
4 Kieran Block	.20	.50
5 Brenden Cuthbert	.20	.50
6 Riley Day	.20	.50
7 Tyler Dietrich	.20	.50
8 Nick Harsulla	.20	.50
9 Ryan Hollweg	.30	.75
10 Daniel Idema	.20	.50
11 Martin Kubaliak	.20	.50
12 Joffrey Lupul	2.00	5.00
13 Steve Marr	.20	.50
14 Tommy Maxwell	.20	.50
15 Stefan Meyer	.20	.50
16 Clarke MacArthur	.40	1.00
17 Kevin Nastiuk	.60	1.50
18 Kyle Pess	.20	.50
19 Adam Redmond	.20	.50
20 Steven Regier	.20	.50
21 Darren Reid	.20	.50
22 Mark Vodden	.20	.50
23 Chris St. Jacques	.20	.50
24 Ryan Stempfle	.20	.50
25 Ben Thomson	.20	.50

2003-04 Medicine Hat Tigers

This checklist is incomplete, but the cards below have been confirmed to exist. If you can help complete this listing, please email hockeymag@beckett.com.

COMPLETE SET (?)		
1 Cam Barker		
2 Riley Day		
3 Ryan Hollweg		
4 Clarke MacArthur		
5 Stefan Meyer		
6 Kevin Nastiuk		
7 Darren Reid		
8 Yannick Seidenberg		

2004-05 Medicine Hat Tigers

COMPLETE SET (25)		20.00
1 Gord Baldwin		.75
2 Cam Barker		1.50
3 Jordan Bendfeld		.75
4 Cody Blanshan		.75
5 Kieran Block		.75
6 Derek Dorsett		.75
7 Nathan Exner		.75
8 Trevor Glass		.75
9 Darren Helm		.75
10 Matt Keetley		.75
11 Jarret Lukin		.75
12 Clarke MacArthur		1.00
13 Steve Marr		.75
14 Tommy Maxwell		.75
15 Stefan Meyer		.75
16 Kevin Nastiuk		1.50
17 Roman Psurny		.75
18 Brett Robertson		.75
19 Kris Russell		.75
20 David Schlemko		.75
21 Daine Todd		.75
22 Devyn Tremblay		.75
23 Kevin Undershute		.75
24 Willie Desjardins CO		.10
25 Shaun Clouston ACO		.10

2005-06 Medicine Hat Tigers

COMPLETE SET (25)	8.00	20.00
1 Gord Baldwin	.30	.75
2 Cam Barker	.60	1.50
3 Jason Battershill	.30	.75
4 Jordan Bendfeld	.30	.75
5 Kieran Block	.30	.75
6 Brennan Bosch	.30	.75
7 Shayne Brown	.30	.75
8 Marek Curilla	.30	.75
9 Derek Dorsett	.30	.75
10 Tyler Ennis	.30	.75
11 Trevor Glass	.30	.75
12 Darren Helm	.30	.75
13 Matt Keetley	.30	.75
14 Tommy Maxwell	.30	.75
15 Blaine Neufeld	.30	.75
16 Roman Psurny	.30	.75
17 Brett Robertson	.30	.75
18 Kris Russell	.30	.75
19 Jerrid Sauer	.30	.75
20 David Schlemko	.30	.75
21 Matt Sokol	.30	.75
22 Chris Stevens	.30	.75
23 Daine Todd	.30	.75
24 Kevin Undershute	.30	.75
25 Scott Wasden	.30	.75

2006-07 Medicine Hat Tigers

COMPLETE SET (25)	12.00	20.00
1 Gord Baldwin	.30	.75
2 Jordan Bendfeld	.30	.75
3 Brennan Bosch	.30	.75
4 Shayne Brown	.30	.75
5 Derek Dorsett	.30	.75
6 Tyler Ennis	.30	.75
7 Trevor Glass	.30	.75
8 Colton Grant	.30	.75
9 Darren Helm	.30	.75
10 Jordan Hickmott	.30	.75
11 Ryan Holfeld	.40	1.00
12 Mark Isherwood	.30	.75
13 Matt Keetley	.40	1.00
14 Matt Lowry	.30	.75
15 Jakub Rumpel	.30	.75
16 Kris Russell	.75	2.00
17 Jerrid Sauer	.30	.75
18 Michael Sauer	.30	.75
19 David Schlemko	.30	.75
20 Chris Stevens	.30	.75
21 Tyler Swystun	.30	.75
22 Daine Todd	.30	.75
23 Kevin Undershute	.30	.75
24 Scott Wasden	.30	.75
25 Willie Desjardins CO	.10	.25

1993-94 Memphis RiverKings

Like most of the CHL sets issued that season, these round cards are approximately the size of a hockey puck. They came in a plastic container with the team logo on the front, and were sold by the booster club for $5..

COMPLETE SET (18)	3.60	9.00
1 Rocco Amonte	.20	.50
2 Peter D'Amario	.20	.50
3 Roydon Gunn	.20	.50
4 Kyle Haviland	.20	.50
5 Mike Jackson	.20	.50
6 Scot Johnston	.20	.50
7 Robert Kelley	.20	.50
8 Mark McGinn	.20	.50
9 Antoine Mindjimba	.30	.75
10 David Moore	.20	.50
11 Glenn Painter	.20	.50
12 Scott Phillips	.20	.50
13 Mike Roberts	.20	.50
14 Andy Ross	.20	.50
15 Steve Shaunessy	.20	.50
16 Ken Venis	.20	.50
17 Bobby Wallwork	.20	.50
18 Randy Boyd CO	.08	.25

1994-95 Memphis RiverKings

Available in 14-card CHL packs that contained an assortment of teams, this 18-card set featured players of the RiverKings.

COMPLETE SET (18)	3.00	8.00
1 Denis Beauchamp	.20	.50
2 Nicolas Brousseau	.20	.50
3 Scott Bower	.30	.75
4 Dan Brown	.20	.50
5 Brian Cook	.20	.50
6 Brent Fleetwood	.20	.50
7 Francois Gagnon	.20	.50
8 Dominic Grand'maison	.20	.50
9 Kyle Haviland	.20	.50
10 Jamie Hearn	.20	.50
11 Mike Jackson	.30	.75
12 Paul Krake	.30	.75
13 Layne LeBel	.20	.50
14 Steve Magnusson	.20	.50
15 Darren Miciak	.20	.50
16 Mark McGinn	.20	.50
17 Bobby Wallwork	.20	.50
18 Herb Boxer CO	.08	.25

1999-00 Memphis RiverKings All-Time

This set features the RiverKings of the CHL. Rather than commemorate the current roster, it features the best players ever to don the River Kings sweater. The set was originally issued as a promotional giveaway, but later was sold by the team as well.

COMPLETE SET (20)	4.00	10.00
1 Tom Mutch	.20	.50
2 Doug Stromback	.20	.50
3 Mike Jackson	.30	.75
4 Mark McGinn	.20	.50
5 Antoine Mindjimba	.30	.75
6 Andrew Miller	.20	.50
7 Dan Brown	.20	.50
8 Hugo Hamelin	.20	.50
9 Derek Grant	.20	.50
10 Steve Thorpe	.20	.50
11 Bobby Wallwork	.20	.50
12 Peter D'Amario	.20	.50
13 John Batten	.20	.50
14 Andy Ross	.20	.50
15 Kyle Haviland	.20	.50
16 Scot Kelsey	.20	.50
17 Scott Brower	.20	.50
18 Jamie Cooke	.30	.75
19 Craig Lindsay	.20	.50
20 Riverthing MAS	.08	.25

2001-02 Memphis RiverKings

This set features the RiverKings of the CHL. The set was sold by the team at home games late in the season, after goalie Sebastien Centomo had moved on to the AHL and later, the NHL. The cards are unnumbered, although they are listed on a checklist. The set is listed in the order it appears on the checklist.

COMPLETE SET (21)	6.00	15.00
1 Team CL Centomo	.30	.75
2 Kahlil Thomas	.20	.50
3 Brad Mueller	.20	.50
4 Kevin Fricke	.20	.50
5 Anthony DiPalma	.20	.50
6 Michal Slastny	.30	.75
7 Jean-Francois Picard	.20	.50
8 Jay Neal	.20	.50
9 Jacques Lariviere	.30	.75
10 Rob Palahnuk	.20	.50
11 Kevin Ryan	.20	.50
12 Sebastien Centomo	2.00	5.00
13 Don Parsons	.20	.50
14 Luch Nasato	.30	.75
15 Mark Richards	.30	.75
16 Brian Tucker	.20	.50
17 Don Martin	.20	.50
18 Ben Gorewich	.20	.50
19 A.J. Aitken	.20	.50
20 Jonathan Gagnon	.20	.50
21 Doug Shedden CO	.20	.50

2003-04 Memphis RiverKings

COMPLETE SET	6.00	15.00
1 Jeremy Cornish	.40	1.00
2 Trent Dickson	.30	.75
3 Juraj Durco	.30	.75
4 Jonathan Gagnon	.30	.75
5 Jasmin Gelinas	.30	.75
6 Jerry Gernander	.30	.75
7 Jeremy Goetzinger	.30	.75
8 Chad Grills	.30	.75
9 Derek Landmesser	.40	1.00
10 Stephen Margeson	.30	.75
11 Alexandre Mathieu	.40	1.00
12 Mike Minard	.40	1.00
13 Brad Mueller	.30	.75
14 Jay Neal	.30	.75
15 Brent Ozarowski	.30	.75
16 Don Parsons	.40	1.00
17 Jean-Francois Racine	.60	1.50
18 Mark Richards	.30	.75
19 Tim Schneider	.30	.75
20 Brian Tucker	.30	.75
21 David Turon	.30	.75

2004-05 Memphis RiverKings

COMPLETE SET (22)		15.00
1 Header Card		.10
2 Aaron Lewis		.50
3 Allan Carr		.50
4 Brad Mueller		.50
5 David Lemanowicz		1.50
6 Derek Landmesser		.50
7 Don Parsons		.75
8 J.F. Racine		1.50
9 Jeremy Goetzinger		.50
10 Jeremy Wray		.50
11 Ken Goetz		1.50
12 Mark Richards		.50
13 Peter Robertson		.50
14 Phil Aucoin		.50
15 Ryan Rome		.50
16 Scott English		2.00
17 Stephen Margeson		.50
18 Ted Crowley		.50
19 Tim Plett		.50
20 Travis Banga		.50
21 Tyson Gajda		.50
22 Wayne Hall		.50

1991-92 Michigan Falcons

This set features the Falcons of the UHL. According to minor league expert Ralph Slate, the set wasn't widely distributed until 1994-95, but based on the players involved and the fact that the manufacturer -- 7th Inning Sketch -- actually went out of business in 1992, this set must have been intended for distribution during that season.

COMPLETE SET (21)	8.00	20.00
1 Christian LaLonde	.40	1.00
2 Victor Posa	.40	1.00
3 Al Murphy	.40	1.00
4 Bill Horn	.40	1.00
5 Rich Sewell	.40	1.00
6 Dan Fowler	.40	1.00
7 Kip Noble	.40	1.00
8 Ange Guzzo	.40	1.00
9 Dean Morton	.40	1.00
10 Jeff Lindsay	.40	1.00
11 Mike Vellucci	.60	1.50
12 Brett Strot	.40	1.00
13 Rick Berens	.40	1.00
14 Kevin Clayton	.40	1.00
15 Todd Humphrey	.40	1.00
16 Terry Christensen CO	.08	.25
16 Tom Viggiano ACO	.08	.25
16 Ray De Grendel ACO	.08	.25
17 Bill Gutenberg	.40	1.00
18 Jamie Stewart	.40	1.00
19 Bob McKillop	.40	1.00
20 Clayton Young	.40	1.00
21 Steve Beadle	.40	1.00

1996-97 Michigan K-Wings

This set features the K-Wings of the IHL. The set was sponsored by BJ Sports, and sold by the team at home games.

COMPLETE SET (27)	4.80	10.00
1 Dan Keczmer	.15	.40
2 Dennis Smith	.15	.40
3 Brad Berry	.15	.40
4 Shane Peacock	.15	.40
5 Jason Lafreniere	.15	.40
6 Collin Bauer	.15	.40
7 Sergei Gusev	.15	.40
8 Igor Korolev/Misspelled Horolev on front		.15
.40		
9 Brent Fedyk	.15	.40
10 Pat Elynuik	.15	.40
11 Jamie Wright	.15	.40
12 Lee Jinman	.15	.40
13 Jeff Mitchell	.15	.40
14 Brad Lukowich	.20	.50
15 Derrick Smith	.15	.40
16 Petr Buzek	.15	.40
17 Patrick Cote	.30	.75
18 Mark Lawrence	.15	.40
19 Jim Storm	.15	.40
20 Roman Turek	.40	1.00
21 Neil Brady	.15	.40
22 Manny Fernandez	.75	2.00
23 Claude Noel CO	.02	.10
24 Jim Playfair CO	.02	.10
25 Checklist		.01
26 PHPA Web Site		.01
27 BJ Sports		.01

1998-99 Michigan K-Wings

This 21-card set features the K-Wings of the IHL on an extra glossy card stock. The cards are not numbered so they appear in the order that was released on the checklist card.

COMPLETE SET (21)	8.00	25.00
1 Mel Angelstad	.40	1.00
2 Jason Botterill	.15	.40
3 Ryan Christie	.15	.40
4 Doug Doull	.75	2.00
5 Kelly Fairchild	.15	.40
6 Marty Flichel	.15	.40
7 Aaron Gavey	.30	.75
8 Greg Leeb	.15	.40
9 Jeff Mitchell	.15	.40
10 Dave Roberts	.15	.40
11 Jon Sim	.30	.75
12 Brad Berry	.15	.40
13 Petr Buzek	.30	.75
14 Richard Jackman	.30	.75
15 Brad Lukowich	.30	.75
16 Matt Martin	.15	.40
17 Evgueni Tsybouk	.15	.40
18 Mike Bales	.30	.75
19 Marty Turco	6.00	15.00
20 IHL Logo card		.01
21 Header/Checklist	.04	.01

1999-00 Michigan K-Wings

This set features the K-Wings of the IHL. The set was produced by EBK Sports and was sold by the team at its souvenir stands. Each card also is serial numbered out of 1,000.

COMPLETE SET (21)	14.00	40.00
1 Jamie Wright	.30	.75
2 Keith Aldridge	.30	.75
3 Steve Gainey	.30	.75
4 Jonathan Sim	.40	1.00
5 Mike Martin	.20	.50
6 Gaetan Royer	.20	.50
7 Jeff MacMillan	.20	.50
8 Aaron Gavey	.20	.50
9 Evgeny Tsybouk	.20	.50
10 Marty Turco	8.00	20.00
11 Matt Martin	.20	.50
12 Ryan Christie	.20	.50
13 Greg Leeb	.20	.50
14 Mark Wotton	.20	.50
15 Kelly Fairchild	.20	.50
16 Gregor Baumgartner	.20	.50
17 Brenden Morrow	4.00	10.00
18 Mel Angelstad	.75	2.00
19 Mike Bales	.30	.75
20 Richard Jackman	.30	.75
21 Roman Lyashenko	.40	1.00

1992-93 Michigan State Spartans

This set features the Spartans of the NCAA. The cards are unnumbered and so are listed below in alphabetical order. The cards were issued as a promotional giveaway.

COMPLETE SET (30)	15.00	40.00
1 Team Photo	.60	1.50
2 Ron Mason HCO	.60	1.50
3 Matt Albers	.60	1.50
4 Michael Burkett	.60	1.50
5 Mike Buzak	.60	1.50
6 Anson Carter	2.50	6.00
7 Brian Clifford	.60	1.50
8 Scott Dean	.60	1.50
9 Ryan Fleming	.60	1.50
10 Ryan Folkening	.60	1.50
11 Steve Guolla	1.25	3.00
12 Kelly Harper	.60	1.50
13 Eric Kruse	.60	1.50
14 James Lambros	.60	1.50
15 Mike Mattis	.60	1.50
16 Wes McCauley	.60	1.50
17 Rem Murray	1.25	3.00
18 Steve Norton	.60	1.50
19 Nicolas Perreault	.60	1.50
20 Bill Shalawylo	.60	1.50
21 Chris Smith	.60	1.50
22 Bryan Smolinski	1.25	3.00
23 Steve Suk	.60	1.50
24 Chris Sullivan	.60	1.50
25 Bart Turner	.60	1.50
26 Bart Vanstaalduinen	.60	1.50
27 Mike Ware	.60	1.50
28 John Weidenbach	.60	1.50
29 Rob Woodward	.60	1.50
30 Scott Worden	.60	1.50

1993-94 Michigan State Spartans

This set features the Spartans of the NCAA. The cards were produced by Phipps Sports Marketing, Inc and were issued as a promotional giveaway. The cards are unnumbered and checklisted below in alphabetical order.

COMPLETE SET (32)	15.00	40.00
1 Matt Albers	.40	1.00
2 Michael Burkett	.40	1.00
3 Mike Buzak	.40	1.00
4 Anson Carter	2.00	5.00
5 Brian Clifford	.75	2.00
6 Brian Crane	.40	1.00
7 Steve Ferranti	.40	1.00
8 Ryan Fleming	.40	1.00
9 Steve Guolla	.75	2.00
10 Kelly Harper	.40	1.00
11 Eric Kruse	.40	1.00
12 Ron Mason CO	.40	1.00
13 Mike Mattis	.40	1.00
14 Rem Murray	.75	2.00
15 Steve Norton	.40	1.00
16 Nicolas Perreault	.40	1.00
17 Tom Ross Spartan Great	.75	2.00
18 Chris Slater	.40	1.00
19 Chris Smith	.40	1.00
20 Bryan Smolinski	1.25	3.00
21 Sparty (Mascot)	.02	.10
22 Chris Sullivan	.40	1.00
23 Steve Suk	.40	1.00
24 Bart Turner	.40	1.00
25 Tony Tuzzolino	1.25	3.00
26 Bart Vanstaalduinen	.40	1.00
27 Mike Ware	.40	1.00
28 John Weidenbach	.40	1.00
29 Josh Wiegand	.40	1.00
30 Scott Worden	.40	1.00
31 Munn Arena	.02	.10
32 Title Card	.02	.10

2000-01 Michigan State Spartans

This set features the Spartans of the NCAA. It was handed out as a promotional giveaway at a pair of home games in 2000. The set is noteworthy for including an early card of hot prospect Ryan Miller.

COMPLETE SET (21)	10.00	35.00
1 Joe Blackburn	.80	2.00
2 Andrew Bogle	.40	1.00
3 Steve Clark	.40	1.00
4 Rustyn Dolyny	.40	1.00
5 Brad Fast	.40	1.00
6 Troy Ferguson	.40	1.00
7 Joe Goodenow	.40	1.00
8 Adam Hall	.40	5.00
9 Andrew Hutchinson	.40	2.00
10 Jon Insana	.40	1.00
11 Steve Jackson	.40	1.00
12 Kris Koski	.40	1.00
13 John-Michael Liles	.40	5.00
14 Brian Maloney	.40	1.00
15 Ryan Miller	6.00	15.00
16 John Nail	.40	1.00
17 Sean Patchell	.40	1.00
18 Damon Whitten	.40	1.00
19 Ron Mason CO	.40	1.00
20 White Out Game 3/2/01	.10	.25
21 Chevy Fans.Com	.04	.01

1990-91 Michigan Tech Huskies

This 31-card standard-size set was sponsored by The Daily Mining Gazette and showcases the Michigan Tech Huskies of the WCHA. Reportedly only 500 sets were produced. The cards are printed on thin cardboard stock. Borderless high gloss player photos grace the fronts, with the jersey number, team name, player name, and position given in a black stripe at the bottom of the card face. On a black and pale yellow background, each back has a black and white head shot, biography, statistics, and career summary. A "Huskies Hockey Quick Fact" completes the card back. The cards are unnumbered and checklisted below in alphabetical order.

COMPLETE SET (31)	6.00	15.00
1 Jim Bonner	.20	.50
2 Newell Brown CO	.08	.25
3 Dwight DeGiacomo	.20	.50
4 Rod Ewacha	.20	.50
5 Peter Grant	.20	.50
6 Tim Hartnett	.20	.50
7 Mike Hauswirth	.20	.50
8 Kelly Hurd	.20	.50
9 Kelly Hurd Red Wings	.20	.50
10 Layne Lebel Jeff Hill	.20	.50
11 Randy Lewis	.20	.50
12 Jay Luknowsky	.20	.50

13 Ken Martel CO .08 .25
Mark Leach CO
14 Darcy Martini .20 .50
15 Reid McDonald .20 .50
16 Hugh McEwen .30 .75
Jim Storm
Kevin Manninen
17 Don Osborne .20 .50
18 Greg Parnell .20 .50
19 Davis Payne .20 .50
20 Kirby Perrault .20 .50
Darren Brkic
21 Ken Plaquin .20 .50
22 Damian Rhodes .75 2.00
23 Geoff Sarjeant .30 .75
24 Jamie Steer .20 .50
25 Rob Tustian .20 .50
26 Scott Vettraino .30 .75
Jamie Ram
27 Tim Watters .20 .50
(black and white)
28 John Young .20 .50
29 John Young .20 .50
Kelly Hurd
30 1991 MacInnes Cup .20 .50
31 1975 NCAA Champions .20 .50

1991-92 Michigan Tech Huskies

This 36-card standard-size set features the 1992-93 Michigan Tech Huskies. Reportedly approximately 2,000 sets were produced. The fronts features full-bleed color action player photos. A gray and yellow stripe at the bottom contains the player's name. The Huskies logo overlaps the picture and the stripe. Some players have two cards, the second of which is distinguished by a subtitle. The cards are unnumbered and checklisted below in alphabetical order.

COMPLETE SET (36) 6.00 15.00
1 Jim Bonner .20 .50
2 Darren Brkic .20 .50
3 Rod Ewacha .20 .50
4 Tim Hartnett .20 .50
5 Mike Hauswirth .20 .50
6 Jeff Hill .20 .50
7 Layne LeBel .20 .50
8 Randy Lewis .20 .50
9 Randy Lewis .20 .50
Hit Squad
10 John MacInnes CO .02 .10
11 Darcy Martini .20 .50
12 Darcy Martini .20 .50
Rink Blaster
13 Reid McDonald .20 .50
14 Hugh McEwen .20 .50
15 Bob Olson ANN .02 .10
16 Don Osborne .20 .50
17 Greg Parnell .20 .50
18 Davis Payne .20 .50
19 Kirby Perrault .20 .50
20 Ken Plaquin .20 .50
21 Jamie Ram .30 .75
22 Geoff Sarjeant .30 .75
23 Geoff Sarjeant .30 .75
WCHA Student-Athlete
24 Jamie Steer .20 .50
25 Jamie Steer .20 .50
Blade Runner
26 Jim Storm .20 .50
27 Scott Vettraino .20 .50
28 John Young .20 .50
29 Credits (Team huddling on Ice) .20 .50
30 Freshman .20 .50
Justin Peca
Liam Garvey
Randy Stevens
Brent Peterson
Travis Seale
31 Great Lakes Invitational .02 .10
32 Home Ice .02 .10
MacInnes Student Ice Arena
33 Team Photo .20 .50
34 NHL Draft .20 .50
Darcy Martini
Davis Payne
Geoff Sarjeant
Ken Plaquin
Jim Storm
Jamie Ram
Jamie Steer
Jim Bonner
35 Pep Band .02 .10
36 Michigan Tech Univ. .02 .10

1993-94 Michigan Tech Huskies

The set features the Huskies of the NCAA. As is the case with most collegiate sets, this is believed to have been issued as a promotional giveaway. Any additional information can be forwarded to hockeymag@beckett.com.

COMPLETE SET (25) 4.80 12.00
1 Pat Mikesch .20 .50
2 Eric Jensen .20 .50
3 Kyle Peterson .20 .50
4 Jay Storm .20 .50
5 Jason Hanchuk .20 .50
6 Mike Figliomeni .20 .50
7 Randy Stevens .20 .50
8 Brent Peterson .20 .50
9 Kirby Perrault .20 .50
10 Brian Hunter .20 .50
11 Travis Seale .20 .50
12 Jamie Ram .30 .75
13 Jeff Hill .20 .50
14 Justin Peca .20 .50
15 Layne LeBel .20 .50
16 Jeff Mikesch .20 .50
17 John Kisil .20 .50
18 Liam Garvey .20 .50
19 Kyle Ferguson .20 .50
20 Jason Wright .20 .50
21 Luciano Caravaggio .20 .50
22 Mitch Lane .20 .50
23 Randy Wakeham .20 .50
24 Martin Machacek .20 .50
25 Winter Carnival .02 .10

2001-02 Michigan Tech Huskies

This set features the Huskies of the NCAA. The set was issued as a promotional giveaway. As the cards are unnumbered, they are listed below in alphabetical order.

COMPLETE SET (33) 8.00 20.00
1 Greg Amadio .30 .75
2 Justin Brown .30 .75
3 Paul Cabana .30 .75
4 Tony DeLorenzo .30 .75
5 Jaron Doetzel .30 .75
6 Chris Durno .30 .75
7 Cam Ellsworth .40 1.00
8 Brett Engelhardt .30 .75
9 Chuck Fabry .30 .75
10 Brady Greco .30 .75
11 John Hartman .30 .75
12 Blizzard T. Husky .04 .10
13 Tom Kaiman .30 .75
14 Bryan Konkel .30 .75
15 Tim Laurila .40 1.00
16 Ryan Lenton .30 .75
17 MacInnes Arena .04 .10
18 Ryan Markham .30 .75
19 Pep Band .04 .10
20 Colin Murphy .30 .75
21 Bob Olson ANN .04 .10
22 Brad Patterson .30 .75
23 Bryan Perez .30 .75
24 Phil Pietila .30 .75
25 Jon Pittis .30 .75
26 Bob Rangus .30 .75
27 Rob Rankin .30 .75
28 Brian Rogers .40 1.00
29 Mike Sertich CO .10 .25
30 Josh Singer .30 .75
31 Brad Sullivan .30 .75
32 Frank Werner .30 .75
33 Clay Wilson .30 .75

1991-92 Michigan Wolverines

Little is known about this set beyond confirmation of the checklist. These cards are unnumbered and checklisted below in alphabetical order. Additional info can be forwarded to hockeymag@beckett.com

COMPLETE SET (25) 6.00 15.00
1 Doug Evans .20 .50
2 Denny Felsner .20 .50
3 Anton Fedorov .20 .50
4 Chris Gordon .20 .50
5 David Harlock .20 .50
6 Mike Helber .20 .50
7 Tim Hogan .20 .50
8 Mike Knuble .30 .75
9 Ted Kramer .20 .50
10 Pat Neaton .20 .50
11 David Oliver .30 .75
12 David Roberts .20 .50
13 Marc Ouimet .20 .50
14 Ron Sacka .20 .50
15 Mark Sakala .20 .50
16 Steve Shields 1.25 3.00
17 Alan Sinclair .20 .50
18 Cam Stewart .30 .75
19 Dan Stiver .20 .50
20 Mike Stone .20 .50
21 Chris Tamer .25 .60
22 Aaron Ward .30 .75
23 Rick Willis .20 .50
24 Brian Wiseman .20 .50
25 Team Card .02 .10

1993-94 Michigan Wolverines

This set features the Wolverines of the NCAA. As is the case with most collegiate sets, this is believed to have been a promotional giveaway. The cards are unnumbered and checklisted below in alphabetical order.

COMPLETE SET (28) 8.00 20.00
1 John Arnold .20 .50
2 Jason Botterill .30 .75
3 Peter Bourke .20 .50
4 Drew Denzin .20 .50
5 Anton Fedorov .20 .50
6 Chris Frescoln .20 .50
7 Chris Gordon .20 .50
8 Steve Halko .20 .50
9 Kevin Hilton .20 .50
10 Tim Hogan .20 .50
11 Mike Knuble .30 .75
12 Mike Legg .20 .50
13 Al Loges .20 .50
14 Warren Luhning .20 .50
15 John Madden 1.50 4.00
16 Brendan Morrison .75 2.00
17 David Oliver .20 .50
18 Ron Sacka .20 .50
19 Mark Sakala .20 .50
20 Harold Schock .20 .50
21 Steve Shields .60 1.50
22 Alan Sinclair .20 .50
23 Ryan Sittler .20 .50
24 Blake Sloan .40 1.00
25 Mike Stone .20 .50
26 Rick Willis .20 .50
27 Brian Wiseman .20 .50
28 Team Photo .20 .50

2002-03 Michigan Wolverines

COMPLETE SET (30) 35.00
1 Billy Powers ACO .10
2 Danny Richmond 2.00
3 Mike Roemensky 1.00
4 David Wyzgowski 1.00
5 Charlie Henderson 1.00
6 Jed Ortmeyer 2.00
7 Jeff Tambellini 3.00
8 David Moss 1.00
9 Gordon Berenson HCO 1.00
10 NCAA Frozen Four .25
11 Eric Nystrom 3.00
12 John Shouneyia 1.00
13 Andrew Ebbett 1.00
14 Michael Woodford 1.00
15 Mel Pearson ACO .25
16 Brandon Rogers 1.00
17 Joe Kautz 1.00
18 Mark Mink 1.00
19 Nick Martens 1.00
20 2002 CCHA Champions .25
21 Jason Ryznar 1.00
22 Andy Burnes 1.00
23 Dwight Helminen 1.00
24 Milan Gajic 1.00
25 Yost Arena .10
26 2002 CCHA Tournament Champs .25
27 J.J. Swistak 1.00
28 Al Montoya 10.00
29 Brandon Kaleniecki 1.00
30 Eric Werner 1.00

2003-04 Michigan Wolverines

This set was issued as a promotional giveaway.

COMPLETE SET (30) 20.00 40.00
1 Jeff Tambellini 1.25 3.00
2 Mike Mayhew .40 1.00
3 David Moss .75 2.00
4 Red Berenson CO .40 1.00
5 Endowed Scholarships .02 .10
6 Jason Ryznar .40 1.00
7 Andy Burnes .40 1.00
8 Dwight Helminen .40 1.00
9 Milan Gajic .40 1.00
10 Reilly Olson .40 1.00
11 Brandon Rogers .40 1.00
12 Joe Kautz .40 1.00
13 Tim Cook .40 1.00
14 Nick Martens .40 1.00
15 T.J. Hensick .75 2.00
16 Eric Werner .40 1.00
17 Brandon Kaleniecki .40 1.00
18 Al Montoya 3.00 8.00
19 Mike Brown .40 1.00
20 Noah Ruden .40 1.00
21 David Rohlfs .40 1.00
22 Eric Nystrom 1.25 3.00
23 Andrew Ebbett .40 1.00
24 Michael Woodford .40 1.00
25 Mel Pearson ACO .02 .10
26 Charlie Henderson .40 1.00
27 David Wyzgowski .40 1.00
28 Jason Dest .40 1.00
29 Matt Hunwick .75 2.00
30 Billy Powers ACO .02 .10

2004-05 Michigan Wolverines

This set was given out at home games in five strips of five cards.

COMPLETE SET (25) 20.00 30.00
1 David Rohlfs .40 1.00
2 Andrew Ebbett .40 1.00
3 Brandon Kaleniecki .40 1.00
4 Al Montoya 2.00 5.00
5 Gameday .02 .10
6 Chad Kolarik .40 1.00
7 Kevin Porter .40 1.00
8 Mike Brown .60 1.50
9 Tim Cook .40 1.00
10 Yost Arena .02 .10
11 Jason Dest .40 1.00
12 Matt Hunwick .60 1.50
13 T.J. Hensick .60 2.00
14 Mike Mayhew .40 1.00
15 Endowed Scholarships .02 .10
16 Nick Martens .40 1.00
17 David Moss 1.25 3.00
18 Eric Nystrom 1.25 3.00
19 Reilly Olson .40 1.00
20 Mel Pearson ACO .02 .10
21 Noah Ruden .40 1.00
22 Jeff Tambellini 1.25 3.00
23 Milan Gajic .40 1.00
24 Charlie Henderson .40 1.00
25 Billy Powers .40 1.00

2004 Michigan Multi-Sport TK Legacy *

This multi-sport series features sporting greats from the University of Michigan. Only those cards depicting hockey players are included in this listing, which includes base cards and autographs.

COMPLETE HOCKEY SET (6) 3.00
1950A John Matchefts AU 10.00
1950B Willard Ikola AU 10.00
1966C Red Berenson 15.00
1996A Marty Turco AU 25.00
1996B Brendan Morrison 20.00
H1 Red Berenson .75
H2 John Matchefts .50
H3 Willard Ikola .50
H4 Brendan Morrison .50
H5 Marty Turco 1.50
H6 Dave Debol .50
HL1 Marty Turco 50.00
Red Berenson AU
HL9 Willard Ikola 20.00
John Matchefts AU
VH1 John Matchefts AU 10.00
VH2 Willard Ikola AU 10.00
VH3 Marty Turco AU 25.00
VH4 Red Berenson AU 15.00
VH5 Brendan Morrison AU 20.00
VH6 Dave Debol AU 10.00

2007-08 Michigan Wolverines

COMPLETE SET (28) 4.00 10.00
1 Louie Caporusso .15 .40
2 Anthony Ciraulo .15 .40
3 Eric Elmblad .15 .40
4 Danny Fardig .15 .40
5 Chris Fragner .15 .40
6 Carl Hagelin .15 .40
7 Bryan Hogan .15 .40
8 Shawn Hunwick .15 .40
9 Steve Kampfer .15 .40
10 Chad Kolarik .15 .40
11 Chad Langlais .15 .40
12 Brian Lebler .15 .40
13 Tristin Llewellyn .15 .40
14 Tim Miller .15 .40
15 Mark Mitera .15 .40
16 Brandon Naurato .15 .40
17 Max Pacioretty .15 .40
18 Aaron Palushaj .15 .40
19 Kevin Porter .15 .40
20 Kevin Quick .15 .40
21 Matt Rust .15 .40
22 Billy Sauer .15 .40
23 Chris Summers .15 .40
24 Travis Turnbull .15 .40
25 Scooter Vaughn .15 .40
26 Ben Winnett .15 .40
27 Red Berenson HC .10 .25
28 Yost Arena .15 .40

1981-82 Milwaukee Admirals

This 15-card standard-size set was produced by TCMA and features the members of the Milwaukee Admirals. The cards are made of thick card stock. On the front, a black-and-white player photo with thin black borders is framed in bright yellow. The team name appears in the yellow border above the photo, while the player's name, jersey number, and position appear below. The horizontal backs carry biography and statistics.

COMPLETE SET (15) 6.00 15.00
1 Pat Rabbitt .40 1.00
2 Real Paiement .40 1.00
3 Fred Berry .40 1.00
4 Blaine Peerless .40 1.00
5 John Flesch .40 1.00
6 Yves Preston .40 1.00
7 Bruce McKay .40 1.00
8 Dale Yakiwchuk .40 1.00
9 Lorne Bokshowan .40 1.00
10 Danny Lecours .40 1.00
11 Sheldon Currie .40 1.00
12 Doug Robb .40 1.00
13 Rob Polman Tuin .60 1.50
14 Bob Collyard .40 1.00
15 Tim Ringler TR .20 .50

1994-95 Milwaukee Admirals

This 28-card standard-size set was manufactured and distributed by Jessen Associates, Inc. for Classic. The fronts display color action player photos with a dark blue marbleized inner border and a black outer border. The player's name, jersey number, and position appear in the teal border on the right edge. The cards are unnumbered and checklisted below in alphabetical order.

COMPLETE SET (28) 3.00 8.00
1 Doug Agnew TR .02 .10
2 Peter Bakovic ACO .02 .10
3 Matt Block .08 .25
4 Gino Cavallini .15 .40
5 Sylvain Couturier .15 .40
6 Brian Dobbin .15 .40
7 Shawn Evans .08 .25
8 Fabulous Fritz .02 .10
9 Chris Govedaris .20 .50
10 Jim Hrivnak .30 .75
11 Tony Hrkac .20 .50
12 Fabian Joseph .20 .50
13 Mark LaForest .20 .50
14 Don MacAdam ACO .02 .10
15 Dave Mackey .08 .25
16 Pat MacLeod .15 .40
17 Dave Marcinyshyn .08 .25
18 Bob Mason .30 .75
19 Mike McNeill .20 .50
20 Kent Paynter .08 .25
21 Ken Sabourin .08 .25
22 Trevor Sim .08 .25
23 Martin Simard .08 .25
24 Mike Tomlak .08 .25
25 Steve Tuttle .08 .25
26 Randy Velischek .15 .40
27 Brad Werenka .15 .40
28 Phil Wittliff CO .02 .10

1995-96 Milwaukee Admirals

This high-quality 25-card set was produced for the team by Collector's Edge and sponsored by Bank One. The card fronts feature color action photography, along with the logos of the club, the bank and the manufacturer. The last card in the set, entitled Dream Ride, features on the back the lyrics to the song of the same name, which apparently is near and dear to the hearts of Admirals fans everywhere. This marks what could be the first ever appropriation of song lyrics for the edification of card collectors. As they cards are unnumbered, they are listed below alphabetically.

COMPLETE SET (25) 4.00 10.00
1 Shawn Anderson .20 .50
2 Jergus Baca .20 .50
3 Gino Cavallini .30 .75
4 Joe Cirella .20 .50
5 Sylvain Couturier .20 .50
6 Tom Draper .30 .75
7 Robert Guillet .20 .50
8 Tony Hrkac .30 .75
9 Fabian Joseph .20 .50
10 Mark LaForest .30 .75
11 Dave MacIsaac .20 .50
12 Mike McNeill .20 .50
13 Dave Mackey .20 .50
14 Kent Paynter .20 .50
15 Ken Sabourin .20 .50
16 Andrew Shier .20 .50
17 Tom Tilley .20 .50
18 Mike Tomlak .20 .50
19 Steve Tuttle .20 .50
20 Terry Yake .30 .75
21 Phil Wittliff CO .02 .10
22 Peter Bakovic ACO .02 .10
23 Rob Irsch ACO .02 .10
24 Doug Agnew TR .02 .10
25 Dream Ride .02 .10

1995-96 Milwaukee Admirals Postcards

Postcard series measures 3 1/2" x 5 1/2" and was sponsored by Sports Medicine Institute.

COMPLETE SET (21) 10.00 25.00
1 Dave MacIsaac .40 1.00
2 Kent Paynter .40 1.00
3 Garry Gulash .40 1.00
4 Jergus Baca .40 1.00
5 Fabian Joseph .40 1.00
6 Sylvain Couturier .40 1.00
7 Mike McNeill .40 1.00
8 Terry Yake .40 1.00
9 David Mackey .40 1.00
10 Bruce Ramsay .40 1.00
11 Tony Hrkac .75 2.00
12 Robert Guillet .40 1.00
13 Shawn Anderson .40 1.00
14 Andrew Shier .40 1.00
15 Steve Tuttle .40 1.00
16 Mike Tomlak .40 1.00
17 Tom Draper .75 2.00
18 Mark Laforest .75 2.00
19 Mikhail Kravets .40 1.00
20 Gino Cavallini .75 2.00
21 Ken Sabourin .40 1.00

1996-97 Milwaukee Admirals

This odd-sized (2 1/2" X 4") 27-card set features the Milwaukee Admirals of the IHL. The cards were produced by the club and sponsored by Bank One as a promotional item. The cards feature action photography on the front surrounded by a thin white border. The logos of Bank One and the PHPA are in the top corners, while the player's name, position and uniform number are listed along the bottom. The cards are unnumbered, and are listed in alphabetical order.

COMPLETE SET (27) 4.00 10.00
1 Doug Agnew TR .02 .10
2 Peter Bakovic ACO .02 .10
3 Sylvain Couturier .15 .40
4 Larry DePalma .15 .40
5 Peter Douris .15 .40
6 Denny Felsner .15 .40
7 Eric Fenton .15 .40
8 Shannon Finn .15 .40
9 Tony Hrkac .30 .75
10 Fabian Joseph ACO .15 .40
11 Jacques Joubert .15 .40
12 Rick Knickle .30 .75
13 Brad Layzell .15 .40
14 Danny Lorenz .30 .75
15 Chris Luongo .15 .40
16 Dave Mackey .15 .40
17 Mike McNeill .15 .40
18 Michel Mongeau .30 .75
19 Kent Paynter .15 .40
20 Christian Proulx .15 .40
21 Patrice Robitaille .15 .40
22 Ken Sabourin .15 .40
23 Steve Strunk .15 .40
24 Tom Tilley .15 .40
25 Mike Tomlak .15 .40
26 Steve Tuttle .15 .40
27 Phil Wittliff CO .02 .10

1997-98 Milwaukee Admirals

Little is known about this set beyond the confirmed checklist. Additional information can be forwarded to hockeymag@beckett.com.

COMPLETE SET (25) 3.60 9.00
1 Jason Cipolla .15 .40
2 Kerry Clark .15 .40
3 Jarrett Deuling .15 .40
4 Kelly Fairchild .20 .50
5 Eric Fenton .15 .40
6 Shannon Finn .15 .40
7 Martin Gendron .30 .75
8 Mike Harder .15 .40
9 Marc Hussey .15 .40
10 Danny Lorenz .30 .75
11 Dave MacIntyre .15 .40
12 Mike McNeill .15 .40
13 Don McSween .15 .40
14 Jeff Nelson .15 .40
15 Brent Peterson .15 .40
16 Christian Proulx .15 .40
17 Ken Sabourin .15 .40
18 Mike Tomlak .15 .40
19 Mike Torchia .30 .75
20 Steve Tuttle .15 .40
21 Mark Visheau .15 .40
22 Al Sims HCO .02 .10
23 Peter Bakovic ACO .02 .10
24 Fabian Joseph ACO .02 .10
25 Doug Agnew TR .02 .10

1998-99 Milwaukee Admirals

Little is known about this set beyond the confirmed checklist. Additional information can be forwarded to hockeymag@beckett.com.

COMPLETE SET (24) 4.00 10.00
1 Al Sims CO .02 .10
2 Jeff Daniels .15 .40
3 Sergei Klimentiev .15 .40
4 Chris Mason .20 .50
5 Eric Fenton .15 .40
6 Shannon Finn .15 .40
7 Jason Cipolla .15 .40
8 Jeff Kealty .15 .40
9 Bobby Russell .15 .40
10 David Gosselin .30 .75
11 Richard Lintner .30 .75
12 Jeff Nelson .20 .50
13 Kay Whitmore .25 .60
14 Claude Noel ACO .02 .10
15 Karlis Skrastins .20 .50
16 Mark Mowers .20 .50
17 Craig Darby .20 .50
18 Roscoe MASCOT .02 .10
19 Doug Friedman .15 .40
20 Matt Henderson .15 .40
21 Marc Moro .30 .75
22 Petr Sykora .30 .75
23 Jeff Staples .15 .40
24 Marian Cisar .40 1.00

1998-99 Milwaukee Admirals Postcards

This set features the Admirals of the IHL. These postcard-sized issues were given out at autograph sessions and other promotional ventures. Anyone knowing of additional cards in the set are encouraged to write hockeymag@beckett.com.

COMPLETE SET (11)
1 Doug Friedman .20 .50
2 Brad Smyth .20 .50
3 Jeff Staples .20 .50
4 Matt Henderson .20 .50
5 Petr Sykora .20 .50
6 Jeff Kealty .20 .50
7 Jason Cipolla .20 .50
8 Richard Lintner .40 1.00
9 Kimmo Timonen .40 1.00
10 Vitali Yachmenev .30 .75
11 Tomas Vokoun 1.25 3.00

1999-00 Milwaukee Admirals Keebler

This set was issued in sheet form as a promotional giveaway.

COMPLETE SET (20)
1 Corey Hirsch
2 Marian Cisar
3 Chris Mason
4 Jayme Filipowicz
5 Bubba Berenzweig
6 Mark Mowers
7 Brent Peterson
8 Phil Crowe
9 Dan Keczmer
10 Jason Dawe
11 Eric Fenton
12 Matt Eldred
13 Alexandre Boikov
14 Marc Moro
15 Paul Healey
16 Daniel Riva
17 Ryan Tobler
18 David Gosselin
19 Al Sims CO
20 Claude Noel ACO

2000-01 Milwaukee Admirals Keebler

This 20-card set features players from the 2000-01 Milwaukee Admirals of the IHL. The cards were issued in perforated sheets of five which consisted of 4 player cards and one coupon for Keebler products. The card fronts carry an action photo with a Keebler logo in the top left corner, the backs carry biographical information, career stats and accomplishments. The cards are not numbered and are listed below in alphabetical order.

COMMON CARD (20) 8.00 20.00
1 Jonas Andersson .60 1.50
2 Denis Arkhipov .60 2.00
3 Bubba Berenzweig .30 .75
4 Greg Classen .40 1.00
5 Mark Eaton .30 .75
6 Jayme Filipowicz .30 .75
7 Sean Haggerty .30 .75
8 Jan Lasak .80 2.00
9 Chris Mason .40 1.00
10 Marc Moro .40 1.00
11 Mark Mowers .40 1.00
12 John Namestnikov .30 .75
13 Ville Peltonen .40 1.00
14 Daniel Riva .30 .75
15 Petr Sachl .30 .75
16 Pavel Skrbek .40 1.00
17 Jeremy Stevenson .40 1.00
18 Ryan Tobler .30 .75
19 Alexei Vasiliev .30 .75
20 Mike Watt .30 .75

2000-01 Milwaukee Admirals Postcards

This set features the Admirals of the IHL. These postcard-like issues were handed out a various games in conjunction with player autograph sessions. They are not numbered and are listed below in alphabetical order.

COMPLETE SET (18) 6.00 15.00
1 Jonas Andersson .60 1.50
2 Andrew Berenzweig .30 .75
3 Alexandre Boikov .30 .75
4 Jayme Filipowicz .30 .75
5 David Gosselin .60 1.50
6 Jason Goulet .30 .75
7 Sean Haggerty .30 .75
8 Jan Lasak .80 2.00
9 Chris Mason .40 1.00
10 Mark Mowers .40 1.00
11 Ville Peltonen .40 1.00
12 Dan Riva .30 .75
13 Petr Sachl .30 .75
14 Pavel Skrbek .40 1.00
15 Ryan Tobler .30 .75
16 Alexei Vasiliev .30 .75
17 Mike Watt .30 .75
18 Alex Westlund .30 .75

2001-02 Milwaukee Admirals

This set features the Admirals of the AHL. The set was issued as a promotional giveaway in the form of five six-card strips. Each strip contains five player cards and one coupon for a product of Keebler, the sponsor of the set. The cards are unnumbered, so they are listed in alphabetical order.

COMPLETE SET (25) 8.00 20.00
1 Erik Anderson .30 .75
2 Jonas Andersson .30 .75
3 Martin Bartek .30 .75
4 Bubba Berenzweig .30 .75
5 Alexandre Boikov .30 .75
6 Frederic Bouchard .30 .75
7 Marian Cisar .40 1.00
8 Kevin Dean .30 .75
9 Steve Dubinsky .30 .75
10 David Gosselin .40 1.00
11 Jason Goulet .30 .75
12 Chris Mason .40 1.00
13 Brett Hauer .30 .75
14 Timo Helbling .30 .75
15 Jan Lasak .80 2.00
16 Jay Legault .30 .75
17 Bryan Lundbohm .30 .75
18 Marc Moro .60 1.50
19 Mark Mowers .40 1.00
20 Konstantin Panov .30 .75
21 Nathan Perrott .60 1.50
22 Petr Sachl .30 .75
23 Yves Sarault .30 .75
24 Robert Schnabel .30 .75
25 Jeremy Stevenson .30 .75

2001-02 Milwaukee Admirals Postcards

This set features the Admirals of the AHL. These cards were given out individually at player autograph sessions, making set building difficult. This checklist is not believed to be complete. If you have information on other singles, please forward it to hockeymag@beckett.com..

COMPLETE SET (11) 2.00 5.00
1 Robert Schnabel .20 .50
2 Bryan Lundbohm .20 .50
3 Yves Sarault .20 .50
4 Timo Helbling .20 .50
5 Martin Bartek .20 .50
6 Kevin Dean .20 .50
7 David Gosselin .30 .75
8 Marc Moro .40 1.00
9 Jason Goulet .20 .50
10 Jonas Andersson .20 .50
11 Roscoe MASCOT .10 .25

2002-03 Milwaukee Admirals

These cards were issued as promotional giveaways in five-card strips over the course of five home games. They were sponsored by Keebler.

COMPLETE SET (25) 35.00
1 Tomas Kloucek 3.00
2 Chris Madden 3.00
3 Wyatt Smith 1.00
4 Brian Finley 3.00
5 Dan Hamhuis 3.00
6 Andrew Hutchinson 2.00
7 Robert Schnabel 1.00
8 Bob Wren 1.00
9 Reid Simpson 1.00
10 Jan Lasak 3.00
11 Cameron Mann 2.00
12 Domenic Pittis 2.00
13 Martin Erat 2.00
14 Jonas Andersson 1.00
15 Greg Koehler 1.00
16 Bubba Berenzweig 1.00
17 Konstantin Panov 1.00
18 Peter Smrek 1.00
19 Vernon Fiddler 1.00
20 Jason Beckett 1.00
21 Greg Classen 1.00
22 Timo Helbling 1.00
23 Darren Haydar 2.00
24 Pascal Trepanier 1.00
25 Bryan Lundbohm 1.00

2002-03 Milwaukee Admirals Postcards

These postcards were issued as singles at player signing sessions. It's likely the checklist is incomplete. Please forward any additional information to hockeymag@beckett.com

COMPLETE SET (15) 15.00
1 Jonas Andersson .75
2 Jason Beckett .75
3 Bubba Berenzweig .75
4 Greg Classen .75
5 Martin Erat 1.50
6 Vern Fiddler .75
7 Dan Hamhuis 2.00
8 Darren Haydar 2.00
9 Tomas Kloucek 2.00
10 Jan Lasak 2.00
11 Chris Madden 2.00
12 Cameron Mann 1.00
13 Konstantin Panov .50
14 Robert Schnabel .50
15 Pascal Trepanier .50

2003-04 Milwaukee Admirals

COMPLETE SET (30) 15.00
1 Kirill Safronov .50
2 Jay Henderson .50
3 Brian Finley .75
4 Timo Helbling .50
5 Cheerleaders .10
6 Darren Haydar .75
7 Curtis Murphy .50
8 Tony Hrkac .50
9 Andrew Hutchinson .75
10 Mascot .10

11 Brad Tiley .50
12 Timofei Shishkanov .50
13 Vernon Fiddler .50
14 Scott Upshall 2.00
15 Claude Noel CO .10
16 Raitis Ivanans .50
17 Mathieu Darche .50
18 Wade Flaherty .75
19 Brandon Segal .50
20 Arena .01
21 Greg Zanon .50
22 Simon Gamache 1.00
23 Greg Classen .50
24 Wyatt Smith .50
25 Team Photo .25
26 Ray Schultz .50
27 Mike Farrell .50
28 Bryan Lundbohm .50
29 Libor Pivko .50
30 Todd Richards ACO .10

2003-04 Milwaukee Admirals Postcards

These oversized cards were issued at team events in singles form.

COMPLETE SET (23) 20.00
1 Greg Classen .75
2 Mathieu Darche .75
3 Mike Farrell .75
4 Vernon Fiddler .75
5 Brian Finley 1.00
6 Wade Flaherty 1.00
7 Simon Gamache 1.50
8 Darren Haydar 1.00
9 Timo Helbling .75
10 Jay Henderson .75
11 Tony Hrkac .75
12 Andrew Hutchinson 1.00
13 Raitis Ivanans .75
14 Bryan Lundbohm .75
15 Curtis Murphy .75
16 Libor Pivko .75
17 Kirill Safronov .75
18 Ray Schultz .75
19 Timofei Shishkanov .75
20 Wyatt Smith .75
21 Brad Tiley .75
22 Scott Upshall 2.50
23 Greg Zanon .75

2004-05 Milwaukee Admirals

These cards were issued as promotional giveaways on various nights throughout the season in five-card strips.

COMPLETE SET (30) 50.00
1 Brian Finley 3.00
2 Jeremy Yablonski 1.00
3 Brad Tiley 1.00
4 Cam Severson 2.00
5 Roscoe MASCOT .10
6 Seamus Kotyk 2.00
7 Paul Brown 1.00
8 Burke Henry 1.00
9 Libor Pivko 1.00
10 Brendan Yarema 1.00
11 Jerred Smithson 1.00
12 Bryan Lundbohm 2.00
13 Ryan Suter 3.00
14 Brandon Segal 1.00
15 Calder Cup Winners 1.00
16 Jordin Tootoo 10.00
17 Scottie Upshall 3.00
18 Dan Hamhuis 2.00
19 Andrew Hutchinson 2.00
20 Admirals Ice Angels 1.00
21 Greg Zanon 1.00
22 Simon Gamache 2.00
23 Kevin Klein 1.00
24 Wyatt Smith 1.00
25 Todd Richards 1.00
26 Darren Haydar 1.00
27 Timofei Shishkanov 1.00
28 Vernon Fiddler 1.00
29 Tony Hrkac 1.00
30 Claude Noel 1.00

2005-06 Milwaukee Admirals Choice

COMPLETE SET (19) 10.00
1 Kris Beech .20 .50
2 Sheldon Brookbank .20 .50
3 Paul Brown .20 .50
4 Greg Classen .20 .50
5 Vern Fiddler .20 .50
6 Brian Finley .30 .75
7 Darren Haydar .20 .50
8 Kevin Klein .20 .50
9 Libor Pivko .20 .50
10 T.J. Reynolds .20 .50
11 Pekka Rinne .40 1.00
12 Marco Rosa .20 .50
13 Brandon Segal .20 .50
14 Timofei Shishkanov .20 .50
15 Jordin Tootoo .75 2.00
16 Shea Weber .20 .50
17 Jeremy Yablonski .20 .50
18 Greg Zanon .20 .50
19 Claude Noel HC .02 .10

2005-06 Milwaukee Admirals Pepsi

COMPLETE SET (26) 25.00
1 Kris Beech .40 1.00
2 Rick Berry .40 1.00
3 Sheldon Brookbank .40 1.00
4 Paul Brown .40 1.00
5 Greg Classen .40 1.00
6 Chris Durno .40 1.00
7 Brian Finley .60 1.50
8 Simon Gamache .40 1.00
9 Darren Haydar .40 1.00
10 Kevin Klein .40 1.00
11 Nathan Lutz .40 1.00
12 Scott May .40 1.00
13 Rich Peverley .40 1.00
14 Libor Pivko .40 1.00
15 T.J. Reynolds .40 1.00
16 Pekka Rinne .75 2.00
17 Brandon Segal .40 1.00
18 Zach Stortini .40 1.00
19 Jordin Tootoo 1.25 3.00
20 Scottie Upshall .75 2.00
21 Shea Weber .40 1.00
22 Jeremy Yablonski .40 1.00
23 Greg Zanon .40 1.00
24 Claude Noel HC .02 .10
25 Todd Richards AC .02 .10
26 Roscoe MASCOT .02 .10

2006-07 Milwaukee Admirals

COMPLETE SET (24) 10.00 18.00
1 Ramzi Abid .30 .75
2 Sheldon Brookbank .40 1.00
3 Chris Durno .30 .75
4 Karl Goehring• .40 1.00
5 Jason Guerriero .30 .75
6 Alex Henry .30 .75
7 Bracken Kearns .30 .75
8 Kevin Klein .30 .75
9 Ville Koistinen .30 .75
10 John Laliberte .30 .75
11 Patrick Leahy .30 .75
12 Cal O'Reilly .30 .75
13 Rich Peverley .30 .75
14 T.J. Reynolds .30 .75
15 Pekka Rinne• .40 1.00
16 Brandon Segal .30 .75
17 Kim Staal .30 .75
18 Victor Uchevatov .30 .75
19 John Vigilante .30 .75
20 Kelsey Wilson .60 1.50
21 Nolan Yonkman .30 .75
22 Claude Noel CO .10 .25
23 Lane Lambert ACO .10 .25
24 Roscoe MASCOT .02 .10

2007-08 Milwaukee Admirals

COMPLETE SET (24) 4.00 10.00
1 Dov Grumet-Morris .50 1.25
2 Bryan Schmidt .15 .40
3 Cody Franson• .50 1.25
4 Ryan Maki .15 .40
5 Mike Santorelli .15 .40
6 John Vigilanti .15 .40
7 Andreas Thuresson .15 .40
8 Jason Guerriero .15 .40
9 John Laliberti .15 .40
10 Cal O'Reilly .15 .40
11 Kelsey Wilson .15 .40
12 Mark Matheson .15 .40
13 Matt Ellison .15 .40
14 Josh Langfeld .15 .40
15 Kevin Ulanski .15 .40
16 Janne Niskala .15 .40
17 Alex Henry .15 .40
18 Pekka Rinne .15 .40
19 Rich Peverley .15 .40
20 Antti Pihlstrom .15 .40
21 Nolan Yonkman .15 .40
22 Alexander Sulzer .15 .40
23 Lane Lambert• .15 .40
24 Brad Lauer .15 .40

1984-85 Minnesota-Duluth Bulldogs

This set features the Bulldogs of the NCAA and was confirmed to exist in 2002 by Ralph Slate of hockeydb.com reknown. The set was produced by Tim and Larry's Sportscards and features the first card of Brett Hull. It is believed that as few as 250 sets were produced.

COMPLETE SET (33) 100.00
1 Ben Duffey .40 1.00
2 Brett Hull 30.00 75.00
3 Danny May .40 1.00
4 Dave Morrow .40 1.00
5 Joe Delisle .40 1.00
6 Brian Nelson .40 1.00
7 Jon Downing .40 1.00
8 Brian Nelson .40 1.00
9 Sean Toomey .40 1.00
10 Brian Durand .40 1.00
11 Jim Plankers .40 1.00
12 Mark Odnokon .40 1.00
13 Jim Sprenger .40 1.00
14 Tom Lorentz .40 1.00
15 Darin Illikainen .40 1.00
16 Rick Kosti .40 1.00
17 Norm Maciver .75 2.00
18 Guy Gosselin .40 1.00
19 Matt Christensen .40 1.00
20 Jim Johnson .75 2.00
21 Mark Baron .40 1.00
22 Bill Watson .40 1.00
23 Bruce Fishback .40 1.00
24 Dave Cowan .40 1.00
25 Mike Cortes .40 1.00
26 Jim Toninato .40 1.00
27 Skeeter Moore .40 1.00
28 Mike DeAngelis .40 1.00
29 Tom Herzig .40 1.00
30 Mike Sertich CO .08 .25
31 Bulldog Cheerleaders .40 1.00
32 Bulldogs Assistants .08 .25
33 Team Photo .08 .25

1985-86 Minnesota-Duluth Bulldogs

This 36-card standard-size set features color action player photos with rounded corners and black borders against a white card face. An oval inset at the lower right shows a head shot. The player's name is printed in black at the bottom. The cards are numbered on the back. It has been reported that this set may have been reprinted to take advantage of the popularity of Brett Hull.

COMPLETE SET (36) 12.00 30.00
1 Skeeter Moore .30 .75
2 Terry Shold .20 .50
3 Mike DeAngelis .20 .50
4 Rob Pallin .20 .50
5 Norm Maciver .30 .75
6 Wayne Smith .20 .50
7 Dave Cowan .20 .50
8 Darin Illikainen .20 .50
9 Rick Hayko .20 .50
10 Guy Gosselin .30 .75
11 Paul Roff .20 .50
12 Jim Toninato .20 .50
13 Tom Hanson .20 .50
14 Mike Cortes .20 .50
15 Matt Christensen .20 .50
16 Bruce Fishback .20 .50
17 Mark Odnokon .20 .50
18 Brian Johnson .20 .50
19 Bob Alexander .20 .50
20 Tom Lorentz .20 .50
21 Roman Sindelar .20 .50
22 Jim Sprenger .20 .50
23 Dan Tousignant .20 .50
24 Sean Toomey .20 .50
25 Brian Durand .20 .50
26 John Hyduke .20 .50
27 Brian Nelson .20 .50
28 Brett Hull 8.00 20.00
29 Joe DeLisle .20 .50
30 Pat Janostin .20 .50
31 Ben Duffy .20 .50
32 Sean Krakiwsky .20 .50
33 Mike Sertich .20 .50
34 Coaching Staff .08 .25
Jim Knapp ACO
Glenn Kulyk ACO
Tim McDonald ACO
Mike Valesano ACO
Rick Menz EQUIP
Dale Hoganson EQUIP
Betty Fleissner TR
35 Cheerleaders .40 1.00
36 Jay Jackson (Mascot) .08 .25
The Maroon Loon

1993-94 Minnesota-Duluth Bulldogs

These 30 standard-size cards feature on their fronts white-bordered color player action shots. The player's name and position, along with the Minnesota Bulldog logo, appear within the brown stripe across the bottom of the photo. The back carries the player's name, position, biography, and statistics on the left. His career highlights appear on the right. The set was produced by Collect-A-Sport and features a card of Chris Marinucci, 1993-94 Hobey Baker winner. The cards are unnumbered and checklisted below in alphabetical order.

COMPLETE SET (30) 4.00 10.00
1 Rod Aldoff .15 .40
2 Niklas Axelson .15 .40
3 David Buck .15 .40
4 Jerome Butler .15 .40
5 Brian Caruso .20 .50
6 Matt Christian .20 .50
Chet Culic
7 Marc Christian .15 .40
8 Joe Ciccarello .15 .40
9 Kyle Erickson .15 .40
Adam Roy
10 Brad Federenko .20 .50
11 Rusty Fitzgerald .20 .50
12 Jason Garatti .15 .40
13 Greg Hanson .20 .50
14 Don Jablonic .15 .40
15 Kraig Karakas .15 .40
16 Brett Larson .20 .50
17 Taras Lendzyk .15 .40
18 Derek Locker .15 .40
19 Chris Marinucci .20 .50
20 Todd Mickolajak .20 .50
Chris Snell
21 Rod Miller .15 .40
22 Rick Mrozik .20 .50
23 Aaron Novak .15 .40
24 Corey Osmak .15 .40
25 Sergei Petrov .15 .40
26 Jeff Romfo .15 .40
27 Mike Sertich CO .02 .10
28 Chris Sittlow .15 .40
29 Joe Tamminen .15 .40
30 Title Card .08 .25
Roster

1993-94 Minnesota-Duluth Commemorative

These four standard-size cards feature black-and-white fronts with color photos on the backs. The set was produced by Collect-A-Sport to commemorate the 1992-93 WCHA champs.

COMPLETE SET (4) 1.50 4.00
1 Chris Marinucci .40 1.00
2 Derek Plante .75 2.00
3 Brett Hauer .40 1.00
4 Jon Rohloff .40 1.00

2004-05 Minnesota-Duluth Bulldogs

The cards came in three packs of seven cards and two packs of six cards and were handed out over five different home games.

COMPLETE SET (33) 30.00
1 Nick Anderson 1.00
2 Tyler Brosz 1.00
3 T.J. Caig 1.00
4 Dan Carlson 1.00
5 Mike Curry 1.00
6 Steve Czech 1.00
7 Travis Gawryletz 1.00
8 Ryan Garis 1.00
9 Tim Hambly 1.00
10 Brett Hammond 1.00
11 Josh Johnson 1.50
12 Blair Lefebvre 1.00
13 Jeff McFarland 1.00
14 Bryan McGregor 1.00
15 Matt McKnight 1.00
16 Josh Miskovich 1.00
17 Marco Peluso 1.00
18 Neil Petruic 1.00
19 Isaac Reichmuth 1.50
20 Jay Rosehill 1.00
21 Evan Schwabe 1.50
22 Todd Smith 1.00
23 Tim Stapleton 1.00
24 Luke Stauffacher 1.00
25 Ryan Swanson 1.00
26 Justin Williams 1.00
27 Lee Davidson ACO#)Scott Sandelin CO#)Steve Rohlik ACO .10
28 Tom Kurvers 1.00
29 Junior Lessard 2.00
30 Chris Marinucci 2.00
31 Bill Watson 1.00
32 Mascots .10
33 Sponsor .01

1991-92 Minnesota Golden Gophers

Sponsored by MCI, this 26-card standard-size set features the 1991-92 Minnesota Golden Gophers. On a maroon background, the horizontal and vertical fronts have color action player photos along with the player's name and the name of the high school he attended. The white backs carry the player's name, number, biography, and profile. The cards are unnumbered and checklisted below in alphabetical order.

COMPLETE SET (26) 6.00 15.00
1 Scott Bell .20 .50
2 Tony Bianchi .20 .50
3 John Brill .20 .50
4 Jeff Callinan .20 .50
5 Joe Dziedzic .30 .75
6 Sean Fabian .20 .50
7 Jed Fiebelkorn .20 .50
8 Nick Gerebi .20 .50
9 Darby Hendrickson .30 .75
10 Craig Johnson .30 .75
11 Trent Klatt .40 1.00
12 Cory Laylin .20 .50
13 Steve Magnusson .30 .75
14 Chris McAlpine .30 .75
15 Justin McHugh .20 .50
16 Eric Means .20 .50
17 Mike Muller .20 .50
18 Tom Newman .20 .50
19 Jeff Nielsen .20 .50
20 John O'Connell .20 .50
21 Larry Olimb .20 .50
22 Travis Richards .20 .50
23 Brandon Steege .20 .50
24 Jeff Stolp .20 .50
25 Todd Westlund .20 .50
26 Doug Zmolek .30 .75

1992-93 Minnesota Golden Gophers

Featuring the 1992-93 Minnesota Golden Gophers hockey team (WCHA), this 25-card measures the standard-size. The fronts feature full-bleed, posed, color player photos. A gray bar at the top (or right edge) displays the school name, while the player's name is printed in maroon lettering in a yellow bar at the bottom. The cards are unnumbered and checklisted below in alphabetical order.

COMPLETE SET (25) 4.00 10.00
1 Scott Bell .15 .40
2 Jesse Bertogliat .40 1.00
Brian Bonin
3 Tony Bianchi .15 .40
4 John Brill .15 .40
5 Jeff Callinan .15 .40
6 Bobby Dustin .15 .40
Dave Larson
7 Joe Dziedzic .20 .50
8 Jed Fiebelkorn .15 .40
9 Darby Hendrickson .20 .50
10 Craig Johnson .15 .40
11 Steve Magnusson .20 .50
12 Chris McAlpine .20 .50
13 Justin McHugh .15 .40
14 Eric Means .15 .40
15 Jeff Moen .15 .40
16 Tom Newman .15 .40
17 Jeff Nielsen .20 .50
18 Travis Richards .15 .40
19 Brandon Steege .15 .40
20 Matt Stelljes .15 .40
Ryan Alstead
21 Dan Trebil .02 .10
Greg Zwakman
22 Charlie Wasley .15 .40
Mike McAlpine
23 Todd Westlund .15 .40
24 Dan Woog .08 .25
Jim Hillman
25 Doug Woog CO .08 .25

1993-94 Minnesota Golden Gophers

This set features the Golden Gophers of the NCAA. The cards were printed by the team and issued as a promotional giveaway. On a maroon background, the fronts feature posed, color action player photos and portraits with a thin yellow border. The player's name is printed in yellow letters with a maroon outline on the bottom of the photo. The cards are unnumbered and checklisted below in alphabetical order.

COMPLETE SET (30) 6.00 100.00
1 Brett Abrahamson 1.50 4.00
2 Jesse Bertogliat 1.50 4.00
3 Tony Bianchi 1.50 4.00
4 Brian Bonin 2.00 5.00
5 Andy Brink 1.50 4.00
6 Jeff Callinan 1.50 4.00
7 Nick Checco 1.50 4.00
8 Bobby Dustin 1.50 4.00
9 Joe Dziedzic 2.00 5.00
10 Jed Fiebelkorn 1.50 4.00
11 Brent Godbout 1.50 4.00
12 Dan Hendrickson 1.50 4.00
13 Jim Hillman 1.50 4.00
14 John Hillman 1.50 4.00
15 Brian LaFleur 1.50 4.00
16 Dave Larson 1.50 4.00
17 Steve Magnusson 1.50 4.00
18 Chris McAlpine 2.00 5.00
19 Mike McAlpine 1.50 4.00
20 Justin McHugh 1.50 4.00
21 Eric Means 1.50 4.00
22 Jeff Moen 1.50 4.00
23 Jeff Nielsen 2.00 5.00
24 Brandon Steege 1.50 4.00
25 Dan Trebil 1.50 4.00
26 Charlie Wasley 1.50 4.00
27 Dan Woog ACO .40 1.00
28 Doug Woog CO .75 2.00
29 Greg Zwakman 1.50 4.00
30 Title Card .02 .10

1994-95 Minnesota Golden Gophers

This set features the Golden Gophers of the NCAA. The cards were sponsored by SuperAmerica and EverReady and issued as a promotional giveaway. On a white card face with team color-coded stripes in the background, the fronts display action shots or water color portraits by artist M.L. Sahlberg. The cards are unnumbered and checklisted below in alphabetical order.

COMPLETE SET (31) 10.00 25.00
1 Will Anderson .30 .75
2 Scott Bell .30 .75
3 Jesse Bertogliat .30 .75
4 Brian Bonin .40 1.00
5 Andy Brink .30 .75
6 Aaron Broten .75 2.00
Neal Broten
Paul Broten
7 Jeff Callinan .30 .75
8 Nick Checco .30 .75
9 Mike Crowley .75 2.00
10 Steve DeBus .30 .75
11 Bobby Dustin .30 .75
12 Jed Fiebelkorn .30 .75
13 Brent Godbout .30 .75
14 Jason Godbout .30 .75
15 Casey Hankinson .30 .75
16 Dan Hendrickson .30 .75
17 Ryan Kraft .30 .75
18 Brian LaFleur .30 .75
19 Dave Larson .30 .75
20 Justin McHugh .30 .75
21 Jeff Moen .30 .75
22 Jay Moser .30 .75
23 Lou Nanne .40 1.00
24 Joe Pankratz .30 .75
25 Jason Seils .30 .75
26 Brandon Steege .30 .75
27 Dan Trebil .40 1.00
28 Charlie Wasley .30 .75
29 Dan Woog .08 .25
30 Doug Woog CO .08 .25
31 Greg Zwakman .30 .75

1995-96 Minnesota Golden Gophers

This set was issued by the team as a promotional giveaway. The cards are unnumbered so the set is checklisted in alphabetical order.

COMPLETE SET (30) 100.00 175.00
1 Checklist .40 1.00
2 Doug Woog CO .75 2.00
3 Brett Abrahamson 3.00 6.00
4 Mike Anderson 3.00 6.00
5 Reggie Berg 3.00 6.00
6 Jesse Bertogliat 3.00 6.00
7 Brian Bonin 5.00 10.00
8 Andy Brink 3.00 6.00
9 Nick Checco 3.00 6.00
10 Nick Crowley 3.00 6.00
11 Steve Debus 3.00 6.00
12 Bobby Dustin 3.00 6.00
13 Jason Godbout 3.00 6.00
14 Casey Hankinson 3.00 6.00
15 Dan Hendrickson 3.00 6.00
16 Clint Johnson 3.00 6.00
17 Bill Kohn 3.00 6.00
18 Ryan Kraft 3.00 6.00
19 Brian LaFleur 3.00 6.00
20 Dave Larson 3.00 6.00
21 Jeff Moen 3.00 6.00
22 Jay Moser 3.00 6.00
23 Tom Nevers 3.00 6.00
24 Erik Rasmussen 5.00 10.00
25 Jason Seils 3.00 6.00
26 Wyatt Smith 3.00 6.00
27 Dan Trebil 3.00 6.00
28 Charlie Wasley 3.00 6.00
29 Dan Woog ACO .75 2.00
30 Greg Zwakman 3.00 6.00

1996-97 Minnesota Golden Gophers

Little is known about this set beyond the confirmed checklist and the fact that it was issued as a promotional giveaway. Any additional information can be forwarded to hockeymag@beckett.com.

COMPLETE SET (27) 25.00 50.00
1 Checklist .02 .10
2 Doug Woog CO .02 .10
3 Brett Abrahamson .60 1.50
4 Mike Anderson .60 1.50
5 Reggie Berg 1.25 3.00
6 Nick Checco 1.25 3.00
7 Ben Clymer 1.25 3.00
8 Mike Crowley 1.25 3.00
9 Eric Day .60 1.50
10 Steve DeBus .60 1.50
11 Brent Godbout .60 1.50
12 Jason Godbout .60 1.50
13 Casey Hankinson 1.25 3.00
14 Dan Hendrickson 1.25 3.00
15 Bill Kohn .60 1.50
16 Ryan Kraft 1.25 3.00
17 Brian LaFleur .60 1.50
18 Mike Lyons .60 1.50
19 Willy Marvin .60 1.50
20 Cory Miller .60 1.50
21 Nate Miller .60 1.50
22 Rico Pagel .60 1.50
23 Erik Rasmussen 1.25 3.00
24 Wyatt Smith 1.25 3.00
25 Dave Spehar .60 1.50
26 Ryan Trebil .60 1.50
27 Dan Woog .02 .10

1997-98 Minnesota Golden Gophers

This set was handed out as a promotional giveaway at one home game, making it quite scarce on the secondary market.

COMPLETE SET (26) 15.00 30.00
1 Checklist .08 .25
2 Doug Woog HCO .20 .50
3 Mike Anderson .40 1.00
4 Slev Debus .40 1.00
5 Ryan Kraft .60 1.50
6 Nate Miller .40 1.00
7 Brett Abrahamson .40 1.00
8 Erik Day .40 1.00
9 Bill Kohn .40 1.00
10 Cory Miller .40 1.00
11 Ben Clymer .75 2.00
12 Casey Hankinson .40 1.00
13 Willy Marvin .40 1.00
14 Reggie Berg .40 1.00
15 Jason Godbout .40 1.00
16 Mike Lyons .40 1.00
17 Ryan Trebil .40 1.00
18 Dylan Mills .40 1.00
19 Dave Spehar .40 1.00
20 Erik Westrum .75 2.00
21 Wyatt Smith .60 1.50
22 Aaron Miskovich .40 1.00
23 Rico Pagel .40 1.00
24 Matt Leimbeck .40 1.00
25 Stuart Senden .40 1.00
26 Goldy Gopher Mascot .20 .50

1998-99 Minnesota Golden Gophers

This set features the Golden Gophers of the NCAA. Like most NCAA issues, this set was handed out as a promotional giveaway at a single home game.

COMPLETE SET (30) 20.00 35.00
1 Header Card .02 .10
2 Doug Woog HCO .20 .50
3 Mark Nenovich .40 1.00
4 Erik Wendell .75 2.00
5 Dylan Mills .40 1.00
6 Nate Miller .40 1.00
7 Rob LaRue .40 1.00
8 Reggie Berg .40 1.00
9 Bill Kohn .40 1.00
10 Mike Lyons .40 1.00
11 Cory Miller .40 1.00
12 Mike Anderson .40 1.00
13 Jordon Leopold 1.50 4.00
14 Ryan Westrum .40 1.00
15 Doug Meyer .40 1.00
16 Rico Pagel .40 1.00
17 Stuart Senden .40 1.00
18 Nick Angell .40 1.00
19 Dave Spehar .40 1.00
20 Pat O'Leary .40 1.00
21 Ryan Trebil .40 1.00
22 Adam Hauser .75 2.00
23 Wyatt Smith .75 2.00
24 Brad Timmons .40 1.00
25 Matt Leimbeck .40 1.00
26 Aaron Miskovich .40 1.00
27 Erik Daly .40 1.00
28 Erik Westrum .75 2.00
29 John Pohl .75 2.00
30 Goldy Gopher Mascot .08 .25

1998-99 Minnesota Golden Gophers Women

Issued as a giveaway at a late-season home game.

COMPLETE SET (25) 10.00 25.00
1 Angela Borek .40 1.00
2 Winny Brodt .40 1.00
3 Emily Buchholz .40 1.00
4 Tracy Donaghue .40 1.00
5 Tracy Engstrom .40 1.00
6 Lacey Franzmeier .40 1.00
7 Laura Halldorson CO .08 .25
8 Amber Hegland .40 1.00
9 David Horn ACO .08 .25
10 Courtney Kennedy .40 1.00
11 Shannon Kennedy .40 1.00
12 Erica Killewald .40 1.00
13 Betsey Kukowski .40 1.00
14 Megan Milbert .40 1.00
15 Nadine Muzerall .40 1.00
16 Crystal Nicholas .40 1.00
17 Kelly Olson .40 1.00
18 Sarma Pone .40 1.00
19 Brittny Ralph .40 1.00
20 Jenny Schmidgall 1.25 3.00
21 Kris Scholz .40 1.00
22 Laura Slominski .40 1.00
23 Ambria Thomas .40 1.00
24 Tai Thorsheim .40 1.00
25 Libby Witchger ACO .08 .25

1999-00 Minnesota Golden Gophers

This set features the Golden Gophers of the NCAA. The cards were issued as a promotional giveaway at a late-season game. The cards are unnumbered, and so are listed in alphabetical order.

COMPLETE SET (30) 8.00 20.00
1 Nick Angell .20 .50
2 Nick Anthony .20 .50
3 Matt DeMarchi .20 .50
4 Goldy Gopher MAS .08 .25
6 Ben Hamilton .20 .50
7 Adam Hauser .75 2.00
8 Matt Leimbeck .20 .50
9 Jordan Leopold 1.25 3.00
10 Don Lucia CO .08 .25
11 Mike Lyons .20 .50
12 Doug Meyer .20 .50
13 Nate Miller .20 .50
14 Dylan Mills .20 .50
15 Aaron Miskovich .20 .50
16 Mark Nenovich .20 .50
17 Pat O'Leary .20 .50
18 Rico Pagel .20 .50
19 John Pohl 1.25 3.00
20 Chad Roberge .20 .50
21 Pete Samargia .20 .50
22 Stuart Senden .20 .50
23 Dave Spehar .20 .50
24 Jeff Taffe 2.00 5.00
25 Ben Tharp .20 .50
26 Ryan Trebil .20 .50
27 University of Minnesota .08 .25
28 Dan Welch .20 .50
29 Erik Young .20 .50
29 Erik Wendell .30 .75
30 Erik Westrum .40 1.00

2000-01 Minnesota Golden Gophers

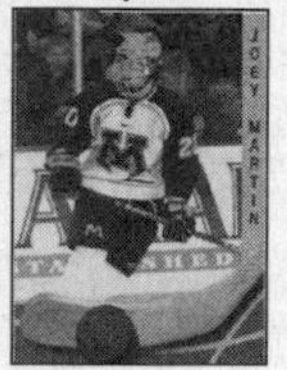

This set features the Golden Gophers of the NCAA. The cards were issued as a promotional giveaway late in the season. The cards are unnumbered, so are listed below in alphabetical order.

COMPLETE SET (28) 15.00 25.00
1 Header Card .04 .01
2 Nick Angell .30 .75
3 Nick Anthony .30 .75
4 Matt DeMarchi .30 .75
5 Goldy Gopher MASCOT .04 .10
6 Adam Hauser .75 2.00
7 Rod Johnson FOOTBALL .30 .75
8 Matt Koalska .30 .75
9 Matt Leimbeck .30 .75
10 Jordan Leopold 1.25 3.00
11 Don Lucia CO .10 .25
12 Joey Martin .30 .75
13 Paul Martin .30 .75
14 Dylan Mills .30 .75
15 Aaron Miskovich .30 .75
16 Mark Nenovich .30 .75
17 Pat O'Leary .30 .75
18 John Pohl .75 2.00
19 Grant Potulny .40 1.00
20 Troy Riddle .30 .75
21 Chad Roberge .30 .75
22 Pete Samargia .30 .75
23 Stuart Senden .30 .75
24 Jeff Taffe 1.25 3.00
25 Ben Tharp .30 .75
26 Jon Waibel .30 .75
27 Erik Wendell .30 .75
28 Erik Westrum .75 2.00

2001-02 Minnesota Golden Gophers

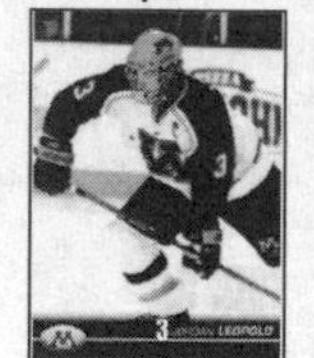

This set features the Golden Gophers of the NCAA in their championship season. The set was issued as a promotional giveaway at a game in January, 2002.

COMPLETE SET (29) 12.00 30.00
1 Header Card .10 .25
2 Don Lucia CO .10 .25
3 Goldy Gopher MASCOT .04 .10
4 Nick Anthony .40 1.00
5 Mike Erickson .40 1.00
6 Chad Roberg .60 1.50
7 Keith Ballard .60 1.50
8 Erik Wendell .60 1.50
9 Paul Martin .40 1.00
10 John Pohl .60 1.50
11 Judd Stevens .40 1.00
12 Jon Waibel .40 1.00
13 Jordan Leopold 1.20 3.00
14 Mark Nenovich .40 1.00
15 Adam Hauser .40 1.00
16 Garrett Smaagaard .40 1.00
17 Grant Potulny .40 1.00
18 Matt DeMarchi .40 1.00
19 Joey Martin .40 1.00
20 Troy Riddle .40 1.00
21 Jeff Taffe 1.20 3.00
22 Matt Koalska .40 1.00
23 Pat O'Leary .40 1.00
24 Nick Angell .40 1.00
25 Barry Tallackson .40 1.00
26 Brett MacKinnon .40 1.00
27 Jake Fleming .40 1.00
28 Travis Weber .40 1.00
29 Justin Johnson .40 1.00

2002-03 Minnesota Golden Gophers

COMPLETE SET (31) 20.00 40.00
1 Nick Anthony .40 1.00
2 P.J. Atherton .40 1.00
3 Keith Ballard 1.00 2.50

4 Matt DeMarchi .40 1.00
5 Mike Erickson .40 1.00
6 Jake Fleming .40 1.00
7 Gino Guyer .60 1.50
8 Chris Harrington .40 1.00
9 Tyler Hirsch .40 1.00
10 Justin Johnson .40 1.00
11 Peter Kennedy .40 1.00
12 Matt Koalska .40 1.00
13 Brett MacKinnon .40 1.00
14 Joey Martin .40 1.00
15 Paul Martin .75 2.00
16 Grant Potulny .60 1.50
17 Jerrid Reinholz .40 1.00
18 Troy Riddle .40 1.00
19 Chad Roberg .40 1.00
20 Andrew Sertich .40 1.00
21 Garrett Smaagaard .40 1.00
22 Dustin Smieja .40 1.00
23 Judd Stevens .40 1.00
24 Barry Tallackson .75 2.00
25 Thomas Vanek 6.00 15.00
26 Jon Waibel .40 1.00
27 Travis Weber .40 1.00
28 Dan Welch .40 1.00
29 Don Lucia HCO .10 .25
30 Goldy Gopher Mascot .02 .10
31 NCAA Champs .20 .50

2003-04 Minnesota Golden Gophers

This set was issued as a promotional giveaway over the course of four home games in the form of four seven-card strips.

COMPLETE SET (28) 20.00 40.00
1 Barry Tallackson .75 2.00
2 Jake Taylor .50 1.25
3 Thomas Vanek 3.00 8.00
4 Mike Vannelli .50 1.25
5 Jon Waibel .50 1.25
6 Dustin Smieja .50 1.25
7 Championship Team Photo .10 .25
8 Don Lucia CO .02 .10
9 P.J. Atherton .50 1.25
10 Keith Ballard 1.00 2.50
11 Kellen Briggs .75 2.00
12 Jake Fleming .50 1.25
13 Gino Guyer 1.00 2.50
14 Chris Harrington .50 1.25
15 Tyler Hirsch .50 1.25
16 Dan Irmen .75 2.00
17 Justin Johnson .75 2.00
18 Peter Kennedy .50 1.25
19 Matt Koalska .60 1.50
20 Brett MacKinnon .50 1.25
21 Joey Martin .50 1.25
22 Grant Potulny .50 1.25
23 Ryan Potulny 1.25 3.00
24 Jerrid Reinholz .50 1.25
25 Troy Riddle .50 1.25
26 Andy Sertich .60 1.50
27 Garrett Smaagaard .50 1.25
28 Judd Stevens .50 1.25

2004-05 Minnesota Golden Gophers

COMPLETE SET (27) 25.00
1 PJ Atherton 1.00
2 Brent Borgen 1.00
3 Kellen Briggs 1.50
4 Kris Chucko 2.00
5 Jake Fleming 1.00
6 Alex Goligoski 3.00
7 Ben Gordon 1.00
8 Gino Guyer 1.00
9 Nate Hagemo 1.00
10 Chris Harrington 1.00
11 Tyler Hirsch 1.00
12 Mike Howe 1.00
13 Danny Irmen 1.00
14 Justin Johnson 1.50
15 Evan Kaufman 1.00
16 Peter Kennedy 1.00
17 Don Lucia 1.00
18 Derek Peltier 1.00
19 Tom Pohl 1.00
20 Ryan Potulny 1.00
21 Jerrid Reinholz 1.00
22 Andy Sertich 2.00
23 Garrett Smaagaard 1.00
24 Brent Solei 1.00
25 Judd Stevens 1.00
26 Barry Tallackson 1.00
27 Mike Vannelli 1.00

2004-05 Minnesota Golden Gophers Women

COMPLETE SET (14) 15.00
1 Natalie Darwitz 2.50
2 Krissy Wendell 2.50
3 Anya Miller 1.00
4 Erica McKenzie 1.00
5 Natalie Lamme 1.00
6 Krista Johnson 1.00
7 Jody Horak 1.00
8 Stacy Troumbly 1.00
9 Becky Wacker 1.00
10 Lyndsay Wall 1.00
11 Whitney Graft 1.00
12 Chelsey Brodt 1.00
13 Ashley Albrecht 1.00
14 Laura Halldorson CO .10

2005-06 Minnesota Golden Gophers

COMPLETE SET (27) 15.00 30.00
1 R.J. Anderson .30 .75
2 P.J. Atherton .30 .75
3 Brent Borgen .30 .75
4 Justin Bostrom .30 .75
5 Kellen Briggs .30 .75
6 Kris Chucko .60 1.50
7 Jeff Frazee 1.25 3.00
8 Alex Goligoski .75 2.00
9 Ben Gordon .30 .75
10 Gino Guyer .40 1.00
11 Nate Hagemo .40 1.00
12 Chris Harrington .30 .75
13 Mike Howe .30 .75
14 Danny Irmen .40 1.00
15 Evan Kaufmann .30 .75
16 Peter Kennedy .30 .75
17 Phil Kessel 10.00
18 Derek Peltier .30 .75
19 Tom Pohl .30 .75
20 Ryan Potulny 1.25 3.00
21 Andy Sertich .30 .75
22 Brent Solei .30 .75
23 Ryan Stoa .60 1.50
24 Mike Vannelli .30 .75
25 Blake Wheeler .75 2.00
26 Don Lucia HC .02 .10
27 Goldy Gopher MASCOT .02 .10

2006-07 Minnesota Golden Gophers

COMPLETE SET (25) 25.00 35.00
1 R.J. Anderson .40 1.00
2 Jay Barriball .60 1.50
3 Justin Bostrom .40 1.00
4 Kellen Briggs .40 1.00
5 Mike Carman .40 1.00
6 David Fischer .40 1.00
7 Ryan Flynn .40 1.00
8 Jeff Frazee .75 2.00
9 Alex Goligoski .75 2.00
10 Ben Gordon .40 1.00
11 Mike Howe .40 1.00
12 Erik Johnson 2.00 5.00
13 Evan Kaufmann .40 1.00
14 Tony Lucia .40 1.00
15 Jim O'Brien .75 2.00
16 Kyle Okposo 2.00 5.00
17 Derek Peltier .40 1.00
18 Tom Pohl .40 1.00
19 Brian Schack .40 1.00
20 Brent Solei .40 1.00
21 Ryan Stoa .75 2.00
22 Mike Vannelli .40 1.00
23 Blake Wheeler .75 2.00
24 Don Lucia CO .10 .25
25 Goldy Gopher MASCOT .10 .25

2007-08 Minnesota Golden Gophers

COMPLETE SET (25) 4.00 10.00
1 R.J. Anderson .15 .40
2 Jay Barriball .15 .40
3 Stu Bickel .15 .40
4 Justin Bostrom .15 .40
5 Mike Carman .15 .40
6 Cade Fairchild .15 .40
7 David Fischer .15 .40
8 Drew Fisher .15 .40
9 Ryan Flynn .15 .40
10 Jeff Frazee .15 .40
11 Ben Gordon .15 .40
12 Mike Hoeffel .15 .40
13 Mike Howe .15 .40
14 Alex Kangas .15 .40
15 Evan Kaufmann .15 .40
16 Tony Lucia .15 .40
17 Derek Peltier .15 .40
18 Tom Pohl .15 .40
19 Brian Schack .15 .40
20 Brent Solei .15 .40
21 Ryan Stoa .15 .40
22 Kevin Wehrs .15 .40
23 Blake Wheeler .15 .40
24 Patrick White .15 .40
25 Don Lucia HC .10 .40

1994-95 Minnesota Moose

This set features the Moose of the IHL. The set was issued as a promotional giveaway in the form of four, four-card perforated strips. It is believed that all were issued on the same night, but that is not yet verified.

COMPLETE SET (16) 8.00 20.00
1 Dave Christian .60 1.50
2 Kris Miller .60 1.50
3 John Young .60 1.50
4 Tom Draper .75 2.00
5 Daniel Shank .60 1.50
6 Dean Kolstad .60 1.50
7 Yvon Corriveau .60 1.50
8 Frank Serratore CO .20 .50
9 Dave Snuggerud .60 1.50
10 Mark Osiecki .60 1.50
11 Brad Miller .60 1.50
12 Frank Pietrangelo .75 2.00
13 Stephane Morin .60 1.50
14 Sean Williams .60 1.50
15 Dave Hakstol .60 1.50
16 Mick E. Moose MAS .20 .50

1995-96 Minnesota Moose

This set features the Moose of the IHL. It is believed to have been issued as a promotional giveaway, but that has not been confirmed. Any additional information can be forwarded to hockeymag@beckett.com

COMPLETE SET (16) 6.00 15.00
1 Dave Christian .40 1.00
2 Chris Jensen .40 1.00
3 Sandy Smith .60 1.50
4 Stephane Morin .60 1.50
5 Dave Gagnon .60 1.50
6 Sean Williams .40 1.00
7 Yvon Corriveau .40 1.00
8 Chris Govedaris .40 1.00
9 Mike Hurlbut .40 1.00
10 Dave Hakstol .40 1.00
11 Bryan Fogarty .40 1.00
12 Dave Morissette .40 1.00
13 Brad Miller .40 1.00
14 Kris Miller .40 1.00
15 Frank Serratore CO .20 .50
16 Mick E. Moose MASCOT .20 .50

2003-04 Minnesota State Mavericks

This set was issued as a promotional giveaway. The cards are unnumbered and so are listed below in alphabetical order.

COMPLETE SET (20) 20.00
1 Cole Bassett 1.00
2 Brock Becker 1.00
3 Jake Brenk 1.00
4 Chad Clower 1.00
5 Jon Dubel 1.00
6 Aaron Forsythe 1.00
7 Adam Gerlach 1.00
8 Jon Hart 1.00
9 Steven Johns 1.00
10 Shane Joseph 1.00
11 Rick Kisskeys 1.00
12 Jeff Marler 1.00
13 Ryan McKelvie 1.00
14 Nate Metcalf 1.00
15 Kyle Nixon 1.50
16 Matt Paluczak 1.00
17 Dana Sorensen 1.00
18 Brad Thompson 1.00
19 Christian Toll 1.00
20 Jon Volp 1.50

2000-01 Mississauga Ice Dogs

This set features the Ice Dogs of the OHL. The set was produced by the team and sold at its souvenir shop. The cards are unnumbered, so the set is listed in alphabetical order. It is noteworthy for including an early card of top prospect Jason Spezza.

COMPLETE SET (28) 8.00 20.00
1 Team CL .04 .01
2 Brett Angel .20 .50
3 Blue and Baby Blue MASCOT .16 .25
4 Grant Buckley .16 .40
5 Don Cherry OWN .80 2.00
6 Steve Cherry CO .04 .10
7 Fraser Clair .16 .40
8 Mark Cranley .16 .40
9 David Dalliday .16 .40
10 Andrew Davis .16 .40
11 Justin Dumont .16 .40
12 Omar Ennaffati .16 .40
13 John Jarram .16 .40
14 Patrick Jarrett .80 1.00
15 Brent Labre .16 .40
16 Brian McGrattan .16 .40
17 Sean McMorrow .16 1.00
18 Michael Mole .20 1.00
19 Chris Osborne .16 .40
20 Jeff Paisley .16 .40
21 Brandon Robinson .16 .40
22 Adam Solnik .16 .40
23 Jason Spezza 4.00 10.00
24 Dan Sullivan .16 .40
25 Chris Thaler .16 .40
26 Rick Vaive CO .16 .25
27 Mike Wehrstedt .16 .40
28 Chad Wiseman .16 .40

2001-02 Mississauga Ice Dogs

COMPLETE SET (26) 12.00
1 Team card .10
2 Matt Tanel .40
3 T.J. Reynolds .40
4 Travis Parent .40
5 Nathan O'Nabigon .40
6 Patrick O'Sullivan 1.50
7 Chris Churran .40
8 Dan Rudisuela .40
9 Mike Wehrstedt .40
10 Tyler Eady .40
11 John Kozoriz .40
12 Adam Sturgeon .40
13 Chris Hawley .40
14 Alexander Skorohod .40
15 Miguel Beaudry .40
16 Andrew Smale .40
17 Bobby Turner .40
18 John Eminger .40
19 Igor Radulov 2.00
20 Greg Jacina .40
21 Mike Barrett .40
22 Daniel Sisca .40
23 Don Cherry OWN 2.00
24 Steve Cherry GM .10
25 Joel Washkurak ACO .10
26 Blue MASCOT .10

2002-03 Mississauga Ice Dogs

COMPLETE SET (23) 15.00
1 Checklist .01
2 Travis Parent .50
3 Ian Maracle .50
4 Scott Hotham .50
5 Derek Lyons .50
6 Chris Curran .50
7 Dan Rudisuela .50
8 Tyler Eady .50
9 Tomas Linhart .75
10 Chris Hawley .50
11 Pavel Voroshin .75
12 Wes Ryplen .50
13 Miquel Beaudry .75
14 Matt Harpwood .75
15 Daniel Buccella .50
16 Rob Schremp 3.00
17 Salvatore Malandrino .50
18 Greg Jacina .50
19 Ryan Stokes .50
20 Patrick O'Sullivan 1.50
21 Dany Revelle .50
22 Blair Jarrett .50
23 Daniel Sisca .50
25 Matt Harpwood .50
26 Steve Ludzik .50
27 Mark Osborne .50
28 Wayne Crawford .50
29 Dave Sweetman .50
30 Kevin Elliot .50
31 Blue the mascot .50

2003-04 Mississauga Ice Dogs

COMPLETE SET (24) 12.00
1 Adam Abraham .50
2 Chris Bain .75
3 Cody Bass .50
4 Anthony Butera .50
5 Rick Caughell .50
6 Chris Chimienti .50
7 Chris Curran .50
8 Brad Efthimiou .50
9 Brandon Elliott .50
10 Lukas Grauwiler .50
11 Doug Groenestege .75
12 Blair Jarrett .50
13 Daryl Knowles .50
14 Mark O'Leary .50
15 Patrick O'Sullivan .75
16 Chad Painchaud .50
17 Kyle Quincey .50
18 Dany Revelle .50
19 Dan Rudisuela .50
20 David Shantz 1.50
21 Ryan Stokes .50
22 Nick Van Herpt .50
23 Tom Zanoski .50
24 Scott Zimmerman .50

2004-05 Mississauga Ice Dogs

A total of 300 team sets were produced.

COMPLETE SET (24) 15.00
1 Anthony Butera .75
2 Bradley Snetsinger .50
3 Adam Abraham .50
4 Cody Bass .50
5 David Shantz 1.50
6 Dustin Jeffrey .50
7 Kyle Quincey .75
8 Michael Swift .50
9 Gianluc Caputi .50
10 Craig Cescon .50
11 Tom Zanoski .50
12 Vladimir Svacina .50
13 Patrick O'Sullivan 1.50
14 Daniel Carcillo .50
15 John Hecimovic .50
16 Paul Merchese .50
17 Michael Ouzas .50
18 David Pszenyczny .50
19 Frankie Santini .50
20 Justin DaCosta 1.00
21 Stefan Legein .50
22 Nathan Hooper .50
23 Jordan Owens .50
24 Aaron Barton .50

2005-06 Mississauga Ice Dogs

COMPLETE SET (24) 6.00 15.00
1 Cody Bass .75
2 Vladimir Svacina .75
3 Jordan Owens .75
4 Drew Schiestel .75
5 Michael Smith .75
6 Keith Wynn .75
7 Lucas Lobsinger 1.00
8 Luca Caputi .75
9 Kyle Lamb .75
10 Justin Gvora .75
11 Jordan Skellett .75
12 Andrew Marcoux .75
13 Andrew Merrett .75
14 Oskar Osala .75
15 Brett Oliphante .75
16 Justin Dacosta .75
17 Kyle Knechtel .75
18 Joshua Day .75
19 Franck Santini .75
20 Nathan Martine .75
21 Drew McAvoy .75
22 Stefan Legein .75
23 Jadran Beljo .75
24 Chris Lawrence .75

2006-07 Mississauga Ice Dogs

COMPLETE SET (23) 8.00 15.00
1 Cody Bass .25 .60
2 Alex Pietrangelo .25 .60
3 Stephan Legein .25 .60
4 Jadran Beljo .25 .60
5 Chris Lawrence .25 .60
6 Jordan Owens .25 .60
7 Brett Oliphant .25 .60
8 Michael Swift .25 .60
9 Luca Caputi .25 .60
10 Barry Sanderson .25 .60
11 Jordan Skellett .25 .60
12 Andrew Merrett .25 .60
13 Travis Fuller .25 .60
14 Oskar Osala .25 .60
15 Steven Manojlovic .25 .60
16 Josh Day .25 .60
17 Franck Santini .25 .60
18 Nathan Martine .25 .60
19 Drew Mcavoy .25 .60
20 Drew Schiestel .25 .60
21 Kyle Lamb .25 .60
22 Lucas Lobsinger .40 1.00
23 Andrew Loverock .40 1.00

1996-97 Mississippi Sea Wolves

This set was sold by the team at home games and was sponsored by Play It Again Sports.

COMPLETE SET (22) 4.00 10.00
1 Frederik Beaubien .30 .75
2 Alexei Budayev .20 .50
3 Sylvain Daigle .20 .50
4 Kevin Evans .20 .50
5 Quinn Fair .20 .50
6 Shawn Frappier .20 .50
7 Kevin Hilton .20 .50
8 Kelly Hurd .20 .50
9 Derek Innanen .20 .50
10 Yanick Jean .20 .50
11 John Kosobud .20 .50
12 Troy Mann .20 .50
13 Roger Maxwell .20 .50
14 Mike Muller .30 .75
15 Simon Oliver .20 .50
16 Patrick Rochon .20 .50
17 Jeff Rohlicek .30 .75
18 Mark Rupnow .20 .50
19 Joaikin Wassberger .20 .50
20 Steven Yule .20 .50
21 Bruce Boudreau HCO .08 .25
22 Hook Mascot .02 .10

1997-98 Mississippi Sea Wolves

Little is known about this set beyond the confirmed checklist. Additional information can be forwarded to hockeymag@beckett.com.

COMPLETE SET (22) 4.00 10.00
1 Sinuhe Wallinheimo .40 1.00
2 Neal Martin .20 .50
3 Don Chase .20 .50
4 John Kosobud .20 .50
5 Jeff Rohlicek .20 .50
6 Kelly Hurd .20 .50
7 Chad Dameworth .20 .50
8 Bruce Boudreau HCO .02 .10
9 Teemu Numminen .20 .50
10 Dan Back .20 .50
11 Dean Hulett .20 .50
12 Mark Rupnow .20 .50
13 Hook Mascot .02 .10
14 Patrick Rochon .20 .50
15 Troy Mann .20 .50
16 Quinn Fair .20 .50
17 Shawn Frappier .20 .50
18 Brian Farrell .20 .50
19 Steve Yule .20 .50
20 Kevin Evans .20 .50
21 Brad Guzda .20 .50
22 Forbes MacPherson .20 .50

1999-00 Mississippi Sea Wolves

This set features the Sea Wolves of the ECHL. The set was produced by Roox and was sold by the team at home games.

COMPLETE SET (25) 20.00 50.00
1 Rob Flahiff EQM .02 .10
2 Marc Potvin HCO .75 2.00
3 Hook MAS .02 .10
4 Team Photo .75 2.00
5 Cynthia Dedeaux TR .02 .10
6 Trevor Gillies .75 2.00
7 Steve Duke .75 2.00
8 Sean Gillam .75 2.00
9 Bob Woods .75 2.00
10 Cody Bowtell .75 2.00
11 Patrick Rochon .75 2.00
12 Jonathan Weaver .75 2.00
13 John Kosobud .75 2.00
14 Brad Essex 1.25 3.00
15 Scott King .75 2.00
16 Ryan Gaucher .75 2.00
17 Brad Goulet .75 2.00
18 Mike Martone .75 2.00
19 J.F. Aube .75 2.00
20 Dave Paradise .75 2.00
21 John Evangelista .75 2.00
22 Mikhail Kravets .75 2.00
23 Chuck Thuss 1.25 3.00
24 Sylvain Daigle 1.25 3.00
25 Mark Rupnow .75 2.00

1999-00 Mississippi Sea Wolves Kelly Cup

This set features the Sea Wolves of the ECHL. The set was produced by the team and features players from the previous season to honor their league championship win. The set was sold by the team at home games for $10.

COMPLETE SET (25) 4.00 10.00
1 Bruce Boudreau CO .20 .50
2 Hook MAS .02 .10
3 James Carey TR .02 .10
4 Cynthia Dedeaux TR .02 .10
5 Karl Infanger .20 .50
6 Sean Blanchard .20 .50
7 Bob Woods .20 .50
8 Cody Bowtell .20 .50
9 Vaclav Nedomansky .20 .50
10 Patrick Rochon .20 .50
11 John Kosobud .20 .50
12 Brad Essex .30 .75
13 Andrew Dale .20 .50
14 Dean Mando .20 .50
15 Kevin Hilton .20 .50
16 Quinn Fair .20 .50
17 Chris Schmidt .20 .50
18 Mike Martone .20 .50
19 Kelly Hurd .20 .50
20 Mikhail Kravets .20 .50
21 Travis Scott .30 .75
22 Mark Rupnow .20 .50
23 Troy Mann .20 .50
24 Chuck Thuss .30 .75
25 Mississippi Sea Wolves .20 .50

2003-04 Mississippi Sea Wolves

These cards were given away as promotional items at several home games. It's believed that other cards exist in this series. If you have additional info, please forward it to hockeymag@beckett.com. Because we could not gather enough confirmed sales data, the cards are not priced.

COMPLETE SET (17)
1 Anthony Battaglia
2 Brent Gauvreau
3 Louis Dumont
4 Greg Gardner
5 Jeff Hutchins
6 Andrei Lupandin
7 Austin Miller
8 Steve O'Rourke
9 John Evangelista
10 Travis Lisabeth
11 Sean Matile
12 Roger Maxwell
13 Patrick Rochon
14 Kerry Ellis-Toddington
15 Steffon Walby
16 Mascot
17 Checklist

1999-00 Missouri River Otters

This set features the River Otters of the UHL. The cards were printed by Roox and sold by the team. They are not numbered, so they are listed below in alphabetical order.

COMPLETE SET (28) 4.00 10.00
1 Team Photo .20 .50
2 Tomas Baluch .15 .40
3 Chris Bernard .15 .40
4 Charles Blyth .15 .40
5 Colin Chaulk .15 .40
6 Randy Gallatin .15 .40
7 Forrest Gore .15 .40
8 Ben Gorewich .15 .40
9 Jay Hebert .15 .40
10 Kiley Hill .15 .40
11 Jan Kobezda .15 .40
12 Lonnie Loach .30 .75
13 Jeremiah McCarthy .20 .50
14 Jeremy Rebek .15 .40
15 Brian Regan .15 .40
16 Allan Roulette .15 .40
17 Alain St. Hilaire .15 .40
18 Curtis Sayler .15 .40
19 Trevor Sherban .15 .40
20 Marty Standish .15 .40
21 Michal Stastny .30 .75
22 Chris Tok .15 .40
23 Dan Tompkins .15 .40
24 Mark Reeds HCO .15 .40
25 Scott Bell CO .15 .40
26 Oscar MASCOT .08 .25
27 Otter Mobile .08 .25
28 Checklist .08 .25

2000-01 Missouri River Otters

This set features the River Otters of the UHL. The cards were issued as promotional giveaways, apparently on three separate occasions, and in subsets of nine cards. Collectors needed to attend all three games to compile the entire set.

COMPLETE SET (27) 7.20 18.00
1 Team CL #1 .04 .10
2 Lonnie Loach .40 1.00
3 Chris Tok .30 .75
4 Colin Chaulk .40 1.00
5 Kiley Hill .40 1.00
6 Jeremy Rebek .30 .75
7 Trevor Sherban .30 .75
8 Jay Hebert .30 .75
9 Randy Gallatin .30 .75
10 Team CL #2 .04 .10
11 Darin Kimble .40 1.00
12 Troy Michalski .30 .75
13 Benoit Thibert .30 .75
14 Eric Murano .40 1.00
15 Lee Cole .30 .75
16 Robert Starke .30 .75
17 Ryan Johnston .30 .75
18 Mark Reeds CO .10 .25
19 Team CL #3 .04 .10
20 Kevin Plager .30 .75
21 Mike Bayrack .30 .75
22 Jay Woodcroft .30 .75
23 Jared Reigstad .30 .75
24 Anthony Cappelletti .30 .75
25 Kiley Hill AS .30 .75
26 Colin Chaulk AS .30 .75
27 John Sheehan TR .04 .10
27 Jim Jeans EM .04 .10

1999-00 Missouri River Otters Sheet

This set features the River Otters of the UHL. The cards were issued as a promotional giveaway in the form of a three-panel perforated sheet. The set was sponsored by a local pub and by Disney.

COMPLETE SET (25) 7.20 18.00
1 Tomas Baluch .30 .75
2 Charlie Blythe .30 .75
3 Colin Chaulk .30 .75
4 Randy Gallatin .30 .75
5 Yuri Gerasimov .30 .75
6 Ben Gorewich .30 .75
7 Jay Hebert .30 .75
8 Kiley Hill .30 .75
9 Jan Kobezda .30 .75
10 Lonnie Loach .40 1.00
11 Jeremiah McCarthy .30 .75
12 Jeremy Rebek .30 .75
13 Brian Regan .30 .75
14 Alan Roulette .30 .75
15 Alain St. Hilaire .30 .75
16 Curtis Sayler .30 .75
17 Trevor Sherban .30 .75
18 Marty Standish .30 .75
19 Michal Stastny .40 1.00
20 Jason Stewart .30 .75
21 Chris Tok .30 .75
22 Dan Tompkins .30 .75
23 Mark Reeds CO .08 .25
24 Scott Bell .30 .75
25 Oscar the Otter MASCOT .02 .10

2001-02 Missouri River Otters

This set features the River Otters of the UHL. The set was issued as a promotional giveaway in two 15-card series, and then was later sold by the team as a complete 30-card issue.

COMPLETE SET (30) 8.00 20.00
1 Missouri River Otters Logo .04 .10
2 Aaron Vickar .30 .75
3 Lonnie Loach .40 1.00
4 Dustin Whitecotton .30 .75
5 Troy Mann .30 .75
6 Anthony Cappelletti .30 .75
7 Casey VanSchagen .30 .75
8 Ben White .30 .75
9 Curtis Voth .40 1.00
10 Charlie Blyth .30 .75
11 Scott Perry .30 .75
12 Kelvin Solari .30 .75
13 Mark Reeds CO .30 .75
14 Oscar the River Otter MASCOT .04 .10
15 Checklist I .04 .10
16 Missouri River Otters .04 .10
17 Brian Regan .30 .75
18 Darin Kimble .60 1.50
19 Eric Murano .40 1.00
20 Jason Gudmundson .30 .75
21 Mike Jaros .30 .75
22 Joe Ritson .30 .75
23 Tony White .30 .75
24 Simon Poirier .30 .75
25 Vaclav Pazourek .30 .75
26 Joe Pecoraro .30 .75
27 Kevin Chabbert .30 .75
28 John Sheehan TR .04 .10
29 Team Photo .30 .75
30 Checklist 2 .04 .10

2003-04 Missouri River Otters

This set was issued in two series as a promotional giveaway.

COMPLETE SET (24) 20.00
1 Checklist .01
2 Anthony Cappelletti 1.00
3 Charlie Blyth 1.00
4 Jesse Heerema 1.00
5 Jeff Cameron 1.00
6 Jeff Petruic 1.00
7 Colin Embley 1.00
8 Bobby Rapoza 1.00
9 Troy Mann 1.00
10 Tony White 1.00
11 Chad Moore 1.00
12 Team Photo .25
13 Checklist .01
14 Ben White 1.00
15 Kevin Chabbert 1.00
16 Forrest Gore 1.00
17 Joe Ritson 1.00
18 Brian Regan 1.50
19 George Cantrall 1.50
20 River Otters Kids Club .10
21 Ryan Gillis 1.00
22 Tim Knudsen 1.50
23 Rob Davidson 1.00
24 Lonnie Loach HCO .25

2004-05 Missouri River Otters

This set was issued in two parts by the River Otters of the UHL. Each 16-card series was sold for $4 at the team's merchandise shop.

COMPLETE SET (32) 12.00
1 Header .01
2 Charlie Blyth .50
3 Jason Tapp .50
4 B.J. Heckendorn .50
5 Barrie Moore .50
6 Mike Dombkiewicz .50
7 Cole Bassett .50
8 Ryan Johnson .75
9 Riku Varjamo .50
10 Mat Snesrud .50
11 Quinten Van Horlick .75
12 Jim Montgomery .75
13 Kevin Kaminski CO .50
14 Ice Zone .01
15 Prize Card .01
16 Checklist Series 1 .01
17 Header .01
18 Bob Rapoza .50
19 Josh Legge .50
20 Kevin Reiter .50
21 Lars Pettersen .50
22 Mark Odut .50
23 George Cantrall .50
24 Justin Quenneville .50
25 Glen Detulleo .50
26 Rod Sundquist .50
27 Brad MacMillan .50
28 Barret Jackman 1.50
29 Team Photo .50
30 Sponsor Card .01
31 Prize Card .01
32 Checklist Series 2 .01

2005-06 Missouri River Otters

COMPLETE SET (24) 20.00
1 Missouri River Otters .10
2 Kevin Kaminski HC .10
3 Richard Paul 1.00
4 Dave Stewart 1.00
5 Martin Vasut 1.00
6 Jim Murphy 1.00
7 J.P. Beilsten 1.00
8 Lars Pettersen 1.00
9 B.J. Heckendorn 1.00
10 Tyler Butler 1.00
11 Mark Lindsay 1.00
12 Brenden Cuthbert 1.00
13 Missouri River Otters .10
14 Brad Church 1.00
15 Tim O'Connell 1.00
16 Jimmy Callahan 1.00
17 Frank Littlejohn 1.00

18 Mark Odut		1.00
19 Brad MacMillan		1.00
20 Kevin Reiter		1.00
21 Damian Surma		1.00
22 Oscar (Mascot)		.10
23 Matt Suderman		1.00
24 Scott Horvath		1.00

1997-98 Mobile Mysticks

This set features the Mysticks of the ECHL. The cards were produced by Starzsports, and were sold by the team at home games.

COMPLETE SET (21)	4.00	10.00
1 Chuck Thuss	.20	.50
2 Mike Mayhew	.20	.50
3 Matt Shaw CO	.08	.25
4 Dave Craievich	.20	.50
5 Jim Jensen	.20	.50
6 Anton Fedorov	.20	.50
7 Russell Monteith	.20	.50
8 Yanick Jean	.20	.50
9 Dave Larson	.20	.50
10 Chris Brooks	.20	.50
11 Brandon Carper	.20	.50
12 Phil Valk	.20	.50
13 Patrice Paquin	.20	.50
14 Kevin Hilton	.20	.50
15 Fredrick Nasvall	.20	.50
16 Andrew Will	.20	.50
17 Steve Suk	.20	.50
18 Mike Lenarduzzi	.30	.75
19 Neil Donovan	.20	.50
20 Hugues Gervais	.20	.50
21 Chad Remackel	.20	.50

1997-98 Mobile Mysticks Kellogg's

This set features the Mysticks of the ECHL. These cards were issued as a promotional giveaway in four-card strips at seven different home games. Each strip contained three player cards and one Kellogg's ad card. The players on cards No. 2 and 4 are not known at this time. Identification should be sent to hockeymag@beckett.com.

COMPLETE SET (21)	6.00	15.00
1 Andrew Will	.40	1.00
2 unknown		
3 Neil Donovan	.40	1.00
4 unknown		
5 Dave Larson	.40	1.00
6 Jim Jensen	.40	1.00
7 Mike Mayhew	.40	1.00
8 Matt Shaw HCO	.15	.40
9 Yanick Jean	.40	1.00
10 Steve Suk	.40	1.00
11 Chad Remackel	.40	1.00
12 Tom Neziol ACO	.08	.25
13 Dave Craievich	.40	1.00
14 Chris Brooks	.40	1.00
15 Fredrick Nasvall	.40	1.00
16 Puck MAS	.08	.25
17 Anton Fedorov	.40	1.00
18 Hugues Gervais	.40	1.00
19 Phil Valk	.40	1.00
20 Mike Lenarduzzi	.60	1.50
21 Russell Monteith	.40	1.00

1998-99 Mobile Mysticks

This 22-card set was handed out as a promotional giveaway at five different home games, making it an extremely difficult set to acquire. The cards were distributed in perforated strips.

COMPLETE SET (22)	6.00	15.00
1 Russell Monteith	.40	1.00
2 Slapshot Mascot	.02	.10
3 Tom Neziol ACO	.02	.10
4 Kevin Kerr	.40	1.00
5 Steve Debus	.40	1.00
6 Steve Chapman GM	.02	.10
7 Puck Mascot	.02	.10
8 Yanick Jean	.40	1.00
9 Dave Craievich	.40	1.00
10 Jason Elders	.40	1.00
11 Alain Savage	.40	1.00
12 Joel Theriault	.40	1.00
13 Chad Alban	.60	1.50
14 John McCabe	.40	1.00
15 Simmons/Jeffreys/Young	.20	.50
16 Hughes Gervais	.40	1.00
17 Brandon Carper	.40	1.00
18 Craig Binns	.40	1.00
19 Jeff Pyle HCO	.08	.25
20 Jim Shepherd	.40	1.00
21 Andrew Will	.40	1.00
22 Francois Page	.40	1.00

1999-00 Mobile Mysticks

This set features the Mysticks of the ECHL. The set was issued as a promotional giveaway at an early-season game.

COMPLETE SET (23)	6.00	50.00
1 Dave Craievich	1.00	2.50
2 David Van Drunen	1.00	2.50
3 Mitch Vig	1.00	2.50
4 Benoit Cotnoir	1.00	2.50
5 Bobby Stewart	1.00	2.50
6 John McCabe	1.00	2.50
7 Hugues Gervais	1.00	2.50
8 Tom Nolan	1.00	2.50
9 Chad Onufrechuk	1.00	2.50
10 Jason Elders	1.00	2.50
11 B.J. Kilbourne	1.00	2.50
12 Mark Turner	1.00	2.50
13 Jeff Kozakowski	1.00	2.50
14 Josh Harrold	1.00	2.50
15 Russ Guzior	1.00	2.50
16 Anders Sorensen	1.00	2.50
17 Jason Clarke	1.00	2.50
18 Chad Alban	2.00	5.00
19 Steve Debus	2.00	6.00
20 Scott Cherrey	1.00	2.50
21 Jeff Pyle CO	1.00	2.50
22 Tom Neziol CO	.08	.25
23 Southern Ford Dealers		.01

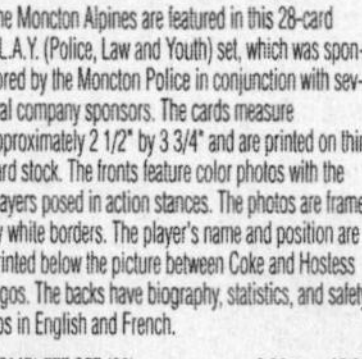

1983-84 Moncton Alpines

The Moncton Alpines are featured in this 28-card P.L.A.Y. (Police, Law and Youth) set, which was sponsored by the Moncton Police in conjunction with several company sponsors. The cards measure approximately 2 1/2" by 3 3/4" and are printed on thin card stock. The fronts feature color photos with the players posed in action stances. The photos are framed by white borders. The player's name and position are printed below the picture between Coke and Hostess logos. The backs have biography, statistics, and safety tips in English and French.

COMPLETE SET (28)	6.00	15.00
1 Doug Messier CO	.20	.50
2 Chris Smith	.20	.50
3 Marco Baron	.40	1.00
4 Mike Zanier	.40	1.00
5 Dwayne Boettger	.20	.50
6 Lowell Loveday	.20	.50
7 Joe McDonnell	.20	.50
8 Peter Dineen	.20	.50
9 John Blum	.30	.75
10 Steve Smith	.75	2.00
11 Reg Kerr	.30	.75
12 Tom Rowe	.20	.50
13 Ross Lambert	.20	.50
14 Pat Conacher	.40	1.00
15 Paul Miller	.20	.50
16 Bert Yachimel	.20	.50
17 Tom Gorence	.30	.75
18 Jeff Crawford	.20	.50
19 Serge Boisvert	.30	.75
20 Todd Strueby	.30	.75
21 Todd Bidner	.20	.50
22 Dean Dachyshyn	.20	.50
23 Ray Cote	.20	.50
24 Shawn Babcock	.20	.50
25 Shawn Dineen	.20	.50
26 Marc Habscheid	.40	1.00
27 Charlie Lavalee TR Kevin Ferris TR	.08	.25
NNO Checklist Card	.20	.50

1984-85 Moncton Golden Flames

The Moncton Golden Flames are featured in this 26-card P.L.A.Y. (Police, Law and Youth) set, which was sponsored by the Moncton Police in conjunction with several company sponsors. The cards measure approximately 2 1/2" by 3 3/4" and are printed on thin card stock. The fronts feature color photos with the players posed in action stances.

COMPLETE SET (26)	10.00	25.00
1 Brian Patafie TR	.08	.25
2 Mike Bianni TR	.08	.25
3 Pierre Page CO	.20	.50
4 Neil Sheehy	.40	1.00
5 George White	.20	.50
6 Mark Lamb	.40	1.00
7 Dan Kane	.20	.50
8 Dan Bolduc	.40	1.00
9 Lou Kiriakou	.20	.50
10 Joel Otto	.75	2.00
11 Dale Degray	.40	1.00
12 Mike Clayton	.20	.50
13 Mickey Volcan	.20	.50
14 Ted Pearson	.20	.50
15 Mario Simioni	.20	.50
16 Keith Hanson	.20	.50
17 Yves Courteau	.20	.50
18 Dan Cormier	.20	.50
19 Todd Hooey	.20	.50
20 Mike Vernon	4.00	10.00
21 Dave Meszaros	.20	.50
22 Bruce Eakin	.20	.50
23 Ed Kastelic	.40	1.00
24 Tony Stiles	.20	.50
25 Pierre Rioux	.20	.50
26 Gino Cavallini	.40	1.00

1985-86 Moncton Golden Flames

The Moncton Golden Flames are featured in this 28-card P.L.A.Y. (Police, Law and Youth) set, which was sponsored by the Moncton Police in conjunction with several company sponsors. The cards measure approximately 2 1/2" by 3 3/4" and are printed on thin card stock. The fronts feature color photos with the players posed in action stances. The photos are framed by white borders. The player's name and position are printed below the picture between Coke and Hostess logos. The backs have biography, statistics, and safety tips in English and French.

COMPLETE SET (28)	8.00	20.00
1 Terry Crisp GM/CO	.40	1.00
2 Dan Bolduc ACO	.08	.25
3 Terry Crisp GM/CO Dan Bolduc ACO	.40	1.00
4 Al Pedersen	.30	.75
5 Dave Meszaros	.20	.50
6 George White	.20	.50
7 Mark Lamb	.60	1.50
8 Doug Kostynski	.20	.50
9 Brian Bradley	.75	2.00
10 Rob Kivell	.20	.50
11 Geoff Courtnall	1.25	3.00
12 Tony Stiles	.20	.50
13 Jim Buettgen	.20	.50
14 Cleon Daskalakis	.40	1.00
15 Rick Kosti	.20	.50
16 Kevan Guy	.20	.50
17 John Blum	.20	.50
18 Brian Patafie TR Mike Bajani Jamie Druet	.08	.25
19 Greg Johnston	.30	.75
20 Dale Degray	.20	.50
21 John Meulenbroeks	.20	.50
22 Dave Reid	.40	1.00
23 Jay Miller	1.25	3.00
24 Yves Courteau	.20	.50
25 Robin Bartel	.20	.50
26 Benoit Doucet	.20	.50
27 Pete Bakovic	.20	.50
28 Team Photo	.40	1.00

1986-87 Moncton Golden Flames

CKCW CKCW CKCW
BRETT HULL
Right Wing
Coke

The Moncton Golden Flames are featured in this 28-card P.L.A.Y. (Police, Law and Youth) set, which was sponsored by the Moncton Police in conjunction with several company sponsors. The cards measure approximately 2 1/2" by 3 3/4" and are printed on thin card stock. The fronts feature color photos with the players posed in action stances. This set includes first pro cards of Brett Hull, Gary Roberts, Bill Ranford, and Lyndon Byers.

COMPLETE SET (28)	30.00	75.00
1 Terry Crisp CO/GM	.40	1.00
2 Danny Bolduc ACO	.08	.25
3 Doug Dadswell	.40	1.00
4 Doug Kostynski	.20	.50
5 Bill Ranford	6.00	15.00
6 Brian Patafie TR	.08	.25
7 Dave Pasin	.30	.75
8 Darwin McCutcheon	.20	.50
9 Team Photo	.40	1.00
10 Kevan Guy	.20	.50
11 Kraig Nienhuis	.30	.75
12 Gary Roberts	2.00	5.00
13 Ken Sabourin	.30	.75
14 Marc D'Amour	.40	1.00
15 Don Mercier	.20	.50
16 Wade Campbell	.20	.50
17 Mark Paterson	.20	.50
18 Cleon Daskalakis	.40	1.00
19 Lyndon Byers	2.00	5.00
20 Brett Hull	15.00	40.00
21 Bob Sweeney	.40	1.00
22 Gord Hynes	.20	.50
23 Peter Bakovic	.20	.50
24 Dave Reid	.40	1.00
25 Mike Rucinski	.20	.50
26 Ray Podloski	.20	.50
27 Bob Bodak	.20	.50
28 John Carter	.30	.75

1987-88 Moncton Hawks

Sponsored by Coke, Shoppers Drug Mart, and CKCW, this 25-card set measures approximately 2 1/2" by 3 3/4" and features posed, color player photos with white studio backgrounds. The fronts have white borders with sponsor names printed in red above and below the picture. The player's name and position are printed in black just below the photo. The cards are unnumbered and checklisted below in alphabetical order.

COMPLETE SET (25)	4.80	12.00
1 Joel Baillargeon	.20	.50
2 Rick Bowness CO	.20	.50
3 Rick Carrano TR Wayne Flemming EQMG	.08	.25
4 Bobby Dollas	.30	.75
5 Peter Douris	.30	.75
6 Iain Duncan	.20	.50
7 Bob Essensa	.75	2.00
8 Todd Flichel	.20	.50
9 Rob Fowler	.20	.50
10 Randy Gilhen	.30	.75
11 Matt Hervey	.20	.50
12 Brent Hughes	.30	.75
13 Jamie Husgen	.20	.50
14 Mike Jeffrey	.20	.50
15 Guy Larose	.20	.50
16 Chris Levasseur	.20	.50
17 Len Nielson	.20	.50
18 Roger Ohman	.20	.50
19 Dave Quigley	.20	.50
20 Ron Pesetti	.20	.50
21 Steve Penney	.40	1.00
22 Scott Schneider	.20	.50
23 Ryan Stewart	.20	.50
24 Gord Whitaker	.20	.50
25 Team Photo	.40	1.00

1990-91 Moncton Hawks

These 25 cards measure approximately 2 7/16" by 3 5/8" and feature on their fronts white-bordered posed-on-ice color shots of the '90-91 Moncton Hawks. The player's name and position appear at the lower left. The logos for the set's sponsors, Hostess, Frito Lay, and CKCW Radio, also appear on the front. The cards are unnumbered and checklisted below in alphabetical order.

COMPLETE SET (25)	4.00	10.00
1 Larry Bernard	.15	.40
2 Lee Davidson	.15	.40
3 Iain Duncan	.15	.40
4 Craig Duncanson	.15	.40
5 Dallas Eakins	.20	.50
6 Dave Farrish CO/GM	.02	.10
7 Wayne Flemming EQMG	.02	.10
8 Todd Flichel	.15	.40
9 Peter Hankinson	.15	.40
10 Matt Hervey	.15	.40
11 Brent Hughes	.20	.50
12 Anthony Joseph	.15	.40
13 Sergei Kharin	.15	.40
14 Denis Larocque	.15	.40
15 Guy Larose	.20	.50
16 Scott Levins	.20	.50
17 Bryan Marchment	.40	1.00
18 Chris Norton	.15	.40
19 Mike O'Neill	.30	.75
20 Grant Richison	.15	.40
21 Scott Schneider	.15	.40
22 Rob Snitzer TR	.02	.10
23 Rick Tabaracci	.40	1.00
24 Simon Wheeldon	.20	.50
25 Team Card	.20	.50

1991-92 Moncton Hawks

This 28-card set measures approximately 2 1/2" by 3 5/8" and was sponsored by the Moncton Police Force, the Sackville Police Force, and the Hostess/Frito Lay company. The fronts feature color photos with the players posed in action stances. The photos are framed by white borders. The player's name and position appear in the lower left corner, while the Hostess/Frito Lay logo is in the lower right corner.The cards are unnumbered and checklisted below in alphabetical order.

COMPLETE SET (28)	4.00	10.00
1 Luciano Borsato	.15	.40
2 Jason Cirone	.15	.40
3 Rob Cowie	.15	.40
4 Lee Davidson	.15	.40
5 Kris Draper	.40	1.00
6 Dallas Eakins	.20	.50
7 Dave Farrish GM/CO	.02	.10
8 Wayne Flemming EQMG	.02	.10
9 Sean Gauthier	.20	.50
10 Ken Gernander	.20	.50
11 Tod Hartje	.15	.40
12 Bob Joyce	.20	.50
13 Claude Julien	.15	.40
14 Chris Kiene	.15	.40
15 Mark Kumpel P/ACO	.15	.40
16 Derek Langille	.15	.40
17 Tyler Larter	.15	.40
18 John LeBlanc	.15	.40
19 Scott Levins	.15	.40
20 Rob Murray	.15	.40
21 Kent Paynter	.15	.40
22 Rudy Poeschek	.20	.50
23 Dave Prior CO	.02	.10
24 Warren Rychel	.20	.50
25 Rob Snitzer TR	.02	.10
26 Rick Tabaracci	.40	1.00
27 The Hawk (Mascot)	.02	.10
28 Darren Veitch	.20	.50

2001-02 Moncton Wildcats

This set features the Wildcats of the QMJHL. The cards were produced by CTM Ste-Foy and were sold at that shop, as well as at the team's home games. It was reported that less than 1,000 sets were produced.

COMPLETE SET (26)	6.00	15.00
1 Bill Ruggiero	.30	.75
2 Andrew Carver	.20	.50
3 James Sanford	.20	.50
4 Kyle Murnaghan	.20	.50
5 Daniel Hudgin	.20	.50
6 Mathieu Betournay	.20	.50
7 Karl Gagne	.20	.50
8 Ian Seguin	.20	.50
9 Michel Dube	.20	.50
10 Francois Caron	.20	.50
11 Nathan Saunders	.20	.50
12 Brad Larter	.20	.50
13 Teddy Kyres	.20	.50
14 Kevin Glode	.20	.50
15 David Philpott	.20	.50
16 Ryan Salvis	.20	.50
17 Collin Circelli	.20	.50
18 Corey Crawford	.30	.75
19 Matt Davis	.30	.75
20 Patrick Thoreson	.80	2.00
21 Maxime Desruisseaux	.20	.50
22 Julien Lavoie	.20	.50
23 Scott English	.20	.50
24 Luke Pelham	.20	.50
25 Steve Bernier	1.00	2.50
NNO Title Card/CL	.04	.10

2002-03 Moncton Wildcats

COMPLETE SET (26)	8.00	15.00
1 Nathan Saunders	.20	.50
2 Matt Davis	.20	.50
3 Francois Caron	.20	.50
4 Evgeni Artukhin	.30	.75
5 Evgeni Artukhin WJC	.30	.75
6 Corey Crawford	.40	1.00
7 Bruce Graham	.30	.75
8 James Sanford	.30	.75
9 Patrick Sampson	.20	.50
10 Mathieu Betournay	.20	.50
11 Ryan Salvis	.20	.50
12 Kevin Glode	.20	.50
13 Luke Pelham	.20	.50
14 Maxime Desruisseaux	.20	.50
15 Kevin Hamel	.20	.50
16 Josh Hepditch	.20	.50
17 Jonathan Favreau	.20	.50
18 Kyle Murnaghan	.20	.50
19 Daniel Hudgin	.20	.50
20 Michel Dube	.20	.50
21 Sebastien Strozynski	.20	.50
22 Yannick Searles	.20	.50
23 Carl McLean	.20	.50
24 Karl Gagne	.20	.50
25 Steve Bernier	1.25	3.00
26 Team Picture	.10	.25

2003-04 Moncton Wildcats

COMPLETE SET (25)	12.00
1 James Sanford	.40
2 Yan Ouimet	.40
3 Bruce Graham	1.00
4 Mathieu Betournay	.40
5 Karl Gagne	.40
6 Christian Gaudet	.40
7 Martin Karsums	1.00
8 Francois Caron	.40
9 Kevin Hamel	.40
10 Nathan Saunders	.40
11 Kevin Glode	.40
12 Thierry Douville	.40
13 Cody Doucette	.40
14 Joshua Hepditch	.40
15 Mathieu Wathier	.40
16 Ryan Salvis	.40
17 Bobby Mazerolle	.40
18 Konstantin Zakharov	.40
19 Corey Crawford	.75
20 Ryan Papaioannou	.75
21 Luke Pelham	.40
22 Maxime Desruisseaux	.40
23 Steve Bernier	1.00
NNO James Sanford TL	.40
NNO Steve Bernier TL	1.00

2004-05 Moncton Wildcats

A total of 1,050 team sets were produced.

COMPLETE SET (25)	12.00
1 Wesley Welcher	.50
2 Oskars Bartulis	.50
3 Corey Crawford	1.00
4 Charles Bergeron	.50
5 Kevin Glode	.50
6 Brad Marchand	.50
7 Adam Blanchette	.50
8 Charles Tanguay	.50
9 Luke Pelham	.50
10 Christian Gaudet	.50
11 Jean-Sebastien Adam	.50
12 Stephane Goulet	.50
13 Jason Demers	.50
14 Ryan Salvis	.50
15 Adam Pineault	.50
16 Yan Ouimet	.50
17 Jean-Christophe Blanchard	1.00
18 Stanson Donovan	.50
19 Martins Karsums	1.00
20 Bruce Graham	.50
21 Steve Bernier	1.00
22 Jerome Samson	.50
23 Josh Hepditch	.50
24 Guillaume Veilleux	.50
25 Nathan Saunders	.50

2005-06 Moncton Wildcats

COMPLETE SET (30)	15.00
1 Adam Pineault	1.00
2 Stephane Goulet	.75
3 Jean Christophe Blanchard	.75
4 Matt Eagles	.75
5 Brad Marchand	.75
6 Christian Gaudet	.75
7 Guillaume Blouin	.75
8 Oskars Bartulis	.75
9 Keith Yandle	.75
10 Josh Hepditch	.75
11 Maxime Belanger	.75
12 Tim Spencer	.75
13 Martins Karsums	1.50
14 Jerome Samson	.75
15 Jean Sebastien Adam	.75
16 Andrew MacDonald	.75
17 Philippe Dupuis	.75
18 Nathan Welton	.75
19 Nick Emanuele	.75
20 Jason Demers	.75
21 Ian-Mathieu Girard	.75
22 Jean-Philip Chabot	.75
23 Matt Marquardt	.75
24 Chris Morehouse	.75
25 Brad Ouskun	.75
26 Brad Smith	.75
27 Jhase Sniderman	.75
28 Josh Tordjman	1.50
29 Luc Bourdon	1.50
30 David MacDonald	.75

2006-07 Moncton Wildcats

COMPLETE SET (24)	8.00	15.00
1 Nicola Riopel	.40	1.00
2 Andrew Macdonald	.25	.60
3 Roopertti Martikainen	.25	.60
4 Matthew Brenton	.25	.60
5 Randy Cameron	.25	.60
6 Jason Lepage	.25	.60
7 Jerome Samson	.25	.60
8 Pierre-Marc Lessard	.25	.60
9 Matt Marquardt	.25	.60
10 Matt Eagles	.25	.60
11 Nathan Welton	.25	.60
12 Murdock Maclellan	.25	.60
13 Jhase Sniderman	.40	1.00
14 Nick Emanuele	.25	.60
15 Alexi Pianosi	.25	.60
16 Brad Smith	.25	.60
17 Marc-Andre Labelle	.25	.60
18 Chris Morehouse	.25	.60
19 Brad Ouskun	.25	.60
20 Patrick Campbell	.25	.60
21 Igor Voroshilov	.25	.60
22 Matt Boyle	.25	.60
23 Kelan Herr	.25	.60
24 Christian Gaudet	.25	.60

1997-98 Moose Jaw Warriors

COMPLETE SET (19)		12.00
1 Jay Ewasiuk	.40	1.00
2 Jordon Flodell	.30	.75
3 Justin Hansen	.30	.75
4 Cory Hintz	.30	.75
5 Chad Hinz	.30	.75
6 Brent Hobday	.30	.75
7 Marek Ivan	.30	.75
8 Trevor Johnson	.30	.75
9 Tim McEachen	.30	.75
10 Donavan Nunweiler	.40	1.00
11 Dustin Paul	.30	.75
12 Nathan Read	.30	.75
13 Scott Schoneck	.30	.75
14 Shawn Skolney	.30	.75
15 Dave Taylor	.30	.75
16 Chris Twerdun	.30	.75
17 Dreu Volk	.30	.75
18 Jason Weitzel	.30	.75
19 Dayle Wilcox	.30	.75

2001-02 Moose Jaw Warriors

This set features the Warriors of the WHL. The set was produced by CTM Ste-Foy and was sold at Warriors home games. The production run for the set was 1,000 copies.

COMPLETE SET (22)	4.80	12.00
1 Ryan Jorde	.20	.50
2 Jarad Bourassa	.20	.50
3 Deryk Engelland	.20	.50
4 Nathan Paetsch	.40	1.00
5 Bobby-Chad Mitchell	.20	.50
6 Kyle Brodziak	.20	.50
7 Derek Krestanovich	.40	1.00
8 Steve Crampton	.20	.50
9 Sean O'Connor	.20	.50
10 Brian Sutherby	.60	1.50
11 Tim Plett	.20	.50
12 Shawn Limpright	.20	.50
13 Lee Zalasky	.20	.50
14 Harlan Anderson	.20	.50
15 Tyler Johnson	.20	.50
16 David Bararuk	.20	.50
17 Mark Kitts	.20	.50
18 Craig Olynick	.30	.75
19 Lane Manson	.20	.50
20 Shaun Landolt	.20	.50
21 Kyle Kettles	.20	.50
22 Blake Grenier	.20	.50

2002-03 Moose Jaw Warriors

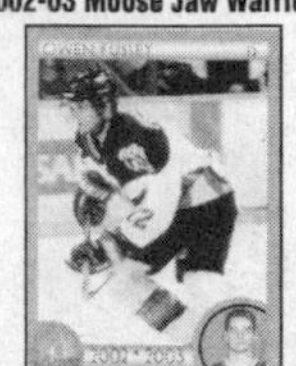

COMPLETE SET (22)	12.00
1 John Boychuk	1.00
2 Jarad Bourassa	.50
3 Deryk Engelland	.50
4 Nathan Paetsch	1.00
5 Michael Busto	.50
6 Kyle Brodziak	.50
7 Tomas Fleischmann	2.00
8 Derek Krestanovich	.75
9 Owen Fussey	.75
10 Petr Jelinek	.50
11 Jon Kress	.50
12 Harlan Anderson	.50
13 Tyler Johnson	.50
14 David Bararuk	.50
15 Troy Brouwer	.50
16 Ashton Rome	.50
17 Lane Manson	.50
18 Dustin Boyd	.50
19 Cam Lilley	.50
20 Blake Grenier	.75
21 Steve Belanger	.75
22 Checklist/Logo	.01

2004-05 Moose Jaw Warriors

COMPLETE SET (24)	20.00
1 Greg Park	.75
2 Jordan Henry	.75
3 Cole Simpson	.75
4 Cole Butterfield	.75
5 Dan Ehrman	.75
6 Dylan Chapman	.75
7 Jacob Dietrich	.75
8 Justin Scott	.75
9 Kenndal McArdle	3.00
10 Blair Jones	.75
11 Garrett Robinson	.75
12 Dustin Boyd	.75
13 Andre Hermanson	.75
14 Brennen Wray	.75
15 Masi Marjamaki	1.00
16 Stuart Kerr	.75
17 Riley Holzapfel	.75
18 Troy Brouwer	.75
19 Steven Gillen	.75
20 Ian McKenzie	.75
21 Carter Smith	.75
22 Joey Perricone	.75
23 Josh Lepp	1.00
24 Checklist	.10

2005-06 Moose Jaw Warriors

COMPLETE SET (25)	15.00
1 Jason Bast	.60
2 Dustin Boyd	1.50
3 Troy Brouwer	.60
4 Dylan Chapman	.00
5 Travis Ehrhardt	.60
6 Kyle Fecho	.60
7 Steven Gillen	.60
8 Martin Grundling	.60
9 Matthew Hansen	.60
10 Andre Herman	.60
11 Riley Holzapfel	.60
12 Blair Jones	.60
13 Andrew Leslie	.50
14 Kendall McArdle	1.50
15 Ian McKenzie	.60
16 Joey Perricone	1.00
17 Garrett Robinson	.60
18 Cole Simpson	.60
19 Carter Smith	.60
20 Bjorn Svensson	.60
21 Brennen Wray	.60
22 Jesse Zetariuk	.60
23 Old Dutch Foods SPONSOR	.01
24 Boston Pizza SPONSOR	.01
25 Air Waves SPONSOR	.01

2006-07 Moose Jaw Warriors

COMPLETE SET (24)	10.00	18.00
1 Jock Sutter	.30	.75
2 Travis Hamonic	.30	.75
3 Ryan Stanton	.30	.75
4 Chad Suer	.30	.75
5 Travis Ehrhardt	.30	.75
6 Martin Grundling	.30	.75
7 Keith Voytechek	.30	.75
8 Neal Prokop	.30	.75
9 Brady Calla	.30	.75
10 Matt Isbister	.30	.75
11 Garrett Robinson	.30	.75
12 Brad Riege	.30	.75
13 Ryley Grantham	.30	.75
14 Jordan Knackstedt	.30	.75
15 Jason Bast	.30	.75
16 Riley Holzapfel	.40	1.00
17 Michael Hengen	.30	.75
18 Steven Gillen	.30	.75
19 Jason Reese	.30	.75
20 Cody Thoring	.30	.75
21 Jason Grecica	.30	.75
22 Joey Perricone	.40	1.00
23 Kurt Jory	.40	1.00
24 Giffen Nyren	.30	.75

1990-91 Montreal-Bourassa AAA

The 25 cards in this oversized set measure approximately 3" by 3 3/4" and feature players from the AAA Midget squad based in Bourassa, a suburb of Montreal. The cards feature a posed color photo on the front, with an anti-drug inscription written in French along the bottom. The crudely designed backs have biographical data, along with the logo celebrating the 15th anniversary of the club.

COMPLETE SET (25)	2.00	5.00
1 Team Card	.02	.10
2 Police Card	.02	.10
3 Coach Card	.02	.10
4 Coach Card	.02	.10
5 Coach Card	.02	.10
6 Peter Arvanitis	.08	.25
7 Luc Bilodeau	.08	.25
8 Luc Corriveau	.08	.25
9 David Desnoyers	.08	.25
10 Alexandre Duchesne	.08	.25
11 Dominic Gagne	.08	.25
12 Benoit Goyer	.08	.25
13 Serge Kiopini	.08	.25
14 Ted Laviolette	.08	.25
15 Ian McIntyre	.08	.25
16 Nathan Morin	.08	.25
17 Valentino Passarelli	.08	.25
18 Jean-Sebastien Perras	.08	.25
19 Sylvain Pinel	.08	.25
20 Sebastien Plouffe	.15	.40
21 Simon Roy	.08	.25
22 Erasmo Saltarelli	.15	.40
23 Alain Savage	.08	.25
24 Christian Sbrocca	.08	.25
25 Patrick Traverse	.30	.75

1979-80 Montreal Juniors

This oversized set (approximately 4X6) features black and white images. Little is known about the set outside of the checklist below, provided by collector Steve Coran. As we have no confirmed sales info, the cards are listed below without pricing.

COMPLETE SET (29)
1 Jeff Barratt
2 Andre Begin
3 Dennis Champagne
4 Denis Cyr
5 Ghyslain Cyr
6 Roland Diotte
7 Pierre Dubois
8 Sylvain Gagne
9 Guy Jacob
10 Mike Krushelnyski
11 Ron Lapointe
12 Richard Lavallee
13 Daniel Laxton
14 Francois Laxton
15 Francois Lecompte
16 Eikke Leime
17 Pierre Martin
18 Bill Mulcahey
19 Gates Orlando
20 Patrice Pare
21 Mario Patry
22 Fabian Pavlin
23 Roger Poitras
24 Constant Prindolo
25 Denis Savard
26 Eric Taylor
27 Denis Tremblay
28 J.J. Vezina
29 Taras Zytynsky

1955-56 Montreal Royals

This set features the Royals, Montreal's top farm team. Cards measure 5 1/4" x 4 1/2" and were issued by Hygrade Franks. Card fronts are black and white and card backs feature an ad for Hygrade Franks that encourages purchasers to collect all six cards.

COMPLETE SET (6)	50.00	350.00
1 Walter Cline	6.00	50.00
2 Andre Corriveau	6.00	50.00
3 Jacques Deslauriers	6.00	50.00

4 Cec Hoekstra 10.00 60.00
5 Gerry McNeil 20.00 100.00
6 Guy Rousseau 10.00 60.00

1993-94 Muskegon Fury

This 20-card set of the Muskegon Fury of the Colonial Hockey League was produced by Rising Star Sports Promotions. The cards feature action photography on the front inside a teal border, along with league logo and player name, number and position. the backs have complete stats but are unnumbered.

COMPLETE SET (20) 10.00 25.00
1 Header Card .08 .25
2 Steve Ludzik CO .50 1.25
3 Bob Jones .50 1.25
4 Darrel Newman .50 1.25
5 Brett Seguin .50 1.25
6 Dan Woodley .75 2.00
7 Jodi Murphy .50 1.25
8 Mark Karpen .50 1.25
9 Robert Melanson .50 1.25
10 Paul Kelly .50 1.25
11 Joey Simon .50 1.25
12 Scott Feasby .50 1.25
13 Scott Campbell .50 1.25
14 Joe Hawley .50 1.25
15 Justin Morrison .50 1.25
16 Roch Belley 1.25 3.00
17 Todd Charlesworth .75 2.00
18 Kevin Barrett .50 1.25
19 Mark Turner .50 1.25
20 Steve Herniman .50 1.25

1994-95 Muskegon Fury

This 18-card set of the Muskegon Fury of the CHL was produced by Rising Star Sports Promotions and sponsored by McDonald's. The cards feature and action photo inside a teal border. The logos of Rising Star and the CHL are prominently displayed alongside the player's name and position. Card backs contain complete career and personal stats, but are unnumbered. These cards are very similar in design to other Muskegon sets; check the stats on the back to determine the year of your set.

COMPLETE SET (18) 3.00 8.00
1 Header Card .02 .10
2 Rich Parent .40 1.00
3 Grant Block .20 .50
4 Justin Morrison .20 .50
5 Scott Feasby .20 .50
6 Scott Campbell .20 .50
7 Mark Vilneff .20 .50
8 Brett Seguin .20 .50
9 Todd Charlesworth .20 .50
10 Marc Saumier .20 .50
11 Norm Krumpschmid .20 .50
12 Darryl Gilmour .30 .75
13 Paul Kelly .20 .50
14 Steve Walker .20 .50
15 Wes McCauley .20 .50
16 Steve Herniman .20 .50
17 Andy Bezeau .20 .50
18 Jamie Black .20 .50

1995-96 Muskegon Fury

This 20-card set produced by Rising Star Promotions and sponsored by McDonald's features the Muskegon Fury of the Colonial Hockey League. The card fronts have a color action photo within a teal border. The league logo is in the lower left, with player name, number and position along the bottom. The back contains career information for each player. The cards are unnumbered. The design for this set is eerily similar to the previous two years; collectors should check the stats on the back to ascertain which year their set is from.

COMPLETE SET (20) 4.00 10.00
1 Team Photo .20 .50
2 Mark Vilneff .20 .50
3 Kyle Haviland .20 .50
4 Brett Seguin .20 .50
5 Rick Girhiny .20 .50
6 Cory Johnson .20 .50
7 Paul Kelly .20 .50
8 Mark Turner .20 .50
9 Scott Feasby .20 .50
10 Stephen Webb .30 .75
11 Bobby Wallwork .20 .50
12 Richard Fatrola .20 .50
13 Steve Walker .20 .50
14 Robert Melanson .20 .50
15 Rich Parent .60 1.50
16 Jamie Hearn .20 .50
17 Brian Greer .20 .50
18 Steve Herniman .20 .50
19 Terry Ficorelli ANN .02 .10
20 McDonald's Sponsor .02 .10

1998-99 Muskegon Fury

This set features the Fury of the UHL. The cards were issued as promotional giveaways over the course of several home games, making the set difficult to complete.

COMPLETE SET (30) 12.00 30.00
1 Terry Ficorelli ANN .02 .10
2 Jason Pain .60 1.50
3 Furious Fred MAS .02 .10
4 Lubos Krajcovic .60 1.50
5 Chris Maillet .60 1.50
6 Robin Bouchard .60 1.50
7 Randy Cantu TR .02 .10
8 Francis Nault .60 1.50
9 Checklist .02 .10
10 Richard Kromm CO .02 .10
11 Joe Dimaline .60 1.50
12 Richard Kromm CO .02 .10
13 David Bouskill .60 1.50
14 Cory Banika .75 2.00
15 Rob Melanson .60 1.50
16 John Vary .80 1.50
17 Gilman Tire AD .01
18 Steve Webb .75 2.00
18 Andy Bezeau .75 2.00
19 Paul Willett .60 1.50
20 Mike Feasby .60 1.50
21 Sergei Kharin .75 2.00
22 Denis Khlopotnov .75 2.00
23 David Beauregard .75 2.00
24 Dmitri Emilyantsev .60 1.50
25 Mark Vilneff .60 1.50
26 Scott Feasby .60 1.50
27 Andrei Petrunin .75 2.00
28 Vadim Podrezov .60 1.50
29 Grant Richison .60 1.50
30 Tony Lisman GM .02 .10

1999-00 Muskegon Fury

This set features the Fury of the UHL. The set was produced by Roox and issued as a promotional giveaway over the course of several games throughout the season.

COMPLETE SET (36) 8.00 20.00
1 Sergei Kharin .30 .75
2 Vadim Podrezov .30 .75
3 Andrei Petrunin .40 1.00
4 Scott Feasby .30 .75
5 Joe Dimaline .40 1.00
6 Rob Melanson .30 .75
7 Robin Bouchard .30 .75
8 Muskegon Fury .30 .75
9 Quinn Hancock .30 .75
10 Francis Nault .30 .75
11 Alex Vasilevski .30 .75
12 Mark Vilneff .30 .75
13 Andrew Luciuk .30 .75
14 Bob Janosz .40 1.00
15 Chris Maillet .30 .75
16 Tomas Kapusta .30 .75
17 Mike McCourt .30 .75
18 Brian Tucker .30 .75
19 Aaron Porter .30 .75
20 Jason Rose .30 .75
21 Alain LaPlante .30 .75
22 Mike Feasby .08 .25
23 Terry Ficorelli .08 .25
24 Furious Fred MAS .08 .25
25 Richard Kromm CO .08 .25
26 Phil Kopinski TR .08 .25
27 Mikhail Nemirovsky .30 .75
28 Don McSween .30 .75
29 Dalen Hrooshkin .30 .75
30 Lucas Nehrling .30 .75
31 1999-00 Fury AS .30 .75
32 Tony Lisman GM .08 .25
33 Checklist .08 .25
34 Rob Hutson .30 .75
35 Joel Gardner .30 .75
36 Muskegon Fury .20 .50

2000-01 Muskegon Fury

This set features the Fury of the UHL. The cards were handed out as promotional giveaways over the course of several games, and were sponsored by a local tire store.

COMPLETE SET (30) 15.00 30.00
1 Robin Bouchard .40 1.00
2 Philippe Roy .60 1.50
3 Alain O'Driscoll .40 1.00
4 Todd Robinson .60 1.50
5 J.F. Tremblay .40 1.00
6 Ed Kowalski .40 1.00
7 Dean Mayrand .40 1.00
8 Glenn Crawford .60 1.50
9 Sergei Kharin .40 1.00
10 Andrew Luciuk .40 1.00
11 Sylvain Daigle .60 1.50
12 Maxim Linnik .60 1.50
13 Andrew Merrick .40 1.00
14 Mark Vilneff .40 1.00
15 Rob Melanson .40 1.00
16 Scott Feasby .60 1.50
17 Quinn Hancock .40 1.00
18 Francis Nault .40 1.00
19 Krikor Arman .40 1.00
20 Richard Kromm CO .40 1.00
21 Joe Dimaline .40 1.00
22 Justin Martin .40 1.00
23 Alexei Krovopuskov .40 1.00
24 Rob Hutson .40 1.00
25 Furious Fred MAS .04 .10
26 Scott Hlady .40 1.00
27 Phil Kopinski TR .04 .10
28 Rick Emmett .40 1.00
29 Scott Myers .40 1.00
30 Terry Ficorelli ANN .04 .10

2002-03 Muskegon Fury

COMPLETE SET (27) 10.00
1 Brant Blackned .50
2 Robin Bouchard .50
3 Josh Burk .50
4 Mike Busniuk HCO .10
5 Sylvain Daigle .75
6 Rustyn Dolyny .50
7 Terry Ficorelli ANN .10
8 John Glavota .50
9 Shane Glover .50
10 Scott Hollis .50
11 Rob Kennedy EQM .10
12 Jeff Kozakowski .50
13 Tony Lisman OWNER .10
14 Andrew Luciuk .50
15 Jeff Lukasak .50
16 Mike Feasby ACO .10
17 Steven MacIntyre .50
18 Philippe Plante .50
19 Chris Porowski TR .10
20 Billy Pugliese .50
21 Gary Ricciardi .50
22 Todd Robinson .50
23 Scott Feasby .50
24 Brandon Snee .50
25 Travis Thiessen .50
26 Furious Fred Mascot .10
NNO Checklist .01

2003-04 Muskegon Fury

COMPLETE SET (23) 10.00
1 David Ambler .50
2 Brant Blackned .50
3 Robin Bouchard .50
4 Sylvain Daigle .75
5 Rustyn Dolyny .50
6 Scott Feasby .50
7 B.J. Gaustad .50
8 Brian Haaland .75
9 Scott Hollis .50
10 Jason Jaworski .50
11 Trevor Johnson .50
12 Jason Lawmaster .75
13 Jeff Nelson .50
14 Dave Noel-Bernier .50
15 Tyler Palmer .50
16 Michal Pinc .50
17 Billy Pugliese .50
18 Todd Robinson .50
19 Petr Suchanek .50
20 Garry Toor .50
21 Todd Nelson CO .10
22 Chris Davidson-Adams EQM .10
23 Brad Chavis TR .10

2005-06 Muskegon Fury

COMPLETE SET (24) 15.00
1 Brett Angel 1.00
2 Robin Bouchard .75
3 Bill Collins .75
4 Rustyn Dolyny .75
5 Ken Fels 1.00
6 Nigel Hawryliw .75
7 Jon Insana .75
8 Trevor Johnson .75
9 Ryan Keller .75
10 Kevin LaPointe 1.00
11 Jason Lawmaster 1.00
12 Jeff Nelson .75
13 Steve O'Rourke .75
14 Jeff Petruic .75
15 Joe Pomaranski .75
16 Clayton Pool 1.00
17 Todd Robinson .75
18 David Van Drunen .75
19 Clay Wilson .75
20 David Wrigley .75
21 Bill Zalba .75
22 Todd Nelson CO .10
23 Furious Fred MASCOT .01
24 Terry Ficorelli VPC .01

1984-85 Nanaimo Clippers

This set features the Clippers of the BCJHL. The cards are oversized (3 X 5) and feature posed shots on the ice. The set was sponsored by the RCMP and local businesses. The cards are unnumbered and so are listed in alphabetical order. Checklist provided by the good folks at Ab. D Cards.

COMPLETE SET (22) 8.00 20.00
1 Team Picture .20 .50
2 Jay Barner .40 1.00
3 Dale Brisco .40 1.00
4 Chris Calverley .40 1.00
5 Jamie Cayford .40 1.00
6 Carey Coroy .40 1.00
7 Brian Deleeuw .40 1.00
8 Frank Furlan .60 1.50
9 Bill Hardy .40 1.00
10 Rick Hunt .40 1.00
11 Rob Jack .60 1.50
12 Al Johnson .40 1.00
13 Gery Keremidschieff .40 1.00
14 Wade Michalenko .40 1.00
15 Mitch Poulin .40 1.00
16 Kevin Rabbitt .40 1.00
17 Rob Schmidt .40 1.00
18 Ron Sparks .40 1.00
19 Joe Stanley .40 1.00
20 Rod Summers .40 1.00
21 Kevin Thorlakson .40 1.00
22 Darren Wourns .60 1.50

1991-92 Nanaimo Clippers

This oversized set features the Nanaimo Clippers of the British Columbia JHL. The cards measure approximately 3 1/2 x 5 and are full color. They were produced by DEC.

COMPLETE SET (22) 3.00 8.00
1 Glenn Calder .15 .40
2 Wade Dayley .15 .40
3 Jason Disiewich .15 .40
4 Andy Faulkner .15 .40
5 Darren Holme .15 .40
6 Casey Hungle .15 .40
7 Jim Ingram .15 .40
8 Chris Jones .15 .40
9 Ryan Keller .15 .40
10 Jade Kersey .15 .40
11 Scott Kowalski .15 .40
12 Sean Krause .15 .40
13 Jim Lessard .15 .40
14 Ryan Loxam .15 .40
15 Mickey McGuire .15 .40
16 Dan Murphy .15 .40
17 Jason Northand .15 .40
18 Trevor Post .15 .40
19 Brian Schiebel .15 .40
20 Sjon Wynia .15 .40
21 Shawn York .15 .40
22 Geordie Young .15 .40

1989-90 Nashville Knights

This 23-card standard-size set was sponsored by Lee's Famous Recipe Country Chicken (a restaurant chain). The fronts feature color photos with the players in a variety of action and still poses. White borders enhance the front, and the player's name appears in the border below the picture. The cards are unnumbered and checklisted below in alphabetical order.

COMPLETE SET (23) 3.00 8.00
1 Pat Bingham .15 .40
2 Andre Brassard .15 .40
3 Mike Bukta .15 .40
4 Chris Cambio .15 .40
5 Chick-E-Lee (Mascot) .08 .25
6 Glen Engevik .15 .40
7 Matt Gallagher .08 .25
Dir. Player Development
Scott Gleer ABM
8 Archie Henderson CO .20 .50
9 Billy Huard .30 .75
10 Craig Jenkins ANN .08 .25
Dave Cavaliere TR
11 Todd Jenkins .15 .40
12 Brock Kelly .15 .40
13 Paul Krayer .15 .40
14 Garth Lamb .15 .40
15 Rob Levasseur .15 .40
16 Dan O'Brien .15 .40
17 Bob Polk OWN .08 .25
Ron Fuller OWN
18 John Reid (In action) .15 .40
19 John Reid (Portrait) .15 .40
20 Jeff Salzbrunn .15 .40
21 Mike Schwalb .20 .50
22 Ron Servatius .15 .40
23 Jason Simon .20 .50

1991-92 Nashville Knights

This 24-card set of the Nashville Knights of the East Coast Hockey League was issued as a game premium. The set is unnumbered; the cards are listed by order of the player's jersey number, which is listed on the front of the card. It was sponsored by TV station WZTV, whose logo is garishly emblazoned across the card fronts.

COMPLETE SET (25) 2.80 50.00
1 Header Card .02 .10
2 San Jose Sharks .40 1.00
3 Chris Harvey 1.25 3.00
4 Chris Grassie .75 2.00
5 Daryll Mitchell .75 2.00
6 Ron Majic .75 2.00
7 Daniel Rolfe .75 2.00
8 Mark Hilton .75 2.00
9 Angelo Russo .75 2.00
10 Jeff Jablonski .75 2.00
11 Rob Dumas .75 2.00
12 Chuck Wiegand .75 2.00
13 Steve Chelios .75 2.00
14 Kevin Sullivan .75 2.00
15 Mike Hiltner .75 2.00
16 Brock Kelly 1.25 3.00
17 Paul Cohen 1.25 3.00
18 Scott Taylor .75 2.00
19 Mike DeCarle .75 2.00
20 Jim Ritchie .75 2.00
21 Michael Seaton .75 2.00
22 Frank Anzalone CO .08 .25
23 Dave Cavaliere TR .02 .10
24 Mike Eruzione OWNER 2.00 5.00
25 Sean Tomalty .75 2.00

1992-93 Nashville Knights

This 25-card set of the Nashville Knights of the ECHL was sponsored by WZTV and issued as a game premium. The cards feature posed photos on the front and cursory stats on the back, along with card number.

COMPLETE SET (25) 3.00 8.00
1 Header Card .08 .25
2 Nick Fotiu CO .20 .50
3 George Kozak ACO .02 .10
4 Tom Cole .15 .40
5 Scott Matusovich .15 .40
6 Chris Grassie .15 .40
7 Bob Creamer .15 .40
8 Ray DeSouza .20 .50
9 Stanislav Tkach .15 .40
10 Don Parsons .15 .40
11 Steve Sullivan .15 .40
12 Brian Ferreira .15 .40
13 Rob Dumas .15 .40
14 Michael Seaton .15 .40
15 Mike DeCarle .15 .40
16 Trevor Jobe .15 .40
17 Brian Horan .15 .40
18 Andrey Dylevsky .15 .40
19 Rob Pallante .15 .40
20 Bryan Krygier .15 .40
21 Troy Mick .20 .50
22 Darcy Kaminski .15 .40
23 Olie Sundstrom .20 .50
24 Dale King TR .02 .10
25 Kevin Krueger MED .02 .10

1995-96 Neepewa Natives

This blank backed set features color photos of each player along with their name and the team logo.

COMPLETE SET (24) 10.00
1 Ryan Anderson .20 .50
2 Ryan Brunel .20 .50
3 Jeff Hudson .20 .50
4 Darren Kirk .20 .50
5 Dwayne Ripley .20 .50
6 Trevor Angus .20 .50
7 Mike Baranyk .20 .50
8 Duane Hoey .20 .50
9 Spencer Platt .20 .50
10 Jeremy Robinson .20 .50
11 Ryan Ogilvie .20 .50
12 Angelo Kokanas .20 .50
13 Craig Anderson .20 .50
14 Dale Isfeld .20 .50
15 Derek Henkelman .20 .50
16 Darcy Pengelly .20 .50
17 Kori Pearson .20 .50
18 Brett Hagberg .20 .50
19 Keith Carson .20 .50
20 Todd Barth .20 .50
21 Craig Martin .20 .50
22 Jason Glover .20 .50
23 Danny Senff .20 .50
24 Billy Joe Stasiuk HCO .08 .25

1996-97 New Hampshire Wildcats

This set was handed out in conjunction with the local DARE program. The cards below are the only ones known to exist, but the numbering suggests that others were released at some point.

COMPLETE SET (10) 9.78 25.00
21 Derek Bekar .75 2.00
22 Eric Boguniecki 2.00 5.00
23 Christian Bragnalo .75 2.00
24 Eric Fitzgerald .75 2.00
25 Jason Krog 1.50 4.00
26 Mark Mowers 1.50 4.00
27 Eric Nickulas 1.50 4.00
28 Tim Murray .75 2.00
29 Tom Nolan .75 2.00
30 Steve O'Brien .75 2.00

1997-98 New Hampshire Wildcats

This set features the Wildcats of the NCAA. The cards were produced by the team and handed out to kids by members of the local police force. The odd numbering suggests other cards might exist in this series. Information on additional singles can be forwarded to hockeymag@beckett.com.

COMPLETE SET (12)
13 Steve O'Brien .40 1.00
14 Dan Enders .40 1.00
15 Jason Krog 1.25 3.00
16 Dylan Dellezay .40 1.00
17 Sean Matile .60 1.50
18 Chad Onufrechuk .40 1.00
19 Tim Walsh .40 1.00
20 Tom Nolan .40 1.00
21 Derek Bekar .60 1.50
22 Erik Johnson .40 1.00
23 Ryan Harris .40 1.00
24 Christian Bragnalo .40 1.00

1998-99 New Hampshire Wildcats

This set features the Wildcats of the NCAA. The singles were handed out to kids by local police officers. The set is noteworthy for including members of the school's men's and women's teams.

COMPLETE SET (18) 10.00 25.00
1 John Sadowski .40 1.00
2 Chad Onufrechuk .40 1.00
3 Dan Enders .40 1.00
4 Jason Krog 1.25 3.00
5 Sean Matile .60 1.50
6 Michelle Thornton .75 2.00
7 Kim Knox .75 2.00
8 Tina Carrabba .75 2.00
9 Megan Hales .75 2.00
10 Allicia Roberts .75 2.00
11 Samantha Holmes .75 2.00
12 Steve O'Brien .40 1.00
13 Ryan Harris .40 1.00
14 Jay Shipulski .40 1.00
15 Tim Walsh .40 1.00
16 Jayme Filipowicz .75 2.00
17 Mike Souza .40 1.00
18 Christian Bragnalo .40 1.00

1998-99 New Haven Beast

This set features the Beast of the AHL. The cards were produced by the team and sold at its souvenir stands.

COMPLETE SET(24) 4.80 10.00
1 Craig Ferguson .15 .40
2 Ian MacNeil .15 .40
3 Marek Malik .15 .40
4 Craig MacDonald .15 .40
5 Byron Ritchie .15 .40
6 Steve Halko .15 .40
7 Shane Willis .40 1.00
8 Todd MacDonald .15 .40
9 Scott Levins .15 .40
10 Dwayne Hay .15 .40
11 Chad Cabana .15 .40
12 Tom Buckley .15 .40
13 Ryan Johnson .15 .40
14 Mike Fountain .30 .75
15 Ashlin Halfnight .15 .40
16 John Jakopin .15 .40
17 Chris Allen .15 .40
17 Peter Ratchuk .15 .40
18 Lance Ward .15 .40
18 Joey Tetarenko .40 1.00
19 Andrew Long .15 .40
19 Greg Koehler .15 .40
20 Tommy Westlund .15 .40
20 Marcus Nilsson .30 .75

1989-90 New Haven Nighthawks

This black-and-white set was issued on the 20th anniversary of the Nighthawks of the ECHL. It commemorates the best players of the team's past. The set was sponsored by Casio. It is unnumbered and is listed alphabetically by player name.

COMPLETE SET (15) 4.00 12.00
1 Ken Baumgartner .75 2.00
2 John Bednarski .20 .50
3 Tom Colley .20 .50
4 Daryl Evans .30 .75
5 Ed Johnstone .30 .75
6 Alain Langlais .20 .50
7 Mark Lofthouse .30 .75
8 Hubie McDonough .60 1.50
9 Bill Plager .75 2.00
10 Ron Scott .30 .75
11 Bobby Sheehan .40 1.00
12 Doug Soetaert .60 1.50
13 Jim Wiemer .30 .75
14 Rick Dudley CO .40 1.00
15 Parker McDonald GM/CO .30 .75

1997-98 New Mexico Scorpions

Little is known about this set beyond the confirmed checklist. It is believed that this set was sold by this WPHL team early in the season. Additional information can be forwarded to hockeymag@beckett.com.

COMPLETE SET (30) 4.80 12.00
1 Team Photo .15 .40
2 Regan Harper .15 .40
3 Eric Ricard .15 .40
4 Darren Wright .15 .40
5 Derek Crawford .15 .40
6 Sylvain Naud .30 .75
7 Mike Sanderson .15 .40
8 Brian Barnes .15 .40
9 Craig Hamelin .15 .40
10 Darcy Pengelly .15 .40
11 Todd Marcellus .15 .40
12 George Dupont .15 .40
13 Jordan Shields .15 .40
14 Francois Chaput .15 .40
15 Nick Hriczov .15 .40
16 Frederik Beaubien .30 .75
17 David Lessard .15 .40
18 Hugh Bertrand .15 .40
19 Kelly Morel .15 .40
20 Derek Shybunka .15 .40
21 Tony Martino .20 .50
22 Marc Sigel .15 .40
23 Brad Wingfield .15 .40
24 Tyler Boucher .15 .40
25 Carl Paradis .15 .40
26 Aldo Iaquinta .15 .40
27 Garry Unger CO .20 .50
28 Spencer MAS .02 .10
29 Team shot .15 .40
30 New Year's Celebration .02 .10

1997-98 New Mexico Scorpions II

This 12-card set was a late-season release, and contains multiple photos of a few of the team's key players.

COMPLETE SET (12) 2.50 6.00
1 Center Ice .08 .25
2 Eric Ricard .20 .50
3 Sylvain Naud .30 .75
4 Sylvain Naud .30 .75
5 Tony Martino .30 .75
6 Tony Martino .30 .75
7 Tyler Boucher .20 .50
8 Tyler Boucher .20 .50
9 Tyler Boucher .20 .50
10 George Dupont .20 .50
11 Aldo Iaquinta .20 .50
12 Spencer the Scorpion .08 .25

2001-02 New Mexico Scorpions

This set features the Scorpions of the WPHL. The set was produced by Choice Marketing and was issued as a promotional giveaway in March, 2002. A total of 2,000 sets were produced.

COMPLETE SET (23) 40.00 80.00
1 Sergei Radchenko .60 4.00
2 Trevor Hammer .60 4.00
3 Jay Banach .60 4.00
4 Shaun Fairweather .60 4.00
5 Mike O'Malley .60 4.00
6 Peter Ambroziak .80 5.00
7 Chris Richards .60 4.00
8 Yann Joseph .60 4.00
9 Jonathan St. Louis .60 4.00
10 Tyler Baines .60 4.00
11 Alek Stojanov .80 5.00
12 Jonathan Delisle .60 4.00
13 Scott Myers .60 4.00
14 Travis Van Tighem .60 4.00
15 Arturs Kupaks .80 4.00
16 David Comacchia .80 4.00
17 Donald Choukalos .80 5.00
18 Steve Zoryk .60 4.00
19 Gatis Tseplis .60 1.50
20 Tony Martino CO .10 .50
21 Robert Haddock ACO .10 .50
22 The Scorpion MASCOT .10 .50
NNO Header Card .04 .10

2002-03 New Mexico Scorpions

COMPLETE SET (23) 20.00
1 Peter Ambroziak 1.00
2 Tyler Baines 1.00
3 Peter Brearley 1.00
4 Luciano Caravaggio 1.50
5 Leigh Dean 1.00
6 Mario Dumoulin 1.00
7 Arturo Kupaks 1.00
8 Stephen Margeson 1.00
9 Nate Mauer 1.00
10 Scott Myers 1.50
11 Mike O'Malley 1.00
12 Shaun Peet 1.00
13 Neil Breen 1.00
14 Tobin Praznik 1.00
15 Chris Richards 1.00
16 Craig Stahl 1.00
17 Dave Bourque 1.00
18 Bill McDonald HCO .10
19 Mike Payne 1.00
21 Travis Van Tighem ACO .10
22 Stanley the Scorpion Mascot .10
NNO Checklist .01

2003-04 New Mexico Scorpions

This set was produced by Choice Marketing and sold at home games.

COMPLETE SET (22) 10.00
1 Checklist .01
2 Erik Adams .50
3 Jeff Alcombrack .50
4 Ben Gorewich .50
5 Brian Barker .50
6 Chris Richards .50
7 Clint Wensley .50
8 Danny Lorenz .75
9 Vladimir Hartinger .50
10 Jaroslav Kerestes .50
11 Kevin Edgar .50
12 Arturs Kupaks .50
13 Matt Mathias .50
14 Miguel Beaudry .75
15 Mike Oliveira .50
17 Shaun Peet .50
18 Peter Ambroziak .50
19 Craig Stahl .50
20 Walker McDonald .50
21 Bill McDonald HCO .10
22 Mascot .10

2004-05 New Mexico Scorpions

These cards were issued in strips of five as stadium giveaways at several home games.

COMPLETE SET (25) 30.00
1 Peter Ambroziak 1.00
2 Miguel Beaudry 2.00
3 Jordan Bianchin 1.00
4 Vladimir Hartinger 1.00
5 Mike Possin 1.00
6 Ladislav Kouba 1.00
7 Alexandre Piche 1.00
8 Aaron Schneekloth 1.00
9 Guy St. Vincent 1.00
10 Matt Weber 1.00
11 Erik Adams 1.00
12 Trevor Hammer 1.00
13 Andrew Katzburg 2.00
14 Konrad McKay 1.00
15 Ivan Svarny 1.00
16 Shawn Legault 2.50
17 Daryl Moor 1.00
18 Randy Murphy 1.00
19 Mike Oliveira 1.00
20 Daniel Tetrault 1.00
21 Ladislav Kouba 1.00
22 Alexandre Piche 1.00
23 Aaron Schneekloth 1.00
24 Guy St. Vincent 2.00
25 Matt Weber 1.00

2006-07 New Mexico Scorpions

COMPLETE SET (21) 20.00 35.00
1 Ray Edwards CO .10 .25
2 Randy Murphy ACO .10 .25
3 Stanley The Scorpion MASCOT .02 .10
4 Chris Robertson .60 1.50
5 Mike Falk .60 1.50
6 Scott Reid .75 2.00
7 Dave Cacciola .75 2.00
8 Andrew Smale .60 1.50
9 Ryan McLeod .60 1.50
10 Rob Guinn .60 1.50
11 Konrad Reeder .60 1.50
12 Mike Prpich .75 2.00
13 Kevin Harvey .60 1.50
14 Craig MacDonald .60 1.50
15 Jamie Herrington .60 1.50
16 Lance Herauf .60 1.50
17 Josh Garbutt .60 1.50
18 Matt Frick .60 1.50
19 Peter Kennedy .60 1.50
20 Aaron MacInnis .60 1.50
21 Vladimir Hartinger .60 1.50

1997-98 New Orleans Brass

Little is known about this set beyond the confirmed checklist. Additional information can be forwarded to hockeymag@beckett.com.

COMPLETE SET (21) 4.00 10.00
1 Jeff Lazaro .30 .75
2 Darryl LaFrance .20 .50
3 Eric Montreuil .20 .50
4 Steve Cheredaryk .30 .75
5 Brad Symes .20 .50
6 Bill McKay .20 .50
7 Martin Villeneuve .20 .50
8 Martin Woods .20 .50
9 Joe Seroski .20 .50
10 Russ Guzior .20 .50
11 Scratch Mo Mascot .02 .10
12 Kevin Pozzo .20 .50
13 Pierre Gendron .20 .50
14 Mike Minard .30 .75
15 Scott Allegrino TR .02 .10
16 Mikhail Nemirovsky .20 .50
17 Kyle Peterson .20 .50
18 Ted Sator HCO .02 .10
19 Scott King .30 .75
20 Jason Downey .20 .50
21 Eric Brule .30 .75

1990-91 Newmarket Saints

This 26-card set features the 1990-91 Newmarket Saints of the AHL (American Hockey League). Measuring approximately 2 1/2" by 3 3/4", the fronts feature on-ice color posed action shots framed by white borders. The cards are unnumbered and checklisted below in alphabetical order.

COMPLETE SET (26) 4.00 10.00
1 Frank Anzalone CO .08 .25
2 Tim Bean .15 .40
3 Brian Blad .15 .40
4 Bryan Cousineau COP .02 .10
5 Alan Hepple .15 .40
6 Donald Hillock COP .02 .10
7 Robert Horyna .15 .40
8 Kent Hulst .15 .40
9 Mike Jackson .15 .40
10 Greg Johnston .20 .50
11 Eldred King MAYOR .02 .10
12 Frank Kovacs COP .02 .10
13 Derek Langille .15 .40
14 Lanny the dog .02 .10
15 Mike Millar .15 .40
16 Mike Moes .15 .40
17 Bill Purcell ACO .02 .10
18 Bobby Reynolds .15 .40
19 Damian Rhodes .60 1.50
20 Bill Root .20 .50
21 Joe Sacco .30 .75
22 Darryl Shannon .30 .75
23 Doug Shedden .30 .75
24 Mike Stevens .20 .50
25 Darren Veitch .20 .50
26 Greg Walters .15 .40

1988-89 Niagara Falls Thunder

This 25-card set measures approximately 2 5/8" by 4 1/8" and was sponsored by the Niagara Falls Fire Department and area businesses. The cards are printed on thin card stock. The fronts have a white card face and feature color action player photos with two thin black lines forming a border.

COMPLETE SET (25) 8.00 20.00
1 Title Card .08 .25
2 Brad May .75 2.00
3 Paul Wolanski .20 .50
4 Keith Primeau 3.00 8.00
5 Mark Lawrence .20 .50
6 Mike Rosati .40 1.00
7 Dennis Vial .30 .75
8 Shawn McCosh .20 .50
9 Jason Soules .20 .50
10 Rob Fournier .20 .50
11 Scott Pearson .20 .50
12 Jamie Leach .20 .50
13 Colin Miller .20 .50
14 Bryan Fogarty .20 .50
15 Keith Osborne .20 .50
16 Stan Drulia .40 1.00
17 Paul Laus .40 1.00

18 Adrian Van Der Sloot .20 .50
19 Greg Allen .20 .50
20 Don Pancoe .20 .50
21 Alain LaForge .20 .50
22 Bill LaForge GM/CO .08 .25
23 Steve Locke .20 .50
24 Benny Rogano ACO .08 .25
25 Heavy Evason ACO .08 .25

1989-90 Niagara Falls Thunder

Sponsored by local Arby's and Pizza Pizza stores, these 25 cards measure approximately 2 5/8" by 4 1/8" and feature on their fronts white-bordered posed-on-ice color shots of the 1989-90 Niagara Falls Thunder. The player's name appears in red lettering within the white bottom margin. The cards are unnumbered and checklisted below in alphabetical order.

COMPLETE SET (25) 6.00 15.00
1 Greg Allen .20 .50
2 Roch Belley .30 .75
3 David Benn .20 .50
4 Andy Bezeau .20 .50
5 George Burnett CO .20 .50
6 Todd Coopman .20 .50
7 Randy Hall ACO .08 .25
8 John Johnson .20 .50
9 Paul Laus .40 1.00
10 Mark Lawrence .20 .50
11 Brad May .40 1.00
12 Don McConnell .20 .50
13 Brian Mueggler .20 .50
14 Don Pancoe .20 .50
15 Keith Primeau 2.00 5.00
16 Geoff Rawson .20 .50
17 Ken Ruddick .20 .50
18 Greg Suchan .20 .50
19 Trainers .08 .25
Paul Bruneau
Dennis Scott
20 Steve Udvari .30 .75
21 Jeff Walker .20 .50
22 Jason Winch .20 .50
23 Paul Wolanski .20 .50
24 Title Card .08 .25
25 Checklist Card .20 .50

1993-94 Niagara Falls Thunder

Printed by Slapshot Images Ltd., this 29-card set features the 1993-94 Niagara Falls Thunder. The cards measure standard size (2 1/2" by 3 1/2"). On a geometrical purple and green background, the fronts feature color action player photos with thin grey borders.

COMPLETE SET (29) 4.00 10.00
1 Title Card/Checklist .02 .10
2 Jimmy Hibbert .15 .40
3 Darryl Foster .15 .40
4 Gerry Skrypec .15 .40
5 Greg de Vries .30 .75
6 Tim Thompson .15 .40
7 Joel Yates .15 .40
8 Yianni Ioannou .15 .40
9 Steve Nimigon .15 .40
10 Jeff Johnstone .15 .40
11 Brandon Convery .15 .40
12 Dale Junkin .15 .40
13 Ethan Moreau .30 .75
14 Derek Grant .15 .40
15 Neil Fewster .15 .40
16 Jason Reesor .15 .40
17 Tom Moores .15 .40
18 Matthew Mayo .15 .40
19 Bogdan Savenko .15 .40
20 Corey Bricknell .15 .40
21 Derek Sylvester .15 .40
22 Anatoli Filatov .15 .40
23 Jason Bonsignore .15 .40
24 Mike Perna .15 .40
25 Manny Legace .40 1.00
26 Randy Hall CO GM .02 .10
27 Chris Johnstone CO .02 .10
28 Jason Bonsignore .20 .50
Ethan Moreau
Brandon Convery
Towering Prospects
NNO Slapshot Ad Card .01

2001-02 Norfolk Admirals

This set features the Admirals of the AHL. It is believed that this set was produced by the team and sold at home games.

COMPLETE SET (27) 4.80 12.00
1 Ajay Baines .20 .50
2 Bill Bowler .30 .75
3 Bobby Russell .14 .35
4 Casey Hankinson .30 .75
5 Chris McAlpine .14 .35
6 Craig Andersson .60 1.50
7 Dmitri Tolkunov .14 .35
8 Jean-Yves Leroux .14 .35
9 Jeff Helperl .14 .35
10 Jim Campbell .14 .35
11 Kent Huskins .14 .35
12 Matt Henderson .14 .35
13 Michael Leighton .80 2.00
14 Mike Peluso .30 .75
15 Mike Souza .14 .35
16 Nolan Baumgartner .14 .35
17 Peter White .14 .35
18 Quintin Laing .14 .35
19 Humun Ndur .14 .35
20 Shawn Thornton .14 .35
21 Steve McCarthy .20 .50
22 Ty Jones .20 .50
23 Tyler Arnason .30 .75
24 Valeri Zelepukin .14 .35
25 Vladimir Chebaturkin .14 .35
26 Trent Yawney CO .04 .10
NNO Team CL .04 .10

2002-03 Norfolk Admirals

COMPLETE SET (26) 15.00
1 Johnathan Aitken .50
2 Craig Andersson 1.00
3 Ajay Baines .50
4 Scotty Balan .50
5 Cam Bristow .50
6 Brandin Cote .50
7 Louie DeBrusk .50
8 Casey Hankinson .50
9 Jeff Helperl .50
10 Matt Henderson .50
11 Burke Henry .50
12 Kent Huskins .50
13 Quintin Laing .50
14 Mike Leighton 1.50
15 Steve McCarthy .75
16 Brett McLean .50
17 Travis Moen .75
18 Mike Peluso .50
19 Igor Radulov 2.00
20 Shawn Thornton 1.00
21 Dmitri Tolkunov .50
22 Yorick Treille .50
23 Marty Wilford .50
24 Mikhail Yakubov 1.00
25 Trent Yawney CO .10
NNO Checklist .01

2003-04 Norfolk Admirals

COMPLETE SET (24) 5.00 12.00
1 Johnathan Aitken .30 .75
2 Craig Andersson .40 1.00
3 Anton Babchuk .20 .50
4 Ajay Baines .20 .50
5 Michal Barinka .20 .50
6 Blake Bellefeuille .30 .75
7 Brandin Cote .20 .50
8 Matt Ellison .20 .50
9 Carsen Germyn .30 .75
10 Burke Henry .20 .50
11 Duncan Keith .30 .75
12 Matt Keith .20 .50
13 Lasse Kukkonen .20 .50
14 Quintin Laing .40 1.00
15 Adam Munro .40 1.00
16 Steve Passmore .40 1.00
17 Bobby Russell .20 .50
18 Shawn Thornton .20 .50
19 Yorick Treille .20 .50
20 Pavel Vorobiev .20 .50
21 Marty Wilford .20 .50
22 Mikhail Yakubov .20 .50
23 Trent Yawney CO .02 .10
24 Checklist .02 .10

2004-05 Norfolk Admirals

COMPLETE SET (26) 15.00
1 Craig Anderson 1.00
2 Anton Babchuk .50
3 Ajay Baines .50
4 Michal Barinka .50
5 Rene Bourque 1.00
6 Mike Brown .50
7 Brandin Cote .50
8 Matt Ellison .50
9 Duncan Keith .50
10 Matt Keith .50
11 Nick Kuiper .50
12 Quintin Laing .50
13 Michael Leighton 1.00
14 Travis Moen .50
15 Jason Morgan .50
16 Eric Nickulas .50
17 Igor Radulov .50
18 Shawn Thornton 1.00
19 Jim Vandermeer 1.00
20 Pavel Vorobiev .50
21 Marty Wilford .50
22 James Wisniewski .50
23 Mikhail Yakubov .50
24 Trent Yawney CO .10
25 Training Staff .10
NNO Checklist .01

2005-06 Norfolk Admirals

COMPLETE SET (30) 12.00
1 Norfolk Admirals .10
2 Steve Munn .50
3 Michal Barinka .50
4 Brian Lee .50
5 Carl Corazzini .50
6 Anton Babchuk .50
7 Martin St. Pierre .50
8 Milan Bartovic .50
9 Mark Cullen .50
10 Colin Fraser .75
11 Dustin Byfuglien 5.00
12 Jason Morgan .50
13 Nathan Barrett .50
14 James Wisniewski .50
15 Mike Brown .50
16 Matt Keith .50
17 Nick Kuiper .50
18 Eric Meloche .50
19 Quintin Laing .50
20 Corey Crawford 1.00
21 Ajay Baines .50
22 Adam Munro 1.00
23 Mikhail Yakubov .50
24 Shawn Thornton 1.00
25 Mike Haviland HC .10
26 Rick Kowalsky AC .10
27 McClung/Bender TR .10
28 Cinq-Mars/Holden EQM .10
29 Al MacIsaac GM .10
30 Pascal Bedard .50

2006-07 Norfolk Admirals

COMPLETE SET (28) 6.00 15.00
1 Patrick Lalime .30 .75
2 Corey Crawford .30 .75
3 Steve Munn .20 .50
4 David Koci .20 .50
5 Brandon Rogers .20 .50
6 Cam Barker .20 .50
7 Jordan Hendry .20 .50
8 Carl Corazzini .20 .50
9 Bruno St. Jacques .20 .50
10 Martin St. Pierre .20 .50
11 Craig MacDonald .20 .50
12 Troy Brouwer .30 .75
13 David Bolland 1.25 3.00
14 Colin Fraser .20 .50
15 Dustin Byfuglien 2.00 5.00
16 Bryan Bickell .20 .50
17 Adam Burish .20 .50
18 Jonas Nordqvist .20 .50
19 Michael Blunden .30 .75
20 Pierre Parenteau .20 .50
21 Reed Low .30 .75
22 Adam Berti .20 .50
23 Brandon Bochenski .20 .50
24 Danny Richmond .20 .50
25 Al MacIsaac GM .05 .10
26 Mike Haviland CO .10 .25
27 Ted Dent ACO .05 .10
28 Trainers .05 .10

2007-08 Norfolk Admirals

COMPLETE SET (30) 6.00 15.00
1 Jonathan Boutin .40 1.00
2 Marc Denis .40 1.00
3 Karri Ramo .40 1.00
4 Jay Leach .20 .50
5 Matt Smaby .20 .50
6 Mario Scalzo .20 .50
7 David Schneider .20 .50
8 Vladimir Mihalik .20 .50
9 Jay Rosehill .20 .50
10 Andy Rogers .20 .50
11 Justin Keller .20 .50
12 Adam Henrich .20 .50
13 Kyle Wanvig .20 .50
14 Norm Milley .20 .50
15 Chris Lawrence .20 .50
16 Junior Lessard .20 .50
17 Paul Szczechura .20 .50
18 Karl Stewart .20 .50
19 Radek Smolenak .40 1.00
20 Rob Klinkhammer .20 .50
21 Bracken Kearns .20 .50
22 Blair Jones .20 .50
23 Justin Fletcher .20 .50
24 Zbynek Hrdel .20 .50
25 Marek Kvapil .20 .50
26 Stanislav Lascek .20 .50
27 Shawn Collymore .20 .50
28 Steve Stirling HC .04 .10
29 Darren Rumble AC .04 .10
30 Tommy Alva .04 .10
Peter Henderson TR

1982-83 North Bay Centennials

This 24-card set was printed on thick card stock. The fronts feature a mix of action poses and portraits bordered in white. The backs carry biographical information and sponsor logos, Aunt May's City Bakery (Northern) Limited and CFCH-600 Radio. The cards are unnumbered and checklisted below in alphabetical order.

COMPLETE SET (24) 8.00 20.00
1 Allen Bishop .30 .75
2 John Capel .30 .75
3 Rob Degagne .30 .75
4 Phil Drouillard .30 .75
5 Jeff Eatough .30 .75
6 Tony Gilliard .30 .75
7 Paul Gillis .60 1.50
8 Pete Handley .30 .75
9 Mark Hatcher .30 .75
10 Tim Helmer .30 .75
11 Craig Kales .30 .75
12 Bob LaForest .30 .75
13 Mark LaForest .75 2.00
14 Bill Maguire .30 .75
15 Andrew McBain .60 1.50
16 Ron Meighan .30 .75
17 Rick Morocco .30 .75
18 Alain Raymond .30 .75
19 Joe Reekie .75 2.00
20 Joel Smith .40 1.00
21 Bert Templeton CO .30 .75
22 Kevin Vescio .30 .75
23 Peter Woodgate .30 .75
24 Don Young .30 .75

1983-84 North Bay Centennials

This 25-card set measures approximately 2 1/2" by 4" and is printed on thin card stock. The fronts carry color, posed action player photos with white borders. The player's name appears in a buttorscotch-colored plaque that is superimposed over the picture. The cards are unnumbered and checklisted below in alphabetical order.

COMPLETE SET (25) 8.00 20.00
1 Sponsor's Card .08 .25
2 Peter Abric .30 .75
3 Richard Benoit .30 .75
4 Scott Birnie .30 .75
5 John Capel .30 .75
6 Curtis Collin .30 .75
7 Rob Degagne .30 .75
8 Kevin Hatcher 1.25 3.00
9 Mark Hatcher .30 .75
10 Tim Helmer .30 .75
11 Jim Hunter .30 .75
12 Kevin Kerr .30 .75
13 Nick Kypreos .60 1.50
14 Mike Larouche .30 .75
15 Greg Larsen .30 .75
16 Mark Lavarre .30 .75
17 Brett MacDonald .30 .75
18 Wayne Macphee .30 .75
19 Peter McGrath .30 .75
20 Rob Nichols .30 .75
21 Ron Sanko .30 .75
22 Kevin Vescio .30 .75
23 Mike Webber .30 .75
24 Peter Woodgate .30 .75
25 Bert Templeton CO/GM .30 .75

1993-94 North Bay Centennials

Co-sponsored by MCTV and Collectors Corner and printed by Slapshot Images Ltd., this standard size 26-card set features the 1993-94 North Bay Centennials. On a geometrical yellow and black background, the fronts feature color action player photos with thin grey borders. The player's name, position and team name, as well as the producer's logo, appear on the front.

COMPLETE SET (26) 4.00 10.00
1 Brad Brown .20 .50
2 Sandy Allan .20 .50
3 Rob Lave .15 .40
4 Steve McLaren .15 .40
5 Andy Delmore .40 1.00
6 Corey Neilson .15 .40
7 Jason Campeau .15 .40
8 Jim Ensom .15 .40
9 Bill Lang .15 .40
10 Ryan Gillis .15 .40
11 Michael Burman .15 .40
12 Stefan Rivard .15 .40
13 B.J. MacPherson .15 .40
14 Lee Jinman .15 .40
15 Scott Cherrey .15 .40
16 Damien Bloye .15 .40
17 Denis Gaudet .15 .40
18 Bob Thornton .15 .40
19 John Guirestante .15 .40
20 Jeff Shevalier .15 .40
21 Scott Roche .20 .50
22 Vitali Yachmenev .30 .75
23 Bert Templeton CO .15 .40
24 Rob Kirsch ACO .02 .10
25 Brad Brown .15 .40
Vitali Yachmenev
Top Prospects
NNO Slapshot Ad Card .01

1994-95 North Bay Centennials

Sponsored by MCTV, Guardian and Wingate Lottery, and printed by Slapshot Images Ltd., this 26-card set features the 1994-95 North Bay Centennials. On a yellow and black background, the fronts feature color action player photos with thin gray borders. The player's name, position and team name, as well as the producer's logo, appear on the front.

COMPLETE SET (26) 4.00 10.00
1 Joel Gagnon .15 .40
2 Scott Roche .20 .50
3 Derek Lahnalampi .15 .40
4 Brad Brown .20 .50
5 Steve McLaren .15 .40
6 Kam White .15 .40
7 Corey Neilson .15 .40
8 Jason Campeau .15 .40
9 Stephen Carpenter .15 .40
10 Trevor Gallant .15 .40
11 Alex Matvichuk .15 .40
12 Ryan Gillis .15 .40
13 Kris Cantu .15 .40
14 Stefan Rivard .15 .40
15 Brian Whitley .15 .40
16 Dustin Virag .15 .40
17 Lee Jinman .20 .50
18 Scott Cherrey .15 .40
19 Damien Bloye .15 .40
20 Justin Robinson .15 .40
21 Kody Grigg .15 .40
22 John Guirestante .15 .40
23 Gary Roach .15 .40
24 Vitali Yachmenev .30 .75
25 Shane Parker CO/GM .02 .10
Tom Hedican ACO
NNO Ad Card .01

1992-93 North Dakota Fighting Sioux

This scarce promotional giveaway set features North Dakota of the NCAA. The cards are unnumbered and checklisted below alphabetically. Thirteen additional cards in this series (28-40) were recently confirmed by collector Dale Sprenger. Cards #28-32, including a key issue of Ed Belfour, were apparently included with the base set. The remaining eight cards feature ND alumni and a design similar to the Belfour and Casey base set cards. These final eight cards were available only with a purchase at local Subway sandwich shops. We have no pricing info on these cards.

COMPLETE SET (32) 8.00 20.00
1 Akil Adams .30 .75
2 Darren Bear .30 .75
3 Sean Beswick .30 .75
4 Brad Bombardir .40 1.00
5 Joby Bond .30 .75
6 Troy Davis .30 .75
7 Chris Gotziaman .30 .75
8 Dean Grillo .30 .75
9 Corey Howe .30 .75
10 Brett Hryniuk .30 .75
11 Greg Johnson .75 2.00
12 Chad Johnson .30 .75
13 Corey Johnson .30 .75
14 Todd Jones .30 .75
15 Scott Kirton .30 .75
16 Page Klostreich .30 .75
17 Jon Larson .30 .75
18 Jeff Lembke .30 .75
19 John McCoy .30 .75
20 Kevin McKinnon .30 .75
21 Darcy Mitani .30 .75
22 Keith Murphy .30 .75
23 Nick Naumenko .40 1.00
24 Jarrod Olson .30 .75
25 Lars Oxholm .30 .75
26 Kevin Powell .30 .75
27 Kevin Rappana .30 .75
28 Don Riendeau
29 Marty Schriner
30 Teeder Wynne
31 Ed Belfour ALUM
32 Jon Casey ALUM
33 Dave Christian ALUM
34 Tony Hrkac ALUM
35 Bob Joyce ALUM
36 Troy Murray ALUM
37 James Patrick ALUM
38 Russ Romaniuk ALUM
39 Garry Valk ALUM
40 Dixon Ward ALUM

2003-04 North Dakota Fighting Sioux

These cards were issued over the course of six home games. A five-card pack was given to the first 1,000 attendees who asked for them at each game. Thanks to collector Dale Sprenger for the info.

COMPLETE SET (30) 20.00 50.00
1 Brandon Bochenski 1.25 3.00
2 Nate Ziegelmann .40 1.00
3 James Massen .40 1.00
4 Quinn Fylling .40 1.00
5 Mike Prpich .40 1.00
6 Ryan Hale .40 1.00
7 Tyler Palmiscno .40 1.00
8 Matt Jones .75 2.00
9 Brad Berry ACO .20 .50
10 Chris Porter .40 1.00
11 Zach Parise 8.00 20.00
12 Drew Stafford 2.00 5.00
13 Colby Genoway .75 2.00
14 Lee Marvin .40 1.00
15 Team Logo .02 .10
16 Andy Schneider .40 1.00
17 Brady Murray 1.25 3.00
18 Engelstad Arena .02 .10
19 Rory McMahon .40 1.00
20 Matt Smaby 1.25 3.00
21 Jordan Parise 1.25 3.00
22 Brian Canady .40 1.00
23 Robbie Bina .40 1.00
24 Jake Brandt .40 1.00
25 Dean Blais CO .20 .50
26 Matt Greene 1.25 3.00
27 Erik Fabian .40 1.00
28 David Lundholm .40 1.00
29 Dave Hakstol .75 2.00
30 Nick Fuher .40 1.00

2004-05 North Dakota Fighting Sioux

These were issued as a stadium giveaway. They were handed out in five-card perforated strips only on Friday night games and only at certain doors. It was stated on the UND website that only the first 1,000 people would receive the cards so there is a potential of just 1,000 sets.

COMPLETE SET (30) 40.00
1 Header Card .10
2 Robbie Bina 1.00
3 Jake Brandt 2.00
4 Brian Canady 1.00
5 Erik Fabian 1.00
6 Scott Foyt 1.00
7 Nick Fuher 1.00
8 Quinn Fylling 1.00
9 Colby Genoway 1.00
10 Matt Greene 3.00
11 Matt Jones 2.00
12 Rylan Kaip 1.00
13 Philippe Lamoureux 2.00
14 Lee Marvin 1.00
15 James Massen 1.00
16 Rory McMahon 2.00
17 Brady Murray 2.00
18 Jordan Parise 3.00
19 Chris Porter 1.00
20 Mike Prpich 1.00
21 Kyle Radke 1.00
22 Andy Schneider 1.00
23 Matt Smaby 2.00
24 Rastislav Smirko 2.00
25 Drew Stafford 3.00
26 Travis Zajac 3.00
27 Brad Berry ACO .50
28 Carey Eades ACO .50
29 Dave Hakstol CO .50
30 Team Photo .50

1995-96 North Iowa Huskies

This 34-card set features color action player photos on the fronts with player information on the backs. The set contains a 1995-96 season schedule of games listed below as card number 33. The cards are unnumbered and so are checklisted below in alphabetical order.

COMPLETE SET (34) 20.00 50.00
1 Dave Boehm .75 2.00
2 Mike Cerniglia .75 2.00
3 Lionel Crump .75 2.00
4 Peter Cullen .75 2.00
5 Nate Dicasmirro .75 2.00
6 D.J. Drayna .75 2.00
7 Andy Fermoyle .75 2.00
8 Matt Fetterman .75 2.00
9 Mike Fryar 1.25 3.00
10 Shane Fukushima .75 2.00
11 Bucky Gruber .75 2.00
12 Jason Helgeson TR .02 .10
13 Mark Hicks ACO .02 .10
14 Huskies CL .02 .10
15 Furlin Husky (Mascot) .02 .10
16 Ryan James .75 2.00
17 Tom Lund .75 2.00
18 Kevin Mackey .75 2.00
19 Erik Macy .75 2.00
20 Josh Mizerek .75 2.00
21 Joe Mussey ACO .02 .10
22 Gregg Naumenko 2.00 5.00
23 Matt Noga .75 2.00
24 P.K. O'Handley CO .02 .10
25 Mark Pannitto 1.25 3.00
26 Matt Romaniski .75 2.00
27 Mike Romano .75 2.00
28 Mike Rucinski 1.25 3.00
29 R.J. Schriefer .75 2.00
30 Mike Skogland .75 2.00
31 Matt Snesrud .75 2.00
32 Team Media .02 .10
33 Season Schedule .02 .10
34 Title Card .02 .10

1992-93 Northern Michigan Wildcats

Little is known about this set beyond the confirmed checklist. Any additional information can be forwarded to hockeymag@beckett.com.

COMPLETE SET (32) 4.80 12.00
1 Brian Barker .20 .50
2 Steve Carpenter .20 .50
3 Chad Dameworth .20 .50
4 Dustin Fahl .20 .50
5 Joe Frederick .20 .50
6 Bryan Ganz .20 .50
7 Scott Green .20 .50
8 Greg Hadden .20 .50
9 Steve Hamilton .20 .50
10 Mike Harding .20 .50
11 Jason Hehr .20 .50
12 Dave Huettl .20 .50
13 Troy Johnson .20 .50
14 Karson Kaebel .20 .50
15 Kory Karlander .20 .50
16 Rob Kruhlak .20 .50
17 Garett MacDonald .20 .50
18 Bill MacGillivray .20 .50
19 Don McCusker .20 .50
20 Brent Riplinger .20 .50
21 Dan Ruoho .20 .50
22 Corwin Saurdiff .20 .50
23 Kyuin Shim .20 .50
24 Geoff Simpson .20 .50
25 Scott Smith .20 .50
26 Paul Taylor .20 .50
27 Steve Woog .20 .50
28 Rick Comley CO .02 .10
29 Pat Ford ACO .02 .10
30 Morey Gare ACO .02 .10
31 Dave Shyiak .20 .50
32 Wildcat Willy .02 .10

1993-94 Northern Michigan Wildcats

This 32-card set was issued at one home game as a promotional giveaway. Any additional information can be forwarded to hockeymag@beckett.com.

COMPLETE SET (32) 6.00 15.00
1 Brian Barker .20 .50
2 Keith Bartholomaus .20 .50
3 Steve Carpenter .20 .50
4 Darcy Dallas .20 .50
5 Chad Dameworth .20 .50
6 Bryan Ganz .20 .50
7 Justin George .20 .50
8 Scott Green .20 .50
9 Greg Hadden .20 .50
10 Steve Hamilton .20 .50
11 Patrick Hansson .20 .50
12 Mike Harding .20 .50
13 Jason Hehr .20 .50
14 Mike Hillock .20 .50
15 Trevor Janicki .20 .50
16 Karson Kaebel .20 .50
17 Kory Karlander .20 .50
18 Dieter Kochan .40 1.00
19 Roger Lewis .20 .50
20 Garett MacDonald .20 .50
21 Bill MacGillivray .20 .50
22 Don McCusker .20 .50
23 Brent Riplinger .20 .50
24 Dean Seymour .20 .50
25 Scott Smith .20 .50
26 Paul Taylor .20 .50
27 Shayne Tomlinson .20 .50
28 Jason Welch .20 .50
29 Steve Woog .20 .50
30 Pat Ford ACO .02 .10
31 Morey Gare ACO .02 .10
32 Rick Comley CO .02 .10

2004-05 Northern Michigan Wildcats

This set was given away over the course of several NMU home games.

COMPLETE SET (27) 30.00
1 Pat Bateman 1.00
2 Matt Ciancio 1.00
3 Dusty Collins 1.00
4 Andrew Contois 1.00
5 Blake Cosgrove 1.00
6 Kevin Gardner 1.00
7 Tim Hartung 1.00
8 Josh Hatinger 1.00
9 Bob Helminen 1.00
10 Clayton Lainsbury 1.00
11 Rob Lehtinen 1.00
12 Matt Maunu 1.00
13 Jamie Milam 1.00
14 John Miller 1.00
15 Patrick Murphy 1.00
16 Dan Olver 2.00
17 Nathan Oystrick 1.00
18 Mike Santorelli 1.00
19 Andrew Sarauer 1.00
20 Bobby Selden 1.00
21 Matt Siddall 1.00
22 Dirk Southern 1.00
23 Alan Swanson 1.00
24 Zach Tarkir 1.00
25 Tuomas Tarkki 2.00
26 Geoff Waugh 1.00
27 Bill Zaniboni 2.00

2001-02 Notre Dame Fighting Irish

This set features the Fighting Irish of the NCAA. Little is known about this set, its distribution or if this is a full checklist. If you have any additional information, please forward it to hockeymag@beckett.com. Thanks to Vinnie Montalbano for updating this information.

COMPLETE SET (?) 15.00 30.00
1 Jeremiah Kimento .75 2.00
2 David Inman .75 2.00
3 Jon Maruk .75 2.00
4 Sam Cornelius .75 2.00
5 Rob Globke 1.25 3.00
6 Neil Komadoski .75 2.00
7 Brett Lebda .75 2.00
8 Connor Dunlop 1.25 3.00
9 Evan Neilsen .75 2.00
10 T.J. Mathieson .75 2.00
11 Brad Wanchulak .75 2.00
12 Ryan Mundt .75 2.00
13 Paul Harris .75 2.00
14 Aaron Gill .75 2.00
15 John Wroblewski .75 2.00
16 Derek Smith .75 2.00
17 Cory McLean .75 2.00
18 Michael Chin .75 2.00

2002-03 Notre Dame Fighting Irish

COMPLETE SET (16) 12.00 20.00
1 Jake Wiegand .60 1.50
2 Connor Dunlop .75 2.00
3 Michael Chin .60 1.50
4 Tony Zasowski .60 1.50
5 John Wroblewski .60 1.50
6 Ad card .01 .01
7 Evan Nielsen .60 1.50
8 team card .02 .10
9 Ad card .01 .01
10 Kyle Dolder .60 1.50
11 Tom Galvin .60 1.50
12 Neil Komadoski .60 1.50
13 Brett Lebda 1.25 3.00
14 Rob Globke .75 2.00
15 Aaron Gill .60 1.50
16 T.J. Mathieson .75 2.00

2003-04 Notre Dame Fighting Irish

These cards were issued as a promotional giveaway. It's believed there could be more cards in this series. Please forward any information to hockeymag@beckett.com.

1 Joe Zurenko 1.00
2 Derek Smith 1.00
3 Cory McLean 1.00
4 Brad Wanchulak 1.00
5 Morgan Cey 1.50
6 T.J. Mathieson 1.00
7 Brett Lebda 1.00
8 Rob Globke 3.00
9 Neil Komadoski 1.00
10 Tom Galvin 1.00
11 Aaron Gill 1.50

2004-05 Notre Dame Fighting Irish

This set was issued as a promotional giveaway. It's possible the checklist is not complete. Please forward additional info to hockeymag@beckett.com.

COMPLETE SET (25) 25.00
1 Wes O'Neill 2.00
2 David Brown 2.00
3 Bryan D'Arcy 1.00
4 Mark Van Guilder 1.00
5 Victor Oreskovich 1.00
6 Evan Rankin 1.00
7 Brock Sheahan 1.00
8 Andrew Eggert 1.00
9 Luke Lucyk 1.00
10 Dave Venard 1.00
11 Michael Bartlett 1.00
12 T.J. Jindra 1.00
13 Matt Williams-Kovacs 1.00
14 Josh Sciba 1.00
15 Noah Babin 1.00
16 Jason Paige 1.00
17 Rory Walsh 2.00
18 Tim Wallace 1.00
19 Tony Gill 1.00
20 Mike Walsh 1.00
21 Matt Amado 1.00
22 Chris Trick 1.00
23 Joe Zurenko 1.00
24 Cory McLean 1.00
25 Morgan Cey 2.00

2005-06 Notre Dame Freshmen

COMPLETE SET (5) 5.00
1 Eric Condra 1.00
2 Justin White 1.00
3 Garrett Regan 1.00
4 Jordan Pierce 1.00
5 Christian Hanson 1.00

1984-85 Nova Scotia Oilers

This 26-card police set features the Nova Scotia Oilers of the American Hockey League. The cards measure approximately 2 1/2" by 3 3/4" and were sponsored by Q104 (an FM radio station), Coca-Cola, Hostess, and the Bedford Town Police, and the Halifax City Police. The cards display posed color player photos on a white card face. The player's name and position appear at the bottom.

COMPLETE SET (26) 6.00 15.00
1 Mark Holden .30 .75
2 Dave Allison .20 .50
3 Dwayne Boettger .20 .50
4 Lowell Loveday .20 .50
5 Rejean Cloutier .20 .50
6 Ray Cote .20 .50

7 Pat Conacher .40 1.00
8 Ken Berry .40 1.00
9 Steve Graves .20 .50
10 Todd Strueby .40 1.00
11 Steve Smith .75 2.00
12 Archie Henderson .30 .75
13 Dean Dachyshyn .20 .50
14 Marc Habscheid .40 1.00
15 Larry Melnyk .30 .75
16 Raimo Summanen .40 1.00
17 Jim Playfair .20 .50
18 Mike Zanier .40 1.00
19 Ian Wood .20 .50
20 Dean Hopkins .20 .50
21 Norm Aubin .20 .50
22 Tony Currie .20 .50
23 Ross Lambert .20 .50
24 Terry Martin .20 .50
25 Ed Chadwick CO .40 1.00
Larry Kish CO
Bob Boucher CO
26 Lou Christian TR .08 .25
Kevin Farris TR

1985-86 Nova Scotia Oilers

This 28-card police set features the Nova Scotia Oilers. The cards measure approximately 2 1/2" by 3 3/4" and were sponsored by Coca-Cola, Hostess, Q104 (an FM radio station), IGA food stores, and the Halifax City Police. The fronts display color action photos on a white card face. The sponsor logos appear across the top and in the lower corners. The player's name and position is below the picture.

COMPLETE SET (28) 6.00 15.00
1 Dean Hopkins .20 .50
2 Jeff Larmer .20 .50
3 Mike Moller .20 .50
4 Dean Dachyshyn .20 .50
5 Bruce Boudreau .30 .75
6 Ken Solheim .20 .50
7 Jeff Beukeboom .30 .75
8 Mark Lavarre .20 .50
9 John Olson .20 .50
10 Lou Crawford .20 .50
11 Warren Skorodenski .40 1.00
12 Dwayne Boettger .20 .50
13 Daryl Reaugh 1.25 3.00
14 John Miner .20 .50
15 Jim Ralph 1.25 3.00
16 Wayne Presley .30 .75
17 Steve Graves .20 .50
18 Tom McMurchy .20 .50
19 Darin Sceviour .20 .50
20 Kent Paynter .20 .50
21 Larry Kish GM/CO .08 .25
22 Jim Playfair .20 .50
23 Kevin Farris TR .08 .25
Ralph Mosher TR
24 Mickey Volcan .20 .50
25 Ron Low ACO .40 1.00
26 Don Biggs .20 .50
27 Bruce Eakin .20 .50
28 Team Photo .30 .75

1976-77 Nova Scotia Voyageurs

Set was sponsored by Farmers Twin Cities Co-op Dairy Ltd. Cards measure 4"x 6". Cards are listed below in alphabetical order. It is not known whether this list is complete and we have no pricing data; additional info can be forwarded to hockeymag@beckett.com. Thanks to collector Dale Sprenger for providing the info below.

COMPLETE SET (?)
1 Bruce Baker
2 Mike Busniuk
3 Jim Cahoon
4 Cliff Cox
5 Dave Elenbaas
6 Brian Engblom
7 Don Howse
8 Pat Hughes
9 Peter Lee
10 Chuck Luksa
11 Gilles Lupien
12 Al MacNeil CO
13 Gord McTavish
14 Pierre Mondou
15 Hal Phillipoff
16 Mike Polich
17 Rod Schutt
18 Ed Walsh
19 Ron Wilson
20 Paul Woods

1977-78 Nova Scotia Voyageurs

Sponsored by the Farmers Twin Cities Co-op Dairy Ltd., this 24-card set measures approximately 3 1/4" by 6" and features the Nova Scotia Voyageurs of the American Hockey League. The fronts feature posed action player photos bordered in white. In the top border appears "Nova Scotia Voyageurs 1977-78," while the player's name, facsimile autograph, sponsor name and logo, and team logo are printed below the picture. The backs are blank. The cards are unnumbered and checklisted below in alphabetical order.

COMPLETE SET (24) 15.00 30.00
1 Bruce Baker .50 1.00
2 Maurice Barrette .50 1.00
3 Barry Borrett .50 1.00
4 Tim Burke .50 1.00
5 Jim Cahoon .50 1.00
6 Norm Dupont .75 1.50
7 Greg Fox .75 1.50
8 Mike Hobin .50 1.00
9 Bob Holland .50 1.00
10 Don Howse .50 1.00
11 Pat Hughes 1.00 2.00
12 Chuck Luksa .50 1.00
13 Dave Lumley 1.00 2.00
14 Al MacNeil CO .75 1.50
15 Gord McTavish .50 1.00
16 Rick Meagher 1.50 3.00
17 Mike Polich .50 1.00
18 Moe Robinson .50 1.00
19 Gaston Rochette .50 1.00
20 Pierre Roy .50 1.00
21 Frank St.Marseille 1.00 2.00
22 Derrick St.Marseille TR .25 .50
23 Rod Schutt .50 1.00
24 Ron Wilson 1.00 2.00

1983-84 Nova Scotia Voyageurs

This 24-card police set features the Nova Scotia Oilers of the American Hockey League. The cards measure approximately 2 1/2" by 3 3/4" and were sponsored by Q104 (an FM radio station), Coca-Cola, and Hostess. The cards display posed color player photos on a white card face. The player's name and jersey number appear at the top. The three sponsors' logos are in the bottom white border.

COMPLETE SET (24) 6.00 15.00
1 Mark Holden .40 1.00
2 Bill Kitchen .20 .50
3 Dave Allison .20 .50
4 Stephane Lefebvre .20 .50
5 Stan Hennigar .20 .50
6 Steve Marengere .20 .50
7 John Goodwin .20 .50
8 John Newberry .20 .50
9 Bill Riley .30 .75
10 Norman Baron .30 .75
11 Brian Skrudland .75 2.00
12 Mike Lalor .40 1.00
13 Blair Barnes .20 .50
14 Remi Gagne .20 .50
15 Steve Penney .75 2.00
16 Michel Therrien .30 .75
17 Dave Stoyanovich .20 .50
18 Brian Patafie TR .08 .25
Lou Christian TR
19 Mike McPhee .75 2.00
20 Wayne Thompson .20 .50
21 Ted Fauss .20 .50
22 Jeff Teal .20 .50
23 Larry Landon .20 .50
24 Greg Moffett .20 .50

1996-97 OCN Blizzard

COMPLETE SET (25) 10.00
1 Rick Gregory .20 .50
2 Reynold Monias .20 .50
3 Dave Patenaude .20 .50
4 Clint Miller .20 .50
5 Alec Durocher .20 .50
6 Peter Bird .20 .50
7 Steve Ford .20 .50
8 Devin Salisbury .20 .50
9 John Brass .20 .50
10 Barrett Labossiere .20 .50
11 Cliff Duchesne .20 .50
12 Mike Stevenson .20 .50
13 Wally Wuttunee .20 .50
14 Don Boyer .20 .50
15 Jay Seymour .20 .50
16 Darren Kirk .20 .50
17 Tobias Hall .20 .50
18 John O'Toole .20 .50
19 Chad Ramsay .20 .50
20 Clayton Debray .20 .50
21 Konrad Mckay .20 .50
22 Ryan Belbas .20 .50
23 John McCusker .20 .50
24 Ryan Person .20 .50
25 Patrick Herman .20 .50

1997-98 OCN Blizzard

COMPLETE SET (24) 20.00
1 Team Picture .20 .50
2 Tucker Madder .20 .50
3 Kevin Wilson .20 .50
4 Larry Willerton .20 .50
5 Terence Tootoo 4.00 10.00
6 Clayton Quinn .20 .50
7 Shaun Rose .20 .50
8 Brad Hicks .20 .50
9 Barrett Labossiere .20 .50
10 Curtis Baldwin .20 .50
11 Jimmie Ronnback .20 .50
12 Wally Wuttunee .20 .50
13 Don Boyer .20 .50
14 Aaron Porter .20 .50
15 Alec Durocher .20 .50
16 Cliff Duchesne .20 .50
17 Devin Salisbury .20 .50
18 Cory Dittmer .20 .50
19 Derek Ernest .20 .50
20 Konrad Mckay .20 .50
21 Ryan Belbas .20 .50
22 John McCusker .20 .50
23 Ryan Person .20 .50
24 Tyler Love .20 .50

1998-99 OCN Blizzard

This set features the first card of the extremely popular Inuit star, Jordin Tootoo.

COMPLETE SET (24) 40.00
1 Team Picture .40 1.00
2 Terence Tootoo 4.00 10.00
3 Kevin Wilson .20 .50
4 Larry Willerton .20 .50
5 Morris Elderkin .20 .50
6 Darcy Johnson .20 .50
7 Shaun Rose .20 .50
8 Brad Hicks .20 .50
9 Barrett Labossiere .20 .50
10 Kevin Stoneman .20 .50
11 Jamie Vossen .20 .50
12 Jordin Tootoo 10.00 25.00
13 Aaron Porter .20 .50
14 Chad Ryan .20 .50
15 Cliff Duchesne .20 .50
16 Devin Salisbury .20 .50
17 Jimmie Ronnback .20 .50
18 Tom Herman .20 .50
19 Konrad Mckay .20 .50
20 Ryan Belbas .20 .50
21 John McCusker .20 .50
22 Ryan Person .20 .50
23 Preston McKay .20 .50
24 Brian Tucker .20 .50

1999-00 OCN Blizzard

COMPLETE SET (24)
1 Team Picture .20 .50
2 Rob Hrabec .20 .50
3 Justin Relland .20 .50
4 Cory Sawatzky .20 .50
5 Justin Seaborg .20 .50
6 Gary Lafreniere .20 .50
7 Darcy Johnson .20 .50
8 Darryl Crumb .20 .50
9 Kirk Zieffle .20 .50
10 Jamie Muswagon .20 .50
11 Michael Young .20 .50
12 Ryan Braun .20 .50
13 Mike Glover .20 .50
14 Dustin Rogers .20 .50
15 Phillip Albert .20 .50
16 Justin Williams .20 .50
17 Dave Splawinski .20 .50
18 Steve Reid .20 .50
19 Clifford Scatch .20 .50
20 Tom Herman .20 .50
21 Terence Tootoo 4.00 10.00
22 Dwayne Twerdin .20 .50
23 Jeff Grandfield .20 .50
24 Preston McKay .20 .50

2000-01 OCN Blizzard

COMPLETE SET (25) 20.00
1 Team Picture .25
2 Marc-Andre Leclerc .50
3 Garrett Hildebrandt .50
4 Matko Malbasa .50
5 Jared Lang .50
6 Darcy Johnson .50
7 Alton Jackson .50
8 Kirk Zieffle .50
9 Jamie Muswagon .50
10 Michael Young .50
11 Ryan Braun .50
12 Shayne Emmons .50
13 Derek Sharp .50
14 Phillip Albert .50
15 Justin Williams .50
16 Curtis Campbell .50
17 Clifford Scatch .50
18 Trevor Len .50
19 Terence Tootoo 10.00
20 Justin Tetrault .50
21 Jeff Grandfield .50
22 Dan Joyal .50
23 Steve Macintyre .50
24 Tim Haun .50
25 Dave Splawinski .50

2001-02 OCN Blizzard

COMPLETE SET (27) 12.00
1 Header Card .01
2 Team Picture .25
3 Louis Chabot .50
4 Mike Gooch .50
5 Garrett Hildebrandt .50
6 Jeff Froese .50
7 Cody Reynolds .50
8 Andy Coates .50
9 Aaron Starr .50
10 Alton Jackson .50
11 Kirk Zieffle .50
12 Jamie Muswagon .50
13 Michael Young .50
14 Ryan Braun .50
15 Russell Spence .50
16 Phillip Albert .50
17 Justin Williams .50
18 Justin Seaborg .50
19 Leighton Alexson .50
20 Trevor Len .50
21 Mark Wallmann .50
22 Justin Tetrault .50
23 Mike Ouellet .50
24 Everett Bear .50
25 Dylan Rochon .50
26 Marc-Andre Leclerc .50
27 Dave Splawinski .50

2002-03 OCN Blizzard

COMPLETE SET (27) 12.00
1 Team Picture .25
2 Andrew Gallant .50
3 Mike Gooch .50
4 Garrett Hildebrandt .50
5 Dallas Jackson .50
6 Paul Wallmann .50
7 Andy Coates .50
8 Aaron Starr .50
9 Alton Jackson .50
10 Jared Lang .50
11 Michael Young .50
12 Ryan Braun .50
13 Kiel Wilgosh .50
14 Daniel Mayer .50
15 Jason Kowalski .50
16 Mike Kaluzny .50
17 Ryan Weistche .50
18 Trevor Len .50
19 Tyler Rhyorchuk .50
20 Jason Marin .50
21 Everett Bear .50
22 Chop Melnyk .50
23 Dylan Rochon .50
24 Ryan Constant .50
25 Jonathon Meyer .50
26 Mark Wallmann .50
27 League Champs .10

2003-04 OCN Blizzard

COMPLETE SET (27) 10.00
1 Header Card .01
2 Everett Bear .50
3 Jason Butler .50
4 Ryan Constant .50
5 Pierre-Olivier Girouard .50
6 Mike Gooch .50
7 Tim Hammell .50
8 Cole Hunter .50
9 Dallas Jackson .50
10 Travis Kotyk .50
11 Jared Lang .50
12 Daniel Mayer .50
13 Lyle McKay .50
14 Don Melnyk .50
15 Jonathon Meyer .50
16 Brett Needham .50
17 Lem Randell .50
18 Jonathon Romic .50
19 Aaron Starr .50
20 Matt Summers .50
21 Stephen Sunderman .50
22 David Victor .50
23 Mark Wallmann .50
24 Paul Wallmann .50
25 Kiel Wilgosh .50
26 Michael Young .50
27 Team Photo .10

1998-99 Odessa Jackalopes

This 22-card set of the WPHL Jackalopes was handed out as a promotional giveaway at a home game in November, 1998.

COMPLETE SET (22) 10.00 25.00
1 Jacque Rodrigue .40 1.00
2 Rob Lukacs .75 2.00
3 Ryan Equale .40 1.00
4 Rick Girhiny .75 2.00
5 Terry Flynn .40 1.00
6 Paul Fioroni .40 1.00
7 Mike Ross .60 1.50
8 Johan Hagman .40 1.00
9 Sami Laine .60 1.50
10 Anders Lindberg .75 2.00
11 Dan Lavergne .40 1.00
12 Bo Anderson .40 1.00
13 Shayne LeBreton .40 1.00
14 Michael Tornquist .60 1.50
15 Christian Wibner .75 2.00
16 Chris Morque .40 1.00
17 Bill Pye .75 2.00
18 Martin Ohrstedt .75 2.00
19 Joe Clark CO .02 .10
20 Pat Kerin EM .02 .10
21 Greg Andis TR .02 .10
22 Golden Corral .02 .10

1999-00 Odessa Jackalopes

This set featuring the Jackalopes of the WPHL was issued as a promotional giveaway at a home game in December of 1999.

COMPLETE SET (21) 5.60 20.00
1 Michael Tornquist .40 1.00
2 Paul Vincent .40 1.00
3 Chris Morque .40 1.00
4 Fredrick Lindh .40 1.00
5 Bill Pye .75 2.00
6 Sami Laine .75 2.00
7 Jason Pellerin .40 1.00
8 Eric Perricone .40 1.00
9 Karson Kaebel .40 1.00
10 Roy Gray .40 1.00
11 Rick Girhiny .40 1.00
12 Mark Smith .40 1.00
13 John Bossio .40 1.00
14 Mike Vandenberghe .40 1.00
15 Gary Coupal .75 2.00
16 Jacque Rodrigue .40 1.00
17 Savo Mitrovic .40 1.00
18 George Umunna .40 1.00
19 Greg Andis TR .02 .10
20 Joe Harrell EQM .02 .10
21 Kentucky Fried Chicken .04 .01

2001-02 Odessa Jackalopes

This set features the Jackalopes of the WPHL. The set was issued as a promotional giveaway at a home game. The cards are unnumbered, so they are listed in alphabetical order.

COMPLETE SET (21) 12.00 30.00
1 Trevor Allman .60 1.50
2 Jeffrey Ambrosio .80 2.00
3 John Bossio .60 1.50
4 Kenny Corupe .80 2.00
5 Matt Cressman .60 1.50
6 Adam Doyle .60 1.50
7 Robert Frid .60 1.50
8 Mike Gorman .60 1.50
9 Joe Harris .60 1.50
10 Jeff Haydar .60 1.50
11 Scott Hillman .60 1.50
12 Doug Johnson .60 1.50
13 Derek Laxdal ACO .10 .25
14 Alexander Lyubimov .60 1.50
15 Don Margettie .60 1.50
16 Don McKee CO .10 .25
17 Jacque Rodrigue .60 1.50
18 Mike Sanderson .80 2.00
19 Mark Smith .60 1.50
20 Tim Slay .60 1.50
21 Team Photo .20 .50

2002-03 Odessa Jackalopes

COMPLETE SET (24) 20.00
1 John Bossio 1.00
2 Matt Carney 1.50
3 Matt Cressman 1.00
4 Jerry Cunningham 1.00
5 Denis Desmarais 1.00
6 Adam Doyle 1.00
7 Ryan Edwards 1.00
8 David Francis 1.00
9 Robert Frid 1.00
10 Greg Gatto 1.00
11 Mike Gorman 1.50
12 Scott Green 1.00
13 Kevin Hansen 1.00
14 Scott Hillman 1.00
15 Don Margettie 1.00
16 Mike Rutter 1.00
17 Sebastien Thinel 1.00
18 Greg Willers 1.00
19 Jami Yoder 1.00
20 Don McKee HCO .25
21 Derek Laxdal ACO .25
22 Joe Harrell EQM .10
23 Greg Andis TR .10
24 Sonic Ad .01

2003-04 Odessa Jackalopes

Produced by Grandstand Cards, this set was sold by the team at home games. The cards are unnumbered and are listed in alphabetical order.

COMPLETE SET (22) 10.00
1 Header Card .01
2 John Bossio .50
3 Mark Cairns .75
4 Matt Cressman .50
5 Adam Doyle .50
6 Shaun Fairweather .50
7 Jeff Goldie .50
8 Mike Gorman .75
9 Scott Green .50
10 Wayne Hall .50
11 Scott Hillman .50
12 Jaroslav Kerestes .50
13 Sal Lettieri .50
14 Joel Martin .75
15 Matt Price .50
16 Mike Rutter .50
17 Pat Stachniak .75
18 Sebastien Thinel .75
19 Danny Williams .50
20 Jami Yoder .50
21 Don McKee HCO .10
22 Greg Gatto ACO .10

2004-05 Odessa Jackalopes

This team set was issued as a stadium giveaway at a late-season home game.

COMPLETE SET (21) 20.00
1 B.J. Adams 1.00
2 Pascal Bedard 1.00
3 Matt Cressman 1.00
4 Paul Davies 1.00
5 Derek Dolson 2.00
6 Adam Doyle 1.50
7 Mike Gorman 2.00
8 Mike Hanson 1.00
9 Scott Hillman 1.00
10 Joel Irving 1.00
11 Tom Kotsopolous 2.00
12 John Kozoriz 1.00
13 R.C. Lyke 1.00
14 Don Margettie 1.00
15 Chris Paradise 1.00
16 Mike Rutter 2.00
17 Sebastien Thinel 2.00
18 Ben Wallace 1.00
19 Don McKee CO .50
20 Slappy MASCOT .10
21 Midland Memorial Hospital .01

2005-06 Odessa Jackalopes

COMPLETE SET (19) 15.00
1 Pascal Bedard .75
2 Chris Brannen .75
3 Mike Carter .75
4 Matt Cressman .75
5 Paul Davies .75
6 Andrew Davis .75
7 Derek Dolson 1.50
8 Jeff Ewasko .75
9 Mike Gorman 1.50
10 Scott Hillman .75
11 John Kozoriz .75
12 Josh Legge .75
13 Dominic Leveille .75
14 Adam Loncan 1.50
15 Jamie Lovell .75
16 Don Margettie .75
17 Mike Rutter .75
18 Sebastien Thinel .75
19 Don McKee HC .25

2006-07 Odessa Jackalopes

COMPLETE SET (21) 15.00 30.00
1 Blaine Bablitz .60 1.50
2 Pascal Bedard .60 1.50
3 Chris Brannen .60 1.50
4 Matt Cressman .60 1.50
5 Andrew Davis .60 1.50
6 Derek Dolson 1.00 2.50
7 Alex Dunn .60 1.50
8 Jeff Ewasko 1.25 3.00
9 Mike Gorman 1.00 2.50
10 Scott Hillman .60 1.50
11 John Kozoriz .60 1.50
12 Jay Latulippe .60 1.50
13 Josh Legge .60 1.50
14 Don Margettie .60 1.50
15 Mike Ramsay .60 1.50
16 Mike Rutter .60 1.50
17 Steve Thurn .60 1.50
18 Brian Swiniarski .60 1.50
19 Nathan Ward .60 1.50
20 Don McKee CO .20 .50
21 Doug Johnson ACO .20 .50

1999-00 Ohio State Buckeyes

This set features the Buckeyes of the NCAA. The set was issued as a promotional giveaway at a home game.

COMPLETE SET (20) 6.00 20.00
1 Ray Aho .60 1.50
2 Peter Broccoli .40 1.00
3 Louie Colsant .40 1.00
4 Jason Crain .40 1.00
5 Yan DesGagne .40 1.00
6 Jean-Francois Dufour .40 1.00
7 Jaisen Freeman .40 1.00
8 Nick Ganga .40 1.00
9 Ryan Jestadt .40 1.00
10 Miguel LaFleche .40 1.00
11 Mike McCormick .40 1.00
12 Eric Meloche .40 1.00
13 Luke Pavlas .60 1.50
14 Jason Selleke .40 1.00
15 Andre Signoretti .40 1.00
16 Ryan Skaleski .40 1.00
17 Ryan Smith .40 1.00
18 Scott Titus .40 1.00
19 Benji Wolke .40 1.00
20 Brutus Buckeye MASCOT .08 .25

2000-01 Ohio State Buckeyes

This set features the Buckeyes of the NCAA. The set was issued as a promotional giveaway in Jan. 2001. The set is noteworthy for featuring the first cards of 2001 first-rounders Dave Steckel and R. J Umberger.

COMPLETE SET (20) 8.00 20.00
1 Andro Signoretti .30 .75
2 Jean-Francois Dufour .30 .75
3 Jaisen Freeman .30 .75
4 Jason Crain .30 .75
5 Mike McCormick .30 .75
6 Scott Titus .30 .75
7 Nick Ganga .30 .75
8 Yan DesGagne .30 .75
9 Miguel LaFleche .30 .75
10 Ryan Smith .30 .75
11 Peter Broccoli .30 .75
12 Luke Pavlas .40 1.00
13 Peter Wishloff .30 .75
14 Mike Betz .30 .75
15 R.J. Umberger 2.00 5.00
16 Dave Steckel 1.20 3.00
17 Scott May .30 .75
18 Doug Andress .30 .75
19 Brutus Buckeye MASCOT .10 .25
20 John Markell CO .10 .25

2001-02 Ohio State Buckeyes

This set features the Buckeyes of the NCAA. It was issued as a promotional giveaway at a last-season home game. The cards, which are slightly smaller than standard size, are unnumbered, and thus are listed in alphabetical order.

COMPLETE SET (20) 12.00 30.00
1 Doug Andress .60 1.50
2 Daymen Bencharski .60 1.50
3 Mike Betz .60 1.50
4 Peter Broccoli .60 1.50
5 Paul Caponigri .60 1.50
6 Jason Crain .60 1.50
7 Yan DesGagne .60 1.50
8 Miguel LaFleche .60 1.50
9 T.J. Latorre .60 1.50
10 Scott May .60 1.50
11 Mike McCormick .60 1.50
12 Chris Olsgard .60 1.50
13 Luke Pavlas .80 2.00
14 Eric Skaug .60 1.50
15 Ryan Smith .60 1.50
16 Dave Steckel 1.20 3.00
17 Scott Titus .60 1.50
18 R.J. Umberger 1.20 3.00
19 Reed Whiting .60 1.50
20 Brutus Buckeye MASCOT .10 .25

2002-03 Ohio State Buckeyes

COMPLETE SET (20) 20.00
1 Doug Andress 1.00
2 Daymen Bencharski 1.00
3 Mike Betz 1.50
4 J.B. Bittner 1.00
5 Peter Broccoli 1.00
6 Paul Caponigri 1.00
7 Miguel LaFleche 1.00
8 Scott May 1.00
9 Chris Olsgard 1.00
10 Luke Pavlas 1.00
11 Eric Skaug 1.00
12 Lee Spector 1.00
13 Dave Steckel 1.50
14 Scott Titus 1.00
15 R.J. Umberger 2.50
16 Thomas Welsh 1.00
17 Reed Whiting 1.00
18 John Markell HCO .25
19 Brutus Buckeye .10
20 Nathan Guenin .50
Ryan Kesler
Dan Knapp(#Rod Pelley
Dave Caruso

2003-04 Ohio State Buckeyes

This set was given away to the first 5,000 fans at the Jan. 17, 2004 home game. The cards are smaller than standard size. They are unnumbered and so are listed below in alphabetical order.

COMPLETE SET (20) 8.00 20.00
1 Doug Andress .40 1.00
2 Daymen Bencharski .40 1.00
3 Mike Betz .60 1.50
4 J.B. Bittner .40 1.00
5 Paul Caponigri .40 1.00
6 Dave Caruso .60 1.50
7 Nathan Guenin .40 1.00
8 Kelly Holowaty .40 1.00
9 Dan Knapp .40 1.00
10 Scott May .40 1.00
11 Chris Olsgard .40 1.00
12 Rod Pelley .40 1.00
13 Lee Spector .40 1.00
14 Dave Steckel .75 2.00
15 Thomas Welsh .40 1.00
16 Reed Whiting .40 1.00
17 Sean Collins .40 1.00
Andrew Cohombri
18 Matt Beaudoin .40 1.00
Kenny Bernard
Matt Waddell
19 Bryce Anderson(#Tyson Strachan .40 1.00
Dave Barton
20 Mascot .10 .25

2004-05 Ohio State Buckeyes

COMPLETE SET (20) 10.00 25.00
1 Bryce Anderson .40 1.00
2 Dave Barton .40 1.00
3 Matt Beaudoin .40 1.00
4 Kenny Bernard .40 1.00
5 J.B. Bittner .40 1.00
6 Dave Carusa .75 2.00
7 Sean Collins .40 1.00
8 Nate Guenin .75 2.00
9 Dan Knapp .40 1.00
10 Rod Pelley .40 1.00
11 Andrew Schembri .40 1.00
12 Lee Spector .40 1.00
13 Tyson Strachan .40 1.00
14 Matt Waddell .40 1.00
15 Thomas Welsh .40 1.00
16 Ian Keserich .75 2.00
Johan Krull
17 Matt McIlvane .40 1.00
Domenic Maiani
18 Tom Fritsche .75 2.00
Kyle Hood
19 John Dingle .40 1.00
Jason DeSantis
20 Sam Campbell .40 1.00
Phil Lauderdale
Zach Pelletier

2004-05 Ohio State Buckeyes Women

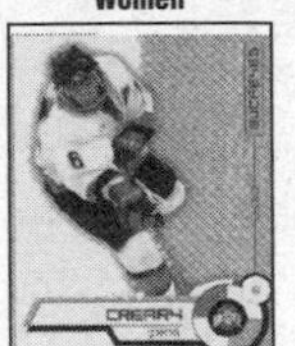

This set was issued as a promotional giveaway. The design mirrors that of the men's set from the same season.

COMPLETE SET (20) 8.00 20.00
1 Melissa Glasser .75 2.00
2 Jennifer Desson .40 1.00
3 Jeni Creary .40 1.00

4 Jaclyn Haines .40 1.00
5 Meaghan Mulvaney .40 1.00
6 Jana Harrigan .40 1.00
7 Crystal Sayther .40 1.00
8 Katie Sershen .40 1.00
9 Tessa Bonhomme .40 1.00
10 Amber Bowman .40 1.00
11 Katie Maroney .40 1.00
12 Lacey Schultz .40 1.00
13 Krysta Skarda .40 1.00
14 Erika Vanderveer .75 2.00
15 Shelby Aldous .75 2.00
Lisa Chesson
16 Jody Heywood .40 1.00
Erin Keyes
17 Jill Mauch .75 2.00
Pamela Patterson
18 Mallory Peckels .40 1.00
Rachel Vanscoy
19 Jackie Barto CO .02 .10
20 Buckeye MASCOT .02 .10

2005-06 Ohio State Buckeyes

COMPLETE SET (25) 8.00 20.00
1 Bryce Anderson .30 .75
2 Dave Barton .30 .75
3 Matt Beaudoin .30 .75
4 Kenny Bernard .30 .75
5 Dave Caruso .60 1.50
6 Sean Collins .30 .75
7 Tom Fritsche .60 1.50
8 Nate Guenin .30 .75
9 Kyle Hood .30 .75
10 Dan Knapp .30 .75
11 Domenic Maiani .30 .75
12 Rod Pelley .60 1.50
13 Andrew Schembri .30 .75
14 Tyson Strachan .30 .75
15 Matt Waddell .30 .75
16 Ian Keserich SO .60 1.50
17 Zach Pelletier SO .30 .75
18 Jason DeSantis SO .30 .75
19 Phil Lauderdale SO .30 .75
20 Johann Kroll SO .30 .75
21 Sam Campbell SO .30 .75
22 Matt McIlvane SO .30 .75
23 John Dingle SO .30 .75
24 Corey Elkins FR .30 .75
25 Nick Biondo FR .30 .75

2006-07 Ohio State Buckeyes

COMPLETE SET (25) 15.00 25.00
1 Bryce Anderson .40 1.00
2 Dave Barton .40 1.00
3 Matt Beaudoin .40 1.00
4 Kenny Bernard .40 1.00
5 Sean Collins .40 1.00
6 Jason DeSantis .40 1.00
7 John Dingle .40 1.00
8 Tommy Goebel .40 1.00
9 Johann Kroll .40 1.00
10 Domenic Maiani .40 1.00
11 Matt McIlvane .40 1.00
12 Andrew Schembri .40 1.00
13 Tyson Strachan .40 1.00
14 Matt Waddell .40 1.00
15 Phil Lauderdale .40 1.00
16 Nick Filion .60 1.50
17 Corey Elkins .40 1.00
18 Nick Biondo .40 1.00
19 Tom Fritsche .60 1.50
20 Zach Pelletier .40 1.00
21 Kyle Hood .40 1.00
22 Sam Campbell .40 1.00
23 Joe Palmer .60 1.50
24 Mathieu Picard .40 1.00
25 Brutus Buckeye MASCOT .10 .25

2006-07 Ohio State Buckeyes Women

COMPLETE SET (20) 15.00 25.00
1 Mallory Peckels .50 1.25
2 Katie Maroney .50 1.25
3 Jody Heywood .50 1.25
4 Tessa Bonhomme .50 1.25
5 Erika Vanderveer .50 1.25
6 Whitney Miller .50 1.25
7 Hayley Klassen .50 1.25
8 Lisa Chesson .50 1.25
9 Liana Bonanno .50 1.25
10 Krysta Skarda .50 1.25
11 Jill Mauch .50 1.25
12 Erin Keys .50 1.25
13 Kelly Cahill .50 1.25
14 Olivia Antognoli .50 1.25
15 Lacey Schultz .50 1.25
16 Morgan Marziali .50 1.25
17 Megan Hostasek .50 1.25
18 Amber Bowman .50 1.25
19 Shelby Aldous .50 1.25
20 The Freshmen .50 1.25

2007-08 Ohio State Buckeyes

1 Nick Biondo .15 .40
2 Jason DeSantis .15 .40
3 John Dingle .15 .40
4 Corey Elkins .15 .40
5 Nick Filion .15 .40
6 Tom Fritsche .15 .40
7 Tommy Goebel .15 .40
8 Kyle Hood .15 .40
9 Johann Kroll .15 .40
10 Phil Lauderdale .15 .40
11 Matt McIlvane .15 .40
12 Joseph Palmer .15 .40
13 Zach Pelletier .15 .40
14 Mathieu Picard .15 .40
15 John Albert .15 .40
Erick Belanger
16 Peter Boyd .15 .40
Dustin Carlson
Brad Gorham
17 Ryan Markell .15 .40
Chris Reed
Kyle Reed
18 Todd Rudasill .15 .40
Patrick Schafer
C.J. Severyn
19 Shane Sims .15 .40
Sergio Somma
Corey Toy
20 Brutus Buckeye MASCOT .10 .40

2005-06 OHL Bell All-Star Classic

COMPLETE SET (38) 8.00 20.00
1 Kevin Lalande .20 .50
2 David Bolland .20 .50
3 Wojtek Wolski .40 1.00
4 Bobby Ryan .40 1.00
5 Matt Lashoff .20 .50
6 John Vigilante .20 .50
7 Cory Emmerton .20 .50
8 Derek Joslin .20 .50
9 Andrej Sekera .20 .50
10 Marc Staal .20 .50
11 Chris Stewart .20 .50
12 Jonathan D'Aversa .20 .50
13 Ryan Parent .20 .50
14 Peter Aston .20 .50
15 Benoit Pouliot .40 1.00
16 Dan Lacosta .20 .50
17 Jordan Owens .40 1.00
18 Patrick McNeill .20 .50
19 Peter Tsimikalis .20 .50
20 Andrew Marshall .20 .50
21 Bobby Sanguinetti .20 .50
22 Michael Blunden .40 1.00
23 Ryan Callahan .20 .50
24 Adam Dennis .40 1.00
25 Justin Donati .20 .50
26 Steve Downie .75 2.00
27 Tyler Haskins .20 .50
28 Dylan Hunter .20 .50
29 Tyler Kennedy .20 .50
30 Scott Lehman .20 .50
31 Bryan Little .40 1.00
32 Ryan MacDonald .20 .50
33 Evan McGrath .40 1.00
34 Ryan O'Marra .40 1.00
35 Chad Painchaud .20 .50
36 Tommy Pyatt .20 .50
37 Robbie Schremp .40 1.00
38 Jordan Staal 1.25 3.00
39 Matt Kelly .20 .50
40 Jamie Tardif .20 .50

1992-93 Oklahoma City Blazers

This 18-card standard-size set was sponsored by TD's Sports Cards (a Tulsa baseball card store) and Planters Nuts and Snacks. Ten thousand sets were produced. Randomly inserted throughout the sets were 350 autographed cards of each player. The cards feature color action player photos with white borders. The player's name is superimposed on the photo at the bottom. The cards are unnumbered and checklisted below in alphabetical order.

COMPLETE SET (18) 3.00 8.00
1 Title Card .08 .25
2 Carl Boudreau .20 .50
3 Joe Burton .20 .50
4 Sylvain Fleury .20 .50
5 Brendan Garvey .20 .50
6 Guy Girouard .20 .50
7 Sean Gorman .20 .50
8 Jamie Hearn .20 .50
9 Craig Johnson .20 .50
10 Paul Krake .30 .75
11 Chris Laganas .20 .50
12 Daniel Larin .20 .50
13 Mark McGinn .20 .50
14 Alan Perry .30 .75
15 Steve Simoni .20 .50
16 Jim Solly .20 .50
17 Boyd Sutton .20 .50
18 Team Photo .20 .50

1993-94 Oklahoma City Blazers

Like each of the CHL sets issued that year, these are round cards approximately the size of a hockey puck. They come in a plastic container with the team logo on the front, and were sold at home games by the booster club for about $5.

COMPLETE SET (18) 3.00 8.00
1 Kent Anderson .20 .50
2 Carl Boudreau .20 .50
3 Joe Burton .20 .50
4 Mike Ciolli .20 .50
5 Guy Girouard .20 .50
6 Jules Jardine .20 .50
7 Craig Johnson .20 .50
8 Chris Laganas .20 .50
9 Jeff Massey .20 .50
10 Derry Menard .20 .50
11 Trent Pankewicz .20 .50
12 Alan Perry .30 .75
13 James Richmond .20 .50
14 Bruce Shoebottom .20 .50
15 Steve Simoni .20 .50
16 Jim Solly .20 .50
17 Mike Williams .20 .50
18 Mike McEwen CO .07 .20

1998-99 Oklahoma City Blazers

This 23-card set of the CHL Blazers was sold by the team late in the season at its souvenir stands.

COMPLETE SET (23) 4.00 10.00
1 Peter Arvanitis .20 .50
2 Dan Fournel .20 .50
3 Dominic Fafard .20 .50
4 Craig Willard .20 .50
5 Simon Olivier .20 .50
6 Joe Burton .30 .75
7 Craig Johnson .20 .50
8 Tom Gomes .20 .50
9 Steve Moore .20 .50
10 Jim Jensen .20 .50
11 Brad Preston .20 .50
12 Rod Butler .20 .50
13 Michael Pozzo .20 .50
14 Chris Johnston .20 .50
15 Hardy Sauter .20 .50
16 Jean-Ian Filiatrault .30 .75
17 Mike Williams .20 .50
18 Doug Sauter HCO .02 .10
19 Corey MacIntyre .20 .50
20 Daniel Larin .20 .50
21 Brandon Rose TR .02 .10
22 Team Photo .20 .50
23 Checklist .02 .10

2003-04 Oklahoma City Blazers

This set was sold at home games. The cards are unnumbered and listed in alphabetical order.

COMPLETE SET (24) 4.00 10.00
1 Header Card .01 .01
2 Peter Arvanitis .20 .50
3 Boyd Ballard .30 .75
4 Les Borsheim .20 .50
5 Ryan Campbell .20 .50
6 Sean Connors .30 .75
7 Qamil Charlie Elezi .30 .75
8 Tyler Fleck .20 .50
9 Bryan Forslund .20 .50
10 Brad Herauf .20 .50
11 Stefan Katalina .20 .50
12 Justin Kot .20 .50
13 Tim Laurila .20 .50
14 Mike Lucci .20 .50
15 Blair Manning .20 .50
16 Peter Robertson .20 .50
17 Jesse Saltmarsh .20 .50
18 Hardy Sauter .20 .50
19 Doug Sheppard .20 .50
20 Marty Standish .30 .75
21 Ryan Watson .20 .50
22 Doug Sauter HCO .02 .10
23 Sponsor .01 .01
24 Sponsor .01 .01

2004-05 Oklahoma City Blazers

COMPLETE SET (24) 10.00 25.00
1 B.J. Ballas .40 1.00
2 Jarad Bourassa .40 1.00
3 Michel Beausoleil .60 1.50
4 Brendon Morrow 4.00 10.00
5 Hardy Sauter .60 1.50
6 Pat Hallett .40 1.00
7 Tyler Fleck .40 1.00
8 Brad Herauf .40 1.00
9 Scott Selig .40 1.00
10 Cody Loughlean .40 1.00
11 Bryan Forslund .40 1.00
12 Garrett Prosofsky .60 1.50
13 Boyd Ballard .60 1.50
14 Jason Goulet .60 1.50
15 Sean Connors .60 1.50
16 Kevin Harris .40 1.00
17 Kahlil Thomas .40 1.00
18 Shawn Weiman .40 1.00
19 Doug Sauter CO .02 .10
20 Team Photo .02 .10
21 Clyde S. Dale MASCOT .01 .01
22 Crash Test Dummies .01 .01
23 Sponsor .01 .01
NNO Header Card .01 .01

1995-96 Oklahoma Coyotes RHI

This set features the Coyotes of Roller Hockey Intl. Only 500 of these 18 card sets were printed. They were available through the Coyotes Booster Club over a several game span at the end of the season. The cards are not numbered, and therefore are listed alphabetically.

COMPLETE SET (18) 6.00 15.00
1 Kevin Barrett .30 .75
2 Joe Burton .40 1.00
3 Scott Drevitch .30 .75
4 George Dupont .30 .75
5 Jason Elders .30 .75
6 Jean-Ian Filiatrault .40 1.00
7 Johan Finnstrom .30 .75
8 Tom Gomes .30 .75
9 Radek Hamr .30 .75
10 Ross Harris .40 1.00
11 Jason Knox .30 .75
12 Perry Neufeld .30 .75
13 Darcy Pengelly .30 .75
14 Trevor Sherban .30 .75
15 Peter Skudra .75 2.00
16 Darren Stolk .30 .75
17 Rob Weingartner .30 .75
18 Guy Gadowsky CO .08 .25

2006-07 Okotoks Oilers

COMPLETE SET (24) 12.00 20.00
1 Nathan Brummit .40 1.00
2 Jesse Budkins .40 1.00
3 Derrick Burnett .40 1.00
4 David Civitarese .40 1.00
5 Dan Conacher .40 1.00
6 Justin Daigle .40 1.00
7 Bradley Eidsness .40 1.00
8 Mark Jensen .40 1.00
9 Curtis Leinweber .40 1.00
10 Zack MacKinnon .40 1.00
11 Spencer Mcelhinney .40 1.00
12 Carter Madsen .40 1.00
13 Jeff Matheson .40 1.00
14 Andrew Owsiak .40 1.00
15 Jesse Perrin .40 1.00
16 Jeff Sapisha .40 1.00
17 Brian Schmautz .40 1.00
18 Kyle Schussler .40 1.00
19 Elliott Sheen .40 1.00
20 Everett Sheen .40 1.00
21 Devin Welsh .40 1.00
22 Garry Vanhereweghe CO .10 .25
23 Trevor McFarlane ACO .10 .25
24 Jeff Totz ACO .10 .25

2007-08 Okotoks Oilers

COMPLETE SET (20) 4.00 10.00
1 James Bannister .25 .60
2 David Civitarese .25 .60
3 Dan Conacher .25 .60
4 Mason Conway .25 .60
5 Justin Daigle .25 .60
6 Brian Doust .25 .60
7 Chris Duszynsky .25 .60
8 Brad Eidsness .25 .60
9 Corbin Gavin .25 .60
10 Brandon Hoogenboom .25 .60
11 Jesse Hudkins .25 .60
12 Curtis Leinweber .25 .60
13 Zak MacKinnon .25 .60
14 Carter Madsen .25 .60
15 Amory Mudrewich .25 .60
16 Jesse Perrin .25 .60
17 Derek Rodwell .25 .60
18 Kyle Schussler .25 .60
19 Elliot Sheen .25 .60
20 Braely Torris .25 .60

1993-94 Omaha Lancers

This set features the Lancers of the USHL. The set was available at hobby shops in the Omaha area and at AK-SAR-BEN arena where the Lancers play. The fronts feature posed action shots inside borders. The team name and player information appears in two stripes immediately below the picture. The cards are unnumbered and checklisted below in alphabetical order.

COMPLETE SET (28) 4.00 10.00
1 Ryan Bencurik .15 .40
2 Jeff Borders .15 .40
3 Sean Bowman .15 .40
4 Doc Del Castillo ACO .02 .10
5 Jeff Edwards .15 .40
6 Tony Gasparini .15 .40
7 Mike Guentzel CO .02 .10
8 Scott Haig .15 .40
9 Ken Hemenway .15 .40
10 Bill Hubbard .15 .40
11 Klage Kaebel .15 .40
12 Rob Klasnick .15 .40
13 Tony Kolozsy .15 .40
14 Tom Kowal .15 .40
15 Charlie Lentz .15 .40
16 Justin Lyle .15 .40
17 Chris Marvel .15 .40
18 Mike Peluso .15 .40
19 Scott Pionk ACO .02 .10
20 Dan Riva .15 .40
21 Nathan Rocheleau .15 .40
22 Eric Runyan .15 .40
23 Joe Russo .15 .40
24 Brian Swanson .40 1.00
25 Scott Swanson .15 .40
26 Justin Theel .15 .40
27 Jamie Thompson .15 .40
28 Brendan Walsh .15 .40

2001-02 Omaha Lancers

We have confirmed the existence of one card in this series. If you have any additional info, please email hockeymag@beckett.com.

COMPLETE SET (?)
1 Yale Lewis

2002-03 Orlando Seals

It's possible this checklist is incomplete. If you have additions, please contact us at hockeymag@beckett.com.

COMPLETE SET (???) 15.00
1 B.J. Stephens 1.00
2 Mike Correia 1.00
3 Stan Drulia HCO 1.00
4 Mascot .10
5 Todd Bennett 1.00
6 Chris LiPuma 1.00
7 Louis Goulet 1.00
8 Zac Boyer 1.00
9 David Goverde 1.50
10 Mark White 1.00
11 Jad Ramsay 1.00
12 Joe Spencer 1.00
13 Sponsor Card .01
14 Ethan Burnes 1.00
15 Ryan Anderson 1.00
16 Mascot .10
17 Chris Cerrella 1.00
18 Todd Nowicki 1.00
19 Joe Seroski 1.00

1998-99 Orlando Solar Bears

This set features the Solar Bears of the IHL. This issue was sold in team set form at home games and is much easier to find than the giveaway cards issued later that season.

COMPLETE SET (19) 4.00 10.00
1 Checklist/Logo card .02 .10
2 Patrick Neaton .20 .50
3 Sean McCann .20 .50
4 Clayton Norris .20 .50
5 Hubie McDonough .30 .75
6 Shawn Carter .20 .50
7 Grigori Panteleyev .30 .75
8 Todd Richards .30 .75
9 Shawn Wansborough .20 .50
10 Mark Beaufait .40 1.00
11 Scott Hollis .20 .50
12 David Mackey .20 .50
13 David Littman .30 .75
14 Grigori Panteleyev AS .30 .75
15 Mark Beaufait AS .40 1.00
16 Curt Fraser CO .20 .50
17 Peter Horachek ACO .20 .50
18 Orlando Arena .20 .50
19 Shades MASCOT .20 .50

1998-99 Orlando Solar Bears II

This set was given away at two different home games. The cards were issued in perforated sheets and are unnumbered. They are extremely difficult to find in complete set form.

COMPLETE SET (22) 25.00
1 David Littman .60 1.50
2 Mark Beaulait .75 2.00
3 Shawn Carter .40 1.00
4 David Mackey .40 1.00
5 Sean McCann .40 1.00
6 Hubie McDonough .60 1.50
7 Patrick Neaton .40 1.00
8 Clayton Norris .40 1.00
9 Grigori Panteleyev .60 1.50
10 Todd Richards .60 1.50
11 Curt Fraser HCO .40 1.00
12 Scott Bailey .60 1.50
13 Rob Bonneau .40 1.00
14 Allan Egeland .40 1.00
15 Todd Krygier .40 1.00
16 Kirby Law .40 1.00
17 Curtis Murphy .40 1.00
18 Mike Nicholishen .40 1.00
19 Frederik Oduya .40 1.00
20 Ken Sabourin .40 1.00
21 Pierre Sevigny .40 1.00
22 Peter Horachek ACO .40 1.00

1980-81 Oshawa Generals

This 25-card P.L.A.Y. (Police, Laws and Youth) set measures approximately 2 5/8" by 4 1/8" and features color posed action player photos and is bordered by white borders accented by a thin red line. The player's name, position, and team are superimposed in white letters on the picture.

COMPLETE SET (25) 62.50 125.00
1 Generals Logo .40 1.00
2 Ray Flaherty .40 1.00
3 Craig Kitchener .40 1.00
4 Dan Revell .40 1.00
5 Bob Kucheran .40 1.00
6 Pat Poulin .40 1.00
7 Dave Andreychuk 7.50 15.00
8 Barry Tabobondung .40 1.00
9 Steve Konroyd 1.25 3.00
10 Paul Edwards .40 1.00
11 Dale Degray 1.25 3.00
12 Joe Cirella 1.25 3.00
13 Norm Schmidt .40 1.00
14 Markus Lehto .60 1.50
15 Mitch Lamoureux .60 1.50
16 Tony Tanti 1.50 4.00
17 Bill Laforge .40 1.00
18 Greg Gravel .40 1.00
19 Mike Lekun .40 1.00
20 Chris Smith .40 1.00
21 Peter Sidorkiewicz 1.50 4.00
22 Greg Stefan 1.50 4.00
23 Tom McCarthy 1.50 4.00
24 Rick Lanz 1.50 4.00
25 Bobby Orr 40.00 80.00

1981-82 Oshawa Generals

This 25-card P.L.A.Y. (Police, Laws and Youth) set measures approximately 2 5/8" by 4 1/8" and features color posed action player photos. The backs carry "Tips from the Generals" that include a hockey tip and its application to a life situation.

COMPLETE SET (25) 24.00 60.00
1 Generals Logo .40 1.00
2 Chris Smith .60 1.50
3 Peter Sidorkiewicz 1.50 4.00
4 Ali Butorac .60 1.50
5 Dan Revell .60 1.50
6 Mitch Lamoureux .75 2.00
7 Norm Schmidt .60 1.50
8 Paul Edwards .60 1.50
9 Dan Nicholson .60 1.50
10 John Hutchings .60 1.50
11 Dave Gans .60 1.50
12 Dave Andreychuk 6.00 15.00
13 Mike Stern .60 1.50
14 Dale Degray .75 2.00
15 Mike Lekun .60 1.50
16 Greg Gravel .60 1.50
17 Dave MacLean .60 1.50
18 Tony Tanti 1.25 3.00
19 John MacLean 6.00 15.00
20 Jim Uens .60 1.50
21 Guy Jacob .60 1.50
22 Jeff Steffan .60 1.50
23 Paul Theriault .60 1.50
24 Sherry Bassin .60 1.50
25 Durham Regional .20 .50
Police Logo

1982-83 Oshawa Generals

This 25-card set measures approximately 2 5/8" by 4 1/8" and features color, posed action player photos framed by thin red border lines that rest on a white card face. The player's name, position, and the team logo are superimposed across the top of the picture in white lettering.

COMPLETE SET (25) 14.00 35.00
1 Generals Logo .20 .50
2 Jeff Hogg .60 1.50
3 Peter Sidorkiewicz 1.25 3.00
4 Dale Degray .60 1.50
5 Joe Cirella .60 1.50
6 Todd Smith .40 1.00
7 Scott Brydges .40 1.00
8 Jeff Steffen .40 1.00
9 Don Biggs .40 1.00
10 Todd Hooey .40 1.00
11 Tony Tanti .75 2.00
12 Danny Gratton .40 1.00
13 Steve King .40 1.00
14 Dan Defazio .40 1.00
15 John MacLean 3.00 8.00
16 Tim Burgess .40 1.00
17 Mike Stern .40 1.00
18 Dan Nicholson .40 1.00
19 David Gans .40 1.00
20 John Hutchings .40 1.00
21 Norm Schmidt .40 1.00
22 Todd Charlesworth .40 1.00
23 Paul Theriault CO .30 .75
24 Sherry Bassin GM .40 1.00
25 Durham Regional .20 .50
Police Logo

1983-84 Oshawa Generals

This 30-card P.L.A.Y. (Police, Laws and Youth) set measures approximately 2 5/8" by 4 1/8" and features color posed action player photos. The backs carry "Tips from the Generals" that include a hockey tip and its application to a life situation.

COMPLETE SET (30) 12.00 30.00
1 Peter Sidorkiewicz .75 2.00
2 Kirk McLean 4.00 10.00
3 Todd Charlesworth .40 1.00
4 Ian Ferguson .30 .75
5 John Hutchings .30 .75
6 Generals Logo .08 .25
7 Mark Haarmann .30 .75
8 Joel Curtis .30 .75
9 Dan Gratton .30 .75
10 Steve Hedington .30 .75
11 Scott Brydges .30 .75
12 CKAR Radio .08 .25
13 Brad Walcot .30 .75
14 Paul Theriault CO .30 .75
15 Jon Jenkins .08 .25
Chief of Police
16 Sherry Bassin GM .40 1.00
17 Craig Morrison .30 .75
18 Bolahood's .08 .25
19 Bruce Melanson .30 .75
20 Mike Stern .30 .75
21 Gary McColgan .30 .75
22 Lee Giffin .40 1.00
23 Brent Maki .30 .75
24 Ronald McDonald .20 .50
25 Jeff Steffen .30 .75
26 John Stevens .30 .75
27 David Gans .30 .75
28 Don Biggs .40 1.00
29 Chip Crandall .30 .75
30 Durham Police Logo .08 .25

1989-90 Oshawa Generals

These over-sized cards (approximately 2 5/8 X 4 1/8 inches) feature color action photos on the front and sponsor logos on the back. Cards were printed by Whitby Business Forms. The Lindros single has been widely counterfeited. Collectors should be wary when purchasing that card in single form. Your best bet is to purchase the complete set if you want a legitimate copy.

COMPLETE SET (35) 14.00 35.00
1 Corey Banika .20 .50
2 David Craievich .20 .50
3 Scott Hollis .20 .50
4 Mike Decoff .20 .50
5 Joe Busillo .20 .50
6 Matt Hoffman .20 .50
7 Craig Donaldson .20 .50
8 Jason Denomme .20 .50
9 Brian Grieve .20 .50
10 Wade Simpson .20 .50
11 Dale Craigwell .40 1.00
12 Mike Lenarduzzi .20 .50
13 Rick Cornacchia CO .02 .10
14 David Edwards .20 .50
15 Kevin Butt .40 1.00
16 Team Photo .07 .20
17 Clair Cornish .20 .50
18 Jarrod Skalde .40 1.00
19 Mark Deazeley .20 .50
20 Jean Paul Davis .20 .50
21 Todd Coopman .02 .10
22 Trevor McIvor .20 .50
23 Mike Craig .40 1.00
24 Paul O'Hagan .20 .50
25 Iain Fraser .20 .50
26 Brent Grieve .20 .50
27 Lions International .02 .10
28 National Sports Centre .02 .10
29 Durham Regional Police .02 .10
30 Oshawa Generals .02 .10
31 Eric Lindros 8.00 20.00
32 Bill Armstrong .20 .50
33 Chris Vanclief .20 .50
34 Scott Luik .20 .50
35 Fred Brathwaite 1.25 3.00

1989-90 Oshawa Generals 7th Inning Sketch

This set of the 1989-90 Oshawa Generals of the OHL was released by 7th Inning Sketch in advance of its full 1989-90 OHL issue. The cards, numbered 1-23, are the same as those found in the larger set. Card #1, featuring Eric Lindros, has been widely counterfeited. Collectors should exercise caution when purchasing this card as a single. Your best precaution is to use a jeweler's loupe to carefully study the print pattern on the front of the card.

COMPLETE SET (23) 4.80 12.00
1 Eric Lindros 2.00 5.00
2 Jarrod Skalde .30 .75
3 Joe Busillo .20 .50
4 Dale Craigwell .30 .75
5 Clair Cornish .20 .50
6 Jean-Paul Davis .20 .50
7 Craig Donaldson .20 .50
8 Wade Simpson .20 .50
9 Mike Craig .30 .75
10 Mark Deazeley .20 .50
11 Scott Hollis .20 .50
12 Brian Grieve .20 .50
13 Dave Craievich .20 .50
14 Paul O'Hagan .20 .50
15 Matt Hoffman .20 .50
16 Trevor McIvor .20 .50
17 Cory Banika .20 .50
18 Kevin Butt .30 .75
19 Iain Fraser .20 .50
20 Bill Armstrong .20 .50
21 Scott Luik .20 .50
22 Brent Grieve .20 .50
23 Fred Brathwaite .60 1.50

1991-92 Oshawa Generals

This 32-card standard-size set was sponsored by Coca-Cola and Domino's Pizza. The cards feature color action player photos framed by a royal blue double line. A white circle at the lower right corner carries the player's jersey number or the season year '91-'92.

COMPLETE SET (32) 8.00 20.00
1 Mike Fountain .30 .75
2 Brian Grieve .15 .40
3 Trevor Burgess .15 .40
4 Wade Simpson .15 .40
5 Ken Shepard .15 .40
6 Stephane Yelle .30 .75
7 Matt Hoffman .15 .40
8 Neil Iserhoff .15 .40
9 Rob Leask .15 .40
10 Kevin Spero .15 .40
11 Scott Hollis .15 .40
12 Sean Brown .20 .50
13 Todd Bradley .15 .40
14 Darryl LaFrance .15 .40
15 Markus Brunner .20 .50
16 B.J. MacPherson .15 .40
17 Jason Campeau .15 .40
18 Jason Weaver .15 .40
19 Jan Benda .20 .50
20 Jason Arnott 1.50 4.00
21 Eric Lindros 3.00 8.00
22 Wayne Daniels .02 .10
Dir. of Operations
23 Joe Cook .15 .40
24 Can't Beat the Real .02 .10
Thing (Coke Ad)
25 Experience the .02 .10
Domino's Effect
(Pizza Ad)
26 Mark Deazeley .15 .40
27 Jean-Paul Davis .15 .40
28 Brian Grieve .15 .40
29 Oshawa Generals .40 1.00
Team Photo
30 Ian Young CO .02 .10
Larry Marson CO5
Rick Cornacchia CO
31 Sponsor Ads .02 .10
Checklist
32 Prosport's Action .02 .10

1991-92 Oshawa Generals Sheet

This 18" by 12" sheet was sponsored by the 8th Annual United Way Face-Off Breakfast. The front features posed, color player cards with the players' names printed in a black stripe that appears below each picture. The center of the sheet carries the words "8th Annual United Way Face-Off Breakfast" in sky blue print. The team name also appears in the center, along with the year, the individual sheet number, and the production run (5,000). The players are checklisted below as they appear from left to right. Although these typically are found in sheet form, we are listing values for singles below as well as the complete sheet price.

COMPLETE SHEET (26) 8.00 20.00
1 Scott Hollis .15 .40
2 Jan Benda .20 .50
3 Joe Cook .15 .40
4 Wade Simpson .15 .40
5 B.J. MacPherson .15 .40
6 David Anderson .15 .40
7 Stephane Yelle .30 .75
8 Troy Sweet .15 .40
9 Matt Hoffman .15 .40
10 Trevor Burgess .15 .40
11 Jason Weaver .15 .40
12 Craig Lutes .15 .40
13 Darryl LaFrance .15 .40
14 Jason Arnott 1.50 4.00
15 Eric Lindros 3.00 8.00
16 Brian Grieve .15 .40
17 Mark Deazeley .15 .40
18 Mike Cote .15 .40
19 Markus Brunner .20 .50
20 Kevin Spero .15 .40
21 Todd Bradley .15 .40
22 Mike Fountain .30 .75
23 Fred Brathwaite .30 .75
24 Jean-Paul Davis .15 .40
25 Jason Campeau .15 .40
26 Neil Iserhoff .15 .40

1992-93 Oshawa Generals Sheet

This 18" by 12" sheet was sponsored by the 9th Annual United Way Face-Off Breakfast. The front features posed, color player cards with the players' names printed in a black stripe that appears below each picture. The center of the sheet carries the words "9th Annual United Way Face-Off Breakfast" in black print. The team name also appears in the center, along with the year, the individual sheet number, and the production run (5,000). Although these typically are found in sheet form, we are listing values for singles below as well as the complete sheet price.

COMPLETE SHEET (26) 6.00 15.00
1 Wade Simpson .20 .50
2 Jamie Kress .20 .50
3 Sean Brown .25 .60
4 Jason Arnott 1.25 3.00
5 Mark Brooks .20 .50
6 Rob McQuat .20 .50
7 Joe Cook .20 .50
8 Chris Hall .20 .50
9 Jason McQuat .20 .50
10 Jason Julian .20 .50
11 Kevin Spero .20 .50
12 Steve Haight .20 .50
13 B.J. MacPherson .20 .50
14 Billy-Jay Johnston .20 .50
15 Stephane Soulliere .20 .50
16 Todd Bradley .20 .50
17 Darryl Lafrance .20 .50
18 Aaron Albright .20 .50
19 Trevor Burgess .20 .50
20 Scott Hollis .20 .50
21 Serge Dunphy .20 .50
22 Joel Gagnon .30 .75
23 Brian Kent .30 .75
24 Stephane Yelle .40 1.00
25 Jason Campeau .20 .50
26 Neil Iserhoff .20 .50

1993-94 Oshawa Generals

Printed by Slapshot Images Ltd., this standard size 27-card set features the 1993-94 Oshawa Generals. Reportedly only 3,000 of these sets were produced; the title card also serves as a Certificate of Authenticity and has the number 3,000 printed in the lower right corner. On a geometrical team color-coded background, the fronts feature color action player photos with thin black borders. The player's name, position and team name, as well as the producer's logo, appear on the front.

COMPLETE SET (27) 4.00 10.00
1 Title Card .02 .10
Checklist
2 Joel Gagnon .20 .50
3 Ken Shepard .20 .50
4 Jan Snopek .20 .50
5 David Froh .15 .40
6 Brandon Gray .15 .40
7 Damon Hardy .15 .40
8 Sean Brown .25 .60
9 Jeff Andrews .15 .40
10 Stephane Yelle .30 .75
11 Stephane Soulliere .15 .40
12 Andrew Power .15 .40
13 Todd Bradley .15 .40
14 Darryl Lafrance .20 .50
15 Darryl Moxam .15 .40
16 Robert Dubois .15 .40
17 Kevin Vaughan .15 .40
18 Rob McQuat .20 .50
19 B.J. Johnston .15 .40
20 Paul Doherty .15 .40
21 Eric Boulton .40 1.00
22 Marc Savard .40 1.00
23 Chris Hall .15 .40
24 Jason McQuat .15 .40
25 Ryan Lindsay .15 .40
26 Rick Cornacchia CO .02 .10
Wayne Daniels DIR
Brian Drumm ACO
NNO Slapshot Ad Card .02 .10

2001-02 Oshawa Generals

We have confirmed the existence of one card in this series. Please forward any additional information you might have to hockeymag@beckett.com.

COMPLETE SET (?)
1 Nathan Horton

2003-04 Oshawa Generals

COMPLETE SET (26) 5.00 12.00
1 Dan Turple .30 .75
3 John Neal .20 .50
4 Chris Petrow .20 .50
6 Bret Nasby .20 .50
7 Clay McFadden .20 .50
8 Fred Hatziioannou .20 .50
10 Tyler Donati .20 .50
11 Andrew Gibbons .20 .50
12 Justin Donati .20 .50
14 Andy Reiss .20 .50
15 Aaron Lobb .20 .50
16 Mike McLean .20 .50
17 Chris Hulit .20 .50
19 Jordan Beirnes .20 .50
20 Justin Wallingford .20 .50
21 Adam Berti .20 .50
22 Mike Kavanagh .20 .50
23 Brandon McBride .20 .50
24 Ryan Kitchen .20 .50
25 Ben Eager .40 1.00
26 Paul Ranger .20 .50
27 Gary Friesen .20 .50
28 Tobias Whelan .20 .50
31 Ryan Gibb .30 .75
NNO Paul Ranger TL .75 2.00
NNO Ben Eager TL .75 2.00

2004-05 Oshawa Generals

COMPLETE SET (22) 5.00 12.00
1 Carlo Di Rienzo .40 1.00
2 Ryan Gibb .40 1.00
3 John Neal .60 1.50
4 Trevor Waddell .20 .50
5 Bret Nasby .20 .50
6 Brett Trudell .20 .50
7 Justin Allen .20 .50
8 Peter Tsimikalis .20 .50
9 Tom Jefferson .20 .50
10 Cal Clutterbuck .40 1.00
11 Matt Piva .20 .50
12 Matt Puntureri .20 .50
13 Jesse Biduke .20 .50
14 Devereaux Heshmatpour .30 .75
15 Adam Berti .40 1.00
16 Mike Kavanaugh .20 .50
17 Brandon McBride .20 .50
18 Chad Thompson .20 .50
19 James DeLory .20 .50
20 David Halasz .20 .50
21 Gary Friesen .20 .50
22 Checklist .01 .01

2004-05 Oshawa Generals Autographs

One autographed player card was inserted into every 2004-05 Oshawa Generals team set. It is believed that every member of the Generals signed for inclusion in this insert. If anyone has information to the contrary, please contact us at hockeymag@beckett.com.

COMPLETE SET (21) 60.00

2006-07 Oshawa Generals

COMPLETE SET (24) 12.00 20.00
1 John Tavares 3.00 8.00
2 Dale Mitchell .40 1.00
3 Tyler Taylor .20 .50
4 Igor Gongalsky .20 .50
5 Cal Clutterbuck .20 .50
6 Dean Howard .20 .50
7 Kory Nagy .20 .50
8 Brett MacLean .40 1.00
9 Corey Cowick .20 .50
10 Kyle Paige .20 .50
11 Kody Musselman .20 .50
12 Shea Kewin .20 .50
13 Brett Parnham .20 .50
14 Ziga Pance .20 .50
15 Trevor Koverko .20 .50
16 Michael Del Zotto .60 1.50
17 Matt Seegmiller .20 .50
18 Peter Aston .20 .50
19 Eric Regan .20 .50
20 Billy Siekris .20 .50
21 James Delory .20 .50
22 Loic Lacasse .30 .75
23 Mark Packwood .30 .75
24 Oshawa Generals .10 .25

1981-82 Ottawa 67's

The cards measure approximately 5 1/2" by 8 1/2" and feature black-and-white player portraits in white borders. A facsimile autograph and player's jersey number are printed in the wide bottom margin. The backs are blank. The cards are unnumbered and checklisted below in alphabetical order. Thanks to collector Stan Mendes for providing additional checklist information.

COMPLETE SET (25) 12.00 30.00
1 James Allison .30 .75
2 John Boland .30 .75
3 Randy Boyd .30 .75
4 Adam Creighton 1.25 3.00
5 Bill Dowd .30 .75
6 Dwayne Davison .30 .75
7 Alan Hepple .30 .75
8 Mike James .30 .75
9 Brian Kilrea CO .75 2.00
10 Moe Lemay .60 1.50
11 Benny Lorige .30 .75
12 Paul Louttit .30 .75
12 Doug Stewart .30 .75
13 Don McLaren .30 .75
13 Fraser Wood .30 .75
14 John Ollson .30 .75
15 Brian Patafie TR .20 .50
16 Mark Paterson .40 1.00
17 Phil Patterson .30 .75
18 Larry Power .30 .75
19 Jim Ralph 2.00 5.00
20 Darcy Roy .40 1.00
21 Brad Shaw 1.25 3.00
22 Brian Small .30 .75
23 Doug Stewart .30 .75
24 Jeff Vaive .30 .75
25 Fraser Wood .30 .75

1982-83 Ottawa 67's

Sponsored by Coke and Channel 12, this 25-card set measures approximately 2 5/8" by 4 1/8" and features posed, color player photos with white borders. The player's name and jersey number are printed in black across the bottom of the picture.The cards are unnumbered and checklisted below in alphabetical order.

COMPLETE SET (25) 12.00 30.00
1 Bruce Cassidy .30 .75
2 Greg Coram .30 .75
3 Adam Creighton .75 2.00
4 Bill Dowd .30 .75
5 Gord Hamilton ACO .20 .50
6 Scott Hammond .30 .75
7 Alan Hepple .30 .75
8 Alan Hepple .30 .75
9 Jim Jackson TR .20 .50
10 Mike James .30 .75
11 Brian Kilrea CO .75 2.00
12 Paul Louttit .30 .75
13 Brian McKinnon .30 .75
14 Don McLaren .30 .75
15 John Ollson .30 .75
16 Darren Pang 2.00 5.00
17 Mark Paterson .30 .75
18 Phil Patterson .30 .75
19 Larry Power .30 .75
20 Gary Roberts 3.00 8.00
21 Brian Rome .30 .75
22 Darcy T. Roy .30 .75
23 Brad Shaw 1.00 2.50
24 Doug Stewart .30 .75
25 Jeff Vaive .30 .75
26 Larry MacAndrew .30 .75
27 Gord Hamilton Jr. .30 .75

1983-84 Ottawa 67's

Sponsored by Coke and Channel 12, this 27-card set measures approximately 2 5/8" by 4 1/8". The fronts feature posed, color player photos with white borders. The player's name and jersey number are printed in black across the bottom of the picture. The cards are unnumbered and checklisted below in alphabetical order.

COMPLETE SET (27) 10.00 25.00
1 Richard Adolfi .20 .50
2 Bill Bennett .20 .50
3 Bruce Cassidy .30 .75
4 Todd Clarke .20 .50
5 Greg Coram .30 .75
6 Adam Creighton .75 2.00
7 Bob Giffin .20 .50
8 Gord Hamilton ACO .08 .25
9 Gord Hamilton Jr. TR .08 .25
10 Scott Hammond .20 .50
11 John Hanna .20 .50
12 Tim Helmer .20 .50
13 Steve Hrynewich .20 .50
14 Jim Jackson TR .08 .25
15 Mike James .20 .50
16 Brian Kilrea CO/MG .40 1.00
17 Larry MacAndrew TR .08 .25
18 Brian McKinnon .20 .50
19 Don McLaren .30 .75
20 Roy Myllari .20 .50
21 Darren Pang 1.50 4.00
22 Mark Paterson .30 .75
23 Phil Patterson .20 .50
24 Gary Roberts 2.00 5.00
25 Darcy Roy .20 .50
26 Brad Shaw .75 2.00
27 Steve Simoni .20 .50

1984-85 Ottawa 67's

This 28-card set was sponsored by Coca-Cola and Focus Photographic Services Commercial Photography. The cards measure approximately 2 5/8" by 4 1/8" and feature color, full-length, posed player photos with white borders. The player's name and jersey number are superimposed on the bottom of the picture. The cards are unnumbered and checklisted below in alphabetical order.

COMPLETE SET (28) 8.00 20.00
1 Tom Allen .30 .75
2 Graydon Almstedt .30 .75
3 Bill Bennett .30 .75
4 Bruce Cassidy .30 .75
5 Greg Coram .40 1.00
6 Bob Ellett CO .08 .25
7 Tony Geesink .30 .75
8 Bob Giffin .30 .75
9 John Hanna .30 .75
10 Tim Helmer .30 .75
11 Andy Helmuth .30 .75
12 Steve Hrynewich .30 .75
13 Rob Hudson .30 .75
14 Jim Jackson TR .08 .25
15 Steve Kayser .30 .75
16 Bill Kuchma .30 .75
17 Mike Larouche .30 .75
18 Tom Lawson MG .08 .25
19 Richard Lessard .30 .75
20 Gary Roberts 1.50 4.00
21 Jerry Scott .30 .75
22 John Shepherd PR .08 .25
23 Steve Simoni .30 .75
24 Greg Sliz .30 .75
25 Gord Thomas TR .08 .25
26 Chris Vickers .30 .75
27 Bert Weir .30 .75
28 Dennis Wigle .30 .75

1992-93 Ottawa 67's

Celebrating the 25th anniversary of the Ottawa 67's, this 24-card standard-size set features color posed and action player photos with purple borders. The player's name, position, and jersey number appear in a black vertical stripe on the left side of the card. The phrase "25th Anniversary" is printed at the bottom in large red and blue letters. The cards are unnumbered and checklisted below in alphabetical order.

COMPLETE SET (24) 4.80 12.00
1 Ken Belanger .30 .75
2 Curt Bowen .20 .50
3 Rich Bronilla .20 .50
4 Mathew Burnett .20 .50
5 Shawn Caplice .20 .50
6 Mike Carr .20 .50
7 Chris Coveny .20 .50
8 Howard Darwin (Founder) .08 .25
9 Shean Donovan .40 1.00
10 Mark Edmundson .20 .50
11 Billy Hall .20 .50
12 Mike Johnson .20 .50
13 Brian Kilrea GM/CO .20 .50
14 Grayson Lafoley .20 .50
15 Grant Marshall .40 1.00
16 Cory Murphy .20 .50
17 Mike Peca 1.25 3.00
18 Greg Ryan .20 .50
19 Jeff Salajko .20 .50
20 Gerry Skrypec .20 .50
21 Sean Spencer .20 .50
22 Steven Washburn .25 .60
23 Mark Yakabuski .20 .50
24 Title Card .08 .25

1999-00 Ottawa 67's

Released in 1999 by JOGO Incorporated, this full-color set features the Ottawa 67's of the OHL. Card backs contain black and white portraits and a short blurb about each player highlighting his career. The checklist card features a shot of the Memorial Cup winning 1998-99 Ottawa 67's.

COMPLETE SET (30) 4.80 12.00
1 Mark Bell .60 1.50
2 Matt Zultek .20 .50
3 Adam Chapman .08 .25
4 Miguel Delisle .30 .75
5 Randy Davidson .08 .25
6 Lance Galbraith .20 .50
7 Ian Jacobs .08 .25
8 Mike James .08 .25
9 Zenon Konopka .20 .50
10 Marc Lefebvre .08 .25
11 Joe Talbot .08 .25
12 Josh Tataryn .08 .25
13 Dan Tessier .20 .50
14 Vincent Grant .20 .50
15 Brendan Bell .08 .25
16 Chris Cava .08 .25
17 Kevin Malcolm .08 .25
18 Mike Gresdal .08 .25
19 Russ Moyer .08 .25
20 Luke Sellars .20 .50
21 Jeremy Van Hoof .20 .50
22 Jon Zion .30 .75
23 Seamus Kotyk .40 1.00
24 Lavente Szuper .40 1.00
25 Jeff Hunt .08 .25
26 Brian Kilrea HCO .20 .50
27 Bert O'Brien ACO .02 .10
28 Vince Mallette ACO .02 .10
29 Jeff Keech TR .02 .10
30 Checklist .02 .10

2000-01 Ottawa 67's

This thick-stock set was produced by Jogo, and sold by the team at its gift shop for $5. Production was limited to 3,000 copies. There are at least two spelling errors on the checklist card, neither of which were corrected.

COMPLETE SET (30) 4.80 12.00
1 Joe Talbot .20 .50
2 Lance Galbraith .20 .50
3 Jeremy Van Hoof .20 .50
4 Jon Zion .20 .50
5 Russ Moyer .16 .40
6 Pierre Mitsou .16 .40
7 Brendan Bell .20 .50
8 Adam Smyth .16 .40
9 Marc Lefebvre .16 .40
10 Sean Scully .16 .40
11 Brett McGrath .16 .40
12 Zenon Konopka .20 .50
13 Rodney Bauman .16 .40
14 Luke Sellars .20 .50
15 Miguel Delisle .20 .50
16 Vadim Sozinov .20 .50
17 Adam Chapman .16 .40
18 Bryan Rodney .16 .40
19 Sebastien Savage .16 .40
20 Seamus Kotyk .30 .75
21 John Ceci .16 .40
22 Vince Mallette CO .10 .25
23 Bert O'Brien CO .10 .25
24 Brian Kilrea CO .20 .50
25 Jeff Hunt OWN .04 .10
26 Riley & Killer Puck MASCOT .04 .10
27 Brian Kilrea 900 .20 .50
28 Doug Wilson .20 .50
29 Team Photo .20 .25
30 Team CL .10 .01

2001-02 Ottawa 67's

This set features the 67's of the OHL. The set was produced by Jogo and sold at the team's souvenir stand.

COMPLETE SET (30) 4.80 12.00
1 J.F. Perras .30 .75
2 Jon Ceci .20 .50
3 Karol Sloboda .20 .50
4 Carter Trevisani .20 .50
5 Jon Zion .30 .75
6 Russ Moyer .20 .50
7 Pierre Mitsou .20 .50
8 Adam Smyth .20 .50
9 Brendan Bell .30 .75
10 Matthew Albiani .20 .50
11 Lane Moodie .20 .50
12 Sean Scully .20 .50
13 Brett McGrath .20 .50
14 Zenon Konopka .30 .75
15 Rodney Bauman .20 .50
16 Miguel Delisle .20 .50
17 Jeremy Akeson .20 .50
18 Mark Mancari .20 .50
19 Adam Chapman .20 .50
20 Bryan Rodney .20 .50
21 Corey Locke .20 .50
22 Vince Mallette ACO .04 .10
23 Bert O'Brien ACO .04 .10
24 Brian Kilrea CO .20 .50
25 Jeff Hunt OWN .04 .10
26 Banner Ceremony .04 .10
27 Brad Marsh .20 .50
28 Riley and Riley Jr. .04 .10
29 Killer Puck .04 .10
30 Dance Team/ CL .20 .50

2002-03 Ottawa 67's

COMPLETE SET 5.00 12.00
1 Chris Hardill .30 .75
2 Karol Sloboda .20 .50
3 Carter Trevisani .20 .50
4 Will Colbert .20 .50
5 Russ Moyer .20 .50
6 Pierre Mitsou .20 .50
7 Adam Smyth .20 .50
8 Brendan Bell .30 .75
9 Matthew Albiani .20 .50
10 Lou Dickenson .20 .50
11 Scott Sheppard .20 .50
12 Bryan Bickell .20 .50
13 Sean Scully .20 .50
14 Peter Tsimikalis .20 .50
15 Rodney Bauman .20 .50
16 Kyle Wharton .20 .50
17 Jeremy Akeson .20 .50
18 Mark Mancari .20 .50
19 Julian Talbot .20 .50
20 Lukas Mensator .40 1.00
21 Matthew Foy .30 .75
22 Corey Locke .60 1.50
23 Jeff Hunt Owner .02 .10
24 Brian Kilrea HCO .10 .25
25 Bert O'Brien ACO .02 .10
26 Vince Malette ACO .02 .10
27 Mascot .02 .10
28 XFM Girls .10 .25
29 Mike Peca .20 .50
Brian Kilrea
30 Girl Guides of Canada .01 .01

2003-04 Ottawa 67's

COMPLETE SET (25) 6.00 15.00
1 Tyson Aitcheson .20 .50
2 Jeremy Akeson .20 .50
3 Matthew Albiani .20 .50
4 Danny Battochio .30 .75
5 Rodney Bauman .20 .50
6 Brodie Beard .20 .50
7 Bryan Bickell .20 .50
8 Will Colbert .20 .50
9 Greg Goodnough .20 .50
10 David Halasz .20 .50
11 Brad Hartley .20 .50
12 Robbie Lawrance .20 .50
13 Corey Locke .40 1.00
14 Mark Mancari .20 .50
15 Phil Mangan .20 .50
16 Lukas Mensator .40 1.00
17 Pierre Mitsou .20 .50
18 Elgin Reid .20 .50
19 Julian Talbot .20 .50
20 Brody Todd .20 .50
21 Peter Tsimikalis .20 .50
22 Kyle Wharton .20 .50
NNO Brian Kilrea CO .02 .10
NNO Corey Locke TL .75 2.00
NNO Lukas Mensator TL .75 2.00

2004-05 Ottawa 67's

A total of 1,000 team sets were produced.

COMPLETE (23) 12.00
1 Lukas Kaspar .50
2 Anthony Guadagnolo 1.00
3 Bryan Bickell .50
4 Brodie Beard .50
5 Pat Ouellette .50
6 Robbie Lawrance .50
7 Jeremy Akeson .50
8 Mark Mancari .50
9 Julian Talbot .50
10 Brad Bonello .50
11 Nick Van Herpt .50
12 Danny Battochio 1.50
13 Will Colbert .50
14 David Jarram .50
15 Brad Staubitz 1.00
16 Jamie Vanderveeken .50
17 Arron Alphonso .50
18 Derek Joslin .50
19 Elgin Reid .50
20 Jamie McGinn 1.00
21 Chris Hulit 1.00
22 Jakub Petruzalek .50
23 Matt Lahey .50

2005-06 Ottawa 67's

COMPLETE SET (25) 8.00 15.00
1 Julian Talbot .20 .50
2 Brodie Beard .20 .50
3 Bryan Bickell .20 .50
4 Pat Campbell .20 .50
5 Shea Kewin .20 .50
6 Thomas Kiriakou .20 .50
7 Robbie Lawrence .20 .50
8 Pat Ouellette .20 .50
9 Sean Ryan .20 .50
10 Jakub Vojta .20 .50
11 Brent MacKie .20 .50
12 Danny Battochio .40 1.00
13 Arron Alphonso .20 .50
14 Logan Couture 1.00 2.50
15 Pat Daley .20 .50
16 Chris Hulit .20 .50
17 Brady Morrison .40 1.00
18 Derek Joslin .20 .50
19 Matt Lahey .20 .50
20 Jamie McGinn .30 .75
21 Joe Pleckaitis .20 .50
22 Tibor Radulay .20 .50
23 Elgin Reid .20 .50
24 Joe Grimaldi .20 .50
25 Brett Liscomb .20 .50

2006-07 Ottawa 67s

COMPLETE SET (22) 8.00 15.00
1 Logan Couture .60 1.50
2 Scott Cowie .25 .60
3 Thomas Kiriakou .25 .60
4 Matt Lahey .25 .60
5 Cody Lindsay .25 .60
6 Brett Liscomb .40 1.00
7 Jamie Mcginn .40 1.00
8 Mathieu Methot .25 .60
9 Thomas Nesbitt .25 .60
10 Matt Ribeiro .25 .60
11 Brodie Beard .25 .60
12 Tyler Cuma .25 .60
13 Julien Demers .25 .60
14 Joe Grimaldi .25 .60
15 Derek Joslin .25 .60
16 Sean Ryan .25 .60
17 Jakub Vojta .25 .60
18 Arron Alphonso .25 .60
19 Jason Bailey .25 .60
20 Julian Cimadamore .25 .60
21 Lukas Flueler .40 1.00
22 Brady Morrison .40 1.00

2000-01 Owen Sound Attack

This set features the Attack of the OHL. The cards were produced by the team and sold at its souvenir stands. The cards are unnumbered and so are listed below in alphabetical order.

COMPLETE SET (26) 4.80 12.00
1 Michael Barrett .20 .50
2 Trevor Blanchard .20 .50
3 Luc Chiasson .20 .50
4 Richard Colwill .20 .50
5 Justin Day .30 .75
6 Kris Fraser .20 .50
7 Justin Hodgins .20 .50
8 Greg Jacina .20 .50
9 Bryan Kazarian .30 .75
10 Josh Legge .20 .50
11 Paul MacDermid CO .10 .25
12 Jason Nobili CO .10 .25
13 Brian O'Leary CO .10 .25
14 Dene Poulin .20 .50
15 Richard Power .20 .50
16 Corey Roberts .30 .75
17 Agris Saviels .30 .75
18 Ryan Sharp .20 .50
19 Daniel Sisca .20 .50
20 Shawn Snider .20 .50
21 Dan Sullivan .20 .50
22 Brandon Verner .20 .50
23 Nick Vukovic .20 .75
24 Joel Ward .20 .50
25 Bill Zalba .20 .50
26 Team Photo .20 .25

2001-02 Owen Sound Attack

This set features the Attack of the OHL. The cards were produced by the team and sold at its souvenir shop. The cards are unnumbered, and are listed below in alphabetical order.

COMPLETE SET (24) 4.80 12.00
1 Robert Chapman .20 .50
2 Richard Colwill .20 .50
3 Ryan Courtney .20 .50
4 David Dalliday .20 .50
5 Justin Day .30 .75
6 Jesse Gimblett .20 .50
7 Fred Hatziioannou .20 .50
8 Greg Jacina .30 .75
9 Michael Jacobsen .20 .50
10 Ladislav Kolda .20 .50
11 Jeff MacDermid .20 .50
12 Kyle McAllister .30 .75
13 Richard Power .20 .50
14 Justin Renner .30 .75
15 Brad Richardson .20 .50
16 Cory Roberts .30 .75
17 Dan Rogers .20 .50
18 Agris Saviels .30 .75
19 Ryan Sharp .20 .50
20 Daniel Sisca .20 .50
21 Sean Stefanski .20 .50
22 Dan Sullivan .20 .50
23 John Wheaton .20 .50
24 Tom Zanoski .20 .50

2002-03 Owen Sound Attack

COMPLETE SET (26) 5.00 12.00
1 Mascot .02 .10
2 Brett Howden .20 .50
3 Pat Sutton .20 .50
4 Jiri Paska .20 .50
5 Mark Giordano .20 .50
6 Patrick Jarrett .40 1.00
7 Dan Rogers .20 .50
8 Matt Passfield .20 .50
9 Tom Zanoski .20 .50
10 Jesse Gimblett .20 .50
11 Michael Gough .20 .50
12 Brad Richardson .20 .50
13 Andrew Maksym .20 .50
14 Steve Henwood .20 .50
15 Brett McGrath .20 .50
16 Justin Renner .20 .50
17 Ladislav Kolda .20 .50
18 John Weathon .20 .50
19 Fred Hatziioannou .20 .50
20 Jeff McDermid .20 .50
21 Miguel Delisle .20 .50
22 David Edgeworth .20 .50
23 Mike Angelidis .20 .50
24 Dan LaCosta .30 .75
25 Marty Magers .30 .75
26 Checklist .02 .10

2003-04 Owen Sound Attack

COMPLETE SET (25) 6.00 15.00
1 The Bear Cubby .01 .05
2 Matt Smyth .20 .50
3 Wes Cunningham .20 .50
4 Pat Sutton .20 .50
5 Justin Dacosta .20 .50
6 Mark Giordano .20 .50
7 Patrick Jarrett .30 .75
8 Bobby Ryan 1.50 4.00
9 Andrew Maksym .20 .50
10 Richard Hornseth .20 .50
11 Brad Richardson .20 .50
12 Kevin Baker .20 .50
13 Kevin Harvey .20 .50
14 Jonathan Lehun .20 .50
15 Pavel Voroshnin .30 .75
16 Andre Deveaux .20 .50
17 Jim Kehoe .20 .50
18 Stefan Ruzicka .40 1.00
19 Jeff MacDermid .20 .50
20 John Wires .20 .50
21 Adam Smyth .20 .50
22 Mike Angelidis .20 .50
23 Dan LaCosta .30 .75
24 Robert Gherson .30 .75
25 Checklist .01 .05

2004-05 Owen Sound Attack

A total of 500 team sets were produced.

COMPLETE SET (24) 6.00 15.00
1 Mike Angelidis .20 .50
2 Neil Conway .40 1.00
3 Igor Gongalsky .20 .50
4 Derek Brochu .20 .50
5 Brad Richardson .20 .50
6 Kevin Baker .20 .50
7 Matthew Kang .20 .50
8 Colin Hanley .20 .50
9 Jonathan Lehun .20 .50
10 Matt Smyth .20 .50
11 Bob Sanguinetti .40 1.00
12 Stefan Ruzicka .40 1.00
13 Theo Peckham .20 .50
14 Payton Liske .20 .50
15 Robin Big Snake .60 1.50
16 Andrej Sekera .20 .50
17 Dan Lacosta .20 .50
18 Wes Cunningham .20 .50
19 Trevor Koverko .40 1.00
20 Justin Dacosta .20 .50
21 Scott Giles .20 .50
22 Patrick Jarrett .30 .75
23 Bobby Ryan 1.50 4.00
24 Cubby MASCOT .02 .10

2005-06 Owen Sound Attack

COMPLETE SET (24) 8.00 15.00
1 Bobby Ryan .75 2.00
2 Neil Conway .40 1.00
3 Andrej Sekera .20 .50
4 Kyle Lamb .20 .50
5 Trevor Koverko .20 .50
6 Jeff Moor .20 .50
7 Scott Giles .20 .50
8 Igor Gongalsky .20 .50
9 Derek Brochu .20 .50
10 Scott Tregunna .20 .50
11 Josh Catto .20 .50
12 Jeff Kyrzakos .20 .50
13 Matthew Kang .20 .50
14 Zach McCullough .20 .50
15 Joshua Bailey .20 .50
16 Marcus Carroll .20 .50
17 Bob Sanguinetti .40 1.00
18 Theo Peckham .40 1.00
19 Marek Bartanus .20 .50
20 Payton Liske .20 .50
21 Mike Angelidis .20 .50
22 Miles Cope .20 .50
23 Justin Allen .20 .50
24 Kyle Knechtel .40 1.00

2006-07 Owen Sound Attack

COMPLETE SET (22) 8.00 15.00
1 Theo Peckham .20 .50
2 Michael D'orazio .20 .50
3 Neil Conway .40 1.00
4 Dalyn Flatt .20 .50
5 Andrew Shorkey .20 .50
6 David Kolomatis .20 .50
7 Guy Carteciano .20 .50
8 Bobby Ryan .75 2.00
9 Derek Brochu .20 .50
10 Scott Tregunna .20 .50
11 Lane Macdermid .20 .50
12 Thomas Stajan .20 .50
13 Wayne Simmonds .20 .50
14 Zach Mccullough .20 .50
15 Josh Bailey .20 .50
16 Michael Farrell .20 .50
17 Marcus Carroll .20 .50
18 Bobby Sanguinetti .40 1.00
19 Marek Bartanus .20 .50
20 Anton Hedman .20 .50
21 Trevor Lewis .60 1.50
22 Scott Bowles .40 1.00

1993-94 Owen Sound Platers

Sponsored by Domino's Pizza, The Eastwood Network, and The Sport Stop, this 36-card set measures the standard size. The fronts feature posed and action color player photos with white borders. The player's name and number appears in a black bar under the picture. The cards are unnumbered and checklisted below in alphabetical order.

COMPLETE SET (36) 8.00 20.00
1 Craig Binns .15 .40
2 Jim Brown .15 .40
3 Andrew Brunette .60 1.50
4 Luigi Calce .15 .40
5 Jason Campbell .15 .40
6 Draft Veterans .15 .40
Rod Hinks
Jason MacDonald
Kevin Weekes
Marian Kacir
7 Paddy Flynn ACO .02 .10
8 Kirk Furey .15 .40
9 Jerry Harrigan CO .02 .10
10 Joe Harris .15 .40
11 Rod Hinks .15 .40
12 Marian Kacir .15 .40
13 Shane Kenny .15 .40
14 Jeff Kostuch .15 .40
15 Dave Lemay .15 .40
16 Jason MacDonald .20 .50
17 Rick Mancini TR .02 .10
18 Kirk Maltby .40 1.00
19 Brian Medeiros .15 .40
20 Mike Morrone .15 .40
21 Ryan Mougenel .15 .40
22 Scott Penton .15 .40

23 Wayne Primeau .40 1.00
24 Jeremy Rebek .15 .40
25 Rob Schweyer .15 .40
26 Willie Skilliter .15 .40
27 Jamie Storr .60 1.50
28 Jamie Storr .60 1.50
Pure Gold
29 Jamie Storr's Mask .60 1.50
30 Jamie Storr .60 1.50
Wayne Primeau
Sure Picks
31 Scott Walker .40 1.00
32 Kevin Weekes .60 1.50
33 Kevin Weekes' Mask .40 1.00
34 Shayne Wright .15 .40
35 Title Card .02 .10
Domino's Ad Card
36 Title Card .02 .10
Eastwood Ad Card

1994-95 Owen Sound Platers

This set features the Platers of the OHL and was sponsored by Domino's Pizza. Frankly, that's about all we know on this one. Have any additional info? Send it to hockeymag@beckett.com.

COMPLETE SET (36) 6.00 15.00
1 Shawn Silver .20 .50
2 Shane Kenny .15 .40
3 Kevin Young .15 .40
4 Kirk Furey .15 .40
5 Peter MacKellar .15 .40
6 Willie Skilliter .15 .40
7 Joe Harris .15 .40
8 Brian Medeiros .15 .40
9 David Zunic .15 .40
10 Jeff Kostuch .15 .40
11 Jason Campbell .15 .40
12 Scott Smith .15 .40
13 Rob Schweyer .15 .40
14 Shayne Wright .15 .40
15 Scott Seiling .15 .40
16 Jeremy Rebek .15 .40
17 Rob Fitzgerald .15 .40
18 Ryan Mougenel .15 .40
19 John Argiropoulos .15 .40
20 Wayne Primeau .20 .50
21 Chris Wismer .15 .40
22 Matt Osborne .15 .40
23 Murray Hogg .15 .40
24 Brent Johnson 2.00 5.00
25 Jamie Storr (Jersey #31) .40 1.00
26 Jamie Storr (Jersey #92 .40 1.00
27 Jamie Storr (King Tut Mask) .40 1.00
28 Jamie Storr Draft .40 1.00
28 Wayne Primeau Draft .20 .50
28 Shayne Wright Draft .15 .40
29 Wayne Primeau Prime Time .20 .50
30 Coaching Staff .04 .10
31 Larry Gibson SB .04 .10
32 Joel Traplin TR .04 .10
33 Broadcast Team .04 .10
34 Ed Schambers Bus Dr. .04 .10
35 Domino's Pizza .01 .02
36 Jim Gardhouse Motors .01 .02

1995-96 Owen Sound Platers

This set features the Platers of the OHL. The set was produced by the team and sold at its souvenir stands.

COMPLETE SET (36) 4.80 12.00
1 Team Photo Card .15 .40
2 Ric Seiling CO .02 .10
3 Gus Eyers CO .02 .10
4 Brian Warrilow CO .02 .10
5 Rick Mancini TR .02 .10
6 Wayne Primeau .20 .50
7 Shawn Gallant .15 .40
8 Shane Kenny .15 .40
9 Chris Biagini .15 .40
10 Marek Babic .15 .40
11 Oleg Tsirkounov .15 .40
12 Peter MacKellar .15 .40
13 Ryan Davis .15 .40
14 John Argiropoulos .15 .40
15 Jason Campbell .15 .40
16 Dan Snyder .40 1.00
17 Steve Gallace .15 .40
18 Scott Seiling .15 .40
19 Jeremy Rebek .15 .40
20 Adam Mair .20 .50
21 Ryan Christie .20 .50
22 Larry Paleczny .20 .50
23 Wayne Primeau .20 .50
24 Chris Wismer .15 .40
25 Matt Osborne .15 .40
26 Mike Loach .15 .40
27 Brent Johnson .75 2.00
28 Jim Ensom .15 .40
29 Brent Johnson .75 2.00
30 Mike Loach .15 .40
31 Jim Ensom .15 .40
32 Wayne Primeau .20 .50
33 Shane Kenny .15 .40
34 Sun Times News .01
35 Jim Gardhouse Motors .01
36 Domino's Pizza .01

1996-97 Owen Sound Platers

This set features the Platers of the OHL. The set was produced by the team and sold at its souvenir stands.

COMPLETE SET (27) 15.00
1 John Lovell CO .02 .10
2 Brian O'Leary CO .02 .10
3 Curtis Sanford .60 1.50
4 Shawn Gallant .15 .40
5 Brent Johnson .75 2.00
6 Joel Dezainde .15 .40
7 Kyle Dafoe .15 .40
8 Kyle Flaxey .15 .40
9 Matt Osborne .15 .40
10 Jamie Sokolsky .15 .40
11 Kurt Walsh .15 .40
12 Andrew Williamson .15 .40
13 Ryan Davis .15 .40
14 Sean Avery .75 2.00
15 Paul Daze .15 .40
16 Dan Snyder .40 1.00
17 Steve Gallace .15 .40
18 Scott Wray .15 .40
19 Adam Mair .30 .75
20 Larry Paleczny .20 .50
21 Ryan Christie .15 .40
22 Chris Wismer .15 .40
23 Todd Miller .15 .40
24 Adam Campbell .15 .40
25 Jason Doyle .30 .75
26 Wes Goldie .15 .40
27 Owen Sound Platers .15 .40

1997-98 Owen Sound Platers

This set features the Platers of the OHL. The set was produced by the team and sold at home games.

COMPLETE SET (26) 4.80 12.00
1 Owen Sound Platers .20 .50
2 Curtis Sanford .30 .75
3 Adam Campbell .20 .50
4 Kyle Dafoe .20 .50
5 Kyle Flaxey .20 .50
6 Chris Hopiavuori .20 .50
7 Jamie Sokolsky .20 .50
8 Colin Beardsmore .20 .50
9 Dave Stephenson .20 .50
10 Ryan Davis .20 .50
11 Ryan Rivard .20 .50
12 Sean Avery .75 2.00
13 Dan Snyder .40 1.00
14 Wes Goldie .20 .50
15 Adam Mair .30 .75
16 Larry Paleczny .20 .50
17 Ryan Christie .20 .50
18 Randy Davidson .20 .50
19 Joel Ward .20 .50
20 Chris Wismer .20 .50
21 Jason Doyle .30 .75
22 Brendan Brooks .20 .50
23 Adam Collins .20 .50
24 Eoin McInerney .40 1.00
25 Brian O'Leary CO .08 .25
26 Kirk Maltby .30 .75

1998-99 Owen Sound Platers

This set features the Platers of the OHL. It is believed that the set was produced by the team and sold at its souvenir stands.

COMPLETE SET (28) 4.80 12.00
1 Owen Sound Platers .08 .25
2 Curtis Sanford .40 1.00
3 Mike Barrett .15 .40
4 Kyle Flaxey .15 .40
5 Chris Hopiavuori .20 .50
6 Mike Dombkiewicz .15 .40
7 Jeff Kaufman .15 .40
8 Dave Stephenson .15 .40
9 Chris Minard .30 .75
10 Stephane Savage .15 .40
11 Sean Avery .40 1.00
12 Peter Campbell .15 .40
13 Dan Snyder .40 1.00
14 Jan Sulc .15 .40
15 Wes Goldie .30 .75
16 Adam Mair .30 .75
17 Chad Woollard .20 .50
18 Stephen Lafleur .20 .50
19 Randy Davidson .20 .50
20 Joel Ward .20 .50
21 Juri Golicic .20 .50
22 Bryan Kazarian .20 .50
23 Nick Vukovic .30 .75
24 Brent Sullivan .15 .40
25 Adam Campbell .15 .40
26 Corey Roberts .15 .40
27 Adam Mair .30 .75
28 Coaches .02 .10

1999-00 Owen Sound Platers

This 31-card set features the OHL's Platers. Cards feature full color action shots and a black border along the bottom that contains the player's name, position, number, and team logo. These cards are not numbered, therefore they appear in the order they came out of the sealed set.

COMPLETE SET (31) 4.00 10.00
1 Brian O'Leary ACO .02 .10
2 Dave Siciliano HCO .02 .10
3 Michael Barrett .15 .40
4 Kenny Corupe .20 .50
5 Tim Hamel .15 .40
6 Curtis Sanford .40 1.00
7 Agris Saviels .20 .50
8 Joel Ward .15 .40
9 Bill Zalba .15 .40
10 Matt Rock .15 .40
11 Mike Lymer .15 .40
12 Adam Campbell .15 .40
13 Chris Hopiavuori .15 .40
14 Mike Dombkiewicz .15 .40
15 Cory Roberts .20 .50
16 Greg Jacina .20 .50
17 Wes Goldie .20 .50
18 Dave Stephenson .15 .40
19 Daniel Sisca .15 .40
20 Bryan Kazarian .30 .75
21 Kyle McAllister .30 .75
22 Shawn Snider .15 .40
23 Trevor Blanchard .15 .40
24 Derek Campbell .15 .40
25 Jason Kowalski .15 .40
26 Brent Sullivan .15 .40
27 Alexei Salaschenko .15 .40
28 Nick Vukovic .15 .40
29 Kris Fraser .15 .40
30 Chris Minard .15 .40
31 Team Photo .02 .10

2003-04 Pacific AHL Prospects

COMPLETE SET 15.00 40.00
1 Ari Ahonen .40 1.00
2 Adrian Foster .20 .50
3 Tuomas Pihlman .20 .50
4 Aleksander Suglobov .20 .50
5 Ray Emery .75 2.00
6 Alexandre Giroux .20 .50
7 Chris Kelly .20 .50
8 Julien Vauclair .20 .50
9 Wade Dubielewicz .40 1.00
10 Jeff Hamilton .20 .50
11 Justin Mapletoft .20 .50
12 Mattias Weinhandl .20 .50
13 Kari Lehtonen 2.00 5.00
14 Tommi Santala .20 .50
15 Karl Stewart .20 .50
16 Ilja Bryzgalov .40 1.00
17 Chris Kunitz .40 1.00
18 Tony Martensson .20 .50
19 Brad Boyes .40 1.00
20 Marcel Goc .30 .75
21 Seamus Kotyk .40 1.00
22 Garrett Stafford .20 .50
23 Miroslav Zalesak .30 .75
24 Jiri Hudler .75 2.00
25 Niklas Kronwall .40 1.00
26 Marc Lamothe .40 1.00
27 Nathan Robinson .20 .50
28 Benoit Gratton .20 .50
29 Alexander Perezhogin .40 1.00
30 Tomas Plekanec .40 1.00
31 Eero Somervuori .20 .50
32 Jozef Balej .40 1.00
33 Jason LaBarbera .60 1.50
34 Dominic Moore .30 .75
35 Fedor Tyutin .30 .75
36 Layne Ulmer .20 .50
37 Chad Wiseman .20 .50
38 Peter Budaj .60 1.50
39 Eric Perrin .40 1.00
40 Dan Cavanaugh .20 .50
41 Kyle Wanvig .40 1.00
42 Patrick DesRochers .30 .75
43 Dany Sabourin .40 1.00
44 Mike Zigomanis .20 .50
45 Scott Barney .20 .50
46 Mathieu Chouinard .40 1.00
47 Noah Clarke .20 .50
48 Denis Grebeshkov .20 .50
49 Adam Hauser .75 2.00
50 Steve Kelly .20 .50
51 Yanick Lehoux .20 .50
52 Pavel Rosa .20 .50
53 Fedor Fedorov .40 1.00
54 Kirill Koltsov .20 .50
55 Brandon Reid .40 1.00
56 Simon Gamache .40 1.00
57 Darren Haydar .40 1.00
58 Andrew Hutchinson .20 .50
59 Timofei Shishkanov .20 .50
60 Scottie Upshall EXISTS?
61 Anton Babchuk .20 .50
62 Matt Ellison .20 .50
63 Kirby Law .20 .50
64 Antero Niittymaki .40 1.00
65 Graham Mink .20 .50
66 Maxime Ouellet .40 1.00
67 Pat Leahy .20 .50
68 Colton Orr .40 1.00
69 Hannu Toivonen .75 2.00
70 Ryan Miller 1.25 3.00
71 Jason Pominville .60 1.50
72 Eric Beaudoin .20 .50
73 Mike Green .20 .50
74 Lukas Krajicek .20 .50
75 Denis Shvidki .20 .50
76 Petr Taticek .20 .50
77 David LeNeveu .40 1.00
78 Fredrik Sjostrom .40 1.00
79 Jeff Taffe .20 .50
80 Brendan Bell .20 .50
81 Sebastien Centomo .40 1.00
82 Mikael Tellqvist .60 1.50
83 Kyle Wellwood .40 1.00
84 Tim Jackman .20 .50
85 Aaron Johnson .20 .50
86 Pascal Leclaire .40 1.00
87 Brad Moran .20 .50
88 Doug Lynch .20 .50
89 Mike Morrison .40 1.00
90 Jani Rita .20 .50
91 Steve Valiquette .40 1.00
92 Jason Bacashihua .40 1.00
93 Dan Jancevski .20 .50
94 Colby Armstrong .40 1.00
95 Andy Chiodo .40 1.00
96 Michel Ouellet .40 1.00
97 Michal Sivek .20 .50
98 Jay McClement .20 .50
99 Johnny Pohl .20 .50
100 Peter Sejna .20 .50

2003-04 Pacific AHL Prospects Gold

*GOLD: 2X TO 5X BASE HI
PRINT RUN 925 SER.#'d SETS

2003-04 Pacific AHL Prospects Autographs

COMMON CARD (1-6)
PRINT RUN 500 SER.#'d SETS
1 Kari Lehtonen 15.00 40.00
2 Ryan Miller 12.50 30.00
3 Wade Dubielewicz 12.50 30.00
4 David LeNeveu 12.50 30.00
5 Ari Ahonen 15.00 40.00
6 Pascal Leclaire 12.50 30.00

2003-04 Pacific AHL Prospects Crease Lightning

STATED ODDS 1:10
1 Ari Ahonen 1.50 4.00
2 Kari Lehtonen 3.00 8.00
3 Phil Sauve 1.50 4.00
4 Alex Auld 1.50 4.00
5 Rastislav Stana 2.50 6.00
6 Andrew Raycroft 3.00 8.00
7 Ryan Miller 2.50 6.00
8 Pascal Leclaire 2.00 5.00

2003-04 Pacific AHL Prospects Destined for Greatness

COMMON CARD (1-10) 1.25 3.00
STATED ODDS 1:5
1 Jason Spezza 3.00 8.00
2 Antoine Vermette 1.25 3.00
3 Rick DiPietro 1.25 3.00
4 Trent Hunter 2.50 6.00
5 Jonathan Cheechoo 3.00 8.00
6 Jiri Hudler 1.50 4.00
7 Michael Ryder 2.00 5.00
8 Jason King 1.25 3.00
9 Carlo Colaiacovo 1.25 3.00
10 Peter Sejna 1.25 3.00

2003-04 Pacific AHL Prospects Jerseys

STATED ODDS ONE PER HOBBY BOX
1 Wade Dubielewicz 10.00 25.00
2 Jeff Hamilton 6.00 15.00
3 Tomas Plekanec 5.00 12.00
4 Denis Shvidki 5.00 12.00
5 David LeNeveu 8.00 20.00
6 Matt Murley 8.00 20.00

1995-96 PEI Senators

This set features the Senators of the AHL. These postcard-sized (5X7) collectibles are blank backed and are believed to have been issued as a promotional giveaway.

COMPLETE SET (24) 6.00 15.00
1 Scott Allison .20 .50
2 Radim Bicanek .20 .50
3 Patrick Charbonneau .20 .50
4 Pavol Demitra 1.25 3.00
5 Cosmo Dupaul .20 .50
6 Daniel Guerard .20 .50
7 Steve Guolla .30 .75
8 Shawn Heaphy .20 .50
9 Justin Hocking .20 .50
10 Martin Lamarche .20 .50
11 Eric Lavigne .20 .50
12 Kaj Linna .30 .75
13 Darrin Madeley .30 .75
14 Chad Penney .20 .50
15 Michel Picard .20 .50
16 Lance Pitlick .30 .75
17 Jean-Yves Roy .30 .75
18 Claude Savoie .20 .50
19 Darcy Simon .20 .50
20 Steve Strunk .20 .50
21 Patrick Traverse .20 .50
22 Jason Zent .20 .50
23 Coaching Staff .08 .25
24 Brutus MAS .02 .10

2003-04 P.E.I. Rocket

COMPLETE SET (24) 5.00 12.00
1 Julien Beaulieu .20 .50
2 Jimmy Bonneru .20 .50
3 Jonathan Boutin .30 .75
4 Pierre-Andre Bureau .20 .50
5 Yanick Charron .20 .50
6 Marc-Andre Gragnani .20 .50
7 Tyler Hawes .20 .50
8 Milan Hruska .20 .50
9 David Laliberte .20 .50
10 Michael Lambert .20 .50
11 Mark Lee .20 .50
12 Fabien Laniel .20 .50
13 Maxim Lapierre .20 .50
14 Jeff Macauley .20 .50
15 Tyler Noye .20 .50
16 Brent Maclellan .20 .50
17 Ryan Mior .30 .75
18 Sebastien Nolet .30 .75
19 Steve Pelletier .20 .50
20 Jonathan Persson .20 .50
21 Jean-Francois Roux .20 .50
22 Dominic Soucy .20 .50
23 Steve Tilley .20 .50
24 Cory Urquhart .20 .50

2004-05 P.E.I. Rocket

A total of 400 team sets were produced. Card #23 does not exist.

COMPLETE SET (30) 5.00 12.00
1 Alexandre Boivin .15 .40
2 Anthony Potobschnik .15 .40
3 Billy Bezeau .15 .40
4 Connor MacDonald .15 .40
5 David Laliberte .15 .40
6 David MacDonald .15 .40
7 Dominic Soucy .15 .40
8 Greg O'Brien .15 .40
9 Jimmy Bonneau .15 .40
10 Jonathan Boutin .40 1.00
11 Julien Beaulieu .15 .40
12 Kris MacDonald .15 .40
13 Marc-Andre Gragnani .15 .40
14 Maxim Lapierre .15 .40
15 Michael Dubuc .15 .40
16 Michel Charette .15 .40
17 Pierre-Andre Bureau .15 .40
18 Riku Korpinen .15 .40
19 Ryan Mior .40 1.00
20 Tyler Hawes .15 .40
21 Viatcheslav Trukhno .30 .75
22 Yanick Charron .15 .40
24 Kevin Hamel .15 .40
25 Alexander Ennaffati .15 .40
26 Pierre Bergeron .15 .40
27 Jean-Francois Boucher .15 .40
28 Jean-Francois Bernard .40 1.00
29 Fabien Laniel .15 .40
30 Louis-Philippe Lachance .15 .40
31 Alain Vigneault CO .15 .40

2005-06 PEI Rocket

COMPLETE SET (29) 6.00 15.00
1 Ryan Mior .40 1.00
2 Stephen Lund .20 .50
3 Louis-Phillippe LaChance .20 .50
4 Travis Mealy .20 .50
5 Nathan Snowie .20 .50
6 Alexandre Boivin .20 .50
7 Geoff Walker .20 .50
8 Slava Trukhno .40 1.00
9 Greg O'Brien .20 .50
10 Stanson Donovan .20 .50
11 David Laliberte .20 .50
12 Devan Praught .20 .50
13 Olivier Gauthier .20 .50
14 Tyler Hawes .20 .50
15 Anton Skorykh .20 .50
16 Lucasz Steciuk .20 .50
17 Nicolas Leduc .20 .50
18 Jean-Claude Milot .20 .50
19 Joseph Haddad .20 .50
20 Michael Dubuc .20 .50
21 Chad Locke .20 .50
22 Steve Nalywary .20 .50
23 Matthew LaChaine .20 .50
24 Antoine Lafleur .40 1.00
25 Simon Bolduc .20 .50
26 David MacDonald .20 .50
27 Pascal Lebel .20 .50
28 Marc-Andre Gragnani .20 .50
29 Danny Stewart .20 .50

2006-07 PEI Rocket

COMPLETE SET (23) 8.00 15.00
1 David Laliberte .25 .60
2 Geoff Walker .25 .60
3 Ryan Mior .30 .75
4 Antoine Lafleur .50 1.25
5 Stephen Lund .25 .60
6 Pierre-Marc Guilbault .25 .60
7 Jordon Southorn .25 .60
8 Pierre-Luc Lessard .25 .60
9 Marc-Andre Gragnani .40 1.00
10 Pascal Boutin .25 .60
11 Chris Doyle .25 .60
12 Martin Latal .25 .60
13 Guillaume Doucet .25 .60
14 Lucas Mckinley .25 .60
15 Devan Praught .25 .60
16 Benoit Levesque .25 .60
17 Tyles Hawes .25 .60
18 Peter Cmorej .25 .60
19 Matthew Lachaine .25 .60
20 Maxim Cliché .25 .60
21 Joey Haddad .25 .60
22 Chad Locke .25 .60
23 Gregory Paynter .25 .60

2002-03 Pee Dee Pride RBI

COMPLETE SET (18) 8.00 20.00
133 B.J. Adams .40 1.00
134 Daniel Carriere .40 1.00
135 Aaron Gates .40 1.00
136 Mike Glumac .60 1.50
137 Wes Goldie .40 1.00
138 Derek Halldorson .40 1.00
139 Kyle Kidney .40 1.00
140 Gregor Krajnc .40 1.00
141 Ryan Knox .40 1.00
142 Eric Naud .40 1.00
143 Jason Metcalfe .40 1.00
144 Matt Reid .40 1.00
145 Jason Robinson .40 1.00
146 Greg Schmidt .40 1.00
147 Allan Sirois .40 1.00
148 Mike Torney .40 1.00
149 Matt Underhill .40 1.00
150 Ron Vogel .75 2.00

1996-97 Pensacola Ice Pilots

This set features the Ice Pilots of the ECHL. The standard-sized cards were produced by DLUX printing and sold by the team at home games.

COMPLETE SET (24) 4.00 10.00
1 Craig Brown .15 .40
2 Stephane Julien .15 .40
3 David Borrozino .15 .40
4 Jeremy Mylymok .15 .40
5 Patrik Alvin .15 .40
6 Rostislav Saglo .15 .40
7 Glen Metropolit .40 1.00
8 Chad Quenneville .15 .40
9 Trevor Buchanan .15 .40
10 Brandon Gray .15 .40
11 Jon Pirrong .30 .75
12 Brent Gretzky .30 .75
13 Martin LaChaine .15 .40
14 Brian Secord .15 .40
15 Hugo Belanger .15 .40
16 Christian Sbrocca .15 .40
17 Tony Prpic .15 .40
18 Shane Calder .15 .40
19 Nick Stajduhar .15 .40
20 Brendan Concannon .15 .40
21 Sean Gauthier .20 .50
22 Al Pederson CO .15 .40
23 George Kozak .15 .40
NNO Header Card .02 .10

1997-98 Pensacola Ice Pilots

This 25-card set features the Ice Pilots of the ECHL. The set apparently was handed out at as a promotional item at several late-season games.

COMPLETE SET (25) 4.80 12.00
1 Team Photo .20 .50
2 J.F. Aube .30 .75
3 Craig Brown .20 .50
4 Michael Burkett .20 .50
5 Shane Calder .20 .50
6 Martin Chouinard .20 .50
7 Brendan Concannon .20 .50
8 Jon Dunmar .20 .50
9 Sean Gauthier .20 .50
10 Christian Gosselin .20 .50
11 Brian LaFleur .20 .50
12 Steven Low .20 .50
13 Scott Malone .20 .50
14 Mike Mayhew .20 .50
15 Keith O'Connell .20 .50
16 Val Passarelli .30 .75
17 Mark Polak .20 .50
18 Chad Quenneville .20 .50
19 Andrew Rodgers .20 .50
20 Nick Stajduhar .20 .50
21 Mike Sullivan .20 .50
22 Kelly Hultgren .20 .50
23 George Kozak ACO .02 .10
24 Allen Pedersen HCO .02 .10
25 D-Lux Printing .02 .10

1998-99 Pensacola Ice Pilots

This set features the Ice Pilots of the ECHL. According to various sources, the sets were intended to be issued as a promotional giveaway, but legal or financial issues forced cancellation of those plans. Several players and team officials were given sets, however, and some have made their way into the secondary market. Because of the nature of this distribution, there is not enough market activity to accurately price these cards. They are checklisted below without values.

COMPLETE SET(27)
1 Shane Calder
2 Nick Stajduhar
3 Etienne Beaudry
4 Bob Wilkie
5 Don Chase
6 Stephen Naughton
7 Chad Quenneville
8 Keith O'Connell
9 Brendan Concannon
10 Keli Corpse
11 Andrew Rodgers
12 Dave Ivaska
13 Rob Phillips
14 Mark Polak
15 Craig Brown
16 Tom Noble
17 Eon MacFarlane
18 Allen Pedersen CO
19 George Kosak CO
20 Iceman MAS
21 Pensacola Ice Pilots
22 The Hangar
23 Pensacola Ice Pilots
24 Kelly Hultgren
25 Mike Sullivan
26 Pensacola Ice Pilots CL
27 PHPA Web Site

2003-04 Pensacola Ice Pilots

This set was produced by RBI Sports with a production run limited to 250 copies. The numbering sequence reflects the entire run of RBI sets that season.

COMPLETE SET (16) 8.00 20.00
337 Tyler Beechey .40 1.00
338 Greg Chambers .40 1.00
339 Brian Collins .40 1.00
340 Brad Cruikshank .40 1.00
341 Brian Eklund .75 2.00
342 Brandon Fleenor .40 1.00
343 Brett Gibson .40 1.00
344 Jade Galbraith .40 1.00
345 Aaron Gionet .40 1.00
346 Dwayne Hay .40 1.00
347 Andreas Holmqvist .40 1.00
348 Evgeny Konstantinov .75 2.00
349 Wes Mason .40 1.00
350 Corey Neilson .75 2.00
351 Aaron Phillips .40 1.00
352 Kent Sauer .40 1.00

2004-05 Penticton Vees

The Vees play in the BC Tier 2 Junior League.

COMPLETE SET (25) 15.00
1 History Card .01 .05
2 Checklist .01 .05
3 Josh Brown .30 .75
4 Aaron Agnew .30 .75
5 Ben Robinson .30 .75
6 Brian Lebler .30 .75
7 Shaun MacDonald .30 .75
8 Ryan Coghlan .60 1.50
9 Jon Cara .30 .75
10 Colin Williams .30 .75
11 Mike Towns .30 .75
12 Jason Harding .30 .75
13 Kevin Borba .60 1.50
14 Cody Collins .30 .75
15 Alex MacLeod .30 .75
16 Chris Rengert .30 .75
17 Peter Farrell .30 .75
18 Justin Coutu .30 .75
19 John Kopp .30 .75
20 Adrian Jack .30 .75
21 Brad Thiessen .30 .75
22 Corey Milan .60 1.50
23 Bruno Campese CO .02 .10
24 Ken Law ACO .02 .10
25 Dan Marshall ANN .02 .10

2005-06 Penticton Vees

COMPLETE SET (24) 10.00 20.00
1 Brennan Barker .40 1.00
2 Jordan Cheveldave .40 1.00
3 Ryan Costanzo .40 1.00
4 Deron Cousens .40 1.00
5 Peter Farrell .40 1.00
6 Tanner House .40 1.00
7 John Kopp .40 1.00
8 Justin Krueger .40 1.00
9 Brian Lebler .40 1.00
10 Alex MacLeod .40 1.00
11 Corey Milan .40 1.00
12 T.J. Miller .40 1.00
13 Ivo Musa .40 1.00
14 Lee Pagee .40 1.00
15 Ben Robinson .40 1.00
16 Robert Skinner .40 1.00
17 Gary Sylvester .40 1.00
18 Mike Towns .40 1.00
19 Evan Trupp .40 1.00
20 Ryan Wagner .40 1.00
21 Mark Walters .40 1.00
22 Jordan White .40 1.00
23 Bruno Campese CO .10 .25
24 1986 Penticton Knights .10 .25

2006-07 Penticton Vees

COMPLETE SET (25) 12.00 20.00
1 Jeremy Beller .30 .75
2 Travis Briard .30 .75
3 Steve Cameron .30 .75
4 Deron Cousens .30 .75
5 Brad Davis .30 .75
6 Dustin Donaghy .30 .75
7 Nigel Dube .30 .75
8 Joel Eisenkirch .30 .75
9 Jordan Funk .30 .75
10 Elias Grossmann .30 .75
11 Michael Guzzo .30 .75
12 Brett Hextall .30 .75
13 Tanner House .30 .75
14 Alex MacLeod .30 .75
15 Kyle McMurphy .30 .75
16 Corey Milan .30 .75
17 Bryant Molle .40 1.00
18 Robert Skinner .30 .75
19 Evan Smith .30 .75
20 Gary Sylvester .30 .75
21 Mike Towns .30 .75
22 Evan Trupp .30 .75
23 Ryan Wagner .30 .75
24 Bruno Campese HC .30 .75
25 72-73 Penticton Broncos Team Photo .30 .75

2007-08 Penticton Vees

COMPLETE SET (21) 5.00 12.00
1 James Bettauer .25 .60
2 Zak Dalpe .25 .60
3 Alex Evin .25 .60
4 Elias Grossmann .25 .60
5 Michael Guzzo .25 .60
6 Michael Hengen .25 .60
7 Brett Hextall .25 .60
8 Zack Josepher .25 .60
9 Nic Knudsen .25 .60
10 Devon Krogh .25 .60
11 Eric Kroshus .25 .60
12 Mitch Labreche .25 .60
13 Denver Manderson .25 .60
14 Kyle McMurphy .25 .60
15 Bryan Mountain .25 .60
16 Trevor Nill .25 .60
17 Cory Schneider .50 1.25
18 Austin Smith .25 .60
19 Ryan Wagner .25 .60
20 Nathan Westover .25 .60
21 Fred Harbinson HC .15 .40

1992-93 Peoria Rivermen

Sponsored by Coca-Cola and Kroger, this 30-card set measures the standard size. The fronts feature color player photos with a white border. The team logo, the player's name, and position appear in a gray bar under the photo, while "1992" is printed in white letters on a blue triangle in the top right corner of the photo. The cards are unnumbered and checklisted below in alphabetical order.

COMPLETE SET (30) 4.00 10.00
1 Jeff Batters .15 .40
2 Parris Duffus .20 .50
3 Greg Eberle TR .02 .10
4 John Faginkrantz MG .02 .10
5 Denny Felsner .15 .40
6 Derek Frenette .15 .40
7 Ron Handy .15 .40
8 Joe Hawley .15 .40
9 Terry Hollinger .15 .40
10 Ron Hoover .15 .40
11 Daniel Laperriere .20 .50
12 Lee J. Leslie .15 .40
13 Dave Mackey .15 .40
14 Jason Marshall .20 .50
15 Brian McKee .15 .40
16 Rick Meagher CO .15 .40
17 Kevin Miehm .15 .40

18 Brian Pellerin ACO	.02	.10
19 Mark Reeds	.15	.40
20 Kyle Reeves	.15	.40
21 Rob Robinson	.15	.40
22 Jason Ruff	.15	.40
23 Geoff Sarjeant	.30	.75
24 Richard Pion	.15	.40
25 Darren Veitch	.15	.40
26 Doug Wickenheiser	.15	.40
27 Shawn Wheeler	.15	.40
28 Checklist	.02	.10
29 Coca Cola Coupon	.02	.10
30 Title Card	.02	.10

1993-94 Peoria Rivermen

Produced by 1993 Hat Tricks, Inc., this 31-card D.A.R.E. (Drug Abuse Resistance Education) set measures approximately 2 3/8" by 3 1/4" and celebrates the tenth anniversary of the Peoria Rivermen (International Hockey League). The fronts feature full-bleed color action photos, except at the bottom where an orange stripe separates a thicker blue stripe carrying player information. The 10th anniversary logo in the lower right corner completes the front. The cards are unnumbered and checklisted below in alphabetical order.

COMPLETE SET (31)	4.00	10.00
1 Mark Bassen	.15	.40
2 Jeff Batters	.15	.40
3 Rene Chapdelaine	.15	.40
4 Doug Crossman	.20	.50
5 Parris Duffus	.30	.75
6 Greg Eberle TR	.02	.10
7 Doug Evans	.15	.40
8 Kevin Evans	.15	.40
9 John Faginkrantz EQMG	.02	.10
10 Denny Felsner	.15	.40
11 Derek Frenette	.15	.40
12 Terry Hollinger	.15	.40
13 Ron Hoover	.15	.40
14 Butch Kaebel	.15	.40
15 Nathan Lafayette	.15	.40
16 Dan Laperriere	.20	.50
17 Dave Mackey	.15	.40
18 Paul MacLean CO	.15	.40
19 Michel Mongeau	.20	.50
20 Brian Pellerin	.15	.40
21 Rick Pion	.15	.40
22 Vitali Prokhorov	.15	.40
23 Mark Reeds ACO	.02	.10
24 John Roderick	.15	.40
25 Geoff Sarjeant	.30	.75
26 Steve Staios	.20	.50
27 Darren Veitch	.15	.40
28 Nick Vitucci	.30	.75
29 Title card	.02	.10
30 Checklist	.02	.10
31 Alcohol Awareness	.02	.10

1995-96 Peoria Rivermen

This standard-sized, 24-card set was produced by the Rivermen and offered for sale through the club at games and by mail. The cards are unnumbered and listed below in alphabetical order.

COMPLETE SET (24)	4.00	10.00
1 Jon Casey	.30	.75
2 Rene Chapdelaine	.20	.50
3 Doug Evans	.20	.50
4 Eric Fenton	.20	.50
5 Shannon Finn	.15	.40
6 Martin Hamrlik	.15	.40
7 Ron Hoover	.15	.40
8 Jacques Joubert	.15	.40
9 Lee J. Leslie	.20	.50
10 Dave MacIntyre	.20	.50
11 Jason Miller	.15	.40
12 Michel Mongeau	.30	.75
13 Glenn Mulvenna	.20	.50
14 Eric Murano	.15	.40
15 Keith Osborne	.20	.50
16 Greg Paslawski	.20	.50
17 Jon Pratt	.15	.40
18 Dan Ratushny	.20	.50
19 Patrice Robitaille	.20	.50
20 Paul Taylor	.15	.40
21 Travis Thiessen	.15	.40
22 Steve Thornton	.15	.40
23 Kirk Tomlinson	.20	.50
24 Steve Wilson	.15	.40

1996-97 Peoria Rivermen

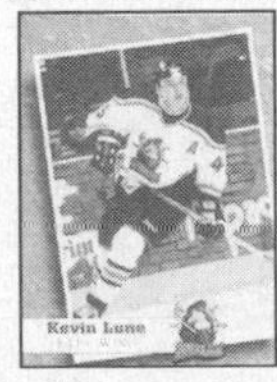

This 25-card set marks the debut of the Rivermen as a member club of the ECHL, but continues the tradition of fine sets. The cards feature action photos on the front, and full stats and bio on the reverse. The unnumbered cards are listed below in alphabetical order.

COMPLETE SET (25)	4.00	10.00
1 Mike Barrie	.20	.50
2 Doug Bonner	.30	.75
3 Greg Eberle/John Krouse	.02	.10
4 Brad Essex	.15	.40
5 Doug Evans ASST CO	.02	.10
6 Liam Garvey	.15	.40
7 Trevor Hanas	.15	.40
8 Jon Hillebrandt	.30	.75
9 Dan Hodge	.20	.50
10 Butch Kaebel	.15	.40
11 Karson Kaebel	.15	.40
12 Justin Krall	.15	.40
13 Jeff Kungle	.15	.40
14 Kevin Lune	.15	.40
15 Darren Maloney	.15	.40
16 Dustin McArthur	.15	.40
17 Jon Pratt	.15	.40
18 Brad Purdie	.15	.40
19 Mark Reeds CO	.02	.10
20 Jason Saal	.30	.75
21 Jan Slavik	.15	.40
22 Marc Terris	.15	.40
23 Jean-Guy Trudel	.20	.50
24 Paul Vincent	.20	.50
25 Title Card	.02	.10

1996-97 Peoria Rivermen Photo Album

This 24-card set was released in perforated album form as a game night promotional giveaway. The cards are unnumbered and therefore are listed below in alphabetical order.

COMPLETE SET (24)	8.00	20.00
1 Mike Barrie	.30	.75
2 Doug Bonner	.60	1.50
3 Greg Eberle TR	.20	.50
4 Brad Essex	.30	.75
5 Doug Evans ASST CO	.20	.50
6 Liam Garvey	.30	.75
7 Trevor Hanas	.30	.75
8 Jon Hillebrandt	.60	1.50
9 Dan Hodge	.30	.75
10 Butch Kaebel	.30	.75
11 Karson Kaebel	.30	.75
12 Justin Krall	.30	.75
13 John Krouse EQUIP	.20	.50
14 Jeff Kungle	.30	.75
15 Kevin Lune	.30	.75
16 Darren Maloney	.30	.75
17 Dustin McArthur	.30	.75
18 Jon Pratt	.30	.75
19 Brad Purdie	.30	.75
20 Jason Saal	.60	1.50
21 Jan Slavik	.30	.75
22 Marc Terris	.30	.75
23 Jean-Guy Trudel	.40	1.00
24 Paul Vincent	.30	.75

1997-98 Peoria Rivermen

Little is known about this set beyond the confirmed checklist. Additional information can be forwarded to hockeymag@beckett.com.

COMPLETE SET (29)	4.00	10.00
1 Garry Gruber	.15	.40
2 Derek Diener	.15	.40
3 Samy Nasreddine	.20	.50
4 Doug Evans	.15	.40
5 Darren Maloney	.15	.40
6 Joe Craigen	.20	.50
7 Rob Phillips	.15	.40
8 Brian Clifford	.15	.40
9 Darcy Smith	.15	.40
10 Butch Kaebel	.20	.50
11 Jean Guy Trudel	.20	.50
12 Brad Essex	.15	.40
13 Justin Krall	.15	.40
14 John Dance	.15	.40
15 Marc Terris	.15	.40
16 Trevor Hanas	.15	.40
17 Dave Paradise	.15	.40
18 David Vallieres	.15	.40
19 Scott Roche	.30	.75
20 Marcel Kuris	.15	.40
21 Jon Pratt	.15	.40
22 Rob Giffin	.20	.50
23 Mark Reeds	.20	.60
24 Greg Eberle	.15	.40
25 John Krouse EQ	.02	.10
26 Mascot	.02	.10
27 Title Card	.02	.10
28 Header Card	.02	.10

1998-99 Peoria Rivermen

This set features the Rivermen of the ECHL. The set was produced by ebk Sports and was sold by the team at home games.

COMPLETE SET (27)	4.80	12.00
1 Darren Maloney	.15	.40
2 Dan Hodge	.15	.40
3 Doug Evans	.15	.40
4 Dan Carney	.15	.40
5 Chris Coveny	.15	.40
6 Alexandre Couture	.15	.40
7 Jamie Thompson	.15	.40
8 Jay Kenney	.15	.40
9 J.F. Boutin	.15	.40
10 Joe Craigen	.30	.75
11 Darcy Smith	.15	.40
12 Dan Murphy	.15	.40
13 Quinn Hancock	.15	.40
14 Mark Reeds CO	.02	.10
15 Marek Ivan	.15	.40
16 Kory Karlander	.15	.40
17 Ken Boone	.15	.40
18 Jeff Trembecky	.15	.40
19 Steve MacKinnon	.15	.40
20 Joe Rybar	.30	.75
21 Peoria Rivermen	.15	.40
22 Scott Roche	.30	.75
23 Chad Lang	.30	.75
24 Kevin Paden	.20	.50
25 Blaine Fitzpatrick	.15	.40
26 Mike Schultz	.15	.40
27 Darren Maloney AS	.02	.10
28 Jamie Thompson AS	.15	.40

1999-00 Peoria Rivermen

This set features the Rivermen of the ECHL. The set was produced by Roox and was issued as a promotional giveaway at a home game.

COMPLETE SET (36)	6.00	100.00
1 Rocky MAS	.08	.25
2 Don Granato CO	.40	1.00
3 Greg Eberle TR	.02	.10
4 Jamie Healy TR	.02	.10
5 Trevor Baker	1.50	4.00
6 Duane Derksen	3.00	8.00
7 Darren Clark	1.50	4.00
8 Jason Christie	1.50	4.00
9 Blaine Fitzpatrick	1.50	4.00
10 John Gurskis	1.50	4.00
11 Alexandre Couture	1.50	4.00
12 Darren Maloney	1.50	4.00
13 Blaz Emersic	1.50	4.00
14 Cody Rudkowsky	3.00	8.00
15 J.F. Boutin	1.50	4.00
16 Joe Rybar	2.00	5.00
17 Matt Smith	1.50	4.00
18 Tomaz Razinger	1.50	4.00
19 Craig Anderson	1.50	4.00
20 Jason Lawmaster	1.50	4.00
21 Bret Meyers	1.50	4.00
22 Sean Farmer	1.50	4.00
23 Darin Kimble	3.00	8.00
24 Dan Hodge	1.50	4.00
25 Luke Gruden	1.50	4.00
26 Tyler McMillan	1.50	4.00
27 Kenzie Homer	1.50	4.00
28 James Desmarais	1.50	4.00
29 John Butler PRES	.02	.10
30 Mike Nelson VP	.02	.10
31 Bart Rogers GM	.02	.10
32 Michael Sauers GM	.02	.10
33 Jim Small GM	.02	.10
34 Norm Ulrich DOB	.02	.10
35 Manda Girard SALES	.02	.10
36 B.J. Stone SALES	.02	.10

2001-02 Peoria Rivermen

This set features the Rivermen of the UHL. We have no additional information besides the checklist. If you can shed some light on this issue, please write to hockeymag@beckett.com.

COMPLETE SET (24)	8.00	20.00
1 Checklist	.04	.10
2 Jason Christie CO	.04	.10
3 Curtis Sanford	.40	2.00
4 Bob Gassoff Jr.	.40	1.00
5 Chad Starling	.40	1.00
6 Blake Evans	.40	1.00
7 Kevin Tucker	.40	1.00
8 Trevor Baker	.40	1.00
9 Jonathan Fauteux	.40	1.00
10 Randy Rowe	.40	1.00
11 Dustin Kuk	.40	1.00
12 Bret Meyers	.40	1.00
13 Kevin Granato	.40	1.00
14 Dan Hodge	.40	1.00
15 Tyler Rennette	.40	1.00
16 Ryan Finnerty	.40	1.00
17 Brad Voth	.40	1.00
18 Joe Rybar	.60	1.50
19 Darren Clark	.40	1.00
20 Matt Golden	.40	1.00
21 Phil Osaer	.40	1.00
22 Jason Lawmaster	.40	1.00
23 Arvid Rekis	.40	1.00
24 Kevin Cloutier	.40	1.00

2000-01 Peoria Rivermen

This set features the Rivermen of the ECHL. The set was produced by Roox and sold by the team at its souvenir stands.

COMPLETE SET (21)	4.00	10.00
1 Curtis Sanford	.30	2.00
2 Didier Tremblay	.20	.50
3 Luke Gruden	.20	.50
4 J.F. Boutin	.20	.50
5 Lauri Kinos	.20	.50
6 Darren Maloney	.20	.50
7 Trevor Baker	.20	.50
8 Tyler Willis	.20	.50
9 Bret Meyers	.20	.50
10 Dustin Kuk	.20	.50
11 Dan Hodge	.20	.50
12 Joe Rybar	.20	.50
13 Blaine Fitzpatrick	.20	.50
14 Darren Clark	.20	.50
15 Matt Golden	.20	.50
16 Kenric Exner	.40	1.00
17 Jason Lawmaster	.20	.50
18 Arvid Rekis	.20	.50
19 Tomaz Razinger	.20	.50
20 Joe Trotta ACO	.10	.25
21 Jason Christie HCO	.10	.25

2002-03 Peoria Rivermen

COMPLETE SET (25)	5.00	12.00
1 Jason Christie HCO	.10	.25
2 Simon Lajeunesse	.40	1.00
3 Trevor Gillies	.20	.50
4 Lauri Kinos	.20	.50
5 Darren Clark	.20	.50
6 Trevor Baker	.20	.50
7 Greg Day	.20	.50
8 Brett DeCecco	.20	.50
9 Randy Rowe	.20	.50
10 Randy Copley	.20	.50
11 Duane Derksen	.40	1.00
12 Kevin Granato	.20	.50
13 Tyler Rennette	.20	.50
14 Ryan Finnerty	.20	.50
15 Brad Voth	.20	.50
16 Brendan Brooks	.20	.50
17 Derek Booth	.20	.50
18 Scott Crawford	.20	.50
19 Jeremy Yablonski	.20	.50
20 Jason Lawmaster	.20	.50
21 Josh Kern	.20	.50
22 Arvid Rekis	.20	.50
23 Anthony Belza	.20	.50
24 Alfie Michaud	.40	1.00
NNO Checklist	.02	.10

2002-03 Peoria Rivermen Photo Pack

These oversized (11X14) photos were sold in set form by the team. Each card in the set is autographed in black Sharpie and is serial numbered out of 100. The cards are unnumbered and so are listed below in alphabetical order.

COMPLETE SET (8)		50.00
1 Trevor Baker		6.00
2 Brendan Brooks		6.00
3 Darren Clark		6.00
4 Duane Derksen		10.00
5 Ryan Finnerty		6.00
6 Jason Lawmaster		6.00
7 Alfie Michaud		10.00
8 Tyler Rennette		6.00

2002-03 Peoria Rivermen RBI Sports

COMPLETE SET (18)	8.00	20.00
151 Trevor Baker	.40	1.00
152 Anthony Belza	.40	1.00
153 Derek Booth	.40	1.00
154 Brendan Brooks	.40	1.00
155 Darren Clark	.40	1.00
156 Randy Copley	.40	1.00
157 Scott Crawford	.40	1.00
158 Greg Day	.40	1.00
159 Duane Derksen	.75	2.00
160 Trevor Gillies	.40	1.00
161 Josh Kern	.40	1.00
162 Jason Lawmaster	.75	2.00
163 Alfie Michaud	.75	2.00
164 Arvid Rekis	.40	1.00
165 Tyler Rennette	.40	1.00
166 Randy Rowe	.40	1.00
167 Rod Taylor	.40	1.00
168 Brad Voth	.40	1.00

2003-04 Peoria Rivermen

This set was produced by Choice Marketing and sold at home games.

COMPLETE SET (24)	4.00	10.00
1 Adam Edinger	.15	.40
2 Brendan Brooks	.15	.40
3 Bret DeCecco	.15	.40
4 Brett Scheffelmaier	.15	.40
5 Chad Starling	.15	.40
6 Colin Hemingway	.15	.40
7 Craig Olynick	.15	.40
8 Doug MacIver	.15	.40
9 George Halkidis	.15	.40
10 Greg Black	.15	.40
11 Joe Pereira	.15	.40
12 Joe Vandermeer	.15	.40
13 Ken Goetz	.30	.75
14 Levente Szuper	.40	1.00
15 Malcolm Hutt	.15	.40
16 Malcolm MacMillan	.15	.40
17 Marty Johnston	.15	.40
18 Mike Valley	.30	.75
19 Randy Rowe	.15	.40
20 Scott Crawford	.15	.40
21 Scott Turner	.15	.40
22 Trevor Baker	.30	.75
23 Tyler Rennette	.15	.40
24 Jason Christie HCO	.02	.10
NNO Checklist	.01	.05

2004-05 Peoria Rivermen

COMPLETE SET (25)	5.00	12.00
1 Chad Starling	.20	.50
2 Warren Toews	.20	.50
3 Mark Jarant	.20	.50
4 Chris Bogas	.20	.50
5 Brian McCullough	.20	.50
6 Randy Rowe	.20	.50
7 Trevor Baker	.20	.50
8 Justin Maiser	.20	.50
9 Travis Rycroft	.20	.50
10 Scott Turner	.20	.50
11 Alfie Michaud	.40	1.00
12 Chris Beckford-Tsue	.40	1.00
13 Kris Kasper	.40	1.00
14 Ed Hill	.20	.50
15 Jake Riddle	.20	.50
16 James Sanford	.20	.50
17 Patrick Wellar	.20	.50
18 David Kaczowka	.20	.50
19 Tyler Rennette	.20	.50
20 Joe Pereira	.20	.50
21 Rejean Stringer	.02	.10
22 Stringer MASCOT	.02	.10
23 Colin Hemingway	.20	.50
24 Trevor Byrne	.20	.50
25 Jason Christie CO	.02	.10

2005-06 Peoria Rivermen

COMPLETE SET (24)		15.00
1 Curtis Sanford	.40	1.00
2 Mike Mottau	.30	.75
3 Rocky Thompson	.20	.50
4 Trevor Byrne	.20	.50
5 Brendan Buckley	.20	.50
6 Gavin Morgan	.20	.50
7 Colin Hemingway	.20	.50
8 Jon DiSalvatore	.20	.50
9 Mike Stuart	.20	.50
10 Blake Evans	.20	.50
11 Mike Glumac	.20	.50
12 D.J. King	.20	.50
13 Aaron MacKenzie	.20	.50
14 Troy Riddle	.20	.50
15 Trent Whitfield	.20	.50
16 Potor Sojna	.20	.50
17 Brendan Brooks	.20	.50
18 Ryan Ramsay	.20	.50
19 Chris Beckford-Tseu	.75	2.00
20 Doug Lynch	.20	.50
21 Jason Bacashihua	.40	1.00
22 Patrick Lalime	.40	1.00
23 Jeff Woywitka	.20	.50
24 Steve Pleau CO	.02	.10

2006-07 Peoria Rivermen

COMPLETE SET (25)	8.00	15.00
1 Chris Beckford-Tseu	.60	1.50
2 Michal Birner	.20	.50
3 Jon DiSalvatore	.20	.50
4 Zack Fitzgerald	.20	.50
5 Mike Glumac	.30	.75
6 Cam Keith	.20	.50
7 D.J. King	.20	.50
8 Charles Linglet	.20	.50
9 Doug Lynch	.20	.50
10 Aaron MacKenzie	.20	.50
11 Ryan MacMurchy	.20	.50
12 Tomas Mojzis	.20	.50
13 Gavin Morgan	.20	.50
14 Roman Polak	.20	.50
15 Ryan Ramsay	.30	.75
16 Marek Schwarz	.75	2.00
17 Peter Sejna	.20	.50
18 Mike Stuart	.20	.50
19 Rocky Thompson	.20	.50
20 Trent Whitfield	.20	.50
21 Stephen Wood	.20	.50
22 Jeff Woywitka	.20	.50
23 Konstantin Zakharov	.20	.50
24 Dave Baseggio	.20	.50
25 Checklist	.02	.10

2007-08 Peoria Rivermen

COMPLETE SET (26)	5.00	12.00
1 Dave Baseggio HC	.15	.40
2 Chris Beckford-Tseu	.25	.60
3 Hans Benson	.25	.60
4 Alex Brooks	.25	.60
5 Nicholas Drazenovic	.25	.60
6 Micki DuPont	.25	.60
7 Ryan Glenn	.25	.60
8 Mike Glumac	.25	.60
9 Alexander Hellstrom	.25	.60
10 Martin Kariya	.25	.60
11 Cam Keith	.25	.60
12 Neil Komadoski	.25	.60
13 Nikolay Lemtyugov	.25	.60
14 Charles Linglet	.25	.60
15 Aaron MacKenzie	.25	.60
16 Roman Polak	.25	.60
17 Chris Porter	.25	.60
18 Ryan Reaves	.25	.60
19 Marek Schwarz	.25	.60
20 Yan Stastny	.25	.60
21 Julian Talbot	.25	.60
22 Jean-Guy Trudel	.25	.60
23 Steve Wagner	.25	.60
24 Trent Whitfield	.25	.60
25 Jeff Woywitka	.25	.60
NNO Checklist	.10	.25

1989-90 Peterborough Petes

This 25-card set paralleled the 7th Inning Sketch OHL league set but featured players of the Peterborough club. The card stock was thicker than the league set and the pictures were sharper.

COMPLETE SET (26)	10.00	25.00
98 Troy Stephens	.40	1.00
99 Dan Brown	.40	1.00
100 Mike Ricci	1.25	3.00
101 Brent Pope	.40	1.00
102 Mike Dagenais	.40	1.00
103 Scott Campbell	.40	1.00
104 Jamie Pegg	.40	1.00
105 Joe Hawley	.40	1.00
106 Jason Dawe	.40	1.00
107 Paul Mitton	.40	1.00
108 Mike Tomlinson	.40	1.00
109 Dave Lorentz	.40	1.00
110 Dale McTavish	.40	1.00
111 Willie McGarvey	.40	1.00
112 Don O'Neill	.40	1.00
113 Mark Myles	.40	1.00
114 Chris Longo	.40	1.00
115 Tom Hopkins	.40	1.00
116 Jassen Cullimore	.40	1.00
117 Geoff Ingram	.40	1.00
118 Twohey Bovair TR	.40	1.00
119 Doug Searle	.40	1.00
120 Bryan Gendron	.40	1.00
121 Andrew Verner	.60	1.50
122 Todd Bocjun	.60	1.50
123 Dick Todd CO	.20	.50

1991-92 Peterborough Petes

This 30-card P.L.A.Y. (Police, Laws and Youth) set measures approximately 2 1/2" by 3 3/4" and features posed, color player photos with bright blue and white borders. The player's name is printed on the picture in white letters in the upper left corner. The team logo appears in the upper right corner.

COMPLETE SET (30)	8.00	20.00
1 Jason Dawe	.30	.75
2 Chris Pronger	3.00	8.00
3 Scott Turner	.20	.50
4 Chad Grills	.20	.50
5 Brent Tully	.20	.50
6 Mike Harding	.20	.50
7 Chris Longo	.20	.50
8 Slapshot MASCOT	.02	.10
9 Doug Searle	.20	.50
10 Mike Tomlinson	.20	.50
11 Bryan Gendron	.20	.50
12 Andrew Verner	.30	.75
13 Ryan Black	.20	.50
14 Don O'Neill	.20	.50
15 Jeff Twohey MG/CO	.02	.10
16 Dale McTavish	.20	.50
17 Jeff Walker	.20	.50
18 Matt St. Germain	.20	.50
19 Dave Roche	.20	.50
20 Colin Wilson	.20	.50
21 Jassen Cullimore	.20	.50
22 Chad Lang	.30	.75
23 Dick Todd MG/CO	.20	.50
24 Geordie Kinnear	.20	.50
25 Shawn Heins	.25	.60
26 John Johnson	.20	.50
27 Kelly Vipond	.20	.50
NNO Police Crest	.02	.10
NNO Kiwanis Sponsor Card	.02	.10
NNO Quaker Sponsor Card	.02	.10

1993-94 Peterborough Petes

Sponsored by Cardboard Heroes and printed by Slapshot Images Ltd., this standard-size 31-card set features the 1993-94 Peterborough Petes. Only 3,000 of these sets have been produced; the first card also serves as a Certificate of Authenticity and has the individual set number printed in the upper left corner. On a grey background, the fronts feature color action player photos with thin maroon borders. The player's name, position and team name, as well as the producer's logo, appear on the front.

COMPLETE SET (31)	6.00	15.00
1 1992-93 OHL Champions	.15	.40
2 Jonathan Murphy	.15	.40
3 Dave Roche	.15	.40
4 Rob Giffin	.15	.40
5 Mike Harding	.15	.40
6 Tim Hill	.15	.40
7 Darryl Moxam	.15	.40
8 Pat Paone	.15	.40
9 Brent Tully	.15	.40
10 Zac Bierk	.30	.75
11 Chad Grills	.15	.40
12 Matt St. Germain	.15	.40
13 Henrik Eppers	.15	.40
14 Rick Emmett	.15	.40
15 Chad Lang	.20	.50
16 Cameron Mann	.40	1.00
17 Steve Hogg	.15	.40
18 Mike Williams	.15	.40
19 Ryan Nauss	.15	.40
20 Jamie Langenbrunner	.40	1.00
21 Ryan Douglas	.15	.40
22 Matt Johnson	.30	.75
23 Kelvin Solari	.15	.40
24 Dan Delmonte	.15	.40
25 Quayde Lightbody	.15	.40
26 Adrian Murray	.15	.40
27 Jason Dawe	.15	.40
28 Mike Harding	.15	.40
29 Chris Pronger	2.00	5.00
30 Sponsor Card Cardboard Heroes Greg Ball Kevin Ball	.02	.10
NNO Slapshot Ad Card	.02	.10

2001-02 Peterborough Petes

This set features the Petes of the OHL. The cards are an oversized 4X6, and feature blurred colour photos on front, with a Gatorade logo upper left and player name and number along the bottom. The cards are not numbered, but are listed in order of jersey number, as they were released. It is believed they were issued as a promotional giveaway by the team.

COMPLETE SET (20)	8.00	20.00
1 Cody Spicer	.60	1.50
2 Dustin Wood	.40	1.00
3 Bryan Hamm	.40	1.00
4 Mark Flood	.40	1.00
5 Trevor Hendrix	.40	1.00
6 James Edgar	.40	1.00
7 Jason Penner	.40	1.00
8 Jon Howse	.40	1.00
9 Ryan Card	.40	1.00
10 Eric Staal	4.00	10.00
11 Josh Patterson	.40	1.00
12 Jim Gagnon	.40	1.00
13 Brad Self	.40	1.00
14 Matt Herneisen	.40	1.00
15 Adam Elzinga	.40	1.00
16 Greg Chambers	.40	1.00
17 Jamie Tardif	.40	1.00
18 Matt Armstrong	.40	1.00
19 David Currie	.60	1.50
20 Lukas Krajicek	.75	2.00

2002-03 Peterborough Petes

COMPLETE SET (24)	6.00	15.00
1 Rick Allain CO	.02	.10
2 Steve Smith ACO	.02	.10
3 Aaron Dawson	.20	.50
4 Mark Flood	.20	.50
5 Shawn Futers	.20	.50
6 Trevor Hendrix	.20	.50
7 Jordan Morrison	.20	.50
8 Jon Howse	.20	.50
9 Ryan Card	.20	.50
10 Eric Staal	2.00	5.00
11 Evgeny Kadatskiy	.20	.50
12 Josh Patterson	.20	.50
13 Jason Penner	.20	.50
14 Greg Williams	.20	.50
15 Chad Robinson	.20	.50
16 Mike Ramsay	.20	.50
17 Patrick Kaleta	.20	.50
18 Adam Elzinga	.20	.50
19 Greg Chambers	.20	.50
20 Jamie Tardif	.20	.50
21 Mike McKeown	.20	.50
22 Jeff MacDougald	.20	.50
23 David Currie	.20	.50
24 Lukas Krajicek	.40	1.00

2004-05 Peterborough Petes Postcards

This set of 5X7 postcard-sized singles were sold in set form by the team.

COMPLETE SET (25)		25.00
1 Jordan Staal		3.00
2 Liam Reddox		1.00
3 Daniel Ryder		1.00
4 Jamie Tardif		1.00
5 Eero Kilpelainen		2.00
6 Patrick Kaleta		1.00
7 Jordan Morrison		1.00
8 Trevor Henrikx		1.00
9 Mark Flood		1.00
10 Niko Vainio		1.00
11 Justin Carauna		1.00
12 Mike Montgomery		1.00
13 Aaron Barton		1.00
14 Patrick Kaleta		1.00
15 Aaron Dawson		1.00
16 Scott Cowie		1.00
17 Justin Soryal		1.00
18 Darryl Flowers		1.00
19 Bryan Young		1.00
20 Peter Aston		1.00
21 Jadran Baljo		1.00
22 Greg Stewart		1.00
23 Greg Williams		1.00
24 Corey Gault		1.00
25 Jeff MacDougald		1.00

2002-03 Philadelphia Phantoms

COMPLETE SET (26)	6.00	15.00
1 Antero Niittymaki	.75	2.00
2 Bruno St. Jacques	.20	.50
3 Dan Peters	.20	.50
4 Mark Greig	.20	.50
5 Kirby Law	.30	.75
6 Peter White	.30	.75
7 Eric Betournay	.20	.50
8 Jack Baker	.20	.50
9 Patrick Sharp	.30	.75
10 Guillaume Lefebvre	.30	.75
11 Pete Vandermeer	.30	.75
12 Andre Savage	.20	.50
13 Jim Vandermeer	.30	.75
14 Mike Siklenka	.30	.75
15 Ian MacNeil	.20	.50
16 Ben Stafford	.20	.50
17 John Slaney	.20	.50
18 Mike Lephart	.20	.50
19 Brad Tiley	.20	.50
20 Wade Skolney	.20	.50
21 Neil Little	.40	1.00
22 David Harlock	.20	.50
23 John Stevens CO	.02	.10
24 Phlex Mascot	.02	.10
25 Subway Coupon	.01	.01
NNO Checklist	.02	.10

2003-04 Philadelphia Phantoms

This set was produced by Choice Marketing and sold at home games.

COMPLETE SET (26)		12.00
1 Checklist		.01
2 Antero Niittymaki		1.50
3 Ben Stafford		.40
4 Boyd Kane		.40
5 Craig Berube		.40
6 Dennis Seidenberg		.40
7 Freddy Meyer		.40
8 Ian MacNeil		.40
9 Jeff Woywitka		.50
10 Joey Hope		.40
11 John Slaney		.40
12 Kirby Law		.75
13 Mark Murphy		.40
14 Mike Peluso		.40
15 Mike Siklenka		.40
16 Neil Little		1.00
17 Nick Deschenes		.40
18 P.J. Stock		1.00
19 Patrick Sharp		.40
20 Pete Vandermeer		.75
21 Peter White		.40
22 Randy Jones		.40
23 Wade Skolney		.40
24 John Stevens		.40
25 Mascot		.10
26 Sponsor		.01

2004-05 Philadelphia Phantoms

COMPLETE SET (25)	6.00	15.00
1 Riley Cote	.20	.50
2 Ben Eager	.30	.75

3 Todd Fedoruk .40 1.00
4 Josh Gratton .60 1.50
5 Joey Hope .20 .50
6 Randy Jones .20 .50
7 Boyd Kane .30 .75
8 Neil Little .40 1.00
9 Eric Meloche .20 .50
10 Freddy Meyer .30 .75
11 Mark Murphy .20 .50
12 Antero Niittymaki .75 2.00
13 Joni Pitkanen .40 1.00
14 David Printz .20 .50
15 Ryan Ready .20 .50
16 Dennis Seidenberg .20 .50
17 Patrick Sharp .30 .75
18 Jon Sim .30 .75
19 Wade Skolney .20 .50
20 John Slaney .20 .50
21 Jeff Smith .20 .50
22 Ben Stafford .20 .50
23 R.J. Umberger .60 1.50
24 Tony Voce .20 .50
NNO Checklist .01 .01

2005-06 Philadelphia Phantoms

COMPLETE SET (26) 5.00 12.00
1 Philadelphia Phantoms CL .01 .01
2 B.J. Abel .20 .50
3 Rejean Beauchemin .40 1.00
4 Marc Cavosie .20 .50
5 Eric Chouinard .20 .50
6 Charlie Cook .20 .50
7 Riley Cote .20 .50
8 Ben Eager .20 .50
9 Triston Grant .20 .50
10 Josh Gratton .40 1.00
11 Joey Hope .20 .50
12 Randy Jones .20 .50
13 Pat Kavanagh .20 .50
14 Eric Meloche .20 .50
15 Freddy Meyer .20 .50
16 Alexandre Picard .20 .50
17 David Printz .20 .50
18 Ryan Ready .20 .50
19 Stefan Ruzicka .20 .50
20 Wade Skolney .20 .50
21 John Slaney .20 .50
22 Jamie Storr .30 .75
23 R.J. Umberger .40 1.00
24 Tony Voce .20 .50
25 John Stevens HC .02 .10
26 Phlex MASCOT .02 .10

2005-06 Philadelphia Phantoms All-Decade Team

COMPLETE SET (12) 8.00 15.00
1 Patrick Sharp .40 1.00
2 Frank Bialowas .75 2.00
3 Mark Greig .40 1.00
4 John Slaney .40 1.00
5 John Stevens .40 1.00
6 Neil Little .75 2.00
7 Peter White .40 1.00
8 Mike Maneluk .40 1.00
9 Kirby Law .40 1.00
10 Freddy Meyer .40 1.00
11 Dennis Seidenberg .40 1.00
12 Antero Niittymaki .75 2.00

2006-07 Philadelphia Phantoms

COMPLETE SET (30) 10.00 18.00
1 Joe Mullen ACO .10 .25
2 Kjell Samuelsson CO .10 .25
3 Ryan Potulny .60 1.50
4 Niko Dimitrakos .30 .75
5 Lars Jonsson .20 .50
6 Denis Tolpeko .20 .50
7 Eric Meloche .20 .50
8 John Slaney .20 .50
9 Martin Houle .40 1.00
10 Rejean Beauchemin .40 1.00
11 Scott Munroe .20 .50
12 Tony Voce .20 .50
13 Triston Grant .40 1.00
14 David Printz .30 .75
15 Nate Guenin .30 .75
16 Ben Eager .30 .75
17 Martin Grenier .20 .50
18 Riley Cote .20 .50
19 Matt Ellison .20 .50
20 Alexandre Picard .20 .50
21 Nolan Baumgartner .20 .50
22 Stefan Ruzicka .30 .75
23 Mark Cullen .20 .50
24 Matt Davis .20 .50
25 Don Morrison .20 .50
26 Jussi Timonen .20 .50
27 Darren Reid .20 .50
28 Frederik Cabana .20 .50
29 Peter Zingoni .20 .50
30 Gino Pisellini .20 .50

1993-94 Phoenix Cobras RHI

This set features the Cobras of Roller Hockey Intl. The set was produced by the team and sold at home games.

COMPLETE SET (20) 3.00 8.00
1 Header Card .02 .10
2 Lee Kasper .20 .50
3 Stuart Silver .20 .50
4 Lou Franceschetti HCO .20 .50
5 Aaron Boh .20 .50
6 Todd Brost .30 .75
7 Michel Couvrette .20 .50
8 Wade Gibson .20 .50
9 Rickard Gronborg .20 .50
10 Hugo Hamelin .20 .50
11 Daniel Larin .20 .50
12 Mike O'Hara .20 .50
13 Sergei Olympiev .20 .50
14 John Redinger .20 .50
15 Brent Sapergia .30 .75
16 Daniel Shank .30 .75
17 Troy Stephens .20 .50
18 Boyd Sutton .20 .50
19 Mike Vukonich .20 .50
20 Alex Zhurik .20 .50

1992-93 Phoenix Roadrunners

Sponsored by Saleway, this 28-card standard-size set features color action photos on the front edged by a blue border on the top and left margins, with full bleed on the bottom and right. The IHL logo is in the top right corner. The player's name and jersey number are printed in red at the bottom while the team name is printed in white immediately above. The team logo is in the lower right and the player's position is printed in red inside a hockey puck in the lower left. The cards are unnumbered and checklisted below in alphabetical order.

COMPLETE SET (28) 4.00 10.00
1 Tim Bothwell CO .15 .40
2 Frank Breault .15 .40
3 Tim Breslin .15 .40
4 Rene Chapdelaine .15 .40
5 Sylvain Couturier .20 .50
6 Phil Crowe .20 .50
7 Darryl Gilmour .20 .50
8 David Goverde .20 .50
9 Ed Kastelic .15 .40
10 Rick Kozuback ACO .02 .10
11 Ted Kramer .15 .40
12 Robert Lang .30 .75
13 Guy Leveque .15 .40
14 Jim Maher .15 .40
15 Brad McCaughey .15 .40
16 Shawn McCosh .15 .40
17 John Mokosak .15 .40
18 Keith Redmond .15 .40
19 Mike Ruark .15 .40
20 Brandy Semchuk .15 .40
21 Dave Stewart .15 .40
22 Brad Tiley .15 .40
23 Dave Trelowicz .15 .40
24 Mike Vukonich .15 .40
25 Tim Watters .20 .50
26 Sean Whyte .15 .40
27 Darryl Williams .15 .40
28 Rocky Roadrunner (Mascot) .02 .10

1993-94 Phoenix Roadrunners

This 25-card set measures the standard size. On a black and white marbleized background, the fronts feature color action player photos with rounded corners and a thin blue border. The player's name, position, and number appear under the photo, along with the team logo. The cards are unnumbered and checklisted below in alphabetical order.

COMPLETE SET (25) 4.00 10.00
1 Tim Breslin .15 .40
2 Brian Chapman .15 .40
3 Stephane Charbonneau .15 .40
4 Dan Currie .20 .50
5 Rick Dudley CO .20 .50
6 Marc Fortier .20 .50
7 David Goverde .20 .50
8 Kevin Grant .15 .40
9 Mark Hardy P/CO .15 .40
10 Dean Hulett .15 .40
11 Pauli Jaks .20 .50
12 Bob Jay .15 .40
13 Rick Knickle .30 .75
14 Guy Leveque .20 .50
15 Eric Lavigne .20 .50
16 Dominic Lavoie .15 .40
17 Jim Maher .15 .40
18 Brian McReynolds .15 .40
19 Rob Murphy .15 .40
20 Keith Redmond .15 .40
21 Dave Stewart .15 .40
22 Dave Thomlinson .15 .40
23 Brad Tiley .15 .40
24 Jim Vesey .15 .40
25 Darryl Williams .15 .40

1995-96 Phoenix Roadrunners

This 24-card set was produced by Jessen Associates for Collector's Edge. The full colour cards were available as a free promotional item at a game; they also were sold through the team's pro shop for $6. Approximately 8,000 sets were made. The cards are unnumbered and are checklisted below in alphabetical order.

COMPLETE SET (24) 4.80 12.00
1 Ruslan Batyrshin .15 .40
2 Frederik Beaubien .30 .75
3 John Blue .30 .75
4 Mike Boback .15 .40
5 Kevin Brown .20 .50
6 Jim Burton .15 .40
7 Dan Bylsma .20 .50
8 Brian Chapman .15 .40
9 Rob Cowie .15 .40
10 Devin Edgerton .15 .40
11 Ken McRae .15 .40
12 Barry Potomski .30 .75
13 Daniel Rydmark .15 .40
14 Jeff Shevalier .20 .50
15 Gary Shuchuk .20 .50
16 Chris Snell .20 .50
17 Jamie Storr .75 2.00
18 Dave Thomlinson .15 .40
19 Nicholas Vachon .15 .40
20 Jan Vopat .20 .50
21 Steve Wilson .15 .40
22 Training staff .02 .10
23 Rob Laird CO .02 .10
24 Rocky Roadrunner .02 .10

1998-99 Phoenix Mustangs

This oversized set was issued in perforated strip form. It was handed out at a home game as a promotional giveaway, and most of the singles were sponsored by local doctors.

COMPLETE SET (25) 150.00
1 Hugo Belanger 3.00 8.00
2 David Goverde 3.00 8.00
3 Dana G. Seltzer MD .08 .25
4 Ianniquc Renaud 2.50 6.00
5 Mark Spence 2.50 6.00
6 Daniel Shank 8.00 20.00
7 Stu Kulak 3.00 8.00
8 Rusty McKie 2.50 6.00
9 Gene Bono 2.50 6.00
10 Jamie Allan 2.50 6.00
11 Michel Couvrette 2.50 6.00
12 Sebastien Fortier 2.50 6.00
13 Corey Laniuk 2.50 6.00
14 Doug McCarthy 2.50 6.00
15 Tom Menicci 2.50 6.00
16 Savo Mitrovic 2.50 6.00
17 Matt Oliver 2.50 6.00
18 Teemu Numminen 3.00 8.00
19 Bobby Rapoza 2.50 6.00
20 Jason Rose 2.50 6.00
21 Darren Veitch 2.50 6.00
22 Sean Whyte 2.50 6.00
23 Brad McCaughey HCO .08 .25
24 Dick Earle TR .08 .25
25 Rusty the Wrangler Mascot .08 .25

1983-84 Pinebridge Bucks

These card are unnumbered and measure 4 1/8" by 2 3/8". There are reports that there may be as many as 20 cards in this set, this checklist represents the 12 that are confirmed.

COMPLETE SET (12) 15.00
1 Dave Burke .60 1.50
2 Dan Burrows .60 1.50
3 Kim Collins .60 1.50
4 Bob Fleming .60 1.50
5 Rick Harris .60 1.50
6 Steve Heittola .60 1.50
7 Ken Latta .60 1.50
8 Tom Madsen .60 1.50
9 Larry Mollard .60 1.50
10 Kelly Rissling .60 1.50
11 Frank Perkins CO .20 .50
12 Frank Juror TR .20 .50

2001-02 Plymouth Whalers

COMPLETE SET (32) 15.00 30.00
1 Libor Ustrnul .30 .75
2 Jared Newman .30 .75
3 Stephen Weiss 1.25 3.00
4 Nathan Tennant .30 .75
5 Damian Surma .30 .75
6 Chad LaRose .60 1.50
7 Jeff Phillips .30 .75
8 Kyle Neufeld .30 .75
9 Brad Yeo .30 .75
10 Paul Drew .30 .75
11 Cole Jarrett .30 .75
12 Nate Kiser .30 .75
13 Karl Stewart .60 1.50
14 John Mitchell .30 .75
15 Greg Campbell .60 1.50
16 George Nistas .30 .75
17 Tim Sestito .30 .75
18 Kris Vernarsky .30 .75
19 James Wisniewski .30 .75
20 Danny McDonald .30 .75
21 Jason Bacashihua 1.25 3.00
22 Jonas Fiedler .30 .75
23 David Liffiton .60 1.50
24 Roberts ACO .02 .10
25 Mike Vellucci CO .02 .10
26 Dan Reed .30 .75
27 Bryan Thompson .30 .75
28 Stephen Weiss AS 1.25 3.00
29 Jason Bacashihua AS 1.25 3.00
30 Chad LaRose AS .60 1.50
31 Greg Campbell TP .40 1.00
32 James Wisniewski TP .30 .75

2002-03 Plymouth Whalers

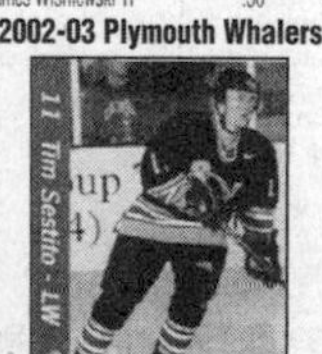

COMPLETE SET (30) 5.00 12.00
1 Cole Jarrett .15 .40
2 Nate Kiser .15 .40
3 Karl Stewart .30 .75
4 John Mitchell .15 .40
5 Jimmy Gagnon .15 .40
6 Sean Thompson .15 .40
7 Chad LaRose .40 1.00
8 John Vigilante .15 .40
9 Taylor Raszka .15 .40
10 Ryan Ramsay .15 .40
11 Mike Letizia .15 .40
12 Steve Phillips .15 .40
13 Paul Drew .30 .75
14 Jonas Fielder .15 .40
15 Brent Mahon .15 .40
16 Cole Jarrett AS .15 .40
17 Tim Sestito .15 .40
18 Martin Cizek .15 .40
19 Chad LaRose AS .40 1.00
20 Chris Thorburn .30 .75
21 James Wisniewski .30 .75
22 Mike Nelson .15 .40
23 Nick Vernelli .15 .40
24 Jeff Weber .30 .75
25 Erik Lundmark .15 .40
26 David Liffiton .30 .75
27 David Liffiton Top Prospect .30 .75
28 Mascot .02 .10
29 Pat Peake RET .10 .25
30 Team Photo .10 .25

2003-04 Plymouth Whalers

COMPLETE SET (28) 6.00 15.00
1 Rane Carnegie .30 .75
2 Dan Collins .20 .50
3 Jonas Fiedler .20 .50
4 Jordan Grant .20 .50
5 Brent Mahon .20 .50
6 Mike Martinelli .20 .50
7 Vaclav Meidl .20 .50
8 John Mitchell .20 .50
9 Gino Pisellini .20 .50
10 Ryan Ramsay .20 .50
11 Tim Sestito .20 .50
12 Sean Thompson .20 .50
13 Nick Vernelli .20 .50
14 John Vigilante .20 .50
15 Craig Cescon .20 .50
16 Mike Knight .20 .50
17 David Liffiton .30 .75
18 Erik Lundmark .20 .50
19 Ryan McGinnis .20 .50
20 Richard Power .20 .50
21 James Wisniewski .30 .75
22 Paul Drew .20 .50
23 Dan Miller .20 .50
24 Ryan Nie .20 .50
25 Michael Vellucci CO .02 .10
26 Coaching Staff .02 .10
27 Alex Roberts .20 .50
28 Mascot .02 .10

2005-06 Plymouth Whalers

COMPLETE SET (29) 8.00 15.00
A01 John Vigilante .20 .50
A02 John Armstrong .20 .50
A03 Jared Boll .30 .75
A04 Steve Ward .20 .50
A05 Cory Tanaka .20 .50
A06 Tom Sestito .20 .50
A07 Gino Pisellini .30 .75
A08 Ryan Nie .20 .50
A09 James Neal .30 .75
A10 Vaclav Meidl .30 .75
A11 Ryan McGinnis .20 .50
A12 Mike Letizia .20 .50
A13 Andrew Fournier .20 .50
A14 Dan Collins .20 .50
B01 Justin Peters .30 .75
B02 Justin Garay .20 .50
B03 Jeremy Smith .30 .75
B04 Ondrej Otcenas .20 .50
B05 Wes Cunningham .20 .50
B06 Derek Merlini .20 .50
B07 Zack Shepley .20 .50
B08 Joe McCann .20 .50
B09 Brett Bellemore .20 .50
B10 Leo Jenner .20 .50
B11 Chris Terry .20 .50
B12 Joe Gaynor .20 .50
B13 Ryan Stephenson .20 .50
B14 Evan Brophey .20 .50
B15 Plymouth Whalers CL .01 .01

2006-07 Plymouth Whalers

COMPLETE SET (29) 12.00 20.00
1 John Armstrong .20 .50
2 Brett Bellemore .20 .50
3 Jared Boll .20 .50
4 Evan Brophey .20 .50
5 Dan Collins .20 .50
6 Vern Cooper .30 .75
7 Wes Cunningham .20 .50
8 Andrew Fournier .20 .50
9 Joe Gaynor .20 .50
10 Kaine Geldart .20 .50
11 A.J. Jenks .20 .50
12 Leo Jenner .20 .50
13 Joe McCann .20 .50
14 Ryan McGinnis .20 .50
15 James Neal .60 1.50
16 Michal Neuvirth .60 1.50
17 Sean O'Connor .20 .50
18 Dan Ryder .40 1.00
19 Tom Sestito .40 1.00
20 Zack Shepley .20 .50
21 Jozef Sladok .20 .50
22 Jeremy Smith .60 1.50
23 Chris Terry .40 1.00
24 Brett Valliquette .20 .50
25 Steve Ward .20 .50
26 Steven Whitely .20 .50
27 James Neal .60 1.50
28 Plymouth Whalers .10 .25
29 Shooter MASCOT .02 .10

2003-04 Port Huron Beacons

This set was issued as a promotional giveaway at several Beacons home games. The cards were issued in perforated strip form.

COMPLETE SET (23) 25.00
1 Michel Beausoleil 1.00
2 David Bell 1.00
3 Aaron Brand 1.00
4 Kory Cooper 1.50
5 Mike Corneau 1.00
6 Adam Dewan 1.00
7 Stu Dunn 1.50
8 Ken Fels 1.00
9 Jason Firth 1.50
10 Benoit Genesse 1.00
11 Matt Goody 1.00
12 Brent Gretzky 1.00
13 Casey Harris 1.00
14 Ian Jacobs 1.00
15 Trevor Karasiewicz 1.00
16 Barry McKinlay 1.00
17 Sam Miller 1.00
18 Simon Poirier 1.00
19 Michael Prochazka 1.00
20 Joey Sewell 1.00
21 Josh Tataryn 1.00
22 John Vary 1.00
23 Wade Winkler 1.00

1998-99 Port Huron Border Cats

This set features the Border Cats of the UHL. The set was produced by ebk Sports, and sold by the team at its souvenir stands.

COMPLETE SET (26) 4.80 12.00
1 Wayne Muir .30 .75
2 Mike O'Grady .20 .50
3 Adam Robbins .20 .50
4 Curtis Sayler .20 .50
5 Olie Sundstrom .20 .50
6 Bob McKillop .20 .50
7 Chris Bergeron .20 .50
8 Lee Cole .20 .50
9 Chad Dameworth .20 .50
10 Mike Zanzarella TR .02 .10
11 Bernie John .20 .50
12 Matt Carmichael .20 .50
13 Kevin Brown .20 .50
14 Kevin Boyd .20 .50
15 Jeff Blum .20 .50
16 Bruce Watson .20 .50
17 Andrei Sryubko .20 .50
18 Paul Polillo .20 .50
19 Kraig Nienhuis .30 .75
20 Brock Myles EM .02 .10
21 Nikolai Syrtsov .20 .50
22 Greg Puhalski CO .08 .25
23 Bridges MASCOT .02 .10
24 Fedor Fedorov .75 2.00
25 Konstantin Simchuk .30 .75
26 Team CL .02 .10

2006-07 Port Huron Flags

COMPLETE SET (25) 12.00 20.00
1 Team Photo .10 .25
2 Craig Mahon .30 .75
3 Pat Sutton .30 .75
4 Mike Olynyk .30 .75
5 Bobby Kukulka .30 .75
6 Kris Vernarsky .30 .75
7 Robert Snowball .75 2.00
8 Jeremy Tucker .30 .75
9 Mike James .30 .75
10 B.J. Adams .30 .75
11 Mark Cadotte .30 .75
12 Ben Gustovson .30 .75
13 Greg Bullock .30 .75
14 Ryan Markham .30 .75
15 Scott Wray .30 .75
16 Trevor Edwards .30 .75
17 John Doherty .30 .75
18 Dustin Traylen .40 1.00
19 Noah Ruden .40 1.00
20 Shayne Tomlinson .30 .75
21 Steve Hildebrand .30 .75
22 Chris Bogas .30 .75
23 Colt King .75 2.00
24 Garett Cameron .30 .75
25 Slapshot MASCOT .02 .10

1993-94 Portland Pirates

This 24-card set of the Portland Pirates of the American Hockey League was sponsored by Pepsi. The glossy cards were available at home games and through the mail. The glossy cards are numbered on the back.

COMPLETE SET (24) 4.80 12.00
1 Randy Pearce .15 .40
2 Crackers MASCOT .02 .10
3 Barry Trotz CO .08 .25
4 Paul Gardner ACO .02 .10
5 Chris Jensen .08 .25
6 Ken Klee .20 .50
7 Steve Poapst .15 .40
8 Jason Woolley .20 .50
9 Jim Mathieson .15 .40
10 Michel Picard .15 .40
11 Jeff Nelson .15 .40
12 Kent Hulst .15 .40
13 Eric Fenton .15 .40
14 Martin Jiranek .15 .40
15 Mike Boback .15 .40
16 Darren McAusland .15 .40
17 Chris Longo .15 .40
18 Kerry Clark .15 .40
19 Jeff Sirkka .15 .40
20 John Slaney .20 .50
21 Kevin Kaminski .20 .50
22 Byron Dafoe .75 2.00
23 Olaf Kolzig 1.25 3.00
24 Todd Nelson .15 .40
NNO Header Card .02 .10

1994-95 Portland Pirates

This 23-card standard-size set was manufactured and distributed by Jessen Associates, Inc. for Classic. The fronts display color action player photos with a red marbleized inner border and a black outer border. The player's name, jersey number, and position appear in the teal border on the right edge. The cards are unnumbered and checklisted below in alphabetical order.

COMPLETE SET (23) 4.00 10.00
1 Norm Batherson .15 .40
2 Mike Boback .15 .40
3 Andrew Brunette .40 1.00
4 Jim Carey .30 .75
5 Jason Christie .15 .40
6 Kerry Clark .15 .40
7 Brian Curran .15 .40
8 Martin Gendron .30 .75
9 Sergei Gonchar .40 1.00
10 Kent Hulst .15 .40
11 Chris Jensen .15 .40
12 Kevin Kaminski .20 .50
13 Ken Klee .15 .40
14 Chris Longo .15 .40
15 Jim Mathieson .15 .40
16 Darren McAusland .15 .40
17 Jeff Nelson .20 .50
18 Todd Nelson .15 .40
19 Mike Parson .20 .50
20 Steve Poapst .15 .40
21 Andre Racicot .20 .50
22 Sergei Tertyshny .15 .40
23 Stefan Ustorf .20 .50

1995-96 Portland Pirates

This 24-card set of the Portland Pirates was sponsored by Dunkin' Donuts and features color action player photos framed in red and shades of gray. The backs carry a small black-and-white player head photo with biographical information and player statistics. The cards are unnumbered and checklisted below in alphabetical order.

COMPLETE SET (24) 6.00 15.00
1 Alexander Alexeev .15 .40
2 Jason Allison .75 2.00
3 Norm Batherson .15 .40
4 Frank Bialowas .40 1.00
5 Patrick Boileau .15 .40
6 Andrew Brunette .60 1.50
7 Stephane Charbonneau .15 .40
8 Jason Christie .15 .40
9 Crackers MASCOT .02 .10
10 Brian Curran .08 .25
11 Martin Gendron .15 .40
12 Kent Hulst .15 .40
13 Alexander Kharlamov .15 .40
14 Jim Mathieson .20 .50
15 Darren McAusland .15 .40
16 Jeff Nelson .15 .40
17 Darryl Paquette .20 .50
18 Rob Pearson .20 .50
19 Steve Poapst .15 .40
20 Joel Poirier .15 .40
21 Sergei Tertyshny .15 .40
22 Barry Trotz CO .08 .25
23 Ron Tugnutt .60 1.50
24 Stefan Ustorf .20 .50

1996-97 Portland Pirates

This 25-card set was produced by Split Second. The set features action photos on the front and a statistical package on the reverse. The unnumbered cards feature the player's sweater number prominently on the back, and are numbered thusly below.

COMPLETE SET (25) 4.80 12.00
1 Robb Stauber .30 .75
3 Steve Poapst .20 .50
4 Stewart Malgunas .20 .50
5 Nolan Baumgartner .20 .50
6 Ron Pascucci .20 .50
7 Norm Batherson .20 .50
9 Marc Potvin .30 .75
10 Kent Hulst .20 .50
12 Brad Church .20 .50
14 Richard Zednik .40 1.00
15 Jaroslav Svejkovsky .30 .75
16 Darren McAusland .20 .50
19 Andrew Brunette .40 1.00
20 Miika Elomo .20 .50
21 Jason Christie .20 .50
22 Alexander Kharlamov .20 .50
24 Daniel Laperriere .20 .50
25 Benoit Gratton .20 .50
27 Patrick Boileau .20 .50
28 Trevor Halverson .20 .50
30 Martin Brochu .40 1.00
33 Anson Carter .60 1.50
NNO Paul Gardner ACO .02 .10
NNO Barry Trotz CO .08 .25
NNO AHL Ad Card .01

1996-97 Portland Pirates Shop N' Save

This set features the Pirates of the AHL. The cards were issued as promotional giveaways at a local grocery store.

COMPLETE SET (10) 4.00 10.00
1 Robb Stauber .50 1.25
2 Steve Poapst .40 1.00
3 Nolan Baumgartner .40 1.00
4 Norm Batherson .40 1.00
5 Kent Hulst .40 1.00
6 Jaroslav Svejkovsky .40 1.00
7 Andrew Brunette .75 2.00
8 Miika Elomo .75 2.00
9 Jason Christie .40 1.00
10 Benoit Gratton .40 1.00

1997-98 Portland Pirates

Little is known about this set beyond the confirmed checklist, but it is believed that the cards were sold in team set form at home games. Additional information can be forwarded to hockeymag@beckett.com.

COMPLETE SET (26) 4.80 12.00
1 Nolan Baumgartner .20 .50
2 Jan Benda .15 .40
3 Patrick Boileau .15 .40
4 Martin Brochu .40 1.00
5 Andrew Brunette .40 1.00
6 Sebastien Charpentier .30 .75
7 Jason Christie .15 .40
8 Brad Church .15 .40
9 Miika Elomo .20 .50
10 Benoit Gratton .30 .75
11 David Harlock .20 .50
12 Dwayne Hay .20 .50
13 Kent Hulst .15 .40
14 Kevin Kaminski .30 .75
15 Mark Major .15 .40
16 Stewart Malgunas .15 .40
17 Rick Mrozik .15 .40
18 Ryan Mulhern .15 .40
19 Mike O'Neill .30 .75
20 Steve Poapst .20 .50
21 Kayle Short .15 .40
22 Alexandre Volchkov .20 .50
23 Jay Wells ACO .02 .10
24 Bryan Trottier HCO .40 1.00
25 PHPA Web Site .01
26 AHL Web Site .01

1998-99 Portland Pirates

This set features the Pirates of the AHL. The set was produced and sold by the team. Research has determined that two versions exist of card #19.

COMPLETE SET (26) 4.80 12.00
1 J-P Dumont .75 2.00
2 Patrick Boileau .15 .40
3 Martin Brochu .30 .75
4 Trevor Halverson .15 .40
5 Matt Herr .20 .50
6 Benoit Gratton .20 .50
7 Nolan Baumgartner .15 .40
8 Casey Hankinson .15 .40
9 Kent Hulst .15 .40
10 Rick Kowalsky .15 .40
11 Daniel Cleary .30 .75
12 Todd Rohloff .15 .40
13 Jeff Toms .15 .40
14 Steve Poapst .15 .40
15 Mike Peluso .30 .75
16 Young/Soutuyo .15 .40
17 Mike Rosati .30 .75
18 Trent Whitfield .30 .75
19 Neil Belland ACO .02 .10
19 Mark Kumpel HCO .02 .10
20 Craig Mills .20 .50
21 Stewart Malgunas .15 .40
22 Rick Mrozik .15 .40
23 Dwight Parrish .15 .40
24 Mark Major .15 .40
25 AHL Web Site .01

1999-00 Portland Pirates

This 25-card set features the Pirates of the AHL. The series was produced by Split Second and sold by the team at home games. Since the cards are not numbered, they are listed below in alphabetical order.

COMPLETE SET (25) 4.00 10.00
1 Nolan Baumgartner .20 .50
2 Alexei Tezikov .30 .75
3 Patrick Boileau .15 .40
4 Martin Brochu .40 1.00
5 Sebastien Charpentier .40 1.00
6 Miika Elomo .20 .50
7 Jakub Ficenec .15 .40
8 J.F. Fortin .20 .50
9 Matt Herr .20 .50
10 Kent Hulst .15 .40
11 Jamie Huscroft .15 .40
12 Martin Kumpel .15 .40
Glen Hanlon
13 Mascot .02 .10
14 Glen Metropolit .30 .75
15 Barrie Moore .15 .40
16 Ryan Mulhern .15 .40
17 Jeff Nelson .15 .40
18 Mike Peluso .20 .50
19 Steve Poapst .15 .40
20 Steve Shirreffs .15 .40
21 Jason Shmyr .15 .40
22 Trainer Card .02 .10
23 Alexandre Volchkov .20 .50
24 Trent Whitfield .30 .75
25 Rob Zettler .15 .40

2000-01 Portland Pirates

This set features the Pirates of the AHL. The set was produced by Choice Marketing and issued initially as a kid's club giveaway. Later, it was available with purchase at a local sub shop.

COMPLETE SET (20) 4.80 12.00
1 Kent Hulst .20 .50
2 Jeff Nelson .20 .50
3 Krys Barch .30 .75
4 Mark Murphy .20 .50
5 Patrick Boileau .20 .50
6 Todd Rohloff .20 .50
7 Jean-Francois Fortin .20 .50
8 Sebastien Charpentier .40 1.00
9 Glen Metropolit .30 .75
10 Remi Royer .30 .75
11 Derek Bekar .20 .50
12 Martin Hlinka .20 .50
13 Corey Hirsch .40 1.00
14 Alexei Tezikov .40 1.00
15 Rob Zettler .20 .50
16 Mike Farrell .20 .50
17 Jakub Ficenec .20 .50
18 Matt Pettinger .40 1.00
19 Jason Shmyr .20 .50
20 Brad Church .30 .75

2004-05 Portland Pirates

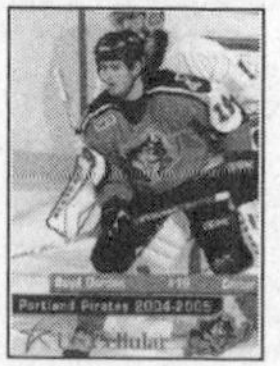

Set was given out in 12-card segments at two home games.

COMPLETE SET (12) 12.00
1 Steve Eminger .50
2 Brian Sutherby .75
3 Boyd Gordon .50
4 Owen Fussey .50
5 Jason Ulmer .50

6 Justin Eddy .50
7 Jeff Paul .50
8 Jared Aulin .75
9 Michel Periard .50
10 Graham Mink 1.00
11 Chris Hajt .50
Mike Amodeo
12 Cam McCaffrey .50
Jonas Johansson
13 Jakub Cutta .50
14 Brooks Laich .75
15 Carlyle Lewis .50
16 Shaone Morrisonn .50
17 Maxime Ouellet 1.00
18 Louis Robitaille .50
19 Garrett Stroshein 1.00
20 Darcy Verot 1.00
21 Trent Whitfield 1.00
22 Nolan Yonkman .50
23 Dwayne Zinger .50
24 Jakub Klepis 1.00
Tomas Fleischmann

2005-06 Portland Pirates

COMPLETE SET (24) 8.00 15.00
1 Geoff Peters .20 .50
2 Aaron Rome .40 1.00
3 Shane O'Brien .20 .50
4 Tim Brent .20 .50
5 Aaron Gavey .20 .50
6 Pierre Parenteau .20 .50
7 Corey Perry .60 1.50
8 Curtis Glencross .20 .50
9 Jordan Smith .20 .50
10 Kenny Smith .20 .50
11 Dieter Kochan .60 1.50
12 Ryan Shannon .20 .50
13 Joel Perrault .20 .50
14 Nathan Saunders .20 .50
15 Ryan Getzlaf .60 1.50
16 Ladislav Smid .40 1.00
17 Igor Pohanka .20 .50
18 Kent Huskins .20 .50
19 Bruno St. Jaques .20 .50
20 Dustin Penner .40 1.00
21 Simon Ferguson .20 .50
22 Nathan Marsters .40 1.00
23 Shane Hynes .20 .50
24 Trevor Gillies .60 1.50

2006-07 Portland Pirates

COMPLETE SET (24) 10.00 18.00
1 Bruce Crowder ACO .10 .25
2 Eric Weinrich ACO .10 .25
3 Zenon Konopka .30 .75
4 Aaron Rome .30 .75
5 Nathan Marsters .30 .75
6 Tim Brent .30 .75
7 Clay Wilson .30 .75
8 Brian Salcido .30 .75
9 Curtis Glencross .30 .75
10 Chris Durno .30 .75
11 Colby Genoway .30 .75
12 Simon Ferguson .30 .75
13 Geoff Peters .30 .75
14 Brett Skinner .30 .75
15 Drew Miller .60 1.50
16 Matt Keith .30 .75
17 Shawn Thornton .40 1.00
18 Petteri Wirtanen .30 .75
19 Bjorn Melin .30 .75
20 Trevor Gillies .40 1.00
21 Ryan Carter .40 1.00
22 Kent Huskins .30 .75
23 Mike Wall .40 1.00
24 Kevin Dineen CO .10 .25

2007-08 Portland Pirates

COMPLETE SET (24) 6.00 15.00
1 Crackers and Salty Pete MASCOTS .30 .75
2 Brendan Mikkelson .30 .75
3 Stephen Dixon .30 .75
4 Darryl Bootland .30 .75
5 Tyler Bouck .30 .75
6 Simon Ferguson .30 .75
7 Brandon Segal .30 .75
8 Joe Callahan .30 .75
9 Bobby Ryan .30 .75
10 Mike McKenna .30 .75
11 Matt Christie .30 .75
12 Drew Miller 1.00 2.50
13 Eric Weinrich .30 .75
14 Jason King .30 .75
15 Bruno St. Jacques .30 .75
16 Mike Hoffman .30 .75
17 Geoff Platt .30 .75
18 Andrew Ebbett .30 .75
19 Brian Salcido .30 .75
20 Michal Birner .30 .75
21 Petteri Wirtanen .30 .75
22 Gerald Coleman .30 .75
23 Brett Festerling .30 .75
24 Andy Schneider .30 .75

1986-87 Portland Winter Hawks

Sponsored by AM-PM Mini-Market, this 24-card set measures the standard size. The white-bordered fronts feature posed-on-ice color player photos. The player's name, number, and position appear in black lettering within the white margin beneath the picture, while the team name is printed vertically along the left border. The sponsor's logo appears at the upper right. The cards are unnumbered and checklisted below in alphabetical order.

COMPLETE SET (24) 15.00 40.00
1 Dave Archibald 1.00 2.50
2 Bruce Basken .60 1.50
3 Thomas Bjuhr .60 1.50
4 Shaun Clouston .60 1.50
5 Jeff Finley .60 1.50
6 Bob Foglietta .60 1.50
7 Brian Gerrits .60 1.50
8 Darryl Gilmour 1.00 2.50
9 Dennis Holland .60 1.50
10 Steve Kloepzig .60 1.50
11 Jim Latos .60 1.50
12 Dave McLay .60 1.50
13 Scott Melnyk .60 1.50
14 Troy Mick .60 1.50
15 Roy Mitchell .60 1.50
16 Jamie Nicolls .60 1.50
17 Trevor Pohl .60 1.50
18 Troy Pohl .60 1.50
19 Glen Seymour 1.00 2.50
20 Jeff Sharples .60 1.50
21 Jay Stark .60 1.50
22 Jim Swan .60 1.50
23 Glen Wesley 2.00 5.00
24 Dan Woodley .60 1.50

1987-88 Portland Winter Hawks

Sponsored by Fred Meyer and Pepsi, this 21-card standard-size set features the 1987-88 Portland Winter Hawks of the Western Hockey League. Inside white borders, the fronts feature posed color player photos shot on the ice at the stadium. The wider left border carries the team name, while the upper right corner of the picture has been cut off to allow space for the sponsor logo. The cards are unnumbered and checklisted below in alphabetical order.

COMPLETE SET (21) 4.80 12.00
1 Wayne Anchikoski .20 .50
2 Eric Badzgon .30 .75
3 Chad Biafore .20 .50
4 James(Hamish) Black .20 .50
5 Terry Black .20 .50
6 Shaun Clouston .20 .50
7 Byron Dafoe 1.25 3.00
8 Brent Fleetwood .20 .50
9 Rob Flintoft .20 .50
10 Bryan Gourlie .20 .50
11 Mark Greyeyes .20 .50
12 Dennis Holland .20 .50
13 Kevin Jorgenson .20 .50
14 Greg Leahy .20 .50
15 Troy Mick .20 .50
16 Roy Mitchell .20 .50
17 Joey Mittelsteadt .20 .50
18 Mike Moore .20 .50
19 Scott Mydan .20 .50
20 Calvin Thudiun .20 .50
21 Pepsi Ad Card .02 .10

1988-89 Portland Winter Hawks

Sponsored by Pepsi and Fred Meyer, this 21-card set measures the standard size. On a white background, the fronts feature posed color player photos with a facsimile autograph in the bottom part of the picture. The player's name, number, and position appear under the picture, while the team name is printed alongside the left border. The cards are unnumbered and checklisted below in alphabetical order.

COMPLETE SET (21) 4.80 12.00
1 Wayne Anchikoski .20 .50
2 Eric Badzgon .30 .75
3 Chad Biafore .20 .50
4 James(Hamish) Black .20 .50
5 Terry Black .20 .50
6 Shaun Clouston .20 .50
7 Byron Dafoe 1.25 3.00
8 Brent Fleetwood .20 .50
9 Rob Flintoft .20 .50
10 Bryan Gourlie .20 .50
11 Mark Greyeyes .20 .50
12 Dennis Holland .20 .50
13 Kevin Jorgenson .20 .50
14 Greg Leahy .20 .50
15 Troy Mick .20 .50
16 Roy Mitchell .20 .50
17 Joey Mittelsteadt .20 .50
18 Mike Moore .20 .50
19 Scott Mydan .20 .50
20 Calvin Thudiun .20 .50
21 Pepsi Coupon .02 .10

1989-90 Portland Winter Hawks

Sponsored by Pepsi and Fred Meyer, this 21-card set measures the standard size. The fronts feature posed color player photos inside a black picture frame and white outer borders. A facsimile autograph is inscribed across the picture. The player's name, number, and position appear under the photo, while the team name is printed alongside the left border. The cards are unnumbered and checklisted below in alphabetical order.

COMPLETE SET (21) 4.80 12.00
1 Jamie Black .20 .50
2 Vince Cocciolo .20 .50
3 Byron Dafoe .75 2.00
4 Cam Danyluk .20 .50
5 Kim Deck .20 .50
6 Dean Dorchak .20 .50
7 Brent Fleetwood .20 .50
8 Rick Fry .20 .50
9 Bryan Gourlie .20 .50
10 Brad Harrison .20 .50
11 Judson Innes .20 .50
12 Dean Intwert .30 .75
13 Kevin Jorgenson .20 .50
14 Todd Kinniburgh .20 .50
15 Greg Leahy .20 .50
16 Jamie Linden .20 .50
17 Scott Mydan .20 .50
18 Mike Ruark .20 .50
19 Jeff Sebastian .20 .50
20 Brandon Smith .25 .60
21 Steve Young .20 .50

1993-94 Portland Winter Hawks

This is a tough team-issued set from the Winter Hawks of the WHL. The cards are unnumbered and are checklisted below in alphabetical order.

COMPLETE SET (27) 8.00 15.00
1 Mike Arbulic .10 .30
2 Lonny Bohonos .20 .50
3 Shannon Briske .10 .30
4 Dave Cammock .10 .30
5 Shawn Collins .10 .30
6 Matt Davidson .10 .30
7 Adam Deadmarsh 1.25 3.00
8 Adam Deadmarsh GM 1.25 3.00
9 Jake Deadmarsh .10 .30
10 Brett Fizzell .10 .30
11 Colin Foley .10 .30
12 Brad Isbister .60 1.50
13 Scott Langkow .40 1.00
14 Mike Little .10 .30
15 Dmitri Markovsky .10 .30
16 Jason McBain .10 .30
17 Scott Nichol .10 .30
18 Brent Peterson .10 .30
19 Nolan Pratt .20 .50
20 Scott Rideout .10 .30
21 Layne Roland .10 .30
22 Dave Scatchard .30 .75
23 Brandon Smith .20 .50
24 Brad Swanson .10 .30
25 Brad Symes .10 .30
26 Jason Wiemer .75 2.00
27 Mike Williamson .10 .30

1997-98 Portland Winter Hawks

This set of standard-sized cards was sold in set form by the team. It features early cards of hobby heroes Marian Hossa and Brenden Morrow.

COMPLETE SET (27) 16.00 40.00
1 Checklist .02 .10
2 Brent Belecki .15 .40
3 Mike Muzechka .15 .40
4 Marian Hossa 6.00 15.00
5 Ken Davis .15 .40
6 Jerad Smith .15 .40
7 Josh Green .40 1.00
8 Bobby Russell .15 .40
9 Kyle Chant .15 .40
10 Brenden Morrow 4.00 10.00
11 Derek MacLean .40 1.00
12 Todd Hornung .15 .40
13 Andrej Podkonicky .30 .75
14 Bobby Duncan .15 .40
15 Todd Robinson .15 .40
16 Chris Jacobson .15 .40
17 Shon Jones-Parry .15 .40
18 Kevin Haupt .15 .40
19 Ryan Thrussell .15 .40
20 Marty Standish .15 .40
21 Jason Labarbera .75 2.00
22 Matt Walker .15 .40
23 Andrew Ference .40 1.00
24 Joey Tetarenko 1.25 3.00
25 Brent Peterson HCO .08 .25
26 Mike Williamson ACO .02 .10
27 Julius Supler ACO .02 .10

2003-04 Portland Winter Hawks

This set was sold by the team at home games.

COMPLETE SET (29) 12.00
1 Dustin Butler .75
2 Tomas Fojtik .40
3 Taylor Sutherlin .40
4 Michael Funk .40
5 Richie Regehr .75
6 Brendan Mikkelson .40
7 Cody McLeod .40
8 Aaron Roberge .40
9 Brian Woolger .40
10 C.J. Jackson .40
11 Chad Wolkowski .40
12 Shane Halifax .40
13 Robin Big Snake .75
14 Alex Aldred .40
15 Brandon Dubinsky 3.00
16 Ivan Dornic .40
17 Dan Da Silva .40
18 Braydon Coburn .75
19 Frazer McLaren .40
20 Derek Poplawski .40
21 Kyle Bailey .40
22 Kevin Opsahl .40
23 Krister Toews .75
24 Ivan Dornic .40
Draft
25 Braydon Coburn 1.50
Draft
26 Mike Williamson HCO .10
27 Blake Wesley ACO .10
28 Mascot .10
29 Checklist .01

2004-05 Portland Winter Hawks

We've confirmed the existence of a handful of cards from this set. If you know of others, please contact us at hockeymag@beckett.com. The three unnumbered bonus cards were available outside of the team set. The Coburn was available only at the Mock Crest Tavern, whose ad is on the back. The other two were available only at the booster club's table.

COMPLETE SET (25)
1 Dustin Butler
2 Cameron Cepek
3 Braydon Coburn
4 Dan DaSilva
5 Brandon Dubinsky
6 Michael Funk
7 Frazer McLaren
8 Mike Sauer
9 Brian Woolger
10 Paul Gaustad
11 Richie Regehr
12 Cody McLeod
13 Robin Big Snake
NNO R. Regehr/P. Gaustad
NNO Braydon Coburn MCT
NNO C. McLeod/R. Big Snake

1984-85 Prince Albert Raiders Stickers

This set of 22 stickers was sponsored by Autotec Oil and Saskatchewan Ronald McDonald House. Each sticker measures 2" by 1 3/4" and could be pasted on a 17" by 11" poster printed in thin glossy paper. The stickers display a black-and-white head shot; the uniform number is also printed on the front. The stickers are unnumbered and checklisted below in alphabetical order.

COMPLETE SET (22) 10.00 25.00
1 Ken Baumgartner 1.25 3.00
2 Brad Bennett .40 1.00
3 Dean Braham .40 1.00
4 Rod Dallman .40 1.00
5 Neil Davey .40 1.00
6 Pat Elynuik .60 1.50
7 Collin Feser .40 1.00
8 Dave Goertz .40 1.00
9 Steve Gotaas .40 1.00
10 Tony Grenier .40 1.00
11 Roydon Gunn .40 1.00
12 Doug Hobson .40 1.00
13 Dan Hodgson .60 1.50
14 Curtis Hunt .40 1.00
15 Kim Issel .40 1.00
16 Ward Komonosky .40 1.00
17 David Manson .40 1.00
18 Dale McFee .40 1.00
19 Ken Morrison .40 1.00
20 Dave Pasin .60 1.50
21 Don Schmidt .40 1.00
22 Emanuel Viveiros .40 1.00

1990-91 Prince Albert Raiders

Sponsored by the High Noon Optimist Club, these 25 standard-size cards of the WHL's Prince Albert Raiders are printed on thin card stock and feature on their fronts color posed-on-ice player photos with white outer borders and yellow and green inner borders. The player's name, jersey number, and position appear in white lettering within the green inner border beneath the picture. The cards are unnumbered and checklisted below in alphabetical order.

COMPLETE SET (25) 4.00 10.00
1 Scott Allison .15 .40
2 Laurie Billeck .15 .40
3 Jeff Gorman .15 .40
4 Donevan Hextall .20 .50
5 Troy Hjertaas .15 .40
6 Dan Kesa .20 .50
7 Jason Kwiatkowski .15 .40
8 Travis Laycock .15 .40
9 Lee J. Leslie .20 .50
10 Jamie Linden .15 .40
11 Dean McAmmond .30 .75
12 Dave Neilson .15 .40
13 Jeff Nelson .20 .50
14 Troy Neumeier .15 .40
15 Pat Odnokon .15 .40
16 Brian Pellerin .15 .40
17 Darren Perkins .15 .40
18 Curt Regnier .20 .50
19 Chad Seibel .15 .40
20 Mark Stowe .15 .40
21 Darren Van Impe .30 .75
22 Shane Zulyniak .15 .40
23 Title Card .02 .10
24 Info Card (Strangers) .02 .10
25 Info Card (Vandalism) .02 .10

1991-92 Prince Albert Raiders

Sponsored by the High Noon Optimist Club, these 24 standard-size cards of the WHL's Prince Albert Raiders are printed on thin card stock and feature on their fronts color posed-on-ice player photos enclosed by green borders. The player's name, jersey number, and position appear in white lettering within the green border near the bottom. The cards are unnumbered and checklisted below in alphabetical order.

COMPLETE SET (24) 3.00 8.00
1 Mike Fedorko CO .02 .10
2 Jeff Gorman .15 .40
3 Merv Haney .15 .40
4 Donevan Hextall .20 .50
5 Troy Hjertaas .15 .40
6 Dan Kesa .20 .50
7 Jason Klassen .15 .40
8 Jason Kwiatkowski .15 .40
9 Jeff Lank .15 .40
10 Travis Laycock .15 .40
11 Lee J. Leslie .15 .40
12 Stan Matwijiw .20 .50
13 Dean McAmmond .20 .50
14 David Neilson .15 .40
15 Jeff Nelson .15 .40
16 Mark Odnokon ACO .02 .10
17 Darren Perkins .15 .40
18 Ryan Pisiak .15 .40
19 Nick Polychronopoulos .15 .40
20 Curt Regnier .20 .50
21 Jason Renard .15 .40
22 Barkley Swenson .15 .40
23 Darren Van Impe .20 .50
24 Shane Zulyniak .15 .40

1993-94 Prince Albert Raiders

This 22-card standard-size set was sponsored by High Noon Prince Albert Optimists and "Stay in School Canada." On a white card face, the fronts feature color action player photos inside a black picture frame. The player's name appears in a yellow bar under the picture. The cards are unnumbered and checklisted below in alphabetical order.

COMPLETE SET (22) 4.00 10.00
1 Ryan Bast .15 .40
2 Rodney Bowers .15 .40
3 Van Burgess .15 .40
4 Brad Church .30 .75
5 Joaquin Gage .30 .75
6 Jeff Gorman .15 .40
7 Merv Haney .15 .40
8 Greg Harvey .15 .40
9 Paul Healey .15 .40
10 Shane Hnidy .30 .75
11 Russell Hogue .15 .40
12 Jason Issel .15 .40
13 Steve Kelly .30 .75
14 Jeff Lank .15 .40
15 Mike McGhan .15 .40
16 Denis Pederson .30 .75
17 Mitch Shawara .15 .40
18 Shayne Toporowski .15 .40
19 David Van Drunen .15 .40
20 Dean Whitney .15 .40
21 Darren Wright .15 .40
22 Shane Zulyniak .10 .40

1994-95 Prince Albert Raiders

This 23-card set of the Prince Albert Raiders of the WHL was sponsored by the Prince Albert Optimists and "Stay in School Canada." The design mirrors that of the 1993-94 set. The set is noteworthy for the inclusion of several NHL first rounders, including Brad Church, Steve Kelly and Dennis Pederson. The cards are unnumbered, and are checklisted below alphabetically.

COMPLETE SET (23) 4.80 12.00
1 Sandy Allan .20 .50
2 Ryan Bast .20 .50
3 Brad Church .30 .75
4 Kris Fizzell .15 .40
5 Paul Healey .15 .40
6 Rob Hegberg .15 .40
7 Shane Hnidy .30 .75
8 Russell Hogue .15 .40
9 Craig Hordal .20 .50
10 Jason Issel .15 .40
11 Neil Johnston .15 .40
12 Steve Kelly .30 .75
13 Jeff Lank .15 .40
14 Mike McGhan .15 .40
15 Denis Pederson .60 1.50
16 Sean Robertson .15 .40
17 Mitch Shawara .15 .40
18 Shayne Toporowski .20 .50
19 Kaleb Toth .15 .40
20 Dave Van Drunen .20 .50
21 Shane Willis .60 1.50
22 Darren Wright .15 .40
23 Shane Zulyniak .15 .40

1995-96 Prince Albert Raiders

This 22-card set of the Prince Albert Raiders of the WHL was sponsored by the Prince Albert Optimists and features color action player photos in a thin back border on a white background. The player's name is printed in a yellow bar with his position in a white star below the picture. This set includes several first round selections, including 1996 first overall selection Chris Phillips. The cards are unnumbered and checklisted below in alphabetical order.

COMPLETE SET (22) 4.80 25.00
1 Rod Branch .40 1.00
2 Curtis Brown .75 2.00
3 Brad Church .40 1.00
4 Kris Fizzell .40 1.00
5 Dallas Flaman .40 1.00
6 Don Halverson .40 1.00
7 Shane Hnidy .40 1.00
8 Russell Hogue .40 1.00
9 Jason Issel .40 1.00
10 Garnet Jacobson .40 1.00
11 Kevin Kellett .40 1.00
12 Steve Kelly .60 1.50
13 Dylan Kemp .40 1.00
14 Michael McGhan .40 1.00
15 Marian Menhart .40 1.00
16 Chris Phillips .75 2.00
17 Blaine Russell .40 1.00
18 Mitch Shawara .40 1.00
19 Dave Van Drunen .40 1.00
20 Roman Vopat .40 1.00
21 Shane Willis .60 1.50
22 Darren Wright .40 1.00

1996-97 Prince Albert Raiders

Sponsored by the Prince Albert Optimists Clubs, this 23-card set features color player photos and jersey numbers on the front, and is checklisted below alphabetically.

COMPLETE SET (23) 4.80 12.00
1 Trevor Baker .20 .50
2 Scott Botterill .20 .50
3 Craig Brunel .20 .50
4 Marco Cefalo .20 .50
5 Dallas Flaman .20 .50
6 Jeremy Goetzinger .20 .50
7 Don Halverson .20 .50
8 Russell Hogue .20 .50
9 Jason Issel .20 .50
10 Garnet Jacobson .20 .50
11 Kevin Kellett .20 .50
12 Dylan Kemp .20 .50
13 Evan Lindsay .30 .75
14 Marian Menhart .20 .50
15 Cory Morgan .20 .50
16 Derek Paget .20 .50
17 Chris Phillips .60 1.50
18 Harlan Pratt .20 .50
19 Blaine Russell .15 .40
20 Adam Stewart .20 .50
21 Dave Van Drunen .30 .75
22 Steve Wilejto .20 .50
23 Shane Willis .40 1.00

1997-98 Prince Albert Raiders

This set features the Raiders of the WHL. The set was sponsored by the Prince Albert Optimists Club and was sold at home games. The cards are unnumbered, and so are listed below in alphabetical order.

COMPLETE SET (21) 4.00 10.00
1 Scott Botterill .20 .50
2 Derek Brandon .20 .50
3 Craig Brunel .20 .50
4 David Cameron .20 .50
5 Clayton Chartrand .20 .50
6 Dallas Flaman .20 .50
7 Jeremy Goetzinger .20 .50
8 Don Halverson .20 .50
9 Trevor Hitchings .20 .50
10 Kevin Kellett .20 .50
11 Evan Lindsay .30 .75
12 Ross Lupaschuk .40 1.00
13 Brady Magneson .20 .50
14 Grant McCune .30 .75
15 Cory Morgan .20 .50
16 Derek Paget .20 .50
17 Harlan Pratt .20 .50
18 Richard Seeley .20 .50
19 Cam Severson .20 .50
20 Brad Swanson .20 .50
21 Steve Wilejto .20 .50

1998-99 Prince Albert Raiders

This 22-card set was produced by Action Printing LTD and is not numbered. The set is listed in alphabetical order.

COMPLETE SET (22) 12.00 20.00
1 Derek Brandon .20 .50
2 Marc Brown .20 .50
3 Craig Brunel .20 .50
4 Clayton Chartrand .20 .50
5 Riley Cote .20 .50
6 Todd Fedoruk .75 2.00
7 Dallas Flaman .20 .50
8 Jeremy Goetzinger .20 .50
9 Scott Hartnell 2.00 5.00
10 Shaun Hill .20 .50
11 Cody Jensen .20 .50
12 Kevin Kellet .20 .50
13 Milan Kraft .75 2.00
14 Evan Lindsay .30 .75
15 Ross Lupachuk .40 1.00
16 Grant McCune .20 .50
17 Cory Morgan .20 .50
18 Kerry Nice .20 .50
19 Derek Paget .20 .50
20 Garrett Prosofsky .20 .50
21 Nick Schultz .75 2.00
22 Richard Seeley .20 .50

2000-01 Prince Albert Raiders

This set features the Raiders of the WHL. The cards were sold by the team at home games. Because they are unnumbered, they are listed below alphabetically.

COMPLETE SET (25) 4.80 12.00
1 Jay Batchelor .20 .50
2 Anton Borodkin .20 .50
3 Kyle Bruce .20 .50
4 Jordan Clarke .20 .50
5 Riley Cote .20 .50
6 Cary Grant TR .04 .11
7 Ryan Haggarty .20 .50
8 J.J. Hunter .20 .50
9 Dustin Kazak .20 .50
10 Jon Kress .20 .50
11 Landon Lillejord .20 .50
12 Connor Lowe .20 .50
13 Grant McCune .31 .78
14 Grant McNeill .20 .50
15 Scott McQueen .20 .50
16 Jon Mirasty .20 .50
17 Chris Harper .20 .50
18 Igor Pohanka .20 .50
19 Garrett Prosofsky .31 .78
20 Riley MASCOT .04 .11
21 Jeff Schmidt .20 .50
22 Nick Schultz .80 2.00
23 Aaron Sorochan .31 .78
24 Blain Stowards .20 .50
25 Greg Watson .31 .78

2001-02 Prince Albert Raiders

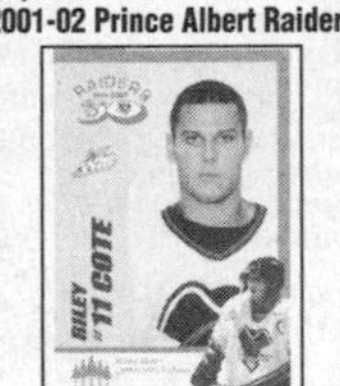

This set features the Raiders of the WHL. The cards are slightly taller than standard-size and feature a pair of photos on the front, accentuated by a red and yellow border. The black and white backs feature stats. It's believed the cards were sold by the team at home games.

COMPLETE SET (24) 6.00 15.00
1 Jay Batchelor .30 .75
2 Kyle Bruce .30 .75
3 Jeremy Colliton .30 1.50
4 Riley Cote .30 .75
5 Justin Cruse .30 .75
6 James Demone .30 .75
7 Paul Deniset .30 .75
8 Perry Faul .30 .75
9 Luke Fritshaw .30 .75
10 Jon Kress .30 .75
11 Wade Klippenstein CO .10 .25
12 Landon Lillejord .30 .75
13 Rastislav Lipka .30 .75
14 Grant McNeill .30 .75
15 Brett Novak .30 .75
16 Igor Pohanka .30 .75
17 Jeff Schmidt .30 .75
18 Drew Schoneck ACO .10 .25
19 Jesse Schultz .30 .75
20 Aaron Sorochan .40 1.00
21 Joe Suderman .30 .75
22 Thomas Vicars .40 1.00
23 Greg Watson .40 1.00
24 Mike Wirll .30 .75

2002-03 Prince Albert Raiders

COMPLETE SET (23) 8.00 20.00
1 Rejean Beauchemin 1.25 3.00
2 Kyle Bruce .30 .75
3 Dane Byers .60 1.50
4 Kyle Chipchura .75 2.00
5 Jeremy Colliton .75 2.00
6 Mark Cress .30 .75
7 Justin Cruse .30 .75
8 Chris Di Ubaldo .30 .75
9 Perry Faul .30 .75
10 Luke Fritshaw .30 .75
11 Kevin Harris .30 .75
12 Jon Kress .30 .75
13 Colin Lafreniere .30 .75
14 Seth Leonard .30 .75
15 Rastislav Lipka .30 .75
16 Grant McNeill .30 .75
17 Brett Novak .30 .75
18 Igor Pohanka .30 .75
19 Rory Rawlyk .30 .75
20 Evan Schafer .30 .75
21 Aaron Sorochan .30 .75
22 Greg Watson .30 .75
23 Andy Zulyniak .30 .75

2003-04 Prince Albert Raiders

This checklist may be incomplete. Please forward additional info to hockeymag@beckett.com.

COMPLETE SET (25) 6.00 15.00
1 Aki Seitsonen .30 .75
2 Brandon Peet .20 .50
3 Brant Hilton .20 .50
4 Brett Novak .20 .50
5 Caine Pearpoint .20 .50
6 Colin Lafreniere .20 .50
7 Dane Byers .60 1.50
8 Dave Manson .20 .50
9 Evan Schafer .20 .50
10 Garth Collins .20 .50
11 Jeff May .20 .50
12 Jeremy Colliton .60 1.50
13 Jordan Morgan .20 .50
14 Justin Cruse .20 .50
15 Kyle Chipchura .60 1.50
16 Luke Fritshaw .20 .50
17 Mark Ardelan .20 .50
18 Michal Polak .20 .50
19 Mike Gauthier .20 .50
20 Mike Hellyer .20 .50
21 Perry Faul .20 .50
22 Peter Anholt .20 .50
23 Rejean Beauchemin .60 1.50
24 Seth Leonard .20 .50
25 Travis Young .20 .50

2004-05 Prince Albert Raiders

COMPLETE SET (24) 8.00 20.00
1 Alex Archibald .30 .75
2 Mike Gauthier .30 .75
3 Jeff May .30 .75
4 Evan Schafer .30 .75
5 Luke Fritshaw .40 1.00
6 Landon Jones .30 .75
7 Scott Doucet .30 .75
8 Mike Hellyer .30 .75
9 Brandon Peet .30 .75
10 Brad Erickson .30 .75
11 Brett Ottmann .30 .75
12 Nolan Waker .30 .75
13 Kyle Chipchura .60 1.50
14 Aki Seitsonen .40 1.00
15 Ryan Depape .30 .75
16 Brett Novak .30 .75
17 Jeremy Colliton .60 1.50
18 Josh Elder .30 .75
19 Caine Pearpoint .30 .75
20 Chris Schlenker .30 .75
21 Dane Byers .60 1.50
22 Garth Collins .30 .75
23 Rejean Beauchemin .75 2.00
24 Peter Anholt CO .02 .10

2005-06 Prince Albert Raiders

COMPLETE SET (26) 8.00 20.00
1 Alex Archibald .40 1.00
2 Dane Byers .60 1.50
3 Kyle Chipchura .60 1.50
4 Peter Cmorej .30 .75
5 Ryan DePape .30 .75
6 Jesse Deckert .40 1.00
7 Scott Doucet .30 .75
8 Jarrid Dowhay .30 .75
9 Josh Elder .30 .75
10 Brad Erickson .30 .75
11 Mike Gauthier .30 .75
12 Mike Hellyer .30 .75
13 Ashton Hewson .30 .75
14 Kyle Howarth .30 .75
15 Jeff May .30 .75
16 Brett Novak .30 .75
17 Brent Ottmann .30 .75
18 Justin Palazzo .30 .75
19 Evan Schafer .30 .75
20 Aki Seitsonen .40 1.00
21 A.J. Thelen .60 1.50
22 Kevin Tipper .30 .75
23 Peter Anholt CO .02 .10
24 Dave Manson ACO .20 .50
25 Mark Odnokon ACO .02 .10
26 Duane Bartley AT .02 .10

2006-07 Prince Albert Raiders

COMPLETE SET (26) 12.00 20.00
1 David Aime .40 1.00
2 Jesse Deckert .40 1.00
3 Mike Gauthier .40 1.00
4 Jeff May .30 .75
5 A.J. Thelen .60 1.50
6 Blaine Tendler .30 .75
7 Cody Vann .30 .75
8 Scott Doucet .30 .75
9 Mike Hellyer .30 .75
10 Jarrid Dowhay .30 .75
11 Matthew Robertson .30 .75
12 Brent Ottmann .30 .75
13 Milan Jurik .30 .75
14 Lukas Zeliska .30 .75
15 Jordan Trach .30 .75
16 Ryan DePape .30 .75
17 Cody Gross .30 .75
18 Andy Smith .40 1.00
19 Josh Elder .30 .75
20 Ashton Hewson .30 .75
21 Justin Palazzo .30 .75
22 Bryce Lamb .30 .75
23 Shane Malone .30 .75
24 Peter Anholt CO .10 .25
25 Dave Manson ACO .20 .50
26 Kris Knoblauch ACO .10 .25

1998-99 Prince George Cougars

This set features the Cougars of the WHL. The set was sponsored by Sight and Sound Music and was sold at home games. The cards are unnumbered and so are listed below in alphabetical order.

COMPLETE SET (27) 7.20 50.00

1 Header card .01
2 Mike Bayrack .40 1.00
3 Blair Betts .75 2.00
4 Tyler Bouck .75 2.00
5 Eric Brewer 4.00 10.00
6 Tyler Brough .40 1.00
7 Justin Cox .40 1.00
8 Travis Eagles .40 1.00
9 Dan Hamhuis 4.00 10.00
10 Trent Hunter 4.00 10.00
11 Michael Kiesman .40 1.00
12 Petr Kubos .40 1.00
13 Adam Loncan .40 1.00
14 Jozef Mrena .40 1.00
15 Scott Myers .75 2.00
16 Mike Olynyk .40 1.00
17 Jonathan Parker .40 1.00
18 Owen Richey .40 1.00
19 Jarrett Smith .75 2.00
20 Kevin Swanson .75 2.00
21 Curtis Tipler .75 2.00
22 Gary Toor .40 1.00
23 Jordan Walker .40 1.00
24 Ian Walterson .40 1.00
25 Tim Wedderburn .40 1.00
26 Jeff Zorn .40 1.00
27 Cougar Coaches .02 .10

1999-00 Prince George Cougars

This set features the Cougars of the WHL. It is believed that the cards were produced by the team and sold at its souvenir stands. The set includes the first card of 2001 first-rounder Dan Hamhuis.

COMPLETE SET (25) 6.00 15.00
1 Scott Meyers .20 .50
2 Tim Wedderburn .20 .50
3 Ryan Chieduch .20 .50
4 Jeff Zorn .20 .50
5 Dan Hamhuis .75 2.00
6 Kevin Seibel .20 .50
7 Gary Toor .20 .50
8 Devin Wilson .20 .50
9 Jozef Mrena .20 .50
10 Aaron Foster .20 .50
11 Tyler Bouck .30 .75
12 Jonathan Parker .20 .50
13 Shon Jones-Parry .20 .50
14 Roman Takac .20 .50
15 Chris Falloon .20 .50
16 Justin Hansen .20 .50
17 Trent Hunter .75 2.00
18 Blair Betts .40 1.00
19 Travis Eagles .20 .50
20 Ed Dempsey CO .02 .10
21 Dallas Thompson CO .02 .10
22 Paul Valaitis .20 .50
23 Billy Thompson .20 .50
24 Justin Cox .30 .75
25 Dan Baum .20 .50

2000-01 Prince George Cougars

This set features the Cougars of the WHL. It is believed that the cards were sponsored by Dairy Queen and sold by the team, but that has not been confirmed. The set is noteworthy for including an early card of 2001 first rounder Dan Hamhuis.

COMPLETE SET (25) 4.80 12.00
1 Team Card .10 .25
2 Billy Thompson .16 .75
3 Tim Wedderburn .16 .40
4 David Koci .16 .40
5 Dan Hamhuis 1.20 2.00
6 Gary Gladue .16 .40
7 Joey Hope .16 .40
8 Devin Wilson .16 .40
9 Chris Falloon .16 .40
10 Nathan Brice .16 .40
11 Christian Chartier .30 .75
12 Berkeley Buchko .30 .75
13 Scott Lynch .16 .40
14 Aaron Foster .16 .40
15 Jon Filewich .16 .40
16 Tomas Tesarek .16 .40
17 Dan Baum .16 .40
18 Adam Stefishen .16 .40
19 Mark Kitts .16 .40
20 Willy Glover .16 .40
21 Brett Allan .16 .40
22 Travis Eagles .16 .40
23 Justin Cox .16 .40
24 Duane Perillat .16 .40
25 Derek Boogaard .16 .50

2001-02 Prince George Cougars

We have confirmed the existence of two cards in this series. If you know of others, please contact us at hockeymag@beckett.com.

COMPLETE SET (?)
1 Jon Filewich
2 Dan Hamhuis

2003-04 Prince George Cougars

COMPLETE SET (25) 10.00 25.00
1 Header Card .02 .10
2 Justin Pogge 3.00 8.00
3 Devin Featherstone .20 .50
4 Curtis Cooper .20 .50
5 Dustin Byfuglien 4.00 10.00
6 Brett Dickie .20 .50
7 Mike Fogolin .20 .50
8 Dennis Rehak .20 .50
9 Chris Falloon .20 .50
10 Nicholas Drazenovic .20 .50
11 Stanislav Bolshakov .20 .50
12 Dylan Yeo .30 .75
13 Brad Priestlay .20 .50
14 Jon Filewich .20 .50
15 Joshua Aspenlind .20 .50
16 Eric Hunter .20 .50
17 Greg Gardiner .20 .50
18 Danny Lapointe .20 .50
19 Myles Zimmer .30 .75
20 Steven Later .20 .50
21 Colin Patterson .20 .50
22 Tyrell Moulton .30 .75
23 Brett Parker .20 .50
24 Todd Ford .20 .50
25 Team Photo .20 .50

1988-89 ProCards AHL

This set of 348 cards features the 14 teams of the American Hockey League. The cards measure the standard size, 2 1/2" by 3 1/2". The fronts feature color player photos accented by a beige-colored hockey stick superimposed on the right and lower sides of the picture. The AHL logo appears in the lower left corner, and the photo is bordered on all sides by red. The cards are unnumbered and checklisted below alphabetically according to teams as follows (teams in alphabetical order and players listed alphabetically within each team): Adirondack Red Wings (1-25), Baltimore Skipjacks (26-48), Binghamton Whalers (49-72), Cape Breton Oilers (73-96), Halifax Citadels (97-119), Hershey Bears (120-147), Maine Mariners (148-169), Moncton Hawks (170-190), New Haven Nighthawks (191-222), Newmarket Saints (223-244), Rochester Americans (245-268), Sherbrooke Canadiens (269-299), Springfield Indians (300-324), and Utica Devils (325-348). Although the team sets were originally packaged individually, they are listed below as one giant set.

COMPLETE SET (348) 32.00 80.00
1 Rob Nichols .07 .20
2 Bill Dineen CO .08 .25
3 Tim Paris Asst.TR .01 .05
4 Glenn Merkosky .05 .15
5 Mike Gober .07 .20
6 Dave Casey TR .01 .05
7 Sam St.Laurent .30 .75
8 Mark Reimer .08 .25
9 Dennis Smith .07 .20
10 Lou Crawford .07 .20
11 John Mokosak .07 .20
12 Murray Eaves .07 .20
13 Dave Korol .07 .20
14 Miroslav Ihnacak .20 .50
15 Dale Krentz .07 .20
16 Brent Fedyk .20 .50
17 Dean Morton .07 .20
18 Jeff Brubaker .15 .40
19 Tim Cheveldae .60 1.50
20 Randy McKay .40 1.00
21 Peter Dineen .07 .20
22 Rob Doyle .07 .20
23 Daniel Shank .40 1.00
24 Joe Ferras .07 .20
25 John Blum .08 .25
26 Tim Bergland .07 .20
27 Robin Bawa .07 .20
28 Shawn Simpson .07 .20
29 Chris Felix .08 .25
30 Jeff Greenlaw .07 .20
31 Frank Dimuzio .07 .20
32 Tyler Larter .07 .20
33 Rob Whistle .07 .20
34 Dallas Eakins .07 .20
35 Mark Hatcher .07 .20
36 Dave Farrish .08 .25
37 Bill Houlder .20 .50
38 Doug Keans .30 .75
39 Lou Franceschetti .08 .25
40 Rob Murray .05 .15
41 Terry Murray GM/CO .20 .50
42 Steve Seftel .07 .20
43 J.P. Mattingly TR .01 .05
44 Mike Richard .07 .20
45 Shawn Cronin .20 .50
46 Scott McCrory .07 .20
47 Mike Millar .07 .20
48 Dave Sherrid TR .01 .05
49 Marc Laforge .07 .20
50 David O'Brien .07 .20
51 Dave Rowbotham .07 .20
52 Kay Whitmore .40 1.00
53 Richard Brodeur .20 .50
54 Mike Vellucci .07 .20
55 Terry Yake .20 .50
56 Roger Kortko .07 .20
57 Jon Smith TR .01 .05
58 Lindsay Carson UER .07 .20
(Misspelled Lindsy on card front)
59 Chris Brant .07 .20
60 Claude Larose CO .08 .25
61 Dallas Gaume .07 .20
62 Charlie Bourgeois .07 .20
63 Todd Krygier .20 .50
64 Gary Callahan .07 .20
65 Mark Reeds .07 .20
66 Al Tuer .07 .20
67 Brian Chapman .07 .20
68 Mark Lavarre .07 .20
69 Mark Dumas .07 .20
70 Jim Culhane .07 .20
71 Larry Trader .07 .20
72 Tom Mitchell GM .01 .05
73 Rob MacInnis .07 .20
74 John B. Hanna .07 .20
75 Dan Currie .20 .50
76 Dave Roach .07 .20
77 Jamie Nicolls .07 .20
78 Alan May .08 .25
79 David Haas .07 .20
80 Daryl Reaugh .60 1.50
81 Mike Ware .07 .20
82 Mike Glover .07 .20
83 Nick Beaulieu .07 .20
84 Mario Barbe .07 .20
85 Darren Beals .07 .20
86 Kim Issel .07 .20
87 Shaun Van Allen .20 .50
88 Jim Ennis .07 .20
89 Mark Lamb .40 1.00
90 Larry Floyd .07 .20
91 Ron Shudra .07 .20
92 Fabian Joseph .08 .25
93 Selmar Odelein .08 .25
94 Don Martin .07 .20
95 Jim Wiemer .08 .25
96 Brad MacGregor .07 .20
97 Gerald Bzdel .07 .20
98 Mike Hough .20 .50
99 Ken McRae .08 .25
100 Bobby Dollas .08 .25
101 Joel Baillargeon .07 .20
102 Ladislav Tresl .05 .15
103 Jacques Mailhot .20 .50
104 Dean Hopkins .07 .20
105 Claude Julien .07 .20
106 Brent Severyn .30 .75
107 Keith Miller .07 .20
108 Scott Shaunessy .07 .20
109 Jaroslav Sevcik .07 .20
110 Darin Kimble .20 .50
111 Jean-Marc Routhier .07 .20
112 Ken Quinney .07 .20
113 Max Middendorf .07 .20
114 Marc Fortier .15 .40
115 Jean-Marc Richard .07 .20
116 Mike Natyshak .07 .20
117 Ron Tugnutt 1.50 4.00
118 Scott Gordon .20 .50
119 Doug Carpenter CO/GM .02 .10
120 Jeff Harding .07 .20
121 Jocelyn Perrault .07 .20
122 Darryl Gilmour .20 .50
123 John Stevens .07 .20
124 Warren Harper .07 .20
125 Chris Jensen .07 .20
126 Mark Freer .08 .25
127 Gordon Paddock .07 .20
128 Bruce Randall .07 .20
129 Glen Seabrooke .07 .20
130 Mike Stothers .07 .20
131 Dave Fenyves .08 .25
132 Mark Lofthouse .07 .20
133 Marc D'Amour .20 .50
134 Shaun Sabol .07 .20
135 Craig Kitteringham .07 .20
136 J.J. Daigneault .20 .50
137 Don Biggs .08 .25
138 Kent Hawley .07 .20
139 Tony Horacek .07 .20
140 Al Hill .08 .25
141 Don Nachbaur .07 .20
142 John Paddock CO .07 .20
143 Kevin McCarthy CO .07 .20
144 Dan Stuck TR .01 .05
145 Doug Yingst .07 .20
146 Frank Mathers PR/GM .07 .20
147 Brian Bucciarelli TR .01 .05
148 Terry Tailefer .07 .20
149 Paul Beraldo .07 .20
150 Jeff Lamb .07 .20
151 Mitch Molloy .07 .20
152 Darren Lowe .07 .20
153 Stephane Quintal .40 1.00
154 Norm Foster .08 .25
155 Jean-Marc Lanthier .07 .20
156 Carl Mokosak .07 .20
157 Mike Neill .07 .20
158 Mike Jeffrey .07 .20
159 Steve Tsujiura .07 .20
160 Scott Drevitch .07 .20
161 Paul Guay .08 .25
162 Scott Wykoff ANN .01 .05
163 John Carter .08 .25
164 Phil Degaetano .07 .20
165 Doug Foerster PB/TKTS .01 .05
166 Bruce Shoebottom .08 .25
167 Ray Podloski .07 .20
168 Greg Hawgood .20 .50
169 Joe Flaherty .07 .20
170 Todd Flichel .07 .20
171 Steven Fletcher .08 .25
172 Len Nielson .07 .20
173 Neil Meadmore .07 .20
174 Gilles Hamel .08 .25
175 Ron Wilson .20 .50
176 Stu Kulak .08 .25
177 Scott Schneider .07 .20
178 Mike Warus .07 .20
179 Jamie Husgen .07 .20
180 Tom Draper .20 .50
181 Guy Gosselin .07 .20
182 Guy Larose .08 .25
183 Stephane Beauregard .30 .75
184 Brent Hughes .15 .40
185 Sean Clement .07 .20
186 Matt Hervey .05 .15
187 Chris Norton .07 .20
188 Rob Snitzer THER .01 .05
189 Rick Bowness CO .20 .50
190 Wayne Flemming MG .01 .05
191 Tim Tookey .08 .25
192 Ken Baumgartner .40 1.00
193 John English .07 .20
194 Darryl Williams .07 .20
195 Hubie McDonough .20 .50
196 Brad Hyatt .07 .20
197 Phil Sykes .05 .15
198 Mario Chitaroni .07 .20
199 Tom Pratt .07 .20
200 Sal Lombardi TR .01 .05
201 Rick Dudley CO .08 .25
202 John Tortorella CO .01 .05
203 Chris Panek .07 .20
204 Scott Green TR .01 .05
205 Eric Germain .07 .20
206 Bob Kudelski .20 .50
207 Joe Paterson .07 .20
208 Al Loring .07 .20
209 Mark Fitzpatrick 1.25 3.00
210 Dan Gratton .07 .20
211 Sylvain Couturier .07 .20
212 Pat Hickey DIR .01 .05
213 Petr Prajsler .05 .15
214 Lyle Phair .07 .20
215 Bob Logan .07 .20
216 Francois Breault .07 .20
217 Paul Kelly .07 .20
218 Steve Richmond .07 .20
219 Denis Larocque .07 .20
220 Brian Wilks .07 .20
221 Dave Pasin .08 .25
222 Gordie Walker .07 .20
223 Marty Dallman .07 .20
224 Jim Ralph .75 2.00
225 Mike Blaisdell .20 .50
226 Sean McKenna .07 .20
227 Mark Kirton .08 .25
228 Greg Hotham .07 .20
229 Bill Root .08 .25
230 Wes Jarvis .07 .20
231 Daryl Evans .07 .20
232 Jack Capuano .07 .20
233 Tim Armstrong .07 .20
234 Alan Hepple .07 .20
235 Brian Blad .07 .20
236 Ken Yaremchuk .08 .25
237 Paul Gagne .15 .40
238 Doug Shedden .20 .50
239 Brian Hoard .07 .20
240 Greg Terrion .15 .40
241 Trevor Jobe .01 .05
242 Jeff Reese .40 1.00
243 Darryl Shannon .20 .50
244 Tim Bernhardt .30 .75
245 The Moose Mascot .02 .10
246 Paul Brydges .07 .20
247 Ken Priestlay .08 .25
248 Jacques Cloutier .20 .50
249 Steve Smith .07 .20
250 Jim Jackson .08 .25
251 Grant Tkachuk .07 .20
252 Kevin Kerr .07 .20
253 Mark Ferner .08 .25
254 Jeff Parker .07 .20
255 Don McSween .08 .25
256 Jim Hofford .07 .20
257 Darcy Wakaluk .60 1.50
258 Scott Metcalfe .07 .20
259 Richie Dunn .07 .20
260 Wayne Van Dorp .15 .40
261 Shawn Anderson .08 .25
262 Jeff Capello .07 .20
263 Mike Donnelly .20 .50
264 Mikael Anderson .20 .50
265 Robert Ray 1.50 4.00
266 Jody Gage .30 .75
267 Francois Guay .05 .15
268 John Van Boxmeer CO .08 .25
269 Jim Nesich .07 .20
270 Jim Nesich .07 .20
271 J.J. Daigneault .20 .50
272 Randy Exelby .08 .25
273 Jyrki Lumme .60 1.50
275 Francois Gravel .07 .20
276 Jacques Parent THER .01 .05
277 Bobby Boulanger MG .01 .05
278 Benoit Brunet .40 1.00
279 Martin Nicoletti .07 .20
280 Mark Pederson .08 .25
281 Stephan Lebeau .40 1.00
282 Claude Larose CO .08 .25
283 Steve Bisson .07 .20
284 Scott Sandelin .07 .20
285 Rocky Dundas .07 .20
286 Serge Roberge .07 .20
287 Rob Bryden .07 .20
288 Marc Saumier .07 .20
289 Jean Hamel CO .07 .20
290 Mario Roberge .08 .25
291 Jocelyn Lemieux .20 .50
292 Ron Chyzowski .07 .20
293 Martin Desjardins .07 .20
294 Steven Martinson .07 .20
295 Jose Charbonneau .08 .25
296 Stephane J.G. Richer .05 .15
297 Sylvain Lefebvre .30 .75
298 Donald Dufresne .08 .25
299 Luc Gauthier .07 .20
300 Shawn Evans .05 .15
301 Mike Stevens .07 .20
302 Bruce Boudreau .20 .50
303 Todd McLellan .07 .20
304 Jeff Hackett 1.50 4.00
305 Bill Berg .20 .50
306 Stu Burnie .07 .20
307 Duncan McPherson .07 .20
308 Jeff Finley .08 .25
309 Ralph Calvanese MG .01 .05
310 Rob DiMaio .40 1.00
311 Chris Pryor .07 .20
312 Jim Roberts CO .07 .20
313 Vern Smith .07 .20
314 Mike Walsh .07 .20
315 Ed Tyburski TR .01 .05
316 Rod Dallman .07 .20
317 George Maneluk .08 .25
318 Richard Kromm .08 .25
319 Kerry Clark .07 .20
320 Hank Lammens .08 .25
321 Tom Fitzgerald .20 .50
322 Dale Henry .07 .20
323 Shawn Byram .07 .20
324 Doug Weiss .07 .20
325 John Walker .07 .20
326 Paul Ysebaert .30 .75
327 Chris Cichocki .07 .20
328 Marc Laniel .07 .20
329 Kevin Todd .20 .50
330 Dan Dellanedis .07 .20
331 Robert Bill TR .01 .05
332 Jeff Croop TR .01 .05
333 Craig Billington .75 2.00
334 Alan Stewart .07 .20
335 Jeff Madill .08 .25
336 Scott Moon TR .01 .05
337 Neil Brady .08 .25
338 Murray Brumwell .07 .20
339 Anders Carlsson .07 .20
340 Dan Dorion .07 .20
341 Tom McVie CO .08 .25
342 David Marcinyshyn .07 .20
343 John Blessman .07 .20
344 Chris Terreri .75 2.00
345 Eric Weinrich .30 .75
346 Janne Ojanen .20 .50
347 Tim Lenardon .07 .20
348 Jamie Huscroft .20 .50

1988-89 ProCards IHL

This set of 119 cards features players from the teams of the International Hockey League. The cards measure the standard size 2 1/2" by 3 1/2". The fronts feature color player photos accented by a beige-colored hockey stick superimposed on the right and lower sides of the picture. The cards are unnumbered and checklisted below alphabetically according to teams as follows: Indianapolis Ice (1-22), Kalamazoo Wings (23-42), Muskegon Lumberjacks (43-65), Peoria Rivermen (66-94), and Saginaw Hawks (95-119). Although the team sets were originally sold with a suggested retail price of 3.00 per team set and packaged individually, they are listed below as one giant set. In many cases that was the way they were advertised and sold, i.e., as a complete set of all the teams in the IHL.

COMPLETE SET (119) 20.00 50.00
1 Bob Lakso .07 .20
2 Rick Boyd .07 .20
3 Alan Perry .20 .50
4 Mark Teevens .07 .20
5 Gary Stewart .07 .20
6 Randy Taylor .07 .20
7 Scott Clements .07 .20
8 Chris McSorley .20 .50
9 Dave Allison .07 .20
10 Shane Doyle .07 .20
11 Darwin McCutcheon .07 .20
12 Geoff Benic .07 .20
13 Rich Oberlin TR .01 .05
14 Glen Johannesen .07 .20
15 Graeme Bonar .07 .20
16 Ron Handy .07 .20
17 Archie Henderson .08 .25
18 Brent Sapergia .07 .20
19 Brad Beck .07 .20
20 Paul Houck .07 .20
21 Jimmy Mann .20 .50
22 Rick Barkovich .07 .20
23 Scott McCrady .07 .20
24 Andy Akervik .07 .20
25 Rob Zettler .20 .50
26 Jarmo Myllys .40 1.00
27 D'Arcy Norton .07 .20
28 Ken Hodge Jr. .20 .50
29 Emanuel Viveiros .07 .20
30 Scott Bjugstad .07 .20
31 Mike Berger .07 .20
32 Joe Lockwood .07 .20
33 Stephane Roy .08 .25
34 Randy Smith .08 .25
35 Mike McHugh .07 .20
36 Warren Babe .07 .20
37 Gary McColgan .07 .20
38 Darin Baker .07 .20
39 Neil Wilkinson .20 .50
40 Kirk Tomlinson .07 .20
41 Larry Dyck .15 .40
42 Dave Schofield .07 .20
43 Brad Aitken .07 .20
44 Jock Callander .40 1.00
45 Todd Charlesworth .07 .20
46 Jeff Cooper .07 .20
47 Jeff Daniels .20 .50
48 Greg Davies .07 .20
49 Lee Giffin .07 .20
50 Dave Goertz .07 .20
51 Steve Gotaas .07 .20
52 Scott Gruhl .40 1.00
53 Doug Hobson .07 .20
54 Kevin MacDonald .07 .20
55 Pat Mayer .07 .20
56 Dave McLlwain .20 .50
57 Dave Michayluk .07 .20
58 Glenn Mulvenna .07 .20
59 Jim Paek .20 .50
60 Frank Pietrangelo .30 .75
61 Bruce Racine .20 .50
62 Mark Recchi 3.00 8.00
63 Troy Vollhoffer .07 .20
64 Jeff Waver .07 .20
65 Mitch Wilson .07 .20
66 Mitch Messier .08 .25
67 Dave Lowry .20 .50
68 Tim Bothwell .08 .25
69 Sheryl Reeves ADM .01 .05
70 Shane MacEachern .08 .25
71 Glen Featherstone .20 .50
72 Charlie Thompson MGR .01 .05
73 Wayne Thomas CO .08 .25
74 Dominic Lavoie .08 .25
75 Team Photo .20 .50
Peoria Rivermen
76 Scott Paluch .07 .20
77 Wayne Gagne .07 .20
78 Dave Thomlinson .20 .50
79 Tony Twist 2.00 5.00
80 Brad McCaughey .07 .20
81 Kelly Chase 1.25 3.00
82 Scott Harlow .07 .20
83 Peter Douris .20 .50
84 Cliff Ronning 1.00 2.50
85 Lyle Odelein .40 1.00
86 Terry MacLean .07 .20
87 Darin Smith .07 .20
88 Skip Probst .07 .20
89 Ed McMurray MGR .01 .05
90 Greg Eberle TR .01 .05
91 Jim Vesey .07 .20
92 Toby Ducolon .07 .20
93 Pat Jablonski .60 1.50
94 Darrell May .07 .20
95 Ed Belfour 10.00 25.00
96 Bruce Cassidy .08 .25
97 Chris Clifford .20 .50
98 Mario Doyon .07 .20
99 Bill Gardner .07 .20
100 Mark Kurzawski .07 .20
101 Lonnie Loach .20 .50
102 Steve Ludzik .08 .25
103 David Mackey .07 .20
104 Dale Marquette .07 .20
105 Gary Moscaluk .07 .20
106 Marty Nanne .07 .20
107 Brian Noonan .40 1.00
108 Mark Paterson .07 .20
109 Kent Paynter .07 .20
110 Guy Phillips .07 .20
111 John Reid .07 .20
112 Mike Rucinski .07 .20
113 Warren Rychel .30 .75
114 Everett Sanipass .20 .50
115 Mike Stapleton .08 .25
116 Darryl Sutter .40 1.00
117 Jari Torkki .07 .20
118 Bill Watson .08 .25
119 Sean Williams .08 .25

1989-90 ProCards AHL

This set of 360 standard-size cards features the 14 teams of the American Hockey League. Although the team sets were originally sold with a suggested retail price of 3.00 per team set and packaged individually, they are listed below as one giant set. In many cases that was the way they were advertised and sold, i.e., as a complete set of all the teams in the AHL. The set is constructed in team order.

COMPLETE SET (360) 36.00 90.00
1 New Haven Checklist .01 .05
2 Francois Breault .08 .25
3 Paul Kelly .08 .25
4 Phil Sykes .15 .40
5 Ron Scott .15 .40
6 Micah Aivazoff .15 .40
7 Sylvain Couturier .08 .25
8 Carl Repp .08 .25
9 Murray Brumwell .08 .25
10 Todd Elik .20 .50
11 Darwin Bozek .08 .25
12 Eric Germain .08 .25
13 Scott Young .40 1.00
14 Chris Kontos .20 .50
15 Scott Bjugstad .15 .40
16 Eric Ricard .08 .25
17 Ross Wilson .08 .25
18 Graham Stanley .08 .25
19 Chris Panek .10 .25
20 Nick Fotiu .40 1.00
21 Rene Chapdelaine .08 .25
22 Gordie Walker .08 .25
23 Tim Bothwell .15 .40
24 Kevin MacDonald .08 .25
25 Darryl Williams .08 .25
26 John Van Kessel .08 .25
27 Paul Brydges .08 .25
28 Moncton Checklist .01 .05
29 Guy Larose .15 .40
30 Danton Cole .15 .40
31 Brent Hughes .15 .40
32 Larry Bernard .08 .25
33 Stu Kulak .08 .25
34 Bob Essensa .75 2.00
35 Luciano Borsato .15 .40
36 Guy Gosselin .08 .25
37 Todd Flichel .08 .25
38 Brian Hunt .08 .25
39 Neil Meadmore .08 .25
40 Matt Hervey .08 .25
41 Dallas Eakins .08 .25
42 Brad Jones .08 .25
43 Chris Norton .08 .25
44 Bryan Marchment .40 1.00
45 Rick Tabaracci .60 1.50
46 Grant Richison .08 .25
47 Brian McReynolds .08 .25
48 Tony Joseph .08 .25
49 Dave Farrish .15 .40
50 Rob Snitzer .01 .05
51 Ron Wilson .15 .40
52 Scott Schneider .08 .25
53 Maine Checklist .01 .05
54 Dave Buda .08 .25
55 Paul Beraldo .30 .75
56 Lou Crawford .08 .25
57 Mark Montanari .08 .25
58 Don Sweeney .40 1.00
59 Jeff Sirkka .08 .25
60 Norm Foster .20 .50
61 Greg Poss .08 .25
62 Gord Cruickshank .08 .25
63 Bruce Shoebottom .08 .25
64 Mark Ziliotto .08 .25
65 Ron Hoover .08 .25
66 Scott Harlow .08 .25
67 Mike Millar .08 .25
68 Bob Beers .20 .50
69 Ray Neufeld .15 .40
70 Graeme Townshend .20 .50
71 Billy O'Dwyer .08 .25
72 Frank Caprice .20 .50
73 John Blum .08 .25
74 Jerry Foster .08 .25
75 Bill Sutherland and .08 .25
Rick Bowness
76 Scott Drevitch .08 .25
77 Baltimore Checklist .01 .05
78 John Purves .08 .25
79 Jeff Greenlaw .08 .25
80 Jim Taylor .08 .25
81 Alfie Turcotte .08 .25
82 Dan Redmond .01 .05
83 Chris Felix .08 .25
84 Bobby Babcock .08 .25
85 Steve Maltais .08 .25
86 Mike Richard .08 .25
87 Team Picture .08 .25
88 Bob Mason .30 .75
89 Mark Ferner .15 .40
90 Steve Seftel .08 .25
91 Brian Tutt .08 .25
92 Terry Murray .15 .40
93 Jim Hrivnak .20 .50
94 Tyler Larter .08 .25
95 Tim Bergland .08 .25
96 Dennis Smith .08 .25
97 Steve Hollett .08 .25
98 Shawn Simpson .08 .25
99 Robin Bawa .08 .25
100 John Druce .20 .50
101 Kent Paynter .08 .25
102 Alain Cote .15 .40
103 J.P. Mattingly .01 .05
104 Newmarket Checklist .01 .05
105 Dean Anderson .08 .25
106 Wes Jarvis .08 .25
107 Brian Blad .08 .25
108 Derek Laxdal .08 .25
109 Kent Hulst .08 .25
110 Tim Bernhardt .20 .50
111 Brian Hoard .08 .25
112 Bill Root .15 .40
113 Paul Gardner .08 .25
114 Tim Armstrong .08 .25
115 Sean McKenna .08 .25
116 Tim Bean .08 .25
117 Alan Hepple .08 .25
118 Greg Hotham .08 .25
119 Scott Pearson .20 .50
120 Peter Ihnacak .15 .40
121 John McIntyre .08 .25
122 Paul Gagne .08 .25
123 Darren Veitch .15 .40
124 Mark LaForest .15 .40
125 Doug Shedden .15 .40
126 Bobby Reynolds .08 .25
127 Tie Domi 3.00 8.00
128 Ken Hammond .15 .40
129 Cape Breton Checklist .01 .05
130 Wade Campbell .08 .25
131 Chris Joseph .15 .40
132 Mario Barbe .08 .25
133 Mike Greenlay .20 .50
134 Peter Soberlak .08 .25
135 Bruce Bell .15 .40
136 Dan Currie .08 .25
137 Fabian Joseph .15 .40
138 Stan Drulia .30 .75
139 Todd Charlesworth .08 .25
140 Norm Maciver .20 .50
141 David Haas .08 .25
142 Tim Tisdale .08 .25
143 Eldon Reddick .20 .50
144 Alexander Tyznych .08 .25
145 Kim Issel .08 .25
146 Corey Foster .08 .25
147 Tomas Kapusta .08 .25
148 Brian Wilks .08 .25
149 John LeBlanc .08 .25
150 Ivan Matulik .08 .25
151 Shaun Van Allen .30 .75
152 Halifax Checklist .01 .05
153 Scott Gordon .20 .50
154 Trevor Steinburg .08 .25
155 Miroslav Ihnacak .15 .40
156 Jamie Baker .15 .40
157 Robbie Ftorek .20 .50
158 C. McQuaid and .01 .05
B.Smith
159 Mario Brunetta .20 .50
160 Jean-Marc Routhier .08 .25
161 David Espe .08 .25
162 Ken Quinney .08 .25
163 Mark Vermette .08 .25
164 Dean Hopkins .08 .25
165 Claude Julien .08 .25
166 Claude Lapointe .20 .50
167 Stephane Morin .20 .50
168 Bryan Fogarty .20 .50
169 Dave Pichette .08 .25
170 Kevin Kaminski .15 .40
171 Brent Severyn .40 1.00
172 Max Middendorf .08 .25
173 Jean-Marc Richard .08 .25
174 Gerald Bzdel .08 .25
175 Ladislav Tresl .08 .25
176 Jaroslav Sevcik .08 .25
177 Greg Smyth .15 .40
178 Joel Baillargeon .08 .25
179 Sherbrooke Checklist .01 .05
180 Andre Racicot .20 .50
181 Jean-Claude Bergeron .20 .50
182 Jim Nesich .08 .25
183 Todd Richards .08 .25
184 Francois Gravel .08 .25
185 Lyle Odelein .40 1.00
186 Benoit Brunet .30 .75
187 Mario Roberge .15 .40
188 Marc Saumier .08 .25
189 Norman Desjardins .08 .25
190 Dan Woodley .08 .25
191 Andrew Cassels .30 .75
192 Roy Mitchell .08 .25
193 Guy Darveau .08 .25
194 Ed Cristofoli .08 .25
195 Stephane J.G. Richer .08 .25
196 Jacques Parent .01 .05
197 Luc Gauthier .08 .25
198 John Ferguson .08 .25
199 Mathieu Schneider .40 1.00
200 Serge Roberge .08 .25
201 Jean Hamel .08 .25
202 Utica Checklist .01 .05
203 Jason Simon .08 .25
204 Jeff Madill .08 .25
205 Kevin Todd .20 .50
206 Myles O'Connor .08 .25
207 Jon Morris .15 .40
208 Bob Hoffmeyer .08 .25

209 Paul Ysebaert .30 .75
210 Steve Rooney .15 .40
211 Claude Vilgrain .20 .50
212 Paul Guay .08 .25
213 Roland Melanson .08 .25
214 Tom McVie .15 .40
215 David Marcinyshyn .08 .25
216 Perry Anderson .08 .25
217 Jamie Huscroft .20 .50
218 Bob Woods .08 .25
219 Pat Conacher .20 .50
220 Jean-Marc Lanthier .08 .25
221 Chris Kiene .08 .25
222 Eric Weinrich .20 .50
223 Brian Fitzgerald .01 .05
224 Craig Billington .60 1.50
225 Jim Thomson .15 .40
226 Tim Budy .08 .25
227 Marc Laniel .08 .25
228 Robert Bill .01 .05
229 Springfield Checklist .01 .05
230 Mike Walsh .08 .25
231 Dale Henry .08 .25
232 Bill Berg .20 .50
233 Hank Lammens .08 .25
234 Rob DiMaio .40 1.00
235 Shawn Byram .08 .25
236 Jeff Hackett .75 2.00
237 Wayne McBean .15 .40
238 Tim Hanley .08 .25
239 Tom Fitzgerald .15 .40
240 Mike Stevens .08 .25
241 George Maneluk .08 .25
242 Dean Ewen .08 .25
243 Dale Kushner .08 .25
244 Shawn Evans .08 .25
245 Rod Dallman .08 .25
246 Mike Keller .08 .25
247 Sean LeBrun .08 .25
248 Kerry Clark .08 .25
249 Ed Tyburski .01 .05
250 Derek King .40 1.00
251 Marc Bergevin .20 .50
252 Jeff Finley .15 .40
253 Jim Roberts .08 .25
254 Chris Pryor .08 .25
255 Rochester Checklist .01 .05
256 Robert Ray 2.00 5.00
257 Ken Priestlay .15 .40
258 Darcy Wakaluk .30 .75
259 Richie Dunn .08 .25
260 Ken Sutton .20 .50
261 Terry Martin .08 .25
262 Scott Metcalfe .08 .25
263 Joel Savage .08 .25
264 Brad Miller .08 .25
265 Donald Audette .75 2.00
266 John Van Boxmeer .08 .25
267 The Moose .01 .05
268 Brian Ford .08 .25
269 Darcy Loewen .08 .25
270 Bob Halkidis .15 .40
271 Steve Ludzik .15 .40
272 Steve Smith .08 .25
273 Francois Guay .08 .25
274 Mike Donnelly .08 .25
275 Darrin Shannon .30 .75
276 Jody Gage .40 1.00
277 Dave Baseggio .08 .25
278 Bob Corkum .30 .75
279 Jim Jackson .08 .25
280 Don McSween .08 .25
281 Jim Hofford .08 .25
282 Scott McCrory .08 .25
283 Binghamton Checklist .01 .05
284 Raymond Saumier .08 .25
285 Mike Berger .08 .25
286 Corey Beaulieu .08 .25
287 Doug McKay .08 .25
288 Blair Atcheynum .08 .25
289 Al Tuer .08 .25
290 Chris Lindberg .15 .40
291 Daryl Reaugh .75 2.00
292 James Black .08 .25
293 Vern Smith .08 .25
294 Todd Krygier .20 .50
295 Bob Bodak .08 .25
296 Jon Smith .01 .05
297 Michel Picard .15 .40
298 Jim Culhane .08 .25
299 Brian Chapman .08 .25
300 Jim Ennis .08 .25
301 Jacques Caron .08 .25
302 Jim McKenzie .15 .40
303 Kay Whitmore .40 1.00
304 Terry Yake .15 .40
305 Mike Moller .08 .25
306 Adirondack Checklist .01 .05
307 Bob Wilkie .08 .25
308 Chris McRae .08 .25
309 Chris Kotsopoulos .15 .40
310 Steve Sumner .01 .05
311 Timothy Abbott .01 .05
312 Gord Kruppke .08 .25
313 Mike Gober .08 .25
314 Al Conroy .08 .25
315 Sam St.Laurent .15 .40
316 Dave Casey .01 .05
317 Yves Racine .20 .50
318 Randy McKay .20 .50
319 Dale Krentz .08 .25
320 Sheldon Kennedy .30 .75
321 Barry Melrose 1.25 3.00
322 Dennis Holland .08 .25
323 Glenn Merkosky .08 .25
324 Murray Eaves .08 .25
325 Mark Reimer .15 .40
326 Tim Cheveldae .40 1.00
327 Peter Dineen .08 .25
328 Dean Morton .08 .25
329 Derek Mayer .15 .40
330 Hershey Checklist .01 .05
331 Don Biggs .08 .25
332 Scott Sandelin .08 .25
333 Shaun Sabol .08 .25
334 Murray Baron .15 .40
335 Dave Fenyves .08 .25
336 Glen Seabrooke .08 .25
337 Mark Freer .15 .40
338 Ray Allison .08 .25
339 Chris Jensen .08 .25
340 Ross Fitzpatrick .08 .25
341 Brian Dobbin .08 .25
342 Darren Rumble .08 .25
343 Mike Stothers .08 .25
344 Jiri Latal .08 .25
345 Don Nachbaur .08 .25
346 John Stevens .08 .25
347 Steven Fletcher .08 .25
348 Kent Hawley .08 .25
349 Bill Armstrong .08 .25
350 Bruce Hoffort .15 .40
351 Gordon Paddock .08 .25
352 Marc D'Amour .20 .50
353 Tim Tookey .08 .25
354 Reid Simpson .08 .25
355 Mark Bassen .08 .25
356 Rocky Trottier .08 .25
357 Harry Bricker .01 .05
358 Dan Stuck .01 .05
359 Al Hill .08 .25
360 Kevin McCarthy .08 .25

1989-90 ProCards IHL

This set of 208 standard-size cards features the nine teams of the International Hockey League. Although the team sets were originally sold with a suggested retail price of 3.00 per team set and packaged individually, they are listed below as one giant set. In many cases that was the way they were advertised and sold, i.e., as a complete set of all the teams in the IHL.

COMPLETE SET (208) 28.00 70.00
1 Peoria Checklist .01 .05
2 Darwin McPherson .08 .25
3 Pat Jablonski .30 .75
4 Scott Paluch .08 .25
5 Guy Hebert 2.00 5.00
6 Rich Pilon .15 .40
7 Curtis Joseph 10.00 20.00
8 Robert Dirk .20 .50
9 Darin Smith .08 .25
10 Terry McLean .08 .25
11 Kevin Miehm .15 .40
12 Toby Ducolon .08 .25
13 Mike Wolak .08 .25
14 Adrien Plavsic .20 .50
15 Dave Thomlinson .15 .40
16 Jim Vesey .15 .40
17 Michel Mongeau .20 .50
18 Tom Nash .01 .05
19 David O'Brien .08 .25
20 Dominic Lavoie .20 .50
21 Keith Osborne .08 .25
22 Rob Robinson .08 .25
23 Wayne Thomas .15 .40
24 Flint Checklist .01 .05
25 Jason Lafreniere .08 .25
26 Rick Knickle .30 .75
27 Jerry Tarrant .08 .25
28 Paul Broten .08 .25
29 Kevin Miller .40 1.00
30 Jim Latos .08 .25
31 Daniel Lacroix .15 .40
32 Dennis Vial .40 1.00
33 Denis Larocque .08 .25
34 Mike Golden .08 .25
35 Mike Hurlbut .08 .25
36 Scott Brower .08 .25
37 Lee Giffin .08 .25
38 Jeff Bloemberg .08 .25
39 Simon Wheeldon .08 .25
40 Rob Zamuner .40 1.00
41 Joe Paterson .08 .25
42 Barry Chyzowski .08 .25
43 Peter Laviolette .08 .25
44 Corey Millen .20 .50
45 Darren Lowe .08 .25
46 Peter Fiorentino .08 .25
47 Soren True .08 .25
48 Mike Richter 4.80 10.00
49 Ice Checklist .01 .05
50 Sean Williams .08 .25
51 Bruce Cassidy .08 .25
52 Mark Kurawski .08 .25
53 Bob Bassen .20 .50
54 Marty Nanne .08 .25
55 Jari Torkki .08 .25
56 Ryan McGill .15 .40
57 Mike Peluso .75 2.00
58 Darryl Sutter .40 1.00
59 Dan Vincelette .08 .25
60 Lonnie Loach .15 .40
61 Mike Rucinski .08 .25
62 Jim Playfair .08 .25
63 Everett Sanipass .08 .25
64 Dale Marquette .08 .25
65 Gary Moscaluk .08 .25
66 Mario Doyon .08 .25
67 Ray LeBlanc .40 1.00
68 Mike Eagles .15 .40
69 Warren Rychel .20 .50
70 Jim Johannson .08 .25
71 Cam Russell .20 .50
72 Mike McNeil .08 .25
73 Jimmy Waite .30 .75
74 Kalamazoo Checklist .01 .05
75 Kevin Schamehorn .08 .25
76 Kevin Evans .08 .25
77 D'Arcy Norton .08 .25
78 Scott Robinson .08 .25
79 Larry DePalma .08 .25
80 Ed Courtenay .15 .40
81 Rob Zettler .20 .50
82 Dusan Pasek .08 .25
83 Gary Emmons .08 .25
84 Peter Lappin .08 .25
85 Mario Thyer .08 .25
86 Mike McHugh .08 .25
87 Randy Smith .15 .40
88 Link Gaetz .40 1.00
89 Ken Hodge Jr. .08 .25
90 Pat MacLeod .20 .50
91 Neil Wilkinson .20 .50
92 Brett Barnett .08 .25
93 Larry Dyck .15 .40
94 Dean Kolstad .08 .25
95 Jarmo Myllys .40 1.00
96 Paul Jerrard .08 .25
97 Jean-Francois Quintin .15 .40
98 Mitch Messier .08 .25
99 Phoenix Checklist UER .01 .05
(110 Jeff Lamb not listed)
100 Bryant Perrier .08 .25
101 Keith Gretzky .40 1.00
102 Don Martin .08 .25
103 David Littman .15 .40
104 Mike DeCarle .08 .25
105 Grant Tkachuk .08 .25
106 Richard Novak .08 .25
107 Chris Luongo .08 .25
108 Bruce Boudreau .15 .40
109 Nick Beaulieu .08 .25
110 Jeff Lamb .08 .25
111 Rob Nichols .08 .25
112 Garry Unger .20 .50
113 Larry Floyd .08 .25
114 Brent Sapergia .08 .25
115 Randy Exelby .20 .50
116 Jim McGeough .08 .25
117 Tom Karalis .08 .25
118 Ken Spangler .08 .25
119 Jacques Mailhot .08 .25
120 Shawn Dineen .08 .25
121 Dave Korol .08 .25
122 Fort Wayne Checklist .01 .05
123 Colin Chin .08 .25
124 Scott Shaunessy .08 .25
125 Bob Lakso .08 .25
126 Duane Joyce .08 .25
127 Joe Stephan .08 .25
128 Ron Shudra .08 .25
129 Bob Fowler .08 .25
130 Steve Bisson .08 .25
131 Craig Endean .08 .25
132 Carl Mokosak .08 .25
133 Carey Lucyk .08 .25
134 Craig Channell .08 .25
135 Frederic Chabot .75 2.00
136 Brian Hannon .08 .25
137 Keith Miller .08 .25
138 Al Sims .20 .50
139 Stephane Beauregard .30 .75
140 Ron Handy .08 .25
141 Byron Lomow .08 .25
142 Muskegon Checklist .01 .05
143 Jamie Leach .08 .25
144 Chris Clifford .08 .25
145 Dave Capuano .15 .40
146 Jeff Daniels .08 .25
147 Dave Goertz .08 .25
148 Perry Ganchar .08 .25
149 Mitch Wilson .08 .25
150 Scott Gruhl .40 1.00
151 Randy Taylor .08 .25
152 Bruce Racine .20 .50
153 Dave Michayluk .15 .40
154 Richard Zemlak .15 .40
155 Brad Aitken .08 .25
156 Paul Stanton .15 .40
157 Darren Stolk .08 .25
158 Jim Paek .15 .40
159 Mark Kachowski .08 .25
160 Dan Frawley .08 .25
161 Mike Mersch .08 .25
162 Glenn Mulvenna .08 .25
163 Phill Russell .15 .40
164 Blair McDonald .08 .25
165 Milwaukee Checklist .01 .05
166 Shaun Clouston .08 .25
167 Steve Veilleux .08 .25
168 Peter Bakovic .08 .25
169 Peter DeBoer .20 .50
170 Ernie Vargas .08 .25
171 Keith Street .08 .25
172 Rob Murphy .15 .40
173 David Bruce .20 .50
174 Shannon Travis .08 .25
175 Jeff Rohlicek .08 .25
176 Jay Mazur .08 .25
177 Kevan Guy .08 .25
178 Troy Gamble .40 1.00
179 Ronnie Stern .20 .50
180 Jim Revenberg .08 .25
181 Jose Charbonneau .08 .25
182 Ian Kidd .08 .25
183 Todd Hawkins .08 .25
184 Carl Valimont .08 .25
185 Jim Agnew .08 .25
186 Curtis Hunt .08 .25
187 Dean Cook .08 .25
188 Ron Wilson .15 .40
189 Ron Lapointe .08 .25
190 Salt Lake City Checklist .01 .05
191 Brian Glynn .15 .40
192 Stephane Matteau .30 .75
193 Rick Barkovich .08 .25
194 Jeff Wenaas .08 .25
195 Darryl Olsen .08 .25
196 Rick Lessard .08 .25
197 Kevin Grant .08 .25
198 Rich Chernomaz .08 .25
199 Stu Grimson 1.25 3.00
200 Jamie Hislop and Bob Francis .08 .25
201 Doug Pickell .08 .25
202 Chris Biotti .08 .25
203 Tim Sweeney .20 .50
204 Ken Sabourin .15 .40
205 Randy Bucyk .08 .25
206 Wayne Cowley .15 .40
207 Rick Hayward .08 .25
208 Marc Bureau .20 .50

1990-91 ProCards AHL/IHL

This 629-card standard-size set features players who started or were expected to start the 1990-91 season in the minors. Players from the American Hockey League and the International Hockey League are included in this set. This set features red borders with a yellow hockey stick on the left side of the card diagonally framing a full-color picture of the player while the backs of the cards feature the basic factual information about the player as well as a complete statistical history. There are two number 99's: and the set is arranged by teams: Binghamton Rangers (1-25), Hershey Bears (26-53), Fredericton Canadiens (54-75), Peoria Rivermen (76-99) Kalamazoo Wings (99-122), Maine Mariners (123-145), Newmarket Saints (146-170), Springfield Indians (171-194), Baltimore Skipjacks (195-219), Cape Breton Oilers (220-242), Moncton Hawks (243-264, 343-344), Rochester Americans (265-295), San Diego Gulls (296-321), Milwaukee Admirals (322-342), Phoenix Roadrunner (345-369), Muskegon Lumberjacks (370-392), Indianapolis Ice (393-414), New Haven Nighthawks (415-441), Halifax Citadels (442-468), Adirondack Red Wings (469-493), Capital District Islanders (494-514), Albany Choppers (515-535), Fort Wayne Komets (536-556), Utica Devils (557-581), Kansas City Blades (582-602), and Salt Lake City Golden Eagles (603-628). Each team has its own team checklist (TC) card as the last card in the team's numbering sequence. Although the team sets were originally sold with a suggested retail price of 4.00 per team set and packaged individually, they are listed below as one giant set.

COMPLETE SET (629) 40.00 100.00
1 Rob Zamuner .30 .75
2 Todd Charlesworth .05 .15
3 Bob Bodak .05 .15
4 Len Hachborn .08 .25
5 Peter Fiorentino .05 .15
6 Kord Cernich .05 .15
7 Daniel Lacroix .20 .50
8 Joe Paterson .05 .15
9 Sam St.Laurent .20 .50
10 Jeff Bloemberg .05 .15
11 Mike Golden .05 .15
12 Mike Hurlbut .08 .25
13 Mark LaForest .20 .50
14 Chris Cichocki .05 .15
15 John Paddock .08 .25
16 Peter Laviolette .20 .50
17 Martin Bergeron .05 .15
18 Rudy Poeschek .40 1.00
19 Eric Germain .05 .15
20 Al Hill ACO .05 .15
21 Rick Bennett .08 .25
22 Tie Domi 2.00 5.00
23 Ross Fitzpatrick .05 .15
24 Brian McReynolds .08 .25
25 Binghamton Rangers TC .01 .05
26 Mike Eaves CO .05 .15
27 Lance Pitlick .15 .40
28 Dale Kushner .05 .15
29 Reid Simpson .08 .25
30 Craig Fisher .08 .25
31 Dominic Roussel .30 .75
32 Dave Fenyves .05 .15
33 Brian Dobbin .05 .15
34 Darren Rumble .15 .40
35 Murray Baron .15 .40
36 Bruce Hoffort .08 .25
37 Steve Beadle .05 .15
38 Chris Jensen .05 .15
39 Mike Stothers .05 .15
40 Kent Hawley .05 .15
41 Scott Sandelin .05 .15
42 Guy Phillips .05 .15
43 Mark Bassen .05 .15
44 Steve Scheifele .05 .15
45 Bill Armstrong .05 .15
46 Shaun Sabol .05 .15
47 Mark Freer .05 .15
48 Claude Boivin .08 .25
49 Len Barrie .08 .25
50 Bill Armstrong .05 .15
51 Tim Tookey .05 .15
52 Harry Bricker ACO .01 .05
53 Hershey Bears TC .01 .05
54 Alain Cote .08 .25
55 Luc Gauthier .05 .15
56 Eric Charron .05 .15
57 Mario Roberge .05 .15
58 Tom Sagissor .05 .15
59 Brent Bobyck .05 .15
60 John Ferguson .05 .15
61 Jim Nesich .05 .15
62 Gilbert Dionne .15 .40
63 Herbert Hohenberger .05 .15
64 Dan Woodley .05 .15
65 Roy Mitchell .05 .15
66 Frederic Chabot .75 2.00
67 Andre Racicot .20 .50
68 Paul DiPietro .20 .50
69 Norman Desjardins .05 .15
70 Martin St.Amour .05 .15
71 Jesse Belanger .20 .50
72 Ed Cristofoli .05 .15
73 Patrick Lebeau .08 .25
74 Paulin Bordeleau CO .05 .15
75 Fredericton Canadiens TC .01 .05
76 Keith Osborne .05 .15
77 Rich Pilon .15 .40
78 Alain Raymond .05 .15
79 Rob Robinson .05 .15
80 Andy Rymsha .05 .15
81 Randy Skarda .08 .25
82 Dave Thomlinson .05 .15
83 Tom Tilley .15 .40
84 Steve Tuttle .05 .15
85 Tony Twist 1.50 4.00
86 David Bruce .08 .25
87 Kelly Chase .40 1.00
88 Nelson Emerson .75 2.00
89 Guy Hebert 1.25 3.00
90 Tony Hejna .05 .15
91 Michel Mongeau .15 .40
92 David O'Brien .15 .40
93 Kevin Miehm .08 .25
94 Darwin McPherson .05 .15
95 Dominic Lavoie .05 .15
96 Yves Heroux .05 .15
97 Pat Jablonski .30 .75
98 Bob Plager CO .20 .50
99A Peoria Rivermen TC .01 .05
99B Jayson More .08 .25
100 Kevin Evans .05 .15
101 Warren Babe .05 .15
102 Mitch Messier .05 .15
103 John Blue .20 .50
104 Larry Dyck .08 .25
105 Duane Joyce .05 .15
106 Kari Takko .15 .40
107 Brett Barnett .05 .15
108 Pat MacLeod .08 .25
109 Peter Lappin .05 .15
110 Link Gaetz .40 1.00
111 Larry DePalma .05 .15
112 Steve Gotaas .05 .15
113 Mike McHugh .05 .15
114 Dan Keczmer .08 .25
115 Jackson Penney .05 .15
116 Ed Courtenay .15 .40
117 Jean-Francois Quintin .05 .15
118 Scott Robinson .05 .15
119 Mario Thyer .05 .15
120 Enrico Ciccone .30 .75
121 Kevin Constantine and John Marks .15 .40
122 Kalamazoo Wings TC .01 .05
123 Shayne Stevenson .20 .50
124 Jeff Lazaro .08 .25
125 Matt DelGuidice .20 .50
126 Ron Hoover .05 .15
127 John Mokosak .05 .15
128 John Blum .05 .15
129 Mike Parson .20 .50
130 Bruce Shoebottom .05 .15
131 Dave Donnelly .05 .15
132 Ralph Barahona .05 .15
133 Graeme Townshend .40 1.00
134 Ken Hodge Jr. .15 .40
135 Norm Foster .20 .50
136 Greg Poss .05 .15
137 Brad James .05 .15
138 Lou Crawford .05 .15
139 Rick Allain .05 .15
140 Bob Beers .15 .40
141 Ken Hammond .08 .25
142 Mark Montanari .05 .15
143 Rick Bowness CO .08 .25
144 Bob Gould P/CO .05 .15
145 Maine Mariners TC .01 .05
146 Mike Stevens .05 .15
147 Greg Walters .05 .15
148 Mike Moes .05 .15
149 Kent Hulst .05 .15
150 Len Esau .05 .15
151 Darryl Shannon .15 .40
152 Bobby Reynolds .05 .15
153 Derek Langille .05 .15
154 Jeff Serowik .08 .25
155 Darren Veitch .15 .40
156 Joe Sacco .15 .40
157 Alan Hepple .15 .40
158 Doug Shedden .15 .40
159 Steve Bancroft .05 .15
160 Greg Johnston .15 .40
161 Trevor Jobe .05 .15
162 Bill Root .15 .40
163 Tim Bean .05 .15
164 Brian Blad .05 .15
165 Robert Hornya .05 .15
166 Dean Anderson .05 .15
167 Damian Rhodes .75 2.00
168 Mike Millar .05 .15
169 Mike Jackson .05 .15
170 Newmarket Saints TC .01 .05
171 Cal Brown .05 .15
172 Michel Picard .15 .40
173 Cam Brauer .05 .15
174 Jim Burke .05 .15
175 Jim McKenzie .15 .40
176 Mike Tomlak .05 .15
177 Ross McKay .05 .15
178 Blair Atcheynum .20 .50
179 Chris Tancill .08 .25
180 Mark Greig .08 .25
181 Joe Day .05 .15
182 Jim Roberts CO .05 .15
183 Emanuel Viveiros .05 .15
184 Daryl Reaugh .75 2.00
185 Tommie Eriksen .05 .15
186 Terry Yake .15 .40
187 Chris Govedaris .05 .15
188 Chris Bright .05 .15
189 John Stevens .05 .15
190 Brian Chapman .05 .15
191 James Black .08 .25
192 Scott Daniels .05 .15
193 Kelly Ens .05 .15
194 Springfield Indians TC .01 .05
195 Ken Lovsin .05 .15
196 Kent Paynter .08 .25
197 Jim Mathieson .20 .50
198 Bob Mendel .05 .15
199 Reggie Savage .08 .25
200 Alfie Turcotte .05 .15
201 Victor Gervais .05 .15
202 Todd Hlushko .20 .50
203 Steve Seftel .05 .15
204 Thomas Sjogren .05 .15
205 Steve Maltais .08 .25
206 Bob Joyce .15 .40
207 Tyler Larter .05 .15
208 Mark Ferner .08 .25
209 Bobby Babcock .05 .15
210 Jeff Greenlaw .05 .15
211 Tim Taylor .30 .75
212 John Purves .05 .15
213 Chris Felix .15 .40
214 Jiri Vykoukal .05 .15
215 Shawn Simpson .05 .15
216 Jim Hrivnak .20 .50
217 Rob Laird CO/GM .01 .05
218 Barry Trotz Asst.CO .20 .50
219 Baltimore Skipjacks TC .01 .05
220 David Haas .05 .15
221 Wade Campbell .05 .15
222 Dan Currie .05 .15
223 Shaun Van Allen .15 .40
224 Norm Maciver .20 .50
225 Mike Greenlay .20 .50
226 Peter Soberlak .05 .15
227 Tim Tisdale .05 .15
228 Mario Barbe .05 .15
229 Shjon Podein .40 1.00
230 Trevor Sim .05 .15
231 Corey Foster .08 .25
232 Mike Ware .05 .15
233 Marc Laforge .05 .15
234 Bruce Bell .08 .25
235 Tomas Kapusta .05 .15
236 Alexander Tyjynch .05 .15
237 Tomas Srsen .05 .15
238 Collin Bauer .05 .15
239 Francois Leroux .20 .50
240 Don MacAdam CO .01 .05
241 Norm Ferguson ACO .01 .05
242 Cape Breton Oilers TC .01 .05
243 Tony Joseph .05 .15
244 Brent Hughes .15 .40
245 Larry Bernard .05 .15
246 Simon Wheeldon .05 .15
247 Todd Flichel .05 .15
248 Craig Duncanson .05 .15
249 Iain Duncan .05 .15
250 Bryan Marchment .20 .50
251 Matt Hervey .05 .15
252 Chris Norton .05 .15
253 Dallas Eakins .05 .15
254 Peter Hankinson .05 .15
255 Grant Richison .05 .15
256 Lee Davidson .05 .15
257 Denis Larocque .05 .15
258 Scott Levins .15 .40
259 Guy Larose .08 .25
260 Scott Schneider .05 .15
261 Sergei Kharin .05 .15
262 Hawk .01 .05
263 Dave Farrish CO .05 .15
264 Moncton Hawks TC .01 .05
265 Kevin Haller .20 .50
266 Joel Savage .05 .15
267 Scott Metcalfe .05 .15
268 Ian Boyce .05 .15
269 David Littman .20 .50
270 Dave Baseggio .05 .15
271 Ken Sutton .15 .40
272 Brad Miller .05 .15
273 Bill Houlder .20 .50
274 Dan Frawley .15 .40
275 Scott McCrory .05 .15
276 Steve Ludzik .15 .40
277 Robert Ray 1.50 4.00
278 Darrin Shannon .20 .50
279 Dale Degray .05 .15
280 Bob Corkum .30 .75
281 Grant Tkachuk .05 .15
282 Kevin Kerr .05 .15
283 Mitch Molloy .05 .15
284 Darcy Loewen .08 .25
285 Jody Gage .20 .50
286 Jiri Sejba .05 .15
287 Steve Smith .05 .15
288 Darcy Wakaluk .20 .50
289 Donald Audette .75 2.00
290 Don McSween .08 .25
291 Francois Guay .05 .15
292 Terry Martin ACO .01 .05
293 Don Lever CO .05 .15
294 The Moose .01 .05
295 Rochester Americans TC .01 .05
296 Mike O'Connell CO .15 .40
297 Paul Marshall .05 .15
298 Darin Bannister .05 .15
299 Rob Nichols .05 .15
300 Charlie Simmer P/CO .20 .50
301 Bob Jones .05 .15
302 Scott Brower .05 .15
303 Taylor Hall .05 .15
304 Carl Mokosak .05 .15
305 Glen Hanlon .20 .50
306 Peter Dineen .20 .50
307 Mike Sullivan .20 .50
308 Steven Martinson .05 .15
309 Dave Korol .05 .15
310 Darren Lowe .05 .15
311 Mark Reimer .08 .25
312 Mike Gober .05 .15
313 Al Tuer .05 .15
314 Dean Morton .05 .15
315 Jim McGeough .05 .15
316 Clark Donatelli .05 .15
317 Steven Dykstra .05 .15
318 Brent Sapergia .05 .15
319 Lloyd Floyd .05 .15
320 D'Arcy Norton .05 .15
321 San Diego Gulls TC .01 .05
322 Garry Valk .20 .50
323 Ian Kidd .05 .15
324 Todd Hawkins .05 .15
325 Carl Valimont .05 .15
326 Peter DeBoer .05 .15
327 Curt Fraser ACO .15 .40
328 David Mackey .05 .15
329 Jim Benning .20 .50
330 Peter Bakovic .05 .15
331 Steve Weeks .20 .50
332 Steve Veilleux .05 .15
333 Shaun Clouston .05 .15
334 Gino Odjick .75 2.00
335 Mike Murphy CO .08 .25
336 Cam Brown .05 .15
337 Patrice LeFebvre .08 .25
338 Eric Murano .05 .15
339 Jim Revenberg .15 .40
340 Don Gibson .05 .15
341 Steve McKichan .05 .15
342 Milwaukee Admirals TC .01 .05
343 Rick Tabaracci .30 .75
344 Mike O'Neill .20 .50
345 Rick Hayward .08 .25
346 Sean Whyte .05 .15
347 Petr Prajsler .05 .15
348 John Van Kessel .05 .15
349 Mario Gosselin .20 .50
350 Kyosti Karjalainen .05 .15
351 Mikael Lindholm .05 .15
352 David Goverde .08 .25
353 Graham Stanley .05 .15
354 Stephane J.G. Richer Defenseman .05 .15
355 Brian Lawton .15 .40
356 Jerome Bechard .05 .15
357 Jeff Rohlicek .05 .15
358 Steve Jacques .06 .15
359 Chris Kontos .20 .50
360 Sylvain Couturier .05 .15
361 Peter Sentner .05 .15
362 Steve Graves .05 .15
363 Daryn McBride .05 .15
364 Steve Rooney .15 .40
365 Mickey Volcan .05 .15
366 Kevin MacDonald .05 .15
367 Ralph Backstrom CO .20 .50
368 Garry Unger ACO .20 .50
369 Phoenix Roadrunners TC .01 .05
370 Rob Dopson .20 .50
371 Jock Callander .40 1.00
372 Chris Clifford .20 .50
373 Sandy Smith .05 .15
374 Jim Kyte .15 .40
375 Mike Needham .15 .40
376 Mitch Wilson .05 .15
377 Dave Goertz .05 .15
378 Mark Kachowski .05 .15
379 Perry Ganchar .05 .15
380 Mark Major .08 .25
381 Joel Gardner .05 .15
382 Scott Gruhl .30 .75
383 Todd Nelson .05 .15
384 Darren Stolk .05 .15
385 Scott Shaunessy .05 .15
386 Mike Mersch .05 .15
387 Glenn Mulvenna .05 .15
388 Brad Aitken .05 .15
389 Dave Michayluk .05 .15
390 Blair MacDonald CO .05 .15
391 Phil Russell ACO .08 .25
392 Muskegon Lumberjacks TC .01 .05
393 Sean Williams .05 .15
394 Ryan McGill .05 .15
395 Mike Eagles .15 .40
396 Jim Johannson .15 .40
397 Marty Nanne .05 .15
398 Jim Playfair .05 .15
399 Warren Rychel .30 .75
400 Cam Russell .20 .50
401 Jimmy Waite .20 .50
402 Mike Stapleton .05 .15
403 Trevor Dam .05 .15
404 Tracy Egeland .05 .15
405 Owen Lessard .05 .15
406 Jeff Sirkka .05 .15
407 Mike Dagenais .05 .15
408 Alex Roberts .05 .15
409 Dominik Hasek 10.00 25.00
410 Martin Desjardins .05 .15
411 Frantisek Kucera .15 .40
412 Carl Mokosak .05 .15
413 Dave McDowell .05 .15
414 Indianapolis Ice TC .01 .05
415 Paul Saundercock .05 .15
416 Darryl Williams .05 .15
417 Micah Aivazoff .05 .15
418 Robb Stauber .20 .50
419 Tom Martin .05 .15
420 Billy O'Dwyer .05 .15
421 Scott Harlow .05 .15
422 Jim Thomson .05 .15
423 Jim Pavese .05 .15
424 Ron Scott .05 .15
425 Dave Pasin .05 .15
426 Serge Roy .05 .15
427 Darryl Gilmour .15 .40
428 Mike Donnelly .20 .50
429 Rene Chapdelaine .05 .15
430 Brandy Semchuk .05 .15
431 Paul Holden .05 .15
432 Bob Berg .05 .15
433 Ladislav Tresl .05 .15
434 Eric Ricard .05 .15
435 Murray Brumwell .05 .15
436 Shawn McCosh .05 .15
437 Ross Wilson .05 .15
438 Scott Young .40 1.00
439 David Moylan .05 .15
440 Marcel Comeau CO .05 .15
441 New Haven Nighthawks TC .01 .05
442 David Espe .05 .15
443 Mario Doyon .05 .15
444 Gerald Bzdel .05 .15
445 Claude Lapointe .20 .50
446 Dean Hopkins .05 .15
447 Clement Jodoin .05 .15
448 Kevin Kaminski .40 1.00
449 Jamie Baker .15 .40
450 Mark Vermette .05 .15
451 Iiro Jarvi .15 .40
452 Kip Miller .40 1.00
453 Greg Smyth .08 .25
454 Serge Roberge .05 .15
455 Stephane Morin .20 .50
456 Brent Severyn .40 1.00
457 Jean-Marc Richard .05 .15
458 Ken Quinney .05 .15
459 Jeff Jackson .15 .40
460 Jaroslav Sevcik .05 .15
461 David Latta .05 .15
462 Trevor Steinburg .05 .15
463 Miroslav Ihnacak .05 .15
464 Jim Sprott .05 .15
465 Mike Bishop .05 .15
466 Stephane Fiset .75 2.00
467 Scott Gordon .20 .50
468 Halifax Citadels TC .01 .05
469 Gord Kruppke .05 .15

470 Glenn Merkosky .15 .40
471 Dennis Holland .05 .15
472 Chris McRae .05 .15
473 Al Conroy .05 .15
474 Yves Racine .20 .50
475 Jim Nill P/CO .05 .15
476 Barry Melrose CO .75 2.00
477 Bob Wilkie .05 .15
478 Guy Dupuis .05 .15
479 Doug Houda .15 .40
480 Tom Bissett .05 .15
481 Bill McDougall .08 .25
482 Glen Goodall .05 .15
483 Kory Kocur .05 .15
484 Chris Luongo .05 .15
485 Serge Anglehart .05 .15
486 Marc Potvin .40 1.00
487 Stewart Malgunas .05 .15
488 John Chabot .20 .50
489 Daniel Shank .20 .50
490 Randy Hansch .20 .50
491 Dave Gagnon .08 .25
492 Scott King .05 .15
493 Adirondack Red Wings TC .01 .05
494 Derek Laxdal .05 .15
495 Sean LeBrun .05 .15
496 Shawn Bryan .05 .15
497 Wayne Doucet .05 .15
498 Rich Kromm .05 .15
499 Chris Pryor P/CO .05 .15
500 George Maneluk .05 .15
501 Brad Lauer .08 .25
502 Wayne McBean .08 .25
503 Jeff Finley .15 .40
504 Jim Culhane .05 .15
505 Paul Cohen .05 .15
506 Brent Grieve .08 .25
507 Kevin Cheveldayoff .05 .15
508 Dennis Vaske .08 .25
509 Dave Chyzowski .05 .15
510 Travis Green .75 2.00
511 Dean Chynoweth .20 .50
512 Rob DiMaio .30 .75
513 Paul Guay .05 .15
514 Capital District Islanders TC .01 .05
515 Rick Knickle .20 .50
516 Curtis Hunt .05 .15
517 Bruce Racine .20 .50
518 Yves Heroux .05 .15
519 Joe Stefan .05 .15
520 Torrie Robertson .20 .50
521 Nick Beaulieu .05 .15
522 Dave Richter .08 .25
523 Jeff Waver .05 .15
524 Gordon Paddock .05 .15
525 Darryl Noren .05 .15
526 Byron Lomow .05 .15
527 Ivan Matulik .05 .15
528 Dan Woodley .05 .15
529 Dale Henry .05 .15
530 Soren True .05 .15
531 Stuart True .05 .15
532 Rob MacInnis .05 .15
533 Vern Smith .05 .15
534 Paul Laus .40 1.00
535 Albany Choppers TC .01 .05
536 Robin Bawa .05 .15
537 Steven Fletcher .05 .15
538 Lonnie Loach .08 .25
539 Al Sims CO .08 .25
540 Collin Chin .05 .15
541 Bruce Boudreau P/CO .05 .15
542 Bob Lakso .05 .15
543 John Anderson .15 .40
544 Kevin Kaminski .40 1.00
545 Bruce Major .05 .15
546 Stephane Brochu .05 .15
547 Peter Hankinson .05 .15
548 Carey Lucyk .05 .15
549 Tom Karalis .05 .15
550 Bob Jay .05 .15
551 Mike Butters .05 .15
552 Brian McKee .05 .15
553 Ray LeBlanc .20 .50
554 Tom Draper .15 .40
555 Steve Laurin .05 .15
556 Fort Wayne Komets TC .01 .05
557 Sergei Starikov .05 .15
558 Claude Vilgrain .15 .40
559 Jeff Sharples .08 .25
560 Bob Woods .05 .15
561 Perry Anderson .08 .25
562 Brennan Maley .05 .15
563 Mike Posma .05 .15
564 Tom McVie GM/CO .05 .15
565 Chris Palmer .05 .15
566 Bill Huard .15 .40
567 Marc Laniel .05 .15
568 Neil Brady .05 .15
569 Jason Simon .08 .25
570 Kevin Todd .20 .50
571 Jeff Madill .08 .25
572 Jeff Christian .05 .15
573 Todd Copeland .05 .15
574 Mike Bodnarchuk .05 .15
575 Chris Kiene .05 .15
576 Myles O'Connor .08 .25
577 Jamie Huscroft .15 .40
578 Mark Romaine .05 .15
579 Rollie Melanson .20 .50
580 Utica Devils Team .08 .25
581 Utica Devils TC .01 .05
582 Ron Handy .05 .15
583 Cam Plante .05 .15
584 Lee Giffin .08 .25
585 Jim Latos .05 .15
586 Stu Kulak .08 .25
587 Claude Julien .05 .15
588 Rick Barkovich .05 .15
589 Randy Exelby .20 .50
590 Mark Vichorek .05 .15
591 Darin Smith .05 .15
592 Mike Kelfer .05 .15
593 Andy Akervik .05 .15
594 Mike Hiltner .05 .15
595 Kevin Sullivan .05 .15
596 Troy Frederick .05 .15
597 Claudio Scremin .05 .15
598 Kurt Semandel .05 .15
599 Mike Colman .05 .15
600 Jeff Odgers .40 1.00
601 Wade Flaherty .20 .50
602 Kansas City Blades TC .01 .05
603 Marc Bureau .20 .50
604 Darryl Olsen .05 .15
605 Rick Lessard .05 .15
606 Kevin Grant .05 .15
607 Rich Chernomaz .05 .15
608 Randy Bucyk .05 .15
609 Wayne Crowley .05 .15
610 Ken Sabourin .05 .15
611 Bob Francis CO .01 .05
612 Jamie Hislop CO .05 .15
613 Kevan Melrose .05 .15
614 Scott McCrady .05 .15
615 Corey Lyons .05 .15
616 Martin Simard .05 .15
617 C.J. Young .08 .25
618 Mark Osiecki .08 .25
619 Bryan Deasley .05 .15
620 Kerry Clark .05 .15
621 Paul Kruse .15 .40
622 Darren Banks .40 1.00
623 Richard Zemlak .08 .25
624 Todd Harkins .05 .15
625 Warren Sharples .05 .15
626 Andrew McKim .15 .40
627 Steve Guenette .08 .25
628 Salt Lake City Golden Eagles TC .01 .05

1991-92 ProCards

This 620-card standard-size set was produced by Pro-Cards and features players from the American, International and Colonial Leagues. Fronts feature a posed color photo enclosed by a white border. The player's name is in black within a gold bar at the top and the team name appears beneath in a yellow bar. The photo appears in a red and black speckled "frame" enclosed by a small blue border. The respective league logo (American Hockey League, Colonial Hockey League, or International Hockey League) appears in the lower right corner. The cards are numbered on the back and checklisted below according to teams as follows: Rochester Americans (1-24), Peoria Rivermen (25-47), Maine Mariners (48-69), Fredericton Canadiens (70-92), Springfield Indians (93-117), Adirondack Red Wings (118-142), Kalamazoo Wings (143-163), Moncton Hawks (164-189), Binghamton Rangers (190-214), Cape Breton Oilers (215-238), Fort Wayne Komets (239-262), Hershey Bears (263-287), Muskegon Lumberjacks (288-310), San Diego Gulls (311-334), St. John's Maple Leafs (335-359), New Haven Nighthawks (360-383), Phoenix Roadrunners (384-407), Utica Devils (408-428), Flint Bulldogs of the Colonial Hockey League (429-451), Capital District Islanders (452-476), Indianapolis Ice (477-504), Kansas City Blades (505-527), Halifax Citadels (528-546), Baltimore Skipjacks (547-573), Salt Lake City Golden Eagles (574-594), and Milwaukee Admirals (595-620). Although the team sets were originally sold with a suggested retail price of 4.00 per team set and packaged individually, they are listed below as one giant set.

COMPLETE SET (620) 40.00 100.00
1 Bill Houlder .15 .40
2 Brian Curran .08 .25
3 Dan Frawley .08 .25
4 Darcy Loewen .08 .25
5 Jiri Sejba .08 .25
6 Lindy Ruff .08 .25
7 Chris Snell .08 .25
8 Bob Corkum .20 .50
9 Dave Baseggio .05 .15
10 Sean O'Donnell .05 .15
11 Brad Rubachuk .05 .15
12 Peter Ciavaglia .05 .15
13 Joel Savage .05 .15
14 Jason Winch .05 .15
15 Steve Ludzik .08 .25
16 Don McSween .08 .25
17 David DaVita .05 .15
18 Greg Brown .08 .25
19 David Littman .20 .50
20 Tom Draper .20 .50
21 Jody Gage .40 1.00
22 Terry Martin .07 .20
23 Don Lever .08 .25
24 Rochester Checklist .01 .05
25 Jason Marshall .08 .25
26 Michel Mongeau .08 .25
27 Derek Frenette .05 .15
28 Kevin Miehm .08 .25
29 Guy Hebert .75 2.00
30 Greg Poss .05 .15
31 Dave Mackey .08 .25
32 Dan Fowler .05 .15
33 Mark Bassen .07 .20
34 Yves Heroux .08 .25
35 Harold Snepsts .40 1.00
36 Bruce Shoebottom .07 .20
37 Jaan Luik .05 .15
38 Alain Raymond .05 .15
39 Kyle Reeves .05 .15
40 Brian McKee .05 .15
41 Steve Tuttle .08 .25
42 Rob Tustian .05 .15
43 Richard Pion .08 .25
44 Joe Hawley .05 .15
45 Brian Pellerin .05 .15
46 Jason Ruff .08 .25
47 Rivermen Checklist .01 .05
48 Wes Walz .30 .75
49 Steve Bancroft .05 .15
50 John Blue .20 .50
51 Rick Allain .05 .15
52 Mike Walsh .05 .15
53 Dave Thomlinson .08 .25
54 Dennis Smith .05 .15
55 Jack Capuano .08 .25
56 Mike Rossetti .05 .15
57 Petr Prajsler .08 .25
58 Matt Glennon .05 .15
59 John Byce .08 .25
60 Howie Rosenblatt .08 .25
61 Brad Tiley .05 .15
62 Lou Crawford .05 .15
63 Matt Hervey .08 .25
64 Peter Douris .08 .25
65 Jeff Lazaro .08 .25
66 David Reid .20 .50
67 E.J. McGuire .05 .15
68 Frank Bathe .07 .20
69 Maine Checklist .01 .05
70 Paul DiPietro .08 .25
71 Darcy Simon .05 .15
72 Patrick Lebeau .20 .50
73 Gilbert Dionne .20 .50
74 John Ferguson .08 .25
75 Norman Desjardins .05 .15
76 Luc Gauthier .07 .20
77 Jean-Claude Bergeron .20 .50
78 Andre Racicot .15 .40
79 Steve Veilleux .05 .15
80 Patrice Brisebois .20 .50
81 Tom Sagissor .05 .15
82 Lindsay Vallis .05 .15
83 Steve Larouche .08 .25
84 Sean Hill .20 .50
85 Jesse Belanger .20 .50
86 Stephane J.G. Richer .08 .25
87 Marc Labelle .05 .15
88 Pierre Sevigny .08 .25
89 Eric Charron .08 .25
90 Ed Ronan .08 .25
91 Paulin Bordeleau .08 .25
92 Fredericton Checklist .01 .05
93 Daryl Reaugh .75 2.00
94 Jergus Baca .08 .25
95 Karl Johnston .05 .15
96 Shawn Evans .05 .15
97 Scott Humeniuk .05 .15
98 Cam Brauer .05 .15
99 Scott Eichstadt .05 .15
100 Paul Cyr .08 .25
101 James Black .08 .25
102 Chris Govedaris .08 .25
103 Joe Day .08 .25
104 Chris Tancill .08 .25
105 Kerry Russell .07 .20
106 Denis Chalifoux .05 .15
107 Blair Atcheynum .08 .25
108 John Stevens .05 .15
109 Brian Chapman .05 .15
110 Chris Bright .05 .15
111 Jim Burke .05 .15
112 Scott Daniels .08 .25
113 Kelly Ens .05 .15
114 Mike Tomlak .08 .25
115 Mario Gosselin .20 .50
116 Jay Leach .05 .15
117 Springfield Checklist .01 .05
118 Allan Bester .20 .50
119 Daniel Shank .20 .50
120 Lonnie Loach .08 .25
121 Mark Reimer .08 .25
122 Kirk Tomlinson .05 .15
123 Stewart Malgunas .08 .25
124 Serge Anglehart .05 .15
125 Chris Luongo .08 .25
126 Keith Primeau 1.25 3.00
127 Ken Quinney .08 .25
128 Dave Flanagan .05 .15
129 Pete Stauber .20 .50
130 Mike Sillinger .20 .50
131 Micah Aivazoff .08 .25
132 Gary Schuchuk .08 .25
133 Bill McDougall .08 .25
134 Sheldon Kennedy .20 .50
135 Derek Mayer .05 .15
136 Darin Bannister .05 .15
137 Guy Dupuis .05 .15
138 Gord Kruppke .05 .15
139 Jason York .20 .50
140 Barry Melrose .40 1.00
141 Glenn Merkosky .08 .25
142 Adirondack Checklist .01 .05
143 Larry Dyck .08 .25
144 Roy Mitchell .05 .15
145 Greg Spenrath .05 .15
146 Steve Herniman .05 .15
147 Brad Berry .08 .25
148 Jim Nesich .05 .15
149 Tim Lenardon .05 .15
150 Steve Guenette .08 .25
151 Paul Jerrard .05 .15
152 Cal McGowan .08 .25
153 Scott Robinson .05 .15
154 Mitch Messier .08 .25
155 Tony Joseph .05 .15
156 Steve Maltais .40 1.00
157 Steve Gotaas .05 .15
158 Doug Barrault .05 .15
159 Dave Moylan .05 .15
160 Mario Thyer .08 .25
161 Bob Hoffmeyer .05 .15
162 Wade Dawson .05 .15
163 Wings Checklist .01 .05
164 Rob Murray .07 .20
165 Chris Kiene .05 .15
166 Lee Davidson .05 .15
167 Rudy Poeschek .40 1.00
168 Kent Paynter .05 .15
169 John LeBlanc .07 .20
170 Dallas Eakins .05 .15
171 Claude Julien .05 .15
172 Bob Joyce .08 .25
173 Derek Langille .05 .15
174 Rob Cowie .08 .25
175 Warren Rychel .40 1.00
176 Tom Karalis .05 .15
177 Kris Draper .40 1.00
178 Ken Gernander .05 .15
179 Tod Hartje .08 .25
180 Sean Gauthier .05 .15
181 Tyler Larter .05 .15
182 Scott Levins .08 .25
183 Jason Cirone .05 .15
184 Mark Kumpel .08 .25
185 Rick Tabaracci .40 1.00
186 Luciano Borsato .08 .25
187 Dave Farrish .08 .25
188 Dave Prior .05 .15
189 Moncton Checklist .01 .05
190 Peter Fiorentino .05 .15
191 Glen Goodall .05 .15
192 John Mokosak .05 .15
193 Sam St.Laurent .20 .50
194 Daniel Lacroix .20 .50
195 Guy Larose .08 .25
196 Mike Hurlbut .08 .25
197 Peter Laviolette .08 .25
198 Eric Bennett .05 .15
199 Steven King .08 .25
200 Boris Rousson .40 1.00
201 Jody Hull .15 .40
202 Shaun Sabol .05 .15
203 Joe Paterson .05 .15
204 Rob Zamuner .30 .75
205 Don Biggs .08 .25
206 Chris Cichocki .07 .20
207 Ross Fitzpatrick .05 .15
208 Mark LaForest .08 .25
209 Brian McReynolds .07 .20
210 Jeff Bloemberg .08 .25
211 Kord Cernich .05 .15
212 Ron Smith .05 .15
213 Al Hill .08 .25
214 Binghamton Checklist .01 .05
215 Francois Leroux .15 .40
216 Marc Laforge .05 .15
217 Max Middendorf .07 .20
218 Shjon Podein .30 .75
219 Jason Soules .07 .20
220 Collin Bauer .05 .15
221 Shaun Van Allen .15 .40
222 Eldon Reddick .20 .50
223 Evgeny Belosheiken .20 .50
224 David Haas .05 .15
225 Norm Foster .20 .50
226 Greg Hawgood .20 .50
227 Steven Rice .15 .40
228 Dan Currie .08 .25
229 Peter Soberlak .05 .15
230 Martin Rucinsky .40 1.00
231 Tomas Kapusta .08 .25
232 Dean Antos .05 .15
233 Craig Fisher .07 .20
234 Tomas Srsen .05 .15
235 Don McAdam .05 .15
236 Norm Ferguson .05 .15
237 Coaching Staff .01 .05
238 Cape Breton Checklist .01 .05
239 Peter Hankinson .05 .15
240 Chris McRae .05 .15
241 Craig Martin .08 .25
242 Carey Lucyk .05 .15
243 Jean-Marc Richard .05 .15
244 Grant Richison .05 .15
245 Mark Turner .05 .15
246 Todd Flichel .05 .15
247 Scott Shaunessy .05 .15
248 Darin Smith .05 .15
249 Ian Boyce .08 .25
250 Colin Chin .07 .20
251 Bob Jones .05 .15
252 Bob Jay .07 .20
253 Kelly Hurd .05 .15
254 Scott Gruhl .40 1.00
255 Kory Kocur .07 .20
256 Steven Fletcher .05 .15
257 Bob Lakso .07 .20
258 Dusty Imoo .20 .50
259 Mike O'Neill .20 .50
260 Bruce Boudreau .08 .25
261 Al Sims .15 .40
262 Komets Checklist .01 .05
263 Ray Letourneau .05 .15
264 Marc D'Amour .20 .50
265 Dominic Roussel .30 .75
266 Bill Armstrong (LW) .07 .20
267 Al Conroy .08 .25
268 Dale Kushner .08 .25
269 Toni Porkka .05 .15
270 Mike Stothers .05 .15
271 Darren Rumble .05 .15
272 Reid Simpson .05 .15
273 Claude Boivin .08 .25
274 Len Barrie .08 .25
275 Chris Jensen .08 .25
276 Pat Murray .08 .25
277 Eric Dandenault .05 .15
278 Rod Dallman .08 .25
279 Mark Freer .05 .15
280 Bill Armstrong (D) .08 .25
281 Tim Tookey .08 .25
282 Jamie Cooke .05 .15
283 Dave Fenyves .05 .15
284 Steve Morrow .05 .15
285 Martin Hostak .05 .15
286 Mike Eaves .08 .25
287 Hershey Checklist .01 .05
288 Dave Michayluk .20 .50
289 Glenn Mulvenna .07 .20
290 Jean Blouin .05 .15
291 Jock Callander .40 1.00
292 Perry Ganchar .05 .15
293 Paul Laus .30 .75
294 Mark Major .05 .15
295 Bruce Racine .20 .50
296 Daniel Gauthier .05 .15
297 Mike Needham .05 .15
298 Jeff Daniels .08 .25
299 Sandy Smith .05 .15
300 Gilbert Delorme .05 .15
301 Rob Dopson .20 .50
302 Eric Brule .05 .15
303 Alain Morissette .05 .15
304 Paul Dyck .05 .15
305 Jason Smart .05 .15
306 Gord Dineen .05 .15
307 Todd Nelson .08 .25
308 Jamie Heward .05 .15
309 Paul Russell .05 .15
310 Lumberjack Checklist .01 .05
311 Soren True .05 .15
312 Murray Duval .05 .15
313 Dmitri Kvartalnov .15 .40
314 Larry Floyd .05 .15
315 Alan Leggett .05 .15
316 Alan Hepple .05 .15
317 Ron Duguay .20 .50
318 Len Hachborn .08 .25
319 Steve Martinson .20 .50
320 Rick Knickle .30 .75
321 Darcy Norton .05 .15
322 Keith Gretzky .20 .50
323 Brian Straub .05 .15
324 Denny Lambert .08 .25
325 Jason Prosofsky .08 .25
326 Bruce Hoffort .08 .25
327 Sergei Starikov .07 .20
328 Dave Korol .05 .15
329 Robbie Nichols .05 .15
330 Kord Cernich .05 .15
331 Brent Sapergia .08 .25
332 Don Waddell .08 .25
333 Charlie Simmer .20 .50
334 San Diego Checklist .01 .05
335 Rob Mendel .05 .15
336 Curtis Hunt .05 .15
337 Jeff Serowik .08 .25
338 Bruce Bell .08 .25
339 Yanic Perreault .30 .75
340 Brad Aitken .05 .15
341 Keith Osborne .05 .15
342 Todd Hawkins .05 .15
343 Andrew McKim .08 .25
344 Kevin McClelland .08 .25
345 Mike Stevens .08 .25
346 Dave Tomlinson .08 .25
347 Kevin Maguire .08 .25
348 Mike MacWilliams .05 .15
349 Greg Walters .05 .15
350 Guy Lehoux .05 .15
351 Todd Gillingham .08 .25
352 Len Esau .05 .15
353 Greg Johnston .08 .25
354 Felix Potvin 2.00 5.00
355 Damian Rhodes .40 1.00
356 Joel Quenneville .05 .15
357 Marc Crawford .30 .75
358 Mike Eastwood .08 .25
359 St.Johns Checklist .01 .05
360 Lou Franceschetti .08 .25
361 John Murray Anderson .05 .15
362 Scott Schneider .05 .15
363 Jerome Bechard .05 .15
364 Mario Doyon .07 .20
365 Jeff Jackson .08 .25
366 John Tanner .08 .25
367 Al Tuer .05 .15
368 Paul Willett .05 .15
369 Darryl Williams .05 .15
370 George Maneluk .05 .15
371 Eric Ricard .05 .15
372 Trevor Stienburg .05 .15
373 Jerry Tarrant .05 .15
374 Michael McEwen .08 .25
375 Brian Dobbin .08 .25
376 David Latta .07 .20
377 Jim Sprott .05 .15
378 Trevor Pochipinski .07 .20
379 Stan Drulia .20 .50
380 Kent Hulst .05 .15
381 Brad Turner .05 .15
382 Doug Carpenter .05 .15
383 New Haven Checklist .01 .05
384 Bob Berg .20 .50
385 Steve Jaques .05 .15
386 Chris Norton .05 .15
387 Vern Smith .05 .15
388 Kevin MacDonald .05 .15
389 Ross Wilson .05 .15
390 Shawn McCosh .05 .15
391 Mike Vukonich .05 .15
392 Marc Saumier .05 .15
393 Mike Ruark .05 .15
394 Kris Miller .05 .15
395 Tim Breslin .05 .15
396 Paul Holden .05 .15
397 Jeff Rohlicek .05 .15
398 Kyosti Karjalainen .08 .25
399 David Goverde .20 .50
400 John Van Kessel .05 .15
401 Sean Whyte .05 .15
402 Brent Thompson .08 .25
403 Darryl Gilmour .20 .50
404 Scott Bjugstad .07 .20
405 Ralph Backstrom .15 .40
406 Rick Kozuback .05 .15
407 Roadrunner Checklist .01 .05
408 Brent Severyn .40 1.00
409 Dean Malkoc .08 .25
410 Matt Ruchty .05 .15
411 Jarrod Skalde .20 .50
412 Brian Sullivan .05 .15
413 Ben Hankinson .20 .50
414 Bill Huard .15 .40
415 Jeff Christian .05 .15
416 Corey Schwab .20 .50
417 Kevin Dean .40 1.00
418 Todd Copeland .05 .15
419 Mike Bodnarchuk .05 .15
420 Jason Miller .05 .15
421 Chad Erickson .20 .50
422 David Craievich .05 .15
423 Jim Dowd .20 .50
424 Jamie Huscroft .15 .40
425 Myles O'Connor .08 .25
426 Jon Morris .08 .25
427 Valeri Zelepukin .20 .50
428 Utica Checklist .01 .05
429 Brad Beck .05 .15
430 Brett MacDonald .05 .15
431 Jacques Mailhot .08 .25
432 Francois Ouellette .05 .15
433 Ron Kinghorn .05 .15
434 Dennis Miller .05 .15
435 Darren Miciak .05 .15
436 Tom Sasso .05 .15
437 Peter Corbett .05 .15
438 Brian Horan .05 .15
439 John Messuri .05 .15
440 E.J. Sauer .05 .15
441 Tom Mutch .05 .15
442 Jason Simon .05 .15
443 Steve Sullivan .05 .15
444 Scott Allen .05 .15
445 Stephane Brochu .08 .25
446 Ken Spangler .08 .25
447 Lee Odelein .05 .15
448 Antti Autere .05 .15
449 John Reid .05 .15
450 Skip Probst CO .01 .05
451 Flint Checklist .05 .15
452 Dean Ewen .05 .15
453 Brent Grieve .15 .40
454 Jim Culhane .05 .15
455 Joni Lehto .05 .15
456 Graeme Townshend .08 .25
457 Danny Lorenz .08 .25
458 Phil Huber .05 .15
459 Kevin Cheveldayoff .07 .20
460 Dennis Vaske .15 .40
461 Wayne Doucet .05 .15
462 Greg Parks .07 .20
463 Dean Chynoweth .05 .15
464 Lee Giffin .08 .25
465 Richard Kromm .08 .25
466 Derek Laxdal .08 .25
467 Travis Green .40 1.00
468 Iain Fraser .08 .25
469 Rick Hayward .08 .25
470 Jeff Finley .08 .25
471 Dave Chyzowski .07 .20
472 Mark Fitzpatrick .40 1.00
473 Hubie McDonough .08 .25
474 Sean LeBrun .05 .15
475 Chris Pryor .05 .15
476 Capital District CL .01 .05
477 Jeff Sirkka .05 .15
478 Owen Lessard .05 .15
479 Jim Playfair .05 .15
480 Dan Vincelette .07 .20
481 Tracey Egeland .05 .15
482 Shawn Byram .05 .15
483 Trevor Dam .05 .15
484 Martin Desjardins .05 .15
485 Milan Tichy .08 .25
486 Cam Russell .15 .40
487 Mike Speer .05 .15
488 Sean Williams .05 .15
489 Paul Gillis .08 .25
490 Brad Lauer .05 .15
491 Trent Yawney .15 .40
492 Craig Woodcroft .08 .25
493 Justin LaFayette .05 .15
494 Rob Conn .08 .25
495 Frantisek Kucera .08 .25
496 Mike Peluso .40 1.00
497 Roch Belley .20 .50
498 Ryan McGill .07 .20
499 Kerry Toporowski .08 .25
500 Dominik Hasek 4.00 8.00
501 Adam Bennett .07 .20
502 Ray LeBlanc .20 .50
503 John Marks .07 .20
504 Ice Checklist .01 .05
505 Mikhail Kravets .07 .20
506 Gary Emmons .05 .15
507 Ed Courtenay .08 .25
508 Claudio Scremin .05 .15
509 Jarmo Myllys .40 1.00
510 Mike Colman .05 .15
511 Kevin Evans .08 .25
512 Troy Frederick .05 .15
513 Ron Handy .05 .15
514 Murray Garbutt .05 .15
515 Gordon Frantti .05 .15
516 Dale Craigwell .20 .50
517 Wade Flaherty .30 .75
518 Dean Kolstad .08 .25
519 Rick Lessard .08 .25
520 Craig Coxe .40 1.00
521 Jeff Madill .08 .25
522 Peter Lappin .08 .25
523 Duane Joyce .05 .15
524 Larry DePalma .08 .25
525 Pat MacLeod .08 .25
526 Andy Akervik .05 .15
527 Blades Checklist .01 .05
528 Mike Dagenais .05 .15
529 Gerald Bzdel .05 .15
530 Stephane Fiset .40 1.00
531 David Espe .05 .15
532 Patrick Labrecque .20 .50
533 Niclas Andersson .08 .25
534 Jon Klemm .30 .75
535 Denis Chasse .20 .50
536 Stephane Charbonneau .05 .15
537 Ivan Matulik .05 .15
538 Serge Roberge .05 .15
539 Daniel Dore .05 .15
540 Sergei Kharin .08 .25
541 Jamie Baker .08 .25
542 Ken McRae .08 .25
543 David Marcinyshyn .07 .20
544 Clement Jodoin .05 .15
545 Dean Hopkins .05 .15
546 Checklist .01 .05
547 Jeff Greenlaw .07 .20
548 Byron Dafoe .40 1.00
549 Jim Hrivnak .20 .50
550 Olaf Kolzig 1.25 3.00
551 John Purves .07 .20
552 Bobby Reynolds .08 .25
553 Simon Wheeldon .20 .50
554 Jim Mathieson .20 .50
555 Trevor Halverson .08 .25
556 Steve Seftel .05 .15
557 Ken Lovsin .08 .25
558 Victor Gervais .05 .15
559 Steve Martell .08 .25
560 Chris Clarke .05 .15
561 Brent Hughes .08 .25
562 Jiri Vykoukal .05 .15
563 Tim Taylor .20 .50
564 Richie Walcott .05 .15
565 Harry Mews .05 .15
566 Craig Duncanson .08 .25
567 Todd Hlushko .08 .25
568 Mark Ferner .08 .25
569 Bobby Babcock .07 .20
570 Reggie Savage .08 .25
571 Rob Laird .05 .15
572 Barry Trotz .01 .05
573 Baltimore Checklist .01 .05
574 Kevan Melrose .05 .15
575 Kevin Grant .05 .15
576 Kevan Guy .08 .25
577 Darryl Olsen .05 .15
578 Kevin Worthman .05 .15
579 Darren Stolk .05 .15
580 Bryan Deasley .05 .15
581 Paul Kruse .08 .25
582 Darren Banks .40 1.00
583 Corey Lyons .05 .15
584 Kenny Clark .05 .15
585 Todd Strueby .08 .25
586 Rich Chernomaz .05 .15
587 Tim Harris .05 .15
588 Shawn Heaphy .05 .15
589 Todd Harkins .08 .25
590 Richard Zemlak .08 .25
591 Warren Sharples .08 .25
592 Jason Muzzatti .20 .50
593 Dennis Holland .05 .15
594 Salt Lake City CL .01 .05
595 Shawn Antoski .15 .40
596 Peter Bakovic .05 .15
597 Robin Bawa .07 .20
598 Cam Brown .05 .15
599 Neil Eisenhut .08 .25
600 Jason Herter .07 .20
601 Ian Kidd .05 .15
602 Troy Neumeier .05 .15
603 Carl Valimont .05 .15
604 Phil Von Stefenelli .08 .25
605 Andrew McBain .08 .25
606 Eric Murano .08 .25
607 Rob Murphy .08 .25
608 Brian Blad .05 .15
609 Randy Boyd .05 .15
610 Don Gibson .05 .15
611 Paul Guay .08 .25
612 Jay Mazur .08 .25
613 Jeff Larmer .08 .25
614 Ladislav Tresl .08 .25
615 Dennis Snedden .05 .15
616 Corrie D'Alessio .08 .25
617 Bob Mason .20 .50
618 Jack McIlhargey .08 .25
619 Curt Fraser .08 .25
620 Admirals Checklist .01 .05

1996-97 Providence Bruins

This 25-card set was produced by SplitSecond for sale by the club at the team shop. It was originally offered for sale for $5. The cards feature the standard SplitSecond design. The cards are listed below according to jersey number, which is displayed prominently on the card.

COMPLETE SET (25) 4.00 10.00
2 Mark Cornforth .15 .40
3 Charles Paquette .15 .40
4 John Gruden .15 .40
6 Peter Laviolette .20 .50
8 Jean-Yves Roy .15 .40
9 Justin Gould .15 .40
10 David Emma .15 .40
11 Davis Payne .20 .50
13 Martin Simard .20 .50
14 Kirk Nielsen .15 .40
17 P.C. Drouin .20 .50
18 Jay Moser .15 .40
19 Bill McCauley .15 .40
21 Tim Sweeney LL .15 .40
22 Mitch Lamoureux .20 .50
23 Yevgeny Shaldybin .15 .40
25 Kevin Sawyer .30 .75
27 Brad Konik .15 .40
28 Milt Mastad .15 .40
29 Rob Tallas .30 .75
34 Bob Beers .20 .50
44 Brett Harkins .15 .40
49 Andre Roy .20 .50
NNO Bob Francis CO .02 .10
NNO AHL Web Site .01

1997-98 Providence Bruins

This set features the Bruins of the AHL. The set was produced by the team and sold at home games for $8.

COMPLETE SET (26) 4.80 12.00
1 Rob Tallas .30 .75
2 Elias Abrahamsson .15 .40
3 Bill Armstrong .15 .40
4 Dean Chynoweth .15 .40
5 Aaron Downey .60 1.50
6 Hal Gill .30 .75
7 John Grahame .60 1.50
8 Antti Laaksonen .20 .50
9 Cameron Mann .20 .50
10 Anders Myrvold .20 .50
11 Eric Naud .15 .40
12 Kirk Nielsen .15 .40
13 Charles Paquette .15 .40
14 Joel Prpic .15 .40
15 Barry Richter .20 .50
16 Randy Robitaille .30 .75
17 Jon Rohloff .15 .40
18 Andre Roy .30 .75
19 Jean-Yves Roy .15 .40
20 Yevgeny Shaldybin .15 .40
21 Landon Wilson .20 .50
22 Andrei Yakhanov .15 .40
23 Tom McVie HCO .02 .10
24 Rod Langway ACO .02 .10
25 PHPA Web Site .01
26 AHL Web Site .01

1998-99 Providence Bruins

This set features the Bruins of the AHL. The set was produced by Split Second and sold by the team at its souvenir stands.

COMPLETE SET (25) 4.80 10.00
1 Peter Laviolette CO .20 .50
2 Elias Abrahamsson .15 .40
3 Johnathan Aitken .15 .40
4 Bill Armstrong .15 .40
5 Steve Bancroft .15 .40
6 Shawn Bates .30 .75
7 Jim Carey .30 .75
8 Aaron Downey .60 1.50
9 John Grahame .60 1.50
10 Joe Harney .15 .40
11 Jay Henderson .20 .50
12 Antti Laaksonen .30 .75
13 Cameron Mann .20 .50
14 Marquis Mathieu .20 .50
15 Eric Nickulas .20 .50
16 Peter Nordstrom .15 .40
17 Joel Prpic .15 .40
18 Randy Robitaille .20 .50
19 Andre Savage .30 .75
20 Brandon Smith .20 .50
21 Mattias Timander .15 .40
22 Joel Trottier .15 .40
23 Terry Virtue .20 .50
24 Landon Wilson .20 .50
25 AHL Web Site .01

1999-00 Providence Bruins

This set features the Bruins of the AHL. The set was produced by SplitSecond and was sold by the team at home games.

COMPLETE SET (25) 4.80 12.00
1 Elias Abrahamsson .15 .40
2 Johnathan Aitken .15 .40
3 Shane Belter .15 .40
4 Nick Boynton .40 1.00
5 Jeremy Brown .15 .40
6 Vratislav Cech .15 .40
7 Jassen Cullimore .15 .40
8 Aaron Downey .60 1.50
9 Peter Ferraro .15 .40
10 Maxime Gingras .30 .75
11 John Grahame .60 1.50
12 Jay Henderson .30 .75
13 Joe Hulbig .15 .40
14 Antti Laaksonen .15 .40
15 Tim Lovell .15 .40
16 Cameron Mann .30 .75
17 Marquis Mathieu .20 .50
18 Keith McCambridge .15 .40
19 Eric Nickulas .30 .75
20 Joel Prpic .15 .40
21 Andre Savage .20 .50
22 Brandon Smith .20 .50
23 Denis Timofeev .15 .40
24 Jeff Wells .15 .40
25 Kay Whitmore .20 .50

2000-01 Providence Bruins

This set features the Bruins of the AHL. The set was produced by Choice Marketing and sold by the team at its souvenir stands.

COMPLETE SET (22) 6.00 10.00
1 Kay Whitmore .30 .75
2 Keith McCambridge .20 .50
3 Nick Boynton .40 1.00
4 Eric Manlow .20 .50
5 Zdenek Kutlak .20 .50
6 Cameron Mann .30 .75
7 Eric Nickulas .30 .50
8 Pavel Kolarik .20 .50
9 Jay Henderson .20 .50
10 Lee Goren .40 .75
11 Peter Vandermeer .20 .75
12 Marquis Mathieu .30 .50
13 Ivan Huml .60 1.00
14 Terry Hollinger .20 .50
15 Elias Abrahamsson .20 .50
16 Jeremy Brown .20 .50
17 Brandon Smith .20 .50
18 Mattias Karlin .30 .50
19 Jon Coleman .20 .50
20 Jonathan Girard .40 1.00
21 Peter Ferraro .20 .50
22 Kay Whitmore .30 .75
NNO Team CL .10 .01

2001-02 Providence Bruins

This set features the Bruins of the AHL. The 21-card set was produced by Choice Marketing and sold by the team at its souvenir shop. It is known that 1,000 of these sets were produced.

COMPLETE SET (21) 4.80 12.00
1 Andrew Raycroft .40 1.00
2 Jeff Maund .20 .50
3 Keith McCambridge .14 .35
4 Bobby Allen .14 .35
5 Chris Kelleher .14 .35
6 Eric Manlow .14 .35
7 Zdenek Kutlak .20 .50
8 Tony Tuzzolino .20 .50
9 Pavel Kolarik .14 .35
10 Lee Goren .40 1.00
11 John Emmons .14 .35
12 Andy Hilbert .60 1.50
13 Joe Hulbig .14 .35
14 Carl Corazzini .14 .35
15 Ivan Huml .40 1.00
16 Sean Haggerty .14 .35
17 Dennis Bonvie .20 .50
18 Mattias Karlin .20 .50
19 Martin Wilde .14 .35
20 Greg Crozier .20 .50
21 Jonathan Girard .40 1.00
NNO Title Card/CL .04 .10

2002-03 Providence Bruins

COMPLETE SET (21) 5.00 12.00
1 Andrew Raycroft .75 2.00
2 Kevin Dallman .20 .50
3 Chris Kelleher .20 .50
4 Keith Aucoin .20 .50
5 Rich Brennan .20 .50
6 Zdenek Kutlak .20 .50
7 Matt Herr .20 .50
8 Martin Samuelsson .40 1.00
9 Kris Vernarsky .30 .75
10 Jay Henderson .20 .50
11 Chris Paradise .20 .50
12 Andy Hilbert .30 .75
13 Shaone Morrisonn .40 1.00
14 Darren Van Oene .20 .50
15 Peter Metcalf .20 .50
16 Lee Goren .30 .75
17 Mike Gellard .20 .50
18 Brantt Myhres .20 .50
19 Pat Leahy .30 .75
20 Tim Thomas .75 2.00
NNO Checklist .01 .05

2003-04 Providence Bruins

This set was produced by Choice Marketing and sold at home games.

COMPLETE SET (24) 5.00 12.00
1 Rich Brennan .15 .40
2 Ed Campbell .15 .40
3 Carl Corazzini .15 .40
4 Kevin Dallman .15 .40
5 Mike Gellard .15 .40
6 Matt Herr .15 .40
7 Andy Hilbert .30 .75
8 Ivan Huml .15 .40
9 Milan Jurcina .30 .75
10 Zdenek Kutlak .15 .40
11 Pat Leahy .30 .75
12 Robert Liscak .15 .40
13 Peter Metcalf .15 .40
14 Brett Nowak .15 .40
15 Colton Orr .40 1.00
16 Martin Samuelsson .15 .40
17 Andre Savage .15 .40
18 Tim Thomas .60 1.50
19 Hannu Toivonen 1.25 3.00
20 Darren Van Oene .15 .40
21 Kris Vernarsky .15 .40
22 Brendan Walsh .15 .40
23 Brian White .15 .40
24 Martin Wilde .15 .40
NNO Checklist .01 .05

2004-05 Providence Bruins

This set was sold by the team at home games.

COMPLETE SET (25) 5.00 12.00
1 Pat Aufiero .20 .50
2 Patrice Bergeron .60 1.50
3 Brad Boyes .40 1.00
4 Carl Corazzini .20 .50
5 Kevin Dallman .20 .50
6 Chris Dyment .20 .50
7 Jayme Filipowicz .20 .50
8 David Gove .20 .50
9 Ben Guite .20 .50
10 Jay Henderson .20 .50
11 Andy Hilbert .20 .50
12 Milan Jurcina .20 .50
13 Pat Leahy .20 .50
14 Steve Munn .20 .50
15 Colton Orr .40 1.00
16 Martin Samuelsson .20 .50
17 Brent Thompson .20 .50
18 Yorick Treille .20 .50
19 Kris Vernarsky .20 .50
20 Brendan Walsh .20 .50
21 Peter Hamerlik .30 .75
22 Hannu Toivonen .75 2.00
23 Scott Gordon CO .02 .10
24 Rob Murray ACO .02 .10
25 Checklist .02 .10

2005-06 Providence Bruins

COMPLETE SET (25) 6.00 15.00
1 Zdenek Blatny .20 .50
2 Sean Curry .20 .50
3 Chris Dyment .20 .50
4 Scott Ford .30 .75
5 Ben Guite .20 .50
6 Eric Healey .20 .50
7 Jay Leach .20 .50
8 David Lundbohm .20 .50
9 Jason MacDonald .20 .50
10 Eric Nickulas .20 .50
11 Pascal Pelletier .30 .75
12 Tyler Redenbach .20 .50
13 Jeremy Reich .20 .50
14 Nathan Robinson .40 1.00
15 Michael Schutte .20 .50
16 Jonathan Sigalet .40 1.00
17 Jordan Sigalet .75 2.00
18 Garrett Stroshein .40 1.00
19 Mark Stuart .40 1.00
20 Tim Thomas .60 1.50
21 Nate Thompson .20 .50
22 Ben Walter .20 .50
23 Scott Gordon HC .02 .10
24 Rob Murray AC .02 .10
NNO Providence Bruins CL .02 .10

2006-07 Providence Bruins

COMPLETE SET (25) 8.00 15.00
1 Bobby Allen .20 .50
2 Chris Collins .30 .75
3 Sean Curry .20 .50
4 Nathan Dempsey .20 .50
5 Nate DiCasmirro .20 .50
6 Brian Finley .30 .75
7 Petr Kalus .30 .75
8 Martin Karsums .20 .50
9 David Krejci .30 .75
10 Matt Lashoff .30 .75
11 Jay Leach .20 .50
12 Dennis Packard .20 .50
13 Pascal Pelletier .20 .50
14 Wacey Rabbit .60 1.50
15 Jeremy Reich .30 .75
16 Jonathan Sigalet .40 1.00
17 Jordan Sigalet .75 2.00
18 Yan Stastny .20 .50
19 Mark Stuart .40 1.00
20 Philippe Sauve .30 .75
21 Nate Thompson .30 .75
22 T.J. Trevelyan .40 1.00
23 Kris Versteeg 2.00 5.00
24 Ben Walter .20 .50
25 Dwayne Zinger .20 .50

1936-37 Providence Reds

Printed on thin card stock, this 10-card set measures approximately 2 1/4" by 3 1/2". The fronts feature black-and-white player photos bordered in white. The player's name and position are printed beneath the picture, along with the statement "A New 'Reds' Picture Every Amateur Hockey Night". Unlike the other nine cards, the name of the player on card 10 is not printed beneath his picture. From his facsimile autograph on the picture, his first name may be "Jacques," but his last name remains unidentified. The backs are blank. The cards are unnumbered and checklisted below in alphabetical order.

COMPLETE SET (10) 200.00 400.00
1 Bobby Bauer 37.50 75.00
2 Paddy Byrne 12.50 25.00
3 Woody Dumart 37.50 75.00
4 Jackie Keating 12.50 25.00
5 Art Lesieur 12.50 25.00
6 Bert McInenly 12.50 25.00
7 Gus Rivers 12.50 25.00
8 Milt Schmidt 75.00 150.00
9 Jerry Shannon 12.50 25.00
10 Player Unidentified 12.50 25.00

1999 QMJHL All-Star Game Program Inserts

We are attempting to compile this checklist with the help of readers. If you have any cards from this set, please send the name, number and scan (if possible) to hockeymag@beckett.com.

COMPLETE SET (?)
1 Samuel St. Pierre

2000 QMJHL All-Star Program Inserts

These oversized cards were issued as perforated inserts inside the 2000 QMJHL All-Star Game program.

COMPLETE SET (46) 20.00 50.00
1 Guy Chouinard CO .20 .50
2 Maxime Ouellet .60 1.50
3 Sebastien Caron .75 2.00
4 Joe Rullier .40 1.00
5 Marc-Andre Bergeron .75 2.00
6 Chris Lyness .40 1.00
7 Jonathan Gautier .40 1.00
8 Francois Beauchemin 1.25 3.00
9 Michel Periard .40 1.00
10 Mike Ribeiro .75 2.00
11 Wesley Scanzano .40 1.00
12 Jonathan Roy .40 1.00
13 Carl Malette .40 1.00
14 Ramzi Abid .40 1.00
15 Simon Gamache .40 1.00
16 Marco Charpentier .40 1.00
17 Marc-Andre Thinel .40 1.00
18 Jerome Tremblay .40 1.00
19 Brandon Reid .75 2.00
20 Benoit Dusablon .40 1.00
21 Eric Chouinard .40 1.00
22 Claude Julien CO .40 1.00
23 Alexei Volkov .40 1.00
24 Drew MacIntyre .40 1.00
25 Joey DiPenta .75 2.00
26 Kirill Safronov .40 1.00
27 Alexander Riazantsev .40 1.00
28 Daniel MacLeod .40 1.00
29 Roustam Bakhriddinov .40 1.00
30 Adam Rivet .40 1.00
31 Miroslav Zalesak .40 1.00
32 Edo Terglav .40 1.00
33 Maxim Potapov .40 1.00
34 Thatcher Bell .40 1.00
35 Radim Vrbata 1.25 3.00
36 Jan-Philippe Cadieux .40 1.00
37 Dmitri Afanassenkov .40 1.00
38 Michael Ryder 2.00 5.00
39 Artem Rybin .40 1.00
40 Andrei Shefer .40 1.00
41 Brad Richards 4.00 10.00
42 Juraj Kolnik .40 1.00
43 Danny Bowie .40 1.00
44 All-Star Game Logo .02 .10
45 Team World Logo .02 .10
46 Team Quebec Logo .02 .10

1996-97 Quad-City Mallards

This 22-card set is circular in design. It was initially released as a giveaway only promotion with two cards inserted in Whitey's Ice Cream Bars, and other cards handed out at the games. Later in the season the entire set was sold at Whitey's.

COMPLETE SET (22) 8.00 20.00
1 Todd Newton .40 1.00
2 Brad Barton .40 1.00
3 Travis Tucker .40 1.00
4 Stephen Sangermano .40 1.00
5 Dave Larson .40 1.00
6 Jim Ensom .40 1.00
7 Justin McHugh .40 1.00
8 Fredrick Nasvall .40 1.00
9 Hugo Proulx .40 1.00
10 Carl LeBlanc .40 1.00
11 Glenn Stewart .40 1.00
12 Brett Strot .40 1.00
13 Andy Faulkner .40 1.00
14 Mark McFarlane .40 1.00
15 Howie Rosenblatt .60 1.50
16 Rick Emmett .40 1.00
17 Sergei Zvyagin .40 1.00
18 David Fletcher .40 1.00
19 John Batten .40 1.00
20 John Anderson HCO .40 1.00
21 Matt Shaw ACO .40 1.00
22 Mo Mallard Mascot .20 .50

1997-98 Quad-City Mallards

This set features the Mallards of the UHL. The cards were produced by Roox, and sold by the team at its souvenir stands.

COMPLETE SET (23) 4.80 12.00
1 Glenn Stewart .20 .50
2 Rick Emmett .20 .50
3 Sergei Zvyagin .20 .50
4 Howie Rosenblatt .30 .75
5 Brad Barton .20 .50
6 Kirk Llano .20 .50
7 Wayne Muir .30 .75
8 Hugo Proulx .20 .50
9 Mark McFarlane .20 .50
10 Steve Chelios .30 .75
11 Travis Tucker .20 .50
12 Carl LeBlanc .20 .50
13 Stas Tkatch .20 .50
14 Andy Faulkner .20 .50
15 Steve Gibson .20 .50
16 Tom Perry .20 .50
17 Matt Mullin .30 .75
18 Bogdan Rudenko .30 .75
19 Ryan Gelinas .30 .75
20 Jim Brown .20 .50
21 Kerry Toporowski .30 .75
22 Corey Neilson .20 .50
23 Quad City Mallards CL .02 .10

1998-99 Quad-City Mallards

This set features the Mallards of the UHL. The set was produced by Roox and was sold by the team at home games.

COMPLETE SET (24) 4.00 10.00
1 Sergei Zvyagin .20 .50
2 Brendan Brooks .20 .50
3 Scott Burfoot .02 .10
4 Matt Carey .20 .50
5 Rick Emmett .20 .50
6 Martin Fillion .20 .50
7 Rusty Fitzgerald .20 .50
8 Chad Ford .20 .50
9 Robert Frid .20 .50
10 Steve Gibson .20 .50
11 Garry Gulash .20 .50
12 Kevin Kerr .30 .75
13 Brian LaFleur .20 .50
14 Carl LeBlanc .20 .50
15 Mark McFarlane .20 .50
16 Stephanie Madore .20 .50
17 Mike Melas .20 .50
18 Hugo Proulx .20 .50
19 Bruce Richardson .20 .50
20 Howie Rosenblatt .30 .75
21 Scott Thompson .20 .50
22 Bill Weir .20 .50
23 Glenn Stewart .20 .50
24 Team CL .02 .10

1999-00 Quad-City Mallards

This set features the Mallards of the UHL. The set was produced by Roox and sold at home games. There are two number one cards in the set.

COMPLETE SET (24) 4.00 10.00
1 Iannique Renaud .20 .50
1 Moe Mallard MAS .02 .10
2 Yannick Latour .20 .50
3 Steve Gibson .20 .50
4 Garry Gulash .20 .50
5 Mike Melas .20 .50
6 Rick Emmett .20 .50
7 Ryan Lindsay .20 .50
8 Patrick Nadeau .20 .50
9 Hugo Proulx .20 .50
10 Paul Johnson .20 .50
11 Brendan Buckley .20 .50
12 Martin Hlinka .20 .50
13 Brendan Brooks .20 .50
14 Rusty Fitzgerald .20 .50
15 Kelly Hultgren .20 .50
16 Mark McFarlane .20 .50
17 Glenn Stewart .20 .50
18 Martin Villeneuve .30 .75
19 Brian LaFleur .20 .50
20 Robert DeClantis .20 .50
21 Kevin Kerr .30 .75
22 Scott Buhler .30 .75
24 Quad City Mallards CL .02 .10

2000-01 Quad-City Mallards

This set features the Mallards of the UHL. The cards were produced by Roox and sold by the team at its souvenir stands.

COMPLETE SET (27) 4.00 10.00
1 Team CL .04 .01
2 Andy Fermoyle .16 .40
3 Garry Gulash .16 .40
4 Frederick Jobin .16 .40
5 Vlad Serov .16 .40
6 Dan Bjornlie .16 .40
7 Peter Armbrust .16 .40
8 Patrick Nadeau .16 .40
9 Ryan Lindsay .16 .40
10 Jason Ulmer .16 .40
11 Hugo Proulx .16 .40
12 Mike Sim .16 .40
13 Chad Power .16 .40
14 Paul Johnson .16 .40
15 Kelly Perrault .16 .40
16 Mark McFarlane .16 .40
17 Etienne Drapeau .20 .50
18 Martin Hlinka .16 .40
19 Rick Emmett .20 .50
20 Martin Villeneuve .16 .40
21 Scott Myers .16 .40
22 Cam Severson .16 .75
23 Steve Gibson .16 .40
24 Kerry Toporowski .20 .50
25 Paul MacLean CO .10 .25
26 Mo Mallard MASCOT .04 .10
27 Ima Duck MASCOT .04 .10

2001-02 Quad-City Mallards

This set features the Mallards of the UHL. The set was sold by the team at home games. The cards are unnumbered and so are listed below in alphabetical order.

COMPLETE SET (24) 4.80 12.00
1 Peter Armbrust .20 .50
2 Dan Bjornlie .20 .50
3 Keli Corpse .30 .75
4 Joe Dimaline .20 .50
5 Andy Fermoyle .20 .50
6 Nick Ganga .20 .50
7 Steve Gibson .30 .75
8 Garry Gulash .20 .50
9 Frederick Jobin .20 .50
10 Kyle Kidney .20 .50
11 Sanny Lindstrom .20 .50
12 Brian McCullough .20 .50
13 Mark McFarlane .20 .50
14 Paul MacLean CO .20 .50
15 Dylan Mills .30 .75
16 Aaron Miskovich .30 .75
17 Patrick Nadeau .20 .50
18 Brant Nicklin .20 .50
19 Hugo Proulx .20 .50
20 Jesse Rooney .20 .50
21 Brandon Sampair .20 .50
22 Kerry Toporowski .30 .75
23 Jason Ulmer .30 .75
24 Mo and Ima MASCOTS .04 .10

2005-06 Quad City Mallards

COMPLETE SET (25) 6.00 12.00
1 Anthony Blumer .20 .50
2 Tom Clayton .20 .50
3 Glenn Detulleo .20 .50
4 Terry Friesen .40 1.00
5 Tom Galvin .20 .50
6 Jason Jaworski .20 .50
7 Andrei Lupandin .20 .50
8 Rafal Martynowski .20 .50
9 Patrick Nadeau .20 .50
10 Samy Nasreddine .40 1.00
11 Mike Olynyk .20 .50
12 Joe Pace .20 .50
13 Joel Pullman .20 .50
14 Matt Radosiovich .20 .50
15 Jesse Rycroft .20 .50
16 Jason Tapp .40 1.00
17 Jonathan Tremblay .20 .50
18 Noah Whyte .20 .50
19 Chad Wolford .20 .50
20 J.J. Wrobel .20 .50
21 Jami Yoder .20 .50
22 Brian Curran CO .02 .10
23 Larry Easter TR .02 .10
24 Jason Rivera TR .02 .10
25 Aaron Roof ANN .02 .10

2006-07 Quad City Mallards

COMPLETE SET (20) 12.00 20.00
1 Justin Chwedoruk .40 1.00
2 Brian Curran CO .20 .50
3 Brent Currie .75 2.00
4 Sergei Durdin .40 1.00
5 Travis Granbois .40 1.00
6 Nick Harloff .40 1.00
7 Andrei Lupandin .40 1.00
8 Patrick Nadeau .40 1.00
9 Don Parsons .40 1.00
10 Jeff Petruic .40 1.00
11 Brett Pilkington .40 1.00
12 Matt Radoslovich .40 1.00
13 Zach Sikich .60 1.50
14 Sean Starke .40 1.00
15 Luke Stauffacher .75 2.00
16 Blake Stewart .40 1.00
17 Jason Tapp .75 2.00
18 Mathieu Wathier .40 1.00
19 Chad Woollard .40 1.00
20 Jami Yoder .40 1.00

2007-08 Quad City Flames

COMPLETE SET (25) 5.00 12.00
1 Ryan McGill HC .15 .40
2 David van der Gulik .25 .60
3 Brett Sutter .25 .60
4 Grant Stevenson .25 .60
5 Brandon Prust .25 .60
6 Warren Peters .25 .60
7 Matt Pelech .25 .60
8 Eric Nystrom .25 .60
9 Dustin Boyd .25 .60
10 Brent Krahn .25 .60
11 Adam Pardy .25 .60
12 Brett Palin .25 .60
13 Tomi Maki .25 .60
14 Krys Kolanos .25 .60
15 Matt Keetley .25 .60
16 Tim Hambly .25 .60
17 Carsen Germyn .25 .60
18 Cam Cunning .25 .60
19 Derek Couture .25 .60
20 Kris Chucko .25 .60
21 Gord Baldwin .25 .60
22 Curtis McElhinney .25 .60
23 Kevin Lalande .25 .60
24 Tim Ramholt .25 .60
25 Team Card .10 .25

2007-08 Quad City Flames Franchise Firsts

COMPLETE SET (5) 2.00 5.00
A Dustin Boyd .40 1.00
B Matt Keetley .40 1.00
C Grant Stevenson .40 1.00
D Eric Nystrom .40 1.00
E Curtis McElhinney .40 1.00

1956-57 Quebec Aces

The set was also issued on a limited basis as a factory set in a black presentation box. This 15-card set measures approximately 5" by 7" and features black-and-white posed action player photos with a white border. The player's name is inscribed across the lower portion of the photo. On a white background, the backs carry the sponsor (Maurice Pollack Limitee) and team logos. The cards are unnumbered and checklisted below in alphabetical order.

COMPLETE SET (16) 75.00 150.00
1 Gene Achtynichuk 3.00 6.00
2 Bob Beckett 6.00 12.00
3 Marcel Bonin 7.50 15.00
4 Joe Crozier 10.00 20.00
5 Jacque Gagne 3.00 6.00
6 Dick Garnelle 3.00 6.00
7 Floyd Hillman 6.00 12.00
8 Jean Paul Lamonde 3.00 6.00
9 Jean-Marie Loisette 3.00 6.00
10 Brent MacNab 3.00 6.00
11 Al Millar 3.00 6.00
12 Willie O'Ree 15.00 30.00
13 Nick Tabuchie 3.00 6.00
14 Skip Teal 3.00 6.00
15 Orval Tessier 7.50 15.00
16 Ludger Tremblay 5.00 10.00

1962-63 Quebec Aces

This 21-card set features the Quebec Aces of the Quebec Senior Hockey League. The cards measure approximately 3 1/2" by 5 1/2" and have black and white posed action photos with white borders. The player's name is printed in black at the bottom. The backs are blank. The cards are unnumbered and checklisted below in alphabetical order. The existence of a corrected version of the Bill Dineen card recently has been confirmed. The set is considered complete with either version.

COMPLETE SET (21) 50.00 100.00
1 Ronald Attwell 2.00 4.00
2 Serge Aubry 3.00 6.00
3 Guy Black 2.00 4.00
4 Skippy Burchell 2.00 4.00
5 Jean Marie Cossette 2.00 4.00
6 Robert Courcy 2.00 4.00
7A Bill Dineen ERR 6.00 12.00
(Misspelled Dinenn)
7B Bill Dineen COR 7.50 15.00
8 Terry Gray 5.00 10.00
9 Reggie Grigg 2.00 4.00
10 John Hanna 2.00 4.00
11 Michel Harvey 2.00 4.00
12 Charlie Hodge 12.50 25.00
13 Ed Hoekstra 3.00 6.00
14 Michel Labadie 2.00 4.00
15 Claude Labrosse 2.00 4.00
16 Danny Lewicki 4.00 8.00
17 Frank Martin 2.00 4.00
18 Jim Morrison 3.00 6.00
19 Guy Rousseau 2.00 4.00
20 Dollard St. Laurent 5.00 10.00
21 Bill Sutherland 3.00 6.00

1963-64 Quebec Aces

This 23-card set features the Quebec Aces of the Quebec Senior Hockey League. The cards measure approximately 3 1/2" by 5 1/2" and have black and white posed action photos with white borders. The player's name is printed in black at the bottom. The backs are blank. The cards are unnumbered and checklisted below in alphabetical order.

COMPLETE SET (23) 75.00 150.00
1 Gilles Banville 1.50 3.00
2 Don Blackburn 1.50 3.00
3 Skippy Burchell 1.50 3.00
4 Billy Carter 1.50 3.00
5 Floyd Curry CO 5.00 10.00
6 Bill Dineen 5.00 10.00
7 Wayne Freitag 1.50 3.00
8 Jean Gauthier 1.50 3.00
9 Terry Gray 2.50 5.00
10 John Hanna 1.50 3.00
11 Doug Harvey 15.00 30.00
12 Wayne Hicks 1.50 3.00
13 Charlie Hodge 7.50 15.00
(Standing before net)
14 Charlie Hodge 7.50 15.00
(Spread out before net in defensive posture)
15 Ed Hoekstra 2.50 5.00
16 Frank Martin 1.50 3.00
17 Rene LaCasse 1.50 3.00
18 Cleland Mortson 1.50 3.00
19 Gerry O'Drowski 2.50 5.00
20 Rino Robazzo 2.50 5.00
21 Leon Rochefort 1.50 3.00
22 Cliff Pennington 2.50 5.00
23 Lorne Worsley 17.50 35.00

1964-65 Quebec Aces

This 19-card set features the Quebec Aces of the Quebec Senior Hockey League. The cards measure approximately 3 1/2" by 5 1/2". The fronts have posed black-and-white player photos with white borders. The player's name is printed in black at the bottom. The backs are blank. The cards are unnumbered and checklisted below in alphabetical order.

COMPLETE SET (19) 62.50 125.00
1 Gilles Banville 1.50 3.00
2 Red Berenson 5.00 10.00
3 Don Blackburn 1.50 3.00
4 Jean Guy Gendron 4.00 8.00
5 Bernard Geoffrion 15.00 30.00
6 Terry Gray 4.00 8.00
7 John Hanna 1.50 3.00
8 Doug Harvey 12.50 25.00
9 Wayne Hicks 1.50 3.00
10 Edward Hoekstra 2.50 5.00
11 Rene Lacasse 1.50 3.00
12 Raymond Larose 1.50 3.00
13 Jimmy Morrison 2.50 5.00
14 Cleland Mortson 1.50 3.00
15 Leon Rochefort 4.00 8.00
16 Guy Rousseau 1.50 3.00
17 Bill Sutherland 2.00 4.00
18 Brian Watson 2.00 4.00
19 Lorne Worsley 12.50 25.00

1965-66 Quebec Aces

This 19-card set measures 3 1/2" by 5 1/2". The fronts feature white-bordered posed action shots. The player's name is printed in the wider white border at the bottom. The backs are blank. The cards are unnumbered and checklisted below in alphabetical order.

COMPLETE SET (19) 37.50 75.00
1 Gilles Banville 1.50 3.00
2 Gary Bauman 1.50 3.00
3 Don Blackburn 1.50 3.00
4 Jean-Guy Gendron 2.50 5.00
5 Bernard Geoffrion CO 12.50 25.00
6 Terry Gray 2.50 5.00
7 John Hanna 1.50 3.00
8 Wayne Hicks 1.50 3.00
9 Ed Hoekstra 2.50 5.00
10 Don Johns 1.50 3.00
11 Gordon Labossiere 2.50 5.00
12 Yvon Lacoste 1.50 3.00
13 Jimmy Morrison 2.50 5.00
14 Cleland Mortson 1.50 3.00
15 Simon Nolet 4.00 8.00
16 Noel Price 2.50 5.00
17 Rino Robazzo 2.50 5.00
18 Leon Rochefort 2.50 5.00
19 Bill Sutherland 2.00 4.00

1950 Quebec Citadelles

These 20 blank-backed photos of the Quebec Citadelles measure 4" by 6" and feature cream-bordered sepia tones of the suited-up players posed on the ice. The players' facsimile autographs appear near the bottom of the pictures. The photos are unnumbered and checklisted below in alphabetical order. These photos were sent as a complete set by the team via postal envelopes. Blue-tinted variations of these cards exist. More difficult to locate, they command a premium of up to two times. This set includes the earliest known card-like element of all-time great, Jean Beliveau.

COMPLETE SET (20) 200.00 400.00
1 Neil Amadio 5.00 10.00
2 Jean Beliveau 125.00 250.00
3 Georges Bergeron CO 4.00 8.00
4 Bruce Cline 6.00 12.00
5 Norm Diviney 4.00 8.00
6 Guy Gervais 4.00 8.00
7 Bernard Guay 4.00 8.00
8 Gord Haworth 5.00 10.00
9 Camille Henry 12.50 25.00
10 Gordie Hudson 4.00 8.00
11 Claude Larochelle 6.00 12.00
12 Bernie Lemonde 4.00 8.00
13 Paul Emile Legault 4.00 8.00
14 Copper Leyte 4.00 8.00
15 Rainer Makila 5.00 10.00
16 Marcel Paille 12.50 25.00
17 Jean-Marie Plante 4.00 8.00
18 Claude Senechal 4.00 8.00
19 Jean Tremblay 12.50 25.00
20 Alphonses Gagnon CO 4.00 8.00

1999-00 Quebec Citadelles

This set features the Citadelles of the AHL. The set was produced by card shop CTM-Ste-Foy and was sold at that store and home games as well.

COMPLETE SET (26) 4.80 12.00
1 Mike McBain .15 .40
2 Gennady Razin .15 .40
3 Chris Albert .15 .40
4 Xavier Delisle .15 .40
5 Darcy Harris .15 .40
6 Marc Beaucage .15 .40
7 Stephane Robidas .15 .40
8 Jason Ward .30 .75
9 Francois Groleau .15 .40
10 Jonathan Delisle .15 .40
11 Stephane Roy .15 .40
12 Patrice Tardif .30 .75
13 Pierre Sevigny .30 .75
14 Jesse Belanger .15 .40
15 Eric Fichaud .30 .75
16 Andre Bashkirov .15 .40
17 Mathieu Garon .60 1.50
18 Dave Morissette .15 .40
19 Miloslav Guren .15 .40
20 Matthieu Descoteaux .15 .40
21 Jeff Shevalier .15 .40
22 Josh DeWolf .15 .40
23 Boyd Olson .15 .40
24 Matt Higgins .15 .40
25 Arron Asham .20 .50
NNO Quebec Citadelles .08 .25

2000-01 Quebec Citadelles

This set features the Citadelles of the AHL. The cards were produced by CTM-Ste-Foy and sold by that card shop, as well as by the team.

COMPLETE SET (24) 6.00 15.00
1 Gennady Razin .20 .50
2 Eric Chouinard .60 1.00
3 Francois Beauchemin .20 .50
4 Xavier Delisle .20 .50
5 Marc Beaucage .20 .50
6 Jason Ward .30 .75
7 Matt Higgins .20 .50
8 Mike McBain .20 .50
9 Miloslav Guren .20 .50
10 Pierre Sevigny .20 .50
11 Michael Ryder .30 2.00
12 Jonathan Delisle .20 .50
13 Eric Fichaud .30 .75
14 Andrei Bashkirov .30 .75
15 Mathieu Garon .60 1.50
16 Matt O'Dette .20 .50
17 Mathieu Raby .20 .50
18 Barry Richter .20 .50
19 Matthieu Descoteaux .20 .50
20 Josh DeWolf .20 .50
21 Eric Bertrand .20 .50
22 Arron Asham .30 .75
23 Mike Ribeiro .40 1.00
NNO Team CL .10 .01

2000-01 Quebec Citadelles Signed

This set is exactly the same as the base Citadelles set from this season, save that every card has been hand signed by the player pictured. Each card also is serial numbered out of just 100. The team CL is not signed.

COMPLETE SET (24) 30.00 75.00
1 Gennady Razin 1.20 3.00
2 Eric Chouinard 4.00 10.00
3 Francois Beauchemin 1.20 3.00
4 Xavier Delisle 1.20 3.00
5 Marc Beaucage 1.20 3.00
6 Jason Ward 2.00 5.00
7 Matt Higgins 1.20 3.00
8 Mike McBain 1.20 3.00
9 Miloslav Guren 1.20 3.00
10 Pierre Sevigny 1.20 3.00
11 Michael Ryder 2.00 20.00
12 Jonathan Delisle 1.20 3.00
13 Eric Fichaud 1.20 3.00
14 Andrei Bashkirov 1.20 3.00
15 Mathieu Garon 6.00 15.00
16 Matt O'Dette 1.20 3.00
17 Mathieu Raby 1.20 3.00
18 Barry Richter 1.20 3.00
19 Matthieu Descoteaux 1.20 3.00
20 Josh DeWolf 1.20 3.00
21 Eric Bertrand 1.20 3.00
22 Arron Asham 1.20 3.00
23 Mike Ribeiro 4.00 10.00
NNO Team CL .10 .25

2001-02 Quebec Citadelles

This set features the Citadelles of the AHL. The set was produced by CTM Ste-Foy and was sold at home games. Production of the set was limited to 1,000 copies.

COMPLETE SET (28) 8.00 20.00
1 Gennady Razin .20 .50
2 Eric Chouinard .30 .75
3 Eric Landry .20 .50
4 Ron Hainsey .60 1.50
5 Jason Ward .20 .50
6 Craig Darby .20 .50
7 Marc-Andre Thinel .30 .75
8 Martti Jarventie .30 .75
9 Francois Bouillon .30 .75
10 Francis Belanger .20 .50
11 Francois Beauchemin .20 .50
12 Pierre Sevigny .20 .50
13 Michael Ryder .40 1.00
14 Jonathan Delisle .20 .50
15 Vadim Tarasov .60 1.50
16 Mathieu Garon .40 1.00
17 Matt O'Dette .20 .50
18 Luc Belanger .30 .75
19 Jayme Filipowicz .20 .50
20 Mathieu Descoteaux .20 .50
21 Benoit Gratton .20 .50
22 Timo Vertala .20 .50
23 Arron Asham .20 .50
24 Andrei Markov .20 .50
25 Xavier Delisle .20 .50
26 Mike Ribeiro .30 .75
27 Marcel Hossa 1.60 4.00
28 Title Card/CL .04 .10

1992 Quebec Pee-Wee Tournament

This set features the best 12 and 13-year-old teams in the world that participated in the annual Quebec Pee-Wee Tournament. Though there are more than 1,900 cards in the set, we list only those players that might be familiar to the average collector.

COMPLETE SET (1903) 50.00 125.00
COMMON CARD (1-1903) .01 .05
495 Daniel Tkaczuk .75 2.00
560 J-P Dumont 1.25 3.00
777 J.F. Damphousse .75 2.00
836 Steve Begin .75 2.00
1002 Bobby Allen .75 2.00
1120 Chris Bala .75 2.00
1403 David Aebischer 2.00 5.00
1464 Dainius Zubrus .40 1.00
1576 Mike York 1.25 3.00
1741 Robert Dome .40 1.00
1776 Sergei Samsonov 4.00 10.00

1993 Quebec Pee-Wee Tournament

This 1808-card set measures the standard size (2 1/2" by 3 1/2") and features posed, color player photos of participants at the Quebec International Pee-Wee Tournament. The pictures are framed by a wide stripe that is purple at the top and blends to a pinkish-purple shade toward the bottom. The player's name is printed in white in the purple border above the photo, while the team name is printed below. The player's country is printed on both sides of the photo. The backs have the same purple color scheme and carry a small, close-up photo along with biographical information and the appropriate national flag. The series was available only as one giant set boxes in acrylic, making singles somewhat difficult to acquire. Because of the vast numbers of players never to be heard from again, we only list players of some note in the book. Card numbers 1446, 1499, 1570, 1736, 1738, 1741, 1744, 1746, 1747, 1757, 1780, 1807 are missing. Card 1758 Donald Pierce is listed as 1757 on the checklist card.

COMPLETE SET (1808) 80.00 200.00
COMMON CARD (1-1808) .01 .05
15 Sebastien Caron 1.25 3.00
30 Wesley Scanzano .20 .50
116 Eric Chouinard .75 2.00
227 Eric Lecompte .20 .50
228 Simon Roy .08 .25
272 Simon Lajeunesse 1.25 3.00
301 Frederic Brindamour .40 1.00
342 Simon Gagne 10.00 25.00
346 Carl Menard .08 .25
348 Jean-Francois Damphousse 1.25 3.00
349 Benoit Dusablon .40 1.00
432 Sebastien Caron 1.25 3.00
523 Alex Tanguay 8.00 20.00
538 Sylvain Plamondon .08 .25
554 Jay Legault .40 1.00
562 Daniel Tkaczuk .75 2.00
565 Peter Sarno .40 1.00
597 Paul Mara 1.25 3.00
664 Tim Connolly 1.25 3.00
673 Chris Madden .20 .50
704 Niklos Tselios .30 .75
836 Shawn Sutter .20 .50
877 Brian Gionta 4.00 10.00
903 Jonathan Girard .75 2.00
911 Eric Bertrand .20 .50
1053 Philippe Sauve 1.25 3.00
1080 Jean-Francois Fortin .08 .25
1152 Mike Comrie 2.00 5.00
1227 Jason Labarbera .75 2.00
1327 Nick Chin .20 .50
1339 Marc Ouimet .08 .25
1391 Mike Ribeiro 1.25 3.00
1398 Patrick Desrosiers .40 1.00
1406 Tommy Kotsopoulos .75 2.00
1408 Adam Colagiacomo .40 1.00
1417 Michael Ryder 2.00 5.00
1441 Matt Zultek .40 1.00
1529 Gregor Baumgartner .20 .50
1554 Marian Hossa 12.00 30.00
1560 Robert Dome .40 1.00
1638 Oliver Aeschlimann .20 .50
1704 Ladislav Nagy 2.00 5.00
1717 Jan Lasak 1.25 3.00
1756 Joseph R. Blackburn .40 1.00
1775 Sascha Goc .30 .75
NNO Manon Rheaume 2.00 5.00

1993 Quebec Pee-Wee Tournament Gold

This three-card insert standard-size set features color player photos with metallic-gold borders on white card stock. The player's name is printed in the border at the top, while the card title is printed below the picture. The backs carry a player profile against a metallic-gold background with white borders. Two of the cards are numbered, while one is not. The listing below reflects this numbering.

COMPLETE SET (3) 4.80 12.00
1 Brad Park .75 2.00
2 Manon Rheaume 4.00 10.00
NNO Guy Chouinard .40 1.00

1994 Quebec Pee-Wee Tournament

This set features the best 12 and 13-year-old teams in the world that participated in the annual Quebec Pee-Wee Tournament. Though there are more than 1,800 cards in the set, we list only those players who might be familiar to the average collector.

COMPLETE SET (1853) 60.00 150.00
COMMON CARD (1-1853) .01 .05
11 Vincent Lecavalier 10.00 25.00
246 John-Michael Liles 1.50 4.00
345 Eric Chouinard .40 1.00
418 Ramzi Abid .40 1.00
497 Mathieu Chouinard .40 1.00
512 Phillipe Sauve 1.25 3.00
565 Seamus Kotyk .40 1.00
573 Rico Fata .40 1.00
617 Jonathan Girard .40 1.00
628 Martin Grenier .40 1.00
649 Tim Connolly .75 2.00
806 Justin Papineau .60 1.50
888 David Legwand 1.25 3.00
902 Junior Lessard 1.50 4.00
934 Marcel Rodman .40 1.00
1025 Norm Milley .75 2.00
1077 Simon Gagne 4.00 10.00
1148 Maxime Ouellet 1.25 3.00
1169 Jordan Krestanovich .40 1.00
1182 Brian Eklund .75 2.00
1202 Freddy Meyer .75 2.00
1211 Rick DiPietro 6.00 15.00
1256 Michael Ryan .40 1.00
1607 Dominic Moore .75 2.00
1717 Sheldon Keefe .40 1.00
1752 Mathieu Biron .40 1.00

1995 Quebec Pee-Wee Tournament

This set features the best 12 and 13-year-old teams in the world that participated in the annual Quebec Pee-Wee Tournament. Though there are more than 1,800 cards in the set, we list only those players who might be familiar to the average collector.

COMPLETE SET (1825) 50.00 125.00
COMMON CARD (1-1825) .01 .05
1 Jozef Balej .40 1.00
109 Brandon Reid 1.25 3.00
234 Simon Gamache .75 2.00
278 Antoine Vermette 2.00 5.00
378 Maxime Ouellet .75 2.00
448 Marc-Andre Thinel .75 2.00
516 Tim Connolly .75 2.00
552 Zenon Konopka .40 1.00
607 Dusty Jamieson .40 1.00
608 Michael Leighton 1.25 3.00
617 Jamie Chamberlain .40 1.00
692 Justin Williams 1.50 4.00
762 Andy Hilbert .75 2.00
764 Damian Surma .40 1.00
834 Luke Sellars .40 1.00
1054 Craig Andersson .75 2.00
1153 Alexandre Giroux .40 1.00
1205 Luca Cereda .40 1.00
1243 Ron Hainsey 1.25 3.00
1318 Jason Pominville 2.00 5.00
1438 Jamie Lundmark .75 2.00

1996 Quebec Pee-Wee Tournament

This set features the best 12 and 13-year-old teams in the world that participated in the annual Quebec Pee-Wee Tournament. Though there are more than 1,400 cards in the set, we list only those players who might be familiar to the average collector. It is worth noting, however, that there are a number of female players in this set. Although they are not worth listing individually, we have confirmed sales for some of these cards anywhere from $1 to $5.

COMPLETE SET (1474) 50.00 125.00
COMMON CARD (1-1474) .01 .05
1 Jozef Balej .40 1.00
2 Michal Barinka .40 1.00
16 Daniel Boisclair .75 2.00
23 Bobby Goepfert 1.50 4.00
32 Ryan Shannon .75 2.00
166 Brett Lebda .75 2.00
245 Jared Aulin 1.25 3.00
328 Pascal Leclaire 2.00 5.00
333 Yanick Lehoux .75 2.00
335 Jason Pominville 1.50 4.00
531 Rob Globke 1.00 2.50
560 J-F Racine 1.25 3.00
578 Gregory Campbell 1.25 3.00
638 Tim Gleason 1.50 4.00
678 Jim Slater .75 2.00
680 Kris Vernarsky .75 2.00
720 Jay Bouwmeester 6.00 15.00
899 Michael Komisarek 2.00 5.00
975 Sean McMorrow .75 2.00
992 Alexandre Vermette 1.50 4.00
1174 Michael Cammalleri 2.00 5.00
1227 M-A Pouliot 2.00 5.00
1288 Charline Labonte 2.00 5.00
1406 Scottie Upshall 2.00 5.00

1997 Quebec Pee-Wee Tournament

This set features the best 12 and 13-year-old teams in the world that participated in the annual Quebec Pee-Wee Tournament. Though there are nearly 1,400 cards in the set, we list only those players who might be familiar to the average collector.

COMMON CARD .05
284 Stephen Werner .40 1.00
290 Scottie Upshall 1.50 4.00
820 Eric Nystrom 2.00 5.00
831 Chris Higgins 2.00 5.00
835 Bobby Goeppert 1.00 2.50
1113 Oliver Setzinger .40 1.00
1118 Thomas Vanek 8.00 20.00
1126 Tobias Stephan 1.50 4.00
1165 Ryan Whitney 2.00 5.00
1234 Sean Collins .40 1.00
1384 Marcel Goc 1.25 3.00

1998 Quebec Pee Wee Tournament

This mammoth set features the best 12 and 13-year-old teams in the world. Several players have achieved some notoriety in the intervening years. We list only those players.

COMPLETE SET
157 Ryan Kesler 1.25 3.00
544 Danny Richmond .40 1.00
1032 Igor Mirnov .40 1.00
1225 Christopher Campoli .75 2.00

1999 Quebec Pee Wee Tournament Collection Souvenir

Sponsored by Compuware, this set features color action photos of many current NHL superstars who played in the Quebec Pee Wee Hockey World Championships before they were famous.

COMPLETE SET (30) 16.00 40.00
1 Brad Park .40 1.00
2 Guy Chouinard .08 .25
3 Manon Rheaume 1.25 3.00
4 Patrick Roy 4.00 10.00
5 Joe Juneau .20 .50
6 Sergei Samsonov 1.25 3.00
7 Dainius Zubrus .20 .50
8 Robert Dome .08 .25
9 Daniel Tkaczuk .20 .50
10 Alex Tanguay 1.25 3.00
11 Jean-Marc Pelletier .40 1.00
12 Oleg Kvasha .20 .50
13 Steve Begin .08 .25
14 Daniel Corso .20 .50
15 Sacha Goc .20 .50
16 Marian Hossa 2.00 5.00
17 Paul Mara .40 1.00
18 J-F Damphousse .40 1.00
19 Philippe Sauve .75 2.00
20 Gregor Baumgartner .08 .25
21 Ladislav Nagy .75 2.00
22 Vincent Lecavalier 2.00 5.00
23 David Legwand .75 2.00
24 Rico Fata .40 1.00
25 Mathieu Chouinard .40 1.00
26 Eric Chouinard .40 1.00
27 Mathieu Biron .20 .50
28 Simon Gagne 1.50 4.00
29 Mike Ribeiro .40 1.00
30 Jonathan Girard .40 1.00

2000 Quebec Pee Wee Tournament

COMPLETE SET
1276 Evan McGrath .75 2.00
1347 Robbie Schremp 4.00 10.00

1980-81 Quebec Remparts

This 22-card set measures approximately 2" by 3" and features posed color player photos. The cards were issued as part of a contest. The pictures are full-bleed except for a white bottom border that contains the team logo, player's name, and jersey number. The backs are blank. The collector who obtained the entire set and turned it in became eligible to enter a contest in which the grand prize was a trip to Disney World. The cards are unnumbered and checklisted below in alphabetical order.

COMPLETE SET (22) 10.00 20.00
1 Marc Bertrand .30 .75
2 Jacques Chouinard .30 .75
3 Roger Cote .30 .75
4 Gaston Drapeau CO .20 .50
5 Claude Drouin .30 .75
6 Gaetan Duchesne .75 2.00
7 Scott Fraser .40 1.00
8 Jean-Marc Lanthier .40 1.00
9 Jean Paul Lariviere .30 .75
10 Andre Larocque .30 .75
11 Roberto Lavoie .30 .75
12 Marc Lemay .30 .75
13 Stephane Lessard .30 .75
14 Paul Levesque .30 .75
15 Richard Linteau .30 .75
16 Patrice Masse .30 .75
17 David Pretty .30 .75
18 Guy Riel .30 .75
19 Daniel Rioux .30 .75
20 Roberto Romano .75 2.00
21 Michel Therrien .75 2.00
22 Gilles Tremblay .60 1.50

1998-99 Quebec Remparts

This 25-card set was produced by Cartes Timbres Monnaies in conjunction with the Quebec Remparts of the QMJHL. It features several top prospects, including Eric Chouinard and Maxime Ouellet.

COMPLETE SET (25) 16.00 40.00
1 David Archambault .20 .50
2 David Bernier .20 .50
3 Nicholas Bilotto .20 .50
4 Tommy Bolduc .20 .50
5 Eric Chouinard .75 2.00
6 Ray Dalton .20 .50
7 Joey Fetta .20 .50
8 Simon Gagne 6.00 15.00
9 Martin Grenier .40 1.00
10 Eric Laplante .20 .50
11 Jeff Leblanc .20 .50
12 Pierre Loiselle .20 .50
13 Jerome Marois .20 .50
14 Andre Martineau .20 .50
15 Martin Moise .20 .50
16 Alexandre Morel .20 .50
17 Maxime Ouellet 4.00 10.00
18 Sylvain Plamondon .20 .50
19 Wesley Scanzano .20 .50
20 Simon Tremblay .20 .50
21 Dmitri Tolkunov .75 2.00
22 Antoine Vermette 1.25 3.00
23 Jonathan Wilhelmy .20 .50
24 Travis Zachary .20 .50
25 Title Card .02 .10

1998-99 Quebec Remparts Signed

This 25-card set was produced by Cartes Timbres Monnaies in conjunction with the Quebec Remparts. Production was limited to just 100 serial #'d sets and the entire set is signed (except for Joey Fetta who was traded). Set is unnumbered and checklisted below in alphabetical order.

COMPLETE SET (25) 40.00 100.00
1 David Archambault 1.25 3.00
2 David Bernier 1.25 3.00
3 Nicholas Bilotto 1.25 3.00
4 Tommy Bolduc 1.25 3.00
5 Eric Chouinard 4.80 10.00
6 Ray Dalton 1.25 3.00
7 Joey Fetta 1.25 3.00
8 Simon Gagne 15.00 40.00
9 Martin Grenier 2.00 5.00
10 Eric Laplante 1.25 3.00
11 Jeff Leblanc 1.25 3.00
12 Pierre Loiselle 1.25 3.00
13 Jerome Marois 1.25 3.00
14 Andre Martineau 1.25 3.00
15 Martin Moise 1.25 3.00
16 Alexandre Morel 1.25 3.00
17 Maxime Ouellet 10.00 25.00
18 Sylvain Plamondon 1.25 3.00
19 Wesley Scanzano 1.25 3.00
20 Simon Tremblay 1.25 3.00
21 Dmitri Tolkunov 2.00 5.00
22 Antoine Vermette 4.00 10.00
23 Jonathan Wilhelmy 1.25 3.00
24 Travis Zachary 1.25 3.00
25 Title Card .08 .25

1999-00 Quebec Remparts

This 25-card set pictures the Remparts of the QMJHL. Base cards feature full-color action photography and a red border along the right edge and bottom of the card which contains player names and the team logo.

COMPLETE SET (25) 4.80 12.00
1 Jean Mallette .15 .40
2 Patrick Chouinard .15 .40
3 Kirill Safronov .30 .75
4 Eric Chouinard .40 1.00
5 Patrick Grandmaitre .15 .40
6 Eric Laplante .15 .40
7 Wesley Scanzano .15 .40
8 Chris Lyness .15 .40
9 Tommy Bolduc .15 .40
10 Jean-Francois Touchette .15 .40
11 Philippe Paris .15 .40
12 Karl Morin .15 .40
13 Andre Martineau .15 .40
14 Sylvain Plamondon .15 .40
15 Martin Moise .15 .40
16 Martin Grenier .30 .75
17 Andre Hart .15 .40
18 Maxime Ouellet 1.25 3.00
19 Martin Pare .15 .40
20 Eric Cloutier .15 .40
21 Kristian Kudroc .30 .75
22 Casey Leggett .15 .40
23 Shawn Collymore .20 .50
24 Mike Ribeiro .40 1.00
25 Header Card/CL .02 .10

1999-00 Quebec Remparts Signed

This 25-card set parallels the base Quebec Remparts set in an autographed version. The cards are signed on a unique ghosted area on the card front, while the backs are serial numbered out of 100. The header card remains in the set, but it is not signed.

COMPLETE SET (25) 30.00 75.00
1 Jean Mallette .75 2.00
2 Patrick Chouinard .75 2.00
3 Kirill Safronov 2.00 5.00
4 Eric Chouinard 4.00 10.00
5 Patrick Grandmaitre .75 2.00
6 Eric Laplante .75 2.00
7 Wesley Scanzano .75 2.00
8 Chris Lyness .75 2.00
9 Tommy Bolduc .75 2.00
10 Jean-Francois Touchette .75 2.00
11 Philippe Paris .75 2.00
12 Karl Morin .75 2.00
13 Andre Martineau .75 2.00
14 Sylvain Plamondon .75 2.00
15 Martin Moise .75 2.00
16 Martin Grenier 2.00 5.00
17 Andre Hart .75 2.00
18 Maxime Ouellet 8.00 20.00
19 Martin Pare .75 2.00
20 Eric Cloutier .75 2.00
21 Kristian Kudroc 2.00 5.00
22 Casey Leggett .75 2.00
23 Shawn Collymore 1.25 3.00
24 Mike Ribeiro 4.00 10.00
25 Header Card/CL .08 .25

2000-01 Quebec Remparts

This set features the Remparts of the QMJHL. The cards were produced by CTM-Ste-Foy and sold by that card shop, as well as by the team.

COMPLETE SET (24) 4.80 12.00
1 Jean Mallette .20 .50
2 Sebastian Bourgon .20 .50
3 Richard Paul .20 .50
4 David Boilard .20 .50
5 Jeff Hadley .20 .50
6 Remi Bergeron .20 .50
7 Sebastian Morissette .20 .50
8 Philippe Paris .20 .50
9 Justin Stewart .20 .50
10 Yannick Searles .20 .50
11 Mike Bray .20 .50
12 Guillaume Fournier .20 .50
13 Robert Pearce .20 .50
14 Petr Preucil .20 .50
15 Philippe Parent .20 .50
16 Didier Bochatay .20 .50
17 Scott Della Vedova .30 .75
18 Alexandre Reuben .30 .75
19 David Masse .20 .50
20 Shawn Collymore .20 .75
21 Guillaume Berube .20 .50
22 Kevin Lachance .30 .75
23 Cory Urquhart .20 .50
NNO Team CL .04 .01

2000-01 Quebec Remparts Signed

This set is exactly the same as the base Remparts set from this season, save that every card has been hand signed by the player pictured. Each card also is serial numbered out of just 100. The team CL is not signed.

COMPLETE SET (24) 14.00 35.00
2 Sebastian Bourgon .80 2.00
3 Richard Paul .80 2.00
5 Jeff Hadley .80 2.00
6 Remi Bergeron .80 2.00
7 Sebastian Morissette .80 2.00
8 Philippe Paris .80 2.00
9 Justin Stewart .80 2.00
10 Yannick Searles .80 2.00
11 Mike Bray .80 2.00
12 Guillaume Fournier .80 2.00
13 Robert Pearce .80 2.00
14 Petr Preucil .80 2.00
15 Philippe Parent .80 2.00
17 Scott Della Vedova 2.00 5.00
20 Shawn Collymore .80 5.00
21 Guillaume Berube .80 2.00
22 Kevin Lachance 2.00 5.00
NNO Team CL .04 .25

2001-02 Quebec Remparts

This set features the Remparts of the QMJHL. The set was produced by CTM Ste-Foy and was sold at Remparts home games. It is believed that less than 1,000 sets were produced.

COMPLETE SET (24) 4.80 12.00
1 Jean-Michel Bolduc .20 .50
2 Sebastien Bourgon .20 .50
3 Yan Turcotte .20 .50
4 Jeff Hadley .20 .50
5 Josh Hennessy .20 .50
6 Mark Hurtubise .20 .50
7 Mathieu Dery .20 .50
8 Robert Pearce .20 .50
9 Yannick Searles .20 .50
10 Mike Bray .20 .50
11 Tomas Spila .20 .50
12 Samuel Duplain .20 .50
13 Petr Preucil .20 .50
14 Daniel Houle .20 .50
15 Didier Bochatay .20 .50
16 Denis Berube .20 .50
17 Jeff MacAulay .20 .50
18 Mario Joly .20 .50
19 David Masse .20 .50
20 Shawn Collymore .20 .50
21 Guillaume Berube .20 .50
22 Kevin Lachance .20 .50
23 Sebastien Thinel .20 .50
24 Cory Urquhart .20 .50

2002-03 Quebec Remparts

Cards U12-U23 available as an update set.

COMPLETE SET (23) 18.00
1 Jean-Michel Bolduc .75
2 Sebastien Bourgon .50
3 Colin Ledaire .50
4 Josh Hennessy .50
5 Mark Hurtubise .50
6 Vladimir Kutny .50
7 Robert Pearce .50
8 Jordan LaVallee .50
9 Timofei Shishkanov 1.00
10 Jason Kostadine .50
11 Curtis Tidball .50
12 Frederic Faucher .50
13 Karl St. Pierre .50
14 Didier Bochatay .50
15 Ben McMullin .75
16 David Masse .50
17 Shawn Collymore .75
18 Guillaume Berube .50
19 Steve Pelletier .50
20 Kevin Lachance .75
21 Pierre-Olivier Beaulieu .50
22 Chris Montgomery .50
U12 Evan Shaw .50
U14 Jean-Michel Filiatrault 2.00
U15 Alexandre Rouleau .75
U16 Aaron Johnson .50
U17 Pierre Morvan .50
U20 Benoit Beauchemin .50
U21 Remy Tremblay .50
U22 Checklist/Logo .10
U23 Jamie McCabe .50
NNO Checklist .10

2003 Quebec Remparts Memorial Cup

Cards are unnumbered and thus are listed in alphabetical order.

COMPLETE SET (21) 18.00
1 Guillaume Berube .75
2 Jean-Michel Bolduc 1.00
3 Sebastien Bourgon .75
4 Frederic Faucher .75
5 Jean-Michel Filiatrault 2.50
6 Josh Hennessy .75
7 Aaron Johnson .75
8 Jason Kostadine .75
9 Vladimir Kutny .75
10 Kevin Lachance 1.00
11 Jordan Lavallee .75
12 David Masse .75
13 Jamie McCabe .75
14 Chris Montgomery .75
15 Pierre Morvan .75
16 Robert Pearce .75
17 Alexandre Rouleau 1.00
18 Evan Shaw .75
19 Timofei Shishkanov 1.25
20 Karl St.Pierre .75
21 Curtis Tidball .75

2003-04 Quebec Remparts

COMPLETE SET (28) 5.00 12.00
1 Andrew Andricopoulos .20 .50
2 Adam Blanchette .20 .50
3 Christian Brideau .20 .50
4 Tyler Chambers .20 .50
5 Jean-Michel Cote .30 .75
6 Kevin Coughlin .20 .50
7 Simon Courcelles .20 .50
8 Jean-Michel Filiatrault .40 1.00
9 Ian Girard .20 .50
10 Stephane Goulet .20 .50
11 Josh Hennessy .30 .75
12 Alexandre Imbeault .20 .50
13 Alexandre Kojevnikov .20 .50
14 Louis-Phillipe Lachance .20 .50
15 Jordan LaVallee .20 .50
16 Justin Laverdiere .20 .50
17 Maxime Lincourt .20 .50
18 Eric L'Italien .20 .50
19 Mathieu Melanson .20 .50
20 Corey Pastershank .20 .50
21 Robert Pearce .20 .50
22 Joey Ryan .20 .50
23 Evan Shaw .20 .50
24 Alexei Shkotov .20 .50
25 Brandon Tidball .20 .50
26 Marc-Edouard Vlasic .60 1.50
27 Nathan Welton .20 .50
28 Checklist/Title Card .01 .05

2004-05 Quebec Remparts

A total of 400 team sets were produced.

COMPLETE SET (25) 6.00 15.00
1 Gennady Churilov .20 .50
2 Jordan LaVallee .20 .50
3 Karl Gagne .20 .50
4 Maxime Lacroix .20 .50
5 Maxime Lincourt .20 .50
6 Simon Courcelles .20 .50
7 Andrew Andricopoulos .20 .50
8 Ian Girard .20 .50
9 Maxime Joyal .20 .50
10 Alexander Radulov 1.50 4.00
11 Brandon Tidball .40 1.00
12 Marc-Edouard Vlasic 1.25 3.00
13 Max Gratchev .20 .50
14 Josh Hennessy .40 1.00
15 Mathieu Melanson .20 .50
16 Drew Paris .20 .50
17 Jonathan Alain-Rochette .20 .50
18 Joey Ryan .20 .50
19 Sebastien Bernier .20 .50
20 Kevin Coughlin .20 .50
21 Jonathan Boutin .30 .75
22 Alexandre Mineault .20 .50
23 Michael Tessier .20 .50
24 Guillaume Veilleux .20 .50
25 Evan Shaw .20 .50

2005-06 Quebec Remparts

COMPLETE SET (25) 10.00 18.00
1 Angelo Esposito 2.00 5.00
2 Alexander Radulov .75 2.00
3 Stephen Valente .20 .50
4 Joey Ryan .20 .50
5 Drew Paris .20 .50
6 Michal Sersen .20 .50
7 Simon Coucelles .20 .50
8 Felix Petit .20 .50
9 Maxime Lacroix .20 .50
10 Alexandre Mineault .20 .50
11 Max Gratchev .20 .50
12 Andrew Andricopoulos .20 .50
13 Jordan Lavallee .20 .50
14 Cedrick Desjardins .30 .75
15 Kevin Desfosses .20 .50
16 Kenzie Sheppard .20 .50
17 Nicolas Robillard .20 .50
18 Pierre Bergeron .20 .50
19 Brent Aubin .20 .50
20 Christophe Poirier .20 .50
21 Guillaume Veilleux .20 .50
22 Marc-Edouard Vlasic .20 .50
23 Todd Chinova .20 .50
24 Yan Ouimet .20 .50
25 Mathieu Melanson .20 .50

2006-07 Quebec Remparts

COMPLETE SET (27) 12.00 20.00
1 Angelo Esposito 2.00 5.00
2 Andrew Andricopoulos .20 .50
3 Joey Ryan .20 .50
4 Pierre Bergeron .20 .50
5 Kelsey Tessier .40 1.00
6 Roman Bashkirov .40 1.00
7 Hubert Genest .20 .50
8 Felix Petit .20 .50
9 Brent Aubin .40 1.00
10 Maxime Sauve .20 .50
11 Loic Lacasse .20 .50
12 Alexandre Mineault .20 .50
13 Ruslan Bashkirov .40 1.00
14 Billy Bezeau .20 .50
15 Kevin Desfosses .40 1.00
16 Boby Fugere .20 .50
17 Maxime Lacroix .20 .50
18 Christophe Poirier .20 .50

19 Philippe Poirier .20 .50
20 Joel Roch .20 .50
21 Benjamin Rubin .20 .50
22 Kenzie Sheppard .20 .50
23 Matthew Smith .40 1.00
24 Marc-Olivier Vallerand .20 .50
25 Guillaume Veilleux .20 .50
26 Mathieu Lavoie .20 .50
EL2 Brent Aubin .20 .50

2007-08 Quebec Remparts

Card #22 does not exist.

1 Kevin Desfosses
2 Jonathan Roy
3 Pierre Bergeron
4 Dominik Bohac
5 Hubert Genest
6 Samuel Groulx
7 Louis-Philippe Lacroix
8 Benjamin Lecomte
9 Mikael Tam
10 Brian Cayouette
11 Angelo Esposito
12 Felix Petit
13 Maxime Sauve
14 Darick Ste-Marie
15 Kelsey Tessier
16 Jonathan Audy-Marchessault
17 Olivier Daunais
18 Joshua Desmarais
19 Maxime Lacroix
20 Mathieu Loisel
21 Christophe Poirier
23 Mikhail Stefanovich
24 Marc-Olivier Vallerand
25 Maxim Cliche
26 Sebastien Trudeau
27 David Gilbert
28 Patrick Roy CO
LE1 Angelo Esposito

2007-08 Quebec Remparts Signature Series

1 Kevin Desfosses
2 Jonathan Roy
3 Pierre Bergeron
4 Dominik Bohac
5 Hubert Genest
6 Samuel Groulx
7 Louis-Philippe Lacroix
8 Benjamin Lecomte
9 Mikael Tam
10 Brian Cayouette
11 Angelo Esposito
12 Felix Petit
13 Darick Ste-Marie
14 Kelsey Tessier
15 Jonathan Audy-Marchessault
16 Maxime Lacroix
17 Mathieu Loisel
18 Christophe Poirier
19 Mikhail Stefanovich
20 Marc-Olivier Vallerand
21 Maxim Cliche
22 Sebastien Trudeau
23 David Gilbert
24 Patrick Roy CO

2008-09 Quebec Remparts

1 Charles Lavigne
2 Jonathan Roy
3 Samuel Carrier
4 Samuel Groulx
5 David Gilbert
6 Guillaume Monast
7 Mikael Tam
8 Kevin Marshall
9 Benjamin Breault
10 Brian Cayouette
11 Frederick Roy
12 Sebastien Trudeau
13 Jean-Simon Allard
14 Mathieu Loisel
15 Yannick Reiber
16 Frederik Roy-Cote
17 Julien Corriveau
18 Kelsey Tessier
19 Hubert Genest
20 Jonathan Audy-Marchessault
21 Marc-Olivier Vallerand
22 Mikhail Stefanovich
23 Dmitry Kugryshev
24 Alexandre Neron
25 Patrick Roy CO
26 Martin Laperriere CO
27 Champion MASCOT

2008-09 Quebec Remparts Signature Series

1 Charles Lavigne
2 Jonathan Roy
3 Frederik Roy-Cote
4 Julien Corriveau
5 Kelsey Tessier
6 Hubert Genest
7 Marc-Olivier Vallerand
8 Mikhail Stefanovich
9 Dmitry Kugryshev
10 Jonathan Audy-Marchessault
11 Yannick Reiber
12 Jean-Simon Allard
13 Sebastien Trudeau
14 Frederick Roy
15 Brian Cayouette
16 Benjamin Breault
17 Alexandre Neron
18 Kevin Marshall
19 Mikael Tam
20 Guillaume Monast
21 David Gilbert
22 Samuel Groulx
23 Samuel Carrier
24 Mathieu Loisel

1992-93 Raleigh Icecaps

This 38-card standard-size set features the Raleigh Icecaps of the ECHL. Inside a blue-and-white border design, the fronts feature on-ice posed color player photos with rounded corners. The player's name and position appear under the photo, while the words "1992-93 Raleigh IceCaps" are printed above the photo. The backs carry biography, stats, and a player profile. The cards were issued in two separate series. The first series cards, produced by Sportsprint (Atlanta, GA), are unnumbered and checklisted below in alphabetical order, whereas the second series cards, produced by RBI Sports Cards Inc. (Greensboro, North Carolina), are numbered on the back.

COMPLETE SET (38) 6.00 15.00
1 Cappy Bear (Mascot) .02 .10
2 Sean Cowan .20 .50
3 Joel Gardner .20 .50
4 Bill Kovacs .20 .50
5 Alan Leggett .20 .50
6 Kirby Lindal .20 .50
7 Derek Linnell .20 .50
8 Jim Mill .20 .50
9 Kris Miller .20 .50
10 Todd Person .20 .50
11 Chic Pojar .20 .50
12 Jim Powers .20 .50
13 Stan(Smokey) Reddick .30 .75
14 Doug Roberts .20 .50
15 Jeff Robison .20 .50
16 Jeff Tomlinson .20 .50
17 Brian Tulik .20 .50
18 Bruno Villeneuve .20 .50
19 Lyle Wildgoose .20 .50
20 Team Photo DP .15 .40
21 Bruno Villeneuve .20 .50
22 Jeff Robison .20 .50
23 Jim Powers .20 .50
24 Derek Linnell .20 .50
25 Chris Marshall .20 .50
26 Kris Miller .20 .50
27 Joel Gardner .20 .50
28 Stan(Smokey) Reddick .30 .75
29 Jim Mill .20 .50
30 Alan Leggett .20 .50
31 Brian Tulik .20 .50
32 Kirby Lindal .20 .50
33 Sean Cowan .20 .50
34 Lyle Wildgoose .20 .50
35 Todd Person .20 .50
36 Chic Pojar .20 .50
37 Mike Lappin .20 .50
38 Doug Bacon .20 .50

1993-94 Raleigh Icecaps

Produced by RBI Sports Cards, this 20-card standard-size set features the Raleigh Icecaps of the ECHL. On a white card face, the fronts feature color action player photos inside purple borders. The player's name appears under the photo.

COMPLETE SET (20) 3.00 8.00
1 Ralph Barahona .15 .40
2 Rick Barkovich .15 .40
3 Matt Delguidice .20 .50
4 Martin D'Orsonnens .15 .40
5 Jamie Erb .15 .40
6 Chad Erickson .20 .50
7 Donevan Hextall .20 .50
8 Shaun Kane .15 .40
9 Al Leggett .15 .40
10 Derek Linnell .15 .40
11 Joe McCarthy .15 .40
12 Chris Nelson .15 .40
13 Barry Nieckar .15 .40
14 Jim Powers .15 .40
15 Stan Reddick .20 .50
16 Kevin Riehl .15 .40
17 Jeff Robison .15 .40
18 David Shute .15 .40
19 Lyle Wildgoose .15 .40
20 Kurt Kleinendorst CO .08 .25

1994-95 Raleigh Icecaps

Produced by RBI Sports Cards, this 19-card standard-size set features the Raleigh Icecaps of the ECHL. Just 1,000 sets were produced. On a black card face, the fronts feature color action and posed player photos inside a white frame. The player's name appears under the photo, while the team name is printed above the photo. There are several production errors in this set. Card number 12 was not produced. Card numbers 9 and 18 were mistakenly duplicated and explains the absence of card numbers 10 and 19.

COMPLETE SET (19) 3.00 8.00
1 John Blessman .20 .50
2 Rick Barkovich CO .08 .25
3 Alexsandr Chunchukov .20 .50
4 Frank Cirone .20 .50
5 Brett Duncan .20 .50
6 Anton Fedorov .20 .50
7 Todd Hunter .20 .50
8 Rodrigo Lavinsh .30 .75
9 Derek Linnell .20 .50
10 Eric Long UER .20 .50
(Card misnumbered 9 on back)
11 Scott MacNair .20 .50
13 Brad Mullahy .20 .50
14 Lenny Pereira .20 .50
15 Jimmy Powers .20 .50
16 Chic Pojar .20 .50
17 Kevin Riehl .20 .50
18 Todd Reirden .30 .75
19 Justin Tomberlin UER .20 .50
(Card misnumbered 18 on back)
20 Lyle Wildgoose .20 .50

1989-90 Rayside-Balfour Jr. Canadians

This 20-card set is printed on thin card stock and measures approximately 2 3/8" by 3 3/8." The cards feature full-bleed, color, posed player photos. The player's name and jersey number are printed in black at the bottom. The team logo and name are printed at the top. The cards are unnumbered and checklisted below in alphabetical order.

COMPLETE SET (20) 3.00 8.00
1 Team Photo .40 1.00
2 Dave Barrett .20 .50
3 Dan Baston .20 .50
4 Rick Chartrand .20 .50
5 Simon Chartrand .20 .50
6 Ron Clark .20 .50
7 Brian Dickinson .20 .50
8 Trevor Duncan .20 .50
9 Don Gauthier .20 .50
10 Shawn Hawkins .20 .50
11 Roy Hildebrandt .20 .50
12 Al Laginski .20 .50
13 Eric Lanteigne .20 .50
14 Mike Leblanc .20 .50
15 Kevin MacDonald .20 .50
16 Mike Mooney .20 .50
17 Rick Potvin .20 .50
18 Rick Poulin .20 .50
19 Steve Prior .20 .50
20 Scott Sutton .20 .50

1990-91 Rayside-Balfour Jr. Canadians

This 23-card set is printed on thin card stock and measures approximately 2 3/8" by 3 1/4." The cards feature full-bleed, color, posed player photos. The player's name and jersey number are printed in black at the bottom. The team logo and name are printed at the top. The cards are unnumbered and checklisted below in alphabetical order.

COMPLETE SET (23) 3.00 8.00
1 Dan Baston .15 .40
2 Jon Boeve .15 .40
3 Jordan Boyle .15 .40
4 Serge Coulombe .15 .40
5 Mike Dore .15 .40
6 Denis Gosselin .15 .40
7 Mike Gratton .15 .40
8 Jason Hall .15 .40
9 Grant Healey .15 .40
10 Marc Lafreniere .15 .40
11 Alain Leclair .15 .40
12 Mike Longo .15 .40
13 Troy Mallette .30 .75
1985-86 rookie photo
14 Matthew Mooney .15 .40
15 Virgil Nose .15 .40
16 Trevor Oystrick .15 .40
17 Steve Proceviat .15 .40
18 Chris Puskas .15 .40
19 Yvon Quenneville .15 .40
20 Michael Sullivan .20 .50
21 Trevor Tremblay .15 .40
22 Sean Van Amburg .15 .40
23 Title Card .02 .10

1991-92 Rayside-Balfour Jr. Canadians

This 23-card set measures approximately 2 3/8" by 3 5/16" and is printed on thin card stock. The fronts feature color, full-bleed, posed action player photos. The player's name and jersey number are printed in black at the bottom. The team logo appears in either red or white at the upper left corner. The cards are unnumbered and checklisted below in alphabetical order.

COMPLETE SET (23) 3.00 8.00
1 Dan Baston .20 .50
2 Don Cucksey .20 .50
3 Dean Cull .20 .50
4 Mike Dore .20 .50
5 Denis Gosselin .20 .50
6 Jason Hall .20 .50
7 Grant Healey .20 .50
8 Marc Lafreniere .20 .50
9 Mike Longo .20 .50
10 Scott Maclellan .20 .50
11 Matt Mooney .20 .50
12 Rob Moxness .20 .50
13 Virgil Nose .20 .50
14 Trent Oystrick .20 .50
15 Jon Stewart .20 .50
16 Jon Slos .20 .50
17 Dave Sutton .20 .50
18 Scott Sutton .20 .50
19 Trevor Tremblay .20 .50
20 Jaak Valiots .20 .50
21 Sean Van Amburg .20 .50
22 Jason Young .02 .10
Stickboy
23 Title Card .02 .10

2002-03 Reading Royals

COMPLETE SET (32) 10.00 25.00
1 Series 1 Header Card .02 .10
2 Francois Drainville .40 1.00
3 David Lohrei CO .20 .50
4 Matt Snesrud .40 1.00
5 Ray DiLauro .40 1.00
6 Chris Bogas .40 1.00
7 Simon Tremblay .40 1.00
8 Jim Dube .40 1.00
9 Series 2 Header Card .02 .10
10 Jonathon Shockey .40 1.00
11 Colin Pepperall .40 1.00
12 Brad Rooney .40 1.00
13 Brandon Dietrich .40 1.00
14 Kris Waltze .40 1.00
15 Hunter Lahache .40 1.00
16 Jeff Giuliano .40 1.00
17 Series 3 Header Card .20 .50
18 Sean Gauthier .40 1.00
19 Steve Rymsha .40 1.00
20 Tom Rouleau .40 1.00
21 Geoff Peters .40 1.00
22 Duilio Grande .40 1.00
23 Keegan McAvoy .40 1.00
24 Brian McCullough .40 1.00
25 Series 4 Header Card .02 .10
26 Steve Shirreffs .40 1.00
27 Ryan Flinn .60 1.50
28 Scott Fankhouser .60 1.50
29 Jeff Sanger .40 1.00
30 Antoine Bergeron .40 1.00
31 Alex Kim .40 1.00
32 Dan Riva .40 1.00

2002-03 Reading Royals RBI Sports

COMPLETE SET (18) 8.00 20.00
169 Antoine Bergeron .40 1.00
170 Craig Brunel .40 1.00
171 Brandon Dietrich .40 1.00
172 Ray DiLauro .40 1.00
173 Jim Dube .40 1.00
174 Jeff Giuliano .40 1.00
175 Duilio Grande .40 1.00
176 Alex Kim .40 1.00
177 Brian McCullough .40 1.00
178 Colin Pepperall .40 1.00
179 Dan Riva .40 1.00
180 Brad Rooney .40 1.00
181 Remi Royer .75 2.00
182 Tom Rouleau .40 1.00
183 Steve Rymsha .40 1.00
184 Jeff Sanger .75 2.00
185 Mat Snesrud .40 1.00
186 Simon Tremblay .40 1.00

2003-04 Reading Royals

This set was issued in four mini-sets as a promotional giveaway over the course of the 2003-04 season.

COMPLETE SET (30) 12.00 30.00
1 Header Card Series One .01 .05
2 Derek Clancey .40 1.00
3 Adam Hauser 1.25 3.00
4 Mat Snesrud .40 1.00
5 Jason Maleyko .40 1.00
6 Tomas Slovak .40 1.00
7 Jonathan Zion .40 1.00
8 Leon Hayward .40 1.00
9 Header Card Series Two .01 .05
10 Judd Medak .40 1.00
11 David Masse .40 1.00
12 Nick Lent .40 1.00
13 Jeff Finger .40 1.00
14 Francis Nault .40 1.00
15 Graig Mischler .40 1.00
16 Header Card Series Three .01 .05
17 Peter Hay .40 1.00
18 Ian Turner .40 1.00
19 Kent Davyduke .40 1.00
20 Dean Arsene .40 1.00
21 Darryl Laplante .40 1.00
22 Dave Stewart .75 2.00
23 Header Card Series Four .01 .05
24 Mascot .02 .10
25 Reading Royals .02 .10
26 Brad Church .40 1.00
27 Cody Rudkowsky .75 2.00
28 Terry Denike .75 2.00
29 Matt Passfield .40 1.00
30 Doug Nolan .40 1.00

2003-04 Reading Royals RBI Sports

This set was produced by RBI Sports and limited to just 250 copies. The numbering sequence reflects the entire run of RBI sets over the course of the season.

COMPLETE SET (18) 15.00
289 Brad Church 1.00
290 Kent Davyduke 1.00
291 Peter Hay 1.00
292 Leon Hayward 1.00
293 Nick Lent 1.00
294 Jason Maleyko 1.00
295 Judd Medak 1.00
296 Graig Mischler 1.00
297 Francis Nault 1.00
298 Doug Nolan 1.00
299 Matt Passfield 1.00
300 Cody Rudkowsky 1.50
301 Tomas Slovak 1.00
302 Scooter Smith 1.00
303 Mat Snesrud 1.00
304 Ian Turner 1.00
305 David Belitski 1.50
306 Josh Barker 1.00

2004-05 Reading Royals

These cards were given away at four separate home games. We do not have a checklist for the first series of six cards. If you know of them, please forward the info to hockeymag@beckett.com.

COMPLETE SET (28
1 unknown
2 unknown
3 unknown
4 unknown
5 unknown
6 unknown
7 David Masse
8 Tom Galvin
9 Cail MacLean
10 Aaron Smith
11 Graig Mischler
12 Barry Brust
13 Ryan Kinasewich
14 Ian Turner
15 Mike Souza
16 Preston Mizzi
17 Dan Welch
18 Larry Courville
19 Slapshot MASCOT
20 Nick Greenough
21 Jeff Miles
22 Martin Wilde
23 Mikko Viitanen
24 Adam Borzecki
NNO Header Card
NNO Header Card
NNO Header Card
NNO Header Card

2005-06 Reading Royals

COMPLETE SET (19) 8.00 15.00
1 Chris Bala .30 .75
2 Doug Christiansen .30 .75
3 Larry Courville .30 .75
4 Jon Francisco .30 .75
5 Yutaka Fukufuji .75 2.00
6 Tyler Hanchuck .30 .75
7 T.J. Kemp .30 .75
8 Mike Kompon .30 .75
9 Malcolm MacMillan .30 .75
10 John Morlang .30 .75
11 Reagan Rome .30 .75
12 Dany Roussin .60 1.50
13 Cody Rudkowsky .60 1.50
14 Jeff State .30 .75
15 Shay Stephenson .30 .75
16 Eric Werner .30 .75
17 Karl Taylor HC .02 .10
18 Slapshot MASCOT .02 .10
19 Reading Royals .02 .10

2006-07 Reading Royals

COMPLETE SET (18) 15.00 30.00
1 Rob Lalonde .75 2.00
2 Shawn German .60 1.50
3 Taylor Christie .60 1.50
4 Reagan Rome .60 1.50
5 Jason Becker .60 1.50
6 Malcolm Macmillan 1.00 2.50
7 Shawn Collymore .60 1.50
8 Joe Zappala .60 1.50
9 John Snowden .60 1.50
10 Jon Francisco .60 1.50
11 Dany Roussin .60 1.50
12 Ned Lukacevic .60 1.50
13 Kevin Saurette .60 1.50
14 Greg Hogeboom .60 1.50
15 Chris Bala .60 1.50
16 Jeff Pietrasiak .75 2.00
17 Yutaka Fukufuji 2.00 5.00
18 Karl Taylor CO .20 .50

2007-08 Reading Royals

COMPLETE SET (22) 4.00 10.00
1 Terry Denike .25 .60
2 Rob LaLonde .25 .60
3 Patrik Hersley .25 .60
4 Shawn Germain .25 .60
5 Victor Uchevatov .25 .60
6 Steven Later .25 .60
7 Ned Lukacevic .25 .60
8 Malcolm MacMillan .25 .60
9 Joe Zappala .25 .60
10 Chris Blight .25 .60
11 Patrick Jarrett .25 .60
12 Dany Roussin .25 .60
13 Brock Hooton .25 .60
14 Mike Salekin .25 .60
15 Kevin Saurette .25 .60
16 Matt Herneisen .25 .60
17 Marc Cavosie .25 .60
18 Brian Boulay .25 .60
19 Charlie Kronschnabel .25 .60
20 Jon Quick .25 .60
21 PJ Atherton .25 .60
22 Karl Taylor .25 .60

1993-94 Red Deer Rebels

This 30-card set measures the standard size. The fronts feature posed action on-ice player photos with hatched borders. The player's name and number are printed in white letters inside a silver bar above the picture, while the team name appears alongside the left side. The cards are unnumbered and checklisted below in alphabetical order.

COMPLETE SET (30) 4.00 10.00
1 Peter Anholt CO .02 .10
2 Byron Briske .15 .40
3 Curtis Cardinal .15 .40
4 Jason Clague .15 .40
5 Dale Donaldson .15 .40
6 Dave Greenway .15 .40
7 Scott Grimwood TR .02 .10
8 Sean Halifax .15 .40
9 Chris Kibermanis .15 .40
10 Pete LeBoutillier .15 .40
11 Pete LeBoutillier .15 .40
In Action
12 Terry Lindgren .15 .40
13 Chris Maillet .15 .40
14 Eddy Marchant .15 .40
15 Mike McBain .15 .40
16 Mike Moller ACO .02 .10
17 Andy Nowicki ACO .02 .10
18 Berkley Pennock .15 .40
19 Tyler Quiring .15 .40
20 Craig Reichert .15 .40
21 Ken Richardson .15 .40
22 Sean Selmser .15 .40
23 Vaclav Slansky .15 .40
24 Mark Toljanich .15 .40
25 Darren Van Impe .20 .50
26 Pete Vandermeer .30 .75
27 Chris Wickenheiser .20 .50
28 Brad Zimmer .15 .40
29 Jonathan Zukiwsky .15 .40
30 The Centrum .02 .10

1995-96 Red Deer Rebels

This 24-card set of the Red Deer Rebels of the WHL features extremely blurry color player photos in gray and black borders. The backs carry a player profile. The cards are unnumbered and checklisted below in alphabetical order.

COMPLETE SET (24) 4.00 10.00
1 Arron Asham .15 .40
2 Bryan Boorman .15 .40
3 Aleksei Boudaev .15 .40
4 Mike Broda .15 .40
5 Mike Brown .20 .50
6 Jay Henderson .30 .75
7 David Hruska .15 .40
8 Chris Kibermanis .15 .40
9 Brad Leeb .30 .75
10 Terry Lindgren .15 .40
11 Mike McBain .20 .50
12 Brent McDonald .15 .40
13 Ken McKay .15 .40
14 Harlan Pratt .15 .40
15 Greg Schmidt .15 .40
16 Pete Vandermeer .30 .75
17 Jesse Wallin .20 .50
18 Lance Ward .20 .50
19 Mike Whitney .15 .40
20 Chris Wickenheiser .30 .75
21 B.J. Young .15 .40
22 Jonathan Zukiwsky .20 .50
23 Drug Awareness Team .02 .10
24 Team Picture .15 .40

1996-97 Red Deer Rebels

Sold by the team at home games. Sponsored by RCMP and Parkland Colour Press.

COMPLETE SET (29) 6.00 15.00
1 Collector Series Card .01 .05
2 Team Photo .08 .25
3 Mike McBain .20 .50
4 Jesse Wallin .20 .50
5 Arron Asham .40 1.00
6 Kyle Kos .20 .50
7 Jonathan Zukiwsky .20 .50
8 Stephen Peat .75 2.00
9 Brent McDonald .20 .50
10 Greg Schmidt .20 .50
11 Chris Ovington .20 .50
12 Martin Tomasek .20 .50
13 Brad Rohrig .20 .50
14 Devin Francon .20 .50
15 B.J. Young .20 .50
16 Mike Broda .20 .50
17 Matt Van Horlick .20 .50
18 Mike Brown .20 .50
19 Lance Ward .20 .50
20 Kris Knoblauch .20 .50
21 Brad Leeb .20 .50
22 Garnet Stevenson .20 .50
23 Lloyd Shaw .20 .50
24 Mike Whitney .20 .50
25 Jesse Wallin .20 .50
26 Lance Ward .20 .50
27 The Centrum .02 .10
28 Drug Awareness .02 .10
29 Rowdy MASCOT .02 .10

1997-98 Red Deer Rebels

This set features the Rebels of the WHL. The set was produced by the team and sold at home games. The cards are unnumbered, and so are listed alphabetically.

COMPLETE SET (25) 4.80 12.00
1 Team photo .15 .40
2 Arron Asham .30 .75
3 Andrew Bergen .15 .40
4 Joel Boschman .15 .40
5 Chris Cederstrand .15 .40
6 Devin Francon .15 .40
7 John Kachur .15 .40
8 Kyle Kos .15 .40
9 Brad Leeb .15 .40
10 Justin Mapletoft .60 1.50
11 Brent McDonald .15 .40
12 Shawn McNeil .15 .40
13 Scott McQueen .15 .40
14 Frank Mrazek .20 .50
15 Cam Ondrik .15 .40
16 Chris Ovington .15 .40
17 Stephen Peat .60 1.50
18 Brad Rohrig .15 .40
19 Robert Schnabel .20 .50
20 Jesse Wallin .30 .75
21 Lance Ward .30 .75
22 Mike Whitney .15 .40
23 Jon Zukiwsky .20 .50
24 Woolly Bully MASCOT .02 .10
25 Drug Awareness .01

1998-99 Red Deer Rebels

This set features the Rebels of the WHL. The cards were sold by the team at home games. They are unnumbered, so they are listed below in alphabetical order.

COMPLETE SET (24) 4.80 12.00
1 Jay Batchelor .20 .50
2 Lukas Bednarik .20 .50
3 Andrew Bergen .20 .50
4 Michael Clague .30 .75
5 Andrew Coates .20 .50
6 Devin Francon .20 .50
7 Kyle Kos .20 .50
8 Brad Leeb .20 .50
9 Justin Mapletoft .60 1.50
10 Kevin Marsh .20 .50
11 Brett McDonald .20 .50
12 Shawn McNeil .20 .50
13 Scott McQueen .20 .50
14 Frank Mrazek .20 .50
15 Rhett Nevill .20 .50
16 Chris Ovington .20 .50
17 Stephen Peat .60 1.50
18 Dustin Schwartz .30 .75
19 Jeff Smith .20 .50
20 Jim Vandermeer .20 .50
21 Justin Wallin .20 .50
22 Jordan Watt .30 .75
23 Wooly Bully MASCOT .02 .10
24 Drug Awareness Card .01

2000-01 Red Deer Rebels

This set features the Rebels of the WHL. The set is noteworthy for capturing the team during its Memorial Cup-winning season. The cards were sold by the team and are unnumbered, so they are listed below in alphabetical order.

COMPLETE SET (24) 4.80 15.00
1 Checklist .04 .10
2 Colby Armstrong .40 1.50
3 Shane Bendera .40 1.00
4 Andrew Bergen .16 .40
5 Devin Francon .16 .40
6 Michael Garnett .16 .40
7 Boyd Gordon .16 .40
8 Shane Grypiuk .16 .40
9 Diarmuid Kelly .16 .40
10 Ladislav Kouba .16 .40
11 Ross Lupaschuk .30 .75
12 Doug Lynch .30 .75
13 Justin Mapletoft .60 1.50
14 Derek Meech .16 .40
15 Donovan Rattray .16 .40
16 Jeff Smith .16 .40
17 Shay Stephenson .16 .40
18 Joel Stepp .16 .40
19 Bryce Thoma .16 .40
20 Jim Vandermeer .16 .75
21 Martin Vymazal .16 .40
22 Justin Wallin .16 .40
23 Kyle Wanvig .60 1.50
24 Jeff Woywitka .40 1.50

2000-01 Red Deer Rebels Signed

This set is exactly the same as the base Rebels set from this season, save that every card has been hand signed by the player pictured. Amazingly, this set was originally made available by the team for the bargain price of $10.

COMPLETE SET (24) 24.00 60.00
1 Checklist .04 .10
2 Colby Armstrong 2.00 7.50
3 Shane Bendera 2.00 5.00
4 Andrew Bergen .80 2.00
5 Devin Francon .80 2.00
6 Michael Garnett .80 2.00
7 Boyd Gordon .80 2.00
8 Shane Grypiuk .80 2.00
9 Diarmuid Kelly .80 2.00
10 Ladislav Kouba .80 2.00
11 Ross Lupaschuk 2.00 5.00
12 Doug Lynch 2.00 5.00
13 Justin Mapletoft 3.00 7.50
14 Derek Meech .80 2.00
15 Donovan Rattray .80 2.00
16 Jeff Smith .80 2.00
17 Shay Stephenson .80 2.00
18 Joel Stepp .80 2.00
19 Bryce Thoma .80 2.00
20 Jim Vandermeer .80 3.00
21 Martin Vymazal .80 2.00
22 Justin Wallin .80 2.00
23 Kyle Wanvig 3.00 7.50
24 Jeff Woywitka 2.00 7.50

2001-02 Red Deer Rebels

COMPLETE SET (21) 6.00 15.00
1 Cover Card .01 .05
2 Colby Armstrong .40 1.00
3 Shane Bendera .40 1.00
4 Andrew Bergen .20 .50
5 Derek Endicott .20 .50
6 Jason Ertl .20 .50
7 Colin Fraser .20 .50
8 Boyd Gordon .40 1.00
9 Diarmuid Kelly .20 .50
10 Ladislav Kouba .20 .50
11 Doug Lynch .30 .75
12 Derek Meech .30 .75
13 Chris Neiszner .20 .50
14 Joel Rupprecht .20 .50
15 Jeff Smith .20 .50
16 Shay Stephenson .20 .50
17 Joel Stepp .20 .50
18 Bryce Thoma .20 .50
19 Cam Ward 4.00 10.00
20 Mikhail Yakubov .40 1.00
21 Woolly Bully MAS .02 .10

2002-03 Red Deer Rebels

This set features the Rebels of the WHL. The cards are listed in the order they appear on the checklist card.

COMPLETE SET (26) 15.00 40.00
1 Cam Ward/CL 2.00 5.00
2 Derek Meech .40 1.00
3 Dion Phaneuf 6.00 15.00
4 Bryce Thoma .20 .50
5 Jeff Woywitka .40 1.00
6 Cody Holzapfel .20 .50
7 Masi Marjamaki .40 1.00
8 Matt Ellison .20 .50
9 Joel Stepp .20 .50
10 Colin Fraser .30 .75
11 Blair Jones .20 .50
12 Jason Ertl .20 .50
13 Jared Walker .20 .50
14 Derek Endicott .20 .50
15 Carsen Germyn .20 .50
16 Boyd Gordon .40 1.00
17 Stuart Kerr .20 .50
18 Ladislav Kouba .20 .50
19 Matt Keith .20 .50
20 Diarmuid Kelly .20 .50
21 Shay Stephenson .20 .50
22 Nathan Brice .20 .50
23 Jesse Zetariuk .20 .50
24 Chris Neiszner .20 .50
25 Cam Ward 2.00 5.00
26 Adam Jennings .30 .75

2003-04 Red Deer Rebels

COMPLETE SET (24) 10.00 25.00
1 Derek Meech .30 .75
2 Dion Phaneuf 6.00 15.00
3 Paul Kurceba .20 .50
4 Dan Mercer .20 .50
5 Mikko Kuukka .20 .50
6 Andre Herman .20 .50
7 Colin Fraser .30 .75
8 Kyle Ross .20 .50
9 Jason Ertl .20 .50
10 Jared Walker .20 .50
11 Derek Endicott .20 .50
12 Justin Taylor .20 .50
13 Ted Vandermeer .20 .50
14 Stuart Kerr .30 .75
15 Blair Jones .20 .50
16 Shay Stephenson .20 .50
17 Nathan Brice .20 .50
18 Jesse Zetariuk .20 .50
19 Chris Neiszner .20 .50
20 Cam Ward 1.50 4.00
21 Trevor Peeters .30 .75
22 Wooly Bully MASCOT .02 .10
23 Brent Sutter CO .20 .50
24 Team Photo .20 .50

2005-06 Red Deer Rebels

COMPLETE SET (25) 8.00 15.00
1 Brennan Chapman .20 .50
2 Matthew Cline .20 .50
3 Luke Egener .20 .50
4 Eric Frere .20 .50
5 Tanner Gillies .20 .50
6 Matthew Hansen .20 .50
7 Garrett Klotz .20 .50
8 Jordan Knackstedt .20 .50
9 Pierre-Paul Lamoureux .20 .50
10 Devon LeBlanc .20 .50
11 Andrew Leslie .40 1.00
12 Vladimir Mihalik .20 .50
13 Karey Pieper .20 .50
14 Alex Poulter .20 .50
15 James Reimer .20 .50
16 Justin Scott .20 .50
17 Jonathon Smith .20 .50
18 Brandon Sutter 1.00 2.50
19 Brett Sutter .40 1.00
20 Ted Vandermeer .20 .50
21 Kris Versteeg 2.00 5.00
22 Roman Wick .20 .50
23 Mike Berube .20 .50
24 Josh Bray .20 .50
25 Red Deer Rebels CL .01 .01

1981-82 Regina Pats

This 25-card set measures approximately 2 5/8" by 4 1/8" and is printed on thin card stock. The fronts feature color, posed action player photos with white borders accented by a thin red line. The player's jersey number, name, and position appear in black print across the bottom of the picture. The cards are unnumbered and checklisted below in alphabetical order.

COMPLETE SET (25) 12.00 30.00
1 Pats Logo .20 .50
2 Garth Butcher .75 2.00
3 Lyndon Byers 2.00 5.00
4 Jock Callander 1.50 4.00
5 Marc Centrone .40 1.00
6 Dave Goertz .40 1.00
7 Evans Dobni .40 1.00
8 Dale Derkatch .40 1.00
9 Jeff Crawford .40 1.00
10 Jim Clarke .40 1.00
11 Jayson Meyer .40 1.00
12 Gary Leeman .75 2.00
13 Bruce Holloway .40 1.00
14 Ken Heppner .40 1.00
15 Taylor Hall .40 1.00
16 Wally Schreiber .60 1.50
17 Kevin Pylypow .40 1.00
18 Ray Plamondon .40 1.00
19 Brent Pascal .40 1.00
20 Dave Michayluk .60 1.50
21 Barry Trotz .40 1.00
22 Al Tuer .60 1.50
23 Tony Vogel .40 1.00
24 Martin Wood .40 1.00
25 Regina Police Logo .20 .50

1982-83 Regina Pats

This 25-card set measures approximately 2 5/8" by 4 1/8" and features color, posed action player photos on white card stock. The pictures are framed by a thin red line. The player's name, jersey number, and position are printed in black on the photo.

COMPLETE SET (25) 10.00 25.00
1 Regina Pats and Police Logo .08 .25
2 Todd Lumbard .40 1.00
3 Jamie Reeve .40 1.00
4 Dave Goertz .30 .75
5 John Miner .30 .75
6 Doug Trapp .30 .75
7 R.J. Dundas .30 .75
8 Stu Grimson 1.50 4.00
9 Al Tuer .30 .75
10 Rick Herbert .30 .75
11 Tony Vogel .30 .75
12 John Bekkers .30 .75
13 Dale Derkatch .60 1.50
14 Gary Leeman .75 2.00
15 Nevin Markwart .40 1.00
16 Kurt Wickenheiser .30 .75
17 Jeff Frank .30 .75
18 Marc Centrone .30 .75
19 Taylor Hall .30 .75
20 Lyndon Byers 1.50 4.00
21 Jayson Meyer .30 .75
22 Jeff Crawford .30 .75
23 Don Boyd CO .20 .50
24 Barry Trapp ACO .20 .50
25 K-9 Big Blue (Mascot) .08 .25

1983-84 Regina Pats

This 25-card set measures approximately 2 5/8" by 4 1/8" and features color, posed action player photos with white borders accented by a thin red line. The player's name is superimposed at the bottom of the picture.

COMPLETE SET (25) 8.00 20.00
1 Title Card .08 .25
2 Todd Lumbard .40 1.00
3 Jamie Reeve .40 1.00
4 Dave Goertz .30 .75
5 John Miner .30 .75
6 Doug Trapp .30 .75
7 R.J. Dundas .30 .75
8 Stu Grimson 1.25 3.00
9 Al Tuer .30 .75
10 Rick Herbert .30 .75
11 Tony Vogel .30 .75
12 John Bekkers .30 .75
13 Dale Derkatch .40 1.00
14 Gary Leeman .60 1.50
15 Nevin Markwart .40 1.00
16 Kurt Wickenheiser .30 .75
17 Jeff Frank .30 .75
18 Marc Centrone .30 .75
19 Taylor Hall .30 .75
20 Lyndon Byers 1.25 3.00
21 Jayson Meyer .30 .75
22 Jeff Crawford .30 .75
23 Don Boyd CO .30 .75
24 Barry Trapp ACO .20 .50
25 K-9 Big Blue (Mascot) .08 .25

1986-87 Regina Pats

Produced by Royal Studios, this 30-card set measures the standard size. The fronts feature color posed action player photos with red and white borders. The player's name and number are printed in red in the bottom white margin along with the team name and year, which are printed in black. The cards are unnumbered and checklisted below in alphabetical order.

COMPLETE SET (30) 6.00 15.00
1 Troy Bakogeorge .20 .50
2 Grant Chorney .20 .50
3 Gary Dickie .20 .50
4 Milan Dragicevic .20 .50
5 Mike Dyck .20 .50
6 Craig Endean .20 .50
7 Mike Gibson .20 .50
8 Erin Ginnell .20 .50
9 Brad Hornung .20 .50
10 Mark Janssens .30 .75
11 K-9 (Mascot) .08 .25
12 Trent Kachur .20 .50
13 Craig Kalawsky .20 .50
14 Dan Logan .20 .50
15 Jim Mathieson .20 .50
16 Darin McInnes .20 .50
17 Darrin McKechnie .20 .50
18 Rob McKinley .30 .75
19 Brad Miller .20 .50
20 Stacy Nickel .20 .50
21 Cregg Nicol .20 .50
22 Ken Nielsen .20 .50
23 Darren Parsons .20 .50
24 Doug Sauter .20 .50
25 Ray Savard .20 .50
26 Dennis Sobchuk .30 .75
27 Chris Tarnowski .20 .50
28 Mike Van Slooten .20 .50
29 Brian Wilkie .20 .50
30 Rod Williams .20 .50

1987-88 Regina Pats

Produced by Royal Studios, this 28-card standard-size set features color, posed action player photos with red and white borders. The player's name is printed in red in the bottom white margin along with the team name and year, which are printed in black. The cards are unnumbered and checklisted below in alphabetical order.

COMPLETE SET (28) 4.80 12.00
1 Kevin Clemens .20 .50
2 Gary Dickie .20 .50
3 Milan Dragicevic .20 .50
4 Mike Dyck .20 .50
5 Craig Endean .20 .50
6 Kevin Gallant PR .08 .25
7 Jamie Heward .20 .50
8 Rod Houk .30 .75
9 Mark Janssens .30 .75
10 Trent Kachur .20 .50
11 Craig Kalawsky .20 .50
12 K-9 (Mascot) .08 .25
13 Frank Kovacs .20 .50
14 Darren Kwiatkowski .20 .50
15 Brian Leibel .20 .50
16 Tim Logan .20 .50
17 Jim Mathieson .20 .50
18 Darrin McKechnie .20 .50
19 Rob McKinley .20 .50
20 Brad Miller .20 .50
21 Cregg Nicol .20 .50
22 Doug Sauter CO .08 .25
23 Dan Sexton .20 .50
24 Mike Sillinger .40 1.00
25 Dennis Sobchuk .30 .75
26 Stanley Szumlak TR .08 .25
27 Mike Van Slooten .20 .50
28 Team Photo .20 .50

1988-89 Regina Pats

This 25-card standard-size set features color, posed action player photos with red and white borders. The player's name is printed in red in the bottom white margin along with the team name and year, which are printed in black. The cards are unnumbered and checklisted below in alphabetical order.

COMPLETE SET (24) 4.00 12.00
1 Shane Bogden .20 .50
2 Cam Brauer .20 .50
3 Scott Daniels .25 .60
4 Gary Dickie .20 .50
5 Mike Dyck .20 .50
6 Dave Gerse .20 .50
7 Kevin Haller .25 .60
8 Jamie Heward .20 .50
9 Terry Hollinger .20 .50
10 Rod Houk .20 .50
11 Frank Kovacs .20 .50
12 Brian Leibel .20 .50
13 Bernie Lynch CO .20 .50
14 Kelly Markwart .20 .50
15 Jim Mathieson .30 .75
16 Brad Mcginnis .20 .50
17 Brad Miller .20 .50
18 Dwayne Montieth TR .08 .25
19 Curtis Nykyforuk .20 .50
20 Darren Parsons .20 .50
21 Cory Paterson .20 .50
22 Jeff Sebastian .20 .50
23 Mike Sillinger .30 .75
24 Chad Silver .20 .50
25 Jamie Splett .20 .50

1989-90 Regina Pats

Sponsored by Mr. Lube, this 22-card set measures approximately 4" by 6" and is printed on thin card stock. The fronts feature black-and-white posed action photos with royal blue borders. The player's jersey number and name are printed in white in the bottom margin along with the team and sponsor logo.The cards are unnumbered and checklisted below in alphabetical order.

COMPLETE SET (21) 4.00 10.00
1 Kelly Chotowetz .20 .50
2 Hal Christiansen .20 .50
3 Scott Daniels .25 .60
4 Wade Fennig .20 .50
5 Jason Glickman .20 .50
6 Kevin Haller .30 .75
7 Jamie Heward .30 .75
8 Terry Hollinger .20 .50
9 Frank Kovacs .20 .50
10 Mike Kirby .20 .50
11 Kelly Markwart .20 .50
12 Jim Mathieson .30 .75
13 Cam McLellan .20 .50
14 Troy Mick .20 .50
15 Greg Pankewicz .20 .50
16 Cory Paterson .20 .50
17 Garry Pearce .20 .50
18 Mike Risdale .20 .50
19 Collin Ruck .20 .50
20 Mike Sillinger .30 .75
21 Jamie Splett .20 .50
22 Heath Weenk .20 .50

1996-97 Regina Pats

This 25-card set features the Regina Pats of the WHL. The cards were produced by the team and offered for sale for $7 at the team shop. The fronts feature a color action photo superimposed over a cutaway rink shot. The player's name and number appear at the top, with the team logo in the bottom right. The set includes several prominent prospects, including NHL first rounders Josh Holden, Dmitri Nabokov, Derek Morris, Kyle Calder and Brad Stuart.

COMPLETE SET (25) 7.20 15.00
1 Josh Holden .30 .75
2 Curtis Tipler .15 .40
3 Shane Lanigan .15 .40
4 Brad Stuart 1.25 3.00
5 David Maruca .15 .40
6 Perry Johnson .15 .40
7 Chad Mercier .15 .40
8 Kyle Calder .40 1.00
9 Josh Dobbyn .15 .40
10 Aaron Mori .15 .40
11 Gerald Adams .15 .40
12 Boyd Kane .20 .50
13 Lars Pattersen .15 .40
14 Dean Arsene .15 .40
15 Andy Adams .15 .40
16 Derek Morris .75 2.00
17 Kyle Freadrich .20 .50
18 Bryan Randall .15 .40
19 Clint Orr .15 .40
20 Brett Lysak .30 .75
21 Joey Bouvier .15 .40
22 Cody Jensen .15 .40
23 Rich Preston CO .08 .25
24 Team Photo .15 .40
25 Dmitri Nabokov .15 .40

1997-98 Regina Pats

This set features the Pats of the WHL. The set was sponsored by local police, and was handed out by officers to kids.

COMPLETE SET (25) 7.20 20.00
1 Gerad Adams .20 .50
2 Kyle Calder .75 2.00
3 Boyd Kane .30 .75
4 Brett Lysak .30 .75
5 Kevin Saurette .20 .50
6 Travis Churchman .20 .50
7 Dean Arsene .20 .50
8 Barret Jackman 2.00 5.00
9 Scott Roles .20 .50
10 John Cirjak .20 .50
11 Ronald Petrovicky .30 .75
12 Kyle Freadrich .30 .75
13 David Maruca .20 .50
14 Drew Kehler .20 .50
15 Bryan Randall .20 .50
16 Joey Bouvier .20 .50
17 Cody Jensen .20 .50
18 Shane Lanigan .20 .50
19 Mark Thompson .20 .50
20 Dennis Bassett .20 .50
21 Chris Kwas .20 .50
22 Derek Morris .75 2.00
23 Aaron Mori .20 .50
24 Brad Stuart 1.25 3.00
25 Josh Holden .40 1.00

2001-02 Regina Pats

This set was produced by the Pats of the WHL. It's uncertain how they were distributed, but it's believed they were issued as a promotional giveaway, based on the wealth of sponsor logos. The set we obtained was signed by every player, save for Bassen and Yacboski. It's not known whether they were widely issued signed, or if this was a limited edition that was made available. Any additional information can be forwarded to hockeymag@beckett.com. The cards are unnumbered, and so are listed in alphabetical order.

COMPLETE SET (24) 10.00 25.00
1 Curtis Austring .40 1.00
2 Chad Bassen .40 1.00
3 Corey Becker .40 1.00
4 Dean Beuker .40 1.00
5 Drew Callender ACO .04 .10
6 Brennan Chapman .40 1.00
7 Chad Davidson .80 2.00
8 Jeff Feniak .40 1.00
9 Josh Harding .80 2.00
10 Grant Jacobsen .40 1.00
11 Kevin Koroll .40 1.00
12 Kyle Ladobruk .40 1.00
13 Bob Lowes CO .10 .25
14 David McDonald .40 1.00
15 Chad Mercier ACO .04 .10
16 Tyson Moulton .40 1.00
17 Garth Murray .80 2.00
18 Filip Novak .80 2.00
19 Zach Roe .40 1.00
20 Chris Schlenker .40 1.00
21 Eric Sonnenberg .40 1.00
22 Matej Trojovsky .40 1.00
23 Daniel Waschuk .40 1.00
24 Darryl Yacboski .40 1.00

2002-03 Regina Pats

COMPLETE SET (23) 8.00 20.00
1 Grant Jacobsen .30 .75
2 Matt Trojovsky .30 .75
3 Petr Dvorak .30 .75
4 Matt Hubbauer .30 .75
5 •Darryl Yacboski .30 .75
6 Jesse Deckert .30 .75
7 Todd Davison .30 .75
8 Rick Rypien .40 1.00
9 David Graden .30 .75
10 Wade Davis .30 .75
11 Britt Dougherty .30 .75
12 Curtis Austring .30 .75
13 Kyle Ladobruk .30 .75
14 Codey Becker .30 .75
15 Chris Schlenker .30 .75
16 Tyson Mulock .30 .75
17 Daniel Waschuk .30 .75
18 David McDonald .30 .75
19 Jordan McGillivray .30 .75
20 Brennan Chapman .30 .75
21 Tyson Moulton .40 1.00
22 Kyle Fecho .30 .75
23 Josh Harding 1.25 3.00

2003-04 Regina Pats

COMPLETE SET (24) 5.00 12.00
1 Paul Albers .20 .50
2 Craig Lineker .20 .50
3 Kyle Deck .20 .50
4 Derek Reinhart .20 .50
5 Landon Jones .20 .50
6 Tanner Stockwell .20 .50
7 Lance Morrison .20 .50
8 Rick Rypien .30 .75
9 David McDonald .20 .50
10 Kyle Lamb .20 .50
11 Dan Waschuk .20 .50
12 Ivo Kratena .20 .50
13 Kamil Vavra .20 .50
14 Kyle Nason .20 .50
15 Chris Schlenker .20 .50
16 Codey Becker .20 .50
17 Jonathan Bubnick .20 .50
18 Mike O'Dwyer .20 .50
19 Jordan McGillivray .20 .50
20 Andrew DeSousa .20 .50
21 Nick Olynyk .20 .50
22 Jesse Deckert .20 .50
23 Josh Harding .75 2.00
24 Britt Dougherty .20 .50

2004-05 Regina Pats

COMPLETE SET (24) 5.00 12.00
1 Regina Pats CL .01 .05
2 Paul Albers .20 .50
3 Craig Lineker .20 .50
4 Kyle Deck .20 .50
5 Derek Reinhart .20 .50
6 Logan Pyett .20 .50
7 Rick Rypien .30 .75
8 Kyle Ross .20 .50
9 Justin Bernhardt .20 .50
10 Braden Appleby .20 .50
11 Dan Waschuk .20 .50
12 Ryan McDonald .20 .50
13 Ian Duval .20 .50
14 Kyle Nason .20 .50
15 Terrance Delaronde .20 .50
16 Brent Hill .20 .50
17 Jonathan Bubnick .20 .50
18 Jordan McGillivray .20 .50
19 Jan Zapletal .20 .50
20 David Reekie .20 .50
21 Jordan Fuder .20 .50
22 Dustin Slade .20 .50
23 Craig Schira .20 .50
24 Preston Mosewich .20 .50

2005-06 Regina Pats

COMPLETE SET (28) 8.00 15.00
1 Justin Bernhardt .20 .50
2 Kyle Deck .20 .50
3 Ian Duval .20 .50
4 Garrett Festerling .20 .50
5 Spencer Fraipont .20 .50
6 Jordan Fuder .20 .50
7 Shane Halifax .20 .50
8 Petr Kalus .60 1.50
9 Brett Leffler .20 .50
10 Levi Lind .20 .50
11 Jason MacDonald .20 .50
12 Jordan McGillivray .20 .50
13 Curtis Patterson .20 .50
14 Logan Pyett .20 .50
15 David Reekie .40 1.00
16 Derek Reinhart .20 .50
17 Matt Robinson .20 .50
18 Kyle Ross .20 .50
19 Nick Ross .20 .50
20 Linden Rowatt .40 1.00
21 Andy Schenn .20 .50
22 Craig Schira .20 .50
23 Michael Senseman .20 .50
24 Tyson Sievert .20 .50
25 Denis Tolpeko .20 .50
26 Ryan McDonald .20 .50
27 Matt MacDermott .20 .50
28 Joshua Fauth .20 .50

2006-07 Regina Pats

COMPLETE SET (23) 12.00 20.00
1 Justin Bernhardt .40 1.00
2 Scott Brownlee .40 1.00
3 Kyle Deck .40 1.00
4 Matt Delahey .40 1.00
5 Ian Duval .40 1.00
6 Jordan Eberle .60 1.50
7 Garrett Festerling .40 1.00
8 Derek Hulak .40 1.00
9 Jared Jagow .40 1.00
10 Brett Leffler .40 1.00
11 Levi Lind .40 1.00
12 Jason MacDonald .40 1.00
13 Ryan McDonald .40 1.00
14 Logan Pyett .40 1.00
15 Derek Reinhart .40 1.00
16 Kyle Ross .40 1.00
17 Nick Ross .40 1.00
18 Linden Rowatt .60 1.50
19 Craig Schira .40 1.00
20 Justin Scott .40 1.00
21 Niko Snellman .40 1.00
22 Colten Teubert .40 1.00
23 Regina Pats .10 .25

1996 RHI Inaugural Edition

This nineteen-card Roller Hockey International set features the logos of all the teams from the hip, new game on the front, with franchise information on the back.

COMPLETE SET (19) 1.25 3.00
1 Los Angeles Blades .08 .25
2 Long Island Jaws .08 .25
3 Empire State Cobras .08 .25
4 Denver DareDevils .08 .25
5 Anaheim Bullfrogs .08 .25
6 Orlando Jackals .08 .25
7 Ottawa Loggers .08 .25
8 Oklahoma Coyotes .08 .25
9 Oakland Skates .08 .25
10 New Jersey Rockin Rollers .08 .25
11 Montreal Roadrunners .08 .25
12 Minnesota Arctic Blast .08 .25
13 Vancouver VooDoo .08 .25
14 St. Louis Vipers .08 .25
15 San Jose Rhinos .08 .25
16 San Diego Barracudas .08 .25
17 Sacramento River Rats .08 .25
18 Philadelphia Bulldogs .08 .25
NNO Checklist .02 .10

1984-85 Richelieu Riverains

This 19-card set of the Richelieu Riverains of the Quebec Midget AAA league measures approximately 4" by 5 1/2". The fronts feature black-and-white posed player portraits with a facsimile autograph and jersey number on the left. The backs are blank. The cards are unnumbered and checklisted below in alphabetical order.

COMPLETE SET (19) 4.80 12.00
1 Miguel Baldris .30 .75
2 Nicolas Beaulieu .30 .75
3 Martin Cole .30 .75
4 Sylvain Coutourier .40 1.00
5 Dominic Edmond .30 .75
6 Yves Gaucher .30 .75
7 Eric Gobel .30 .75
8 Carl Lemieux .30 .75
9 Michel Levesque .30 .75
10 Brad Loi .30 .75
11 Eric Primeau .30 .75
12 Stephane Quintal .60 1.50
13 Jean Michel Ray .30 .75
14 Serge Richard .30 .75
15 Stephane Robinson .30 .75
16 Danny Rochefort .30 .75
17 Martin Savaria .30 .75
18 Sylvain Senecal .30 .75
19 Eric Sharron .30 .75

1988-89 Richelieu Riverains

Cards measure approximately 3" x 4" with card fronts featuring color posed photos. Card backs have players name and number along with safety tips in French.

COMPLETE SET (30) 4.80 12.00
1 Header Card .07 .20
2 Marc Beaurivage .20 .50
3 Denis Benoit .20 .50
4 Jonathan Black .20 .50
5 Richard Boisvert .20 .50
6 Hugues Bouchard .20 .50
7 Francois Bourdeau .20 .50
8 Guy Caplette .20 .50
9 Bertrand Cournoyer .20 .50
10 Yves Cournoyer .20 .50
11 Michel Deguise .20 .50
12 Patrick Grise .20 .50
13 Robert Guillet .20 .50
14 Jimmy Lachance .20 .50
15 Roger Laporte .20 .50
16 Frederic Lefebvre .20 .50
17 Frederic Maltais .20 .50
18 Andre Kid Millette .20 .50
19 Joseph Napolitano .20 .50
20 Remy Patoine .20 .50
21 Jean Plamondon .20 .50
22 Steve Plasse .20 .50
23 Jean Francois Poirier .20 .50
24 Jacques Provencal .20 .50
25 Alain Rancourt .20 .50
26 Francois St.Germain .20 .50
27 Frederic Savard .20 .50
28 Martin Tanguay .20 .50
29 Richard Valois .20 .50
30 Stephane Valois .20 .50

1990-91 Richmond Renegades

Produced by 7th Inning Sketch and sponsored by Richmond Comix and Cardz Inc., this 18-card standard-size set features posed color player photos with red borders. The player's name appears at the bottom.

COMPLETE SET (18) 3.00 8.00
1 Brad Turner .20 .50
2 Victor Posa .20 .50
3 Antti Autere .20 .50
4 Phil Huber .20 .50
5 Steve Spott .20 .50
6 Kelly Mills .20 .50
7 Paul Cain .20 .50
8 Shawn Lillie .20 .50
9 Kirby Lindal .20 .50
10 Dave Aiken .20 .50
11 Terry McCutcheon .20 .50
12 Jordan Fois .20 .50
13 Brad Beck .20 .50
14 Doug Pickell .20 .50
15 Frank Lascala .20 .50
16 John Haley .20 .50
17 Peter Harris .20 .50
18 Chris McSorley CO .30 .75

1991-92 Richmond Renegades

Sponsored by "Bleacher Bums" Sports Cards Inc. and Domino's Pizza, this 20-card set was issued as a trifold sheet, one 12 1/2" by 7" team photo and two sheets with ten standard-size player cards per sheet. The fronts feature color action player photos accented by a border design that shades from orange at the top to black at the bottom. The player's name and position appear below the picture, as do sponsor names.

COMPLETE SET (20) 3.60 9.00
1 Rob Vanderydt .20 .50
2 Larry Rooney .15 .40
3 Brendan Flynn .15 .40
4 Scott Drevitch .15 .40
5 Joni Lehto .15 .40
6 Todd Drevitch .15 .40
7 Paul Rutherford .15 .40
8 Dave Aiken .15 .40
9 Pat Bingham .15 .40
10 Trevor Jobe .15 .40
11 Bob Berg .15 .40
12 Mark Kuntz .15 .40
13 Joe Cappirini .15 .40
14 Trevor Converse .15 .40
15 Steve Scheifele .15 .40
16 Jon Gustafson .20 .50
17 Marco Fuster .15 .40
18 Guy Gadowsky .15 .40
19 Dave Allison CO .08 .25
20 Jamie McLennan .40 1.00
NNO Large Team Photo .75 2.00

1992-93 Richmond Renegades

Sponsored by "Bleacher Bums" Sports Cards Inc. and Kellogg's, this 20-card set was issued as a trifold sheet, one 12 1/2" by 7" team photo and two sheets with ten standard-size player cards per sheet. The fronts feature color action player photos accented by a black and orange border design. The picture itself is rimmed by an orange and white frame. Outside the frame is an orange design with varying sizes of stripes against a black background. The player's name and position appear below the picture as do sponsor names. The cards are unnumbered and checklisted below in alphabetical order.

COMPLETE SET (20) 3.00 8.00
1 Will Averill .15 .40
2 Frank Bialowas .20 .50
3 Scott Drevitch .15 .40
4 Brendan Flynn .15 .40
5 Guy Gadowsky ACO .02 .10
6 Jon Gustafson .15 .40
7 Phil Huber .15 .40
8 Mike James .15 .40
9 Jeffery Kampersal .15 .40
10 Mark Kuntz .15 .40
11 Sean LeBrun .15 .40
12 Kevin Malgunas .15 .40
13 Jim McGeough .20 .50
14 Ed Sabo .15 .40
15 Jeff Saterdalen .15 .40
16 Alan Schuler .15 .40
17 Martin Smith .15 .40
18 Roy Sommer CO .02 .10
19 Jeff Torrey .15 .40
20 Ben Wyzansky .15 .40
NNO Large Team Photo 1.00 2.50

1993-94 Richmond Renegades

Sponsored by "Bleacher Bum" Collectibles, Inc., radio station XL102, and Kellogg's, this 20-card set features the 1993-94 Richmond Renegades. The standard-size cards are printed on thin card stock. On a team color-coded background, the fronts feature color action player photos with purple borders, along with the player's name, position and team name.

COMPLETE SET (20) 3.00 8.00
1 Ken Weiss .15 .40
2 Guy Phillips .15 .40
3 Alexander Zhdan .15 .40
4 Alan Schuler .15 .40
5 John Craighead .15 .40
6 Colin Gregor .15 .40
7 Rob MacInnis .15 .40
8 Devin Derksen .20 .50
9 Jason Renard .15 .40
10 Peter Allen .15 .40
11 Roy Sommer CO .08 .25
12 Milan Hnilicka .60 1.50
13 Oleg Santurian .15 .40
14 Brendan Flynn .15 .40
15 Ken Blum .15 .40
16 Steve Bogoyevac .15 .40
17 Eric Germain .15 .40
18 Chris Foy .15 .40
19 Darren Colbourne .15 .40
20 Jon Gustafson .20 .50

1994-95 Richmond Renegades

This 20-card set produced by Bleacher Bums and sponsored by Q-94 features the Richmond Renegades of the ECHL. The sets were available through the team. The fronts feature dynamic action shots over a blurred background, while the backs include player stats. The cards are unnumbered and are listed below as they came out of the team bag. Reportedly, production was significantly shorter for this set than the previous two Richmond issues.

COMPLETE SET (20) 4.00 10.00
1 Andrew Shier .20 .50
2 Shane Henry .20 .50
3 Shawn Snesar .20 .50
4 Steve Bogoyevac .20 .50
5 Chris Foy .20 .50
6 Scott Gruhl .30 .75
7 Blaine Moore .20 .50
8 Don Lester .20 .50
9 Kurt Mallett .20 .50
10 Garett MacDonald .20 .50
11 Jay Murphy .20 .50
12 Darren Wetherill .20 .50
13 Grant Sjerven .20 .50
14 Jan Benda .30 .75
15 Lou Body .20 .50
16 Mike Taylor .20 .50
17 Sean O'Brien .20 .50
18 Chris Tucker .20 .50
19 Jason Currie .20 .50
20 Roy Sommer CO .08 .25

1995-96 Richmond Renegades

This 25-card set of the Richmond Renegades of the ECHL was produced by Bleacher Bum and was supported by a wealth of sponsors. The cards were originally issued in a strip, thus single cards will have perforated edges. The cards feature a dynamic front design including an action photo and the Riley Cup Championship logo in the bottom right. The cards are unnumbered, and are ordered as they appeared on the strips.

COMPLETE SET (25) 3.60 9.00
1 Greg Hadden .15 .40
2 Mike Taylor .15 .40
3 Jay Murphy .15 .40
4 Todd Sparks .15 .40
5 Lou Body .15 .40
6 Sandy Allan .30 .75
7 Darren Wetherill .15 .40
8 Brian Goudie .15 .40
9 Brendan Flynn .15 .40
10 Kurt Mallett .15 .40
11 Dmitri Pankov .15 .40
12 Steve Carpenter .15 .40
13 Jason Mallon .15 .40
14 Scott Gruhl .40 1.00
15 Trevor Senn .15 .40
16 Garett MacDonald .15 .40
17 Martin Roy .15 .40
18 Michael Burman .15 .40
19 Grant Sjerven .15 .40
20 Mike Morin .15 .40
21 Andy Davis ANN .02 .10
22 The Gade -- Mascot .02 .10
23 Rob Jones TR .02 .10
24 Roy Sommer CO .02 .10
25 C.Laughlin GM H.Feuerstein CEO .02 .10

1996-97 Richmond Renegades

These cards feature full-color fronts with statistical information and a profile photo on the back. Cards are unnumbered and checklisted below in alphabetical order.

COMPLETE SET (25) 3.00 8.00
1 Scott Burfoot .20 .50
2 Taylor Clarke .15 .40
3 David Dartsch .15 .40
4 Freezer .02 .10
5 Gade .02 .10
6 Matt Garzone .15 .40
7 Brian Goudie .15 .40
8 Scott Gruhl CO .20 .50
9 Garry Gulash .15 .40
10 Mike Harding .15 .40
11 Tommy Holmes .15 .40
12 Rod Langway ACO .20 .50
13 Paul Lepler .15 .40
14 Jay McNeill .15 .40
15 Craig Paterson .15 .40
16 Chris Pittman .15 .40
17 Mike Rucinski .15 .40
18 Brian Secord .15 .40
19 Trevor Senn .15 .40
20 Grant Sjerven .15 .40
21 Andrew Shier .15 .40
22 Mike Taylor .15 .40
23 Tripp Tracy .30 .75
24 Jason Wright .15 .40
25 Title Card .02 .10

2000-01 Richmond Renegades

This set features the Renegades of the ECHL. The set was produced as a promotional giveaway and was handed out after the All-Star break. The cards are slightly oversized and are printed on very thin card-stock. The cards are unnumbered, and so are listed below in alphabetical order.

COMPLETE SET (19) 8.00 20.00
1 Gerad Adams .40 1.00

2 Brian Goudie .40 1.00
3 Nathan Forster .40 1.00
4 Joe Blaznek .40 1.00
5 Bob Thornton .40 1.00
6 Forrest Gore .40 1.00
7 Dan Vandermeer .40 1.00
8 Joe Vandermeer .40 1.00
9 Rod Taylor .40 1.00
10 Richard Pitirri .40 1.00
11 George Awada .40 1.00
12 Ryan Skaleski .40 1.00
13 Derek Schutz .40 1.00
14 Frank Novock .40 1.00
15 Matt Noga .40 1.00
16 Mike Siklenka .40 1.00
17 Sean Matile .60 1.50
18 Rastislav Stana .80 2.00
19 Brian McCullough .40 1.00

2006-07 Richmond Renegades

COMPLETE SET (20) 8.00 15.00
1 Jay Chrapala .40 1.00
2 Scott Corbett .30 .75
3 Brett Cross .30 .75
4 Andre Gill .30 .75
5 Mat Goody .75 2.00
6 Brian Goudie .30 .75
7 Doug Groenestege .40 1.00
8 Dean Jackson .30 .75
9 Don Melnyk .30 .75
10 David Mitchell .30 .75
11 Mike Owens .30 .75
12 Joe Pace .30 .75
13 Richard Reichenbach .30 .75
14 Tyler Schremp .30 .75
15 Danny White .30 .75
16 Duane Whitehead .30 .75
17 J.J. Wrobel .30 .75
18 Phil Youngclaus .30 .75
19 John Brophy CO .10 .25
20 Graffiti Ink Gallery SPONSOR .01 .01

2004-05 Richmond Riverdogs

This set features the Riverdogs of the UHL.

COMPLETE SET (28) 5.00 12.00
1 Checklist .01 .05
2 Donny Martin CO .02 .10
3 Glenn Morelli OWN .02 .10
4 Jim Duhart .40 1.00
5 Simo Pulkki .20 .50
6 Brian Goudie .20 .50
7 Ivan Curic .40 1.00
8 Francis Belanger .40 1.00
9 Ryan Prentice .20 .50
10 David Hymovitz .40 1.00
11 Mark Turner .20 .50
12 Mark Langdon .20 .50
13 David Brosseau .20 .50
14 Luch Nasato .20 .50
15 Trevor Senn .20 .50
16 Brian Herbert .20 .50
17 J.J. Wrobel .20 .50
18 Dennis Vial .40 1.00
19 Derek Shutz .20 .50
20 Brett Cross .20 .50
21 Anthony Dipalma .20 .50
22 Brent Belecki .20 .50
23 Dan McIntyre .20 .50
24 Semir Ben-Amor .20 .50
25 Razz MASCOT .02 .10
26 Team Photo .02 .10
27 Zamboni .02 .10
28 Richmond Coliseum .02 .10

1996-97 Rimouski Oceanic

This 28-card set was the first of two this season to feature the Oceanic of the QMJHL. The cards featured a color action photo and jersey number on the front, with a head shot and statistical data on the back. It was sold through the team and at convenience stores in the region. The set is unnumbered, and listed in alphabetical order. The most noteworthy player in the set is Vincent Lecavalier, a forward looked upon as an early favorite for the top pick in the 1998 NHL Entry Draft. Less than 3,000 of these sets were produced.

COMPLETE SET (28) 12.00 25.00
1 Jonathan Beaulieu .15 .40
2 Martin Bedard .15 .40
3 Eric Belzile .15 .40
4 Denis Boily .15 .40
5 Dave Bolduc .15 .40
6 Yan Bouchard .20 .50
7 Nicolas Chabot .15 .40
8 Eryc Collin .15 .40
9 Eric Drouin .15 .40
10 Yannick Dupont .15 .40
11 Frederic Girard .15 .40
12 Jimmy Grondin .15 .40
13 Bobby Lebel CO .08 .25
14 Vincent Lecavalier 7.50 15.00
15 Frederic Levac .15 .40
16 Francois Levesque .15 .40
17 Philippe Lord .15 .40
18 Dave Malenfant .15 .40
19 Eric Normandin .20 .50
20 Mathieu Normandin .15 .40
21 Philippe Plante .15 .40
22 Martin Poitras .20 .50
23 Saison 1996-1997 .08 .25
24 Philippe Sauve 1.25 3.00
25 Sebastien Simard .15 .40
26 David St-Onge .15 .40
27 Mathieu Sunderland .20 .50
28 Gaston Therrien CO .08 .25

1996-97 Rimouski Oceanic Quebec Provincial Police

Card fronts feature color photos, along with players jersey number and the Rimouski logo. Card backs feature statistical information and all text is in French. Each card also bears a serial number. Cards are unnumbered and checklisted below alphabetically.

COMPLETE SET (26) 16.00 40.00
1 Jonathan Beaulieu .20 .50
2 Martin Bedard .20 .50
3 Eric Belzile .20 .50
4 Maxime Blouin .20 .50
5 Denis Boily .20 .50
6 Yan Bouchard .20 .50
7 Nicolas Chabot .20 .50
8 Eryc Collin .20 .50
9 Eric Drouin .20 .50
10 Yannick Dupont .20 .50
11 Frederic Girard .20 .50
12 Jimmy Grondin .20 .50
13 Vincent Lecavalier 12.00 25.00
14 Frederic Levac .20 .50
15 Francois Levesque .20 .50
16 Philipe Lord .20 .50
17 Dave Malenfant .20 .50
18 Eric Normandin .20 .50
19 Mathieu Normandin .20 .50
20 Philippe Plante .20 .50
21 Martin Poitras .20 .50
22 Philippe Sauve 2.00 5.00
23 Nicola Spaccucci .20 .50
24 David St-Onge .20 .50
25 Sebastien Tremblay .20 .50
26 Title Card .02 .10

1996-97 Rimouski Oceanic Update

This 10-card set was produced as a companion set to the basic Rimouski series issued earlier in the season. The design for both series is identical. The players featured in the update were late arrivals due to trades. Less than 1200 of these sets were produced. The cards are unnumbered and thus are listed in alphabetical order.

COMPLETE SET (10) 2.50 6.00
1 Eric Belanger (LW) .20 .50
2 Eric Belanger (C) .60 1.50
3 Philippe Grondin .20 .50
4 Jason Lehoux .20 .50
5 Jonathan Levesque .20 .50
6 Louki MASCOT .08 .25
7 Guillaume Rodrigue .20 .50
8 Joe Rullier .40 1.00
9 Russell Smith .20 .50
10 Derrick Walser .30 .75

1997-98 Rimouski Oceanic

This set was produced by the team and sold at home games. It is noteworthy for including early cards of Vincent Lecavalier and Brad Richards.

COMPLETE SET (25) 10.00 25.00
4 Vincent Lecavalier 4.00 10.00
7 Joe Rullier .30 .75
9 Jonathan Beaulieu .15 .40
10 David Bilodeau .15 .40
11 Jimmy Crondin .15 .40
14 Dave Malenfant .15 .40
17 Kevin Bolduc .15 .40
19 Eric Normandin .15 .40
20 Francois Drainville .15 .40
21 Eric Belanger .30 .75
22 Eric Drouin .15 .40
24 Julien Desrosiers .15 .40
25 David St-Onge .15 .40
27 Phillippe Grondin .15 .40
33 Phillippe Sauve 1.25 3.00
35 Jean-Marc Pelletier .60 1.50
36 Jonathan St-Louis .15 .40
39 Brad Richards 5.00 12.00
44 Guillaume Couture .15 .40
45 Chad Gagnon .15 .40
55 Casey Leggett .15 .40
79 Denis Boily .15 .40
91 Derrick Walser .30 .75
98 Adam Borzecki .15 .40
NNO Team Card .15 .40

1999-00 Rimouski Oceanic

This 24-card set features the QMJHL's Oceanic, the Memorial Cup winners for that season. Base cards contain full color action photography and have purple borders along the top and the right hand side which feature the player's name and team logo.

COMPLETE SET (24) 6.00 15.00
1 Nicolas Pilote .15 .40
2 Joe Rullier .30 .75
3 Jonathan Beaulieu .15 .40
4 Nicolas Poirier .15 .40
5 Thatcher Bell .20 .50
6 Brent Maclellan .15 .40
7 Alexandre Tremblay .15 .40
8 Jean-Francois Babin .15 .40
9 Benoit Martin .15 .40
10 Jan Philippe Cadieux .15 .40
11 Jean-Philippe Briere .15 .40
12 Alexis Castonguay .15 .40
13 Rene Vydareny .15 .40
14 Ronnie Decontie .15 .40
15 Shawn Scanzano .15 .40
16 Michel Ouellet .15 .40
17 Jacques Lariviere .15 .40
18 Eric Salvail .15 .40
19 Sebastien Caron .40 1.00
20 Brad Richards 2.00 5.00
21 Aaron Johnson .15 .40
22 Juraj Kolnik .60 1.50
23 Michel Periard .30 .75
24 Header Card/CL .02 .10

1999-00 Rimouski Oceanic Signed

This set of 23 cards parallels the base Rimouski Oceanic Set. The main differences are that the cards are signed on a specially imprinted area on the front of the card, while the backs are serial numbered out of 100.

COMPLETE SET (24) 30.00 75.00
1 Nicolas Pilote .75 2.00
2 Joe Rullier 1.50 4.00
3 Jonathan Beaulieu .75 2.00
4 Nicolas Poirier .75 2.00
5 Thatcher Bell 1.50 4.00
6 Brent Maclellan .75 2.00
7 Alexandre Tremblay .75 2.00
8 Jean-Francois Babin .75 2.00
9 Benoit Martin .75 2.00
10 Jan Philippe Cadieux .75 2.00
11 Jean-Philippe Briere .75 2.00
12 Alexis Castonguay .75 2.00
13 Rene Vydareny .75 2.00
14 Ronnie Decontie .75 2.00
15 Shawn Scanzano .75 2.00
16 Michel Ouellet .75 2.00
17 Jacques Lariviere .75 2.00
18 Eric Salvail .75 2.00
19 Sebastien Caron 2.00 5.00
20 Brad Richards 10.00 25.00
21 Aaron Johnson .75 2.00
22 Juraj Kolnik 3.00 8.00
23 Michel Periard 1.50 4.00
24 Header Card/CL .08 .25

2000-01 Rimouski Oceanic

This set features the Oceanic of the QMJHL. The set was produced by CTM-Ste-Foy, and was sold both by that card shop, as well as by the team.

COMPLETE SET (26) 5.00 12.00
1 Phillippe Lauze .20 .75
2 Tim Sinasac .20 .50
3 Jonathan Beaulieu .20 .50
4 Nichola Pilote .20 .50
5 Nicolas Poirier .20 .50
6 Thatcher Bell .30 .50
7 Tomas Malec .20 .50
8 Brent MacLellan .20 .50
9 Jean-Francois Plourde .20 .50
10 Jean-Francois Babin .20 .50
11 Benoit Martin .20 .50
12 Daniel Petiquay .20 .75
13 Jean-Phillippe Briere .20 .50
14 Ryan Clowe .75 2.00
15 Mathieu Fournier .20 .50
16 Gabriel Balasescu .20 .50
17 Mathieu Simard .20 .50
18 Samuel Gibbons .20 .50
19 Michel Ouellet .20 .50
20 Jonathan Pelletier .30 .75
21 Eric Salvail .30 .75
22 Aaron Johnson .20 .50
23 Sebastien Bolduc .20 .75
24 Louky MASCOT .04 .10
25 Doris Labonte CO .04 .10
NNO Team CL .04 .01

2000-01 Rimouski Oceanic Signed

This set is exactly the same as the base Oceanic set from this season, save that every card has been hand signed by the player pictured. Each card also is serial numbered out of just 100.

COMPLETE SET (26) 16.00 40.00
1 Phillippe Lauze .80 4.00
2 Tim Sinasac .80 2.00
3 Jonathan Beaulieu .80 2.00
4 Nichola Pilote .80 2.00
5 Nicolas Poirier .80 2.00
6 Thatcher Bell 1.20 3.00
7 Tomas Malec .80 2.00
8 Brent MacLellan .80 2.00
9 Jean-Francois Plourde .80 2.00
10 Jean-Francois Babin .80 2.00
11 Benoit Martin .80 2.00
12 Daniel Petiquay .80 4.00
13 Jean-Phillippe Briere .80 2.00
14 Ryan Clowe 4.00 10.00
15 Mathieu Fournier .80 2.00
16 Gabriel Balasescu .80 2.00
17 Mathieu Simard .80 2.00
18 Samuel Gibbons .80 2.00
19 Michel Ouellet .80 2.00
20 Jonathan Pelletier 1.20 4.00
21 Eric Salvail 1.20 4.00
22 Aaron Johnson .80 2.00
23 Sebastien Bolduc .80 4.00
24 Louky MASCOT .04 .10
25 Doris Labonte CO .04 .10
NNO Team CL .04 .10

2001-02 Rimouski Oceanic

This set features the Oceanic of the QMJHL. The set was produced by CTM Ste-Foy and was sold at Oceanic home games. It was reported that less than 1,000 sets were produced.

COMPLETE SET (23) 4.80 12.00
1 Chaz Johnson .20 .50
2 Philippe Lauze .20 .50
3 Dany Stewart .20 .50
4 Michel Gavalier .20 .50
5 Nicolas Poirier .40 1.00
6 Thatcher Bell .30 .75
7 Thomas Malec .30 .75
8 Brent Maclellan .20 .50
9 Jean-Francois Plourde .20 .50
10 Benoit Martin .20 .50
11 Daniel Petiquay .20 .50
12 Jean-Philippe Briere .20 .50
13 Ryan Clowe .30 .75
14 Mathieu Fournier .20 .50
15 Gabriel Balasescu .20 .50
16 Samuel Gibbons .20 .50
17 Michel Ouellet .20 .50
18 Eric Neilson .20 .50
19 Patrick Lepage .40 1.00
20 Eric Salvail .40 1.00
21 Aaron Johnson .40 1.00
22 Sebastien Bolduc .40 1.00
23 Marc-Antoine Pouliot 1.25 3.00

2002-03 Rimouski Oceanic

COMPLETE SET (22) 5.00 12.00
1 Guillaume Chicoine .20 .50
2 Patrick Coulombe .20 .50
3 Jason D'Ascanio .20 .50
4 Francois Gauthier .20 .50
5 Michel Gavalier .20 .50
6 Zbynek Hrdel .20 .50
7 Danick Jasmin-Riel .20 .50
8 Philippe Lauze .20 .50
9 Mattews Lemaire .20 .50
10 Eric Neilson .20 .50
11 Sebastien Nolet .20 .50
12 Daniel Petiquay .20 .50
13 Marc-Antoine Pouliot .75 2.00
14 Jonathan Robert .20 .50
15 Dany Roussin .40 1.00
16 Eric Salvail .20 .50
17 Christopher Sorensen .20 .50
18 Dany Stewart .20 .50
19 Mark Tobin .20 .50
20 Erick Tremblay .20 .50
21 Jeremy Turgeon .20 .50
22 Alexander Vachon .40 1.00

2003-04 Rimouski Oceanic

This regulation-sized set was produced by CTM Ste-Foy and Extreme Cards and features the first two licensed cards of Sidney Crosby. Not every set includes the NNO cards, so the set is considered complete without them.

COMPLETE SET (25) 15.00 30.00
1 Benoit Arsenault .20 .50
2 Charles Bergeron .20 .50
3 Francois Bolduc .20 .50
4 Jean-Michel Bolduc .20 .50
5 Jean-Sebastien Cote .20 .50
6 Patrick Coulombe .20 .50
7 Sidney Crosby 8.00 20.00
8 Cedrick Desjardins .40 1.00
9 Olivier Didier .20 .50
10 Zbynek Hrdel .20 .50
11 Danick Jasmin-Riel .20 .50
12 Philippe Lauze .20 .75
13 Guillaume Lavallee .20 .50
14 Mattews Lemaire .20 .50
15 Eric Neilson .20 .50
16 Marc-Antoine Pouliot .40 1.00
17 Michal Sersen .20 .50
18 Danny Stewart .20 .50
19 Mark Tobin .20 .50
20 Erick Tremblay .20 .50
21 Alexandre Vachon .20 .50
22 Guillaume Veilleux .20 .50
23 Hubert Veilleux .20 .50
NNO Sidney Crosby TL 12.00 30.00
NNO Marc-Antoine Pouliot TL .75 2.00

2003-04 Rimouski Oceanic Sheets

This team issued set of 5 sheets featured players of the Oceanic from the 2003-04 season. Sheets measured approximately 17" x 6".

COMPLETE SET (5) 20.00 40.00
1 Mattews Lemaire 2.00 5.00
Charles Bergeron
Eric Nelson
Olivier Didier
Danick Jasmin Riel
2 Erick Tremblay 2.00 5.00
Dany Roussin
Philippe Lauze
Jean-Sebastien Cote
Michal Sersen
3 Mark Tobin 2.00 5.00
Patrick Coulombe
Marc-Antone Pouliot
Francois Bolduc
Cedrik Desjardins
4 Guillame Veilleux 10.00 25.00
Sidney Crosby
Guillame Lavallee
Alexandre Vachon
5 Jean-Michal Bolduc 2.00 5.00
Hubert Veilleux
Zbynek Hrdel
Dany Stewart
Benoit Arsenault

2004-05 Rimouski Oceanic

A total of 5,000 team sets were produced, with additional cards being available in wax form. The Limited Edition cards of Crosby and Pouliot were available in random team sets.

COMPLETE SET (23) 10.00 25.00
1 Sidney Crosby 4.00 10.00
2 Alexandre Vachon .40 1.00
3 Dany Roussin .40 1.00
4 Graham Bona .20 .50
5 Sebastien Aspirot .20 .50
6 Nicolas Bachand .20 .50
7 Jamie Blom .20 .50
8 Francois Bolduc .20 .50
9 Francois Charette .20 .50
10 Jean-Sebastien Cote .20 .50
11 Patrick Coulombe .20 .50
12 Cedrik Desjardins .40 1.00
13 Maxime Desruisseaux .20 .50
14 Zbynek Hrdel .20 .50
15 Sebastien Laferriere .20 .50
16 Eric Neilson .40 1.00
17 Marc-Antoine Pouliot .40 1.00
18 Michal Sersen .20 .50
19 Danny Stewart .20 .50
20 Mark Tobin .20 .50
21 Erick Tremblay .20 .50
22 Jean-Michel Filiatrault .75 2.00
23 Jean-Michel Bolduc .20 .50
LE1 Sidney Crosby LTD/300 15.00 40.00
LE2 Marc-Antoine Pouliot LTD/300 4.00 10.00

2004-05 Rimouski Oceanic Season Ticket

This set of six cards was available only to purchasers of season tickets to the 2004-05 Oceanic. The cards are printed on clear plastic, are horizontally oriented, and have a serial number on the back. They are unnumbered, and so are listed below in alphabetical order.

COMPLETE SET (6) 20.00 50.00
1 Jonathan Beaulieu .75 2.00
2 Sebastien Caron 1.50 4.00
3 Sidney Crosby 15.00 40.00
4 Vincent Lecavalier 4.00 10.00
5 Brad Richards 4.00 10.00
6 Allan Sirois .75 2.00

2005-06 Rimouski Oceanic

COMPLETE SET (30) 6.00 15.00
1 Patrick Coulombe .20 .50
2 Erick Tremblay .20 .50
3 Jean-Michel Bolduc .20 .50
4 Jamie Blom .20 .50
5 Mark Tobin .20 .50
6 Sebastien Aspirot .20 .50
7 Francois Bolduc .20 .50
8 Jean-Sebastien Cote .20 .50
9 Sebastien Laferriere .20 .50
10 Graham Bona .20 .50
11 Francis Charette .20 .50
12 Maxime Lincourt .20 .50
13 Philippe Roberge .40 1.00
14 David Skokan .40 1.00
15 Pierre-Alexandre Joncas .20 .50
16 Maxime Macenauer .20 .50
17 David Bouchard .40 1.00
18 Jason Caron .20 .50
19 Nicholas Goyens .20 .50
20 Guillaume Mailloux .20 .50
21 Dave Plante .20 .50
22 Michael Chiasson .20 .50
23 Marc-Andre Laroche .20 .50
24 Guillaume Letourneau .20 .50
25 Olivier Fortier .20 .50
26 Philippe Garnier .20 .50
27 Drew Paris .20 .50
28 Max Gratchev .20 .50
29 Maxime Tanguay .20 .50
30 Tommy Legault .20 .50

2006-07 Rimouski Oceanic

COMPLETE SET (24) 8.00 15.00
1 Olivier Fortier .25 .60
2 Maxime Tanguay .40 1.00
3 Philippe Garnier .25 .60
4 Maxime Gratchev .40 1.00
5 François Bolduc .25 .60
6 Graham Bona .25 .60
7 David Skokan .25 .60
8 Pierre-Alexandre Joncas .25 .60
9 David Bouchard .25 .60
10 Nicholas Goyens .25 .60
11 Dave Plante .25 .60
12 Marc-André Laroche .25 .60
13 Philippe Cornet .25 .60
14 Patrice Cormier .25 .60
15 Alexandre Néron .25 .60
16 Jordan Caron .25 .60
17 Alexandre Brunet .25 .60
18 Louis-Philippe Lachance .25 .60
19 Christopher Stevens .25 .60
20 Frédéric Desrochers .25 .60
21 Michal Frolik .60 1.50
22 Kevin Cormier .25 .60
23 Tommy Legault .40 1.00
24 Michael Chiasson .40 1.00

1993-94 Roanoke Express

Sponsored by Advance Auto Parts, First Virginia Bank, radio station J93.5 FM and WJPR TV 27, this 25-card standard-size set commemorates the inaugural season of the Roanoke Express. The fronts feature borderless color action player photos. The team logo appears on the bottom left with the player's name, position and number in two red bars next to it. The cards are unnumbered and checklisted below in alphabetical order.

COMPLETE SET (25) 3.00 8.00
1 Frank Anzalone CO .08 .25
2 Will Averill .15 .40
3 Claude Barthe .15 .40
4 Lev Berdichevsky .15 .40
5 Hughes Bouchard .15 .40
6 Reggie Brezeault .15 .40
7 Ilja Dubkov .15 .40
8 Pat Ferschweiler .15 .40
9 Kyle Galloway .15 .40
10 Jeff Jestadt .15 .40
11 Roger Larche .15 .40
12 Dana McGuane TR .02 .10
13 Jim Mill .15 .40
14 Dave Morissette .15 .40
15 Chris Potter .15 .40
16 Dan Ryder .15 .40
17 Gairin Smith .15 .40
18 Michael Smith .15 .40
19 Tony Szabo .15 .40
20 Stephen Tepper .15 .40
21 Oleg Yashin .15 .40
22 Team Photo .15 .40
23 Dave Morissette .02 .10
First Franchise Goal
24 Sponsor Card .02 .10
Advance Auto Parts
25 Sponsor Card .02 .10
First Virginia Bank

1994-95 Roanoke Express

This 24-card set features the Roanoke Express of the ECHL. The cards -- which were printed on extremely thin paper -- were available through the team, and possibly offered as a game night promotion. The fronts feature a blurry action photo, with team logo and player name and position. The unnumbered backs include stats and the logos of several sponsors.

COMPLETE SET (24) 4.00 10.00
1 Team Photo .20 .50
2 Dave Gagnon .30 .75
3 Chris Potter .20 .50
4 Dave Stewart .20 .50
5 Michael Smith .20 .50
6 Jon Larson .20 .50
7 Carl Fleury .20 .50
8 Jeff Jestadt .20 .50
9 Marty Schriner .20 .50
10 Rouslan Toujikov .20 .50
11 Jason Clarke .20 .50
12 Stephane Desjardins .20 .50
13 Robin Bouchard .20 .50
14 Oleg Yashin .20 .50
15 Ilja Dubkov .20 .50
16 Derek Laxdal .30 .75
17 Mark Luger .20 .50
18 Pat Ferschweiler .20 .50
19 Dan Ryder .20 .50
20 Frank Anzalone CO .08 .25
21 Dana McGuane TR .02 .10
22 Loco Mascot .02 .10
23 Board of Directors .02 .10
24 Fan Card .01

1995-96 Roanoke Express

This 25-card set of the Roanoke Express of the ECHL was a team-produced issue, and available only through the club. The fronts feature sharp, pseudo-action shots with the player's name in a red border along the left, and position and number in a green border along the top. A gold foil Express logo graces the lower right corner.

COMPLETE SET (25) 4.00 10.00
1 Jeff Jestadt .15 .40
2 Dave Stewart .15 .40
3 Matt DelGuidice .30 .75
4 Dave Holum .15 .40
5 Mike Stacchi .15 .40
6 Paul Croteau .15 .40
7 Marty Schriner .15 .40
8 L.P. Charbonneau .15 .40
9 Michael Smith .15 .40
10 Ilja Dubkov .20 .50
11 Tim Christian .15 .40
12 Brian Gallentine .15 .40
13 Jeff Jablonski .15 .40
14 Daniel Berthiaume .40 1.00
15 Duane Harmer .15 .40
16 Jason Clarke .15 .40
17 Tim Hanley .15 .40
18 Jon Larson .15 .40
19 Nick Jones .15 .40
20 Chris Potter .15 .40
21 Craig Herr .15 .40
22 Frank Anzalone CO .08 .25
23 Chris Pollack TR .02 .10
24 Loco MASCOT .02 .10
25 Team Photo .02 .10

1996-97 Roanoke Express

This 24-card set features the Roanoke Express of the ECHL was team issued. The cards feature action photography on the front, along with a comprehensive stats package on the reverse. The cards prominently feature the player's jersey number on the back, and are listed below thusly.

COMPLETE SET (24) 3.00 8.00
1 Dave Gagnon .20 .50
2 Dave Stewart .15 .40
3 Eric Landry .15 .40
5 Michael Smith .15 .40
7 Jeff Loder .15 .40
8 Duane Harmer .15 .40
10 Bobby Brown .15 .40
11 J.F. Tremblay .15 .40
12 Ryan Equale .15 .40
14 Doug Searle .15 .40
15 Jeff Jablonski .15 .40
17 Jeff Cowan .20 .50
18 Sean Brown .20 .50
21 Ilya Dubkov .15 .40
22 Matt O'Dette .15 .40
23 Chris Lipsett .15 .40
24 Tim Christian .15 .40
35 Larry Moberg .20 .50
NNO Frank Anzalone CO .02 .10
NNO Checklist .02 .10
NNO Mike Holden TR .02 .10
NNO Team Photo .15 .40
NNO Elmer the Engine .02 .10
NNO Loco the Railyard Dog .02 .10

1998-99 Roanoke Express

These card were handed out at Express home games. They are numbered on the back on the lower left hand corner in small print. Card #7 is unconfirmed to date, but is believed to exist. Anyone with additional information is urged to forward it to the publisher.

COMPLETE SET (26) 25.00
1 Tony Mancuso GM .20 .50
2 Scott Gordon HCO .20 .50
3 Perry Florio ACO .20 .50
4 Darren Abbott DOB .20 .50
5 Dave Gagnon .60 1.50
6 Daniel Berthiaume .75 2.00
7 Unknown .40 1.00
8 Doug Searle .40 1.00
9 Jason Dailey .40 1.00
10 Duane Harmer .40 1.00
11 Mike Peron .40 1.00
12 Kris Cantu .40 1.00
13 Travis Smith .40 1.00
14 J.C. Ruid .40 1.00
15 Ben Schust .40 1.00
16 Jeremy Schaefer .40 1.00
17 J.F. Tremblay .40 1.00
18 Mike Mader .40 1.00
19 Nicholas Windsor .40 1.00
20 Peter Brearley .40 1.00
21 Nic Beaudoin .40 1.00
22 Chris Lipsett .40 1.00
23 Tim Christian .40 1.00
24 Dru Burgess .40 1.00
25 Chris Wismer .40 1.00
26 Loco Mascot .20 .50

2000-01 Roanoke Express

This set features the Express of the ECHL. The set was issued as a promotional giveaway. Local police officers attended several games, handing out a different card to children at each one. That makes accumulating a complete set a difficult task, indeed.

COMPLETE SET (22) 8.00 20.00
1 Roanoke Express .40 .50
2 Mike Peron .40 1.00
3 Joe Dusbabek .40 1.00
4 Troy Lake .40 1.00
5 Jeff Burgoyne .40 1.00
6 Ben Schust .40 1.00
7 Dave Gagnon .60 1.50
8 Calvin Elfring .40 1.00
9 Colin Anderson .40 1.00
10 Todd Compeau .40 1.00
11 Daniel Berthiaume .60 1.50
12 Loco MASCOT .10 .25
13 Aaron Gates .40 1.00
14 Travis Smith .40 1.00
15 John Sadowski .40 1.00
16 Perry Florio CO .10 .25
17 Nate Handrahan .40 1.00
18 Jeff Sproat .40 1.00
19 Jay Shipulski .40 1.00
20 Doug Sheppard .40 1.00
21 George McMillan SHERIFF .04 .01
22 Adam Dewan .40 1.00

2001-02 Roanoke Express

This set features the Express of the ECHL. The cards were handed out to children, one card at a time, from police officers at Express games. Because of this, complete sets are nearly impossible to compile.

COMPLETE SET (24) 20.00 50.00
1 Daniel Berthiaume 1.20 3.00
2 Chris Cava .80 2.00
3 Steve Chabbert .80 2.00
4 Duncan Dalmao .80 2.00
5 Brett DeCecco 1.20 3.00
6 Joe Dusbabek .80 2.00
7 Brad Essex .80 2.00
8 Vernon Fiddler .80 2.00
9 Pete Gardiner .80 2.00
10 Jeff Helperl .80 2.00
11 Marty Hughes .80 2.00
12 Rick Kowalsky .80 2.00
13 Troy Lake .80 2.00
14 Frank Novock .80 2.00
15 Mike Omicioli 1.20 3.00
16 Mike Peron .80 2.00
17 Guy Ricciardi 1.20 3.00
18 Travis Smith .80 2.00
19 Jeff Sproat .80 2.00
20 Terence Tootoo 2.00 5.00
21 Jordan Willis 1.60 4.00
22 Perry Florio CO .20 .50
23 Mark Bernard ACO .20 .50
24 George McMillan .80 2.00

2002-03 Roanoke Express

COMPLETE SET (25) 15.00 40.00
1 Sebastien Laplante .75 2.00
2 Sheriff McMillan .10 .25
3 Dan Sullivan .75 2.00
4 Loco Mascot .10 .25
5 Cole Fischer .75 2.00
6 Perry Florio HCO .10 .25
7 Tony MacAulay ACO .10 .25
8 Scotty Balan .75 2.00
9 Josh Barker .75 2.00
10 Dan Carlson .75 2.00
11 Adam Colagiacomo .75 2.00
12 Duncan Dalmao .75 2.00
13 Joe Dusbabek .75 2.00
14 Brad Essex .75 2.00
15 Dylan Gyori 1.25 3.00
16 Jason Jaffray .75 2.00
17 Rick Kowalsky .75 2.00
18 Shawn Limpright .75 2.00
19 Evan Lindsay .75 2.00
20 Chad Mazurak .75 2.00
21 Frank Novock .75 2.00
22 Mike Peron .75 2.00
23 Doug Schueller .75 2.00
24 David Silverstone .75 2.00
25 Tim O'Connell .75 2.00

2002-03 Roanoke Express RBI Sports

COMPLETE SET (18) 10.00 18.00
187 Josh Barker .40 1.00

188 Scotty Balan .40 1.00
189 Cam Bristow .40 1.00
190 Dan Carlson .40 1.00
191 Duncan Dalmao .40 1.00
192 Joe Dusbabek .40 1.00
193 Brad Essex .40 1.00
194 Cole Fisher .40 1.00
195 Dylan Gyori .60 1.50
196 Jason Jaffray .40 1.00
197 Rick Kowalsky .40 1.00
198 Sebastien Laplante .60 1.50
199 Chad Mazurak .40 1.00
200 Frank Novock .40 1.00
201 Tim O'Connell .40 1.00
202 Mike Peron .40 1.00
203 Doug Schueller .40 1.00
204 David Silverstone .40 1.00

2003-04 Roanoke Express

COMPLETE SET (16) 6.00 15.00
305 Josh Barker .40 1.00
306 David Belitski .60 1.50
307 Kevin Bergin .40 1.00
308 Dan Carlson .40 1.00
309 Dan Carney .40 1.00
310 Duncan Dalmao .40 1.00
311 Joe Dusbabek .40 1.00
312 Rick Kowalsky .40 1.00
313 Shawn Limpright .40 1.00
314 Andrew McPherson .40 1.00
315 Andrew Oke .40 1.00
316 Bryan Perez .40 1.00
317 Doug Scatchard .40 1.00
318 Robert Snowball .40 1.00
319 Blair Stayzer .40 1.00
320 Jason Wolfe .60 1.50

2005-06 Roanoke Valley Vipers

We have no pricing information on this set.

1 David Beauregard
2 Jonathan Charette
3 Shawn Conschafter
4 Michael Krelove
5 Gray Shaneberger
6 Matt Miller
7 Rico Fatticci
8 Jan Jas
9 Branislav Kvetan
10 Mark Scott
11 Travis Smith

1963-64 Rochester Americans

Printed on thin paper stock, this set of twenty photos, was issued in two series and measures approximately 4" by 6". This set features borderless black-and-white posed or action shots of the AHL (American Hockey League) Amerks. The white back carries the player's name, age, height, weight, and statistics from previous years in the minors. The cards are unnumbered and checklisted below in alphabetical order.

COMPLETE SET (20) 100.00 200.00
1 Lou Angotti 4.00 8.00
2 Al Arbour 10.00 20.00
3 Norm Armstrong 2.50 5.00
4 Ed Babiuk 2.50 5.00
5 Wally Boyer 4.00 8.00
6 Arnie Brown 4.00 8.00
7 Gerry Cheevers UER 25.00 50.00
(Misspelled Jerry on card back)
8 Don Cherry 30.00 60.00
9 Mike Corbett 2.50 5.00
10 Joe Crozier CO 2.50 5.00
11 Jack Curran TR 2.50 5.00
12 Les Duff 2.50 5.00
13 Gerry Ehman 2.50 5.00
14 Dick Gamble 4.00 8.00
15 Larry Hillman 2.50 5.00
16 Bronco Horvath 7.50 15.00
17 Eddie Lawson 2.50 5.00
18 Jim Pappin 4.00 8.00
19 Darryl Sly 2.50 5.00
20 Stan Smrke 3.00 6.00

1971-72 Rochester Americans

Cards measure 5" x 7" and feature black and white glossy photos on the front, along with a facsimile autograph. Backs are blank. Cards are unnumbered and checklisted below alphabetically.

COMPLETE SET (18) 37.50 75.00
1 Red Armstrong 2.50 5.00
2 Guy Burrowes 2.50 5.00
3 Gaye Cooley 2.50 5.00
4 Bob Craig 2.50 5.00
5 Bob Ellett 2.50 5.00
6 Ron Fogal 2.50 5.00
7 Rod Graham 2.50 5.00
8 Dave Hrechkosy 3.50 7.00
9 Herman Karp 2.50 5.00
10 Bob Kelly 5.00 10.00
11 Larry McKillop 2.50 5.00
12 Bob Malcolm 2.50 5.00
13 Barry Merrell 2.50 5.00
14 Wayne Morusyk 2.50 5.00
15 Rick Pagnutti 2.50 5.00
16 Gerry Sillers 2.50 5.00
17 Gene Sobchuk 2.50 5.00
18 Lynn Zimmerman 2.50 5.00

1977-78 Rochester Americans

These cards feature black and white front photos with a facsimile autograph. Front also features players name, position, biographical information, and statistics. Cards are unnumbered and checklisted below in alphabetical order.

COMPLETE SET (24) 12.50 25.00
1 Team Photo .50 1.00
2 Duane Rupp .75 1.50
3 Nate Angelo TR .25 .50
4 Earl Anderson .75 1.50
5 Bill Bennett .50 1.00
6 Daryl Drader .50 1.00
7 Rene Drolet .50 1.00
8 Rene Drolet .50 1.00
9 Darryl Edestrand .75 1.50
10 Ron Garwasiuk .50 1.00
11 Rod Graham .50 1.00
12 Rod Graham .50 1.00
13 Doug Halward .75 1.50
14 Bjorn Johansson .50 1.00
15 Steve Langdon .50 1.00
16 Ray Maluta .50 1.00
17 Brian McGregor .50 1.00
18 Clayton Pachal .50 1.00
19 Dave Parro .75 1.50
20 Jim Pettie .50 1.00
21 Sean Shanahan .50 1.00
22 Al Sims 1.00 2.00
23 Barry Smith .75 1.50

1979-80 Rochester Americans

These cards are oversized, measuring 8-by-10.5 inches. They are blank backed and unnumbered. The set was sponsored by Wendy's.

1 Mike Boland 2.00 5.00
2 Mike Breen 2.00 5.00
3 Paul Crowley 2.00 5.00
4 Daryl Drader 2.00 5.00
5 Ron Garwasiuk 2.00 5.00
6 Chris Halyk 2.00 5.00
7 Bill Inglis CO 1.50 4.00
8 Randy Ireland 2.00 5.00
9 Joe Kowal 2.00 5.00
10 Normand Lefebvre 2.00 5.00
11 Bob Mongrain 2.00 5.00
12 Wayne Ramsey 2.00 5.00
13 Jacques Richard 3.00 8.00
14 Geordie Robertson 2.00 5.00
15 Andre Savard 3.00 10.00
16 Ron Schock 3.00 8.00
17 Dave Schultz 12.00 30.00
18 Barry Smith 2.00 5.00
19 Bill Stewart 2.00 5.00
20 Richard Suwek 2.00 5.00
21 Mark Toffolo 2.00 5.00
22 Jim Turkiewicz 2.00 5.00
23 Ed Walsh 2.00 5.00
24 Jim Walsh 2.00 5.00

1991-92 Rochester Americans Dunkin' Donuts

Sponsored by Dunkin' Donuts, this 20-card set measures the standard size. It was issued in four perforated strips, each consisting of four player cards and a Dunkin' Donuts coupon. On white card stock, the fronts feature color action player photos. Blue and red border stripes edge the picture on the bottom and half way on each side. The player's name is printed in a red-lined box above the picture, while logos and additional player information appear beneath it. In black print on a white background, the backs carry biography, statistics, and sponsor logo. The cards are unnumbered and checklisted below in alphabetical order.

COMPLETE SET (20) 4.00 10.00
1 Greg Brown .20 .50
2 Peter Ciavaglia .30 .75
3 Bob Corkum .30 .75
4 Brian Curran .20 .50
5 David DiVita .20 .50
6 Tom Draper .30 .75
7 Jody Gage .40 1.00
8 Dan Frawley .20 .50
9 Dave Littman .30 .75
10 Darcy Loewen .20 .50
11 Don McSween .30 .75
12 Brad Rubachuk .20 .50
13 Lindy Ruff .40 1.00
14 Joel Savage .20 .50
15 Jiri Sejba .20 .50
16 Chris Snell .20 .50
17 Coupon Dunkin' Donuts .01 .05
18 Coupon Dunkin' Donuts .01 .05
19 Coupon Dunkin' Donuts .01 .05
20 Coupon Dunkin' Donuts .01 .05

1991-92 Rochester Americans Kodak

The 1991-92 Rochester American Team Photo and Trading Card Set was co-sponsored by Kodak and Wegmons Photo Center. It consists of three 11 1/4" by 9 1/2" sheets joined together and tri-folded. The first sheet displays a team photo of the players dressed in street clothes. The second and third sheets consist of 15 cards each arranged in three rows of five cards. The last four slots of the third sheet display sponsor coupons. After perforation, the cards would measure approximately 2 1/4" by 3 1/8". The player photos on the fronts have rounded corners and are poses shot from the waist up against a studio background. Team color-coded (red and blue) stripes edge the pictures on the bottom and each side. The player's name, position, and the team logo are above the picture, while sponsor logos and the uniform number are below it. In red and blue print, the backs carry biography and statistics. The cards are checklisted below as they are arranged in the album, with coaches presented first and then the players in alphabetical order.

COMPLETE SET (26) 4.80 12.00
1 Don Lever CO .08 .25
2 Terry Martin ACO .08 .25
3 Ian Boyce .20 .50
4 John Bradley .20 .50
5 Greg Brown .20 .50
6 Keith Carney .20 .50
7 Peter Ciavaglia .20 .50
8 Bob Corkum .30 .75
9 Brian Curran .20 .50
10 David DiVita .20 .50
11 Lou Franceschetti .30 .75
12 Dan Frawley .20 .50
13 Jody Gage .40 1.00
14 Kevin Haller .30 .75
15 Dave Littman .25 .60
16 Darcy Loewen .20 .50
17 Steve Ludzik .20 .50
18 Don McSween .20 .50
19 Brad Miller .20 .50
20 Sean O'Donnell .30 .75
21 Brad Rubachuk .20 .50
22 Lindy Ruff .40 1.00
23 Joel Savage .20 .50
24 Jiri Sejba .20 .50
25 Chris Snell .20 .50
26 Jason Winch .20 .50

1991-92 Rochester Americans Postcards

Sponsored by Genny Light, this 21-card set measures approximately 3 1/2" by 5 1/2" and features the 1991-92 Rochester Americans of the American Hockey League. The fronts have black-and-white action player photos with rounded corners and black borders. The player's name, uniform number, position, biography and last amateur club appear beneath the photo, along with the team logo. The backs are in postcard format and carry the sponsor's logo along with the words "STOP DWI. Don't Drink and Drive". The cards are unnumbered and checklisted below in alphabetical order.

COMPLETE SET (21) 4.00 10.00
1 Dave Baseggio .20 .50
2 John Bradley .20 .50
3 Greg Brown .20 .50
4 Keith Carney .20 .50
5 Peter Ciavaglia .20 .50
6 Bob Corkum .30 .75
7 David DiVita .20 .50
8 Tom Draper .30 .75
9 Lou Franceschetti .30 .75
10 Dan Frawley .20 .50
11 Bill Houlder .30 .75
12 Don Lever CO .08 .25
13 David Littman .30 .75
14 Terry Martin ACO .08 .25
15 Don McSween .20 .50
16 Sean O'Donnell .30 .75
17 Lindy Ruff .20 .50
18 Joel Savage .20 .50
19 Jiri Sejba .20 .50
20 Chris Snell .20 .50
21 Ed Zawatsky .20 .50

1992-93 Rochester Americans Dunkin' Donuts

Sponsored by Dunkin' Donuts, this 20-card set measures the standard size. It was issued in four perforated strips, each consisting of five player cards. On white card stock, the fronts feature color action player photos framed by team color-coded (red and blue) border stripes. Logos, jersey number, and position are printed above the picture, while the player's name is printed on the wider blue stripe beneath the picture. In black print on a white background, the backs carry biography, statistics, and sponsor logo. The cards are unnumbered and checklisted below in alphabetical order.

COMPLETE SET (20) 6.00 15.00
1 Peter Ambroziak .20 .50
2 Greg Brown .20 .50
3 Peter Ciavaglia .25 .60
4 Jozef Cierny .20 .50
5 David DiVita .20 .50
6 Dan Frawley .20 .50
7 Jody Gage .30 .75
8 Andrei Jakovenko .20 .50
9 Olaf Kolzig 2.00 5.00
10 Doug Macdonald .20 .50
11 Mike McLaughlin .20 .50
12 Sean O'Donnell .30 .75
13 Bill Pye .30 .75
14 Brad Rubachuk .20 .50
15 Bruce Shoebottom .20 .50
16 Todd Simon .20 .50
17 Jeff Sirkka .20 .50
18 Chris Snell .20 .50
19 Scott Thomas .30 .75
20 Jason Young .20 .50

1992-93 Rochester Americans Kodak

The 1992-93 Rochester American Team Photo and Trading Card Set was co-sponsored by Kodak and Wegmons Photo Center. It consists of three 11 1/4" by 9 1/2" sheets joined together and tri-folded. The first sheet displays a team photo of the players in uniform. The second and third sheets consist of 15 cards each arranged in three rows of five cards. (The last four slots of the third sheet display sponsor coupons.) After perforation, the cards would measure approximately 2 1/4" by 3 1/8". The player photos on the fronts have rounded corners and are poses shot from the waist up against a studio background. The player's name, position, and the team logo are above the picture, while sponsor logos and the uniform number are below it. In red and blue print, the backs carry biography and statistics. The cards are checklisted below as they are arranged in the album, with coaches presented first and then the players in alphabetical order.

COMPLETE SET (26) 15.00 40.00
1 John Van Boxmeer CO .40 1.00
2 Terry Martin ACO .08 .25
3 Peter Ambroziak .40 1.00
4 Greg Brown .40 1.00
5 Peter Ciavaglia .40 1.00
6 Jozef Cierny .40 1.00
7 David DiVita .40 1.00
8 Dan Frawley .40 1.00
9 Jody Gage 1.00 2.50
10 The Moose (mascot) .08 .25
11 Tony Iob .40 1.00
12 Olaf Kolzig 4.00 10.00
13 Doug MacDonald .40 1.00
14 Mike McLaughlin .40 1.00
15 Sean O'Donnell 1.00 2.50
16 Brad Pascall 1.00 2.50
17 Bill Pye 1.00 2.50
18 Brad Rubachuk .40 1.00
19 Joel Savage .40 1.00
20 Bruce Shoebottom .75 2.00
21 Todd Simon .40 1.00
22 Jeff Sirkka .40 1.00
23 Chris Snell .40 1.00
24 Scott Thomas 1.00 2.50
25 Jason Winch .40 1.00
26 Jason Young .40 1.00

1993-94 Rochester Americans Kodak

This 25-card set of the Rochester Americans of the AHL was sponsored by Kodak and distributed by the team's booster club. The set was issued in sheet form, with each card measuring 2 1/2" by 3 1/4". The card fronts carry a posed photo, player name and position and logos of the club and sponsors. The backs are unnumbered, but carry comprehensive stats.

COMPLETE SET (25) 4.80 12.00
1 John Van Boxmeer CO .20 .50
2 Terry Martin ACO .08 .25
3 Peter Ambroziak .25 .60
4 Mike Bavis .25 .60
5 James Black .25 .60
6 Derek Booth .25 .60
7 Philippe Boucher .25 .60
8 David Cooper .25 .60
9 Todd Flichel .25 .60
10 Jody Gage .40 1.00
11 Viktor Gordiouk .25 .60
12 Bill Horn .25 .60
13 Markus Ketterer .30 .75
14 Mark Krys .25 .60
15 Doug MacDonald .25 .60
16 Dean Melanson .25 .60
17 Moose -- Mascot .08 .25
18 Sean O'Donnell .30 .75
19 Brad Pascall .25 .60
20 Sergei Petrenko .25 .60
21 Brad Rubachuk .25 .60
22 Todd Simon .25 .60
23 Scott Thomas .30 .75
24 Mikhail Volkov .25 .60
25 Jason Young .25 .60

1995-96 Rochester Americans

This 25-card set of the Rochester Americans of the AHL was produced for the team by Split Second. The sets were available at games and by mail through the club. The set features a blurry action photo on the front and complete stats on the back. As they are unnumbered, the cards are presented in alphabetical order.

COMPLETE SET (25) 6.00 15.00
1 Craig Charron .20 .50
2 David Cooper .20 .50
3 Dan Frawley .20 .50
4 Jody Gage .40 1.00
5 Terry Hollinger .25 .60
6 Dane Jackson .20 .50
7 Ladislav Karabin .20 .50
8 Sergei Klimentiev .20 .50
9 Jamie Leach .20 .50
10 Jay Mazur .20 .50
11 Dean Melanson .20 .50
12 Scott Metcalfe .20 .50
13 Barrie Moore .20 .50
14 Scott Nichol .20 .50
15 Rumun Ndur .25 .60
16 Scott Pearson .20 .50
17 Serge Roberge .20 .50
18 Steve Shields .75 2.00
19 Robb Stauber .30 .75
20 Mikhail Volkov .20 .50
21 Dixon Ward .30 .75
22 Bob Westerby .20 .50
23 Mike Wilson .20 .50
24 Shayne Wright .20 .50
25 John Tortorella CO .08 .25

1996-97 Rochester Americans

This set features the Americans of the AHL. The set was produced by SplitSecond and was sold at home games for $5.

COMPLETE SET (26) 4.00 10.00
1 Rochester Americans .15 .40
2 Sergei Klimentiev .15 .40
3 Craig Charron .15 .40
4 Craig Millar .15 .40
5 Scott Metcalfe .15 .40
6 Ed Ronan .15 .40
7 Terry Hollinger .15 .40
8 Shayne Wright .15 .40
9 Barrie Moore .15 .40
10 Scott Nichol .15 .40
11 Charlie Huddy .15 .40
12 Vaclav Varada .20 .50
13 Wayne Primeau .30 .75
14 Terry Yake .15 .40
15 Dan Frawley .15 .40
16 Frederic Deschenes .15 .40
17 Steve Shields .40 1.00
18 Paul Rushforth .15 .40
19 Dane Jackson .15 .40
20 Rumun Ndur .20 .50
21 Greg Walters .15 .40
22 Eric Lavigne .15 .40
23 John Tortorella CO .02 .10
24 Moose MAS .02 .10
25 AHL Web Site .01
26 PHPA Web Site .01

1997-98 Rochester Americans

This set features the Amerks of the AHL. The cards were sponsored by Pepsi and issued as a promotional giveaway. The cards came in five-card sheets, and were given out at five different games.

COMPLETE SET (25) 8.00 20.00
1-1 Dane Jackson .30 .75
1-2 Scott Metcalfe .30 .75
1-3 Denis Hamel .30 .75
1-4 Mark Dutiaume .30 .75
1-5 Daniel Bienvenue .30 .75
2-1 Craig Charron .30 .75
2-2 Scott Nichol .30 .75
2-3 Martin Menard .30 .75
2-4 Erik Rasmussen .40 1.00
2-5 Mike Zanutto .30 .75
3-1 Vaclav Varada .40 1.00
3-2 Dan Frawley .30 .75
3-3 Patrice Tardif .40 1.00
3-4 Greg Walters .30 .75
3-5 Matt Davidson .30 .75
4-1 Mike Hurlbut .30 .75
4-2 Shayne Wright .30 .75
4-3 Mike McKee .30 .75
4-4 Dean Melanson .30 .75
4-5 Eric Lavigne .30 .75
5-1 Martin Biron 2.00 5.00
5-2 Sergei Klimentiev .30 .75
5-3 Mike Bales .40 1.00
5-4 Rumun Ndur .30 .75
5-5 Jean-Luc Grand-Pierre .30 .75

1998-99 Rochester Americans

This set features the Amerks of the AHL. The set was issued in five-card strips at five home games late in the season.

COMPLETE SET (25) 6.00 15.00
1 Craig Fisher .20 .50
2 Greg Walters .20 .50
3 Matt Davidson .20 .50
4 Randy Cunneyworth .20 .50
5 Martin Biron 1.25 3.00
6 Mike Hurlbut .20 .50
7 Tom Draper .30 .75
8 Mike Harder .20 .50
9 Denis Hamel .20 .50
10 Jean-Luc Grand-Pierre .20 .50
11 Scott Nichol .20 .50
12 Francois Methot .20 .50
13 Dean Melanson .20 .50
14 Jason Mansoff .20 .50
15 Jason Holland .20 .50
16 Darren Van Oene .20 .50
17 Dean Sylvester .30 .75
18 Cory Sarich .20 .50
19 Erik Rasmussen .30 .75
20 Dominic Pittis .20 .50
21 The Moose MAS .02 .10
22 Darwin McCutcheon CO .02 .10
23 Jody Gage .30 .75
24 Shane Kenny .20 .50
25 Steffon Walby .20 .50

2000-01 Rochester Americans

This set features the Americans of the AHL. The set was produced by Choice Marketing, and sold by the team at its souvenir stands.

COMPLETE SET (29) 4.80 12.00
1 Jeremy Adduono .14 .35
2 Tom Askey .20 .50
3 Martin Biron .80 2.00
4 Kevin Bolibruck .14 .35
5 Craig Brunel .14 .35
6 Brian Campbell .14 .35
7 Craig Charron .14 .35
8 Jason Cipolla .14 .35
9 Jason Holland .14 .35
10 Doug Houda .14 .35
11 Mike Hurlbut .14 .35
12 Dane Jackson .14 .35
13 Jaroslav Kristek .30 .50
14 Mike Mader .14 .35
15 Francois Methot .14 .35
16 Norm Milley .30 .75
17 Joe Murphy .14 .35
18 Todd Nelson .14 .35
19 Mika Noronen .80 1.50
20 Andrew Peters .14 1.00
21 Chris Taylor .14 .35
22 Paul Traynor .14 .35
23 Darren Van Oene .14 .35
24 Randy Cunneyworth CO .10 .25
25 Jon Christiano CO .04 .10
26 Dave A. Williams EM .04 .10
27 Kent Weisbeck TR .04 .10
28 The Moose MASCOT .04 .10
NNO Team CL .04 .01

2002-03 Rochester Americans

COMPLETE SET (26) 8.00 20.00
1 Tom Askey .30 .75
2 Milan Bartovic .20 .50
3 Jason Botterill .20 .50
4 Rory Fitzpatrick .20 .50
5 Paul Gaustad .30 .75
6 Denis Hamel .20 .50
7 Radoslav Hecl .20 .50
8 Doug Houda .20 .50
9 Doug Janik .20 .50
10 Ryan Jorde .20 .50
11 Jaroslav Kristek .30 .75
12 Sean McMorrow .30 .75
13 Francois Methot .20 .50
14 Ryan Miller 2.00 5.00
15 Norm Milley .20 .50
16 Karel Mosovsky .20 .50
17 Jiri Novotny .30 .75
18 Andrew Peters .60 1.50
19 Jason Pominville .60 1.50
20 Peter Ratchuk .20 .50
21 Chris Taylor .20 .50
22 Ryan Miller 2.00 5.00
23 Randy Cunneyworth HCO .02 .10
24 Jon Christiano ACO .02 .10
25 The Moose Mascot .02 .10
NNO Checklist .01 .05

2003-04 Rochester Americans

This set was produced by Choice Marketing and sold at home games.

COMPLETE SET (29) 6.00 15.00
1 Doug Houda ACO .02 .10
2 Tom Askey .30 .75
3 Milan Bartovic .12 .30
4 Jason Botterill .12 .30
5 Brian Chapman .12 .30
6 David Cullen .12 .30
7 Randy Cunneyworth .12 .30
8 Pete Gardiner .12 .30
9 Paul Gaustad .20 .50
10 Doug Janik .12 .30
11 Ryan Jorde .12 .30
12 Steve Lingren .12 .30
13 Sean McMorrow .30 .75
14 Ryan Miller 1.25 3.00
15 Jason Dawe .12 .30
16 Norm Milley .30 .75
17 Karel Mosovsky .12 .30
18 Rick Mrozik .12 .30
19 Jiri Novotny .30 .75
20 Nathan Paetsch .30 .75
21 Geoff Peters .30 .75
22 Domenic Pittis .20 .50
23 Jason Pominville .75 2.00
24 Scott Ricci .12 .30
25 Derek Roy .75 2.00
26 Derek Roy .75 2.00
27 Michael Ryan .20 .50
28 Mascot .02 .10
29 Chris Thorburn .12 .30
NNO Checklist .01 .05

2004-05 Rochester Americans

COMPLETE SET (30) 8.00 20.00
1 Checklist .01 .05
2 Tom Askey .30 .75
3 Milan Bartovic .20 .50
4 Jason Botterill .20 .50
5 David Cullen .20 .50
6 Paul Gaustad .20 .50
7 Doug Janik .20 .50
8 Jeff Jillson .20 .50
9 Ryan Jorde .20 .50
10 Steve Lingren .20 .50
11 Sean McMorrow .30 .75
12 Ryan Miller .75 2.00
13 Norm Milley .20 .50
14 Jiri Novotny .20 .50
15 Nathan Paetsch .20 .50
16 Daniel Paille .40 1.00
17 Geoff Peters .60 1.50
18 Jason Pominville .40 1.00
19 Todd Rohloff .20 .50
20 Derek Roy .40 1.00
21 Michael Ryan .20 .50
22 Brandon Smith .20 .50
23 Chris Taylor .20 .50
24 Chris Thorburn .20 .50
25 Thomas Vanek .75 2.00
26 The Moose MASCOT .02 .10
27 Ryan Miller .75 2.00
28 Derek Roy .40 1.00
29 Thomas Vanek .75 2.00
30 Randy Cunneyworth CO .02 .10
Doug Houda CO

1999-00 Rockford IceHogs

This set features the IceHogs of the UHL. The set was produced by Roox and was sold by the team at home games. Because of the obtuse numbering system on the card backs, they have been listed below in alphabetical order.

COMPLETE SET (26) 4.00 50.00
1 Brant Blackned .75 2.00
2 Peter Cava 1.25 3.00
3 Patrice Charbonneau .75 2.00
4 Mike Correia .75 2.00
5 Dan Davies .75 2.00
6 Raymond Delarosbil .75 2.00
7 Mike Figliomeni 1.25 3.00
8 Jason Firth 1.25 3.00
9 Sheldon Gorski 1.25 3.00
10 Jeff Kostuch .75 2.00
11 Evgeny Krivomaz .75 2.00
12 Derek Landmesser .75 2.00
13 Alexandre Makombo 1.25 3.00
14 Barry McKinley .75 2.00
15 Normand Paquet .75 2.00
16 Jean-Francois Rivard .75 2.00
17 Shawn Smith .75 2.00
18 Carlos Soke .75 2.00
19 Wayne Strachan .75 2.00
20 Curtis Tipler .75 2.00
21 Jesse Welling .75 2.00
22 Scott Burfoot CO .08 .25
23 Dale DeGray CO .08 .25
24 Hamilton E. Hog MASCOT .02 .10
25 Mike Figliomeni AS 1.25 3.00
26 Jason Firth AS 1.25 3.00

2000-01 Rockford IceHogs

This set features the IceHogs of the UHL. The set was produced by the team and sold at its souvenir stands. The cards are unnumbered and are listed below alphabetically.

COMPLETE SET (25) 4.00 10.00
1 Curtis Bois .20 .50
2 Patrice Charbonneau .20 .50
3 Nick Checco .30 .75
4 Curtis Cruickshank .30 .75
5 Jeff DaCosta .20 .50
6 Dan Davies .20 .50
7 Steve Dumonski .20 .50
8 Chris Fattey .20 .50
9 Mike Figliomeni .20 .50
10 Justin Kearns .30 .75
11 Evgeny Krivomaz .20 .50
12 Jocelyn Langlois .20 .50
13 Michel Periard .20 .50
14 Jean-Francois Rivard .20 .50
15 David Runge .20 .50
16 Francois Sasseville .20 .50
17 Shawn Smith .20 .50
18 Mike Tobin .20 .50
19 Yan Turgeon .20 .50
20 Eduard Zankovets .20 .50
21 Dale DeGray CO .10 .25
22 Scott Burfoot CO .10 .25
23 Hamilton E. Hog MASCOT .10 .25
24 Logo Card .04 .01
25 Header Card .04 .01

2001-02 Rockford IceHogs

COMPLETE SET (25) 8.00 20.00
1 Ben Christopherson .40 1.00
2 Clint Wensley .40 1.00
3 Dan Davies .40 1.00
4 Darwin Murray .40 1.00
5 David Hoogsteen .40 1.00
6 Ernie Thorp .40 1.00
7 Forrest Gore .40 1.00
8 Hamilton E. Hog .40 1.00
9 Harold Hersh .10 .25
10 J.F. Rivard .40 1.00
11 Jared Reigstad .40 1.00
12 Jeff Antonovich .40 1.00
13 Jeff Dacosta .40 1.00
14 Jeremy Vokes .40 1.00
15 Joe Statkus .40 1.00
16 Mike Sgroi .40 1.00
17 Nick Checco .40 1.00
18 Oak Hewer .40 1.00
19 Quinten Van Horlick .40 1.00
20 Scott Bell CO .10 .25
21 Sergei Petrov .40 1.00
22 Steve Debus .40 1.00
23 T.J. Guidarelli .40 1.00
24 Wes Blevins .40 1.00
NNO Team CL .40 1.00

2002-03 Rockford Ice Hogs

COMPLETE SET (25) 8.00 20.00
1 Scott Bell CO .02 .10
2 Darwin Murray .40 1.00
3 Raitis Ivanans .40 1.00
4 Kenzie Homer .40 1.00
5 Alexander Alexeev .40 1.00
6 Oak Hewer .40 1.00
7 Erik Wendell .40 1.00
8 Jeff Antonovich .40 1.00
9 Matt Loen .40 1.00
10 Jeremy Rebek .40 1.00
11 Steve Cygan .40 1.00
12 Clint Wensley .40 1.00
13 Quinten Van Horlick .40 1.00
14 Steve Dumonski .40 1.00
15 Nick Angell .40 1.00
16 Joe Statkus .40 1.00
17 Jay Hebert .40 1.00
18 Dan Davies .40 1.00
19 Brad Olsen .40 1.00
20 Jeff Dacosta .40 1.00
21 Brant Nicklin .40 1.00
22 Ryan McIntosh .40 1.00
23 Mascot .02 .10
24 Mascot .02 .10
25 Team card/CL .02 .10

2003-04 Rockford Ice Hogs

This set was produced by Choice Marketing and sold at home games. Minor league collector Ralph Slate reports just 300 sets were produced.

COMPLETE SET (20) 6.00 15.00
1 B.J. Adams .30 .75
2 Justin Cardwell .30 .75
3 Steve Cygan .30 .75
4 Dan Davies .30 .75
5 Jeff Ewasko .40 1.00
6 John Glavota .30 .75
7 Kenzie Homer .30 .75
8 Dale Junkin .30 .75
9 Nathan Lutz .30 .75
10 Don Margettie .40 1.00
11 Kelly Miller .30 .75
12 Bob Nardella .30 .75
13 Dave Paradise .30 .75
14 Gary Ricciardi .30 .75
15 Paul Schonfelder .40 1.00
16 Adam Solnik .30 .75
17 Ron Vogel .40 1.00
18 Owen Walter .30 .75
19 Maris Ziedins .30 .75
20 Mark Bernard HCO .10 .25

2005-06 Rockford Ice Hogs

COMPLETE SET (27) 8.00 15.00
1 Greg Barber .20 .50
2 Robin Big Snake .75 2.00
3 Dan Boeser .20 .50
4 Ryan Carrigan .20 .50
5 Matt Gens .20 .50
6 Corey Hessler .20 .50
7 Chaz Johnson .40 1.00
8 Nathan Lutz .20 .50
9 Preston Mizzi .20 .50
10 Bob Nardella .20 .50
11 Jason Notermann .40 1.00
12 Steve Pelletier .20 .50
13 Olivier Proulx .20 .50
14 Jason Ralph .40 1.00
15 Billy Tibbetts .40 1.00
16 Yannick Tifu .20 .50
17 Rob Voltera .20 .50
18 Bruce Watson .40 1.00
19 Steve Yetman .20 .50
20 Tom Zabkowicz .20 .50
21 Josh Mizerek .20 .50
22 Ron Vogel .40 1.00
23 Michel Robinson .20 .50
24 Steve Martinson .20 .50
25 Hammer Hog MASCOT .02 .10
26 Hamilton E. Hog MASCOT .02 .10
NNO Rockford Ice Hogs CL .02 .10

2006-07 Rockford IceHogs

COMPLETE SET (27) 12.00 20.00
1 Jesse Bennefield .30 .75
2 Kaleb Betts .40 1.00
3 Robin Big Snake .75 2.00
4 Dan Boeser .30 .75
5 Paul Brown .30 .75
6 Frederic Cloutier• .60 1.50
7 Bryce Cockburn .30 .75
8 Nicolas Corbeil .30 .75
9 Mike Doyle .30 .75
10 Luke Fritshaw .30 .75
11 Matt Gens .30 .75

12 Corey Hessler .30 .75
13 Chaz Johnson .30 .75
14 Mike Letizia .30 .75
15 Erik Lizon .30 .75
16 Nathan Lutz .30 .75
17 Preston Mizzi .40 1.00
18 Jake Moreland .40 1.00
19 Jason Notermann .30 .75
20 Jason Ralph .30 .75
21 Kevin Ulanski .30 .75
22 Bruce Watson .30 .75
23 Tim Wedderburn .30 .75
24 Steve Martinson CO .20 .50
25 Hammer Hog MASCOT .02 .10
26 Hamilton E. Hog MASCOT .02 .10
27 Team Card .10 .25

1995-96 Roller Hockey Magazine RHI

This 6-card set was inserted as a promotional enticement into the September 1996 issue of Roller Hockey Magazine.

COMPLETE SET (6) 2.00 5.00
1 Oleg Yashin .40 1.00
2 Frankie Ouellette .40 1.00
3 Nick Vitucci .60 1.50
4 Mike Martens .40 1.00
5 Alain Morissette .40 1.00
6 Simon Roy .40 1.00

1999-00 Rouyn-Noranda Huskies

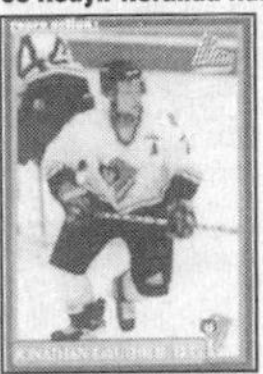

This set features the Huskies of the QMJHL. The set was produced by card shop CTM-Ste-Foy and was sold at the store and at home games.

COMPLETE SET (26) 4.80 12.00
1 Kyrill Alexeev .15 .40
2 Marc-Andre Binette .15 .40
3 Maxime Bouchard .15 .40
4 Bruno Cadieux .15 .40
5 Sebastien Centomo .60 1.50
6 Kevin Cloutier .15 .40
7 Jonathan Gauthier .15 .40
8 Patrick Gilbert .15 .40
9 Andre Hart .15 .40
10 Robert Horak .15 .40
11 Eric L'Italien .15 .40
12 Mathieu Leclerc .15 .40
13 Jason Lehoux .15 .40
14 Jonathan Pelletier .15 .40
15 Bertrand-Pierre Plouffe .15 .40
16 Matthew Quinn .15 .40
17 Mike Ribeiro .60 1.50
18 Shawn Scanzano .15 .40
19 Jason Jessiel .15 .40
20 Jerome Tremblay .15 .40
21 Alain Turcotte .15 .40
22 Steve Vandal .15 .40
23 Guy Boucher CO .02 .10
24 Andre Parke CO .02 .10
25 Jean Pronovost CO .15 .40
26 Michel Maroux TR .02 .10

2000-01 Rouyn-Noranda Huskies

This set features the Huskies of the QMJHL. The cards were produced by CTM-Ste-Foy, and were sold both by that card shop and by the team.

COMPLETE SET (27) 6.00 15.00
1 Dominic D'Amour .20 .50
2 Jonathan Gauthier .20 .50
3 Matthew Quinn .20 .50
4 Kirill Alexeev .20 .50
5 Sebastian Strozynski .20 .50
6 Bertrand Pierre Plouffe .20 .50
7 Maxime Talbot .20 .50
8 Guillaume Lefebvre .40 1.00
9 Alexandre Morel .20 .50
10 Michal Pinc .20 .50
12 Mathieu Leclerc .20 .50
13 Jerome Marois .20 .50
14 Patrice Theriault .20 .50
15 Patrick Gilbert .20 .50
16 Maxime Ouellet .80 2.00
17 Louis Mandeville .20 .50
18 Wesley Scanzano .30 .75
19 Sebastien Centomo 1.20 1.00
20 Maxime Bouchard .20 .50
21 Bruno Cadieux .20 .50
22 Jean-Philippe Hamel .20 .50
23 Shawn Scanzano .20 .50
24 Jonathan Gagnon .20 .50
25 Marc-Andre Binette .20 .50
26 Jean Pronovost CO .20 .25
NNO Lappy MASCOT .04 .10

2000-01 Rouyn-Noranda Huskies Signed

This set is exactly the same as the base Huskies set from this season, save that every card has been hand signed by the player pictured. Each card also is serial numbered out of just 100.

COMPLETE SET (27) 24.00 60.00
1 Dominic D'Amour .80 2.00
2 Jonathan Gauthier .80 2.00
3 Matthew Quinn .80 2.00
4 Kirill Alexeev .80 2.00
5 Sebastian Strozynski .80 2.00
6 Bertrand Pierre Plouffe .80 2.00
7 Maxime Talbot .80 2.00
8 Guillaume Lefebvre 2.00 5.00
9 Alexandre Morel .80 2.00
10 Michal Pinc .80 2.00
12 Mathieu Leclerc .80 2.00
13 Jerome Marois .80 2.00
14 Patrice Theriault .80 2.00
15 Patrick Gilbert .80 2.00
16 Maxime Ouellet 4.00 10.00
17 Louis Mandeville .80 2.00
18 Wesley Scanzano 1.20 3.00
19 Sebastien Centomo 6.00 7.50
20 Maxime Bouchard .80 2.00
21 Bruno Cadieux .80 2.00
22 Jean-Philippe Hamel .80 2.00
23 Shawn Scanzano .80 2.00
24 Jonathan Gagnon .80 2.00
25 Marc-Andre Binette .80 2.00
26 Jean Pronovost CO .80 2.00
NNO Lappy MASCOT .04 .10

1993-94 RPI Engineers

This 31-card set of the RPI Engineers was produced by Collect-A-Sport. Reportedly, production was limited to 2,000 sets, all of which were offered for sale at the arena on game nights.

COMPLETE SET (31) 4.00 10.00
1 Kelly Askew .15 .40
2 Adam Bartell .15 .40
3 Kobie Boykins .15 .40
4 Jeff Brick .15 .40
5 Tim Carvel .15 .40
6 Wayne Clarke .15 .40
7 Cam Cuthbert .15 .40
8 Steve Duncan ACO .02 .10
9 Dan Fridgen ACO .02 .10
10 Jeff Gabriel .15 .40
11 Craig Hamelin .15 .40
12 Chris Kiley .15 .40
13 Ken Kwasniewski .15 .40
14 Brad Layzell .15 .40
15 Neil Little .30 .75
16 Xavier Majic .20 .50
17 Jeff Matthews .15 .40
18 Chris Maye .15 .40
19 Jeff O'Connor .15 .40
20 Ron Pasco .15 .40
21 Eric Perardi .15 .40
22 Jon Pirrong .15 .40
23 Buddy Powers CO .02 .10
24 Tim Regan .15 .40
25 Bryan Richardson .15 .40
26 Patrick Rochon .15 .40
27 Mike Rolanti .15 .40
28 Tim Spadafore .15 .40
29 Mike Tamburro .15 .40
30 1993-94 Team .15 .40
31 Checklist .02 .10

1976-77 Saginaw Gears

This set features black and white player photos on slightly oversized stock. It's possible that the checklist is not complete. If you have additional information, please forward it to hockeymag@beckett.com.

COMPLETE SET (13) 17.50 35.00
1 Rick Chinnick 1.50 3.00
2 Marcel Comeau 1.50 3.00
3 Michel DeGuise 1.50 3.00
4 Marc Gaudreault 1.50 3.00
5 Greg Hotham 1.50 3.00
6 Stu Irving 1.50 3.00
7 Kevin Kemp 1.50 3.00
8 Mario Lessard 1.50 3.00
9 Gord Malinoski 1.50 3.00
10 Mike Ruest 1.50 3.00
11 D'Arcy Ryan 1.50 3.00
12 Dave Westner 1.50 3.00
13 Wayne Zuk 1.50 3.00

1978-79 Saginaw Gears

This 20-card set features black-and-white posed player photos. The team name and year appear in the top white border with the player's name printed in the bottom border. The player's position is listed on a puck at the bottom left of the photo. The backs are blank. The cards are unnumbered and checklisted below in alphabetical order. This set was the subject of a number of fierce bidding wars over the past two years, leading to a tremendous value increase in this edition.

COMPLETE SET (20) 12.50 300.00
1 Wren Blair .75 15.00
2 Marcel Comeau .75 15.00
3 Dennis Desrosiers .50 15.00
4 Jon Fontas .50 15.00
5 Bob Froese 2.00 25.00
6 Gunnar Garrett TR .25 1.00
7 Bob Gladney .50 15.00
8 Warren Holmes .50 15.00
9 Stu Irving .50 15.00
10 Larry Hopkins .50 15.00
11 Scott Jessee .50 15.00
12 Lynn Jorgenson .50 15.00
13 Doug Keans 1.50 25.00
14 Claude Larochelle .50 15.00
15 Paul McIntosh .50 15.00
16 Don Perry .50 15.00
17 Greg Steel .50 15.00
18 Mark Suzor .50 15.00
19 Mark Toffolo .50 15.00
20 Dave Westner .50 15.00

1999-00 Saginaw Gears

This set features the Gears of the UHL. Little is known about this set, other than that it was produced by Roox as part of a series of promotional giveaways. The Loder issue is actually a magnet, while the others are traditional cards. Any additional information can be forwarded to hockeymag@beckett.com.

COMPLETE SET (4) 2.00 5.00
1 Brian Mueller .40 1.00
2 Derek Pinfold .40 1.00
3 Jeff Loder .75 2.00
4 Keith Osborne .40 1.00

2002-03 Saginaw Spirit

We have confirmed the existence of one card in this series. If you have information about others, please contact us at hockeymag@beckett.com.

COMPLETE SET (?)
1 Colt King
2 Chris Thorburn

2003-04 Saginaw Spirit

COMPLETE SET (28) 5.00 12.00
1 Patrick Asselin .20 .50
2 Paul Bissonnette .20 .50
3 Daniel Borges .20 .50
4 Mike Brown .30 .75
5 Chase Crowder .20 .50
6 Steve Dix .20 .50
7 Adam Gibson .20 .50
8 Jesse Gimblett .20 .50
9 Jesse Jenish .20 .50
10 Phil Kozak .20 .50
11 Nick Lees .20 .50
12 Justin McCutcheon .20 .50
13 Patrick McNeill .20 .50
14 Georgi Misharin .20 .50
15 Mike Pain .20 .50
16 Eric Pfligler .20 .50
17 Geoff Platt .20 .50
18 Tom Pyatt .30 .75
19 Taylor Raszka .20 .50
20 Jean-Michel Rizk .30 .75
21 Marc-Andre Rizk .20 .50
22 Adam Sturgeon .20 .50
23 Mike Suggs .20 .50
24 Stephen Sunderman .20 .50
25 Team Card .02 .10
26 Rick Brothers .20 .50
27 Moe Mantha CO .02 .10
28 Bryan and Jose .02 .10

2004-05 Saginaw Spirit

COMPLETE SET (24) 5.00 12.00
1 Patrick McNeill .20 .50
2 Marek Kvapil .20 .50
3 Jean-Michel Rizk .20 .50
4 Paul Bissonnette .20 .50
5 Patrick Asselin .20 .50
6 Peter Franchin .20 .50
7 Rick Caughell .20 .50
8 Kevin Tuckey .20 .50
9 Gary Klapkowski .20 .50
10 Scott Fletcher .20 .50
11 Daniel Borges .20 .50
12 Jamie Klie .20 .50
13 Chris Ferguson .20 .50
14 Taylor Raszka .20 .50
15 Dan Idema .20 .50
16 Chase Crowder .20 .50
17 Tom Pyatt .30 .75
18 Thomas Harrison .20 .50
19 Sean Courtney .20 .50
20 Aaron Rock .20 .50
21 Jesse Gimblett .20 .50
22 Matt Corrente .40 1.00
23 Mike Brown .30 .75
24 Mascot .02 .10

2005-06 Saginaw Spirit

COMPLETE SET (24) 6.00 12.00
1 Patrick Asselin .20 .50
2 Michal Birner .20 .50
3 Chris Chappell .20 .50
4 Jack Combs .20 .50
5 Matt Corrente .40 1.00
6 Tom Craig .20 .50
7 Ryan Daniels .20 .50
8 Chris Ferguson .20 .50
9 Scott Fletcher .20 .50
10 Jesse Gimblett .20 .50
11 Tyson Gimblett .20 .50
12 Jamie Klie .20 .50
13 Erik Lundmark .20 .50
14 Tom Mannino .20 .50
15 Joe McCann .20 .50
16 Ryan McDonough .20 .50
17 Patrick McNeill .20 .50
18 Tim Priamo .20 .50
19 Tom Pyatt .40 1.00
20 Garrett Sinfield .20 .50
21 Anthony Soboczynski .20 .50
22 Francois Thuot .40 1.00
23 Zack Torquato .20 .50
24 Steven Whitely .20 .50

2006-07 Saginaw Spirit

COMPLETE SET (25) 8.00 16.00
1 Tom Pyatt .40 1.00
2 Patrick Mcneill .30 .75
3 Garrett Sinfield .20 .50
4 Curtis Cooper .20 .50
5 Nick Crawford .20 .50
6 Tommy Mannino .20 .50
7 Christopher Breen .20 .50
8 Tomas Zaborsky .20 .50
9 Jan Mursak .20 .50
10 Matt Corrente .30 .75
11 Tyler Haskins .20 .50
12 Andrew Cloutier .20 .50
13 Tom Craig .20 .50
14 Chris Chappell .20 .50
15 Ryan Daniels .40 1.00
16 Jack Combs .20 .50
17 Zack Torquato .40 1.00
18 Patrick Asselin .20 .50
19 Jovica Zelenbaba .20 .50
20 T.J. Brodie .20 .50
21 Ryan Berard .20 .50
22 Ryan Mcdonough .20 .50
23 Sammy Spirit MASCOT .10 .25
24 Steagle Colbeagle MASCOT .40 1.00
LE1 Patrick Mcneill .75 2.00

1994-95 Saint John Flames

This 26-card standard-size set was manufactured and distributed by Jessen Associates, Inc. for Classic. The fronts display color action player photos with a red marbleized inner border and a black outer border. The player's name, jersey number, and position appear in the teal border on the right edge. The cards are unnumbered and checklisted below in alphabetical order.

COMPLETE SET (26) 3.00 8.00
1 Joel Bouchard .20 .50
2 Rick Carriere ACO .02 .10
3 Ryan Duthie .08 .25
4 Neil Eisenhut .08 .25
5 Leonard Esau .08 .25
6 Bob Francis CO .02 .10
7 Mark Greig .08 .25
8 Francois Groleau .08 .25
9 Sami Helenius .30 .75
10 Todd Hlushko .20 .50
11 Dale Kushner .08 .25
12 Bobby Marshall .08 .25
13 Scott Morrow .08 .25
14 Michael Murray .08 .25
15 Jason Muzzatti .30 .75
16 Barry Nieckar .08 .25
17 Nicolas Perreault .08 .25
18 Jeff Perry .08 .25
19 Dwayne Roloson .30 .75
20 Todd Simpson .08 .25
21 Harbour Station .02 .10
22 Cory Stillman .30 .75
23 David Struch .08 .25
24 Niklas Sundblad .08 .25
25 Andrei Trefilov .20 .50
26 Vesa Viitakoski .08 .25

1996-97 Saint John Flames

This set features the Flames of the AHL. The cards were produced by SplitSecond and sold at home games. The cards are unnumbered, and so are listed below alphabetically.

COMPLETE SET (26) 4.00 10.00
1 Jamie Allison .15 .40
2 Chris Dingman .20 .50
3 Scott Fraser .15 .40
4 Denis Gauthier .15 .40
5 Ian Gordon .15 .40
6 Patrik Haltia .20 .50
7 Sami Helenius .30 .75
8 Marc Hussey .15 .40
9 Marko Jantunen .20 .50
10 Ladislav Kohn .15 .40
11 Martin Lamarche .15 .40
12 Jesper Mattsson .20 .50
13 Keith McCambridge .15 .40
14 Dale McTavish .15 .40
15 Burke Murphy .15 .40
16 Marty Murray .30 .75
17 Paxton Schulte .15 .40
18 Jarrod Skalde .30 .75
19 Jason Smith .30 .75
20 Clarke Wilm .20 .50
21 Ravil Yakubov .15 .40
22 Paul Baxter CO .08 .25
23 Jeff Perry CO .08 .25
24 Fleaburn MAS .02 .10
25 AHL Web Site .01
26 PHPA Web Site .01

1995-96 Saint John Flames

This 25-card set features borderless color action player photos of the Saint John Flames of the AHL. The backs carry player information and statistics. The cards are unnumbered and checklisted below in alphabetical order.

COMPLETE SET (25) 4.00 50.00
1 Jamie Allison .60 1.50
2 Paul Baxter CO .02 .10
3 Joel Bouchard .60 1.50
4 Tom Coolen CO .02 .10
5 Brett Duncan .60 1.50
6 Ian Gordon .60 1.50
7 Sami Helenius 1.25 3.00
8 Todd Hlushko .60 1.50
9 Marc Hussey .60 1.50
10 Ladislav Kohn .60 1.50
11 Frank Kovacs .60 1.50
12 David Ling .75 2.00
13 Jesper Mattsson .60 1.50
14 Keith McCambridge .60 1.50
15 Marty Murray .75 2.00
16 Michael Murray .60 1.50
17 David Neilson .60 1.50
18 Jeff Perry .60 1.50
19 Darren Ritchie .60 1.50
20 Dwayne Roloson 6.00 15.00
21 Todd Simpson .60 1.50
22 Jarrod Skalde .75 2.00
23 David Struch .60 1.50
24 Niklas Sundblad .75 2.00
25 Vesa Viitakoski .60 1.50

1997-98 Saint John Flames

This set features the Flames of the AHL. The cards were produced by the team and sold at home games and via mail.

COMPLETE SET (25) 8.00 15.00
1 Jamie Allison .15 .40
2 Erik Andersson .15 .40
3 Ryan Bast .15 .40
4 Travis Brigley .15 .40
5 Eric Charron .15 .40
6 Jeff Cowan .30 .75
7 Hnat Domenichelli .20 .50
8 Jim Dowd .20 .50
9 Denis Gauthier .30 .75
10 Jean-Sebastien Giguere 2.00 5.00
11 Sami Helenius .30 .75
12 Ladislav Kohn .15 .40
13 Eric Landry .15 .40
14 Jesper Mattsson .15 .40
15 Keith McCambridge .15 .40
16 Tyler Moss .20 .50
17 Burke Murphy .15 .40
18 Marty Murray .20 .50
19 Chris O'Sullivan .15 .40
20 Paxton Schulte .20 .50
21 Rocky Thompson .15 .40
22 John Tripp .20 .50
23 Clarke Wilm .15 .40
24 Bill Stewart HCO .08 .25
25 Jeff Perry CO .08 .25

2005-06 Saint John's Sea Dogs

COMPLETE SET (24) 6.00 12.00
1 Jason Churchill .40 1.00
2 Alex Grant .20 .50
3 Alexandre Monahan .20 .50
4 Alexandre Labonte .20 .50
5 Brett Gallant .20 .50
6 Cedric Archambault .20 .50
7 Charles Bergeron .40 1.00
8 Felix Schulz .40 1.00
9 Jean-Philippe Cote .20 .50
10 Jeff Caron .20 .50
11 Jevin Maclellan .20 .50
12 Jonathan Laberge .20 .50
13 Kevin Coughlin .20 .50
14 Martin Bartos .20 .50
15 Maxime Dubuc .20 .50
16 Mike Neil .20 .50
17 Patrick Leask .20 .50
18 Riley Whitlock .40 1.00
19 Ryan Moore .20 .50
20 Ryan Sparling .20 .50
21 Sebastien Rioux .20 .50
22 Vincent Lambert .20 .50
23 Matthew Block .20 .50
24 Luc Melanson .20 .50

2006-07 Saint Johns Sea Dogs

COMPLETE SET (25) 8.00 15.00
1 Alex Grant .40 1.00
2 Mike Noyes .25 .60
3 Ryan Sparling .25 .60
4 Felix Schulz .40 1.00
5 David Macdonald .25 .60
6 Dave Bouchard .25 .60
7 Bruce Crawford .25 .60
8 Sebastien Rioux .25 .60
9 Jonathan Laberge .25 .60
10 Mike Thomas .25 .60
11 Charles Bergeron .25 .60
12 Shayne Tremblay .25 .60
13 Maxime Dubuc .25 .60
14 Alexandre Labonte .25 .60
15 Olivier Painchaud .25 .60
16 David Stich .25 .60
17 Chris Didomenico .25 .60
18 Alexandre Monohan .25 .60
19 Anthony Bergin .25 .60
20 Maxime Joyal .40 1.00
21 Aaron Barton .40 1.00
22 Pascal Amyot .25 .60
23 Brett Gallant .25 .60
24 Yann Sauve .25 .60
LE1 Alex Grant .75 2.00

2003-04 Salmon Arm Silverbacks

The set features the Silverbacks of the BCJHL, including two 2004 first rounders in Chucko and Zajac. The set is unnumbered and listed in alphabetical order.

COMPLETE SET (25) 8.00 20.00
1 Evan Barlow .20 .50
2 Jay Birnie .40 1.00
3 Steve Christie .40 1.00
4 Kris Chucko 1.25 3.00
5 Rick Cleaver .20 .50
6 Spencer Dillon .20 .50
7 Bryn Gagnon .20 .50
8 Trevor Geiger .20 .50
9 Blaine Jarvis .20 .50
10 Jaye Judd .20 .50
11 Patrick Lepage .40 1.00
12 Julian Marcuzzi .20 .50
13 Tyrell Mason .20 .50
14 Ryan McLeod .20 .50
15 Jason Miller .20 .50
16 Travis Ramsey .20 .50
17 Chris Shudo .20 .50
18 Kiel Sonne .40 1.00
19 Ben Street .20 .50
20 Craig Switzer .20 .50
21 Travis Zajac 2.00 5.00
22 Header Card .01 .05
23 Award Winners .40 1.00
24 Header Card .01 .05
25 Team Photo .20 .50

2004-05 Salmon Arm Silverbacks

COMPLETE SET (24) 5.00 12.00
1 Jamie Silverson .30 .75
2 Brendon Nash .30 .75
3 Dustin Degagne .30 .75
4 Robbie Rodgers .30 .75
5 Mark Santorelli .30 .75
6 Brodie Sheahan .30 .75
7 Ben Stroot .30 .75
8 Tyrell Mason .30 .75
9 Darcy Zajac .40 1.00
10 Bryn Gagnon .30 .75
11 Trevor Geiger .30 .75
12 Luke Cain .30 .75
13 Ryan Duncan .30 .75
14 Ernie Stewart .30 .75
15 Kiel Sonne .30 .75
16 Jesse Deckert .30 .75
17 Brad Atkinson .30 .75
18 Evan Barlow .30 .75
19 Julian Marcuzzi .30 .75
20 Jesse Griffith .30 .75
21 Kong MASCOT .02 .10
22 Team Card .02 .10
23 Logo Card .02 .10
24 Logo Card .30 .75

2005-06 Salmon Arm Silverbacks

COMPLETE SET (25) 10.00 20.00
1 Logo .01 .01
2 Logo .01 .01
3 August Aiken .40 1.00
4 Billy Blase .40 1.00
5 Luke Cain .40 1.00
6 Dustin Degagne .40 1.00
7 Matt Dyck .40 1.00
8 Jesse Griffith .40 1.00
9 Travis Holloway .40 1.00
10 Damon Kipp .40 1.00
11 Josh Lund .40 1.00
12 Cam Macintyre .40 1.00
13 Brendon Nash .40 1.00
14 Evan Pighin .40 1.00
15 Chris Rawlings .40 1.00
16 Rob Rodgers .40 1.00
17 Brodie Sheahan .40 1.00
18 Erik Spady .40 1.00
19 Ernie Stewart .40 1.00
20 Justin Taylor .40 1.00
21 Ben Winnet .40 1.00
22 Shaun Witschen .40 1.00
23 Darcy Zajac .40 1.00
24 Kong MASCOT .01 .01
25 Ad Card .01 .01

1988-89 Salt Lake Golden Eagles

Commemorating the 20th anniversary of the Salt Lake Golden Eagles, this 24-card standard-size set features color close-up shots against a light blue background. The player's name and position are printed diagonally in black across the front. The set was sponsored by the USDA Forest Service and Utah State Lands and Forestry agency. Card number 10 was never issued.

COMPLETE SET (24) 12.00 30.00
1 Rick Barkovich .20 .50
2 Michael Dark .20 .50
3 Terry Perkins .20 .50
4 Peter Lappin .20 .50
5 Wayne Cowley .20 .50
6 Rich Chernomaz .20 .50
7 Steve Smith .40 1.00
8 Theo Fleury 8.00 20.00
9 Dave Reierson .20 .50
10 Not Issued .20 .50
11 Martin Simard .20 .50
12 Stu Grimson 1.25 3.00
13 Darwin McCutcheon .20 .50
14 Doug Clarke .20 .50
15 Doug Pickell .20 .50
16 Randy Bucyk .20 .50
17 Jim Johannson .20 .50
18 Rick Lessard .20 .50
19 Ken Sabourin .20 .50
20 Chris Biotti .20 .50
21 Jeff Wenaas .20 .50
22 Mark Holmes .20 .50
23 Bob Bodak .20 .50
24 Marc Bureau .40 1.00
NNO Smokey the Bear .20 .50

1992-93 Salt Lake Golden Eagles

Little is known about this set beyond the confirmed checklist. Any additional information should be forwarded to hockeymag@beckett.com.

COMPLETE SET (26) 4.00 10.00
1 Todd Brost .15 .40
2 Rod Buskas .15 .40
3 Rich Chernomaz .15 .40
4 Kerry Clark .15 .40
5 Tomas Forslund .15 .40
6 Todd Gillingham .15 .40
7 Todd Harkins .15 .40
8 Tim Harris .15 .40
9 Shawn Heaphy .15 .40
10 Paul Holden .15 .40
11 Trevor Kidd .40 1.00
12 Paul Kruse .20 .50
13 Patrick Lebeau .20 .50
14 Sandy McCarthy .30 .75
15 Kris Miller .15 .40
16 Jason Muzzatti .20 .50
17 Alex Nikolic .15 .40
18 Ken Sabourin .15 .40
19 David St. Pierre .15 .40
20 Darren Stolk .15 .40
21 David Struch .15 .40
22 Andrei Trefilov .20 .50
23 Kevin Wortman .15 .40
24 Bob Francis CO .08 .25
25 Brian Patafie TR .02 .10
26 Team card .15 .40

1998-99 San Angelo Outlaws

This 27-card set was handed out early in the season over the span of several home games.

COMPLETE SET (27) 7.20 18.00
1 Jason Abel .30 .75
2 Jean Blouin .30 .75
3 Carl Boudreau .40 1.00
4 Daniel Chaput .30 .75
5 Ryan Connolly .30 .75
6 Brad Cook .30 .75
7 Marty Diamond .30 .75
8 Chad Erickson .40 1.00
9 Sandis Girvitch .30 .75
10 Ross Harris .40 1.00
11 Kevin McKinnon .30 .75
12 Aigars Mironovics .30 .75
13 Skeeter Moore .30 .75
14 Carl Paradis .40 1.00
15 Ryan Reid .30 .75
16 Al Rooney .30 .75
17 Shayne Stevenson .40 1.00
18 Mike Vandenberghe .30 .75
19 Kris Waltze .30 .75
20 Tom Nurre .30 .75
21 Rich Van Patten EM .08 .25
22 Shaun Clouston CO .08 .25
23 Ransom Mascot .08 .25
24 Rusty Mascot .08 .25
25 Jay Willman ANNC .08 .25
26 Jonathan Luce .30 .75
27 Joe Briley TR .08 .25

1999-00 San Angelo Outlaws

This 31-card set was sold by the team at the rink and through the mail. The set is numbered on the back up to 35, however, card numbers 16,20,25,and 30 do not exist.

COMPLETE SET (31) 30.00 75.00
1 Mike Bajurny 1.50 4.00
2 Scott Chartier 1.25 3.00
3 Jamie Garrick 1.25 3.00
4 Sandis Girvitch 1.25 3.00
5 Corey Isen 1.25 3.00
6 Ed Kowalski 1.25 3.00
7 Kevin Kreutzer 1.50 4.00
8 Adam Lord 1.50 4.00
9 Dave Lylyk 1.25 3.00
10 Kevin McKinnon 1.25 3.00
11 Skeeter Moore 1.25 3.00
12 Erik Noack 1.25 3.00
13 Carl Paradis 1.50 4.00
14 Pavel Evstigneev 1.25 3.00
15 Robby Sandrock 1.25 3.00
17 Kris Waltze 1.50 4.00
18 Dion Wandler 1.25 3.00
19 Darren Wright 1.25 3.00
21 San Angelo Coliseum .40 1.00
22 Frank Froio EQM .40 1.00
23 Jeff Smith 1.25 3.00
24 Harvard/Henry .40 1.00
26 Mike Collins CO .40 1.00
27 Off-Ice Officials .40 1.00
28 Ransom Mascot .40 1.00
29 Rusty Mascot .40 1.00
31 Inflatable Rusty .40 1.00
32 Side Rink Action .40 1.00
33 Team Photo .40 1.00
34 Jay Willman 1.25 3.00
35 Booster Club .40 1.00

1998-99 San Antonio Iguanas

This 21-card set was sold by the team at games and via mail order. The Jason MacIntyre card may have been pulled from some of the sets due to his lifetime ban from the WCHL that was issued during this season.

COMPLETE SET (21) 4.80 12.00
1 Ken Shepard .20 .50
2 John Hultberg .40 1.00
3 Brian Shantz .40 1.00
4 Paul Jackson .40 1.00
5 Iggy Mascot .02 .10
6 Jason MacIntyre .75 2.00
7 Pat Caron .20 .50
8 Mike Tobin .20 .50
9 Dave Doucette .20 .50
10 Marc Laforge .20 .50
11 Kevin Lune .20 .50
12 Jay Pylypuik .20 .50
13 Johnny Brdarovic .20 .50
14 Roy Gray .20 .50
15 Ricky Jacob .20 .50
16 Blair Rota .20 .50
17 Cheyne Lazar .20 .50
18 Trevor Matschke .20 .50
19 Fred Goltz .20 .50
20 Todd Gordon HCO .02 .10
21 Iguanas Cheerleaders .40 1.00

1999-00 San Antonio Iguanas

This set features the Iguanas of the CHL. The set was produced and sold by the team at home games.

COMPLETE SET (25) 4.00 10.00
1 San Antonio Iguanas .20 .50
2 Church's Chicken .01
3 Jason MacIntyre .20 .50
4 Trevor Matschke .20 .50
5 Johnny Brdarovich .20 .50
6 Scott Green .20 .50
7 Brian Shantz .30 .75
8 Henry Kuster .30 .75
9 Bob Westerby .30 .75
10 Blair Rota .20 .50
11 Garnet Jacobson .20 .50
12 Ricky Jacob .20 .50
13 Jeff Boettger .20 .50
14 Wade Gibson .20 .50
15 Sam Fields .20 .50
16 Marc Laforge .30 .75
17 Trevor Anderson .20 .50
18 Corwin Saurdiff .30 .75
19 Mitch Shawara .20 .50
20 Chris Stewart CO .08 .25
21 Craig Coxe CO .30 .75
22 Manny Sanchez TR .02 .10
23 Chad Daniels TR .02 .10
24 Iggy MAS .02 .10
25 San Antonio Iguanas CL .02 .10

2003-04 San Antonio Rampage

COMPLETE SET (24) 5.00 12.00
1 Scott Allen HCO .02 .10
2 Ian Herbers ACO .02 .10
3 Lukas Krajicek .30 .75
4 Daryl Andrews .30 .75
5 Mascot .02 .10
6 Kent Huskins .20 .50
7 Paul Elliott .20 .50
8 Grant McNeill .20 .50
9 Vaclav Nedorost .20 .50
10 Greg Campbell .30 .75
11 Sean O'Connor .20 .50
12 Ryan Jardine .20 .50
13 Brent Cullaton .20 .50

14 Denis Shvidki .20 .50
15 Josh Olson .20 .50
16 Eric Beaudoin .20 .50
17 Matt Dzieduszycki .20 .50
18 Petr Taticek .40 1.00
19 Michel Periard .20 .50
20 Simon Lajeunesse .40 1.00
21 Kristian Kudroc .20 .50
22 Lee Goren .30 .75
23 Travis Scott .30 .75
24 Sponsor .01 .05

2004-05 San Antonio Rampage

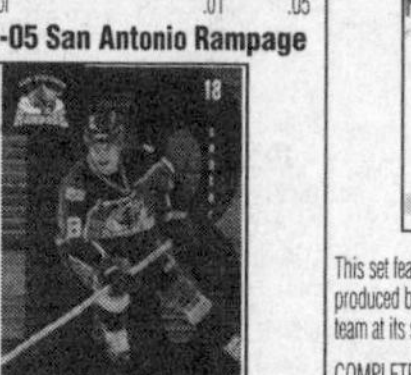

These cards are not numbered. Issued as a stadium giveaway.

COMPLETE SET (22) 10.00 25.00
1 Mascot .02 .10
2 Lukas Krajicek .40 1.00
3 T.J. Reynolds .40 1.00
4 Jay Bouwmeester .75 2.00
5 Filip Novak .40 1.00
6 Joel Kwiatkowski .40 1.00
7 Serge Payer .40 1.00
8 Stephen Weiss .75 2.00
9 Chris Nielsen .40 1.00
10 Gregory Campbell .75 2.00
11 Joe Cullen .40 1.00
12 Ryan Jardine .40 1.00
13 Rob Globke .75 2.00
14 Nathan Horton .75 2.00
15 Juraj Kolnik .40 1.00
16 Jeff Brown .40 1.00
17 Petr Taticek .40 1.00
18 Kamil Kreps .40 1.00
19 Patrick DesRochers 2.00
20 Victor Uchevatov .40 1.00
21 Travis Scott .40 1.00
22 Greg Jacina .40 1.00

1995-96 San Diego Barracudas RHI

This 14-card set is blank-backed, and features card fronts with varying border colours. Any additional information can be forwarded to hockeymag@beckett.com.

COMPLETE SET (14) 2.00 5.00
1 Dan Elsener .20 .50
2 Sandy Gasseau .20 .50
3 Brad Belland .20 .50
4 Stephen Grogg .20 .50
5 Frankie Ouellette .30 .75
6 Alan Leggett .20 .50
7 Soren True .20 .50
8 John Spoltore .30 .75
9 Ralph Barahona .20 .50
10 Oleg Yashin .20 .50
11 Stephane St. Amour .20 .50
12 Max Middendorf .30 .75
13 Clark Polgase .20 .50
14 Steve Martinson HCO .08 .25

1992-93 San Diego Gulls

This 24-card standard-size set features full-bleed, color player photos. The player's name is superimposed on the picture in red lettering. The player's position appears in a black circle in the lower left corner. The cards are unnumbered and checklisted below in alphabetical order.

COMPLETE SET (24) 4.00 10.00
1 John Anderson .20 .50
2 Perry Anderson .15 .40
3 Scott Arniel .20 .50
4 Michael Brewer .15 .40
5 Dale DeGray .15 .40
6 Gord Dineen .15 .40
7 Rick Dudley CO .15 .40
8 Larry Floyd .15 .40
9 Keith Gretzky .20 .50
10 Peter Hankinson .15 .40
11 Bill Houlder .20 .50
12 Andrei Iakovenko .15 .40
13 Rick Knickle .30 .75
14 Denny Lambert .20 .50
15 Mitch Lamoureux .20 .50
16 Clint Malarchuk .30 .75
17 Steve Martinson .15 .40
18 Hubie McDonough .15 .40
19 Don McSween .15 .40
20 Mitch Molloy .15 .40
21 Robbie Nichols .15 .40
22 Lindy Ruff .20 .50
23 Daniel Shank .30 .75
24 Sergei Starikov .15 .40

1999-00 San Diego Gulls

This set features the Gulls of the WCHL. The unnumbered cards were handed out in two different packs of 10 at a single home game late in the season.

COMPLETE SET (20) 6.00 15.00
1 Rod Aldoff .20 .50
2 Brad Belland .20 .50
3 Jamie Black .30 .75
4 Frederick Jobin .20 .50
5 Olaf Kjenstadt .30 .75
6 Brett Larson .20 .50
7 Steven Low .20 .50
8 B.J. MacPherson .20 .50
9 Petr Marek .20 .50
10 Taj Melson .20 .50
11 Sergei Naumov .60 1.50
12 Barry Potomski .60 1.50
13 Dennis Purdie .60 1.50
14 Martin St. Amour .30 .75
15 Stephane St. Amour .30 .75
16 Mark Woolf .30 .75
17 Steve Martinson HCO .30 .75
18 Gulls Win .20 .50
19 Goal Celebration .20 .50
20 Gulls Girls Cheerleaders .40 1.00

2000-01 San Diego Gulls

This set features the Gulls of the WCHL. The set was produced by Grandstand Cards and was sold by the team at its souvenir stands.

COMPLETE SET (22) 3.60 10.00
1 Jamie Black .16 .40
2 Cris Classen .16 .75
3 Serge Crochetiere .16 .40
4 Dan Gravelle .16 .40
5 Trevor Koenig .16 .75
6 Ashley Langdone .16 1.00
7 Brett Larson .16 .40
8 Cory Laylin .16 .40
9 B.J. MacPherson .16 .40
10 Kevin Mackie .16 .40
11 Petr Marek .16 .40
12 Taj Melson .16 .40
13 Brian Morrison .16 .40
14 Samy Nasreddine .16 .40
15 Jeff Petruic .16 .40
16 Dennis Purdie .30 .75
17 Mark Stitt .16 .40
18 Mike Taylor .16 .40
19 Chad Wagner .16 .40
20 Mark Woolf .16 .40
21 Gulls Score! .10 .25
22 San Diego Gulls Bench .16 .40

2001-02 San Diego Gulls

This set features the Gulls of the WCHL. These cards were handed out at a game on December 28, 2001. The set is unnumbered and is listed in alphabetical order.

COMPLETE SET (24) 10.00 25.00
1 Boyd Ballard .40 1.00
2 Jamie Black .40 1.00
3 Clint Cabana .40 1.00
4 Serge Crochetiere .40 1.00
5 Jaisen Freeman .40 1.00
6 Dan Gravelle .40 1.00
7 Trevor Koenig .40 1.00
8 Ashley Langdone .40 1.00
9 Shawn Mansoff .40 1.00
10 Petr Marek .40 1.00
11 Taj Melson .40 1.00
12 Brian Morrison .40 1.00
13 Samy Nasreddine .60 1.50
14 Billy Pugliese .40 1.00
15 Dennis Purdie .80 2.00
16 Trevor Sherban .40 1.00
17 John Spollore .80 2.00
18 Mark Stitt .40 1.00
19 Mark Woolf .80 2.00
20 B.J. MacPherson .60 1.50
21 Gulls Girls .80 2.00
22 Sandy MASCOT .04 .10
23 Gulls Bench .04 .10
24 Gulls Score! .20 .50

1994-95 San Jose Rhinos RHI

This set features the Rhinos of Roller Hockey Intl. The cards were sold in set form by the team at home games.

COMPLETE SET (16) 3.00 8.00
1 Rocky Mascot .08 .25
2 Ken Blum .20 .50
3 Steve Carpenter .20 .50
4 Will Clarke .20 .50
5 Darren Colbourne .20 .50
6 Bart Cote .20 .50
7 Brian Goudie .20 .50
8 Jon Gustafson .30 .75
9 Greg Hadden .20 .50
10 Blaine Moore .20 .50
11 Jay Murphy .20 .50
12 Dennis Purdie .40 1.00
13 Roy Sommer CO .08 .25
14 Mike Taylor .20 .50
15 Darren Wetherill .20 .50
16 Mark Woolf .30 .75

1994-95 Sarnia Sting

Sponsored by Big V Drug Stores and Pizza Hut and printed by Slapshot Images Ltd., this 31-card set commemorates the Sting's inaugural year. On a black and silver background, the fronts feature color action player photos with thin grey borders. The player's name, position and team name, as well as the producer's logo, also appear on the front.

COMPLETE SET (31) 4.00 10.00
1 Checklist .02 .10
2 Ken Carroll .10 .30
3 Scott Hay .10 .30
4 Kam White .10 .30
5 Joe Doyle .10 .30
6 Tom Brown .10 .30
7 Jeremy Miculinic .10 .30
8 Darren Mortier .10 .30
9 Aaron Brand .20 .50
10 Chris George .10 .30
11 Stephane Soulliere .10 .30
12 Paul McInnes .10 .30
13 Trevor Letowski .40 1.00
14 Dustin McArthur .10 .30
15 Rob Massa .10 .30
16 Brendan Yarema .10 .30
17 Dan DelMonte .10 .30
18 B.J. Johnston .10 .30
19 Wes Mason .10 .30
20 Rob Guinn .10 .30
21 Jeff Brown .10 .30
22 Dennis Maxwell .10 .30
23 Damon Hardy .10 .30
24 Alan Letang .20 .50
25 Matt Hogan .10 .30
26 Sasha Cucuz .10 .30
27 Rich Brown CO .02 .10
28 Gord Hamilton TR .02 .10
29 Dino Ciccarelli Shawn Burr .20 .50
30 Buzz MASCOT .02 .10
NNO Ad Card .04 .01

1995-96 Sarnia Sting

COMPLETE SET (25) 5.00 12.00
1 Jeff Salajko .20 .50
2 Patrick DesRochers .30 .75
3 Gerald Moriarity .30 .75
4 Allan Carr .20 .50
5 Tom Brown .20 .50
6 Andy Delmore .30 .75
7 Darren Mortier .20 .50
8 Aaron Brand .20 .50
9 Eric Boulton .60 1.50
10 Jonathan Sim .30 .75
11 Trevor Letowski .30 .75
12 Mike Hanson .20 .50
13 Todd Miller .20 .50
14 Brendan Yarema .20 .50
15 Brad Simms .20 .50
16 David Nemirovsky .20 .50
17 Jeff Brown .20 .50
18 Andrew Proskurnicki .20 .50
19 Wes Mason .20 .50
20 Scott Corbett .20 .50
21 Dave Bourque .20 .50
22 Sean Brown .20 .50
23 Marcin Snita .20 .50
24 Rich Brown ACO .02 .10
25 Mark Hunter HCO .08 .25

1996-97 Sarnia Sting

This attractive 31-card set was produced by Haines Printing for the Sting and was distributed by the club at the rink. The cards feature action photography on the front, with the player's name and number, and the insignia of the sponsor, Bayview Chrysler, along the bottom. The set is noteworthy for the inclusion of a special card of captain Trevor Letowski as a member of the Canadian National Junior team.

COMPLETE SET (31) 6.00 10.00
1 Bill Abercrombie ACO .02 .10
2 Louie Blackbird .15 .40
3 Bryan Blair .15 .40
4 Dave Bourque .15 .40
5 Joe Canale CO .08 .25
6 Scott Corbett .15 .40
7 Andy Delmore .30 .75
8 Patrick DesRochers .30 .75
9 Michael Hanson .15 .40
10 Abe Herbst .20 .50
11 Shane Kenny .15 .40
12 Darryl Knight .15 .40
13 Trevor Letowski .40 1.00
14 Trevor Letowski Team Canada .40 1.00
15 Wes Mason .20 .50
16 Darren Mortier .15 .40
17 Kevin Mota .15 .40
18 Eoin McInerney .30 .75
19 Lucas Nehrling .15 .40
20 Dan Pawlaczyk .15 .40
21 Andrew Proskurnicki .15 .40
22 Richard Rochefort .15 .40
23 Bogdan Rudenko .15 .40
24 Jon Sim .40 1.00
25 Brad Simms .15 .40
26 Marcin Snita .15 .40
27 Casey Wolak .15 .40
28 Season Line-Up .01
29 Title Card .01
30 Team Logo .02 .10
31 Calendar Card .01

2000-01 Sarnia Sting

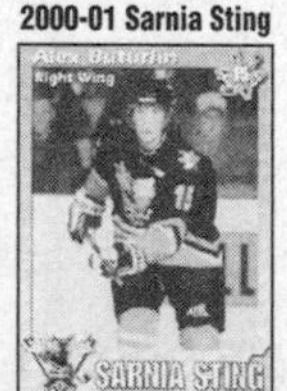

This set features the Sting of the OHL. The set was produced by the team and sold at home games. The cards are unnumbered, and are listed below alphabetically.

COMPLETE SET (24) 4.80 12.00
1 Header Card .04 .01
2 Larry Bernard CO .10 .25
3 Chris Berti .20 .50
4 Cory Brekelmans .20 .50
5 Rick Brown CO .10 .25
6 Alex Buturlin .30 .50
7 Adam Campbell .20 .50
8 Tyler Coleman .20 .50
9 Ryan Fraser .20 .50
10 Robert Gherson .30 1.00
11 Julius Halfkenny .20 .50
12 Ryan Hare .20 .50
13 John Hecimovic .20 .50
14 Scott Heffernan .20 .50
15 Eric Himelfarb .30 1.00
16 Dusty Jamieson .30 .75
17 Jeff Luckovitch .20 .50
18 Preston Mizzi .20 .50
19 Kris Newbury .30 .75
20 Robb Palahnuk .20 .50
21 Jason Penner .30 .75
22 Tom Rogerson .20 .50
23 Maxim Rybin .30 .75
24 Reg Thomas .20 .50

2003-04 Sarnia Sting

COMPLETE SET (23) 5.00 12.00
1 Charles Amodeo .20 .50
2 John Barrow .30 .75
3 Marco Caprara .30 .75
4 Daniel Carcillo .75 2.00
5 Marek Chvatal .20 .50
6 Richard Clune .20 .50
7 Craig Foster .20 .50
8 Dan Fritsche .75 2.00
9 Micheal Haley .20 .50
10 John Hecimovic .20 .50
11 Anton Kadeykin .20 .50
12 Colt King .30 .75
13 Drew Larman .20 .50
14 Matt Manias .20 .50
15 Ryan Munce .60 1.50
16 Matt Pelech .20 .50
17 David Pszenyczny .20 .50
18 Daniel Sisca .20 .50
19 Trevor Solomon .20 .50
20 Joey Tenute .30 .75
21 Steve Ward .20 .50
22 Jeff Whitfield .20 .50
23 Kelsey Wilson .20 .50

2006-07 Sarnia Sting

COMPLETE SET (22) 12.00 20.00
1 Steven Stamkos 2.00 5.00
2 Trevor Kell .30 .75
3 Tomas Pospisil .30 .75
4 Steven Reese .30 .75
5 Steve Ferry .30 .75
6 Sebastian Dahm .40 1.00
7 Ryan Wilson .30 .75
8 Parker Van Buskirk .40 1.00
9 Mike Roelofsen .30 .75
10 Matt Martin .30 .75
11 Mark Katic .50 1.25
12 Kyle Tront .30 .75
13 Justin DiBenedetto .30 .75
14 Jared Gomes .30 .75
15 Harrison Reed .30 .75
16 Danny Anger .30 .75
17 Daniel Lombardi .30 .75
18 Dalton Prout .30 .75
19 Christian Steingraber .30 .75
20 Chris Mifflen .30 .75
21 Brandon Mashinter .30 .75
22 Bobby Davey .30 .75

2007-08 Sarnia Sting

COMPLETE SET (25) 5.00 12.00
1 Tomi Karhunen .15 .40
2 Peter DiSalvo .15 .40
3 Ryan Berard .15 .40
4 Justin DiBenedetto .15 .40
5 Devin Didiomete .15 .40
6 Steve Ferry .15 .40
7 Jared Gomes .15 .40
8 Jordan Hill .15 .40
9 Marek Indra .15 .40
10 Mark Katic .15 .40
11 Colt Kennedy .15 .40
12 Dan Lombardi .15 .40
13 Matt Martin .15 .40
14 Brett Oliphant .15 .40
15 Ben O'Quinn .15 .40
16 Dalton Prout .15 .40
17 Harrison Reed .15 .40
18 Steve Reese .15 .40
19 Joe Rogalski .15 .40
20 Matt Smyth .15 .40
21 Steven Stamkos 1.00 2.50
22 Steve Whitely .15 .40
23 Ryan Wilson .15 .40
24 Aaron Snow .15 .40
25 Jamie Arniel .15 .40

1992-93 Saskatchewan JHL

This 168-card set features players in the Saskatchewan Junior Hockey League. The cards are slightly larger than standard size, measuring 2 9/16" by 3 9/16." The fronts feature color action player photos with team color-coded borders at the top and bottom. The player's name and position appear in the top border. The team name and logo appear in the wider bottom border.

COMPLETE SET (168) 8.00 20.00
1 Troy Edwards .05 .15
2 Simon Oliver .05 .15
3 Gerald Tallaire .05 .15
4 Blair Allison .05 .15
5 Mads True .05 .15
6 Steve Brent .05 .15
7 Jay Dobrescu .05 .15
8 Dave Debusschere .05 .15
9 Bryan Cossette .05 .15
10 Brooke Battersby .05 .15
11 Kyle Niemegeers .05 .15
12 Darren McLean .05 .15
13 Carson Cardinal .05 .15
14 Bill McKay .05 .15
15 Chris Hatch .05 .15
16 Nolan Weir .05 .15
17 Karl Johnson .05 .15
18 Jason Brown .05 .15
19 Tyler Kuhn .05 .15
20 Daniel Dennis .05 .15
21 Wally Spence .05 .15
22 Rob Beck .05 .15
23 Aaron Cain .20 .50
24 Darryl Dickson .05 .15
25 Travis Cheyne .05 .15
26 Mark Leoppky .05 .15
27 Jason Ahenakew .05 .15
28 Kyle Paul .05 .15
29 Dean Normand .05 .15
30 Brett Kinaschuk .05 .15
31 Darren Schmidt .05 .15
32 Chris Schinkel .05 .15
33 David Foster .05 .15
34 Jason Zimmerman .05 .15
35 Tom Perry .05 .15
36 Kent Kinaschuk .05 .15
37 Collin Froese .05 .15
38 Shawn Zimmerman .05 .15
39 Larry Empey .05 .15
40 Curtis Knight .05 .15
41 Blake Shipley .05 .15
42 Cory Heon .05 .15
43 Steve Pashulka .05 .15
44 Rob Kinch .05 .15
45 Dean Gerard .05 .15
46 Matt Desmarais .05 .15
47 Chad Rusnak .05 .15
48 Brad Bagu .05 .15
49 Cam Bristow .05 .15
50 Derek Simonson .05 .15
51 Ken Ruddock .05 .15
52 Tyler Deis .05 .15
53 Steve Tansowny .05 .15
54 Bill Stait .05 .15
55 Garfield Henderson .05 .15
56 Lonny Deobald .05 .15
57 Lyle Ehrmantraut .05 .15
58 Layne Humenny .05 .15
59 Darren Balcombe .05 .15
60 Jeff McCutheon .05 .15
61 Trevor Wathen .05 .15
62 Derek Wynne .05 .15
63 Matt Russo .05 .15
64 Bruce Matatall .05 .15
65 Derek Crimin .05 .15
66 Chad Crumley .05 .15
67 Mike Hillock .05 .15
68 Art Houghton .05 .15
69 Lee Materi .05 .15
70 Nick Dyhr .05 .15
71 Darren Maloney .05 .15
72 Kurtise Souchotte .05 .15
73 Noel Kamel .05 .15
74 Trent Harper .05 .15
75 Ted Grayling .05 .15
76 Keith Harris .05 .15
77 Corri Moffat .05 .15
78 Travis Vantighem .05 .15
79 Darren Houghton .05 .15
80 Wade Welte .05 .15
81 Dave Doucet .05 .15
82 Jason Prokopetz .05 .15
83 Gordon McCann .05 .15
84 Clint Hooge .05 .15
85 Glen McGillvary .05 .15
86 Regan Simpson .05 .15
87 Mike Masse .05 .15
88 Jeremy Procyshyn .05 .15
89 Jim Nellis .05 .15
90 Todd Kozak .05 .15
91 Brent Hoiness .05 .15
92 Josh Welter .05 .15
Jason Welter
93 Eldon Barker .05 .15
94 Duane Vandale .05 .15
95 Brad McEwen .05 .15
96 Trent Tibbatts .05 .15
97 Jody Reiter .05 .15
98 Greg Moore .05 .15
99 Jon Rowe .05 .15
100 Mike Evans .05 .15
101 Jason Krug .05 .15
102 Jon Bracco .05 .15
103 Ryan Sandholm .05 .15
104 Darryl Sangster .05 .15
105 Brett Colborne .05 .15
106 Dean Moore .05 .15
107 Chris Dechaine .05 .15
108 Steve McKenna .05 .15
109 Tony Bergin .05 .15
110 Tim Murray .05 .15
111 Casey Kesselring .05 .15
112 Todd Barth .05 .15
113 Ryan McConnell .05 .15
114 Ian Adamson .05 .15
115 Warren Pickford .05 .15
116 Todd Murphy .05 .15
117 Rob Phillips .05 .15
118 Trevor Demmans .05 .15
119 Jeff Greenwood .05 .15
120 Kevin Messer .05 .15
121 Dion Johnson .05 .15
122 Rejean Stringer .05 .15
123 Scott Mead .05 .15
124 Jeff Lawson .05 .15
125 Scot Newberry .05 .15
126 Bill Reid .05 .15
127 Chris Winkler .05 .15
128 Kyle Girgan .05 .15
129 Trevor Warrener .05 .15
130 Richard Boscher .05 .15
131 Tom Thomson .05 .15
132 Mike Wevers .05 .15
133 Barton Holt .05 .15
134 Kent Rogers .05 .15
135 Richard Gibbs .05 .15
136 Jared Witt .05 .15
137 Jamie Stelmak .05 .15
138 Greg Wahl .05 .15
139 J. Sotropa .05 .15
140 Mark Pivetz .05 .15
141 Travis Kirby .05 .15
142 Jason Scanzano .05 .15
143 Tyson Balog .05 .15
144 Daryl Krauss .05 .15
145 Mike Harder .05 .15
146 Tyler McMillan .05 .15
147 Darcy Herlick .05 .15
148 Dave Zwyer .05 .15
149 Craig McKechnie .05 .15
150 Cam Cook .05 .15
151 Derek Bruselinck .05 .15
152 Travis Smith .05 .15
153 Daryl Jones .05 .15
154 Mike Savard .05 .15
155 Jeremy Matthies .05 .15
156 Michel Cook .05 .15
157 Leigh Brookbank .05 .15
158 Christian Dutil .05 .15
159 Scott Heshka .05 .15
160 Danny Galarneau .05 .15
161 Jamie Dunn .05 .15
162 Nigel Werenka .05 .15
163 Steve Sabo .05 .15
164 Tony Toth .05 .15
165 Sebastien Moreau .05 .15
166 Tim Slukynsky .05 .15
167 Sheldon Bylsma .05 .15
168 Stacy Prevost .10 .30

1981-82 Saskatoon Blades

This 25-card P.L.A.Y. (Police, Laws and Youth) set was sponsored by the Saskatoon Police Department and area businesses. The cards measure approximately 2 1/2" by 3 3/4" and are printed on thin card stock. The fronts feature white-bordered color photos with the player's posed in action stances. The player's name, biographical information, and position appear in the bottom white margin. The team logo appears in the lower left corner.

COMPLETE SET (25) 10.00 25.00
1 Blades Team Photo .75 2.00
2 Daryl Stanley .30 .75
3 Leroy Gorski .30 .75
4 Donn Clark .30 .75
5 Brad Duggan .30 .75
6 Dave Chartier .30 .75
7 Dave Brown 1.25 3.00
8 Adam Thompson .30 .75
9 Bruce Eakin .30 .75
10 Brian Skrudland 1.25 3.00
11 Roger Kortko .30 .75
12 Ron Dreger .30 .75
13 Daryl Lubiniecki .30 .75
14 Marc Habscheid .75 2.00
15 Saskatoon Police Logo .20 .50
16 Todd Strueby .40 1.00
17 Craig Hurley .30 .75
18 Bill Hlynsky .30 .75
19 Lane Lambert .75 2.00
20 Mike Bloski .30 .75
21 Bruce Gordon .30 .75
22 Perry Ganchar .40 1.00
23 Ron Loustel .30 .75
24 Blades Logo .20 .50
25 Checklist Card .20 .50

1983-84 Saskatoon Blades

This set contains 24 P.L.A.Y. (Police, Law and Youth) cards and features the Saskatoon Blades of the Western Hockey League. The cards measure approximately 2 7/16" by 3 3/4". The fronts feature a color posed action shot with white borders. The team logo appears in the lower left corner, with player information to the right in black lettering.

COMPLETE SET (24) 12.00 30.00
1 Team Photo .40 1.00
2 Trent Yawney .40 1.00
3 Grant Jennings .40 1.00
4 Duncan MacPherson .20 .50
5 Greg Holtby .20 .50
6 Dan Leier .20 .50
7 Dwaine Hutton .20 .50
8 Wendel Clark 6.00 15.00
9 Kerry Laviolette .20 .50
10 Dave Chartier .20 .50
11 Dale Henry .20 .50
12 Randy Smith .20 .50
13 Kevin Kowalchuk .20 .50
14 Todd McLellan .20 .50
15 Title Card Saskatoon Police .08 .25
16 Larry Korchinski .20 .50
17 Curtis Chamberlain .20 .50
18 Greg Lebsack .20 .50
19 Ron Dreger .20 .50
20 Doug Kyle .20 .50
21 Rick Smith .20 .50
22 Joey Kocur 2.00 5.00
23 Allan Larochelle .20 .50
24 Mark Thietke .20 .50

1984-85 Saskatoon Blades Stickers

This set of 20 stickers was sponsored by Autotec Oil and Saskatchewan Ronald McDonald House. Each sticker measures approximately 2" by 1 3/4" and could be pasted on a 17" by 11" poster printed in thin glossy paper. The stickers display a black-and-white head shot; the uniform number is also printed on the front. The stickers are unnumbered and checklisted below in alphabetical order.

COMPLETE SET (20) 10.00 25.00
1 Jack Bowkus .30 .75
2 Curtis Chamberlain .30 .75
3 Wendel Clark 6.00 15.00
4 Ron Dreger .30 .75
5 Randy Hoffart .30 .75
6 Mark Holick .30 .75
7 Greg Holtby .30 .75
8 Grant Jennings .40 1.00
9 Kevin Kowalchuk .30 .75
10 Bryan Larkin .30 .75
11 James Latos .30 .75
12 Duncan MacPherson .30 .75
13 Rod Matechuk .30 .75
14 Todd McLellan .30 .75
15 Darren Moren .30 .75
16 Mike Morin .30 .75
17 Devon Oleniuk .30 .75
18 Grant Tkachuk .30 .75
19 Troy Vollhoffer .30 .75
20 Trent Yawney .40 1.00

1986-87 Saskatoon Blades Photos

This set is comprised of 25 photos of members of the WHL's Saskatoon Blades. The photos measure a large 8 X 11.5 inches, and bear the mark of sponsor Shell Oil.

COMPLETE SET (24) 14.00 35.00
1 Blair Atcheynum .75 2.00
2 Colin Bayer .40 1.00
3 Jack Bowkus .40 1.00
4 Mike Butkas .40 1.00
5 Kelly Chase 2.00 5.00
6 Tim Cheveldae .75 2.00
7 Blaine Chrest .40 1.00
8 Kerry Clark .40 1.00
9 Brian Glynn .40 1.00
10 Mark Holick .40 1.00
11 Kevin Kaminski .75 2.00
12 Tracey Katelnikoff .40 1.00
13 Kory Kocur .40 1.00
14 Bryan Larkin .40 1.00
15 Curtis Leschyshyn .75 2.00
16 Dan Logan .40 1.00
17 Todd MacLellan .40 1.00
18 Devon Oleniuk .40 1.00
19 Marty Prazma .40 1.00
20 Marty Weimer .40 1.00
21 Walter Shutter .40 1.00
22 Grant Tkachuk .40 1.00
23 Tony Twist 2.00 5.00
24 Shaun Van Allen .75 2.00

1988-89 Saskatoon Blades

This standard size set features posed color photos on the front, and safety tips and logos on the back. Cards are numbered as seen below.

COMPLETE SET (25) 4.00 10.00
1 Joe Penkala .20 .50
2 Saskatoon Police Emblem .07 .20
3 Marcel Comeau .20 .50
4 Dean Kuntz .20 .50
5 Mike Greenlay .20 .50
6 Jody Praznik .20 .50
7 Ken Sutton .20 .50
8 Sawn Snesar .20 .50
9 Shane Langager .20 .50
10 Dean Holdien .20 .50
11 Rob Lelacheur .20 .50
12 David Struch .20 .50
13 Collin Bauer .20 .50
14 Kevin Yellowaga .20 .50
15 Drew Sawtell .20 .50
16 Brian Gerrits .20 .50
17 Kirk Roworth .20 .50
18 Tracey Katelnikoff .20 .50
19 Scott Scissons .20 .50
20 Jason Smart .20 .50
21 Jason Christie .20 .50
22 Daren Bader .20 .50
23 Kevin Kaminski .20 .50
24 Kory Kocur .20 .50
25 Darwin McPherson .20 .50

1989-90 Saskatoon Blades

These standard-sized cards feature the Blades of the Western Hockey League. It is believed that they were issued individually by members of the local police, rather than issued in team set form.

COMPLETE SET (25) 6.00 15.00
1 Terry Ruskowski .30 .75
2 Cam Moon .20 .50
3 Damon Kustra .20 .50
4 Trevor Robins .20 .50
5 Mark Raiter .20 .50
6 Mark Wotton .30 .75
7 Shawn Snesar .20 .50
8 Trevor Sherban .20 .50
9 Shane Langager .20 .50
10 Dean Holdien .20 .50
11 Rob Lelacheur .20 .50
12 David Struch .20 .50
13 Derek Tibbatts .20 .50
14 Drew Sawtell .20 .50
15 Richard Matvichuk .60 1.50
16 Trent Coghill .20 .50
17 Jeff Buchanan .20 .50
18 Grant Chorney .20 .50
19 Shawn Yakimishyn .20 .50
20 Scott Scissons .20 .50
21 Jason Smart .20 .50
22 Jason Christie .20 .50
23 Darin Bader .20 .50
24 Dean Rambo .20 .50
25 Collin Bauer .20 .50

1990-91 Saskatoon Blades

This 27-card P.L.A.Y. (Police, Laws and Youth) set was sponsored by the Saskatoon Police Department and area businesses. The cards measure approximately 2 1/2" by 3 3/4" and are printed on thin card stock. On a blue card face, the fronts feature white-bordered posed action color photos. The player's name, position, and biographical information appear in the bottom blue margin. The yellow and blue team logo appears in the lower right corner.

COMPLETE SET (27) 4.80 12.00
1 Terry Ruskowski CO .25 .60
2 Trevor Robins .20 .50
3 Cam Moon .20 .50
4 Jeff Buchanan .20 .50
5 Mark Raiter .20 .50
6 Trevor Sherban .20 .50
7 Jason Knox .20 .50
8 Dean Rambo .20 .50
9 Rob LeLacheur .20 .50
10 David Struch .20 .50
11 Greg Leahy .20 .50
12 Derek Tibbatts .20 .50
13 Shane Calder .20 .50
14 Richard Matvichuk .40 1.00
15 Trent Coghill .20 .50
16 Mark Wotton .25 .60
17 Kelly Markwart .20 .50
18 Mark Franks .20 .50
19 Scott Scissons .20 .50
20 Tim Cox .20 .50
21 Gaetan Blouin .20 .50
22 Darin Bader .20 .50
23 Shawn Yakimishyn .20 .50
24 Ryan Strain .20 .50
25 Jason Peters .20 .50
26 Team Card .20 .50
27 Title Card .20 .50

1991-92 Saskatoon Blades

This 25-card P.L.A.Y. (Police, Laws and Youth) set was issued as a sheet measuring approximately 12 1/2" by 17 1/2", with five rows of five cards each. If cut, the individual cards would measure the standard size. On a black card face, the fronts feature posed color player photos with thin white borders. The player's name and biography along with the team's 25th anniversary logo appear below the picture.

COMPLETE SET (25) 4.80 12.00
1 Lorne Molleken CO .08 .25
2 Trevor Robins .20 .50
3 Norm Maracle .40 1.00
4 Jeff Buchanan .20 .50
5 Mark Raiter .20 .50
6 Bryce Goebel .20 .50
7 Rhett Trombley .30 .75
8 Chad Rusnak .20 .50
9 Jason Knight .20 .50
10 David Struch .20 .50
11 Shane Calder .20 .50
12 Derek Tibbatts .20 .50
13 Glen Gulutzan .20 .50
14 Richard Matvichuk .60 1.50
15 Chad Michalchuk .20 .50
16 Mark Wotton .30 .75
17 Mark Franks .20 .50
18 Andy MacIntyre .20 .50
19 Ryan Fujita .20 .50
20 Sean McFatridge .20 .50
21 Jason Becker .20 .50
22 Shawn Yakimishyn .20 .50
23 James Startup .20 .50
24 Paul Buczkowski .20 .50
NNO McGruff .02 .10

1993-94 Saskatoon Blades

Sponsored by Coca-Cola, this is an oversized 24-card set measuring approximately 8 1/2" by 5 1/2". The borderless fronts feature posed color player photos on the ice surrounded by a Coca-Cola advertising display. The player's name and number in black letters appear in the lower left corner. The words "Best on Ice - Blades and Coca-Cola" are printed over the top of the photo in red, white, and blue. The backs are blank. The cards are unnumbered and checklisted below in alphabetical order.

COMPLETE SET (24) 4.80 12.00
1 Chad Allan .20 .50
2 Frank Banham .25 .60
3 Frank Banham .25 .60
Mark Deyell
Ivan Salon
4 Wade Belak .20 .50
5 Paul Buczkowski .20 .50
6 Shane Calder .25 .60
7 Mark Deyell .30 .75
8 Jason Duda .20 .50
9 Trevor Ethier .20 .50
10 Mike Gray .20 .50
11 Trevor Hanas .20 .50
12 Devon Hanson .20 .50
13 Andrew Kemper .20 .50
14 Kirby Law .20 .50
15 Andy Macintyre .20 .50
16 Norm Maracle .40 1.00
17 Ivan Salon .20 .50
18 Todd Simpson .20 .50
19 Derek Tibbatts .20 .50
20 Derek Tibbatts .20 .50
Clarke Wilm
Andy Macintyre
21 Rhett Warrener .30 .75
22 Clarke Wilm .30 .75
23 Mark Wotton .25 .60
24 Team Photo .20 .50

1995-96 Saskatoon Blades

The 27 oversized (2 1/2" by 4 1/2") cards set feature the Saskatoon Blades of the WHL. Apparently, the cards were issued as a promotional giveaway at PW Pharmacies in Saskatoon. The front displays a color action photo, along with the player's name and number and the Blades logo. A Carlton cards logo appears in the upper right. The backs contain biographical information as well as the logos of all participating sponsors. Complete cards also included a coupon for savings on various products at PW. The cards are worth 50 percent of the value below without the coupon. The cards are unnumbered and thus are checklisted below in alphabetical order.

COMPLETE SET (27) 4.80 12.00
1 Chad Allan .20 .50
2 Frank Banham .30 .75
3 Dennis Bassett .20 .50
4 Wade Belak .30 .75
5 Ryan Bonni .30 .75
6 Paul Buczkowski .20 .50
7 Don Clark CO .20 .50
8 Mathieu Cusson .20 .50
9 Mark Deyell .30 .75
10 Pavel Kriz .20 .50
11 Jeromie Kufflick .20 .50
12 Laird Laluk .20 .50
13 Erik Leelle .20 .50
14 Richard Peacock .20 .50
15 Greg Phillips .20 .50
16 Garrett Prosofsky .30 .75
17 Nathan Rempel .20 .50
18 Cory Sarich .40 1.00
19 Jeremy Schaefer .20 .50
20 Mark Smith .20 .50
21 Martin Sonnenberg .20 .50
22 Randy Weinberger .20 .50
23 Clark Wilm .30 .75
24 Team Logo CL .02 .10
25 Crime Stoppers Logo .02 .10
26 Celebration 30 Years .02 .10
27 Assistant Coaches .02 .10
Chartier
Engele
Federke

1996-97 Saskatoon Blades

This set of the Saskatoon Blades features 28 oversized (2 1/2" X 4 1/2") cards. The fronts display color photos, with the player's name, jersey number and Blades logo inscribed along the bottom. The backs feature biographical data, a safety tip, and the locations of every PW Pharmacy in Saskatoon. PW sponsored the set as a promotional giveaway at local stores. Interestingly, the backs exhort fans to collect all 27 cards, but the set contains 28. The cards come attached to money-saving coupons from PW; if the coupon is removed, the value is 50 percent that listed below. The unnumbered cards are checklisted below alphabetically.

COMPLETE SET (28) 4.80 12.00
1 Stewart Bacharuk .20 .50
2 Jon Barkman .20 .50
3 Justin Bekkering .20 .50
4 Derek Bjornson .20 .50
5 Ryan Bonni .20 .50
6 Christian Chartier .30 .75
7 Matt Cockell .20 .50
8 Mathieu Cusson .20 .50
9 Jared Dumba .20 .50
10 Ryan Gaucher .20 .50
11 Ryan Henderson .20 .50
12 Ryan Johnston .20 .50
13 Vladislav Klochkov .20 .50
14 Laird Laluk .20 .50
15 Tyler Love .20 .50
16 Sheldon Nedielski .20 .50
17 Greg Phillips .20 .50
18 Garrett Prosofsky .20 .50
19 Nathan Rempel .20 .50
20 Cory Sarich .20 .50
21 Brian Skrudland .20 .50
22 Martin Sonnenberg .20 .50
23 Lyle Steenbergen .20 .50
24 Rhett Warrener .30 .75
25 Kyle Werner .20 .50
26 Team Logo CL .08 .25
27 Action/Goal .08 .25
28 Team(Reebok) .08 .25

1997-98 Saskatoon Blades

Released by the Blades in conjunction with Coca-Cola, this 25-card set features oversized cards with full color action photography and blank backs. The fronts also feature a ghosted area to facilitate autographing. One card remains unidentified in this set. If you have information on their identities, please forward them to hockeymag@beckett.com. The set is not numbered, therefore it appears in alphabetical order.

COMPLETE SET (25) 4.80 12.00
1 Jon Barkman .20 .50
2 Derek Bjornson .20 .50
3 Ryan Bonni .30 .75
4 Christian Chartier .30 .75
5 Matt Cockell .20 .50
6 Mathieu Cusson .20 .50
7 Chad Elmy .20 .50
8 Ryan Gaucher .20 .50
9 Derek Halldorson .20 .50
10 Ryan Johnston .20 .50
11 Dylan Kemp .20 .50
12 Tyler Mackay .20 .50
13 Kevin McKay .30 .75
14 Matt Miller .20 .50
15 Dennis Mullen .20 .50
16 Greg Phillips .20 .50
17 Petja Pietilainen .20 .50
18 Garrett Prosofsky .30 .75
19 Nathan Rempel .20 .50
20 Darcy Robinson .20 .50
21 Cory Sarich .30 .75
22 Martin Sonnenberg .30 .75
23 Mascot .08 .25
24 Header Card .08 .25
25 unknown .20 .50

2000-01 Saskatoon Blades

This set features the Blades of the WHL. The cards were sold at the team's home games.

COMPLETE SET (32) 4.80 12.00
1 Logo Card .04 .11
2 Team Photo .16 .40
3 Kevin Dickie CO .10 .25
4 Bruno Baseotto ACO .10 .25
5 Tim Cheveldae ACO .16 .40
6 Jason Goulet .16 .40
7 Matt Suderman .16 .40
8 Scotty Balan .20 .50
9 Ryan Stempfle .16 .40
10 Kane Ludwar .16 .40
11 Adrian Foster .40 1.00
12 Martin Erat .40 1.00
13 Garrett Bembridge .16 .40
14 Davin Heintz .16 .40
15 Justin Wallin .16 .40
16 Trent Adamus .16 .40
17 Jeff Coulter .16 .40
18 Chris Manchakowski .16 .40
19 Justin Kanigan .16 .40
20 David Cameron .16 .40
21 Derek Halldorson .16 .40
22 Aaron Starr .16 .40
23 Ryan Kehrig .16 .40
24 Rob Woods .16 .40
25 Warren Peters .16 .40
26 Petr Prochazka .16 .40
27 Justin Kelly .16 .40
28 Michael Garnett .16 .40
29 Tony Kolewaski .16 .40
30 Martin Vymazal .16 .40
31 Helmutt MASCOT .04 .11
32 Jay Richards DJ .04 .11

2001-02 Saskatoon Blades

This set features the Blades of the WHL. Little has been confirmed to date regarding this set, but it is believed that they were sold at home games.

COMPLETE SET (32) 6.00 15.00
1 Header .04 .10
2 Derek Couture .20 .50
3 Paul Gentile .20 .50
4 Willy Glover .20 .50
5 Kyle Harris .20 .50
6 Davin Heintz .20 .50
7 Adam Huxley .20 .50
8 Justin Keller .20 .50
9 Ryan Keller 1.00 2.00
10 Justin Kelly .20 .50
11 Richard Mueller .20 .50
12 Warren Peters .20 .50
13 Tim Preston .20 .50
14 Daniel Volrab .20 .50
15 Trent Adamus .20 .50
16 Tiger Williams/Kelly Hrudey .40 1.00
17 Scotty Balan .20 .50
18 Mike Green .60 1.50
19 Kane Ludwar .20 .50
20 Stephen Mann .20 .50
21 Sean Moir .20 .50
22 Ryan Stempfle .20 .50
23 Matt Suderman .20 .50
24 Rob Woods .20 .50
25 Michael Garnett .50 1.00
26 Ryan Senft .20 .50
27 Helmutt .04 .10
28 Steve Hildebrand TR .04 .10
29 Kevin Dickie CO .04 .10
30 Bruno Baseotto .04 .10
31 Wendel Clark Night .40 1.00
32 Team Photo .20 .50

2002-03 Saskatoon Blades

COMPLETE SET (30)
1 Evan Haw .50
2 Sean Moir .50
3 Matt Suderman .50
4 Matt Bergen .50
5 Steven Later .50
6 Denny Johnston .50
7 Trent Adamus .50
8 Michael Bubnick .50
9 Marcus Paulsson .50
10 Adam Houle .50
11 Daniel Volrab .50
12 Wacey Rabbit .50
13 Derek Couture .50
14 Joe Barnes .50
15 Rob Woods .50
16 Warren Peters .50
17 Adam Huxley .75
18 Mike Green 1.00
19 John Dahl .50
20 Stephen Mann .50
21 Adam Ward .75
22 Brett Jaeger .75
23 Ryan Keller .50
24 Tanner Shultz .50
25 Jack Brodsky PRES .10
26 Brent McEwan GM .10
27 Kevin Dickie CO .10
28 Bruno Baseotto ACO .10
29 Stev Hildebrand TR .10
30 Team Photo/CL .10

2003-04 Saskatoon Blades

COMPLETE SET (23) 6.00 15.00
1 Mascot .02 .10
2 Team Photo .02 .10
3 Boris Lekovic .30 .75
4 Adam Ward .30 .75
5 Joel Eisenkirch .30 .75
6 Dane Crowley .30 .75
7 Evan Haw .30 .75
8 Nicolaus Knudsen .30 .75
9 Ben Van Lare .30 .75
10 Richard Kelly .30 .75
11 Rob Woods .30 .75
12 Matt Fetznei .30 .75
13 Mike Green .40 1.00
14 Bjorn Svensson .30 .75
15 Ryan Cyr .30 .75
16 Dayln Flatt .30 .75
17 Joe Barnes .30 .75
18 Trent Adamus .30 .75
19 Derek Couture .30 .75
20 Tanner Shultz .30 .75
21 Wacey Rabbit .75 2.00
22 Devin Setoguchi .75 2.00
23 Ryan Keller .30 .75

2004-05 Saskatoon Blades

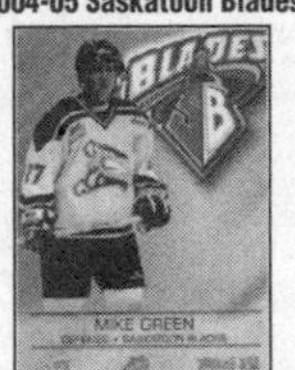

This set was issued in two parts: a 12-card first series and a 10-card second series.

COMPLETE SET (22) 8.00 20.00
1 Nicolaus Knudsen .30 .75
2 Joel Eisenkirch .30 .75
3 Justin McCrae .30 .75
4 Russell Monette .30 .75
5 Tyson Sievert .30 .75
6 Aaron Bader .30 .75
7 Daniel Waschuk .30 .75
8 Chris Cloud .30 .75
9 Ben Van Lare .30 .75
10 Tyler Boldt .30 .75
11 Mike Green .40 1.00
12 Zdenek Bahensky .40 1.00
13 Ryan Cyr .30 .75
14 Ryan Keller .30 .75
15 Devin Setoguchi .75 2.00
16 Joe Barnes .30 .75
17 Dayln Flatt .40 1.00
18 Dane Crowley .30 .75
19 Evan Haw .30 .75
20 Wacey Rabbit .75 2.00
21 Ryan Menei .30 .75
22 Bjorn Svensson .30 .75

2005-06 Saskatoon Blades

COMPLETE SET (24) 10.00 20.00
1 Aaron Bader .30 .75
2 Zdenek Bahensky .30 .75
3 Joe Barnes .30 .75
4 Chris Cloud .30 .75
5 Brad Cole .30 .75
6 Ryan Funk .30 .75
7 Adam Geric .30 .75
8 Colton Gillies .30 .75
9 Michael Hengen .30 .75
10 Anton Khudobin .40 1.00
11 Chad Klassen .30 .75
12 Joe Logan .30 .75
13 Michael MacAngus .30 .75
14 Blair MacAulay .30 .75
15 Justin McCrae .30 .75
16 Ryan Menei .30 .75
17 Todd Panchyson .30 .75
18 Derek Price .30 .75
19 Wacey Rabbit .60 1.50
20 David Schulz .30 .75
21 Devin Setoguchi .60 1.50
22 Brett Ward .30 .75
23 Jim Watt .40 1.00
24 Brennan Zasitko .30 .75

2006-07 Saskatoon Blades

COMPLETE SET (24) 8.00 15.00
1 Dustin Cameron .25 .60
2 Chris Cloud .25 .60
3 Brad Cole .25 .60
4 Troy Crowley .25 .60
5 Craig Cuthbert .25 .60
6 Kenton Dulle .25 .60
7 Ryan Funk .25 .60
8 Adam Geric .25 .60
9 Colton Gillies .25 2.00
10 Braden Holtby .25 .60
11 Derek Hulak .25 .60
12 Sam Klassen .25 .60
13 Garrett Klotz .25 .60
14 Rastislav Konecny .25 .60
15 Joe Logan .25 .60
16 Blair MacAulay .25 .60
17 Justin McCrae .25 .60
18 Ryan Menei .25 .60
19 Gaelan Patterson .25 .60
20 Bohdan Visnak .25 .60
21 Brett Ward .25 .60
22 Walker Wintoneak .25 .60
23 Teigan Zahn .25 .60
24 Garrett Zemlak .25 .60

1980-81 Sault Ste. Marie Greyhounds

Sponsored by Blue Bird Bakery Limited and Coke, this 25-card set captures the 1980-81 Soo Greyhounds of the OHL. The cards measure approximately 2 1/2" by 4" and feature posed, color player photos. Of interest to collectors are the first cards of current NHL stars John Vanbiesbrouck and Ron Francis.

COMPLETE SET (25) 37.50 75.00
1 Ken Porteous .30 .75
2 Brian Petterle .30 .75
3 Gord Dineen .40 1.00
4 Tony Cella .30 .75
5 Doug Shedden .60 1.50
6 Terry Tait .30 .75
7 Greyhounds Logo .20 .50
8 Steve Smith .30 .75
9 Huey Larkin .30 .75
10 Steve Gatzos .30 .75
11 Tim Zwijack .30 .75
12 Vic Morin .30 .75
13 John Vanbiesbrouck 12.50 25.00
14 Ron Francis 12.50 25.00
15 Tony Butorac .30 .75
16 John Goodwin .30 .75
17 Ron Handy .30 .75
18 Jim Pavese .40 1.00
19 Sault Ste. Marie .20 .50
Police Logo
20 Rick Morocco .30 .75
21 Ken Latta .30 .75
22 Kirk Rueter .30 .75
23 OMJHL Logo .20 .50
24 Terry Crisp 1.00 2.50
25 Marc D'Amour .75 2.00

1981-82 Sault Ste. Marie Greyhounds

Sponsored by Blue Bird Bakery Limited, Coke, 920 CKCY radio, and Canadian Tire, this 28-card set measures approximately 2 1/8" by 4 1/8" and features posed, color player photos with white borders. The player's name is printed in white on the picture, above the player's head. His position and the team name are printed in fuchsia at the bottom. The cards are unnumbered and checklisted below in alphabetical order. This set contains early cards of Rick Tocchet, John Vanbiesbrouck and Ron Francis.

COMPLETE SET (28) 32.00 80.00
1 Jim Aldreda .30 .75
2 Dave Andreoli .30 .75
3 Richard Beaulne .30 .75
4 Bruce Bell .30 .75
5 Chuck Brimmer .30 .75
6 Tony Cella .30 .75
7 Kevin Conway .30 .75
8 Terry Crisp CO .75 2.00
9 Marc D'Amour .60 1.50
10 Gord Dineen .40 1.00
11 Chris Felix .40 1.00
12 Ron Francis 10.00 25.00
13 Steve Graves .30 .75
14 Wayne Groulx .30 .75
15 Huey Larkin .30 .75
16 Ken Latta .30 .75
17 Mike Lococo .30 .75
18 Jim Pavese .40 1.00
19 Dirk Rueter .30 .75
20 Steve Smith .30 .75
21 Terry Tait .30 .75
22 Rick Tocchet 8.00 20.00
23 John Vanbiesbrouck 10.00 25.00
24 Harry Wolfe ANN .20 .50
25 J.D. Yari .02 .10
26 Bluebird Bakery .02 .10
Limited Logo
27 Canadian Tire Logo .02 .10
28 Coca-Cola Ad .02 .10

1982-83 Sault Ste. Marie Greyhounds

Sponsored by Blue Bird Bakery Limited and 920 CKCY radio station, this 25-card set measures approximately 2 1/2" by 4" and feature color, posed player photos with white borders. The player's name is superimposed on the photo in white lettering. His position is in black at the bottom. The cards are unnumbered and checklisted below in alphabetical order.

COMPLETE SET (25) 16.00 40.00
1 Jim Aldred .30 .75
2 John Armelin .30 .75
3 Richard Beaulne .30 .75
4 Jeff Beukeboom .60 1.50
5 Tony Cella .30 .75
6 Kevin Conway .30 .75
7 Terry Crisp .60 1.50
8 Chris Felix .40 1.00
9 Steve Graves .30 .75
10 Gus Greco .30 .75
11 Wayne Groulx .30 .75
12 Sam Haidy .30 .75
13 Tim Hoover .30 .75
14 Pat Lahey .30 .75
15 Huey Larkin .30 .75
16 Mike Lococo .30 .75
17 Mike Neill .30 .75
18 Ken Sabourin .30 .75
19 Steve Smith .30 .75
20 Terry Tait .30 .75
21 Rick Tocchet 4.00 10.00
22 John Vanbiesbrouck 6.00 15.00
23 Harry Wolfe ANN .20 .50
24 Station Mall Sponsor .02 .10
25 Bluebird Bakery Ltd. .02 .10

1983-84 Sault Ste. Marie Greyhounds

Sponsored by 920 CKCY radio, Coke, and IGA, the cards in this 25-card set measure approximately 2 1/2" by 4" and feature color, posed player photos with white borders. The player's name appears in an orange bar at the bottom of the picture. The cards are unnumbered and checklisted below in alphabetical order.

COMPLETE SET (25) 8.00 20.00
1 Jeff Beukeboom .40 1.00
2 Graeme Bonar .20 .50
3 Chris Brant .20 .50
4 John English .20 .50
5 Chris Felix .40 1.00
6 Rick Fera .20 .50
7 Marc Tournier .20 .50
8 Steve Graves .20 .50
9 Gus Greco .20 .50
11 Wayne Groulx .20 .50
11 Sam Haidy .20 .50
12 Tim Hoover .20 .50
13 Jerry Iuliano .20 .50
14 Pat Lahey .20 .50
15 Mike Lococo .20 .50
16 Jean-Marc MacKenzie .20 .50
17 Mike Oliverio .20 .50
18 Brit Peer .20 .50
19 Joey Rampton .20 .50
20 Ken Sabourin .40 1.00
21 Jim Samec .20 .50
22 Rick Tocchet 3.00 8.00
23 Harry Wolfe ANN .20 .50
24 IGA Sponsor Card .02 .10
25 Coke Sponsor Card .02 .10

1984-85 Sault Ste. Marie Greyhounds

Sponsored by 920 CKCY radio, Coke, and IGA, this 25-card set measures approximately 2 1/2" by 4" and features white-bordered, posed, color photos of the players on ice with a blue studio background. The player's name appears on a bright red plaque near the bottom. The cards are unnumbered and checklisted below in alphabetical order.

COMPLETE SET (25) 8.00 20.00
1 Marty Abrams .20 .50
2 Jeff Beukeboom .30 .75
3 Graeme Bonar .20 .50
4 Chris Brant .20 .50
5 Terry Crisp CO .40 1.00
6 Chris Felix .40 1.00
7 Scott Green .20 .50
8 Wayne Groulx .20 .50
9 Steve Hollett .20 .50
10 Tim Hoover .20 .50
11 Derek King .60 1.50
12 Tyler Larter .20 .50
13 Jean-Marc MacKenzie .20 .50
14 Scott Mosey .20 .50
15 Mike Oliverio .20 .50
16 Brit Peer .20 .50
17 Wayne Presley .40 1.00
18 Bob Probert 2.50 6.00
19 Brian Rome .20 .50
20 Ken Sabourin .30 .75
21 Rob Veccia .20 .50
22 Harry Wolfe ANN .08 .25
23 Rob Zettler .40 1.00
24 IGA Ad .08 .25
25 Coca-Cola Ad .08 .25

1987-88 Sault Ste. Marie Greyhounds

Printed on thin card stock, this 35-card set features players from the 1987-88 season of the Sault Ste. Marie Greyhounds and also past Greyhounds players who have gone on to NHL fame, such as Wayne Gretzky. The fronts feature white-bordered posed-on-ice color player photos. The player's name appears in white lettering near the top; his position and the team name appear in blue lettering near the bottom.

COMPLETE SET (35) 50.00 125.00
1 Barry King .08 .25
Chief of Police
2 Dan Currie .20 .50
3 Mike Glover .20 .50
4 Tyler Larter .20 .50
5 Bob Jones .20 .50
6 Lyndon Slewidge .08 .25
National Anthem Singer
7 Brad Jones .20 .50
8 Ron Francis 3.00 8.00
9 Dale Turnbull .20 .50
10 Don McConnell .20 .50
11 Chris Felix .30 .75
12 Steve Udvari .20 .50
13 Shawn Simpson .20 .50
14 Rob Zettler .40 1.00
15 Phil Esposito 6.00 15.00
Co-owner
16 John Vanbiesbrouck 6.00 15.00
17 Mike Oliverio .20 .50
18 Colin Ford .20 .50
19 Steve Herniman .20 .50
20 Troy Mallette .40 1.00
21 Craig Hartsburg .40 1.00
22 Don Boyd CO/GM .08 .25
23 Peter Fiorentino .20 .50
24 Jeff Columbus .20 .50
25 Brad Stepan .20 .50
26 Rick Tocchet 2.00 5.00
27 Shane Sargant .20 .50
28 Wayne Muir .20 .50
29 Wayne Gretzky 40.00 100.00
30 Gary Luther .20 .50
31 Harry Wolfe ANN .08 .25
32 Rod Thacker .20 .50
33 Coaches Card .08 .25
Terry Tait
Ted Nolan
Mark Pavoni
34 Brian Hoard .20 .50
35 Glen Johnston .20 .50

1989-90 Sault Ste. Marie Greyhounds

This 30-card P.L.A.Y. (Police, Law and Youth) set measures 2 3/4" by 3 1/2". The fronts feature posed on-ice player photos with black and white borders. The player's name and number appear on the bottom. The backs carry sponsor logos at the bottom and "Tips from the Hounds."

COMPLETE SET (30) 8.00 20.00
1 Barry King CL .08 .25
Chief of Police
2 Sault Ste. Marie .08 .25
Police Logo
3 Ted Nolan CO .30 .75
4 Team Logo .20 .50
5 Sherry Bassin GM .20 .50
6 Jim Ritchie .20 .50
7 Bob Boughner .30 .75
8 Denny Lambert .40 1.00
9 Doug Minor .20 .50
10 Rick Pracey .20 .50
11 Colin Miller .20 .50
12 Kevin King .20 .50
13 Ron Francis 2.00 5.00
14 Rick Kowalsky .20 .50
15 Adam Foote .75 2.00
16 Wade Whitten .20 .50
17 Dale Turnbull .20 .50
18 Bob Jones .20 .50
19 David Carrie .20 .50
20 Brad Tiley .20 .50
21 Wayne Muir .20 .50
22 Dave Babcock .20 .50
23 David Matsos .20 .50
24 Dan Ferguson .20 .50
25 Jeff Szeryk .20 .50
26 Mike Zuke ACO .08 .25
27 Dave Doucette .20 .50
28 John Campbell .08 .25
Constable
29 Graeme Harvey .20 .50
30 John Fuselli ACO .08 .25

1993-94 Sault Ste. Marie Greyhounds

Sponsored by Pino's Food Trunk Road and Sault Ste. Marie Public Utilities Commission, and printed by Slapshot Images Ltd., this standard-size 30-card set features the 1993-94 Sault Ste. Marie Greyhounds. On a geometrical team color-coded background, the fronts feature color action player photos with thin black borders. The player's name, position and team name, as well as the producer's logo, also appear on the front.

COMPLETE SET (30) 4.80 10.00
1 Andrea Carpano .15 .40
2 Ryan Douglas .15 .40
3 Dan Cloutier .75 2.00
4 Oliver Pastinsky .15 .40
5 Scott King .25 .60
6 Drew Bannister .25 .60
7 Sean Gagnon .15 .40
8 Andre Payette .15 .40
9 Peter MacKellar .15 .40
UER Name spelled
Mackellar on front
10 Richard Uniacke .15 .40
11 Steve Zoryk .15 .40
12 Brad Baber .15 .40
13 Gary Roach .15 .40
14 Jeff Gies .15 .40
15 Tom MacDonald .15 .40
16 Rhett Trombley .15 .40
17 Joe Van Volsen .15 .40
18 Andrew Clark .15 .40
19 Briane Thompson .15 .40
20 Aaron Gavey .25 .60
21 Wade Gibson .15 .40
22 Chad Grills .15 .40
23 Jeff Toms .15 .40
24 Steve Sullivan .60 1.50
25 Jeremy Stevenson .15 .40
26 Corey Moylan .15 .40
27 Steve Spina .15 .40
28 Dave Mayville GM .02 .10
29 Ted Nolan CO .30 .75
30 Dan Flynn ACO .02 .10
Mike Zuke ACO

1993-94 Sault Ste. Marie Greyhounds Memorial Cup

This 32-card standard-size set was printed by Precision Litho. The fronts feature color action player photos with rounded corners and gray-and-red team color-coded borders. The team name and logo are printed above the photos, while the player's name and number appear below. The backs present biography, 1992-93 statistics, an anti-drug or alcohol slogan, and sponsor logos.

COMPLETE SET (32) 6.00 15.00
1 Memorial Cup .40 1.00
2 Dan Tanevski .15 .40
3 Mark Matier .15 .40
4 Oliver Pastinsky .15 .40
5 Peter MacKellar .15 .40
6 Drew Bannister .20 .50
7 Sean Gagnon .20 .50
8 Joe Clarke .15 .40
9 Chad Penney .15 .40
10 Neal Martin .15 .40
11 Perry Pappas .15 .40
12 David Matsos .15 .40
13 Rick Kowalsky .15 .40
14 Gary Roach .15 .40
15 Jarret Reid .15 .40
16 Steve Sullivan .60 1.50
17 Tom MacDonald .15 .40
18 Jodie Murphy .15 .40
19 Ralph Intranuovo .15 .40
20 Brad Baber .15 .40
21 Briane Thompson .15 .40
22 Aaron Gavey .20 .50
23 Wade Gibson .15 .40
24 Kiley Hill .15 .40
25 Jeff Toms .15 .40
26 Joe Van Volsen .15 .40
27 Dan Cloutier .75 2.00
28 Kevin Hodson .60 1.50
29 David Mayville DIR .02 .10
Sherry Bassin GM
30 Ted Nolan CO .20 .50
Danny Flynn ACO
31 Executive Staff .02 .10
32 Mike Zuke ACO .02 .10
Forrest Varcoe TR
John Mayne TR
Maurice Sicard TR

1995-96 Sault Ste. Marie Greyhounds

This 30-card set was produced by the Greyhounds for distribution at the rink, by mail, and through the team's web page. The cards feature action photography on the front, with player name, number and bio superimposed over a Hounds logo on the back. The cards are unnumbered, and are listed below alphabetically. The set is noteworthy for including the first cards ever of several outstanding prospects, including Joe Thornton, Rico Fata and Richard Jackman.

COMPLETE SET (30) 10.00 25.00
1 Peter Cava .15 .40
2 Scott Cherrey .15 .40
3 Dan Cloutier .60 1.50
4 Lee Cole .15 .40
5 Jason Doyle .20 .50
6 Rico Fata .30 .75
7 Blaine Fitzpatrick .15 .40
8 Jeff Gies .15 .40
9 Richard Jackman .30 .75
10 Steve Lowe .15 .40
11 Dave Mayville GM .02 .10
12 Robert Mulick .15 .40
13 Kevin Murnaghan .15 .40
14 Cory Murphy .15 .40
15 Joe Paterson CO .02 .10
16 Andre Payette .15 .40
17 Michal Podolka .30 .75
18 Ben Schust .15 .40
19 Brian Stacey .15 .40
20 Brian Stewart .15 .40
21 Joe Thornton 6.00 15.00
22 Trevor Tokarczyk .15 .40
23 Richard Uniacke .20 .50
24 Joe Van Volsen .15 .40
25 Jamie Wentzell .15 .40
26 M.Zuke/B.Jones ACO .02 .10
27 Greyhounds Staff .02 .10
28 Toronto Bank and Trust .02 .10
29 School of Business .02 .10
30 Team Photo .02 .10

1996-97 Sault Ste. Marie Greyhounds

This 30-card set may stand as the top junior issue of the year. The cards feature color action photography, along with the player's name and number. The backs feature comprehensive stats, but are unnumbered, hence the alphabetical listing below. The set is noteworthy for the inclusion of two cards of Joe Thornton, the top pick in the '97 NHL draft. The second card features him as a member of the Canadian National Junior Team.

COMPLETE SET (30) 10.00 25.00
1 Wes Booker .15 .40
2 Bill Browne .15 .40
3 Peter Cava .15 .40
4 Justin Davis .15 .40
5 J.J. Dickie .15 .40
6 Oak Hewer .15 .40
7 Richard Jackman .20 .50
8 Richard Jackman .20 .50
Team Canada 1997
9 Matt Lahey .15 .40
10 David Mayville .02 .10
Director of Operations
11 Jake McCracken .30 .75
12 Marc Moro .30 .75
13 Robert Mulick .15 .40
14 Joe Paterson CO .02 .10
15 Daniel Passero .15 .40
16 Nathan Perrott .30 .75
17 Michael Podolka .30 .75
18 Nick Robinson .15 .40
19 Ben Schust .15 .40
20 Joe Seroski .15 .40
21 Chad Spurr .15 .40
22 Brian Stewart .15 .40
23 Joe Thornton 4.00 10.00
24 Joe Thornton 4.00 10.00
Team Canada 1997
25 Trevor Tokarczyk .15 .40
26 Richard Uniacke .15 .40
27 David Wight .15 .40
28 Chad Woollard .15 .40
29 Mike Zuke ACO .02 .10
B.Jones ACO
30 Team Photo .02 .10

1996-97 Sault Ste. Marie Greyhounds Autographed

Along with the regular version of the team set, the Hounds also offered a completely signed version for $15. This set includes two signed cards from 1997 top pick Joe Thornton. The cards do not bear any authenticating marks, so it is possible that an autographed set could be compiled individually.

COMPLETE SET (24) 40.00 100.00
1 Wes Booker .75 2.00
2 Bill Browne .75 2.00
3 Peter Cava .75 2.00
4 Justin Davis .75 2.00
5 J.J. Dickie .75 2.00
6 Oak Hewer .75 2.00
7 Richard Jackman 1.25 3.00
8 Richard Jackman 1.25 3.00
Team Canada 1997
9 Matt Lahey .75 2.00
11 Jake McCracken 1.50 4.00
12 Marc Moro 2.00 5.00
13 Robert Mulick .75 2.00
14 Joe Paterson CO .75 2.00
15 Daniel Passero .75 2.00
16 Nathan Perrott 2.00 5.00
17 Michael Podolka 1.50 4.00
18 Nick Robinson .75 2.00
19 Ben Schust .75 2.00
20 Joe Seroski 1.25 3.00
21 Chad Spurr .75 2.00
22 Brian Stewart .75 2.00
23 Joe Thornton 15.00 40.00
24 Joe Thornton 15.00 40.00
Team Canada 1997
25 Trevor Tokarczyk .75 2.00
26 Richard Uniacke 1.25 3.00
27 David Wight .75 2.00
28 Chad Woollard .75 2.00
29 Mike Zuke ACO .75 2.00
B.Jones ACO

2002-03 Sault Ste. Marie Greyhounds

COMPLETE SET (23) 8.00 20.00
1 Adam Munro .40 1.00
2 Joey Biasucci .30 .75
3 Trevor Daley .40 1.00
4 Jeff Carter 3.00 8.00
5 Michael Krelove .20 .50
6 Matt Herneisen .20 .50
7 Jeff Doyle .20 .50
8 Mike Moher .20 .50
9 Tyler Kennedy .20 .50
10 Tyler Dutchyshen .20 .50
11 Brian Rempel .20 .50
12 Petr Taticek .40 1.00
13 Jeff Larsh .20 .50
14 Sean Stefanski .20 .50
15 Jordan Smith .20 .50
16 Mike Amodeo .20 .50
17 Jiri Drtina .20 .50
18 Niko Tuomi .20 .50
19 Ryan Kitchen .20 .50
20 Scott Dobben .20 .50
21 Brad Staubitz .20 .50
22 Jordan Kennedy .20 .50
23 Ryan McKay .20 .50

2003-04 Sault Ste. Marie Greyhounds

COMPLETE SET (32) 6.00 15.00
1 Jakub Cechs .30 .75
2 Travis Chapman .20 .50
3 Brett Connolly .20 .50
4 Andrew Desjardins .20 .50
5 Scott Dobben .20 .50
6 Jeffrey Doyle .20 .50
7 Kevin Druce .30 .75
8 Brad Good .20 .50
9 Jeff Carter 1.50 4.00
10 David Jarram .20 .50
11 Tyler Kennedy .20 .50
12 Jacob King .20 .50
13 Jeff Larsh .20 .50
14 Chris Lawrence .20 .50
15 Matt Leszczynski .20 .50
16 Aaron Lewicki .20 .50
17 Mike Looby .20 .50
18 Jason Pitton .20 .50
19 Matt Puntureri .20 .50
20 Jordan Smith .20 .50
21 Brad Staubitz .20 .50
22 Reg Thomas .20 .50
23 Martin Tuma .20 .50
24 Marty Abrams CO .02 .10
25 Denny Lambert ACO .02 .10
26 Terry Barbeau ACO .02 .10
27 Andy Martin EQM .02 .10
28 Dave Torrie GM .02 .10
29 Rod Bogart TR .02 .10
30 Header Card .01 .05
31 Header Card .01 .05
32 Checklist .01 .05

2004-05 Sault Ste. Marie Greyhounds

COMPLETE SET (25) 6.00 15.00
1 Jakub Cech .20 .50
2 Kyle Gajewski .20 .50
3 Brad Good .20 .50
4 David Jarram .20 .50
5 Joshua Day .20 .50
6 Jeff Carter 1.25 3.00
7 Tyler Cuthbert .20 .50
8 Chris Lawrence .20 .50
9 Ryan McInerny .20 .50
10 Brandon MacLean .20 .50
11 Tyler Kennedy .20 .50
12 Tyler McKinley .20 .50
13 Jason Pitton .20 .50
14 Jeff Larsh .20 .50
15 Jordan Smith .20 .50
16 Jacob King .20 .50
17 Andrew Desjardins .20 .50
18 Matt Puntureri .30 .75
19 Matthew Leszczynski .20 .50
20 Blair Jarrett .20 .50
21 Brad Staubitz .20 .50
22 Martin Tuma .20 .50
23 Jacob Lalonde .20 .50
24 Reg Thomas .20 .50
25 Checklist .01 .05

1993-94 Seattle Thunderbirds

This 30-card standard-size set features the 1993-94 Seattle Thunderbirds of the Western Hockey League (WHL). On a white card face, the fronts display posed color player photos. The pictures are edged by a row of blue stars on the left and by "Thunderbirds" in green print on the right. The top left corner appears the team logo, while the player's name and position are printed in black beneath the photo.

COMPLETE SET (30) 4.80 12.00
1 Mike Barrie .20 .50
2 Doug Bonner .20 .50
3 Davie Carson .20 .50
4 Jeff Dewar .20 .50
5 Brett Duncan .20 .50
6 Shawn Gervais .20 .50
7 Chris Herperger .30 .75
8 Troy Hyatt .20 .50
9 Curt Kamp TR .02 .10
10 Olaf Kjenstadt .20 .50
11 Walt Kyle CO .02 .10
12 Milt Mastad .20 .50
13 Larry McMorran .20 .50
14 Jim McTaggart ACO .02 .10
15 Regan Mueller .20 .50
16 Kevin Mylander .20 .50
17 Drew Palmer .20 .50
18 Jeff Peddigrew .20 .50
19 Darryl Plandowski ACO .02 .10
20 Deron Quint .30 .75
21 Darrell Sandback .20 .50
22 Chris Schmidt .20 .50
23 Lloyd Shaw .20 .50
24 Alexandre Matvichuk .20 .50
25 Darcy Smith .20 .50
26 Rob Tallas .30 .75
27 Paul Vincent .20 .50
28 Chris Wells .20 .50
29 Brendan Witt .30 .75
30 Team photo .20 .50

1995-96 Seattle Thunderbirds

This 32-card set was produced and sold by the club. The fronts feature action photography, while the backs include a headshot, stats and bio. The set is noteworthy for including the first appearance of Patrick Marleau, the second player selected in the 1997 Entry Draft. The cards are unnumbered and are listed below in alphabetical order.

COMPLETE SET (32) 10.00 30.00
1 Perry Andrusiak ACO .02 .10
2 Shane Belter .20 .50
3 Rick Berry .30 .75
4 Jeff Blair .20 .50
5 Doug Bonner .30 .75
6 Kevin Borris .15 .40
7 Torrey DiRoberto .20 .50
8 Michal Divisek .15 .40
9 Paul Ferone .15 .40
10 Shawn Gervais .15 .40
11 Jan Hrdina .75 2.00
12 Curt Kamp TR .02 .10
13 Greg Kuznik .15 .40
14 Blair Manning .15 .40
15 Patrick Marleau 8.00 20.00
16 Jim McTaggart ACO .02 .10
17 Tony Mohagen .15 .40
18 Don Nachbaur CO .02 .10
19 Jason Norrie .15 .40
20 Drew Palmer .15 .40
21 Tyler Perry .15 .40
22 Jamie Pollock .15 .40
23 Kevin Popp .15 .40
24 Jeremy Reich .20 .50
25 Cody Rudkowsky .40 1.00
26 Chris Schmidt .15 .40
27 Lloyd Shaw .15 .40
28 Chris Thompson .15 .40
29 Dan Tompkins .15 .40
30 Cool Bird MASCOT .02 .10
32 Seattle Key Arena .04 .01
NNO Title Card .04 .01

1996-97 Seattle Thunderbirds

This 28-card set was produced by S&H Ltd. The cards were available through the team at the rink or through the mail. The cards feature action photos on the front, and statistical analysis on the backs. The player's sweater number is displayed in the lower right hand corner. As the cards themselves are unnumbered, they are listed below according to the sweater number. The set is noteworthy for the inclusion of Patrick Marleau, the second overall pick in the 1997 NHL Entry Draft.

COMPLETE SET (28) 8.00 20.00
1 Jeff Blair .20 .50
3 Rod LeRoux .20 .50
4 Nathan Forster .20 .50
5 Brad Swanson .20 .50
6 Rick Berry .30 .75
7 Paul Ferone .20 .50
8 Jame Pollock .20 .50
9 Tyler Willis .20 .50
11 Chris Thompson .20 .50
12 Patrick Marleau 3.00 8.00
13 Jouni Kuokkanen .20 .50
14 Martin Cerven .20 .50
15 Jeremy Reich .30 .75
16 Bret DeCecco .40 1.00
17 Tony Mohagen .20 .50
18 Torrey DiRoberto .20 .50
19 Nick Szadkowski .20 .50
21 Brian Ballman .20 .50
22 Greg Kuznik .20 .50
23 Randy Perry .20 .50
24 Shawn Skolney .20 .50
30 Cody Rudkowsky .40 1.00
31 Kris Cantu .20 .50
32 Shane Belter .20 .50
NNO Cool Bird MASCOT .02 .10
NNO Rob Sumner ACO .02 .10
NNO Thunderbirds .02 .10
Through the Years
NNO Don Nachbaur CO .02 .10

1997-98 Seattle Thunderbirds

This set features the Thunderbirds of the WHL. It was sold in set form by the team. It features early cards of NHL young star Mark Parrish.

COMPLETE SET (1-27) 7.20 15.00
1 Header Card .02 .10
2 Cool Bird Mascot .02 .10
3 Rod Leroux .20 .50
4 Nathan Forster .20 .50
5 Jason Beckett .20 .50
6 Rick Berry .30 .75
7 Chris Thompson .20 .50
8 Jame Pollock .20 .50
9 David Morisset .30 .75
10 Jeff Blair .20 .50
11 Jouni Kuokkanen .20 .50
12 Scott Kelman .30 .75
13 Jeremy Reich .30 .75
14 Brett DeCecco .30 .75
15 Tim Preston .20 .50
16 Torrey DiRoberto .30 .75
17 Petr Vala .20 .50
18 Ryan Tresk .20 .50
19 Greg Kuznik .20 .50
20 Matt Demarski .20 .50
21 Mark Parrish .75 2.00
22 Stanislav Gron .60 1.50
23 Cody Rudkowsky .40 1.00
24 A.J. Van Bruggen .20 .50
25 Don Nachbaur HCO .08 .25
26 Rob Sumner ACO .04 .10
27 Curt Kamp TR .02 .10

1969-70 Seattle Totems

This set features the Totems of the old WHL. A White Front Stores exclusive at stores in Aurora, Tacoma, Burien, and Bellevue, this set of 20 team photos measures approximately 8" by 10". Printed on thin paper, the front features a posed color player photo with a studio background. The pictures have white borders, and the player's signature is inscribed in the lower right corner. In black print on white, the backs present biography and statistics from the past season.

COMPLETE SET (20) 60.00 150.00
1 Don Head 8.00 20.00
2 Chuck Holmes 3.00 8.00
3 Bob Courcy 3.00 8.00
4 Marc Boileau 3.00 8.00
5 Garry Leonard 3.00 8.00
6 Art Stratton 3.00 8.00
7 Gary Kilpatrick 3.00 8.00
8 Don Ward 3.00 8.00
9 Jack Michie 3.00 8.00
10 Ronald Ingram 3.00 8.00
11 John Hanna 3.00 8.00
12 Ray Larose 3.00 8.00
13 Jack Dale 3.00 8.00
14 Tom McVie 3.00 8.00
15 Gerry Meehan 6.00 15.00
16 Chris Worthy 3.00 8.00
17 Bobby Schmautz 8.00 20.00
18 Dwight Carruthers 3.00 8.00
19 Patrick Dunn TR .75 2.00
20 Bill MacFarland CO .75 2.00

1989-90 7th Inn. Sketch OHL

This 200-card standard-size set was issued by 7th Inning Sketch featuring members of the Ontario Hockey League. The fronts of the cards have yellow borders which surround the player's photo and on the bottom of the front is the player's name. In the upper right hand corner, the team's name is featured. The set has been popular with collectors since it features early cards of Eric Lindros. The set was also issued on a limited basis (a numbered edition of 3000) as a factory set; however, the factory set only included 167 cards as 33 cards were dropped for unspecified reasons.

COMPLETE SET (200) 12.00 30.00
COMPLETE FACT.SET (167) 12.00 30.00
1 Eric Lindros 1.50 4.00
(Beware counterfeits)
2 Jarrod Skalde .20 .50
3 Joe Busillo .02 .10
4 Dale Craigwell .08 .25
5 Clair Cornish .02 .10
6 Jean-Paul Davis .02 .10
7 Craig Donaldson .02 .10
8 Wade Simpson .02 .10
9 Mike Craig .08 .25
10 Mark Deazeley .02 .10
11 Scott Hollis .02 .10
12 Brian Grieve .02 .10
13 Dave Craievich .02 .10
14 Paul O'Hagan .02 .10
15 Matt Hoffman .02 .10
16 Trevor McIvor .02 .10
17 Cory Banika .02 .10
18 Kevin Butt .07 .20
19 Iain Fraser .02 .10
20 Bill Armstrong .07 .20
21 Scott Luik .02 .10
22 Brent Grieve .02 .10
23 Fred Brathwaite .40 1.00
24 Paul Holden .02 .10
25 Trevor Dam .02 .10
26 Chris Taylor .02 .10
27 Mark Guy .02 .10
28 Louie DeBrusk .30 .75
29 John Battice .02 .10
30 Chris Crombie .02 .10
31 Sean Basilio .07 .20
32 Aaron Nagy .02 .10
33 Greg Ryan .02 .10
34 Steve Martell .02 .10
35 Scott MacKay .02 .10
36 Dennis Purdie .30 .75
37 Steve Boyd .02 .10
38 John Tanner .08 .25
39 David Anderson .02 .10
40 Rick Corriveau .02 .10
41 Todd Hlushko .08 .25
42 Doug Synish .02 .10
43 Dan LeBlanc .07 .20
44 Dave Noseworthy .02 .10
45 Karl Taylor .02 .10
46 Jeff Hodgen .02 .10
47 Mike Kelly .01 .05
Gary Agnew CO
48 Wayne Maxner .02 .10
49 Brett Seguin .02 .10
50 Greg Walters .02 .10
51 Chris Snell .02 .10
52 Troy Binnie .02 .10
53 Joni Lehto .02 .10
54 Steve Kluczkowski .02 .10
55 Ryan Kuwabara .07 .20
56 Chris Simon .40 1.00
57 Jerrett DeFazio .07 .20
58 Rob Sangster .02 .10
59 Greg Clancy .02 .10
60 Peter Ambroziak .02 .10
61 Jeff Ricciardi .02 .10
62 John East .02 .10
63 Joey McTamney .02 .10
64 Dan Poirier .02 .10
65 Gairin Smith .02 .10
66 Wade Gibson .02 .10
67 Checklist Card .01 .05
68 Andrew Brodie .02 .10
69 Craig Wilson .02 .10
70 Peter McGlynn .02 .10
71 George Dourian .02 .10
72 Bob Berg .07 .20
73 Richard Fatrola .02 .10
74 Craig Fraser .02 .10
75 Brent Gretzky .20 .50
76 Jake Grimes .02 .10
77 Darren McCarty .75 2.00
78 Ted Miskolczi .02 .10
79 Rob Pearson .08 .25
80 Gordon Pell .02 .10
81 John Porco .02 .10
82 Ken Rowbotham .02 .10
83 Scott Thornton .20 .50
84 Shawn Way .02 .10
85 Steve Bancroft .02 .10
86 Greg Bignell .02 .10
87 Scott Boston .02 .10
88 Scott Feasby .02 .10
89 Derek Morin .07 .20
90 Sean O'Reilly .07 .20
91 Jason Skelet .02 .10
92 Greg Dreveny .02 .10
93 Jeff Fife .02 .10
94 Rob Slopar .02 .10
95 Joe Desrosiers .01 .05
96 Danny Flynn .02 .10
97 Dr. R.L. Vaughan .01 .05
98 Troy Stephens .02 .10
99 Dan Brown .02 .10
100 Mike Ricci .40 1.00
101 Brent Pope .02 .10
102 Mike Dagenais .07 .20
103 Scott Campbell .02 .10
104 Jamie Pegg .02 .10
105 Joe Hawley .02 .10
106 Jason Dawe .08 .25
107 Paul Mitton .02 .10
108 Mike Tomlinson .02 .10
109 Dave Lorentz .02 .10
110 Dale McTavish .02 .10
111 Willie McGarvey .02 .10
112 Don O'Neill .02 .10
113 Mark Myles .02 .10
114 Chris Longo .07 .20
115 Tom Hopkins .02 .10
116 Jassen Cullimore .02 .10
117 Geoff Ingram .02 .10
118 Twohey .01 .05
Bovair TR
119 Doug Searle .02 .10
120 Bryan Gendron .02 .10
121 Andrew Verner .08 .25
122 Todd Bocjun .07 .20
123 Dick Todd .02 .10
124 George Burnett .02 .10
125 Brad May .30 .75
126 David Benn .02 .10
127 Brian Mueggler .02 .10
128 Todd Coopman .02 .10
129 Geoff Rawson .02 .10
130 Keith Primeau .75 2.00
131 Mark Lawrence .07 .20
132 Randy Hall .02 .10
133 Greg Suchan .02 .10
134 Ken Ruddick .02 .10
135 Jason Winch .07 .20
136 Paul Wolanski .02 .10
137 Dennis Scott .01 .05
138 Steve Udvari .02 .10
139 Roch Belley .07 .20
140 Don Pancoe .02 .10
141 Paul Bruneau .01 .05
142 Paul Laus .20 .50
143 Mike St. John .02 .10
144 John Johnson .02 .10
145 Greg Allen .02 .10
146 Don McConnell .02 .10
147 Andy Bezeau .02 .10
148 Jeff Walker .02 .10
149 John Spoltore .02 .10
150 Derek Switzer .07 .20
151 Tyler Ertel .02 .10
152 Shawn Antoski .08 .25
153 Jason Corrigan .02 .10
154 Derian Hatcher .30 .75
155 John Vary .02 .10
156 Jamie Caruso .02 .10
157 Trevor Halverson .02 .10
158 Robert Deschamps .02 .10
159 Jeff Gardiner .07 .20
160 Gary Miller .02 .10
161 Shayne Antoski .08 .25
162 John Van Kessel .02 .10
163 Colin Austin .02 .10
164 Tom Purcell .02 .10
165 Joel Morin .02 .10
166 Tim Favot .02 .10
167 Checklist Card .01 .05
168 Jason Beaton .02 .10
169 Chris Ottmann .02 .10
170 Mike Matuszek .02 .10
171 Rob Fournier .02 .10
172 Ron Bertrand .07 .20
173 Bert Templeton .02 .10
174 Casey Jones .01 .05
175 Robert Frayn .02 .10
176 Claude Noel .02 .10
177 Sean Basilio Award .02 .10
178 Chris Longo Rookie .02 .10
179 Cory Keenan AS .02 .10
180 Owen Nolan Award .40 1.00
181 Steven Rice AS .08 .25
182 Shayne Stevenson .08 .25
Scorer
183 Mike Ricci Award .20 .50
184 Jason Firth Award .02 .10
185 John Slaney Award .02 .10
186 Iain Fraser Award .02 .10
187 Steven Rice Star .08 .25
188 Eric Lindros Scorer 1.25 3.00
189 Keith Primeau Scorer .40 1.00
190 Mike Ricci Award .20 .50
191 Mike Torchia AS .08 .25
192 Mike Torchia Star .07 .20
193 Jarrod Skalde Champs .08 .25
194 Paul O'Hagan Award .02 .10
195 Eric Lindros 1.25 3.00
(Where in 1991)
196 Eric Lindros AS 1.25 3.00
197 Jeff Fife Award .02 .10
198 Iain Fraser MVP .02 .10
199 Bill Armstrong Winner .02 .10
200 Checklist Card .01 .05

1990-91 7th Inn. Sketch OHL

The 7th Inning Sketch OHL Hockey set contains 400 standard-size cards. The front features a full color photo, enframed by different color borders. The player's position appears in a star at the lower left hand corner, with his name and "OHL" in the bar below the picture. The back has another color photo, with biographical information and career summary in a box running the length of the card. This set features a regular card (1) as well as a promo card of hockey star Eric Lindros. The promo version has the same front as Lindros' card number 1 but has an asterisk in the card number position on the card back. Players from the following teams are represented in this set: Oshawa Generals (1, 325-339, 341-345, 347-350), Belleville Bulls (2 10, 12-21, 23, 340, 346), Kingston Frontenacs (11, 51-75), Cornwall Royals (22, 24-50), Ottawa 67's (76-100, 230), Detroit Compuware Ambassadors (101-121, 123-125), North Bay Centennials (122, 301-324), London Knights (126-149), Sault Ste. Marie Greyhounds (150-173, 175-176), Windsor Spitfires (174, 177-200), Dukes of Hamilton (201-225), Kitchener Rangers (226-229, 231-250, 370), Niagara Falls Thunder (251-275), Owen Sound Platers (276-299), Peterborough Petes (351-369, 371-376), and Sudbury Wolves (377-400). First round picks (1991 NHL Draft) in this set include Eric Lindros (1), Alex Stojanov (7), Pat Peake (14), Glen Murray (18), and Trevor Halverson (21). First round picks (1992 NHL Draft rank indicated in parenthesis) in this set include Todd Warriner (4), Cory Stillman (6), Brandon Convery (8), Curtis Bowen (22), and Grant Marshall (23). A factory set, a numbered edition of 9000 sets, was produced and marketed separately.

COMPLETE SET (400) 8.00 20.00
COMPLETE FACT.SET (400) 10.00 25.00
1 Eric Lindros 1.50 4.00
2 Greg Dreveny .02 .10
3 Belleville Checklist UER .01 .05
4 Richard Fatrola .02 .10
5 Craig Fraser .02 .10
6 Robert Frayn .02 .10
7 Brent Gretzky .15 .40
8 Jake Grimes .02 .10
9 Darren Hurley .02 .10
10 Rick Marshall .02 .10
11 Checklist UER .01 .05
12 Darren McCarty .75 2.00
13 Derek Morin .02 .10
14 Sean O'Reilly .02 .10
15 Rob Pearson UER .08 .25
(Listed on Oshawa CL but reverse says Belleville Bulls)
16 John Porco .02 .10
17 Ken Rowbotham .02 .10
18 Ken Ruddick .02 .10
19 Jim Sonmez .02 .10
20 Brad Teichmann .02 .10
21 Chris Varga .02 .10
22 Checklist Card .01 .05
23 Larry Mavety CO .01 .05
24 Rival Fullum .02 .10
25 Nathan Lafayette .02 .10
26 Darren Bell .02 .10
27 Craig Brocklehurst .02 .10
28 Shawn Caplice .02 .10
29 Mike Cavanaugh .02 .10
30 Jason Cirone .02 .10
31 Chris Clancy .02 .10
32 Mark DeSantis .02 .10
33 Rob Dykeman .02 .10
34 Shayne Gaffar .02 .10
35 Ilpo Kauhanen .02 .10
36 Rob Kinghan .02 .10
37 Dave Lemay .02 .10
38 Guy Leveque .02 .10
39 Matt McGuffin .02 .10
40 Marcus Middleton .02 .10
41 Thomas Nemeth .02 .10
42 Rod Pasma .02 .10
43 Richard Raymond .02 .10
44 Jeff Reid .02 .10
45 Jerry Ribble .02 .10
46 Jean-Alain Schneider .02 .10
47 John Slaney .02 .10
48 Jeremy Stevenson .02 .10
49 Ryan VandenBussche .40 1.00
50 Marc Crawford CO .20 .50
51 Tony Bella .02 .10
52 Drake Berehowsky .20 .50
53 Jason Chipman .02 .10
54 Tony Cimellaro .02 .10
55 Keli Corpse .02 .10
56 Mike Dawson .02 .10
57 Sean Gauthier UER .02 .10
58 Fred Goltz .02 .10
59 Gord Harris .02 .10
60 Tony Iob .02 .10
61 John Bernie .02 .10
62 Dale Junkin .02 .10
63 Nathan Lafayette .02 .10
64 Blake Martin .02 .10
65 Mark McCague .02 .10
66 Bob McKillop .02 .10
67 Justin Morrison .02 .10
68 Bill Robinson .02 .10
69 Joel Sandie .02 .10
70 Kevin King .02 .10
71 Dave Stewart .02 .10
72 Joel Washkurak .02 .10
73 Brock Woods .02 .10
74 Randy Hall CO .02 .10
75 John Vary .02 .10
76 Peter Ambroziak .02 .10
77 Troy Binnie .02 .10
78 Curt Bowen .02 .10
79 Andrew Brodie .02 .10
80 Ottawa Checklist .02 .10
81 Greg Clancy .02 .10
82 Jerrett DeFazio .02 .10
83 Kris Draper .40 1.00
84 Wade Gibson .02 .10
85 Ryan Kuwabara .02 .10
86 Joni Lehto .02 .10
87 Donald MacPherson .02 .10
88 Grant Marshall .20 .50
89 Peter McGlynn .02 .10
90 Maurice O'Brien .02 .10
91 Jeff Ricciardi .02 .10
92 Brett Seguin .02 .10
93 Len DeVuono .02 .10
94 Gerry Skrypec .02 .10
95 Chris Snell .02 .10
96 Jason Snow .02 .10
97 Sean Spencer .02 .10
98 Brad Spry .02 .10
99 Matt Stone .02 .10
100 Brian Kilrea CO .08 .25
101 Kevin Butt .08 .25
102 Glen Craig .02 .10
103 Paul Doherty .02 .10
104 Mark Donahue .02 .10
105 Jeff Gardiner .02 .10
106 Trent Gleason .02 .10
107 Troy Gleason .02 .10
108 Mark Lawrence .08 .25
109 Trevor McIvor .02 .10
110 Paul Mitton .02 .10
111 David Myles .02 .10
112 Jeffery Nolan .02 .10
113 Rob Papineau .02 .10
114 Pat Peake .02 .10
115 Chris Phelps .02 .10
116 John Pinches .02 .10
117 James Shea .02 .10
118 James Sheehan .02 .10
119 John Stos .02 .10
120 Tom Sullivan .02 .10
121 John Wynne .02 .10
122 Robert Thorpe .02 .10
123 David Benn .02 .10
124 Andy Weidenbach CO UER .01 .05
125 Detroit Checklist .01 .05
126 David Anderson .02 .10
127 Sean Basilio .08 .25
128 Brent Brownlee .02 .10
129 Rick Corriveau .02 .10
130 Derrick Crane .02 .10
131 Chris Crombie .02 .10
132 Louie DeBrusk .40 1.00
133 Mark Guy .02 .10
134 Brett Marrietti .02 .10
135 Steve Martell .02 .10
136 Scott McKay .02 .10
137 Aaron Nagy .02 .10
138 Brett Nicol .02 .10
139 Barry Potomski .40 1.00
140 Dennis Purdie .40 1.00
141 Kelly Reed .02 .10
142 Gregory Ryan .02 .10
143 Brad Smyth .02 .10
144 Nick Stajduhar .02 .10
145 John Tanner .08 .25
146 Chris Taylor .02 .10
147 Mark Visheau .02 .10
148 Gary Agnew CO .08 .25
149 London Checklist .02 .10
150 Sault Ste. Marie .02 .10
Checklist
151 David Babcock .02 .10
152 Drew Bannister .02 .10
153 Bob Boughner .30 .75
154 Joe Busillo .02 .10
155 Mike DeCoff .02 .10
156 Jason Denomme .02 .10
157 Adam Foote .75 2.00
158 Kevin Hodson .30 .75
159 Shaun Imber .02 .10
160 Ralph Intranuovo .02 .10
161 Kevin King .02 .10
162 Rick Kowalsky .02 .10
163 Chris Kraemer .02 .10
164 Dan Lambert .08 .25
165 Mike Lenarduzzi .08 .25
166 Tom MacDonald .02 .10
167 Mark Matier .02 .10
168 David Matsos .02 .10
169 Colin Miller .02 .10
170 Perry Pappas .02 .10
171 Jarrett Reid .02 .10
172 Kevin Reid .02 .10
173 Brad Tiley UER .02 .10
174 Windsor Checklist .01 .05
175 Wade Whitten .02 .10
176 Ted Nolan CO .20 .50
177 Sean Burns .02 .10
178 Jason Cirone .02 .10
179 John Copley .02 .10
180 Tyler Ertel .02 .10
181 Brian Forestell .02 .10
182 Rival Fullum .02 .10
183 Steve Gibson .02 .10
184 Leonard MacDonald .02 .10
185 Mike Speer .02 .10
186 Kevin MacKay .02 .10
187 Ryan Merritt .02 .10
188 Doug Minor .02 .10
189 Rick Morton .02 .10
190 Sean O'Hagan .08 .25
191 Mike Polano .02 .10
192 Cory Stillman .20 .50
193 Jason Stos .02 .10
194 Trevor Walsh .02 .10
195 Todd Warriner .20 .50
196 Jeff Wilson .02 .10
197 Jason York .20 .50
198 Jason Zohil .02 .10
199 Steve Smith .02 .10
200 Brad Smith CO .02 .10
201 Jeff Bes .02 .10
202 Mike Blum .02 .10
203 Sean Brown .02 .10
204 Darcy Cahill .02 .10
205 Dale Chokan .02 .10
206 Chris Code .02 .10
207 George Dourion .02 .10
208 Todd Gleason .02 .10
209 Hamilton Checklist UER .01 .05
210 Michael Hartwick .02 .10
211 Scott Jenkins .02 .10
212 Rob Leask .02 .10
213 Gordon Pell .02 .10
214 Michael Reier .02 .10
215 Kayle Short .02 .10
216 Jason Skellett .02 .10
217 Gairin Smith .02 .10
218 Jeff Smith .02 .10
219 Jason Soules .02 .10
220 Alex Stojanov .02 .10
221 Dan Tanevski .02 .10
222 Gary Taylor .02 .10
223 Brent Watson .02 .10
224 Steve Woods .02 .10
225 Jay Johnston CO UER .01 .05
226 Mike Allen .02 .10
227 Brad Barton .02 .10
228 Richard Borgo .02 .10
229 Justin Cullen .02 .10
230 Lenny DeVuono .02 .10
231 Norman Dezainde .02 .10
232 Jason Firth .02 .10
233 Derek Gauthier .02 .10
234 Jamie Israel .02 .10
235 Chris LiPuma .02 .10
236 Tony McCabe .02 .10
237 Paul McCallion .02 .10
238 Shayne McCosh .02 .10
239 Rod Saarinen .02 .10
240 Steve Smith .02 .10
241 Joey St.Aubin .02 .10
242 Rob Stopar .02 .10
243 Jason Zohil UER .02 .10

244 Mike Torchia .08 .25
245 Gib Tucker .02 .10
246 John Uniac .02 .10
247 Jack Williams .02 .10
248 Joe McDonnell CO .02 .10
249 Steven Rice .02 .10
250 Mike Polano .02 .10
251 Greg Allen .02 .10
252 Roch Belley .08 .25
253 Andy Bezeau .02 .10
254 Derek Booth .02 .10
255 Kevin Brown .02 .10
256 Mark Cardiff .02 .10
257 Jason Coles .02 .10
258 Todd Coopman .02 .10
259 Richard Girhiny .02 .10
260 Brian Holk .02 .10
261 John Johnson .02 .10
262 Dan Krisko .02 .10
263 Manny Legace .75 2.00
264 Brad May .30 .75
265 Don McConnell .02 .10
266 Niagara Falls Checklist UER (Nigara& sic) .01 .05
267 Aaron Morrison .02 .10
268 Cory Pageau .02 .10
269 Geoff Rawson .02 .10
270 Todd Simon .02 .10
271 Steve Staios .08 .25
272 Jeff Walker .02 .10
273 Todd Wetzel .02 .10
274 Jason Winch .02 .10
275 Paul Wolanski .02 .10
276 Owen Sound Checklist .01 .05
277 Andrew Brunette .40 1.00
278 Wyatt Buckland .02 .10
279 Jason Buetow .02 .10
280 Jason Castellan .02 .10
281 Trent Cull .02 .10
282 Robert Deschamps .02 .10
283 Chris Driscoll .02 .10
284 Bryan Drury .02 .10
285 Todd Hunter .02 .10
286 Troy Hutchinson .02 .10
287 Kirk Maltby .30 .75
288 Geordie Maynard .02 .10
289 Kevin McDougall .02 .10
290 Ted Miskolczi .02 .10
291 Steve Parson .02 .10
292 Jeff Perry .02 .10
293 Grayden Reid .02 .10
294 Mike Speer .02 .10
295 Mark Strohack .02 .10
296 Mark Vilneff .02 .10
297 Keith Whitmore .02 .10
298 Jim Brown .02 .10
299 Len McNamara CO .01 .05
300 David Branch COMM .02 .10
301 Shayne Antoski .02 .10
302 Jason Beaton .02 .10
303 Ron Bertrand .02 .10
304 Michael Burman .02 .10
305 Jamie Caruso .02 .10
306 Allan Cox .02 .10
307 Tim Favot .02 .10
308 Trevor Halverson .02 .10
309 Derian Hatcher .40 1.00
310 Bill Lang .02 .10
311 Jason MacDonald .02 .10
312 Gary Miller .02 .10
313 Chris Ottmann .02 .10
314 Chad Penney .02 .10
315 Rick Pollard .02 .10
316 Bradley Shepard .02 .10
317 John Spoltore .08 .25
318 Derek Switzer .02 .10
319 Karl Taylor .02 .10
320 John Vary .02 .10
321 Kevin White .02 .10
322 Billy Wright .02 .10
323 Bert Templeton CO .02 .10
324 North Bay Checklist .01 .05
325 Oshawa Checklist UER .01 .05
326 Jan Benda .02 .10
327 Fred Brathwaite .40 1.00
328 Markus Brunner .02 .10
329 Trevor Burgess .02 .10
330 Clair Cornish .02 .10
331 Mike Cote .02 .10
332 Dave Craievich .02 .10
333 Dale Craigwell .20 .50
334 Jean-Paul Davis .02 .10
335 Mark Deazeley .02 .10
336 Mike Fountain .08 .25
337 Brian Grieve .02 .10
338 Matt Hoffman .02 .10
339 Scott Hollis .02 .10
340 Scott Boston .02 .10
341 Scott Luik .02 .10
342 Craig Lutes .02 .10
343 William MacPherson .02 .10
344 Paul O'Hagan .02 .10
345 Wade Simpson .02 .10
346 Jarrod Skalde UER .20 .50
(Listed on Belleville CL but reverse says Oshawa Generals)
347 Troy Sweet .02 .10
348 Jason Weaver .02 .10
349 Rick Cornacchia CO .02 .10
350 The Trophy .02 .10
351 Greg Bailey .02 .10
352 Ryan Black .02 .10
353 Todd Bocjun UER .08 .25
(Reversed negative on card front)
354 Toby Burkitt .02 .10
355 Scott Campbell .02 .10
356 Jassen Cullimore .02 .10
357 Jason Dawe .08 .25
358 Dan Ferguson .02 .10
359 Bryan Gendron .02 .10
360 Michael Harding .02 .10
361 Joe Hawley .02 .10
362 Peterborough Checklist UER .01 .05
363 Geordie Kinnear .02 .10
364 Chris Longo UER .02 .10
365 Dale McTavish .02 .10
366 Mark Myles .02 .10
367 Don O'Neill .02 .10
368 Jamie Pegg .02 .10
369 Brent Pope .02 .10
370 Kitchener Checklist UER .01 .05
371 Doug Searle .02 .10
372 Troy Stephens .02 .10
373 Mike Tomlinson .02 .10
374 Brent Tully .02 .10
375 Andrew Verner .08 .25
376 Dick Todd CO .02 .10
377 John Tanner .08 .25
378 Adam Bennett .02 .10
379 Kyle Blacklock .02 .10
380 Terry Chitaroni .02 .10
381 Brandon Convery .02 .10
382 J.D. Eaton .02 .10
383 Derek Etches .02 .10
384 Rod Hinks .02 .10
385 Bill Kovacs .02 .10
386 Alain Laforge .02 .10
387 Jamie Matthews .02 .10
388 Glen Murray .75 2.00
389 Dean Cull .02 .10
390 Sean O'Donnell .20 .50
391 Sudbury Checklist UER .01 .05
392 Mike Peca .75 2.00
393 Shawn Rivers .02 .10
394 Dan Ryder .02 .10
395 Alastair Still .02 .10
396 Michael Yeo .02 .10
397 Barry Young .02 .10
398 Jason Young .02 .10
399 Ken MacKenzie CO .02 .10
400 Bob Berg UER .02 .10
(Missing draft eligibility information)
NNO Eric Lindros promo 2.00 5.00

1990-91 7th Inn. Sketch QMJHL

This 268-card standard-size set was produced by 7th Inning Sketch featuring players from the Quebec Major Junior Hockey League. First round picks (1991 NHL Draft) in this set include Patrick Poulin (9), Martin Lapointe (10), and Philippe Boucher (13). The best known players in the set, however, are 1990 second-rounder Felix Potvin and 1991 first-rounder Martin Brodeur. A factory set, a numbered edition of 4,800, was produced and marketed separately.

COMPLETE SET (268) 8.00 20.00
COMPLETE FACT.SET (268) 10.00 25.00
1 Patrick Poulin .08 .25
2 Steve Lupien .08 .25
3 Pierre Gagnon .08 .25
4 Eric Plante .02 .10
5 Stephane Desjardins .02 .10
6 Peter Valenta .02 .10
7 Alexander Legault .02 .10
8 Patrice Brisebois .20 .50
9 Martin Charrois .02 .10
10 Fric Dandenault .02 .10
11 Claude Jutras Jr. .02 .10
12 David Pekarek .02 .10
13 Denis Chasse .08 .25
14 Ian Laperriere .08 .25
15 Roger Larche .02 .10
16 Dave Paquet .02 .10
17 Pascal Lebrasseur .02 .10
18 Eric Meloche .02 .10
19 The Face Off .01 .05
20 Sylvain Rodrigue .08 .25
21 Dary Giarard .02 .10
22 Eric Rochette .02 .10
23 Steve Gosselin .02 .10
24 Martin Lavalle .02 .10
25 Martin Lapointe .75 2.00
26 Eric Brule .02 .10
27 Richard Boivin .02 .10
28 Patrice Martineau .02 .10
29 Dave Tremblay .02 .10
30 Steve Larouche .02 .10
31 Danny Beauregard .02 .10
32 Francois Belanger .02 .10
33 Michel St.Jacques .02 .10
34 Patric Sissillan .02 .10
35 Felix Potvin 1.50 4.00
36 Sebastien Parent .02 .10
37 Eric Duchesne .02 .10
38 Gilles Bouchard .02 .10
39 Martin Gagne .02 .10
40 Stephane Charbonneau .02 .10
41 Martin Beaupre .02 .10
42 Daniel Paradis .02 .10
43 Joe Canale .02 .10
44 Georges Vezina Arena .02 .10
45 Francois Leblanc .08 .25
46 Martin Chaput .02 .10
47 Marc Beaucage .02 .10
48 Carl Mantha .02 .10
49 Jim Bermingham .02 .10
50 Philippe Boucher .08 .25
51 Denis Chalifoux .02 .10
52 Sylvain Naud .02 .10
53 Jean Roberge .02 .10
54 Sandy McCarthy .40 1.00
55 Eric Dubois .02 .10
56 Jean Blouin .02 .10
57 Jason Brousseau .02 .10
58 Pierre Sandke .02 .10
59 Benoit Larose .02 .10
60 Yanick Frechette .02 .10
61 Pierre Calder .02 .10
62 Patric Grise .02 .10
63 Martin Dalfoux .02 .10
64 [illegible] .40 1.00
65 Martin Trudel .02 .10
66 Carl Leblanc .02 .10
67 Martin Brochu .40 1.00
68 Benoit Terrien .02 .10
69 QMJHL Action .02 .10
70 Pascal Vincent .02 .10
71 Christian Tardi .02 .10
72 Christian Campeau .02 .10
73 Eric Raymond .08 .25
74 John Kovacs .02 .10
75 Steve Areas .02 .10
76 Pascal Dufalt .02 .10
77 Greg MacEachern .02 .10
78 Remi Belliveau .02 .10
79 Jocelyn Langlois .02 .10
80 Carl Menard .02 .10
81 Sebastein Foneir .02 .10
82 Jean-Franco Gregoire .02 .10
83 Normand Demers .02 .10
84 Nicolas Lefebvre .02 .10
85 Dominic Maltais .02 .10
86 Mario Therrien .02 .10
87 Daniel Thibault .02 .10
88 Jean-Francois Labbe .40 1.00
89 Alain Cote .02 .10
90 Eric Prillo .02 .10
91 Patrick Nadeau .02 .10
92 Claude Poner .02 .10
93 Stephane Julier .02 .10
94 Patrice Rene .02 .10
95 Francis Coutineir .02 .10
96 Guy Lefebvre .02 .10
97 Carl Boudreau .02 .10
98 Jacques Parent .02 .10
99 Stephane Bouquet .02 .10
100 Yanic Perreault .20 .50
101 Yvan Bergeron .02 .10
102 Jean-Francois Rivard .08 .25
103 Daniel Laflamme .02 .10
104 Francois Bourdeau .02 .10
105 Yvan Charrois .02 .10
106 Patric Genest .02 .10
107 Herve Lapointe .02 .10
108 Jean-Francois Jomphe .08 .25
109 Marc Tardif .02 .10
110 Eric Cardinal .02 .10
111 Denis Cloutier .02 .10
112 QMJHL Action .02 .10
113 Alain Samscartier .01 .05
114 Marquis Mathieu .08 .25
115 Stephan Tartari .02 .10
116 QMJHL Action .02 .10
117 QMJHL Action .02 .10
118 Martin Ray .02 .10
119 David Boudreault .02 .10
120 Mario Durroulin .02 .10
121 Jean-Francis Dieard .02 .10
122 QMJHL Action .02 .10
123 QMJHL Action .02 .10
124 Mausime Gagne .02 .10
125 Stephane Guellet .02 .10
126 Steven Paiement .02 .10
127 Francois Olympique .02 .10
128 Eric Coci .02 .10
129 Simon Toupin .02 .10
130 Shane Doirrin .02 .10
131 Todd Sparks .02 .10
132 Bruno Lajeunesse .02 .10
133 Marcel Cousineau .20 .50
134 Claude-Charl Sauirol .02 .10
135 Eric Bellerose .02 .10
136 QMJHL Action .02 .10
137 QMJHL Action .02 .10
138 Martin Lepage .02 .10
139 Michael Langauer .02 .10
140 Fredric Boivin .02 .10
141 Steven Dinn .02 .10
142 QMJHL Action .02 .10
143 QMJHL Action .02 .10
144 Dan Paolucci .02 .10
145 Bruno Villeneuve .02 .10
146 Checklist Card .08 .25
(Yanic Perreault)
147 Checklist Card .01 .05
148 Stefan Simoes .02 .10
149 Joel Blain .02 .10
150 Eric Lavigne .02 .10
151 Checklist Card .01 .05
152 Checklist Card .01 .05
(Patrick Poulin)
153 Robert Melanson .02 .10
154 Brian Rogger .02 .10
155 Checklist Card .01 .05
156 Checklist Card .01 .05
157 Francois Ouellette .08 .25
158 QMJHL Action .02 .10
159 Checklist Card .75 2.00
(Felix Potvin)
160 Checklist Card .01 .05
161 Checklist Card .01 .05
162 Checklist Card .01 .05
163 QMJHL Action .02 .10
164 QMJHL Action .02 .10
165 Checklist Card .01 .05
166 Checklist Card .01 .05
167 QMJHL Action .02 .10
168 QMJHL Action .02 .10
169 Pierre Fillon .02 .10
170 Yanick Degrace .08 .25
171 Paul Daigneault .02 .10
172 Stacy Dellaire .02 .10
173 Steve Searles .02 .10
174 Todd Gillingham .02 .10
175 Yves Sarault .02 .10
176 Jason Downey .02 .10
177 Paul Brousseau .02 .10
178 Raymond Delarosbi .02 .10
179 Yvan Corbin .02 .10
180 Gaston Drapeau .02 .10
181 Celebration .02 .10
182 Reginald Brezeault .02 .10
183 Eric Lafrance .02 .10
184 Martin Lavalle .02 .10
185 Sebastein Lavallee .02 .10
186 Sebastien Bordeleau .02 .10
187 Richard Hamelin .02 .10
188 Eric Beaulieu .02 .10
189 Hughes Mongeon .02 .10
190 Alaine Cole .02 .10
191 Eric Desrochers .08 .25
192 Eric Joyal .02 .10
193 Steve Dortigny .02 .10
194 Fredrick Lefebvre .02 .10
195 Patrick Hebert .02 .10
196 Johnny Lorenzo .08 .25
197 Sylvain Cornier .02 .10
198 QMJHL Action .02 .10
199 Dave Morissette .02 .10
200 Yanick Dupre .02 .10
201 Eric Marcoux .02 .10
202 Bruno Ducharme .02 .10
203 Martin Caron .02 .10
204 Yves Meunier .02 .10
205 Eric Bissonette .02 .10
206 Jason Underhill .02 .10
207 Dave Belliveau .02 .10
208 Steve Lapointe .02 .10
209 Dean Melanson .02 .10
210 Trevor Dehaime .02 .10
211 Jacques Leblanc .02 .10
212 Normand Pacquet .02 .10
213 Huges Laliberte .02 .10
214 Craig Prior .02 .10
215 Patrick Labrecque .08 .25
216 Patrick Cloutier .02 .10
217 Michael Bazinet .02 .10
218 Christian Proulx .02 .10
219 QMJHL Action .02 .10
220 Charles Poulin .02 .10
221 Christian Larivierre .02 .10
222 Martin Brodeur 3.00 8.00
223 Yanick Lemay .02 .10
224 Dennis Leblanc .02 .10
225 Francois Groleau .02 .10
226 Pierre Sevigny .02 .10
227 Pierre Allard .02 .10
228 Craig Martin .02 .10
229 Karl Dykhuis .08 .25
230 Etienne Lavoie .02 .10
231 Stan Melanson .02 .10
232 Dominic Rheaume .02 .10
233 Mario Nobili .02 .10
234 Martin Gendron .08 .25
235 Stephane Menard .02 .10
236 David St.Pierre .02 .10
237 Yan Arsenault .02 .10
238 Norman Flynn .01 .05
239 QMJHL Action .02 .10
240 David Chouinard .02 .10
241 Robert Guilliet .02 .10
242 Martin Lajeunesse .02 .10
243 Nichol Cloutier .02 .10
244 Joel Brouchard .08 .25
245 Donald Brashear .40 1.00
246 Sebastien Tremblay .02 .10
247 Dominique Grandmaison .02 .10
248 Nicolas Lefebvre .02 .10
249 Joseph Napolitano .02 .10
250 Marc Savard .02 .10
251 Alain Gauthier .02 .10
252 Patrick Cole .02 .10
253 Richard Aimonette .02 .10
254 Martin Laitre .02 .10
255 Carl Lamonthe .02 .10
256 QMJHL Action .02 .10
257 Andre Durocher .02 .10
258 Jocelyn Martel .02 .10
259 Jeanot Ferlard .02 .10
260 Claude Savoie .02 .10
262 Denis Beauchamp .02 .10
263 Jean-Francois Gagnon .02 .10
264 Andre Boulaine .02 .10
265 Paul-Emile Exantus .02 .10
266 Danny Nolet .02 .10
267 Jean Lebreau .02 .10
268 Claude Barthe .02 .10

1990-91 7th Inn. Sketch WHL

The 7th Inning Sketch WHL Hockey set contains 347 standard-size cards. The front features a full color photo, framed by different color borders, with the player's name and "WHL" in the bar below the picture. The set includes noteworthy cards of Scott Niedermayer and, Chris Osgood. A factory set, (a numbered edition of 6,000), was produced and marketed separately. Card number 120 was never issued.

COMPLETE SET (347) 7.20 18.00
COMPLETE FACT.SET (347) 8.00 20.00
1 Brent Bilodeau .08 .25
2 Craig Chapman .01 .05
3 Jeff Jubenville .02 .10
4 Al Kinisky .02 .10
5 Kevin Malgunas .02 .10
6 Andy MacIntyre .02 .10
7 Darren McAusland .01 .05
8 Mike Seaton .01 .05
9 Turner Stevenson .20 .50
10 Lindsay Valis .02 .10
11 Dave Wilkie .08 .25
12 Jesse Wilson .02 .10
13 Dody Wood .02 .10
14 Bradley Zavisha .02 .10
15 Vince Boe .02 .10
16 Scott Davis .02 .10
17 Troy Hyatt .02 .10
18 Trevor Pennock .02 .10
19 Corey Schwab .20 .50
20 Scott Bellefontaine .08 .25
21 Travis Kelln .02 .10
22 Peter Anholt CO/GM .01 .05
23 Sonny Mignacca UER .08 .25
24 Chris Osgood .75 2.00
25 Murray Garbutt .02 .10
26 Kalvin Knibbs .02 .10
27 Jason Krywulak .02 .10
28 Jason Miller .02 .10
29 Rob Niedermayer .30 .75
30 Clayton Norris .02 .10
31 Jason Prosofsky .08 .25
32 Dana Rieder .02 .10
33 Kevin Riehl .02 .10
34 Tyler Romanchuk .02 .10
35 Dave Shute .02 .10
36 Lorne Toews .02 .10
37 Scott Townsend .02 .10
38 David Cooper .08 .25
39 Jon Duval .02 .10
40 Dan Kordic .08 .25
41 Mike Rathje .20 .50
42 Tim Bothwell CO .02 .10
43 Brent Thompson .08 .25
44 Jeff Knight .02 .10
45 Van Burgess .02 .10
46 Kimbi Daniels .08 .25
47 Curtis Friesen .02 .10
48 Todd Holt .02 .10
49 Blake Knox .02 .10
50 Trent McCleary .02 .10
51 Mark McFarlane .02 .10
52 Eddie Patterson .02 .10
53 Lloyd Pellitier .02 .10
54 Geoff Sanderson .30 .75
55 Andrew Schneider .02 .10
56 Tyler Wright .08 .25
57 Joel Dyck .02 .10
58 Len MacAusland .02 .10
59 Evan Marble .02 .10
60 David Podlubny .02 .10
61 Kurt Seher .02 .10
62 Jason Smith .02 .10
63 Justin Burke .08 .25
64 Kelly Thiessen .08 .25
65 Todd Esselmont .02 .10
66 Graham James CO/GM .01
67 Chris Herperger .02 .10
68 Mark McCoy .02 .10
69 Dean Malkoc .08 .25
70 Dennis Sproxton .08 .25
71 Centennial Civic Center .02 .10
72 Kimbi Daniels .08 .25
73 Shane Calder .02 .10
74 Mark Franks .02 .10
75 Greg Leahy .02 .10
76 Dean Rambo .02 .10
77 Scott Scissons .02 .10
78 David Struch .02 .10
79 Derek Tibbatts .02 .10
80 Shawn Yakimishyn .02 .10
81 Trent Coghill .02 .10
82 Robert Lelacheur .02 .10
83 Richard Matvichuk .30 .75
84 Mark Raiter .02 .10
85 Trevor Sherban .02 .10
86 Mark Wotton .08 .25
87 Cam Moon .08 .25
88 Trevor Robins .08 .25
89 Jeff Buchanan .02 .10
90 Ryan Strain .02 .10
91 Tim Cox .02 .10
92 Terry Ruskowski CO .02 .10
93 Saskatchewan Place .02 .10
94 Darin Bader .02 .10
95 Gaetan Blouin .02 .10
96 Rick Kozuback CO/GM .01 .05
97 Jason Bowen .02 .10
98 Fran Deferenza .02 .10
99 Terry Degner .02 .10
100 Devin Derksen .02 .10
101 Martin Svetlik .02 .10
102 Jeremy Warring .08 .25
103 Corey Jones .08 .25
104 Dean Tiltgen UER .02 .10
105 Ryan Fujita .02 .10
106 Jeff Fancy .02 .10
107 Terry Virtue .20 .50
108 Dennis Pinfold .02 .10
109 Kyle Reeves .02 .10
110 Steve McNutt UER .02 .10
111 Todd Klassen .02 .10
112 Darren Hastman .02 .10
113 Bill Lindsay .20 .50
114A Brian Sakic ERR .02 .10
(Misspelled Buan on card front)
114B Brian Sakic COR .02 .10
115 Dan Sherstenka .02 .10
116 Don Blishen .08 .25
117 Jason Marshall .02 .10
118 Dean Zayonce .02 .10
119 Brad Loring .02 .10
121 Darcy Austin UER .08 .25
122 Darcy Werenka .02 .10
123 Shane Peacock .02 .10
124 Rob Hartnell UER .02 .10
125 Brad Zimmer .02 .10
126 Allan Egeland .02 .10
127 Brad Rubachuk .02 .10
128 Jamie Pushor .20 .50
129 Jamie McLennan UER .30 .75
130 Lance Burns .02 .10
131 Ryan Smith .02 .10
132 Jason McBain .02 .10
133 Duane Maruschak UER .02 .10
134 Kevin St.Jacques .02 .10
135 Jason Sorochan .02 .10
136 Jason Widmer .02 .10
137 Bob Loucks CO .02 .10
138 Jason Ruff .02 .10
139 Pat Pylypuik .02 .10
140 Scott Adair .02 .10
141 Radek Sip .02 .10
142 Russ West .02 .10
143 Scott Thomas .02 .10
144 Kent Staniforth .02 .10
145 Travis Thiessen .02 .10
146 Mark Hussey .02 .10
147 Kevin Masters .02 .10
148 Todd Johnson .02 .10
149 Bob Loucks .02 .10
150A Rob Reimer ERR .02 .10
(Numbered 149 on back)
150B Rob Reimer COR .02 .10
151 Jeff Petruic .02 .10
152 Chris Schmidt .02 .10
153 Scott Barnstable .02 .10
154 Ian Layton .02 .10
155 Kevin Smyth .02 .10
156 Kim Deck .02 .10
157 Jason White .02 .10
158 Peter Cox .02 .10
159 Jeff Calvert UER .08 .25
160 Paul Dyck UER .02 .10
161 Derek Kletzel .02 .10
162 Jason Fitzsimmons UER .08 .25
163 Darcy Jerome .02 .10
164 Hal Christiansen .02 .10
165 Terry Hollinger .02 .10
166 Mike Risdale .08 .25
167 Jamie Heward .02 .10
168 Louis Dumont .02 .10
169 Cory Dosdall .02 .10
170 Terry Bendera .02 .10
171 Jamie Hayden .02 .10
172 Kelly Chotowetz .02 .10
173 Brad Scott .02 .10
174 Jeff Shantz .30 .75
175 Kelly Markwart .02 .10
176 Gary Pearce .02 .10
177 Kerry Biette .02 .10
178 Jamie Splett .02 .10
179 Frank Kovacs .02 .10
180 Greg Pankewicz .02 .10
181 Colin Ruck .02 .10
182 Brad Tippett CO .02 .10
183 Dusty Imoo .08 .25
184 Derek Eberle .02 .10
185 Heath Weenk .02 .10
186 Mike Sillinger .20 .50
187 Erin Thornton .02 .10
188 Mike Chrun .02 .10
189 Pat Falloon .20 .50
190 Bobby House UER .02 .10
191 Mike Jickling .02 .10
192 Trevor Tovall UER .02 .10
193 Steve Junker .02 .10
194 Shane Maitland .02 .10
195 Chris Lafreniere .02 .10
196 Frank Evans .02 .10
197 Jon Klemm .30 .75
198 Shawn Dietrich UER .08 .25
199 Dennis Saharchuk UER .02 .10
200 Mark Woolf .02 .10
201 Ray Whitney .20 .50
202 Scott Bailey .08 .25
203 Mark Ruark .02 .10
204 Brent Thurston .02 .10
205 Dan Faassen .02 .10
206 Kerry Toporowski .02 .10
207 Des Christopher .08 .25
208 Geoff Grandberg .02 .10
209 Bryan Maxwell CO .02 .10
210 Cam Danyluk .02 .10
211 Brian Vanderkracht .02 .10
212 Calvin Thudium .02 .10
213 Mark Szoke UER .02 .10
214 Kelly McCrimmon CO/GM .02 .10
215 Kevin Robertson UER .02 .10
216A Brian Purdy ERR .02 .10
(Misspelled Puroy on card front)
216B Brian Purdy COR .02 .10
217 Hardy Sauter .02 .10
218 Dwayne Gylywoychuk .02 .10
219 Bart Cote .02 .10
220 Merv Priest .02 .10
221 Jeff Hoad .02 .10
222 Glen Gulutzan .02 .10
223 Johan Skillgard .02 .10
224 Byron Penstock .08 .25
225A Mike Vadenberghe ERR .02 .10
(Misspelled Vandenberghe on card front)
225B Mike Vadenberghe COR .02 .10
226 Trevor Kidd .40 1.00
227 Dan Kopec .02 .10
228 Greg Hutchings .02 .10
229 Chris Constant .02 .10
230 Glen Webster .02 .10
231 Rob Puchniak .02 .10
232 Calvin Flint .02 .10
233 Stuart Scantlebury .02 .10
234 Jason White .02 .10
235 Gary Audette .02 .10
236 Kevin Schmalz .02 .10
237 Dwayne Newman .02 .10
238 Chris Catellier .02 .10
239 Todd Harris .02 .10
240 Mike Shemko .02 .10
241 John Badduke .02 .10
242 Mark Cipriano .02 .10
243 Brad Bagu .02 .10
244 Ross Harris .02 .10
245 Dino Caputo .02 .10
246 Cam Bristow .02 .10
247 Jarret Zukiwsky UER .02 .10
248 Jason Knox .02 .10
249 Gerry St.Cyr .02 .10
250 Larry Woo .02 .10
251 Jason Peters .02 .10
252 Shane Stangby .02 .10
253 Dave McMillen .02 .10
254 Colin Gregor UER .02 .10
255 Steve Passmore .40 1.00
256 Shayne Green UER .02 .10
257 Kevin Koopman .08 .25
258 Larry Watkins UER .02 .10
259 Scott Fukami UER .02 .10
260 Rick Hopper CO .01 .05
261 Laurie Billeck .02 .10
262 Rob Daum CO/GM UER .01 .05
263 Mark Stowe .02 .10
264 Curtis Regnier .02 .10
265 David Neilson .02 .10
266 Brian Pellerin .02 .10
267 Dean McAmmond .20 .50
268 Darren Van Impe .15 .40
269 Troy Neumeier .02 .10
270 Mike Langen .08 .25
271 Dan Kesa .02 .10
272 Travis Laycock .08 .25
273 Scott Allison .02 .10
274 Jeff Gorman .02 .10
275 Lee J. Leslie .02 .10
276 Jason Kwiatkowski .02 .10
277 Donevan Hextall UER .02 .10
278 Shane Zulyniak .02 .10
279 Darren Perkins .02 .10
280 Chad Seibel .02 .10
281 Jeff Nelson .02 .10
282 Troy Hjertas .02 .10
283 Jamie Linden .02 .10
284 Zac Boyer .02 .10
285 Jarret Bousquet .02 .10
286 Steven Yule .02 .10
287 Tommy Renney CO UER .08 .25
(Renny on back)
288 Lance Johnson .02 .10
289 Scott Niedermayer .75 2.00
290 Ryan Harrison .02 .10
291 Ed Patterson .08 .25
292 Jeff Watchorn .02 .10
293 Cal McGowan .02 .10
294 Dale Masson .08 .25
295 Joey Mittelsteadt UER .02 .10
296 Scott Loucks .02 .10
297 Shea Esselmont .02 .10
298 Craig Bonner .02 .10
299 Mike Mathers .02 .10
300 Fred Hettle .02 .10
301 Craig Lyons .02 .10
302 Murray Duval .02 .10
303 Jamie Barnes .02 .10
304 Bryan Gourlie .02 .10
305 Chad Bereznuik .02 .10
306 Corey Hirsch .20 .50
307 Darryl Sydor .30 .75
308 Jarrett Deuling .02 .10
309 Cory Stock .02 .10
310 Chris Rowland .02 .10
311 Mike Ruark .02 .10
312 Steve Konowalchuk .30 .75
313 Jeff Sebastian .02 .10
314 Brandon Smith .08 .25
315 Greg Gatto .02 .10
316 Brad Harrison .02 .10
317 Brantt Myhres .40 1.00
318 Jamie Black .02 .10
319 Colin Foley .02 .10
320 Cam Danyluk .02 .10
321 Dean Dorchak .02 .10
322 Ryan Slemko .02 .10
323 Kim Deck .02 .10
324 Kelly Harris .02 .10
325 Murray Bokenfohr .02 .10
326 Dean Intwert .08 .25
327 Dennis Saharchuk UER .02 .10
328 Shane Seiker UER .02 .10
329 Terry Virtue .20 .50
330 Josh Erdman .02 .10
331 Layne Roland .02 .10
332 Michel Michon .02 .10
333 Scott Mydan UER .02 .10
334 Brandon Wheat Kings .01 .05
335 Moose Jaw Warriors .01 .05
336 Swift Current Broncos .01 .05
337 Regina Pats UER .01 .05
338 Saskatoon Blades .01 .05
339 Medicine Hat Tigers .01 .05
340 The Goalmouth .01 .05
341 Portland Winter Hawks .01 .05
342 Kamloops Blazers UER .01 .05
343 Victoria Cougars .01 .05
344 Tri City Americans .01 .05
345 Spokane Chiefs .01 .05
346 Seattle Thunderbirds .01 .05
347 Lethbridge Hurricanes .01 .05
348 Prince Albert Raiders .01 .05

1990 7th Inn. Sketch Memorial Cup

ERIC LINDROS

The 7th Inn. Sketch Memorial Cup Hockey set consists of 100 standard-size cards. The front features a borderless color posed photo of the player against an aqua blue background. The upper right corner of the picture is cut off and various hockey league logos are placed there. The set features players from the four semi-final teams in the 1990 Memorial Cup playoffs, Kamloops Blazers (1-25), Kitchener Rangers (26-49), Laval Titans (50-74), and Oshawa Generals (75-100). These cards were only issued as factory sets, with a numbered edition of 3,000 sets. The set features cards of future NHL players Corey Hirsch, Eric Lindros, Martin Lapointe, Scott Niedermayer, and Darryl Sydor.

COMPLETE SET (100) 30.00 50.00
1 Len Barrie .20 .50
2 Zac Boyer .20 .50
3 Dave Chyzowski .20 .50
4 Shea Esselmont .20 .50
5 Todd Esselmont .20 .50
6 Phil Huber .20 .50
7 Lance Johnson .20 .50
8 Paul Kruse .20 .50
9 Cal McGowan .20 .50
10 Mike Needham .20 .50
11 Brian Shantz .20 .50
12 Darryl Sydor .75 2.00
13 Jeff Watchorn .20 .50
14 Jarrett Bousquet .20 .50
15 Todd Harris .20 .50
16 Deen Malkoc .20 .50
17 Joey Mittelstadt .20 .50
18 Scott Niedermayer 1.25 3.00
19 Clayton Young .20 .50
20 Trevor Sim .20 .50
21 Murray Duval .20 .50
22 Steve Yule .20 .50
23 Craig Bonner .20 .50
24 Dale Masson .20 .50
25 Corey Hirsch .40 1.00
26 Joe McDonnell .20 .50
27 Rick Chambers .20 .50
28 John Finnie .20 .50
29 Randy Pearce .20 .50

30 Mark Montanari .20 .50
31 Mike Torchia .20 .50
32 Jason York .30 .75
33 Jason Firth .20 .50
34 Jamie Israel .20 .50
35 Richard Borgo .20 .50
36 John Uniac .20 .50
37 Steve Smith .20 .50
38 Steven Rice .20 .50
39 Gilbert Dionne .30 .75
40 Cory Keenan .20 .50
41 Rick Allain .20 .50
42 John Copley .20 .50
43 Gib Tucker .20 .50
44 Chris LiPuma .20 .50
45 Brad Barton .20 .50
46 Rival Fullum .20 .50
47 Joey St.Aubin .20 .50
48 Jack Williams .20 .50
49 Shayne Stevenson .20 .50
50 Pierre Creamer .20 .50
51 Carl Mantha .20 .50
52 Julian Cameron .20 .50
53 Sandy McCarthy .75 2.00
54 Gino Odjick .40 1.00
55 Eric Raymond .20 .50
56 Carl Boudreau .20 .50
57 Greg MacEachern .20 .50
58 Allen Kerr .20 .50
59 Patrice Brisebois .30 .75
60 Eric Bissonette .20 .50
61 Martin Lapointe 1.25 3.00
62 Michel Gingras .20 .50
63 Sylvain Naud .20 .50
64 Pat Caron .20 .50
65 Regis Tremblay .20 .50
66 Francois Pelletier .20 .50
67 Jason Brousseau .20 .50
68 Eric Dubois .20 .50
69 Claude Boivin .20 .50
70 Denis Chalifoux .20 .50
71 Jim Bermingham .20 .50
72 Daniel Arsenault .20 .50
73 Normand Demers .20 .50
74 Serge Anglehart .20 .50
75 Rick Cornacchia .20 .50
76 Kevin Butt .20 .50
77 Fred Brathwaite 1.25 3.00
78 Paul O'Hagan .20 .50
79 Craig Donaldson .20 .50
80 Jean-Paul Davis .20 .50
81 Brian Grieve .20 .50
82 Bill Armstrong .20 .50
83 Wade Simpson .20 .50
84 Dave Craievich .20 .50
85 Dale Craigwell .30 .75
86 Joe Busillo .20 .50
87 Cory Banika .20 .50
88 Eric Lindros 10.00 20.00
89 Iain Fraser .20 .50
90 Mike Craig .20 .50
91 Jarrod Skalde .30 .75
92 Brent Grieve .20 .50
93 Scott Luik .20 .50
94 Matt Hoffman .20 .50
95 Trevor McIvor .20 .50
96 Scott Hollis .20 .50
97 Mark Deazeley .20 .50
98 Clair Cornish .20 .50
99 Oshawa Wins 2.00 5.00
(Eric Lindros holding
up Memorial Cup)
100 Checklist Card .02 .10

1991-92 7th Inn. Sketch OHL

Brent Gretzky

This 384-card standard-size set was issued by 7th Inning Sketch and features players of the Ontario Hockey League. The production run was limited to 9,000 factory sets, with each set individually numbered "X of 9,000." On a white card face, the fronts feature color action player photos enclosed by different color frames. The player's name, the year and league, and the team name appear below the picture. The cards are numbered on the back and checklisted below according to teams. Cards numbered 98, 147, 293 and 360 were never produced.

COMPLETE SET (384) 8.00 20.00
1 John Slaney .07 .20
2 Jason Meloche .02 .10
3 Mark DeSantis .02 .10
4 Richard Raymond .02 .10
5 Dave Lemay .02 .10
6 Matt McGuffin .02 .10
7 Sam Oliveira .02 .10
8 Jeremy Stevenson .05 .15
9 Todd Walker .02 .10
10 Jean-Alain Schneider .02 .10
11 Guy Leveque .05 .15
12 Shayne Gaffar .02 .10
13 Mike Prokopec .05 .15
14 Nathan LaFayette .07 .20
15 Larry Courville .08 .25
16 Chris Clancy .02 .10
17 Tom Nemeth .05 .15
18 Jeff Reid .02 .10
19 Ilpo Kauhanen .08 .25
20 Rob Dykeman .08 .25
21 Rival Fullum .05 .15
22 Ryan VandenBussche .08 .25
23 Jordan Bell .05 .15
24 Paul Andrea UER .02 .10
Team affiliation says
Generals; should
say Royals
25 John Lovell CO UER .01 .05
Team affiliation says
Generals; should
say Royals
26 Alan Letang .02 .10
27 Chris Phelps .02 .10
28 John Wynne .02 .10
29 Rob Kinghan .02 .10
30 Glen Craig .02 .10
31 Eric Cairns .40 1.00
32 John Pinches .02 .10
33 Todd Harvey .20 .50
34 Craig Fraser .02 .10
35 Pat Peake .08 .25
36 Chris Skoryna .02 .10
37 Bob Wren .05 .15
38 Chris Varga .02 .10
39 David Benn .02 .10
40 Mark Lawrence .05 .15
41 Jeff Kostuch .02 .10
42 J.D. Eaton .02 .10
43 Derek Etches .02 .10
44 Jeff Gardiner .02 .10
45 James Shea .08 .25
46 Brad Teichmann .08 .25
47 Jim Rutherford CO .05 .15
48 Derek Wilkinson .05 .15
49 OHL Action .02 .10
50 OHL Action .02 .10
51 Sandy Allan .08 .25
52 Ron Bertrand .08 .25
53 Brad Brown .08 .25
54 Dennis Bonvie .40 1.00
55 Bradley Shepard .02 .10
56 Allan Cox .02 .10
57 Jack Williams .05 .15
58 Chad Penney .02 .10
59 Jason Firth .02 .10
60 Bill Lang .02 .10
61 Ryan Merritt .02 .10
62 Michael Burman .02 .10
63 Billy Wright .02 .10
64 Dave Szabo .02 .10
65 James Sheehan .02 .10
66 John Spoltore .02 .10
67 Paul Rushforth .02 .10
68 Jeff Shevalier .07 .20
69 Robert Thorpe .02 .10
70 Drake Berehowsky .08 .25
71 Patrick Barton .02 .10
72 Bert Templeton CO .05 .15
73 Wade Gibson .02 .10
74 C.J. Denomme UER .08 .25
Name spelled C. Jay
on back
75 Mike Torchia .08 .25
76 Mike Polano .02 .10
77 Tony McCabe .02 .10
78 Chris Kraemer .02 .10
79 Tim Spitzig .02 .10
80 Trevor Gallant .02 .10
81 Yvan Corbin .02 .10
82 Norman Dezainde .05 .15
83 Marc Robillard .02 .10
84 Derek Gauthier .02 .10
85 Gib Tucker .02 .10
86 Paul McCallion .02 .10
87 Eric Manlow .05 .15
88 Jamie Caruso .02 .10
89 Gary Miller .02 .10
90 Jason Stevenson .02 .10
91 Shayne McCosh .02 .10
92 Jason Gladney .02 .10
93 Brad Barton .02 .10
94 Chris LiPuma .07 .20
95 Justin Cullen .02 .10
96 Bill Smith SCOUT .01 .05
97 Joe McDonnell CO .01 .05
99 Brent Gretzky .08 .25
100 Gairin Smith .02 .10
101 Blair Scott .02 .10
102 Daniel Godbout .02 .10
103 Dan Preston .02 .10
104 Ian Keiller .02 .10
105 Rick Marshall .02 .10
106 Aaron Morrison .02 .10
107 Dominic Belanger .02 .10
108 Kevin Brown .05 .15
109 Tony Cimellaro .02 .10
110 Larry Mavety CO .01 .05
111 Jake Grimes .05 .15
112 Greg Dreveny .08 .25
113 Darren McCarty .75 2.00
114 Doug Doull .02 .10
115 Scott Boston .05 .15
116 Dale Chokan .02 .10
117 Darren Hurley .02 .10
118 Brian Mielko UER .02 .10
Card misnumbered 61
119 Richard Gallace UER .02 .10
Card misnumbered 65
120 Shayne Antoski .08 .25
121 Greg Bailey .02 .10
122 Keith Redmond .02 .10
123 Dick Todd CO .05 .15
124 Scott Turner .02 .10
125 Colin Wilson .02 .10
126 Mike Tomlinson .02 .10
127 Dale McTavish .02 .10
128 Chris Longo .02 .10
129 Chad Lang .08 .25
130 Brent Tully .05 .15
131 Shawn Heins .05 .15
132 Geordie Kinnear .05 .15
133 Jeff Walker .02 .10
134 Chris Pronger 1.25 3.00
135 Chad Grills .02 .10
136 Michael Harding .02 .10
137 Matt St.Germain .02 .10
138 Don O'Neill .02 .10
139 Dave Roche .08 .25
140 Doug Searle .02 .10
141 Bryan Gendron .02 .10
142 Kelly Vipond .05 .15
143 Andrew Verner .08 .25
144 Ryan Black .05 .15
145 Jason Dawe .08 .25
146 Jassen Cullimore .08 .25
148 Jason Arnott .40 1.00
149 Jan Benda .05 .15
150 Todd Bradley .02 .10
151 Markus Brunner .05 .15
152 Jason Campeau .02 .10
153 Mark Deazeley .02 .10
154 Matt Hoffman .02 .10
155 Scott Hollis .02 .10
156 Neil Iserhoff .02 .10
157 Darryl Lafrance .02 .10
158 B.J. MacPherson .05 .15
159 Troy Sweet .02 .10
160 Jason Weaver .02 .10
161 Stephane Yelle .20 .50
162 Trevor Burgess .02 .10
163 Joe Cook .02 .10
164 Jean-Paul Davis .02 .10
165 Brian Grieve .02 .10
166 Rob Leask .07 .20
167 Wade Simpson .02 .10
168 Kevin Spero .02 .10
169 Fred Brathwaite .40 1.00
170 Mike Fountain .08 .25
171 Rick Cornacchia .05 .15
172 Checklist 1-98 .01 .05
173 Todd Warriner .08 .25
174 Reuben Castella .02 .10
175 Cory Stillman .20 .50
176 Steve Gibson .02 .10
177 Trent Cull .02 .10
178 John Copley .02 .10
179 Craig Binns .02 .10
180 Ryan O'Neill .02 .10
181 Matthew Mullin .08 .25
182 Todd Hunter .02 .10
183 Jason Stos .02 .10
184 Robert Frayn .02 .10
185 Leonard MacDonald .02 .10
186 Tom Sullivan .02 .10
187 Steve Smith .02 .10
188 Bill Bowler .08 .25
189 James Allison .02 .10
190 Kevin MacKay .02 .10
191 David Myles .02 .10
192 Wayne Maxner GM CO .02 .10
193 Dave Prpich CO UER .01 .05
Windsor on front;
should say Spitfires
194 Brady Blain .02 .10
195 Eric Stamp UER .02 .10
Windsor on front;
should say Spitfires
196 OHL Action .02 .10
197 David Babcock .02 .10
198 Brad Love .02 .10
199 Jade Junkin .02 .10
200 Rick Corriveau .02 .10
201 Scott Campbell .02 .10
202 Jason Clarke .02 .10
203 George Burnett .02 .10
204 Ryan Tocher .02 .10
205 Dennis Maxwell .08 .25
206 Greg Scott .02 .10
207 Mark Tardiff .02 .10
208 Neil Fewster .02 .10
209 Jason Coles .02 .10
210 Randy Hall CO .01 .05
211 Todd Simon .05 .15
212 Ethan Moreau .30 .75
213 Todd Wetzel .02 .10
214 Tom Moores .02 .10
215 Geoff Rawson .02 .10
216 Dan Krisko .02 .10
217 Manny Legace .40 1.00
218 Kevin Brown .05 .15
219 Steve Staios .07 .20
220 Checklist 99-196 .01 .05
221 Checklist 197-290 .01 .05
222 Tony Bella .02 .10
223 Shawn Caplice .02 .10
224 Keli Corpse .05 .15
225 Chris Gratton .40 1.00
226 Gord Harris .02 .10
227 Cory Johnson .02 .10
228 Kevin King .02 .10
229 Justin Morrison .05 .15
230 Alastair Still .02 .10
231 Chris Scharf .02 .10
232 Brian Stagg .02 .10
233 Mike Dawson .02 .10
234 Rod Pasma .02 .10
235 Craig Rivet .08 .25
236 Dave Stewart .02 .10
237 John Vary .02 .10
238 Jason Wadel .02 .10
239 Joel Yates .02 .10
240 Mark Lamothe .08 .25
241 Pete McGlynn .08 .25
242 Gilmour OHL Action .02 .10
243 Checklist 291-383 .01 .05
244 Joel Sandie .02 .10
245 Glen Murray .40 1.00
246 Derek Armstrong .02 .10
247 Michael Peca .40 1.00
248 Barry Young .02 .10
249 Bernie John .02 .10
250 Terry Chitaroni .05 .15
251 Jason Young .02 .10
252 Rod Hinks .02 .10
253 Michael Yeo .02 .10
254 Kyle Blacklock .05 .15
255 Dan Ryder .08 .25
256 Doug Mason CO .01 .05
257 Jamie Rivers .08 .25
258 Brandon Convery .07 .20
259 Barrie Moore .02 .10
260 Shawn Rivers .05 .15
261 Jamie Matthews .07 .20
262 Tim Favot .02 .10
263 Bob MacIsaac .02 .10
264 Sean Gagnon .02 .10
265 Ken MacKenzie GM CO .01 .05
266 George Dourion .02 .10
267 Brian MacKenzie .02 .10
268 Jason Zohil .02 .10
269 Rick Tarasuk .02 .10
270 Jamie Storr .30 .75
271 Sean Basilio .08 .25
272 Rick Morton .02 .10
273 Jason Hughes .02 .10
274 Scott Walker .40 1.00
275 Willie Skilliter .02 .10
276 Shawn Krueger .02 .10
277 Jason MacDonald .02 .10
278 Kirk Maltby .20 .50
279 Brock Woods .02 .10
280 Troy Hutchinson .02 .10
281 Geordie Maynard .02 .10
282 Luigi Calce .02 .10
283 Steven Parson .20 .50
284 Andrew Brunette .20 .50
285 Robert MacKenzie .02 .10
286 Jason Buetow .02 .10
287 Wyatt Buckland .02 .10
288 Jim Brown .02 .10
289 Gord Dickie .02 .10
290 Jeff Smith .02 .10
291 Peter Ambroziak .05 .15
292 Mark O'Donnell UER .02 .10
Name spelled
O'donnell on back
294 Grayden Reid .05 .15
295 Sean Spencer .08 .25
296 Gerry Skrypec .02 .10
297 Billy Hall .02 .10
298 Sean Gawley .02 .10
299 Grant Marshall .08 .25
300 Michael Johnson .02 .10
301 Brett Seguin .02 .10
302 Chris Coveny .02 .10
303 Ryan Kuwabara .05 .15
304 Jeff Ricciardi .02 .10
305 Curt Bowen .05 .15
306 Zbynek Kukacka .02 .10
307 Chris Gignac .02 .10
308 Steve Washburn .08 .25
309 Brian Kilrea CO .05 .15
310 Mike Lenarduzzi .08 .25
311 Matt Stone .02 .10
312 Ken Belanger .02 .10
313 Chris Simon .20 .50
314 Kiley Hill .02 .10
315 Chris Grenville .02 .10
316 Aaron Gavey .08 .25
317 Briane Thompson .02 .10
318 Ted Nolan CO .08 .25
319 Perry Pappas .02 .10
320 Kevin Hodson .20 .50
321 Colin Miller .02 .10
322 Tom MacDonald .02 .10
323 Shaun Imber .02 .10
324 Jarret Reid .02 .10
325 Tony Iob .02 .10
326 Mark Matier .02 .10
327 Drew Bannister .07 .20
328 Jason Denomme .02 .10
329 David Matsos .02 .10
330 Rick Kowalsky .02 .10
331 Tim Bacik .08 .25
332 Ralph Intranuovo .07 .20
333 Jonas Rudberg .02 .10
334 Jeff Toms .02 .10
335 Jason Julian .02 .10
336 Brian Goudie .02 .10
337 Gary Roach .02 .10
338 Brad Baber .02 .10
339 Todd Gleason UER .05 .15
Team affiliation says
Greyhounds; should
say Storm
340 Chris McMurtry .02 .10
341 Matt Turek .02 .10
342 Shane Johnson .02 .10
343 Grant Pritchett .02 .10
344 Mike Cote .02 .10
345 Duane Harmer .02 .10
346 Jeff Bes .05 .15
347A Wade Whitten .02 .10
347B Dan Tanevski UER .02 .10
(Should be number 360)
348 Bill Kovacs .05 .15
349 Kayle Short .02 .10
350 Sylvain Cloutier .07 .20
351 Brent Watson .02 .10
352 Brent Pope .02 .10
353 Craig Lutes .02 .10
354 Michael Hartwick .02 .10
355 Kevin Reid .02 .10
356 Toby Burkitt .02 .10
357 Todd Bertuzzi .75 2.00
358 Angelo Amore .08 .25
359 Jeff Pawluk .02 .10
361 Gordon Ross .02 .10
362 Dennis Purdie .30 .75
363 Dave Gilmore .02 .10
364 Brent Brownlee .08 .25
365 Aaron Nagy .02 .10
366 Barry Potomski .40 1.00
367 Steve Smillie .02 .10
368 Kelly Reed .02 .10
369 Gary Agnew CO .01 .05
370 Chris Taylor .05 .15
371 Brett Marietti .02 .10
372 Cory Evans .02 .10
373 Brian Stacey .02 .10
374 Chris Crombie .02 .10
375 Derrick Crane .02 .10
376 Scott McKay .05 .15
377 Gregory Ryan .02 .10
378 Mark Visheau .02 .10
379 Gerry Arcella .02 .10
380 Nick Stajduhar .05 .15
381 Jason Allison .75 2.00
382 Sean O'Reilly .02 .10
383 Paul Wolanski .02 .10
XXX Chris Schushack .05 .15
numbered 000

1991-92 7th Inn. Sketch QMJHL

This 298-card standard-size set was issued by 7th Inning Sketch and features players of the Quebec Major Junior Hockey League. The production run was limited to 4,000 factory sets, with each set individually numbered "X of 4,000." On a white card face, the fronts feature color action player photos enclosed by different color frames. The corners of the picture are cut out to permit space for gold stars. The player's name, the year and league, and the team name appear below the picture. In a horizontal format, the backs have biography, statistics, and player profile in French and English. The cards are numbered on the back and checklisted below according to teams as follows: St. Hyacinthe Laser (1-28), Granby Bisons (29-52), Shawinigan Cataractes (53-77), Chicoutimi Sagueneens (78-101), Trois Rivieres Draveurs (102-125), Verdun College Francais (126-150), St. Jean Lynx (151-172), Beauport Harfangs (173-198), Hull Olympiques (199-223), Laval Titan (224-248), Victoriaville Tigres (249-273), and Drummondville Voltigeurs (274-296). Card number 256 was never produced.

COMPLETE SET (297) 6.00 15.00
1 Martin Brodeur 1.50 4.00
2 Normand Paquet .02 .10
3 David Desnoyers .02 .10
4 Carlo Colombi .02 .10
5 Stephane Menard .08 .25
6 Sebastien Berube .02 .10
7 Marc Desgagne .02 .10
8 Mil Sukovic .02 .10
9 Patrick Belisle .02 .10
10 Patrick Poulin .08 .25
11 Martin Trudel .02 .10
12 Charles Poulin .05 .15
13 Etienne Thibault .02 .10
14 Pierre Allard .02 .10
15 Francois Gagnon .02 .10
16 Stephane Huard .02 .10
17 Yannik Lemay .02 .10
18 Dany Fortin .02 .10
19 Carl Menard .02 .10
20 Serge Labelle .02 .10
21 Dean Melanson .02 .10
22 Yves Meunier .02 .10
23 Pierre Petroni CO .01 .05
24 Mario Pouliot CO UER .01 .05
(Team affiliation says
Bisons; should say Laser)
25 Alain Cote UER .05 .15
(Team affiliation on
front says Bisons;
should say Lasers;
Back erroneously says
Kingston Frontenancs)
26 Hugues Laliberte .02 .10
27 Martin Gendron .08 .25
28 Stan Melanson .02 .10
29 Carl Lebianc .02 .10
30 Patrick Grise .02 .10
31 Yves Charron .02 .10
32 Hughes Mongeon .02 .10
33 Christian Tardif .02 .10
34 Patrick Tessier .02 .10
35 Christian Campeau .02 .10
36 Mario Therrien .02 .10
37 Martin Balleux .02 .10
38 Joel Brassard .02 .10
39 Sebastien Fortier .02 .10
40 Jocelyn Langlois .02 .10
41 Giuseppe Argentos .02 .10
42 Sylvain Brisson .02 .10
43 Philippe Boucher .08 .25
44 Martin Brochu .40 1.00
45 Marc Rodgers .02 .10
46 Pascal Gagnon .02 .10
47 Benoit Therrien .02 .10
48 Robin Bouchard .02 .10
49 Michel Savoie .02 .10
50 Jean-Sebastien Boileau .02 .10
51 Patrick Lamoureux .02 .10
52 Stephane Giard .08 .25
53 Maxime Jean .02 .10
54 Alain Cote .05 .15
55 Francois Groleau .05 .15
56 Richard Hamelin .05 .15
57 Eric Beauvis UER .05 .15
(Name misspelled
Beavis on back)
58 Steve Laplante .02 .10
59 Yves Meunier .02 .10
60 Steve Dontigny .02 .10
61 Simon Roy .02 .10
62 Jean-Francois Laroche .02 .10
63 Patrick Traverse .08 .25
64 Eric Joyal .02 .10
65 Jean-Francois .02 .10
Gregoire UER
(Name misspelled
Jean-Fracois on front)
66 Jocelyn Charbonneau .05 .15
67 Jean Imbeau .05 .15
68 Francois Bourdeau .02 .10
69 Alain Savage Jr. .02 .10
70 Johnny Lorenzo .08 .25
71 Patrick Lalime .75 2.00
72 Patrick Melfi .02 .10
73 Marc Tardif .02 .10
74 Marc Savard .02 .10
75 Alain Sanscartier CO .01 .05
76 Pascal Lebrasseur .05 .15
77 Checklist 1-101 .01 .05
78 Dany Girard .02 .10
79 Eddy Gervais .02 .10
80 Dave Tremblay .02 .10
81 Dany Larochelle .02 .10
82 Michel St.Jacques .02 .10
83 Rodney Petawabano .02 .10
84 Eric Duchesne .02 .10
85 Patrick Clement .02 .10
86 Steve Gosselin .02 .10
87 Patrick Lapointe .02 .10
88 Patrice Martineau .02 .10
89 Danny Beauregard .02 .10
90 Martin Lamarche .02 .10
91 Sebastien Parent .02 .10
92 Christian Caron .02 .10
93 Sylvain Careau .08 .25
94 Martin Beaupre .02 .10
95 Daniel Paradis .02 .10
96 Sylvain Rodrigue .08 .25
97 Joe Canale CO .01 .05
98 Patrick Lampron .02 .10
99 Carl Blondin .02 .10
100 Carl Wiseman .02 .10
101 Hugo Hamelin .08 .25
102 Claude Poirier .02 .10
103 Charles Paquette .02 .10
104 Carl Fleury UER .05 .15
(Name spelled FLeury
on front)
105 Paolo Racicot .02 .10
106 Sebastien Moreau .02 .10
107 Pascal Trepanier .02 .10
108 Dominic Maltais .05 .15
109 Steve Ares .02 .10
110 Daniel Thibault .02 .10
111 Eric Messier .20 .50
112 Stephane Julien .02 .10
113 Dave Paquet .02 .10
114 Nicolas Turmel .02 .10
115 Pascal Rheaume .20 .50
116 Carl Boudreau .02 .10
117 Dave Boudreault .02 .10
118 Eric Bellerose .05 .15
119 Steve Searles .02 .10
120 Patrick Nadeau .05 .15
121 Stephan Viens .02 .10
122 Jean-Francois Labbe .40 1.00
123 Jocelyn Thibault 1.25 3.00
124 Gaston Drapeau CO .01 .05
125 Checklist 102-198 .01 .05
126 Martin Lajeunesse .02 .10
127 Etienne Lavoie .02 .10
128 Dominic Rheaume .02 .10
129 Robert Guillet .02 .10
130 Francois Rivard .02 .10
131 Phillippe DeRouville .15 .40
132 Andrej Dobrota .02 .10
133 Pierre Gendron .02 .10
134 Dave Chouinard .02 .10
135 Martin Tanguay .05 .15
136 Jacques Blouin .02 .10
137 Martin Larochelle .02 .10
138 Jean-Martin Morin .02 .10
139 Donald Brashear .40 1.00
140 Stephane Paradis .02 .10
141 Jan Simcik .02 .10
142 Yan Arsenault .02 .10
143 Joel Bouchard .08 .25
144 Jean-Sebastien .02 .10
Lefebvre
145 David St. Pierre UER .05 .15
(Name misspelled
St-Pierre on front)
146 Mario Nobili .02 .10
147 Stacy Dallaire .02 .10
148 Carl Lamothe .05 .15
149 Andre Bouliane .08 .25
150 Simon Arial .02 .10
151 Stephane Madore .02 .10
152 Hughes Bouchard .02 .10
153 Steve Decaen .02 .10
154 Jason Downey .02 .10
155 Raymond Delarosbil .02 .10
156 Lino Salvo .02 .10
157 Reginald Brezeault .02 .10
158 Nathan Morin .02 .10
159 Samuel Groleau .05 .15
160 Patrick Carignan .02 .10
161 Stephane St-Amour .02 .10
162 Marquis Mathieu .05 .15
163 Yves Sarault .05 .15
164 Dave Belliveau .02 .10
165 Trevor Duhaime .02 .10
166 Eric O'Connor .02 .10
167 Christian Proulx .05 .15
168 Martin Lavallee .08 .25
169 Jean-Francois Gagnon .08 .25
170 Eric Lafrance .05 .15
171 Enrico Scardocchio .02 .10
172 David Bergeron .02 .10
173 Guillaume Morin .08 .25
174 Charlie Boucher .02 .10
175 Martin Rozon .02 .10
176 Brandon Piccarreto .02 .10
177 Simon Toupin .05 .15
178 Jamie Bird .02 .10
179 Herve Lapointe .02 .10
180 Ian MacIntyre .02 .10
181 Jean-Francois Rivard .08 .25
182 Alain Chainey CO .01 .05
183 Daniel Laflamme .02 .10
184 Patrice Paquin .02 .10
185 Patrick Deraspe .02 .10
186 Martin Roy .02 .10
187 Jeannot Ferland .02 .10
188 Patrick Genest .02 .10
189 Matthew Barnaby .40 1.00
190 Jean-Guy Trudel .02 .10
191 Eric Moreau .02 .10
192 Eric Cool .05 .15
193 Alexandre Legault .02 .10
194 Gregg Pineo .02 .10
195 LHJMQ Action .02 .10
196 Radoslav Balaz .02 .10
197 Stefan Simoes .02 .10
198 LHJMQ Action .02 .10
199 Francois Paquette .02 .10
200 Paul Macdonald .02 .10
201 Shane Doiron .02 .10
202 Michal Longauer .02 .10
203 Joe Crowley .02 .10
204 Joey Deliva .02 .10
205 Pierre-Francois .02 .10
Lalonde
206 Paul Brousseau .05 .15
207 Martin Lepage .02 .10
208 Yanick DeGrace .08 .25
209 Jim Campbell .08 .25
210 Sebastien Bordeleau .08 .25
211 Marc Legault .08 .25
212 Joel Blain .02 .10
213 Claude Jutras .02 .10
214 Eric Lavigne .05 .15
215 Todd Sparks .02 .10
216 Sylvain Lapointe .02 .10
217 Eric Lecompte .08 .25
218 Thierry Mayer .02 .10
219A Harold Hersh ERR .08 .25
(Jim Campbell photo
on back)
219B Harold Hersh COR .02 .10
220 Frederic Boivin .02 .10
221 Steven Dion .02 .10
222 Alain Vigneault .15 .40
223 Checklist 199-298 .01 .05
224 Petr Valenta .02 .10
225 LHJMQ Action .02 .10
226 Jim Bermingham .02 .10
227 Yanick Dube .08 .25
228 Sandy McCarthy .40 1.00
229 Dany Michaud .02 .10
230 Jason Brousseau .02 .10
231 Marc Beaucage .02 .10
232 Eric Cardinal .02 .10
233 Martin Chaput .02 .10
234 Jean Roberge .02 .10
235 Philip Gathercole .02 .10
236 Michael Gaul .02 .10
237 Yannick Frechette .02 .10
238 Sylvain Blouin .02 .10
239 David Pekarek .02 .10
240 John Kovacs .02 .10
241 Eric Raymond .08 .25
242 Emmanuel Fernandez 1.25 3.00
243 Yan St. Pierre .02 .10
244 Brant Blackned .02 .10
245 Eric Veilleux .02 .10
246 Pascal Vincent .02 .10
247 Benoit Larose .02 .10
248 Olivier Guillaume .02 .10
249 Alain Gauthier .08 .25
250 Bruno Ducharme .08 .25
251 Patrick Charbonneau .08 .25
252 Daniel Germain .02 .10
253 Pascal Chiasson .02 .10
254 Marc Thibeault .02 .10
255 Martin Woods .02 .10
257 Dominic Grand'maison .02 .10
258 Carl Poirer .02 .10
259 Stephane Larocque .02 .10
260 Mario Dumoulin .02 .10
261 Yan Laterreur .02 .10
262 Claude Savoie .05 .15
263 Denis Beauchamp .02 .10
264 Patrick Bisaillon .02 .10
265 Pascal Bernier .02 .10
266 Nicolas Lefebvre .02 .10
267 LHJMQ Action .02 .10
268 Joseph Napolitano .02 .10
269 Sebastien Tremblay .02 .10
270 Alexandre Daigle .20 .50
271 Pierre Pillion .02 .10
272 Yves Lambert .02 .10
273 Pierre Aubry CO .01 .05
274 Yves Loubier .08 .25
275 Pierre Sandke UER .02 .10
(First name Peter
on back)
276 Louis Bernard .02 .10
277 Alain Nasreddine .05 .15
278 Sylvain Ducharme .02 .10
279 Jeremy Caissie .02 .10
280 Eric Meloche .02 .10
281 Ian Laperriere .20 .50
282 Hugo Proulx .07 .20
283 Dave Whittom .02 .10
284 Yanick Dupre .05 .15
285 Eric Plante .02 .10
286 Stephane Desjardins .02 .10
287 Rene Corbet .20 .50
288 David Lessard .02 .10
289 Eric Marcoux .02 .10
290 Alexandre Duchesne .02 .10
291 Maxime Petitclerc UER .02 .10
(Name misspelled
Peticlerc on front)
292 Pierre Gagnon .08 .25
293 Roger Larche UER .02 .10
(Name misspelled
Larache on front)
294 Jean Hamel .02 .10
295 Alexandre Gaumond .02 .10
296 Paul-Emile Exentus .02 .10
297 LHJMQ Action .02 .10
298 LHJMQ Action .02 .10

1991-92 7th Inn. Sketch WHL

This 361-card standard-size set was issued by 7th Inning Sketch and features players of the Western Hockey League. The production run was limited to 7,000 factory sets, with each set individually numbered "X of 7,000." On a white card face, the fronts feature color action player photos enclosed by different color frames. The corners of the picture are cut out to permit space for gold stars. The player's name, the year and league, and the team name appear below the picture. The cards are numbered on the back and checklisted below according to team order.

COMPLETE SET (361) 6.00 15.00
1 Valeri Bure .30 .75
2 Hardy Sauter .02 .10
3 Bryan Maxwell CO .02 .10
4 Scott Bailey .08 .25
5 Mike Gray .02 .10
6 Mark Szoke .02 .10
7 Mike Jickling .02 .10
8 Frank Evans .02 .10
9 Steve Junker .07 .20
10 Greg Gatto .02 .10
11 Jared Bednar .02 .10
12 Justin Hocking .07 .20
13 Paxton Schulte .07 .20
14 Brad Toporowski .02 .10
15 Shane Maitland .02 .10
16 Aaron Boh .02 .10
17 Ryan Duthie .05 .15
18 Craig Reichert .05 .15
19 Danny Faassen .02 .10
20 Randy Toye .02 .10

21 Geoff Grandberg	.02	.10
22 Jeremy Warring	.08	.25
23 Tyler Romanchuck	.02	.10
24 Jamie Linden	.05	.15
25 1990-91 Champs	.02	.10
26 Corey Jones	.08	.25
27 Brandon Smith	.02	.10
28 Mike Williamson	.02	.10
29 Adam Murray	.02	.10
30 Steve Konowalchuk	.20	.50
31 Shawn Stone	.02	.10
32 Adam Deadmarsh	.40	1.00
33 Rick Mearns	.02	.10
34 Chris Rowland	.02	.10
35 Brandon Coates	.02	.10
36 Dave Cammock	.02	.10
37 Colin Foley	.02	.10
38 Dennis Saharchuk	.02	.10
39 Jiri Beranek	.02	.10
40 Chad Seibel	.02	.10
41 Kelly Harris	.02	.10
42 Layne Roland	.02	.10
43 Cale Hulse	.05	.15
44 Ken Hodge CO	.02	.10
45 Peter Cox	.02	.10
46 Joaquin Gage	.20	.50
47 Brent Peterson CO	.02	.10
48 Jason McBain	.02	.10
49 John Badduke	.02	.10
50 Rick Hopper	.01	.05
51 Dave Hamilton	.08	.25
52 Dwayne Newman	.02	.10
53 Chris Catellier	.02	.10
54 Fran Defrenza	.02	.10
55 Randy Chadney	.02	.10
56 David Hebky	.02	.10
57 Craig Fletcher	.02	.10
58 Kane Chaloner	.02	.10
59 Ross Harris	.02	.10
60 Mike Barrie	.02	.10
61 Steve Lingren	.02	.10
62 Shea Esselmont	.02	.10
63 Matt Smith	.02	.10
64 Gerry St.Cyr	.05	.15
65 Andrew Laming	.02	.10
66 Jeff Fancy	.02	.10
67 Ryan Pellaers	.02	.10
68 Steve Passmore	.40	1.00
69 Scott Fukami	.02	.10
70 Darcy Mattersdorfer	.02	.10
71 Chris Hawes	.02	.10
72 The Goalies I	.05	.15
73 Checklist 1-97	.01	.05
74 Riverside Coliseum	.02	.10
75 Tom Renney	.07	.20
76 Corey Hirsch	.20	.50
77 Scott Ferguson	.02	.10
78 Steve Yule	.02	.10
79 Todd Johnson	.02	.10
80 Jarrett Bousquet	.02	.10
81 Mike Mathers	.02	.10
82 Rod Stevens	.02	.10
83 Lance Johnson	.02	.10
84 Zac Boyer	.02	.10
85 Craig Lyons	.05	.15
86 Dale Masson	.08	.25
87 Scott Loucks	.05	.15
88 Darcy Tucker	.20	.50
89 Shayne Green	.05	.15
90 Michal Sup	.02	.10
91 Craig Bonner	.02	.10
92 Jeff Watchorn	.02	.10
93 Jarrett Dueling	.05	.15
94 Ed Patterson	.07	.20
95 David Wilkie	.08	.25
96 The Goalies III	.05	.15
97 A Goal	.02	.10
98 Andy MacIntyre	.02	.10
99 Rhett Trombley	.07	.20
100 Lorne Molleken CO	.01	.05
101 Trevor Robins	.08	.25
102 Jeff Buchanan	.02	.10
103 Mark Raiter	.02	.10
104 Bryce Goebel	.02	.10
105 Paul Buczkowski	.02	.10
106 James Startup	.02	.10
107 Chad Rusnak	.02	.10
108 Sean McFatridge	.02	.10
109 Shane Calder	.05	.15
110 Ryan Fujita	.02	.10
111 Derek Tibbatts	.02	.10
112 Glen Gulutzan	.02	.10
113 Richard Matvichuk	.20	.50
114 Chad Michalchuk	.02	.10
115 Mark Wotton	.07	.20
116 Mark Franks	.02	.10
117 Norm Maracle	.20	.50
118 Jason Becker	.02	.10
119 Shawn Yakimishyn	.02	.10
120 Ed Chynoweth PRES	.05	.15
121 Checklist 98-195	.01	.05
122 Craig Chapman	.02	.10
123 Jeff Jubenville	.02	.10
124 George Zajankala	.02	.10
125 Turner Stevenson	.20	.50
126 Rob Tallas	.20	.50
127 Ryan Brown	.02	.10
128 Andrew Kemper	.02	.10
129 Brendan Witt	.20	.50
130 Troy Hyatt	.02	.10
131 Mike Kennedy	.08	.25
132 Jesse Wilson	.02	.10
133 Kurt Seher	.05	.15
134 Dody Wood	.05	.15
135 Darren McAusland	.02	.10
136 Jeff Sebastian	.02	.10
137 Eric Bouchard	.02	.10
138 Joel Dyck	.02	.10
139 Blake Knox	.02	.10
140 Peter Anholt CO	.01	.05
141 Chris Wells	.08	.25
142 Andrew Reimer	.07	.20
143 Along the Boards	.02	.10
144 Which Way Is Up	.01	.05
145 Checklist 196-287	.01	.05
146 Tacoma Dome	.02	.10
147 Opening Ceremonies	.02	.10
148 Marcel Comeau CO	.02	.10
149 Donn Clark CO	.01	.05
150 John Varga	.05	.15
151 Joey Young	.02	.10
152 Laurie Billeck	.02	.10
153 Jeff Calvert	.08	.25
154 Tuomas Gronman	.08	.25
155 Jason Knox	.02	.10
156 Kevin Malgunas	.02	.10
157 Dave McMillen	.02	.10
158 Darryl Onofrychuk	.08	.25
159 Mike Piersol	.02	.10
160 Lasse Pirjeta	.02	.10
161 Drew Schoneck	.02	.10
162 Corey Stock	.02	.10
163 Ryan Strain	.02	.10
164 Michal Sykora	.05	.15
165 Scott Thomas	.05	.15
166 Toby Weishaar	.02	.10
167 Jeff Whittle	.05	.15
168 The Rockettes	.02	.10
169 Allan Egeland	.05	.15
170 Van Burgess	.02	.10
171 Trever Fraser	.02	.10
172 Jamie Black	.05	.15
173 WHL Action	.02	.10
174 Andy Schneider	.05	.15
175 John McMulkin	.02	.10
176 Rick Girard	.05	.15
177 Shane Hnidy	.02	.10
178 Jason Krywulak	.05	.15
179 Jeremy Riehl	.05	.15
180 Brent Bilodeau	.08	.25
181 Mark McCoy	.02	.10
182 Malt Young	.02	.10
183 Dan Sherstenka	.02	.10
184 Jarrod Daniel	.08	.25
185 Lennie MacAusland	.02	.10
186 Keith McCambridge	.02	.10
187 Jason Horvath	.02	.10
188 Kevin Koopman	.08	.25
189 Chris Herperger	.05	.15
190 Trent McCleary	.08	.25
191 Tyler Wright	.08	.25
192 Todd Holt	.05	.15
193 Ashley Buckberger	.05	.15
194 Bram Vanderkracht	.02	.10
195 Ken Zilka	.02	.10
196 Chris Osgood	.75	2.00
197 Rob Puchniak	.02	.10
198 Todd Dutiaume	.02	.10
199 Mike Maneluk	.07	.20
200 Shawn Dietrich	.08	.25
201 Chris Johnston	.02	.10
202 Brian Purdy	.05	.15
203 Mike Chrun	.02	.10
204 Dan Kopec	.02	.10
205 Ryan Smith	.05	.15
206 Marty Murray	.08	.25
207 Merv Priest	.02	.10
208 Bobby House	.05	.15
209 Chris Constant	.02	.10
210 Dwayne Gylywoychuk	.02	.10
211 Stu Scantlebury	.02	.10
212 Mark Kolesar	.07	.20
213 Craig Geekie	.02	.10
214 Terran Sandwith	.02	.10
215 Jeff Hoad	.02	.10
216 Kelly McCrimmon	.02	.10
217 Carlos Bye	.02	.10
218 Trevor Hanas	.02	.10
219 Jeff Shantz	.20	.50
220 Heath Weenk	.02	.10
221 Nathan Dempsey	.02	.10
222 Louis Dumont	.02	.10
223 Garry Pearce	.02	.10
224 Terry Bendera	.02	.10
225 Hal Christiansen	.02	.10
226 Jason Smith	.20	.50
227 Kerry Biette	.02	.10
228 Barry Becker	.08	.25
229 Derek Eberle	.02	.10
230 Ken Richardson	.02	.10
231 Niklas Barklund	.02	.10
232 Frank Kovacs	.02	.10
233 Not Issued	.01	.05
234 Not Issued	.01	.05
235 Lloyd Pelletier	.08	.25
236 Dale Vossen	.01	.05
237 A.J. Kelham	.02	.10
238 Mike Risdale	.08	.25
239 Brad Bagu	.02	.10
240 Niko Ovaska	.02	.10
241 Brad Tippett CO	.01	.05
242 The Goalies II	.05	.15
243 Lee J. Leslie	.05	.15
244 Darren Perkins	.02	.10
245 Jason Kwiatkowski	.05	.15
246 Jason Renard	.02	.10
247 Dan Kesa	.07	.20
248 Jason Klassen	.02	.10
249 Nick Polychronopoulus	.02	.10
250 David Neilson	.02	.10
251 Merv Haney	.02	.10
252 Troy Hjertaas	.02	.10
253 Curt Regnier	.07	.20
254 Dean McAmmond	.20	.50
255 Travis Laycock	.08	.25
256 Jeff Lank	.02	.10
257 Barkley Swenson	.02	.10
258 Darren Van Impe	.08	.25
259 Ryan Pisiak	.02	.10
260 Jeff Gorman	.02	.10
261 Stan Matwijiw	.08	.25
262 Mike Fedorko	.02	.10
263 Mark Odnokon	.01	.05
264 Shane Zulyniak	.02	.10
265 Jeff Nelson	.07	.20
266 Donevan Hextall	.07	.20
267 Kevin Masters	.02	.10
268 Chris Schmidt	.02	.10
269 Jeff Budai	.02	.10
270 Bill Hooson	.02	.10
271 Fred Hettle	.02	.10
272 Kent Staniforth	.02	.10
273 Travis Stevenson	.02	.10
274 David Jesiolowksi	.02	.10
275 Mike Babcock CO	.01	.05
276 Scott Allison	.02	.10
277 Travis Thiessen	.02	.10
278 Marc Hussey	.02	.10
279 Kevin Smyth	.05	.15
280 Jason Fitzsimmons	.08	.25
281 Jeff Petruic	.02	.10
282 Russ West	.02	.10
283 Derek Kletzel	.05	.15
284 Jarret Zukiwsky	.02	.10
285 Jason Carey	.02	.10
286 Close Checking	.02	.10
287 Checklist 288-360	.01	.05
288 Jason Bowen	.05	.15
289 Dean Tiltgen	.05	.15
290 Terry Degner	.07	.20
291 Jodie Murphy	.02	.10
292 Brian Sakic	.05	.15
293 Jamie Barnes	.02	.10
294 Darren Hastman	.02	.10
295 Todd Klassen	.05	.15
296 Mirsad Mujcin	.02	.10
297 Trevor Sherban	.02	.10
298 Chadden Cabana	.02	.10
299 Adam Rettschlag	.02	.10
300 Mark Toljanich	.02	.10
301 Kory Mullin	.02	.10
302 Byron Penstock	.08	.25
303 Vladimir Vujtek	.07	.20
304 Bill Lindsay	.08	.25
305 Jeff Cej	.02	.10
306 Mike Busniak CO	.02	.10
307 Todd Harris	.02	.10
308 Cory Dosdall	.02	.10
309 Jason Smith	.20	.50
310 Mark Dawkins	.08	.25
311 Dan O'Rourke	.02	.10
312 Darby Walker	.02	.10
313 Olaf Kjenstadt	.05	.15
314 Sonny Mignacca	.08	.25
315 Jon Duval	.02	.10
316 Lorne Toews	.02	.10
317 Dana Rieder	.02	.10
318 Clayton Norris	.05	.15
319 David Cooper	.07	.20
320 Larry Watkins	.02	.10
321 Evan Marble	.02	.10
322 Scott Lindsay	.05	.15
323 Ryan Petz	.02	.10
324 Jeramie Heistad	.02	.10
325 Scott Townsend	.02	.10
326 Stacy Roest	.20	.50
327 Rob Niedermayer	.30	.75
328 Tim Bothwell CO	.05	.15
329 Kevin Riehl	.07	.20
330 Mike Rathje	.08	.25
331 Bryan McCabe	.20	.50
332 MHT Tiger MASCOT	.02	.10
333 Dean Intwert	.08	.25
334 Mike Vandenberghe	.02	.10
335 Cam Danyluk	.02	.10
336 Darcy Austin	.08	.25
337 Jason Knight	.02	.10
338 Lee Sorochan	.08	.25
339 Al Kinisky	.02	.10
340 Rob Hartnell	.02	.10
341 Radek Sip	.02	.10
342 Jamie Pushor	.08	.25
343 Shane Peacock	.02	.10
344 Cadrin Smart	.02	.10
345 Maurice Meagher	.02	.10
346 Lance Burns	.02	.10
347 Dominic Pittis	.20	.50
348 Todd MacIsaac	.02	.10
349 Brad Zimmer	.02	.10
350 Jason Sorochan	.02	.10
351 Darcy Werenka	.07	.20
352 Kevin St.Jacques	.05	.15
353 David Trofimenkoff	.02	.10
354 Terry Hollinger	.05	.15
355 Travis Munday	.02	.10
356 Slade Stephenson	.02	.10
357 Jason Widmer	.07	.20
358 Brad Zavisha	.05	.15
359 Bob Loucks CO	.01	.05
360 Brantt Myhres	.40	1.00
0 Garfield Henderson	.05	.15
Numbered 000		

1991 7th Inn. Sketch CHL Award Winners

This 30-card boxed standard-size set features Canadian Hockey League Award Winners. Each box has on its back a checklist and the set serial number. The cards feature action color player photos with gray borders against a black card face. The player's specific achievement is printed in gray in the black margin at the top. His name and team appear in white at the bottom.

COMPLETE SET (30)	4.00	10.00
1 Eric Lindros	.75	2.00
2 Dale Craigwell	.08	.25
3 Nathan Lafayette	.07	.20
4 Chris Snell	.08	.25
5 Cory Stillman	.20	.50
6 Mike Torchia	.20	.50
7 George Burnett	.07	.20
8 Eric Lindros	.75	2.00
9 Sherwood Bassin	.07	.20
10 Eric Lindros	.75	2.00
11 Scott Niedermayer	.20	.50
12 Pat Falloon	.08	.25
13 Scott Niedermayer	.20	.50
14 Darryl Sydor	.20	.50
15 Donevan Hextall	.07	.20
16 Jamie McLennan	.15	.40
17 Tom Renney	.08	.25
18 Frank Evans	.07	.20
19 Bob Brown	.07	.20
20 Ray Whitney	.20	.50
21 Philippe Boucher	.07	.20
22 Yanic Perreault	.15	.40
23 Benoit Larose	.07	.20
24 Patrice Brisebois	.08	.25
25 Philippe Boucher	.07	.20
26 Felix Potvin	.40	1.00
27 Joe Canale	.07	.20
28 Christian Lariviere	.07	.20
29 Roland Janelle	.07	.20
30 Yanic Perreault	.15	.40

1991 7th Inn. Sketch Memorial Cup

The 1991 7th Inn. Sketch Memorial Cup Hockey set captures the four teams that participated in the Canadian junior hockey championship, with one team each from the OHL and WHL, and two from the QMJHL (the host league). The cards measure the standard size and feature on the fronts color action player photos enclosed by silver borders. The upper right and lower left corners are cut off to permit space for the CHL and '91 Memorial Cup logos, respectively. The player's name in the bottom silver border rounds out the card face. The set is skip-numbered due to the fact that several cards were withdrawn from the set after only a few sets had been released. These 17 card numbers are 21, 36 (Rob Dykeman), 96 (Eric Lindros), 106 (Pat Peake), 107 (Steve Staios), 110 (Alex Stojanov), 111 (Glen Murray), 113 (Jason Dawe), 114 (Nathan Lafayette), 116 (Guy Leveque), 118 (Shayne Antoski), 119 (Eric Lindros), 120 (Dennis Purdie), 121 (Terry Chitaroni), and 124 (Jamie Matthews).

COMPLETE SET (130)	50.00	100.00
COMPLETE SHORT SET (113)	6.00	15.00
1 Mike Lenarduzzi	.08	.25
2 Kevin Hodson	.20	.50
3 OHL Action Sault Ste. Marie vs. Oshawa	.05	.15
4 Bob Boughner	.20	.50
5 Adam Foote	.30	.75
6 Brad Tiley	.05	.15
7 Brian Goudie	.05	.15
8 Wade Whitten	.05	.15
9 Jason Denomme	.05	.15
10 David Matsos	.05	.15
11 Rick Kowalsky	.05	.15
12 Jarret Reid	.05	.15
13 Perry Pappas	.05	.15
14 Tom MacDonald	.05	.15
15 Mike DeCoff	.05	.15
16 Joe Busillo	.05	.15
17 Denny Lambert	.08	.25
18 Mark Matier	.05	.15
19 Shaun Imber	.05	.15
20 Ralph Intranuovo	.08	.25
21 Chris Snell SP	.75	2.00
22 Tony Iob	.05	.15
23 Colin Miller	.05	.15
24 Ted Nolan	.20	.50
25 Sylvain Rodrigue	.05	.15
26 Felix Potvin	1.50	4.00
27 Martin Lavallee	.05	.15
28 Eric Brule	.05	.15
29 Steve Larouche	.05	.15
30 Michel St-Jacques	.05	.15
31 Patrick Clement	.05	.15
32 Patrick Bisaillon	.05	.15
33A Checklist 62-131 SP	.75	2.00
33B Checklist 62-131 (Withdrawn numbers omitted)	.08	.25
34 Gilles Bouchard	.05	.15
35 Eric Rochette	.05	.15
36 Rob Dykeman SP	.75	2.00
37A Checklist 1-61 SP	.75	2.00
37B Checklist 1-61 (Withdrawn numbers omitted)	.08	.25
38 Patrice Martineau	.05	.15
39 Danny Beauregard	.05	.15
40 Francois Belanger	.05	.15
41 Sebastien Parent	.08	.25
42 Martin Gagne	.05	.15
43 Stephane Charbonneau	.05	.15
44 Martin Beaupre	.05	.15
45 Daniel Paradis	.05	.15
46 Joe Canale	.05	.15
47 OHL Action Sault Ste. Marie vs. Oshawa	.05	.15
48 Jubilation	.05	.15
49 Steve Lupien	.05	.15
50 Pierre Gagnon	.05	.15
51 Alexandre Legault	.05	.15
52 Martin Charrois	.05	.15
53 Eric Dandenault	.05	.15
54 Denis Chasse	.08	.25
55 Guy Lehoux	.05	.15
56 Ian Laperriere	.20	.50
57 Hugo Proulx	.05	.15
58 Dave Whittom	.05	.15
59 Yanick Dupre UER	.08	.25
60 Eric Plante	.05	.15
61 Stephane Desjardins	.08	.25
62 Patrice Brisebois	.08	.25
63 Rene Corbet	.20	.50
64 Marc Savard	.05	.15
65 Claude Jutras Jr.	.05	.15
66 David Pekarek	.05	.15
67 Roger Larche UER (Name misspelled Larohe on front)	.05	.15
68 Dave Paquet	.08	.25
69 Eric Meloche	.05	.15
70 CHL Action Spokane vs. Lethbridge	.05	.15
71 Celebration Ed Chynoweth PRES Jon Klemm	.15	.40
72 Felix Potvin MVP	1.50	4.00
73 Scott Bailey	.20	.50
74 Trevor Kidd	.30	.75
75 Chris Lafreniere	.05	.15
76 Frank Evans	.05	.15
77 Jon Klemm	.20	.50
78 Brent Thurston	.05	.15
79 Jamie McLennan	.20	.50
80 Steve Junker	.05	.15
81 Mark Szoke	.05	.15
82 Ray Whitney	.40	1.00
83 Geoff Grandberg	.05	.15
84 Cam Danyluk	.05	.15
85 Kerry Toporowski	.05	.15
86 Trevor Tovell	.05	.15
87 Pat Falloon	.20	.50
88 Bram Vanderkracht	.05	.15
89 Mike Jickling	.05	.15
90 Murray Garbutt	.05	.15
91 Calvin Thudium	.05	.15
92 Mark Woolf	.05	.15
93 Shane Maitland	.05	.15
94 Bart Cote	.05	.15
95 Bryan Maxwell	.05	.15
96 Eric Lindros SP	15.00	30.00
97 Scott Niedermayer	.40	1.00
98 Patrick Poulin	.08	.25
99 Brent Bilodeau	.08	.25
100 Pat Falloon	.20	.50
101 Darcy Werenka	.08	.25
102 Martin Lapointe	.60	1.50
103 Philippe Boucher	.08	.25
104 Jeff Nelson	.08	.25
105 Rene Corbet	.20	.50
106 Pat Peake SP	.75	2.00
107 Steve Staios SP	.75	2.00
108 Richard Matvichuk	.20	.50
109 Dean McAmmond	.20	.50
110 Alex Stojanov SP	.75	2.00
111 Glen Murray SP	1.50	4.00
112 Tyler Wright	.08	.25
113 Jason Dawe SP	1.25	3.00
114 Nathan Lafayette SP	.75	2.00
115 Yanic Perreault	.20	.50
116 Guy Leveque SP	.75	2.00
117 Darren Van Impe	.08	.25
118 Shawn Antoski SP	.75	2.00
119 Eric Lindros SP	15.00	30.00
120 Dennis Purdie SP	.75	2.00
121 Terry Chitaroni SP	.75	2.00
122 Jamie Pushor	.08	.25
123 Chris Osgood	1.50	4.00
124 Jamie Matthews SP	.75	2.00
125 Yves Sarault	.05	.15
126 Yanic Dupre UER	.08	.25
127 Brad Zimmer	.05	.15
128 Copps Coliseum	.05	.15
129 Jason Widmer	.08	.25
130 Marc Savard	.05	.15
131 Mike Torchia		
132 Andrew Verner		

1999-00 Shawinigan Cataractes

This 24-card set features the QMJHL Cataractes. Base cards feature full-color action photography and have green borders along the right side and the bottom of the card where the team logo is also pictured.

COMPLETE SET (24)	4.00	10.00
1 Jonathan Lessard	.15	.40
2 Philippe Gelinas	.15	.40
3 Jonathan Bellemare	.15	.40
4 Anthony Quessy	.20	.50
5 Alexandre Blackburn	.15	.40
6 Pascal Dupuis	.15	.40
7 Marc-Andre Bergeron	.20	.50
8 Francis Desaluriers	.15	.40
9 Jean-Sebastien Trudelle	.15	.40
10 Jean-Philippe Pare	.20	.50
11 Jean-Francois David	.15	.40
12 Philippe Deblois	.15	.40
13 Dave Verville	.15	.40
14 Mathieu Chouinard	.60	1.50
15 Gilbert Lefrancois	.15	.40
16 Denis Desmarais	.15	.40
17 Yannick Noiseux	.15	.40
18 Dominic Forget	.15	.40
19 Conor McGuire	.15	.40
20 Jean-Francois Dufort	.15	.40
21 Andre Landry	.15	.40
22 David Chicoine	.15	.40
23 Jason Pominville	.60	1.50
24 Header Card/CL	.02	.10

1999-00 Shawinigan Cataractes Signed

This 24-card set parallels the base Shawinigan Cataractes set in an autographed version. The fronts feature autographs on a ghosted-out portion of the photo, while the backs are serial numbered out of 100.

COMPLETE SET (24)	20.00	50.00
1 Jonathan Lessard	.75	2.00
2 Philippe Gelinas	.75	2.00
3 Jonathan Bellemare	.75	2.00
4 Anthony Quessy	.75	2.00
5 Alexandre Blackburn	.75	2.00
6 Pascal Dupuis	.75	2.00
7 Marc-Andre Bergeron	1.50	4.00
8 Francis Desaluriers	.75	2.00
9 Jean-Sebastien Trudelle	.75	2.00
10 Jean-Philippe Pare	1.50	4.00
11 Jean-Francois David	.75	2.00
12 Philippe Deblois	.75	2.00
13 Dave Verville	.75	2.00
14 Mathieu Chouinard	4.00	10.00
15 Gilbert Lefrancois	.75	2.00
16 Denis Desmarais	.75	2.00
17 Yannick Noiseux	.75	2.00
18 Dominic Forget	.75	2.00
19 Conor McGuire	.75	2.00
20 Jean-Francois Dufort	.75	2.00
21 Andre Landry	.75	2.00
22 David Chicoine	.75	2.00
23 Jason Pominville	4.00	10.00
24 Header Card/CL	.20	.50

2000-01 Shawinigan Cataractes

This set features the Cataractes of the QMJHL. The set was produced by CTM Ste-Foy and was sold both by that card shop and by the team.

COMPLETE SET (24)	6.00	15.00
1 Denis Desmarais	.16	.40
2 Zbynek Michalek	.16	.40
3 Jonathan Beaulieu	.16	.40
4 Jonathan Lessard	.16	.40
5 Jonathan Bellemare	.16	.40
6 Patrick Bolduc	.16	.40
7 Anthony Quessy	.16	.40
8 David Chicoine	.16	.40
9 Gilbert Lefrancois	.16	.40
10 Radim Vrbata	.60	1.00
11 Yannick Noiseux	.16	.40
12 Marc-Andre Bergeron	.16	.50
13 Jimmy Cuddihy	.20	1.00
14 Kevin Bergin	.16	.40
15 Francois Gagnon	.16	.40
16 Olivier Michaud	2.00	3.00
17 Frederic Cloutier	.16	1.00
18 Jean-Francois David	.16	.40
19 Alexandre Menard Burrows	.16	.40
20 Jason Pominville	.40	1.50
21 Dominic Forget	.16	.40
22 Trevor Ettinger	.16	.40
23 Jean-Francois Dufort	.16	.40
NNO Coaches	.10	.25

2000-01 Shawinigan Cataractes Signed

This set is exactly the same as the base Cataractes set from this season, save that every card has been hand signed by the player pictured. Each card also is serial numbered out of just 100.

COMPLETE SET (24)	24.00	60.00
1 Denis Desmarais	.80	2.00
2 Michalek Zbynek	.80	2.00
3 Jonathan Beaulieu	.80	2.00
4 Jonathan Lessard	.80	2.00
5 Jonathan Bellemare	.80	2.00
6 Patrick Bolduc	.80	2.00
7 Anthony Quessy	.80	2.00
8 David Chicoine	.80	2.00
9 Gilbert Lefrancois	.80	2.00
10 Radim Vrbata	3.20	8.00
11 Yannick Noiseux	.80	2.00
12 Marc-Andre Bergeron	.80	4.00
13 Jimmy Cuddihy	1.20	5.00
14 Kevin Bergin	.80	2.00
15 Francois Gagnon	.80	2.00
16 Olivier Michaud	6.00	15.00
17 Frederic Cloutier	.80	5.00
18 Jean-Francois David	.80	2.00
19 Alexandre Menard Burrows	.80	2.00
20 Jason Pominville	2.00	10.00
21 Dominic Forget	.80	2.00
22 Trevor Ettinger	.80	2.00
23 Jean-Francois Dufort	.80	2.00
NNO Coaches	.10	.25

2001-02 Shawinigan Cataractes

This set features les Cataractes of the QMJHL. The set was produced by well-known card store CTM Ste-Foy, and was sold by that shop and at the team's souvenir stand. Production was limited to no more than 1,000 sets.

COMPLETE SET (24)	6.00	15.00
1 Denis Desmarais	.20	.50
2 Zbynek Michalek	.20	.50
3 Paul-Andre Bourgoin	.20	.50
4 Jimmy Fillion	.30	.75
5 Jonathan Lessard	.20	.50
6 Jonathan Bellemore	.20	.50
7 Mathieu Gravel	.20	.50
8 Jonathan Villeneuve	.20	.50
9 David Chicoine	.20	.50
10 Armands Berzins	.20	.50
11 Philippe Bastarache	.20	.50
12 Jimmy Cuddihy	.40	1.00
13 Chris Hodgson	.20	.50
14 Thiery Poudrier	.20	.50
15 Olivier Michaud	2.00	5.00
16 Guillaume Lavallee	.20	.50
17 David Leroux	.20	.50
18 Jean-Francois David	.20	.50
19 Jonathan Boutin	.20	.50
20 Alexandre Burrows	.20	.50
21 Mathieu Payette	.20	.50
22 Jason Pominville	.30	.75
23 Jean-Francois Dufort	.20	.50
NNO Title Card/CL	.04	.10

2002-03 Shawinigan Cataractes

COMPLETE SET (25)	5.00	12.00
1 Julien Ellis	.30	.75
2 Dave Grenier	.20	.50
3 Paul-Andre Bourgouin	.20	.50
4 Frederic Gariepy	.20	.50
5 Mathieu Gravel	.20	.50
6 Karl Morin	.20	.50
7 Armands Berzins	.20	.50
8 Danick Bouchard	.20	.50
9 Jimmy Cuddihy	.30	.75
10 Mathieu Fournier	.20	.50
11 Kevin Deslauriers	.20	.50
12 Thiery Poudrier	.20	.50
13 David Leroux	.20	.50
14 Sebastien Gauthier	.20	.50
15 Jonathan Villeneuve	.20	.50
16 Michel Bergevin-Robinson	.30	.75
17 Jonathan Boutin	.20	.50
18 Justin Vienneau	.20	.50
19 Marek Hascak	.20	.50
20 Simon-Pierre Sauve	.20	.50
21 Dominic Plante	.20	.50
22 Benoit Mondou	.30	.75
23 Nicolas Desilets	.20	.50
24 Charles Gauthier	.20	.50
25 Checklist	.02	.10

2003-04 Shawinigan Cataractes

COMPLETE SET (23)	5.00	12.00
1 Eric Begin	.20	.50
2 Steve Bellefleur	.20	.50
3 Danick Bouchard	.20	.50
4 Jonathan Boutin	.20	.50
5 Ben Chaisson	.20	.50
6 Jimmy Cuddihy	.30	.75
7 Marty Doyle	.30	.75
8 Nicolas Desilets	.20	.50
9 Julien Ellis	.30	.75
10 Charles Gauthier	.20	.50
11 Sebastien Gauthier	.20	.50
12 Michal Gavalier	.20	.50
13 Marc-Olivier Gignac	.30	.75
14 Mathieu Gravel	.20	.50
15 Pierre-Marc Guilbault	.20	.50
16 Marek Hascak	.20	.50
17 Jonathan Jolette	.20	.50
18 Benoit Mondou	.30	.75
19 Jean-Philippe Paquet	.20	.50
20 Pascal Pelletier	.30	.75
21 Thiery Poudrier	.20	.50
22 Simon-Pierre Sauve	.20	.50
23 Justin Vienneau	.20	.50

2005-06 Shawinigan Cataractes

COMPLETE SET (23)	6.00	12.00
1 Julien Ellis	.30	.75
2 Ben MacFarlane	.20	.50
3 Alex Bourret	.40	1.00
4 Benoit Mondou	.30	.75
5 Jean-Philippe Paquet	.20	.50
6 Justin Vienneau	.20	.50
7 Eric Begin	.20	.50
8 Steve Bellefleur	.20	.50
9 Patrick Bernier	.20	.50
10 Danick Bouchard	.20	.50
11 Nicolas Desilets	.20	.50
12 Guillaume Durand	.20	.50
13 Pierre-Marc Guilbault	.20	.50
14 Kyell Henegan	.20	.50
15 Cedric Lalonde-McNicoll	.20	.50
16 Triston Manson	.20	.50
17 Francis Pare	.20	.50
18 Mathieu Petrin	.20	.50
19 Egor Egorov	.20	.50
20 Charles Milette	.20	.50
21 Guillaume Lahreque	.20	.50
22 Jan Danecek	.20	.50
23 Sean Smyth	.20	.50

1986-87 Sherbrooke Canadiens

This 30-card set of the Sherbrooke Canadiens of the AHL was produced by Graphique Estrie, Inc. The cards feature action photos on the front, surrounded by a white border. The team logo, player name and sweater name appear along the bottom, along with the position in French. These unnumbered cards are listed below in alphabetical order.

COMPLETE SET (30)	4.00	10.00
1 Entraineurs 1986-87	.02	.10
2 Soigneurs 1986-87	.02	.10
3 Coupe Stanley 1986	.20	.50
4 Joel Baillargeon	.15	.40
5 Daniel Berthiaume	.30	.75
6 Serge Boisvert	.15	.40
7 Graeme Bonar	.15	.40
8 Randy Bucyk	.15	.40
9 Bill Campbell	.15	.40
10 Jose Charbonneau	.15	.40
11 Rejean Cloutier	.15	.40
12 Bobby Dollas	.15	.40
13 Peter Douris	.15	.40
14 Steven Fletcher	.15	.40
15 Perry Ganchar	.15	.40
16 Luc Gauthier	.15	.40
17 Randy Gilhen	.15	.40
18 Scott Harlow	.15	.40
19 Rick Hayward	.15	[illegible]
20 Kevin Houle	.15	[illegible]
21 Rick Knickle	.30	[illegible]
22 Vincent Riendeau	.30	[illegible]
23 Guy Rouleau	.15	[illegible]
24 Scott Sandelin	.15	[illegible]
25 Karel Svoboda	.15	[illegible]
26 Peter Taglianetti	[illegible]	[illegible]
27 Gilles Thibaudeau	[illegible]	[illegible]
28 Ernie Vargas	[illegible]	[illegible]
29 Andre Villeneuve	[illegible]	[illegible]
30 Brian Williams	[illegible]	[illegible]

2000-01 Sherbroo[illegible]

This set features the Castors of the QMJHL and was produced by CTM- Ste-Foy. They were made available through that card shop, as well as at the team's home games. Although the set is numbered to 23, it apparently contains just 19 cards. It's not known whether certain cards were pulled, or never produced.

COMPLETE SET (19)	3.60	10.00
1 Drew MacIntyre	.20	.75
2 Sebastien Courcelles	.20	.50
3 Simon Tremblay	.20	.50
4 Eric Lavigne	.20	.50
5 Patrick Gosselin	.20	.50
6 Steve Morency	.20	.50
7 Francis Trudel	.20	.50
9 Jonathan Robert	.20	.50
11 Eric Dagenais	.20	.50
12 Louis-Philip Lemay	.20	.75
13 Artem Trmavski	.20	.50
14 Joey Neale	.20	.50
15 Benoit Genesse	.20	.50
16 Pierre-Luc Courchesne	.20	.50
17 Mathieu Thibodeau	.20	.50
18 Nicolas Corbeil	.40	1.00
21 Francois Belanger	.20	.50
22 Cajou MAS	.04	.10
23 Jos Canale CO	.20	.50

2000-01 Sherbrooke Castors Signed

This set is exactly the same as the base Castors set from this season, save that every card has been hand signed by the player pictured. Each card also is serial numbered out of just 100.

COMPLETE SET (19)	16.00	40.00
1 Drew MacIntyre	1.00	5.00
2 Sebastien Courcelles	1.00	2.50
3 Simon Tremblay	1.00	2.50
4 Eric Lavigne	1.00	2.50
5 Patrick Gosselin	1.00	2.50
6 Steve Morency	1.00	2.50
7 Francis Trudel	1.00	2.50
9 Jonathan Robert	1.00	2.50
11 Eric Dagenais	1.00	2.50
12 Louis-Philip Lemay	1.00	5.00
13 Artem Trmavski	1.00	2.50
14 Joey Neale	1.00	2.50
15 Benoit Genesse	1.00	2.50
16 Pierre-Luc Courchesne	1.00	2.50
17 Mathieu Thibodeau	1.00	2.50
18 Nicolas Corbeil	2.00	5.00
21 Francois Belanger	1.00	2.50
22 Cajou MAS	.04	.10
23 Jos Canale CO	1.00	2.50

2001-02 Sherbrooke Castors

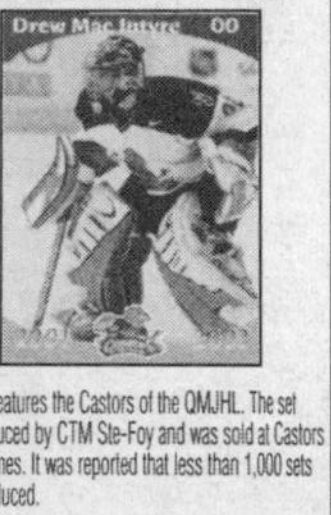

This set features the Castors of the QMJHL. The set was produced by CTM Ste-Foy and was sold at Castors home games. It was reported that less than 1,000 sets were produced.

COMPLETE SET (21)	4.80	12.00
1 Drew MacIntyre	.30	.75
2 Eric Dagenais	.20	.50
3 Dany Roussin	.20	.50
4 Juha-Pekka Ketola	.20	.50
5 Patrik Levesque	.20	.50
6 David Chicoine	.20	.50
7 Jonathan Paiement	.20	.50
8 Cedrick Duhamel	.20	.50
9 Yan Gaudette	.20	.50
10 Francis Trudel	.20	.50
11 Maxime Boisclair	.30	.75
12 Jonathan Robert	.20	.50
13 Mathieu Wathier	.20	.50
14 Louis-Philip Lemay	.30	.75
15 Bertrand-Pierre Plouffe	.30	.75
16 Sebastien Courcelles	.20	.50
17 Patrick Mbaraga	.20	.50
18 Pierre-Luc Courchesne	.20	.50
19 Nicolas Corbeil	.40	1.00
20 Bruno D'Amico	.20	.50
21 Francois Belanger	.20	.50

1993-94 Sherbrooke Faucons

...tly confirmed set features unnumbered cards. ...listed below by jersey number.

...T	6.00	15.00
	2.00	5.00
	.40	1.00
	.20	.50
	.20	.50
	.20	.50
	.20	.50
		.50
		.50
		.50

1974-75 Sioux City Musketeers

This 20-card set is printed on yellow stock. According to the producer, the cards were intended to be standard size but actually came out a little larger. The fronts feature bordered, posed player photos that have a dark green tint to them. In dark green lettering, the team name is printed above the picture while the player's name is printed below it. The cards are unnumbered and checklisted below in alphabetical order. Reportedly only 250 sets were made and they were originally sold at home games for $2.50.

COMPLETE SET (20)	50.00	100.00
1 Steve Boyle	2.50	5.00
2 Dave Davies	2.50	5.00
3 Steve Desloges	2.50	5.00
4 Greg Gilbert	2.50	5.00
5 Barry Head	2.50	5.00
6 Steve Heathwood	2.50	5.00
7 Dave Kartio	2.50	5.00
8 Ralph Kloiber	2.50	5.00
9 Pete Maxwell	2.50	5.00
10 Randy McDonald	2.50	5.00
11 Terry Mulroy	2.50	5.00
12 Sam Nelligan	2.50	5.00
13 Julian Nixon	2.50	5.00
14 Mike Noel	2.50	5.00
15 Jim Peck	2.50	5.00
16 Bogdan Podwysocki	2.50	5.00
17 John Saville P/CO	2.50	5.00
18 Alex Shibicky Jr.	5.00	10.00
19 Bob Thomerson	2.50	5.00
20 Jim White	5.00	10.00

1998-99 Sioux City Musketeers

This set features the Musketeers of the USHL. The oversized (5X6) cards feature an action photo and bio info on the front, along with a blank back. They were issued by the team and sold at the rink. The set is noteworthy for featuring top prospects Rostislav Klesla, David Hale and Ruslan Fedotenko. The set is unnumbered and listed below alphabetically.

COMPLETE SET (25)	8.00	15.00
1 Lee Arnold	.20	.50
2 Michael Betz	.20	.50
3 Mark Bry	.20	.50
4 Chad Dahlen	.20	.50
5 Ruslan Fedotenko	.75	2.00
6 Cullen Flaherty	.20	.50
7 David Hale	.40	1.00
8 Tim Judy	.20	.50
9 Rostislav Klesla	2.00	5.00
10 Nathan Kotewa	.20	.50
11 A.J. Kratofil	.20	.50
12 Jordan Lashmett	.20	.50
13 Brendan McCartin	.20	.50
14 Jake Moreland	.20	.50
15 Trent Mozak	.20	.50
16 Chad Nordhagen	.20	.50
17 Pat O'Leary	.20	.50
18 Chris Olsgard	.20	.50
19 Tyler Palmiscno	.20	.50
20 Luke Pavlas	.30	.75
21 Morgan Roach	.20	.50
22 Tim Skarperud	.20	.50
23 Jeff Van Dyke	.20	.50
24 Adam Wallace	.20	.50
25 B.J. Willis	.20	.50

1999-00 Sioux City Musketeers

This set features the Musketeers of the USHL. It is believed the set was produced by the team and sold at its souvenir stands. The set is noteworthy for including the first card of David Hale, a 2000 first-round choice of the New Jersey Devils.

COMPLETE SET (21)	4.00	10.00
1 Mike Betz	.20	.50
2 Max Bull	.20	.50
3 Matt Ciancio	.20	.50
4 Chad Dahlen	.20	.50
5 Henry Dryden	.20	.50
6 Lukas Fiala	.20	.50
7 David Hale	.40	1.00
8 Eric Helstedt	.20	.50
9 Justin Hillier	.20	.50
10 Steve Jones	.20	.50
11 Tim Judy	.20	.50
12 A.J. Kratofil	.20	.50
13 Brendan McCartin	.20	.50
14 John Miller	.20	.50
15 Trent Mozak	.20	.50
16 Chad Nordhagen	.20	.50
17 Chris Olsgard	.20	.50
18 Tyler Palmiscno	.20	.50
19 Scott Palaski	.20	.50
20 Brandon Schmitt	.20	.50
21 Jeff Van Dyke	.20	.50

2000-01 Sioux City Musketeers

This set features the Musketeers of the USHL. Little is known about the set beyond the confirmed checklist. ...dditional information can be forwarded to hockey-...@beckett.com.

...E SET (30)	8.00	20.00
	.04	.10
	.30	.75
	.30	.75
	.30	.75
	.30	.75
	.30	.75
	.30	.75
	.30	.75
	.30	.75
	.30	.75
	.30	.75
	.10	.25
13 Tim Judy	.30	.75
14 Erik Johnson	.30	.75
15 Brian Kerr	.30	.75
16 Zechariah Klann	.30	.75
17 Patrick Knutson	.30	.75
18 Jack Kowal CO	.10	.25
19 Brendan McCartin	.30	.75
20 Trent Mozak	.30	.75
21 Brian Panik	.30	.75
22 Scott Polaski	.30	.75
23 Brandon Schmitt	.30	.75
24 Brandon Schwartz	.30	.75
25 Dave Siciliano CO	.10	.25
26 Bryan Smith	.30	.75
27 Mitch Thortsen	.30	.75
28 Aaron Venasky	.30	.75
29 David Vychodil	.30	.75
30 John Zeiler	.30	.75

2004-05 Sioux City Musketeers

COMPLETE SET (30)	8.00	20.00
1 Brian Bales	.30	.75
2 Justin Bostrom	.30	.75
3 Kent Bostrom	.30	.75
4 Chris Butler	.30	.75
5 John Cartera	.30	.75
6 Joe Charlebois	.30	.75
7 Adam Davis	.30	.75
8 Phil DeSimone	.30	.75
9 Corey Elkins	.30	.75
10 Steve Kampfer	.30	.75
11 Nick Kemp	.30	.75
12 Tim Kennedy	.30	.75
13 Peter Lenes	.30	.75
14 Louis Liotti	.30	.75
15 Blake Martin	.30	.75
16 Dennis McCauley	.60	1.50
17 Josh Meyers	.30	.75
18 Christian Minella UER	.30	.75
19 Jon Ralph	.30	.75
20 Chris Spicer	.30	.75
21 Jimmy Spratt	.60	1.50
22 Travis Turnbull	.30	.75
23 Jeff Zatkoff	.60	1.50
24 Team Picture	.30	.75
25 Schedule	.02	.10
26 Mascot	.02	.10
27 Dave Siciliano CO	.02	.10
28 Marty Quarters ACO	.02	.10
29 Chris Brandenberger TR	.02	.10
30 Bill Danderand EQM	.02	.10

2000-01 Sioux Falls Stampede

Set was produced by the team and sponsored by Wells Fargo Bank. The cards are oversized (5" X 6"). The cards are unnumbered and are listed alphabetically. The checklist may be incomplete. If you know of other cards, please contact us at hockeymag@beckett.com.

COMPLETE SET (21)	10.00	25.00
1 Robbie Barker	.30	.75
2 J.B. Bittner	.30	.75
3 Jon Booras	.30	.75
4 Kellen Briggs	.30	.75
5 Jeff Corey	.30	.75
6 Donny DeMars	.30	.75
7 Mike Doyle	.30	.75
8 Jon Dubel	.30	.75
9 John Funk	.30	.75
10 Dave Iannazzo	.30	.75
11 Joe Jensen	.30	.75
12 Josh Grahn	.30	.75
13 Dustan Lick	.30	.75
14 James Massen	.30	.75
15 Jamie Mattie	.30	.75
16 Zach Sikich	.30	.75
17 Dinos Stamoulis	.30	.75
18 Thomas Vanek	4.00	10.00
19 Eric Werner	.30	.75
20 Tom Zaleski	.30	.75
21 Stomp MASCOT	.02	.10

2001-02 Sioux Falls Stampede

These cards are unnumbered. They measure 5 X 6. The set features the first card of Marty Sertich, the 2005 Hobey Baker winner.

COMPLETE SET (19)	10.00	25.00
1 Cody Blanshan	.30	.75
2 Kellen Briggs	.75	2.00
3 Mike Forconi	.30	.75
4 Alex Foster	.30	.75
5 Quinn Fylling	.60	1.50
6 Joe Jensen	.30	.75
7 Jacob Micflikier	.30	.75
8 Jason Moul	.30	.75
9 Eric Przepiorka	.30	.75
10 Layne Sedevie	.40	1.00
11 Marty Sertich	1.50	4.00
12 Jeremy Smith	.30	.75
13 Jesse Stokke	.30	.75
14 Kelly Sullivan	.30	.75
15 Thomas Vanek	3.00	8.00
16 Mike Vannelli	.30	.75
17 Merit Waldrop	.30	.75
18 Jake Wilkens	.30	.75
19 Chris Wothe	.30	.75

2004-05 Sioux Falls Stampede

Set features the Stampede of the USHL. They measure 3"x 4" and are unnumbered. They were issued on four six-card perforated sheets. Set includes 2005 first-rounder T. J. Oshie and Patrick Mullen, son of HOFer Joe Mullen. Thanks to collector Dale Spengler for the list.

COMPLETE SET (24)	15.00	30.00
1-1 Andrew Carroll	.40	1.00
1-2 Tom Gorowsky	.40	1.00
1-3 Nate Prosser	.40	1.00
1-4 Greg Barrett	.75	2.00
1-5 Ryan Thang	.40	1.00
1-6 T.J. Oshie	2.00	5.00
2-1 Chris Peluso	.40	1.00
2-2 Stewart Carlin	.40	1.00
2-3 Aleksanders Jerofejevs	.40	1.00
2-4 Joe Vitale	.40	1.00
2-5 Justin White	.40	1.00
2-6 Andreas Nodl	.40	1.00
3-1 Evan Stephens	.40	1.00
3-2 Warren Byrne	.40	1.00
3-3 Joe Finley	.75	2.00
3-4 John Murray	.75	2.00
3-5 Ben Holmstrom	.40	1.00
3-6 Blake Friesen	.40	1.00
4-1 Justin Milo	.40	1.00
4-2 Jacob Hipp	.40	1.00
4-3 Jon Globke	.40	1.00
4-4 Patrick Mullen	.75	2.00
4-5 Buffalo Wild Wings ad	.02	.10
4-6 Brandon Harrington	.40	1.00

2006-07 Sioux Falls Stampede

COMPLETE SET (24)	12.00	20.00
1 Brad Malone	.40	1.00
2 Patrick Tiesling	.40	1.00
3 Drew Fisher	.40	1.00
4 Ryan Guentzel	.40	1.00
5 David Grun	.40	1.00
6 Matt Lundin	.75	2.00
7 Joey Miller	.40	1.00
8 David Solway	.40	1.00
9 Eric Peterson	.40	1.00
10 Robbie Vrolyk	.40	1.00
11 Doug Schueller ACO	.10	.25
12 Nick Dineen	.40	1.00
13 Stu Bickel	.40	1.00
14 Jake Bauer	.40	1.00
15 Sam Zabkowicz	.40	1.00
16 Zach Redmond	.40	1.00
17 Chris Huxley	.40	1.00
18 Zach Hansen	.40	1.00
19 Dan Sexton	.40	1.00
20 Stomp Mascot	.02	.10
21 Alexi Dostoinov	.40	1.00
22 Jake Drewiske	.40	1.00
23 Kevin Hartzell CO	.10	.25
24 Corey Tropp	.75	2.00

2001-02 Sorel Royaux

This set features the Royaux of the Quebec Senior League. The cards are standard sized and, because they are unnumbered, are listed below alphabetically. Note: the Patrick Roy listed below is not the famous NHL goaltender.

COMPLETE SET (28)	4.80	12.00
1 Daniel Archambault	.20	.50
2 Francois Bourdeau	.20	.50
3 Michel Caron	.20	.50
4 L.P. Charbonneau	.20	.50
5 Georges-Etienne Cote	.20	.50
6 Dany Couette	.20	.50
7 Christian Deschenes	.20	.50
8 Stephane Groleau	.20	.50
9 Eric Joyal	.20	.50
10 Patrick Labrecque	.40	1.00
11 Martin Lacroix	.20	.50
12 Stephane Larocque	.20	.50
13 Jamie Leinhos	.20	.50
14 Justin Leinhos	.20	.50
15 Yanick Levesque GM	.04	.10
16 Dominic Maltais	.40	1.00
17 Francois Paquette	.20	.50
18 Guillaume Rodrigue	.20	.50
19 Patrick Roy	.20	.50
20 Carl St. Germain	.20	.50
21 Yannick Theriault	.20	.50
22 Dan Tice	.20	.50
23 Steve Vincent	.20	.50
24 Sponsor Card	.04	.10
25 Coaching Staff	.04	.10
26 Rink Staff	.04	.10
27 Team Photo	.20	.50
28 History Card	.20	.50

1995-96 South Carolina Stingrays

This 24-card set of the South Carolina Stingrays of the ECHL was produced for the team by Multi-Ad Services. The set was distributed through the team as well. The fronts feature a blurry action photo, along with team and player name. The numbered backs include a portrait and stats.

COMPLETE SET (24)	3.60	9.00
1 Rick Vaive CO	.20	.50
2 Dan Wiebe ACO	.02	.10
3 Joseph Cramp TR	.02	.10
4 Aaron Fackler EQMG	.02	.10
5 Mikhail Volkov	.15	.40
6 Jason Cipolla	.15	.40
7 Mike Ross	.15	.40
8 Rob Concannon	.15	.40
9 Dan Fournel	.15	.40
10 Mark Bavis	.15	.40
11 Darren Ritchie	.15	.40
12 Mike Barrie	.15	.40
13 Marc Tardif	.15	.40
14 Chris Foy	.15	.40
15 Scott Boston	.20	.50
16 Carl LeBlanc	.15	.40
17 Brett Marietti	.15	.40
18 Jared Bednar	.15	.40
19 Paul Rushforth	.15	.40
20 Kevin Knopp	.15	.40
21 Todd Sullivan	.20	.50
22 Justin Duberman	.15	.40
23 Sean Gauthier	.20	.50
24 Mark Rupnow	.15	.40
NNO Header Card	.02	.10

1996-97 South Carolina Stingrays

This 27-card set features the South Carolina Stingrays of the ECHL, and was produced by the team, in conjunction with Marvin Foy Marketing, Inc. The cards feature action photography on the front, complemented by a pair of Stingrays logos on the left side, and the player's name along the lower right border. The back contains two more photos, as well as statistical and biographical data. The set is noteworthy for the rare inclusion of a card depicting a fight in progress (Dan Fournel). The cards boldly feature the player's sweater number on the back of the card, precipitating their numbering thusly below.

COMPLETE SET (28)	4.00	10.00
9 Mike Ross	.15	.40
10 Marc Genest	.15	.40
11 Dan Fournel	.40	1.00
12 David Mayes	.15	.40
14 David Seitz	.15	.40
15 Jeff Romfo	.15	.40
16 Kyle Ferguson	.15	.40
17 Marc Tardif	.15	.40
18 Steve Parson	.15	.40
19 Doug Wood	.15	.40
20 Scott Boston	.30	.75
21 Rob Concannon	.15	.40
22 Rob Butler	.15	.40
24 Brett Marietti	.15	.40
25 Jared Bednar	.15	.40
27 Ed Courtenay	.20	.50
28 Kevin Knopp	.15	.40
29 Jay Moser	.15	.40
30 Corey Cadden	.15	.40
31 Jason Fitzsimmons	.15	.40
33 Chris Hynnes	.15	.40
35 Taras Lendzyk	.15	.40
NNO Header card		
NNO Rick Vaive CO	.20	.50
NNO Aaron Fackler EQMG	.02	.10
NNO Randy Page ANN	.02	.10
NNO Rick Adduono ACO	.02	.10
NNO Kenny Snider TR	.02	.10

2001-02 South Carolina Stingrays

This set features the Stingrays of the ECHL. The set was handed out over the course of several games during the season. The cards are unnumbered and are listed below in alphabetical order.

COMPLETE SET (20)	12.00	30.00
1 Rick Adduono CO	.20	.50
2 Jared Bednar	.80	2.00
3 Ryan Brindley	.60	1.50
4 Adam Calder	.60	1.50
5 Marty Clapton	.60	1.50
6 Jason Fitzsimmons ACO	.20	.50
7 Alan Fyfe	.60	1.50
8 Zach Ham	.60	1.50
9 Jamie Hodson	.80	2.00
10 Joel Irving	.60	1.50
11 Trevor Johnson	.60	1.50
12 Jody Lehman	.60	1.50
13 Hugo Marchand	.60	1.50
14 Brett Marietti	.60	1.50
15 David Seitz	.60	1.50
16 Jason Sessa	.80	2.00
17 Paul Traynor	.80	2.00
18 Buddy Wallace	.60	1.50
19 Chris Wheaton	.60	1.50
20 Brad Williamson	.60	1.50

2002-03 South Carolina Stingrays

This set was sponsored by Mills Printing and was issued as a promotional giveaway at a Stingrays home game.

COMPLETE SET (24)	8.00	20.00
1 Peter Armbrust	.40	1.00
2 Jeff Boulanger	.40	1.00
3 Ryan Brindley	.40	1.00
4 Adam Calder	.40	1.00
5 Marty Clapton	.40	1.00
6 Kirk Daubenspeck	.60	1.50
7 Matt Desrosiers	.40	1.00
8 Robin Gomez	.60	1.50
9 Brent Henley	.60	1.50
10 Curtis Huppe	.40	1.00
11 Joel Irving	.40	1.00
12 Mike Jickling	.40	1.00
13 Trevor Johnson	.40	1.00
14 Brett Marietti	.40	1.00
15 Andy Powers	.40	1.00
16 Aaron Schneekloth	.40	1.00
17 David Seitz	.40	1.00
18 Rod Taylor	.40	1.00
19 Dean Weasler	.40	1.00
20 Brad Williamson	.40	1.00
21 Jason Fitzsimmons CO	.10	.25
22 Jared Bednar ACO	.10	.25
23 DJ Church TR	.01	.05
24 Jocko Cayer EQM	.10	.25

2002-03 South Carolina Stingrays RBI

COMPLETE SET (18)	8.00	20.00
205 Ryan Brinkley	.40	1.00
206 David Brumby	.60	1.50
207 Adam Calder	.40	1.00
208 Marty Clapton	.40	1.00
209 Matt Desrosiers	.40	1.00
210 Kirk Daubenspeck	.60	1.50
211 Robin Gomez	.60	1.50
212 Brent Henley	.60	1.50
213 Curtis Huppe	.40	1.00
214 Joel Irving	.40	1.00
215 Mike Jickling	.40	1.00
216 Trevor Johnson	.40	1.00
217 Brett Marietti	.40	1.00
218 Andy Powers	.40	1.00
219 Aaron Schneekloth	.40	1.00
220 David Seitz	.40	1.00
221 Rod Taylor	.40	1.00
222 Brad Williamson	.40	1.00

2003-04 South Carolina Stingrays

COMPLETE SET (16)	6.00	15.00
321 Chris Allen	.40	1.00
322 Jeff Boulanger	.40	1.00
323 David Brumby	.60	1.50
324 Ed Courtenay	.40	1.00
325 Kirk Daubenspeck	.60	1.50
326 Robin Gomez	.60	1.50
327 Curtis Huppe	.40	1.00
328 Mike Jickling	.40	1.00
329 Colin Johnson	.40	1.00
330 Trevor Johnson	.60	1.50
331 Jim Lorentz	.40	1.00
332 Aaron Power	.40	1.00
333 David Seitz	.40	1.00
334 Shawn Skiehar	.40	1.00
335 Steven Spencer	.40	1.00
336 Kevin Spiewak	.40	1.00

2005-06 South Carolina Stingrays

COMPLETE SET (16)	10.00	20.00
1 Matt Reid	.75	2.00
2 Jeff Legue	.75	2.00
3 Chick-Fil-A Cow	.01	.01
4 Ticket Voucher Card	.01	.01
5 Trevor Johnson	.75	2.00
6 Robin Gomez	.75	2.00
7 Maxime Daigneault	1.50	4.00
8 Ticket Voucher Card	.01	.01
9 Cail McLean	.75	2.00
10 Marty Clapton	.75	2.00
11 Steve Spencer	.75	2.00
12 Ticket Voucher Card	.01	.01
13 Brad Parsons	.75	2.00
14 Nate Kiser	.75	2.00
15 Aaron Power	.75	2.00
16 Ticket Voucher Card	.01	.01

1989-90 Spokane Chiefs

Sponsored by the Spokane Teachers Credit Union, this 20-card standard-size set of the 1989-90 Spokane Chiefs features color posed-on-ice player photos on its fronts. The photos are bordered in team colors (red, white, and blue). The player's name, uniform number, and position appear within the blue border below the picture. The cards are unnumbered and checklisted below in alphabetical order. Reportedly only 3,600 sets were made.

COMPLETE SET (20)	6.00	15.00
1 Mike Chrun	.20	.50
2 John Colvin	.20	.50
3 Shawn Dietrich	.20	.50
4 Milan Dragicevic	.20	.50
5 Frank Evans	.20	.50
6 Pat Falloon	.40	1.00
7 Scott Farrell	.20	.50
8 Jeff Ferguson	.20	.50
9 Travis Green	1.25	3.00
10 Mike Hawes	.20	.50
11 Bobby House	.20	.50
12 Mike Jickling	.20	.50
13 Steve Junker	.20	.50
14 Jon Klemm	.40	1.00
15 Chris Rowland	.20	.50
16 Dennis Saharchuk	.20	.50
17 Kerry Toporowski	.20	.50
18 Trevor Tovell	.20	.50
19 Bram Vanderkracht	.20	.50
20 Ray Whitney	1.25	3.00

1993-94 Spokane Chiefs

This set features the Chiefs of the WHL. The set was produced by the team and sold at home games for $5. The cards are unnumbered and so are listed below in alphabetical order.

COMPLETE SET (30)	6.00	15.00
1 Barry Becker	.30	.75
2 Maxim Bets	.20	.50
3 Valeri Bure	.75	2.00
4 Shaun Byrne	.20	.50
5 Joe Cardarelli	.20	.50
6 John Cirjak	.20	.50
7 Dion Darling	.20	.50
8 Derek Descoteau	.20	.50
9 Ryan Duthie	.20	.50
10 Randy Favaro	.20	.50
11 Craig Geekie	.20	.50
12 Sean Gillam	.20	.50
13 Hugh Hamilton	.20	.50
14 David Jesiolowski	.20	.50
15 Dmitri Leonov	.20	.50
16 Bryan Maxwell CO	.02	.10
17 Bryan McCabe	.40	1.00
18 Memorial Cup Champs	.20	.50
19 Rick More TR	.02	.10
20 Jason Podollan	.20	.50
21 Kevin Popp	.20	.50
22 Kevin Sawyer	.75	2.00
23 Trevor Shoaf	.20	.50
24 Darren Sinclair	.20	.50
25 Darren Smadis	.30	.75
26 Jeremy Stasiuk	.20	.50
27 Scott Townsend	.20	.50
28 Spokane Coliseum	.02	.10
29 Checklist	.02	.10
30 Clover Club Cheerleaders	.20	.50

1994-95 Spokane Chiefs

This set features the Chiefs of the WHL. The cards are standard-sized and were sold at home games. Any additional information can be forwarded to hockeymag@beckett.com.

COMPLETE SET (32)	6.00	15.00
1 Randy Favaro	.20	.50
2 Jarrod Daniel	.20	.50
3 Jason Podollan	.40	1.00
4 Trent Whitfield	.40	1.00
5 Greg Leeb	.20	.50
6 Jay Bertsch	.20	.50
7 Joe Cardarelli	.20	.50
8 Robby Sandrock	.20	.50
9 Kevin Sawyer	.40	1.00
10 Sean Gillam	.20	.50
11 Ryan Berry	.20	.50
12 Mike Haley	.20	.50
13 John Cirjak	.20	.50
14 Jared Hope	.20	.50
15 Joel Boschman	.20	.50
16 Derek Descoteau	.20	.50
17 Jeremy Stasiuk	.20	.50
18 Tomas Pisa	.20	.50
19 Darren Sinclair	.20	.50
20 Paul Bailley	.20	.50
21 Dmitri Leonov	.20	.50
22 Bryan McCabe	.40	1.00
23 Hugh Hamilton	.20	.50
24 Scott Fletcher	.20	.50
25 David Lemanowicz	.40	1.00
26 Mike Babcock CO	.04	.10
27 Parry Schockey CO	.04	.10
28 T.D. Forbes EQMG	.04	.10
29 Ted Schott EQMG	.04	.10
30 Veterans Memorial	.04	.10
31 Veterans Memorial	.04	.10
32 Veterans Memorial	.04	.10

1995-96 Spokane Chiefs

This 30-card set features color player photos in a thin red border on a silver background. The backs carry player information.

COMPLETE SET (30)	4.80	12.00
1 David Lemanowicz	.30	.75
2 Scott Fletcher	.20	.50
3 Hugh Hamilton	.20	.50
4 Chris Lane	.20	.50
5 Dmitri Leonov	.20	.50
6 Darren Sinclair	.20	.50
7 Ty Jones	.30	.75
8 Kris Graf	.20	.50
9 Trent Whitfield	.30	.75
10 Martin Cerven	.30	.75
11 Randy Favaro	.20	.50
12 Jason Podollan	.30	.75
13 Joel Boschman	.20	.50
14 Jared Hope	.20	.50
15 Greg Leeb	.20	.50
16 John Cirjak	.20	.50
17 Mike Haley	.20	.50
18 Ryan Berry	.20	.50
19 Sean Gillam	.20	.50
20 Derek Schutz	.20	.50
21 Joe Cardarelli	.20	.50
22 Adam Magarrell	.20	.50
23 Jay Bertsch	.20	.50
24 John Shockey	.20	.50
25 Mike Babcock CO	.15	.40
26 Parry Shockey ACO	.02	.10
27 T.D. Forss EQMG	.02	.10
28 Ted Schott AEQMG	.02	.10
29 Dan Mitchell	.02	.10
30 Aren Miller	.30	.75

1996-97 Spokane Chiefs

This set features the Chiefs of the WHL. It is believed to have been produced and distributed by the team. Any additional information pertinent to this set can be forwarded to hockeymag@beckett.com.

COMPLETE SET (30)	6.00	15.00
1 Aren Miller	.30	.75
2 Brad Ference	.40	1.00
3 Hugh Hamilton	.20	.50
4 Chris Lane	.20	.50
5 Yegor Mikhailov	.20	.50
6 Ty Jones	.30	.75
7 Kris Graf	.20	.50
8 Trent Whitfield	.30	.75
9 Blake Evans	.20	.50
10 Jared Smyth	.20	.50
11 Joel Boschman	.20	.50
12 Greg Leeb	.30	.75
13 John Cirjak	.20	.50
14 Mike Haley	.20	.50
15 Kyle Rossiter	.30	.75
16 Derek Schutz	.40	1.00
17 Marian Cisar	.40	1.00
18 Joe Cardarelli	.20	.50
19 Adam Magarrell	.20	.50
20 Jay Bertsch	.20	.50
21 Curtis Suter	.20	.50
22 Marc Brown	.20	.50
23 Marc Magliarditi	.30	.75
24 Boomer Mascot	.02	.10
25 Mike Babcock HCO	.02	.10
26 Brett Cox ACO	.02	.10
27 T.D. Forss TR	.02	.10
28 Ted Schott EM	.02	.10
29 Dan Mitchell DRM	.02	.10
30 Spokane All-Star Game	.02	.10

1997-98 Spokane Chiefs

This set features the Chiefs of the WHL. It is believed to have been produced and distributed by the team. Any additional information pertinent to this set can be forwarded to hockeymag@beckett.com.

COMPLETE SET (30)		15.00
1 Aren Miller	.30	.75
2 Brad Ference	.40	1.00
3 Perry Johnson	.20	.50
4 Mark Forth	.20	.50
5 Zenith Komarniski	.30	.75
6 Justin Ossachuk	.20	.50
7 Cole Fischer	.20	.50
8 Brandin Cote	.20	.50
9 Ty Jones	.30	.75
10 Kris Graf	.20	.50
11 Trent Whitfield	.30	.75
12 Jared Smyth	.20	.50
13 Marc Brown	.20	.50
14 Greg Leeb	.30	.75
15 Justin Kelly	.20	.50
16 Ben Johnson	.20	.50
17 Kyle Rossiter	.30	.75
18 Derek Schutz	.30	.75
19 Marian Cisar	.40	1.00
20 Lynn Loyns	.40	1.00
21 Kris Waltze	.20	.50

22 Curtis Suter .20 .50
23 Josh Maser .20 .50
24 Ron Grimard .20 .50
25 Dan Vandermeer .20 .50
26 Shaun Fleming .20 .50
27 Mike Babcock HCO .02 .10
28 Mike Pelino ACO .02 .10
29 T.D. Forss TR .02 .10
30 Dan Mitchell DRM .02 .10

1998-99 Spokane Chiefs

COMPLETE SET (28) 6.00 15.00
1 Mike Babcock CO .20 .50
2 Daniel Bohac .20 .50
3 Kris Callaway .20 .50
4 Brandin Cote .20 .50
5 Jeremy Farr .20 .50
6 Brad Ference .30 .75
7 Cole Fischer .20 .50
8 Mark Forth .20 .50
9 David Hajek .20 .50
10 Chris Harper .20 .50
11 David Haun .20 .50
12 Simon Jones .20 .50
13 Ty Jones .30 .75
14 Tim Krymusa .20 .50
15 Bobby Leavins .20 .50
16 Mike Lencucha .20 .50
17 Lynn Loyns .30 .75
18 Josh Maser .20 .50
19 Mike Pelino .20 .50
20 Kyle Rossiter .20 .50
21 Derek Schutz .20 .50
22 Cam Severson .40 1.00
23 Tim Smith .20 .50
24 Jared Smyth .20 .50
25 Curtis Suter .20 .50
26 Shawn Thompson .20 .50
27 Dan Vandermeer .20 .50
28 Mason Wallin .20 .50

1999-00 Spokane Chiefs

This set features the Chiefs of the WHL. It is believed that the cards were sold in set form by the team. The cards are unnumbered, and are listed below in alphabetical order.

COMPLETE SET (28) 12.00
1 Mike Babcock CO .08 .25
2 Chris Barr .20 .50
3 Daniel Bohac .20 .50
4 Boomer MASCOT .02 .10
5 David Boychuk .20 .50
6 Kris Callaway .20 .50
7 Brandin Cote .20 .50
8 Jeremy Farr .20 .50
9 T.D. Forss EQMG .02 .10
10 Chris Heid .20 .50
11 Matt Keith .20 .50
12 Tim Krymusa .20 .50
13 Mike Lencucha .30 .75
14 Lynn Loyns .30 .75
15 Jeff Lucky .20 .50
16 Tyler MacKay .20 .50
17 Dan Mitchell STAFF .02 .10
18 Bill Peters ACO .02 .10
19 Scott Roles .20 .50
20 Kyle Rossiter .40 1.00
21 Kurt Sauer .30 .75
22 Beau Schott EQMG .02 .10
23 Derek Schutz .20 .50
24 Tim Smith .20 .50
25 Shawn Thompson .20 .50
26 Ryan Thorpe .20 .50
27 Roman Tvrdon .20 .50
28 Mason Wallin .20 .50
29 Spokane Arena .02 .10

2000-01 Spokane Chiefs

This set features the Chiefs of the WHL. It is believed that the cards were sold in set form by the team. The cards are unnumbered and so are listed below in alphabetical order.

COMPLETE SET (30) 4.80 12.00
1 Chris Barr .20 .50
2 David Boychuk .20 .50
3 Barry Brust .30 .75
4 Brandin Cote .20 .50
5 Jevon Desautels .20 .50
6 T.D. Forss EQMG .04 .10
7 Perry Ganchar CO .04 .10
8 Chris Heid .20 .50
9 Barry Horman .20 .50
10 Joff Kehler .20 .50
11 Matt Keith .20 .50
12 Justin Keller .20 .50
13 Tim Krymusa .20 .50
14 Ratislav Lipka .20 .50
15 Lynn Loyns .40 1.00
16 Jeff Lucky .20 .50
17 Tyler MacKay .30 .75
18 Stephen Mann .20 .50
19 Dan Mitchell STAFF .04 .10
20 Chris Ovington .20 .50
21 Craig Perry .20 .50
22 Bill Peters ACO .04 .10
23 Kurt Sauer .30 .75
24 Brad Schell .20 .50
25 Tim Smith .20 .50
26 Shawn Thompson .20 .50
27 Ryan Thorpe .20 .50
28 Roman Tvrdon .20 .50
29 Mason Wallin .20 .50
30 Boomer MASCOT .04 .10

2001-02 Spokane Chiefs

COMPLETE SET (28) 5.00 12.00
1 Header Card .02 .10
2 Chris Barr .20 .50
3 David Boychuk .20 .50
4 Barry Brust .40 1.00
5 Jordan Clarke .20 .50
6 Brandin Cote .20 .50
7 Curtis Darling .40 1.00
8 Jevon Desautels .20 .50
9 Ivan Garcia .20 .50
10 Chris Heid .20 .50
11 Barry Horman .20 .50
12 Joff Kehler .20 .50
13 Matt Keith .30 .75
14 Stuart Kerr .20 .50
15 Chad Klassen .20 .50
16 Tim Krymusa .20 .50
17 Jeff Lucky .20 .50
18 Jeff Lynch .20 .50
19 Kurt Sauer .30 .75
20 Brad Schell .20 .50
21 Scott Scherger .20 .50
22 Mason Wallin .20 .50
23 Perry Ganchar CO .02 .10
24 Bill Peters ACO .02 .10
25 Dan Mitchell TR .02 .10
26 Darcy Bishop TR .02 .10
27 Boomer MASCOT .02 .10
28 Overagers .20 .50

2002-03 Spokane Chiefs

COMPLETE SET (30) 5.00 12.00
1 Chris Barr .20 .50
2 Ryan Blatchford .20 .50
3 Barry Brust .40 1.00
4 Liam Couture .20 .50
5 Andrew DeSousa .20 .50
6 Jevon Desautels .20 .50
7 Chris Heid .20 .50
8 Barry Horman .20 .50
9 Joff Kehler .20 .50
10 Chad Klassen .20 .50
11 Tim Krymusa .20 .50
12 Jakub Langhammer .20 .50
13 Darren Lefebvre .20 .50
14 Jeff Lucky .20 .50
15 Ned Lukacevic .20 .50
16 Doug Lynch .30 .75
17 Jeff Lynch .20 .50
18 Joel Rupprecht .20 .50
19 Brad Schell .20 .50
20 Andy Schenn .20 .50
21 Scott Scherger .20 .50
22 Miroslav Stolc .20 .50
23 Mason Wallin .20 .50
24 Jim Watt .20 .50
25 Colby Zavisha .20 .50
26 Al Conroy CO .02 .10
27 Jamie Huscroft ACO .02 .10
28 Dan Mitchell TR .02 .10
29 Boomer MASCOT .02 .10
30 Darcy Bishop TR .02 .10

2004-05 Spokane Chiefs Magnets

These cards have magnetic backs and were handed out one per night at Wednesday home games.

1 Gary Gladue .75 2.00
2 Jevon Desautels .75 2.00
3 Scott Lynch .75 2.00
4 Chad Klassen .75 2.00
5 Jim Watt .75 2.00
6 Ned Lukacevic .75 2.00
7 Gustav Engman .75 2.00
8 Jeff Lynch .75 2.00

1996-97 Springfield Falcons

This 21-card set was produced by Split Second. These unnumbered cards feature an action photo on the front with a stats package on the reverse. The cards were available through the club at the rink or by mail order.

COMPLETE SET (21) 4.00 10.00
3 Brent Thompson .30 .75
4 Deron Quint .30 .75
5 Steve Cheredaryk .15 .40
10 Kent Manderville .15 .40
11 Hnat Domenichelli .30 .75
12 Steve Martins .30 .75
14 Tom Buckley .15 .40
15 Juha Ylonen .30 .75
16 Chris Longo .15 .40
17 Rhett Gordon .15 .40
19 Tavis Hansen .15 .40
20 Steve Halko .15 .40
22 Scott Levins .15 .40
23 Rob Murray .15 .40
25 Jason McBain .15 .40
27 Jeff Daniels .15 .40
28 Ryan Risidore .20 .50
30 Manny Legace .60 1.50
33 Reggie Savage .15 .40
34 Nolan Pratt .20 .50
35 Scott Langkow .30 .75
44 Kevin Brown .15 .40
NNO AHL Ad Card .01

1997-98 Springfield Falcons

This set features the Falcons of the AHL. The set was produced by SplitSecond and was sold by the team at home games.

COMPLETE SET (26) 4.00 12.00
1 Daniel Briere .75 2.00
2 Ruslan Batyrshin .15 .40
3 Ted Crowley .15 .40
4 Sylvain Daigle .15 .40
5 Andrew Dale .15 .40
6 Shane Doan .75 2.00
7 Jason Doig .20 .50
8 Dan Focht .15 .40
9 Sean Gagnon .15 .40
10 Rhett Gordon .15 .40
11 Tavis Hansen .15 .40
12 Chad Kilger .30 .75
13 Scott Langkow .30 .75
14 Trevor Letowski .40 1.00
15 Scott Levins .20 .50
16 Richard Lintner .20 .50
17 Jason Morgan .15 .40
18 Rob Murray .15 .40
19 Mike Pomichter .15 .40
20 Jeff Shevalier .15 .40
21 Martin Simard .15 .40
22 Brad Tiley .15 .40
23 Dave Farrish CO .08 .25
24 Ron Wilson CO .08 .25
25 PHPA Web Site .01
26 AHL Web Site .01

2002-03 Springfield Falcons

COMPLETE SET (24) 6.00 15.00
1 Ramzi Abid .30 .75
2 Dmitry Afanasenkov .30 .75
3 Nikita Alexeev .40 1.00
4 Frank Banham .20 .50
5 Goran Bezina .20 .50
6 Zac Bierk .40 1.00
7 Jason Bonsignore .20 .50
8 Martin Cibak .20 .50
9 Dan Focht .20 .50
10 Corey Foster .20 .50
11 Martin Grenier .30 .75
12 Jason Jaspers .20 .50
13 Boyd Kane .40 1.00
14 Evgeny Konstantinov .30 .75
15 Kristian Kudroc .20 .50
16 Norm Maciver ACO .02 .10
17 Marty McSorley HCO .20 .50
18 Rob Murray .20 .50
19 Darren Rumble .20 .50
20 Michael Schutte .20 .50
21 Dan Smith .20 .50
22 Jeff Taffe .40 1.00
23 Erik Westrum .40 1.00
24 Shane Willis .20 .50

2003-04 Springfield Falcons Postcards

These singles were recently confirmed. If you have any additional information about this set, please contact us at hockeymag@beckett.com.

COMPLETE SET (28) 15.00 30.00
1 Goran Bezina .40 1.00
2 Trevor Gillies .40 1.00
3 Kiel McLeod .40 1.00
4 Erik Westrum .75 2.00
5 Dustin Wood .40 1.00
6 Igor Knyazev .40 1.00
7 Nikos Tselios .40 1.00
8 Martin Podlesak .40 1.00
9 Darren McLachlin .40 1.00
10 Frederik Sjostrom .40 1.00
11 Jason Jaspers .40 1.00
12 Bryan Helmer .40 1.00
13 Mike Stutzel .40 1.00
14 Peter Ferraro .40 1.00
15 Gary Shuchuk .40 1.00
16 Frank Lukes .40 1.00
17 Chris Ferraro .40 1.00
18 Chris Dyment .40 1.00
19 Frank Banham .75 2.00
20 Jean-Marc Pelletier .75 2.00
21 Mike Wilson .40 1.00
22 Ladislav Kouba .40 1.00
23 Jeremiah McCarthy .40 1.00
24 David LeNeveu .75 2.00
25 Michael Schutte .40 1.00
26 Marty McSorley CO .40 1.00
27 Gord Dineen ACO .20 .50
28 MASCOT .02 .10

2004-05 Springfield Falcons

COMPLETE SET (27) 6.00 15.00
1 Adam Henrich .20 .50
2 Andre Deveaux .20 .50
3 Andreas Holmqvist .20 .50
4 Brian Chapman .20 .50
5 Brian Eklund .30 .75
6 Craig Darby .20 .50
7 Darren Reid .20 .50
8 Dennis Packard .20 .50
9 Derek Bekar .20 .50
10 Doug O'Brien .20 .50
11 Evgeny Artukhin .20 .50
12 Gerard DiCaire .20 .50
13 Harlan Pratt .20 .50
14 Jamie Storr .30 .75
15 Jason Jaspers .20 .50
16 Marc Busenburg .20 .50
17 Mike Egener .20 .50
18 Mitch Fritz .40 1.00
19 Nick Tarnasky .40 1.00
20 Nikita Alexeev .20 .50
21 Nikos Tselios .20 .50
22 Paul Ranger .20 .50
23 Ryan Craig .75 2.00
24 Shane Willis .20 .50
25 Steve McLaren .20 .50
26 Phil Russell ACO .02 .10
27 Dirk Graham CO .02 .10

2005-06 Springfield Falcons

COMPLETE SET (27) 8.00 15.00
1 Adam Henrich .20 .50
2 Andre Deveaux .20 .50
3 Brad Tiley .20 .50
4 Brian Eklund .30 .75
5 Darren Reid .20 .50
6 Dennis Packard .20 .50
7 Doug O'Brien .20 .50
8 Evgeny Artyukhin .20 .50
9 Gerald Coleman .40 1.00
10 Gerard Dicaire .20 .50
11 Harlan Pratt .20 .50
12 Jason Jaspers .20 .50
13 Jim Campbell .20 .50
14 Marek Kvapil .20 .50
15 Mike Egener .40 1.00
16 Mitch Fritz .40 1.00
17 Nick Tarnasky .30 .75
18 Norm Milley .20 .50
19 Paul Ranger .20 .50
20 Steve McLaren .20 .50
21 Ryan Craig .40 1.00
22 Ryan Vesce .20 .50
23 Timo Helbling .20 .50
24 Todd Rohloff .20 .50
25 Dirk Graham CO .02 .10
26 Phil Russell ACO .02 .10
27 Darren Rumble ACO .02 .10

1983-84 Springfield Indians

Produced by Card Collectors Closet (Springfield, MA), this 25-card standard-size set features black-and-white player portraits on a white card face. The team name and year are printed in black at the top. The player's name and position appear at the bottom.

COMPLETE SET (25) 7.20 18.00
1 Gil Hudon .30 .75
2 Jim Ralph 1.25 3.00
3 Todd Bergen .30 .75
4 Len Hachborn .40 1.00
5 John Ollson .20 .50
6 Steve Tsujiura .40 1.00
7 Gordie Williams .20 .50
8 Dave Brown 1.25 3.00
9 Dan Frawley .20 .50
10 Tom McMurchy .20 .50
11 Dave Michayluk .30 .75
12 Bob Mormina .20 .50
13 Perry Pelensky .20 .50
14 Andy Brickley .40 1.00
15 Ross Fitzpatrick .20 .50
16 Florent Robidoux .20 .50
17 Jeff Smith .20 .50
18 Rod Willard .20 .50
19 Darrell Anholt .20 .50
20 Steve Blyth .20 .50
21 Don Dietrich .20 .50
22 Steve Smith .20 .50
23 Daryl Stanley .40 1.00
24 Taras Zytynsky .20 .50
25 Doug Sauter CO .20 .50

1984-85 Springfield Indians

Produced by Card Collectors Closet (Springfield, MA), this 25-card standard-size set features black-and-white player portraits on a white card face. The team name and year are printed in black at the top. The player's name and position appear at the bottom. The pictures are framed by a royal blue border while a red border encloses the photo and the text.

COMPLETE SET (25) 6.00 15.00
1 Mike Sands .40 1.00
2 Lorne Molleken .20 .50
3 Todd Lumbard .20 .50
4 Randy Velischek .30 .75
5 David Jensen .30 .75
6 Ken Leiter .20 .50
7 Vern Smith .20 .50
8 Alan Kerr .30 .75
9 Scott Howson .20 .50
10 Tim Coulis .20 .50
11 Terry Tait .20 .50
12 Tim Trimper .20 .50
13 Rob Flockhart .30 .75
14 Ron Handy .20 .50
15 Jiri Poner .20 .50
16 Chris Pryor .20 .50
17 Dale Henry .20 .50
18 Mark Hamway .20 .50
19 Monty Trottier .20 .50
20 Miroslav Maly .20 .50
21 Dirk Graham 1.25 3.00
22 Roger Kortko .20 .50
23 Bob Bodak .20 .50
24 Lorne Henning CO .30 .75
25 Checklist Card .20 .50

2003-04 St. Georges de Beauce Garaga

This set was produced by Extreme Sports Cards. The Shantz card is incorrectly identified as Daniel Shank.

COMPLETE SET (20) 4.00 10.00
1 Philippe Audet .20 .50
2 Kevin Cloutier .20 .50
3 Philippe Deblois .20 .50
4 Raymond Delarosbil .20 .50
5 Jonathan Delisle .20 .50
6 Carl Fleury .20 .50
7 Francois Garand .20 .50
8 Steve Gosselin .20 .50
9 Jason Groleau .20 .50
10 Jean-Francois Labbe .30 .75
11 Daniel Laflamme .20 .50
12 Jean-Yves Leroux .20 .50
13 Dannick Lessard .20 .50
14 Claude Morin .20 .50
15 Normand Rochefort .20 .50
16 Paul Shantz UER .20 .50
17 Steve Tardif .20 .50
18 Hugo Turcotte .20 .50
19 Mathieu Vachon .20 .50
20 Frederic Vermette .20 .50

2004-05 St Georges de Beauce Garaga

COMPLETE SET (24) 6.00 15.00
1 Steve Tardif .30 .75
2 Jonathan Forest .30 .75
3 Paul Shantz .30 .75
4 Nicolas Poirier .30 .75
5 Claude Morin .30 .75
6 Raymond Delarosbil .30 .75
7 Martin Fillion .30 .75
8 Eric Bertrand .30 .75
9 David Lessard .30 .75
10 Jonathan Delisle .30 .75
11 Mathieu Vachon .30 .75
12 Tommy Bolduc .30 .75
13 Daniel Laflamme .30 .75
14 Kevin Cloutier .30 .75
15 Jean-Philippe Soucy .40 1.00
16 Mike Bajurny .60 1.50
17 Carl Paradis .30 .75
18 John Murphy .30 .75
19 Hugo Levesque .30 .75
20 Jason Rushton .30 .75
21 Didier Tremblay .30 .75
22 Rejean Dufour .30 .75
23 Brandon Christian .30 .75
24 Randy Copley .30 .75

1957-58 St. Catherine's Tee Pees

This set features the Tee Pees of the old OHA. The set features players who were in the Chicago Blackhawks farm system. The set is also known as the Murray's Potato Chips set, due to that name appearing on top of these undersized, black and white issues. The cards apparently were distributed in conjunction with the purchase of a bag of chips. The checklist is known to be incomplete, so no set price is listed. Any additional information can be forwarded to hockeymag@beckett.com. While the cards are numbered, we were able to confirm the numbering on just four of the eight singles. Until the rest of the numbering is confirmed, the remaining cards will be listed as NNOs.

1 Roy Edwards 20.00 40.00
16 Chico Maki 20.00 40.00
17 Don Grosso 10.00 20.00
18 Bob Corupe 10.00 20.00
NNO Matt Ravlich 15.00 30.00
NNO Ed Hoekstra 15.00 30.00
NNO John McKenzie 30.00 60.00
NNO Stan Mikita 100.00 200.00

1993-94 St. Cloud State Huskies

This set features the Huskies of the NCAA. The set was issued as a promotional giveaway at a single home game in the form of a large perforated sheet. The cards have traded hands in both complete and singles form, so both values are listed.

COMPLETE SHEET (30) 15.00
1 Randy Best .20 .50
2 Chad Brennan .20 .50
3 Neil Cooper .20 .50
4 Chris Dopp .20 .50
5 Marc Gagnon .20 .50
6 Sandy Gasseau .20 .50
7 Jay Geisbaur .20 .50
8 Tony Gruba .20 .50
9 Dave Holum .20 .50
10 Kelly Hultgren .20 .50
11 Jason Jiskra .20 .50
12 Eric Johnson .20 .50
13 P.J. Lepler .20 .50
14 Brett Lievers .20 .50
15 Billy Lund .20 .50
16 Mike Maristuen .20 .50
17 Chris Markstrom .20 .50
18 Taj Melson .20 .50
19 Brad Nelson .20 .50
20 Mike O'Connell .20 .50
21 Dave Paradise .20 .50
22 Dan Reimann .20 .50
23 Kelly Rieder .20 .50
24 Adam Rodak .20 .50
25 Gino Santerre .20 .50
26 Jeff Schmidt .20 .50
27 Grant Sjerven .20 .50
28 Coaching Staff .20 .50
29 Marc Gagnon IA .20 .50
30 Kelly Rieder IA .20 .50

2003-04 St. Cloud State Huskies

These cards were issued as a promotional giveaway at a late-season home game.

COMPLETE SET (31) 8.00 20.00
1 Casey Borer .30 .75
2 Tim Boron .40 1.00
3 Grant Clafton .30 .75
4 Tim Conboy .30 .75
5 Adam Coole .40 1.00
6 Mike Doyle .30 .75
7 Justin Fletcher .30 .75
8 Matt Gens .30 .75
9 Matt Hendricks .30 .75
10 Billy Hengen .30 .75
11 Brock Hooton .30 .75
12 Gary Houseman .30 .75
13 Dave Iannazzo .30 .75
14 Joe Jensen .30 .75
15 Ryan LaMere .30 .75
16 Garrett Larson .30 .75
17 Bille Luger .30 .75
18 Andy Lundbohm .30 .75
19 Brian McCormack .30 .75
20 T.J. McElroy .30 .75
21 Jason Montgomery .40 1.00
22 Colin Peters .30 .75
23 Nate Raduns .30 .75
24 Konrad Reeder .30 .75
25 Peter Szabo .30 .75
26 Nate Wright .30 .75
27 Craig Dahl CO .02 .10
28 Brad Willner ACO .02 .10
29 Fred Harbinson ACO .02 .10
30 Mascot .02 .10
31 Team Photo .10 .25

2004-05 St. Cloud State Huskies

Issued as a promotional giveaway. Cards are unnumbered so they're listed below in alphabetical order.

COMPLETE SET (32) 10.00 25.00
1 Chris Anderson .40 1.00
2 Casey Borer .40 1.00
3 Tim Boron .40 1.00
4 Aaron Brocklehurst .40 1.00
5 Grant Clafton .40 1.00
6 Nate Dey .40 1.00
7 Mike Doyle .40 1.00
8 Justin Fletcher .40 1.00
9 Matt Francis .40 1.00
10 Sean Garrity .40 1.00
11 Matt Gens .40 1.00
12 Andrew Gordon .40 1.00
13 Matt Hartman .40 1.00
14 Billy Hengen .40 1.00
15 Brock Hooton .40 1.00
16 Gary Houseman .40 1.00
17 Dave Iannazzo .40 1.00
18 Joe Jensen .40 1.00
19 Ethan Lyerly .40 1.00
20 T.J. McElroy .40 1.00
21 Marty Mjelleli .40 1.00
22 Jason Montgomery .40 1.00
23 Nate Raduns .40 1.00
24 Konrad Reeder .40 1.00
25 Josh Singer .40 1.00
26 Matt Stephenson .40 1.00
27 Peter Szabo .40 1.00
28 Craig Dahl CO .10 .25
29 Fred Harbinson ACO .10 .25
30 Brad Willner ACO .10 .25
31 Sean Donley TR .10 .25
32 Jeremiah Minkel EQM .10 .25

2005-06 St. Cloud State Huskies

COMPLETE SET (33) 10.00 20.00
1 Chris Anderson .30 .75
2 Casey Borer .30 .75
3 Tim Boron .30 .75
4 Aaron Brocklehurst .30 .75
5 David Carlisle .30 .75
6 Grant Clafton .30 .75
7 Nate Dey .30 .75
8 Justin Fletcher .30 .75
9 Matt Francis .30 .75
10 Sean Garrity .30 .75
11 Bobby Goepfert .60 1.50
12 Andrew Gordon .30 .75
13 Matt Hartman .30 .75
14 Billy Hengen .30 .75
15 Brock Hooton .30 .75
16 Gary Houseman .30 .75
17 Joe Jensen .30 .75
18 Dan Kronick .30 .75
19 T.J. McElroy .30 .75
20 Marty Mjelleli .30 .75
21 Jason Montgomery .30 .75
22 Michael Olson .30 .75
23 Nate Raduns .30 .75
24 Konrad Reeder .30 .75
25 Josh Singer .30 .75
26 Matt Stephenson .30 .75
27 John Swanson .30 .75
28 Bob Motzko CO .02 .10
29 Fred Harbinson ACO .02 .10
30 Eric Rud ACO .02 .10
31 Bryan Demaine TR .02 .10
32 Jeremiah Minkel EQM .02 .10
33 Blizzard MASCOT .02 .10

2003-04 St. Francis Xavier X-Men

St. Francis plays in the CIS.

COMPLETE SET (30) 5.00 12.00
1 Ryan White .20 .50
2 Ryan Armstrong .20 .50
3 Stuart MacRae .20 .50
4 Wes Jarvis .20 .50
5 Mike Martone .20 .50
6 Bobby Reed .20 .50
7 Blake Robson .20 .50
8 Ben Berthiaume .20 .50
9 Troy Smith .20 .50
10 Mike Smith .20 .50
11 Danny White .20 .50
12 Graham Power .20 .50
13 Patrick Grandmaitre .20 .50
14 Dustin Russell .20 .50
15 Darren MacMillan .20 .50
16 Alan Dwyer .20 .50
17 Colin Circelli .20 .50
18 Dwayne Baleman .20 .50
19 Ryan Walsh .20 .50
20 Omar Ennaffati .20 .50
21 Eric Braff .20 .50
22 Mike Mole .40 1.00
23 Shawn Snider .20 .50
24 Chris Brannen .20 .50
25 Dallas Flaman .20 .50
26 Todd Norman .20 .50
27 Danny Flynn CO .02 .10
28 Greg MacDonald ACO .02 .10
29 John Kibyuk ACO .02 .10
30 Kyle MacIsaac ACO .02 .10

2004-05 St. Francis Xavier X-Men

COMPLETE SET (24) 5.00 12.00
1 Ryan Armstrong .20 .50
2 Eric Braff .20 .50
3 Collin Circelli .20 .50
4 Alan Dwyer .20 .50
5 Tyler Dyck .20 .50
6 Omar Ennaffati .20 .50
7 Patrick Grandmaitre .20 .50
8 Wes Jarvis .30 .75
9 Jim Kehoe .20 .50
10 Tyson Kellerman .20 .50
11 Matthew Lynn .20 .50
12 Ryan MacKay .20 .50
13 Stuart MacRae .20 .50
14 Darren McMillan .20 .50
15 Michael Mole .40 1.00
16 Graham Power .20 .50
17 Bobby Reed .20 .50
18 Blake Robson .20 .50
19 Mike Smith .20 .50
20 Shawn Snider .20 .50
21 Niko Tuomi .20 .50
22 Ryan Walsh .20 .50
23 Danny White .20 .50
24 Ryan White .20 .50

2003-04 St. Jean Mission

The Mission played in the LNAH, the Quebec semi-pro circuit. The cards were sold at home games.

COMPLETE SET (28) 6.00 15.00
1 Luc Bilodeau .20 .50
2 Murray Cobb .20 .50
3 Alain Cote .20 .50
4 Greg Davis .20 .50
5 Mario DeBenedictis .20 .50
6 Martin Dicaire .20 .50
7 Bobby Dollas .20 .50
8 Corey Foster .20 .50
9 Link Gaetz .75 2.00
10 Pierre Gendron .20 .50
11 Victor Gervais .20 .50
12 Daniel Guerard .20 .50
13 Hugo Hamelin .20 .50
14 Eric Lachapelle .20 .50
15 Steven Low .20 .50
16 Dominique Maltais .20 .50
17 Eric McIntyre .20 .50
18 Rob Murphy .20 .50
19 Charles Paquette .30 .75
20 Pierre Pelletier .20 .50
21 Jean-Francois Piche .20 .50
22 Guillaume Richard .20 .50
23 Sebastien Roger .20 .50
24 Christian Sbrocca .20 .50
25 Dan Tice .20 .50
26 Ronny Valenti .20 .50
27 Steve Vezina .30 .75
28 Dan Zimmerman .20 .50

1992-93 St. John's Maple Leafs

Measuring approximately 2 1/2" by 3 3/4", this 25-card set features the St. John's Maple Leafs of the American Hockey League. The fronts display color action player photos framed by white borders. In the wider bottom border, the player's name, uniform number, position, and logos are printed in black. The cards are unnumbered and checklisted below in alphabetical order.

COMPLETE SET (25) 4.00 10.00
1 Patrik Augusta .15 .40
2 Drake Berehowsky .20 .50
3 Robert Cimetta .15 .40
4 Marc Crawford CO .20 .50
5 Ted Crowley .15 .40
6 Mike Eastwood .30 .75
7 Todd Hawkins .15 .40
8 Curtis Hunt .15 .40
9 Eric Lacroix .20 .50
10 Guy Lehoux .15 .40
11 Kent Manderville .20 .50
12 Kevin McClelland .15 .40
13 Ken McRae .15 .40
14 Brad Miller .15 .40
15 Yanic Perreault .40 1.00
16 Rudy Poeschek .30 .75
17 Joel Quenneville ACO .08 .25
18 Damian Rhodes .40 1.00
19 Joe Sacco .15 .40
20 Jeff Serowik .15 .40
21 Scott Sharples .15 .40
22 Dave Tomlinson .15 .40
23 Nick Wohlers .15 .40
24 Team Photo .15 .40
25 Buddy (Mascot) .02 .10

1993-94 St. John's Maple Leafs

This 25-card standard-size set features the St. John's Maple Leafs of the American Hockey League. The fronts feature color action player photos with white borders and a gray shadow border. The team name "Leafs" in blue lettering edges the left side of the picture. The cards are unnumbered and checklisted below in alphabetical order.

COMPLETE SET (25) 4.00 10.00
1 Patrik Augusta .15 .40
2 Frank Bialowas .20 .50
3 Buddy (Mascot) .02 .10
4 Rich Chernomaz .15 .40
5 Terry Chitaroni .15 .40
6 Marcel Cousineau .20 .50
7 Marc Crawford CO .20 .50
8 Todd Gillingham .15 .40
9 Chris Govedaris .15 .40
10 Paul Holden .15 .40
11 Curtis Hunt .15 .40
12 Alexei Kudashov .15 .40
13 Eric Lacroix .40 1.00
14 Guy Lehoux .15 .40
15 Matt Mallgrave .15 .40
16 Grant Marshall .20 .50
17 Ken McRae .15 .40
18 Yanic Perreault .30 .75
19 Bruce Racine .20 .50
20 Damian Rhodes .40 1.00
21 Chris Snell .15 .40
22 Dan Stiver .15 .40
23 Andy Sullivan .15 .40
24 Ryan Vandenbussche .20 .50
25 Steffon Walby .15 .40

1994-95 St. John's Maple Leafs

This 24-card standard-size set was manufactured and distributed by Jessen Associates, Inc. for Classic. The fronts display color action player photos with a dark blue marbleized inner border and a black outer border. The player's name, jersey number, and position appear in the teal border on the right edge. The cards are unnumbered and checklisted below in alphabetical order.

COMPLETE SET (24) 3.60 9.00
1 Patrik Augusta .08 .25
2 Ken Belanger .08 .25
3 Frank Bialowas .40 1.00
4 Rich Chernomaz .08 .25
5 Brandon Convery .08 .25
6 Marcel Cousineau .20 .50
7 Trent Cull .08 .25
8 Nathan Dempsey .20 .50
9 Kelly Fairchild .20 .50
10 Janne Gronvall .08 .25
11 David Harlock .08 .25
12 Darby Hendrickson .08 .25
13 Marc Hussey .08 .25
14 Kenny Jonsson .40 1.00
15 Mark Kolesar .08 .25
16 Alexei Kudashov .08 .25
17 Guy Lehoux .08 .25
18 Guy Leveque .08 .25

19 Matt Martin .08 .25
20 Robb McIntyre .08 .25
21 Bruce Racine .20 .50
22 Ryan Vandenbussche .30 .75
23 Steffon Walby .08 .25
24 Todd Warriner .20 .50

1995-96 St. John's Maple Leafs

This 25-card set of the St. John's Maple Leafs of the AHL was produced by Split Second for distribution by the team at home games and via mail order.

COMPLETE SET (25) 4.00 10.00
1 Team Photo .15 .40
2 Ken Belanger .30 .75
3 Rob Butz .15 .40
4 Brandon Convery .20 .50
5 Marcel Cousineau .20 .50
6 Trent Cull .15 .40
7 Nathan Dempsey .15 .40
8 Kelly Fairchild .15 .40
9 Brent Gretzky .20 .50
10 Janne Gronvall .15 .40
11 David Harlock .20 .50
12 Jamie Heward .15 .40
13 Mark Kolesar .15 .40
14 Guy Lehoux .15 .40
15 Kent Manderville .30 .75
16 Kory Mullin .15 .40
17 Jason Saal .20 .50
18 Shayne Toporowski .15 .40
19 Paul Vincent .15 .40
20 Steffon Walby .15 .40
21 Mike Ware .15 .40
22 Todd Warriner .30 .75
23 Tom Watt CO .02 .10
24 Mike Foligno CO .08 .25
25 Buddy -- Mascot .02 .10

1996-97 St. John's Maple Leafs

This standard size set features color action photos on the front and backs are loaded with biographical information. The players name and position are featured in a triangle in the lower right corner of the card front. Cards are unnumbered and checklisted below in alphabetical order. This set was sponsored in part by the Royal Canadian Mounted Police.

COMPLETE SET (25) 4.00 10.00
1 Don Beaupre .30 .75
2 Jared Bednar .15 .40
3 Aaron Brand .20 .50
4 Rich Brown CO .15 .40
5 Buddy MAS .02 .10
6 Greg Bullock .15 .40
7 Rob Butz .15 .40
8 Shawn Carter .15 .40
9 Jason Cipolla .15 .40
10 Brandon Convery .20 .50
11 David Cooper .15 .40
12 John Craighead .30 .75
13 Trent Cull .15 .40
14 Nathan Dempsey .20 .50
15 Mark Deyell .20 .50
16 Jamie Heward .15 .40
17 Mark Hunter CO .15 .40
18 Mark Kolesar .20 .50
19 Guy Lehoux .20 .50
20 Sgt. Randy Mercer .15 .40
21 Jason Saal .30 .75
22 Greg Smyth .15 .40
23 Shayne Toporowski .15 .40
24 Yannick Tremblay .20 .50
25 Brian Wiseman .15 .40

1997-98 St. John's Maple Leafs

This set features the Leafs of the AHL. It was produced by the team and sold at home games.

COMPLETE SET (25) 4.00 10.00
1 Kevyn Adams .30 .75
2 Lonny Bohonos .20 .50
3 Aaron Brand .15 .40
4 Rich Brown ACO .02 .10
5 Buddy .02 .10
6 Shawn Carter .15 .40
7 David Cooper .15 .40
8 Marcel Cousineau .30 .75
9 Nathan Dempsey .15 .40
10 Mark Deyell .20 .50
11 Todd Gillingham .15 .40
12 Per Gustafsson .15 .40
13 Mike Kennedy .15 .40
14 Francis Larivee .30 .75
15 Al MacAdam CO .02 .10
16 Daniil Markov .30 .75
17 Zdenek Markov .15 .40
18 Clayton Norris .15 .40
19 Warren Norris .15 .40
20 Ryan Pepperall .15 .40
21 Jason Podollan .15 .40
22 D.J. Smith .20 .50
23 Greg Smyth .15 .40
24 Shawn Thornton .15 .40
25 Jeff Ware .15 .40

1999-00 St. John's Maple Leafs

This 25-card set features players of the St. John's Maple Leafs of the AHL. The front of the card features an action photo with the left edge colored purple and carrying the players last name and the team logo.

COMPLETE SET (25) 4.00 10.00
1 Kevyn Adams .30 .75
2 Vladimir Antipov .15 .40
3 Syl Apps .15 .40
4 Jason Bonsignore .20 .50
5 Aaron Brand .15 .40
6 Craig Charron .15 .40
7 Nathan Dempsey .30 .75
8 Tyler Harlton .15 .40
9 Justin Hocking .15 .40
10 Bobby House .15 .40
11 Konstantin Kalmikov .20 .50
12 Alan MacAdam CO .08 .25
13 Dennis Maxwell .15 .40
14 David Nemirovsky .20 .50
15 Adam Mair .20 .50
16 Ryan Pepperall .15 .40
17 Marek Posmyk .20 .50
18 Marc Robitaille .15 .40
19 Terry Ryan .20 .50
20 Terran Sandwith .15 .40
21 Darrin Shannon .15 .40
22 D.J. Smith .20 .50
23 Shawn Thornton .15 .40
24 Jimmy Waite .30 .75
25 Dimitri Yakushin .15 .40

2000-01 St. John's Maple Leafs

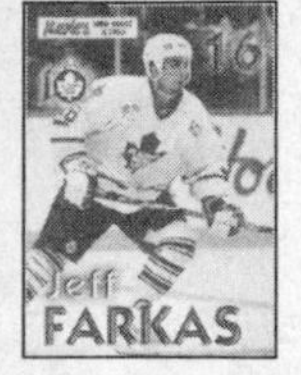

This set features the Maple Leafs of the AHL. The set was produced by the team and sold at home games. The set also features five former AHL All-Stars who once toiled on the Rock.

COMPLETE SET (30) 4.80 12.00
1 Chad Allan .14 .35
2 Syl Apps .14 .35
3 Patrik Augusta .20 .50
4 Buddy The Puffin MASCOT .04 .10
5 Rich Chernomaz .20 .50
6 David Cooper .14 .35
7 Lou Crawford CO .10 .25
8 Nathan Dempsey .30 .75
9 Jeff Farkas .30 .75
10 Mikael Hakanson .14 .35
11 Tyler Harlton .14 .35
12 Bobby House .14 .35
13 Konstantin Kalmikov .30 .75
14 Jacques Lariviere .14 .35
15 Don MacLean .20 .50
16 Adam Mair .20 .50
17 Kevin McClelland CO .10 .25
18 Mike Minard .20 .50
19 Frank Mrazek .14 .35
20 Yanic Perreault .30 .75
21 Alexei Ponikarovsky .30 .75
22 Felix Potvin .40 1.00
23 Alan Rourke .14 .35
24 D.J. Smith .20 .75
25 Chris Snell .14 .35
26 Shawn Thornton .14 .35
27 Michal Travnicek .14 .35
28 Jimmy Waite .20 .75
29 Morgan Warren .14 .35
30 Dmitri Yakushin .14 .35

2001-02 St. John's Maple Leafs

This set features the Leafs of the AHL. The set was sold by the team at its souvenir stands. The set included a contest card that would allow winners to enjoy a special weekend at the AHL All-Star Game, held that season in St. John's. The cards are unnumbered, and are listed alphabetically.

COMPLETE SET (30) 7.20 18.00
1 Russ Adam ACO .04 .10
2 Nikolai Antropov .40 1.00
3 Francois Bouchard .20 .50
4 Luca Cereda .40 1.00
5 Christian Chartier .20 .50
6 Lou Crawford CO .10 .25
7 Nathan Dempsey .30 .75
8 Doug Doull .20 .50
9 Jeff Farkas .40 1.00
10 Paul Healey .20 .50
11 Bobby House .20 .50
12 Jacques Lariviere .20 .50
13 Donald MacLean .20 .50
14 Kevin McClelland ACO .10 .25
15 Craig Mills .20 .50
16 Mike Minard .30 .75
17 Frank Mrazek .20 .50
18 Karel Pilar .40 1.00
19 Alexei Ponikarovsky .40 1.00
20 Alan Rourke .20 .50
21 D.J. Smith .40 1.00
22 Petr Svoboda .20 .50
23 Mikael Tellqvist 1.20 3.00
24 Michal Travnicek .30 .75
25 Morgan Warren .20 .50
26 Marty Wilford .30 .75
27 Bob Wren .30 .75
28 Mile One Stadium .04 .10
29 Buddy the Puffin MASCOT .04 .10
30 All-Star Game PROMO .04 .10

2001-02 St. John's Maple Leafs Police

Each card features a player and a local police officer. Banner across the top reads 'Clarenville Area Citizens' Crime Prevention'. These cards were given out one at a time at a sick childrens hospital about 175 miles from St.John's. Reportedly, just 100 of each card were produced.

COMPLETE SET (16) 15.00 30.00
1 Luca Cereda .75 2.00
2 Christian Chartier .75 2.00
3 Nathan Dempsey 1.25 3.00
4 Doug Doull 2.00 5.00
5 Jeff Farkas .75 2.00
6 Paul Healey .75 2.00
7 Bobby House .75 2.00
8 Donald MacLean .75 2.00
9 Craig Mills .75 2.00
10 Mike Minard .75 2.00
11 Alexei Ponikarovsky 1.25 3.00
12 Allan Rourke .75 2.00
13 D.J.Smith 1.25 3.00
14 Petr Svoboda .75 2.00
15 Morgan Warren .75 2.00
16 Marty Wilford .75 2.00

2002-03 St. John's Maple Leafs Aliant

The cards in this oversized set appear similar to a bookmark. The checklist is possibly incomplete. If you have additional info, please forward to hockeymag@beckett.com.

COMPLETE SET (6) 10.00
1 Doug Doull 2.00
2 Aaron Gavey 1.00
3 Mikael Tellqvist UER 5.00
(Misspelled Mikeal
4 Brad Boyes 2.00
5 Josh Holden 1.00
6 Craig Mills 1.00

1996-97 St. Louis Vipers RHI

This 16-card set was originally supposed to be a 3-series issue, but printer problems forced the third series to be cancelled. The set (except for checklists and headers) is serial numbered out of 500.

COMPLETE SET (16) 75.00 125.00
1 Frank LaScala 4.00 10.00
2 Russ Parent 4.00 10.00
3 Jeff Beaudin 4.00 10.00
4 Perry Turnbull HCO 2.00 5.00
5 Chris Skoryna 4.00 10.00
6 Chris Rogles 6.00 15.00
7 Kevin Plager 4.00 10.00
8 Wayne Anchikoski 6.00 15.00
9 Vipers Record Holders 4.00 10.00
10 Frank Cirone 4.00 10.00
11 C.J. Yoder 4.00 10.00
12 Victor Viper Mascot 2.00 5.00
13 Series 1 Checklist 2.00 5.00
14 Series 2 Checklist 2.00 5.00
15 Series 1 Header 2.00 5.00
16 Series 2 Header 2.00 5.00

1952-53 St. Lawrence Sales

This 108-card black and white set put out by St. Lawrence Sales Agency featured members of the QSHL. The card backs are written in French. The cards measure approximately 1 15/16" by 2 15/16" and are numbered on the back. The key cards in the set are those of future (at that time) NHL greats Jean Beliveau and Jacques Plante. The complete set price includes both versions of card number 17.

COMPLETE SET (108) 700.00 1400.00
1 Jacques Plante 175.00 350.00
2 Glen Harmon 5.00 10.00
3 Jimmy Moore 5.00 10.00
4 Gerard Desaulniers 5.00 10.00
5 Les Douglas 5.00 10.00
6 Fred Burchell 6.00 12.00
7 Ed Litzenberger 7.50 15.00
8 Rollie Rousseau 5.00 10.00
9 Roger Leger 5.00 10.00
10 Phil Samis 5.00 10.00
11 Paul Masnick 6.00 12.00
12 Walter Clune 5.00 10.00
13 Louis Denis 5.00 10.00
14 Gerry Plamondon 6.00 12.00
15 Cliff Malone 5.00 10.00
16 Pete Morin 6.00 12.00
17A Jack Schmidt 6.00 12.00
17B Aldo Guidolin 10.00 20.00
18 Paul Leclerc 5.00 10.00
19 Larry Kwong 6.00 12.00
20 Rosario Joanette 5.00 10.00
21 Tom Smelle 5.00 10.00
22 Gordie Haworth 6.00 12.00
23 Bruce Cline 6.00 12.00
24 Andre Corriveau 5.00 10.00
25 Jacques Deslauriers 5.00 10.00
26 Bingo Ernst 5.00 10.00
27 Jacques Chartrand 5.00 10.00
28 Phil Vitale 5.00 10.00
29 Renald Lacroix 5.00 10.00
30 J.P. Bisaillon 5.00 10.00
31 Jack Irvine 5.00 10.00
32 Georges Bougie 5.00 10.00
33 Paul Larivee 5.00 10.00
34 Carl Smelle 5.00 10.00
35 Walter Pawlyschyn 5.00 10.00
36 Jean Marois 5.00 10.00
37 Jack Gelineau 5.00 10.00
38 Danny Nixon 5.00 10.00
39 Jean Beliveau 200.00 400.00
40 Phil Renaud 5.00 10.00
41 Leon Bouchard 5.00 10.00
42 Dennis Smith 5.00 10.00
43 Joe Crozier 7.50 15.00
44 Al Baccari 5.00 10.00
45 Murdo MacKay 6.00 12.00
46 Gordie Hudson 5.00 10.00
47 Claude Robert 5.00 10.00
48 Yogi Kraiger 6.00 12.00
49 Ludger Tremblay 6.00 12.00
50 Pierre Brillant 5.00 10.00
51 Frank Mario 5.00 10.00
52 Copper Leyth 5.00 10.00
53 Herbie Carnegie 20.00 50.00
54 Punch Imlach 20.00 40.00
55 Howard Riopelle 5.00 10.00
56 Ken Laufman 5.00 10.00
57 Jackie Leclair 7.50 15.00
58 Bill Robinson 5.00 10.00
59 George Ford 5.00 10.00
60 Bill Johnson 5.00 10.00
61 Leo Gravelle 5.00 10.00
62 Jack Giesebrecht 5.00 10.00
63 John Arundel 5.00 10.00
64 Vic Gregg 5.00 10.00
65 Bep Guidolin 7.50 15.00
66 Al Kuntz 5.00 10.00
67 Emile Dagenais 5.00 10.00
68 Bill Richardson 5.00 10.00
69 Bob Robertson 5.00 10.00
70 Ray Fredericks 5.00 10.00
71 James O'Flaherty 5.00 10.00
72 Butch Stahan 5.00 10.00
73 Roger Roberge 5.00 10.00
74 Guy Labrie 5.00 10.00
75 Gilles Dube 5.00 10.00
76 Pete Wywrot 5.00 10.00
77 Tod Campeau 6.00 12.00
78 Roger Bessette 5.00 10.00
79 Martial Pruneau 5.00 10.00
80 Nils Tremblay 5.00 10.00
81 Jacques Locas 5.00 10.00
82 Rene Pepin 5.00 10.00
83 Bob Pepin 5.00 10.00
84 Tom McDougall 5.00 10.00
85 Peter Wright 5.00 10.00
86 Ronnie Matthews 5.00 10.00
87 Irene St-Hilaire 5.00 10.00
88 Dewar Thompson 5.00 10.00
89 Bob Dainville 5.00 10.00
90 Marcel Pelletier 5.00 10.00
91 Delphis Franche 5.00 10.00
92 Georges Roy 5.00 10.00
93 Andy McCallum 5.00 10.00
94 Lou Smrke 5.00 10.00
95 J.P. Lamirande 5.00 10.00
96 Normand Dussault 5.00 10.00
97 Stan Smrke 6.00 12.00
98 Jack Bownass 5.00 10.00
99 Billy Arcand 5.00 10.00
100 Lyall Wiseman 5.00 10.00
101 Jack Hamilton 5.00 10.00
102 Bob Leger 5.00 10.00
103 Larry Regan 6.00 12.00
104 Erwin Grosse 5.00 10.00
105 Roger Bedard 5.00 10.00
106 Ted Hodgson 5.00 10.00
107 Dave Gatherum 7.50 15.00

2000-01 St. Michaels Majors

This set features the Majors of the OHL. The set was produced by the team and sold at its souvenir stands. The cards are unnumbered, so are listed in alphabetical order.

COMPLETE SET (27) 4.80 12.00
1 Team CL .04 .10
2 Team Photo .16 .40
3 Majors Review .10 .25
4 Matt Bacon .16 .40
5 Matt Bannan .16 .40
6 Darryl Bootland .16 .75
7 Chris Boucher .16 .40
8 Tim Brent .30 .75
9 Peter Budaj .60 1.50
10 Dave Cameron CO .10 .25
11 Andy Chiodo .40 2.00
12 Tyler Cook .16 .40
13 Adam Deleeuw .30 .75
14 Matt Ellis .16 .40
15 Steve Farquharson .16 .40
16 Drew Fata .30 .75
17 Michael Gough .16 .40
18 Bob Jones CO .04 .10
19 Kevin Klein .16 1.00
20 Frantisek Lukes .16 .40
21 Lorne Misita .16 .40
22 Lindsay Plunkett .16 .40
23 Mark Popovic .40 1.00
24 T.J. Reynolds .16 .40
25 Ryan Robert .16 .40
26 Mike Sellan .16 .40
27 Ryan Walsh .16 .40

2001-02 St. Michaels Majors

Set was produced and sold by the team. The cards are unnumbered, and so are listed in order of jersey number.

COMPLETE SET (28) 6.00 15.00
1 Logo Checklist .01 .05
2 Team Photo .02 .10
3 Geoff Patton .20 .50
4 Scott Heffernan .20 .50
5 Tyson Gimblett .20 .50
6 Steven Rawski .20 .50
7 Kevin Klein .30 .75
8 Mark Popovic .30 .75
9 Tim Brent .40 1.00
10 Drew Fata .20 .50
11 Jordan Freeland .20 .50
12 Jerrod Smith .20 .50
13 Michael Gouch .20 .50
14 Kyle Spurr .20 .50
15 Ryan Rorabeck .20 .50
16 Matt Bacon .20 .50
17 Frantisek Lukes .20 .50
18 Matt Ellis .20 .50
19 Darryl Boyce .20 .50
20 Daryl Knowles .20 .50
21 Matt Seymour .20 .50
22 Joe Guenther .20 .50
23 Darryl Bootland .30 .75
24 Peter Budaj .60 1.50
25 Andy Chiodo .75 2.00
26 Dave Cameron .20 .50
27 Bob Jones .20 .50
28 Mascot .02 .10

2002-03 St. Michaels Majors

COMPLETE SET (28) 5.00 12.00
1 Justin Peters .30 .75
2 Ted Perry .15 .40
3 Martin Karafiat .15 .40
4 Tyson Gimblett .15 .40
5 Steven Rawski .15 .40
6 Kevin Klein .40 1.00
7 Nathan McIver .15 .40
8 Tim Brent .40 1.00
9 Drew Fata .40 1.00
10 Scott Lehman .15 .40
11 Scott Horvath .15 .40
12 Chris Rebernik .15 .40
13 Kyle Spurr .15 .40
14 Ryan Rorabeck .15 .40
15 Matt Bacon .15 .40
16 Frantisek Lukes .15 .40
17 Connor Cameron .15 .40
18 Darryl Boyce .15 .40
19 Alan Nolan .15 .40
20 Matt Seymour .15 .40
21 Cory Vitarelli .15 .40
22 Darryl Knowles .15 .40
23 Sal Peralta .15 .40
24 Andy Chiodo .75 2.00
25 Dave Cameron CO .02 .10
26 Bob Jones CO .02 .10
27 Mascot .02 .10
28 Logo/CL .01 .05

2003-04 St. Michael's Majors

Cards are unnumbered, so they're listed below in the order they appear on the checklist card.

COMPLETE SET (27) 5.00 12.00
1 Justin Peters .30 .75
2 Ted Perry .20 .50
3 Jamie Vanderveeken .20 .50
4 Ryan Wilson .20 .50
5 Nathan McIver .20 .50
6 Tim Brent .30 .75
7 Ryan Rorabeck .20 .50
8 Chris Cunningham .20 .50
9 Scott Lehman .20 .50
10 Cal Clutterbuck .40 1.00
11 Colin Power .30 .75
12 Tyler Haskins .20 .50
13 Brent Small .20 .50
14 Ian Maracle .20 .50
15 Conner Cameron .20 .50
16 Richard Kelly .20 .50
17 Thomas Waugh .20 .50
18 Darryl Boyce .20 .50
19 Joe Rand .20 .50
20 Cory Vitarelli .20 .50
21 Dustin Vanballegooie .20 .50
22 Sal Peralta .20 .50
23 Michael Ouzas .30 .75
24 Dave Cameron CO .02 .10
25 Bob Jones ACO .02 .10
26 Mikey MASCOT .02 .10
27 Checklist .01 .05

2004-05 St. Michael's Majors

Cards are unnumbered and so are listed below in checklist order.

COMPLETE SET (24) 5.00 12.00
1 Justin Peters .30 .75
2 Steve Whitely .20 .50
3 Jamie Vanderveeken .20 .50
4 Ryan Wilson .20 .50
5 Dale Good .20 .50
6 Nathan McIver .20 .50
7 Matt Halischuk .20 .50
8 John Adamsa .20 .50
9 Chris Cunningham .20 .50
10 Scott Lehman .20 .50
11 Cal Clutterbuck .30 .75
12 Colin Power .20 .50
13 Tyler Haskins .20 .50
14 Cassidy Preston .20 .50
15 Justin DiBenedetto .20 .50
16 Alexei Ivanov .20 .50
17 Scott Levigne .20 .50
18 Travis Elder .20 .50
19 Darryl Boyce .20 .50
20 Joe Rand .20 .50
21 Cory Vitarelli .20 .50
22 Jaroslav Mrazek .20 .50
23 Wayne Savage .20 .50
24 Checklist .01 .05

2005-06 Stockton Thunder

COMPLETE SET (25) 6.00 15.00
1 Likit Andersson .30 .75
2 Casey Bartzen .30 .75
3 Landon Bathe .30 .75
4 Derek Campbell .30 .75
5 Aaron Foster .30 .75
6 Nick Greenough .30 .75
7 Joel Irwin .30 .75
8 Tony Johnson .30 .75
9 Jason Kostadine .30 .75
10 Mike Lalonde .30 .75
11 Aaron MacInnis .30 .75
12 Nathan Martz .30 .75
13 Dave McCulloch .30 .75
14 Jason Metcalfe .30 .75
15 Jake Moreland .30 .75
16 Geno Parrish .30 .75
17 Steve Slonina .30 .75
18 Dean Stork .30 .75
19 Jeff Weber .30 .75
20 Maris Ziedins .30 .75
21 Opening Night .10
22 Chris Cichocki HC .02 .10
23 Stockton Arena .02 .10
24 Thor MASCOT .02 .10
NNO Stockton Thunder CL .02 .10

2006-07 Stockton Thunder

COMPLETE SET (25) 15.00 30.00
1 Jason Beckett .75 2.00
2 Devan Dubnyk• .75 2.00
3 Stephane Goulet .40 1.00
4 Jeff Lang .40 1.00
5 Fans Tribute Card .02 .10
6 Beau Geisler .40 1.00
7 Mike Lalonde .40 1.00
8 Tim Sestito .40 1.00
9 Tyler Spurgeon .40 1.00
10 Thor MASCOT .02 .10
16 Tim Verbeek .75 2.00
17 Eric Main .40 1.00
18 Bryan Young .40 1.00
19 Jim Dahl .40 1.00
20 Adam Huxley .40 1.00
11a Troy Bodie .40 1.00
11b Stephen Slonina .40 1.00
12a Cam Ellsworth• .40 1.00
12b Liam Reddox .40 1.00
13a Brendon Hodge .40 1.00
13b Mark Adamek .40 1.00
14a Nathan Martz .40 1.00
14b Frank Rediker .40 1.00
15a Chris Cichocki CO .40 1.00
15b Tim O'Connell .02 .10

1962-63 Sudbury Wolves

These 22 blank-backed cards measure approximately 4" by 6" and feature white-bordered, posed black-and-white studio head shots of Wolves players (Eastern Professional Hockey League). The player's name and position appear above the team name within the broad white bottom border. The imprint, "Crown Life Hockey School," rounds out the card at the bottom. The cards are unnumbered and checklisted below in alphabetical order.

COMPLETE SET (22) 40.00 100.00
1 Paul Andrea 2.50 5.00
2 Norm Armstrong 1.50 3.00
3 Ed Babiuk 2.00 5.00
4 Hub Beaudry ANN .75 1.50
5 Vern Buffey REF 1.50 3.00
6 Murph Chamberlain CO 1.50 3.00
7 Gerry Cheevers UER 20.00 50.00
(Misspelled Jerry on card front)
8 Wally Chevrier 1.50 3.00
9 Marc Dufour 2.00 4.00
10 Edgar Ehrenverth 1.50 3.00
11 Bill Friday REF 2.50 5.00
12 Jim Johnson 1.50 3.00
13 Chico Kozurok TR .75 1.50
14 Gord Labossiere 2.00 4.00
15 Dunc McCallum 4.00 8.00
16 Dave McComb 1.50 3.00
17 Hugh McLean REF 1.50 3.00
18 Mike McMahon 1.50 3.00
19 Dave Richardson 1.50 3.00
20 Joe Spence ANN .75 1.50
21 Ted Taylor 1.50 3.00
22 Bob Woytowich 4.00 8.00

1984-85 Sudbury Wolves

This 16-card set measures approximately 3 1/2" by 6" and features color, action player photos accented by a hockey stick graphic design in white, green, gray, and red. The player's name and sponsor logos are printed on the design. A discount coupon for 2.50 off any children's admission to a game is attached at the bottom and can be torn along perforations. The card measures approximately 5 1/4" tall when the coupon is removed. The backs carry biographical information and sponsor logos. The cards are numbered on the front near the right edge.

COMPLETE SET (16) 6.00 15.00
1 Andy Spruce CO .20 .50
2 Sean Evoy .60 1.50
3 Mario Martini .40 1.00
4 Brent Daugherty .40 1.00
5 Mario Chitaroni .40 1.00
6 Dan Chiasson .40 1.00
7 Jeff Brown .75 2.00
8 Todd Sepkowski .40 1.00
9 Brad Belland .40 1.00
10 Glenn Greenough .40 1.00
11 John Landry .40 1.00
12 Max Middendorf .40 1.00
13 David Moylan .40 1.00
14 Jamie Nadjiwan .40 1.00
15 Warren Rychel .75 2.00
16 Ed Smith .40 1.00

1985-86 Sudbury Wolves

This 26-card set measures approximately 2 3/4" by 4" and features color, posed player photos with white borders. A facsimile autograph is inscribed across the bottom of the picture.

COMPLETE SET (26) 4.80 12.00
1 Sudbury Police Crest .10 .01
2 Sponsor Card .10 .01
3 Logo Checklist .20 .50
4 Chief of Police .02 .10
5 Wayne Maxner CO .20 .50
6 Sean Evoy .20 .50
7 Todd Lalonde .20 .50
8 Costa Papista .20 .50
9 Robin Rubic .20 .50
10 Dave Moylan .20 .50
11 Brent Daugherty .20 .50
12 Glenn Greenough .20 .50
13 Mario Chitaroni .30 .75
14 Ken McRae .30 .75
15 Mike Hudson .40 1.00
16 Andy Paquette .20 .50
17 Ed Lemaire .20 .50
18 Mark Turner .20 .50
19 Craig Duncanson .20 .50
20 Jeff Brown .40 1.00
21 Team Photo .40 1.00
22 Max Middendorf .20 .50
23 Keith Van Rooyen .20 .50
24 Brad Walcot .20 .50
25 Rob Wilson .20 .50
26 Bill White .20 .50

1986-87 Sudbury Wolves

Cards measure approximately 3" x 4" and feature color action photos and a facsimile autograph on the front. The card backs feature biographical information along with P.L.A.Y. public service messages.

COMPLETE SET (33) 4.80 12.00
1 Ted Mielczarek .30 .75
2 Todd Lalonde .20 .50
3 Costa Papista .20 .50
4 Justin Corbeil .20 .50
5 Dave Moylan .20 .50
6 Brent Daugherty .20 .50
8 Mario Chitaroni .30 .75
9 Jim Way .20 .50
10 Dean Jalbert .20 .50
11 Joe Dragon .20 .50
12 Ken McRae .20 .50
14 Steve Hedington .20 .50
15 Mike Hudson .30 .75
16 Pierre Gagnon .20 .50
17 Peter Hughes .20 .50
18 Mark Turner .20 .50
19 Sudbury Police Logo .08 .25
20 Wayne Doucet .20 .50
21 Paul Dipietro .25 .60
22 Max Middendorf .30 .75
23 Phil Paquette .20 .50
25 Rob Wilson .20 .50
26 Checklist .08 .25
27 Chief of Police .08 .25
28 Claude D'Amour .20 .50
29 Guy Blanchard .20 .50
30 Joe Desrosiers .20 .50
31 Jake Disschops .20 .50
33 Bill White .30 .75
34 Anders Hogberg .20 .50

1987-88 Sudbury Wolves

This 26-card set measures approximately 3" by 4 1/8" and features color, posed action player photos with white borders. The player's name, jersey number, and position are superimposed on the photo at the bottom.

COMPLETE SET (26) 4.00 10.00
1 Checklist Card .08 .25
2 Ted Mielczarek .30 .75
3 Dan Gatenby .20 .50
4 Todd Lalonde .20 .50
5 Justin Corbeil .20 .50
6 Jordan Fois .20 .50
7 Rodney Lapointe .20 .50
8 Dave Akey .20 .50
9 Jim Smith .20 .50
10 Fred Pennell .20 .50
11 Joey Simon .20 .50
12 Luciano Fagioli .20 .50
13 Robb Graham .20 .50
14 John Uniac .20 .50
15 Dave Carrie .20 .50
16 Pierre Gagnon .20 .50
17 Peter Hughes .20 .50
18 Scott McCullough .20 .50
19 Dean Guitard .20 .50
20 Pat Holley .20 .50
21 Chad Badaway .20 .50
22 Paul DiPietro .20 .50
23 Derek Thompson .20 .50
24 Scott Luce .20 .50
25 Rob Wilson .20 .50
26 R. Zanibbi .02 .10
Chief of Police

1988-89 Sudbury Wolves

This 26-card set measures approximately 3" by 4 1/8" and features color, action player photos with white borders. The player's name, jersey number, and position are superimposed on the photo at the bottom.

COMPLETE SET (26) 4.00 10.00
1 Checklist .08 .25
2 David Goverde .30 .75
3 Ted Mielczarek .30 .75

4 Adam Bennett .20 .50
5 Kevin Grant .20 .50
6 Jordan Fois .20 .50
7 Sean O'Donnell .30 .75
8 Kevin Meisner .20 .50
9 Jim Smith .20 .50
10 Red Pennell .20 .50
11 Tyler Pella .20 .50
12 Dean Pella .20 .50
13 Darren Bell .20 .50
14 Derek Thompson .20 .50
15 Terry Chitaroni .20 .50
16 Sean Stansfield .20 .50
17 Alastair Still .20 .50
18 Jim Sonmez .20 .50
19 Shannon Bolton .20 .50
20 Andy Paquette .20 .50
21 Mark Turner .20 .50
22 Paul DiPietro .20 .50
23 Robert Knesaurek .20 .50
24 Todd Lalonde .20 .50
25 Scott Herniman .20 .50
26 R. Zanibbi .08 .25
Chief of Police

1989-90 Sudbury Wolves

This 25-card set measures approximately 3" by 4 1/8" and features color, posed action player photos with white borders. The player's name, jersey number, and position are superimposed on the photo at the bottom.

COMPLETE SET (25) 4.80 12.00
1 Checklist NNO .08 .25
2 Alastair Still .20 .50
3 Bill Kovacs .20 .50
4 Darren Bell .20 .50
5 Scott Mahoney .20 .50
6 Glen Murray .75 2.00
7 Alain Laforge .20 .50
8 Jamie Matthews .20 .50
9 Jon Boeve .30 .75
10 Adam Bennett .20 .50
11 Derek Etches .20 .50
12 Marcus Middleton .20 .50
13 Jim Sonmez .20 .50
14 Leonard MacDonald .20 .50
15 Paul DiPietro .30 .75
16 Neil Ethier .20 .50
17 Sean O'Donnell .20 .50
18 Andy MacVicar .20 .50
19 David Goverde .30 .75
20 Jason Young .20 .50
21 Wade Bartley .20 .50
22 Barry Young .20 .50
23 R. Zanibbi .08 .25
Chief of Police
24 Terry Chitaroni .20 .50
25 Rob Knesaurek .20 .50

1990-91 Sudbury Wolves

This 25-card P.L.A.Y. (Police, Law and Youth) set measures approximately 3" by 4 1/8" and features color posed action player photos with white borders. The player's name and position is superimposed on the picture at the bottom. For the most part, the cards are numbered on both sides after the player's jersey number (except for card number 7 and 18).

COMPLETE SET (25) 4.80 12.00
1 Darryl Paquette .25 .60
2 Adam Bennett .20 .50
3 Barry Young .20 .50
4 Jon Boeve .20 .50
5 Kyle Blacklock .20 .50
6 Sean O'Donnell .25 .60
7 Dan Ryder .25 .60
8 Wade Bartley .20 .50
9 Jamie Matthews .20 .50
10 Rod Hinks .20 .50
11 Derek Etches .20 .50
12 Brandon Convery .20 .50
13 Glen Murray .75 2.00
14 Bill Kovacs .20 .50
15 Terry Chitaroni .20 .50
16 Jason Young .20 .50
17 Alastair Still .20 .50
18 Shawn Rivers .20 .50
19 Alain Laforge .20 .50
20 J.D. Eaton .20 .50
21 Mike Peca .75 2.00
22 Howler (Mascot) .02 .10
23 Mike Yeo .20 .50
24 L'il Rookie .02 .10
Checklist
25 R. Zanibbi .02 .10
Chief of Police

1991-92 Sudbury Wolves

This 25-card set measures approximately 3" by 4 1/8" and features color, posed action player photos with white borders. The player's name, jersey number, and position are superimposed on the photo at the bottom.

COMPLETE SET (25) 4.80 12.00
1 R. Zanibbi .02 .10
Chief of Police
2 Howler (Mascot) .02 .10
3 Team Photo .20 .50
4 Kyle Blacklock .15 .40
5 Sean Gagnon .20 .50
6 Bernie John .15 .40
7 Bob MacIsaac .15 .40
8 Jamie Rivers .20 .50
9 Shawn Rivers .15 .40
10 Joel Sandie .15 .40
11 Barry Young .15 .40
12 George Dourian .15 .40
13 Dan Ryder .30 .75
14 Derek Armstrong .15 .40
15 Terry Chitaroni .15 .40
16 Brandon Convery .20 .50
17 Tim Favot .15 .40
18 Rod Hinks .15 .40
19 Jamie Matthews .20 .50
20 Barrie Moore .20 .50
21 Glen Murray .40 1.00
22 Michael Peca .75 2.00
23 Michael Yeo .15 .40
24 Jason Young .15 .40
25 Jason Zohil .15 .40

1992-93 Sudbury Wolves

These 27 oversized bilingual cards measure approximately 3" by 4 3/16" and feature on their fronts white-bordered color posed-on-ice player photos. The player's name, jersey number, and position are displayed on each card in white lettering at the bottom of the photo.

COMPLETE SET (27) 4.80 12.00
1 Howler and Lil Rookie .02 .10
2 Sudbury Regional Police .02 .10
3 Bob MacIsaac .20 .50
4 Joel Sandie .20 .50
5 Rory Fitzpatrick .20 .50
6 Mike Wilson .20 .50
7 Shawn Frappier .20 .50
8 Bernie John .20 .50
9 Jamie Rivers .30 .75
10 Jamie Matthews .20 .50
11 Zdenek Nedved .20 .50
12 Ryan Shanahan .20 .50
13 Corey Crane .20 .50
14 Matt Kiereck .20 .50
15 Rick Bodkin .20 .50
16 Derek Armstrong .20 .50
17 Barrie Moore .20 .50
18 Rod Hinks .20 .50
19 Kayle Short .20 .50
20 Michael Yeo .20 .50
21 Gary Coupal .20 .50
22 Dennis Maxwell .20 .50
23 Steve Potvin .20 .50
24 Joel Poirier .20 .50
25 Greg Dreveny .20 .50
26 Mark Gowan .30 .75
27 Steve Staios .25 .60

1993-94 Sudbury Wolves

Sponsored by The Sudbury Star, CoverStory, and Sudbury Sports North, and printed by Slapshot Images Ltd., this standard-size 25-card set features the 1993-94 Sudbury Wolves. On a geometrical team color-coded background, the fronts feature color action player photos with thin grey borders. The player's name, position and team name, as well as the producer's logo, also appear on the front.

COMPLETE SET (25) 4.00 10.00
1 Shawn Silver .20 .50
2 Jeff Melnechuk .15 .40
3 Jay McKee .30 .75
4 Chris McMurtry .15 .40
5 Rory Fitzpatrick .20 .50
6 Mike Wilson .20 .50
7 Shawn Frappier .15 .40
8 Jamie Rivers .30 .75
9 Zdenek Nedved .20 .50
10 Ryan Shanahan .20 .50
11 Sean Venedam .20 .50
12 Andrew Dale .15 .40
13 Mark Giannetti .15 .40
14 Rick Bodkin .20 .50
15 Barrie Moore .20 .50
16 Jamie Matthews .20 .50
17 Gary Coupal .15 .40
18 Ilya Lysenko .15 .40
19 Simon Sherry .15 .40
20 Steve Potvin .15 .40
21 Joel Poirier .20 .50
22 Mike Yeo .15 .40
23 Bob MacIsaac .15 .40
24 Paul DiPietro .20 .50
NNO Slapshot Ad Card .02 .10

1993-94 Sudbury Wolves Police

This traditional over-sized issue was released in conjunction with the Sudbury Police. It features color photos on the front, with safety tips and player info on the back.

COMPLETE SET (26) 4.00 10.00
1 Chief of Police .07 .20
2 The Howler .07 .20
3 Jay McKee .30 .75
4 Chris McMurtry .15 .40
5 Rory Fitzpatrick .20 .50
6 Mike Wilson .20 .50
7 Shawn Frappier .15 .40
8 Jamie Rivers .30 .75
9 Jamie Matthews .20 .50
10 Zdenek Nedved .20 .50
11 Ryan Shanahan .20 .50
12 Andrew Dale .15 .40
13 Mark Giannetti .15 .40
14 Rick Bodkin .20 .50
15 Barrie Moore .20 .50
16 Gary Coupal .15 .40
17 Ilya Lysenko .15 .40
18 Simon Sherry .15 .40
19 Steve Potvin .15 .40
20 Joel Poirier .20 .50
21 Shawn Silver .20 .50
22 Micheal Yeo .15 .40
23 Jeff Melnechuk .15 .40
24 Sean Venedam .20 .50
25 Bob MacIsaac .15 .40
26 Sudbury Police .07 .20

1994-95 Sudbury Wolves

Sponsored by The Sudbury Star CoverStory, Sudbury Sports North and Nick's Sports Cards, and printed by Slapshot Images Ltd., this 26-card set features the 1994-95 Sudbury Wolves. On a silver and blue background, the fronts feature color action player photos with thin black borders. The player's name, position and team name, as well as the producer's logo, also appear on the front.

COMPLETE SET (26) 4.00 10.00
1 Checklist .02 .10
2 Dave MacDonald .15 .40
3 Rory Fitzpatrick .15 .40
4 Mike Wilson .15 .40
5 Neal Martin .15 .40
6 Shawn Frappier .15 .40
7 Jamie Rivers .20 .50
8 Zdenek Nedved .15 .40
9 Ryan Shanahan .15 .40
10 Sean Venedam .20 .50
11 Andrew Dale .15 .40
12 Rick Bodkin .15 .40
13 Luc Gagne .15 .40
14 Barrie Moore .15 .40
15 Richard Rochefort .15 .40
16 Krystof Secemski .15 .40
17 Jason Bonsignore .15 .40
18 Liam MacEachern .15 .40
19 Simon Sherry .15 .40
20 Ethan Moreau .30 .75
21 Matt Mullin .20 .50
22 Aaron Starnyski .15 .40
23 Ron Newhook .30 .75
24 Glenn Merkosky CO/GM .02 .10
Todd Lalonde ACO/MG
25 Dan Lebold TR .02 .10
Jason Allen ATR
NNO Ad Card .02 .10

1994-95 Sudbury Wolves Police

Card fronts feature a posed color photo surrounded by a white border. The card number is located in a star in the upper left corner. Card backs contain hockey and safety tips in French and English.

COMPLETE SET (27) 4.80 12.00
1 Chief of Police .02 .10
2 The Howler .02 .10
3 Rick Bodkin .15 .40
4 Gary Coupal .15 .40
5 Andrew Dale .15 .40
6 Luc Gagne .15 .40
7 Chester Gallant .02 .10
8 Kiley Hill .15 .40
9 Liam MacEachern .15 .40
10 Barrie Moore .15 .40
11 Zdenek Nedved .20 .50
12 Ron Newhook .40 1.00
13 Richard Rochefort .15 .40
14 Krysztof Secemski .15 .40
15 Ryan Shanahan .15 .40
16 Simon Sherry .15 .40
17 Sean Venedam .40 1.00
18 Rory Fitzpatrick .15 .40
19 Shawn Frappier .15 .40
20 Gregg Lalonde .15 .40
21 Neal Martin .15 .40
22 Jay McKee .40 1.00
23 Jamie Rivers .20 .50
24 Mike Wilson .20 .50
25 Dave Macdonald .15 .40
26 Matt Mullin .30 .75
27 Steve Valiquette .40 1.00

1995-96 Sudbury Wolves

This 25-card set was one of two produced to commemorate the '95-96 Wolves. This one was released by the team, in conjunction with sponsors Four Star Sports and Belanger's. The set is standard size with an action photo on the front, while the backs contain a player bio.

COMPLETE SET (25) 4.00 10.00
1 Sean Venedam .20 .50
2 Brad Domonsky .20 .50
3 Joe Lombardo .15 .40
4 Tyson Flinn .15 .40
5 Luc Gagne .15 .40
6 Ryan Shanahan .15 .40
7 Simon Sherry .15 .40
8 Kevin Hansen .15 .40
9 Gregg Lalonde .15 .40
10 Liam MacEachern .15 .40
11 Jeremy Adduono .20 .50
12 Ron Newhook .30 .75
13 Noel Burkitt .15 .40
14 Neal Martin .15 .40
15 Tim Swartz .15 .40
16 Rob Butler .15 .40
17 Darryl Moxam .15 .40
18 Steve Valiquette .30 .75
19 Ryan Sly .15 .40
20 Dave MacDonald .20 .50
21 Andrew Dale .15 .40
22 Belanger's All-Star Team .02 .10
23 Four Star Sports .02 .10
24 Richard Rochefort .15 .40
25 Title Card .02 .10

1995-96 Sudbury Wolves Police

This 24-card P.L.A.Y. set measures approximately 3" by 4 1/8" and features color posed player photos augmented by a white border. The player's name and position is superimposed on the photo along the bottom.

COMPLETE SET (24) 4.00 10.00
1 Chief Alex McCauley .02 .10
2 The Howler .02 .10
Mascot
3 Jeremy Adduono .20 .50
4 Noel Burkitt .15 .40
5 Rob Butler .15 .40
6 Andrew Dale .15 .40
7 Brad Domonsky .20 .50
8 Tyson Flinn .15 .40
9 Luc Gagne .15 .40
10 Kevin Hansen .15 .40
11 Gregg Lalonde .15 .40
12 Joe Lombardo .15 .40
13 Dave MacDonald .20 .50
14 Liam MacEachern .15 .40
15 Neal Martin .15 .40
16 Darryl Moxam .15 .40
17 Ron Newhook .30 .75
18 Richard Rochefort .15 .40
19 Ryan Shanahan .15 .40
20 Simon Sherry .15 .40
21 Ryan Sly .15 .40
22 Shawn Sobush .15 .40
23 Steve Valiquette .30 .75
24 Sean Venedam .20 .50

1996-97 Sudbury Wolves

One of two sets issued to commemorate the Wolves' 25th anniversary season, this 27-card standard sized issue was produced by the team and sponsored by Play It Again Sports, The Great Canadian Card Co. and the Sudbury Star. The cards were produced by the team and sold through arena concessions. The cards feature action photography on the front complemented by a black border containing the player's name and the team logo on the left.

COMPLETE SET (27) 4.80 12.00
1 Title card .08 .25
2 Jeremy Adduono .20 .50
3 Louie Blackbird .15 .40
4 Tom Brown .20 .50
5 Peter Campbell .15 .40
6 Brad Domonsky .15 .40
7 Jason Gaggi .20 .50
8 Luc Gagne .15 .40
9 Kevin Hansen .15 .40
10 Jason Hurlbut .15 .40
11 Konstantin Kalmikov .20 .50
12 Robin LaCour .15 .40
13 Paul Mara .40 1.00
14 Norm Milley .60 1.50
15 Gerald Moriarty .15 .40
16 Scott Page .15 .40
17 Steve Reid .15 .40
18 Richard Rochefort .15 .40
19 Brian Scott .15 .40
20 Chris Shanahan .15 .40
21 Ryan Sly .15 .40
22 Jonas Soling .15 .40
23 Steve Valiquette .60 1.50
24 Sean Venedam .20 .50
25 Great Canadian Card Co. .01
26 LaSalle Court Plaza .01
27 Derek Chartrand .08 .25

1996-97 Sudbury Wolves Police

This oversized (3" by 4 3/16"), 26-card set was issued in conjunction with the Sudbury Police Department. The card fronts feature a posed color photo surrounded by a white border. The player's name, number and position are along the bottom, with the card number is displayed in a star in the upper left corner.

COMPLETE SET (26) 4.80 12.00
1 Chief Alex McCauley .02 .10
2 The Howler MASCOT .02 .10
3 Sudbury Wolves 25th .02 .10
4 Jeremy Adduono .20 .50
5 Louie Blackbird .15 .40
6 Tom Brown .20 .50
7 Peter Campbell .15 .40
8 Brad Domonsky .15 .40
9 Tyson Flinn .15 .40
10 Jason Gaggi .15 .40
11 Luc Gagne .15 .40
12 Kevin Hansen .15 .40
13 Konstantin Kalmikov .20 .50
14 Robin Lacour .15 .40
15 Joe Lombardo .15 .40
16 Paul Mara .40 1.00
17 Norm Milley .60 1.50
18 Scott Page .15 .40
19 Richard Rochefort .15 .40
20 Brian Scott .15 .40
21 Chris Shanahan .15 .40
22 Ryan Sly .15 .40
23 Jonas Soling .15 .40
24 Tim Swartz .15 .40
25 Steve Valiquette .60 1.50
26 Sean Venedam .15 .40

1997-98 Sudbury Wolves Police

Card fronts feature a posed color photo surrounded by a white border. The card number is located in a star in the upper left corner. Card backs contain hockey and safety tips in French and English.

COMPLETE SET (25) 8.00 20.00
1 Chief of Police .02 .10
2 Jeremy Adduono .15 .40
3 Ryan Barnes .15 .40
4 Peter Campbell .15 .40
5 Konstantin Kalmikov .20 .50
6 Tom Watt .15 .40
7 Norm Milley .60 1.50
8 Scott Page .15 .40
9 Jonas Soling .15 .40
10 Mike Fisher .75 2.00
11 Taylor Pyatt .40 1.00
12 Derek MacKenzie .40 1.00
13 Nevin Patterson .15 .40
14 Jason Sands .15 .40
15 Colin Scotland .15 .40
16 Paul Mara .40 1.00
17 David Cornacchia .15 .40
18 Ryan McKie .15 .40
19 Michael Tilson .15 .40
20 Brad Morgan .15 .40
21 Matthew Hodges .15 .40
22 Brad Simms .15 .40
23 Steve Valiquette .60 1.50
24 Andrew Raycroft 1.50 4.00
25 The Howler .02 .10

1998-99 Sudbury Wolves

This set features the Wolves of the OHL. The slightly oversized cards were handed out by local police officers.

COMPLETE SET (25) 7.20 18.00
1 Alex McCauley POLICE .02 .10
2 Ken MacKenzie CO .02 .10
3 Alexei Salashchenko .20 .50
4 Kevin Beaumont .20 .50
5 Norm Milley .40 1.00
6 Derek MacKenzie .40 1.00
7 Reg Higgs CO .02 .10
8 Matt Barnhardt .20 .50
9 Mike Fisher .60 1.50
10 Tom Kotsopoulos .40 1.00
11 Marc Long .20 .50
12 Kyle Dafoe .20 .50
13 Jason Jaspers .40 1.00
14 Glenn Crawford .20 .50
15 Ryan McKie .20 .50
16 Corey Sabourin .20 .50
17 Kip Brennan .75 2.00
18 Serge Dube .20 .50
19 Brad Morgan .20 .50
20 Brian McGrattan .20 .50
21 Taylor Pyatt .40 1.00
22 Abe Herbst .20 .50
23 Kevin Mota .20 .50
24 Mark Aggio .20 .50
25 Andrew Raycroft 1.25 3.00

1999-00 Sudbury Wolves

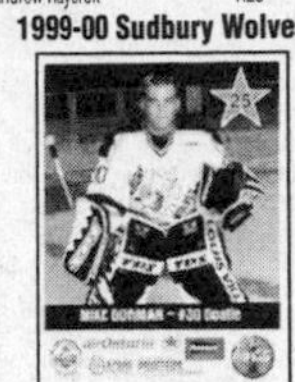

This slightly oversized set features the Wolves of the OHL. The set was sold by the team at the rink, and features 1999 first-rounders Taylor Pyatt and Mike Fisher.

COMPLETE SET (26) 4.80 12.00
1 Chief Alex McCauley .02 .10
2 Bert Templeton CO .08 .25
3 Darren Keily ACO .02 .10
4 Corey Sabourin .15 .40
5 Kyle Dafoe .15 .40
6 Abe Herbst .15 .40
7 Dennis Wideman .15 .40
8 Kevin Mota .15 .40
9 Norm Milley .40 1.00
10 Taylor Pyatt .40 1.00
11 Mike Fisher .60 1.50
12 Alexei Semenov .40 1.00
13 Alexei Salashchenko .15 .40
14 Derek MacKenzie .40 1.00
15 Steve Ellis .15 .40
16 Warren Helford .15 .40
17 Jason Jaspers .40 1.00
18 Brian Mcgrattan .15 .40
19 Drew Kivell .15 .40
19B Tom Kotsopoulos .40 1.00
21 Brad Morgan .15 .40
22 Scott Smith .15 .40
23 R.A. Mobile .02 .10
24 Mike Vaillancourt .15 .40
25 Mike Gorman .15 .40
26 Miguel Beaudry .15 .40

2000-01 Sudbury Wolves

This set features the Wolves of the OHL. The cards are slightly oversized and were produced as part of the P.L.A.Y. series. They were apparently distributed primarily by police officers to school-aged children.

COMPLETE SET (26) 8.00 20.00
1 Chief Alex McCauley .04 .01
2 Bert Templeton CO .20 .50
3 Darren Keily CO .10 .25
4 T.J. Warkus .30 .75
5 Dave Csumrik .30 .75
6 Jason Hicks .30 .75
7 Wally Prawdzik .30 .75
8 Dennis Wideman .30 .75
9 Mike Vaillancourt .30 .75
10 Troy Duncan .30 .75
11 Ladislav Reznicek .30 .75
12 Alexei Semenov .60 1.50
13 Chad Starling .30 .75
14 Nathan Harrington .30 .75
15 Derek MacKenzie .40 1.00
16 Jerry Connell .30 .75
17 Steve Ellis .30 .75
18 Adam Keefe .30 .75
19 Jason Jaspers .60 1.00
20 Jason Bone .30 .75
21 Drew Kivell .30 .75
22 Tom Kotsopoulos .60 1.00
23 Fedor Fedorov .40 1.50
24 Mike Smith .30 .75
25 Miguel Beaudry .30 .75
26 Howler MASCOT .04 .10

2001-02 Sudbury Wolves

This set features the Wolves of the OHL. It measures the standard size and was sold by the team at home games. It is believed that less than 1,000 sets were produced.

COMPLETE SET (30) 6.00 15.00
1 Shandor Alphonso .24 .60
2 Trevor Blanchard .24 .60
3 Travis Chapman .24 .60
4 Bob Chaumont .24 .60
5 Jerry Connell .24 .60
6 Ryan Hastings .24 .60
7 Jim Kehoe .24 .60
8 Darren Kelly ACO .04 .10
9 Josh Legge .24 .60
10 Tyler Leggo .24 .60
11 Andrei Mikhnov .60 1.50
12 Dave Poulin .24 .60
13 Jean-Francois Seguin .24 .60
14 Jeff Shaw .24 .60
15 Rob Shilton .24 .60
16 Sam Skwarchuk .24 .60
17 Mike Smith .40 1.00
18 Shawn Snider .24 .60
19 Dan Speer .24 .60
20 Zach Stortini .24 .60
21 Bert Templeton CO .20 .50
22 Brody Todd .24 .60
23 Joel Whitmarsh .40 1.00
24 John Winstanley .24 .60
25 Sudbury Wolves Card .10 .25
26 Wolves Season Line-Up .10 .25
27 Randy Carlyle No. Retired .20 .50
28 Sudbury Carpetland .01
29 Sudbury City Centre .04 .10
30 Sudbury King Sportswear .01

2001-02 Sudbury Wolves Police

This set features the Wolves of the OHL. The cards are slightly oversized, and were issued as promotional giveaways by the team and the Sudbury Police. It is believed that less than 1,000 sets exist.

COMPLETE SET (26) 6.00 15.00
1 Chief Alex McCauley .01
2 Bert Templeton CO .04 .10
3 Darren Keily ACO .04 .10
4 Brody Todd .30 .75
5 Travis Chapman .30 .75
6 Jim Kehoe .30 .75
7 Josh Legge .30 .75
8 J.F. Seguin .30 .75
9 Andrei Mikhnov .60 1.00
10 John Winstanley .30 .75
11 Shawn Snider .30 .75
12 Jeff Shaw .30 .75
13 Bobby Chaumont .30 .75
14 Rob Shilton .30 .75
15 Tyler Leggo .30 .75
16 Shandor Alphonso .30 .75
17 Jerry Connell .30 .75
18 Zack Stortini .30 .75
19 Dan Speer .30 .75
20 Trevor Blanchard .30 .75
21 Sam Skwarchuk .30 .75
22 Dene Poulin .30 .75
23 Ryan Hastings .30 .75
24 Mike Smith .40 1.00
25 Joel Whitmarsh .40 1.00
26 Howler MASCOT .04 .10

2003-04 Sudbury Wolves

COMPLETE SET (25) 6.00 15.00
1 Header Card .01 .05
2 Shandor Alphonso .25 .60
3 Kevin Beech .40 1.00
4 Stefan Blaho .25 .60
5 Bobby Chaumont .25 .60
6 Jonathan D'Aversa .25 .60
7 Luke Dubbin .25 .60
8 Alexander Eaton .30 .75
9 Patrick Ehelechner .60 1.50
10 Chanse Fitzpatrick .25 .60
11 Ryan Hastings .25 .60
12 Kyle Lamb .25 .60
13 Sean Langdon .25 .60
14 Eric Larochelle .25 .60
15 Matt Maccarone .25 .60
16 Rafal Martynowski .25 .60
17 Adam McQuaid .25 .60
18 Mike Mills .25 .60
19 Dene Poulin .25 .60
20 Jordan Prevost .25 .60
21 Chris Robertson .25 .60
22 Marc Staal .75 2.00
23 Sean Stefanski .25 .60
24 Zach Stortini .25 .60
25 Mike Foligno CO .10 .25

2004-05 Sudbury Wolves

A total of 1,000 team sets were produced.

COMPLETE SET (26) 8.00 20.00
1 Luke Dubbin .30 .75
2 Bobby Chaumont .40 1.00
3 Tomas Sample .30 .75
4 Marc Staal .75 2.00
5 Nicholas Foligno .75 2.00
6 Kevin Beech .30 .75
7 Zach Stortini .30 .75
8 Stefan Blaho .30 .75
9 Devin Didiomete .30 .75
10 Kyle Musselman .30 .75
11 Patrick Ehelechner .60 1.50
12 Alexander Eaton .30 .75
13 Stephen Miller .30 .75
14 Ryan Hastings .30 .75
15 Adam McQuaid .30 .75
16 Ryan McDonough .30 .75
17 Benoit Pouliot 1.25 3.00
18 Mike Mills .30 .75
19 Jonathan D'Aversa .30 .75
20 Rafal Martynowski .30 .75
21 Troy Murray .30 .75
22 Kevin Baker .30 .75
23 Mike Foligno CO .02 .10
24 Bob Jones ACO .02 .10
25 Bryan Verrault ACO .02 .10
26 Howler MASCOT .02 .10

2005-06 Sudbury Wolves

COMPLETE SET (26) 8.00 15.00
1 Marc Staal .60 1.50
2 Kevin Beech .20 .50
3 Chris Abbey .20 .50
4 Ryan Hastings .20 .50
5 Adam McQuaid .20 .50
6 Troy Murray .20 .50
7 Jonathan D'Aversa .20 .50
8 Ryan Crouch .20 .50
9 Kevin Baker .20 .50
10 Matt Dias .20 .50
11 Nicholas Foligno .60 1.50
12 Devin Didiomete .20 .50
13 Anton Hedman .20 .50
14 Akim Aliu .20 .50
15 Mike Mills .20 .50
16 Mark Versteeg-Lytwyn .20 .50
17 Gary Friesen .20 .50
18 Ryan Donally .20 .50
19 Nicholas Tuzzolino .20 .50
20 Justin Allen .20 .50
21 Gerome Giudice .20 .50
22 Mike Foligno .10 .25
23 Bob Jones .20 .50
24 Bryan Verreault .20 .50
25 Howler .02 .10
26 Benoit Pouliot .60 1.50

2006-07 Sudbury Wolves

COMPLETE SET (27) 8.00 20.00
1 Marc Staal .60 1.50
2 Andrew Self .20 .50
3 J.K. Gill .20 .50
4 Matt Dias .20 .50
5 Nick Foligno .60 1.50
6 Gerome Giudice .20 .50
7 Kyle Tarini .20 .50
8 Gary Friesen .20 .50
9 Geoff Guimond .20 .50
10 Devin Didiomete .20 .50
11 Jared Staal 2.00 5.00
12 Patrik Lusnak .20 .50
13 Justin Larson .20 .50
14 Akim Aliu .60 1.50
15 Justin Donati .20 .50
16 Kevin Baker .20 .50
17 Ryan Crouch .20 .50
18 Stephen Miller .20 .50
19 Zach Mccullough .20 .50
20 Adam Mcquaid .40 1.00
21 Tyler Arps .20 .50
22 Jonathan D'Aversa .20 .50
23 Sebastien Dahm .40 1.00
24 Michael Swick .40 1.00
25 Mike Foligno CO .20 .50
26 Bob Jones .10 .25
27 Bryan Verreault .10 .25

1996-97 Surrey Eagles

We have confirmed just this one card from this set that appears to feature the BCJHL Eagles. If you have any additional information, please contact us at hockeymag@beckett.com.

COMPLETE SET (?)
NNO Scott Gomez

2004-05 Surrey Eagles

Features the Eagles of the BCJHL. Set was produced by Upper Deck through its personalized card set division.

COMPLETE SET (23) 6.00 15.00
1 Tyson Angus .30 .75
2 Tim Crowder .30 .75
3 Korey Diehl .30 .75
4 Chris Difrancescantonio .30 .75
5 Tyler Eckford .30 .75
6 Matt Girling .30 .75
7 Rick Hillier CO .02 .10
8 Dan Idema .30 .75
9 Andrew Kozek .30 .75
10 Kyle Kuehner .30 .75
11 Aaron McKenzie .40 1.00
12 Brock Meadows .30 .75
13 T.J. Miller .30 .75
14 David Moncour .30 .75
15 Tyson Moulton .40 1.00
16 T.J. Mulock .40 1.00
17 Kyle Nason .30 .75
18 A Blake Reilly ERR .30 .75
Defence
19 David Rutherford .30 .75
20 Corey Rymut .30 .75
21 Dustin Slade .40 1.00
22 Stewart Thiessen .30 .75
23 Matt Wiest .30 .75
18B Blake Rielly COR

1995-96 Swift Current Broncos

This 20-card set features color player photos on a blue-and-green background. The backs carry player information. The cards are unnumbered and so are checklisted below in alphabetical order.

COMPLETE SET (20) 3.00 8.00
1 Derek Arbez .15 .40
2 Chad Beagle .15 .40
3 Kurt Drummond .15 .40
4 Terry Friesen .30 .75
5 Ryan Geremia .15 .40
6 Jeff Henkelman .15 .40
7 Jeff Kirwan .15 .40
8 Brad Larsen .30 .75
9 Aaron MacDonald .20 .50
10 Craig Millar .15 .40
11 Jaroslav Obsut .20 .50
12 Colin O'Hara .15 .40
13 Jeff Schaeffer .15 .40
14 Brent Sopel .15 .40
15 Josh St. Louis .15 .40
16 Chris Szysky .15 .40
17 Jesse Rezansoff .15 .40
18 Jeremy Rondeau .15 .40
19 Sergei Varlamov .20 .50
20 Tyler Willis .15 .40

1996-97 Swift Current Broncos

This 24-card set was produced by the club for distribution at the rink and by mail. The cards feature an action photograph surrounded by a blue, white and green borders. The black and white backs feature a mug shot, team logo, personal stats and bio and an anti-drug tip.

COMPLETE SET (24) 4.00 10.00
1 Terry Friesen .30 .75
2 Lindsey Materi .20 .50
3 Kevin Mackie .15 .40
4 Jeff Henkelman .15 .40
5 Michal Rozsival .30 .75
6 Brent Sopel .30 .75
7 Lawrence Nycholat .15 .40
8 Chad Beagle .15 .40
9 Jeff Schaeffer .15 .40
10 Tyler Shybunka .15 .40
11 Josh St. Louis .15 .40
12 Chris Szysky .20 .50
13 Tyler Perry .15 .40
14 Dreu Volk .15 .40
15 Nathan Strueby .15 .40
16 Kurt Drummond .15 .40
17 Brad Larsen .30 .75

18 Ryan Tobler .30 .75
19 Jeremy Rondeau .15 .40
20 Jeff Kirwan .15 .40
21 Brett Allan .15 .40
22 Andrew Milne .15 .40
23 Sergei Varlamov .30 .75
24 Derek Arbez .20 .50

1997-98 Swift Current Broncos

This set features the Broncos of the WHL. It is believed to have been produced and distributed by the team. Any additional information pertinent to this set can be forwarded to hockeymag@beckett.com.

COMPLETE SET (22) 4.80 12.00
1 Terry Friesen .30 .75
2 Lindsey Materi .20 .50
3 Tyson Motz .20 .50
4 Jeffrey Beatch .20 .50
5 Jeff Henkelman .20 .50
6 Michal Rozsival .30 .75
7 Dan Hulak .20 .50
8 Lawrence Nycholat .20 .50
9 Toni Bader .20 .50
10 Chad Beagle .20 .50
11 Jeff Schaeffer .20 .50
12 Tyler Shybunka .20 .50
13 Tyler Murray .20 .50
14 Tony Mohagen .20 .50
15 Layne Ulmer .30 .75
16 Dean Serdachny .20 .50
17 Brent Twordik .20 .50
18 Quinn Sherdahl .20 .50
19 Jeff Kirwan .20 .50
21 Brett Allan .20 .50
22 Sergei Varlamov .30 .75

1998-99 Swift Current Broncos

This set features the Chiefs of the WHL. It is believed to have been produced and distributed by the team. Because of the players featured, it is though to have been sold late in the season. Any additional information pertinent to this set can be forwarded to hockeymag@beckett.com.

COMPLETE SET (24) 4.80 12.00
1 Chad Beagle .20 .50
2 Brett Allan .20 .50
3 Quinn Sherdahl .20 .50
4 Bryce Wandler .20 .50
5 Dean Serdachny .20 .50
6 Danis Zaripov .20 .50
7 Kurt Drummond .20 .50
8 Tyler Murray .20 .50
9 Toni Bader .20 .50
10 Brent Twordik .20 .50
11 Nathan Smith .20 .50
12 Jakub Cutta .40 1.00
13 Lawrence Nycholat .20 .50
14 Ben Ondrus .20 .50
15 Tyson Motz .20 .50
16 Jay Langager .20 .50
17 Brad Rohrig .20 .50
18 Jeremy Reich .30 .75
19 Layne Ulmer .40 1.00
20 Chris Sotiropolous .20 .50
21 Josh Maser .20 .50
22 Dan Hulak .20 .50
23 Dustan Heintz .20 .50
24 Jeremy Rondeau .20 .50

1999-00 Swift Current Broncos

This set features the Broncos of the WHL. The set features standard-sized cards with a purple border. The cards are unnumbered, and so are listed below in alphabetical order.

COMPLETE SET (25) 6.00 15.00
1 Brett Allan .20 .50
2 Jay Batchelor .20 .50
3 Jakub Cutta .30 .75
4 Houston Hair .20 .50
5 Scott Henkelman .20 .50
6 James Hiebert .20 .50
7 Todd Hornung .20 .50
8 Dan Hulak .20 .50
9 Jay Langager .20 .50
10 Duncan Milroy .40 1.00
11 Tyson Motz .40 1.00
12 Lawrence Nycholat .20 .50
13 Ben Ondrus .20 .50
14 Colton Orr .40 1.00
15 Craig Priestlay .20 .50
16 Jeremy Reich .20 .50
17 Dean Serdachny .20 .50
18 Nathan Smith .30 .75
19 Matt Sommerfeld .20 .50
20 Clay Thoring .20 .50
21 Brent Twordik .20 .50
22 Layne Ulmer .40 1.00
23 Igor Valeev .20 .50
24 Brendan Vanthuyne .20 .50
25 Bryce Wandler .30 .75

2000-01 Swift Current Broncos

This set features the Broncos of the WHL. The cards were issued by the team and sold at home games. As they are unnumbered, they are listed below in alphabetical order.

COMPLETE SET (24) 4.80 15.00
1 B.J. Boxma .40 1.00
2 Ales Cerny .20 .50
3 Jakub Cutta .40 1.00
4 John Dahl .20 .50
5 Paul Deniset .20 .50
6 Adam Dumbrowski .20 .50
7 Todd Ford .40 1.00
8 Dustin Friesen .30 .75
9 Scott Henkelman .20 .50
10 James Hiebert .20 .50
11 Jay Langager .20 .50
12 Duncan Milroy .60 1.50
13 Tyson Motz .40 1.00
14 Ben Ondrus .20 .50
15 Craig Priestlay .20 .50
16 Kevin Seibel .20 .50
17 Dean Serdachny .20 .50
18 Nathan Smith .30 .75
19 Matt Sommerfeld .20 .50
20 Clay Thoring .20 .50
21 Ian White .80 2.00
22 Header Card .04 .10
23 Checklist .04 .10
24 Charlie MASCOT .04 .10

2001-02 Swift Current Broncos

COMPLETE SET (24) 5.00 12.00
1 Steven Spencer .20 .50
2 Ales Cerny .20 .50
3 Kevin Seibel .20 .50
4 Travis Friedley .20 .50
5 Ian White .40 1.00
6 Aaron Richards .20 .50
7 James Hiebert .20 .50
8 Nathan Smith .20 .50
9 Tim Smith .20 .50
10 Dustin Friesen .20 .50
11 Jason Roberts .20 .50
12 Ben Ondrus .40 1.00
13 John Dahl .20 .50
14 Luke Hunter .20 .50
15 Mitch Love .20 .50
16 Brent Twordik .20 .50
17 Torrie Wheat .20 .50
18 Colin Slobodian .20 .50
19 Ivan Usenko .20 .50
20 Duncan Milroy .40 1.00
21 Matt Sommerfeld .20 .50
22 Todd Ford .20 .50
23 B.J. Boxma .20 .50
24 Mascot .02 .10

2002-03 Swift Current Broncos

COMPLETE SET (24) 5.00 12.00
1 John Dahl .20 .50
2 Todd Ford .20 .50
3 Travis Friedlay .20 .50
4 Dustin Friesen .20 .50
5 Jeff Harvey .20 .50
6 Marian Havel .20 .50
7 James Hiebert .20 .50
8 Luke Hunter .20 .50
9 Alex Lentowich .20 .50
10 Mitch Love .20 .50
11 Darryl Moscaluk .20 .50
12 Ben Ondrus .20 .50
13 Derek Poplawski .20 .50
14 Aaron Richards .20 .50
15 Jason Roberts .20 .50
16 Aaron Rome .40 1.00
17 David Schulz .20 .50
18 Dennis Sergeyev .20 .50
19 Steven Spencer .20 .50
20 Colin Stone .20 .50
21 Torrie Wheat .20 .50
22 Ian White .40 1.00
23 Jeremy Williams .40 1.00
24 Charlie Horse MASCOT .02 .10

2003-04 Swift Current Broncos

COMPLETE SET (24) 6.00 15.00
1 Bryn Brucks .20 .50
2 Jason Fransoo .20 .50
3 Dustin Friesen .20 .50
4 Davin Heintz .20 .50
5 Michael Hengen .20 .50
6 Luke Hunter .20 .50
7 Alex Leavitt .20 .50
8 Alex Lentowich .20 .50
9 Kyle Moir .30 .75
10 Ty Morris .20 .50
11 Darryl Moscaluk .20 .50
12 Tyler Redenbach .30 .75
13 Aaron Richards .20 .50
14 Aaron Rome .30 .75
15 Myles Rumsey .20 .50
16 Jerrid Sauer .20 .50
17 David Schulz .20 .50
18 Colin Stone .20 .50
19 Michael Szczachor .20 .50
20 Matej Trojovsky .30 .75
21 Brent Walker .30 .75
22 Ian White .40 1.00
23 Bobby Williams .20 .50
24 Jeremy Williams .40 1.00

2004-05 Swift Current Broncos

COMPLETE SET (24) 8.00 15.00
1 Travis Brisebois .30 .75
2 Marc Defoe .30 .75
3 Marc Desloges .30 .75
4 Tyler Feakes .30 .75
5 Jason Fransoo .30 .75
6 Michael Hengen .30 .75
7 Barry Horman .30 .75
8 Luke Hughson .30 .75
9 Luke Hunter .30 .75
10 Marek Knebl .30 .75
11 Brady Leavold .30 .75
12 Andrew Leslie .30 .75
13 Don Lloyd .30 .75
14 Kyle Moir .40 1.00
15 Tyler Redenbach .40 1.00
16 Myles Rumsey .30 .75
17 Jerrid Sauer .30 .75
18 Jeremy Schenderling .30 .75
19 David Schulz .30 .75
20 Blair Stengler .30 .75
21 Colin Stone .30 .75
22 Michael Szczachor .30 .75
23 Matej Trojovsky .40 1.00
24 Andrew Wasmuth .30 .75

2005-06 Swift Current Broncos

COMPLETE SET (24) 8.00 15.00
1 Karl Benke .30 .75
2 Michael Hengen .30 .75
3 Derek Price .30 .75
4 Thomas Raffl .30 .75
5 Andrew Wasmuth .30 .75
6 Daniel Rakos .30 .75
7 R.J. Larochelle .30 .75
8 Travis Yonkman .30 .75
9 Kyle Bortis .30 .75
10 Kyle Moir .30 .75
11 Luke Hunter .30 .75
12 Spencer McAvoy .30 .75
13 Donny Lloyd .30 .75
14 Josh Aspenlind .30 .75
15 Levi Nelson .40 1.00
16 Grant Toulmin .30 .75
17 Dale Weise .30 .75
18 Charlie Horse .02 .10
19 Paul Postma .30 .75
20 Jeremy Schenderling .30 .75
21 Myles Rumsey .30 .75
22 Ned Lukacevic .30 .75
23 Marc Desloges .30 .75
24 Zack Smith .30 .75

2006-07 Swift Current Broncos

COMPLETE SET (24) 12.00 20.00
1 Travis Yonkman .60 1.50
2 Kyle Moir .60 1.50
3 David Stieler .30 .75
4 Grant Toulmin .30 .75
5 R.J Larochelle .30 .75
6 Ryan Molle .30 .75
7 Levi Nelson .60 1.50
8 Geordie Wudrick .30 .75
9 Dale Weise .30 .75
10 Kyle Bortis .30 .75
11 Phil Gervais .30 .75
12 Michael Wilson .30 .75
13 Daniel Rakos .30 .75
14 Brady Leavold .30 .75
15 Spencer Mcavoy .30 .75
16 Matt Tassone .30 .75
17 Paul Postma .30 .75
18 Derek Claffey .30 .75
19 Zack Smith .30 .75
20 Myles Rumsey .30 .75
21 Dane Crowley .30 .75
22 Jeremy Schenderling .30 .75
23 Levi Nelson .60 1.50
Dane Crowley
24 Charlie Horse .10 .25

2007-08 Swift Current Broncos

COMPLETE SET (24) 12.00 20.00
1 Mike Brown .30 .75
2 Derek Claffey .30 .75
3 Ian Curtis .60 1.50
4 Jan Dalecky .30 .75
5 Keegan Dansereau .30 .75
6 Justin Dowling .30 .75
7 Eric Doyle .30 .75
8 Cody Eakin .30 .75
9 Erik Felde .30 .75
10 Brad Hoban .30 .75
11 R.J. LaRochelle .30 .75
12 Spencer McAvoy .30 .75
13 Ryan Molle .30 .75
14 Levi Nelson .60 1.50
15 Joel Rogers .30 .75
16 Zack Smith .30 .75
17 Dave Stieler .30 .75
18 Matt Tassone .30 .75
19 Dale Weise .30 .75
20 Michael Wilson .30 .75
21 George Wudrick .30 .75
22 Travis Younkman .60 1.50
23 Charlie Horse MASCOT .02 .10
24 Team Checklist .02 .10

1996-97 Syracuse Crunch

This 25-card set was produced by Split Second and sponsored by Y94 radio and Healthsource. The set features action photos on the front, and statistical information on the back. The cards were sold by the club at the rink or through the mail. The unnumbered cards are listed below according to their sweater numbers, which are displayed prominently in the upper left hand corner of each card back.

COMPLETE SET (25) 4.80 12.00
1 Mike Fountain .30 .75
4 Mark Wotton .15 .40
5 Mark Krys .15 .40
9 Robb Gordon .30 .75
10 Darren Sinclair .15 .40
11 Ian McIntyre .15 .40
14 John Badduke .15 .40
16 Doug Ast .15 .40
17 Brian Loney .15 .40
18 Tyson Nash .60 1.50
19 Lonny Bohonos .20 .50
21 Dave Scatchard .30 .75
23 Chad Allan .15 .40
25 Bogdan Savenko .15 .40
26 John Namestnikov .15 .40
27 Bert Robertsson .20 .50
28 Chris McAllister .20 .50
30 Frederic Cassivi .30 .75
35 Larry Courville .20 .50
37 Rick Girard .15 .40
38 Rod Stevens .15 .40
44 Brent Tully .15 .40
NNO Jack McIlhargey CO .02 .10
NNO AHL Ad Card .01
NNO Crunchman (Mascot) .02 .10

1999-00 Syracuse Crunch

This set features the Crunch of the AHL. The set was released as a promotional giveaway. Sixteen of the cards were given out in sets of eight at two Crunch home games. The remaining cards were available at Tully's Restaurant.

COMPLETE SET (25) 10.00 25.00
1 Harold Druken .40 1.00
2 Matt Cooke .75 2.00
3 Brian Bonin .40 1.00
4 Zenith Komarniski .40 1.00
5 Chad Allan .40 1.00
6 Crunchman MASCOT .08 .25
7 Ryan Ready .40 1.00
8 Brad Leeb .40 1.00
9 Reggie Savage .40 1.00
10 Trent Klatt .40 1.00
11 Martin Gendron .40 1.00
12 Lubomir Vaic .40 1.00
13 Ryan Bonni .40 1.00
14 Brent Sopel .60 1.50
15 Christian Bronsard .60 1.50
16 Barry Smith CO .20 .50
17 Sean Smyl CO .40 1.00
18 Alfie Michaud .60 1.50
19 Trevor Doyle .40 1.00
20 Jarkko Ruutu .40 1.00
21 Chris O'Sullivan .40 1.00
22 Ryan Shannon .40 1.00
23 Pat Kavanagh .40 1.00
24 Mike Brown .40 1.00
25 Tully's Restaurant .02 .10

2000-01 Syracuse Crunch

This set features the Crunch of the AHL. The set was produced by Choice Marketing and apparently was distributed in two 12-card subsets at a pair of home games.

COMPLETE SET (24) 10.00 25.00
1 Marc Lamothe .60 1.50
2 Jean-Francois Labbe .60 1.50
3 Andrei Sryubko .40 1.00
4 Jonas Junkka-Andersson .40 1.00
5 Mike Gaul .40 1.00
6 Dan Watson .40 1.00
7 Bill Bowler .60 1.50
8 Chris Nielsen .40 1.00
9 Jody Shelley 2.00 5.00
10 Mathieu Darche .60 1.50
11 Blake Bellefeuille .60 1.50
12 Jeremy Reich .40 1.00
13 Jeff Williams .40 1.00
14 Martin Spanhel .60 1.50
15 Brad Moran .40 1.00
16 Scott Hollis 1.00
17 Jeff Ware .40 1.00
18 Matt Davidson .40 1.00
19 Sean Selmser .40 1.00
20 Radim Bicanek .40 1.00
21 Reggie Savage .40 1.00
22 Gary Agnew CO .10 .25
23 Ross Yates CO .10 .25
24 Al MASCOT .04 .10

2001-02 Syracuse Crunch

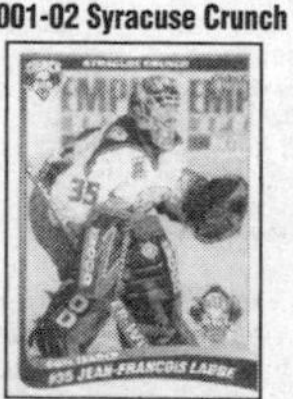

This set features the Crunch of the AHL. The cards were produced by Choice Marketing and were sold at home games.

COMPLETE SET (25) 6.00 15.00
1 Jean-Francois Labbe .30 .75
2 Andrei Sryubko .20 .50
3 Dan Watson .20 .50
4 Paul Manning .20 .50
5 Matt Davidson .30 .75
6 Duvie Westcott .30 .75
7 Jody Shelley .60 3.00
8 Mathieu Darche .30 .75
9 Blake Bellefeuille .30 .75
10 Jeremy Reich .20 .50
11 Martin Spanhel .30 .75
12 David Ling .30 .75
13 Sean Pronger .20 .50
14 Brad Moran .30 .75
15 Derrick Walser .30 .75
16 Jeff Ware .20 .50
17 Martin Paroulek .20 .50
18 Darrel Scoville .20 .50
19 Kent McDonell .20 .50
20 Adam Borzecki .20 .50
21 Andrej Nedorost .30 .75
22 Brett Harkins .20 .50
23 Jonathan Schill .20 .50
24 Tully's Ad Card .01
25 Al MASCOT .04 .10

2002-03 Syracuse Crunch

COMPLETE SET (25) 12.00
1 Karl Goehring .75
2 Pascal Leclaire 1.50
3 Tyler Sloan .50
4 Dan Watson .50
5 Paul Manning .50
6 Matt Davidson .50
7 Mathieu Darche .75
8 Blake Bellefeuille .50
9 Jeremy Reich .50
10 Tim Jackman .50
11 David Ling .50
12 Jonathan Schill .50
13 Brad Moran .50
14 Pauli Levokari .50
15 Darrel Scoville .50
16 Kent McDonell .50
17 Adam Borzecki .50
18 Andrej Nedorost .50
19 Radim Bicanek .50
20 Trevor Ettinger .50
21 Matt Dzieduszycki .50
22 Mike Pandolfo .50
23 Trent Cull .50
24 Al the Gorilla Mascot .10
NNO Quickway Ad .01

2002-03 Syracuse Crunch Sheets

These sheets measure 8/5 X 11 and likely were issued as program inserts. The checklist is incomplete. If you know of others, please write us at hockeymag@beckett.com. Thanks to collector Dale Spengler for this list.

COMPLETE SET (20)
1 Unknown
2 Unknown
3 Kent McDonnell
4 David Ling
5 Unknown
6 Jeremy Reich
7 Duvie Westcott
8 Brad Moran
9 Trent Cull
10 Darrel Scoville
11 Chris Neilson
12 Blake Bellefeuille
13 Mathieu Darche
14 Adam Borzecki
15 Pascal Leclaire
16 Dan Watson
17 Tim Jackman
18 Karl Goehring
19 Andrej Nedorost
20 Mike Pandolfo

2003-04 Syracuse Crunch

This set was produced by Choice Marketing and sold at home games.

COMPLETE SET (24) 4.00 10.00
1 Karl Goehring .30 .75
2 Jamie Pushor .15 .40
3 Mark Hartigan .20 .50
4 Darrel Scoville .15 .40
5 Zenith Komarniski .15 .40
6 Ben Knopp .15 .40
7 Todd Rohloff .15 .40
8 Paul Traynor .15 .40
9 Donald MacLean .15 .40
10 Jeremy Reich .20 .50
11 Tim Jackman .15 .40
12 Joe Motzko .15 .40
13 Brad Moran .15 .40
14 Derrick Walser .15 .40
15 Pauli Levokari .15 .40
16 Aaron Johnson .15 .40
17 Kent McDonell .15 .40
18 Tyler Sloan .15 .40
19 Brandon Sugden .30 .75
20 Pascal Leclaire .40 1.00
21 Anders Eriksson .15 .40
22 Mike Pandolfo .15 .40
23 Trent Cull .15 .40
24 Mascot .01 .05

2004-05 Syracuse Crunch

Produced by Choice Marketing and sold at home games.

COMPLETE SET (25) 5.00 12.00
1 Header/Checklist .01 .05
2 Karl Goehring .30 .75
3 Jamie Pushor .20 .50
4 Mark Hartigan .20 .50
5 Zenith Komarniski .20 .50
6 Ole-Kristian Tollefsen .20 .50
7 Prestin Ryan .20 .50
8 Matthias Trattnig .20 .50
9 Jeremy Reich .20 .50
10 Tim Jackman .20 .50
11 Steven Goertzen .20 .50
12 Alexander Svitov .20 .50
13 Joe Motzko .20 .50
14 Brad Moran .20 .50
15 Andre Lakos .20 .50
16 Aaron Johnson .20 .50
17 Francois Beauchemin .30 .75
18 Brandon Sugden .40 1.00
19 Raffaele Sannitz .20 .50
20 Pascal Leclaire .40 1.00
21 Greg Mauldin .20 .50
22 Jeff Panzer .20 .50
23 Mike Pandolfo .20 .50
24 Al MASCOT .01 .05
25 Sponsor card .01 .05

2005-06 Syracuse Crunch

COMPLETE SET (26) 8.00 15.00
1 Mike Ayers .20 .50
2 Marc Methot .30 .75
3 Mark Hartigan .20 .50
4 Darcy Verot .20 .50
5 Ben Simon .20 .50
6 Geoff Platt .30 .75
7 Andrew Murray .20 .50
8 Tyler Kolarik .20 .50
9 Steven Goertzen .20 .50
10 Peter Sarno .30 .75
11 Joe Motzko .20 .50
12 Brett Nowak .20 .50
13 Alexandre Picard .60 1.50
14 Jeff MacMillan .20 .50
15 Jamie Pushor .20 .50
16 Andy Canzanello .20 .50
17 Ole-Kristian Tollefsen .20 .50
18 Brandon Sugden .40 1.00
19 Martin Prusek .30 .75
20 Tim Konsorada .20 .50
21 Andrew Penner .40 1.00
22 Joakim Lindstrom .30 .75
23 Greg Mauldin .20 .50
24 Aaron Johnson .20 .50
25 Andy Delmore .20 .50
26 Al MASCOT .02 .10

2006-07 Syracuse Crunch

COMPLETE SET (26) 8.00 15.00
1 Tomas Popperle .30 .75
2 Marc Methot .20 .50
3 Mark Hartigan .20 .50
4 Filip Novak .20 .50
5 Darcy Verot .30 .75
6 Ben Simon .20 .50
7 Geoff Platt .30 .75
8 Andrew Murray .20 .50
9 Adam Pineault .30 .75
10 Philippe Dupuis .20 .50
11 Steven Goertzen .20 .50
12 Janne Hauhtonen .20 .50
13 Joe Motzko .20 .50
14 Alexandre Picard .30 .75
15 Tomas Kloucek .20 .50
16 Jeff Szwez .20 .50
17 Ryan Caldwell .20 .50
18 Jamie Pushor .20 .50
19 Andy Canzanello .20 .50
20 Derrick Walser .20 .50
21 Dan LaCosta .20 .50
22 Jekabs Redlihs .20 .50
23 Ty Conklin .30 .75
24 Joakim Lindstrom .30 .75
25 Olivier Labelle .20 .50
26 Al MASCOT .02 .10

1992-93 Tacoma Rockets

This 30-card standard-size set features hatch-bordered, posed-on-ice color player photos. In a white field under the photo are the player's name, and in the right corner, the team logo of crossed red rockets. The team name appears in a diagonal across the top left corner of the photo and the player's position is in blue letters across the top. The cards are unnumbered and checklisted below in alphabetical order.

COMPLETE SET (30) 4.00 10.00
1 Alexander Alexeev .15 .40
2 Jamie Black .20 .50
3 Jamie Butt .20 .50
4 Jeff Calvert .15 .40
5 Don Clark ACO .02 .10
6 Marcel Comeau CO .15 .40
7 Duane Crouse TR .02 .10
8 Allan Egeland .15 .40
9 Marty Flichel .15 .40
10 Trever Fraser .15 .40
11 Jason Kwiatkowski .15 .40
12 Todd MacDonald .15 .40
13 Dave McMillen .15 .40
14 Tony Pechthalt TR .02 .10
15 Ryan Phillips .15 .40
16 Mike Piersol .15 .40
17 Dennis Pinfold .15 .40
18 Kevin Powell .15 .40
19 Tyler Prosofsky .15 .40
20 Stu Scantlebury .15 .40
21 Drew Schoneck .15 .40
22 Adam Smith .15 .40
23 Corey Stock .15 .40
24 Barkley Swenson .15 .40
25 Michal Sykora .20 .50
26 Dallas Thompson .15 .40
27 John Varga .15 .40
28 Toby Weishaar .15 .40
29 Michal Sykora IA .20 .50
30 Cover Card (Team Logo) .08 .25

1993-94 Tacoma Rockets

This 30-card standard-size set features the 1993-94 Tacoma Rockets. The set is printed on thin card stock. The fronts have hatch-bordered color action player photos, with the player's name and position printed in white letters in a dark turquoise shadowed border above the photo. The team name also appears in a dark turquoise shadowed bar to the left of the photo. The cards are unnumbered and checklisted below in alphabetical order.

COMPLETE SET (30) 4.80 12.00
1 Alexander Alexeev .20 .50
2 Jamie Butt .20 .50
3 Trevor Cairns .15 .40
4 Jeff Calvert .15 .40
5 Marcel Comeau CO .15 .40
6 Jason Deleurme .15 .40
7 Allan Egeland .20 .50
8 Marty Flichel .15 .40
9 Trever Fraser .15 .40
10 Michal Grosek .40 1.00
11 Lada Hampeis .15 .40
12 Tavis Hansen .20 .50
13 Burt Henderson .15 .40
14 Jeff Jubenville .15 .40
15 Todd MacDonald .20 .50
16 Kyle McLaren .60 1.50
17 Kory Mullin .15 .40
18 Steve Oviatt TR .02 .10
19 Ryan Phillips .15 .40
20 Mike Piersol .15 .40
21 Dennis Pinfold .15 .40
22 Tyler Prosofsky .20 .50
23 Jamie Reeve ACO .02 .10
24 Adam Smith .15 .40
25 Corey Stock .15 .40
26 Dallas Thompson .15 .40
27 John Varga .20 .50
28 Team Photo .20 .50
29 The Tacoma Dome .02 .10
30 The Tacoma Rockets .15 .40
In Action
Marty Flichel

1998-99 Tacoma Sabercats

This set of the WCHL Sabercats was handed out as a promotional giveaway at one home game, making it extremely difficult to find on the secondary market.

COMPLETE SET (25) 8.00 20.00
1 Blair Allison .30 .75
2 Jergis Bertins .30 .75
3 Scott Boston .60 1.50
4 Dampy Brar .30 .75
5 Jamie Butt .60 1.50
6 Scott Drevitch .60 1.50
7 Brett Duncan .30 .75
8 Jim Gattolliat .30 .75
9 Scott Green .30 .75
10 Casey Hungle .30 .75
11 Tim Lovell .60 1.50
12 Kim Maier .30 .75
13 Trevor Matter .30 .75
14 Brad Mehalko .40 1.00
15 Alex Mukhanov .40 1.00
16 Chris Nelson .30 .75
17 Alex Podalinski .30 .75
18 Chad Richard .30 .75
19 Kevin Smyth .30 .75
20 Paul Taylor .30 .75
21 Edgar Zaltkovskis .30 .75
22 John Oliver HCO .20 .50
23 Sponsor Card .02 .10
24 Mike Carey TR .08 .25
25 Sponsor Card .02 .10

1999-00 Tacoma Sabercats

This set features the Sabercats of the WCHL. The set was produced by Grandstand and issued as a promotional giveaway at one home game.

COMPLETE SET (25) 6.00 15.00
1 Scott Boston .40 1.00
2 Alexander Alexeev .40 1.00
3 Pavel Mikulchik .30 .75
4 Trever Fraser .30 .75
5 Chad Richard .30 .75
6 Cory Morgan .30 .75
7 Brian Leitza .30 .75
8 Alexander Kharlamov .40 1.00
9 Craig Chapman .30 .75
10 Ashley Buckberger .30 .75
11 Trevor Roenick .30 .75
12 Scott Drevitch .40 1.00
13 Jim Gattolliat .30 .75
14 Dampy Brar .30 .75
15 Blair Allison .30 .75
16 Brandon Fleenor .30 .75
17 Kim Maier .30 .75
18 Edgars Zaltkovskis .30 .75
19 Shayne Green .30 .75
20 Brett Duncan .30 .75
21 Local Electician .01
22 Local Electrician .01
23 Local Electrician .01
24 John Olver CO .08 .25
25 Mike Carey TR .08 .25

2000-01 Tacoma Sabercats

This set features the Sabercats of the WCHL. The set was produced by Grandstand and was used as a promotional giveaway at a late-season game.

COMPLETE SET (24) 8.00 20.00
1 Cory Morgan .40 1.00
2 Scott Boston .50 1.25
3 Trever Fraser .40 1.00
4 Jarrett Whidden .40 1.00
5 Charlie Blyth .40 1.00
6 Rob Dumas .40 1.00
7 Alexei Deev .40 1.00
8 Danny Lorenz .50 1.25
9 Alexander Alexeev .40 1.00
10 Ashley Buckberger .50 1.25
11 Brandon Fleenor .40 1.00
12 Luke Curtin .40 1.00
13 Gavin Hodgson .40 1.00
14 Dampy Brar .40 1.00
15 Steve Lowe .40 1.00
16 Dennis Pinfold .40 1.00
17 Scott Drevitch .40 1.00
18 Curtis Menzul .40 1.00
19 Phil Husak .40 1.00
20 Robert Dirk CO .10 .25
21 Jason Kirkman TR .04 .10
22 Sponsor .01
23 Sponsor .01
24 Sponsor .04 .10

2001-02 Tacoma Sabercats

This set features the Sabercats of the WCHL. It was handed out at a game in late February, 2002 and is very difficult to find on the secondary market.

COMPLETE SET (24)	8.00	20.00
1 Alexander Alexeev	.40	1.00
2 Eric Bowen	.40	1.00
3 Dampy Brar	.60	1.50
4 Mike Brusseau	.40	1.00
5 Etienne Drapeau	.40	1.00
6 Scott Drevitch	.60	1.50
7 Marty Flichel	.60	1.50
8 Trever Fraser	.40	1.00
9 David Goverde	.60	1.50
10 Nathan Horne	.40	1.00
11 Yannick Latour	.40	1.00
12 Matt Loen	.40	1.00
13 Casson Masters	.40	1.00
14 Dennis Pinfold	.40	1.00
15 Clayton Read	.40	1.00
16 Francois Sasseville	.40	1.00
17 Brian Stacey	.40	1.00
18 Jarrett Whidden	.40	1.00
19 Jeff Winter	.40	1.00
20 Dampy Brar	.60	1.50
21 Scott Drevitch	.60	1.50
22 Robert Dirk CO	.10	.25
23 Fang MASCOT	.10	.25
24 Saberkitty MASCOT	.10	.25

1995-96 Tallahassee Tiger Sharks

This 27-card set of the Tallahassee Tiger Sharks of the ECHL was sponsored by Burger King and features color action player photos. The backs carry player information.

COMPLETE SET (27)	3.00	8.00
1 Rodrigo Lavinsh	.15	.40
2 Jon Engfer	.15	.40
3 Rod Aldoff	.15	.40
4 Aaron Kriss	.15	.40
5 Ron Pasco	.15	.40
6 Mark Deazley	.20	.50
7 Sean O'Brien	.20	.50
8 Kevin Paden	.15	.40
9 Darren Schwartz	.20	.50
10 Jim Paradise	.15	.40
11 John Uniac	.15	.40
12 Cal Ingraham	.15	.40
13 Matt Oslecki	.15	.40
14 Greg Geldart	.15	.40
15 Alexander Savchenkov	.15	.40
16 Casey Hungle	.15	.40
17 Mark Richards	.20	.50
18 Bob Bell	.20	.50
19 Frenzy (Mascot)	.02	.10
20 Jim Mirabello ANN	.02	.10
21 Mark Richards Bob Bell	.20	.50
22 Terry Christensen CO	.02	.10
23 Jack Capuano ACO	.02	.10
24 Jerry Hilker TR	.02	.10
25 Walter Edwards VP/GM	.02	.10
26 Tony Mancuso AGM	.02	.10
27 John Summers ANN	.02	.10

1999-00 Tallahassee Tiger Sharks

This set features the Tiger Sharks of the ECHL. The set was produced by the team and issued as a promotional giveaway.

COMPLETE SET (26)	6.00	15.00
1 Kevin Kellett	.25	.60
2 Derek Paget	.25	.60
3 Jason Reid	.25	.60
4 Darren McAusland	.25	.60
5 Adam Copeland	.25	.60
6 David Thibeault	.25	.60
7 Matt Oates	.25	.60
8 Paul Buczkowski	.25	.60
9 Alexandre LaPorte	.25	.60
10 Mike Thompson	.25	.60
11 Kimbi Daniels	.25	.60
12 Ian Perkins	.25	.60
13 Chris Wickenheiser	.40	1.00
14 Larry Shapley	.25	.60
15 Chad Hinz	.30	.75
16 Brent Cullaton	.25	.60
17 Jean-Francois Houle	.25	.60
18 Jason Weinrich	.25	.60
19 Maxim Spiridonov	.30	.75
20 Pavel Smirnov	.25	.60
21 Marc-Andre Gaudet	.25	.60
22 Terry Christensen CO	.08	.25
23 Jim Paradise CO	.08	.25
24 Cory Paterson	.25	.60
24 Kyle Schultz	.25	.60
25 Frenzy MAS	.08	.25

1994 Tampa Bay Tritons RHI

This set features the Tritons of Roller Hockey Intl. The cards were sold in an oversized package featuring team information. The set is noteworthy for featuring what is one of the scarcest cards of Mark Messier, who was part-owner of the club.

COMPLETE SET (21)	7.20	25.00
1 Paul Messier HCO	.08	.25
2 Mark Messier	6.00	15.00
3 Mike Jickling	.15	.40
4 John Spoltore	.40	1.00
5 Todd Goodwin	.15	.40
6 Craig Streu	.15	.40
7 Dennis Sproxton	.15	.40
8 Norman Dezainde	.40	1.00
9 Peter Esdale ACO	.08	.25
10 Trevor Sherban	.15	.40
11 Duane Dennis	.15	.40
12 Jarret Zukiwsky	.15	.40
13 Dion Darling	.40	1.00
14 Sean Basilio	.40	1.00
15 Jeff MacLeod	.15	.40
16 Cheerleaders	.20	.50
17 Sean Rowe	.20	.50
18 George Dupont	.15	.40
19 Team Photo	.15	.40
20 Doug Messier ACO	.08	.25
21 Brad Woods	.15	.40

2006-07 Texas Tornados

COMPLETE SET (25)	15.00	25.00
1 Thomas Murphy	.40	1.00
2 Lyon Messier	2.00	5.00
3 Troy Puente	.40	1.00
4 Jake Newton	.40	1.00
5 Nielsson Arcibal	.40	1.00
6 Dylan Cooper	.40	1.00
7 Justin King	.40	1.00
8 Julian Mikola	.40	1.00
9 Ryan Fuller	.40	1.00
10 Colin Long	.40	1.00
11 Tom Brooks	.40	1.00
12 Sean Roadhouse	.40	1.00
13 Adam Flink	.40	1.00
14 John Bullis	.40	1.00
15 Brendan Brickley	.40	1.00
16 Ben Miller	.40	1.00
17 Rob Blanchette	.40	1.00
18 Brian Reagan	.40	1.00
19 Stephane Da Costa	.40	1.00
20 Paul Yovanic	.40	1.00
21 Mike Cifelli	.40	1.00
22 Corson Cramer	.40	1.00
23 Thomas Tragust	.60	1.50
24 Tony Curtale CO	.02	.10
25 Tom Murphy ACO	.02	.10

1998-99 Thetford Mines Coyotes

This set features players from the Thetford Mines Coyotes of the Quebec Semi-Professional Hockey League, one of the most entertaining leagues in all of hockey.

COMPLETE SET (23)	4.00	10.00
1 Steven Paiement	.20	.50
2 Marco Sevigny	.20	.50
3 Stephane Nepveu	.20	.50
4 Jean-Pierre Tardif	.20	.50
5 Eric Roy	.20	.50
6 Eric Deblois	.20	.50
7 Nick Perreault	.20	.50
8 Sebastian Vallee	.20	.50
9 Yohan Bedard	.20	.50
10 Francois Allaire	.20	.50
11 Bernard Bouffard	.20	.50
12 Philippe Morin	.20	.50
13 Pierre Perron	.20	.50
14 Michel Dodier	.20	.50
15 Frederic Barbeau	.20	.50
16 Yves Loubier	.20	.50
17 Michel Bisson	.20	.50
18 David Desnoyers	.20	.50
19 Dominic Cote	.20	.50
20 Jean Roberge	.20	.50
21 Pierre Marcoux	.20	.50
22 Nathan Morin	.20	.50
23 Marc Rodrigue	.20	.50

2001-02 Thetford Mines Coyotes

This set features the Coyotes of the Quebec Senior League. The set sold by the team at home games. The set we received did not include card #14, but the checklist indicates this card pictures Daniel Payette. If anyone has a set and can verify this, please contact us at hockeymag@beckett.com

COMPLETE SET (25)	10.00	25.00
1 Sebastian Bety	.60	1.50
2 Louis Bernard	.40	1.00
3 Terry Bartlett	.40	1.00
4 Stephane Thivierge	.40	1.00
5 Mathieu Gagne	.40	1.00
6 Frederic Barbeau	.40	1.00
7 Jean-Francois Brunelle	.40	1.00
8 Martin Fillion	.40	1.00
9 Pierre Perron	.40	1.00
10 Eric Roy	.40	1.00
11 Francois Page	.40	1.00
12 Eric Drouin	.40	1.00
13 Jean Roberge	.40	1.00
14 Daniel Payette		1.00
15 Marc-Andre Gaudet	.40	1.00
16 Denis Desbiens	.40	1.00
17 Yves Loubier	.40	1.00
18 Daniel Poudrier	.40	1.00
19 Pierre Marcoux	.40	1.00
20 Hugo Poulin	.40	1.00
21 Patrice Tardif	.80	2.00
22 Bryan Faucher	.40	1.00
23 David Thibeault	.40	1.00
24 Martin Lamarche	.40	1.00
NNO Checklist	.10	.25

2002-03 Thetford Mines Coyotes

COMPLETE SET (23)	5.00	12.00
1 Benoit Beausoleil	.20	.50
2 Louis Bernard	.20	.50
3 Sebastien Bety	.30	.75
4 Jean-Francois Brunelle	.20	.50
5 Christian Caron	.20	.50
6 Denis Desbiens	.20	.50
7 Frederic Deschenes	.20	.50
8 Jason Disher	.20	.50
9 Eric Drouin	.20	.50
10 Martin Fillion	.20	.50
11 Marc-Andre Gaudet	.20	.50
12 Guy Loranger	.20	.50
13 Pierre Marcoux	.20	.50
14 Andre Martineau	.20	.50
15 Francois Page	.20	.50
16 Daniel Payette	.20	.50
17 Daniel Poudrier	.20	.50
18 Hugo Poulin	.20	.50
19 Jean Roberge	.20	.50
20 Eric Roy	.20	.50
21 Claude Savoie	.20	.50
22 Patrice Tardif	.30	.75
23 David Thibeault	.20	.50

2003-04 Thetford Mines Prolab

COMPLETE SET (24)	4.00	10.00
1 Benoit Beausoleil	.20	.50
2 Louis Bernard	.20	.50
3 Eric Betournay	.20	.50
4 Sebastien Bety	.20	.50
5 Patrick Bolduc	.20	.50
6 Denis Desbiens	.20	.50
7 Frederic Deschenes	.20	.50
8 Martin Fillion	.20	.50
9 Marc-Andre Gaudet	.20	.50
10 Eric Lavigne	.20	.50
11 David Lessard	.20	.50
12 Pierre Marcoux	.20	.50
13 Andre Martineau	.20	.50
14 Simon Olivier	.20	.50
15 Francois Page	.20	.50
16 Daniel Poudrier	.20	.50
17 Hugo Poulin	.20	.50
18 Christian Proulx	.20	.50
19 Jean Roberge	.20	.50
20 Eric Roy	.20	.50
21 Claude Savoie	.20	.50
22 Pierre Sevigny	.20	.50
23 Patrice Tardif	.20	.50
24 David Thibeault	.20	.50

2004-05 Thetford Mines Prolab

COMPLETE SET (24)	6.00	15.00
1 David Thibeault	.20	.50
2 Benoit Deschamps	.20	.50
3 Marc-Andre Gaudet	.20	.50
4 Dany Lavoie	.20	.50
5 Patrice Tardif	.20	.50
6 Michel Picard	.30	.75
7 Frederic Deschenes	.30	.75
8 Andre Martineau	.20	.50
9 Serge Poudrier	.20	.50
10 Marquis Mathieu	.40	1.00
11 Francois Page	.20	.50
12 Eric Lavigne	.20	.50
13 Samuel Groleau	.20	.50
14 Yves Racine	.20	.50
15 Hugo Poulin	.20	.50
16 Glen Kjernisted	.20	.50
17 Frederic Henry	.20	.50
18 Jean-Francois Beliveau	.20	.50
19 Samuel Gagnon	.20	.50
20 Simon Olivier	.20	.50
21 Mathieu Biron	.20	.50
22 Matt Holmes	.20	.50
23 Dennis Leblanc	.20	.50
24 Benoit Beausoleil	.20	.50
25 Ryan Pisiak	.20	.50
26 Link Gaetz	.75	2.00
27 Gaetan Royer	.20	.50
28 Frederic Deschenes	.30	.75

2004-05 Thetford Mines Prolab Autographs

It is thought that these cards were issued as inserts with the purchase of a base Thetford Mines set. We have confirmed the existence only of the cards listed below. If you know of others, please contact us at hockeymag@beckett.com.

COMPLETE SET (?)		
7 Frederic Deschenes		

1993-94 Thunder Bay Senators

This 19-card set of the Thunder Bay Senators of the Colonial Hockey League was produced for the team by Rising Star Sports Promotions. The set was available through the club, and may have been offered as a game night premium.

COMPLETE SET (19)	4.00	10.00
1 Jean-Francois Labbe	.40	1.00
2 Jamie Hayden	.20	.50
3 Llew NcWana	.20	.50
4 Chris Hynnes	.20	.50
5 Trent McCleary	.40	1.00
6 Richard Borgo	.20	.50
7 Bryan Wells	.20	.50
8 Don Osborne	.20	.50
9 Todd Howarth	.20	.50
10 Bruce Ramsay	.20	.50
11 Brian Downey	.20	.50
12 Barry McKinley	.20	.50
13 Ron Talakowki	.20	.50
14 Tom Warden	.20	.50
15 Mel Angelstad	.30	.75
16 Tommi Hietala	.20	.50
17 Vern Ray	.20	.50
18 Gerry St. Cyr	.20	.50
19 Jerry Menard	.20	.50

1994-95 Thunder Bay Senators

This 20-card set of the Thunder Bay Senators of the CHL was produced by Rising Star Sports Promotions. The cards were available through the team and may have been issued as a game night giveaway.

COMPLETE SET (20)	3.00	8.00
1 Todd Howarth	.15	.40
2 Darren Perkins	.15	.40
3 Derek Scanlan	.15	.40
4 Pat Szturm	.20	.50
5 Barry McKinley	.15	.40
6 Jake Grimes	.15	.40
7 Alain Cote	.15	.40
8 Rival Fullum	.15	.40
9 Terry Menard	.20	.50
10 Mike McCourt	.15	.40
11 Mel Angelstad	.40	1.00
12 Jason Firth	.15	.40
13 Llew NcWana	.15	.40
14 Lance Leslie	.15	.40
15 Neal Purdon	.15	.40
16 Steve Parson	.15	.40
17 Chris Rowland	.15	.40
18 Bruce Ramsay	.15	.40
19 Don Osborne	.15	.40
20 Jean Blouin	.15	.40

1995-96 Thunder Bay Senators

This 20-card set of the Thunder Bay Senators of the Colonial Hockey League was produced by Rising Star Sports Promotions. The cards were only available through Shoppers Drug Mart stores in Thunder Bay, making hobby acquisition difficult. The cards feature a blurry action photo on the front, an complete stats on the back, along with the Shoppers logos. The cards are unnumbered and are listed below alphabetically.

COMPLETE SET (20)	6.00	15.00
1 Team Photo	.30	.75
2 Mel Angelstad	.40	1.00
3 Omer Belisle	.30	.75
4 Frederic Cassivi	.60	1.50
5 Brandon Christian	.30	.75
6 Jason Disher	.30	.75
7 Jason Firth	.30	.75
8 Rival Fullum	.30	.75
9 Todd Howarth	.30	.75
10 Chris Hynnes	.30	.75
11 Barry McKinley	.30	.75
12 Terry Menard	.30	.75
13 Derek Nicolson	.30	.75
14 Llew NcWana	.30	.75
15 Steve Parson	.30	.75
16 Darren Perkins	.30	.75
17 Dan Poirier	.30	.75
18 Neal Purdon	.30	.75
19 Bruce Ramsay	.30	.75
20 Pat Szturm	.40	1.00

1998-99 Thunder Bay Thunder Cats

This set features the Thunder Cats of the UHL. The singles were given away with issues of the local paper. There also have been reports that the complete set could be purchased directly through the paper at the end of the season.

COMPLETE SET (21)	4.00	10.00
1 Jason Lehman	.20	.50
2 Barry McKinlay	.20	.50
3 David Mayes	.20	.50
4 Darrin Szczygiel	.20	.50
5 Allan Roulette	.20	.50
6 Normand Paquet	.20	.50
7 Wayne Strachan	.20	.50
8 Kevin Holliday	.20	.50
9 Dan Brenzavich	.20	.50
10 Mike Henderson	.20	.50
11 Neal Purdon	.20	.50
12 Nikolai Pronin	.20	.50
13 Dan Myre	.20	.50
14 Derek Landmesser	.30	.75
15 Jason Firth	.30	.75
16 Shawn Smith	.20	.50
17 Jean-Francois Rivard	.20	.50
18 Brant Blackned	.20	.50
19 Darrell Clarke TR	.02	.10
20 Tom Warden CO	.02	.10
21 Sean McEachran	.20	.50

1992-93 Thunder Bay Thunder Hawks

This set features the Thunder Hawks of the UHL. The cards were sold by the team at its souvenir stands, and are notable for being slightly smaller than typical cards.

COMPLETE SET (30)		15.00
1 Checklist	.02	.10
2 Bill McDonald CO	.02	.10
3 Larry Wintoneak ACO	.02	.10
4 Mark Michaud	.20	.50
5 Marc Lyons	.20	.50
6 Jamie Hayden	.20	.50
7 Llew Ncwana	.20	.50
8 Marc LaBelle	.20	.50
9 Gary Callaghan	.20	.50
10 Jason Firth	.30	.75
11 Mike Martens	.30	.75
12 Gerry St. Cyr	.30	.75
13 Everton Blackwin	.20	.50
14 Bryan Wells	.20	.50
15 Brian Downey	.20	.50
16 Todd Howarth	.20	.50
17 Bruce Rendall	.20	.50
18 Vern Ray	.20	.50
19 Bruce Ramsay	.20	.50
20 Chris Rowland	.20	.50
21 Barry McKinlay	.20	.50
22 Vincent Faucher	.20	.50
23 Tom Warden	.20	.50
24 Brock Shyiak	.20	.50
25 Mel Angelstad	.40	1.00
26 Harijs Vitolinsh	.20	.50
27 Steve Hogg	.30	.75
28 Terry Menard	.30	.75
29 Mark Woolf	.30	.75
30 Darrell Clarke TR	.02	.10

1992-93 Toledo Storm

This 25-card set features the Toledo Storm of the ECHL. The set features action photography -- which often suffers from the poor quality -- on the front, with stats and bio on the back. The cards were offered for sale by the club at the rink on game nights.

COMPLETE SET (25)	3.00	8.00
1 Checklist	.02	.10
2 Chris McSorley CO	.20	.50
3 Scott Luhrmann EQMG	.02	.10
4 Barry Soskin GM	.02	.10
5 Tim Mouser PR	.02	.10
6 Jeff Gibbons PR	.02	.10
7 Claude Scott The Happy Trumpeter	.02	.10
8 Scott King	.20	.50
9 Andy Suhy	.15	.40
10 Pat Pylypuik	.15	.40
11 Alex Roberts	.15	.40
12 Mark Deazley	.15	.40
13 John Johnson	.15	.40
14 Jeff Rohlicek	.15	.40
15 Dan Wiebe	.15	.40
16 Jeff Jablonski	.15	.40
17 Greg Puhalski	.15	.40
18 Bruce MacDonald	.15	.40
19 Iain Duncan	.15	.40
20 Rick Judson	.15	.40
21 Alex Hicks	.20	.50
22 Barry Potomski	.20	.50
23 Derek Booth	.15	.40
24 Rick Corriveau	.15	.40
25 Mark Richards	.15	.40

1992-93 Toledo Storm Team Issue

Little is known about this set beyond the confirmed checklist. Any additional information can be forwarded to hockeymag@beckett.com.

COMPLETE SET (30)	3.00	8.00
1 Logo Card	.02	.10
2 Chris McSorley CO	.20	.50
3 Scott Luhrmann EQMG	.02	.10
4 Barry Soskin GM	.20	.50
5 Tim Mouser PR	.02	.10
6 Jeff Gibbons PR	.15	.40
7 Mike Williams	.15	.40
8 Scott King	.20	.50
9 Alex Hicks	.20	.50
10 Rick Judson	.15	.40
11 Brent Sapergia	.08	.25
12 Iain Duncan	.15	.40
13 Mark Deazeley	.15	.40
14 Jeff Jablonski	.15	.40
15 Bruce MacDonald	.15	.40
16 Rick Corriveau	.15	.40
17 Pat Pylypuik	.15	.40
18 Alex Roberts	.15	.40
19 Derek Booth	.15	.40
20 Andy Suhy	.15	.40
21 Jason Stos	.15	.40
22 Greg Puhalski	.15	.40
23 Wade Bartley	.08	.25
24 Distillery Crew	.02	.10
25 The Dawnbusters	.02	.10
26 Becky Shock	.02	.10
27 Don Davis	.02	.10
28 Beth Daniels	.02	.10
29 Dennis O'Brien	.02	.10
30 Will Worster	.02	.10

1993-94 Toledo Storm

This 29-card standard-size set features the 1992-93 Riley Cup Champions Toledo Storm of the ECHL (East Coast Hockey League). Inside a white and a thin red border, the fronts feature color action player photos with the player's name and position in a red border at the bottom of the card. The team logo also appears in the bottom.

COMPLETE SET (29)	4.00	10.00
1 Checklist Card	.02	.10
2 Chris McSorley CO	.20	.50
3 Barry Soskin PRES	.02	.10
4 Tim Mouser MG	.02	.10
5 Jeff Gibbons ANN	.02	.10
6 Scott Luhrmann TR	.02	.10
7 Nick Vitucci	.20	.50
8 Andy Suhy	.08	.25
9 Pat Pylypuik	.08	.25
10 Chris Belanger	.08	.25
11 Mike Markovich	.08	.25
12 Darren Perkins	.08	.25
13 Dennis Snedden	.08	.25
14 Mark Deazeley	.20	.50
15 Mark McCreary	.08	.25
16 Jeff Rohlicek	.08	.25
17 Chris Bergeron	.08	.25
18 John Hendry	.08	.25
19 Greg Puhalski	.08	.25
20 Bruce MacDonald	.08	.25
21 Marc Lyons	.08	.25
22 Rick Judson	.08	.25
23 Alex Hicks	.30	.75
24 Barry Potomski	.30	.75
25 Rick Corriveau	.20	.50
26 Kyle Reeves	.20	.50
27 Erin Whitten	1.25	3.00
28 Brian Schoen	.08	.25
29 Riley Cup Champions	.08	.25

1994-95 Toledo Storm

This 24-card standard-size set features the 1993-94 Riley Cup Champion Storm of the ECHL. The borderless fronts have color action player photos with the player's name, number and position across the bottom. The words "Toledo Hockey" are printed vertically down the right edge, while the team logo appears in the upper left corner. The cards are unnumbered and checklisted below in alphabetical order.

COMPLETE SET (24)	3.00	8.00
1 Dave Bankoske	.15	.40
2 Wyatt Buckland	.15	.40
3 Rick Corriveau	.15	.40
4 Norm Dezainde	.20	.50
5 Iain Duncan	.15	.40
6 Jeff Gibbons	.15	.40
7 Alain Harvey	.20	.50
8 John Hendry	.15	.40
9 Ed Henrich	.15	.40
10 Rick Judson	.15	.40
11 Mike Latendresse	.15	.40
12 Scott Luhrmann TR	.02	.10
13 B.J. MacPherson	.15	.40
14 Jim Maher	.15	.40
15 Jay Neal	.15	.40
16 Marquis Mathieu	.15	.40
17 Shawn Penn	.15	.40
18 Darren Perkins	.15	.40
19 Greg Puhalski CO	.02	.10
20 Barry Soskin PR/GM	.02	.10
21 Gerry St. Cyr	.15	.40
22 Rhett Trombley	.20	.50
23 Nick Vitucci	.20	.50
24 1993-94 Riley Cup Champions	.20	.50

1995-96 Toledo Storm

This 26-card set of the Toledo Storm of the ECHL was sponsored by Frito-Lay and available through the team and its booster club. The fronts feature an action photo along with team, league and sponsor logos. The unnumbered backs contain player analysis and stats.

COMPLETE SET (26)	3.00	8.00
1 Rob Laurie	.15	.40
2 Nicolas Perreault	.20	.50
3 Brandon Carper	.15	.40
4 Paul Koch	.15	.40
5 Glen Mears	.15	.40
6 Dan Carter	.15	.40
7 Patrick Gladu	.15	.40
8 Todd Wetzel	.15	.40
9 B.J. MacPherson	.15	.40
10 Mark [illegible]	.15	.40
11 Dennis Purdie	.20	.50
12 Rick Judson	.15	.40
13 Mike Whitton	.15	.40
14 Norm Dezainde	.15	.40
15 Jason Gladney	.15	.40
16 Wade Bartley	.15	.40
17 Jason Smart	.15	.40
18 Mike Kolenda	.15	.40
19 Shawn Penn	.15	.40
20 David Goverde	.20	.50
21 Barry Soskin OWN	.02	.10
22 Greg Puhalski CO	.02	.10
23 Chuck Imburgia DIR	.02	.10
24 Scott Luhrmann EQMG	.02	.10
25 Mark Kelly ANN	.02	.10
26 Sponsor Card	.02	.10

1996-97 Toledo Storm

This 23-card set was produced by Split Second. The unnumbered cards feature an action photo on the front, with a brief statistical package on the back. The club offered them for sale at games and through the mail.

COMPLETE SET (23)	3.00	8.00
1 Ryan Bach	.30	.75
5 Paul Koch	.15	.40
6 Ryan Bast	.15	.40
11 Brian Clifford	.15	.40
14 Mike Sullivan	.15	.40
17 Alex Matvichuk	.15	.40
18 Arturs Kupaks	.15	.40
19 Dennis Purdie	.20	.50
20 Rick Judson	.15	.40
22 Norm Dezainde	.15	.40
23 Jason Gladney	.15	.40
24 Chris Bergeron	.15	.40
25 Mike Whitton	.15	.40
27 Mike Kolenda	.15	.40
28 Dan Pawlaczyk	.15	.40
29 Jeremy Mylymok	.15	.40
32 Don Larner	.15	.40
33 Rob Thorpe	.15	.40
35 David Goverde	.30	.75
NNO Scott Luhrmann TR	.02	.10
NNO Greg Puhalski CO	.02	.10
NNO Barry Soskin PRES	.02	.10
NNO Mark Kelly ANN	.02	.10

1997-98 Toledo Storm

This set was made by Grandstand and were sold by the team at home games. The cards are unnumbered, and are listed below in the order they were inserted in the pack.

COMPLETE SET (30)	3.00	8.00
1 Louis Bernard	.10	.30
2 Robert Thorpe	.10	.30
3 Greg Lakovic	.10	.30
4 Alexandre Jacques	.10	.30
5 Gordy Hunt	.10	.30
6 Andrei Sryubko	.10	.30
7 Sean Venedam	.10	.30
8 Jeremy Rebek	.10	.30
9 Sean Ortiz	.10	.30
10 Tony Prpic	.10	.30
11 Brian Blad	.10	.30
12 Ron Newhook	.20	.50
13 Nick Vitucci	.20	.50
14 Dennis Holland	.10	.30
15 Mark Deazeley	.10	.30
16 Rick Judson	.10	.30
17 Lee Cole	.10	.30
18 Mike Kolenda	.10	.30
19 Dave Arsenault	.10	.30
20 Jason Gladney	.10	.30
21 Bruce MacDonald	.10	.30
22 Kevin Brown	.10	.30
23 Andrew Williamson	.10	.30
24 Shawn Maltby	.10	.30
25 Mike Loach	.10	.30
26 Greg Puhalski HCO	.02	.10
27 Barry Soskin PR	.02	.10
28 Team Staff	.02	.10
29 Mark Kelly	.02	.10
30 Matt Bresnan EM	.02	.10

2003-04 Toledo Storm

These cards were issued as promotional giveaways throughout the 2003-04 season. The cards came in four-card perforated strips. It's believed this checklist is incomplete. If you have further info, please email us at hockeymag@beckett.com.

COMPLETE SET (12)	4.00	10.00
1 Toledo Storm	.02	.10
2 Doug Teskey	.60	1.50
3 Mike Nelson	.40	1.00
4 Josh Legge	.40	1.00
5 Morten Ask	.40	1.00
6 Nick Parillo	.40	1.00
7 Tom Nemeth	.40	1.00
8 Alexandre Jacques	.40	1.00
9 Rick Judson	.40	1.00
10 Landon Bathe	.40	1.00
11 Kris Waltze	.40	1.00
12 Jim Abbott	.40	1.00

2006-07 Toledo Storm

COMPLETE SET (26)	8.00	15.00
1 Andrew Martin	.30	.75
2 Jamie Tardif	.30	.75
3 Jason Maleyko	.30	.75
4 Tom Songin	.30	.75
5 P.J. Martin	.30	.75
6 Paul Crosty	.40	1.00
7 Jon Sitko	.30	.75
8 Jason Schweinsberg EQ MGR	.02	.10
9 Mike Brodeur	.40	1.00
10 Dominic Vicari	.40	1.00
11 Scooter Smith	.30	.75
12 Chris Blight	.30	.75
13 Logan Koopmans	.40	1.00
14 Mike James	.30	.75
15 Taylor Raszka	.30	.75
16 Ken Magowan	.30	.75
17 Nick Parillo	.30	.75
18 Jeff Attard	.30	.75
19 Gerry Burke	.30	.75
20 Dan Watson	.30	.75
21 Mike Walsh	.30	.75
22 Matt Zultek	.30	.75
23 Nick Vitucci CO	.20	.50
24 Rick Judson CO	.02	.10
25 Barry Soskin PRES	.02	.10
26 Dukes MASCOT	.02	.10

1998-99 Topeka Scarecrows

This 23-card set of the WPHL Scarecrows was sold at home games. Note: there are two versions of card #21. It is not known whether either version is scarcer than the other.

COMPLETE SET (23)	4.00	10.00
1 Topeka Scarecrows CL	.02	.10
2 Michal Podolka	.30	.75
3 Shawn Randall	.20	.50
4 Mike Rusk	.20	.50
5 Brett Seguin	.20	.50
6 Tom Stewart	.20	.50
7 Andy Adams	.20	.50
8 Chad Antonishyn	.20	.50
9 Chris Bowen	.20	.50
10 Joe Coombs	.20	.50
11 Scott Dickson	.20	.50
12 Troy Frederick	.20	.50
13 Dave Gregory	.20	.50
14 Trevor Hanas	.20	.50
15 Kyle Haviland	.20	.50
16 Haywire Mascot	.02	.10
17 Kevin Lune	.20	.50
18 Sergei Olympiev	.20	.50
19 Ryan Phillips	.20	.50
20 Paul Kelly HCO	.02	.10
21 Andy Adams NM	.40	1.00
21 Michael Podolka NM	.40	1.00
22 Team Photo	.20	.50

1999-00 Topeka Scarecrows

This set features the Scarecrows of the CHL. The set was produced by Roox and was sold by the team at home games.

COMPLETE SET (21)	4.00	10.00
1 Topeka Scarecrows	.20	.50
2 John Vary	.20	.50
3 Oleg Tsirkounov	.20	.50
4 Bill Monkman	.20	.50
5 Sergei Deschevvy	.20	.50
6 Randy Best	.20	.50
7 Blair Manning	.20	.50
8 Steve Moore	.20	.50
9 Kirk Llano	.20	.50
10 Joey Beaudry	.20	.50
11 Trevor Hanas	.20	.50
12 David Bouskill	.20	.50
13 Rod Branch	.20	.50
14 Joe Coombs	.20	.50
15 Mike Rusk	.20	.50
16 Scot Bell	.20	.50
17 Michal Podolka	.30	.75
18 Brett Seguin	.30	.75
19 Haywire MAS	.08	.25
20 Paul Kelly CO	.08	.25
21 Topeka Scarecrows	.20	.50

2002-03 Topeka Scarecrows

COMPLETE SET (30)	10.00	25.00
1 Layne Sedevie	.40	1.00
2 Slavomir Tomko	.40	1.00
3 Tony Gliniany	.40	1.00
4 Phil Angell	.40	1.00
5 Jeff Balvin	.40	1.00
6 Ryan Peterson	.40	1.00
7 Nick Pernula	.40	1.00
8 J.P. Platisha	.40	1.00
9 Justin White	.40	1.00
10 Luke Erickson	.40	1.00
11 Wade Harstad	.40	1.00
12 James Unger	.40	1.00
13 Steve Eastman	.40	1.00
14 Ryan Miller	.40	1.00
15 Erik Fabian	.40	1.00
16 Eric Vesely	.40	1.00
17 Brent Cummings	.40	1.00
18 Nick Miller	.40	1.00
19 Rob Rankin	.40	1.00
20 Mark Buchholz	.40	1.00
21 Adam Bartholomay	.40	1.00
22 Michael Zacharias	.40	1.00
23 Mascots	.02	.10
24 Zambeauty-Taumi	.20	.50
25 Zambeauty-Janea	.20	.50
26 Zambeauty-Audrey	.20	.50
27 Zambeauty-Tara	.20	.50
28 Zambeauty-Melissa	.20	.50
29 Zambeauty-Amanda	.20	.50
30 Scarecrows logo	.02	.10

2006-07 Toronto Marlies

COMPLETE SET (34)	12.00	20.00
1 J.S. Aubin	.30	.75
2 Bates Battaglia	.20	.50
3 Brendan Bell	.20	.50
4 Brad Brown	.20	.50
5 Carlo Colaiacovo	.20	.50
6 Jeff Corey	.20	.50
7 Dominic D'Amour	.20	.50
8 Duke The Dog MASCOT	.02	.10
9 Robbie Earl	.40	1.00
10 Brett Engelhardt	.20	.50
11 Alex Foster	.20	.50
12 Owen Fussey	.20	.50
13 Greg Gilbert CO	.02	.10
14 Jay Harrison	.20	.50
15 Staffan Kronwall	.20	.50
16 Brad Leeb	.20	.50
17 John Mitchell	.20	.50
18 Marc Moro	.30	.75
19 Colin Murphy	.20	.50
20 Kris Newbury	.20	.50

21 Ben Ondrus .20 .50
22 Justin Pogge .75 2.00
23 John Pohl .30 .75
24 J.F. Racine .30 .75
25 Martin Sagat .20 .50
26 Justin Sawyer .20 .50
27 Jamie Sifers .20 .50
28 Chris St. Jacques .20 .50
29 Alexander Suglobov .20 .50
30 Jiri Tlusty .40 1.00
31 Erik Westrum .40 1.00
32 Ian White .20 .50
33 Jeremy Williams .20 .50
34 Andy Wozniewski .20 .50

2007-08 Toronto Marlies

COMPLETE SET (23) 15.00 25.00
1 Justin Pogge 2.00 5.00
2 Bryan Muir .75 2.00
3 Chris Harrington .40 1.00
4 Anton Stralman .60 1.50
5 Simon Gamache .40 1.00
6 Robbie Earl .60 1.50
7 Kris Newbury .40 1.00
8 David Ling .75 2.00
9 Brent Aubin .40 1.00
10 Jeremy Williams .40 1.00
11 Jay Harrison .40 1.00
12 Alex Foster .40 1.00
13 Ben Ondrus .40 1.00
14 Jaime Sifers .40 1.00
15 Scott Clemmensen .60 1.50
16 Michel Leveille .40 1.00
17 Derrick Walser .40 1.00
18 Collin Murphy .40 1.00
19 Darryl Boyce .40 1.00
20 John Mitchell .10 .25
21 Greg Gilbert .10 .25
22 Dance Park .02 .10
23 Duke .02 .10

2003-04 Toronto Star

Available through select retailers in late October 2003, fans could purchase packs consisting of four random cards from the 100-card base set plus the special foil insert card for that day. The cost of each pack was $3.49 (Canadian funds) plus taxes. A coupon was inserted into each daily issue of the Toronto Star offering one dollar off on a pack of cards. Each coupon was specific to the day's special pack. The promotion ran for 30 days. The cards were produced by In the Game,Inc for the paper.

COMPLETE SET (100) 10.00 25.00
1 Jean-Sebastien Giguere .20 .50
2 Petr Sykora .08 .20
3 Stanislav Chistov .08 .20
4 Dany Heatley .30 .75
5 Ilya Kovalchuk .40 1.00
6 Glen Murray .08 .20
7 Joe Thornton .40 1.00
8 Sergei Samsonov .20 .50
9 Martin Biron .20 .50
10 Miroslav Satan .08 .20
11 Ryan Miller .40 1.00
12 Rod Brind'Amour .08 .20
13 Jeff O'Neill .08 .20
14 Ron Francis .08 .20
15 Rick Nash .40 1.00
16 Rostislav Klesla .08 .20
17 Jarome Iginla .40 1.00
18 Eric Daze .08 .20
19 Jocelyn Thibault .20 .50
20 Alex Tanguay .20 .50
21 Joe Sakic .50 1.25
22 Milan Hejduk .20 .50
23 Patrick Roy 1.50 4.00
24 Peter Forsberg .75 1.50
25 Rob Blake .20 .50
26 Bill Guerin .08 .20
27 Marty Turco .20 .50
28 Mike Modano .25 .60
29 Brendan Shanahan .25 .60
30 Brett Hull .30 .75
31 Chris Chelios .20 .50
32 Dominik Hasek .40 1.00
33 Henrik Zetterberg .20 .50
34 Nicklas Lidstrom .20 .50
35 Pavel Datsyuk .20 .50
36 Steve Yzerman 1.25 3.00
37 Mike Comrie .08 .20
38 Ryan Smyth .20 .50
39 Jay Bouwmeester .08 .20
40 Kristian Huselius .08 .20
41 Roberto Luongo .25 .60
42 Olli Jokinen .08 .20
43 Alexander Frolov .08 .20
44 Jason Allison .08 .20
45 Zigmund Palffy .08 .20
46 Marian Gaborik .40 1.00
47 Manny Fernandez .20 .50
48 Jose Theodore .25 .60
49 Saku Koivu .20 .50
50 Jeff Friesen .08 .20
51 Martin Brodeur 1.00 2.50
52 Patrik Elias .08 .20
53 Scott Niedermayer .08 .20
54 Scott Stevens .08 .20
55 Jamie Langenbrunner .08 .20
56 Alexei Yashin .08 .20
57 Rick DiPietro .20 .50
58 Alexei Kovalev .08 .20
59 Anson Carter .08 .20
60 Eric Lindros .25 .60
61 Mark Messier .25 .60
62 Mike Dunham .20 .50
63 Pavel Bure .25 .60
64 Daniel Alfredsson .08 .20
65 Jason Spezza .25 .60
66 Marian Hossa .20 .50
67 Martin Havlat .20 .50
68 Patrick Lalime .20 .50
69 Jeremy Roenick .25 .60
70 John LeClair .08 .20
71 Simon Gagne .08 .20
72 Tony Amonte .08 .20
73 Sean Burke .20 .50
74 Mario Lemieux 1.50 4.00
75 Evgeni Nabokov .25 .60
76 Pavol Demitra .08 .20
77 Al MacInnis .08 .20
78 Barret Jackman .08 .20
79 Chris Pronger .08 .20
80 Doug Weight .08 .20
81 Keith Tkachuk .20 .50
82 Brad Richards .25 .60
83 Nikolai Khabibulin .25 .60
84 Vincent Lecavalier .25 .60
85 Martin St.Louis .25 .60
86 Owen Nolan .08 .20
87 Alexander Mogilny .08 .20
88 Carlo Colaiacovo .08 .20
89 Nikolai Antropov .08 .20
90 Ed Belfour .25 .60
91 Gary Roberts .08 .20
92 Mats Sundin .25 .60
93 Tie Domi .08 .20
94 Tomas Kaberle .08 .20
95 Ed Jovanovski .08 .20
96 Markus Naslund .08 .20
97 Todd Bertuzzi .08 .20
98 Jaromir Jagr .40 1.00
99 Olaf Kolzig .20 .50
100 Peter Bondra .08 .20

2003-04 Toronto Star Foil

These foil cards were inserted one per pack and the available card changed each day of the promotion.

ONE PER PACK
1 Mario Lemieux 2.00 5.00
2 Steve Yzerman 1.50 4.00
3 Peter Forsberg 1.25 3.00
4 Marian Gaborik .75 2.00
5 Dominik Hasek .75 2.00
6 Joe Thornton .75 2.00
7 Henrik Zetterberg .40 1.00
8 Mike Modano .75 2.00
9 Ed Belfour .40 1.00
10 Marian Hossa .40 1.00
11 Owen Nolan .40 1.00
12 Pavel Bure .75 2.00
13 Jose Theodore .75 2.00
14 Mike Comrie .40 1.00
15 Tie Domi .40 1.00
16 Roberto Luongo .75 2.00
17 Saku Koivu .40 1.00
18 Jarome Iginla .75 2.00
19 Brett Hull .75 2.00
20 Markus Naslund .40 1.00
21 Jaromir Jagr 1.25 3.00
22 Jason Spezza .75 2.00
23 Rick Nash 1.25 3.00
24 Jean-Sebastien Giguere .40 1.00
25 Mats Sundin .75 2.00
26 Ilya Kovalchuk 1.25 3.00
27 Dany Heatley .75 2.00
28 Joe Sakic 1.25 3.00
29 Martin Brodeur 1.50 4.00
30 Patrick Roy 2.00 5.00

2000-01 Trenton Titans

This set features the Titans of the ECHL. The cards were actually distributed in the form of two 12-card sets at different points of the season. Each set had a retail price of $15.

COMPLETE SET (24) 12.00 30.00
1 Scott Bertoli .60 1.50
2 Sandy Cohen .80 2.00
3 Aniket Dhadphale .60 1.50
4 Mike Hall .60 1.50
5 Cail MacLean .60 1.50
6 Steve O'Brien .60 1.50
7 Alain St. Hilaire .60 1.50
8 Scott Stirling .60 1.50
9 Jed Whitchurch .60 1.50
10 Vince Williams .60 1.50
11 Mike Haviland ACO .10 .25
12 Troy Ward HCO .10 .25
13 Dennis Bassett .60 1.50
14 Shane Belter .60 1.50
15 Sasha Cucuz .60 1.50
16 Ian Forbes .60 1.50
17 Butch Kaebel .60 1.50
18 Sean Molina .60 1.50
19 Benoit Morin .60 1.50
20 Jeff Potter .60 1.50
21 Paul Spadafora .60 1.50
22 Kam White .60 1.50
23 David Whitworth .60 1.50
24 Clash MASCOT .10 .25

2001-02 Trenton Titans

This set features the Titans of the ECHL. The set was sold by the team at home games in two 12-card series. The first was released in Jan. 2002, the second in March. Both series retailed for $15 each. The cards are unnumbered and so they are listed alphabetically by 12-card series.

COMPLETE SET (24) 12.00 30.00
1-1 Syl Apps .80 2.00
1-2 Marco Charpentier .60 1.50
1-3 Aniket Dhadphale .60 1.50
1-4 Kirk Lamb .60 1.50
1-5 Matt Libby .60 1.50
1-6 Cail MacLean .60 1.50
1-7 John Nail .60 1.50
1-8 Geoff Peters .60 1.50
1-9 Scott Ricci .60 1.50
1-10 David St. Germain .60 1.50
1-11 Chuck Weber ACO .10 .25
1-12 Matt Zultek .80 2.00
2-1 Graham Belak .80 2.00
2-2 Scott Bertoli .60 1.50
2-3 Ian Forbes .60 1.50
2-4 Peter Horachek CO .20 .50
2-5 Pat Leahy .60 1.50
2-6 Andreas Moborg .60 1.50
2-7 Dan Murphy .60 1.50
2-8 Steve O'Brien .60 1.50
2-9 Alain St. Hilaire .80 2.00
2-10 Ben Stafford .60 1.50
2-11 Kam White .60 1.50
2-12 Rivet MASCOT .10 .25

2002-03 Trenton Titans

COMPLETE SET (24) 20.00
A1 Scott Bertoli 1.00
A2 Adam Edinger 1.00
A3 Andy Hedlund 1.00
A4 Yann Joseph 1.00
A5 B.J. Kilbourne 1.00
A6 John Nail 1.00
A7 Cody Rudkowsky 3.00
A8 Kam White 1.00
A9 Dustin Wood 1.00
A10 Matt Zultek 1.50
A11 Bill Armstrong CO .10
A12 Rivet MASCOT .10
B1 Syl Apps 1.00
B2 Tyler Beechey 1.00
B3 Sean Connolly 1.00
B4 Shaun Fisher 1.00
B5 Ian Forbes 1.00
B6 Mike Hurley 1.00
B7 Steve O'Brien 1.00
B8 David St. Germain 1.00
B9 Jeff Smith 1.00
B10 Daniel Tetrault 1.00
B11 Vince Williams 1.00
B12 Clash MASCOT .10

2003-04 Trenton Titans

This set was produced by RBI Sports and reportedly limited to just 250 copies. The number sequencing includes all sets produced by RBI that season.

COMPLETE SET (16) 6.00 15.00
353 B.J. Abel .40 1.00
354 Andrew Allen .50 1.25
355 Scott Bertoli .40 1.00
356 Mathieu Brunelle .40 1.00
357 Bill Cass .40 1.00
358 Bryce Cockburn .40 1.00
359 Nick Deschenes .40 1.00
360 Peter Fregoe .40 1.00
361 Jay Leach .40 1.00
362 P.J. Martin .40 1.00
363 Devin Rask .40 1.00
364 Dan Riva .40 1.00
365 Jeff Smith .50 1.25
366 Pete Summerfelt .40 1.00
367 Vince Williams .40 1.00
368 Matt Zultek .60 1.50

1994-95 Tri-City Americans

This unusual series was produced by Summit. Four of the cards (#4-7) are standard size, while the other four are slightly oversized, suggesting that they may have been released at different times, or in two separate series. The larger four cards also have a slightly darker blue border around the posed studio shot. All of the cards appear to be laminated, or made strictly from a plastic-type material. The checklist below may be incomplete. Additional information from the readership would be appreciated.

COMPLETE SET (8) 10.00 25.00
1 Dorian Anneck .40 1.00
2 Brent Ascroft .20 .50
3 Brian Boucher 6.00 15.00
4 Rob Butz .20 .50
5 Chad Cabana .30 .75
6 Daymond Langkow 2.00 5.00
7 Ryan Marsh .20 .50
8 Terry Ryan .75 2.00

1995-96 Tri-City Americans

This 31-card set was produced by S&H Ltd. The cards feature action photos on the front, with a mug shot and bio on the back. Unnumbered, the cards are listed below in alphabetical order. The set is noteworthy for the inclusion of three first round selections from the 1995 Entry Draft: Daymond Langkow (TB), Terry Ryan (MTL) and Brian Boucher (PHI).

COMPLETE SET (31) 8.00 20.00
1 Chris Anderson .15 .40
2 Dorian Anneck .20 .50
3 Brent Ascroft .15 .40
4 Aaron Baker .20 .50
5 Alexandre Boikov .15 .40
6 Brian Boucher 2.00 5.00
7 Byron Briske .20 .50
8 Bob Brown GM .02 .10
9 Jerry Fredericksen TR .02 .10
10 Dan Focht .20 .50
11 Dylan Gyori .30 .75
12 Mark Hurley .15 .40
13 Mike Hurley .15 .40
14 Zenith Komarniski .20 .50
15 Daymond Langkow .75 2.00
16 Jody Lapeyre .15 .40
17 Bob Loucks CO .02 .10
18 Scott McCallum .15 .40
19 Boyd Olson .15 .40
20 Warren Renden ACO .02 .10
21 Terry Ryan .30 .75
22 Eric Schneider .15 .40
23 Dan Smith .15 .40
24 Craig Stahl .15 .40
25 Jaroslav Svejkovsky .30 .75
26 Jeremy Thompson .15 .40
27 Gary Toor .15 .40
28 Tom Zavediuk .15 .40
29 Eddie the Eagle (Mascot) .02 .10
30 Brian Boucher 1.25 3.00
(Daymond Langkow
Terry Ryan)
31 Logo Card .02 .10

1998-99 Tri-City Americans

This set of the WHL Americans was issued by the team and sold at its souvenir stands. It features several promising NHLers including Josef Melichar, Jaroslav Kristek and 1999 Rookie of the Year Scott Gomez.

COMPLETE SET (28) 8.00 20.00
1 Jeff Blair .20 .50
2 Josef Melichar .40 1.00
3 Andrew DeSousa .30 .75
4 Darrell Hay .40 1.00
5 Jeff Katcher .20 .50
6 Toni Bader .20 .50
7 Jaroslav Kristek .40 1.00
8 Ken McKay .20 .50
9 Eric Johannson .20 .50
10 Scott Gomez 1.25 3.00
11 Ryley Layden .20 .50
12 Tim Green .20 .50
13 Blake Evans .20 .50
14 K.C. Timmons .20 .50
15 Jordan Landry .20 .50
16 Dylan Gyori .40 1.00
17 Brad Ference .60 1.50
18 Mike Muzechka .20 .50
19 Stephen Peat .60 1.50
20 Curtis Huppe .30 .75
21 Mike Lee .20 .50
22 Jody Lapeyre .20 .50
23 Andrew Guindon .20 .50
24 Blake Ward .30 .75
25 Terry Bangen ACO/AGM .02 .10
26 Training Staff .02 .10
27 Don Hay HCO/GM .20 .50
28 Craig West BR .02 .10

2002-03 Tri-City Stormfront

COMPLETE SET (25) 20.00 40.00
1 Cover Card .10 .25
2 Stormy MASCOT .10 .25
3 Brian Kilburg .75 2.00
4 Nick Klaren .75 2.00
5 Luke Lucyk 1.25 3.00
6 Mark Agnew .75 2.00
7 Tim Madsen .75 2.00
8 Geoff Paukovich .75 2.00
9 Chris Nathe .75 2.00
10 Ryan Dingle .75 2.00
11 Josh Leddy .75 2.00
12 Matt Scherer .75 2.00
13 Bill Thomas .75 2.00
14 Scott Parse .75 2.00
15 Steve Wagner .75 2.00
16 Tom Pohl .75 2.00
17 David Boguslawski .75 2.00
18 James Martin .75 2.00
19 Chad Anderson .75 2.00
20 Mark Van Guilder .75 2.00
21 T.J. Dahl .75 2.00
22 Casey Mapes .75 2.00
23 Eric Aarnio .75 2.00
24 Tom Kowal .75 2.00
25 Regg Simon .75 2.00

1997-98 Tucson Gila Monsters

This set features the Gila Monsters of the WCHL. These postcard-sized singles are blank backed, and were issued by the team as a promotional giveaway.

COMPLETE SET (10) 4.00 10.00
1 Jon Rowe .40 1.00
2 Dan Marcotte .40 1.00
3 David Piirto .40 1.00
4 Peter Romeo .40 1.00
5 Patrick Bisaillon .40 1.00
6 Jason Crane .40 1.00
7 Chris Everett .40 1.00
8 Sam Fields .40 1.00
9 Pierre Gagnon .40 1.00
10 Aigars Mironovics .40 1.00

1966-67 Tulsa Oilers

Little is known about this set featuring the Oilers of the old CHL beyond the confirmed checklist. The cards were oversized black and white images and likely were issued in photo-pack form. Any additional information can be forwarded to hockeymag@beckett.com.

COMPLETE SET (12) 25.00 50.00
1 Ken Campbell 1.50 3.00
2 Andrew Champagne 1.50 3.00
3 Doug Dunville 1.50 3.00
4 Bill Flett 5.00 10.00
5 Nick Harbaruk 1.50 3.00
6 Lowell MacDonald 5.00 10.00
7 Jim McKenny 2.50 5.00
8 Al Millar 1.50 3.00
9 Marc Reaume 2.00 4.00
10 Harry Shaw 1.50 3.00
11 Gary Venneruzzo 2.50 5.00
12 Ron Ward 2.00 4.00

1972-73 Tulsa Oilers Milk Panels

This recently discovered collectible is a 3 1/2" X 6" card cut from the side of a milk carton. The words "Carnation Introduces Your Tulsa Oilers - Meet The Oilers" are prominently displayed, along with player information. Based on Lundrigan's data and the info on the card, we've placed the season of issue at 1972-73. It seems very likely that other panels exist in this series. Any information on them can be sent to hockeymag@beckett.com.

COMPLETE SET (?)
1 Joe Lundrigan

1992-93 Tulsa Oilers

This 18-card standard-size set was sponsored by Crown Auto World. Ten thousand were sets were reportedly produced. Randomly inserted throughout the sets were 350 autographed cards of each player. The cards feature color photos of players in action and still poses. The pictures have white borders, and the player's name is printed in black on the photo at the bottom. The cards are unnumbered and checklisted below in alphabetical order.

COMPLETE SET (18) 3.00 8.00
1 Mike Berger .20 .50
2 Pat Cavanagh .20 .50
3 Shaun Clouston .20 .50
4 Brian Fiatt .20 .50
Tony Martino
5 Tony Fiore .20 .50
6 Taylor Hall .30 .75
7 Tom Karalis .20 .50
8 Greg MacEachern .20 .50
9 Terry MacLean .20 .50
10 Al Murphy .20 .50
11 Sylvain Naud .30 .75
12 Mario Nobili .20 .50
13 Jody Praznik .20 .50
14 E.J. Sauer .20 .50
15 Craig Shepherd .20 .50
16 Garry Unger .40 1.00
17 Team Photo .20 .50
18 Title Card .20 .50

1993-94 Tulsa Oilers

As with the other teams sets issued throughout the Central Hockey League this season, these are round cards approximately the size of a hockey puck. They come in a plastic container with the team logo on the front, and were sold by the booster club at home games for $5 per set.

COMPLETE SET (18) 3.00 8.00
1 Luc Beausoleil .30 .75
2 Mike Berger .20 .50
3 Shaun Clouston .20 .50
4 Craig Coxe .30 .75
5 Brian Flatt .20 .50
6 Taylor Hall .20 .50
7 Tom Karalis .20 .50
8 Doug Lawrence .30 .75
9 Jamie Loewen .20 .50
10 Mike MacWilliam .20 .50
11 Al Murphy .20 .50
12 Sylvain Naud .30 .75
13 Jody Praznik .20 .50
14 Chad Seibel .20 .50
15 Brian Shantz .20 .50
16 Sean Whyte .20 .50
17 Garry Unger CO .30 .75
18 Crown Auto World .02 .10
Sponsor

2003-04 Tulsa Oilers

These cards are unnumbered and thus are listed below in alphabetical order.

COMPLETE SET (24) 4.00 10.00
1 Header Card .01 .05
2 Jason Bermingham .20 .50
3 Rod Branch .30 .75
4 Anthony D'Arpino .20 .50
5 Jordon Flodell .20 .50
6 Dan Gravelle .20 .50
7 Regan Harper .20 .50
8 Tim Kelleher .30 .75
9 Cam Kuzyk .20 .50
10 Branislav Kvetan .20 .50
11 Todd Marcellus .20 .50
12 Rob Meanchoff .20 .50
13 Aaron Millar .20 .50
14 Chris Page .20 .50
15 Derek Reynolds .20 .50
16 Jordan Roach .20 .50
17 Shawn Scanzano .20 .50
18 Wes Scanzano .20 .50
19 Lukas Sedlacek .20 .50
20 Butch Kaebel CO .02 .10
21 Steve Enlow EQM .02 .10
22 Ad card .01 .05
23 Ad card .01 .05
24 Stuart Nichols TR .02 .10

2004-05 Tulsa Oilers

Cards are listed below in alphabetical order. Set is noteworthy for inclusion of Angela Ruggiero, the member of the American women's team who played briefly with the Oilers. The print run was reported to be 2,500 copies.

COMPLETE SET (24) 6.00 15.00
1 Cover Card .01 .05
2 Jason Birmingham .30 .75
3 Cameron Breitkreuz .30 .75
4 Mike Brusseau .30 .75
5 Jeff Cameron .30 .75
6 Jaroslav Cesky .30 .75
7 Lucas Dora .30 .75
8 Steve Enlow .30 .75
9 John Glavota .30 .75
10 Dan Gravelle .30 .75
11 Malcolm Hutt .30 .75
12 Mario Joly .30 .75
13 Butch Kaebel CO .02 .10
14 Klage Kaebel .30 .75
15 Justin Laird .30 .75
16 Todd Marcellus .30 .75
17 Justin Ossachuk .30 .75
18 Todd Paul .30 .75
19 Chris Pelletier .30 .75
20 Doug Pirnak .30 .75
21 Angela Ruggiero 1.25 3.00
22 Bill Ruggiero .40 1.00
23 Dallas Steward .30 .75
24 Oklahoma Trooper .01 .05

1999-00 Tupelo T-Rex

This set features the T-Rex of the WPHL. The cards were produced by SuperCard and were sold by the team at $2 each or a complete set for $30. The cards are very low quality, with a computer-generated bio glued to the back.

COMPLETE SET (19) 12.00 30.00
1 Brent Scott 1.25 3.00
2 Trevor Amundrud 1.25 3.00
3 Bob Brandon 1.25 3.00
4 Jay Pecora .75 2.00
5 Marc Vachon .75 2.00
6 Dave Szabo .75 2.00
7 Joe Van Volsen .75 2.00
8 Regan Harper .75 2.00
9 Jeff Mercer .75 2.00
10 Dave Wilejto .75 2.00
11 Clint Black .75 2.00
12 Pat Powers .75 2.00
13 Roby Gropp 1.25 3.00
14 Casey Hungle .75 2.00
15 Mike Mayhew .75 2.00
16 Jason Dexter .75 2.00
17 Kevin Evans .75 2.00
18 Martin Belanger .75 2.00
19 Ryan Rintoul .75 2.00

1998-99 UHL All-Stars

This set features players who earned a spot in the 1999 UHL All-Star Game. The cards were produced by ebk Sports and were supposed to be sold at the rink the day of the game. Apparently, that was not the case, but a few sets have leaked out onto the secondary market.

COMPLETE SET (22) 16.00 40.00
1 Ross Wilson .75 2.00
2 Stephane Brochu .75 2.00
3 Brian Downey .75 2.00
4 Mark Bultje .75 2.00
5 David Beauregard .75 2.00
6 Joe Dimaline .75 2.00
7 John Vary .75 2.00
8 Paul Willett .75 2.00
9 Vadim Podrezov .75 2.00
10 Wayne Muir .75 2.00
11 Brian Mueller .75 2.00
12 Alexei Deev .75 2.00
13 Lindsay Vallis .75 2.00
14 Patrice Robitaille .75 2.00
15 Jean-Francois Rivard .75 2.00
16 Jason Firth .75 2.00
17 Wayne Strachan .75 2.00
18 Brian LaFleur .75 2.00
19 Kevin Kerr .75 2.00
20 Garry Gulash .75 2.00
21 Mike Melas .75 2.00
22 Glenn Stewart .75 2.00

1999-00 UHL All-Stars East

This set, produced by ebk Sports, was sold at the rink during the 2000 UHL All-Star Game. Due to various production problems, #6T was also released as #2T, #15T released as #6T and #18T released as #1T. It is not known whether any variation is printed in shorter quantities than the others.

COMPLETE SET (22) 4.80 12.00
1T Yevgeny Shaldybin .20 .50
2T Stephan Brochu .20 .50
3T Nick Stajduhar .20 .50
4T Sam Myre .20 .50
5T Mike Maurice .20 .50
6T Chris Palmer .20 .50
7T Chris Grenville .20 .50
8T Gary Roach .20 .50
9T David Mayes .20 .50
10T John Vecchiarelli .40 1.00
11T Nic Beaudoin .20 .50
12T Peter Cermak .20 .50
13T Jay Neal .20 .50
14T Alexei Deev .20 .50
15T Chad Grills .20 .50
16T Dieter Kochan .75 2.00
17T Mark Richards .20 .50
18T Lindsay Vallis .20 .50
19T Ross Wilson .20 .50
20T Doug Searle .20 .50
21T Brent Gretzky .40 1.00
22T Header/Checklist .08 .25

1999-00 UHL All-Stars West

This set was produced by ebk Sports and was offered for sale during the 2000 UHL All-Star Game.

COMPLETE SET (22) 4.80 12.00
1T Kelly Hurd .20 .50
2T Frederic Bouchard .20 .50
3T Jim Durhart .20 .50
4T Jeff Winter .20 .50
5T Lonnie Loach .40 1.00
6T Brian Regan .30 .75
7T Ryan Lindsay .20 .50
8T Jeremy Rebek .20 .50
9T Colin Chaulk .20 .50
10T Scott Feasby .20 .50
11T Joe Dimaline .20 .50
12T Quinn Hancock .20 .50
13T Mike McCourt .20 .50
14T Keith Osborne .30 .75
15T Jeff Loder .20 .50
16T Garry Gulash .20 .50
17T Hugo Proulx .20 .50
18T Glenn Stewart .20 .50
19T Kevin Kerr .40 1.00
20T Jason Firth .30 .75
21T Mike Figliomeni .20 .50
22T Header/Checklist .08 .25

1990 UMD Hull Collection

This 12-card standard-size set (The Brett Hull Collection), was issued by University Minnesota-Duluth in conjunction with World Class Marketing and Collect-A-Sport. The cards have maroon and gold borders on the top and the bottom and are borderless on the side. Cards numbered 10 and 11 are in black and white while the rest of the set was issued with color photos. The set was issued in a special white box with a photo of Brett Hull on the front as well. The sets are numbered (out of 5,000) on the backs of the number 1 card.

COMPLETE SET (12) 6.00 15.00
COMMON CARD (1-12) .60 1.50
1 Hull Portrait 1.25 3.00

1999-00 Utah Grizzlies

This set features the Grizzlies of the IHL. The set was produced by the team and handed out as a promotional giveaway in the form of seven cards at five different home games.

COMPLETE SET (36) 8.00 20.00
1 Volkswagon Golf .01
2 Rich Parent .75 2.00
3 Richard Park .30 .75
4 John Purves .75 2.00
5 Jarrod Skalde .75 2.00
6 Bob Bourne CO .20 .50
7 Checklist .02 .10
8 Volkswagon Jetta .01
9 Gord Dineen .08 .25
10 Sean Tallaire .30 .75
11 Micah Aivazoff .75 2.00
12 Shawn Penn .30 .75
13 Larry Ness TR .08 .25
14 Utah Grizzlies .08 .25
15 Volkswagon New Beetle .01
16 Joe Frederick .30 .75
17 Stewart Malgunas .30 .75
18 Mick Vukota .30 .75
19 Patrick Neaton .30 .75
20 Dean Chynoweth .30 .75
21 Gord Dineen .08 .25
21 Micah Aivazoff .75 2.00
22 Volkswagon Passat .01
23 Rob Bonneau .30 .75
24 Ian Gordon .30 .75
25 Brad Lauer .30 .75
26 Neil Brady .30 .75
27 Grizbee MAS .08 .25
28 Mick Vukota .30 .75
29 Volkswagon GTI .01
30 Brad Miller .30 .75
31 Jeff Sharples .30 .75
32 Darcy Werenka .30 .75
33 Zarley Zalapski .30 .75
34 Greg Payette TR .08 .25
35 Utah Freezz Indoor Soccer .02 .10

2000-01 Utah Grizzlies

This set features the Grizzlies of the IHL. The set was issued as a promotional giveaway at three home games. The cards were issued in perforated strips.

COMPLETE SET (37) 10.00 25.00
1 Volkswagon GTI SPONSOR .01
2 Mike Bales .40 1.50
3 Steve Gainey .80 1.50
4 Brad Lauer .30 1.00
5 Jeff MacMillan .30 1.00
6 Bob Bourne CO .20 .50
7 Utah Grizzlies CL .10 .10
8 Passat SPONSOR .01
9 Patrick Neaton .30 1.00
10 John Erskine .80 2.00
11 John Purves .40 1.50
12 Greg Leeb .40 1.00
13 Jason Taylor CO .10 .25
14 Team Photo .30 1.00
15 New Beetle SPONSOR .01
16 Rick Tabaracci .40 1.50
17 Chris Wells .30 1.00
18 Ryan Christie .60 1.00
19 Alan Letang .30 1.00
20 Craig Ludwig CO .30 1.00
21 1997-98 Team Photo .10 .25
22 Jetta SPONSOR .01
23 Evgeny Tsybouk .40 1.00
24 Eric Houde .40 1.00
25 David Ling .40 1.50
26 Gavin Morgan .30 1.00
27 Payette/Ness/Lund STAFF .04 .10
28 1996-97 Team Photo .10 .25
29 Golf SPONSOR .01
30 Richard Jackman .40 1.00
31 Gregor Baumgartner .40 1.00
32 Jamie Wright .40 1.00
33 Mark Wotton .30 1.00
34 Grizzbee MASCOT .04 .10
35 1995-96 Team Photo .10 .25
36 1998-99 Team Photo
37 1999-00 Team Photo

2001-02 Utah Grizzlies

This set features the Grizzlies of the AHL. The cards were handed out over the course of the season in 6-card strips, one strip at different games. Each strip featured five player cards and one ad card featuring a Volkswagen car. The series features several former Grizzlies, as well as current players.

COMPLETE SET (35) 14.22 35.56
1 Paul Elliott .40 1.00
2 John Erskine .80 2.00
3 Gregor Baumgartner .40 1.00
4 Jon Sim .62 1.56
5 Tommy Salo 1.20 3.00
6 Mascot .04 .11
7 The New Beetle .01 .02
8 Greg Hawgood .40 1.00
9 John Purves .80 2.00
10 Steve Gainey .80 2.00
11 Serge Payer .40 1.00
12 Zigmund Palffy 1.20 3.00
13 Equipment Assistants .04 .11
14 The Cabrino GL .01 .02
15 Mark Wotton .40 1.00
16 Marc Kristoffersson .62 1.56
17 Eric Beaudoin .40 1.00
18 Roman Lyashenko .62 1.56
19 Vladimir Orszagh .40 1.00
20 Bob Bassen ACO .04 .11
21 The GTI .01 .02
22 Jeff MacMillan .40 1.00
23 Cameron Mann .62 1.56
24 Ryan Jardine .62 1.56
25 Jim Montgomery .62 1.56
26 Chad Alban .80 2.00
27 EQMG and TR .04 .11

28 The New Passat .01 .02
29 Dan Jancevski .62 1.56
30 Justin Cox .40 1.00
31 Kyle Rossiter .62 1.56
32 Gavin Morgan .40 1.00
33 Wade Flaherty .62 1.56
34 Don Hay CO .04 .11
35 The Jetta Wagon .01 .02

2002-03 Utah Grizzlies

COMPLETE SET (30) 15.00 40.00
1 Jonathan Sim .60 1.50
2 Steve Ott 3.00 8.00
3 Dan Jancevski .40 1.00
4 Eric Chouinard .40 1.00
5 Justin Cox .40 1.00
6 Checklist .02 .10
7 John Erskine .40 1.00
8 Corey Hirsch .60 1.50
9 Barrett Heisten .40 1.00
10 David Gosselin .40 1.00
11 Jim Montgomery .40 1.00
12 Don Hay HCO .02 .10
13 Steve Gainey .40 1.00
14 Marc-Andre Thinel .40 1.00
15 Jeff Bateman .40 1.00
16 Greg Hawgood .40 1.00
17 David Oliver .40 1.00
18 Bob Bassen ACO .02 .10
19 Jason Bacashihua 2.00 5.00
20 Marc Kristoffersson .60 1.50
21 Jeff MacMillan .40 1.00
22 Alexei Komarov .40 1.00
23 Matthieu Descoteaux .40 1.00
24 Richard Krouse EM .02 .10
25 Gavin Morgan .40 1.00
26 Mark Wotton .40 1.00
27 Mike Smith .40 1.00
28 Eric Landry .40 1.00
29 Mascot .02 .10
30 Greg Payette .40 1.00

1998-99 Val d'Or Foreurs

Card measure 8 1/2 x 11 and feature color action photos on the front and stats and biographical information on the back. Back also features a white box to obtain autographs. Card #S3 features a complete checklist with the dates the cards were made available at Val d'Or Foreurs games.

COMPLETE SET (29) 16.00 40.00
1 Christian Daigle .40 1.00
2 Benoit Dusablon 1.25 3.00
3 Guillaume Lamoureux .40 1.00
4 Danny Groulx .40 1.00
5 Alain Charbonneau .40 1.00
6 Jonathan Fauteux .40 1.00
7 Didier Tremblay .40 1.00
8 Dynamit MASCOT .40 1.00
9 Roberto Luongo 6.00 15.00
10 Nick Greenough .40 1.00
11 Lucio DeMartinis .40 1.00
12 Gaston Therien .40 1.00
13 Francois Hardy .40 1.00
14 David St. Germain .40 1.00
15 Sebastien Laprise .40 1.00
16 Luc Girard .40 1.00
17 Simon Gamache 1.50 4.00
18 Steve Morency .40 1.00
19 Seneque Hyacinthe .40 1.00
20 Dave Verville .40 1.00
21 Alexandre Page .40 1.00
22 Denis Boily .40 1.00
23 Dwight Wolfe .40 1.00
24 Jerome Petit .40 1.00
25 Eric Dubois .40 1.00
26 Jonathan Charron .40 1.00
S1 Anthony Quessy .40 1.00
S2 Mathieu Lendick .40 1.00
S3 Philippe Ouellette .40 1.00

2000-01 Val d'Or Foreurs

This set features les Foreurs of the QMJHL. The set was produced by CTM-Ste-Foy, and was sold by that card shop, as well as by the team.

COMPLETE SET (25) 6.00 15.00
1 Mathieu Roy .16 .40
2 Yan Hallee .16 .40
3 Chris Lyness .16 .40
4 Hugo Levesque .16 .40
5 Luc Girard .16 .40
6 David Cloutier .16 .40
7 Tomas Psenka .16 .40
8 Nicolas Pelletier .30 .75
9 Kory Baker .16 .40
10 Steve Pelletier .16 .40
11 Alex Turcotte .16 .40
12 Simon Gamache .80 3.00
13 Simon Lajeunesse .80 2.00
14 Alexandre Rouleau .16 .40
15 Samuel Duplain .16 .40
16 Pierre Morvan .16 .40
17 Brandon Reid .40 3.00
18 Mathieu Bastien .16 .40
19 Maxime Daigneault 1.20 2.00
20 Jerome Bergeron .16 .40
21 Frederic Bedard .16 .40
22 Eric Fortier .16 .40
23 Stephane Veilleux .16 .40
24 Seneque Hyacinthe .16 .40
NNO Team CL .04 .01

2000-01 Val d'Or Foreurs Signed

This set is exactly the same as the base Foreurs set from this season, save that every card has been hand signed by the player pictured. Each card also is serial numbered out of just 100.

COMPLETE SET (25) 30.00 75.00
1 Mathieu Roy .80 2.00
2 Yan Hallee .80 2.00
3 Chris Lyness .80 2.00
4 Hugo Levesque .80 2.00
5 Luc Girard .80 2.00
6 David Cloutier .80 2.00
7 Tomas Psenka .80 2.00
8 Nicolas Pelletier 1.60 4.00
9 Kory Baker .80 2.00
10 Steve Pelletier .80 2.00
11 Alex Turcotte .80 2.00
12 Simon Gamache 4.00 15.00
13 Simon Lajeunesse 4.00 10.00
14 Alexandre Rouleau .80 2.00
15 Samuel Duplain .80 2.00
16 Pierre Morvan .80 2.00
17 Brandon Reid 4.00 15.00
18 Mathieu Bastien .80 2.00
19 Maxime Daigneault 6.00 10.00
20 Jerome Bergeron .80 2.00
21 Frederic Bedard .80 2.00
22 Eric Fortier .80 2.00
23 Stephane Veilleux .80 2.00
24 Seneque Hyacinthe .80 2.00
NNO Team CL .04 .25

2001-02 Val d'Or Foreurs

This set features the Foreurs of the QMJHL. The set was produced by CTM Ste-Foy and was sold at Foreurs home games. There were 1,000 copies produced of this set.

COMPLETE SET (24) 4.80 12.00
1 Philippe Seguin .20 .50
2 Hugo Levesque .20 .50
3 Chaz Johnson .20 .50
4 Remy Tremblay .20 .50
5 Steve Richards .20 .50
6 Jonathan Gautier .20 .50
7 Vincent Duriau .20 .50
8 Jeff Cotton .20 .50
9 Patrice Bilodeau .20 .50
10 Frederic Bedard .20 .50
11 Nicolas Pelletier .20 .50
12 Francois Gagnon .20 .50
13 Alexandre Rouleau .20 .50
14 Pierre Morvan .20 .50
15 Mathieu Roy .20 .50
16 Samuel Gibbons .20 .50
17 Jonathan Charette .20 .50
18 Kyle Schutte .20 .50
19 Steve Pelletier .20 .50
20 Maxime Daigneault .40 1.00
21 Eric Fortier .30 .75
22 Mathieu Simard .20 .50
23 Adam Morreau .20 .50
24 David Rodman .20 .50

2002-03 Val d'Or Foreurs

COMPLETE SET (24) 5.00 12.00
1 Eric Glaude .20 .50
2 Pierre-Luc Laprise .20 .50
3 Patrice Bilodeau .20 .50
4 Vincent Duriau .20 .50
5 Mark Hurtubise .20 .50
6 Frederic Bedard .20 .50
7 Artem Kozitsyn .20 .50
8 Mathieu Curadeau .20 .50
9 Francois Gagnon .20 .50
10 Erik Lajoie .20 .50
11 Mathieu Dumas .20 .50
12 Denis Berube .30 .75
13 Olivier Latendresse .30 .75
14 Mathieu Roy .60 1.50
15 Benoit Genesse .20 .50
16 Jonathan Charette .20 .50
17 Shawn Collymore .30 .75
18 Didier Bochatay .20 .50
19 Maxime Daigneault .30 .75
20 Jeff Cotton .20 .50
21 Dominic Lachaine .20 .50
22 David Rodman .20 .50
23 Chaz Johnson .20 .50
24 Checklist .01 .05

2003-04 Val d'Or Foreurs

Created by Extreme Sportscards, this 23-card set was sold a home games and by Cartes Timbres Ste-Foy. Cards are unnumbered and are listed below by jersey number.

COMPLETE SET (23) 5.00 12.00
1 Benoit Lessard .20 .50
2 Etienne Grandmont .20 .50
3 Dominic Lachaine .20 .50
4 Patrice Bilodeau .20 .50
5 Mark Hurtubise .20 .50
6 Luc Bourdon .75 2.00
7 Vladimir Kutny .20 .50
8 Artem Kozitsyn .20 .50
9 Jonathan Charette .20 .50
10 Francois Gagnon .20 .50
11 Erik Lajoie .20 .50
12 Mathieu Dumas .20 .50
13 Francois Thuot .30 .75
14 Olivier Latendresse .20 .50
15 Benoit Piche .20 .50
16 Shawn Collymore .20 .50
17 Guillaume Chicoine .20 .50
18 Maxime Daigneault .40 1.00
19 Jeff Cotton .20 .50
20 Patrick Bordeleau .20 .50
21 Mathieu Curadeau .20 .50
22 Sebastien Bisaillon .20 .50
23 Chaz Johnson .20 .50

2001-02 Vancouver Giants

This set features the expansion Giants of the WHL. The cards were produced by the team and sold at souvenir stands for $10 per set. The cards came in a sealed wrapper with an image that emulates the title card. The cards themselves feature an action photo on the front, and black and white player data on the back. Although jersey numbers appear on the front, the cards are unnumbered and thus are listed below alphabetically.

COMPLETE SET (25) 4.80 12.00
1 Title Card .10 .25
2 Mark Ardelan .20 .50
3 Mark Ashton .20 .50
4 Chad Bassen .20 .50
5 Jeff Beatch .20 .50
6 Robin Big Snake .20 1.00
7 Josh Bonar .20 .50
8 Pat Brandreth .20 .50
9 Jeff Coulter .20 .50
10 Don Choukalos .30 .75
11 Andrew Davidson .20 .50
12 Andrew DeSousa .20 .50
13 Marian Havel .30 .75
14 Jeremy Jackson .20 .50
15 Brett Jaeger .20 .50
16 Robin Kovar .20 .50
17 Darren Lynch .30 .75
18 Nick Marach .20 .50
19 Tyson Marsh .20 .50
20 T.J. Mulock .20 .50
21 Jack Redlick .20 .50
22 Dave Selthun .20 .50
23 Chris Stubel .20 .50
24 Ryan Thomas .20 .50
25 Clay Thoring .20 .50

2003-04 Vancouver Giants

COMPLETE SET (25) 10.00 25.00
1 Title Card .01 .05
2 Jordan McLaughlin .20 .50
3 Aaron Sorochan .20 .50
4 Ryan Mayko .20 .50
5 Chad Scharff .20 .50
6 Mark Fistric .30 .75
7 Brennan Chapman .20 .50
8 Joe Logan .20 .50
9 Marcin Kolusz .20 .50
10 Adam Courchaine .20 .50
11 Triston Grant .20 .50
12 Kyle Bruce .20 .50
13 Darrell May .20 .50
14 Gilbert Brule 6.00 15.00
15 Kevin Hayman .20 .50
16 Mitch Bartley .20 .50
17 Braden Appleby .20 .50
18 Matt Kassian .20 .50
19 Tyson Marsh .30 .75
20 Darren Lynch .20 .50
21 Tim Kraus .20 .50
22 Ty Morris .20 .50
23 Lukas Pulpan .20 .50
24 Dean Evason HCO .02 .10
25 Team Photo .20 .50

2004-05 Vancouver Giants

COMPLETE SET 8.00 20.00
1 Luke Egener .20 .50
2 Mark Fistric .30 .75
3 Cody Franson .20 .50
4 Stewart Thiessen .20 .50
5 Jason Reese .20 .50
6 Matt Robinson .20 .50
7 J.D. Watt .20 .50
8 Adam Courchaine .20 .50
9 Triston Grant .20 .50
10 Keith Voytechek .20 .50
11 Shaun Vey .20 .50
12 Andrej Meszaros .40 1.00
13 Gilbert Brule 2.00 5.00
14 Mitch Bartley .20 .50
15 Matt Kassian .20 .50
16 Max Gordichuk .20 .50
17 Garet Hunt .20 .50
18 Paul Albers .20 .50
19 Kyle Lamb .20 .50
20 Tim Kraus .20 .50
21 Chad Scharff .20 .50
22 Marek Schwarz .75 2.00
23 Conlan Seder .20 .50
24 Adam Jennings .20 .50

2005-06 Vancouver Giants

COMPLETE SET (25) 20.00
1 Paul Albers .75
2 Mitchell Bartley .75
3 Mario Bliznak .75
4 Jonathan Blum .75
5 Gilbert Brule 5.00
6 Mitch Czibere .75
7 Brett Festerling .75
8 Mark Fistric 1.00
9 John Flatters .75
10 Cody Franson .75
11 Garet Hunt .75
12 Tim Kraus .75
13 Kyle Lamb .75
14 Milan Lucic 5.00
15 Spencer Machacek .75
16 Brendan Mikkelson 1.00
17 Jason Reese .75
18 Michal Repik .75
19 David Rutherford .75
20 Chad Scharff .75
21 Tyson Sexsmith .75
22 Dustin Slade .75
23 Tommy Tartaglione .75
24 J.D. Wall .76
25 Vancouver Giants .10

1995 Vancouver VooDoo RHI

This 25-card set from Slapshot Images features the Vancouver VooDoo of Roller Hockey International. The cards feature color player photos in a thin gray frame on a black background with a purple zigzag stripe down the left. The backs carry player information.

COMPLETE SET (25) 3.00 8.00
1 Title Card CL .02 .10
2 Dave Tiger Williams .40 1.00
3 James Jenson .20 .50
4 Laurie Billeck .15 .40
5 Doug McCarthy .15 .40
6 Jason Knox .15 .40
7 Brent Thurston .15 .40
8 Dave Cairns CO .02 .10
9 Jason Jennings .15 .40
10 Shayne Green .15 .40
11 Rob Dumas .15 .40
12 Ivan Matulik .15 .40
13 Rob Stewart .15 .40
14 Doug Ast .20 .50
15 Chris Morrison .15 .40
17 Ryan Harrison .15 .40
17 Kevin Hoffman .15 .40
18 Ken Kinney .20 .50
19 Merv Priest .15 .40
20 Steve Brown .15 .40
21 Ryan Harrison .15 .40
1994 All Star Card
22 VooDoo Dolls .15 .40
23 1995 Season Schedules .02 .10
24 VooDoo Merchandise Card .02 .10
25 Titan (Mascot) .02 .10

2003-04 Vernon Vipers

This set features the Vipers of the BCJHL.

COMPLETE SET (22) 4.00 10.00
1 Checklist .01 .05
2 Steve Belanger .20 .50
3 David Boudreau .20 .50
4 Cole Byers .20 .50
5 Dustin Claffey .20 .50
6 Dallas Costanzo .20 .50
7 Scott Dafoe .20 .50
8 Ryan Kindret .20 .50
9 Reed Kipp .20 .50
10 Andrew Lord .20 .50
11 Mark Nelson .20 .50
12 Luke Pierce .20 .50
13 Les Reaney .20 .50
14 Mike Santorelli .20 .50
15 Mark Sibbald .20 .50
16 Aaron Volpatti .20 .50
17 Jake Wilkens .20 .50
18 Mark Wilson .20 .50
19 Andy Zulyniak .20 .50
20 Mike Vandekamp CO .02 .10
21 Bob Dever ACO .02 .10
22 Shawn Bourgeois ACO .02 .10

2004-05 Vernon Vipers

This set features the Vipers from the BCJHL.

COMPLETE SET (25) 6.00 15.00
1 Checklist Card .01 .05
2 Mark Nelson .30 .75
3 Mark Sibbald .30 .75
4 Dean Strong .30 .75
5 Matt Watkins .30 .75
6 History Card .01 .05
7 Sssniper MASCOT .01 .05
8 Andy Zulyniak .30 .75
9 Ryan Whitfield .30 .75
10 Scott Wallace .30 .75
11 Aaron Volpatti .30 .75
12 Mike Ullrich .30 .75
13 Rob Turville .30 .75
14 Lyle Tassone .30 .75
15 Matt Swerhone .30 .75
16 Aaron Schepers .30 .75
17 Mick McCrimmon .30 .75
18 Reed Kipp .30 .75
19 Corey Gannon .30 .75
20 Jeff Fedyk .30 .75
21 Wade Davison .30 .75
22 Dallas Costanzo .30 .75
23 Kurtis Colling .30 .75
24 Troy Cherwinski .30 .75
25 Matt Bourdreau .30 .75

2005-06 Vernon Vipers

COMPLETE SET (25) 6.00 15.00
1 Vernon Vipers CL .02 .10
2 David Arduin .30 .75
3 Hunter Bishop .30 .75
4 Travis Brisebois .30 .75
5 Patrick Cey .30 .75
6 Troy Cherwinski .30 .75
7 Andrew Coburn .30 .75
8 Chris Crowell .30 .75
9 Wade Davison .30 .75
10 Korey Gannon .30 .75
11 Chay Genoway .30 .75
12 Jerry Holden .30 .75
13 Kevyn Kirbyson .30 .75
14 Mickey McCrimmon .30 .75
15 Cody McMullin .30 .75
16 Mike Nichol .30 .75
17 Jon Olthuis .30 .75
18 Shawn Overton .30 .75
19 Matt Swerhone .30 .75
20 Mike Ullrich .30 .75
21 Aaron Volpatti .30 .75
22 Chad Wren .30 .75
23 Andy Zulyniak .30 .75
24 Viper History .02 .10
25 Sniper MASCOT .02 .10

2007-08 Vernon Vipers

COMPLETE SET (25) 10.00 20.00
1 History Card .02 .10
2 Kyle Bigos .40 1.00
3 Hunter Bishop .40 1.00
4 Travis Brisebois .40 1.00
5 Bryce Christianson .40 1.00
6 Chris Crowell .40 1.00
7 Matt Cumming .40 1.00
8 John Digness .40 1.00
9 Trent Dorais .40 1.00
10 Dallas Goodrunning .40 1.00
11 Lucas Gore .40 1.00
12 Cody Ikkala .40 1.00
13 Conner Jones .40 1.00
14 Kellen Jones .40 1.00
15 Ryan Kakoske .40 1.00
16 Brock Palasty .40 1.00
17 Braden Pimm .40 1.00
18 Eliot Raibl .40 1.00
19 Patrick Raley .40 1.00
20 Patrick Rogan .40 1.00
21 Rob Short .40 1.00
22 Evan Witt .40 1.00
23 Scott Zurevinski .40 1.00
24 SS Sniper MASCOT .02 .10
25 Checklist .02 .10

1981-82 Victoria Cougars

This 16-card set was sponsored by the West Coast Savings Credit Union and Saanich Police Department Community Services. The cards measure approximately 3" by 5" and feature posed, color player photos with white borders. The player's name, position, and biographical information appear at the bottom. The cards are unnumbered and checklisted below in alphabetical order.

COMPLETE SET (16) 8.00 20.00
1 Bob Bales .40 1.00
2 Greg Barber .40 1.00
3 Ray Benik .40 1.00
4 Rich Chernomaz .60 1.50
5 Daryl Coldwell .40 1.00
6 Geoff Courtnall 3.00 8.00
7 Paul Cyr .75 2.00
8 Wade Jenson .40 1.00
9 Stu Kulak .60 1.50
10 Peter Martin .40 1.00
11 John Mokosak .40 1.00
12 Mark Morrison .40 1.00
13 Bryant Seaton .40 1.00
14 Jack Shupe .40 1.00
15 Eric Thurston .40 1.00
16 Randy Wickware .40 1.00

1982-83 Victoria Cougars

Featuring current and past players, this 24-card set features the Cougars of the WHL. The cards measure approximately 3" by 5" and feature color player portraits with red and blue borders on a white card face. Past player cards have the words "Graduation Series" stamped in the lower right corner of the picture (card numbers 7, 8, 13, 20-21). The cards are unnumbered and checklisted below in alphabetical order. The Doug Hannesson card has recently been confirmed. It apparently was pulled from the set before release and most copies destroyed. Because we have not yet confirmed one of these cards ever actually appearing in a team set, we no longer recognize it as part of the complete set.

COMPLETE SET (23) 20.00 40.00
1 Steve Bayliss .20 .50
2 Ray Benik .20 .50
3 Rich Chernomaz .40 1.00
4 Geoff Courtnall 1.25 3.00
5 Russ Courtnall 2.00 5.00
6 Paul Cyr .40 1.00
7 Curt Fraser .60 1.50
8 Grant Fuhr 10.00 25.00
9 Shawn Green .20 .50
10 Fabian Joseph .40 1.00
11 Stu Kulak .40 1.00
12 Brenn Leach .20 .50
13 Gary Lupul .20 .50
14 Jack MacKeigan .20 .50
15 Dave Mackey .40 1.00
16 Mark McLeary .20 .50
17 Dan Moberg .20 .50
18 John Mokosak .20 .50
19 Mark Morrison .20 .50
20 Brad Palmer .40 1.00
21 Barry Pederson .75 2.00
22 Eric Thurston .20 .50
23 Ron Viglasi .20 .50
24 Doug Hannesson 10.00 25.00

1983-84 Victoria Cougars

Featuring current and past players, this 24-card set was sponsored by the West Coast Savings Credit Union, CFAX 1070 Radio, and the Greater Victoria Police Departments. The cards measure approximately 3" by 5" and feature color player portraits with red and blue borders on a white card face. The player's name, position, and biographical information appear at the bottom. Past player cards have the words "Graduation Series" stamped in the lower right corner of the picture (card number 2 and 20). The cards are unnumbered and checklisted below in alphabetical order.

COMPLETE SET (24) 8.00 20.00
1 Misko Antisin .40 1.00
2 Murray Bannerman .75 2.00
3 Steve Baylis .20 .50
4 Paul Bilano .20 .50
5 Russ Courtnall 2.00 5.00
6 Greg Davies .20 .50
7 Dean Drozdiak .20 .50
8 Jim Gunn .20 .50
9 Richard Hajdu .20 .50
10 Randy Hansch .40 1.00
11 Matt Hervey .20 .50
12 Fabian Joseph .40 1.00
13 Rob Kivell .20 .50
14 Brenn Leach .20 .50
15 Jack Mackeigan .20 .50
16 Dave Mackey .20 .50
17 Tom Martin .20 .50
18 Darren Moren .30 .75
19 Adam Morrison .20 .50
20 Gord Roberts .20 .50
21 Dan Sexton .20 .50
22 Randy Siska .20 .50
23 Eric Thurston .20 .50
24 Simon Wheeldon .40 1.00

1984-85 Victoria Cougars

Featuring current and past players, this 24-card set was sponsored by the West Coast Savings Credit Union, CFAX 1070 Radio, and the Greater Victoria Police Departments. The cards measure approximately 3" by 5" and feature color player portraits with red and blue borders on a white card face. The player's name, position, and biographical information appear at the bottom. Past player cards have the words "Graduation Series" stamped in the lower right corner of the picture (card numbers 6 and 20). The cards are unnumbered and checklisted below in alphabetical order.

COMPLETE SET (24) 6.00 15.00
1 Misko Antisin .30 .75
2 Greg Batters .20 .50
3 Mel Bridgman .60 1.50
4 Chris Calverley .20 .50
5 Darin Choquette .20 .50
6 Geoff Courtnall .75 2.00
7 Russ Courtnall 1.25 3.00
8 Rick Davidson .20 .50
9 Bill Gregoire .20 .50
10 Richard Hajdu .30 .75
11 Randy Hansch .30 .75
12 Rob Kivell .20 .50
13 Brad Melin .20 .50
14 Jim Mentis .20 .50
15 Adam Morrison .20 .50
16 Mark Morrison .20 .50
17 Kodie Nelson .20 .50
18 Ken Priestlay .30 .75
19 Bruce Pritchard .20 .50
20 Torrie Robertson .40 1.00
21 Trevor Semeniuk .20 .50
22 Dan Sexton .20 .50
23 Randy Siska .20 .50
24 Chris Tarnowski .20 .50

1989-90 Victoria Cougars

Sponsored by Saleway and Romeo's, this 21-card set measures approximately 2 3/4" by 4" and was sponsored by Flynn Printing and other area businesses. The cards feature color, posed action player photos with rounded corners on a yellow card face. The lower right corner of the picture is cut off and the words "Keeper Card" are written diagonally. The cards are unnumbered and checklisted below in alphabetical order.

COMPLETE SET (21) 4.00 10.00
1 John Badduke .20 .50
2 Terry Bendera .20 .50
3 Trevor Buchanan .20 .50
4 Jaret Burgoyne .30 .75
5 Dino Caputo .20 .50
6 Chris Catellier .20 .50
7 Mark Cipriano .20 .50
8 Milan Drag .20 .50
9 Dean Dyer .20 .50
10 Shayne Green .20 .50
11 Ryan Harrison .20 .50
12 Corey Jones .30 .75
13 Terry Klapstein .20 .50
14 Jason Knox .20 .50
15 Curtis Nykyforuk .20 .50
16 Jason Peters .20 .50
17 Blair Scott .20 .50
18 Mike Seaton .20 .50
19 Rob Sumner .20 .50
20 Larry Woo .20 .50
21 Jarret Zukiwsky .20 .50

2000-01 Victoriaville Tigres

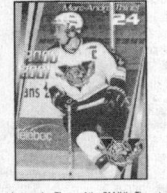

This set features les Tigres of the QMJHL. The set was produced by CTM-Ste-Foy and was sold by that card shop, as well as by the team.

COMPLETE SET (24) 4.80 12.00
1 James Sanford .20 .50
2 Carl Mallette .30 .75
3 Matthew Lombardi .20 .50
4 Teddy Kyres .20 .50
5 Martin Autotte .20 .50
6 Simon St-Pierre .20 .50
7 Pierre-Luc Daneau .20 .50
8 Antoine Vermette .40 1.00
9 Marc-Andre Thinel .40 1.00
10 Mathieu Wathier .20 .50
11 Pierre-Luc Sleigher .20 .50
12 Sandro Sbrocca .20 .50
13 Jonathan Fauteux .20 .50
14 Sergei Kaltygen .20 .50
15 Adam Wojcik .20 .50
16 Jean-Francois Nogues .30 .75
17 Richard Paul .20 .50
18 David Masse .20 .50
19 Luc Levesque .20 .50
20 Mathieu Brunelle .20 .50
21 Sebastien Morissette .20 .50
22 Sebastien Thinel .20 .50
23 Danny Groulx .20 .50
24 Mario Durocher CO .10 .25

2000-01 Victoriaville Tigres Signed

This set is exactly the same as the base Tigres set from this season, save that every card has been hand signed by the player pictured. Each card also is serial numbered out of just 100.

COMPLETE SET (24) 20.00 50.00
1 James Sanford .80 2.00
2 Carl Mallette 1.20 3.00
3 Matthew Lombardi .80 2.00
4 Teddy Kyres .80 2.00
5 Martin Autotte .80 2.00
6 Simon St-Pierre .80 2.00
7 Pierre-Luc Daneau .80 2.00
8 Antoine Vermette 2.00 5.00
9 Marc-Andre Thinel 2.00 5.00
10 Mathieu Wathier .80 2.00
11 Pierre-Luc Sleigher .80 2.00
12 Sandro Sbrocca .80 2.00
13 Jonathan Fauteux .80 2.00
14 Sergei Kaltygen .80 2.00
15 Adam Wojcik .80 2.00
16 Jean-Francois Nogues 1.20 3.00
17 Richard Paul .80 2.00
18 David Masse .80 2.00
19 Luc Levesque .80 2.00
20 Mathieu Brunelle .80 2.00
21 Sebastien Morissette .80 2.00
22 Sebastien Thinel .80 2.00
23 Danny Groulx .80 2.00
24 Mario Durocher CO .80 2.00

2003-04 Victoriaville Tigres

COMPLETE SET (29) 6.00 15.00
1 Matthew Augustine .20 .50
2 Justin Belanger .20 .50
3 Gabriel Boies .20 .50
4 Francis Charland .20 .50
5 Renaud Des Alliers .20 .50
6 Benoit Doucet .20 .50
7 Kyle Doucet .20 .50
8 Jeremy Duchesne .30 .75
9 Cole Fetzner .20 .50
10 Benoit Fournier .20 .50
11 Guillaume Fournier .20 .50
12 Scott Gibson .20 .50

13 Ryan Jenner .20 .50
14 Martin Kasik .20 .50
15 Arthur Kiyaga .20 .50
16 Tommy Lafontaine .20 .50
17 Christian Laroche .20 .50
18 Daniel Manzato .30 .75
19 Olivier Plouffe .20 .50
20 Michael Ramsay .20 .50
21 Robin Richards .20 .50
22 Jonathan Ryan .20 .50
23 Mario Scalzo .40 1.00
24 Daniel Sparre .20 .50
25 Simon St-Pierre .20 .50
26 Josh Tordjman .60 1.50
27 Guillaume Trudel .20 .50
NNO Mario Scalzo TL .20 .50
NNO Francis Charland TL .20 .50

2004-05 Victoriaville Tigres

A total of 350 team sets were produced.

COMPLETE SET (30) 6.00 15.00
1 Maxim Noreau .20 .50
2 Jeremy Duchesne .20 .50
3 Justin Belanger .20 .50
4 Jan Danecek .20 .50
5 Gabriel Boies .20 .50
6 Pierre-Olivier Dupere .20 .50
7 Danny Hollet .20 .50
8 Alexandre Imbeault .20 .50
9 Josh Tordjman .60 1.50
10 Jason Legault .20 .50
11 Tommy Lafontaine .20 .50
12 Bruce Noivo .20 .50
13 Mike Ramsay .20 .50
14 Arthur Kiyaga .20 .50
15 Matt Nickerson .40 1.00
16 Renaud Des Alliers .20 .50
17 Mario Scalzo Jr .40 1.00
18 Samuel Hounsell .20 .50
19 Benoit Doucet .20 .50
20 Francis Guerette-Charland .20 .50
21 Kyle Doucet .20 .50
22 Trevor Mock .20 .50
23 Erick Lizon .20 .50
24 Ryan Jenner .20 .50
25 Maxime Desruisseaux .20 .50
26 Brant Miller .20 .50
27 Nicolas Laplante .20 .50
28 Gabriel Houde-Brisson .20 .50
29 Toby Lafrance .20 .50
30 Alexandre Vachon .20 .50

2005-06 Victoriaville Tigres

COMPLETE SET (22) 6.00 15.00
1 Keven Guerette-Charland .30 .75
2 Jason Legault .30 .75
3 Ryan Jenner .30 .75
4 Benoit Doucet .30 .75
5 Josh Tordjman .60 1.50
6 Benoit Massicotte .30 .75
7 Toby Lafrance .30 .75
8 Gabriel Boies .30 .75
9 Jan Danecek .30 .75
10 Renaud Des Alliers .30 .75
11 Philippe Brisebois .30 .75
12 Alexandre Imbeault .30 .75
13 Maxim Noreau .30 .75
14 Brant Miller .60 1.50
15 Carl Chamberland .30 .75
16 Pierre-Olivier Duperre .30 .75
17 Matthew David .30 .75
18 Erick Lizon .30 .75
19 Trevor Mock .30 .75
20 Francis Guerette-Charland .30 .75
21 Adam Ross .30 .75
22 Stephan Lebeau .30 .75

2006-07 Victoriaville Tigres

COMPLETE SET (24) 5.00 12.00
1 Morten Madsen .40 1.00
2 Keven Veilleux .40 1.00
3 Jean-Christophe Blanchard .20 .50
4 Kevin Poulin .20 .50
5 Maxim Noreau .20 .50
6 Carl Chamberland .20 .50
7 Erick Tremblay .20 .50
8 Jan Kolarik .20 .50
9 Sansdrick Lavoie .20 .50
10 Dave Nolin .20 .50
11 Maxime Robichaud .20 .50
12 Jason Demers .20 .50
13 Jason Legault .20 .50
14 David Foucher .20 .50
15 Keven Guerette-Charland .20 .50
16 Dany Roch .20 .50
17 Adam Ross .20 .50
18 Vincent Zaore-Vanie .20 .50
19 Philippe-Michael Devos .20 .50
20 Kyle Kelly .20 .50
21 Kyle Mcneil .20 .50
22 Benoit Doucet .20 .50
23 Francis Guerette-Charland .20 .50
24 Toby Lafrance .20 .50

1993-94 Waterloo Black Hawks

This 27-card standard-size set features the Waterloo Black Hawks of the USHL. The fronts feature color action player photos, with the team name and logo in a red border above the photo, and the player's name, number, and position beneath it. The cards are unnumbered and checklisted below in alphabetical order.

COMPLETE SET (27) 3.60 9.00
1 Brent Bessey .15 .40
2 Jason Blake .30 .75
3 Scott Brand GM .02 .10
4 Eric Brown .15 .40
5 Rod Butler .15 .40
6 Chris Coakley .15 .40
7 Austin Crawford .15 .40
8 Doug Dietz ACO .02 .10
9 Jon Garver .15 .40
10 Brian Folden .15 .40
11 Bobby Hayes .15 .40
12 Jake Jacoby .15 .40
13 Terry Jarkowsky .15 .40
14 Jeff Kozakowski UER .15 .40
(Misspelled Kozakowski on front)
15 Josh Lampman .15 .40
16 Marty Laurila .15 .40
17 Steve McCall ANN .02 .10
18 Bill McNelis .15 .40
19 Rich Metro .15 .40
20 Scott Mikesch CO .02 .10
21 Barry Soskin PR .02 .10
22 Ben Stadey .15 .40
23 Ed Stanek .15 .40
24 Todd Steinmetz .15 .40
25 Scott Swanjord .20 .50
26 Miles Van Tassel .15 .40
27 Supporting Staff .02 .10
Dave Christians
Mike Christians
Bill Eggers

1995-96 Waterloo Blackhawks

Thanks to collector Dale Sprenger for providing this checklist and the information for many other unusual minor and junior sets.

COMPLETE SET (26) 25.00 50.00
1 Jayme Adduono 1.00 2.50
2 Chris Cerrella 1.00 2.50
3 Mark Eaton 1.25 3.00
4 Jason Furness 1.00 2.50
5 Joe Gray UER .08 .25
6 Zach Ham 1.00 2.50
7 Trevor Hanger 1.00 2.50
8 Kris Harris 1.00 2.50
9 Steve Holeczy 1.00 2.50
10 Lubos Krajcovic 1.00 2.50
11 Jeff Melnechuk 1.00 2.50
12 Jimmy Mroz 1.00 2.50
13 Bobby Owen 1.00 2.50
14 Anthony Perardi 1.00 2.50
15 Chad Poliquin 1.00 2.50
16 Dan Ragusett 1.00 2.50
17 Ryan Rentz 1.00 2.50
18 Ryan Sarazin 1.00 2.50
19 Doug Schmidt 1.00 2.50
20 Andrew Tortorella 1.00 2.50
21 Roger Trudeau 1.00 2.50
22 Mark Wilkinson 1.00 2.50
23 Scott Mikesch CO .08 .25
24 Barry Soskin Owner .08 .25
25 Scott Brand GM .08 .25
26 Jason Shaver PR .08 .25

2003-04 Waterloo Blackhawks

Team-issued set features the Blackhawks of the USHL. The checklist below may not be complete. The cards are unnumbered. Checklist courtesy of collector Vinnie Montalbano.

COMPLETE SET (21) 8.00 20.00
1 Joel Hanson .40 1.00
2 Joe Pavelski 4.00 10.00
3 Matt Fornataro .40 1.00
4 Kevin Regan .75 2.00
5 Garrett Regan .40 1.00
6 Zach Bearson .40 1.00
7 Dan Sturges .40 1.00
8 Tim Filangieri .40 1.00
9 Mike Radja .40 1.00
10 Michael Annett .40 1.00
11 Andrew Thomas .40 1.00
12 Aaron Johnson .75 2.00
13 John Vadnais .40 1.00
14 Jesse Vesel .40 1.00
15 Jake Schwan .40 1.00
16 Josh Duncan .40 1.00
17 Jon-Paul Testwuide .40 1.00
18 Mike Dagenais .40 1.00
19 Dustin Molle .40 1.00
20 David Meckler .40 1.00
21 Peter MacArthur .40 1.00

2004-05 Waterloo Blackhawks

This unnumbered set was issued as a game-night giveaway over the course of several nights. It's likely that the checklist is incomplete. Additional information can be forwarded to hockeymag@beckett.com.

COMPLETE SET (15?)
1 Drew Dobson
2 Tomas Petruska
3 Michael Annett
4 Nathan Lawrence
5 Zach Bearson
6 Matt Arhontas
7 Dustin Molle
8 Joe Grossman
9 Mike Testwuide
10 Jesse Vesel
11 Thomas Fortney
12 Garrett Regan
13 Drew O'Connell
14 Chris Tok ACO
15 Zac Headrick ACO

2005-06 Waterloo Blackhawks

COMPLETE SET (30) 6.00 15.00
1 Ricky Akkerman .20 .50
2 Matt Arhontas .20 .50
3 Zach Bearson .20 .50
4 Eric Bennett .20 .50
5 Andy Bohmbach .20 .50
6 Mike Borisnok .20 .50
7 Cody Chupp .20 .50
8 Kurt Davis .20 .50
9 Drew Dobson .20 .50
10 Tim Gilbert .20 .50
11 Joe Grossman .20 .50
12 Brad Hoelzer .20 .50
13 Christian Jensen .20 .50
14 Vincent LeVerde .20 .50
15 James Marcou .20 .50
16 Clark Oliver .20 .50
17 Kyle Reeds .20 .50
18 mitch Ryan .40 1.00
19 Pasko Skarica .20 .50
20 Joe Sova .20 .50
21 Jeremy Tejchma .20 .50
22 Mike Testwuide .20 .50
23 Isak Tranvik .20 .50
24 Kenny Wochele .40 1.00
25 P K O'Handley CO .20 .50
26 Chris Tok ACO .20 .50
27 Zac Headrick ACO .20 .50
28 Derrick Johnson ACO .20 .50
29 Dave Graham EQM .20 .50
30 Todd Klein TR .20 .50

1992-93 Western Michigan Broncos

These 30 standard-size cards feature color player photos on their fronts, some are action shots, others are posed. These photos are borderless on the sides. The player's name and position appear in a brown bar upon a yellow stripe across the bottom. His uniform number appears within a brown stripe across the top. The cards are unnumbered and checklisted below in alphabetical order.

COMPLETE SET (30) 4.80 12.00
1 Chris Belanger .20 .50
2 Joe Bonnett .15 .40
3 Brent Brekke .20 .50
4 Chris Brooks .15 .40
5 Craig Brown .15 .40
6 Jeremy Brown .15 .40
7 Tom Carriere .15 .40
8 Scott Chartier .20 .50
9 Ryan D'Arcy .15 .40
10 Pat Ferschweiler .15 .40
11 Brian Gallentine .15 .40
12 Jim Holman .15 .40
13 Derek Innanen .15 .40
14 Jason Jennings .20 .50
15 Mikhail Lapin .20 .50
16 Francois Leroux .20 .50
17 Jamal Mayers .60 1.50
18 Kevin McCaffrey ACO .02 .10
19 Dave Mitchell .15 .40
20 Brian Renfrew .15 .40
21 Mike Schafer ACO .02 .10
22 Derek Schooley .15 .40
23 Neil Smith .20 .50
WMU Hall of Fame
24 Colin Ward .15 .40
25 Dave Weaver .15 .40
26 Mike Whitton .15 .40
27 Bill Wilkinson CO .02 .10
28 Peter Wilkinson .15 .40
29 Byron Witkowski .15 .40
30 Lawson Arena .02 .10

1993-94 Western Michigan Broncos

These 30 standard-size cards feature color player photos on their fronts, some are action shots, others are posed. These photos are borderless on three sides. The player's name and uniform number appear vertically in the brown left margin. The cards are unnumbered and checklisted below in alphabetical order.

COMPLETE SET (30) 6.00 15.00
1 David Agnew .20 .50
2 Brent Brekke .30 .75
3 Chris Brooks .20 .50
4 Craig Brown .20 .50
5 Jeremy Brown .20 .50
6 Justin Cardwell .20 .50
7 Tom Carriere .20 .50
8 Tony Code .20 .50
9 Matt Cressman .20 .50
10 Jim Culhane ACO .02 .10
11 Ryan D'Arcy .20 .50
12 Brian Gallentine .20 .50
13 Matt Greene .20 .50
14 Rob Hodge .20 .50
WMU Hall of Fame
15 Jim Holman .20 .50
16 Derek Innanen .20 .50
17 Mark Jodoin .20 .50
18 Brendan Kenny .20 .50
19 Misha Lapin .20 .50
20 Darren Maloney .20 .50
21 Jamal Mayers .75 2.00
22 Dave Mitchell .20 .50
23 Brian Renfrew .20 .50
24 Mike Schafer ACO .02 .10
25 Derek Schooley .20 .50
26 Colin Ward .20 .50
27 Mike Whitton .20 .50
28 Bill Wilkinson CO .02 .10
29 Peter Wilkinson .20 .50
30 Shawn Zimmerman .20 .50

2001-02 Western Michigan Broncos

This set features the Broncos of the NCAA. Little is known about the set and its distribution, or even if the checklist is complete. If you have any additional information, please forward it to hockeymag@beckett.com.

COMPLETE SET (10) 4.00 10.00
1 Anthony Battaglia .40 1.00
2 Mike Bishai .40 1.00
3 Ryan Crane .40 1.00
4 Bryan Farquhar .40 1.00
5 Chad Kline .40 1.00
6 Austin Miller .40 1.00
7 Jeff Reynaert .40 1.00
8 Wayne Gagne ATG .40 1.00
9 Harry Lawson CO .40 1.00
10 Team Photo .40 1.00

2006-07 Westside Warriors

COMPLETE SET (21) 6.00 15.00
1 The General MASCOT .02 .10
2 Mark Howell CO .02 .10
3 Stephen Caple .30 .75
4 Eric Fraser .30 .75
5 Brock Meadows .30 .75
6 Joel Wozniakoski .30 .75
7 Chris Santiago .30 .75
8 Denis Semenov .30 .75
9 Craig Eisenhut .30 .75
10 Kevin Walrod .30 .75
11 Tommy Grant .30 .75
12 Micah Anderson .30 .75
13 Chris Vassos .30 .75
14 Ron Kelly .30 .75
15 Brad Plumton .30 .75
16 Trevor Bailey .30 .75
17 Brendan Ellis .30 .75
18 August Aiken .30 .75
19 Konrad Becker .30 .75
20 Bryce Kakoske .30 .75
21 Sam Huston .30 .75
22 Milrod Kos .30 .75
23 Marcel Bruinsma .30 .75
24 Mark Howell CO .02 .10

1996-97 Wheeling Nailers

This 23-card set of the Wheeling Nailers of the ECHL was produced by Split Second. The cards feature action photography on the front, along with the player's name and number and the team logo. The backs have a brief stats package, along with a larger interpretation of the player's number. As these cards are unnumbered otherwise, they are listed alphabetically below.

COMPLETE SET (23) 3.00 8.00
1 Scotty Allegrino TR .02 .10
2 John Badduke .20 .50
3 Frederic Barbeau .15 .40
4 John Blessman .15 .40
5 Francois Bouillon .15 .40
6 Greg Callahan .15 .40
7 Don Chase .15 .40
8 Jason Clark .15 .40
9 Keli Corpse .15 .40
10 Chad Dameworth .15 .40
11 Ryan Haggerty .20 .50
12 Martin LePage .15 .40
13 Ian McIntyre .15 .40
14 Greg McLean .15 .40
15 Mike Minard .20 .50
16 Perry Pappas .15 .40
17 Eric Royal .15 .40
18 Brad Symes .15 .40
19 John Tanner .20 .50
20 Rob Trumbley .15 .40
21 John Varga .30 .75
22 Tom McVie CO .15 .40
23 Spike Mascot .02 .10

1997-98 Wheeling Nailers

This 25-card set was given out at games as a sheet of perforated cards in a photo pack. The cards measure 2x3". The set was sponsored by TV-WTOV, Nickles, and Undo's. The cards are listed in the order they appear on the sheet.

COMPLETE SET (25) 3.00 8.00
1 J.F. Boutin .15 .40
2 Chris Jensen .15 .40
3 Dan Jablonic .15 .40
4 Dmitri Tarabrin .15 .40
5 Matt Garzone .15 .40
6 Jeremy Brown .15 .40
7 Joe Harney .15 .40
8 Scott Kirton .15 .40
9 Patrick Charbonneau .15 .40
10 Matt Van Horlick .15 .40
11 Mike Latendresse .20 .50
12 Karl Infanger .15 .40
13 Olie Sundstrom .20 .50
14 Stefan Brannare .15 .40
15 Fredrik Svensson .15 .40
16 Marquis Mathieu .30 .75
17 Sergei Radchenko .20 .50
18 Alex Matvichuk .15 .40
19 Kurt Brown .15 .40
20 Quinten Van Horlick .15 .40
21 Nailers Logo .02 .10
22 Swaze Armstrong TR .02 .10
23 Vinny Ferraiuolo EM .02 .10
24 Spike Mascot .02 .10
25 Peter Laviolette HCO .20 .50

1997-98 Wheeling Nailers Photo Pack

This 25-card set measures 2 1/8" X 3 1/8". It was a game-night giveaway sponsored by Nickles Bread. The set is attached as a single sheet. The set is not numbered so the cards appear in sheet order.

COMPLETE SET (25) 4.80 12.00
1 J.F. Boutin .20 .50
2 Chris Jensen .20 .50
3 Dan Jablonic .20 .50
4 Dimitri Tarabrin .30 .75
5 Matt Garzone .20 .50
6 Jeremy Brown .20 .50
7 Joe Harney .20 .50
8 Scott Kirton .20 .50
9 Patrick Charbonneau .20 .50
10 Matt Van Horlick .20 .50
11 Mike Latendresse .30 .75
12 Karl Infanger .20 .50
13 Olie Sundstrom .30 .75
14 Stefane Brannare .20 .50
15 Fredrik Svensson .20 .50
16 Marquis Mathieu .40 1.00
17 Sergei Radchenko .30 .75
18 Alex Matvichuk .20 .50
19 Kurt Brown .20 .50
20 Quinten Van Horlick .20 .50
21 Nailers History Card .02 .10
22 Swaze Armstrong TR .02 .10
23 Vinny Ferraiuolo MGR .02 .10
24 Spike Mascot .02 .10
25 Peter Laviolette HCO .20 .50

2003-04 Wheeling Nailers

COMPLETE SET (16) 20.00
81 Nick Boucher 2.00
82 Steven Crampton 1.25
83 Jean-Francois Dufour 1.25
84 Drew Fata 1.50
85 Brendon Hodge 1.25
86 Jason Jaffray 1.25
87 Mark Kosick 1.25
88 Kamil Kuriplach 1.25
89 Mario Larocque 1.25
90 Brad Mehalko 1.25
91 Jake Ortmeyer 1.25
92 Eduard Pershin 1.25
93 T.J. Reynolds 2.00
94 Alexandre Rouleau 1.25
95 Bogdan Rudenko 1.25
96 J.C. Ruid 1.25

2004-05 Wheeling Nailers Riesbeck's

This set was available with a minimum food purchase at Riesbeck's Food Market in Wheeling.

COMPLETE SET (20) 8.00 20.00
1 Team Card .20 .50
2 Alexandre Rouleau .40 1.00
3 Armands Berzins .40 1.00
4 Team Staff .20 .50
5 Cam Paddock .40 1.00
6 Cliff Loya .40 1.00
7 Curtiss Patrick .40 1.00
8 Dany Sabourin 1.25 3.00
9 Ed McGrane .40 1.00
10 Evgeny Lazarev .40 1.00
11 Brendon Hodge .40 1.00
12 James Laux .40 1.00
13 Joe Exter .40 1.00
14 Kenny Corupe .75 2.00
15 Pascal Morency .40 1.00
16 Randy Perry .40 1.00
17 Ray DiLauro .40 1.00
18 Steve Crampton .40 1.00
19 Kraft Sponsor .02 .10
20 FritoLay Sponsor .02 .10

2004-05 Wheeling Nailers SGA

These cards were given away at home games. We have confirmed the cards given away at two such games on Nov. 14 and March 15. It's likely that others exist. Please contact us at hockeymag@beckett.com if you have further information.

COMPLETE SET(?)
1 Mark Kosick
2 Ben Blais
3 Brendon Hodge
4 Pat Bingham CO
5 AAP Sponsor
6 KoSports Sponsor
7 Joe Exter
8 Randy Perry
9 Pascal Morency
10 McDonald's Sponsor
11 Newspaper Sponsor

1992-93 Wheeling Thunderbirds

This 24-card standard-size set features color, posed action player photos. The pictures are set on a gray card face with a red banner above the photo that contains the year and the manufacturer name (Those Guys Productions). The player's name, position, and team name are printed below the picture.

COMPLETE SET (24) 3.00 8.00
1 Title Card .02 .10
2 Claude Barthe .15 .40
3 Joel Blain .15 .40
4 Derek DeCosty .15 .40
5 Marc Deschamps .15 .40
6 Tom Dion .15 .40
7 Devin Edgerton .15 .40
8 Pete Heine .15 .40
9 Kim Maier .15 .40
10 Mike Millham .20 .50
11 Cory Paterson .15 .40
12 Trevor Pochipinski .15 .40
13 Tim Roberts .15 .40
14 Mark Rodgers .15 .40
15 Darren Schwartz .15 .40
16 Trevor Senn .15 .40
17 Tim Tisdale .15 .40
18 John Uniac .20 .50
19 Denny Magruder MG .02 .10
20 Chuck Greenwood .02 .10
Jim Smith (Producers)
21 Larry Kish VP/MG .02 .10
22 Doug Sauter CO .02 .10
23 T-Bird (Mascot) .02 .10
24 Doug Bacon .15 .40

1993-94 Wheeling Thunderbirds

Minor league expert Ralph Slate reports that these cards were distributed in three different manners: Cards 1-21 were the standard team set, available all season long at home games. Cards PC1-PC4 were handed out as premiums at games. Cards UD1-UD10 comprise a late-season update set which was sold separately. The three are combined here for cataloguing purposes, but may be found on the market as separate entities.

COMPLETE SET (21) 10.00 25.00
1 Header Card CL .02 .10
2 Darren Schwartz .15 .40
3 Cory Paterson .15 .40
4 Derek DeCosty .15 .40
5 Jim Bermingham .15 .40
6 Brock Woods .15 .40
7 Tim Roberts .15 .40
8 Eric Raymond .15 .40
9 Brett Abel .15 .40
10 Sebastien Fortier .15 .40
11 John Johnson .15 .40
12 Brent Pope .15 .40
13 Marquis Mathieu .30 .75
14 Terry Virtue .20 .50
15 Vadim Slivchenko .20 .50
16 Clayton Gainer .15 .40
17 Sylvain LaPointe .15 .40
18 Doug Sauter CO .02 .10
19 Larry Kish VP GM .02 .10
20 Denny Magruder GM .02 .10
21 Bill Cordery ASST TR .02 .10
PC1 Wheeling Thunderbirds 2.00 5.00
PC2 Darren Schwartz 2.00 5.00
PC3 Tim Tisdale 2.00 5.00
PC4 Cory Paterson 2.00 5.00
UD1 Update Checklist .02 .10
UD2 Tim Tisdale .40 1.00
UD3 John Van Kessel .40 1.00
UD4 Rival Fullum .40 1.00
UD5 Steve Gibson .40 1.00
UD6 Dave Goucher .02 .10
Director of Communication
UD7 Gary Zearott .02 .10
Photographer
UD8 Darren Schwartz .02 .10
T-Bird Leader
UD9 Vadim Slivchenko .40 1.00
T-Bird Leader
UD10 Brock Woods .40 1.00
T-Bird Leader

1994-95 Wheeling Thunderbirds

This 25-card set of the Wheeling Thunderbirds of the ECHL was produced by Those Guys for the team. The set was available through the club at games. The stylish fronts featured a player photo, name, number and position, along with team logo.

COMPLETE SET (25) 2.00 5.00
1 Checklist .08 .25
2 Tim Tisdale .20 .50
3 Brock Woods .20 .50
4 Vadim Slivchenko .20 .50
5 Tim Roberts .20 .50
6 Derek DeCosty .20 .50
7 Steve Gibson .20 .50
8 Xavier Majic .25 .60
9 Peter Marek .20 .50
10 Greg Louder .20 .50
11 Gairin Smith .20 .50
12 Darren McAusland .20 .50
13 Brent Pope .08 .25
14 Dominic Fafard .08 .25
15 Pat Barton .08 .25
16 Patrick Labrecque .08 .25
17 Lorne Toews .08 .25
18 Scott Matusovich .08 .25
19 Louis Bernard .08 .25
20 Doug Sutter .08 .25
21 Scott Allegrino TR .08 .25
22 Bill Cordery .08 .25
23 Mark Landini .08 .25
PC1 Xavier Majic .30 .75
PC2 Vadim Slivchenko .30 .75

1995-96 Wheeling Thunderbirds

Sponsored by Nickles Bread, this 24-card set was produced by Zee Productions. The cards measure 2 1/8" X 3 1/8" and were released as part of a perforated sheet, with a large team photo at the top of the set.

COMPLETE SET (24) 4.00 10.00
1 Rob Trumbley .15 .40
2 Geoff Finch .15 .40
3 Samuel Groleau .15 .40
4 Keli Corpse .15 .40
5 Tomas Vokoun .60 1.50
6 Steve Gibson .15 .40
7 Eric Royal .15 .40
8 Brock Woods .15 .40
9 Derek Decosty .15 .40
10 Lorne Toews .15 .40
11 Gairin Smith .15 .40
12 Tony Prpic .20 .50
13 Brent Pope .15 .40
14 Martin Sychra .15 .40
15 Martin LePage .15 .40
16 John Blessman .15 .40
17 Louis Dumont .15 .40
18 Pat Barton .15 .40
19 Ron Wilson .15 .40
20 Martin Brochu .40 1.00
21 Tim Tisdale .15 .40
22 Larry Kish HCO .02 .10
23 Scott Allegrino TR .02 .10
24 T Bird Mascot .02 .10

1995-96 Wheeling Thunderbirds Series II

Sponsored by Nickles Bread, this 20-card set was produced by Zee Productions. The cards measure 2 1/8" X 3 1/8" and came attached with large photos of the two goalies Geoff Finch and Tomas Vokoun.

COMPLETE SET (20) 3.00 8.00
1 John Badduke .20 .50
2 Pat Barton .15 .40
3 John Blessman .15 .40
4 Keli Corpse .15 .40
5 Louis Dumont .15 .40
6 Geoff Finch .30 .75
7 Steve Gibson .15 .40
8 Samuel Groleau .15 .40
9 Martin LePage .15 .40
10 Kevin Lune .15 .40
11 Brent Pope .15 .40
12 Tim Roberts .15 .40
13 Eric Royal .15 .40
14 Gairin Smith .15 .40
15 Lorne Toews .15 .40
16 Tim Tisdale .15 .40
17 Rob Trumbley .15 .40
18 Tomas Vokoun .60 1.50
19 Ron Wilson .15 .40
20 Brock Woods .15 .40

1993-94 Wichita Thunder

As with all CHL sets issued this season, these are round cards approximately the size of a hockey puck. They come in a plastic container with the team logo on the front, and were sold by the team's booster club for about $5 per set.

COMPLETE SET (18) 3.00 8.00
1 Bob Berg .20 .50
2 Mark Bourgeois .20 .50
3 Steve Chelios .20 .50
4 Robert Desjardins .20 .50
5 Paul Dukovac .20 .50
6 Yannick Gosselin .20 .50
7 Ron Handy .20 .50
8 Jamie Hearn .20 .50
9 Roger Hunt .20 .50
10 Paul Jackson .20 .50
11 James Latos .20 .50
12 Greg Neish .20 .50
13 Brent Sapergia .20 .50
14 Darren Srochenski .20 .50
15 Stephane Venne .20 .50
16 Rob Weingartner .20 .50
17 Jack Williams .20 .50
18 Doug Shedden CO .07 .20

1998-99 Wichita Thunder

This 25-card set was given out at a game late in the season and then was sold at the merchandise stand.

COMPLETE SET (25) 4.80 12.00
1 Checklist .02 .10
2 Vernon Beardy .20 .50
3 Travis Clayton .20 .50
4 Chris Dashney .20 .50
5 Mike Donaghue .20 .50
6 Jason Duda .20 .50
7 Rhett Dudley .20 .50
8 Trevor Folk .20 .50
9 Todd Howarth .20 .50
10 John Kachur .20 .50
11 Mark Karpen .20 .50
12 Lance Leslie .30 .75
13 Brad Link .20 .50
14 Mark Macera .30 .75
15 Walker McDonald .20 .50
16 John McGeough .20 .50
17 Thomas Migdal .20 .50
18 Aaron Novak .20 .50
19 Sean O'Reilly .30 .75
20 Kevin Powell .20 .50
21 Greg Smith .30 .75
22 Travis Tipler .20 .50
23 Troy Yarosh .20 .50
24 Bryan Wells HCO .02 .10
25 Goodwrench Dealer Logo .01

1999-00 Wichita Thunder

This set features the Thunder of the CHL. The cards feature full color fronts with name and position on the lower front of the card. Backs feature statistical and biographical information. The cards are unnumbered and checklisted below in alphabetical order.

COMPLETE SET (25) 4.00 10.00
1 Vern Beardy .15 .40
2 Travis Clayton .30 .75
3 Chris Dashney .15 .40
4 Mike Donaghue .15 .40
5 Jason Duda .15 .40
6 Rhett Dudley .15 .40
7 Trevor Folk .15 .40
8 Todd Howarth .15 .40
9 John Kachur .15 .40
10 Mark Karpen .15 .40
11 Lance Leslie .30 .75
12 Brad Link .15 .40
13 Mark Macera .15 .40
14 Walker McDonald .15 .40
15 Jim McGeough .15 .40
16 Thomas Migdal .15 .40
17 Aaron Novak .15 .40
18 Sean O'Reilly .15 .40
19 Kevin Powell .15 .40
20 Greg Smith .30 .75
21 Travis Tipler .15 .40
22 Troy Yarosh .15 .40
23 Bryan Wells .15 .40
24 Title Card .02 .10
25 Dealer Logo Card .02 .10

2000-01 Wichita Thunder

This set features the Thunder of the CHL. Little is known about the set beyond the confirmed checklist. Any additional information can be forwarded to hockeymag@beckett.com.

COMPLETE SET (22) 6.00 15.00
1 Jerod Bina .30 .75
2 Troy Caley .30 .75
3 Travis Clayton .30 .75
4 Trevor Converse .30 .75
5 Mike Donaghue .30 .75
6 Jason Duda .30 .75
7 Rhett Dudley .30 .75
8 Rocky Florio .30 .75
9 Trevor Folk .30 .75
10 Dwayne Gylywoychuk .30 .75
11 Derrek Harper .30 .75
12 Mike Hiebert .30 .75
13 Mark Karpen .30 .75
14 Lance Leslie .30 .75

15 Jim McGeough	.30	.75
16 Aaron Novak	.30	.75
17 Sean O'Reilly	.30	.75
18 Kevin Powell	.30	.75
19 Kris Schultz	.30	.75
20 Greg Smith	.30	.75
21 Mark Strohack	.30	.75
22 Checklist	.02	.10

2000-01 Wilkes-Barre Scranton Penguins

This set features the Penguins of the AHL. The set was produced by Choice Marketing and handed out as a game night promotion late in the season.

COMPLETE SET (28)	5.00	20.00
1 Dennis Bonvie	.20	1.50
2 Brendan Buckley	.20	.75
3 Sven Butenschon	.20	.75
4 Sebastien Caron	.40	1.50
5 Greg Crozier	.20	1.00
6 Trent Cull	.20	.75
7 Andrew Ference	.30	1.00
8 Dylan Gyori	.20	1.00
9 Chris Kelleher	.20	.75
10 Tom Kostopoulos	.20	1.00
11 Joel Laing	.20	.75
12 Jim Leger	.20	.75
13 Jason MacDonald	.20	.75
14 Alexandre Mathieu	.20	.75
15 Josef Melichar	.20	.75
16 Eric Meloche	.20	.75
17 Rich Parent	.30	1.00
18 Glenn Patrick HCO	.08	.25
19 Toby Petersen	.20	1.00
20 John Slaney	.20	.75
21 Martin Sonnenberg	.20	.75
22 Jean-Philippe Soucy	.30	1.00
23 Billy Tibbetts	.40	1.50
24 Darcy Verot	.20	.75
25 Mike Yeo ACO	.20	.10
26 Alexander Zevakhin	.20	.75
27 Tux MASCOT	.20	.10
28 Checklist	.20	.01

2001-02 Wilkes-Barre Scranton Penguins

This set features the Penguins of the AHL. The set was produced by Choice Marketing and was sold at home games.

COMPLETE SET (26)	4.80	12.00
1 Robbie Tallas	.30	.75
2 Robert Scuderi	.20	.50
3 David Koci	.20	.50
4 Brooks Orpik	.30	.75
5 Darcy Robinson	.30	.75
6 Mike Wilson	.20	.50
7 Darcy Verot	.20	.50
8 Ross Lupaschuk	.20	.50
9 Martin Sonnenberg	.20	.50
10 Jan Fadrny	.20	.50
11 Alexander Zevakhin	.20	.50
12 Shane Endicott	.40	1.00
13 Brendan Buckley	.20	.50
14 Jason MacDonald	.20	.50
15 Tomas Surovy	.20	.50
16 Tom Kostopoulos	.30	.75
17 Alexandre Mathieu	.20	.50
18 Peter Ratchuk	.20	.50
19 Sebastien Caron	.30	.75
20 Steve Parsons	.30	.75
21 Robert Dome	.30	.75
22 Eric Meloche	.30	.75
23 Glenn Patrick CO	.04	.10
24 Mike Yeo ACO	.04	.10
25 Tux MASCOT	.04	.10
NNO Checklist		.01

2002-03 Wilkes-Barre Scranton Penguins

COMPLETE SET (27)		12.00
1 Rob Scuderi		.50
2 Brooks Orpik		.75
3 Darcy Robinson		.50
4 Mike Wilson		.50
5 Michel Ouellet		.50
6 Ross Lupaschuk		.50
7 Matt Hussey		.50
8 Milan Kraft		.75
9 Alexander Zevakhin		.50
10 Kris Beech		.75
11 Shane Endicott		.75
12 Toby Petersen		.50
13 Colby Armstrong		.75
14 Michal Sivek		.75
15 Matt Murley		.50
16 Brendan Buckley		.50
17 Jason MacDonald		.50
18 Tomas Surovy		.75
19 Francois Leroux		.75
20 Konstantin Koltsov		.75
21 Tom Kostopoulos		.50
22 Rob Tallas		.75
23 Sebastien Caron		.75
24 Eric Meloche		.50
25 Glen Patrick HCO		.10
26 Mike Yeo ACO		.10
NNO Checklist		.01

2003-04 Wilkes-Barre Scranton Penguins

This set was produced by Choice Marketing and sold at home games.

COMPLETE SET (30)		10.00
1 Checklist		.01
2 Colby Armstrong		.75
3 Jean-Sebastien Aubin		.75
4 Kris Beech		.75
5 Patrick Boileau		.40
6 Martin Brochu		.75
7 Brendan Buckley		.40
8 Andy Chiodo		1.50
9 Shane Endicott		.40
10 Drew Fata		.40
11 Matt Hussey		.40
12 David Koci		.75
13 Tom Kostopoulos		.40
14 Guillaume Lefebvre		.40
15 Ross Lupaschuk		.40
16 Marquis Mathieu		.40
17 Eric Meloche		.40
18 Matt Murley		.40
19 Michel Ouellet		.40
20 Toby Petersen		.40
21 Darcy Robinson		.40
22 Alexandre Rouleau		.40
23 Rob Scuderi		.40
24 Reid Simpson		.40
25 Michal Sivek		.40
26 Tomas Surovy		.40
27 Steve Webb		.40
28 Michel Therrien CO		.10
29 Mike Yeo ACO		.10
30 Mascot		.10

2004-05 Wilkes-Barre Scranton Penguins

COMPLETE SET (30)	6.00	15.00
1 Checklist	.01	.05
2 Rob Scuderi	.20	.50
3 David Koci	.20	.50
4 Chris Kelleher	.20	.50
5 Darcy Robinson	.20	.50
6 Ryan Whitney	.30	.75
7 Michel Ouellet	.20	.50
8 Ross Lupaschuk	.20	.50
9 Colby Armstrong	.30	.75
10 Kris Beech	.20	.50
11 Ben Eaves	.30	.75
12 Shane Endicott	.20	.50
13 Cam Paddock	.20	.50
14 Erik Christensen	.30	.75
15 Guillaume Lefebvre	.20	.50
16 Ramzi Abid	.20	.50
17 Mike Sgroi	.20	.50
18 Maxime Talbot	.20	.50
19 Matt Murley	.20	.50
20 Tomas Surovy	.20	.50
21 Drew Fata	.20	.50
22 Matt Hussey	.20	.50
23 Marc-Andre Fleury	1.00	2.50
24 Alain Nasreddine	.20	.50
25 Dany Sabourin	.40	1.00
26 Andy Chiodo	.40	1.00
27 Tux MASCOT	.02	.10
28 Michel Therrien CO	.02	.10
29 Mike Yeo ACO	.02	.10
30 Wachovia Arena	.01	.05

2005-06 WBS Penguins

COMPLETE SET (29)	6.00	15.00
1 Colby Armstrong	.40	1.00
2 Dennis Bonvie	.40	1.00
3 Daniel Carcillo	.20	.50
4 Sebastien Caron	.40	1.00
5 Erik Christensen	.40	1.00
6 Kenny Corupe	.20	.50
7 Stephen Dixon	.20	.50
8 Ben Eaves	.20	.50
9 Rico Fata	.20	.50
10 Daniel Fernholm	.20	.50
11 Jon Filewich	.20	.50
12 Marc-Andre Fleury	.75	2.00
13 Matt Hussey	.20	.50
14 Chris Kelleher	.20	.50
15 David Koci	.20	.50
16 Konstantin Koltsov	.20	.50
17 Ryan Lannon	.20	.50
18 Guillaume Lefebvre	.30	.75
19 Arpad Mihaly	.20	.50
20 Alain Nasreddine	.20	.50
21 Michel Ouellet	.40	1.00
22 Dany Sabourin	.40	1.00
23 Andy Schneider	.20	.50
24 Ryan Stone	.20	.50
25 Tomas Surovy	.20	.50
26 Noah Welch	.30	.75
27 Ryan Whitney	.40	1.00
28 Joe Mullen ACO	.08	.20
29 Al Sims CO	.07	.20

2006-07 Wilkes-Barre Scranton Penguins

COMPLETE SET (25)	5.00	12.00
1 Alain Nasreddine	.30	.75
2 Alexei Mikhnov	.20	.50
3 Andrew Penner	.30	.75
4 Connor James	.20	.50
5 Daniel Carcillo	.30	.75
6 Dennis Bonvie	.40	1.00
7 Erik Christensen	.30	.75
8 Jeff Deslauriers	.30	.75
9 Jon Filewich	.30	.75
10 Kyle Brodziak	.20	.50
11 Marc-Antoine Pouliot	.30	.75
12 Matt Carkner	.20	.50
13 Maxime Talbot	.30	.75
14 Micki DuPont	.20	.50
15 Noah Welch	.20	.50
16 Rob Schremp	.40	1.00
17 Ryan Lannon	.30	.75
18 Ryan Stone	.40	1.00
19 Stephen Dixon	.20	.50
20 Tom Gilbert	.20	.50
21 Tyler Kennedy	.20	.50
22 Wade Skolney	.20	.50
23 Dan Bylsma ACO	.02	.10
24 Todd Richards CO	.02	.10
NNO Checklist	.01	.01

2006-07 Wilkes-Barre Scranton Penguins Jerseys

COMPLETE SET (22)	125.00	300.00
1 Jeff Deslauriers	8.00	20.00
2 Andrew Penner	8.00	20.00
3 Micki DuPont	6.00	15.00
4 Kyle Brodziak	6.00	15.00
5 Jon Filewich	6.00	15.00
6 Ryan Lannon	6.00	15.00
7 Connor James	6.00	15.00
8 Noah Welch	6.00	15.00
9 Tom Gilbert	6.00	15.00
10 Stephen Dixon	6.00	15.00
11 Tyler Kennedy	6.00	15.00
12 Daniel Carcillo	8.00	20.00
13 Dennis Bonvie	10.00	25.00
14 Tim Sesito	6.00	15.00
15 Erik Christensen	10.00	25.00
16 Maxime Talbot	10.00	25.00
17 Matt Carkner	6.00	15.00
18 Ryan Stone	10.00	25.00
19 Marc Antoine Pouliot	10.00	25.00
20 Wade Skolney	6.00	15.00
21 Alain Nasreddine	6.00	15.00
22 Rob Schremp	10.00	25.00

2007-08 Wilkes-Barre Scranton Penguins

COMPLETE SET (29)	10.00	20.00
1 Mark Ardelan	.30	.75
2 Dennis Bonvie	.60	1.50
3 Aaron Boogaard	.40	1.00
4 Tim Brent	.30	.75
5 Ty Conklin	.40	1.00
6 John Curry	.30	.75
7 Jon D'Aversa	.30	.75
8 Deryk Engelland	.30	.75
9 Jon Filewich	.30	.75
10 Alex Goligoski	.60	1.50
11 Ned Havern	.40	1.00
12 Connor James	.30	.75
13 Joe Jensen	.30	.75
14 Tyler Kennedy	.30	.75
15 Ryan Lannon	.30	.75
16 Kris Letang	.30	.75
17 Mark Letestu	.30	.75
18 Ben Lovejoy	.30	.75
19 Kurtis McLean	.30	.75
20 Chris Minard	.30	.75
21 Alain Nasreddine	.30	.75
22 Nathan Smith	.30	.75
23 Ryan Stone	.30	.75
24 Jeff Taffe	.30	.75
25 Tim Wallace	.30	.75
26 Dan Bylsma ACO	.02	.10
27 Todd Richards CO	.02	.10
28 Tux MASCOT	.02	.10
29 Team Photo	.02	.10

2007-08 Wilkes Barre Scranton Penguins Jersey Edition

1 Ryan Lannon	3.00	8.00
2 Deryk Engelland	3.00	8.00
3 Ben Lovejoy	3.00	8.00
4 Nathan Smith	3.00	8.00
5 Tim Brent	3.00	8.00
6 Connor James	3.00	8.00
7 Tyler Kennedy	4.00	10.00
8 Mark Ardelan	3.00	8.00
9 Alex Goligoski	5.00	12.00
10 Chris Minard	3.00	8.00
11 Joe Jensen	3.00	8.00
12 Kurtis McLean	3.00	8.00
13 Jon Filewich	3.00	8.00
14 Jeff Taffe	3.00	8.00
15 Ryan Stone	3.00	8.00
16 Tim Wallace	3.00	8.00
17 Dennis Bonvie	6.00	15.00
18 Alain Nasreddine	3.00	8.00
19 Ty Conklin	5.00	12.00
20 Karl Goehring	5.00	12.00
21 Kris Letang	5.00	12.00
27 Dennis Bonvie LE	8.00	20.00

2004-05 Williams Lake Timberwolves

Set from the BCJHL is noteworthy for the inclusion of the first card of Fabio Luongo, younger brother of NHL All-Star Roberto Luongo.

COMPLETE SET (28)	8.00	20.00
1 Andrew Braithwaite	.40	1.00
2 Cody Brookwell	.30	.75
3 Matt Crowell	.30	.75
4 Bryce Dale	.30	.75
5 Mark Ehl	.30	.75
6 Kevin Galan	.30	.75
7 Zach Gieszler	.30	.75
8 Alex Greenlay	.30	.75
9 Dustin Honing	.30	.75
10 Dave Krisky	.30	.75
11 Mike Leidl	.30	.75
12 Fabio Luongo	1.25	3.00
13 Trent Manchur	.30	.75
14 Tyler Mazzei	.30	.75
15 Josh Murray	.30	.75
16 Brad Reaney	.30	.75
17 Les Reaney	.40	1.00
18 Trevor Turner	.30	.75
19 Steve Van Oosten	.30	.75
20 Duane Whitehead	.30	.75
21 Shaun Witschen	.30	.75
22 Josh Murray	.30	.75
23 Dave Krisky	.30	.75
24 Rick Pitta CO	.02	.10
25 Peter Martin ACO	.02	.10
26 Zamboni	.02	.10
27 Action photo	.02	.10
28 T.H. Wolf MASCOT	.02	.10

1989-90 Windsor Spitfires

This 22-card standard-size set features members of the 1989-90 Windsor Spitfires of the Ontario Hockey league (OHL). The fronts feature posed shots of the players in front of their lockers. The cards are unnumbered and checklisted below in alphabetical order.

COMPLETE SET (22)	4.00	10.00
1 Sean Burns	.20	.50
2 Glen Craig	.20	.50
3 Brian Forestell	.20	.50
4 Chris Fraser	.20	.50
5 Trent Gleason	.20	.50
6 Jon Hartley	.20	.50
7 Ron Jones	.20	.50
8 Bob Leeming	.20	.50
9 Kevin MacKay	.20	.50
10 Kevin McDougall	.20	.50
11 Ryan Merritt	.20	.50
12 David Myles	.20	.50
13 Sean O'Hagan	.30	.75
14 Mike Polano	.20	.50
15 Jason Snow	.20	.50
16 Brad Smith CO	.30	.75
17 Jason Stos	.20	.50
18 Jon Stos	.20	.50
19 Jamie Vargo	.20	.50
20 Trevor Walsh	.20	.50
21 K.J. White	.20	.50
22 Jason Zohl	.20	.50

1992-93 Windsor Spitfires

Sponsored by the Devonshire Mall, these 31 cards measure approximately 2 5/8" by 3 5/8" and feature on their fronts posed-on-ice color shots of the 1992-93 Windsor Spitfires bordered in red, white, and blue. The player's name and the Spitfires logo appear in the white area above the photo.

COMPLETE SET (31)	4.80	12.00
1 Team Card/Checklist	.08	.25
2 Mike Martin	.15	.40
3 Luke Clowes	.15	.40
4 Jason Haelzle	.15	.40
5 Adam Graves	1.25	3.00
6 Craig Lutes	.15	.40
7 David Pluck	.15	.40
8 Colin Wilson	.15	.40
9 Bill Bowler	.30	.75
10 Ryan O'Neill	.15	.40
11 Adam Young	.15	.40
12 Gerrard Masse	.15	.40
13 Daryl Lavoie	.15	.40
14 Peter Allison	.15	.40
15 Ernie Godden RET	.15	.40
16 Brady Blain	.15	.40
17 Todd Warriner	.30	.75
18 Rick Marshall	.15	.40
19 Craig Johnson	.15	.40
20 Kelly Vipond	.15	.40
21 Devy Bear MASCOT	.02	.10
22 Stephen Webb	.20	.50
23 Scott Miller RET	.15	.40
24 Dennis Purdie	.20	.50
25 Steve Gibson	.15	.40
26 Mike Hartwick	.15	.40
27 Shawn Heins	.30	.75
28 David Benn	.15	.40
29 Matt Mullin	.20	.50
30 David Mitchell	.15	.40
31 The Dynamic Duo Todd Warriner Cory Stillman	.20	.50

1993-94 Windsor Spitfires

Co-sponsored by Pizza Hut and radio station CKLW AM 800, and printed by Slapshot Images Ltd., this 27-card standard-size set features the 1993-94 Windsor Spitfires. On a geometrical team color-coded background, the fronts feature color action player photos with thin grey borders. The player's name, position and team name, as well as the producer's logo, also appear on the front.

COMPLETE SET (27)	4.80	12.00
1 Ed Jovanovski	.75	2.00
2 Shawn Silver	.20	.50
3 Travis Scott	.20	.50
4 Mike Martin	.20	.50
5 Daryl Lavoie	.15	.40
6 Craig Lutes	.15	.40
7 David Pluck	.15	.40
8 Bill Bowler	.20	.50
9 David Green	.15	.40
10 Adam Young	.15	.40
11 Mike Loach	.15	.40
12 Brady Blain	.15	.40
13 Shayne McCosh	.15	.40
14 Rob Shearer	.20	.50
15 Joel Poirier	.15	.40
16 Cory Evans	.15	.40
17 Vladimir Kretchine	.15	.40
18 Dave Roche	.20	.50
19 Ryan Stewart	.15	.40
20 Dave Geris	.15	.40
21 Dan West	.15	.40
22 Luke Clowes	.15	.40
23 John Cooper	.15	.40
24 Akil Adams	.15	.40
25 Sponsor Card Pizza Hut	.02	.10
26 Sponsor Card Steve Dell Radio station AM 800	.02	.10
NNO Slapshot Ad Card	.02	.10

1994-95 Windsor Spitfires

Sponsored by Pizza Hut, Mr. Lube, CKLW AM 800, and printed by Slapshot Images Ltd., this 29-card set features the 1994-95 Windsor Spitfires. On a red and blue background, the fronts feature color player action photos with thin black borders. The player's name, position and team name, as well as the producer's logo, also appear on the front.

COMPLETE SET (29)	5.60	14.00
1 Checklist		.01
2 Jamie Storr	.30	.75
3 Travis Scott	.20	.50
4 Paul Beazley	.15	.40
5 Mike Martin	.15	.40
6 Chris Van Dyk	.15	.40
7 Denis Smith	.20	.50
8 Glenn Crawford	.15	.40
9 David Pluck	.15	.40
10 Bill Bowler	.30	.75
11 David Green	.15	.40
12 Adam Young	.15	.40
13 Wes Ward	.15	.40
14 Ed Jovanovski	1.25	3.00
15 Kevin Paden	.15	.40
16 Rob Shearer	.20	.50
17 Joel Poirier	.15	.40
18 Cory Evans	.15	.40
19 Vladimir Kretchine	.15	.40
20 David Roche	.20	.50
21 Rick Emmett	.15	.40
22 David Geris	.15	.40
23 Caleb Ward	.15	.40
24 Luke Clowes	.15	.40
25 John Cooper	.15	.40
26 Tim Findlay	.20	.50
27 Pizza Hut		.01
28 Radio station AM 800		.01
NNO Ad Card		.01

1998-99 Windsor Spitfires

This set features the Spitfires of the OHL. It is believed that they were issued as part of a fire safety program, and may only have been available to school children. Additional information can be forwarded to us at hockeymag@beckett.com.

COMPLETE SET (9)	3.00	8.00
1 Fire Chief	.04	.10
2 Coaches	.04	.10
3 Duke MASCOT	.04	.10
4 Michael Hanson	.40	1.00
5 Jeff Kapitanchuk	.40	1.00
6 Michael Leighton	1.25	3.00
7 Jason Polera	.40	1.00
8 Blair Stayzer	.75	2.00
9 Curtis Watson	.40	1.00

2002-03 Windsor Spitfires

This oversized set was sold at Spitfires home games. The cards are unnumbered, but are listed in the order they were issued in (roughly by jersey number, with non-team members interspersed throughout.)

COMPLETE SET (30)	4.80	20.00
1 Title Card/Checklist		.01
2 Ryan Aschaber	.30	1.00
3 Frank Rediker	.30	1.00
4 David Lomas	.16	.40
5 Iain McPhee	.16	.40
6 Mitchell Maunu	.30	1.50
7 Tim Gleason	.40	2.00
8 Mike James	.16	.40
9 David Bowman	.16	.40
10 Chief of Police		.01
11 Jason Dixon	.16	.40
12 Rob Hennigar	.20	.75
13 Craig Kennedy	.20	.75
14 Elmer Mascot	.04	.10
15 Ahren Nittel	.20	.50
17 Phil Gibson	.16	.40
18 Ryan Donnally	.16	.75
19 Paul Giallonardo	.16	.40
20 Josh Gratton	.16	.40
21 Alexander Shevchenko	.16	.40
22 Darryl Lloyd	.16	.40
23 Jeff Leavitt	.16	.40
24 Duke Mascot	.04	.10
25 Ryan Dickie	.16	.40
26 Matt Anthony	.16	.40
27 John-Scott Dickson	.16	.40
28 Denis Khudyakov	.20	1.00
29 Mike Self	.16	.40
30 Kyle Wellwood	.60	4.00
116 Cam Janssen	.30	2.00

2007-08 Windsor Spitfires

This set includes two 2008 first rounders (Josh Bailey and Greg Nemisz) and likely top-10 pick in 2009, Taylor Hall.

1 Team Checklist	.02	.10
2 Joshua Bailey	1.25	3.00
3 Ryan Baldwin	.40	1.00
4 Marek Biro	.40	1.00
5 Jesse Blacker	.40	1.00
6 Matthew Bragg	.40	1.00
7 Mark Cundari	.40	1.00
8 Ryan Ellis	.40	1.00
9 Andrew Engelage	.60	1.50
10 Richard Greenop	.40	1.00
11 Taylor Hall	1.25	3.00
12 Adam Henrique	.40	1.00
13 Tom Kane	.40	1.00
14 Greg Nemisz	.60	1.50
15 Michal Neuvirth	.75	2.00
16 Jordan Nolan	.60	1.50
17 Blake Parlett	.40	1.00
18 Elgin Reid	.40	1.00
19 Mickey Renaud	.75	2.00
20 Bradley Snetsinger	.40	1.00
21 Eric Wellwood	.40	1.00
22 Andrew Yogan	.40	1.00
23 Harry Young	.40	1.00
24 Bob Boughner PRES	.10	.25
25 Warren Rychel VP/GM	.10	.25
26 Bob Jones AC	.02	.10
27 D.J. Smith AC	.02	.10
28 Bomber Spitfire MASCOT	.02	.10
29 Glenn Stannard CHIEF OF POLICE	.02	.10
30 Elmer Windsor POLICE MASCOT	.02	.10

2003-04 Wisconsin Badgers

Two cards from this set were handed out at Badger home games over the course of the 2003-04 season. The cards are unnumbered and thus are listed below in alphabetical order.

COMPLETE SET (30)	20.00	40.00
1 Dan Boeser	.30	.75
2 Rene Bourque	1.50	4.00
3 Andy Brandt	.75	2.00
4 Bernd Bruckler	.60	1.50
5 Adam Burish	.75	2.00
6 A.J. Degenhardt	.30	.75
7 Jake Dowell	.30	.75
8 Robbie Earl	1.25	3.00
9 John Eichelberger	.30	.75
10 Brian Elliott	.60	1.50
11 John Funk	.30	.75
12 Brent Gibson	.30	.75
13 Tom Gilbert	1.25	3.00
14 Mark Heatley	.75	2.00
15 Andrew Joudrey	.30	.75
16 Chris Julka	.30	.75
17 Luke Kohtala	.60	1.50
18 Jon Krall	.30	.75
19 Nick Licari	.30	.75
20 Jeff Likens	.30	.75
21 Ryan MacMurchy	.30	.75
22 Joey McElroy	.30	.75
23 Matt Olinger	.30	.75
24 Ken Rowe	.30	.75
25 Tom Sawatske	.30	.75
26 Ryan Suter	1.50	4.00
27 Pete Talafous	.30	.75
28 Andy Wozniewski	.60	1.50
29 Mike Eaves HCO	.20	.50
30 Mascot	.02	.10

2004-05 Wisconsin Badgers

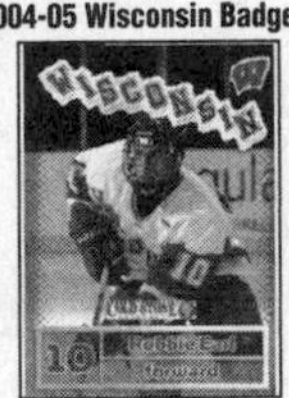

Set was issued as a promotional giveaway at a home game. The cards are not numbered.

COMPLETE SET (28)	15.00	30.00
1 Brian Elliott	.40	1.00
2 Matt Olinger	.40	1.00
3 Matt Auffrey	.40	1.00
4 Robbie Earl	1.25	3.00
5 Pete Talafous	.40	1.00
6 Matt Ford	.75	2.00
7 Davis Drewiske	.40	1.00
8 Bernd Bruckler	.75	2.00
9 Ken Rowe	.40	1.00
10 Jeff Likens	.40	1.00
11 John Funk	.40	1.00
12 Andy Brandt	.40	1.00
13 Jake Dowell	.40	1.00
14 Kyle Klubertanz	.40	1.00
15 Joe Pavelski	.40	1.00
16 Mike Eaves CO	.20	.50
17 Joe Piskula	.40	1.00
18 Ryan MacMurchy	.40	1.00
19 Ross Carlson	.40	1.00
20 A.J. Degenhardt	.40	1.00
21 Josh Engel	.40	1.00
22 Tom Gilbert	1.25	3.00
23 Andrew Joudrey	.40	1.00
24 Nick Licari	.40	1.00
25 Jeff Slinde	.40	1.00
26 Luke Kohtala	.75	2.00
27 Mark Heatley	.75	2.00
28 Adam Burish	.75	2.00

2004-05 Wisconsin Badgers Women

Issued as a promotional giveaway.

COMPLETE SET (24)	10.00	25.00
1 Sara Bauer	.40	1.00
2 Nikki Burish	.40	1.00
3 Sharon Cole	.40	1.00
4 Vicki Davis	.40	1.00
5 Christine Dufour	.40	1.00
6 Molly Engstrom	.40	1.00
7 Jackie Friesen	.40	1.00
8 Meghan Horras	.40	1.00
9 Grace Hutchins	.40	1.00
10 Mark Johnson CO	.40	1.00
11 Cyndy Kenyon	.40	1.00
12 Heidi Kletzien	.40	1.00
13 Carla MacLeod	.75	2.00
14 Lindsay Macy	.40	1.00
15 Meaghan Mikkelson	.40	1.00
16 Phoebe Monteleone	.40	1.00
17 Emily Morris	.40	1.00
18 Mikka Nordby	.40	1.00
19 Bobbi-Jo Slusar	.40	1.00
20 Nicole Uliasz	.40	1.00
21 Amy Vermeulen	.40	1.00
22 Jesse Vetter	.40	1.00
23 Kristen Witting	.40	1.00
24 Jinelle Zaugg	.40	1.00

2005-06 Wisconsin Badgers

COMPLETE SET (27)	15.00	30.00
1 Andy Brandt	.40	1.00
2 Adam Burish	.40	1.00
3 Ross Carlson	.40	1.00
4 Shane Connelly	.75	2.00
5 A.J. Degenhardt	.40	1.00
6 Jake Dowell	.40	1.00
7 Davis Drewiske	.40	1.00
8 Robbie Earl	.75	2.00
9 Brian Elliott	.75	2.00
10 Josh Engel	.40	1.00
11 Matthew Ford	.40	1.00
12 Tom Gilbert	.40	1.00
13 Tom Gorowsky	.40	1.00
14 Ryan Jeffery	.40	1.00
15 Andrew Joudrey	.40	1.00
16 Kyle Klubertanz	.40	1.00
17 Nick Licari	.40	1.00
18 Jeff Likens	.40	1.00
19 Ryan MacMurchy	.40	1.00
20 Matt Olinger	.40	1.00
21 Joe Pavelski	.40	1.00
22 Joe Piskula	.40	1.00
23 Jack Skille	2.00	5.00
24 Jeff Slinde	.40	1.00
25 Ben Street	.40	1.00
26 Mike Eaves HC	.20	.50
27 Bucky Badger MASCOT	.02	.10

2007-08 Wisconsin Badgers

These cards were given away at three separate home games. The cards were issued in perforated strips. The first had 10 cards, the others nine. The cards are standard size and have color fronts and black and white backs. The fronts also feature the logo of the set sponsor, Quaker Steak and Lube Restaurant. The set features three 2007 NHL first rounders, including the third overall Pick, Kyle Turris. The cards are not numbered and are listed below alphabetically.

COMPLETE SET (27)	25.00	40.00

2007-08 Wisconsin Badgers

1 Tom Bardis	.60	1.50
2 Zach Bearson	.60	1.50
3 Aaron Bendickson	.60	1.50
4 Andy Bohmbach	.60	1.50
5 Shane Connelly	.60	1.50
6 Michael Davies	.60	1.50
7 Sean Dolan	.60	1.50
8 Davis Drewiske	.60	1.50
9 Josh Engel	.60	1.50
10 Matthew Ford	.60	1.50
11 Blake Geoffrion	1.00	2.50
12 Cody Goloubef	.60	1.50
13 Tom Gorowsky	.60	1.50
14 Ben Grotting	.60	1.50
15 Scott Gudmandson	.60	1.50
16 Jeff Henderson	.60	1.50
17 Ryan Jeffery	.60	1.50
18 Craig Johnson	.60	1.50
19 Patrick Johnson	.60	1.50
20 Kyle Klubertanz	.60	1.50
21 Jamie McBain	.75	2.00
22 Ryan McDonagh	1.00	2.50
23 John Mitchell	.60	1.50
24 Brendan Smith	.60	1.50
25 Podge Turnbull	.60	1.50
26 Kyle Turris	4.00	10.00
27 Mike Eaves HC	.60	1.50

2000-01 Worcester Icecats

This set features the IceCats of the AHL. The set was produced by Choice Marketing and was handed out over the course of two games as a promotional giveaway.

COMPLETE SET (30)	8.00	20.00
1 Ed Campbell	.20	.50
2 Daniel Corso	.40	1.00
3 Justin Papineau	.40	1.00
4 Jaroslav Obsut	.20	.50
5 Ladislav Nagy	.80	2.00
6 Marc Brown	.20	.50
7 Pascal Rheaume	.20	.50
8 Mike Van Ryn	.40	1.00
9 Cody Rudkowsky	.40	1.50
10 Andrei Troschinsky	.20	.50
11 Mark Rycroft	.40	1.00
12 Matt Walker	.20	.50
13 Jamie Thompson	.20	.50
14 Darren Rumble	.30	.75
15 Scratch MASCOT	.04	.10
16 Team CL	.04	.01
17 Dwayne Roloson	.40	2.00
18 Jame Pollock	.20	.50
19 Eric Boguniecki	.40	1.50
20 Chris Murray	.40	1.00
21 Tyler Rennette	.20	.50
22 Marty Reasoner	.40	1.00
23 Dale Clarke	.30	.75
24 Tyler Willis	.30	.75
25 Jan Horacek	.30	.75
26 Peter Smrek	.30	.75
27 Mike Peluso	.30	.75
28 Doug Friedman	.20	.50
29 Shawn Mamane	.20	.50
30 Don Granato CO	.10	.25

2001-02 Worcester Icecats

This set features the Icecats of the AHL and actually features two separately released series of cards. The sets -- one issued early in the season, another late -- weres produced by Choice Marketing and was sold by the team at its souvenir shop. Each series was limited to 2,000 copies.

COMPLETE SET (15) 10.00 25.00
1 Darren Rumble .30 .75
2 Marc Brown .30 .75
3 Ed Campbell .30 .75
4 Jeff Panzer .30 .75
5 Cody Rudkowsky .40 1.00
6 Igor Valeev .30 .75
7 Dale Clarke .40 .75
8 Mike Van Ryn .40 1.00
9 Barret Jackman .40 2.00
10 Jame Pollock .30 .75
11 Daniel Tkaczuk .30 .75
12 Greg Davis .30 .75
13 Jamie Thompson .30 .75
14 Tyson Nash .60 1.50
15 Scratch MASCOT .10 .10
16 Team Photo/CL .10 .25
17 Reinhard Divis .40 1.50
18 Andrei Troschinsky .30 .75
19 Steve Halko .30 .75
20 Matt Walker .30 .75
21 Eric Boguniecki .40 1.00
22 Justin Papineau .40 1.00
23 Christian Laflamme .30 .75
24 Brad Voth .30 .75
25 Mark Rycroft .40 .75
26 Steve McLaren .30 .75
27 Eric Nickulas .30 .75
28 Justin Papineau .30 .75
Jeff Panzer
Eric Boguniecki AS
29 Brent Johnson .80 2.00
30 Don Granato CO .10 .25

2002-03 Worcester IceCats

COMPLET SET (28) 6.00 15.00
1 Checklist .01 .05
2 Terry Virtue .20 .50
3 Steve Bancroft .20 .50
4 Aris Brimanis .20 .50
5 John Pohl .75 2.00
6 Jame Pollock .20 .50
7 Eric Nickulas .20 .50
8 Jason Dawe .20 .50
9 Blake Evans .20 .50
10 Greg Davis .20 .50
11 Marc Brown .10 .50
12 Steve Dubinsky .20 .50
13 Steve McLaren .20 .50
14 Brett Scheffelmaier .20 .50
15 Mark Rycroft .20 .50
16 Christian Laflamme .20 .50
17 Justin Papineau .20 .50
18 Igor Valeev .20 .50
19 Matt Walker .20 .50
20 Jeff Panzer .20 .50
21 Sergei Varlamov .20 .50
22 Christian Backman .20 .50
23 Curtis Sanford .60 1.50
24 Phil Osaer .20 .50
25 Reinhard Divis .40 1.00
26 Eric Boguniecki MVP .20 .50
27 Don Granato HCO .02 .10
28 Scratch Mascot .02 .10

2003-04 Worcester Ice Cats

This set was produced by Choice Marketing and sold at home games.

COMPLETE SET (28) 4.00 10.00
1 Checklist .01 .05
2 Curtis Sanford .40 1.00
3 Joe Vandermeer .15 .40
4 Terry Virtue .15 .40
5 Jon Coleman .15 .40
6 Trevor Byrne .15 .40
7 Aris Brimanis .15 .40
8 Johnny Pohl .40 1.00
9 Tom Koivisto .15 .40
10 Jame Pollock .15 .40
11 Greg Black .15 .40
12 Mike Stuart .15 .40
13 Blake Evans .15 .40
14 Mike Glumac .15 .40
15 Chris Corrinet .15 .40
16 Marc Brown .15 .40
17 Jay McClement .15 .40
18 Steve McLaren .30 .75
19 Aaron MacKenzie .15 .40
20 Colin Hemingway .15 .40
21 Ernie Hartlieb .15 .40
22 Steve Martins .15 .40
23 Brett Scheffelmaier .15 .40
24 Jeff Panzer .15 .40
25 Sergei Varlamov .15 .40
26 Reinhard Divis .30 .75
27 Don Granato CO .02 .10
28 Steve Pleau ACO .02 .10

2003-04 Worcester Ice Cats 10th Anniversary

This special set was produced by Choice Marketing to commemorate the team's anniversary and was sold at home games.

COMPLETE SET (20) 4.00 10.00
1 Checklist .01 .05
2 Dwayne Roloson .40 1.00
3 Brent Johnson .40 1.00
4 Barret Jackman .30 .75
5 Bryce Salvador .15 .40
6 Terry Virtue .30 .75
7 Matt Walker .15 .40
8 Ed Campbell .15 .40
9 Rory Fitzpatrick .15 .40
10 Ricard Persson .15 .40
11 Eric Boguniecki .15 .40
12 Justin Papineau .15 .40
13 Marty Reasoner .15 .40
14 Ladislav Nagy .30 .75
15 Jeff Panzer .15 .40
16 Stephane Roy .15 .40
17 Jochen Hecht .15 .40
18 Johnny Pohl .30 .75
19 Michal Handzus .15 .40
20 Reed Low .15 .40

2004-05 Worcester IceCats

COMPLETE SET (26) 5.00 12.00
1 Curtis Sanford .40 1.00
2 Mike Mottau .20 .50
3 Trevor Byrne .20 .50
4 Aris Brimanis .20 .50
5 Brendan Buckley .20 .50
6 Johnny Pohl .40 1.00
7 Jon DiSalvatore .20 .50
8 Mike Stuart .20 .50
9 Blake Evans .20 .50
10 Mike Glumac .20 .50
11 Erkki Rajamaki .20 .50
12 Jay McClement .20 .50
13 D.J. King .20 .50
14 Aaron MacKenzie .20 .50
15 Alexei Shkotov .20 .50
16 Peter Sejna .20 .50
17 Dennis Wideman .20 .50
18 Brendan Brooks .20 .50
19 Jason Bacashihua .60 1.50
20 Jeff Hoggan .40 1.00
21 Ryan Ramsay .20 .50
22 Robin Gomez .20 .50
23 Don Granato CO .02 .10
24 Steve Pleau ACO .02 .10
25 Mascots .02 .10
NNO Checklist .01 .05

2007-08 Worcester Sharks

COMPLETE SET (27) 12.00 20.00
1 Riley Armstrong .30 .75
2 Marc Busenburg .30 .75
3 Tom Cavanagh .30 .75
4 Taylor Dakers• .60 1.50
5 Brennan Evans .30 .75
6 T.J. Fox .30 .75
7 Thomas Greiss .60 1.50
8 Mike Iggulden .30 .75
9 Derek Joslin .30 .75
10 Lukas Kaspar .30 .75
11 Graham Mink .60 1.50
12 Mike Morris .30 .75
13 Dennis Packard .30 .75
14 Dimitri Patzold .60 1.50
15 Tomas Plihal .30 .75
16 Nate Raduns• .30 .75
17 Ashton Rome .30 .75
18 Devin Setoguchi .60 1.50
19 Dan Spang .30 .75
20 Brad Staubitz .30 .75
21 Patrick Traverse .30 .75
22 Jonathan Tremblay .30 .75
23 Craig Valette .30 .75
24 Tom Walsh .30 .75
25 Roy Sommer HC .02 .10
26 David Cunniff AC .02 .10
27 Finz MASCOT .02 .10

2003-04 Yarmouth Mariners

COMPLETE SET (31) 4.00 10.00
1 Checklist .01 .05
2 Travis Antler .20 .50
3 Todd Ballah .20 .50
4 Jamie Barbour .20 .50
5 Brent Boardman .20 .50
6 Jarrett Bottomley .20 .50
7 Tim Clayton .20 .50
8 Georges d'Entremont .20 .50
9 Justin d'Entremont .20 .50
10 Jason Hedges .20 .50
11 Steve Holland .20 .50
12 Grant Kenny .20 .50
13 Brad Larter .20 .50
14 Jordan McMullen .20 .50
15 Jody Mosher .20 .50
16 Matt Oxtoby .20 .50
17 David Philpott .20 .50
18 Mark Plenzich .20 .50
19 Jason Robichaud .20 .50
20 Curtis Thorne .20 .50
21 Michael Dilorenzo .02 .10
22 Josh Vanderbreggen .20 .50
23 Sean Wadden .20 .50
24 Steve Yetman .20 .50
25 Paul Currie CO .02 .10
26 Laurie Barron ACO .02 .10
27 Mark Muise EQM .02 .10
28 Mark Wheeler TR .02 .10
29 One Team One Goal .02 .10
30 Mariner Pressure .02 .10
31 Hard to the Net .02 .10

1991 Arena Draft Picks

The 1991 Arena Draft Picks boxed set consists of 33 standard-size cards. The set was produced in English as well as French versions, with both versions currently carrying the same values. One thousand cards (numbered out of 667 for the English version, 333 for the French) signed by each player were randomly inserted throughout the sets with one autograph per approximately ten sets or two per case. Moreover, a Pat Falloon hologram was produced in conjunction with this set, although its release came much later. The Falloon hologram is not included in the complete set price below. The production run was reported to be 198,000 English and 99,000 French sets, and each set was issued with a numbered certificate of authenticity. The full-bleed fronts have a white background and show the hockey player in an action pose wearing a tuxedo.

COMPLETE SET (33) 1.25 3.00
1 Pat Falloon .02 .10
2 Scott Niedermayer .08 .25
3 Scott Lachance .01 .05
4 Peter Forsberg UER .40 1.00
5 Alek Stojanov .01 .05
6 Richard Matvichuk .02 .10
7 Patrick Poulin .01 .05
8 Martin Lapointe .20 .50
9 Tyler Wright .01 .05
10 Philippe Boucher .01 .05
11 Pat Peake .01 .05
12 Markus Naslund UER .20 .50
13 Brent Bilodeau .01 .05
14 Glen Murray .20 .50
15 Niklas Sundblad .01 .05
16 Trevor Halverson .01 .05
17 Dean McAmmond .02 .10
18 Rene Corbet .01 .05
19 Eric Lavigne .01 .05
20 Steve Staios .01 .05
21 Jim Campbell .02 .10
22 Jassen Cullimore .01 .05
23 Jamie Pushor .02 .10
24 Donevan Hextall .01 .05
25 Andrew Verner .02 .10
26 Jason Dawe .01 .05
27 Jeff Nelson .01 .05
28 Darcy Werenka .01 .05
29 Francois Groleau .01 .05
30 Guy Leveque .01 .05
31 Yanic Perreault .05 .15
32 Pat Falloon and .02 .10
Scott Lachance
NNO Checklist Card .02 .01
HOLO Pat Falloon .08 .25
Hologram

1991 Arena Draft Picks Autographs

The 1991 Arena Draft Picks autographs consists of 33 standard-size cards. One thousand cards (numbered out of 667 for the English version, 333 for the French) signed by each player were randomly inserted throughout the sets with one autograph per approximately ten sets or two per case. The full-bleed fronts have a white background and show the hockey player in an action pose wearing a tuxedo.

COMPLETE SET (33) 75.00 125.00
1 Pat Falloon 2.00 5.00
2 Scott Niedermayer 6.00 15.00
3 Scott Lachance 1.25 3.00
4 Peter Forsberg UER 30.00 75.00
5 Alek Stojanov 1.25 3.00
6 Richard Matvichuk 2.00 5.00
7 Patrick Poulin 1.25 3.00
8 Martin Lapointe 6.00 15.00
9 Tyler Wright 1.25 3.00
10 Philippe Boucher 1.25 3.00
11 Pat Peake 1.25 3.00
12 Markus Naslund UER 6.00 15.00
13 Brent Bilodeau 1.25 3.00
14 Glen Murray 6.00 15.00
15 Niklas Sundblad 1.25 3.00
16 Trevor Halverson 1.25 3.00
17 Dean McAmmond 2.00 5.00
18 Rene Corbet 2.00 5.00
19 Eric Lavigne 1.25 3.00
20 Steve Staios 1.25 3.00
21 Jim Campbell 1.25 3.00
22 Jassen Cullimore 1.25 3.00
23 Jamie Pushor 1.25 3.00
24 Donevan Hextall 1.25 3.00
25 Andrew Verner 2.00 5.00
26 Jason Dawe 1.25 3.00
27 Jeff Nelson 1.25 3.00
28 Darcy Werenka 1.25 3.00
29 Francois Groleau 1.25 3.00
30 Guy Leveque 1.25 3.00
31 Yanic Perreault 2.00 5.00

1994-95 Assets

Produced by Classic, the 1994 Assets set features stars from basketball, hockey, football, baseball, and auto racing. The set was released in two series of 50 cards each. 1,994 cases were produced of each series. This standard-sized card set features a player photo with his name in silver letters on the lower left corner and the Assets logo on the upper right. The back has a color photo on the left side along with a biography on the right side of the card. A Sprint phone card is randomly inserted in each five-card pack.

COMPLETE SET (100) 6.00 15.00
8 Ed Jovanovski .05 .15
20 Radek Bonk .08 .25
21 Manon Rheaume .50 1.25
33 Ed Jovanovski .05 .15
45 Radek Bonk .08 .25
46 Manon Rheaume .50 1.25
57 Jeff O'Neill .05 .15
60 Petr Sykora .08 .25
62 Eric Fichaud .07 .20
72 Manon Rheaume .50 1.25
82 Jeff O'Neill .05 .15
85 Petr Sykora .08 .25
87 Eric Fichaud .07 .20
97 Manon Rheaume .50 1.25

1994-95 Assets Die Cuts

This 25-card standard-size set was randomly inserted into packs. DC1-10 were included in series one while DC11-25 were included in series two packs. These cards feature the player on the card and the ability to separate the player's photo. The back contains information about the player on the section of the card that is separable.

COMPLETE SET (25) 30.00 80.00
DC9 Ed Jovanovski .60 1.50
DC10 Manon Rheaume 4.00 10.00
DC24 Eric Fichaud .60 1.50

1994-95 Assets Phone Cards $1000

Measuring 2" by 3 1/4", these rounded-corner cards were randomly inserted in first-series packs. The fronts feature color player photos, with "One Thousand Dollars" in cursive script along the left edge. The backs give instructions on how to use the phone cards. The cards expired December 1, 1995. There was a Shaquille O'Neal $1000 promotional phone card issued for the Assets set. The Front is stamped "Sample" and the back gives a description about the set--it is not a usable phone card.

*PIN NUMBER REVEALED: HALF VALUE
4 Manon Rheaume 40.00 80.00

1994-95 Assets Phone Cards $2000

These rounded-corner cards measuring 2" by 3 1/4" were randomly inserted into second series packs. Just four of each of these cards were produced. The front features the player's photo, with "Two Thousand Dollars" written in cursive script along the left edge. In the bottom left corner is the Assets logo. The back gives instructions on how to use the phone card. The cards are unnumbered and checklisted below in alphabetical order. The cards expired on March 31, 1996.

3 Manon Rheaume

1994-95 Assets Phone Cards $5

These cards measure 2" by 3 1/4", have rounded corners and were randomly inserted into packs. Cards 1-5 were inserted into first series packs while 6-15 were in second series packs. The front features the player's photo, with "Five Dollars" written in cursive script along the left edge. In the bottom left corner is the Assets logo. The back gives instructions on how to use the phone card. Series one cards expired on December 1, 1995 while second series cards expired on March 31, 1996.

COMPLETE SET (15) 8.00 20.00
*PIN NUMBER REVEALED: 2X TO .5X
14 Manon Rheaume .75 1.50

1994-95 Assets Phone Cards One Minute

Measuring 2" by 3 1/4", these cards have rounded corners and were inserted one per pack. Cards 1-24 were in first series packs while 25-48 were included with second series packs. The front features the player's photo and on the side is how long the card is good for. The Assets logo is in the bottom left corner. The back gives instructions on how to use the phone card. The first series cards expired on December 1, 1995 while the second series cards expired on March 31, 1996. The cards with a $2 logo are worth a mulitple of the regular cards. Please refer to the values below for these cards.

COMPLETE SET (48) 7.50 20.00
*PIN NUMB.REVEALED: .2X to .5X BASIC INS.
*TWO DOLLAR: .5X TO 1.2X BASIC INSERTS
4 Radek Bonk .15 .40
10 Ed Jovanovski .15 .40
18 Manon Rheaume .60 1.50
28 Eric Fichaud .15 .40
41 Jeff O'Neill .15 .40
42 Manon Rheaume .60 1.50
48 Petr Sykora .20 .50

1994-95 Assets Silver Signature

This 48-card standard-size set was randomly inserted at a rate of four per box. The cards are identical to the first twenty-four cards in the each series, except that these show a silver facsimile autograph on their fronts. The first 24 cards correspond to cards 1-24 in the first series while the second 24 cards correspond to cards 51-74 in the second series.

*SILVER SIGS: 1.2X TO 3X BASIC CARDS

1996 Assets

The 1996 Classic Assets was issued in one set totalling 50 cards. This 50-card premium set has a tremendous selection of the top athletes in the world headlines. Each card features action photos, up-to-date statistics and is printed on high-quality, foil-stamped stock. Hot Print cards are parallel cards randomly inserted in Hot Packs and are valued at a multiple of the regular cards below.

COMPLETE SET (50) 5.00 10.00
8 Radek Dvorak .05 .15
14 Brian Holzinger .05 .15
17 Ed Jovanovski .05 .15
45 Petr Sykora .05 .15

1996 Assets A Cut Above

The even cards were randomly inserted in retail packs at a rate of one in eight, and the odd cards were inserted in clear asset packs at a rate of one in 20, this 20-card die-cut set is composed of 10 phone cards and 10 trading cards. The cards have rounded corners except for one which is cut in a straight corner design. The fronts feature a color action player cut-out superimposed over a gray background with the words "cut above" printed throughout and resembled to be cut so it displays a basketball game behind it. The backs carry a color action player photo with the player's name and a short career summary.

COMPLETE SET (20) 20.00 50.00
CA4 Brian Holzinger .50 1.25

1996 Assets Hot Prints

These parallel cards were randomly seeded in 1996 Assets Hot Packs. Each card is marked Hot Print on the cardfront.

*HOT PRINTS: .8X TO 2X BASIC CARDS

1996 Assets Phone Cards $2

This 30-card set was inserted in retail packs at a rate of 1 per pack with a minimum value of $2 per phone card. The cards measure approximately 2 1/8" by 3 3/8" with rounded corners. The fronts display color aciton player photos with the player's name in a red bar below. The backs carry the instructions on how to use the cards and the expiration date of 1/31/97. Hot Print Cards parallel cards were randomly inserted in Hot Packs. These cards are valued as a mulitple of the cards below.

COMPLETE SET (30) 12.50 30.00
*$2 CARDS: .6X TO 1.5X $1 CARDS
*PIN NUMBER REVEALED: HALF VALUE

1995 Assets Gold

This 50-card set measures the standard size. The fronts feature borderless player action photos with the player's name printed in gold at the bottom. The backs carry a portrait of the player with his name, career highlights, and statistics. The Dale Earnhardt card was pulled from circulation early in the product's release. It is considered a Short Print (SP) but is not included in the complete set price.

COMPLETE SET (49) 6.00 15.00
2 Jeff O'Neill .05 .15
3 Jeff Friesen .07 .20
4 Aki-Petteri Berg .05 .15
5 Todd Marchant .07 .20
6 Blaine Lacher .07 .20
7 Petr Sykora .08 .25
8 David Oliver .05 .15
9 Manon Rheaume .20 .50
10 Ed Jovanovski .07 .20

1995 Assets Gold Printer's Proofs

These parallel cards were randomly seeded at the rate of 1:18 packs. They feature the words "Printer's Proof" on the cardfronts.

*PRINT PROOF: 2X TO 5X BASIC CARDS

1995 Assets Gold Die Cuts Silver

This 20-card set was randomly inserted in packs at a rate of one in 18. The fronts feature a borderless player color action photo with a diamond-shaped top and the player's action taking place in front of the card name. The backs carry the card name, player's name and career highlights. The cards are numbered on the backs. Gold versions were inserted at a rate of one in 72 packs.

COMPLETE SET (20) 10.00 25.00
*GOLDS: 1.2X to 3X SILVERS
STATED ODDS 1:72
SDC13 Manon Rheaume .75 2.00

1995 Assets Gold Phone Cards $2

This 47-card set was randomly inserted in packs and measures 2 1/8" by 3 3/8". The fronts feature color action player photos with the player's name below. The $2 calling value is printed vertically down the left. The backs carry the instructions on how to use the cards which expired on 7/31/96. The cards are unnumbered.

COMPLETE SET (47) 15.00 40.00
*PIN NUMBER REVEALED: HALF VALUE
2 Jeff O'Neill .30 .75
3 Jeff Friesen .40 1.00
4 Aki-Petteri Berg .30 .75
5 Todd Marchant .30 .75
6 Blaine Lacher .30 .75
7 Petr Sykora .60 1.50
8 David Oliver .30 .75
9 Manon Rheaume .75 2.00
10 Ed Jovanovski .30 .75

1995 Assets Gold Phone Cards $5

This 16-card set measures 2 1/8" by 3 3/8" and was randomly inserted in packs. The fronts feature color action player photos with the player's name below. The $5 calling value is printed vertically down the left. The backs carry the instructions on how to use the cards which expired on 7/31/96. The cards are unnumbered. The Microlined versions are inserted at a rate of one in 18 packs versus one in six packs for the basic $5 card.

COMPLETE SET (16) 25.00 60.00
*MICROLINED: .6X TO 1.5X BASIC INSERTS
STATED ODDS 1:18
*PIN NUMBER REVEALED: HALF VALUE
3 Manon Rheaume 1.00 2.50

1995 Assets Gold Silver Signatures

These parallel cards were inserted one per pack. They feature a silver foil facsimile signature on the cardfronts.

COMP. SILVER SIG SET (50) 15.00 40.00
*SILVER SIGS: .8X TO 2X BASIC CARDS

1997 Bowman CHL

The 1997-98 Bowman CHL set was issued in one series totaling 165 cards and was distributed in eight-card packs with a suggested retail price of $1.89. It marks Topps first venture into minor league hockey. The set features color photos of established CHL stars as well as 40 NHL 1997 Draft Prospects. The 40 Draft Prospects each autographed cards that were distributed at the rate of one in 24 to form the Bowman CHL Prospects Autographs insert set. Each of these cards is authenticated by the Topps Certified Autograph Issue stamp.

COMPLETE SET (160) 10.00 25.00
1 Jan Bulis .15 .40
2 Daniel Cleary .15 .40
3 Dave Duerden .07 .20
4 Cameron Mann .07 .20
5 Alyn McCauley .15 .40
6 Tyler Rennette .07 .20
7 Marc Savard .20 .50
8 Daniel Tkaczuk .15 .40
9 John Tripp .07 .20
10 Joel Trottier .07 .20
11 Sean Yenedam .07 .20
12 Alexander Volchkov .07 .20
13 Sean Blanchard .07 .20
14 Kevin Bolibruck .07 .20
15 Nick Boynton .20 .50
16 Paul Mara .15 .40
17 Marc Moro .07 .20
18 Marty Wilford .07 .20
19 Zac Bierk .20 .50
20 Kory Cooper .07 .20
21 Richard Rochefort .07 .20
22 Matt Cooke .20 .50
23 Boyd Devereaux .20 .50
24 Rico Fata .15 .40
25 Dwayne Hay .07 .20
26 Trevor Letowski .07 .20
27 Ryan Mougenel .07 .20
28 Todd Norman .07 .20
29 Larry Paleczny .07 .20
30 Colin Pepperall .07 .20
31 Jonathan Sim .07 .20
32 Joe Thornton 1.50 4.00
33 Brian Wesenberg .07 .20
34 Andy Delmore .07 .20
35 Chris Hajt .07 .20
36 Richard Jackman .07 .20
37 Denis Smith .07 .20
38 Jamie Sokolsky .07 .20
39 Paul Traynor .07 .20
40 Patrick DesRochers .15 .40
41 Robert Esche .40 1.00
42 Roberto Luongo 1.50 4.00
43 Frederic Henry .07 .20
44 Marc Oliver Roy .07 .20
45 Samy Nasreddine .07 .20
46 Jean-Francois Fortin .07 .20
47 Martin Ethier .07 .20
48 Jason Doig .07 .20
49 Dominic Perna .07 .20
50 Daniel Briere .30 .75
51 Pavel Rosa .07 .20
52 Philippe Audet .07 .20
53 Gordie Dwyer .07 .20
54 Martin Menard .07 .20
55 Jonathan Delisle .07 .20
56 Peter Worrell .20 .50
57 Francois Methot .07 .20
58 Steve Begin .07 .20
59 Karol Bartanus .07 .20
60 J-P Dumont .40 1.00
61 Marc Denis .40 1.00
62 Jean-Sebastien Giguere .75 2.00
63 Jason Gorleau .07 .20
64 Radoslav Suchy .07 .20
65 Stephane Robidas .07 .20
66 Marc-Andre Gaudet .07 .20
67 Eric Drouin .07 .20
68 Derrick Walser .07 .20
69 Vincent Lecavalier 1.25 3.00
70 Denis Hamel .07 .20
71 Daniel Corso .07 .20
72 Martin Moise .07 .20
73 Eric Belanger .07 .20
74 Olivier Morin .07 .20
75 Jerome Tremblay .07 .20
76 Jody Shelley .30 .75
77 Eric Normandin .07 .20
78 David Thibeault .07 .20
79 Christian Daigle .15 .40
80 Alexandre Jacques .07 .20
81 Brian Boucher .40 1.00
82 Randy Petruk .15 .40
83 Hugh Hamilton .07 .20
84 Joel Kwiatkowski .07 .20
85 Zenith Komarniski .07 .20
86 Joey Tetarenko .20 .50
87 Tyler Willis .07 .20
88 Patrick Marleau .75 2.00
89 Trent Whitfield .07 .20
90 Martin Cerven .07 .20
91 Donnie Kinney .07 .20
92 Brad Isbister .15 .40
93 Todd Robinson .07 .20
94 Greg Leeb .07 .20
95 John Cirjak .07 .20
96 Randy Perry .07 .20
97 Derek Schutz .07 .20
98 Brenden Morrow .40 1.00
99 Shawn McNeil .07 .20
100 Brad Ference .07 .20
101 Ryan Hoople .07 .20
102 Brian Elder .07 .20
103 Mike McBain .07 .20
104 Jesse Wallin .07 .20
105 Chris Phillips .20 .50
106 Kelly Smart .07 .20
107 Arron Asham .07 .20
108 Byron Ritchie .20 .50
109 Derek Morris .20 .50
110 Travis Brigley .07 .20
111 Justin Kurtz .07 .20
112 B.J. Young .07 .20
113 Shane Willis .07 .20
114 Josh Holden .07 .20
115 Cory Sarich .07 .20
116 Brad Larsen .07 .20
117 Stefan Cherneski .07 .20
118 Peter Schaefer .07 .20
119 Dmitri Nabokov .07 .20
120 Sergei Varlamov .20 .50
121 Daniel Cleary TP .07 .20
122 Jarrett Smith TP .07 .20
123 Alexandre Mathieu TP .07 .20
124 Matt Elich TP .07 .20
125 Joe Thornton TP .75 2.00
126 Mike Brown TP .07 .20
127 Derek Schutz TP .07 .20
128 Benoit Cote TP .07 .20
129 Jason Ward TP .07 .20
130 Karol Bartanus TP .07 .20
131 Tyler Rennette TP .07 .20
132 Matt Zultek TP .15 .40
133 Brad Ference TP .15 .40
134 Daniel Tetrault TP .07 .20
135 Ray Bonni TP .07 .20
136 Kevin Grimes TP .07 .20
137 Paul Mara TP .15 .40
138 Nikos Tselios TP .07 .20
139 Curtis Cruickshank TP .07 .20
140 Pierre-Luc Therrien TP .07 .20
141 Patrick Marleau TP .40 1.00
142 Ty Jones TP .07 .20
143 Jeremy Reich TP .07 .20
144 Adam Mair TP .15 .40
145 Adam Colagiacomo TP .07 .20
146 Harold Druken TP .15 .40
147 Brenden Morrow TP .30 .75
148 Jay Legault TP .07 .20
149 Jeff Zehr TP .07 .20
150 Scott Barney TP .07 .20
151 Gregor Baumgartner TP .07 .20
152 Daniel Tkaczuk TP .20 .50
153 Eric Brewer TP .20 .50
154 Nick Boynton TP .20 .50
155 Vratislav Cech TP .07 .20
156 Kyle Kos TP .07 .20
157 Jean-Francois Fortin TP .07 .20
158 Wes Jarvis TP .07 .20
159 Roberto Luongo TP .75 2.00
160 J-F Damphousse TP .07 .20
NNO B.B.Redempt. .40 1.00
NNO Ref.Redempt. .40 1.00
NNO Ato.Ref.Redempt. .40 1.00
NNO Auto.Redempt. .40 1.00

1997 Bowman CHL OPC

Randomly inserted in packs at the rate of 1:6, this 160 card set is an O-Pee-Chee parallel version of the basic Bowman CHL issue.

COMPLETE SET (160) 300.00 600.00
*STARS: 4X TO 10X BASIC CARDS

1997 Bowman CHL Autographs

Randomly inserted at the rate of 1:46, this 37-card set features cards signed by the top NHL draft picks. Each of these cards is authenticated by the Topps Certified Autograph Issue stamp.

COMPLETE SET (40) 150.00 200.00
2 Jarrett Smith 2.00 5.00
3 Alexandre Mathieu 2.00 5.00
4 Matt Elich 2.00 5.00
10 Karol Bartanus 2.00 5.00
11 Tyler Rennette 2.00 5.00
13 Brad Ference 2.00 5.00
14 Daniel Tetrault 2.00 5.00
15 Ray Bonni 2.00 5.00
16 Kevin Grimes 2.00 5.00
18 Nikos Tselios 2.00 5.00
19 Curtis Cruickshank 2.00 5.00
20 Pierre-Luc Therrien 2.00 5.00
22 Ty Jones 2.00 5.00
23 Jeremy Reich 2.00 5.00
24 Adam Mair 2.00 5.00
25 Adam Colagiacomo 2.00 5.00
26 Harold Druken 2.00 5.00
28 Jay Legault 2.00 5.00
29 Jeff Zehr 4.00 10.00
30 Scott Barney 2.00 5.00
31 Gregor Baumgartner 2.00 5.00
33 Eric Brewer 5.00 12.00
34 Nick Boynton 5.00 12.00
35 Vratislav Cech 2.00 5.00
36 Kyle Kos 2.00 5.00
37 Jean Francois Fortin 2.00 5.00
38 Wes Jarvis 2.00 5.00
39 Roberto Luongo 8.00 20.00
121 Daniel Cleary 2.00 5.00
125 Joe Thornton 20.00 40.00
126 Mike Brown 2.00 5.00
127 Derek Schutz 2.00 5.00
128 Benoit Cote 2.00 5.00
129 Jason Ward 4.00 10.00
132 Matt Zultek 2.00 5.00
147 Brenden Morrow 10.00 20.00
160 Jean-Francois Damphousse 5.00 12.00
149 Jeff Zehr

1997 Bowman CHL Bowman's Best

This 20-card set was randomly inserted in packs at the rate of one in 12 and features color player photos printed on laser-cut cards using chromium technology. Refractor and atomic refractor parallels were also created and randomly inserted. Refractors were inserted at a rate of 1:24 and atomic refractors at 1:48.

COMPLETE SET (20) 25.00 35.00
*REF.STARS: 1.5X TO 3X BASIC BOWMAN'S BEST
*ATOMIC REF: 2.5X TO 5X BASIC BOWMAN'S BEST
1 Joe Thornton 4.00 10.00
2 Patrick Marleau 1.50 4.00
3 Paul Mara .60 1.50
4 Daniel Tkaczuk .60 1.50
5 Jason Ward .60 1.50
6 Nick Boynton .75 2.00
7 Daniel Cleary .60 1.50
8 Eric Brewer .75 2.00
9 Brad Ference .60 1.50
10 Stefan Cherneski .60 1.50
11 Ryan Bonni .60 1.50
12 Adam Colagiacomo .60 1.50
13 Mike Brown .60 1.50
14 Scott Barney .60 1.50
15 Jarrett Smith .60 1.50
16 Brenden Morrow 1.25 3.00
17 Jean-Francois Fortin .60 1.50
18 Roberto Luongo 4.00 10.00
19 Curtis Cruickshank .60 1.50
20 Pierre-Luc Therrien .60 1.50

1998 Bowman CHL

The 1998 Bowman CHL set was issued in one series totaling 165 cards and was distributed in eight-card packs with a suggested retail price of $1.89. The set features action color photos of established CHL stars as well as 40 NHL 1998 Draft Prospects. The backs carry player information and statistics.

COMPLETE SET (165) 20.00 50.00
1 Robert Esche .20 .50
2 Chris Hajt .07 .20
3 Mark McMahon .07 .20
4 Jeff Brown .07 .20
5 Richard Jackman .07 .20
6 Greg Labenski .07 .20
7 Marek Posmyk .07 .20
8 Brian Willsie .07 .20
9 Jason Ward .07 .20
10 Manny Malhotra .07 .20
11 Matt Cooke .40 1.00
12 Mike Gorman .07 .20
13 Rodney Richard .07 .20
14 David Legwand .40 1.00
15 Jon Sim .07 .20
16 Peter Sarno .07 .20
17 Andrew Long .07 .20
18 Peter Cava .07 .20
19 Colin Pepperall .07 .20
20 Jay Legault .07 .20
21 Brian Finley .20 .50
22 Martin Skoula .07 .20
23 Brian Campbell .07 .20
24 Sean Blanchard .07 .20
25 Bryan Allen .07 .20
26 Peter Hogan .07 .20
27 Nick Boynton .40 1.00
28 Matt Bradley .07 .20
29 Jeremy Adduono .07 .20
30 Mike Henrich .07 .20
31 Justin Papineau .20 .50
32 Bujar Amidovski .40 1.00
33 Robert Mailloux .07 .20
34 Daniel Tkaczuk .07 .20
35 Sean Avery .40 1.00
36 Mark Bell .20 .50
37 Kevin Colley .07 .20
38 Norm Milley .40 1.00
39 Scott Barney .07 .20
40 Joel Trottier .07 .20
41 Brent Belecki .07 .20
42 Randy Petruk .20 .50
43 Brad Ference .07 .20
44 Perry Johnson .07 .20
45 Joel Kwiatkowski .07 .20
46 Zenith Komarniski .07 .20
47 Greg Kuznik .07 .20
48 Andrew Ference .07 .20
49 Jason Deleurme .07 .20
50 Trent Whitfield .07 .20
51 Dylan Gyori .07 .20
52 Todd Robinson .07 .20
53 Marian Hossa .40 1.00
54 Mike Hurley .07 .20
55 Greg Leeb .07 .20
56 Andrej Podkonicky .20 .50
57 Quinn Hancock .07 .20
58 Marian Cisar .07 .20
59 Bret DeCecco .07 .20
60 Brenden Morrow .20 .50
61 Evan Lindsay .20 .50
62 Terry Friesen .20 .50
63 Ryan Shannon .07 .20
64 Michal Rozsival .07 .20
65 Luc Theoret .07 .20
66 Brad Stuart .40 1.00
67 Burke Henry .07 .20
68 Cory Sarich .07 .20
69 Martin Sonnenberg .07 .20
70 Mark Smith .20 .50
71 Shawn McNeil .07 .20
72 Brad Moran .07 .20
73 Josh Holden .07 .20
74 Cory Cyrenne .07 .20
75 Shane Willis .07 .20
76 Stefan Cherneski .07 .20
77 Jay Henderson .07 .20
78 Ronald Petrovicky .07 .20
79 Sergei Varlamov .07 .20
80 Chad Hinz .07 .20
81 Mathieu Garon .20 .50
82 Mathieu Chouinard .20 .50
83 Dominic Perna .07 .20
84 Didier Tremblay .07 .20
85 Mike Ribeiro .20 .50
86 Marty Johnston .07 .20
87 Remi Royer .07 .20
88 Patrick Pelchat .07 .20
89 Daniel Corso .07 .20
90 Francois Fortier .07 .20
91 Marc-Andre Gaudet .07 .20
92 Francois Beauchemin .07 .20
93 Michel Tremblay .07 .20
94 Jean-Philippe Pare .07 .20
95 Francois Methot .07 .20
96 David Thibeault .07 .20
97 Jonathan Girard Jr. .20 .50
98 Karol Bartanus .07 .20
99 Peter Ratchuk .07 .20
100 Pierre Dagenais .20 .50
101 Philippe Sauve .40 1.00
102 Remi Bergeron .07 .20
103 Vincent Lecavalier .20 .50
104 Eric Chouinard .40 1.00
105 Oleg Timchenko .07 .20
106 Sebastien Roger .07 .20
107 Simon Gagne .40 1.00
108 Alex Tanguay .40 1.00
109 David Gosselin .07 .20
110 Ramzi Abid .20 .50
111 Eric Drouin .07 .20
112 Dominic Auger .07 .20
113 Martin Moise .07 .20
114 Randy Copley .07 .20
115 Alexandre Mathieu .07 .20
116 Brad Richards .20 .50
117 Dmitri Tolkunov .07 .20
118 Alexei Tezikov .07 .20
119 Derrick Walser .07 .20
120 Adam Borzecki .07 .20
121 Ramzi Abid .20 .50
122 Brett Allan .07 .20
123 Mark Bell .20 .50
124 Blair Betts .07 .20
125 Randy Copley .07 .20
126 Simon Gagne .40 1.00
127 Mike Henrich .07 .20
128 Vincent Lecavalier .20 .50
129 Norman Milley .40 1.00
130 Chris Neilsen .07 .20
131 Rico Fata .20 .50
132 Mike Ribeiro .20 .50
133 Bryan Allen .07 .20
134 John Erskine .20 .50
135 Jonathan Girard Jr. .20 .50
136 Stephen Peat .40 1.00
137 Robyn Regehr .30 .75
138 Brad Stuart .40 1.00
139 Patrick Desrochers .20 .50
140 Jason Labarbera .20 .50
141 David Cameron .07 .20
142 Jonathan Cheechoo .40 1.00
143 Eric Chouinard .40 1.00
144 Brent Gauvreau .07 .20
145 Scott Gomez .20 .50
146 Jeff Heerema .07 .20
147 David Legwand .40 1.00
148 Manny Malhotra .20 .50
149 Justin Papineau .07 .20
150 Andrew Peters .07 .20
151 Michael Rupp .40 1.00
152 Alex Tanguay .40 1.00
153 Francois Beauchemin .07 .20
154 Mathieu Biron .07 .20
155 Jiri Fischer .40 1.00
156 Alex Henry .20 .50
157 Kyle Rossiter .07 .20
158 Martin Skoula .07 .20
159 Mathieu Chouinard .20 .50
160 Philippe Sauve .40 1.00
161 Brian Finley .20 .50
162 Brent Belecki .07 .20
163 Dominic Perna .07 .20
164 Jonathan Cheechoo .40 1.00
165 Checklist .07 .20

1998 Bowman CHL Golden Anniversary

Randomly inserted in packs at the rate of 1:57, this 165-card set is a gold-foil parallel version of the base set and is sequentially numbered to 50 in honor of the 50 years of Bowman cards.

*STARS: 12.5X TO 30X BASIC CARDS

1998 Bowman CHL OPC International

Inserted one in every pack, this 165-card set is parallel to the base set and features color player photos with a national indication in the background by way of a map printed on 16 pt. mirror board. Each back is written in the language of that player's native country.

*STARS: .75X TO 2X BASIC CARDS

1998 Bowman CHL Autographs Blue

Randomly inserted in packs at the rate of 1:39, this 40-card set features cards signed by the top 40 NHL draft prospects and authenticated by a blue foil "Topps Certified Issue" stamp. Silver and blue variations were also created and inserted randomly. Silver autos were inserted at a rate of 1:157 and gold at 1:470.

*SILVER AU's: .75X TO 2X BASIC AU
*GOLD AU's: 2X TO 5X BASIC AU
A1 Justin Papineau 2.50 6.00
A2 Jason Labarbera 4.00 10.00
A3 Michael Rupp 4.00 10.00
A4 Stephen Peat 5.00 12.00
A5 Manny Malhotra 2.50 6.00
A6 Michael Henrich 2.50 6.00
A7 Kyle Rossiter 2.50 6.00
A8 Mark Bell 5.00 12.00
A9 Mathieu Chouinard 5.00 12.00
A10 Vincent Lecavalier 8.00 20.00
A11 David Legwand 5.00 12.00
A12 Bryan Allen 2.50 6.00
A13 Francois Beauchemin 2.50 6.00
A14 Robyn Regehr 5.00 12.00
A15 Eric Chouinard 4.00 10.00
A16 Norman Milley 4.00 10.00
A17 Alex Henry 2.50 6.00
A18 Ramzi Abid 2.50 6.00
A19 Jiri Fischer 5.00 12.00
A20 Patrick Desrochers 4.00 10.00
A21 Mathieu Biron 2.50 6.00
A22 Brad Stuart 5.00 12.00
A23 Philippe Sauve 8.00 20.00
A24 John Erskine 4.00 10.00
A25 Jonathan Cheechoo 8.00 20.00
A26 Brett Allan 2.50 6.00
A27 Scott Gomez 6.00 15.00
A28 Chris Neilsen 2.50 6.00
A29 David Cameron 2.50 6.00
A30 Jonathan Girard Jr. 5.00 12.00
A31 Jeff Heerema 2.50 6.00
A32 Blair Betts 2.50 6.00
A33 Andrew Peters 2.50 6.00
A34 Randy Copley 4.00 10.00
A35 Alex Tanguay 6.00 15.00
A36 Simon Gagne 6.00 15.00
A37 Brent Gauvreau 2.50 6.00
A38 Mike Ribeiro 5.00 12.00
A39 Martin Skoula 2.50 6.00
A40 Rico Fata 4.00 10.00

1998 Bowman CHL Scout's Choice

Randomly inserted in packs at the rate of 1:12, this 21-card set features color photos of players picked by Bowman Hockey Scouts and printed on borderless, double-etched foil cards.

COMPLETE SET (21) 30.00 60.00
SC1 Bryan Allen .40 1.00
SC2 Manny Malhotra .40 1.00
SC3 Daniel Tkaczuk .40 1.00
SC4 Bujar Amidovski .40 1.00
SC5 Patrick Desrochers .40 1.00
SC6 Brad Ference .40 1.00
SC7 Marian Hossa .60 1.50
SC8 Brad Stuart .40 1.00
SC9 Sergei Varlamov .40 1.00
SC10 Randy Petruk .40 1.00
SC11 Karol Bartanus .40 1.00
SC12 Vincent Lecavalier .50 1.25
SC13 Jonathan Girard .40 1.00
SC14 Peter Ratchuk .40 1.00
SC15 Alex Tanguay .60 1.50
SC16 Rico Fata .40 1.00
SC17 Brian Finley .50 1.25
SC18 Jonathan Cheechoo .40 1.00
SC19 Scott Gomez .40 1.00
SC20 Michal Rozsival .40 1.00
SC21 Mathieu Garon .40 1.00

1998 Bowman Chrome CHL

The 1998-99 Bowman Chrome CHL hobby-only set was issued in one series totaling 165 cards. The 4-card packs retail for $3.00 each. The fronts feature color action photography on chromium technology. The Bowman Rookie Card stamp appears on all cards for players making their first appearance in the set. The scheduled release date was September, 1998.

COMPLETE SET (165) 30.00 60.00
1 Robert Esche .60 1.50
2 Chris Hajt .15 .40
3 Mark McMahon .15 .40
4 Jeff Brown .15 .40
5 Richard Jackman .15 .40
6 Greg Labenski .15 .40
7 Marek Posmyk .15 .40
8 Brian Willsie .15 .40
9 Jason Ward .15 .40
10 Manny Malhotra .15 .40
11 Matt Cooke .75 2.00
12 Mike Gorman .15 .40
13 Rodney Richard .15 .40
14 David Legwand .75 2.00
15 Jon Sim .15 .40
16 Peter Sarno .60 1.50
17 Andrew Long .15 .40
18 Peter Cava .15 .40
19 Colin Pepperall .15 .40
20 Jay Legault .15 .40
21 Brian Finley .60 1.50
22 Martin Skoula .15 .40
23 Brian Campbell .15 .40
24 Sean Blanchard .15 .40
25 Bryan Allen .15 .40
26 Peter Hogan .15 .40
27 Nick Boynton .75 2.00
28 Matt Bradley .15 .40
29 Jeremy Adduono .15 .40
30 Mike Henrich .15 .40
31 Justin Papineau .15 .40
32 Bujar Amidovski .60 1.50
33 Robert Mailloux .15 .40
34 Daniel Tkaczuk .15 .40
35 Sean Avery .75 2.00
36 Mark Bell .75 2.00
37 Kevin Colley .15 .40
38 Norman Milley .60 1.50
39 Scott Barney .15 .40
40 Joel Trottier .15 .40
41 Brent Belecki .15 .40
42 Randy Petruk .60 1.50
43 Brad Ference .15 .40
44 Perry Johnson .15 .40
45 Joel Kwiatkowski .15 .40
46 Zenith Komarniski .15 .40
47 Greg Kuznik .15 .40
48 Andrew Ference .60 1.50
49 Jason Deleurme .15 .40
50 Trent Whitfield .15 .40
51 Dylan Gyori .15 .40
52 Todd Robinson .15 .40
53 Marian Hossa .75 2.00
54 Mike Hurley .15 .40
55 Greg Leeb .15 .40
56 Andrej Podkonicky .15 .40
57 Quinn Hancock .15 .40
58 Marian Cisar .15 .40
59 Bret DeCecco .15 .40
60 Brenden Morrow .60 1.50
61 Evan Lindsay .60 1.50
62 Terry Friesen .60 1.50
63 Ryan Shannon .15 .40
64 Michal Rozsival .15 .40
65 Luc Theoret .15 .40
66 Brad Stuart .75 2.00
67 Burke Henry .15 .40
68 Cory Sarich .15 .40
69 Martin Sonnenberg .15 .40
70 Mark Smith .60 1.50
71 Shawn McNeil .15 .40
72 Brad Moran .15 .40
73 Josh Holden .15 .40
74 Cory Cyrenne .15 .40
75 Shane Willis .15 .40
76 Stefan Cherneski .15 .40
77 Jay Henderson .15 .40
78 Ronald Petrovicky .15 .40
79 Sergei Varlamov .15 .40
80 Chad Hinz .15 .40
81 Mathieu Garon .40 1.00
82 Mathieu Chouinard .60 1.50
83 Dominic Perna .15 .40
84 Didier Tremblay .15 .40
85 Mike Ribeiro .40 1.00
86 Marty Johnston .15 .40
87 Remi Royer .15 .40
88 Patrick Pelchat .15 .40
89 Daniel Corso .15 .40
90 Francois Fortier .15 .40
91 Marc-Andre Gaudet .15 .40
92 Francois Beauchemin .15 .40
93 Michel Tremblay .15 .40
94 Jean-Philippe Pare .15 .40
95 Francois Methot .15 .40
96 David Thibeault .15 .40
97 Jonathan Girard Jr. .60 1.50
98 Karol Bartanus .15 .40
99 Peter Ratchuk .15 .40
100 Pierre Dagenais .60 1.50
101 Philippe Sauve .75 2.00
102 Remi Bergeron .15 .40
103 Vincent Lecavalier .60 1.50
104 Eric Chouinard .60 1.50
105 Oleg Timchenko .15 .40
106 Sebastien Roger .15 .40
107 Simon Gagne .75 2.00
108 Alex Tanguay .75 2.00
109 David Gosselin .15 .40
110 Ramzi Abid .15 .40
111 Eric Drouin .15 .40
112 Dominic Auger .15 .40
113 Martin Moise .15 .40
114 Randy Copley .15 .40
115 Alexandre Mathieu .15 .40
116 Brad Richards .60 1.50
117 Dmitri Tolkunov .15 .40
118 Alexei Tezikov .15 .40
119 Derrick Walser .15 .40
120 Adam Borzecki .15 .40
121 Ramzi Abid .15 .40
122 Brett Allan .15 .40
123 Mark Bell .40 1.00
124 Blair Betts .40 1.00
125 Randy Copley .60 1.50
126 Simon Gagne .75 2.00
127 Mike Henrich .15 .40
128 Vincent Lecavalier .60 1.50
129 Norman Milley .60 1.50
130 Chris Nielsen .15 .40
131 Rico Fata .60 1.50
132 Mike Ribeiro .40 1.00
133 Bryan Allen .15 .40
134 John Erskine .60 1.50
135 Jonathan Girard Jr. .60 1.50
136 Stephen Peat .75 2.00
137 Robyn Regehr .60 1.50
138 Brad Stuart .75 2.00
139 Patrick Desrochers .60 1.50
140 Jason Labarbera .60 1.50
141 David Cameron .15 .40
142 Jonathan Cheechoo 1.25 3.00
143 Eric Chouinard .60 1.50
144 Brent Gauvreau .15 .40
145 Scott Gomez .40 1.00
146 Jeff Heerema .15 .40
147 David Legwand .75 2.00
148 Manny Malhotra .15 .40
149 Justin Papineau .15 .40
150 Andrew Peters .15 .40
151 Michael Rupp .60 1.50
152 Alex Tanguay .75 2.00
153 Francois Beauchemin .15 .40
154 Mathieu Biron .15 .40
155 Jiri Fischer .75 2.00
156 Alex Henry .15 .40
157 Kyle Rossiter .15 .40
158 Martin Skoula .60 1.50
159 Mathieu Chouinard .60 1.50
160 Philippe Sauve .75 2.00
161 Brian Finley .60 1.50
162 Brent Belecki .15 .40
163 Dominic Perna .15 .40
164 Jonathan Cheechoo .75 2.00
165 Checklist .15 .40
NNO Puck Redemption .15 .40

1998 Bowman Chrome CHL Golden Anniversary

Randomly inserted in packs at a rate of 1:39, this 165-card parallel offers the same players as in the Bowman Chrome CHL base set. The set is sequentially numbered to 50. Cards are randomly inserted into packs. A refractor variation was also created and inserted randomly. Refractors were serial numbered to just 5 and are not priced due to scarcity.

*STARS: 10X TO 25X BASIC CARDS

1998 Bowman Chrome CHL OPC International

Randomly inserted in packs at a rate of 1:8, this 165-card parallel features the same players as in the Bowman Chrome CHL base set. The set also offers background map designs of the player's homeland and vital statistics written in that player's native language. A refractor variation was also created and inserted at a rate of 1:48.

*STARS: 2.5X TO 5X BASIC CARDS
*REF.STARS: 8X TO 20X BASIC CARDS

1998 Bowman Chrome CHL Refractors

Randomly inserted in packs at a rate of 1:12, this 165-card parallel offers a refractive version of the same players as in the Bowman Chrome CHL base set.

REF.STARS: 4X TO 10X BASIC CARD

1999 Bowman CHL

Released as a 165-card set, 1999 Bowman CHL set features 122 CHL superstars, 40 NHL draft prospects, two dual player cards of stars from the WHL, OHL, QMJHL and Prospects All-Star Game, and one checklist.

COMPLETE SET (165) 20.00 50.00
1 Alex Auld .30 .75
2 Maxime Ouellet .30 .75
3 Nolan Yonkman .07 .20
4 Jeff Beatch .07 .20
5 Pavel Brendl .20 .50
6 Jamie Chamberlain .07 .20
7 Kyle Wanvig .07 .20
8 Chris Kelly .07 .20
9 Scott Kelman .07 .20
10 Derek MacKenzie .07 .20
11 Tim Connolly .20 .50
12 Alexandre Giroux .07 .20
13 Oleg Saprykin .20 .50
14 Sheldon Keefe .20 .50
15 Branislav Mezei .20 .50
16 Brett Lysak .07 .20
17 Peter Reynolds .07 .20
18 Ross Lupaschuk .07 .20
19 Mirko Murovic .07 .20
20 Steve McCarthy .20 .50
21 Radim Vrbata .20 .50
22 Dusty Jamieson .07 .20
23 Matt Carkner .07 .20
24 Denis Shvidki .20 .50
25 Jonathan Fauteux .07 .20
26 Martin Grenier .07 .20
27 Marc-Andre Thinel .20 .50
28 Luke Sellars .07 .20
29 Brad Ralph .07 .20
30 Scott Cameron .07 .20
31 Charlie Stephens .07 .20
32 Jamie Lundmark .20 .50
33 Justin Mapletoft .20 .50
34 Kristopher Beech .20 .50
35 Taylor Pyatt .20 .50
36 Michael Zigomanis .20 .50
37 Edward Hill .07 .20
38 Barret Jackman .40 1.00
39 Simon LaJeunesse .30 .75
40 Brian Finley .30 .75
41 Maxime Ouellet .30 .75
42 Alexei Volkov .30 .75
43 Roberto Luongo .40 1.00
44 Chris Lyness .07 .20
45 Simon Tremblay .07 .20
46 Eric Tremblay .07 .20
47 Jonathan Girard .20 .50
48 Dimitri Tolkunov .07 .20
49 Philippe Plante .07 .20
50 Eric Chouinard .20 .50
51 Wesley Scanzano .07 .20
52 Vincent Dionne .07 .20
53 Sebastien Roger .07 .20
54 Ladislav Nagy .40 1.00
55 Alex Tanguay .40 1.00
56 Martin Moise .07 .20
57 Brad Richards .40 1.00
58 Juraj Kolnik .20 .50
59 Simon Gagne .40 1.00
60 Gregor Baumgartner .07 .20
61 Mathieu Benoit .07 .20
62 Pierre-Luc Therrien .07 .20
63 Danny LaVoie .07 .20
64 Mathieu Chouinard .07 .20
65 Andrew Carver .07 .20
66 Jiri Fischer .20 .50
67 Alexander Ryazantsev .07 .20
68 Didier Tremblay .07 .20
69 Mathieu Biron .07 .20
70 Michel Periard .07 .20
71 Mike Ribeiro .30 .75
72 Francois Fortier .07 .20
73 Benoit Dusablon .07 .20
74 Jerome Tremblay .07 .20
75 Samuel St.Pierre .07 .20
76 Marc-Andre Thinel .20 .50
77 Alexandre Tremblay .07 .20
78 Patrick Grandmaitre .07 .20
79 Christian Daigle .07 .20
80 David Thibeault .07 .20
81 Dominic Forget .07 .20
82 James Desmarais .07 .20
83 Pavel Brendl .20 .50
84 Kyle Calder .20 .50
85 Jason Chimera .20 .50
86 Chad Hinz .07 .20
87 Curtis Huppe .07 .20
88 Milan Kraft .20 .50
89 Brad Leeb .07 .20
90 Jamie Lundmark .20 .50
91 Brett Lysak .07 .20
92 Brad Moran .20 .50
93 Frantisek Mrazek .07 .20
94 Brad Twordik .07 .20
95 Kurt Drummond .07 .20
96 Burke Henry .07 .20
97 Steve McCarthy .20 .50
98 Richard Seeley .07 .20
99 Brad Stuart .30 .75
100 Luc Theoret .07 .20
101 Alexandre Fomitchev .07 .20
102 Brady Block .07 .20
103 Ajay Baines .07 .20
104 Blair Betts .20 .50
105 Tyler Bouck .20 .50
106 Mike Brown .07 .20
107 Bret DeCecco .07 .20
108 Scott Gomez .30 .75
109 Dylan Gyori .07 .20
110 Donnie Kinney .07 .20
111 Ken McKay .07 .20
112 Brett McLean .07 .20
113 Brenden Morrow .30 .75
114 Marty Standish .07 .20
115 Andrew Ference .20 .50
116 Brad Ference .07 .20
117 Scott Hannan .30 .75
118 Darrell Hay .07 .20
119 Robyn Regehr .30 .75
120 Chris St. Croix .07 .20
121 Kenric Exner .30 .75
122 Cody Rudkowsky .30 .75
123 Scott Barney .07 .20
124 Kevin Colley .07 .20
125 Sheldon Keefe .20 .50
126 Norman Milley .20 .50
127 Scott Page .07 .20
128 Justin Papineau .20 .50
129 Ryan Ready .07 .20
130 Denis Shvidki .20 .50
131 Chris Stanley .07 .20
132 Dan Tessier .07 .20
133 Daniel Tkaczuk .20 .50
134 Michael Zigomanis .20 .50
135 Jim Baxter .07 .20
136 Branislav Mezei .20 .50
137 Brian Campbell .07 .20
138 Greg Labenski .07 .20
139 Jeff McKercher .07 .20
140 Martin Skoula .20 .50
141 Brian Finley .30 .75
142 Seamus Kotyk .30 .75
143 Adam Colagiacomo .07 .20
144 Tim Connolly .20 .50
145 Harold Druken .20 .50
146 Rico Fata .20 .50
147 David Legwand .30 .75
148 Adam Mair .07 .20
149 Kent McDonell .20 .50
150 Ivan Novoseltsev .20 .50
151 Peter Sarno .20 .50
152 Dan Snyder .40 1.00
153 Jason Spezza 1.25 3.00
154 Jason Ward .07 .20
155 Alex Henry .07 .20
156 Wes Jarvis .07 .20
157 Paul Mara .07 .20
158 Kevin Mitchell .07 .20
159 Dan Passero .07 .20
160 Dan Watson .07 .20
161 Gene Chiarello .07 .20
162 Chris Madden .30 .75
163 M.Ouellet/B.DeCecco .07 .20
164 S.Barney/M.Thinel .07 .20
165 Checklist .07 .20

1999 Bowman CHL Gold

Randomly inserted in packs, this 165-card set parallels the base Bowman CHL set on cards enhanced with a "Bowman Gold" stamp on the card front. Each card is randomly inserted at a rate of one in eight packs and sequentially numbered to 99.

*STARS: 6X TO 15X BASIC CARDS

1999 Bowman CHL OPC International

Randomly seeded in packs, this 165-card set parallels the base Bowman CHL set on cards with enhanced backgrounds featuring a monument from the player's home province or country. Card backs contain relevant stats written in the featured player's native language.

COMPLETE SET (165) 50.00 100.00
*STARS: .75X TO 2X BASIC CARDS

1999 Bowman CHL Autographs

Randomly inserted in packs at the rate of 1:16, this 40-card set features authentic autographs coupled with action photography. Each card contains the gold foil "Bowman Certified Autograph" stamp in the upper right hand corner. Silver and gold variations were also created and inserted randomly. Silver autos were inserted at a rate of 1:43 and gold at 1:128. Note: Card #BA19, long thought not to exist, has been confirmed. We do not have any pricing information, however.

*SILVER: 1X TO 2X BASIC CARDS
*GOLD: 2.5X TO 5X BASIC CARDS
BA1 Brian Finley 4.00 10.00
BA2 Simon Lajeunesse 4.00 10.00
BA3 Barret Jackman 5.00 12.00
BA4 Edward Hill 2.00 5.00
BA5 Michael Zigomanis 4.00 10.00
BA6 Taylor Pyatt 4.00 10.00
BA7 Kristopher Beech 4.00 10.00
BA8 Justin Mapletoft 4.00 10.00
BA9 Jamie Lundmark 4.00 10.00
BA10 Charlie Stephens 2.00 5.00
BA11 Scott Cameron 2.00 5.00
BA12 Brad Ralph 2.00 5.00
BA13 Luke Sellars 2.00 5.00
BA14 Marc-Andre Thinel 4.00 10.00
BA15 Martin Grenier 4.00 10.00
BA16 Jonathan Fauteux 2.00 5.00
BA17 Denis Shvidki 2.00 5.00
BA18 Matt Carkner 2.00 5.00
BA19 Dusty Jamieson
BA20 Radim Vrbata 5.00 12.00
BA21 Alex Auld 6.00 15.00
BA22 Maxime Ouellet 4.00 10.00
BA23 Nolan Yonkman 2.00 5.00
BA24 Jeff Beatch 2.00 5.00
BA25 Pavel Brendl 4.00 10.00
BA26 Jamie Chamberlain 2.00 5.00
BA27 Kyle Wanvig 4.00 10.00
BA28 Chris Kelly 2.00 5.00
BA29 Scott Kelman 2.00 5.00
BA30 Derek MacKenzie 2.00 5.00
BA31 Tim Connolly 4.00 10.00
BA32 Alexandre Giroux 2.00 5.00
BA33 Oleg Saprykin 4.00 10.00
BA34 Sheldon Keefe 2.00 5.00
BA35 Branislav Mezei 2.00 5.00
BA36 Brett Lysak 4.00 10.00
BA37 Peter Reynolds 4.00 10.00
BA38 Ross Lupaschuk 2.00 5.00
BA39 Mirko Murovic 2.00 5.00
BA40 Steve McCarthy 2.00 5.00

1999 Bowman CHL Scout's Choice

Randomly inserted in packs at the rate of 1:12, this 21-card set features double-etched foil and identifies top ranked CHL players. Card backs carry an "SC" prefix.

SC1 Tim Connolly 1.25 3.00
SC2 Scott Kelman .75 2.00
SC3 Pavel Brendl .75 2.00
SC4 Maxime Ouellet 1.25 3.00
SC5 Brian Finley 1.25 3.00
SC6 Denis Shvidki .75 2.00
SC7 Michael Zigomanis .75 2.00
SC8 Taylor Pyatt .75 2.00
SC9 Kris Beech .75 2.00
SC10 Jamie Lundmark .75 2.00
SC11 Jason Spezza 2.00 5.00
SC12 Rico Fata .75 2.00
SC13 David Legwand 1.25 3.00
SC14 Daniel Tkaczuk .75 2.00
SC15 Brad Stuart .75 2.00
SC16 Jiri Fischer .75 2.00
SC17 Simon Gagne 1.50 4.00
SC18 Alex Tanguay 1.25 3.00
SC19 Scott Gomez .75 2.00

SC20 Ladislav Nagy .75 2.00
SC21 Roberto Luongo 1.50 4.00

1991 Classic

The set features 50 of the top 60 NHL draft picks. The set was issued in a run of 360,000 factory sets and included an individually numbered certificate of authenticity. The cards were issued in both English and French and carry the same value.

COMPLETE SET (50) 1.25 3.00
*FRENCH: SAME VALUE
1 Eric Lindros .60 1.50
2 Pat Falloon .02 .10
3 Scott Niedermayer
4 Scott Lachance .02 .10
5 Peter Forsberg .75 2.00
6 Alek Stojanov .02 .10
7 Richard Matvichuk .02 .10
8 Patrick Poulin .02 .10
9 Martin Lapointe .08 .25
10 Tyler Wright .02 .10
11 Philippe Boucher .02 .10
12 Pat Peake .02 .10
13 Markus Naslund
14 Brent Bilodeau .02 .10
15 Glen Murray
16 Niklas Sundblad .02 .10
17 Martin Rucinsky .08 .25
18 Trevor Halverson .02 .10
19 Dean McAmmond .02 .10
20 Ray Whitney .08 .25
21 Rene Corbet .02 .10
22 Eric Lavigne .02 .10
23 Zigmund Palffy .15 .40
24 Steve Staios .02 .10
25 Jim Campbell .02 .10
26 Jassen Cullimore .02 .10
27 Martin Hamrlik .02 .10
28 Jamie Pushor .02 .10
29 Donevan Hextall .02 .10
30 Andrew Verner .02 .10
31 Jason Dawe .02 .10
32 Jeff Nelson .02 .10
33 Darcy Werenka .02 .10
34 Jozef Stumpel .08 .25
35 Francois Groleau .02 .10
36 Guy Leveque .02 .10
37 Jamie Matthews .02 .10
38 Dody Wood .02 .10
39 Yanic Perreault .08 .25
40 Jamie McLennan .08 .25
41 Yanic Dupre UER .02 .10
42 Sandy McCarthy .08 .25
43 Chris Osgood .20 .50
44 Fredrik Lindquist .02 .10
45 Jason Young .02 .10
46 Steve Konowalchuk .08 .25
47 Michael Nylander UER .08 .25
48 Shane Peacock .02 .10
49 Yves Sarault .02 .10
50 Marcel Cousineau .08 .25
NNO Patrick Poulin AU/1100 .75 2.00
NNO Rocket Ismail .08 .25

1991 Classic Promos

The two standard size promo cards were issued by Classic to show collectors and dealers the style of their new hockey draft picks set.

COMPLETE SET (2) 1.20 3.00
1 Eric Lindros 1.25 3.00
2 Pat Falloon .08 .25

1992 Classic

The 1992 Classic Hockey Draft Picks set consists of 120 standard-size cards. The production run for the regular issue cards was reportedly 9,966 ten-box cases. Classic also issued the 1992 Draft Pick set in a Gold version. The Gold factory sets were packaged in a walnut display case. The Gold sets also included an individually numbered card signed by Valeri and Pavel Bure. The set included the first card of female goaltender Manon Rheaume.

COMPLETE SET (120) 5.00 10.00
1 Roman Hamrlik .02 .10
2 Alexei Yashin .02 .10
3 Mike Rathje .02 .10
4 Darius Kasparaitis .02 .10
5 Cory Stillman .02 .10
6 Robert Petrovicky .02 .10
7 Andrei Nazarov .02 .10
8 Cory Stillman CL .02 .10
9 Jason Bowen .02 .10
10 Jason Smith .02 .10
11 David Wilkie .02 .10
12 Curtis Bowen .02 .10
13 Grant Marshall .02 .10
14 Valeri Bure .10 .30
15 Jeff Shantz .02 .10
16 Justin Hocking .02 .10
17 Mike Peca .20 .50
18 Marc Hussey .02 .10
19 Sandy Allan .10 .30
20 Kirk Maltby .10 .30
21 Cale Hulse .02 .10
22 Sylvain Cloutier .10 .30
23 Martin Gendron .02 .10
24 Kevin Smyth .02 .10
25 Jason McBain .02 .10
26 Lee J. Leslie .02 .10
27 Ralph Intranuovo .02 .10
28 Martin Reichel .02 .10
29 Stefan Ustorf .02 .10
30 Jarkko Varvio .02 .10
31 Jere Lehtinen .15 .40
32 Janne Gronvall .02 .10
33 Martin Straka .15 .40
34 Libor Polasek .02 .10
35 Jozef Cierny .02 .10
36 Jan Vopat .02 .10
37 Ondrej Steiner .02 .10
38 Jan Caloun .02 .10
39 Petr Hrbek .02 .10
40 Richard Smehlik .02 .10
41 Sergei Gonchar CL .02 .10
42 Sergei Krivokrasov .02 .10
43 Sergei Gonchar .10 .30
44 Boris Mironov .02 .10
45 Denis Metlyuk .02 .10
46 Sergei Klimovich .02 .10
47 Sergei Brylin .02 .10
48 Andrei Nikolishin .02 .10
49 Alexander Cherbayev .02 .10
50 Sergei Zholtok .02 .10
51 Vitali Prokhorov .02 .10
52 Nikolai Borschevsky .02 .10
53 Vitali Tomilin .02 .10
54 Alexander Alexeyev .02 .10
55 Roman Zolotov .02 .10
56 Konstantin Korotkov .02 .10
57 Laperriere Family .02 .10
58 Lacroix Family .02 .10
59 Manon Rheaume 1.50 4.00
60 Hamrlik/Yashin/Rathje CL .02 .10
61 Viktor Kozlov CL .02 .10
62 Viktor Kozlov .10 .30
63 Denny Felsner CL .02 .10
64 Denny Felsner .02 .10
65 Darrin Madeley .02 .10
66 Mario Lemieux FLB .60 1.50
67 Sandy Moger .02 .10
68 Dave Karpa .02 .10
69 Martin Jiranek .02 .10
70 Dwayne Norris .02 .10
71 Michael Stewart .02 .10
72 Joby Messier .02 .10
73 Mike Bales .10 .30
74 Scott Thomas .02 .10
75 Dan Laperriere .02 .10
76 Mike Lappin .02 .10
77 Eric Lacroix .02 .10
78 Martin Lacroix .02 .10
79 Scott LaGrand .02 .10
80 Jean-Yves Roy .02 .10
81 Scott Pellerin .02 .10
82 Rob Gaudreau .02 .10
83 Mike Boback .02 .10
84 Dixon Ward .02 .10
85 Jeff McLean .02 .10
86 Dallas Drake .02 .10
87 Bret Hedican .02 .10
88 Doug Zmolek .02 .10
89 Trent Klatt .02 .10
90 Larry Olimb .02 .10
91 Duane Derksen .10 .30
92 Doug MacDonald .02 .10
93 Dmitri Kvartalnov CL .02 .10
94 Jim Cummins .02 .10
95 Lonnie Loach .02 .10
96 Keith Jones .02 .10
97 Jason Woolley .02 .10
98 Rob Zamuner .10 .30
99 Brad Werenka .02 .10
100 Brent Grieve .02 .10
101 Sean Hill .10 .30
102 Keith Carney .02 .10
103 Peter Ciavaglia .02 .10
104 David Littman .10 .30
105 Bill Guerin .25 .60
106 Mikhail Kravets .02 .10
107 J.F. Quintin .02 .10
108 Mike Needham .02 .10
109 Jason Ruff .02 .10
110 Mike Vukonich .02 .10
111 Shawn McCosh .02 .10
112 Dave Tretowicz .02 .10
113 Todd Harkins .02 .10
114 Jason Muzzatti .02 .10
115 Paul Kruse .02 .10
116 Kevin Wortman .02 .10
117 Sean Burke .10 .30
118 Keith Gretzky .02 .10
119 Ray Whitney .10 .30
120 Dmitri Kvartalnov .02 .10
SP Mario Lemieux FLB 2.00 5.00
AU1 M.Lemieux AU/2000 40.00 80.00
AU2 Bure Brothers AU/6000 10.00 20.00

1992 Classic Gold

Classic also issued the 1992 Draft Picks set in a Gold version. The singles sell for between three and eight times the corresponding regular cards. Reportedly only 6,000 sets and 7,500 uncut sheets were produced. The sets were packaged in a walnut display case. The Gold factory sets also included an individually numbered card signed by Valeri and Pavel Bure.

*GOLD STARS: 1.5X TO 4X BASIC CARDS

1992 Classic Autographs

COMPLETE SET (?)
NNO David Wilkie 2.00 5.00
NNO Petr Hrbek 2.00 5.00
NNO Jeff McLean 2.00 5.00

1992 Classic Gold Promo

The front features a black-and-white action player photo bordered in white. The player's name is printed in a gold foil stripe beneath the picture, with the position given on a short black bar. On a gold background, the back has draft information, statistics, player profile, and a second black-and-white photo that is horizontally oriented. The card is unnumbered and has the disclaimer "For Promotional Purposes Only" printed on the back.

NNO Mario Lemieux 3.00 8.00

1992 Classic LPs

This ten-card standard-size set features hockey draft picks. The cards are numbered on the back with an "LP" prefix. The cards were random inserts in packs of 1992 Classic Hockey Draft Picks.

COMPLETE SET (10) 2.50 6.00
LP1 Roman Hamrlik .20 .50
LP2 Alexei Yashin .20 .50
LP3 Mike Rathje .20 .50
LP4 Darius Kasparaitis .20 .50
LP5 Cory Stillman .20 .50
LP6 Dmitri Kvartalnov .20 .50
LP7 David Wilkie .20 .50
LP8 Curtis Bowen .20 .50
LP9 Valeri Bure .40 1.00
LP10 Joby Messier .20 .50

1992 Classic Promos

These three cards measure the standard size and feature color action player photos with white borders, except for the Lemieux card, which has a black and white picture with the words "Flash Back 92" printed at the top. The player's name is printed in a gold stripe at the bottom, which intersects the Classic logo at the lower left corner. The gold backs have horizontally oriented player photos, again the Lemieux being black and white and the others color. The text on the back is vertically oriented, except for the biography, and includes draft information, career highlights, and the words "For Promotional Purposes Only". The cards are unnumbered and checklisted below in alphabetical order.

COMPLETE SET (3) 3.00 8.00
1 Roman Hamrlik 1.25 3.00
2 Mario Lemieux 2.00 5.00
(Flash Back 92)
3 Ray Whitney .40 1.00

1992-93 Classic Manon Rheaume C3 Presidential

This standard-size card pictures Rheaume holding a hockey stick and carrying an equipment bag over her shoulder. The picture is bordered in white, and her name and position are printed on the wider right border. The Classic "C3 Presidential" logo is gold foil stamped across the top of the picture. The back has a color close-up photo and a player quote. Reportedly only 5,000 of these cards were produced.

1 Manon Rheaume 4.00 10.00

1992-93 Classic Manon Rheaume Promo

Manon Rheaume, professional hockey's first female player, signed her trading card for fans before the Atlanta Braves playoff game Wednesday, October 7, 1992. Sponsored by Power 99, a local radio station, this promotion was aimed at benefiting "Pennies from Heaven," an urban renewal movement championed by former President Jimmy Carter and Atlanta Braves third baseman Terry Pendleton. Fans who brought a jar of pennies or a 10.00 donation were given the autographed Rheaume promotional card; close to 1,000 cards were signed and about 2,500 promo bags were given away. The front of this standard size card features a posed color player photo with white borders. Her name appears in a gold stripe across the bottom of the picture. The words "A Classic First" are printed in gold at the upper right corner of the picture. The center back shows the yellow and green Classic logo. The disclaimer "For Promotional Purposes Only" is printed in black at the top and bottom and in gray over the rest of the card back.

NNO Manon Rheaume 4.00 10.00

1993 Classic

The 1993 Classic Hockey Draft set consists of 150 standard-size cards. Production was reported to be 14,500 sequentially-numbered ten-box cases. More than 15,000 autographed cards from Manon Rheaume, Doug Gilmour, Mark Recchi, Mike Bossy, Jeff O'Neill and other hockey stars were randomly inserted throughout the packs. Subsets featuring foil-stamped cards are Top 10, The Class of '94, The Daigle File, Flashbacks, College Champions, Manon Rheaume, and Hockey Art.

COMPLETE SET (150) 4.00 10.00
1 Alexandre Daigle .02 .10
2 Chris Pronger .20 .50
3 Chris Gratton .08 .25
4 Paul Kariya .40 1.00
5 Rob Niedermayer .02 .10
6 Viktor Kozlov .08 .25
7 Jason Arnott .20 .50
8 Niklas Sundstrom .02 .10
9 Todd Harvey .02 .10
10 Jocelyn Thibault .20 .50
11 Checklist 1 .02 .10
Top Draft Picks
12 Pat Peake .02 .10
1993 CHL POY
13 Jason Allison .25 .60
14 Todd Bertuzzi .20 .50
15 Maxim Bets .02 .10
16 Curtis Bowen .02 .10
17 Kevin Brown .02 .10
18 Valeri Bure .08 .25
19 Jason Dawe .02 .10
20 Adam Deadmarsh .20 .50
21 Aaron Gavey .02 .10
22 Nathan Lafayette .02 .10
23 Eric Lecompte .02 .10
24 Manny Legace .20 .50
25 Mike Peca .20 .50
26 Denis Pederson .02 .10
27 Jeff Shantz .02 .10
28 Nick Stadjuhar .02 .10
29 Cory Stillman .02 .10
30 Michal Sykora .02 .10
31 Brent Tully .02 .10
32 Mike Wilson .02 .10
33 Junior Production Line .02 .10
Kevin Brown
Pat Peake
Bob Wren
34 Checklist 2 .02 .10
Dynamic Duo
Alexandre Daigle
Alexei Yashin
35 Antti Aalto .02 .10
36 Radim Bicanek .02 .10
37 Vladimir Chebaturkin .02 .10
38 Alexander Cherbayev .02 .10
39 Markus Ketterer .02 .10
40 Saku Koivu .20 .50
41 Vladimir Kretchine .02 .10
42 Alexei Kudashov .02 .10
43 Janne Laukkanen .02 .10
44 Janne Niinimaa .02 .10
45 Juha Riihijarvi .02 .10
46 Nikolai Tsulygin .02 .10
47 Vesa Viitakoski .02 .10
48 David Vyborny .02 .10
49 Nikolai Zavarukhin .02 .10
50 Alexandre Daigle .02 .10
1991 QMJHL Draft
51 Alexandre Daigle .02 .10
1991-92 QMJHL Rookie
52 Alexandre Daigle .02 .10
1992 CHL ROY
53 Alexandre Daigle .02 .10
Emerging Superstar
1992-93
54 Alexandre Daigle .02 .10
First Draft Pick
55 Jim Montgomery .02 .10
56 Mike Dunham .02 .10
57 Matt Martin .02 .10
58 Garth Snow .08 .25
59 Shawn Walsh .02 .10
60 Mark Bavis .02 .10
Mike Davis
61 Scott Chartier .02 .10
62 Craig Darby .02 .10
63 Ted Drury .02 .10
64 Steve Dubinsky .02 .10
65 Joe Frederick .02 .10
66 Cammi Granato .20 .50
67 Brett Hauer .02 .10
68 Jon Hillebrandt .02 .10
69 Ryan Hughes .02 .10
70 Dean Hulett .02 .10
71 Kevin O'Sullivan .02 .10
72 Dan Plante .02 .10
73 Derek Plante .02 .10
74 Travis Richards .02 .10
75 Barry Richter .02 .10
76 David Roberts .02 .10
77 Chris Rogles .02 .10
78 Jon Rohloff .02 .10
79 Brian Rolston .02 .10
80 David Sacco .02 .10
81 Brian Savage .08 .25
82 Mike Smith .02 .10
83 Chris Tamer .02 .10
84 Chris Therien .02 .10
85 Aaron Ward .02 .10
86 Russian Celebration .02 .10
87 Vyacheslav Butsayev .02 .10
88 Jan Kaminsky .02 .10
89 Alexander Karpovtsev .02 .10
90 Valeri Karpov .02 .10
91 Sergei Petrenko .02 .10
92 Andrei Sapozhnikov .02 .10
93 Sergei Sorokin .02 .10
94 German Titov .02 .10
95 Andrei Trefilov .02 .10
96 Alexei Yashin .02 .10
97 Dimitri Yushkevich .02 .10
98 Radek Bonk .02 .10
99 Jason Bonsignore .02 .10
100 Brad Brown .02 .10
101 Chris Drury .40 1.00
102 Jeff Friesen .02 .10
103 Sean Haggerty .02 .10
104 Jeff Kealty .02 .10
105 Alexander Kharlamov .02 .10
106 Stanislav Neckar .02 .10
107 Tom O'Connor .02 .10
108 Jeff O'Neill .20 .50
109 Deron Quint .02 .10
110 Vadim Sharifianov .02 .10
111 Oleg Tverdovsky .08 .25
112 Manon Rheaume COMIC .30 .75
113 Paul Kariya COMIC .20 .50
114 Alexandre Daigle COMIC .02 .10
115 Jeff O'Neill COMIC .02 .10
116 Mike Bossy .20 .50
117 Pavel Bure .20 .50
118 Chris Chelios .20 .50
119 Doug Gilmour .08 .25
120 Roman Hamrlik .08 .25
121 Jari Kurri .20 .50
122 Alexander Mogilny .08 .25
123 Felix Potvin .20 .50
124 Teemu Selanne .40 1.00
125 Tommy Soderstrom .08 .25
126 Mike Bales .02 .10
127 Jozef Cierny .02 .10
128 Ivan Droppa .02 .10
129 Anders Eriksson .02 .10
130 Anatoli Fedotov .02 .10
131 Martin Gendron .02 .10
132 Daniel Guerard .02 .10
133 Corey Hirsch .02 .10
134 Milos Holan .02 .10
135 Kenny Jonsson .02 .10
136 Steven King .02 .10
137 Alexei Kovalev .20 .50
138 Sergei Krivokrasov .02 .10
139 Mats Lindgren .02 .10
140 Grant Marshall .02 .10
141 Jesper Mattsson .02 .10
142 Sandy McCarthy .02 .10
143 Dean Melanson .02 .10
144 Robert Petrovicky .02 .10
145 Mike Rathje .02 .10
146 Manon Rheaume .40 1.00
147 Claude Savoie .02 .10
148 Mikhail Shtalenkov .08 .25
149 Manon Rheaume .40 1.00
A Season To Remember
150 Manon Rheaume .40 1.00
Up Close And Personal
MR1 Manon Rheaume Acetate 10.00 25.00

1993 Classic Autographs

AU1 Mike Bossy AU/975 12.50 30.00
AU2 Pavel Bure AU/900 20.00 50.00
AU3 Chris Chelios AU/1800 15.00 40.00
AU4 Doug Gilmour AU/1850 15.00 40.00
AU5 Alexander Mogilny/950 12.50 30.00
AU6 Jim Montgomery AU/1800 2.00 5.00
AU7 Rob Niedermayer AU/2500 12.50 30.00
AU8 Jeff O'Neill AU/2225 8.00 20.00
AU9 Pat Peake AU/790 2.00 5.00
AU10 Mark Recchi AU/1725 12.00 30.00
AU11 Manon Rheaume AU/1500 20.00 50.00
AU12 Geoff Sanderson AU/875 2.00 5.00

1993 Classic Class of '94

These standard size cards were randomly inserted throughout the foil packs. The cards are acetates and the player's last name is in capital letters in the clear potion. The fronts also have a color action photo of the player. The backs have player statistics. The cards are numbered on the back with a "CL" prefix.

COMPLETE SET (7) 3.00 8.00
CL1 Jeff O'Neill .60 1.50
CL2 Jason Bonsignore .40 1.00
CL3 Jeff Friesen .40 1.00
CL4 Radek Bonk .40 1.00
CL5 Deron Quint .40 1.00
CL6 Vadim Sharifianov .40 1.00
CL7 Tom O'Connor .40 1.00

1993 Classic Crash Numbered

This 10-card standard-size set was randomly inserted throughout the foil packs and 15,000 individually numbered copies were made of each. The fronts have a color action photo with the player's name at the bottom in the icy border. The backs have a color photo on the right-side and player information and statistics on the left. The cards are numbered on the back with a "N" prefix.

COMPLETE SET (10) 30.00 80.00
N1 Alexandre Daigle 2.00 5.00
N2 Paul Kariya 6.00 15.00
N3 Jeff O'Neill 1.25 3.00
N4 Jason Bonsignore 2.00 5.00
N5 Teemu Selanne 6.00 15.00
N6 Pavel Bure 2.00 5.00
N7 Alexander Mogilny 2.00 5.00
N8 Manon Rheaume 5.00 12.00
N9 Felix Potvin 2.00 5.00
N10 Radek Bonk 1.25 3.00

1993 Classic Manon Rheaume Promo

This standard-size promo card features then-Atlanta Knights goaltender, Manon Rheaume. Inside a light gray border, the fronts features Rheaume in a sleeveless white blouse. The horizontal back has player information on the left and a second picture on the right with Rheaume dressed in black. The disclaimer "For Promotional Purposes Only" appears on the left beneath the text. The card is unnumbered.

NNO Manon Rheaume 2.00 5.00
Up Close and Personal

1993 Classic Previews

These five standard-size cards were inserted on an average of three per case of 1993 Classic Basketball Draft Picks. The fronts have a color action photo with the player's name at the bottom in the icy border. The backs say "preview" and tells that it is one of 17,500 preview cards of that player. The cards are unnumbered.

COMPLETE SET (5) 2.00 5.00
HK1 Alexandre Daigle .20 .50
HK2 Manon Rheaume 1.50 4.00
HK3 Barry Richter .20 .50
HK4 Teemu Selanne .75 2.00
HK5 Alexei Yashin .20 .50

1993 Classic Promos

These four standard-size promo cards feature gray-bordered glossy color player action shots on the fronts. The player's name and position appears in blue lettering within the bottom border. The back carries another color player action shot, but bordered in white. The player's biography and draft status are printed in black lettering within the broad lower border. The unnumbered Paul Kariya card was distributed at the San Francisco Labor Day Sports Collectors Convention, held in September 1993. The cards are numbered on the back with a "PR" prefix.

COMPLETE SET (4) 8.00 20.00
1 Alexandre Daigle 2.00 5.00
2 Jeff O'Neill 2.00 5.00
Jason Bonsignore
Jeff Friesen
The Class of '94
3 Pavel Bure 2.00 5.00
NNO Paul Kariya 2.00 5.00

1993 Classic Team Canada

This seven-card standard size set was randomly inserted throughout the foil packs. These acetate cards have a color action photo on the left clear portion with player name at the bottom. The right-side has a letter so the complete set spells Canada. The backs have the player's name and statistics. The cards are numbered on the back with a "TC" prefix.

COMPLETE SET (7) 7.50 15.00
TC1 Greg Johnson .75 2.00
TC2 Paul Kariya 2.00 5.00
TC3 Brian Savage .75 2.00
TC4 Bill Ranford .75 2.00
TC5 Mark Recchi .75 2.00
TC6 Geoff Sanderson .75 2.00
IC7 Adam Graves .75 2.00

1993 Classic Top Ten

Measuring the standard-size, these ten acetate cards were randomly inserted throughout the foil packs. The cards have a color action photo, visible on both sides. the backs also have player statistics. The cards are numbered on the back with a "DP" prefix.

COMPLETE SET (10) 10.00 20.00
DP1 Alexandre Daigle .40 1.00
DP2 Chris Pronger 1.00 2.50
DP3 Chris Gratton .40 1.00
DP4 Paul Kariya 2.00 5.00
DP5 Rob Niedermayer .40 1.00
DP6 Viktor Kozlov .40 1.00
DP7 Jason Arnott .40 1.00
DP8 Niklas Sundstrom .40 1.00
DP9 Todd Harvey .40 1.00
DP10 Jocelyn Thibault 1.00 2.50

1994 Classic

The 1994 Classic Hockey set consists of 120 standard-size cards. Production was reported at 6,000 U.S. and 2,000 Canadian 10-box foil cases. The Jason Arnott Canada World Champs card (numbered TC1) was randomly inserted into Canadian packs. Classic also offered a redemption program in which a collector sending in wrappers received various prizes. For each 216 wrappers redeemed a collector received either a Cam Neely or a Doug Gilmour autographed card. For each 360 wrappers redeemed, a Manon Rheaume autograph card was sent by Classic.

COMPLETE SET (120) 4.00 10.00
1 Ed Jovanovski .02 .10
2 Oleg Tverdovsky .01 .05
3 Radek Bonk .01 .05
4 Jason Bonsignore .01 .05
5 Jeff O'Neill .01 .05
6 Ryan Smyth .08 .25
7 Jamie Storr .02 .10
8 Jason Wiemer .01 .05
9 Nolan Baumgartner .01 .05
10 Jeff Friesen .01 .05
11 Wade Belak .01 .05
12 Ethan Moreau .02 .10
13 Alexander Kharlamov .01 .05
14 Eric Fichaud .02 .10
15 Wayne Primeau .01 .05
16 Brad Brown .01 .05
17 Chris Dingman .01 .05
18 Evgeni Ryabchikov .01 .05
19 Yan Golubovsky .01 .05
20 Chris Wells .01 .05
21 Vadim Sharifjanov .01 .05
22 Dan Cloutier .08 .25
23 Checklist .01 .05
24 Jamie Langenbrunner .01 .05
25 Kenny Jonsson .01 .05
26 Curtis Bowen .01 .05
27 Sergei Gonchar .02 .10
28 Stefan Bergqvist .01 .05
29 Vaclav Prospal .01 .05
30 Valeri Bure .01 .05
31 Richard Shulmistra .01 .05
32 Chris Armstrong .01 .05
33 Brian Farrell .01 .05
34 Brian Savage .02 .10
35 Blaine Lacher .01 .05
36 Kevin Brown .01 .05
37 Joe Dziedzic .01 .05
38 Peter Ferraro .01 .05
39 Chris Ferraro .01 .05
40 Todd Harvey .02 .10
41 Eric Lecompte .01 .05
42 Dean Grillo .01 .05
43 Valeri Karpov .01 .05
44 Andrew Shier .01 .05
45 Vesa Viitakoski .01 .05
46 Xavier Majic .01 .05
47 Kevin Smyth .01 .05
48 Jeff Nelson .01 .05
49 Cory Stillman .01 .05
50 Clayton Beddoes .01 .05
51 Craig Conroy .01 .05
52 Dean Fedorchuk .01 .05
53 John Gruden .01 .05
54 Chris McAlpine .01 .05
55 Sean McCann .01 .05
56 Derek Maguire .01 .05
57 David Oliver .01 .05
58 Mike Pomichter .01 .05
59 Jamie Ram .01 .05
60 Shawn Reid .01 .05
61 Dwayne Roloson .01 .05
62 Steve Shields .08 .25
63 Brian Wiseman .01 .05
64 Drew Bannister .01 .05
65 Matt Johnson .01 .05
66 Scott Malone .01 .05
67 Sergei Berezin .01 .05
68 Chad Penney .01 .05
69 Ian Laperriere .01 .05
70 Andrei Nikolishin .01 .05
71 Kelly Fairchild .01 .05
72 Jere Lehtinen .08 .25
73 Ravil Gusmanov .01 .05
74 Checklist .01 .05
75 Neil Little .01 .05
76 Brian Rolston .02 .10
77 David Vyborny .01 .05
78 Nikolai Tsulygin .01 .05
79 Niklas Sundstrom .01 .05
80 Patrik Juhlin .01 .05
81 Dan Plante .01 .05
82 Brandon Convery .01 .05
83 Nick Stajduhar .01 .05
84 Garth Snow .02 .10
85 Corey Hirsch .02 .10
86 Craig Darby .01 .05
87 Andrei Nazarov .01 .05
88 Todd Marchant .01 .05
89 Jeff Neilson .01 .05
90 Brendan Witt .01 .05
91 Denis Metlyuk .01 .05
92 Maxim Bets .01 .05
93 Sean Pronger .01 .05
94 Chris Tamer .01 .05
95 Saku Koivu .08 .25
96 Mattias Norstrom .02 .10
97 Ville Peltonen .02 .10
98 Rene Corbet .01 .05
99 Brent Gretzky .01 .05
100 Chris Marinucci .01 .05
101 Ian Moran .01 .05
102 Janne Laukkanen .01 .05
103 Todd Bertuzzi .08 .25
104 Darby Hendrickson .01 .05
105 Janne Niinimaa .01 .05
106 David Roberts .01 .05
107 Pat Neaton .01 .05
108 Mats Lindgren .01 .05
109 Todd Warriner .01 .05
110 Jason Allison .08 .25
111 Radim Bicanek .01 .05
112 Denis Pederson .02 .10
113 Viktor Kozlov .02 .10
114 Mike Murray .01 .05
115 Aaron Gavey .01 .05
116 Mike Peca .08 .25
117 Jason Zent .01 .05
118 Jason MacDonald .01 .05
119 Aaron Israel .01 .05
120 Manon Rheaume .60 1.50
TC1 Jason Arnott CWC .75 2.00
AU1 Doug Gilmour AU 8.00 20.00
AU2 Cam Neely AU 12.50 30.00
AU3 Manon Rheaume AU 12.50 30.00

1994 Classic Gold

Each of the 120 regular issue cards was issued as a parallel set with a gold-foil stamp and inserted at a rate of one gold card per pack. The card design is identical to the regular issue, except that the city name is printed in gold-foil stamped letters. In addition, collectors could acquire gold cards by mail. If Classic received either 36 or 54 wrappers in their redemption program from any collector, the collector received 10 gold cards. If a collector mailed in 108 wrappers, there were 25 gold cards sent from Classic. Also, a complete gold factory set was available to collectors who redeemed the Field card from the "Rookie of the Year?" insert set/contest.

*STARS: 1.25X TO 3X BASIC CARDS

1994 Classic All-Americans

Found only in U.S. cases and inserted at a rate of one card per box, this ten-card standard-size set spotlights first team NCAA All-Americans. The cards are serially numbered out of 6,000 on the back.

COMPLETE SET (10) 3.00 8.00
AA1 Craig Conroy .40 1.00
AA2 John Gruden .40 1.00
AA3 Chris Marinucci .40 1.00
AA4 Chris McAlpine .40 1.00
AA5 Sean McCann .40 1.00
AA6 David Oliver .40 1.00
AA7 Mike Pomichter .40 1.00
AA8 Jamie Ram .40 1.00
AA9 Shawn Reid .40 1.00
AA10 Dwayne Roloson .75 2.00

1994 Classic All-Rookie Team

Inserted in both U.S. and Canadian cases at a rate of one card per box. Each card is serially numbered out of 13,500.

COMPLETE SET (6) 4.00 10.00
AR1 Martin Brodeur 4.00 10.00
AR2 Jason Arnott .20 .50
AR3 Alexei Yashin .20 .50
AR4 Oleg Petrov .08 .25
AR5 Chris Pronger .75 2.00
AR6 Alexander Karpovtsev .08 .25

1994 Classic Autographs

Inserted at a rate of one card per box, this 36-card set measures the standard size. The backs carry a congratulatory message which serves to authenticate the signature. The autograph cards that correspond to the regular draft cards are listed in numerical order while those autograph cards not in the regular set are listed in alphabetical order. In addition to the insertion of one per box, these cards were redeemable on a random basis in exchange for sending 72 wrappers to Classic.

3 Radek Bonk/4940 1.50 4.00
4 Jason Bonsignore/4300 .75 2.00
5 Jeff O'Neill/5380 1.50 4.00
10 Jeff Friesen/6145 4.00 10.00
34 Brian Savage/4930 1.50 4.00
38 Peter Ferraro/4875 .75 2.00
39 Chris Ferraro/4770 .75 2.00
76 Brian Rolston/2400 1.50 4.00
86 Craig Darby/1915 .75 2.00
94 Chris Tamer/1900 .75 2.00
106 David Roberts/1970 .75 2.00
NNO Chris Rogles/1920 .75 2.00
NNO Ryan Hughes/1940 .75 2.00
NNO Travis Richards/1950 .75 2.00
NNO Chris Gratton/2000 6.00 15.00
NNO Derek Plante/1970 1.50 4.00
NNO Cam Stewart/970 .75 2.00
NNO Chris Marinucci .75 2.00
NNO Brett Harkins/1885 .75 2.00
NNO Scott Chartier/1930 .75 2.00
NNO Rob Niedermayer/950 8.00 20.00
NNO Doug Gilmour/1950 15.00 30.00
NNO Fred Knipscheer/1945 .75 2.00
NNO Ted Drury/1920 .75 2.00
NNO Mike Dunham/1955 4.00 10.00
NNO Mike Bavis/1955 4.00 10.00
NNO Jon Hillebrandt/1570 .75 2.00
NNO Brett Hauer/1930 .75 2.00
NNO Stanislav Neckar/4645 .75 2.00
NNO Manon Rheaume/2400 15.00 40.00
NNO Dan Plante .75 2.00
NNO Jim Storm/1950 .75 2.00

NNO David Sacco/1975 .75 2.00
NNO Dean Hulett/1955 .75 2.00
NNO Aaron Ward/1965 .75 2.00
NNO Dallas Drake/960 .75 2.00
NNO John Lilley/2460 .75 2.00
NNO Jon Rohloff/2010 .75 2.00
NNO Barry Richter/1935 .75 2.00
NNO Eric Fenton/1845 .75 2.00

1994 Classic CHL All-Stars

This 10-card standard-size set was randomly inserted in Canadian foil packs only. The fronts have a color action photo with the player's name at the top along with the CHL emblem. The backs have a full-color action photo with player information and the number printed out of 2,000. The cards are numbered on the back with a "C" prefix.

COMPLETE SET (10) 7.50 20.00
C1 Jason Allison 1.25 3.00
C2 Yanick Dube .40 1.00
C3 Eric Fichaud .75 2.00
C4 Jeff Friesen .40 1.00
C5 Aaron Gavey .40 1.00
C6 Ed Jovanovski .75 2.00
C7 Jeff O'Neill 1.25 3.00
C8 Ryan Smyth 1.25 3.00
C9 Jamie Storr .75 2.00
C10 Brendan Witt .40 1.00

1994 Classic CHL Previews

Randomly inserted in Canadian foil packs only, this six-card standard-size set was created to preview Classic's 1995 CHL set. Unfortunately, the company was unable to complete negotiations with the league, and the full set was never created.

COMPLETE SET (6) 15.00 25.00
CP1 Wayne Primeau 1.25 3.00
CP2 Eric Fichaud 2.50 6.00
CP3 Wade Redden 2.50 5.00
CP4 Jason Doig 1.25 3.00
CP5 Vitali Yachmenev 1.25 3.00
CP6 Nolan Baumgartner 1.25 3.00

1994 Classic Draft Day

Issued in a ten-card cello pack, these cards were issued on the occasion of the NHL draft, which took place on June 28-29, 1994. The cards measure the standard size, and were available through a wrapper redemption offer. The fronts feature borderless color action player photos; the player's name is printed in a bar at the bottom that intersects the Classic logo at the lower left corner. The city (or state) of the teams that were likely to draft the player is printed vertically in block lettering along the right edge. The backs carry the "Draft Day 94" logo superimposed over a color painting of a hockey player. A tagline at the bottom rounds out the back and gives the production figures "1 of 10,000". The cards are unnumbered and checklisted below in alphabetical order.

COMPLETE SET (10) 12.50 30.00
1 Radek Bonk 1.50 4.00
Anaheim Mighty Ducks
2 Radek Bonk 1.50 4.00
Florida Panthers
3 Radek Bonk 1.50 4.00
Ottawa Senators
4 Jason Bonsignore 1.50 4.00
Edmonton Oilers
5 Ed Jovanovski 1.50 4.00
Anaheim Mighty Ducks
6 Ed Jovanovski 1.50 4.00
Florida Panthers
7 Ed Jovanovski 1.50 4.00
Ottawa Senators
8 Jeff O'Neill 1.50 4.00
Anaheim Mighty Ducks
9 Jeff O'Neill 1.50 4.00
Florida Panthers
10 Jeff O'Neill 1.50 4.00
Ottawa Senators

1994 Classic Draft Prospects

Found only in U.S. cases and inserted at a rate of one card per box, this ten-card standard-size set features players expected to be selected early in the 1995 NHL entry draft. The fronts feature the player's name in capital letters on the top with a small notation underneath that he is a 1995 Draft Prospect. The majority of the card is devoted to the player's photo. The reverse of the card features the player's photo on the left side of the cards with a biography on the right side. The cards are numbered in the top left corner. Each card is serially numbered out of 6,000 on the bottom.

COMPLETE SET (10) 5.00 12.00
DP1 Bubba Berenzweig .40 1.00
DP2 Aki Berg .40 1.00
DP3 Chad Kilger .40 1.00
DP4 Daymond Langkow .75 2.00
DP5 Alyn McCauley .75 2.00
DP6 Igor Melyakov .40 1.00
DP7 Erik Rasmussen .40 1.00
DP8 Marty Reasoner .75 2.00
DP9 Scott Roche .75 2.00
DP10 Petr Sykora 2.00 5.00

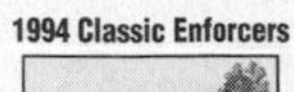

1994 Classic Enforcers

Featured in both U.S. and Canadian cases and inserted on average of three cards per box, this ten-card standard-size set captures the toughest players in the minor leagues. The horizontal fronts feature color action player photos with the player's name in a black bar at the bottom. The set name also appears at the bottom. On a background consisting of a crude drawing of the front photo, the back carries a player profile.

COMPLETE SET (10) 7.50 15.00
E1 Donald Brashear 1.25 3.00
E2 Daniel Lacroix .60 1.50
E3 Dale Henry .60 1.50
E4 John Badduke .60 1.50
E5 Corey Schwab 1.25 3.00
E6 Craig Martin .60 1.50
E7 Kerry Clark .60 1.50
E8 Kevin Kaminski .60 1.50
E9 Jim Kyte .60 1.50
E10 Mark DeSantis .60 1.50

1994 Classic Enforcers Promo

This standard-size card was issued to promote the 1994 Classic hockey series. The horizontal front features Richard Zemlak preparing to fight another player. On a background consisting of a crude drawing of the front photo, the back presents an advertisement for Classic hockey cards. The card is numbered on the back in the upper right corner.

PR1 Richard Zemlak .40 1.00

1994 Classic Picks

This five-card standard-size set was randomly inserted in packs. The fronts feature color action photos with the player's name and the Classic logo at the bottom. The backs carry the player's name in the upper left, card number in the upper right, career and biographical information, logos, and a small color player photo.

COMPLETE SET (5) 6.00 15.00
CP11 Ed Jovanovski 2.00 5.00
CP12 Oleg Tverdovsky .75 2.00
CP13 Radek Bonk .75 2.00
CP14 Jason Allison 2.00 5.00
CP15 Manon Rheaume 2.00 5.00

1994 Classic Previews

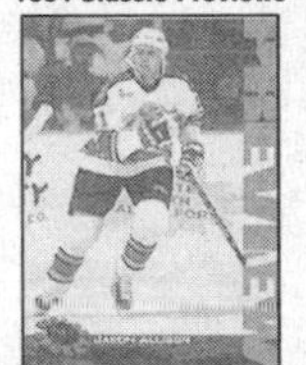

Randomly inserted in 1994 Classic basketball packs, this 5-card set measures the standard-size. The fronts feature full-bleed color action photos, except at the bottom where a color stripe carries the player's name. The word "PREVIEW" is printed vertically in large block letters running down the right edge. On a purple-tinted action photo, the backs display the Classic logo and a short congratulatory message. The cards are unnumbered and checklisted below in alphabetical order.

COMPLETE SET (5) 10.00 20.00
HK1 Jason Allison 1.50 4.00
HK2 Radek Bonk .75 2.00
HK3 Xavier Majic .75 2.00
HK4 Manon Rheaume 7.50 15.00
HK5 Oleg Tverdovsky 1.50 4.00

1994 Classic ROY Sweepstakes

This 20-card standard-size set was featured in U.S. and Canadian cases and inserted on average of five cards per case. Holders of the winning Field Card could redeem it for a complete set of 1994 Classic Hockey Gold cards. The fronts feature a color action player cutout superimposed over a large hockey puck. The words "Rookie of the Year?" and the player's name appear along the right. The backs carry the checklist, along with information on how to claim the prize. The deadline for redeeming cards was September 1, 1995.

COMPLETE SET (20) 4.00 10.00
R1 Jason Allison .60 1.50
R2 Radek Bonk .20 .50
R3 Jason Bonsignore .08 .25
R4 Valeri Bure .20 .50
R5 Jeff Friesen .20 .50
R6 Aaron Gavey .08 .25
R7 Todd Harvey .20 .50
R8 Kenny Jonsson .20 .50
R9 Ed Jovanovski .60 1.50
R10 Patrik Juhlin .08 .25
R11 Valeri Karpov .08 .25
R12 Viktor Kozlov .20 .50
R13 Blaine Lacher .20 .50
R14 Andrei Nikolishin .20 .50
R15 Jeff O'Neill .40 1.00
R16 David Oliver .08 .25
R17 Garth Snow .20 .50
R18 Jamie Storr .20 .50
R19 Oleg Tverdovsky .20 .50
R20 Field Card WIN G .08 .25

1994 Classic Tri-Cards

Featured in both U.S. and Canadian cases and inserted at a rate of two cards per box, this 26-card standard-size set showcases the top three prospects from each NHL city. The horizontal fronts feature three borderless color player photos next to each other, with the player's name in a black bar under each photo, and the team name in a purple bar directly below. The backs carry three small color player portraits with a brief player profile. The cards are arranged alphabetically by city name. Each card has three numbers.

COMPLETE SET (26) 30.00 60.00
T1 Valeri Karpov 1.25 3.00
T2 Nikolai Tsulygin
T3 Oleg Tverdovsky
T4 Fred Knipscheer 1.25 3.00
T5 Blaine Lacher
T6 Evgeni Ryabchikov
T7 David Cooper .75 2.00
T8 Wayne Primeau
T9 Steve Shields
T10 Chris Dingman .75 2.00
T11 Cory Stillman
T12 Vesa Viitakoski
T13 Eric Lecompte .75 2.00
T14 Ethan Moreau
T15 Mike Pomichter
T16 Todd Harvey 1.25 3.00
T17 Jamie Langenbrunner
T18 Jere Lehtinen
T19 Curtis Bowen .75 2.00
T20 Yan Golubovsky
T21 Kevin Hodson
T22 Jason Bonsignore 1.25 3.00
T23 Mats Lindgren
T24 David Oliver
T25 Chris Armstrong 1.50 4.00
T26 Ed Jovanovski
T27 Jason Podollan
T28 Andrei Nikolishin .75 2.00
T29 Jeff O'Neill
T30 Kevin Smyth
T31 Kevin Brown 1.25 3.00
T32 Matt Johnson
T33 Jamie Storr
T34 Valeri Bure 3.00 8.00
T35 Saku Koivu
T36 Brian Savage
T37 Denis Pederson .75 2.00
T38 Brian Rolston
T39 Vadim Sharifijanov
T40 Todd Bertuzzi .75 2.00
T41 Chris Marinucci
T42 Dan Plante
T43 Corey Hirsch .75 2.00
T44 Niklas Sundstrom
T45 Scott Malone
T46 Radim Bicanek 1.25 3.00
T47 Radek Bonk
T48 Chad Penney
T49 Patrik Juhlin .75 2.00
T50 Denis Metlyuk
T51 Janne Niinimaa
T52 Greg Andrusak .75 2.00
T53 Pat Neaton
T54 Chris Wells
T55 Rene Corbet .75 2.00
T56 Adam Deadmarsh
T57 Garth Snow
T58 David Roberts .75 2.00
T59 Ian Laperriere
T60 Patrice Tardiff
T61 Jeff Friesen 1.50 4.00
T62 Viktor Kozlov
T63 Ville Peltonen
T64 Aaron Gavey .75 2.00
T65 Brent Gretzky
T66 Jason Weimer
T67 Brandon Convery 1.50 4.00
T68 Eric Fichaud
T69 Kenny Jonsson
T70 Mike Fountain .75 2.00
T71 Rick Girard
T72 Mike Peca
T73 Jason Allison .75 2.00
T74 Alexander Kharlamov
T75 Brendan Witt
T76 Mika Alatalo .75 2.00
T77 Ravil Gusmanov
T78 Deron Quint

1994 Classic Women of Hockey

Inserted in both U.S. and Canadian product at a rate of one card per pack, this 40-card standard-size set features female hockey players who represented Canada (1-21) and the U.S.A. (22-40) at the 1994 World Women's Ice Hockey Championships. The fronts have color action player cutouts superimposed over a Canadian or American flag with a metallic sheen. The words "Team Canada Women" or "Team USA Women" appear alongside the right, while the player's name is printed at the bottom. The backs carry a close-up color player photo, along with stats from the tournament (won by Canada) and player profile.

COMPLETE SET (40) 8.00 20.00
W1 Manon Rheaume 1.25 3.00
W2 France St. Louis .20 .50
W3 Cheryl Pounder .20 .50
W4 Therese Brisson .20 .50
W5 Cassie Campbell .75 2.00
W6 Angela James .20 .50
W7 Danielle Goyette .40 1.00
W8 Jane Robinson .20 .50
W9 Stacy Wilson .20 .50
W10 Margot Page .20 .50
W11 Laura Leslie .20 .50
W12 Judy Diduck .20 .50
W13 Hayley Wickenheiser 2.00 5.00
W14 Nathalie Picard .20 .50
W15 Leslie Reddon .20 .50
W16 Marianne Grnak .20 .50
W17 Andria Hunter .20 .50
W18 Nancy Drolet .40 1.00
W19 Geraldine Heaney .20 .50
W20 Karen Nystrom .20 .50
W21 Manon Rheaume CL .40 1.00
W22 Kelly Dyer .20 .50
W23 Vicki Movsessian .20 .50
W24 Lisa Brown .20 .50
W25 Shawna Davidson .20 .50
W26 Colleen Coyne .20 .50
W27 Karyn Bye .75 2.00
W28 Suzanne Merz .20 .50
W29 Gretchen Ulion .20 .50
W30 Sandra Whyte .20 .50
W31 Cindy Curley .20 .50
W32 Michele DiFronzo .20 .50
W33 Stephanie Boyd .20 .50
W34 Shelley Looney .20 .50
W35 Jeanine Sobek .20 .50
W36 Beth Beagan .20 .50
W37 Cammi Granato .75 2.00
W38 Christina Bailey .20 .50
W39 Kelly O'Leary .20 .50
W40 Erin Whitten .30 .75

1995 Classic

This 100-card standard-size set marked the conclusion of the fifth (and so far, final) set Classic issued featuring hockey prospects. 3,990 sequentially numbered American cases and 999 Canadian cases were issued with 12 boxes in a case, 36 packs in a box and 10 cards in a pack. There were also a special Manon Rheaume autograph card issued on the average of one per case. One Hot Box, containing nothing but inserts, was inserted one every five cases.

COMPLETE SET (100) 3.00 8.00
1 Bryan Berard .05 .15
2 Wade Redden .01 .05
3 Aki Berg .01 .05
4 Chad Kilger .01 .05
5 Daymond Langkow .05 .15
6 Steve Kelly .01 .05
7 Shane Doan .08 .25
8 Terry Ryan .01 .05
9 Mike Martin .01 .05
10 Radek Dvorak .08 .25
11 Jarome Iginla .08 .25
12 Teemu Riihijarvi .01 .05
13 Jean-Sebastien Giguere .08 .25
14 Peter Schaefer .01 .05
15 Jeff Ware .01 .05
16 Martin Biron .60 1.50
17 Brad Church .01 .05
18 Petr Sykora .08 .25
19 Denis Gauthier .01 .05
20 Sean Brown .01 .05
21 Brad Isbister .20 .50
22 Miikka Elomo .01 .05
23 Mathieu Sunderland .01 .05
24 Marc Moro .01 .05
25 Jan Hlavac .08 .25
26 Brian Wesenberg .01 .05
27 Mike McBain .01 .05
28 Georges Laraque .08 .25
29 Marc Chouinard .08 .25
30 Donald MacLean .01 .05
31 Jason Doig .01 .05
32 Aaron MacDonald .01 .05
33 Patrick Cote .01 .05
34 Christian Dube .01 .05
35 Chris McAllister .01 .05
36 Denis Smith .01 .05
37 Mark Dutiaume .01 .05
38 Dwayne Hay .01 .05
39 Nathan Perrott .01 .05
40 Christian Laflamme .01 .05
41 Paxton Schafer .01 .05
42 Shane Kenny .01 .05
43 Nic Beaudoin .01 .05
44 Philippe Audet .01 .05
45 Brad Larsen .01 .05
46 Ryan Pepperall .01 .05
47 Mike Leclerc .05 .15
48 Shane Willis .10 .30
49 Darryl Laplante .01 .05
50 Larry Courville .01 .05
51 Mike O'Grady .01 .05
52 Petr Buzek .01 .05
53 Alyn McCauley .01 .05
54 Scott Roche .01 .05
55 John Tripp .01 .05
56 Johnathan Aitken .01 .05
57 Blake Bellefeuille .01 .05
58 Daniel Briere .08 .25
59 Josh DeWolf .01 .05
60 Josh Green .01 .05
61 Chris Hajt .01 .05
62 Josh Holden .01 .05
63 Henry Kuster .01 .05
64 Dan Lacouture .01 .05
65 Oleg Orekhovsky .01 .05
66 Andrei Petrunin .01 .05
67 Tom Poti .01 .05
68 Peter Ratchuk .01 .05
69 Andrei Zyuzin .01 .05
70 George Breen .01 .05
71 Greg Bullock .01 .05
72 Kent Fearns .01 .05
73 Eric Flinton .01 .05
74 Brian Holzinger .01 .05
75 Chris Kenady .01 .05
76 Kaj Linna .01 .05
77 Brian Mueller .01 .05
78 Brent Peterson .01 .05
79 Chad Quenneville .01 .05
80 Randy Stevens .01 .05
81 Adam Wiesel .01 .05
82 Barrie Colts .01 .05
83 Belleville Bulls .01 .05
84 Detroit Jr. Whalers .01 .05
85 Guelph Storm .01 .05
86 Kingston Frontenacs .01 .05
87 Kitchener Rangers .01 .05
88 London Knights .01 .05
89 Niagara Falls Thunder .01 .05
90 North Bay Centennials .01 .05
91 Oshawa Generals .08 .25
92 Ottawa 67's .01 .05
93 Owen Sound Platers .01 .05
94 Peterborough Petes .01 .05
95 S.S. Marie Greyhounds .50 1.25
96 Sarnia Sting .01 .05
97 Sudbury Wolves .01 .05
98 Windsor Spitfires .01 .05
99 Bryan Berard CL .01 .05
100 Wade Redden CL .01 .05

1995 Classic Gold

This 100 card set is a parallel to the regular Classic issue. The cards are inserted one per American pack.

COMPLETE SET (100) 20.00 40.00
*STARS: 1.25X TO 3X BASIC CARDS

1995 Classic Printer's Proofs

These cards were inserted approximately one per box. The cards are numbered out of 749.

COMPLETE SET (100) 150.00 300.00
*STARS: 8X TO 20X BASIC CARDS

1995 Classic Printer's Proofs Gold

These 100 cards are a parallel to the Classic Gold set. The cards were inserted one every three boxes and are numbered out of 249.

*STARS:12.5X TO 30X BASIC CARDS

1995 Classic Silver

This 100 card standard-size set is a parallel to the regular Classic issue. The cards were inserted one per Canadian pack.

COMPLETE SET (100) 20.00 40.00
*STARS: .6X TO 1.5X BASIC CARDS

1995 Classic Autographs

These 24 standard-size cards were inserted on the average of one per box. Classic guaranteed that there would be one autographed card in each box. The front is a picture of the card along with the signature. The back is a congratulatory message that you have received an authentic signed card.

1 George Breen/2400 .75 2.00
2 Greg Bullock/2485 .75 2.00
3 Petr Buzek/3978 1.50 4.00
4 Radek Dvorak/4022 2.00 5.00
5 Kent Fearns/4034 .75 2.00
6 Eric Flinton/2495 .75 2.00
7 Josh Green/4293 .75 2.00
8 Josh Holden/4994 .75 2.00
9 Brian Holzinger/2599 .75 2.00
10 Ed Jovanovski/2584 1.50 4.00
11 Chris Kenady/2500 .75 2.00
12 Henry Kuster/2490 .75 2.00
13 Josef Marha/2584 .75 2.00
14 Brian Mueller/2488 .75 2.00
15 Angel Nikolov/2500 .75 2.00
16 Oleg Orekhovsky/5090 .75 2.00
17 Brent Peterson/2468 .75 2.00
18 Andrei Petrunin/4764 .75 2.00
19 Chad Quenneville/2594 .75 2.00
20 Miroslav Satan/2487 12.50 30.00
21 Randy Stevens/2591 .75 2.00
22 Petr Sykora/792 12.50 30.00
23 Adam Wiesel/2511 .75 2.00
24 Andrei Zyuzin/5076 .75 2.00
NNO Manon Rheaume/6300 12.50 30.00

1995 Classic CHL All-Stars

These cards feature all-stars of the CHL. They were inserted into Canadian packs at a ratio of 1:72. The cards are numbered with a "AS" prefix.

COMPLETE SET (18) 25.00 50.00
AS1 Nolan Baumgartner .75 2.00
AS2 Wade Redden 1.50 4.00
AS3 Henry Kuster .75 2.00
AS4 Daymond Langkow 1.50 4.00
AS5 Shane Doan 2.00 5.00
AS6 Steve Kelly .75 2.00
AS7 Tyler Moss .75 2.00
AS8 Bryan Berard 1.50 4.00
AS9 Ed Jovanovski 1.50 4.00
AS10 Chad Kilger .75 2.00
AS11 Daniel Cleary .75 2.00
AS12 Ethan Moreau .75 2.00
AS13 Jean-Sebastien Giguere 1.50 4.00
AS14 Denis Gauthier .75 2.00
AS15 Jason Doig .75 2.00
AS16 Etienne Drapeau .75 2.00
AS17 Daniel Briere 1.50 4.00
AS18 Mark Chouinard .75 2.00

1995 Classic Five Sport

The 1995 Classic Five Sport set was issued in one series of 200 standard-size cards. Cards were issued in 10-card regular packs (SRP $1.99). Boxes contained 36 packs. One autographed card was guaranteed in each pack and one certified autograph card (with an embossed logo) appeared in each box. There were also memorabilia redemption cards included in some packs and were guaranteed in at least one pack per box. The cards are numbered and divided into the five sports as follows: Basketball (1-42), Football (43-92), Baseball (93-122), Hockey (123-160), Racing (161-180), Alma Maters (181-190), Picture Perfect (191-200).

COMPLETE SET (200) 6.00 15.00
COMP. SILVER DIE CUT(200) 12.50 30.00
*SILVER DCs: .75X TO 2X BASIC CARDS
COMP. RED DIE CUT (200) 40.00 100.00
*RED DCs: 2X TO 5X BASIC CARDS
*PROOFS: 4X TO 10X BASIC CARDS
123 Bryan Berard .05 .15
124 Wade Redden .05 .15
125 Aki-Petteri Berg .05 .15
126 Nolan Baumgartner .05 .15
127 Jason Bonsignore .05 .15
128 Steve Kelly .05 .15
129 George Breen .05 .15
130 Terry Ryan .05 .15
131 Greg Bullock .05 .15
132 Jarome Iginla .30 .75
133 Petr Buzek .05 .15
134 Brad Church .05 .15
135 Jay McKee .05 .15
136 Jan Hlavac .08 .25
137 Petr Sykora .15 .40
138 Ed Jovanovski .05 .15
139 Chris Kenady .05 .15
140 Marc Moro .05 .15
141 Kaj Linna .05 .15
142 Aaron MacDonald .05 .15
143 Chad Kilger .05 .15
144 Tyler Moss .05 .15
145 Christian Laflamme .05 .15
146 Brian Mueller .05 .15
147 Daymond Langkow .15 .40
148 Brent Peterson .05 .15
149 Chad Quenneville .05 .15
150 Chris Van Dyk .05 .15
151 Kent Fearns .05 .15
152 Adam Wiesel .05 .15
153 Marc Chouinard .05 .15
154 Jason Doig .05 .15
155 Denis Smith .05 .15
156 Radek Dvorak .05 .15
157 Donald MacLean .05 .15
158 Shane Kenny .05 .15
159 Brian Holzinger .05 .15
160 Eric Flinton .05 .15
189 Eric Williams .05 .15
George Breen

1995 Classic Five Sport Silver Die Cuts

These cards are identical to the regular set with the exception of a die-cut around the balls that are printed on the right side. They were inserted one per regular pack.

COMPLETE SET (200) 12.00 30.00
*SILVER DC: .8X TO 2X BASIC CARDS

1995 Classic Five Sport Red Die Cuts

*RED DIE CUT: 1.2X TO 3X BASIC CARDS
RED DIE CUT STATED ODDS 1:8

1995 Classic Five Sport Printer's Proofs

*PRINTER PROOF/75: 4X TO 10X BASIC CARDS
STATED PRINT RUN 795 SETS

1995 Classic Five Sport Autographs

This set was randomly inserted into packs and is a signed version of the basic issue cards. The backs carry a "Congratulations" message stating that it is an autographed 1995 Five Sport Autograph Edition Card with the sport's ball pictured at the bottom. The cards are unnumbered. Many of these autographed cards were later re-issued in 1995-96 Classic Five Sport Signings with a slightly different cardback that reads "...Received a Limited-Edition Autographed Card." This message is the same one used on the Hot Box Autographs but these Five Sport Signings Autographs are not serial numbered on the back.

*SIGNINGS VERSION: .4X TO 1X
126 Nolan Baumgartner 2.00 5.00
127 Jason Bonsignore 2.00 5.00
128 Steve Kelly 2.00 5.00
129 George Breen 2.00 5.00
131 Greg Bullock 2.00 5.00
132 Jarome Iginla 10.00 20.00
133 Petr Buzek 2.00 5.00
135 Jay McKee 2.00 5.00
136 Jan Hlavac 2.00 6.00
137 Petr Sykora SP 10.00 20.00
138 Ed Jovanovski 2.50 6.00
139 Chris Kenady 2.00 5.00
140 Marc Moro 2.00 5.00
141 Kaj Linna 2.00 5.00
142 Aaron MacDonald 2.00 5.00
144 Tyler Moss 2.00 5.00
145 Christian Laflamme 2.00 5.00
146 Brian Mueller 2.00 5.00
148 Brent Peterson 2.00 5.00
149 Chad Quenneville 2.00 5.00
150 Chris Van Dyk SP 2.00 5.00
151 Kent Ferns 2.00 5.00
152 Adam Wiesel 2.00 5.00
153 Marc Chouinard SP 3.00 8.00
154 Jason Doig 2.00 5.00
155 Denis Smith 2.00 5.00
156 Radek Dvorak 2.00 5.00
157 Don MacLean 2.00 5.00
158 Shane Kenny 2.00 5.00

1995 Classic Five Sport Autographs Numbered

Cards in this set were issued primarily in 1995-96 Classic Five Sport Signings packs and are essentially a parallel version of the basic 1995 Classic Five Sport Autographs insert. The only differences are in the hand serial numbering on the cardbacks (of 225 or 295) and the embossing crimp on the card's corner.

STATED PRINT RUN 225 SER.#'d SETS
137 Petr Sykora/225 5.00 12.00

1995 Classic Five Sport Classic Standouts

Randomly inserted in regular packs at a rate of one in 216, this 10-card standard-size set features both the hot new stars and the established elite of all five sports. Fronts have full-color player cutouts set against a gold and black foil background. The player's name is printed in gold foil at the top. Backs contain a full-color action shot with the player's name printed in yellow and a career highlights box. The cards are numbered with a "CS" prefix.

COMPLETE SET (10) 15.00 40.00
CS5 Bryan Berard .75 2.00

1995 Classic Five Sport Fast Track

Randomly inserted in retail packs, this 20-card standard-size set spotlights the young stars of sports who are fast becoming major stars. Borderless fronts contain a player in full-color action while the rest of the shot is printed in colored foil. Backs have a color action shot in one box and two color separated boxes with the rest of the photo. A player profile appears underneath the photo. The cards are numbered with a "FT" prefix.

COMPLETE SET (20) 15.00 40.00
FT5 Bryan Berard .40 1.00
FT14 Petr Sykora 1.00 2.50

1995 Classic Five Sport On Fire

Ten of the 20-cards in this set were released in Hobby Hot Packs while the other ten were released in retail Hot packs. Fronts have full-color player cutouts set against a flame background with the On Fire logo printed at the bottom. The player's name is printed vertically in white type on the left side. backs feature biography and players's statistics.

COMPLETE SET (20) 30.00 80.00
R9 Bryan Berard 2.00 5.00

1995 Classic Five Sport Phone Cards $3

The five-card set of $3 Foncards were found one per 72 retail packs. The credit-card size plastic pieces have a borderless front with a full-color action player photo and the $3 emblem printed on the upper right in blue. The player's name is printed in white type vertically on the lower left. The Sprint logo appears on the bottom also. White backs carry information of how to place calls using the card.

COMPLETE SET (5) 4.00 8.00
3 Brian Holzinger .40 1.00

1995 Classic Five Sport Phone Cards $4

These cards were inserted randomly into packs at a rate of one in 72 and featured the five top prospects or performers of the individual sports. The borderless fronts feature full-color action photos with the athlete's name printed in white across the bottom. The Sprint logo and $4 are printed along the top. White backs contain information about placing calls using the card.

COMPLETE SET (5) 6.00 15.00
3 Wade Redden .50 1.25

1995 Classic Five Sport Previews

Randomly inserted in Classic hockey packs, this five-card standard-size set features the leaders and the up-and-coming rookies of the five sports. Borderless fronts have a full-color action shot with gold foil stamp of "preview" and the player's name, school and position printed vertically on the right side of the card. The player's sport's ball (or tire) is printed in a montage on the right. Backs have another full-color action shot and also a biography, statistics and profile. The cards are numbered with a "SP" prefix.

COMPLETE SET (5) 3.00 8.00
SP4 Bryan Berard .40 1.00

1995 Classic Five Sport Record Setters

This 10-card standard-size set was inserted in retail packs and feature the stars and rookies of the five sports. The fronts display full-bleed color action photos; the title "Record Setters" in prismatic block lettering appears toward the bottom. On a sepia-tone photo, the backs carry a player profile. The cards are numbered on the back with an "RS" prefix and hand-numbered out of 1250.

COMPLETE SET (10) 12.00 30.00
RS2 Bryan Berard .60 1.50

1995 Classic Five Sport Strive For Five

This interactive game card set consists of 65 cards to be used like playing cards. Collector's gained a full suit of cards to redeem prizes. The odds of finding the card in packs were one in 10. Fronts are bordered in metallic silver foil and picture the player in full-color action. The cards are numbered on both top and bottom in silver foil and the player's name is printed vertically in silver foil. Backs have green backgrounds with the game rules printed in white type.

COMPLETE SET (65) 12.00 30.00
HK1 Wade Redden .20 .50
HK2 Jan Hlavac .20 .50
HK3 Brad Church .20 .50
HK4 Steve Kelly .20 .50
HK5 Radek Dvorak .20 .50
HK6 Jason Bonsignore .20 .50
HK7 Petr Sykora .20 .50
HK8 Daymond Langkow .20 .50
HK9 Chad Kilger .20 .50
HK10 Nolan Baumgartner .20 .50
HK11 Brian Holzinger .20 .50
HK12 Aki-Petteri Berg .20 .50
HK13 Ed Jovanovski .20 .50

1995-96 Classic Five Sport Signings

COMPLETE SET (100) 6.00 15.00
70 Bryan Berard .07 .20
71 Wade Redden .07 .20
72 Aki-Petteri Berg .07 .20
73 Nolan Baumgartner .07 .20
74 Jason Bonsignore .07 .20
75 Ed Jovanovski .07 .20
76 Radek Dvorak .07 .20
77 Brian Holzinger .07 .20
78 Brad Church .07 .20

1995-96 Classic Five Sport Signings Die Cuts

These parallel cards were randomly inserted into one in every four packs. The cards feature a die cut design on the front right edge.

*DIE CUT: .8X TO 2X BASIC CARDS
STATED ODDS 1:4

1995-96 Classic Five Sport Signings Red Signature

The Red Signature parallels were randomly inserted in regular Classic Five Sport Hot Boxes and are identical to the regular cards with the exception of a red foil facsimile signature on the front (basic cards feature silver foil signatures).

*RED SIGN: 1.5X TO 4X BASIC CARDS

1995-96 Classic Five Sport Signings Blue Signature

The Blue Signature parallels were randomly inserted in regular Classic Five Sport Hot Boxes and are identical to the regular card with the exception of a blue foil facsimile signature on the front (basic cards feature silver foil signatures).

*BLUE SIGN: 1.5X TO 4X BASIC CARDS

1995-96 Classic Five Sport Signings Freshly Inked

This 30-card set was randomly inserted in 1995 Classic Five Sport Signings packs. The fronts feature borderless player color action photos with the player's name printed in gold foil across the bottom. The backs carry an artist's drawing of the player with the player's name at the top.

COMPLETE SET (30) 12.00 30.00
STATED ODDS 1:10
FS23 Brian Holzinger .40 1.00
FS24 Radek Dvorak .40 1.00
FS25 Petr Sykora .60 1.50
FS26 Daymond Langkow .40 1.00

1991 Classic Four Sport

This 230-card multi-sport standard-size set includes all 200 draft picks players from the four Classic Draft Picks sets (football, baseball, basketball, and hockey), plus an additional 30 draft picks not previously found in these other sets. A subset within the 230 cards consists of five cards highlighting the publicized one-on-one game between Billy Owens and Larry Johnson. As an additional incentive to collectors, Classic randomly inserted over 60,000 autographed cards into the 15-card foil packs; it is claimed that each case should contain two or more autographed cards. The autographed cards feature 61 different players, approximately two-thirds of whom were hockey players. The production run for the English version was 25,000 cases, and a bilingual (French) version of the set was also produced at 20 percent of the English production. The major subdivisions of set are according to sport: hockey (2-50), baseball (51-101), football (102-148), and basketball (149-202).

COMPLETE SET (230) 5.00 12.00
1 Larry Johnson .15 .40
Brien Taylor
Russell Maryland
Eric Lindros
2 Pat Falloon .05 .15
3 Scott Niedermayer .08 .25
4 Scott Lachance .05 .15
5 Peter Forsberg .60 1.50
6 Alek Stojanov .05 .15
7 Richard Matvichuk .05 .15
8 Patrick Poulin .05 .15
9 Martin Lapointe .05 .15
10 Tyler Wright .05 .15
11 Philippe Boucher .05 .15
12 Pat Peake .05 .15
13 Markus Naslund .05 .15
14 Brent Bilodeau .05 .15
15 Glen Murray .05 .15
16 Niklas Sundblad .05 .15
17 Martin Rucinsky .05 .15
18 Trevor Halverson .05 .15
19 Dean McAmmond .05 .15
20 Ray Whitney .07 .20
21 Rene Corbet .05 .15
22 Eric Lavigne .05 .15
23 Zigmund Palffy .20 .50
24 Steve Staios .05 .15
25 Jim Campbell .05 .15
26 Jassen Cullimore .05 .15
27 Martin Hamrlik .05 .15
28 Jamie Pushor .05 .15
29 Donevan Hextall .05 .15
30 Andrew Verner .05 .15
31 Jason Dawe .05 .15
32 Jeff Nelson .05 .15
33 Darcy Werenka .05 .15
34 Jozef Stumpel .07 .20
35 Francois Groleau .05 .15
36 Guy Leveque .05 .15
37 Jamie Matthews .05 .15
38 Dody Wood .05 .15
39 Yanic Perreault .05 .15
40 Jamie McLennan .05 .15
41 Yanick Dupre UER .05 .15
(Yanic misspelled
on both sides)
42 Sandy McCarthy .05 .15
43 Chris Osgood .30 .75
44 Fredrik Lindqvist .05 .15
45 Jason Young .05 .15
46 Steve Konowalchuk .05 .15
47 Michael Nylander UER .05 .15
48 Shane Peacock .05 .15
49 Yves Sarault .05 .15
50 Marcel Cousineau .05 .15

1991 Classic Four Sport Autographs

The 1991 Classic Draft Collection Autograph set consists of 61 standard-size cards. They were randomly inserted throughout the foil packs. Listed after the player's name is how many cards were autographed by that player. An "A" suffix after card number is used here for convenience.

2A Pat Falloon/1100 2.50 6.00
3A Scott Niedermayer/1250 6.00 12.00
4A Scott Lachance/1100 2.00 5.00
6A Alek Stojanov/950 2.00 5.00
8A Patrick Poulin/1100 2.00 5.00
10A Tyler Wright/950 2.00 5.00
11A Philippe Boucher/1150 2.00 5.00
12A Pat Peake/1100 2.50 6.00
14A Brent Bilodeau/1000 2.00 5.00
15A Glen Murray/1100 2.00 5.00
16A Niklas Sundblad/900 2.00 5.00
17A Martin Rucinsky/1100 2.00 5.00
18A Trevor Halverson/1100 2.00 5.00
19A Dean McAmmond/1100 2.00 5.00
20A Ray Whitney/2600 2.50 6.00
21A Rene Corbet/950 2.00 5.00
22A Eric Lavigne/1100 2.00 5.00
24A Steve Staios/1100 2.00 5.00
25A Jim Campbell/1100 2.50 6.00
26A Jassen Cullimore/1000 2.00 5.00
28A Jamie Pushor/1050 2.00 5.00
29A Donevan Hextall/1100 2.50 6.00
30A Andrew Verner/1200 2.00 5.00
31A Jason Dawe/950 2.00 5.00
32A Jeff Nelson/1100 2.00 5.00
33A Darcy Werenka/1150 2.00 5.00
35A Francois Groleau/1150 2.00 5.00
36A Guy Leveque/1150 2.00 5.00
37A Jamie Matthews/1100 2.00 5.00
38A Dody Wood/1050 2.00 5.00
39A Yanic Perreault/1100 2.00 5.00
40A Jamie Matthews/1100 2.00 5.00
41A Yanick Dupre/1050 2.00 5.00
42A Sandy McCarthy/1150 2.50 6.00
43A Chris Osgood/1100 30.00 60.00
44A F.Lindqvist/1100 3.00 8.00
45A Jason Young/1200 2.00 5.00
46A Steve Konowalchuk/1350 2.50 6.00
47A Michael Nylander/1100 2.00 5.00
48A Shane Peacock/1150 2.00 5.00
49A Yves Sarault/1150 2.00 5.00
50A Marcel Cousineau/1100 2.00 5.00

1991 Classic Four Sport French

COMPLETE SET (230) 6.00 15.00
*FRENCH VERSION: .4X TO 1X

1992 Classic Four Sport

The 1992 Classic Draft Picks Collection consists of 325 standard-size cards, featuring the top picks from football, basketball, baseball, and hockey drafts. According to Classic, 40,000 12-box foil cases were produced. Randomly inserted in the 12-card packs were over 100,000 autograph cards from over 50 of the top draft picks from basketball, football, baseball, and hockey, including cards autographed by Shaquille O'Neal, Desmond Howard, Roman Hamrlik, and Phil Nevin. Also inserted in the packs were "Instant Win Giveway Cards" that entitled the collector to the 500,000.00 sports memorabilia giveway that Classic offered in this contest. There was also a factory set produced with gold parallel cards.

COMPLETE SET (325) 6.00 15.00
151 Roman Hamrlik .05 .15
152 Alexei Yashin .05 .15
153 Mike Rathje .05 .15
154 Darius Kasparaitis .05 .15
155 Cory Stillman .05 .15
156 Robert Petrovicky .05 .15
157 Andrei Nazarov .05 .15
158 Jason Bowen .05 .15
159 Jason Smith .05 .15
160 David Wilkie .05 .15
161 Curtis Bowen .05 .15
162 Grant Marshall .05 .15
163 Valeri Bure .08 .25
164 Jeff Shantz .05 .15
165 Justin Hocking .05 .15
166 Mike Peca .25 .60
167 Marc Hussey .05 .15
168 Sandy Allan .05 .15
169 Kirk Maltby .05 .15
170 Cale Hulse .05 .15
171 Sylvain Cloutier .05 .15
172 Martin Gendron .05 .15
173 Kevin Smyth .05 .15
174 Jason McBain .05 .15
175 Lee J. Leslie .05 .15
176 Ralph Intranuovo .05 .15
177 Martin Reichel .05 .15
178 Stefan Ustorf .05 .15
179 Jarkko Varvio .05 .15
180 Martin Straka .20 .50
181 Libor Polasek .05 .15
182 Jozef Cierny .05 .15
183 Sergei Krivokrasov .15 .40
184 Sergei Gonchar .15 .40
185 Boris Mironov .05 .15
186 Denis Metlyuk .05 .15
187 Sergei Klimovich .05 .15
188 Sergei Brylin .05 .15
189 Andrei Nikolishin .05 .15
190 Alexander Cherbayev .05 .15
191 Vitali Tomilin .05 .15
192 Sandy Moger .05 .15
193 Darrin Madeley .05 .15
194 Denny Felsner .05 .15
195 Dwayne Norris .05 .15
196 Joby Messier .05 .15
197 Michael Stewart .05 .15
198 Scott Thomas .05 .15
199 Daniel Laperriere .05 .15
200 Martin Lacroix .05 .15
201 Scott LaGrand .05 .15
202 Scott Pellerin .05 .15
203 Jean-Yves Roy .05 .15
204 Rob Gaudreau .05 .15
205 Jeff McLean .05 .15
206 Dallas Drake .05 .15
207 Doug Zmolek .05 .15
208 Duane Derksen .05 .15
209 Jim Cummins .05 .15
210 Lonnie Loach .05 .15
211 Rob Zamuner .05 .15
212 Brad Werenka .05 .15
213 Brent Grieve .05 .15
214 Sean Hill .05 .15
215 Peter Ciavaglia .05 .15
216 Jason Ruff .05 .15
217 Shawn McCosh .05 .15
218 Dave Tretowicz .05 .15
219 Mike Vukonich .05 .15
220 Kevin Wortman .05 .15
221 Jason Muzzatti .05 .15
222 Dmitri Kvartalnov .05 .15
223 Ray Whitney .07 .20
224 Manon Rheaume .40 1.00
225 Viktor Kozlov .08 .25

1992 Classic Four Sport Gold

Issued in factory set form, these cards parallel the basic Classic Four-Sport set. Each cards features gold foil highlights and are valued as a multiple of the basic Four-Sport cards. The factory sealed set also included an additional "Future Superstars" autographed card. Only 9,500 sequentially numbered factory sets were produced and each was packaged in a walnut display case.

COMP.FACT.SET (326) 60.00 120.00
*GOLD: 1.2X TO 3X BASIC CARDS
AU Future Superstars AU 50.00 80.00
Phil Nevin
Shaquille O'Neal
Desmond Howard
Roman Hamrlik
(Certified AUTO/9500)

1992 Classic Four Sport Autographs

The 1992 Classic Four Sport Autograph set consists of base cards hand signed by the featured player with a congratulatory message on the backs. . They were randomly inserted throughout the foil packs. Each card also included a hand written serial number on the front and the checklist below reflects the quantity of cards each player signed. We've assigned card number according to the player's base card. Jan Caloun and Jan Vopat were not included in the regular set and hence are listed as unnumbered.

151 Roman Hamrlik/1550 2.50 6.00
153A Mike Rathje/2075 2.00 5.00
155 Cory Stillman/2125 2.00 5.00
158 Jason Bowen/2075 2.00 5.00
159 Jason Smith/2075 2.00 5.00
165 Justin Hocking/2075 2.00 5.00
170 Cale Hulse/1850 2.00 5.00
181 Libor Polasek/1950 2.00 5.00
185 Boris Mironov/2075 2.00 5.00
192 Sandy Moger/1075 2.00 5.00
195 Dwayne Norris/1075 2.00 5.00
196 Joby Messier/1075 2.00 5.00
207 Doug Zmolek/1075 2.00 5.00
224 Manon Rheaume/1992 12.50 30.00
NNO Jan Vopat/1775 2.00 5.00
NNO Jan Caloun/1975 2.00 5.00

1992 Classic Four Sport BCs

Inserted one per jumbo pack, these 20 bonus cards measure the standard size. The cards are numbered on the dark gray stripe and arranged according to sport as follows: basketball (1-6), hockey (7-12), football (13-17), and baseball (18-20). A randomly inserted Future Superstars card has a picture of all four players on its front, shot against a horizon with dark clouds and lightning; the back indicates that just 10,000 of these cards were produced.

COMPLETE SET (20) 3.00 8.00
BC7 Roman Hamrlik .08 .25
BC8 Valeri Bure .08 .25
BC9 Dallas Drake .08 .25
BC10 Dmitri Kvartalnov .08 .25
BC11 Manon Rheaume .75 2.00
BC12 Viktor Kozlov .08 .25

1992 Classic Four Sport LPs

Randomly inserted in foil packs, this 25-card standard-size insert set features full-bleed glossy color action player photos on the fronts. The sports represented are football (1-7, 16), basketball (8-14), baseball (17-21), and hockey (22-25). An 8 1/2" by 11" version of Shaquille O'Neal is known to exist.

LP15 Phil Nevin 1.50 4.00
Shaquille O'Neal
Roman Hamrlik
Desmond Howard
LP22 Roman Hamrlik .20 .50
LP23 Mike Rathje .20 .50
LP24 Valeri Bure .20 .50
LP25 Alexei Yashin .30 .75

1992 Classic Four Sport Previews

These five preview standard-size cards were randomly inserted in baseball and hockey draft picks foil packs. According to the backs, just 10,000 of each card were produced. The fronts display the full-bleed glossy color player photos. At the upper right corner, the word "Preview" surmounts the Classic logo. This logo overlays a black stripe that runs down the left side and features the player's name and position. The gray backs have the word "Preview" in red lettering at the top and are accented by short purple diagonal stripes on each side. Between the stripes are a congratulations and an advertisement. The cards are numbered on the back with a "CC" prefix.

COMPLETE SET (5) 6.00 15.00
CC3 Roman Hamrlik .40 1.00

1992 Classic Four Sport Promos

These five promo cards were packaged in a cello pack and distributed to dealers. The cards measure the standard size (2 1/2" by 3 1/2"). The fronts display the same full-bleed glossy color player photos as the above-mentioned preview cards. They differ in that the Classic logo at the upper left corner is not surmounted by the word Preview." The promo backs have a different design than the preview backs, displaying a second color player photo on the right side as well as biography and player profile in black print on a silver background. The cards are numbered on the back.

COMPLETE SET (5) 6.00 15.00
PR3 Roman Hamrlik .40 1.00

1993 Classic Four Sport

The 1993 Classic Four-Sport Draft Pick Collection set consists of 325 standard-size cards of the top 1993 draft picks from football, basketball, baseball, and hockey. Just 49,500 sequentially numbered 12-box cases were produced. The set includes two topical subsets: John R. Wooden Award (310-314) and All-Rookie Basketball Team (315-319).

COMPLETE SET (325) 4.00 10.00
185 Alexandre Daigle .05 .15
186 Chris Pronger .20 .50
187 Chris Gratton .05 .15
188 Paul Kariya .40 1.00
189 Rob Niedermayer .08 .25
190 Viktor Kozlov .08 .25
191 Jason Arnott .20 .50
192 Niklas Sundstrom .05 .15
193 Todd Harvey .05 .15
194 Jocelyn Thibault .20 .50
195 Kenny Jonsson .05 .15
196 Denis Pederson .05 .15
197 Adam Deadmarsh .08 .25
198 Mats Lindgren .05 .15
199 Nick Stajduhar .05 .15
200 Jason Allison .08 .25
201 Jesper Mattsson .05 .15
202 Saku Koivu .20 .50
203 Anders Eriksson .05 .15
204 Todd Bertuzzi .05 .15
205 Eric Lecompte .05 .15
206 Nikolai Tsulygin .05 .15
207 Janne Niinimaa .05 .15
208 Maxim Bets .05 .15
209 Rory Fitzpatrick .05 .15
210 Eric Manlow .05 .15
211 David Roche .05 .15
212 Vladimir Chebaturkin .05 .15
213 Bill McCauley .05 .15
214 Chad Lang .05 .15
215 Cosmo DuPaul .05 .15
216 Bob Wren .05 .15
217 Chris Simon .05 .15
218 Ryan Brown .05 .15
219 Mikhail Shtalenkov .05 .15
220 Vladimir Krechine .05 .15
221 Jason Saal .05 .15
222 Dion Darling .05 .15
223 Chris Helleher .05 .15
224 Antti Aalto .05 .15
225 Alain Nasreddine .05 .15
226 Paul Vincent .05 .15
227 Manny Legace .05 .15
228 Igor Chibirev .05 .15
229 Tom Noble .05 .15
230 Mike Bales .05 .15
231 Jozef Cierny .05 .15
232 Ivan Droppa .05 .15
233 Anatoli Fedotov .05 .15
234 Martin Gendron .05 .15
235 Daniel Guerard .05 .15
236 Corey Hirsch .07 .20
237 Steven King .05 .15
238 Sergei Krivokrasov .05 .15
239 Darrin Madeley .05 .15
240 Grant Marshall .05 .15
241 Sandy McCarthy .07 .20
242 Bill McDougall .05 .15
243 Dean Melanson .05 .15
244 Roman Oksiuta .05 .15
245 Robert Petrovicky .05 .15
246 Mike Rathje .05 .15
247 Eldon Reddick .05 .15
248 Andrei Trefilov .05 .15
249 Jiri Slegr .05 .15
250 Leonid Toropchenko .05 .15
251 Dody Wood .05 .15
252 Kevin Paden .05 .15
253 Manon Rheaume .30 .75
254 Cammi Granato .08 .25
255 Patrick Charbonneau .05 .15
256 Curtis Bowen .05 .15
257 Kevin Brown .05 .15
258 Valeri Bure .08 .25
259 Janne Laukkanen .05 .15

1993 Classic Four Sport Gold

This parallel issue to the 1993 Classic Four Sport set consists of 325 Gold foil versions of the regular set, plus four player autograph cards that were inserted into each factory gold set. Each of the four players autographed 3900 cards. Aside from the special gold-foil highlights (such as the ghosted stripe carrying the player's name being offset by gold-foil lines) the cards are identical to the regular 1993 Classic Four Sport base cards.

COMP.FACT.SET (332) 150.00 250.00
*GOLD: 1.5X TO 4X BASIC CARDS
AU2 Chris Gratton AU/3900 4.00 10.00

1993 Classic Four Sport Acetates

Randomly inserted throughout the 1993 Classic Four-Sport foil packs, this 12-card standard-size acetate set features on its fronts clear-bordered color player action cutouts set on basketball, football, baseball, or hockey stick backgrounds. The cards are unnumbered but carry letter designations. They are checklisted in the order that spells '93 Rookie Class.

COMPLETE SET (12) 6.00 15.00
11 Alexandre Daigle .40 1.00
12 Chris Pronger .40 1.00

1993 Classic Four Sport Autographs

Randomly inserted in '93 Classic Four-Sport packs, these standard-size cards feature on their fronts borderless color player action shots. The back carries a congratulatory message. The cards are listed below by their corresponding regular card numbers, except for Jennings and Klippenstein, which are shown as unnumbered cards (NNO) at the end of the checklist since they are not in the regular set. The number of cards each player signed is shown. The Rider card may have been autopenned.

189A Rob Niedermayer/4500 2.00 5.00
196A Denis Pederson/2050 1.50 4.00
197A Adam Deadmarsh/4250 2.00 5.00
218A Ryan Brown/900 1.50 4.00
222A Dion Darling/1050 1.50 4.00
253A Manon Rheaume/1250 30.00 60.00
NNO Wade Klippenstein/800 1.50 4.00
NNO Jason Jennings/1475 1.50 4.00

1993 Classic Four Sport Chromium Draft Stars

Inserted one per jumbo pack, these 20 standard-size cards feature color player action cutouts on their borderless metallic fronts. The player's name, along with the production number (1 of 80,000), appear vertically in gold foil at the lower left. The cards are numbered on the back with a "DS" prefix.

COMPLETE SET (20) 8.00 20.00
DS58 Alexandre Daigle .40 1.00
DS59 Chris Pronger .40 1.00
DS60 Chris Gratton .40 1.00

1993 Classic Four Sport LP Jumbos

Random inserts in hobby boxes, these five oversized cards measure approximately 3 1/2" by 5" and feature on their fronts borderless color player action shots. The player's name, statistics, biography, and career highlights, along with the card's production number out of 8,000 produced, appear on a gray lithic background to the left. The cards are numbered on the back as "X of 5."

COMPLETE SET (5) 12.00 30.00
2 Alexandre Daigle 1.25 3.00

1993 Classic Four Sport LPs

Randomly inserted throughout the 1993 Classic Four-Sport foil packs, this 25-card standard-size set features the hottest draft pick players in 1993. The borderless fronts feature color player action shots. The player's name appears vertically at the lower left. The production number (1 of 63,400) appears in gold foil at the lower right. The cards are numbered on the back with an "LP" prefix.

COMPLETE SET (25) 20.00 40.00
LP1 Four-in-One Card 1.50 4.00
Chris Webber
Drew Bledsoe
Alex Rodriguez
Alexandre Daigle
LP22 Alexandre Daigle .40 1.00
LP23 Chris Pronger .60 1.50
LP24 Chris Gratton .40 1.00
LP25 Paul Kariya .75 2.00

1993 Classic Four Sport MBNA Promos

This two-card set uses Classic's designs from its Four-Sport LPs "Four in One" insert number LP1. Card number 1 reproduces the Chris Webber/Alex Rodriguez side of LP1, card number 2 reproduces the Drew Bledsoe/Alexandre Daigle side. This set was issued exclusively to cardholders of the MBNA/ScoreBoard VISA. The backs contain congratulatory messages, information about the players depicted, and a notation than 10,000 sets were issued. Although the design and copyright reads 1993, these cards probably were first issued in 1994.

2 Drew Bledsoe 2.00 5.00
Alexander Daigle

1993 Classic Four Sport McDonald's

Classic produced this 35-card four-sport standard-size set for a promotion at McDonald's restaurants in central and southeastern Pennsylvania, southern New Jersey, Delaware, and central Florida. The cards were distributed in five-card packs. A five-card "limited production" subset was randomly inserted throughout these packs. The promotion also featured instant win cards awarding 2,000 pieces of autographed Score Board memorabilia. An autographed Chris Webber card was also randomly inserted in the packs on a limited basis. The set is arranged according to sports as follows: football (1-10), baseball (11, 26, 31-35), hockey (12-20), and basketball (21-25, 27-30). The cards are numbered on the back in the upper left, and the McDonald's trademark is gold foil stamped toward the bottom.

COMPLETE SET (35) 4.00 10.00
13 Kevin Dineen .05 .15
14 Andre Faust .05 .15
15 Roman Hamrlik .08 .25
16 Mark Recchi .20 .50
17 Manon Rheaume .50 1.25
18 Dominic Roussel .10 .30
19 Teemu Selanne .40 1.00
20 Tommy Soderstrom .10 .30

1993 Classic Four Sport McDonald's LPs

Measuring the standard size, these five limited production cards were randomly inserted in 1993 Classic McDonald's five-card packs. Chris Webber, the number one pick in the NBA draft, autographed 1,250 of his cards. Printed vertically, and parallel and next to the gold foil band, "1 of 16,750" appears in gold foil. The Classic Four Sport logo appears in the upper right. The cards are numbered on the back in gold foil with an "LP" prefix.

COMPLETE SET (5) 3.00 8.00
LP4 Manon Rheaume 1.50 4.00

1993 Classic Four Sport Power Pick Bonus

Issued one per jumbo sheet, these 20 standard-size cards feature on their borderless fronts color player action shots, the backgrounds for which are faded to black-and-white. The player's name and the sets production number (1 of 80,000) appear in green-foil cursive lettering near the bottom. The cards are numbered on the back with a "PP" prefix.

COMPLETE SET (20) 10.00 25.00
PP18 Alexandre Daigle .40 1.00
PP19 Chris Pronger .60 1.50
PP20 Chris Gratton .40 1.00
NNO Four in One Special 1.50 4.00

1993 Classic Four Sport Previews

Issued as unnumbered inserts in '93 Classic hockey packs, these five cards measure the standard size. The fronts are similar in design to regular 1993 Classic Four-Sport cards. The backs carry a congratulatory message. The cards are unnumbered and checklisted below in alphabetical order.

COMPLETE SET (5) 2.50 6.00
CC1 Alexandre Daigle .30 .75

1993 Classic Four Sport Tri-Cards

Randomly inserted throughout the 1993 Classic Four-Sport foil packs, this set features five standard-size cards with three players on each card separated by perforations. The cards are numbered on the back with a "TC" prefix.

COMPLETE SET (5) 10.00 25.00
TC4 Alexandre Daigle 1.50 4.00
TC9 Chris Pronger
TC14 Chris Gratton

1994 Classic Four Sport

Featuring top rookies from basketball, baseball, football and hockey, the 1994 Classic Four-Sport set consists of 200 standard-size cards. No more than 25,000 cases were produced. Over 100 players signed 100,000 cards that were randomly inserted four per case. Collectors who found one of 100 Glenn Robinson Instant Winner Cards received a complete Classic Four-Sport autographed card set. Also inserted on an average of one in every five cases were 4,695 hand-numbered 4-in-1 cards featuring all four number 1 picks. Classic's wrapper redemption program offered four levels of participation: 1) bronze-collect 20 wrappers and receive a 4-card Classic Player of the Year set, featuring Grant Hill, Shaquille O'Neal, Emmitt Smith, and Steve Young; 2) silver-collect 30 wrappers and receive the Classic Player of the Year set and a random autograph card; 3) gold-collect 144 wrappers and receive the Classic Player of the Year set and an autograph card by Muhammad Ali; and 4) platinum-collect 216 wrappers and receive the Classic Player of the Year set plus an autograph card by Shaquille O'Neal. The cards are numbered on the back and checklisted below by sport as follows: basketball (1-50), football (51-114), hockey (115-160), baseball (161-188), and Wooden Award Contenders (189-197).

COMPLETE SET (200) 6.00 15.00
115A Ed Jovanovski ERR .08 .25
115B Ed Jovanovski COR .08 .25
116 Oleg Tverdovsky .08 .25
117 Radek Bonk .08 .25
118 Jason Bonsignore .05 .15
119 Jeff O'Neill .07 .20
120 Ryan Smyth .05 .15
121 Jamie Storr .15 .40
122 Jason Wiemer .05 .15
123 Evgeny Ryabchikov .05 .15
124 Nolan Baumgartner .05 .15
125 Jeff Friesen .10 .30
126 Wade Belak .05 .15
127 Maxim Bets .05 .15
128 Ethan Moreau .05 .15
129 Alexander Kharlamov .05 .15
130 Eric Fichaud .05 .15
131 Wayne Primeau .05 .15
132 Brad Brown .05 .15
133 Chris Dingman .05 .15
134 Craig Darby .05 .15
135 Darby Hendrickson .05 .15
136 Yan Golubovsky .05 .15
137 Chris Wells .05 .15
138 Vadim Sharifijanov .05 .15
139 Dan Cloutier .05 .15
140 Todd Marchant .08 .25
141 David Roberts .05 .15
142 Brian Rolston .05 .15
143 Garth Snow .15 .40
144 Cory Stillman .05 .15
145 Chad Penney .05 .15
146 Jeff Nelson .05 .15
147 Michael Stewart .05 .15
148 Mike Dunham .08 .25
149 Joe Frederick .05 .15
150 Mark DeSantis .05 .15
151 David Cooper .05 .15
152 Andrei Buschan .05 .15
153 Mike Greenlay .05 .15
154 Geoff Sarjeant .05 .15
155 Pauli Jaks .05 .15
156 Greg Andrusak .05 .15
157 Denis Metlyuk .05 .15
158 Mike Fountain .05 .15
159 Brent Gretzky .05 .15
160 Jason Allison .20 .50
F01 4-in-1 1.00 2.50
Glenn Robinson
Dan Wilkinson
Paul Wilson
Ed Jovanovski
Number One Draft Picks

1994 Classic Four Sport Gold

Seeded one per pack and featuring top rookies from basketball, baseball, football and hockey, the 1994 Classic Four-Sport gold set consists of 200 standard-size cards. The player's name and the Classic Four-Sport logo is on the right side of the picture along with the information that this is a gold card.

COMPLETE SET (200) 12.00 30.00
*GOLD: .8X TO 2X BASIC CARDS

1994 Classic Four Sport Printer's Proofs

Randomly inserted in packs and featuring top rookies from basketball, baseball, football and hockey, the 1994 Classic Four-Sport Printer's Proofs set consists of 200 standard-size cards. The information that this is a printer's proof card is directly above the player's name. Both the printer's proof logo and the name of the player are in red.

*PRINT PROOFS: 2.5X TO 6X BASIC CARDS

1994 Classic Four Sport Autographs

Randomly inserted in packs at a rate of one in 103, this standard-size set features players from the 1994 Classic Four-Sport set who autographed cards within the set. The fronts feature full-bleed color action player photos. The player's name is gold-foil stamped across the bottom of the picture. The backs have a congratulatory message about receiving an autographed card. Though the cards are unnumbered, we have assigned them the same number as their four-sport regular issue counterpart.

115A Ed Jovanovski/1180 6.00 15.00
119A Jeff O'Neill/3000 3.00 8.00
124A Nolan Baumgartner/2900 2.00 5.00
134A Craig Darby/2990 2.00 5.00
139A Dan Cloutier/2980 2.50 6.00
140A Todd Marchant/3100 2.50 6.00
143A Garth Snow/3050 2.50 6.00
144A Cory Stillman/3000 2.00 5.00
148A Mike Dunham/2960 3.00 8.00
149A Joe Frederick/3000 2.00 5.00
150A Mark DeSantis/3000 2.00 5.00
154A Geoff Sarjeant/3000 2.00 5.00
156A Greg Andrusak/2970 2.00 5.00
157A Denis Metlyuk/2960 2.00 5.00
158A Mike Fountain/3000 2.00 5.00

1994 Classic Four Sport BCs

This 20-card bonus standard-size set was inserted one per '94 Classic Four-Sport jumbo packs. The fronts feature full color player photos. The backs carry biographical and statistical information about the player.

COMPLETE SET (20) 6.00 15.00
BC17 Ed Jovanovski .20 .50
BC18 Radek Bonk .20 .50
BC19 Jeff O'Neill .20 .50
BC20 Ethan Moreau .20 .50

1994 Classic Four Sport Classic Picks

This 10-card standard-size set was randomly inserted in packs at rate of one in 72. The fronts feature full-color action player photos with the player's name and card title below. The backs carry a small player photo, the player's name, biographical information, and career highlights printed over a ghosted photo of the same player.

COMPLETE SET (10) 6.00 15.00
25 Ethan Moreau .40 1.00

1994 Classic Four Sport High Voltage

This 20-card sequentially-numbered standard-size set features the top draft picks. The cards are printed on holographic foil board with a striking design. 2,995 of each even-numbered card and 5,495 of each odd-numbered cards were produced. The cards were inserted on an average of 3 per case and had stated odds of one in 144 hobby packs. The fronts feature the players against a background of lightning while the backs feature a biography on the left side of the card. The right side shows more lightning and the player's photo.

COMPLETE SET (20) 40.00 100.00
COMMON CARD (HV1-HV20) .75 2.00
COMMON SP (HV1-HV20)
HV4 Ed Jovanovski SP 2.50 6.00
HV8 Oleg Tverdovsky SP 2.00 5.00
HV12 Radek Bonk SP 4.00 10.00
HV16 Jason Bonsignore SP 2.00 5.00
HV19 Jeff O'Neill .75 2.00

1994 Classic Four Sport Phone Cards $1

This set of eight phone cards was randomly inserted in Four-Sport packs. Printed on hard plastic, each card measures 2 1/8" by 3 3/8" and has rounded corners. The fronts display full-bleed color action photos, with the phone time value ($1, $2, $3, $4 or $5) and the player's name printed vertically in red along the right edge. The horizontal backs carry instructions for use of the cards. The cards are unnumbered and checklisted below in alphabetical order. The $3 and $5 cards were inserted into retail packs. The phone cards could be used until November 30, 1995.

COMPLETE SET (8) 3.00 8.00
*TWO DOLLAR: .5X TO 1.2X $1 CARDS
*THREE DOLLAR: .6X TO 1.5X $1 CARDS
*FOUR DOLLAR: .8X TO 2X $1 CARDS
*FIVE DOLLAR: 1X TO 2.5X $1 CARDS
*PIN NUMBER REVEALED: HALF VALUE
4 Ed Jovanovski .20 .50
6 Jeff O'Neill .20 .50

1994 Classic Four Sport Previews

Randomly inserted in 1994-95 Classic hockey foil packs at a rate of three per case, these five standard-size preview cards show the design of the 1994-95 Classic Four-Sport series. The full-bleed color action photos are gold-foil stamped with the "4-Sport Preview" emblem and the player's name. The backs feature another full-bleed closeup photo, with biography and statistics displayed on a ghosted panel.

COMPLETE SET (5) 6.00 15.00
P1 Jeff O'Neill .40 1.00

1994 Classic Four Sport Tri-Cards

Inserted one in every three cases, this five-card standard-size set features three top running backs, linebackers, hockey centers, pitchers and basketball guards and compares their individual skills. Every card is sequentially-numbered out of 2,695. The horizontal fronts feature the three players equally while the backs gives a brief biography of why the three players are grouped together.

COMPLETE SET (5) 4.00 10.00
TC4 Radek Bonk .40 1.00
Chris Wells
Jeff O'Neill

1995 Classic Ice Breakers

These cards were randomly inserted into packs at a ratio of approximately one every other box. The cards are sequentially numbered an less than 2,000 of each card were printed. The cards feature some of the leading prospects which included Bryan Berard, Nolan Baumgartner and Wade Redden. A die-cut version of these cards were issued as well. These cards were sequentially numbered to 495. The cards are numbered with a "BK" prefix.

COMPLETE SET (20) 30.00 60.00
*DIE CUT STARS: 2X TO 4X BASIC CARDS
BK1 Bryan Berard 2.00 5.00
BK2 Wade Redden 2.00 5.00
BK3 Aki Berg .75 2.00
BK4 Chad Kilger .75 2.00
BK5 Daymond Langkow 2.00 5.00
BK6 Steve Kelly .75 2.00
BK7 Shane Doan 2.50 6.00
BK8 Terry Ryan .75 2.00
BK9 Radek Dvorak 2.50 6.00
BK10 Miikka Elomo .75 2.00
BK11 Teemu Riihijarvi .75 2.00
BK12 Jean-Sebastien Giguere 2.00 5.00
BK13 Martin Biron 5.00 12.00
BK14 Jeff Ware .75 2.00

5 Brad Church .75 2.00
6 Petr Sykora 2.50 6.00
7 Jason Bonsignore .75 2.00
8 Brian Holzinger .75 2.00
9 Ed Jovanovski 2.00 5.00
10 Nolan Baumgartner .75 2.00

1993 Classic Pro Prospects

The 1993 Classic Pro Hockey Prospects set features 150 standard-size cards. The production run was 6,500 sequentially numbered cases, and female hockey phenom Manon Rheaume autographed 6,500 cards for random insertion into the foil packs.

COMPLETE SET (150) 4.00 10.00
1 Manon Rheaume .40 1.00
Draveurs Promote
Female Goaltender
2 Manon Rheaume .40 1.00
Quebec League Welcomes
Female Netminder
3 Manon Rheaume .40 1.00
4 Manon Rheaume .40 1.00
5 Manon Rheaume .40 1.00
6 Manon Rheaume .40 1.00
7 Manon Rheaume .40 1.00
8 Oleg Petrov .01 .05
9 Shjon Podein .01 .05
10 Alexei Kovalev AS .08 .25
11 Roman Oksiuta .01 .05
12 Dave Tomlinson .01 .05
13 Jason Miller .01 .05
14 Andrew McKim .01 .05
15 Dallas Drake .01 .05
16 Rob Gaudreau .01 .05
17 Darrin Madeley .01 .05
18 Scott Pellerin .01 .05
19 Scott Thomas .01 .05
20 Chris Tancill AS .01 .05
21 Patrick Kjellberg .01 .05
22 Jim Dowd .01 .05
23 Daniel Gauthier .01 .05
24 Mark Beaufait .01 .05
25 Milan Tichy AS .01 .05
26 Chris Osgood .50 1.25
27 Charles Poulin .01 .05
28 Patrick Lebeau .01 .05
29 Chris Govedaris .01 .05
30 Andrei Trefilov AS .01 .05
31 Kevin Stevens MLG .08 .25
32 Dmitri Kvartalnov MLG .01 .05
33 Patrick Roy MLG .60 1.50
34 Mark Recchi MLG .20 .50
35 Adam Oates MLG .20 .50
36 Patrick Augusta .01 .05
37 Gerry Fleming .01 .05
38 Sergei Krivokrasov .01 .05
39 Mike O'Neill .01 .05
40 Darrin Madeley AS .01 .05
41 Lindsay Vallis .01 .05
42 Todd Nelson .01 .05
43 Keith Jones .01 .05
44 Howie Rosenblatt .01 .05
45 Jason Ruff AS .01 .05
46 Robert Lang .01 .05
47 Andre Faust .01 .05
48 Steve Bancroft .01 .05
49 Iain Fraser .01 .05
50 Roman Hamrlik AS .01 .05
51 Pierre Sevigny .01 .05
52 Jeff Levy .01 .05
53 Len Barrie .01 .05
54 David Goverde .01 .05
55 Vladimir Malakhov AS .01 .05
56 Scott White .01 .05
57 Dmitri Motkov .01 .05
58 Jason Herter .01 .05
59 Drake Berehowsky .01 .05
60 Steve King AS .01 .05
61 Doug Barrault .01 .05
62 Martin Hamrlik .01 .05
63 Kevin Miehm .01 .05
64 Shaun Van Allen .01 .05
65 Corey Hirsch AS .01 .05
66 Dwayne Norris .01 .05
67 Petr Hrbek .01 .05
68 Philippe Boucher .01 .05
69 Denis Chervyakov .01 .05
70 Sergei Zubov AS .01 .05
71 Geoff Sarjeant .01 .05
72 Les Kuntar .01 .05
73 Byron Dafoe .20 .50
74 Checklist .01 .05
Alexei Kovalev
Sergei Zubov
Steve King
Corey Hirsch
75 Alexander Andrievski AS .01 .05
76 Checklist .01 .05
Joby Messier
Mitch Messier
77 Brian Sullivan .01 .05
78 Steve Larouche .01 .05
79 Denis Chasse .01 .05
80 Felix Potvin AS .20 .50
81 Josef Beranek .01 .05
82 Ken Klee .01 .05
83 Jozef Stumpel .08 .25
84 Andrew Verner .01 .05
85 Keith Osborne AS .01 .05
86 Igor Malykhin .01 .05
87 Gilbert Dionne .01 .05
88 Viktor Gordiouk .01 .05
89 Glen Murray .01 .05
90 Scott Pellerin AS .01 .05
91 Tommy Soderstrom .08 .25
92 Terry Chitaroni .01 .05
93 Viktor Kozlov .08 .25
94 Mikhail Shtalenkov .08 .25
95 Leonid Toropchenko .01 .05
96 Alex Galchenyuk .01 .05
97 Anatoli Fedotov .01 .05
98 Igor Chibirev .01 .05
99 Keith Gretzky .01 .05
100 Manon Rheaume .60 1.50
101 Sean Whyte .01 .05
102 Steve Konowalchuk .08 .25
103 Richard Borgo .01 .05
104 Paul DiPietro .01 .05
105 Patrik Carnback AS .01 .05
106 Mike Fountain .01 .05
107 Jamie Heward .01 .05
108 David St. Pierre .01 .05
109 Sean O'Donnell .01 .05
110 Greg Andrusak AS .01 .05
111 Damian Rhodes .08 .25
112 Ted Crowley .01 .05
113 Chris Taylor .01 .05
114 Terran Sandwith .01 .05
115 Jesse Belanger AS .01 .05
116 Justin Duberman .01 .05
117 Arturs Irbe .20 .50
118 Chris LiPuma .01 .05
119 Mike Torchia .01 .05
120 Niclas Andersson AS .01 .05
121 Rick Knickle .01 .05
122 Scott Gruhl .01 .05
123 Dave Michayluk .01 .05
124 Guy Leveque .01 .05
125 Scott Thomas AS .01 .05
126 Travis Green .01 .05
127 Joby Messier .01 .05
128 Victor Ignatjev .01 .05
129 Brad Tiley .01 .05
130 Grigori Panteleyev AS .01 .05
131 Vyatcheslav Butsayev .01 .05
132 Danny Lorenz .01 .05
133 Marty McInnis .01 .05
134 Ed Ronan .01 .05
135 Slava Kozlov AS .20 .50
136 Kevin St. Jacques .01 .05
137 Pavel Kostichkin .01 .05
138 Mike Hurlbut .01 .05
139 Tomas Forslund .01 .05
140 Rob Gaudreau AS .01 .05
141 Shawn Heaphy .01 .05
142 Radek Hamr .01 .05
143 Jaroslav Otevrel .01 .05
144 Keith Redmond .01 .05
145 Tom Pederson AS .01 .05
146 Jaroslav Modry .01 .05
147 Darren McCarty .20 .50
148 Terry Yake .01 .05
149 Ivan Droppa .01 .05
150 The VCR Line .01 .05
Shaun Van Allen
Dan Currie
Steven Rice
AU1 Dmitri Kvartalnov 2.00 5.00
AU/4000
(Certified Autograph)
AU2 Manon Rheaume 20.00 40.00
AU/6500
(Certified Autograph)

1993 Classic Pro Prospects BCs

One BC card was inserted in each jumbo pack. The cards are numbered on the back with a "BC" prefix.

COMPLETE SET (20) 15.00 30.00
BC1 Alexei Kovalev .40 1.00
BC2 Andrei Trefilov .20 .50
BC3 Roman Hamrlik .20 .50
BC4 Vladimir Malakhov .20 .50
BC5 Corey Hirsch .30 .75
BC6 Sergei Zubov .20 .50
BC7 Felix Potvin .40 1.00
BC8 Tommy Soderstrom .30 .75
BC9 Viktor Kozlov .30 .75
BC10 Manon Rheaume 1.50 4.00
BC11 Jesse Belanger .20 .50
BC12 Rick Knickle .20 .50
BC13 Joby Messier .20 .50
BC14 Vyacheslav Butsayev .20 .50
BC15 Tomas Forslund .20 .50
BC16 Jozef Stumpel .30 .75
BC17 Dmitri Kvartalnov MLG .20 .50
BC18 Adam Oates MLG .40 1.00
BC19 Dallas Drake .20 .50
BC20 Mark Recchi MLG .40 1.00

1993 Classic Pro Prospects LPs

The cards are numbered on the back with an "LP" prefix.

COMPLETE SET (5) 12.50 25.00
LP1 Manon Rheaume 6.00 15.00
LP2 Alexei Kovalev 1.25 3.00
LP3 Rob Gaudreau .75 2.00
LP4 Viktor Kozlov 1.25 3.00
LP5 Dallas Drake .75 2.00

1993 Classic Pro Prospects Prototypes

These three standard-size promo cards were issued to show the design of the 1993 Classic Pro Hockey Prospects set. Inside white borders, the fronts display color action player photos. A color bar edges the top of each picture and carries the player's name, team, and position. Also a black bar edges the bottom of each picture. On a gray background, the backs feature a color close-up photo, logos, biographical information, statistics, and career summary. A black bar that accents the top carries the card number and the disclaimer "For Promotional Purposes Only".

COMPLETE SET (3) 3.00 8.00
PR1 Steve King .60 1.50
PR2 Manon Rheaume 2.50 6.00
PR3 Rob Gaudreau .60 1.50

1994 Classic Pro Prospects

This 250-card set includes more than 100 foil-stamped subset cards. Randomly inserted throughout the foil packs were 25 limited print clear acetate cards and over 10,000 randomly inserted autographed cards of Radek Bonk, Alexei Yashin, Chris Pronger, Manon Rheaume, Joe Juneau, and more.

COMPLETE SET (250) 3.00 8.00
1 Radek Bonk .01 .05
2 Radek Bonk .01 .05
3 Radek Bonk .01 .05
4 Vlastimil Kroupa .01 .05
5 Mattias Norstrom .01 .05
6 Jaroslav Nedved .01 .05
7 Steve Dubinsky .01 .05
8 Christian Proulx .01 .05
9 Michal Grosek .01 .05
10 Pat Neaton .01 .05
11 Jason Arnott .01 .05
12 Martin Brodeur .40 1.00
13 Alexandre Daigle .01 .05
14 Ted Drury .01 .05
15 Iain Fraser .01 .05
16 Chris Gratton .08 .25
17 Greg Johnson .01 .05
18 Paul Kariya .40 1.00
19 Alexander Karpovtsev .01 .05
20 Chris Lipuma .01 .05
21 Kirk Maltby .01 .05
22 Sandy McCarthy .01 .05
23 Darren McCarty .01 .05
24 Jaroslav Modry .01 .05
25 Jim Montgomery .01 .05
26 Markus Naslund .20 .50
27 Rob Niedermayer .08 .25
28 Chris Osgood .30 .75
29 Pat Peake .01 .05
30 Derek Plante .01 .05
31 Chris Pronger .20 .50
32 Mike Rathje .01 .05
33 Mikael Renberg .08 .25
34 Damian Rhodes .08 .25
35 Garth Snow .08 .25
36 Cam Stewart .01 .05
37 Jim Storm .01 .05
38 Michal Sykora .01 .05
39 Jocelyn Thibault .20 .50
40 Alexei Yashin .01 .05
41 Checklist 1 .01 .05
42 Vesa Viitakoski .01 .05
43 Jake Grimes .01 .05
44 Jim Dowd .01 .05
45 Craig Ferguson .01 .05
46 Mike Boback .01 .05
47 Francois Groleau .01 .05
48 Juha Riihijarvi .01 .05
49 Mikhail Shtalenkov .08 .25
50 Zigmund Palffy .08 .25
51 Felix Potvin .20 .50
52 Alexei Kovalev .08 .25
53 Larry Robinson .08 .25
54 John LeClair .30 .75
55 Dominic Roussel .08 .25
56 Geoff Sanderson .08 .25
57 Greg Pankewicz .01 .05
58 Brent Bilodeau .01 .05
59 Brandon Convery .01 .05
60 Fred Knipscheer .01 .05
61 Igor Chibirev .01 .05
62 Anatoli Fedotov .01 .05
63 Bob Kellogg .01 .05
64 Mike Maurice .01 .05
65 Chad Penney .01 .05
66 Mike Bavis .01 .05
67 Eric Veilleux .01 .05
68 Parris Duffus .01 .05
69 Daniel Lacroix .01 .05
70 Milos Holan .01 .05
71 Mike Muller .01 .05
72 Micah Aivazoff .01 .05
73 Krzysztof Oliwa .01 .05
74 Ryan Hughes .01 .05
75 Christian Soucy .01 .05
76 Keith Redmond .01 .05
77 Mark De Santis .01 .05
78 Craig Martin .01 .05
79 Mike Kennedy .01 .05
80 Pauli Jaks .01 .05
81 Colin Chin .01 .05
82 Jody Gage .01 .05
83 Don Biggs .01 .05
84 Tim Tookey .01 .05
85 Clint Malarchuk .08 .25
86 Jozef Cierny .01 .05
87 Radek Hamr .01 .05
88 Jason Dawe .01 .05
89 Chris Longo .01 .05
90 Brian Rolston .08 .25
91 Mike McKee .01 .05
92 Vitali Prokhorov .01 .05
93 Chris Snell .01 .05
94 Martin Brochu .08 .25
95 Dan Plante .01 .05
96 Darcy Werenka .01 .05
97 Steffon Walby .01 .05
98 David Emma .01 .05
99 Dan Stiver .01 .05
100 Radek Bonk .01 .05
101 Mark Visheau .01 .05
102 Dean Melanson .01 .05
103 Vladimir Tsyplakov .01 .05
104 Mikhail Volkov .01 .05
105 Aaron Miller .01 .05
106 Alexei Kudashov .01 .05
107 Shawn Rivers .01 .05
108 Ladislav Karabin .01 .05
109 Matt Mallgrave .01 .05
110 Craig Darby .01 .05
111 Marcel Cousineau .01 .05
112 Jamie McLennan .08 .25
113 Yanic Perreault .08 .25
114 Zac Boyer .01 .05
115 Sergei Zubov .01 .05
116 Dan Kesa .01 .05
117 Jim Hiller .01 .05
118 Dmitri Starostenko .01 .05
119 Chris Tamer .01 .05
120 Aaron Ward .01 .05
121 Claude Savoie .01 .05
122 Jamie Black .01 .05
123 Jean-Francois Jomphe .01 .05
124 Paxton Schulte .01 .05
125 Jarkko Varvio .01 .05
126 Jaroslav Otevrel .01 .05
127 Dane Jackson .01 .05
128 Brent Grieve .01 .05
129 Checklist .30 .75
Pascal Rheaume
Manon Rheaume
130 Rene Corbet .01 .05
131 Joe Frederick .01 .05
132 Martin Tanguay .01 .05
133 Fredrik Jax .01 .05
134 Jamie Linden .01 .05
135 Jason Smith .01 .05
136 Rick Kowalsky .01 .05
137 Dino Grossi .01 .05
138 Aris Brimanis .01 .05
139 Jeff McLean .01 .05
140 Tyler Wright .01 .05
141 Roman Gorev .01 .05
142 Dean Hulett .01 .05
143 Niklas Sundblad .01 .05
144 Jeff Bes .01 .05
145 Pascal Rheaume .01 .05
146 Donald Brashear .01 .05
147 Hugo Belanger .01 .05
148 Blair Scott .01 .05
149 Steve Staios .01 .05
150 Matt Martin .01 .05
151 Richard Matvichuk .01 .05
152 Paul Brousseau .01 .05
153 Evgeny Namestnikov .01 .05
154 Mike Peca .20 .50
155 Jeff Nelson .01 .05
156 Greg Andrusak .01 .05
157 Norm Batherson .01 .05
158 Martin Bakula .01 .05
159 Ed Patterson .01 .05
160 Steve Larouche .01 .05
161 Libor Polasek .01 .05
162 Jon Hillebrandt .01 .05
163 Guy Leveque .01 .05
164 Eric Lacroix .01 .05
165 Scott Walker .01 .05
166 Robert Burakovsky .01 .05
167 Markus Ketterer .01 .05
168 Mike Speer .01 .05
169 Martin Jiranek .01 .05
170 Andy Schneider .01 .05
171 Terry Hollinger .01 .05
172 Mark Lawrence .01 .05
173 Martin Lapointe .20 .50
174 Vaclav Prospal .01 .05
175 Mike Fountain .01 .05
176 Alexander Kerch .01 .05
177 Oleg Petrov .01 .05
178 Derek Armstrong .01 .05
179 Matthew Barnaby .01 .05
180 Andrei Nazarov .01 .05
181 Andrei Trefilov .01 .05
182 Jean-Yves Roy .01 .05
183 Boris Rousson .01 .05
184 Dan Laperriere .01 .05
185 Yan Kaminsky .01 .05
186 Ralph Intranuovo .01 .05
187 Sandy Moger .01 .05
188 Grant Marshall .01 .05
189 Denny Felsner .01 .05
190 Cory Stillman .01 .05
191 Eric Lavigne .01 .05
192 Jarrod Skalde .01 .05
193 Steve Junker .01 .05
194 Alexander Cherbayev .01 .05
195 Nathan Lafayette .01 .05
196 Ed Ward .01 .05
197 Harijs Vitolinsh .01 .05
198 Jarmo Kekalainen .01 .05
199 Neil Eisenhut .01 .05
200 Radek Bonk .01 .05
201 Jason Bonsignore .01 .05
202 Jeff Friesen .01 .05
203 Ed Jovanovski .08 .25
204 Brett Lindros .01 .05
205 Jeff O'Neill .20 .50
206 Deron Quint .01 .05
207 Vadim Sharifjanov .01 .05
208 Oleg Tverdovsky .01 .05
209 Checklist .01 .05
Jeff O'Neill
Jeff Friesen
210 David Cooper .01 .05
211 Doug McDonald .01 .05
212 Leonid Toropchenko .01 .05
213 Chris Rogles .01 .05
214 Slava Kozlov .08 .25
215 Denis Metlyuk .01 .05
216 Scott McKay .01 .05
217 Brian Loney .01 .05
218 Kevin Hodson .01 .05
219 Bobby House .01 .05
220 Sergei Krivokrasov .01 .05
221 Brett Harkins .01 .05
222 Cale Hulse .01 .05
223 Marc Tardif .01 .05
224 Jon Rohloff .01 .05
225 Kevin Smyth .01 .05
226 Jason Young .01 .05
227 Sergei Zholtok .01 .05
228 Todd Simon .01 .05
229 Jerome Bechard .01 .05
230 Matt Robbins .01 .05
231 Joe Cook .01 .05
232 John Brill .01 .05
233 Dan Goldie .01 .05
234 Dan Gravelle .01 .05
235 Shawn Wheeler .01 .05
236 Brad Harrison .01 .05
237 Joe Dragon .01 .05
238 Jason Jennings .01 .05
239 Manon Rheaume .75 2.00
240 Jamie Steer .01 .05
241 Scott Rogers .01 .05
242 Lyle Wildgoose .01 .05
243 Darren Colbourne .01 .05
244 Mike Smith .01 .05
245 Chris Bright .01 .05
246 Chris Belanger .01 .05
247 Darren Schwartz .01 .05
248 Cammi Granato .60 1.50
249 Erin Whitten .20 .50
250 Manon Rheaume .75 2.00
NNO Arnott/Yashin ROY .40 1.00

1994 Classic Pro Prospects Autographs

This 9-card set includes over 10,000 randomly inserted autographed cards of Radek Bonk, Alexei Yashin, Chris Pronger, Manon Rheaume, Joe Juneau, and more.

AU1 Radek Bonk/2400 5.00 10.00
AU2 Jason Bonsignore/2450 5.00 10.00
AU3 Jeff Friesen/2450 10.00 25.00
AU4 Joe Juneau/1370 8.00 20.00
AU5 Alexei Kovalev/1900 5.00 10.00
AU6 Chris Pronger/1400 12.50 30.00
AU7 Manon Rheaume/1900 30.00 80.00
AU8 Erin Whitten/1800 12.50 30.00
AU9 Alexei Yashin/1400 6.00 15.00

1994 Classic Pro Prospects Ice Ambassadors

This standard-size set features young players from all over the world. The cards were inserted one per jumbo sheet in a late-season, retail-only repackaging configuration. The fronts feature a player photo with a stripe down the right side carrying the player's name. On the bottom of the card in gold lettering is the identification of the team. The reverse of the card features a player photo on the top half with statistical information on the bottom half.

COMPLETE SET (20) 3.00 8.00
IA1 Adrian Aucoin .08 .25
IA2 Corey Hirsch .15 .40
IA3 Paul Kariya 1.00 2.50
IA4 David Harlock .08 .25
IA5 Manny Legace .30 .75
IA6 Chris Therien .08 .25
IA7 Todd Warriner .08 .25
IA8 Todd Marchant .08 .25
IA9 Matt Martin .08 .25
IA10 Peter Ferraro .08 .25
IA11 Brian Rolston .15 .40
IA12 Jim Campbell .08 .25
IA13 Mike Dunham .30 .75
IA14 Craig Johnson .08 .25
IA15 Saku Koivu 1.00 2.50
IA16 Jere Lehtinen .30 .75
IA17 Viktor Kozlov .15 .40
IA18 Andrei Nikolishin .08 .25
IA19 Sergei Gonchar .15 .40
IA20 Valeri Karpov .08 .25

1994 Classic Pro Prospects International Heroes

Randomly inserted through the foil packs, these 25 clear acetate standard-size cards predominantly feature the U.S. and Canadian National Teams. The cards are numbered on the back with an "LP" prefix. The nationalities of the players are as follows: U.S. (1-10); Canadian (11-20, 24); Czech (21); Russian (22, 25); and Finnish (23).

COMPLETE SET (25) 20.00 40.00
LP1 Jim Campbell .75 2.00
LP2 Ted Drury .75 2.00
LP3 Mike Dunham 1.25 3.00
LP4 Chris Ferraro .75 2.00
LP5 Peter Ferraro .75 2.00
LP6 Darby Hendrickson .75 2.00
LP7 Craig Johnson .75 2.00
LP8 Todd Marchant .75 2.00
LP9 Matt Martin .75 2.00
LP10 Brian Rolston .75 2.00
LP11 Adrian Aucoin .75 2.00
LP12 Martin Gendron .75 2.00
LP13 David Harlock .75 2.00
LP14 Corey Hirsch .75 2.00
LP15 Paul Kariya 3.00 8.00
LP16 Manny Legace 1.25 3.00
LP17 Brett Lindros .75 2.00
LP18 Brian Savage .75 2.00
LP19 Chris Therien .75 2.00
LP20 Todd Warriner .75 2.00
LP21 Radek Bonk .75 2.00
LP22 Pavel Bure 1.25 3.00
LP23 Teemu Selanne 3.00 8.00
LP24 Mark Recchi 1.50 4.00
LP25 Alexei Yashin 1.50 4.00

1994 Classic Pro Prospects Promo

This standard-size promo card was issued to show the design of the 1994 Classic Pro Hockey Prospects set. Inside white borders, the front displays a color action player photo. The player's name, team, and position appear in a black bar at the bottom of the card. Also inside white borders, the back features another color player photo, logos, biographical information, and scoring totals. The disclaimer "For Promotional Purposes Only" is printed on the back.

1 Radek Bonk 1.50 4.00

1994 Classic Pro Prospects Prototype

Given away at the 1994 National Sports Convention in Houston, this prototype card measures the standard size. The front features a borderless color action player photo, with the player's name at the bottom. The word "PROTOTYPE" is written vertically in red block lettering along the right edge. On a screened background, the back carries an advertisement for the convention in gold foil lettering. The card is unnumbered.

NNO Jason Arnott 2.00 5.00

1996 Clear Assets

The 1996 Clear Assets set was issued in one series totaling 70 cards. The set features 75 upscale acetate cards of the most collectible athletes from baseball, basketball, football, hockey and auto racing. Also included is the debut appearance by many of the top players entering the 1996 football draft. Release date was April 1996.

COMPLETE SET (70) 6.00 15.00
51 Manon Rheaume .20 .50
56 Bryan Berard .08 .25
57 Petr Sykora .10 .30
58 Ed Jovanovski .10 .30
59 Radek Dvorak .08 .25

1996 Clear Assets Phone Cards $1

COMPLETE SET (30) 5.00 12.00
*PIN NUMBER REVEALED: HALF VALUE
$1 CARDS ONE PER RETAIL PACK
*$2 CARDS: .6X TO 1.5X $1 CARDS
ONE PER HOBBY PACK
CARDS EXPIRED 10/1/97
5 Wade Redden .10 .30
11 Manon Rheaume .30 .75
22 Petr Sykora .15 .40

1996 Clear Assets Phone Cards $5

Inserted at a rate of 1:10 packs, this 20-card set of acetate phone cards features many of the biggest names in sports. The Sprint phone cards carry expiration dates of 10/1/97.

COMPLETE SET (20) 12.00 30.00
*PIN NUMBER REVEALED:HALF VALUE
16 Petr Sykora .40 1.00

1996 Collector's Edge Future Legends

This set features top performers from the AHL and IHL. The cards were sold in wax pack form and featured thin card stock with stylized metallic etching on the front.

COMPLETE SET (50) 6.00 15.00
1 Brad Bombardir .07 .20
2 Niklas Andersson .07 .20
3 Mike Dunham .20 .50
4 Anders Eriksson .07 .20
5 Kelly Fairchild .07 .20
6 Chris Ferraro .07 .20
7 Peter Ferraro .07 .20
8 Eric Fichaud .15 .40
9 Manny Legace .20 .50
10 David Ling .07 .20
11 Jim Montgomery .07 .20
12 Chris Murray .07 .20
13 Rob Brown .07 .20
14 Rem Murray .07 .20
15 Rob Murray .07 .20
16 Jan Caloun .07 .20
17 Frederic Chabot .15 .40
18 Craig Fisher .07 .20
19 Dwayne Roloson .15 .40
20 Brad Smyth .07 .20
21 Steve Sullivan .20 .50
22 Petr Sykora .07 .20
23 Darcy Tucker .15 .40
24 London Wilson .15 .40
25 Greg Hawgood .07 .20
26 Stephane Beauregard .15 .40
27 Aki Berg .07 .20
28 Matt Johnson .07 .20
29 Curtis Joseph .20 .50
30 Dan Lambert .07 .20
31 Eric LeCompte .07 .20
32 Brett Lievers .07 .20
33 Mark McArthur .15 .40
34 Ethan Moreau .15 .40
35 Marty Murray .07 .20
36 Wayne Primeau .07 .20
37 John Purves .07 .20
38 Manon Rheaume 1.00 2.50
39 Barry Richter .07 .20
40 Jamie Rivers .07 .20
41 Tommy Salo .20 .50
42 Jamie Storr .20 .50
43 Tom Tilley .07 .20
44 Derek Wilkinson .15 .40
45 Mike Wilson .07 .20
46 Sandis Ozolinsh .07 .20
47 Andrew Brunette .15 .40
48 James Black .07 .20
49 Terry Yake .07 .20
50 Mike Prokopec .07 .20

1996 Collector's Edge Future Legends Autographed Hot Picks

Randomly inserted at 2 per box, these cards carry full color photos and autographs of the featured player.

COMPLETE SET (4) 10.00 20.00
1 Chris Phillips 2.00 5.00
2 Boyd Devereaux 2.00 5.00
3 Richard Jackman 2.00 5.00
4 Marcus Nilsson 2.00 5.00

1996 Collector's Edge Ice

This 200 card standard-size set features members of the America Hockey League and the International Hockey League. The cards are sequenced in alphabetical order within alphabetical team order. A parallel prismatic version of these cards were issued, they are valued as a multiple of the regular cards.

COMPLETE SET (200) 15.00 30.00
1 Curtis Bowen .02 .10
2 Anders Eriksson .02 .10
3 Kevin Hodson .08 .25
4 Martin Lapointe .20 .50
5 Aaron Ward .02 .10
6 Mike Dunham .20 .50
7 Chris McAlpine .02 .10
8 Brian Rolston .20 .50
9 Corey Schwab .08 .25
10 Steve Sullivan .20 .50
11 Petr Sykora .20 .50
12 Darren Van Impe .02 .10
13 Mike Maneluk .02 .10
14 David Sacco .02 .10
15 Jarrod Skalde .08 .25
16 Nikolai Tsulygin .02 .10
17 Peter Ferraro .02 .10
18 Chris Ferraro .02 .10
19 Corey Hirsch .08 .25
20 Mattias Norstrom .08 .25
21 Jamie Ram .08 .25
22 Chris Armstrong .02 .10
23 Alexei Kudashov .02 .10
24 Todd MacDonald .02 .10
25 Steve Washburn .02 .10
26 Kevin Weekes .20 .50
27 Rene Corbet .02 .10
28 Janne Laukkanen .02 .10
29 Aaron Miller .02 .10
30 Landon Wilson .08 .25
31 Fred Brathwaite .20 .50
32 Ryan Haggerty .02 .10
33 Ralph Intranuovo .02 .10
34 Todd Marchant .20 .50
35 David Oliver .02 .10
36 Marko Tuomainen .02 .10
37 Peter White .02 .10
38 Sebastien Bordeleau .02 .10
39 Martin Brochu .08 .25
40 Valeri Bure .08 .25
41 Craig Conroy .08 .25
42 Darcy Tucker .20 .50
43 David Wilkie .02 .10
44 Paul Healey .02 .10
45 Chris Herperger .02 .10
46 Jim Montgomery .02 .10
47 Chris Therien .02 .10
48 Pavol Demitra .20 .50
49 Michel Picard .02 .10
50 Jason Zent .02 .10
51 Patrick Boileau .02 .10
52 Jim Carey .08 .25
53 Sergei Gonchar .08 .25
54 Jeff Nelson .02 .10
55 Stefan Ustorf .02 .10
56 Alexander Kharlamov .02 .10
57 Ron Tugnutt .20 .50
58 Scott Bailey .08 .25
59 Clayton Beddoes .02 .10
60 Andre Roy .02 .10
61 Evgeny Ryabchikov .08 .25
62 Mark Astley .02 .10
63 Jody Gage .08 .25
64 Sergei Klimentiev .02 .10
65 Barrie Moore .02 .10
66 Mike Wilson .02 .10
67 Shayne Wright .02 .10
68 Michal Grosek .08 .25
69 Tavis Hansen .02 .10
70 Nikolai Khabibulin .30 .75
71 Scott Langkow .08 .25
72 Jason McBain .02 .10
73 Dwayne Roloson .08 .25
74 Cory Stillman .08 .25
75 Jamie Allison .02 .10
76 Jesper Mattson .02 .10
77 David Ling .02 .10
78 Brandon Convery .02 .10
79 Darby Hendrickson .02 .10
80 Janne Gronvall .02 .10
81 Jason Saal .02 .10
82 Brent Gretzky .02 .10
83 Kent Manderville .02 .10
84 Shayne Toporowski .02 .10
85 Paul Vincent .02 .10
86 Mark Kolesar .02 .10
87 Lonny Bohonos .02 .10
88 Larry Courville .02 .10
89 Jassen Cullimore .02 .10
90 Scott Walker .08 .25
91 Mike Buzak .02 .10
92 Craig Darby .02 .10
93 Eric Fichaud .08 .25
94 Andreas Johansson .02 .10
95 Jamie Rivers .02 .10
96 Jason Strudwick .02 .10
97 Patrice Tardif .02 .10
98 Alex Vasilevskii .02 .10
99 Drew Bannister .02 .10
100 Stan Drulia .02 .10
101 Aaron Gavey .02 .10
102 Reggie Savage .02 .10
103 Derek Wilkinson .08 .25
104 Rob Brown .02 .10
105 Dan Currie .02 .10
106 Kevin MacDonald .02 .10
107 Steve Maltais .08 .25
108 Shawn Rivers .02 .10
109 Wendell Young .08 .25
110 Don Biggs .02 .10
111 Dale DeGray .02 .10
112 Paul Lawless .02 .10
113 Danny Lorenz .02 .10
114 Dave Tomlinson .02 .10
115 Jock Callander .08 .25
116 Phillipe DeRouville .02 .10
117 Ryan Savoia .02 .10
118 Mike Stevens .02 .10
119 Chris Tamer .08 .25
120 Peter Bondra .20 .50
121 Peter Ciavaglia .02 .10
122 Rick Knickle .02 .10
123 Lonnie Loach .02 .10
124 Michal Pivonka .02 .10
125 Andy Bezeau .02 .10
126 Bob Essensa .08 .25
127 Andrew McBain .02 .10
128 Kevin Miehm .02 .10
129 Scott Arniel .02 .10
130 Kevin Dineen .08 .25
131 Rob Dopson .08 .25
132 Mark Freer .02 .10
133 Troy Gamble .08 .25
134 Ethan Moreau .00 .25
135 Sergei Klimovich .02 .10
136 Eric Lecompte .02 .10
137 Eric Manlow .02 .10
138 Kip Miller .02 .10

139 Manny Fernandez	.20	.50
140 Mike Kennedy	.02	.10
141 Jamie Langenbrunner	.20	.50
142 Derrick Smith	.02	.10
143 Jordan Willis	.08	.25
144 Jan Caloun	.02	.10
145 Viktor Kozlov	.08	.25
146 Andrei Nazarov	.02	.10
147 Geoff Sarjeant	.02	.10
148 Patrik Augusta	.02	.10
149 Viktor Gordiouk	.02	.10
150 Dave Littman	.08	.25
151 Todd Gillingham	.02	.10
152 Greg Hawgood	.02	.10
153 Patrice Lefebvre	.02	.10
154 Pokey Reddick	.08	.25
155 Manon Rheaume	.75	2.00
156 Jeff Sharples	.02	.10
157 Todd Simon	.02	.10
158 Radek Bonk	.20	.50
159 Gino Cavallini	.02	.10
160 Tom Draper	.08	.25
161 Tony Hrkac	.08	.25
162 Fabian Joseph	.02	.10
163 Mark Laforest	.02	.10
164 Dave Christian	.02	.10
165 Bryan Fogarty	.02	.10
166 Chris Govedaris	.02	.10
167 Mike Hurlbut	.02	.10
168 Chris Imes	.02	.10
169 Stephane Morin	.02	.10
170 Allan Bester	.08	.25
171 Kerry Clark	.02	.10
172 Neil Eisenhut	.02	.10
173 Craig Fisher	.02	.10
174 Patrick Neaton	.02	.10
175 Todd Richards	.02	.10
176 Jon Casey	.08	.25
177 Doug Evans	.02	.10
178 Michel Mongeau	.02	.10
179 Greg Paslawski	.02	.10
180 Darren Veitch	.02	.10
181 Frederick Beaubien	.02	.10
182 Kevin Brown	.02	.10
183 Rob Cowie	.02	.10
184 Yanic Perreault	.08	.25
185 Chris Snell	.02	.10
186 Jan Vopat	.02	.10
187 Robin Bawa	.02	.10
188 Stephane Beauregard	.08	.25
189 Dale Craigwell	.02	.10
190 John Purves	.08	.25
191 Jeff Madill	.02	.10
192 Gord Dineen	.02	.10
193 Chris Marinucci	.08	.25
194 Mark McArthur	.02	.10
195 Zigmund Palffy	.20	.50
196 Tommy Salo	.20	.50
197 Checklist	.02	.10
198 Checklist	.02	.10
199 Checklist	.02	.10
200 Checklist	.02	.10

1996 Collector's Edge Ice Crucibles

This 25 card standard-size set was randomly inserted into packs. The fronts feature the players photo along with the word "Crucible" on the top and his name on the bottom. The cards are numbered with a "C" prefix. The backs include a player head shot as well as recent stats.

COMPLETE SET (25)	15.00	30.00
C1 David Roberts	.40	1.00
C2 Ian Laperriere	.40	1.00
C3 Kevin Dineen	.40	1.00
C4 Kenny Jonsson	.40	1.00
C5 Jim Carey	.75	2.00
C6 Todd Marchant	.40	1.00
C7 David Oliver	.40	1.00
C8 Yanic Perreault	.75	2.00
C9 Chris Therien	.40	1.00
C10 Viktor Kozlov	.75	2.00
C11 Valeri Bure	.40	1.00
C12 Nikolai Khabibulin	1.00	2.50
C13 Steven Rice	.40	1.00
C14 Mike Kennedy	.40	1.00
C15 Peter Bondra	.75	2.00
C16 Sergei Zubov	.40	1.00
C17 Slava Kozlov	.75	2.00
C18 Chris Osgood	.75	2.00
C19 Darren McCarty	.40	1.00
C20 Jason Dawe	.40	1.00
C21 Trevor Kidd	1.00	2.50
C22 Tommy Salo	1.00	2.50
C23 Michal Pivonka	.40	1.00
C24 Zigmund Palffy	.75	2.00
NNO Checklist	.40	1.00

1996 Collector's Edge Ice Livin' Large

This set was randomly inserted into packs. The cards feature top players. The cards are numbered with a "L" prefix.

COMPLETE SET (11)	20.00	40.00
L1 Adam Graves	.75	2.00
L2 Marty McSorley	.75	2.00
L3 Adam Oates	1.25	3.00
L4 Keith Primeau	.75	2.00
L5 Bill Ranford	1.25	3.00
L6 Curtis Joseph	1.50	4.00
L7 Felix Potvin	1.50	4.00
L8 Mike Vernon	1.25	3.00
L9 Theo Fleury	.75	2.00
L10 Kevin Stevens	.75	2.00
L11 Martin Brodeur	8.00	20.00
NNO Checklist	.75	2.00

1996 Collector's Edge Ice Platinum Club

Random inserts in packs of Collectors Edge Ice.

COMPLETE SET (8)	10.00	25.00
1 Mike Dunham	2.00	5.00
2 Eric Fichaud	.75	2.00
3 Manny Legace	2.00	5.00
4 Steve Sullivan	.75	2.00
5 Darcy Tucker	.75	2.00
6 Jamie Langenbrunner	.75	2.00
7 Ethan Moreau	.75	2.00
8 Jamie Storr	.75	2.00

1996 Collector's Edge Ice Prism

This 200-card set was issued as a parallel to the base set. They weren't issued as inserts, however. Instead, they were sold in team set form on a localized basis across the AHL and IHL. These cards are actually quite scarce, and provide a real challenge for player collectors.

*PRISM CARDS: 2X to 5X BASIC CARDS

1996 Collector's Edge Ice Promos

This 7-card set was issued as a promotional device to entice dealers to purchase the upcoming Collector's Edge Ice set of minor league stars. The cards mirror the design of the regular issue cards, save for the numbering, which comes with a PR-prefix.

COMPLETE SET (7)	.75	2.00
PR1 Todd Marchant	.08	.25
PR2 Tommy Salo	.20	.50
PR3 Michael Dunham	.20	.50
PR4 Viktor Kozlov	.15	.40
PR5 Dwayne Roloson	.15	.40
PR6 Tony Hrkac	.08	.25
NNO Title Card	.20	.50

1996 Collector's Edge Ice QuantumMotion

This 13 card set was randomly inserted into packs. The full-bleed cards feature a player photo over most of it. The words "Quantum Motion" are located in the lower right corner.

COMPLETE SET (13)	15.00	30.00
1 Manny Fernandez	1.50	4.00
2 Pokey Reddick	.75	2.00
3 Yanic Perreault	.75	2.00
4 Rob Brown	.75	2.00
5 Hubie McDonough	.75	2.00
6 Stan Drulia	.75	2.00
7 Michel Picard	.75	2.00
8 Jim Carey	1.25	3.00
9 Martin Lapointe	1.25	3.00
10 Valeri Bure	.75	2.00
11 Martin Brochu	1.25	3.00
12 Corey Schwab	1.25	3.00
NNO Checklist	.75	2.00

1996 Collector's Edge Ice Signed, Sealed and Delivered

This 8-card set highlights youngsters set to make their power known in the NHL. Cards were randomly inserted in packs at an unknown ratio.

COMPLETE SET (8)	8.00	20.00
1 Alexandre Volchkov	1.25	3.00
2 Chris Allen	1.25	3.00
3 Brian Bonin	1.25	3.00
4 Josh Green	1.25	3.00
5 Chris Hajt	1.25	3.00
6 Josh Holden	1.25	3.00
8 Andrei Zyuzin	1.25	3.00
NNO Alexandre Volchkov	1.25	3.00

1996 Collector's Edge Ice The Wall

This 13 card die-cut set was inserted as a set in each sealed foil box. The cards feature goaltenders and their masks are on the front. The backs are devoted to a player photo. Also on the backs are vital statistics, and a brief biography. The cards are numbered with a "TW" prefix.

COMPLETE SET (12)	6.00	12.00
TW1 Ray LeBlanc	.40	1.00
TW2 Manny Fernandez	.75	2.00
TW3 Rick Knickle	.40	1.00
TW4 Troy Gamble	.40	1.00
TW5 Pokey Reddick	.40	1.00
TW6 Wendell Young	.40	1.00
TW7 Jim Carey	.40	1.00
TW8 Dwayne Roloson	.40	1.00
TW9 Les Kuntar	.40	1.00
TW10 Mike Dunham	.75	2.00
TW11 Eric Fichaud	.40	1.00
TW12 Kevin Hodson	.40	1.00

1995 Images

This 100-card set features top NHL prospects currently playing in the juniors, minors or overseas. The standard-sized cards feature full-bleed color photography over a metallic sheen background. The Classic logo is in the upper left corner, while the Images logo, player name and position rest on a blue and silver bar near the bottom. The backs feature another color photo, stats and the logos of the licensing bodies. One autographed card was found in each box. A total of 1995 individually numbered 12-box cases were produced.

COMPLETE SET (100)	5.00	12.00
1 Bryan Berard	.07	.20
2 Jeff Friesen	.02	.10
3 Tommy Salo	.25	.60
4 Jim Carey	.07	.20
5 Wade Redden	.07	.20
6 Jocelyn Thibault	.15	.40
7 Ian Laperriere	.02	.10
8 Todd Marchant	.02	.10
9 Blaine Lacher	.02	.10
10 Pavel Bure	.15	.40
11 Alex Vasilevskii	.02	.10
12 Jason Doig	.02	.10
13 Eric Fichaud	.07	.20
14 Eric Daze	.07	.20
15 Ed Jovanovski	.07	.20
16 Alexander Selivanov	.02	.10
17 Brent Gretzky	.02	.10
18 Terry Ryan	.02	.10
19 Chris Wells	.02	.10
20 Wade Belak	.02	.10
21 Kevin Dineen	.02	.10
22 Craig Fisher	.02	.10
23 Jan Caloun	.02	.10
24 Manny Fernandez	.15	.40
25 Radek Bonk	.02	.10
26 Dave Christian	.02	.10
27 Patrice Tardif	.02	.10
28 Kevin Brown	.02	.10
29 Hubie McDonough	.02	.10
30 Yan Golubovsky	.02	.10
31 Steve Larouche	.02	.10
32 Chris Therien	.02	.10
33 Craig Darby	.02	.10
34 Dwayne Norris	.02	.10
35 Roman Oksiuta	.02	.10
36 Steve Washburn	.02	.10
37 Todd Bertuzzi	.15	.40
38 Cory Stillman	.07	.20
39 Steve Kelly	.02	.10
40 Nathan LaFayette	.02	.10
41 Dwayne Roloson	.07	.20
42 Nikolai Khabibulin	.15	.40
43 Radim Bicanek	.02	.10
44 Jeff O'Neill	.02	.10
45 Jason Bonsignore	.02	.10
46 Shean Donovan	.02	.10
47 Wayne Primeau	.02	.10
48 Jamie Langenbrunner	.02	.10
49 Dan Cloutier	.15	.40
50 Ethan Moreau	.07	.20
51 Brad Bombardir	.02	.10
52 Jason Muzzatti	.02	.10
53 Jassen Cullimore	.02	.10
54 Jason Zent	.02	.10
55 Sergei Gonchar	.07	.20
56 Steve Rucchin	.02	.10
57 Rob Cowie	.02	.10
58 Miroslav Satan	.40	1.00
59 Kenny Jonsson	.07	.20
60 Adam Deadmarsh	.02	.10
61 Mike Dunham	.15	.40
62 Corey Hirsch	.02	.10
63 Janne Laukkanen	.02	.10
64 Craig Conroy	.02	.10
65 Ryan Sittler	.02	.10
66 Jeff Nelson	.02	.10
67 Michel Picard	.02	.10
68 Mark Astley	.02	.10
69 Lonny Bohonos	.02	.10
70 Evgeny Ryabchikov	.02	.10
71 Chris Osgood	.07	.20
72 Manon Rheaume	1.00	2.50
73 Mike Kennedy	.02	.10
74 Deron Quint	.02	.10
75 Jamie Storr	.07	.20
76 Aris Brimanis	.02	.10
77 Valeri Bure	.02	.10
78 Rene Corbet	.02	.10
79 David Oliver	.02	.10
80 Chris McAlpine	.02	.10
81 Petr Sykora	.15	.40
82 Brad Church	.07	.20
83 Daymond Langkow	.15	.40
84 Chad Kilger	.02	.10
85 Shane Doan	.20	.50
86 Jeff Ware	.02	.10
87 Christian Laflamme	.02	.10
88 Cory Cross	.02	.10
89 Al Secord	.02	.10
90 Jason Woolley	.02	.10
91 Bryan McCabe	.02	.10
92 Travis Richards	.02	.10
93 Andrei Nazarov	.02	.10
94 Mike Pomichter	.02	.10
95 Chris Marinucci	.02	.10
96 Jean-Yves Roy	.02	.10
97 Brian Rolston	.07	.20
98 Aaron Ward	.02	.10
99 Jim Carey CL	.02	.10
100 Pavel Bure CL	.07	.20

1995 Images Gold

These 100 standard-size cards were issued as a one-per-pack parallel to the Images set. The card design is identical to the standard Images card, except for the metallic background being a golden tone rather than the standard silver.

*STARS: 1.25X TO 2.5X BASIC CARDS

1995 Images Autographs

These 22 standard-size cards were random inserts throughout the packs. The card design is identical to the standard Images card except for the facsimile autograph inscribed across the picture. The number of cards signed is indicated in parenthesis.

2A Jeff Friesen/1500	4.00	10.00
6A Jocelyn Thibault/1185	4.00	10.00
9A Blaine Lacher/1500	2.00	5.00
25A Radek Bonk/970	3.00	8.00
30A Yan Golubovsky/1500	.75	2.00
36A Steve Washburn/1500	.75	2.00
41A Dwayne Roloson/1115	.75	2.00
45A Jason Bonsignore/1500	2.00	5.00
46A Shean Donovan/1500	.75	2.00
48A J.Langenbrunner/1500	5.00	12.00
54A Jason Zent/1125	.75	2.00
59A Kenny Jonsson/1180	2.00	5.00
60A Adam Deadmarsh/1500	6.00	15.00
64A Craig Conroy/1170	.75	2.00
74A Deron Quint/1500	.75	2.00
76A Aris Brimanis/1500	.75	2.00
79A David Oliver/1500	.75	2.00
80A Chris McAlpine/1185	.75	2.00
81A Petr Sykora/1500	3.00	8.00
94A Mike Pomichter/1175	.75	2.00
95A Chris Marinucci/1500	.75	2.00
98A Aaron Ward/1190	.75	2.00

1995 Images Clear Excitement

This 20-card standard-size set was randomly inserted only in Hot boxes. Essentially, the odds of finding one of these cards was 1, 152 packs. Each pack in a Hot box has 3 cards from any of the five insert sets. These clear cards feature color player action cutouts on their fronts. The player's name appears in a blue bar on the left. The backs carry the reverse image as a shadow with the player's name in an oval across it. The blue bar on the left contains information about the player and the card number at the top.

COMPLETE SET (20)	75.00	150.00
CE1 Bryan Berard	2.50	6.00
CE2 Jeff Friesen	2.00	5.00
CE3 Tommy Salo	3.00	8.00
CE4 Jim Carey	2.50	6.00
CE5 Wade Redden	2.50	6.00
CE6 Jocelyn Thibault	3.00	8.00
CE7 Ian Laperriere	2.00	5.00
CE8 Todd Marchant	2.00	5.00
CE9 Blaine Lacher	2.00	5.00
CE10 Pavel Bure	3.00	8.00
CE11 Petr Sykora	3.00	8.00
CE12 Daymond Langkow	2.50	6.00
CE13 Radek Bonk	2.00	5.00
CE14 Patrice Tardif	2.00	5.00
CE15 Jeff Nelson	2.00	5.00
CE16 Jeff O'Neill	2.00	5.00
CE17 Ed Jovanovski	2.50	6.00
CE18 Jason Doig	2.00	5.00
CE19 Chris Marinucci	2.00	5.00
CE20 Manon Rheaume	12.50	30.00

1993-94 Images Four Sport

These 150 standard-size cards feature on their borderless fronts color player action shots with backgrounds that have been thrown out of focus. On the white background to the left, career highlights, biography and statistics are displayed. Just 6,500 of each card were produced. The set closes with Classic Headlines (128-147) and checklists (148-150). A redemption card inserted one per case entitled the collector to one set of basketball draft preview cards. This offered expired 9/30/94.

COMPLETE SET (150)	6.00	15.00
4 Alexandre Daigle	.10	.30
8 Chris Pronger	.20	.50
16 Jim Montgomery	.08	.25
17 Todd Marchant	.08	.25
20 Mike Dunham	.08	.25
21 Garth Snow	.10	.30
24 Barry Richter	.08	.25
30 Rob Niedermayer	.15	.50
32 Jesse Belanger	.08	.25
35 Peter Ferraro	.08	.25
38 Ted Drury	.08	.25
43 Derek Plante	.08	.25
46 Jim Campbell	.08	.25
56 Chris Osgood	.60	1.50
62 Jason Arnott	.15	.40
74 Jocelyn Thibault	.10	.30
86 Chris Gratton	.08	.25
92 Mike Rathje	.08	.25
101 Martin Brodeur	.40	1.00
106 Paul Kariya	.60	1.50
111 Manon Rheaume	.40	1.00
121 Felix Potvin	.15	.40
125 Alexei Yashin	.10	.30
130 Alexei Yashin B/W	.08	.25
135 Chris Pronger BW	.08	.25
138 Chris Gratton BW	.08	.25
142 Jason Arnott B/W	.10	.30
147 Manon Rheaume B/W	.25	.60

1993-94 Images Four Sport Chrome

Randomly inserted one in every fourteen 1994 Classic Images packs, these 20 limited print (9,750 of each) cards measure the standard size and feature color player action shots on their borderless metallic fronts. The cards are numbered on the back with a "CC" prefix. This set was also available in uncut sheet form as a redeemed prize for the Marshall Faulk M5 card.

COMPLETE SET (20)	15.00	40.00
CC12 Cammi Granato	.75	2.00
CC13 Alexei Yashin	.50	1.25
CC14 Alexandre Daigle	.60	1.50
CC15 Manon Rheaume	1.25	3.00
CC16 Radek Bonk	.40	1.00
NNO Uncut Sheet	30.00	80.00

1993-94 Images Four Sport Sudden Impact

Inserted one per '94 Classic Images pack, these 20 gold foil-board cards measure the standard-size. The gold metallic fronts feature borderless color player action shots on backgrounds that have been thrown out of focus. The player's name and position appear in vertical lettering within a black strip across the card near the right edge. The back carries a color player action shot at the top, followed below by career highlights on a white panel. The player's name appears in vertical black lettering within a ghosted action strip at the left edge. The cards are numbered on the back with an "SI" prefix.

COMPLETE SET (20)	4.00	10.00
SI5 Alexandre Daigle	.40	1.00
SI6 Rob Niedermayer	.30	.75
SI7 Jocelyn Thibault	.30	.75
SI8 Derek Plante	.20	.50

1995 Images Four Sport

Printed on 18-point micro-lined foil board, the 1995 Classic Images set consists of 120 standard-size cards, featuring the top draft picks from the four major sports. Classic produced 1,995 sequentially-numbered 16-box hobby cases. This series also features one "Hot Box" in every four cases; each pack in it included at least one card from five insert sets, plus the special Clear Excitement chase cards not found anywhere else, for a total of 24 inserts per Hot Box. There was a promotional card issued, not inserted into '94-95 Assets packs, for Grant Hill numbered HP1. The front is the same as the card in the set, but the back has an orange background and describes the product's features.

COMPLETE SET (120)	6.00	15.00
94 Ed Jovanovski	.15	.40
95 Oleg Tverdovsky	.10	.30
96 Radek Bonk	.20	.50
97 Jason Bonsignore	.10	.30
98 Jeff O'Neill	.10	.30
99 Ryan Smyth	.30	.75
100 Jamie Storr	.20	.50
101 Jason Wiemer	.10	.30
102 Nolan Baumgartner	.10	.30
103 Jeff Friesen	.20	.50
104 Wade Belak	.10	.30
105 Ethan Moreau	.10	.30
106 Alexander Kharlamov	.10	.30
107 Eric Fichaud	.20	.50
108 Wayne Primeau	.10	.30
109 Brad Brown	.10	.30
110 Chris Dingman	.10	.30
111 Chris Wells	.10	.30
112 Vadim Sharifijanov	.10	.30
113 Dan Cloutier	.10	.30
114 Jason Allison	.20	.50
115 Todd Marchant	.10	.30
116 Brent Gretzky	.10	.30
117 Petr Sykora	.30	.75
118 Manon Rheaume	.20	.50
120 Marshall Faulk CL	.15	.40

1995 Images Four Sport Classic Performances

Randomly inserted in hobby boxes at a rate of one in every 12 packs, this 20-card standard-size set relives great moments from the careers of 20 top athletes. Each card is numbered out of 4,495. The fronts feature the player against a gold background. The back contains on the left side a description of the great moment and on the right side a color player photo. The cards are numbered with a "CP" prefix.

COMPLETE SET (20)	20.00	50.00
CP19 Ed Jovanovski	.40	1.00
CP20 Eric Fichaud	.50	1.25

1995 Images Four Sport Clear Excitement

Randomly inserted at a rate of one in every 24 packs in hobby and retail hot boxes (1:1536 over the product run), these two five-card acetate sets each feature five notable athletes from different sports. Cards with the prefix "E" were inserted in hobby hot boxes, while cards with the prefix "C" were found in retail hot boxes. The cards are numbered out of 300.

COMPLETE SET (10)	60.00	150.00
E5 Manon Rheaume	5.00	12.00

1995 Images Four Sport Previews

Randomly inserted one per 24 packs in second-series '94-95 Assets packs, this five-card standard-size set was issued to promote the Classic Images series. Just 5,000 of each card were produced. The cards display the player's photo showcased against a metallic background. The backs are devoted on the left side to the player's identification and a note saying you have received a limited edition preview card. The right side of the reverse has a full-color photo of the player and the card is numbered at the upper right corner. The cards are numbered with an "IP" prefix.

COMPLETE SET (5)	6.00	15.00
IP4 Manon Rheaume	.75	2.00

1995 Images Platinum Players

The cards in this 10 card standard-size set were randomly inserted at a rate of one per 36 packs. The fronts have a color action photo with a green and silver foil background. The word "Images" is at the top and "Platinum Player" is at the bottom. The backs have a color action photo with a green tint in the background. Player information appears at the bottom and each card is numbered out of 1,995.

COMPLETE SET (10)	10.00	20.00
PL1 Pavel Bure	1.50	4.00
PL2 Tony Granato	.40	1.00
PL3 Kevin Dineen	.40	1.00
PL4 Ron Hextall	1.25	3.00
PL5 Claude Lemieux	.40	1.00
PL6 Mark Recchi	1.50	4.00
PL7 Benoit Hogue	.40	1.00
PL8 Tim Cheveldae	.40	1.00
PL9 Darcy Wakaluk	.40	1.00
PL10 Todd Gill	.40	1.00

1995 Images Platinum Premier Draft Choice

One card from this 10 standard-size set was randomly inserted in every 48 packs. The card of Bryan Berard, the no. 1 draft choice, was redeemable for a 25.00 Manon Rheaume autographed phone card. The offer expired 12/31/95. The fronts feature a player action photo on a borderless blue and silver background with the player's name printed vertically down the left side. The backs carry the card number and players name in a marble blue stripe at the top with the redemption directions below. A checklist of the 10 cards is printed at the bottom.

COMPLETE SET (10)	10.00	20.00
PD1 Bryan Berard	1.00	2.50
PD2 Wade Redden	1.00	2.50
PD3 Steve Kelly	.40	1.00
PD4 Petr Sykora	3.00	8.00
PD5 Brad Church	.40	1.00
PD6 Daymond Langkow	1.50	4.00
PD7 Chad Kilger	.40	1.00
PD8 Terry Ryan	.40	1.00
PD9 Jason Doig	.40	1.00
PD10 Field Card	.40	1.00

1995 Images Platinum Prospects

The ten cards in this set (found 1:36 packs) feature some of the top prospects for NHL stardom. The cards feature a color player photo over a diagonally split silver and blue metallic background. The Images logo is in the top left corner, while the Platinum Prospects logo rests in the bottom right, beside the player's name in stylized script. The backs feature another color photo and a blurb assessing the player's chances. Each card is serially numbered out of 1,995 at the bottom left corner.

COMPLETE SET (10)	10.00	20.00
PR1 Jeff Nelson	.40	1.00
PR2 Jim Carey	1.25	3.00
PR3 Ian Laperriere	.40	1.00
PR4 Chris Osgood	1.25	3.00
PR5 Todd Marchant	.40	1.00
PR6 Radek Bonk	.40	1.00
PR7 Chris Marinucci	.40	1.00
PR8 Tommy Salo	2.50	5.00
PR9 Manny Fernandez	1.50	4.00
PR10 Jan Caloun	.40	1.00

1990-91 Michigan State Collegiate Collection 200

This 200-card standard-size set was produced by Collegiate Collection. The fronts feature black and white shots for earlier players or color shots for later players, with borders in the team's colors white and green. Since most cards are football, we've noted below which cards feature other sports. Although some players were famous in others sports, like Kirk Gibson and Steve Garvey, they do have football cards in this set.

COMPLETE SET (200)	6.00	15.00
52 Don(Zippy) Thompson HK	.05	.15
55 Doug Roberts HK	.05	.15
64 Tom Ross HK	.05	.15
69 John Chandik HK	.05	.15
75 Weldon Olson HK	.05	.15
84 Joe Selinger HK	.05	.15
95 Norm Barnes HK	.05	.15
97 Craig Simpson HK	.07	.20
125 Craig Simpson	.05	.15
137 Bob Essensa HK	.08	.25
197 Rod Brind'Amour HK	.20	.50

1990-91 Michigan State Collegiate Collection Promos

This ten-card standard size set features some of the great athletes from Michigan State History. Most of the cards in the set feature an action photograph on the front of the card along with either statistical or biographical information on the back of the card. Since this set involves more than one sport we have put a two-letter abbreviation to indicate the sport played.

COMPLETE SET (10)	1.50	4.00
1 Ron Scott HK	.08	.25

1996-97 Score Board All Sport PPF

The 1996-97 All Sport Past Present and Future set was issued in two series in six-card packs. The product contains original vintage and rookie cards of the top athletes from baseball, basketball, football and hockey as well as new cards of tomorrow's stars from each sport. Release date for series one was October 1996; series two was February 1997. There was also a gold parallel produced for this set. Series one gold cards were inserted 1:10 packs while series two had gold cards inserted at a 1:5 ratio.

COMPLETE SET (200)	6.00	15.00
71 Ed Jovanovski	.07	.20
72 Chris Phillips	.07	.20
73 Alexander Volchkov	.07	.20
74 Adam Colagiacomo	.07	.20
75 Jonathan Aitken	.07	.20
76 Rico Fata	.07	.20
77 Andrei Zyuzin	.07	.20
78 Josh Holden	.07	.20
79 Boyd Devereaux	.07	.20
97 Bryan Berard	.07	.20
98 Dainius Zubrus	.07	.20
99 Radek Dvorak	.07	.20
170 Dainius Zubrus	.07	.20
171 Joe Thornton	.15	.40
172 Daniel Briere	.07	.20
173 Radek Dvorak	.07	.20
174 Richard Jackman	.07	.20
175 Robert Dome	.07	.20
176 Sergei Samsonov	.15	.40
177 Jarome Iginla	.15	.40
178 Dan Cleary	.07	.20
199 Andrei Zyuzin	.07	.20

1996-97 Score Board All Sport PPF Gold

*GOLDS: 1.2X TO 3X BASIC CARDS
GOLD STATED ODDS SER.1 1:10/SER.2 1:5

1996-97 Score Board Autographed Collection

Each box of Score Board Autographed Collection contains 16 packs containing six cards. The 50-card regular set includes top athletes from all four major team sports. According to Score Board, a total of 1,500 sequentially numbered cases were produced.

COMPLETE SET (50)	5.00	12.00
45 Joe Thornton	.15	.40
46 Dan Cleary	.07	.20
47 Robert Dome	.07	.20
48 Alexander Volchkov	.07	.20
49 Adam Colagiacomo	.07	.20
50 Andrei Zyuzin	.07	.20

1996-97 Score Board Autographed Collection Autographs

Each box of Autographed Collection contains an average of four autographed cards. There are two different varieties: silver foil stamped cards with no individual serial numbering inserted at a rate of 1:7 packs, and Gold foil serial numbered autographs inserted at a rate of 1:16 packs.

9 Dan Cleary	1.50	4.00
10 Adam Colagiacomo	1.50	4.00
13 Robert Dome	1.50	4.00
40 Sergei Samsonov	5.00	12.00
45 Joe Thornton	6.00	15.00
53 Dainius Zubrus	2.00	5.00
54 Andrei Zyuzin	1.50	4.00

1996-97 Score Board Autographed Collection Autographs Gold

These Gold foil parallel signed cards were seeded at the rate of 1:16 packs. They are Score Board Certified and individually numbered out of 250, 300 or 350 except for Stepfret Williams.

*UNLISTED GOLD: .6X TO 1.5X BASIC AU

1996-97 Score Board Autographed Collection Game Breakers

This 30-card insert set was printed on metallic stock and has two versions-- regular and gold. The insertion ratio is 1:10 packs for regular inserts and 1:50 for the gold foil version.

COMPLETE SET (30)	25.00	60.00
*GOLD: .8X TO 2X BASIC INSERTS		
GOLD STATED ODDS 1:50		
GB29 Joe Thornton	1.25	3.00
GB30 Alexander Volchkov	.60	1.50

1997-98 Score Board Autographed Collection

The 1998 Autographed Collection set was issued in one series totaling 50 cards with players from baseball, basketball, football and hockey. The product's major draw was an average of five autographed cards and one memorabilia redemption card per 18-pack box. The regular autographs were inserted 1:4.5 packs, the Blue Ribbon autographs were inserted 1:18 packs. The one per box memorabilia redemption cards were not all redeemed due to the fact that Score Board, Inc. filed for bankruptcy a few months after the product's release. Score Board also released a "Strongbox Collection" that original retailed for around $125. Each Strongbox included a parallel of this 50 card set, one star player autographed ball with holder, one star player autographed 8" x 10", one Athletic Excellence card and One Sports City USA card.

COMPLETE SET (50)	5.00	12.0
4 Joe Thornton	.07	.2
27 Robert Dome	.07	.2
36 Sergei Samsonov	.10	.3

1997-98 Score Board Autographed Collection Athletic Excellence

These 3 1/2" x 5" cards, were inserted one per Score Board "Strongbox Collection" box that originally retailed for around $125. Each Strongbox also included parallel of the 1998 Autograph Collection 50 card set, one star player autographed baseball with holder, one star player autographed 8" x 10" and one Sports City USA card. Each card is sequentially numbered out of 750.

COMPLETE SET (12)	10.00	25.00
AE2 Joe Thornton	.75	2.00

1997-98 Score Board Autographed Collection Autographs

One autographed card was available in one in every 4.5 Score Board Autograph Collection packs. The cards have a circular player photograph in the middle with a white oval below that includes a player's autograph. The card backs read, "Congratulations! You have received an authentic Score Board autographed card." There was also a Kerry Wood card produced that made its way into the marketplace although it was not inserted into packs. The cards are unnumbered and listed below in alphabetical order.

4 Daniel Briere	1.50	4.00
5 Dan Cleary	1.50	4.00
7 Robert Dome	1.50	4.00
11 Richard Jackman	1.50	4.00

1997-98 Score Board Autographed Collection Blue Ribbon Autographs

One Blue Ribbon autographed card was available in one in every 18 Score Board Autograph Collection packs. The cards have a circular player photograph with a blue ribbon border in the middle with a white oval below that includes a player's autograph. The cards are hand numbered out of the amounts listed below in the upper right hand corner. The card backs read, "Congratulations! You have received an authentic Score Board autographed card." The cards are unnumbered and listed below in alphabetical order. A Warrick Dunn card was later released through a home shopping network show. Some Kobe Bryant cards have surfaced in un-signed form and can often be found with forged autographs on the front. No authentic Kobe signed and numbered cards are known although the Congratulations Score Board message is included on the card-backs.

14 Joe Thornton/1950	4.00	10.00

1997-98 Score Board Autographed Collection Sports City USA

These multi-player, city-themed cards were inserted one in nine Autographed Collection packs. There is also a Strongbox parallel found one per Score Board "Strongbox Collection" box that originally retailed for around $125. Each Strongbox also included a parallel of the 1998 Autograph Collection 50 card set, one star player autographed baseball with holder, one star player autographed 8" x 10" and one Athletic Excellence jumbo card.

COMPLETE SET (15)	10.00	25.00
*STRONGBOX/600: .8X to 2X BASIC INSERTS		
SC10 Emmitt Smith Troy Aikman Richard Jackman	1.50	4.00
SC11 Kordell Stewart Robert Dome	.50	1.25

1997-98 Score Board Autographed Collection Strongbox

*STRONGBOX: .8X TO 2X BASIC CARDS

1997 Score Board Players Club

The 70 cards that make-up this set are a grouping from baseball, basketball, football and hockey players. Card fronts are full colored action shots, with professional team names air-brushed out. The card backs contain 1997 projected statistics and biographical information. Along with the number 1 Die-Cuts and Play Back inserts, vintage cards were the major draw to this product. One in 32 packs contained a vintage card from 1909-1979 from any of the four sports. An original Honus Wagner T206 card was offered as a redemption in 1:153,600 packs. Also, one vintage wax pack was available via redemption card in one in every 32 packs.

COMPLETE SET (70)	5.00	12.00
6 Robert Dome	.07	.20
12 Daniel Briere	.07	.20
22 Joe Thornton	.07	.20
32 Dainius Zubrus	.07	.20
42 Sergei Samsonov	.15	.40
57 Dan Cleary	.07	.20
60 Richard Jackman	.07	.20
65 Alexander Volchkov	.07	.20

1997 Score Board Players Club #1 Die-Cuts

Each player in this 20 card set, inserted one in 32 packs, was at one time selected as a first round selection in the professional draft. The cards are die-cut in the shape of a "1" and have gold foil on the left border. The backs contain pre-professional biographical information and (if applicable) statistics from their last college or minor league season. The card numbers have a "D" prefix.

COMPLETE SET (20) 25.00 60.00
D4 Joe Thornton 1.50 4.00

1997 Score Board Players Club Play Backs

This 15-card set highlights stars form all four major U.S. sports. The card fronts have a player photo superimposed on a photo of the player's jersey. To the left is a movie reel design with individual action shots. The backs have another player photograph and biographical information. The cards are numbered with a "PB" prefix.

COMPLETE SET (15) 30.00 80.00
STATED ODDS 1:32
PB8 Dainius Zubrus 1.25 3.00

1997 Score Board Talk N' Sports

This product features phone cards with a couple twists, including trivia contests to win memorabilia and to check current sports scores. The 50-card regular set includes stars and prospects from all four major team sports. According to Score Board, a total of 1,500 sequentially numbered cases were produced.

COMPLETE SET (50) 4.00 10.00
46 Dainius Zubrus .07 .20
47 Sergei Samsonov .20 .50
48 Jay McKee .07 .20
49 Marcus Nilsson .07 .20
50 Joe Thornton .20 .50

1997 Score Board Talk N' Sports Essentials

These 10 plastic acetate cards were randomly inserted at a rate of 1:24 Talk N' Sports packs.

COMPLETE SET (10) 25.00 60.00
E10 Dainius Zubrus 1.50 4.00

1997 Score Board Talk N' Sports Phone Cards $1

The $1 phone cards were inserted one per pack. The checklist of this 50-card set parallels the regular set. The phone time on these $1 phone cards could be combined. They expired on 7/31/1998.

COMPLETE SET (50) 8.00 20.00
*PIN NUMBER REVEALED: HALF VALUE

1997 Score Board Talk N' Sports Phone Cards $20

These $20 phone cards allow users to choose sports updates in lieu of the phone time. The time on the card can be used interchangably for either phone calls or sports updates. The $20 cards were inserted at a rate of 1:36 packs and expired on 7/31/1998. Each card is sequentially numbered out of 1,440.

COMPLETE SET (10) 25.00 60.00
*PIN NUMBER REVEALED: HALF VALUE
10 Dainius Zubrus 2.00 5.00

1995 Signature Rookies

This 70-card standard-size set features a number of NHL draft picks from 1994 as well as several future draft prospects. With a suggested retail price of 5.00, each foil pack contained five regular cards, a mail-in offer or a chase card, and an autographed card. Each player signed 7,750 of their cards. The fronts feature borderless color action player cut-outs on a colorful, computerized background. The player's name in gold-foil appears in a black bar at the bottom, while the production number "1 of 45,000" is printed in a gold-foil bar at the left. The backs carry a small color player photo, along with a short biography and player profile. 1,995 cases were produced; 1,000 cases were supposedly sold out of the country, with the remaining 995 cases available in the U.S. Several error cards exist in the set. Limited numbers of corrected versions exist for four of them, as noted below.

COMPLETE SET (70) 5.00 12.00
1 Vaclav Varada .02 .10
2 Roman Vopat .02 .10
3 Yannick Dube .02 .10
4 Colin Cloutier .02 .10
5 Scott Cherrey .02 .10
6 Johan Finnstrom .02 .10
7 Fredrik Modin .20 .50
8 Stephane Roy .02 .10
9 Yevgeni Ryabchikov .02 .10
10 Jose Theodore .50 1.25
11 Jason Holland .02 .10
12 Richard Park .02 .10
13 Jason Podollan .02 .10
14 Mattias Ohlund .20 .50
15 Chris Wells .02 .10
16 Hugh Hamilton .02 .10
17 Edvin Frylen .02 .10
18 Wade Belak .02 .10
19 Sebastien Bety .02 .10
20 Chris Dingman .02 .10
21 Peter Nylander .02 .10
22 Daymond Langkow .40 1.00
23 Kelly Fairchild .02 .10
24 Norm Dezainde .02 .10
25 Nolan Baumgartner .02 .10
26 Deron Quint .02 .10
27 Sheldon Souray .02 .10
28 Stefan Ustorf .02 .10
29 Juha Vuorivirta .02 .10
30 Marc Seliger .02 .10
31 Ryan Smyth .50 1.25
32 Dimitri Tabarin .02 .10
33 Nikolai Tsulygin .02 .10
34 Paul Vincent .02 .10
35 Rhett Warrener .02 .10
36 Jamie Rivers .02 .10
37 Rumun Ndur .02 .10
38 Phil Huber .02 .10
39 Radek Dvorak .20 .50
40 Mike Barrie .02 .10
41 Chris Hynnes .02 .10
42 Mike Dubinsky .02 .10
43 Steve Cheredaryk .02 .10
44 Jim Carey .08 .25
45A Dorian Anneck ERR .02 .10
45B Dorian Anneck COR .02 .10
46 Jorgen Jonsson .02 .10
47 Alyn McCauley .02 .10
48 Corey Nielson .02 .10
49 Daniel Tjarnqvist .08 .25
50 Vadim Yepanchintsev .02 .10
51 Sean Haggerty .02 .10
52A Milan Hejduk 1.00 2.50
52B Milan Hejduk COR 1.00 2.50
53 Adam Magarrell .02 .10
54 Dave Scatchard .08 .25
55 Sebastien Vallee .02 .10
56 Milos Guren .02 .10
57 Johan Davidsson .02 .10
58 Byron Briske .02 .10
59 Sylvain Blouin .02 .10
60 Bryan Berard UER .60 1.50
(Name misspelled Brian on front)
61 Tim Findlay .02 .10
62 Doug Bonner .02 .10
63 Curtis Brown .08 .25
64A Brad Symes ERR .02 .10
64B Brad Symes COR .02 .10
65 Andrew Taylor .02 .10
66 Brad Bombardir .02 .10
67 Joe Dziedzic .02 .10
68 Valentin Morozov .02 .10
69A Mark McArthur ERR .02 .10
69B Mark McArthur COR .02 .10
70 Checklist .02 .10
CS1 Martin Brodeur

1995 Signature Rookies Auto-Phonex

This 41-card set measures standard size. The fronts feature a color action player photo made to look as if breaking out of a blue background. The backs carry a small close-up photo of the player with the team name, position, biographical information and statistics. Each 6-card pack consisted of five regular cards and one hand-signed phone card.

COMPLETE SET (41) 2.00 5.00
1 Mika Alatalo .02 .10
2 Chad Allan UER .02 .10
(Text reads four year veteran of pro hockey; should be junior hockey)
3 Jonas Andersson-Junkka .02 .10
4 Serge Aubin .08 .25
5 David Belitski .05 .15
6 Aki Berg .02 .10
7 Zac Bierk .08 .25
8 Lou Body .02 .10
9 Kevin Bolibruck .02 .10
10 Brian Boucher .30 .75
11 Jack Callahan .02 .10
12 Jake Deadmarsh .02 .10
13 Andy Delmore .02 .10
14 Shane Doan .30 .75
15 Daniel Cleary .02 .10
16 Ian Gordon .02 .10
17 Jochen Hecht .08 .25
18 Martin Hohenberger .02 .10
19 Thomas Holmstrom .30 .75
20 Cory Keenan .02 .10
21 Shane Kenney .02 .10
22 Pavel Kriz .02 .10
23 Justin Kurtz .02 .10
24 Jan Labraaten .02 .10
25 Brad Larsen .02 .10
26 Donald MacLean .02 .10
27 Tavis MacMillan .02 .10
28 Mike Martin .02 .10
29 Bryan Berard .08 .25
30 Dimitri Nabokov .02 .10
31 Todd Norman .02 .10
32 Cory Peterson .02 .10
33 Johan Ramstedt .02 .10
34 Wade Redden .08 .25
35 Kevin Riehl .02 .10
36 David Roberts .02 .10
37 Terry Ryan .02 .10
38 Brian Scott .02 .10
39 Alexander Selivanov .08 .25
40 Peter Wallin .02 .10
NNO Checklist .01 .01

1995 Signature Rookies Auto-Phonex Beyond 2000

Inserted 1:6 packs, this set features five players who were thought to have a great shot at excelling well into the 21st century. The fronts feature the player's photo against a futuristic background. The back has a player portrait along with his position, his '93-94 stats and a quote about that player's abilities. 5,000 sets were produced, and each player signed 200 cards. Signed versions are worth 10X to 20X basic cards.

COMPLETE SET (5) 2.00 5.00
B1 Jamie Rivers .20 .50
B2 Terry Ryan .20 .50
B3 Ryan Smyth .75 2.00
B4 Nolan Baumgartner .20 .50
B5 Jose Theodore 1.25 3.00

1995 Signature Rookies Auto-Phonex Jaromir Jagr

Inserted 1:6 packs, this 5-card standard-size set showcases Jaromir Jagr. 5,000 sets were produced, and Jagr signed 500 of each card. The front features color photos picturing Jagr in action; the irregular fuchsia borders mimic the effect of water splattering on a surface. The back has a photo of Jagr along with biographical details and personal information located at the upper right corner.

COMPLETE SET (5) 3.00 8.00
COMMON JAGR (JJ1-JJ5) .75 2.00
JAGR SIGNATURE (JJ1-JJ5) 40.00 100.00

1995 Signature Rookies Auto-Phonex Phone Cards

Inserted one per pack, this 39-phone card set features a number of top NHL prospects. Each phone card bears an authentic signature and is serially numbered on the front. Shane Doan, card 14, did not sign. The backs explain how to use the card. Values below are for unused $3 cards. Scratching the back to reveal the PIN number decreases the value by 50 percent. The higher value NNO phone cards listed at the bottom were random inserts at indeterminate odds.

COMPLETE SET (40) 60.00 120.00
1 Mika Alatalo 1.50 4.00
2 Chad Allan .75 2.00
3 Jonas Andersson-Junkka .75 2.00
4 Serge Aubin 1.50 4.00
5 David Belitski .75 2.00
6 Aki Berg 1.25 3.00
7 Zac Bierk 1.25 3.00
8 Lou Body .75 2.00
9 Kevin Bolibruck .75 2.00
10 Brian Boucher 8.00 20.00
11 Jack Callahan .75 2.00
12 Jake Deadmarsh .75 2.00
13 Andy Delmore 1.25 3.00
14 Shane Doan 2.00 5.00
15 Daniel Cleary 1.25 3.00
16 Ian Gordon .75 2.00
17 Jochen Hecht 5.00 12.00
18 Martin Hohenberger .75 2.00
19 Thomas Holmstrom 2.00 5.00
20 Cory Keenan .75 2.00
21 Shane Kenney .75 2.00
22 Pavel Kriz .75 2.00
23 Justin Kurtz .75 2.00
24 Jan Labraaten .75 2.00
25 Brad Larsen .75 2.00
26 Donald MacLean .75 2.00
27 Tavis MacMillan .75 2.00
28 Mike Martin .75 2.00
29 Bryan Berard 1.50 4.00
30 Dimitri Nabokov .75 2.00
31 Todd Norman .75 2.00
32 Cory Peterson .75 2.00
33 Johan Ramstedt .75 2.00
34 Wade Redden 1.25 3.00
35 Kevin Riehl .75 2.00
36 David Roberts .75 2.00
37 Terry Ryan .75 2.00
38 Brian Scott .75 2.00
39 Alexander Selivanov .75 2.00
40 Peter Wallin .75 2.00
NNO D. Langkow $30 card 1.50 4.00
NNO Wade Redden $6 card 1.50 4.00
NNO Nolan Baumgartner $6 card 1.50 4.00
NNO Terry Ryan $6 card 1.50 4.00

1995 Signature Rookies Auto-Phonex Prodigies

Inserted 1:6 packs, this five-card standard-size set features five young guns. The front features the player showcased in action. The player's name is in red while the word "Prodigies" is printed in big, black bold letters against a yellow background on the bottom. The back features biographical information in the upper left corner. The rest of the reverse features a black-and-white player photo with his '93-94 stats and a quote about the player also placed on the bottom half. 5,000 sets were produced, and each player signed 200 of his cards. Signed versions are worth 5X to 8X basic cards.

COMPLETE SET (5) 2.00 5.00
P1 Bryan Berard UER .40 1.00
(Name misspelled Brian)
P2 Daymond Langkow .75 2.00
P3 Daniel Cleary .40 1.00
P4 Aki Berg .40 1.00
P5 Wade Redden .75 2.00

1995 Signature Rookies Club Promos

These five standard-size cards were sent to members of the Signature Rookies Club. The fronts feature the players photo occupying most of the right side of the card. The player's are identified underneath the photos. The cards are autographed just above the player's name while the sequential autograph number is under the player's name. The words Club Promo go vertically down the left side of the card while the Signature Rookies Hockey logo is in the lower left corner. The backs have a smaller duplication of the front photo on the left side while all relevant vital stats and biographical information are on the right side. The Signature Rookies authentic signature sticker is right above their logo on the back. Reports suggest that unsigned versions of these cards exist as well. These cards are marked PROMO, and are numbered One of 2,000. As these are rarely seen, no values have been tracked. It is fair to suggest, however, that they are worth considerably less than the signed versions.

COMPLETE SET (5) 20.00 20.00
1 Sergei Luchinkin 2.00 5.00
2 Stefan Ustorf 2.00 5.00
3 Brad Brown 2.00 5.00
4 Yanick Dube 2.00 5.00
5 Vitali Yachmenev 2.00 5.00

1995 Signature Rookies Cool Five

The five cards in this standard-size set were randomly inserted into packs. The left side of the front identifies the card as being 1 of 7,000, with the Cool Five logo in the lower left corner. The remainder is devoted to a full-color player photo which bleeds to the corner. The back has a head-and-shoulders portrait on the left side along with his biography on the right side. Signatures from this 5-card set were randomly inserted throughout the packs.

COMPLETE SET (5) 10.00 10.00
CF1 Radek Bonk .20 .50
CF2 Brad Park .75 2.00
CF3 Brian Leetch .75 2.00
CF4 Maurice Richard 2.00 5.00
CF5 Henri Richard .75 2.00

1995 Signature Rookies Cool Five Signatures

The five cards in this standard-size set were randomly inserted into packs. The left side of the front identifies the set as 1 of 7,000 and the Cool Five logo is in the lower left corner. The card is autographed over the player's photo and the serial number of the autograph is on the bottom. The remainder of the card is devoted to a full-color player photo that bleeds to the corner. In the middle of the back is the Signature Rookies authentic signature logo. The remainder of the back features a head-and-shoulders player portrait on the left side along with his biography on the right side. The card is numbered in the upper right corner.

CF1 Radek Bonk 2.00 5.00
CF2 Brad Park 6.00 15.00
CF3 Brian Leetch 5.00 10.00
CF4 Maurice Richard 40.00 80.00
CF5 Henri Richard 10.00 25.00

1995 Signature Rookies Future Flash

The ten cards in this standard-size set were randomly inserted into packs. The left side of the front identifies the card as being one of 7,000, with the Future Flash logo in the lower left corner. The remainder of the card is devoted to a full-color player photo with a multiple exposure effect that bleeds to the corner. The back has a head-and-shoulders player portrait on the left side along with his biography on the right side. The card is numbered in the upper right corner. Signatures from this 10-card set were randomly inserted throughout the packs.

COMPLETE SET (10) 2.00 5.00
FF1 Jeff Ambrosio .40 1.00
FF2 Brad Brown .40 1.00
FF3 Patrick Juhlin .40 1.00
FF4 Sergei Gorbachev .40 1.00
FF5 Vasili Kamenev 1.50 4.00
FF6 Oleg Orekhovski .40 1.00
FF7 Maxim Kuznetsov .40 1.00
FF8 Sergei Luchinkin .40 1.00
FF9 Scott Roche .75 2.00
FF10 Alexei Morozov .75 2.00

1995 Signature Rookies Future Flash Signatures

The ten cards in this standard-size set were randomly inserted into packs. The left side of the front identifies the card as being 1 of 2,100, with the Future Flash logo in the lower left corner. The autograph is on the player's photo and is sequentially identified underneath the player's name. The remainder of the card is devoted to a full-color player photo with a multiple exposure effect that bleeds to the corner. The Signature Rookies Authentic Signature Logo is on the right side near the bottom. Other aspects of the back include a head-and-shoulders player portrait on the left side along with his biography on the right side. The cards are numbered in the upper right corner.

COMPLETE SET (10) 60.00 120.00
FF1 Jeff Ambrosio 6.00 15.00
FF2 Brad Brown 6.00 15.00
FF3 Patrick Juhlin 6.00 15.00
FF4 Sergei Gorbachev 6.00 15.00
FF5 Vasili Kamenev 6.00 15.00
FF6 Oleg Orekhovski 6.00 15.00
FF7 Maxim Kuznetsov 8.00 20.00
FF8 Sergei Luchinkin 6.00 15.00
FF9 Scott Roche 8.00 20.00
FF10 Alexei Morozov 8.00 20.00

1995 Signature Rookies Miracle on Ice

This 50-card standard-size set features 20 players, two coaches, and special action shots. Just 299 cases were produced, and each six-card pack contained an autograph card. The fronts display color action player photos that are edged on the left and bottom by a red, white and blue American flag design. Also the lower left corner of each card has a small oblique photo of the American team celebrating. The production run ("1 of 24,000"), a special "Miracle On Ice, 1980" emblem, and the player's name are gold foil-stamped on the front. On a ghosted red, white and blue flag design, the backs carry a color close-up photo, biography, and player profile.

COMPLETE SET (50) 10.00 20.00
1 Bill Baker .07 .20
2 Bill Baker .07 .20
3 Neal Broten .30 .75
4 Neal Broten .30 .75
5 Dave Christian .20 .50
6 Dave Christian .20 .50
7 Steve Christoff .07 .20
8 Steve Christoff .07 .20
9 Jim Craig .60 1.50
10 Jim Craig .60 1.50
11 Mike Eruzione .60 1.50
12 Mike Eruzione .60 1.50
13 John Harrington .07 .20
14 John Harrington .07 .20
15 Steve Janasak .07 .20
16 Steve Janasak .07 .20
17 Mark Johnson .07 .20
18 Mark Johnson .07 .20
19 Rob McClanahan .07 .20
20 Rob McClanahan .07 .20
21 Ken Morrow .20 .50
22 Ken Morrow .20 .50
23 Jack O'Callahan .07 .20
24 Jack O'Callahan .07 .20
25 Mark Pavelich .07 .20
26 Mark Pavelich .07 .20
27 Mike Ramsey .08 .25
28 Mike Ramsey .08 .25
29 Buzz Schneider .07 .20
30 Buzz Schneider .07 .20
31 Dave Silk .07 .20
32 Dave Silk .07 .20
33 Bob Suter .07 .20
34 Bob Suter .07 .20
35 Eric Strobel .07 .20
36 Eric Strobel .07 .20
37 Phil Verchota .07 .20
38 Phil Verchota .07 .20
39 Marc Wells .07 .20
40 Marc Wells .07 .20
41 Herb Brooks CO .60 1.50
42 Herb Brooks CO .60 1.50
43 Craig Patrick ACO .20 .50
44 Craig Patrick ACO .20 .50
45 Clinching The Gold .20 .50
46 Do You Believe In Miracles .20 .50
47 Eruzione Decides It .20 .50
48 Celebration .20 .50
49 A Dream Becomes Reality .20 .50
50 Checklist .07 .20

1995 Signature Rookies Miracle on Ice Signatures

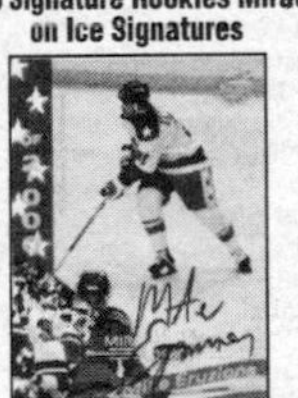

This 43-card standard-size set features 20 players, two coaches, and special action shots. The cards are identical to the regular issue with the addition of authentic signatures inscribed across the fronts. Two thousand of each card were signed. Card numbers 41 and 45-50 were not issued in signed form. Cards are numbered out of 2,000 on front. Both an Eruzione and Brooks celebration promos exist.

COMPLETE SET (43) 175.00 350.00
1 Bill Baker 5.00 12.00
2 Bill Baker 5.00 12.00
3 Neal Broten 5.00 12.00
4 Neal Broten 5.00 12.00
5 Dave Christian 5.00 12.00
6 Dave Christian 5.00 12.00
7 Steve Christoff 5.00 12.00
8 Steve Christoff 5.00 12.00
9 Jim Craig 10.00 25.00
10 Jim Craig 10.00 25.00
11 Mike Eruzione 20.00 50.00
12 Mike Eruzione 20.00 50.00
13 John Harrington 5.00 12.00
14 John Harrington 5.00 12.00
15 Steve Janasak 5.00 12.00
16 Steve Janasak 5.00 12.00
17 Mark Johnson 10.00 25.00
18 Mark Johnson 10.00 25.00
19 Rob McClanahan 5.00 12.00
20 Rob McClanahan 5.00 12.00
21 Ken Morrow 4.00 10.00
22 Ken Morrow 4.00 10.00
23 Jack O'Callahan 12.50 30.00
24 Jack O'Callahan 12.50 30.00
25 Mark Pavelich 5.00 12.00
26 Mark Pavelich 5.00 12.00
27 Mike Ramsey 5.00 12.00
28 Mike Ramsey 5.00 12.00
29 Buzz Schneider 10.00 25.00
30 Buzz Schneider 10.00 25.00
31 Dave Silk 4.00 10.00
32 Dave Silk 4.00 10.00
33 Bob Suter 5.00 12.00
34 Bob Suter 5.00 12.00
35 Eric Strobel 10.00 25.00
36 Eric Strobel 10.00 25.00
37 Phil Verchota 5.00 12.00
38 Phil Verchota 5.00 12.00
39 Marc Wells 5.00 12.00
40 Marc Wells 5.00 12.00
42 Herb Brooks CO 20.00 50.00
43 Craig Patrick ACO 4.00 10.00
44 Craig Patrick ACO 4.00 10.00
NNO Celebration Promo 30.00 80.00
Herb Brooks/7500
NNO Celebration Promo
Mike Eruzione/60

1995 Signature Rookies Signatures

Inserted one per foil pack, this 69-card issue is a parallel set and features the same design as the regular issue. Each player signed 7,750 of his cards which are hand numbered. The fronts feature borderless color action player cut-outs on a colorful, computerized background. The player's name in gold-foil appears in a black bar at the bottom. The backs carry a small color player photo, along with a short biography and player profile. Because several players could not fulfill their signing commitments in time for packaging, Signature Rookies inserted some redemption cards which specifically identified the player for whom the card could be redeemed. Once the redemption period expires, these cards will have limited market value.

COMPLETE SET (69) 50.00 100.00
1 Vaclav Varada .40 1.00
2 Roman Vopat .40 1.00
3 Yanick Dube .40 1.00
4 Colin Cloutier .40 1.00
5 Scott Cherrey .40 1.00
6 Johan Finnstrom .40 1.00
7 Fredrik Modin 2.00 5.00
8 Stephane Roy .40 1.00
9 Evgeni Ryabchikov .40 1.00
10 Jose Theodore 6.00 15.00
11 Jason Holland .40 1.00
12 Richard Park .40 1.00
13 Jason Podollan .40 1.00
14 Mattias Ohlund 2.00 5.00
15 Chris Wells .40 1.00
16 Hugh Hamilton .40 1.00
17 Edvin Frylen .40 1.00
18 Wade Belak .40 1.00
19 Sebastien Bety .40 1.00
20 Chris Dingman .40 1.00
21 Peter Nylander .40 1.00
22 Daymond Langkow 2.00 5.00
23 Kelly Fairchild .40 1.00
24 Norm Dezainde .40 1.00
25 Nolan Baumgartner .40 1.00
26 Deron Quint .40 1.00
27 Sheldon Souray .40 1.00
28 Stefan Ustorf .40 1.00
29 Juha Vuorvirta .40 1.00
30 Marc Seliger 1.25 3.00
31 Ryan Smyth 4.00 10.00
32 Dimitri Tabarin .40 1.00
33 Nikolai Tsulygin .40 1.00
34 Paul Vincent .40 1.00
35 Rhett Warrener .40 1.00
36 Jamie Rivers .40 1.00
37 Rumun Ndur 1.25 3.00
38 Phil Huber .40 1.00
39 Radek Dvorak 2.00 5.00
40 Mike Barrie .40 1.00
41 Chris Hynnes .40 1.00
42 Mike Dubinsky .40 1.00
43 Steve Cheredaryk .40 1.00
44 Jim Carey 2.00 5.00
45 Brad Symes .40 1.00
46 Jorgen Jonsson .40 1.00
47 Alyn McCauley .40 1.00
48 Corey Nielson .40 1.00
49 Daniel Tjarnqvist 1.25 3.00
50 Vadim Epanchintsev .40 1.00
51 Sean Haggerty .40 1.00
52 Mark McArthur .40 1.00
53 Adam Magarrell .40 1.00
54 Dave Scatchard 1.25 3.00
55 Sebastien Vallee .40 1.00
56 Milos Guren .40 1.00
57 Johan Davidsson .40 1.00
58 Byron Briske .40 1.00
59 Sylvain Blouin .40 1.00
60 Bryan Berard UER 1.25 3.00
61 Tim Findlay .40 1.00
62 Doug Bonner 1.25 3.00
63 Curtis Brown .40 1.00
64 Dorian Anneck .40 1.00
65 Andrew Taylor .40 1.00
66 Brad Bombardir .40 1.00
67 Joe Dziedzic .40 1.00
68 Valentin Morozhov .40 1.00
69 Milan Hejduk 6.00 15.00

1995 Signature Rookies Fame and Fortune #1 Pick

Randomly inserted in packs at a rate of three in 16, this five-card set features the No. 1 pick in the NHL, the NFL, the NBA and Major leagues. The No. 5 card pictures all four of the picks. Fronts have a psychedelic background and feature the player in a full-color action cutout. "#1 Pick" appears in a sky blue and green type at the top and the bottom has a gold foil strip that contains the player's name, or names in the case of the #5 card, in raised white letters. Backs continue with the psychedelic background and picture the player or players in action. Player stats and biographies also appear on the back.

COMPLETE SET (5) 1.00 2.50
P1 Bryan Berard .20 .50
P5 Brian Berard .30 .75
K-Jana Carter
Darin Erstad
Joe Smith

1994 Signature Rookies Gold Standard

This multi-sport set consists of 100 standard-size cards. The fronts feature color action players photos with a circular gold foil seal at the upper left corner. The player's name appears on a diagonal black stripe edged by yellow. The horizontal backs carry a narrowly-cropped closeup photo and, on a ghosted panel, biography and player profile. The set is subdivided according to sport as follows: basketball (1-25), football (26-50), baseball (51-75), and hockey (76-100). Each sport is sequenced in alphabetical order.

COMPLETE SET (100) 5.00 12.00
76 Nolan Baumgartner .07 .20
77 Wade Belak .07 .20
78 Radek Bonk .10 .30
79 Brad Brown .07 .20
80 Dan Cloutier .10 .30
81 Johan Davidsson .07 .20
82 Yannick Dube .07 .20
83 Eric Fichaud .10 .30
84 Johann Finnstrom .07 .20
85 Edvin Frylen .07 .20
86 Patrik Juhlin .07 .20
87 Valeri Karpov .07 .20
88 Nikolai Khabibulin .30 .75
89 Mattias Ohlund .10 .30
90 Jason Podollan .07 .20
91 Vadim Sharifjanov .10 .30
92 Ryan Smyth .20 .50
93 Dimitri Tabarin .07 .20
94 Nikolai Tsulygin .07 .20
95 Stefan Ustorf .07 .20
96 Paul Vincent .07 .20
97 Roman Vopat .07 .20
98 Rhett Warrener .07 .20
99 Vitali Yachmenev .07 .20
100 Vadim Yepenchinstev .07 .20

1994 Signature Rookies Gold Standard Facsimile

This 20-card standard-size set was inserted one per pack. The fronts display full-bleed color player photos. A facsimile autograph, the "Gold Standard" seal, and another emblem are gold-foil stamped on the fronts. Also a diagonal line carrying the player's name (also in gold foil) is edged by gold foil stripes. On the left side, the horizontal backs show a narrowly-cropped closeup of the front photo. The remainder of the backs carry biography, statistics, and player profile, all on a ghosted background. In addition to card number, each back carries a serial number.

COMPLETE SET (20) 5.00 12.00
GS3 Radek Bonk .30 .75
GS4 Nolan Baumgartner .30 .75
GS7 Valeri Karpov .30 .75
GS18 Ryan Smyth .40 1.00

1994 Signature Rookies Gold Standard HOF

COMPLETE SET (24) 8.00 20.00
STATED PRINT RUN 20,000 SETS
ISSUED VIA MAIL REDEMPTION
HOF3 Mike Bossy .60 1.50
HOF7 Tony Esposito .50 1.25

1994 Signature Rookies Gold Standard HOF Autographs

Inserted at a rate of one per box, this 24-card standard-sized set is identical to the regular set except for the signatures inscribed across the front and the expression "Hall of Fame" gold-foil stamped at the upper left. Each card is numbered out of 2500. The collector could obtain unsigned versions by mailing in a redemption card that was randomly inserted in packs. These redemption cards are valued at 1/10 the value of the signed cards. The cards are numbered with an "HOF" prefix.

3 Mike Bossy 10.00 25.00
7 Tony Esposito 12.00 30.00

1994 Signature Rookies Gold Standard Legends

This five-card standard size set was randomly inserted into packs. This set has great athletes past and present from all sports. The fronts have the word "Legends" on the top and the player's name on the bottom printed in silver ink against a black background. Meanwhile, the player's photo is shown against a gold background. The backs contain the player's photo on the left quarter with a biography about that player on the remainder of the card.

COMPLETE SET (5) 3.00 8.00
L5 Brian Leetch .40 1.00

1994 Signature Rookies Tetrad

These 120 standard-size cards feature borderless color player action shots on their fronts. The player's name appears in gold-foil lettering near the bottom. The words "1 of 45,000" appear in vertical gold-foil lettering within a simulated marble column near the left edge. The cards of this four-sport set are numbered on the back in Roman numerals and organized as follows: Football (1-40), Basketball (41-83), Baseball (84-103), and Hockey (104-118).

COMPLETE SET (120) 3.00 8.00
104 Sven Butenschon .07 .20
105 Dan Cloutier .10 .30
106 Pat Jablonski .07 .20
107 Valeri Karpov .07 .20
108 Nikolai Khabibulin .20 .50
109 Sergei Klimentiev .07 .20
110 Krzysztol Oliwa .07 .20
111 Dmitri Riabykin .07 .20

112 Ryan Risidore .07 .20
113 Shawn Rivers .07 .20
114 Vadim Sharifjanov .10 .30
115 Mika Stromberg .07 .20
116 Tim Taylor .07 .20
117 Vitali Yachmenev .07 .20
118 Wendell Young .07 .20

1994 Signature Rookies Tetrad Autographs

Inserted one card (or trade coupon) per pack, these 117 standard-size autographed cards comprise a parallel set to the regular '94 Tetrad set. Aside from the autographs and each card's numbering out of 7,750 produced, they are identical in design to their regular issue counterparts. The cards of this four-sport set are numbered on the back in Roman numerals and organized as follows: Football (1-40), Basketball (41-83), Baseball (84-103), and Hockey (104-118). Bernard Williams (card number 11) did not sign his cards.

104 Sven Butenschon 1.50 4.00
105 Dan Cloutier 2.50 6.00
106 Pat Jablonski 1.50 4.00
107 Valeri Karpov 1.50 4.00
108 Nikolai Khabibulin 3.00 8.00
109 Sergei Klimentiev 1.50 4.00
110 Krzysztof Oliwa 1.50 4.00
111 Dmitri Riabykin 1.50 4.00
112 Ryan Risidore 1.50 4.00
113 Shawn Rivers 1.50 4.00
114 Vadim Sharifjanov 2.50 6.00
115 Mika Stromberg 1.50 4.00
116 Tim Taylor 1.50 4.00
117 Vitali Yachmenev 1.50 4.00
118 Wendell Young 1.50 4.00

1994 Signature Rookies Tetrad Previews

Randomly inserted in Signature Rookies Football packs, these seven standard-size cards feature borderless color player action shots on their fronts. The player's name and position appear in gold-foil lettering near the bottom. The words "Promo, 1 of 10,000" appear in vertical gold-foil lettering within a simulated marble column near the left edge. On a ghosted background drawing of a Greek temple, the back carries the player's name, position, team, height and weight, and career highlights. The cards of this multisport set are numbered on the back with a "T" prefix.

COMPLETE SET (7) 1.25 3.00
T2 Tim Taylor .08 .25

1994 Signature Rookies Tetrad Titans

Randomly inserted in packs, these 12 standard-size cards feature borderless color player action shots on their fronts. The player's name appears in gold-foil lettering near the bottom. The words "1 of 10,000" appear in vertical gold-foil lettering within a simulated marble column near the left edge. On a ghosted background drawing of a Greek temple, the back carries the player's name, position, team, height and weight, and career highlights. The cards of this multisport set are numbered on the back in Roman numerals.

COMPLETE SET (12) 3.00 8.00
122 Bobby Hull .60 1.50

1994 Signature Rookies Tetrad Titans Autographs

Randomly inserted in packs, these 12 standard-size autographed cards comprise a parallel set to the regular 1994 Tetrad Titans set. Aside from the autographs (some cards issued as redemptions in packs) and each card's numbering out of 1,050 produced (except the 2,500 signed O.J. cards), they are identical in design to their regular issue counterparts. The cards of this multisport set are numbered on the back in Roman numerals.

COMPLETE SET (12) 125.00 250.00
122 Bobby Hull/1050 20.00 40.00

1995 Signature Rookies Tetrad

This 76-card standard-size set features borderless fronts with color action player photos. The named player stands out on a faded background with his name printed in gold below. The backs carry an elongated color action player photo on one side while a head photo, biographical information, position, college, and career statistics round out the backs.

COMPLETE SET (76) 5.00 12.00
61 Alexei Morozov .15 .40
62 Radek Dvorak .05 .15
66 Terry Ryan .05 .15
67 Shane Doan .15 .40
68 Brad Church .05 .15
69 Brian Boucher .40 1.00
70 Dmitri Nabokov .05 .15

1995 Signature Rookies Tetrad Autobilia

The 1995 Signature Rookies Tetrad Autobilia set was issued in one series with a total of 100 cards. The fronts feature a color action player cut-out on a background of a repeated action player photo with the player's name printed in a gold bar at the bottom. The words" Club Set" are printed in gold foil on the fronts as well. The backs carry two player photos with the player's name, position, biographical information, career statistics, and a player fact.

COMPLETE SET (100) 10.00 25.00
*SILVER: 4X TO 1X GOLD
38 Nolan Baumgartner .08 .25
39 Bryan Berard .15 .40
40 Aki-Petteri Berg .10 .30
41 Dan Cleary .08 .25
42 Radek Dvorak .08 .25
43 Patrick Juhlin .08 .25
44 Jan Labraaten .08 .25
45 Daymond Langkow .15 .40
46 Sergei Luchinkin .08 .25
47 Cameron Mann .15 .40
48 Alexei Morozov .15 .40
49 Oleg Tverdovsky .15 .40
50 Johan Ramstedt .08 .25
51 Wade Redden .15 .40
52 Sami-Ville Salomaa .08 .25
53 Alexei Vasiljev .08 .25
54 Peter Wallin .08 .25
94 Brian Boucher .60 1.50
95 Martin Brodeur .50 1.25
96 Brad Church .08 .25
97 Shane Doan .30 .75
98 Terry Ryan .08 .25
99 Ryan Smyth .15 .40

1995 Signature Rookies Tetrad Autobilia Auto-Phonex Test

This 3-card set was issued in packs of 1995 Signature Rookies Autobilia packs. Each card follows a similar design to the base cards except for the addition of the words "Auto-Phonex Test Issue" on the left hand side of the cardfronts. The title "Autobilia" at the top was also replaced with "Tetrad."

COMPLETE SET (3) 1.25 3.00
T1 Jim Carey .50 1.25

1995 Signature Rookies Tetrad Autobilia Autographed Cards

These cards are an autographed parallel to the base set. Signature Rookies reported that players signed the following items: 1000 cards, 3000 photos, 500 pennants, 500 hats, 3000 baseballs, 550 basketballs, 1000 footballs. Special items included 100 Darin Erstad signed bats and an undisclosed amount of the following issues: Muhammad Ali signed boxing glove, Joe DiMaggio signed cards, Jaromir Jagr signed hockey stick, Jaromir Jagr signed practice jersey, and Jim Carey signed mask.

38 Nolan Baumgartner 1.25 3.00
39 Bryan Berard 2.00 5.00
40 Aki-Petteri Berg 1.50 4.00
41 Dan Cleary 1.50 4.00
42 Radek Dvorak 1.25 3.00
43 Patrick Juhlin 1.25 3.00
44 Jan Labraaten 1.25 3.00
45 Daymond Langkow 1.25 3.00
46 Sergei Luchinkin 1.25 3.00
47 Cameron Mann 1.25 3.00
48 Alexei Morozov 1.25 3.00
49 Oleg Tverdovsky 1.25 3.00
50 Johan Ramstedt 1.25 3.00
51 Wade Redden 1.25 3.00
52 Sami-Ville Salomaa 1.25 3.00
53 Alexei Vasiljev 1.25 3.00
54 Peter Wallin 1.25 3.00
94 Brian Boucher 2.50 6.00
95 Martin Brodeur 6.00 15.00
96 Brad Church 1.25 3.00
97 Shane Doan 1.50 4.00
98 Terry Ryan 1.25 3.00
99 Ryan Smyth 4.00 10.00

1995 Signature Rookies Tetrad Autobilia Autographed Photos

*SIGNED PHOTOS: 4X TO 10X BASIC CARDS
38 Nolan Baumgartner 1.25 3.00
39 Bryan Berard 2.00 5.00
40 Aki-Petteri Berg 1.50 4.00
41 Dan Cleary 1.50 4.00
42 Radek Dvorak 1.25 3.00
43 Patrick Juhlin 1.25 3.00
44 Jan Labraaten 1.25 3.00
45 Daymond Langkow 1.25 3.00
46 Sergei Luchinkin 1.25 3.00
47 Cameron Mann 1.25 3.00
48 Alexei Morozov 1.25 3.00
49 Oleg Tverdovsky 1.25 3.00
50 Johan Ramstedt 1.25 3.00
52 Sami-Ville Salomaa 1.25 3.00
53 Alexei Vasiljev 1.25 3.00
54 Peter Wallin 1.25 3.00
94 Brian Boucher 2.50 6.00
95 Martin Brodeur 6.00 15.00
96 Brad Church 1.25 3.00
97 Shane Doan 1.50 4.00
98 Terry Ryan 1.25 3.00
99 Ryan Smyth 4.00 10.00

1995 Signature Rookies Tetrad Autographs

SIGS NUMBERED OUT OF 5000
61 Alexei Morozov 1.25 3.00
62 Radek Dvorak 1.25 3.00
66 Terry Ryan 1.25 3.00
67 Shane Doan 1.50 4.00
68 Brad Church 1.25 3.00
69 Brian Boucher 2.50 6.00
70 Dmitri Nabokov 1.25 3.00

1995 Signature Rookies Tetrad Mail-In

This five-card standard size set was available through the mail from Signature Rookies. The set highlights the 1995 first overall draft picks in basketball, football, baseball and hockey. The fronts picture color action photos blended with a fractal-swirling design. In a gold foil stamp, the players name is found vertically on the right. "Mail In" and "#1 Pick" adorn the top and bottom respectively on the left. The back has another color action photo in the upper-right corner. The rest is devoted to a player biography and statistics set on top of the same fractal-swirling design. The cards are numbered with a "P" prefix (P1-P5).

COMPLETE SET (5) 1.50 4.00
P4 Bryan Berard .40 1.00
P5 Joe Smith .60 1.50
Ki-Jana Carter
Darin Erstad
Bryan Berard

1995 Signature Rookies Tetrad Previews

This five-card standard-size set was randomly inserted in SR BK autobilia packs. The fronts display borderless color action player photos. The named player stands out on a faded background with his name printed in gold below. The backs carry an elongated color action player photo on one side while a head photo, biographical information, position, college, and career statistics round out the backs.

COMPLETE SET (5) 1.00 2.50
2 Jim Carey .20 .50

1995 Signature Rookies Tetrad SR Force

This 35-card standard-size set features color action player photos on the front on a white background. Pictures of one foot, the head, and one arm are set out as separate photos on the side of the main picture. The words, "SR Force," are printed in the white border at the top, while the player's name is in gold at the bottom of the picture. The backs carry the same photo as a faded background with photos of the head and parts of one leg. The player's name, position, team, biographical information, and statistics round out the back. The cards are numbered with an "F" prefix.

COMPLETE SET (35) 6.00 15.00
F1 Nolan Baumgartner .10 .30
F2 Bryan Berard .10 .30
F3 Aki-Petteri Berg .15 .40
F4 Daymond Langkow .20 .50
F5 Wade Redden .10 .30
F6 Martin Brodeur .60 1.50
F7 Jim Carey .20 .50
F8 Jaromir Jagr .75 2.00
F9 Maxim Kuznetsov .10 .30
F10 Terry Ryan .10 .30

1995 Signature Rookies Tetrad SR Force Autographs

RANDOM INSERTS IN PACKS
F1 Nolan Baumgartner 1.25 3.00
F2 Bryan Berard 1.50 4.00
F3 Aki-Petteri Berg 1.50 4.00
F4 Daymond Langkow 1.25 3.00
F5 Wade Redden 1.25 3.00
F6 Martin Brodeur 6.00 15.00
F7 Jim Carey 4.00 10.00
F8 Jaromir Jagr 10.00 25.00
F9 Maxim Kuznetsov 1.25 3.00
F10 Terry Ryan 1.25 3.00

1995 Slapshot Memorial Cup

Produced by Slapshot Images Ltd., this 110-card standard-size set commemorates the 1995 Memorial Cup of the Canadian Hockey League. The set includes the champions of the three member leagues (Detroit/OHL; Hull/LMJHQ; Kamloops/WHL) as well as the host team (Brandon). On a simulated wood background, the fronts feature color action photos inside a jagged black or blue picture frame. The player's name is printed above the photo, while the team name is printed vertically running down the left edge. The backs have biography, a color headshot, and a player profile. The set is arranged according to teams as follows: Kamloops Blazers (1-25), Brandon Wheat Kings (26-50), Hull Olympiques (51-75), and Detroit Jr. Red Wings (76-100).

COMPLETE SET (110) 12.00 30.00
1 Rod Branch .07 .20
2 Jeff Oldenborger .07 .20
3 Jason Holland .07 .20
4 Nolan Baumgartner .15 .40
5 Keith McCambridge .07 .20
6 Ivan Vologjaninov .07 .20
7 Aaron Keller .07 .20
8 Greg Hart .07 .20
9 Jarome Iginla 2.00 5.00
10 Ryan Huska .07 .20
11 Jeff Ainsworth .07 .20
12 Darcy Tucker .40 1.00
13 Hnat Domenichelli .15 .40
14 Tyson Nash .75 2.00
15 Shane Doan 1.25 3.00
16 Jeff Antonovich .07 .20
17 Bonnie Kinney .07 .20
18 Ashley Buckberger .07 .20
19 Brad Lukowich .30 .75
20 Bob Westerby .07 .20
21 Jason Strudwick .15 .40
22 Bob Maudie .07 .20
23 Randy Petruk .20 .50
24 Shawn McNeil .07 .20
25 Don Hay CO .07 .20
26 Bryon Penstock .07 .20
27 Brian Elder .07 .20
28 Jeff Staples .07 .20
29 Scott Laluk .07 .20
30 Kevin Pozzo .07 .20
31 Wade Redden .40 1.00
32 Justin Kurtz .15 .40
33 Sven Butenschon .07 .20
34 Bryan McCabe .20 .50
35 Kelly Smart .07 .20
36 Bobby Brown .07 .20
37 Mike Dubinsky .07 .20
38 Mike LeClerc .30 .75
39 Dean Kletzel .07 .20
40 Darren Ritchie .07 .20
41 Mark Dutiaume .07 .20
42 Ryan Robson .07 .20
43 Chris Dingman .15 .40
44 Darren Van Oene .07 .20
45 Colin Cloutier .07 .20
46 Darryl Stockham .07 .20
47 Peter Schaefer .20 .50
48 Marty Murray .20 .50
49 Alex Vasilevski .07 .20
50 Bob Lowes CO .07 .20
51 Michael Coveny .07 .20
52 Jan Nemecek .15 .40
53 Chris Hall .07 .20
54 Jason Groleau .07 .20
55 Alex Rodrigue .07 .20
56 Jamie Bird .07 .20
57 Harold Hersh .07 .20
58 Carl Prud'Homme .07 .20
59 Sean Farmer .07 .20
60 Carl Beaudoin .07 .20
61 Gordie Dwyer .07 .20
62 Richard Safarik .07 .20
63 Carl Charland .07 .20
64 Jean-Guy Trudel .15 .40
65 Francois Cloutier .07 .20
66 Roddie MacKenzie .07 .20
67 Colin White .30 .75
68 Martin Menard .07 .20
69 Sebastien Bordeleau .07 .20
70 Jonathan Delisle .07 .20
71 Peter Worrell .40 1.00
72 Louis-Philippe Charbonneau .15 .40
73 Jose Theodore 2.00 5.00
74 Neil Savary .15 .40
75 Michael McKay .15 .40
76 Darryl Foster .07 .20
77 Quade Lightbody .07 .20
78 Ryan MacDonald .07 .20
79 Mike Rucinski .07 .20
80 Murray Sheehan .07 .20
81 Matt Ball .07 .20
82 Gerry Lanigan .07 .20
83 Mike Morrone .07 .20
84 Tom Buckley .07 .20
85 Eric Manlow .07 .20
86 Bill McCauley .07 .20
87 Andrew Taylor .07 .20
88 Scott Blair .07 .20
89 Jeff Mitchell .07 .20
90 Jason Saal .15 .40
91 Jamie Allison .15 .40
92 Bryan Berard .20 .50
93 Dan Pawlaczyk .07 .20
94 Milan Kostolny .07 .20
95 Duane Harmer .07 .20
96 Shayne McCosh .07 .20
97 Sean Haggerty .07 .20
98 Nic Beaudoin .07 .20
99 Paul Maurice CO/GM .07 .20
100 Pete Deboer ACO .07 .20
101 Kamloops Checklist .07 .20
102 Brandon Checklist .07 .20
103 Hull Checklist .07 .20
104 Detroit Checklist .07 .20
105 OHL Champions Detroit Jr. Red Wings .07 .20
106 WHL Champions Kamloops Blazers .07 .20
107 LMJHQ Champions Hull Olympiques .07 .20
NNO OHL Playoff Summary .07 .20
NNO LHJMQ Playoff Summary .07 .20
NNO WHL Playoff Summary .07 .20

1991 South Carolina Collegiate Collection

This 200-card set measures standard sized and features cards of all-time great South Carolina athletes. The fronts have a black border with color action shots on each one. The school name and logo are found across the top border of the card. The featured player's name is found along the bottom border set against a red background. The backs carry a small bio of the player and his/her statistics.

COMPLETE SET (200) 5.00 12.00
72 Chris Boyle HK .05 .15

1991 Star Pics

This 72 card standard-size set contained 18 1991 first round draft picks. The cards have glossy action color player photos, with a thin white border on a background picturing a hockey mask. The player's name appears in a white lettering below the picture. The print run was supposed to be 225, 000 individually numbered sets. Autographed cards were randomly inserted into the sets. The autograph cards are valued at 20X to 100X the prices below for Flashback cards and 20X to 50X for the other cards.

SEALED SET (72) 2.00 10.00
1 Al Morganti .02 .10
2 Pat Falloon .02 .10
3 Jamie Pushor .02 .10
4 Jean Beliveau FLB .08 .25
5 Martin Lapointe .20 .50
6 Jamie Matthews .02 .10
7 Rod Gilbert FLB .08 .25
8 Niklas Sundblad .02 .10
9 Steve Konowalchuk .02 .10
10 Alex Delvecchio FLB .08 .25
11 Donevan Hextall .02 .10
12 Dody Wood .02 .10
13 Scott Niedermayer .20 .50
14 Trevor Halverson .02 .10
15 Terry Chitaroni .02 .10
16 Tyler Wright .02 .10
17 Andrei Lomakin UER .02 .10
18 Martin Hamrlik .02 .10
19 Dimitri Filimonov UER .02 .10
20 Ed Belfour FLB .20 .50
21 Andrew Verner .02 .10
22 Yanic Perreault .02 .10
23 Michael Nylander .02 .10
24 Scott Lachance .02 .10
25 Pavel Bure .60 1.50
26 Mike Torchia .02 .10
27 Frank Mahovlich FLB .08 .25
28 Philippe Boucher .02 .10
29 Jiri Slegr .02 .10
30 Sergei Fedorov FLB .30 .75
31 Rene Corbet .02 .10
32 Jamie McLennan .02 .10
33 Shane Peacock .02 .10
34 Mario Nobili .02 .10
35 Peter Forsberg .75 2.00
36 All-Rookie Team .02 .10
Pat Falloon
Tyler Wright
Philippe Boucher
Andrew Verner
Scott Lachance
37 Arturs Irbe .20 .50
38 Alexei Zhitnik .02 .10
39 Pat Peake .02 .10
40 Adam Oates FLB .08 .25
41 Markus Naslund .20 .50
42 Eric Lavigne .02 .10
43 Jeff Nelson .02 .10
44 Yanic Dupre UER .02 .10
45 Justin Morrison .02 .10
46 Alek Stojanov .02 .10
47 Marcel Cousineau .02 .10
48 Alexei Kovalev .08 .25
49 Andrei Trefilov .02 .10
50 Mats Sundin FLB .20 .50
51 Steve Staios .02 .10
52 Glenn Hall FLB .08 .25
53 Brent Bilodeau .02 .10
54 Darcy Werenka .02 .10
55 Chris Osgood .40 1.00
56 Nathan Lafayette .02 .10
57 Richard Matvichuk .02 .10
58 Dimitri Mironov UER .02 .10
59 Jason Dawe .02 .10
60 Mike Ricci FLB .02 .10
61 Gerry Cheevers FLB .08 .25
62 Jim Campbell .02 .10
63 Francois Groleau .02 .10
64 Glen Murray .20 .50
65 Jason Young .02 .10
66 Dean McAmmond .02 .10
67 Guy Leveque .02 .10
68 Patrick Poulin .02 .10
69 Bobby House .02 .10
70 Jaromir Jagr FLB .40 1.00
71 Jassen Cullimore .02 .10
72 Checklist Card .02 .10

2000-01 UD CHL Prospects

This 100-card base set was released in March 2001 with a SRP of $2.49 for a 5-card pack. There was a subset of 10 Draft Prospects included in the base set.

COMPLETE SET (100) 20.00 25.00
1 Jay Harrison .10 .20
2 Jay McClement .10 .20
3 Adam Henrich .10 .20
4 Carlo Colaiacovo .30 .50
5 Nikita Alexeev .30 .50
6 Brad Boyes .40 1.00
7 Peter Hamrlik .30 .50
8 Cory Stillman .10 .20
9 Derek Roy .40 .75
10 Michael Zigomanis .30 .50
11 Jason Spezza 1.50 2.00
12 Chad Wiseman .10 .20
13 Patrick Jarrett .30 .50
14 Chris Thorburn .30 .50
15 John Kozoriz .10 .20
16 Brandon Cullen .10 .20
17 Jonathan Zion .10 .20
18 Miguel Delisle .10 .20
19 Ryan Ramsay .10 .20
20 Marcel Rodman .10 .20
21 Stephen Weiss 1.25 1.50
22 Libor Ustrnul .10 .20
23 Rob Zepp .30 .50
24 Kris Vernarsky .30 .50
25 Jason Penner .10 .20
26 Trevor Daley .30 .50
27 Alexei Semenov .30 .50
28 Mark Popovic .10 .20
29 Tim Gleason .40 .75
30 Craig Kennedy .10 .20
31 Steve Ott .40 .75
32 Brian Finley .30 .50
33 Kyle Wellwood .40 1.00
34 Raffi Torres .30 .50
35 Chris Kelly .10 .20
36 Scott Cameron .10 .20
37 Cole Jarrett .10 .20
38 Maxim Rybin .10 .20
39 Derek MacKenzie .10 .20
40 Ryan Held .10 .20
41 Colt King .10 .20
42 Rick Nash 2.00 5.00
43 Greg Jacina .10 .20
44 Branko Radivojevic .40 .75
45 Jordin Tootoo 1.25 3.00
46 Pavel Brendl .10 .20
47 Ryan Craig .10 .20
48 Owen Fussey .10 .20
49 Brent Krahn .40 .75
50 Erik Christensen .10 .20
51 Jared Aulin .30 .50
52 Kiel McLeod .10 .20
53 Dan Blackburn .40 .75
54 Jeff Woywitka .30 .50
55 Ryan Hollweg .10 .20
56 Jay Bouwmeester 2.00 1.50
57 Ben Knopp .10 .20
58 Marcel Hossa .30 .50
59 Greg Watson .10 .20
60 Justin Mapletoft .30 .50
61 Matt Hubbauer .10 .20
62 Garth Murray .10 .20
63 Matthew Spiller .30 .50
64 Barrett Heisten .40 .75
65 Gerard Dicaire .10 .20
66 Jamie Lundmark .40 .75
67 Duncan Milroy .10 .20
68 Nathan Smith .10 .20
69 Konstantin Panov .10 .20
70 Mike Comrie 1.25 1.00
71 Tomas Kopecky .10 .20
72 Jozef Balej .30 1.00
73 Shane Bendera .30 .50
74 Blake Evans .10 .20
75 Igor Pohanka .10 .20
76 Robin LeBlanc .10 .20
77 Yanick Lehoux .30 .50
78 Jean-Francois Racine .30 .50
79 Pascal LeClaire .40 .75
80 Chris Montgomery .10 .20
81 Brent MacLellan .10 .20
82 Thatcher Bell .10 .20
83 Antoine Vermette .40 .75
84 Carl Mallette .10 .20
85 Nicolas Poirier .10 .20
86 Radim Vrbata .30 .50
87 Maxime Ouellet .40 .75
88 Brandon Reid .40 .75
89 Jason Spezza 1.50 2.00
90 Pascal LeClaire .40 .75
91 Dan Blackburn .40 .75
92 Stephen Weiss 1.25 1.00
93 Tim Gleason .40 .75
94 Duncan Milroy .40 .75
95 Kiel McLeod .30 .50
96 Jay McClement .10 .20
97 Jay Harrison .10 .20
98 Greg Watson .40 .75
99 Jason Spezza 1.50 2.00
100 Jay Bouwmeester 2.00 1.50

2000-01 UD CHL Prospects Autographs

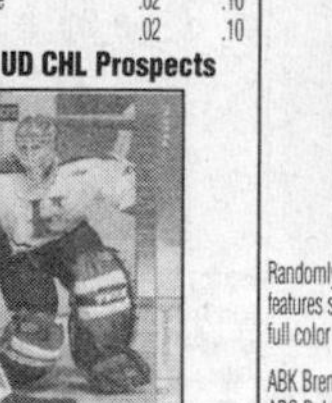

Randomly inserted at a rate of 1:107, this 9-card set features some of the hottest prospects from the CHL in full color photos and player autographs.

ABK Brent Krahn 15.00
ABO Bobby Orr 125.00 250.00
ADB Dan Blackburn 8.00 20.00
AJB Jay Bouwmeester 10.00 25.00
AJS Jason Spezza 12.50 30.00
APB Pavel Brendl 8.00 10.00
APL Pascal LeClaire 15.00
ART Raffi Torres 8.00 10.00
ARZ Rob Zepp 15.00

2000-01 UD CHL Prospects CHL Class

Inserted at a rate of 1:17, this 10-card set featured elite CHL performers on silver foil card stock. The card fronts carry the player's name and jersey number in red foil.

COMPLETE SET (10) 12.50 25.00
CC1 Brian Finley .75 2.00
CC2 Michael Zigomanis .40 1.00
CC3 Jason Spezza 3.00 8.00
CC4 Jay Bouwmeester 2.00 5.00
CC5 Rob Zepp .75 2.00
CC6 Pavel Brendl .40 1.00
CC7 Dan Blackburn 1.25 3.00
CC8 Mike Comrie .75 2.00
CC9 Pascal LeClaire .75 2.00
CC10 Maxime Ouellet .75 2.00

2000-01 UD CHL Prospects Destination the Show

Inserted at a rate of 1:33, this 6-card set features players who are considered locks for the NHL. Each card carries a color action photo and is highlighted by silver and red foil accents.

COMPLETE SET (6) 12.50 15.00
D1 Jason Spezza 4.00 8.00
D2 Dan Blackburn 1.50 3.00
D3 Pavel Brendl 1.25 1.00
D4 Jay Bouwmeester 2.50 5.00
D5 Zdenek Blatny 1.25 1.00
D6 Pascal LeClaire 2.00

2000-01 UD CHL Prospects Future Leaders

Inserted at 1:17, this 10-card set features player's of the CHL considered to be the future of the NHL. Each card is printed on silver foil card stock with red foil highlights.

COMPLETE SET (10) 12.50 12.00
FL1 Jason Spezza 3.00 5.00
FL2 Raffi Torres .75 2.00
FL3 Brad Boyes .75 2.00
FL4 Stephen Weiss .75 2.00
FL5 Michael Zigomanis .40 1.00
FL6 Jamie Lundmark .40 1.00
FL7 Mike Comrie .75 2.00
FL8 Nathan Smith .40 1.00
FL9 Radim Vrbata .40 1.00
FL10 Brandon Reid .40 1.00

2000-01 UD CHL Prospects Game Jerseys

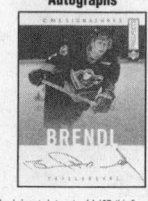

Inserted a rate of 1:18, these cards carry game-worn jersey swatches of some of the biggest names in the CHL. Card fronts carry a color action photo on mostly white stock, the player's name appears vertically on the right side and his jersey number is in grey at the bottom right. The swatch is in the shape of a maple leaf in the center of the card. Autographed parallels were also inserted and numbered to 100 sets.

DBL.JSY STAT.PRINT RUN 250 SER.#'d SETS
BK Brent Krahn 15.00
DB Dan Blackburn 8.00 20.00
JA Jason Spezza Windsor Jersey 10.00 25.00
JB Jay Bouwmeester 8.00 20.00
JL Jamie Lundmark 5.00 12.00
JS Jason Spezza Mississauga Jersey 10.00 25.00
NE Nikita Alexeev 5.00 12.00
PB Pavel Brendl 5.00 12.00
RT Raffi Torres 5.00 12.00
RZ Rob Zepp 5.00 12.00
BB D.Blackburn/B.Krahn 12.50 30.00
BZ D.Blackburn/R.Zepp 10.00 25.00
LB J.Lundmark/D.Blackburn 12.50 30.00
LK J.Lundmark/B.Krahn 8.00 20.00
SB J.Spezza/J.Bouwmeester 25.00 60.00
SL J.Spezza/J.Lundmark 20.00 50.00
SS J.Spezza/J.Spezza 25.00 60.00
ST J.Spezza/R.Torres 20.00 50.00
SZ J.Spezza/R.Zepp 12.50 30.00
TZ R.Torres/R.Zepp 8.00 20.00

2000-01 UD CHL Prospects Great Desire

Inserted at a rate of 1:33, this 6-card set features a small color action photo in the top right hand corner, and a larger photo of the player's eyes in the center surrounded by the words "Great Desire" in red foil. The player's jersey number is in the left bottom corner in silver foil.

COMPLETE SET (6) 12.50 25.00
GD1 Jason Spezza 4.00 8.00
GD2 Jay Bouwmeester 2.50 5.00
GD3 Mike Comrie 3.00
GD4 Raffi Torres 1.25 2.00
GD5 Brandon Reid 1.25 2.00
GD6 Pascal LeClaire 3.00

2000-01 UD CHL Prospects Supremacy

Randomly inserted at 1:17, this 10-card set features elite players of the CHL on silver foil stock. The player's name and jersey number on the card front in red foil. The card back explains why the player was chosen for the set.

COMPLETE SET (10) 12.50 20.00
CS1 Jason Spezza 3.00 8.00
CS2 Brian Finley .75 2.00
CS3 Raffi Torres .40 1.00
CS4 Rob Zepp .75 2.00
CS5 Pavel Brendl .40 1.00
CS6 Justin Mapletoft .40 1.00
CS7 Barrett Heisten .40 1.00
CS8 Mike Comrie .75 2.00
CS9 Jay Bouwmeester 2.00 5.00
CS10 Pascal LeClaire .75 2.00

1999-00 UD Prospects

The 1999-00 Upper Deck Prospects set was released as a 90-card set that featured 67 NHL prospects, 22

nada's Best, and 1 checklist card. Each pack con-
ned 5-cards and carried a suggested retail price of
99.

MPLETE SET (90)	25.00	30.00
Wayne Gretzky	1.25	3.00
Jason Spezza	1.25	3.00
Sheldon Keefe	.08	.25
Mark Bell	.20	.50
Justin Papineau	.15	.40
Denis Shvidki	.15	.40
Darryl Bootland	.20	.50
Michael Zigomanis	.15	.40
Chris Eade	.08	.25
Brad Boyes	.60	1.50
Michael Henrich	.08	.25
2 Nikita Alexeev	.08	.25
3 Libor Ustrnul	.08	.25
Brian Finley	.15	.40
5 Chris Berti	.08	.25
6 Agris Saviels	.08	.25
7 Kris Newbury	.08	.25
3 Jared Newman	.08	.25
Samu Isosalo	.08	.25
Mike Van Ryn	.15	.40
Miguel Delisle	.08	.25
2 Rostislav Klesla	.20	.50
3 Raffi Torres	.20	.50
4 Kurtis Foster	.08	.25
5 Lou Dickenson	.08	.25
6 Milan Kraft	.15	.40
7 Jamie Lundmark	.20	.50
8 Scott Hartnell	.20	.50
9 Ben Knopp	.08	.25
0 Mike Wirll	.08	.25
1 Ryan Craig	.08	.25
2 Kris Beech	.15	.40
3 Pavel Brendl	.15	.40
4 Blake Robson	.08	.25
5 Jarret Stoll	.15	.40
6 Oleg Saprykin	.15	.40
7 Eric Johannson	.08	.25
8 Warren Peters	.08	.25
9 Marcel Hossa	.30	.75
0 Shane Endicott	.08	.25
1 Craig Olynick	.08	.25
2 Brent Krahn	.30	.75
3 Matt Pettinger	.15	.40
4 Jaroslav Kristek	.08	.25
5 Milan Bartovic	.08	.25
6 Jared Aulin	.15	.40
7 Jakub Cutta	.15	.40
48 Blake Ward	.08	.25
49 Lynn Lyons	.15	.40
50 Jay Bouwmeester	.75	2.00
51 Nick Schultz	.15	.40
52 Filip Novak	.08	.25
53 Michael Bubnick	.08	.25
54 Charline Labonte	.75	2.00
55 Thatcher Bell	.08	.25
56 Yanick Lehoux	.08	.25
57 Antoine Vermette	.20	.50
58 Alexei Volkov	.15	.40
59 Michal Sivek	.15	.40
60 Carl Mallette	.08	.25
61 Maxime Ouellet	.30	.75
62 Simon Lagace-Daigle	.08	.25
63 Andrei Shefer	.08	.25
64 Mathieu Chouinard	.15	.40
65 Philippe Sauve	.20	.50
66 Daniel Sedin	.30	.75
67 Henrik Sedin	.30	.75
68 Thatcher Bell	.08	.25
69 Brad Boyes	.60	1.50
70 Jared Aulin	.15	.40
71 Dany Heatley	1.25	3.00
72 Ryan Hare	.08	.25
73 Scott Hartnell	.30	.75
74 Jay Bouwmeester	.75	2.00
75 Kiel McLeod	.08	.25
76 Kris Newbury	.08	.25
77 Blake Robson	.08	.25
78 Jarret Stoll	.15	.40
79 Antoine Vermette	.20	.50
80 Mike Wirll	.08	.25
81 Jason Spezza	1.25	3.00
82 Jay Harrison	.08	.25
83 Brandon Janes	.08	.25
84 Craig Olynick	.08	.25
85 Mark Popovic	.08	.25
86 Nick Schultz	.15	.40
87 Karl St. Pierre	.08	.25
88 Pascal Leclaire	.30	.75
89 Blake Ward	.08	.25
90 Checklist	.08	.25

1999-00 UD Prospects CHL Class

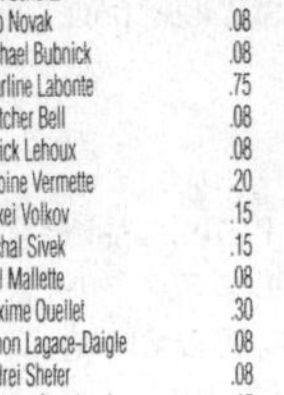

Randomly inserted in packs at 1:4, this 10-card insert set showcases ten of the hottest talents in the CHL. Card backs carry a "C" prefix.

COMPLETE SET (10)	15.00	15.00
C1 Jason Spezza	2.00	5.00
C2 Justin Papineau	.60	1.50
C3 Mark Bell	.75	2.00
C4 Kris Beech	.60	1.50
C5 Jay Bouwmeester	1.25	3.00
C6 Denis Shvidki	.60	1.50
C7 Pavel Brendl	.60	1.50
C8 Brian Finley	.75	2.00
C9 Jamie Lundmark	.75	2.00
C10 Thatcher Bell	.60	1.50

1999-00 UD Prospects Destination the Show

Randomly inserted in packs at 1:17, this 10-card insert set features ten prospects that are preparing for their trip to "The Show". Card backs carry a "DS" prefix.

COMPLETE SET (10)	30.00	35.00
DS1 Jason Spezza	4.00	10.00
DS2 Pavel Brendl	1.25	3.00
DS3 Henrik Sedin	1.50	4.00
DS4 Daniel Sedin	1.50	4.00
DS5 Jamie Lundmark	1.50	4.00
DS6 Taylor Pyatt	1.25	3.00
DS7 Brian Finley	1.50	4.00
DS8 Kris Beech	1.50	4.00
DS9 Denis Shvidki	1.25	3.00
DS10 Jay Bouwmeester	2.00	5.00

1999-00 UD Prospects Game Jerseys

Randomly inserted in packs at 1:215, this 12-card insert features twelve of some of the most collectable phenoms in the game. Card backs are numbered using the players initials.

CL Charline Labonte	40.00	50.00
HS Henrik Sedin	15.00	30.00
JB Jay Bouwmeester	40.00	50.00
JS Jason Spezza	60.00	100.00
KB Kris Beech	15.00	30.00
LD Lou Dickenson	10.00	20.00
PB Pavel Brendl	10.00	20.00
TB Thatcher Bell	10.00	20.00
DSD Daniel Sedin	15.00	30.00

1999-00 UD Prospects International Stars

Randomly inserted in packs at 1:9, this 10-card insert set features the next generation of international superstars. Card backs carry an "IN" prefix.

COMPLETE SET (10)	20.00	40.00
IN1 Daniel Sedin	.75	2.00
IN2 Henrik Sedin	.75	2.00
IN3 Pavel Brendl	.60	1.50
IN4 Alexei Volkov	.75	2.00
IN5 Denis Shvidki	.60	1.50
IN6 Milan Kraft	.75	2.00
IN7 Nikita Alexeev	.60	1.50
IN8 Oleg Saprykin	.75	2.00
IN9 Jaroslav Kristek	.60	1.50
IN10 Marcel Hossa	.75	2.00

1999-00 UD Prospects Signatures of Tradition

Randomly inserted in packs at 1:17, this 30-card insert set features autographed cards of future NHL stars. Card backs are numbered using the player's initials.

AV Alexei Volkov	6.00	15.00
BF Brian Finley	6.00	15.00
BM Branislav Mezei	4.00	10.00
CL Charline Labonte	12.50	30.00
DS Daniel Sedin	6.00	15.00
HS Henrik Sedin	6.00	15.00
JB Jay Bouwmeester	12.50	30.00
JL Jamie Lundmark	6.00	15.00
JS Jason Spezza	15.00	40.00
KB Kris Beech	6.00	15.00
MB Mark Bell	6.00	15.00
MC Mathieu Chouinard	6.00	15.00
MO Maxime Ouellet	6.00	15.00
MV Mike Van Ryn	4.00	10.00
PB Pavel Brendl	4.00	10.00
TP Taylor Pyatt	4.00	10.00
WG Wayne Gretzky	250.00	400.00
DSH Denis Shvidki	4.00	10.00

2001-02 UD Prospects

Released in mid-August 2001, this 45-card set focused on young prospects of the CHL.

COMPLETE SET (45)	40.00	30.00
1 Jason Spezza	2.50	3.00
2 Dan Blackburn	.75	1.00
3 Daniel Boisclair	.40	.75
4 Jeff Woywitka	.30	.50
5 Matthew Spiller	.30	.50
6 Nathan Paetsch	.30	.50
7 Mark Popovic	.30	.50
8 Jay McClement	.30	.50
9 Garth Murray	.30	.50
10 Aaron Lobb	.30	.50
11 Derek Roy	.75	1.00
12 Jean-Francois Soucy	.40	.75
13 Nicolas Corbeil	.30	.50
14 Colt King	.30	.50
15 Robin Leblanc	.30	.50
16 Jay Harrison	.30	.50
17 Jiri Jakes	.30	.50
18 Lukas Krajicek	.40	.75
19 Jason Pominville	.40	.75
20 Shawn Collymore	.30	.50
21 Michael Garnett	.40	.75
22 Adam Munro	.40	.75
23 Dan Hamhuis	.40	.75
24 Doug Lynch	.30	.50
25 Shaone Morrisonn	.40	.75
26 Carlo Colaiacovo	.40	.75
27 Stephen Weiss	.40	.75
28 Joel Stepp	.30	.50
29 Jeff Lucky	.30	.50
30 Cory Stillman	.30	.50
31 Chris Thorburn	.30	.50
32 Colby Armstrong	.40	.75
33 Brent Maclellan	.30	.50
34 Jordin Tootoo	4.00	5.00
35 Greg Watson	.30	.50
36 Martin Podlesak	.30	.50
37 Duncan Milroy	.40	.75
38 Frantisek Bakrlik	.30	.50
39 Brendan Bell	.30	.50
40 Kiel McLeod	.30	.50
41 Jason Spezza	2.50	3.00
42 Jason Spezza	2.50	3.00
43 Jason Spezza	2.50	3.00
44 Jason Spezza	2.50	3.00
45 2001 Top Prospects Summary	.30	.50

2001-02 UD Prospects Autographs

Randomly inserted at 1:6 packs, this 23-card set featured authentic player autographs.

AAM Adam Munro	8.00	20.00
ABK Brent Krahn	6.00	15.00
ABO Bobby Orr	125.00	250.00
ACK Colt King	4.00	10.00
ACS Cory Stillman	4.00	10.00
ACT Chris Thorburn	4.00	10.00
ADB Dan Blackburn	6.00	15.00
ADH Dan Hamhuis	8.00	20.00
ADM Duncan Milroy	4.00	10.00
AGW Greg Watson	4.00	10.00
AJB Jay Bouwmeester	12.50	25.00
AJH Jay Harrison	4.00	10.00
AJL Jamie Lundmark	6.00	15.00
AJM Jay McClement	4.00	10.00
AJS Jason Spezza	12.50	30.00
AKM Kiel McLeod	4.00	10.00
AMG Michael Garnett	6.00	15.00
AMP Mark Popovic	4.00	10.00
APL Pascal Leclaire	6.00	15.00
ARK Rostislav Klesla	6.00	15.00
ART Raffi Torres	8.00	20.00
ASW Stephen Weiss	8.00	20.00
AWG Wayne Gretzky	125.00	300.00

2001-02 UD Prospects Jersey Autographs

Limited to just 30 serial-numbered copies each, this 17-card set featured both game-worn jersey swatches and authentic player autographs.

SAM Adam Munro	20.00	50.00
SCK Colt King	15.00	40.00
SCS Cory Stillman	15.00	40.00
SCT Chris Thorburn	15.00	40.00
SDB Dan Blackburn	15.00	40.00
SDH Dan Hamhuis	30.00	80.00
SDM Duncan Milroy	15.00	40.00
SGW Greg Watson	15.00	40.00
SJH Jay Harrison	15.00	40.00
SJM Jay McClement	15.00	40.00
SJS Jason Spezza	60.00	150.00
SKM Kiel McLeod	15.00	40.00
SMG Michael Garnett	20.00	50.00
SMP Mark Popovic	15.00	40.00
SSW Stephen Weiss	30.00	60.00
SWA Jason Spezza	60.00	150.00
SWH Jason Spezza	60.00	150.00

2001-02 UD Prospects Jerseys

Inserted at overall odds of 1 per pack, this 62 card set featured swatches of jerseys worn by the pictured player(s) during the 2001 CHL Top Prospects Game. Dual jersey cards were serial-numbered to 125 copies each. A gold parallel of this set was also created and each card was serial-numbered out of 75.

COMMON CARD	4.00	10.00
JAL Aaron Lobb	4.00	10.00
JAM Adam Munro	5.00	12.00
JBB Brendan Bell	4.00	10.00
JBM Brent Maclellan	4.00	10.00
JBO Daniel Boisclair	5.00	12.00
JCA Colby Armstrong	4.00	10.00
JCK Colt King	4.00	10.00
JCS Cory Stillman	4.00	10.00
JCT Chris Thorburn	4.00	10.00
JDB Dan Blackburn	6.00	15.00
JDH Dan Hamhuis	5.00	12.00
JDL Doug Lynch	4.00	10.00
JDM Duncan Milroy	4.00	10.00
JDR Derek Roy	5.00	12.00
JFB Frantisek Bakrlik	4.00	10.00
JGM Garth Murray	4.00	10.00
JGW Greg Watson	4.00	10.00
JJF Jean-Francois Soucy	5.00	12.00
JJH Jay Harrison	4.00	10.00
JJJ Jiri Jakes	4.00	10.00
JJL Jeff Lucky	4.00	10.00
JJM Jay McClement	4.00	10.00
JJP Jason Pominville	5.00	12.00
JJS Jason Spezza	10.00	25.00
JJT Jordin Tootoo	15.00	40.00
JJW Jeff Woywitka	5.00	12.00
JKM Kiel McLeod	4.00	10.00
JLK Lukas Krajicek	5.00	12.00
JMG Michael Garnett	4.00	10.00
JMP Mark Popovic	4.00	10.00
JMS Matthew Spiller	4.00	10.00
JNC Nicolas Corbeil	4.00	10.00
JNP Nathan Paetsch	4.00	10.00
JPO Martin Podlesak	4.00	10.00
JRL Robin Leblanc	4.00	10.00
JSC Shawn Collymore	4.00	10.00
JSM Shaone Morrisonn	5.00	12.00
JST Joel Stepp	4.00	10.00
JSW Stephen Weiss	4.00	10.00
JWA Jason Spezza	10.00	25.00
JWH Jason Spezza	10.00	25.00
CBD D. Blackburn/D. Milroy	8.00	20.00
CBG D. Boisclair/M. Garnett	8.00	20.00
CBM D. Blackburn/A. Munro	8.00	20.00
CBS D. Blackburn/J. Spezza	15.00	40.00
CBW D. Blackburn/S. Weiss	10.00	25.00
CHM J. Harrison/K. McLeod	8.00	20.00
CHW D. Hamhuis/S. Weiss	8.00	20.00
CKP L. Krajicek/M. Podlesak	5.00	12.00
CKW C. King/G. Watson	8.00	20.00
CMS J. McClement/C. Stillman	8.00	20.00
CMT G. Murray/C. Thorburn	8.00	20.00
CPM M. Popovic/D. Milroy.	8.00	20.00
CRT D. Roy/J. Tootoo	50.00	125.00
CSA J. Spezza/J. Spezza	15.00	40.00
CSB J. Spezza/J. Spezza	15.00	40.00
CSH J. Spezza/D. Hamhuis	12.50	30.00
CSM J. Spezza/D. Milroy	10.00	25.00
CSS J. Spezza/J. Spezza	15.00	40.00
CSW J. Spezza/S. Weiss	15.00	40.00
CWA J. Woywitka/C. Armstrong	8.00	20.00
CWM S. Weiss/D. Milroy	10.00	25.00

1991 Ultimate Draft

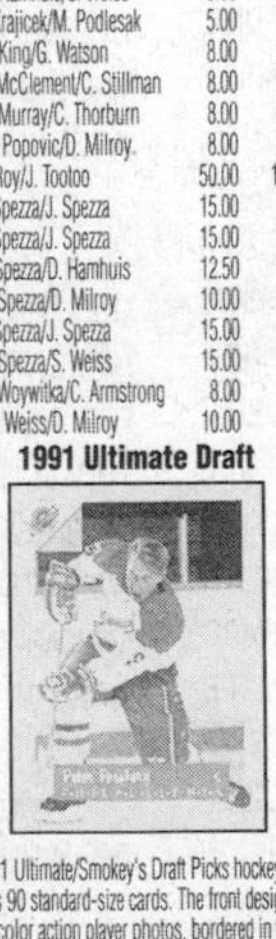

The 1991 Ultimate/Smokey's Draft Picks hockey set contains 90 standard-size cards. The front design has glossy, color action player photos, bordered in white. The upper left corner of the picture is cut off to allow space for a logo with the words "Sportcards Ultimate Hockey". The player's name, position, and team appear in white lettering in a blue-gray rectangle near the card bottom. Reportedly production quantities were as follows: 6,000 American set cases equaling 120,000 sets, 750 French set cases equaling 15,000 sets, 5,000 American ten-box wax cases, 1,500 French ten-box wax cases, and 500 autographed sets. Currently the French and English cards are valued equally. Autographed versions are worth 30X to 50X basic cards.

COMPLETE SET (90)	3.00	8.00
1 Ultimate/Preview	.01	.05
2 Pat Falloon	.02	.10
3 Scott Niedermayer	.02	.10
4 Scott Lachance	.01	.05
5 Peter Forsberg	.40	1.00
6 Alek Stojanov	.01	.05
7 Richard Matvichuk	.02	.10
8 Patrick Poulin	.01	.05
9 Martin Lapointe	.08	.25
10 Tyler Wright	.01	.05
11 Philippe Boucher	.01	.05
12 Pat Peake	.01	.05
13 Markus Naslund	.08	.25
14 Brent Bilodeau	.01	.05
15 Glen Murray	.08	.25
16 Niklas Sundblad	.01	.05
17 Trevor Halverson	.01	.05
18 Dean McAmmond UER	.01	.05
19 Jim Campbell	.01	.05
20 Rene Corbet	.01	.05
21 Eric Lavigne	.01	.05
22 Steve Staios	.01	.05
23 Jassen Cullimore	.01	.05
24 Jamie Pushor	.01	.05
25 Donevan Hextall	.01	.05
26 Andrew Verner	.02	.10
27 Jason Dawe	.01	.05
28 Jeff Nelson	.01	.05
29 Darcy Werenka	.01	.05
30 Francois Groleau	.01	.05
31 Guy Leveque	.01	.05
32 Jamie Matthews	.01	.05
33 Dody Wood	.02	.10
34 Yanic Perreault	.01	.05
35 Jamie McLennan UER	.02	.10
36 Yanic Dupre	.01	.05
37 1st Round Checklist	.01	.05
38 Chris Osgood	.40	1.00
39 Fredrik Lindquist	.01	.05
40 Jason Young	.01	.05
41 Steve Konowalchuk	.02	.10
42 Michael Nylander	.02	.10
43 Shane Peacock	.01	.05
44 Yves Sarault	.01	.05
45 Marcel Cousineau	.02	.10
46 Nathan Lafayette	.01	.05
47 Bobby House	.01	.05
48 Kerry Toporowski	.01	.05
49 Terry Chitaroni	.01	.05
50 Mike Torchia	.02	.10
51 Mario Nobili	.01	.05
52 Justin Morrison	.01	.05
53 Grayden Reid	.01	.05
54 Yanic Perreault Underdog	.01	.05
55 2nd Round Checklist	.01	.05
56 Niedermayer& Falloon& and Lachance	.02	.10
57 The Goalies	.02	.10
58 Pat Falloon FDP	.02	.10
59 Scott Niedermayer FDP	.02	.10
60 Scott Lachance FDP	.01	.05
61 Peter Forsberg FDP	.40	1.00
62 Alek Stojanov FDP	.01	.05
63 Richard Matvichuk FDP	.02	.10
64 Patrick Poulin FDP	.01	.05
65 Martin Lapointe FDP	.08	.25
66 Tyler Wright FDP	.01	.05
67 Philippe Boucher FDP	.01	.05
68 Pat Peake FDP	.01	.05
69 Markus Naslund FDP	.08	.25
70 Brent Bilodeau FDP	.01	.05
71 Glen Murray FDP	.08	.25
72 Niklas Sundblad FDP	.01	.05
73 Trevor Halverson FDP	.01	.05
74 Dean McCammond FDP	.01	.05
75 Award Winners Philippe Doucher Jeff Nelson Scott Niedermayer	.01	.05
76 The Swedes Markus Naslund Peter Forsberg	.08	.25
77 3rd and 4th Round Checklist	.01	.05
78 Pat Falloon BW	.02	.10
79 Scott Niedermayer BW	.02	.10
80 Falloon/Niedermayer BW	.02	.10
81 Scott Lachance BW	.01	.05
82 Philippe Boucher BW	.01	.05
83 Markus Naslund BW	.08	.25
84 Glen Murray BW	.08	.25
85 Niklas Sundblad BW	.01	.05
86 Jason Dawe BW	.01	.05
87 Yanic Perreault BW	.02	.10
88 Offensive Threats Yanic Dupre Mikael Nylander	.01	.05
89 Group Shot/Overview	.01	.05
90 Face the Future/ Ultimate	.01	.05

1991 Ultimate Draft Promos

This three-card standard-size set was given out to dealers and collectors to promote the new Ultimate hockey draft picks cards. The front design is basically the same as the regular issue. The Torchia card displays a different player photo, while the Stojanov card is cropped differently. Also the promos have the team name below the player's name rather than city name as with their regular issue. The backs of the promos differ from those of the regular issue in that the photos on the back are more ghosted and the word "Sample" is stenciled over them. Also the player information on the Stojanov card back is arranged differently on the promo. The cards are unnumbered and checklisted below in alphabetical order.

COMPLETE SET (3)	.40	1.00
1 Pat Falloon	.20	.50
2 Alex Stojanov	.08	.25
3 Mike Torchia	.08	.25

1996 Visions

The 1996 Classic Visions set consists of 150 standard-size cards. The fronts feature full-bleed color action player photos. The player's position and name are presented in blue foil, while the Classic logo and set title "96 Visions" are stamped in gold foil. The back carries a second color photo, college statistics, biography, and a player fact.

COMPLETE SET (150)	6.00	15.00
82 Bryan Berard	.15	.40
83 Jeff Friesen	.15	.40
84 Petr Buzek	.15	.40
85 Nolan Baumgartner	.08	.25
86 Jason Bonsignore	.08	.25
87 Jan Hlavac	.15	.40
88 Ethan Moreau	.08	.25
89 Radek Dvorak	.08	.25
90 Brian Holzinger	.08	.25
91 Petr Sykora	.20	.50
92 Ed Jovanovski	.15	.40
93 Jeff O'Neill	.08	.25
94 Manon Rheaume	.20	.50
123 Petr Sykora	.20	.50

1996 Visions Signings

The 1996 Visions Signings set consists of 100 standard-size cards. The fronts feature full-bleed color action player photos. The player's position and name are stamped in prismatic foil along with the Classic logo and set title "96 Visions Signings." This set contains standouts from five sports grouped together in this order: basketball, football, hockey, baseball and racing. Cards were distributed in six-card packs. Release date was June 1996. The main allure to this product, in addition to the conventional inserts, were autographed memorabilia redemption cards inserted one per 10 packs.

COMPLETE SET (100)	6.00	15.00
61 Boyd Devereaux	.08	.25
62 Alexandre Volchkov	.08	.25
63 Trevor Wasyluk	.08	.25
64 Luke Curtin	.08	.25
65 Richard Jackman	.08	.25
66 Jonathan Zukiwsky	.08	.25
67 Geoff Peters	.08	.25
68 Daniel Briere	.15	.40
69 Chris Allen	.08	.25
70 Jason Sweitezer	.08	.25
71 Steve Nimigon	.08	.25
72 Jay McKee	.08	.25
73 Henry Kuster	.08	.25
74 Johnathan Aitken	.08	.25
75 Ed Jovanovski	.08	.25
76 Petr Sykora	.15	.40
77 Bryan Berard	.08	.25
78 Manon Rheaume	.20	.50
79 Radek Dvorak	.08	.25

1996 Visions Signings Artistry

This 10-card insert set was printed on thick 24-point stock. Cards were inserted at a rate of 1:60 Vision Signings packs.

COMPLETE SET (10)	20.00	50.00
6 Petr Sykora	2.00	5.00

1996 Visions Signings Autographs Gold

Certified autographed cards were inserted in Visions Signings packs at an overall rate of 1:12. Some players signed only the silver version while others signed both gold and silver cards. The Gold foil cards were not individually serial numbered. The quantity signed is unknown but assumed to be significantly higher than the corresponding number signed for the silver foil cards. We've listed the unnumbered cards alphabetically.

2 Jonathan Aitken	1.50	4.00
4 Chris Allen	1.50	4.00
8 Daniel Briere	2.50	6.00
14 Luke Curtin	1.50	4.00
17 Boyd Devereaux	2.00	5.00
31 Richard Jackman	2.00	5.00
33 Ed Jovanovski	3.00	8.00
35 Henry Kuster	1.50	4.00
37 Jay McKee	1.50	4.00
44 Steve Nimigon	1.50	4.00
49 Geoff Peters	1.50	4.00
62 Jason Sweitezer	1.50	4.00
66 Alexandre Volchkov	2.00	5.00
68 Trevor Wasyluk	1.50	4.00
73 Jonathan Zukiwsky	1.50	4.00

1996 Visions Signings Autographs Silver

Certified autographed cards were inserted in Visions Signings packs at an overall rate of 1:12. Some players signed only silver cards while others signed gold and silver foil cards. The Silver cards were individually serial numbered as noted below. We've listed the unnumbered cards alphabetically.

3 Jonathan Aitken/360	2.00	5.00
5 Chris Allen/385	2.00	5.00
11 Daniel Briere/390	2.00	5.00
17 Luke Curtin/370	2.00	5.00
20 Boyd Devereaux/350	2.00	5.00
36 Richard Jackman/400	2.00	5.00
38 Ed Jovanovski/405	4.00	10.00
40 Henry Kuster/415	2.00	5.00
43 Jay McKee/385	2.00	5.00
50 Steve Nimigon/380	2.00	5.00
55 Geoff Peters/390	2.00	5.00
70 Jason Sweitezer/355	2.00	5.00
75 Alexandre Volchkov/375	2.00	5.00
78 Trevor Wasyluk/365	2.00	5.00
84 Jonathan Zukiwsky/375	2.00	5.00

1997 Visions Signings

Score Board's follow-up to the 1996 Visions Signings debut product was released in June 1997. The second-year product had more of a memorabilia emphasis. According to Score Board, 1,700 sequentially numbered cases were produced with five cards per pack, 16 packs per box and 10 boxes per case. Each pack contains either an autographed card or an insert card. The 50-card regular set includes stars and prospects from all four major team sports. Also, one in every two packs contained a gold parallel card to the base set.

COMPLETE SET (50)	5.00	10.00
40 Dainius Zubrus	.05	.15
41 Joe Thornton	.15	.40
42 Dan Cleary	.05	.15
43 Sergei Samsonov	.08	.25

1997 Visions Signings Gold

COMPLETE SET (50)	10.00	25.00

*GOLD: .8X TO 2X BASIC CARDS
GOLD STATED OSS 1:2

1997 Visions Signings Artistry

The cards in this 20-card set feature Score Board's "exclusive printing technology" and were inserted at a rate of 1:6 Vision Signings packs.

COMPLETE SET (20)	20.00	40.00
A20 Dainius Zubrus	.40	1.00

1997 Visions Signings Artistry Autographs

These certified autographed cards feature Score Board's "exclusive printing technology" and were inserted at a rate of 1:18 packs. These 20 cards are autographed parallels of the Artistry insert set.

A20 Dainius Zubrus	2.50	6.00

1997 Visions Signings Autographs

Each 1997 Visions Signings pack contained either an autographed card or an insert card. One in six packs contain a regular autograph card. Four cards, Troy Aikman, Brett Favre, Allen Iverson, and Emmitt Smith were never issued, therefore the complete set only contains 62 cards.

28 Josh Holden	1.50	4.00
51 Sergei Samsonov	4.00	10.00
55 Joe Thornton	3.00	8.00
65 Dainius Zubrus	2.00	5.00
66 Andrei Zyuzin	1.50	4.00

1993 Fax Pax World of Sport*

Issued in Great Britain, and part of a multi-sport set. Each card was standard size, and was full color. Card backs feature stats and biographical information.

COMPLETE SET (3)	2.00	5.00
25 Wayne Gretzky	2.00	5.00
26 Brett Hull	.40	1.00
27 Eric Lindros	.40	1.00

1993 FCA 50*

This 50-card standard-size set was sponsored by Fellowship of Christian Athletes. The color player photos on the fronts are accented on three sides by a thin pink stripe; the card face itself shades from blue to white as one moves toward the bottom. The FCA logo, featuring a cross with two olive branches, is superimposed in the upper left corner, while the player's name is printed beneath the picture and his sport in the pink stripe on the left. On a blue background, the backs carry a close-up photo, biography, and the player's testimony.

17 Mike Gartner HK	.30	.75

1997-98 Pinnacle Collector's Club Team Pinnacle *

This 9-card set was part of a much larger multi-sport set available with membership to Pinnacle's Collector's Club. Promo cards carried the player's name across the top of the card not the side like the regular cards.

COMPLETE SET (9)		100.00
H1 Wayne Gretzky	8.00	20.00
H2 Patrick Roy	6.00	15.00
H3 Eric Lindros	3.00	8.00
H4 Paul Kariya	5.00	12.00
H5 Peter Forsberg	5.00	12.00
H6 John Vanbiesbrouck	2.00	5.00
H7 Martin Brodeur	6.00	15.00
H8 Steve Yzerman	6.00	15.00
H9 Jaromir Jagr	4.00	10.00
H10 Mark Messier	3.00	8.00
NNO Wayne Gretzky PROMO	10.00	25.00
NNO Peter Forsberg PROMO	6.00	15.00

ACKNOWLEDGMENTS

A GREAT DEAL OF DILIGENCE, HARD WORK, AND DEDICATED EFFORT WENT INTO THIS YEAR'S VOLUME. THE HIGH STANDARDS TO WHICH WE HOLD OURSELVES, HOWEVER, COULD NOT HAVE BEEN MET WITHOUT THE EXPERT INPUT AND GENEROUS AMOUNT OF TIME CONTRIBUTED BY MANY PEOPLE. OUR SINCERE THANKS ARE EXTENDED TO EACH AND EVERY ONE OF YOU.

EACH YEAR WE REFINE THE PROCESS OF DEVELOPING THE MOST ACCURATE AND UP-TO-DATE INFORMATION FOR THIS BOOK. I BELIEVE THIS YEAR'S PRICE GUIDE IS OUR BEST YET. THANKS AGAIN TO ALL OF THE CONTRIBUTORS NATIONWIDE (LISTED BELOW) AS WELL AS OUR STAFF HERE IN DALLAS.

THOSE WHO HAVE WORKED CLOSELY WITH US ON THIS AND MANY OTHER BOOKS, HAVE AGAIN PROVEN THEMSELVES INVALUABLE IN EVERY ASPECT OF PRODUCING THIS BOOK: MIKE ARONSTEIN, PETE BELANGER, ERWIN BORAU, BILL BOSSERT, JOHN BRENNER, CARTOMANIA (JOSEPH E. FILION), COLLECTION DE SPORT AZ (RONALD VILLANUEVE), BILL AND DIANE DODGE, GERVISE FORD, STEVE FREEDMAN, LARRY AND JEFF FRITSCH, JOHN FURNISS, GARY GAGEN, DICK GARIEPY, DICK GILKESON, MIKE AND HOWARD GORDON, GEORGE GRAUER, GENE GUARNERE, JERRY AND ETTA HERSH, MIKE HERSH, GERALD HIGGS, IN THE GAME, SEAN ISAACS, DENNIS KANNOKKO, PAUL AND ANNA KANNOKKO, LEW LIPSET, PAUL MARCHANT, MICHAEL MORETTO, JEAN-GUY PICHETTE, JACK POLLARD, GAVIN RILEY, ROTMAN PRODUCTIONS, JOHN RUMIERZ, KEVIN SAVAGE, ANGELO SAVELLI, MIKE SCHECHTER (MSA), RICHARD SHERMAN, BRAD SHRABIN, GARY SILKSTONE, GERRY SOBIE, JOHN SPALDING, PHIL AND JOAN SPECTOR, NIGEL SPILL, MURVIN STERLING, TOPPS, UPPER DECK, ROB UNLUS, MICHEL VAILLANCOURT, SHIRL VOLK, PETE WOOTEN, KIT YOUNG, AND ROBERT ZANZE. FINALLY, WE GIVE A SPECIAL ACKNOWLEDGMENT TO DENNIS W. ECKES, MR. SPORT AMERICANA, WHOSE UNTIMELY PASSING IN 1991 WAS A REAL LOSS TO THE HOBBY AND TO ME PERSONALLY. THE SUCCESS OF THE BECKETT PRICE GUIDES HAVE ALWAYS BEEN THE RESULT OF A TEAM EFFORT.

MANY OTHER INDIVIDUALS HAVE PROVIDED PRICE INPUT, ILLUSTRATIVE MATERIAL, CHECKLIST VERIFICATIONS, ERRATA, AND/OR BACKGROUND INFORMATION. AT THE RISK OF INADVERTENTLY OVERLOOKING OR OMITTING THESE MANY CONTRIBUTORS, WE SHOULD LIKE TO PERSONALLY THANK AB D CARDS (DALE WESOLEWSKI), JERRY ADAMIC, BREN ADAMS, MURRAY AKBART, NEIL ARMSTRONG, ALAN APPLEGATE, ROLAND J. ATLAS, ART BAKER, BRENT BARNES, FRANK AND VIVIAN BARNING, ROBERT BEAUDOIN, AL BEHARRELL, TODD BELLEROSE, GARY BENTON, BEULAH SPORTS (JEFF BLATT), KI BILLY, CHAD BLICK, MICHEL BOLDUC, JOSEPH BONETT, PETER BORKOWSKI, LUC BOUCHER, B. JACK BOURLAND III, TONY BOUWMAN, JIM BOYNE, ELIO BRANDELLI, TIM BRAHMER, MARCO BRIZUELA, DOUGLAS BROWN, BOB BRUNER, DAN BRUNER, JACEY BUEL, DAVE BULLIS, ERIC BURGOYNE, SCOTT BURKE, JASON CAINES, JIM CAPPELLO, DANNY CARISEO, GREG CASKEY, RICK CHAMBERS, DWIGHT CHAPIN, JEFF CHAPMAN, MICHAEL CHARK, STEVE CHIARAMONTE, SUSAN CHRISTENSEN, LARRY CIANCONE, SCOTT COATES, ALLAN E. COHEN, SHANE COHEN (GRAND SLAM), BARRY COLLA, MATT COLLETT, KEN COLLINS, SHELBY COLSON, JOE CONTE, DAN CONWAY, RYAN COPE, MICHAEL J. COX, TAYLOR CRANE, WIL CURTIS, ALLEN CUSTER, KENNETH DANIELS, STEVEN DANVER, LEO DAVIS, SCOTT DEAN, JIM DECORSO, MARY DEMPSTER, DEERQUOTES BASEBALL CARDS, NORMAND DESROCHES, LARRY DETIENNE, DAVE DEVENEY, KARLOS DIEGO, LEON DILL, MARIO DIPASTENA, MARC DIXON, GERARD DOLCI, BENOIT DOYON, MICHEL DUBOIS, CHARLES DUGRE, JOHN DUPLISEA, DON ELLIS, DANNY ELLWOOD, MICHAEL ESPOSITO, BRYAN EPSTEIN, DOAK EWING, DAVE FELTHAM, LARRY FLEMING, DON FORSEY, FRANK FOX, CRAIG FRANK, MARK FRANKE, KATHRYN FRIEDLANDER, BOB FRIEDMAN, BOB FRYE, JAMES FUNKE JR., TOM GALANIS, JIM GALUSHA, RICHARD, GARIEPY, NEIL GARVEY, RON AND DAVE GIBARA, MICHAEL R. GIONET, DAVE GIOVE, MIKE GOGAL, HARVEY GOLDFARB, BRIAN GOLDSTEIN, JEFF GOLDSTEIN, RENVEL GONSALVES, RYNEL GONSALVES, SETH GORDON, JOHN GOSNEY, ERIK GRAVEL, PIERRE-LUC GRAVEL, GREAT CANADIAN SPORTCARD CO., HALL'S NOSTALGIA, GERALD HAMELIN, TOM HARRETT, RON HELLER, BILL HENDERSON, TOM HENDRICKSON, WAYNE HEPBURN, CHICK HERSHBERGER, CLAY HILL, GARY HLADY, SHAWN HOAGLAND, KEITH HOLTZMANN, JOSEPH HORGAN, DAN HORTON, TERESA HORTON, D. HOWERY JR., RICHARD IRVING, TORSTEIN H. JACOBSEN, JOHN JAMES, ROBERT JANSING, CLIFF JANZEN, PETER JEFFREY, LESLIE JEZUIT, SCOTT JUGAN, ROBERT KANTOR, JAY AND MARY KASPER, SAM KASSAM, JOHN KELLY, RICK KEPLINGER, LARRY KERRIGAN, JOHN KILLAN, DEAN KONIECZKA, BOB KRAWETZ, CHUCK KUCERA, GEORGE KUMAGAI, ROB KUHLMAN, THOMAS KUNNECKE, ROGER LAMPERT, TED LARKINS, BRENT LEE, SCOTT LELIEVRE, IRV LERNER, HOWIE LEVY, MIKE LEWANDOSKI, STEPHANE LIZOTTE, NICHOLAS LOCASTO, THE LOCKER ROOM, TIM LOOP, FRANK PEZ, KAROLINE K. LOWRY, DOUG LOWTHER, STEVEN J. LOY, THIERRY LUBENEC, JIM MACIE, MARASCO, ADAM MARTIN, JASON MARTIN, CHRIS MAYHEW, MICHAEL MCDONALD, BLAKE MEYER, JOHN MEYER, DICK MILLERD, BEN MITCHELL, PAUL V. MOHRLE, JOE MORANO, MICHAEL MORETTO, MICHEL MORIN, BRIAN MORRIS, KEVIN MUDRAK, LARRY MURRAY, TODD NELKIN, ROB NICHOLLS, DAVE NICKLAS, PAUL NOBLE, LEANDRE NORMAND, DAVID NYSTROM, JOHN O'HARA, JOHN O' MARA, GLENN OLSON, NELSON PAINE, ANDREW PAK, DAVID PAOLICELLI, TOM PARKER, CLAY PASTERNACK, ALAN PEACE, JOE PELLICIO, ALAN PHILPOT, DALE PINNEY, RICHARD PLETT, LEN POTTIE, RED RIVER COINS AND CARDS, RANDALL REESE, TOM REID, DAVE AND SHAWN REDDEN, PAULA REINKE, RALPH REITSMA, RON RESSLER, DOROTHY REZNIK, OWEN RICKER, MARK ROGERS, JOHN WAYNE ROMAN, PAUL ROMERO, CHARLES ROOKE, JIM ROUTLY, GRANT ROWLAND, JOE RUBERT II, TERRY SACK, JOE SAK, LINDA SANTIAGO, CHERYL SAUVE, MIKE SHAFER, CHRIS SKLENER, LYLE SKRAPEK, SLAPSHOT SPORTS COLLECTIBLES, STEVE SMITH, DON SPAGNOLA, CARL SPECHT, DAVE STALLINGS, CARY STEPHENSON, DAN STICKNEY, ANDY STOLTZ, RAY STONEHOUSE, CHERYL SUAVE, MARK SUCHAWERICZ, DAVE SULARZ, WALT SUSKI, FRED SUZMAN, DANNY TARQUINI, PAUL S. TAYLOR, LEE TEMANSON, TERESA TEWELL, CHUCK THOMAS, TIM THOMPSON, JOE TOMASIK, DARREN TURCOTTE, MICHEL VAILLANCOURT, VARIETE SPORTS, ROB VERES, VERVILLE ENR., ERNIE VICKERS, CLAYTON VIGENT, SHIRL VOLK, JONATHAN WALDMAN, JONATHAN WATTS, DAVID WEINER, ANDREW B. WEISENFELD, KERMIT B. WELLS, BRIAN WENTZ, BILL WESSLUND, FRANK AND JASON WILDER, KELLY WIONZEK, BRIAN WOBBEKING, TED WOO, THOMAS L. WUJEK, ANDRE YIP HOI, YAZ'S SPORTS MEMORABILIA, GERARD YODICE, CHRISTINA ZAWADZKI, AND BILL ZIMPLEMAN.

A SPECIAL THANKS ALSO GOES OUT TO THOSE WHO GRACIOUSLY DONATED THEIR KNOWLEDGE AND EXPERTISE (AND THEIR CARDS) IN ADDING TO THE COMPREHENSIVENESS OF THIS YEAR'S VOLUME: RALPH SLATE (WHOSE WEB SITE WWW.HOCKEYDB.COM IS ONE OF THE HOBBY'S GREAT MINOR LEAGUE RESOURCES), VINNIE MONTALBANO AND DALE SPRENGER (FOR THEIR EFFORTS IN IMPROVING THE SCOPE OF OUR MINOR LEAGUE AND COLLEGE COVERAGE), CASPAR FRIBERG (FINNISH ISSUES), MAREK PANDOSCAK (SLOVAKIAN ISSUES), JIRI KUCA AND JIRI PETERKA (CZECH ISSUES), HOLGER PETERSEN (GERMAN ISSUES), HOCKEY HEAVEN, CHRISTIAN OLANDER, AND PER VEDIN (SWEDISH ISSUES), JOE BONNETT, STEWART ETLINGER, DINO FAZIO, STEVE FRASER, CTM STE-FOY, GERRY GARLAND, GARY GIOVANE, IAN GREEN (ARMCHAIR SPORTS UK), JOHN IGNATO, CHAD KITZMAN, TROY MOORE, JEREMY POCLITAR, J.D. PORTER, GUS SAUNDERS, ANDRE YIP HOI (TIME-OUT SPORTSCARDS), DAVE WESELOWSKI.

EVERY YEAR WE MAKE ACTIVE SOLICITATIONS FOR EXPERT INPUT. WE ARE PARTICULARLY APPRECIATIVE OF THE HELP (HOWEVER EXTENSIVE OR CURSORY) PROVIDED FOR THIS VOLUME. WE RECEIVE MANY INQUIRIES, COMMENTS AND QUESTIONS REGARDING MATERIAL WITHIN THIS BOOK. IN FACT, EACH AND EVERY ONE IS READ AND DIGESTED. TIME CONSTRAINTS, HOWEVER, PREVENT US FROM PERSONALLY REPLYING. BUT KEEP SHARING YOUR KNOWLEDGE. EVEN THOUGH WE CANNOT RESPOND TO EACH LETTER, YOU ARE MAKING SIGNIFICANT CONTRIBUTIONS TO THE HOBBY THROUGH YOUR INTEREST AND COMMENTS.

THE EFFORT TO CONTINUALLY REFINE AND IMPROVE THIS BOOK ALSO INVOLVES A GROWING NUMBER OF PEOPLE AND TYPES OF EXPERTISE ON OUR HOME TEAM. OUR COMPANY BOASTS A SUBSTANTIAL SPORTS COLLECTIBLES PUBLISHING TEAM, WHICH STRENGTHENS OUR ABILITY TO PROVIDE COMPREHENSIVE ANALYSIS OF THE MARKETPLACE. OUR HOCKEY ANALYSTS PLAYED A MAJOR PART IN COMPILING THIS YEARS BOOK, TRAVELLING THOUSANDS OF MILES DURING THE PAST YEAR TO ATTEND SPORTS CARD SHOWS AND VISIT CARD SHOPS AROUND THE UNITED STATES AND CANADA. THEIR BASELINE ANALYSIS AND CAREFUL PROOFREADING WERE KEY CONTRIBUTIONS TO THE ACCURACY OF THIS ANNUAL.

OUR PRICE GUIDE TEAM PLAYED A MAJOR PART IN COMPILING THIS YEAR'S BOOK THROUGH DEDICATED EFFORTS TO COMPILE THE MOST COMPLETE AND ACCURATE CHECKLISTS AND PRICING DATA AVAILABLE. THE MAJORITY OF ADDITIONS, CORRECTIONS, AND CHANGES TO THIS EDITION WERE MADE BY BECKETT HOCKEY SENIOR MARKET ANALYST TIM TROUT. HIS EFFORTS WERE ABLY ASSISTED BY THE REST OF THE PRICE GUIDE TEAM: JEFF CAMAY, RUSS ENCONTRO, BRIAN FLEISCHER, DAN HITT, BRYAN HORNBECK, KEITH HOWER, ALDOUS LLANOS AND AR TAN. FINALLY, THIS BOOK COULD NOT HAVE BEEN PRODUCED WITHOUT THE FINE WORK OF OUR PREPRESS AND DESIGN STAFF OF GEAN PAUL FIGARI AND TOM CARROLL.

THE WHOLE BECKETT MEDIA TEAM HAS MY THANKS FOR JOBS WELL DONE. THANK YOU, EVERYONE.

BECKETT®

THE #1 AUTHORITY ON COLLECTIBLES

HOCKEY CARD PRICE GUIDE

Number 20

THE HOBBY'S MOST RELIABLE AND RELIED UPON SOURCE™

Founder & Advisor: Dr. James Beckett III • **Edited By** Tim Trout with the staff of **BECKETT HOCKEY**
Beckett Media LP - Dallas, Texas

Prices in this guide reflect current retail rates determined just prior to printing. They do not reflect for-sale prices by the author, publisher, distributors, advertisers, or any card dealers associated with this guide. Every effort has been made to eliminate errors. Readers are invited to write us noting any errors which may be researched and corrected in subsequent printings. The publisher will not be held responsible for losses which may occur in the sale or purchase of cards because of information contained herein.

BECKETT is a registered trademark of
BECKETT MEDIA LP
DALLAS, TEXAS

Manufactured in the United States of America
Published by Beckett Media LP

Beckett Media LP
4635 McEwen Road
Dallas, TX 75244
(972) 991-6657
www.beckett.com

First Printing
ISBN 1-930692-89-7

The Beckett Hockey Card Price Guide and Checklist #21 already is being researched and prepared for release in November, 2011. In order for it to be the best resource on the market, it requires your help. If you know of any sets or singles not listed in this edition, or if you have pricing data to update the information herein, please contact us. You can send your information by email to hockeymag@beckett.com, or via the regular mail at Beckett Hockey Annual, 4635 McEwen Rd. Dallas, TX 75244. Please be sure to include your full contact information. We'll forward a complimentary copy of next year's book to 10 randomly selected hobbyists who make a contribution to that edition.